# LEGACY STANDARD BIBLE

## — PORTABLE PARAGRAPH REFERENCE RED LETTER —

STEADFAST BIBLES

**LEGACY STANDARD BIBLE**

Portable Paragraph Reference Red Letter

Typesetting by 2K / DENMARK. Printed in Korea ◊ 28 27 26 25 24 / 1 2 3 4 5

STEADFAST BIBLES
*Is a division of*
THREE SIXTEEN PUBLISHING

Southern California

978-1-63664-358-8 978-1-63664-361-8 978-1-63664-364-9 978-1-63664-367-0 978-1-63664-373-1
978-1-63664-359-5 978-1-63664-362-5 978-1-63664-365-6 978-1-63664-368-7 978-1-63664-374-8
978-1-63664-360-1 978-1-63664-363-2 978-1-63664-366-3 978-1-63664-369-4

# FOREWORD

### *Scriptural Promise*

"The grass withers, the flower fades,
But the word of our God stands forever."
Isaiah 40:8

The Legacy Standard Bible has been produced with the conviction that the words of Scripture as originally penned in Hebrew, Aramaic, and Greek are the eternal Word of God. The Holy Scriptures speak with authority to each generation, giving wisdom that leads to salvation, that people may serve Christ to the glory of God. Because it is God-breathed (2Ti 3:16), every word of it is inspired, every word is true, and every word must be conveyed to every nation, tribe, people, and tongue (Rev 7:9), so that every word can be taught and obeyed (Jos 23:14; Mt 28:20; Jn 17:17).

### *The Fourfold Aim of The Lockman Foundation*

1. These publications shall be true to the original Hebrew, Aramaic, and Greek.
2. They shall be grammatically correct.
3. They shall be understandable.
4. They shall give the Lord Jesus Christ His proper place, the place which the Word gives Him; therefore, no work will ever be personalized.

### *Preface to the Legacy Standard Bible*

In the history of English Bible translations, the King James Version is the most well known. This time-honored version of 1611, itself a revision of the Bishops' Bible of 1568, became the basis for the English Revised Version, which appeared in 1881 (New Testament) and 1885 (Old Testament). Its American counterpart, a product of both British and American scholarship, was published in 1901. Recognizing the values of the American Standard Version, The Lockman Foundation felt an urgency to preserve the ASV while incorporating recent discoveries of Hebrew and Greek textual sources and rendering it into more current English. This resulted in the New American Standard Bible, a translation based upon the time-honored principles of translation of the ASV and KJV, along with other linguistic tools and biblical scholarship.

The Legacy Standard Bible reflects another iteration of such preservation and refinement. Worked on by a core translation team in conjunction with pastors and educators from different countries, it is designed to honor, maintain, and advance the tradition represented by the NASB.

### *Principles of Translation*

**Key Principles:** The Legacy Standard Bible has worked to uphold the style and translational choices of the NASB as much as possible. Even more, it has endeavored to follow through on the NASB's stated intent to be true to the original Hebrew, Aramaic, and Greek. While the interpreter, teacher, and pastor have the goal of understanding what the text means, the translator is to provide them with what the text says. Consistently, the goal of this translation is to be a window into the original text. Within that goal, this revision has focused upon accuracy and consistency. It has checked that words and grammar have been carried over properly. It also established rules for the consistent translation of terms within their various nuances. This allows the reader to more easily reconstruct what the original texts said. It also helps the reader more easily trace the flow of argument within a text, identify when the same word is used in another passage, and make connections between texts.

There are limits to the application of this philosophy. In this edition, a word might not be translated consistently in order to maintain a highly familiar rendering of a text or to preserve a wordplay in the text that advances the inspired author's message. Moreover, because Scripture is a literary masterpiece, some linguistic features could not be transferred to this translation, not even by a note. Nevertheless, ensuring that the original languages are precisely rendered paves the way for careful readers to discover these insights for themselves.

In this way, the LSB upholds the philosophy that a translation does not replace pastors or teachers but rather depends upon faithful believers and the church to study and live out what has been written (Ac 8:30-31). Translation is a tool for the church and must be done in that context so that each word of Scripture may be taught and lived.

**Modern English Usage:** The attempt has been made to render the grammar and terminology in contemporary English. When word-for-word literalness was determined unacceptable to the modern reader, a change was made in the direction of a more current English idiom. In the instances where this has been done, the more literal rendering has been indicated in the notes. There are a few exceptions to this procedure. Of note, while an effort has been made to incorporate conjunctions as much as possible, the conjunction "and" is occasionally not translated at the beginning of sentences because of differences in style between ancient and modern writing. Punctuation is a relatively modern invention, and ancient writers often linked most of their sentences with "and" or other connectives.

**Alternative Readings:** In addition to the more literal renderings, notations have been made to include readings of variant manuscripts, explanatory equivalents of the text, and alternate translations that may bring out a play on words difficult to maintain in the text. These notations have been used specifically to assist the reader in comprehending the terms used by the original author.

**Names of God:** In the Scriptures, the name of God is significant and understandably so. Traditionally, the translation "God" renders the Hebrew word *Elohim*. Likewise, the word "Lord" is a translation of *Adonai*. In the LSB, God's covenant name is rendered as *Yahweh*. The meaning and implication of this name is God's self-deriving, ongoing, and never-ending existence. Exodus 3:14-15 shows that God Himself considered it important for His people to know His name. The effect of revealing God's name is His distinction from other gods and His expression of intimacy with the nation of Israel. Such a dynamic is a prevalent characteristic of the Scriptures as Yahweh appears in the OT over 6,800 times.

In addition to Yahweh, the full name of God, the OT also includes references to God by a shorter version of His name, Yah. By itself, God's name "Yah" may not be as familiar, but the appearance of it is recognizable in Hebrew names and words (e.g. Zechar-*iah*, meaning Yah remembers, and Hallelu-*jah*, meaning praise Yah!). God's shortened name "Yah" is predominantly found in poetry and praise.

The translation "Yahweh" is substantiated by scholarly reconstruction as well as by historical discussions in Theodoret, Epiphanius, Clement of Alexandria, Origen, and Aquila. Consequently, those latter individuals affirm the usage of God's covenant name in the period of the early church. Preserving this in translation foundationally records what is present in the OT text. It also allows proper distinction between God's personal name and the title "Lord" (*Adonai*), which emphasizes God's authority. Even more, it helps the reader to engage God with the name which He gifted to His people. Thus, the reintroduction of God's personal name into the translation of the OT is a feature that enhances the precision, intensity, and clarity of the biblical text in English.

The NT uses the term "Lord" (*Kurios*) to translate Yahweh. The LSB maintains the translation "Lord" and does not change those instances to Yahweh. In cases when "Lord" explicitly translates Yahweh in a quotation of the OT, a footnote is provided stating such. Nevertheless, the LSB maintains the translation of "Lord" in the NT for the same reason it upholds Yahweh in the OT: because that is what is written in the original text. Just as translations preserve the distinct wording between an OT passage and its quotation in the NT, so this distinction is preserved.

While there may be several factors behind this shift from Yahweh to Lord, for the apostles, one purpose centers on the declaration that Jesus Christ is Lord. Because the NT writers rendered Yahweh as Lord, they showed that Jesus is both Lord over all (even over Caesar, Ac 25:26) and none other than Yahweh Himself (Ac 2:25, 34, 36). Hence, the term "Lord" is a profound title showing Christ's supremacy in heaven and earth. That being said, the significance of this title presumes that one understands the movement from Yahweh to Lord. By rendering what is written in both the OT and NT, one can observe this shift and the fullness of its theological import.

**The Terminology of Slave:** The NASB has already translated the Greek term *doulos* frequently as "slave" in the NT. The LSB made this consistent across the NT. This upholds the lexical definition of the term, its consistent translation, and its distinction from other terms that do denote a "servant." Such consistency also highlights a biblical theological reality that Christians were slaves of sin but now are slaves of Christ (Ro 6:16-22). Biblical writers did not shy from this term because it condemned a wicked form of slavery (i.e., to sin, Satan, and death), highlighted the power of redemption, and affirmed one's total submission to the lordship of Christ.

In the OT, the Hebrew term *ebed* has more flexibility than *doulos* in the NT. For the word *ebed*, the notion of servant and slave can be present in describing one's relationship with God and man. The Messiah is the suffering Servant (Is 52:13; cf. Ac 3:26) even as Israel was a slave of Egypt (Dt 5:15) but now a slave of God (Lv 25:55). Likewise, Joseph's brothers call themselves Joseph's servants (Ge 44:9; *ebed*) but later in the same verse they say they are willing to become Joseph's slaves (Ge 44:9; again *ebed*). All of this demonstrates that *ebed* can have both the notion of servant and slave. For this reason, the NT translates *ebed* not merely with *doulos* but other words (e.g., *pais*). The apostles recognized that *ebed* can have different nuances that go beyond "slave." Accordingly, in human relationships, the term "servant" is used for *ebed* when talking about one's general submission to another as opposed to economic ownership (slave). In relationships between man and God, slave is used unless *ebed* occurs with a personal name (e.g., My servant David). This formulation conforms to the nuances of the word and also connects well with NT usage of slave. This translation principle also often brings out that God's people emphasize their total subjection to their loving God (by calling themselves His slaves) even as He uses them uniquely as His servants in His plan.

**Units of Measurement and Currency:** Because this translation is designed to bring the reader to what was originally written, the LSB maintains the unit of measurement and currency used in the original writing. For clarity, conversions into both American and metric units are provided in the notes for measurements. This allows for the LSB to serve the entire English-speaking world by not choosing one country's unit of measurement or currency over another.

**Hebrew Text:** The Legacy Standard Bible utilizes the latest edition of Rudolf Kittel's *Biblia Hebraica* together with the most recent light from lexicography, cognate languages, and the Dead Sea Scrolls.

**Hebrew Tenses, Aspect, and Stem:** While recognizing the challenges of the Hebrew verbal system, the approach of the LSB has been guided by the Hebrew verb's form in light of its immediate and broad contexts. Thus, fundamentally, the LSB works to express distinctively the various verb forms. When appropriate, the translators have brought out various emphases of the verbal stem such as simple active, simple middle-passive, factitive, causative, and iterative. The translation has also attempted to capture the complete, ongoing, habitual, inceptive, and resultative aspect of the verb. Finally, the translators took into account temporal adverbials and the syntactic constructions surrounding the verb to identify its tense.

**Greek Text:** The Legacy Standard Bible has the benefit of a number of critical Greek texts in determining the best variant reading to translate. The 27th edition of Eberhard Nestle's *Novum Testamentum Graece*, supplemented by the 28th edition in the General Epistles, serve as the base text.

On every variant reading the *Society of Biblical Literature GNT* as well as the *Tyndale House GNT* were also consulted. In the end, each decision was based upon the current available manuscript evidence.

**Greek Tenses, Moods, and Syntax:** A distinction was observed in the treatment of the Greek aorist tense and the Greek imperfect tense. Aorists are usually simple past tense in the indicative (e.g., "He did."). Imperfects are usually rendered as English past progressive (e.g., "He was doing") or inceptive (e.g., "He began to do"). "Began to" is italicized if it renders an imperfect tense, in order to distinguish it from the Greek verb for "begin." In some contexts the Greek imperfect is conveyed better as a simple past tense (e.g., "had an illness for many years" would be preferable to "was having an illness for many years" and would be understood in the same way).

On the other hand, not all aorists have been rendered as English pasts ("He did"). Judging from the context in which they occur, some needed to be rendered as English perfects ("He has done"), or even as past perfects ("He had done") to make proper sense.

In addition to aorists and imperfects, the translators have been sensitive to bring out in English the perfect tense indicative and participle as conveying a current state initiated in the past ("one who has been born of God," cf. 1Jn 5:1).

*Imperatives:* As for the distinction between aorist and present imperatives, the translators have usually rendered these imperatives as simple commands, rather than attempting a fine distinction as "Begin to do!" (for the aorist imperative), or, "Continually do!" (for the present imperative).

*Participles:* The LSB has also tried to convey the presence and function of each Greek participle. They often are translated temporally ("After Jesus entered Capernaum, he entered the synagogue"). This limits a translation reflecting what grammarians call the "attendant circumstance" function of the participle. While the translators do not question that function, the desire is to show the reader when there is a dependent participle which usually leads to a temporal or causal idea as conveyed in context.

*Questions:* In the rendering of negative questions introduced by the particle *me-* (which always expects the answer "No"), the LSB maintains the wording of the Greek text as opposed to adding a phrase at the end of the question (e.g., "He will not do this, will he?"). This allows for questions that truly have such phrasing to stand out (Jn 18:25). Readers are trusted to determine, given the context and the wording of the question, that a negative response is intended.

**Hebrew Acrostics:** At times, the biblical authors structured their writings where each section of poetry begins with a successive letter of the Hebrew alphabet. Psalm 119 is a well-known example of this, but far from the only one (see Pss 9-10, 25, 34, 37, 111, 112, 119, 145; Pr 31:10-31; Lam 1, 2, 3, 4; and Na 1:2-8). Because the Legacy Standard Bible endeavors to be a window into the original text, all known acrostics are labeled with each section having its respective Hebrew letter and English transliteration. While some acrostics correspond with the complete alphabet (e.g., Pss 34, 119; Lam 3), others reflect a part of the Hebrew alphabet (Na 1:2-8) or extend over chapter divisions (Pss 9-10). Nevertheless, acrostics bring out the artistic beauty of God's Word, reflect the completeness of thought and theology in the passage, and provide ease of memory for the original hearers. It is a feature intended by the inspired writer and so deserves the attention of the modern reader.

**Gender Language:** The Legacy Standard Bible is committed to precisely representing what was written in the original languages. Accordingly, while the translation recognizes that the Hebrew and Greek terms for "man" can legitimately mean "mankind" or "humanity" and renders such when appropriate, it does not add in phrases like "and sister" because they are not in the original text (cf. Jas 2:15 where the Greek word for "sister" is actually used). This abides with the LSB's commitment to being a word-for-word translation and honoring what was originally written in its exact formulation. Since there are highly interpretative matters involved in "gender-neutral" language, the Legacy Standard Bible allows the pastor and teacher to explain the text. Overall, the Legacy Standard Bible's commitment to focus upon authorial intent directs the translation concerning this issue. Doing so aligns the translation with its predecessors, an important goal as a legacy translation.

### *The Commitments of the Legacy Standard Bible*

**The Legacy Standard Bible aspires to be a legacy preserved**—to uphold the work and tradition that is found in translations from the KJV, ASV, to NASB.

**The Legacy Standard Bible aspires to be a legacy performed**—to advance the commitments of past translations by bringing forth features of the original text relative to accuracy and consistency.

**The Legacy Standard Bible aspires to be a legacy passed on**—to equip generations to study Scripture and continue the philosophy of being a window into the original text for the glory of God.

**The Lockman Foundation**

# EXPLANATION OF GENERAL FORMAT FOR THIS EDITION

**Superior Numbers and Letters** denote notes and cross references, respectively. Notes can refer to literal renderings, alternate translations, or explanations. Cross references in italics are parallel passages.
**Paragraphs** are designated by boldface verse numbers or letters.
**Quotation Marks** are used in the text in accordance with modern English usage.
**Personal Pronouns** are capitalized when pertaining to Deity. While descriptions about God are not capitalized, those which are used indisputably as direct titles for God are.
**Italics** are used in the text to indicate words which are not found in the original Hebrew, Aramaic, or Greek but implied by it. Italics are used in the footnotes to signify alternate readings for the text. Unitalicized text in the footnote alternate readings is the same as italics in the Bible text.
**Small Caps** in the NT are used in the text to indicate OT quotations or obvious references to OT texts. Variations of OT wording are found in NT citations depending on whether the NT writer translated from a Hebrew text, used existing Greek or Aramaic translations, or paraphrased the material. It should be noted that modern rules for the indication of direct quotation were not used in biblical times; thus, the ancient writer would use exact quotations or references to quotation without specific indication of such.
**Asterisks** are used to mark present tense verbs in Greek which have been translated with an English past tense in order to conform to modern usage (i.e., historical presents). The translators recognized that in some contexts the present tense seems more unexpected and unjustified to the English reader than a past tense would have been. For the sake of heightened vividness, Greek authors frequently used the present tense thereby transporting their readers in imagination to the actual scene at the time of occurrence. However, the translators felt that it would be wise to change these historical presents to English past tenses.

# ABBREVIATIONS AND SPECIAL MARKINGS

| | | |
|---|---|---|
| **Aram** | = | Aramaic |
| **DSS** | = | Dead Sea Scrolls |
| **Eng** | = | English |
| **Gr** | = | Greek translation of OT (Septuagint or LXX) or Greek text of NT |
| **Heb** | = | Hebrew text, usually Masoretic |
| **Lat** | = | Latin |
| **LXX** | = | Septuagint, the Greek translation of OT |
| **M.T.** | = | Masoretic text |
| **Syr** | = | Syriac |
| **Vg.** | = | Vulgate, the Latin translation of the Bible |
| **Lit** | = | A literal translation |
| **Or** | = | An alternate translation justified by the Hebrew, Aramaic, or Greek |
| [ ] | = | In text, brackets indicate words probably not in the original writings |
| [ ] | = | In notes, brackets indicate references to a name, place, or thing similar to, but not identical with that in the text |
| **Approx.** | = | Approximately |
| **cf.** | = | compare |
| **f, ff** | = | following verse or verses |
| **mg** | = | Refers to a marginal reading on another verse |
| **ms, mss** | = | manuscript, manuscripts |
| **v, vv** | = | verse, verses |

# BOOKS OF THE BIBLE

### *THE OLD TESTAMENT*



### *THE NEW TESTAMENT*

# THE OLD TESTAMENT

LEGACY STANDARD BIBLE

# GENESIS

### *Creation*

1 [a]In the beginning [b]God [c]created
the heavens and the earth. **2** And
the earth was [a,1]formless and void,
and [b]darkness was over the [2]surface
of the deep, and [c]the Spirit of God
[d]was hovering over the [2]surface of
the waters. **3** Then [a]God said, "Let
there be light"; and there was light.
**4** And God saw that the light was
[a]good; and God [b]separated the light
from the darkness. **5** [a]And God called
the light day, and the darkness He
called night. And [b]there was evening
and there was morning, one day.
**6** Then God said, "Let there be [1]an
[a]expanse in the midst of the waters,
and let it separate the waters from
the waters." **7** So God made the
[1]expanse and separated [a]the waters
which were below the [1]expanse from
the waters [b]which were above the
[1]expanse; and it was so. **8** And God
called the [1]expanse heaven. And
there was evening and there was
morning, a second day.
**9** Then God said, "[a]Let the waters
below the heavens be gathered into
one place, and let [b]the dry land
appear"; and it was so. **10** And God
called the dry land earth, and the
[a]gathering of the waters He called
seas; and God saw that it was good.
**11** Then God said, "Let the earth
sprout [a,1]vegetation, [2]plants yield-
ing seed, *and* fruit trees on the earth
bearing fruit after [3]their kind [4]with
seed in them"; and it was so. **12** And
the earth brought forth [1]vegetation,
[2]plants yielding seed after [3]their
kind, and trees bearing fruit [4]with
seed in them, after [3]their kind; and
God saw that it was good. **13** And
there was evening and there was
morning, a third day.
**14** Then God said, "Let there be
[a,1]lights in the [b,2]expanse of the
heavens to separate the day from
the night, and let them be for [c]signs
and for [d]seasons and for days and
years; **15** and let them be for [1]lights
in the [2]expanse of the heavens to
give light on the earth"; and it was
so. **16** So God made the two [1]great
lights, the [a]greater [2]light [3]to rule
the day, and the lesser [2]light [3]to rule
the night, and *also* [b]the stars. **17** [a]And
God placed them in the [1]expanse of
the heavens to give light on the earth,
**18** and [1]to [a]rule the day and the night,
and to separate the light from the
darkness; and God saw that it was
good. **19** And there was evening and
there was morning, a fourth day.

◆ **1:1** [a]Ps 102:25; Is 40:21; Jn 1:1, 2; Heb 1:10 [b]Ps 89:11; 90:2; Ac 17:24; Ro 1:20; Heb 11:3 [c]Job 38:4; Is 42:5; 45:18; Rev 4:11 **1:2** [a]Jer 4:23 [b]Job 38:9 [c]Ps 104:30; Is 40:13, 14 [d]Dt 32:11; Is 31:5 [1]Or *a waste and emptiness* [2]Lit *face* **1:3** [a]Ps 33:6, 9; 2Co 4:6 **1:4** [a]Ps 145:9, 10 [b]Is 45:7 **1:5** [a]Ps 74:16 [b]Ps 65:8 **1:6** [a]Is 40:22; Jer 10:12; 2Pe 3:5 [1]Or *a firmament* **1:7** [a]Job 38:8-11 [b]Ps 148:4 [1]Or *firmament* **1:8** [1]Or *firmament* **1:9** [a]Ps 104:6-9; Jer 5:22; 2Pe 3:5 [b]Ps 24:1, 2; 95:5 **1:10** [a]Ps 33:7; 95:5; 146:6 **1:11** [a]Ps 65:9-13; 104:14; Heb 6:7 [1]Or *grass* [2]Or *herbs* [3]Lit *its* [4]Lit *in which is its seed* **1:12** [1]Or *grass* [2]Or *herbs* [3]Lit *its* [4]Lit *in which is its seed* **1:14** [a]Ps 74:16; 136:7 [b]Ps 19:1; 150:1 [c]Jer 10:2 [d]Ps 104:19 [1]Or *luminaries, light-bearers* [2]Or *firmament* **1:15** [1]Or *luminaries, light-bearers* [2]Or *firmament* **1:16** [a]Ps 136:8, 9 [b]Job 38:7; Ps 8:3; Is 40:26 [1]Or *luminaries, light-bearers* [2]Or *luminary, light-bearer* [3]Lit *for the dominion of* **1:17** [a]Jer 33:20, 25 [1]Or *firmament* **1:18** [a]Jer 31:35 [1]Lit *for the dominion of*

**20** Then God said, "Let the waters
swarm with swarms of living crea-
tures, and let birds fly above the
earth [1]across the face of the [2]expanse
of the heavens." **21** And God created
[a]the great sea monsters and every
living creature that moves, with
which the waters swarmed after
their kind, and every winged bird
after its kind; and God saw that it
was good. **22** Then God blessed them,
saying, "Be fruitful and multiply, and
fill the waters in the seas, and let the
birds multiply on the earth." **23** And
there was evening and there was
morning, a fifth day.

**24** [a]Then God said, "Let the earth
bring forth living creatures after
[1]their kind: cattle and creeping things
and beasts of the earth after [1]their
kind"; and it was so. **25** God made the
[a]beasts of the earth after [1]their kind,
and the cattle after [1]their kind, and
every creeping thing of the ground
after its kind; and God saw that it was
good.

**26** Then God said, "Let [a]Us make
[b]man in Our image, according to
Our likeness, so that they will have
[c]dominion over the fish of the sea
and over the birds of the [1]sky and
over the cattle and over all the earth
and over every creeping thing that
creeps on the earth." **27** And God
created man [a]in His own image, in
the image of God He created him;
[b]male and female He created them.
**28** God blessed them, and God said to
them, "[a]Be fruitful and multiply, and
fill the earth, and subdue it; and have
dominion over the fish of the sea and
over the birds of the [1]sky and over
every living thing that creeps on the
earth." **29** Then God said, "Behold,
[a]I have given to you every plant
yielding seed that is on the [1]surface
of all the earth, and every tree [2]which
has *the* fruit of *the* tree yielding seed;
it shall be food for you; **30** and [a]to
every beast of the earth and to every
bird of the [1]sky and to every thing
that creeps on the earth [2]which has
life, *I have given* every green plant for
food"; and it was so. **31** And God saw
all that He had made, and behold,
it was very [a]good. And there was
evening and there was morning, the
sixth day.

**2** Thus the heavens and the earth
were completed, and all [a]their
hosts. **2** And [1]on [a]the seventh day
God completed His work which He
had done, and [b]He rested on the
seventh day from all His work which
He had done. **3** Then God blessed
the seventh day and sanctified it,
because on it He rested from all His
work which God had created [1]in
making *it*.

### *The Generations of the Heavens and the Earth*

**4** [a]These are the generations of
the heavens and the earth when
they were created, in [b]the day that
[1]Yahweh God made earth and heaven.

**1:20** [1]Lit *on* [2]Or *firmament* **1:21** [a]Ps 104:25-28 **1:24** [a]Ge 2:19; 6:20; 7:14; 8:19 [1]Lit *its* **1:25** [a]Ge 7:21, 22; Jer 27:5 [1]Lit *its* **1:26** [a]Ge 3:22; 11:7 [b]Ge 5:1; 9:6; 1Co 11:7; Eph 4:24; Jas 3:9 [c]Ps 8:6-8 [1]Lit *heavens* **1:27** [a]Ge 5:1f; 1Co 11:7; Eph 4:24; Col 3:10 [b]Mt 19:4; Mk 10:6 **1:28** [a]Ge 9:1, 7; Lv 26:9; Ps 127:3, 5 [1]Lit *heavens* **1:29** [a]Ps 104:14; 136:25 [1]Lit *face of* [2]Lit *in which is the fruit of a tree yielding seed* **1:30** [a]Ps 145:15, 16; 147:9 [1]Lit *heavens* [2]Lit *in which is a living soul* **1:31** [a]Ps 104:24, 28; 119:68; 1Ti 4:4 ◆ **2:1** [a]Dt 4:19; 17:3 **2:2** [a]Ex 20:8-11; 31:17 [b]Heb 4:4, 10 [1]Or *by* **2:3** [1]Lit *to make* **2:4** [a]Job 38:4-11 [b]Ge 1:3-31 [1]The personal covenant name of God, a form of I AM WHO I AM, cf. Ex 3:14-15

5 [a]Now no shrub of the field was yet
in the earth, and no plant of the field
had yet grown, [b]for Yahweh God had
not caused it to rain upon the earth,
and there was no man to [1]cultivate
the ground. 6 But a [1]stream would rise
from the earth and water the whole
[2]surface of the ground. 7 Then Yahweh
God formed man of [a]dust from the
ground and breathed into his nostrils
the breath of life; and so the [b]man
became a living [1]being. 8 And Yah-
weh God planted a [a]garden in Eden,
toward the east; and there He placed
the man whom He had formed. 9 And
out of the ground Yahweh God caused
to grow [a]every tree that is [b]desirable
in appearance and good for food; [c]the
tree of life also in the midst of the
garden, and the tree of the knowledge
of good and evil.

10 Now a [a]river went out of Eden
to water the garden; and from there
it divided and became four [1]rivers.
11 The name of the first is Pishon; it is
the one that [1]went around the whole
land of [a]Havilah, where there is gold.
12 Now the gold of that land is good;
the bdellium and the onyx stone are
there. 13 And the name of the second
river is Gihon; it is the one that [1]went
around the whole land of Cush.
14 And the name of the third river is
[a,1]Tigris; it is the one that went east
of [2]Asshur. And the fourth river is
the [b,3]Euphrates.

15 Then Yahweh God took the man
and [1]set him in the garden of Eden to
cultivate it and keep it. 16 And Yahweh
God [a]commanded the man, saying,
"From any tree of the garden you may
surely eat; 17 but from the tree of the
knowledge of good and evil, you shall
not eat from it; for in the day that you
eat from it [a]you will surely die."

18 Then Yahweh God said, "It is not
good for the man to be alone; [a]I will
make him a helper [1]suitable for him."
19 [a]And out of the ground Yahweh
God had formed every beast of the
field and every bird of the [1]sky, and
He [b]brought *each* to the man to see
what he would call it; and whatever
the man called a living creature, that
was its name. 20 And the man gave
names to all the cattle and to the
birds of the [1]sky and to every beast
of the field; but for [2]Adam there was
not found [a]a helper [3]suitable for him.
21 So Yahweh God caused a [a]deep
sleep to fall upon the man, and he
slept; then He took one of his ribs
and closed up the flesh at that place.
22 And Yahweh God [1]fashioned [a]the
rib, which He had taken from the
man, into a woman, and He brought
her to the man. 23 Then the man said,

"[a]This one finally is
    bone of my bones,
And flesh of my flesh;
This one shall be
    called [1]Woman,
Because this one was
    taken out of [2]Man."

24 [a]Therefore a man shall leave his
father and his mother, and cleave

**2:5** [a]Ge 1:11 [b]Ps 65:9, 10; Jer 10:12, 13 [1]Lit *serve* **2:6** [1]Or *mist* [2]Lit *face of* **2:7** [a]Ge 3:19 [b]1Co 15:45 [1]Lit *soul* **2:8** [a]Ge 13:10; Is 51:3; Eze 28:13 **2:9** [a]Eze 47:12 [b]Ge 3:6 [c]Ge 3:22; Rev 2:7; 22:2, 14 **2:10** [a]Ps 46:4 [1]Lit *heads* **2:11** [a]Ge 25:18 [1]Lit *surrounds* **2:13** [1]Lit *surrounds* **2:14** [a]Da 10:4 [b]Ge 15:18 [1]Heb *Hiddekel* [2]Or *Assyria* [3]Heb *Perath* **2:15** [1]Or *caused him to rest* **2:16** [a]Ge 3:2, 3 **2:17** [a]Dt 30:15, 19, 20; Ro 6:23; 1Ti 5:6; Jas 1:15 **2:18** [a]1Co 11:9 [1]Lit *corresponding to* **2:19** [a]Ge 1:24 [b]Ge 1:26 [1]Lit *heavens* **2:20** [a]Ge 2:18 [1]Lit *heavens* [2]Or *man* [3]Lit *corresponding to* **2:21** [a]Ge 15:12 **2:22** [a]1Co 11:8, 9 [1]Lit *built* **2:23** [a]Ge 29:14; Eph 5:28, 29 [1]Heb *Ishshah* [2]Heb *Ish* **2:24** [a]Mt 19:5; Mk 10:7, 8; 1Co 6:16; Eph 5:31

to his wife; and they shall become
one flesh. 25 [a]And the man and his
wife were both naked and were not
ashamed.

### *Adam and Eve Sent Out from the Garden*

3 Now [a]the serpent was more crafty
than any beast of the field which
Yahweh God had made. And he said
to the woman, "Indeed, has God said,
'[1]You shall not eat from [2]any tree of
the garden'?" 2 And the woman said
to the serpent, "[a]From the fruit of the
trees of the garden we may eat; 3 but
from the fruit of the tree which is in
the midst of the garden, God said, 'You
shall not eat from it, and you shall not
touch it, lest you die.'" 4 [a]And the ser-
pent said to the woman, "You surely
will not die! 5 For God knows that in
the day you eat from it your eyes will
be opened, and [a]you will be like God,
knowing good and evil." 6 [a]Then the
woman saw that the tree was good for
food, and that it was a delight to the
eyes, and that the tree was desirable
to make *one* wise, so she took from its
fruit and ate; and she gave also to her
husband with her, and he ate. 7 And
the eyes of both of them were opened,
and they [a]knew that they were naked;
and they sewed fig leaves together and
made themselves [1]loin coverings.

8 Then they heard the sound of
[a]Yahweh God walking in the garden
in the [1]cool of the day, [b]and the man
and his wife hid themselves from the
presence of Yahweh God in the midst
of the trees of the garden. 9 Yahweh
God called to the man and said to
him, "[a]Where are you?" 10 And he
said, "[a]I heard the sound of You in
the garden, and I was afraid because
I was naked; so I hid." 11 And He said,
"Who told you that you were naked?
Have you eaten from the tree of which
I commanded you not to eat?" 12 [a]And
the man said, "The woman whom You
gave *to be* with me, she gave to me
from the tree, and I ate." 13 Then Yah-
weh God said to the woman, "What is
this you have done?" And the woman
said, "[a]The serpent deceived me, and
I ate." 14 And Yahweh God said to the
serpent,

"[a]Because you have done this,
Cursed are you more
  than any of the cattle,
And more than every
  beast of the field;
On your belly you will go,
And [b]dust you will eat
All the days of your life;
15 And I will put [a]enmity
Between you and the woman,
And between your seed
  and her seed;
[b]He shall [1]bruise you
  on the head,
And you shall bruise
  him on the heel."

16 To the woman He said,
"I will greatly multiply
Your pain and [1]conception,
In pain you will
  [a,2]bear children;
Your desire will be
  for your husband,
And [b]he will rule over you."

---

**2:25** [a]Ge 3:7, 10, 11 ◆ **3:1** [a]2Co 11:3; Rev 12:9; 20:2 [1]Lit *you* (plural) [2]Or *every* **3:2** [a]Ge 2:16, 17
**3:4** [a]Jn 8:44; 2Co 11:3 **3:5** [a]Is 14:14; Eze 28:2, 12-17 **3:6** [a]Ro 5:12-19; 1Ti 2:14; Jas 1:14, 15; 1Jn 2:16
**3:7** [a]Is 47:3; Lam 1:8 [1]Or *girdles* **3:8** [a]Ge 18:33; Lv 26:12; Dt 23:14 [b]Job 31:33; Ps 139:1-12; Hos 10:8;
Am 9:3; Rev 6:15-17 [1]Lit *wind, breeze* **3:9** [a]Ge 4:9; 18:9 **3:10** [a]Ex 20:18, 19; Dt 5:25 **3:12** [a]Job 31:33;
Pr 28:13 **3:13** [a]2Co 11:3; 1Ti 2:14 **3:14** [a]Dt 28:15-20 [b]Is 65:25; Mic 7:17 **3:15** [a]Rev 12:17 [b]Ro 16:20
[1]Or *crush* **3:16** [a]Jn 16:21; 1Ti 2:15 [b]1Co 14:34 [1]Or *childbirth* [2]Or *give birth to*, cf. 4:1, 2, 17, 20, 22

**17** Then to Adam He said, "Because
you have listened to the voice of
your wife and have eaten from the
tree about which I commanded you,
saying, 'You shall not eat from it';
[a]Cursed is the ground
because of you;
[b]In [1]pain you will eat of it
All the days of your life.
**18** "Both thorns and thistles
it shall [a]grow for you;
And you will eat the
[1]plants of the field;
**19** By the sweat of your [1]face
You will eat bread,
Till you [a]return to the ground,
Because [b]from it
you were taken;
For you are dust,
And to dust you shall return."
**20** Now the man called his wife's
name [a,1]Eve, because she was the
mother of all *the* living. **21** Then Yah-
weh God made garments of skin for
Adam and his wife, and He clothed
them.
**22** Then Yahweh God said, "Behold,
the man has become like one of [a]Us
[1]to know good and evil; and now,
lest he send forth his hand and take
also from [b]the tree of life and eat and
live forever"— **23** therefore Yahweh
God sent him out from the garden
of Eden, to [1]cultivate the ground
from which he was taken. **24** So [a]He
drove the man out; and at the [b]east
of the garden of Eden He stationed
the [c]cherubim and the flaming sword
which turned every direction to
[1]guard the way to [d]the tree of life.

### *Cain and Abel*

**4** Now the man [1]knew his wife
Eve, and she conceived and
[2]gave birth to [3]Cain, and she said,
"I have gotten a [4]man with *the help
of* Yahweh." **2** And again, she [1]gave
birth to his brother Abel. [a]Abel was
[b]a keeper of flocks, but Cain was a
cultivator of the ground. **3** So it hap-
pened [1]in the course of time that Cain
brought an offering to Yahweh of the
fruit of the ground. **4** [a]Abel, on his
part, also brought of the firstborn of
his flock and of their fat portions.
And [b]Yahweh had regard for Abel
and for his offering; **5** but [a]for Cain
and for his offering He had no regard.
So [b]Cain became very angry, and his
countenance fell. **6** Then Yahweh said
to Cain, "[a]Why are you angry? And
why has your countenance fallen?
**7** [a]If you do well, [1]will not *your
countenance* be lifted up? [b]And if
you do not do well, sin is lying at
the door; and its desire is for you,
[c]but you must rule over it." **8** Then
Cain [1]spoke to Abel his brother; and
it happened when they were in the
field, that Cain rose up against Abel
his brother and [a]killed him.
**9** Then Yahweh said to Cain,
"[a]Where is Abel your brother?" And he
said, "I do not know. Am I my brother's

---

**3:17** [a]Ge 5:29; Ro 8:20-22; Heb 6:8 [b]Job 5:7; 14:1; Ecc 2:23 [1]Or *sorrow* **3:18** [a]Ge 2:5 [1]Lit *plant* **3:19** [a]Ps 90:3; 104:29; Ecc 12:7 [b]Ge 2:7 [1]Lit *nose* **3:20** [a]2Co 11:3; 1Ti 2:13 [1]Lit *living, life* **3:22** [a]Ge 1:26 [b]Ge 2:9; Rev 22:14 [1]Or *knowing* **3:23** [1]Lit *serve* **3:24** [a]Eze 31:11 [b]Ge 2:8 [c]Ex 25:18-22; Ps 104:4; Eze 10:1-20; Heb 1:7 [d]Ge 2:9 [1]Lit *keep*, cf. 2:15 ◆ **4:1** [1]Or *had relations with* [2]Or *bore Cain*, cf. 3:16 [3]Lit *gotten one* [4]Or *man, Yahweh* **4:2** [a]Lk 11:50, 51 [b]Ge 46:32; 47:3 [1]Or *bore his brother Abel*, cf. 3:16 **4:3** [1]Lit *at the end of days* **4:4** [a]Heb 11:4 [b]1Sa 15:22 **4:5** [a]1Sa 16:7 [b]Is 3:9; Jd 11 **4:6** [a]Jon 4:4 **4:7** [a]Jer 3:12; Mic 7:18 [b]Nu 32:23 [c]Job 11:14, 15; Ro 6:12, 16 [1]Or *surely you will be accepted.* **4:8** [a]Mt 23:35; Lk 11:51; 1Jn 3:12-15; Jd 11 [1]Lit *said*; ancient versions add *let us go into the field* **4:9** [a]Ge 3:9

keeper?" **10** And He said, "What have
you done? [a]The voice of your broth-
er's blood is crying out to Me from the
ground. **11** And now, [a]cursed are you
from the ground, which has opened
its mouth to receive your brother's
blood from your hand. **12** [a]When you
cultivate the ground, it will no longer
yield its strength to you; [b]you will
be a vagrant and a wanderer on the
earth." **13** And Cain said to Yahweh,
"My punishment is too great to bear!
**14** Behold, You have [a]driven me this
day from the face of the ground; and
from Your face I will be hidden, and [b]I
will be a vagrant and a wanderer on
the earth, and it will be that [c]whoever
finds me will kill me." **15** So Yahweh
said to him, "Therefore whoever kills
Cain, vengeance will be taken on him
[a]sevenfold." And Yahweh [b,1]appointed
a sign for Cain, so that no one who
found him would strike him.

**16** Then Cain went out from the
presence [a]of Yahweh and [1]settled in
the land of [2]Nod, east of Eden.

**17** Then Cain [1]knew his wife, and
she conceived and [2]gave birth to
Enoch; and he built a city and called
the name of the city Enoch, after the
name of his son. **18** Now to Enoch was
born Irad, and Irad [1]was the father of
Mehujael, and Mehujael [1]was the fa-
ther of Methushael, and Methushael
[1]was the father of Lamech. **19** And
Lamech took for himself [a]two wives:
the name of the one was Adah, and
the name of the other, Zillah. **20** And
Adah [1]gave birth to Jabal; he was the
father of those who live in tents and
*have* livestock. **21** And his brother's
name was Jubal; he was the father
of all those who play the lyre and
pipe. **22** As for Zillah, she also [1]gave
birth to Tubal-cain, the forger of all
implements of bronze and iron; and
the sister of Tubal-cain was Naamah.

**23** And Lamech said to his wives,
"Adah and Zillah,
Hear my voice,
You wives of Lamech,
Give ear to my word,
[a]For I [1]have killed a man
for [2]striking me;
And a boy for wounding me;
**24** If Cain is avenged [a]sevenfold,
Then Lamech
seventy-sevenfold."

**25** [a]Then Adam [1]knew his wife
again; and she [2]gave birth to a son
and named him [3]Seth, for *she said,*
"God [4]has set for me another [5]seed
in place of Abel, [b]for Cain killed him."
**26** And to Seth, to him also, [a]a son
was born; and he called his name
Enosh. Then *men* began [b]to call
[1]upon the name of Yahweh.

### *The Generations of Adam*

**5** This is the book of the generations
of Adam. In the day when God
created man, He made him [a]in the
likeness of God. **2** He created them
[a]male and female, and He [b]blessed
them and named them [1]Man in the
day when they were created.

---

**4:10** [a]Nu 35:33; Dt 21:1-9; Heb 12:24; Rev 6:9, 10 **4:11** [a]Ge 3:14; Dt 28:15-20; Ga 3:10 **4:12** [a]Dt 28:15-24; Joel 1:10-20 [b]Lv 26:17, 36 **4:14** [a]Ge 3:24; Jer 52:3 [b]Dt 28:64-67 [c]Nu 35:19 **4:15** [a]Ge 4:24 [b]Eze 9:4, 6 [1]Or *set a mark on* **4:16** [a]2Ki 24:20; Jer 23:39; 52:3 [1]Lit *dwelt* [2]Wandering **4:17** [1]Or *had relations* [2]Or *bore Enoch*, cf. 3:16 **4:18** [1]Lit *begot* **4:19** [a]Ge 2:24 **4:20** [1]Or *bore Jabal*, cf. 3:16 **4:22** [1]Or *bore Tubal-cain*, cf. 3:16 **4:23** [a]Ex 20:13; Lv 19:18; Dt 32:35; Ps 94:1 [1]Or *kill* [2]Or *bruising*, cf. Ex 21:25 **4:24** [a]Ge 4:15 **4:25** [a]Ge 5:3 [b]Ge 4:8 [1]Or *had relations* [2]Or *bore* [3]Heb *Sheth* [4]Heb *shath* [5]Or *offspring* **4:26** [a]Lk 3:38 [b]Ge 12:8; 26:25; 1Ki 18:24; Ps 116:17; Joel 2:32; Zep 3:9; 1Co 1:2 [1]Or *by*
◆ **5:1** [a]Ge 1:26, 27; Eph 4:24; Col 3:10 **5:2** [a]Mt 19:4; Mk 10:6 [b]Ge 1:28 [1]Lit *Adam*

**3** When Adam had lived 130 years,
he [1]became the father of *a son* in his
own likeness, according to his image,
and named him Seth. **4** Then the
days of Adam after he became the
father of Seth were 800 years, and
he became the father of *other* sons
and daughters. **5** So all the days that
Adam lived were 930 years, and he
died.

**6** And Seth lived 105 years and
became the father of Enosh. **7** Then
Seth lived 807 years after he became
the father of Enosh, and he had *other*
sons and daughters. **8** So all the days
of Seth were 912 years, and he died.

**9** And Enosh lived 90 years and
became the father of Kenan. **10** Then
Enosh lived 815 years after he became
the father of Kenan, and he became
the father of *other* sons and daugh-
ters. **11** So all the days of Enosh were
905 years, and he died.

**12** And Kenan lived 70 years and
became the father of Mahalalel.
**13** Then Kenan lived 840 years after
he became the father of Mahalalel,
and he became the father of *other*
sons and daughters. **14** So all the days
of Kenan were 910 years, and he died.

**15** And Mahalalel lived 65 years
and became the father of Jared.
**16** Then Mahalalel lived 830 years
after he became the father of Jared,
and he became the father of *other*
sons and daughters. **17** So all the days
of Mahalalel were 895 years, and he
died.

**18** And Jared lived 162 years and
became the father of Enoch. **19** Then
Jared lived 800 years after he be-
came the father of Enoch, and he
became the father of *other* sons and
daughters. **20** So all the days of Jared
were 962 years, and he died.

**21** And Enoch lived 65 years and
became the father of Methuselah.
**22** Then Enoch [a]walked with God
300 years after he became the father
of Methuselah, and he became the
father of *other* sons and daughters.
**23** So all the days of Enoch were 365
years. **24** [a]Enoch walked with God;
and he was not, for God [b]took him.

**25** And Methuselah lived 187 years
and became the father of Lamech.
**26** Then Methuselah lived 782
years after he became the father of
Lamech, and he became the father
of *other* sons and daughters. **27** So
all the days of Methuselah were 969
years, and he died.

**28** And Lamech lived 182 years and
became the father of a son. **29** Now he
called his name Noah, saying, "This
one will [1]give us rest from our work
and from the pain of our hands *aris-
ing* from [a]the ground which Yahweh
has cursed." **30** Then Lamech lived
595 years after he became the father
of Noah, and he became the father
of *other* sons and daughters. **31** So all
the days of Lamech were 777 years,
and he died.

**32** And Noah was [a]500 years old,
and Noah became the father of Shem,
Ham, and Japheth.

### *The Nephilim and the Daughters of Men*

**6** Now it happened, when men
began to multiply on the face of
the land, and daughters were born
to them, **2** that the sons of God saw
that the daughters of men were
good *in appearance*; and they took

**5:3** [1]Lit *begot*, so in ch **5:22** [a]Ge 6:9; 17:1; 24:40; 48:15; Mic 6:8; Mal 2:6; 1Th 2:12 **5:24** [a]2Ki 2:11; Jd 14 [b]2Ki 2:10; Ps 49:15; 73:24; Heb 11:5 **5:29** [a]Ge 3:17-19; 4:11 [1]Lit *comfort us in* **5:32** [a]Ge 7:6

wives for themselves, whomever
they chose. **3** Then Yahweh said,
"[a]My Spirit shall not [1]strive with
man forever [b,2]because he indeed
is flesh; [3]nevertheless his days shall
be 120 years." **4** The [a]Nephilim were
on the earth in those days, and also
afterward, when the sons of God
came in to the daughters of men, and
they bore *children* to them. Those
were the mighty men who *were* of
old, men of renown.

**5** Then Yahweh saw that the evil
of man was great on the earth, and
that [a]every intent of the thoughts of
his heart was only evil continually.
**6** [a]And Yahweh regretted that He
had made man on the earth, and
He was [b]grieved [1]in His heart. **7** And
Yahweh said, "[a]I will blot out man
whom I have created from the face
of the land, from man to animals to
creeping things and to birds of the
[1]sky; for [b]I regret that I have made
them." **8** But [a]Noah [b]found favor in
the eyes of Yahweh.

### *The Generations of Noah*

**9** These are the generations of
Noah. Noah was a [a]righteous man,
[b,1]blameless among *those in* his
generations; Noah [c]walked with God.
**10** And Noah [1]became the father of
three sons: Shem, Ham, and Japheth.

**11** Now the earth was [a]corrupt
before God, and the earth was [b]filled
with violence. **12** And God saw the
earth, and behold, it was corrupt;
for [a]all flesh had corrupted their
way upon the earth.

**13** Then God said to Noah, "[a]The
end of all flesh has come before Me;
for the earth is filled with violence
because of them; and behold, I am
about to destroy them with the earth.
**14** Make for yourself an ark of gopher
wood; you shall make the ark with
rooms, and you shall [1]cover it inside
and out with pitch. **15** Now this is
how you shall make it: the length of
the ark [1]300 cubits, its breadth 50
cubits, and its height 30 cubits. **16** You
shall make a [1]window for the ark, and
complete it to one [2]cubit from [3]the
top; and set the door of the ark in the
side of it; you shall make it with low-
er, second, and third decks. **17** As for
Me, behold [a]I am bringing the flood
of water upon the earth, to destroy
all flesh in which is the breath of life,
from under heaven; everything that
is on the earth shall breathe its last.
**18** But I will establish [a]My covenant
with you; and [b]you shall enter the
ark—you and your sons and your
wife and your sons' wives with you.
**19** [a]And of every living thing of all
flesh, you shall bring two of every
*kind* into the ark, to keep *them* alive
with you; they shall be male and
female. **20** [a]Of the birds after their
kind, and of the animals after their
kind, of every creeping thing of the
ground after its kind, two of every

◆ **6:3** [a]Ga 5:16, 17; 1Pe 3:20 [b]Ps 78:39 [1]Or *rule in*; some ancient versions *abide in* [2]Or *in his going astray he is flesh* [3]Or *therefore* **6:4** [a]Nu 13:33 **6:5** [a]Ge 8:21; Ps 14:1-3; Pr 6:18; Mt 15:19; Ro 1:28-32 **6:6** [a]Ge 6:7; Jer 18:7-10 [b]Is 63:10; Eph 4:30 [1]Lit *to* **6:7** [a]Dt 28:63; 29:20 [b]Ge 6:6; Am 7:3, 6 [1]Lit *heavens* **6:8** [a]Mt 24:37; Lk 17:26; 1Pe 3:20 [b]Ge 19:19; Ex 33:17; Lk 1:30 **6:9** [a]Ps 37:39; 2Pe 2:5 [b]Ge 17:1; Dt 18:13; Job 1:1 [c]Ge 5:24 [1]Or *having integrity*; lit *complete, perfect* **6:10** [1]Lit *begot* **6:11** [a]Dt 31:29; Jdg 2:19 [b]Eze 8:17 **6:12** [a]Ps 14:1-3 **6:13** [a]Is 34:1-4; Eze 7:2, 3; Am 8:2; 1Pe 4:7 **6:14** [1]Or *pitch* **6:15** [1]Approx. 450 ft. long, 75 ft. wide, and 45 ft. high or 135 m, 23 m, and 14 m **6:16** [1]Or *roof* [2]A cubit was approx. 18 in. or 45 cm [3]Lit *above* **6:17** [a]2Pe 2:5 **6:18** [a]Ge 9:9-16; 17:7 [b]Ge 7:7 **6:19** [a]Ge 7:2, 14, 15 **6:20** [a]Ge 7:3

*kind* will come to you to keep *them*
alive. **21** As for you, take for yourself
some of all [a]food which is edible,
and gather *it* to yourself; and it shall
be for food for you and for them."
**22** [a]Thus Noah did; according to all
that God had commanded him, so
he did.

### *Noah and the Flood*

**7** Then Yahweh said to Noah,
"Enter the ark, you and all your
household, for you *alone* I have
seen *to be* [a]righteous before Me
in this generation. **2** You shall take
[1]with you of every [a]clean animal [2]by
sevens, a male and his female; and of
the animals that are not clean, two,
a male and his female; **3** also of the
birds of the [1]sky, [2]by sevens, male
and female, to keep *their* seed alive
on the face of all the earth. **4** For after
[a]seven more days, I will send rain
on the earth [b]forty days and forty
nights; and I will blot out from the
face of the land [c]every living thing
that I have made." **5** [a]And Noah did
according to all that Yahweh had
commanded him.

**6** Now Noah was [a]six hundred
years old when the flood of water
[1]came upon the earth. **7** Then [a]Noah
and his sons and his wife and his
sons' wives with him entered the
ark because of the water of the flood.
**8** [a]Of clean animals and animals that
are not clean and birds and every-
thing that creeps on the ground,
**9** [1]by twos they came to Noah into
the ark, male and female, as God
had commanded Noah. **10** Now it
happened after [a]the seven days, that
the water of the flood [1]came upon the
earth. **11** In the [a]six hundredth year of
Noah's life, in the second month, on
the seventeenth day of the month, on
this day all [b]the fountains of the great
deep split open, and the [1]floodgates
of the sky were opened. **12** [a]Then the
rain [1]came upon the earth for forty
days and forty nights.

**13** On this very day [a]Noah and
Shem and Ham and Japheth, the sons
of Noah, and Noah's wife and the
three wives of his sons with them,
entered the ark, **14** they and every
beast after its kind, and all the cattle
after [1]their kind, and every creeping
thing that creeps on the earth after its
kind, and every bird after its kind—
every [2]fowl, every winged creature.
**15** So they came to Noah into the ark,
[a]by twos of all flesh in which was
the breath of life. **16** And those that
entered, male and female of all flesh,
entered as God had commanded him;
and Yahweh closed *it* behind him.

**17** Then the flood [1]came upon the
earth for [a]forty days, and the water
multiplied and lifted up the ark, so
that it rose above the earth. **18** And
the water prevailed and multiplied
greatly upon the earth, and the ark
went on the [1]surface of the water.
**19** And the water prevailed more
and more upon the earth, so that
all the high mountains under all the
heavens were covered. **20** The water
prevailed [1]fifteen cubits higher, [a]and
the mountains were covered. **21** [a]And

---

**6:21** [a]Ge 1:29, 30 **6:22** [a]Ge 7:5; Heb 11:7 ♦**7:1** [a]Ge 6:9 **7:2** [a]Lv 11:1-31; Dt 14:3-20 [1]Lit *to* [2]Lit *seven seven* **7:3** [1]Lit *heavens* [2]Lit *seven seven* **7:4** [a]Ge 7:10 [b]Ge 7:12, 17 [c]Ge 6:7, 13 **7:5** [a]Ge 6:22 **7:6** [a]Ge 5:32 [1]Lit *was* **7:7** [a]Ge 6:18; 7:13; Mt 24:38f; Lk 17:27 **7:8** [a]Ge 6:19, 20; 7:2, 3 **7:9** [1]Lit *two two* **7:10** [a]Ge 7:4 [1]Lit *were* **7:11** [a]Ge 7:6 [b]Ge 8:2 [1]Or *windows of the heavens* **7:12** [a]Ge 7:4, 17 [1]Lit *was* **7:13** [a]Ge 6:18; 7:7 **7:14** [1]Lit *its* [2]Lit *bird* **7:15** [a]Ge 6:19; 7:9 **7:17** [a]Ge 7:4 [1]Lit *was* **7:18** [1]Lit *face* **7:20** [a]Ge 8:4 [1]Approx. 22.5 ft. or 6.75 m **7:21** [a]Ge 6:7, 13, 17; 7:4

all flesh that [1]moved on the earth breathed its last, that is birds and cattle and beasts and every swarming thing that swarms upon the earth, as well as all mankind. **22** All [a]in whose nostrils was the breath of the spirit of life—of all that was on the dry land—died. **23** Thus He blotted out [1]every living thing that was upon the face of the land, from man to animals to creeping things and to birds of the [2]sky, and they were blotted out from the earth; and only [a]Noah remained, and those that were with him in the ark. **24** [a]And the water prevailed upon the earth 150 days.

### *The Water Dries Up*

**8** Then [a]God remembered Noah and all the beasts and all the cattle that were with him in the ark; and [b]God caused a wind to pass over the earth, and the water subsided. **2** Also [a]the fountains of the deep and the [1]floodgates of the sky were closed, and [b]the rain from the sky was restrained; **3** and the water receded from the earth, going *forth* and returning, and at the end [a]of 150 days the water decreased. **4** In the seventh month, on the seventeenth day of the month, [a]the ark rested upon the mountains of Ararat. **5** Now the water decreased steadily until the tenth month; in the tenth *month*, on the first day of the month, the tops of the mountains appeared.

**6** Then it happened at the end of forty days, that Noah opened the [a]window of the ark which he had made; **7** and he sent out a raven, and it went out *flying* back and forth until the water was dried up [1]from the earth. **8** Then he sent out a dove from him, to see if the water was abated from the face of the land; **9** but the dove found no resting place for the sole of its foot, so it returned to him into the ark, for the water was on the [1]surface of all the earth. Then he stretched out his hand and took it and brought it into the ark to himself. **10** Then he waited yet another seven days; and again he sent out the dove from the ark. **11** And the dove came to him toward [1]evening, and behold, in its [2]beak was a freshly picked olive leaf. So Noah knew that the water was abated from the earth. **12** Then he waited yet another seven days and sent out [a]the dove; but it did not return to him again.

**13** Now it happened in the [a]six hundred and first year, in the first *month*, on the first of the month, the water was dried up [1]from the earth. Then Noah removed the covering of the ark and looked, and behold, the [2]surface of the ground was dried up. **14** In the second month, on the twenty-seventh day of the month, the earth was dry. **15** Then God spoke to Noah, saying, **16** "Go out of the ark, you and your wife and your sons and your sons' wives with you. **17** Bring out with you every living thing of all flesh that is with you, birds and animals and every creeping thing that creeps on the earth, that they may [a]swarm on the earth, and that they may be fruitful and multiply on the earth." **18** So Noah went out, and

---

**7:21** [1]Or *crept* **7:22** [a]Ge 2:7 **7:23** [a]Mt 24:38, 39; Lk 17:26, 27; Heb 11:7; 1Pe 3:20; 2Pe 2:5 [1]Lit *all existence* [2]Lit *heavens* **7:24** [a]Ge 8:3 ◆ **8:1** [a]Ge 19:29; Ex 2:24; 1Sa 1:19; Ps 105:42 [b]Ex 14:21; 15:10; Job 12:15; Ps 29:10; Is 44:27; Na 1:4 **8:2** [a]Ge 7:11 [b]Ge 7:4, 12 [1]Or *windows of the heavens* **8:3** [a]Ge 7:24 **8:4** [a]Ge 7:20 **8:6** [a]Ge 6:16 **8:7** [1]Lit *from upon* **8:9** [1]Lit *face* **8:11** [1]Lit *the time of evening* [2]Lit *mouth* **8:12** [a]Jer 48:28 **8:13** [a]Ge 7:6 [1]Lit *from upon* [2]Lit *face* **8:17** [a]Ge 1:22, 28

his sons and his wife and his sons'
wives with him. **19** Every beast, every
creeping thing, and every bird, every-
thing that moves on the earth, went
out [1]by their families from the ark.

### *Yahweh's Covenant with Noah*

**20** Then Noah built [a]an altar to Yah-
weh and took of every [b]clean animal
and of every clean bird and offered
[c]burnt offerings on the altar. **21** And
Yahweh [a]smelled the [1]soothing aro-
ma; and Yahweh said [2]to Himself, "I
will never again [b]curse the ground
because of man, for [c]the [3]intent of
man's heart is evil from his youth;
[d]and I will never again strike down
every living thing as I have done.
**22** "While all the days
of the earth *remain*,
Seedtime and harvest,
And cold and heat,
And [a]summer and winter,
And [b]day and night
Shall not cease."

**9** And God blessed Noah and his
sons and said to them, "[a]Be
fruitful and multiply, and fill the
earth. **2** And the fear of you and the
terror of you will be on every beast
of the earth and on every bird of the
[1]sky; with everything that creeps on
the ground, and all the fish of the
sea, into your hand they are given.
**3** Every moving thing that is alive
shall be food for you; [a]as *with* the
green plant, I give all to you. **4** How-
ever, flesh with its life, *that is*, [a]its
blood, you shall not eat. **5** Surely I
will require [a,1]your lifeblood; [b,2]from
every living thing I will require it.
And [2]from *every* man, [2]from each
man's brother I will require the life
of man.
**6** "[a]Whoever sheds man's blood,
By man his blood
shall be shed,
For [b]in the image of God
He made man.
**7** "As for you, [a]be fruitful
and multiply;
[1]Swarm on the earth
and multiply in it."
**8** Then God spoke to Noah and to
his sons with him, saying, **9** "As for
Me, behold, [a]I establish My covenant
with you and with your seed after
you; **10** and with every living creature
that is with you, the birds, the cattle,
and every beast of the earth with you;
of all that comes out of the ark, even
every beast of the earth. **11** Indeed I
establish My covenant with you; and
all flesh shall [a]never again be cut off
by the water of the flood, [b]and there
shall never again be a flood to destroy
the earth." **12** Then God said, "This is
[a]the sign of the covenant which I am
giving *to be* between Me and you and
every living creature that is with you,
for [1]all successive generations; **13** I put
My [a]bow in the cloud, and it shall be
for a sign of a covenant between Me
and the earth. **14** And it will be, when
I bring a cloud over the earth, that
the bow will be seen in the cloud,

---

**8:19** [1]Or *according to their kind* **8:20** [a]Ge 12:7, 8; 13:18; 22:9 [b]Ge 7:2; Lv 11:1-47 [c]Ge 22:2; Ex 10:25 **8:21** [a]Ex 29:18, 25 [b]Ge 3:17; 6:7, 13, 17; Is 54:9 [c]Ge 6:5; Ps 51:5; Jer 17:9; Ro 1:21; 3:23; Eph 2:1-3 [d]Ge 9:11, 15 [1]Or *resting*; related to Noah, cf. 5:29 [2]Lit *to His heart* [3]Or *inclination* **8:22** [a]Ps 74:17 [b]Jer 33:20, 25 ◆**9:1** [a]Ge 1:28; 9:7 **9:2** [1]Lit *heavens* **9:3** [a]Ge 1:29 **9:4** [a]Lv 7:26f; 17:10-16; 19:26; Dt 12:16, 23; 15:23; 1Sa 14:34; Ac 15:20, 29 **9:5** [a]Ex 20:13; 21:12 [b]Ex 21:28, 29 [1]Lit *your blood of your lives* [2]Lit *from the hand of* **9:6** [a]Ex 21:12-14; Lv 24:17; Nu 35:33; Mt 26:52 [b]Ge 1:26, 27 **9:7** [a]Ge 9:1 [1]Or *increase*, cf. Ex 1:7 **9:9** [a]Ge 6:18 **9:11** [a]Ge 8:21 [b]Is 54:9 **9:12** [a]Ge 9:13, 17; 17:11 [1]Or *everlasting generations* **9:13** [a]Eze 1:28

15 and [a]I will remember My covenant,
which is between Me and you and
every living creature of all flesh;
and [b]never again shall the water
become a flood to destroy all flesh.
16 So the bow shall be in the cloud,
and I will look upon it, to remember
the [a]everlasting covenant between
God and every living creature of all
flesh that is on the earth." 17 And God
said to Noah, "This is the sign of the
covenant which I have established
between Me and all flesh that is on
the earth."

### *Noah's Three Sons*

18 Now the sons of Noah who went
out of the ark were Shem and Ham
and Japheth; and [a]Ham was the
father of Canaan. 19 These three
*were* the sons of Noah, and [a]from
these the whole earth was scattered
abroad.
20 Then Noah began *to be* [1]a man
of the land and planted a vineyard.
21 And he drank of the wine and
[a]became drunk and uncovered
himself inside his tent. 22 Then
Ham, the father of Canaan, [a]saw
the nakedness of his father and told
his two brothers outside. 23 But Shem
and Japheth took the garment and
laid it upon both their shoulders and
walked backward and covered the
nakedness of their father; and their
faces were turned backward, so that
they did not see their father's naked-
ness. 24 Then Noah awoke from his
wine, and he knew what his youngest
son had done to him. 25 So he said,

"[a]Cursed be Canaan;
[b,1]A servant of servants
He shall be to his brothers."
26 And he said,
"[a]Blessed be Yahweh,
The God of Shem;
And let Canaan be
[1]his servant.
27 "[a]May God enlarge Japheth,
And let him dwell
in the tents of Shem;
And let Canaan be
[1]his servant."

28 And Noah lived 350 years after
the flood. 29 So all the days of Noah
were 950 years, and he died.

### *The Generations of Shem, Ham, and Japheth*

10 Now these are the generations
of Shem, Ham, and Japheth,
the sons of Noah; and sons were born
to them after the flood.
2 [a]The sons of Japheth *were* [b]Gomer
and Magog and [c]Madai and [d]Javan and
Tubal and [e]Meshech and Tiras. 3 The
sons of Gomer *were* [a]Ashkenaz and
[1]Riphath and [b]Togarmah. 4 The sons
of Javan *were* Elishah and [a]Tarshish,
Kittim and [1]Dodanim. 5 From these
the coastlands of the nations [1]were
separated into their lands, every one
according to his tongue, according to
their families, into their nations.
6 [a]The sons of Ham *were* Cush
and [1]Mizraim and Put and Canaan.
7 The sons of Cush *were* [a]Seba and
Havilah and Sabtah and [b]Raamah
and Sabteca; and the sons of Raamah
*were* [b]Sheba and [c]Dedan. 8 Now Cush

---

**9:15** [a]Lv 26:42, 45; Dt 7:9; Eze 16:60 [b]Ge 9:11 **9:16** [a]Ge 17:13, 19; 2Sa 23:5 **9:18** [a]Ge 9:25-27; 10:6 **9:19** [a]Ge 9:1, 7; 10:32; 1Chr 1:4 **9:20** [1]Or *a farmer* **9:21** [a]Pr 20:1 **9:22** [a]Hab 2:15 **9:25** [a]Dt 27:16 [b]Jos 9:23 [1]The lowest of servants **9:26** [a]Ge 14:20; 24:27 [1]Or *their* **9:27** [a]Ge 10:2-5; Is 66:19 [1]Or *their* ◆**10:2** [a]1Chr 1:5-7 [b]Eze 38:2, 6 [c]2Ki 17:6 [d]Is 66:19 [e]Eze 38:2 **10:3** [a]Jer 51:27 [b]Eze 27:14 [1]In 1Chr 1:6, *Diphath* **10:4** [a]Eze 27:12, 25 [1]In 1Chr 1:7, *Rodanim* **10:5** [1]Or *separated themselves* **10:6** [a]1Chr 1:8-10 [1]Or *Egypt* **10:7** [a]Is 43:3 [b]Eze 27:22 [c]Eze 27:15, 20

[1]was the father of Nimrod; he began to be a mighty one on the earth. **9** He was a mighty hunter before Yahweh; therefore it is said, "Like Nimrod a mighty hunter before Yahweh." **10** The beginning of his kingdom was [a,1]Babel and Erech and Accad and Calneh, in the land of [b]Shinar. **11** From that land he went out [a]to Assyria and built Nineveh and Rehoboth-Ir and Calah, **12** and Resen between Nineveh and Calah; that is the great city. **13** Mizraim [1]was the father of [a]Ludim and Anamim and Lehabim and Naphtuhim **14** and [a]Pathrusim and Casluhim (from whom came the Philistines) and Caphtorim.

**15** Canaan [1]was the father of [a]Sidon, his firstborn, and [b]Heth **16** and [a]the Jebusite and the Amorite and the Girgashite **17** and the Hivite and the Arkite and the Sinite **18** and the Arvadite and the Zemarite and the Hamathite; and afterward the families of the Canaanite were scattered. **19** [a]The border of the Canaanite [1]extended from Sidon as you go toward Gerar, as far as Gaza; as you go toward [b]Sodom and Gomorrah and Admah and Zeboiim, as far as Lasha. **20** These are the sons of Ham, according to their families, according to their tongues, by their lands, by their nations.

**21** Also to Shem, the father of all the children of Eber, *and* the [1]older brother of Japheth, children were born. **22** [a]The sons of Shem *were* [b]Elam and Asshur and [c]Arpachshad and [d]Lud and Aram. **23** The sons of Aram *were* [a]Uz and Hul and Gether and Mash. **24** Arpachshad [1]was the father of [a]Shelah; and Shelah [1]was the father of Eber. **25** [a]Now two sons were born to Eber; the name of the one *was* [1]Peleg, for in his days the earth was divided; and his brother's name *was* Joktan. **26** And Joktan [1]was the father of Almodad and Sheleph and Hazarmaveth and Jerah **27** and Hadoram and Uzal and Diklah **28** and [1]Obal and Abimael and Sheba **29** and Ophir and Havilah and Jobab; all these were the sons of Joktan. **30** Now their [1]settlement [2]extended from Mesha as you go toward Sephar, the hill country of the east. **31** These are the sons of Shem, according to their families, according to their tongues, by their lands, according to their nations.

**32** These are the families of the sons of Noah, according to their generations, by their nations; and [a]out of these the nations were separated on the earth after the flood.

### *The Tower of Babel*

**11** Now the whole earth [1]had the same language and [2]the same words. **2** And it happened as they journeyed east, that they found a plain in the land [a]of Shinar and [1]settled there. **3** Then they said to one another, "Come, let us make bricks and burn *them* thoroughly." And they had brick for stone, and they had [a]tar for mortar. **4** And they

---

**10:8** [1]Lit *begot* **10:10** [a]Ge 11:9 [b]Ge 11:2; 14:1 [1]Or *Babylon* **10:11** [a]Mic 5:6 **10:13** [a]Jer 46:9 [1]Lit *begot* **10:14** [a]1Chr 1:12 **10:15** [a]1Chr 1:13; Jer 47:4 [b]Ge 23:3 [1]Lit *begot* **10:16** [a]Ge 15:19-21 **10:19** [a]Nu 34:2-12 [b]Ge 14:2, 3 [1]Lit *was* **10:21** [1]Or *the brother of Japheth the elder* **10:22** [a]1Chr 1:17 [b]Ge 14:1, 9 [c]Ge 11:10 [d]Is 66:19 **10:23** [a]Job 1:1; Jer 25:20 **10:24** [a]Ge 11:12; Lk 3:35 [1]Lit *begot* **10:25** [a]1Chr 1:19 [1]Lit *division* **10:26** [1]Lit *begot* **10:28** [1]In 1Chr 1:22, *Ebal* **10:30** [1]Lit *dwelling* [2]Lit *was* **10:32** [a]Ge 9:19 ♦**11:1** [1]Lit *was one lip* [2]Or *one* set of *words* **11:2** [a]Ge 10:10; 14:1; Da 1:2 [1]Lit *dwelt* **11:3** [a]Ge 14:10

said, "Come, let us build for ourselves
a city, and a tower whose top [a]*will
reach* into heaven, and let us make
for ourselves [b]a name, lest we [c]be
scattered over the face of the whole
earth." **5** [a]Then Yahweh came down
to see the city and the tower which
the sons of men had built. **6** And
Yahweh said, "Behold, they are one
people, and they all have [a,1]the same
language. And this is what they have
begun to do. So now nothing which
they purpose to do will be [2]impossi-
ble for them. **7** Come, [a]let Us go down
and there [b]confuse their [1]language,
so that they will not understand one
another's [1]language." **8** So Yahweh
[a]scattered them from there over the
face of the whole earth; and they
stopped building the city. **9** Therefore
its name was called [a,1]Babel, because
there Yahweh confused the [2]language
of the whole earth; and from there
Yahweh scattered them over the face
of the whole earth.

### *The Generations of Shem*

**10** [a]These are the generations of
Shem. Shem was 100 years old and
[1]became the father of Arpachshad
two years after the flood; **11** and Shem
lived 500 years after he became the
father of Arpachshad, and he became
the father of *other* sons and daugh-
ters.

**12** And Arpachshad lived 35 years
and became the father of Shelah;
**13** and Arpachshad lived 403 years
after he became the father of Shelah,
and he became the father of *other*
sons and daughters.

**14** And Shelah lived 30 years and
became the father of Eber; **15** and
Shelah lived 403 years after he
became the father of Eber, and he
became the father of *other* sons and
daughters.

**16** And Eber lived 34 years and be-
came the father of Peleg; **17** and Eber
lived 430 years after he became the
father of Peleg, and he became the
father of *other* sons and daughters.

**18** And Peleg lived 30 years and
became the father of Reu; **19** and
Peleg lived 209 years after he became
the father of Reu, and he became the
father of *other* sons and daughters.

**20** And Reu lived 32 years and be-
came the father of Serug; **21** and Reu
lived 207 years after he became the
father of Serug, and he became the
father of *other* sons and daughters.

**22** And Serug lived 30 years and
became the father of Nahor; **23** and
Serug lived 200 years after he be-
came the father of Nahor, and he
became the father of *other* sons and
daughters.

**24** Nahor lived 29 years and became
the father of [a]Terah; **25** and Nahor
lived 119 years after he became the
father of Terah, and he became the
father of *other* sons and daughters.

**26** And Terah lived 70 years and
became [a]the father of Abram, Nahor,
and Haran.

### *The Generations of Terah*

**27** Now these are the generations of
Terah. Terah became the father of
Abram, Nahor, and Haran; and [a]Ha-
ran became the father of [b]Lot. **28** And

---

**11:4** [a]Dt 1:28; 9:1; Ps 107:26 [b]Ge 6:4; 2Sa 8:13 [c]Dt 4:27 **11:5** [a]Ge 18:21; Ex 3:8; 19:11, 18, 20
**11:6** [a]Ge 11:1 [1]Lit *one lip* [2]Lit *withheld from* **11:7** [a]Ge 1:26 [b]Ge 42:23; Ex 4:11; Dt 28:49; Is 33:19; Jer 5:15 [1]Lit *lip* **11:8** [a]Ge 11:4; Ps 92:9; Lk 1:51 **11:9** [a]Ge 10:10 [1]Or *Babylon* [2]Lit *lip*
**11:10** [a]Ge 10:22-25 [1]Lit *begot*, so in ch **11:24** [a]Jos 24:2 **11:26** [a]Jos 24:2 **11:27** [a]Ge 11:31; 12:4 [b]Ge 13:10; 14:12; 19:1, 29

Haran died [1]in the presence of Terah
his father in the land of his birth, in
[a]Ur of the Chaldeans. **29** Abram and
[a]Nahor took wives for themselves.
The name of Abram's wife was [b]Sarai;
and the name of Nahor's wife was
[c]Milcah, the daughter of Haran, the
father of Milcah and the father of
Iscah. **30** [a]And Sarai was barren; she
had no child.

**31** And Terah took Abram his
son, and Lot the son of Haran, his
grandson, and Sarai his daughter-in-
law, his son Abram's wife; and they
went out [1]together from [a]Ur of the
Chaldeans in order to go to the land
of Canaan; and they came as far as
Haran and [2]settled there. **32** And the
days of Terah were 205 years; and
Terah died in Haran.

### *Yahweh Appears to Abram*

**12** And [a]Yahweh said to Abram,
"[1]Go forth from your land,
And from your kin
And from your father's house,
To the land which I
will show you;
**2** And [a]I will make you
a great nation,
And [b]I will bless you,
And make your name great;
And so [c,1]you shall
be a blessing;
**3** And [a]I will bless those
who bless you,
And the one who [1]curses
you I will [2]curse.
[b]And in you all the families
of the earth will be blessed."

**4** So Abram went forth as Yahweh
had spoken to him; and [a]Lot went
with him. Now Abram was seventy-
five years old when he departed
from Haran. **5** So Abram took Sarai
his wife and Lot his brother's son,
and all their [a]possessions which they
had accumulated, and [b]the [1]persons
which they had acquired in Haran,
and they departed to go forth to the
land of Canaan; [c]thus they came to
the land of Canaan. **6** And Abram
passed through the land as far as
the site of [a]Shechem, to the [1]oak of
Moreh. Now the Canaanite *was* then
in the land. **7** Then Yahweh [a]appeared
to Abram and said, "[b]To your seed I
will give this land." So he built [c]an
altar there to Yahweh who had ap-
peared to him. **8** Then he proceeded
from there to the mountain on the
east of Bethel, and he pitched his tent
with [a]Bethel on the west and Ai on
the east; and there he built an altar to
Yahweh and [b]called upon the name
of Yahweh. **9** And Abram journeyed
on, continuing toward [a]the [1]Negev.

### *Abram and Sarai in Egypt*

**10** Now there was [a]a famine in the
land; so Abram went down to Egypt
to sojourn there, for the famine was
[b]severe in the land. **11** And it hap-
pened as he drew near to entering
Egypt, that he said to Sarai his wife,
"Now behold, I know that you are

**11:28** [a]Ge 11:31 [1]Or *during the lifetime of* **11:29** [a]Ge 24:10 [b]Ge 17:15; 20:12 [c]Ge 22:20, 23; 24:15 **11:30** [a]Ge 16:1 **11:31** [a]Ge 15:7; Ne 9:7; Ac 7:4 [1]Lit *with them* [2]Lit *dwelt* ◆ **12:1** [a]Ge 15:7; Ac 7:3; Heb 11:8 [1]Lit *Go for yourself* **12:2** [a]Ge 17:4-6; 18:18; 46:3; Dt 26:5 [b]Ge 22:17 [c]Zec 8:13 [1]Lit *be a blessing* **12:3** [a]Ge 24:35; 27:29; Nu 24:9 [b]Ge 22:18; 26:4; 28:14; Ac 3:25; Ga 3:8 [1]Or *declares you insignificant, declares you contemptible* [2]Or *bind under a curse* **12:4** [a]Ge 11:27, 31 **12:5** [a]Ge 13:6 [b]Ge 14:14; Lv 22:11 [c]Ge 11:31; Heb 11:8 [1]Lit *souls* **12:6** [a]Ge 35:4; Dt 11:30 [1]Or *terebinth* **12:7** [a]Ge 17:1; 18:1 [b]Ge 13:15; 15:18; Dt 34:4; Ps 105:9-12; Ac 7:5; Ga 3:16 [c]Ge 13:4, 18; 22:9 **12:8** [a]Jos 8:9, 12 [b]Ge 4:26; 21:33 **12:9** [a]Ge 13:1, 3; 20:1; 24:62 [1]South country **12:10** [a]Ge 26:1 [b]Ge 43:1

a woman [a]beautiful in appearance;
**12** [a]and it will be when the Egyptians
see you, that they will say, 'This is
his wife'; and they will kill me,
but they will let you live. **13** Please
say that you are [a]my sister so that
it may go well with me because of
you, and that [b,1]I may live on account
of you." **14** Now it happened when
Abram came into Egypt, that the
Egyptians [1]saw that the woman was
very beautiful. **15** And Pharaoh's
officials saw her and praised her to
Pharaoh; and [a]the woman was taken
into Pharaoh's house. **16** Therefore
[a]he treated Abram well because of
her; and sheep and oxen and donkeys
and male and female servants and
female donkeys and camels [b,1]came
into his possession.

**17** But Yahweh [a]struck Pharaoh and
his house with great plagues because
of Sarai, Abram's wife. **18** Then Phar-
aoh called Abram and said, "[a]What
is this you have done to me? Why
did you not tell me that she was your
wife? **19** Why did you say, 'She is my
sister,' so that I took her for myself
as a wife? So now, [1]here is your wife,
take her and go." **20** So Pharaoh
commanded *his* men concerning
him; and they [1]sent him away with
his wife and all that belonged to him.

### *Abram and Lot Separate*

**13** So Abram went up from Egypt
to [a]the [1]Negev, he and his wife
and all that belonged to him, and Lot
with him.
**2** Now Abram was [a]very rich
in livestock, in silver and in gold.
**3** And he went [1]on his journeys from
the [2]Negev as far as Bethel, to the
place where his tent had been at the
beginning, [a]between Bethel and Ai,
**4** to the place of the [a]altar which he
had made there formerly; and there
Abram called upon the name of
Yahweh.

**5** Now [a]Lot, who was going with
Abram, also had flocks and herds
and tents. **6** And [a]the land could not
[1]sustain them [2]while living togeth-
er, [b]for their possessions were so
abundant that they were not able to
live together. **7** [a]And there was strife
between the herdsmen of Abram's
livestock and the herdsmen of Lot's
livestock. Now [b]the Canaanite and
the Perizzite were living then in the
land.

**8** [a]So Abram said to Lot, "Please let
there be no strife between you and
me, nor between my herdsmen and
your herdsmen, for we are brothers.
**9** Is not the whole land before you?
Please separate from me; if *to* the
left, then I will go to the right; or if
*to* the right, then I will go to the left."
**10** Then Lot lifted up his eyes and saw
all the [a,1]valley of the Jordan, that it
was well watered everywhere—
*this was* before Yahweh [b]destroyed
Sodom and Gomorrah—like [c]the
garden of Yahweh, [d]like the land of
Egypt as you go to [e]Zoar. **11** So Lot
chose for himself all the [1]valley of the
Jordan, and Lot journeyed eastward.

---

**12:11** [a]Ge 26:7; 29:17 **12:12** [a]Ge 20:11 **12:13** [a]Ge 20:2, 5, 12; 26:7 [b]Jer 38:17, 20 [1]Lit *my soul*
**12:14** [1]Lit *saw the woman that she was* **12:15** [a]Ge 20:2 **12:16** [a]Ge 20:14 [b]Ge 13:2 [1]Lit *he had*
**12:17** [a]Ge 20:18; 1Chr 16:21; Ps 105:14 **12:18** [a]Ge 20:9, 10; 26:10 **12:19** [1]Or *behold* **12:20** [1]Or *let him go*, cf. Ex 3:20; 4:21 ◆ **13:1** [a]Ge 12:9 [1]South country **13:2** [a]Ge 24:35 **13:3** [a]Ge 12:8 [1]Lit *by his stages* [2]South country **13:4** [a]Ge 12:7, 8 **13:5** [a]Ge 12:5 **13:6** [a]Ge 36:7 [b]Ge 12:5, 16; 13:2 [1]Lit *bear* [2]Lit *to dwell* **13:7** [a]Ge 26:20 [b]Ge 12:6; 15:20, 21 **13:8** [a]Pr 15:18; 20:3 **13:10** [a]Ge 19:17-29; Dt 34:3 [b]Ge 19:24 [c]Ge 2:8, 10 [d]Ge 47:6 [e]Ge 14:2, 8; 19:22; Dt 34:3 [1]Lit *circle* **13:11** [1]Lit *circle*

Thus they separated from each other.
12 Abram lived in the land of Canaan,
while Lot lived in [a]the cities of the
[1]valley and moved his tents as far as
Sodom. 13 Now [a]the men of Sodom
were evil and [b]sinners, exceedingly
so, against Yahweh.
14 And Yahweh said to Abram, after
Lot had separated from him, "[a]Now
lift up your eyes and look from the
place where you are, [b]northward
and southward and eastward and
westward; 15 [a]for all the land which
you see, [b]I will give it to you and to
your seed forever. 16 And I will make
your seed [a]as the dust of the earth, so
that if anyone can number the dust of
the earth, then your seed can also be
numbered. 17 Arise, [a]walk about the
land through its length and breadth;
for [b]I will give it to you." 18 Then
Abram moved his tent and came and
lived by the [a,1]oaks of Mamre, which
are in Hebron, and there he built [b]an
altar to Yahweh.

### *Kings of the Valley Take Lot*

14 And it happened in the days
of Amraphel king of [a]Shinar,
Arioch king of Ellasar, Chedorlao-
mer king of [b]Elam, and Tidal king
of [1]Goiim, 2 *that* they made war with
Bera king of Sodom, and with Birsha
king of Gomorrah, Shinab king of
[a]Admah, and Shemeber king of
[b]Zeboiim, and the king of Bela (that
is, [c]Zoar). 3 All these [1]came as allies
to [a]the valley of Siddim (that is, [b]the
Salt Sea). 4 Now for twelve years they
had served Chedorlaomer, but the
thirteenth year they rebelled. 5 So in
the fourteenth year Chedorlaomer
and the kings that were with him,
came and struck the [a]Rephaim in
[b]Ashteroth-karnaim and the Zuzim
in Ham and the Emim in [c,1]Shaveh-
kiriathaim, 6 and the [a]Horites in
their Mount Seir, as far as [b]El-paran,
which is by the wilderness. 7 Then
they turned back and came to En-
mishpat (that is, [a]Kadesh). And
they struck all the country of the
Amalekites, and also the Amorites,
who were living in [b]Hazazon-tamar.
8 And the king of Sodom and the
king of Gomorrah and the king of
Admah and the king of Zeboiim and
the king of Bela (that is, Zoar) came
out; and they arranged *themselves*
for battle against them in [a]the valley
of Siddim, 9 against Chedorlaomer
king of Elam and Tidal king of [1]Goiim
and Amraphel king of Shinar and
Arioch king of Ellasar, four kings
against five— 10 now the valley of
Siddim was full of tar pits—and
[a]the kings of Sodom and Gomorrah
fled, and they fell [1]into them; but
those who remained behind fled
to the [b]hill country. 11 Then they
took all the possessions of Sodom
and Gomorrah and all their food
supply and departed. 12 They also
took Lot, [a]Abram's nephew, and his
possessions and departed; [b]now he
was living in Sodom.

**13:12** [a]Ge 14:2; 19:24, 25, 29 [1]Lit *circle* **13:13** [a]Ge 18:20; Eze 16:49 [b]Ge 39:9; Nu 32:23; 2Pe 2:7, 8
**13:14** [a]Dt 3:27; 34:1-4; Is 49:18 [b]Ge 28:14 **13:15** [a]Ge 12:7 [b]Ge 13:17; 15:7; 17:8; 2Chr 20:7; Ac 7:5
**13:16** [a]Ge 16:10; 28:14; Nu 23:10 **13:17** [a]Nu 13:17-24 [b]Ge 13:15 **13:18** [a]Ge 14:13 [b]Ge 8:20; 12:7, 8
[1]Or *terebinths* ◆**14:1** [a]Ge 10:10; 11:2 [b]Ge 10:22; Is 11:11; Da 8:2 [1]Or *nations* **14:2** [a]Ge 10:19 [b]Dt 29:23
[c]Ge 13:10; 19:22 **14:3** [a]Ge 14:8, 10 [b]Nu 34:12; Dt 3:17; Jos 3:16 [1]Lit *joined together* **14:5** [a]Dt 3:11, 13
[b]Dt 1:4; Jos 9:10 [c]Nu 32:37 [1]Or *the plain of Kiriathaim* **14:6** [a]Ge 36:20; Dt 2:12, 22 [b]Ge 21:21; Nu 10:12
**14:7** [a]Nu 13:26 [b]2Chr 20:2 **14:8** [a]Ge 14:3 **14:9** [1]Or *nations* **14:10** [a]Ge 14:17, 21, 22 [b]Ge 19:17 [1]Lit
*there* **14:12** [a]Ge 11:27 [b]Ge 13:12

**13** Then [1]a fugitive came and told
Abram the [a]Hebrew. Now he was
dwelling by the [b,2]oaks of Mamre
the Amorite, brother of Eshcol and
brother of Aner, and these were
[c,3]in a covenant with Abram. **14** So
Abram heard that [a]his [1]relative had
been taken captive, and he [2]led out
his trained men, [b]born in his house,
318 *in number*, and went in pursuit
as far as [c]Dan. **15** [a]And he divided [1]his
*men* against them by night, he and
his servants, and struck them and
pursued them as far as Hobah, which
is [2]north of [b]Damascus. **16** And he
[a]brought back all the possessions,
and he also brought back [b]his [1]rela-
tive Lot with his possessions and also
the women and the people.

### *Melchizedek Blesses Abram*

**17** Then after he came back from
striking down Chedorlaomer and the
kings who were with him, [a]the king of
Sodom went out to meet him at the
valley of Shaveh (that is, [b]the King's
Valley). **18** And [a]Melchizedek king of
Salem brought out [b]bread and wine;
now he was a [c]priest of [1]God Most
High. **19** Then he blessed him and said,

"Blessed be Abram
 of [1]God Most High,
[a,2]Possessor of heaven
 and earth;
**20** And blessed be [1]God Most High,
Who has delivered your
 enemies into your hand."

[a]Then he gave him a tenth of all.
**21** And the king of Sodom said to
Abram, "Give the [1]people to me, but
take the possessions for yourself."
**22** Then Abram said to the king of
Sodom, "I have [1]raised my hand to
Yahweh [a,2]God Most High, [b,3]posses-
sor of heaven and earth, **23** that [a]I will
not take a thread or a sandal strap or
anything that is yours, so that you
would not say, 'I have made Abram
rich.' **24** [1]I will take nothing except
what the young men have eaten, and
the share of the men who went with
me, [a]Aner, Eshcol, and Mamre; let
them take their share."

### *Yahweh Cuts a Covenant with Abram*

**15** After these things [a]the word
of Yahweh came to Abram in
a vision, saying,

"[b]Do not fear, Abram,
 I am [c]a shield to you;
[1]Your [d]reward shall
 be very great."

**2** And Abram said, "O Lord Yahweh,
what will You give me, as I go on
being childless, and the [1]heir of
my house is Eliezer of Damascus?"
**3** And Abram said, "[1]Since You have
given no seed to me, behold, [2]one
[a]born in my house is my heir." **4** Then
behold, the word of Yahweh came
to him, saying, "This one will not be
your heir; [a]but one who will come
forth from your own [1]body, he shall
be your heir." **5** And He brought

---

**14:13** [a]Ge 40:15; Ex 3:18 [b]Ge 13:18; 14:24 [c]Ge 21:27, 32 [1]Lit *the* [2]Or *terebinths* [3]Lit *possessors of the covenant* **14:14** [a]Ge 14:12 [b]Ge 12:5; 15:3; 17:27; Ecc 2:7 [c]Dt 34:1; Jdg 18:29; 1Ki 15:20 [1]Lit *brother* [2]Or *mustered* **14:15** [a]Jdg 7:16 [b]Ge 15:2 [1]Lit *himself* [2]Lit *on the left* **14:16** [a]1Sa 30:8, 18, 19 [b]Ge 14:12, 14 [1]Lit *brother* **14:17** [a]Ge 14:10 [b]2Sa 18:18 **14:18** [a]Heb 7:1-10 [b]Ps 104:15 [c]Ps 110:4; Heb 5:6, 10 [1]Heb *El Elyon* **14:19** [a]Ge 14:22 [1]Heb *El Elyon* [2]Or *Creator* **14:20** [a]Heb 7:4 [1]Heb *El Elyon* **14:21** [1]Lit *soul* **14:22** [a]Ge 14:19 [b]Ps 24:1 [1]Or *sworn* [2]Heb *El Elyon* [3]Or *Creator* **14:23** [a]2Ki 5:16 **14:24** [a]Ge 14:13 [1]Lit *Not to me except* ◆ **15:1** [a]Ge 15:4; 46:2; 1Sa 15:10 [b]Ge 21:17; 26:24; Is 41:10 [c]Dt 33:29 [d]Nu 18:20; Ps 58:11 [1]Or *Your very great reward* **15:2** [1]Lit *son of acquisition* **15:3** [a]Ge 14:14 [1]Lit *Behold* [2]Lit *a son of* **15:4** [a]Ga 4:28 [1]Lit *inward parts*

him outside and said, "Now look
toward the heavens, and [a]number
the stars, if you are able to number
them." And He said to him, "[b]So shall
your seed be." **6** [a]Then he believed in
Yahweh; and He counted it to him
as righteousness. **7** And He said to
him, "I am Yahweh who brought you
out of [a]Ur of the Chaldeans, to [b]give
you this land to [1]possess it." **8** And
he said, "O Lord Yahweh, [a]how may
I know that I will [1]possess it?" **9** So He
said to him, "[1]Bring Me a three year
old heifer, and a three year old female
goat, and a three year old ram, and
a turtledove, and a young pigeon."
**10** Then he [1]brought all these to Him
and [a]split them into parts [2]down the
middle and laid each part opposite
the other; but he [b]did not split apart
the birds. **11** Then the birds of prey
came down upon the carcasses, and
Abram drove them away.

**12** Now it happened that when
the sun was going down, [a]a deep
sleep fell upon Abram; and behold,
[1]terror *and* great darkness fell upon
him. **13** Then *God* said to Abram,
"Know for certain that [a]your seed
will be sojourners in a land that is not
theirs, [1]and [b]they will be enslaved
and mistreated [c]four hundred years.
**14** But I will also judge the nation to
whom they are enslaved, and after-
ward they will come out [a]with [1]many
possessions. **15** As for you, [a]you shall
go to your fathers in peace; you will
be buried at a good old age. **16** Then
in [a]the fourth generation they will
return here, for [b]the iniquity of the
Amorite is not yet complete."

**17** Now it happened that the sun
had set, and it was very dark, and
behold, *there appeared* a smoking
oven and a flaming torch which
[a]passed between these pieces. **18** On
that day Yahweh cut a covenant with
Abram, saying,

"[a]To your seed I have
given this land,
From [b]the river of Egypt
as far as the great river,
the river Euphrates:

**19** [a]the Kenite and the Kenizzite and
the Kadmonite **20** and the Hittite
and the Perizzite and the Rephaim
**21** and the Amorite and the Canaanite
and the Girgashite and the Jebusite."

### *Sarai and Hagar*

**16** Now [a]Sarai, Abram's wife, had
borne him no *children,* and she
had [b]an Egyptian servant-woman
whose name was Hagar. **2** So Sarai said
to Abram, "Now behold, Yahweh has
shut my *womb* from bearing *children.*
[a]Please go in to my servant-woman;
perhaps I will [1]obtain children
through her." And Abram listened to
the voice of Sarai. **3** And after Abram
had [1]lived [a]ten years in the land of Ca-
naan, Abram's wife Sarai took Hagar
the Egyptian, her servant-woman,
and gave her to her husband Abram
as his wife. **4** So he went in to Hagar,
and she conceived. Then she saw that

---

**15:5** [a]Ge 22:17; 26:4; Dt 1:10 [b]Ex 32:13; Ro 4:18; Heb 11:12 **15:6** [a]Ro 4:3, 20-22; Ga 3:6; Jas 2:23
**15:7** [a]Ge 11:31 [b]Ge 13:15, 17 [1]Or *inherit* **15:8** [a]Jdg 6:36-40; Lk 1:18 [1]Or *inherit* **15:9** [1]Lit *Take*
**15:10** [a]Ge 15:17 [b]Lv 1:17 [1]Lit *took* [2]Lit *in the midst* **15:12** [a]Ge 2:21; 28:11; Job 33:15 [1]Or *a terror of great darkness* **15:13** [a]Ac 7:6, 17 [b]Ex 1:11; Dt 5:15 [c]Ex 12:40; Ga 3:17 [1]Lit *and shall serve them; and they shall afflict them* **15:14** [a]Ex 12:32-38 [1]Lit *great* **15:15** [a]Ge 25:8; 47:30 **15:16** [a]Ge 15:13
[b]Lv 18:24-28 **15:17** [a]Jer 34:18, 19 **15:18** [a]Ge 17:8; Jos 21:43; Ac 7:5 [b]Ex 23:31; Nu 34:1-15; Dt 1:7, 8
**15:19** [a]Ex 3:17; 23:28; Jos 24:11; Ne 9:8 ◆ **16:1** [a]Ge 11:30 [b]Ge 12:16 **16:2** [a]Ge 30:3, 4, 9, 10 [1]Lit *be built from her* **16:3** [a]Ge 12:4 [1]Lit *dwelt*

she had conceived, so her mistress
became [1]contemptible in her sight.
**5** And Sarai said to Abram, "[a]May the
violence done to me be upon you. I
gave my servant-woman into your
[1]embrace, but she saw that she had
conceived, so I became [2]contempt-
ible in her [3]sight. [b]May Yahweh judge
between [4]you and me." **6** But Abram
said to Sarai, "Behold, your servant-
woman is in your [1]hand; do to her
what is good in your [2]sight." So Sarai
afflicted her, and [a]she fled from her
presence.

**7** Now [a]the angel of Yahweh found
her by a spring of water in the wil-
derness, by the spring on the way to
[b]Shur. **8** And he said, "Hagar, Sarai's
servant-woman, [a]where have you
come from and where are you
going?" And she said, "I am fleeing
from the presence of my mistress
Sarai." **9** Then the angel of Yahweh
said to her, "Return to your mistress
and [1]humble yourself under her
hands." **10** Moreover, the [a]angel of
Yahweh said to her, "[b]I will greatly
multiply your seed so that [1]they
will be too many to be counted."
**11** And the angel of Yahweh said to
her further,

"Behold, you [1]are with child,
And you will bear a son;
And you shall call his
name [2]Ishmael,
Because [a]Yahweh has
heard your affliction.

**12** "And he will be a [a]wild
donkey of a man,
His hand *will be*
against everyone,
And everyone's hand
*will be* against him;
And he will dwell [b,1]in the
face of all his brothers."

**13** Then she called the name of Yah-
weh who spoke to her, "[1]You are [2]a
God who sees"; for she said, "[a]Have
I even [3]remained alive here after
seeing Him?" **14** Therefore the well
was called [1]Beer-lahai-roi; behold,
it is between [a]Kadesh and Bered.

**15** So Hagar bore Abram a son; and
Abram called the name of his son,
whom Hagar bore, Ishmael. **16** Now
Abram was [a]eighty-six years old
when Hagar bore Ishmael to [1]him.

### *Circumcision, the Sign of the Covenant*

**17** Now it happened that when
Abram was ninety-nine years
old, [a]Yahweh appeared to Abram and
said to him,

"I am [1]God [b]Almighty;
Walk before Me
and be [c,2]blameless,
**2** so that I may [1]confirm
My [a]covenant
between Me and you,
And that I may [b]multiply
you exceedingly."

**3** Then Abram [a]fell on his face, and
God spoke with him, saying,

---

**16:4** [1]Or *cursed*, cf. 12:3 **16:5** [a]Jer 51:35 [b]Ge 31:53; Ex 5:21 [1]Lit *bosom* [2]Or *cursed*, cf. 12:3 [3]Lit *eyes* [4]Lit *me and you* **16:6** [a]Ge 16:9 [1]Or *power* [2]Lit *eyes* **16:7** [a]Ge 21:17, 18; 22:11, 15; 31:11 [b]Ge 20:1; 25:18 **16:8** [a]Ge 3:9; 1Ki 19:9, 13 **16:9** [1]Lit *afflict*, cf. 16:6 **16:10** [a]Ge 22:15-18 [b]Ge 17:20 [1]Or *it shall not be counted for multitude* **16:11** [a]Ex 2:23, 24; 3:7, 9 [1]Or *have conceived*, cf. 3:16; 21:2; 25:21; Ex 2:2; 1Sa 1:20; Lk 1:31, 36 [2]Lit *God hears* **16:12** [a]Job 24:5; 39:5-8 [b]Ge 25:18 [1]Or *to the east of, in defiance of* **16:13** [a]Ge 32:30; Ps 139:1-12 [1]Or *You, O God, see me* [2]Heb *El roi* [3]Lit *seen here after the one who saw me* **16:14** [a]Ge 14:7 [1]Lit *the well of the living one who sees me* **16:16** [a]Ge 12:4; 16:3 [1]Lit *Abram* ◆ **17:1** [a]Ge 12:7; 18:1 [b]Ge 28:3; 35:11 [c]Ge 6:9; Dt 18:13 [1]Heb *El Shaddai* [2]Or *having integrity*; lit *complete, perfect* **17:2** [a]Ge 15:18 [b]Ge 13:16; 15:5 [1]Lit *give* **17:3** [a]Ge 17:17; 18:2

4 "As for Me, behold, My
covenant is with you,
And you will be the father
of a [a]multitude of nations.
5 "And no longer shall your
name be called [1]Abram,
But [a]your name shall
be [2]Abraham;
For [b]I have made you the
father of a multitude
of nations.
6 "And I will make you exceedingly
fruitful, and I will make nations
of you, and [a]kings will go forth
from you. 7 And I will establish My
covenant between Me and you and
your seed after you throughout
their generations for an [a]everlasting
covenant, [b]to be God to you and [c]to
your seed after you. 8 [a]And I will give
to you and to your seed after you,
the land of your sojournings, all the
land of Canaan, for an everlasting
possession; and [b]I will be their God."
9 God said further to Abraham,
"Now as for you, [a]you shall keep My
covenant, you and your seed after
you throughout their generations.
10 [a]This is My covenant, which you
shall keep, between Me and you
and your seed after you: every male
among you shall be circumcised.
11 And [a]you shall be circumcised
in the flesh of your foreskin, and
it shall be the sign of the covenant
between Me and you. 12 And every
male among you who is [a]eight days
old shall be circumcised throughout
your generations, one who is born in
the house or one who is bought with
money from any foreigner, who is
not of your seed. 13 A *servant* who is
born in your house or [a]who is bought
with your money shall surely be cir-
cumcised; thus shall My covenant
be in your flesh for an everlasting
covenant. 14 But an uncircumcised
male who is not circumcised in the
flesh of his foreskin, that person shall
be [a]cut off from his people; he has
broken My covenant."

### *Sarah Will Bear Isaac*

15 Then God said to Abraham, "As
for Sarai your wife, you shall not
call her name Sarai, but [1]Sarah *shall
be* her name. 16 And I will bless her,
and indeed I will give you [a]a son by
her. Then I will bless her, and she
shall be *a mother of* nations; [b]kings
of peoples will [1]come from her."
17 Then Abraham [a]fell on his face
and laughed and said in his heart,
"Will *a son* be born to a man one
hundred years old? And [b]will Sarah,
who is ninety years old, bear *a son*?"
18 And Abraham said to God, "Oh
that Ishmael might live before You!"
19 But God said, "No, but Sarah your
wife will bear you [a]a son, and you
shall call his name [1]Isaac; and [b]I will
establish My covenant with him for
an everlasting covenant for his seed
after him. 20 As for Ishmael, I have
heard you; behold, I will bless him
and [a]will make him fruitful and will
multiply him exceedingly. [b]He shall
[1]become the father of twelve princes,

**17:4** [a]Ge 35:11; 48:19 **17:5** [a]Ne 9:7 [b]Ro 4:17 [1]Lit *exalted father* [2]Lit *father of a multitude*
**17:6** [a]Ge 17:16; 35:11 **17:7** [a]Ge 17:13, 19; Ps 105:9, 10; Lk 1:55 [b]Ge 26:24; Lv 11:45; 26:12, 45; Heb 11:16 [c]Ge 28:13; Ga 3:16 **17:8** [a]Ge 12:7; 13:15, 17; Ac 7:5 [b]Ex 6:7; 29:45; Lv 26:12; Dt 29:13; Rev 21:7
**17:9** [a]Ex 19:5 **17:10** [a]Jn 7:22; Ac 7:8; Ro 4:11 **17:11** [a]Ex 12:48; Dt 10:16; Ac 7:8; Ro 4:11 **17:12** [a]Lv 12:3
**17:13** [a]Ex 12:44 **17:14** [a]Ex 4:24-26 **17:15** [1]Lit *princess* **17:16** [a]Ge 18:10 [b]Ge 17:6; 36:31 [1]Lit *be*
**17:17** [a]Ge 17:3; 18:12; 21:6 [b]Ge 21:7 **17:19** [a]Ge 17:16; 18:10; 21:2 [b]Ge 26:2-5 [1]Lit *he laughs*
**17:20** [a]Ge 16:10 [b]Ge 25:12-16 [1]Lit *beget twelve princes*

and I will make him a [c]great nation.
**21** But My covenant I will establish
with [a]Isaac, whom [b]Sarah will bear
to you at this season next year." **22** So
He finished talking with him, and
[a]God went up from Abraham.

**23** Then Abraham took Ishmael
his son, and all who were [a]born in
his house and all who were bought
with his money, every male among
the men of Abraham's household,
and circumcised the flesh of their
foreskin in the very same day, [b]as
God had spoken with him. **24** Now
Abraham was ninety-nine years old
when [a]he was circumcised in the
flesh of his foreskin. **25** And [a]Ishmael
his son was thirteen years old when
he was circumcised in the flesh of
his foreskin. **26** In the very same
day Abraham was circumcised, and
Ishmael his son. **27** Now all the men
of his household, who were [a]born
in the house or bought with money
from a foreigner, were circumcised
with him.

### *Yahweh Appears to Abraham*

**18** Then [a]Yahweh appeared to
him by the [b,1]oaks of Mamre,
while he was sitting at the tent door
in the heat of the day. **2** And he lifted
up his eyes and looked, and behold,
three [a]men were standing nearby; he
saw, and he ran from the tent door to
meet them, and he bowed himself
to the earth, **3** and he said, "[1]My
Lord, if now I have found favor in
Your sight, please do not [2]pass Your
servant by. **4** Please let a little water
be brought and [a]wash your feet, and
[1]rest yourselves under the tree; **5** and
let me [a,1]bring a piece of bread, that
you may [2]refresh your hearts; after
that you may pass on, since in such
a manner you have passed *by* your
servant." And they said, "So you shall
do, as you have said." **6** So Abraham
hurried into the tent to Sarah and
said, "[1]Hurry, prepare [2]three seahs of
fine flour, knead *it*, and make bread
cakes." **7** Abraham also ran to the
herd and took a tender and [1]choice
calf and gave *it* to *his* young man,
and he hurried to prepare it. **8** Then
he took curds and milk and the calf
which he had prepared, and placed
*it* before them; and he was standing
by them under the tree, and they ate.

**9** Then they said to him, "Where
is Sarah your wife?" And he said,
"There, in the tent." **10** And He said,
"[a]I will surely return to you [1]at this
time next year; and behold, Sarah
your wife will have a son." And Sarah
was listening at the tent door which
was behind him. **11** Now [a]Abraham
and Sarah were old, advanced in age;
Sarah was [b]past [1]childbearing. **12** And
Sarah laughed [1]to herself, saying,
"[a]After I am worn out, shall I have
pleasure, my [b]lord being old also?"
**13** And Yahweh said to Abraham,
"Why did Sarah laugh, saying, 'Shall
I indeed [1]bear *a son*, when I am *so*
old?' **14** [a]Is anything too [1]difficult for

**17:20** [c]Ge 21:18 **17:21** [a]Ge 17:19; 18:10, 14 [b]Ge 21:2 **17:22** [a]Ge 18:33; 35:13 **17:23** [a]Ge 14:14 [b]Ge 17:9-11 **17:24** [a]Ro 4:11 **17:25** [a]Ge 16:16 **17:27** [a]Ge 14:14 ◆ **18:1** [a]Ge 12:7; 17:1 [b]Ge 13:18; 14:13 [1]Or *terebinths* **18:2** [a]Ge 18:16, 22; 32:24; Jos 5:13; Jdg 13:6-11; Heb 13:2 **18:3** [1]Or *O Lord* [2]Lit *pass away from Your servant* **18:4** [a]Ge 19:2; 24:32; 43:24 [1]Lit *support* **18:5** [a]Jdg 6:18, 19; 13:15, 16 [1]Lit *take* [2]Lit *sustain your heart* **18:6** [1]Lit *Hasten 3 measures* [2]Approx. 21 qt. or 23 l, a seah was approx. 7 qt. or 7.7 l **18:7** [1]Lit *good* **18:10** [a]Ge 21:2; Ro 9:9 [1]Lit *when the time revives* **18:11** [a]Ge 17:17; Ro 4:19 [b]Heb 11:11 [1]Lit *the manner of women* **18:12** [a]Ge 17:17; Lk 1:18 [b]1Pe 3:6 [1]Lit *within* **18:13** [1]Lit *surely bear* **18:14** [a]Jer 32:17, 27; Zec 8:6; Mt 19:26; Lk 1:37; Ro 4:21 [1]Or *marvelous*

Yahweh? At the [b]appointed time I will
return to you, [2]at this time next year,
and Sarah will have a son." **15** Then
Sarah denied *it* however, saying, "I
did not laugh"; for she was afraid.
And He said, "No, but you did laugh."

### *Yahweh and Abraham Speak About Sodom*

**16** Then [a]the men rose up from there
and looked down toward Sodom; and
Abraham was walking with them to
send them off. **17** [a]Now Yahweh said,
"Shall I conceal from Abraham [b]what
I am about to do, **18** since Abraham
will surely become a great and
[1]mighty nation, and in him [a]all the
nations of the earth will be blessed?
**19** For I have [a,1]known him, so that
he may [b]command his children and
his household after him, [c]that they
keep the way of Yahweh to do righ-
teousness and justice, so that Yahweh
may bring upon Abraham [d]what He
has spoken about him." **20** So Yah-
weh said, "[a]The outcry of Sodom
and Gomorrah is indeed great, and
their sin is exceedingly grave. **21** I will
[a]go down now and see whether they
have done entirely according to its
outcry, which has come to Me; and
if not, I will know."

**22** Then [a]the men turned away
from there and went toward Sodom,
while Abraham was still standing
before [b]Yahweh. **23** Then Abraham
came near and said, "[a]Will You in-
deed sweep away the righteous with
the wicked? **24** Suppose there are fifty
righteous within the city; will You
indeed sweep *it* away and not [1]spare
the place for the sake of the fifty
righteous who are in it? **25** Far be it
from You to do [1]such a thing, to put to
death the righteous with the wicked,
so that the righteous and the wicked
are *treated* alike. Far be it from You!
Shall not [a]the Judge of all the earth
do justice?" **26** So Yahweh said, "[a]If I
find in Sodom fifty righteous within
the city, then I will [1]spare the whole
place on their account." **27** And
Abraham answered and said, "Now
behold, I have [1]ventured to speak to
the Lord, although I am *but* [a]dust and
ashes. **28** Suppose the fifty righteous
are lacking five, will You destroy the
whole city because of five?" And He
said, "I will not destroy *it* if I find
forty-five there." **29** Then he spoke
to Him yet again and said, "Suppose
forty are found there?" And He said,
"I will not do *it* on account of the
forty." **30** Then he said, "Oh may the
Lord not be angry, and I shall speak;
suppose thirty are found there?" And
He said, "I will not do *it* if I find thirty
there." **31** And he said, "Now behold,
I have [1]ventured to speak to the Lord;
suppose twenty are found there?"
And He said, "I will not destroy *it*
on account of the twenty." **32** Then
he said, "[a]Oh may the Lord not be
angry, and I shall speak only this
once; suppose ten are found there?"
And He said, "I will not destroy *it*
on account of the ten." **33** And as
soon as He had finished speaking to

---

**18:14** [b]Ge 17:21; 18:10 [2]Lit *when the time revives* **18:16** [a]Ge 18:2, 22; 19:1 **18:17** [a]Ge 18:22, 26, 33; Am 3:7 [b]Ge 18:21; 19:24 **18:18** [a]Ge 12:3; 22:18; Ac 3:25; Ga 3:8 [1]Or *populous* **18:19** [a]Ne 9:7; Am 3:2 [b]Dt 6:6, 7 [c]Ge 17:9 [d]Ge 12:2, 3 [1]Or *chosen* **18:20** [a]Ge 19:13; Eze 16:49, 50 **18:21** [a]Ge 11:5; Ex 3:8; Ps 14:2 **18:22** [a]Ge 18:16; 19:1 [b]Ge 18:1, 17 **18:23** [a]Ex 23:7; Nu 16:22; 2Sa 24:17; Ps 11:4-7 **18:24** [1]Or *forgive* **18:25** [a]Dt 1:16, 17; 32:4; Job 8:3, 20; Ps 58:11; 94:2; Is 3:10, 11; Ro 3:5, 6 [1]Lit *after this manner* **18:26** [a]Jer 5:1 [1]Or *forgive* **18:27** [a]Ge 3:19; Job 30:19; 42:6 [1]Lit *undertaken* **18:31** [1]Lit *undertaken* **18:32** [a]Jdg 6:39

Abraham, [a]Yahweh departed, and
Abraham returned to his place.

### *Yahweh Destroys Sodom and Gomorrah*

**19** Then the [a]two angels came to
Sodom in the evening as Lot
was sitting in the gate of Sodom. [b]Lot
saw *them* and rose to meet them and
[1]bowed down *with his* [2]face to the
ground. **2** And he said, "Now behold,
my lords, please turn aside into your
servant's house, and spend the night,
and wash your feet; then you may rise
early and go on your way." They said
however, "No, but we shall spend the
night in the square." **3** Yet he pressed
them strongly, so they turned aside
to him and entered his house; [a]and
he made a feast for them and baked
unleavened bread, and they ate. **4** Be-
fore they lay down, [a]the men of the
city, the men of Sodom, surrounded
the house, from young to old, all the
people [1]from every quarter; **5** and
they called to Lot and said to him,
"[a]Where are the men who came to
you tonight? Bring them out to us
that we may [1]know them." **6** But Lot
went out to them at the doorway
and shut the door behind him, **7** and
said, "Please, my brothers, do not
act wickedly. **8** Now behold, [a]I have
two daughters who have not known
a man; please let me bring them out
to you, and do to them what is good
in your eyes; only do nothing to these
men, inasmuch as they have come
under the [1]shelter of my roof." **9** But
they said, "Step aside." Furthermore,
they said, "This one came to sojourn,
and already [a]he is persistently acting
like a judge; now we will treat you
more wickedly than them." So they
pressed hard against [1]Lot and stepped
up to break the door. **10** But [a]the men
reached out their [1]hands and brought
Lot into the house [2]with them and
shut the door. **11** [a]And they [1]struck
the men who were at the doorway of
the house with blindness, from small
to great, so that they wearied *them-*
*selves trying* to find the doorway.

**12** Then the *two* men said to Lot,
"Whom else have you here? A son-
in-law, and your sons, and your
daughters, and everyone you have
in the city, bring *them* out of the
place; **13** for we are about to destroy
this place because [a]their outcry has
become great before Yahweh, so
[b]Yahweh has sent us to destroy it."
**14** And Lot went out and spoke to his
sons-in-law, who [1]were to marry his
daughters, and said, "Get up, [a]get out
of this place, for Yahweh will destroy
the city." [b]But he appeared to his
sons-in-law [2]to be jesting.

**15** Now at the [1]breaking of dawn,
the angels urged Lot, saying, "Get
up, take your wife and your two
daughters who are here, lest you
be swept away in the [2]punishment
of the city." **16** But he hesitated. So
the men [a]seized his hand and the
hand of his wife and the [1]hands of
his two daughters, for [b]the compas-
sion of Yahweh *was* upon him; and

---

**18:33** [a]Ge 17:22; 35:13 ◆**19:1** [a]Ge 18:2, 22 [b]Ge 18:2-5 [1]Lit *bowed himself* [2]Lit *nose* **19:3** [a]Ge 18:6-8 **19:4** [a]Ge 13:13; 18:20 [1]Or *without exception*; lit *from every end* **19:5** [a]Lv 18:22; Jdg 19:22 [1]Have intercourse **19:8** [a]Jdg 19:24 [1]Lit *shadow* **19:9** [a]Ex 2:14 [1]Lit *the man, against Lot* **19:10** [a]Ge 19:1 [1]Lit *hand* [2]Lit *to* **19:11** [a]Dt 28:28, 29; 2Ki 6:18; Ac 13:11 [1]Lit *smote* **19:13** [a]Ge 18:20 [b]Lv 26:30-33; Dt 4:26; 28:45; 1Chr 21:15 **19:14** [a]Nu 16:21, 45; Rev 18:4 [b]Jer 43:1, 2 [1]Or *had married*; lit *were taking* [2]Lit *like one who was jesting* **19:15** [1]Lit *rising* [2]Or *iniquity* **19:16** [a]Dt 5:15; 6:21; 7:8; 2Pe 2:7 [b]Ex 34:7; Ps 32:10; 33:18, 19 [1]Lit *hand*

they brought him out and put him outside the city. **17** Now it happened, as they brought them outside, [1]one said, "[a]Escape for your life! [b]Do not look behind you, and do not stay [2]anywhere in the [c]valley; escape to [d]the [3]mountains, lest you be swept away." **18** But Lot said to them, "Oh no, my lords! **19** Now behold, your servant has found favor in your sight, and you have magnified your lovingkindness, which you have shown me by preserving my life; but I cannot escape to the [1]mountains, lest calamity overtake me and I die; **20** now behold, this town is near *enough* to flee to, and it is small. Please, let me escape there (is it not small?) [1]that my life may be preserved." **21** And he said to him, "Behold, I grant you this [1]request also, that I will not overthrow the city of which you have spoken. **22** Hurry, escape there, for I cannot do anything until you arrive there." Therefore the name of the city was called [a,1]Zoar.

**23** The sun had risen over the earth when Lot came to Zoar. **24** And Yahweh [a]rained on Sodom and Gomorrah brimstone and fire from Yahweh out of heaven, **25** and [a]He overthrew those cities, and all the [1]valley, and all the inhabitants of the cities, and what grew on the ground. **26** Then his wife, from behind him, [a]looked *back*, and she became a pillar of salt.

**27** Now Abraham arose early in the morning *and went* to [a]the place where he had stood before Yahweh; **28** and he looked down toward Sodom and Gomorrah, and toward all the land of the [1]valley, and he saw, and behold, [a]the smoke of the land went up like the smoke of a [2]furnace.

**29** Thus it happened, when God destroyed the cities of the [1]valley, that [a]God remembered Abraham and [b]sent Lot out of the midst of the overthrow, when He overthrew the cities in which Lot lived.

### *Lot and His Daughters*

**30** And Lot went up from Zoar and [a,1]stayed in the [2]mountains, and his two daughters with him; for he was afraid to [3]stay in Zoar; and he [1]stayed in a cave, he and his two daughters. **31** Then the firstborn said to the younger, "Our father is old, and there is not a man [1]on earth to [a]come in to us after the manner of the earth. **32** Come, [a]let us make our father drink wine, and let us lie with him that we may preserve *our* seed through our father." **33** So they made their father drink wine that night, and the firstborn went in and lay with her father; and he did not know when she lay down or when she arose. **34** Now it happened on the following day, that the firstborn said to the younger, "Behold, I lay last night with my father; let us make him drink wine tonight also; and you go in and lie with him, that we may preserve *our* seed through our father." **35** So they made their father drink wine that night also, and the younger arose and lay with him; and he did not know when she lay down

**19:17** [a]Jer 48:6 [b]Ge 19:26 [c]Ge 13:10 [d]Ge 14:10 [1]Lit *he* [2]Lit *in all the circle* [3]Lit *mountain* **19:19** [1]Lit *mountain* **19:20** [1]Lit *and my soul will live* **19:21** [1]Lit *thing* **19:22** [a]Ge 13:10; 14:2 [1]Lit *small* **19:24** [a]Dt 29:23; Ps 11:6; Is 13:19; Eze 16:49, 50; Lk 17:29; Jd 7 **19:25** [a]Dt 29:23; Ps 107:34; Is 13:19; Lam 4:6; 2Pe 2:6 [1]Lit *circle* **19:26** [a]Ge 19:17; Lk 17:32 **19:27** [a]Ge 18:22 **19:28** [a]Rev 9:2; 18:9 [1]Lit *circle* [2]Lit *kiln* **19:29** [a]Dt 7:8; 9:5, 27 [b]2Pe 2:7 [1]Lit *circle* **19:30** [a]Ge 19:17, 19 [1]Lit *dwelt* [2]Lit *mountain* [3]Lit *dwell* **19:31** [a]Ge 16:2, 4; 38:8; Dt 25:5 [1]Or *in the land* **19:32** [a]Lk 21:34

or when she arose. **36** Thus both the
daughters of Lot conceived by their
father. **37** And the firstborn bore a
son and called his name [a]Moab; he
is the father of the Moabites to this
day. **38** As for the younger, she also
bore a son and called his name Ben-
ammi; he is the father of the [1]sons of
[a]Ammon to this day.

### *Abraham Lies to Abimelech*

**20** And Abraham journeyed
from [a]there toward the land
of [b]the [1]Negev and settled between
Kadesh and Shur; then he sojourned
in [c]Gerar. **2** And Abraham said of
Sarah his wife, "[a]She is my sister."
So [b]Abimelech king of Gerar sent
and took Sarah. **3** [a]But God came to
Abimelech in a dream of the night and
said to him, "Behold, [b]you are a dead
man because of the woman whom
you have taken, for she is [1]married."
**4** (Now Abimelech had not come near
her.) Then he said, "Lord, [a]will You
kill a nation, even *though* righteous?
**5** Did he not himself say to me, 'She is
my sister'? And she [a]herself also said,
'He is my brother.' In [b]the integrity of
my heart and the innocence of my
[1]hands I have done this." **6** Then God
said to him in the dream, "Indeed,
I know that in the integrity of your
heart you have done this, and I also
[a,1]held you back from sinning against
Me; therefore I did not let you touch
her. **7** So now, return the man's wife,
for [a]he is a prophet, and he will pray
for you, and you will live. But if you
do not return *her*, know that you shall
surely die, you and all who are yours."
**8** So Abimelech arose early in the
morning and called all his servants
and told all these things in their hear-
ing; and the men were greatly afraid.
**9** [a]Then Abimelech called Abraham
and said to him, "What have you done
to us? And [1]how have I sinned against
you, that you have brought on me and
on my kingdom [b]a great sin? You have
done to me [2]things that ought not
to be done." **10** And Abimelech said
to Abraham, "What have you seen,
that you have done this thing?" **11** And
Abraham said, "Because I said, surely
there is no [a]fear of God in this place,
and [b]they will kill me because of my
wife. **12** Besides, she actually is my sis-
ter, the daughter of my father, but not
the daughter of my mother, and she
became my wife; **13** and it happened
when [a]God caused me to wander
from my father's house, that I said
to her, 'This is [1]the lovingkindness
which you will show to me: [2]every-
where we go, [b]say of me, "He is my
brother."'" **14** [a]Abimelech then took
sheep and oxen and male and female
slaves and gave them to Abraham and
returned his wife Sarah to him. **15** And
Abimelech said, "[a]Behold, my land is
before you; [1]settle wherever it is good
in your sight." **16** To Sarah he said,
"Behold, I have given your [a]brother
one thousand pieces of silver; behold,
it is [1]your vindication before all who
are with you, and before all you are
[2]cleared." **17** [a]And Abraham prayed to

**19:37** [a]Dt 2:9 **19:38** [a]Dt 2:19 [1]Heb *Bene-Ammon* ◆ **20:1** [a]Ge 18:1 [b]Ge 12:9 [c]Ge 26:1, 6 [1]South country **20:2** [a]Ge 12:11-13; 20:12; 26:7 [b]Ge 12:15 **20:3** [a]Ge 12:17, 18 [b]Ge 20:7 [1]Lit *married to a husband* **20:4** [a]Ge 18:23-25 **20:5** [a]Ge 20:13 [b]1Ki 9:4; Ps 7:8; 26:6 [1]Lit *palms* **20:6** [a]1Sa 25:26, 34 [1]Lit *restrained* **20:7** [a]1Sa 7:5; 2Ki 5:11; Job 42:8 **20:9** [a]Ge 12:18 [b]Ge 39:9 [1]Lit *what* [2]Lit *deeds* **20:11** [a]Ne 5:15; Pr 16:6 [b]Ge 12:12; 26:7 **20:13** [a]Ge 12:1-9 [b]Ge 12:13; 20:5 [1]Lit *your* [2]Lit *at every place where* **20:14** [a]Ge 12:16 **20:15** [a]Ge 13:9; 34:10; 47:6 [1]Lit *dwell* **20:16** [a]Ge 20:5 [1]Lit *for you a covering of the eyes* [2]Lit *decided* **20:17** [a]Nu 12:13; 21:7; Jas 5:16

God, and God healed Abimelech and
his wife and his maidservants, so that
they bore *children*. **18** [a]For Yahweh
had utterly shut all the wombs of the
household of Abimelech because of
Sarah, Abraham's wife.

### *Isaac Is Born*

**21** [a]Now Yahweh visited Sarah
as He had said, and Yahweh
did for Sarah as He had [1]promised.
**2** [a]So Sarah conceived and bore a son
to Abraham in his old age, at [b]the
appointed time of which God had
spoken to him. **3** And Abraham called
the name of his son who was born to
him, whom Sarah bore to him, [a]Isaac.
**4** Then Abraham circumcised his son
Isaac when he was [a]eight days old,
as God had commanded him. **5** Now
Abraham was [a]one hundred years
old when his son Isaac was born
to him. **6** And Sarah said, "God has
made [a]laughter for me; everyone
who hears will laugh [1]with me."
**7** And she said, "[a]Who would have
said to Abraham that Sarah would
nurse children? Yet I have borne *him*
a son in his old age."

### *Sarah Sends Hagar Away*

**8** And the child grew and was weaned,
and Abraham made a great feast
on the day that Isaac was weaned.
**9** And Sarah saw [a]the son of Hagar
the Egyptian, whom she had borne
to Abraham, [b,1]laughing *in jest*.
**10** Therefore she said to Abraham,
"[a]Drive out this maidservant and
her son! The son of this maidservant
shall not be an heir with my son, with
Isaac." **11** [a]And the matter [1]distressed
Abraham greatly because of his son.
**12** So God said to Abraham, "[1]Do not
be distressed because of the boy
and your maidservant; whatever
Sarah tells you, listen to her voice,
for [a]through Isaac your seed shall
be named. **13** And of [a]the son of the
maidservant I will make a nation
also, because he is your seed." **14** So
Abraham rose early in the morning
and took bread and a [1]skin of water
and gave *them* to Hagar, putting
*them* on her shoulder, and *gave her*
the child, and sent her away. So she
went and wandered about in the
wilderness of Beersheba.

**15** When the water in the skin was
finished, she [1]put the child under
one of the bushes. **16** Then she went
and sat down opposite him, about a
bowshot away, for she said, "Do not
let me [1]see when the child dies." And
she sat opposite him and [a]lifted up
her voice and wept. **17** Then God
[a]heard the voice of the boy crying;
and the angel of God called to Hagar
from heaven and said to her, "What
is the matter with you, Hagar? [b]Do
not fear, for God has heard the voice
of the boy where he is. **18** Arise, lift
up the boy, and hold him by [1]the
hand, [a]for I will make a great nation
of him." **19** Then God [a]opened her
eyes, and she saw [b]a well of water;
and she went and filled the skin with
water and gave the boy a drink.

---

**20:18** [a]Ge 12:17 ◆ **21:1** [a]Ge 17:16, 21; 18:10, 14; Ga 4:23 [1]Lit *spoken* **21:2** [a]Ac 7:8; Ga 4:22; Heb 11:11 [b]Ge 17:21; 18:10, 14 **21:3** [a]Ge 17:19, 21 **21:4** [a]Ge 17:12; Ac 7:8 **21:5** [a]Ge 17:17 **21:6** [a]Ge 18:13; Ps 126:2; Is 54:1 [1]Lit *for* **21:7** [a]Ge 18:11, 13 **21:9** [a]Ge 16:1, 4, 15 [b]Ga 4:29 [1]Or *playing* **21:10** [a]Ga 4:30 **21:11** [a]Ge 17:18 [1]Lit *was very grievous in Abraham's sight* **21:12** [a]Ro 9:7; Heb 11:18 [1]Lit *Do not let it be grievous in your sight* **21:13** [a]Ge 16:10; 21:18; 25:12-18 **21:14** [1]A skin used as a bottle **21:15** [1]Lit *cast* **21:16** [a]Jer 6:26; Am 8:10 [1]Lit *look upon the death of the child* **21:17** [a]Ex 3:7; Dt 26:7; Ps 6:8 [b]Ge 26:24 **21:18** [a]Ge 16:10; 21:13; 25:12-16 [1]Lit *your* **21:19** [a]Nu 22:31; 2Ki 6:17 [b]Ge 16:7, 14

**20** [a]And God was with the boy,
and he grew; and he [1]lived in the wil-
derness and was an archer. **21** [a]And
he [1]lived in the wilderness of Paran,
and his mother took a wife for him
from the land of Egypt.

### *A Covenant with Abimelech*

**22** Now it happened at that time,
that [a]Abimelech and Phicol, the
commander of his army, spoke to
Abraham, saying, "[b]God is with you
in all that you do; **23** so now, [a]swear
to me here by God that you will not
deal falsely with me or with my
offspring or with my posterity, but
according to the lovingkindness that
I have shown you, you shall show
me and the land in which you have
sojourned." **24** And Abraham said, "I
swear it." **25** But Abraham reproved
Abimelech about the well of water
which the servants of Abimelech
[a]had seized. **26** And Abimelech said,
"I do not know who has done this
thing; you did not tell me, nor did I
hear of it [1]until today."

**27** So Abraham took sheep and
oxen and gave them to Abimelech,
and [a]the two of them cut a covenant.
**28** Then Abraham set seven ewe
lambs of the flock by themselves.
**29** And Abimelech said to Abraham,
"What do these seven ewe lambs
mean, which you have set by them-
selves?" **30** He said, "You shall take
these seven ewe lambs from my hand
so that it may be a [a]witness to me,
that I dug this well." **31** Therefore
he called that place [a]Beersheba,
because there the two of them swore
*an oath.* **32** So they cut a covenant
at Beersheba; and Abimelech and
Phicol, the commander of his army,
arose and returned to the land of the
Philistines. **33** And *Abraham* planted
a tamarisk tree at Beersheba, and
there [a]he called upon the name of
Yahweh, the [b]Everlasting God. **34** And
Abraham sojourned [a]in the land of
the Philistines for many days.

### *The Offering of Isaac*

**22** Now it happened after these
things, that [a]God tested Abra-
ham and said to him, "[b]Abraham!"
And he said, "Here I am." **2** Then He
said, "Take now [a]your son, your only
one, whom you love, Isaac, and [b]go
forth to the land of [c]Moriah, and offer
him there as a [d]burnt offering on one
of the mountains of which I will tell
you." **3** So Abraham rose early in the
morning and saddled his donkey and
took two of his young men with him
and Isaac his son; and he split wood
for the burnt offering and arose and
went to the place of which God had
told him. **4** On the third day Abraham
lifted up his eyes and saw the place
from a distance. **5** And Abraham said
to his young men, "Stay here with the
donkey while I and the boy go over
there; and we will worship, and we
will return to you." **6** Then Abraham
took the wood of the burnt offering
and [a]put it on Isaac his son, and he
took in his hand the fire and the
knife. So the two of them walked on
together.

**7** Then Isaac spoke to Abraham his
father and said, "My father!" And he

---

**21:20** [a]Ge 28:15; 39:2, 3, 21 [1]Lit *dwelt* **21:21** [a]Ge 25:18 [1]Lit *dwelt* **21:22** [a]Ge 20:2, 14; 26:26 [b]Ge 26:28; Is 8:10 **21:23** [a]Jos 2:12; 1Sa 24:21 **21:25** [a]Ge 26:15, 18, 20-22 **21:26** [1]Lit *except* **21:27** [a]Ge 26:31 **21:30** [a]Ge 31:48 **21:31** [a]Ge 21:14; 26:33 **21:33** [a]Ge 12:8 [b]Ex 15:18; Dt 32:40; Ps 90:2; 93:2; Is 40:28; Jer 10:10; Hab 1:12; Heb 13:8 **21:34** [a]Ge 22:19 ◆ **22:1** [a]Dt 8:2, 16; Heb 11:17; Jas 1:12-14 [b]Ge 22:11 **22:2** [a]Ge 22:12, 16; Jn 3:16; 1Jn 4:9 [b]Ge 12:1 [c]2Chr 3:1 [d]Ge 8:20 **22:6** [a]Jn 19:17

said, "Here I am, my son." And he said, "Behold, the fire and the wood, but where is the [a]lamb for the burnt offering?" **8** And Abraham said, "God will [1]provide for Himself the lamb for the burnt offering, my son." So the two of them walked on together.

**9** Then they came to [a]the place of which God had told him; and Abraham built [b]the altar there and arranged the wood and bound his son Isaac and [c]put him on the altar, on top of the wood. **10** And Abraham stretched out his hand and took the knife to slay his son. **11** But [a]the angel of Yahweh called to him from heaven and said, "Abraham, Abraham!" And he said, "Here I am." **12** And He said, "Do not stretch out your hand against the boy, and do nothing to him; for now [a]I know that you [1]fear God, since you have not withheld [b]your son, your only one, from Me." **13** Then Abraham lifted up his eyes and saw, and behold, *there was* a ram after *it had been* caught in the thicket by its horns; and Abraham went and took the ram and offered it up for a burnt offering in the place of his son. **14** And Abraham called the name of that place [1]Yahweh Will Provide, as it is said this day, "In the mount of Yahweh [a]it will [2]be provided."

**15** Then the angel of Yahweh called to Abraham a second time from heaven, **16** and said, "[a]By Myself I have sworn, declares Yahweh, because you have done this thing and have not spared your son, your only one, **17** indeed I will greatly bless you, and I will greatly [a]multiply your seed as the stars of the heavens and as [b]the sand which is on the seashore; and [c]your seed shall possess the gate of his enemies. **18** [a]In your [1]seed all the nations of the earth shall [2]be blessed, because you have [b]listened to My voice." **19** [a]So Abraham returned to his young men, and they arose and walked together to Beersheba; and Abraham lived at Beersheba.

**20** Now it happened after these things, that it was told to Abraham, saying, "Behold, [a]Milcah [1]also has borne children to your brother Nahor: **21** Uz his firstborn and Buz his brother and Kemuel the father of Aram **22** and Chesed and Hazo and Pildash and Jidlaph and Bethuel." **23** And Bethuel [1]was the father of [a]Rebekah. These eight Milcah bore to Nahor, Abraham's brother. **24** And his concubine, whose name was Reumah, [1]also bore Tebah and Gaham and Tahash and Maacah.

### *Sarah's Death and Burial*

**23** And [1]Sarah lived 127 years; *these were* the years of the life of Sarah. **2** Sarah died in [a]Kiriath-arba (that is, Hebron) in the land of Canaan; and Abraham [1]came to mourn for Sarah and to weep for her. **3** Then Abraham rose from before his dead and spoke to the [a]sons of Heth, saying, **4** "I am

---

**22:7** [a]Ex 29:38-42; Jn 1:29, 36; Rev 13:8 **22:8** [1]Lit *see* **22:9** [a]Ge 22:2 [b]Ge 12:7, 8; 13:18 [c]Heb 11:17-19; Jas 2:21 **22:11** [a]Ge 16:7-11; 21:17, 18 **22:12** [a]Jas 2:21, 22 [b]Ge 22:2, 16 [1]Or *reverence*; lit *are a fearer of God* **22:14** [a]Ge 22:8 [1]Heb *Yahweh-jireh* [2]Lit *be seen* **22:16** [a]Ps 105:9; Lk 1:73; Heb 6:13, 14 **22:17** [a]Ge 15:5; 26:4; Jer 33:22; Heb 11:12 [b]Ge 32:12 [c]Ge 24:60 **22:18** [a]Ge 12:3; 18:18; Ac 3:25; Ga 3:8, 16 [b]Ge 18:19; 22:3, 10; 26:5 [1]Or *descendants* [2]Or *experience blessing repeatedly, bless themselves* **22:19** [a]Ge 22:5 **22:20** [a]Ge 11:29 [1]Lit *she also* **22:23** [a]Ge 24:15 [1]Lit *begot* **22:24** [1]Lit *she also* ◆ **23:1** [1]Lit *the life of Sarah was* **23:2** [a]Jos 14:15; 15:13; 21:11 [1]Or *proceeded* **23:3** [a]Ge 10:15; 15:20

[a]a sojourner and a foreign resident
among you; [b]give me a [c]possession
for a burial site among you that I may
bury my dead out of my sight." **5** And
the sons of Heth answered Abraham,
saying to him, **6** "Hear us, my lord,
you are a [a,1]mighty prince among us;
bury your dead in the choicest of our
burial sites; none of us will refuse
you his burial sites for burying your
dead." **7** So Abraham rose and bowed
to the people of the land, the sons
of Heth. **8** And he spoke with them,
saying, "If it is your [1]desire *for me* to
bury my dead out of my sight, hear
me, and meet with [a]Ephron the son
of Zohar for me, **9** that he may give
me the cave of Machpelah which
belongs to him, which is at the end
of his field; for the full price let him
give it to me in [1]your presence as a
possession for a burial site." **10** Now
Ephron was sitting among the sons
of Heth; and Ephron the Hittite
answered Abraham in the hearing
of the sons of Heth, *even* [a]of all who
went in at the gate of his city, saying,
**11** "No, my lord, hear me; [a]I give you
the field, and I give you the cave
that is in it. In the sight of the sons
of my people I give it to you; bury
your dead." **12** And Abraham bowed
before the people of the land. **13** And
he spoke to Ephron in the hearing
of the people of the land, saying, "If
you will only please hear me; I will
give the silver for the field, accept
*it* from me that I may bury my dead
there." **14** Then Ephron answered
Abraham, saying to him, **15** "My lord,
hear me; a piece of land worth [1]four
hundred [a]shekels of silver, what is
that between me and you? So bury
your dead." **16** So Abraham heard
Ephron; and Abraham [a]weighed out
for Ephron the silver which he had
named in the [1]hearing of the sons of
Heth, four hundred shekels of silver,
[2]commercial standard.

**17** So [a]Ephron's field, which was in
Machpelah, which faced Mamre, the
field and the cave which was in it, and
all the trees which were in the field,
that were [1]within all the confines of
its border, [2]were deeded over **18** to
Abraham as purchased [a]in the sight
of the sons of Heth, before all who
came in at the gate of his city. **19** After
this, Abraham buried Sarah his wife
in the cave of the field at Machpelah
facing Mamre (that is, Hebron) in the
land of Canaan. **20** So the field and
the cave that is in it [1]were [a]deeded
over to Abraham for a possession for
a burial site by the sons of Heth.

### *A Wife for Isaac*

**24** Now [a]Abraham was old, ad-
vanced in age; and Yahweh had
[b]blessed Abraham in every way. **2** And
Abraham said to his servant, the
oldest of his household, who [a]ruled
over all that he owned, "[b]Please place
your hand under my thigh, **3** and I will
make you swear by Yahweh, [a]the God
of heaven and the God of earth, that
you [b]shall not take a wife for my son
from the daughters of [c]the Canaanites,

**23:4** [a]Ge 17:8; Lv 25:23; 1Chr 29:15; Ps 39:12; 105:12; 119:19; Heb 11:9, 13 [b]Ac 7:16 [c]Ge 49:30 **23:6** [a]Ge 14:14; 20:7 [1]Lit *prince of God* **23:8** [a]Ge 25:9 [1]Lit *soul* **23:9** [1]Lit *the midst of you* **23:10** [a]Ge 23:18; 34:20, 24; Ru 4:1, 11 **23:11** [a]2Sa 24:21-24 **23:15** [a]Ex 30:13; Eze 45:12 [1]Approx. 10 lb. or 4.4 kg, a shekel was approx. 0.4 oz. or 11 gm **23:16** [a]2Sa 14:26; Jer 32:9, 10; Zec 11:12 [1]Lit *ears* [2]Lit *current according to the merchant* **23:17** [a]Ge 25:9; 49:29, 30; 50:13 [1]Lit *in all its border around* [2]Or *were ratified* **23:18** [a]Ge 23:10 **23:20** [a]Jer 32:10-14 [1]Lit *were confirmed* ◆ **24:1** [a]Ge 18:11 [b]Ge 12:2; 13:2; 24:35; Ga 3:9 **24:2** [a]Ge 39:4-6 [b]Ge 24:9; 47:29 **24:3** [a]Ge 14:19, 22 [b]Dt 7:3; 2Co 6:14-17 [c]Ge 10:15-19; 26:34, 35; 28:1, 8

among whom I live, **4** but you will go
to [a]my land and to my kin, and take
a wife for my son Isaac." **5** And the
servant said to him, "Suppose the
woman is not willing to follow me to
this land; should I indeed take your
son back to the land from where you
came?" **6** Then Abraham said to him,
"[a]Beware lest you take my son back
there! **7** [a]Yahweh, the God of heaven,
who took me from my father's house
and from the land of my kin, and who
spoke to me and who swore to me,
saying, '[b]To your seed I will give this
land,' He will send [c]His angel before
you, and you will take a wife for my
son from there. **8** But if the woman
is not willing to follow you, then
you will [a]be free from this oath of
mine; [b]only do not take my son back
there." **9** So the servant [a]placed his
hand under the thigh of Abraham his
master and swore to him concerning
this matter.

**10** Then the servant took ten cam-
els from the camels of his master,
and he went with all kinds of [a]good
things of his master's in his hand. So
he arose and went to [1]Mesopotamia,
to [b]the city of Nahor. **11** And he made
the camels kneel down outside the
city by [a]the well of water at evening
time, [b]the time when the women go
out to draw water. **12** And he said,
"[a]O Yahweh, the God of my master
Abraham, please [b]cause *this* to
happen before me today, and show
lovingkindness to my master Abra-
ham. **13** Behold, [a]I am standing by the
spring of water, and the daughters
of the men of the city are coming
out to draw water; **14** now may it be
that the young woman to whom I
say, 'Please let down your jar so that
I may drink,' and she says, 'Drink,
and I will give *water* to your camels
to drink also'—*may* she *be the one*
whom You have decided for Your
servant Isaac; and by this I will know
that You have shown lovingkindness
to my master."

### *Rebekah Goes with Abraham's Servant*

**15** [a]And before he had finished speak-
ing, behold, [b]Rebekah who was born
to Bethuel the son of [c]Milcah, the
wife of Abraham's brother Nahor,
was coming out with her jar on her
shoulder. **16** Now the young woman
was [a]very beautiful in appearance, a
virgin, and no man had [1]known her;
and she went down to the spring and
filled her jar and came up. **17** Then
the servant ran to meet her and
said, "[a]Please give me a little water
to drink from your jar." **18** [a]And she
said, "Drink, my lord"; and she quick-
ly lowered her jar to her hand and
gave him a drink. **19** Now when she
had finished giving him a drink, [a]she
said, "I will draw also for your camels
until they have finished drinking."
**20** So she hurried and emptied her
jar into the watering channel and ran
again to the well to draw, and she drew
for all his camels. **21** [a]Meanwhile, the
man was gazing at her [1]in silence, to
know whether Yahweh had made his
journey successful or not.

---

**24:4** [a]Ge 12:1; Heb 11:15 **24:6** [a]Ge 24:8 **24:7** [a]Ge 24:3 [b]Ge 12:7; 13:15; 15:18; Ex 32:13 [c]Ge 16:7; 21:17; 22:11; Ex 23:20, 23 **24:8** [a]Jos 2:17-20 [b]Ge 24:6 **24:9** [a]Ge 24:2 **24:10** [a]Ge 24:22, 53 [b]Ge 11:31, 32 [1]Heb *Aram-naharaim*; lit *Aram of the two rivers* **24:11** [a]Ge 24:42 [b]Ex 2:16; 1Sa 9:11 **24:12** [a]Ge 24:27, 42, 48; 26:24; Ex 3:6, 15 [b]Ge 27:20 **24:13** [a]Ge 24:43 **24:15** [a]Ge 24:45 [b]Ge 22:20, 23 [c]Ge 11:29 **24:16** [a]Ge 12:11; 26:7; 29:17 [1]Or *relations with* **24:17** [a]Jn 4:7 **24:18** [a]Ge 24:14, 46 **24:19** [a]Ge 24:14 **24:21** [a]Ge 24:12-14, 27, 52 [1]Lit *keeping silent*

**22** Now it happened that when
the camels had finished drinking,
the man took a [a]gold ring weighing
a [1]half-shekel and two bracelets for
her [2]wrists weighing ten shekels in
gold, **23** and said, "Whose daughter
are you? Please tell me, is there a
place for us to lodge in your father's
house?" **24** And she said to him, "[a]I
am the daughter of Bethuel, the son
of Milcah, whom she bore to Nahor."
**25** And she said to him, "We have
plenty of both straw and feed, and a
place to lodge in." **26** Then the man
[a]bowed low and worshiped Yahweh.
**27** And he said, "[a]Blessed be Yahweh,
the God of my master Abraham, who
has not forsaken [b]His lovingkindness
and His truth toward my master; as
for me, [c]Yahweh has guided me in
the way to the house of my master's
brothers."

**28** Then [a]the young woman ran and
told her mother's household about
these things. **29** Now Rebekah had
a brother whose name was [a]Laban;
and Laban ran outside to the man
at the spring. **30** Now it happened,
when he saw the ring and the brace-
lets on his sister's [1]wrists, and when
he heard the words of Rebekah his
sister, saying, "[2]This is what the man
said to me," he came out to the man;
and behold, he was standing by the
camels at the spring. **31** And he said,
"[a]Come in, [b]blessed of Yahweh! Why
do you stand outside since [c]I have
prepared the house and a place for
the camels?" **32** So the man came into
the house. Then [a,1]Laban unloaded
the camels, and he gave straw and
feed to the camels, and water to wash
his feet and the feet of the men who
were with him. **33** Then *food* was
set before him to eat, but he said, "I
will not eat until I have spoken my
words." And he said, "Speak!" **34** So
he said, "I am [a]Abraham's servant.
**35** And Yahweh has greatly [a]blessed
my master, so he has become great;
and He has given him [b]flocks and
herds, and silver and gold, and
male slaves and female slaves, and
camels and donkeys. **36** Now [a]Sarah
my master's wife bore a son to my
master [1]in her old age, and [b]he has
given him all that he has. **37** [a]And my
master made me swear, saying, 'You
shall not take a wife for my son from
the daughters of the Canaanites, in
whose land I [1]live; **38** but you shall
go to my father's house and to my
family, and take a wife for my son.'
**39** [a]Then I said to my master, 'Sup-
pose the woman does not follow me.'
**40** And he said to me, '[a]Yahweh, be-
fore whom I have [b]walked, will send
[c]His angel with you and will make
your journey successful, and you will
take a wife for my son from my family
and from my father's house. **41** [a]Then
you will be free from my oath, when
you come to my relatives. Now if they
do not give her to you, you will be
free from my oath.'

**42** "So [a]I came today to the spring
and said, 'O Yahweh, the God of my
master Abraham, if now You will

**24:22** [a]Ge 24:47; Ex 32:2, 3 [1]A shekel was approx. 0.4 oz. or 11 gm [2]Lit *hands* **24:24** [a]Ge 24:15
**24:26** [a]Ge 24:48, 52; Ex 4:31 **24:27** [a]Ge 24:12, 42, 48; Ex 18:10; Ru 4:14; 1Sa 25:32; 2Sa 18:28; Lk 1:68
[b]Ge 32:10; Ps 98:3 [c]Ge 24:21, 48 **24:28** [a]Ge 29:12 **24:29** [a]Ge 29:5, 13 **24:30** [1]Lit *hands* [2]Lit *Thus
the man* **24:31** [a]Ge 29:13 [b]Ge 26:29; Ru 3:10; Ps 115:15 [c]Ge 18:3-5; 19:2, 3 **24:32** [a]Ge 43:24; Jdg 19:21
[1]Lit *he* **24:34** [a]Ge 24:2 **24:35** [a]Ge 24:1 [b]Ge 13:2 **24:36** [a]Ge 21:1-7 [b]Ge 25:5 [1]Lit *after she was old*
**24:37** [a]Ge 24:2-4 [1]Lit *dwell* **24:39** [a]Ge 24:5 **24:40** [a]Ge 24:7 [b]Ge 5:22, 24; 17:1 [c]Ex 23:20
**24:41** [a]Ge 24:8 **24:42** [a]Ge 24:11, 12

make my journey on which I go
[b]successful; **43** behold, [a]I am stand-
ing by the spring of water, and may it
be that the [7]maiden who comes out to
draw, and to whom I say, "[b]Please let
me drink a little water from your jar";
**44** and she will say to me, "You drink,
and I will draw for your camels also";
she is the woman whom Yahweh has
decided upon for my master's son.'
**45** "Before I had finished [a]speaking
in my heart, behold, [b]Rebekah was
coming out with her jar on her shoul-
der, and she went down to the spring
and drew, and [c]I said to her, 'Please
give me a drink.' **46** Then she hurried
and lowered her jar from her *shoul-
der* and said, '[a]Drink, and I will also
give *water* to your camels to drink';
so I drank, and she also gave *water* to
the camels to drink. **47** [a]Then I asked
her and said, 'Whose daughter are
you?' And she said, 'The daughter of
Bethuel, Nahor's son, whom Milcah
bore to him'; and I put the [b]ring on her
nose and the bracelets on her [7]wrists.
**48** And I [a]bowed low and worshiped
Yahweh; and I blessed Yahweh, the
God of my master Abraham, [b]who
had guided me in the true way to take
the daughter of my master's [7]relative
for his son. **49** So now if you are going
to [a]show lovingkindness and truth
with my master, tell me; and if not,
tell me, that I may turn to the right
or to the left."
**50** Then Laban and Bethuel an-
swered and said, "[a]The matter comes
from Yahweh; [b]*so* we cannot speak to
you bad or good. **51** Behold, Rebekah
is before you, take *her* and go, and let
her be the wife of your master's son,
as Yahweh has spoken."
**52** Now it happened that when
Abraham's servant heard their words,
he [a]bowed himself to the ground
[7]before Yahweh. **53** The servant
brought out [a]articles of silver and
articles of gold, and garments, and
gave them to Rebekah; he also gave
precious things to her brother and to
her mother. **54** Then he and the men
who were with him ate and drank and
spent the night. And then they arose
in the morning, and he said, "[a]Send
me away to my master." **55** But her
brother and her mother said, "[a]Let
the young woman stay with us *a few*
days, or *even* ten; afterward she will
go." **56** And he said to them, "Do not
delay me, since [a]Yahweh has made
my way successful. Send me away
that I may go to my master." **57** And
they said, "We will call the young
woman and ask about [7]her wishes."
**58** Then they called Rebekah and said
to her, "Will you go with this man?"
And she said, "I will go." **59** Thus they
sent away their sister Rebekah and
[a]her nurse with Abraham's servant
and his men. **60** And they blessed
Rebekah and said to her,

"May you, our sister,
[a]Become thousands
of ten thousands,
And may [b]your seed possess
The gate of those
who hate him."

**61** Then Rebekah arose with her
young women, and they mounted

---

**24:42** [b]Ne 1:11 **24:43** [a]Ge 24:13 [b]Ge 24:14 [7]Or *virgin* **24:45** [a]1Sa 1:13 [b]Ge 24:15 [c]Ge 24:17 **24:46** [a]Ge 24:18, 19 **24:47** [a]Ge 24:23, 24 [b]Eze 16:11, 12 [7]Lit *hands* **24:48** [a]Ge 24:26, 52 [b]Ge 24:27; Ps 32:8; 48:14; Is 48:17 [7]Lit *brother* **24:49** [a]Ge 47:29; Jos 2:14 **24:50** [a]Ps 118:23; Mk 12:11 [b]Ge 31:24, 29 **24:52** [a]Ge 24:26, 48 [7]Lit *to* **24:53** [a]Ge 24:10, 22; Ex 3:22; 11:2; 12:35 **24:54** [a]Ge 24:56, 59; 30:25 **24:55** [a]Jdg 19:4 **24:56** [a]Ge 24:40 **24:57** [7]Lit *her mouth* **24:59** [a]Ge 35:8 **24:60** [a]Ge 17:16 [b]Ge 22:17

the camels and went after the man.
So the servant took Rebekah and
went.

### *Rebekah Becomes Isaac's Wife*

**62** Now Isaac had come from going
to [a]Beer-lahai-roi, for he [1]was living
in [b]the land of the [2]Negev. **63** And
Isaac went out [a]to [1]muse in the field
toward evening; and [b]he lifted up his
eyes and looked, and behold, camels
were coming. **64** And Rebekah lifted
up her eyes and saw Isaac and dis-
mounted from the camel. **65** Then she
said to the servant, "Who is that man
walking in the field to meet us?" And
the servant said, "He is my master."
Then she took her [1]veil and covered
herself. **66** And the servant recounted
to Isaac all the things that he had
done. **67** Then Isaac brought her into
his mother Sarah's tent, and [a]he took
Rebekah, and she became his wife,
and [b]he loved her. Thus, Isaac was
comforted after [c]his mother's *death.*

### *The Death of Abraham*

**25** Now Abraham took another
wife, [1]whose name was
Keturah. **2** [a]And she bore to him
Zimran and Jokshan and Medan and
Midian and Ishbak and Shuah. **3** Now
Jokshan [1]was the father of Sheba
and Dedan. And the sons of Dedan
were Asshurim and Letushim and
Leummim. **4** And the sons of Midian
*were* Ephah and Epher and Hanoch
and Abida and Eldaah. All these *were*
the sons of Keturah. **5** [a]And Abraham
gave all that he had to Isaac; **6** but
to the sons of the concubines which
Abraham had, Abraham gave gifts
while he was still living, and he
[a]sent them away from his son Isaac
eastward, to the land of the east.
**7** These are the days of the years
of Abraham's life that he lived, [a]175
years. **8** And Abraham breathed his
last and died [a]in a good old age, an
old man and full *of days*; and he was
[b]gathered to his people. **9** Then his
sons Isaac and Ishmael buried him
in [a]the cave of Machpelah, in the
field of Ephron the son of Zohar the
Hittite, facing Mamre, **10** [a]the field
which Abraham bought from the
sons of Heth; there Abraham was
buried with Sarah his wife. **11** Now
it happened after the death of Abra-
ham, that [a]God blessed his son Isaac;
and Isaac [1]lived by [b]Beer-lahai-roi.

### *The Generations of Ishmael*

**12** Now these are the generations
of [a]Ishmael, Abraham's son, whom
Hagar the Egyptian, Sarah's servant-
woman, bore to Abraham; **13** and
these are the names of [a]the sons of
Ishmael, by their names, [1]in the order
of their birth: Nebaioth, the firstborn
of Ishmael, and Kedar and Adbeel and
Mibsam **14** and Mishma and Dumah
and Massa, **15** Hadad and Tema, Jetur,
Naphish, and Kedemah. **16** These
are the sons of Ishmael and these
are their names, by their villages,
and by their camps; [a]twelve princes
according to their [1]tribes. **17** These are

**24:62** [a]Ge 16:14; 25:11 [b]Ge 20:1 [1]Lit *was dwelling* [2]South country **24:63** [a]Jos 1:8; Ps 1:2; 77:12; 119:15, 27, 48; 143:5; 145:5 [b]Ge 18:2 [1]Or *stroll*; meaning uncertain **24:65** [1]Or *shawl* **24:67** [a]Ge 25:20 [b]Ge 29:18 [c]Ge 23:1, 2 ◆ **25:1** [1]Lit *and her name* **25:2** [a]1Chr 1:32, 33 **25:3** [1]Lit *begot* **25:5** [a]Ge 24:35, 36 **25:6** [a]Ge 21:14 **25:7** [a]Ge 12:4 **25:8** [a]Ge 15:15; 47:8, 9 [b]Ge 25:17; 35:29; 49:29, 33 **25:9** [a]Ge 23:17, 18; 49:29, 30; 50:13 **25:10** [a]Ge 23:3-16 **25:11** [a]Ge 12:2, 3; 22:17; 26:3 [b]Ge 16:14; 24:62 [1]Lit *dwelt* **25:12** [a]Ge 16:15 **25:13** [a]1Chr 1:29-31 [1]Lit *in regard to their generations* **25:16** [a]Ge 17:20 [1]Or *peoples*

the years of the life of Ishmael, [a]137
years; and he breathed his last and
died and was [b]gathered to his people.
**18** And they dwelt from [a]Havilah to
[b]Shur which is [1]east of Egypt [2]as one
goes toward Assyria; [c]he [3]settled in
the face of all his brothers.

### *The Generations of Isaac*

**19** Now these are [a]the generations
of Isaac, Abraham's son: Abraham
[1]became the father of Isaac; **20** and
Isaac was forty years old when he took
[a]Rebekah, the [b]daughter of Bethuel
the [1]Aramean of Paddan-aram, the
[c]sister of Laban the [1]Aramean, to
be his wife. **21** And Isaac entreated
Yahweh on behalf of his wife because
she was barren; and [a]Yahweh [1]was
moved by his entreaty. So Rebekah
his wife [b]conceived. **22** But the chil-
dren struggled together within her;
and she said, "If it is so, why then am
I this *way*?" So she went to [a]inquire
of Yahweh. **23** And Yahweh said to
her,

"[a]Two nations are
in your womb;
[b]And two peoples will be
separated from your body;
And one people shall be
stronger than the other;
And [c]the older shall
serve the younger."

**24** And her days to give birth were
fulfilled, and behold, there were
twins in her womb. **25** And the first
came forth red, [a]all over like a hairy
garment; and they named him Esau.
**26** Afterward his brother came forth
with [a]his hand holding on to Esau's
heel, so [b]his name was called [1]Jacob;
and Isaac was [c]sixty years old when
she gave birth to them.

### *Esau Sells His Birthright*

**27** And the boys grew up; Esau became
a skillful hunter, a man of the field, but
Jacob was a [1]peaceful man, [a,2]living
in tents. **28** Isaac loved Esau because
[1]he had [a]an appetite for *hunted* game,
[b]but Rebekah loved Jacob.

**29** And Jacob had cooked [a]stew. And
Esau came in from the field, and he
was [1]famished. **30** Then Esau said to
Jacob, "Please give me a swallow from
the red stuff—[1]this red stuff, for I am
[2]famished." Therefore his name was
called [3]Edom. **31** But Jacob said, "[1]First
sell me your [a]birthright." **32** And Esau
said, "Behold, I am about to die; so
of what *use* then is the birthright to
me?" **33** And Jacob said, "[1]First swear
to me"; so he swore to him and [a]sold
his birthright to Jacob. **34** So Jacob gave
Esau bread and lentil stew; and he ate
and drank and rose and went away.
Thus Esau despised his birthright.

### *Yahweh Establishes the Oath with Isaac*

**26** Now there was [a]a famine in
the land, besides the previous
famine that had occurred in the days
of Abraham. So Isaac went to Gerar,
to [b]Abimelech king of the Philistines.

**25:17** [a]Ge 16:16 [b]Ge 25:8; 49:33 **25:18** [a]1Sa 15:7 [b]Ge 20:1 [c]Ge 16:12 [1]Lit *before* [2]Lit *as you go* [3]Lit *fell over against* **25:19** [a]Mt 1:2 [1]Lit *begot* **25:20** [a]Ge 24:15, 29, 67 [b]Ge 22:23 [c]Ge 24:29 [1]Syrian **25:21** [a]1Sa 1:17; 1Chr 5:20; 2Chr 33:13; Ezr 8:23; Ps 127:3 [b]Ro 9:10 [1]Lit *was entreated of him* **25:22** [a]1Sa 9:9; 10:22 **25:23** [a]Ge 17:4-6, 16; Nu 20:14; Dt 2:4, 8 [b]Ge 27:29 [c]Ge 27:40; Mal 1:2, 3; Ro 9:12 **25:25** [a]Ge 27:11 **25:26** [a]Hos 12:3 [b]Ge 27:36 [c]Ge 25:20 [1]Lit *one who takes by the heel, supplants* **25:27** [a]Heb 11:9 [1]Lit *complete* [2]Lit *dwelling* **25:28** [a]Ge 27:19 [b]Ge 27:6-10 [1]Lit *game was in his mouth* **25:29** [a]2Ki 4:38 [1]Lit *weary* **25:30** [1]Lit *the red, this red* [2]Lit *weary* [3]Lit *red* **25:31** [a]Dt 21:16, 17; 1Chr 5:1, 2 [1]Lit *Today* **25:33** [a]Heb 12:16 [1]Lit *Today* ◆**26:1** [a]Ge 12:10 [b]Ge 20:1, 2

**2** And Yahweh [a]appeared to him and
said, "Do not go down to Egypt;
[b]dwell in the land of which I shall
tell you. **3** Sojourn in this land, and [a]I
will be with you and [b]bless you, for
[c]to you and to your seed I will give all
these lands, and I will establish [d]the
oath which I swore to your father
Abraham. **4** [a]And I will multiply
your seed as the stars of heaven, and
I will give your seed all these lands;
and [b]by your seed all the nations of
the earth [1]shall be blessed; **5** because
Abraham [a]listened to My voice and
kept My charge, My commandments,
My statutes, and My laws."

### *Isaac and Abimelech*

**6** So Isaac [1]lived in Gerar. **7** Then
the men of the place asked about
his wife. And he said, "[a]She is my
sister," for he was [b]afraid to say, "my
wife," *thinking*, "lest the men of the
place kill me on account of Rebekah,
for she is [c]beautiful in appearance."
**8** Now it happened, when he had
been there a long time, that Abim-
elech king of the Philistines looked
out through a window and saw, and
behold, Isaac was [1]caressing his wife
Rebekah. **9** Then Abimelech called
Isaac and said, "Behold, surely she
is your wife! How then did you say,
'She is my sister'?" And Isaac said to
him, "Because I said, 'Lest I die on
account of her.'" **10** [a]And Abimelech
said, "What is this you have done to
us? One of the people might easily
have lain with your wife, and you
would have brought guilt upon us."
**11** So Abimelech commanded all the
people, saying, "He who [a]touches
this man or his wife shall surely be
put to death."

**12** And Isaac sowed in that land
and [1]reaped in the same year one
hundredfold. And [a]Yahweh blessed
him, **13** and the man [a]became great
and continued to grow greater until
he became very great; **14** and [a]he had
possessions of flocks and posses-
sions of herds and many servants,
so that the Philistines were jealous
of him. **15** Now [a]all the wells which
his father's servants had dug in the
days of Abraham his father, the Phi-
listines stopped up [1]by filling them
with earth. **16** Then Abimelech said
to Isaac, "Go away from us, for you
are [a,1]too mighty for us." **17** And Isaac
departed from there and camped in
the valley of Gerar and [1]settled there.

### *The Quarrel over the Wells*

**18** Then Isaac dug again the wells of
water which [1]had been dug in the
days of his father Abraham, but the
Philistines had stopped them up after
the death of Abraham; and he [2]called
them by the same names by which
his father had called them. **19** Then
Isaac's servants dug in the valley
and found there a well of [1]flowing
water. **20** And the herdsmen of Gerar
[a]contended with the herdsmen of
Isaac, saying, "The water is ours!"
So he named the well [1]Esek, because
they quarreled with him. **21** Then

---

**26:2** [a]Ge 12:7; 17:1; 18:1 [b]Ge 12:1 **26:3** [a]Ge 26:24; 28:15; 31:3 [b]Ge 12:2 [c]Ge 12:7; 13:15; 15:18 [d]Ge 22:16-18; Ps 105:9 **26:4** [a]Ge 15:5; 22:17; Ex 32:13 [b]Ge 22:18; Ga 3:8 [1]Or *experience blessing repeatedly, bless themselves* **26:5** [a]Ge 22:16 **26:6** [1]Lit *dwelt* **26:7** [a]Ge 12:13; 20:2, 12 [b]Pr 29:25 [c]Ge 12:11; 24:16; 29:17 **26:8** [1]Lit *laughing with* **26:10** [a]Ge 20:9 **26:11** [a]Ps 105:15 **26:12** [a]Ge 24:1; 26:3; Job 42:12; Pr 10:22 [1]Lit *found* **26:13** [a]Pr 10:22 **26:14** [a]Ge 24:35; 25:5 **26:15** [a]Ge 21:25, 30 [1]Lit *and filled them* **26:16** [a]Ex 1:9 [1]Lit *much mightier than we* **26:17** [1]Lit *dwelt* **26:18** [1]Lit *they had dug* [2]Lit *called their names as the names* **26:19** [1]Lit *living* **26:20** [a]Ge 21:25 [1]Contention

they dug another well, and they
contended over it also, so he called it
[1]Sitnah. **22** Then he moved away from
there and dug another well, and they
did not contend over it; so he named
it [1]Rehoboth, and he said, "[a,2]At last
Yahweh has made [3]room for us, and
we will be [b]fruitful in the land."

**23** And he went up from there
to [a]Beersheba. **24** And Yahweh
[a]appeared to him that night and said,

"[b]I am the God of your
father Abraham;
[c]Do not fear, for I am with you.
I [d]will bless you
and multiply your seed,
For the sake of My
servant Abraham."

**25** So he built an [a]altar there and
called upon the name of Yahweh
and pitched his tent there; and there
Isaac's servants dug out a well.

### *Isaac's Oath with Abimelech*

**26** Now [a]Abimelech came to him
from Gerar [1]with his adviser Ahuz-
zath and Phicol the commander of
his army. **27** And Isaac said to them,
"[a]Why have you come to me, since
you hate me and have sent me away
from you?" **28** Then they said, "We
see plainly [a]that Yahweh has been
with you; so we said, 'Let there now
be an oath between us—between
[1]you and us—and let us cut a cov-
enant with you, **29** that you will do us
no harm, just as we have not touched
you [1]and have done to you nothing
but good and have sent you away in
peace. You are now the [a]blessed of
Yahweh.'" **30** Then [a]he made them a
feast, and they ate and drank. **31** In the
morning they arose early, and [a]each
swore to [1]the other; then Isaac sent
them away, and they departed from
him in peace. **32** Now it happened on
that day, that Isaac's servants came
in and told him about the well which
they had dug and said to him, "We
have found water." **33** So he called it
Shibah; therefore the name of the
city is [a]Beersheba to this day.

**34** And Esau was forty years old,
[a]and he took as a wife Judith the
daughter of Beeri the Hittite, and
*also* Basemath the daughter of Elon
the Hittite; **35** and [a]they [1]brought
bitterness to Isaac and Rebekah.

### *Isaac Calls to Bless Esau*

**27** Now it happened that when
Isaac was old and [a]his eyes
were too dim to see, that he called his
[b]older son Esau and said to him, "My
son." And he said to him, "Here I am."
**2** [a,1]And Isaac said, "Behold now, I am
old, *and* I do not know the day of my
death. **3** So now, please take up your
gear, your quiver and your bow, and
go out to the field and [a]hunt game
for me; **4** and prepare a savory dish
for me such as I love, and bring it to
me that I may eat, so that [a]my soul
may bless you before I die."

**5** Now Rebekah was listening while
Isaac was speaking to his son Esau.
Then Esau went to the field to hunt
for game to bring *to Isaac*. **6** [a]But

---

**26:21** [1]Enmity **26:22** [a]Ps 4:1; Is 54:2, 3 [b]Ge 17:6; Ex 1:7 [1]Broad places [2]Lit *Truly now* [3]Or *broad*
**26:23** [a]Ge 22:19 **26:24** [a]Ge 26:2 [b]Ge 17:7, 8; 24:12; Ex 3:6; Ac 7:32 [c]Ge 15:1 [d]Ge 22:17; 26:3, 4
**26:25** [a]Ge 12:7, 8; 13:4, 18; Ps 116:17 **26:26** [a]Ge 21:22 [1]Lit *and his confidential friend* **26:27** [a]Jdg 11:7
**26:28** [a]Ge 21:22, 23 [1]Lit *us and you* **26:29** [a]Ge 24:31; Ps 115:15 [1]Lit *and just as we* **26:30** [a]Ge 19:3
**26:31** [a]Ge 21:31 [1]Lit *his brother* **26:33** [a]Ge 21:31 **26:34** [a]Ge 28:8; 36:2 **26:35** [a]Ge 27:46
[1]Lit *were a bitterness of spirit to* ◆ **27:1** [a]Ge 48:10; 1Sa 3:2 [b]Ge 25:25, 33, 34 **27:2** [a]Ge 47:29 [1]Lit *He*
**27:3** [a]Ge 25:28 **27:4** [a]Ge 27:19, 25, 31; 48:9, 15, 16; Dt 33:1; Heb 11:20 **27:6** [a]Ge 25:28

Rebekah spoke to her son Jacob,
saying, "Behold, I heard your father
speaking to your brother Esau, saying,
**7** 'Bring me *some* game and prepare a
savory dish for me, that I may eat and
bless you in the presence of Yahweh
before my death.' **8** So now, my son,
[a]listen to my voice [1]as I command
you. **9** Go now to the flock and [1]get
for me two choice [2]young goats from
there, that I may prepare them *as* a
savory dish for your father, such as
he loves. **10** Then you shall bring *it* to
your father, that he may eat, so that
he may bless you before his death."
**11** Then Jacob [1]answered his mother
Rebekah, "Behold, Esau my brother
is a [a]hairy man, and I am a smooth
man. **12** [a]Perhaps my father will feel
me, then I will be as a mocker in his
sight, and I will bring upon myself a
curse and not a blessing." **13** But his
mother said to him, "Your curse be on
me, my son; only [a]listen to my voice,
and go, get *them* for me." **14** So he went
and got *them* and brought *them* to his
mother; and his mother made a savory
dish such as his father loved. **15** Then
Rebekah took the [1]best [a]garments of
Esau her elder son, which were with
her in the house, and she put them on
Jacob her younger son. **16** And she put
the skins of the [1]young goats on his
hands and on the smooth part of his
neck. **17** She also gave the savory dish
and the bread, which she had prepared
into the hand of her son Jacob.

### *Isaac Blesses Jacob and Esau*

**18** Then he came to his father and
said, "My father." And he said, "Here
I am. Who are you, my son?" **19** And
Jacob said to his father, "I am Esau
your firstborn; I have done as you
told me. [a]Rise up, please, sit and eat
of my game, that [b]your soul may
bless me." **20** Then Isaac said to his
son, "How is it that you have found
*it* so quickly, my son?" And he said,
"[a]Because Yahweh your God caused
*it* to happen to me." **21** Then Isaac
said to Jacob, "Please come near, that
[a]I may feel you, my son, whether you
are really my son Esau or not." **22** So
Jacob came near to Isaac his father,
and he felt him and said, "The voice
is the voice of Jacob, but the hands
are the hands of Esau." **23** And he did
not recognize him because his hands
were [a]hairy like his brother Esau's
hands; so he blessed him. **24** And he
said, "Are you really my son Esau?"
And he said, "I am." **25** So he said,
"Bring *it* near to me, and I will eat of
my son's game, that [a]my soul may
bless you." And he brought *it* near
to him, and he ate; he also brought
him wine, and he drank. **26** Then his
father Isaac said to him, "Please come
near and kiss me, my son." **27** So he
came near and kissed him; and he
smelled the smell of his garments,
and then he [a]blessed him and said,

"See, [b]the smell of my son
Is like the smell of a field
[c]which Yahweh has blessed;
**28** Now may [a]God give you
of the dew of heaven,
And of the [b]fatness
of the earth,
And an abundance
of grain and new wine;

**27:8** [a]Ge 27:13, 43 [1]Lit *according to what* **27:9** [1]Lit *take* [2]Lit *kids of goats* **27:11** [a]Ge 25:25 [1]Lit *said to* **27:12** [a]Ge 27:21, 22 **27:13** [a]Ge 27:8 **27:15** [a]Ge 27:27 [1]Or *choice*, cf. 3:6; lit *desirable* **27:16** [1]Lit *kids of the goats* **27:19** [a]Ge 27:31 [b]Ge 27:4 **27:20** [a]Ge 24:12 **27:21** [a]Ge 27:12 **27:23** [a]Ge 27:16 **27:25** [a]Ge 27:4 **27:27** [a]Heb 11:20 [b]SS 4:11 [c]Ps 65:10 **27:28** [a]Ge 27:39; Dt 33:13, 28; Pr 3:20; Zec 8:12 [b]Nu 18:12

29 [a]May peoples serve you,
And nations bow
down to you;
[b]Be master of your brothers,
[c]And may your mother's
sons bow down to you.
[d]Cursed be those
who curse you,
And blessed be those
who bless you."

30 Now it happened that as soon
as Isaac had finished blessing Jacob,
and Jacob had hardly gone out from
the presence of Isaac his father,
that Esau his brother came in from
his hunting. 31 Then he also made
a savory dish and brought it to his
father; and he said to his father,
"[a]Let my father arise and eat of his
son's game, that [b]your soul may bless
me." 32 And Isaac his father said to
him, "[a]Who are you?" And he said, "I
am your son, [b]your firstborn, Esau."
33 Then Isaac [1]trembled exceedingly
violently and said, "[a]Who was he
then that hunted game and brought
*it* to me, so that I ate of all *of it* before
you came and blessed him? [b]Indeed,
he shall be blessed." 34 As Esau heard
the words of his father, [a]he cried out
with an exceedingly great and bitter
cry and said to his father, "Bless me,
me also, O my father!" 35 And he
said, "[a]Your brother came deceitfully
and has taken away your blessing."
36 Then he said, "[1]Is he not rightly
named [a]Jacob, for he has supplanted
me these two times? He took away
my birthright, and behold, now he
has taken away my blessing." And
he said, "Have you not reserved a
blessing for me?" 37 But Isaac an-
swered and said to Esau, "Behold,
I have made him [a]your master, and
all his *fellow* brothers I have given to
him [1]as servants; and with grain and
new wine I have sustained him. Now
as for you then, what can I do, my
son?" 38 And Esau said to his father,
"Do you have only one blessing, my
father? Bless me, *even* me also, O my
father." So Esau lifted his voice and
[a]wept.

39 Then [a]Isaac his father answered
and said to him,

"Behold, [b,1]away from the
fatness of the earth shall
be your habitation,
And [1]away from the dew
of heaven from above.
40 "By your sword you shall live,
And your brother
[a]you shall serve;
But it shall be [b]when you
become restless,
That you will [1]break his
yoke from your neck."

41 So Esau [a]bore a grudge against
Jacob because of the blessing with
which his father had blessed him;
and Esau said in his heart, "[b]The
days of mourning for my father
are near; then I will kill my brother
Jacob." 42 Then the words of her elder
son Esau were told to Rebekah. So
she sent and called her younger son
Jacob and said to him, "Behold, your
brother Esau is consoling himself
concerning you *by planning* to kill
you. 43 So now, my son, [a]listen to

**27:29** [a]Ge 25:23; Is 45:14; 49:7, 23; 60:12, 14 [b]Ge 9:26, 27; 27:37 [c]Ge 37:7, 10 [d]Ge 12:3; Nu 24:9
**27:31** [a]Ge 27:19 [b]Ge 27:4 **27:32** [a]Ge 27:18 [b]Ge 25:33, 34 **27:33** [a]Ge 27:35 [b]Ge 25:23; 28:3, 4; Nu 23:20 [1]Lit *trembled with a very great trembling* **27:34** [a]Heb 12:17 **27:35** [a]Ge 27:19
**27:36** [a]Ge 25:26, 32-34 [1]Or *Was he then named Jacob that he has* **27:37** [a]Ge 27:28, 29 [1]Lit *for* **27:38** [a]Heb 12:17 **27:39** [a]Heb 11:20 [b]Ge 27:28; Dt 33:13, 28 [1]Or *of* **27:40** [a]Ge 25:23; 27:29 [b]2Ki 8:20-22 [1]Lit *tear off* **27:41** [a]Ge 32:3-11; 37:4, 8 [b]Ge 50:2-4, 10 **27:43** [a]Ge 27:8, 13

my voice, and arise, [1]flee to [b]Haran,
to my brother [c]Laban! **44** Stay with
him [a]a few days, until your brother's
wrath [1]subsides, **45** until your broth-
er's anger [1]against you subsides and
he forgets [a]what you did to him.
Then I will send and get you from
there. Why should I be bereaved of
you both in one day?"
**46** Then Rebekah said to Isaac, "I
am tired of [1]living because of [a]the
daughters of Heth; [b]if Jacob takes a
wife from the daughters of Heth, like
these, from the daughters of the land,
what good will my life be to me?"

### *Jacob Is Sent to Laban*

**28** So Isaac called Jacob and
[a]blessed him and commanded
him and said to him, "[b]You shall not
take a wife from the daughters of Ca-
naan. **2** Arise, go to Paddan-aram, to
the house of [a]Bethuel your mother's
father; and from there take to yourself
a wife from the daughters of Laban
your mother's brother. **3** May [a,1]God
Almighty [b]bless you and [c]make you
fruitful and [d]multiply you, that you
may become an [e]assembly of peoples.
**4** May He also give you the [a]blessing
of Abraham, to you and to your seed
with you, that you may [b]possess the
land of your [c]sojournings, which God
gave to Abraham." **5** Then [a]Isaac sent
Jacob away, and he went to Paddan-
aram to Laban, son of Bethuel the
Aramean, the brother of Rebekah,
the mother of Jacob and Esau.

**6** And Esau saw that Isaac had
blessed Jacob and sent him away to
Paddan-aram to take for himself a
wife from there, *and that* when he
blessed him he commanded him,
saying, "[a]You shall not take a wife
from the daughters of Canaan,"
**7** and that Jacob had listened to
his father and his mother and had
gone to Paddan-aram. **8** So Esau saw
that [a]the daughters of Canaan were
displeasing [1]in the sight of his father
Isaac; **9** and Esau went to Ishmael
and took Mahalath, the daughter of
Ishmael, Abraham's son, the sister of
Nebaioth, to be his wife, [a]besides the
wives that he had.

### *Jacob's Dream*

**10** Then Jacob departed from [a]Beer-
sheba and went toward [b]Haran.
**11** And he reached [1]a [a]certain place
and spent the night there because the
sun had set; and he took one of the
stones of the place and put it [2]under
his head and lay down in that place.
**12** [a]Then he had a dream, and behold,
a [1]ladder stood on the earth with its
top touching heaven; and behold,
[b]the angels of God were ascending
and descending on it. **13** And behold,
[a]Yahweh stood [1]above it and said, "I
am Yahweh, [b]the God of your father
Abraham and the God of Isaac; the
land on which you lie, I will give it
[c]to you and to [d]your seed. **14** And your
seed will also be like [a]the dust of the
earth, and you will [1]spread out [b]to the

**27:43** [b]Ge 11:31 [c]Ge 24:29 [1]Lit *flee for yourself* **27:44** [a]Ge 31:41 [1]Lit *turns away* **27:45** [a]Ge 27:12, 19, 35 [1]Lit *turns away from you* **27:46** [a]Ge 26:34, 35; 28:8 [b]Ge 24:3 [1]Lit *my life* ◆ **28:1** [a]Ge 27:33 [b]Ge 24:3, 4 **28:2** [a]Ge 25:20 **28:3** [a]Ge 17:1; 35:11; 48:3 [b]Ge 22:17 [c]Ge 17:6, 20 [d]Ge 17:2; 26:4, 24 [e]Ge 35:11; 48:4 [1]Heb *El Shaddai* **28:4** [a]Ge 12:2; 22:17 [b]Ge 15:7, 8; 17:8 [c]1Chr 29:15; Ps 39:12 **28:5** [a]Ge 27:43 **28:6** [a]Ge 28:1 **28:8** [a]Ge 24:3; 26:34, 35; 27:46 [1]Lit *in the eyes of his* **28:9** [a]Ge 26:34; 36:2 **28:10** [a]Ge 26:23 [b]Ge 12:4, 5; 27:43 **28:11** [a]Ge 28:19 [1]Lit *the place* [2]Lit *at his head-place* **28:12** [a]Ge 41:1; Nu 12:6 [b]Jn 1:51 [1]Or *stairway* **28:13** [a]Ge 35:1; Am 7:7 [b]Ge 26:3, 24 [c]Ge 13:15, 17; 26:3 [d]Ge 12:7; 15:18 [1]Or *beside him* **28:14** [a]Ge 13:16; 22:17 [b]Ge 13:14, 15 [1]Lit *break through*

west and to the east and to the north
and to the south; and [c]in you and in
your seed all the families of the earth
shall be blessed. **15** Behold, [a]I am with
you and [b]will keep you wherever you
go. And [c]I will bring you back to this
land; for [d]I will not forsake you until
I have done what I have [1]promised
you." **16** Then Jacob [a]awoke from his
sleep and said, "[b]Surely Yahweh is
in this place, and I did not know it."
**17** And he was afraid and said, "[a]How
fearsome is this place! This is none
other than the house of God, and this
is the gate of heaven."

**18** So Jacob rose early in the morn-
ing and took [a]the stone that he had
put [1]under his head and set it up as
a pillar and poured oil on its top.
**19** And he called the name of that
place [a,1]Bethel; however, [2]previously
the name of the city had been [b]Luz.
**20** Then Jacob [a]made a vow, saying,
"[b]If God will be with me and will
keep me on this journey on which I
am going, and will give me [c,1]food to
eat and garments to wear, **21** and [a]I
return to my father's house in peace,
[b]then Yahweh will be my God. **22** Now
this stone, which I have set up as a
pillar, [a]will be God's house, and [b]of
all that You give me I will surely give
a tenth to You."

### *Jacob's Love for Rachel*

**29** Then Jacob [1]took up his jour-
ney and came to the land of
[a]the sons of the east. **2** And he looked,
and behold, [a]a well in the field, and
behold, three flocks of sheep were
lying there beside it, for from that
well they gave *water* to the flocks to
drink. Now the stone on the mouth
of the well was large. **3** And all the
flocks would be gathered there, and
they would roll the stone from the
mouth of the well and give *water* to
the sheep to drink and return the
stone back to its place on the mouth
of the well.

**4** And Jacob said to them, "My
brothers, where are you from?" And
they said, "We are from [a]Haran."
**5** Then he said to them, "Do you
know Laban the [a]son of Nahor?" And
they said, "We know *him*." **6** And he
said to them, "Is it well with him?"
And they said, "It is well, and here
is [a]Rachel his daughter coming with
the sheep." **7** And he said, "Behold, it
is still high day; it is not time for the
livestock to be gathered. Give *water*
to the sheep to drink, and go, pasture
them." **8** But they said, "We cannot,
until all the flocks are gathered, and
they roll the stone from the mouth
of the well; then we give *water* to the
sheep to drink."

**9** While he was still speaking with
them, Rachel came with her father's
sheep, for she was a shepherdess.
**10** Now it happened, when Jacob
saw Rachel the daughter of Laban
his mother's brother and the sheep
of Laban his mother's brother, Jacob
came near and rolled the stone from
the mouth of the well and gave *water*
to the flock of Laban his mother's
brother to drink. **11** Then Jacob
[a]kissed Rachel and lifted his voice

**28:14** [c]Ge 12:3; 18:18; 22:18; 26:4 **28:15** [a]Ge 26:3, 24; 31:3 [b]Nu 6:24; Ps 121:5, 7, 8 [c]Ge 48:21; Dt 30:3 [d]Nu 23:19; Dt 7:9; 31:6, 8 [1]Lit *spoken to* **28:16** [a]1Ki 3:15; Jer 31:26 [b]Ex 3:4-6; Jos 5:13-15; Ps 139:7-12 **28:17** [a]Ps 68:35 **28:18** [a]Ge 28:11; 35:14 [1]Lit *at his head-place* **28:19** [a]Jdg 1:23 [b]Ge 35:6; 48:3 [1]Lit *the house of God* [2]Lit *at the first* **28:20** [a]Ge 31:13; Jdg 11:30; 2Sa 15:8 [b]Ge 28:15 [c]1Ti 6:8 [1]Lit *bread* **28:21** [a]Jdg 11:31 [b]Dt 26:17 **28:22** [a]Ge 35:7 [b]Lv 27:30; Dt 14:22 ◆**29:1** [a]Jdg 6:3, 33 [1]Lit *lifted up his feet* **29:2** [a]Ge 24:10, 11; Ex 2:15, 16 **29:4** [a]Ge 28:10 **29:5** [a]Ge 24:24, 29 **29:6** [a]Ex 2:16 **29:11** [a]Ge 33:4

and wept. **12** And Jacob told Rachel
that he was a [a,1]relative of her father
and that he was Rebekah's son, and
[b]she ran and told her father.

**13** So it happened that when
[a]Laban heard the report of Jacob
his sister's son, he ran to meet him,
and he [b]embraced him and kissed
him and brought him to his house.
Then he recounted to Laban all
these things. **14** And Laban said to
him, "Surely you are [a]my bone and
my flesh." And he stayed with him
one month.

**15** Then Laban said to Jacob, "Be-
cause you are my [1]relative, should
you therefore serve me for nothing?
Tell me, what shall [a]your wages be?"
**16** Now Laban had two daughters; the
name of the older was Leah, and the
name of the younger was Rachel.
**17** And Leah's eyes were weak, but
Rachel was [a]beautiful in form and
beautiful in appearance. **18** Now
Jacob [a]loved Rachel, so he said, "[b]I
will serve you seven years for your
younger daughter Rachel." **19** And
Laban said, "It is better that I give
her to you than to give her to anoth-
er man; stay with me." **20** So Jacob
served seven years for Rachel, and
they were in his sight but a few days
[a]because of his love for her.

### *Laban Deceives Jacob*

**21** Then Jacob said to Laban, "Give *me*
my wife, for my days are fulfilled, that
I may [a]go in to her." **22** And Laban
gathered all the men of the place and
made a feast. **23** Now it happened in
the evening that he took his daughter
Leah and brought her to him; and
*Jacob* went in to her. **24** Laban also
gave his servant-woman Zilpah to his
daughter Leah as a servant-woman.
**25** Now it happened in the morning
that, behold, it was Leah! And he
said to Laban, "[a]What is this you
have done to me? Was it not for
Rachel that I served with you? Why
then have you [b]deceived me?" **26** But
Laban said, "It is not [1]the practice in
our place to give the younger before
the firstborn. **27** Fulfill the week of
this one, and we will give you the
other also for the service which [a]you
shall serve with me for another seven
years." **28** And Jacob did so and ful-
filled her week, and he gave him his
daughter Rachel as his wife. **29** Laban
also gave his servant-woman Bilhah
to his daughter Rachel as her servant-
woman. **30** So *Jacob* went in to Rachel
also, and indeed [a]he loved Rachel
more than Leah, and he served with
[1]Laban for [b]another seven years.

**31** And Yahweh saw that Leah was
[1]unloved, and He opened her womb,
but Rachel was barren. **32** So Leah
conceived and bore a son and named
him [1]Reuben, for she said, "Because
Yahweh has [a,2]seen my affliction;
surely now my husband will love me."
**33** Then she conceived again and bore
a son and said, "[a]Because Yahweh
has [1]heard that I am [2]unloved, He has
therefore given me this *son* also." So
she named him Simeon. **34** And she
conceived again and bore a son and
said, "Now this time my husband will

**29:12** [a]Ge 28:5 [b]Ge 24:28 [1]Lit *brother* **29:13** [a]Ge 24:29-31 [b]Ge 33:4 **29:14** [a]Ge 2:23; Jdg 9:2; 2Sa 5:1; 19:12, 13 **29:15** [a]Ge 31:41 [1]Lit *brother* **29:17** [a]Ge 12:11, 14; 26:7 **29:18** [a]Ge 24:67 [b]Hos 12:12 **29:20** [a]SS 8:7 **29:21** [a]Jdg 15:1 **29:25** [a]Ge 12:18; 20:9; 26:10 [b]1Sa 28:12 **29:26** [1]Lit *done thus in* **29:27** [a]Ge 31:41 **29:30** [a]Ge 29:17, 18 [b]Ge 31:41 [1]Lit *him* **29:31** [1]Lit *hated* **29:32** [a]Ge 16:11; 31:42; Ex 3:7; 4:31; Dt 26:7; Ps 25:18 [1]Lit *see, a son* [2]Lit *looked upon* **29:33** [a]Dt 21:15 [1]Heb *shama*, related to Simeon [2]Lit *hated*

be [1]joined to me because I have borne
him three sons." Therefore he was
named [a]Levi. **35** And she conceived
again and bore a son and said, "This
time I will [1]praise Yahweh." Therefore
she named him [a,2]Judah. Then she
stopped bearing.

### *The Sons of Jacob*

**30** Then Rachel saw that [a]she
bore Jacob no children, so
[1]she became jealous of her sister;
and she said to Jacob, "[b]Give me
children, or else I die." **2** Then Ja-
cob's anger burned against Rachel,
and he said, "Am I in the place of
God, who has [a]withheld from you
the fruit of the womb?" **3** And she
said, "[a]Here is my maidservant
Bilhah, go in to her that she may
[b]bear on my knees, that [a,1]through
her I too may obtain children." **4** So
[a]she gave him her servant-woman
Bilhah as a wife, and Jacob went in
to her. **5** And Bilhah conceived and
bore Jacob a son. **6** Then Rachel said,
"God has [a,1]rendered justice to me
and has indeed listened to my voice
and has given me a son." Therefore
she named him [2]Dan. **7** And Rachel's
servant-woman Bilhah conceived
again and bore Jacob a second son.
**8** So Rachel said, "With [1]mighty
wrestlings I have [2]wrestled with my
sister, *and* I have indeed prevailed."
And she named him Naphtali.
**9** Then Leah saw that she had
stopped bearing, so she took her
servant-woman Zilpah and gave
her to Jacob as a wife. **10** And Leah's
servant-woman Zilpah bore Jacob
a son. **11** Then Leah said, "[1]How
fortunate!" So she named him [2]Gad.
**12** And Leah's servant-woman Zilpah
bore Jacob a second son. **13** Then Leah
said, "[1]Happy am I! For women [a]will
call me happy." So she named him
[2]Asher.
**14** And in the days of the wheat
harvest, Reuben went and found
[a]mandrakes in the field and brought
them to his mother Leah. Then Rachel
said to Leah, "Please give me some
of your son's mandrakes." **15** But she
said to her, "Is it a small matter for
you to take my husband? And would
you take my son's mandrakes also?"
So Rachel said, "Therefore he will lie
with you tonight in return for your
son's mandrakes." **16** Then Jacob
came in from the field in the evening.
And Leah went out to meet him and
said, "You must come in to me, for I
have surely hired you with my son's
mandrakes." So he lay with her that
night. **17** And God listened to Leah,
and she conceived and bore Jacob a
fifth son. **18** And Leah said, "God has
given me my [1]wages because I gave
my servant-woman to my husband."
So she named him Issachar. **19** Then
Leah conceived again and bore a sixth
son to Jacob. **20** And Leah said, "God
has gifted me a good gift; this time
my husband [1]will honor me because
I have borne him six sons." So she
named him Zebulun. **21** Afterward she
bore a daughter and named her Dinah.

**29:34** [a]Ge 49:5 [1]Heb *lavah*, related to Levi **29:35** [a]Ge 49:8; Mt 1:2 [1]Heb *jadah*, related to Judah [2]Heb *Jehudah* ◆ **30:1** [a]Ge 29:31 [b]1Sa 1:5, 6 [1]Lit *Rachel* **30:2** [a]Ge 20:18; 29:31 **30:3** [a]Ge 16:2 [b]Ge 50:23; Job 3:12 [1]Lit *from her I too may be built* **30:4** [a]Ge 16:3, 4 **30:6** [a]Ps 35:24; 43:1; Lam 3:59 [1]Lit *judged* [2]He judged **30:8** [1]Lit *wrestlings of God* [2]Heb *niphtal*, related to Naphtali **30:11** [1]Lit *With fortune!*; some versions *Fortune has come* [2]Fortune **30:13** [a]Lk 1:48 [1]Lit *With my happiness!* [2]Happy **30:14** [a]SS 7:13 **30:18** [1]Heb *sachar*, related to Issachar **30:20** [1]Heb *zabal*, related to Zebulun

22 Then [a]God remembered Rachel,
and God listened to her and [b]opened
her womb. 23 So she conceived and
bore a son and said, "God has [a]tak-
en away my reproach." 24 And she
named him Joseph, saying, "[a]May
Yahweh [1]give me another son."

### *Jacob Names His Wages*

25 Now it happened when Rachel
had borne Joseph, that Jacob said to
Laban, "[a]Send me away, that I may go
to my own place and to my own land.
26 Give *me* my wives and my children
[a]for whom I have served you, and
let me go; for you yourself know my
service which I have [1]rendered you."
27 But Laban said to him, "If now I
have found favor in your sight, *stay
with me*; I have interpreted an omen
[a]that Yahweh has blessed me on your
account." 28 And he *continued* to say,
"[a]Name me your wages, and I will
give it." 29 But he said to him, "[a]You
yourself know how I have served you
and how your livestock have [1]fared
with me. 30 For you had little before
[1]I came, but it has [a]spread out to a
multitude, and Yahweh has blessed
you [2]at *every* step of mine. But now,
when shall I provide for my own
household also?" 31 So he said, "What
shall I give you?" And Jacob said, "You
shall not give me anything. If you will
do this *one* thing for me, I will again
pasture *and* keep your flock: 32 let
me pass through your entire flock
today, removing from there every
[a]speckled and spotted sheep and
every black [1]one among the lambs
and the spotted and speckled among
the goats; and *such* shall be my wages.
33 So my righteousness will answer
for me later, when you come con-
cerning my [1]wages. Every one that
is not speckled and spotted among
the goats and black among the lambs,
*if found* with me, will be considered
stolen." 34 And Laban said, "Behold,
[1]let it be according to your word."
35 So he removed on that day the
striped and spotted male goats and
all the speckled and spotted female
goats, every one with white in it, and
all the black ones among the sheep,
and gave them into the [1]care of his
sons. 36 And he put *a distance of*
three days' journey between himself
and Jacob, and Jacob was pasturing
the rest of Laban's flocks.

37 Then Jacob [1]took fresh rods of
poplar and almond and plane trees,
and he peeled white stripes in them,
exposing the white which *was* [2]in the
rods. 38 And he set the rods which he
had peeled in front of the flocks in
the trough, *that is*, in the watering
channels, where the flocks came
to drink; and they [1]mated when
they came to drink. 39 So the flocks
[1]mated by the rods, and the flocks
brought forth striped, speckled, and
spotted. 40 And Jacob separated the
lambs, and he [1]made the flocks face
toward the striped and all the black
in the flock of Laban; and he set his
own herds apart and did not set them
with Laban's flock. 41 Now it would
be that, whenever the [1]stronger of
the flock [2]were mating, Jacob would

**30:22** [a]1Sa 1:19, 20 [b]Ge 29:31 **30:23** [a]Is 4:1; Lk 1:25 **30:24** [a]Ge 35:17 [1]Lit *add to me*; Heb *Joseph*
**30:25** [a]Ge 24:54, 56 **30:26** [a]Ge 29:18, 20, 27; Hos 12:12 [1]Lit *served* **30:27** [a]Ge 26:24; 39:3, 5; Is 61:9
**30:28** [a]Ge 29:15; 31:7, 41 **30:29** [a]Ge 31:6 [1]Lit *been* **30:30** [a]Ge 28:14 [1]Lit *me* [2]Lit *at my foot*
**30:32** [a]Ge 31:8 [1]Lit *sheep* **30:33** [1]Lit *wages which are before you* **30:34** [1]Lit *would that it might be*
**30:35** [1]Lit *hand* **30:37** [1]Lit *took to himself* [2]Lit *on* **30:38** [1]Or *conceived* **30:39** [1]Or *conceived*
**30:40** [1]Lit *set the faces* **30:41** [1]Firm and compact; lit *bound ones* [2]Or *conceived*

place the rods in the sight of the flock
in the trough, so that they might
[3]mate by the rods; **42** but when the
flock was feeble, he did not put
*them* in; so the feebler were Laban's
and the [1]stronger Jacob's. **43** So [a]the
man [b]spread out exceedingly and
had large flocks and female and male
servants and camels and donkeys.

### *Jacob Leaves While Laban Is Gone*

**31** Then [1]Jacob heard the words
of Laban's sons, saying, "Jacob
has taken away all that belonged to
our father, and from what belonged
to our father he has made all this
[2]wealth." **2** And Jacob saw the face of
Laban, and behold, it was not *friend-*
*ly* toward him as formerly. **3** Then
Yahweh said to Jacob, "[a]Return to the
land of your fathers and to your kin,
and [b]I will be with you." **4** So Jacob
sent and called Rachel and Leah to
his flock in the field, **5** and he said to
them, "[a]I see your father's face, that it
is not *friendly* toward me as formerly,
but [b]the God of my father has been
with me. **6** [a]You also know that I have
served your father with all my power.
**7** Yet your father has [a]cheated me
and [b]changed my wages ten times;
however, [c]God did not allow him to
harm me. **8** If [a]he spoke thus, 'The
speckled shall be your wages,' then
all the flock bore speckled; and if
he spoke thus, 'The striped shall be
your wages,' then all the flock bore
striped. **9** Thus God has [a]delivered
your father's livestock and given
*them* to me. **10** Now it happened at
the time when the flock were [1]mating
that I lifted up my eyes and saw in a
dream, and behold, the male goats
which were [2]mating *were* striped,
speckled, and mottled. **11** Then [a]the
angel of God said to me in the dream,
'Jacob,' and I said, 'Here I am.' **12** He
said, 'Lift up now your eyes and see
*that* all the male goats which are
[1]mating are striped, speckled, and
mottled; for [a]I have seen all that
Laban has been doing to you. **13** I
am [a]the God *of* Bethel, where you
[b]anointed a pillar, where you made
a vow to Me; now arise, [1]leave this
land, and [c]return to the land of your
kin.'" **14** Then Rachel and Leah said
to him, "Do we still have any por-
tion or inheritance in our father's
house? **15** Are we not counted by
him as foreigners? For [a]he has sold
us and has also [1]entirely consumed
[2]our purchase price. **16** Surely all the
riches which God has delivered *over*
*to us* from our father belong to us and
our children; now then, do whatever
God has said to you."

**17** Then Jacob arose and put his
children and his wives upon camels;
**18** and he drove away all his livestock
and all his possessions which he had
accumulated, his acquired livestock
which he had accumulated in Paddan-
aram, in order [a]to go to the land of
Canaan to his father Isaac. **19** Now
Laban had gone to shear his flock.
Then Rachel stole the [a,1]household
idols that were her father's. **20** And

---

**30:41** [3]Or *conceive* **30:42** [1]Firm and compact; lit *bound ones* **30:43** [a]Ge 12:16; 13:2; 24:35; 26:13, 14; 30:30 [b]Ge 28:14 ◆ **31:1** [1]Lit *he* [2]Lit *glory* **31:3** [a]Ge 32:9 [b]Ge 28:15 **31:5** [a]Ge 31:2 [b]Ge 21:22; 28:13, 15; 31:29, 42, 53; Is 41:10; Heb 13:5 **31:6** [a]Ge 30:29 **31:7** [a]Ge 29:25 [b]Ge 31:41 [c]Ge 15:1; 31:29 **31:8** [a]Ge 30:32 **31:9** [a]Ge 31:1, 16 **31:10** [1]Or *conceiving* [2]Lit *leaping upon the flock* **31:11** [a]Ge 16:7-11; 22:11, 15; 31:13; 48:16 **31:12** [a]Ex 3:7 [1]Lit *leaping upon the flock* **31:13** [a]Ge 28:13, 19 [b]Ge 28:18, 20 [c]Ge 28:15; 32:9 [1]Lit *go out from* **31:15** [a]Ge 29:20, 23, 27 [1]Enjoyed the benefit of [2]Lit *our money* **31:18** [a]Ge 35:27 **31:19** [a]Ge 31:30, 34; 35:2; Jdg 17:5; 1Sa 19:13; Hos 3:4 [1]Heb *teraphim*

Jacob [1]deceived Laban the Aramean
by not telling him that he was fleeing.
**21** So he fled with all that he had; and
he arose and crossed the [1]River and
set his face toward the hill country
of [a]Gilead.

### *Laban Pursues Jacob*

**22** Then it was told to Laban on the
third day that Jacob had fled; **23** so
he took his [1]relatives with him and
pursued him *a distance of* seven
days' journey, and he overtook him
in the hill country of Gilead. **24** [a]And
God came to Laban the Aramean in
a [b]dream of the night and said to
him, "[c,1]Beware lest you speak to
Jacob either good or bad."

**25** So Laban caught up with Jacob.
Now Jacob had pitched his tent in the
hill country, and Laban with his [1]rela-
tives camped in the hill country of
Gilead. **26** Then Laban said to Jacob,
"What have you done [1]by deceiving
me and carrying away my daughters
like captives of the sword? **27** Why
did you flee secretly and [1]deceive
me and not tell me—so that I might
have sent you away with gladness
and with songs, with [a]tambourine
and with [b]lyre—**28** and not allow me
[a]to kiss my sons and my daughters?
Now you have acted foolishly. **29** It
is in my hand to do evil against you,
but [a]the God of your father spoke to
me last night, saying, '[b,1]Beware of
speaking either good or evil to Jacob.'
**30** So now you have indeed gone away
because you longed greatly for your
father's house; *but* why did you steal
[a]my gods?" **31** Then Jacob answered
and said to Laban, "Because I was
afraid, because I said, 'Lest you take
your daughters from me by force.'
**32** [a]The one with whom you find
your gods shall not live; in the pres-
ence of our [1]relatives recognize what
is yours [2]among my belongings and
take *it* for yourself." But Jacob did not
know that Rachel had stolen them.

**33** So Laban went into Jacob's tent
and into Leah's tent and into the tent
of the two maidservants, but he did
not find *them*. Then he went out
of Leah's tent and entered Rachel's
tent. **34** Now Rachel had taken the
[1]household idols and put them in
the camel's saddle, and she sat on
them. And Laban felt through all the
tent but did not find *them*. **35** And she
said to her father, "Let not my lord be
angry that I cannot [a]rise before you,
for the manner of women is upon
me." So he searched but did not find
the [b,1]household idols.

**36** Then Jacob became angry and
contended with Laban; and Jacob
answered and said to Laban, "What
is my transgression? What is my sin
that you have hotly pursued me?
**37** Though you have felt through all
my goods, what have you found of
all your household goods? Place *it*
here before my [1]relatives and your
[1]relatives, that they may decide
between us two. **38** These twenty
years I *have been* with you; your
ewes and your female goats have
not miscarried, nor have I eaten the
rams of your flocks. **39** That which

---

**31:20** [1]Lit *stole the heart of* **31:21** [a]Ge 37:25 [1]The Euphrates River **31:23** [1]Lit *brothers*
**31:24** [a]Ge 20:3; 31:29 [b]Ge 20:3, 6; 31:11 [c]Ge 24:50; 31:7, 29 [1]Lit *Take heed to yourself* **31:25** [1]Lit *brothers* **31:26** [1]Lit *and you have stolen my heart* **31:27** [a]Ex 15:20 [b]Ge 4:21 [1]Lit *steal me*
**31:28** [a]Ge 31:55 **31:29** [a]Ge 31:5, 24, 42, 53 [b]Ge 31:24 [1]Lit *Take heed to yourself* **31:30** [a]Ge 31:19; Jos 24:2; Jdg 18:24 **31:32** [a]Ge 44:9 [1]Lit *brothers* [2]Lit *with me* **31:34** [1]Heb *teraphim*
**31:35** [a]Lv 19:32 [b]Ge 31:19 [1]Heb *teraphim* **31:37** [1]Lit *brothers*

was torn *of beasts* I did not bring to
you; I bore the loss of it myself. You
required it of my hand *whether* sto-
len by day or stolen by night. **40** *Thus*
I was: by day the [1]heat consumed me
and the frost by night, and my sleep
fled from my eyes. **41** These twenty
years I have been in your house; [a]I
served you fourteen years for your
two daughters and six years for
your flock, and you [b]changed my
wages ten times. **42** If [a]the God of
my father, the God of Abraham, and
the dread of Isaac, had not been for
me, surely now you would have sent
me away empty. [b]God has seen my
affliction and the toil of my hands,
so He [c]rendered *the* decision last
night."

### *The Covenant at Mizpah*

**43** Then Laban answered and said to
Jacob, "The daughters are my daugh-
ters, and the children are my chil-
dren, and [a]the flocks are my flocks,
and all that you see is mine. But what
can I do this day to these daughters
of mine or to their children whom
they have borne? **44** So now come,
let us [a]cut a covenant, [1]you and I,
and [b]let it be a witness between
[2]you and me." **45** Then Jacob took
[a]a stone and raised it up *as* a pillar.
**46** And Jacob said to his [1]relatives,
"Gather stones." So they took stones
and made a heap, and they ate there
by the heap. **47** And Laban [a]called it
[1]Jegar-sahadutha, but Jacob called it
[2]Galeed. **48** Then Laban said, "[a]This
heap is a witness between [1]you
and me this day." Therefore it was
named Galeed, **49** and [a,1]Mizpah, for
he said, "May Yahweh watch between
[2]you and me when we are [3]absent
one from the other. **50** If you afflict
my daughters, or if you take wives
besides my daughters, *although* no
man is with us, see, [a]God is witness
between [1]you and me." **51** And Laban
said to Jacob, "Behold this heap and
behold the pillar which I have set
between [1]you and me. **52** This heap is
a witness, and the pillar is a witness,
that I will not pass by this heap to
you *for harm*, and you will not pass
by this heap and this pillar to me for
harm. **53** [a]The God of Abraham and
the God of Nahor, the God of their
father, [b]judge between us." So Jacob
swore by [c]the dread of his father
Isaac. **54** Then Jacob [a]offered a sac-
rifice on the mountain and called his
[1]relatives to eat a [2]meal; and they ate
[2]the meal and spent the night on the
mountain. **55** [1]And Laban arose early
in the morning and [a]kissed his sons
and his daughters and blessed them.
Then Laban departed and returned
to his place.

### *Jacob's Fear of Esau*

**32** Now Jacob went on his way,
[a]and the angels of God met
him. **2** Then Jacob said when he saw
them, "This is God's [1]camp." So he
named that place [a,2]Mahanaim.

---

**31:40** [1]Or *drought* **31:41** [a]Ge 29:27, 30 [b]Ge 31:7 **31:42** [a]Ge 31:5, 29, 53 [b]Ge 29:32; Ex 3:7 [c]Ge 31:24, 29 **31:43** [a]Ge 31:1 **31:44** [a]Ge 21:27, 32; 26:28 [b]Jos 24:27 [1]Lit *I and you* [2]Lit *me and you* **31:45** [a]Ge 28:18; Jos 24:26, 27 **31:46** [1]Lit *brothers* **31:47** [a]Jos 22:34 [1]Lit *the heap of witness* in Aram [2]Lit *the heap of witness* in Heb **31:48** [a]Jos 24:27 [1]Lit *me and you* **31:49** [a]Jdg 11:29; 1Sa 7:5, 6 [1]Lit *the watchtower* [2]Lit *me and you* [3]Lit *hidden* **31:50** [a]Jer 29:23; 42:5 [1]Lit *me and you* **31:51** [1]Lit *me and you* **31:53** [a]Ge 28:13 [b]Ge 16:5 [c]Ge 31:42 **31:54** [a]Ex 18:12 [1]Lit *brothers* [2]Lit *bread* **31:55** [a]Ge 31:28, 43 [1]Ch 32:1 in Heb ◆ **32:1** [a]2Ki 6:16, 17; Ps 34:7 **32:2** [a]Jos 21:38; 2Sa 2:8 [1]Or *company* [2]Lit *Two Camps, Two Companies*

**3** Then Jacob [a]sent messengers
before him to his brother Esau in the
land of [b]Seir, the [1]country of [c]Edom.
**4** He also commanded them saying,
"Thus you shall say to my lord, to
Esau: 'Thus says your servant Jacob,
"I have sojourned with Laban and
have been [a]delayed until now; **5** [a]and
I have oxen and donkeys *and* flocks
and male and female slaves; and I
have sent to tell my lord, [b]that I may
find favor in your sight."'"

**6** Then the messengers returned
to Jacob, saying, "We came to your
brother, to Esau, and furthermore
[a]he is coming to meet you, and four
hundred men are with him." **7** Then
Jacob was [a]greatly afraid and dis-
tressed; and he divided the people
who were with him, and the flocks
and the herds and the camels, into
two camps. **8** And he said, "If Esau
comes to the one camp and strikes
it, then the camp which remains will
escape."

**9** And Jacob said, "O [a]God of my
father Abraham and God of my father
Isaac, O Yahweh, who said to me,
'[b]Return to your land and to your
kin, and I will [1]prosper you,' **10** [1]I am
unworthy [a]of all the lovingkindness
and of all the truth which You have
shown to Your slave; for with my staff
*only* I crossed this Jordan, and now I
have become two camps. **11** [a]Deliver
me, I pray, [b]from the hand of my
brother, from the hand of Esau; for
I fear him, lest he come and strike
me down *with* the [c]mothers and
the children. **12** For You said, '[a]I will
surely [1]prosper you and [b]make your
seed as the sand of the sea, which is
too great to be numbered.'"

**13** So he spent the night there.
Then he took from what [1]he had
with him a [a]present for his brother
Esau: **14** two hundred female goats
and twenty male goats, two hundred
ewes and twenty rams, **15** thirty
milking camels and their colts, forty
cows and ten bulls, twenty female
donkeys and ten male donkeys.
**16** And he gave *them* into the hand
of his servants, every flock by itself,
and said to his servants, "Pass on
before me and put a space between
flocks." **17** And he commanded the
first one in front, saying, "When
my brother Esau meets you and
asks you, saying, 'To whom do you
belong, and where are you going,
and to whom do these *animals* in
front of you belong?' **18** then you
shall say, '*These* belong to your ser-
vant Jacob; it is a present sent to my
lord, to Esau. And behold, he also is
behind us.'" **19** Then he commanded
also the second and the third and
all those who followed the flocks,
saying, "After this manner you shall
speak to Esau when you find him;
**20** and you shall say, 'Behold, your
servant Jacob also is behind us.'" For
he said, "I will appease his face with
the present that goes before me.
Then afterward I will see his face;
perhaps he will lift up my face." **21** So
the present passed on before him,
while he himself spent that night
in the camp.

**22** And he arose that same night and
took his two wives and his two servant-

**32:3** [a]Ge 27:41, 42; 32:7, 11 [b]Ge 14:6; 33:14 [c]Ge 25:30; 36:8, 9 [1]Lit *field* **32:4** [a]Ge 31:41
**32:5** [a]Ge 30:43 [b]Ge 33:8 **32:6** [a]Ge 33:1 **32:7** [a]Ge 32:11 **32:9** [a]Ge 28:13; 31:42 [b]Ge 28:15; 31:3, 13
[1]Lit *do good with you* **32:10** [a]Ge 24:27 [1]Lit *I am less than all* **32:11** [a]Ps 59:1, 2 [b]Ge 27:41, 42; 33:4
[c]Hos 10:14 **32:12** [a]Ge 28:14 [b]Ge 22:17 [1]Lit *do good with* **32:13** [a]Ge 43:11 [1]Lit *had come to his hand*

women and his eleven children and
crossed the ford of the [a]Jabbok. 23 And
he took them and sent them across the
stream. And he sent across whatever
he had.

### *Jacob Wrestles with God*

24 Then Jacob was left alone, and a
man [a]wrestled with him until the
[1]breaking of dawn. 25 And he saw
that he had not prevailed against
him, so he touched the socket of his
thigh; and so the socket of Jacob's
thigh was dislocated while he wres-
tled with him. 26 Then he said, "Let
me go, for the dawn is [1]breaking."
But he said, "[a]I will not let you go
unless you bless me." 27 So he said
to him, "What is your name?" And
he said, "Jacob." 28 [a]Then He said,
"Your name shall no longer be Ja-
cob, but [1]Israel; for you have striven
with God and with men and have
prevailed." 29 Then [a]Jacob asked
him and said, "Please tell me your
name." But he said, "Why is it that
you ask my name?" And he blessed
him there. 30 So Jacob named the
place [1]Peniel, for *he said,* "[a]I have
seen God face to face, yet my [2]life
has been delivered." 31 And the sun
rose upon him just as he crossed
over [a]Penuel, and he was limping
on his thigh. 32 Therefore, to this
day the sons of Israel do not eat
the sinew of the hip which is on
the socket of the thigh because he
touched the socket of Jacob's thigh
in the sinew of the hip.

### *Jacob Meets Esau*

33 Then Jacob lifted up his eyes
and saw, and behold, [a]Esau
was coming, and four hundred men
with him. So he divided the children
[1]among Leah and Rachel and the two
servant-women. 2 And he put the
servant-women and their children
first, and Leah and her children after
*them,* and Rachel and Joseph after
*them.* 3 But he himself passed on
ahead of them and [a]bowed down
to the ground seven times, until he
[b]came near to his brother.

4 Then Esau ran to meet him and
embraced him and [a]fell on his neck
and kissed him, and they wept. 5 And
he lifted up his eyes and saw the
women and the children and said,
"[1]Who are these with you?" And
he said, "[a]The children whom God
has graciously given your servant."
6 Then the servant-women came near
[1]with their children, and they bowed
down. 7 Leah likewise came near with
her children, and they bowed down;
and afterward Joseph came near with
Rachel, and they bowed down. 8 And
he said, "What do you mean by [a]all
[1]these camps which I have met?" And
he said, "[b]To find favor in the sight
of my lord." 9 But Esau said, "[a]I have
plenty, my brother; let what you have
be your own." 10 And Jacob said, "No,
please, if now I have found favor in
your sight, then take my present
from my hand, [1]for I see your face
as one sees the face of God, and you
have received me favorably. 11 Please

**32:22** [a]Dt 3:16; Jos 12:2 **32:24** [a]Hos 12:3, 4 [1]Lit *rising* **32:26** [a]Hos 12:4 [1]Lit *rising*
**32:28** [a]Ge 35:10; 1Ki 18:31 [1]Lit *he who strives with God, God strives* **32:29** [a]Jdg 13:17, 18
**32:30** [a]Ge 16:13; Ex 24:10, 11; 33:20; Nu 12:8; Jdg 6:22; 13:22 [1]Lit *the face of God* [2]Lit *soul*
**32:31** [a]Jdg 8:8 ◆ **33:1** [a]Ge 32:6 [1]Or *to* **33:3** [a]Ge 42:6; 43:26 [b]Ge 27:21-22 **33:4** [a]Ge 45:14, 15
**33:5** [a]Ge 48:9; Ps 127:3; Is 8:18 [1]Or *What relation are these to you?* **33:6** [1]Lit *they and*
**33:8** [a]Ge 32:13-16 [b]Ge 32:5 [1]Lit *this camp* **33:9** [a]Ge 27:39, 40 **33:10** [1]Lit *for therefore I have seen your face like seeing God's face*

take my [a]blessing which has been
brought to you, [b]because God has
dealt graciously with me and because
I have [1]everything." Thus he urged
him, and he took *it*.
12 Then [1]Esau said, "Let us take our
journey and go, and I will go before
you." 13 But he said to him, "My lord
knows that the children are weak
and that the flocks and herds which
are nursing are [1]a care to me. And if
they are driven hard one day, all the
flocks will die. 14 Please let my lord
pass on before his servant, and I will
lead on slowly, according to the pace
of the cattle that are before me and
according to the pace of the children,
until I come to my lord at [a]Seir."
15 Then Esau said, "Please let me
leave with you some of the people
who are with me." But he said, "Why
*do* this? [a]Let me find favor in the sight
of my lord." 16 So Esau returned that
day on his way to Seir. 17 But Jacob
journeyed to [a,1]Succoth and built for
himself a house and made booths for
his livestock; therefore the place is
named Succoth.

### *Jacob Camps in Shechem*

18 Now Jacob came safely to the city
of [a]Shechem, which is in the land
of Canaan, when he came from
[b]Paddan-aram, and he camped before
the city. 19 [a]Then he bought a portion
of a field where he had pitched his tent
from the hand of the sons of Hamor,
Shechem's father, for one hundred
[1]qesitah. 20 Then he set up there an
altar and called it [1]El-Elohe-Israel.

### *Simeon and Levi Deceive Shechem*

34 Now [a]Dinah the daughter of
Leah, whom she had borne to
Jacob, went out to see the daughters
of the land. 2 Then Shechem the son
of Hamor [a]the Hivite, the prince of
the land, saw her and took her and
lay with her and violated her. 3 [1]And
he was deeply attracted to Dinah the
daughter of Jacob, and he loved the
young woman and spoke to the heart
of the young woman. 4 So Shechem
[a]spoke to his father Hamor, saying,
"Get me this girl as a wife." 5 Now
Jacob heard that he had defiled Dinah
his daughter; but his sons were with
his livestock in the field, so Jacob
kept silent until they came in. 6 Then
Hamor the father of Shechem went
out to Jacob to speak with him. 7 Now
the sons of Jacob came in from the
field when they heard *it*; and the
men were grieved, and they were
very angry because he had done
a [a,1]disgraceful thing in Israel [2]by
lying with Jacob's daughter, for such
a thing ought not to be done.
8 But Hamor spoke with them,
saying, "The soul of my son Shechem
longs for your daughter; please give
her to him as a wife. 9 And intermarry
with us; give your daughters to us
and take our daughters for your-
selves. 10 Thus you shall [1]live with
us, and [a]the land shall be *open* before
you; [1]live and [b]trade in it and [c]take
possession of property in it." 11 And
Shechem also said to her father and
to her brothers, "If I find favor in your
sight, then I will give whatever you

**33:11** [a]Ge 27:35; 1Sa 25:27 [b]Ge 30:43 [1]Lit *all* **33:12** [1]Lit *he* **33:13** [1]Lit *upon me* **33:14** [a]Ge 32:3 **33:15** [a]Ru 2:13 **33:17** [a]Jos 13:27; Jdg 8:5, 14; Ps 60:6 [1]Lit *booths* **33:18** [a]Ge 12:6; Jos 24:1; Jdg 9:1 [b]Ge 25:20; 28:2 **33:19** [a]Jos 24:32; Jn 4:5 [1]Ancient currency, cf. Jos 24:32; Job 42:11 **33:20** [1]God, the God of Israel ◆ **34:1** [a]Ge 30:21 **34:2** [a]Ge 34:30 **34:3** [1]Lit *His soul clung* **34:4** [a]Jdg 14:2 **34:7** [a]Dt 22:20-30; Jdg 20:6; 2Sa 13:12 [1]Lit *senseless* [2]Lit *to lie* **34:10** [a]Ge 13:9; 20:15 [b]Ge 42:34 [c]Ge 47:27 [1]Lit *dwell*

say to me. **12** Ask me ever so much bridal payment and gift, and I will give according as you say to me; but give me the girl as a wife."

**13** But Jacob's sons answered Shechem and his father Hamor with deceit, and *thus* they spoke, because he had defiled Dinah their sister. **14** And they said to them, "We cannot do this thing, to give our sister to [a]one who is uncircumcised, for that would be a reproach to us. **15** Only on this *condition* will we consent to you: if you will become like us, in that every male among you be circumcised, **16** then we will give our daughters to you, and we will take your daughters for ourselves, and we will [1]live with you and become one people. **17** But if you will not listen to us to be circumcised, then we will take our daughter and go."

**18** Now their words seemed good in the sight of Hamor and Shechem, Hamor's son. **19** So the young man did not delay to do the thing because he was delighted with Jacob's daughter. Now he was more honored than all the household of his father. **20** So Hamor and his son Shechem came to the [a]gate of their city and spoke to the men of their city, saying, **21** "These men are peaceful with us; therefore let them [1]live in the land and trade in it, for behold, the land is [2]large enough for them. Let us take their daughters for us as wives and give our daughters to them. **22** Only on this *condition* will the men consent to us to [1]live with us, to become one people: that every male among us be circumcised as they are circumcised. **23** Will not their livestock and what they acquire and all their cattle be ours? Only let us consent to them, and they will [1]live with us." **24** [a]And all who went out of the gate of his city listened to Hamor and to his son Shechem, and every male was circumcised, all who went out of the gate of his city.

**25** Now it happened on the third day, when they were in pain, that two of Jacob's sons, [a]Simeon and Levi, Dinah's brothers, each took his sword and came upon the unsuspecting city and killed every male. **26** And they killed Hamor and his son Shechem with the edge of the sword and took Dinah from Shechem's house and went away. **27** Jacob's sons came upon the slain and plundered the city because they had defiled their sister. **28** They took their flocks and their herds and their donkeys and that which was in the city and that which was in the field; **29** and they captured and plundered all their wealth and all their little ones and their wives, even all that *was* in the houses. **30** Then Jacob said to Simeon and Levi, "You have [a]brought trouble on me by [b]making me odious among the inhabitants of the land, among [c]the Canaanites and the Perizzites; and [d,1]my men being few in number, they will gather together against me and strike me, and I will be destroyed, I and my household." **31** But they said, "Should he [1]treat our sister as a harlot?"

---

**34:14** [a]Ge 17:14 **34:16** [1]Lit *dwell* **34:20** [a]Ru 4:1; 2Sa 15:2 **34:21** [1]Lit *dwell* [2]Lit *wide of hands before them* **34:22** [1]Lit *dwell* **34:23** [1]Lit *dwell* **34:24** [a]Ge 23:10 **34:25** [a]Ge 49:5-7 **34:30** [a]Jos 7:25 [b]Ex 5:21; 1Sa 13:4; 2Sa 10:6 [c]Ge 13:7; 34:2 [d]Ge 46:26, 27; Dt 4:27; 1Chr 16:19; Ps 105:12 [1]Lit *I, few in number* **34:31** [1]Or *make*

### *Jacob Goes Up to Bethel*

35 Then God said to Jacob, "Arise,
go up to [a]Bethel and [1]live there,
and make an altar there to [b]God, who
appeared to you [c]when you fled [2]from
your brother Esau." **2** So Jacob said to
his [a]household and to all who were
with him, "Put away [b]the foreign gods
which are among you and [c]cleanse
yourselves and change your gar-
ments; **3** and let us arise and go up to
Bethel, and I will make [a]an altar there
to God, [b]who answered me in the day
of my distress and [c]has been with me
[1]wherever I have gone." **4** So they gave
to Jacob all the foreign gods which
[1]they had and the rings which were in
their ears, and Jacob hid them under
the [2]oak which was near Shechem.
**5** Then they journeyed on, and
there was [a,1]a terror from God upon
the cities which were around them,
and they did not pursue the sons of
Jacob. **6** So Jacob came to [a]Luz (that
is, Bethel), which is in the land of
Canaan, he and all the people who
were with him. **7** [a]And he built an
altar there and called the place
[1]El-bethel, because there God had
revealed Himself to him when he fled
[2]from his brother. **8** Then [a]Deborah,
Rebekah's nurse, died, and she was
buried below Bethel under the oak;
it was named [1]Allon-bacuth.

### *Jacob Is Renamed Israel*

**9** Then God appeared to Jacob again
when he came from Paddan-aram,
and He [a]blessed him. **10** [a]And God
said to him,

"Your name is Jacob;
Your name shall no longer
be called Jacob,
But Israel shall be your name."

Thus He called his name Israel. **11** God
also said to him,

"I am [a,1]God Almighty;
[b]Be fruitful and multiply;
A nation and an [c]assembly
of nations shall
[2]come from you,
And [d]kings shall [2]come
forth from your loins.
**12** "[a]And the land which I gave
to Abraham and Isaac,
I will give it to you,
And I will give the land to
your seed after you."

**13** Then [a]God went up from him in
the place where He had spoken with
him. **14** And Jacob set up [a]a pillar in
the place where He had spoken with
him, a pillar of stone, and he poured
out a drink offering on it; he also
poured oil on it. **15** So Jacob named
the place where God had spoken with
him, [a,1]Bethel.
**16** Then they journeyed from Beth-
el; and there was still some distance
to go to [a]Ephrath, and Rachel gave
birth, and she [1]suffered severely in
her labor. **17** Now it happened that
when she was in severe labor the
midwife said to her, "Do not fear,
for now [a]you have another son."
**18** Now it happened as her soul was

◆ **35:1** [a]Ge 28:19 [b]Ge 28:13 [c]Ge 27:43 [1]Lit *dwell* [2]Lit *from the face of* **35:2** [a]Ge 18:19; Jos 24:15 [b]Ge 31:19, 30, 34 [c]Ex 19:10, 14 **35:3** [a]Ge 28:20-22 [b]Ps 107:6 [c]Ge 28:15; 31:3, 42 [1]Lit *in the way which* **35:4** [1]Lit *were in their hand* [2]Or *terebinth* **35:5** [a]Ex 15:16; 23:27; Dt 2:25 [1]Or *a terror of God* **35:6** [a]Ge 28:19; 48:3 **35:7** [a]Ge 35:3 [1]The God of Bethel [2]Lit *from the face of* **35:8** [a]Ge 24:59 [1]Lit *oak of weeping* **35:9** [a]Ge 32:29 **35:10** [a]Ge 17:5; 32:28 **35:11** [a]Ge 17:1; 28:3; Ex 6:3 [b]Ge 9:1, 7 [c]Ge 48:4 [d]Ge 17:6, 16; 36:31 [1]Heb *El Shaddai* [2]Or *come into being* **35:12** [a]Ge 12:7; 13:15; 26:3, 4; 28:13; Ex 32:13 **35:13** [a]Ge 17:22; 18:33 **35:14** [a]Ge 28:18, 19; 31:45 **35:15** [a]Ge 28:19 [1]Lit *the house of God* **35:16** [a]Ge 35:19; 48:7; Ru 4:11; Mic 5:2 [1]Lit *had difficulty in her giving birth* **35:17** [a]Ge 30:24

departing (for she died), that she
named him [1]Ben-oni; but his father
called him [2]Benjamin. **19** So [a]Rachel
died and was buried on the way to
[b]Ephrath (that is, Bethlehem). **20** And
Jacob set up a pillar over her grave;
that is the [a]pillar of Rachel's grave
to this day. **21** Then Israel journeyed
on and pitched his tent beyond the
[a,1]tower of [2]Eder.

### *The Sons of Jacob*

**22** Now it happened while Israel was
dwelling in that land, that [a]Reuben
went and lay with Bilhah his father's
concubine, and Israel heard *of it.*
And there were twelve sons of
Jacob—
**23** [a]the sons of Leah:
Reuben, Jacob's firstborn,
then Simeon and Levi and
Judah and Issachar and
Zebulun;
**24** [a]the sons of Rachel:
Joseph and Benjamin;
**25** and [a]the sons of Bilhah,
Rachel's servant-woman:
Dan and Naphtali;
**26** and [a]the sons of Zilpah,
Leah's servant-woman:
Gad and Asher.
These are the sons of Jacob who were
born to him in Paddan-aram.
**27** And Jacob came to his father
Isaac at [a]Mamre of [b]Kiriath-arba
(that is, Hebron), where Abraham
and Isaac had sojourned.
**28** Now the days of Isaac were [a]180
years. **29** And Isaac breathed his last
and died and was [a]gathered to his
people, an [b]old man and full of days;
and [c]his sons Esau and Jacob buried
him.

### *The Generations of Esau*

**36** Now these are the generations
of [a]Esau (that is, Edom).
**2** Esau [a]took his wives from the
daughters of Canaan: Adah the
daughter of Elon the Hittite, and
[b]Oholibamah the daughter of Anah
and the [c]granddaughter of Zibeon
the Hivite; **3** also Basemath, Ishmael's
daughter, the sister of Nebaioth.
**4** And Adah bore [a]Eliphaz to Esau,
and Basemath bore Reuel, **5** and
Oholibamah bore Jeush and Jalam
and Korah. These are the sons of
Esau who were born to him in the
land of Canaan.
**6** [a]Then Esau took his wives and
his sons and his daughters and all
[1]his household, and his livestock
and all his cattle and all his acquired
goods, which he had accumulated in
the land of Canaan, and he went to
a land away from his brother Jacob.
**7** [a]For their possessions had become
too great for them to [1]live together,
and the [b]land where they [c]sojourned
could not sustain them because of
their livestock. **8** So Esau lived in the
hill country of [a]Seir; Esau is [b]Edom.
**9** These then are the generations
of Esau the father of [1]the Edomites
in the hill country of Seir. **10** These
are the names of Esau's sons: Eliphaz
the son of Esau's wife Adah, Reuel

**35:18** [1]Lit *the son of my sorrow* [2]Lit *the son of the right hand* **35:19** [a]Ge 48:7 [b]Ru 1:2; 4:11; Mic 5:2 **35:20** [a]1Sa 10:2 **35:21** [a]Mic 4:8 [1]Heb *Migdal-eder* [2]Or *flock* **35:22** [a]Ge 49:4; 1Chr 5:1 **35:23** [a]Ge 29:31-35; 30:18-20; 46:8; Ex 1:1-4 **35:24** [a]Ge 30:22-24; 35:18 **35:25** [a]Ge 30:5-8 **35:26** [a]Ge 30:10-13 **35:27** [a]Ge 13:18; 18:1; 23:19 [b]Jos 14:15 **35:28** [a]Ge 25:26 **35:29** [a]Ge 25:8; 49:33 [b]Ge 15:15 [c]Ge 25:9 ◆ **36:1** [a]Ge 25:30 **36:2** [a]Ge 28:9 [b]Ge 36:25 [c]Ge 36:24 **36:4** [a]1Chr 1:35 **36:6** [a]Ge 12:5 [1]Lit *the souls of his house* **36:7** [a]Ge 13:6 [b]Ge 17:8; Heb 11:9 [c]1Chr 29:15; Ps 39:12 [1]Lit *dwell* **36:8** [a]Ge 32:3 [b]Ge 36:1, 19 **36:9** [1]Lit *Edom*

the son of Esau's wife Basemath.
11 The sons of Eliphaz were Teman,
Omar, [1]Zepho and Gatam and Kenaz.
12 Timna was a concubine of Esau's
son Eliphaz, and she bore [a]Amalek
to Eliphaz. These are the sons of
Esau's wife Adah. 13 These are the
sons of Reuel: Nahath and Zerah,
Shammah and Mizzah. These were
the sons of Esau's wife Basemath.
14 These were the sons of Esau's wife
Oholibamah, the daughter of Anah
and the [1]granddaughter of Zibeon:
[2]she bore to Esau, Jeush and Jalam
and Korah.

15 These are the chiefs of the sons
of Esau. The sons of Eliphaz, the
firstborn of Esau, are chief Teman,
chief Omar, chief Zepho, chief
Kenaz, 16 chief Korah, chief Gatam,
chief Amalek. These are the chiefs
[1]*descended* from Eliphaz in the land
of Edom; these are the sons of Adah.
17 These are the sons of Reuel, Esau's
son: chief Nahath, chief Zerah, chief
Shammah, chief Mizzah. These are
the chiefs [1]*descended* from Reuel in
the land of Edom; these are the sons
of Esau's wife Basemath. 18 These are
the sons of Esau's wife Oholibamah:
chief Jeush, chief Jalam, chief Korah.
These are the chiefs [1]*descended* from
Esau's wife Oholibamah, the daugh-
ter of Anah. 19 These are the sons of
Esau (that is, Edom), and these are
their chiefs.

20 These are the sons of Seir [a]the
Horite, the inhabitants of the land:
Lotan and Shobal and Zibeon and
Anah, 21 and Dishon and Ezer and
Dishan. These are the chiefs [1]*de-
scended* from the Horites, the sons of
Seir in the land of Edom. 22 The sons
of Lotan were Hori and [1]Hemam; and
Lotan's sister was Timna. 23 These
are the sons of Shobal: [1]Alvan and
Manahath and Ebal, [2]Shepho and
Onam. 24 These are the sons of
Zibeon: Aiah and Anah—he is the
Anah who found the hot springs in
the wilderness when he was pastur-
ing the donkeys of his father Zibeon.
25 These are the children of Anah:
Dishon and Oholibamah, the daugh-
ter of Anah. 26 These are the sons
of [a,1]Dishon: [2]Hemdan and Eshban
and Ithran and Cheran. 27 These are
the sons of Ezer: Bilhan and Zaavan
and [1]Akan. 28 These are the sons
of Dishan: Uz and Aran. 29 These
are the chiefs of the Horites: chief
Lotan, chief Shobal, chief Zibeon,
chief Anah, 30 chief Dishon, chief
Ezer, chief Dishan. These are the
chiefs [1]*descended* from the Horites,
according to their *various* chiefs in
the land of Seir.

31 Now these are the kings who
reigned in the land of Edom before
*any* [a]king of the sons of Israel
reigned. 32 [a]And Bela the son of
Beor became king in Edom, and
the name of his city was Dinhabah.
33 Then Bela died, and Jobab the son
of Zerah of Bozrah became king in
his place. 34 Then Jobab died, and
Husham of the land of the Temanites
became king in his place. 35 Then
Husham died, and Hadad the son
of Bedad, who struck down Midian

---

**36:11** [1]In 1Chr 1:36, *Zephi* **36:12** [a]Ex 17:8-16; Nu 24:20; Dt 25:17-19; 1Sa 15:2, 3 **36:14** [1]Gr *son* [2]Lit *and she* **36:16** [1]Lit *of Eliphaz* **36:17** [1]Lit *of Reuel* **36:18** [1]Lit *of Oholibamah, Esau's wife* **36:20** [a]Ge 14:6; Dt 2:12, 22; 1Chr 1:38-42 **36:21** [1]Lit *of the Horites* **36:22** [1]In 1Chr 1:39, *Homam* **36:23** [1]In 1Chr 1:40, *Alian* [2]In 1Chr 1:40, *Shephi* **36:26** [a]1Chr 1:41 [1]Heb *Dishan* [2]In 1Chr 1:41, *Hamran* **36:27** [1]In 1Chr 1:42, *Jaakan* **36:30** [1]Lit *of the Horites* **36:31** [a]Ge 17:6, 16; 35:11; 1Chr 1:43 **36:32** [a]1Chr 1:43

in the field of Moab, became king in
his place; and the name of his city
was Avith. **36** Then Hadad died, and
Samlah of Masrekah became king
in his place. **37** Then Samlah died,
and Shaul of Rehoboth on the [1]River
became king in his place. **38** Then
Shaul died, and Baal-hanan the son
of Achbor became king in his place.
**39** Then Baal-hanan the son of Ach-
bor died, and [1]Hadar became king in
his place; and the name of his city
was [2]Pau; and his wife's name was
Mehetabel, the daughter of Matred,
daughter of Mezahab.
**40** Now these are the names of
the chiefs [1]*descended* from Esau,
according to their families *and* their
places, by their names: chief Timna,
chief [2]Alvah, chief Jetheth, **41** chief
Oholibamah, chief Elah, chief Pinon,
**42** chief Kenaz, chief Teman, chief
Mibzar, **43** chief Magdiel, chief Iram.
These are the chiefs of Edom (that is,
Esau, the father of [1]the Edomites), ac-
cording to their *places of* habitation
in the land of their possession.

### *The Generations of Jacob*

**37** Now Jacob lived in [a]the land
[1]where his father had sojourned,
in the land of Canaan. **2** These are the
generations of Jacob.
Joseph, when [a]seventeen years of
age, was pasturing *the flock with* his
brothers while he was *still* a youth,
along with [b]the sons of Bilhah and
the sons of Zilpah, his father's wives.
And Joseph brought back an [c]evil
report about them to their father.
**3** Now Israel loved Joseph more than
all his sons because he was [a]the son
of his old age; and he made him a
[b,1]varicolored tunic. **4** And his broth-
ers saw that their father loved him
more than all his brothers, and *so*
they [a]hated him and could not speak
to him in peace.

### *Joseph's Dreams*

**5** Then Joseph [a,1]had a dream, and
he told it to his brothers; so they
hated him even more. **6** And he said
to them, "Please listen to this dream
which I have [1]had: **7** Indeed, behold,
we were binding sheaves in the
field, and behold, my sheaf rose up
and also stood upright; and behold,
your sheaves gathered around and
[a]bowed down to my sheaf." **8** Then
his brothers said to him, "[a]Are you
really going to reign over us? Or are
you really going to rule over us?" So
they hated him even more for his
dreams and for his words.
**9** Then he [1]had still another dream
and recounted it to his brothers and
said, "Behold, I have [1]had still another
dream; and behold, the sun and the
moon and eleven stars were bowing
down to me." **10** And he recounted
*it* to his father and to his brothers;
and his father rebuked him and said
to him, "What is this dream that you
*have* [1]had? Shall I and your mother
and [a]your brothers really come to
bow ourselves down before you to
the ground?" **11** [a]And his brothers
were jealous of him, but his father
[b]kept the saying *in mind.*

**36:37** [1]The Euphrates River **36:39** [1]In 1Chr 1:50, *Hadad* [2]In 1Chr 1:50, *Pai* **36:40** [1]Lit *of Esau* [2]In 1Chr 1:51, *Aliah* **36:43** [1]Heb *Edom* ◆ **37:1** [a]Ge 17:8; 28:4 [1]Lit *of his father's sojournings* **37:2** [a]Ge 41:46 [b]Ge 35:25, 26 [c]1Sa 2:22-24 **37:3** [a]Ge 44:20 [b]Ge 37:23, 32 [1]Or *full-length robe, long-sleeved garment*; cf. 2Sa 13:18; SS 5:3 **37:4** [a]Ge 27:41; 1Sa 17:28 **37:5** [a]Ge 28:12; 31:10, 11, 24 [1]Lit *dreamed* **37:6** [1]Lit *dreamed* **37:7** [a]Ge 42:6, 9; 43:26; 44:14 **37:8** [a]Ge 49:26; Dt 33:16 **37:9** [1]Lit *dreamed* **37:10** [a]Ge 27:29 [1]Lit *dreamed* **37:11** [a]Ac 7:9 [b]Da 7:28; Lk 2:19, 51

**12** Then his brothers went to pas-
ture their father's flock in Shechem.
**13** And Israel said to Joseph, "Are not
your brothers pasturing *the flock* in
[a]Shechem? Come, and I will send
you to them." And he said to him,
"[1]I will go." **14** Then he said to him,
"Go now and see about the welfare of
your brothers and the welfare of the
flock, and bring word back to me."
So he sent him from the valley of
[a]Hebron, and he came to Shechem.
**15** And a man found him, and be-
hold, he was wandering in the field;
and the man asked him, "[1]What are
you seeking?" **16** And he said, "I am
seeking my brothers; please tell me
where they are pasturing *the flock*."
**17** Then the man said, "They have
journeyed from here; for I heard
*them* saying, 'Let us go to [a]Dothan.'"
So Joseph went after his brothers and
found them at Dothan.

### *Joseph Sold by His Brothers*

**18** And they saw him from a distance,
and before he came close to them,
they [a]plotted against him to put
him to death. **19** Then they said to
one another, "[1]Here comes this
dreamer! **20** So now, come and let us
kill him and cast him into one of the
pits; and [a]we will say, 'A wild beast
devoured him.' Then let us see what
will become of his dreams!" **21** But
[a]Reuben heard *this* and delivered
him out of their hands and said, "Let
us not strike down his life." **22** Reu-
ben further said to them, "Shed no
blood. Cast him into this pit that is in
the wilderness, but do not put forth
your hands against him"—that he
might deliver him out of their hands
to return him to his father. **23** Now it
happened, when Joseph [1]reached his
brothers, that they stripped Joseph of
his [2]tunic, the varicolored tunic that
was on him; **24** and they took him and
cast him into the pit. Now the pit was
empty, without any water in it.
**25** And they sat down to eat [1]a
meal. Then they lifted up their eyes
and saw, and behold, a caravan of
[a]Ishmaelites was coming from
Gilead, with their camels bearing
[b,2]aromatic gum and [c,3]balm and
[4]myrrh, going to bring *them* down
to Egypt. **26** And Judah said to his
brothers, "What gain is it that we
kill our brother and [a]cover up his
blood? **27** [a]Come and let us sell him
to the Ishmaelites and not lay our
hands on him, for he is our brother,
our *own* flesh." And his brothers
listened. **28** Then some [a]Midianite
traders passed by, so they pulled *him*
up and lifted Joseph out of the pit and
[b]sold Joseph to the Ishmaelites for
[1]twenty *shekels* of silver. Thus [c]they
brought Joseph into Egypt.
**29** Then Reuben returned to the
pit, and behold, Joseph was not in
the pit; so he [a]tore his garments.
**30** Then he returned to his brothers
and said, "[a]The boy is not *there*; as
for me, where am I to go?" **31** So [a]they
took Joseph's tunic and slaughtered a
male goat and dipped the tunic in the

---

**37:13** [a]Ge 33:18-20 [1]Lit *Behold me* **37:14** [a]Ge 13:18; 23:2, 19; 35:27; Jos 14:14, 15; Jdg 1:10 **37:15** [1]Lit *saying, "What...?"* **37:17** [a]2Ki 6:13 **37:18** [a]Ps 31:13; 37:12, 32; Mk 14:1; Jn 11:53; Ac 23:12 **37:19** [1]Lit *Behold, this master of dreams comes* **37:20** [a]Ge 37:32, 33 **37:21** [a]Ge 42:22 **37:23** [1]Lit *came to* [2]Or *full-length robe* **37:25** [a]Ge 16:11, 12; 37:28; 39:1 [b]Ge 43:11 [c]Jer 8:22; 46:11 [1]Lit *bread* [2]Or *ladanum spice* [3]Or *mastic* [4]Or *resinous bark* **37:26** [a]Ge 37:20 **37:27** [a]Ge 42:21 **37:28** [a]Ge 37:25; Jdg 6:1-3; 8:22, 24 [b]Ge 45:4, 5; Ps 105:17; Ac 7:9 [c]Ge 39:1 [1]Approx. 8 oz. or 220 gm, a shekel was approx. 0.4 oz. or 11 gm **37:29** [a]Ge 37:34; 44:13 **37:30** [a]Ge 42:13, 36 **37:31** [a]Ge 37:3, 23

blood; 32 and they sent the varicol-
ored tunic and brought it to their fa-
ther and said, "We found this; please
recognize *it*—whether it is your son's
tunic or not." 33 And he recognized
it and said, "It is my son's tunic. [a]A
wild beast has devoured him; [b]Joseph
has surely been torn to pieces!" 34 So
Jacob [a]tore his clothes and put sack-
cloth on his loins and mourned for
his son many days. 35 Then all his
sons and all his daughters arose to
comfort him, but he refused to be
comforted. And he said, "Surely I will
[a]go down to Sheol in mourning for
my son." So his father wept for him.
36 Meanwhile, the [1]Midianites [a]sold
him in Egypt to Potiphar, Pharaoh's
officer, the captain of the bodyguard.

### *Judah and Tamar*

38 Now it happened at that time
that Judah went down from his
brothers and turned aside to a certain
[a]Adullamite, whose name was Hirah.
2 And Judah saw there a daughter of
a certain Canaanite whose name was
[a]Shua; and he took her and went in
to her. 3 So she conceived and bore a
son, and he named him [a]Er. 4 Then
she conceived again and bore a son,
and she named him [a]Onan. 5 And
she bore still another son, and she
named him [a]Shelah; and it was at
Chezib [1]that she bore him.
6 Then Judah took a wife for Er his
firstborn, and her name *was* Tamar.
7 But [a]Er, Judah's firstborn, was evil
in the sight of Yahweh, so Yahweh
put him to death. 8 Then Judah said
to Onan, "[a]Go in to your brother's
wife, and perform your duty as a
brother-in-law to her, and raise up a
seed for your brother." 9 And Onan
knew that the [a]seed would not be
his; and it happened that when he
went in to his brother's wife, he
wasted it on the ground in order not
to give seed to his brother. 10 But
what he did was displeasing in the
sight of Yahweh; so He [a]put him to
death also. 11 Then Judah said to his
daughter-in-law Tamar, "[a]Live as a
widow in your father's house until
my son Shelah grows up"; for he
[1]thought, "*I am afraid* lest he also
die like his brothers." So Tamar went
and lived in her father's house.
12 And [1]after a considerable time,
Shua's daughter, the wife of Judah,
died. Then Judah was comforted,
and he went up to his sheepshearers
at [a]Timnah, he and his friend Hirah
the Adullamite. 13 Then it was told to
Tamar, "[1]Behold, your father-in-law
is going up to [a]Timnah to shear his
sheep." 14 So she removed her widow's
garments from herself and [a]covered
*herself* with a [1]veil and wrapped
herself. And she sat at the entrance
of [2]Enaim, which is on the road to
Timnah; for she saw that Shelah had
grown up, and [b]she had not been giv-
en to him as a wife. 15 Then Judah saw
her, and he thought she *was* a harlot,
for she had covered her face. 16 So he
turned aside to her by the road and
said, "Here now, let me come in to
you"; for he did not know that she was
his daughter-in-law. And she said,

---

**37:33** [a]Ge 37:20 [b]Ge 44:28 **37:34** [a]Ge 37:29 **37:35** [a]Ge 25:8; 35:29; 42:38; 44:29, 31
**37:36** [a]Ge 39:1 [1]Lit *Medanites* ◆ **38:1** [a]Jos 15:35; 1Sa 22:1 **38:2** [a]1Chr 2:3 **38:3** [a]Ge 46:12; Nu 26:19 **38:4** [a]Ge 46:12 **38:5** [a]Nu 26:20 [1]Lit *when* **38:7** [a]Ge 46:12; Nu 26:19; 1Chr 2:3
**38:8** [a]Dt 25:5, 6; Mt 22:24 **38:9** [a]Dt 25:6 **38:10** [a]Ge 46:12; Nu 26:19 **38:11** [a]Ru 1:12, 13 [1]Lit *said*
**38:12** [a]Jos 15:10, 57 [1]Lit *the days became many and* **38:13** [a]Jos 15:10, 57; Jdg 14:1 [1]Lit *saying, Behold*
**38:14** [a]Ge 24:65 [b]Ge 38:11, 26 [1]Or *shawl* [2]In Jos 15:34, *Enam*

"What will you give me, that you may
come in to me?" **17** He said, therefore,
"I will send you a [1]young goat from
the flock." She said, moreover, "Will
you give a pledge until you send *it*?"
**18** Then he said, "What pledge shall I
give you?" And she said, "[a]Your signet
and your cord and your staff that is in
your hand." So he gave *them* to her
and went in to her, and she conceived
by him. **19** Then she arose and went.
And she removed her [1]veil from her-
self and put on her widow's garments.
**20** Then Judah sent the [1]young
goat by his friend the Adullamite to
take the pledge from the woman's
hand, but he did not find her. **21** So
he asked the men of her place,
saying, "Where is the cult prostitute
who was by the road at Enaim?" But
they said, "There has been no cult
prostitute here." **22** So he returned
to Judah and said, "I did not find her;
and furthermore, the men of the
place said, 'There has been no cult
prostitute here.'" **23** Then Judah said,
"Let her [1]keep them, lest we become
a laughingstock. Behold, I sent this
young goat, but you did not find her."
**24** Now it happened about three
months later that it was told to Judah
saying, "[1]Your daughter-in-law Tamar
has played the harlot, and behold,
she is also with child by harlotry."
Then Judah said, "Bring her out and
[a]let her be burned!" **25** It was while
she was being brought out that she
sent to her father-in-law, saying, "I
am with child by the man to whom
these things belong." And she said,
"[a]Please recognize *this* and see,
whose signet ring and cords and staff
are these?" **26** And Judah recognized
*them* and said, "[a]She is more righ-
teous than I, inasmuch as [b]I did not
give her to my son Shelah." And he
did not [1]know her again.
**27** Now it happened at the time she
was giving birth, that behold, there
were [a]twins in her womb. **28** And it
happened, while she was giving birth,
one put out a hand, and the midwife
took and tied a scarlet *thread* on his
hand, saying, "This one came out
first." **29** And then it happened, as
he drew back his hand, that behold,
his brother came out. So she said,
"What a breach you have made for
yourself!" So he was named [a,1]Perez.
**30** Afterward his brother came out
who had the scarlet *thread* on his
hand; and he was named [a,1]Zerah.

### *Joseph in Potiphar's House*

**39** Now Joseph was brought
down to Egypt; and Potiphar,
an Egyptian official of Pharaoh, the
captain of the bodyguard, bought
him [1]from the [a]Ishmaelites, who had
brought him down there. **2** [a]And Yah-
weh was with Joseph, so he became
a [1]successful man. And he was in the
house of his master, the Egyptian.
**3** Now his master [a]saw that Yahweh
was with him and *how* Yahweh
[b]caused all that he did to succeed in
his hand. **4** So Joseph [a]found favor
in his sight and [1]attended on him;
and he appointed him overseer over
his house, and [b]all that he owned he

**38:17** [1]Lit *kid of goats* **38:18** [a]Ge 38:25; 41:42 **38:19** [1]Or *shawl* **38:20** [1]Lit *kid of goats by the hand of* **38:23** [1]Lit *take for herself* **38:24** [a]Lv 21:9 [1]Lit *saying, Your* **38:25** [a]Ge 37:32 **38:26** [a]1Sa 24:17 [b]Ge 38:14 [1]Or *have relations with* **38:27** [a]Ge 25:24-26 **38:29** [a]Ge 46:12; Ru 4:12 [1]Lit *a breach* **38:30** [a]1Chr 2:4 [1]Lit *a dawning, brightness* ◆ **39:1** [a]Ge 37:25, 28, 36; Ps 105:17 [1]Lit *from the hand of* **39:2** [a]Ge 39:3, 21, 23; Ac 7:9 [1]Or *prosperous* **39:3** [a]Ge 21:22; 26:28 [b]Ps 1:3 **39:4** [a]Ge 18:3; 19:19 [b]Ge 24:2; 39:8, 22 [1]Or *ministered*

gave in his hand. **5** Now it happened
that from the time he appointed
him overseer in his house and over
all that he owned, Yahweh [a]blessed
the Egyptian's house on account of
Joseph; thus [b]the blessing of Yahweh
was upon all that he owned, in the
house and in the field. **6** So he left
everything he owned in Joseph's
hand; and with him *there* he did
not [1]concern himself with anything
except the [2]food which he [3]ate.

Now Joseph was [a]beautiful in form
and beautiful in appearance.

**7** And it happened after these
events [a]that his master's wife [1]set
her eyes on Joseph and said, "[b]Lie
with me." **8** But [a]he refused and
said to his master's wife, "Behold,
with me *here*, my master [1]does not
concern himself with anything in
the house, and he has given all that
he owns into my hand. **9** [a,1]There is
no one greater in this house than I,
and he has withheld nothing from
me except you, because you are his
wife. How then could I do this great
evil and [b]sin against God?" **10** So it
happened that as she spoke to Joseph
day after day, he did not listen to her
to lie beside her *or* be with her.

**11** Now it happened [1]one day that
he went into the house to do his work,
and none of the men of the household
was there inside. **12** Then she seized
him by his garment, saying, "Lie with
me!" And he left his garment in her
hand and fled and went outside.
**13** Now it happened, when she saw
that he had left his garment in her
hand and had fled outside, **14** that she
called to the men of her household
and spoke to them, saying, "See, he
has brought in a [1]Hebrew to us to
laugh at us; he came in to me to lie
with me, and I [2]screamed. **15** Now it
happened that when he heard that
I raised my voice and [1]screamed,
he left his garment beside me and
fled and went outside." **16** And she
placed his garment beside her until
his master came home. **17** Then she
[a]spoke to him [1]with these words, say-
ing, "The Hebrew slave, whom you
brought to us, came in to me to laugh
at me; **18** and as I raised my voice and
[1]screamed, he left his garment beside
me and fled outside."

### *Joseph Is Put into Jail*

**19** Now it happened that when his
master heard the words of his wife,
which she spoke to him, saying,
"[1]This is what your slave did to me,"
[a]his anger burned. **20** So Joseph's
master took him and [a]put him into
the jail, the place where the king's
prisoners were confined; and he
was there in the jail. **21** But [a]Yahweh
was with Joseph and [1]extended lov-
ingkindness to him and [b]gave him
favor in the sight of the chief jailer.
**22** So the chief jailer [a]gave into the
hand of Joseph all the prisoners who
were in the jail; so that whatever was
done there, he was [1]the one who did
*it*. **23** [a]The chief jailer did not super-
vise anything under Joseph's hand

**39:5** [a]Ge 30:27 [b]Dt 28:3, 4, 11 **39:6** [a]Ge 29:17; 1Sa 16:12 [1]Lit *know* [2]Lit *bread* [3]Or *used to eat* **39:7** [a]Pr 7:15-20 [b]2Sa 13:11 [1]Lit *lifted up her eyes at* **39:8** [a]Pr 6:23, 24 [1]Lit *does not know what is in the house* **39:9** [a]Ge 41:40 [b]Ge 20:6; 42:18; 2Sa 12:13; Ps 51:4 [1]Or *He is not greater* **39:11** [1]Lit *about this day* **39:14** [1]Lit *Hebrew man* [2]Lit *called with a great voice* **39:15** [1]Lit *called out* **39:17** [a]Ex 23:1; Pr 26:28 [1]Lit *according to* **39:18** [1]Lit *called out* **39:19** [a]Pr 6:34 [1]Lit *According to these things your slave* **39:20** [a]Ge 40:3; Ps 105:18 **39:21** [a]Ge 39:2; Ps 105:19; Ac 7:9 [b]Ex 3:21; 11:3; 12:36 [1]Or *turned aside*, cf. 38:1, 16 **39:22** [a]Ge 39:4; 40:3, 4 [1]Lit *the doer* **39:23** [a]Ge 39:3, 8

because [b]Yahweh was with him; and whatever he did, [c]Yahweh made to succeed.

### *Joseph Interprets the Officials' Dreams*

**40** Now it happened that after these things, [a]the cupbearer and the baker for the king of Egypt offended their lord, the king of Egypt. **2** And Pharaoh was [a]furious with his two officials, the chief cupbearer and the chief baker. **3** So he put them in confinement in the house of the [a]captain of the bodyguard, in the jail, the *same* place where Joseph was imprisoned. **4** And the captain of the bodyguard appointed Joseph as overseer over them, and he [1]attended to them; and they were in confinement for [2]some time. **5** Then the cupbearer and the baker for the king of Egypt, who were confined in jail, both had a dream the same night, each man with his *own* dream *and* each dream with its *own* interpretation. **6** Now Joseph came to them in the morning and saw them, and behold, they were dejected. **7** So he asked Pharaoh's officials who were with him in confinement in his master's house, saying, "[a]Why are your faces so sad today?" **8** Then they said to him, "[a]We have [1]had a dream, and there is no one to interpret it." Then Joseph said to them, "[b]Do not interpretations belong to God? Recount *it* to me, please."

**9** So the chief cupbearer recounted his dream to Joseph and said to him, "In my dream, [1]behold, *there was* a vine in front of me; **10** and on the vine *were* three branches. And as it was budding, its blossoms came out, *and* its clusters produced ripe grapes. **11** Now Pharaoh's cup was in my hand; so I took the grapes and squeezed them into Pharaoh's cup, and I put the cup into Pharaoh's [1]hand." **12** Then Joseph said to him, "This is the [a]interpretation of it: the three branches are three days; **13** within three more days Pharaoh will [1]lift up your head and restore you to your [2]office; and you will put Pharaoh's cup into his hand according to your former custom when you were his cupbearer. **14** Only remember me when it goes well with you, and please [a]show me lovingkindness by remembering me to Pharaoh and getting me out of this house. **15** For [a]I was in fact stolen from the land of the Hebrews, and even here I have done nothing that they should have put me into the pit."

**16** And the chief baker saw that he had interpreted favorably, so he said to Joseph, "I also *saw* in my dream, and behold, *there were* three baskets of white bread on my head; **17** and in the top basket *there were* some of all [1]sorts of baked food for Pharaoh, and the birds were eating them out of the basket on my head." **18** Then Joseph answered and said, "This is its interpretation: the three baskets are three days; **19** within three more days Pharaoh will lift up your head off of you and will hang you on a tree, and the birds will eat your flesh off of you."

**39:23** [b]Ge 39:2, 3 [c]Ge 39:3 ◆ **40:1** [a]Ge 40:11, 13; Ne 1:11 **40:2** [a]Pr 16:14 **40:3** [a]Ge 39:1, 20 **40:4** [1]Or *ministered to* [2]Lit *days* **40:7** [a]Ne 2:2 **40:8** [a]Ge 41:15 [b]Ge 41:16; Da 2:27, 28 [1]Lit *dreamed* **40:9** [1]Lit *and behold* **40:11** [1]Lit *palm* **40:12** [a]Da 2:36; 4:18, 19 **40:13** [1]Or possibly *forgive you* [2]Lit *place* **40:14** [a]Jos 2:12; 1Sa 20:14; 1Ki 2:7 **40:15** [a]Ge 37:26-28 **40:17** [1]Lit *food for Pharaoh made by a baker*

**20** Thus it happened on the third
day, *which was* [a]Pharaoh's birthday,
that he made a feast for all his ser-
vants; [b]and he lifted up the head of
the chief cupbearer and the head of
the chief baker among his servants.
**21** And he restored the chief cup-
bearer to his [1]office, and [a]he put the
cup into Pharaoh's [2]hand; **22** but [a]he
hanged the chief baker, just as Joseph
had interpreted to them. **23** Yet the
chief cupbearer did not remember
Joseph, but [a]forgot him.

### *Joseph Interprets Pharaoh's Dream*

**41** Now it happened at the end of
two full years that Pharaoh had
a dream, and behold, he was standing
by the Nile. **2** And behold, from the
Nile there came up seven cows,
sleek and [1]fat; and they grazed in the
[a]reeds. **3** Then behold, seven other
cows came up after them from the
Nile, [1]ugly and [2]thin, and they stood
by the *other* cows on the bank of the
Nile. **4** And the ugly and [1]thin cows
ate up the seven sleek and fat cows.
Then Pharaoh awoke. **5** He again fell
asleep and dreamed a second time;
and behold, seven ears of grain came
up on a single stalk, plump and good.
**6** And behold, seven ears, thin and
scorched by the east wind, sprouted
up after them. **7** And the thin ears
swallowed up the seven plump and
full ears. Then Pharaoh awoke, and
behold, *it was* a dream. **8** Now it
happened that in the morning [a]his
spirit was troubled, so he sent and
called for all the [b,1]magicians of Egypt
and all its [c]wise men. And Pharaoh
recounted to them his dream, but
[d]there was no one who could inter-
pret them to Pharaoh.
**9** Then the chief cupbearer spoke
to Pharaoh, saying, "I would bring
to remembrance today [a]my *own*
[1]offenses. **10** Pharaoh was [a]furious
with his servants, and [b]he put me
in confinement in the house of the
captain of the bodyguard, *both* me
and the chief baker. **11** [a]And we had
a dream [1]on the same night, [2]he and
I; each of us dreamed according to
the interpretation of his *own* dream.
**12** Now there *was* with us a Hebrew
youth, a [a]slave of the captain of the
bodyguard, and we recounted *them*
to him, and [b]he interpreted our
dreams for us. To each one he inter-
preted according to his *own* dream.
**13** And just [a]as he interpreted for us,
so it happened; he restored me in my
[1]office, but he hanged him."
**14** Then Pharaoh sent and [a]called
for Joseph, and they [b]rushed him out
of the pit; and he shaved himself and
changed his clothes, and he came
to Pharaoh. **15** And Pharaoh said to
Joseph, "I have had a dream, [a]but no
one can interpret it; yet [b]I have heard
[1]it said about you, that [2]you hear a
dream *and that* you can interpret
it." **16** Joseph then answered Phar-
aoh, saying, "[a,1]It is not in me; [b]God
will [2]answer *concerning* the welfare

**40:20** [a]Mt 14:6 [b]2Ki 25:27; Jer 52:31 **40:21** [a]Ge 40:13 [1]Lit *wine-pouring* [2]Lit *palm*
**40:22** [a]Ge 40:19; Es 7:10 **40:23** [a]Job 19:14; Ps 31:12; Ecc 9:15 ◆ **41:2** [a]Job 8:11; Is 19:6, 7
[1]Lit *fat of flesh* **41:3** [1]Lit *bad*, so in ch [2]Lit *lean of flesh* **41:4** [1]Lit *lean of flesh* **41:8** [a]Da 2:1, 3
[b]Ex 7:11, 22; Da 1:20; 2:2 [c]Mt 2:1 [d]Da 2:27; 4:7 [1]Or *soothsayer priests* **41:9** [a]Ge 40:14, 23 [1]Or *sins*
**41:10** [a]Ge 40:2, 3 [b]Ge 39:20 **41:11** [a]Ge 40:5 [1]Lit *one night* [2]Lit *I and he* **41:12** [a]Ge 37:36 [b]Ge 40:12
**41:13** [a]Ge 40:21, 22 [1]Lit *place* **41:14** [a]Ps 105:20 [b]Da 2:25 **41:15** [a]Ge 41:8 [b]Da 5:16 [1]Lit *about you, saying* [2]Lit *you hear a dream to interpret it* **41:16** [a]Da 2:30; Zec 4:6; Ac 3:12; 2Co 3:5 [b]Ge 40:8; 41:25, 28, 32; Dt 29:29; Da 2:22, 28, 47 [1]Lit *Apart from me* [2]Lit *answer the peace of Pharaoh*

of Pharaoh." 17 So Pharaoh spoke to
Joseph, "In my dream, behold, I was
standing on the bank of the Nile;
18 and behold, seven cows, [1]fat and
sleek came up out of the Nile, and
they grazed in the reeds. 19 And be-
hold, seven other cows came up after
them, poor and very ugly and lean,
such as I had never seen in all the
land of Egypt, in regard to [1]ugliness;
20 and the lean and ugly cows ate up
the first seven fat cows. 21 But they
[1]devoured them, and yet it could not
be known that they had [1]devoured
them. [2]For they were just as ugly
as [3]before. Then I awoke. 22 Then I
saw also in my dream, and behold,
seven ears, full and good, came up
on a single stalk; 23 and behold, seven
ears, withered, thin, *and* scorched
by the east wind, sprouted up after
them; 24 and the thin ears swallowed
the seven good ears. So [a]I told it to
the [1]magicians, but there was no one
who could declare it to me."

25 Then Joseph said to Pharaoh,
"Pharaoh's [1]dreams are one *and the
same*; [a]God has declared to Pharaoh
what He is about to do. 26 The seven
good cows are seven years; and the
seven good ears are seven years; the
[1]dreams are one *and the same*. 27 And
the seven lean and ugly cows that
came up after them are seven years,
and the seven lean ears scorched by
the east wind [a]will be seven years of
famine. 28 [1]It is as I have spoken to
Pharaoh: [a]God has shown to Pharaoh
what He is about to do. 29 Behold,
[a]*seven years* of great abundance
are coming in all the land of Egypt;
30 and after them [a]seven years of
famine will arise, and all the abun-
dance will be forgotten in the land of
Egypt, and the famine will [1]ravage the
land, 31 so that the abundance will be
unknown in the land because of that
subsequent famine; for it *will be* very
heavy. 32 Now as for the repeating of
the dream to Pharaoh twice, *it means*
that [a]the matter is confirmed by God,
and God will quickly bring it about.
33 So now let Pharaoh look for a
man [a]understanding and wise, and
set him over the land of Egypt. 34 Let
Pharaoh take action and appoint
overseers over the land, and let him
exact a fifth *of the produce* of the
land of Egypt in the seven years of
abundance. 35 Then let them [a]gather
all the food of these good years that
are coming, and let them store up
the grain for food in the cities under
Pharaoh's authority, and let them
keep watch over *it*. 36 And let the
food be appointed for the land for
the seven years of famine which will
happen in the land of Egypt, so that
the land will not be cut off during
the famine."

### *Joseph Is Set over Egypt*

37 And the [1]proposal seemed good
[2]to Pharaoh and [2]to all his servants.
38 Then Pharaoh said to his servants,
"Can we find a man like this, [a]in whom
is a divine spirit?" 39 So Pharaoh said
to Joseph, "Since God has made you
know all of this, there is no one so
[a]understanding and wise as you are.

**41:18** [1]Lit *fat of flesh* **41:19** [1]Lit *badness* **41:21** [1]Lit *entered their inward parts* [2]Lit *And* [3]Lit *in the beginning* **41:24** [a]Is 8:19; Da 4:7 [1]Or *soothsayer priests* **41:25** [a]Ge 41:28, 32; Da 2:28, 29, 45 [1]Lit *dream is* **41:26** [1]Lit *dream is* **41:27** [a]2Ki 8:1 **41:28** [a]Ge 41:25, 32 [1]Lit *That is the thing which I spoke* **41:29** [a]Ge 41:47 **41:30** [a]Ge 41:54, 56; 47:13; Ps 105:16 [1]Lit *destroy* **41:32** [a]Ge 41:25, 28 **41:33** [a]Ge 41:39 **41:35** [a]Ge 41:48 **41:37** [1]Lit *word* [2]Lit *in the sight of* **41:38** [a]Job 32:8; Da 4:8, 9, 18; 5:11, 14 **41:39** [a]Ge 41:33

**40** [a]You shall be over my house, and
according to your [1]command all my
people shall [2]do homage; only in the
throne I will be greater than you."
**41** And Pharaoh said to Joseph, "See,
I have set you [a]over all the land of
Egypt." **42** Then Pharaoh [a]removed
his signet ring from his hand and
put it on Joseph's hand and clothed
him in garments of fine linen and
[b]put the gold necklace around his
neck. **43** And he had him ride in [1]his
second chariot; and they called out
before him, "[2]Bow the knee!" And
he set him over all the land of Egypt.
**44** Moreover, Pharaoh said to Joseph,
"*Though* I am Pharaoh, yet [a]without
[1]your permission no one shall raise
his hand or foot in all the land of
Egypt." **45** Then Pharaoh named
Joseph [1]Zaphenath-paneah; and he
gave him Asenath, the daughter of
Potiphera priest of [a,2]On, as a wife.
And Joseph went forth over the land
of Egypt.

**46** Now Joseph was [a]thirty years old
when he [1]stood before Pharaoh, king
of Egypt. And Joseph went out from
the presence of Pharaoh and passed
through all the land of Egypt. **47** And
during the seven years of plenty the
land brought forth [1]abundantly. **48** So
he gathered all the food of *these*
seven years which happened in the
land of Egypt and placed the food
in the cities; he placed in every city
the food from its own surrounding
fields. **49** Thus Joseph stored up grain
[1]in great abundance like the sand of
the sea, until he stopped [2]measuring
*it*, for it was [3]beyond measure.

### *The Sons of Joseph*

**50** Now before the year of famine
came, [a]two sons were born to Joseph,
whom Asenath, the daughter of
Potiphera priest of [1]On, bore to him.
**51** And Joseph named the firstborn
[1]Manasseh, "For," *he said*, "God has
made me forget all my trouble and
all my father's household." **52** And he
named the second [1]Ephraim, "For,"
*he said*, "[a]God has made me fruitful
in the land of my affliction."

**53** Then the seven years of plenty
which had been in the land of Egypt
came to an end, **54** and [a]the seven
years of famine began to come, just as
Joseph had said. So there was famine
in all the lands, but in all the land of
Egypt there was bread. **55** Then all the
land of Egypt was famished, and the
people cried out to Pharaoh for bread;
and Pharaoh said to all the Egyptians,
"Go to Joseph; [a]whatever he says to
you, you shall do." **56** Now the famine
was over all the face of the land. And
Joseph opened all [1]the storehouses
and sold to the Egyptians; and the
famine was severe in the land of Egypt.
**57** Now all the earth *also* came to Egypt
to buy grain from Joseph because [a]the
famine was severe in all the earth.

### *Joseph's Brothers Sent to Egypt*

**42** Now [a]Jacob saw that there
was grain in Egypt, and Jacob
said to his sons, "Why are you staring

---

**41:40** [a]Ps 105:21; Ac 7:10 [1]Lit *mouth* [2]Lit *kiss* **41:41** [a]Ge 42:6; Ps 105:21; Da 6:3; Ac 7:10 **41:42** [a]Es 3:10; 8:2 [b]Da 5:7, 16, 29 **41:43** [1]Lit *the second...which was his* [2]Or *Attention, Make way*; Heb *Abreck* **41:44** [a]Ps 105:22 [1]Lit *you no one* **41:45** [a]Jer 43:13; Eze 30:17 [1]Probably Egyptian for "God speaks; he lives" [2]Or *Heliopolis* **41:46** [a]Ge 37:2 [1]Or *entered the service of* **41:47** [1]Lit *by handfuls* **41:49** [1]Lit *very much* [2]Lit *numbering* [3]Or *without number* **41:50** [a]Ge 48:5 [1]Or *Heliopolis* **41:51** [1]Lit *making to forget* **41:52** [a]Ge 17:6; 28:3; 49:22 [1]Lit *fruitfulness* **41:54** [a]Ge 41:30; Ps 105:16; Ac 7:11 **41:55** [a]Jn 2:5 **41:56** [1]Lit *that which was in them* **41:57** [a]Ge 12:10 ◆ **42:1** [a]Ac 7:12

at one another?” **2** Then he said,
“Behold, [a]I have heard that there is
grain in Egypt; go down there and
buy *some* for us from there, [b]so that
we may live and not die.” **3** So ten
brothers of Joseph went down to
buy grain from Egypt. **4** But Jacob did
not send Joseph’s brother [a]Benjamin
with his brothers, for he said, “[b]Lest
*any* harm befall him.” **5** So the sons of
Israel came to buy grain among those
who were coming, [a]for the famine
was in the land of Canaan *also*.

**6** Now [a]Joseph was the one in pow-
er over the land; he was the one who
sold to all the people of the land. And
Joseph’s brothers came and [b]bowed
down to him with *their* [1]faces to
the ground. **7** And Joseph saw his
brothers and recognized them, but
he disguised himself to them and
[a]spoke to them harshly. And he said
to them, “Where have you come
from?” And they said, “From the land
of Canaan, to buy food.”

**8** But Joseph recognized his broth-
ers, although [a]they did not recognize
him. **9** And Joseph [a]remembered the
dreams which he [1]had about them
and said to them, “You are spies; you
have come to look at the [2]nakedness
of the land.” **10** Then they said to him,
“No, [a]my lord, but your servants have
come to buy food. **11** We are all sons
of one man; we are [a]honest men;
your servants are not spies.” **12** And
he said to them, “No, but you have
come to look at the [1]nakedness of
our land!” **13** So they said, “Your
servants are twelve brothers *in all*,
the sons of one man in the land of
Canaan; and behold, the youngest
is with [a]our father today, and [b]one
is no more.” **14** And Joseph said to
them, “It is as I said [1]to you, you are
spies; **15** by this you will be tested: [a]by
the life of Pharaoh, you shall not go
from this place unless your youngest
brother comes here! **16** Send one of
you that he may get your brother,
while you remain confined, that your
words may be tested, whether there
is [a]truth in you. But if not, by the life
of Pharaoh, surely you are spies.”
**17** Then he put them all together in
[a]prison for three days.

**18** And Joseph said to them on the
third day, “Do this and live, for [a]I
fear God: **19** if you are honest men,
let one of your brothers be confined
in [1]your prison; but as for *the rest of*
you, go, bring grain for the famine
of your households, **20** and [a]bring
your youngest brother to me, so your
words may be proven true, and you
will not die.” And they did so. **21** Then
they said to one another, “[a]Surely we
are guilty concerning our brother be-
cause we saw the distress of his soul
when he begged us, yet we would
not listen; therefore this distress has
come upon us.” **22** And Reuben an-
swered them, saying, “[a]Did I not tell
you, saying, ‘Do not sin against the
boy’; yet you would not listen? [b]So
also his blood, behold, it is required
*of us*.” **23** Now they did not know that
Joseph was listening, for there was an

---

**42:2** [a]Ac 7:12 [b]Ge 43:8; Ps 33:18, 19 **42:4** [a]Ge 35:24 [b]Ge 42:38 **42:5** [a]Ge 12:10; 26:1; 41:57; Ac 7:11 **42:6** [a]Ge 41:41, 55 [b]Ge 37:7-10; 41:43; Is 60:14 [1]Lit *noses* **42:7** [a]Ge 42:30 **42:8** [a]Ge 37:2; 41:46 **42:9** [a]Ge 37:6-9 [1]Lit *had dreamed* [2]Or *undefended parts* **42:10** [a]Ge 37:8 **42:11** [a]Ge 42:16, 19, 31, 34 **42:12** [1]Or *undefended parts* **42:13** [a]Ge 43:7 [b]Ge 37:30; 42:32; 44:20 **42:14** [1]Lit *to you, saying* **42:15** [a]1Sa 17:55 **42:16** [a]Ge 42:11 **42:17** [a]Ge 40:4, 7 **42:18** [a]Ge 39:9; Lv 25:43; Ne 5:15 **42:19** [1]Lit *the house of your prison* **42:20** [a]Ge 42:34; 43:5; 44:23 **42:21** [a]Ge 37:26-28; 45:3; Hos 5:15 **42:22** [a]Ge 37:21, 22 [b]Ge 9:5, 6; 1Ki 2:32; 2Chr 24:22; Ps 9:12

interpreter between them. **24** And he
turned away from them and [a]wept.
Then he returned to them and spoke
to them. And he [b]took Simeon from
them and bound him before their
eyes. **25** [a]Then Joseph gave a com-
mand to fill their bags with grain and
to restore every man's money in his
sack and to give them provisions for
the journey. And thus it was done
for them.

**26** So they loaded their donkeys
with their grain and went from
there. **27** Then one *of them* opened
his sack to give his donkey fodder
at the lodging place. And he saw his
[a]money; and behold, it was in the
mouth of his sack. **28** So he said to
his brothers, "My money has been
returned, and behold, it is even in
my sack." And their hearts [1]sank,
and they *turned* [2]trembling to one
another, saying, "[a]What is this that
God has done to us?"

### *Jacob Is Bereaved*

**29** Then they came to their father
Jacob in the land of Canaan and told
him all that had happened to them,
saying, **30** "The man, the lord of the
land, [a]spoke harshly with us and
took us for spies of the country. **31** So
we said to him, 'We are [a]honest men;
we are not spies. **32** We are twelve
brothers, sons of our father; one is no
more, and the youngest is with our
father today in the land of Canaan.'
**33** Then the man, the lord of the land,
said to us, '[a]By this I will know that
you are honest men: leave one of
your brothers with me and take *grain*
*for* the famine of your households,
and go. **34** But bring your youngest
brother to me that I may know that
you are not spies, but [1]honest men.
I will give your brother to you, and
you may [a]trade in the land.'"

**35** Now it happened that they were
emptying their sacks, and behold,
[a]every man's bundle of money *was*
in his sack; and they and their father
saw their bundles of money, and they
feared. **36** And their father Jacob said
to them, "You have [a]bereaved me of
my children: Joseph is no more, and
Simeon is no more, and you would
take Benjamin; all these things are
against me." **37** Then Reuben spoke
to his father, saying, "You may put
my two sons to death if I do not bring
him *back* to you; put him in my hand,
and I will return him to you." **38** But
[1]Jacob said, "My son shall not go
down with you; for his [a]brother is
dead, and he alone remains. [b]If harm
should befall him on the journey on
which you are going, then you will
[c]bring my gray hair down to Sheol
in sorrow."

### *The Brothers Return to Egypt*

**43** [a]Now the famine was heavy
in the land. **2** And it happened
when they had finished eating the
grain which they had brought from
Egypt, that their father said to them,
"Go back, buy us a little food." **3** Judah
spoke to him, however, saying, "[a]The
man solemnly warned us, saying,
'You shall not see my face unless your
brother is with you.' **4** If you send our
brother with us, we will go down and

---

**42:24** [a]Ge 43:30; 45:14, 15 [b]Ge 43:14, 23 **42:25** [a]Ge 44:1; Ro 12:17, 20, 21; 1Pe 3:9 **42:27** [a]Ge 43:21, 22 **42:28** [a]Ge 43:23 [1]Lit *went out* [2]Lit *trembled* **42:30** [a]Ge 42:7 **42:31** [a]Ge 42:11 **42:33** [a]Ge 42:19, 20 **42:34** [a]Ge 34:10 [1]Lit *you are honest* **42:35** [a]Ge 43:12, 15, 21 **42:36** [a]Ge 43:14 **42:38** [a]Ge 37:33, 34; 42:13; 44:27, 28 [b]Ge 42:4 [c]Ge 37:35; 44:29, 31 [1]Lit *he* ◆ **43:1** [a]Ge 12:10; 26:1; 41:56, 57 **43:3** [a]Ge 43:5; 44:23

buy you food. **5** But if you do not
send *him*, we will not go down; for
the man said to us, 'You will not see
my face unless your brother is with
you.'" **6** Then Israel said, "Why did
you treat me so badly [1]by telling the
man whether you still had *another*
brother?" **7** But they said, "The man
questioned particularly about us and
our kin, saying, '[a]Is your father still
alive? Have you *another* brother?' So
we told him concerning these things.
Could we possibly have known that
he would say, 'Bring your brother
down'?" **8** Then Judah said to his
father Israel, "Send the boy with me,
and we will arise and go, [a]that we
may live and not die, we as well as
you and our little ones. **9** [a]I myself
will be *the* guarantee for him; from
my hand you may require him. If I
do not bring him *back* to you and set
him before you, then [1]I shall bear the
sin before you all *my* days. **10** For if we
had not delayed, surely by now we
could have returned twice."
**11** Then their father Israel said to
them, "If *it must be* so, then do this:
take some of the best products of the
land in your [1]bags, and bring *them*
down to the man [a]as a present, a little
[b,2]balm and a little honey, [3]aromatic
gum and [4]myrrh, pistachio nuts and
almonds. **12** Now take double *the*
money in your hand, and take back
in your hand [a]the money that was
put back in the mouth of your sacks;
perhaps it was a mistake. **13** And take
your brother also, and arise, return to
*the man;* **14** and may [a,1]God Almighty
[b]grant you compassion before the
man, so that he will release to you
[c]your other brother and Benjamin.
And as for me, [d]if I am bereaved of
my children, I am bereaved." **15** So
the men took [a]this present, and they
took double *the* money in their hand,
and Benjamin; and they arose and
went down to Egypt and stood before
Joseph.

### *Joseph Sees Benjamin*

**16** Then Joseph saw Benjamin with
them and said to his [a]house steward,
"Bring the men into the house, and
slay an animal and prepare *it*; for
the men are to eat with me at noon."
**17** So the man did as Joseph said and
[1]brought the men to Joseph's house.
**18** And the men were afraid because
they were brought to Joseph's
house; and they said, "*It is* because
of the money that was returned in
our sacks the first time that we are
being brought in, that he may [1]seek
occasion against us and fall upon
us and take us for slaves with our
donkeys." **19** So they came near to
Joseph's house steward and spoke
to him at the entrance of the house,
**20** and they said, "Oh, my lord, we
indeed came down the first time to
buy food, **21** and it happened when
we came to the lodging place, that we
opened our sacks, and behold, [a]each
man's money was in the mouth of
his sack, our money in [1]full. So [b]we
have brought it back in our hand.
**22** We have also brought down other
money in our hand to buy food; we

**43:6** [1]Lit *to tell* **43:7** [a]Ge 42:13; 43:27 **43:8** [a]Ge 42:2 **43:9** [a]Ge 42:37; 44:32; Phm 18, 19 [1]Lit *I shall have sinned before you all the days* **43:11** [a]Ge 32:20; 43:25, 26 [b]Ge 37:25; Jer 8:22; Eze 27:17 [1]Or *vessels* [2]Or *mastic* [3]Or *ladanum spice* [4]Or *resinous bark* **43:12** [a]Ge 42:25, 35; 43:21, 22 **43:14** [a]Ge 17:1; 28:3; 35:11 [b]Ps 106:46 [c]Ge 42:24 [d]Ge 42:36 [1]Heb *El Shaddai* **43:15** [a]Ge 43:11 **43:16** [a]Ge 44:1 **43:17** [1]Lit *the man brought* **43:18** [1]Lit *roll himself upon us* **43:21** [a]Ge 42:27, 35 [b]Ge 43:12, 15 [1]Lit *its weight*

do not know who put our money in our sacks." **23** And he said, "[1]Be well, do not be afraid. [a]Your God and the God of your father has given you treasure in your sacks; your money has come to me." Then [b]he brought Simeon out to them. **24** Then the man brought the men into Joseph's house and [a]gave them water, and they [b]washed their feet; and he gave their donkeys fodder. **25** So they prepared [a]the present [1]for Joseph's coming at noon; for they had heard that they were to eat [2]a meal there.

**26** Then Joseph came home, and they brought into the house to him the present which was in their hand and [a]bowed to the ground before him. **27** And he asked them about their [1]well-being and said, "[a]Is your old father [1]well, of whom you spoke? Is he still alive?" **28** And they said, "Your servant our father is well; he is still alive." [a]They bowed down and prostrated themselves. **29** Then he lifted his eyes and saw his brother Benjamin, his mother's son. And he said, "Is this [a]your youngest brother, of whom you spoke to me?" And he said, "[b]May God be gracious to you, my son." **30** And Joseph hurried *out* for [a,1]he was deeply stirred with compassion over his brother, and he sought *a place* to weep; and he entered his chamber and [b]wept there. **31** Then he washed his face and came out; and he [a]restrained himself and said, "Set the [1]meal." **32** So they set *the meal* for him by himself, and for them by themselves, and for the Egyptians who ate with him by themselves, because the Egyptians could not eat bread with the Hebrews, for that is [a]an abomination to the Egyptians. **33** And they [1]were seated before him, [a]the firstborn according to his birthright and the youngest according to his youth, and the men looked at one another in astonishment. **34** And he took portions to them from [1]his own table, [a]but Benjamin's portion was five times greater than any of theirs. So they feasted and drank freely with him.

### *The Brothers Fall Before Joseph*

**44** [a]Then he commanded his house steward, saying, "Fill the men's sacks with food, as much as they can carry, and put each man's money in the mouth of his sack. **2** Now put my cup, the silver cup, in the mouth of the sack of the youngest, and his money for the grain." And he did [1]as Joseph had told *him*. **3** [1]As the morning light *broke*, the men were sent away, they with their donkeys. **4** Now they had *just* gone out of [a]the city *and* were not far off when Joseph said to his house steward, "Arise, pursue the men; you shall overtake them and say to them, 'Why have you repaid evil for good? **5** Is not this the one from which my lord drinks and which he indeed uses to interpret [a]omens? You have done evil in doing this.'"

**43:23** [a]Ge 42:28 [b]Ge 42:24 [1]Lit *Peace be to you* **43:24** [a]Ge 18:4; 19:2; 24:32 [b]Lk 7:44; Jn 13:5; 1Ti 5:10 **43:25** [a]Ge 43:11, 15 [1]Lit *until* [2]Lit *bread* **43:26** [a]Ge 37:7, 10 **43:27** [a]Ge 43:7; 45:3 [1]Lit *peace*, cf. 43:23 **43:28** [a]Ge 37:7, 10 **43:29** [a]Ge 42:13 [b]Nu 6:25; Ps 67:1 **43:30** [a]1Ki 3:26 [b]Ge 42:24; 45:2, 14, 15; 46:29 [1]Lit *his compassion grew warm* **43:31** [a]Ge 45:1 [1]Lit *bread* **43:32** [a]Ge 46:34; Ex 8:26 **43:33** [a]Ge 42:7 [1]Lit *sat* **43:34** [a]Ge 35:24; 45:22 [1]Lit *his face* ◆ **44:1** [a]Ge 42:25 **44:2** [1]Or *according to the word* **44:3** [1]Lit *The morning was light* **44:4** [a]Ge 44:13 **44:5** [a]Ge 30:27; 44:15; Lv 19:26; Dt 18:10-14

**6** So he overtook them and spoke
these words to them. **7** And they said
to him, "Why does my lord speak
such words as these? Far be it from
your servants to do such a thing. **8** Be-
hold, [a]the money which we found
in the mouth of our sacks we have
brought back to you from the land
of Canaan. How then could we steal
silver or gold from your lord's house?
**9** [a]With whomever of your servants it
is found, let him die, and we also will
be my lord's [b]slaves." **10** So he said,
"Now let it also be according to your
words; he with whom it is found shall
be my slave, but *the rest of* you shall
be innocent." **11** Then they hurried,
each man brought his sack down to
the ground, and each man opened
his sack. **12** So he searched, beginning
with the oldest and ending with the
youngest, and [a]the cup was found in
Benjamin's sack. **13** Then they [a]tore
their clothes, and each man loaded
his donkey and returned to [b]the city.

**14** Then Judah and his brothers
came to Joseph's house, and he was
still there. So [a]they fell to the ground
before him. **15** And Joseph said to
them, "What is this deed that you
have done? Do you not know that
such a man as I can indeed interpret
[a]omens?" **16** So Judah said, "What
can we say to my lord? What can
we speak? And how can we justify
ourselves? God has found out the
iniquity of your servants; behold, we
are my lord's [a]slaves, both we and the
one in whose [1]possession the cup
*has been* found." **17** But he said, "Far
be it from me to do this. The man in
whose [1]possession the cup has been
found, he shall be my slave; but as for
you, go up in peace to your father."

### *Judah Remains Instead of Benjamin*

**18** Then Judah came near to him and
said, "O my lord, may your servant
please speak a word in my lord's ears,
and [a,1]do not be angry with your ser-
vant; for [b]you are equal to Pharaoh.
**19** [a]My lord asked his servants, say-
ing, 'Have you a father or a brother?'
**20** And we said to my lord, 'We have
an old father and [a]a little child of *his*
old age. Now [b]his brother is dead, so
he alone is left of his mother, and his
father loves him.' **21** Then you said to
your servants, '[a]Bring him down to
me that I may set my eyes on him.'
**22** And we said to my lord, 'The boy
cannot leave his father; if he should
leave his father, [1]his father would
die.' **23** You said to your servants,
however, '[a]If your youngest brother
does not come down with you, you
will not see my face again.' **24** Thus
it happened that when we went up
to your servant my father, we told
him the words of my lord. **25** [a]And
our father said, 'Go back, buy us a
little food.' **26** But we said, 'We cannot
go down. If our youngest brother is
with us, then we will go down; for
we cannot see the man's face if our
youngest brother is not with us.'
**27** And your servant my father said
to us, 'You know that [a]my wife bore
me two sons; **28** and the one went
out from me, and [a]I said, "Surely
he is torn to pieces," and I have not
seen him since. **29** If you take this one

**44:8** [a]Ge 43:21 **44:9** [a]Ge 31:32 [b]Ge 44:16 **44:12** [a]Ge 44:2 **44:13** [a]Ge 37:29, 34; Nu 14:6; 2Sa 1:11 [b]Ge 44:4 **44:14** [a]Ge 37:7, 10 **44:15** [a]Ge 44:5 **44:16** [a]Ge 44:9 [1]Lit *hand* **44:17** [1]Lit *hand* **44:18** [a]Ge 18:30, 32; Ex 32:22 [b]Ge 37:7, 8; 41:40-44 [1]Lit *let not your anger burn against* **44:19** [a]Ge 43:7 **44:20** [a]Ge 37:3; 43:8; 44:30 [b]Ge 37:33; 42:13, 38 **44:21** [a]Ge 42:15, 20 **44:22** [1]Lit *he would* **44:23** [a]Ge 43:3, 5 **44:25** [a]Ge 43:2 **44:27** [a]Ge 46:19 **44:28** [a]Ge 37:31-35

also from [1]me and harm befalls him, you will [a]bring my gray hair down to Sheol in [2]evil.’ **30** So now, when I come to your servant my father, and the boy is not with us—[a,1]and his life is bound up in the *boy’s* life— **31** so it will be that when he sees that the boy is not *with us*, he will die. Thus your servants will [a]bring the gray hair of your servant our father down to Sheol in sorrow. **32** For your servant [a]became a guarantee for the boy to my father, saying, ‘If I do not bring him *back* to you, [1]then I shall bear the sin before my father all *my* days.’ **33** So now, please let your servant remain instead of the boy as a slave to my lord, and let the boy go up with his brothers. **34** For how shall I go up to my father if the boy is not with me, lest I see the evil that would [1]overtake my father?”

### *Joseph Sends for Jacob*

**45** Then Joseph could not restrain himself before all those who stood by him, and he called out, “Have everyone go out from me.” So there [1]was no man with him [a]when Joseph made himself known to his brothers. **2** [a]Then he [1]wept loudly. And the Egyptians heard *it*, and the household of Pharaoh heard *it*. **3** Then Joseph said to his brothers, “[a]I am Joseph! [b]Is my father still alive?” But his brothers could not answer him, for [c]they were terrified at his presence.

**4** Then Joseph said to his brothers, “Please come near to me.” And they came near. And he said, “I am Joseph, your brother, whom you [a]sold into Egypt. **5** So now do not be grieved or angry [1]with yourselves because [a]you sold me here, for [b]God sent me before you to preserve life. **6** For the famine *has been* in the land [a]these two years, and there are still five years in which there will be neither plowing nor harvesting. **7** [a]So God sent me before you to establish for you a remnant in the earth and to keep you alive for a great *remnant* of survivors. **8** So now, it was not you who sent me here, but God; and He has set me as a [a]father to Pharaoh and lord of all his household and ruler over all the land of Egypt. **9** Hurry and go up to my father, and [a]say to him, ‘Thus says your son Joseph, “God has set me as lord of all Egypt; come down to me, do not delay. **10** And you shall [1]live in the land of [a]Goshen, and you shall be near me, you and your children and your children’s children and your flocks and your herds and all that you have. **11** There I will also [a]provide for you, for there are still five years of famine *to come*, lest you and your household and all that you have be impoverished.”’ **12** And behold, your eyes see, and the eyes of my brother Benjamin *see*, that it is my mouth which is speaking to you. **13** So you must tell my father of all my glory in Egypt and all that you have seen; and you must hurry and [a]bring my father down here.” **14** Then he fell on his brother Benjamin’s neck and [a]wept, and Benjamin wept on his neck. **15** He

---

**44:29** [a]Ge 42:38; 44:31 [1]Lit *my face* [2]Or *sorrow* **44:30** [a]1Sa 18:1 [1]Lit *his soul is bound with his soul* **44:31** [a]Ge 44:29 **44:32** [a]Ge 43:9 [1]Lit *and I shall have sinned for all the days before my father* **44:34** [1]Lit *find* ◆ **45:1** [a]Ac 7:13 [1]Lit *stood* **45:2** [a]Ge 45:14, 15; 46:29 [1]Lit *gave forth his voice in weeping* **45:3** [a]Ac 7:13 [b]Ge 43:27 [c]Ge 37:20-28; 42:21, 22 **45:4** [a]Ge 37:28 **45:5** [a]Ge 37:28 [b]Ge 45:7, 8; 50:20; Ps 105:17 [1]Lit *in your eyes* **45:6** [a]Ge 37:2; 41:46, 53 **45:7** [a]Ge 45:5 **45:8** [a]Jdg 17:10 **45:9** [a]Ac 7:14 **45:10** [a]Ge 46:28, 34; 47:1 [1]Lit *dwell* **45:11** [a]Ge 47:12 **45:13** [a]Ac 7:14 **45:14** [a]Ge 45:2

kissed all his brothers and wept on
them, and afterward his brothers
talked with him.
**16** Now [a]the [1]news was heard in
Pharaoh's house, saying, "Joseph's
brothers have come." And it was good
in the sight of Pharaoh and in the
sight of his servants. **17** Then Pharaoh
said to Joseph, "Say to your brothers,
'Do this: load your beasts and [1]go to
the land of Canaan, **18** and take your
father and your households and
come to me, and [a]I will give you the
[1]best of the land of Egypt, and you
will eat the fat of the land.' **19** Now
you are commanded, 'Do this: [1]take
[a]wagons from the land of Egypt for
your little ones and for your wives,
and bring your father and come.
**20** Now do not [1]concern yourselves
with your goods, for the [2]best of all
the land of Egypt is yours.'"
**21** Then the sons of Israel did
so; and Joseph gave them [a]wagons
according to the [1]command of Phar-
aoh, and he gave them provisions
for the journey. **22** To [1]each of them
he gave [a]changes of garments, but
to Benjamin he gave three hundred
*pieces of* silver and [b]five changes of
garments. **23** Now to his father he
sent [1]as follows: ten donkeys loaded
with the [2]best things of Egypt and
ten female donkeys loaded with grain
and bread and sustenance for his
father [3]on the journey.
**24** So he sent his brothers away, and
they departed. And he said to them,
"Do not be stirred up on the journey."
**25** Then they went up from Egypt,
and came to the land of Canaan to
their father Jacob. **26** And they told
him, saying, "Joseph is still alive, and
indeed he is ruler over all the land of
Egypt." But [1]his heart was stunned,
for [a]he did not believe them. **27** Yet
they told him all the words of Joseph
that he had spoken to them, and he
saw the [a]wagons that Joseph had sent
to carry him. Then the spirit of their
father Jacob revived. **28** And Israel
said, "It is enough! My son Joseph is
still alive. I will go and see him before
I die."

### *Jacob Moves to Egypt*

**46** So Israel set out with all that
he had and came to [a]Beershe-
ba and offered sacrifices to the [b]God
of his father Isaac. **2** [a]And God spoke
to Israel [1]in visions of the night and
said, "[b]Jacob, Jacob." And he said,
"Here I am." **3** And He said, "[a]I am
God, the God of your father; do not
be afraid to go down to Egypt, for I
will [b]make you a great nation there.
**4** [a]I Myself will go down with you to
Egypt, and [b]I Myself will also bring
you up again; and [c]Joseph will [1]close
your eyes with his hand."
**5** Then Jacob arose from Beershe-
ba; and the sons of Israel carried
their father Jacob and their little ones
and their wives in the [a]wagons which
Pharaoh had sent to carry him. **6** And
they took their livestock and their
possessions, which they had accu-
mulated in the land of Canaan, and

---

**45:16** [a]Ac 7:13 [1]Lit *voice* **45:17** [1]Lit *come, go* **45:18** [a]Ge 27:28 [1]Lit *good* **45:19** [a]Ge 45:21, 27; 46:5; Nu 7:3-8 [1]Lit *take for yourselves* **45:20** [1]Lit *let your eye look with regret upon your vessels* [2]Lit *good* **45:21** [a]Ge 45:19 [1]Lit *mouth* **45:22** [a]2Ki 5:5 [b]Ge 43:34 [1]Lit *all of them he gave each man* **45:23** [1]Lit *like this* [2]Lit *good* [3]Lit *for* **45:26** [a]Ge 37:31-35 [1]Lit *his heart grew numb* **45:27** [a]Ge 45:19 ◆ **46:1** [a]Ge 21:31; 28:10 [b]Ge 26:24; 28:13; 31:42 **46:2** [a]Ge 15:1; Nu 12:6; Job 33:14, 15 [b]Ge 22:11; 31:11 [1]Lit *in the visions* **46:3** [a]Ge 17:1; 28:13 [b]Ge 12:2; Ex 1:9; Dt 26:5 **46:4** [a]Ge 28:15; 48:21 [b]Ge 50:24; Ex 3:8 [c]Ge 50:1 [1]Lit *put his hand on* **46:5** [a]Ge 45:21

they [a]came to Egypt, Jacob and all
his seed with him: **7** his sons and his
grandsons with him, his daughters
and his granddaughters, and all his
seed he brought with him to Egypt.

**8** Now these are the [a]names of
the sons of Israel—of Jacob and his
sons—who were coming to Egypt:
Reuben, Jacob's firstborn. **9** The sons
of Reuben: Hanoch and Pallu and
Hezron and Carmi. **10** The [a]sons of
Simeon: [1]Jemuel and Jamin and Ohad
and [2]Jachin and [3]Zohar and Shaul
the son of a Canaanite woman. **11** The
sons of Levi: [1]Gershon, Kohath, and
Merari. **12** The sons of Judah: Er
and Onan and Shelah and Perez
and Zerah (but Er and Onan died in
the land of Canaan). And the [a]sons of
Perez were Hezron and Hamul. **13** The
sons of Issachar: Tola and [1]Puvvah
and [2]Iob and Shimron. **14** The sons of
Zebulun: Sered and Elon and Jahleel.
**15** These are the sons of Leah, whom
she bore to Jacob in Paddan-aram,
with his daughter Dinah; [1]all his
sons and his daughters *numbered*
thirty-three.

**16** The [a]sons of Gad: [1]Ziphion and
Haggi, Shuni and [2]Ezbon, Eri and
[3]Arodi and Areli. **17** The [a]sons of
Asher: Imnah and Ishvah and Ishvi
and Beriah and their sister Serah.
And the [b]sons of Beriah: Heber
and Malchiel. **18** These are the sons
of Zilpah, whom Laban gave to his
daughter Leah; and she bore to Jacob
these sixteen persons.

**19** The sons of Jacob's wife Rachel:
Joseph and Benjamin. **20** [a]Now to
Joseph in the land of Egypt were
born Manasseh and Ephraim, whom
Asenath, the daughter of Potiphera,
priest of On, bore to him. **21** The
[a]sons of Benjamin: Bela and Becher
and Ashbel, Gera and Naaman, [1]Ehi
and Rosh, [2]Muppim and [3]Huppim and
Ard. **22** These are the sons of Rachel,
who were born to Jacob; *there were*
fourteen persons in all.

**23** The sons of Dan: [1]Hushim.
**24** The sons of Naphtali: [1]Jahzeel
and Guni and Jezer and [2]Shillem.
**25** These are the [a]sons of Bilhah,
whom [b]Laban gave to his daughter
Rachel, and she bore these to Jacob;
*there were* seven persons in all. **26** [a]All
the persons belonging to Jacob, who
came to Egypt, who came out of his
loins, excluding the wives of Jacob's
sons, *were* sixty-six persons in all,
**27** and the sons of Joseph, who were
born to him in Egypt were [1]two; [a]all
the persons of the house of Jacob,
who came to Egypt, *were* seventy.

**28** Now he sent Judah before him
to Joseph, to point out *the way* before
him to [a]Goshen; and they came into
the land of Goshen. **29** And Joseph
harnessed his chariot and went up
to Goshen to meet his father Israel;
as soon as he appeared [1]before him,
he fell on his neck and [a]wept on his
neck a long time. **30** Then Israel said
to Joseph, "Now I can die, since I have
seen your face, that you are still alive."

**46:6** [a]Dt 26:5; Jos 24:4; Ps 105:23; Is 52:4; Ac 7:15 **46:8** [a]Ex 1:1-4; Nu 26:4, 5; 1Chr 2:1ff **46:10** [a]Ex 6:15 [1]In Nu 26:12 and 1Chr 4:24, *Nemuel* [2]In 1Chr 4:24, *Jarib* [3]In Nu 26:13 and 1Chr 4:24, *Zerah* **46:11** [1]In 1Chr 6:16, *Gershom* **46:12** [a]1Chr 2:5 **46:13** [1]In Nu 26:23, *Puvah*; in 1Chr 7:1, *Puah* [2]In Nu 26:24 and 1Chr 7:1, *Jashub* **46:15** [1]Lit *all the souls of* **46:16** [a]Nu 26:15-18 [1]In Nu 26:15, *Zephon* [2]In Nu 26:16, *Ozni* [3]In Nu 26:17, *Arod* **46:17** [a]1Chr 7:30 [b]1Chr 7:31 **46:20** [a]Ge 41:50-52 **46:21** [a]1Chr 7:6 [1]In Nu 26:38, *Ahiram* [2]In Nu 26:39, *Shephupham*; in 1Chr 7:12, *Shuppim* [3]In Nu 26:39, *Hupham* **46:23** [1]In Nu 26:42, *Shuham* **46:24** [1]In 1Chr 7:13, *Jahziel* [2]In 1Chr 7:13, *Shallum* **46:25** [a]Ge 30:5, 7 [b]Ge 29:29 **46:26** [a]Ex 1:5 **46:27** [a]Ex 1:5; Dt 10:22; Ac 7:14 [1]Lit *two souls* **46:28** [a]Ge 45:10 **46:29** [a]Ge 45:14, 15 [1]Lit *to*

**31** And Joseph said to his brothers and
to his father's household, "[a]I will go
up and tell Pharaoh and say to him,
'My brothers and my father's house-
hold, who *were* in the land of Canaan,
have come to me; **32** and the men
are shepherds, for they have been
[1]keepers of livestock; and they have
brought their flocks and their herds
and all that they have.' **33** And it will
be when Pharaoh calls you and says,
'[a]What is your occupation?' **34** then
you shall say, 'Your servants have
been [a,1]keepers of livestock from our
youth and until now, both we and
our fathers,' that you may [2]live in the
land of [b]Goshen; for every shepherd
is [c]an abomination to the Egyptians."

### *Jacob's Family Settles in Goshen*

**47** Then [a]Joseph went in and told
Pharaoh and said, "My father
and my brothers and their flocks and
their herds and all that they have,
have come out of the land of Canaan;
and behold, they are in the land of
[b]Goshen." **2** And he took five men
from among his brothers and [a]set
them before Pharaoh. **3** Then Pharaoh
said to his brothers, "[a]What is your
occupation?" So they said to Phar-
aoh, "Your servants are [b]shepherds,
both we and our fathers." **4** And they
said to Pharaoh, "[a]We have come to
sojourn in the land, for there is no
pasture for your servants' flocks, for
[b]the famine is heavy in the land of
Canaan. So now, please let your ser-
vants [c,1]live in the land of Goshen."
**5** Then Pharaoh said to [1]Joseph, "Your
father and your brothers have come
to you. **6** The land of Egypt is [1]at
your disposal; have your father and
your brothers settle in [a]the best of
the land, let them settle in the land
of Goshen; and if you know any
[b]excellent men among them, then
[2]put them in charge of my livestock."
**7** Then Joseph brought his father
Jacob and stood him before Pharaoh;
and Jacob [a]blessed Pharaoh. **8** And
Pharaoh said to Jacob, "How many
are the days of the years of your life?"
**9** So Jacob said to Pharaoh, "The days
[a]of the years of my sojourning are
[1]130; few and evil have been the
days of the years of my life, and they
have not [2]attained to [b]the days of the
years [3]that my fathers lived during
the days of their sojourning." **10** And
Jacob [a]blessed Pharaoh and went out
from the presence of Pharaoh. **11** So
Joseph settled his father and his
brothers and gave them a possession
in the land of Egypt, in [a]the best of
the land, in the land of [b]Rameses,
as Pharaoh had commanded. **12** And
Joseph [a]provided his father and his
brothers and all his father's house-
hold with [1]food, according to their
little ones.

### *Joseph and the Famine*

**13** Now there was no [1]food in all the
land because the famine was very
heavy, so that [a]the land of Egypt and
the land of Canaan languished be-
cause of the famine. **14** [a]And Joseph

---

**46:31** [a]Ge 47:1 **46:32** [1]Lit *men* **46:33** [a]Ge 47:2, 3 **46:34** [a]Ge 13:7, 8; 26:20; 37:2 [b]Ge 45:10, 18; 47:6, 11 [c]Ge 43:32; Ex 8:26 [1]Lit *men* [2]Lit *dwell* ◆ **47:1** [a]Ge 46:31 [b]Ge 45:10; 46:28 **47:2** [a]Ac 7:13 **47:3** [a]Ge 46:33 [b]Ge 46:34 **47:4** [a]Ge 15:13; Dt 26:5; Ps 105:23 [b]Ge 43:1; Ac 7:11 [c]Ge 46:34 [1]Lit *dwell* **47:5** [1]Lit *Joseph, saying* **47:6** [a]Ge 45:10, 18; 47:11 [b]Ex 18:21, 25; 1Ki 11:28; Pr 22:29 [1]Lit *before you* [2]Lit *appoint them rulers* **47:7** [a]Ge 47:10; 2Sa 14:22; 1Ki 8:66 **47:9** [a]Heb 11:9, 13 [b]Ge 25:7; 35:28 [1]Lit *130 years* [2]Lit *reached* [3]Lit *of the life of my fathers* **47:10** [a]Ge 47:7 **47:11** [a]Ge 47:6, 27 [b]Ex 1:11; 12:37 **47:12** [a]Ge 45:11 [1]Or *bread* **47:13** [a]Ge 41:30; Ac 7:11 [1]Or *bread* **47:14** [a]Ge 41:56

gathered all the money that was found in the land of Egypt and in the land of Canaan for the grain which they bought, and Joseph brought the money into Pharaoh's house. **15** Then the money came to an end in the land of Egypt and in the land of Canaan. So all the Egyptians came to Joseph [1]and said, "Give us [2]food, for [a]why should we die in your presence? For *our* money [3]is gone." **16** Then Joseph said, "Give up your livestock, and I will give you *food* for your livestock, since *your* money [1]is gone." **17** So they brought their livestock to Joseph, and Joseph gave them [1]food in exchange for the horses and the [2]flocks and the herds and the donkeys; and he [3]fed them with [1]food in exchange for all their livestock [4]that year. **18** Then that year came to an end. And they came to him the [1]next year and said to him, "We will not hide from my lord that our money has come to an end, and the [2]livestock are my lord's. There is nothing left [3]for my lord except our bodies and our land. **19** Why should we die before your eyes, both we and our land? Buy us and our land for [1]food, and we and our land will be slaves to Pharaoh. So give us seed, that we may live and not die, and that the land may not be desolate."

**20** So Joseph bought all the land of Egypt for Pharaoh, for [1]every Egyptian sold his field because the famine was severe upon them. Thus the land became Pharaoh's. **21** As for the people, he moved them to the cities from one end of Egypt's border to the other end. **22** Only the land of the priests he did not buy, for the priests had an allotment from Pharaoh, and they ate off the allotment which Pharaoh gave them. Therefore, they did not sell their land. **23** Then Joseph said to the people, "Behold, I have today bought you and your land for Pharaoh; now, *here* is seed for you, and you may sow the land. **24** And it will be, at the harvest you shall give a [a]fifth to Pharaoh, and [1]four-fifths shall be your own for seed of the field and for your food and for those of your households and as food for your little ones." **25** So they said, "You have kept us alive! Let us find favor in the sight of my lord, and we will be Pharaoh's slaves." **26** And Joseph made it a statute concerning the land of Egypt *valid* to this day, that Pharaoh should have the fifth; [a]only the land of the priests [1]did not become Pharaoh's.

**27** Now Israel [1]lived in the land of Egypt, [2]in Goshen, and they [a]took possession of property in it and [b]were fruitful and became very numerous. **28** And Jacob lived in the land of Egypt [a]seventeen years; so the days of Jacob, the years of his life, were 147 years.

**29** Then [a]the days for Israel to die drew near, and he called his son Joseph and said to him, "Please, if I have found favor in your sight, [b]place now your hand under my thigh and [c]deal with me in lovingkindness and truth. Please do not bury me in Egypt. **30** But I will [a]lie down with my fathers, and you will carry me out of Egypt and

**47:15** [a]Ge 47:19 [1]Lit *saying* [2]Or *bread* [3]Lit *ceases* **47:16** [1]Lit *ceases* **47:17** [1]Or *bread* [2]Lit *livestock of the flocks and livestock of the herds* [3]Lit *led them as a shepherd* [4]Lit *in that year* **47:18** [1]Lit *second* [2]Lit *livestock of the cattle* [3]Lit *in the presence of* **47:19** [1]Or *bread* **47:20** [1]Lit *Egypt, every man* **47:24** [a]Ge 41:34 [1]Lit *four parts* **47:26** [a]Ge 47:22 [1]Lit *alone did* **47:27** [a]Ge 47:11 [b]Ge 17:6; 26:4; 35:11; Ex 1:7; Dt 26:5; Ac 7:17 [1]Lit *dwelt* [2]Lit *in the land of Goshen* **47:28** [a]Ge 47:9 **47:29** [a]Dt 31:14; 1Ki 2:1 [b]Ge 24:2 [c]Ge 24:49 **47:30** [a]Ge 15:15; Dt 31:16

bury me in [b]their burial place." And
he said, "I will do as you have said."
**31** Then he said, "[a]Swear to me." So he
swore to him. Then [b]Israel bowed *in*
*worship* at the head of the bed.

### *Israel Blesses Manasseh and Ephraim*

**48** Now it happened after these
things that [1]Joseph was told,
"Behold, your father is sick." So he
took his two sons [a]Manasseh and
Ephraim with him. **2** Then [1]it was told
to Jacob, "Behold, your son Joseph has
come to you," so Israel strengthened
himself and sat [2]up in the bed. **3** Then
Jacob said to Joseph, "[a,1]God Almighty
appeared to me at [b]Luz in the land
of Canaan and blessed me, **4** and He
said to me, 'Behold, I will make you
fruitful and multiply, and I will make
you an assembly of peoples, and I will
give this land to your seed after you
for [a]an everlasting possession.' **5** So
now your two sons, who were born to
you in the land of Egypt before I came
to you in Egypt, are mine; [a]Ephraim
and Manasseh shall be mine, as
[b]Reuben and Simeon are. **6** But your
kin that [1]have been born after them
shall be yours; they shall be called by
the [2]names of their brothers in their
inheritance. **7** Now as for me, when
I came from [a]Paddan, [b]Rachel died,
[1]to my sorrow, in the land of Canaan
on the journey, when there was still
some distance to go to Ephrath; and
I buried her there on the way to
Ephrath (that is, Bethlehem)."
**8** Then Israel [a]saw Joseph's sons
and said, "Who are these?" **9** And
Joseph said to his father, "[a]They
are my sons, whom God has given
me here." So he said, "Bring them to
me, please, that [b]I may bless them."
**10** Now [a]the eyes of Israel were *so* dim
from age *that* he could not see. Then
[1]Joseph brought them close to him,
and he [b]kissed them and embraced
them. **11** Then Israel said to Joseph, "I
never [1]expected to see your face, and
behold, God has let me see your seed
as well." **12** Then Joseph [1]took them
from his knees and [a]bowed with his
face to the ground. **13** And Joseph
took them both, Ephraim with his
right hand toward Israel's left, and
Manasseh with his left hand toward
Israel's right, and brought them close
to him. **14** But Israel stretched out his
right hand and laid it on the head
of Ephraim, who was the younger,
and his left hand on Manasseh's
head, [1]crossing his hands, [2]although
[a]Manasseh was the firstborn. **15** And
he blessed Joseph and said,

"[a]May the God before whom
my fathers Abraham
and Isaac walked,
[b]The God who has been my
shepherd [1]throughout
my life to this day,
**16** [a]The angel who has redeemed
me from all evil,
[b]Bless *these* boys;
And may my name
[1]live on in them,

**47:30** [b]Ge 23:17-20; 25:9, 10; 35:29; 49:29-32; 50:5, 13; Ac 7:15, 16 **47:31** [a]Ge 21:23, 24; 24:3; 31:53; 50:25 [b]1Ki 1:47 ◆ **48:1** [a]Ge 41:51, 52; Jos 14:4 [1]Lit *one said to Joseph* **48:2** [1]Lit *one told Jacob and said* [2]Lit *upon the bed* **48:3** [a]Ge 28:13f; 35:9-12 [b]Ge 28:19; 35:6 [1]Heb *El Shaddai* **48:4** [a]Ge 17:8 **48:5** [a]Ge 41:50-52; 46:20; 48:1; Jos 14:4 [b]1Chr 5:1, 2 **48:6** [1]Lit *you have begotten* [2]Lit *name* **48:7** [a]Ge 33:18 [b]Ge 35:19, 20 [1]Lit *upon me* **48:8** [a]Ge 48:10 **48:9** [a]Ge 33:5 [b]Ge 27:4 **48:10** [a]Ge 27:1 [b]Ge 27:27 [1]Lit *he* **48:11** [1]Lit *meditated, judged* **48:12** [a]Ge 42:6 [1]Lit *made them come out* **48:14** [a]Ge 41:51, 52 [1]Or *consciously directing* [2]Lit *when* **48:15** [a]Ge 17:1 [b]Ge 49:24 [1]Lit *from the continuance of me* **48:16** [a]Ge 22:11, 15-18; 28:13-15; 31:11 [b]Heb 11:21 [1]Lit *be called*

And the [2]names of my fathers
Abraham and Isaac;
And [c]may they grow
into a multitude in the
midst of the earth."

17 But Joseph saw that his father
[a]set his right hand on Ephraim's
head, and it was displeasing in his
sight; so he took hold of his father's
hand to remove it from Ephraim's
head to Manasseh's head. 18 And
Joseph said to his father, "Not so, my
father, for this one is the firstborn.
Place your right hand on his head."
19 But his father refused and said,
"I know, my son, I know; he also
will become a people, and he also
will be great. However, his younger
brother shall be greater than he, and
[a]his seed shall become the fullness
of nations." 20 [a]And he blessed them
that day, saying,

"By you Israel will pronounce
blessing, saying,
'May God make you like
Ephraim and Manasseh!'"

Thus he put Ephraim before Manas-
seh. 21 Then Israel said to Joseph,
"Behold, I am about to die, but [a]God
will be with you and [b]will bring you
back to the land of your fathers.
22 And I give you one [1]portion more
than your brothers, [a]which I took
from the hand of the Amorite with
my sword and my bow."

### *Jacob Assembles His Sons*

49 Then Jacob summoned his
sons and said, "Gather togeth-
er that I may tell you what will befall
you [a]in the last days.

2 "Assemble together and hear,
O sons of Jacob;
And [a]listen to Israel
your father.

3 "Reuben, you are my firstborn;
My might and [a]the
beginning of my vigor,
[1]Preeminent in dignity
and [1]preeminent in strength.
4 "[1]Uncontrolled as water, you
shall not have preeminence,
[a]Because you went up to
your father's bed;
Then you defiled *it*—he
went up to my couch.

5 "[a]Simeon and Levi are brothers;
Their swords are
implements of violence.
6 "[a]Let my soul not enter
into their council;
Let not my glory be united
with their assembly;
Because in their anger
they killed [1]men,
And in their self-will they
hamstrung [2]oxen.
7 "Cursed be their anger,
for it is strong;
And their wrath, for it is cruel.
[a]I will divide them
amongst Jacob,
And scatter them in Israel.

8 "Judah, as for you, your
brothers shall praise you;
Your hand shall be on the
neck of your enemies;
[a]Your father's sons shall
bow down to you.

**48:16** [c]Ge 28:14; 46:3 [2]Lit *name* **48:17** [a]Ge 48:14 **48:19** [a]Ge 28:14; 46:3 **48:20** [a]Heb 11:21 **48:21** [a]Ge 26:3 [b]Ge 28:15; 46:4; 50:24 **48:22** [a]Jos 24:32; Jn 4:5 [1]Or *ridge*; lit *shoulder*; Heb *Shechem* ◆ **49:1** [a]Nu 24:14 **49:2** [a]Ps 34:11 **49:3** [a]Dt 21:17; Ps 78:51; 105:36 [1]Lit *preeminence* **49:4** [a]Ge 35:22; Dt 27:20; 1Chr 5:1 [1]Or *Boiling over*; lit *Recklessness* **49:5** [a]Ge 34:25-30 **49:6** [a]Ps 64:2 [1]Lit *a man* [2]Lit *an ox* **49:7** [a]Jos 19:1, 9; 21:1-42 **49:8** [a]Ge 27:29; 1Chr 5:2

9 "Judah is a [a]lion's whelp;
From the prey, my son,
you have gone up.
[b]He [1]crouches, he lies
down as a lion,
And as a lioness,
who [2]dares rouse him up?
10 "[a]The scepter shall not
depart from Judah,
Nor the ruler's staff from
between his feet,
[1]Until Shiloh comes,
And [b]to him *shall be* the
obedience of the peoples.
11 "[a,1]He ties *his* foal to the vine,
And his donkey's colt
to the choice vine;
[b]He washes his
garments in wine,
And his robes in the blood
of grapes.
12 "His eyes are [1]dark from wine,
And his teeth [2]white
from milk.

13 "[a]Zebulun will dwell
at the seashore;
And he *shall be* a
shore for ships,
And his flank *shall be*
toward Sidon.

14 "Issachar is [1]a strong donkey,
[a]Lying down
between the [2]sheepfolds.
15 "And he saw that a resting
place was good
And that the land
was pleasant,
So he bowed his shoulder
to bear *burdens*,
And became a slave
at forced labor.

16 "[a]Dan shall [b]render
justice to his people,
As one of the tribes of Israel.
17 "Dan shall be a serpent
in the way,
A horned snake in the path,
That bites the horse's heels,
So that his rider falls
backward.
18 "[a]For Your salvation I
hope, O Yahweh.
19 "[a]As for Gad, [1]raiders
shall raid him,
But he will raid
*at* their [2]heels.

20 "[a,1]As for [b]Asher, his
[2]food shall be [3]rich,
And he will yield
royal dainties.

21 "[a]Naphtali is a doe let loose,
He gives beautiful words.

22 "[a]Joseph is a fruitful [1]bough,
A fruitful [1]bough
by a spring;
*Its* [2]branches run over a wall.
23 "And the archers bitterly
attacked him
and shot *at him*,
And they bore a grudge
against him;

**49:9** [a]Eze 19:5-7; Mic 5:8 [b]Nu 24:9 [1]Lit *bows down* [2]Lit *shall* **49:10** [a]Nu 24:17; Ps 60:7; 108:8 [b]Ps 2:6-9; 72:8-11; Is 42:1, 4; 49:6 [1]Or *Until he comes to Shiloh, Until he comes to whom it belongs* **49:11** [a]Dt 8:7, 8; 2Ki 18:32 [b]Is 63:2 [1]Lit *Binding of* **49:12** [1]Or *darker than* [2]Or *whiter than* **49:13** [a]Dt 33:18, 19 **49:14** [a]Jdg 5:16; Ps 68:13 [1]Lit *a donkey of bone* [2]Or *saddlebags* **49:16** [a]Dt 33:22; Jdg 18:26, 27 [b]Ge 30:6 **49:18** [a]Ex 15:2; Ps 25:5; 40:1-3; 119:166, 174; Is 25:9; Mic 7:7 **49:19** [a]Dt 33:20 [1]Lit *a raiding band* [2]Lit *heel* **49:20** [a]Dt 33:24, 25 [b]Ge 30:13 [1]Lit *From* [2]Or *bread* [3]Lit *fat* **49:21** [a]Dt 33:23 **49:22** [a]Dt 33:13-17 [1]Lit *son* [2]Lit *daughters*

24 But his [a]bow remained [1]firm,
And [b,2]his arms were agile,
From the hands of the
[c]Mighty One of Jacob,
From there is [d]the Shepherd,
[e]the Stone of Israel,
25 From [a]the God of your
father who helps you,
And [b,1]by the [2]Almighty
who blesses you
*With* [c]blessings
of heaven above,
Blessings of the deep
that lies beneath,
Blessings of the breasts
and of the womb.
26 "The blessings of your father
Have surpassed the blessings
of my ancestors
Up to the [1]utmost bound
of [a]the everlasting hills;
May they be on the
head of Joseph,
And on the top of the head
of the one distinguished
among his brothers.

27 "Benjamin is a [1]ravenous wolf;
In the morning he
devours the prey,
And in the evening he
divides the spoil."

### *Jacob Breathes His Last*

28 All these are the twelve tribes of
Israel, and this is what their father
spoke to them. So he blessed them.
He blessed them, every one [1]with the
blessing appropriate to him. 29 Then
he commanded them and said to
them, "I am about to be [a]gathered
to my people; [b]bury me with my fa-
thers in the cave that is in [c]the field
of Ephron the Hittite, 30 in the [a]cave
that is in the field of Machpelah,
which is before Mamre, in the land
of Canaan, which Abraham bought
along with the field from Ephron the
Hittite as a possession for a burial
site. 31 There they buried [a]Abraham
and his wife [b]Sarah, there they
buried [c]Isaac and his wife Rebekah,
and there I buried Leah— 32 the field
and the cave that is in it, purchased
from the sons of Heth." 33 So Jacob
finished commanding his sons. And
he drew his feet into the bed and
[a]breathed his last and was [b]gathered
to his people.

50 Then Joseph fell on his father's
face and wept over him and
kissed him. 2 And Joseph command-
ed his servants the physicians to
embalm his father. So the physicians
[a]embalmed Israel. 3 Then *the* forty
days *to do this* were fulfilled, because
in this manner the days of embalm-
ing are fulfilled. And the Egyptians
[a]wept for him seventy days.

4 Then the days of weeping for him
were past, and Joseph spoke to the
household of Pharaoh, saying, "If
now I have found favor in your sight,
please speak in the ears of Pharaoh,
saying, 5 '[a]My father made me swear,
saying, "Behold, I am about to die; in
my grave [b]which I dug for myself in
the land of Canaan, there you shall

**49:24** [a]Job 29:20 [b]Ps 18:34; 73:23; Is 41:10 [c]Ps 132:2, 5; Is 1:24; 49:26 [d]Ps 23:1; 80:1 [e]Ps 118:22; Is 28:16; 1Pe 2:6-8 [1]In an unyielding position [2]Lit *the arms of his hands* **49:25** [a]Ge 28:13; 32:9 [b]Ge 28:3; 48:3 [c]Ge 27:28 [1]Or *with* [2]Heb *Shaddai* **49:26** [a]Dt 33:15, 16 [1]Or *desire*; lit *limit* **49:27** [1]Lit *a wolf that tears* **49:28** [1]Lit *according to his blessing* **49:29** [a]Ge 25:8 [b]Ge 47:30 [c]Ge 23:16-20; 50:13 **49:30** [a]Ge 23:3-20 **49:31** [a]Ge 25:9 [b]Ge 23:19 [c]Ge 35:29 **49:33** [a]Ge 25:8; Ac 7:15 [b]Ge 49:29 ◆ **50:2** [a]Ge 50:26; 2Chr 16:14; Mt 26:12; Mk 16:1; Jn 19:39, 40 **50:3** [a]Ge 50:10; Nu 20:29; Dt 34:8 **50:5** [a]Ge 47:29-31 [b]2Chr 16:14; Is 22:16; Mt 27:60

bury me." So now, please let me go
up and bury my father; then I will
return.'" 6 And Pharaoh said, "Go up
and bury your father, as he made you
swear."

7 So Joseph went up to bury his
father, and with him went up all the
servants of Pharaoh, the elders of his
household, and all the elders of the
land of Egypt, 8 and all the household
of Joseph and his brothers and his
father's household; they left only
their little ones and their flocks and
their herds in the land of Goshen.
9 There also went up with him both
chariots and horsemen; and it was
a very [1]immense camp. 10 And they
came to the [1]threshing floor of Atad,
which is beyond the Jordan, and they
[a]lamented there with a very great
and [2]immense lamentation; and he
[3]observed seven days of mourning
for his father. 11 Now the inhabi-
tants of the land, the Canaanites,
saw the mourning at [1]the threshing
floor of Atad, and they said, "This
is an [2]immense [3]mourning for the
Egyptians." Therefore it was named
[4]Abel-mizraim, which is beyond the
Jordan.

### *Jacob's Burial at Machpelah*

12 Thus his sons did for him as he
had commanded them. 13 Indeed,
his sons carried him to the land of
Canaan and buried him in [a]the cave
of the field of Machpelah before
Mamre, which Abraham had bought
along with the field for *his* possession
*as* a burial site from Ephron the Hit-
tite. 14 *After he had buried his father,*
Joseph returned to Egypt, he and his
brothers, and all who had gone up
with him to bury his father.

15 Then Joseph's brothers saw
that their father was dead, and they
said, "[a]What if Joseph bears a grudge
against us and returns back to us all
the evil which we dealt against him!"
16 So they [1]sent *a message* to Joseph,
saying, "Your father commanded
before he died, saying, 17 'Thus you
shall say to Joseph, "Please forgive,
I beg you, the transgression of your
brothers and their sin, for they dealt
evil against you."' So now, please
forgive the transgression of the
slaves of the God of your father."
And Joseph wept when they spoke to
him. 18 Then his brothers also came
and [a]fell down before him and said,
"Behold, we are your slaves." 19 But
Joseph said to them, "Do not be
afraid, for am I in God's place? 20 As
for you, [a]you meant evil against me,
*but* God meant it for good in order
to do [1]*what has happened on* this
day, to keep many people alive. 21 So
now, do not be afraid; [a]I will provide
for you and your little ones." And he
comforted them and spoke to their
heart.

### *The Death of Joseph*

22 Now Joseph stayed in Egypt, he
and his father's household, and Jo-
seph lived 110 years. 23 And Joseph
saw the third generation of Ephraim's
sons; also the sons of Machir, the
son of Manasseh, were [a]born on
Joseph's knees. 24 And Joseph said to
his brothers, "[a]I am about to die, but

**50:9** [1]Lit *heavy* **50:10** [a]Ac 8:2 [1]Heb *Goren ha-Atad* [2]Lit *heavy* [3]Lit *made a mourning for seven days* **50:11** [1]Heb *Goren ha-Atad* [2]Lit *heavy* [3]Heb *ebel* [4]The meadow (or mourning) of Egypt **50:13** [a]Ge 23:16-20; Ac 7:16 **50:15** [a]Ge 37:28; 42:21, 22 **50:16** [1]Lit *commanded* **50:18** [a]Ge 37:8-10; 41:43 **50:20** [a]Ge 37:26, 27; 45:5, 7 [1]Lit *as it is this day* **50:21** [a]Ge 45:11; 47:12 **50:23** [a]Ge 30:3 **50:24** [a]Ge 48:21; Ex 3:16, 17; Heb 11:22

God will surely [1]take care of you and bring you up from this land to the land which He swore to [b]Abraham, to [c]Isaac, and to [d]Jacob." **25** Then Joseph made the sons of Israel swear, saying, "God will surely [1]take care of you, and [a]you shall carry my bones up from here." **26** So Joseph died at the age of 110 years; and [a]they embalmed him, and he was placed in a coffin in Egypt.

# EXODUS

### *Israel Multiplies in Egypt*

**1** Now these are the [a]names of the sons of Israel who came to Egypt with Jacob; they came each one [1]with his household: **2** Reuben, Simeon, Levi, and Judah; **3** Issachar, Zebulun, and Benjamin; **4** Dan and Naphtali, Gad and Asher. **5** And all the [1]persons who came from the loins of Jacob were [a]seventy [2]in number, but Joseph was *already* in Egypt. **6** [a]Then Joseph died, and all his brothers and all that generation. **7** But the sons of Israel [a]were fruitful and [1]increased and multiplied and became exceedingly [2]mighty, so that the land was filled with them.

**8** And a new [a]king arose over Egypt, who did not know Joseph. **9** [a]And he said to his people, "Behold, the people of the sons of Israel are [1]more and mightier than we. **10** Come, let us [a]deal wisely with them, lest they multiply and it be [1]in the event of war, that they also join themselves to those who hate us and fight against us and [b]go up from the land." **11** So they appointed [a]taskmasters over them to afflict them with [b,1]hard labors. And they built for Pharaoh [c]storage cities, Pithom and [d]Raamses. **12** But the more they afflicted them, [a]the more they multiplied and the more they [1]spread out, so that they were in dread of the sons of Israel. **13** So the Egyptians brutally compelled the sons of Israel [a]to slave labor; **14** and they made [a]their lives bitter with [1]hard slave labor in mortar and bricks and in all *kinds* of slave labor in the field, all their slave labor which they brutally [2]compelled them to do.

**15** Then the king of Egypt spoke to the Hebrew midwives, one of whom [1]was named Shiphrah and the other [1]was named Puah; **16** and he said, "When you are helping the Hebrew women to give birth and see *them* upon the birthstool, [a]if it is a son, then you shall put him to death; but if it is a daughter, then she shall live." **17** But the midwives [a,1]feared God and [b]did not do as the king of Egypt had spoken to them, but let

**50:24** [b]Ge 13:15, 17; 15:7, 8, 18 [c]Ge 26:3 [d]Ge 28:13; 35:12 [1]Or *visit* **50:25** [a]Ge 47:29, 30; Ex 13:19; Jos 24:32; Heb 11:22 [1]Or *visit* **50:26** [a]Ge 50:2 ◆ **1:1** [a]Ge 46:8-27 [1]Lit *and* **1:5** [a]Ge 46:26, 27; Dt 10:22 [1]Lit *souls* [2]Lit *as to souls* **1:6** [a]Ge 50:26 **1:7** [a]Ge 12:2; 28:3; 35:11; 46:3; 47:27; 48:4; Dt 26:5; Ps 105:24; Ac 7:17 [1]Lit *swarmed*, cf. Ge 1:21; Ex 8:2 [2]Or *numerous* **1:8** [a]Ac 7:18, 19 **1:9** [a]Ps 105:24, 25 [1]Or *too many and too mighty for us* **1:10** [a]Ac 7:19 [b]Ge 50:24 [1]Lit *when war befalls that* **1:11** [a]Ge 15:13; Ex 3:7; 5:6 [b]Ex 1:14; 2:11; 5:4-9; 6:6f [c]1Ki 9:19; 2Chr 8:4 [d]Ge 47:11 [1]Lit *their burdens* **1:12** [a]Ex 1:7 [1]Lit *broke forth* **1:13** [a]Ge 15:13; Dt 4:20 **1:14** [a]Ex 2:23; 6:9; Nu 20:15; Ac 7:19 [1]Lit *stiff* [2]Lit *worked through them* **1:15** [1]Lit *the name was* **1:16** [a]Ac 7:19 **1:17** [a]Ex 1:21; Pr 16:6 [b]Ac 4:18-20; 5:29 [1]Or *reverenced*

the boys live. **18** So the king of Egypt
called for the midwives and said
to them, “Why have you done this
thing, and let the boys live?” **19** Then
the midwives said to Pharaoh, “Be-
cause the Hebrew women are not as
the Egyptian women; for they are
vigorous and give birth before the
midwife can come to them.” **20** So
[a]God was good to the midwives, and
[b]the people multiplied and became
very [1]mighty. **21** Now it happened
that because the midwives [a,1]feared
God, He [b]made [2]households for
them. **22** And Pharaoh commanded
all his people, saying, “[a]Every son
who is born [1]you are to cast into [b]the
Nile, and every daughter you are to
keep alive.”

### *The Birth of Moses*

**2** And a man from [a]the house of
Levi went and took a daughter of
Levi *as a wife.* **2** And the woman con-
ceived and bore a son; and she saw
[1]that he was [a,2]beautiful, so she hid
him for three months. **3** But she could
not hide him any longer. So she took
for him [1]an [a]ark of papyrus reeds and
covered it over with tar and pitch.
Then she put the child into it and
put *it* among the [b]reeds by the bank
of the Nile. **4** [a]And his sister stood at
a distance to know what would be
done to him.

**5** And the daughter of Pharaoh
came down [a]to bathe at the Nile, with
her young women walking alongside
the Nile; and she saw the [1]ark among
the reeds and sent her maidservant,
and she took it *to her.* **6** Then she
opened *it* and [1]saw the child. And
behold, *the* [2]boy was crying. And she
had pity on him and said, “This is
one of the Hebrews’ children.” **7** Then
his sister said to Pharaoh’s daughter,
“Shall I go and call [1]a nurse for you
from the Hebrew women that she
may nurse the child for you?” **8** And
Pharaoh’s daughter said to her, “Go.”
So the [1]girl went and called the child’s
mother. **9** Then Pharaoh’s daughter
said to her, “Take this child away
and nurse him for me, and I will give
*you* your wages.” So the woman took
the child and nursed him. **10** And the
child grew, and she brought him to
Pharaoh’s daughter, and [a]he became
her son. And she named him [1]Moses
and said, “Because I [2]drew him out of
the water.”

### *Moses Flees to Midian*

**11** Now it happened in those days,
[a]that Moses had grown up. And he
went out to his brothers and looked
on their [b,1]hard labors. And [c]he saw
an Egyptian striking a Hebrew, one of
his brothers. **12** So he turned this way
and that, and he saw that there was
no one *around.* So he [a]struck down
the Egyptian and hid him in the sand.
**13** Then he went out [a]the next day, and
behold, two Hebrews were struggling
with each other; and he said to the
[1]wicked one, “Why are you striking
your companion?” **14** But he said,
“[a]Who made you a [1]ruler or a judge

---

**1:20** [a]Pr 11:18; Ecc 8:12; Heb 6:10 [b]Ex 1:12; Is 3:10 [1]Or *numerous* **1:21** [a]Ex 1:17 [b]1Sa 2:35; 2Sa 7:11, 27; 1Ki 2:24; 11:38 [1]Or *reverenced* [2]Or *families* **1:22** [a]Ac 7:19 [b]Ge 41:1 [1]Some versions insert *to the Hebrews* ◆ **2:1** [a]Ex 6:16, 18, 20 **2:2** [a]Ac 7:20; Heb 11:23 [1]Lit *him that* [2]Lit *good* **2:3** [a]Is 18:2 [b]Is 19:6 [1]Or *a basket* **2:4** [a]Ex 15:20; Nu 26:59 **2:5** [a]Ex 7:15; 8:20 [1]Or *basket* **2:6** [1]Lit *saw it, the child* [2]Or *lad* **2:7** [1]Lit *a woman giving suck* **2:8** [1]Or *virgin* **2:10** [a]Ac 7:21 [1]Heb *Mosheh*, related to *mashah*; lit *to draw out* [2]Heb *mashah* **2:11** [a]Ac 7:23; Heb 11:24-26 [b]Ex 1:11; 5:4, 5; 6:6, 7 [c]Ac 7:24 [1]Lit *burdens* **2:12** [a]Ac 7:24, 25 **2:13** [a]Ac 7:26-28 [1]Or *the guilty one* **2:14** [a]Ge 19:9; Ac 7:27, 28 [1]Lit *man, a prince*

over us? Are you [2]intending to kill
me as you killed the Egyptian?" Then
Moses was afraid and said, "Surely the
matter has become known." **15** And
Pharaoh heard of this matter, so he
sought to kill Moses. But [a]Moses fled
from the presence of Pharaoh and
settled in the land of Midian, and
he [1]sat down [b]by a well. **16** Now [a]the
priest of Midian had seven daughters;
and [b]they came and drew water and
filled the troughs to give *water* to their
father's flock to drink. **17** Then the
shepherds came and drove them away,
but [a]Moses rose up and saved them
and gave *water* to their flock to drink.
**18** Then they came to [a]Reuel their fa-
ther, and he said, "Why have you come
*back* so soon today?" **19** So they said,
"An Egyptian delivered us from the
hand of the shepherds, and he actually
even drew the water for us and gave
*water* to the flock to drink." **20** And
he said to his daughters, "Where is
he then? Why is it that you have left
the man behind? Call him so that he
may eat bread." **21** [a]And Moses was
willing to settle down with the man,
and he gave his daughter [b]Zipporah
to Moses. **22** Then she gave birth to [a]a
son, and he named him [1]Gershom, for
he said, "I have been [b]a [2]sojourner in
a foreign land."

### *God Hears Israel's Groaning*

**23** Now it happened in *the course*
*of* those many days that the king of
Egypt died. And the sons of Israel
[a]sighed because of the slavery, and
they cried out; and [b]their cry for help
because of *their* slavery rose up to
God. **24** So [a]God heard their groaning;
and God remembered [b]His covenant
with Abraham, Isaac, and Jacob.
**25** [a]And God saw the sons of Israel,
and God knew *them*.

### *God Calls Moses at the Burning Bush*

**3** Now Moses was pasturing the
flock of [a]Jethro his father-in-law,
the priest of Midian; and he led the
flock to the [1]west side of the wil-
derness and came to [b]Horeb, the
[c]mountain of God. **2** [a]And the angel of
[1]Yahweh appeared to him in a blazing
fire from the midst of the [b]bush; and
he looked, and behold, the bush was
burning with fire, yet the bush was
not consumed. **3** So Moses said, "[a,1]I
must turn aside now and see this
[2]marvelous sight. Why is the bush
not burned up?" **4** And Yahweh saw
that he turned aside to look, so [a]God
called to him from the midst of the
bush and said, "Moses, Moses!" And
he said, "Here I am." **5** Then He said,
"Do not come near here. [a]Remove
your sandals from your feet, for the
place on which you are standing is
holy ground." **6** He said also, "[a]I am
the God of your father, the God of
Abraham, the God of Isaac, and the
God of Jacob." [b]Then Moses hid his
face, for he was [c]afraid to look at God.

---

**2:14** [2]Lit *saying* in your heart **2:15** [a]Ac 7:29; Heb 11:27 [b]Ge 24:11; 29:2 [1]Lit *settled*, cf. 2:15a, 21 **2:16** [a]Ex 3:1; 18:12 [b]Ge 24:11, 13, 19; 29:9, 10; 1Sa 9:11 **2:17** [a]Ge 29:3, 10 **2:18** [a]Ex 3:1; Nu 10:29 **2:21** [a]Ac 7:29 [b]Ex 4:25; 18:2 **2:22** [a]Ex 4:20; 18:3, 4 [b]Ge 23:4; Lv 25:23; Ac 7:29; Heb 11:13, 14 [1]Lit *a stranger there* [2]Heb *ger* **2:23** [a]Ex 6:5, 9 [b]Ex 3:7, 9; Dt 26:7; Jas 5:4 **2:24** [a]Ex 6:5; Ac 7:34 [b]Ge 15:13f; 22:16-18; 26:2-5; 28:13-15; Ps 105:8, 42 **2:25** [a]Ex 3:7; 4:31; Ac 7:34 ◆ **3:1** [a]Ex 2:18; 4:18; 18:12; Nu 10:29 [b]Ex 3:12; 17:6; 33:6; 1Ki 19:8 [c]Ex 4:27; 18:5; 24:13 [1]Or *rear part* **3:2** [a]Ge 16:7-11; 21:17; 22:11, 15; Ex 3:4-11, 16; Jdg 13:13-21; Ac 7:30 [b]Dt 33:16; Mk 12:26; Lk 20:37; Ac 7:30 [1]The personal covenant name of God, a form of I AM WHO I AM, cf. Ex 3:14-15 **3:3** [a]Ac 7:31 [1]Lit *Let me turn* [2]Lit *great* **3:4** [a]Ex 4:5 **3:5** [a]Jos 5:15; Ac 7:33 **3:6** [a]Ge 28:13; Ex 3:16; 4:5; Mt 22:32; Mk 12:26; Lk 20:37 [b]Ac 7:32 [c]Jdg 13:22; Rev 1:17

7 And Yahweh said, "I have surely
[a]seen the affliction of My people who
are in Egypt, and I have heard their
cry because of their taskmasters, for
I know their sufferings. 8 So I have
come down [a]to deliver them from the
hand of the Egyptians and to bring
them up from that land to a [b]good
and spacious land, to a land flowing
with milk and honey, to the place of
[c]the Canaanite and the Hittite and
the Amorite and the Perizzite and
the Hivite and the Jebusite. 9 So now,
behold, [a]the cry of the sons of Israel
has come to Me; and I have also seen
the oppression with which the Egyp-
tians are oppressing them. 10 So now,
come and I will send you to Pharaoh,
[a]and so you shall bring My people,
the sons of Israel, out of Egypt." 11 But
Moses said to God, "[a]Who am I, that
I should go to Pharaoh, and that I
should bring the sons of Israel out
of Egypt?" 12 And He said, "Certainly
[a]I will be with you, and this shall be
the sign to you that it is I who have
sent you: [b]when you have brought
the people out of Egypt, [c]you shall
[1]serve God at this mountain."

13 Then Moses said to God, "Be-
hold, I am about to come to the sons
of Israel, and I will say to them, 'The
God of your fathers has sent me to
you.' And they will say to me, 'What is
His name?' What shall I say to them?"
14 And God said to Moses, "[a,1]I AM
WHO [1]I AM"; and He said, "Thus
you shall say to the sons of Israel, '[1]I
AM has sent me to you.'" 15 And God
furthermore said to Moses, "Thus
you shall say to the sons of Israel,
'[a]Yahweh, the God of your fathers,
the God of Abraham, the God of
Isaac, and the God of Jacob, has sent
me to you.' This is My name forever,
and this is My [b]memorial-name from
generation to generation. 16 Go and
[a]gather the elders of Israel together
and say to them, '[b]Yahweh, the God
of your fathers, the God of Abraham,
Isaac, and Jacob, has appeared to me,
saying, "[c,1]I indeed care about you
and what has been done to you in
Egypt. 17 So [a]I said, I will bring you
up out of the affliction of Egypt to the
land of [b]the Canaanite and the Hit-
tite and the Amorite and the Perizzite
and the Hivite and the Jebusite, to a
land [c]flowing with milk and honey."'
18 [a]And they will listen to your voice;
and [b]you with the elders of Israel will
come to the king of Egypt, and you
*all* will say to him, 'Yahweh, the God
of the Hebrews, has met with us. So
now, please, let us go a [c]three days'
journey into the wilderness, that we
may sacrifice to Yahweh our God.'
19 But I know that the king of Egypt
[a]will not give you *permission* to go,
[b]except by a strong hand. 20 So I
will stretch out [a]My hand and strike
Egypt with all My [b]wondrous deeds
which I shall do in the midst of it; and
[c]after that he will let you go. 21 And

**3:7** [a]Ex 2:25; Ne 9:9; Ps 106:44; Is 63:9; Ac 7:34 **3:8** [a]Ge 15:13-16; 46:4; 50:24, 25; Ex 6:6-8; 12:51 [b]Ex 3:17; *13:5; Nu 13:27; Dt 1:25; 8:7-9;* Jer 11:5; Eze 20:6 [c]Ge 15:19-21; Jos 24:11 **3:9** [a]Ex 2:23 **3:10** [a]Ge 15:13, 14; Ex 12:40, 41; Mic 6:4; Ac 7:6, 7 **3:11** [a]Ex 4:10; 6:12; 1Sa 18:18 **3:12** [a]Ge 31:3; Ex 4:12, 15; 33:14-16; Dt 31:23; Jos 1:5; Is 43:2 [b]Ex 19:1 [c]Ex 19:2, 3; Ac 7:7 [1]Or *be a slave for* **3:14** [a]Ex 6:3; Jn 8:24, 28, 58; Heb 13:8; Rev 1:8; 4:8 [1]Related to the name of God, *Yahweh*, which is derived from the verb *hayah*; lit *to be* **3:15** [a]Ex 3:6, 13 [b]Ps 30:4; 97:12; 102:12; 135:13; Hos 12:5 **3:16** [a]Ex 4:29 [b]Ge 28:13; 48:15; Ex 3:2, 6; 4:5 [c]Ex 4:31; Ps 33:18f [1]Lit *Visiting I have visited* **3:17** [a]Ge 15:13-21; 46:4; 50:24, 25 [b]Jos 24:11 [c]Ex 3:8 **3:18** [a]Ex 4:31 [b]Ex 5:1 [c]Ex 5:3; 8:27 **3:19** [a]Ex 5:2 [b]Ex 6:1 **3:20** [a]Ex 6:1; 7:4, 5; 9:15; 13:3, 9, 14 [b]Ex 7:3; 15:11; Dt 6:22; Ne 9:10; Ps 105:27; 135:9; Jer 32:20; Ac 7:36 [c]Ex 11:1; 12:31-33

I will give this people [a]favor in the
sight of the Egyptians; and it shall
be that when you go, you will not go
empty. **22** But *every* woman [a]shall ask
of her neighbor and of the woman
who lives in her house, for articles
of silver and articles of gold, and
clothing; and you will put them on
your sons and daughters. Thus you
will [b]plunder the Egyptians."

### *If They Will Not Believe These Signs*

**4** Then Moses answered and said,
"What if they will not believe
me and will not [a]listen to my voice?
For they may say, '[b]Yahweh has not
appeared to you.'" **2** And Yahweh said
to him, "What is this in your hand?"
And he said, "[a]A staff." **3** Then He
said, "Throw it on the ground." So
he threw it on the ground, and [a]it
became a serpent; and Moses fled
from it. **4** And Yahweh said to Moses,
"Stretch out your hand and grasp
*it* by its tail"—so he stretched out
his hand and took hold of it, and it
became a staff in his [1]hand— **5** "that
[a]they may believe that [b]Yahweh, the
God of their fathers, the God of Abra-
ham, the God of Isaac, and the God
of Jacob, has appeared to you."

**6** And Yahweh furthermore said
to him, "Now put your hand into
your bosom." So he put his hand
into his bosom; then he took it out,
and behold, his hand was [a]leprous
like snow. **7** Then He said, "Return
your hand into your bosom." So he
returned his hand into his bosom,
and when he took it out of his bosom,
behold, [a]it returned *to being* like *the*
*rest of* his flesh. **8** "And so it will be,
if they will not believe you or listen
to the [1]witness of the first sign, they
may believe the [1]witness of [2]this last
sign. **9** But if it will be that they will
not believe even these two signs and
that they will not listen to your voice,
then you shall take some water from
the Nile and pour it on the dry land;
and the water which you take from
the Nile [a]will become blood on the
dry land."

### *Aaron to Speak for Moses*

**10** Then Moses said to Yahweh,
"Please, Lord, [a]I have never been
a man of words, neither [1]recently
nor in time past, nor since You have
spoken to Your slave; for I am *one*
with a [2]hard mouth and a [2]hard
tongue." **11** And Yahweh said to him,
"Who has made man's mouth? Or
[a]who makes *him* mute or deaf, or
seeing or blind? Is it not I, Yahweh?
**12** So now, go, and [a]I, even I, will be
with your mouth and will [b]instruct
you what you shall speak." **13** But he
said, "Please, Lord, [1]send now *the*
*message* by whomever You will."
**14** Then the anger of Yahweh burned
against Moses, and He said, "Is there
not your brother Aaron the Levite?
I know that [1]he can certainly speak.
And moreover, behold, [a]he is coming
out to meet you. And he will see you
and be glad in his heart. **15** And you
are to speak to him and [a]put the

---

**3:21** [a]Ex 11:3; 12:36; 1Ki 8:50; Ps 105:37f; 106:46; Pr 16:7 **3:22** [a]Ge 15:14; Ex 11:2; 12:35 [b]Eze 39:10
◆ **4:1** [a]Ex 3:18; 6:30 [b]Ex 3:15, 16 **4:2** [a]Ex 4:17, 20 **4:3** [a]Ex 7:10-12 **4:4** [1]Lit *palm* **4:5** [a]Ex 4:31; 19:9 [b]Ge 28:13; 48:15; Ex 3:6, 15 **4:6** [a]Nu 12:10; 2Ki 5:27 **4:7** [a]Nu 12:13-15; Dt 32:39; 2Ki 5:14; Mt 8:3; Lk 17:12-14
**4:8** [1]Lit *voice*, cf. 4:9 [2]Lit *the* **4:9** [a]Ex 7:19, 20 **4:10** [a]Ex 3:11; 4:1; 6:12; Jer 1:6 [1]Lit *yesterday* [2]Lit *heavy*
**4:11** [a]Ps 94:9; 146:8; Mt 11:5; Lk 1:20, 64 **4:12** [a]Ex 4:15, 16; Dt 18:18; Is 50:4; Jer 1:9 [b]Mt 10:19, 20; Mk 13:11; Lk 12:11, 12; 21:14, 15 **4:13** [1]Lit *send by the hand which You send* **4:14** [a]Ex 4:27 [1]Lit *speaking he speaks* **4:15** [a]Ex 4:12, 30; 7:1f; Nu 23:5, 12, 16; Dt 18:18; Is 51:16; 59:21; Jer 1:9

words in his mouth; and I, even I,
will be with your mouth and with
his mouth, and I will instruct [1]you in
what you shall do. **16** Moreover, [a]he
shall speak for you to the people; and
he will become as a mouth for you,
and you will become as God to him.
**17** And you shall take in your hand
[a]this staff, [b]with which you shall do
the signs."

### *Moses Returns to Egypt*

**18** Then Moses went and returned to
[1]Jethro [a]his father-in-law and said to
him, "Please, let me go, that I may
return to my brothers who are in
Egypt and see if they are still alive."
And Jethro said to Moses, "Go in
peace." **19** And Yahweh said to Moses
in Midian, "Go, return to Egypt, for
[a]all the men who were seeking your
life are dead." **20** So Moses took his
wife and his [a]sons and mounted
them on a donkey and returned to
the land of Egypt. Moses also took
the [b]staff of God in his hand.
**21** And Yahweh said to Moses,
"When you go to return to Egypt, see
*to it* that all [a]the miraculous wonders
which I have put in your hand, that
you do them before Pharaoh; but as
for Me, [b]I will [1]harden his heart with
strength so that he will not let the
people go. **22** Then you shall say to
Pharaoh, 'Thus says Yahweh, "[a]Israel
is My son, My firstborn. **23** So I said
to you, '[a]Let My son go that he may
serve Me'; but you have refused to let
him go. Behold, [b]I will kill your son,
your firstborn."'"
**24** Now it happened at the lodg-
ing place on the way that Yahweh
encountered him and [a]sought to
put him to death. **25** Then Zipporah
took [a]a flint and cut off her son's
foreskin and touched [1]his feet with
it, and she said, "You are indeed a
bridegroom of blood to me!" **26** So He
let him alone. At that time she said,
"*You are* a bridegroom of blood" with
reference to the circumcision.
**27** [a]Then Yahweh said to Aaron,
"Go to meet Moses in the wilderness."
So he went and encountered him at
the [b]mountain of God and kissed
him. **28** [a]And Moses told Aaron all
the words of Yahweh with which
He had sent him, and [b]all the signs
that He had commanded him *to do.*
**29** Then Moses and Aaron went and
[a]gathered all the elders of the sons
of Israel; **30** and [a]Aaron spoke all the
words which Yahweh had spoken to
Moses. He then did the [b]signs in the
sight of the people. **31** So [a]the people
believed; and they heard that Yahweh
[b,1]cared about the sons of Israel and
that He had seen their affliction. So
[c]they bowed low and worshiped.

### *Pharaoh Will Not Let the People Go*

**5** And afterward Moses and Aaron
came and said to Pharaoh, "[a]Thus
says Yahweh, the God of Israel, '[b]Let
My people go that they may celebrate
a feast to Me in the wilderness.'" **2** But

**4:15** [1]Lit *you* (plural) **4:16** [a]Ex 7:1, 2 **4:17** [a]Ex 4:2, 20; 17:9 [b]Ex 7:9-20; 14:16 **4:18** [a]Ex 2:21; 3:1 [1]Heb *Jether* **4:19** [a]Ex 2:15, 23 **4:20** [a]Ex 18:3, 4; Ac 7:29 [b]Ex 4:17; 17:9; Nu 20:8, 9, 11 **4:21** [a]Ex 3:20; 11:9, 10 [b]Ex 7:3, 13; 9:12, 35; 10:1, 20, 27; 14:4, 8; Dt 2:30; Jos 11:20; 1Sa 6:6; Is 63:17; Jn 12:40; Ro 9:18 [1]Lit *strengthen* **4:22** [a]Is 63:16; 64:8; Jer 31:9; Hos 11:1; Ro 9:4 **4:23** [a]Ex 5:1; 6:11; 7:16 [b]Ex 11:5; 12:29; Ps 105:36; 135:8; 136:10 **4:24** [a]Nu 22:22 **4:25** [a]Ge 17:14; Jos 5:2, 3 [1]Moses' feet **4:27** [a]Ex 4:14 [b]Ex 3:1; 18:5; 24:13 **4:28** [a]Ex 4:15f [b]Ex 4:8f **4:29** [a]Ex 3:16 **4:30** [a]Ex 4:15, 16 [b]Ex 4:1-9 **4:31** [a]Ex 3:18; 4:8f; 19:9 [b]Ge 50:24; Ex 3:16 [c]Ge 24:26; Ex 12:27; 1Chr 29:20 [1]Lit *had visited*
◆ **5:1** [a]Ex 3:18 [b]Ex 4:23; 6:11; 7:16

Pharaoh said, "[a]Who is Yahweh that I should listen to His voice to let Israel go? I do not know Yahweh, and also, [b]I will not let Israel go." **3** Then they said, "[a]The God of the Hebrews has met with us. Please, let us go a three days' journey into the wilderness that we may sacrifice to Yahweh our God, lest He confront us with pestilence or with the sword." **4** But the king of Egypt said to them, "Moses and Aaron, why do you [1]draw the people away from their [2]work? Get *back* to your [a,3]hard labors!" **5** And Pharaoh said, "Look, [a]the people of the land are now many, and you would have them cease from their hard labors!" **6** So on that day Pharaoh commanded [a]the taskmasters over the people and their [b]foremen, saying, **7** "You are no longer to give the people straw to make brick as previously; let them go and gather straw for themselves. **8** But the quota of bricks which they were making previously, you shall set upon them; you are not to reduce any of it. Because they are [a]lazy, therefore they are crying out, '[1]Let us go and sacrifice to our God.' **9** Let *their* slavery be hard on the men, and let them work at it so that they will have no regard for false words."

**10** So [a]the taskmasters of the people and their foremen went out and spoke to the people, saying, "Thus says Pharaoh, 'I am not going to give you *any* straw. **11** You go *and* get straw for yourselves wherever you can find *it*, but no amount of your slave labor will be reduced.'" **12** So the people scattered through all the land of Egypt to gather stubble for straw. **13** And the taskmasters were pressing them, saying, "Complete your [1]work quota, [2]the daily amount, just as when there was straw." **14** Moreover, [a]the foremen of the sons of Israel, whom Pharaoh's taskmasters had set over them, [b]were beaten [1]and were asked, "Why have you not completed your required amount either yesterday or today in making brick as previously?"

**15** Then the foremen of the sons of Israel came and cried out to Pharaoh, saying, "Why do you deal this way with your slaves? **16** There is no straw given to your slaves, yet they keep saying to us, 'Make bricks!' And behold, your slaves are being beaten; but it is the [1]sin of your *own* people." **17** But he said, "You are [a]lazy—lazy! Therefore you say, 'Let us go *and* sacrifice to Yahweh.' **18** So now, go *and* labor; but straw will not be given to you, yet you must deliver the quota of bricks." **19** Then the foremen of the sons of Israel saw that they were in trouble [1]because they were told, "You must not reduce [2]your daily amount of bricks." **20** When they left Pharaoh's presence, they confronted Moses and Aaron, [1]standing there to meet them. **21** [a]And they said to them, "[b]May Yahweh look upon you and judge, for you have [c]made [1]us a foul smell in Pharaoh's sight and in the sight of his servants, to put a sword in their hand to kill us."

**5:2** [a]2Ki 18:35; 2Chr 32:14; Job 21:15 [b]Ex 3:19 **5:3** [a]Ex 3:18 **5:4** [a]Ex 1:11; 2:11; 6:5-7 [1]Lit *loose* [2]Lit *works* [3]Lit *burdens* **5:5** [a]Ex 1:7, 9 **5:6** [a]Ex 1:11; 3:7; 5:10, 13, 14 [b]Ex 5:10, 14, 15, 19 **5:8** [a]Ex 5:17 [1]Lit *saying, 'Let* **5:10** [a]Ex 1:11; 3:7; 5:6 **5:13** [1]Lit *works* [2]Lit *the matter of a day in its day* **5:14** [a]Ex 5:6 [b]Is 10:24 [1]Lit *saying* **5:16** [1]Or *fault* **5:17** [a]Ex 5:8 **5:19** [1]Lit *saying* [2]Lit *from your bricks the matter of a day in its day* **5:20** [1]Lit *taking their stand* **5:21** [a]Ex 14:11; 15:24; 16:2 [b]Ge 16:5; 31:53 [c]Ge 34:30; 1Sa 13:4; 27:12; 2Sa 10:6; 1Chr 19:6 [1]Lit *our savor to stink*

**22** Then Moses returned to Yahweh
and said, "[a]O Lord, why have You
brought harm to this people? Why did
You ever send me? **23** Ever since I came
to Pharaoh to speak in Your name, he
has done harm to this people, [a]and You
have not delivered Your people at all."

### *Yahweh Remembers His Covenant*

**6** Then Yahweh said to Moses,
"Now you shall see what I will do
to Pharaoh; for [a]by a strong hand he
will let them go, and by a strong hand
he will drive them out of his land."
**2** God spoke further to Moses and
said to him, "I am [a]Yahweh; **3** and I
appeared to Abraham, Isaac, and Ja-
cob, as [a,1]God Almighty, but *by* [b]My
name, Yahweh, I was not known to
them. **4** And I also established [a]My
covenant with them, to give them the
land of Canaan, the [1]land in which
they sojourned. **5** Furthermore I have
[a]heard the groaning of the sons of
Israel because the Egyptians are
holding them in slavery, and I have
remembered My covenant. **6** Say,
therefore, to the sons of Israel, '[a]I
am Yahweh, and [b]I will bring you
out from under the hard labors of the
Egyptians, and I will deliver you from
their slavery. I will also [c]redeem you
with [d]an outstretched arm and with
great judgments. **7** Then I will take
you [a,1]for My people, and [b]I will be
[2]your God; and [c]you shall know that
I am Yahweh your God, who brought
you out from under the hard labors of
the Egyptians. **8** And I will bring you
to the land which [a]I [1]swore to give to
Abraham, to Isaac, and to Jacob, and
[b]I will give it to you *for* a possession; [c]I
am Yahweh.'" **9** So Moses spoke thus
to the sons of Israel, but they did not
listen to Moses on [a]account of *their*
weakness of spirit and [1]hard slavery.
**10** Now Yahweh spoke to Moses,
saying, **11** "[a]Come, [1]tell Pharaoh king
of Egypt [2]to let the sons of Israel go
out of his land." **12** But Moses spoke
before Yahweh, saying, "Behold, the
sons of Israel have not listened to
me; [a]how then will Pharaoh listen to
me, for I am of [b]uncircumcised lips?"
**13** Then Yahweh spoke to Moses and
to Aaron and gave them a command
for the sons of Israel and for Pharaoh
king of Egypt, to bring the sons of
Israel out of the land of Egypt.

### *The Heads of Israel's Households*

**14** These are the heads of their fa-
thers' households.
[a]The sons of Reuben, Israel's
firstborn:
Hanoch and Pallu, Hezron
and Carmi; these are
the families of Reuben.
**15** The [a]sons of Simeon:
Jemuel and Jamin and Ohad
and Jachin and Zohar
and Shaul the son of
a Canaanite woman; these are
the families of Simeon.

---

**5:22** [a]Nu 11:11; Jer 4:10 **5:23** [a]Ex 3:8 ◆ **6:1** [a]Ex 3:19, 20; 7:4, 5; 11:1; 12:31, 33, 39; 13:3 **6:2** [a]Ex 3:14, 15
**6:3** [a]Ge 17:1; 35:11; 48:3 [b]Ps 68:4; 83:18; Is 52:6; Jer 16:21; Eze 37:6, 13 [1]Heb *El Shaddai* **6:4** [a]Ge 12:7;
15:18; 17:4, 7; 26:3, 4; 28:4, 13 [1]Lit *land of their sojournings in which...* **6:5** [a]Ex 2:24 **6:6** [a]Ex 13:3, 14;
20:2; Dt 6:12 [b]Ex 3:17; 7:4; 12:51; 16:6; 18:1; Dt 26:8; Ps 136:11 [c]Ex 15:13; Dt 7:8; 1Chr 17:21; Ne 1:10
[d]Dt 4:34; 5:15; 26:8; Ps 136:11f **6:7** [a]Ex 19:5; Dt 4:20; 7:6; 2Sa 7:24 [b]Ge 17:7f; Ex 29:45f; Lv 11:45;
26:12, 13, 45; Dt 29:13 [c]Ex 16:12; Is 41:20; 49:23, 26; 60:16 [1]Lit *to Me for a people* [2]Lit *to you for a God*
**6:8** [a]Ge 15:18; 26:3; Nu 14:30; Ne 9:15; Eze 20:5, 6 [b]Jos 24:13; Ps 136:21, 22 [c]Ex 6:6 [1]Lit *lifted up My hand*
**6:9** [a]Ex 2:23 [1]Lit *stiff* **6:11** [a]Ex 4:22, 23 [1]Lit *speak to* [2]Lit *that he let* **6:12** [a]Ex 4:1, 10; 6:30 [b]Jer 1:6
**6:14** [a]Ge 46:9; Nu 26:5-11; 1Chr 5:3 **6:15** [a]Ge 46:10; 1Chr 4:24

16 These are the names of
[a]the sons of Levi according to
their generations:
Gershon and Kohath
and Merari; and the years of
Levi's life were 137 years.
17 [a]The sons of Gershon:
[1]Libni and Shimei, according
to their families.
18 [a]The sons of Kohath:
Amram and Izhar and Hebron
and Uzziel; and the years of
Kohath's life were 133 years.
19 [a]The sons of Merari:
Mahli and Mushi.
These are the families of the
Levites according to their
generations.
20 [a]And Amram took his father's
sister Jochebed as a wife,
and she bore him Aaron
and Moses; and the years of
Amram's life were 137 years.
21 [a]The sons of Izhar:
Korah and Nepheg and Zichri.
22 [a]The sons of Uzziel:
Mishael and [1]Elzaphan
and Sithri.
23 And Aaron took Elisheba,
the daughter of [a]Amminadab,
the sister of [b]Nahshon, as a
wife, and she bore him [c]Nadab
and Abihu, Eleazar and
Ithamar.
24 *The [a]sons of Korah:*
Assir and Elkanah and
[1]Abiasaph; these are the
families of the Korahites.

**25** And Aaron's son [a]Eleazar took
one of the daughters of Putiel as a
wife, and she bore him [b]Phinehas.
These are the heads of the fathers'
*households* of the Levites according
to their families. **26** It was *the same*
Aaron and Moses to whom Yahweh
said, "[a]Bring out the sons of Israel
from the land of Egypt according to
their [b]hosts." **27** They were the ones
[a]who spoke to Pharaoh king of Egypt
to bring out the sons of Israel from
Egypt; it was *the same* Moses and
Aaron.

### *Aaron Will Speak for Moses*

**28** Now it happened on the day when
Yahweh spoke to Moses in the land of
Egypt, **29** that Yahweh spoke to Mo-
ses, saying, "[a]I am Yahweh; [b]speak
to Pharaoh king of Egypt all that I
am speaking to you." **30** But Moses
said before Yahweh, "Behold, I am of
[a]uncircumcised lips; how then will
Pharaoh listen to me?"

**7** Then Yahweh said to Moses,
"[a]See, I [1]set you *as* God to Phar-
aoh, and your brother Aaron shall
be your prophet. **2** You shall speak
all that I command you, and your
brother [a]Aaron shall speak to Phar-
aoh that he let the sons of Israel go
out of his land. **3** But [a]I will harden
Pharaoh's heart with stiffness that
I may [b]multiply My signs and My
[1]wonders in the land of Egypt. **4** But
[a]Pharaoh will not listen to you. And
I will [1]set My hand upon Egypt and

---

**6:16** [a]Ge 46:11; Nu 3:17; 26:57f; 1Chr 6:1, 16-19 **6:17** [a]Nu 3:18-20; 1Chr 6:17-19 [1]In 1Chr 23:7, *Ladan* **6:18** [a]Nu 3:19; 1Chr 6:2, 18 **6:19** [a]Nu 3:20; 1Chr 6:19; 23:21 **6:20** [a]Ex 2:1, 2; Nu 26:59 **6:21** [a]Nu 16:1; 1Chr 6:37, 38 **6:22** [a]Lv 10:4; Nu 3:30 [1]In Nu 3:30, *Elizaphan* **6:23** [a]Ru 4:19, 20; 1Chr 2:10 [b]Nu 1:7; 2:3 [c]Lv 10:1; Nu 3:2; 26:60; 1Chr 6:3; 24:1 **6:24** [a]Nu 26:11; 1Chr 6:22, 23, 37 [1]In 1Chr 6:23 and 9:19, *Ebiasaph* **6:25** [a]Jos 24:33 [b]Nu 25:7-13; Jos 24:33; Ps 106:30 **6:26** [a]Ex 3:10; 6:13 [b]Ex 7:4; 12:17, 51 **6:27** [a]Ex 5:1 **6:29** [a]Ex 6:2, 6, 8 [b]Ex 6:11; 7:2 **6:30** [a]Ex 4:10; 6:12; Jer 1:6 ◆**7:1** [a]Ex 4:16 [1]Lit *give* **7:2** [a]Ex 4:15 **7:3** [a]Ex 4:21 [b]Ex 11:9; Ac 7:36 [1]Or *miraculous wonders*, cf. 7:9 **7:4** [a]Ex 3:19, 20; 7:13, 16, 22; 8:15, 19; 9:12; 11:9 [1]Lit *give*

[b]bring out My hosts, My people
the sons of Israel, from the land of
Egypt by [c]great judgments. **5** [a]Then
the Egyptians shall know that I am
Yahweh, when I [b]stretch out My
hand against Egypt and bring out the
sons of Israel from their midst." **6** So
Moses and Aaron did *it*; [a]as Yahweh
commanded them, thus they did.
**7** Now Moses was [a]eighty years old
and Aaron eighty-three years old,
when they spoke to Pharaoh.

### *Aaron's Staff Becomes a Serpent*

**8** And Yahweh spoke to Moses and
Aaron, saying, **9** "When Pharaoh
speaks to you, saying, '[a,1]Work a
miraculous wonder,' then you shall
say to Aaron, '[b]Take your staff and
throw *it* down before Pharaoh, *that*
it may become a [2]serpent.'" **10** So
Moses and Aaron came to Pharaoh,
and thus they did just as Yahweh had
commanded; and Aaron threw his
staff down before Pharaoh and [1]his
[2]servants, and it [a]became a [3]serpent.
**11** Then Pharaoh also [a]called for the
wise men and the sorcerers, and
they also, the [b,1]magicians of Egypt,
did [2]the same with [c]their secret arts.
**12** And each one threw down his staff,
and they became [1]serpents. But Aar-
on's staff swallowed up their staffs.
**13** Yet [a]Pharaoh's heart was [1]hardened
with strength, and he did not listen to
them, as Yahweh had spoken.

### *The Plague of Water Turning to Blood*

**14** Then Yahweh said to Moses,
"Pharaoh's heart is [1]hard with firm-
ness; he refuses to let the people go.
**15** Go to Pharaoh in the morning [1]as
[a]he is going out to the water, and
station yourself to meet him on the
bank of the Nile; and you shall take
in your hand [b]the staff that was
turned into a serpent. **16** [a]And you
shall say to him, 'Yahweh, the God
of the Hebrews, sent me to you,
saying, "[b]Let My people go, that
they may serve Me in the wilderness.
But behold, you have not listened
until now." **17** Thus says Yahweh,
"[a]By this you shall know that I am
Yahweh: behold, I am about to strike
[1]the water that is in the Nile with
the staff that is in my hand, and [b]it
will be turned to blood. **18** [a]And the
fish that are in the Nile will die, and
the Nile will [1]become foul, and the
Egyptians will [b]be weary of drinking
water from the Nile."'" **19** Then Yah-
weh said to Moses, "Say to Aaron,
'Take your staff and [a]stretch out
your hand over the waters of Egypt,
over their rivers, over their [1]streams,
and over their pools and over all
their reservoirs of water, that they
may become blood; and there will
be blood throughout all the land of
Egypt, both in *vessels of* wood and
in *vessels of* stone.'"

---

**7:4** [b]Ex 12:51; 13:3, 9 [c]Ex 6:6 **7:5** [a]Ex 7:17; 8:19, 22; 10:7; 14:4, 18, 25 [b]Ex 3:20 **7:6** [a]Ge 6:22; 7:5; Ex 7:2 **7:7** [a]Dt 29:5; 31:2; 34:7; Ac 7:23, 30 **7:9** [a]Is 7:11; Jn 2:18; 6:30 [b]Ex 4:2, 17 [1]Lit *Show a wonder for yourselves* [2]Or *dragon, sea monster, supernatural foe* **7:10** [a]Ex 4:3; 7:9 [1]Lit *before his* [2]Or *slaves*; see Foreword, "The Terminology of Slave" [3]Or *dragon, sea monster, supernatural foe* **7:11** [a]Da 2:2; 4:6; 5:7 [b]Ge 41:8; Ex 7:22; Da 2:2; 2Ti 3:8 [c]Ex 7:22; 8:7, 18; 2Ti 3:9; Rev 13:13, 14 [1]Or *soothsayer priests* [2]Lit *thus* **7:12** [1]Or *dragon, sea monster, supernatural foe* **7:13** [a]Ex 4:21; 7:3, 22; 8:15, 19, 32; 9:7, 12, 34, 35; 10:1, 20, 27 [1]Lit *strengthened* **7:14** [1]Or *glorified*, cf. 14:4; lit *heavy* **7:15** [a]Ex 2:5; 8:20 [b]Ex 4:2, 3; 7:10 [1]Lit *behold* **7:16** [a]Ex 3:13, 18; 4:22; 5:1 [b]Ex 4:23; 5:1, 3 **7:17** [a]Ex 5:2; 7:5; 10:2; Ps 9:16; Eze 25:17 [b]Ex 4:9; 7:20; Rev 11:6; 16:4, 6 [1]Lit *upon the waters* **7:18** [a]Ex 7:21 [b]Ex 7:24 [1]Or *have a bad smell* **7:19** [a]Ex 8:5, 6, 16; 9:22; 10:12, 21; 14:21, 26 [1]Or *canals*

**20** So Moses and Aaron did thus, as Yahweh had commanded. And he raised up [a,1]the staff and struck the water that *was* in the Nile, in the sight of Pharaoh and in the sight of his servants, and [b]all the water that *was* in the Nile was turned to blood. **21** And the fish that *were* in the Nile died, and the Nile [1]became foul, so that the Egyptians could not drink water from the Nile. And the blood was through all the land of Egypt. **22** [a]Yet the [1]magicians of Egypt did [2]the same with their secret arts; and Pharaoh's heart was [3]hardened with strength, and he did not listen to them, as Yahweh had spoken. **23** Then Pharaoh turned and went into his house, and he did not set his heart even on this. **24** So all the Egyptians dug around the Nile for water to drink, for they could not drink of the water of the Nile. **25** And seven full days [1]passed after Yahweh had struck the Nile.

### *The Plague of Frogs*

**8** [1]Then Yahweh said to Moses, "Come to Pharaoh and say to him, 'Thus says Yahweh, "[a]Let My people go, that they may serve Me. **2** But if you refuse to let *them* go, behold, I [1]will smite your whole territory with frogs. **3** And the Nile will [a]swarm with frogs, and they will go up and come into your house and into your bedroom and on your bed and into the houses of your servants and on your people and into your ovens and into your kneading bowls. **4** So the frogs will come up on you and on your people and on all your servants."'" **5** [1]Then Yahweh said to Moses, "Say to Aaron, '[a]Stretch out your hand with your staff over the rivers, over the [2]streams and over the pools, and cause the frogs to come up on the land of Egypt.'" **6** So Aaron stretched out his hand over the waters of Egypt, and the [a,1]frogs came up and covered the land of Egypt. **7** [a]And the [1]magicians did [2]the same with their secret arts; they caused the frogs to come up on the land of Egypt.

**8** Then Pharaoh [a]called for Moses and Aaron and said, "[b]Entreat Yahweh that He may cause the frogs to depart from me and from my people; and [c]I will let the people go, that they may sacrifice to Yahweh." **9** And Moses said to Pharaoh, "[1]May the honor be yours to tell me: when shall I entreat for you and for your servants and for your people, that the frogs be cut off from you and your houses, *that* they may remain only in the Nile?"

**10** Then he said, "Tomorrow." So he said, "*May it be* according to your word, that you may know that there is [a]no one like Yahweh our God. **11** And the [a]frogs will depart from you and your houses and your servants and your people; they will remain only in the Nile." **12** Then Moses and Aaron went out from Pharaoh, and [a]Moses cried out to Yahweh concerning the frogs which He had set upon

**7:20** [a]Ex 17:5 [b]Ps 78:44; 105:29 [1]Lit *with the staff* **7:21** [1]Had a bad smell **7:22** [a]Ex 7:11; 8:7 [1]Or *soothsayer priests* [2]Lit *thus* [3]Lit *strengthened* **7:25** [1]Lit *were fulfilled* ◆ **8:1** [a]Ex 3:18; 4:23; 5:1, 3 [1]Ch 7:26 in Heb **8:2** [1]Or *am about to*, cf. 3:13; 7:17 **8:3** [a]Ps 105:30 **8:5** [a]Ex 7:19 [1]Ch 8:1 in Heb [2]Or *canals* **8:6** [a]Ps 78:45; 105:30 [1]Lit *frog* **8:7** [a]Ex 7:11, 22 [1]Or *soothsayer priests* [2]Lit *thus* **8:8** [a]Ex 8:25; 9:27; 10:16 [b]Ex 8:28; 9:28; 10:17; Nu 21:7; 1Ki 13:6 [c]Ex 8:15, 29, 32 **8:9** [1]Lit *Glory over me* **8:10** [a]Ex 9:14; Dt 4:35, 39; 33:26; 2Sa 7:22; 1Chr 17:20; Ps 86:8; Is 46:9; Jer 10:6, 7 **8:11** [a]Ex 8:13 **8:12** [a]Ex 8:30; 9:33; 10:18

Pharaoh. **13** So Yahweh did according
to the word of Moses, and the frogs
died out of the houses, the courts,
and the fields. **14** So they piled them
in heaps, and the land [1]became foul.
**15** Then Pharaoh saw that there was
relief, and he [1]hardened his heart
with firmness and [a]did not listen to
them, as Yahweh had spoken.

### *The Plague of Gnats*

**16** Then Yahweh said to Moses, "Say
to Aaron, 'Stretch out your staff and
strike the dust of the earth, that it
may become [1]gnats through all the
land of Egypt.'" **17** And they did so;
and Aaron stretched out his hand
with his staff and struck the dust of
the earth, and there were [1]gnats on
man and beast. All the dust of the
earth became [a,1]gnats through all the
land of Egypt. **18** Then [1]the magicians
did the same with their secret arts in
order to bring forth [2]gnats, but [a]they
could not; so there were [2]gnats on
man and beast. **19** And the [1]magicians
said to Pharaoh, "[a]This is the finger
of God." But Pharaoh's heart was
[2]hardened with strength, and he
did not listen to them, as Yahweh
had spoken.

### *The Plague of Flies*

**20** And Yahweh said to Moses, "[a]Rise
early in the morning and stand be-
fore Pharaoh [1]as [b]he comes out to
the water, and you shall say to him,
'Thus says Yahweh, "[c]Let My people
go, that they may serve Me. **21** For if
you do not let My people go, behold,
I will send swarms of flies on you
and on your servants and on your
people and into your houses; and the
houses of the Egyptians will be full of
swarms of flies, and also the ground
on which they *stand*. **22** [a]But on that
day I will make a distinction for the
land of Goshen, where My people
are [1]living, so that no swarms of
flies will be there, that you may know
that [b,2]I, Yahweh, am in the midst of
the land. **23** And I will [1]put a division
between My people and your people.
Tomorrow this sign will happen."'"
**24** Then Yahweh did so. And there
came heavy swarms of flies into the
house of Pharaoh and the houses of
his servants, and the land was [a]laid
waste because of the swarms of flies
in all the land of Egypt.

**25** And Pharaoh [a]called for Moses
and Aaron and said, "[b]Go, sacrifice
to your God within the land." **26** But
Moses said, "It is not right to do so,
for we will sacrifice to Yahweh our
God [1]what is [a]an abomination to the
Egyptians. If we sacrifice [1]what is an
abomination to the Egyptians before
their eyes, will they not then stone
us? **27** We must go a [a]three days' jour-
ney into the wilderness and sacrifice
to Yahweh our God as He says to us."
**28** And Pharaoh said, "[a]I will let you
go, that you may sacrifice to Yahweh
your God in the wilderness; only you
shall not go very far away. [b]Entreat
for me." **29** Then Moses said, "Behold,
I am going out from you, and I shall

---

**8:14** [1]Had a bad smell **8:15** [a]Ex 7:4 [1]Or *glorified*, cf. 14:4; lit *made heavy* **8:16** [1]Or *lice* **8:17** [a]Ps 105:31 [1]Or *lice* **8:18** [a]Ex 7:11, 12; 8:7; 9:11 [1]Or *soothsayer priests* [2]Or *lice* **8:19** [a]Ex 7:5; 10:7; Ps 8:3; Lk 11:20 [1]Or *soothsayer priests* [2]Lit *strengthened* **8:20** [a]Ex 7:15; 9:13 [b]Ex 2:5; 7:15 [c]Ex 3:18; 4:23; 5:1, 3; 8:1 [1]Lit *behold* **8:22** [a]Ex 9:4, 6, 24; 10:23; 11:7 [b]Ex 9:29; 19:5; 20:11 [1]Lit *standing* [2]Or *I am Yahweh in the midst of the earth* **8:23** [1]Lit *set redemption* **8:24** [a]Ps 78:45; 105:31 **8:25** [a]Ex 8:8; 9:27; 10:16 [b]Ex 9:28; 10:8, 24; 12:31 **8:26** [a]Ge 43:32; 46:34; Dt 7:25f [1]Lit *the abomination of Egypt* **8:27** [a]Ex 3:18; 5:3 **8:28** [a]Ex 8:8, 15, 29, 32 [b]Ex 8:8; 9:28; 1Ki 13:6

entreat Yahweh that the swarms of
flies may depart from Pharaoh, from
his servants, and from his people
tomorrow; only may Pharaoh not
[a]deal deceitfully again in not letting
the people go to sacrifice to Yahweh."
**30** So [a]Moses went out from Phar-
aoh and entreated Yahweh. **31** And
Yahweh did according to the word
of Moses and caused the swarms of
flies to depart from Pharaoh, from his
servants, and from his people; not one
remained. **32** Then Pharaoh [1]hardened
his heart with firmness this time also,
and [a]he did not let the people go.

### *The Plague of Dying Egyptian Livestock*

**9** Then Yahweh said to Moses,
"Come to Pharaoh and speak to
him, 'Thus says Yahweh, the God of
the Hebrews, "[a]Let My people go,
that they may serve Me. **2** For [a]if you
refuse to let *them* go and [1]continue
to hold them, **3** behold, [a]the hand of
Yahweh [1]will come *with* a very heavy
pestilence on your livestock which
are in the field, on the horses, on the
donkeys, on the camels, on the herds,
and on the flocks. **4** [a]But Yahweh will
make a distinction between the live-
stock of Israel and the livestock of
Egypt, so that [b]nothing will die of all
that belongs to the sons of Israel."'"
**5** Yahweh also set a definite time,
saying, "Tomorrow Yahweh will do
this thing in the land." **6** So Yahweh
did this thing on the next day, and
[a]all the livestock of Egypt died; [b]but
of the livestock of the sons of Israel,
not one died. **7** And Pharaoh sent,
and behold, there was not even one
of the livestock of Israel dead. But
[a]the heart of Pharaoh was [1]hardened
with firmness, and he did not let the
people go.

### *The Plague of Boils*

**8** Then Yahweh said to Moses and
Aaron, "Take for yourselves handfuls
of soot from a kiln, and let Moses
toss it toward the sky in the sight of
Pharaoh. **9** And it will become fine
dust over all the land of Egypt, and it
will become [a]boils breaking out with
sores on man and beast through all
the land of Egypt." **10** So they took the
soot from the kiln and stood before
Pharaoh; and Moses tossed it toward
the sky, and it became boils breaking
out with sores on man and beast.
**11** [a]And the [1]magicians could not
stand before Moses because of the
boils, for the boils were on the magi-
cians [2]as well as on all the Egyptians.
**12** And [a]Yahweh [1]hardened Pharaoh's
heart with strength, and he did not
listen to them, just as Yahweh had
spoken to Moses.

### *The Plague of Hail*

**13** And Yahweh said to Moses, "[a]Rise
up early in the morning and stand
before Pharaoh, and you shall say
to him, 'Thus says Yahweh, the God
of the Hebrews, "[b]Let My people go,
that they may serve Me. **14** For this
time I will send all My plagues against
your heart and amongst your ser-
vants and your people, so that [a]you

---

**8:29** [a]Ex 8:8, 15 **8:30** [a]Ex 8:12 **8:32** [a]Ex 4:21; 8:8, 15 [1]Or *glorified*, cf. 14:4; lit *made heavy*
◆ **9:1** [a]Ex 4:23; 8:1 **9:2** [a]Ex 8:2 [1]Lit *still hold* **9:3** [a]Ex 7:4; 1Sa 5:6; Ps 39:10; Ac 13:11 [1]Lit *will be*
**9:4** [a]Ex 8:22 [b]Ex 9:6 **9:6** [a]Ex 9:19, 20, 25; Ps 78:48 [b]Ex 9:4 **9:7** [a]Ex 7:14; 8:32 [1]Or *glorified*,
cf. 14:4; lit *heavy* **9:9** [a]Dt 28:27; Rev 16:2 **9:11** [a]Ex 8:18 [1]Or *soothsayer priests* [2]Lit *and on*
*all* **9:12** [a]Ex 4:21; 10:1, 20; 14:8; Jos 11:20; Jn 12:40 [1]Lit *strengthened* **9:13** [a]Ex 8:20 [b]Ex 4:23
**9:14** [a]Ex 8:10; Dt 3:24; 2Sa 7:22; 1Chr 17:20; Ps 86:8; Is 45:5-8; 46:9; Jer 10:6, 7

may know that there is no one like
Me in all the earth. 15 For *if by* now
I had sent forth My hand and struck
you and your people with pestilence,
you would then have been wiped
out from the earth. 16 But, indeed,
[a]for this reason I have caused you
to stand, in order to show you My
power and in order to recount My
name through all the earth. 17 Still
you [1]exalt yourself against My people
[2]by not letting them go. 18 Behold,
about this time tomorrow, [a]I will
rain down very heavy hail, such as
has not been *seen* in Egypt from the
day it was founded [1]until now. 19 So
now, send, bring [a]your livestock and
whatever you have in the field to
safety. [b]Every man and beast that is
found in the field and is not brought
home, the hail will come down on
them, and they will die."'" 20 [a]The
one among the servants of Pharaoh
who [1]feared the word of Yahweh
made his servants and his livestock
flee into the houses; 21 but he who
did not [1]consider in his heart the
word of Yahweh [2]left his servants
and his livestock in the field.

22 Now Yahweh said to Moses,
"Stretch out your hand toward the
sky, that [a]there may be hail on all
the land of Egypt, on man and on
beast and on every plant of the
field, throughout the land of Egypt."
23 So Moses stretched out his staff
toward the sky, and Yahweh gave
forth [1]thunder and [a]hail, and fire
went down to the earth. And Yah-
weh rained down hail on the land of
Egypt. 24 So there was hail, and fire
[1]flashing continually in the midst of
the hail, very heavy, such as had not
been in all the land of Egypt since
it became a nation. 25 [a]And the
hail struck all that was in the field
through all the land of Egypt, from
man to beast; the hail also struck
every plant of the field and shattered
every tree of the field. 26 [a]Only in the
land of Goshen, where the sons of
Israel *were*, there was no hail.

27 Then Pharaoh [a]sent and called
for Moses and Aaron and said to
them, "[b]I have sinned this time;
Yahweh is the righteous one, and
I and my people are the wicked
ones. 28 [a]Entreat Yahweh, for God's
[1]thunder and hail are too much; and
[b]I will let you go, and you shall stay
no longer." 29 And Moses said to him,
"As soon as I go out of the city, I will
[a]spread out my [1]hands to Yahweh;
the [2]thunder will cease, and there
will be hail no longer, that you may
know that [b]the earth is Yahweh's.
30 [a]But as for you and your servants,
I know that [b]you do not yet [1]fear
[2]Yahweh God." 31 (Now the flax and
the [a]barley were struck down, for the
barley was in the ear and the flax was
in bud. 32 But the wheat and the spelt
were not struck down, for they are
late-ripening.) 33 [a]And Moses went
out of the city from Pharaoh and
spread out his [1]hands to Yahweh; and

**9:16** [a]Pr 16:4; Ro 9:17 **9:17** [1]Or *build up* [2]Lit *so as not to let* **9:18** [a]Ex 9:23, 24 [1]Lit *and until now* ***9:19*** [a]*Ex 9:6* [b]*Ex 9:25* **9:20** [a]Pr 13:13 [1]Or *reverenced* **9:21** [1]Lit *set* [2]Lit *then left* **9:22** [a]Rev 16:21 **9:23** [a]Ge 19:24; Jos 10:11; Ps 18:13; 78:47; 105:32; Is 30:30; Eze 38:22; Rev 8:7 [1]Lit *sounds* **9:24** [1]Lit *taking hold of itself* **9:25** [a]Ex 9:19; Ps 78:47, 48; 105:32, 33 **9:26** [a]Ex 8:22; 9:4, 6; 11:7 **9:27** [a]Ex 8:8 [b]Ex 10:16, 17; 2Chr 12:6; Ps 129:4; 145:17; Lam 1:18 **9:28** [a]Ex 8:8, 28; 10:17 [b]Ex 8:25; 10:8, 24 [1]Lit *sounds* **9:29** [a]1Ki 8:22, 38; Ps 143:6; Is 1:15 [b]Ex 8:22; 19:5; 20:11; Ps 24:1; 1Co 10:26 [1]Lit *palms* [2]Lit *sounds* **9:30** [a]Ex 8:29 [b]Is 26:10 [1]Or *reverence* [2]Lit *before Yahweh God* **9:31** [a]Ru 1:22; 2:23 **9:33** [a]Ex 8:12; 9:29 [1]Lit *palms*

the [2]thunder and the hail ceased, and
rain [3]no longer poured on the earth.
**34** But Pharaoh saw that the rain and
the hail and the [1]thunder had ceased.
So he sinned again and [2]hardened
his heart with firmness, he and his
servants. **35** And Pharaoh's heart was
[1]hardened with strength, and he did
not let the sons of Israel go, just as
[a]Yahweh had spoken by the hand of
Moses.

### *The Plague of Locusts*

**10** Then Yahweh said to Moses,
"Come to Pharaoh, for [a]I have
[1]hardened his heart and the heart
of his servants with firmness, that I
may [2]set these signs of Mine [3]among
them, **2** and [a]that you may recount
in the [1]hearing of your son and of
your grandson, how I dealt severely
with the Egyptians, and how I [2]put
My signs among them, [b]that you may
know that I am Yahweh."

**3** Then Moses and Aaron came to
Pharaoh and said to him, "Thus says
Yahweh, the God of the Hebrews,
'How long will you refuse to [a]humble
yourself before Me? [b]Let My people
go, that they may serve Me. **4** For if
you refuse to let My people go, be-
hold, tomorrow I will bring locusts
into your territory. **5** And they shall
cover the [1]surface of the land, so
that no one will be able to see the
land. [a]They will also eat the rest of
what has escaped—what remains for
you from the hail—and they will eat
every tree which sprouts for you out
of the field. **6** Then [a]your houses and
the houses of all your servants and
the houses of all the Egyptians shall
be filled, *something* which neither
your fathers nor your grandfathers
have seen, from the day that they
[1]came upon the earth until this day.'"
And he turned and went out from
Pharaoh. **7** [a]And Pharaoh's servants
said to him, "How long will this man
be [b]a snare to us? Let the men go,
that they may serve Yahweh their
God. Do you not yet know that Egypt
is destroyed?" **8** So Moses and Aaron
[a]were brought back to Pharaoh, and
he said to them, "[b]Go, serve Yahweh
your God! [1]Who are the ones that are
going?" **9** And Moses said, "[a]We shall
go with our young and our old; with
our sons and our daughters, [b]with
our flocks and our herds we shall
go, for it is a feast of Yahweh for us."
**10** Then he said to them, "Thus may
Yahweh be with you, [1]if ever I let you
and your little ones go! See, for evil is
[2]on your faces. **11** Not so! Go now, the
men *among you*, and serve Yahweh,
for [1]that is what you are seeking." So
[a]they were driven out from Pharaoh's
presence.

**12** Then Yahweh said to Moses,
"[a]Stretch out your hand over the land
of Egypt for the locusts, that they
may come up on the land of Egypt
and [b]eat every plant of the land, all
that the hail has left remaining." **13** So
Moses stretched out his staff over the
land of Egypt, and Yahweh directed
an east wind on the land all that day

---

**9:33** [2]Lit *sounds* [3]Lit *was not poured* **9:34** [1]Lit *sounds* [2]Or *glorified*, cf. 14:4; lit *made heavy*
**9:35** [a]Ex 4:21 [1]Lit *strengthened* ◆**10:1** [a]Ex 4:21; 7:13; Jos 11:20; Jn 12:40; Ro 9:18 [1]Or *glorified*, cf. 14:4; lit *made heavy* [2]Or *perform* [3]Lit *in his midst* **10:2** [a]Ex 12:26, 27; 13:8, 14, 15; Dt 4:9; Ps 44:1; 78:5; Joel 1:3 [b]Ex 7:5, 17 [1]Lit *ears* [2]Or *perform* **10:3** [a]1Ki 21:29; 2Chr 34:27; Jas 4:10; 1Pe 5:6 [b]Ex 4:23
**10:5** [a]Joel 1:4; 2:25 [1]Lit *eye* **10:6** [a]Ex 8:3, 21 [1]Lit *were* **10:7** [a]Ex 7:5; 8:19; 12:33 [b]Ex 23:33; Jos 23:13; 1Sa 18:21; Ecc 7:26 **10:8** [a]Ex 8:8 [b]Ex 8:25 [1]Lit *Who and who are* **10:9** [a]Ex 12:37, 38 [b]Ex 10:26
**10:10** [1]Lit *when I* [2]Lit *before your face* **10:11** [a]Ex 10:28 [1]Lit *you seek it* **10:12** [a]Ex 7:19 [b]Ex 10:5, 15

and all that night; *and when* it was morning, the east wind [1]brought the [a]locusts. **14** [a]And the locusts came up over all the land of Egypt and rested on all the territory of Egypt; *they were* very heavy. There had never been so *many* [1]locusts, nor would there be so *many* [2]again. **15** For they covered the surface of the whole land, so that the land was darkened; and they [a]ate every plant of the land and all the fruit of the trees that the hail had left. Thus nothing green was left on tree or plant of the field through all the land of Egypt. **16** Then Pharaoh hurriedly [a]called for Moses and Aaron, and he said, "[b]I have sinned against Yahweh your God and against you. **17** So now, please forgive my sin only this once and [a]entreat Yahweh your God, that He would only cause this death to depart from me." **18** [a]And he went out from Pharaoh and entreated Yahweh. **19** So Yahweh changed *the wind* to a very strong west wind which took up the locusts and drove them into the [1]Red Sea; not one locust remained in all the territory of Egypt. **20** But [a]Yahweh [1]hardened Pharaoh's heart with strength, and he did not let the sons of Israel go.

### The Plague of Darkness

**21** Then Yahweh said to Moses, "[a]Stretch out your hand toward the sky, that there may be darkness over the land of Egypt, even a darkness [b]which may be felt." **22** So Moses stretched out his hand toward the sky, and there was [a]thick darkness in all the land of Egypt for three days. **23** They did not see one another, nor did anyone rise from his place for three days, [a]but all the sons of Israel had light in their *places of* habitation. **24** Then Pharaoh [a]called to Moses and said, "Go, serve Yahweh; only let your flocks and your herds be detained. Even [b]your little ones may go with you." **25** But Moses said, "You must also [1]let us have in our hand sacrifices and burnt offerings, that we may [2]sacrifice *them* to Yahweh our God. **26** [a]Therefore, our livestock too shall go with us; not a hoof shall remain behind, for we shall take some of them to serve Yahweh our God. And until we come there, we ourselves do not know with what we shall serve Yahweh." **27** But [a]Yahweh [1]hardened Pharaoh's heart with strength, and he was not willing to let them go. **28** Then Pharaoh said to him, "[a]Get away from me! [1]Beware, do not see my face again, for in the day you see my face you shall die!" **29** And Moses said, "As you have spoken; [a]I shall never see your face again!"

### Yahweh Says One More Plague

**11** Then Yahweh said to Moses, "One more plague I will bring on Pharaoh and on Egypt; [a]after that he will let you go from here. When he lets you go, he will surely drive you out from here completely. **2** Speak now in the [1]hearing of the people so that [a]each man may ask from his

***10:13*** [a]*Ps 78:46; 105:34* [1]Lit *carried* **10:14** [a]Dt 28:38; Ps 78:46; 105:34; Joel 1:4, 7; 2:1-11; Rev 9:3 [1]Lit *locusts like them before them* [2]Lit *after them* **10:15** [a]Ex 10:5; Ps 105:34f **10:16** [a]Ex 8:8 [b]Ex 9:27 **10:17** [a]Ex 8:8, 28; 9:28; 1Ki 13:6 **10:18** [a]Ex 8:30 **10:19** [1]Lit *Sea of Reeds* **10:20** [a]Ex 4:21; 11:10 [1]Lit *strengthened* **10:21** [a]Ex 9:22 [b]Dt 28:29 **10:22** [a]Ps 105:28; Rev 16:10 **10:23** [a]Ex 8:22 **10:24** [a]Ex 8:8, 25 [b]Ex 10:10 **10:25** [1]Lit *give into* [2]Lit *make* **10:26** [a]Ex 10:9 **10:27** [a]Ex 4:21; 10:20; 14:4, 8 [1]Lit *strengthened* **10:28** [a]Ex 10:11 [1]Lit *Take heed to yourself* **10:29** [a]Ex 11:8; Heb 11:27 ◆ **11:1** [a]Ex 12:31, 33, 39 **11:2** [a]Ex 3:22; 12:35, 36 [1]Lit *ears*

neighbor and each woman from her
neighbor for articles of silver and
articles of gold." **3** [a](And Yahweh
gave the people favor in the sight of
the Egyptians. [b]Moreover, the man
Moses *himself* was very great in the
land of Egypt, *both* in the sight of
Pharaoh's servants and in the sight
of the people.)
**4** So Moses said, "Thus says Yah-
weh, 'About [a]midnight I am going out
into the midst of Egypt, **5** and [a]all the
firstborn in the land of Egypt shall
die, from the firstborn of the Pharaoh
who sits on his throne, even to the
firstborn of the servant-girl who is
behind the millstones; and all the
firstborn of the cattle. **6** Moreover,
there shall be [a]a great cry in all the
land of Egypt, such as there has not
been *before* and such as shall never
be again. **7** [a]But for any of the sons
of Israel a dog will not *even* [1]bark,
whether against man or beast,
that you may know how Yahweh
makes a distinction between Egypt
and Israel.' **8** [a]Then all these your
servants will come down to me and
bow themselves [1]before me, saying,
'Go out, you and all the people who
[2]follow you,' and after that I will go
out." [b]And he went out from Pharaoh
in hot anger.
**9** Then Yahweh said to Moses,
"[a]Pharaoh will not listen to you, so
[b]that My miraculous wonders will
be multiplied in the land of Egypt."
**10** [a]Now Moses and Aaron did all
these miraculous wonders before
Pharaoh; yet [b]Yahweh [1]hardened
Pharaoh's heart with strength, and
he did not let the sons of Israel go
out of his land.

### *The Passover Lamb*

**12** Now Yahweh said to Moses
and Aaron in the land of
[1]Egypt, **2** "[a]This month shall be the
beginning of months for you; it is
to be the first month of the year to
you. **3** Speak to all the congregation
of Israel, saying, 'On the tenth of this
month they are each one to take a
[1]lamb for themselves, according to
their fathers' households, a [1]lamb
for [2]each household. **4** Now if the
household is too small for a [1]lamb,
then he and his neighbor nearest to
his house are to take one according
to the [2]number of persons *in them*;
according to [3]what each man should
eat, you are to [4]apportion the lamb.
**5** Your [1]lamb shall be [a]a male, with-
out blemish, a year old; you may take
it from the sheep or from the goats.
**6** [1]And you shall keep it until the
[a]fourteenth day of the same month,
then the whole assembly of the con-
gregation of Israel shall slaughter it
[b,2]at twilight. **7** [a]Moreover, they shall
take some of the blood and put it on
the two doorposts and on the lintel
[1]of the houses in which they eat it.
**8** And they shall eat the flesh [a]that
night, [b]roasted with fire, and they
shall eat it with [c]unleavened bread

**11:3** [a]Ex 3:21; 12:36; Ps 106:46 [b]Dt 34:10-12 **11:4** [a]Ex 12:29 **11:5** [a]Ex 12:12, 29; Ps 78:51; 105:36; 135:8; 136:10 **11:6** [a]Ex 12:30 **11:7** [a]Ex 8:22; Jos 10:21 [1]Lit *sharpen his tongue* **11:8** [a]Ex 12:31-33 [b]Heb 11:27 [1]Lit *to* [2]Lit *are at your feet* **11:9** [a]Ex 7:4 [b]Ex 7:3 **11:10** [a]Ex 4:21 [b]Ex 7:3; 9:12; 10:20, 27; Jos 11:20; Is 63:17; Jn 12:40 [1]Lit *strengthened* ◆ **12:1** [1]Lit *Egypt, saying* **12:2** [a]Ex 13:4; 23:15; 34:18; Dt 16:1 **12:3** [1]Or *kid* [2]Lit *the* **12:4** [1]Or *kid* [2]Or *amount* [3]Lit *each man's eating* [4]Lit *compute for* **12:5** [a]Lv 22:18-21; 23:12; Heb 9:14; 1Pe 1:19 [1]Or *kid* **12:6** [a]Ex 12:14, 17; Lv 23:5; Nu 9:1-3, 11; 28:16 [b]Ex 16:12; Dt 16:4, 6 [1]Lit *It shall be to you for a guarding* [2]Lit *between the two evenings* **12:7** [a]Ex 12:22 [1]Lit *upon* **12:8** [a]Ex 34:25; Nu 9:12 [b]Dt 16:7 [c]Dt 16:3, 4; 1Co 5:8

[d,1]and bitter herbs. **9** Do not eat any
of it raw or boiled at all with water,
but rather [a]roasted with fire, *both*
its head and its legs along with [b]its
entrails. **10** [a]And you shall not leave
any of it over until morning, but
whatever is left of it until morning,
you shall burn with fire. **11** Now you
shall eat it in this manner: *with* your
loins girded, your sandals on your
feet, and your staff in your hand;
and you shall eat it in haste—it is
[a]the Passover of Yahweh. **12** And [a]I
will go through the land of Egypt on
that night and will strike down all
the firstborn in the land of Egypt,
both man and beast; and [b]against
all the gods of Egypt I will execute
judgments—[c]I am Yahweh. **13** [a]And
the blood shall be a sign for you on
the houses where you are; and I will
see the blood, and I will pass over
you, and there shall be no plague
among you [1]to destroy *you* when I
strike the land of Egypt.

### *The Feast of Unleavened Bread*

**14** 'Now [a]this day will be [b]a memorial
to you, and you shall celebrate it *as*
a feast to Yahweh; throughout your
generations you are to celebrate it *as*
[c,1]a perpetual statute. **15** [a]Seven days
you shall eat unleavened bread, but on
the first day you shall [1]remove leaven
from your houses; for whoever eats
anything leavened from the first day
until the seventh day, [b]that [2]person
shall be cut off from Israel. **16** [a]Now
on the first day there shall be a holy
convocation, and on the seventh day
there shall be a holy convocation for
you; no work at all shall be done on
them, except what must be eaten [1]by
every person, that alone may be done
by you. **17** You shall also keep [a]the
*Feast of* Unleavened Bread, for on this
[b]very day I brought your hosts out
of the land of Egypt; therefore you
shall keep this day throughout your
generations as [c,1]a perpetual statute.
**18** [a]In the first *month*, on the four-
teenth day of the month at evening,
you shall eat unleavened bread until
the twenty-first day of the month at
evening. **19** [a]Seven days there shall
be no leaven found in your houses;
for whoever eats what is leavened,
that [b,1]person shall be cut off from
the congregation of Israel, whether
*he is* a sojourner or a native of the
land. **20** You shall not eat anything
leavened; in all your *places of* habita-
tion you shall eat unleavened bread.'"

**21** Then [a]Moses called for all the
elders of Israel and said to them,
"[1]Bring out and [b]take for yourselves
[2]lambs according to your families
and slaughter [c]the Passover *lamb*.
**22** [a]And you shall take a bunch of
hyssop and dip it in the blood which
is in the basin, and [1]touch some of
the blood that is in the basin to the
lintel and the two doorposts; and
none of you shall go outside the
doorway of his house until morning.
**23** And [a]Yahweh will pass through

---

**12:8** [d]Nu 9:11 [1]Lit *in addition to* **12:9** [a]Ex 12:8 [b]Ex 29:13, 17, 22 **12:10** [a]Ex 16:19; 23:18; 34:25 **12:11** [a]Ex 12:13, 21, 27, 43 **12:12** [a]Ex 11:4, 5 [b]Nu 33:4; Ps 82:1 [c]Ex 6:2 **12:13** [a]Heb 11:28 [1]Lit *for destruction* **12:14** [a]Ex 12:6; Lv 23:4, 5; 2Ki 23:21 [b]Ex 13:9 [c]Ex 12:17, 24; 13:10 [1]Or *an eternal* **12:15** [a]Ex 13:6, 7; 23:15; 34:18; Lv 23:6; Nu 28:17; Dt 16:3, 8 [b]Ge 17:14; Ex 12:19; Nu 9:13 [1]Lit *cause to cease* [2]Lit *soul* **12:16** [a]Lv 23:7, 8; Nu 28:18, 25 [1]Lit *pertaining to* **12:17** [a]Dt 16:3-8 [b]Ex 12:41 [c]Ex 12:14; 13:3, 10 [1]Or *an eternal* **12:18** [a]Ex 12:2; Lv 23:5-8; Nu 28:16-25 **12:19** [a]Ex 12:15; 23:15; 34:18 [b]Nu 9:13 [1]Lit *soul* **12:21** [a]Nu 9:4; Heb 11:28 [b]Ex 12:3 [c]Ex 12:11 [1]Lit *Draw out* [2]Lit *sheep* **12:22** [a]Ex 12:7 [1]Lit *cause to touch* **12:23** [a]Ex 11:4; 12:12, 13

to smite the Egyptians; and He will
see the blood on the lintel and on
the two doorposts, and Yahweh
will pass over the doorway and will
[b]not allow the [c]destroyer to come
into your houses to smite *you*. **24** And
[a]you shall keep this event as a statute
for you and your children forever.
**25** And it will be, when you enter the
land which Yahweh will give you, as
He has [1]promised, you shall keep this
*new* [2]slavery. **26** [a]And it will be when
your children say to you, '[1]What is
the meaning of this *new* slavery to
you?' **27** that you shall say, 'It is a
Passover sacrifice to [a]Yahweh who
passed over the houses of the sons
of Israel in Egypt when He smote
the Egyptians, but delivered our
homes.'" [b]And the people bowed
low and worshiped.

**28** Then the sons of Israel went and
did *so*; just as Yahweh had command-
ed Moses and Aaron, so they did.

### *Death of the Firstborn of Egypt*

**29** Now it happened at [a]midnight that
[b]Yahweh struck all [c]the firstborn in
the land of Egypt, from the firstborn
of Pharaoh who sat on his throne to
the firstborn of the captive who was
in the [1]dungeon, and all the firstborn
of [d]cattle. **30** Then Pharaoh arose in
the night, he and all his servants and
all the Egyptians, and there was [a]a
great cry in Egypt, for there was no
home where there was not someone
dead. **31** Then [a]he called for Moses
and Aaron at night and said, "Rise up,
[b]get out from among my people, both
you and the sons of Israel; and go,
[1]serve Yahweh, as you have spoken.
**32** Take [a]both your flocks and your
herds, as you have spoken, and go,
and bless me also."

### *Israel Goes Out from Egypt*

**33** [a]And the Egyptians strongly
pressed the people to send them
out of the land in haste, for they
said, "We will all be dead." **34** So the
people took up [a]their dough before
it was leavened, *with* their kneading
bowls bound up in the clothes on
their shoulders.

**35** [a]Now the sons of Israel had
done according to the word of
Moses—they had asked from the
Egyptians for articles of silver and
articles of gold, and clothing; **36** and
Yahweh had given the people favor
in the sight of the Egyptians, so that
they let them have what they asked.
Thus they [a]plundered the Egyptians.

**37** And the [a]sons of Israel jour-
neyed from [b]Rameses to Succoth,
about [c]six hundred thousand men
on foot, aside from the little ones.
**38** A [a,1]foreign multitude also went
up with them, [2]along with flocks and
herds, a [b]very [3]large number of live-
stock. **39** And they baked the dough
which they had brought out of Egypt
into cakes of unleavened bread. For it
had not become leavened, since they
were [a]driven out of Egypt and could

---

**12:23** [b]Rev 7:3; 9:4 [c]1Co 10:10; Heb 11:28 **12:24** [a]Ex 12:14, 17; 13:5, 10 **12:25** [1]Lit *spoken* [2]Or *service*
**12:26** [a]Ex 10:2; 13:8, 14, 15; Dt 32:7; Jos 4:6; Ps 78:6 [1]Lit *What is this service to you?* **12:27** [a]Ex 12:11
[b]Ex 4:31 **12:29** [a]Ex 11:4, 5 [b]Nu 8:17; 33:4; Ps 135:8; 136:10 [c]Ex 4:23; Ps 78:51; 105:36 [d]Ex 9:6 [1]Lit *house of the pit*, cf. Ge 37:20; 40:15 **12:30** [a]Ex 11:6 **12:31** [a]Ex 8:8 [b]Ex 8:25 [1]Or *worship* **12:32** [a]Ex 10:9, 26 **12:33** [a]Ex 10:7; 11:1; 12:39; Ps 105:38 **12:34** [a]Ex 12:39 **12:35** [a]Ex 3:21, 22; 11:2, 3; Ps 105:37
**12:36** [a]Ex 3:22 **12:37** [a]Nu 33:3, 5 [b]Ge 47:11 [c]Ex 38:26; Nu 1:46; 2:32; 11:21; 26:51 **12:38** [a]Nu 11:4
[b]Ex 17:3; Nu 20:19; 32:1; Dt 3:19 [1]Or *mixed*, cf. Ne 13:3; Jer 25:20; 50:37 [2]Lit *and* [3]Or *glorious*, cf. 9:24; lit *heavy* **12:39** [a]Ex 6:1; 11:1; 12:31-33

not delay, nor had they [1]prepared any provisions for themselves.

**40** Now the time [1]that the sons of Israel lived in Egypt was [a]430 years. **41** And it happened at the end of 430 years, [1]to [a]the very day, that [b]all the hosts of Yahweh went out from the land of Egypt. **42** [a]It is a night to be kept for Yahweh for having brought them out from the land of Egypt; this night is for Yahweh, to be kept [1]by all the sons of Israel throughout their generations.

### *The Statute of the Passover*

**43** And Yahweh said to Moses and Aaron, "This is the statute of [a]the Passover: no [b,1]foreigner shall eat of it; **44** but every man's [a]slave purchased with money, after you have circumcised him, then he may eat of it. **45** [a]A foreign resident or a hired person shall not eat of it. **46** It shall be eaten in a single house; you shall not bring forth any of the flesh outside of the house, [a]and you shall not break any bone of it. **47** [a]All the congregation of Israel shall [1]celebrate this. **48** But [a]if a sojourner sojourns with you and [1]celebrates the Passover to Yahweh, let all his males be circumcised, and then let him come near to [2]celebrate it; and he shall be like a native of the land. But no uncircumcised person may eat of it. **49** [a,1]The same law shall [2]apply to the native as to the sojourner who sojourns among you."

**50** So all the sons of Israel did; as Yahweh had commanded Moses and Aaron, thus they did. **51** And on that same day [a]Yahweh brought the sons of Israel out of the land of Egypt [b,1]by their hosts.

### *Sanctifying the Firstborn*

**13** Then Yahweh spoke to Moses, saying, **2** "[a]Sanctify to Me every firstborn, the first [1]offspring of every womb among the sons of Israel, both of man and beast; it belongs to Me."

### *The Feast of Unleavened Bread*

**3** And Moses said to the people, "[a]Remember this day in which you went out from Egypt, from the house of [1]slavery; for [b]by a strong hand Yahweh brought you out from this place. [c]And nothing leavened shall be eaten. **4** This day, in the [a]month of Abib, you are going out. **5** And it shall be when Yahweh [a]brings you to the land of the Canaanite, the Hittite, the Amorite, the Hivite, and the Jebusite, which [b]He swore to your fathers to give you, a land flowing with milk and honey, [c]that you shall [1]do this service in this month. **6** For [a]seven days you shall eat unleavened bread, and on the seventh day *there shall be* a feast to Yahweh. **7** Unleavened bread shall be eaten throughout the seven days; and [a]nothing leavened shall be seen [1]among you, nor shall any leaven be seen [1]among you in all your borders.

---

**12:39** [1]Lit *made* **12:40** [a]Ge 15:13, 16; Ac 7:6; Ga 3:17 [1]Or *of the sons of Israel who dwelt* **12:41** [a]Ex 12:17 [b]Ex 3:8, 10; 6:6 [1]Lit *that it happened on this very day* **12:42** [a]Ex 13:10; 34:18; Dt 16:1 [1]Lit *to the sons* **12:43** [a]Ex 12:11; Nu 9:14 [b]Ex 12:48 [1]Lit *son of a stranger* **12:44** [a]Ge 17:12, 13; Lv 22:11 **12:45** [a]Lv 22:10 **12:46** [a]Nu 9:12; Ps 34:20; Jn 19:33, 36 **12:47** [a]Ex 12:6; Nu 9:13, 14 [1]Lit *do* **12:48** [a]Nu 9:14 [1]Lit *does* [2]Lit *do* **12:49** [a]Lv 24:22; Nu 15:15, 16, 29 [1]Lit *One law* [2]Lit *be* **12:51** [a]Ex 12:41 [b]Ex 6:26 [1]Lit *according to* ◆ **13:2** [a]Ex 13:12, 13, 15; 22:29; Lv 27:26; Nu 3:13; 8:16f; 18:15; Dt 15:19; Lk 2:23 [1]Lit *opening* **13:3** [a]Ex 12:42; Dt 16:3 [b]Ex 3:20; 6:1 [c]Ex 12:19 [1]Lit *slaves* **13:4** [a]Ex 12:2; 23:15; 34:18; Dt 16:1 **13:5** [a]Ex 3:8, 17; Jos 24:11 [b]Ex 6:8 [c]Ex 12:25 [1]Lit *serve this service* **13:6** [a]Ex 12:15-20 **13:7** [a]Ex 12:19 [1]Lit *to*

**8** [a]And you shall tell your son on that
day, saying, 'It is because of what
Yahweh did for me when I came out
of Egypt.' **9** And [a]it will be as a sign to
you on your hand and as a memorial
between your eyes, that the law of
Yahweh may be in your mouth; for
with [b]a strong hand Yahweh brought
you out of Egypt. **10** Therefore, you
shall [a]keep this statute at its appoint-
ed time from [1]year to year.

**11** "And it will be when [a]Yahweh
brings you to the land of the Ca-
naanite, as [b]He swore to you and
to your fathers, and gives it to you,
**12** [a]and you shall [1]devote to Yahweh
the first [2]offspring of every womb
and [3]the first offspring of every beast
that you own; the males belong to
Yahweh. **13** But [a]every first [1]offspring
of a donkey you shall redeem with
a lamb, but if you do not redeem *it*,
then you shall break its neck; and
[b]every firstborn of man among your
sons you shall redeem. **14** [a]And it
will be when your son asks you in
time to come, saying, 'What is this?'
then you shall say to him, '[b]With a
strong hand Yahweh brought us out
of Egypt, from the house of [1]slavery.
**15** And it happened, when Pharaoh
hardened *his heart* with stiffness
about letting us go, that [a]Yahweh
killed every firstborn in the land of
Egypt, both the firstborn of man and
the firstborn of beast. Therefore, I
sacrifice to Yahweh the males, the
first [1]offspring of every womb, but
every firstborn of my sons I redeem.'
**16** So [a]it will be as a sign on your hand
and as [1]phylacteries between your
eyes, for with a strong hand Yahweh
brought us out of Egypt."

### *Pillars of Cloud and Fire*

**17** Now it happened that when Phar-
aoh had let the people go, God did
not guide them by the way of the land
of the Philistines, even though it was
near; for God said, "[a]Lest the people
change their minds when they see
war, and return to Egypt." **18** Hence
God turned the people to the way of
the wilderness to the [1]Red Sea; and
the sons of Israel went up [a]in battle
array from the land of Egypt. **19** And
Moses took [a]the bones of Joseph
with him, for he had made the sons
of Israel solemnly swear, saying, "God
will surely [1]take care of you, and you
shall bring up my bones from here
with you." **20** Then they set out from
[a]Succoth and camped in Etham on
the edge of the wilderness. **21** [a]And
Yahweh was going before them in a
pillar of cloud by day to guide them
on the way, and in a pillar of fire by
night to give them light, that they
might go by day and by night. **22** [1]He
[a]did not take away the pillar of cloud
by day, nor the pillar of fire by night,
from before the people.

---

**13:8** [a]Ex 10:2; 12:26f; 13:14; Ps 44:1 **13:9** [a]Ex 12:14; 13:16; Nu 15:39; Dt 6:8; 11:18 [b]Ex 13:3 **13:10** [a]Ex 12:24, 25; 13:5 [1]Lit *days to days* **13:11** [a]Ex 13:5 [b]Ge 15:18; 17:8; 28:15; Ps 105:42-45 **13:12** [a]Ex 13:1, 2; 22:29; 34:19; Lv 27:26; Nu 18:15; Eze 44:30; Lk 2:23 [1]Lit *cause to pass over* [2]Lit *opening* [3]Lit *every issue the offspring of a beast* **13:13** [a]Ex 34:20; Nu 18:15 [b]Nu 3:46 [1]Lit *opening* **13:14** [a]Ex 10:2; 12:26, 27; 13:8; Dt 6:20; Jos 4:6, 21 [b]Ex 13:3, 9 [1]Lit *slaves* **13:15** [a]Ex 12:29 [1]Lit *opening* **13:16** [a]Ex 13:9; Dt 6:8 [1]Or *frontlet-bands* **13:17** [a]Ex 14:11, 12; Nu 14:1-4; Dt 17:16 **13:18** [a]Jos 1:14; 4:12, 13 [1]Lit *Sea of Reeds* **13:19** [a]Ge 50:24, 25; Jos 24:32; Ac 7:15, 16 [1]Lit *visit* **13:20** [a]Ex 12:37; Nu 33:6 **13:21** [a]Ex 14:19, 24; 33:9, 10; Nu 9:15; 14:14; Dt 1:33; Ne 9:12; Ps 78:14; 99:7; 105:39; Is 4:5; 1Co 10:1 **13:22** [a]Ne 9:19 [1]Or *The pillar of cloud by day and the pillar of fire by night did not depart*

### *Israel Crosses the Red Sea*

**14** Now Yahweh spoke to Moses, saying, **2** "Speak to the sons of Israel so that they turn back and camp before [a]Pi-hahiroth, between [b]Migdol and the sea; you shall camp in front of Baal-zephon, opposite it, by the sea. **3** And Pharaoh will say of the sons of Israel, 'They are wandering in confusion in the land; the wilderness has shut them in.' **4** Thus [a]I will [1]harden Pharaoh's heart with strength, and [b]he will pursue them; and I will be glorified through Pharaoh and all his army, so that [c]the Egyptians will know that I am Yahweh." And they did so.

**5** Then the king of Egypt was told that the people had fled, and the heart of Pharaoh and his servants was changed toward the people, and they said, "What is this we have done, that we have let Israel go from serving us?" **6** So he made his chariot ready and took his people with him; **7** and he took six hundred choice chariots and all the *other* chariots of Egypt with officers over all of them. **8** [a]And Yahweh [1]hardened the heart of Pharaoh, king of Egypt, with strength, and he pursued the sons of Israel as the sons of Israel were going out with an [b,2]exalted hand. **9** Then [a]the Egyptians pursued them *with* all the horses *and* chariots of Pharaoh, his horsemen and his army, and they overtook them camping by the sea, [b]beside Pi-hahiroth, in front of Baal-zephon.

**10** Now Pharaoh drew near, and the sons of Israel lifted up their eyes, and behold, the Egyptians were marching after them, and they became very afraid; [a]so the sons of Israel cried out to Yahweh. **11** Then [a]they said to Moses, "Is it because there were no graves in Egypt that you have taken us away to die in the wilderness? What is this you have done against us in [1]bringing us out of Egypt? **12** [a]Is this not the word that we spoke to you in Egypt, saying, '[1]Leave us alone that we may serve the Egyptians'? For it would have been better for us to serve the Egyptians than for us to die in the wilderness." **13** But Moses said to the people, "[a]Do not fear! [1]Stand by and see [b]the salvation of Yahweh which He will accomplish for you today; for the Egyptians whom you have seen today, you will never see them again forever. **14** [a]Yahweh will fight for you, and [b]you will keep silent."

**15** Then Yahweh said to Moses, "Why are you crying out to Me? Speak to the sons of Israel so that they go forward. **16** As for you, raise up [a]your staff and stretch out your hand over the sea and split it, and the sons of Israel shall [1]go through the midst of the sea on dry land. **17** As for Me, behold, [a]I will [1]harden the hearts of the Egyptians with strength so that they will go in after them; and I will be glorified through Pharaoh and all his army, through his chariots and his horsemen. **18** [a]Then the Egyptians will know that I am

---

◆ ***14:2*** [a]*Nu 33:7* [b]*Jer 44:1* **14:4** [a]Ex 4:21; 7:3; 14:17 [b]Ex 14:23 [c]Ex 7:5; 14:25 [1]Lit *strengthen*
**14:8** [a]Ex 14:4 [b]Nu 33:3; Ac 13:17 [1]Lit *strengthened* [2]Lit *high hand* **14:9** [a]Ex 15:9; Jos 24:6 [b]Ex 14:2
**14:10** [a]Jos 24:7; Ne 9:9; Ps 34:17; 107:6 **14:11** [a]Ex 5:21; 15:24; 16:2; Ps 106:7, 8 [1]Lit *so as to bring*
**14:12** [a]Ex 6:9 [1]Lit *Cease from us* **14:13** [a]Ge 15:1; 46:3; Ex 20:20; 2Chr 20:15, 17; Is 41:10, 13, 14 [b]Ex 14:30; 15:2 [1]Or *Take your stand* **14:14** [a]Ex 14:25; 15:3; Dt 1:30; 3:22; Jos 23:3; 2Chr 20:29; Ne 4:20 [b]Is 30:15
**14:16** [a]Ex 4:17, 20; 7:19; 14:21, 26; 17:5, 6, 9; Nu 20:8, 9, 11; Is 10:26 [1]Lit *enter the* **14:17** [a]Ex 14:4, 8 [1]Lit *strengthen* **14:18** [a]Ex 14:25

Yahweh, when I am glorified through
Pharaoh, through his chariots and
his horsemen."
**19** [a]Then the angel of God, who had
been going before the camp of Israel,
moved and went behind them; and
the pillar of cloud moved from before
them and stood behind them. **20** So it
came between the camp of Egypt and
the camp of Israel; and there was the
cloud [1]along with the darkness, yet it
gave light at night. Thus the one did
not come near the other all night.
**21** [a]Then Moses stretched out
his hand over the sea; and Yahweh
[1]swept the sea *back* by a strong east
wind all night and made the sea into
[b]dry ground, so [c]the waters were
split. **22** [a]So the sons of Israel [1]went
through the midst of the sea on the
dry land, and [b]the waters *were* a wall
to them on their right hand and on
their left. **23** Then [a]the Egyptians pur-
sued *them*, and all Pharaoh's horses,
his chariots and his horsemen went
in after them into the midst of the
sea. **24** Then at the morning watch,
[a]Yahweh looked down on the camp
of the Egyptians [1]through the pillar
of fire and cloud and brought the
camp of the Egyptians into confu-
sion. **25** And He [1]caused their chariot
wheels to swerve, and He made them
drive with difficulty; so the Egyptians
said, "Let [2]us flee from Israel, [a]for
Yahweh is fighting for them against
the Egyptians."
**26** Then Yahweh said to Moses,
"[a]Stretch out your hand over the
sea so that the waters may come
back over the Egyptians, over their
chariots and their horsemen." **27** So
Moses stretched out his hand over
the sea, and [a]the sea returned to its
normal state at daybreak while the
Egyptians were fleeing [1]right into it;
then Yahweh [b,2]overthrew the Egyp-
tians in the midst of the sea. **28** And
the waters returned and covered the
chariots and the horsemen, [1]even
Pharaoh's entire army that had gone
into the sea after them; [a]not even
one of them remained. **29** But the
sons of Israel walked on [a]dry land
through the midst of the sea, and the
waters *were* a wall to them on their
right hand and on their left.
**30** [a]Thus Yahweh saved Israel that
day from the hand of the Egyptians,
and Israel [b]saw the Egyptians dead on
the seashore. **31** Then Israel saw the
great hand which Yahweh had [1]used
against the Egyptians; and the people
[2]feared Yahweh, and [a]they believed
in Yahweh and in His servant Moses.

### *The Song of Moses and Israel*

**15** [a]Then Moses and the sons of
Israel sang this song to Yahweh
[1]and said,

"[b,2]I will sing to Yahweh,
for He [3]is highly exalted;
[c]The horse and its rider He
has hurled into the sea.

**14:19** [a]Ex 13:21, 22 **14:20** [1]Lit *and the darkness* **14:21** [a]Ex 7:19; 14:16 [b]Ps 66:6; 106:9; 136:13, 14 [c]Ex 15:8; Jos 3:16; 4:23; Ne 9:11; Ps 74:13; 78:13; 114:3, 5; Is 63:12, 13 [1]Lit *caused to go* **14:22** [a]Ex 15:19; Jos 3:17; 4:22; Ne 9:11; Ps 66:6; 78:13; Heb 11:29 [b]Ex 14:29; 15:8 [1]Lit *entered the* **14:23** [a]Ex 14:4, 17 **14:24** [a]Ex 13:21 [1]Or *in* **14:25** [a]Ex 14:4, 14, 18 [1]Or *removed* [2]Lit *me* **14:26** [a]Ex 14:16 **14:27** [a]Jos 4:18 [b]Ex 15:1, 7; Dt 11:4; Ne 9:11; Ps 78:53; Heb 11:29 [1]Lit *to meet it* [2]Lit *shook off* **14:28** [a]Ps 78:53; 106:11 [1]Lit *in respect to* **14:29** [a]Ex 14:22; Ps 66:6; Is 11:15 **14:30** [a]Ex 14:13; Ps 106:8, 10; Is 63:8, 11 [b]Ps 58:10; 59:10 **14:31** [a]Ex 4:31; 19:9; Ps 106:12; Jn 2:11; 11:45 [1]Lit *done* [2]Or *reverenced* ◆ **15:1** [a]Ps 106:12; Rev 15:3 [b]Is 12:5; 42:10-12 [c]Jer 51:21 [1]Lit *and said, saying* [2]Or *Let me sing* [3]Or *triumphed gloriously*

2 “[a,1]Yah is my strength
and song,
And He has become
my salvation;
[b]This is my God,
and I will praise Him;
[c]My father’s God,
and I will [d]extol Him.
3 “[a]Yahweh is a warrior;
[b]Yahweh is His name.
4 “[a]Pharaoh’s chariots
and his army He has
cast into the sea;
And the choicest
of his officers are sunk
in the [1]Red Sea.
5 “The deeps cover them;
[a]They went down into
the depths like a stone.
6 “[a]Your right hand, O Yahweh,
is majestic in power,
[b]Your right hand, O Yahweh,
shatters the enemy.
7 “And in the greatness
of Your [1]exaltation
You [a]pull down those
who rise up against You;
[b]You send forth Your
burning anger, *and* it
[c]devours them as chaff.
8 “[a]And at the blast of Your
nostrils the waters
were piled up,
[b]The flowing waters
stood up like a heap;
The deeps were congealed
in the heart of the sea.
9 “[a]The enemy said,
‘I will pursue, I will overtake,
I will [b]divide the spoil;
My [1]desire shall be
fulfilled against them;
I will draw out my sword,
my hand will
dispossess them.’
10 “[a]You blew with Your wind,
the sea covered them;
[b]They sank like lead
in the [1]mighty waters.
11 “[a]Who is like You among
the gods, O Yahweh?
Who is like You,
[b]majestic in holiness,
[c]Fearsome in praises,
[d]working wonders?
12 “[a]You stretched out
Your right hand,
The earth swallowed them.
13 “In Your lovingkindness You
have [a]guided the people
whom You have [b]redeemed;
In Your strength You
have led *them* [c]to Your
holy habitation.
14 “[a]The peoples have heard,
they tremble;
Anguish has seized the
inhabitants of Philistia.
15 “Then the [a]chiefs of Edom
were dismayed;
[b]The leaders of Moab,
trembling seizes them;
[c]All the inhabitants
of Canaan have melted away.

---

**15:2** [a]Ps 18:1, 2; Is 12:2; Hab 3:18f [b]Ps 48:14 [c]Ex 3:6, 15, 16 [d]2Sa 22:47; Ps 99:5; Is 25:1 [1]The shortened form of Yahweh, found in poetry and praise (e.g. Hallel*ujah*), and in names (e.g. Zechar*iah*)
**15:3** [a]Ex 14:14; Rev 19:11 [b]Ex 3:15; 6:2, 3, 7, 8; Ps 24:8; 83:18 **15:4** [a]Ex 14:6, 7, 17, 28 [1]Lit *Sea of Reeds*
**15:5** [a]Ex 15:10; Ne 9:11 **15:6** [a]Ex 3:20; 6:1 [b]Ps 118:15, 16 **15:7** [a]Ex 14:27 [b]Ps 78:49, 50 [c]Dt 4:24; Is 5:24; Heb 12:29 [1]Or *loftiness* **15:8** [a]Ex 14:22, 29; Job 4:9 [b]Ps 78:13 **15:9** [a]Ex 14:5, 8, 9 [b]Jdg 5:30; Is 53:12; Lk 11:22 [1]Lit *soul* **15:10** [a]Ex 14:27, 28 [b]Ex 15:5 [1]Or *majestic* **15:11** [a]Ex 8:10; 9:14; Dt 3:24; 2Sa 7:22; 1Ki 8:23; Ps 71:19; 86:8; Mic 7:18 [b]Is 6:3; Rev 4:8 [c]Ps 22:23 [d]Ps 72:18; 136:4
**15:12** [a]Ex 15:6 **15:13** [a]Ne 9:12; Ps 77:20 [b]Ex 15:16; Ps 77:15 [c]Ex 15:17; Ps 78:54 **15:14** [a]Dt 2:25; Hab 3:7
**15:15** [a]Ge 36:15, 40 [b]Nu 22:3, 4 [c]Jos 2:9, 11, 24; 5:1

16 “[a]Terror and dread
fall upon them;
[b]By the greatness of Your
arm they are still as stone;
Until Your people pass
over, O Yahweh,
Until the people pass
over whom You
[c]have purchased.
17 “[a]You will bring them
and [b]plant them
in [c]the mountain
of Your inheritance,
[d]The place, O Yahweh,
which You have made
for You to inhabit,
[e]The sanctuary, O Lord,
which Your hands
have established.
18 “[a]Yahweh shall reign
forever and ever.”

19 [a]For the horses of Pharaoh with
his chariots and his horsemen went
into the sea, and Yahweh brought
back the waters of the sea on them,
but the sons of Israel walked on [b]dry
land through the midst of the sea.

20 [a]And Miriam the prophetess,
Aaron’s sister, took the [b]tambourine
in her hand, and all the women went
out after her with tambourines and
with [c,1]dancing. 21 And Miriam an-
swered them,

“[a]Sing to Yahweh,
for He [1]is highly exalted;
The horse and his rider He
has hurled into the sea.”

### *Yahweh Sweetens the Water*

22 [a]Then Moses [1]had Israel set out
from the [2]Red Sea, and they went
out into [b]the wilderness of [c]Shur;
and they went three days in the wil-
derness and found no water. 23 And
they came to [a]Marah, but they could
not drink the waters [1]of Marah, for
they were [2]bitter; therefore it was
named [3]Marah. 24 So the people
[a]grumbled at Moses, saying, “What
shall we drink?” 25 Then he [a]cried
out to Yahweh, and Yahweh showed
him [b]a tree; and he threw *it* into the
waters, and the waters became sweet.

There He [c]set for them a statute
and a judgment, and there He
[d]tested them. 26 And He said, “[a]If
you will earnestly listen to the voice
of Yahweh your God, and do what
is right in His sight, and give ear [b]to
His commandments, and keep all
His statutes, [c]I will put none of the
diseases on you which I have put on
the Egyptians; for I, [d]Yahweh, am
your healer.”

27 Then they came to [a]Elim where
there *were* twelve springs of water
and seventy date palms, and they
camped there beside the waters.

### *Yahweh Rains Bread from Heaven*

16 Then they set out from Elim,
and all the congregation of the
sons of Israel came to the wilderness
of [a]Sin, which is between Elim and
Sinai, on [b]the fifteenth day of the

**15:16** [a]Ex 23:27; Dt 2:25; Jos 2:9 [b]Ex 15:5, 6 [c]Ex 15:13; Ps 74:2; Is 43:1; Jer 31:11; Tit 2:14; 2Pe 2:1
**15:17** [a]Ex 23:20; 32:34 [b]Ps 44:2; 80:8, 15 [c]Ps 2:6; 78:54, 68 [d]Ps 68:16; 76:2; 132:13, 14 [e]Ps 78:69
**15:18** [a]Ps 10:16; 29:10; Is 57:15 **15:19** [a]Ex 14:23, 28 [b]Ex 14:22, 29 **15:20** [a]Ex 2:4; Nu 26:59; 1Chr 6:3; Mic 6:4 [b]Jdg 11:34; 1Sa 18:6; 1Chr 15:16; Ps 68:25; 81:2; 149:3; Jer 31:4 [c]Jdg 11:34; 21:21; 1Sa 18:6; Ps 30:11; 150:4 [1]Lit *dances* **15:21** [a]Ex 15:1 [1]Or *has triumphed gloriously* **15:22** [a]Ps 77:20; 78:52, 53 [b]Nu 33:8 [c]Ge 16:7; 20:1; 25:18 [1]Lit *caused Israel to journey* [2]Lit *Sea of Reeds* **15:23** [a]Nu 33:8; Ru 1:20 [1]Lit *from* [2]Heb *Marim* [3]Bitterness **15:24** [a]Ex 14:11; 16:2; Ps 106:13 **15:25** [a]Ex 14:10 [b]Eze 47:7, 8 [c]Jos 24:25 [d]Ex 16:4; Dt 8:2, 16; Jdg 2:22; 3:1, 4; Ps 66:10 **15:26** [a]Ex 19:5, 6; Dt 7:12 [b]Ex 20:2-17 [c]Dt 7:15; 28:58, 60 [d]Ex 23:25; Dt 32:39; Ps 41:3, 4; 103:3; 147:3 **15:27** [a]Nu 33:9 ◆ **16:1** [a]Nu 33:10, 11; Eze 30:15 [b]Ex 12:6, 51; 19:1

second month after their departure from the land of Egypt. **2** And the whole congregation of the sons of Israel [a]grumbled against Moses and Aaron in the wilderness. **3** And the sons of Israel said to them, "[a]Would that we had died by the hand of Yahweh in the land of Egypt, [b]when we sat by the pots of [1]meat, when we ate bread to the full; for you have brought us out into this wilderness to put this whole assembly to death with hunger."

**4** Then Yahweh said to Moses, "Behold, [a]I will rain bread from heaven for you; and the people shall go out and gather a day's portion every day, that I may [b]test them, whether or not they will walk in My [1]law. **5** [a]Now it will be on the sixth day, they shall prepare what they bring in, and it will be twice as much as they gather daily." **6** So Moses and Aaron said to all the sons of Israel, "At evening [a,1]you will know that Yahweh has brought you out of the land of Egypt; **7** and in the morning [1]you will see [a]the glory of Yahweh, for [b]He hears your grumblings against Yahweh; and [c]what are we, that you grumble against us?"

### *Yahweh Gives Meat and Bread*

**8** And Moses said, "*This will happen* when Yahweh gives you [1]meat to eat in the evening and bread to the full in the morning; for Yahweh hears your grumblings which you grumble against Him. And what are we? Your grumblings are [a]not against us but against Yahweh."

**9** Then Moses said to Aaron, "Say to all the congregation of the sons of Israel, '[a]Come near before Yahweh, for He has heard your grumblings.'" **10** Now it happened as Aaron spoke to the whole congregation of the sons of Israel, that they turned toward the wilderness, and behold, [a]the glory of Yahweh appeared in the cloud. **11** And Yahweh spoke to Moses, saying, **12** "[a]I have heard the grumblings of the sons of Israel; speak to them, saying, '[1]At twilight you shall eat [2]meat, and in the morning you shall be filled with bread, so that [b]you shall know that I am Yahweh your God.'"

**13** So it happened at evening that [a]the quails came up and covered the camp, and in the morning [b]there was a layer of dew around the camp. **14** [a]Then the layer of dew [1]evaporated, and behold, on the [2]surface of the wilderness [b]there was a fine flake-like thing, fine as the frost on the ground. **15** And the sons of Israel saw *it* and said to one another, "[1]What is it?" For they did not know what it was. And Moses said to them, "[a]It is the bread which Yahweh has given you to eat. **16** This is [1]what Yahweh has commanded, 'Gather of it every man [2]as much as he should eat; you shall take an [a,3]omer apiece according to

**16:2** [a]Ex 14:11; 15:24; Ps 106:25; 1Co 10:10 **16:3** [a]Ex 17:3; Nu 14:2, 3; 20:3; Lam 4:9 [b]Nu 11:4, 5 [1]Or *flesh* **16:4** [a]Ne 9:15; Ps 78:23-25; 105:40; Jn 6:31; 1Co 10:3 [b]Ex 15:25; Dt 8:2, 16 [1]Or *instruction* **16:5** [a]Ex 16:22 **16:6** [a]Ex 6:7 [1]Lit *and you* **16:7** [a]Ex 16:10, 12; Is 35:2; 40:5; Jn 11:4, 40 [b]Nu 14:27; 17:5 [c]Nu 16:11 [1]Lit *and you* **16:8** [a]1Sa 8:7; Lk 10:16; Ro 13:2; 1Th 4:8 [1]Or *flesh* **16:9** [a]Nu 16:16 **16:10** [a]Ex 13:21; 16:7; Nu 16:19; 1Ki 8:10f **16:12** [a]Ex 16:8; Nu 14:27 [b]Ex 6:7; 16:7; 1Ki 20:28; Joel 3:17 [1]Lit *Between the two evenings* [2]Or *flesh* **16:13** [a]Nu 11:31; Ps 78:27-29; 105:40 [b]Nu 11:9 **16:14** [a]Nu 11:7-9 [b]Ex 16:31; Ne 9:15; Ps 78:24; 105:40 [1]Lit *had gone up* [2]Lit *face of* **16:15** [a]Ex 16:4; Ne 9:15; Ps 78:24; Jn 6:31; 1Co 10:3 [1]Heb *Man hu*, sounds similar to *manna*; cf. 16:31 **16:16** [a]Ex 16:32, 36 [1]Lit *the thing which* [2]Lit *according to his eating* [3]Lit *an omer for a head*; an omer was approx. 2.1 qt. or 2.3 l

the number of persons each of you
has in his tent.'" **17** And the sons of
Israel did so; *some* gathered much
and *some* little. **18** And they measured
it with an [1]omer, and [a]he who had
gathered much had no excess, and
he who had gathered little had no
lack; every man gathered [2]as much
as he should eat. **19** And Moses said
to them, "[a]Let no man leave any of
it until morning." **20** But they did not
listen to Moses, and some left part of
it until morning, and it bred worms
and became foul; and Moses was an-
gry with them. **21** So they gathered it
morning by morning, every man [1]as
much as he should eat; but the sun
would grow hot, and it would melt.

### *Yahweh Gives Bread for Two Days*

**22** [a]Now it happened that on the
sixth day they gathered twice as
much bread, two omers for each
one. Then all the [b]leaders of the
congregation came and told Moses.
**23** And he said to them, "This is what
Yahweh has spoken: [a]Tomorrow is a
sabbath observance, a holy sabbath
to Yahweh. Bake what you will bake
and boil what you will boil, and [b]all
that is in excess [1]put aside to be
kept until morning." **24** So they [1]put
it aside until morning, as Moses had
commanded, and [a]it did not become
foul nor was there any worm in it.
**25** And Moses said, "Eat it today, for
today is a sabbath to Yahweh; today
you will not find it in the field. **26** [a]Six
days you shall gather it, but on the
seventh day, *the* sabbath, there will
be [1]none."

**27** Now it happened on the seventh
day, that some of the people went
out to gather, but they found none.
**28** Then Yahweh said to Moses,
"[a]How long do you refuse to keep
My commandments and My [1]laws?
**29** See, Yahweh has given you the
sabbath; therefore He gives you
bread for two days on the sixth day.
Remain every man in his place; let
no man go out of his place on the
seventh day." **30** So the people rested
on the seventh day.

**31** And the house of [a]Israel named
it [1]manna, and it was like [b]coriander
seed, white, and its taste was like
wafers with honey. **32** Then Moses
said, "This is [1]what Yahweh has com-
manded, 'Let an omerful of it be kept
throughout your generations, that
they may see the bread that I fed you
in the wilderness, when I brought
you out of the land of Egypt.'" **33** And
Moses said to Aaron, "[a]Take a jar and
put an omerful of manna in it, and
place it before Yahweh to be kept
throughout your generations." **34** As
Yahweh commanded Moses, so Aar-
on placed it before [a]the Testimony
to be kept. **35** [a]And the sons of Israel
ate the manna forty years, until they
came to an inhabited land; they ate
the manna until they came to the
border of the land of Canaan. **36** (Now
[a]an [1]omer is a tenth of an [2]ephah.)

---

**16:18** [a]2Co 8:15 [1]An omer was approx. 2.1 qt. or 2.3 l [2]Lit *according to his eating* **16:19** [a]Ex 12:10; 16:23; 23:18 **16:21** [1]Lit *according to his eating* **16:22** [a]Ex 16:5 [b]Ex 34:31 **16:23** [a]Ge 2:3; Ex 20:8-11; 23:12; 31:15; 35:2; Lv 23:3; Ne 9:13, 14 [b]Ex 16:19 [1]Lit *lay up for you* **16:24** [a]Ex 16:20 [1]Lit *laid it up* **16:26** [a]Ex 20:9, 10 [1]Lit *none on it* **16:28** [a]2Ki 17:14; Ps 78:10; 106:13 [1]Or *instructions* **16:31** [a]Nu 11:7-9; Dt 8:3, 16 [b]Ex 16:14 [1]Heb *man*, cf. 16:15 **16:32** [1]Lit *the thing which* **16:33** [a]Heb 9:4; Rev 2:17 **16:34** [a]Ex 25:16, 21; 27:21; 40:20; Nu 17:10 **16:35** [a]Dt 8:2f; Jos 5:12; Ne 9:20, 21 **16:36** [a]Ex 16:16 [1]An omer was approx. 2.1 qt. or 2.3 l [2]An ephah was approx. 21 qt. or 23 l

### *Water from the Rock*

17 Then all the congregation of
the sons of Israel journeyed
by [1]stages from the wilderness of
[a]Sin, according to the [2]command
of Yahweh, and they camped at
[b]Rephidim, and there was no water
for the people to drink. **2** Therefore
the people [a]contended with Moses
and said, "Give us water that we may
drink." And Moses said to them,
"[b]Why do you contend with me?
[c]Why do you test Yahweh?" **3** But the
people thirsted there for water; and
[1]they [a]grumbled against Moses and
said, "Why, now, have you brought us
up from Egypt, to put [2]us and [3]our
children and [b,3]our livestock to death
with thirst?" **4** So Moses cried out to
Yahweh, saying, "What shall I do to
this people? A [a]little more and they
will stone me." **5** Then Yahweh said
to Moses, "Pass before the people
and take with you some of [a]the
elders of Israel; and take in your
hand your staff with which [b]you
struck the Nile, and go. **6** Behold, I
will stand before you there on the
rock at [a]Horeb; and [b]you shall strike
the rock, and water will come out
of it, that the people may drink."
And Moses did so in the sight of the
elders of Israel. **7** So he named the
place [a,1]Massah and [b,2]Meribah be-
cause of the contending of the sons
of Israel, and because they [c]tested
Yahweh, saying, "Is Yahweh among
us or not?"

### *Israel Overwhelms Amalek*

**8** Then [a]Amalek came and fought
against Israel at [b]Rephidim. **9** So Mo-
ses said to [a]Joshua, "Choose men for
us and go out, fight against Amalek.
Tomorrow I will take my stand on the
top of the hill with [b]the staff of God in
my hand." **10** And Joshua did as Moses
[1]told him, to fight against Amalek; and
Moses, Aaron, and [a]Hur went up to
the top of the hill. **11** So it happened
when Moses raised his hand up, that
Israel prevailed, and when he let his
hand [1]down, Amalek prevailed. **12** But
Moses' hands were heavy. Then they
took a stone and put it under him,
and he sat on it; and Aaron and Hur
[a]supported his hands, one on one side
and one on the other. Thus his hands
were steady until the sun set. **13** So
Joshua [1]overwhelmed Amalek and
his people with the edge of the sword.
**14** Then Yahweh said to Moses,
"[a]Write this in [1]a book as a memorial
and [2]recite it in Joshua's hearing, [3]that
[b]I will utterly blot out the memory of
Amalek from under heaven." **15** And
Moses built an [a]altar and named it
[b]Yahweh is My Banner; **16** and he
said, "[a]Because He *has sworn* with a
hand upon the throne of Yah, Yahweh
will have war against Amalek from
generation to generation."

### *Jethro's Counsel*

18 Now [a]Jethro, the priest of
Midian, Moses' father-in-law,
heard of all that God had done for

◆**17:1** [a]Ex 16:1; Nu 33:12 [b]Ex 19:2; Nu 33:14 [1]Lit *their journeyings* [2]Lit *mouth* **17:2** [a]Ex 14:11; Nu 20:2, 3, 13 [b]Ex 16:8 [c]Dt 6:16; Ps 78:18, 41; Mt 4:7; 1Co 10:9 **17:3** [a]Ex 16:2, 3 [b]Ex 12:38 [1]Lit *the people* [2]Lit *me* [3]Lit *my* **17:4** [a]Nu 14:10; 1Sa 30:6 **17:5** [a]Ex 3:16, 18 [b]Ex 7:20 **17:6** [a]Ex 3:1 [b]Nu 20:10, 11; Dt 8:15; Ne 9:15; Ps 78:15; 105:41; 114:8; 1Co 10:4 **17:7** [a]Dt 6:16; 9:22; Ps 95:8 [b]Nu 20:13, 24; 27:14; Ps 81:7 [c]Nu 14:22; Dt 33:8 [1]Lit *test* [2]Lit *quarrel* **17:8** [a]Ge 36:12; Nu 24:20; Dt 25:17-19; 1Sa 15:2 [b]Ex 17:1 **17:9** [a]Ex 24:13 [b]Ex 4:20 **17:10** [a]Ex 24:14; 31:2 [1]Lit *said to* **17:11** [1]Lit *rest* **17:12** [a]Is 35:3 **17:13** [1]Lit *weakened* **17:14** [a]Ex 24:4; 34:27; Nu 33:2 [b]Dt 25:19; 1Sa 15:3 [1]Lit *the book* [2]Lit *place it in the ears of* [3]Or *for* **17:15** [a]Ex 24:4 [b]Ge 22:14; Jdg 6:24 **17:16** [a]Ge 22:16 ◆**18:1** [a]Ex 2:16, 18; 3:1

Moses and for Israel His people, how
Yahweh had brought Israel out of
Egypt. **2** And Jethro, Moses' father-
in-law, took Moses' wife [a]Zipporah,
after he had sent her away, **3** and
her [a]two sons, of whom [1]one was
named Gershom, for Moses said, "I
have been [b]a [2]sojourner in a foreign
land." **4** [1]And the other was named
[a,2]Eliezer, for *he said*, "[b]The God of
my father was my help and delivered
me from the sword of Pharaoh."

**5** Then Jethro, Moses' father-in-
law, came with his sons and his wife
to Moses [1]in the wilderness where
he was camped, at [a]the mount of
God. **6** And he [1]sent word to Moses,
"I, your father-in-law Jethro, am
coming to you with your wife and
her two sons with her." **7** Then Moses
went out to meet his father-in-law,
and [a]he bowed down and [b]kissed
him; and they [c]asked each other of
their welfare and went into the tent.
**8** And Moses recounted to his father-
in-law all that Yahweh had done to
Pharaoh and to the Egyptians [a]for
Israel's sake, all the [b]hardship that
had befallen them on the journey,
and *how* [c]Yahweh had delivered
them. **9** And Jethro rejoiced over all
[a]the goodness which Yahweh had
done to Israel, that He had delivered
[1]them from the hand of the Egyp-
tians. **10** So Jethro said, "[a]Blessed be
Yahweh who delivered you from the
hand of the Egyptians and from the
hand of Pharaoh, *and* who delivered
the people from under the hand of
the Egyptians. **11** Now I know that
[a]Yahweh is greater than all the gods;
[1]for [b]in this matter they acted pre-
sumptuously against [2]the people."
**12** [a]Then Jethro, Moses' father-in-law,
took a burnt offering and sacrifices
for God, and Aaron came with all the
elders of Israel to eat [1]a meal with
Moses' father-in-law before God.

**13** Now it happened the next day
that Moses sat to judge the people,
and the people stood about Moses
from the morning until the evening.
**14** And Moses' father-in-law saw all
that he was doing for the people,
so he said, "What is this thing that
you are doing for the people? Why
do you alone sit *as judge* and all the
people stand about you from morn-
ing until evening?" **15** And Moses
said to his father-in-law, "Because
the people come to me [a]to inquire
of God. **16** When they have a [a]matter,
it comes to me, and I judge between
a man and his neighbor and make
known the statutes of God and His
laws." **17** And Moses' father-in-law
said to him, "The thing that you
are doing is not good. **18** [a]You will
surely wear out, both yourself and
[1]these people who are with you, for
the [2]task is too heavy for you; [b]you
cannot do it alone. **19** Now listen to
my voice: I will give you counsel, and
God be with you. [1]You be the people's
representative before God, and you
[a]bring the matters to God; **20** [a]then

---

**18:2** [a]Ex 2:21; 4:25 **18:3** [a]Ex 2:22; 4:20; Ac 7:29 [b]Ex 2:22 [1]Lit *the name of the one was* [2]Heb *ger* **18:4** [a]1Chr 23:15, 17 [b]Ge 49:25 [1]Lit *The name of the other was* [2]Lit *My God is help* **18:5** [a]Ex 3:1, 12; 4:27; 24:13 [1]Lit *unto* **18:6** [1]Lit *said* **18:7** [a]Ge 43:26, 28 [b]Ge 29:13; Ex 4:27 [c]Ge 43:27; 2Sa 11:7 **18:8** [a]Ex 4:23; 7:4, 5 [b]Nu 20:14; Ne 9:32 [c]Ex 15:6, 16 **18:9** [a]Is 63:7-14 [1]Lit *him* **18:10** [a]Ge 14:20; 2Sa 18:28; 1Ki 8:56; Ps 68:19, 20 **18:11** [a]Ex 12:12; 15:11; 2Chr 2:5; Ps 95:3; 97:9; 135:5 [b]Lk 1:51 [1]Lit *indeed, in the thing in which they* [2]Lit *them* **18:12** [a]Ge 31:54; Ex 24:5 [1]Lit *bread* **18:15** [a]Nu 9:6, 8; 27:5; Dt 17:8-13 **18:16** [a]Ex 24:14 **18:18** [a]Nu 11:14, 17; Dt 1:12 [b]Dt 1:9 [1]Lit *this* [2]Lit *matter* **18:19** [a]Nu 27:5 [1]Lit *You be for the people in front of God* **18:20** [a]Dt 1:18; 4:1, 5; 5:1

warn them about the statutes and
the laws, and make known to them
[b]the way in which they shall go and
the work they shall do. **21** But you
shall [1]select [a]excellent men out of
all the people, [b]those who fear God,
men of truth, those who [c]hate greedy
gain; and you shall place *these men*
over them *as* leaders of thousands,
[2]of hundreds, [2]of fifties, and [2]of tens.
**22** And they will judge the people at all
times. And it will be [a]that every ma-
jor matter they will bring to you, but
every minor matter they themselves
will judge. So it will be easier for you,
and [b]they will bear *the burden* with
you. **23** If you do this thing and God
*so* commands you, then you will be
able to [1]endure, and all [2]these people
also will go to [3]their place in peace."

**24** So Moses listened to the voice
of his father-in-law and did all that
he had said. **25** And Moses chose
[a]excellent men out of all Israel and
made them heads over the people,
leaders of thousands, [1]of hundreds,
[1]of fifties, and [1]of tens. **26** And they
judged the people at all times; [a]the
difficult matter they would bring to
Moses, but every minor matter they
themselves would judge. **27** Then Mo-
ses [a,1]let his father-in-law depart, and
he went his way into his own land.

### *Israel at Sinai*

**19** [a]In the third month after the
sons of Israel had gone out of
the land of Egypt, on this day they
came into the wilderness of [b]Sinai.
**2** Then they set out from [a]Rephidim
and came to the wilderness of Sinai
and camped in the wilderness; and
there Israel camped in front of [b]the
mountain.

**3** Now Moses went up to God,
and [a]Yahweh called to him from the
mountain, saying, "Thus you shall
say to the house of Jacob and tell the
sons of Israel: **4** '[a]You yourselves have
seen what I did to the Egyptians, and
*how* I lifted you up on [b]eagles' wings
and brought you to Myself. **5** So now
then, [a]if you will indeed listen to My
voice and [b]keep My covenant, then
you shall be [c]My treasured posses-
sion among all the peoples, for [d]all
the earth is Mine; **6** and you shall be
to Me [a]a kingdom of priests and [b]a
holy nation.' These are the words that
you shall speak to the sons of Israel."

**7** [a]So Moses came and called the
elders of the people and set before
them all these words which Yahweh
had commanded him. **8** [a]And all
the people answered together and
said, "All that Yahweh has spoken we
will do!" And Moses brought back
the words of the people to Yahweh.
**9** Yahweh said to Moses, "Behold, I
will come to you in [a]a thick cloud,
so that the [b]people may hear when I
speak with you and may also believe
in you forever." Then Moses told the
words of the people to Yahweh.

**10** Yahweh also said to Moses, "Go
to the people and [a]set them apart

---

**18:20** [b]Ps 143:8 **18:21** [a]Ex 18:25; Dt 1:13, 15; 2Chr 19:5-10; Ps 15:1-5; Ac 6:3 [b]Ge 42:18; 2Sa 23:3 [c]Dt 16:19 [1]Lit *see* [2]Lit *leaders of* **18:22** [a]Dt 1:17, 18 [b]Nu 11:17 **18:23** [1]Lit *stand* [2]Lit *this* [3]Lit *his* **18:25** [a]Ex 18:21; Dt 1:15 [1]Lit *leaders of* **18:26** [a]Ex 18:22 **18:27** [a]Nu 10:29, 30 [1]Lit *sent off his father-in-law* ◆ **19:1** [a]Ex 12:6, 51; 16:1 [b]Dt 1:6; 4:10, 15; 5:2 **19:2** [a]Ex 17:1; Nu 33:15 [b]Ex 3:1, 12; 18:5 **19:3** [a]Ex 3:4 **19:4** [a]Dt 29:2 [b]Dt 32:11; Rev 12:14 **19:5** [a]Ex 15:26; Dt 5:2f [b]Ps 78:10 [c]Dt 4:20; 7:6; 14:2; 26:18; Ps 135:4; Tit 2:14; 1Pe 2:9 [d]Ex 9:29; Dt 10:14; Job 41:11; Ps 50:12; 1Co 10:26 **19:6** [a]1Pe 2:5, 9; Rev 1:6; 5:10 [b]Dt 7:6; 14:21; 26:19; Is 62:12 **19:7** [a]Ex 4:29, 30 **19:8** [a]Ex 4:31; 24:3, 7; Dt 5:27; 26:17 **19:9** [a]Ex 19:16; 24:15, 16; Dt 4:11; Ps 99:7 [b]Dt 4:12, 36 **19:10** [a]Lv 11:44, 45

as holy today and tomorrow, and let them [b]wash their garments; **11** and let them be ready for the third day, for on [a]the third day Yahweh will come down on Mount Sinai in the sight of all the people. **12** And you shall set bounds for the people all around, saying, '[1]Beware that you do not go up on the mountain or touch the border of it; [a]whoever touches the mountain shall surely be put to death. **13** No hand shall touch him, but [a]he shall surely be stoned or surely [1]shot through; whether beast or man, he shall not live.' When the ram's horn sounds a long blast, they shall come up to [b]the mountain." **14** So Moses went down from the mountain to the people and set the people apart as holy, and they washed their garments. **15** And he said to the people, "Be ready for the third day; do not go near a woman."

**16** [a]So it happened on the third day, when it was morning, that there were [1]thunder and lightning flashes and a [2]thick cloud upon the mountain and a very loud trumpet sound, so that all the people who *were* in the camp trembled. **17** And Moses brought the people out of the camp to meet God, and they stood at the [1]foot of the mountain.

### *Yahweh Descends on Mount Sinai*

**18** [a]Now Mount Sinai *was* all in smoke because Yahweh descended upon it [b]in fire; and its smoke ascended like [c]the smoke of a furnace, and [d]the whole mountain trembled violently. **19** And the sound of the trumpet grew louder and louder; *then* Moses spoke and [a]God answered him with [1]thunder. **20** [a]And Yahweh came down on Mount Sinai, to the top of the mountain; and Yahweh called Moses to the top of the mountain, and Moses went up. **21** Then Yahweh spoke to Moses, "Go down, [1]warn the people, lest [a]they break through to Yahweh to see, and many of them [2]perish. **22** Also let the [a]priests who come near to Yahweh set themselves apart as holy, lest Yahweh break out against them." **23** And Moses said to Yahweh, "The people cannot come up to Mount Sinai, for You [1]warned us, saying, '[a]Set bounds about the mountain, and set it apart as holy.'" **24** Then Yahweh said to him, "[1]Go down and come up *again*, [a]you and Aaron with you; but do not let the [b]priests and the people break through to come up to Yahweh, lest He break out against them." **25** So Moses went down to the people and told them.

### *The Commandments of Yahweh*

**20** Then God spoke all these words, saying,

2 "[a]I am Yahweh your God, [b]who
brought you out of the land
of Egypt, out of the house of
[1]slavery.

3 "[a]You shall have no other [b]gods
[1]before Me.

---

**19:10** [b]Ge 35:2; Lv 15:5; Nu 8:7, 21; 19:19; Rev 22:14 **19:11** [a]Ex 19:16 **19:12** [a]Heb 12:20 [1]Lit *Take heed to yourselves* **19:13** [a]Heb 12:20 [b]Ex 19:17 [1]With arrows **19:16** [a]Heb 12:18, 19, 21 [1]Lit *sounds* [2]Lit *heavy* **19:17** [1]Lit *lower part* **19:18** [a]Dt 4:11; Ps 104:32; 144:5 [b]Ex 3:2; 24:17; Dt 5:4; 2Chr 7:1-3; Heb 12:18 [c]Ge 15:17; 19:28 [d]Jdg 5:5; Ps 68:7, 8; Jer 4:24 **19:19** [a]Ps 81:7 [1]Or *a voice*; lit *a sound* **19:20** [a]Ne 9:13 **19:21** [a]Ex 3:5; 1Sa 6:19 [1]Lit *testify to* [2]Lit *fall* **19:22** [a]Ex 19:24; 24:5; Lv 10:3; 21:6-8 **19:23** [a]Ex 19:12 [1]Lit *testified to* **19:24** [a]Ex 24:1, 9, 12 [b]Ex 19:22 [1]Lit *Go, descend* ◆ **20:2** [a]Lv 26:1; Dt 5:6; Ps 81:10 [b]Ex 13:3; 15:13, 16; Dt 7:8 [1]Lit *slaves* **20:3** [a]Dt 6:14; 2Ki 17:35; Jer 25:6; 35:15 [b]Ex 15:11; 20:23 [1]Or *besides Me*

4 "[a]You shall not make for yourself [1]an idol, or any likeness of what is in heaven above or on the earth beneath or in the water under the earth.
5 "[a]You shall not worship them or serve them; for I, Yahweh your God, am a [b]jealous God, [c]visiting the iniquity of the fathers on the children, on the third and the fourth generations of those who hate Me,
6 but showing lovingkindness to [a]thousands, to those who love Me and keep My commandments.

7 "[a]You shall not take the name of Yahweh your God in vain, for Yahweh will not [1]leave him unpunished who takes His name in vain.

8 "Remember [a]the sabbath day, to keep it holy.
9 "[a]Six days you shall labor and do all your work,
10 but the seventh day is a sabbath of Yahweh your God; *in it* [a]you shall not do any work, you or your son or your daughter, your male or your female slave or your cattle or your sojourner who is within your gates.
11 "[a]For in six days Yahweh made the heavens and the earth, the sea and all that is in them, and rested on the seventh day; therefore Yahweh blessed the sabbath day and made it holy.

12 "[a]Honor your father and your mother, that your [b]days may be prolonged in the land which Yahweh your God gives you.

13 "[a]You shall not murder.

14 "[a]You shall not commit adultery.

15 "[a]You shall not steal.

16 "[a]You shall not bear false witness against your [b]neighbor.

17 "[a]You shall not covet your neighbor's house; [b]you shall not covet your neighbor's wife or his male slave or his female slave or his ox or his donkey or anything that belongs to your neighbor."

18 [a]And all the people perceived the [1]thunder and the lightning flashes and the sound of the trumpet and the mountain smoking; and the people perceived *it*, and they shook

**20:4** [a]Lv 19:4; 26:1; Dt 4:15-19; 27:15 [1]Or *a graven image* **20:5** [a]Ex 23:24; Jos 23:7; 2Ki 17:35 [b]Ex 34:14; Dt 4:24; Jos 24:19; Na 1:2 [c]Ex 34:6, 7; Nu 14:18, 33; Dt 5:9, 10; 1Ki 21:29; Jer 32:18 **20:6** [a]Dt 7:9
**20:7** [a]Lv 19:12; Dt 6:13; 10:20 [1]Or *hold him guiltless* **20:8** [a]Ex 23:12; 31:13-16; Lv 26:2; Dt 5:12
**20:9** [a]Ex 34:21; 35:2, 3; Lv 23:3; Dt 5:13; Lk 13:14 **20:10** [a]Ne 13:16-19 **20:11** [a]Ge 2:2, 3; Ex 31:17
**20:12** [a]Lv 19:3; Dt 27:16; Mt 15:4; 19:19; Mk 7:10; 10:19; Lk 18:20; Eph 6:2 [b]Dt 5:16, 33; 6:2; 11:8, 9; Jer 35:7
**20:13** [a]Ge 9:6; Ex 21:12; Lv 24:17; Mt 5:21; 19:18; Mk 10:19; Lk 18:20; Ro 13:9; Jas 2:11 **20:14** [a]Lv 20:10; Dt 5:18; Mt 5:27; 19:18; Ro 13:9 **20:15** [a]Ex 21:16; Lv 19:11, 13; Mt 19:18; Ro 13:9 **20:16** [a]Ex 23:1, 7; Dt 5:20; Mt 19:18 [b]Lv 19:18 **20:17** [a]Dt 5:21; Ro 7:7; 13:9; Eph 5:3, 5 [b]Pr 6:29; Mt 5:28 **20:18** [a]Ex 19:16, 18; Heb 12:18, 19 [1]Lit *sounds*

and stood at a distance. **19** [a]Then they
said to Moses, "Speak [1]to us yourself,
and we will listen; but let not God
speak [1]to us, lest we die." **20** And
Moses said to the people, "[a]Do not be
afraid; for God has come in order [b]to
test you, and in order that [c]the fear of
Him may [1]be with you, so that you
may not sin." **21** So the people stood
at a distance, but Moses came near
[a]the dense gloom where God *was.*
**22** Then Yahweh said to Moses,
"Thus you shall say to the sons of
Israel, 'You yourselves have seen that
[a]I have spoken [1]to you from heaven.
**23** [a]You shall not make *other gods*
besides Me; [b]gods of silver or gods
of gold, you shall not make for yourselves.
**24** You shall make [a]an altar of
earth for Me, and you shall sacrifice
on it your [b]burnt offerings and your
[c]peace offerings, [d]your sheep and
your oxen; in every place [e]where I
cause My name to be remembered, I
will come to you and bless you. **25** And
if you make an altar of stone for Me,
[a]you shall not build it of cut stones,
for if you wield your tool on it, you
will profane it. **26** And you shall not go
up by steps to My altar, so that [a]your
nakedness will not be exposed on it.'

### *Judgments About Slaves*

**21** "Now these are the [a]judgments
which you are to set before
*them:*
**2** "If you buy [a]a Hebrew slave, he
shall serve for six years; but on the
seventh he shall go out as a free
man without payment. **3** If he comes
[1]alone, he shall go out [1]alone; if he is
the husband of a wife, then his wife
shall go out with him. **4** If his master
gives him a wife, and she bears him
sons or daughters, the wife and her
children shall belong to her master,
and he shall go out [1]alone. **5** But [a]if the
slave plainly says, 'I love my master,
my wife, and my children; I will not go
out as a free man,' **6** then his master
shall bring him to [1]God, and he shall
bring him to the door or the doorpost.
Then his master shall pierce his ear
with an awl; and he shall serve him
permanently.
**7** "[a]And if a man sells his daughter
as a female slave, she is not to [1]go free
[b]as the male slaves [1]do. **8** If she is
[1]displeasing in the eyes of her master
[2]who designated her for himself, then
he shall let her be redeemed. He does
not have authority to sell her to a foreign
people because of his treachery
to her. **9** And if he designates her for
his son, he shall do to her according
to the custom of daughters. **10** If he
takes for himself another woman, he
may not reduce her [1]food, her clothing,
or [a]her conjugal rights. **11** And if
he will not do these three *things* for
her, then she shall go out for nothing,
without *payment of* money.

### *Judgments About Personal Injuries*

**12** "[a]He who strikes a man so that
he dies shall surely be put to death.

---

**20:19** [a]Dt 5:5, 23-27; Ga 3:19; Heb 12:19 [1]Lit *with* **20:20** [a]Ex 14:13; Is 41:10, 13 [b]Ex 15:25; Dt 13:3 [c]Dt 4:10; 6:24; Pr 3:7; 16:6; Is 8:13 [1]Lit *be before* **20:21** [a]Ex 19:16; Dt 5:22 **20:22** [a]Dt 4:36; 5:24, 26; Ne 9:13 [1]Lit *with* **20:23** [a]Ex 20:3 [b]Ex 32:1, 2, 4; Dt 29:17 **20:24** [a]Ex 20:25; 27:1-8 [b]Ex 10:25; 18:12 [c]Ex 24:5; Lv 1:2 [d]Dt 12:5; 16:6, 11; 26:2; 2Chr 6:6 [e]Dt 12:5; 26:2 **20:25** [a]Dt 27:5, 6; Jos 8:31 **20:26** [a]Ex 28:42, 43 ♦**21:1** [a]Ex 24:3, 4; Dt 4:14; 6:1 **21:2** [a]Lv 25:39-43; Dt 15:12-18; Jer 34:14 **21:3** [1]Lit *by himself* **21:4** [1]Lit *by himself* **21:5** [a]Dt 15:16, 17 **21:6** [1]Or *the judges who acted in God's name* **21:7** [a]Ne 5:5 [b]Ex 21:2, 3 [1]Lit *go out* **21:8** [1]Lit *bad* [2]Or *so that he did not designate her* **21:10** [a]1Co 7:3, 5 [1]Lit *flesh* **21:12** [a]Ge 9:6; Lv 24:17; Nu 35:30; Mt 26:52

**13** [a]But [1]if he did not lie in wait *for*
*him,* but [b]God let *him* fall into his
hand, then I will appoint you a place
to which he may flee. **14** [a]If, however,
a man acts presumptuously toward
his neighbor, so as to kill him by
deceit, you shall take him *even* from
My altar, that he may die.
**15** "And he who strikes his father
or his mother shall surely be put to
death.
**16** "[a]He who [1]kidnaps a man,
whether he sells him or he is found in
his hand, shall surely be put to death.
**17** "[a]And he who curses his father
or his mother shall surely be put to
death.
**18** "And if men contend *with each*
*other* and one strikes the other with a
stone or with *his* fist, and he does not
die but [1]remains in bed, **19** if he gets
up and walks around outside on his
staff, then he who struck him shall go
unpunished; he shall only pay for [1]his
loss of time, and [2]he shall take care
of him until he is completely healed.
**20** "And if a man strikes his male
or female slave with a rod and he
dies [1]at his hand, he shall surely [2]be
punished. **21** But if for a day or two he
*is able to* stand, no punishment shall
be taken; [a]for he is his [1]property.
**22** "And if men struggle with each
other and [1]strike a woman with child
so that [2]she gives birth prematurely,
yet there is no injury, he shall surely
be fined as the woman's husband
[3]will set for him, and he shall [a]pay
[4]as the judges *decide.* **23** But if there
is *any further* injury, [a]then you shall
pay life for life, **24** [a]eye for eye, tooth
for tooth, hand for hand, foot for
foot, **25** burn for burn, bruise for
bruise, wound for wound.
**26** "And if a man strikes the eye of
his male or female slave and ruins it,
he shall let him go free on account
of his eye. **27** And if he [1]knocks out
a tooth of his male or female slave,
he shall let him go free on account
of his tooth.
**28** "And if an ox gores a man or a
woman [1]to death, [a]the ox shall surely
be stoned and its flesh shall not be
eaten; but the owner of the ox shall
go unpunished. **29** If, however, an ox
was previously in the habit of goring
and its owner has been warned, yet
he does not confine it and it puts a
man or a woman to death, the ox
shall be stoned and its owner also
shall be put to death. **30** If a ransom is
[1]demanded of him, then he shall give
for the redemption of his life whatev-
er is [1]demanded of him. **31** Whether it
gores a son or [1]a daughter, it shall be
done to him according to [2]the same
judgment. **32** If the ox gores a male
or female slave, [1]the owner shall give
his *or her* master [a,2]thirty shekels of
silver, and the ox shall be stoned.
**33** "And if a man opens a pit, or if a
man digs a pit and does not cover it
over, and an ox or a donkey falls into
it, **34** the owner of the pit shall make
restitution; he shall [1]give money to

---

**21:13** [a]Nu 35:10-34; Dt 19:1-13; Jos 20:1-9 [b]1Sa 24:4, 10, 18 [1]Lit *he who* **21:14** [a]Dt 19:11, 12; 1Ki 2:28-34 **21:16** [a]Dt 24:7 [1]Lit *steals* **21:17** [a]Lv 20:9; Pr 20:20; Mt 15:4; Mk 7:10 **21:18** [1]Lit *lies* **21:19** [1]Lit *his sitting* [2]Lit *healing, he shall cause to be healed* **21:20** [1]Lit *under* [2]Lit *suffer vengeance* **21:21** [a]Lv 25:44-46 [1]Lit *money* **21:22** [a]Ex 21:30; Dt 22:18, 19 [1]Lit *smote* [2]Or *an untimely birth occurs;* lit *her children come out* [3]Lit *lays on him* [4]Lit *by arbitration* **21:23** [a]Lv 24:19; Dt 19:21 **21:24** [a]Lv 24:20; Dt 19:21; Mt 5:38 **21:27** [1]Lit *causes to fall* **21:28** [a]Ge 9:5; Ex 21:32 [1]Lit *so that he dies* **21:30** [1]Lit *laid on him* **21:31** [1]Lit *gores a daughter* [2]Lit *this* **21:32** [a]Zec 11:12; Mt 26:15; 27:3, 9 [1]Lit *he* [2]Approx. 12 oz. or 330 gm, a shekel was approx. 0.4 oz. or 11 gm **21:34** [1]Lit *give back*

its owner, and the dead *animal* shall
become his.
**35** "And if one man's ox [1]hurts an-
other's so that it dies, then they shall
sell the live ox and divide its price
equally; and also they shall divide
the dead *ox*. **36** Or *if* it is known that
the ox was previously in the habit of
goring, yet its owner has not confined
it, he shall surely pay ox for ox, and
the dead *animal* shall become his.

### *Judgments About Property Rights*

**22** "[1]If a man steals an ox or a
sheep and slaughters it or sells
it, he shall pay five oxen for the ox
and [a]four sheep for the sheep.
**2** "[1]If the [a]thief is [2]caught while
breaking in and is struck so that he
dies, there will be no bloodguiltiness
on his account. **3** *But* if the sun has
risen on him, there will be bloodguilt-
iness on his account. He shall surely
make restitution; if he owns nothing,
then he shall be [a]sold for his theft. **4** If
what he stole is actually found alive in
his hand, whether an ox or a donkey
or a sheep, [a]he shall pay double.
**5** "If a man lets a field or vineyard
be grazed *bare* and lets his animal
loose so that it grazes in another
man's field, he shall make restitution
from the best of his own field and the
best of his own vineyard.
**6** "If a fire breaks out and spreads
to thorn bushes, so that stacked grain
or the standing grain or the field *itself*
is consumed, he who started the fire
shall surely make restitution.
**7** "[a]If a man gives his neighbor
money or goods to keep *for him* and
it is stolen from the man's house,
if the thief is [1]caught, he shall pay
double. **8** If the thief is not [1]caught,
then the owner of the house shall
[2]appear before [a,3]the judges *to* deter-
mine whether he [4]laid his hands on
his neighbor's property. **9** For every
[1]breach of trust, *whether it is* for ox,
for donkey, for sheep, for clothing,
*or* for any lost thing about which one
says, 'This is it,' the [2]case of both par-
ties shall come before [a,3]the judges;
he whom [3]the judges condemn shall
pay double to his neighbor.
**10** "If a man gives his neighbor
a donkey, an ox, a sheep, or any
animal to keep *for him*, and it dies
or is injured or is driven away while
no one is looking, **11** then an [a]oath
before Yahweh shall be made by the
two of them [1]that he has not [2]laid
hands on his neighbor's property;
and its owner shall accept *it*, and
he shall not make restitution. **12** But
if it is actually stolen from him, he
shall make restitution to its owner.
**13** Now if it is all torn to pieces, let
him bring it as evidence; he shall not
make restitution for what has been
torn to pieces.
**14** "If a man [1]borrows *anything*
from his neighbor, and it is injured
or dies while its owner is not with it,
he shall make full restitution. **15** But if
its owner is with it, he shall not make
restitution; if it is hired, it came for
its hire.

### *Various Judgments*

**16** "[a]If a man seduces a virgin who
is not engaged and lies with her,

---

**21:35** [1]Lit *smites* ◆ **22:1** [a]2Sa 12:6; Lk 19:8 [1]Ch 21:37 in Heb **22:2** [a]Mt 6:19; 24:43; 1Pe 4:15 [1]Ch 22:1 in Heb [2]Lit *found* **22:3** [a]Mt 18:25 **22:4** [a]Ex 22:7 **22:7** [a]Lv 6:1-7 [1]Lit *found* **22:8** [a]Ex 22:9; Dt 17:8, 9; 19:17 [1]Lit *found* [2]Lit *approach to* [3]Or *God* [4]Lit *stretched his hand* **22:9** [a]Ex 22:8, 28; Dt 25:1 [1]Or *matter of transgression* [2]Lit *matter* [3]Or *God* **22:11** [a]Heb 6:16 [1]Lit *whether* [2]Lit *stretched his hand* **22:14** [1]Lit *asks* **22:16** [a]Dt 22:28, 29

he must pay a dowry for her *to be*
his wife. **17** If her father absolutely
refuses to give her to him, he shall
[1]pay money equal to the [a]dowry for
virgins.

**18** "You shall not allow a [a]sorceress
to live.

**19** "[a]Whoever lies with an animal
shall surely be put to death.

**20** "[a]And he who sacrifices to [1]any
god, other than to Yahweh alone,
shall be [2]devoted to destruction.

**21** "[a]You shall not mistreat a
sojourner or oppress him, for you
were sojourners in the land of Egypt.
**22** [a]You shall not afflict any widow or
orphan. **23** And if you indeed afflict
him, *and* [a]if he earnestly cries out to
Me, [b]I will surely hear his cry; **24** and
My anger will burn, and I will kill you
with the sword, [a]and your wives shall
become widows and your children
fatherless.

**25** "[a]If you lend money to My peo-
ple, to the afflicted [1]among you, you
are not to [2]act as a creditor to him;
you shall not [3]charge him [b]interest.
**26** If you ever take your neighbor's
cloak [a]as a pledge, you shall return it
to him before the sun sets, **27** for that
is his only covering; it is his cloak for
his [1]body. What else shall he sleep in?
And it shall be that [a]when he cries
out to Me, I will hear *him*, for [b]I am
gracious.

**28** "You shall not [a,1]curse God, [b]nor
curse a ruler of your people.

**29** "[a]You shall not delay *the offer-
ing from* [1]the fullness of your harvest
and the juice of your wine vat. [b]The
firstborn of your sons you shall give
to Me. **30** [a]And you shall do the same
with your oxen *and* with your sheep.
It shall be with its mother seven days;
[b]on the eighth day you shall give it
to Me.

**31** "[a]You shall be holy men to Me,
therefore [b]you shall not eat *any* flesh
torn to pieces in the field; you shall
throw it to the dogs.

**23** "[a]You shall not bear a false
report; do not join your hand
with a wicked man to be a [b]malicious
witness. **2** You shall not follow [1]the
masses in doing evil, nor shall you
[2]testify in a case so as to turn aside
after [1]the masses in order to [a,3]cause
*justice* to be turned aside; **3** [a]nor shall
you [1]be partial to a poor man in his
case.

**4** "[a]If you meet your enemy's ox
or his donkey wandering away, you
shall surely return it to him. **5** [a]If
you see the donkey of one who hates
you lying *helpless* under its load, you
shall refrain from leaving it to him,
you shall surely release *it* with him.

**6** "[a]You shall not cause the justice
*due* to your needy *brother* to be
turned aside in his case. **7** [a]Keep far

---

**22:17** [a]Ge 34:12; 1Sa 18:25 [1]Lit *weigh out silver* **22:18** [a]Lv 19:31; 20:6, 27; Dt 18:10, 11; 1Sa 28:3; Jer 27:9, 10 **22:19** [a]Lv 18:23; 20:15, 16; Dt 27:21 **22:20** [a]Ex 32:8; 34:15; Lv 17:7; Nu 25:2; Dt 17:2, 3, 5; 1Ki 18:40; 2Ki 10:25 [1]Lit *the gods* [2]Lit *put under the ban* **22:21** [a]Ex 23:9; Lv 19:33, 34; 25:35; Dt 1:16; 10:19; 27:19; Zec 7:10 **22:22** [a]Dt 24:17, 18; Pr 23:10, 11; Jer 7:6, 7 **22:23** [a]Dt 15:9; Job 35:9; Lk 18:7 [b]Dt 10:18; *Job 34:28; Ps 10:14, 17, 18; 18:6*; 68:5; Jas 5:4 **22:24** [a]Ps 109:2, 9 **22:25** [a]Lv 25:35-37; Dt 15:7-11 [b]Dt 23:19, 20; Ne 5:7; Ps 15:5; Eze 18:8 [1]Lit *with* [2]Lit *be* [3]Lit *lay upon* **22:26** [a]Dt 24:6, 10-13; Job 24:3; Pr 20:16; Am 2:8 **22:27** [a]Ex 22:23 [b]Ex 34:6 [1]Lit *skin* **22:28** [a]Lv 24:15, 16 [b]Ecc 10:20; Ac 23:5 [1]Or *revile* **22:29** [a]Ex 23:16, 19; Dt 26:2-11; Pr 3:9 [b]Ex 13:2, 12 [1]Lit *your fullness and your tears* **22:30** [a]Dt 15:19; Lv 22:27 [b]Ge 17:12; Lv 12:3 **22:31** [a]Ex 19:6; Lv 11:44; 19:2 [b]Lv 7:24; 17:15; Eze 4:14 ◆ **23:1** [a]Ex 20:16; Lv 19:11f; Dt 5:20; Ps 101:5; Pr 10:18 [b]Dt 19:16-21; Ps 35:11; Pr 19:5; Ac 6:11 **23:2** [a]Dt 16:19; 24:17 [1]Lit *many men* [2]Or *answer* [3]Or *pervert* justice, cf. 23:6 **23:3** [a]Ex 23:6; Lv 19:15; Dt 1:17; 16:19 [1]Lit *honor* **23:4** [a]Dt 22:1-4 **23:5** [a]Dt 22:4 **23:6** [a]Ex 23:2, 3; Lv 19:15 **23:7** [a]Ex 20:16; Ps 119:29; Eph 4:25

from a [1]false charge, and [b]do not kill
the innocent or the righteous, for [c]I
will not justify the guilty.
8 "[a]And you shall not take a bribe,
for a bribe blinds the clear-sighted
and [1]subverts the cause of the [2]just.
9 "[a]And you shall not oppress a
sojourner, since you yourselves know
the soul of a sojourner, for you *also*
were sojourners in the land of Egypt.

### *Judgments About Work and Rest*

10 "[a]Now you shall sow your land for
six years and gather in its produce,
11 but *on* the seventh year you shall
let it [1]rest and lie fallow, so that the
needy of your people may eat; and
whatever they leave the beast of the
field may eat. Thus you shall do with
your vineyard *and* your olive grove.
12 "[a]Six days you are to do your
work, but on the seventh day you
shall [1]rest so that your ox and your
donkey may [2]rest, and the son of
your maidservant, as well as your
sojourner, may refresh themselves.
13 Now [a]concerning everything
which I have said to you, beware; and
[b]do not mention the name of other
gods, nor let *them* be heard [1]from
your mouth.

### *Judgments About National Feasts*

14 "[a]Three times a year you shall
celebrate a feast to Me. 15 You shall
keep [a]the Feast of Unleavened
Bread; for seven days you are to eat
unleavened bread, as I commanded
you, at the appointed time in the
[b]month Abib, for in it you came out
of Egypt. And [c,1]none shall appear
before Me empty-handed. 16 Also *you*
*shall keep* [a]the Feast of the Harvest
*of* the first fruits of your labors *from*
what you sow in the field; also the
Feast of the Ingathering at the end
of the year [b]when you gather in *the*
*fruit of* your labors from the field.
17 [a]Three times a year all your males
shall appear before the Lord Yahweh.
18 "[a]You shall not offer the blood
of My sacrifice with leavened bread;
[b]nor is the fat of My [1]feast to remain
overnight until morning.
19 "You shall bring [a]the choice first
fruits of your ground into the house
of Yahweh your God.
"[b]You shall not boil a young goat
in the milk of its mother.

### *Yahweh Will Drive Out Israel's Enemies*

20 "Behold, I am going to send [a]an
angel before you to keep you along
the way and [b]to bring you into the
place which I have prepared. 21 Keep
watch *of yourself* before him and lis-
ten to his voice; [a]do not be rebellious
toward him, for he will not pardon
your transgression, since [b]My name
is in him. 22 But if you truly listen
to his voice and do all that I speak,
then [a]I will be an enemy to your
enemies and an adversary to your

**23:7** [b]Ex 20:13; Dt 27:25 [c]Ex 34:7; Dt 25:1; Ro 1:18 [1]Lit *lying word* **23:8** [a]Dt 10:17; 16:19; Pr 15:27; 17:8, 23; Is 5:22, 23 [1]Or *distorts the words* [2]Or *righteous* **23:9** [a]Ex 22:21; Lv 19:33f; Dt 24:17f; 27:19 **23:10** [a]Lv 25:1-7 **23:11** [1]Lit *drop* **23:12** [a]Ex 20:8-11; 31:15; 34:21; 35:2, 3; Lv 23:3; Dt 5:13f [1]Related to sabbath, cf. Ge 2:2 [2]Related to Noah, cf. Ge 2:15; 5:29 **23:13** [a]Dt 4:9, 23; 1Ti 4:16 [b]Jos 23:7; Ps 16:4; Hos 2:17 [1]Lit *on* **23:14** [a]Ex 23:17; 34:22-24; Dt 16:16 **23:15** [a]Ex 12:14-20; Lv 23:6-8; Nu 28:16-25 [b]Ex 12:2; 13:4 [c]Ex 22:29; 34:20 [1]Lit *they shall not* **23:16** [a]Ex 34:22; Lv 23:10; Nu 28:26 [b]Lv 23:39 **23:17** [a]Ex 23:14; 34:23; Dt 16:16 **23:18** [a]Ex 34:25; Lv 2:11 [b]Ex 12:10; Lv 7:15; Dt 16:4 [1]Or *festival* **23:19** [a]Ex 22:29; 34:26; Dt 26:2, 10; Ne 10:35; Pr 3:9 [b]Dt 14:21 **23:20** [a]Ex 3:2; 14:19; 23:23; 32:34; 33:2 [b]Ex 15:16, 17 **23:21** [a]Dt 9:7; Ps 78:40, 56 [b]Ex 3:14; 6:3; 34:5-7 **23:22** [a]Ge 12:3; Nu 24:9; Dt 30:7

adversaries. **23** [a]For My angel will go
before you and bring you in to *the*
*land of* the Amorites, the Hittites,
the Perizzites, the Canaanites, the
Hivites, and the Jebusites; and I will
annihilate them. **24** [a]You shall not
worship their gods, you shall not
serve them, and you shall not do
according to their deeds; [b]but you
shall utterly pull them down and
shatter their [c]*sacred* pillars in pieces.
**25** [a]But you shall serve Yahweh your
God, [1]and He will bless your bread
and your water; and [b]I will remove
sickness from your midst. **26** There
shall be no one miscarrying or
[a]barren in your land; [b]I will fulfill the
number of your days. **27** I will [a]send
My terror ahead of you and [b]throw
into confusion all the people among
whom you come, and I will [c]make
all your enemies [1]turn *their* backs
to you. **28** And I will send [a]hornets
ahead of you so that they will [b]drive
out the Hivites, the Canaanites, and
the Hittites before you. **29** [a]I will not
drive them out before you in a single
year, lest the land become desolate
and the beasts of the field become
too numerous for you. **30** I will drive
them out before you [a]little by little,
until you become fruitful and take
the land as an inheritance. **31** [a]And I
will set your boundary from the [1]Red
Sea to the sea of the Philistines, and
from the wilderness to the [2]River;
[b]for I will give the inhabitants of the
land into your hand, and you will
[c]drive them out from before you.
**32** [a]You shall cut no covenant with
them [b]or with their gods. **33** [a]They
shall not live in your land, lest they
make you sin against Me; for *if* you
serve their gods, [b]it will surely be a
snare to you."

### *Yahweh Cuts His Covenant with Israel*

**24** Then He said to Moses,
"[a]Come up to Yahweh, you
and Aaron, [b]Nadab and Abihu and
[c]seventy of the elders of Israel, and
you *all* shall worship at a distance.
**2** Moses alone, however, shall come
near to Yahweh, but they shall not
come near, and the people shall not
come up with him."

**3** Then Moses came and recounted
to the people all the words of Yahweh
and all the judgments; and all the
people answered with one voice and
said, "[a]All the words which Yahweh
has spoken we will do!" **4** [a]And Moses
wrote down all the words of Yahweh.
Then he arose early in the morning
and built an [b]altar [1]at the foot of the
mountain with twelve pillars for the
twelve tribes of Israel. **5** And he sent
young men of the sons of Israel,
[a]and they offered burnt offerings
and sacrificed young bulls as peace
offerings to Yahweh. **6** [a]And Moses
took half of the blood and put *it*
in basins, and the *other* half of the

---

**23:23** [a]Ex 23:20; Jos 24:8, 11 **23:24** [a]Ex 20:5; 23:13, 33; Dt 12:30f [b]Nu 33:52; Dt 7:5; 12:3; 2Ki 18:4 [c]Ex 34:13; Lv 26:1; 2Ki 3:2 **23:25** [a]Lv 26:3-13; Dt 6:13; 10:12; 28:1-14; Jos 22:5; 1Sa 12:20; Mt 4:10 [b]Ex 15:26; Dt 7:15 [1]Or *that He may bless* **23:26** [a]Dt 7:14 [b]Dt 4:40; Job 5:26 **23:27** [a]Ge 35:5; Ex 15:16; Dt 2:25; Jos 2:9 [b]Dt 7:23 [c]Ps 18:40; 21:12 [1]Lit *offer their necks* **23:28** [a]Dt 7:20; Jos 24:12 [b]Ex 33:2; 34:11 **23:29** [a]Dt 7:22 **23:30** [a]Dt 7:22 **23:31** [a]Ge 15:18; Dt 1:7, 8; 11:24 [b]Dt 2:36; Jos 21:44 [c]Jos 24:12, 18 [1]Lit *Sea of Reeds* [2]The Euphrates River **23:32** [a]Ex 34:12; Dt 7:2 [b]Ex 23:13, 24 **23:33** [a]Dt 7:1-5, 16 [b]Ex 34:12; Dt 12:30; Jos 23:13; Jdg 2:3; Ps 106:36 ◆ **24:1** [a]Ex 19:24 [b]Ex 6:23; 28:1; Lv 10:1, 2 [c]Nu 11:16 **24:3** [a]Ex 19:8; 24:7; Dt 5:27 **24:4** [a]Ex 17:14; 34:27; Dt 31:9 [b]Ex 17:15 [1]Lit *under* **24:5** [a]Ex 18:12 **24:6** [a]Heb 9:18

blood he [1]sprinkled on the altar.
**7** Then he took [a]the book of the
covenant and read *it* in the hearing
of the people; and they said, "[b]All
that Yahweh has spoken we will do,
and we will be obedient!" **8** So [a]Moses
took the blood and [1]sprinkled *it* on
the people and said, "Behold [b]the
blood of the covenant, which Yahweh
has cut with you [2]in accordance with
all these words."

**9** Then Moses went up [1]with Aar-
on, [a]Nadab and Abihu, and seventy
of the elders of Israel, **10** and [a]they
saw the God of Israel; and under His
feet [b,1]there appeared to be a pave-
ment of sapphire, [2]as clear as the sky
itself. **11** Yet He did not stretch out His
hand against the nobles of the sons
of Israel; and [a]they beheld God, and
they ate and drank.

**12** Now Yahweh said to Moses,
"Come up to Me on the mountain and
[1]remain there, and [a]I will give you the
stone tablets [2] with the [3]law and the
commandment which I have written
for their instruction." **13** So Moses
arose [1]with [a]Joshua his [2]attendant,
and Moses went up to [b]the moun-
tain of God. **14** But to the elders he
said, "[a]Remain here for us until we
return to you. And behold, [b]Aaron
and Hur are with you; whoever [1]has
a *legal* matter, let him approach
them." **15** Then Moses went up to the
mountain, and [a]the cloud covered
the mountain. **16** [a]And the glory of
Yahweh dwelt on Mount Sinai, and
the cloud covered it for six days;
and on the seventh day He [b]called
to Moses from the midst of the cloud.
**17** [a]And the appearance of the glory
of Yahweh was like a [b]consuming fire
on the mountain top, in the eyes of
the sons of Israel. **18** Then Moses
entered the midst of the cloud [1]as
he went up to the mountain; and
Moses was on the mountain [a]forty
days and forty nights.

### *Contributions for the Sanctuary*

**25** Then Yahweh spoke to Moses,
saying, **2** "[a]Speak with the
sons of Israel so that they take a
[1]contribution for Me; [b]from every
man whose heart is willing you shall
take My [1]contribution. **3** And this is
the [1]contribution which you shall
take from them: gold, silver, and
bronze, **4** [a,1]blue, purple, and scarlet
*material*, fine linen, goat *hair*, **5** rams'
skins dyed red, porpoise skins, acacia
wood, **6** [a]oil for lighting, [b]spices for
the anointing oil and for the fragrant
incense, **7** onyx stones, and setting
stones for the [a]ephod and for the
[b,1]breastpiece. **8** And let them [a]make
a sanctuary for Me, [b]that I may dwell
among them. **9** [a]According to all that
I am going to show you, *as* the pattern
of the tabernacle and the pattern of all
its furniture, just so you shall make *it*.

---

**24:6** [1]Lit *threw, splashed* **24:7** [a]Ex 24:4; Heb 9:19 [b]Ex 24:3 **24:8** [a]Heb 9:19, 20 [b]Zec 9:11; Mt 26:28; Mk 14:24; Lk 22:20; 1Co 11:25; Heb 13:20 [1]Lit *threw, splashed* [2]Lit *on all* **24:9** [a]Ex 24:1 [1]Lit *and* **24:10** [a]Ex 24:11; Nu 12:8; Is 6:5; Jn 1:18; 6:46 [b]Eze 1:26; 10:1; Rev 4:3 [1]Lit *like a pavement* [2]Lit *and as* **24:11** [a]Ge 16:13; 32:30; Ex 24:10 **24:12** [a]Ex 31:18; 32:15; Dt 5:22 [1]Lit *be* [2]Lit *and* [3]Or *instruction*, cf. 24:12b **24:13** [a]Ex 17:9-14; 33:11 [b]Ex 3:1 [1]Lit *and* [2]Or *minister* **24:14** [a]Ge 22:5 [b]Ex 17:10, 12 [1]Lit *is a master of matters* **24:15** [a]Ex 19:9 **24:16** [a]Ex 16:10; Nu 14:10 [b]Ps 99:7 **24:17** [a]Ex 3:2; Eze 1:28 [b]Dt 4:24; 9:3; Heb 12:29 **24:18** [a]Ex 34:28; Dt 9:9; 10:10 [1]Lit *and* ◆ **25:2** [a]Ex 35:4-9 [b]Ex 35:21; 1Chr 29:3, 5, 9; Ezr 2:68; 2Co 8:11, 12; 9:7 [1]Or *heave offering* **25:3** [1]Or *heave offering* **25:4** [a]Ex 28:5, 6, 8 [1]Or *violet* **25:6** [a]Ex 27:20 [b]Ex 30:23f **25:7** [a]Ex 28:4, 6-14 [b]Ex 28:4, 15-30 [1]Or *pouch* **25:8** [a]Ex 36:1-5 [b]Ex 29:45, 46; Nu 5:3; Dt 12:11; 1Ki 6:13; 2Co 6:16; Rev 21:3 **25:9** [a]Ex 25:40; 26:30; Ac 7:44; Heb 8:2, 5

### *The Ark of the Testimony*

**10** "[a]And they shall make an ark of
acacia wood two and a half [1]cubits
[2]long, and one and a half cubits [3]wide,
and one and a half cubits [4]high. **11** You
shall [a]overlay it with pure gold, inside
and out you shall overlay it, and you
shall make a gold molding [1]around it.
**12** You shall cast four gold rings for
it and [1]fasten them on its four feet,
and two rings shall be on one side of
it and two rings on the other side of
it. **13** You shall make poles of acacia
wood and overlay them with gold.
**14** You shall put the poles into the
rings on the sides of the ark, to carry
the ark with them. **15** The [a]poles shall
[1]remain in the rings of the ark; they
shall not be removed from it. **16** You
shall [a]put into the ark the testimony
which I shall give you.

**17** "You shall [a]make a [1]mercy seat
of pure gold, two and a half [2]cubits
[3]long and one and a half cubits [4]wide.
**18** You shall make two cherubim of
gold; make them of hammered work
[1]at the two ends of the mercy seat.
**19** Make one cherub [1]at one end and
one cherub [1]at the other end; from
*one piece* you shall make the mercy
seat *with* the cherubim at its two
ends. **20** [a]The cherubim shall have
*their* wings spread upward, covering
the mercy seat with their wings,
with their faces toward one another;
the faces of the cherubim are to be
toward the mercy seat. **21** [a]You shall
put the mercy seat [1]on top of the
ark, and [b]in the ark you shall put
the testimony which I will give to
you. **22** [a]There I will meet with you;
and from above the mercy seat, from
[b]between the two cherubim which
are upon the ark of the testimony,
I will speak to you about all which
I will command you for the sons of
Israel.

### *Bread of the Presence*

**23** "[a]You shall make a table of acacia
wood, two [1]cubits [2]long and one cu-
bit [3]wide and one and a half cubits
[4]high. **24** You shall overlay it with
pure gold and make a gold [a]border
around it. **25** You shall make for it
a rim of a [1]handbreadth around *it*;
and you shall make a gold border for
the rim around it. **26** You shall make
four gold rings for it and put rings
on the four corners which are on its
four feet. **27** The rings shall be close
to the rim as holders for the poles
to carry the table. **28** You shall make
the poles of acacia wood and overlay
them with gold, so that with them
the table may be carried. **29** You shall
make its [a,1]dishes and its pans and
its jars and its offering bowls with
which to pour drink offerings; you
shall make them of pure gold. **30** You
shall set [a]the bread of the [1]Presence
on the table before Me [2]at all times.

**25:10** [a]Ex 37:1-9; Dt 10:3; Heb 9:4 [1]A cubit was approx. 18 in. or 45 cm [2]Lit *its length* [3]Lit *its width* [4]Lit *its height* **25:11** [a]Heb 9:4 [1]Lit *on it round about* **25:12** [1]Or *put* **25:15** [a]1Ki 8:8 [1]Lit *be* **25:16** [a]Ex 40:20; Dt 10:2; 31:26; 1Ki 8:9; Heb 9:4 **25:17** [a]Ex 37:6 [1]Or *propitiatory seat*, *place of atonement*, so through v 22 [2]A cubit was approx. 18 in. or 45 cm [3]Lit *its length* [4]Lit *its width* **25:18** [1]Lit *from* **25:19** [1]Lit *from* **25:20** [a]1Ki 8:7; 1Chr 28:18; Heb 9:5 **25:21** [a]Ex 26:34; 40:20 [b]Ex 25:16 [1]Lit *above, upon* **25:22** [a]Ex 29:42, 43; 30:6, 36; Lv 16:2; Nu 17:4 [b]Nu 7:89; 1Sa 4:4; 2Sa 6:2; 2Ki 19:15; Ps 80:1; Is 37:16 **25:23** [a]Ex 37:10-16 [1]A cubit was approx. 18 in. or 45 cm [2]Lit *its length* [3]Lit *its width* [4]Lit *its height* **25:24** [a]Ex 25:11 **25:25** [1]A handbreadth was approx. 3 in. or 7.6 cm **25:29** [a]Ex 37:16; Nu 4:7 [1]Or *platters* **25:30** [a]Ex 39:36; 40:23; Lv 24:5-9 [1]Lit *Face* [2]Or *continually*

### *The Golden Lampstand*

**31** “[a] Then you shall make a lamp-
stand of pure gold. The lampstand, its
base, and its shaft are to be made of
hammered work; its cups, its [1]bulbs,
and its flowers shall be [2]of *the same*
*piece.* **32** [a]Six branches shall go out
from its sides; three branches of the
lampstand from its one side and three
branches of the lampstand from its
[1]other side. **33** [a]Three cups *shall be*
shaped like almond *blossoms* in the
one branch, a [1]bulb and a flower, and
three cups shaped like almond *blos-*
*soms* in the [2]other branch, a [1]bulb
and a flower—so for the six branches
going out from the lampstand; **34** and
[a]in the lampstand four cups shaped
like almond *blossoms,* its [1]bulbs and
its flowers. **35** [a]And a [1]bulb shall be
under the *first* pair of branches
*coming* out of it, and a [1]bulb under
the *second* pair of branches *coming*
out of it, and a [1]bulb under the *third*
pair of branches *coming* out of it, for
the six branches coming out of the
lampstand. **36** [a] Their [1] bulbs and
their branches shall be [2]of *the same*
*piece*; all of it shall be one piece of
hammered work of pure gold. **37** Then
you shall make its lamps seven *in*
*number*; and [a]they shall [1]mount its
lamps so as to shed light on the space
in front of it. **38** And its tongs and
[1]their trays *shall be* of pure gold. **39** It
shall be made from a [1]talent of pure
gold, with all these utensils. **40** [a]And
see that you make *them* [b]after the
pattern for them, which was shown
to you on the mountain.

### *Instructions for Making the Tabernacle*

**26** “[a]Moreover you shall make
the tabernacle with ten cur-
tains of fine twisted linen and [1]blue
and purple and scarlet *material*;
you shall make them with cheru-
bim, the work of a skillful designer.
**2** The length of each curtain shall be
[1]twenty-eight cubits, and the width
of each curtain four [2]cubits; all the
curtains shall have [3]the same mea-
surements. **3** Five curtains shall be
[1]joined to one another, and *the other*
five curtains *shall be* [1]joined to one
another. **4** And you shall make loops
of [1]blue on the edge of the [2]outermost
curtain in the one set, and likewise
you shall make *them* on the edge of
the curtain that is outermost in the
second [3]set. **5** You shall make fifty
loops in the one curtain, and you
shall make fifty loops on the [1]edge
of the curtain that is in the second
[2]set; the loops shall be opposite each
other. **6** You shall make fifty clasps of
gold, and you shall [1]join the curtains
to one another with the clasps so that
the [2]tabernacle will be a unit.

**7** “Then [a]you shall make curtains
of goats’ *hair* for a tent over the
tabernacle; you shall make eleven
curtains in all. **8** The length of each
curtain *shall be* [1]thirty cubits, and
the width of each curtain four cubits;

**25:31** [a]Ex 37:17-24; 1Ki 7:49; Zec 4:2 [1]Or *calyx* [2]Lit *of itself* **25:32** [a]Ex 37:18 [1]Lit *second* **25:33** [a]Ex 37:19 [1]Or *calyx* [2]Lit *one branch* **25:34** [a]Ex 37:20 [1]Or *calyxes* **25:35** [a]Ex 37:21 [1]Or *calyx* **25:36** [a]Ex 37:22 [1]Or *calyxes* [2]Lit *of itself* **25:37** [a]Nu 8:2 [1]Lit *raise up* **25:38** [1]Lit *its snuff dishes* **25:39** [1]A talent was approx. 75 lb. or 34 kg **25:40** [a]Heb 8:5 [b]Ex 25:9; 26:30; Nu 8:4; Ac 7:44 ◆ **26:1** [a]Ex 36:8-19 [1]Or *violet* **26:2** [1]Approx. 42 ft. Or 12.6 m [2]A cubit was approx. 18 in. or 45 cm [3]Lit *one measure* **26:3** [1]Or *coupled* **26:4** [1]Or *violet* [2]Lit *one curtain from the end in the coupling* [3]Lit *coupling* **26:5** [1]Lit *end* [2]Lit *coupling* **26:6** [1]Or *couple* [2]Or *dwelling place,* so in ch **26:7** [a]Ex 36:14 **26:8** [1]Approx. 45 ft. or 13.5 m the eleven curtains shall have [2]the same measurements. **9** And you shall [1]join five curtains by themselves and the *other* six curtains by themselves, and you shall double over the sixth curtain [2]at the front of the tent. **10** You shall make fifty loops on the edge of the [1]curtain that is outermost in the one [2]set, and fifty loops on the edge of the curtain *that is outermost in* the second [2]set.

**11** "You shall make fifty clasps of [1]bronze, and you shall put the clasps into the loops and [2]join the tent together so that it will be one unit. **12** The [1]overlapping part that is left over in the curtains of the tent, the half curtain that is left over, shall lap over the back of the tabernacle. **13** The cubit on one side and the cubit on the other, of what is left over in the length of the curtains of the tent, shall lap over the sides of the tabernacle on one side and on the other to cover it. **14** [a]You shall make a covering for the tent of rams' skins [1]dyed red and a covering of porpoise skins above.

**15** "Then you shall make [a]the boards for the tabernacle of acacia wood, standing upright. **16** Ten cubits *shall be* the length of [1]each board, and one and a half cubits the width of each board. **17** *There shall be* two [1]tenons for each board, [2]fitted to one another; thus you shall do for all the boards of the tabernacle. **18** You shall make the boards for the tabernacle: twenty boards [1]for the south side. **19** You shall make forty [a]bases of silver under the twenty boards, two bases under one board for its two tenons, and two bases under another board for its two tenons; **20** and for the second side of the tabernacle, on the north side, twenty boards, **21** and their forty bases of silver; two bases under one board and two bases under another board. **22** For the [1]rear of the tabernacle, to the west, you shall make six boards. **23** You shall make two boards for the corners of the tabernacle at the [1]rear. **24** They shall be [1]separated beneath, but together at their completion [2]at its top, [3]at the first ring; thus it shall be with both of them: they shall form the two corners. **25** There shall be eight boards with their bases of silver, sixteen bases; two bases under one board and two bases under another board.

**26** "Then you shall make [a]bars of acacia wood, five for the boards of one side of the tabernacle, **27** and five bars for the boards of the [1]other side of the tabernacle, and five bars for the boards of the side of the tabernacle for the [2]rear *side* to the west. **28** The middle bar in the [1]center of the boards shall pass through from end to end. **29** You shall overlay the boards with gold and make their rings of gold *as* holders for the bars; and you shall overlay the bars with gold. **30** Then you shall erect the tabernacle [a]according to its [1]plan which you have been shown in the mountain.

**31** "You shall make [a]a veil of [1]blue and purple and scarlet *material* and

---

**26:8** [2]Lit *one measure* **26:9** [1]Or *couple* [2]Lit *toward the front of the face of the tent* **26:10** [1]Lit *one curtain* [2]Lit *coupling* **26:11** [1]Or *copper* [2]Or *couple* **26:12** [1]Lit *excess* **26:14** [a]Ex 36:19 [1]Or *tanned* **26:15** [a]Ex 36:20-34 **26:16** [1]Lit *the* **26:17** [1]Lit *hands* [2]Lit *bound* **26:18** [1]Lit *toward the side of the Negev to the south* **26:19** [a]Ex 38:27 **26:22** [1]Lit *extreme parts* **26:23** [1]Lit *extreme parts* **26:24** [1]Lit *twins* [2]Or *at its head* [3]Or *with reference to* **26:26** [a]Ex 36:31 **26:27** [1]Lit *second* [2]Lit *extreme parts* **26:28** [1]Lit *midst* **26:30** [a]Ex 25:9, 40; Ac 7:44; Heb 8:5 [1]Lit *judgment* **26:31** [a]Ex 36:35, 36; 2Chr 3:14; Mt 27:51; Heb 9:3 [1]Or *violet*

fine twisted linen; it shall be made
with cherubim, the work of a skill-
ful designer. **32** You shall [1]hang it on
four pillars of acacia overlaid with
gold, their hooks *also being of* gold,
on four bases of silver. **33** You shall
[1]hang up the veil under the clasps,
and you shall bring in [a]the ark of the
testimony there within the veil; and
the veil shall separate for you [b]the
holy place and the Holy of Holies.
**34** [a]You shall put the mercy seat on
the ark of the testimony in the Holy
of Holies. **35** [a]You shall set the table
outside the veil and the [b]lampstand
opposite the table on the side of the
tabernacle toward the south; and you
shall put the table on the north side.
**36** "[a]You shall make a screen for
the doorway of the tent of [1]blue and
purple and scarlet *material* and fine
twisted linen, the work of a [2]weaver.
**37** [a]You shall make five pillars of aca-
cia for the screen and overlay them
with gold, their hooks *also being of*
gold; and you shall cast five bases of
[1]bronze for them.

### The Bronze Altar

**27** "And you shall make [a]the altar
of acacia wood, five [1]cubits
long and five cubits wide; the altar
shall be square, and its height shall
be three cubits. **2** You shall make [a]its
horns on its four corners; its horns
shall be [1]of the *same piece*, and
you shall overlay it with [2]bronze.
**3** You shall make its pots for remov-
ing its ashes, and its shovels and
its bowls and its flesh hooks and
its firepans; you shall make all its
utensils of bronze. **4** You shall make
for it a grating, a network of bronze,
and on the net you shall make four
bronze rings [1]at its four corners.
**5** You shall put it beneath, under
the ledge of the altar, so that the net
will reach halfway down the altar.
**6** You shall make poles for the altar,
poles of acacia wood, and overlay
them with bronze. **7** Its poles shall
be inserted into the rings, so that the
poles shall be on the two sides of the
altar [a]when it is carried. **8** You shall
make it hollow with planks; [a]as it
was shown to you in the mountain,
so they shall make *it*.

### The Court of the Tabernacle

**9** "You shall make [a]the court of the
[1]tabernacle. [2]On the south side *there*
*shall be* hangings for the court of fine
twisted linen [3]one hundred cubits
long for one side; **10** and its pillars
*shall be* twenty, with their twenty
bases of bronze; the hooks of the
pillars and their [1]bands *shall be* of
silver. **11** Likewise for the north side
in length *there shall be* hangings one
hundred *cubits* long, and its twenty
pillars with their twenty bases of
bronze; the hooks of the pillars and
their bands *shall be* of silver. **12** *For*
the width of the court on the west
side *shall be* hangings of fifty cubits
*with* their ten pillars and their ten
bases. **13** The width of the court on
the east side toward the sunrise
*shall be* fifty cubits. **14** The hangings
for the *one* [1]side *of the gate shall be*

**26:32** [1]Lit *put* **26:33** [a]Ex 25:16; 40:21 [b]Heb 9:2f [1]Lit *put* **26:34** [a]Ex 25:21; 40:20; Lv 16:2 **26:35** [a]Ex 40:22 [b]Ex 40:24 **26:36** [a]Ex 36:37 [1]Or *violet* [2]A weaver in colors; lit *variegator* **26:37** [a]Ex 36:38 [1]Or *copper* ◆ **27:1** [a]Ex 38:1-7 [1]A cubit was approx. 18 in. or 45 cm **27:2** [a]Ps 118:27 [1]Lit *from itself* [2]Or *copper*, so in ch **27:4** [1]Lit *on* **27:7** [a]Nu 4:15 **27:8** [a]Ex 25:40; 26:30; Ac 7:44; Heb 8:5 **27:9** [a]Ex 38:9-20 [1]Or *dwelling place* [2]Lit *For the side of the Negev to the south* [3]Approx. 150 ft. or 45 m **27:10** [1]Or *fillets, rings* **27:14** [1]Lit *shoulder*

[2]fifteen cubits *with* their three pillars and their three bases. **15** And for the [1]other [2]side *shall be* hangings of fifteen cubits *with* their three pillars and their three bases. **16** And as for the gate of the court *there shall be* a screen of [1]twenty cubits, of [2]blue and purple and scarlet *material* and fine twisted linen, the work of a [3]weaver, *with* their four pillars and their four bases. **17** All the pillars around the court shall be furnished with silver bands *with* their hooks of silver and their bases of bronze. **18** The length of the court *shall be* one hundred cubits, and the width fifty throughout, and the height five cubits of fine twisted linen, and their bases of bronze. **19** All the utensils of the tabernacle *used* in all its service, and all its pegs, and all the pegs of the court, *shall be* of bronze.

**20** "And you shall command the sons of Israel, that they bring you [a]clear oil of beaten olives for the [1]light, to make a lamp [2]burn continually. **21** In the [a]tent of meeting, outside [b]the veil which is before the testimony, [c]Aaron and his sons shall keep it in order from evening to morning before Yahweh; *it shall be* a perpetual [d]statute throughout their generations [1]for the sons of Israel.

### The Priests' Garments

**28** "Now as for you, [a]bring near to yourself Aaron your brother, and his sons with him, from among the sons of Israel, to minister as priests to Me—Aaron, [b]Nadab and Abihu, Eleazar and Ithamar, Aaron's sons. **2** You shall make [a]holy garments for Aaron your brother, for glory and for beauty. **3** You shall speak to all those [a,1]wise at heart [b]whom I have filled with [2]the spirit of wisdom, that they make Aaron's garments to set him apart as holy, in order for him to minister as priest to Me. **4** These are the garments which they shall make: a [a,1]breastpiece and an ephod and a robe and a tunic of checkered work, a turban and a sash, and they shall make holy garments for Aaron your brother and his sons, in order for him to minister as priest to Me. **5** They shall take [a]the gold and the [1]blue and the purple and the scarlet *material* and the fine linen.

**6** "They shall also make [a]the ephod of gold, of [1]blue and purple *and* scarlet *material* and fine twisted linen, the work of the skillful designer. **7** It shall have two shoulder pieces joined to its two ends, that it may be joined. **8** The skillfully woven band, which is on it, shall be like its workmanship, [1]of the same material: of gold, of [2]blue and purple and scarlet *material* and fine twisted linen. **9** You shall take two onyx stones and engrave on them the names of the sons of Israel, **10** six of their names on the one stone and the names of the remaining six on the second stone, according to their birth. **11** [1]As a jeweler engraves a signet, you shall engrave the two stones according to

---

**27:14** [2]Approx. 22.5 ft. or 6.75 m **27:15** [1]Lit *second* [2]Lit *shoulder* **27:16** [1]Approx. 30 ft. or 9 m [2]Or *violet* [3]A weaver in colors; lit *variegator* **27:20** [a]Ex 35:8, 28; Lv 24:1-4 [1]Or *luminary* [2]Lit *ascend* **27:21** [a]Ex 25:22; 29:42; 30:36 [b]Ex 26:31, 33 [c]Ex 30:8; 1Sa 3:3; 2Chr 13:11 [d]Ex 28:43; 29:9; Lv 3:17; 16:34; Nu 18:23; 19:21; 1Sa 30:25 [1]Lit *from* ◆ **28:1** [a]Nu 18:7; Ps 99:6; Heb 5:1, 4 [b]Ex 24:1, 9 **28:2** [a]Ex 29:5, 29; 31:10; 39:1-31; Lv 8:7-9, 30 **28:3** [a]Ex 31:6; 35:25, 31-35; 36:1 [b]Ex 31:3; Is 11:2; 1Co 12:7-11; Eph 1:17 [1]Or *skillful* [2]Artistic skill **28:4** [a]Ex 28:15-43 [1]Or *pouch* **28:5** [a]Ex 25:3 [1]Or *violet* **28:6** [a]Ex 39:2-7; Lv 8:7 [1]Or *violet* **28:8** [1]Lit *from it* [2]Or *violet* **28:11** [1]Lit *Work of a craftsman of stone*

the names of the sons of Israel; you
shall set them all around in filigree
*settings* of gold. **12** You shall put the
two stones on the shoulder pieces of
the ephod, *as* stones of remembrance
for the sons of Israel, and Aaron shall
[a]bear their names before Yahweh on
his two shoulders [b]for remembrance.
**13** [a]You shall make filigree *settings* of
gold, **14** and two chains of pure gold;
you shall make them a twisted work
of cords, and you shall put the chains
of cords on the filigree *settings*.

**15** "[a]You shall make a [1]breastpiece
of judgment, the work of a skillful
designer; like the work of the ephod
you shall make it: of gold, of [2]blue and
purple and scarlet *material* and fine
twisted linen you shall make it. **16** It
shall be square, *having been* folded
double, a [1]span [2]in length and a [1]span
in width. **17** You shall [1]mount on it
four rows of stones; the first row *shall
be* a row of ruby, topaz, and emerald;
**18** and the second row a turquoise,
a sapphire, and a diamond; **19** and
the third row a jacinth, an agate, and
an amethyst; **20** and the fourth row a
beryl and an onyx and a jasper; they
shall be [1]set in gold settings. **21** The
stones shall be according to the
names of the sons of Israel: twelve,
according to their names; they shall
be *like* the engravings of a signet,
*each* [a]*according* to his name for the
twelve tribes. **22** You shall make on
the [1]breastpiece chains of a twisted
work of cords in pure gold. **23** You
shall make on the breastpiece two
rings of gold, and you shall put the
two rings on the two ends of the
breastpiece. **24** You shall put the two
cords of gold on the two rings at the
ends of the breastpiece. **25** You shall
put the two ends of the two cords
on the two filigree *settings*, and you
shall put them on the shoulder pieces
of the ephod at the front of it. **26** You
shall make two rings of gold and shall
place them on the two ends of the
breastpiece, on the edge of it, which
is toward the inner side of the ephod.
**27** You shall make two rings of gold
and put them on the bottom of the
two shoulder pieces of the ephod,
on the front of it close to the place
where it is joined, above the skillfully
woven band of the ephod. **28** They
shall bind the breastpiece by its rings
to the rings of the ephod with a [1]blue
cord, so that it will be on the skillfully
woven band of the ephod, and that
the breastpiece will not come loose
from the ephod. **29** Aaron shall carry
the names of the sons of Israel in the
breastpiece of judgment over his
heart when he comes into the holy
place, for a remembrance before
Yahweh continually. **30** [a]You shall put
in the breastpiece of judgment the
[b,1]Urim and the Thummim, and they
shall be over Aaron's heart when he
comes in before Yahweh; and Aaron
shall carry the judgment of the sons
of Israel over his heart before Yahweh
continually.

**31** "[a]You shall make the robe of
the ephod entirely of [1]blue. **32** There
shall be an opening [1]at its top in the
middle of it; around the edge of its

---

**28:12** [a]Ex 28:29; 39:6f [b]Ex 39:7; Lv 24:7; Nu 31:54; Jos 4:7; 1Co 11:24f **28:13** [a]Ex 39:16-18
**28:15** [a]Ex 39:8-21 [1]Or *pouch* [2]Or *violet* **28:16** [1]A span was approx. 9 in. or 23 cm [2]Lit *its*
**28:17** [1]Lit *fill in a setting of stones, four rows of stones* **28:20** [1]Lit *interwoven with gold in their settings* **28:21** [a]Rev 7:4-8; 21:12 **28:22** [1]Or *pouch*, so through v 30 **28:28** [1]Or *violet*
**28:30** [a]Lv 8:8 [b]Nu 27:21; Dt 33:8; Ezr 2:63; Ne 7:65 [1]Lit *lights and perfections* **28:31** [a]Ex 39:22-26
[1]Or *violet* **28:32** [1]Or *for his head*

opening there shall be a binding of woven work, like the opening of a coat of mail, so that it will not be torn. **33** You shall make on its hem pomegranates of blue and purple and scarlet *material*, all around on its hem, and bells of gold between them all around: **34** a golden bell and a pomegranate, a golden bell and a pomegranate, all around on the hem of the robe. **35** It shall be on Aaron [1]when he ministers; and its sound shall be heard when he comes into the holy place before Yahweh and when he goes out, so that he will not die.

**36** "You shall also make [a]a plate of pure gold and shall engrave on it, like the engravings of a signet, '[b]Holy to Yahweh.' **37** You shall [1]fasten it on a [2]blue cord, and it shall be on the turban; it shall be at the front of the turban. **38** It shall be on Aaron's forehead, and Aaron shall [a,1]take away the iniquity of the holy things which the sons of Israel set apart as holy, with regard to all their holy gifts; and it shall continually be on his forehead, that [b]they may be accepted before Yahweh.

**39** "You shall weave [a]the tunic of checkered work of fine linen, and you shall make a turban of fine linen, and you shall make a sash, the work of a [1]weaver.

**40** "For Aaron's sons you shall make [a]tunics; you shall also make sashes for them, and you shall make [b,1]caps for them, for glory and for beauty. **41** You shall put them on Aaron your brother and on his sons with him; and you shall [a]anoint them and [1]ordain them and set them apart as holy, that they may minister to Me as priests. **42** You shall make for them [a]linen undergarments to cover *their* bare flesh; they shall [1]reach from the loins even to the thighs. **43** They shall be on Aaron and on his sons when they come into the tent of meeting or [a]when they approach the altar to minister in the holy place, so that they do not incur [1]guilt and die. [b]It *shall be* a perpetual statute to him and to his seed after him.

### *Setting Apart the Priests*

**29** "[a]Now this is [1]what you shall do to them to set them apart as holy to minister as priests to Me: take one bull from the herd and two rams without blemish, **2** and [a]unleavened bread and unleavened cakes mixed with oil, and unleavened wafers [1]spread with oil; you shall make them of fine wheat flour. **3** And you shall put them in one basket and bring them near in the basket along with the bull and the two rams. **4** Then [a]you shall bring Aaron and his sons near to the doorway of the tent of meeting and wash them with water. **5** And you shall take the garments, and put on Aaron the [a]tunic and [b]the robe of the ephod and [c]the ephod and [d]the [1]breastpiece, and gird him with the skillfully [e]woven band of the ephod; **6** and you shall set the

**28:35** [1]Lit *for ministering* **28:36** [a]Ex 39:30, 31; Lv 8:9 [b]Zec 14:20 **28:37** [1]Lit *place* [2]Or *violet* **28:38** [a]Lv 10:17; 22:16; Nu 18:1 [b]Lv 1:4; 22:27; 23:11; Is 56:7 [1]Or *bear* **28:39** [a]Ex 39:27-29 [1]A weaver in colors; lit *variegator* **28:40** [a]Ex 28:4; 39:27, 41 [b]Ex 29:9; 39:28; Lv 8:13; Eze 44:18 [1]Lit *headgear* **28:41** [a]Ex 29:7, 9; 30:30; 40:15; Lv 8:1-36; 10:7 [1]Lit *fill their hand* **28:42** [a]Ex 39:28; Lv 6:10; 16:4; Eze 44:18 [1]Lit *be* **28:43** [a]Ex 20:26 [b]Ex 27:21 [1]Or *iniquity* ◆ **29:1** [a]Lv 8:1-34 [1]Lit *the thing which* **29:2** [a]Lv 2:4; 6:19-23 [1]Or *anointed* **29:4** [a]Ex 40:12; Lv 8:6 **29:5** [a]Ex 28:39; Lv 8:7 [b]Ex 28:31 [c]Ex 28:6 [d]Ex 28:15 [e]Ex 28:8 [1]Or *pouch*

[a]turban on his head and put [b]the
holy crown on the turban. **7** Then
you shall take [a]the anointing oil
and pour it on his head and anoint
him. **8** And you shall bring his sons
near and put [a]tunics on them. **9** You
shall gird them with [a]sashes, Aaron
and his sons, and bind [1]caps on them,
and they shall have [b]the priesthood
by a perpetual statute. So you shall
[c,2]ordain Aaron and his sons.

### *Slaughtering the Offerings*

**10** "Then you shall bring the bull
near before the tent of meeting,
and Aaron and his sons shall [a]lay
their hands on the head of the bull.
**11** You shall slaughter the bull before
Yahweh at the doorway of the tent
of meeting. **12** You shall [a]take some
of the blood of the bull and put *it*
on [b]the horns of the altar with your
finger; and you shall pour out all the
blood at the base of the altar. **13** You
shall [a]take all the fat that covers the
entrails and the [1]lobe of the liver and
the two kidneys and the fat that is on
them, and you shall offer them up in
smoke on the altar. **14** But [a]the flesh
of the bull and its hide and its refuse,
you shall burn with fire outside the
camp; it is a sin offering.

**15** "[a]You shall also take the one
ram, and Aaron and his sons shall
lay their hands on the head of the
ram; **16** and you shall slaughter the
ram, and you shall take its blood
and splash it around on the altar.
**17** Then you shall cut the ram into
its pieces, and wash its entrails and
its legs, and put *them* [1]with its pieces
and [2]its head. **18** You shall offer up in
smoke the whole ram on the altar; it
is a burnt offering to Yahweh: [a]it is a
soothing aroma, an offering by fire
to Yahweh.

**19** "Then [a]you shall take the second
ram, and Aaron and his sons shall lay
their hands on the head of the ram.
**20** You shall slaughter the ram, and
take some of its blood and put *it* on
the lobe of Aaron's right ear and on
the lobes of his sons' right ears and
on the thumbs of their right hands
and on the big toes of their right
feet, and splash the *rest of the* blood
around on the altar. **21** Then you shall
take some of the blood that is on the
altar and some of the [a]anointing oil,
and sprinkle *it* on Aaron and on his
garments and on his sons and on
his sons' garments with him; so he
and his garments shall be set apart
as holy, as well as his sons and his
sons' garments with him.

**22** "You shall also take the fat from
the ram and the fat tail and the fat
that covers the entrails and the [1]lobe
of the liver and the two kidneys and
the fat that is on them and the right
thigh (for it is a ram of [2]ordination),
**23** and one cake of bread and [a]one
cake of bread *mixed with* oil and one
wafer from the basket of unleavened
bread which is *set* before Yahweh;
**24** and you shall put [1]all these [2]in the
[3]hands of Aaron and [2]in the [3]hands
of his sons, and you shall wave them
as a wave offering before Yahweh.
**25** [a]You shall take them from their

---

**29:6** [a]Ex 28:4, 39 [b]Ex 28:36, 37; Lv 8:9 **29:7** [a]Ex 30:25; Lv 8:12; 21:10; Nu 35:25; Ps 133:2
**29:8** [a]Ex 28:39, 40; Lv 8:13 **29:9** [a]Ex 28:40 [b]Ex 40:15; Nu 3:10; 18:7; 25:13; Dt 18:5 [c]Ex 28:41; Lv 8:1-36
[1]Lit *headgear* [2]Lit *fill the hand of* **29:10** [a]Lv 1:4; 8:14 **29:12** [a]Lv 8:15 [b]Ex 27:2; 30:2 **29:13** [a]Lv 3:3, 4
[1]Or *appendage on* **29:14** [a]Lv 4:11, 12, 21; Heb 13:11 **29:15** [a]Lv 8:18 **29:17** [1]Lit *on* [2]Lit *on its*
**29:18** [a]Ge 8:21; Ex 29:25 **29:19** [a]Lv 8:22f **29:21** [a]Ex 30:25, 31; Lv 8:30 **29:22** [1]Or *appendage on*
[2]Lit *filling* **29:23** [a]Lv 8:26 **29:24** [1]Lit *the whole* [2]Lit *on* [3]Lit *palms* **29:25** [a]Lv 8:28

hands and offer them up in smoke on
the altar on the burnt offering for a
soothing aroma before Yahweh; it is
an offering by fire to Yahweh.
**26** "Then you shall take [a]the
breast of Aaron's ram of [1]ordination
and wave it as a wave offering before
Yahweh; and it shall be your portion.
**27** You shall set apart as holy the
breast of the wave offering and the
thigh of the [1]contribution offering
which was waved and which was
[2]raised up *as a contribution* from
the ram of [3]ordination, from the
one which was for Aaron and from
the one which was for his sons. **28** It
shall be for Aaron and his sons as a
perpetual statute from the sons of
Israel, for it is a [1]contribution offer-
ing; and it shall be a [1]contribution
offering from the sons of Israel from
the sacrifices of their peace offerings,
*even* their [1]contribution offering to
Yahweh.
**29** "[a]The holy garments of Aaron
shall be for his sons after him, [1]that
in them they may be anointed and
ordained. **30** For seven days the one
of his sons who is priest in his stead
shall put them on when he comes
into the tent of meeting to minister
in the holy place.

### *Yahweh Will Meet and Speak to Israel*

**31** "You shall take the ram of [1]ordina-
tion and [a]boil its flesh in a holy place.
**32** Aaron and his sons shall eat the
flesh of the ram and the bread that is
in the basket, at the doorway of the
tent of meeting. **33** Thus [a]they shall
eat [1]those things by which atonement
was made [2]to ordain them, [3]to set
them apart as holy; but a [b,4]layman
shall not eat *them*, because they are
holy. **34** [a]If any of the flesh of [1]ordi-
nation or any of the bread remains
until morning, then you shall burn
the remainder with fire; it shall not
be eaten, because it is holy.
**35** "Thus you shall do to Aaron
and to his sons, according to all that
I have commanded you; you shall
[1]ordain them through [a]seven days.
**36** [a]Each day you shall offer a bull
as a sin offering for atonement, and
you shall [1]purify the altar when you
make atonement [2]for it, and [b]you
shall anoint it to set it apart as holy.
**37** For seven days you shall make
atonement [1]for the altar and set it
apart as holy; then [a]the altar shall
be most holy, *and* whatever touches
the altar shall be holy.
**38** "Now [a]this is what you shall
offer on the altar: two one year old
lambs each day, continuously. **39** The
[a]one lamb you shall offer in the
morning, and the second lamb you
shall offer [1]at twilight; **40** and there
*shall be* [1]one-tenth *of an ephah* of
fine flour mixed with one-fourth of a
[2]hin of beaten oil, and one-fourth of
a hin of wine for a drink offering with
the one lamb. **41** The second lamb you
shall offer [1]at twilight, and you shall
offer with it [2]the same grain offering

**29:26** [a]Lv 7:31, 34; 8:29 [1]Lit *filling* **29:27** [1]Or *heave offering* [2]Or *heaved up* [3]Lit *filling* **29:28** [1]Or *heave offering* **29:29** [a]Nu 20:26, 28 [1]Lit *for anointing in them and filling their hand in them*
**29:31** [a]Lv 8:31 [1]Lit *filling* **29:33** [a]Lv 10:14 [b]Lv 22:10, 13 [1]Lit *them* [2]Lit *to fill their hand* [3]Or *to sanctify them* [4]Lit *stranger* **29:34** [a]Ex 12:10; 23:18; 34:25; Lv 8:32 [1]Lit *filling* **29:35** [a]Lv 8:33 [1]Lit *fill their hand*
**29:36** [a]Heb 10:11 [b]Ex 40:10 [1]Or *offer a sin offering on the altar* [2]Lit *upon* **29:37** [a]Ex 30:28f [1]Lit *upon*
**29:38** [a]Nu 28:3-31; 29:6-38 **29:39** [a]Eze 46:13-15 [1]Lit *between the two evenings* **29:40** [1]Approx. 2.1 qt. or 2.3 l, an ephah was approx. 21 qt. or 23 l [2]Approx. 1 qt. or 0.9 l, a hin was approx. 1 gal. or 3.8 l
**29:41** [1]Lit *between the two evenings* [2]Lit *according to the grain offering of the morning*

and [3]the same drink offering as in the morning, for a soothing aroma, an offering by fire to Yahweh. **42** It shall be a continual burnt offering throughout your generations at the doorway of the tent of meeting before Yahweh, [a]where I will meet with you, to speak to you there. **43** I will meet there with the sons of Israel, and it shall be set apart as holy by My glory. **44** I will set the tent of meeting and the altar apart as holy; I will also set Aaron and his sons apart as holy to minister as priests to Me. **45** [a]I will dwell among the sons of Israel and will be their God. **46** They shall know that [a]I am Yahweh their God who brought them out of the land of Egypt, that I might dwell among them; I am Yahweh their God.

### *The Altar of Incense*

**30** "Moreover, you shall make [a]an altar as a place for burning incense; you shall make it of acacia wood. **2** Its length *shall be* a [1]cubit, and its width a cubit; it shall be square. And its height *shall be* two cubits; its horns *shall be* [2]of the same piece. **3** You shall overlay it with pure gold, its top and its [1]sides all around, and its horns; and you shall make a gold molding all around for it. **4** You shall make two gold rings for it under its molding; you shall make *them* on its two side walls—on [1]opposite sides—and [2]they shall be holders for poles with which to carry it. **5** You shall make the poles of acacia wood and overlay them with gold. **6** You shall put [1]this altar in front of the veil that is [2]near the ark of the testimony, in front of the [a,3]mercy seat that is over the testimony, where I will meet with you. **7** Aaron shall burn fragrant incense on it; he shall burn it every morning when he trims the lamps. **8** When Aaron [1]trims the lamps [2]at twilight, he shall burn incense. *There shall be* continual incense before Yahweh throughout your generations. **9** You shall not offer any strange incense on [1]this altar or burnt offering or grain offering; and you shall not pour out a drink offering on it. **10** Aaron shall [a]make atonement on its horns once a year; he shall make atonement on it with the blood of the sin offering of atonement once a year throughout your generations. It is most holy to Yahweh."

### *The Census and the Atonement Price*

**11** Yahweh also spoke to Moses, saying, **12** "When you take [a]a [1]census of the sons of Israel [2]to number them, then each one of them shall give [b]a *price of* atonement for [3]himself to Yahweh when you [4]number them, so that there will be no plague among them when you [4]number them. **13** This is what everyone who [1]is numbered shall give: half a [2]shekel according to the shekel of the sanctuary ([a]the shekel is twenty [3]gerahs), half a

**29:41** [3]Lit *according to its* **29:42** [a]Ex 25:22; Nu 17:4 **29:45** [a]Ex 25:8; Lv 26:12; Nu 5:3; Dt 12:11; Zec 2:10; 2Co 6:16; Rev 21:3 **29:46** [a]Ex 20:2 ◆ **30:1** [a]Ex 37:25-29 **30:2** [1]A cubit was approx. 18 in. or 45 cm [2]Lit *from itself* **30:3** [1]Lit *walls* **30:4** [1]Lit *its two* [2]Lit *it* **30:6** [a]Ex 25:21f [1]Lit *it* [2]Or *over;* lit *upon* [3]Or *propitiatory seat, place of atonement* **30:8** [1]Lit *causes to ascend* [2]Lit *between the two evenings* **30:9** [1]Lit *it* **30:10** [a]Lv 16:18 **30:12** [a]Ex 38:25, 26; Nu 1:2; 26:2 [b]Nu 31:50 [1]Lit *sum* [2]Lit *for their being mustered* [3]Lit *his soul* [4]Lit *muster* **30:13** [a]Lv 27:25; Nu 3:47; Eze 45:12 [1]Lit *passes over to those who are mustered* [2]A shekel was approx. 0.4 oz. or 11 gm [3]Approx. 0.5 oz. or 14 gm, a gerah was approx. 0.025 oz. or 0.7 gm

shekel as a [4]contribution to Yahweh. 14 Everyone who [1]is numbered, from twenty years old and over, shall give the [2]contribution to Yahweh. 15 The rich shall not pay more and the poor shall not pay less than the half shekel when you give the [1]contribution to Yahweh to make atonement for your souls. 16 And you shall take the atonement money from the sons of Israel and shall give it for the service of the tent of meeting, that it may be a remembrance for the sons of Israel before Yahweh, to make atonement for your souls."

### *The Laver for the Priestly Washing*

17 And Yahweh spoke to Moses, saying, 18 "You shall also make [a]a laver of [1]bronze, with its stand of bronze, for washing; and you shall [b]put it between the tent of meeting and the altar, and you shall put water in it. 19 And Aaron and his sons shall [a]wash their hands and their feet from it; 20 when they come into the tent of meeting, they shall wash with water, so that they will not die; or when they approach the altar to minister, by offering up in smoke a fire *sacrifice* to Yahweh. 21 So they shall wash their hands and their feet, so that they will not die; and [a]it shall be a perpetual statute for them, for [1]Aaron and his seed throughout their generations."

### *The Holy Anointing Oil*

22 Moreover, Yahweh spoke to Moses, saying, 23 "But as for you, take for yourself the finest of spices: of flowing myrrh 500 *shekels*, and of fragrant cinnamon half as much, 250, and of fragrant cane 250, 24 and of cassia 500, according to the shekel of the sanctuary, and of olive oil a [1]hin. 25 And you shall make [1]of these a holy anointing oil, a perfume mixture, the work of a perfumer; it shall be [a]a holy anointing oil. 26 And with it [a]you shall anoint the tent of meeting and the ark of the testimony, 27 and the table and all its utensils, and the lampstand and its utensils, and the altar of incense, 28 and the altar of burnt offering and all its utensils, and the laver and its stand. 29 You shall also set them apart as holy, that they may be most holy; whatever touches them shall be holy. 30 [a]And you shall anoint Aaron and his sons, and you shall set them apart as holy, that they may minister as priests to Me. 31 And you shall speak to the sons of Israel, saying, 'This shall be a holy anointing oil to Me throughout your generations. 32 It shall not be poured on [1]anyone's body, nor shall you make *any* like it in [2]the same specifications; [a]it is holy, *and* it shall be holy to you. 33 [a]Whoever shall mix *any* like it or whoever puts any of it on a [1]layman [b,2]shall be cut off from his people.'"

### *The Incense*

34 Then Yahweh said to Moses, "Take for yourself fragrances, stacte and onycha and galbanum, fragrances with pure frankincense; there shall be an equal part of each. 35 With it

---

**30:13** [4]Lit *heave offering* **30:14** [1]See v 13, note 1 [2]Lit *heave offering of Yahweh* **30:15** [1]Lit *heave offering of Yahweh* **30:18** [a]Ex 38:8 [b]Ex 40:30 [1]Or *copper* **30:19** [a]Ex 40:31f; Is 52:11 **30:21** [a]Ex 28:43 [1]Lit *him* **30:24** [1]A hin was approx. 1 gal. or 3.8 l **30:25** [a]Ex 37:29; 40:9; Lv 8:10 [1]Lit *it* **30:26** [a]Ex 40:9; Lv 8:10; Nu 7:1 **30:30** [a]Ex 29:7; Lv 8:12 **30:32** [a]Ex 30:25, 37 [1]Lit *the flesh of man* [2]Lit *its proportion* **30:33** [a]Ex 30:38 [b]Ge 17:14; Ex 12:15; Lv 7:20f [1]Lit *stranger* [2]Lit *even he shall*

you shall make incense, a perfume, the work of a perfumer, salted, pure, *and* holy. **36** You shall beat some of it very fine, and you shall put part of it before the testimony in the tent of meeting [a]where I will meet with you; it shall be most holy to you. **37** The incense which you shall make, [a]you shall not make in [1]the same specifications for yourselves; it shall be holy to you for Yahweh. **38** [a]Whoever shall make *any* like it, to [1]use as perfume, [2]shall be cut off from his people."

### *Bezalel and Oholiab*

**31** [a]And Yahweh spoke to Moses, saying, **2** "See, I have called by name Bezalel, the [a]son of Uri, the son of Hur, of the tribe of Judah. **3** And I have [a]filled him with the Spirit of God in wisdom, in discernment, in knowledge, and in all *kinds of* [1]craftsmanship, **4** to devise artistic designs for work in gold, in silver, and in [1]bronze, **5** and in the cutting of stones [1]for settings, and in the carving of wood, in order *for him* to work in all *kinds of* [2]craftsmanship. **6** And behold, I Myself have [1]appointed with him [a]Oholiab, the son of Ahisamach, of the tribe of Dan; and in the hearts of all who are [2]wise at heart I have put [3]wisdom, that they may make all that I have commanded you: **7** [a]the tent of meeting, and [b]the ark of testimony, and [c]the [1]mercy seat upon it, and all the furniture of the tent, **8** [a]the table also and its [1]utensils, and the [b]pure *gold* lampstand with all its [1]utensils, and [c]the altar of incense, **9** [a]the altar of burnt offering also with all its [1]utensils, and [b]the laver and its stand, **10** the [a,1]woven garments as well, and the holy garments for Aaron the priest, and the garments of his sons, *with which* to minister as priests; **11** [a]the anointing oil also, and the [b]fragrant incense for the holy place, they shall make *them* according to all that I have commanded you."

### *The Sign of the Sabbath*

**12** Yahweh spoke to Moses, saying, **13** "But as for you, speak to the sons of Israel, saying, '[a]You shall surely keep My sabbaths; for *this* is [b]a sign between Me and you throughout your generations, that you may know that I am Yahweh who makes you holy. **14** Therefore you shall keep the sabbath, for it is holy to you. [a]Everyone who profanes it shall surely be put to death; for whoever does any work on it, that person shall be cut off from among his people. **15** [a]Six days work may be done, but on the seventh day there is a [b]sabbath of complete rest, holy to Yahweh; [c]whoever does any work on the sabbath day shall surely be put to death. **16** So the sons of Israel shall keep the sabbath, to [1]celebrate the sabbath throughout their generations as an everlasting covenant.' **17** [a]It is a sign between Me and the sons of Israel forever; [b]for in

---

**30:36** [a]Ex 29:42 **30:37** [a]Ex 30:32 [1]Lit *its proportion* **30:38** [a]Ex 30:33 [1]Lit *smell of it* [2]Lit *even he shall* ◆ **31:1** [a]Ex 35:30-36:1 **31:2** [a]1Chr 2:20 **31:3** [a]Ex 35:31; 1Ki 7:14; 1Co 12:4-8 [1]Or *workmanship* **31:4** [1]Or *copper* **31:5** [1]Lit *to fill in (for a setting)* [2]Or *workmanship* **31:6** [a]Ex 35:34 [1]Lit *given* [2]Or *skillful* [3]Or *skill* **31:7** [a]Ex 36:8-38 [b]Ex 37:1-5 [c]Ex 37:6-9 [1]Or *propitiatory seat, place of atonement* **31:8** [a]Ex 37:10-16 [b]Ex 37:17-24; Lv 24:4 [c]Ex 37:25-29 [1]Or *vessels* **31:9** [a]Ex 38:1-7 [b]Ex 38:8 [1]Or *vessels* **31:10** [a]Ex 39:1 [1]Or *service garments* **31:11** [a]Ex 30:23-32 [b]Ex 30:34-38 **31:13** [a]Ex 20:8 [b]Ex 31:17; Eze 20:12, 20 **31:14** [a]Ex 31:15; 35:2; Nu 15:32, 35; Jn 7:23 **31:15** [a]Ex 20:9-11; 23:12; 34:21; 35:2; Lv 23:3; Dt 5:12-14 [b]Ge 2:2f; Ex 16:23; 20:8; 35:2, 3 [c]Ex 31:14 **31:16** [1]Lit *do* **31:17** [a]Ex 31:13; Eze 20:12 [b]Ge 1:31; 2:2, 3; Ex 20:11

six days Yahweh made heaven and
earth, but on the seventh day He
rested and was refreshed."
**18** When He had finished speaking
with him upon Mount Sinai, He gave
Moses [a]the two tablets of the testi-
mony, tablets of stone, [b]written by
the finger of God.

### *The Golden Calf*

**32** Then the people saw that Mo-
ses [a]delayed to come down
from the mountain. So the people
assembled about Aaron and said to
him, "Arise, [b]make us [1]gods who will
go before us; as for [c]this Moses, the
man who brought us up from the land
of Egypt, we do not know what has
become of him." **2** And Aaron said to
them, "[a]Tear off the gold rings which
are in the ears of your wives, your
sons, and your daughters, and bring
*them* to me." **3** Then all the people
tore off the gold rings which were
in their ears and brought *them* to
Aaron. **4** And he took *this* from their
hand and fashioned it with a graving
tool and made it into a [a]molten calf;
and they said, "[1]These are your gods,
O Israel, who brought you up from
the land of Egypt." **5** And Aaron
looked and built an altar before it;
and Aaron made a proclamation and
said, "Tomorrow *shall be* a feast to
Yahweh." **6** So the next day they rose
early and [a]offered burnt offerings
and brought peace offerings; and
[b]the people sat down to eat and to
drink and rose up [c]to play.
**7** Then Yahweh spoke to Moses,
"Go! Go down at once, for your peo-
ple, whom [a]you brought up from
the land of Egypt, have [b]corrupted
*themselves.* **8** They have quickly
turned aside from the way which
I commanded them. [a]They have
made for themselves a molten calf
and have worshiped it and [b]have
sacrificed to it and said, '[c,1]These are
your gods, O Israel, who brought you
up from the land of Egypt!'" **9** [a]And
Yahweh said to Moses, "I have seen
this people, and behold, they are [b]a
stiff-necked people. **10** Now then [a]let
Me alone, that My anger may burn
against them and that I may consume
them; and [b]I will make you a great
nation."
**11** Then [a]Moses entreated [1]the
favor of Yahweh his God and said,
"O Yahweh, why does Your anger
burn against Your people whom You
have brought out of the land of Egypt
with great power and with a strong
hand? **12** Why should [a]the Egyptians
speak, saying, 'With evil *intent* He
brought them out to kill them in the
mountains and to consume them
from the face of the earth'? Turn
from Your burning anger and relent
concerning *doing* harm to Your peo-
ple. **13** Remember Abraham, Isaac,
and Israel, Your servants to whom
You [a]swore by Yourself, and You said
to them, 'I will [b]multiply your seed as
the stars of the heavens, and [c]all this
land of which I have spoken I will give
to your seed, and they shall inherit

**31:18** [a]Ex 24:12; 34:29; Dt 4:13; 5:22; 9:10f [b]Ex 32:15, 16; 34:1, 28; Dt 9:10 ◆ **32:1** [a]Ex 24:18; Dt 9:11, 12 [b]Ac 7:40 [c]Ex 14:11 [1]Or *a god* **32:2** [a]Ex 35:22 **32:4** [a]Dt 9:16; Ne 9:18; Ps 106:19; Ac 7:41 [1]Or *This is your god* **32:6** [a]Ac 7:41 [b]1Co 10:7 [c]Ex 32:17-19; Nu 25:2 **32:7** [a]Ex 32:4, 11; Dt 9:12 [b]Ge 6:11f **32:8** [a]Ex 20:3, 4, 23 [b]Ex 22:20; 34:15; Dt 32:17 [c]1Ki 12:28 [1]Or *This is your god* **32:9** [a]Nu 14:11-20 [b]Ex 33:3, 5; 34:9; Is 48:4; Ac 7:51 **32:10** [a]Dt 9:14 [b]Nu 14:12 **32:11** [a]Dt 9:18, 26 [1]Lit *the face of Yahweh* **32:12** [a]Nu 14:13-19; Dt 9:28; Jos 7:9 **32:13** [a]Ge 22:16-18; Heb 6:13 [b]Ge 15:5; 26:4 [c]Ge 12:7; 13:15; 15:18; 17:8; 35:12; Ex 13:5, 11; 33:1

*it* forever.'" **14** [a]So Yahweh relented
concerning the harm which He said
He would do to His people.

**15** [a]Then Moses turned and went
down from the mountain. And the
two tablets of the testimony were in
his hand, [b]tablets which were written
on both [1]sides; they were written on
one *side* and the other. **16** Now the
tablets were the work of God, and
the writing was the writing of God
engraved on the tablets. **17** Then Josh-
ua heard the sound of the people [1]as
they shouted. And he said to Moses,
"There is a sound of war in the camp."
**18** But he said,

"It is not the sound
  of the cry of triumph,
Nor is it the sound
  of the cry of defeat;
But the sound
  of singing I hear."

**19** Now it happened, as soon as
[1]Moses came near the camp, that
[a]he saw the calf and *the* dancing;
and Moses' anger burned, and [b]he
threw the tablets from his hands and
shattered them [2]at the foot of the
mountain. **20** [a]Then he took the calf
which they had made and burned
*it* with fire and ground it to powder
and scattered it over the surface of
the water and made the sons of Israel
drink *it*.

**21** *Then* Moses said to Aaron,
"What did this people do to you, that
you have brought *such* great sin upon
them?" **22** And Aaron said, "Do not let
the anger of my lord burn; you know
the people yourself, [a]that they are
[1]prone to evil. **23** Indeed [a]they said
to me, 'Make [1]gods for us who will
go before us; for this Moses, the man
who brought us up from the land of
Egypt, we do not know what has be-
come of him.' **24** And I said to them,
'Whoever has any gold, let them tear
it off.' So they gave *it* to me, and [a]I
threw it into the fire, and out came
this calf."

**25** Now Moses saw that the people
were [1]out of control—for Aaron had
[a]let them [2]get out of control to be
a derision among [3]their enemies—
**26** so Moses stood in the gate of the
camp and said, "Whoever is for Yah-
weh, *come* to me!" And all the sons of
Levi gathered together to him. **27** And
he said to them, "Thus says Yahweh,
the God of Israel, 'Every man *among
you* put his sword upon his thigh, and
go back and forth from gate to gate
in the camp, and kill every man his
brother and every man his friend
and every man his [1]neighbor.'" **28** So
[a]the sons of Levi did according to
the word of Moses, and about three
thousand men of the people fell
that day. **29** Then Moses said, "[1]Be
ordained today to Yahweh—for every
man has been against his son and
against his brother—in order that
He may bestow a blessing upon you
today."

**30** Now it happened on the next
day, that Moses said to the people,
"[a]You yourselves have [1]committed
a great sin; but now I am going up
to Yahweh, perhaps I can [b]make
atonement for your sin." **31** Then
Moses returned to Yahweh and said,
"Alas, this people has [1]committed a

---

**32:14** [a]Ps 106:45 **32:15** [a]Dt 9:15 [b]Ex 31:18 [1]Lit *their sides* **32:17** [1]Lit *in its shouting*
**32:19** [a]Ex 32:6; Dt 9:16 [b]Dt 9:17 [1]Lit *he* [2]Lit *beneath* **32:20** [a]Dt 9:21 **32:22** [a]Dt 9:24 [1]Lit *in evil*
**32:23** [a]Ex 32:1-4 [1]Or *a god* **32:24** [a]Ex 32:4 **32:25** [a]1Ki 12:28-30; 14:16 [1]Lit *let loose* [2]Lit *go loose*
[3]Lit *those who rise against them* **32:27** [1]Or *kin* **32:28** [a]Nu 25:7-13; Dt 33:9 **32:29** [1]Lit *Fill your
hand* **32:30** [a]1Sa 12:20, 23 [b]Nu 25:13 [1]Lit *sinned* **32:31** [1]Lit *sinned*

great sin, and they have made [a,2]gods
of gold for themselves. **32** But now, if
You will forgive their sin—but if not,
please blot me out from Your [a]book
which You have written!" **33** And
Yahweh said to Moses, "Whoever
has sinned against Me, [a]I will blot
him out of My book. **34** But now go,
guide the people [a]where I told you.
Behold, [b]My angel shall go before
you; nevertheless [c]in the day when
I [1]punish, [d]I will [2]punish them for
their sin." **35** [a]Then Yahweh smote
the people because of [b]what they did
with the calf which Aaron had made.

### *Moses and the Tent of Meeting*

**33** Then Yahweh spoke to Moses,
"Go! Go up from here, you and
the people whom you have brought
up from the land of Egypt, to the
land of which [a]I swore to Abraham,
[b]to Isaac, and [c]to Jacob, saying, '[d]To
your seed I will give it.' **2** And I will
send [a]an angel before you, and [b]I will
drive out the Canaanite, the Amorite,
the Hittite, the Perizzite, the Hivite,
and the Jebusite. **3** *Go up* to a land
[a]flowing with milk and honey; for I
will not go up in your midst because
you are [b]a stiff-necked people, lest [c]I
consume you on the way."

**4** Then the people heard this [1]sad
word and [a]went into mourning; and
none of them put on his ornaments.
**5** So Yahweh said to Moses, "Say to the
sons of Israel, 'You are [a]a stiff-necked
people; should I go up in your midst
for one moment, I would consume
you. So now, put off your ornaments
from you, that I may know what I
shall do with you.'" **6** So the sons of
Israel stripped themselves of their
ornaments, from Mount Horeb
*onward.*

**7** Now Moses used to take [a]the
tent and pitch it outside the camp,
a good distance from the camp,
and he called it the tent of meeting.
And [b]everyone who sought Yahweh
would go out to the tent of meeting
which was outside the camp. **8** And it
happened whenever Moses went out
to the tent, that all the people would
arise and stand, each at the entrance
of his tent, and gaze after Moses until
he entered the tent. **9** And it hap-
pened whenever Moses entered the
tent, that [a]the pillar of cloud would
descend and stand at the entrance
of the tent; [b]and [1]Yahweh would
speak with Moses. **10** And all the
people would see the pillar of cloud
standing at the entrance of the tent.
And all the people would arise and
worship, each at the entrance of his
tent. **11** Thus [a]Yahweh used to speak
to Moses face to face, just as a man
speaks to his friend. Then [1]Moses
would return to the camp, and [b]his
attendant Joshua the son of Nun, a
young man, would not depart from
the tent.

### *Moses and the Glory of Yahweh*

**12** Then Moses said to Yahweh,
"See, You say to me, '[a]Bring up this
people!' But You Yourself have not
let me know [b]whom You will send
with me. [c]Moreover, You have said,

---

**32:31** [a]Ex 20:23 [2]Or *a god* **32:32** [a]Ps 69:28; Is 4:3; Da 12:1; Mal 3:16, 17; Php 4:3; Rev 3:5; 21:27
**32:33** [a]Ex 17:14; Dt 29:20; Ps 9:5; Rev 3:5 **32:34** [a]Ex 3:17 [b]Ex 23:20 [c]Dt 32:35; Ro 2:5, 6 [d]Ps 99:8
[1]Lit *visit* [2]Lit *visit their sin upon them* **32:35** [a]Ex 32:28 [b]Ex 32:4, 24 ◆ **33:1** [a]Ex 32:13 [b]Ge 26:1-3
[c]Ge 28:10 [d]Ge 12:7 **33:2** [a]Ex 32:34 [b]Ex 23:27-31; Jos 24:11 **33:3** [a]Ex 3:8, 17 [b]Ex 32:9; 33:5 [c]Ex 32:10
**33:4** [a]Nu 14:1, 39 [1]Lit *evil* **33:5** [a]Ex 33:3 **33:7** [a]Ex 18:7, 12-16 [b]Ex 29:42f **33:9** [a]Ex 13:21 [b]Ps 99:7
[1]Lit *He* **33:11** [a]Nu 12:8; Dt 34:10 [b]Ex 24:13 [1]Lit *he* **33:12** [a]Ex 3:10; 32:34 [b]Ex 33:2 [c]Ex 33:17

'I have known you by name, and
you have also found favor in My
sight.' **13** So now, I pray You, if I have
found favor in Your sight, [a]let me
know Your ways that I may know
You, so that I may find favor in Your
sight. [b]See also, that this nation is
Your people." **14** And He said, "[a]My
presence shall go *with you,* and [b]I
will give you rest." **15** Then he said to
Him, "[a]If Your presence does not go
*with us,* do not lead us up from here.
**16** Indeed, how then can it be known
that I have found favor in Your sight,
I and Your people? Is it not by Your
going with us, so that [a]we, I and Your
people, may be distinguished from all
the *other* people who are upon the
face of the [1]earth?"

**17** Then Yahweh said to Moses, "I
will also do this thing of which you
have spoken; [a]for you have found
favor in My sight, and I have known
you by name." **18** [a]Then [1]Moses said,
"I pray You, show me Your glory!"
**19** And He said, "[a]I Myself will make
all My goodness pass before you, and
I will proclaim the name of Yahweh
before you; and [b]I will be gracious to
whom I will be gracious, and I will
show compassion on whom I will
show compassion." **20** But He said,
"You cannot see My face, [a]for no
man can see Me and live!" **21** Then
Yahweh said, "Behold, there is a place
[1]by Me, and [a]you shall stand *there* on
the rock; **22** and it will come about,
while My glory is passing by, that I
will put you in the cleft of the rock
and [a]cover you with My hand until I
have passed by. **23** Then I will remove
My hand, and you shall see My back,
but [a]My face shall not be seen."

### *Stone Tablets like the Former Ones*

**34** Now Yahweh said to Moses,
"Carve out for yourself [a]two
stone tablets like the former ones,
and [b]I will write on the tablets the
words that were on the former
tablets which you shattered. **2** So be
prepared by morning, and come up
in the morning to [a]Mount Sinai, and
[1]present yourself there to Me on the
top of the mountain. **3** [a]And no man is
to come up with you, nor let any man
be seen [1]anywhere on the mountain;
even the flocks and the herds may
not graze in front of that mountain."
**4** So he carved out [a]two stone tablets
like the former ones, and Moses rose
up early in the morning and went
up to Mount Sinai, as Yahweh had
commanded him, and he took two
stone tablets in his hand. **5** [a]Then
Yahweh descended in the cloud and
stood there with him, and [1]He called
upon the name of Yahweh. **6** Then
Yahweh passed by in front of him and
called out, "Yahweh, Yahweh God,
[a]compassionate and gracious, slow
to anger, and abounding in loving-
kindness and [1]truth; **7** who [a]keeps
lovingkindness for thousands, who
forgives iniquity, transgression, and
sin; yet He [b]will by no means leave

---

**33:13** [a]Ps 25:4; 27:11; 51:13; 86:11; 119:33 [b]Ex 3:7, 10; 5:1; 32:12, 14; Dt 9:26, 29 **33:14** [a]Dt 4:37; Is 63:9 [b]Dt 12:10; 25:19; Jos 21:44; 22:4 **33:15** [a]Ps 80:3, 7, 19 **33:16** [a]Lv 20:24, 26 [1]Lit *ground* **33:17** [a]Ex 33:12 **33:18** [a]Ex 33:20-23 [1]Lit *he* **33:19** [a]Ex 34:6, 7 [b]Ro 9:15 **33:20** [a]Is 6:5; 1Ti 6:16 **33:21** [a]Ps 18:2, 46; 27:5; 61:2; 62:7 [1]Lit *with* **33:22** [a]Ps 91:1, 4; Is 49:2; 51:16 **33:23** [a]Ex 33:20; Jn 1:18 ◆ **34:1** [a]Ex 24:12; 31:18; 32:16, 19 [b]Dt 10:2, 4 **34:2** [a]Ex 19:11, 18, 20 [1]Or *place yourself before* **34:3** [a]Ex 19:12, 13 [1]Lit *on all* **34:4** [a]Ex 34:1 **34:5** [a]Ex 19:9; 33:9 [1]Or possibly *he* (Moses), but cf. 33:19 **34:6** [a]Nu 14:18; Dt 4:31; Ne 9:17; Ps 86:15; 103:8; 108:4; 145:8; Joel 2:13; Ro 2:4 [1]Or *faithfulness* **34:7** [a]Ex 20:5, 6; Dt 5:10; 7:9; Ps 103:3; 130:3, 4; 1Jn 1:9 [b]Ex 23:7; Dt 7:10; Job 10:14; Na 1:3

*the guilty* unpunished, [c]visiting the
iniquity of fathers on the children
and on the grandchildren to the third
and fourth generations." **8** And Moses
made haste [a,1]to bow low toward the
earth and worship. **9** And he said, "[a]If
now I have found favor in Your sight,
O Lord, I pray, let the Lord go along in
our midst, even though [b,1]they are a
stiff-necked people, and [c]pardon our
iniquity and our sin, and [d]take us as
Your own inheritance."

### *Yahweh Cuts a Covenant with Israel*

**10** Then [1]God said, "Behold, [a]I am
going to cut a covenant. Before all
your people [b]I will do wondrous
deeds which have not been created
in all the earth nor among any of the
nations; and all the people [2]among
whom you live will see the working
of Yahweh, for it is a fearful thing that
I am going to do with you.

**11** "[1]Be sure to keep what I am
commanding you this day: behold,
[a]I am going to drive out the Amorite
before you, and the Canaanite, the
Hittite, the Perizzite, the Hivite, and
the Jebusite. **12** [a]Beware lest you cut
a covenant with the inhabitants of
the land into which you are going,
lest it become a snare in your midst.
**13** [a]But *rather*, you are to tear down
their altars and shatter their *sacred*
pillars and cut down their [b,1]Asherim
**14**—for [a]you shall not worship any
other god, for Yahweh, whose name is
Jealous, is a jealous God— **15** lest you
cut a covenant with the inhabitants
of the land, and they play the harlot
with their gods and [a]sacrifice to their
gods, and one *of them* [b]invite you
[1]to eat of his sacrifice, **16** and [a]you
take some of his daughters for your
sons, and his daughters play the
harlot with their gods and cause your
sons *also* to play the harlot with their
gods. **17** [a]You shall make for yourself
no molten gods.

**18** "You shall keep [a]the Feast of Un-
leavened Bread. For [b]seven days you
shall eat unleavened bread, which I
commanded you, at the appointed
time in the [c]month of Abib, for in
the month of Abib you came out of
Egypt.

**19** "[a]The first offspring from every
womb belongs to Me, even of all your
male livestock, the first offspring
from [1]cattle and sheep. **20** [a]And you
shall redeem with a lamb the [1]first
offspring from a donkey; and if you
do not redeem *it*, then you shall break
its neck. You shall redeem [b]all the
firstborn of your sons. [c,2]None shall
appear before Me empty-handed.

**21** "You shall work [a]six days, but on
the seventh day you shall rest; *even*
during plowing time and harvest you
shall rest. **22** And you shall celebrate
[a]the Feast of Weeks, *that is*, the first
fruits of the wheat harvest, and the
Feast of Ingathering at the turn of the
year. **23** [a]Three times a year all your

---

**34:7** [c]Dt 5:9 **34:8** [a]Ex 4:31 [1]Lit *and bowed...worshiped* **34:9** [a]Ex 33:13 [b]Ex 32:9 [c]Ex 34:7 [d]Dt 4:20; 9:26, 29; 32:9; Ps 33:12 [1]Lit *it is* **34:10** [a]Ex 34:27, 28; Dt 5:2 [b]Dt 4:32; Ps 72:18; 136:4 [1]*Lit He* [2]*Lit in whose midst you are* **34:11** [a]Ex 33:2 [1]Lit *Keep for yourself* **34:12** [a]Ex 23:32, 33 **34:13** [a]Ex 23:24; Dt 12:3 [b]Dt 16:21; Jdg 6:25, 26; 2Ki 18:4; 2Chr 34:3f [1]Wooden symbols of a female deity **34:14** [a]Ex 20:3, 5; Dt 4:24 **34:15** [a]Ex 22:20; 32:8 [b]Nu 25:1, 2; Dt 32:37, 38 [1]Lit *and you eat* **34:16** [a]Dt 7:3; Jos 23:12, 13; 1Ki 11:1-4 **34:17** [a]Ex 20:4, 23; Lv 19:4; Dt 5:8 **34:18** [a]Ex 12:17; Lv 23:6; Nu 28:16f [b]Ex 12:15, 16 [c]Ex 12:2; 13:4 **34:19** [a]Ex 13:2; 22:29f [1]Or *oxen* **34:20** [a]Ex 13:13 [b]Ex 13:15; Nu 3:45 [c]Ex 22:29; 23:15; Dt 16:16 [1]Lit *first opening of* [2]Lit *They shall not* **34:21** [a]Ex 20:9f; 23:12; 31:15; 35:2; Lv 23:3; Dt 5:13f **34:22** [a]Ex 23:16; Nu 28:26 **34:23** [a]Ex 23:14-17

males are to appear before the Lord
Yahweh, the God of Israel. **24** For I will
[a]dispossess nations before you and
enlarge your borders, and no man
shall covet your land when you go up
three times a year to appear before
Yahweh your God.
**25** "[a]You shall not [1]offer the blood
of My sacrifice with leavened bread,
[b]and the sacrifice of the Feast of the
Passover shall not [2]be left over until
morning.
**26** "You shall bring [a]the very first
of the first fruits of your ground into
the house of Yahweh your God.
"You shall not boil a young goat in
its mother's milk."
**27** Then Yahweh said to Moses,
"[a]Write [1]down these words, for in
accordance with these words I have
cut [b]a covenant with you and with
Israel." **28** So he was there with Yah-
weh [a]forty days and forty nights;
he did not eat bread or drink water.
And [b,1]he wrote on the tablets the
words of the covenant, [c]the Ten
[2]Commandments.

### *The Shining Face of Moses*

**29** Now it happened when Moses was
coming down from Mount Sinai (and
the [a]two tablets of the testimony
*were* in Moses' hand as he was com-
ing down from the mountain), that
Moses did not know that [b]the skin of
his face shone because of his speak-
ing with Him. **30** Then Aaron and all
the sons of Israel saw Moses, and
behold, the skin of his face shone,
and [a]they were afraid to come near
him. **31** Then Moses called to them,
and Aaron and all the rulers in the
congregation returned to him; and
Moses spoke to them. **32** And after-
ward all the sons of Israel came near,
and he commanded them everything
that Yahweh had spoken [1]to him on
Mount Sinai. **33** Then Moses finished
speaking with them and [a]put a veil
over his face. **34** But whenever Moses
went in before Yahweh to speak with
Him, [a]he would take off the veil until
he came out; and then he would
come out and speak to the sons of
Israel what he had been commanded,
**35** [a]and the sons of Israel would see
the face of Moses, that the skin of
Moses' face shone. So Moses would
return the veil over his face until he
went in to speak with Him.

### *The Sabbath Command*

**35** Then Moses assembled all
the congregation of the sons
of Israel and said to them, "[a]These
are the things that Yahweh has com-
manded *you* to [1]do:
**2** "[a]Six days work may be done, but
on the seventh day you shall have a
holy *day*, [b]a sabbath of complete rest
to Yahweh; [c]whoever does any work
on it shall be put to death.

### *Willing Hearts Contribute to Yahweh*

**3** "[a]You shall not kindle a fire in any
of your *places of* habitation on the
sabbath day."
**4** And Moses spoke to all the con-
gregation of the sons of Israel, saying,
"This is the thing which Yahweh has

---

**34:24** [a]Ex 33:2; Ps 78:55 **34:25** [a]Ex 23:18 [b]Ex 12:10 [1]Lit *slaughter* [2]Lit *remain overnight*
**34:26** [a]Ex 23:19; Dt 26:2 **34:27** [a]Ex 17:14; 24:4 [b]Ex 34:10 [1]Lit *for yourself* **34:28** [a]Ex 24:18
[b]Ex 31:18; 34:1 [c]Dt 4:13; 10:4 [1]Or *He*, Yahweh [2]Lit *Words* **34:29** [a]Ex 32:15 [b]Mt 17:2; 2Co 3:7
**34:30** [a]2Co 3:7 **34:32** [1]Lit *with* **34:33** [a]2Co 3:13 **34:34** [a]2Co 3:16 **34:35** [a]2Co 3:13
◆ **35:1** [a]Ex 34:32 [1]Lit *do them* **35:2** [a]Ex 20:9, 10; 23:12; 31:15; 34:21; Lv 23:3; Dt 5:13f [b]Ex 16:23
[c]Nu 15:32-36 **35:3** [a]Ex 12:16; 16:23

commanded, saying, **5** '[a]Take from
among you a [1]contribution to Yah-
weh; whoever is of a willing heart,
let him bring it as a [1]contribution to
Yahweh: gold, silver, and [2]bronze,
**6** and [1]blue, purple, and scarlet *ma-
terial*, fine linen, goats' *hair*, **7** and
rams' skins [1]dyed red, and porpoise
skins, and acacia wood, **8** and oil for
lighting, and spices for the anointing
oil, and for the fragrant incense, **9** and
onyx stones and setting stones for
the ephod and for the [1]breastpiece.
**10** '[a]And let everyone [1]wise at
heart among you come and make all
that Yahweh has commanded: **11** the
[a,1]tabernacle, its tent and its cover-
ing, its clasps and its boards, its bars,
its pillars, and its bases; **12** the [a]ark
and its poles, the [1]mercy seat, and the
curtain of the screen; **13** the [a]table
and its poles, and all its [1]utensils,
and the bread of the [2]Presence; **14** the
[a]lampstand also for the light and its
utensils and its lamps and the oil for
the light; **15** and the [a]altar of incense
and its poles, and the [b]anointing
oil and the [c]fragrant incense, and
the screen for the doorway at the
[1]entrance of the tabernacle; **16** [a]the
altar of burnt offering with its
[1]bronze grating, its poles, and all
its [2]utensils, the laver and its stand;
**17** [a]the hangings of the court, its
pillars and its bases, and the screen
for the gate of the court; **18** the pegs
of the tabernacle and the pegs of the
court and their cords; **19** the [a,1]woven
garments for ministering in the holy
place, the holy garments for Aaron
the priest and the garments of his
sons, to minister as priests.'"

### *Contributions Brought by the People*

**20** Then all the congregation of the
sons of Israel went out from Moses'
presence. **21** [a]And everyone whose
heart [1]stirred him and everyone
whose spirit was willing came *and*
brought the [2]contribution to Yahweh
for the work of the tent of meeting
and for all its service and for the
holy garments. **22** Then all whose
hearts were willing, both men and
women, came *and* brought brooches
and [1]earrings and signet rings and
bracelets, all articles of gold; so
*did* every man who waved it as a
wave offering of gold to Yahweh.
**23** And every man, [1]who had in his
possession [2]blue and purple and
scarlet *material* and fine linen and
goats' *hair* and rams' skins [3]dyed red
and porpoise skins, brought them.
**24** Everyone who could raise up a
[1]contribution of silver and [2]bronze
brought the [1]contribution to Yahweh;
and every man [3]who had in his pos-
session acacia wood for any work
of the service brought it. **25** All the
women [1]wise at heart spun with their
hands and brought what they had
spun, *in* [2]blue and purple *and* scarlet
*material* and *in* fine linen. **26** And
all the women whose heart [1]stirred
with wisdom spun the goats' *hair*.

---

**35:5** [a]Ex 25:1-9 [1]Or *heave offering* [2]Or *copper* **35:6** [1]Or *violet* **35:7** [1]Or *tanned* **35:9** [1]Or *pouch* **35:10** [a]Ex 31:6 [1]Or *skillful* **35:11** [a]Ex 26:1-30 [1]Lit *dwelling place* **35:12** [a]Ex 25:10-22 [1]Or *propitiatory seat, place of atonement* **35:13** [a]Ex 25:23-30 [1]Or *vessels* [2]Lit *Face* **35:14** [a]Ex 25:31ff **35:15** [a]Ex 30:1-6 [b]Ex 30:25 [c]Ex 30:34-38 [1]Or *doorway* **35:16** [a]Ex 27:1-8 [1]Or *copper* [2]Or *vessels* **35:17** [a]Ex 27:9-18 **35:19** [a]Ex 31:10; 39:1 [1]Or *service garments* **35:21** [a]Ex 25:2; 35:5, 22, 26, 29; 36:2 [1]Lit *lifted up* [2]Or *heave offering* **35:22** [1]Or *nose rings* **35:23** [1]Lit *with whom was found* [2]Or *violet* [3]Or *tanned* **35:24** [1]Or *heave offering* [2]Or *copper* [3]Lit *with whom was found* **35:25** [1]Or *skilled* [2]Or *violet* **35:26** [1]Lit *lifted them up in wisdom*

**27** And the rulers brought the onyx
stones and the stones for setting for
the ephod and for the [1]breastpiece;
**28** and [a]the spice and the oil for the
light and for the anointing oil and
for the fragrant incense. **29** The sons
of Israel—all the men and women
whose heart was willing to bring *ma-
terial* for all the work, which Yahweh
had commanded through the hand
of Moses to do—brought a [a]freewill
offering to Yahweh.

**30** [a]Then Moses said to the sons
of Israel, "See, Yahweh has called
by name Bezalel the son of Uri, the
son of Hur, of the tribe of Judah.
**31** And He has filled him with the
Spirit of God, in wisdom, in discern-
ment, and in knowledge, and in all
[1]craftsmanship; **32** to devise [1]designs
for working in gold and in silver and
in [2]bronze, **33** and in the cutting of
stones for settings and in the carving
of wood, so as to do *well* in every
work of thoughtful design. **34** He also
has put in his heart to teach, both he
and [a]Oholiab, the son of Ahisamach,
of the tribe of Dan. **35** [a]He has filled
them with [1]wisdom *in their* heart to
do every work of an engraver and of
a designer and of an embroiderer,
in [2]blue and in purple *and* in scarlet
*material* and in fine linen, and of a
weaver, as those who do every work
and make designs.

**36** "Now Bezalel and Oholiab and
every person [1]wise at heart, to
whom Yahweh has given [2]wisdom
and discernment to know how to
do all the work of the service of
*constructing* the sanctuary, shall do
in accordance with all that Yahweh
has commanded."

### *Making the Tabernacle*

**2** Then Moses called Bezalel and
Oholiab and every person [1]wise at
heart to whom Yahweh had given
[2]wisdom, [a]everyone whose heart
stirred him, to come to the work to
do it. **3** And they received from Moses
the entire [1]contribution which the
sons of Israel had brought [2]to do the
work in the service of the sanctuary.
And they still *continued* bringing to
him freewill offerings every morning.
**4** And all the [1]wise men who were
doing all the work of the sanctuary
came, each from [2]the work which [3]he
was doing, **5** and they said to [1]Moses,
"[a]The people are bringing much
more than enough for the service of
the work which Yahweh commanded
*us* to [2]do." **6** So Moses commanded
and a [1]proclamation was passed
throughout the camp, saying, "Let
no man or woman any longer do the
work for the [2]contributions of the
sanctuary." Thus the people were
restrained from bringing *any more.*
**7** [a]Indeed, the [1]material they had was
sufficient and more than enough for
all the work, to do it.

**8** [a]And all those [1]wise at heart
among those who were doing the
work made the [2]tabernacle with
ten curtains; of fine twisted linen
and [3]blue and purple and scarlet
*material*, with cherubim, the work
of a skillful designer, [4]Bezalel made

**35:27** [1]Or *pouch* **35:28** [a]Ex 30:23ff **35:29** [a]Ex 35:21; 1Chr 29:9 **35:30** [a]Ex 31:1-6 **35:31** [1]Or *work* **35:32** [1]Lit *devices* [2]Or *copper* **35:34** [a]Ex 31:6 **35:35** [a]Ex 31:3, 6; 35:31; 1Ki 7:14 [1]Or *skill* [2]Or *violet* ◆ **36:1** [1]Or *skillful* [2]Or *skill* **36:2** [a]Ex 35:21, 26 [1]Or *skillful* [2]Or *skill* **36:3** [1]Lit *heave offering* [2]Lit *to perform it for the work* **36:4** [1]Or *skillful* [2]Lit *his* [3]Lit *they were* **36:5** [a]2Chr 24:14; 31:6-10 [1]Lit *Moses, saying,* [2]Lit *do it* **36:6** [1]Lit *voice* [2]Lit *heave offering* **36:7** [a]1Ki 8:64 [1]Lit *work* **36:8** [a]Ex 26:1-14 [1]Or *skillful* [2]Lit *dwelling place* [3]Or *violet* [4]Lit *he*

them. **9** The length of each curtain
was [1]twenty-eight cubits and the
width of each curtain four [2]cubits;
all the curtains had [3]the same
measurements. **10** He [1]joined five
curtains to one another, and *the*
*other* five curtains he [1]joined to one
another. **11** He made loops of [1]blue on
the edge of the [2]outermost curtain in
the first [3]set; he did likewise on the
edge of the curtain that was [2]outer-
most in the second [3]set. **12** He made
[a]fifty loops in the one curtain, and he
made fifty loops on the [1]edge of the
curtain that was in the second [2]set;
the loops were opposite each other.
**13** He made [a]fifty clasps of gold and
[1]joined the curtains to one another
with the clasps, so the tabernacle was
one unit.

**14** Then [a]he made curtains of goats'
*hair* for a tent over the tabernacle; he
made eleven curtains [1]in all. **15** The
length of each curtain *was* [1]thirty
cubits and four cubits the width of
each curtain; the eleven curtains
had [2]the same measurements. **16** He
[1]joined five curtains by themselves
and *the other* six curtains by them-
selves. **17** Moreover, he made fifty
loops on the edge of the curtain that
was outermost in the *first* [1]set, and
he made fifty loops on the edge of
the curtain *that was outermost in* the
second [1]set. **18** He made fifty clasps of
[1]bronze to [2]join the tent together so
that it would be [3]a unit. **19** He made
a covering for the tent of rams' skins
[1]dyed red and a covering of porpoise
skins above.

**20** [a]Then he made the boards
for the tabernacle of acacia wood,
standing *upright*. **21** Ten cubits *was*
the length of [1]each board and one
and a half cubits the width of each
board. **22** *There were* two tenons for
each board, [1]fitted to one another;
thus he did for all the boards of
the tabernacle. **23** And he made the
boards for the tabernacle: twenty
boards [1]for the south side; **24** and
he made forty bases of silver under
the twenty boards; two bases under
one board for its two tenons and two
bases under another board for its two
tenons. **25** Then for the second side
of the tabernacle, on the north side,
he made twenty boards, **26** and their
forty bases of silver; two bases un-
der one board and two bases under
another board. **27** For the [1]rear of the
tabernacle, to the west, he made six
boards. **28** And he made two boards
for the corners of the [1]tabernacle at
the [2]rear. **29** And they were [1]sepa-
rated beneath, but were together
at their completion at the [2]top, [3]at
the first ring; thus he did with both
of them for the two corners. **30** And
there were eight boards with their
bases of silver, sixteen bases, two
bases under every board.

**31** Then he made [a]bars of acacia
wood, five for the boards of one side
of the tabernacle, **32** and five bars
for the boards of the [1]other side of

**36:9** [1]Approx. 43 ft. or 12.6 m [2]A cubit was approx. 18 in. or 45 cm [3]Lit *one measure* **36:10** [1]Or *coupled* **36:11** [1]Or *violet* [2]Lit *one curtain from the end in the coupling* [3]Lit *coupling* **36:12** [a]Ex 26:5 [1]Lit *end* [2]Lit *coupling* **36:13** [a]Ex 26:6 [1]Or *coupled* **36:14** [a]Ex 26:7-14 [1]Lit *in number* **36:15** [1]Approx. 45 ft. or 13.5 m [2]Lit *one measure* **36:16** [1]Or *coupled* **36:17** [1]Lit *coupling* **36:18** [1]Or *copper* [2]Or *couple* [3]Lit *one* **36:19** [1]Or *tanned* **36:20** [a]Ex 26:15-29 **36:21** [1]Lit *the* **36:22** [1]Lit *bound* **36:23** [1]Lit *to the side of the Negev, to the south* **36:27** [1]Lit *extreme parts* **36:28** [1]Lit *dwelling place* [2]Lit *extreme parts* **36:29** [1]Lit *twins* [2]Or *head* [3]Or *with reference to* **36:31** [a]Ex 26:26-29 **36:32** [1]Or *second*

the tabernacle, and five bars for the
boards of the tabernacle for the [2]rear
*side* to the west. **33** And he made the
middle bar to pass through in the
[1]center of the boards from end to
end. **34** He also overlaid the boards
with gold and made their rings of
gold *as* holders for the bars and
overlaid the bars with gold.

**35** [a]Moreover, he made the veil of
[1]blue and purple and scarlet *materi-
al* and fine twisted linen; he made it
with cherubim, the work of a skillful
designer. **36** And he made four pillars
of acacia for it and overlaid them
with gold, with their hooks of gold;
and he cast four bases of silver for
them. **37** And he made a [a]screen for
the doorway of the tent, of [1]blue and
purple and scarlet *material* and fine
twisted linen, the work of a [2]weaver;
**38** and *he made* its [a]five pillars with
their hooks, and he overlaid their
tops and their [1]bands with gold; but
their five bases were of [2]bronze.

### *Making the Ark of the Testimony*

**37** [a]And Bezalel made the ark of
acacia wood; its length was two
and a half [1]cubits, and its width one and
a half cubits, and its height one and
a half cubits; **2** and he overlaid it
with pure gold inside and out, and
made a gold molding for it all around.
**3** He cast four rings of gold for it on
its four feet; even two rings on one
side of it, and two rings on the [1]other
side of it. **4** He made poles of acacia
wood and overlaid them with gold.
**5** He put the poles into the rings on
the sides of the ark to carry [1]it. **6** He
made a [1]mercy seat of pure gold, two
and a half [2]cubits [3]long and one and
a half cubits [4]wide. **7** He made two
cherubim of gold; he made them of
hammered work [1]at the two ends of
the mercy seat; **8** one cherub [1]at the
one end and one cherub [1]at the other
end; from *one piece* he made the mer-
cy seat *with* the cherubim [1]at its two
ends. **9** The cherubim had *their* wings
spread upward, covering the mercy
seat with their wings, with their faces
toward each other; the faces of the
cherubim were toward the mercy seat.

### *Making the Table*

**10** [a]Then he made the table of acacia
wood, two [1]cubits [2]long and a cubit
[3]wide and one and a half cubits [4]high.
**11** He overlaid it with pure gold and
made a gold molding for it all around.
**12** He made a rim for it of a hand-
breadth all around and made a gold
molding for its rim all around. **13** He
cast four gold rings for it and put the
rings on the four corners that were on
its four feet. **14** Close to the rim were
the rings, the holders for the poles to
carry the table. **15** He made the poles
of acacia wood and overlaid them with
gold, to carry the table. **16** He made the
utensils which were on the table, its
[1]dishes and its pans and its offering
bowls and its jars, with which to pour
out drink offerings, of pure gold.

### *Making the Lampstand*

**17** [a]Then he made the lampstand of
pure gold. He made the lampstand

---

**36:32** [2]Lit *extreme parts* **36:33** [1]Lit *midst* **36:35** [a]Ex 26:31-37 [1]Or *violet* **36:37** [a]Ex 26:36 [1]Or *violet* [2]A weaver in colors; lit *variegator* **36:38** [a]Ex 26:37 [1]Or *fillets, rings* [2]Or *copper*
◆ **37:1** [a]Ex 25:10-20 [1]A cubit was approx. 18 in. or 45 cm **37:3** [1]Lit *second* **37:5** [1]Lit *the ark*
**37:6** [1]Or *propitiatory seat, place of atonement*, so through v 9 [2]A cubit was approx. 18 in. or 45 cm [3]Lit *its length* [4]Lit *its width* **37:7** [1]Lit *from* **37:8** [1]Lit *from* **37:10** [a]Ex 25:23-29 [1]A cubit was approx. 18 in. or 45 cm [2]Lit *its length* [3]Lit *its width* [4]Lit *its height* **37:16** [1]Or *platters* **37:17** [a]Ex 25:31-39

of hammered work, its base and
its shaft; its cups, its [1]bulbs, and
its flowers were [2]of *the same piece.*
**18** There were six branches going out
of its sides; three branches of the
lampstand from the one side of it
and three branches of the lampstand
from the [1]other side of it; **19** three cups
shaped like almond *blossoms,* a [1]bulb
and a flower in one branch, and three
cups shaped like almond *blossoms,*
a [1]bulb and a flower in the other
branch—so for the six branches
coming out of the lampstand. **20** In
the lampstand *there were* four cups
shaped like almond *blossoms,* its
[1]bulbs and its flowers; **21** and a [1]bulb
was under the *first* pair of branches
*coming* out of it, and a [1]bulb under
the *second* pair of branches *coming*
out of it, and a [1]bulb under the *third*
pair of branches *coming* out of it, for
the six branches coming out of the
lampstand. **22** Their [1]bulbs and their
branches were *of one piece* with it;
the whole of it *was* a single ham-
mered work of pure gold. **23** He made
its seven lamps with its tongs and
its [1]trays of pure gold. **24** He made it
and all its utensils from a [1]talent of
pure gold.

### *Making the Altar of Incense*

**25** [a]Then he made the altar of in-
cense of acacia wood: a cubit [1]long
and a cubit [2]wide, square, and two
cubits [3]high; its horns were *of one*
*piece* with it. **26** He overlaid it with
pure gold, its top and its [1]sides all
around, and its horns; and he made
*a gold molding for it all* around. **27** He
made two golden rings for it under
its molding, on its two sides—on
opposite sides—as holders for poles
with which to carry it. **28** He made the
poles of acacia wood and overlaid
them with gold. **29** [a]And he made
the holy anointing oil and the pure,
fragrant incense of spices, the work
of a perfumer.

### *Making the Altar of Burnt Offering*

**38** [a]Then he made the altar
of burnt offering of acacia
wood, five [1]cubits [2]long, and five
cubits [3]wide, square, and three
cubits [4]high. **2** He made its horns
on its four corners, its horns [1]being
*of one piece* with it, and he overlaid
it with [2]bronze. **3** He made all the
utensils of the altar, the pots and
the shovels and the bowls, the flesh
hooks and the firepans; he made all
its utensils of bronze. **4** He made
for the altar a grating of a network
of bronze beneath, under its ledge,
reaching halfway down. **5** He cast
four rings on the four ends of the
bronze grating *as* holders for the
poles. **6** He made the poles of aca-
cia wood and overlaid them with
bronze. **7** He inserted the poles into
the rings on the sides of the altar,
with which to carry it. He made it
hollow with planks.

### *Making the Laver of Bronze*

**8** [a]Moreover, he made the laver of
bronze with its base of bronze, [1]from
the mirrors of the serving women
who served at the doorway of the
tent of meeting.

---

**37:17** [1]Or *calyxes* [2]Lit *of itself* **37:18** [1]Lit *second* **37:19** [1]Or *calyx* **37:20** [1]Or *calyxes* **37:21** [1]Or *calyx* **37:22** [1]Or *calyxes* **37:23** [1]Lit *snuff dishes* **37:24** [1]A talent was approx. 75 lb. or 34 kg **37:25** [a]Ex 30:1-5 [1]Lit *its length* [2]Lit *its width* [3]Lit *its height* **37:26** [1]Lit *walls* **37:29** [a]Ex 30:23-25, 34, 35 ◆ **38:1** [a]Ex 27:1-8 [1]A cubit was approx. 18 in. or 45 cm [2]Lit *its length* [3]Lit *its width* [4]Lit *its height* **38:2** [1]Lit *were* [2]Or *copper,* so in ch **38:8** [a]Ex 30:18 [1]Lit *with*

### *Making the Court*

**9** [a]Then he made the court: [1]for the
south side the hangings of the court
were of fine twisted linen, [2]one hun-
dred cubits; **10** their twenty pillars,
and their twenty bases, *made* of
bronze; the hooks of the pillars and
their [1]bands *were* of silver. **11** For the
north side *there were* one hundred
cubits; their twenty pillars and their
twenty bases *were* of bronze, the
hooks of the pillars and their bands
*were* of silver. **12** For the west side
*there were* hangings of [1]fifty cubits
*with* their ten pillars and their ten
bases; the hooks of the pillars and
their bands *were* of silver. **13** For the
east side toward the sunrise fifty
cubits. **14** The hangings for the *one*
[1]side *of the gate were* [2]fifteen cubits,
*with* their three pillars and their
three bases, **15** and so for the [1]other
[2]side. [3]On both sides of the gate of
the court *were* hangings of fifteen cu-
bits, *with* their three pillars and their
three bases. **16** All the hangings of the
court all around *were* of fine twisted
linen. **17** The bases for the pillars *were*
of bronze, the hooks of the pillars
and their bands *were* of silver; and
the overlaying of their tops *were* of
silver, and all the pillars of the court
were furnished with silver bands.
**18** The screen of the gate of the court
was the work of the [1]weaver, of [2]blue
and purple and scarlet *material* and
fine twisted linen. And the length
*was* [3]twenty cubits and the [4]height
*was* five cubits, corresponding to the
hangings of the court. **19** Their four
pillars and their four bases *were* of
bronze; their hooks *were* of silver,
and the overlaying of their tops and
their bands *were* of silver. **20** All the
pegs of the [1]tabernacle and of the
court all around *were* of bronze.

### *The Things Numbered for the Tabernacle*

**21** These are the things numbered for
the [1]tabernacle, the [1]tabernacle of
the testimony, as they were [2]num-
bered according to the [3]command of
Moses, for the service of the Levites,
by the hand of Ithamar the son of
Aaron the priest. **22** Now [a]Bezalel
the son of Uri, the son of Hur, of the
tribe of Judah, made all that Yahweh
had commanded Moses. **23** With him
*was* [a]Oholiab the son of Ahisamach,
of the tribe of Dan, a craftsman and
a skillful designer and a [1]weaver in
[2]blue and in purple and in scarlet
*material* and fine linen.

**24** All the gold that was used for
the work, in all the work of the
sanctuary, even the gold of the wave
offering, was [1]29 talents and [2]730
shekels, according to [a]the shekel
of the sanctuary. **25** [a]The silver
of those of the congregation who
were [1]numbered was [2]100 talents
and [3]1,775 shekels, according to the
shekel of the sanctuary; **26** [a]a beka a

**38:9** [a]Ex 27:9-19 [1]Lit *to the side of the Negev, to the south* [2]Approx. 150 ft. or 45 m **38:10** [1]Or *fillets, rings*; so in ch **38:12** [1]Approx. 75 ft. or 22.5 m **38:14** [1]Lit *shoulder* [2]Approx. 22.5 ft. or 6.75 m **38:15** [1]Lit *second* [2]Lit *shoulder* [3]Lit *On this side and on that side* **38:18** [1]A weaver in colors; lit *variegator* [2]Or *violet* [3]Approx. 30 ft. or 9 m [4]Lit *height in width* **38:20** [1]Lit *dwelling place* **38:21** [1]Lit *dwelling place* [2]Lit *appointed* [3]Lit *mouth* **38:22** [a]Ex 31:2 **38:23** [a]Ex 31:6 [1]A weaver in colors; lit *variegator* [2]Or *violet* **38:24** [a]Ex 30:13; Lv 27:25; Nu 3:47; 18:16 [1]Approx. 1.08 tons or 0.98 metric tons, a talent was approx. 75 lb. or 34 kg [2]Approx. 18 lb. or 8 kg, a shekel was approx. 0.4 oz. or 11 gm **38:25** [a]Ex 30:11-16 [1]Lit *mustered* [2]Approx. 3.75 tons or 3.4 metric tons [3]Approx. 44.3 lb. or 19.5 kg **38:26** [a]Ex 30:13, 15

head (*that is,* half a shekel according
to the shekel of the sanctuary), for
each one who passed over to those
who were [1]numbered, from twenty
years old and upward, for [b]603,550
men. **27** One hundred talents of silver
were for casting the bases of the
sanctuary and the bases of the veil;
one hundred bases for one hundred
talents, a talent for a base. **28** Of the
1,775 *shekels,* he made hooks for the
pillars and overlaid their tops and
made bands for them. **29** The bronze
of the wave offering was 70 talents
and 2,400 shekels. **30** With it he
made the bases to the doorway of
the tent of meeting, and the bronze
altar and its bronze grating, and all
the utensils of the altar, **31** and the
bases of the court all around and the
bases of the gate of the court, and
all the pegs of the [1]tabernacle and
all the pegs of the court all around.

### *Making the Holy Garments*

**39** Moreover, from the [a,1]blue and
purple and scarlet *material,*
they made finely [b]woven garments
for ministering in the holy place [2]as
well as the holy garments which
were for Aaron, just as Yahweh had
commanded Moses.

**2** [a]He made the ephod of gold,
*and* of blue and purple and scarlet
*material,* and fine twisted linen.
**3** Then they hammered out gold
sheets and cut *them* into threads
[1]to be woven in *with* the blue and
the purple and the scarlet *material*
and the fine linen, the work of a
*skillful* designer. **4** They made joining
shoulder pieces for [1]the ephod; it was
joined at its two *upper* ends. **5** The
skillfully woven band which was on
it was like its workmanship, [1]of the
same material: of gold, *and* of blue
and purple and scarlet *material,* and
fine twisted linen, just as Yahweh had
commanded Moses.

**6** [a]They made the onyx stones,
set all around in filigree *settings* of
gold; they were engraved *like* the en-
gravings of a signet, according to the
names of the sons of Israel. **7** And [a]he
placed them on the shoulder pieces
of the ephod, *as* stones of remem-
brance for the sons of Israel, just as
Yahweh had commanded Moses.

**8** [a]He made the breastpiece, the
work of a skillful designer, like the
workmanship of the ephod: of gold,
*and* of blue and purple and scarlet
*material,* and fine twisted linen. **9** It
was square; they made the breast-
piece, *having been* folded double, a
[1]span [2]long and a span [3]wide when
folded double. **10** And they [1]mounted
four rows of stones on it. The first
row *was* a row of ruby, topaz, and
emerald; **11** and the second row, a tur-
quoise, a sapphire, and a diamond;
**12** and the third row, a jacinth, an
agate, and an amethyst; **13** and the
fourth row, a beryl, an onyx, and a
jasper. They were set in their filigree
*settings* with gold filigree. **14** The
stones were corresponding to the
names of the sons of Israel; they
were twelve, corresponding to their
names, *engraved with* the engravings
of a signet, each with its name for
the twelve tribes. **15** They made on

**38:26** [b]Ex 12:37; Nu 1:46; 26:51 [1]Lit *mustered* **38:31** [1]Lit *dwelling place* ◆ **39:1** [a]Ex 35:23 [b]Ex 31:10; 35:19 [1]Or *violet,* so in ch [2]Lit *and they made* **39:2** [a]Ex 28:6-12 **39:3** [1]Lit *to work* **39:4** [1]Lit *it* **39:5** [1]Lit *from it* **39:6** [a]Ex 28:9-11 **39:7** [a]Ex 28:12 **39:8** [a]Ex 28:15-28 **39:9** [1]A span was approx. 9 in. or 23 cm [2]Lit *its length* [3]Lit *its width* **39:10** [1]Lit *filled*

the breastpiece chains of a twisted work of cords in pure gold. **16** They made two gold filigree *settings* and two gold rings, and put the two rings on the two ends of the breastpiece. **17** Then they put the two gold cords in the two rings at the ends of the breastpiece. **18** They put the *other* two ends of the two cords on the two filigree *settings* and put them on the shoulder pieces of the ephod at the front of it. **19** They made two gold rings and placed *them* on the two ends of the breastpiece, on its inner edge which was next to the ephod. **20** Furthermore, they made two gold rings and placed them on the bottom of the two shoulder pieces of the ephod, on the front of it, close to the place where it joined, above the skillfully woven band of the ephod. **21** They bound the breastpiece by its rings to the rings of the ephod with a blue cord, so that it would be on the skillfully woven band of the ephod, and that the breastpiece would not come loose from the ephod, just as Yahweh had commanded Moses.

**22** [a]Then he made the robe of the ephod of woven work entirely of blue; **23** [a]and the opening of the robe was *at the top* in the center, as the opening of a coat of mail, with a binding all around its opening, so *that it would not* be torn. **24** They made pomegranates of blue and purple and scarlet *material and* twisted *linen* on the hem of the robe. **25** They also made bells of pure gold and put the bells between the pomegranates all around on the hem of the [l]robe, **26** [l]alternating a bell and a pomegranate all around on the hem of the robe for the ministry, just as Yahweh had commanded Moses.

**27** [a]They made the tunics of finely woven linen for Aaron and his sons, **28** and the turban of fine linen, and the headdresses of the [l]caps of fine linen, and the linen undergarments of fine twisted linen, **29** and the sash of fine twisted linen, and blue and purple and scarlet *material*, the work of the [l]weaver, just as Yahweh had commanded Moses.

**30** [a]They made the plate of the holy crown of pure gold and [l]wrote upon it *with* engraved writing *as found on* a signet, "Holy to Yahweh." **31** They [l]fastened a blue cord to it, to [l]fasten it on the turban above, just as Yahweh had commanded Moses.

**32** Thus all the service of *constructing* the [l]tabernacle of the tent of meeting was [a]completed; and the sons of Israel did according to all that Yahweh had commanded Moses; so they did. **33** They brought the tabernacle to Moses, the tent and all its [l]furnishings: its clasps, its boards, its bars, and its pillars and its bases; **34** and the covering of rams' skins [l]dyed red, and the covering of porpoise skins, and the screening veil; **35** the ark of the testimony and its poles and the [l]mercy seat; **36** the table, all its utensils, and the bread of the [l]Presence; **37** the pure *gold* lampstand, [l]with its arrangement of lamps and all its utensils, and the oil for the light; **38** and the gold altar, and the anointing oil and the fragrant

---

**39:22** [a]Ex 28:31, 34 **39:23** [a]Ex 28:32 **39:25** [l]Lit *robe, between the pomegranates* **39:26** [l]Lit *a bell and a pomegranate, a bell...* **39:27** [a]Ex 28:39, 40, 42 **39:28** [l]Lit *headgear* **39:29** [l]A weaver in colors; lit *variegator* **39:30** [a]Ex 28:36, 37 [l]Lit *wrote on it a writing* **39:31** [l]Lit *put* **39:32** [a]Ge 2:1 [l]Lit *dwelling place* **39:33** [l]Or *utensils* **39:34** [l]Or *tanned* **39:35** [l]Or *propitiatory seat, place of atonement* **39:36** [l]Lit *Face* **39:37** [l]Lit *its lamps, the lamps set in order*

incense, and the veil for the doorway
of the tent; **39** the [1]bronze altar and
its [1]bronze grating, its poles and all
its utensils, the laver and its stand;
**40** the hangings for the court, its pil-
lars and its bases, and the screen for
the gate of the court, its cords and its
pegs, and all the [1]equipment for the
service of the tabernacle, for the tent
of meeting; **41** the woven garments
for ministering in the holy place
and the holy garments for Aaron
the priest and the garments of his
sons, to minister as priests. **42** Thus,
according to all that Yahweh had
commanded Moses, so the sons of
Israel did in all their service. **43** And
Moses saw all the work, and behold,
they had done it; just as Yahweh had
commanded, so they had done. Then
Moses [a]blessed them.

### *Setting Up the Tabernacle*

**40** Then Yahweh spoke to Moses,
saying, **2** "[a]On the first day of
the first month you shall set up the
[1]tabernacle of the tent of meeting.
**3** [a]You shall place the ark of the testi-
mony there, and you shall screen the
ark with the veil. **4** You shall [a]bring
in the table and [b,1]arrange what
belongs on it; and you shall [c]bring
in the lampstand and [2]mount its
lamps. **5** Moreover, you shall [a]set
the gold altar of incense before the
ark of the testimony and set up the
veil for the doorway to the taberna-
cle. **6** You shall set the altar of burnt
offering in front of the doorway of
the tabernacle of the tent of meeting.
**7** You shall [a]set the laver between the
tent of meeting and the altar and put
water [1]in it. **8** You shall set up the
court all around and [1]hang up the
screen for the gateway of the court.
**9** Then you shall take the anointing
oil and [a]anoint the tabernacle and
all that is in it and set it apart as holy
and all its [1]furnishings; and it shall
be holy. **10** You shall anoint the altar
of burnt offering and all its utensils,
and set the altar apart as holy, and
[a]the altar shall be most holy. **11** You
shall anoint the laver and its stand,
and set it apart as holy. **12** Then you
shall [a]bring Aaron and his sons to
the doorway of the tent of meeting
and wash them with water. **13** [a]You
shall put the holy garments on Aaron
and anoint him and set him apart
as holy, that he may minister as a
priest to Me. **14** You shall bring his
sons and put tunics on them; **15** and
you shall anoint them even as you
have anointed their father, that they
may minister as priests to Me; and
their anointing will be for them for
a [a]perpetual priesthood throughout
their generations." **16** Thus Moses
did; according to all that Yahweh had
commanded him, so he did.

**17** Now [a]it happened, in the first
month [1]of the second year, on the
first *day* of the month, the [2]taber-
nacle was erected. **18** Moses erected
the tabernacle and [1]laid its bases
and set up its boards and [1]inserted
its bars and erected its pillars. **19** He
spread the tent over the tabernacle
and placed the covering of the tent

**39:39** [1]Or *copper* **39:40** [1]Or *utensils* **39:43** [a]Lv 9:22, 23; Nu 6:23-26 ◆ **40:2** [a]Ex 19:1; 40:17; Nu 1:1 [1]Lit *dwelling place* **40:3** [a]Ex 26:33; 40:21; Nu 4:5 **40:4** [a]Ex 26:35; 40:22 [b]Ex 25:30; 40:23 [c]Ex 40:24f [1]Lit *arrange its arrangement* [2]Or *light* **40:5** [a]Ex 40:26 **40:7** [a]Ex 30:18; 40:30 [1]Lit *there* **40:8** [1]Lit *put* **40:9** [a]Ex 30:26; Lv 8:10 [1]Or *utensils* **40:10** [a]Ex 29:37 **40:12** [a]Lv 8:1-6 **40:13** [a]Ex 28:41; Lv 8:13 **40:15** [a]Ex 29:9; Nu 25:13 **40:17** [a]Ex 40:2 [1]Lit *in* [2]Lit *dwelling place* **40:18** [1]Lit *put*

[1]on top of it, just as Yahweh had
commanded Moses. **20** Then he took
[a]the testimony and put *it* into the
ark and [1]attached the poles to the
ark and put the [2]mercy seat [3]on top
of the ark. **21** He brought the ark into
the tabernacle and [a]placed the veil of
the screen and screened off the ark
of the testimony, just as Yahweh had
commanded Moses. **22** Then he [a]put
the table in the tent of meeting on the
north side of the tabernacle, outside
the veil. **23** He set the arrangement of
[a]bread in order on it before Yahweh,
just as Yahweh had commanded
Moses. **24** Then he placed the lamp-
stand in the tent of meeting, opposite
the table, on the south side of the
tabernacle. **25** He [a]lighted the lamps
before Yahweh, just as Yahweh had
commanded Moses. **26** Then he
[a]placed the gold altar in the tent of
meeting in front of the veil; **27** and he
[a]burned fragrant incense on it, just
as Yahweh had commanded Moses.
**28** Then he placed the screen at the
doorway of the tabernacle. **29** He
[a]placed the altar of burnt offering
*before* the doorway of the taberna-
cle of the tent of meeting, and he
[b]offered on it the burnt offering and
the meal offering, just as Yahweh had
commanded Moses. **30** He placed the
laver between the tent of meeting
and the altar and put water in it for
washing. **31** [a]From it Moses and Aar-
on and his sons washed their hands
and their feet. **32** When they entered
the tent of meeting, and when they
approached the altar, they washed,
just as Yahweh had commanded
Moses. **33** He [a]erected the court
all around the [1]tabernacle and the
altar, and he put up the screen for
the gateway of the court. Thus Moses
finished the work.

### *The Glory of Yahweh*

**34** [a]Then the cloud covered the tent
of meeting, and the [b]glory of Yahweh
[c]filled the tabernacle. **35** And Moses
[a]was not able to enter the tent of
meeting because the cloud had dwelt
on it, and the glory of Yahweh filled
the tabernacle. **36** Now throughout
all their journeys [a]whenever the
cloud was taken up from over the
tabernacle, the sons of Israel would
set out; **37** but [a]if the cloud was not
taken up, then they did not set out
until the day when it was taken up.
**38** For throughout all their journeys,
[a]the cloud of Yahweh was on the
tabernacle by day, and there was fire
in it by night, in the sight of all the
house of Israel.

---

**40:19** [1]Lit *over it above* **40:20** [a]Ex 25:16; Dt 10:5; 1Ki 8:9; 2Chr 5:10; Heb 9:4 [1]Lit *set* [2]Or propitiatory *seat, place of atonement* [3]Lit *over the ark above* **40:21** [a]Ex 26:33 **40:22** [a]Ex 26:35 **40:23** [a]Ex 25:30; Lv 24:5, 6 **40:25** [a]Ex 25:37; 40:4 **40:26** [a]Ex 30:6; 40:5 **40:27** [a]Ex 30:7 **40:29** [a]Ex 40:6 [b]Ex 29:38-42 **40:31** [a]Ex 30:19, 20 **40:33** [a]Ex 27:9-18; 40:8 [1]Or *dwelling place* **40:34** [a]Nu 9:15-23 [b]1Ki 8:11; Eze 43:4f; Rev 15:8 [c]Ge 1:22, 28 **40:35** [a]1Ki 8:11; 2Chr 5:13, 14 **40:36** [a]Nu 9:17; Ne 9:19 **40:37** [a]Nu 9:19-22 **40:38** [a]Ex 13:21; Nu 9:12, 15; Ps 78:14; Is 4:5

# LEVITICUS

### *The Statutes of Burnt Offerings*

**1** Then [a,1]Yahweh called to Moses
and spoke to him from the tent
of meeting, saying, **2** "Speak to the
sons of Israel and say to them, 'When
any man from among you brings an
[a,1]offering near to Yahweh, you shall
bring your [1]offering of animals from
[b]the herd or the flock. **3** If his offering
is a [a]burnt offering from the herd, he
shall bring it near, a male [b]without
blemish; he shall bring it near [c]to the
doorway of the tent of meeting, that
he may be accepted before Yahweh.
**4** [a]And he shall lay his hand on the
head of the burnt offering, that it
may be accepted for him to make
[b]atonement on his behalf. **5** [a]Then
he shall slaughter the [1]young bull
before Yahweh; and Aaron's sons the
priests shall bring near [b]the blood
and [c]splash the blood around on
the altar that is at the doorway of
the tent of meeting. **6** [a]And he shall
then skin the burnt offering and cut
it into its pieces. **7** [a]And the sons of
Aaron the priest shall put fire on the
altar and arrange wood on the fire.
**8** Then Aaron's sons the priests shall
arrange the pieces, the head, and the
[a]suet over the wood which is on the
fire that is on the altar. **9** Its [a]entrails,
however, and its legs he shall wash
with water. And [b]the priest shall offer
up in smoke all of it on the altar for a
burnt offering, an offering by fire of
[c]a soothing aroma to Yahweh.

**10** 'But if his offering is from the
flock, of the sheep or of the goats, for
a burnt offering, he shall bring near
a [a]male without blemish. **11** [a]And he
shall slaughter it on the side of the
altar northward before Yahweh, and
Aaron's sons the priests shall splash
its blood around on the altar. **12** He
shall then cut it into its pieces with
its head and its [a]suet, and the priest
shall arrange them on the wood
which is on the fire that is on the al-
tar. **13** The entrails, however, and the
legs he shall wash with water. And
[a]the priest shall bring all of it near
and offer it up in smoke on the altar;
it is a burnt offering, an offering by
fire of a soothing aroma to Yahweh.

**14** 'But if his offering to Yahweh
is a burnt offering of birds, then he
shall bring near his offering from the
[a]turtledoves or from young pigeons.
**15** And the priest shall bring it near to
the altar and wring off its head and
offer it up in smoke on the altar; and
its blood is to be drained out [a]on the
side of the altar. **16** He shall also take
away its crop with its feathers and
cast it beside the altar eastward, to
the place of the [a,1]ashes. **17** Then he
shall tear it by its wings, *but* [a]he shall

---

◆ ***1:1*** [a]*Ex 19:3; 25:22; Nu 7:89* [1]The personal covenant name of God, a form of I AM WHO I AM, cf. Ex 3:14-15 **1:2** [a]Mk 7:11 [b]Lv 22:18f [1]Heb *qorban* **1:3** [a]Lv 6:8-13 [b]Ex 12:5; Lv 22:20-24; Dt 15:21; 17:1 [c]Lv 17:8, 9; Dt 12:5, 6, 11 **1:4** [a]Ex 29:10, 15, 19; Lv 3:2, 8 [b]Ex 29:33; Lv 4:20, 26, 31; 2Chr 29:23, 24 **1:5** [a]Ex 29:11, 16, 20 [b]Lv 17:11 [c]Lv 1:11; 3:2, 8, 13; Heb 12:24; 1Pe 1:2 [1]Or *one of the herd*; lit *son of the herd* **1:6** [a]Lv 7:8 **1:7** [a]Lv 6:8-13 **1:8** [a]Lv 1:12; 3:3, 4; 8:20 **1:9** [a]Ex 12:9 [b]Nu 15:8-10; 28:11-14 [c]Ge 8:21; Ex 29:18, 25; Lv 1:13; Nu 15:3; Eph 5:2 **1:10** [a]Ex 12:5; Lv 1:3; Eze 43:22; 1Pe 1:19 **1:11** [a]Ex 24:6; Lv 1:5; 8:19; 9:12 **1:12** [a]Lv 3:3, 4 **1:13** [a]Nu 15:4-7; 28:11-14 **1:14** [a]Ge 15:9; Lv 5:7, 11; 12:8; Lk 2:24 **1:15** [a]Lv 5:9 **1:16** [a]Lv 6:10 [1]Soaked with fat; or *fat ashes* **1:17** [a]Ge 15:10; Lv 5:8

not separate *it.* And the priest shall
offer it up in smoke on the altar on
the wood which is on the fire; [b]it is a
burnt offering, an offering by fire of
a soothing aroma to Yahweh.

### *The Statutes of Grain Offerings*

2 'Now when anyone brings near
a [a]grain offering as an offering
to Yahweh, his offering shall be of
fine flour, and he shall pour oil on
it and put frankincense on it. **2** He
shall then bring it to Aaron's sons the
priests; and he shall take from it [a]his
handful of its fine flour and of its oil
with all of its frankincense. And the
priest shall offer *it* up in smoke *as* its
[b]memorial portion on the altar, an
offering by fire of a soothing aroma
to Yahweh. **3** [a]And the remainder of
the grain offering belongs to [b]Aaron
and his sons: a thing most holy of the
offerings to Yahweh by fire.
**4** 'Now when you bring near an
offering of a grain offering baked
in an oven, *it shall be* [a]unleavened
cakes of fine flour mixed with oil or
unleavened wafers [1]spread with oil.
**5** And if your offering is a grain offer-
ing *made* [a]on the griddle, *it shall be*
of fine flour, unleavened, mixed with
oil; **6** you shall break it into bits and
pour oil on it; it is a grain offering.
**7** Now if your offering is a grain offer-
ing *made* [a]in a [1]pan, it shall be made
of fine flour with oil. **8** And you will
bring in the grain offering which is
made of these things to Yahweh, and
it shall be brought near to the priest,
and he shall bring it to the altar. **9** The
priest then shall raise up from the
grain offering [a]its memorial portion,
and he shall offer *it* up in smoke on
the altar *as* an offering by fire of a
soothing aroma to Yahweh. **10** [a]And
the remainder of the grain offering
belongs to Aaron and his sons: a
thing most holy of the offerings to
Yahweh by fire.
**11** '[a]No grain offering, which you
bring near to Yahweh, shall be made
with leaven, for you shall not offer [1]up
in smoke any leaven or any honey as
an [b]offering by fire to Yahweh. **12** [a]As
an offering of first fruits you shall
bring them near to Yahweh, but they
shall not ascend for a soothing aroma
on the altar. **13** Every grain offering
of yours, moreover, you shall season
with salt, so that [a]the salt of the cov-
enant of your God shall not be lacking
from your grain offering; with all your
offerings you shall bring salt near.
**14** 'Also if you bring near a grain
offering of early ripened things to
Yahweh, you shall bring near [a]fresh
heads of grain roasted in the fire,
grits of new growth, for the grain
offering of your early ripened things.
**15** You shall then put oil on it and
place frankincense on it; it is a grain
offering. **16** And the priest shall offer
up in smoke [a]its memorial portion,
part of its grits and its oil with all its
frankincense as an offering by fire
to Yahweh.

### *The Statutes of Peace Offerings*

3 'Now if his offering is a [a]sacrifice
of peace offerings, if he is going
to bring near one from the herd,
whether male or female, he shall

---

**1:17** [b]Lv 9:13 ◆ **2:1** [a]Lv 6:14-18; Nu 15:4 **2:2** [a]Lv 5:12; 6:15 [b]Lv 2:9, 16; 5:12; 24:7; Ac 10:4 **2:3** [a]Lv 2:10; 6:16 [b]Lv 10:12, 13 **2:4** [a]Ex 29:2 [1]Lit *anointed* **2:5** [a]Lv 6:21; 7:9 **2:7** [a]Lv 7:9 [1]Lit *lidded cooking pan* **2:9** [a]Lv 2:2, 16; 5:12 **2:10** [a]Lv 2:3; 6:16 **2:11** [a]Ex 23:18; 34:25; Lv 6:16, 17 [b]Ex 29:25; Lv 1:13 [1]Lit *up from it* **2:12** [a]Ex 34:22; Lv 7:13; 23:10, 17, 18 **2:13** [a]Nu 18:19; 2Chr 13:5; Eze 43:24 **2:14** [a]Lv 23:14 **2:16** [a]Lv 2:2 ◆ **3:1** [a]Lv 7:11-34; 17:5

bring it near [b]without blemish be-
fore Yahweh. **2** [a]Then he shall lay his
hand on the head of his offering and
[b]slaughter it at the doorway of the
tent of meeting, and Aaron's sons the
priests shall splash the blood around
on the altar. **3** From the sacrifice of
the peace offerings he shall bring an
offering by fire near to Yahweh, the
fat that covers the entrails and all
the fat that is on the entrails, **4** and
the two kidneys with the fat that is
on them, which is on the loins, and
the [1]lobe of the liver, which he shall
remove with the kidneys. **5** Then
[a]Aaron's sons shall offer *it* up in
smoke on the altar [b]on the burnt
offering, which is on the wood that
is on the fire; [c]it is an offering by
fire of a soothing aroma to Yahweh.
**6** But if his offering for a sacrifice of
peace offerings to Yahweh is from the
flock, he shall bring it near, male or
female, [a]without blemish. **7** If he is
going to bring near [a]a lamb for his
offering, then he shall bring it near
[b]before Yahweh, **8** and [a]he shall lay
his hand on the head of his offering
and [b]slaughter it before the tent
of meeting, and Aaron's sons shall
[c]splash its blood around on the altar.
**9** And from the [a]sacrifice of peace
offerings he shall bring near as an
offering by fire to Yahweh its fat, [1]the
entire fat tail which he shall remove
close to the backbone, and the fat
that covers the entrails and all the
fat that is on the entrails, **10** and the
two kidneys with the fat that is on
them, which is on the loins, and the
[1]lobe of the liver, which he shall
remove [a]with the kidneys. **11** Then
the priest shall offer *it* up in smoke
[a]on the altar *as* [b]food, an offering by
fire to Yahweh.

**12** 'Moreover, if his offering is
[a]a goat, then he shall bring it near
before Yahweh, **13** and he shall lay
his hand on its head and slaughter
it before the tent of meeting, and the
sons of Aaron shall splash its blood
around on the altar. **14** And from it
he shall bring near his offering as
an offering by fire to Yahweh the
fat that covers the entrails and all
the fat that is on the entrails, **15** and
the two kidneys with the fat that is
on them, which is on the loins, and
the [1]lobe of the liver, which he shall
remove [a]with the kidneys. **16** And the
priest shall offer them up in smoke
on the altar *as* food, an offering by
fire for a soothing aroma; [a]all fat is
Yahweh's. **17** It is a [a]perpetual statute
throughout your generations in all
your *places of* habitation: you shall
not eat any fat [b]or any blood.'"

### *The Statutes of Sin Offerings*

**4** Then Yahweh spoke to Moses,
saying, **2** "Speak to the sons
of Israel, saying, 'If a person sins
[a]unintentionally in any of the [1]things
which Yahweh has [b]commanded not
to be done, and he does any one of
them, **3** [a]if the anointed priest sins
so as to bring guilt on the people,
then let him bring near to Yahweh a

**3:1** [b]Lv 1:3; 22:20-24 **3:2** [a]Lv 1:4 [b]Ex 29:11, 16, 20 **3:4** [1]Or *appendage on* **3:5** [a]Lv 7:28-34 [b]Ex 29:38-42; Nu 28:3-10 [c]Nu 15:8-10; 28:12-14 **3:6** [a]Lv 3:1; 22:20-24 **3:7** [a]Nu 15:4, 5; 28:4-8 [b]Lv 17:8, 9; 1Ki 8:62 **3:8** [a]Lv 1:4 [b]Lv 3:2 [c]Lv 1:5 **3:9** [a]Lv 17:5; Nu 7:88; 1Sa 10:8; 2Sa 6:17; 1Ki 3:15; 8:63, 64; 1Chr 16:1 [1]Lit *the fat tail, entire* **3:10** [a]Lv 3:4, 15 [1]Or *appendage on* **3:11** [a]Lv 3:5 [b]Lv 3:16; 21:6, 8, 17, 22 **3:12** [a]Nu 15:6-11 **3:15** [a]Lv 3:4; 7:4 [1]Or *appendage on* **3:16** [a]Lv 7:23-25 **3:17** [a]Lv 6:18, 22; 7:34, 36; 10:9, 15; 16:29; 17:7; 23:14, 21; 24:3 [b]Lv 7:26; 17:10-16 ◆ **4:2** [a]Lv 4:22, 27; 5:15-18; 22:14 [b]Lv 4:13 [1]Lit *commands of Yahweh which are not to be done* **4:3** [a]Lv 4:14, 23, 28

bull from the herd without blemish as a sin offering for the sin he has [1]committed. **4** Then he shall bring the bull to the doorway of the tent of meeting before Yahweh, and [a]he shall lay his hand on the head of the bull and slaughter the bull before Yahweh. **5** Then the [a]anointed priest shall take some of the blood of the bull and bring it to the tent of meeting, **6** and the priest shall dip his finger in the blood and sprinkle some of the blood seven times before Yahweh in front of [a]the veil of the sanctuary. **7** The priest shall also put some of the blood on the horns of [a]the altar of fragrant incense which is before Yahweh in the tent of meeting; and all the blood of the bull he shall pour out at the base of the altar of burnt offering which is at the doorway of the tent of meeting. **8** [a]Then he shall raise up from it all the fat of the bull of the sin offering: the fat that covers the entrails and all the fat which is on the entrails, **9** and the two kidneys with the fat that is on them, which is on the loins, and the [1]lobe of the liver, which he shall remove [a]with the kidneys **10** (just as it is raised up from the ox of the sacrifice of peace offerings), and the priest shall offer them up in smoke on the altar of burnt offering. **11** But [a]the hide of the bull and all its flesh with its head and its legs and its entrails and its refuse, **12** [1]that is, all *the rest of* the bull, he shall bring out to [a]a clean place outside the camp where the [2]ashes are poured out, and he shall burn it on wood with fire; where the [2]ashes are poured out it shall be burned.

**13** ‘[a]Now if the whole congregation of Israel commits error, and the matter is hidden from the sight of the assembly, and they commit any of the [1]things which Yahweh has commanded not to be done, and they become guilty; **14** [a]when the sin [1]which they have [2]committed becomes known, then the assembly shall bring near [b]a bull from the herd for a sin offering and bring it before the tent of meeting. **15** Then [a]the elders of the congregation shall lay their hands on the head of the bull before Yahweh, and the bull shall be slaughtered [b]before Yahweh. **16** Then the anointed priest shall bring some of the blood of the bull to the tent of meeting; **17** and [a]the priest shall dip his finger in the blood and sprinkle *it* seven times before Yahweh in front of the veil. **18** And he shall put some of the blood on the horns of [a]the altar which is before Yahweh [1]in the tent of meeting; and all the blood he shall pour out at the base of the altar of burnt offering which is at the doorway of the tent of meeting. **19** [a]He shall then raise up all its fat from it and offer it up in smoke on the altar. **20** He shall also do with the bull just as he did with [a]the bull of the sin offering; thus he shall do with it. So [b]the priest shall make atonement for them, and they will be forgiven. **21** Then he shall bring out the bull to *a place* outside the camp and burn it

---

**4:3** [1]Lit *sinned* **4:4** [a]Lv 1:4; 4:15; Nu 8:12 **4:5** [a]Lv 4:3, 17 **4:6** [a]Ex 40:21, 26 **4:7** [a]Lv 4:18, 25, 30, 34; 8:15; 9:9; 16:18 **4:8** [a]Lv 3:3, 4 **4:9** [a]Lv 3:4 [1]Or *appendage on* **4:11** [a]Lv 9:11; Nu 19:5 **4:12** [a]Lv 4:21; 6:10, 11; 16:27 [1]Lit *and* [2]Soaked with fat; or *fat ashes* **4:13** [a]Nu 15:24-26 [1]Lit *commands of Yahweh which are not to be done* **4:14** [a]Lv 4:3 [b]Lv 4:3, 23, 28 [1]Lit *concerning which* [2]Lit *sinned* **4:15** [a]Lv 8:14, 18, 22; Nu 8:10, 12 [b]Lv 1:3 **4:17** [a]Lv 4:6 **4:18** [a]Lv 4:7, 25, 30, 34 [1]Lit *which is in* **4:19** [a]Lv 4:8 **4:20** [a]Lv 4:8, 21 [b]Nu 15:25, 28

as he burned the first bull; it is [a]the sin offering for the assembly.

**22** ‘When [a]a leader [b]sins and unintentionally does any one of all the [1]things which Yahweh his God has commanded not to be done, and he becomes guilty, **23** [a]or if his sin [1]which he has committed is made known to him, he shall bring for his offering a [b,2]goat, [c]a male without blemish. **24** Then he shall lay his hand on the head of the male goat and slaughter it in the place where [1]they slaughter the burnt offering before Yahweh; it is a sin offering. **25** Then the priest shall take some of the blood of the sin offering with his finger and put it on [a]the horns of the altar of burnt offering; and *the rest of* its blood he shall pour out at the base of the altar of burnt offering. **26** [a]And all its fat he shall offer up in smoke on the altar as *in the case of* the fat of the sacrifice of peace offerings. Thus [b]the priest shall make atonement for him in regard to his sin, and he will be forgiven.

**27** ‘Now if [1]anyone of [2]the common people sins [a]unintentionally in doing any of the [3]things which Yahweh has commanded not to be done, and becomes guilty, **28** [a]or if his sin which he has [1]committed is made known to him, then he shall bring for his offering a [b,2]goat, a [c]female without blemish, for his sin which he has [1]committed. **29** [a]And he shall lay his hand on the head of the sin offering and [b]slaughter the sin offering at the place of the burnt offering. **30** And the priest shall take some of its blood with his finger and put it on the horns of [a]the altar of burnt offering; and [b]all *the rest of* its blood he shall pour out at the base of the altar. **31** [a]Then he shall remove all its fat, just as the fat was removed from the sacrifice of peace offerings; and the priest shall offer it up in smoke on the altar for [b]a soothing aroma to Yahweh. Thus the priest shall make atonement for him, [1]and he will be forgiven.

**32** ‘But if he brings [a]a lamb as his offering for a sin offering, he shall bring it, a female without blemish. **33** [a]And he shall lay his hand on the head of the sin offering and slaughter it for a sin offering [b]in the place where [1]they slay the burnt offering. **34** And the priest shall take some of the blood of the sin offering with his finger and put it on the horns of [a]the altar of burnt offering, and [b]all *the rest of* its blood he shall pour out at the base of the altar. **35** Then he shall remove [a]all its fat, just as the fat of the lamb is removed from the sacrifice of the peace offerings, and the priest shall offer them up in smoke on the altar, on the offerings by fire to Yahweh. Thus [b]the priest shall make atonement for him in regard to his sin which he has [1]committed, and he will be forgiven.

---

**4:21** [a]Lv 4:13f; 16:15-17; Nu 15:24-26 **4:22** [a]Nu 31:13; 32:2 [b]Lv 4:2, 27 [1]Lit *commands of Yahweh which are not to be done* **4:23** [a]Lv 4:3 [b]Lv 4:3, 14, 28 [c]Lv 4:28 [1]Lit *in which he has sinned* [2]Lit *buck of the goats* **4:24** [1]Lit *one slaughters* **4:25** [a]Lv 4:7, 18, 30, 34 **4:26** [a]Lv 4:19 [b]Lv 4:20, 31; 5:10, 13, 16, 18; 6:7 **4:27** [a]Lv 4:2; Nu 15:27 [1]Lit *one soul* [2]Lit *the people of the land* [3]Lit *commands of Yahweh which are not to be done* **4:28** [a]Lv 4:3 [b]Lv 4:3, 14, 23, 32 [c]Lv 4:23 [1]Lit *sinned* [2]Or *female goat* **4:29** [a]Lv 1:4; 4:4, 24 [b]Lv 1:5, 11 **4:30** [a]Lv 4:7, 18, 25, 34 [b]Lv 4:7 **4:31** [a]Lv 4:8 [b]Ge 8:21; Ex 29:18; Lv 1:9, 13; 2:2, 9, 12 [1]Or *so that he may be* **4:32** [a]Lv 4:28 **4:33** [a]Lv 1:4, 5 [b]Lv 4:29 [1]Lit *one slays* **4:34** [a]Lv 4:7, 18, 25, 30 [b]Lv 4:7 **4:35** [a]Lv 4:26, 31 [b]Lv 4:20 [1]Lit *sinned*

5 'Now if a person sins after he
hears a [1]public [a]oath *to testify*
when he is a witness, whether he
has seen or *otherwise* known, if he
does not tell *it*, then he will bear his
[2]guilt. 2 Or a person who touches
[a]any unclean thing, whether a
carcass of an unclean beast or the
carcass of unclean cattle or a carcass
of unclean swarming things—
*though* it is hidden from him, yet
he is unclean—will be guilty. 3 Or if
he touches human uncleanness, of
whatever *sort* his uncleanness *may*
be with which he becomes unclean,
and it is hidden from him, and then
he comes to know *it*, he will be guilty.
4 Or if a person [a]swears thoughtlessly
with his lips to do evil or to do good,
in whatever matter a man may speak
thoughtlessly with a *sworn* oath, and
it is hidden from him, and then he
comes to know *it*, he will be guilty in
one of these. 5 So it shall be, when he
becomes guilty in one of these, that
he shall [a]confess that in which he
has sinned. 6 He shall also bring his
guilt offering to Yahweh for his sin
which he has [1]committed, [a]a female
from the flock, a lamb or a [2]goat, as a
sin offering. So the priest shall make
atonement on his behalf for his sin.

7 'But if [1]he cannot afford a lamb,
then he shall bring to Yahweh his
*guilt offering* for that in which he has
sinned, two turtledoves or two young
pigeons, [a]one for a sin offering and
the other for a burnt offering. 8 And
he shall bring them to the priest, who
shall bring near first that which is for
the sin offering and shall nip its head
at the front of its neck, but he [a]shall
not separate *it*. 9 He shall also sprinkle
some of the blood of the sin offering
[a]on the side of the altar, while the rest
of the blood shall be drained out [b]at
the base of the altar: it is a sin offering.
10 The second he shall then prepare
as a burnt offering [a]according to the
*legal* judgment. [b]So the priest shall
make atonement on his behalf for his
sin which he has [1]committed, and it
will be forgiven him.

11 'But [a]if his [1]means are insufficient for two turtledoves or two
young pigeons, then for his offering
for that which he has sinned, he shall
bring the tenth of an [2]ephah of fine
flour for a sin offering; [b]he shall not
place oil on it or put frankincense
on it, for it is a sin offering. 12 He
shall then bring it to the priest, and
the priest shall take his handful of it
as its memorial portion and offer *it*
up in smoke on the altar, [1]with the
offerings of Yahweh by fire: it is a sin
offering. 13 So the priest shall make
atonement for him concerning his
sin which he has [1]committed from
[a]one of these, and it will be forgiven
him; then [b]*the rest* shall become the
priest's, like the grain offering.'"

### *The Statutes of Guilt Offerings*

14 Then Yahweh spoke to Moses, saying, 15 "[a]If a person acts unfaithfully
and sins [b]unintentionally against the
holy things of Yahweh, then he shall
bring his [c]guilt offering to Yahweh: [d]a
ram without blemish from the flock,

---

◆ **5:1** [a]Pr 29:24; Jer 23:10 [1]Lit *voice of an oath* [2]Or *iniquity* **5:2** [a]Lv 11:8, 11, 24-40; Nu 19:11-16; Dt 14:8 **5:4** [a]Nu 30:6, 8; Ps 106:33 **5:5** [a]Lv 16:21; 26:40; Nu 5:7; Pr 28:13 **5:6** [a]Lv 4:28, 32 [1]Lit *sinned* [2]Lit *female goat* **5:7** [a]Lv 12:6, 8; 14:22, 30, 31 [1]Lit *his hand does not reach enough for* **5:8** [a]Lv 1:17 **5:9** [a]Lv 1:15 [b]Lv 4:7, 18 **5:10** [a]Lv 1:14-17 [b]Lv 4:20, 26; 5:13, 16 [1]Lit *sinned* **5:11** [a]Lv 14:21-32; 27:8 [b]Lv 2:1, 2 [1]Lit *hand does not reach* [2]An ephah was approx. 21 qt. or 23 l **5:12** [1]Lit *upon* **5:13** [a]Lv 5:4, 5 [b]Lv 2:3 [1]Lit *sinned* **5:15** [a]Nu 5:5-8 [b]Lv 4:2; 22:14 [c]Lv 7:1-10 [d]Lv 6:6

according to your valuation in silver
by [1]shekels, in *terms of* the [e]shekel
of the sanctuary, for a guilt offering.
**16** [a]And he shall make restitution for
that which he has sinned against
the holy thing, and he shall add to
it a fifth part of it and give it to the
priest. [b]The priest shall then make
atonement for him with the ram
of the guilt offering, and it will be
forgiven him.

**17** "Now if a person sins and does
any one of the things [1]which Yahweh
has commanded not to be done, [a]but
he was unaware, still he is guilty and
shall bear his punishment. **18** He is
then to bring to the priest [a]a ram
without blemish from the flock,
according to your valuation, for
a guilt offering. So the priest shall
make atonement for him concern-
ing his error in which he sinned
[b]unintentionally and did not know
*it*, and it will be forgiven him. **19** It
is a guilt offering; he was certainly
guilty before Yahweh."

**6** [1]Then Yahweh spoke to Moses,
saying, **2** "[a]If a person sins and
acts unfaithfully against Yahweh and
deals falsely with his companion
in regard to a deposit or a security
entrusted *to him* or through robbery,
or *if* he has extorted from his com-
panion, **3** or [a]has found what was lost
and dealt falsely about it and sworn
falsely, so that he sins in regard to
any one of the things a man may do;
**4** then it shall be, when he sins and
becomes guilty, that he shall [a]return
what he took by robbery or what
he got by extortion, or the deposit
which was [1]entrusted to him or the
lost thing which he found, **5** or any-
thing about which he swore falsely;
[a]he shall make restitution for it [1]in
full and add to it one-fifth more. [b]He
shall give it to the one to whom it be-
longs on the day *he presents* his guilt
offering. **6** Then he shall bring to the
priest his guilt offering to Yahweh,
[a]a ram without blemish from the
flock, according to your valuation,
for a guilt offering, **7** and [a]the priest
shall make atonement for him before
Yahweh, and he will be forgiven for
any one of the things which he may
have done to incur guilt."

### *Statutes for the Priest in the Offerings*

**8** [1]Then Yahweh spoke to Moses,
saying, **9** "Command Aaron and his
sons, saying, 'This is [a]the law for the
burnt offering: the burnt offering
itself *shall remain* on the hearth on
the altar all night until the morning,
and [b]the fire on the altar shall be
kept burning on it. **10** And the priest
shall put on [a]his linen robe, and he
shall put on undergarments next to
his flesh; and he shall raise up the
[1]ashes *to* which the fire [2]reduces the
burnt offering on the altar and place
them beside the altar. **11** Then he
shall take off his garments and put on
other garments and carry the [1]ashes
outside the camp to a clean place.
**12** And the fire on the altar shall be
kept burning on it. It shall not go out,
but the priest shall burn wood on it

---

**5:15** [e]Ex 30:13 [1]A shekel was approx. 0.4 oz. or 11 gm **5:16** [a]Lv 6:5; 22:14; Nu 5:7, 8 [b]Lv 7:2-7 **5:17** [a]Lv 4:2; 5:19 [1]Lit *the commands of Yahweh which are* **5:18** [a]Lv 5:15 [b]Lv 5:17 ◆ **6:1** [1]Ch 5:20 in Heb **6:2** [a]Ex 22:7-15 **6:3** [a]Ex 23:4; Dt 22:1-4 **6:4** [a]Lv 24:18, 21 [1]Or *deposited with* **6:5** [a]Lv 5:16 [b]Nu 5:8 [1]Lit *in its sum* **6:6** [a]Lv 5:15 **6:7** [a]Lv 7:2-5 **6:8** [1]Ch 6:1 in Heb **6:9** [a]Ex 29:38-42; Nu 28:3-10 [b]Lv 6:12, 13 **6:10** [a]Ex 28:39, 42; 39:27, 28 [1]Soaked with fat; or *fat ashes* [2]Lit *consumes* **6:11** [1]Soaked with fat; or *fat ashes*

every morning; and he shall lay out the burnt offering on it and offer up in smoke the fat portions of the peace offerings [a]on it. **13** Fire shall be kept burning continually on the altar; it shall not go out.

**14** 'Now this is the law of the grain offering: the sons of Aaron shall bring it near before Yahweh in front of the altar. **15** [a]Then one *of them* shall raise up from it a handful of the fine flour of the grain offering, [1]with its oil and all the frankincense that is on the grain offering, and he shall offer *it* up in smoke on the altar, a soothing aroma, as its memorial offering to Yahweh. **16** [a]What is left of it Aaron and his sons shall eat. It shall be eaten as unleavened cakes in a holy place; they shall eat it in the court of the tent of meeting. **17** [a]It shall not be baked with leaven. I have given it as their share from My offerings by fire; [b]it is most holy, like the sin offering and [c]the guilt offering. **18** [a]Every male among the sons of Aaron may eat it; it is a perpetual statute throughout your generations, from the offerings by fire to Yahweh. [b]Whoever touches them will be set apart as holy.'"

**19** Then Yahweh spoke to Moses, saying, **20** "This is the offering which Aaron and his sons shall bring near to Yahweh on the day when he is anointed; the [1]tenth of an [a]ephah of fine flour as [b]a [2]regular grain offering, half of it in the morning and half of it in the evening. **21** It shall be prepared with oil on a [a]griddle. When it is *well* stirred, you shall bring it. You shall bring near the grain offering in baked pieces as a soothing aroma to Yahweh. **22** And the anointed priest, who will be in his place [1]among his sons, shall [2]offer it. By a perpetual statute it shall be entirely offered up in smoke to Yahweh. **23** So every grain offering of the priest shall be burned entirely. It shall not be eaten."

**24** Then Yahweh spoke to Moses, saying, **25** "Speak to Aaron and to his sons, saying, 'This is the law of the sin offering: [a]in the place where the burnt offering is slaughtered, the sin offering shall be slaughtered before Yahweh; it is most holy. **26** [a]The priest who offers it for sin shall eat it. It shall be eaten in a holy place, in the court of the tent of meeting. **27** [a]Anyone who touches its flesh will be set apart as holy; and when any of its blood sprinkles on a garment, in a holy place you shall wash what was sprinkled on. **28** Also [a]the earthenware vessel in which it was boiled shall be broken; and if it was boiled in a bronze vessel, then it shall be scoured and rinsed in water. **29** [a]And every male among the priests may eat of it; [b]it is most holy. **30** But no sin offering, [a]of which any of the blood is brought into the tent of meeting to make atonement [b]in the holy place, shall be eaten; [c]it shall be burned with fire.

**7** 'Now this is the law of the [a]guilt offering; it is most holy. **2** In [a]the place where they slaughter the burnt offering they are to slaughter the guilt offering, and he shall splash its

**6:12** [a]Lv 3:5 **6:15** [a]Lv 2:2, 9 [1]Lit *and some of* **6:16** [a]Lv 2:3; 10:12-14; Eze 44:29 **6:17** [a]Lv 2:11 [b]Ex 40:10; Lv 6:25, 26, 29, 30; Nu 18:9 [c]Lv 7:7; 10:16-18 **6:18** [a]Lv 6:29; 7:6; Nu 18:10; 1Co 9:13 [b]Lv 6:27 **6:20** [a]Lv 5:11 [b]Nu 4:16 [1]Approx. 2.1 qt. or 2.3 l, an ephah was approx. 21 qt. or 23 l [2]Lit *grain offering continually* **6:21** [a]Lv 2:5 **6:22** [1]Lit *from among* [2]Lit *do* **6:25** [a]Lv 1:11 **6:26** [a]Lv 6:29 **6:27** [a]Lv 7:19 **6:28** [a]Lv 11:33; 15:12 **6:29** [a]Lv 6:18 [b]Lv 6:17, 25 **6:30** [a]Lv 4:1-21 [b]Lv 4:7, 18 [c]Lv 4:11, 12, 21 ◆**7:1** [a]Lv 5:14-6:7 **7:2** [a]Lv 1:11

blood around on the altar. **3** Then
he shall bring near from it all its fat:
the [a]fat tail and the fat that covers
the entrails, **4** and the two kidneys
with the fat that is on them, which
is on the loins, and the lobe on
the liver he shall remove [a]with the
kidneys. **5** And the priest shall offer
them up in smoke on the altar as an
offering by fire to Yahweh; it is a guilt
offering. **6** [a]Every male among the
priests may eat of it. It shall be eaten
in a holy place; it is most holy. **7** The
guilt offering is like the [a]sin offering,
there is one law for them; the [b]priest
who makes atonement with it [1]shall
have it. **8** Also the priest who brings
near any man's burnt offering, [1]that
priest shall have for himself the skin
of the burnt offering which he has
brought near. **9** Likewise, every grain
offering that is baked in the oven and
everything prepared in a [1]pan or on
a [a]griddle [2]shall belong to the priest
who brings it near. **10** And every grain
offering, mixed with oil or dry, shall
[1]belong to all the sons of Aaron, [2]to
all alike.

**11** 'Now this is the law of the [a]sacri-
fice of peace offerings which shall
be brought near to Yahweh. **12** If he
brings it near for [a]thanksgiving, then
along with the sacrifice of thanksgiv-
ing he shall bring near [b]unleavened
cakes mixed with oil and unleavened
wafers [1]spread with oil and cakes *of*
*well* stirred fine flour mixed with
oil. **13** With the sacrifice of his peace
offerings for thanksgiving, he shall
bring near his offering with cakes of
[a]leavened bread. **14** Of [1]this he shall
bring near, one of every offering as
a [2]contribution to Yahweh; [a]it shall
[3]belong to the priest who splashes
the blood of the peace offerings.

**15** '[a]Now *as for* the flesh of the
sacrifice of his thanksgiving peace
offerings, it shall be eaten on the day
of his offering; he shall not leave any
of it over until morning. **16** But if the
sacrifice of his offering is a [a]votive or
a freewill offering, it shall be eaten
on the day that he brings near his
sacrifice, and on the [1]next day what
is left of it may be eaten; **17** [a]but
what is left over from the flesh of
the sacrifice on the third day shall
be burned with fire. **18** So if any of
the flesh of the sacrifice of his peace
offerings should *ever* be eaten on the
third day, he who brings it near will
not be accepted, *and* it will not be
counted to his *benefit*. It shall be an
[a]offensive thing, and the person who
eats of it will bear his *own* iniquity.

**19** 'Also the flesh that touches
anything unclean shall not be eaten;
it shall be burned with fire. [1]As for
*other* flesh, anyone who is clean may
eat *such* flesh. **20** [a]But the person
who eats the flesh of the sacrifice
of peace offerings which belong to
Yahweh, [1]in his uncleanness, that
person [b]shall be cut off from his
people. **21** [a]When anyone touches
anything unclean, whether human
uncleanness or an unclean animal
or any unclean [1]detestable thing,

---

**7:3** [a]Lv 3:9 **7:4** [a]Lv 3:4 **7:6** [a]Lv 6:18, 29; Nu 18:9 **7:7** [a]Lv 6:25, 26, 30 [b]1Co 9:13; 10:18 [1]Lit *it shall be for him* **7:8** [1]Lit *for the priest, it shall be for him* **7:9** [a]Lv 2:5 [1]Lit *lidded cooking pan* [2]Lit *for the priest, it shall be for him* **7:10** [1]Lit *be* [2]Lit *a man as his brother* **7:11** [a]Lv 3:1 **7:12** [a]Lv 7:15 [b]Lv 2:4; Nu 6:15 [1]Or *anointed* **7:13** [a]Lv 2:12; 23:17, 18; Am 4:5 **7:14** [a]Nu 18:8, 11, 19 [1]Lit *it* [2]Or *heave offering* [3]Lit *be for* **7:15** [a]Lv 22:29, 30 **7:16** [a]Lv 19:5-8 [1]Lit *morrow and what* **7:17** [a]Ex 12:10 **7:18** [a]Lv 19:7; Pr 15:8 **7:19** [1]Lit *And the flesh* **7:20** [a]Lv 22:3-7; Nu 19:13 [b]Lv 7:25 [1]Lit *and his uncleanness is on him* **7:21** [a]Lv 5:2, 3 [1]Some mss *swarming thing*

and eats of the flesh of the sacrifice
of peace offerings which belong to
Yahweh, that person shall be cut off
from his people.'"
**22** Then Yahweh spoke to Moses,
saying, **23** "Speak to the sons of Is-
rael, saying, 'You shall not eat [a]any
fat *from* an ox, a sheep, or a goat.
**24** Also the fat of *an animal* which
dies and the fat of an animal [a]torn
*by beasts* may be put to any other
use, but you must certainly not eat
it. **25** For whoever eats the fat of the
animal from which [1]an offering by
fire is brought near to Yahweh, even
the person who eats shall be cut off
from his people. **26** [a]And you shall
not eat any blood, either of bird
or animal, in any of your *places of*
habitation. **27** Any person who eats
any blood, even that person shall be
cut off from his people.'"
**28** Then Yahweh spoke to Moses,
saying, **29** "Speak to the sons of Israel,
saying, 'He who brings [a]the sacrifice
of his peace offerings near to Yahweh
shall bring his offering to Yahweh
from the sacrifice of his peace offer-
ings. **30** His own hands are to bring
offerings by fire to Yahweh. He shall
bring the fat with the breast, that the
[a]breast may be waved as a wave offer-
ing before Yahweh. **31** And the priest
shall offer up the fat in smoke on the
altar, but [a]the breast shall belong to
Aaron and his sons. **32** And you shall
give [a]the right thigh to the priest as
a [1]contribution from the sacrifices
of your peace offerings. **33** The one
among the sons of Aaron who brings
near the blood of the peace offerings
and the fat, the right thigh shall be
his as *his* portion. **34** For I have taken
[a]the breast of the wave offering and
the thigh of the [1]contribution from
the sons of Israel from the sacrifices
of their peace offerings, and I have
given them to Aaron the priest and to
his sons as a perpetual statute *taken*
from the sons of Israel.
**35** 'This is [1]the share for Aaron and
[1]the [a]share for his sons from the of-
ferings by fire to Yahweh, in that day
when he brought them near to min-
ister as priests to Yahweh. **36** [1]These
Yahweh had commanded to be given
them from the sons of Israel in the
day that He [a]anointed them. It is a
perpetual statute throughout their
generations.'"
**37** This is the law of the burnt offer-
ing, the grain offering and the sin of-
fering and the guilt offering and [a]the
ordination offering and the sacrifice
of peace offerings, **38** [a]which Yahweh
commanded Moses at Mount Sinai in
the day that He commanded the sons
of Israel to bring their offerings near
to Yahweh in the wilderness of Sinai.

### *The Ordination of Aaron and His Sons*

**8** Then Yahweh spoke to Moses,
saying, **2** "[a]Take Aaron and his
sons with him, and the [b]garments
and [c]the anointing oil and the bull
of the sin offering and the two
rams and the basket of unleavened
bread, **3** and assemble all the con-
gregation at the doorway of the tent

**7:23** [a]Lv 3:17 **7:24** [a]Ex 22:31; Lv 17:15; 22:8 **7:25** [1]Lit *he offers an offering by fire* **7:26** [a]Ge 9:4; Lv 17:10-16; 19:26; Dt 12:23; 1Sa 14:33; Ac 15:20 **7:29** [a]Lv 3:1 **7:30** [a]Ex 29:26, 27; Lv 8:29; Nu 6:20 **7:31** [a]Nu 18:11; Dt 18:3 **7:32** [a]Ex 29:27; Lv 7:34; 9:21; Nu 6:20 [1]Or *heave offering* **7:34** [a]Ex 29:27; Lv 10:14, 15; Nu 18:18 [1]Or *heave offering* **7:35** [a]Nu 18:8 [1]Or *the anointed portion of* **7:36** [a]Ex 40:13-15; Lv 8:12, 30 [1]Lit *Which* **7:37** [a]Ex 29:22-34; Lv 8:22, 23 **7:38** [a]Lv 1:1; 26:46; 27:34; Dt 4:5 ◆ **8:2** [a]Ex 28:1 [b]Lv 6:10 [c]Ex 30:25

of meeting." **4** So Moses did just as
Yahweh commanded him. Then
the congregation was assembled at
the doorway of the tent of meeting,
**5** and Moses said to the congregation,
"This is the thing which Yahweh has
commanded to do."

**6** Then [a]Moses had Aaron and
his sons come near and [b]washed
them with water. **7** And he [a]put the
tunic on him and girded him with
the sash and clothed him with the
robe and put the ephod on him; and
he girded him with the skillfully
woven band of the ephod, [1]with
which he tied *it* to him. **8** He then
placed the [1]breastpiece on him, and
in the [1]breastpiece he put [a,2]the Urim
and the Thummim. **9** He also placed
the turban on his head, and on the
turban, at its front, he placed [a]the
golden plate, the holy crown, just as
Yahweh had commanded Moses.

**10** Moses then took [a]the anointing
oil and anointed the [1]tabernacle and
all that was in it and set them apart
as holy. **11** And he sprinkled some of it
on the altar seven times and anointed
the altar and all its utensils and the
laver and its stand, to [a]set them apart
as holy. **12** Then he poured some of
the [a]anointing oil on Aaron's head
and anointed him, to set him apart as
holy. **13** [a]Next Moses brought Aaron's
sons near and clothed them with tu-
nics and girded them with sashes and
bound [1]caps on them, just as Yahweh
had commanded Moses.

**14** Then he brought [a]the bull of
the sin offering, and Aaron and his
sons laid their hands on the head of
the bull of the sin offering. **15** Next
[1]Moses slaughtered *it* and took the
blood and with his finger [a]put *some
of it* around on the horns of the
altar and purified the altar. Then he
poured out *the rest of* the blood at the
base of the altar and set it apart as
holy, to make atonement for it. **16** He
also [a]took all the fat that was on the
entrails, and the [1]lobe of the liver,
and the two kidneys and their fat;
and Moses offered it up in smoke on
the altar. **17** [a]But the bull and its hide
and its flesh and its refuse he burned
in the fire outside the camp, just as
Yahweh had commanded Moses.

**18** Then he brought near [a]the ram
of the burnt offering, and Aaron
and his sons laid their hands on the
head of the ram. **19** [1]Then Moses
slaughtered *it* and splashed the
blood around on the altar. **20** And
he cut the ram into its pieces. Then
Moses [a]offered up the head and the
pieces and the suet in smoke. **21** And
he washed the entrails and the legs
with water. Then Moses [a]offered
up the whole ram in smoke on the
altar. It was a burnt offering for a
soothing aroma; it was an offering
by fire to Yahweh, just as Yahweh had
commanded Moses.

**22** Then he brought near the sec-
ond ram, [a]the ram of [1]ordination, and
Aaron and his sons laid their hands

**8:6** [a]Ex 29:4-6 [b]Ex 30:19, 20; Ps 26:6; 1Co 6:11; Eph 5:26 **8:7** [a]Ex 28:4 [1]Lit *and with it he girded* **8:8** [a]Ex 28:30; Nu 27:21; Dt 33:8; 1Sa 28:6; Ezr 2:63; Ne 7:65 [1]Lit *pouch* [2]Lit *the lights and perfections* **8:9** [a]Ex 28:36 **8:10** [a]Ex 30:26-29; Lv 8:2 [1]Or *dwelling place* **8:11** [a]Ex 29:36, 37; 30:29 **8:12** [a]Ex 29:7; 30:30; Lv 21:10, 12; Ps 133:2 **8:13** [a]Ex 29:8, 9 [1]Lit *headgear* **8:14** [a]Ex 29:10; Lv 4:4; Ps 66:15; Eze 43:19 **8:15** [a]Ex 29:12; Lv 4:7; Eze 43:20 [1]Lit *he slaughtered it and Moses took* **8:16** [a]Ex 29:13 [1]Or *appendage on* **8:17** [a]Ex 29:14; Lv 4:11, 12 **8:18** [a]Ex 29:15; Lv 8:2 **8:19** [1]Lit *He slaughtered it and Moses sprinkled* **8:20** [a]Lv 1:8 **8:21** [a]Ex 29:18 **8:22** [a]Ex 29:31; Lv 8:2 [1]Lit *filling*, so in ch

on the head of the ram. **23** [1]And Moses slaughtered *it* and took some of its blood and [a]put it on the lobe of Aaron's right ear and on the thumb of his right hand and on the big toe of his right foot. **24** He also brought Aaron's sons near; and Moses put some of the blood on the lobe of their right ear and on the thumb of their right hand and on the big toe of their right foot. Moses then [a]splashed *the rest of* the blood around on the altar. **25** And he took the fat, and the fat tail, and all the fat that was on the entrails, and the [1]lobe of the liver, and the two kidneys and their fat, and the right thigh. **26** [a]From the basket of unleavened bread that was before Yahweh, he took one unleavened cake and one cake of bread *mixed with* oil and one wafer, and he placed *them* on the portions of fat and on the right thigh. **27** He then [a]put all *these* on the hands of Aaron and on the hands of his sons, and waved them as a wave offering before Yahweh. **28** Then Moses [a]took them from their hands and offered them up in smoke on the altar with the burnt offering. They were an ordination offering for [b]a soothing aroma; it was an offering by fire to Yahweh. **29** Moses also took [a]the breast and waved it as a wave offering before Yahweh; it was [b]Moses' portion of the ram of ordination, just as Yahweh had commanded Moses.

**30** So Moses [a]took some of the anointing oil and some of the blood which was on the altar and sprinkled it on Aaron, on his garments, on his sons, and on the garments of his sons with him; and he set Aaron apart as holy, his garments and his sons and the garments of his sons with him.

**31** Then Moses said to Aaron and to his sons, "[a]Boil the flesh at the doorway of the tent of meeting, and eat it there together with the bread which is in the basket of the ordination offering, just as I commanded, [b]saying, 'Aaron and his sons shall eat it.' **32** [a]And the remainder of the flesh and of the bread you shall burn in the fire. **33** [a]And you shall not go outside the doorway of the tent of meeting for seven days, until the day that the period of your ordination is fulfilled; for he will [1]ordain you through seven days. **34** Yahweh has commanded to do as has been done this day, to make atonement on your behalf. **35** At the doorway of the tent of meeting, moreover, you shall remain day and night for seven days and [a]keep the charge of Yahweh, so that you will not die, for so I have been commanded." **36** Thus Aaron and his sons did all the things which Yahweh had commanded through Moses.

### *Aaron Brings Offerings*

**9** Now it happened [a]on the eighth day that Moses called Aaron and his sons and the elders of Israel; **2** and he said to Aaron, "[a]Take for yourself a calf, a bull, for a sin offering, and a ram for a burnt offering, *both* without blemish, and bring *them* near before Yahweh. **3** Then to the sons of Israel you shall speak, saying, 'Take a male

**8:23** [a]Ex 29:20, 21 [1]Lit *He slaughtered it and Moses took* **8:24** [a]Heb 9:18-22 **8:25** [1]Or *appendage on* **8:26** [a]Ex 29:23 **8:27** [a]Ex 29:24 **8:28** [a]Ex 29:25 [b]Ge 8:21 **8:29** [a]Lv 7:31-34 [b]Ex 29:26; Ps 99:6 **8:30** [a]Ex 29:21 **8:31** [a]Ex 29:31 [b]Ex 29:32 **8:32** [a]Ex 29:34 **8:33** [a]Ex 29:35 [1]Lit *fill your hands* **8:35** [a]Nu 3:7; 9:19; Dt 11:1; 1Ki 2:3; Eze 48:11 ◆ **9:1** [a]Eze 43:27 **9:2** [a]Eze 29:1; Lv 4:3

goat for a sin offering, and a calf and
a lamb, both one year old, without
blemish, for a burnt offering, **4** and
an ox and a ram for peace offerings,
to sacrifice before Yahweh, and a
grain offering mixed with oil; for
today [a]Yahweh will appear to you.'"
**5** So they took what Moses had com-
manded to the front of the tent of
meeting, and the whole congregation
came near and stood before Yahweh.
**6** And Moses said, "This is the thing
which Yahweh has commanded you
to do, that [a]the glory of Yahweh may
appear to you." **7** Moses then said to
Aaron, "Come near to the altar and
[a]offer your sin offering and your
burnt offering, that you may make
atonement for yourself and for the
people; then offer the offering [1]for
the people, that you may make
atonement for them, just as Yahweh
has commanded."

**8** [a]So Aaron came near to the
altar and slaughtered the calf of the
sin offering which was for himself.
**9** [a]Then Aaron's sons brought the
blood near to him; and he dipped his
finger in the blood and [b]put *some* on
the horns of the altar and poured
out *the rest of* the blood at the base
of the altar. **10** The fat and the kidneys
and the [1]lobe of the liver of the sin
offering he then offered up in smoke
on the altar just as Yahweh had com-
manded Moses. **11** [a]The flesh and the
skin, however, he burned with fire
outside the camp.

**12** Then he slaughtered the burnt
offering; and Aaron's sons handed
the blood to him, and he splashed
it around on the altar. **13** And they
handed the burnt offering to him in
[1]pieces, with the head, and he offered
*them* up in smoke on the altar. **14** He
also washed the entrails and the legs
and offered *them* up in smoke with
the burnt offering on the altar.

**15** Then he brought near the
people's offering and took the [a]goat
of the sin offering which was for
the people and slaughtered it and
offered it for sin, like the first. **16** He
also brought near the burnt offering
and [1]offered it according to [a]the *legal*
judgment. **17** Next he brought near
[a]the grain offering and filled his
[1]hand with some of it and offered *it*
up in smoke on the altar, [b]besides the
burnt offering of the morning.

**18** Then [a]he slaughtered the ox
and the ram, the sacrifice of peace
offerings which was for the people;
and Aaron's sons handed the blood
to him, and he splashed it around
on the altar. **19** As for the portions
of fat from the ox and from the ram,
the fat tail and the *fat* [a]covering and
the kidneys and the [1]lobe of the liver,
**20** they now placed the portions of fat
on the breasts; and he offered [1]them
up in smoke on the altar. **21** But [a]the
breasts and the right thigh Aaron
waved as a wave offering before Yah-
weh, just as Moses had commanded.

**22** Then Aaron lifted up his hands
toward the people and [a]blessed them,
and he stepped down after offering
the sin offering and the burnt offer-
ing and the peace offerings. **23** And
Moses and Aaron went into the tent
of meeting. Then they came out and

**9:4** [a]Ex 29:43 **9:6** [a]Ex 24:16; Lv 9:23 **9:7** [a]Heb 5:3; 7:27 [1]Lit *of* **9:8** [a]Lv 4:1-12 **9:9** [a]Lv 9:12, 18 [b]Lv 4:7 **9:10** [1]Or *appendage on* **9:11** [a]Lv 4:11, 12; 8:17 **9:13** [1]Lit *its pieces* **9:15** [a]Lv 4:27-31 **9:16** [a]Lv 1:1-13 [1]Lit *made* **9:17** [a]Lv 2:1-3 [b]Lv 3:5 [1]Lit *palm* **9:18** [a]Lv 3:1-11 **9:19** [a]Lv 3:9 [1]Or *appendage on* **9:20** [1]Lit *the portions of fat* **9:21** [a]Ex 29:26, 27; Lv 7:30-34 **9:22** [a]Nu 6:22-26; Dt 21:5; Lk 24:50

blessed the people. And [a]the glory of
Yahweh appeared to all the people.
**24** [a]Then fire came out from before
Yahweh and consumed the burnt
offering and the portions of fat on
the altar. And all the people saw *it*
and shouted and fell on their faces.

### *Nadab and Abihu Offer Strange Fire*

**10** Then [a]Nadab and Abihu, the
sons of Aaron, took their
respective [b]firepans and put fire in
them. Then they placed incense on
it and offered strange fire before Yah-
weh, which He had not commanded
them. **2** [a]And fire came out from the
presence of Yahweh and consumed
them, and they died before Yahweh.
**3** Then Moses said to Aaron, "It is
what Yahweh spoke, saying,

'By those who [a]come near Me
I [b,1]will be treated as holy,
And before all the people
I will [c]be glorified.'"

So Aaron kept silent.
**4** Then Moses called to [a]Mishael
and Elzaphan, the sons of Aaron's
uncle Uzziel, and said to them,
"Come near, carry your [1]relatives
away from the front of the sanctuary
to the outside of the camp." **5** So they
came near and carried them still in
their [a]tunics to the outside of the
camp, as Moses had said. **6** Then
Moses said to Aaron and to his
sons Eleazar and Ithamar, "[a]Do not
[1]uncover your heads nor tear your
clothes, so that you will not die and
that He will not [b]become wrathful
against all the congregation. But your
[2]relatives, the whole house of Israel,
shall weep over the burning which
Yahweh has [3]brought about. **7** You
shall not even go out from the door-
way of the tent of meeting, lest you
die; for [a]the anointing oil of Yahweh
is upon you." So they did according
to the word of Moses.

**8** Yahweh then spoke to Aaron, say-
ing, **9** "[a]Do not drink wine or strong
drink, neither you nor your sons with
you, when you come into the tent of
meeting, so that you will not die—it
is a perpetual statute throughout
your generations— **10** and [a]so as to
separate between the holy and the
profane, and between the unclean
and the clean, **11** and [a]so as to instruct
the sons of Israel in all the statutes
which Yahweh has spoken to them
through Moses."

**12** Then Moses spoke to Aaron
and to his remaining sons, [a]Eleazar
and Ithamar, "[b]Take the remaining
grain offering from the offerings to
Yahweh by fire and eat it unleavened
beside the altar, for it is most holy.
**13** And you shall eat it in a holy place
because it is a statute for you and a
statute for your sons *taken* out of the
offerings of Yahweh by fire; for thus
I have been commanded. **14** [a]The
breast of the wave offering, however,
and the thigh of the [1]contribution
offering you may eat in a clean
place, you and your sons and your
daughters with you; for they have
been given as a statute for you and

**9:23** [a]Lv 9:6; Nu 16:19 **9:24** [a]1Ki 18:38, 39; 2Chr 7:1 ◆ **10:1** [a]Ex 24:1, 9; Nu 3:2; 26:61 [b]Lv 16:12
**10:2** [a]Nu 3:4; 16:35; 26:61 **10:3** [a]Ex 19:22; Lv 21:6 [b]Ex 30:30; Eze 38:16 [c]Ex 14:4, 17; Is 49:3; Eze 28:22
[1]Or *will show Myself holy* **10:4** [a]Ex 6:22 [1]Lit *brothers* **10:5** [a]Ex 29:5; Lv 8:13 **10:6** [a]Lv 21:1-5, 10-12 [b]Nu 1:53; 16:22, 46; 18:5; Jos 7:1; 22:18, 20; 2Sa 24:1 [1]Lit *unbind* [2]Lit *brothers* [3]Lit *burned*
**10:7** [a]Ex 28:41; Lv 21:12 **10:9** [a]Pr 20:1; 31:5; Is 28:7; Eze 44:21; Hos 4:11; Lk 1:15; Eph 5:18; 1Ti 3:3; Tit 1:7
**10:10** [a]Lv 11:47; 20:25; Eze 22:26 **10:11** [a]Dt 17:10, 11; 33:10 **10:12** [a]Ex 6:23; Nu 3:2 [b]Lv 6:14-18
**10:14** [a]Lv 7:30-34; Nu 18:11 [1]Or *heave offering*

a statute for your sons *taken* out of
the sacrifices of the peace offerings
of the sons of Israel. **15** [a]The thigh
contributed by [1]raising up and the
breast offered by waving they shall
bring along with the offerings by
fire of the portions of fat, to wave
as a wave offering before Yahweh;
so it shall be a perpetual statute for
you and your sons with you, just as
Yahweh has commanded."
**16** But Moses searched carefully
for the [a]goat of the sin offering, and
behold, it had been burned up! So he
was angry with Aaron's remaining
sons Eleazar and Ithamar, saying,
**17** "Why [a]did you not eat the sin of-
fering at the holy place? For it is most
holy, and [1]He gave it to you to bear
away [b]the guilt of the congregation,
to make atonement for them before
Yahweh. **18** Behold, [a]since its blood
had not been brought inside, into the
sanctuary, you should certainly have
[b]eaten it in the sanctuary, just as I
commanded." **19** But Aaron spoke to
Moses, "Behold, this very day they
[a]brought near their sin offering and
their burnt offering before Yahweh.
Then things like these happened to
me. So if I had eaten a sin offering
today, would it have been good in the
sight of Yahweh?" **20** So Moses heard
*this*, and it was good in his sight.

### *Clean and Unclean Animals*

**11** Yahweh spoke again to Moses
and to Aaron, saying to them,
**2** "Speak to the sons of Israel, saying,
'[a]These are the creatures which you
*may* eat from all the animals that are
on the earth. **3** Whatever divides a
hoof, thus making split hoofs, *and*
chews the cud, among the animals,
that you may eat. **4** Nevertheless,
[a]you shall not eat of these, among
those which chew the cud or among
those which divide the hoof: the
camel, for though it chews cud, it
does not divide the hoof; it is unclean
to you. **5** Likewise, the [1]shaphan, for
though it chews cud, it does not
divide the hoof; it is unclean to you;
**6** the [1]rabbit also, for though it chews
cud, it does not divide the hoof; it
is unclean to you; **7** and the pig, for
though it divides the hoof, thus
making a split hoof, it does not chew
cud; it is unclean to you. **8** You shall
not eat of their flesh, and you shall
not touch their carcasses; they are
unclean to you.
**9** '[a]These you may eat, whatever
is in the water: all that have fins and
scales, those in the water, in the seas,
or in the rivers, you may eat. **10** [a]But
whatever is in the seas and in the
rivers that does not have fins and
scales among all the swarming life
of the water, and among all the living
creatures that are in the water, they
are detestable things to you, **11** and
they shall be detestable to you; you
may not eat of their flesh, and their
carcasses you shall detest. **12** Whatev-
er in the water does not have fins and
scales is detestable to you.
**13** 'These, moreover, [a]you shall
detest among the birds; they shall
not be eaten; they are detestable:
the [1]eagle and the vulture and the
[2]buzzard, **14** and the kite and the

**10:15** [a]Lv 7:34 [1]Or *heaving up* **10:16** [a]Lv 9:3, 15 **10:17** [a]Lv 6:24-30 [b]Ex 28:38; Lv 22:16; Nu 18:1 [1]Or *was given* **10:18** [a]Lv 6:30 [b]Lv 6:26 **10:19** [a]Lv 9:8, 12 ◆**11:2** [a]Dt 14:3-21 **11:4** [a]Ac 10:14 **11:5** [1]A small, shy, furry animal *(Hyrax syriacus)* found in the peninsula of the Sinai, northern Israel, and the region round the Dead Sea; KJV *coney*, orig NASB *rock badger* **11:6** [1]Or *hare* **11:9** [a]Dt 14:9 **11:10** [a]Dt 14:10 **11:13** [a]Dt 14:12-19 [1]Or *vulture* [2]Or *black vulture*

falcon in its kind, **15** every raven in its
kind, **16** and the ostrich and the owl
and the gull and the hawk in its kind,
**17** and the little owl and the cormorant
and the [1]great owl, **18** and the white
owl and the [1]pelican and the carrion
vulture, **19** and the stork, the heron
in its kinds, and the hoopoe, and
the bat.

**20** 'All the swarming things that
fly *and* that walk on *all* fours are
detestable to you. **21** Yet these you
may eat among all the swarming
things that fly *and* that walk on *all*
fours: those which have above their
feet jointed legs with which to jump
on the earth. **22** These of them you
may eat: the locust in its kinds and
the devastating locust in its kinds
and the cricket in its kinds and the
grasshopper in its kinds. **23** But all
other swarming things that fly *and*
that are four-footed are detestable
to you.

**24** 'By these, moreover, you will
be made unclean: whoever touches
their carcasses becomes unclean
until evening, **25** and [a]whoever
picks up any of their carcasses shall
wash his clothes and be unclean
until evening. **26** Concerning all the
animals which divide the hoof but
do not make a split *hoof* or which do
not chew cud, they are unclean to
you: whoever touches them becomes
unclean. **27** Also whatever walks on
its paws, among all the creatures that
walk on *all* fours, are unclean to you;
whoever touches their carcasses be-
comes unclean until evening, **28** and
the one who picks up their carcasses
shall wash his clothes and be unclean
until evening; they are unclean to
you.

**29** 'Now these are to you the un-
clean among the swarming things
which swarm on the earth: the mole
and the mouse and the [1]great lizard
in its kinds, **30** and the gecko and
the [1]crocodile and the lizard and the
[2]sand reptile and the chameleon.
**31** These are to you the unclean
among all the swarming things;
whoever touches them when they
are dead becomes unclean until
evening. **32** Also anything on which
one of them may fall when they are
dead becomes unclean, including
any wooden article or clothing or a
skin or a sack—any article by which
work is done—[a]it shall be put in the
water and be unclean until evening,
then it becomes clean. **33** As for any
[a]earthenware vessel into which one
of them may fall, whatever is in it
becomes unclean, and you shall break
[1]the vessel. **34** Any of the [1]food which
may be eaten, on which water comes,
shall become unclean, and any [1]liquid
which may be drunk in every vessel
shall become unclean. **35** Everything,
moreover, on which part of their
carcass may fall becomes unclean;
an oven or a [1]stove shall be smashed;
they are unclean and shall continue
as unclean to you. **36** Nevertheless a
spring or a cistern [1]collecting water
shall be clean, though the one who
touches their carcass shall be unclean.
**37** And if a part of their carcass falls on
any seed for sowing which is to be
sown, it is clean. **38** Though if water
is put on the seed and a part of their
carcass falls on it, it is unclean to you.

---

**11:17** [1]Specifically, *great horned owl* **11:18** [1]Or *owl, jackdaw* **11:25** [a]Lv 11:40 **11:29** [1]Or *thorn-tailed lizard* **11:30** [1]Or *lizard* [2]Species unknown **11:32** [a]Lv 15:12 **11:33** [a]Lv 6:28; 15:12 [1]Lit *it* **11:34** [1]If touched by a carcass, cf. 11:29-32 **11:35** [1]A hearth for supporting two pots **11:36** [1]Lit *of a gathering of*

**39** 'Also if one of the animals dies
which you have for food, the one who
touches its carcass becomes unclean
until evening. **40** [a]He too, who eats
some of its carcass shall wash his
clothes and be unclean until evening,
and the one who picks up its carcass
shall wash his clothes and be unclean
until evening.

**41** '[a]Now every swarming
thing that swarms on the earth is
detestable; it shall not be eaten.
**42** Whatever goes on its belly, and
whatever goes on *all* fours, whatever
has many feet, in respect to every
swarming thing that swarms on
the earth, you shall not eat them,
for they are detestable. **43** [a]Do
not render [1]yourselves detestable
through any of the swarming things
that swarm; and you shall not make
yourselves unclean with them so
that you become unclean. **44** For [a]I
am Yahweh your God. Therefore,
set yourselves apart as holy and [b]be
holy, for I am holy. And you shall not
make yourselves unclean with any
of the swarming things that move
on the earth. **45** [a]For I am Yahweh
who brought you up from the land
of Egypt to be your God; thus [b]you
shall be holy, for I am holy.'"

**46** This is the law regarding the
animal and the bird and every living
thing that moves in the waters and
everything that swarms on the earth,
**47** [a]to separate between the unclean
and the clean, and between the edi-
ble creature and the creature which
is not to be eaten.

### *Atonement After Giving Birth*

**12** Then Yahweh spoke to Moses,
saying, **2** "Speak to the sons of
Israel, saying:

'When a woman [1]gives birth and
bears a male *child*, then she shall be
unclean for seven days, [a]as in the
days of [2]her menstruation she shall
be unclean. **3** Now on [a]the eighth
day the flesh of his foreskin shall
be circumcised. **4** Then she shall
remain in the blood of *her* cleansing
for thirty-three days; she shall not
touch any holy thing; and she shall
not enter the sanctuary until the days
of her cleansing are fulfilled. **5** But if
she bears a female *child*, then she
shall be unclean for two weeks, as
in her [1]menstruation; and she shall
remain in the blood of *her* cleansing
for sixty-six days.

**6** '[a]When the days of her cleansing
are fulfilled, for a son or for a daugh-
ter, she shall bring to the priest at the
doorway of the tent of meeting a one
year old lamb for a burnt offering and
a young pigeon or a turtledove [b]for
a sin offering. **7** Then he shall bring
it near before Yahweh and make
atonement for her, and she shall be
cleansed from the [1]flow of her blood.
This is the law for her who bears *a
child*, whether a male or a female.
**8** But if [1]she cannot afford a lamb,
then she shall take [a]two turtledoves
or two young pigeons, [b]the one for a
burnt offering and the other for a sin
offering; and the [c]priest shall make
atonement for her, and she will be
clean.'"

**11:40** [a]Lv 17:15; 22:8; Dt 14:21; Eze 44:31 **11:41** [a]Lv 11:29 **11:43** [a]Lv 20:25 [1]Lit *your souls*
**11:44** [a]Ex 6:7; 16:12; 23:25; Is 43:3; 51:15 [b]Lv 19:2; 1Pe 1:16 **11:45** [a]Ex 6:7; 20:2; Lv 22:33; 25:38; 26:45
[b]Lv 19:2; 1Pe 1:16 **11:47** [a]Lv 10:10; Eze 22:26; 44:23 ◆ **12:2** [a]Lv 15:19; 18:19 [1]Lit *produces seed* [2]Lit
*the impurity of her sickness* **12:3** [a]Ge 17:12; Lk 1:59; 2:21 **12:5** [1]Lit *impurity* **12:6** [a]Lk 2:22 [b]Lv 5:7
**12:7** [1]Lit *fountain* **12:8** [a]Lk 2:22-24 [b]Lv 5:7 [c]Lv 4:26 [1]Lit *her hand does not find a sufficiency of a
lamb*

### *Statutes About Leprosy*

**13** Then Yahweh spoke to Moses
and to Aaron, saying, **2** "When
a man has on the skin of his [1]body a
swelling or a scab or a bright spot, and
it becomes [2]an infection of leprosy
on the skin of his [1]body, [a]then he
shall be brought to Aaron the priest
or to one of his sons the priests.
**3** Then the priest shall look at the
mark on the skin of the [1]body, and
if the hair in the infection has turned
white and the infection appears to be
deeper than the skin of his [1]body, it
is an infection of leprosy; when the
priest has looked at him, he shall
pronounce him unclean. **4** But if the
bright spot is white on the skin of his
[1]body, and [2]it does not appear to be
deeper than the skin, and the hair
on it has not turned white, then the
priest shall [3]isolate *him who has*
the infection for seven days. **5** Then
the priest shall look at him on the
seventh day, and if in his eyes the
infection [1]has not changed *and*
the infection has not spread on the
skin, then the priest shall [2]isolate him
for seven more days. **6** And the priest
shall look at him again on the seventh
day, and if the infection has faded and
the mark has not spread on the skin,
then the priest shall pronounce him
clean; it is *only* a scab. And he shall
[a]wash his clothes and be clean.
**7** "But if the scab spreads farther
on the skin after he has shown him-
self to the priest for his cleansing,
he shall appear again to the priest.
**8** And the priest shall look, and if the
scab has spread on the skin, then the
priest shall pronounce him unclean;
it is leprosy.
**9** "When the infection of leprosy
is on a man, then he shall be brought
to the priest. **10** The priest shall then
look, and if there is a [a]white swelling
in the skin, and it has turned the
hair white, and there is raw flesh *still*
alive in the swelling, **11** it is [1]a chron-
ic leprosy on the skin of his [2]body,
and the priest shall pronounce him
unclean; he shall not [3]isolate him,
for he is unclean. **12** But if the lep-
rosy breaks out farther on the skin,
and the leprosy covers all the skin
of *him who has* the infection from
his head even to his feet, [1]as far as
the priest can see, **13** then the priest
shall look, and behold, *if* the leprosy
has covered all his [1]body, he shall
pronounce clean *him who has* the
infection; it has all turned white,
*and* he is clean. **14** But whenever
raw flesh appears on him, he shall be
unclean. **15** And the priest shall look
at the raw flesh, and he shall pro-
nounce him unclean; the raw flesh
is unclean; it is leprosy. **16** Or if the
raw flesh turns again and is changed
to white, then he shall [a]come to the
priest, **17** and the priest shall look
at him, and behold, *if* the infection
has turned to white, then the priest
shall pronounce clean *him who has*
the infection; he is clean.
**18** "When the [1]body has a boil on
its skin and it is healed, **19** and in
the place of the boil there is a white
swelling or a reddish-white bright
spot, then it shall be shown to the
priest; **20** and the priest shall look,

◆ **13:2** [a]Dt 24:8 [1]Lit *flesh* [2]Lit *a mark, a stroke;* so in ch **13:3** [1]Lit *flesh* **13:4** [1]Lit *flesh* [2]Lit *the appearance of it is not deeper* [3]Lit *shut up* **13:5** [1]Lit *has stood* [2]Lit *shut up* **13:6** [a]Lv 11:25; 14:8 **13:10** [a]Nu 12:10; 2Ki 5:27; 2Chr 26:19, 20 **13:11** [1]Lit *an old* [2]Lit *flesh* [3]Lit *shut up* **13:12** [1]Lit *with regard to the whole sight of the priest's eyes* **13:13** [1]Lit *flesh* **13:16** [a]Lk 5:12-14 **13:18** [1]Lit *flesh*

and behold, *if* [1]it appears to be lower than the skin, and the hair on it has turned white, then the priest shall pronounce him unclean; it is the infection of leprosy; it has broken out in the boil. **21** But if the priest looks at it, and behold, there are no white hairs in it, and it is not lower than the skin and is faded, then the priest shall [1]isolate him for seven days; **22** and if it spreads farther on the skin, then the priest shall pronounce him unclean; it is an infection. **23** But if the bright spot remains in its place and does not spread, it is *only* the scar of the boil; and the priest shall pronounce him clean.

**24** "Or if the [1]body sustains in its skin a burn by fire, and the raw *flesh* of the burn becomes a bright spot, reddish-white, or white, **25** then the priest shall look at it. And if the hair in the bright spot has [a]turned white and it appears to be deeper than the skin, it is leprosy; it has broken out in the burn. Therefore, the priest shall pronounce him unclean; it is an infection of leprosy. **26** But if the priest looks at it, and behold, there is no white hair in the bright spot, and it is no [1]deeper than the skin but is faded, then the priest shall [2]isolate him for seven days; **27** and the priest shall look at him on the seventh day. If it spreads farther in the skin, then the priest shall pronounce him unclean; it is an infection of leprosy. **28** But if the bright spot remains in its place and has not spread in the skin but is faded, it is the swelling from the burn; and the priest shall pronounce him clean, for it is *only* the scar of the burn.

**29** "Now if a man or woman has an infection on the head or on the beard, **30** then the priest shall look at the infection, and if it appears to be deeper than the skin, and there is thin yellowish hair in it, then the priest shall pronounce him unclean; it is a scale; it is leprosy of the head or of the beard. **31** But if the priest looks at the infection of the scale, and behold, it appears to be no deeper than the skin, and there is no black hair in it, then the priest shall [1]isolate *the person* with the scaly infection for seven days. **32** Now on the seventh day the priest shall look at the infection, and if the scale has not spread, and there is no yellowish hair in it, and the appearance of the scale is no deeper than the skin, **33** then he shall shave himself, but he shall not shave the scale; and the priest shall [1]isolate *the person* with the scale seven more days. **34** Then on the seventh day the priest shall look at the scale, and if the scale has not spread in the skin and it appears to be no deeper than the skin, the priest shall pronounce him clean; and he shall wash his clothes and be clean. **35** But if the scale spreads farther in the skin after his cleansing, **36** then the priest shall look at him, and if the scale has spread in the skin, the priest need not seek for the yellowish hair; he is unclean. **37** If in his sight the scale has remained, however, and black hair has grown in it, the scale has healed, he is clean; and the priest shall pronounce him clean.

**38** "When a man or a woman has bright spots on the skin of the [1]body, *even* white bright spots, **39** then the

**13:20** [1]Lit *the appearance of it is lower* **13:21** [1]Lit *shut up* **13:24** [1]Lit *flesh* **13:25** [a]Ex 4:6; Nu 12:10; 2Ki 5:27 **13:26** [1]Lit *lower* [2]Lit *shut up* **13:31** [1]Lit *shut up* **13:33** [1]Lit *shut up* **13:38** [1]Lit *flesh*

priest shall look, and if the bright spots on the skin of their [1]bodies are a faded white, it is [2]eczema that has broken out on the skin; he is clean.

**40** "Now if a [1]man loses the hair of his head, he is [a]bald; he is clean. **41** And if his head becomes bald at the [1]front and sides, he is bald on the forehead; he is clean. **42** But if on the bald head or the bald forehead, there occurs a reddish-white infection, it is leprosy breaking out on his bald head or on his bald forehead. **43** Then [a]the priest shall look at him; and if the swelling of the infection is reddish-white on his bald head or on his bald forehead, like the appearance of leprosy in the skin of the [1]body, **44** he is a leprous man; he is unclean. The priest shall surely pronounce him unclean; his infection is on his head.

**45** "As for the leper who has the infection, his clothes shall be torn, and [a]the hair of his head shall be [1]uncovered, and he shall [b]cover his mustache and call out, '[c]Unclean! Unclean!' **46** He shall remain unclean all the days during which he has the infection; he is unclean. He shall live alone; his *place of* habitation shall be [a]outside the camp.

**47** "When a garment has a [1]mark of leprosy in it, whether it is a wool garment or a linen garment, **48** whether in [1]warp or woof, of linen or of wool, whether in leather or in any article made of leather, **49** if the mark is greenish or reddish in the garment or in the leather or in the [1]warp or in the woof or in any article of leather, it is a leprous mark and shall be shown to the priest. **50** Then [a]the priest shall look at the mark and shall [1]isolate the article with the mark for seven days. **51** He shall then look at the mark on the seventh day; if the mark has spread in the garment, whether in the warp or in the woof or in the leather, whatever the purpose for which the leather is used, the mark is a [1]leprous malignancy; it is unclean. **52** So he shall burn the garment, whether the warp or the woof, in wool or in linen, or any article of leather in which the mark occurs, for it is a [1]leprous malignancy; it shall be burned in the fire.

**53** "But if the priest shall look, and indeed the mark has not spread in the garment, either in the warp or in the woof or in any article of leather, **54** then the priest shall command them to wash the thing in which the mark occurs, and he shall [1]isolate it for seven more days. **55** After the article with the mark has been washed, the priest shall again look, and if the mark has not changed its appearance, even though the mark has not spread, it is unclean; you shall burn it in the fire, whether an eating away has produced bareness on the top or on the front of it.

**56** "Then if the priest looks, and if the mark has faded after it has been washed, then he shall tear it out of the garment or out of the leather, whether from the warp or from the woof; **57** and if it appears again in the garment, whether in the warp or in the woof or in any article of

**13:39** [1]Lit *flesh* [2]Lit *tetter* **13:40** [a]2Ki 2:23; Is 15:2; Am 8:10 [1]Lit *man's head becomes bald* **13:41** [1]Lit *border of his face* **13:43** [a]Lv 10:10; Eze 22:26 [1]Lit *flesh* **13:45** [a]Lv 10:6 [b]Eze 24:17, 22; Mic 3:7 [c]Lam 4:15 [1]Or *disheveled* **13:46** [a]Nu 5:1-4; 12:14 **13:47** [1]Lit *infection*, so in ch **13:48** [1]Or *weaving or texture* **13:49** [1]Or *weaving or texture* **13:50** [a]Eze 44:23 [1]Lit *shut up* **13:51** [1]Lit *malignant leprosy* **13:52** [1]Lit *malignant leprosy* **13:54** [1]Lit *shut up*

leather, it is an outbreak; you shall
burn the article with the mark in the
fire. **58** Now the garment, whether
the warp or the woof or any article
of leather from which the mark has
departed when you washed it, shall
then be washed a second time and
will be clean."

**59** This is the law for the mark
of leprosy in a garment of wool or
linen, whether in the warp or in the
woof or in any article of leather, for
pronouncing it clean or unclean.

### *Statutes for Cleansing a Leper*

**14** Then Yahweh spoke to Moses,
saying, **2** "This shall be the law
of the leper in the day of his cleans-
ing. [a]Now he shall be brought to the
priest, **3** and the priest shall go [a]out
to the outside of the camp. Thus the
priest shall look, and if the [1]infection
of leprosy has been healed in the
leper, **4** then the priest shall give a
command to take two live clean birds
and [a]cedar wood and a [1]scarlet string
and hyssop for the one who is to be
cleansed. **5** The priest shall also give
a command to slaughter the one
bird in an earthenware vessel over
[1]running water. **6** *As for* the live bird,
he shall take it together with [a]the
cedar wood and the [1]scarlet string
and the [b]hyssop, and he shall dip
them and the live bird in the blood
of the bird that was slaughtered over
the [2]running water. **7** [a]He shall then
sprinkle seven times the one who is
to be cleansed from the leprosy and
shall pronounce him clean, and he
shall let the live bird go free over the
open field. **8** [a]The one to be cleansed
shall then wash his clothes and shave
off all his hair and bathe in water and
[b]be clean. Now afterward, he may
enter the camp, but he [c]shall stay
outside his tent for seven days. **9** And
it will be on the seventh day that he
shall shave off all his hair: he shall
shave his head and his beard and his
eyebrows, even all his hair. He shall
then wash his clothes and bathe his
[1]body in water and [a]be clean.

**10** "Now on the eighth day he
shall take two male lambs without
blemish, and a yearling ewe lamb
without blemish, and three-tenths *of
an* [1]*ephah* of fine flour mixed with oil
for a grain offering, and one [a,2]log of
oil; **11** and the priest who pronounces
him clean shall present the man to
be cleansed as well as [1]these things
before Yahweh at the doorway of the
tent of meeting. **12** Then the priest
shall take the one male lamb and
bring it near for a [a]guilt offering, with
the [b,1]log of oil, and wave them as a
[c]wave offering before Yahweh. **13** Next
he shall slaughter the male lamb in
[a]the place where they slaughter the
sin offering and the burnt offering, at
the place of the sanctuary—for the
guilt offering, [b]like the sin offering,
belongs to the priest; it is most holy.
**14** The priest shall then take some of
the blood of the [a]guilt offering, and
the priest shall put *it* on [b]the lobe
of the right ear of the one to be

◆ ***14:2*** [a]*Mt 8:4*; Mk 1:44; Lk 5:14; 17:14 **14:3** [a]Lv 13:46 [1]Lit *mark, stroke*; so in ch **14:4** [a]Lv 14:6, 49, 51, 52; Nu 19:6 [1]Lit *scarlet color and* **14:5** [1]Lit *living* **14:6** [a]Lv 14:4 [b]Ps 51:7 [1]Lit *scarlet color and* [2]Lit *living* **14:7** [a]Eze 36:25 **14:8** [a]Lv 11:25; 13:6; Nu 8:7 [b]Lv 14:9, 20 [c]Nu 5:2, 3; 12:14, 15; 2Chr 26:21 **14:9** [a]Lv 14:8, 20 [1]Lit *flesh* **14:10** [a]Lv 14:12, 15, 21, 24 [1]Approx. 6.3 qt. or 6.9 l, an ephah was approx. 21 qt. or 23 l [2]A log was approx. 10 oz. or 300 ml **14:11** [1]Lit *them* **14:12** [a]Lv 5:6, 18; 6:6; 14:19 [b]Lv 14:10 [c]Ex 29:22-24, 26 [1]A log was approx. 10 oz. or 300 ml **14:13** [a]Ex 29:11; Lv 1:11; 4:24 [b]Lv 6:24-30; 7:7 **14:14** [a]Lv 14:19 [b]Ex 29:20; Lv 8:23, 24

cleansed and on the thumb of his
right hand and on the big toe of his
right foot. **15** The priest shall also take
some of the [a,1]log of oil and pour *it*
into his left palm; **16** the priest shall
then dip his right-hand finger into
the oil that is in his left palm, and
with his finger sprinkle some of
the oil seven times before Yahweh.
**17** Of the remaining oil which is in
his palm, the priest shall put some
on the right ear lobe of the one to
be cleansed and on the thumb of his
right hand and on the big toe of his
right foot, on the blood of the guilt
offering; **18** but the rest of the oil that
is in the priest's palm, he shall put on
the head of the one to be cleansed.
So the priest shall make [a]atonement
on his behalf before Yahweh. **19** The
priest shall next offer the [a]sin offer-
ing and make atonement for the one
to be cleansed from his uncleanness.
Then afterward, he shall slaughter
the burnt offering. **20** And the priest
shall offer up the burnt offering and
the grain offering on the altar. Thus
the priest shall make atonement for
him, and [a]he will be clean.

**21** "[a]But if he is poor and his
[1]means are insufficient, then he is
to take one male lamb for a [b]guilt
offering as a wave offering to make
atonement for him, and one-tenth
*of an* [2]*ephah* of fine flour mixed
with oil for a grain offering, and a
[c,3]log of oil, **22** and two turtledoves
or two young pigeons which [1]are
within his means, [a]the one shall be
a [b]sin offering and the other a burnt
offering. **23** [a]Then the eighth day he
shall bring them for his cleansing to
the priest, at the doorway of the tent
of meeting, before Yahweh. **24** And
the priest shall take the lamb of the
guilt offering and [a]the [1]log of oil, and
the priest shall wave them as a wave
offering before Yahweh. **25** Next he
shall slaughter the lamb of the guilt
offering; and the priest shall take
some of the blood of the guilt offering
and put *it* on [a]the lobe of the right ear
of the one to be cleansed and on the
thumb of his right hand and on the
big toe of his right foot. **26** The priest
shall also pour some of the oil into
his left palm; **27** and with his right-
hand finger the priest shall sprinkle
some of the oil that is in his left palm
seven times before Yahweh. **28** The
priest shall then put some of the oil
that is in his palm on the lobe of the
right ear of the one to be cleansed
and on the thumb of his right hand
and on the big toe of his right foot,
on the place of the blood of the guilt
offering. **29** Moreover, the rest of the
oil that is in the priest's palm he
shall put on the head of the one to
be cleansed, to make atonement on
his behalf before Yahweh. **30** He shall
then offer one of the turtledoves or
young pigeons, [1]which are within
his means. **31** *He shall offer* what [1]he
can afford, [a]the one for a sin offering
and *the other* for a burnt offering,
together with the grain offering. So
the priest shall make atonement
before Yahweh on behalf of the one
to be cleansed. **32** This is the law *for*

**14:15** [a]Lv 14:10 [1]A log was approx. 10 oz. or 300 ml **14:18** [a]Lv 4:26; Nu 15:28; Heb 2:17
**14:19** [a]Lv 14:12 **14:20** [a]Lv 14:8, 9 **14:21** [a]Lv 5:11; 12:8; 27:8 [b]Lv 14:22 [c]Lv 14:10 [1]Lit *hand is not reaching* [2]An ephah was approx. 21 qt. or 23 l [3]A log was approx. 10 oz. or 300 ml **14:22** [a]Lv 5:7 [b]Lv 14:21, 24, 25 [1]Lit *his hand reaches* **14:23** [a]Lv 14:10, 11 **14:24** [a]Lv 14:10 [1]A log was approx. 10 oz. or 300 ml **14:25** [a]Lv 14:14 **14:30** [1]Lit *from those which his hand can reach* **14:31** [a]Lv 5:7 [1]Lit *his hand can reach*

*him* in whom there is an infection of
leprosy, whose [1]means are limited for
his cleansing."

### *Statute for Cleansing a Leprous House*

**33** Yahweh further spoke to Moses
and to Aaron, saying:
**34** "[a]When you enter the land of
Canaan, which I am giving you for
a possession, and I put a mark of
leprosy on a house in the land of
your possession, **35** then the one who
owns the house shall come and tell
the priest, saying, '*Something* like [a]a
mark *of leprosy* has become visible to
me in the house.' **36** The priest shall
then command that they empty the
house before the priest goes in to look
at the mark, so that everything in the
house need not become unclean;
and afterward the priest shall go in
to look at the house. **37** So he shall
look at the mark, and if the mark on
the walls of the house has greenish
or reddish depressions and appears
deeper than the *surface of* the wall,
**38** then the priest shall come out of
the house, to the [1]doorway, and [2]put
the house under isolation for seven
days. **39** And the priest shall return
on the seventh day and look *again.*
If the mark has indeed spread in the
walls of the house, **40** then the priest
shall command them to tear out the
stones with the mark in them and
throw them away [1]at an unclean place
outside the city. **41** And he shall have
the house scraped all around [1]inside,
and they shall pour out the plaster
that they scrape off at an unclean
place outside the city. **42** Then they
shall take other stones and replace
*those* stones, and he shall take other
plaster and replaster the house.
**43** "If, however, the mark breaks
out again in the house after he has
torn out the stones and scraped the
house, and after it has been replas-
tered, **44** then the priest shall come
in and look *again.* If he sees that the
mark has indeed spread in the house,
it is [a]a [1]leprous malignancy in the
house; it is unclean. **45** He shall there-
fore tear down the house, its stones
and its timbers and all the plaster of
the house, and he shall take *them*
outside the city to an [a]unclean place.
**46** Moreover, whoever goes into the
house during the time that he has
[1]put it under isolation becomes
[a]unclean until evening. **47** Likewise,
whoever lies down in the house shall
wash his clothes, and whoever eats
in the house shall wash his clothes.
**48** "If, on the other hand, the priest
comes in and looks *again*, and the
mark has not indeed spread in the
house after the house has been
replastered, then the priest shall
pronounce the house clean because
the mark has [1]not reappeared. **49** To
cleanse the house then, he shall
take [a]two birds and cedar wood
and a [1]scarlet string and hyssop,
**50** and he shall slaughter the one
bird in an earthenware vessel over
[1]running water. **51** Then he shall take
the cedar wood and the [a]hyssop and
the [1]scarlet string, with the live bird,
and he shall dip them in the blood
of the slaughtered bird as well as

---

**14:32** [1]Lit *hand does not reach* **14:34** [a]Ge 17:8; Nu 32:22; Dt 7:1; 32:49 **14:35** [a]Ps 91:10 **14:38** [1]Lit *doorway of the house* [2]Lit *shut up* **14:40** [1]Lit *to* **14:41** [1]Lit *from the house around* **14:44** [a]Lv 13:51 [1]Lit *malignant leprosy* **14:45** [a]Lv 14:41 **14:46** [a]Nu 19:7, 10, 21, 22 [1]Lit *shut up* **14:48** [1]Lit *healed* **14:49** [a]Lv 14:4 [1]Lit *scarlet color* **14:50** [1]Lit *living* **14:51** [a]1Ki 4:33; Ps 51:7 [1]Lit *scarlet color*

in the [2]running water, and he shall
sprinkle the house seven times.
**52** He shall thus cleanse the house
with the blood of the bird and with
the [1]running water, along with the
live bird and with the cedar wood
and with the hyssop and with the
[2]scarlet string. **53** However, he shall
let the live bird go free outside the
city into the open field. So he shall
make atonement for the house, and
it will be clean."

**54** This is the law for any mark of
leprosy—even for a [a]scale, **55** and
for the [a]leprous garment or house,
**56** and [a]for a swelling and for a scab
and for a bright spot— **57** to instruct
[1]when they are unclean and [2]when
they are clean. This is the law of
leprosy.

### *Statute for Cleansing Bodily Discharges*

**15** Yahweh also spoke to Moses
and to Aaron, saying, **2** "Speak
to the sons of Israel and say to them,
'[a]When any man has a discharge
from his [1]body, [2]his discharge is un-
clean. **3** This, moreover, shall be his
uncleanness in his discharge: it is his
uncleanness whether his body allows
its discharge to flow or whether his
body obstructs its discharge. **4** Every
bed on which the person with the
discharge lies becomes unclean, and
everything on which he sits becomes
unclean. **5** Anyone, moreover, who
touches his bed shall wash his
clothes and bathe in water and be
unclean until evening; **6** and whoever
sits on the thing on which the man
with the discharge has been sitting
shall wash his clothes and bathe in
water and be unclean until evening.
**7** Also whoever touches the [1]person
with the discharge shall wash his
clothes and bathe in water and be
unclean until evening. **8** Or if the man
with the discharge spits on one who
is clean, he too shall wash his clothes
and bathe in water and be unclean
until evening. **9** Every saddle on
which the person with the discharge
rides becomes unclean. **10** Whoever
then touches any of the things which
were under him shall be unclean un-
til evening, and he who carries them
shall wash his clothes and bathe in
water and be unclean until evening.
**11** Likewise, whomever the one with
the discharge touches without having
rinsed his hands in water shall wash
his clothes and bathe in water and be
unclean until evening. **12** However,
an [a]earthenware vessel which the
person with the discharge touches
shall be broken, and every wooden
vessel shall be rinsed in water.

**13** 'Now when the man with the
discharge becomes cleansed from his
discharge, then he [a]shall count off for
himself seven days for his cleansing;
he shall then wash his clothes and
bathe his body in [1]running water
and will become clean. **14** Then on
the eighth day he shall take for him-
self [a]two turtledoves or two young
pigeons and come before Yahweh to
the doorway of the tent of meeting
and give them to the priest; **15** and
the priest shall offer them, [a]one for
a sin offering and the other for a

---

**14:51** [2]Lit *living* **14:52** [1]Lit *living* [2]Lit *scarlet color* **14:54** [a]Lv 13:30 **14:55** [a]Lv 13:47-52 **14:56** [a]Lv 13:2 **14:57** [1]Lit *in the day of uncleanness* [2]Lit *in the day of cleanness* ◆ **15:2** [a]Lv 22:4; Nu 5:2; 2Sa 3:29 [1]Lit *flesh*, so in ch [2]Or *by his discharge, he is unclean* **15:7** [1]Lit *flesh* **15:12** [a]Lv 6:28; 11:33 **15:13** [a]Lv 8:33; 14:8 [1]Lit *living* **15:14** [a]Lv 14:22, 23 **15:15** [a]Lv 5:7; 14:31

burnt offering. So [b]the priest shall
make atonement on his behalf before
Yahweh because of his discharge.
16 ‘[a]Now if a [1]man has a seminal
emission, he shall bathe all his body
in water and be unclean until eve-
ning. 17 As for any garment or any
leather on which there is seminal
emission, it shall be washed with
water and be unclean until evening.
18 If *there is* a woman with whom a
man lies *so that* there is a seminal
emission, they shall both bathe in
water and be [a]unclean until evening.
19 ‘[a]If a woman has a discharge,
*and* her discharge in her body is
blood, she shall continue in her men-
strual impurity for seven days; and
whoever touches her shall be unclean
until evening. 20 Everything also on
which she lies during her menstrual
impurity shall be unclean, and ev-
erything on which she sits shall be
unclean. 21 And anyone who touches
her bed shall wash his clothes and
bathe in water and be unclean until
evening. 22 And whoever touches any
thing on which she sits shall wash
his clothes and bathe in water and
be unclean until evening. 23 Whether
it be on the bed or on the thing on
which she is sitting, when he touches
it, he shall be unclean until evening.
24 [a]If a man actually lies with her so
that her menstrual impurity is on
him, he shall be unclean seven days,
and every bed on which he lies shall
be unclean.
25 ‘[a]Now if a woman has a dis-
charge of her blood many days, not at
the period of her menstrual impurity,
or if she has a discharge beyond [1]that
period, all the days of her unclean
discharge she shall continue as
though [2]in her menstrual impurity;
she is unclean. 26 Any bed on which
she lies all the days of her discharge
shall be to her like [1]her bed at men-
struation; and every thing on which
she sits shall be unclean, like her
uncleanness from her menstrual im-
purity. 27 Likewise, whoever touches
them shall be unclean and shall wash
his clothes and bathe in water and be
unclean until evening. 28 Now if she
becomes clean from her discharge,
she shall count off for herself seven
days; and afterward she will be clean.
29 Then on the eighth day she shall
take for herself two turtledoves or
two young pigeons and bring them
in to the priest, to the doorway of
the tent of meeting. 30 And the priest
shall [1]offer the [a]one for a sin offering
and the other for a burnt offering. So
the priest shall make atonement on
her behalf before Yahweh because of
her unclean discharge.’
31 “Thus you shall keep the sons
of Israel separated from their un-
cleanness, so that they will not die
in their uncleanness by [a]making
My [1]tabernacle that is among them
unclean.” 32 This is the law for the
one with a discharge, and for the
man [1]who has a seminal emission
so that he is unclean by it, 33 and
for the woman who is ill because of
menstrual impurity, and for the one
who has a discharge, whether a male
or a female, or a man who lies with
an unclean woman.

---

**15:15** [b]Lv 14:19, 31 **15:16** [a]Lv 22:4; Dt 23:10, 11 [1]Lit *man's...goes out from him* **15:18** [a]1Sa 21:4
**15:19** [a]Lv 12:2 **15:24** [a]Lv 18:19; 20:18 **15:25** [a]Mt 9:20; Mk 5:25; Lk 8:43 [1]Lit *her menstrual impurity* [2]Lit *in the days of* **15:26** [1]Lit *the bed of her menstrual impurity* **15:30** [a]Lv 5:7 [1]Lit *make*
**15:31** [a]Lv 20:3; Nu 19:13, 20; Eze 5:11; 36:17 [1]Lit *dwelling place* **15:32** [1]Lit *whose seminal emission goes out from him*

### The Day of Atonement

**16** Now Yahweh spoke to Moses after [a]the death of the two sons of Aaron, when they came near the presence of Yahweh and died. **2** And Yahweh said to Moses:

"Tell your brother Aaron that he shall not enter [a]at any time into the holy place inside the veil, before the [1]mercy seat which is on the ark, so that he will not die; for [b]I will appear in the cloud over the mercy seat. **3** Aaron shall enter the holy place with this: with a bull from the herd for a [a]sin offering and a ram for a burnt offering. **4** He shall put on the [a]holy linen tunic, and the linen undergarments shall be next to his [1]body, and he shall be girded with the linen sash and attired with the linen turban (these are holy garments). Then he shall [b]bathe his [1]body in water and put them on. **5** And he shall take from the congregation of the sons of Israel [a]two male goats for a sin offering and one ram for a burnt offering. **6** Then [a]Aaron shall bring near the bull for the sin offering which is for himself, that he may make atonement for himself and for his household. **7** And he shall take the two goats and present them before Yahweh at the doorway of the tent of meeting. **8** And Aaron shall cast lots for the two goats, one lot for Yahweh and the other lot for the [1]scapegoat. **9** Then Aaron shall bring near the goat on which the lot for Yahweh fell, and he shall offer it as a sin offering. **10** But the goat on which the lot for the [1]scapegoat fell shall be presented alive before Yahweh, to make [a]atonement upon it, to send it out into the wilderness as the [1]scapegoat.

**11** "Then Aaron shall bring near the bull of the sin offering, [a]which is for himself, and make atonement for himself and [b]for his household, and he shall slaughter the bull of the sin offering which is for himself. **12** And he shall take a [a]firepan full of coals of fire from upon the altar before Yahweh and [1]two handfuls of finely ground [b]fragrant incense, and bring *it* inside the veil. **13** And he shall put the incense on the fire before Yahweh, that the cloud of incense may cover the [a]mercy seat that is on *the ark of* the testimony, [b]so that he will not die. **14** Moreover, [a]he shall take some of the blood of the bull and sprinkle *it* [b]with his finger on the mercy seat on the east *side*; also in front of the mercy seat he shall sprinkle some of the blood with his finger seven times.

**15** "Then he shall slaughter the goat of the sin offering [a]which is for the people and bring its blood inside the veil and do with its blood as he did with the blood of the bull. And he shall sprinkle it on the mercy seat and in front of the mercy seat. **16** [a]So he shall make atonement for the holy place because of the uncleanness of the sons of Israel and because of their transgressions in regard to all

◆ **16:1** [a]Lv 10:1, 2 **16:2** [a]Ex 30:10; Heb 6:19; 9:7, 25 [b]Ex 25:21, 22; 40:34; 1Ki 8:10-12 [1]Or *propitiatory seat, place of atonement*; so in ch **16:3** [a]Lv 4:1-12; 16:6; Heb 9:7 **16:4** [a]Ex 28:39, 42 [b]Ex 30:20; Lv 16:24; Heb 10:22 [1]Lit *flesh* **16:5** [a]Lv 4:13-21; 2Chr 29:21; Eze 45:22 **16:6** [a]Heb 5:3 **16:8** [1]Lit *goat of removal*; or possibly a name: *Azazel* **16:10** [a]Is 53:4-10; Ro 3:25; 1Jn 2:2 [1]Lit *goat of removal*; or possibly a name: *Azazel* **16:11** [a]Heb 7:27; 9:7 [b]Lv 16:33 **16:12** [a]Lv 10:1; Nu 16:18 [b]Ex 30:34-38 [1]Lit *the filling of the hollow of his hands* **16:13** [a]Ex 25:21 [b]Ex 28:43; Lv 22:9; Nu 4:15, 20 **16:14** [a]Heb 9:25 [b]Lv 4:6, 17 **16:15** [a]Heb 7:27; 9:7, 12 **16:16** [a]Ex 29:36, 37; 30:10; Heb 2:17

their sins; and thus he shall do for
the tent of meeting which abides
with them in the midst of their un-
cleanness. **17** Now when he goes in to
make atonement in the holy place, no
one shall be in the tent of meeting
until he comes out, that he may make
atonement for himself and for his
household and for all the assembly of
Israel. **18** Then he shall go out to the
altar that is before Yahweh and make
atonement for it. And he shall take
some of the blood of the bull and of
the blood of the goat, and [a]put it on
the horns of the altar on all sides.
**19** [a]With his finger he shall sprinkle
some of the blood on it seven times
and cleanse it and set it apart as holy
from the uncleanness of the sons of
Israel.

**20** "And when he finishes making
atonement for the holy place and the
tent of meeting and the altar, he shall
bring near the live goat. **21** Then Aar-
on shall lay both of his hands on the
head of the live goat, and [a]confess
over it all the iniquities of the sons of
Israel and all their transgressions [1]in
regard to all their sins; and he shall
lay them on the head of the goat and
send *it* out into the wilderness by
the hand of a man ready *to do this.*
**22** And the goat shall bear on itself all
their iniquities to an isolated land;
and he shall send out the goat in the
wilderness.

**23** "Then Aaron shall come into
the tent of meeting and take off
[a]the linen garments which he put
on when he went into the holy place
and shall leave them there. **24** [a]And
he shall bathe his [1]body with water in
a holy place and put on [b]his clothes
and come forth, and offer his burnt
offering and the burnt offering of
the people and make atonement for
himself and for the people. **25** Then
he shall offer up in smoke the fat of
the sin offering on the altar. **26** And
the one who sent the goat out as the
[1]scapegoat [a]shall wash his clothes
and bathe his [2]body with water;
then afterward he shall come into
the camp. **27** But the bull of the sin
offering and the goat of the sin offer-
ing, [a]whose blood was brought in to
make atonement in the holy place,
shall be taken outside the camp, and
they shall burn their hides, their
flesh, and their refuse in the fire.
**28** Then the [a]one who burns them
shall wash his clothes and bathe his
body with water, and afterward he
shall come into the camp.

**29** "And *this* shall be a perpetual
statute for you: [a]in the seventh
month, on the tenth day of the
month, you shall humble your souls
and not [b]do any work, whether the
native or the sojourner who sojourns
among you; **30** for it is on this day
that [1]atonement shall be made for
you to [a]cleanse you; you will be clean
from all your sins before Yahweh.
**31** It is to be a sabbath of solemn
rest for you, that you may [a]humble
your souls; it is a perpetual statute.
**32** So the priest who is anointed and
[1]ordained to minister as a priest in
his father's place shall make atone-
ment: he shall thus put on [a]the linen
garments, the holy garments, **33** and

---

**16:18** [a]Lv 4:25; Eze 43:20, 22 **16:19** [a]Lv 16:14; Eze 43:20 **16:21** [a]Lv 5:5 [1]Lit *in addition to*
**16:23** [a]Lv 16:4; Eze 42:14; 44:19 **16:24** [a]Lv 16:4 [b]Ex 28:40, 41 [1]Lit *flesh* **16:26** [a]Lv 11:25, 40 [1]Lit *goat of removal*; or possibly a name: *Azazel* [2]Lit *flesh* **16:27** [a]Lv 6:30; Heb 13:11 **16:28** [a]Nu 19:8
**16:29** [a]Lv 23:27; Nu 29:7 [b]Ex 31:14, 15 **16:30** [a]Ps 51:2; Jer 33:8; Eph 5:26 [1]Lit *he shall make atonement*
**16:31** [a]Lv 23:32; Ezr 8:21; Is 58:3, 5; Da 10:12 **16:32** [a]Lv 16:4 [1]Lit *whose hand is filled*

make atonement for the holy sanctuary, and he shall make atonement for the tent of meeting and for the altar. He shall also make atonement for [a]the priests and for all the people of the assembly. **34** Now you shall have this as a [a]perpetual statute, to [b]make atonement for the sons of Israel for all their sins once every year." And just as Yahweh had commanded Moses, *so* he did.

### *Statutes Against Eating Blood*

**17** Then Yahweh spoke to Moses, saying, **2** "Speak to Aaron and to his sons and to all the sons of Israel and say to them, 'This is what Yahweh has commanded, saying, **3** "Any man from the house of Israel who slaughters an ox or a lamb or a goat in the camp, or who slaughters it outside the camp, **4** and [a]has not brought it to the doorway of the tent of meeting to bring *it* near as an offering to Yahweh before the [1]tabernacle of Yahweh, it will be counted as bloodguiltiness to that man. He has shed blood, and that man shall be cut off from among his people. **5** [1]*The reason is* so that the sons of Israel may bring their sacrifices which they were sacrificing in the open field, that they may bring them in to Yahweh, at the doorway of the tent of meeting to the priest, and sacrifice them as sacrifices of peace offerings to Yahweh. **6** And the priest shall splash the blood on the altar of Yahweh at the doorway of the tent of meeting and [a]offer up the fat in smoke as a soothing aroma to Yahweh. **7** [a]And they shall no longer sacrifice their sacrifices to the [1]goat demons with which they play the harlot. This shall be a perpetual statute to them throughout their generations."'

**8** "Then you shall say to them, 'Any man from the house of Israel, or from the sojourners who sojourn among them, who offers a burnt offering or sacrifice, **9** and [a]does not bring it to the doorway of the tent of meeting to [1]offer it to Yahweh, that man also shall be cut off from his people.

**10** '[a]And any man from the house of Israel, or from the sojourners who sojourn among them, who eats any blood, [b]I will set My face against that person who eats blood and will cut him off from among his people. **11** For [a]the [1]life of the flesh is in the blood, and I have given it to you on the altar to make atonement for your souls; for [b]it is the blood that makes atonement by the [1]life.' **12** Therefore I said to the sons of Israel, 'No person among you may eat blood, and no sojourner who sojourns among you may eat blood.' **13** So any man from the sons of Israel, or from the sojourners who sojourn among them, who *in* hunting catches a beast or a bird which may be eaten, [a]shall pour out its blood and cover it with earth.

**14** "[a]For *as for the* [1]life of all flesh, its blood is *identified* with its [1]life. Therefore I said to the sons of Israel, 'You are not to eat the blood of any flesh, for the [1]life of all flesh is its blood; whoever eats it shall be cut off.' **15** [a]And when any person eats *an animal* which dies or is torn *by*

---

**16:33** [a]Lv 16:11 **16:34** [a]Lv 23:31 [b]Heb 9:7 ◆**17:4** [a]Dt 12:5-21 [1]Lit *dwelling place* **17:5** [1]Lit *In order that* **17:6** [a]Nu 18:17 **17:7** [a]Ex 22:20; 32:8; 34:15; Dt 32:17; 2Chr 11:15; Ps 106:37f; 1Co 10:20 [1]Or *goat-idols* **17:9** [a]Ex 20:24; Lv 17:4 [1]Lit *do* **17:10** [a]Ge 9:4; Lv 3:17; 7:26, 27; Dt 12:16, 23-25; 1Sa 14:33 [b]Lv 20:3, 6; Jer 44:11 **17:11** [a]Ge 9:4; Lv 17:14 [b]Heb 9:22 [1]Lit *soul* **17:13** [a]Dt 12:16 **17:14** [a]Ge 9:4; Lv 17:11 [1]Lit *soul* **17:15** [a]Ex 22:31; Lv 7:24; 22:8; Dt 14:21

*beasts*, whether he is a native or a sojourner, he shall wash his clothes and bathe in water and remain unclean until evening; then he will become clean. **16** But if he does not wash *them* or bathe his body, then [a]he shall bear his [1]guilt."

### *Statutes on the Nakedness of Relatives*

**18** Then Yahweh spoke to Moses, saying, **2** "Speak to the sons of Israel and say to them, '[a]I am Yahweh your God. **3** You shall not do according to what is [a]done in the land of Egypt where you lived, nor are you to do according to what is [b]done in the land of Canaan where I am bringing you; you shall not walk in their statutes. **4** You are to do My judgments and keep My statutes, to walk in them; [a]I am Yahweh your God. **5** So you shall keep My statutes and My judgments, [a]which if a man does them, he shall live by them; I am Yahweh.

**6** 'None of you shall approach any blood relative [1]of his to uncover nakedness; I am Yahweh. **7** [a]You shall not uncover the nakedness of your father, that is, the nakedness of your mother. She is your mother; you are not to uncover her nakedness. **8** [a]You shall not uncover the nakedness of your father's wife; it is your father's nakedness. **9** [a]The nakedness of your sister, *either* your father's daughter or your mother's daughter, whether born at home or born outside, their nakedness you shall not uncover. **10** The nakedness of your son's daughter or your daughter's daughter, their nakedness you shall not uncover; for [1]their nakedness is yours. **11** The nakedness of your father's wife's daughter, [1]born to your father, she is your sister; you shall not uncover her nakedness. **12** [a]You shall not uncover the nakedness of your father's sister; she is your father's blood relative. **13** You shall not uncover the nakedness of your mother's sister, for she is your mother's blood relative. **14** [a]You shall not uncover the nakedness of your father's brother; you shall not approach his wife; she is your aunt. **15** [a]You shall not uncover the nakedness of your daughter-in-law; she is your son's wife; you shall not uncover her nakedness. **16** [a]You shall not uncover the nakedness of your brother's wife; it is your brother's nakedness. **17** [a]You shall not uncover the nakedness of a woman and of her daughter, nor shall you take her son's daughter or her daughter's daughter, to uncover her nakedness; they are blood relatives. It is [1]lewdness. **18** And you shall not [1]marry a woman in addition to [2]her sister [3]as a rival while she is alive, to uncover her nakedness.

**19** '[a]Also you shall not approach a woman to uncover her nakedness during her [b]menstrual impurity. **20** [a]And you shall not lie sexually with your neighbor's wife, to be

***17:16*** [a]*Nu 19:20* [1]*Or iniquity* ◆**18:2** [a]Ex 6:7; Lv 11:44; Eze 20:5 **18:3** [a]Eze 20:7, 8 [b]Lv 18:24-30; 20:23 **18:4** [a]Lv 18:2 **18:5** [a]Ne 9:29; Eze 18:9; 20:11; Lk 10:28; Ro 10:5; Ga 3:12 **18:6** [1]Lit *of his flesh* **18:7** [a]Lv 20:11; Dt 27:20; Eze 22:10 **18:8** [a]Lv 20:11; Dt 22:30; 27:20; 1Co 5:1 **18:9** [a]Lv 18:11; 20:17; Dt 27:22 **18:10** [1]Lit *they are your nakedness* **18:11** [1]Lit *begotten of* **18:12** [a]Lv 20:19 **18:14** [a]Lv 20:20 **18:15** [a]Lv 20:12 **18:16** [a]Lv 20:21 **18:17** [a]Lv 20:14 [1]Or *wickedness* **18:18** [1]Lit *take a wife* [2]Or *another* [3]Lit *to be* **18:19** [a]Lv 15:24; 20:18 [b]Lv 12:2 **18:20** [a]Lv 20:10; Pr 6:29; Mt 5:27, 28; 1Co 6:9; Heb 13:4

defiled with her. **21** And you shall
not give any of your seed [a]to pass
them over to Molech, nor shall you
[b]profane the name of your God; I am
Yahweh. **22** [a]And you shall not lie with
a male as [1]one lies with a female; it
is an abomination. **23** [a]Also you shall
not lie with any animal to be defiled
with it, nor shall any woman stand
before an animal to [1]mate with it; it
is a perversion.

**24** 'So do not defile yourselves by
any of these things; for by all these
[a]the nations which I am casting out
before you have become defiled.
**25** So the land has become defiled,
[a]and I have brought its [1]punish-
ment upon it. And the land [b]has
vomited out its inhabitants. **26** But
as for you, you shall keep My stat-
utes and My judgments and shall
not do any of these abominations,
*neither* the native nor the sojourner
who sojourns among you **27** (for the
men of the land who have been
before you have done all these
abominations, and the land has
become defiled); **28** so that the land
will not vomit you out, should you
defile it, as it has vomited out the
nation which has been before you.
**29** For whoever does any of these
abominations, [1]those persons who
do *so* shall be cut off from among
*their people.* **30** Thus you are to
keep [a]My charge, that you do not
do any of the abominable statutes
which have been done before you,
so as not to defile yourselves with
them; [b]I am Yahweh your God.'"

### *Yahweh Is Holy*

**19** Then Yahweh spoke to Moses,
saying:

**2** "Speak to all the congregation of
the sons of Israel and say to them,
'[a]You shall be holy, for I, Yahweh
your God, am holy. **3** Every one of you
[a]shall fear his mother and his father,
and you shall keep [b]My sabbaths; [c]I
am Yahweh your God. **4** Do not turn
to [a]idols or make for yourselves
molten [b]gods; I am Yahweh your God.

**5** 'Now when you offer a sacrifice of
peace offerings to Yahweh, you shall
offer it so that you may be accepted.
**6** It shall be eaten the same day you
offer *it* and the next day; but what
remains until the third day shall be
burned with fire. **7** So if it is eaten at
all on the third day, it is an offense; it
will not be accepted. **8** And everyone
who eats it will bear his iniquity, for
he has profaned the holy thing of
Yahweh; and that person shall be cut
off from his people.

### *Various Statutes*

**9** '[a]Now when you reap the harvest
of your land, you shall not reap to
the very corners of your field, nor
shall you gather the gleanings of
your harvest. **10** Nor shall you glean
your vineyard, nor shall you gather
the fallen fruit of your vineyard; you
shall leave them for the afflicted
and for the sojourner. I am Yahweh
your God.

**11** '[a]You shall not steal, nor deal
falsely, [b]nor lie to one another.
**12** [a]And you shall not swear falsely

---

**18:21** [a]Lv 20:2-5; Dt 12:31 [b]Lv 19:12; 20:3; 21:6; Eze 36:20; Mal 1:12 **18:22** [a]Lv 20:13; Dt 23:18 mg; Ro 1:27 [1]Lit *those who lie* **18:23** [a]Ex 22:19; Lv 20:15, 16; Dt 27:21 [1]Or *lie* **18:24** [a]Lv 18:3; Dt 18:12 **18:25** [a]Lv 20:23; Dt 9:5; 18:12 [b]Lv 18:28; 20:22 [1]Lit *iniquity* **18:29** [1]Or *and the* **18:30** [a]Lv 22:9; Dt 11:1 [b]Lv 18:2 ◆ **19:2** [a]Ex 19:6; Lv 11:44; 20:7, 26; Eph 1:4; 1Pe 1:16 **19:3** [a]Ex 20:12; 31:13; Dt 5:16 [b]Ex 20:8 [c]Lv 11:44 **19:4** [a]Lv 26:1; Ps 96:5; 115:4-7 [b]Ex 20:23; 34:17 **19:9** [a]Lv 23:22; Dt 24:20-22 **19:11** [a]Ex 20:15, 16 [b]Jer 9:3-5; Eph 4:25 **19:12** [a]Ex 20:7; Dt 5:11; Mt 5:33

by My name, so as to [b]profane the
name of your God; I am Yahweh.
**13** '[a]You shall not oppress your
neighbor nor rob *him.* [b]The wages
of a hired man shall not remain with
you overnight until morning. **14** You
shall not curse a deaf man nor [a]place
a stumbling block before the blind,
but you shall fear your God; I am
Yahweh.
**15** '[a]You shall do no injustice in
judgment; you shall not be partial
to the poor nor defer to the great,
but you shall judge your neighbor
in righteousness. **16** You shall not go
about as [a]a slanderer among your
people, and you shall not stand
against the [b,1]life of your neighbor;
I am Yahweh.
**17** 'You [a]shall not hate your brother
in your heart; you [b]may surely re-
prove your neighbor, and so not bear
sin because of him. **18** [a]You shall not
take vengeance, [b]and you shall not
keep *your anger* against the sons of
your people, but [c]you shall love your
neighbor as yourself; I am Yahweh.
**19** 'You are to keep My statutes. You
shall not breed together two kinds of
your cattle; [a]you shall not sow your
field with two kinds of seed nor wear
a garment upon you of two kinds of
material mixed together.
**20** '[a]Now if a man lies sexually
with a woman who is a slave assigned
to *another* man, but who has in no
way been redeemed nor given her
freedom, there shall be punishment;
they shall not, *however*, be put to
death because she was not free.
**21** And he shall bring his guilt offer-
ing to Yahweh to the doorway of the
tent of meeting, [a]a ram for a guilt
offering. **22** The priest shall also make
atonement for him with the ram of
the guilt offering before Yahweh for
his sin which he has committed, and
the sin which he has committed will
be forgiven him.
**23** 'When you enter the land and
plant all kinds of trees for food,
then you shall designate their fruit
as [1]forbidden. Three years it shall
be [1]forbidden to you; *it* shall not be
eaten. **24** But in the fourth year all
its fruit shall be holy, an offering of
praise to Yahweh. **25** Now in the fifth
year you shall eat of its fruit, that its
produce may increase for you; I am
Yahweh your God.
**26** 'You shall not eat *anything* [a]with
the blood nor interpret [b]omens or
soothsaying. **27** [a]You shall not round
off the side-growth of your heads nor
harm the edges of your beard. **28** And
you shall not make any cuts in your
[1]body for the [2]dead nor make any tat-
too marks on yourselves: I am Yahweh.
**29** '[a]Do not [1]profane your daughter
by making her a harlot, so that the
land will not fall to harlotry and the
land become full of lewdness. **30** You
shall [a]keep My sabbaths and [b]fear My
sanctuary; I am Yahweh.
**31** 'Do not turn to [a,1]mediums or
spiritists; do not seek them out to be
defiled by them. I am Yahweh your
God.

---

**19:12** [b]Lv 18:21 **19:13** [a]Ex 22:7-15, 21-27 [b]Dt 24:15; Jas 5:4 **19:14** [a]Dt 27:18 **19:15** [a]Ex 23:3, 6; Dt 1:17; 10:17; 16:19 **19:16** [a]Ps 15:3; Jer 6:28; 9:4; Eze 22:9 [b]Ex 23:7; Dt 27:25 [1]Lit *blood* **19:17** [a]1Jn 2:9, 11; 3:15 [b]Mt 18:15; Lk 17:3 **19:18** [a]Dt 32:35; Ro 12:19; Heb 10:30 [b]Ps 103:9 [c]Mt 19:19; Mk 12:31; Lk 10:27; Ro 13:9; Ga 5:14; Jas 2:8 **19:19** [a]Dt 22:9, 11 **19:20** [a]Dt 22:23-27 **19:21** [a]Lv 6:1-7 **19:23** [1]Lit *uncircumcised* **19:26** [a]Ge 9:4; Lv 7:26f; 17:10; Dt 12:16, 23 [b]Dt 18:10; 2Ki 17:17 **19:27** [a]Lv 21:5; Dt 14:1 **19:28** [1]Lit *flesh* [2]Lit *soul* **19:29** [a]Lv 21:9; Dt 22:21; 23:17, 18 [1]Or *degrade* **19:30** [a]Lv 19:3 [b]Lv 26:2 **19:31** [a]Lv 20:6, 27; Dt 18:11; 1Sa 28:3; Is 8:19 [1]Or *ghosts or spirits*

**32** '[a]You shall rise up before the
gray-haired and honor the [1]aged, and
you shall fear your God; I am Yahweh.
**33** '[a]And when a sojourner sojourns
with you in your land, you shall not
mistreat him. **34** The sojourner who
sojourns with you shall be to you as
the native among you, and [a]you shall
love him as yourself, for you were
sojourners in the land of Egypt; I am
Yahweh your God.
**35** '[a]You shall do no wrong in
judgment, in measurement of
weight, or in volume. **36** You shall
have [a,1]just balances, [1]just weights,
a [1]just [2]ephah, and a [1]just [3]hin; I am
Yahweh your God, who brought you
out from the land of Egypt. **37** You
shall thus keep all My statutes and
all My judgments and do them; I am
Yahweh.'"

### *Set Yourselves Apart as Holy*

**20** Then Yahweh spoke to Moses,
saying, **2** "You shall also say to
the sons of Israel:
'Any man from the sons of Israel
or from the sojourners sojourning in
Israel [a]who gives any of his seed to
Molech shall surely be put to death;
[b]the people of the land shall stone
him with stones. **3** I will also set My
face against that man and will cut him
off from among his people because
he has given some of *those who are*
his seed to Molech, [a]so as to defile
My sanctuary and [b]to profane My
holy name. **4** If the people of the land,
however, [1]should ever turn a blind
eye to that man when he gives any
of *those who are* his seed to Molech,
so as not to put him to death, **5** then
I Myself will set My face against that
man and against his family, and I will
cut off from among their people both
him and all those who play the harlot
after him, in playing the harlot after
Molech.
**6** 'As for the person who turns to
[a,1]mediums and to spiritists, to play
the harlot after them, I will also set
My face against that person and will
cut him off from among his people.
**7** Therefore, you shall set yourselves
apart as holy and [a]be holy, for I am
Yahweh your God. **8** [a]And you shall
keep My statutes and do them; I am
Yahweh who makes you holy.
**9** '[a]If *there is* anyone who curses
his father or his mother, he shall
surely be put to death; he has cursed
his father or his mother. His blood-
guiltiness is upon him.
**10** '[a]If *there is* a man who commits
adultery with another man's wife,
one who commits adultery with
his friend's wife, the adulterer and
the adulteress shall surely be put
to death. **11** [a]If *there is* a man who
lies with his father's wife, he has
uncovered his father's nakedness;
both of them shall surely be put to
death. Their bloodguiltiness is upon
them. **12** [a]If *there is* a man who lies
with his daughter-in-law, both of
them shall surely be put to death;
they have committed [1]perversion.
Their bloodguiltiness is upon them.
**13** [a]If *there is* a man who lies with a
male as those who lie with a woman,

---

**19:32** [a]Pr 23:22; Lam 5:12; 1Ti 5:1 [1]Lit *face of the aged* **19:33** [a]Ex 22:21; Dt 24:17, 18 **19:34** [a]Lv 19:18 **19:35** [a]Dt 25:13-16; Eze 45:10 **19:36** [a]Dt 25:13-15; Pr 20:10 [1]Or *righteous* [2]An ephah was approx. 21 qt. or 23 l [3]A hin was approx. 1 gal. or 3.8 l ◆ **20:2** [a]Lv 18:21 [b]Lv 20:27; 24:14-23; Nu 15:35, 36; Dt 21:21 **20:3** [a]Lv 15:31 [b]Lv 18:21 **20:4** [1]Lit *hiding they hide their eyes from* **20:6** [a]Lv 19:31 [1]Or *ghosts and spirits* **20:7** [a]Eph 1:4; 1Pe 1:16 **20:8** [a]Ex 31:13 **20:9** [a]Ex 21:17; Dt 27:16 **20:10** [a]Ex 20:14; Lv 18:20; Dt 5:18 **20:11** [a]Lv 18:7, 8; Dt 27:20 **20:12** [a]Lv 18:15 [1]Or *incest* **20:13** [a]Lv 18:22

both of them have committed an abomination; they shall surely be put to death. Their bloodguiltiness is upon them. **14** [a]If *there is* a man who [1]marries a woman and her mother, it is lewdness; both he and they shall be burned with fire so that there will be no lewdness in your midst. **15** [a]If *there is* a man who lies with an animal, he shall surely be put to death; you shall also kill the animal. **16** If *there is* a woman who approaches any animal to [1]mate with it, you shall kill the woman and the animal; they shall surely be put to death. Their bloodguiltiness is upon them.

**17** '[a]If *there is* a man who takes his sister, his father's daughter, or his mother's daughter, so that he sees her nakedness and she sees his nakedness, it is a disgrace; and they shall be cut off in the sight of the sons of their people. He has uncovered his sister's nakedness; he bears his guilt. **18** [a]If *there is* a man who lies with a [1]menstruous woman and uncovers her nakedness, he has laid bare her flow, and she has uncovered the flow of her blood; thus both of them shall be cut off from among their people. **19** [a]You shall also not uncover the nakedness of your mother's sister or of your father's sister, for such a one has made naked his [1]blood relative; they will bear their guilt. **20** [a]If *there is* a man who lies with his aunt, he has uncovered his uncle's nakedness; they will bear their sin. They will die childless. **21** [a]If *there is* a man who takes his brother's wife, it is an [1]impure act; he has uncovered his brother's nakedness. They will be childless.

**22** 'You shall therefore keep all My statutes and all My judgments and do them, so that the land to which I am bringing you to [1]inhabit will not [a]vomit you out. **23** Moreover, you shall not walk in [a]the statutes of the nation which I will cast out before you, for they did all these things, and [b]therefore I have loathed them. **24** Hence I have said to you, "[a]You yourselves shall possess their land, and I Myself will give it to you to possess it, a land flowing with milk and honey." I am Yahweh your God, who has [b]separated you from the peoples. **25** [a]You are therefore to separate between the clean animal and the unclean, and between the unclean bird and the clean; and you shall not make [1]yourselves detestable by animal or by bird or by anything [2]that creeps on the ground, which I have separated for you as unclean. **26** Thus you shall be holy to Me, for I Yahweh am holy; and I [a]have separated you from the peoples to be Mine.

**27** 'Now a man or a woman [a]who is a medium or a [1]spiritist shall surely be put to death. They shall be stoned with stones. Their bloodguiltiness is upon them.'"

### *The Holiness of the Priests*

**21** Then Yahweh said to Moses, "Speak to the priests, the sons of Aaron, and say to them:

'[a]No one shall defile himself for a *dead* person among his people,

**20:14** [a]Lv 18:17; Dt 27:23 [1]Lit *takes* **20:15** [a]Lv 18:23; Dt 27:21 **20:16** [1]Lit *lie* **20:17** [a]Lv 18:9; Dt 27:22 **20:18** [a]Lv 15:24; 18:19 [1]Lit *sick* **20:19** [a]Lv 18:12, 13 [1]Lit *flesh* **20:20** [a]Lv 18:14 **20:21** [a]Lv 18:16 [1]Or *abhorrent* **20:22** [a]Lv 18:28 [1]Lit *dwell in it* **20:23** [a]Lv 18:3 [b]Lv 18:25 **20:24** [a]Ex 13:5; 33:1-3 [b]Ex 33:16; Lv 20:26 **20:25** [a]Lv 10:10; 11:1-47; Dt 14:3-21 [1]Lit *your souls* [2]Lit *with which the ground creeps* **20:26** [a]Lv 20:24 **20:27** [a]Lv 19:31 [1]Lit *spiritist among them* ◆ **21:1** [a]Lv 19:28; Eze 44:25

**2** [a]except for his [1]blood relatives who are nearest to him, his mother and his father and his son and his daughter and his brother, **3** also for his virgin sister, who is near to him [1]because she has had no husband; for her he may defile himself. **4** He shall not defile himself as a [1]relative by marriage among his people, and so profane himself. **5** [a]They shall not make any baldness on their heads [b]nor shave off the edges of their beards [c]nor make any cuts in their flesh. **6** They shall be holy to their God and [a]not profane the name of their God, for they bring near the offerings [1]to Yahweh by fire, [b]the food of their God; so they shall be holy. **7** [a]They shall not take a woman who is profaned by harlotry, nor shall they take a woman divorced from her husband; for he is holy to his God. **8** Therefore, you shall set him apart as holy, for he brings near [a]the food of your God; he shall be holy to you; for I Yahweh, who makes you holy, am holy. **9** [a]Also the daughter of any priest, if she profanes herself by harlotry, she profanes her father; she shall be burned with fire.

**10** 'And the priest who is the highest among his brothers, on whose head the anointing oil has been poured and [1]who has been ordained to wear the garments, [a]shall not [2]uncover his head nor tear his clothes; **11** [a]nor shall he approach any dead person nor defile himself *even* for his father or his mother; **12** [a]nor shall he go out of the sanctuary nor profane the sanctuary of his God, for [b]the dedication of the anointing oil of his God is on him; I am Yahweh. **13** And he shall take a wife in her virginity. **14** [a]A widow or a divorced woman or one who is profaned by harlotry, these he may not take; but rather he shall take a virgin of his own people as a wife, **15** so that he will not profane his seed among his people; for I am Yahweh who makes him holy.'"

**16** Then Yahweh spoke to Moses, saying, **17** "Speak to Aaron, saying, 'No man of your seed throughout their generations who has a defect shall come near to offer the [a]food of his God. **18** [a]For no one who has a defect shall come near: a blind man or a lame man or he who has a [a,1]disfigured *face* or any deformed *limb*, **19** or a man who has a broken foot or broken hand, **20** or a hunchback or a dwarf, or *one who has* a [1]defect in his eye or eczema or scabs or [a]crushed testicles. **21** No man among the seed of Aaron the priest who has a defect shall approach to bring near the offerings to Yahweh by fire; *since* he has a defect, he shall not approach to bring near [a]the food of his God. **22** He may eat [a]the food of his God, *both* of the most holy and of the holy, **23** only he shall not go in to the veil or approach the altar because he has a defect, so that he will not profane My sanctuaries. For I am Yahweh who makes them holy.'" **24** So Moses spoke to Aaron and to his sons and to all the sons of Israel.

**21:2** [a]Lv 21:11 [1]Lit *flesh* **21:3** [1]Or *whom no man has had* **21:4** [1]Lit *husband among* **21:5** [a]Dt 14:1; Eze 44:20 [b]Lv 19:27 [c]Dt 14:1 **21:6** [a]Lv 18:21 [b]Lv 3:11 [1]Lit *of* **21:7** [a]Lv 21:13, 14 **21:8** [a]Lv 21:6 **21:9** [a]Ge 38:24; Lv 19:29 **21:10** [a]Lv 10:6 [1]Lit *whose hand has been filled* [2]Lit *unbind* **21:11** [a]Lv 19:28; Nu 19:14 **21:12** [a]Lv 10:7 [b]Ex 29:6, 7 **21:14** [a]Lv 21:7; Eze 44:22 **21:17** [a]Lv 21:6 **21:18** [a]Lv 22:19-25 [1]Lit *slit* **21:20** [a]Dt 23:1; Is 56:3-5 [1]Lit *obscurity* **21:21** [a]Lv 21:6 **21:22** [a]1Co 9:13

### *Various Statutes for Priests*

**22** Then Yahweh spoke to Moses, saying, **2** "Tell Aaron and his sons to be careful with the holy *gifts* of the sons of Israel, which they set apart to Me as holy, so as not to profane My holy name; I am Yahweh. **3** Say to them, '[a]If any man among all your seed throughout your generations comes near to the holy *gifts* which the sons of Israel set apart as holy to Yahweh, and he has an uncleanness, that person shall be cut off from before Me; I am Yahweh. **4** [a]No man of the seed of Aaron, who is a leper or who has a discharge, may eat of the holy *gifts* until he is clean. [b]And if one touches anything made unclean by a corpse, or if [c]a man has a seminal emission, **5** or [a]if a man touches any teeming things by which he is made unclean or any man by whom he is made unclean, whatever his uncleanness, **6** a [1]person who touches any such thing shall be unclean until evening and shall not eat of the holy *gifts* unless he has bathed his [2]body in water. **7** But the sun will set, and he will be clean. And afterward he shall eat of the holy *gifts*, for [a]it is his [1]food. **8** He shall not eat [a]*an animal* which dies or is torn *by beasts*, becoming unclean by it; I am Yahweh. **9** They shall therefore keep [a]My charge so that [b]they will not bear sin because of it and die thereby because they profane it; I am Yahweh who makes them holy.

**10** '[a]No [1]layman, however, is to eat the holy *gift*; a foreign resident with the priest or a hired man shall not eat of the holy *gift*. **11** [a]But if a priest buys a person as *his* property with his money, [1]that one may eat of it, and those who are born in his house may eat of his [2]food. **12** If a priest's daughter is married to a [1]layman, she shall not eat of the [2]contribution of the holy *gifts*. **13** But if a priest's daughter becomes a widow or divorced, and has no seed, and returns to her father's house as in her youth, she shall eat of her father's [1]food; [a]but no [2]layman shall eat of it. **14** [a]But if a man eats a holy *gift* unintentionally, then he shall add to it a fifth of it and shall give the holy *gift* to the priest. **15** [a]They shall not profane the holy *gifts* of the sons of Israel which they raise up to Yahweh, **16** and *so* cause them [a]to bear [1]punishment for guilt by eating their holy *gifts*; for I am Yahweh who makes them holy.'"

### *Offerings Without Blemish*

**17** Then Yahweh spoke to Moses, saying, **18** "Speak to Aaron and to his sons and to all the sons of Israel and say to them, '[a]Any man of the house of Israel or of the sojourners in Israel who brings near his offering, whether it is any of their [1]votive or any of their freewill offerings, which they bring near to Yahweh for a burnt offering— **19** [a]for you to be accepted—*it must be* a male without blemish from the cattle, the sheep, or the goats. **20** [a]Whatever has a defect, you shall not bring *it* near, for it will not be accepted for you.

◆ **22:3** [a]Lv 7:20, 21; Nu 19:13 **22:4** [a]Lv 14:1-32 [b]Lv 11:24-28, 39, 40 [c]Lv 15:16, 17 **22:5** [a]Lv 11:23-28 **22:6** [1]Lit *soul* [2]Lit *flesh* **22:7** [a]Nu 18:11 [1]Lit *bread* **22:8** [a]Lv 7:24; 11:39, 40; 17:15 **22:9** [a]Lv 18:30 [b]Ex 28:43; Lv 22:16; Nu 18:22 **22:10** [a]Ex 29:33; Lv 22:13; Nu 3:10 [1]Lit *stranger* **22:11** [a]Ge 17:13; Ex 12:44 [1]Lit *he may* [2]Lit *bread* **22:12** [1]Lit *stranger* [2]Or *heave offering* **22:13** [a]Lv 22:10 [1]Lit *bread* [2]Lit *stranger* **22:14** [a]Lv 5:15, 16 **22:15** [a]Nu 18:32 **22:16** [a]Lv 10:17; 22:9 [1]Or *iniquity requiring a guilt offering* **22:18** [a]Nu 15:14 [1]Lit *vows* **22:19** [a]Lv 21:18-21; Dt 15:21 **22:20** [a]Dt 15:21; 17:1; Mal 1:8, 14; Heb 9:14; 1Pe 1:19

21 And when a man brings a sacrifice
of peace offerings near to Yahweh [a]to
[1]fulfill a special vow or for a freewill
offering, of the herd or of the flock,
it must be without blemish to be ac-
cepted; there shall be no defect in it.
22 Those *that are* blind or fractured
or maimed or *have* a running sore
or eczema or scabs, you shall not
bring near to Yahweh nor make of
them an offering by fire on the altar
to Yahweh. 23 Now in respect to an ox
or a lamb which has [1]an overgrown
or stunted *member*, you may offer
it for a freewill offering, but for a
votive offering it will not be accepted.
24 Also [a]anything *with its testicles*
bruised or crushed or torn or cut, you
shall not bring near to Yahweh, and
you shall not do *thus* in your land,
25 nor shall you bring near any such
thing from the hand of a foreigner for
offering [a]as the [1]food of your God; for
their corruption is in them, they have
a defect; they shall not be accepted
for you.'"

26 Then Yahweh spoke to Moses,
saying, 27 "When an ox or a sheep or
a goat is born, it shall [1]remain [a]seven
days [2]with its mother, and from the
eighth day on it shall be accepted as
a sacrifice of an offering by fire to
Yahweh. 28 [a]But, *whether* it is an ox
or a sheep, you shall not slaughter
*both* it and its young in one day.
29 And when you sacrifice [a]a sacri-
fice of thanksgiving to Yahweh, you
shall sacrifice it so that you may be
accepted. 30 It shall be eaten on the
same day; you shall leave none of it
until morning; I am Yahweh. 31 [a]So
you shall keep My commandments
and do them; I am Yahweh.

32 "And you shall not profane My
holy name, but I will be treated as
holy among the sons of Israel; I am
Yahweh who makes you holy, 33 [a]who
brought you out from the land of
Egypt to be your God; I am Yahweh."

### *Yahweh's Appointed Times*

23 And Yahweh spoke again to
Moses, saying, 2 "Speak to
the sons of Israel and say to them,
'[a]The appointed times of Yahweh
which you shall [b]proclaim as holy
convocations—My appointed times
are these:

### *The Sabbath*

3 '[a]For six days work may be done,
but on the seventh day there is a
sabbath of complete rest, a holy
convocation. You shall not do any
work; it is a sabbath to Yahweh in all
your *places of* habitation.

### *The Passover*

4 'These are the [a]appointed times of
Yahweh, holy convocations which
you shall proclaim at the times
appointed for them. 5 [a]In the first
month, on the fourteenth day of the
month [1]at twilight is the Passover of
Yahweh. 6 Then on the fifteenth day
of the same month there is the [a]Feast
of Unleavened Bread to Yahweh; for
seven days you shall eat unleavened
bread. 7 On the first day you shall have
a holy convocation; you shall [a]not do

---

**22:21** [a]Nu 15:3, 8 [1]Or *make a special votive offering* **22:23** [1]Or *a deformed* **22:24** [a]Lv 21:20
**22:25** [a]Lv 21:22 [1]Lit *bread* **22:27** [a]Ex 22:30 [1]Lit *be* [2]Lit *under* **22:28** [a]Dt 22:6, 7 **22:29** [a]Lv 7:12
**22:31** [a]Lv 19:37; Nu 15:40; Dt 4:40 **22:33** [a]Lv 11:45 ◆ **23:2** [a]Lv 23:4, 37, 44; Nu 29:39 [b]Lv 23:21
**23:3** [a]Ex 20:9, 10; 23:12; 31:13-17; 35:2, 3; Lv 19:3; Dt 5:13, 14 **23:4** [a]Ex 23:14; Lv 23:2 **23:5** [a]Ex 12:18, 19;
Nu 28:16-25; Dt 16:1; Jos 5:10 [1]Lit *between the two evenings* **23:6** [a]Ex 12:14-20; 23:15; 34:18; Dt 16:3-8
**23:7** [a]Lv 23:8, 21, 25, 35, 36

any laborious work. 8 But for seven days you shall bring near an offering by fire to Yahweh. On the seventh day is a holy convocation; you shall not do any laborious work.'"

### *The Feast of the Harvest*

9 Then Yahweh spoke to Moses, saying, 10 "Speak to the sons of Israel and say to them, 'When you enter the land which I am going to give to you and [a]reap its harvest, then you shall bring in the sheaf of the first fruits of your harvest to the priest. 11 And he shall wave the sheaf before Yahweh for you to be accepted; on the day after the sabbath the priest shall wave it. 12 Now on the day when you wave the sheaf, you shall offer a male lamb one year old without blemish for a burnt offering to Yahweh. 13 Its [a]grain offering shall then be two-tenths *of an* [1]*ephah* of fine flour mixed with oil, an offering by fire to Yahweh *for* a soothing aroma, with its drink offering, a fourth of a [2]hin of wine. 14 Until this same day, until you have brought in the offering of your God, [a]you shall eat neither bread nor roasted grain nor new growth. It is to be a perpetual statute throughout your generations in all your *places of* habitation.

### *The Feast of Weeks*

15 '[a]You shall also count for yourselves from the day after the sabbath, from the day when you brought in the sheaf of the wave offering; there shall be seven complete sabbaths. 16 You shall count fifty days to the day after the seventh sabbath; then you shall bring a [a]new grain offering near to Yahweh. 17 You shall bring in from your *places of* habitation two *loaves* of bread for a wave offering, made of two-tenths *of an* [1]*ephah*; they shall be of a fine flour, baked [a]with leaven as first fruits to Yahweh. 18 Along with the bread you shall bring near seven one year old male lambs without blemish and a bull from the herd and two rams; they shall be a burnt offering to Yahweh, with their grain offering and their drink offerings, an offering by fire of a soothing aroma to Yahweh. 19 You shall also offer [a]one male goat for a sin offering and two male lambs one year old for a sacrifice of peace offerings. 20 The priest shall then wave them with the bread of the first fruits for a wave offering with two lambs before Yahweh; they shall be holy to Yahweh for the priest. 21 On this same day you shall [a]make a proclamation as well; it shall be a holy convocation for you. You shall do no laborious [b]work. It is to be a perpetual statute in all your *places of* habitation throughout your generations.

22 '[a]When you reap the harvest of your land, moreover, you shall not reap to the very corners of your field nor gather the gleaning of your harvest; you are to leave them for the afflicted and the sojourner. I am Yahweh your God.'"

### *The Feast of Trumpets*

23 Again Yahweh spoke to Moses, saying, 24 "Speak to the sons of Israel,

---

**23:10** [a]Ex 23:19; 34:26 **23:13** [a]Lv 6:20 [1]An ephah was approx. 21 qt. or 23 l [2]A hin was approx. 1 gal. or 3.8 l **23:14** [a]Ex 34:26; Nu 15:20, 21 **23:15** [a]Nu 28:26-31; Dt 16:9-12 **23:16** [a]Nu 28:26 **23:17** [a]Lv 2:12; 7:13 [1]An ephah was approx. 21 qt. or 23 l **23:19** [a]Lv 4:23; Nu 28:30 **23:21** [a]Lv 23:2, 4 [b]Lv 23:7 **23:22** [a]Lv 19:9, 10; Dt 24:19; Ru 2:15f

saying, '[a]In the seventh month on
the first of the month you shall have
a [1]rest, a [b]memorial by blowing *of*
*trumpets*, a holy convocation. **25** You
shall [a]not do any laborious work, but
you shall bring an offering by fire
near to Yahweh.'"

### *The Day of Atonement*

**26** And Yahweh spoke to Moses, say-
ing, **27** "On exactly [a]the tenth day of
this seventh month is [b]the day of
atonement; it shall be a holy convo-
cation for you, and you shall humble
your souls and bring an offering by
fire near to Yahweh. **28** And you shall
not do any work on this same day, for
it is a [a]day of atonement, [b]to make
atonement on your behalf before
Yahweh your God. **29** If there is any
[1]person who will not humble himself
on this same day, [a]he shall be cut off
from his people. **30** And as for any
person who does any work on this
same day, that person I will cause
to perish from among his people.
**31** You shall do no work at all. It is
to be a perpetual statute throughout
your generations in all your *places of*
habitation. **32** It is to be a sabbath of
complete rest to you, and you shall
humble your souls; on the ninth of
the month at evening, from evening
until evening you shall keep your
sabbath."

### *The Feast of Booths*

**33** Again Yahweh spoke to Moses,
saying, **34** "Speak to the sons of Israel,
saying, 'On [a]the fifteenth of this sev-
enth month is the [b]Feast of Booths
for seven days to Yahweh. **35** On the
first day is a holy convocation; you
shall do [a]no laborious work of any
kind. **36** [a]For seven days you shall
bring an offering by fire near to Yah-
weh. On [b]the eighth day you shall
have a holy convocation and bring
an offering by fire near to Yahweh;
it is a solemn assembly. You shall do
no laborious work.

**37** "These are [a]the appointed times
of Yahweh which you shall proclaim
as holy convocations, to bring offer-
ings by fire near to Yahweh—burnt
offerings and grain offerings, sacri-
fices and drink offerings, [b]*each* day's
matter on its own day— **38** besides
*those of* the sabbaths of Yahweh and
besides your gifts and besides all
your [1]votive and freewill offerings,
which you give to Yahweh.

**39** 'On exactly the fifteenth day of
the seventh month, [a]when you have
gathered in the produce of the land,
you shall celebrate the feast of Yah-
weh for seven days, with a [1]rest on
the first day and a [1]rest on the eighth
day. **40** And on the first day you shall
take for yourselves the [1]foliage of
beautiful trees, palm branches and
boughs of leafy trees and willows
of the brook, and you shall be glad
before Yahweh your God for seven
days. **41** You shall thus celebrate it
*as* a feast to Yahweh for seven days
in the year. It *shall be* a perpetual
statute throughout your generations;
you shall celebrate it in the seventh
month. **42** You shall [1]live [a]in booths
for seven days; all the native-born
in Israel shall [1]live in booths, **43** so

---

**23:24** [a]Nu 29:1 [b]Nu 10:9, 10 [1]Lit *sabbath rest* **23:25** [a]Lv 23:21 **23:27** [a]Lv 16:29; 25:9; Nu 29:7 [b]Ex 30:10; Lv 16:30; 23:28; Nu 29:7-11 **23:28** [a]Lv 23:27 [b]Lv 16:34 **23:29** [a]Ge 17:14; Lv 13:46; Nu 5:2 [1]Lit *soul* **23:34** [a]Nu 29:12 [b]Lv 23:42, 43; Dt 16:13, 16; Ezr 3:4; Ne 8:14; Zec 14:16; Jn 7:2 **23:35** [a]Lv 23:25 **23:36** [a]Nu 29:12-34 [b]Nu 29:35-38 **23:37** [a]Lv 23:2 [b]Nu 28:1-29:38 **23:38** [1]Lit *vows, and besides all your* **23:39** [a]Ex 23:16 [1]Lit *sabbath rest* **23:40** [1]Lit *products, fruit* **23:42** [a]Lv 23:34 [1]Lit *dwell*

that [a]your generations may know
that I had the sons of Israel live in
booths when I brought them out
from the land of Egypt. I am Yahweh
your God.'" **44** So Moses spoke to the
sons of Israel [a]the appointed times of
Yahweh.

### *The Lamps and the Bread Before Yahweh*

**24** Then Yahweh spoke to Moses,
saying, **2** "Command the sons
of Israel that they bring to you [a]clear
oil from beaten olives for the [1]light,
to make a lamp [2]burn continually.
**3** Outside the veil of testimony in the
tent of meeting, Aaron shall keep it
in order from evening to morning
before Yahweh continually; *it shall be*
a perpetual statute throughout your
generations. **4** He shall keep the lamps
in order on the [a]pure *gold* lampstand
before Yahweh continually.
**5** "[a]Then you shall take fine flour
and bake twelve cakes with it; two-
tenths *of an ephah* shall be *in* each
cake. **6** And you shall set them *in* two
rows, six *to* a row, on the [a]pure *gold*
table before Yahweh. **7** And you shall
put pure frankincense on each row
that it may be [a]a memorial portion
for the bread, *even* an offering by fire
to Yahweh. **8** [a]Every sabbath day he
shall set it in order before Yahweh
[b]continually; it is an everlasting
covenant [1]for the sons of Israel.
**9** [a]And it shall be for Aaron and his
sons, and they shall eat it in a holy
place; for it is most holy to him from
the offerings to Yahweh by fire, *his*
portion forever."
**10** Now the son of an Israelite
woman, whose father was an Egyp-
tian, went out among the sons of
Israel; and the Israelite woman's
son and a man of Israel struggled
with each other in the camp. **11** And
the son of the Israelite woman blas-
phemed the [a]Name and cursed. So
they brought him to Moses. (Now
his mother's name was Shelomith,
the daughter of Dibri, of the tribe of
Dan.) **12** And they put him in [1]custo-
dy [2]so that [a]the command of Yahweh
might be made clear to them.
**13** Then Yahweh spoke to Moses,
saying, **14** "Bring the one who has
cursed outside the camp, and let all
who heard him [a]lay their hands on
his head; then [b]let all the congre-
gation stone him. **15** And you shall
speak to the sons of Israel, saying,
'[a]If anyone curses his God, then he
will bear his sin. **16** Moreover, the
one who [a]blasphemes the name of
Yahweh shall surely be put to death;
all the congregation shall certainly
stone him. The sojourner as well as
the native, when he blasphemes the
Name, shall be put to death.

### *An Eye for an Eye*

**17** '[a]If a man strikes down the life of
any human being, he shall surely be
put to death. **18** [a]And the one who
strikes down the life of an animal shall
make restitution for it, life for life. **19** If
a man [1]injures his neighbor, just as he

**23:43** [a]Dt 31:13; Ps 78:5f **23:44** [a]Lv 23:37 ◆ **24:2** [a]Ex 27:20, 21 [1]Or *luminary* [2]Lit *ascend* **24:4** [a]Ex 25:31; 31:8; 37:17 **24:5** [a]Ex 25:30; 39:36; 40:23 **24:6** [a]Ex 25:24; 1Ki 7:48 **24:7** [a]Lv 2:2, 9, 16 **24:8** [a]Mt 12:5 [b]Ex 25:30; Nu 4:7; 2Chr 2:4 [1]Lit *from* **24:9** [a]Mt 12:4; Mk 2:26; Lk 6:4 **24:11** [a]Ex 3:15; 22:28; Job 2:5, 9; Is 8:21 **24:12** [a]Ex 18:15; Nu 15:34 [1]Or *prison* [2]Lit *to declare distinctly to them according to the mouth of Yahweh* **24:14** [a]Dt 13:9; 17:7 [b]Lv 20:2, 27; Dt 21:21 **24:15** [a]Ex 22:28 **24:16** [a]1Ki 21:10; Mt 12:31; Mk 3:28f **24:17** [a]Ge 9:6; Ex 21:12; Nu 35:30, 31; Dt 27:24 **24:18** [a]Lv 24:21 **24:19** [1]Lit *gives a blemish*

has done, so it shall be done to him:
**20** [a]fracture for fracture, [b]eye for eye,
tooth for tooth; just as he has [1]injured
a man, so it shall be [2]inflicted on him.
**21** Thus the one who strikes down an
animal shall make restitution for it,
but [a]the one who strikes down a man
shall be put to death. **22** There shall be
[a]one *standard of* judgment for you;
it shall be for the sojourner as well
as the native, for I am Yahweh your
God.'" **23** Then Moses spoke to the
sons of Israel, and they brought the
one who had cursed outside the camp
and stoned him with stones. Thus the
sons of Israel did, just as Yahweh had
commanded Moses.

### *The Sabbatical Year*

**25** Yahweh then spoke to Mo-
ses [1]at Mount Sinai, saying,
**2** "Speak to the sons of Israel and say
to them, 'When you come into the
land which I am giving to you, then
the land shall have a sabbath to Yah-
weh. **3** [a]Six years you shall sow your
field, and six years you shall prune
your vineyard and gather in its pro-
duce, **4** but during [a]the seventh year
the land shall have a sabbath rest, a
sabbath to Yahweh; you shall not sow
your field nor prune your vineyard.
**5** [1]What grows of its own accord from
your harvest you shall not reap, and
your grapes of untrimmed vines you
*shall* not gather; the land shall have
a sabbatical year. **6** [a]And the sabbath
*produce* of the land shall be for food;
for you and your male and female
slaves and your hired man and your
foreign resident, those who sojourn
with you. **7** Even your cattle and the
beasts that are in your land shall have
all its produce to eat.

### *The Year of Jubilee*

**8** 'You are also to count off seven
sabbaths of years for yourself, seven
times seven years, so that you have
the time of the seven sabbaths of
years, *namely*, forty-nine years. **9** You
shall then sound a ram's horn abroad
on [a]the tenth day of the seventh
month; on the day of atonement you
shall sound a horn all through your
land. **10** You shall thus set apart as
holy the fiftieth year and [a]proclaim
[1]a release through the land to all its
inhabitants. It shall be a jubilee for
you, [2]and [b]each of you shall return
to his own possession *of land*, [2]and
each of you shall return to his family.
**11** You shall have the fiftieth year as a
jubilee; you shall not sow; you shall
not reap what grows of its own ac-
cord; you shall not gather in *from* its
untrimmed vines. **12** For it is a jubilee;
it shall be holy to you. You shall eat
its produce out of the field.

**13** '[a]On this year of jubilee, each of
you shall return to his own posses-
sion *of land*. **14** If you make a sale,
moreover, to your companion or
buy from your friend's hand, [a]you
shall not mistreat one another.
**15** Corresponding to the number of
years after the jubilee, you shall buy
from your [1]companion; he is to sell
to you according to the number of
years of produce. **16** [a]In proportion
to the [1]extent of the years you shall
increase its price, and in proportion

---

**24:20** [a]Ex 21:23; Dt 19:21 [b]Mt 5:38 [1]Lit *given a blemish* [2]Lit *given* **24:21** [a]Lv 24:17 **24:22** [a]Ex 12:49; Nu 9:14; 15:15, 16, 29 ◆ **25:1** [1]Or *on* **25:3** [a]Ex 23:10, 11 **25:4** [a]Lv 25:20 **25:5** [1]Lit *The growth from spilled kernels* **25:6** [a]Lv 25:20, 21 **25:9** [a]Lv 23:27 **25:10** [a]Jer 34:8, 15, 17 [b]Lv 25:13, 28, 54 [1]Or *liberty* [2]Or *when* **25:13** [a]Lv 25:10; 27:24 **25:14** [a]Lv 25:17 **25:15** [1]Lit *companion's hands* **25:16** [a]Lv 25:27, 51, 52 [1]Lit *multitude*

to the fewness of the years you shall
diminish its price, for *it is the* number
of *crops it* produces *that* he is selling
to you. **17** So [a]you shall not mistreat
one another, but you shall [1]fear your
God; for I am Yahweh your God.

**18** 'You shall thus observe My
statutes and keep My judgments,
so as to do them, that [a]you may live
securely on the land. **19** Then the land
will yield its fruit, so that you can eat
your fill and live securely on it. **20** But
if you say, "[a]What are we going to eat
on the seventh year [1]if we do not sow
or gather in our produce?" **21** then [a]I
will command My blessing for you in
the sixth year that it will bring forth
the produce for three years. **22** So
you shall sow the eighth year and eat
[a]old things from that produce, eating
*the old* until the ninth year when its
produce comes in.

### *The Redemption of Land*

**23** 'The land, moreover, shall not be
sold permanently, for [a]the land is
Mine; for [b]you are *but* sojourners
and foreign residents with Me.
**24** Thus for every [1]piece of land of
your possession, you shall provide
for the redemption of the land.

**25** '[a]If a brother of yours becomes
so poor he has to sell part of his
possession *of land*, then his nearest
kinsman redeemer is to come and
redeem what his brother has sold.
**26** Or in case a man has no kinsman
redeemer, but [1]recovers his means
and finds sufficient *payment* for
its redemption, **27** [a]then he shall
calculate the years since its sale
and return the balance to the man
to whom he sold it, and so return to
his possession *of land*. **28** But if [1]he
has not found sufficient means to
return it to himself, then what he has
sold shall remain in the hands of its
purchaser until the year of jubilee;
but at the jubilee it shall [2]revert, that
[a]he may return to his possession *of
land*.

**29** 'Likewise, if a man sells a house
for habitation in a walled city, then
his redemption right remains valid
until a full year from its sale; his
right of redemption lasts a full year.
**30** But if it is not redeemed for him
within the space of a full year, then
the house that is in the walled city
passes permanently to its purchaser
throughout his generations; it does
not [1]revert in the jubilee. **31** The
houses of the villages, however,
which have no surrounding wall,
shall be considered [1]as open fields;
they have redemption rights and
[2]revert in the jubilee. **32** As for [a]cities
of the Levites, the Levites have a
permanent right of redemption for
the houses of the cities which are
their possession. **33** What, therefore,
[1]belongs to the Levites may be re-
deemed, and a house sale [2]in the city
of [3]their possession [4]reverts in the
jubilee, for the houses of the cities
of the Levites are their possession
among the sons of Israel. **34** [a]But
pasture fields of their cities shall not
be sold, for that is their perpetual
possession.

**25:17** [a]Lv 25:14; Pr 14:31; 22:22; Jer 7:5, 6; 1Th 4:6 [1]Or *reverence* **25:18** [a]Lv 26:5; Dt 12:10; Jer 23:6 **25:20** [a]Lv 25:4 [1]Or *behold* **25:21** [a]Dt 28:8 **25:22** [a]Lv 26:10 **25:23** [a]Ex 19:5 [b]Ge 23:4; 1Chr 29:15; Ps 39:12; Heb 11:13; 1Pe 2:11 **25:24** [1]Lit *land* **25:25** [a]Ru 2:20; 4:4, 6 **25:26** [1]Lit *his hand reaches* **25:27** [a]Lv 25:16 **25:28** [a]Lv 25:10, 13 [1]Lit *his hand has not found sufficient to* [2]Lit *go out* **25:30** [1]Lit *go out* **25:31** [1]Lit *according to* [2]Lit *go out* **25:32** [a]Nu 35:1-8; Jos 21:2 **25:33** [1]Lit *is from* [2]Lit *and* [3]Lit *his* [4]Lit *goes out* **25:34** [a]Nu 35:2-5

### *Redemption Rights for Poor Brothers*

**35** '[a]Now if a brother of yours be-
comes poor and his [1]means with
regard to you falter, then you are
to sustain him, like a sojourner or
a foreign resident, that he may live
with you. **36** [a]Do not take [1]usurious
interest from him, but fear your God,
that your brother may live with you.
**37** You shall not give him your silver
at interest nor your food for gain. **38** [a]I
am Yahweh your God, who brought
you out of the land of Egypt to give
you the land of Canaan *and* [b]to be
your God.

**39** '[a]If a brother of yours becomes
so poor with regard to you that he
sells himself to you, you shall not
subject him to a slave's service. **40** He
shall be with you as a hired man, as
[a]if he were a foreign resident; he
shall serve with you until the year of
jubilee. **41** He shall then go out from
you, he and his sons with him, and
shall return to his family, that he may
return to the possession *of the land* of
his fathers. **42** For they are My slaves
whom I brought out from the land of
Egypt; they shall not be sold *in* a slave
sale. **43** [a]You shall not have dominion
over him with brutality, but you shall
fear your God. **44** As for your male
and female slaves whom you may
have—you may acquire male and
female slaves from the nations that
are around you. **45** And also you may
acquire from the sons of the foreign
residents who sojourn among you,
from them and their families who
are with you; as for those whom they
have begotten in your land, they also
may become your possession. **46** You
may even give them as an inheritance
to your sons after you, to receive as
a possession; you can use them as
permanent slaves. [a]But in respect to
your brothers, the sons of Israel, you
shall not have dominion over one
another with brutality.

### *Kindness Toward a Poor Sojourner*

**47** 'Now if the [1]means of a sojourner
or of a foreign resident with you
becomes sufficient, and a brother of
yours becomes so poor with regard to
him as to sell himself to a sojourner
who resides with you or to the descen-
dants of a sojourner's family, **48** then
he shall have redemption right after
he has been sold. One of his brothers
may redeem him, **49** or his uncle or
his uncle's son may redeem him, or
one of his blood relatives from his
family may redeem him; or [a,1]if he
prospers, he may redeem himself.
**50** He then with his purchaser shall
calculate from the year when he
sold himself to him up to the year of
jubilee; and the price of his sale shall
correspond to the number of years.
*It is* like the days of a hired man *that*
he shall be with him. **51** If there are
still many years, [a]he shall return part
of his purchase price in proportion
to them for his own redemption;
**52** and if few years remain until the
year of jubilee, he shall so calculate
with him. In proportion to his years
he shall return *the amount for* his
redemption. **53** Like a man hired year
by year he shall be with him; [a]he shall
not have dominion over him with

---

**25:35** [a]Dt 15:7-11; 24:14, 15 [1]Lit *hand* **25:36** [a]Ex 22:25; Dt 23:19, 20 [1]Lit *interest and usury* **25:38** [a]Lv 11:45 [b]Ge 17:7 **25:39** [a]Ex 21:2-6; Dt 15:12-18; 1Ki 9:22 **25:40** [a]Ex 21:2 **25:43** [a]Ex 1:13, 14; Lv 25:46, 53; Eze 34:4; Col 4:1 **25:46** [a]Lv 25:43 **25:47** [1]Lit *hand...reaches* **25:49** [a]Lv 25:26, 27 [1]Lit *if his hand has reached and* **25:51** [a]Lv 25:16 **25:53** [a]Lv 25:43

brutality in your sight. **54** Even if he is not redeemed by [1]these *means*, [a]he shall still go out in the year of jubilee, he and his sons with him. **55** For the sons of Israel are My slaves; they are My slaves whom I brought out from the land of Egypt. I am Yahweh your God.

### *He Walks Among Those Who Walk in His Statutes*

**26** 'You shall not make for yourselves [a,1]idols, nor shall you set up for yourselves [b]a graven image or [c]a *sacred* pillar, nor shall you [2]place a [d]carved stone in your land to bow down [3]to it; for I am Yahweh your God. **2** [a]You shall keep My sabbaths and fear My sanctuary; I am Yahweh. **3** [a]If you walk in My statutes and keep My commandments so as to do them, **4** then [a]I shall give you rains in their season, so that the land will give forth its produce and the trees of the field will give forth their fruit. **5** [a]Indeed, your threshing will last for you until grape gathering, and grape gathering will last until sowing time. You will thus eat your [1]food to the full and [b]live securely in your land. **6** [a]I shall also give *you* peace in the land so that [b]you may lie down, with no one making *you* tremble. [c]I shall also eliminate wild beasts from the land, and [d]no sword will pass through your land. **7** But you will pursue your enemies, and they will fall before you by the sword; **8** [a]and five of you will pursue one hundred, and one hundred of you will pursue ten thousand, and your enemies will fall before you by the sword. **9** So I will turn toward you and [a]make you fruitful and multiply you, and I will [b]confirm My covenant with you. **10** [a]And you will eat the old supply and clear out the old because of the new. **11** [a]Moreover, I will [1]make My [2]dwelling among you, and My soul will not loathe you. **12** [a]I will also walk among you and be your God, and you shall be My people. **13** [a]I am Yahweh your God, who brought you out of the land of Egypt so that *you* would not be their slaves, and [b]I broke the bars of your yoke and made you walk erect.

### *Reject His Statutes and He Will Strike You*

**14** '[a]But if you do not obey Me and do not do all these commandments, **15** if, instead, you [a]reject My statutes, and if your soul loathes My judgments so as not to do all My commandments *and* so [b]break My covenant, **16** I, in turn, will do this to you: I will appoint over you a [a]sudden terror, consumption and fever that will waste away the eyes and cause the [b]soul to pine away; also, [c]you will sow your seed uselessly, for your enemies will eat it up. **17** And I will [1]set My face against you so that you will be [2]defeated before your enemies; and [a]those who hate you will have dominion over

---

**25:54** [a]Lv 25:10, 13, 28 [1]Or *these years* ◆ **26:1** [a]Lv 19:4; Dt 5:8 [b]Ex 20:4; Dt 16:21f [c]Ex 23:24 [d]Nu 33:52 [1]Or *graven images* [2]Lit *give* [3]Lit *over* **26:2** [a]Lv 19:30 **26:3** [a]Dt 7:12-26; 11:13; 28:1-14 **26:4** [a]Dt 11:14 **26:5** [a]Dt 11:15; Joel 2:19, 26; Am 9:13 [b]Lv 25:18, 19; Eze 34:25 [1]Lit *bread* **26:6** [a]Ps 29:11; 85:8; 147:14 [b]Zep 3:13 [c]Lv 26:22 [d]Lv 26:25 **26:8** [a]Dt 32:30 **26:9** [a]Ge 17:6; 22:17; 48:4 [b]Ge 17:7 **26:10** [a]Lv 25:22 **26:11** [a]Ex 25:8; 29:45, 46; Eze 37:26 [1]Lit *give* [2]Or *tabernacle* **26:12** [a]Ge 3:8; Dt 23:14; 2Co 6:16 **26:13** [a]Ex 20:2 [b]Eze 34:27 **26:14** [a]Dt 28:15-68; Jos 23:15 **26:15** [a]Lv 26:11; 2Ki 17:15 [b]Lv 26:9 **26:16** [a]Dt 28:22; Ps 78:33 [b]1Sa 2:33; Eze 24:23; 33:10 [c]Jdg 6:3-6; Job 31:8 **26:17** [a]Ps 106:41 [1]Lit *give* [2]Lit *smitten*

you, and [b]you will flee when no one
is pursuing you. 18 If also after these
things you do not obey Me, then I will
discipline you [a]seven times more for
your sins. 19 I will also [a]break down
your pride of strength; I will also
give your sky over *to become* like iron
and your earth like bronze. 20 [a]And
your power will be spent uselessly,
for your land will not give forth its
produce and the trees of the land will
not give forth their fruit.

21 'If then, you [a]walk in hostility
against Me and are unwilling to obey
Me, I will increase the plague on you
[b]seven times according to your sins.
22 [a]And I will send out among you the
beasts of the field, which will bereave
you of your children and cut down
your cattle and reduce your number
so that [b]your roads lie desolate.

23 '[a]And if by these things you do
not accept My discipline, but walk
in hostility against Me, 24 then I will
[a]walk in hostility against you; and I,
even I, will strike you [b]seven times
for your sins. 25 I will also bring
upon you a sword which will execute
[a]vengeance for the covenant; and
when you gather together into your
cities, I will send [b]pestilence among
you so that you shall be given over
into enemy hands. 26 [a]When I break
your staff of bread, ten women will
bake your bread in one oven, and
they will bring back your bread by
*rationed* weight so that you will [b]eat
and not become full.

27 'Yet, if in spite of this you do not
obey Me, but walk in hostility against
Me, 28 then [a]I will walk in wrathful
hostility against you, and I, even I,
will discipline you seven times for
your sins. 29 Further, [a]you will eat the
flesh of your sons, and the flesh of
your daughters you will eat. 30 I then
[a]will destroy your high places and cut
down your [b]incense altars and give
your corpses *to lie* on the corpses of
your idols, for My soul shall loathe
you. 31 And I will give your cities
over as a [a]waste and will make your
[b]sanctuaries desolate, and I will not
[c]smell your soothing aromas. 32 And
I will make [a]the land desolate, [b]so
that your enemies who inhabit it will
*themselves* feel desolate because of it.
33 You, however, I [a]will scatter among
the nations and will draw out a sword
after you, as your land becomes desolate and your cities become waste.

34 '[a]Then the land will make up for
its sabbaths all the days of the desolation, and you will be in your enemies'
land; then the land will rest and make
up for its sabbaths. 35 All the days
of *its* desolation it will observe the
rest which it did not observe on your
sabbaths, while you were living on
it. 36 As for those of you who may
remain, I will also bring [a]weakness
into their hearts in the lands of their
enemies. And the sound of a driven
leaf will pursue them, and even when
no one is pursuing they will flee [1]as
though from the sword, and they will

---

**26:17** [b]Lv 26:36, 37; Ps 53:5; Pr 28:1 **26:18** [a]Lv 26:21, 24, 28 **26:19** [a]Is 28:1-3; Eze 24:21 **26:20** [a]Ps 127:1; Is 17:10, 11; 49:4; Jer 12:13 **26:21** [a]Lv 26:23, 27, 40 [b]Lv 26:18 **26:22** [a]2Ki 17:25 [b]Jdg 5:6 **26:23** [a]Lv 26:21; Jer 5:3 **26:24** [a]Lv 26:28, 41 [b]Lv 26:21 **26:25** [a]Jer 50:28; 51:11 [b]Nu 14:12 **26:26** [a]Is 3:1; Eze 4:16, 17; 5:16 [b]Mic 6:14 **26:28** [a]Lv 26:24, 41; Is 59:18 **26:29** [a]2Ki 6:29 **26:30** [a]2Ki 23:20; Eze 6:3, 6; Am 7:9 [b]2Chr 34:4, 7; Is 27:9 **26:31** [a]Ne 2:3; Jer 44:2, 6, 22 [b]Is 63:18; Lam 2:7 [c]Am 5:21 **26:32** [a]Jer 9:11; 12:11; 25:11; 33:10 [b]Jer 18:16; 19:8 **26:33** [a]Dt 4:27; 28:64; Ps 44:11; 106:27; Jer 31:10; Eze 12:15; 20:23; Zec 7:14 **26:34** [a]Lv 26:43; 2Chr 36:21 **26:36** [a]Is 30:17; Lam 1:3, 6; 4:19; Eze 21:7 [1]Lit *the flight of the sword*

fall. **37** [a]They will therefore stumble over each other as if *running* from the sword, although no one is pursuing; and you will have *no strength* [1]to stand up before your enemies. **38** But [a]you will perish among the nations, and your enemies' land will consume you. **39** [a]So those of you who may remain will rot away in their iniquity in the lands of your enemies; and also in the iniquities of their fathers they will rot away with them.

**40** '[a]If they confess their iniquity and the iniquity of their fathers, in their unfaithfulness which they committed against Me, and also how they walked in hostility against Me— **41** I also was walking in hostility against them, to bring them into the land of their enemies—[a]or if their uncircumcised heart becomes humbled so that [b]they then make up for their iniquity, **42** then I will remember [a]My covenant with Jacob, and I will remember also [b]My covenant with Isaac and [c]My covenant with Abraham as well, and I will remember the land. **43** [a]For the land will be forsaken by them and will make up for its sabbaths while it is made desolate without them. They, meanwhile, will be making up for their iniquity [1]because they rejected My judgments and their [b]soul loathed My statutes. **44** Yet in spite of this, when they are in the land of their enemies, I will not reject them, nor will I so [a]loathe them as [b]to bring an end to them, [c]breaking My covenant with them; for I am Yahweh their God. **45** But I will remember for them the [a]covenant with their ancestors, whom I brought out of the land of Egypt in the sight of the nations, that [b]I might be their God. I am Yahweh.'"

**46** [a]These are the statutes and judgments and laws which Yahweh has given *to be* between Himself and the sons of Israel by the hand of Moses at Mount Sinai.

### *Holy to Yahweh*

**27** Then Yahweh spoke to Moses, saying, **2** "Speak to the sons of Israel and say to them, '[a]When a man makes a difficult vow, he *shall be valued* according to your valuation of persons belonging to Yahweh. **3** If your valuation is of the male from twenty years even to sixty years old, then your valuation shall be [1]fifty shekels of silver, according to [a]the shekel of the sanctuary. **4** Or if it is a female, then your valuation shall be thirty shekels. **5** If it be from five years even to twenty years old then your valuation for the male shall be twenty shekels and for the female ten shekels. **6** But if *they are* from a month even up to five years old, then your valuation shall be [a]five shekels of silver for the male, and for the female your valuation shall be three shekels of silver. **7** If *they are* from sixty years old and upward, if it is a male, then your valuation shall be fifteen shekels, and for the female ten shekels. **8** But if he is poorer than your valuation, then he shall be [1]presented before the priest, and

**26:37** [a]Jer 6:21; Na 3:3 [1]Lit *you will stand* **26:38** [a]Dt 4:26 **26:39** [a]Eze 4:17; 33:10 **26:40** [a]Jer 3:12-15; 14:20; Hos 5:15 **26:41** [a]Jer 4:4; 9:25, 26; Eze 44:7, 9; Ac 7:51 [b]Eze 20:43 **26:42** [a]Ge 28:13-15; 35:11, 12 [b]Ge 26:2-5 [c]Ge 22:15-18 **26:43** [a]Lv 26:34 [b]Lv 26:11 [1]Lit *because and by the cause* **26:44** [a]Lv 26:11 [b]Dt 4:31; Jer 30:11 [c]Jer 33:20-26 **26:45** [a]Ex 6:6-8 [b]Ge 17:7 **26:46** [a]Lv 7:38; 27:34; Dt 4:5; 29:1
◆ **27:2** [a]Nu 6:2; Dt 23:21-23 **27:3** [a]Ex 30:13; Lv 27:25; Nu 3:47; 18:16 [1]Approx. 1.25 lb. or 550 gm, a shekel was approx. 0.4 oz. or 11 gm **27:6** [a]Nu 18:16 **27:8** [1]Lit *made to stand*

the priest shall value him; [a]according
to [2]the means of the one who vowed,
the priest shall value him.
**9** 'Now if it is an animal of the
kind which [1]men can bring near
as an offering to Yahweh, any such
that one gives to Yahweh shall be
holy. **10** [a]He shall not replace it or
exchange it, a good for a bad, or a
bad for a good; or if he does exchange
animal for animal, then both it and
its substitute shall become holy. **11** If,
however, it is any unclean animal of
the kind which [1]men do not bring
near as an offering to Yahweh, then
he shall [2]present the animal before
the priest. **12** And the priest shall
value it [1]as either good or bad; as
you, the priest, value it, so it shall
be. **13** But if he should ever *wish to*
redeem it, then he shall add one-fifth
of it to your valuation.
**14** 'Now if a man sets his house
apart as holy to Yahweh, then the
priest shall value it [1]as either good
or bad; as the priest values it, so it
shall stand. **15** Yet if the one who
sets it apart as holy should *wish to*
redeem his house, then he shall add
one-fifth of your valuation price to
it, so that it may be his.
**16** 'Again, if a man sets apart as
holy to Yahweh a portion of the fields
of his own possession, then your
valuation shall be [1]proportionate to
the seed needed for it: a [2]homer of
barley seed at [3]fifty shekels of silver.
**17** If he sets apart his field as holy
from the year of jubilee, according
to your valuation it shall stand. **18** If
he sets apart his field as holy after
the jubilee, however, then the priest
shall calculate the price for [1]him
[2]proportionate to the years that are
left until the year of jubilee; and it
shall be deducted from your valu-
ation. **19** If the one who sets it apart
as holy should ever wish to redeem
the field, then he shall add one-fifth
of your valuation price to it so that
it may stand as his own. **20** Yet if he
will not redeem the field, [1]but has
sold the field to another man, it may
no longer be redeemed; **21** and it will
be that when it [1]reverts in the jubilee,
the field shall be holy to Yahweh, like
a field *that is* [2]devoted; [a]it shall be
for the priest as his possession. **22** Or
if he sets apart as holy to Yahweh a
field which he has bought, which is
not a portion of the field of his own
possession, **23** then the priest shall
calculate for [1]him the amount of your
valuation up to the year of jubilee;
and he shall on that day give your
valuation as holy to Yahweh. **24** In the
year of jubilee the field shall return
to the one from whom he bought it,
to whom the possession of the land
belongs. **25** Every valuation of yours,
moreover, shall be according to [a]the
shekel of the sanctuary. The shekel
shall be twenty [1]gerahs.
**26** '[a]However, a firstborn among
animals, which as a firstborn belongs
to Yahweh, no man may set it apart
as holy; whether ox or sheep, it is
Yahweh's. **27** But if *it is* among the un-
clean animals, then he shall [1]ransom
it according to your valuation and

**27:8** [a]Lv 5:11; 14:21-24 [2]Lit *what the hand reaches* **27:9** [1]Lit *they* **27:10** [a]Lv 27:33 **27:11** [1]Lit *they* [2]Lit *make the animal stand* **27:12** [1]Lit *between* **27:14** [1]Lit *between* **27:16** [1]Lit *according to its seed* [2]A homer was approx. 6.5 bu. or 230 l [3]Approx. 1.25 lb. or 0.55 kg **27:18** [1]Or *it* [2]Lit *according to the years* **27:20** [1]Or *if he* **27:21** [a]Nu 18:14; Eze 44:29 [1]Lit *goes out* [2]Lit *possession* **27:23** [1]Or *it* **27:25** [a]Ex 30:13; Lv 27:3; Nu 3:47; 18:16 [1]A gerah was approx. 0.025 oz. or 0.7 gm **27:26** [a]Ex 13:2 **27:27** [1]Or *redeem*

add to it one-fifth of it; and if it is
not redeemed, then it shall be sold
according to your valuation.
28 'Nevertheless, [a]anything which
a man [1]devotes to Yahweh out of all
that he has, of man or animal or of
the fields of his own possession, shall
not be sold or redeemed. Anything
[2]devoted to destruction is most holy
to Yahweh. 29 No [1]one who may have
been [2]devoted among men shall be
[3]ransomed; he shall surely be put to
death.
30 'Thus [a]all the tithe of the land,
of the seed of the land or of the fruit
of the tree, belongs to Yahweh; it is
holy to Yahweh. 31 If, therefore, a man
wishes to redeem part of his tithe, he
shall add to it one-fifth of it. 32 For
every tenth part of herd or flock,
whatever [a]passes under the rod, the
tenth one shall be holy to Yahweh.
33 [a]He shall not inquire whether *it is*
good or bad, nor shall he exchange it;
or if he does exchange it, then both it
and its substitute shall become holy.
It shall not be redeemed.'"
34 [a]These are the commandments
which Yahweh commanded Moses
for the sons of Israel at Mount Sinai.

# NUMBERS

### *The Census of Israel's Warriors*

1 Then [1]Yahweh spoke to Moses
in the wilderness of Sinai, in the
tent of meeting, on [a]the first of the
second month, in the second year
after they had come out of the land
of Egypt, saying, 2 "[a]Take a [1]census
of all the congregation of the sons of
Israel, by their families, by their
fathers' households, according to
the number of names, every male,
head by head 3 from [a]twenty years
old and upward, whoever *is able to*
go out to war in Israel, you and Aaron
shall [1]number them by their armies.
4 With you, moreover, there shall be a
man of each tribe, [a]each one head of
his father's household. 5 These then
are the names of the men who shall
stand with you:

[a]of Reuben, Elizur the son of Shedeur;
6 of Simeon, Shelumiel the son of Zurishaddai;
7 of Judah, [a]Nahshon the son of Amminadab;
8 of Issachar, Nethanel the son of Zuar;
9 of Zebulun, Eliab the son of Helon;
10 of the sons of Joseph:
of Ephraim, Elishama the son of Ammihud;
of Manasseh, Gamaliel the son of Pedahzur;
11 of Benjamin, Abidan the son of Gideoni;
12 of Dan, Ahiezer the son of Ammishaddai;
13 of Asher, Pagiel the son of Ochran;

---

**27:28** [a]Nu 18:14; Jos 6:17-19 [1]Or *banned* [2]Or *put under the ban* **27:29** [1]Or *banned* [2]Or *put under the ban* [3]Or *redeemed* **27:30** [a]Ge 28:22; 2Chr 31:5; Ne 13:12 **27:32** [a]Jer 33:13; Eze 20:37 **27:33** [a]Lv 27:10 **27:34** [a]Lv 26:46; Dt 4:5 ◆ **1:1** [a]Ex 40:2, 17 [1]The personal covenant name of God, a form of I AM WHO I AM, cf. Ex 3:14-15 **1:2** [a]Ex 12:37; 38:25, 26; Nu 26:2 [1]Lit *sum* **1:3** [a]Ex 30:14; 38:26 [1]Lit *muster*, so in ch **1:4** [a]Ex 18:21, 25; Nu 1:16; Dt 1:15 **1:5** [a]Ge 29:32; Ex 1:2; Dt 33:6; Rev 7:5 **1:7** [a]Ru 4:20; 1Chr 2:10; Lk 3:32

14 of Gad, Eliasaph the son of
[a]Deuel;
15 of Naphtali, Ahira the son of
Enan.
16 "These are they who were [a]called
*upon* by the congregation, the leaders
of their fathers' tribes; they were the
[b]heads of [1]divisions of Israel."
17 So Moses and Aaron took these
men who had been designated by
name, 18 and they assembled all the
congregation together on the [a]first
of the second month. Then they
registered by [b]genealogy in their
families, by their fathers' households,
according to the number of names,
from twenty years old and upward,
head by head, 19 just as [a]Yahweh had
commanded Moses. So he numbered
them in the wilderness of Sinai.
20 [a]Now the sons of Reuben, Is-
rael's firstborn, their genealogical
registration by their families, by their
fathers' households, according to the
number of names, head by head,
every male from twenty years old
and upward, whoever *was able to* go
out to war, 21 their numbered men of
the tribe of Reuben *were* 46,500.
22 [a]Of the sons of Simeon, their
genealogical registration by their
families, by their fathers' households,
their numbered men, according to
the number of names, head by head,
every male from twenty years old
and upward, [b]whoever *was able to*
go out to war, 23 their numbered men
of the tribe of Simeon *were* 59,300.
24 [a]Of the sons of Gad, their ge-
nealogical registration by their fam-
ilies, by their fathers' households,
according to the number of names,
from twenty years old and upward,
whoever *was able to* go out to war,
25 their numbered men of the tribe
of Gad *were* 45,650.
26 [a]Of the sons of Judah, their
genealogical registration by their
families, by their fathers' households,
according to the number of names,
from twenty years old and upward,
whoever *was able to* go out to war,
27 their numbered men of the tribe
of Judah *were* 74,600.
28 [a]Of the sons of Issachar, their
genealogical registration by their
families, by their fathers' households,
according to the number of names,
from twenty years old and upward,
whoever *was able to* go out to war,
29 their numbered men of the tribe
of Issachar *were* 54,400.
30 [a]Of the sons of Zebulun, their
genealogical registration by their
families, by their fathers' households,
according to the number of names,
from twenty years old and upward,
whoever *was able to* go out to war,
31 their numbered men of the tribe
of Zebulun *were* 57,400.
32 [a]Of the sons of Joseph, *namely*,
of the sons of Ephraim, their gene-
alogical registration by their fami-
lies, by their fathers' households,
according to the number of names,
from twenty years old and upward,
whoever *was able to* go out to war,
33 their numbered men of the tribe
of Ephraim *were* 40,500.
34 [a]Of the sons of Manasseh, their
genealogical registration by their
families, by their fathers' households,

---

**1:14** [a]Nu 2:14 **1:16** [a]Ex 18:21; Nu 7:2; 16:2; 26:9 [b]Ex 18:25 [1]Or *clans*; lit *thousands* **1:18** [a]Nu 1:1 [b]Ezr 2:59; Heb 7:3 **1:19** [a]2Sa 24:1 **1:20** [a]Nu 26:5-7 **1:22** [a]Nu 26:12-14 [b]Ps 144:1 **1:24** [a]Ge 30:11; Nu 26:15-18; Jos 4:12; Jer 49:1 **1:26** [a]Ge 29:35; Nu 26:19-22; 2Sa 24:9; Ps 78:68; Mt 1:2 **1:28** [a]Nu 26:23-25 **1:30** [a]Nu 26:26, 27 **1:32** [a]Nu 26:35-37; Dt 33:13-17; Jer 7:15; Ob 19 **1:34** [a]Nu 26:28-34

according to the number of names,
from twenty years old and upward,
whoever *was able to* go out to war,
35 their numbered men of the tribe
of Manasseh *were* 32,200.
36 [a]Of the sons of Benjamin, their
genealogical registration by their
families, by their fathers' households,
according to the number of names,
from twenty years old and upward,
whoever *was able to* go out to war,
37 their numbered men of the tribe
of Benjamin *were* 35,400.
38 [a]Of the sons of Dan, their ge-
nealogical registration by their fam-
ilies, by their fathers' households,
according to the number of names,
from twenty years old and upward,
whoever *was able to* go out to war,
39 their numbered men of the tribe
of Dan *were* 62,700.
40 [a]Of the sons of Asher, their
genealogical registration by their
families, by their fathers' households,
according to the number of names,
from twenty years old and upward,
whoever *was able to* go out to war,
41 their numbered men of the tribe
of Asher *were* 41,500.
42 [a]Of the sons of Naphtali, their
genealogical registration by their
families, by their fathers' households,
according to the number of names,
from twenty years old and upward,
whoever *was able to* go out to war,
43 their numbered men of the tribe
of Naphtali *were* 53,400.
44 These are the ones who were
numbered, whom Moses and Aaron
*numbered*, with the leaders of Israel,
twelve men, each of whom was of
his father's household. 45 So all the
numbered men of the sons of Israel
by their fathers' households, from
twenty years old and upward, whoev-
er *was able to* go out to war in Israel,
46 even all the numbered men were
[a]603,550.

### *Levites Not Numbered in the Census*

47 [a]The Levites, however, were not
numbered among them by their
fathers' tribe. 48 Yahweh had spoken
to Moses, saying, 49 "Only the tribe
of Levi [a]you shall not number, nor
shall you take their [1]census among
the sons of Israel. 50 But you shall
[a]appoint the Levites over the [1]taber-
nacle of the testimony and over all its
furnishings and over all that belongs
to it. They shall carry the tabernacle
and all its furnishings, and they
shall attend to it; they shall also
camp around the tabernacle. 51 [a]So
when the tabernacle is to set out, the
Levites shall take it down; and when
the tabernacle encamps, the Levites
shall set it up. But [b]the [1]layman who
comes near shall be put to death.
52 [a]And the sons of Israel shall camp,
each man by his own camp, and each
man by his own standard, according
to their armies. 53 [a]But the Levites
shall camp around the tabernacle
of the testimony so that there will
be [b]no wrath on the congregation
of the sons of Israel. [c]So the Levites
shall keep charge of the tabernacle
of the testimony." 54 Thus the sons
of Israel did; according to all which
Yahweh had commanded Moses, so
they did.

---

**1:36** [a]Ge 49:27; Nu 26:38-41; 2Chr 17:17; Rev 7:8 **1:38** [a]Ge 30:6; 46:23; Nu 2:25; 26:42, 43 **1:40** [a]Nu 26:44-47 **1:42** [a]Nu 26:48-50 **1:46** [a]Ex 12:37; 38:26; Nu 2:32; 26:51 **1:47** [a]Nu 2:33; 3:14-39; 4:49; 26:57-64 **1:49** [a]Nu 26:62 [1]Lit *sum* **1:50** [a]Ex 38:21; Nu 3:6-8, 25-37; 4:15, 25-27, 31, 32 [1]Lit *dwelling place*, so in ch **1:51** [a]Nu 4:1-33 [b]Nu 3:10, 38; 4:15, 19, 20 [1]Lit *stranger* **1:52** [a]Nu 2:2, 34 **1:53** [a]Nu 3:23, 29, 35, 38 [b]Lv 10:6; Nu 16:46; 18:5 [c]Nu 8:24; 18:2-4; 1Chr 23:32

### *Israel Camped by Their Standards*

**2** Now Yahweh spoke to Moses
and to Aaron, saying, **2** “[a]The
sons of Israel shall camp, each by his
own standard, with the [1]banners of
their fathers’ households; they shall
camp around the tent of meeting [2]at
a distance. **3** Now those who camp on
the east side toward the sunrise *shall
be* of the standard of the camp of
Judah, by their armies, and the leader
of the sons of Judah: [a]Nahshon the
son of Amminadab, **4** and his army,
even their [1]numbered men, 74,600.
**5** Those who camp next to him *shall
be* the tribe of Issachar, and the lead-
er of the sons of Issachar: [a]Nethanel
the son of Zuar, **6** and his army, even
his numbered men, 54,400. **7** *Then*
the tribe of Zebulun, and the leader
of the sons of Zebulun: [a]Eliab the
son of Helon, **8** and his army, even his
numbered men, 57,400. **9** The total
of the numbered men of the camp
of Judah: 186,400, by their armies.
[a]They shall set out first.

**10** “On the south side *shall be* the
standard of the camp of Reuben by
their armies, and the leader of the
sons of Reuben: [a]Elizur the son of
Shedeur, **11** and his army, even his
numbered men, 46,500. **12** And those
who camp next to him *shall be* the
tribe of Simeon, and the leader of the
sons of Simeon: [a]Shelumiel the son
of Zurishaddai, **13** and his army, even
their numbered men, 59,300. **14** Then
the tribe of Gad, and the leader of
the sons of Gad: [a]Eliasaph the son
of [1]Deuel, **15** and his army, even their
numbered men, 45,650. **16** The total
of the numbered men of the camp of
Reuben: 151,450 by their armies. And
[a]they shall set out second.

**17** “[a]Then the tent of meeting shall
set out *with* the camp of the Levites
in the midst of the camps; just as they
camp, so they shall set out, every
man in his place by their standards.

**18** “On the west side *shall be* the
standard of the camp of [a]Ephraim
by their armies, and the leader of
the sons of Ephraim: [b]Elishama the
son of Ammihud, **19** and his army,
even their numbered men, 40,500.
**20** Next to him *shall be* the tribe of
Manasseh, and the leader of the sons
of Manasseh: [a]Gamaliel the son of
Pedahzur, **21** and his army, even their
numbered men, 32,200. **22** Then the
tribe of [a]Benjamin, and the leader of
the sons of Benjamin: [b]Abidan the
son of Gideoni, **23** and his army, even
their numbered men, 35,400. **24** The
total of the numbered men of the
camp of Ephraim: 108,100, by their
armies. And [a]they shall set out third.

**25** “On the north side *shall be* the
standard of the camp of Dan by their
armies, and the leader of the sons
of Dan: [a]Ahiezer the son of Ammi-
shaddai, **26** and his army, even their
numbered men, 62,700. **27** Those
who camp next to him *shall be* the
tribe of Asher, and the leader of the
sons of Asher: [a]Pagiel the son of
Ochran, **28** and his army, even their
numbered men, 41,500. **29** Then the
tribe of [a]Naphtali, and the leader of
the sons of Naphtali: [b]Ahira the son
of Enan, **30** and his army, even their
numbered men, 53,400. **31** The total

◆ **2:2** [a]Nu 1:52; 24:2 [1]Lit *signs* [2]Or *facing it* **2:3** [a]Nu 1:7; 10:14; Ru 4:20; 1Chr 2:10; Lk 3:32, 33 **2:4** [1]Lit *mustered*, so in ch **2:5** [a]Nu 1:8; 7:18, 23 **2:7** [a]Nu 1:9 **2:9** [a]Nu 10:14 **2:10** [a]Nu 1:5 **2:12** [a]Nu 1:6 **2:14** [a]Nu 1:14; 7:42 [1]Many mss *Reuel* **2:16** [a]Nu 10:18 **2:17** [a]Nu 1:53 **2:18** [a]Ge 48:14-20; Jer 31:9, 18-20 [b]Nu 1:10 **2:20** [a]Nu 1:10 **2:22** [a]Ps 68:27 [b]Nu 1:11 **2:24** [a]Nu 10:22 **2:25** [a]Nu 1:12 **2:27** [a]Nu 1:13 **2:29** [a]Ge 30:8 [b]Nu 1:15

of the numbered men of the camp of
Dan *was* 157,600. [a]They shall set out
last by their standards."
32 These are the numbered men
of the sons of Israel by their fathers'
households; the total of the num-
bered men of the camps by their
armies, [a]603,550. 33 [a]The Levites,
however, were not numbered among
the sons of Israel, just as Yahweh had
commanded Moses. 34 Thus the sons
of Israel did; according to all that
Yahweh commanded Moses, so they
camped by their standards, and so
they set out, every one by his family
according to his father's household.

### *Priests and Levites*

3 [a]Now these are the generations
of Aaron and Moses at the time
when Yahweh spoke with Moses on
Mount Sinai. 2 [a]These then are the
names of the sons of Aaron: Nadab
the firstborn, and Abihu, Eleazar and
Ithamar. 3 These are the names of the
sons of Aaron, the [a]anointed priests,
whom he [1]ordained to minister as
priests. 4 [a]But Nadab and Abihu died
before Yahweh when they offered
strange fire before Yahweh in the
wilderness of Sinai; and they had
no children. So Eleazar and Ithamar
ministered as priests [1]in the lifetime
of their father Aaron.
5 Then Yahweh spoke to Moses,
saying, 6 "[a]Bring the tribe of Levi
near and have them stand before
Aaron the priest, that they may min-
ister to him. 7 And they shall keep his
*responsibility* and the *responsibility*
for the whole congregation before
the tent of meeting, to perform the
[a]service of the tabernacle. 8 They
shall also keep all the furnishings
of the tent of meeting, along with
the responsibility of the sons of
Israel, to perform the service of the
[1]tabernacle. 9 You shall thus [a]give
the Levites to Aaron and to his sons;
they are wholly given to him from
among the sons of Israel. 10 So you
shall appoint Aaron and his sons that
[a]they may keep their priesthood, but
[b]the [1]outsider who comes near shall
be put to death."
11 Then Yahweh spoke to Moses,
saying, 12 "Now, behold, I [a]have taken
the Levites from among the sons of
Israel instead of every [b]firstborn, the
first offspring of the womb among
the sons of Israel. So the Levites shall
be Mine. 13 For [a]all the firstborn are
Mine; on the day that I struck down
all the firstborn in the land of Egypt,
I sanctified to Myself all the firstborn
in Israel, from man to beast. They
shall be Mine; I am Yahweh."
14 Then Yahweh spoke to Moses
[a]in the wilderness of Sinai, saying,
15 "[a,1]Number the sons of Levi by
their fathers' households, by their
families; every male from a month
old and upward you shall [2]number."
16 So Moses numbered them accord-
ing to the [1]word of Yahweh, just as
he had been commanded. 17 [a]These
then are the sons of Levi by their
names:

Gershon and Kohath and
Merari.

---

**2:31** [a]Nu 10:25 **2:32** [a]Ex 38:26; Nu 1:46 **2:33** [a]Nu 1:47; 26:57-62 ◆ **3:1** [a]Ex 6:20-27
**3:2** [a]Ex 6:23; Nu 26:60 **3:3** [a]Ex 28:41 [1]Lit *filled their hand* **3:4** [a]Lv 10:1, 2; Nu 26:61 [1]Lit *before the face* **3:6** [a]Nu 8:6-22; 18:1-7; Dt 10:8 **3:7** [a]Nu 1:50 **3:8** [1]Lit *dwelling place*, so in ch
**3:9** [a]Nu 18:6 **3:10** [a]Ex 29:9 [b]Nu 1:51 [1]Lit *stranger* **3:12** [a]Nu 3:45; 8:14 [b]Ex 13:2 **3:13** [a]Ex 13:2; Lv 27:26; Ne 10:36 **3:14** [a]Ex 19:1 **3:15** [a]Nu 1:47 [1]Lit *Muster* [2]Lit *muster*, so in ch **3:16** [1]Lit *mouth*
**3:17** [a]Ex 6:16-22

18 And these are the names of
the [a]sons of Gershon by their
families:
Libni and Shimei;
19 and the sons of Kohath by
their families:
Amram and Izhar, Hebron and
Uzziel;
20 and the sons of Merari by
their families:
Mahli and Mushi. These are
the families of the Levites
according to their fathers'
households.
21 Of Gershon *was* the family of
the Libnites and the family of the
Shimeites; these *were* the families of
the Gershonites. 22 Their numbered
men, in the numbering of every male
from a month old and upward, *even*
their numbered men *were* 7,500.
23 The families of the Gershonites
were to camp behind the tabernacle
westward, 24 and the leader of the fa-
thers' households of the Gershonites
*was* Eliasaph the son of Lael.

### *Responsibilities of the Priests*

25 Now [a]the responsibility of the sons
of Gershon in the tent of meeting *in-
volved* the tabernacle and [b]the tent,
its covering, and [c]the screen for the
doorway of the tent of meeting, 26 and
[a]the hangings of the court, and [b]the
screen for the doorway of the court
which is around the tabernacle and
the altar, and its cords, according to
all the service [1]concerning them.
27 Of Kohath *was* the family of
the Amramites and the family of
the Izharites and the family of the
Hebronites and the family of the
Uzzielites; these were the families of
the Kohathites. 28 In the numbering
of every male from a month old and
upward, *there were* 8,600, keeping
the responsibility of the sanctuary.
29 The families of the sons of Kohath
were to camp on the southward side
of the tabernacle, 30 and the leader
of the fathers' households of the Ko-
hathite families was [1]Elizaphan the
son of Uzziel. 31 Now [a]their respon-
sibility *involved* [b]the ark, [c]the table,
[d]the lampstand, [e]the altars, and the
utensils of the sanctuary with which
they minister, and the screen, and
all the service [1]concerning them;
32 and Eleazar the son of Aaron the
priest *was* the chief of the leaders of
Levi *and had* the oversight of those
who keep the responsibility of the
sanctuary.
33 Of Merari *was* the family of
the Mahlites and the family of the
Mushites; these *were* the families
of Merari. 34 And their numbered
men, in the numbering of every
male from a month old and upward,
*were* 6,200. 35 And the leader of the
fathers' households of the families of
Merari *was* Zuriel the son of Abihail.
They *were* to [a]camp on the north-
ward side of the tabernacle. 36 Now
the appointed responsibility of the
sons of Merari *involved* the boards
of the tabernacle, its bars, its pillars,
its bases, all its equipment, and the
service concerning them, 37 and the
pillars around the court with their
bases and their pegs and their cords.
38 Now those who were to [a]camp
before the tabernacle eastward,
before the tent of meeting toward

---

**3:18** [a]Ex 6:17 **3:25** [a]Nu 4:24-26 [b]Ex 26:1, 7, 14 [c]Ex 26:36 **3:26** [a]Ex 27:9, 12, 14, 15 [b]Ex 27:16 [1]Lit *of it*
**3:30** [1]In Ex 6:22, *Elzaphan* **3:31** [a]Nu 4:15 [b]Ex 25:10-22 [c]Ex 25:23-28 [d]Ex 25:31-40 [e]Ex 27:1, 2; 30:1-5
[1]Lit *of it* **3:35** [a]Nu 1:53; 2:25 **3:38** [a]Nu 1:53; 2:3

the sunrise, are Moses and Aaron and
his sons, keeping the responsibility
of the sanctuary for the responsi-
bility of the sons of Israel; but [b]the
[1]outsider coming near was to be put
to death. **39** All the numbered men
of the Levites, whom Moses and
Aaron numbered at the [1]command
of Yahweh by their families, every
male from a month old and upward,
*were* [a]22,000.

### *Redemption of the Firstborn*

**40** Then Yahweh said to Moses,
"[a]Number every firstborn male
of the sons of Israel from a month
old and upward, and [1]make a list of
their names. **41** And you [a]shall take
the Levites for Me, I am Yahweh,
instead of all the firstborn among
the sons of Israel, and the cattle of
the Levites instead of all the first-
born among the cattle of the sons of
Israel." **42** So Moses numbered all the
firstborn among the sons of Israel,
just as Yahweh had commanded him;
**43** and all the firstborn males by the
number of names from a month old
and upward, for their numbered men
were [a]22,273.

**44** Then Yahweh spoke to Moses,
saying, **45** "[a]Take the Levites instead
of all the firstborn among the sons of
Israel and the cattle of the Levites.
And the Levites shall be Mine; I am
Yahweh. **46** [a]For the redemption price
of the 273 of the firstborn of the sons
of Israel who are in excess beyond
the Levites, **47** you shall take [a]five
[1]shekels apiece, per head; you shall
take *them* in [b]terms of the shekel of
the sanctuary ([c]the shekel is twenty
[2]gerahs), **48** and give the money, the
redemption price of those who are
in excess among them, to Aaron
and to his sons." **49** So Moses took
the money of the redemption price
from those who were in excess, be-
yond those redeemed by the Levites;
**50** from the firstborn of the sons of
Israel he took the money in terms
of the shekel of the sanctuary, 1,365.
**51** Then Moses gave the money of the
redemption price to Aaron and to his
sons, at the [1]command of Yahweh,
just as Yahweh had commanded
Moses.

### *Duties of the Kohathites*

**4** Then Yahweh spoke to Moses
and to Aaron, saying, **2** "Take [1]a
census of the [2]descendants of Ko-
hath from among the sons of Levi,
by their families, by their fathers'
households, **3** from [a]thirty years
and upward, even to fifty years old,
all who enter the duty of doing the
work in the tent of meeting. **4** This is
the service of the sons of Kohath in
the tent of meeting, *concerning* the
most holy things.

**5** "And *when* the camp sets out,
Aaron and his sons shall go in and
they shall take down [a]the veil of
the screen and cover the [b]ark of the
testimony with it; **6** and they shall put
a [a]covering of porpoise skin on it and
shall spread over *it* a cloth of pure
[1]blue and shall insert its poles. **7** Over
the table of the bread of the Presence

**3:38** [b]Nu 1:51 [1]Lit *stranger* **3:39** [a]Nu 3:43; 4:48; 26:62 [1]Lit *word* **3:40** [a]Nu 3:15 [1]Lit *take the number* **3:41** [a]Nu 3:12, 45 **3:43** [a]Nu 3:39 **3:45** [a]Nu 3:12 **3:46** [a]Ex 13:13, 15; Nu 18:15, 16 **3:47** [a]Lv 27:6; Nu 18:16 [b]Ex 30:13 [c]Lv 27:25; Eze 45:12 [1]A shekel was approx. 0.4 oz. or 11 gm [2]A gerah was approx. 0.025 oz. or 0.7 gm **3:51** [1]Lit *mouth* ◆ **4:2** [1]Lit *the sum* [2]Lit *sons* **4:3** [a]Nu 4:23, 30, 35; 8:24; 1Chr 23:3, 24, 27; Ezr 3:8 **4:5** [a]Ex 40:5; Lv 16:2; 2Chr 3:14; Mt 27:51; Heb 9:3 [b]Ex 25:10-16 **4:6** [a]Nu 4:25 [1]Or *violet*

they shall also spread a cloth of [1]blue
and put on it the dishes and the pans
and the offering bowls and the jars for
the drink offering, and [a]the continual
bread shall be on it. **8** And they shall
spread over them a cloth of scarlet
*material* and cover the same with a
covering of porpoise skin, and they
shall insert its poles. **9** Then they
shall take a [1]blue cloth and cover
the [a]lampstand for the light, [b]along
with its lamps and its tongs, and
its [2]trays and all its oil vessels, by
which they minister in connection
to it; **10** and they shall put it and all
its utensils in a covering of porpoise
skin and shall put it on the carrying
bars. **11** And over the golden altar they
shall spread a [1]blue cloth and cover
it with a covering of porpoise skin
and shall insert its poles; **12** and they
shall take all the utensils of ministry,
with which they minister in the sanc-
tuary, and put them in a [1]blue cloth
and cover them with a covering of
porpoise skin and put them on the
carrying bars. **13** Then they shall take
away the [1]ashes from the [a]altar and
spread a purple cloth over it. **14** They
shall also put on it all its utensils by
which they minister in connection
with it: the firepans, the flesh hooks
and shovels and the bowls, all the
utensils of the altar; and they shall
spread a cover of porpoise skin
over it and insert its poles. **15** When
Aaron and his sons have finished
covering the holy *objects* and all the
furnishings of the sanctuary, when
the camp is to set out, after that the
sons of Kohath shall come to carry
*them*, so that they will not touch the
holy *objects* [a]and die. These are the
[1]things in the tent of meeting which
the sons of Kohath are to carry.
**16** "And the assignment of Eleazar
the son of Aaron the priest is [a]the oil
for the light and the [b]fragrant incense
and [c]the continual grain offering and
[d]the anointing oil—the assignment
of all the [1]tabernacle and of all that
is in it, with the sanctuary and its
furnishings."
**17** Then Yahweh spoke to Moses
and to Aaron, saying, **18** "Do not
let the tribe of the families of the
Kohathites be cut off from among the
Levites. **19** But do this to them that
they may live and [a]not die when
they approach the most holy *objects*:
Aaron and his sons shall go in and
set each of them to his service and
to his load; **20** but [a]they shall not go
in to see the holy *objects* even for a
moment, or they will die."

### *Duties of the Gershonites*

**21** Then Yahweh spoke to Moses,
saying, **22** "Take [1]a census of the sons
of Gershon [2]also, by their fathers'
households, by their families; **23** from
[a]thirty years and upward to fifty years
old, you shall [1]number them; all who
enter to perform the duty of perform-
ing the service in the tent of meeting.
**24** This is the service of the families
of the Gershonites, in serving and
in carrying: **25** they shall carry [a]the
curtains of the tabernacle and the
tent of meeting *with* its covering
and [b]the covering of porpoise skin
that is on top of it, and the screen for

**4:7** [a]Ex 25:30; Lv 24:5-9 [1]Or *violet* **4:9** [a]Ex 25:31 [b]Ex 25:37, 38 [1]Or *violet* [2]Lit *snuff dishes* **4:11** [1]Or *violet* **4:12** [1]Or *violet* **4:13** [a]Ex 27:1-8 [1]Soaked with fat; or *fat ashes* **4:15** [a]Nu 1:51; 4:19, 20; 2Sa 6:6, 7 [1]Lit *burden...of the sons* **4:16** [a]Lv 24:1-3 [b]Ex 30:34-38 [c]Lv 6:20 [d]Ex 30:22-33 [1]Lit *dwelling place*, so in ch **4:19** [a]Nu 4:15 **4:20** [a]Ex 19:21; 1Sa 6:19 **4:22** [1]Lit *the sum* [2]Lit *also them* **4:23** [a]Nu 4:3; 1Chr 23:3, 24, 27 [1]Lit *muster*, so in ch **4:25** [a]Ex 40:19 [b]Ex 26:14; Nu 4:6

the doorway of the tent of meeting,
**26** and [a]the hangings of the court,
and the screen for the doorway of the
gate of the court which is around the
tabernacle and the altar, and their
cords and all the equipment for their
service; and all that is to be done,
[l]they shall perform. **27** All the service
of the sons of the Gershonites, in all
their loads and in all their service,
shall be *performed* at the [l]command
of Aaron and his sons; and you shall
assign to them as a responsibility all
their loads. **28** This is the service of
the families of the sons of the Ger-
shonites in the tent of meeting, and
their responsibilities *shall be* [l]under
the direction of Ithamar the son of
Aaron the priest.

### *Duties of the Merarites*

**29** "*As for* the sons of Merari, you
shall number them by their families,
by their fathers' households; **30** from
[a]thirty years and upward even to fifty
years old, you shall number them,
everyone who enters the duty of
performing the service of the tent
of meeting. **31** Now this is the respon-
sibility of their loads, for all their
service in the tent of meeting: the
boards of the tabernacle and its bars
and its pillars and its bases, **32** and
the pillars around the court and their
bases and their pegs and their cords,
with all their equipment and with all
their service; and you shall assign
*each man* by name the items of the
responsibility of [l]his load. **33** This
is the service of the families of the
*sons of Merari,* according to all their
service in the tent of meeting, [l]under
the direction of Ithamar the son of
Aaron the priest."

**34** So Moses and Aaron and the
leaders of the congregation num-
bered the sons of the Kohathites by
their families and by their fathers'
households, **35** from [a]thirty years
and upward even to fifty years old,
everyone who entered the duty
of service in the tent of meeting.
**36** Their numbered men by their
families were 2,750. **37** These are
the numbered men of the Kohathite
families, everyone who was serving
in the tent of meeting, whom Moses
and Aaron numbered according to
the [l]commandment of Yahweh by the
hand of Moses.

**38** The numbered men of the sons
of Gershon by their families and by
their fathers' households, **39** from
thirty years and upward even to
fifty years old, everyone who en-
tered the duty of service in the tent
of meeting, **40** their numbered men
by their families, by their fathers'
households, were 2,630. **41** These are
the numbered men of the families of
the sons of Gershon, everyone who
was serving in the tent of meeting,
whom Moses and Aaron numbered
according to the [l]commandment of
Yahweh.

**42** The numbered men of the fam-
ilies of the sons of Merari by their
families, by their fathers' households,
**43** from [a]thirty years and upward
even to fifty years old, everyone who
entered the duty of service in the tent
of meeting, **44** their numbered men
by their families were 3,200. **45** These
are the numbered men of the families

---

**4:26** [a]Ex 38:9 [l]Lit *so they shall serve* **4:27** [l]Lit *mouth* **4:28** [l]Lit *in the hand* **4:30** [a]Nu 4:3; 8:24-26
**4:32** [l]Lit *their* **4:33** [l]Lit *in the hand* **4:35** [a]1Chr 23:24 **4:37** [l]Lit *mouth* **4:41** [l]Lit *mouth*
**4:43** [a]Nu 8:24-26

of the sons of Merari, whom Moses and Aaron numbered according to the [1]commandment of Yahweh by the hand of Moses.

**46** All the numbered men of the Levites, whom Moses and Aaron and the leaders of Israel numbered, by their families and by their fathers' households, **47** from thirty years and upward even to fifty years old, everyone who could enter to perform the work of service and the service of carrying in the tent of meeting, **48** their numbered men were [a]8,580. **49** According to the [1]word of Yahweh by the hand of Moses, they [a]were numbered, everyone by his serving or carrying; thus *these were* his numbered men, just as Yahweh had commanded Moses.

### *Unclean Sent Outside the Camp*

**5** Then Yahweh spoke to Moses, saying, **2** "Command the sons of Israel that they [a]send away from the camp every leper and everyone having a [b]discharge and everyone who is [c,1]unclean because of a *dead* person. **3** You shall send away both male and female; you shall send them outside the camp so that they will not defile their camp where I dwell [a]in their midst." **4** And the sons of Israel did so and sent them outside the camp; just as Yahweh had spoken to Moses, thus the sons of Israel did.

### *Restitution for Sins*

**5** Then Yahweh spoke to Moses, saying, **6** "Speak to the sons of Israel, '[a]When a man or woman commits any of the sins of mankind, acting unfaithfully against Yahweh, and that person is guilty, **7** then [1]he shall [a]confess [2]his sins which [3]he has committed, and he [b]shall make restitution in full for his wrong and add to it one-fifth of it and give *it* to him whom he has [4]wronged. **8** But if the man has no *kinsman* redeemer to whom restitution may be made for the wrong, the restitution which is made for the wrong *must go* to Yahweh for the priest, besides the ram of atonement, by which atonement is made for him. **9** [a]Also every [1]contribution pertaining to all the holy *gifts* of the sons of Israel, which they bring near to the priest, shall be his. **10** So every man's holy *gifts* shall be his; whatever any man gives to the priest, it [a]becomes his.'"

### *The Statutes of Jealousy*

**11** Then Yahweh spoke to Moses, saying, **12** "Speak to the sons of Israel and say to them, 'If any man's wife [a]goes astray and is unfaithful to him, **13** and a man lies [a]sexually with her, and it is hidden from the eyes of her husband, and she is [1]undetected; but she has defiled herself, and there is no witness against her, and she has not been caught in the act, **14** [1]if a spirit of [a]jealousy comes over him and he is jealous of his wife and she has defiled herself, or if a spirit of jealousy comes over him and he is jealous of his wife but she has not defiled herself, **15** the man shall then bring his wife to the priest and shall bring *as* [1]an offering for her

---

**4:45** [1]Lit *mouth* **4:48** [a]Nu 3:39 **4:49** [a]Nu 1:47 [1]Lit *mouth* ◆ **5:2** [a]Lv 13:8, 46; Nu 12:10, 14, 15 [b]Lv 15:2 [c]Lv 21:1; Nu 9:6-10; 19:11 [1]Or *defiled*, cf. 5:3, 13, 14 **5:3** [a]Lv 26:12; Nu 35:34 **5:6** [a]Lv 5:14-6:7 **5:7** [a]Lv 5:5; 26:40, 41; Jos 7:19 [b]Lv 6:4, 5 [1]Lit *they* [2]Lit *their* [3]Lit *they have* [4]Lit *guilty* **5:9** [a]Lv 7:32, 34; 10:14, 15 [1]Lit *heave offering* **5:10** [a]Lv 10:13 **5:12** [a]Nu 5:19-21, 29 **5:13** [a]Lv 18:20; 20:10 [1]Lit *concealed* **5:14** [a]Pr 6:34; SS 8:6 [1]Lit *and* **5:15** [1]Lit *her*

one-tenth of an [2]ephah of barley
meal; he shall not pour oil on it nor
put frankincense on it, for it is a grain
offering of jealousy, a grain offering
of remembrance, [a]a reminder of
iniquity.
**16** 'Then the priest shall bring
her near and have her stand before
Yahweh, **17** and the priest shall take
holy water in an earthenware vessel;
and the priest shall take some of
the dust that is on the floor of the
tabernacle and put *it* into the water.
**18** The priest shall then have the
woman stand before Yahweh and
let *the hair of* the woman's head go
loose, and he shall place the grain
offering of remembrance [1]in her
hands, which is the grain offering of
jealousy; and in the hand of the priest
is to be the water of bitterness that
brings curses. **19** Then the priest shall
have her swear *an oath* and shall say
to the woman, "If no man has lain
with you, and if you have not [a]gone
astray into [1]defilement, *being* under
*the authority of* your husband, be
free from this water of bitterness
that brings curses; **20** if you, howev-
er, have [a]gone astray, *being* under
*the authority of* your husband, and
if you have defiled yourself, and a
man other than your husband has
lain with you" **21** (then the priest
shall have the woman [a]swear with
the oath of the curse, and the priest
shall say to the woman), "Yahweh
make you a curse and an oath among
your people by Yahweh making your
thigh fall away and your abdomen
*swell;* **22** *and this* water that brings
curses shall go into your [1]stomach
and make your abdomen swell and
your thigh fall away." And the woman
[a]shall say, "Amen. Amen."
**23** 'The priest shall then write these
curses on a scroll, and he shall [1]wash
them off into the water of bitterness.
**24** Then he shall make the woman
drink the water of bitterness that
brings curses, so that the water which
brings a curse will go into her to cause
bitterness. **25** And the priest shall take
the grain offering of jealousy from the
woman's hand, and he shall wave the
grain offering before Yahweh and
bring it near to the altar; **26** and [a]the
priest shall take a handful of the grain
offering as its memorial offering and
offer *it* up in smoke on the altar, and
afterward he shall make the woman
drink the water. **27** So he will have her
drink the water, and it will be that, if
she has defiled herself and has been
unfaithful to her husband, that the
water which brings curses will go
into her to *cause* bitterness, and her
abdomen will swell and her thigh will
fall away, and the woman will become
[a]a curse among her people. **28** But if
the woman has not defiled herself
and is clean, she will then be free and
conceive a seed.
**29** 'This is the law of jealousy: when
a wife, *being* under *the authority of*
her husband, [a]goes astray and defiles
herself, **30** or when a spirit of jealousy
comes over a man and he is jealous
of his wife, he shall then make the
woman stand before Yahweh, and
the priest shall apply all this law to
her. **31** Moreover, the man will be free
from [1]guilt, but that woman shall
[a]bear her [1]guilt.'"

---

**5:15** [a]1Ki 17:18; Eze 29:16 [2]An ephah was approx. 21 qt. or 23 l **5:18** [1]Lit *on her palms* **5:19** [a]Nu 5:12 [1]Or *uncleanness* **5:20** [a]Nu 5:12 **5:21** [a]Jos 6:26; 1Sa 14:24; Ne 10:29 **5:22** [a]Dt 27:15 [1]Or *inward parts* **5:23** [1]Lit *wipe* **5:26** [a]Lv 2:2, 9 **5:27** [a]Jer 29:18; 42:18; 44:12 **5:29** [a]Nu 5:12 **5:31** [a]Lv 20:17 [1]Or *iniquity*

### *The Nazirite Vow*

6 Again Yahweh spoke to Moses,
saying, 2 “Speak to the sons of
Israel and say to them, ‘When a man
or woman makes a [1]special vow, the
vow of [a]a [2]Nazirite, to dedicate
himself as a Nazirite to Yahweh, 3 he
shall [a]abstain as a Nazirite from wine
and strong drink; he shall drink no
vinegar, whether made from wine
or strong drink, nor shall he drink
any grape juice nor eat fresh or dried
grapes. 4 All the days of his [1]Nazirite
*vow* he shall not eat anything that is
produced by the grape vine, from *the*
seeds even to *the* skin.

5 ‘All the days of his vow as a Naz-
irite [a]no razor shall pass over his
head. He shall be holy until the days
are fulfilled for which he dedicated
himself as a Nazirite to Yahweh; he
shall let the locks of hair on his head
grow long.

6 ‘[a]All the days of his dedication
as a Nazirite to Yahweh he shall not
go near to a dead person. 7 He [a]shall
not defile himself for his father or
for his mother, for his brother or for
his sister, when they die, because
the Nazirite *vow* to his God is on his
head. 8 All the days of his Nazirite
*vow* he is holy to Yahweh.

9 ‘But if a man dies very suddenly
beside him and he defiles the head
*of hair during* his Nazirite *vow*, then
[a]he shall shave his head on the day
when he becomes clean; [b]he shall
shave it on the seventh day. 10 Then
on the eighth day he shall bring [a]two
turtledoves or two young pigeons to
the priest, to the doorway of the tent
of meeting. 11 And the priest shall
offer [a]one for a sin offering and *the*
other for a burnt offering and make
atonement for him [1]concerning his
sin because of the *dead* person. And
that same day he shall set apart his
head as holy, 12 and shall dedicate
to Yahweh the days of his [1]Nazirite
*vow* and shall bring a male lamb a
year old for a guilt offering; but the
former days will be void because his
Nazirite *vow* was defiled.

13 ‘Now this is the law of the Naz-
irite [a]when the days of his Nazirite
*vow* are fulfilled: he shall bring [1]the
offering to the doorway of the tent
of meeting. 14 And he shall bring his
offering near to Yahweh: one male
lamb a year old without blemish for
a burnt offering and one [a]ewe-lamb
a year old without blemish for a
sin offering and one ram without
blemish for a peace offering, 15 and
a basket of [a]unleavened cakes of fine
flour mixed with oil and unleavened
wafers spread with oil, along with
[b]their grain offering and their drink
offering. 16 Then the priest shall bring
*them* near before Yahweh and shall
offer his sin offering and his burnt
offering. 17 He shall also offer with
the ram a sacrifice of peace offerings
to Yahweh, together with the basket
of unleavened cakes; the priest shall
likewise offer its grain offering and
its drink offering. 18 [a]The Nazirite
shall then shave the head *of hair* for
his Nazirite *vow* at the doorway of
the tent of meeting and take the hair
of his head of his Nazirite *vow* and
put *it* on the fire which is under the

◆ **6:2** [a]Jdg 13:5; 16:17; Am 2:11, 12 [1]Or *difficult* [2]Lit *one separated* **6:3** [a]Lk 1:15 **6:4** [1]Or *living as a Nazirite*, so through v 21 **6:5** [a]1Sa 1:11 **6:6** [a]Lv 21:1-3; Nu 19:11-22 **6:7** [a]Nu 9:6 **6:9** [a]Lv 14:8, 9 [b]Nu 6:18 **6:10** [a]Lv 5:7; 14:22 **6:11** [a]Lv 5:7 [1]Lit *because of that which he sinned* **6:12** [1]Lit *one separated* **6:13** [a]Ac 21:26 [1]Lit *it* **6:14** [a]Lv 14:10; Nu 15:27 **6:15** [a]Ex 29:2; Lv 2:4 [b]Nu 15:1-7 **6:18** [a]Nu 6:9; Ac 21:23, 24

sacrifice of peace offerings. **19** [a]And
the priest shall take the ram's
shoulder *when it has been* boiled,
and one unleavened cake out of the
basket and one unleavened wafer,
and shall put *them* on the [1]hands
of the Nazirite after he has shaved
the *hair* of his Nazirite *vow*. **20** Then
the priest shall wave them for a wave
offering before Yahweh. It is holy for
the priest, together with the breast
offered by waving and the thigh of-
fered by [1]raising up; and [a]afterward
the Nazirite may drink wine.'
**21** "This is the law of the Nazirite
who vows his offering to Yahweh
according to his Nazirite *vow*, in
addition to what *else* [1]he can afford;
according to his vow which he takes,
so he shall do according to the law of
his Nazirite *vow*."

### *Yahweh Blesses the Sons of Israel*

**22** Then Yahweh spoke to Moses,
saying, **23** "Speak to Aaron and to his
sons, saying, 'Thus [a]you shall bless the
sons of Israel. You shall say to them:

**24** Yahweh [a]bless you,
   and [b]keep you;

**25** Yahweh [a]make His face
   shine on you,
And [b]be gracious to you;

**26** Yahweh [a]lift up His
   [1]face on you,
And [b]give you peace.'

**27** "So they shall [a,1]invoke My name
on the sons of Israel, and I *then* will
bless them."

### *Offerings of the Leaders*

**7** Now it happened on [a]the day
that Moses had finished setting
up the tabernacle, that he [b]anointed
it and set it apart as holy with all its
furnishings and the altar and all
its utensils; he anointed them and
set them apart as holy. **2** Then [a]the
leaders of Israel, the heads of their
fathers' households, [b]brought an
offering near (they were the leaders
of the tribes; they were the ones who
[1]were over the [2]numbered men).
**3** And they brought their offering
before Yahweh, six [a]covered carts
and twelve oxen, a cart for *every* two
of the leaders and an ox for each one,
and they brought them near before
the tabernacle. **4** Then Yahweh spoke
to Moses, saying, **5** "Accept *these
things* from them, that they may be
[1]used in the service of the tent of
meeting, and you shall give them to
the Levites, *to* each man according
to his service." **6** So Moses took the
carts and the oxen and gave them
to the Levites. **7** Two carts and four
oxen he gave to the sons of Gershon,
according to [a]their service, **8** and
four carts and eight oxen he gave
to the sons of Merari, according to
[a]their service, under the [1]direction of
Ithamar the son of Aaron the priest.
**9** But he did not give *any* to the sons
of Kohath because theirs *was* [a]the
service of the holy *objects, which*
they carried on the shoulder.
**10** And the leaders brought near
the dedication *offering* [1]for the al-
tar [2]when [a]it was anointed, so the

**6:19** [a]Lv 7:28-34 [1]Lit *palms* **6:20** [a]Ecc 9:7 [1]Or *heaving up* **6:21** [1]Lit *his hand can reach*
**6:23** [a]1Chr 23:13 **6:24** [a]Dt 28:3-6; Ps 28:9 [b]1Sa 2:9; Ps 17:8 **6:25** [a]Ps 80:3, 7, 19 [b]Ps 86:16
**6:26** [a]Ps 4:6; 44:3 [b]Ps 29:11; 37:37 [1]Or *countenance* **6:27** [a]2Sa 7:23; 2Chr 7:14 [1]Lit *put*
◆ **7:1** [a]Ex 40:17 [b]Ex 40:9-11; Nu 7:10, 84, 88 **7:2** [a]Nu 1:5-16 [b]2Chr 35:8 [1]Lit *stood* [2]Lit *mustered*
**7:3** [a]Is 66:20 **7:5** [1]Lit *for serving* **7:7** [a]Nu 4:24-26 **7:8** [a]Nu 4:31, 32 [1]Lit *hand* **7:9** [a]Nu 4:5-15
**7:10** [a]Nu 7:1; 2Chr 7:9 [1]Lit *of* [2]Lit *in the day that*

leaders brought their offering near
before the altar. **11** Then Yahweh
said to Moses, "Let them bring their
offering near, one leader each day, for
the dedication of the altar."

**12** Now the one who brought his
offering near on the first day was
Nahshon the son of Amminadab, of
the tribe of Judah; **13** and his offering
*was* one silver [a,1]dish whose weight
*was* 130 *shekels*, one silver bowl of 70
shekels, [b]according to the [2]shekel of
the sanctuary, both of them full of
fine flour mixed with oil for a grain
offering; **14** one gold pan of 10 *shekels*,
full of incense; **15** one bull from the
herd, one ram, one male lamb one
year old, for a burnt offering; **16** [a]one
male goat for a sin offering; **17** and for
the sacrifice of peace offerings, two
oxen, five rams, five male goats, five
male lambs one year old. This *was*
the offering of [a]Nahshon the son of
Amminadab.

**18** On the second day Nethanel
the son of Zuar, leader of Issachar,
brought *an offering* near; **19** he
brought near as his offering one
silver dish whose weight *was* 130
*shekels*, one silver bowl of 70 shekels,
according to the shekel of the sanc-
tuary, both of them full of fine flour
mixed with oil for a grain offering;
**20** one gold pan of 10 *shekels*, full of
incense; **21** one bull from the herd,
one ram, one male lamb one year
old, for a burnt offering; **22** one male
goat for a sin offering; **23** and for the
sacrifice of [a]peace offerings, two
oxen, five rams, five male goats, five
male lambs one year old. This *was*
the offering of Nethanel the son of
Zuar.

**24** On the third day *it was* Eliab
the son of Helon, leader of the sons
of Zebulun; **25** his offering *was* one
silver dish whose weight *was* 130
*shekels*, one silver bowl of 70 shekels,
according to the shekel of the sanc-
tuary, both of them full of fine flour
mixed with oil for a grain offering;
**26** one gold pan of 10 *shekels*, full of
incense; **27** one bull from the herd,
one ram, one [a]male lamb one year
old, for a burnt offering; **28** one male
goat for a sin offering; **29** and for the
sacrifice of peace offerings, two oxen,
five rams, five male goats, five male
lambs one year old. This *was* the
offering of Eliab the son of Helon.

**30** On the fourth day *it was* Elizur
the son of Shedeur, leader of the
sons of Reuben; **31** his offering *was*
one silver dish whose weight *was*
130 *shekels*, one silver bowl of 70
shekels, according to the shekel of
the sanctuary, both of them full of
fine flour mixed with oil for a grain
offering; **32** one gold pan of 10 *shekels*,
full of incense; **33** one bull from the
herd, one ram, one [a]male lamb one
year old, for a burnt offering; **34** one
male goat for a sin offering; **35** and
for the sacrifice of peace offerings,
two oxen, five rams, five male goats,
five male lambs one year old. This
*was* the offering of Elizur the son of
Shedeur.

**36** On the fifth day *it was* Shelu-
miel the son of Zurishaddai, leader
of the sons of Simeon; **37** his offering
*was* one silver dish whose weight
*was* 130 *shekels*, one silver bowl of
70 shekels, according to the shekel
of the sanctuary, both of them full of
fine flour mixed with oil for a grain

**7:13** [a]Ex 25:29; 37:16 [b]Nu 3:47 [1]Or *platter*, so in ch [2]A shekel was approx. 0.4 oz. or 11 gm, so in ch
**7:16** [a]Lv 4:23 **7:17** [a]Lk 3:32, 33 **7:23** [a]Lv 7:11-13 **7:27** [a]Is 53:7; Jn 1:29; 1Pe 1:19 **7:33** [a]Heb 9:28

offering; **38** one gold pan of 10 *shekels,*
full of incense; **39** one bull from the
herd, one ram, one male lamb one
year old, for a burnt offering; **40** one
male goat for a sin offering; **41** and for
the sacrifice of peace offerings, two
oxen, five rams, five male goats, five
male lambs one year old. This *was*
the offering of Shelumiel the son of
Zurishaddai.

**42** On the sixth day *it was* [a]Eliasaph
the son of Deuel, leader of the sons
of Gad; **43** his offering *was* one silver
dish whose weight *was* 130 *shekels,*
one silver bowl of 70 shekels, accord-
ing to the shekel of the sanctuary,
both of them full of [a]fine flour mixed
with oil for a grain offering; **44** one
gold pan of 10 *shekels,* full of incense;
**45** [a]one bull from the herd, one ram,
one male lamb one year old, for a
burnt offering; **46** one male goat for a
sin offering; **47** and for the sacrifice of
peace offerings, two oxen, five rams,
five male goats, five male lambs one
year old. This *was* the offering of
Eliasaph the son of Deuel.

**48** On the seventh day *it was*
[a]Elishama the son of Ammihud,
leader of the sons of Ephraim; **49** his
offering *was* one silver dish whose
weight *was* 130 *shekels,* one silver
bowl of 70 shekels, according to the
shekel of the sanctuary, both of them
full of fine flour mixed with oil for
a grain offering; **50** one gold pan of
10 *shekels,* full of [a]incense; **51** [a]one
bull from the herd, one ram, one
male lamb one year old, for a burnt
offering; **52** one male goat for a sin
offering; **53** and for the sacrifice of
peace offerings, two oxen, five rams,
five male goats, five male lambs one
year old. This *was* the offering of
Elishama the son of Ammihud.

**54** On the eighth day *it was* [a]Gama-
liel the son of Pedahzur, leader of the
sons of Manasseh; **55** his offering *was*
one silver dish whose weight *was* 130
*shekels,* one silver bowl of 70 shekels,
according to the shekel of the sanc-
tuary, both of them full of fine flour
mixed with oil for a grain offering;
**56** one gold pan of 10 *shekels,* full of
[a]incense; **57** one bull from the herd,
one ram, one [a]male lamb one year
old, for a burnt offering; **58** one male
goat for a sin offering; **59** and for the
[a]sacrifice of peace offerings, two
oxen, five rams, five male goats, five
male lambs one year old. This *was*
the offering of Gamaliel the son of
Pedahzur.

**60** On the ninth day *it was* [a]Abidan
the son of Gideoni, leader of the
sons of Benjamin; **61** his offering *was*
one silver dish whose weight *was*
130 *shekels,* one silver bowl of 70
shekels, according to the shekel of
the sanctuary, both of them full of
fine flour mixed with oil for a grain
offering; **62** one gold pan of 10 *shekels,*
full of [a]incense; **63** one bull from the
herd, one ram, one male lamb one
year old, for a burnt offering; **64** one
male goat for a [a]sin offering; **65** and for
the sacrifice of [a]peace offerings, two
oxen, five rams, five male goats, five
male lambs one year old. This *was* the
offering of Abidan the son of Gideoni.

**66** On the tenth day *it was* [a]Ahiezer
the son of Ammishaddai, leader of

**7:42** [a]Nu 1:14; 10:20 **7:43** [a]Lv 2:5; 14:10 **7:45** [a]Ps 50:8-14; Is 1:11 **7:48** [a]Nu 1:10; 2:18; 1Chr 7:26 **7:50** [a]Dt 33:10; Eze 8:11; Lk 1:10 **7:51** [a]Mic 6:6-8 **7:54** [a]Nu 2:20 **7:56** [a]Ex 30:7 **7:57** [a]Ex 12:5; Ac 8:32; Rev 5:6 **7:59** [a]Lv 3:1-17 **7:60** [a]Nu 1:11; 2:22 **7:62** [a]Rev 5:8; 8:3, 4 **7:64** [a]2Co 5:21 **7:65** [a]Col 1:20 **7:66** [a]Nu 1:12; 2:25

the sons of Dan; 67 his offering *was*
one silver dish whose weight *was*
130 *shekels*, one silver bowl of 70
shekels, according to the [a]shekel of
the sanctuary, both of them full of
fine flour mixed with oil for a grain
offering; 68 one gold pan of 10 *shekels*,
full of [a]incense; 69 one bull from the
herd, one ram, one male lamb one
year old, for a burnt offering; 70 one
male goat for a sin offering; 71 and
for the sacrifice of peace offerings,
two oxen, five rams, five male goats,
five male lambs one year old. This
*was* the offering of Ahiezer the son
of Ammishaddai.

72 On the eleventh day *it was*
[a]Pagiel the son of Ochran, leader
of the sons of Asher; 73 his offering
*was* one silver dish whose weight
*was* 130 *shekels*, one silver bowl of
70 shekels, according to the shekel
of the sanctuary, both of them full of
fine flour mixed with oil for a grain
offering; 74 one gold pan of 10 *shekels*,
full of [a]incense; 75 one bull from the
herd, one ram, one male lamb one
year old, for a burnt offering; 76 one
male goat for a sin offering; 77 and
for the sacrifice of peace offerings,
two oxen, five rams, five male goats,
five male lambs one year old. This
*was* the offering of Pagiel the son of
Ochran.

78 On the twelfth day *it was* [a]Ahira
the son of Enan, leader of the sons
of Naphtali; 79 his offering *was* one
[a]silver dish whose weight *was* 130
*shekels*, one silver bowl of 70 shekels,
according to the shekel of the sanc-
tuary, both of them full of fine flour
mixed with oil for a grain offering;
80 one gold pan of 10 *shekels*, full of
incense; 81 one bull from the herd,
one ram, one male lamb one year
old, for a burnt offering; 82 one male
goat for a sin offering; 83 and for the
sacrifice of peace offerings, two oxen,
five rams, five male goats, five male
lambs one year old. This *was* the
offering of Ahira the son of Enan.

84 This *was* [a]the dedication *offer-
ing* [1]for the altar from the leaders of
Israel [2]when [b]it was anointed: twelve
silver dishes, twelve silver bowls,
twelve gold pans, 85 each silver dish
*weighing* 130 *shekels* and each bowl
70; all the silver of the utensils *was*
2,400 *shekels*, according to the shek-
el of the sanctuary; 86 the twelve
gold pans, full of incense, *weighing*
10 *shekels* apiece, according to the
[a]shekel of the sanctuary, all the gold
of the pans 120 *shekels*; 87 all the
oxen for the burnt offering twelve
bulls, *all* the rams twelve, the male
lambs one year old with their grain
offering twelve, and the male goats
for a sin offering twelve; 88 and all
the oxen for the sacrifice of peace
offerings 24 bulls, *all* the rams 60,
the male goats 60, the male lambs
one year old 60. [a]This *was* the ded-
ication *offering* for the altar after it
was anointed.

89 Now when [a]Moses went into
the tent of meeting to speak with
Him, he heard the voice speaking to
him from above [b]the [1]mercy seat that
was on the ark of the testimony, from
[c]between the two cherubim, so He
spoke to him.

---

**7:67** [a]Ex 30:13; Lv 27:25 **7:68** [a]Ps 141:2 **7:72** [a]Nu 1:13; 2:27 **7:74** [a]Mal 1:11 **7:78** [a]Nu 1:15; 2:29 **7:79** [a]Ezr 1:9, 10; Da 5:2 **7:84** [a]Nu 7:10 [b]Nu 7:1 [1]Lit *of* [2]Lit *in the day that* **7:86** [a]Ex 30:13 **7:88** [a]Nu 7:1, 10 **7:89** [a]Ex 40:34, 35 [b]Ex 25:21, 22 [c]Ps 80:1; 99:1 [1]Or *propitiatory seat, place of atonement*

### *The Seven Lamps*

8 Then Yahweh spoke to Moses,
saying, 2 “Speak to Aaron and say
to him, ‘When you [1]mount the lamps,
the seven lamps will [a]give light in
the front of the lampstand.’” 3 Aaron
therefore did so; he [1]mounted its
lamps at the front of the lampstand,
just as Yahweh had commanded Moses.
4 [a]Now this was the workmanship
of the lampstand, hammered work of
gold; from its base to its flowers it
was hammered work; [b]according to
the pattern which Yahweh had shown
Moses, so he made the lampstand.

### *Cleansing of the Levites*

5 Again Yahweh spoke to Moses, saying,
6 “Take the Levites from among
the sons of Israel and [a]cleanse them.
7 Thus you shall do to them, for
their [1]cleansing: *sprinkle* [2]purifying
[a]water on them, and let them [b,3]use
a razor over their whole [4]body and
[c]wash their clothes, and they will
be clean. 8 Then let them take a bull
from the herd with [a]its grain offering,
fine flour mixed with oil; and a
second bull from the herd you shall
take for a sin offering. 9 So [a]you shall
bring the Levites near before the tent
of meeting. [b]You shall also assemble
the whole congregation of the sons
of Israel, 10 and bring the Levites
near before Yahweh; and the sons of
Israel [a]shall lay their hands on the
Levites. 11 Aaron then shall [1]present
the Levites before Yahweh as a [a]wave
offering from the sons of Israel, that
they may be *qualified* to perform
the service of Yahweh. 12 Now [a]the
Levites shall lay their hands on the
heads of the bulls; then offer the one
for a sin offering and the other for a
burnt offering to Yahweh, to make
atonement for the Levites. 13 And you
shall have the Levites stand before
Aaron and before his sons so as to
present them as a wave offering to
Yahweh.

14 “Thus you shall separate the
Levites from among the sons of Israel,
and [a]the Levites shall be Mine.
15 Then after that the Levites may go
in to serve the tent of meeting. But
you shall cleanse them and [a]present
them as a wave offering; 16 for they
are [a]wholly given to Me from among
the sons of Israel. I have taken them
for Myself [b]instead of every first
issue of the womb, the firstborn of
all the sons of Israel. 17 For [a]every
firstborn among the sons of Israel
is Mine, among the men and among
the animals; on the day that I struck
down all the firstborn in the land of
Egypt I sanctified them for Myself.
18 But I have taken the Levites instead
of every firstborn among the sons
of Israel. 19 [a]And I have given the
Levites as [1]a gift to Aaron and to his
sons from among the sons of Israel,
to perform the service of the sons
of Israel at the tent of meeting and
to make atonement on behalf of the
sons of Israel, so that there will be no
[b]plague among the sons of Israel by
[2]their coming near to the sanctuary.”

20 Thus did Moses and Aaron and
all the congregation of the sons of

◆ **8:2** [a]Ex 25:37; Lv 24:2, 4 [1]Lit *raise up* **8:3** [1]Lit *raised up* **8:4** [a]Ex 25:31-40 [b]Ex 25:9, 31-40; 26:30; 37:17-24 **8:6** [a]Is 52:11 **8:7** [a]Nu 19:9, 13, 20 [b]Lv 14:8, 9 [c]Nu 8:21 [1]Lit *this their cleansing* [2]Lit *water of sin* [3]Lit *cause to pass* [4]Lit *flesh* **8:8** [a]Lv 2:1; Nu 15:8-10 **8:9** [a]Ex 29:4; 40:12 [b]Lv 8:3 **8:10** [a]Lv 1:4 **8:11** [a]Lv 7:30, 34 [1]Lit *wave*, so in ch **8:12** [a]Ex 29:10 **8:14** [a]Nu 3:12; 16:9 **8:15** [a]Ex 29:24 **8:16** [a]Nu 3:9 [b]Ex 13:2; Nu 3:12, 45 **8:17** [a]Ex 13:2, 12, 13, 15; Lk 2:23 **8:19** [a]Nu 3:9 [b]Nu 1:53; 16:46 [1]Lit *given ones* [2]Lit *the sons of Israel's*

Israel to the Levites; according to all that Yahweh had commanded Moses concerning the Levites, so the sons of Israel did to them. **21** [a]The Levites, too, purified themselves from sin and washed their clothes; and Aaron presented them as a wave offering before Yahweh. Aaron also made atonement for them to cleanse them. **22** Then after that the Levites went in to perform their service in the tent of meeting before Aaron and before his sons; just as Yahweh had commanded Moses concerning the Levites, so they did to them.

### *Retirement of the Levites*

**23** Now Yahweh spoke to Moses, saying, **24** "This is what *applies* to the Levites: from [a]twenty-five years old and upward [1]they shall enter to perform *their* duty in the service of the tent of meeting. **25** But at the age of fifty years they shall [1]retire from *their* duty in the service and not serve anymore. **26** They may, however, minister to their brothers in the tent of meeting [a]in order to keep *up* their responsibility, but they *themselves* shall perform no service. Thus you shall deal with the Levites concerning their responsibilities."

### *The Passover*

**9** Thus Yahweh spoke to Moses in the wilderness of Sinai, in [a]the first month of the second year after they had come out of the land of Egypt, saying, **2** "Now, let the sons of Israel observe the Passover at [a]its appointed time. **3** On the fourteenth day of this month, [1]at twilight, you shall observe it at its appointed time; you shall observe it according to all its statutes and according to all its judgments." **4** So Moses [1]told the sons of Israel to celebrate the Passover. **5** [a]And they celebrated the Passover in the first *month*, on the fourteenth day of the month, at twilight, in the wilderness of Sinai; [b]according to all that Yahweh had commanded Moses, so the sons of Israel did. **6** But there were *some* men who were [a]unclean because of a [1]dead person, so that they could not celebrate Passover on that day; so [b]they came near before Moses and Aaron on that day. **7** And those men said to him, "We are unclean because of a [1]dead person. *But* why are we restrained from bringing near the offering of Yahweh at its appointed time among the sons of Israel?" **8** Moses therefore said to them, "[a,1]Wait, and I will listen to what Yahweh will command concerning you."

**9** Then Yahweh spoke to Moses, saying, **10** "Speak to the sons of Israel, saying, 'If any one of you or of your generations becomes unclean because of a *dead* [1]person, or is on a distant journey, he may, however, celebrate the Passover to Yahweh. **11** In the second month on the [a]fourteenth day at twilight, they shall observe it; they [b]shall eat it with unleavened bread and bitter herbs. **12** They [a]shall leave none of it until morning [b]nor break a bone of it; according to all the statute of the Passover they shall celebrate it.

---

**8:21** [a]Nu 8:7 **8:24** [a]Nu 4:3; 1Chr 23:3, 24, 27 [1]Lit *he* **8:25** [1]Lit *return* **8:26** [a]Nu 1:53
◆ **9:1** [a]Ex 40:2, 17; Nu 1:1 **9:2** [a]Ex 12:6; Lv 23:5; Dt 16:1, 2 **9:3** [1]Lit *between the two evenings*, so in ch
**9:4** [1]Lit *spoke to* **9:5** [a]Jos 5:10 [b]Ex 12:1-13 **9:6** [a]Nu 5:2; 19:11-22 [b]Ex 18:15; Nu 27:2 [1]Lit *soul of man*
**9:7** [1]Lit *soul of man* **9:8** [a]Ex 18:15; Ps 85:8 [1]Lit *Stand* **9:10** [1]Lit *soul* **9:11** [a]2Chr 30:2, 15 [b]Ex 12:8
**9:12** [a]Ex 12:10 [b]Ex 12:46; Jn 19:36

**13** [a]But the man who is clean and is
not on a journey, and yet [1]neglects to
celebrate the Passover, that [2]person
shall then be cut off from his people,
for he did not bring near the offering
of Yahweh at its appointed time.
That man [b]will bear his sin. **14** [a]If a
sojourner sojourns among you and
[1]celebrates the Passover to Yahweh,
according to the statute of the Pass-
over and according to its judgment,
so he shall do; you shall have [b]one
statute, both for the sojourner and
for the native of the land.'"

### *The Cloud Covering the Tabernacle*

**15** Now on [a]the day that the taberna-
cle was erected [b]the cloud covered
the tabernacle, the [c]tent of the
testimony, and [d]in the evening it
was like the appearance of fire over
the tabernacle until morning. **16** So it
was continuously; [a]the cloud would
cover it *by day*, and the appearance
of fire by night. **17** [a]Now whenever
the cloud would go up from over
the tent, afterward the sons of Israel
would then set out; and in the place
where the cloud settled down, there
the sons of Israel would camp. **18** At
the [1]command of Yahweh the sons of
Israel would set out, and at the [1]com-
mand of Yahweh they would camp;
[a]as long as the cloud settled over the
tabernacle, they remained camped.
**19** Even when the cloud lingered over
the tabernacle for many days, [1]the
sons of Israel would keep the charge
of Yahweh and not set out. **20** If
[1]sometimes the cloud remained a few
days over the tabernacle, [a]according
to the [2]command of Yahweh they
remained camped. Then according
to the [2]command of Yahweh they
set out. **21** If [1]sometimes the cloud
[2]remained from evening until morn-
ing, when the cloud was lifted in the
morning, they would move out; or
*if it remained* in the daytime and at
night, whenever the cloud was lifted,
they would set out. **22** Whether it was
two days or a month or a year that the
cloud lingered over the tabernacle,
dwelling above it, the sons of Israel
remained camped and did not set out;
but [a]when it was lifted, they did set
out. **23** [a]At the [1]command of Yahweh
they camped, and at the [1]command
of Yahweh they set out; they kept the
charge of Yahweh, according to the
[1]command of Yahweh by the hand
of Moses.

### *The Silver Trumpets*

**10** Yahweh spoke further to Moses,
saying, **2** "Make yourself two
trumpets of silver, of hammered work
you shall make them; and you shall
use them for [a]summoning the con-
gregation and for having the camps
set out. **3** [a]So both will be blown,
and all the congregation shall gather
themselves to you at the doorway of
the tent of meeting. **4** Yet if *only* one is
blown, then the [a]leaders, the heads of
the [1]divisions of Israel, shall assemble
before you. **5** But *when* you blow an
alarm, the camps that are pitched [a]on
the east side shall set out. **6** Then you
will blow an alarm the second time,

**9:13** [a]Ge 17:14; Ex 12:15, 47 [b]Nu 5:31 [1]Or *ceases* [2]Lit *soul* **9:14** [a]Ex 12:48 [b]Ex 12:49; Lv 24:22; Nu 15:15, 16, 29 [1]Or *would celebrate* **9:15** [a]Ex 40:2, 17 [b]Ex 40:34 [c]Nu 17:7 [d]Ex 13:21, 22
**9:16** [a]Ex 40:34; Ne 9:12 **9:17** [a]Ex 40:36-38; Nu 10:11, 12 **9:18** [a]1Co 10:1 [1]Lit *mouth* **9:19** [1]Lit *and the* **9:20** [a]Ps 48:14; Pr 3:5, 6 [1]Lit *it was that* [2]Lit *mouth* **9:21** [1]Lit *it was that* [2]Lit *was*
**9:22** [a]Ex 40:36, 37 **9:23** [a]Ps 73:24; 107:7; Is 63:14 [1]Lit *mouth* ◆ **10:2** [a]Is 1:13 **10:3** [a]Jer 4:5; Joel 2:15 **10:4** [a]Ex 18:21; Nu 1:16; 7:2 [1]Or *clans*; lit *thousands* **10:5** [a]Nu 10:14

and the camps that are pitched on
[a]the south side shall set out; an alarm
is to be blown for them to set out.
**7** When convening the assembly,
however, you shall blow without
[a]sounding an alarm. **8** [a]The priestly
sons of Aaron, moreover, shall blow
the trumpets; and [1]this shall be for
you a perpetual statute throughout
your generations. **9** Now when you
go to war in your land against the
adversary who [a]attacks you, then
you shall sound an alarm with the
trumpets, that you may be [b]remem-
bered before Yahweh your God and
be saved from your enemies. **10** Also
in the day of your gladness and in
your appointed [1]feasts, and on the
first *days* of your months, [a]you shall
blow the trumpets over your burnt
offerings and over the sacrifices of
your peace offerings; and they shall
be as a remembrance of you before
your God. I am Yahweh your God."

### *Israel Sets Out from Sinai*

**11** Now it happened in [a]the second
year, in the second month, on
the twentieth of the month, *that*
the cloud was lifted from over the
[1]tabernacle of the testimony; **12** and
the sons of Israel set out on [a]their
journeys from the wilderness of
Sinai. Then the cloud settled down
in the [b]wilderness of Paran. **13** [a]So
*they moved out* for the first time ac-
cording to the [1]command of Yahweh
by the hand of Moses. **14** And the
standard of the camp of the sons
of Judah, according to their armies,
[a]set out first, with Nahshon the son
of Amminadab, over its army, **15** and
Nethanel the son of Zuar, over the
tribal army of the sons of Issachar;
**16** and Eliab the son of Helon over the
tribal army of the sons of Zebulun.

**17** [a]Then the tabernacle was taken
down; and the sons of Gershon and
the sons of Merari, who were carry-
ing the tabernacle, set out. **18** Next
[a]the standard of the camp of Reuben,
according to their armies, set out
with Elizur the son of Shedeur, over
its army, **19** and Shelumiel the son of
Zurishaddai over the tribal army of
the sons of Simeon, **20** and Eliasaph
the son of Deuel over the tribal army
of the sons of Gad.

**21** [a]Then the Kohathites set out,
carrying the holy *objects*; and [b]the
tabernacle was set up before their
arrival. **22** [a]Next the standard of the
camp of the sons of Ephraim, ac-
cording to their armies, set out, with
Elishama the son of Ammihud over
its army, **23** and Gamaliel the son of
Pedahzur over the tribal army of the
sons of Manasseh; **24** and Abidan the
son of Gideoni over the tribal army
of the sons of Benjamin.

**25** [a]Then the standard of the camp
of the sons of Dan, according to
their armies, *which formed* the [b]rear
guard for all the camps, set out, with
Ahiezer the son of Ammishaddai
over its army, **26** and Pagiel the son
of Ochran over the tribal army of the
sons of Asher; **27** and Ahira the son of
Enan over the tribal army of the sons
of Naphtali. **28** [1]This was the order of
march of the sons of Israel by their
armies as they set out.

---

**10:6** [a]Nu 10:18 **10:7** [a]Joel 2:1 **10:8** [a]Nu 31:6; Jos 6:4; 2Chr 13:12 [1]Lit *it* **10:9** [a]Jdg 2:18; 1Sa 10:18; Ps 106:42 [b]Ge 8:1; Ps 106:4 **10:10** [a]Ps 81:3-5 [1]Or *times* **10:11** [a]Ex 40:17 [1]Lit *dwelling place*, so in ch **10:12** [a]Ex 40:36 [b]Ge 21:21; Nu 12:16 **10:13** [a]Dt 1:6 [1]Lit *mouth* **10:14** [a]Nu 2:3-9 **10:17** [a]Nu 4:21-32 **10:18** [a]Nu 2:10-16 **10:21** [a]Nu 4:4-20 [b]Nu 10:17 **10:22** [a]Nu 2:18-24 **10:25** [a]Nu 2:25-31 [b]Jos 6:9, 13 **10:28** [1]Lit *These are the settings out of the sons*

29 Then Moses said to [a]Hobab the
son of [b]Reuel the Midianite, Moses'
father-in-law, "We are setting out
to the place of which Yahweh said,
'[c]I will give it to you'; [d]come with us
and we will do you good, for Yahweh
[e]has [1]promised good concerning Is-
rael." 30 But he said to him, "[a]I will
not come, but rather will go to my
*own* land and kin." 31 Then he said,
"Please do not leave us, inasmuch
as you know where we should camp
in the wilderness, and you [a]will be
as eyes for us. 32 So it will be, if you
go with us, that [a,1]whatever good
Yahweh [2]does for us, [b]we will [3]do
for you."

33 [a]Thus they set out from the
mount of Yahweh three days' jour-
ney, with [b]the ark of the covenant
of Yahweh journeying in front of
them for the [1]three days, to spy out
[c]a resting place for them. 34 [a]Now
the cloud of Yahweh was over them
by day when they set out from the
camp.

35 Then it happened when the ark
set out that Moses said,

"[a]Rise up, O Yahweh!
And let Your enemies
be scattered,
And let those [b]who
hate You flee
[1]before You."

36 And when it came to rest, he said,
"[a]Return, O Yahweh,
*To* the myriad [b]thousands
of Israel."

### *The People Complain*

11 Now the people became like
[a]those who complain of ca-
lamity [b]in the ears of Yahweh. And
Yahweh heard *it* and His anger was
kindled, and the fire of Yahweh
burned among them and consumed
*some* of the outskirts of the camp.
2 [a]The people therefore cried out to
Moses, and Moses prayed to Yahweh,
and the fire [1]died out. 3 So the name
of that place was called [a,1]Taberah
because the fire of Yahweh burned
among them.

4 And the [a]rabble who were among
them [1]had greedy desires; and also
the sons of Israel wept again and said,
"[b]Who will give us [2]meat to eat? 5 [a]We
remember the fish which we used to
eat free in Egypt, the cucumbers and
the melons and the leeks and the
onions and the garlic, 6 but now [a]our
[1]appetite is dried up. There is nothing
at all [2]to look at except this manna."

7 [a]Now the manna was like cori-
ander seed, and its appearance like
that of [b]bdellium. 8 The people would
go about and gather *it* and grind *it*
[1]between two millstones or beat *it* in
the mortar, and boil *it* in the pot and
make cakes with it; and its taste was
as the taste of [2]cakes baked with oil.
9 [a]And when the dew fell on the camp
at night, the manna would fall [1]with it.

### *Moses Complains*

10 Now Moses heard the people
weeping throughout their families,

**10:29** [a]Jdg 4:11 [b]Ex 2:18; 3:1; 18:12 [c]Ge 12:7; Ex 6:4-8 [d]Ps 95:1-7; 100:1-5 [e]Dt 4:40; 30:5 [1]Lit *spoken* **10:30** [a]*Jdg 1:16; Mt 21:28, 29* **10:31** [a]Job 29:15 **10:32** [a]Ps 22:27-31; 67:5-7 [b]Lv 19:34; Dt 10:18 [1]Lit *that good which* [2]Lit *does good* [3]Lit *do good* **10:33** [a]Nu 10:12 [b]Dt 1:33 [c]Is 11:10 [1]Lit *3 days' journey* **10:34** [a]Nu 9:15-23 **10:35** [a]Ps 68:1, 2; Is 17:12-14 [b]Dt 7:10; 32:41 [1]Or *from Your presence* **10:36** [a]Is 63:17 [b]Dt 1:10 ◆ **11:1** [a]Nu 14:2; 16:11; 17:5 [b]Nu 11:18; 14:28 **11:2** [a]Nu 12:11, 13; 21:7 [1]Lit *sank down* **11:3** [a]Dt 9:22 [1]Lit *burning* **11:4** [a]Ex 12:38; 1Co 10:6 [b]Ps 78:20 [1]Lit *desired a desire* [2]Lit *flesh*, so in ch **11:5** [a]Ex 16:3 **11:6** [a]Nu 21:5 [1]Lit *soul* [2]Lit *for our eyes* **11:7** [a]Ex 16:31 [b]Ge 2:12 **11:8** [1]Lit *with* [2]Lit *juice of oil* **11:9** [a]Ex 16:13, 14 [1]Lit *on*

each man at the doorway of his
tent; and the anger of Yahweh was
kindled greatly, and it was evil in the
sight of Moses. **11** [a]So Moses said to
Yahweh, "Why have You [1]allowed
this evil toward Your slave? And
why have I not found favor in Your
sight, that You have laid the burden
of all this people on me? **12** Was it I
who conceived all this people? Was
it I who gave birth to them, that You
should say to me, 'Carry them in your
bosom as a [a,1]nurse carries a nursing
baby, to the land which [b]You swore
to their fathers'? **13** Where am I to get
meat to give to [a]all this people? For
they weep before me, saying, 'Give
us meat that we may eat!' **14** [a]I alone
am not able to carry all this people
because it is too heavy for me. **15** [a]So
if You are going to deal thus with me,
please kill me at once, if I have found
favor in Your sight, and do not let me
see my wretchedness."

### *The Spirit Rests upon the Elders*

**16** Yahweh therefore said to Moses,
"Gather for Me [a]seventy men from
the elders of Israel, [b]whom you know
to be the elders of the people and
their officers, and take them to the
tent of meeting, and let them take
their stand there with you. **17** [a]Then
I will come down and speak with you
there, and I will take of [b]the Spirit
*who is upon you, and will* put *Him*
upon them; and they shall bear the
burden of the people with you, so that
you will not bear *it* all alone. **18** And
say to the people, '[a]Set yourselves
apart as holy for tomorrow, and you
shall eat meat; for you have wept
[b]in the ears of Yahweh, saying, "Oh
that someone would give us meat to
eat! For it was good for us in Egypt."
Therefore Yahweh will give you meat,
and you shall eat. **19** You shall eat, not
one day, nor two days, nor five days,
nor ten days, nor twenty days, **20** [1]but
a whole month, until it comes out of
your nostrils and becomes loathsome
to you; because [a]you have rejected
Yahweh who is among you and have
wept before Him, saying, "Why did
we ever go out from Egypt?"'" **21** But
Moses said, "The people, among
whom I am, are 600,000 on foot;
yet You have said, 'I will give them
meat, so that they may eat for a
whole month.' **22** Should flocks and
herds be slaughtered for them, to be
sufficient for them? Or should all the
fish of the sea be gathered together
for them, to be sufficient for them?"
**23** And Yahweh said to Moses, "Is
[a]Yahweh's [1]power limited? Now you
shall see whether [b]My word will
happen for you or not."

**24** So Moses went out and [a]told the
people the words of Yahweh. Also, he
gathered seventy men of the elders
of the people and had them stand
around the tent. **25** [a]Then Yahweh
came down in the cloud and spoke
to him; and He took of the Spirit
who was upon him and placed *Him*
upon the seventy elders. And when
the Spirit rested upon them, they
prophesied. But they did not do *it*
again.

**26** But two men had remained in
the camp; the name of one was Eldad

---

**11:11** [a]Ex 5:22; Dt 1:12 [1]Lit *dealt ill with* **11:12** [a]2Ki 10:1, 5; Is 49:23 [b]Ge 24:7; Ex 13:5, 11; 33:1 [1]Or *foster-father* **11:13** [a]Nu 11:21, 22; Jn 6:5-9 **11:14** [a]Ex 18:18; Dt 1:12 **11:15** [a]Ex 32:32 **11:16** [a]Ex 24:1, 9 [b]Ex 18:25 **11:17** [a]Nu 11:25 [b]1Sa 10:6; Joel 2:28 **11:18** [a]Ex 19:10, 22 [b]Nu 11:1 **11:20** [a]Jos 24:27; 1Sa 10:19 [1]Lit *until* **11:23** [a]Is 50:2; 59:1 [b]Eze 12:25; 24:14 [1]Lit *hand short* **11:24** [a]Nu 11:16 **11:25** [a]Nu 11:17; 12:5

and the name of the [1]other Medad.
And [a]the Spirit rested upon them
(now they were among those who
had been registered, but had not
gone out to the tent), and they proph-
esied in the camp. **27** So a young man
ran and told Moses and said, "Eldad
and Medad are prophesying in the
camp." **28** Then [a]Joshua the son of
Nun, the attendant of Moses from
his youth, said, "[b]Moses, my lord,
restrain them." **29** But Moses said to
him, "Are you jealous for my sake?
[a]Would that all the people of Yahweh
were prophets, that Yahweh would
put His Spirit upon them!" **30** Then
Moses [1]returned to the camp, *both*
he and the elders of Israel.

### *The Quail and the Plague*

**31** [a]Now there went forth a wind
from Yahweh, and it brought quail
from the sea, and let *them* fall beside
the camp, about a day's journey on
this side and a day's journey on the
other side, all around the camp and
[1]about two [2]cubits over the surface
of the ground. **32** And the people
[1]spent all day and all night and all
the next day, and gathered the quail
(he who gathered least gathered [2]ten
[a]homers), and they spread *them* out
for themselves all around the camp.
**33** [a]While the meat was still between
their teeth, before it was chewed, the
anger of Yahweh was kindled against
the people, and Yahweh struck the
people with a very severe plague.
**34** So the name of that place was
called [a,1]Kibroth-hattaavah because
there they buried the people who
had been greedy. **35** From Kibroth-
hattaavah [a]the people set out for
Hazeroth, and they [1]remained at
Hazeroth.

### *Miriam and Aaron Speak Against Moses*

**12** Then Miriam and Aaron spoke
against Moses because of the
Cushite woman whom he had taken
*as a wife* (for he had taken a [a]Cushite
woman); **2** [a]and they said, "Has Yah-
weh indeed spoken only through
Moses? Has He not spoken through
us as well?" And Yahweh heard it.
**3** (Now the man Moses was [a]very
humble, more than any man who was
on the face of the earth.) **4** Suddenly
Yahweh said to Moses and Aaron and
to Miriam, "You three come out to
the tent of meeting." So the three of
them came out. **5** [a]Then Yahweh came
down in a pillar of cloud and stood at
the doorway of the tent, and He called
[1]Aaron and Miriam. And then both
came forward, **6** and He said,

"Hear now My words:
If there is a prophet
among you,
I, Yahweh, shall make Myself
known to him in a [a]vision.
I shall speak with him
in a [b]dream.

**7** "Not so, with [a]My
servant Moses,
[b]He is faithful in all
My household;

---

**11:26** [a]*Nu 24:2;* 1Sa 10:6; 2Chr 15:1; Ne 9:30 [1]Lit *second* **11:28** [a]Ex 33:11; Jos 1:1 [b]Mk 9:38-40
**11:29** [a]1Co 14:5 **11:30** [1]Lit *removed himself* **11:31** [a]Ex 16:13; Ps 78:26-28; 105:40 [1]Or from *about two cubits above* [2]A cubit was approx. 18 in. or 45 cm **11:32** [a]Eze 45:11 [1]Lit *rose* [2]Approx. 65 bu. or 2,300 l, a homer was approx. 6.5 bu. or 230 l **11:33** [a]Ps 78:29-31; 106:15 **11:34** [a]Dt 9:22 [1]Lit *the graves of greediness* **11:35** [a]Nu 33:17 [1]Lit *were* ◆**12:1** [a]Ex 2:21 **12:2** [a]Nu 16:3 **12:3** [a]Mt 11:29
**12:5** [a]Ex 19:9; 34:5 [1]Or *"Aaron and Miriam!"* **12:6** [a]Ge 46:2; 1Sa 3:15 [b]Ge 31:11; 1Ki 3:5, 15
**12:7** [a]Jos 1:1 [b]Heb 3:2, 5

8 [a]With him I speak
mouth to mouth,
Indeed clearly,
and not in riddles,
And he beholds
[b]the form of Yahweh.
Why then were you not afraid
To speak against My servant,
against Moses?"
**9** So the anger of Yahweh burned
against them, and [a]He went away. **10** But
the cloud withdrew from over the tent,
and behold, [a]Miriam *was* leprous, as
[b]*white as* snow. And Aaron turned
toward Miriam, and behold, she *was*
leprous. **11** Then Aaron said to Moses,
"Oh, my lord, I beg you, [a]do not place
*this* sin on us, in which we have acted
foolishly and in which we have sinned.
**12** Oh, do not let her be like one dead,
whose flesh is half eaten away when
he comes from his mother's womb!"
**13** And Moses cried out to Yahweh,
saying, "O God, [a]heal her, I pray!"
**14** But Yahweh said to Moses, "If her
father had but [a]spit in her face, would
she not bear her dishonor for seven
days? Let her be shut up for seven days
[b]outside the camp, and afterward she
may be received again." **15** So [a]Miriam
was shut up outside the camp for seven
days, and the people did not set out
until Miriam was received again.
**16** Afterward, however, the people
set out from Hazeroth and camped
in the *wilderness of Paran.*

### *The Spies Sent into Canaan*

**13** Then [a]Yahweh spoke to Moses saying, **2** "[a]Send out for
yourself men so that they may spy
out the land of Canaan, which I am
going to give to the sons of Israel;
you shall send a man from each
of their fathers' tribes, every one
a leader among them." **3** So Moses
sent them from the wilderness of
Paran at the [1]command of Yahweh,
all of them men who were heads of
the sons of Israel. **4** These then *were*
their names:
from the tribe of Reuben,
Shammua the son of Zaccur;
5 from the tribe of Simeon,
Shaphat the son of Hori;
6 from the tribe of Judah, [a]Caleb
the son of Jephunneh;
7 from the tribe of Issachar,
Igal the son of Joseph;
8 from the tribe of Ephraim,
[a]Hoshea the son of Nun;
9 from the tribe of Benjamin,
Palti the son of Raphu;
10 from the tribe of Zebulun,
Gaddiel the son of Sodi;
11 from the tribe of Joseph,
from the tribe of Manasseh,
Gaddi the son of Susi;
12 from the tribe of Dan,
Ammiel the son of Gemalli;
13 from the tribe of Asher,
Sethur the son of Michael;
14 from the tribe of Naphtali,
Nahbi the son of Vophsi;
15 from the tribe of Gad,
*Geuel the* son of Machi.
**16** These are the names of the men
whom Moses sent to spy out the
land; but Moses called [a]Hoshea the
son of Nun, Joshua.
**17** So Moses sent them to spy out
the land of Canaan and said to them,

**12:8** [a]Dt 34:10; Hos 12:13 [b]Ex 20:4; 24:10, 11; Dt 5:8; Ps 17:15 **12:9** [a]Ge 17:22; 18:33 **12:10** [a]Dt 24:9 [b]Ex 4:6; 2Ki 5:27 **12:11** [a]2Sa 19:19; 24:10 **12:13** [a]Ps 30:2; 41:4; Is 30:26; Jer 17:14 **12:14** [a]Dt 25:9; Job 17:6; 30:10; Is 50:6 [b]Nu 5:1-4 **12:15** [a]Dt 24:9 ◆ **13:1** [a]Dt 1:22, 23 **13:2** [a]Dt 1:22; 9:23 **13:3** [1]Lit *mouth* **13:6** [a]Nu 14:6, 30; Jos 14:6 **13:8** [a]Nu 13:16; Dt 32:44 **13:16** [a]Nu 13:8; Dt 32:44

"Go up [1]there into [a]the [2]Negev; then
go up into the hill country. **18** And see
what the land is like, and whether
the people who live in it are strong *or*
weak, whether they are few or many.
**19** And how is the land in which they
live, is it good or bad? And how are
the cities in which they live, are *they*
[1]like *open* camps or with fortifica-
tions? **20** [a]And how is the land, is it
fat or lean? Are there trees in it or
not? [1]Make an [b]effort then to get
some of the fruit of the land." Now
the time was the time of the first ripe
grapes.

**21** So they went up and spied out
the land from [a]the wilderness of Zin
as far as Rehob, [b,1]at Lebo-hamath.
**22** And they had gone up into [a]the
Negev and [1]came to Hebron where
[b]Ahiman, Sheshai, and Talmai, the
[2]descendants of [c]Anak were. (Now
Hebron was built seven years before
[d]Zoan in Egypt.)

**23** Then they came to the [1]valley
of [a,2]Eshcol and from there cut down
a branch with a single cluster of
grapes; and they carried it on a pole
between two *men* with some of the
pomegranates and the figs. **24** That
place was called the valley of [1]Eshcol,
because of the cluster which the sons
of Israel cut down from there.

### *The Spies Recount What They Saw*

**25** Then they returned from spying
out the land, at the end of forty days,
**26** and went and came to Moses and
Aaron and to all the congregation of
the sons of Israel [1]in the wilderness
of Paran, at [a]Kadesh; and they
brought back word to them and to all
the congregation and showed them
the fruit of the land. **27** Thus they
recounted to him and said, "We went
in to the land where you sent us; and
[a]it certainly does flow with milk and
honey, and [b]this is its fruit. **28** Never-
theless, [a]the people who live in the
land are strong, and the cities are
fortified *and* very large; and more-
over, we saw [b]the [1]descendants of
Anak there. **29** Amalek is living in the
land of [a]the Negev and the Hittites
and the Jebusites and [b]the Amorites
are living in the hill country, and [c]the
Canaanites are living by the sea and
by the side of the Jordan."

**30** Then Caleb quieted the people
[1]before Moses and said, "We should
by all means go up and take posses-
sion of it, for we are surely able to
overcome it." **31** But the men who
had gone up with him said, "[a]We
are not able to go up against the
people, for they are too strong for
us." **32** So they gave out to the sons
of Israel [a]a bad report of the land
which they had spied out, saying,
"The land, which we have passed
through to spy out on, is [b]a land that
devours its [1]inhabitants; and [c]all the
people whom we saw in it are men of
*great* size. **33** There also we saw the
[a]Nephilim (the sons of Anak are part
of the Nephilim); and [b]we became
like grasshoppers in our own sight,
and so we were in their sight."

---

**13:17** [a]*Ge 12:9; 13:1, 3* [1]Lit *here* [2]South country, so in ch **13:19** [1]Lit in **13:20** [a]Dt 1:24, 25 [b]Dt 31:6, 23 [1]Lit *Use your strength* **13:21** [a]*Nu 20:1; 27:14; 33:36* [b]Jos 13:5 [1]Or *to the entrance of* Hamath
**13:22** [a]Nu 13:17 [b]Jos 15:14 [c]Nu 13:28, 33 [d]*Ps 78:12, 43* [1]*Lit one came; some mss they came* [2]Lit *children*
**13:23** [a]Ge 14:13; Nu 13:24; 32:9; Dt 1:24 [1]Or *wadi* [2]Lit *cluster* **13:24** [1]Lit *cluster* **13:26** [a]*Nu 20:1, 14; 32:8* [1]Lit *to* **13:27** [a]Ex 3:8, 17; 13:5 [b]Dt 1:25 **13:28** [a]Dt 1:28; 9:1, 2 [b]Nu 13:33 [1]Lit *born ones*
**13:29** [a]Nu 13:17; 14:25, 45 [b]Jos 10:6 [c]Nu 14:43, 45 **13:30** [1]Lit *toward* **13:31** [a]Dt 1:28; 9:1-3
**13:32** [a]Nu 14:36, 37; Ps 106:24 [b]Eze 36:13, 14 [c]Am 2:9 [1]Or *settlers* **13:33** [a]Ge 6:4 [b]Dt 1:28; 9:2; Jos 11:21

### *The People Rebel*

**14** Then all the congregation [1]lifted
up their voices and cried, and
the people wept [2]that night. **2** And all
the sons of Israel [a]grumbled against
Moses and Aaron; and the whole
congregation said to them, "[b]Would
that we had died in the land of Egypt!
Or would that we had died in this
wilderness! **3** And why is Yahweh
bringing us into this land, [a]to fall by
the sword? [b]Our wives and our little
ones will become plunder; would
it not be better for us to return to
Egypt?" **4** So they said to one another,
"[a]Let us appoint a leader and return
to Egypt."
**5** [a]Then Moses and Aaron fell on
their faces in the presence of all the
assembly of the congregation of the
sons of Israel. **6** And Joshua the son of
Nun and Caleb the son of Jephunneh,
of those who had spied out the land,
tore their clothes; **7** and they spoke
to all the congregation of the sons
of Israel, saying, "[a]The land which
we passed through to spy out is an
exceedingly good land. **8** [a]If Yahweh
is pleased with us, then He will bring
us into this land and give it to us—[b]a
land which flows with milk and hon-
ey. **9** But as for you, only [a]do not rebel
against Yahweh; and do not [b]fear the
people of the land, for they are our
[1]bread. Their [2]protection has been
*removed from* them, and Yahweh is
with us; do not fear them." **10** [a]But
all the congregation said to stone
them with stones. Then [b]the glory
of Yahweh appeared in the tent of
meeting to all the sons of Israel.

### *Moses Prays for the People*

**11** [a]Yahweh said to Moses, "How long
will this people spurn Me? And how
long will [b]they not believe in Me,
despite all the signs which I have
done in their midst? **12** I will strike
them with [a,1]pestilence and dispos-
sess them, and I [b]will make you into
a nation greater and mightier than
they."
**13** [a]But Moses said to Yahweh,
"Then the Egyptians will hear of it,
for by Your power You brought up
this people from their midst, **14** and
they will tell *it* to the inhabitants of
this land. They have heard that You,
O Yahweh, are in the midst of this
people, for [a]You, O Yahweh, are seen
eye to eye, while Your cloud stands
over them; and You go before them in
a pillar of cloud by day and in a pillar
of fire by night. **15** Now if You put this
people to death as one man, [a]then
the nations who have heard of Your
fame will [1]say, **16** 'Because Yahweh
[a]was not able to bring this people
into the land which He swore to
them, therefore He slaughtered them
in the wilderness.' **17** So now, I pray,
let the power of the Lord be great, just
as You have [1]declared, **18** '[a]Yahweh
*is slow to anger and* abundant in
lovingkindness, forgiving iniquity
and transgression; but [b]He will by
no means clear *the guilty*, [c]visiting
the iniquity of the fathers on the

◆ **14:1** [1]Lit *lifted and gave their voice* [2]Lit *in that* **14:2** [a]Nu 11:1 [b]Nu 11:5; 16:13; 20:3, 4; 21:5
**14:3** [a]Ex 5:21; 16:3 [b]Nu 14:31; Dt 1:39 **14:4** [a]Ne 9:17 **14:5** [a]Nu 16:4 **14:7** [a]Nu 13:27; Dt 1:25
**14:8** [a]Dt 10:15 [b]Ex 3:8; Nu 13:27 **14:9** [a]Dt 1:26; 9:23, 24 [b]Dt 1:21, 29 [1]Or *food* [2]Lit *shadow*
**14:10** [a]Ex 17:4 [b]Ex 16:10; Lv 9:23 **14:11** [a]Ex 32:9-13 [b]Ps 106:24 **14:12** [a]Lv 26:25; Dt 28:21 [b]Ex 32:10
[1]Lit *the pestilence* **14:13** [a]Ex 32:11-14; Ps 106:23 **14:14** [a]Ex 13:21; Dt 5:4 **14:15** [a]Ex 32:12 [1]Lit *speak, saying* **14:16** [a]Jos 7:7 **14:17** [1]Lit *spoken, saying* **14:18** [a]Ex 20:6; 34:6, 7; Dt 5:10; 7:9; Ps 103:8; 145:8;
Jon 4:2 [b]Ex 20:5; Dt 5:9; 7:10 [c]Ex 34:7

children [1]to the third and the fourth
*generations.*' **19** [a]Pardon, I pray, the
iniquity of this people according to
the greatness of Your lovingkindness,
just as You also have forgiven this
people, from Egypt even until now."

### *Evil Complainers*

**20** So Yahweh said, "[a]I have pardoned
*them* according to your word; **21** but
indeed, [a]as I live, [b,1]all the earth will
be filled with the glory of Yahweh.
**22** Surely [a]all the men who have seen
My glory and My signs which I have
done in Egypt and in the wilderness,
yet [b]have put Me to the test these ten
times and have not listened to My
voice, **23** [a]shall by no means see the
land which I swore to their fathers,
nor shall any of those who spurned
Me see it. **24** But My servant Caleb,
[a]because he has had a different
spirit and has followed Me fully,
[b,1]I will bring into the land [2]which
he entered, and his seed shall take
possession of it. **25** [a]Now the Ama-
lekites and the Canaanites live in the
valleys; turn tomorrow and set out
to the wilderness by the way of the
[1]Red Sea."

**26** Yahweh spoke to Moses and
Aaron, saying, **27** "How long *shall I
bear* with this evil congregation who
are [a]grumbling against Me? I have
heard the complaints of the sons
of Israel, which they are [1]making
against Me. **28** Say to them, '[a]As I
live,' declares Yahweh, 'just as [b]you
have spoken in My hearing, so I will
surely do to you; **29** [a]your corpses will
fall in this wilderness, even all [b]your
[1]numbered men, according to your
complete number from twenty years
old and upward, who have grumbled
against Me. **30** Surely you shall not
come into the land in which I [1]swore
to make you dwell, [a]except Caleb the
son of Jephunneh and Joshua the son
of Nun. **31** [a]Your little ones, however,
who you said would become plun-
der—I will bring them in, so that
they will know the land which you
have rejected. **32** [a]But as for you, your
corpses will fall in this wilderness.
**33** And your sons shall be shepherds
for [a]forty years in the wilderness, and
they will [1]suffer *for* your [2]unfaithful-
ness, until your corpses come to an
end in the wilderness. **34** According
to the [a]number of days which you
spied out the land, forty days, for
every day you shall bear your [1]guilt
a year, *even* forty years, and you will
know My opposition. **35** [a]I, Yahweh,
have spoken, surely this I will do to
all this evil congregation who are
gathered together against Me. In this
wilderness they shall come to an end,
and there they will die.'"

**36** [a]As for the men whom Moses
sent to spy out the land and who
returned and made all the congrega-
tion grumble against him by bringing
out a bad report concerning the land,
**37** even [a]those men who brought out
the very bad report of the land died

---

**14:18** [1]Lit *on* **14:19** [a]Ex 32:32; 34:9 **14:20** [a]Mic 7:18-20 **14:21** [a]Nu 14:28; Dt 32:40; Is 49:18 [b]Is 6:3; Hab 2:14 [1]Lit *and all* **14:22** [a]1Co 10:5 [b]Ex 5:21; 14:11; 15:24; 16:2; 17:2, 3; 32:1; Nu 11:1, 4; 12:1; 14:2 **14:23** [a]Nu 26:65; 32:11; Heb 3:18 **14:24** [a]Nu 14:6-9 [b]Nu 26:65; 32:12; Dt 1:36; Jos 14:6-15 [1]Lit *him* [2]Lit *where* **14:25** [a]Nu 13:29 [1]Lit *Sea of Reeds* **14:27** [a]Nu 11:1 [1]Lit *complaining* **14:28** [a]Nu 14:21 [b]Nu 14:2; Dt 2:14, 15; Heb 3:17 **14:29** [a]Heb 3:17 [b]Nu 1:45, 46 [1]Lit *mustered* **14:30** [a]Nu 14:24 [1]Lit *lifted up My hand* **14:31** [a]Nu 14:3 **14:32** [a]Nu 26:64, 65; 32:13; 1Co 10:5 **14:33** [a]Dt 2:7; 8:2, 4; 29:5 [1]Lit *bear* [2]Lit *fornications* **14:34** [a]Nu 13:25 [1]Or *iniquities* **14:35** [a]Nu 23:19 **14:36** [a]Nu 13:4-16, 32 **14:37** [a]1Co 10:10; Heb 3:17, 18

by a [b]plague before Yahweh. 38 But
Joshua the son of Nun and Caleb the
son of Jephunneh remained alive out
of those men who went to spy out
the land.

### *Israel Struck Down*

39 Then Moses spoke [a]these words to
all the sons of Israel, and [b]the people
mourned greatly. 40 In the morning,
however, they rose up early and went
up to the [1]ridge of the hill country,
saying, "[a]Here we are; we will go
up to the place which Yahweh has
promised because we have indeed
sinned." 41 But Moses said, "[a]Why
then do you trespass against the
[1]command of Yahweh, when it will
not succeed? 42 [a]Do not go up, for
Yahweh is not among you, so that
you are not [1]defeated before your
enemies. 43 For the Amalekites and
the Canaanites will be there in front
of you, and you will fall by the sword,
inasmuch as you have turned back
from following Yahweh. And Yahweh
will not be with you." 44 But they
went up heedlessly to the [1]ridge of
the hill country; neither [a]the ark of
the covenant of Yahweh nor Moses
moved from the camp. 45 Then the
Amalekites and the Canaanites who
lived in that hill country came down,
and struck them and beat them down
as far as [a]Hormah.

### *Offerings When Entering Canaan*

15 Now Yahweh spoke to Moses,
saying, 2 "[a]Speak to the sons
of Israel and say to them, 'When
you enter the land of your places
of habitation, which I am going to
give you, 3 then make [a]an offering by
fire to Yahweh, a burnt offering or a
sacrifice to [b,1]fulfill a special vow, or
as a freewill offering or in your [c]ap-
pointed times, to make a [d]soothing
aroma to Yahweh, from the herd or
from the flock. 4 [a]And the one who
brings his offering near shall bring
near to Yahweh a grain offering of
one-tenth *of an* [1]*ephah* of fine flour
mixed with one-fourth of a [2]hin of
oil, 5 and you shall prepare wine for
the drink offering, one-fourth of a
hin, with the burnt offering or for
the sacrifice, for [a]each lamb. 6 Or for
a ram you shall prepare as a grain
offering two-tenths *of an ephah* of
fine flour mixed with one-third of a
hin of oil; 7 and for the drink offering
you shall bring near one-third of a
hin of wine as a soothing aroma to
Yahweh. 8 And when you prepare [a]a
*bull* from the herd as a burnt offering
or a sacrifice, to [1]fulfill a special vow,
or for peace offerings to Yahweh,
9 then you shall bring near with the
*bull* from the herd a grain offering
of three-tenths *of an ephah* of fine
flour mixed with one-half a hin of
oil; 10 and you shall bring near as the
drink offering one-half a hin of wine
as an offering by fire, as a soothing
aroma to Yahweh.

11 'Thus it shall be done for each
ox, or for each ram, or for each of
the male lambs, or of the goats.
12 According to the number that you
prepare, so you shall do for everyone

**14:37** [b]Nu 16:49 **14:39** [a]Nu 14:28-35 [b]Ex 33:4 **14:40** [a]Dt 1:41-44 [1]Or *top of the mountain*
**14:41** [a]2Chr 24:20 [1]Lit *mouth* **14:42** [a]Dt 1:42 [1]Lit *smitten* **14:44** [a]Nu 31:6 [1]Or *top of the mountain*
**14:45** [a]Nu 21:3 ◆ **15:2** [a]Lv 23:10 **15:3** [a]Lv 1:2, 3 [b]Lv 22:21 [c]Lv 23:1-44 [d]Ge 8:21; 2Co 2:15, 16;
Php 4:18 [1]Or *make a special votive offering* **15:4** [a]Nu 28:1-29:40 [1]An ephah was approx. 21 qt. or 23 l
[2]A hin was approx. 1 gal. or 3.8 l **15:5** [a]Lv 1:10; 3:6; Nu 15:11 **15:8** [a]Lv 1:3; 3:1 [1]Or *make a special votive offering*

according to their number. 13 All who
are native shall do these things in
this manner, in bringing near an
offering by fire, as a soothing aroma
to Yahweh.

### *Statute for the Sojourner*

14 'And if a sojourner sojourns with
you, or one who may be among you
throughout your generations, and he
[1]offers an offering by fire as a soothing
aroma to Yahweh, just as you do so he
shall do. 15 *As for* the assembly, there
shall be [a]one statute for you and for
the sojourner who sojourns *with you*,
a perpetual statute throughout your
generations; as you are, so shall the
sojourner be before Yahweh. 16 There
shall be [a]one law and one judgment
for you and for the sojourner who
sojourns with you.'"

17 Then Yahweh spoke to Moses,
saying, 18 "Speak to the sons of
Israel and say to them, 'When you
enter the land where I am going to
bring you, 19 then it shall be, that
when you eat of the [a,1]food of the
land, you shall [2]raise up [3]a contri-
bution offering to Yahweh. 20 [a]Of the
first of your [1]dough you shall [2]raise
up a cake as a [3]contribution offer-
ing; as [b]the [3]contribution offering
of the threshing floor, so you shall
raise it up. 21 From the first of your
[1]dough you shall give to Yahweh a
[2]contribution offering throughout
your generations.

22 'But when you [a]unintentionally
fail and do not observe all these com-
mandments, which Yahweh has spo-
ken to Moses, 23 *even* all that Yahweh
has commanded you by the hand of
Moses, from the day when Yahweh
commanded and onward throughout
your generations, 24 then it will be, if
it is done [a]unintentionally, *hidden*
from the sight of the congregation,
that all the congregation shall offer
one bull from the herd for a burnt
offering as a soothing aroma to Yah-
weh, [b]with its grain offering and its
drink offering, according to the *legal*
judgment, and one male goat for a
sin offering. 25 Then [a]the priest shall
make atonement for all the congre-
gation of the sons of Israel, and they
will be pardoned; for it was an error,
and they have brought their offering,
an offering by fire to Yahweh, and
their sin offering before Yahweh, for
their error. 26 So all the congregation
of the sons of Israel will be pardoned,
with the sojourner who sojourns
among them, for *it happened* to all
the people through [a]error.

27 'Also if one person sins [a]unin-
tentionally, then he shall bring near
a one year old female goat for a sin of-
fering. 28 [a]And the priest shall make
atonement before Yahweh for the
person who goes astray when he sins
unintentionally, making atonement
for him [1]that he may be pardoned.
29 You shall have one law for him who
does *anything* unintentionally, for
him who is native among the sons
of Israel and for the sojourner who
sojourns among them. 30 But the
person who does *anything* with a
[a]high hand, whether he is native or
a sojourner, that one is blaspheming
Yahweh; and that person shall be cut

**15:14** [1]Lit *does* **15:15** [a]Nu 9:14; 15:29 **15:16** [a]Lv 24:22 **15:19** [a]Jos 5:11, 12 [1]Lit *bread* [2]Or *heave up* [3]Or *a heave offering* **15:20** [a]Ex 34:26; Lv 23:14 [b]Dt 14:22, 23; 16:13 [1]Or *coarse meal* [2]Or *heave up* [3]Or *heave offering* **15:21** [1]Or *coarse meal* [2]Or *heave offering* **15:22** [a]Lv 4:2 **15:24** [a]Lv 4:2, 22, 27; 5:15, 18 [b]Nu 15:8-10 **15:25** [a]Lv 4:20; Heb 2:17 **15:26** [a]Nu 15:24 **15:27** [a]Lv 4:27-31; Lk 12:48 **15:28** [a]Lv 4:35 [1]Or *and he shall* **15:30** [a]Nu 14:40-44; Dt 1:43; 17:12, 13

off from among his people. **31** Because
he has [a]despised the word of Yahweh
and has broken His commandment,
that person shall be completely cut
off; [b]his [1]guilt *will be* on him.'"

### *A Sabbath-Breaker Put to Death*

**32** Now the sons of Israel were in the
wilderness, and they found a man
[a]gathering wood on the sabbath
day. **33** And those who found him
gathering wood brought him near
to Moses and Aaron and to all the
congregation; **34** and they put him
in [1]custody [a]because it had not been
[2]declared what should be done to
him. **35** Then Yahweh said to Moses,
"The man shall surely be put to
death; [a]all the congregation shall
stone him with stones outside the
camp." **36** So all the congregation
brought him outside the camp and
stoned him [1]to death with stones,
just as Yahweh had commanded
Moses.

**37** Yahweh also spoke to Moses,
saying, **38** "Speak to the sons of Israel,
and tell them that they shall make for
themselves [a]tassels on the corners
of their garments throughout their
generations, and that they shall put
on the tassel of each corner a cord
of blue. **39** And it shall be a tassel for
you [1]to look at and [a]remember all
the commandments of Yahweh, so
*as to do them and not* [2]follow after
your own heart and your own eyes,
after which you played the harlot,
**40** so that you may remember to do
all My commandments and [a]be holy
to your God. **41** I am Yahweh your God
who brought you out from the land
of Egypt to be your God; I am Yahweh
your God."

### *Korah Rises Up Against Moses*

**16** Now [a]Korah the son of Izhar,
the son of Kohath, the son
of Levi, with [b]Dathan and Abiram,
the sons of Eliab, and On the son of
Peleth, sons of Reuben, took *others*,
**2** and they rose up before Moses,
[1]together with some of the sons of
Israel, 250 leaders of the congre-
gation, [a,2]*those* called *upon* by the
assembly, men of renown. **3** Then
they assembled together [a]against
Moses and Aaron, and said to them,
"[b,1]You have gone far enough, for
all the congregation are holy, every
one of them, and [c]Yahweh is in
their midst; so why do you exalt
yourselves above the assembly of
Yahweh?"

**4** And Moses heard *this* and [a]fell
on his face; **5** and he spoke to Korah
and all his congregation, saying, "To-
morrow morning Yahweh will show
who is His, and [a]who is holy, and will
bring *him* near to Himself; even [b]the
one whom He will choose, He will
bring near to Himself. **6** Do this: take
censers for yourselves, Korah and all
[1]your congregation, **7** and put fire in
them, and lay incense upon them in
the presence of Yahweh tomorrow;
and the man whom Yahweh chooses
*shall be* the one who is holy. [a,1]You
have gone far enough, you sons of
Levi!"

---

**15:31** [a]2Sa 12:9; Pr 13:13 [b]Eze 18:20 [1]Or *iniquity* **15:32** [a]Ex 31:14, 15; 35:2, 3 **15:34** [a]Nu 9:8 [1]Or *prison* [2]Lit *declared distinctly* **15:35** [a]Lv 20:2, 27; 24:14-23; Dt 21:21 **15:36** [1]Lit *with stones and he died* **15:38** [a]Dt 22:12; Mt 23:5 **15:39** [a]Dt 4:23; 6:12; 8:11, 14, 19 [1]Lit *and you shall look at it* [2]Lit *seek* **15:40** [a]Lv 11:44, 45 ◆ **16:1** [a]Ex 6:21; Jd 11 [b]Nu 26:9; Dt 11:6 **16:2** [a]Nu 1:16; 26:9 [1]Lit *and men from* [2]Lit *called ones of* **16:3** [a]Nu 12:2; Ps 106:16 [b]Nu 16:7 [c]Nu 5:3 [1]Lit *It is much for you* **16:4** [a]Nu 14:5 **16:5** [a]Lv 10:3; Ps 65:4 [b]Nu 17:5, 8 **16:6** [1]Lit *his* **16:7** [a]Nu 16:3 [1]Lit *It is much for you*

**8** Then Moses said to Korah, "Hear
now, you sons of Levi, **9** [a]is it [1]not
enough for you that the God of Israel
has separated you from the *rest of* the
congregation of Israel, [b]to bring you
near to Himself, to perform the ser-
vice of the tabernacle of Yahweh, and
to stand before the congregation to
minister to them; **10** and that He has
brought you near, *Korah*, and all your
brothers, sons of Levi, with you? And
are you [a]seeking for the priesthood
also? **11** Therefore you and all your
congregation are gathered together
[a]against Yahweh; but as for Aaron,
[1]who is he that [b]you grumble against
him?"

**12** Then Moses sent [1]a summons
to Dathan and Abiram, the sons of
Eliab; but they said, "We will not
come up. **13** Is it [1]not enough that you
have brought us up out of a [a]land
flowing with milk and honey [b]to put
us to death in the wilderness, but you
would also lord it over us? **14** Indeed,
you have not brought us [a]into a land
flowing with milk and honey, nor
have you given us an inheritance of
[b]fields and vineyards. Would you
[c,1]put out the eyes of [2]these men?
We will not come up!"

**15** Then Moses became very angry
and said to Yahweh, "[a]Do not regard
their offering! [b]I have not taken a
single donkey from them, nor have
I done harm to any of them." **16** And
Moses said to Korah, "You and
all your congregation be present
before Yahweh tomorrow, both you
and they along with Aaron. **17** And
each of you take his firepan and put
incense on [1]it, and each of you bring
his censer near before Yahweh, 250
firepans; also you and Aaron *shall*
each *bring* his firepan." **18** So they
each took his *own* censer and put
fire on [1]it, and laid incense on [1]it;
and they stood at the doorway of
the tent of meeting, with Moses and
Aaron. **19** Thus Korah assembled all
the congregation against them at the
doorway of the tent of meeting. And
[a]the glory of Yahweh appeared to all
the congregation.

**20** Then Yahweh spoke to Moses
and Aaron, saying, **21** "[a]Separate
yourselves from among this congre-
gation, [b]that I may consume them
instantly." **22** But they fell on their
faces and said, "O God, [a]God of the
spirits of all flesh, [b]when one man
sins, will You be angry with the entire
congregation?"

**23** Then Yahweh spoke to Moses,
saying, **24** "Speak to the congregation,
saying, '[a]Get back from around the
dwellings of Korah, Dathan and
Abiram.'"

**25** Then Moses arose and went to
Dathan and Abiram, with the elders
of Israel following him, **26** and he
spoke to the congregation, saying,
"[a]Turn aside now from the tents of
these wicked men, and touch noth-
ing that belongs to them, [b]lest you be
swept away in all their sin." **27** So they
got back from around the dwellings
of Korah, Dathan and Abiram; but
Dathan and Abiram came out *and*
stood at the doorway of their tents,

---

**16:9** [a]Is 7:13 [b]Nu 3:6, 9; Dt 10:8 [1]Or *too little for you* **16:10** [a]Nu 3:10; 18:1-7 **16:11** [a]Ex 16:7 [b]1Co 10:10 [1]Lit *what* **16:12** [1]Lit *to call* **16:13** [a]Ex 16:3; Nu 11:4-6 [b]Nu 14:2, 3 [1]Lit *a little thing* **16:14** [a]Nu 13:27; 14:8 [b]Ex 22:5; 23:10, 11; Nu 20:5 [c]Jdg 16:21; 1Sa 11:2 [1]Lit *bore out* [2]Lit *those* **16:15** [a]Ge 4:4, 5 [b]1Sa 12:3 **16:17** [1]Lit *them* **16:18** [1]Lit *them* **16:19** [a]Nu 14:10; 16:42; 20:6 **16:21** [a]Nu 16:45 [b]Ex 32:10, 12 **16:22** [a]Nu 27:16 [b]Ge 18:23-32; Lv 4:3 **16:24** [a]Nu 16:45 **16:26** [a]Is 52:11 [b]Ge 19:15, 17

along with their wives and [a]their
sons and their little ones. **28** And Mo-
ses said, "By this you shall know that
[a]Yahweh has sent me to do all these
deeds; for this is not from my heart.
**29** If these men die [1]the death of all
men or [2]if they suffer the [a]fate of all
men, *then* Yahweh has not sent me.
**30** But [a]if Yahweh creates an entirely
new thing and the ground opens its
mouth and swallows them up with all
that is theirs, and they [b]go down to
Sheol alive, then you will know that
these men have spurned Yahweh."

**31** And it happened that as he
finished speaking all these words,
the ground that was under them
split open; **32** and [a]the earth opened
its mouth and swallowed them up,
and their households, and [b]all the
men who belonged to Korah with
*their* possessions. **33** So they and all
that belonged to them went down
to Sheol alive; and the earth closed
over them, and they perished from
the midst of the assembly. **34** Then
all Israel who *were* around them fled
at their [1]outcry, for they said, "Lest
the earth swallow us up!" **35** [a]Fire
also came forth from Yahweh and
consumed the [b]250 men who were
bringing near the incense.

**36** [1]Then Yahweh spoke to Moses,
saying, **37** "Say to Eleazar, the son of
Aaron the priest, that he shall take
up the censers out of the midst of the
[1]blaze, and *you* scatter [2]the burning
coals abroad; for they are holy. **38** As
for the censers of these [1]men who
have sinned at the cost of their lives,
make them into hammered sheets
for a plating of the altar, since they
brought them near before Yahweh,
and they are holy; and [a]they shall be
for a sign to the sons of Israel." **39** So
Eleazar the priest took the bronze
censers which the men who were
burned had brought near, and they
hammered them out as a plating for
the altar, **40** as a [1]memorial to the
sons of Israel that [a]no [2]outsider who
is not of the seed of Aaron should
come near [b]to burn incense before
Yahweh; so that he will not become
like Korah and his congregation—
just as Yahweh had spoken to him by
the hand of Moses.

### *Grumbling and Plague*

**41** But on the next day all the congre-
gation of the sons of Israel [a]grumbled
against Moses and Aaron, saying,
"You are the ones who have caused
the death of the people of Yahweh."
**42** It came about, however, when the
congregation had assembled against
Moses and Aaron, that they turned
toward the tent of meeting, and be-
hold, the cloud covered it and [a]the
glory of Yahweh appeared. **43** Then
Moses and Aaron came to the front
of the tent of meeting, **44** and Yahweh
spoke to Moses, saying, **45** "[a,1]Get
away from among this congregation,
that I may consume them instantly."
Then they fell on their faces. **46** And
Moses said to Aaron, "Take your
censer and put in it fire from the
altar, and lay incense *on it*; then
bring it quickly to the congregation

---

**16:27** [a]Nu 26:11 **16:28** [a]Ex 3:12-15; 4:12, 15 **16:29** [a]Ecc 3:19 [1]Lit *like the death* [2]Lit *the visitation of all men be visited upon them* **16:30** [a]Job 31:2, 3 [b]Ps 55:15 **16:32** [a]Nu 26:10; Dt 11:6; Ps 106:17 [b]Nu 26:11 **16:34** [1]Or *voice* **16:35** [a]Nu 11:1-3; 26:10 [b]Nu 16:2 **16:36** [1]Ch 17:1 in Heb **16:37** [1]Or *place of burning* [2]Lit *the fire* **16:38** [a]Eze 14:8; 2Pe 2:6 [1]Lit *sinners against their lives* **16:40** [a]Nu 1:51 [b]Ex 30:7-10 [1]Or *reminder* [2]Lit *stranger* **16:41** [a]Nu 16:3 **16:42** [a]Nu 16:19 **16:45** [a]Nu 16:21, 24 [1]Or *Arise*

and [a]make atonement for them, for
[b]wrath has gone forth from Yahweh,
the plague has begun!" **47** Then Aaron
took *it* as Moses had spoken, and ran
into the midst of the assembly, for
behold, the plague had begun among
the people. [a]So he put *on* the incense
and made atonement for the people.
**48** And he took his stand between
the dead and the living, so that the
plague was checked. **49** [a]But those
who died by the plague were 14,700,
besides those who [b]died on account
of Korah. **50** Then Aaron returned
to Moses at the doorway of the tent
of meeting, for the plague had been
checked.

### *Aaron's Rod Buds*

**17** [1]Then Yahweh spoke to Moses,
saying, **2** "Speak to the sons of
Israel, and get from them a rod for
each father's household: twelve rods
from all their leaders according to
their fathers' households. You shall
write each name on his rod, **3** and
write Aaron's name on the rod of
Levi; for there is one rod for the head
*of each* of their fathers' households.
**4** You shall then deposit them in
the tent of meeting in front of [a]the
testimony, where I meet with you.
**5** And it will come about that the
rod of [a]the man whom I choose will
sprout. Thus I will rid Myself of the
grumblings of the sons of Israel, who
are grumbling against you." **6** Moses
therefore spoke to the sons of Israel,
and all their leaders gave him a rod
apiece, for each leader according to
their fathers' households, twelve
rods, with the rod of Aaron among
their rods. **7** So Moses deposited the
rods before Yahweh in [a]the tent of
the testimony.

**8** Now it happened on the next
day Moses went into the tent of the
testimony; and behold, [a]the rod of
Aaron for the house of Levi had
sprouted and put forth buds and
produced flowers, and it bore ripe
almonds. **9** Moses then brought out
all the rods from the presence of
Yahweh to all the sons of Israel; and
they looked, and each man took his
rod. **10** But Yahweh said to Moses,
"Put back the rod of Aaron [a]before
the testimony [1]to be kept as a sign
against the [b,2]rebels, that you may put
an end to their grumblings against
Me, so that they will not die." **11** Thus
Moses did; just as Yahweh had com-
manded him, so he did.

**12** Then the sons of Israel spoke
to Moses, saying, "[a]Behold, we are
breathing our last breath, we are
perishing, we are all perishing!
**13** [a]Everyone who comes near, who
comes near to the tabernacle of
Yahweh, must die. Are we to breathe
our utter last?"

### *Responsibilities of the Levites*

**18** So Yahweh said to Aaron, "You
and your sons and your father's
household with you shall [a]bear the
guilt [1]in connection with the sanctu-
ary, and you and your sons with you
shall bear the guilt [2]in connection
with your priesthood. **2** But bring
near with you also your brothers,
the tribe of Levi, the tribe of your

---

**16:46** [a]Nu 25:13; Is 6:6, 7 [b]Nu 18:5; Dt 9:22 **16:47** [a]Nu 25:6-8, 13 **16:49** [a]Nu 25:9 [b]Nu 16:32, 35
◆ **17:1** [1]Ch 17:16 in Heb **17:4** [a]Ex 25:16, 21, 22; Nu 17:7 **17:5** [a]Nu 16:5 **17:7** [a]Nu 1:50, 53; 9:15
**17:8** [a]Eze 17:24; Heb 9:4 **17:10** [a]Nu 17:4 [b]Dt 9:7, 24 [1]Lit *for preserving* [2]Lit *sons of rebellion* **17:12** [a]Is 6:5
**17:13** [a]Nu 1:51 ◆ **18:1** [a]Ex 28:38; Lv 10:17; 22:16 [1]Lit *of the sanctuary* [2]Lit *of your priesthood*

father, that they may be [a]joined with
you and minister to you, while you
and your sons with you are before
the tent of the testimony. **3** And they
shall thus keep your responsibility
and the responsibility of all the tent,
but [a]they shall not come near to the
furnishings of the sanctuary and [b]the
altar, so that neither they nor you will
die. **4** And they shall be joined with
you and keep the responsibility of
the tent of meeting, for all the service
of the tent; but [1]an outsider may not
come near you. **5** So you shall keep
the [a]responsibility of the sanctuary
and the responsibility of the altar,
[b]so that there will no longer be wrath
on the sons of Israel. **6** And behold,
I Myself [a]have taken your brothers
the Levites from among the sons of
Israel; they are [b]a gift to you, given
to Yahweh, to perform the service
for the tent of meeting. **7** But you
and your sons with you shall [a]keep
your priesthood in everything that
concerns the altar and inside the
veil, and you are to perform service.
I am giving you the priesthood as [b]a
[1]bestowed service, but [c]the [2]outsid-
er who comes near shall be put to
death."

### *The Priests' Portion*

**8** Then Yahweh spoke to Aaron, "Now
behold, I Myself have given you *the
responsibility* of My [a,1]contributions,
even all the holy gifts of the sons of
Israel I have given them to you as a
portion and to your sons as a per-
petual statute. **9** This shall be yours
from the most holy *gifts reserved*
from the fire; every offering of theirs,
even [a]every grain offering and every
[b]sin offering and every guilt offering,
which they shall render to Me, shall
be most holy for you and for your
sons. **10** As the most holy *gifts* you
shall eat it; every male shall eat it.
It shall be holy to you. **11** This also is
yours, [a]the contribution from their
gift, even all the wave offerings of
the sons of Israel; I have [b]given
them to you and to your sons and
daughters with you as a perpetual
statute. Everyone of your household
who is clean may eat it. **12** [a]All the
[1]best of the fresh oil and all the [1]best
of the fresh wine and of the grain,
the first fruits of those which they
give to Yahweh, I give them to you.
**13** [a]The first ripe fruits of all that is
in their land, which they bring to
Yahweh, shall be yours; everyone of
your household who is clean may eat
it. **14** [a]Every devoted thing in Israel
shall be yours. **15** [a,1]Every first issue of
the womb of all flesh, whether man
or animal, which they bring near to
Yahweh, shall be yours; nevertheless
the firstborn of man you shall surely
redeem, and the firstborn of unclean
animals you shall redeem. **16** Now
as to their redemption price, from a
month old you shall redeem them,
*by your valuation*, five [1]shekels in
silver, according to the [1]shekel of the
sanctuary, which is twenty gerahs.
**17** But [a]the firstborn of an ox or the
firstborn of a sheep or the firstborn
of a goat, you shall not redeem; they

---

**18:2** [a]Nu 3:5-10 **18:3** [a]Nu 4:15-20 [b]Nu 1:51; 18:7 **18:4** [1]Lit *a stranger* **18:5** [a]Ex 27:21; Lv 24:3 [b]Nu 16:46 **18:6** [a]Nu 3:12, 45 [b]Nu 3:9 **18:7** [a]Ex 29:9 [b]Nu 18:20; Dt 18:2; Mt 10:8; 1Pe 5:2, 3 [c]Nu 1:51 [1]Lit *service of gift* [2]Lit *stranger* **18:8** [a]Lv 6:16, 18; 7:28-34 [1]Or *heave offerings*, so in ch **18:9** [a]Lv 2:1-16 [b]Lv 6:30 **18:11** [a]Nu 18:1; Dt 18:3 [b]Lv 22:1-16 **18:12** [a]Dt 18:4; 32:14; Ps 81:16; 147:14 [1]Lit *fat* **18:13** [a]Ex 22:29; 23:19; 34:26 **18:14** [a]Lv 27:1-33 **18:15** [a]Ex 13:13, 15; Nu 3:46 [1]Lit *Everything that opens* **18:16** [1]A shekel was approx. 0.4 oz. or 11 gm **18:17** [a]Dt 15:19

are holy. [b]You shall splash their blood
on the altar and shall offer up their
fat in smoke *as* an offering by fire, for
a soothing aroma to Yahweh. **18** And
their [1]meat shall be yours; it shall be
yours like the [a]breast of a wave offer-
ing and like the right thigh. **19** [a]All the
contributions of the holy *gifts*, which
the sons of Israel raise up to Yahweh,
I have given to you and your sons
and your daughters with you, as a
perpetual statute. It is [b]an everlasting
covenant of salt before Yahweh to
you and your seed with you." **20** Then
Yahweh said to Aaron, "[a]You shall
have no inheritance in their land nor
own any portion among them; [b]I am
your portion and your inheritance
among the sons of Israel.

**21** "Now to the sons of Levi, behold, I
have given all the [a]tithe in Israel for an
inheritance, in return for their service
which they perform, the service of the
tent of meeting. **22** [a]And the sons of
Israel shall not come near the tent of
meeting again, or they will bear sin and
die. **23** Only the Levites shall perform
the service of the tent of meeting, and
they shall [a]bear their iniquity; it shall
be a perpetual statute throughout your
generations, and among the sons of
Israel [b]they shall have no inheritance.
**24** For the tithe of the sons of Israel,
which they raise up as a contribution
offering to Yahweh, I have given to the
Levites for an inheritance; therefore
I have said concerning them, '[a]They
shall have no inheritance among the
sons of Israel.'"

**25** Then Yahweh spoke to Moses,
saying, **26** "Moreover, *you* shall speak
to the Levites and say to them, 'When
you take from the sons of Israel [a]the
tithe which I have given you from
them for your inheritance, then you
shall raise up a contribution offering
from it to Yahweh, a [b]tithe of the tithe.
**27** And your contribution offering shall
be reckoned to you as the grain from
the threshing floor or the full produce
from the wine vat. **28** So you shall also
raise up a contribution offering to Yah-
weh from all your tithes, which you
receive from the sons of Israel; and
from it you shall give the contribution
offering of Yahweh to Aaron the priest.
**29** Out of all your gifts you shall raise
up every contribution offering due to
Yahweh, from all the [1]best of them,
[2]the sacred part from them.' **30** And
you shall say to them, 'When you have
raised up from it the best of it, then *the
rest* shall be accounted to the Levites
as the product of the threshing floor
and as the product of the wine vat.
**31** And you may eat it anywhere, you
and your households, for it is your
compensation in return for your ser-
vice in the tent of meeting. **32** And you
will bear no sin by reason of it when
you have raised up the [1]best of it. But
you shall not [a]profane the sacred gifts
of the sons of Israel, so that you will
not die.'"

### *Statute of the Red Heifer*

**19** Then Yahweh spoke to Moses
and Aaron, saying, **2** "This is
the statute of the law which Yahweh
has commanded, saying, 'Speak to
the sons of Israel that they take to
you a [a]red heifer without blemish,

**18:17** [b]Lv 3:2 **18:18** [a]Lv 7:31 [1]Lit *flesh* **18:19** [a]Nu 18:11 [b]2Chr 13:5 **18:20** [a]Dt 10:9; 12:12; 14:27, 29 [b]Dt 18:2; Jos 13:33; Eze 44:28 **18:21** [a]Lv 27:30-33; Dt 14:22-29 **18:22** [a]Nu 1:51 **18:23** [a]Nu 18:1 [b]Nu 18:20 **18:24** [a]Dt 10:9 **18:26** [a]Nu 18:21 [b]Ne 10:38 **18:29** [1]Lit *fat* [2]Lit *its* **18:32** [a]Lv 22:15, 16 [1]Lit *fat* ◆**19:2** [a]Lv 22:20-25

in which is no defect *and* [b]on which
a yoke has never [1]been placed. **3** And
you shall give it to [a]Eleazar the priest,
and it shall [b]be brought outside the
camp and be slaughtered in his
presence. **4** Next Eleazar the priest
shall take some of its blood with
his finger and [a]sprinkle some of its
blood toward the front of the tent
of meeting seven times. **5** Then the
heifer shall be burned in his sight;
[a]its hide and its flesh and its blood,
with its refuse, shall be burned. **6** And
the priest shall take [a]cedar wood and
hyssop and scarlet *material* and cast
it into the midst of the [1]burning heif-
er. **7** The priest [a]shall then wash his
clothes and bathe his [1]body in water
and afterward come into the camp,
but the priest shall be unclean until
evening. **8** The one who burns it shall
also wash his clothes in water and
bathe his [1]body in water and shall
be unclean until evening. **9** Now a
man who is clean shall gather up the
ashes of the heifer and deposit them
outside the camp in a clean place,
and [1]the congregation of the sons
of Israel shall keep it as [a]water to
remove impurity; it is [2]purification
from sin. **10** And the one who gathers
the ashes of the heifer [a]shall wash
his clothes and be unclean until
evening; and it shall be a perpetual
statute to the sons of Israel and to
*the sojourner who* sojourns among
them.

**11** '[a]The one who touches the
corpse of any [1]person shall be
unclean for seven days. **12** That one
shall [a]purify himself from unclean-
ness with [1]the water on the third day
and on the seventh day, *and then* he
will be clean; but if he does not purify
himself on the third day and on the
seventh day, he will not be clean.
**13** [a]Anyone who touches a corpse,
the [1]body of a man who has died,
and does not purify himself, [b,2]makes
the [3]tabernacle of Yahweh unclean;
and that person shall be cut off from
Israel. Because the water for impurity
was not [c,4]splashed on him, he shall
be unclean; his uncleanness is still
on him.

**14** 'This is the law when a man dies
in a tent: everyone who comes into
the tent and everyone who is in the
tent shall be unclean for seven days.
**15** And every open vessel, which has
no covering [1]tied down on it, shall
be unclean. **16** [a]Also, anyone who in
the open field touches one who has
been slain with a sword or who has
died *naturally*, or a human bone or
a grave, shall be unclean for seven
days. **17** Then for the unclean *person*
they shall take some of the [1]ashes of
the [2]burnt [a,3]purification from sin
and [4]flowing water shall be [5]added
to them in a vessel. **18** And a clean
person shall take hyssop and dip *it* in
the water and sprinkle *it* on the tent
*and on all the* furnishings and on the
persons who were there and on the
one who touched the bone or the one
slain or the one dying *naturally* or
the grave. **19** Then the clean *person*

---

**19:2** [b]Dt 21:3 [1]Lit *come up* **19:3** [a]Nu 3:4 [b]Lv 4:11, 12, 21; Nu 19:9 **19:4** [a]Lv 4:6, 17; 16:14
**19:5** [a]Ex 29:14; Lv 4:11, 12 **19:6** [a]Lv 14:4 [1]Lit *burning of the heifer* **19:7** [a]Lv 16:26, 28; 22:6 [1]Lit *flesh*
**19:8** [1]Lit *flesh* **19:9** [a]Nu 8:7; 31:23 [1]Lit *it shall be to the congregation...Israel, for a guarding as water of impurity* [2]Or *a sin offering* **19:10** [a]Nu 19:7 **19:11** [a]Lv 21:1, 11; Nu 5:2; 6:6; Ac 21:26, 27 [1]Lit *soul of man* **19:12** [a]Nu 19:19; 31:19 [1]Lit *it* **19:13** [a]Lv 7:21; 22:3-7 [b]Lv 15:31; 20:3; Nu 19:20 [c]Nu 19:19 [1]Lit *soul* [2]Or *defiles*, cf. Lv 20:3; Eze 23:28 [3]Lit *dwelling place* [4]Lit *thrown* **19:15** [1]Lit *cord* **19:16** [a]Nu 31:19
**19:17** [a]Nu 19:9 [1]Lit *dust* [2]Lit *burning of the* [3]Or *sin offering* [4]Lit *living* [5]Lit *put*

[a]shall sprinkle on the unclean on the
third day and on the seventh day; and
on the seventh day he shall purify
him from uncleanness, and he shall
wash his clothes and bathe *himself* in
water and shall be clean by evening.
**20** 'But the man who is unclean
and does not purify himself from
uncleanness, that person shall be cut
off from the midst of the assembly
because he has [a,1]made the sanctuary
of Yahweh unclean; the water for
impurity has not been [2]splashed
on him; he is unclean. **21** So it shall
be a perpetual statute for them.
And he [a]who sprinkles the water
for impurity shall wash his clothes,
and he who touches the water for
impurity shall be unclean until eve-
ning. **22** [a]Furthermore, anything that
the unclean *person* touches shall be
unclean; and the person who touches
*it* shall be unclean until evening.'"

### *No Water for the Congregation*

**20** Then the sons of Israel, the
whole congregation, came
to the [a]wilderness of Zin in the first
month; and the people stayed at
Kadesh. And Miriam died there and
was buried there.
**2** [a]Now there was no water for the
congregation, [b]and they assembled
themselves against Moses and Aaron.
**3** [a]The people thus contended with
Moses and spoke, saying, "[b]If only
we had breathed our last [c]when our
brothers breathed their last before
Yahweh! **4** [a]Why then have you
brought the assembly of Yahweh
into this *wilderness,* for us and our
beasts to die [1]here? **5** And why have
you made us come up from Egypt,
to bring us into this evil place? [a]It is
not a place of [1]grain or figs or vines
or pomegranates, nor is there water
to drink." **6** Then Moses and Aaron
came in from the presence of the
assembly to the doorway of the tent
of meeting and [a]fell on their faces.
Then the glory of Yahweh appeared to
them; **7** and Yahweh spoke to Moses,
saying, **8** "Take [a]the rod; and you and
your brother Aaron assemble the
congregation and speak to the rock
before their eyes, that it may yield its
water. You shall thus bring forth water
for them out of the rock and let the
congregation and their beasts drink."

### *Moses Strikes the Rock*

**9** So Moses took the rod [a]from before
Yahweh, just as He had commanded
him; **10** and Moses and Aaron gath-
ered the assembly before the rock.
And he said to them, "[a]Listen now,
you rebels; shall we bring forth water
for you out of this rock?" **11** Then Mo-
ses raised high his hand and struck
the rock twice with his rod; and
[a]water came forth abundantly, and
the congregation and their beasts
drank. **12** But Yahweh said to Moses
and Aaron, "[a]Because you did not
believe Me, to treat Me as holy in the
sight of the sons of Israel, therefore
you shall not bring this assembly
into the land which I have given
them." **13** Those *were* the waters of
[a,1]Meribah [2]because the sons of
Israel contended with Yahweh, and
He proved Himself holy among them.

---

**19:19** [a]Eze 36:25; Heb 10:22 **19:20** [a]Nu 19:13 [1]Or *defiled*, cf. Lv 20:3; Eze 23:28 [2]Lit *thrown* **19:21** [a]Nu 19:7 **19:22** [a]Lv 5:2, 3; 7:21; 22:5, 6 ◆ **20:1** [a]Nu 13:21; 27:14; 33:36 **20:2** [a]Ex 17:1 [b]Nu 16:19, 42 **20:3** [a]Ex 17:2 [b]Nu 14:2, 3 [c]Nu 16:31-35 **20:4** [a]Ex 17:3 [1]Lit *there* **20:5** [a]Nu 16:14 [1]Lit *seed* **20:6** [a]Nu 14:5 **20:8** [a]Ex 4:17, 20; 17:5, 6 **20:9** [a]Nu 17:10 **20:10** [a]Ps 106:33 **20:11** [a]Ps 78:16; Is 48:21; 1Co 10:4 **20:12** [a]Nu 20:24; 27:14; Dt 1:37; 3:26, 27 **20:13** [a]Ex 17:7; Ps 95:8 [1]Lit *contention* [2]Or *where*

### *Edom Refuses Passage*

14 From Kadesh Moses then sent
messengers to [a]the king of Edom:
"Thus your brother Israel has said,
'You [b]know all the hardship that has
befallen us, 15 that our fathers went
down to Egypt, and we stayed in
Egypt a long time, and the Egyptians
treated us and our fathers badly. 16 So
[a]we cried out to Yahweh, and He
heard our voice and sent [b]an angel
and brought us out from Egypt; now
behold, we are at Kadesh, a town on
the edge of your territory. 17 Please
[a]let us pass through your land. We
will not pass through field or through
vineyard; we will not even drink
water from a well. We will go along
the king's highway; we will not turn
to the right or to the left until we pass
through your territory.'"
18 [a]Edom, however, said to him,
"You shall not pass through [1]us, lest
I come out to meet you with the
sword." 19 Again, the sons of Israel
said to him, "We will go up by the
highway, and if I and [a]my livestock
do drink any of your water, [b]then I
will [1]pay its price. Let me only pass
through on my feet, [2]nothing *else*."
20 But he said, "[a]You shall not pass
through." And Edom came out to
meet him with a heavy [1]force and
with a strong hand. 21 [a]Thus Edom
refused to allow Israel to pass through
*his territory;* [b]*so Israel* turned away
from him.
22 Then they set out from [a]Kadesh,
and the sons of Israel, the whole
congregation, came to Mount Hor.

### *The Death of Aaron*

23 And Yahweh spoke to Moses and
Aaron at [a]Mount Hor by the border
of the land of Edom, saying, 24 "Aaron
will be [a]gathered to his people, for he
shall not enter the land which I have
given to the sons of Israel because
[b]you rebelled against My [1]command
at the waters of Meribah. 25 Take
Aaron and his son [a]Eleazar and
bring them up to Mount Hor; 26 and
strip Aaron of his garments and put
them on his son Eleazar. So Aaron
will be [a]gathered *to his people* and
will die there." 27 So Moses did just as
Yahweh had commanded, and they
went up to Mount Hor in the sight
of all the congregation. 28 And Moses
stripped Aaron of his garments and
[a]put them on his son Eleazar, and
[b]Aaron died there on the mountain
top. Then Moses and Eleazar came
down from the mountain. 29 So all
the congregation saw that Aaron
breathed his last, and all the house
of Israel wept for Aaron thirty [a]days.

### *Destruction of Canaanite Cities*

21 Then the Canaanite, the king of
[a]Arad, who lived in the [1]Negev,
heard that Israel was coming by the
way of [2]Atharim, and he fought
against Israel and took some of them
captive. 2 So [a]Israel made a vow to
Yahweh *and said,* "If You will indeed
give this people into my hand, then
I will devote their cities to destruc-
tion." 3 Then Yahweh heard the voice
of Israel and gave the Canaanites
over; so they devoted them and their

---

**20:14** [a]Ge 36:31-39; Dt 2:4 [b]Jos 2:9, 10; 9:9, 10, 24 **20:16** [a]Ex 2:23; 3:7 [b]Ex 14:19 **20:17** [a]Nu 21:22 **20:18** [a]Nu 24:18 [1]Lit *me* **20:19** [a]Ex 12:38 [b]Dt 2:6, 28 [1]Lit *give* [2]Or *no great thing* **20:20** [a]Jdg 11:17 [1]Lit *people* **20:21** [a]Jdg 11:17 [b]Dt 2:8 **20:22** [a]Nu 20:1, 14 **20:23** [a]Nu 33:37 **20:24** [a]Ge 25:8 [b]Nu 20:5, 10 [1]Lit *mouth* **20:25** [a]Nu 3:4 **20:26** [a]Nu 20:24 **20:28** [a]Ex 29:29 [b]Nu 33:38; Dt 10:6; 32:50 **20:29** [a]Ge 1:5; 50:3, 10; Dt 34:8 ◆ **21:1** [a]Nu 33:40; Jos 12:14; Jdg 1:16 [1]South country [2]Or *the spies* **21:2** [a]Ge 28:20; Jdg 11:30

cities to destruction. Thus the name
of the place was called [a,1]Hormah.
**4** Then they set out from Mount
Hor by the way to the [1]Red Sea, to
[a]go around the land of Edom; and
the [2]people became impatient on the
way. **5** And the people spoke against
God and against Moses, "[a]Why have
you brought us up out of Egypt to
die in the wilderness? For there is no
[1]food and no water, and [b,2]we loathe
this miserable food."

### *The Bronze Serpent*

**6** [a]So Yahweh sent fiery serpents
among the people, and [b]they bit
the people so that [c]many people of
Israel died. **7** [a]Then the people came
to Moses and said, "We have sinned
because we have spoken against
Yahweh and against you; [b]pray to
Yahweh, that He may remove the
serpents from us." And Moses prayed
for the people. **8** Then Yahweh said to
Moses, "[1]Make a [a]fiery *serpent* and
set it on a standard; and it will be that
everyone who is bitten and looks at
it, will live." **9** And Moses made a
[a]bronze serpent and set it on the
standard; and it happened, that if a
serpent bit any man, when he looked
to the bronze serpent, he lived.
**10** [a]Then the sons of Israel set out
and camped in Oboth. **11** They then
set out from Oboth and camped at
Iye-abarim, in the wilderness which
is opposite Moab, *east* toward the
sunrise. **12** [a]From there they set out
and camped in [1]Wadi Zered. **13** From
there they set out and camped on
the other side of the Arnon, which
is in the wilderness that comes out
of the border of the Amorites, [a]for
the Arnon is the border of Moab,
between Moab and the Amorites.
**14** Therefore it is said in the Book of
the Wars of Yahweh,

"Waheb in Suphah,
And the wadis of the Arnon,
**15** And the slope of the wadis
That extends to the site of [a]Ar,
And leans to the border
of Moab."

**16** [a]And from there *they continued*
to [1]Beer, that is the well where Yah-
weh said to Moses, "Assemble the
people, that I may give them water."
**17** [a]Then Israel sang this song:

"Spring up, O well! Sing to it!
**18** "The well, which the
leaders dug,
Which the nobles of the
people carved out,
With the scepter *and*
with their staffs."

And from the wilderness *they con-
tinued* to Mattanah, **19** and from Mat-
tanah to Nahaliel, and from Nahaliel
to Bamoth, **20** and from Bamoth to
the valley that is in the land of Moab,
at the top of Pisgah which overlooks
the [1]wasteland.

### *Sihon and Og Struck Down*

**21** [a]Then Israel sent messengers
to Sihon, king of the Amorites,
saying, **22** "[a]Let me pass through
your land. We will not turn off into

**21:3** [a]Nu 14:45 [1]Lit *a devoted thing, destruction* **21:4** [a]Dt 2:8 [1]Lit Sea of Reeds [2]Lit soul of the *people was short* **21:5** [a]Nu 14:2, 3 [b]Nu 11:6 [1]Lit *bread* [2]Lit *our soul loathes* **21:6** [a]Dt 8:15 [b]Jer 8:17 [c]1Co 10:9 **21:7** [a]Nu 11:2; Ps 78:34; Is 26:16; Hos 5:15 [b]Ex 8:8; 1Sa 12:19; Ac 8:24 **21:8** [a]Is 14:29; 30:6; Jn 3:14 [1]Lit *Make for yourself* **21:9** [a]2Ki 18:4; Jn 3:14, 15 **21:10** [a]Nu 33:43, 44 **21:12** [a]Nu 33:45 [1]A dry ravine except during rainy season **21:13** [a]Nu 22:36; Jdg 11:18 **21:15** [a]Nu 21:28; Dt 2:9, 18, 29 **21:16** [a]Nu 33:46-49 [1]Lit *a well* **21:17** [a]Ex 15:1; Ps 105:2 **21:20** [1]Or *Jeshimon* **21:21** [a]Dt 2:26-37; Jdg 11:19 **21:22** [a]Nu 20:16, 17

field or vineyard; we will not drink
water from wells. We will go by the
king's highway until we have passed
through your border." **23** [a]But Sihon
would not allow Israel to pass through
his border. So Sihon gathered all his
people and went out to meet Israel
in the wilderness and came to [b]Jahaz
and fought against Israel. **24** Then
[a]Israel [1]struck him with the edge of
the sword and took possession of his
land from the Arnon to the Jabbok,
as far as the sons of Ammon; for the
[b]border of the sons of Ammon *was*
[2]Jazer. **25** And Israel took all these
cities, and [a]Israel lived in all the
cities of the Amorites, in Heshbon,
and in all her [1]towns. **26** For Hesh-
bon was the city of Sihon, king of
the Amorites. Now it was he who
had fought against the former king
of Moab and had taken all his land
out of his hand, as far as the Arnon.
**27** Therefore those who use proverbs
say,

"Come to Heshbon!
Let it be built!
So let the city of Sihon
be established.

**28** "[a]For a fire went forth
from Heshbon,
A flame from the town
of Sihon;
It devoured [b]Ar of Moab,
The [c,1]dominant [2]heights
*of the Arnon.*

**29** "[a]Woe to you, O Moab!
You perish, O people
of [b]Chemosh!
[c]He has given his sons
as fugitives,
[d]And his daughters
into captivity,
To an Amorite king, Sihon.

**30** "But we have cast them down,
Heshbon perishes
as far as [a]Dibon,
And we have made desolate
even to Nophah,
Which *reaches* to Medeba."

**31** Thus Israel lived in the land of
the Amorites. **32** And Moses sent to
spy out [a]Jazer, and they captured its
towns and dispossessed the Amo-
rites who *were* there.

**33** [a]Then they turned and went up
by the way of Bashan, and Og the king
of Bashan went out to meet them, he
and all his people for battle at [b]Edrei.
**34** But Yahweh said to Moses, "[a]Do
not fear him, for I have given him into
your hand, and all his people and his
land; and you shall do to him as you
did to Sihon, king of the Amorites,
who lived at Heshbon." **35** So [a]they
struck down him and his sons and
all his people, until [1]there was no
survivor remaining for him; and they
possessed his land.

### *Balak Sends for Balaam*

**22** [a]Then the sons of Israel set
out and camped in the plains
of Moab beyond the Jordan *opposite*
Jericho.

**2** And [a]Balak the son of Zippor saw
all that Israel had done to the Am-
orites. **3** [a]So Moab was in great fear
because of the people, for they were
numerous; and Moab was in dread
of the sons of Israel. **4** Then Moab
said to the elders of [a]Midian, "Now

**21:23** [a]Nu 20:21 [b]Dt 2:32 **21:24** [a]Am 2:9 [b]Dt 2:37 [1]Lit *smote*, as in Gr and Lat [2]M.T. *strong*
**21:25** [a]Am 2:10 [1]Lit *daughters* **21:28** [a]Jer 48:45 [b]Nu 21:15 [c]Nu 22:41; Is 15:2; 16:12 [1]Lit *lords of the* [2]Or *Bamoth* **21:29** [a]Jer 48:46 [b]Jdg 11:24; 1Ki 11:33; 2Ki 23:13 [c]Is 15:5 [d]Is 16:2 **21:30** [a]Nu 32:3, 34; Jer 48:18, 22 **21:32** [a]Nu 32:1, 3, 35; Jer 48:32 **21:33** [a]Dt 3:1-7 [b]Jos 13:12 **21:34** [a]Dt 3:2 **21:35** [a]Dt 3:3, 4 [1]Lit *he had no survivor* ◆ **22:1** [a]Nu 33:48, 49 **22:2** [a]Jdg 11:25 **22:3** [a]Ex 15:15 **22:4** [a]Nu 25:15-18; 31:1-3

this assembly will lick up all that is
around us, as the ox licks up the grass
of the field." And Balak the son of
Zippor was king of Moab at that time.
**5** So he sent messengers to [a]Balaam
the son of Beor, at [b]Pethor, which
is near the [1]River, *in* the land of the
sons of his people, to call him, saying,
"Behold, a people came out of Egypt;
behold, they cover the surface of the
land, and they are settled opposite
me. **6** [a]So now, please come, [b]curse
this people for me since they are
too [1]mighty for me; perhaps I may
be able to strike them down and drive
them out of the land. For I know that
he whom you bless is blessed, and he
whom you curse is cursed."

**7** So the elders of Moab and the
elders of Midian went away with
the *fees for* [a]divination in their
hand; and they came to Balaam and
spoke Balak's words to him. **8** And he
said to them, "Spend the night here,
and I will bring word back to you as
Yahweh may speak to me." And the
leaders of Moab stayed with Balaam.
**9** Then [a]God came to Balaam and
said, "Who are these men with you?"
**10** And Balaam said to God, "Balak
the son of Zippor, king of Moab,
has sent *word* to me, **11** 'Behold,
there is a people who came out of
Egypt, and they cover the surface of
the land; now come, curse them for
me; perhaps I may be able to fight
against them and drive them out.'"
**12** And God said to Balaam, "Do not
go with them; [a]you shall not curse
the people, for they [b]are blessed."
**13** *So Balaam arose* in the morning
and said to Balak's leaders, "Go back
to your land, for Yahweh has refused
to allow me to go with you." **14** And
the leaders of Moab arose and came
to Balak and said, "Balaam refused
to go with us."

**15** Then Balak again sent leaders,
more numerous and more [1]honor-
able than [2]the former. **16** And they
came to Balaam and said to him,
"Thus says Balak the son of Zippor,
'Let nothing, I beg you, withhold
you from coming to me; **17** for I will
indeed honor you richly, and I will
do whatever you say to me. [a]Please
come then, curse this people for me.'"
**18** And Balaam replied to the servants
of Balak, "[a]Though Balak were to give
me his house full of silver and gold,
I could not do anything, either small
or great, to trespass the [1]command of
Yahweh my God. **19** So now, please,
you also stay here tonight, and I will
know what else Yahweh will speak
to me." **20** And God came to Balaam
at night and said to him, "If the men
have come to call you, rise up *and* go
with them; but [a]only the word which
I speak to you shall you do."

**21** [a]So Balaam arose in the morn-
ing and saddled his donkey and went
with the leaders of Moab.

### *Balaam's Donkey and the Angel*

**22** But God was angry because he was
going, [a]so the angel of Yahweh took
his stand in the way as an adversary
against him. Now he was riding on
his donkey, and his two young men
were with him. **23** Then the donkey
saw the angel of Yahweh standing in

**22:5** [a]Jos 24:9; 2Pe 2:15f; Jd 11 [b]Dt 23:4 [1]The Euphrates River **22:6** [a]Nu 22:17; 23:7, 8 [b]Nu 22:12; 24:9 [1]Or *numerous* **22:7** [a]Nu 23:23; 24:1; Jos 13:22 **22:9** [a]Ge 20:3 **22:12** [a]Nu 23:8; 24:9 [b]Ge 12:2; 22:17 **22:15** [1]Or *distinguished* [2]Lit *these* **22:17** [a]Nu 22:6 **22:18** [a]Nu 22:38; 24:13; 1Ki 22:14; 2Chr 18:13 [1]Lit *mouth* **22:20** [a]Nu 22:35; 23:5, 12, 16, 26; 24:13 **22:21** [a]2Pe 2:15 **22:22** [a]Ex 23:20

the way with his drawn sword in his
hand, and the donkey turned off from
the way and went into the field; so
Balaam struck the donkey to turn it
back into the way. **24** Then the angel
of Yahweh stood in a narrow path
of the vineyards, *with* a wall on this
side and a wall on that side. **25** And
the donkey saw the angel of Yahweh,
and it pressed itself to the wall and
pressed Balaam's foot against the wall,
so he struck it again. **26** And the angel
of Yahweh passed on ahead and stood
in a narrow place where there was
no way to turn to the right hand or
the left. **27** Then the donkey saw the
angel of Yahweh and lay down under
Balaam; so [a]Balaam was angry and
struck the donkey with his stick.
**28** And [a]Yahweh opened the mouth
of the donkey, and it said to Balaam,
"What have I done to you, that you
have struck me these three times?"
**29** Then Balaam said to the donkey,
"Because you have made a mockery
of me! If there had been a sword in
my hand, [a]I would have killed you
by now." **30** And the donkey said to
Balaam, "Am I not your donkey on
which you have ridden all your life to
this day? Have I ever been accustomed
to do so to you?" And he said, "No."

**31** Then Yahweh opened the eyes
of Balaam, and he saw [a]the angel
of Yahweh standing in the way with
*his drawn* sword in his hand; and he
bowed his head down [1]and prostrated
himself to the ground. **32** And the angel
of Yahweh said to him, "Why have you
struck your donkey these three times?
Behold, I have come out as an adver-
sary because your way was [a,1]contrary
to me. **33** And the donkey saw me and
turned aside from me these three
times. If it had not turned aside from
me, I would surely have killed you just
now, and let it live." **34** And Balaam
said to the angel of Yahweh, "[a]I have
sinned, for I did not know that you
were standing in the way against me.
So now, if it is evil in your sight, I will
turn back." **35** But the angel of Yahweh
said to Balaam, "Go with the men, but
[a]you shall speak only the word which
I [1]tell you." So Balaam went along with
the leaders of Balak.

**36** Then Balak heard that Balaam
was coming and went out to meet
him at the city of Moab, which is on
the Arnon border, [1]at the end of the
border. **37** Then Balak said to Balaam,
"Did I not urgently send to you to call
you? Why did you not come to me?
Am I indeed unable to honor you?"
**38** So Balaam said to Balak, "Behold,
I have come now to you! [a]Am I able
to speak anything at all? The word
that God puts in my mouth, that I
shall speak." **39** And Balaam went
with Balak, and they came to Kiriath-
huzoth. **40** And Balak sacrificed oxen
and sheep, and sent *some* to Balaam
and the leaders who were with him.

**41** Then it happened in the morn-
ing that Balak took Balaam and
brought him up to [a,1]the high places
of Baal, and he saw from there the
[b]end of *the camp* of the people.

### *Yahweh Speaks Through Balaam*

**23** Then Balaam said to Balak,
"Build seven altars for me
here, and prepare seven bulls and
seven rams for me here." **2** So Balak

**22:27** [a]Jas 1:19 **22:28** [a]2Pe 2:16 **22:29** [a]Pr 12:10; Mt 15:19 **22:31** [a]Jos 5:13-15 [1]Lit *and prostrated himself to his nose* **22:32** [a]2Pe 2:15 [1]Lit *reckless* **22:34** [a]Nu 14:40 **22:35** [a]Nu 22:20 [1]Or *speak to* **22:36** [1]Lit *which is at* **22:38** [a]Nu 22:18 **22:41** [a]Nu 21:28 [b]Nu 23:13 [1]Or *Bamoth-baal*

did just as Balaam had spoken, and
Balak and Balaam offered up a bull
and a ram on each altar. **3** Then
Balaam said to Balak, "Stand beside
your burnt offering, and I will go;
perhaps Yahweh will come to meet
me, and whatever He shows me I will
tell you." So he went to a bare hill.
**4** Now God met Balaam, and he
said to Him, "I have set up the seven
altars, and I have offered up a bull
and a ram on each altar." **5** Then Yah-
weh [a]put a word in Balaam's mouth
and said, "Return to Balak, and you
shall speak thus." **6** So he returned
to him, and behold, he was standing
beside his burnt offering, he and all
the leaders of Moab. **7** Then he took
up his [1]discourse and said,

"From [a]Aram Balak
has brought me,
Moab's king from the
mountains of the East,
'[b]Come curse Jacob for me,
And come, denounce Israel!'
**8** "[a]How shall I curse whom
God has not cursed?
And how can I denounce
whom Yahweh has
not denounced?
**9** "For I see him from the
top of the rocks,
And I look at him
from the hills;
[a]Behold, a people
*who* dwells alone,
And will not be reckoned
among the nations.
**10** "[a]Who can number the
dust of Jacob,
Or count the fourth
part of Israel?
[b]Let [1]me die the death
of the upright,
[c]And let my end be like his!"

**11** Then Balak said to Balaam,
"What have you done to me? [a]I took
you to curse my enemies, but behold,
you have blessed them repeatedly!"
**12** And he replied, "Must I not be
careful to speak [a]what Yahweh puts
in my mouth?"

### *Balaam's Discourse*

**13** Then Balak said to him, "Please
come with me to another place from
where you may see them, but you will
only see the end of them and will not
see all of them; and curse them for me
from there." **14** So he took him to the
field of Zophim, to the top of Pisgah,
and built seven altars and offered a
bull and a ram on *each* altar. **15** And he
said to Balak, "Stand here beside your
burnt offering while I myself meet
*Yahweh* over there." **16** Then Yahweh
met Balaam and [a]put a word in his
mouth and said, "Return to Balak,
and thus you shall speak." **17** So he
came to him, and behold, he was
standing beside his burnt offering,
and the leaders of Moab with him.
And Balak said to him, "What has
Yahweh spoken?" **18** Then he took
up his [1]discourse and said,

"Arise, O Balak, and hear;
Give ear to me,
O son of Zippor!
**19** "[a]God is not a man,
that He should lie,
Nor a son of man,
that He should repent;
[b]Has He said, and will
He not do it?

---

◆ **23:5** [a]Nu 22:20; Dt 18:18; Jer 1:9 **23:7** [a]Nu 22:5; Dt 23:4 [b]Nu 22:6 [1]Lit *parable* **23:8** [a]Nu 22:12
**23:9** [a]Dt 32:8; 33:28 **23:10** [a]Ge 13:16; 28:14 [b]Is 57:1 [c]Ps 37:37 [1]Lit *my soul* **23:11** [a]Ne 13:2
**23:12** [a]Nu 22:20 **23:16** [a]Nu 22:20 **23:18** [1]Lit *parable* **23:19** [a]1Sa 15:29 [b]Is 40:8; 55:11

Or has He spoken, and will
He not establish it?
20 “Behold, I have received *a*
*command* to bless;
[a]When He has blessed,
then [b]I cannot revoke it.
21 “[a]He has not observed
[1]misfortune in Jacob;
[b]Nor has He seen
trouble in Israel;
[c]Yahweh his God is with him,
[d]And the shout of a king
is among them.
22 “[a]God brings them
out of Egypt,
He is for them like
the [b]horns of the wild ox.
23 “[a]For there is no omen
against Jacob,
Nor is there any divination
against Israel;
At the proper time it
shall be said to Jacob
And to Israel,
what God has done!
24 “[a]Behold, a people rises
like a lioness,
And as a lion it lifts itself;
It will not lie down
until it devours the prey,
And drinks the blood
of the slain.”

25 Then Balak said to Balaam, “Do
not curse them at all nor bless them
at all!” 26 But Balaam replied to Balak,
“Did I not tell you, saying, ‘[a]Whatever
Yahweh speaks, that I must do’?”

27 Then Balak said to Balaam,
“Please come, I will take you to another place; perhaps it will be right in
the eyes of God that you curse them
for me from there.” 28 So Balak took
Balaam to the top of Peor which
overlooks the [1]wasteland. 29 And
Balaam said to Balak, “Build seven
altars for me here and prepare seven
bulls and seven rams for me here.”
30 And Balak did just as Balaam had
said and offered up a bull and a ram
on *each* altar.

### *Spirit of God Comes upon Balaam*

24 And Balaam saw that it was
good in the eyes of Yahweh
to bless Israel, so he did not go as at
other times to [1]encounter [a]omens,
but he set his face toward the [b]wilderness. 2 And Balaam lifted up his
eyes and saw Israel dwelling tribe by
tribe; and [a]the Spirit of God came
upon him. 3 Then he took up his
[1]discourse and said,

“[a]The oracle of Balaam
the son of Beor,
And the oracle of the man
whose eye is uncovered;
4 The oracle of him who
[a]hears the [1]words of God,
Who beholds the [b]vision
of [2]the Almighty,
Falling down, yet having
his eyes opened,
5 How fair are your
tents, O Jacob,
Your dwellings, O Israel!
6 “Like [1]valleys that stretch out,
Like gardens beside the river,
Like [a]aloes planted
by Yahweh,
Like [b]cedars beside the waters.

---

**23:20** [a]Ge 12:2; 22:17; Nu 22:12 [b]Is 43:13 **23:21** [a]Nu 14:18, 19, 34; Ps 32:2, 5 [b]Dt 9:24; 32:5; Jer 50:20 [c]Ex 3:12; Dt 31:23 [d]Dt 33:5; Ps 89:15-18 [1]Or *wickedness* **23:22** [a]Nu 24:8 [b]Dt 33:17
**23:23** [a]Nu 22:7; 24:1; Jos 13:22 **23:24** [a]Ge 49:9; Na 2:11, 12 **23:26** [a]Nu 22:18 **23:28** [1]Or *Jeshimon*
◆ **24:1** [a]Nu 22:7; 23:23 [b]Nu 23:28 [1]Or *meet*, cf. 21:33; 22:34, 36; 23:3 **24:2** [a]Nu 11:26; 1Sa 19:20; Rev 1:10
**24:3** [a]Nu 24:15, 16 [1]Lit *parable*, so in ch **24:4** [a]Nu 22:20 [b]Ge 15:1; Nu 12:6 [1]Lit *sayings* [2]Heb *Shaddai*
**24:6** [a]Ps 45:8 [b]Ps 1:3 [1]Or possibly *palm trees*

7 "Water will flow
from his buckets,
And his seed *will be*
by many waters,
And his king shall be lifted
up higher than [a]Agag,
[b]And his kingdom
shall be exalted.
8 "[a]God brings him out of Egypt,
He is for him like the
horns of the wild ox.
[b]He will devour the nations
*who are* his adversaries,
And will gnaw their
bones in pieces,
And [1]shatter *them*
with his [c]arrows.
9 "[a]He [1]crouches, he lies
down as a lion,
And as a [2]lion,
who [3]dares rouse him?
[b]Blessed is everyone
who blesses you,
And cursed is everyone
who curses you."

10 Then Balak's anger burned
against Balaam, and he struck his
[1]hands together; and Balak said to
Balaam, "I called you to curse my en-
emies, but behold, you have blessed
them repeatedly these three times!
11 So now, [1]flee to your place. I said I
would honor you greatly, but behold,
Yahweh has held you back from hon-
or." 12 And Balaam said to Balak, "[a]Did
I not tell your messengers whom you
had sent to me, saying, 13 'Though
Balak were to give me his house full
of silver and gold, I could not do
anything to trespass the [1]command
of Yahweh, either good or bad, [a]of my
own [2]accord. [b]What Yahweh speaks,
that I will speak'? 14 So now, behold,
[a]I am going to my people; come, *and*
I will advise you what this people will
do to your people in the last days."

### *Oracle of Balaam*

15 Then he took up his discourse and
said,
"[a]The oracle of Balaam
the son of Beor,
And the oracle of the man
whose eye is uncovered,
16 The oracle of him who hears
the [1]words of God,
And knows the knowledge
of the [2]Most High,
Who beholds the vision
of the [3]Almighty,
Falling down, yet having
his eyes opened.
17 "I see him, but not now;
I behold him, but not near;
A star shall come forth
from Jacob,
[a]A scepter shall rise
from Israel,
[b]And shall crush through
the [1]forehead of Moab,
And [2]tear down all
the sons of [3]Sheth.
18 "[a]And Edom shall be
a possession,
[b]Seir, its enemies, also
will be a possession,
While Israel performs
valiantly.
19 "And one from Jacob shall
have dominion,

**24:7** [a]Nu 24:20; 1Sa 15:8 [b]Ps 145:11-13 **24:8** [a]Nu 23:22 [b]Nu 23:24; Ps 2:9 [c]Ps 45:5 [1]Or *crush*, cf. 24:17 **24:9** [a]Ge 49:9; Nu 23:24 [b]Ge 12:3; 27:29 [1]Lit *bows down* [2]Or *lioness* [3]Lit *shall* **24:10** [1]Lit *palms* **24:11** [1]Lit *flee for yourself* **24:12** [a]Nu 22:18 **24:13** [a]Nu 16:28 [b]Nu 22:20 [1]Lit *mouth* [2]Lit *heart* **24:14** [a]Nu 31:8, 16; Jos 13:22 **24:15** [a]Nu 24:3, 4 **24:16** [1]Lit *sayings* [2]Heb *Elyon* [3]Heb *Shaddai* **24:17** [a]Ge 49:10 [b]Nu 21:29; Is 15:1-16:14 [1]Lit *corners* [2]Or *the skull of the head of* [3]Lit *tumult* **24:18** [a]Ge 27:29; Am 9:11, 12 [b]Ge 32:3

And will make the survivor
perish from the city."
**20** Then he looked at Amalek and
took up his discourse and said,
"Amalek was the first
of the nations,
[a]But his end *shall be*
[1]destruction."
**21** Then he looked at the [a]Kenite
and took up his discourse and said,
"Your habitation is enduring,
And your nest is set in the cliff.
**22** "Nevertheless Kain will
be consumed;
How long will [a]Asshur
[1]keep you captive?"
**23** Then he took up his discourse
and said,
"Woe, who can live except
when God has ordained it?
**24** "But ships *shall come* from
the coast of [a]Kittim,
And they shall afflict Asshur
and will afflict [b]Eber;
[c]So they also *will come*
to destruction."
**25** Then Balaam arose and went
and returned to [a]his place, and Balak
also went his way.

### *Israel Sacrifices to Baal*

**25** And Israel remained at
[a]Shittim, and the people began
[b]to play the harlot with the daugh-
ters of Moab. **2** Indeed [a]they called
the people to the sacrifices of their
gods, and the people ate and bowed
down to their gods. **3** So [a]Israel joined
themselves to [1]Baal of Peor, and the
anger of Yahweh burned against
Israel. **4** And Yahweh said to Moses,
"Take all *who are* the heads of the
people and execute them [1]in broad
daylight before Yahweh, [a]so that the
burning anger of Yahweh may turn
away from Israel." **5** So Moses said to
the judges of Israel, "Each of you [a]kill
his men who have joined themselves
to [1]Baal of Peor."
**6** Then behold, one of the sons
of Israel came and brought near to
his brothers a [a]Midianite woman, in
the sight of Moses and in the sight of
all the congregation of the sons of
Israel, [b]while they were weeping at
the doorway of the tent of meeting.
**7** [a]And Phinehas the son of Eleazar,
the son of Aaron the priest, saw it,
so he arose from the midst of the
congregation and took a spear in his
hand, **8** and he went after the man of
Israel into the [1]tent and pierced both
of them through, the man of Israel
and the woman, through the [2]body.
[a]Then the plague on the sons of
Israel was checked. **9** [a]So those who
died by the plague were 24,000.

### *The Jealousy of Phinehas*

**10** Then Yahweh spoke to Moses,
saying, **11** "[a]Phinehas the son of
Eleazar, the son of Aaron the priest,
has turned away My wrath from the
sons of Israel in that he was jealous
with My jealousy among them, so
that I did not consume the sons of Is-
rael [b]in My jealousy. **12** Therefore say,
'[a]Behold, I give him My [b]covenant of
peace; **13** and it shall be for him and
his seed after him, a covenant of a

**24:20** [a]Nu 24:24 [1]Lit *to destroying* **24:21** [a]Ge 15:19 **24:22** [a]Ge 10:21, 22 [1]Lit *take*
**24:24** [a]Ge 10:4; Eze 27:6 [b]Ge 10:21 [c]Nu 24:20 **24:25** [a]Nu 24:14 ◆ **25:1** [a]Nu 33:49; Jos 2:1
[b]Nu 31:16; 1Co 10:8; Rev 2:14 **25:2** [a]Ex 34:15; Dt 32:38 **25:3** [a]Ps 106:28, 29; Hos 9:10 [1]Or *Baal-peor*
**25:4** [a]Dt 13:17 [1]Lit *in front of the sun* **25:5** [a]Ex 32:27 [1]Or *Baal-peor* **25:6** [a]Nu 22:4 [b]Joel 2:17
**25:7** [a]Ps 106:30 **25:8** [a]Nu 16:46-48 [1]Or *inner rooms* [2]Or *belly* **25:9** [a]Nu 14:37; 16:48-50; 31:16
**25:11** [a]Ps 106:30 [b]Ex 20:5 **25:12** [a]Ps 106:30, 31 [b]Is 54:10; Eze 34:25; 37:26

[a]perpetual priesthood, because he
was jealous for his God and [b]made
atonement for the sons of Israel.'"
**14** Now the name of the [1]slain
man of Israel who was [1]slain with
the Midianite woman, was Zimri
the son of Salu, a leader of a father's
household among the Simeonites.
**15** And the name of the Midianite
woman, who was struck down, was
[a]Cozbi the daughter of [b]Zur, [1]who
was head of the people of a father's
household in Midian.
**16** Then Yahweh spoke to Moses,
saying, **17** "[a]Be hostile to the Midi-
anites and strike them, **18** for they
have been hostile to you with their
deceptive tricks, with which they
have deceived you in the affair of
Peor and in the affair of Cozbi, the
daughter of the leader of Midian,
their sister who was slain on the day
of the plague because of Peor."

### *Census of the Sons of Israel*

**26** [1]Then it happened after the
[a]plague, [2]that Yahweh spoke to
Moses and to Eleazar the son of Aaron
the priest, saying, **2** "[a]Take a [1]census of
all the congregation of the sons of Isra-
el from twenty years old and upward,
by their fathers' households, whoever
is able to go out to war in Israel." **3** So
Moses and Eleazar the priest spoke
with them [a]in the plains of Moab by
the Jordan at Jericho, saying, **4** "*Take
a census of the people* from twenty
years old and upward, as Yahweh has
commanded Moses."
Now the sons of Israel who came
*out of the land of Egypt were*:

**5** Reuben, Israel's firstborn,
the sons of Reuben:
*of* Hanoch, the family of
the Hanochites;
of Pallu, the family of
the Palluites;
**6** of Hezron, the family of
the Hezronites;
of Carmi, the family of
the Carmites.
**7** These are the families of
the Reubenites, and those
who were numbered of them
were [a]43,730.
**8** And the son of Pallu: Eliab.
**9** And the sons of Eliab:
Nemuel and Dathan and
Abiram. These are the Dathan
and Abiram who were [a]called
*upon* by the congregation,
who contended against
Moses and against Aaron in
the congregation of Korah,
when they contended against
Yahweh,
**10** and [a]the earth opened its
mouth and swallowed them
up along with Korah, when
that congregation died,
[b]when the fire consumed 250
men, so that they became a
[1]warning.
**11** [a]The sons of Korah, however,
did not die.

**12** The sons of Simeon according
to their families:
of [1]Nemuel, the family of the
Nemuelites;
of Jamin, the family of the
Jaminites;

---

**25:13** [a]Ex 29:9 [b]Nu 16:46 **25:14** [1]Lit *smitten* **25:15** [a]Nu 25:18 [b]Nu 31:8 [1]Lit *he* **25:17** [a]Nu 25:1; 22:4; 31:1-3 ◆ **26:1** [a]Nu 25:9 [1]Ch 25:19 in Heb [2]Ch 26:1 in Heb **26:2** [a]Ex 30:11-16; 38:25, 26; Nu 1:2 [1]Lit *sum* **26:3** [a]Nu 22:1; 33:48; 35:1 **26:7** [a]Nu 1:21 **26:9** [a]Nu 1:16; 16:2 **26:10** [a]Nu 16:32 [b]Nu 16:35, 38 [1]Lit *sign* **26:11** [a]Nu 16:27, 33; Dt 24:16 **26:12** [1]In Ge 46:10 and Ex 6:15, *Jemuel*

of [2]Jachin, the family of
the Jachinites;
13 of [1]Zerah, the family of
the Zerahites;
of Shaul, the family of
the Shaulites.
14 These are the families of
the Simeonites, [a]22,200.

15 The sons of Gad according to
their families:
of [1]Zephon, the family of
the Zephonites;
of Haggi, the family of
the Haggites;
of Shuni, the family of
the Shunites;
16 of [1]Ozni, the family of
the Oznites;
of Eri, the family of the Erites;
17 of [1]Arod, the family of
the Arodites;
of Areli, the family of
the Arelites.
18 These are the families of
the sons of Gad according to
those who were numbered of
them, [a]40,500.

19 The [a]sons of Judah *were* Er
and Onan, but Er and Onan
died in the land of Canaan.
20 And the [a]sons of Judah
according to their families
were:
of Shelah, the family of
the Shelanites;
of Perez, the family of
the Perezites;
of Zerah, the family of
the Zerahites.
21 And the sons of Perez were:
of Hezron, the family of
the Hezronites;
of Hamul, the family of
the Hamulites.
22 These are the families of
Judah according to those
who were numbered of them,
[a]76,500.

23 The [a]sons of Issachar
according to their families:
*of* Tola, the family of
the Tolaites;
of [1]Puvah, the family of
the Punites;
24 of [1]Jashub, the family of
the Jashubites;
of Shimron, the family of
the Shimronites.
25 These are the families of
Issachar according to those
who were numbered of them,
[a]64,300.

26 The [a]sons of Zebulun
according to their families:
of Sered, the family of
the Seredites;
of Elon, the family of
the Elonites;
of Jahleel, the family of
the Jahleelites.
27 These are the families of
the Zebulunites according to
those who were numbered of
them, [a]60,500.

28 The [a]sons of Joseph according
to their families: Manasseh
and Ephraim.

**26:12** [2]In 1Chr 4:24, *Jarib* **26:13** [1]In Ge 46:10, *Zohar* **26:14** [a]Nu 1:23 **26:15** [1]In Ge 46:16, *Ziphion* **26:16** [1]In Ge 46:16, *Ezbon* **26:17** [1]In Ge 46:16, *Arodi* **26:18** [a]Nu 1:25 **26:19** [a]Ge 38:2; 46:12 **26:20** [a]Ge 49:8; 1Chr 2:3; Rev 7:5 **26:22** [a]Nu 1:27 **26:23** [a]Ge 46:13; 1Chr 7:1 [1]In Ge 46:13, *Puvvah*; in 1Chr 7:1, *Puah* **26:24** [1]In Ge 46:13, *Iob* **26:25** [a]Nu 1:29 **26:26** [a]Ge 46:14 **26:27** [a]Nu 1:31 **26:28** [a]Ge 46:20; Dt 33:16f

29 The sons of Manasseh:
of Machir, the family of
the Machirites; and [a]Machir
[1]became the father of Gilead:
of Gilead, the family of the
Gileadites.
30 These are the sons of Gilead:
*of* [1]Iezer, the family of
the [a]Iezerites;
of Helek, the family of
the Helekites;
31 and *of* Asriel, the family of
the Asrielites;
and *of* Shechem, the family of
the Shechemites;
32 and *of* Shemida, the family of
the Shemidaites;
and *of* Hepher, the family of
the Hepherites.
33 Now Zelophehad the son of
Hepher had no sons,
but only daughters;
and [a]the names of the
daughters of Zelophehad were
Mahlah, Noah, Hoglah, Milcah
and Tirzah.
34 These are the families of
Manasseh; and those who
were numbered of them were
[a]52,700.

35 These are the sons of Ephraim
according to their families:
of Shuthelah, the family of
the Shuthelahites;
of [1]Becher, the family of
the Becherites;
of Tahan, the family of
the Tahanites.
36 And these are the sons of
*Shuthelah:*
of Eran, the family of
the Eranites.
37 These are the families of
the sons of Ephraim according
to those who were numbered
of them, [a]32,500.
These are the sons of
Joseph according to their
families.

38 The sons of Benjamin
according to their families:
of Bela, the family of
the Belaites;
of Ashbel, the family of
the Ashbelites;
of [1]Ahiram, the family of
the Ahiramites;
39 of [1]Shephupham, the family of
the Shuphamites;
of [2]Hupham, the family of
the Huphamites.
40 And the sons of Bela were
[1]Ard and Naaman:
*of Ard*, the family of
the Ardites;
of Naaman, the family of
the Naamites.
41 These are the sons of
Benjamin according to their
families; and those who were
numbered of them were
[a]45,600.

42 These are the sons of Dan
according to their families:
of [1]Shuham, the family of
the Shuhamites.
These are the families of
Dan according to their
families.

**26:29** [a]Jos 17:1; 1Chr 7:14f [1]Lit *begot* **26:30** [a]Jdg 6:11, 24, 34 [1]In Jos 17:2, *Abiezer* **26:33** [a]Nu 27:1 **26:34** [a]Nu 1:35 **26:35** [1]In 1Chr 7:20, *Bered* **26:37** [a]Nu 1:33 **26:38** [1]In Ge 46:21, *Ehi*; in 1Chr 8:1, *Aharah* **26:39** [1]In Ge 46:21, *Muppim*; in 1Chr 7:12, *Shuppim* [2]In Ge 46:21, *Muppim* and *Huppim* **26:40** [1]In 1Chr 8:3, *Addar* **26:41** [a]Nu 1:37 **26:42** [1]In Ge 46:23, *Hushim*

43 All the families of the
Shuhamites, according to
those who were numbered of
them, were [a]64,400.
44 The [a]sons of Asher according
to their families:
of Imnah, the family of
the Imnites;
of Ishvi, the family of
the Ishvites;
of Beriah, the family of
the Beriites.
45 Of the sons of Beriah:
of Heber, the family of
the Heberites;
of Malchiel, the family of
the Malchielites.
46 And the name of the daughter
of Asher *was* Serah.
47 These are the families of the
sons of Asher according to
those who were numbered of
them, [a]53,400.

48 The [a]sons of Naphtali
according to their
families:
of Jahzeel, the family of
the Jahzeelites;
of Guni, the family of
the Gunites;
49 of Jezer, the family of
the Jezerites;
of [a]Shillem, the family of
the Shillemites.
50 These are the families of
Naphtali according to their
families; and those who were
numbered of them were
[a]45,400.

51 These are those who were num-
bered of the sons of Israel, [a]601,730.
52 Then Yahweh spoke to Moses,
saying, 53 "[1]Among these the land
shall be divided for an inheritance
according to the number of names.
54 [a]To the larger *group* you shall
increase their inheritance, and to
the smaller *group* you shall diminish
their inheritance; each shall be given
their inheritance according to those
who were numbered of them. 55 But
the land shall be [a]divided by lot.
They shall [1]receive their inheritance
according to the names of the tribes
of their fathers. 56 According to the
selection by lot, their inheritance
shall be divided between the larger
and the smaller *groups*."
57 [a]And these are those who were
numbered of the Levites according
to their families:
of Gershon, the family of
the Gershonites;
of Kohath, the family of
the Kohathites;
of Merari, the family of
the Merarites.
58 These are the families of Levi:
the family of the Libnites,
the family of the Hebronites,
the family of the Mahlites,
the family of the Mushites,
the family of the Korahites.
[a]Kohath [1]became the father of
Amram.
59 And the name of Amram's wife
[a]was Jochebed, the daughter of Levi,
who was born to Levi in Egypt; and
she bore to Amram: Aaron and Moses
and their sister Miriam. 60 [a]And to

**26:43** [a]Nu 1:39 **26:44** [a]Ge 46:17; 1Chr 7:30 **26:47** [a]Nu 1:41 **26:48** [a]Ge 46:24; 1Chr 7:13 **26:49** [a]1Chr 7:13 **26:50** [a]Nu 1:43 **26:51** [a]Ex 12:37; 38:26; Nu 1:46; 11:21 **26:53** [1]Lit *To* **26:54** [a]Nu 33:54 **26:55** [a]Nu 33:54; 34:13 [1]Lit *inherit according to* **26:57** [a]Ge 46:11; Ex 6:16; 1Chr 6:1, 16 **26:58** [a]Ex 6:20 [1]Lit *begot* **26:59** [a]Ex 2:1, 2; 6:20 **26:60** [a]Nu 3:2

Aaron were born Nadab and Abihu,
Eleazar and Ithamar. **61** [a]But Nadab
and Abihu died when they offered
strange fire before Yahweh. **62** And
those who were numbered of them
were [a]23,000, every male from a
month old and upward, for [b]they
were not numbered among the sons
of Israel [c]since no inheritance was
given to them among the sons of
Israel.

**63** These are those who were
numbered by Moses and Eleazar
the priest, who numbered the sons
of Israel in the plains of Moab by
the Jordan at Jericho. **64** [a]But among
these there was not a man of those
who were numbered by Moses and
Aaron the priest, who numbered
the sons of Israel in the wilderness
of Sinai. **65** For Yahweh had said [1]of
them, "[a]They shall surely die in the
wilderness." And not a man was left
of them, [b]except Caleb the son of Je-
phunneh and Joshua the son of Nun.

### *The Daughters of Zelophehad*

**27** Then [a]the daughters of Zelo-
phehad, the son of Hepher, the
son of Gilead, the son of Machir, the
son of Manasseh, of the families of
Manasseh the son of Joseph, came
near; and these are [b]the names of
his daughters: Mahlah, Noah and
Hoglah and Milcah and Tirzah. **2** And
they stood before Moses and before
Eleazar the priest and before the
leaders and all the congregation, at
the doorway of the tent of meeting,
saying, **3** "Our father [a]died in the *wil-
derness, yet he was* not among the
congregation of those who gathered
themselves together against Yahweh
in the congregation of Korah; but he
died in his own sin, and [b]he had no
sons. **4** Why should the name of our
father be withdrawn from among his
family because he had no son? Give
us a possession among our father's
brothers." **5** [a]So Moses brought their
case near before Yahweh.

**6** Then Yahweh spoke to Moses,
saying, **7** "[a]The daughters of Zelo-
phehad are right in *their* statements.
You shall surely give them a posses-
sion for an inheritance among their
father's brothers, and you shall have
the inheritance of their father pass
on to them. **8** Further, you shall
speak to the sons of Israel, saying,
'If a man dies and has no son, then
you shall have his inheritance pass
on to his daughter. **9** And if he has
no daughter, then you shall give his
inheritance to his brothers. **10** And
if he has no brothers, then you shall
give his inheritance to his father's
brothers. **11** And if his father has no
brothers, then you shall give his in-
heritance to his blood relative in his
own family, and he shall possess it;
and it shall be a [a]statutory judgment
to the sons of Israel, just as Yahweh
commanded Moses.'"

**12** [a]Then Yahweh said to Moses,
"Go up to this [b]mountain of Abarim,
and see the land which I have given to
the sons of Israel. **13** So *when* you have
seen it, you too [a]will be gathered to
your people, [b]as Aaron your brother
[1]*was*, **14** for in the wilderness of Zin,
during the strife of the congregation,

---

**26:61** [a]Lv 10:1, 2; Nu 3:4 **26:62** [a]Nu 3:39 [b]Nu 1:47 [c]Nu 18:23, 24 **26:64** [a]Nu 14:29-35; Dt 2:14-16; Heb 3:17 **26:65** [a]Nu 14:26-35; Ps 90:3-10; 1Co 10:5 [b]Dt 1:36; Jos 14:6-10 [1]Or *to* ◆**27:1** [a]Nu 26:33; 36:1 [b]Nu 26:33 **27:3** [a]Nu 26:64, 65 [b]Nu 26:33 **27:5** [a]Nu 9:8; 27:21 **27:7** [a]Nu 36:2; Jos 17:4 **27:11** [a]Nu 35:29 **27:12** [a]Dt 3:23-27; 32:48-52 [b]Nu 33:47, 48 **27:13** [a]Nu 31:2 [b]Nu 20:24, 28; Dt 10:6
[1]Lit *was gathered*

[a]you rebelled against My [1]command
[2]to treat Me as holy before their eyes
at the water." (These are the waters of
Meribah of Kadesh in the wilderness
of Zin.)

### *Moses Commissions Joshua*

**15** Then Moses spoke to Yahweh,
saying, **16** "[a]May Yahweh, the God of
the spirits of all flesh, appoint a man
over the congregation, **17** who [a]will
go out [1]and come in before them, and
who will lead them out and [2]bring
them in, so that the congregation of
Yahweh will not be [b]like sheep which
have no shepherd." **18** So Yahweh said
to Moses, "[1]Take Joshua the son of
Nun, a man [a]in whom is the Spirit,
and [b]lay your hand on him; **19** and
have him stand before Eleazar the
priest and before all the congrega-
tion, and [a]commission him in their
sight. **20** And you shall put some of
your [1]splendor on him, in order that
all the congregation of the sons of
Israel may obey *him.* **21** Moreover,
he shall stand before Eleazar the
priest, who shall inquire for him
[a]by the judgment of the Urim be-
fore Yahweh. At his [1]command they
shall go out, and at his [1]command
they shall come in, *both* he and the
sons of Israel with him, even all the
congregation." **22** So Moses did just
as Yahweh commanded him; and he
took Joshua and had him stand be-
fore Eleazar the priest and before all
the congregation. **23** Then he laid his
hands on him and [a]commissioned
him, just as Yahweh had spoken by
the hand of Moses.

### *Daily Offerings*

**28** Then Yahweh spoke to Moses,
saying, **2** "Command the sons
of Israel and say to them, 'You shall
[1]be careful to bring near My offering,
My [a]food for My offerings by fire, of
a soothing aroma to Me, at their
appointed time.' **3** [a]And you shall
say to them, 'This is the offering by
fire which you shall bring near to
Yahweh: two male lambs one year old
without blemish *as* a continual burnt
offering every day. **4** You shall offer
the one lamb in the morning, and the
other lamb you shall offer [1]at twilight,
**5** also [a]a tenth of an [1]ephah of fine
flour for a [b]grain offering, mixed with
a fourth of a [2]hin of beaten oil. **6** It is
a continual burnt offering which was
ordained in Mount Sinai as a soothing
aroma, an offering by fire to Yahweh.
**7** Then the drink offering with it *shall
be* a fourth of a hin for each lamb,
[a]in the holy place you shall pour out
a drink offering of strong drink to
Yahweh. **8** And the other lamb you
shall offer [1]at twilight; as the grain
offering of the morning and as its
drink offering, you shall offer it, an
offering by fire, a soothing aroma to
Yahweh.

### *Sabbath Offerings*

**9** 'Then on the sabbath day two male
lambs one year old without blemish,
and two-tenths *of an* [1]*ephah* of fine

**27:14** [a]Nu 20:12; Dt 32:51; Ps 106:32 [1]Lit *mouth* [2]Lit *for My sanctity* **27:16** [a]Nu 16:22 **27:17** [a]Dt 31:2; 2Chr 1:10 [b]1Ki 22:17; Eze 34:5; Mt 9:36; Mk 6:34 [1]Lit *before them and who will* [2]Lit *who will bring* **27:18** [a]Nu 11:25-29; Dt 34:9 [b]Nu 27:23 [1]Lit *Take for yourself* **27:19** [a]Dt 3:28; 31:3, 7, 8, 23 **27:20** [1]Or *authority* **27:21** [a]Ex 28:30; 1Sa 28:6 [1]Lit *mouth* **27:23** [a]Dt 31:23 ◆ **28:2** [a]Lv 3:11 [1]Lit *watch* **28:3** [a]Ex 29:38-42 **28:4** [1]Lit *between the two evenings* **28:5** [a]Ex 16:36; Nu 15:4 [b]Lv 2:1 [1]An ephah was approx. 21 qt. or 23 l [2]A hin was approx. 1 gal. or 3.8 l **28:7** [a]Ex 29:42 **28:8** [1]Lit *between the two evenings* **28:9** [1]An ephah was approx. 21 qt. or 23 l

flour mixed with oil as a grain offer-
ing, and its drink offering: **10** *This is*
the burnt offering of every sabbath
in addition to the [a]continual burnt
offering and its drink offering.

### *Monthly Offerings*

**11** 'Then [a]at the beginning of each of
your months you shall bring near a
burnt offering to Yahweh: two bulls
from the herd and one ram, seven
male lambs one year old without
blemish; **12** [a]and three-tenths *of an*
[1]*ephah* of fine flour mixed with oil
for a grain offering, for each bull; and
two-tenths of fine flour mixed with
oil for a grain offering, for the one
ram; **13** and a tenth *of an* [1]*ephah* of
fine flour mixed with oil for a grain
offering for each lamb, for a burnt
offering of a soothing aroma, an of-
fering by fire to Yahweh. **14** And their
drink offerings shall be half a hin of
wine for a bull and a third of a hin
for the ram and a fourth of a hin for
a lamb; this is the burnt offering of
each month throughout the months
of the year. **15** And one male goat for
a sin offering to Yahweh; it shall be
offered with its drink offering in
addition to the [a]continual burnt
offering.

### *Passover Offerings*

**16** '[a]Then on the fourteenth day of
the first month shall be the Passover
of Yahweh. **17** [a]And on the fifteenth
day of this month *shall be* a [b]feast;
unleavened bread *shall be* eaten
for seven days. **18** On the [a]first day
*shall be* a holy convocation; you
shall do no laborious work. **19** And
you shall bring near an offering by
fire, a burnt offering to Yahweh: two
bulls from the herd and one ram and
seven male lambs one year old; [a]they
shall be for you without blemish.
**20** Now as for their grain offering,
you shall offer fine flour mixed with
oil: three-tenths *of an* [1]*ephah* for a
bull and two-tenths for the ram. **21** A
tenth *of an* [1]*ephah* you shall offer for
[2]each of the seven lambs; **22** and one
male goat for a [a]sin offering to make
atonement for you. **23** You shall offer
these besides [a]the burnt offering of
the morning, which is for a continual
burnt offering. **24** After this manner
you shall offer daily, for seven days,
[a]the food of the offering by fire, of a
soothing aroma to Yahweh; it shall
be offered with its drink offering
in addition to the [b]continual burnt
offering. **25** Now on the seventh day
you shall have a holy convocation;
[a]you shall do no laborious work.

### *Offerings for the Feast of Weeks*

**26** 'Also on [a]the day of the first fruits,
when you bring near a new grain
offering to Yahweh in your *Feast of*
Weeks, you shall have a holy convo-
cation; [b]you shall do no laborious
work. **27** And you shall bring near a
burnt offering for a soothing aroma
to Yahweh: two bulls from the herd,
one ram, seven male lambs one year
old; **28** and their grain offering, fine
flour mixed with oil: three-tenths *of*
*an* [1]*ephah* for each bull, two-tenths

---

**28:10** [a]Nu 28:3 **28:11** [a]Nu 10:10; Eze 46:6, 7 **28:12** [a]Nu 15:4-12 [1]An ephah was approx. 21 qt. or 23 l **28:13** [1]An ephah was approx. 21 qt. or 23 l **28:15** [a]Nu 28:3 **28:16** [a]Ex 12:1-20; Lv 23:5-8; Dt 16:1-8 **28:17** [a]Lv 23:6 [b]Ex 23:15; 34:18; Dt 16:3-8 **28:18** [a]Lv 23:7 **28:19** [a]Dt 15:21 **28:20** [1]An ephah was approx. 21 qt. or 23 l **28:21** [1]An ephah was approx. 21 qt. or 23 l [2]Lit *each lamb* **28:22** [a]Lv 16:18; Ro 8:3; Ga 4:4f **28:23** [a]Nu 28:3 **28:24** [a]Lv 3:11 [b]Nu 28:3 **28:25** [a]Nu 28:18 **28:26** [a]Ex 23:16; 34:22; Lv 23:15-21; Dt 16:9-12 [b]Nu 28:18 **28:28** [1]An ephah was approx. 21 qt. or 23 l

for the one ram, **29** a tenth for [1]each of the seven lambs; **30** *also* one male goat to make atonement for you. **31** [a]Besides the continual burnt offering and its grain offering, you shall offer *them* with their drink offerings. They shall be [1]without blemish.

### *The Various Offerings of the Seventh Month*

**29** '[a]Now in the seventh month, on the first day of the month, you shall also have a holy convocation; [b]you shall do no laborious work. It will be to you a day for blowing trumpets. **2** And you shall offer a burnt offering as a soothing aroma to Yahweh: one bull from the herd, one ram, *and* seven male lambs one year old without blemish; **3** also their grain offering, fine flour mixed with oil: three-tenths *of an* [1]*ephah* for the bull, two-tenths for the ram, **4** and one-tenth for [1]each of the seven lambs. **5** And *offer* one male goat for a sin offering, to make atonement for you, **6** [a]besides the burnt offering of the new moon and its grain offering, and the [b]continual burnt offering and its grain offering, and their drink offerings, according to their *legal* judgment, for a soothing aroma, an offering by fire to Yahweh.

**7** 'Then on [a]the tenth day of this seventh month you shall have a holy convocation, and you shall humble yourselves; you shall not do any work. **8** And you shall bring near a burnt offering to Yahweh *as* a soothing aroma: one bull from the herd, one ram, seven male lambs one year old, [a]having them without blemish; **9** and their grain offering, fine flour mixed with oil: three-tenths *of an* [1]*ephah* for the bull, two-tenths for the one ram, **10** a tenth for each of the seven lambs; **11** one male goat for a sin offering, besides [a]the sin offering of atonement and [b]the continual burnt offering and its grain offering and their drink offerings.

**12** 'Then on [a]the fifteenth day of the seventh month you shall have a holy convocation; you [b]shall do no laborious work, and you shall celebrate a feast to Yahweh for seven days. **13** And you shall bring near a burnt offering, an offering by fire as a soothing aroma to Yahweh: thirteen bulls from the herd, two rams, fourteen male lambs one year old, which are without blemish; **14** and their grain offering, fine flour mixed with oil: three-tenths *of an* [1]*ephah* for [2]each of the thirteen bulls, two-tenths for [3]each of the two rams, **15** and a tenth for each of the fourteen lambs; **16** and one male goat for a sin offering, [a]besides the continual burnt offering, its grain offering, and its drink offering.

**17** 'Then on [a]the second day: twelve bulls from the herd, two rams, fourteen male lambs one year old without blemish; **18** and their grain offering and their drink offerings for the bulls, for the rams and for the lambs, by their number [a]according to the *legal* judgment;

**28:29** [1]Lit *each lamb* **28:31** [a]Nu 28:3 [1]Lit *without blemish to you* ◆ **29:1** [a]Ex 23:16; 34:22; Lv 23:23-25 [b]Nu 28:26 **29:3** [1]An ephah was approx. 21 qt. or 23 l **29:4** [1]Lit *each lamb*, so in ch **29:6** [a]Nu 28:27 [b]Nu 28:3 **29:7** [a]Lv 16:29-34; 23:26-32 **29:8** [a]Lv 22:20; Dt 15:21; 17:1 **29:9** [1]An ephah was approx. 21 qt. or 23 l **29:11** [a]Lv 16:3, 5 [b]Nu 28:3 **29:12** [a]Lv 23:33-35; Dt 16:13-15 [b]Nu 29:1 **29:14** [1]An ephah was approx. 21 qt. or 23 l [2]Lit *each bull* [3]Lit *each ram* **29:16** [a]Nu 28:3 **29:17** [a]Lv 23:36 **29:18** [a]Lv 2:1-16

19 and one male goat for a sin offer-
ing, [a]besides the continual burnt
offering and its grain offering and
their drink offerings.
20 'Then on the third day: eleven
bulls, two rams, fourteen male lambs
one year old without blemish; 21 and
their grain offering and their drink
offerings for the bulls, for the rams
and for the lambs, by their number
according to the *legal* judgment;
22 and one male goat for a sin of-
fering, besides the continual burnt
offering and its grain offering and its
drink offering.
23 'Then on the fourth day: ten
bulls, two rams, fourteen male lambs
one year old without blemish; 24 their
grain offering and their drink offerings
for the bulls, for the rams and for the
lambs, by their number according to
the *legal* judgment; 25 and one male
goat for a sin offering, besides the
continual burnt offering, its grain
offering and its drink offering.
26 'Then on the fifth day: nine
bulls, two rams, fourteen male
lambs one year old [a]without blem-
ish; 27 and their grain offering and
their drink offerings for the bulls,
for the rams and for the lambs, by
their number according to the *legal*
judgment; 28 and one male goat for
a sin offering, besides the continual
burnt offering and its grain offering
and its drink offering.
29 'Then on the sixth day: eight
bulls, two rams, fourteen male
lambs one year old without blem-
ish; 30 and their grain offering and
their drink offerings for the bulls,
for the rams and for the lambs, by
their number according to the *legal*
judgment; 31 and one male goat for
a sin offering, besides the continual
burnt offering, its grain offering and
its drink offerings.
32 'Then on the seventh day: seven
bulls, two rams, fourteen male lambs
one year old without blemish; 33 and
their grain offering and their drink
offerings for the bulls, for the rams and
for the lambs, by their number accord-
ing to the *legal* judgment; 34 and one
male goat for a sin offering, besides
the continual burnt offering, its grain
offering and its drink offering.
35 '[a]On the eighth day you shall
have a solemn assembly; you shall
do no laborious work. 36 But you
shall bring near a burnt offering, an
offering by fire, as a soothing aroma
to Yahweh: one bull, one ram, seven
male lambs one year old without
blemish; 37 their grain offering and
their drink offerings for the bull,
for the ram and for the lambs, by
their number according to the *legal*
judgment; 38 and one male goat for
a sin offering, besides the continual
burnt offering and its grain offering
and its drink offering.
39 'You shall offer these to Yahweh
at your [a]appointed times, besides your
[1]votive offerings and your freewill of-
ferings, for your burnt offerings and
for your grain offerings and for your
drink offerings and for your peace
offerings.'" 40 [1]And Moses spoke to
the sons of Israel according to all that
Yahweh had commanded Moses.

### *The Statutes for Vows*

30 Then Moses spoke to [a]the
heads of the tribes of the sons
of Israel, saying, "This is the word

**29:19** [a]Nu 28:8 **29:26** [a]Heb 7:26 **29:35** [a]Lv 23:36 **29:39** [a]Lv 23:2 [1]Lit *vows* **29:40** [1]Ch 30:1 in Heb ◆ **30:1** [a]Nu 1:4, 16; 7:2

which Yahweh has commanded.
2 [a]If a man makes a vow to Yahweh
or swears an oath to bind himself
with a binding obligation, he shall
not violate his word; he shall do
according to all that proceeds out of
his mouth.

3 "Also if a woman makes a vow
to Yahweh and binds herself by an
obligation in her father's house in her
youth, 4 and her father hears her vow
and her obligation by which she has
bound herself, and her father [1]says
nothing to her, then all her vows shall
stand, and every obligation by which
she has bound herself shall stand.
5 But if her father should forbid her
on the day he hears *of it*, none of her
vows or her obligations by which she
has bound herself shall stand; and
Yahweh will pardon her because her
father had forbidden her.

6 "However, if she should [1]marry
while [2]under her vows or the rash
statement of her lips by which she
has bound herself, 7 and her husband
hears of it and says nothing to her on
the day he hears *it*, then her vows
shall stand, and her obligations by
which she has bound herself shall
stand. 8 But if, on the day her hus-
band hears *of it*, he forbids her, then
he shall annul her vow which [1]she is
under and the rash statement of her
lips by which she has bound herself;
and Yahweh will pardon her.

9 "But the vow of a widow or of
a divorced woman, everything by
which she has bound herself, shall
stand against her. 10 However, if
she vowed in her husband's house
or bound herself by an obligation
with an oath, 11 and her husband
heard *it* but said nothing to her *and*
did not forbid her, then all her vows
shall stand, and every obligation by
which she bound herself shall stand.
12 But if her husband indeed annuls
them on the day he hears *them*, then
whatever proceeds out of her lips
concerning her vows or concerning
the obligation of herself shall not
stand; her husband has annulled
them, and Yahweh will pardon her.

13 "Every vow and every binding
oath to humble herself, her hus-
band may cause it to stand, or her
husband may annul it. 14 But if her
husband indeed says nothing to
her from day to day, then he causes
all her vows or all her obligations
which are on her to stand; he has
caused them to stand because he said
nothing to her on the day he heard
them. 15 But if he indeed annuls them
after he has heard them, then he
shall bear her guilt."

16 These are the statutes which
Yahweh commanded Moses, *as*
between a man and his wife, *and as*
between a father and his daughter,
*while she is* in her youth in her fa-
ther's house.

### *Vengeance on Midian*

31 Then Yahweh spoke to Moses,
saying, 2 "[a]Take full vengeance
for the sons of Israel on the Midian-
ites; afterward you will be [b]gathered
to your people." 3 And Moses spoke
to the people, saying, "Arm men from
among you for the war, that they
may [1]go against Midian to execute
[a]Yahweh's vengeance on Midian.
4 One thousand from each tribe of all
the tribes of Israel you shall send to

**30:2** [a]Dt 23:21-23; Mt 5:33 **30:4** [1]Lit *is silent to her*, so in ch **30:6** [1]Lit *be to a husband* [2]Lit *her vows are on her* **30:8** [1]Lit *is on her* ◆ **31:2** [a]Nu 25:1, 16, 17 [b]Nu 20:24, 26; 27:13 **31:3** [a]Lv 26:25 [1]Lit *be*

the war." **5** So there were [1]furnished from the thousands of Israel, one thousand from each tribe, twelve thousand armed for war. **6** And Moses sent them, one thousand from each tribe, to the war, and Phinehas the son of Eleazar the priest, to the war with them, [a]and the holy vessels and [b]the trumpets for the alarm in his hand. **7** So they made war against Midian, just as Yahweh had commanded Moses, and [a]they killed every male. **8** They killed the kings of Midian along with the *rest of* their slain: [a]Evi and Rekem and [b]Zur and Hur and Reba, the five kings of Midian; they also killed [c]Balaam the son of Beor with the sword. **9** And the sons of Israel captured the women of Midian and their little ones; and all their cattle and all their flocks and all their goods they plundered. **10** Then they burned all their cities where they lived and all their camps with fire. **11** [a]And they took all the spoil and all the loot, both of man and of beast. **12** And they brought the captives and the loot and the spoil to Moses and to Eleazar the priest and to the congregation of the sons of Israel, to the camp at the plains of Moab, which are by the Jordan *opposite* Jericho.

**13** And Moses and Eleazar the priest and all the leaders of the congregation went out to meet them outside the camp. **14** And Moses was angry with the officers of the army, the commanders of thousands and the commanders of hundreds, who had come from service in the war. **15** So Moses said to them, "Have you [1]spared [a]all the women? **16** [a]Behold, these [1]caused the sons of Israel, through the word of [b]Balaam, to [2]act unfaithfully against Yahweh in the matter of Peor, so the plague was among the congregation of Yahweh. **17** [a]So now, kill every male among the little ones, and kill every woman who has known man [1]intimately. **18** But all the [1]girls who have not known man [2]intimately, [3]spare for yourselves. **19** [a]And you, camp outside the camp seven days; whoever has killed any person and whoever has touched any slain, purify yourselves, you and your captives, on the third day and on the seventh day. **20** And you shall purify for yourselves every garment and every article of [1]leather and all the work of goats' *hair* and all articles of wood."

**21** Then Eleazar the priest said to the men of war who had gone to battle, "This is the statute of the law which Yahweh has commanded Moses: **22** only the gold and the silver, the bronze, the iron, the tin and the lead, **23** everything that can stand the fire, you shall pass through the fire, and it shall be clean, but it shall be purified with [a]water for impurity. But whatever cannot stand the fire you shall pass through the water. **24** And you shall wash your clothes on the seventh day and be clean, and afterward you may enter the camp."

### *Division of the Loot*

**25** Then Yahweh spoke to Moses, saying, **26** "You and Eleazar the priest and the heads of the fathers'

**31:5** [1]Lit *delivered* **31:6** [a]Nu 14:44 [b]Nu 10:8, 9 **31:7** [a]Dt 20:13; Jdg 21:11; 1Ki 11:15, 16 **31:8** [a]Jos 13:21 [b]Nu 25:15 [c]Nu 31:16; Jos 13:22 **31:11** [a]Dt 20:14 **31:15** [a]Dt 20:14 [1]Lit *let...live* **31:16** [a]Nu 25:1-9 [b]Nu 31:8 [1]Lit *were to* [2]Or possibly *defect from Yahweh* **31:17** [a]Dt 7:2; 20:16-18 [1]Lit *by lying with a man* **31:18** [1]Lit *female children* [2]Lit *by lying with a man* [3]Lit *keep alive* **31:19** [a]Nu 19:11-22 **31:20** [1]Or *skin* **31:23** [a]Nu 19:9, 17

*households* of the congregation take a count of the loot [1]that was captured, both of man and of animal; **27** and [a]divide the loot between the warriors who went out to battle and all the congregation. **28** [a]And you shall exact a levy for Yahweh from the men of war who went out to battle, one [1]in five hundred of the persons and of the cattle and of the donkeys and of the sheep; **29** take it from their half and give it to Eleazar the priest, as a [1]contribution to Yahweh. **30** And from the sons of Israel's half, you shall take one drawn out of every fifty of the persons, of the cattle, of the donkeys, and of the sheep, from all the animals, and give them to the Levites who [a]keep charge of the tabernacle of Yahweh." **31** Moses and Eleazar the priest did just as Yahweh had commanded Moses.

**32** Now the loot that remained from the plunder which the [1]men of war had plundered was 675,000 sheep, **33** and 72,000 cattle, **34** and 61,000 donkeys, **35** and of human beings, of the women who had not known man [1]intimately, all the persons were 32,000.

**36** And the half, the portion of those who went out to war, was *as follows*: the number of sheep was 337,500; **37** and the levy of Yahweh from the sheep was 675; **38** and the cattle were 36,000, from which the levy of Yahweh was 72; **39** and the donkeys were 30,500, from which the levy of Yahweh was 61; **40** and the human beings were 16,000, from whom the levy of Yahweh was 32 persons. **41** And Moses gave the levy, *which was* the contribution to Yahweh, to Eleazar the priest, just [a]as Yahweh had commanded Moses.

**42** As for the sons of Israel's half, which Moses [1]separated from the men who had gone to war— **43** now the congregation's half was 337,500 sheep, **44** and 36,000 cattle, **45** and 30,500 donkeys, **46** and the human beings were 16,000— **47** and from the sons of Israel's half, Moses took one drawn out of every fifty, both of man and of animals, and gave them to the Levites, who kept the responsibility of the tabernacle of Yahweh, just as Yahweh had commanded Moses.

**48** Then the officers who were over the thousands of the army, the commanders of thousands and the commanders of hundreds, came near to Moses, **49** and they said to Moses, "Your servants have taken a census of men of war who are in our charge, and no man of us is missing. **50** So we have brought near as an offering to Yahweh what each man found—articles of gold, armlets and bracelets, signet rings, earrings and necklaces—[a]to make atonement for ourselves before Yahweh." **51** And Moses and Eleazar the priest took the gold from them, all *kinds of* crafted articles. **52** And all the gold from the contribution offering which they raised up *in offering* to Yahweh, from the commanders of thousands and the commanders of hundreds, was 16,750 [1]shekels. **53** [a]The men of war had taken plunder, every man for himself. **54** So Moses and Eleazar

**31:26** [1]Lit *of captives* **31:27** [a]Jos 22:8 **31:28** [a]Nu 18:21-30 [1]Lit *soul from* **31:29** [1]Lit *heave offering*, so in ch **31:30** [a]Nu 3:7, 8, 25, 26, 31, 36, 37; 18:3, 4 **31:32** [1]Lit *people* **31:35** [1]Lit *by lying with a man* **31:41** [a]Nu 5:9, 10; 18:19 **31:42** [1]Or *divided* **31:50** [a]Ex 30:12-16 **31:52** [1]A shekel was approx. 0.4 oz. or 11 gm **31:53** [a]Nu 31:32; Dt 20:14

the priest took the gold from the commanders of thousands and of hundreds, and they brought it to the tent of meeting as [a]a memorial for the sons of Israel before Yahweh.

### *Reuben and Gad Possess Gilead*

**32** Now the sons of Reuben and the sons of Gad had an [a]exceedingly large number of livestock. And they saw the land of [b]Jazer and the land of Gilead, that [1]it was indeed a place suitable for livestock, **2** so the sons of Gad and the sons of Reuben came and spoke to Moses and to Eleazar the priest and to the leaders of the congregation, saying, **3** "[a]Ataroth, Dibon, Jazer, Nimrah, Heshbon, Elealeh, Sebam, Nebo, and Beon, **4** the land, [a]which Yahweh struck before the congregation of Israel, is a land for livestock, and your servants have livestock." **5** And they said, "If we have found favor in your sight, let this land be given to your servants as a possession; do not take us across the Jordan."

**6** But Moses said to the sons of Gad and to the sons of Reuben, "Shall your brothers go to war while you yourselves sit here? **7** [a]Now why are you [1]discouraging the sons of Israel from crossing over into the land which Yahweh has given them? **8** [1]This is what your fathers did when I sent them from [a]Kadesh-barnea to see the land. **9** Indeed they went up to [a]the [1]valley of Eshcol and saw the land, and they [2]discouraged the sons of Israel so that they did not go into the land which Yahweh had given them. **10** So [a]Yahweh's anger burned in that day, and He swore *an oath*, saying, **11** '[a]None of the men who came up from Egypt, from twenty years old and upward, shall see the land which I swore to Abraham, to Isaac, and to Jacob; for they did not follow Me fully, **12** except Caleb the son of Jephunneh the Kenizzite and Joshua the son of Nun, [a]for they have followed Yahweh fully.' **13** [a]So Yahweh's anger burned against Israel, and He made them wander in the wilderness forty years, until the entire generation of those who had done evil in the sight of Yahweh was brought to an end. **14** Now behold, you have risen up in your fathers' place, a brood of sinful men, to add still more to the burning [a]anger of Yahweh against Israel. **15** For if you [a]turn away from following Him, He will once more abandon them in the wilderness, and you will destroy all these people."

**16** Then they came near to him and said, "We will build here sheepfolds for our livestock and cities for our little ones; **17** [a]but we ourselves will be armed ready *to go* before the sons of Israel, until we have brought them to their place, and our little ones live in the fortified cities because of the inhabitants of the land. **18** [a]We will not return to our homes until every one of the sons of Israel has possessed his inheritance. **19** For we will not have an inheritance with them on the other side of the Jordan and beyond because our inheritance has fallen to us [a]on this side of the Jordan east."

---

**31:54** [a]Ex 30:16 ◆ **32:1** [a]Ex 12:38 [b]Nu 21:32 [1]Lit *behold, the place, a place for* **32:3** [a]Nu 32:34-38 **32:4** [a]Nu 21:34 **32:7** [a]Nu 13:27-14:4 [1]Lit *restraining the hearts of* **32:8** [a]Nu 13:3, 26; Dt 1:19-25 [1]Lit *Thus your fathers* **32:9** [a]Nu 13:24; Dt 1:24 [1]Or *wadi* [2]Lit *restrained the hearts of* **32:10** [a]Nu 14:11f; Dt 1:34 **32:11** [a]Nu 14:28-30 **32:12** [a]Dt 1:36; Jos 14:8f **32:13** [a]Nu 14:33-35 **32:14** [a]Dt 1:34f **32:15** [a]Dt 30:17, 18; 2Chr 7:19, 20 **32:17** [a]Jos 4:12, 13 **32:18** [a]Jos 22:1-4 **32:19** [a]Jos 12:1; 13:8

**20** [a]So Moses said to them, "If
you will do [1]this, if you will arm
yourselves before Yahweh for the
war, **21** and all of you armed men
cross over the Jordan before Yah-
weh until He has dispossessed His
enemies from before Him, **22** [a]and
the land is subdued before Yahweh,
then afterward you shall return and
be free of obligation toward Yahweh
and toward Israel, and this land shall
be yours for a possession before
Yahweh. **23** But if you will not do so,
behold, you have sinned against Yah-
weh, and be sure [a]your sin will find
you out. **24** Build yourselves cities for
your little ones and sheepfolds for
your sheep, and [a]do [1]what you have
promised."

**25** And the sons of Gad and the
sons of Reuben spoke to Moses,
saying, "Your servants will do just
as my lord commands. **26** [a]Our little
ones, our wives, our livestock, and all
our cattle shall [1]remain there in the
cities of Gilead; **27** but your servants,
everyone who is armed for war, will
[a]cross over in the presence of Yahweh
to battle, just as my lord says."

**28** So Moses gave a command con-
cerning them to Eleazar the priest
and to Joshua the son of Nun and to
the heads of the fathers' *households*
of the tribes of the sons of Israel.
**29** And Moses said to them, "If the
sons of Gad and the sons of Reuben,
everyone who is armed for battle,
will cross with you over the Jordan
in the presence of Yahweh, and the
land is subdued before you, then you
shall give them the land of Gilead
for a possession; **30** but if they will
not cross over with you armed, they
shall have possessions among you
in the land of Canaan." **31** And the
sons of Gad and the sons of Reuben
answered, saying, "As Yahweh has
said to your servants, so we will do.
**32** We ourselves will cross over armed
in the presence of Yahweh into the
land of Canaan, and the possession
of our inheritance *shall remain* with
us across the Jordan."

**33** [a]So Moses gave to them, to
the sons of Gad and to the sons
of Reuben and to the half-tribe of
Joseph's son Manasseh, the kingdom
of Sihon, king of the Amorites and
the kingdom of Og, the king of
Bashan, the land with its cities with
*their* [1]territories, the cities of the
surrounding land. **34** And the sons
of Gad built Dibon and Ataroth and
[a]Aroer, **35** and Atroth-shophan and
Jazer and Jogbehah, **36** and [a]Beth-
nimrah and Beth-haran as fortified
cities, and sheepfolds for sheep.
**37** And the sons of Reuben built
Heshbon and Elealeh and Kiriatha-
im, **38** and [a]Nebo and Baal-meon—
*their* names being changed—and
Sibmah, and they gave *other* names
to the cities which they built. **39** And
the sons of [a]Machir the son of
Manasseh went to Gilead and took it
and dispossessed the Amorites who
were in it. **40** So Moses gave [a]Gilead
to Machir the son of Manasseh, and
he lived in it. **41** And Jair the son of
Manasseh went and took its [1]towns
and called them [a,2]Havvoth-jair.
**42** And Nobah went and took Kenath

**32:20** [a]Dt 3:18 [1]Lit *this thing* **32:22** [a]Dt 3:20 **32:23** [a]Ge 4:7; 44:16; Is 59:12 **32:24** [a]Nu 30:2 [1]Lit *that which has come out of your mouth* **32:26** [a]Jos 1:14 [1]Lit *be* **32:27** [a]Jos 4:12 **32:33** [a]Dt 3:8-17; Jos 12:1-6 [1]Lit *borders* **32:34** [a]Dt 2:36 **32:36** [a]Nu 32:3 **32:38** [a]Is 46:1 **32:39** [a]Ge 50:23 **32:40** [a]Dt 3:12, 13, 15; Jos 17:1 **32:41** [a]Dt 3:14; Jdg 10:4 [1]Lit *tent villages* [2]Lit *the towns of Jair*

and its towns and called it Nobah
after [a]his own name.

### *The Journey from Egypt to Jordan*

**33** These are the journeys of the
sons of Israel, by which they
came out from the land of Egypt by
their armies, by [a]the hand of Moses
and Aaron. **2** And Moses wrote down
their starting places according to
their journeys by the [1]command of
Yahweh, and these are their journeys
according to their starting places.

3 [a]They journeyed from
Rameses in the first month, on
the fifteenth day of the first
month; on the [1]next day after
the Passover the sons of Israel
[b]started out [2]with a high
hand in the sight of all the
Egyptians,

4 but the Egyptians were
burying all their firstborn
whom Yahweh had struck
down among them. Yahweh
had also executed judgments
[a]on their gods.

5 Then [a]the sons of Israel
journeyed from Rameses and
camped in Succoth.

6 [a]They journeyed from
Succoth and camped in
Etham, which is on the edge
of the
wilderness.

7 [a]They journeyed from
Etham and turned back to
Pi-hahiroth, which faces Baal-
zephon, and they camped
before Migdol.

8 [a]They journeyed [1]from before
Hahiroth and passed through
the midst of the sea into the
wilderness; and [b]they went
three days' journey in the wil-
derness of Etham and camped
at Marah.

9 [a]They journeyed from Marah
and came to Elim; and in Elim
there were twelve springs of
water and seventy palm trees,
and they camped there.

10 They journeyed from Elim
and camped by
the [1]Red Sea.

11 They journeyed from the
[1]Red Sea and camped in
[a]the wilderness of Sin.

12 They journeyed from the
wilderness of Sin and camped
at Dophkah.

13 They journeyed from
Dophkah and camped at
Alush.

14 They journeyed from
Alush and camped [a]at
Rephidim; now it was there
that the people had no
water to drink.

15 They journeyed from
Rephidim and camped
in [a]the wilderness
of Sinai.

16 They journeyed from the
wilderness of Sinai and
camped at [a]Kibroth-
hattaavah.

17 They journeyed from Kibroth-
hattaavah and camped at
[a]Hazeroth.

---

**32:42** [a]2Sa 18:18; Ps 49:11 ◆ **33:1** [a]Ps 77:20; 105:26; Mic 6:4 **33:2** [1]Lit *mouth* **33:3** [a]Ex 12:37 [b]Ex 14:8 [1]Lit *morrow* [2]Or *boldly* **33:4** [a]Ex 12:12 **33:5** [a]Ex 12:37 **33:6** [a]Ex 13:20 **33:7** [a]Ex 14:1, 2 **33:8** [a]Ex 14:22 [b]Ex 15:22, 23 [1]Many mss *from Pi-hahiroth* **33:9** [a]Ex 15:27 **33:10** [1]Lit *Sea of Reeds* **33:11** [a]Ex 16:1 [1]Lit *Sea of Reeds* **33:14** [a]Ex 17:1 **33:15** [a]Ex 19:1 **33:16** [a]Nu 11:34 **33:17** [a]Nu 11:35

18 They journeyed from
Hazeroth and camped at
Rithmah.
19 They journeyed from Rithmah
and camped at Rimmon-
perez.
20 They journeyed from
Rimmon-perez and camped
at [a]Libnah.
21 They journeyed from Libnah
and camped at Rissah.
22 They journeyed from Rissah
and camped in Kehelathah.
23 They journeyed from
Kehelathah and camped at
Mount Shepher.
24 They journeyed from Mount
Shepher and camped at
Haradah.
25 They journeyed from Haradah
and camped at Makheloth.
26 They journeyed from
Makheloth and camped at
Tahath.
27 They journeyed from Tahath
and camped at Terah.
28 They journeyed from Terah
and camped at Mithkah.
29 They journeyed from Mithkah
and camped at Hashmonah.
30 They journeyed from
Hashmonah and camped at
[a]Moseroth.
31 They journeyed from
Moseroth and camped at
Bene-jaakan.
32 They journeyed from
[a]Bene-jaakan and camped at
Hor-haggidgad.
33 They journeyed from Hor-
haggidgad and camped at
[a]Jotbathah.
34 They journeyed from
Jotbathah and camped at
Abronah.
35 They journeyed from Abronah
and camped at [a]Ezion-geber.
36 They journeyed from Ezion-
geber and camped in the
wilderness of [a]Zin, that is,
Kadesh.
37 They journeyed from Kadesh
and camped at [a]Mount Hor,
[b]at the edge of the land of
Edom.
38 [a]Then Aaron the priest
went up to Mount Hor at the
[1]command of Yahweh, and he
died there in the fortieth year
after the sons of Israel had
come from the land of Egypt,
on the first *day* in the fifth
month.
39 Now Aaron was 123 years
old when he died on
Mount Hor.

40 Now the Canaanite, the king
of [a]Arad [1]who lived in the
[2]Negev in the land of Canaan,
heard when the sons of Israel
were coming.

41 Then they journeyed from
Mount Hor and camped at
Zalmonah.
42 They journeyed from
Zalmonah and camped at
Punon.
43 They journeyed from Punon
and camped at [a]Oboth.
44 They journeyed from Oboth
and camped at Iye-abarim, at
the border of Moab.

---

**33:20** [a]Dt 1:1 **33:30** [a]Dt 10:6 **33:32** [a]Ge 36:27; Dt 10:6; 1Chr 1:42 **33:33** [a]Dt 10:7 **33:35** [a]Dt 2:8
**33:36** [a]Nu 20:1 **33:37** [a]Nu 20:22 [b]Nu 20:16 **33:38** [a]Nu 20:28; Dt 10:6 [1]Lit *mouth* **33:40** [a]Nu 21:1
[1]Lit *and he* [2]South country **33:43** [a]Nu 21:10, 11

45 They journeyed from Iyim and camped at Dibon-gad.

46 They journeyed from Dibon-gad and camped at Almon-diblathaim.

47 They journeyed from Almon-diblathaim and camped in the mountains of [a]Abarim, before Nebo.

48 They journeyed from the mountains of Abarim and [a]camped in the plains of Moab by the Jordan *opposite* Jericho.

49 They camped by the Jordan, from Beth-jeshimoth as far as [a]Abel-shittim in the plains of Moab.

### *Statutes of Possessing the Land*

**50** Then Yahweh spoke to Moses in
the plains of Moab by the Jordan
*opposite* Jericho, saying, **51** "Speak to
the sons of Israel and say to them,
'[a]When you cross over the Jordan
into the land of Canaan, **52** then you
shall dispossess all the inhabitants of
the land from before you and [a]destroy
all their carved stones and destroy
all their molten images and demol-
ish all their high places; **53** [a]and you
shall take possession of the land and
inhabit it, for I have given the land to
you to possess it. **54** [a]And you shall
inherit the land by lot according to
your families; to the larger you shall
give a larger inheritance, and to
the smaller you shall give a smaller
inheritance. Wherever the lot falls
*to anyone,* that shall be his. You
shall inherit according to the tribes
of your fathers. **55** But if you do not
dispossess the inhabitants of the land
from before you, then it will be that
those whom you let remain of them
*will become* [a]as pricks in your eyes
and as thorns in your sides, and they
will trouble you in the land which you
inhabit. **56** And it will be as I plan to
do to them, so I will do to you.'"

### *Apportioning Canaan*

**34** Then Yahweh spoke to Moses,
saying, **2** "Command the sons
of Israel and say to them, 'When
you enter [a]the land of Canaan, this
is the land that shall fall to you as an
inheritance, *even the* land of Canaan
according to its borders. **3** [a]And your
southern [1]sector shall [2]extend from
the wilderness of Zin along the side
of Edom, and your southern border
shall [2]extend from the end of the Salt
Sea [b]eastward. **4** Then your border
shall turn from the south to the as-
cent of Akrabbim and [1]continue to
Zin, and its [2]termination shall be to
the south of [a]Kadesh-barnea; and it
shall [3]reach Hazaraddar and [1]contin-
ue to Azmon. **5** And the border shall
turn from Azmon to the brook of
Egypt, and its termination shall be
at [a]the sea.

**6** 'And as for the west border, you
shall have the Great Sea, that is, *its*
[1]coastline; this shall be your west
border.

**7** '[a]And this shall be your north
border: you shall draw your *border*
line from the Great Sea to Mount Hor.
**8** You shall draw a line from Mount
Hor to [a,1]Lebo-hamath, and the

---

**33:47** [a]Nu 27:12 **33:48** [a]Nu 22:1 **33:49** [a]Nu 25:1 **33:51** [a]Jos 3:17 **33:52** [a]Ex 23:24; Lv 26:1; Dt 7:5; 12:3, 30; Ps 106:34-36 **33:53** [a]Dt 11:31; 17:14; Jos 21:43 **33:54** [a]Nu 26:53-56 **33:55** [a]Jos 23:13 ◆**34:2** [a]Ge 17:8; Ps 78:54, 55; 105:11 **34:3** [a]Jos 15:1-3 [b]Jos 15:5 [1]Lit *side* [2]Lit *be* **34:4** [a]Nu 32:8 [1]Lit *pass along* [2]Lit *goings out*, so in ch [3]Lit *go forth to* **34:5** [a]Jos 15:4 **34:6** [1]Lit *border* **34:7** [a]Eze 47:15-17 **34:8** [a]Jos 13:5 [1]Or *the entrance of Hamath*

termination of the border shall be at
Zedad; **9** and the border shall proceed
to Ziphron, and its termination shall
be at Hazar-enan. This shall be your
north border.
**10** 'For your east border you shall
also draw a line from Hazar-enan
to Shepham, **11** and the border shall
go down from Shepham to [a]Riblah
on the east side of Ain; and the
border shall go down and reach to
the [1]slope on the east side of the Sea
of [b,2]Chinnereth. **12** And the border
shall go down to the Jordan, and its
termination shall be at the Salt Sea.
This shall be your land according to
its borders all around.'"
**13** So Moses commanded the sons
of Israel, saying, "[a]This is the land
that you shall inherit by lot among
you as a possession, which Yahweh
has commanded to give to the nine
and a half tribes. **14** [a]For the tribe of
the sons of Reuben have received
*theirs* according to their fathers'
households, and the tribe of the sons
of Gad according to their fathers'
households, and the half-tribe of
Manasseh have received their inher-
itance. **15** The two and a half tribes
have received their inheritance
across the Jordan opposite Jericho
to the east toward the sunrise."
**16** Then Yahweh spoke to Moses,
saying, **17** "[a]These are the names of
the men who shall apportion the
land to you for inheritance: Eleazar
the priest and Joshua the son of Nun.
**18** And you shall take one leader of
every tribe to apportion the land for
inheritance. **19** Now these are the
names of the men:
Of the tribe of [a]Judah, [b]Caleb
the son of Jephunneh.
**20** "Of the tribe of the sons of
[a]Simeon, Samuel the son of
Ammihud.
**21** "Of the tribe of [a]Benjamin,
Elidad the son of Chislon.
**22** "Of the tribe of the sons of
Dan a leader, Bukki the son of
Jogli.
**23** "Of the sons of Joseph: of the
tribe of the sons of Manasseh
a leader, Hanniel the son of
Ephod.
**24** "Of the tribe of the sons of
Ephraim a leader, Kemuel the
son of Shiphtan.
**25** "Of the tribe of the sons of
Zebulun a leader, Elizaphan
the son of Parnach.
**26** "Of the tribe of the sons of
Issachar a leader,
Paltiel the son of Azzan.
**27** "Of the tribe of the sons of
Asher a leader, Ahihud the
son of Shelomi.
**28** "Of the tribe of the sons of
Naphtali a leader, Pedahel the
son of Ammihud."
**29** These are those whom Yahweh
commanded to apportion the inheri-
tance to the sons of Israel in the land
of Canaan.

### *Cities for the Levites*

**35** [a]Now Yahweh spoke to Mo-
ses in the plains of Moab by
the Jordan *opposite* Jericho, saying,
**2** "Command the sons of Israel that
they give to the Levites from the
inheritance of their possession cities
to live in; and you shall give to the

**34:11** [a]2Ki 23:33 [b]Dt 3:17; Jos 13:27 [1]Lit *shoulder* [2]Galilee **34:13** [a]Ge 15:18; Nu 26:52-56; Dt 11:24; Jos 14:1-5 **34:14** [a]Nu 32:33 **34:17** [a]Jos 14:1, 2 **34:19** [a]Ge 29:35; Dt 33:7; Ps 60:7 [b]Nu 13:6, 30; 26:65; Dt 1:36 **34:20** [a]Ge 29:33; 49:5; Eze 48:24 **34:21** [a]Ge 49:27; Dt 33:12; Ps 68:27 ◆ **35:1** [a]Lv 25:32-34

Levites pasture lands around the cities. 3 And the cities shall be theirs to live in; and their pasture lands shall be for their cattle and for their herds and for all their beasts.

4 "And the pasture lands of the cities which you shall give to the Levites *shall extend* from the wall of the city [1]outward [2]one thousand cubits around. 5 You shall also measure outside the city on the east side [1]two thousand cubits, and on the south side two thousand cubits, and on the west side two thousand cubits, and on the north side two thousand cubits, with the city in the center. This shall become theirs as pasture lands for the cities.

### *Cities of Refuge*

6 "And the cities which you shall give to the Levites *shall be* the [a]six cities of refuge, which you shall give for the manslayer to flee to; and in addition to them you shall give forty-two cities. 7 All the cities which you shall give to the Levites *shall be* [a]forty-eight cities, [1]together with their pasture lands. 8 [a]Now as for the cities which you shall give from the possession of the sons of Israel, you shall take more from the larger, and you shall take less from the smaller; each shall give some of his cities to the Levites in proportion to his possession which he inherits."

9 Then Yahweh spoke to Moses, saying, 10 "[a]Speak to the sons of Israel and say to them, 'When you cross the Jordan into the land of Canaan, 11 [a]then you shall select for yourselves cities to be your [b]cities of refuge, that the manslayer who has struck down any person [c]unintentionally may flee there. 12 [a]And the cities shall be for you as a refuge from the avenger, so that the manslayer will not die until he stands before the congregation for judgment. 13 And the cities which you are to give shall be your six cities of refuge. 14 You [a]shall give three cities across the Jordan and three cities [1]in the land of Canaan; they are to be cities of refuge. 15 These six cities shall be for refuge for the sons of Israel and for the sojourner and for the foreign resident among them; that anyone who strikes a person down [a]unintentionally may flee there.

16 '[a]But if he struck him down with an iron object, so that he died, he is a murderer; the murderer shall surely be put to death. 17 And if he struck him down with a stone in the hand, by which he would die, and *as a result* he died, he is a murderer; the murderer [a]shall surely be put to death. 18 Or if he struck him with a wooden object in the hand, by which he would die, and *as a result* he died, he is a murderer; the murderer shall surely be put to death. 19 The blood avenger himself shall put the murderer to death; he shall put him to death when he meets him. 20 [a]And if he pushed him of hatred or threw something at him [b]lying in wait and *as a result* he died, 21 or if he struck him down with his hand in enmity, and *as a result* he died, the one who struck him shall surely be put to

**35:4** [1]Lit *and outward* [2]Approx. 500 yd. or 450 m **35:5** [1]Approx. 1000 yd. or 900 m
**35:6** [a]Jos 20:7-9 **35:7** [a]Jos 21:41 [1]Lit *them* **35:8** [a]Lv 25:32-34; Nu 26:54; 33:54; Jos 21:1-42
**35:10** [a]Jos 20:1-9 **35:11** [a]Dt 19:1-13 [b]Jos 20:2f [c]Ex 21:13; Lv 4:2f, 22f; Nu 35:22-25 **35:12** [a]Dt 19:4-6; Jos 20:2, 3 **35:14** [a]Dt 4:41 [1]Lit *you shall give in* **35:15** [a]Nu 35:11 **35:16** [a]Ex 21:12, 14; Lv 24:17
**35:17** [a]Nu 35:31 **35:20** [a]Ge 4:8; 2Sa 3:27; 20:10 [b]Ex 21:14; Dt 19:11

death; he is a murderer; the blood
avenger shall put the murderer to
death when he meets him.
**22** '[a]But if he pushed him suddenly
without enmity or threw something
at him without lying in wait, **23** or
with any stone—by which one might
die, *yet* without seeing—and it fell
upon him, and he died, but he was
not his enemy nor seeking his injury,
**24** then [a]the congregation shall judge
between the [1]slayer and the blood
avenger according to these *legal*
judgments. **25** And the congregation
shall deliver the manslayer from the
hand of the blood avenger, and the
congregation shall restore him to his
city of refuge to which he fled; and he
shall live in it until the death of the
high priest who was anointed with
the holy oil. **26** But if the manslayer
at any time goes beyond the border
of his city of refuge to which he may
flee, **27** and the blood avenger finds
him outside the border of his city
of refuge, and the blood avenger
kills the manslayer, he will not be
guilty of blood **28** because he should
have remained in his city of refuge
until the death of the high priest. But
after the death of the high priest the
manslayer shall return to the land of
his possession.
**29** 'And these things shall be
for a [a]statutory judgment to you
throughout your generations in all
your *places of* habitation.
**30** '[a]If anyone strikes down a
person, the murderer shall be put
to death at the mouth of witnesses,
but [b]no person shall be put to death
on the testimony of one witness.
**31** Moreover, you shall not take
ransom for the life of a murderer
who is guilty of death, but he shall
surely be put to death. **32** And you
shall not take ransom for him who
has fled to his city of refuge, that he
may return to live in the land [1]before
the death of the priest. **33** [a]So you
shall not pollute the land in which
you are; for blood pollutes the land,
and no propitiation can be made for
the land for the blood that is shed
on it, except [b]by the blood of him
who shed it. **34** And you shall not
[a]defile the land in which you live,
in the midst of which [b]I dwell; for I
Yahweh am dwelling in the midst of
the sons of Israel.'"

### *Inheritance Through Marriage*

**36** [a]And the heads of the fathers'
*households* of the family of the
sons of Gilead, the son of Machir, the
son of Manasseh, of the families of
the sons of Joseph, came near and
spoke before Moses and before the
leaders, the heads of the fathers'
*households* of the sons of Israel, **2** and
they said, "Yahweh commanded my
lord to give the land by lot to the sons
of Israel as an inheritance, and my
lord [a]was commanded by Yahweh to
give the inheritance of Zelophehad
our brother to his daughters. **3** But
if they [1]marry one of the sons of the
*other* tribes of the sons of Israel, their
inheritance will be withdrawn from
the inheritance of our fathers and
will be added to the inheritance of
the tribe to which they belong; thus

**35:22** [a]Nu 35:11 **35:24** [a]Jos 20:6 [1]Or *one who strikes down*, cf. 35:21 **35:29** [a]Nu 27:11 **35:30** [a]Nu 35:16 [b]Dt 17:6; 19:15; Mt 18:16; Jn 7:51; 8:17, 18 **35:32** [1]Or *until* **35:33** [a]Dt 21:7, 8; Ps 106:38 [b]Ge 9:6 **35:34** [a]Lv 18:24, 25 [b]Nu 5:3 ◆ **36:1** [a]Nu 27:1 **36:2** [a]Nu 27:5-7 **36:3** [1]Lit *become wives to*, so in ch

it will be withdrawn from our allotted
inheritance. **4** And when the [a]jubilee
of the sons of Israel [1]comes, then
their inheritance will be added to the
inheritance of the tribe to which they
belong; so their inheritance will be
withdrawn from the inheritance of
the tribe of our fathers."

**5** Then Moses commanded the
sons of Israel according to the [1]word
of Yahweh, saying, "The tribe of
the sons of Joseph are right in *their*
statements. **6** [a]This is [1]what Yahweh
has commanded concerning the
daughters of Zelophehad, saying, 'Let
them marry whoever is good in their
sight; only they must marry within
the family of the tribe of their father.'
**7** Thus [a]no inheritance of the sons
of Israel shall [1]be transferred from
tribe to tribe, for the sons of Israel
shall each [2]hold to the inheritance of
the tribe of his fathers. **8** [a]And every
daughter who comes into possession
of an inheritance of any tribe of the
sons of Israel shall be wife to one of
the family of the tribe of her father,
so that the sons of Israel each may
possess the inheritance of his fathers.
**9** Thus no inheritance shall [1]be trans-
ferred from one tribe to another tribe,
for the tribes of the sons of Israel shall
each [2]hold to his own inheritance."

**10** Just as Yahweh had commanded
Moses, so the daughters of Zelophe-
had did: **11** [a]And Mahlah, Tirzah,
Hoglah, Milcah, and Noah, the
daughters of Zelophehad married
their uncles' sons. **12** They married
*those* from the families of the sons
of Manasseh the son of Joseph, and
their inheritance [1]remained with the
tribe of the family of their father.

**13** [a]These are the commandments
and the judgments which Yahweh
commanded to the sons of Israel by
the hand of Moses in the plains of
Moab by the Jordan *opposite* Jericho.

# DEUTERONOMY

### *Israel from Seir to Kadesh-barnea*

**1** These are the words which Mo-
ses spoke to all Israel [a]across
the Jordan in the wilderness, in the
[b]Arabah opposite [1]Suph, between
Paran and Tophel and Laban and
Hazeroth and Dizahab. **2** It is eleven
days' *journey* from [a]Horeb by the
way of Mount [b]Seir to [c]Kadesh-
barnea. **3** Now it happened, in the
[a]*fortieth* year, on the first *day* of
the eleventh month, Moses spoke
to the children of Israel, [b]according
to all that [1]Yahweh had commanded
him *to give* to them, **4** after he had
[a]struck down Sihon the king of the
Amorites, who lived in Heshbon,
and [b]Og the king of Bashan, who
lived in [c]Ashtaroth [1]and Edrei.
**5** Across the Jordan in the land of
Moab, Moses undertook to expound
this law, saying,

**36:4** [a]Lv 25:10 [1]Lit *shall be* **36:5** [1]Lit *mouth* **36:6** [a]Nu 27:7 [1]Lit *the thing which* **36:7** [a]1Ki 21:3 [1]Lit *turn about* [2]Lit *cleave* **36:8** [a]1Chr 23:22 **36:9** [1]Lit *turn about* [2]Lit *cleave* **36:11** [a]Nu 26:33 **36:12** [1]Lit *was* **36:13** [a]Lv 26:46; 27:34; Nu 22:1 ◆ **1:1** [a]Dt 4:46 [b]Dt 2:8 [1]Possibly the Red Sea **1:2** [a]Ex 3:1; 17:6 [b]Ge 32:3 [c]Nu 13:26; 32:8; Dt 9:23 **1:3** [a]Nu 33:38 [b]Dt 4:1, 2 [1]The personal covenant name of God, a form of I AM WHO I AM, cf. Ex 3:14-15 **1:4** [a]Nu 21:21-26; Dt 2:26-35; Jos 13:10; Ne 9:22 [b]Nu 21:33-35; Jos 13:12 [c]Jos 12:4 [1]As in ancient versions; M.T. omits *and*

6 "Yahweh our God [a]spoke to us at
Horeb, saying, 'You have [1]stayed long
enough at this mountain. 7 Turn and
set out, and go to [a]the hill country
of the Amorites, and to all their
neighbors in the Arabah, in the hill
country and in the [1]Shephelah and in
[b]the [2]Negev and by the seacoast, the
land of the Canaanites, and Lebanon,
as far as the great river, the river Eu-
phrates. 8 See, I have given over the
land before you; go in and possess the
land which Yahweh [a]swore to give to
your fathers, to Abraham, to Isaac,
and to Jacob, to them and to their
seed after them.'

9 "And I spoke to you at that time,
saying, '[a]I am not able to bear *the
burden* of you alone. 10 Yahweh your
God has [a]multiplied you, and behold,
you are this day like the stars of heav-
en in number. 11 May Yahweh, the
God of your fathers, increase you a
thousand-fold more than you are and
bless you, [a]just as He has [1]promised
you! 12 How can I alone bear the load
and burden of you and your strife?
13 [a,1]Choose wise and understanding
and experienced men from your
tribes, and I will appoint them as
your heads.' 14 Then you answered
me and said, 'The thing which you
have said to do is good.' 15 So I took
the heads of your tribes, wise and
*experienced men*, and gave them as
heads over you, leaders of thousands
and [1]of hundreds, [1]of fifties and [1]of
tens, and officers for your tribes.

16 "Then I commanded your judges
at that time, saying, 'Hear *the cases*
between your brothers, and [a]judge
righteously between a man and his
brother or the sojourner who is with
him. 17 [a]You shall not show partiality
in judgment; you shall hear the small
and the great alike. You shall [b]not fear
[1]man, for the judgment is God's. [c]The
case that is too hard for you, you shall
bring to me, and I will hear it.' 18 [a]And
I commanded you at that time all the
things that you should do.

19 "Then we set out from [a]Horeb
and went through all that [b]great and
fearsome wilderness which you saw
on the way to the [c]hill country of the
Amorites, just as Yahweh our God
had commanded us; and we came to
[a]Kadesh-barnea. 20 And I said to you,
'You have come to the hill country of
the Amorites which Yahweh our God
is about to give us. 21 See, Yahweh
your God has given over the land
before you; go up, take possession,
as Yahweh, the God of your fathers,
has spoken to you. [a]Do not fear or
be dismayed.'

22 "[a]Then all of you came near to
me and said, 'Let us send men before
us, that they may search out the land
for us and bring back to us word of
the way by which we should go up
and the cities which we shall enter.'
23 And the thing was good in my
sight, and I took twelve of your men,
one man for each tribe. 24 [a]Then
they turned and went up into the
hill country and came to the valley
of Eshcol and spied it out. 25 Then
they took *some* of the fruit of the land
in their hands and brought it down

**1:6** [a]Nu 10:11-13 [1]Lit *dwelt* **1:7** [a]Ge 15:18; Dt 11:24; Jos 10:40 [b]Ge 12:9 [1]Or *lowland* [2]South country **1:8** [a]Ge 12:7; 26:3; 28:13; Ex 33:1; Nu 14:23; 32:11; Heb 6:13, 14 **1:9** [a]Ex 18:18, 24; Nu 11:14 **1:10** [a]Ge 15:5; 22:17; Ex 32:13; Dt 7:7; 10:22; 26:5; 28:62 **1:11** [a]Dt 1:8, 10 [1]Lit *spoken to* **1:13** [a]Ex 18:21 [1]Lit *Give for yourselves* **1:15** [1]Lit *leaders of* **1:16** [a]Dt 16:18; Jn 7:24 **1:17** [a]Dt 10:17; 16:19; 24:17; 2Chr 19:5, 6; Pr 24:23-26; Ac 10:34; Jas 2:1, 9 [b]Pr 29:25 [c]Ex 18:22, 26 [1]Lit *because of man* **1:18** [a]Ex 18:20 **1:19** [a]Dt 1:2 [b]Dt 2:7; 8:15; 32:10; Jer 2:6 [c]Dt 1:7 **1:21** [a]Jos 1:6, 9 **1:22** [a]Nu 13:1-3 **1:24** [a]Nu 13:21-25

to us; and they brought word back to
us and said, 'It is a good land which
Yahweh our God is about to give us.'
**26** "[a]Yet you were not willing
to go up, but [b]rebelled against the
[1]command of Yahweh your God;
**27** and [a]you grumbled in your tents
and said, 'Because Yahweh hates us,
He has brought us out of the land
of Egypt to give us into the hand of
the Amorites to destroy us. **28** Where
can we go up? Our brothers have
made our hearts melt, saying, "The
people are bigger and taller than we;
the cities are large and fortified to
heaven. And moreover, we saw [a]the
sons of the Anakim there."' **29** Then
I said to you, 'Do not be in dread, nor
fear them. **30** Yahweh your God, who
goes before you, will [a]Himself fight
on your behalf, [1]just as He did for you
in Egypt before your eyes, **31** and in
the wilderness where you saw how
[a]Yahweh your God carried you, just
as a man carries his son, in all the
way which you have walked until
you came to this place.' **32** But [a,1]for
all this, you did not believe Yahweh
your God, **33** [a]who goes before you
on *your* way, [b]to spy out a place for
you to encamp, in fire by night and
cloud by day, to show you the way in
which you should go.
**34** "Then Yahweh heard the sound
of your words, and He was angry and
[a]swore *an oath*, saying, **35** '[a]Not one
of these men, this evil generation,
shall see the good land which I swore
to give your fathers, **36** except Caleb
the son of Jephunneh; he shall see it,
and [a]to him and to his sons I will give
the land on which he has set foot,
because he has followed Yahweh
fully.' **37** [a]Yahweh was angry with me
also on your account, saying, '[b]Not
even you shall enter there. **38** Joshua
the son of Nun, who stands before
you, [a]he shall enter there; strength-
en him, for [b]he will cause Israel to
inherit it. **39** Moreover, [a]your little
ones who you said would become
plunder, and your sons, who this day
have [b]no knowledge of good or evil,
shall enter there, and I will give it to
them, and they shall possess it. **40** But
as for you, [a]turn around and set out
for the wilderness by the way to the
[1]Red Sea.'
**41** "[a]Then you said to me, 'We
have sinned against Yahweh; we
will indeed go up and fight, just as
Yahweh our God commanded us.'
And every man of you girded on his
weapons of war and regarded it as
easy to go up into the hill country.
**42** [a]And Yahweh said to me, 'Say
to them, "Do not go up and do not
fight—for I am not among you—so
that you are not [1]defeated before your
enemies."' **43** So I spoke to you, but
you would not listen. Instead [a]you
rebelled against the [1]command of
Yahweh and acted presumptuously
and went up into the hill country.
**44** [a]And the Amorites who [1]lived in
that hill country came out to meet

---

***1:26*** [a]Nu 14:1-4 [b]Dt 9:23 [1]Lit *mouth* **1:27** [a]Dt 9:28; Ps 106:25 **1:28** [a]Nu 13:28, 33; Dt 9:2
**1:30** [a]Ex 14:14; Dt 3:22; 20:4; Ne 4:20 [1]Lit *according to all that* **1:31** [a]Dt 32:10-12; Is 46:3, 4; 63:9;
Hos 11:3; Ac 13:18 **1:32** [a]Nu 14:11; Ps 106:24; Heb 3:19; 4:2; Jd 5 [1]Lit *in this matter* **1:33** [a]Ex 13:21;
Nu 9:15-23; Ne 9:12; Ps 78:14 [b]Nu 10:33 **1:34** [a]Nu 14:28-30; Heb 3:18 **1:35** [a]Ps 95:11; 106:26; Eze 20:15;
1Co 10:5; Heb 3:14-19 **1:36** [a]Nu 14:24; Jos 14:9 **1:37** [a]Nu 20:12; Dt 3:26; 4:21 [b]Nu 27:13, 18
**1:38** [a]Nu 14:30 [b]Nu 34:17; Dt 3:28; 31:7; Jos 11:23 **1:39** [a]Nu 14:3, 31 [b]Is 7:15, 16 **1:40** [a]Nu 14:25
[1]Lit *Sea of Reeds* **1:41** [a]Nu 14:40 **1:42** [a]Nu 14:41-43 [1]Lit *smitten* **1:43** [a]Nu 14:40 [1]Lit *mouth*
**1:44** [a]Nu 14:45 [1]Lit *dwelt*

you and pursued you [b]as bees do and
crushed you from Seir to Hormah.
**45** Then you returned and wept be-
fore Yahweh; but [a]Yahweh did not
listen to your voice nor give ear to
you. **46** So you remained in [a]Kadesh
many days, according to the days that
you remained *there.*

### *Wanderings in the Wilderness*

**2** "[a]Then we turned and set out
for the wilderness by the way
to the [1]Red Sea, as Yahweh spoke
to me, and circled [b]Mount Seir for
many days. **2** And Yahweh spoke to
me, saying, **3** 'You have circled this
mountain long enough. *Now* turn
north, **4** [a]and command the people,
saying, "You are going to pass through
the [b]territory of your brothers the
sons of Esau who live in Seir; and
[c]they will be afraid of you. So be very
careful; **5** do not [1]provoke them, for
I will not give you any of their land,
even *as little as* a [2]footstep [a]because
I have given Mount Seir to Esau as a
possession. **6** You shall buy food from
them with money so that you may
eat, and you shall also bargain with
them for water with money so that
you may drink. **7** For Yahweh your
God has blessed you in all the work
of your hand; He has known your
[1]wanderings through this [a]great wil-
*derness. These* [b]*forty years* Yahweh
your God has been with you; you
have not lacked a thing."'
**8** "So we passed beyond our broth-
ers the sons of Esau, who live in Seir,
away from the [a]Arabah road, away
from Elath and [b]from Ezion-geber.
And we turned and passed through
by the way of the wilderness of
Moab. **9** Then Yahweh said to me,
'Do not harass Moab, nor provoke
them to war, for I will not give you
any of [1]their land as a possession
because I have given [a]Ar to [b]the
sons of Lot as a possession.' **10** (The
[a]Emim lived there formerly, a people
as great, numerous, and tall as the
Anakim. **11** Like the Anakim, they are
also regarded as [a]Rephaim, but the
Moabites call them Emim. **12** [a]Now
the Horites formerly lived in Seir,
but the sons of Esau dispossessed
them and destroyed them from be-
fore them and settled in their place,
[b]just as Israel would do to the land
of [1]their possession which Yahweh
gave to them.) **13** 'Now arise and cross
over the [1]brook Zered yourselves.' So
we crossed over the [1]brook Zered.
**14** Now the [1]time that it took for us to
come from Kadesh-barnea until we
crossed over the [2]brook Zered was
[a]thirty-eight years, until [b]all the
generation of the men of war came
to an end from within the camp,
as [c]Yahweh had sworn to them.
**15** [a]Moreover the hand of Yahweh
was against them, to bring them
into confusion from within the camp
until they all came to an end.
**16** "So it happened when [a]all the
men of war had come to an end
in death from among the people,
**17** that Yahweh spoke to me, saying,

**1:44** [b]Ps 118:12 **1:45** [a]Job 27:8, 9; Ps 66:18; Jn 9:31 **1:46** [a]Nu 20:1, 22; Dt 2:7, 14; Jdg 11:17
◆ **2:1** [a]Nu 21:4 [b]Dt 1:2 [1]Lit *Sea of Reeds* **2:4** [a]Nu 20:14-21 [b]Ge 36:8 [c]Ex 15:15, 16 **2:5** [a]Ge 36:8; Jos 24:4 [1]Or *engage in strife with* [2]Lit *treading of a sole of a foot* **2:7** [a]Dt 1:19 [b]Nu 14:33, 34; 32:13; Dt 2:14 [1]Lit *goings* **2:8** [a]Dt 1:1 [b]Nu 33:35; 1Ki 9:26 **2:9** [a]Nu 21:15, 28; Dt 2:18, 29 [b]Ge 19:36, 37 [1]Lit *his* **2:10** [a]Ge 14:5 **2:11** [a]Ge 14:5; Dt 2:20 **2:12** [a]Ge 36:20; Dt 2:22 [b]Nu 21:25, 35 [1]Lit *his* **2:13** [1]Or *wadi* **2:14** [a]Dt 2:7 [b]Nu 14:29-35; 26:64, 65; Ps 106:26; 1Co 10:5 [c]Dt 1:34, 35 [1]Lit *days in which we went* [2]Or *wadi* **2:15** [a]Jd 5 **2:16** [a]Dt 2:14

**18** 'Today you are about to cross over
[a]Ar, the border of Moab. **19** And you
will come opposite the [a]sons of
Ammon. Do not harass them nor
provoke them, for I will not give you
any of the land of the sons of Ammon
as a possession because I have given
it to [b]the sons of Lot as a possession.'
**20** (It is also regarded as the land of
the [a]Rephaim, *for* Rephaim formerly
lived in it, but the Ammonites call
them Zamzummin, **21** a people as
great, numerous, and tall as the
Anakim, but Yahweh destroyed them
before them. And they dispossessed
them and settled in their place, **22** just
as He did for the sons of Esau, who
[a]live in Seir, when He destroyed [b]the
Horites from before them; they dis-
possessed them and settled in their
place even to this day. **23** And the
[a]Avvim, who lived in villages as far
as Gaza, the [b,1]Caphtorim who came
from [c,2]Caphtor, destroyed them and
lived in their place.) **24** 'Arise, set
out, and pass through the [a,1]valley
of Arnon. Look! I have given Sihon
the Amorite, king of Heshbon, and
his land into your hand; begin to
take possession and provoke him
to battle. **25** This day I will begin to
put [a]the dread and fear of you [1]upon
the peoples [2]everywhere under the
heavens, who, when they hear the
report of you, [b]will tremble and be
in anguish because of you.'

**26** "[a]So I sent messengers from the
wilderness of Kedemoth to Sihon
king of Heshbon with words of peace,
saying, **27** 'Let me pass through your
land, I will [1]go only on the highway;
I will not turn aside to the right or to
the left. **28** You will sell me food for
money so that I may eat, and give me
water for money so that I may drink;
[a]only let me pass through on [1]foot,
**29** just as the sons of Esau who live
in Seir and the Moabites who live in
[a]Ar did for me, until I cross over the
Jordan into the land which Yahweh
our God is giving to us.' **30** But [a]Sihon
king of Heshbon was not willing
for us to pass [1]through his land,
for [b]Yahweh your God stiffened his
spirit and made his heart obstinate,
in order to give him over into your
hand, as *he is* today. **31** And Yahweh
said to me, 'See, I have begun to give
Sihon and his land [1]over to you. Be-
gin to possess, so that you may *fully*
possess his land.'

**32** "Then Sihon [1]with all his people
came out to meet us in battle at Jahaz.
**33** [a]But Yahweh our God gave him [1]over
to us, and we [b]struck him down with
his sons and all his people. **34** So we
captured all his cities at that time and
[a,1]devoted to destruction [2]the men,
women, and little ones of every city.
We left no survivor remaining. **35** We
took [a]only the animals as our plunder
and the spoil of the cities which we
had captured. **36** From [a]Aroer which
is on the edge of the [1]valley of Arnon
and *from* the city which is in the
[1]valley, even to Gilead, there was

**2:18** [a]Dt 2:9 **2:19** [a]Ge 19:38 [b]Dt 2:9 **2:20** [a]Dt 2:11 **2:22** [a]Ge 36:8; Dt 2:5 [b]Dt 2:12
**2:23** [a]Jos 13:3 [b]Ge 10:14; 1Chr 1:12 [c]Jer 47:4; Am 9:7 [1]Possibly ancestors to the Philistines, cf. Ge 10:14; Jer 47:4 [2]Possibly Crete **2:24** [a]Nu 21:13, 14; Jdg 11:18 [1]Or *wadi* **2:25** [a]Ex 23:27; Dt 11:25; Jos 2:9 [b]Ex 15:14-16 [1]Lit *in front of* [2]Lit *under all the heavens* **2:26** [a]Nu 21:21-32; Dt 1:4; Jdg 11:19-21
**2:27** [1]Lit *go by the way* **2:28** [a]Nu 20:19 [1]Lit *my feet* **2:29** [a]Dt 2:9 **2:30** [a]Nu 21:23 [b]Ex 4:21; Jos 11:20 [1]Lit *by him* **2:31** [1]Lit *before you* **2:32** [1]Lit *he and* **2:33** [a]Ex 23:31; Dt 7:2 [b]Dt 29:7 [1]Lit *before us* **2:34** [a]Dt 3:6; 7:2 [1]Or *put them under the ban* [2]Lit *every city of men...* **2:35** [a]Dt 3:7
**2:36** [a]Dt 3:12; 4:48; Jos 12:2; 13:9 [1]Or *wadi*

not a town that was too high for us;
Yahweh our God gave all [2]over to us.
**37** [a]Only you did not go near to the
land of the sons of Ammon, all along
the [1]river [b]Jabbok and the cities of the
hill country, and wherever Yahweh
our God had commanded us.

### *Israel Takes Possession of the Land*

**3** “[a]Then we turned and went up
the road to Bashan, and Og king
of Bashan, [1]with all his people, came
out to meet us in battle at Edrei. **2** But
Yahweh said to me, ‘Do not fear him,
for I have given him and all his people
and his land over into your hand; and
you shall do to him just as you did
to Sihon king of the Amorites, who
lived at Heshbon.’ **3** So Yahweh our
God also gave Og, king of Bashan, with
all his people over into our hand, and
we struck [1]them until [2]there was no
survivor remaining for him. **4** And
we captured all his cities at that time;
there was not a town which we did
not take from them: sixty cities, all the
region of [a]Argob, the kingdom of Og in
Bashan. **5** All these were cities fortified
with high walls, gates and bars, besides
a great many [1]unwalled towns. **6** And
we [1]devoted them to destruction, as
we did to [a]Sihon king of Heshbon,
[b,2]devoting to destruction [3]the men,
women, and little ones of every city.
**7** [a]But all the animals and the spoil of
the cities we took as our plunder.
**8** “[a]Thus we took the land at that
time from the hand of the two kings
of the Amorites who were beyond
the Jordan, from the [1]valley of Arnon
to Mount Hermon **9** (Sidonians [a]call
Hermon [b]Sirion, and the Amorites
call it [c]Senir): **10** all the cities of the
plateau and all Gilead and [a]all Bashan,
as far as Salecah and Edrei, cities of
the kingdom of Og in Bashan. **11** (For
only Og king of Bashan remained
of the remnant of the [a]Rephaim.
Behold, his [1]bedstead was an iron
[1]bedstead; it is in [b]Rabbah of the
sons of Ammon. Its length was [2]nine
cubits, and its width four cubits [3]by
ordinary cubit.)
**12** “So we took possession of this
land at that time. From [a]Aroer, which
is by the [1]valley of Arnon, and half
the hill country of [b]Gilead and its
cities I gave to the Reubenites and
to the Gadites. **13** And the rest of
Gilead and all Bashan, the kingdom
of Og, I gave to the half-tribe of
Manasseh, all the region of Argob.
(Concerning all Bashan, it is called
the land of Rephaim. **14** [a]Jair the son
of Manasseh took all the region of
Argob as far as the border of the
Geshurites and the Maacathites and
called [1]it—*that is,* Bashan—after his
own name, [2]Havvoth-jair, *as it is* to
this day.) **15** [a]And to Machir I gave
Gilead. **16** And to the Reubenites
and to the Gadites I gave from Gilead
even as far as the [1]valley of Arnon,
the middle of the [1]valley [2]as a border
and as far as the [1]river [a]Jabbok, the
border of the sons of Ammon; **17** the

**2:36** [2]Lit *before us* **2:37** [a]Dt 2:19 [b]Ge 32:22; Nu 21:24; Dt 3:16 [1]Or *wadi* ◆ **3:1** [a]Nu 21:33-35 [1]Lit *he and* **3:3** [1]Lit *him* [2]Lit *he had no survivor* **3:4** [a]Dt 3:13, 14; 1Ki 4:13 **3:5** [1]Or *rural* **3:6** [a]Dt 1:4 [b]Dt 2:34 [1]Or *put them under the ban* [2]Or *putting under the ban* [3]Lit *every city of men...* **3:7** [a]Dt 2:35 **3:8** [a]Nu 32:33; Jos 12:1-7; 13:8-12 [1]Or *wadi* **3:9** [a]Dt 4:48; Jos 11:17; Ps 42:6; 133:3 [b]Ps 29:6 [c]1Chr 5:23 **3:10** [a]Jos 13:11 **3:11** [a]Ge 14:5; Dt 2:11, 20 [b]2Sa 11:1; 12:26; Jer 49:2 [1]Or *couch* [2]Approx. 14 ft. long and 6 ft. wide or 4 m and 1.8 m [3]Lit *by a man's forearm* **3:12** [a]Dt 2:36 [b]Nu 32:32-38; Jos 13:8-13 [1]Or *wadi* **3:14** [a]Nu 32:41; 1Chr 2:22 [1]Lit *them* [2]Lit *the towns of Jair* **3:15** [a]Nu 32:39, 40 **3:16** [a]Nu 21:24; Dt 2:37 [1]Or *wadi* [2]Lit *and*

Arabah also, with the Jordan [1]as *a*
border, from [a,2]Chinnereth [b]even
as far as the sea of the Arabah, [c]the
Salt Sea, [3]at the foot of the slopes of
Pisgah on the east.
**18** "Then I commanded you at that
time, saying, '[a]Yahweh your God has
given you this land to possess it; [b]all
you men of valor shall cross over
armed before your brothers, the sons
of Israel. **19** [a]But your wives and your
little ones and your livestock (I know
that you have [b]much livestock) shall
remain in your cities which I have
given you, **20** [a]until Yahweh gives rest
to your brothers as to you, and they
also possess the land which Yahweh
your God will give them beyond the
Jordan. [b]Then you may return, every
man to his possession which I have
given you.' **21** And I commanded
Joshua at that time, saying, 'Your
eyes have seen all that Yahweh your
God has done to these two kings; so
Yahweh shall do to all the kingdoms
into which you are about to cross.
**22** Do not fear them, for Yahweh your
God [a]is the one fighting for you.'

### *Moses Pleads to Cross the Jordan*

**23** "I also pleaded with Yahweh at that
time, saying, **24** 'O Lord Yahweh, You
have begun to show Your slave [a]Your
greatness and Your strong hand; for
what [b]god is there in heaven or on
earth who can do such works and
mighty acts as Yours? **25** Let me, I
pray, cross over and see the [a]good
land that is beyond the Jordan, [1]that
good hill country and Lebanon.'
**26** But [a]Yahweh was angry with me
on your account and would not
listen to me; and Yahweh said to
me, '[1]Enough! Speak to Me no more
of this matter. **27** Go up to the top
of [a]Pisgah and lift up your eyes to
the west and north and south and
east, and see *it* with your eyes, [b]for
you shall not cross over this Jor-
dan. **28** [a]But command Joshua and
strengthen him and encourage him,
[b]for he shall go across [1]at the head of
this people, and he will cause them
to inherit the land which you will
see.' **29** So we remained in the valley
opposite [a]Beth-peor.

### *Keep the Commandments of Yahweh*

**4** "So now, O Israel, listen to the
statutes and the judgments
which [a]I am teaching you to do, so
that [b]you may live and go in and take
possession of the land which Yah-
weh, the God of your fathers, is giving
you. **2** [a]You shall not add to the word
which [b]I am commanding you, nor
take away from it, that you may keep
the commandments of Yahweh your
God which I am commanding you.
**3** [a]Your eyes have seen what Yahweh
has done in the case of Baal-peor,
for all the men who walked after
Baal-peor, Yahweh your God has
destroyed [1]them from among you.
**4** But you who clung to Yahweh your
God are alive today, every one of you.
**5** "See, I have taught you statutes
and judgments [a]just as Yahweh

**3:17** [a]Nu 34:11; Jos 13:27 [b]Jos 12:3 [c]Ge 14:3; Jos 3:16 [1]Lit *and* [2]The Sea of Galilee [3]Lit *under*
**3:18** [a]Jos 1:13 [b]Nu 32:20; Jos 4:12, 13 **3:19** [a]Jos 1:14 [b]Ex 12:38 **3:20** [a]Jos 1:15 [b]Jos 22:4
**3:22** [a]Ex 14:14; Dt 1:30; 20:4; Ne 4:20 **3:24** [a]Dt 11:2 [b]Ex 8:10; 15:11; 2Sa 7:22; Ps 71:19; 86:8
**3:25** [a]Dt 4:22 [1]Lit *this* **3:26** [a]Dt 1:37 [1]Lit *Enough for you* **3:27** [a]Nu 23:14; 27:12 [b]Dt 1:37
**3:28** [a]Nu 27:18; Dt 31:3, 7, 8, 23 [b]Dt 1:38 [1]Lit *before this people* **3:29** [a]Nu 25:1-3; Dt 4:46; 34:6
◆ **4:1** [a]Dt 1:3 [b]Lv 18:5; Dt 5:33; 8:1; 16:20; 30:16, 19; Eze 20:11; Ro 10:5 **4:2** [a]Dt 12:32; Pr 30:6; Rev 22:18
[b]Dt 4:5, 14, 40 **4:3** [a]Nu 25:1-9 [1]Lit *him* **4:5** [a]Lv 26:46; 27:34

my God commanded me, that you
should do thus in the land where
you are entering to possess it. **6** You
shall keep and do *them*, [a]for that is
your wisdom and your understand-
ing in the sight of the peoples who
will hear all these statutes and say,
'Surely this great nation is a wise
and understanding people.' **7** For
[a]what great nation is there that has
a god [b]so near to it as is Yahweh our
God [c]whenever we call on Him? **8** Or
what great nation is there that has
[a]statutes and judgments as righteous
as this whole law which I am setting
before you today?

**9** "Only [a]keep yourself and keep
your soul very carefully, lest you for-
get the things which your eyes have
seen and lest they depart from your
heart [b]all the days of your life. But
[c]make them known to your sons and
to your grandsons. **10** *Remember* the
day you stood before Yahweh your
God at Horeb, when Yahweh said to
me, 'Assemble the people to Me, that I
may cause them to hear My words [a]so
they may learn to [1]fear Me all the days
they live on the earth, and that they
may [b]teach their children.' **11** And
you came near and stood at the foot
of the mountain, [a]and the mountain
burned with fire to the *very* heart of
the heavens: darkness, cloud, and
dense gloom. **12** Then Yahweh spoke
to you from the midst of the fire; you
heard the sound of words, but you
saw no form—only a voice. **13** So He
declared to you His covenant which
He commanded you to do, *that is*,
[a]the Ten [1]Commandments; and [b]He
wrote them on two tablets of stone.
**14** And Yahweh commanded me at
that time to teach you statutes and
judgments, that you might do them
in the land where you are going over
to possess it.

**15** "So [a]keep your souls very care-
fully, since you did not see any [b]form
on the day Yahweh spoke to you at
Horeb from the midst of the fire,
**16** lest you [a]act corruptly and [b]make
a graven image for yourselves in the
form of any figure, the likeness of
male or female, **17** the likeness of
any animal that is on the earth, the
likeness of [a]any winged bird that flies
in the sky, **18** the likeness of anything
that creeps on the ground, the like-
ness of any fish that is in the water
below the earth, **19** and lest you lift up
your eyes to heaven and see the sun
and the moon and the stars, [a]all the
host of heaven, [b]and be drawn away
and worship them and serve them,
those which Yahweh your God has
apportioned for all the peoples under
the whole heaven. **20** But Yahweh has
taken you and brought you out of
[a]the iron furnace, from Egypt, to [b]be
a people for His own inheritance, as
today.

**21** "[a]Now Yahweh was angry with
me on your account and swore that I
would not cross the Jordan, and that I
would not enter the good land which

---

**4:6** [a]Dt 30:19, 20; 32:46, 47; Job 28:28; Ps 19:7; 111:10; Pr 1:7; 2Ti 3:15 **4:7** [a]Dt 4:32-34; 2Sa 7:23 [b]Ps 34:17, 18; 145:18; 148:14; Is 55:6 [c]Ps 34:18; 85:9 **4:8** [a]Ps 89:14; 97:2; 119:144, 160, 172 **4:9** [a]Dt 4:23; 6:12; 8:11, 14, 19; Pr 4:23; 23:19 [b]Dt 6:2; 12:1; 16:3 [c]Ge 18:19; Dt 4:10; 6:7, 20-25; 11:19; 32:46; Ps 78:5, 6; Pr 22:6; Eph 6:4 **4:10** [a]Dt 14:23; 17:19; 31:12, 13 [b]Dt 4:9 [1]Or *reverence* **4:11** [a]Ex 19:18; Heb 12:18, 19 **4:13** [a]Ex 34:28; Dt 10:4 [b]Ex 31:18; 34:1, 28 [1]Lit *Words* **4:15** [a]Jos 23:11 [b]Is 40:18 **4:16** [a]Dt 4:25; 9:12; 31:29 [b]Ex 20:4; Lv 26:1; Dt 5:8, 9; 27:15; Ro 1:23 **4:17** [a]Ro 1:23 **4:19** [a]Ge 2:1; Dt 17:3; 2Ki 17:16; 21:3 [b]Dt 13:5, 10; Job 31:26-28 **4:20** [a]1Ki 8:51; Jer 11:4 [b]Ex 19:5; Dt 7:6; 14:2; 26:18; Tit 2:14; 1Pe 2:9 **4:21** [a]Nu 20:12; Dt 1:37

Yahweh your God is giving you as an inheritance. **22** For [a]I will die in this land, I shall not cross the Jordan, but you shall cross and take possession of this [b]good land. **23** So keep yourselves, [a]lest you forget the covenant of Yahweh your God which He cut with you and [b]make for yourselves a graven image in the form of anything *against* which Yahweh your God has commanded you. **24** For Yahweh your God is a [a]consuming fire, a [b]jealous God.

**25** "When you [1]become the father of children and children's children and remain long in the land and [a]act corruptly and [b]make [2]a graven image in the form of anything and [c]do that which is evil in the sight of Yahweh your God *so as* to provoke Him to anger, **26** I [a]call heaven and earth to witness against you today, that you will [b]surely perish quickly from the land where you are going over the Jordan to possess it. You shall not prolong your days on it, but will be utterly destroyed. **27** And Yahweh will [a]scatter you among the peoples, and you will remain few in number among the nations where Yahweh drives you. **28** [a]And there you will serve gods, the work of man's hands, [b]wood and stone, [c]which neither see nor hear nor eat nor smell. **29** [a]But from there you will seek Yahweh your God, and you will find *Him*, for you will search for Him [b]with all your heart and all your soul. **30** When you [a]are in distress and all these things have come upon you, [b]in the last days [c]you will return to Yahweh your God and listen to His voice. **31** For Yahweh your God is a [a]compassionate God; [b]He will not fail you nor [c]destroy you nor [d]forget the covenant with your fathers which He swore to them.

**32** "Indeed, [a]ask now concerning the former days which were before you, since the [b]day that God created [1]man on the earth, and *inquire* [c]from one end of the heavens to the other. [d]Has *anything* been done like this great thing, or has *anything* been heard like it? **33** [a]Has *any* people heard the voice of God speaking from the midst of the fire, as you have heard *it*, and lived? **34** [a]Or has a god tried to go to take for himself a nation from within *another* nation [b]with trials, with signs and wonders and with war and [c]with a mighty hand and with an outstretched arm and with great terrors, [1]as Yahweh your God did for you in Egypt before your eyes? **35** To you it was shown that you might know that Yahweh, He is God; [a]there is no other besides Him. **36** [a]Out of the heavens He caused you to hear His voice [b]to discipline you; and on earth He caused you to see His great fire, and you heard His words from the midst of the fire.

**4:22** [a]Nu 27:13, 14 [b]Dt 3:25 **4:23** [a]Dt 4:9 [b]Dt 4:16 **4:24** [a]Ex 24:17; Dt 9:3; Is 30:27; 33:14; Heb 12:29 [b]Dt 5:9; 6:15 **4:25** [a]Dt 4:16 [b]Dt 4:23 [c]2Ki 17:17 [1]Lit *beget* [2]Or *an idol* **4:26** [a]Dt 30:19; 31:28; 32:1; Is 1:2; Mic 6:2 [b]Dt 7:4; 8:19, 20 **4:27** [a]Lv 26:33; Dt 28:64; 29:28; Ne 1:8 **4:28** [a]Dt 28:36, 64; Jer 16:13 [b]Dt 29:17 [c]Ps 115:4-8; 135:15-18; Is 44:12-20 **4:29** [a]Dt 30:1-3, 10; 2Chr 15:4; Is 55:6; Jer 29:13 [b]Dt 6:5; 10:12 **4:30** [a]Ps 18:6; 59:16; 107:6, 13 [b]Dt 31:29; Jer 23:20; Hos 3:5; Heb 1:2 [c]Jer 4:1, 2 **4:31** [a]Ex 34:6; 2Chr 30:9; Ne 9:31; Ps 103:8; 111:4; 116:5; Jon 4:2 [b]Dt 31:6, 8; Jos 1:5; 1Chr 28:20; Heb 13:5 [c]Jer 30:11 [d]Lv 26:45 **4:32** [a]Dt 32:7; Job 8:8 [b]Ge 1:27; Is 45:12 [c]Dt 28:64; Mt 24:31 [d]Dt 4:7; 2Sa 7:23 [1]Or *Adam* **4:33** [a]Ex 20:22; Dt 5:24, 26 **4:34** [a]Ex 14:30; Dt 33:29 [b]Dt 7:19 [c]Dt 5:15; 6:21; Ps 136:12 [1]Lit *according to all that* **4:35** [a]Ex 8:10; 9:14; Dt 4:39; 32:12, 39; 1Sa 2:2; Is 43:10-12; 44:6-8; 45:5-7; Mk 12:32 **4:36** [a]Ex 19:9, 19; 20:18, 22; Dt 4:33; Ne 9:13; Heb 12:25 [b]Dt 8:5

**37** [a,1]Because He loved your fathers,
therefore He chose their seed after
them. And He [b,2]personally brought
you from Egypt by His great power,
**38** dispossessing before you nations
greater and mightier than you, to
bring you in *and* [a]to give you their
land for an inheritance, as it is to-
day. **39** Know therefore today, and
take it to your heart, that [a]Yahweh,
He is God in heaven above and on
the earth below; there is no other.
**40** [a]So you shall keep His statutes
and His commandments which I
am commanding you today, that [b]it
may go well with you and with your
children after you, and [c]that you may
prolong *your* days on the land which
Yahweh your God is giving you for all
the days."

**41** [a]Then Moses set apart three
cities across the Jordan to the *east*
toward the sunrise, **42** that a man-
slayer might flee there, who slew
his neighbor [1]without premedita-
tion, [2]not hating him previously; so
he shall flee to one of these cities
that he might live: **43** [a]Bezer in the
wilderness on the plateau for the
Reubenites, and Ramoth in Gilead
for the Gadites, and Golan in Bashan
for the Manassites.

**44** Now this is the law which Moses
set before the sons of Israel; **45** these
are the testimonies and the statutes
*and the* judgments which Moses spoke
to the sons of Israel when they came
out from Egypt, **46** across the Jordan,
in the valley [a]opposite Beth-peor, in
the land of [b]Sihon king of the Am-
orites who lived at Heshbon, whom
Moses and the sons of Israel struck
down when they came out from Egypt.
**47** And they took possession of his land
and the land of [a]Og king of Bashan, the
two kings of the Amorites, *who were*
across the Jordan to the *east* toward
the sunrise, **48** from [a]Aroer, which is
on the edge of the [1]valley of Arnon,
even as far as [b]Mount Sion (that is,
Hermon), **49** with all the Arabah across
the Jordan to the east, even as far as
the sea of the Arabah, [1]at the foot
of the slopes of Pisgah.

### *The Ten Commandments Repeated*

**5** Then Moses summoned all Israel
and said to them:

"Hear, O Israel, the statutes and
the judgments which I am speaking
today in your [1]hearing, that you may
learn them and be careful to do them.
**2** Yahweh our God cut [a]a covenant
with us at Horeb. **3** [a]Yahweh did not
cut this covenant with our fathers,
but with us, *with* all those of [1]us
alive here today. **4** Yahweh spoke to
you [a]face to face at the mountain
[b]from the midst of the fire. **5** [a]I was
standing between Yahweh and you
at that time, to declare to you the
word of Yahweh; [b]for you were afraid
because of the fire and did not go up
the mountain. [1]He said,

**6** '[a]I am Yahweh your God who
brought you out of the land
of Egypt, out of the house of
[1]slavery.

---

**4:37** [a]Dt 7:7, 8; 10:15; 33:3 [b]Ex 33:14; Is 63:9 [1]Lit *And instead, because* [2]Lit *with His presence* **4:38** [a]Nu 32:4; 34:14, 15 **4:39** [a]Dt 4:35; Jos 2:11 **4:40** [a]Lv 22:31; Dt 4:2; Ps 105:45 [b]Dt 4:1; 5:16, 29, 33; 6:3, 18; 12:25, 28; 22:7 [c]Ex 23:26; Dt 32:47 **4:41** [a]Nu 35:6; Dt 19:2-13; Jos 20:7-9 **4:42** [1]Lit *without knowledge* [2]Lit *and he was not hating him previously* **4:43** [a]Jos 20:8 **4:46** [a]Dt 3:29 [b]Nu 21:21-25 **4:47** [a]Dt 1:4; 3:3, 4 **4:48** [a]Dt 2:36; 3:12 [b]Dt 3:9; Ps 133:3 [1]Or *wadi* **4:49** [1]Lit *under* ◆ **5:1** [1]Lit *ears* **5:2** [a]Ex 19:5; Mal 4:4 **5:3** [a]Jer 31:32; Heb 8:9 [1]Lit *us ourselves* **5:4** [a]Nu 14:14; Dt 34:10 [b]Dt 4:33 **5:5** [a]Ga 3:19 [b]Ex 19:16, 21-24; 20:18; Heb 12:18-21 [1]Lit *saying* **5:6** [a]Ex 20:2-17; Lv 26:1; Dt 6:4; Ps 81:10 [1]Lit *slaves*

7 '[a]You shall have no other gods
[1]before Me.

8 '[a]You shall not make for
yourself [1]an idol—any
likeness *of* what is in heaven
above [2]or on the earth
beneath [2]or in the water under
the earth.

9 'You shall not worship them
or serve them; for I, Yahweh
your God, am a jealous God,
[a]visiting the iniquity of the
fathers on the children and
on the third and the fourth
*generations* of those who
hate Me,

10 but [a]showing lovingkindness
to thousands, to those
who love Me and keep My
commandments.

11 '[a]You shall not take the name
of Yahweh your God in vain,
for Yahweh will not [1]leave him
unpunished who takes His
name in vain.

12 '[a]Observe the sabbath day to
keep it holy, as Yahweh your
God commanded you.

13 'Six days you shall labor and
do all your work,

14 but [a]the seventh day is a
sabbath of Yahweh your God;
*in it* you shall not do any
work, you or your son or your
daughter or your male slave
or your female slave or your
ox or your donkey or any of
your cattle or your sojourner
who is within your gates, so
that your male slave and your
female slave may rest as well
as you.

15 '[a]You shall remember that
you were a slave in the land
of Egypt, and Yahweh your
God brought you out of there
with a mighty hand and
with an outstretched arm;
therefore Yahweh your God
commanded you to observe
the sabbath day.

16 '[a]Honor your father and your
mother, as Yahweh your God
has commanded you, [b]that
your days may be prolonged
and that it may go well with
you on the land which Yahweh
your God gives you.

17 '[a]You shall not murder.

18 '[a]You shall not commit
adultery.

19 '[a]You shall not steal.

20 '[a]You shall not bear false
witness against your
neighbor.

21 '[a]You shall not covet your
neighbor's wife, and you shall
not desire your neighbor's
house, his field, or his male

---

**5:7** [a]Ex 20:3 [1]*Or besides* **5:8** [a]Ex 20:4-6; Lv 26:1; Dt 4:15-18; 27:15; Ps 97:7 [1]Or a graven image [2]Lit *or what is* **5:9** [a]Ex 34:7; Nu 14:18; Dt 7:10 **5:10** [a]Nu 14:18; Dt 7:9; Jer 32:18 **5:11** [a]Ex 20:7; Lv 19:12; Dt 6:13; 10:20; Mt 5:33 [1]Or *hold him guiltless* **5:12** [a]Ex 16:23-30; 20:8-11; 31:13f; Mk 2:27f **5:14** [a]Ge 2:2; Heb 4:4 **5:15** [a]Ex 20:11 **5:16** [a]Ex 20:12; Lv 19:3; Dt 27:16; Mt 15:4; 19:19; Mk 7:10; 10:19; Lk 18:20; Eph 6:2, 3; Col 3:20 [b]Dt 4:40 **5:17** [a]Ge 9:6; Ex 20:13; Lv 24:17; Mt 5:21f; 19:18; Mk 10:19; Ro 13:9; Jas 2:11 **5:18** [a]Ex 20:14; Lv 20:10; Mt 5:27f; 19:18; Mk 10:19; Lk 18:20; Ro 13:9; Jas 2:11 **5:19** [a]Ex 20:15; Lv 19:11 **5:20** [a]Ex 20:16; 23:1; Mt 19:18 **5:21** [a]Ex 20:17; Ro 7:7; 13:9

slave or his female slave,
his ox or his donkey or
anything that belongs to your
neighbor.'
**22** "These words Yahweh spoke to
all your assembly at the mountain
from the midst of the fire, *of* the
cloud and *of* the dense gloom,
with a great voice, and He added
no more. [a]He wrote them on two
tablets of stone and gave them to
me. **23** Now it happened that when
you heard the voice from the midst
of the darkness, while the mountain
was burning with fire, you came
near to me, all the heads of your
tribes and your elders. **24** And you
said, 'Behold, Yahweh our God
has shown us His glory and His
greatness, and we have heard His
voice from the midst of the fire; we
have seen today that God speaks
with man, yet he lives. **25** [a]So now
then why should we die? For this
great fire will consume us; if we
hear the voice of Yahweh our God
any longer, then we will die. **26** For
[a]who is there of all flesh who has
heard the voice of the living God
speaking from the midst of the fire,
as we *have*, and lived? **27** As for you,
go near and hear all that Yahweh
our God says; then speak to us all
that Yahweh our God speaks to you,
and we will hear and do *it*.'
**28** "And Yahweh heard the voice
of your words when you spoke to
me, [a]and Yahweh said to me, 'I have
heard the voice of the words of this
people which they have spoken to
you. They have done well in all
that they have spoken. **29** [a]Oh that
they had such a heart in them, that
they would fear Me and [b]keep all
My commandments all the days,
that [c]it may be well with them and
with their sons forever! **30** Go, say
to them, "Return to your tents."
**31** [a]But as for you, stand here by
Me, that I may speak to you all the
commandments and the statutes
and the judgments which you
shall teach them, that they may
do *them* in the land which I give
them to possess.' **32** So you shall be
careful to do just as Yahweh your
God has commanded you; [a]you
shall not turn aside to the right or
to the left. **33** [a]In all the way which
Yahweh your God has commanded
you, you shall walk, [b]that you may
live and that it may be well with you
and that you may prolong *your* days
in the land which you will possess.

### *Love Yahweh Your God*

**6** "Now this is the commandment,
the statutes and the judgments,
which Yahweh your God has com-
manded *me* to teach you, that you
might do *it* in the land where you
are going over to possess it, **2** so
that you and your son and your
grandson might [a]fear Yahweh your
God, to keep all His statutes and
His commandments which I am
commanding you, [b]all the days of
your life, and that your days may be
prolonged. **3** O Israel, you shall listen
and [1]be careful to do *it*, that [a]it may
be well with you and that you may
multiply greatly, just as Yahweh, the

**5:22** [a]Ex 24:12; 31:18; Dt 4:13 **5:25** [a]Ex 20:18, 19; Dt 18:16 **5:26** [a]Dt 4:33 **5:28** [a]Dt 18:17 **5:29** [a]Ps 81:13; Is 48:18 [b]Dt 11:1 [c]Dt 5:16, 33 **5:31** [a]Ex 24:12 **5:32** [a]Dt 17:20; 28:14; Jos 1:7; 23:6; Pr 4:27 **5:33** [a]Dt 10:12; Jer 7:23; Lk 1:6 [b]Dt 4:1, 40; 12:25, 28; 22:7; Eph 6:3 ◆ **6:2** [a]Ex 20:20; Dt 10:12; Ps 111:10; 128:1; Ecc 12:13 [b]Dt 4:9 **6:3** [a]Dt 5:33 [1]Lit *keep*

God of your fathers, has promised
you, *in* [b]a land flowing with milk and
honey.

**4** "[a]Hear, O Israel! [1]Yahweh is our
God, [b]Yahweh is one! **5** [a]You shall
love Yahweh your God [b]with all
your heart and with all your soul and
with all your might. **6** [a]These words,
which I am commanding you today,
shall be on your heart. **7** [a]You shall
teach them diligently to your sons
and shall speak of them when you
sit in your house and when you walk
by the way and when you lie down
and when you rise up. **8** [a]You shall
bind them as a sign on your hand,
and they shall be as [1]phylacteries
between your eyes. **9** [a]You shall write
them on the doorposts of your house
and on your gates.

**10** "Then it will be, when Yahweh
your God brings you into the land
which He swore to your fathers, to
Abraham, to Isaac, and to Jacob,
to give you, [a]great and good cities
which you did not build, **11** and
houses full of all good things which
you did not fill, and hewn cisterns
which you did not dig, vineyards
and olive trees which you did not
plant, and [a]you will eat and be
satisfied, **12** then beware, lest [a]you
forget Yahweh who brought you
from the land of Egypt, out of the
house of [1]slavery. **13** [a]Yahweh your
God you shall [1]fear; and Him you
shall serve; and by His name you
shall [b]swear. **14** [a]You shall not walk
after other gods, any of the gods of
the peoples who surround you, **15** for
Yahweh your God in the midst of you
is a [a]jealous God—lest the anger of
Yahweh your God be kindled against
you, and He destroy you from the
face of the earth.

**16** "[a]You shall not put Yahweh your
God to the test, [b]as you tested *Him*
at Massah. **17** [a]You should diligently
keep the commandments of Yahweh
your God and His testimonies and
His statutes which He has com-
manded you. **18** And you shall do
what is right and good in the sight of
Yahweh, that [a]it may be well with you
and that you may go in and possess
the good land which Yahweh swore
to *give* your fathers, **19** by driving out
all your enemies from before you, as
Yahweh has spoken.

**20** "[a]When your son asks you in
time to come, saying, 'What *do* the
testimonies and the statutes and the
judgments *mean* which Yahweh our
God commanded you?' **21** then you
shall say to your son, 'We were slaves
to Pharaoh in Egypt, and Yahweh
brought us from Egypt with a strong
hand. **22** Moreover, Yahweh showed
great and calamitous signs and won-
ders before our eyes against Egypt,
Pharaoh, and all his household;
**23** But He brought us out from there
in order to bring us in, to give us the
land which He had sworn to our
fathers.' **24** So Yahweh commanded
us to do all these statutes, [a]to fear
Yahweh our God for our good all *our*
days and [b]for our survival, as *it is*

---

**6:3** [b]Ex 3:8, 17 **6:4** [a]Mt 22:37; Mk 12:29, 30; Lk 10:27 [b]Dt 4:35, 39; Jn 10:30; 1Co 8:4; Eph 4:6 [1]Or *Yahweh our God is one Yahweh, Yahweh our God, Yahweh is unique*; cf. Mk 12:29 **6:5** [a]Mt 22:37; Mk 12:30; Lk 10:27 [b]Dt 4:29; 10:12 **6:6** [a]Dt 11:18 **6:7** [a]Dt 4:9; 11:19; Eph 6:4 **6:8** [a]Ex 12:14; 13:9, 16; Dt 11:18; Pr 3:3; 6:21; 7:3 [1]Or *frontlet bands* **6:9** [a]Dt 11:20 **6:10** [a]Dt 9:1; 19:1; Jos 24:13; Ps 105:44 **6:11** [a]Dt 8:10; 11:15; 14:29 **6:12** [a]Dt 4:9 [1]Lit *slaves* **6:13** [a]Dt 13:4; Mt 4:10; Lk 4:8 [b]Dt 5:11; 10:20; Ps 63:11; Mt 5:33 [1]Or *reverence* **6:14** [a]Jer 25:6 **6:15** [a]Dt 4:24; 5:9 **6:16** [a]Mt 4:7; Lk 4:12 [b]Ex 17:7 **6:17** [a]Dt 11:22; Ps 119:4 **6:18** [a]Dt 4:40 **6:20** [a]Ex 13:8, 14 **6:24** [a]Dt 10:12; Jer 32:39 [b]Ps 41:2; Lk 10:28

today. **25** [a]And it will be righteous-
ness for us if we [1]are careful to do all
this commandment before Yahweh
our God, just as He commanded us.

### *Devote the Nations to Destruction*

**7** "[a]When Yahweh your God brings
you into the land where you are
entering to possess it, and He clears
away many nations before you, the
Hittites and the Girgashites and
the Amorites and the Canaanites
and the Perizzites and the Hivites
and the Jebusites, [b]seven nations
more numerous and stronger than
you, **2** and when Yahweh your God
gives them over before you and you
strike them down, [a]then you shall
devote them to destruction. [b]You shall
cut no covenant with them [c]and show
no favor to them. **3** Furthermore, [a]you
shall not intermarry with them; you
shall not give your [1]daughters to
[2]their sons, nor shall you take [3]their
daughters for your [4]sons. **4** For [1]they
will turn your [2]sons away from
[3]following Me, and they will serve
other gods; then the anger of Yahweh
will be kindled against you, and [a]He
will quickly destroy you. **5** But thus
you shall do to them: [a]you shall tear
down their altars and shatter their *sa-
cred* pillars and cut their [1]Asherim in
pieces and burn their graven images
with fire. **6** For you are [a]a holy people
to Yahweh your God; Yahweh your
God has chosen you to be [b]a people
for His [1]own treasured possession out
of all the peoples who are on the face
of the [2]earth.

**7** "[a]Yahweh did not set His affec-
tion on you nor choose you because
you were more in number than any of
the peoples, for you were the fewest
of all peoples, **8** but because Yahweh
loved you and kept the [a]oath which
He swore to your fathers, [b]Yahweh
brought you out with a strong hand
and redeemed you from the house
of [1]slavery, from the hand of Phar-
aoh king of Egypt. **9** You shall know
therefore that Yahweh your God,
[a]He is God, [b]the faithful God, [c]who
keeps [1]His covenant and [1]His loving-
kindness to a thousand generations
with those who [d]love Him and keep
His commandments; **10** but [a]repays
those who hate Him to [1]their faces, to
make [2]them perish; He will not delay
[3]with him who hates Him, He will
repay him to his face. **11** Therefore,
you shall keep the commandment
and the statutes and the judgments
which I am commanding you today,
to do them.

### *Yahweh's Covenant Blessings*

**12** "[a]Then it will be, because you
listen to these judgments and keep
and do them, that Yahweh your God
will keep with you [1]His covenant and
[1]His lovingkindness which He swore
to your fathers. **13** And He will [a]love
you and bless you and [b]multiply you;
He will also bless the fruit of your
womb and the fruit of your ground,

---

**6:25** [a]Dt 24:13; Ro 10:3 [1]Lit *keep* ◆**7:1** [a]Dt 20:16-18 [b]Ac 13:19 **7:2** [a]Nu 31:17; Jos 11:11 [b]Ex 23:32 [c]Dt 7:16; 13:8 **7:3** [a]Ex 34:15, 16; Jos 23:12; Ezr 9:2 [1]Lit *daughter* [2]Lit *his son* [3]Lit *his daughter* [4]Lit *son* **7:4** [a]Dt 4:26 [1]Lit *he* [2]Lit *son* [3]Lit *after* **7:5** [a]Ex 23:24; 34:13; Dt 12:3 [1]Wooden symbols of a female deity **7:6** [a]Ex 19:6; Dt 14:2, 21; Ps 50:5; Jer 2:3 [b]Ex 19:5; Dt 4:20; 14:2; 26:18; Ps 135:4; Tit 2:14; 1Pe 2:9 [1]Or *special treasure* [2]Lit *ground* **7:7** [a]Dt 4:37 **7:8** [a]Ex 32:13 [b]Ex 13:3 [1]Lit *slaves* **7:9** [a]Dt 4:35, 39 [b]Is 49:7; 1Co 1:9; 1Th 5:24; 2Ti 2:13 [c]Ex 20:6; Da 9:4 [d]Dt 5:10 [1]Lit *the* **7:10** [a]Is 59:18; Na 1:2 [1]Lit *his face* [2]Lit *him* [3]Lit *to* **7:12** [a]Lv 26:3-13; Dt 28:1-14 [1]Lit *the* **7:13** [a]Ps 146:8; Pr 15:9; Jn 14:21 [b]Lv 26:9; Dt 13:17; 30:5

your grain and your new wine and your oil, the increase of your herd and the young of your flock, [1]in the land which He swore to your fathers to give you. **14** You shall be blessed above all peoples; there will be no male or female [a]barren among you or among your cattle. **15** [a]And Yahweh will take away from you all sickness; and He will not put on you any of the harmful diseases of Egypt which you have known, but He will give them to all who hate you. **16** And you shall consume all the peoples whom Yahweh your God will give over to you; [a]your eye shall not pity them, nor shall you serve their gods, for that *would be* [b]a snare to you.

**17** "If you should say in your heart, 'These nations are more numerous than I; how can I [a]dispossess them?' **18** you shall not be afraid of them; you shall well [a]remember what Yahweh your God did to Pharaoh and to all Egypt: **19** [a]the great trials which your eyes saw and the signs and the wonders and the mighty hand and the outstretched arm by which Yahweh your God brought you out. So shall Yahweh your God do to all the peoples of whom you are afraid. **20** Moreover, Yahweh your God will send [a]the hornet against them until those who remain and hide themselves from you perish. **21** You shall not dread [1]them, for [a]Yahweh your God is in your midst, [b]a great and fearsome God. **22** [a]And Yahweh your God will clear away these nations before you little by little; you will not be able to put an end to them quickly, lest the [1]wild beasts become too numerous for you. **23** [a]But Yahweh your God will give them over before you and will [1]throw them into great confusion until they are destroyed. **24** [a]And He will give their kings into your hand so that you will make their name perish from under heaven; [b]no man will be able to stand before you until you have destroyed them. **25** The graven images of their gods you are to [a]burn with fire; you shall [b]not covet the silver or the gold that is on them, nor take it for yourselves, lest you be [c]snared by it, for it is an [d]abomination to Yahweh your God. **26** And you shall not bring an abomination into your house and become devoted to [a]destruction like it; you shall utterly detest it, and you shall utterly abhor it, for it is devoted to destruction.

### *Do Not Forget Yahweh Your God*

**8** "The entire commandment that I am commanding you today you shall be careful to do, that you [a]may live and multiply, and go in and possess the land which Yahweh swore *to give* to your fathers. **2** [a]And you shall remember all the way which Yahweh your God has [b]led you in the wilderness these forty years, that He might humble you, [c]testing you, to know what was in your heart, whether you would keep His commandments or not. **3** And He humbled you and let you be hungry and fed you with manna

---

**7:13** [1]Lit *on the ground* **7:14** [a]Ex 23:26 **7:15** [a]Ex 15:26 **7:16** [a]Dt 7:2 [b]Ex 23:33; Jdg 8:27; Ps 106:36 **7:17** [a]Nu 33:53 **7:18** [a]Ps 105:5 **7:19** [a]Dt 4:34 **7:20** [a]Ex 23:28; Jos 24:12 **7:21** [a]Ex 29:45; Jos 3:10 [b]Dt 10:17; Ne 1:5; 9:32 [1]Lit *from before them* **7:22** [a]Ex 23:29, 30 [1]Lit *beasts of the field* **7:23** [a]Ex 23:27; Jos 10:10 [1]Lit *confuse them with* **7:24** [a]Jos 6:2; 10:23-25 [b]Dt 11:25; Jos 1:5; 10:8; 23:9 **7:25** [a]Ex 32:20; Dt 12:3; 1Chr 14:12 [b]Ex 20:17 [c]Dt 7:16; Jdg 8:27 [d]Dt 17:1 **7:26** [a]Lv 27:28f ◆ **8:1** [a]Dt 4:1 **8:2** [a]Dt 8:16 [b]Ps 136:16; Am 2:10 [c]Ex 15:25; 20:20; 2Chr 32:31

which you did not know, nor did your
fathers know, that He might make
you know that [a]man does not live
by bread alone, but by everything
that proceeds out of the mouth of
Yahweh. **4** [a]Your clothing did not
wear out on you, nor did your foot
swell these forty years. **5** [a]Thus you
shall know in your heart that Yahweh
your God was disciplining you just
as a man disciplines his son. **6** So
you shall keep the commandments
of Yahweh your God, to walk in His
ways and to [1]fear Him. **7** For [a]Yahweh
your God is bringing you into a good
land, a land of brooks of water, of
fountains and springs, flowing forth
in valleys and hills; **8** a land of wheat
and barley, of vines and fig trees and
pomegranates, a land of olive oil and
honey; **9** a land where you will eat
food without scarcity, in which you
will not lack anything; a land whose
stones are iron, and out of whose
hills you can dig copper. **10** And so
[a]you will eat and be satisfied, and
you shall bless Yahweh your God for
the good land which He has given
you.

**11** "[1]Beware lest you [a]forget Yahweh
your God by not keeping His com-
mandments and His judgments and
His statutes which I am commanding
you today; **12** lest [a]you eat and are sat-
isfied and build good houses and live
*in them,* **13** and your herds and your
flocks multiply, and your silver and
gold multiply, and all that you have
multiplies, **14** and your heart becomes
[1]lifted up and you [a]forget Yahweh
your God who brought you out from
the land of Egypt, out of the house
of [2]slavery. **15** He led you through
[a]the great and fearsome wilderness,
*with its* [b]fiery serpents and scorpions
and thirsty ground where there was
no water; He [c]brought water for you
out of the rock of flint. **16** In the wil-
derness He fed you manna [a]which
your fathers did not know, that He
might humble you and that He might
[b]test you, to do good for you [1]in the
end, **17** lest [a]you say in your heart,
'My power and the might of my hand
made me this wealth.' **18** But you shall
remember Yahweh your God, for [a]it
is He who is giving you power to
make wealth, that He may confirm
His covenant which He swore to
your fathers, as *it is* this day. **19** Now
it will be, if you ever forget Yahweh
your God and walk after other gods
and serve them and worship them,
[a]I testify against you today that you
will surely perish. **20** Like the nations
that Yahweh makes to perish before
you, so [a]you shall perish, because
you would not listen to the voice of
Yahweh your God.

### *Israel Provoked Yahweh*

**9** "Hear, O Israel! You are crossing
over the Jordan today to go in
to dispossess [a]nations greater and
mightier than you, great cities [b,1]forti-
fied to heaven, **2** a people great and
tall, the sons of the Anakim, whom
you know and of whom you have
heard *it said,* '[a]Who can stand be-
fore the sons of Anak?' **3** So you shall

**8:3** [a]Mt 4:4; Lk 4:4 **8:4** [a]Dt 29:5; Ne 9:21 **8:5** [a]Dt 4:36; 2Sa 7:14; Pr 3:12; Heb 12:6; Rev 3:19 **8:6** [1]Or *reverence* **8:7** [a]Dt 11:9-12; Jer 2:7 **8:10** [a]Dt 6:11 **8:11** [a]Dt 4:9 [1]Lit *Take heed to yourself* **8:12** [a]Pr 30:9; Hos 13:6 **8:14** [a]Dt 8:11; Ps 106:21 [1]Or *proud* [2]Lit *slaves* **8:15** [a]Dt 1:19; Jer 2:6 [b]Nu 21:6 [c]Ex 17:6; Nu 20:11; Dt 32:13; Ps 78:15; 114:8 **8:16** [a]Ex 16:15 [b]Dt 8:2 [1]Lit *at your end* **8:17** [a]Dt 9:4 **8:18** [a]Pr 10:22; Hos 2:8 **8:19** [a]Dt 4:26; 30:18 **8:20** [a]Eze 5:5-17 ◆ **9:1** [a]Dt 4:38; 7:1; 11:23 [b]Dt 1:28 [1]Lit *and fortified* **9:2** [a]Nu 13:22, 28, 33; Jos 11:21, 22

know today that [a]it is Yahweh your God who is crossing over before you as [b]a consuming fire. He will destroy them, and He will subdue them before you, so that [c]you may dispossess them and make them perish quickly, just as Yahweh has spoken to you.

**4** "[a]Do not say in your heart when Yahweh your God has driven them out before you, saying, 'Because of my righteousness Yahweh has brought me in to possess this land,' but *it is* [b]because of the wickedness of these nations *that* Yahweh is dispossessing them before you. **5** It is [a]not for your righteousness or for the uprightness of your heart that you are going to possess their land, but *it is* because of the wickedness of these nations *that* Yahweh your God is dispossessing them before you, in order to confirm [b]the [1]oath which Yahweh swore to your fathers, to Abraham, to Isaac, and to Jacob.

**6** "So you shall know *it is* not because of your righteousness *that* Yahweh your God is giving you this good land to possess, for you are [a]a [1]stiff-necked people. **7** Remember, do not forget how you provoked Yahweh your God to wrath in the wilderness; [a]from the day that you went out of the land of Egypt until you came to this place, you have been rebellious against Yahweh. **8** Even [a]at Horeb you provoked Yahweh to wrath, and Yahweh was so angry with you that He would have destroyed you. **9** When I went up to the mountain to receive the tablets of stone, the tablets of the covenant which Yahweh had cut with you, then I remained on the mountain forty days and nights; [a]I neither ate bread nor drank water. **10** And Yahweh gave me the two tablets of stone [a]written by the finger of God; and on them *were* all the words which Yahweh had spoken with you at the mountain from the midst of the fire on the day of the assembly. **11** Now it happened [a]at the end of forty days and nights, that Yahweh gave me the two tablets of stone, the tablets of the covenant. **12** [a]Then Yahweh said to me, 'Arise, go down from here quickly, for your people whom you brought out of Egypt have acted corruptly. They have [b]quickly turned aside from the way which I commanded them; they have made a molten image for themselves.' **13** [a]Yahweh spoke further to me, saying, 'I have seen this people, and indeed, [1]they are a [b,2]stiff-necked people. **14** [a]Let Me alone, that I may destroy them and [b]blot out their name from under heaven; and I will make of you a nation mightier and more numerous than they.'

**15** "[a]So I turned and came down from the mountain while the mountain was burning with fire, and the two tablets of the covenant were in my two hands. **16** And I saw that you had indeed sinned against Yahweh your God. You had made for yourselves a molten calf; you had turned aside quickly from the way which Yahweh had commanded you. **17** And I took hold of the two tablets and threw them from my hands and shattered them before your eyes.

---

**9:3** [a]Dt 31:3; Jos 3:11 [b]Dt 4:24; Heb 12:29 [c]Ex 23:31; Dt 7:24 **9:4** [a]Dt 8:17; 9:7, 24; 31:27 [b]Lv 18:3, 24-30; Dt 12:31; 18:9-14 **9:5** [a]Tit 3:5 [b]Ge 12:7; 13:15; 15:7; 17:8; 26:4; 28:13 [1]Lit *word* **9:6** [a]Dt 9:13; 10:16; 31:27 [1]Or *stubborn* **9:7** [a]Ex 14:10f; Nu 14:22 **9:8** [a]Ex 32:7-10; Ps 106:19 **9:9** [a]Ex 24:18; 34:28; Dt 8:3; 9:18 **9:10** [a]Dt 4:13 **9:11** [a]Dt 9:9 **9:12** [a]Ex 32:7, 8 [b]Jdg 2:17 **9:13** [a]Ex 32:9 [b]Dt 10:16; 31:27; 2Ki 17:14 [1]Lit *he is* [2]Or *stubborn* **9:14** [a]Ex 32:10 [b]Ps 9:5; 109:13 **9:15** [a]Ex 32:15-19

**18** [a]And I fell down before Yahweh, [b]as at the first, forty days and nights; [c]I neither ate bread nor drank water [d]because of all your sin which you had committed in doing what was evil in the sight of Yahweh to provoke Him to anger. **19** For [a]I was afraid of the anger and the wrath with which Yahweh was provoked against you in order to destroy you, [b]but Yahweh listened to me that time also. **20** And Yahweh was angry enough with Aaron to destroy him; so I also prayed for Aaron at the same time. **21** [a]Now I took your [1]sinful *thing*, the calf which you had made, and burned it with fire and crushed it, grinding it very small until it was as fine as dust; and I threw its dust into the brook that came down from the mountain.

**22** "Again at [a]Taberah and at [b]Massah and at [c]Kibroth-hattaavah you provoked Yahweh to wrath. **23** When Yahweh sent you from [a]Kadesh-barnea, saying, '[b]Go up and possess the land which I have given you,' then you rebelled against the [1]command of Yahweh your God; [c]you did not believe Him, and you did not listen to His voice. **24** [a]You have been rebellious against Yahweh from the day I knew you.

**25** "[a]So I fell down before Yahweh the forty days and the forty nights, which I [1]did because Yahweh had *said He would* destroy you. **26** [a]And I prayed to Yahweh and said, 'O Lord Yahweh, do not destroy Your people, even Your inheritance, whom You have redeemed through Your greatness, whom You have brought out of Egypt with a strong hand. **27** Remember Your servants, Abraham, Isaac, and Jacob; do not look at the stiff-*neck* of this people or at their wickedness or their sin, **28** lest the land from which You brought us say, "[a]Because Yahweh was not able to bring them into the land which He had [1]promised them and because He hated them He has brought them out to put them to death in the wilderness." **29** Yet they are Your people, even [a]Your inheritance, whom You have brought out by Your [b]great power and Your outstretched arm.'

### *The Tablets Rewritten*

**10** "At that time Yahweh said to me, '[a]Carve out for yourself two tablets of stone like the former ones, and come up to Me on the mountain, and [b]make an ark of wood for yourself. **2** [a]And I will write on the tablets the words that were on the former tablets which you shattered, and [b]you shall put them in the ark.' **3** So [a]I made an ark of acacia wood and [b]carved out two tablets of stone like the former ones and went up on the mountain with the two tablets in my hand. **4** And He wrote on the tablets, like the former writing, [a]the Ten [1]Commandments [b]which Yahweh had spoken to you on the mountain from the midst of the fire [c]on the day of the assembly; and Yahweh gave them to me. **5** Then I turned and [a]came down from the mountain and [b]put the tablets in the ark which

---

**9:18** [a]Ex 34:28 [b]Dt 10:10 [c]Dt 9:9 [d]Ex 34:9 **9:19** [a]Ex 32:10f; Heb 12:21 [b]Ex 34:10; Dt 10:10 **9:21** [a]Ex 32:20 [1]Lit *sin* **9:22** [a]Nu 11:3 [b]Ex 17:7 [c]Nu 11:34 **9:23** [a]Dt 1:2 [b]Dt 1:21 [c]Dt 1:26; Ps 106:24 [1]Lit *mouth* **9:24** [a]Dt 9:7; 31:27 **9:25** [a]Dt 9:18 [1]Lit *fell down* **9:26** [a]Ex 32:11-13; 1Sa 7:9; Jer 15:1 **9:28** [a]Ex 32:12; Nu 14:16 [1]Lit *spoken to* **9:29** [a]Dt 4:20; 1Ki 8:51; Ne 1:10; Ps 106:40 [b]Dt 4:34 ◆ **10:1** [a]Ex 34:1 [b]Ex 25:10 **10:2** [a]Dt 4:13 [b]Ex 25:16 **10:3** [a]Ex 25:5; 37:1-9 [b]Ex 34:4 **10:4** [a]Ex 34:28; Dt 4:13 [b]Ex 20:1 [c]Dt 9:10; 18:16 [1]Lit *Words* **10:5** [a]Ex 34:29 [b]Ex 40:20

I had made; [c]and there they are, as
Yahweh commanded me."

**6** (Now the sons of Israel set out
from [1]Beeroth [a]Bene-jaakan to
Moserah. [b]There Aaron died, and
there he was buried, and Eleazar
his son ministered as priest in his
place. **7** [a]From there they set out to
Gudgodah, and from Gudgodah to
Jotbathah, a land of brooks of water.
**8** [a]At that time Yahweh set apart
the tribe of Levi to carry the ark of
the covenant of Yahweh, to stand
before Yahweh [b]to minister for Him
and to bless in His name to this day.
**9** [a]Therefore, Levi does not have
a portion or inheritance with his
brothers; Yahweh is his inheritance,
just as Yahweh your God spoke to
him.)

**10** "[a]I, moreover, stayed on the
mountain forty days and forty nights
like the first time, and Yahweh lis-
tened to me that time also; Yahweh
was not willing to destroy you.
**11** Then Yahweh said to me, 'Arise, go
on your journey ahead of the people,
that they may go in and possess the
land which I swore to their fathers
to give them.'

### *Circumcise Your Heart*

**12** "[a]So now, Israel, what does Yahweh
your God ask from you, but to [1]fear
Yahweh your God, to walk in all His
ways and [b]love Him, and to serve Yah-
weh your God with [c]all your heart and
with all your soul, **13** *and* to keep the
commandments of Yahweh and His
statutes which I am commanding you
today for your good? **14** Behold, [a]to
Yahweh your God belong heaven and
the [1]highest heavens, [b]the earth and
all that is in it. **15** [a]Yet on your fathers
did Yahweh set His affection to love
them, and He chose their seed after
them, *even* you above all peoples,
as *it is* this day. **16** [a]So circumcise
[1]your heart, and [b]stiffen your neck
no longer. **17** [a]For Yahweh your God
is the God of gods and the [b]Lord of
lords, the great, the mighty, and the
fearsome God [c]who does not show
partiality nor [d]take a bribe. **18** He
executes justice for [a]the orphan and
the widow, and shows love for the
sojourner by giving him food and
clothing. **19** [a]So show love for the
sojourner, for you were sojourners in
the land of Egypt. **20** Yahweh your God
you shall fear; Him you shall serve,
and to Him you shall [a]cling, and by
His name [b]you shall swear. **21** He is
[a]your praise, and He is your God, who
has done these great and fearsome
things for you which your eyes have
seen. **22** [a]Your fathers went down to
Egypt seventy persons *in all*, [b]and
now Yahweh your God has made you
as numerous as the stars of heaven.

### *Love and Serve Yahweh*

**11** "You shall therefore [a]love Yah-
weh your God, and [b]keep His
charge, His statutes, His judgments,
and His commandments all *your*

---

**10:5** [c]1Ki 8:9 **10:6** [a]Nu 33:30, 31 [b]Nu 20:25-28; 33:38 [1]Or *the wells of the sons of Jaakan*
**10:7** [a]Nu *33:33, 34* **10:8** [a]Nu 3:6; 18:1-7; Dt 31:9 [b]Dt 17:12; 18:5; 21:5 **10:9** [a]Nu 18:20, 24; Dt 18:1, 2;
Eze 44:28 **10:10** [a]Ex 34:28; Dt 9:18 **10:12** [a]Mic 6:8 [b]Dt 6:5; Mt 22:37; 1Ti 1:5 [c]Dt 4:29 [1]Or
*reverence* **10:14** [a]1Ki 8:27; Ne 9:6; Ps 68:33; 115:16 [b]Ps 24:1 [1]Lit *heaven of heavens* **10:15** [a]Dt 4:37
**10:16** [a]Lv 26:41; Jer 4:4 [b]Dt 9:6 [1]Lit *the foreskin of your heart* **10:17** [a]Jos 22:22; Ps 136:2; Da 2:47; 1Ti 6:15;
Rev 19:16 [b]Rev 17:14 [c]Dt 1:17; Ac 10:34; Ro 2:11; Ga 2:6; Eph 6:9 [d]Dt 16:19 **10:18** [a]Ex 22:22-24; Ps 68:5;
146:9 **10:19** [a]Lv 19:34; Eze 47:22, 23 **10:20** [a]Dt 11:22; 13:4 [b]Dt 5:11; 6:13; Ps 63:11 **10:21** [a]Ps 109:1;
148:14; Jer 17:14 **10:22** [a]Ge 46:27 [b]Ge 15:5; 22:17; Dt 1:10 ◆ **11:1** [a]Dt 6:5; 10:12 [b]Lv 18:30; 22:9

days. 2 So know this day [a]that I *am*
not *speaking* with your sons who
have not known and who have not
seen the [1]discipline of Yahweh your
God—His greatness, His strong hand
and His outstretched arm, 3 and [a]His
signs and His works which He did
in the midst of Egypt to Pharaoh
the king of Egypt and to all his land;
4 and what He did to Egypt's army,
to its horses and its chariots, [a]when
He made the water of the [1]Red Sea
to [2]engulf them while they were
pursuing you, and Yahweh made
them perish [3]utterly; 5 and what He
did to you in the wilderness until you
came to this place; 6 and [a]what He
did to Dathan and Abiram, the sons
of Eliab, the son of Reuben, when the
earth opened its mouth and swal-
lowed them, their households, their
tents, and [b]every living thing that
[1]followed them, among all Israel—
7 but your own eyes have seen all the
great work of Yahweh which He did.
8 "You shall therefore keep every
commandment which I am com-
manding you today, [a]so that you
may be strong and go in and possess
the land into which you are about
to cross to possess it; 9 [a]so that you
may prolong *your* days on the land
which Yahweh swore to your fathers
to give to them and to their seed, [b]a
land flowing with milk and honey.
10 For the land, into which you are
entering to possess it, is not like the
land of Egypt from which you came
out, where you used to sow your seed
and water it with your [1]foot like a
vegetable garden. 11 But [a]the land
into which you are about to cross to
possess it, a land of hills and valleys,
drinks water from the rain of heaven,
12 a land for which Yahweh your God
cares; [a]the eyes of Yahweh your God
are always on it, from the [1]beginning
even to the end of the year.
13 "And it will be that, [a]if you listen
obediently to my commandments
which I am commanding you today,
[b]to love Yahweh your God and to
serve Him [c]with all your heart and
all your soul, 14 that [a,1]I, *Yahweh*,
will give the rain for your land in its
season, the [b,2]early and [3]late rains,
that you may gather in your grain and
your new wine and your oil. 15 [a]And
[1]I will give [2]grass in your fields for
your cattle, and [b]you will eat and be
satisfied. 16 [a,1]Beware lest your hearts
be deceived, and you turn away
and serve other gods and worship
them, 17 and [a]the anger of Yahweh
will be kindled against you, and He
will [b]shut up the heavens [c]so that
there will be no rain and the ground
will not yield its fruit; and [d]you will
perish quickly from the good land
which Yahweh is giving you.
18 "[a]You shall therefore place these
words of mine on your heart and on
your soul; and you shall bind them
as a sign on your hand, and they
shall be as [1]phylacteries between
your eyes. 19 [a]And you shall teach

**11:2** [a]Dt 4:34 [1]Or *instruction* **11:3** [a]Ex 7:8-21 **11:4** [a]Ex 14:28; Dt 1:40; 2:1 [1]Lit *Sea of Reeds* [2]Lit *flow over their faces* [3]Lit *to this day* **11:6** [a]Nu 16:1-35; Ps 106:16-18 [b]Nu 26:10, 11 [1]Lit *was at their feet* **11:8** [a]Dt 31:6, 7, 23; Jos 1:6, 7 **11:9** [a]Dt 4:40; 5:16, 33; 6:2; Pr 10:27 [b]Ex 3:8 **11:10** [1]Probably a treadmill **11:11** [a]Dt 8:7 **11:12** [a]1Ki 9:3 [1]Lit *beginning of the year* **11:13** [a]Lv 26:3; Dt 7:12 [b]Dt 11:1 [c]Dt 4:29 **11:14** [a]Lv 26:4; Dt 28:12 [b]Joel 2:23; Jas 5:7 [1]Some ancient versions *He* [2]Autumn [3]Spring **11:15** [a]Ps 104:14 [b]Dt 6:11 [1]Some ancient versions *He* [2]Or *plants*, cf. Ge 2:15 **11:16** [a]Job 31:27 [1]Lit *Watch yourselves* **11:17** [a]Dt 6:15; 9:19 [b]1Ki 8:35; 2Chr 6:26; 7:13 [c]Dt 28:24 [d]Dt 4:26 **11:18** [a]Ex 13:9, 16; Dt 6:8 [1]Lit *frontlet bands* **11:19** [a]Dt 4:9, 10; 6:7; Pr 22:6

them to your sons, speaking of them
when you sit in your house and when
you walk along the road and when
you lie down and when you rise up.
**20** [a]And you shall write them on the
doorposts of your house and on your
gates, **21** so that [a]your days and the
days of your sons may be multiplied
on the land which Yahweh swore to
your fathers to give them, as [b,1]long
as the heavens *remain* above the
earth. **22** For if you are [a]careful to
keep this entire commandment
which I am commanding you to do,
[b]to love Yahweh your God, to walk
in all His ways, and to [c]cling to Him,
**23** then Yahweh will [a]dispossess all
these nations from before you, and
you will [b]dispossess nations greater
and mightier than you. **24** [a]Every
place on which the sole of your
foot treads shall be yours; [b]your
border will be from the wilderness
to Lebanon, *and* from the river, the
river Euphrates, as far as the [1]western
sea. **25** [a]No man will be able to stand
before you; Yahweh your God will put
the dread of you and the fear of you
on all the land on which you set foot,
as He has spoken to you.

### *A Blessing and a Curse*

**26** “[a]See, I am setting before you
today a blessing and a curse: **27** the
[a]blessing, if you listen to the com-
mandments of Yahweh your God,
which I am commanding you today;
**28** and the [a]curse, if you do not listen
to the commandments of Yahweh
your God, but turn aside from the
way which I am commanding you
today, by walking after other gods
which you have not known.
**29** “And it will be, when Yahweh
your God brings you into the land
where you are entering to possess
it, [a]that you shall set the blessing
on Mount Gerizim and the curse
on Mount Ebal. **30** Are they not
across the Jordan, west of the way
toward the sunset, in the land of the
Canaanites who live in the Arabah,
opposite [a]Gilgal, beside [b]the [1]oaks
of Moreh? **31** For you are about to
cross the Jordan to go in to possess
the land which Yahweh your God is
giving you, and [a]you shall possess
it and live in it, **32** and you shall be
careful to do all the statutes and the
judgments which I am setting before
you today.

### *Yahweh's Chosen Place of Worship*

**12** “These are the statutes and
the judgments which you shall
be careful to do in the land which
Yahweh, the God of your fathers,
has given you to possess [a]all the
days you live on the [1]earth. **2** You
shall utterly destroy all the places
where the nations whom you shall
dispossess serve their gods, on the
[a]high mountains and on the hills
and under every green tree. **3** [a]And
you shall tear down their altars and
shatter their *sacred* pillars and burn
their [1]Asherim with fire, and you shall
cut the graven images of their gods
in pieces and [b]destroy their name
from that place. **4** You shall not do

**11:20** [a]Dt 6:9 **11:21** [a]Pr 3:2; 4:10; 9:11 [b]Ps 72:5 [1]Lit *the days of the heavens* **11:22** [a]Dt 6:17 [b]Dt 11:1 [c]Dt 10:20 **11:23** [a]Dt 4:38 [b]Dt 9:1 **11:24** [a]Jos 1:3; 14:9 [b]Ge 15:18; Ex 23:31; Dt 1:7, 8 [1]Mediterranean Sea **11:25** [a]Ex 23:27; Dt 7:24 **11:26** [a]Dt 30:1, 19 **11:27** [a]Dt 28:1-14 **11:28** [a]Dt 28:15-68 **11:29** [a]Dt 27:12; Jos 8:33 **11:30** [a]Jos 4:19 [b]Ge 12:6 [1]Lit *terebinths* **11:31** [a]Dt 17:14; Jos 21:43 ◆ **12:1** [a]Dt 4:9, 10; 1Ki 8:40 [1]Lit *ground* **12:2** [a]2Ki 16:4; 17:10, 11 **12:3** [a]Nu 33:52; Dt 7:5; Jdg 2:2 [b]Ex 23:13; Ps 16:4; Zec 13:2 [1]Wooden symbols of a female deity

thus toward Yahweh your God. **5** [a]But
you shall seek *Yahweh* at the place
which Yahweh your God will choose
from all your tribes, to establish His
name there for His dwelling, and
there you shall come. **6** And there you
shall bring your burnt offerings, your
sacrifices, [a]your tithes, the [1]contri-
bution of your hand, your votive
offerings, your freewill offerings,
and the firstborn of your herd and of
your flock. **7** There also you and your
households shall eat before Yahweh
your God, and [a]be glad in all that you
send forth your hand *to do*, in which
Yahweh your God has blessed you.

**8** "You shall not do at all what
we are doing here today, [a]every
man *doing* whatever is right in his
own eyes; **9** for you have not as yet
come to [a]the resting place and the
[b]inheritance which Yahweh your
God is giving you. **10** Now you will
cross the Jordan and live in the land
which Yahweh your God is giving you
to inherit. And [a]He will give you rest
from all your enemies around *you*
so that you live in security. **11** [a]Then
it will be that the place in which
Yahweh your God will choose for His
name to dwell, there you shall bring
all that I am commanding you: your
burnt offerings and your sacrifices,
your tithes and the [1]contribution of
your hand, and all your choice votive
*offerings which* you will vow to Yah-
weh. **12** And you shall [a]be glad before
Yahweh your God, you and your sons
and daughters, your male and female
slaves, and the [b]Levite who is within
your gates, since [c]he has no portion
or inheritance with you.

**13** "[a]Beware, lest you offer your
burnt offerings in every *cultic* place
you see, **14** but in the place which
Yahweh chooses in one of your
tribes, there you shall offer your
burnt offerings, and there you shall
do all that I am commanding you.

**15** "[a]However, you may sacrifice
and eat meat within any of your
gates, [1]whatever you desire, accord-
ing to the blessing of Yahweh your
God which He has given you; the
unclean and the clean may eat of
it, as of [b]the gazelle and the deer.
**16** [a]Only you shall not eat the blood;
[b]you are to pour it out on the ground
like water. **17** [a]You are not allowed to
eat within your gates the tithe of
your grain or new wine or oil, or the
firstborn of your herd or flock, or any
of your votive offerings which you
vow, or your freewill offerings, or the
[1]contribution of your hand. **18** But
[a]you shall eat them before Yahweh
your God in [b]the place which Yahweh
your God will choose, you and your
son and daughter, and your male and
female slaves, and the [c]Levite who is
within your gates; and you shall [d]be
glad before Yahweh your God in all
that you send forth your hand *to do*.
**19** [a]Beware lest you forsake the Levite
all your days upon your land.

**20** "When Yahweh your God
enlarges your territory [a]as He has
promised you, and you say, 'I will

**12:5** [a]Ex 20:24; Dt 12:11, 13; 2Chr 7:12; Ps 78:68 **12:6** [a]Dt 14:22 [1]Or *heave offering* **12:7** [a]Lv 23:40; Dt 12:12, 18; 14:26; 28:47; Ecc 3:12, 13; 5:18-20 **12:8** [a]Jdg 17:6; 21:25 **12:9** [a]Dt 3:20; 25:19; Ps 95:11 [b]Dt 4:21 **12:10** [a]Jos 11:23 **12:11** [a]Dt 12:5; 15:20; 16:2; 17:8; 18:6 [1]Or *heave offering* **12:12** [a]Dt 12:7 [b]Dt 12:18, 19; 26:11-13 [c]Dt 10:9; 14:29 **12:13** [a]Dt 12:5, 11 **12:15** [a]Dt 12:20-23 [b]Dt 12:22; 14:5; 15:22 [1]Lit *in every desire of your soul* **12:16** [a]Ge 9:4; Lv 7:26; 17:10-12; 1Sa 14:33f; Ac 15:20, 29 [b]Dt 15:23 **12:17** [a]Dt 12:26 [1]Lit *heave offering* **12:18** [a]Dt 14:23 [b]Dt 12:5 [c]Dt 12:12 [d]Dt 12:7; Ecc 3:12f; 5:18-20 **12:19** [a]Dt 14:27 **12:20** [a]Ge 15:18; Dt 11:24; 19:8

eat meat,' because [1]you desire to eat
meat, *then* you may eat meat, [2]what-
ever you desire. **21** If the place where
Yahweh your God chooses to set His
name is too far away from you, then
you may sacrifice of your herd and
flock which Yahweh has given you,
as I have commanded you; and you
may eat within your gates [1]whatever
you desire. **22** Just as a gazelle or a
deer is eaten, so you will eat it; the
unclean and the clean alike may eat
of it. **23** Only be strong *in yourselves*
[a]not to eat the blood, for the blood
is the [1]life, and you shall not eat the
[1]life with the flesh. **24** You shall not
eat it; you shall pour it out on the
ground like water. **25** You shall not
eat it, so that [a]it may be well with you
and your sons after you, for [b]you will
be doing what is right in the sight of
Yahweh. **26** [a]Only your holy things
which you may have and your votive
offerings, you shall take and go to the
place which Yahweh chooses. **27** And
[a]you shall offer your burnt offerings,
the flesh and the blood, on the altar
of Yahweh your God; and the blood
of your sacrifices shall be poured out
on the altar of Yahweh your God, and
[b]you shall eat the flesh.

**28** “Be careful to listen to all these
words which I command you, so that
[a]it may be well with you and your
sons after you forever, for you will be
doing what is good and right in the
sight of Yahweh your God.

**29** “When [a]Yahweh your God cuts
off before you the nations which you
are going in to dispossess, and you
dispossess them and inhabit their
land, **30** beware lest you be ensnared
[1]to follow them, after they are de-
stroyed before you, and lest you
inquire after their gods, saying, ‘How
do these nations serve their gods,
that I also may do likewise?’ **31** [a]You
shall not do thus toward Yahweh
your God, for every abominable act
which Yahweh hates they have done
for their gods; for [b]they even burn
their sons and daughters in the fire
to their gods.

**32** “[a,1]Whatever I am commanding
you, you shall be careful to do; [b]you
shall not add to nor take away from it.

### *Stone Those Who Prophesy Against Yahweh*

**13** “[a,1]If a prophet or a dreamer of
dreams arises among you and
gives you a sign or a wonder, **2** and
the sign or the wonder comes true,
concerning which he spoke to you,
saying, ‘[a]Let us walk after other gods
(whom you have not known) and let
us serve them,’ **3** you shall not listen
to the words of that prophet or that
dreamer of dreams; for Yahweh your
God is [a]testing you to find out if [b]you
love Yahweh your God with all your
heart and with all your soul. **4** [a]You
shall walk after Yahweh your God
and fear Him; and you shall keep
His commandments, listen to His
voice, serve Him, and [b]cling to Him.
**5** But that prophet or that dreamer of
dreams shall be [a]put to death because

---

**12:20** [1]Lit *your soul desires* [2]Lit *in every desire of your soul* **12:21** [1]Lit in every desire of your soul
**12:23** [a]Ge 9:4; Lv 17:10-14; Dt 12:16 [1]Lit *soul* **12:25** [a]Dt 4:40; Is 3:10 [b]Ex 15:26; 1Ki 11:38
**12:26** [a]Nu 5:9f; 18:19; Dt 12:17 **12:27** [a]Lv 1:9, 13 [b]Lv 3:1-17 **12:28** [a]Dt 4:40; Ecc 8:12 **12:29** [a]Jos 23:4
**12:30** [1]Lit *after them* **12:31** [a]Dt 9:5 [b]Lv 18:21; Dt 18:10; Ps 106:37; Jer 32:35 **12:32** [a]Dt 4:2;
Jos 1:7 [b]Pr 30:6; Rev 22:18 [1]Lit *Everything that* ◆ **13:1** [a]Mt 24:24; Mk 13:22; 2Th 2:9 [1]Ch 13:2 in
Heb **13:2** [a]Dt 13:6, 13 **13:3** [a]Ex 20:20; Dt 8:2, 16; 1Co 11:19 [b]Dt 6:5 **13:4** [a]2Ki 23:3; 2Chr 34:31; 2Jn 6
[b]Dt 10:20 **13:5** [a]Dt 13:9, 15; 17:5; 1Ki 18:40

he has [1]counseled [2]rebellion against
Yahweh your God who brought you
from the land of Egypt and redeemed
you from the house of [3]slavery, [b]to
drive you from the way in which
Yahweh your God commanded you
to walk. [c]So you shall purge the evil
from among you.
**6** "[a]If your brother, your mother's
son, or your son or daughter, or the
wife [1]you cherish, or your friend
who is as your own soul, entices you
secretly, saying, '[b]Let us go and serve
other gods' (whom neither you nor
your fathers have known, **7** of the
gods of the peoples who are around
you, near you or far from you, from
one end of the earth to the other
end), **8** [a]you shall not be willing to
accept him or listen to him; [b]and your
eye shall not pity him; and you shall
not spare him or conceal him. **9** [a]But
you shall surely kill him; [b]your hand
shall be first against him to put him
to death, and afterwards the hand of
all the people. **10** So you shall stone
him [1]to death because he has sought
[a]to drive you from Yahweh your God
who brought you out from the land
of Egypt, out of the house of [2]slavery.
**11** Thus [a]all Israel will hear and be
afraid and will never again do such
an evil thing among you.
**12** "If you hear in one of your cities,
which Yahweh your God is giving you
to live in, *anyone* saying *that* **13** some
vile men have gone out from among
you and have driven the inhabitants
of their city *astray*, saying, '[a]Let us
go and serve other gods' (whom
you have not known), **14** then you
shall inquire and search out and ask
thoroughly. Behold, if it is true *and*
the matter is confirmed, that this
abomination has been done among
you, **15** [a]you shall surely strike the
inhabitants of that city with the edge
of the sword, [1]devoting it to destruc-
tion and all that is in it and its cattle
with the edge of the sword. **16** [a]Then
you shall gather all its spoil into the
middle of its open square and burn
the city and all its spoil with fire as
a whole burnt offering to Yahweh
your God; and it shall be a [b,1]ruin
forever. It shall never be rebuilt.
**17** Now nothing from that which is
devoted to destruction shall cling
to your hand, in order that Yahweh
may turn from [a]His burning anger
and [b]grant compassion to you and
show compassion to you and [c]make
you multiply, just [d]as He has sworn
to your fathers, **18** [1]if you will listen
to the voice of Yahweh your God,
[2]keeping all His commandments
which I am commanding you today,
[3]and doing what is right in the sight
of Yahweh your God.

### *Clean and Unclean Animals*

**14** "You are [a]the sons of Yahweh
your God; [b]you shall not gash
yourselves nor [1]shave your forehead
for the sake of the dead. **2** For you are
[a]a holy people to Yahweh your God,
and Yahweh has chosen you to be a
[b]people for His [1]treasured possession

**13:5** [b]Dt 4:19; 13:10 [c]1Co 5:13 [1]Lit *spoken* [2]Lit *turning aside* [3]Lit *slaves* **13:6** [a]Dt 17:2-7; 29:18 [b]Dt 13:2 [1]Lit *of your bosom* **13:8** [a]Pr 1:10 [b]Dt 7:2 **13:9** [a]Dt 13:5 [b]Lv 24:14; Dt 17:7 **13:10** [a]Dt 13:5 [1]Lit *with stones so that he dies* [2]Lit *slaves* **13:11** [a]Dt 19:20 **13:13** [a]Dt 13:2 **13:15** [a]Dt 13:5 [1]Or *putting it under the ban* **13:16** [a]Dt 7:25, 26 [b]Jos 8:28; Is 17:1; 25:2; Jer 49:2 [1]Lit *mound* **13:17** [a]Ex 32:12; Nu 25:4 [b]Dt 30:3 [c]Dt 7:13 [d]Ge 22:17; 26:4, 24; 28:14 **13:18** [1]Or *for* [2]Lit *to keep* [3]Lit *to do* ◆ **14:1** [a]Ro 8:16; 9:8, 26; Ga 3:26; 1Jn 3:1 [b]Lv 19:28; 21:5; Jer 16:6; 41:5 [1]Lit *make a baldness between your eyes* **14:2** [a]Lv 20:26; Dt 7:6; Ro 12:1 [b]Ex 19:5; Dt 4:20; 26:18; Tit 2:14; 1Pe 2:9 [1]Or *special treasure*

out of all the peoples who are on the
face of the earth.

**3** "[a]You shall not eat any abomina-
ble thing. **4** [a]These are the animals
which you may eat: the ox, the sheep,
the goat, **5** [1]the deer, the gazelle, the
roebuck, the wild goat, the ibex, the
antelope, and the mountain sheep.
**6** And any animal that divides the
hoof and has the hoof split in [1]two
*and* [2]chews the cud, among the
animals, that *one* you may eat. **7** Nev-
ertheless, you are not to eat of these
among those which [1]chew the cud or
among those that divide the hoof in
[2]two: the camel and the [3]rabbit and
the [4]shaphan, for though they [1]chew
the cud, they do not divide the hoof;
they are unclean for you. **8** And the
pig, because it divides the hoof but
*does* not *chew* the cud, it is unclean
for you. You shall not eat any of their
flesh nor touch their carcasses.

**9** "These you may eat of all that are
in water: anything that has fins and
scales you may eat, **10** but anything
that does not have fins and scales you
shall not eat; it is unclean for you.

**11** "You may eat any clean bird.
**12** But [a]these are the ones which
you shall not eat: the [1]eagle and the
vulture and the [2]buzzard, **13** and the
red kite, the falcon, and the kite in
their kinds, **14** and every raven in its
kind, **15** and the ostrich, the owl, the
gull, and the hawk in their kinds,
**16** the little owl, the [1]great owl, the
white owl, **17** the pelican, the carrion
vulture, the cormorant, **18** the stork,
and the heron in their kinds, and the
hoopoe and the bat. **19** And all the
[1]teeming life with wings are unclean
to you; they shall not be eaten. **20** You
may eat any clean bird.

**21** "[a]You shall not eat anything
which dies *of itself*. You may give it
to the sojourner who is within your
gates, so that he may eat it, or you
may sell it to a foreigner, for you are
[b]a holy people to Yahweh your God.
[c]You shall not boil a young goat in its
mother's milk.

**22** "You [a]shall surely tithe all the
produce from [1]what you sow, which
comes out of the field every year.
**23** And you shall eat in the presence of
Yahweh your God, [a]at the place where
He chooses for His name to dwell, the
tithe of your grain, your new wine,
your oil, and the firstborn of your
herd and your flock, so that you may
[b]learn to fear Yahweh your God all
*your* days. **24** And if the [1]distance is
so great for you that you are not able
to [2]bring *the tithe*, since the place
where Yahweh your God chooses [a]to
set His name is too far away from
you when Yahweh your God blesses
you, **25** then you shall [1]exchange *it*
for money and bind the money in
your hand and go to the place which
Yahweh your God chooses. **26** And
you may spend the money for what-
ever your [1]heart desires: for oxen
or sheep or wine or strong drink or
whatever your [1]heart [2]desires; and

**14:3** [a]Eze 4:14 **14:4** [a]Lv 11:2-45; Ac 10:14 **14:5** [1]Exact identification of these animals is uncertain **14:6** [1]Lit *two hoofs* [2]Lit *brings up* **14:7** [1]Lit *brings up* [2]Lit *a cleaving* [3]Or *hare* [4]A small, shy, furry animal *(Hyrax syriacus)* found in the peninsula of the Sinai, northern Israel, and the region round the Dead Sea; KJV *coney*, orig NASB *rock badger* **14:12** [a]Lv 11:13 [1]Or *vulture* [2]Or *black vulture* **14:16** [1]Or *great horned owl* **14:19** [1]Flying insects **14:21** [a]Lv 17:15; 22:8; Eze 4:14; 44:31 [b]Dt 14:2 [c]Ex 23:19; 34:26 **14:22** [a]Lv 27:30; Dt 12:6, 17; Ne 10:37 [1]Lit *your seed* **14:23** [a]Dt 12:5 [b]Dt 4:10; Ps 2:11; 111:10; 147:11; Is 8:13; Jer 32:38-40 **14:24** [a]Dt 12:5, 21 [1]Lit *way* [2]Lit *carry it* **14:25** [1]Lit *give in money* **14:26** [1]Lit *soul* [2]Lit *asks of you*

[a]there you shall eat in the presence of Yahweh your God and be glad, you and your household. **27** Also you shall not forsake [a]the Levite who is within your gates, [b]for he has no portion or inheritance among you.

**28** "[a]At the end of every third year you shall bring out all the tithe of your produce in that year and shall deposit *it* within your gates. **29** And the Levite, [a]because he has no portion or inheritance among you, and [b]the sojourner, the [1]orphan, and the widow who are within your gates, shall come and [c]eat and be satisfied, in order that [d]Yahweh your God may bless you in all the work of your hand which you do.

### *Remission of Debt Every Seven Years*

**15** "[a]At the end of *every* seven years you shall [1]grant a remission *of debts.* **2** And this is the manner of remission: every creditor shall release what he has loaned to his neighbor; he shall not exact it of his neighbor and his brother because the remission from Yahweh has been proclaimed. **3** [a]From a foreigner you may exact *it,* but your hand shall release whatever of yours is with your brother. **4** However, there will be no needy one among you, since [a]Yahweh will surely bless you in the land which Yahweh your God is giving you as an inheritance to possess, **5** *if only* you listen obediently to the voice of Yahweh your God, to be careful to do all this commandment which I am commanding you today. **6** [a]For Yahweh your God will bless you as He has promised you, and you will lend to many nations, but you will not borrow; and you will rule over many nations, but they will not rule over you.

**7** "If there is [a]a needy one among you, one of your brothers, in any of your gates *of the towns* in your land which Yahweh your God is giving you, [b]you shall not harden your heart nor close your hand from your needy brother; **8** but [a]you shall freely open your hand to him and shall generously lend him sufficient for his need *in* whatever he lacks. **9** Beware lest there be a vile [1]thought in your heart, saying, '[a]The seventh year, the year of the remission of debts, is near,' and [b]your eye is hostile toward your needy brother, and you give him nothing; then he [c]may cry to Yahweh against you, and it will be a sin in you. **10** You shall generously give to him, and your heart shall not be grieved when you give to him, because [a]for this thing Yahweh your God will bless you in all your work and in all that you send forth your hand *to do.* **11** [a]For the needy will never cease *to be* [1]in the land; therefore I am commanding you, saying, 'You shall freely open your hand to your brother, to your afflicted and needy in your land.'

**12** "[a]If your brother, a Hebrew man or woman, *is* sold to you, then he shall serve you six years, but in the seventh year you shall [1]let him go *to be* free from you. **13** When you [1]let him go *to be* free from you, you shall not [1]let him go empty-handed. **14** You

---

**14:26** [a]Dt 12:7 **14:27** [a]Dt 12:12 [b]Nu 18:20; Dt 10:9; 18:12 **14:28** [a]Dt 26:12 **14:29** [a]Dt 10:9 [b]Dt 16:11, 14; 24:19-21; 26:12; Ps 94:6; Is 1:17 [c]Dt 6:11 [d]Dt 15:10; Mal 3:10 [1]Or *fatherless* ◆ **15:1** [a]Dt 31:10 [1]Lit *make a release* **15:3** [a]Dt 23:20 **15:4** [a]Dt 28:8 **15:6** [a]Dt 28:12, 13 **15:7** [a]Lv 25:35; Dt 15:11 [b]1Jn 3:17 **15:8** [a]Mt 5:42; Lk 6:34; Ga 2:10 **15:9** [a]Dt 15:1 [b]Mt 20:15 [c]Ex 22:23; Dt 24:15; Job 34:28; Ps 12:5; Jas 5:4 [1]Lit *word* **15:10** [a]Dt 14:29; Ps 41:1; Pr 22:9 **15:11** [a]Mt 26:11; Mk 14:7; Jn 12:8 [1]Lit *in the midst of* **15:12** [a]Ex 21:2-6; Lv 25:39-43; Jer 34:14 [1]Lit *send him out* **15:13** [1]Lit *send him out*

shall furnish him generously from
your flock and from your threshing
floor and from your wine vat; you
shall give to him as Yahweh your
God has blessed you. **15** And you shall
remember that you were a slave in
the land of Egypt, and Yahweh your
God redeemed you; therefore I am
commanding you [1]this today. **16** And
it will be that, [a]if he says to you, 'I
will not go out from you,' because he
loves you and your household, since
he fares well with you; **17** then you
shall take an awl and pierce it through
his ear into the door, and he shall be
your servant forever. Also you shall
do likewise to your maidservant.

**18** "It shall not seem hard in your
sight when you [1]let him go *to be* free
from you, for he has given you six
years *with* [2]double the service of a
hired man; so Yahweh your God will
bless you in whatever you do.

**19** "[a]You shall set apart as holy to
Yahweh your God all the firstborn
males that are born of your herd and
of your flock; you shall not work with
the firstborn of your herd nor shear
the firstborn of your flock. **20** [a]You
and your household shall eat it every
year before Yahweh your God in the
place which Yahweh chooses. **21** [a]But
if it has any defect, *such as* lameness
or blindness, *or* any serious defect,
you shall not sacrifice it to Yahweh
your God. **22** You shall eat it within
your gates; [a]the unclean and the
clean alike *may eat it,* as [a]a gazelle
or a deer. **23** Only [a]you shall not eat
its blood; you are to pour it out on
the ground *like* water.

### *The Passover*

**16** "Keep [a]the month of Abib and
[b,1]celebrate the Passover to
Yahweh your God, for in the month
of Abib Yahweh your God brought
you out of Egypt by night. **2** And
you shall sacrifice the Passover to
Yahweh your God from the flock
and the herd, in the place where
Yahweh chooses for His name to
dwell. **3** [a]You shall not eat leavened
bread with it; seven days you shall
eat with it unleavened bread, the
bread of affliction (for you came out
of the land of Egypt in haste), so that
you may remember the day when
you came out of the land of Egypt
[b]all the days of your life. **4** For seven
days no leaven shall be seen with
you in all your territory, and [a]none
of the flesh which you sacrifice on
the evening of the first day shall
remain overnight until morning.
**5** You are not allowed to sacrifice
the Passover in any of your gates *of
the towns* which Yahweh your God
is giving you; **6** but [a]at the place
where Yahweh your God chooses for
His name to dwell, there you shall
sacrifice the Passover in the evening
at sunset, at the appointed time that
you came out of Egypt. **7** And you
shall [a]cook and eat *it* in the place
which Yahweh your God chooses.
In the morning you are to return
to your tents. **8** Six days you shall
eat unleavened bread, and [a]on the
seventh day there shall be [b]a solemn
assembly to Yahweh your God; you
shall do no work *on it.*

**15:15** [1]Lit *this thing* **15:16** [a]Ex 21:5, 6 **15:18** [1]Lit *send him out* [2]Lit *double the amount*
**15:19** [a]Ex 13:2, 12 **15:20** [a]Lv 7:15-18; Dt 12:5; 14:23 **15:21** [a]Lv 22:19-25; Dt 17:1 **15:22** [a]Dt 12:15, 16, 22
**15:23** [a]Ge 9:4; Lv 7:26; 17:10; 19:26; Dt 12:16, 23 ◆**16:1** [a]Ex 12:2 [b]Nu 28:16 [1]Lit *do* **16:3** [a]Ex 12:8,
15, 19, 39; 13:3; 34:18 [b]Dt 4:9 **16:4** [a]Ex 12:8, 10; 34:25 **16:6** [a]Dt 12:5 **16:7** [a]Ex 12:8; 2Chr 35:13
**16:8** [a]Nu 28:25 [b]Ex 12:16; 13:6; Lv 23:8, 36

### *The Feast of Weeks*

**9** "[a]You shall count seven weeks for
yourself; you shall begin to count
seven weeks from the time you begin
to put the sickle to the standing grain.
**10** Then you shall [1]celebrate the Feast
of Weeks to Yahweh your God with a
tribute of a freewill offering of your
hand, which you shall give just as
Yahweh your God blesses you; **11** and
you shall [a]be glad before Yahweh
your God, you and your son and your
daughter and your male and female
slaves and [b]the Levite who is within
your gates and [c]the sojourner and
the [1]orphan and the widow who are
in your midst, in the place where Yah-
weh your God chooses for His name
to dwell. **12** [a]And you shall remember
that you were a slave in Egypt, and
you shall be careful to observe these
statutes.

### *The Feast of Booths*

**13** "[a]You shall [1]celebrate the Feast
of Booths seven days after you have
gathered in from your threshing floor
and your wine vat; **14** and you shall
[a]be glad in your feast, you and your
son and your daughter and your male
and female slaves and the Levite and
the sojourner and the [1]orphan and
the widow who are within your gates.
**15** Seven days you shall celebrate a
feast to Yahweh your God in the place
which Yahweh chooses, because
Yahweh your God will bless you in
all your produce and in all the work
of your hands, so that you will be
altogether glad.

**16** "[a]Three times in a year all your
males shall appear before Yahweh
your God in the place which He
chooses, at the Feast of Unleavened
Bread and at the Feast of Weeks and
at the Feast of Booths, and [b]they shall
not appear before Yahweh empty-
handed. **17** Every man [1]shall give as
he is able, according to the blessing
of Yahweh your God which He has
given you.

### *Do Not Distort Justice*

**18** "You shall appoint for yourself
judges and officers in all your gates *of
the towns* which Yahweh your God is
giving you, according to your tribes,
and they shall judge the people with
righteous judgment. **19** [a]You shall
not distort justice; [b]you shall not
[1]be partial, and [c]you shall not take
a bribe, for a bribe blinds the eyes
of the wise and perverts the words
of the righteous. **20** Righteousness!
Righteousness, you shall pursue, that
[a]you may live and possess the land
which Yahweh your God is giving
you.

**21** "[a]You shall not plant for yourself
an [1]Asherah of any kind of tree beside
the altar of Yahweh your God, which
you shall make for yourself. **22** [a]And
you shall not set up for yourself a
*sacred* pillar which Yahweh your God
hates.

**17** "[a]You shall not sacrifice to Yah-
weh your God an ox or a sheep
which has a defect *or* any [1]blemish,
for that is an abominable thing to
Yahweh your God.

---

**16:9** [a]Ex 23:16; 34:22; Lv 23:15; Nu 28:26 **16:10** [1]Lit *do* **16:11** [a]Dt 12:7 [b]Dt 12:12 [c]Dt 14:29 [1]Or *fatherless* **16:12** [a]Dt 15:15 **16:13** [a]Lv 23:34-43 [1]Lit *do* **16:14** [a]Dt 16:11 [1]Or *fatherless* **16:16** [a]Ex 23:14-17; 34:23, 24 [b]Ex 34:20 **16:17** [1]Lit *according to the gift of his hand* **16:19** [a]Ex 23:2; Lv 19:15; Dt 1:17; 10:17 [b]Pr 24:23 [c]Ex 23:8; Pr 17:23; Ecc 7:7 [1]Lit *regard persons* **16:20** [a]Dt 4:1 **16:21** [a]Dt 7:5; 2Ki 17:16; 21:3; 2Chr 33:3 [1]A wooden symbol of a female deity **16:22** [a]Lv 26:1
◆ **17:1** [a]Dt 15:21 [1]Lit *evil thing*

2 “[a]If there is found in your midst,
in any of your gates *of the towns*
which Yahweh your God is giving
you, a man or a woman who does
what is evil in the sight of Yahweh
your God, by trespassing against His
covenant, 3 and has gone and [a]served
other gods and worshiped them, [b]or
the sun or the moon or any of the
heavenly host, [c]which I have not
commanded, 4 and if it is told to you
and you have heard of it, then you
shall inquire thoroughly. Behold, if
it is true and the matter is confirmed
that this abomination has been done
in Israel, 5 then you shall bring out
that man or that woman who has
done this evil deed to your gates, *that
is*, the man or the woman, and [a]you
shall stone them, and they will die.
6 [a]On the mouth of two witnesses or
three witnesses, he who is to die shall
be put to death; he shall not be put to
death on the mouth of one witness.
7 [a]The hand of the witnesses shall
be first against him to put him to
death, and afterward the hand of all
the people. [b]So you shall purge the
evil from your midst.

### *Judging Cases*

8 “[a]If any case is too difficult for you
to judge, between [1]one kind of homi-
cide or another, between [2]one kind
of lawsuit or another, and between
[3]one kind of assault or another, being
cases of dispute in your gates, then
you shall arise and go up to [b]the place
which Yahweh your God chooses.
9 So you shall come to [a]the Levitical
priest or the judge who is *in office* in
those days, and you shall inquire *of
them*, and they will declare to you
the judgment in the case. 10 And you
shall do according to the [1]terms of
the judgment which they declare to
you from that place which Yahweh
chooses; and you shall be careful to
do according to all that they teach
you. 11 [a]According to the [1]terms of
the law which they teach you, and
according to the judgment which
they tell you, you shall do; you shall
not turn aside from the word which
they declare to you, to the right or
the left. 12 And the man who acts
[a]presumptuously by not listening
to the priest who stands there to
minister to Yahweh your God, or to
the judge, that man shall die; thus
you shall purge the evil from Israel.
13 Then all the people will hear and
be afraid and will not act [a]presump-
tuously again.

### *Statutes for the King*

14 “When you enter the land which
Yahweh your God gives you, and you
[a]possess it and live in it, and you say,
‘[b]I will set a king over me like all the
nations who are around me,’ 15 you
shall surely set a king over you whom
Yahweh your God chooses, *one* [a]from
among your brothers you shall set as
king over yourselves; you may not
put a foreigner over yourselves who
is not your brother. 16 [a]Moreover, he
shall not multiply horses for himself,
nor shall he [b]cause the people to
return to Egypt to multiply horses.

**17:2** [a]Dt 13:6-11 **17:3** [a]Ex 22:20 [b]Job 31:26-28 [c]Jer 7:22 **17:5** [a]Lv 24:14; Jos 7:25 **17:6** [a]Nu 35:30; Dt 19:15; Mt 18:16; Jn 8:17; 2Co 13:1; 1Ti 5:19; Heb 10:28 **17:7** [a]Lv 24:14; Dt 13:9 [b]1Co 5:13
**17:8** [a]2Chr 19:10; Hag 2:11 [b]Dt 12:5; Ps 122:5 [1]Lit *blood to blood* [2]Lit *judgment to judgment* [3]Lit *stroke to stroke* **17:9** [a]Dt 19:17 **17:10** [1]Lit *mouth* **17:11** [a]Dt 25:1 [1]Lit *mouth* **17:12** [a]Nu 15:30; Dt 1:43; 17:13; 18:20; Hos 4:4 **17:13** [a]Dt 17:12 **17:14** [a]Dt 11:31; Jos 21:43 [b]1Sa 8:5, 19, 20; 10:19 **17:15** [a]Jer 30:21
**17:16** [a]1Ki 4:26; 10:26-29; Ps 20:7 [b]Is 31:1; Eze 17:15

[c]Yahweh has said to you, 'You shall
never again return that way.' **17** [a]And
he shall not multiply wives for him-
self, [1]or else his heart will turn away;
nor shall he greatly increase silver
and gold for himself.

**18** "Now it will be when he sits on
the throne of his kingdom, that he
shall write for himself a copy of this
law on a scroll [a,1]in the presence of
the Levitical priests. **19** And it shall
be with him, and he shall read it [a]all
the days of his life, that he may learn
to fear Yahweh his God, [1]to carefully
observe all the words of this law and
these statutes, **20** that his heart may
not be lifted up above his brothers
[a]and that he may not turn aside from
the commandment, to the right or
the left, so that he may prolong *his*
days in his kingdom, he and his sons
in the midst of Israel.

### *The Portion of the Levites*

**18** "[a]The Levitical priests, the
whole tribe of Levi, shall have
no portion or inheritance with Israel;
they shall eat of the offerings to Yah-
weh by fire and of His inheritance.
**2** [a]And they shall have no inheritance
among their brothers; Yahweh is their
inheritance, as He [1]promised them.

**3** "[a]Now this shall be the *legal*
judgment for the priests *taken* from
the people, from those who offer a
*sacrifice*, either an ox or a sheep: they
shall give to the priest the shoulder
and the two cheeks and the stomach.
**4** You shall give him the [a]first fruits
of your grain, your new wine and
your oil and the first shearing of
your sheep. **5** [a]For Yahweh your God
has chosen him and his sons from
all your tribes, to [b]stand to minister
in the name of Yahweh all the days.

**6** "Now if a Levite comes from any
of your gates *of the towns* through-
out Israel where he [a]sojourns and
comes [1]whenever he desires to the
place which Yahweh chooses, **7** then
he shall minister in the name of
Yahweh his God like all his brothers
the Levites who stand there before
Yahweh. **8** [a]They shall eat [1]equal
portions, except *what they receive*
from the sale of their fathers' *estates*.

### *Do Not Imitate Abominations*

**9** "When you enter the land which
Yahweh your God gives you, you shall
not learn to [a,1]imitate the abomina-
tions of those nations. **10** There shall
not be found among you anyone
[a]who makes his son or his daugh-
ter pass through the fire, one who
uses divination, one [b]who practices
soothsaying or one who interprets
omens or a sorcerer, **11** or one who
is an enchanter [a]or a medium or a
spiritist or one who inquires of the
dead. **12** For whoever does these
things is an abomination to Yahweh;
and [a]because of these abominations
Yahweh your God will dispossess
them from before you. **13** [a]You shall
be [1]blameless before Yahweh your
God. **14** For those nations, which you
shall dispossess, listen to those who

---

**17:16** [c]Ex 13:17, 18; Hos 11:5 **17:17** [a]2Sa 5:13; 12:11; 1Ki 11:3, 4 [1]Lit *nor* **17:18** [a]Dt 31:24-26 [1]Lit *from before* **17:19** [a]Dt 4:9, 10; Jos 1:8 [1]Lit *to keep to do them* **17:20** [a]Dt 5:32; 1Ki 15:5 ◆ **18:1** [a]Dt 10:9; 1Co 9:13 **18:2** [a]Nu 18:20 [1]Lit *spoke to* **18:3** [a]Lv 7:32-34; Nu 18:11, 12 **18:4** [a]Nu 18:12 **18:5** [a]Ex 29:9 [b]Dt 10:8 **18:6** [a]Nu 35:2, 3 [1]Lit *with all the desire of his soul* **18:8** [a]Lv 27:30-33; Nu 18:21-24; 2Chr 31:4; Ne 12:44 [1]Lit *portion like portion* **18:9** [a]Dt 9:5 [1]Lit *do according to* **18:10** [a]Dt 12:31 [b]Ex 22:18; Lv 19:26, 31; 20:6; Jer 27:9, 10; Mal 3:5 **18:11** [a]Lv 19:31 **18:12** [a]Lv 18:24 **18:13** [a]Ge 6:9; 17:1; Mt 5:48 [1]Or *having integrity*; lit *complete, perfect*

[a]practice soothsaying and to divin-
ers, but as for you, Yahweh your God
has not allowed you *to do* so.

### *Yahweh Will Raise Up a Prophet*

**15** "[a]Yahweh your God will raise
up for you a prophet like me from
among you, from your brothers;
you shall listen to him. **16** This is
[a]according to all that you asked of
Yahweh your God in Horeb on the
day of the assembly, saying, 'Let me
not hear again the voice of Yahweh
my God; let me not see this great fire
anymore, or I will die.' **17** [a]And Yah-
weh said to me, 'They have [1]spoken
well. **18** I will raise up a prophet from
among their brothers like you, and
[a]I will put My words in his mouth,
and [b]he shall speak to them all that
I command him. **19** [a]And it will be
that whoever will not listen to My
words which he shall speak in My
name, I Myself will require *it* of him.
**20** But the prophet who speaks a
word [a]presumptuously in My name
which I have not commanded him
to speak, or [b]which he speaks in the
name of other gods, [1]that prophet
shall die.' **21** Now [1]you may say in
your heart, 'How will we know the
word which Yahweh has not spo-
ken?' **22** [a]When a prophet speaks
in the name of Yahweh, if the thing
does not come about or come true,
that is the thing which Yahweh has
not spoken. The prophet has spoken
it [b]presumptuously; you shall not be
afraid of him.

### *Statutes About Cities of Refuge*

**19** "[a]When Yahweh your God
cuts off the nations, whose
land Yahweh your God gives you,
and you dispossess them and settle
in their cities and in their houses,
**2** [a]you shall set apart three cities for
yourself in the midst of your land,
which Yahweh your God gives you
to [1]possess. **3** You shall prepare the
[1]roads for yourself, and divide into
three parts the territory of your land
which Yahweh your God will give you
to inherit, [2]so that any manslayer
may flee there.

**4** "[a]Now this is the case of the
manslayer who may flee there and
live: when he strikes down his friend
[1]without premeditation, [2]not hating
him previously— **5** as when *a man*
goes into the forest with his friend
to cut wood, and his hand [1]swings
the axe to cut down the tree, and the
iron *head* slips off the [2]handle and
[3]strikes his friend so that he dies—
he may flee to one of these cities
and live; **6** lest the avenger of blood
pursue the manslayer when his heart
is [1]angry, and overtake him, because
the way is long, and [2]strike down his
life, though he was not deserving of
death, since he had not hated him
previously. **7** Therefore, I am com-
manding you, saying, 'You shall set
apart three cities for yourself.'

**8** "Now if Yahweh your God
[a]enlarges your territory, just as He
has sworn to your fathers, and gives
you all the land which He [1]promised

---

**18:14** [a]2Ki 21:6 **18:15** [a]Mt 21:11; Lk 2:25-34; 7:16; 24:19; Jn 1:21, 25; 4:19; Ac 3:22; 7:37 **18:16** [a]Ex 20:18, 19; Dt 5:23-27 **18:17** [a]Dt 5:28 [1]Lit *done well what they have spoken* **18:18** [a]Is 51:16; Jn 17:8 [b]Jn 4:25; 8:28; 12:49, 50 **18:19** [a]Ac 3:23; Heb 12:25 **18:20** [a]Dt 13:5; 17:12 [b]Dt 13:1, 2; Jer 14:14; Zec 13:3 [1]Lit *and that* **18:21** [1]Lit *if you say* **18:22** [a]Jer 28:9 [b]Dt 18:20 ◆ **19:1** [a]Dt 6:10, 11 **19:2** [a]Dt 4:41; Jos 20:2 [1]Lit *possess it* **19:3** [1]Lit *road* [2]Lit *and it shall be for every manslayer to flee there* **19:4** [a]Nu 35:9-34 [1]Lit *without knowledge* [2]Lit *and he was not hating him previously* **19:5** [1]Lit *is thrust with* [2]Lit *wood* [3]Lit *finds* **19:6** [1]Or *hot* [2]Lit *strike him in the soul* **19:8** [a]Ge 15:18 [1]Lit *spoke*

to give to your fathers— **9** if you [1]be
careful to do all this commandment
which I am commanding you today,
[a]to love Yahweh your God and to
walk in His ways all *your* days—[b]then
you shall add three more cities for
yourself, besides these three. **10** So
innocent blood will not be shed in
the midst of your land which Yahweh
your God gives you as an inheritance,
and [a]bloodguiltiness be on you.

**11** "But [a]if there is a man who hates
his neighbor and lies in wait for him
and rises up against him and strikes
down [1]his life so that he dies, and he
flees to one of these cities, **12** then the
elders of his city shall send and take
him from there and give him over
into the hand of the avenger of blood,
that he may die. **13** [a,1]You shall not
pity him, but [b]you shall purge the
blood of the innocent from Israel,
that it may go well with you.

### *Statutes About Boundaries and Witnesses*

**14** "[a]You shall not move your neigh-
bor's boundary mark, which the an-
cestors have set, in your inheritance
which you will inherit in the land
that Yahweh your God gives you to
[1]possess.

**15** "[a]A single witness shall not rise
up against a man on account of any
iniquity or any sin [1]which he has
committed; at the mouth of two or
three witnesses a matter shall be es-
tablished. **16** [a]If a malicious witness
rises up against a man to [1]accuse him
of [2]wrongdoing, **17** then both the men
who have the dispute shall stand
[a]before Yahweh, before the priests
and the judges who will be *in office* in
those days. **18** And the judges [a]shall
inquire thoroughly, and behold, *if* the
witness is a false witness *and* he has
[1]accused his brother falsely, **19** then
[a]you shall do to him just as he had
intended to do to his brother. Thus
you shall purge the evil from among
you. **20** [a]And the rest will hear and be
afraid and will never again do such
an evil thing among you. **21** Thus
[a]your eye shall not show pity: [b]life
for life, [c]eye for eye, tooth for tooth,
hand for hand, foot for foot.

### *Statutes About Warfare*

**20** "If you go out to battle against
your enemies and see [a]horses
and chariots *and* people more nu-
merous than you, [b]do not be afraid
of them; for Yahweh your God, who
brought you up from the land of
Egypt, is with you. **2** Now it will be,
when you are drawing near to the
battle, the priest shall approach and
speak to the people. **3** And he shall
say to them, 'Hear, O Israel, you are
drawing near to the battle against
your enemies today. Do not let your
heart be faint. [a]Do not be afraid, nor
be alarmed, nor be in dread before
them, **4** for Yahweh your God [a]is the
one who goes with you, to fight for
you against your enemies, to save
you.' **5** The officers also shall speak
to the people, saying, 'Who is the

---

**19:9** [a]Dt 6:5 [b]Jos 20:7 [1]Lit *keep...to do it* **19:10** [a]Nu 35:33; Dt 21:1-9 **19:11** [a]Ex 21:12; Nu 35:16; 1Jn 3:15 [1]Lit *him in the soul* **19:13** [a]Dt 7:2 [b]1Ki 2:31 [1]Lit *Your eye* **19:14** [a]Dt 27:17; Job 24:2; Pr 22:28; Hos 5:10 [1]Lit *possess it* **19:15** [a]Nu 35:30; Dt 17:6; Mt 18:16; Jn 8:17; 2Co 13:1; 1Ti 5:19; Heb 10:28 [1]Lit *in any sin, which he sins* **19:16** [a]Ex 23:1; Ps 27:12 [1]Lit *testify against* [2]Lit *turning aside* **19:17** [a]Dt 17:9 **19:18** [a]Dt 25:1 [1]Lit *testified against* **19:19** [a]Pr 19:5 **19:20** [a]Dt 17:13; 21:21 **19:21** [a]Dt 19:13 [b]Ex 21:23; Lv 24:20 [c]Mt 5:38 ◆ **20:1** [a]Dt 3:22; 7:18; 31:6, 8; Ps 20:7; Is 31:1 [b]2Chr 32:7, 8; Ps 23:4; Is 41:10 **20:3** [a]Dt 20:1; Jos 23:10 **20:4** [a]Dt 1:30; 3:22; Jos 23:10

man that has built a new house and
has not [a]dedicated it? Let him go and
return to his house, lest he die in the
battle and another man dedicate it.
6 Who is the man that has planted a
vineyard and has not [1]begun to use
its fruit? Let him go and return to
his house, lest he die in the battle
and another man [1]begin to use its
fruit. 7 [a]And who is the man that is
engaged to a woman and has not
[1]married her? Let him go and return
to his house, lest he die in the battle
and another man [2]marry her.' 8 Then
the officers shall speak further to the
people and say, '[a]Who is the man that
is afraid and whose heart is faint? Let
him go and return to his house, so
that [1]he might not make his brothers'
hearts melt like his heart.' 9 Now it
will be that when the officers have
finished speaking to the people, they
shall appoint commanders of armies
at the head of the people.

10 "If you come near a city to fight
against it, you shall call for *terms*
of peace. 11 Now it will be that if it
[1]agrees to make peace with you and
opens to you, then all the people
who are found in it shall become
your [a]forced labor and shall serve
you. 12 However, if it does not make
peace with you, but makes war
against you, then you shall besiege it.
13 And Yahweh your God shall give it
into your hand, [a]and you shall strike
all the males in it with the edge of
the sword. 14 Only the women and
the little ones and [a]the animals and
all that is in the city, all its spoil,
you shall plunder for yourself; and
you shall consume the spoil of your
enemies which Yahweh your God has
given you. 15 Thus you shall do to all
the cities that are very far from you,
which are not of the cities of these
nations [1]nearby. 16 [a]Only in the cities
of these peoples that Yahweh your
God is giving you as an inheritance,
you shall not leave alive anything
that breathes. 17 But you shall devote
them to destruction, the Hittite and
the Amorite, the Canaanite and the
Perizzite, the Hivite and the Jebusite,
as Yahweh your God has commanded
you, 18 so that they may not teach you
to do [a]according to all their abomina-
tions which they have done for their
gods, so that you would [b]sin against
Yahweh your God.

19 "If you besiege a city for many
days, to make war against it in order
to capture it, you shall not destroy
its trees by swinging an axe against
them; for you may eat from them,
and you shall not cut them down.
[1]For is the tree of the field a man,
that it should [2]be besieged by you?
20 Only the trees which you know are
not trees for food you shall destroy
and cut down, that you may build
siegeworks against the city that is
making war with you until it falls.

### *Atonement for Innocent Blood*

21 "If a slain person is found
fallen in the open country in
the land which Yahweh your God
gives you to [1]possess, *and* it is not
known who has struck him, 2 then
your elders and your judges shall go
out and measure *the distance* to the

---

**20:5** [a]Ne 12:27 **20:6** [1]Lit *treat(ed) it as common* **20:7** [a]Dt 24:5 [1]Lit *taken* [2]Lit *take*
**20:8** [a]Jdg 7:3 [1]As in Gr and other ancient versions **20:11** [a]1Ki 9:21 [1]Lit *answers peace*
**20:13** [a]Nu 31:7 **20:14** [a]Jos 8:2 **20:15** [1]Lit *here* **20:16** [a]Ex 23:31-33; Nu 21:2, 3; Dt 7:1-5;
Jos 11:14 **20:18** [a]Ex 34:12-16; Dt 7:4; 9:5; 12:30, 31 [b]Ex 23:33; 2Ki 21:3-15; Ps 106:34-41 **20:19** [1]Read as
interrogative with ancient versions [2]Lit *come before you in the siege* ◆ **21:1** [1]Lit *possess it*

cities which are around the slain one.
3 And it shall be that the city which is
nearest to the slain man, that is, the
elders of that city, shall take a heifer
of the herd, which has not been
worked and which has not pulled
in a yoke; 4 and the elders of that
city shall bring the heifer down to a
valley with running water, which has
not been plowed or sown, and they
shall break the heifer's neck there in
the valley. 5 Then [a]the priests, the
sons of Levi, shall come near, for
Yahweh your God has chosen them to
minister for Him and to bless in the
name of Yahweh; and every dispute
and every [1]assault [2]shall be settled
by them. 6 And all the elders of that
city [1]who are nearest to the slain
man shall [a]wash their hands over
the heifer whose neck was broken
in the valley; 7 and they shall answer
and say, 'Our hands did not shed this
blood, nor did our eyes see *it*. 8 Atone
for Your people Israel whom You have
redeemed, O Yahweh, and do not
place the guilt of [a]innocent blood in
the midst of Your people Israel.' And
the bloodguiltiness shall be atoned
for them. 9 [a]So you shall purge the
guilt of innocent blood from your
midst, when you do what is right in
the eyes of Yahweh.

### *Statutes About Domestic Relations*

10 "*If* you go out to battle against your
enemies, and [a]Yahweh your God
gives them over into your hands and
you take them away captive, 11 and
see among the captives a beautiful
woman and set your affection on
her and would take her as a wife for
yourself, 12 then you shall bring her
home to your house, and she shall
[a]shave her head and [1]trim her nails.
13 She shall also [1]remove the clothes
of her captivity and shall remain in
your house and [a]weep for her father
and mother a full month; and after
that you may go in to her and be her
husband, and she shall be your wife.
14 And it will be that, if you do not
desire her, then you shall let her go
[1]wherever she wishes; but you shall
certainly not sell her for money; you
shall not [2]mistreat her because you
have [a]humbled her.

15 "If a man has two wives, the one
loved and [a]the other [1]unloved, and
*both* the loved and the [1]unloved have
borne him sons, if the firstborn son
belongs to the [1]unloved, 16 then it
shall be in the day he [1]wills what he
has to his sons, he cannot make the
son of the loved the firstborn before
the son of the [2]unloved, who is the
firstborn. 17 But he shall recognize
the firstborn, the son of the [1]unloved,
by giving him a double portion of
all that [2]he has, for he is the [a]first
of his vigor; [b]the *legal* judgment for
the firstborn belongs to him.

18 "If any man has a stubborn and
rebellious son who will [a]not obey
his father or his mother, and when
they discipline him, he will not even
listen to them, 19 then his father and
mother shall seize him and bring him
out to the elders of his city [1]at the
gateway of his hometown. 20 Then

**21:5** [a]Dt 17:9-11; 19:17; 1Chr 23:13 [1]Lit *stroke* [2]Lit *shall be according to their mouth* **21:6** [a]Mt 27:24 [1]Lit *which is* **21:8** [a]Nu 35:33, 34; Jon 1:14 **21:9** [a]Dt 19:13 **21:10** [a]Jos 21:44 **21:12** [a]Lv 14:8, 9; Nu 6:9 [1]Lit *do* **21:13** [a]Ps 45:10 [1]Lit *remove from her* **21:14** [a]Ge 34:2 [1]Lit *according to her soul* [2]Or *enslave* **21:15** [a]Ge 29:33 [1]Lit *hated* **21:16** [1]Lit *makes to inherit* [2]Lit *hated* **21:17** [a]Ge 49:3 [b]Ge 25:31 [1]Lit *hated* [2]Lit *is found with him* **21:18** [a]Ex 20:12; Lv 19:3; Pr 1:8; Eph 6:1-3 **21:19** [1]Lit *and to the gate of his place*

they shall say to the elders of his city,
'This son of ours is stubborn and
rebellious; he will not listen to our
voice; he is a glutton and a drunkard.'
**21** [a]Then all the men of his city shall
stone him, and he will die; so [b]you
shall purge the evil from your midst,
and [c]all Israel will hear *of it* and fear.

### *A Man Hanged on a Tree Is Cursed*

**22** "And if a man has committed
a sin, [a]the judgment of which is
death, and he is put to death, and
you hang him on a tree, **23** [a]his corpse
shall not hang all night on the tree,
but you shall surely bury him on the
same day (because [b]cursed of God is
he who is hanged), so that you [c]do
not make unclean your land which
Yahweh your God gives you as an
inheritance.

### *Various Statutes*

**22** "[a]You shall not see your brother's ox or his sheep straying
away and [1]ignore them; you shall
certainly bring them back to your
brother. **2** And if your brother is not
near you, or if you do not know him,
then you shall bring it home to your
house, and it shall be with you until
your brother searches for it; then you
shall give it back to him. **3** Thus you
shall do with his donkey, and you shall
do likewise with his garment, and you
shall do likewise with anything lost by
your brother, which he has lost and
you have found. You are not allowed
to [1]ignore *them.* **4** You shall not see
your brother's donkey or his ox fallen
down on the way and [1]ignore *them;*
you shall certainly help him to raise
*them* up.

**5** "A woman shall not wear man's
clothing, nor shall a man put on a
woman's clothing; for whoever does
these things is an abomination to
Yahweh your God.

**6** "If you happen to come upon a
bird's nest along the way, in any tree
or on the ground, with young ones
or eggs, and the mother sitting on
the young or on the eggs, [a]you shall
not take the mother with the young;
**7** you shall certainly let the mother
go, but the young you may take for
yourself, [a]in order that it may be well
with you and that you may prolong
your days.

**8** "When you build a new house,
you shall make a parapet for your
roof, so that you will not bring
bloodguilt on your house if anyone
falls from it.

**9** "[a]You shall not sow your vineyard with two kinds of seed, lest [1]all
the produce of the seed which you
have sown and the increase of the
vineyard become defiled.

**10** "[a]You shall not plow with an ox
and a donkey together.

**11** "[a]You shall not wear a material
mixed of wool and flax together.

**12** "[a]You shall make yourself tassels
on the four corners of your garment
with which you cover yourself.

### *Statutes About Sexual Immorality*

**13** "[a]If any man takes a wife and goes
in to her and *then* [1]turns against her,
**14** and charges her with shameful
deeds and brings forth against her a

---

**21:21** [a]Lv 20:2, 27; 24:14-23; Nu 15:25, 36 [b]Dt 19:19 [c]Dt 13:11 **21:22** [a]Dt 22:26; Mt 26:66; Mk 14:64; Ac 23:29 **21:23** [a]Jos 8:29; 10:26, 27; Jn 19:31 [b]Ga 3:13 [c]Lv 18:25; Nu 35:34 ◆ **22:1** [a]Ex 23:4, 5; Pr 27:10; Zec 7:9 [1]Lit *hide yourself* **22:3** [1]Lit *hide yourself* **22:4** [1]Lit *hide yourself* **22:6** [a]Lv 22:28 **22:7** [a]Dt 4:40 **22:9** [a]Lv 19:19 [1]Lit *the fullness* **22:10** [a]2Co 6:14-16 **22:11** [a]Lv 19:19 **22:12** [a]Nu 15:37-41; Mt 23:5 **22:13** [a]Ge 29:21; Dt 24:1; Jdg 15:1 [1]Lit *hates her*

bad name and says, 'I took this woman, *but* when I came near her, I did not find her a virgin,' **15** then the girl's father and her mother shall take and bring out the *evidence* of the girl's virginity to the elders of the city at the gate. **16** Then the girl's father shall say to the elders, 'I gave my daughter to this man as a wife, but he [1]turned against her; **17** and behold, he has charged her with shameful deeds, saying, "I did not find your daughter a virgin." But [1]this is the evidence of my daughter's virginity.' And they shall spread the garment before the elders of the city. **18** So [a]the elders of that city shall take the man and chastise him, **19** and they shall fine him [1]one hundred *shekels* of silver and give it to the girl's father because he brought forth a bad name against a virgin of Israel. And she shall be his wife; he cannot [2]divorce her all his days.

**20** "But if this [a,1]charge is true, that the girl was not found a virgin, **21** then they shall bring out the girl to the doorway of her father's house, and the men of her city shall stone her, and she will die because she has [a]committed a disgraceful act in Israel by playing the harlot in her father's house; thus [b]you shall purge the evil from among you.

**22** "[a]If a man is found lying with a married woman, then both of them shall die, the man who lay with the woman, and the woman; thus you shall purge the evil from Israel.

**23** "[a]If there is a girl who is a virgin engaged to a man, and *another* man finds her in the city and lies with her, **24** then you shall bring them both out to the gate of that city, and you shall stone them, and they will die; the girl, because she did not cry out in the city, and the man, because he has violated his neighbor's wife. Thus you shall purge the evil from among you.

**25** "But if in the field the man finds the girl who is engaged, and the man forces her and lies with her, then only the man who lies with her shall die. **26** But you shall do nothing to the girl; there is no sin in the girl worthy of death, for just as a man rises against his neighbor and murders him, so is this case. **27** When he found her in the field, the engaged girl cried out, but there was no one to save her.

**28** "[a]If a man finds a girl who is a virgin, who is not engaged, and seizes her and lies with her and they are found, **29** then the man who lay with her shall give to the girl's father fifty *shekels* of silver, and she shall become his wife because he has violated her; he cannot divorce her all his days.

**30** "[a,1]A man shall not take his father's wife so that he will not uncover his father's skirt.

### *Those Who May Not Enter the Assembly*

**23** "[a]No one who is [1]emasculated or has his male organ cut off shall enter the assembly of Yahweh. **2** No one of illegitimate birth shall enter the assembly of Yahweh; even to the tenth generation, none of his *seed*

---

**22:16** [1]Lit *hated her* **22:17** [1]Lit *these are* **22:18** [a]Ex 18:21; Dt 1:9-18 **22:19** [1]Approx. 2.5 lb. or 1.1 kg [2]Lit *send her away* **22:20** [a]Dt 17:4 [1]Lit *matter* **22:21** [a]Ge 34:7; Lv 19:29; 21:9; Dt 23:17, 18; Jdg 20:5-10; 2Sa 13:12, 13 [b]Dt 13:5; 17:7; 19:19 **22:22** [a]Lv 20:10; Eze 16:38; Mt 5:27, 28; Jn 8:5; 1Co 6:9; Heb 13:4 **22:23** [a]Lv 19:20-22; Mt 1:18, 19 **22:28** [a]Ex 22:16 **22:30** [a]Lv 18:8; 20:11; Dt 27:20; 1Co 5:1 [1]Ch 23:1 in Heb ◆ **23:1** [a]Lv 21:20; 22:24 [1]Lit *wounded by crushing* of testicles

shall enter the assembly of Yahweh.
**3** [a]No Ammonite or Moabite shall
enter the assembly of Yahweh; even
to the tenth generation, none of their
*seed* shall ever enter the assembly
of Yahweh, **4** [a]because they did not
meet you with [1]food and water on
the way when you came out of Egypt,
and because they hired against you
[b]Balaam the son of Beor from Pe-
thor of [2]Mesopotamia, to curse you.
**5** Nevertheless, Yahweh your God
was not willing to listen to Balaam,
but Yahweh your God [a]turned the
curse into a blessing for you because
Yahweh your God [b]loves you. **6** [a]You
shall never seek their peace or their
prosperity all your days.

**7** "You shall not abhor an Edomite,
for [a]he is your brother; you shall not
abhor an Egyptian, [b]for you were a
sojourner in his land. **8** The sons of the
third generation who are born to them
may enter the assembly of Yahweh.

**9** "When you go out as [1]an army
against your enemies, you shall keep
yourself from every evil thing.

**10** "[a]If there is among you any
man who is unclean because of a
nocturnal emission, then he must
go outside the camp; he may not
[1]reenter the camp. **11** But it shall be
when evening approaches, he shall
bathe himself with water, and at
sundown he may [1]reenter the camp.

**12** "You shall also have a place
outside the camp and go out there,
**13** and you shall have a [1]spade among
your tools, and it shall be when you
sit down outside, you shall dig with
it and shall turn [2]to cover up your
excrement. **14** Since [a]Yahweh your
God walks in the midst of your camp
to deliver you and to give your ene-
mies over to you, therefore your camp
must be [b]holy; and He must not see
[1]anything indecent among you, [2]or
He will turn away from you.

**15** "[a]You shall not hand over to his
master a slave who has [1]escaped from
his master to you. **16** He shall live with
you in your midst, in the place which
he shall choose in one of your gates *of
the towns* where it pleases him; [a]you
shall not mistreat him.

**17** "[a]None of the daughters of
Israel shall be a cult prostitute, [b]nor
shall any of the sons of Israel be a
cult prostitute. **18** You shall not bring
the hire of a harlot or the wages of
a [a,1]dog into the house of Yahweh
your God for any votive offering, for
both of these are an abomination to
Yahweh your God.

**19** "[a]You shall not charge interest
to your brother: interest on money,
food, *or* anything that may be loaned
at interest. **20** [a]You may charge inter-
est to a foreigner, but to your brother
you shall not charge interest, so that
[b]Yahweh your God may bless you in
all [1]that you send forth your hand *to
do* in the land which you are about
to enter to [2]possess.

**21** "[a]When you make a vow to
Yahweh your God, you shall not delay

***23:3*** [a]*Ne 13:1, 2* **23:4** [a]Ne 13:2 [b]Nu 22:5; 23:7; Jos 24:9; 2Pe 2:15; Jd 11 [1]Lit *bread* [2]Heb *Aram-naharaim* **23:5** [a]*Pr 26:2* [b]*Dt 4:37* ***23:6*** [a]*Ezr 9:12* ***23:7*** [a]*Ge 25:24-26; Ob 10, 12* [b]Ex 22:21; 23:9; Lv 19:34; Dt 10:19 **23:9** [1]Or *a camp* **23:10** [a]Lv 15:16 [1]Lit *come to the midst of* **23:11** [1]Lit *come to the midst of* **23:13** [1]Lit *peg* [2]Lit *and* **23:14** [a]Lv 26:12 [b]Ex 3:5 [1]Lit *nakedness of anything* [2]Lit *and* **23:15** [a]1Sa 30:15 [1]Lit *delivered himself* **23:16** [a]Ex 22:21; Pr 22:22 **23:17** [a]Lv 19:29; Dt 22:21 [b]Ge 19:5; 2Ki 23:7 **23:18** [a]Lv 18:22; 20:13 [1]Male prostitute, sodomite **23:19** [a]Ex 22:25; Lv 25:35-37; Ne 5:2-7; Ps 15:5 **23:20** [a]Dt 28:12 [b]Dt 15:10 [1]Lit *the putting forth of your hand* [2]Lit *possess it* **23:21** [a]Nu 30:1, 2; Job 22:27; Ps 61:8; Ecc 5:4, 5; Mt 5:33

to pay it, for Yahweh your God will
surely require it of you; and it will
be a sin in you. **22** However, if you
refrain from vowing, it will not be
a sin in you. **23** You shall be careful
and do what goes out from your lips,
just as you have voluntarily vowed
to Yahweh your God that which you
spoke with your mouth.

**24** "When you enter your neighbor's vineyard, then you may eat
grapes [1]until you are fully satisfied,
but you shall not put any in your
[2]basket.

**25** "[a]When you enter your neighbor's standing grain, then you may
pluck the heads with your hand, but
you shall not wield a sickle in your
neighbor's standing grain.

### *Statutes About Divorce*

**24** "If a man takes a wife and
marries her, and it happens
[1]that she finds no favor in his eyes
because he has found some [a]indecency in her, and [b]he writes her a
certificate of divorce and puts *it* in
her hand and sends her out from
his house, **2** and she goes out of his
house and goes and becomes another
man's *wife*, **3** and if the latter husband
[1]turns against her and writes her a
certificate of divorce and puts *it* in
her hand and sends her out of his
house, or if the latter husband dies
*who took* her to be his wife, **4** *then*
her [a]former husband who sent her
away is not allowed to take her again
to be his wife, since she has been
defiled; for that is an abomination
before Yahweh, and you shall not
bring sin on the land which Yahweh
your God gives you as an inheritance.

**5** "[a]When a man takes a new wife,
he shall not go out with the army nor
be charged with any duty; he shall
be free at home one year and shall
[b]give gladness to his wife whom he
has taken.

### *Remember You Were Slaves in Egypt*

**6** "No one shall take a handmill or
an upper millstone in pledge, for he
would be taking a life in pledge.

**7** "[a]If a man is [1]caught kidnapping
any of his brothers of the sons of
Israel, and he mistreats him or sells
him, then that thief shall die; so you
shall purge the evil from among you.

**8** "[a]Take care against [1]an infection
of leprosy, to be very careful and to
do according to all that the Levitical
priests instruct you; as I have commanded them, so you shall be careful
to do. **9** Remember what Yahweh your
God did [a]to Miriam on the way as
you came out of Egypt.

**10** "[a]When you make your neighbor a loan of any sort, you shall not
enter his house to take his deposit.
**11** You shall stand outside, and the
man to whom you make the loan shall
bring the deposit out to you. **12** Now
if he is an afflicted man, you shall
not sleep with his deposit. **13** [a]When
the sun goes down you shall surely
return the deposit to him, that he
may sleep in his cloak and bless you;
and [b]it will be righteousness for you
before Yahweh your God.

**14** "[a]You shall not oppress a hired
person *who is* afflicted and needy,

**23:24** [1]Lit *according to your satisfaction of your soul* [2]Or *vessel* **23:25** [a]Mt 12:1; Mk 2:23; Lk 6:1
◆ **24:1** [a]Nu 5:12, 28; Dt 22:13-21 [b]Mt 5:31; 19:7-9; Mk 10:4, 5 [1]Lit *if* **24:3** [1]Lit *hates her* **24:4** [a]Jer 3:1
**24:5** [a]Dt 20:7 [b]Pr 5:18 **24:7** [a]Ex 21:16 [1]Lit *found stealing* **24:8** [a]Lv 13:1-14, 57 [1]Lit *a mark, a stroke*
**24:9** [a]Nu 12:10 **24:10** [a]Ex 22:26, 27 **24:13** [a]Ex 22:26 [b]Dt 6:25; Ps 106:31; Da 4:27 **24:14** [a]Lv 19:13;
25:35-43; Dt 15:7-18; Pr 14:31; Am 4:1; 1Ti 5:18

whether *he is* one of your brothers
or one of your sojourners who is in
your land within your gates. **15** [a]You
shall give him his wages on his day
[1]before the sun goes down, for he is
afflicted and sets his soul on it, so
that [b]he will not cry against you to
Yahweh and it become sin in you.

**16** "[a]Fathers shall not be put to
death [1]for *their* sons, nor shall sons
be put to death [1]for *their* fathers; each
shall be put to death for his own sin.

**17** "[a]You shall not pervert the
justice [1]due a sojourner *or* [2]an orphan,
nor [b]take a widow's garment
in pledge. **18** But you shall remember
that you were a slave in Egypt and
that Yahweh your God redeemed you
from there; therefore I am commanding
you to do this thing.

**19** "[a]When you reap your harvest in
your field and have forgotten a sheaf
in the field, you shall not go back to
get it; it shall be [b]for the sojourner,
for the [1]orphan, and for the widow,
in order that Yahweh your God [c]may
bless you in all the work of your hands.
**20** [a]When you beat your olive tree, you
shall not go over the boughs after you
*finish*; it shall be [b]for the sojourner,
for the [1]orphan, and for the widow.

**21** "When you gather the grapes of
your vineyard, you shall not glean it
after you *finish*; it shall be for the sojourner,
for the [1]orphan, and for the
widow. **22** And you shall remember
that you were a slave in the land of
Egypt; therefore I am commanding
you to do this thing.

**25** "[a]If there is a dispute between
men and they go to court *for
judgment*, and [1]the judges judge their
case, [b]and they justify the righteous
and condemn the wicked, **2** then it
shall be if the wicked man [a,1]deserves
to be struck, the judge shall then
make him lie down and be struck
in his presence with the number of
stripes according to his [2]guilt. **3** [a]He
may strike him forty times *but* no
more, lest he strike him with many
more stripes than these and your
brother be [b]dishonored in your eyes.

**4** "[a]You shall not muzzle the ox
while it is threshing.

**5** "If brothers live together and one
of them dies and has no son, then
the wife of the one who died shall
not be *married* outside *the family*
to a strange man. [a]Her husband's
brother shall go in to her and take
her to himself as wife and perform
the duty of a husband's brother to
her. **6** And it will be that the firstborn
whom she bears shall [1]assume the
name of his dead brother, so that
[a]his name will not be blotted out
from Israel. **7** [a]But if the man does
not desire to take his brother's wife,
then his brother's wife shall go up
to the gate to the elders and say, 'My
husband's brother refuses to raise
up a name for his brother in Israel;
he is not willing to perform the duty
of a husband's brother to me.' **8** Then
the elders of his city shall summon
him and speak to him. And *if* he
stands and says, 'I do not desire to

**24:15** [a]Lv 19:13; Jer 22:13; Jas 5:4 [b]Ex 22:23; Dt 15:9; Job 35:9; Jas 5:4 [1]Lit *that the sun shall not go down on it* **24:16** [a]2Ki 14:6; 2Chr 25:4; Jer 31:29, 30; Eze 18:20 [1]Or *with* **24:17** [a]Ex 23:9; Lv 19:33; Dt 1:17; 10:17; 16:19; 27:19 [b]Ex 22:22 [1]Lit *of* [2]Or *the fatherless* **24:19** [a]Lv 19:9, 10; 23:22 [b]Dt 14:29 [c]Pr 19:17 [1]Or *fatherless* **24:20** [a]Lv 19:10 [b]Dt 24:19 [1]Or *fatherless* **24:21** [1]Or *fatherless* ◆ **25:1** [a]Dt 17:8-13; 19:17 [b]Dt 1:16, 17 [1]Lit *they judge them* **25:2** [a]Pr 19:29; Lk 12:48 [1]Lit *is a son of beating* [2]Or *wickedness* **25:3** [a]2Co 11:24 [b]Job 18:3 **25:4** [a]Pr 12:10; 1Co 9:9; 1Ti 5:18 **25:5** [a]Mt 22:24; Mk 12:19; Lk 20:28 **25:6** [a]Ru 4:5, 10 [1]Lit *stand on* **25:7** [a]Ru 4:5, 6

take her,' **9** [a]then his brother's wife
shall come to him in the sight of the
elders and pull his sandal off his foot
and [b]spit in his face; and she shall
answer and say, 'Thus it is done to
the man who does not build up his
brother's house.' **10** And in Israel his
name shall be called, 'The house of
him whose sandal is removed.'
**11** "If *two* men, a man and his
brother, are struggling together, and
the wife of one comes near to deliver
her husband from the hand of the
one who is striking him, and she puts
out her hand and seizes his genitals,
**12** then you shall cut off her [1]hand;
[a,2]you shall not show pity.
**13** "[a]You shall not have in your bag
[1]differing weights, a large and a small.
**14** You shall not have in your house
[1]differing measures, a large and a
small. **15** You shall have a full and
just weight; you shall have a full and
just [1]measure, [a]that your days may be
prolonged in the [2]land which Yahweh
your God gives you. **16** For [a]everyone
who does these things, everyone who
acts unjustly, is an abomination to
Yahweh your God.
**17** "[a]Remember what Amalek did
to you along the way when you came
out from Egypt, **18** how he met you
along the way and attacked among
you all the stragglers at your rear,
but you were faint and weary; and
he [a]did not [1]fear God. **19** Therefore
it will be, when Yahweh your God
has given you [a]rest from all your
surrounding enemies, in the land
which Yahweh your God gives you as
an inheritance to [1]possess, you shall
blot out the memory of Amalek from
under heaven; you must not forget.

### *Bringing First Fruits and Tithes*

**26** "Then it will be, when you
enter the land which Yahweh
your God gives you as an inheritance
and you possess it and live in it, **2** that
you shall take some of [a]the first of all
the fruit of the ground which you
bring in from your land that Yahweh
your God gives you, and you shall
put *it* in a basket and [b]go to the place
where Yahweh your God chooses for
His name to dwell. **3** And you shall go
to the priest who is in office in those
days and say to him, 'I declare this
day to Yahweh [1]my God that I have
entered the land which Yahweh swore
to our fathers to give us.' **4** Then the
priest shall take the basket from your
hand and set it down before the altar
of Yahweh your God. **5** And you shall
answer and say before Yahweh your
God, '[a]My father was a [1]wandering
Aramean, and he went down to Egypt
and [2]sojourned there, [b]few in num-
ber; but there he became a [c]great,
mighty, and populous nation. **6** And
the [a]Egyptians treated us harshly
and afflicted us and imposed hard
slave labor on us. **7** Then [a]we cried
out to Yahweh, the God of our fa-
thers, and Yahweh heard our voice
and saw our affliction and our toil
and our oppression; **8** [a]and Yahweh
brought us out of Egypt with a strong
hand and an outstretched arm and
with great terror and with signs and

---

**25:9** [a]Ru 4:7, 8 [b]Nu 12:14 **25:12** [a]Dt 7:2; 19:13 [1]Lit *palm* [2]Lit *your eye* **25:13** [a]Lv 19:35-37; Pr 11:1; 20:23; Eze 45:10; Mic 6:11 [1]Lit *a stone and a stone* **25:14** [1]Lit *an ephah and an ephah* **25:15** [a]Ex 20:12 [1]Lit *ephah* [2]Lit *ground* **25:16** [a]Pr 11:1 **25:17** [a]Ex 17:8-16 **25:18** [a]Ps 36:1; Ro 3:18 [1]Or *reverence* **25:19** [a]Dt 12:9 [1]Lit *possess it* ◆ **26:2** [a]Ex 22:29; 23:16, 19; Nu 18:13; Pr 3:9 [b]Dt 12:5 **26:3** [1]As in Gr; Heb *your* **26:5** [a]Ge 43:1-14 [b]Ge 46:27 [c]Dt 1:10; 10:22 [1]Or *perishing* [2]Or *lived as an sojourner* **26:6** [a]Ex 1:8-11 **26:7** [a]Ex 2:23-25; 3:9 **26:8** [a]Dt 4:34; 34:11, 12

wonders; **9** and He has brought us to
this place and has given us this land,
[a]a land flowing with milk and honey.
**10** So now behold, I have brought the
first of the fruit of the ground [a]which
You, O Yahweh, have given me.' And
you shall set it down before Yahweh
your God and worship before Yahweh
your God; **11** and you and [a]the Levite
and the sojourner who is among you
shall [b]be glad in all the good which
Yahweh your God has given you and
your household.

**12** "[a]When you have finished
[1]paying all the tithe of your produce
in the third year, the year of tithing,
then you shall give it to the Levite, to
the sojourner, to the [2]orphan, and to
the widow, that they may eat within
your gates and be satisfied. **13** Then
you shall say before Yahweh your
God, 'I have purged the sacred *portion*
from *my* house, and I also have given
it to the Levite and the sojourner, the
[1]orphan and the widow, according to
all Your commandments which You
have commanded me; [a]I have not tres-
passed against or forgotten any of Your
commandments. **14** I have not eaten of
it [1]while mourning, nor have I purged
any of it while I was unclean, nor have
I given any of it to the dead. I have
listened to the voice of Yahweh my
God; I have done according to all that
You have commanded me. **15** [a]Look
down from Your holy habitation, from
heaven, and bless Your people Israel
and the ground which You have given
to us, [b]a land flowing with milk and
honey, as You swore to our fathers.'

**16** "This day Yahweh your God
commands you to do these statutes
and judgments. You shall therefore
be careful to do them [a]with all your
heart and with all your soul. **17** [a]You
have today declared Yahweh to be
your God, and [1]that you would walk
in His ways and keep His statutes, His
commandments, and His judgments,
and listen to His voice. **18** And Yahweh
has today declared you to be [a]His
people, a treasured possession, as He
promised you, and [1]that you should
keep all His commandments; **19** and
[1]that He will [a]set you high above
all nations which He has made, for
praise, a name, and beauty; and that
you shall be [b]a holy people to Yahweh
your God, as He has spoken."

### *Curses on Mount Ebal*

**27** Then Moses and the elders of
Israel commanded the people,
saying, "Keep the entire command-
ment which I am commanding you
today. **2** [a]So it will be on the day
when you cross the Jordan to the
land which Yahweh your God gives
you, that you shall set up for yourself
large stones and coat them with lime
**3** and write on them all the words
of this law when you cross over, so
that you may enter the land which
Yahweh your God gives you, [a]a land
flowing with milk and honey, as
Yahweh, the God of your fathers,
[1]promised you. **4** So it will be when
you cross the Jordan, you shall set
up [a]on Mount Ebal, these stones,
[1]as I am commanding you today,

**26:9** [a]Ex 3:8, 17 **26:10** [a]Dt 8:18; Pr 10:22 **26:11** [a]Dt 12:12 [b]Dt 12:7; 16:11; Ecc 3:12, 13; 5:18-20 **26:12** [a]Lv 27:30; Nu 18:24; Dt 14:28, 29; Heb 7:5, 9, 10 [1]Lit *tithing* [2]Or *fatherless* **26:13** [a]Ps 119:141, 153, 176 [1]Or *fatherless* **26:14** [1]Lit *while in my* **26:15** [a]Ps 80:14; Is 63:15; Zec 2:13 [b]Dt 26:9 **26:16** [a]Dt 4:29 **26:17** [a]Ps 48:14 [1]Lit *to walk in* **26:18** [a]Ex 6:7; 19:5; Dt 4:20; 7:6; 14:2; 28:9; 29:13; Tit 2:14; 1Pe 2:9 [1]Lit *to keep all* **26:19** [a]Dt 4:7, 8; 28:1, 13 [b]Ex 19:6; Dt 7:6; Is 62:12; Jer 2:3; 1Pe 2:9 [1]Lit *to set you* ◆ **27:2** [a]Jos 8:30-32 **27:3** [a]Dt 26:9 [1]Lit *spoke to* **27:4** [a]Dt 11:29; Jos 8:30 [1]Lit *which*

and you shall coat them with lime.
5 Moreover, you shall build there an
altar to Yahweh your God, an altar of
stones; you [a]shall not [1]wield an iron
*tool* on them. 6 You shall build the
altar of Yahweh your God of [1]uncut
stones, and you shall offer on it burnt
offerings to Yahweh your God; 7 and
you shall sacrifice peace offerings
and eat there and [a]be glad before
Yahweh your God. 8 And you shall
write on the [1]stones all the words
of this law very distinctly."

9 Then Moses and the Levitical
priests spoke to all Israel, saying, "Be
silent and listen, O Israel! This day
you have become a people for Yah-
weh your God. 10 You shall therefore
listen to the voice of Yahweh your
God and do His commandments and
His statutes which I am commanding
you today."

11 Moses also commanded the
people on that day, saying, 12 "When
you cross the Jordan, these shall
stand on [a]Mount Gerizim to bless
the people: [b]Simeon, Levi, Judah,
Issachar, Joseph, and Benjamin.
13 For the curse, these shall stand
on Mount Ebal: Reuben, Gad, Asher,
Zebulun, Dan, and Naphtali. 14 The
Levites shall then answer and say
to all the men of Israel with a loud
voice,

15 'Cursed is the man who makes
[a]a graven image or a molten image,
an abomination to Yahweh, the
work of the hands of the craftsman,
and sets *it* up in secret.' And [b]all
the people shall answer and say,
'Amen.'

16 '[a]Cursed is he who dishonors
his father or mother.' And all the
people shall say, 'Amen.'

17 '[a]Cursed is he who moves his
neighbor's boundary mark.' And all
the people shall say, 'Amen.'

18 '[a]Cursed is he who leads a blind
*person* astray on the road.' And all the
people shall say, 'Amen.'

19 '[a]Cursed is he who perverts the
justice due a sojourner, [1]orphan, and
widow.' And all the people shall say,
'Amen.'

20 '[a]Cursed is he who lies with his
father's wife because he has uncov-
ered his father's skirt.' And all the
people shall say, 'Amen.'

21 '[a]Cursed is he who lies with any
animal.' And all the people shall say,
'Amen.'

22 '[a]Cursed is he who lies with his
sister, the daughter of his father or
the daughter of his mother.' And all
the people shall say, 'Amen.'

23 '[a]Cursed is he who lies with his
mother-in-law.' And all the people
shall say, 'Amen.'

24 '[a]Cursed is he who strikes his
neighbor in secret.' And all the peo-
ple shall say, 'Amen.'

25 '[a]Cursed is he who takes a bribe
to strike down [1]innocent blood.' And
all the people shall say, 'Amen.'

26 '[a]Cursed is he who does not
confirm the words of this law by
doing them.' And all the people shall
say, 'Amen.'

**27:5** [a]Ex 20:25; Jos 8:31 [1]Lit *lift up* **27:6** [1]Lit *whole* **27:7** [a]Dt 26:11 **27:8** [1]Stones coated with lime, cf. 27:4 **27:12** [a]Dt 11:29 [b]Jos 8:33-35 **27:15** [a]Ex 20:4, 23; 34:17; Lv 19:4; 26:1; Dt 4:16, 23; 5:8; Is 44:9 [b]1Co 14:16 **27:16** [a]Ex 20:12; 21:17; Lv 19:3; 20:9; Dt 5:16; Eze 22:7 **27:17** [a]Dt 19:14; Pr 22:28 **27:18** [a]Lv 19:14 **27:19** [a]Ex 22:21; 23:9; Lv 19:33; Dt 10:18; 24:17 [1]Or *fatherless* **27:20** [a]Lv 18:8; 20:11; Dt 22:30; 1Co 5:1 **27:21** [a]Ex 22:19; Lv 18:23; 20:15 **27:22** [a]Lv 18:9; 20:17 **27:23** [a]Lv 20:14 **27:24** [a]Ex 21:12; Lv 24:17; Nu 35:30, 31 **27:25** [a]Ex 23:7; Dt 10:17; Ps 15:5; Eze 22:12 [1]Lit *soul of innocent blood* **27:26** [a]Ps 119:21; Jer 11:3; Ga 3:10

### *Blessings for Keeping the Commandments*

28 "[a]Now it will be, if you dili-
gently listen to the voice of
Yahweh your God, being careful to
do all His commandments which I
am commanding you today, Yahweh
your God [b]will set you high above
all the nations of the earth. 2 And all
these blessings will come upon you
and [a]overtake you if you listen to the
voice of Yahweh your God:
3 "Blessed *shall* you *be* in the city,
and blessed *shall* you *be* [a]in the [1]field.
4 "Blessed *shall be* the [1]offspring
of your [2]body and the [1]produce of
your ground and the [1]offspring of
your beasts, the increase of your herd
and the young of your flock.
5 "Blessed *shall be* your basket and
your kneading bowl.
6 "Blessed *shall* you *be* [a]when you
come in, and blessed *shall* you *be*
when you go out.
7 "Yahweh shall cause your ene-
mies who rise up against you to be
[1]defeated before you; they will come
out against you one way and will flee
before you seven ways. 8 Yahweh will
command the blessing upon you in
your barns and in [a]all that *you* send
forth your hand *to do*, and He will
bless you in the land which Yahweh
your God gives you. 9 [a]Yahweh will
establish you as a holy people to
Himself, as He swore to you, if you
keep the commandments of Yahweh
your God and walk in His ways. 10 So
all the peoples of the earth will see
that [a,1]you are called by the name
of Yahweh, and they will be afraid
of you. 11 [a]And Yahweh will make
you abound in prosperity, in the
[1]offspring of your [2]body and in the
[1]offspring of your beast and in
the [1]produce of your ground, in
the land which Yahweh swore to your
fathers to give you. 12 Yahweh will
open for you His good storehouse,
the heavens, to give rain to your land
in its season and to bless all the work
of your hand; and [a]you shall lend
to many nations, but you shall not
borrow. 13 [a]And Yahweh will make
you the head and not the tail, and
you only will be above, and you will
not be underneath, if you listen to
the commandments of Yahweh your
God, which I am commanding you
today, to keep and to do, 14 and [a]do
not turn aside from any of the words
which I am commanding you today,
to the right or to the left, to walk
after other gods to serve them.

### *Curses for Not Keeping the Commandments*

15 "[a]But it will be, if you do not listen
to the voice of Yahweh your God, to
keep *and* to do all His command-
ments and His statutes with which I
am commanding you today, that all
these curses will come upon you and
overtake you:
16 "[a]Cursed *shall* you *be* in the city,
and cursed *shall* you *be* in the [1]field.
17 "[a]Cursed *shall be* your basket
and your kneading bowl.
18 "[a]Cursed *shall be* the [1]offspring
of your [2]body and the [1]produce of

◆ **28:1** [a]Ex 15:26; 23:22-27; Lv 26:3-13; Dt 7:12-26; 11:13 [b]Dt 28:13; 26:19; 1Chr 14:2 **28:2** [a]Zec 1:6
**28:3** [a]Ge 39:5 [1]Or *country* **28:4** [1]Lit *fruit* [2]Lit *womb* **28:6** [a]Ps 121:8 **28:7** [1]Lit *smitten*
**28:8** [a]Dt 15:10 **28:9** [a]Ex 19:5 **28:10** [a]2Chr 7:14 [1]Lit *the name of Yahweh is called upon you*
**28:11** [a]Dt 28:4; Pr 10:22 [1]Lit *fruit* [2]Or *womb* **28:12** [a]Dt 23:20 **28:13** [a]Dt 28:1, 44 **28:14** [a]Dt 5:32;
Jos 1:7 **28:15** [a]Lv 26:14-43; Jos 23:15; Da 9:11 **28:16** [a]Dt 28:3 [1]Or *country* **28:17** [a]Dt 28:5
**28:18** [a]Dt 28:4 [1]Lit *fruit* [2]Or *womb*

your ground, the increase of your
herd and the young of your flock.
19 “[a]Cursed *shall* you *be* when
you come in, and cursed *shall* you
*be* when you go out.
20 “[a]Yahweh will send upon you
the curse, confusion, and [b]rebuke, in
all [1]that you send forth your hand to
do, until you are destroyed and until
[c]you perish quickly, on account of
the evil of your deeds, because you
have forsaken Me. 21 [a]Yahweh will
make the pestilence cling to you until
He has consumed you from the land
where you are entering to possess it.
22 [a]Yahweh will strike you with con-
sumption and with fever and with
inflammation and with fiery heat and
with [1]the sword and [b]with scorching
wind and with mildew, and they will
pursue you until [c]you perish. 23 And
[1]the heaven which is over your head
shall be bronze, and the earth which
is under you, iron. 24 [a]Yahweh will
make the rain of your land powder
and dust; from heaven it shall come
down on you until you are destroyed.
25 “[a]Yahweh shall cause you to be
[1]defeated before your enemies; you
will go out one way against them, but
you will flee seven ways before them
and you will [b]become *an exampl*
*of* terror to all the kingdoms of th
earth. 26 [a]And your carcasses will b
food to all birds of the sky and to th
beasts of the earth, and there will b
no one to frighten *them* away.
27 “[a]Yahweh will strike you wit
the boils of Egypt and with [b]tumo
and with the scab and with the itch,
from which you cannot be healed.
28 Yahweh will strike you with mad-
ness and with blindness and with
bewilderment of heart; 29 and you
will [a,1]grope at noon, as the blind
man gropes in darkness, and you will
not succeed in your ways; but you
shall only be oppressed and robbed
all *your* days, with none to save you.
30 [a]You shall betroth a wife, but
another man will violate her; [b]you
shall build a house, but you will not
live in it; you shall plant a vineyard,
but you will not [1]use its fruit. 31 Your
ox shall be slaughtered before your
eyes, but you will not eat of it;
your donkey shall be torn away from
you and will not be returned to you;
your sheep shall be given to your
enemies, and you will have none
to save you. 32 [a]Your sons and your
daughters shall be given to another
people, while your eyes look on and
yearn for them all the day *long*; but
there will be nothing [1]you can do.
33 [a]A people whom you do not know
shall eat up the produce of your
ground and all your labors, and you
will never be anything but oppressed
and crushed all *your* days. 34 And you
shall be driven mad by the sight of
what your eyes see. 35 [a]Yahweh will
strike you on the knees and legs with
sore boils, from which you cannot
be healed, from the sole of your foot
to the top of your head. 36 [a]Yahweh
will lead you and your king, whom
you set over you, to a nation which

**28:19** [a]Dt 28:6 **28:20** [a]Dt 28:8; Mal 2:2 [b]Ps 6; Is 51:20; 66:15 [c]Dt 4:26 [1]Lit *the putting forth of your hand which you do* **28:21** [a]Lv 26:25; Nu12; Jer 24:10; Am 4:10 **28:22** [a]Lv 26:16 [b]Am 4:9 [c]Dt 4:26 [1]Or *drought* **28:23** [1]Lit *your* **28:2**t 11:17; 28:12 **28:25** [a]Dt 28:7; Is 30:17 [b]2Chr 29:8; Jer 15:4; 24:9; Eze 23:46 [1]Lit *smitten* **28:26** [a]J33; 16:4; 19:7; 34:20 **28:27** [a]Ex 9:9; Dt 7:15; 28:60, 61 [b]1Sa 5:6 **28:29** [a]Ex 10:21 [1]Lit *be grg* **28:30** [a]Job 31:10; Jer 8:10 [b]Am 5:11 [1]Lit *begin it* **28:32** [a]Dt 28:41 [1]Lit *in the strength ur hand* **28:33** [a]Jer 5:15, 17 **28:35** [a]Dt 28:27 **28:36** [a]2Ki 17:4, 6; 24:12, 14; 25:7, 11; 2Chr 36:1-2139:1-9

neither you nor your fathers have
known, and there you shall serve
other gods, [b]wood and stone. **37** [a]You
shall become an object of horror, a
proverb, and a byword among all the
people where Yahweh drives you.
**38** "[a]You shall bring out much seed
to the field, but you will gather in
little, for [b]the locust will consume
it. **39** [a]You shall plant and cultivate
vineyards, but you will neither drink
of the wine nor gather *the grapes*, for
the worm will devour them. **40** [a]You
shall have olive trees throughout
your territory, but you will not anoint
yourself with the oil, for your olives
will drop off. **41** [a]You shall become
the father of sons and daughters,
but they will not be yours, for they
will go into captivity. **42** [a]The cricket
shall possess all your trees and the
produce of your ground. **43** [a]The so-
journer who is among you shall rise
above you higher and higher, but you
will go down lower and lower. **44** [a]He
shall lend to you, but you will not
lend to him; [b]he shall be the head,
and you will be the tail.
**45** "So all these curses shall come
on you and pursue you and overtake
you [a]until you are destroyed, because
you would not listen to the voice of
Yahweh your God to keep His com-
mandments and His statutes which
He commanded you. **46** And they
shall become [a]a sign and a wonder
on you and your seed forever.
**47** "[a]Because you did not serve
Yahweh your God with gladness
and a merry heart—because of the
abundance of all things, **48** therefore
you shall serve your enemies whom
Yahweh will send against you, [a]in
hunger, in thirst, in nakedness, and
in the lack of all things; and He [b]will
put an iron yoke on your neck until
He has destroyed you.
**49** "[a]Yahweh will bring a nation
against you from afar, from the end
of the earth, [b]as the eagle swoops
down, a nation whose tongue you
shall not understand, **50** a nation of
fierce countenance who will [a]have
no respect for the old, nor show
favor to the young. **51** Moreover, it
shall eat the [1]offspring of your herd
and the produce of your ground
until you are destroyed, who also
will not allow grain, new wine, or
oil, *and* the increase of your herd
or the young of your flock to remain
for you until they have caused you to
perish. **52** [a]And it shall besiege you
in all your gates until your high and
fortified walls in which you trusted
come down throughout your land,
and it shall besiege you in all your
gates throughout your land which
Yahweh your God has given you.
**53** [a]Then you shall eat the [1]offspring
of your own body, the flesh of your
sons and of your daughters whom
Yahweh your God has given you,
during the siege and the distress
by which your enemy will [2]oppress
you. **54** The man who is [1]refined
and very delicate among you [2]shall
be hostile toward his brother and

---

**28:36** [b]Dt 4:28; Jer 16:13 **28:37** [a]1Ki 9:7, 8; Jer 1924:9; 25:9; 29:18 **28:38** [a]Is 5:10; Mic 6:15; Hag 1:6 [b]Ex 10:4; Joel 1:4 **28:39** [a]Is 5:10; 17:10, 11 **8:40** [a]Jer 11:16; Mic 6:15 **28:41** [a]Dt 28:32 **28:42** [a]Dt 28:38 **28:43** [a]Dt 28:13 **28:44** [a]Dt 2 [b]Dt 28:13 **28:45** [a]Dt 4:25, 26 **28:46** [a]Nu 26:10; Is 8:18; Eze 5:15; 14:8 **28:47** [a]D7; Ne 9:35-37 **28:48** [a]Lam 4:4-6 [b]Jer 28:13, 14 **28:49** [a]Is 5:26-30; 7:18-20; Jer 5:15; 6:22, 23 [b]Jer 4; 49:22; Lam 4:19; Hos 8:1 **28:50** [a]Is 47:6 **28:51** [1]Lit *fruit* **28:52** [a]Jer 10:17, 18; Zep 1:15, 16 **:53** [a]Lv 26:29; 2Ki 6:28, 29; Jer 19:9; Lam 2:20; 4:10 [1]Lit *fruit* [2]Or *distress* **28:54** [1]Lit *tender* [2]Lit *his hall be evil toward*

toward the wife [3]he cherishes and
toward the rest of his children who
remain, **55** so that he will not give
*even* one of them any of the flesh
of his children which he will eat,
since he has nothing *else* remaining,
during the siege and the distress by
which your enemy will [1]oppress you
in all your gates. **56** [a]The [1]refined
and delicate woman among you,
who would not venture to set the
sole of her foot on the ground for
delicateness and [2]refinement, [3]shall
be hostile toward the husband [4]she
cherishes and toward her son and
daughter, **57** and toward her after-
birth which issues from between her
[1]legs and toward her children whom
she bears; for [a]she will eat them
secretly for lack of anything *else*,
during the siege and the distress by
which your enemy will [2]oppress you
in your gates.

**58** "If you are not careful to do
all the words of this law which
are written in this book, to [a,1]fear
this glorious and fearsome [b]name,
Yahweh your God, **59** then Yahweh
will bring wondrous plagues on
you and plagues on *those who are*
your seed, even great and enduring
plagues, and miserable and en-
during sicknesses. **60** [a]And He will
bring back on you all the diseases
of Egypt of which you were afraid,
and they will cling to you. **61** Also
every sickness and every plague,
which is not written in the book of
this law, Yahweh will bring on you
[a]until you are destroyed. **62** Then
you shall remain few in number,
[a]whereas you were as numerous
as the stars of heaven, because
you did not listen to the voice of
Yahweh your God. **63** And it will be
that as Yahweh [a]delighted over you
to prosper you and multiply you,
so Yahweh will [b]delight over you to
make you perish and destroy you;
and you will be [c]torn from the land
where you are entering to possess
it. **64** Moreover, Yahweh will [a]scatter
you among all peoples, from one end
of the earth to the other end of the
earth; and there you shall [b]serve
other gods, wood and stone, which
you or your fathers have not known.
**65** [a]Moreover, among those nations
you shall find no relief, and there
will be no resting place for the sole
of your foot; but there [b]Yahweh will
give you a trembling heart, failing
of eyes, and despair of soul. **66** So
your life shall [1]hang in doubt before
you; and you will be in dread night
and day and shall not have *any* faith
in your life. **67** [a]In the morning you
shall say, 'Would that it were eve-
ning!' And at evening you shall
say, 'Would that it were morning!'
because of the dread of your heart
which you dread, and because of the
sight of your eyes which you will see.
**68** And Yahweh will bring you back
to Egypt in ships, by the way about
which I spoke to you, 'You will never
see it again!' And there you will offer
yourselves for sale to your enemies
as male and female slaves, but there
will be no buyer."

**28:54** [3]Lit *of his bosom* **28:55** [1]Or *distress* **28:56** [a]Lam 4:10 [1]Lit *tender* [2]Lit *tenderness* [3]Lit *her eye shall be evil toward* [4]Lit *of her bosom* **28:57** [a]2Ki 6:28, 29; Lam 4:10 [1]Lit *feet* [2]Or *distress* **28:58** [a]Ps 99:3; Mal 1:14 [b]Is 42:8 [1]Or *reverence* **28:60** [a]Dt 28:27 **28:61** [a]Dt 4:25, 26 **28:62** [a]Dt 1:10; Ne 9:23 **28:63** [a]Jer 32:41 [b]Pr 1:26 [c]Jer 12:14; 45:4 **28:64** [a]Lv 26:33; Dt 4:27; Ne 1:8 [b]Dt 4:28; 29:26; 32:17 **28:65** [a]Lam 1:3 [b]Lv 26:36 **28:66** [1]Lit *be hung for you in front* **28:67** [a]Job 7:4

### The Covenant in Moab

29 [a,1] These are the words of
the covenant which Yahweh
commanded Moses to cut with the
sons of Israel in the land of Moab,
besides the [b]covenant which He had
cut with them at Horeb.
**2** [1]And Moses summoned all Israel
and said to them, "You have seen all
that Yahweh did before your eyes in
the land of Egypt to Pharaoh and all
his servants and all his land; **3** [a]the
great trials which your eyes have
seen, those great signs and wonders.
**4** Yet to this day [a]Yahweh has not
given you a heart to know, nor eyes
to see, nor ears to hear. **5** And I have
led you forty years in the wilderness;
[a]your clothes have not worn out on
you, and your sandal has not worn
out on your foot. **6** [a]You have not
eaten bread, nor have you drunk
wine or strong drink, in order that
you might know that I am Yahweh
your God. **7** [a]Then you came to this
place, and Sihon the king of Heshbon
and Og the king of Bashan came out
to meet us for battle, but we struck
them down; **8** and we took their land
and [a]gave it as an inheritance to the
Reubenites, the Gadites, and the
half-tribe of the Manassites. **9** [a]So
you shall keep the words of this
covenant to do them, [b]that you may
prosper in all that you do.
**10** "You stand today, all of you,
before Yahweh your God: your heads,
your tribes, your elders, and your
officers, *even* all the men of Israel,
**11** your little ones, your wives, and
the sojourner who is within your
camps, from [a]the one who chops
your wood to the one who draws
your water, **12** that you may enter
into the covenant with Yahweh your
God and into His oath, which Yahweh
your God is cutting with you today,
**13** in order that He may establish you
today as His people and that [a]He may
be your God, just as He spoke to you
and as He swore to your fathers, to
Abraham, to Isaac, and to Jacob.
**14** "Now not with you alone am I
[a]cutting this covenant and this oath,
**15** [a]but both with those who stand
here with us today in the presence of
Yahweh our God and with those who
are not with us here today— **16** for
you know how we lived in the land of
Egypt, and how we came through the
midst of the nations through which
you passed; **17** moreover, you have
seen their detestable things and their
idols *of* [a]wood, stone, silver, and gold,
which *they had* with them— **18** [a]lest
there be among you a man or wom-
an, or family or tribe, whose heart
turns away today from Yahweh our
God, to go to serve the gods of those
nations; lest there be among you [b]a
root bearing poisonous fruit and
wormwood. **19** And it will be when
he hears the words of this curse, that
he will [1]bless himself in his heart,
saying, 'I have peace though I walk in
the stubbornness of my heart in or-
der [2]to sweep away the watered *land*
with the dry.' **20** Yahweh shall not be
willing to pardon him, but rather the
anger of Yahweh and [a]His jealousy

◆ **29:1** [a]Lv 26:46; 27:34 [b]Dt 5:2, 3 [1]Ch 28:69 in Heb **29:2** [1]Ch 29:1 in Heb **29:3** [a]Dt 4:34; 7:19 **29:4** [a]Is 6:9, 10; Eze 12:2; Mt 13:14; Ac 28:26, 27; Ro 11:8 **29:5** [a]Dt 8:4 **29:6** [a]Dt 8:3 **29:7** [a]Nu 21:21-24, 33, 35; Dt 2:26-3:17 **29:8** [a]Nu 32:32, 33; Dt 3:12, 13 **29:9** [a]Dt 4:6; 1Ki 2:3 [b]Jos 1:7 **29:11** [a]Jos 9:21, 23, 27 **29:13** [a]Ge 17:7; Ex 6:7 **29:14** [a]Jer 31:31; Heb 8:7, 8 **29:15** [a]Ac 2:39 **29:17** [a]Ex 20:23; Dt 4:28; 28:36 **29:18** [a]Dt 13:6 [b]Dt 32:32; Heb 12:15 **29:19** [1]Or *consider himself blessed* [2]To destroy everything **29:20** [a]Ps 79:5; Eze 23:25

will [b,1]burn against that man, and
every curse which is written in this
book will [2]rest on him, and Yahweh
will [c]blot out his name from under
heaven. **21** Then Yahweh will separate
him out for [1]adversity from all the
tribes of Israel, according to all the
curses of the covenant [a]which are
written in this book of the law.
**22** "And the generation to come,
your sons who rise up after you and
[a]the foreigner who comes from a
distant land, shall see the plagues of
the land and the diseases with which
Yahweh has [1]afflicted it, and they will
say, **23** 'All its land is [a]brimstone and
salt, [b]a burning waste, [1]unsown and
nothing sprouting, and no grass
grows in it, like the overthrow of
[c]Sodom and Gomorrah, Admah and
Zeboiim, which Yahweh overthrew in
His anger and in His wrath.' **24** And
all the nations will say, '[a]Why has
Yahweh done thus to this land? Why
this great burning anger?' **25** Then
*men* will say, '[a]Because they forsook
the covenant of Yahweh, the God
of their fathers, which He cut with
them when He brought them out of
the land of Egypt. **26** And they went
and served other gods and wor-
shiped them, gods whom they have
not known and whom He had not
apportioned to them. **27** Therefore,
*the anger of* Yahweh was kindled
against that land, [a]to bring upon it
every curse which is written in this
book; **28** and [a]Yahweh uprooted them
from their land in anger and in fury
and in great wrath, and He cast them
into another land, as *it is* this day.'
**29** "[a]The secret things belong to
Yahweh our God, but [b]the things
revealed belong to us and to our sons
forever, that we may do all the words
of this law.

### *Yahweh Will Take You Back*

**30** "So it will be, when all of these
things have come upon you,
[a]the blessing and the curse which I
have set before you, and you cause
*these things* to return to your heart
[b]in all the nations where Yahweh
your God has banished you, **2** and
you [a]return to Yahweh your God
and listen to His voice [b]with all your
heart and soul according to all that I
am commanding you today, you and
your sons, **3** then Yahweh your God
will [a,1]return [2]you from captivity and
return *His* compassion on you, and
He [b]will gather you again from all the
peoples where Yahweh your God has
[c]scattered you. **4** If those of you who
are banished are at the ends of the
sky, [a]from there Yahweh your God
will gather you, and from there He
will take you *back*. **5** [a]And Yahweh
your God will bring you into the
land which your fathers possessed,
and you shall possess it; and He will
prosper you and [b]multiply you more
than your fathers.
**6** "Moreover [a]Yahweh your God will
circumcise your heart and the heart

---

**29:20** [b]Ps 74:1; 80:4 [c]Ex 32:33; Dt 9:14; 2Ki 14:27 [1]Lit *smoke* [2]Lit *lie down* **29:21** [a]Dt 30:10 [1]Lit *evil* **29:22** [a]Jer 19:8; 49:17; 50:13 [1]Lit *made it sick* **29:23** [a]Ge 19:24; Is 34:9; Jer 17:6; Zep 2:9 [b]Is 1:7; 64:11 [c]Jd 7 [1]Lit *it is not sown and does not cause to sprout* **29:24** [a]1Ki 9:8; Jer 22:8 **29:25** [a]2Ki 17:9-23; 2Chr 36:13-21 **29:27** [a]Da 9:11 **29:28** [a]2Chr 7:20; Ps 52:5; Pr 2:22; Eze 19:12, 13 **29:29** [a]Ac 1:7 [b]Jn 5:39; Ac 17:11; 2Ti 3:16 ♦ **30:1** [a]Dt 11:26; 30:15, 19 [b]Lv 26:40-45; Dt 28:64; 29:28; 1Ki 8:47 **30:2** [a]Dt 4:29, 30; Ne 1:9 [b]Dt 4:29 **30:3** [a]Ge 28:15; 48:21; Ps 126:1, 4; Jer 29:14 [b]Ps 147:2; Jer 32:37; Eze 34:13 [c]Dt 4:27 [1]Or *restore* [2]Lit *your captivity* **30:4** [a]Ne 1:9; Is 43:6; 48:20; 62:11 **30:5** [a]Jer 29:14; 30:3 [b]Dt 7:13; 13:17 **30:6** [a]Dt 10:16

of your seed, [b]to love Yahweh your
God with all your heart and with all
your soul, so that you may live. **7** [a]And
Yahweh your God will [1]inflict all these
curses on your enemies and on those
who hate you, who persecuted you.
**8** And you shall return and listen to
the voice of Yahweh, and you shall
do all His commandments which I
am commanding you today. **9** [a]Then
Yahweh your God will [1]prosper you
abundantly in all the work of your
hand, in the [2]offspring of your [3]body
and in the [2]offspring of your cattle
and in the [2]produce of your ground,
for [b]Yahweh will return to rejoice over
you for good, just as He rejoiced over
your fathers, **10** [1]when you listen to
the voice of Yahweh your God to keep
His commandments and His statutes
which [a]are written in this book of the
law, [1]when you return to Yahweh your
God [b]with all your heart and soul.

**11** "For this commandment which I
am commanding you today is not too
difficult for you, nor is it far *from you.*
**12** It is not in heaven, [1]that you should
say, '[a]Who will go up to heaven for us
and get it for us and make us hear it,
that we may do it?' **13** Nor is it beyond
the sea, [1]that you should say, 'Who
will cross the sea for us and get it for
us and make us hear it, that we may
do it?' **14** But the word is very near
you, in your mouth and in your heart,
that you may do it.

### *Choose Life*

**15** "See, [a]I have set before you today
life and [1]prosperity, and death and
[2]calamity; **16** in that I am command-
ing you today [a]to love Yahweh your
God, to walk in His ways, and to keep
His commandments and His statutes
and His judgments, that you [b]may
live and multiply, and that Yahweh
your God may bless you in the land
where you are entering to possess it.
**17** But if your heart turns away and
you will not listen, but are drawn
away and worship other gods and
serve them, **18** I declare to you today
that [a]you shall surely perish. You will
not prolong *your* days in the land
where you are crossing the Jordan
to enter [1]and possess it. **19** [a]I call
heaven and earth to witness against
you today, that I have set before you
life and death, [b]the blessing and the
curse. So choose life in order that you
may live, you and your seed, **20** [a]by
loving Yahweh your God, by listening
to His voice, and [b]by holding fast to
Him; [c]for [1]this is your life and the
length of your days, [2]that you may
live in [d]the land which Yahweh swore
to your fathers, to Abraham, to Isaac,
and to Jacob, to give them."

### *Be Strong and Courageous*

**31** So Moses went and spoke these
words to all Israel. **2** And he
said to them, "I am [a]120 years old
today; [b]I am no longer able to come
and go, and Yahweh has said to me,
'[c]You shall not cross this Jordan.'
**3** [a]It is Yahweh your God who will
cross ahead of you; He will destroy
these nations before you, and you
shall dispossess them. [b]Joshua is

---

**30:6** [b]Dt 6:5 **30:7** [a]Dt 7:15 [1]Lit *put* **30:9** [a]Jer 31:27, 28 [b]Jer 32:41 [1]Lit *make you have excess for good* [2]Lit *fruit* [3]Lit *womb* **30:10** [a]Dt 29:21 [b]Dt 4:29 [1]Or *for you will* **30:12** [a]Ro 10:6-8 [1]Lit *to say* **30:13** [1]Lit *to say* **30:15** [a]Dt 11:26 [1]Lit *good* [2]Lit *evil* **30:16** [a]Dt 6:5 [b]Dt 4:1; 30:19 **30:18** [a]Dt 4:26; 8:19 [1]Lit *to* **30:19** [a]Dt 4:26 [b]Dt 30:1 **30:20** [a]Dt 6:5 [b]Dt 10:20 [c]Dt 4:1; 32:47; Ac 17:25, 28 [d]Ge 12:7; 17:1-8 [1]Lit *that* [2]Lit *to dwell* ◆ **31:2** [a]Dt 34:7 [b]Nu 27:17; 1Ki 3:7 [c]Dt 1:37; 3:27 **31:3** [a]Dt 9:3 [b]Nu 27:18

the one who will cross ahead of you,
just as Yahweh has spoken. **4** And
Yahweh will do to them just as He
did to Sihon and Og, the kings of the
Amorites, and to their land, when
He destroyed them. **5** [a]And Yahweh
will give them over before you, and
you shall do to them according to all
the commandments which I have
commanded you. **6** [a]Be strong and
courageous. [b]Do not be afraid or be
in dread of them, for [c]Yahweh your
God is the one who goes with you.
[d]He will not fail you or forsake you."

**7** Then Moses called to Joshua and
said to him in the sight of all Israel,
"[a]Be strong and courageous, for you
shall go with this people into the land
which Yahweh has sworn to their fa-
thers to give them, and you shall give
it to them as an inheritance. **8** [a]And
Yahweh is the one who goes ahead of
you; He will be with you. [b]He will not
fail you or forsake you. Do not fear or
be dismayed."

**9** So Moses wrote this law and gave
it to the priests, the sons of Levi [a]who
carried the ark of the covenant of
Yahweh, and to all the elders of Israel.
**10** Then Moses commanded them,
saying, "At the end of *every* seven
years, at the time of [a]the year of the
remission of debts, at the [b]Feast of
Booths, **11** when all Israel comes [a]to
appear before Yahweh your God at
[b]the place which He will choose,
[c]you shall read this law in front of
all Israel in their hearing. **12** Assemble
the people, the men and the women
and little ones and [1]the sojourner
who is within your gates, so that they
may hear and so that they may [a]learn
and fear Yahweh your God and be
careful to do all the words of this law.
**13** And their children, who have not
known, will hear and learn to fear
Yahweh your God, all the days you
live on the land [1]which you are about
to cross the Jordan to [2]possess."

### *Yahweh Has Moses Write a Song*

**14** Then Yahweh said to Moses, "Be-
hold, [a,1]the time for you to die is near;
call Joshua and present yourselves at
the tent of meeting, that I may com-
mission him." [b]So Moses and Joshua
went and presented themselves at the
tent of meeting. **15** [a]And Yahweh ap-
peared in the tent in a pillar of cloud,
and the pillar of cloud stood at the
doorway of the tent. **16** And Yahweh
said to Moses, "Behold, [a]you are
about to lie down with your fathers;
and [b]this people will arise and play
the harlot with the foreign gods of
the land, into the midst of which they
are going, and they [c]will forsake Me
and break My covenant which I have
cut with them. **17** [a]Then My anger will
be kindled against them in that day,
and [b]I will forsake them and [c]hide My
face from them, and they will be con-
sumed, and many evils and troubles
will find them, so that they will say in
that day, '[d]Is it not because our God
is not among us that these evils have
found us?' **18** But I will surely hide My
face in that day because of all the evil
which they will do, for they will turn
to other gods.

**31:5** [a]Dt 7:2 **31:6** [a]Jos 10:25; 1Chr 22:13 [b]Dt 1:29; 7:18; 20:1 [c]Dt 20:4 [d]Jos 1:5; Heb 13:5 **31:7** [a]Dt 1:38; 3:28 **31:8** [a]Ex 13:21; 33:14 [b]Dt 31:6; Jos 1:5; Heb 13:5 **31:9** [a]Nu 4:5, 6, 15; Dt 10:8; 31:25, 26; Jos 3:3 **31:10** [a]Dt 15:1, 2 [b]Lv 23:34; Dt 16:13 **31:11** [a]Dt 16:16 [b]Dt 12:5 [c]Jos 8:34; 2Ki 23:2 **31:12** [a]Dt 4:10 [1]Lit *your sojourner* **31:13** [1]Lit *where* [2]Lit *possess it* **31:14** [a]Nu 27:12, 13; Dt 4:22; 32:50 [b]Ex 33:9-11 [1]Lit *your days to die are* **31:15** [a]Ex 33:9 **31:16** [a]Ge 15:15 [b]Ex 34:15; Dt 4:25-28; Jdg 2:11, 12, 17 [c]Jdg 10:6; 1Ki 18:18; 19:10; Jer 2:13 **31:17** [a]Jdg 2:14; 6:13 [b]2Chr 15:2; 24:20 [c]Ps 104:29; Is 8:17 [d]Nu 14:42

19 "So now, [a]write this song for
yourselves and teach it to the sons
of Israel; put it in their mouths, so
that this song may be a witness for
Me against the sons of Israel. 20 [a]For
when I bring them into the land
flowing with milk and honey, which
I swore to their fathers, and they have
eaten and are satisfied and [b]become
fat, then they will turn to other gods
and serve them and spurn Me and
break My covenant. 21 Then it will
be, [a]when many evils and troubles
have found them, that this song will
answer them as a witness (for it shall
not be forgotten from the mouths of
their seed); for [b]I know their intent
which they are [1]developing today,
before I have brought them into the
land which I swore." 22 [a]So Moses
wrote this song the same day and
taught it to the sons of Israel.

### *Joshua Is Commissioned*

23 [a]Then He commissioned Joshua
the son of Nun and said, "[b]Be strong
and courageous, for you shall bring
the sons of Israel into the land which
I swore to them, and [c]I will be with
you."
24 And it happened, when Moses
finished writing the words of this law
in a book until they were complete,
25 that Moses commanded the Levites
[a]who carried the ark of the covenant
of Yahweh, saying, 26 "Take this
book of the law and place it beside
the ark of the covenant of Yahweh
your God, that it may be there as a
witness against you. 27 For I know
[a]your rebellion and [b]your [1]stiff-neck;
behold, while I am still alive with
you today, you have been rebellious
against Yahweh; how much more,
then, after my death? 28 Assemble
to me all the elders of your tribes and
your officers, that I may speak these
words in their hearing and [a]call the
heavens and the earth to witness
against them. 29 For I know that af-
ter my death you will [a]act corruptly
and turn away from the way which I
have commanded you; and evil will
befall you in the last days, for you
will do that which is evil in the sight
of Yahweh, provoking Him to anger
with the work of your hands."

### *The Song of Moses*

30 Then Moses spoke in the hearing
of all the assembly of Israel the
words of this song, until they were
complete:

32 "[a]Give ear, O heavens,
and let me speak;
And let the earth hear the
words of my mouth.
2 "[a]Let what I have learned
drop as the rain,
My speech distill as the dew,
[b]As the droplets on
the fresh grass
And as the showers
on the herb.
3 "[a]For I proclaim the
name of Yahweh;
[b]Ascribe greatness to our God!
4 "[a]The Rock! His work
is [1]perfect,
[b]For all His ways are [2]just;

**31:19** [a]Dt 31:22 **31:20** [a]Dt 6:10-12; 8:10, 19; 11:16, 17 [b]Dt 32:15-17 **31:21** [a]Lv 26:41; Dt 4:30 [b]1Chr 28:9; Jn 2:24, 25 [1]Lit *making* **31:22** [a]Dt 31:19 **31:23** [a]Nu 27:23; Dt 31:7 [b]Jos 1:6 [c]Ex 3:12 **31:25** [a]Dt 31:9 **31:27** [a]Dt 9:7, 24 [b]Ex 32:9; Dt 9:6, 13 [1]Or *stubbornness* **31:28** [a]Dt 4:26; 30:19; 32:1 **31:29** [a]Jdg 2:19 ◆ **32:1** [a]Dt 4:26; Ps 50:4; Is 1:2; Jer 6:19 **32:2** [a]Is 55:10, 11 [b]Ps 72:6 **32:3** [a]Ex 33:19; 34:5, 6 [b]Dt 3:24; 5:24 **32:4** [a]Dt 32:15, 18, 30; 2Sa 22:31 [b]Ge 18:25; Da 4:37 [1]Or *blameless*, cf. 2Sa 22:31; Ps 18:30 [2]Or *judgment*

[c]A God of faithfulness
and without injustice,
Righteous and upright is He.
5 "[a,1]They have acted
corruptly toward Him,
*They are* not His children
because of their defect;
[b]*But are* a perverse
and crooked generation.
6 "Do you thus [a]repay Yahweh,
[b]O people who are
wickedly foolish
and without wisdom?
[c]Is not He your Father
who has bought you?
[d]He has made you
and established you.
7 "Remember the
ancient days,
Consider the years from
generation to generation.
[a]Ask your father, and he
will declare to you,
Your elders, and they
will speak to you.
8 "[a]When the Most High
gave the nations
their inheritance,
When He separated
the sons of [1]man,
He set the boundaries
of the peoples
[b]According to the number
of the [2]sons of Israel.
9 "[a]*For Yahweh's portion*
is His people;
Jacob is the allotment
of His inheritance.
10 "[a]He found him
in a desert land,
And in the howling waste
of a wilderness;
He encircled him;
He cared for him;
He guarded him
as [b]the pupil of His eye.
11 "[a]Like an eagle that
stirs up its nest,
That hovers over its young,
[b]He spread His wings
and caught them;
He carried them
on His pinions.
12 "[a]Yahweh alone guided him,
[b]And there was no foreign
god with him.
13 "[a]He made him ride
on the high places of the earth,
And he ate the produce
of the field;
[b]And He made him suck
honey from the rock,
And [c]oil from the
flinty rock,
14 Curds of cows,
and milk of the flock,
With fat of lambs,
And rams, the breed
of Bashan, and goats,
[a]With the finest
of the wheat—
And of the [b]blood of grapes
you drank wine.

15 "[a]But [1]Jeshurun grew
fat and kicked—
You grew fat, thick,
and sleek—
[b]Then he abandoned
God [c]who made him,

**32:4** [c]Dt 7:9 **32:5** [a]Dt 4:25; 31:29 [b]Mt 17:17 [1]Lit *It has* **32:6** [a]Ps 116:12 [b]Dt 32:28 [c]Dt 1:31; Ps 74:2; Is 63:16 [d]Dt 32:15 **32:7** [a]Ex 12:26; Ps 78:5-8 **32:8** [a]Ac 17:26 [b]Nu 23:9; Dt 33:28 [1]Or *Adam* [2]Gr *angels of God*; DSS *number of the sons of God* **32:9** [a]1Sa 10:1; 1Ki 8:51, 53; Jer 10:16 **32:10** [a]Dt 1:19 [b]Ps 17:8; Pr 7:2; Zec 2:8 **32:11** [a]Ex 19:4; Dt 33:12 [b]Ps 18:10-18 **32:12** [a]Dt 4:35, 39 [b]Dt 32:39; Is 43:12 **32:13** [a]Is 58:14 [b]Dt 8:8; Ps 81:16 [c]Job 29:6 **32:14** [a]Ps 81:16; 147:14 [b]Ge 49:11 **32:15** [a]Dt 31:20 [b]Jdg 10:6 [c]Dt 32:6 [1]A poetic name for Israel, cf. 33:5, 26; Is 44:2

And treated [d]the Rock
of his salvation with
wicked foolishness.
16 “[a]They made Him jealous
with strange *gods*;
[b]With abominations they
provoked Him to anger.
17 “[a]They sacrificed to demons
who were not God,
[b]To gods whom they
have not known,
[c]New *gods* who
came lately,
Whom your fathers
did not dread.
18 “You neglected [a]the Rock
who begot you,
[b]And forgot the God who
brought you forth.

19 “[a]And Yahweh saw *this*
and spurned *them*
[b]Because of the provocation
of His sons and daughters.
20 “Then He said, ‘I will hide
My face from them;
[a]I will see what their
end *shall be*;
[b]For they are a perverse
generation,
[c]Sons in whom is no
faithfulness.
21 ‘[a]They have made Me jealous
with *what* is not God;
They have provoked
Me to anger
with their [b,1]idols.
[c]So I will make them
jealous with *those*
*who* are not a people;
I will provoke them
to anger with a wickedly
foolish nation,
22 [a]For a fire is kindled
in My anger,
And it burns to the
lowest part of Sheol,
[b]And it consumes the
earth with its produce,
And it sets on fire the
foundations of the
mountains.
23 ‘[a]I will heap calamities
on them;
[b]I will exhaust My
arrows on them.
24 ‘[a]*They will be* wasted
by famine, and
consumed by [1]plague
[b]And bitter destruction;
[c]And the teeth of beasts I
will send upon them,
[d]With the venom of crawling
things of the dust.
25 ‘[a]Outside the sword
will bereave,
And inside terror—
[b]Both choice man
and virgin,
The nursing baby
with the man of gray hair.
26 ‘I would have said, “[a]I will
cut them to pieces;
[b]I will cause the memory
of them to cease from men,”
27 Had I not feared the
provocation by the enemy,
Lest their adversaries
misjudge,

---

**32:15** [d]Dt 32:4; Ps 89:26 **32:16** [a]Ps 78:58 [b]Ps 106:29 **32:17** [a]Lv 17:7; 1Co 10:20 [b]Dt 28:64 [c]Jdg 5:8 **32:18** [a]Dt 32:4 [b]Ps 106:21 **32:19** [a]Lv 26:30; Ps 106:40 [b]Jer 44:21-23 **32:20** [a]Dt 31:29 [b]Dt 32:5 [c]Dt 9:23 **32:21** [a]Dt 32:16; 1Co 10:22 [b]Dt 32:17; 1Ki 16:13, 26 [c]Ro 10:19 [1]Lit *vanities* **32:22** [a]Nu 16:33-35; Ps 18:7, 8; Lam 4:11 [b]Lv 26:20 **32:23** [a]Dt 29:21 [b]Ps 18:14; 45:5 **32:24** [a]Dt 28:22, 48 [b]Ps 91:6 [c]Lv 26:22 [d]Am 5:18, 19 [1]Lit *burning heat* **32:25** [a]Lam 1:20; Eze 7:15 [b]2Chr 36:17; Lam 2:21 **32:26** [a]Dt 4:27; 28:64 [b]Dt 9:14

Lest they say, "[a]Our hand
is [1]triumphant,
And Yahweh has not
done all this."'
28 "[a]For they are a nation
where counsel perishes,
And there is no
discernment in them.
29 "[a]Would that they were wise,
that they had insight into this,
[b]That they would understand
their [1]future!
30 "[a]How could one pursue
one thousand,
And two put ten
thousand to flight,
Unless their [b]Rock
had sold them,
And Yahweh had handed
them over?
31 "Indeed their rock is
not like our Rock,
[a]Even our enemies
[1]themselves judge this.
32 "For their vine is from
the vine of Sodom,
And from the fields
of Gomorrah;
Their grapes are grapes
of [a]poison,
Their clusters, bitter.
33 "Their wine is the venom
of [1]serpents,
And the [2]deadly
poison of cobras.

34 '[a]Is it not laid up
in store with Me,
Sealed up in My treasuries?
35 '[a]Vengeance is Mine,
and retribution,
[b]In due time their foot
will stumble;
[c]For the day of their
disaster is near,
And the impending things
are hastening upon them.'
36 "[a]For Yahweh will render
justice to His people,
[b]And will have compassion
on His slaves,
When He sees that *their*
[1]strength is gone,
And there is none
*remaining*, bond or free.
37 "And He will say,
'[a]Where are their gods,
The rock in which they
sought refuge?
38 '[a]Who ate the fat
of their sacrifices,
*And* drank the wine
of their drink offering?
[b]Let them rise up
and help you,
Let them be your
hiding place!
39 '[a]See now that I, I am He,
[b]And there is no god
besides Me;
[c]It is I who put to death
and give life.
[d]I have wounded,
and it is I who heal,
[e]And there is no one who can
deliver from My hand.
40 'Indeed, [a]I lift up My
hand to heaven,
And say, as I live forever,

**32:27** [a]Nu 15:30 [1]Lit *high* **32:28** [a]Dt 32:6 **32:29** [a]Dt 5:29 [b]Dt 31:29 [1]Or *latter end*
**32:30** [a]Lv 26:7, 8 [b]Dt 32:4; Ps 44:12 **32:31** [a]Ex 14:25 [1]Lit *are judges* **32:32** [a]Dt 29:18 **32:33** [1]Lit *dragons* [2]Lit *cruel* **32:34** [a]Job 14:17; Jer 44:21 **32:35** [a]Ps 94:1; Ro 12:19; Heb 10:30 [b]Jer 23:12 [c]Eze 7:5-10 **32:36** [a]Ps 135:14; Heb 10:30 [b]Lv 26:43-45; Dt 30:1-3 [1]Lit *hand* **32:37** [a]Jdg 10:14; Jer 2:28 **32:38** [a]Nu 25:1, 2 [b]Jer 11:12 **32:39** [a]Is 41:4; 43:10 [b]Dt 32:12; Is 45:5 [c]1Sa 2:6; Ps 68:20 [d]Ps 51:8 [e]Ps 50:22 **32:40** [a]Eze 20:5, 6; 21:4, 5

41 [a]If I sharpen My
[1]flashing sword,
And My hand takes
hold on judgment,
[b]I will render vengeance
on My adversaries,
And I will repay those
who hate Me.
42 '[a]I will make My arrows
drunk with blood,
[b]And My sword will
devour flesh,
With the blood of the
slain and the captives,
From the long-haired
[1]leaders of the enemy.'
43 "[a]O nations, cause His
people to shout for joy;
[b]For He will avenge the
blood of His slaves,
[c]And He will render vengeance
on His adversaries,
[d]And He will atone for His
land *and* His people."

**44** Then Moses came and spoke all
the words of this song in the hearing
of the people, he and [a,1]Joshua the
son of Nun. **45** Then Moses finished
speaking all these words to all Israel,
**46** and he said to them, "[a]Place in your
heart all the words with which I am
warning you today, which you shall
command [b]your sons to be careful
to do, *even* all the words of this law.
**47** For it is not an idle word for you;
indeed [a]it is your life. And [b]by this
word you will prolong your days in
the land, [1]which you are about to
cross the Jordan to [2]possess."

### *Moses to Go Up Mount Nebo*

**48** [a]And Yahweh spoke to Moses that
very same day, saying, **49** "[a]Go up to
this mountain of the Abarim, Mount
Nebo, which is in the land of Moab
[1]opposite Jericho, and look at the
land of Canaan, which I am giving
to the sons of Israel for a possession.
**50** Then die on the mountain where
you ascend, and be [a]gathered to your
people, as Aaron your brother died
on Mount Hor and was gathered to
his people, **51** [a]because you *both* act-
ed unfaithfully with Me in the midst
of the sons of Israel at the waters of
Meribah-kadesh, in the [b]wilderness
of Zin, because you *both* did not
treat Me as holy in the midst of the
sons of Israel. **52** [a]For you shall see
the land at a distance, but [b]you shall
not go there, into the land which I
am giving the sons of Israel."

### *The Blessing of Moses*

**33** Now this is the blessing with
which Moses [a]the man of God
blessed the sons of Israel before his
death. **2** And he said,
"[a]Yahweh came from Sinai,
[b]And He [1]dawned
on them from Seir;
[c]He shone forth
from Mount Paran,
And He came
from [d]the [2]midst of ten
thousand holy ones;
[e]At His right hand there
was [3]flashing lightning
for them.

---

**32:41** [a]Is 34:6-8 [b]Jer 50:28-32 [1]Or *lightning* **32:42** [a]Dt 32:23 [b]Jer 12:12; 46:10, 14 [1]Lit head
**32:43** [a]Ro 15:10 [b]2Ki 9:7; Rev 6:10; 19:2 [c]Is 1:24, 25 [d]Ps 65:3; 79:9; 85:1 **32:44** [a]Nu 13:8, 16 [1]Lit
*Hoshea* **32:46** [a]Eze 40:4; 44:5 [b]Dt 4:9 **32:47** [a]Dt 8:3; 30:20 [b]Dt 4:40; 33:25 [1]Lit *where* [2]Lit
*possess it* **32:48** [a]Nu 27:12 **32:49** [a]Nu 27:12-14; Dt 3:27 [1]Lit *which is opposite* **32:50** [a]Ge 25:8
**32:51** [a]Nu 20:12 [b]Nu 27:14 **32:52** [a]Dt 34:1-3 [b]Dt 1:37; 3:27 ◆ **33:1** [a]Jos 14:6 **33:2** [a]Ex 19:18, 20;
Ps 68:8, 17 [b]Jdg 5:4 [c]Nu 10:12; Hab 3:3 [d]Da 7:10; Ac 7:53 [e]Ex 23:20-22 [1]Lit *rose to* [2]Lit *myriads of
holiness* [3]Or *a fiery law*

3 “[a]Indeed, He loves [1]the people;
[b]All [2]Your holy ones
are in Your hand,
[c]And they [3]followed
in Your steps;
*Everyone* is bearing
up Your words.
4 “[a]Moses commanded
us with a law,
[b]A possession for the
assembly of Jacob.
5 “[a]And He was king in Jeshurun,
When the heads of the
people were gathered,
The tribes of Israel together.

6 “[a]May Reuben live and not die,
Nor his men be few.”

7 [a]And this regarding Judah; so he
said,
“Hear, O Yahweh,
the voice of Judah,
And bring him
to his people.
With his hands he
contended for [1]them,
And may You be a help
against his adversaries.”

8 Of Levi he said,
“*Let* Your [a]Thummim
and Your Urim *belong*
to [1]Your [b]holy one,
[c]Whom You tested at Massah,
[2]With whom You contended
at the waters of Meribah;
9 [a]Who said of his father
and his mother,
‘I did not consider them’;
And he did not recognize
his brothers,
Nor did he know his own sons,
For [b]they kept Your word,
And they observed
Your covenant.
10 “[a]They shall [1]teach Your
judgments to Jacob,
And Your law to Israel.
[b]They shall put incense
[2]before You,
And [c]whole burnt offerings
on Your altar.
11 “O Yahweh, bless his substance,
And accept the work
of his hands;
Crush the loins of those
who rise up against him,
And those who hate
him, so that they will
not rise *again*.”

12 Of Benjamin he said,
“[a]May the beloved of Yahweh
dwell in security by Him,
[b]Who shields him all the day,
[c]And he dwells between
His shoulders.”

13 Of Joseph he said,
“[a]Blessed of Yahweh
*be* his land,
With the choice things
of heaven, with the dew,
And from the deep
lying beneath,
14 And with the choice
produce of the sun,
And with the choice
yield of the months,

---

**33:3** [a]Dt 4:37; Mal 1:2 [b]Dt 7:6; 14:2 [c]Dt 6:1-9; Lk 10:39 [1]Lit *peoples* [2]Lit *His* [3]Or *lie down at Your feet*
**33:4** [a]Dt 4:2; Jn 7:19 [b]Ps 119:111 **33:5** [a]Nu 23:21 **33:6** [a]Ge 49:3, 4 **33:7** [a]Ge 49:8-12 [1]Lit *him*
**33:8** [a]Ex 28:30; Lv 8:8 [b]Ps 106:16 [c]Ex 17:7; Nu 20:13, 24; Dt 6:16 [1]Lit *him* [2]Or *For* **33:9** [a]Ex 32:27-29 [b]Mal 2:5 **33:10** [a]Lv 10:11; Dt 31:9-13 [b]Lv 16:12, 13 [c]Ps 51:19 [1]Or *instruct* [2]Lit *in Your nostrils*
**33:12** [a]Dt 4:37f; 12:10 [b]Dt 32:11 [c]Ex 28:12 **33:13** [a]Ge 27:27, 28; 49:22-26

15 And with the [1]best things
of [a]the ancient mountains,
And with the choice things
of the everlasting hills,
16 And with the choice things
of the earth and its fullness,
And the favor [a]of Him
who dwelt in the bush.
Let it come to the
head of Joseph,
And to the top of the head
of the one distinguished
among his brothers.
17 "As the firstborn of his
ox, splendor is his,
And his horns are the
horns of [a]the wild ox;
With them he will
[b]push the peoples,
All [1]at once, *to* the
ends of the earth.
And those are the ten
thousands of Ephraim,
And those are the thousands
of Manasseh."

18 [a]Of Zebulun he said,
"Be glad, Zebulun,
in your going forth,
And, Issachar,
in your tents.
19 "[a]They will call peoples
*to* the mountain;
There they will offer
[b]righteous sacrifices;
For they will [1]draw
out [c]the abundance
of the seas,
And the hidden treasures
of the sand."

20 [a]Of Gad he said,
"Blessed is the one
who enlarges Gad;
He lies down [b]as a [1]lion,
And tears the arm, also
the top of the head.
21 "[a]Then he [1]provided the
first *part* for himself,
[b]For there the ruler's
portion was [2]reserved;
[c]And he came *with* the
heads of the people;
[d]He did the righteousness
of Yahweh,
And His judgments
with Israel."

22 [a]Of Dan he said,
"Dan is [b]a lion's whelp,
That leaps forth
from Bashan."

23 Of Naphtali he said,
"[a]O Naphtali, satisfied
with favor,
And full of the blessing
of Yahweh,
Take possession of the
sea and the south."

24 [a]Of Asher he said,
"More blessed than sons
is Asher;
May he be favored
by his brothers,
[b]And may he dip his foot in oil.
25 "[a]Your locks will be
iron and bronze,
[b]And according to your days,
so your fortitude will be.

**33:15** [a]Hab 3:6 [1]Or *chief* **33:16** [a]Ex 2:2-6; 3:2, 4 **33:17** [a]Nu 23:22 [b]1Ki 22:11; Ps 44:5 [1]Or *together* **33:18** [a]Ge 49:13-15 **33:19** [a]Ex 15:17; Ps 2:6; Is 2:3 [b]Ps 4:5; 51:19 [c]Is 60:5 [1]Lit *suck* **33:20** [a]Ge 49:19 [b]Ge 49:9 [1]Or *lioness* **33:21** [a]Nu 32:1-5 [b]Nu 34:14 [c]Jos 4:12 [d]Jos 22:1-3 [1]Lit *saw* [2]Or *covered up* **33:22** [a]Ge 49:16 [b]Eze 19:2, 3 **33:23** [a]Ge 49:21 **33:24** [a]Ge 49:20 [b]Job 29:6 **33:25** [a]Ps 147:13 [b]Dt 4:40; 32:47

26 “[a]There is none like
the God of [1]Jeshurun,
[b]Who rides the heavens
[2]to your help,
And through the skies
in His majesty.
27 “[a]The eternal God
is a [1]dwelling place,
[b]And underneath are
the everlasting arms;
[c]And He drove out
the enemy from before you,
[d]And said, ‘Destroy!’
28 “[a]So Israel dwells in security,
[b]The fountain of
Jacob secluded,
[c]In a land of grain
and new wine;
[d]His heavens also
drop down dew.
29 “[a]Blessed are you, O Israel;
[b]Who is like you, a people
saved by Yahweh,
[c]Who is the shield of your help
[d]And the sword
of your majesty!
[e]So your enemies will
cower before you,
[f]And you will tread
upon their high places.”

### *The Death of Moses*

34 [a]Then Moses went up from
the plains of Moab to Mount
Nebo, to the top of Pisgah, which
*is* opposite Jericho. And Yahweh
[b]showed him all the land, Gilead
as far as Dan, 2 and all Naphtali and
the land of Ephraim and Manasseh,
and all the land of Judah as far as
the [a,1]western sea, 3 and the [1]Negev
and the plain in the valley of Jericho,
[a]the city of palm trees, as far as Zoar.
4 Then Yahweh said to him, “This is
the land which [a]I swore to Abraham,
to Isaac, and to Jacob, saying, ‘I will
give it to your seed’; I have let you see
*it* with your eyes, but you shall not go
over there.” 5 So Moses [a]the servant
of Yahweh [b]died there in the land of
Moab, according to the [1]command of
Yahweh. 6 And He buried him in the
valley in the land of Moab, [a]opposite
Beth-peor; but [b]no man knows his
burial place to this day. 7 Now Moses
was [a]120 years old when he died;
[b]his eye was not dim, nor his vigor
abated. 8 So the sons of Israel wept
for Moses in the plains of Moab thirty
days. Then the days of weeping *and*
mourning for Moses came to an end.
9 Now Joshua the son of Nun was
[a]filled with the spirit of wisdom, for
Moses had laid his hands on him; and
the sons of Israel listened to him and
did as Yahweh had commanded Mo-
ses. 10 [a]And there has not yet arisen
a prophet in Israel like Moses, whom
[b]Yahweh knew face to face, 11 [1]in
regard to all the signs and wonders
which Yahweh sent him to do in the
land of Egypt against Pharaoh, all his
*servants*, and all his land, 12 and [1]in
regard to all the mighty [2]power and
[1]in regard to all the great terror which
Moses did in the sight of all Israel.

**33:26** [a]Ex 15:11; Dt 4:35; Ps 86:8; Jer 10:6 [b]Dt 10:14; Ps 68:33, 34; 104:3; Hab 3:8 [1]A poetic name for Israel, cf. 33:5, 26; Is 44:2 [2]Lit *in* **33:27** [a]Ps 90:1, 2 [b]Ge 49:24 [c]Ex 34:11; Jos 24:18 [d]Dt 7:2 [1]Or *refuge* **33:28** [a]Dt 33:12; Jer 23:6 [b]Nu 23:9; Dt 32:8 [c]Ge 27:28, 37 [d]Dt 33:13 **33:29** [a]Ps 1:1; 32:1, 2 [b]Dt 4:32; 2Sa 7:23 [c]Ge 15:1; Ps 33:20; 115:9-11 [d]Ps 68:34 [e]Ps 66:3 [f]Nu 33:52 ◆ **34:1** [a]Dt 32:49 [b]Dt 32:52 **34:2** [a]Dt 11:24 [1]Mediterranean Sea **34:3** [a]Jdg 1:16; 3:13; 2Chr 28:15 [1]South country **34:4** [a]Ge 12:7; 26:3; 28:13 **34:5** [a]Nu 12:7; Jos 1:1, 2 [b]Dt 32:50 [1]Lit *mouth* **34:6** [a]Dt 3:29; 4:46 [b]Jd 9 **34:7** [a]Dt 31:2 [b]Ge 27:1; 48:10 **34:9** [a]Nu 27:18, 23; Is 11:2 **34:10** [a]Dt 18:15, 18 [b]Ex 33:11; Nu 12:8; Dt 5:4 **34:11** [1]Lit *to* **34:12** [1]Lit *to* [2]Lit *hand*

*The Book of*

# JOSHUA

### *Yahweh's Commands to Joshua*

**1** Now it came about after the death
of Moses the servant of [1]Yahweh,
that Yahweh spoke to Joshua the son
of Nun, Moses' [2]attendant, saying,
**2** "Moses [a]My servant is dead; so now
arise, [b]cross this Jordan, you and all
this people, to the land which I am
giving to them, to the sons of Israel.
**3** [a]Every place on which the sole of
your foot treads, I have given it to
you, just as I spoke to Moses. **4** [a]From
the wilderness and this Lebanon,
even as far as the great river, the
river Euphrates, all the land of the
Hittites, and as far as the Great Sea
toward the setting of the sun will
be your territory. **5** [a]No man will *be
able to* stand before you all the days
of your life. Just as I have been with
Moses, I will be with you; [b]I will not
fail you or forsake you. **6** [a]Be strong
and courageous, for you shall cause
this people to inherit the land which
I swore to their fathers to give them.
**7** Only be strong and very courageous
to [a,1]be careful to do according to all
the law which Moses My servant
commanded you; do not turn aside
from it to the right or to the left, so
that you may [2]be prosperous wher-
ever you go. **8** [a]This book of the law
shall not depart from your mouth,
but you shall meditate on it day and
night, so that you may [1]be careful to
do according to all that is written in
it; [b]for then you will make your way
successful, and then you will [2]be
prosperous. **9** Have I not commanded
you? [a]Be strong and courageous! [b]Do
not be in dread or be dismayed, for
Yahweh your God is with you wher-
ever you go."

### *Joshua's Command to the Officers*

**10** Then Joshua commanded the of-
ficers of the people, saying, **11** "Pass
through the midst of the camp and
command the people, saying, 'Pre-
pare provisions for yourselves, for
within [a]three days you are to cross
this Jordan, to go in to possess the
land which Yahweh your God is
giving you, to possess it.'"

**12** [a]To the Reubenites and to
the Gadites and to the half-tribe
of Manasseh, Joshua [1]said, **13** "Re-
member the word which Moses
the servant of Yahweh commanded
you, saying, '[a]Yahweh your God gives
you rest and will give you this land.'
**14** Your wives, your little ones, and
your cattle shall remain in the land
which Moses gave you beyond the
Jordan, but you shall cross before
your brothers in battle array, all your
valiant warriors, and shall help them
**15** until Yahweh gives your brothers
rest as *He gives* you, and they also
possess the land which Yahweh your
God is giving them. [a]Then you shall
return to the land of your possession
and possess it, which Moses [b]the
servant of Yahweh gave you beyond

◆ **1:1** [1]The personal covenant name of God, a form of I AM WHO I AM, cf. Ex 3:14-15 [2]Or *minister*
**1:2** [a]Nu 12:7; Dt 34:5 [b]Jos 1:11 **1:3** [a]Dt 11:24 **1:4** [a]Ge 15:18; Nu 34:3 **1:5** [a]Dt 7:24 [b]Dt 31:6, 7; Heb 13:5 **1:6** [a]Dt 31:6, 7, 23 **1:7** [a]Dt 5:32 [1]Lit *observe* [2]Or *act wisely* **1:8** [a]Dt 31:24; Jos 8:34 [b]Dt 29:9; Ps 1:1-3 [1]Lit *observe* [2]Or *act wisely* **1:9** [a]Jos 1:7 [b]Dt 31:8 **1:11** [a]Jos 3:2 **1:12** [a]Nu 32:20-22 [1]Lit *said, saying* **1:13** [a]Dt 3:18-20 **1:15** [a]Jos 22:4 [b]Jos 1:1

the Jordan *to the east* toward the sunrise."

**16** And they answered Joshua, saying, "All that you have commanded us we will do, and wherever you send us we will go. **17** Just as we listened to Moses in all things, so we will listen to you; only [a]may Yahweh your God be with you as He was with Moses. **18** Anyone who rebels against your [1]command and does not listen to your words, in all that you command him, shall be put to death; only be strong and courageous."

### *Rahab Hides the Spies*

**2** Then Joshua the son of Nun sent two men as spies secretly from [a]Shittim, saying, "Go, see the land, especially Jericho." So they went and came into the house of [b]a harlot whose name was Rahab and [1]lodged there. **2** And it was told to the king of Jericho, saying, "Behold, men from the sons of Israel have come here tonight to search out the land." **3** And the king of Jericho sent *word* to Rahab, saying, "Bring out the men who have come to you, who have entered your house, for they have come to search out all the land." **4** But the [a]woman had taken the two men and hidden them, and she said, "Yes, the men came to me, but I did not know where they were from. **5** Now it happened when *it was time* to shut the gate at dark, that the men went out; I do not know where the men went. Pursue them quickly, for you may overtake them." **6** But [a]she had brought them up to the roof and concealed them in the stalks of flax which she had laid in order on the roof. **7** So the men pursued them on the road to the Jordan to the fords; and as soon as those who were pursuing them had gone out, they shut the gate.

**8** Now before they lay down, [1]she came up to them on the roof **9** and said to the men, "[a]I know that Yahweh has given you the land, and that the [b]terror of you has fallen on us, and that all the inhabitants of the land have [1]melted away before you. **10** [a]For we have heard how Yahweh dried up the water of the [1]Red Sea before you when you came out of Egypt and [b]what you did to the two kings of the Amorites who were beyond the Jordan, to Sihon and Og, whom you [2]devoted to destruction. **11** Indeed we heard *it*, [a]and our hearts melted, and a *courageous* spirit no longer rose up in *any* man because of you; for [b]Yahweh your God, He is God in heaven above and on earth beneath. **12** So now, please swear to me by Yahweh, since I have shown lovingkindness to you, that you also will show lovingkindness to my father's household and give me a [a]pledge of [1]truth, **13** and preserve my father and my mother and my brothers and my sisters alive, with all who belong to them, and deliver our [1]lives from death." **14** So the men said to her, "Our [1]life [2]for yours if you do not tell this business of ours; and it will be when Yahweh gives us the land that we will [a]show lovingkindness and truth to you."

**1:17** [a]Jos 1:5, 9 **1:18** [1]Lit *mouth* ◆ **2:1** [a]Nu 25:1; Jos 3:1 [b]Heb 11:31; Jas 2:25 [1]Lit *lay down* **2:4** [a]2Sa 17:19 **2:6** [a]Jas 2:25 **2:8** [1]Lit *then she* **2:9** [a]Nu 20:24; Jos 9:24 [b]Ex 23:27; Dt 2:25; Jos 9:9, 10 [1]Or *become demoralized* **2:10** [a]Ex 14:21; Nu 23:22; 24:8 [b]Nu 21:21-35 [1]Lit *Sea of Reeds* [2]Or *put under the ban* **2:11** [a]Jos 5:1; 7:5; Ps 22:14; Is 13:7; 19:1 [b]Dt 4:39 **2:12** [a]Jos 2:18, 19 [1]Or *faithfulness* **2:13** [1]Lit *souls* **2:14** [a]Ge 24:49 [1]Lit *soul* [2]Lit *instead of you to die*

### The Oath to Rahab

**15** Then she let them down by a rope
through the window, for her house
was on the city wall, so that she was
living on the wall. **16** And she said to
them, "[a]Go to the hill country, lest
the pursuers reach you. And hide
yourselves there for three days until
the pursuers return. Then afterward
you may go on your way." **17** And the
men said to her, "[a]We *shall be* free
from this oath [1]to you which you
have made us swear, **18** [1]unless, when
we come into the land, you tie this
cord of scarlet thread in the window
through which you let us down, and
[a]gather to yourself into the house
your father and your mother and
your brothers and all your father's
household. **19** And it will be that any-
one who goes out of the doors of your
house into the street, his blood *shall
be* on his own head, and we *shall be*
free; but anyone who is with you in
the house, [a]his blood *shall be* on our
head if a hand is *laid* on him. **20** But
if you tell this business of ours, then
we shall be free from the oath which
you have made us swear." **21** And she
said, "According to your words, so be
it." So she sent them away, and they
went; and she tied the scarlet cord in
the window.

**22** And they went and came to
the hill country and remained there
for three days until the pursuers
returned. The pursuers had sought
*them* [1]all along the road but had not
found *them*. **23** Then the two men
returned and came down from the
hill country and crossed over and
came to Joshua the son of Nun,
and they recounted to him all that
had happened to them. **24** And they
said to Joshua, "Surely Yahweh has
given all the land into our hands;
moreover, [a]all the inhabitants of
the land have [1]melted away before
us."

### Israel Crosses the Jordan

**3** Then Joshua rose early in the
morning; and he and all the sons
of Israel set out from [a]Shittim and
came to the Jordan, and they lodged
there before they crossed. **2** [a]Now it
happened that at the end of three
days the officers went through the
midst of the camp; **3** and they com-
manded the people, saying, "When
you see the [a]ark of the covenant of
Yahweh your God with the Levitical
priests carrying it, then you shall set
out from your place and go after it.
**4** However, there shall be between
you and it a distance of about [1]2,000
cubits by measure. Do not come near
it, that you may know the way by
which you shall go, for you have not
passed this way before."

**5** Then Joshua said to the people,
"[a]Set yourselves apart as holy, for
tomorrow Yahweh will do wondrous
deeds among you." **6** And Joshua
spoke to the priests, saying, "Carry
the ark of the covenant and cross
over ahead of the people." So they
carried the ark of the covenant and
went ahead of the people.

**7** Then Yahweh said to Joshua,
"This day I will begin to [a]magnify
you in the sight of all Israel, that

---

**2:16** [a]Jas 2:25 **2:17** [a]Ge 24:8 [1]Lit *of yours* **2:18** [a]Jos 2:12 [1]Lit *behold* **2:19** [a]Mt 27:25 **2:22** [1]Lit *through all the road* **2:24** [a]Jos 2:9 [1]Or *become demoralized* ◆ **3:1** [a]Jos 2:1 **3:2** [a]Jos 1:11 **3:3** [a]Dt 31:9 **3:4** [1]Approx. 3,000 ft. or 914 m, a cubit was approx. 18 in. or 45 cm **3:5** [a]Ex 19:10, 11; Jos 7:13 **3:7** [a]Jos 4:14

they may know that just as I have
been with Moses, I will be with you.
**8** Moreover, you shall command the
priests who are carrying the ark of
the covenant, saying, 'When you
come to the edge of the waters of
the Jordan, you shall stand *still* in the
Jordan.'" **9** Then Joshua said to the
sons of Israel, "Come near, and hear
the words of Yahweh your God."
**10** And Joshua said, "By this you
shall know that [a]the living God is
among you, and that He will assured-
ly [b]dispossess from before you the
Canaanite, the Hittite, the Hivite, the
Perizzite, the Girgashite, the Amo-
rite, and the Jebusite. **11** Behold, the
ark of the covenant of [a]the Lord of
all the earth is crossing over ahead of
you into the Jordan. **12** So now, [a]take
for yourselves twelve men from the
tribes of Israel, one man for each
tribe. **13** And it will be that when the
soles of the feet of the priests who
carry the ark of Yahweh, the Lord
of all the earth, rest in the waters of
the Jordan, the waters of the Jordan
will be cut off, *and* the waters which
are [1]flowing down from above [2]will
[a]stand in one heap."

**14** So it happened that when the
people set out from their tents to
cross the Jordan with the priests car-
rying [a]the ark of the covenant before
the people, **15** and when those who
carried the ark came into the Jordan,
and the feet of the priests carrying
the ark were dipped in the edge of
the water (for the [a]Jordan overflows
all its banks all the days of harvest),
**16** [a]the waters which were [1]flowing
down from above stood *and* rose up
in [b]one heap, a great distance away
at Adam, the city that is beside Zare-
than; and those which were [1]flowing
down toward the sea of the [c]Arabah,
the Salt Sea, were completely cut off.
So the people crossed opposite Jeri-
cho. **17** And the priests who carried
the ark of the covenant of Yahweh
stood firm [a]on dry ground in the
middle of the Jordan while all Israel
crossed on dry ground until all the
nation had completed crossing the
Jordan.

### *Memorial Stones from the Jordan*

**4** Now it happened when all the na-
tion had completed crossing the
[a]Jordan, that Yahweh spoke to Joshua,
saying, **2** "[a]Take for yourselves twelve
men from the people, one man from
each tribe, **3** and command them,
saying, 'Carry for yourselves twelve
stones from here out of the middle
of the Jordan, from the place where
the priests' feet are standing firm,
and carry them over with you and
lay them down in [a]the lodging place
where you will lodge tonight.'" **4** So
Joshua called the twelve men whom
he had appointed from the sons of
Israel, one man from each tribe;
**5** and Joshua said to them, "[1]Cross
again before the ark of Yahweh your
God into the middle of the Jordan,
and each of you carry a stone on his
shoulder, according to the number
of the tribes of the sons of Israel, **6** in
order that this would be a sign among
you, so that [a]when your children ask
[1]later, saying, 'What do these stones

---

**3:10** [a]Dt 5:26; 1Th 1:9 [b]Ex 33:2; Dt 7:1 **3:11** [a]Job 41:11; Ps 24:1; Zec 6:5 **3:12** [a]Jos 4:2 **3:13** [a]Ex 15:8 [1]Lit *going* [2]Lit *and they will* **3:14** [a]Ps 132:8; Ac 7:44f **3:15** [a]1Chr 12:15; Jer 12:5; 49:19 **3:16** [a]Ps 66:6; 74:15; 114:3, 5 [b]Jos 3:13 [c]Dt 1:1 [1]Lit *going* **3:17** [a]Ex 14:21, 22, 29 ◆ **4:1** [a]Dt 27:2; Jos 3:17 **4:2** [a]Jos 3:12 **4:3** [a]Jos 4:20 **4:5** [1]Lit *Cross before the ark* **4:6** [a]Ex 12:26; 13:14; Jos 4:21 [1]Lit *tomorrow*

mean to you?' **7** then you shall say
to them, 'Because the [a]waters of the
Jordan were cut off before the ark
of the covenant of Yahweh; when it
crossed the Jordan, the waters of the
Jordan were cut off.' So these stones
shall become a [b]memorial to the sons
of Israel forever."
**8** Thus the sons of Israel did as
Joshua commanded and carried
twelve stones from the middle of
the Jordan, just as Yahweh spoke to
Joshua, according to the number of
the tribes of the sons of Israel; and
they carried them over with them
to [a]the lodging place and laid them
down there. **9** But Joshua set up
twelve [a]stones in the middle of the
Jordan at the place where the feet
of the priests who carried the ark
of the covenant were standing, and
they are there to this day. **10** Now
the priests who carried the ark were
standing in the middle of the Jordan
until everything was completed that
Yahweh had commanded Joshua to
speak to the people, according to all
that Moses had commanded Joshua.
And the people hurried and crossed.
**11** And it happened when all the
people had completed crossing, that
the ark of Yahweh and the priests
crossed before the people. **12** [a]And
the sons of Reuben and the sons of
Gad and the half-tribe of Manasseh
crossed over in battle array before
the sons of Israel, just as Moses had
spoken to them; **13** about 40,000
equipped for war crossed for battle
before Yahweh to the desert plains
of Jericho.
**14** [a]On that day, Yahweh magnified
Joshua in the sight of all Israel, so
that they [1]feared him, just as they
had [1]feared Moses all the days of his
life.
**15** Then Yahweh said to [1]Joshua,
**16** "Command the priests who carry
[a]the ark of the testimony that they
come up from the Jordan." **17** So
Joshua commanded the priests,
saying, "Come up from the Jordan."
**18** So it happened when the priests
who carried the ark of the covenant
of Yahweh had come up from the
middle of the Jordan, and the soles
of the priests' feet were [1]lifted up to
the dry ground, that the waters of the
Jordan returned to their place and
went over all its banks as before.
**19** Now the people came up from
the Jordan on the [a]tenth of the first
month and camped at Gilgal on the
eastern edge of Jericho. **20** [a,1]And
those twelve stones which they had
taken from the Jordan, Joshua set up
[b]at Gilgal. **21** Then he said to the sons
of [1]Israel, "When your children ask
their fathers in time to come, saying,
'What do these stones mean?' **22** then
you shall make your children know,
saying, 'Israel crossed this Jordan on
[a]dry land.' **23** For Yahweh your God
dried up the waters of the Jordan
before you until you had crossed, just
as Yahweh your God had done to the
[1]Red Sea, [a]which He dried up before
us until we had crossed, **24** that [a]all
the peoples of the earth may know
that the [b]hand of Yahweh is strong,
so that you may [c,1]fear Yahweh your
God [2]forever."

---

**4:7** [a]Jos 3:13 [b]Ex 12:14; Nu 16:40 **4:8** [a]Jos 4:20 **4:9** [a]Ge 28:18; Jos 24:26f; 1Sa 7:12 **4:12** [a]Nu 32:17
**4:14** [a]Jos 3:7 [1]Or *reverenced* **4:15** [1]Lit *Joshua, saying* **4:16** [a]Ex 25:16 **4:18** [1]Lit *drawn out*
**4:19** [a]Dt 1:3 **4:20** [a]Jos 4:8 [b]Jos 4:3, 8 [1]Lit *these* **4:21** [1]Lit *Israel, saying,* **4:22** [a]Jos 3:17
**4:23** [a]Ex 14:21 [1]Lit *Sea of Reeds* **4:24** [a]1Ki 8:42; 2Ki 19:19; Ps 106:8 [b]Ex 15:16; 1Chr 29:12; Ps 89:13
[c]Ex 14:31; Ps 76:7f; Jer 10:7 [1]Or *reverence* [2]Lit *all the days*

### *The Men of Israel Circumcised*

**5** Now it happened when all the kings of the Amorites who *were* beyond the Jordan to the west, and all the kings of the [a]Canaanites who *were* by the sea, [b]heard how Yahweh had dried up the waters of the Jordan before the sons of Israel until [1]they had crossed, that their hearts melted, and there was no spirit in them any longer because of the sons of Israel.

**2** At that time Yahweh said to Joshua, "Make for yourself [a]flint knives and circumcise again the sons of Israel the second time." **3** So Joshua made himself flint knives and circumcised the sons of Israel at [1]Gibeath-haaraloth. **4** Now this is the reason why Joshua circumcised them: [a]all the people who came out of Egypt who were males, all the men of war, died in the wilderness along the way when they came out of Egypt. **5** For all the people who came out were circumcised, but all the people who were born in the wilderness along the way as they came out of Egypt had not been circumcised. **6** For the sons of Israel had walked [a]forty years in the wilderness, until all the nation, *that is,* the men of war who came out of Egypt, were completely *destroyed* because they did not listen to the voice of Yahweh, [b]to whom Yahweh had sworn that He would not let them see the land which Yahweh had sworn to their fathers to give us, a land flowing with milk and honey. **7** And their sons whom He raised up in their place, Joshua [1]circumcised; for they were uncircumcised because they had not circumcised them along the way.

**8** Now it happened that when they had completed circumcising all the nation, they remained in their places in the camp until they were [1]healed. **9** Then Yahweh said to Joshua, "Today I have rolled away [a]the reproach of Egypt from you." So the name of that place is called [1]Gilgal to this day.

**10** Then the sons of Israel camped at Gilgal and [a]celebrated the Passover on the evening of the [b]fourteenth day of the month on the desert plains of Jericho. **11** And on the [1]day after the Passover, on [2]that very day, they ate some of the yield of the land, unleavened cakes and roasted *grain.* **12** [a]Then the manna ceased on the [1]day after they had eaten some of the produce of the land, so that the sons of Israel no longer had manna, but they ate some of the produce of the land of Canaan during that year.

### *Commander of Yahweh's Host*

**13** Now it happened when Joshua was by Jericho, that he lifted up his eyes and looked, and behold, [a]a man was standing opposite him with his sword drawn in his hand, and Joshua went to him and said to him, "Are you for us or fo our adversaries?" **14** He said, "No! Rther I indeed come now *as* commander of the host of Yahweh." And Jdhua [a]fell on his face to the earth ad bowed down and said to him, "hat has my lord to say to his slave?" **15** The commander of the host of Yaleh said to Joshua, "[a]Remove yourndals from your feet, for the

◆ **5:1** [a]Nu 13:29 [b]Jos 2:10, 11 [1]Other mss *we* **5:2** [a]Ex 4:25 **5:3** [1]Lit *the hill of the foreskins*
**5:4** [a]Dt 2:14 **5:6** [a]Dt 2:7, 14 [b]Nu 14:29-35; 26:63-65 **5:7** *circumcised them* **5:8** [1]Lit *revived*
**5:9** [a]Zep 2:8 [1]Lit *Rolling* **5:10** [a]Ex 12:18 [b]Jos 4:19 **5:11** *morrow* [2]Lit *this* **5:12** [a]Ex 16:35
[1]Lit *morrow* **5:13** [a]Ge 18:1, 2; 32:24, 30; Nu 22:31 **5:14** [a](3 **5:15** [a]Ex 3:5

place where you are standing is holy."
And Joshua did so.

### *The Destruction of Jericho*

6 Now Jericho was tightly shut be-
cause of the sons of Israel; no one
went out, and no one came in. 2 And
Yahweh said to Joshua, "See, I have
given Jericho into your hand, with
[a]its king *and* the valiant warriors.
3 And you shall march around the
city, all the men of war circling the
city once. You shall do so for six days.
4 Also seven priests shall carry seven
[a]trumpets of rams' horns before the
ark; then on the seventh day you
shall march around the city seven
times, and the priests shall blow the
trumpets. 5 And it will be that when
they make a long blast with the ram's
horn, and when you hear the sound
of the trumpet, all the people shall
shout with a great shout; and the wall
of the city will fall down [1]beneath
itself, and the people will go up every
man [2]straight ahead."

6 So Joshua the son of Nun called
the priests and said to them, "Carry
the ark of the covenant, and let seven
priests carry seven trumpets of rams'
horns before the ark of Yahweh."
7 Then [1]he said to the people, "Go for-
ward, and march around the city, and
let the armed men go on before the
ark of Yahweh." 8 And so it happened
that, when Joshua had spoken to the
people, the seven priests carrying
the seven trumpets of rams' horns
before Yahweh passed on forward
and blew the trumpets; and the ark
of the covenant of Yahweh came
after them. 9 And the armed men
went before the priests who blew the
trumpets, and [a]the rear guard came
after the ark, while they continued
to blow the trumpets. 10 But Joshua
commanded the people, saying, "You
shall not shout nor let your voice be
heard nor let a word proceed out of
your mouth, until the day I tell you,
'Shout!' Then you shall shout!" 11 So
he had the ark of Yahweh [1]taken
around the city, circling *it* once; then
they came into the camp and spent
the night in the camp.

12 Then Joshua rose early in the
morning, and the priests carried
the ark of Yahweh. 13 [a]And the
seven priests carrying the seven
trumpets of rams' horns before the
ark of Yahweh went on continually
and blew the trumpets; and the
armed men went before them, and
[b]the rear guard came after the ark of
Yahweh, and they continued to blow
the trumpets. 14 Thus the second day
they marched around the city once
and returned to the camp; they did
so for six days.

15 Then it happened that on the
seventh day they rose early at the
[1]breaking of dawn and marched
around the city in the same manner
seven times; only on that day they
marched around the city seven
times. 16 Now it happened that on
the seventh time, the priests blew
the trumpets, and Joshua said to the
people, "[a]Shout! For Yahweh has giv-
en you the city. 17 And the city shall
be [a]devoted to destruction, it and
all that is in it belongs to Yahweh;
only Rahab the harlot [1]and all who
are with her in the house shall live

◆ **6:2** [a]Dt 7:24 **6:4** [a]Lv 25:9 **6:5** [1]Or *in place* [2]Lit *before himself* **6:7** [1]Or *they* **6:9** [a]Jos 6:13; Is 52:12 **6:11** [1]Lit *to go around* **6:13** [a]Jo [b]Jos 6:9 **6:15** [1]Lit *rising* **6:16** [a]2Chr 13:14f **6:17** [a]Lv 27:28; Dt 20:17 [1]Lit *she and all*

because she hid the messengers whom we sent. **18** But as for you, only keep yourselves from the things devoted to destruction, lest *as* you are devoting *them* to destruction, you also [a]take some of the things devoted to destruction and make the camp of Israel devoted to destruction and bring trouble on it. **19** [a]But all the silver and gold and articles of bronze and iron are holy to Yahweh; they shall go into the treasury of Yahweh." **20** So the people shouted, and [1]*the priests* blew the trumpets; and when the people heard the sound of the trumpet, the people shouted with a great shout, and the [a]wall fell down [2]beneath itself, so that the people went up into the city, every man straight [3]ahead, and they took the city. **21** [a]And they devoted to destruction everything in the city, both man and woman, young and old, and ox and sheep and donkey, with the edge of the sword.

**22** Now to the two men who had spied out the land, Joshua said, "[a]Go into the harlot's house and bring the woman and all she has out of there, as you have sworn to her." **23** So the young men who were spies went in and [a]brought out Rahab and her father and her mother and her brothers and all she had; they also brought out all her relatives and placed them outside the camp of Israel. **24** [a]But they burned the city with fire, and all that was in it. Only the silver and gold, and articles of bronze and iron, they put into the treasury of the [1]house of Yahweh. **25** However, [a]Rahab the harlot and her father's household and all she had, Joshua preserved alive; and she has lived in the midst of Israel to this day, for [b]she hid the messengers whom Joshua sent to spy out Jericho.

**26** Then Joshua made them swear *an oath* at that time, saying, "[a]Cursed before Yahweh is the man who rises up and builds this city Jericho; with *the loss of* his firstborn he shall lay its foundation, and with *the loss of* his youngest son he shall set up its gates." **27** So [a]Yahweh was with Joshua, and the [b]report about him was in all the land.

### *Israel Struck Down at Ai*

**7** [a]But the sons of Israel acted unfaithfully in regard to the things devoted to destruction. Achan, the son of Carmi, the son of Zabdi, the son of Zerah, from the tribe of Judah, took some of the devoted things; therefore the anger of Yahweh burned against the sons of Israel.

**2** Now Joshua sent men from Jericho to Ai, which is near [a]Beth-aven, east of Bethel, and said to them, "[1]Go up and spy out the land." So the men went up and spied out Ai. **3** Then they returned to Joshua and said to him, "Do not have all the people go up; *only* about two or three thousand men need go up to strike down Ai; do not have all the people toil up there, for they are few." **4** So about three thousand men from the people went up there, but [a]they fled [1]from the men of Ai. **5** And the men of Ai struck down about thirty-six of their

**6:18** [a]Jos 7:1 **6:19** [a]Nu 31:11, 12, 21-23 **6:20** [a]Heb 11:30 [1]Or *they* [2]Lit *in its place* [3]Lit *before himself* **6:21** [a]Dt 20:16 **6:22** [a]Jos 2:12-19 **6:23** [a]Heb 11:31 **6:24** [a]Dt 20:16-18 [1]The tabernacle **6:25** [a]Heb 11:31 [b]Jos 2:6 **6:26** [a]1Ki 16:34 **6:27** [a]Ge 39:2; Jdg 1:19 [b]Jos 9:1, 3 ◆ **7:1** [a]Jos 6:17-19 **7:2** [a]Jos 18:12; 1Sa 13:5; 14:23 [1]Lit *saying, Go* **7:4** [a]Lv 26:17; Dt 28:25 [1]Lit *before*

men and pursued them [1]from the
gate as far as Shebarim and struck
them down on the descent, so the
[a]hearts of the people melted and
became as water.
**6** Then Joshua [a]tore his clothes
and fell to the earth on his face
before the ark of Yahweh until the
evening, *both* he and the elders of
Israel; and [b]they put dust on their
heads. **7** Joshua said, "Alas, O Lord
Yahweh, why did You ever bring this
people over the Jordan, *only* to give
us into the hand of the Amorites, to
make us perish? If only we had been
willing [1]to live beyond the Jordan!
**8** O Lord, what can I say since Israel
has turned *their* [1]back before their
enemies? **9** [a]And the Canaanites and
all the inhabitants of the land will
hear of it, and they will surround us
and cut off our name from the earth.
And what will You do for Your great
name?"
**10** So Yahweh said to Joshua, "Rise
up! Why is it that you have fallen on
your face? **11** Israel has sinned, and
[a]they have also trespassed against My
covenant which I commanded them.
And they have even taken some of
the things devoted to destruction and
have both stolen and dealt falsely.
Moreover, they have also put *them*
among their own things. **12** Therefore
the [a]sons of Israel cannot rise before
their enemies; they turn *their* [1]backs
before their enemies, for they have
become devoted to destruction. I
will not be with you anymore unless
you destroy the things devoted to
destruction from your midst. **13** Rise
up! [a]Set the people apart as holy
and say, 'Set yourselves apart as
holy for tomorrow, for thus Yahweh,
the God of Israel, has said, "[b]There
are things devoted to destruction
in your midst, O Israel. You cannot
rise before your enemies until you
have removed the things devoted to
destruction from your midst." **14** In
the morning then you shall come
near by your tribes. And it will be
that the tribe which [a]Yahweh takes
*by lot* shall come near by families,
and the family which Yahweh takes
shall come near by households,
and the household which Yahweh
takes shall come near man by man.
**15** [a]And it will be that the one who
is taken with the things devoted to
destruction shall be burned with
fire, he and all that belongs to him,
because he has trespassed against the
covenant of Yahweh, and because he
[b]has committed a disgraceful thing
in Israel.'"

### *The Sin of Achan*

**16** So Joshua arose early in the
morning and brought Israel near
by [1]tribes, and the tribe of Judah
was taken. **17** And he brought the
family of Judah near, and he took
the family of the Zerahites; and he
brought the family of the Zerahites
near man by man, and Zabdi was
taken. **18** And he brought his house-
hold near man by man; and [a]Achan,
son of Carmi, son of Zabdi, son of
Zerah, from the tribe of Judah, was
taken. **19** Then Joshua said to Achan,
"My son, I implore you, [a]give glory

**7:5** [a]Lv 26:36; Jos 2:11; Eze 21:7; Na 2:10 [1]Or *before* **7:6** [a]Job 2:12 [b]Job 42:6; Lam 2:10; Rev 18:19
**7:7** [1]Lit *and had lived* **7:8** [1]Lit *neck* **7:9** [a]Ex 32:12; Dt 9:28 **7:11** [a]Jos 6:18, 19 **7:12** [a]Nu 14:39, 45; Jdg 2:14 [1]Lit *necks* **7:13** [a]Jos 3:5 [b]Jos 6:18 **7:14** [a]Pr 16:33 **7:15** [a]1Sa 14:38f [b]Ge 34:7; Jdg 20:6
**7:16** [1]Lit *its tribes* **7:18** [a]Nu 32:23; Ac 5:1-10 **7:19** [a]1Sa 6:5; 2Chr 30:22; Jer 13:16; Jn 9:24

to Yahweh, the God of Israel, and
give praise to Him; and declare to
me now what you have done. Do
not hide it from me." 20 So Achan
answered Joshua and said, "Truly,
I have sinned against Yahweh, the
God of Israel, and [1]this is what I did:
21 I saw among the spoil a beautiful
mantle from Shinar and two hun-
dred [1]shekels of silver and a bar of
gold fifty shekels in weight; then I
[a,2]coveted them and took them; and
behold, they are concealed in the
earth inside my tent with the silver
underneath it."
22 So Joshua sent messengers, and
they ran to the tent; and behold, it
was concealed in his tent with the
silver underneath it. 23 And they
took them from inside the tent and
brought them to Joshua and to all the
sons of Israel, and they poured them
out before Yahweh. 24 Then Joshua
and all Israel with him, took Achan
the son of Zerah, the silver, the
mantle, the bar of gold, his sons, his
daughters, his [1]oxen, his donkeys, his
sheep, his tent, and all that belonged
to him; and they brought them up to
[a]the valley of [2]Achor. 25 And Joshua
said, "Why have you [a]troubled us?
Yahweh will trouble you this day."
And all Israel stoned him with stones;
and they burned them with fire [1]after
*they* had stoned them with stones.
26 Then they raised over him a great
heap of stones that stands to this day,
and Yahweh turned from His burning
anger. Therefore the name of that
place has been called [a]the valley of
[1]Achor to this day.

### *Ai Given to Israel*

8 Now Yahweh said to Joshua, "[a]Do
not fear or be dismayed. Take all
the people of war with you and arise,
go up to Ai; see, [b]I have given into
your hand the king of Ai, his people,
his city, and his land. 2 So you shall
do to Ai and its king just as you did to
Jericho and its king; you shall [a]take
only its spoil and its cattle as plunder
for yourselves. [1]Set an ambush for
the city behind it."
3 So Joshua rose with all the peo-
ple of war to go up to Ai; and Joshua
chose 30,000 men, valiant warriors,
and sent them out at night. 4 And he
commanded them, saying, "See, you
are [a]going to ambush the city from
behind [1]it. Do not go very far from
the city, but all of you be ready. 5 Then
I and all the people who are with me
will come near the city. And it will be
that when they come out to meet us as
at the first, [a]we will flee before them.
6 And they will come out after us until
we have drawn them away from the
city, for they will say, '*They* are fleeing
before us as at the first.' So we will flee
before them. 7 And you shall rise from
*your* ambush and take possession of
the city, for Yahweh your God will
give it into your hand. 8 Then it will
be that when you have seized the
city, that you shall set the city on fire.
You shall do *it* [a]according to the word
of Yahweh. See, I have commanded
you." 9 So Joshua sent them away, and
they went to the place of ambush and
remained between Bethel and Ai, on
the west side of Ai; but Joshua spent
that night among the people.

**7:20** [1]Lit *thus and thus I did* **7:21** [a]Eph 5:5; 1Ti 6:10 [1]A shekel was approx. 0.4 oz. or 11 gm [2]Or *desired*, cf. Ge 3:6-8 **7:24** [a]Jos 15:7 [1]Or *cattle* [2]Lit *trouble*, cf. 6:18; 7:25 **7:25** [a]Jos 6:18 [1]Lit *and they stoned* **7:26** [a]Is 65:10; Hos 2:15 [1]Lit *trouble*, cf. 6:18; 7:25 ◆ **8:1** [a]Jos 1:9; 10:8 [b]Jos 6:2 **8:2** [a]Dt 20:14; Jos 8:27 [1]Lit *Set for yourself* **8:4** [a]Jdg 20:29 [1]Lit *the city* **8:5** [a]Jdg 20:32 **8:8** [a]Dt 20:16-18; Jos 8:2

**10** Now Joshua [a]rose early in the
morning and mustered the people,
and he went up with the elders of
Israel before the people to Ai. **11** Then
all the people of war who *were* with
him went up and drew near and ar-
rived in front of the city and camped
on the north side of Ai. Now *there
was* a valley between him and Ai.
**12** And he took about 5,000 men
and set them in ambush between
[a]Bethel and Ai, on the west side of
the [1]city. **13** So they set the people, all
the army that was on the north side
of the city, and its rear guard on the
west side of the city, and Joshua went
that night into the midst of the valley.
**14** Now it happened that when the
king of Ai saw *it*, the men of the city
hurried and rose up early and went
out to meet Israel in battle, he and
all his people at the appointed place
before the desert plain. But he did
not know that *there was* an ambush
against him behind the city. **15** And
Joshua and all Israel pretended to
be beaten before them and fled [a]by
the way of the wilderness. **16** And
all the people who were in the city
were called together to pursue them,
and they pursued Joshua and [a]were
drawn away from the city. **17** So not
a man remained in Ai or Bethel who
had not gone out after Israel, and
they forsook the city, *leaving it* open,
and pursued Israel.

**18** Then Yahweh said to Joshua,
"[a]Stretch out the javelin that is in
your hand toward Ai, for I will give it
into your hand." So Joshua stretched
out the javelin that was in his hand
toward the city. **19** Then the *men in*
ambush rose quickly from their place,
and when he had stretched out his
hand, they ran and entered the city
and captured it, and they quickly set
the city on fire. **20** Then the men of Ai
turned [1]back and looked, and behold,
the smoke of the city ascended to
the sky, and they had no place to flee
this way or that, for the people who
had been fleeing to the wilderness
turned against the pursuers. **21** But
Joshua and all Israel saw that the
*men in* ambush had captured the
city and that the smoke of the city
ascended. So they turned back and
struck down the men of Ai. **22** [1]And
the others came out from the city to
meet them, so that they were *trapped*
in the midst of Israel, [2]some on this
side and some on that side; and they
struck them down until [3]there was
[a]no one remaining for him who sur-
vived or escaped. **23** But they seized
the king of Ai alive and brought him
to Joshua.

**24** Now it happened that when
Israel had finished killing all the
inhabitants of Ai in the field in the
wilderness where they pursued
them, and all of them fell by the
edge of the sword until they were
completely *destroyed*, then all Israel
turned back to Ai and struck it with
the edge of the sword. **25** [a]So all who
fell that day, both men and women,
were 12,000—all the [1]people of Ai.
**26** For Joshua [a]did not withdraw his
hand with which he stretched out
the javelin until he had devoted to
destruction all the inhabitants of
Ai. **27** [a]Israel took only the cattle and
the spoil of that city as plunder for

---

**8:10** [a]Ge 22:3 **8:12** [a]Ge 12:8; 28:19; Jdg 1:22 [1]Ai **8:15** [a]Jos 15:61; 16:1; 18:12 **8:16** [a]Jdg 20:31
**8:18** [a]Ex 14:16; 17:9-13; Jos 8:26 **8:20** [1]Lit *behind them* **8:22** [a]Jos 8:8 [1]Lit *These came* [2]Lit
*these...those* [3]Lit *he had no one* **8:25** [a]Dt 20:16-18 [1]Lit *men* **8:26** [a]Ex 17:11, 12 **8:27** [a]Jos 8:2

themselves, according to the word of
Yahweh which He had commanded
Joshua. **28** So Joshua burned Ai and
made it [a]a heap forever, a desolation
until this day. **29** [a]And he hanged the
king of Ai on a tree until evening; and
at sunset Joshua gave a command,
and they took his body down from
the tree and threw it at the entrance
of the city gate and raised over it a
great heap of stones *that stands* to
this day.

**30** Then Joshua built an altar to
Yahweh, the God of Israel, on [a]Mount
Ebal, **31** just as Moses the servant of
Yahweh had commanded the sons
of Israel, as it is written in the book
of the law of Moses, [a]an altar of
uncut stones on which no man had
wielded an iron *tool*; and they offered
burnt offerings on it to Yahweh and
sacrificed peace offerings. **32** And he
[a]wrote there on the stones a copy
of the law of Moses, which [1]he had
written, in the presence of the sons
of Israel. **33** [a]And all Israel with their
elders and officers and their judges
were standing on both sides of the
ark before the Levitical priests who
carried the ark of the covenant of
Yahweh, the sojourner as well as
the native. Half of them *stood* in
front of [b]Mount Gerizim and half
of them in front of Mount Ebal, just
as Moses the servant of Yahweh had
given a command at first to bless the
people of Israel. **34** Then afterward
he read all the words of the law, the
blessing and the curse, according to
all that is written in [a]the book of the
law. **35** There was not a word of all
that Moses had commanded which
Joshua did not read before all the
assembly of Israel [a]with the women
and the little ones and the sojourners
who were [1]going among them.

### *The Gibeonites Act Craftily*

**9** Now it happened when [a]all the
kings who were beyond the Jor-
dan, in the hill country and in the
[1]Shephelah and on all the [b]coast of
the Great Sea toward Lebanon, [c]the
Hittite and the Amorite, the Ca-
naanite, the Perizzite, the Hivite and
the Jebusite, heard of it, **2** that they
gathered themselves together with
[a,1]one accord to fight with Joshua and
with Israel.

**3** Now the inhabitants of [a]Gibeon
heard what Joshua had done to Jer-
icho and to Ai. **4** So they also acted
craftily and went and traveled as
envoys and took worn-out sacks on
their donkeys, and wineskins worn-
out and torn and [1]mended, **5** and
worn-out and patched sandals on
their feet, and worn-out clothes on
themselves; and all the bread of their
provision *was* dry *and* was crumbled.
**6** And they went to Joshua to the
[a]camp at Gilgal and said to him and
to the men of Israel, "We have come
from a far country; so now, cut a
covenant with us." **7** Then the men of
Israel said to the [a]Hivites, "Perhaps
you are living [1]within our land; [b]how
then shall we cut a covenant with
you?" **8** But they said to Joshua, "[a]We
are your servants." Then Joshua said
to them, "Who are you and where do
you come from?" **9** They said to him,

**8:28** [a]Dt 13:16 **8:29** [a]Dt 21:22, 23 **8:30** [a]Dt 27:2-8 **8:31** [a]Ex 20:25 **8:32** [a]Dt 27:2, 3, 8 [1]Moses **8:33** [a]Dt 27:11-14 [b]Dt 11:29 **8:34** [a]Jos 1:8 **8:35** [a]Ex 12:38; Dt 31:12; Zec 8:23 [1]Lit *walking*
◆ **9:1** [a]Nu 13:29; Jos 3:10 [b]Nu 34:6 [c]Ex 3:17; 23:23 [1]Or *lowland* **9:2** [a]Ps 83:3, 5 [1]Lit *one mouth*
**9:3** [a]Jos 9:17, 22; 10:2; 21:17 **9:4** [1]Lit *tied up* **9:6** [a]Jos 5:10 **9:7** [a]Jos 9:1; 11:19 [b]Ex 23:32; Dt 7:2 [1]Lit *among us* **9:8** [a]Dt 20:11; 2Ki 10:5

"Your servants have come from [a]a very far country because of the [1]fame of Yahweh your God; for [b]we have heard the report of Him and all that He did in Egypt, **10** and all that He did to the two kings of the Amorites who were beyond the Jordan, to Sihon king of Heshbon and to Og king of Bashan who was at Ashtaroth. **11** So our elders and all the inhabitants of our country spoke to us, saying, 'Take provisions in your hand for the journey, and go to meet them and say to them, "[a]We are your servants; now then, cut a covenant with us."' **12** This bread of ours *was* warm *when* we took it for our provisions out of our houses on the day that we left to come to you; but now behold, it is dry and has become crumbled. **13** And these wineskins which we filled were new, and behold, they are torn; and these clothes of ours and our sandals are worn out because of the very long journey." **14** So the men *of Israel* took some of their provisions, but [a]they did not ask for the [1]command of Yahweh. **15** [a]And Joshua made peace with them and cut a covenant with them, to let them live; and the leaders of the congregation swore *an oath* to them.

**16** Now it happened at the end of three days after they had cut a covenant with them, that they heard that they were near them and that they were living [1]nearly among them. **17** Then the sons of Israel set out and came to their cities on the third day. Now their cities *were* [a]Gibeon and Chephirah and Beeroth and Kiriath-jearim. **18** But the sons of Israel did not strike them down because the leaders of the congregation had sworn to them by Yahweh the God of Israel. And the whole congregation grumbled against the leaders. **19** Then all the leaders said to the whole congregation, "We have sworn to them by Yahweh, the God of Israel, so now we cannot touch them. **20** This we will do to them, even let them live, so that wrath will not be upon us for the oath which we swore to them." **21** So the leaders said to them, "Let them live." Thus they became [a]hewers of wood and drawers of water for the whole congregation, just as the leaders had spoken to them.

**22** Then Joshua called for them and spoke to them, saying, "Why have you deceived us, saying, 'We are very far from you,' [a]when you are living nearly in the midst of us? **23** So now, you are [a]cursed, and [1]you shall never be cut loose from being slaves, both hewers of wood and drawers of water for the house of my God." **24** So they answered Joshua and said, "[a]Because it was certainly told to your slaves that Yahweh your God had commanded His servant Moses to give you all the land and to destroy all the inhabitants of the land before you; therefore we feared greatly for our lives because of you and have done this thing. **25** So now, behold, [a]we are in your hands; do as it seems good and right in your sight to do to us." **26** Thus he did to them and delivered them from the hands of the sons of Israel, and they did not kill them. **27** But Joshua made them that day hewers of wood and drawers of water for the congregation and for

---

**9:9** [a]Jos 9:16, 17 [b]Jos 2:9; 9:24 [1]Or *name* **9:11** [a]Jos 9:8 **9:14** [a]Nu 27:21 [1]Lit *mouth*
**9:15** [a]Ex 23:32 **9:16** [1]Or *in the midst of them* **9:17** [a]Jos 18:25 **9:21** [a]Dt 29:11 **9:22** [a]Jos 9:16
**9:23** [a]Ge 9:25 [1]Lit *a slave shall not be cut off from you* **9:24** [a]Jos 9:9 **9:25** [a]Ge 16:6

the altar of Yahweh, to this day, [a]in the place which He would choose.

### *The Sun Stands Still*

**10** Now it happened that when Adoni-zedek king of Jerusalem heard that Joshua had captured Ai and had devoted it to destruction (just [a]as he had done to Jericho and its king, so he had done to Ai and its king), and that the inhabitants of Gibeon had [b]made peace with Israel and were [1]within their land, **2** they [a]feared exceedingly because Gibeon *was* a great city, like one of the royal cities, and because it was greater than Ai, and all its men *were* mighty. **3** Therefore Adoni-zedek king of Jerusalem sent *word* [a]to Hoham king of Hebron and to Piram king of Jarmuth and to Japhia king of Lachish and to Debir king of Eglon, saying, **4** "Come up to me and help me, and let us strike Gibeon, for it has [a]made peace with Joshua and with the sons of Israel." **5** So the five kings of [a]the Amorites, the king of Jerusalem, the king of Hebron, the king of Jarmuth, the king of Lachish, *and* the king of Eglon, gathered together and went up, they with all their armies, and camped by Gibeon and fought against it.

**6** Then the men of Gibeon sent *word* to Joshua to the camp at Gilgal, saying, "Do not [1]abandon your slaves; come up to us quickly and save us and help us, for all the kings of the Amorites that live in the hill country have assembled against us." **7** So Joshua went up from Gilgal, he and [a]all the people of war with him and all the valiant warriors. **8** And Yahweh said to Joshua, "[a]Do not fear them, for I have given them into your hands; not [1]one of them shall stand before you." **9** So Joshua came upon them suddenly—he had gone up, *marching* all night from Gilgal. **10** [a]And Yahweh threw them into confusion before Israel, and He struck them with a great slaughter at Gibeon and pursued them by the way of the ascent of Beth-horon and struck them as far as Azekah and Makkedah. **11** Now it happened as they fled from before Israel, *while* they were at the descent of Beth-horon, that [a]Yahweh threw down large stones from heaven on them as far as Azekah, and they died; *there were* more who died [1]from the hailstones than those whom the sons of Israel killed with the sword.

**12** Then Joshua spoke to Yahweh in the day when Yahweh gave over the Amorites before the sons of Israel, and he said in the sight of Israel,

"O [a]sun, stand still at Gibeon,
And O moon in the valley
of Aijalon."

**13** [a]So the sun stood still, and
the moon stopped,
Until the nation avenged
themselves of their enemies.

Is it not written in [b]the book of Jashar? And [c]the sun stood in the middle of the sky and did not hasten to go *down* for about a whole day. **14** And there was no day like that before it or after it, when Yahweh listened to the voice of a man; for [a]Yahweh fought for Israel.

**9:27** [a]Dt 12:5 ◆ **10:1** [a]Jos 8:21f [b]Jos 9:15 [1]Lit *among them* **10:2** [a]Ex 15:14-16 **10:3** [a]Jos 10:23 **10:4** [a]Jos 9:15 **10:5** [a]Nu 13:29 **10:6** [1]Lit *slacken your hands from* **10:7** [a]Jos 8:1 **10:8** [a]Jos 1:5, 9 [1]Lit *a man* **10:10** [a]Dt 7:23 **10:11** [a]Ps 18:12f; Is 28:2 [1]Lit *with* **10:12** [a]Hab 3:11 **10:13** [a]Hab 3:11 [b]2Sa 1:18 [c]Is 38:8 **10:14** [a]Ex 14:14; Dt 1:30; Jos 10:42

15 Then Joshua and all Israel with
him returned to the camp to Gilgal.

### *Joshua Captures Makkedah*

16 And these [a]five kings fled and hid
themselves in the cave at Makkedah.
17 Then it was told Joshua, saying,
"The five kings have been found hid-
den in the cave at Makkedah." 18 And
Joshua said, "Roll large stones against
the mouth of the cave and assign men
by it to keep watch over them, 19 but
as for you, do not stand *there*; pursue
your enemies and [1]attack them in the
rear. Do not allow them to enter their
cities, for Yahweh your God has given
them into your hand." 20 Now it
happened when Joshua and the sons
of Israel had finished striking them
with a very great slaughter [a]until
they were completely *destroyed*, and
the survivors—*those* of them *who*
survived—[1]had entered the fortified
cities, 21 that all the people returned
to the camp to Joshua at Makkedah
in peace. No one *so much as* [1]lifted
his tongue against any of the sons
of Israel.

22 Then Joshua said, "Open the
mouth of the cave and bring these
five kings out to me from the cave."
23 And they did so and [a]brought
these five kings out to him from
the cave: the king of Jerusalem, the
king of Hebron, the king of Jarmuth,
the king of Lachish, *and* the king
of Eglon. 24 Now it happened that
when they brought these kings out to
Joshua, Joshua called for all the men
*of Israel and said* to the chiefs of the
men of war who had gone with him,
"Come near, [a]put your feet on the
necks of these kings." So they came
near and put their feet on their necks.
25 Joshua then said to them, "[a]Do not
fear or be dismayed! Be strong and
courageous, for thus Yahweh will
do to all your enemies with whom
you fight." 26 So afterward Joshua
struck them and put them to death,
and he [a]hanged them on five trees;
and they hung on the trees until
evening. 27 Now it happened that at
[1]sunset Joshua gave a command, and
[a]they took them down from the trees
and threw them down into the cave
where they had hidden themselves,
and they put large stones over the
mouth of the cave, to this very day.

28 Now Joshua captured Makkedah
on that day and struck it and its
king with the edge of the sword;
[a]he [1]devoted [2]it to destruction and
every [3]person who was in it. He left
no survivor. Thus he did to the king
of Makkedah [b]just as he had done to
the king of Jericho.

### *Israel Captures Kings by Yahweh's Sword*

29 Then Joshua and all Israel with
him passed on from Makkedah to
[a]Libnah and fought against Libnah.
30 And Yahweh gave it also with its
king into the hands of Israel, and he
struck it and every person who was
in it with the edge of the sword. He
left no survivor remaining in it. Thus
he did to its king just as he had done
to the king of Jericho.

31 And Joshua and all Israel with
him passed on from Libnah to

---

**10:16** [a]Jos 10:5 **10:19** [1]Lit *smite their tail* **10:20** [a]Dt 20:16 [1]Lit *and had* **10:21** [1]Lit *sharpened* **10:23** [a]Dt 7:24 **10:24** [a]Mal 4:3 **10:25** [a]Jos 10:8 **10:26** [a]Jos 8:29 **10:27** [a]Dt 21:22, 23 [1]Lit *the time of the going of the sun* **10:28** [a]Dt 20:16 [b]Jos 6:21 [1]Or *put under the ban*, so in ch [2]Some mss *them* [3]Lit *soul*, so in ch **10:29** [a]Jos 15:42; 21:13

Lachish, and they camped by it and
fought against it. **32** And Yahweh gave
Lachish into the hands of Israel; and
he captured it on the second day
and struck it and every person who
was in it with the edge of the sword,
according to all that he had done to
Libnah.

**33** Then Horam king of [a]Gezer
came up to help Lachish, and Joshua
struck him and his people down until
[1]there was no survivor remaining for
him.

**34** And Joshua and all Israel with
him passed on from Lachish to Eglon,
and they camped by it and fought
against it. **35** And they captured it on
that day and struck it with the edge
of the sword; and every person who
was in it, he devoted to destruction
*on* that day according to all that he
had done to Lachish.

**36** Then Joshua and all Israel with
him went up from Eglon to [a]Hebron,
and they fought against it. **37** And they
captured it and struck it and its king
and all its cities and all the persons
who *were* in it with the edge of the
sword. He left no survivor remaining,
according to all that he had done to
Eglon. And he devoted it and every
person who *was* in it to destruction.

**38** Then Joshua and all Israel with
him returned to [a]Debir, and they
fought against it. **39** And he captured
it and its king and all its cities, and
they struck them with the edge of
the sword and devoted every person
who was in it to destruction. He left
no survivor remaining. Just as he had
done to Hebron, so he did to Debir
and its king, as he had also done to
Libnah and its king.

**40** Thus Joshua struck all the
land—[a]the hill country and the
[1]Negev and the [2]Shephelah and the
slopes—as well as [b]all their kings.
He left no survivor remaining, but
[c]he devoted to destruction all who
breathed, just as Yahweh, the God
of Israel, had commanded. **41** And
Joshua struck them from Kadesh-
barnea even as far as Gaza, and all
the country of [a]Goshen even as far
as Gibeon. **42** And Joshua captured
all these kings and their lands at one
time because [a]Yahweh, the God of
Israel, fought for Israel. **43** So Joshua
and all Israel with him returned to
the camp at Gilgal.

### *Joshua Takes the Whole Land*

**11** Now it happened, when Jabin
king of [a]Hazor heard *of it*, that
he sent to Jobab king of Madon and to
the king of Shimron and to the king
of Achshaph, **2** and to the kings who
were of the north in the hill coun-
try and in the [a]Arabah—south of
[1]Chinneroth and in the [2]Shephelah
and on the [3]heights of Dor on the
west— **3** to the Canaanite on the east
and on the west, and the Amorite
and the Hittite and the Perizzite and
the Jebusite in the hill country, and
[a]the Hivite [1]at the foot of [b]Hermon
in the land of [c]Mizpeh. **4** Then they
came out, they and all their armies
with them, [a]*as* many people as the
sand that is on the seashore, with
very many horses and chariots. **5** So
all of these kings agreed to meet, and

**10:33** [a]Jos 16:3, 10; Jdg 1:29; 1Ki 9:16f [1]Lit *he had no survivor* **10:36** [a]Nu 13:22; Jdg 1:10, 20; 2Sa 5:1, 3, 5, 13; 2Chr 11:10 **10:38** [a]Jos 15:15; Jdg 1:11; 1Chr 6:58 **10:40** [a]Dt 1:7 [b]Dt 7:24 [c]Dt 20:16 [1]South country [2]Or *lowland* **10:41** [a]Jos 11:16; 15:51 **10:42** [a]Jos 10:14 ♦ **11:1** [a]Jos 11:10 **11:2** [a]Jos 12:3; 13:27 [1]Sea of Galilee [2]Or *lowland* [3]Heb *Naphoth-dor* **11:3** [a]Dt 7:1; Jdg 3:3, 5; 1Ki 9:20 [b]Jos 11:17; 13:5, 11 [c]Jos 15:38; 18:26 [1]Lit *under* **11:4** [a]Jdg 7:12

they came and encamped together at
the waters of Merom, to fight against
Israel.

6 Then Yahweh said to Joshua,
"[a]Do not be afraid because of them,
for tomorrow at this time I will give
all of them over, slain, before Israel;
you shall [b]hamstring their horses
and burn their chariots with fire."
7 So Joshua and all the people of war
with him came upon them suddenly
by the waters of Merom, and they
fell upon them. 8 And Yahweh gave
them into the hand of Israel, so that
they struck them down, and they
pursued them as far as Great Sidon
and [a]Misrephoth-maim and the
valley of [b]Mizpeh to the east; and
they struck them until [1]there was no
survivor remaining for them. 9 And
Joshua did to them as Yahweh had
said to him; he [a]hamstrung their
horses and burned their chariots
with fire.

10 Then Joshua turned back at
that time and captured [a]Hazor
and struck its king with the sword;
for Hazor formerly was the head
of all these kingdoms. 11 [a]And they
struck every person who was in it
with the edge of the sword, [1]devot-
ing *them* to destruction; there was
no one left who breathed. And he
burned Hazor with fire. 12 And
Joshua captured all the cities of
these kings and all their kings,
and he struck them with the edge
of the sword, *and* he devoted them
to destruction, just [a]as Moses the
servant of Yahweh had commanded.
13 However, Israel did not burn any
cities that stood on their mounds,
except Hazor alone, *which* Joshua
burned. 14 [a]Now all the spoil of
these cities and the cattle, the sons
of Israel took as their plunder; but
they struck every man with the
edge of the sword until they had
destroyed them. They left no one
remaining who breathed. 15 Just as
Yahweh had commanded Moses
His servant, so Moses commanded
Joshua, and so Joshua did; he left
nothing undone of all that Yahweh
had commanded Moses.

16 Thus Joshua took all that land:
[a]the hill country and all the [1]Negev,
all that land of Goshen, the [2]Sheph-
elah, [b]the Arabah, the hill country
of Israel and its [2]Shephelah 17 from
[a]Mount Halak, that rises toward Seir,
even as far as Baal-gad in the valley
of Lebanon [1]at the foot of Mount
Hermon. And he captured [b]all their
kings and struck them down and
put them to death. 18 Joshua waged
war a long time with all these kings.
19 There was not a city which made
peace with the sons of Israel except
[a]the Hivites living in Gibeon; they
took them all in battle. 20 [a]For it
was of Yahweh to strengthen their
hearts, to meet Israel in battle in
order that he might [b]devote them to
destruction, that they might [1]receive
no mercy, but that he might destroy
them, just as Yahweh had command-
ed Moses.

21 Then Joshua came at that time
and cut off [a]the Anakim from the
hill country, from Hebron, from
Debir, from Anab and from all the

**11:6** [a]Jos 10:8 [b]2Sa 8:4 **11:8** [a]Jos 13:6 [b]Jos 11:3 [1]Lit *he had no survivor* **11:9** [a]Jos 11:6
**11:10** [a]Jos 11:1 **11:11** [a]Dt 20:16 [1]Or *putting them under the ban*, so in ch **11:12** [a]Nu 33:50-52;
Dt 7:2; 20:16f **11:14** [a]Nu 31:11, 12 **11:16** [a]Jos 10:40, 41 [b]Jos 11:2 [1]South country [2]Or *lowland*
**11:17** [a]Jos 12:7 [b]Dt 7:24 [1]Lit *under* **11:19** [a]Jos 9:3, 7 **11:20** [a]Ex 14:17 [b]Dt 7:16 [1]Lit *have*
**11:21** [a]Nu 13:33; Dt 9:2

hill country of Judah and from all
the hill country of Israel. Joshua de-
voted them to destruction with their
cities. **22** There were no Anakim left
in the land of the sons of Israel; only
in Gaza, in [a]Gath, and in [b]Ashdod
some remained. **23** So Joshua took
the whole land, according to all that
Yahweh had spoken to Moses, and
[a]Joshua gave it for an inheritance to
Israel according to their divisions by
their tribes. [b]Thus the land was quiet
from war.

### *The Kings of the East Struck Down*

**12** Now these are the [a]kings of
the land whom the sons of
Israel struck down, and whose land
they possessed beyond the Jordan
*to the east* toward the sunrise, from
the valley of the Arnon as far as
Mount Hermon, and all the Arabah
to the east: **2** Sihon king of the Am-
orites, who lived in Heshbon *and*
ruled [a]from Aroer, which is on the
edge of the valley of the Arnon, both
the middle of the valley and half
of Gilead, even as far as the brook
Jabbok, the border of the sons of
Ammon; **3** and the [a]Arabah as far
as the Sea of [1]Chinneroth toward
the east, and as far as the sea of the
Arabah, *even* the Salt Sea, eastward
[2]toward [b]Beth-jeshimoth, and on
*the south*, [3]*at the foot* of the slopes
of Pisgah; **4** and the territory of Og
king of Bashan, one of [a]the rem-
nant of the Rephaim, who lived at
[b]Ashtaroth and at Edrei **5** and ruled
over Mount Hermon and [a]Salecah
and all Bashan, as far as [b]the border
of the Geshurites and the Maaca-
thites, and half of Gilead, *as far as*
the border of Sihon king of Hesh-
bon. **6** Moses the servant of Yahweh
and the sons of Israel struck them
down; and [a]Moses the servant of
Yahweh gave it to the Reubenites
and the Gadites and the half-tribe
of Manasseh as a possession.

### *The Kings of the West Struck Down*

**7** Now these are the kings of the
land whom Joshua and the sons of
Israel struck down beyond the Jordan
toward the west, from Baal-gad in
the valley of Lebanon even as far as
[a]Mount Halak, which rises toward
Seir; and Joshua gave it to the tribes
of Israel as a possession according to
their divisions, **8** in [a]the hill country
and in the [1]Shephelah and in the
Arabah and on the slopes and in
the wilderness and in the [2]Negev;
the Hittite, the Amorite and the
Canaanite, the Perizzite, the Hivite
and the Jebusite:

**9** the [a]king of Jericho, one;
the [b]king of Ai, which is
beside Bethel, one;
**10** the [a]king of Jerusalem, one;
the king of Hebron, one;
**11** the king of Jarmuth, one;
the king of Lachish, one;
**12** the king of Eglon, one;
the king of Gezer, one;
**13** the king of Debir, one;
the king of Geder, one;
**14** the king of Hormah, one;
the king of [a]Arad, one;
**15** the king of Libnah, one;
the king of Adullam, one;

**11:22** [a]1Sa 17:4; 1Ki 2:39; 1Chr 8:13 [b]Jos 15:46f; 1Sa 5:1; Is 20:1 **11:23** [a]Dt 1:38 [b]Dt 12:9, 10; 25:19; Heb 4:8
◆ **12:1** [a]Nu 32:33; Dt 3:8-17 **12:2** [a]Dt 2:36 **12:3** [a]Jos 11:2 [b]Jos 13:20 [1]Galilee [2]Lit *the way of* [3]Lit
*under* **12:4** [a]Dt 3:11 [b]Dt 1:4 **12:5** [a]Dt 3:10; Jos 13:11; 1Chr 5:11 [b]Dt 3:14; 1Sa 27:8 **12:6** [a]Nu 32:33;
Dt 3:12 **12:7** [a]Jos 11:17 **12:8** [a]Jos 11:16 [1]Or *lowland* [2]South country **12:9** [a]Jos 6:2 [b]Jos 8:29
**12:10** [a]Jos 10:23 **12:14** [a]Nu 21:1

16 the king of Makkedah, one;
the king of Bethel, one;
17 the king of Tappuah, one;
the [a]king of Hepher, one;
18 the king of [a]Aphek, one;
the king of Lasharon, one;
19 the king of Madon, one;
the king of Hazor, one;
20 the king of Shimron-meron, one;
the king of Achshaph, one;
21 the king of Taanach, one;
the king of Megiddo, one;
22 the king of [a]Kedesh, one;
the king of Jokneam in Carmel, one;
23 the king of Dor in the [1]heights of Dor, one;
the king of [a]Goiim in Gilgal, one;
24 the king of Tirzah, one:
[a]in all, thirty-one kings.

### *Land That Remains to Be Possessed*

13 Now [a]Joshua was old, advanced in years, and Yahweh
said to him, "You are old, advanced
in years, and very much of the land
remains to be possessed. 2 This is
the land that remains: all the regions
*of* the Philistines and all *those of*
the [a]Geshurites; 3 from the Shihor
which is [1]east of Egypt, even as far
as the border of Ekron to the north
(it is counted as Canaanite); the [a]five
lords of the Philistines: the Gazite,
the Ashdodite, the Ashkelonite, the
Gittite, the Ekronite; and the Avvite
4 [1]to the south, all the land of the
*Canaanite*, *and* Mearah that belongs
to the Sidonians, as far as [a]Aphek,
to the border of the [b]Amorite; 5 and
the land of the [a]Gebalite, and all of
Lebanon, *to the east* toward the sunrise, [b]from Baal-gad below Mount
Hermon as far as [1]Lebo-hamath.
6 All the inhabitants of the hill
country from Lebanon as far as
[a]Misrephoth-maim, all the Sidonians, I will dispossess them from
before the sons of Israel; [b]only allot
it to Israel for an inheritance as I
have commanded you. 7 So now, apportion this land for an inheritance
to the nine tribes and the half-tribe
of Manasseh."

### *The Inheritance East of the Jordan*

8 With [1]the other half-tribe, the
Reubenites and the Gadites received
their inheritance which Moses gave
them [a]beyond the Jordan to the
east, just as Moses the servant of
Yahweh gave to them; 9 from Aroer,
which is on the edge of the valley
of the Arnon, with the city which
is in the middle of the valley, and
all the plain of Medeba, as far as
Dibon; 10 and all the cities of Sihon
king of the Amorites, who reigned
in Heshbon, as far as the border of
the sons of Ammon; 11 and [a]Gilead,
and the [1]territory of the Geshurites
and Maacathites, and all Mount
Hermon, and all Bashan as far as
Salecah; 12 all the kingdom of [a]Og
in Bashan, who reigned in Ashtaroth
and in Edrei (he alone remained of
the remnant of the Rephaim); for
Moses [b]struck them and dispossessed them. 13 But the sons of Israel
did not dispossess the Geshurites

**12:17** [a]1Ki 4:10 **12:18** [a]Jos 13:4; 2Ki 13:17 **12:22** [a]Jos 19:37; 20:7; 21:32 **12:23** [a]Ge 14:1 [1]Or *Naphath-dor* **12:24** [a]Dt 7:24 ◆ **13:1** [a]Jos 14:10 **13:2** [a]Jos 13:11; 1Sa 27:8 **13:3** [a]1Sa 6:4, 16 [1]Lit *on the face of* **13:4** [a]Jos 12:18; 19:30; 1Sa 4:1; 1Ki 20:26, 30 [b]Eze 16:3; Am 2:10 [1]Or *from the Teman* **13:5** [a]1Ki 5:18 [b]Jos 12:7 [1]Or *the entrance of Hamath* **13:6** [a]Jos 11:8 [b]Nu 33:54 **13:8** [a]Jos 12:1-6 [1]Lit *it, the* **13:11** [a]Ge 37:25; Nu 32:29; Jos 13:25; 17:5f [1]Or *border* **13:12** [a]Dt 3:11 [b]Nu 21:24

or the Maacathites; so Geshur and
Maacath live among Israel until this
day. **14** [a]Only to the tribe of Levi he
did not give an inheritance; the
offerings by fire to Yahweh, the God
of Israel, are [1]their inheritance, as
He spoke to him.

**15** So Moses gave *an inheritance* to
the tribe of the sons of Reuben ac-
cording to their families. **16** And their
[1]territory was [a]from Aroer, which
is on the edge of the valley of the
Arnon, with the city which is in the
middle of the valley and all the plain
by Medeba; **17** Heshbon, and all its
cities which are on the plain: Dibon
and Bamoth-baal and Beth-baal-
meon, **18** and [a]Jahaz and Kedemoth
and Mephaath, **19** and [a]Kiriathaim
and Sibmah and Zereth-shahar on
the hill of the valley, **20** and Beth-
peor and the slopes of Pisgah and
Beth-jeshimoth, **21** even all the cities
of the plain and all the kingdom of
Sihon king of the Amorites who
reigned in Heshbon, whom Moses
struck with the leaders of Midian,
[a]Evi and Rekem and Zur and Hur
and Reba, the princes of Sihon, who
lived in the land. **22** The sons of Israel
also killed [a]Balaam the son of Beor,
the diviner, with the sword among
*the rest of* their slain. **23** And the
border of the sons of Reuben was
the [1]Jordan. This was the inheritance
of the sons of Reuben according to
their families, the cities and their
villages.

**24** Moses also gave *an inheritance*
to the tribe of Gad, to the sons of
Gad, according to their families.
**25** And their territory was [a]Jazer,
and all the cities of Gilead, and half
the land of the sons of Ammon, as
far as Aroer which is before Rab-
bah; **26** and from Heshbon as far as
Ramath-mizpeh and Betonim, and
from Mahanaim as far as the bor-
der of [1]Debir; **27** and in the valley,
Beth-haram and Beth-nimrah and
Succoth and Zaphon, the rest of
the kingdom of Sihon king of Hesh-
bon, with the Jordan [1]as a border, as
far as the *lower* end of the Sea of
[a,2]Chinnereth beyond the Jordan to
the east. **28** This is the inheritance
of the sons of Gad according to
their families, the cities and their
villages.

**29** Moses also gave *an inheritance*
to the half-tribe of Manasseh; and
it was for the half-tribe of the sons
of Manasseh according to their
families. **30** And their territory was
from Mahanaim, all Bashan, all the
kingdom of Og king of Bashan, and
all of [a,1]Havvoth-jair, which are in
Bashan, sixty cities; **31** also half of
Gilead, with [a]Ashtaroth and Edrei,
the cities of the kingdom of Og in
Bashan, *were* for the sons of Machir
the son of Manasseh, for half of the
sons of Machir according to their
families.

**32** These are *the territories* which
Moses apportioned for an inheritance
in the plains of Moab, beyond the
Jordan at Jericho to the east. **33** But
[a]to the tribe of Levi, Moses did not
give an inheritance; Yahweh, the God
of Israel, is their inheritance, as He
had [1]promised to them.

---

**13:14** [a]Dt 18:1, 2 [1]Lit *his* **13:16** [a]Jos 13:9 [1]Or *border* **13:18** [a]Nu 21:23; Jdg 11:20; Is 15:4; Jer 48:34
**13:19** [a]Nu 32:37; Jer 48:1, 23; Eze 25:9 **13:21** [a]Nu 31:8 **13:22** [a]Nu 31:8 **13:23** [1]Lit *Jordan and border*
**13:25** [a]Nu 21:32; Jos 21:39; 2Sa 24:5; 1Chr 6:81; 26:31; Is 16:8f; Jer 48:32 **13:26** [1]Or *Lidebir*
**13:27** [a]Nu 34:11; Dt 3:17 [1]Lit *and border* [2]Galilee **13:30** [a]Nu 32:41 [1]Or *the towns of Jair*
**13:31** [a]Jos 9:10; 12:4; 13:12; Jdg 10:6; 1Sa 7:3f; 12:10; 1Chr 6:71 **13:33** [a]Dt 18:1f; Jos 13:14 [1]Lit *spoken to*

### *The Inheritance Beyond the Jordan*

**14** Now these are *the territories*
which the sons of Israel inher-
ited in the land of Canaan, which
[a]Eleazar the priest and Joshua the
son of Nun and the heads of the
[1]households of the tribes of the sons
of Israel apportioned to them for an
inheritance, **2** by the [a]lot of their in-
heritance, as Yahweh commanded by
the hand of Moses, for the nine tribes
and the half-tribe. **3** For [a]Moses had
given the inheritance of the two tribes
and the half-tribe beyond the Jordan;
but [b]he did not give an inheritance to
the Levites among them. **4** For the sons
of Joseph were two tribes, [a]Manasseh
and Ephraim, and they did not give
a portion to the Levites in the land,
except cities to live in, with their pas-
ture lands for their livestock and for
their property. **5** Thus the sons of Israel
did just [a]as Yahweh had commanded
Moses, and they divided the land.

### *Caleb's Inheritance*

**6** Then the sons of Judah drew near
to Joshua in Gilgal, and [a]Caleb the
son of Jephunneh the Kenizzite said
to him, "You know the word which
Yahweh spoke to Moses the man
of God concerning [1]you and me in
Kadesh-barnea. **7** I was forty years
old when [a]Moses the servant of Yah-
weh sent me from Kadesh-barnea
to spy out the land, and I brought
word back to him as *it was* in my
heart. **8** Nevertheless, my brothers
who went up with me made the heart
*of the people* [1]melt *with fear*; but [a]I
followed Yahweh my God fully. **9** So
Moses swore on that day, saying,
'Surely [a]the land on which your foot
has trodden will be an inheritance
to you and to your children forever
because you have followed Yahweh
my God fully.' **10** So now behold,
Yahweh has let me live, just as He
spoke, these forty-five years, from
the time that Yahweh spoke this
word to Moses, when Israel walked
in the wilderness; so now behold, I
am eighty-five years old today. **11** [a]I
am still as strong today as I was
in the day Moses sent me; as my
strength was then, so my strength is
now, for war and for [b]going out and
coming in. **12** So now, give me this hill
country about which Yahweh spoke
on that day, for you heard on that
day that [a]Anakim *were* there, with
great fortified cities; perhaps Yahweh
will be with me, and I will dispossess
them as Yahweh has spoken."
**13** So Joshua [a]blessed him and
[b]gave Hebron to Caleb the son
of Jephunneh for an inheritance.
**14** Therefore, Hebron became the
inheritance of Caleb the son of Je-
phunneh the Kenizzite until this day
because he fully followed Yahweh,
the God of Israel. **15** Now the name of
Hebron was formerly [1]Kiriath-arba;
*for Arba* was the greatest man among
the Anakim. [a]Then the land was qui-
et from war.

### *Judah's Inheritance*

**15** Now [a]the lot for the tribe of
the sons of Judah according to
their families [1]reached the [b]border of
Edom, southward to the [c]wilderness

---

◆ **14:1** [a]Nu 34:16-29 [1]Lit *fathers* **14:2** [a]Nu 26:55; 33:54; 34:13 **14:3** [a]Nu 32:33 [b]Jos 13:14
**14:4** [a]Ge 41:51f; 46:20; 48:1, 5; Nu 26:28; 2Chr 30:1 **14:5** [a]Nu 35:1f; Jos 21:2 **14:6** [a]Nu 13:6, 30; 14:6,
24, 30 [1]Lit *me and concerning you* **14:7** [a]Nu 13:1-31 **14:8** [a]Nu 14:24; Dt 1:36 [1]Lit *become demoralized*
**14:9** [a]Dt 1:36 **14:11** [a]Dt 34:7 [b]Dt 31:2 **14:12** [a]Nu 13:33 **14:13** [a]Jos 22:6 [b]Jdg 1:20; 1Chr 6:55f
**14:15** [a]Jos 11:23 [1]Lit *the city of Arba* ◆ **15:1** [a]Nu 34:3, 4 [b]Nu 20:16 [c]Dt 32:51 [1]Lit *was to*

of Zin at the *far* end *toward the*
south. **2** And their south border was
from the *lower* end of the Salt Sea,
from the bay that turns to the south.
**3** Then it went out southward to the
ascent of Akrabbim and passed on
to Zin and went up by the south
of Kadesh-barnea and continued
to Hezron and went up to Addar
and turned about to Karka. **4** And
it [a]passed on to Azmon and went
out to the [b,1]brook of Egypt, and the
[2]border ended at the sea. This shall
be your south border. **5** And the [a]east
border *was* the Salt Sea, as far as
the [1]mouth of the Jordan. And the
[b]border of the north side was from
the bay of the sea at the [1]mouth of
the Jordan. **6** Then the border went
up to Beth-hoglah and passed by on
the north of Beth-arabah; and the
border went up to the stone of Bohan
the son of Reuben. **7** Then the border
went up to Debir from [a]the valley of
Achor and turned northward toward
Gilgal which is opposite the ascent of
Adummim, which is on the south of
the valley; and the border continued
to the waters of En-shemesh and [1]it
ended at En-rogel. **8** Then the border
went up the valley of Ben-hinnom
to the slope of the [a]Jebusite on the
south (that is, Jerusalem); and the
border went up to the top of the
*mountain which is* before the valley
of Hinnom to the west, which is at
the end of the valley of Rephaim
toward the north. **9** From the top of
the mountain the border curved to
the spring of the waters of Nephtoah
and proceeded to the cities of Mount
Ephron; then the border curved to
[a]Baalah (that is, [b]Kiriath-jearim).
**10** Then the border turned about
from Baalah westward to Mount
Seir and continued to the slope of
Mount Jearim on the north (that is,
Chesalon) and went down to Beth-
shemesh and continued through
[a]Timnah. **11** Then the border went
out to the side of Ekron northward.
Then the border curved to Shikkeron
and passed on to Mount Baalah and
went out to Jabneel, and the [1]border
ended at the sea. **12** And the west bor-
der *was* [a]at the Great Sea, even *its*
[1]coastline. This is the border around
the sons of Judah according to their
families.

**13** Now [a]he gave to Caleb the son
of Jephunneh a portion [b]among
the sons of Judah, according to the
[1]command of Yahweh to Joshua,
*namely*, [2]Kiriath-arba, *Arba being*
the father of Anak (that is, Hebron).
**14** [a]And Caleb dispossessed from
there the three [b]sons of Anak:
Sheshai and Ahiman and Talmai,
the children of Anak. **15** Then [a]he
went up from there against the in-
habitants of Debir; now the name of
Debir formerly was Kiriath-sepher.
**16** And Caleb said, "The one who
strikes down Kiriath-sepher and
captures it, [1]I will give him Achsah
my daughter as a wife." **17** [a]And Oth-
niel the son of Kenaz, the brother
of Caleb, captured it; so he gave
him Achsah his daughter as a wife.
**18** [a]Now it happened that when she
came *to him*, she enticed him to ask
her father for a field. So she alighted

**15:4** [a]Nu 34:5 [b]Ge 15:18; 1Ki 8:65 [1]Or *wadi* [2]Lit *goings out of the border were* **15:5** [a]Nu 34:3, 10-12 [b]Jos 18:15-19 [1]Lit *end* **15:7** [a]Jos 7:24 [1]Lit *the goings out of it were* **15:8** [a]Jos 15:63 **15:9** [a]1Chr 13:6 [b]Jdg 18:12 **15:10** [a]Ge 38:13; Jdg 14:1 **15:11** [1]Lit *goings out of the border were* **15:12** [a]Nu 34:6 [1]Lit *border* **15:13** [a]Jos 14:13-15 [b]Nu 13:6 [1]Lit *mouth* [2]Lit *the city of Arba* **15:14** [a]Jos 11:21, 22 [b]Nu 13:33; Dt 9:2 **15:15** [a]Jos 10:38 **15:16** [1]Lit *and I* **15:17** [a]Jdg 1:13; 3:9 **15:18** [a]Jdg 1:14

from the donkey, and Caleb said to
her, “What do you want?” **19** Then
she said, “Give me a blessing; since
you have given me the land of the
[1]Negev, give me also springs of
water.” So he gave her the upper
springs and the lower springs.
**20** This is the inheritance of the
tribe of the sons of Judah according
to their families.
**21** Now the cities at the *far* end
of the tribe of the sons of Judah
toward the border of Edom in the
south were Kabzeel and [a]Eder and
Jagur, **22** and Kinah and Dimonah and
Adadah, **23** and Kedesh and Hazor
and Ithnan, **24** Ziph and Telem and
Bealoth, **25** and Hazor-hadattah
and Kerioth-hezron (that is, Hazor),
**26** Amam and Shema and Moladah,
**27** and Hazar-gaddah and Heshmon
and Beth-pelet, **28** and Hazar-shual
and [a]Beersheba and Biziothiah,
**29** Baalah and Iim and Ezem, **30** and
Eltolad and Chesil and Hormah,
**31** and [a]Ziklag and Madmannah
and Sansannah, **32** and Lebaoth and
Shilhim and Ain and Rimmon; in all,
twenty-nine cities with their villages.
**33** In the [1]Shephelah: [a]Eshtaol and
Zorah and Ashnah, **34** and Zanoah
and En-gannim, Tappuah and Enam,
**35** Jarmuth and [a]Adullam, Socoh and
Azekah, **36** and Shaaraim and Aditha-
im and Gederah and Gederothaim;
fourteen cities with their villages.
**37** Zenan and Hadashah and
Migdal-gad, **38** and Dilean and Miz-
peh and Joktheel, **39** [a]Lachish and
Bozkath and Eglon, **40** and Cabbon
and Lahmas and Chitlish, **41** and
Gederoth, Beth-dagon and Naamah
and Makkedah; sixteen cities with
their villages.
**42** Libnah and Ether and Ashan,
**43** and Iphtah and Ashnah and Nezib,
**44** and Keilah and Achzib and Mare-
shah; nine cities with their villages.
**45** Ekron, with its towns and its vil-
lages; **46** from Ekron even to the sea,
all that were by the [1]side of Ashdod,
with their villages.
**47** Ashdod, its towns and its vil-
lages; Gaza, its towns and its villages;
as far as [a]the [1]brook of Egypt and the
Great Sea, even *its* [2]coastline.
**48** And in the hill country: Shamir
and Jattir and Socoh, **49** and Dannah
and Kiriath-sannah (that is, Debir),
**50** and Anab and Eshtemoh and
Anim, **51** and Goshen and Holon
and Giloh; eleven cities with their
villages.
**52** Arab and Dumah and Eshan,
**53** and Janum and Beth-tappuah
and Aphekah, **54** and Humtah and
Kiriath-arba (that is, Hebron) and
Zior; nine cities with their villages.
**55** Maon, Carmel and Ziph and
Juttah, **56** and Jezreel and Jokdeam
and Zanoah, **57** Kain, Gibeah and
Timnah; ten cities with their villages.
**58** Halhul, Beth-zur and Gedor,
**59** and Maarath and Beth-anoth and
Eltekon; six cities with their villages.
**60** Kiriath-baal (that is, Kiriath-
jearim) and Rabbah; two cities with
their villages.
**61** In the wilderness: Beth-arabah,
Middin and Secacah, **62** and Nibshan
and the City of Salt and Engedi; six
cities with their villages.
**63** Now as for the [a]Jebusites, the
inhabitants of Jerusalem, the sons

---

**15:19** [1]South country **15:21** [a]Ge 35:21 **15:28** [a]Ge 21:31 **15:31** [a]1Sa 27:6; 30:1 **15:33** [a]Jdg 13:25; 16:31 [1]Or *lowland* **15:35** [a]1Sa 22:1 **15:39** [a]Jos 10:3; 2Ki 14:19 **15:46** [1]Lit *hand* **15:47** [a]Jos 15:4 [1]Or *wadi* [2]Lit *border* **15:63** [a]Jdg 1:21; 2Sa 5:6; 1Chr 11:4

of Judah could not dispossess them;
so the Jebusites live with the sons of
Judah at Jerusalem until this day.

### *Ephraim's Inheritance*

16 Then the lot for the sons of Jo-
seph went out from the Jordan
at Jericho to the waters of Jericho
on the east into [a]the wilderness,
going up from Jericho through the
hill country to Bethel. 2 And it went
out from Bethel to Luz and [a]passed
on to the border of the Archites
at Ataroth. 3 Then it went down
westward to the territory of the
Japhletites, as far as the territory of
lower [a]Beth-horon even to [b]Gezer,
and [1]it ended at the sea.
4 So the [a]sons of Joseph, Manasseh
and Ephraim, received their inheri-
tance. 5 Now *this* was the territory
of the sons of Ephraim according
to their families: the border of their
inheritance eastward was [a]Ataroth-
addar, as far as upper Beth-horon.
6 Then the border went westward
at [a]Michmethath on the north, and
the border turned about eastward
to Taanath-shiloh and passed on
*beyond* it to the east of Janoah. 7 And
it went down from Janoah to Ataroth
and to [a]Naarah and reached Jericho
and came out at the Jordan. 8 From
[a]Tappuah the border continued
westward *to the* [1]brook of Kanah,
and [2]it ended at the sea. This is the
inheritance of the tribe of the sons of
Ephraim according to their families,
9 *together* with the cities which were
set apart for the sons of Ephraim in
the midst of the inheritance of the
sons of Manasseh, all the cities with
their villages. 10 [a]But they did not
dispossess the Canaanites who lived
in Gezer, so [b]the Canaanites live in
the midst of Ephraim to this day, and
they became forced laborers.

### *Manasseh's Inheritance*

17 And *this* was the lot for the
tribe of [a]Manasseh, for he was
the firstborn of Joseph. To Machir
the firstborn of Manasseh, the father
of Gilead, [1]were allotted Gilead and
Bashan, because he was a man of
war. 2 So *the lot* was *made* for the rest
of the sons of Manasseh according to
their families: for the sons of Abiezer
and for the sons of Helek and for the
sons of Asriel and for the sons of
Shechem and for the sons of Hepher
and for the sons of Shemida; these
*were* the sons of Manasseh the son of
Joseph, the males according to their
families.
3 However, [a]Zelophehad, the son
of Hepher, the son of Gilead, the son
of Machir, the son of Manasseh, had
no sons, only daughters; and these
are the names of his daughters:
Mahlah and Noah, Hoglah, Milcah
and Tirzah. 4 And they came near
before Eleazar the priest and before
Joshua the son of Nun and before the
leaders, saying, "Yahweh command-
ed Moses to give us an inheritance
among our brothers." So [a]according
to the [1]word of Yahweh he gave
them an inheritance among their
father's brothers. 5 Thus there fell
ten portions to Manasseh, besides
the land of Gilead and Bashan, which

◆ **16:1** [a]Jos 8:15; 18:12 **16:2** [a]Jos 18:13 **16:3** [a]Jos 18:13; 1Ki 9:17 [b]Jos 10:33 [1]Lit *the goings out of it were* **16:4** [a]Jos 17:14 **16:5** [a]Jos 18:13 **16:6** [a]Jos 17:7 **16:7** [a]1Chr 7:28 **16:8** [a]Jos 17:8 [1]Or *wadi* [2]Lit *the goings out of it were* **16:10** [a]Jdg 1:29; 1Ki 9:16 [b]Jos 17:12, 13 ◆ **17:1** [a]Ge 41:51; 46:20; 48:17f [1]Lit *and there was to him* **17:3** [a]Nu 26:33; 27:1-7 **17:4** [a]Nu 27:5-7 [1]Lit *mouth*

is beyond the Jordan, **6** because the
daughters of Manasseh received an
inheritance among his sons. And the
[a]land of Gilead belonged to the rest
of the sons of Manasseh.

**7** And the border of Manasseh [1]ran
from Asher to Michmethath which
was east of Shechem; then the border
went [2]southward to the inhabitants
of En-tappuah. **8** The land of Tappuah
belonged to Manasseh, but [a]Tappuah
on the border of Manasseh *belonged*
to the sons of Ephraim. **9** And the
[a]border went down to the [1]brook
of Kanah, southward of the [1]brook
(these cities *belonged* to Ephraim
among the cities of Manasseh), and
the border of Manasseh *was* on the
north side of the [1]brook, and [2]it
ended at the sea. **10** The south side
*belonged* to Ephraim and the north
side to Manasseh, and the sea was
[1]their border; and they reached to
Asher on the north and to Issachar
on the east. **11** And in Issachar and in
Asher, [a]Manasseh had Beth-shean
and its towns, and Ibleam and its
towns, and the inhabitants of Dor
and its towns, and the inhabitants of
En-dor and its towns, and the inhab-
itants of Taanach and its towns, and
the inhabitants of Megiddo and its
towns, the third is [b]Napheth. **12** [a]But
the sons of Manasseh could not take
possession of these cities because the
Canaanites persisted in living in that
land. **13** Now it happened that when
the sons of Israel became strong,
[a]they put the Canaanites to forced
labor, but they did not dispossess
them completely.

**14** Then the [a]sons of Joseph spoke
to Joshua, saying, "Why have you
given me only one lot and one por-
tion for an inheritance, since I am
a numerous people whom Yahweh
has thus far blessed?" **15** And Joshua
said to them, "If you are a numerous
people, go [1]up to the forest and [2]clear
a place for yourself there in the land
of the Perizzites and of the Rephaim,
since the hill country of Ephraim is
too narrow for you." **16** And the sons
of Joseph said, "The hill country is
not enough for us, and all the Ca-
naanites who live in the valley land
have [a]chariots of iron, both those
who are in Beth-shean and its towns
and those who are in the valley of
Jezreel." **17** Then Joshua spoke to the
house of Joseph, to Ephraim and
Manasseh, saying, "You are a nu-
merous people and have great power;
you shall not have one lot *only*, **18** but
the hill country shall be yours. For
though it is a forest, you shall [1]clear
it, and to its [2]farthest borders it shall
be yours; for you shall dispossess the
Canaanites, even though they have
[a]chariots of iron *and* even though
they are strong."

### *The Remaining Land Divided*

**18** Then the whole congregation
of the sons of Israel assembled
themselves at [a]Shiloh and set up the
tent of meeting there; and the land
was subdued before them.

**2** And there remained among the
sons of Israel seven tribes who had
not divided their inheritance. **3** So
Joshua said to the sons of Israel,

---

**17:6** [a]Jos 13:30, 31 **17:7** [1]Lit *was* [2]Lit *to the right hand* **17:8** [a]Jos 16:8 **17:9** [a]Jos 16:8f [1]Or *wadi* [2]Lit *the goings out of it were* **17:10** [1]Lit *its* **17:11** [a]1Chr 7:29 [b]Jos 11:2; 12:23 **17:12** [a]Jdg 1:27 **17:13** [a]Jos 16:10 **17:14** [a]Nu 13:7 **17:15** [1]Lit *up for yourself* [2]Lit *cut down* **17:16** [a]Jos 17:18; Jdg 1:19; 4:3, 13 **17:18** [a]Jos 17:16 [1]Lit *cut it down* [2]Lit *goings out* ◆ **18:1** [a]Jdg 21:19; Jer 7:12; 26:6, 9

"[a]How long will you put off entering
to take possession of the land which
Yahweh, the God of your fathers, has
given you? **4** Provide for yourselves
three men from [1]each tribe that I may
send them, and that they may arise
and walk through the land and write
*a description of* it according to their
inheritance; then they shall [2]return
to me. **5** And they shall divide it into
seven portions; [a]Judah shall stay in its
territory on the south, and the house
of Joseph shall stay in their territory
on the north. **6** So you shall write *a*
*description of* the land in seven divi-
sions and bring *the description* here
to me. [a]I will cast lots for you here
before Yahweh our God. **7** For [a]the
Levites have no portion among you
because the priesthood of Yahweh is
[1]their inheritance. Gad and Reuben
and the half-tribe of Manasseh also
have received their inheritance east-
ward beyond the Jordan, which Moses
the servant of Yahweh gave them."
**8** Then the men arose and went,
and Joshua commanded those who
went to write *the description of* the
land, saying, "Go and walk through
the land and write *a description of*
it, and return to me; then I will cast
lots for you here before Yahweh in
[a]Shiloh." **9** So the men went and
passed through the land and wrote
*a description of* it by cities in seven
divisions in a book; and they came to
Joshua to the camp at Shiloh. **10** And
[a]Joshua cast lots for them in Shiloh
before Yahweh, and there Joshua
divided the land to the sons of Israel
according to their divisions.

### *Benjamin's Inheritance*

**11** Now the lot of the tribe of the
sons of Benjamin came up according
to their families, and the territory
of their lot [1]lay between the sons
of Judah and the sons of Joseph.
**12** [a]And their border on the north
side was from the Jordan; then
the border went up to the side of
Jericho on the north and went up
through the hill country westward,
and [1]it ended at the wilderness of
Beth-aven. **13** From there the border
passed on to [a]Luz, to the side of Luz
(that is, Bethel) southward; and the
border went down to Ataroth-addar,
near the hill which *lies* on the south
of [b]lower Beth-horon. **14** Then the
border curved *from there* and turned
round on the west side southward,
from the hill which *lies* before Beth-
horon southward; and [1]it ended at
Kiriath-baal (that is, Kiriath-jearim),
a city of the sons of Judah. This *was*
the west side. **15** Then the [a]south side
*was* from the edge of Kiriath-jearim,
and the border went out westward
and went out to the fountain of
the waters of Nephtoah. **16** Then
the border went down to the edge
of the hill which is in the [a]valley of
Ben-hinnom, which is in the valley
of Rephaim northward; and it went
down to the valley of Hinnom, to
the slope of the Jebusite southward,
and went down to En-rogel. **17** Then
it curved northward and went out to
En-shemesh and went out to Geli-
loth, which is opposite the ascent of
Adummim, and it went down to the
[a]stone of Bohan the son of Reuben.

**18:3** [a]Jdg 18:9 **18:4** [1]Lit *the* [2]Lit *come* **18:5** [a]Jos 15:1 **18:6** [a]Jos 14:2 **18:7** [a]Nu 18:7, 20; Jos 13:33 [1]Lit *his* **18:8** [a]Jos 18:1 **18:10** [a]Nu 34:16-29; Jos 19:51 **18:11** [1]Lit *went out* **18:12** [a]Jos 16:1 [1]Lit *the goings out of it were* **18:13** [a]Ge 28:19; Jdg 1:23 [b]Jos 16:3 **18:14** [1]Lit *the goings out of it were* **18:15** [a]Jos 15:5-9 **18:16** [a]2Ki 23:10 **18:17** [a]Jos 15:6

**18** Then it continued to the side in
front of the Arabah northward and
went down to the Arabah. **19** And the
border passed on to the side of Beth-
hoglah northward; and the [1]border
ended at the north bay of the Salt Sea,
at the south end of the Jordan. This
*was* the south border. **20** Moreover,
the Jordan was its border on the east
side. This *was* the inheritance of the
sons of Benjamin, according to their
families *and* according to its borders
all around.

**21** Now the cities of the tribe of
the sons of Benjamin according to
their families were Jericho and Beth-
hoglah and Emek-keziz, **22** and Beth-
arabah and Zemaraim and Bethel,
**23** and Avvim and Parah and Ophrah,
**24** and Chephar-ammoni and Ophni
and [a]Geba; twelve cities with their
villages. **25** Gibeon and Ramah and
Beeroth, **26** and Mizpeh and Che-
phirah and Mozah, **27** and Rekem and
Irpeel and Taralah, **28** and [a]Zelah,
Haeleph and the Jebusite (that is,
Jerusalem), Gibeah, Kiriath; fourteen
cities with their villages. This is the
inheritance of the [b]sons of Benjamin
according to their families.

### *Simeon's Inheritance*

**19** Then the second lot came out
for Simeon, for the tribe of the
sons of Simeon according to their
families, and their inheritance was
in the midst of the inheritance of the
sons of Judah. **2** So they had as their
inheritance Beersheba or [1]Sheba
and Moladah, **3** and Hazar-shual and
Balah and Ezem, **4** and Eltolad and
Bethul and Hormah, **5** and Ziklag
and Beth-marcaboth and Hazar-susah,
**6** and Beth-lebaoth and Sharuhen;
thirteen cities with their villages; **7** Ain,
Rimmon and Ether and Ashan; four
cities with their villages; **8** and all the
villages which *were* around these cities
as far as Baalath-beer, Ramah of the
[1]Negev. This *was* the inheritance of
the tribe of the sons of Simeon accord-
ing to their families. **9** The inheritance
of the sons of Simeon *was taken* from
the portion of the sons of Judah, for
the share of the sons of Judah was too
large for them; so the sons of Simeon
received *an* inheritance in the midst
of [1]Judah's inheritance.

### *Zebulun's Inheritance*

**10** Now the third lot came up for
the sons of Zebulun according to
their families. And the territory
of their inheritance was as far as
Sarid. **11** Then their border went up
to the west and to Maralah; it then
reached Dabbesheth and reached
the [1]brook that is before Jokneam.
**12** Then it turned from Sarid to the
east toward the sunrise as far as
the border of Chisloth-tabor, and
it went out to Daberath and [1]up to
Japhia. **13** From there it passed on to
the east toward the sunrise to Gath-
hepher, to Eth-kazin, and it went out
to Rimmon [1]which curves to Neah.
**14** And the border circled around
it on the north to Hannathon, and
[1]it ended at the valley of Iphtahel.
**15** *Included* also *were* Kattah and
Nahalal and Shimron and Idalah and
Bethlehem; twelve cities with their
villages. **16** This *was* the inheritance
of the sons of Zebulun according to

---

**18:19** [1]Lit *goings out of the border were* **18:24** [a]Ezr 2:26; Is 10:29 **18:28** [a]2Sa 21:14 [b]Nu 26:38
◆ **19:2** [1]In Jos 15:26, *Shema* **19:8** [1]South country **19:9** [1]Lit *their* **19:11** [1]Or *wadi* **19:12** [1]Lit *went up* **19:13** [1]Or *and is marked off* **19:14** [1]Lit *the goings out of it were*

their families, these cities with their
villages.

### *Issachar's Inheritance*

**17** The fourth lot came out for Issachar,
for the sons of Issachar according to
their families. **18** And their territory
*included* Jezreel and Chesulloth and
[a]Shunem, **19** and Hapharaim and
Shion and Anaharath, **20** and Rabbith
and Kishion and Ebez, **21** and Remeth
and En-gannim and En-haddah and
Beth-pazzez. **22** And the border
reached to [a]Tabor and Shahazumah
and Beth-shemesh, and [1]their border
ended at the Jordan; sixteen cities
with their villages. **23** This *was* the
inheritance of the tribe of the sons of
Issachar according to their families,
the cities with their villages.

### *Asher's Inheritance*

**24** Now the fifth lot came out for the
tribe of the sons of Asher according
to their families. **25** And their terri-
tory was Helkath and Hali and Beten
and Achshaph, **26** and Allammelech
and Amad and Mishal; and it reached
to Carmel on the west and to Shihor-
libnath. **27** Then it turned *east* toward
the sunrise to Beth-dagon and
reached to Zebulun and to the valley
of Iphtahel northward to Beth-emek
and Neiel; then it went out [1]to the
north to [a]Cabul, **28** and Ebron and
Rehob and Hammon and Kanah,
as far as Great [a]Sidon. **29** Then the
border turned to Ramah and to the
fortified city of Tyre; then the bor-
der turned to Hosah, and [1]it ended
at the sea by the region of [a]Achzib.
**30** *Included* also *were* Ummah and
Aphek and Rehob; twenty-two cities
with their villages. **31** This *was* the
inheritance of the tribe of the sons
of Asher according to their families,
these cities with their villages.

### *Naphtali's Inheritance*

**32** The sixth lot came out for the sons
of Naphtali, for the sons of Naphtali
according to their families. **33** And their
border was from Heleph, from the oak
in Zaanannim and Adami-nekeb and
Jabneel, as far as Lakkum, and [1]it end-
ed at the Jordan. **34** Then the border
turned westward to Aznoth-tabor and
went out from there to Hukkok; and
it reached to Zebulun on the south
and reached to Asher on the west
and to Judah at the Jordan *to the east*
toward the sunrise. **35** Now the
fortified cities *were* Ziddim, Zer and
[a]Hammath, Rakkath and [b]Chinnereth,
**36** and Adamah and Ramah and Hazor,
**37** and Kedesh and Edrei and En-hazor,
**38** and Yiron and Migdal-el, Horem
and Beth-anath and Beth-shemesh;
nineteen cities with their villages.
**39** This *was* the inheritance of the
tribe of the sons of Naphtali according
to their families, the cities with their
villages.

### *Dan's Inheritance*

**40** The seventh lot came out for the
tribe of the sons of Dan according to
their families. **41** And the territory
of their inheritance was Zorah and
Eshtaol and Ir-shemesh, **42** and
Shaalabbin and Aijalon and Ithlah,
**43** and Elon and Timnah and Ekron,
**44** and Eltekeh and Gibbethon and
Baalath, **45** and Jehud and Bene-berak

---

**19:18** [a]1Sa 28:4; 2Ki 4:8 **19:22** [a]Jdg 4:6; Ps 89:12 [1]Lit *the goings out of their border were*
**19:27** [a]1Ki 9:13 [1]Lit *from the left hand* **19:28** [a]Ge 10:19; Jdg 1:31; Ac 27:3 **19:29** [a]Jdg 1:31 [1]Lit *the goings out of it were* **19:33** [1]Lit *the goings out of it were* **19:35** [a]Ge 10:18; 1Ki 8:65 [b]Dt 3:17

and Gath-rimmon, **46** and Me-jarkon and Rakkon, with the territory over against [1]Joppa. **47** And the territory of the [a]sons of Dan went out from them; for the sons of Dan went up and fought with Leshem and captured it. Then they struck it with the edge of the sword and possessed it and [1]settled in it; and they called [b,2]Leshem Dan after the name of Dan their father. **48** This *was* the inheritance of the tribe of the sons of Dan according to their families, these cities with their villages.

**49** So they finished *apportioning* the land for inheritance by its borders. Then the sons of Israel gave an inheritance in their midst to Joshua the son of Nun. **50** In accordance with the [1]command of Yahweh they gave him the city for which he asked, [a]Timnath-serah in the hill country of Ephraim. So he built the city and [2]settled in it.

**51** [a]These are the inheritances which Eleazar the priest and Joshua the son of Nun and the heads of the [1]households of the tribes of the sons of Israel distributed by lot in Shiloh before Yahweh at the doorway of the tent of meeting. So they finished dividing the land.

### *The Cities of Refuge*

**20** Then Yahweh spoke to Joshua, saying, **2** "Speak to the sons of Israel, saying, '[1]Designate [a]the cities of refuge, of which I spoke to you by the hand of Moses, **3** that the manslayer who strikes down any person unintentionally, without premeditation, may flee there, and they shall become for you as a refuge from the avenger of blood. **4** And he shall flee to one of these cities and shall stand at the entrance of the [a]gate of the city and speak his case in the hearing of the elders of that city; and they shall [1]take him into the city to them and give him a place, so that he may live among them. **5** Now [a]if the avenger of blood pursues him, then they shall not surrender the manslayer into his hand because he struck his neighbor without premeditation and did not hate him beforehand. **6** And he shall live in that city [a]until he stands before the congregation for judgment, until the death of the one who is high priest in those days. Then the manslayer shall return and come to his own city and to his own house, to the city from which he fled.'"

**7** So they [1]set apart [a]Kedesh in [2]Galilee in the hill country of Naphtali and Shechem in the hill country of Ephraim and Kiriath-arba (that is, Hebron) in [b]the hill country of Judah. **8** Now beyond the Jordan east of Jericho, they [1]designated Bezer in the wilderness on the plain from the tribe of Reuben and Ramoth in Gilead from the tribe of Gad and Golan in Bashan from the tribe of Manasseh. **9** [a]These were the appointed cities for all the sons of Israel and for the sojourner who sojourns among them, that whoever strikes down any person unintentionally may flee there and

**19:46** [1]Heb *Japho* **19:47** [a]Jdg 18:1 [b]Jdg 18:29 [1]Lit *dwelt* [2]Laish **19:50** [a]Nu 13:8; Jos 24:30 [1]Lit *mouth* [2]Lit *dwelt* **19:51** [a]Jos 18:10 [1]Lit *fathers* ◆ **20:2** [a]Nu 35:6-34; Dt 4:41-43; 19:2ff [1]Lit *Set for yourselves* **20:4** [a]Ru 4:1; Job 5:4; Jer 38:7 [1]Lit *gather* **20:5** [a]Nu 35:12 **20:6** [a]Nu 35:12 **20:7** [a]Jos 21:32; 1Chr 6:76 [b]Jos 21:11; Lk 1:39 [1]Lit *sanctified* [2]Heb *Galil* **20:8** [1]Lit *set* **20:9** [a]Nu 35:13ff

not die by the hand of the avenger of blood until he stands before the congregation.

### *The Cities of the Levites*

**21** Then the heads of [1]households of [a]the Levites came near to Eleazar the priest and to Joshua the son of Nun and to the heads of [1]households of the tribes of the sons of Israel. **2** And they spoke to them at Shiloh in the land of Canaan, saying, "[a]Yahweh commanded by the hand of Moses to give us cities to live in, with their pasture lands for our cattle." **3** So the sons of Israel gave the Levites from their inheritance these cities with their pasture lands, according to the [1]command of Yahweh. **4** Then the lot came out for the families of the Kohathites. And the sons of Aaron the priest, who were of the Levites, [1]received thirteen cities by lot from the tribe of Judah and from the tribe of the Simeonites and from the tribe of Benjamin.

**5** Now the rest of the sons of Kohath [1]received ten cities by lot from the families of the tribe of Ephraim and from the tribe of Dan and from the half-tribe of Manasseh.

**6** And the sons of Gershon [1]received thirteen cities by lot from the families of the tribe of Issachar and from the tribe of Asher and from the tribe of Naphtali, and from the half-tribe of Manasseh in Bashan.

**7** The sons of Merari according to their families [1]received twelve cities from the tribe of Reuben and from the tribe of Gad and from the tribe of Zebulun.

**8** So the [a]sons of Israel gave by lot to the Levites these cities with their pasture lands, as Yahweh had commanded by the hand of Moses.

**9** They also gave from the tribe of the sons of Judah and from the tribe of the sons of Simeon these cities which are *here* mentioned by name; **10** and they were for the sons of Aaron, one of the families of the Kohathites, of the sons of Levi, for the lot was theirs first. **11** So [a]they gave them Kiriath-arba (*Arba being* the [b]father of Anak), that is, Hebron, in the hill country of Judah, with its pasture lands all around it. **12** But the fields of the city and its villages they gave to Caleb the son of Jephunneh as his possession.

**13** Thus [a]to the sons of Aaron the priest they gave [b]Hebron, the city of refuge for the manslayer, with its pasture lands, [c]Libnah also with its pasture lands, **14** [a]Jattir with its pasture lands, [b]Eshtemoa with its pasture lands, **15** [1]Holon with its pasture lands, and [a]Debir with its pasture lands, **16** and [1]Ain with its pasture lands, and [a]Juttah with its pasture lands, *and* [b]Beth-shemesh with its pasture lands; nine cities from these two tribes. **17** From the tribe of Benjamin, [a]Gibeon with its pasture lands, [b]Geba with its pasture lands, **18** Anathoth with its pasture lands and [1]Almon with its pasture lands; four cities. **19** All the cities of the sons of Aaron, the priests, were thirteen cities with their pasture lands.

◆ **21:1** [a]Nu 35:1-8 [1]Lit *fathers* **21:2** [a]Nu 35:2 **21:3** [1]Lit *mouth* **21:4** [1]Lit *had* **21:5** [1]Lit *had* **21:6** [1]Lit *had* **21:7** [1]Lit *had* **21:8** [a]Ge 49:5ff **21:11** [a]1Chr 6:55 [b]Jos 14:15; 15:13 **21:13** [a]1Chr 6:57 [b]Jos 15:54 [c]Jos 15:42 **21:14** [a]Jos 15:48 [b]Jos 15:50 **21:15** [a]Jos 15:49 [1]In 1Chr 6:58, *Hilen* **21:16** [a]Jos 15:55 [b]Jos 15:10 [1]In 1Chr 6:59, *Ashan* **21:17** [a]Jos 18:25 [b]Jos 18:24 **21:18** [1]In 1Chr 6:60, *Allemeth*

20 Then the cities from the tribe
of Ephraim were allotted to the
[a]families of the sons of Kohath, the
Levites, *even to* the rest of the sons
of Kohath. 21 And they gave them
[a]Shechem, the city of refuge for the
manslayer, with its pasture lands,
in the hill country of Ephraim, and
Gezer with its pasture lands, 22 and
Kibzaim with its pasture lands,
and Beth-horon with its pasture
lands; four cities. 23 From the tribe
of Dan, Elteke with its pasture lands,
Gibbethon with its pasture lands,
24 Aijalon with its pasture lands, and
Gath-rimmon with its pasture lands;
four cities. 25 From the half-tribe of
Manasseh, *they gave* Taanach with
its pasture lands and Gath-rimmon
with its pasture lands; two cities.
26 All the cities with their pasture
lands for the families of the rest of
the sons of Kohath were ten.

27 [a]Now to the sons of Gershon,
one of the families of the Levites,
from the half-tribe of Manasseh,
*they gave* Golan in Bashan, the city of
refuge for the manslayer, with its pas-
ture lands, and Be-eshterah with its
pasture lands; two cities. 28 From the
tribe of Issachar, *they gave* Kishion
with its pasture lands, Daberath with
its pasture lands, 29 Jarmuth with its
pasture lands, En-gannim with its
pasture lands; four cities. 30 From
the tribe of Asher, *they gave* Mishal
with its pasture lands, Abdon with
its pasture lands, 31 Helkath with
its pasture lands and Rehob with its
pasture lands; four cities. 32 From the
tribe of Naphtali, *they gave* [a]Kedesh
in Galilee, the city of refuge for the
manslayer, with its pasture lands
and Hammoth-dor with its pasture
lands and Kartan with its pasture
lands; three cities. 33 All the cities of
the Gershonites according to their
families were thirteen cities with
their pasture lands.

34 Now to the families of [a]the sons
of Merari, the rest of the Levites, *they
gave* from the tribe of Zebulun, Jok-
neam with its pasture lands *and* Kar-
tah with its pasture lands. 35 Dimnah
with its pasture lands, Nahalal with
its pasture lands; four cities. 36 From
the tribe of Reuben, *they gave* [a]Bezer
with its pasture lands and Jahaz with
its pasture lands, 37 Kedemoth with its
pasture lands and Mephaath with
its pasture lands; four cities. 38 From
the tribe of Gad, *they gave* [a]Ramoth
in Gilead, the city of refuge for the
manslayer, with its pasture lands and
[b]Mahanaim with its pasture lands,
39 Heshbon with its pasture lands,
Jazer with its pasture lands; four cities
in all. 40 All *these were* the cities of
the sons of Merari according to their
families, the rest of the families of
the Levites; and their lot was twelve
cities.

41 [a]All the cities of the Levites in
the midst of the possession of the
sons of Israel were forty-eight cities
with their pasture lands. 42 These
cities each had its surrounding pas-
ture lands; thus *it was* with all these
cities.

43 [a]So Yahweh gave Israel all the
land which He had sworn to give to
their fathers, and [b]they possessed it
and lived in it. 44 And Yahweh [a]gave
them rest on every side, according

**21:20** [a]1Chr 6:66 **21:21** [a]Jos 20:7 **21:27** [a]1Chr 6:71 **21:32** [a]Jos 20:7 **21:34** [a]1Chr 6:77
**21:36** [a]Dt 4:43; Jos 20:8 **21:38** [a]Dt 4:43; 1Ki 4:13 [b]Ge 32:2; 2Sa 2:8 **21:41** [a]Nu 35:7 **21:43** [a]Dt 34:4
[b]Nu 33:53; Dt 11:31; 17:14 **21:44** [a]Jos 1:13; 23:1

to all that He had sworn to their
fathers, and [b]no one of all their en-
emies stood before them; [c]Yahweh
gave all their enemies into their
hand. **45** [a]Not [1]*one* promise of the
good promises which Yahweh had
[2]promised to the house of Israel
failed; all came to pass.

### *Reuben, Gad, and Manasseh*

**22** [a]Then Joshua summoned the
Reubenites and the Gadites
and the half-tribe of Manasseh,
**2** and said to them, "You have kept
all that Moses the servant of Yahweh
commanded you [a]and have listened
to my voice in all that I commanded
you. **3** You have not forsaken your
brothers these many days to this day,
but have kept the responsibility of
the commandment of Yahweh your
God. **4** And now [a]Yahweh your God
has given rest to your brothers, as He
spoke to them; so now turn and go to
your tents, to the land of your pos-
session, which Moses the servant of
Yahweh gave you beyond the Jordan.
**5** Only keep yourselves very carefully
to do the commandment and the law
which Moses the servant of Yahweh
commanded you, to [a]love Yahweh
your God and walk in all His ways
and keep His commandments and
cling to Him and serve Him [b]with
all your heart and with all your
soul." **6** Then Joshua [a]blessed them
and sent them away, and they went
to their tents.

**7** Now [a]to the one half-tribe of
Manasseh Moses had given *a posses-
sion* in Bashan, but [b]to the other half
Joshua gave *a possession* among their
brothers westward beyond the Jor-
dan. So when Joshua sent them away
to their tents, he blessed them, **8** and
spoke to them, saying, "Return to
your tents with great riches and with
very much livestock, with silver, gold,
bronze, iron, and with very many
clothes; [a]divide the spoil of your
enemies with your brothers." **9** Then
the sons of Reuben and the sons of
Gad and the half-tribe of Manasseh
returned *home* and departed from the
sons of Israel at Shiloh which is in the
land of Canaan, to go to the [a]land of
Gilead, to the land of their possession
which they had possessed, according
to the [1]command of Yahweh by the
hand of Moses.

### *An Altar Called Witness*

**10** And they came to the region of the
Jordan which is in the land of Canaan,
and the sons of Reuben and the sons
of Gad and the half-tribe of Manasseh
built an altar there by the Jordan, a
large altar in appearance. **11** And the
sons of Israel heard *it* [1]said, "Behold,
the sons of Reuben and the sons of
Gad and the half-tribe of Manasseh
have [a]built an altar at the [2]entrance
of the land of Canaan, in the region
of the Jordan, on the side *belonging to*
the sons of Israel." **12** Then the sons
of Israel heard *of it*, and the whole
congregation of the sons of Israel
assembled themselves at [a]Shiloh to
go up against them in war.

**13** Then the sons of Israel sent to
the sons of Reuben and to the sons of
Gad and to the half-tribe of Manasseh,

**21:44** [b]Dt 7:24 [c]Ex 23:31 **21:45** [a]Jos 23:14; 1Ki 8:56 [1]Lit *a word from every good word* [2]Lit *spoken*
◆ **22:1** [a]Nu 32:20-22 **22:2** [a]Jos 1:12-18 **22:4** [a]Nu 32:18; Dt 3:20 **22:5** [a]Dt 5:10 [b]Dt 4:29
**22:6** [a]Ge 47:7; Jos 14:13; 2Sa 6:18; Lk 24:50 **22:7** [a]Nu 32:33 [b]Jos 17:1-13 **22:8** [a]Nu 31:27; 1Sa 30:16
**22:9** [a]Nu 32:1, 26, 29 [1]Lit *mouth* **22:11** [a]Dt 12:5; Jos 22:19 [1]Lit *saying* [2]Lit *front* **22:12** [a]Jos 18:1

into the land of Gilead, [a]Phinehas
the son of Eleazar the priest, **14** and
with him ten leaders, one leader for
each father's household from each
of the tribes of Israel; and [a]each one
of them *was* the head of his father's
household among the [1]thousands of
Israel. **15** So they came to the sons of
Reuben and to the sons of Gad and
to the half-tribe of Manasseh, to the
land of Gilead, and they spoke with
them saying, **16** "Thus says the whole
congregation of Yahweh, 'What is
this unfaithful act which you have
committed against the God of Israel,
turning away from following Yahweh
this day, by [a]building yourselves an
altar, to rebel against Yahweh this
day? **17** Is [a]the iniquity of Peor too
small *a thing* for us, from which we
have not cleansed ourselves to this
day, although there was a plague on
the congregation of Yahweh? **18** Yet
you are turning away this day from
following Yahweh. Now it will be
that, if you rebel against Yahweh
today, [a]He will be angry with the
whole congregation of Israel tomor-
row. **19** If, however, the land of your
possession is unclean, then [1]cross
into the land of the possession of
Yahweh, where the tabernacle of
Yahweh dwells, and take possession
among us. But do not rebel against
Yahweh, nor rebel against us by
[a]building an altar for yourselves,
besides the altar of Yahweh our God.
**20** Did not [a]Achan the son of Zerah
act unfaithfully in the things devoted
to destruction, and indignation fall
on all the congregation of Israel? But
he was not the only man to breathe
his last in his iniquity.'"

**21** Then the sons of Reuben and
the sons of Gad and the half-tribe
of Manasseh answered and spoke to
the heads of the thousands of Israel.
**22** "The [a]Mighty One, God, Yahweh,
the Mighty One, God, Yahweh! [b]He
knows, and may Israel itself know.
If *it was* in rebellion or if in an un-
faithful act against Yahweh, do not
save us this day! **23** If we have built for
ourselves an altar to turn away from
following Yahweh, or if to [a]perform
a burnt offering or grain offering on
it, or if to offer sacrifices of peace
offerings on it, may Yahweh Himself
require it. **24** But truly we have done
this out of concern, [1]for a reason,
saying, 'In time to come your sons
may say to our [2]sons, "What have
you to do with Yahweh, the God of
Israel? **25** And Yahweh has made the
Jordan a border between us and you,
*you* sons of Reuben and sons of Gad;
you have no portion in Yahweh." So
your sons may make our sons stop
fearing Yahweh.'

**26** "Therefore we said, 'Let us
[1]build an altar, not for burnt offering
or for sacrifice; **27** rather it shall be
[a]a witness between us and you and
between our generations after us,
that we are to [b]perform the service
of Yahweh before Him with our burnt
offerings and with our sacrifices and
with our peace offerings, so that your
sons will not say to our sons in time
to come, "You have no portion in
Yahweh."' **28** Therefore we said, 'It
will also be that if they say *this* to

---

**22:13** [a]Nu 25:7, 11; 31:6 **22:14** [a]Nu 1:4 [1]Or *families* **22:16** [a]Jos 22:11 **22:17** [a]Nu 25:1-9
**22:18** [a]Nu 16:22 **22:19** [a]Jos 22:11 [1]Lit *cross for yourselves* **22:20** [a]Jos 7:1-26 **22:22** [a]Dt 10:17
[b]1Ki 8:39; Job 10:7; Ps 44:21 **22:23** [a]Dt 12:11 **22:24** [1]Lit *from* [2]Lit *sons, saying* **22:26** [1]Lit *prepare to build for ourselves* **22:27** [a]Ge 31:48; Jos 24:27 [b]Dt 12:6, 11, 26f

us or to our generations in time to
come, then we shall say, "See the
copy of the altar of Yahweh which
our fathers made, not for burnt
offering or for sacrifice; rather it is a
witness between us and you."' **29** Far
be it from us to rebel against Yahweh
and turn away from following Yah-
weh this day, by [a]building an altar
for burnt offering, for grain offering
or for sacrifice, besides the altar of
Yahweh our God which is before His
[1]tabernacle."

**30** So Phinehas the priest and
the leaders of the congregation,
even the heads of the thousands of
Israel who *were* with him, heard the
words which the sons of Reuben
and the sons of Gad and the sons of
Manasseh spoke. And it was good in
their sight. **31** And Phinehas the son
of Eleazar the priest said to the sons
of Reuben and to the sons of Gad and
to the sons of Manasseh, "Today we
know that [a]Yahweh is in our midst
because you have not committed
this unfaithful act against Yahweh;
so then you have delivered the sons
of Israel from the hand of Yahweh."

**32** Then Phinehas the son of
Eleazar the priest and the leaders
returned from the sons of Reuben
and from the sons of Gad, from the
land of Gilead to the land of Canaan,
to the sons of Israel, and brought
back word to them. **33** And the word
was good in the sight of the sons of
Israel, and the sons of Israel [a]blessed
God; and they did not speak of going
up against them in war to destroy the
land in which the sons of Reuben and
the sons of Gad were living. **34** And
the sons of Reuben and the sons of
Gad [a]called the altar *Witness*; "For,"
*they said*, "it is a witness between us
that Yahweh is God."

### *Joshua Calls All Israel*

**23** Now it happened after many
days, after Yahweh had given
[a]rest to Israel from all their enemies
[1]on every side, and Joshua was old,
advanced in years, **2** that [a]Joshua
called for all Israel, for their elders
and their heads and their judges and
their officers, and said to them, "I am
old, advanced in years. **3** And you
have seen all that Yahweh your God
has done to all these nations because
of you, for [a]Yahweh your God is He
who has been fighting for you. **4** See,
[a]I have allotted to you these nations
which remain as an inheritance for
your tribes, with all the nations which
I have cut off, from the Jordan even
to the Great Sea toward the setting
of the sun. **5** And Yahweh your God,
He will thrust them out from before
you and [a]dispossess them before you;
and [b]you will possess their land, just
as Yahweh your God [1]promised you.
**6** [a]Be very strong, then, to keep and
to do all that is written in the book
of the law of Moses, so that you may
not turn aside from it to the right
hand or to the left, **7** so that you will
not go *along* with these nations,
these which remain among you, and
you will not [a]mention the name of
their gods, and you will not [b]make
*anyone* swear *by them*, and you will
not [c]serve them, and you will not

---

**22:29** [a]Dt 12:13f [1]Lit *dwelling place* **22:31** [a]Ex 25:8; Lv 26:11f; 2Chr 15:2 **22:33** [a]1Chr 29:20; Da 2:19; Lk 2:28 **22:34** [a]Ge 31:47-49 ◆ **23:1** [a]Jos 21:44 [1]Lit *from round about* **23:2** [a]Jos 24:1 **23:3** [a]Dt 1:30 **23:4** [a]Ex 23:30 **23:5** [a]Ex 23:20 [b]Nu 33:53 [1]Lit *spoke to* **23:6** [a]Dt 5:32; Jos 1:7 **23:7** [a]Ex 23:13; Ps 16:4 [b]Dt 6:13; 10:20 [c]Ex 20:5

bow down to them. **8** But you are to
cling to Yahweh your God, as you
have done to this day. **9** [a]For Yahweh
has dispossessed great and mighty
nations from before you; and as for
you, [b]no man has stood before you
to this day. **10** [a]One of your men will
pursue one thousand, for Yahweh
your God is [b]He who fights for you,
just as He [1]promised you. **11** So keep
your souls very carefully to love Yah-
weh your God. **12** For if you ever turn
back and [a]cling to the rest of these
nations, these which remain among
you, and [b]intermarry with them, so
that you go *along* with them and they
with you, **13** know with certainty that
Yahweh your God will not continue to
dispossess these nations from before
you; but they will be a [a]snare and a
trap to you and a whip on your sides
and thorns in your eyes, until you
perish from off this good land which
Yahweh your God has given you.

**14** "Now behold, today [a]I am going
the way of all the earth, and you know
in all your hearts and in all your souls
that [b]not one word of all the good
words which Yahweh your God spoke
concerning you has failed; all have
come to pass for you; not one word of
them has failed. **15** And it will be that
just as all the good words which Yah-
weh your God spoke to you have come
upon you, so [a]Yahweh will bring upon
you all the calamitous words, until He
has destroyed you from off this good
land which Yahweh your God has giv-
en you. **16** [a]When you trespass against
the covenant of Yahweh your God,
which He commanded you, and go
and serve other gods and bow down
to them, then the anger of Yahweh
will burn against you, and you will
perish quickly from off the good land
which He has given you."

### *Joshua Gathers Israel*

**24** Then [a]Joshua gathered all the
tribes of Israel to Shechem
and called for the elders of Israel and
for their heads and their judges and
their officers; and they presented
themselves before God. **2** And Josh-
ua said to all the people, "Thus says
Yahweh, the God of Israel, 'From
ancient times your fathers lived be-
yond the [1]River, *namely*, [a]Terah, the
father of Abraham and the father of
Nahor, and they served other gods.
**3** Then [a]I took your father Abraham
from beyond the [1]River and led him
through all the land of Canaan and
[b]multiplied his seed and gave him
[c]Isaac. **4** To Isaac I gave [a]Jacob and
Esau, and [b]to Esau I gave Mount
Seir to possess it; but [c]Jacob and his
sons went down to Egypt. **5** Then [a]I
sent Moses and Aaron, and I smote
Egypt [1]by what I did in its midst;
and afterward I brought you out.
**6** And I brought your fathers out of
Egypt, and [a]you came to the sea;
and Egypt pursued your fathers
with chariots and horsemen to the
[1]Red Sea. **7** Then they cried out to
Yahweh; He put darkness between
you and the Egyptians and brought
the sea upon them and covered
them; and your own eyes saw what

---

**23:9** [a]Ex 23:23, 30 [b]Dt 7:24 **23:10** [a]Lv 26:8; Dt 28:7; 32:20 [b]Dt 3:22; Jos 23:3 [1]Lit *spoke to*
**23:12** [a]Ex 34:15, 16; Ps 106:34, 35 [b]Dt 7:3, 4; Ezr 9:2; Ne 13:25 **23:13** [a]Ex 23:33; 34:12; Dt 7:16
**23:14** [a]1Ki 2:2 [b]Jos 21:45 **23:15** [a]Lv 26:14-33; Dt 28:15 **23:16** [a]Dt 4:25, 26 ◆ **24:1** [a]Jos 23:2
**24:2** [a]Ge 11:27-32 [1]The Euphrates River **24:3** [a]Ge 12:1; 24:7 [b]Ge 15:5 [c]Ge 21:3 [1]The Euphrates River
**24:4** [a]Ge 25:25, 26 [b]Ge 36:8; Dt 2:5 [c]Ge 46:6, 7 **24:5** [a]Ex 4:14-17 [1]Lit *according to* **24:6** [a]Ex 14:2-31
[1]Lit *Sea of Reeds*

I did in Egypt. And [a]you lived in the
wilderness for many days. **8** Then
[a]I brought you into the land of the
Amorites who lived beyond the
Jordan, and they fought with you;
and I gave them into your hand, and
you took possession of their land,
and I destroyed them before you.
**9** Then [a]Balak the son of Zippor,
king of Moab, arose and fought
against Israel, and he sent and sum-
moned Balaam the son of Beor to
curse you. **10** But I [a]was not willing
to listen to Balaam. So he blessed
you repeatedly, and I delivered you
from his hand. **11** [a]And you crossed
the Jordan and came to Jericho;
and the citizens of Jericho fought
against you, *and* [b]the Amorite and
the Perizzite and the Canaanite
and the Hittite and the Girgashite,
the Hivite and the Jebusite. Thus [c]I
gave them into your hand. **12** Then
I [a]sent the hornet before you, and
it [1]drove out the two kings of the
Amorites from before you, *but* [b]not
by your sword or your bow. **13** [a]And
I gave you a land on which you had
not labored and cities which you
had not built, and you have lived in
them; you are eating of vineyards
and olive groves which you did not
plant.'

### *We Will Serve Yahweh Our God*

**14** "So now, [a,1]fear Yahweh and serve
Him in integrity and [2]truth; and put
away the gods which your fathers
served beyond the [3]River and in
Egypt, and serve Yahweh. **15** If it is evil
in your sight to serve Yahweh, choose
for yourselves today whom you will
serve: whether the gods which your
fathers served which were beyond
the River or [a]the gods of the Am-
orites in whose land you are living;
but as for me and my house, we will
serve Yahweh."

**16** And the people answered and
said, "Far be it from us that we should
forsake Yahweh to serve other gods;
**17** for Yahweh our God is He who
brought us and our fathers up out of
the land of Egypt, from the house of
slavery, and who did these great signs
in our sight and kept us through all
the way in which we went and among
all the peoples through whose midst
we passed. **18** And Yahweh drove out
from before us all the peoples, even
the Amorites who lived in the land.
We also will serve Yahweh, for He is
our God."

**19** Then Joshua said to the people,
"You will not be able to serve Yah-
weh, [a]for He is a holy God. He is [b]a
jealous God; [c]He will not forgive your
transgression or your sins. **20** [a]If you
forsake Yahweh and serve foreign
gods, then He will turn and do you
harm and consume you after He has
done good to you." **21** And the people
said to Joshua, "No, but we will serve
Yahweh." **22** And Joshua said to the
people, "You are witnesses against
yourselves that [a]you have chosen for
yourselves Yahweh, to serve Him."
And they said, "We are witnesses."
**23** "So now, put away the foreign gods
which are in your midst, and [a]incline
your hearts to Yahweh, the God of
Israel." **24** [a]And the people said to

---

**24:7** [a]Dt 1:46; 2:14 **24:8** [a]Nu 21:21-32 **24:9** [a]Nu 22:2-6 **24:10** [a]Dt 23:5 **24:11** [a]Jos 3:14-17 [b]Ex 23:23, 28; Dt 7:1 [c]Ex 23:31 **24:12** [a]Ex 23:28; Dt 7:20 [b]Ps 44:3 [1]Lit *drove them out* **24:13** [a]Dt 6:10, 11 **24:14** [a]Dt 10:12; 18:13; 1Sa 12:24 [1]Or *reverence* [2]Or *faithfulness* [3]The Euphrates River **24:15** [a]Jdg 6:10 **24:19** [a]Lv 19:2; 20:7, 26 [b]Ex 20:5; 34:14 [c]Ex 23:21 **24:20** [a]Dt 4:25, 26 **24:22** [a]Ps 119:173 **24:23** [a]1Ki 8:57, 58; Ps 119:36; 141:4 **24:24** [a]Ex 19:8; 24:3, 7; Dt 5:27

Joshua, "We will serve Yahweh our
God, and we will listen to His voice."
**25** [a]So Joshua cut a covenant with the
people that day and made for them a
statute and a judgment in Shechem.
**26** And Joshua [a]wrote these words
in the book of the law of God; and
he took a large stone and set it up
there under the oak that was by the
sanctuary of Yahweh. **27** And Joshua
said to all the people, "Behold, [a]this
stone shall be for a witness against
us, for it has heard all the words of
Yahweh which He spoke [1]to us; thus
it shall be for a witness against you,
lest you deny your God." **28** Then
Joshua dismissed the people, each
to his inheritance.

### *Joshua's Death and Burial*

**29** Now it happened that after these
things, Joshua the son of Nun, the
servant of Yahweh, died, being 110
years old. **30** And they buried him
in the territory of his inheritance in
[a]Timnath-serah, which is in the hill
country of Ephraim, on the north of
Mount Gaash.
**31** [a]And Israel served Yahweh all
the days of Joshua and all the days of
the elders who [1]survived Joshua, who
knew all the work of Yahweh which
He had done for Israel.
**32** Now [a]they buried the bones
of Joseph, which the sons of Israel
brought up from Egypt, at Shechem,
in the portion of the field [b]which
Jacob had bought from the sons of
Hamor the father of Shechem for
one hundred [1]qesitah; and they
became the inheritance of Joseph's
sons. **33** And Eleazar the son of
Aaron died; and they buried him [1]at
Gibeah of [a]Phinehas his son, which
was given him in the hill country of
Ephraim.

# *The Book of* JUDGES

### *The Fight Against the Canaanites*

**1** Now it happened after the death
of Joshua that the sons of Israel
[a]asked of [1]Yahweh, saying, "Who
shall go up first for us [b]against the
Canaanites, to fight against them?"
**2** And Yahweh said, "[a]Judah shall
go up; behold, I have given the land
into his hand." **3** Then Judah said
to Simeon his brother, "Come up
with me into [1]the territory allotted
me, that we may fight against the
Canaanites; and [2]I in turn will go
with you into [3]the territory allotted
you." So Simeon went with him. **4** So
Judah went up, and [a]Yahweh gave
the Canaanites and the Perizzites
into their hands, and they struck
down 10,000 men at Bezek. **5** Then
they found Adoni-bezek in Bezek
and fought against him, and they
struck down the Canaanites and the
Perizzites. **6** But Adoni-bezek fled;
and they pursued him and seized

---

**24:25** [a]Ex 24:8 **24:26** [a]Dt 31:24 **24:27** [a]Jos 22:27, 34 [1]Lit *with* **24:30** [a]Jos 19:50
**24:31** [a]Jdg 2:6f [1]Lit *prolonged days after* **24:32** [a]Ge 50:24, 25; Ex 13:19 [b]Ge 33:19; Jn 4:5; Ac 7:15f
[1]Ancient currency, cf. Ge 33:19; Job 42:11 **24:33** [a]Jos 22:13 [1]Or *on the hill* ◆ **1:1** [a]Nu 27:21
[b]Jdg 1:27; 2:21-23; 3:1-6 [1]The personal covenant name of God, a form of I AM WHO I AM, cf. Ex 3:14-15
**1:2** [a]Ge 49:8 **1:3** [1]Lit *my lot* [2]Lit *I, even I* [3]Lit *your lot* **1:4** [a]Ps 44:2; 78:55

him and cut off his [1]thumbs and big
toes. **7** And Adoni-bezek said, "Sev-
enty kings with their thumbs and
their big toes cut off used to gather
up *scraps* under my table; [a]as I have
done, so God has repaid me." So they
brought him to Jerusalem, and he
died there.

**8** Then the sons of Judah fought
against [a]Jerusalem and captured
it and struck it with the edge of
the sword and set the city on
fire. **9** And afterward the sons of
Judah went down to fight against
the Canaanites living in the hill
country and in the [1]Negev and in
the [2]Shephelah. **10** [a]So Judah went
against the Canaanites who lived in
Hebron (now the name of Hebron
formerly *was* Kiriath-arba); and
they struck Sheshai and Ahiman
and Talmai.

**11** Then [a]from there he went
against the inhabitants of Debir
(now the name of Debir formerly
*was* Kiriath-sepher). **12** And Caleb
said, "The one who strikes Kiriath-
sepher and captures it, I will even
give him my daughter Achsah as
a wife." **13** [a]Then Othniel the son
of Kenaz, Caleb's younger brother,
captured it; so he gave him his
daughter Achsah as a wife. **14** Now
[a]it happened that when she came
*to him,* she enticed him to ask her
father for the field. Then she alight-
ed from [1]her donkey, and Caleb said
to her, "What [2]do you want?" **15** And
she said to him, "Give me a blessing,
since you have given me the land
of the [1]Negev, so you shall give me
also springs of water." So Caleb gave
her the upper springs and the lower
springs.

**16** Now the sons of [a]the Kenite,
Moses' father-in-law, went up from
the [b]city of palms with the sons of
Judah, to the wilderness of Judah
which is in the south of [c]Arad; and
they went and lived with the people.
**17** Then Judah went with Simeon his
brother, and they struck the Canaan-
ites living in Zephath and devoted it
to destruction. So the name of the
city was called [a]Hormah. **18** And
Judah captured [a]Gaza with its terri-
tory and Ashkelon with its territory
and Ekron with its territory. **19** Now
Yahweh was with Judah, and they
took possession of the hill country;
but they *could* not dispossess the
inhabitants of the valley because
they had [a]iron chariots. **20** Then they
gave Hebron to Caleb, [a]as Moses had
[1]promised; and he dispossessed
from there [b]the three sons of Anak.
**21** [a]But the sons of Benjamin did not
dispossess the [b]Jebusites who lived
in Jerusalem; so the Jebusites have
lived with the sons of Benjamin in
Jerusalem to this day.

**22** Likewise the house of Joseph
went up against Bethel, and Yahweh
was with them. **23** And the house of
Joseph spied out Bethel ([a]now the
name of the city was formerly Luz).
**24** Then the [1]spies saw a man coming
out of the city, and they said to him,
"Please show us the entrance to the
city, and [a]we will treat you with
lovingkindness." **25** So he showed
them the entrance to the city, and

---

**1:6** [1]Lit *thumbs of his hands and his feet* **1:7** [a]Lv 24:19 **1:8** [a]Jos 15:63; Jdg 1:21 **1:9** [1]South country [2]Or *lowland* **1:10** [a]Jos 15:13-19 **1:11** [a]Jos 15:15 **1:13** [a]Jdg 3:9 **1:14** [a]Jos 15:18 [1]Lit *the* [2]Lit *for yourself* **1:15** [1]South country **1:16** [a]Nu 10:29-32; Jdg 4:11 [b]Dt 34:3; Jdg 3:13 [c]Nu 21:1 **1:17** [a]Nu 21:3 **1:18** [a]Jos 11:22 **1:19** [a]Jos 17:16; Jdg 4:3, 13 **1:20** [a]Jos 14:9 [b]Jos 15:14; Jdg 1:10 [1]Lit *spoken* **1:21** [a]Jos 15:63; Jdg 1:8 [b]1Chr 11:4 **1:23** [a]Ge 28:19 **1:24** [a]Jos 2:12 [1]Lit *the ones keeping watch*

they struck the city with the edge of the sword, [a]but they let the man and all his family go free. **26** So the man went into the land of the Hittites and built a city and named it Luz [1]which is its name to this day.

### *Israel Fails to Complete the Conquest*

**27** [a]But Manasseh did not take possession of Beth-shean and its towns or Taanach and its towns or the inhabitants of Dor and its towns or the inhabitants of Ibleam and its towns or the inhabitants of Megiddo and its towns; so [b]the Canaanites persisted to live in that land. **28** And it happened when Israel became strong, that they put the Canaanites to forced labor, but they did not dispossess them completely.

**29** [a]Also Ephraim did not dispossess the Canaanites who were living in Gezer; so the Canaanites lived in Gezer among them.

**30** Zebulun did not dispossess the inhabitants of Kitron or the inhabitants of [1]Nahalol; so the Canaanites lived among them and became subject to forced labor.

**31** Asher did not dispossess the inhabitants of Acco or the inhabitants of Sidon, or of Ahlab or of Achzib or of Helbah or of Aphik or of Rehob. **32** So the Asherites lived among the Canaanites, the inhabitants of the land; for they did not dispossess them.

**33** Naphtali did not dispossess the inhabitants of Beth-shemesh or the inhabitants of Beth-anath, but lived among the Canaanites, the inhabitants of the land; and the inhabitants of Beth-shemesh and Beth-anath became forced labor for them.

**34** Then the Amorites pressed the sons of Dan into the hill country, for they did not allow them to come down to the valley; **35** and the Amorites persisted in [1]living in Mount Heres, in Aijalon, and in Shaalbim; but the hand of the house of Joseph became heavy, and they became forced labor. **36** Now the border of the Amorites ran from the [a]ascent of Akrabbim, from Sela and upward.

### *The Angel of Yahweh Speaks to Israel*

**2** Then [a]the angel of Yahweh came up from Gilgal to [b]Bochim. And he said, "[c]I brought you up out of Egypt and led you into the land which I have sworn to your fathers; and I said, '[d]I will never break My covenant with you, **2** and as for you, [a]you shall cut no covenant with the inhabitants of this land; [b]you shall tear down their altars.' But you have not listened to My voice; what is this you have done? **3** Therefore I also said, '[a]I will not drive them out before you; but they will [1]become [b]*as thorns* in your sides, and their gods will become a snare to you.'" **4** So it happened that when the angel of Yahweh spoke these words to all the sons of Israel, the people lifted up their voices and wept. **5** So they named that place [1]Bochim; and there they sacrificed to Yahweh.

### *Joshua's Death and Burial*

**6** [a]Then Joshua sent the people away, and the sons of Israel went each to

---

**1:25** [a]Jos 6:25 **1:26** [1]Lit *it* **1:27** [a]Jos 17:12 [b]Jdg 1:1 **1:29** [a]Jos 16:10 **1:30** [1]Possibly same as *Nahalal* **1:35** [1]Lit *dwelling* **1:36** [a]Jos 15:3 ◆ **2:1** [a]Jdg 6:11; 13:2-21 [b]Jdg 2:5 [c]Ex 20:2 [d]Ge 17:7, 8; Lv 26:42, 44; Dt 7:9 **2:2** [a]Ex 23:32; Dt 7:2-5 [b]Ex 34:12, 13 **2:3** [a]Jos 23:13 [b]Nu 33:55 [1]Some ancient mss *be adversaries, and* **2:5** [1]Lit *weepers* **2:6** [a]Jos 24:28-31

his inheritance to possess the land.
**7** And the people served Yahweh all
the days of Joshua and all the days
of the elders who [1]survived Joshua,
who saw all the great work of Yahweh
which He had done for Israel. **8** Then
Joshua the son of Nun, the servant of
Yahweh, died at the age of 110. **9** And
they buried him in the territory of
[a]his inheritance in Timnath-heres,
in the hill country of Ephraim, north
of Mount Gaash. **10** And all that gen-
eration also were gathered to their
fathers; and there arose another
generation after them who [a]did
not know Yahweh or even the work
which He had done for Israel.

### *Israel Serves Baals*

**11** Then the sons of Israel did [a]what
was evil in the eyes of Yahweh and
[1]served the [b]Baals, **12** and [a]they
forsook Yahweh, the God of their
fathers, who had brought them out
of the land of Egypt, and followed
other gods from *among* the gods of
the peoples who were around them
and bowed themselves down to
them; thus they provoked Yahweh
to anger. **13** So they forsook Yahweh
and [a]served Baal and the Ashtaroth.
**14** [a]And the anger of Yahweh burned
against Israel, and He gave them
into the hands of plunderers who
plundered them; and [b]He sold them
*into the hands* of their enemies
around *them*, so that they could no
longer stand before their enemies.
**15** Wherever they went, the hand of
Yahweh was against them for evil, as
Yahweh had spoken and [a]as Yahweh
had sworn to them, so that they were
severely distressed.

### *Yahweh Raises Up Judges*

**16** [a]Then Yahweh raised up judges
[1]who saved them from the hands
of those who plundered them. **17** Yet
they did not listen to their judges ei-
ther, for they played the harlot after
other gods and bowed themselves
down to them. They turned aside
quickly from the way [a]in which their
fathers had walked in obeying the
commandments of Yahweh; they did
not do as *their fathers*. **18** Now when
Yahweh raised up judges for them,
[a]Yahweh was with the judge and
saved them from the hand of their
enemies all the days of the judge;
for Yahweh was [b]moved to pity by
their groaning because of those who
oppressed and suppressed them.
**19** But it happened when the judge
died, that they would turn back and
act more corruptly than their fathers,
in following other gods to serve them
and bow down to them; they did
not abandon their practices or their
stubborn ways. **20** [a]So the anger of
Yahweh burned against Israel, and He
said, "Because this nation has tres-
passed against My covenant which
I commanded their fathers and has
not listened to My voice, **21** [a]I also
will no longer dispossess before them
any of the nations which Joshua left
when he died, **22** in order to [a]test
Israel by them, whether they will
keep the way of Yahweh to walk in
it as their fathers [1]did, or not." **23** So
Yahweh allowed those nations to

**2:7** [1]Lit *prolonged days after* **2:9** [a]Jos 19:49f **2:10** [a]Ex 5:2; 1Sa 2:12 **2:11** [a]Jdg 3:7, 12; 4:1; 6:1 [b]Jdg 6:25; 8:33; 10:6 [1]Or *worshiped* **2:12** [a]Dt 31:16 **2:13** [a]Jdg 10:6 **2:14** [a]Dt 31:17; Ps 106:40-42 [b]Dt 28:25; 32:30 **2:15** [a]Lv 26:14-39; Dt 28:15-68 **2:16** [a]Ps 106:43-45 [1]Lit *and they* **2:17** [a]Jdg 2:7 **2:18** [a]Jos 1:5 [b]Dt 32:36; Ps 106:44 **2:20** [a]Jdg 2:14 **2:21** [a]Jos 23:4, 5, 13 **2:22** [a]Dt 8:2; 13:3 [1]Lit *kept*

rest, not dispossessing them quickly; and He did not give them into the hand of Joshua.

### *Yahweh Tests Israel*

**3** [a]Now these are the nations which Yahweh *allowed* to remain, to test Israel by them (*that is,* all who had not known any of the wars of Canaan; **2** [1]however, *God tested them* in order that the generations of the sons of Israel would know *war,* by learning war, [1]especially those who had not known it formerly). **3** *These nations are:* the five lords of the Philistines and all the Canaanites and the Sidonians and [a]the Hivites who lived in Mount Lebanon, from Mount Baal-hermon as far as [1]Lebo-hamath. **4** And they were for [a,1]testing Israel, to know if they would [2]obey the commandments of Yahweh, which He had commanded their fathers by the hand of Moses. **5** [a]Now the sons of Israel lived among the Canaanites, the Hittites, the Amorites, the Perizzites, the Hivites, and the Jebusites; **6** and [a]they took their daughters for themselves as wives and gave their own daughters to their sons and served their gods.

### *Yahweh Raises Up Othniel*

**7** Thus the sons of Israel did [a]what was evil in the eyes of Yahweh and [b]forgot Yahweh their God and [c]served the Baals and the [1]Asheroth. **8** Then the anger of Yahweh burned against Israel, so that He sold them *into the hands of* Cushan-rishathaim king of [1]Mesopotamia; and the sons of Israel served Cushan-rishathaim eight years. **9** Then the sons of Israel cried to Yahweh, and Yahweh raised up a savior for the sons of Israel to save them, [a]Othniel the son of Kenaz, Caleb's younger brother. **10** [a]And the Spirit of Yahweh came upon him, and he judged Israel. And he went out to war, and Yahweh gave Cushan-rishathaim king of [1]Mesopotamia into his hand. So his hand was strong against Cushan-rishathaim. **11** Then the land was quiet for forty years. And Othniel the son of Kenaz died.

**12** Then the sons of Israel again [a]did what was evil in the eyes of Yahweh. So [b]Yahweh strengthened Eglon the king of Moab against Israel because they had done what was evil in the eyes of Yahweh. **13** And he gathered to himself the sons of Ammon and Amalek; and he went and struck Israel, and they possessed [a]the city of the palm trees. **14** So the sons of Israel served Eglon the king of Moab eighteen years.

### *Yahweh Raises Up Ehud and Shamgar*

**15** Then the sons of Israel [a]cried to Yahweh, and Yahweh raised up a savior for them, Ehud the son of Gera, the Benjamite, a left-handed man. And the sons of Israel sent tribute by his hand to Eglon the king of Moab. **16** And Ehud made himself a sword which had two edges, a [1]cubit in length, and he bound it on his right

◆ **3:1** [a]Jdg 1:1; 2:21, 22 **3:2** [1]Lit *only* **3:3** [a]Jos 9:7; 11:19 [1]Or *the entrance of Hamath* **3:4** [a]Dt 8:2 [1]Lit *testing by them* [2]Lit *hear* **3:5** [a]Ps 106:35 **3:6** [a]Ex 34:15, 16; Dt 7:3, 4; Jos 23:12 **3:7** [a]Jdg 2:11 [b]Dt 4:9 [c]Jdg 2:13 [1]Wooden symbols of a female deity **3:8** [1]Heb *Aram-naharaim* **3:9** [a]Jdg 1:13 **3:10** [a]Nu 11:25-29; 24:2 [1]Heb *Aram* **3:12** [a]Jdg 2:11 [b]Jdg 2:14 **3:13** [a]Dt 34:3; Jdg 1:16 **3:15** [a]Ps 78:34 **3:16** [1]A cubit was approx. 18 in. or 45 cm

thigh under his cloak. 17 Then he
brought the tribute near to Eglon
king of Moab. Now Eglon was a very
fat man. 18 And it happened when
he had finished bringing the tribute
near, that he sent away the people
who had carried the tribute. 19 But
he himself turned back from the
graven images which were at Gilgal
and said, "I have a secret message
for you, O king." And he said, "Keep
silence." And all who stood by him
left him. 20 But Ehud came to him
while he was sitting alone in his
cool roof chamber. And Ehud said,
"I have a message from God for you."
And he arose from his seat. 21 Then
Ehud sent forth his left hand, took
the sword from his right thigh, and
thrust it into his belly. 22 The handle
also went in after the blade, and the
fat closed over the blade, for he did
not draw the sword out of his belly;
and the refuse came out. 23 Then
Ehud went out into the vestibule and
shut the doors of the roof chamber
behind him and locked *them*.

24 Now he went out, and his
servants came in and looked, and
behold, the doors of the roof cham-
ber were locked; and they said, "[a]He
is surely [1]relieving himself in the cool
room." 25 Then they waited until
they were ashamed; but behold, he
did not open the doors of the roof
chamber. Therefore they took the
key and opened them, and behold,
their master had fallen to the [1]floor
dead.

26 Now Ehud escaped while they
were delaying, and he passed by the
graven images and escaped to Seirah.
27 And it happened when he had
arrived, that [a]he blew the trumpet
in the hill country of Ephraim; and
the sons of Israel went down with
him from the hill country, and he *was*
in front of them. 28 Then he said to
them, "Pursue *them*, for Yahweh has
given your enemies the Moabites into
your hands." So they went down af-
ter him and captured [a]the fords of
the Jordan opposite Moab and did
not allow anyone to cross. 29 And
they struck down at that time about
10,000 Moabites, all robust and val-
iant men; and no one escaped. 30 So
Moab was subdued that day under
the hand of Israel. And the land was
quiet for eighty years.

31 Now after him was [a]Shamgar
the son of Anath. And he struck down
600 Philistines with an oxgoad; and
he also saved Israel.

### *Yahweh Raises Up Deborah and Barak*

4 Then [a]the sons of Israel again
did what was evil in the eyes of
Yahweh. Now Ehud had died. 2 And
Yahweh sold them into the hand of
[a]Jabin king of Canaan, who reigned
in Hazor; and the commander of
his army was Sisera, who lived in
[b]Harosheth-hagoyim. 3 Then the
sons of Israel cried to Yahweh; for
he had 900 [a]iron chariots, and he
oppressed the sons of Israel severely
for twenty years.

4 Now Deborah, a [1]prophetess,
the wife of Lappidoth, was judging
Israel at that time. 5 And she used to
[1]sit under the [a]palm tree of Deborah
between Ramah and Bethel in the

---

**3:24** [a]1Sa 24:3 [1]Lit *covering his feet* **3:25** [1]Lit *earth* **3:27** [a]Jdg 6:34; 1Sa 13:3 **3:28** [a]Jdg 7:24; 12:5 **3:31** [a]Jdg 5:6 ◆ **4:1** [a]Jdg 2:19 **4:2** [a]Jos 11:1, 10 [b]Jdg 4:13, 16 **4:3** [a]Jdg 1:19 **4:4** [1]Lit *woman prophetess* **4:5** [a]Ge 35:8 [1]Or *live*

hill country of Ephraim; and the
sons of Israel came up to her for
judgment. **6** Then she sent and sum-
moned [a]Barak the son of Abinoam
from Kedesh-naphtali and said to
him, "Has not Yahweh, the God of
Israel, commanded, 'Go and march
to Mount Tabor, and take with you
10,000 men from the sons of Naph-
tali and from the sons of Zebulun?
**7** And I will draw out to you Sisera,
the commander of Jabin's army, with
his chariots and his [1]many *troops* to
the river Kishon, and [a]I will give him
into your hand.'" **8** Then Barak said
to her, "If you will go with me, then
I will go; but if you will not go with
me, I will not go." **9** So she said, "I
will surely go with you; nevertheless,
the honor shall not be yours on the
journey that you are about to take,
[a]for Yahweh will sell Sisera into the
hand of a woman." Then Deborah
arose and went with Barak to Kedesh.
**10** Then Barak called [a]Zebulun and
Naphtali together to Kedesh, and
10,000 men went up [b,1]with him;
Deborah also went up with him.

**11** Now Heber [a]the Kenite had sep-
arated himself from the Kenites, from
the sons of Hobab the father-in-law
of Moses, and had pitched his tent as
far away as the [1]oak in [b]Zaanannim,
which is near Kedesh.

**12** Then they told Sisera that Barak
the son of Abinoam had gone up
to Mount Tabor. **13** So Sisera called
together all his chariots, [a]900 iron
chariots, and all the people who *were*
with him, from [b]Harosheth-hagoyim
to the river Kishon. **14** And Deborah
said to Barak, "Arise! For this is the
day in which Yahweh has given Sis-
era into your hand; has not [a]Yahweh
gone out before you?" So Barak went
down from Mount Tabor with 10,000
men following him. **15** [a]And Yahweh
threw Sisera and all *his* chariots and
all *his* camp into confusion with the
edge of the sword before Barak; and
Sisera came down from *his* chariot
and fled away on foot. **16** But Barak
pursued the chariots and *all those*
*in* the camp as far as Harosheth-
hagoyim, and all the camp of Sisera
fell by the edge of the sword; [a]not
even one remained.

**17** Now Sisera fled away on foot to
the tent of Jael the wife of Heber the
Kenite, for *there was* peace between
Jabin the king of Hazor and the house
of Heber the Kenite. **18** And Jael went
out to meet Sisera and said to him,
"Turn aside, my master, turn aside to
me! Do not be afraid." And he turned
aside to her into the tent, and she
covered him with a [1]rug. **19** [a]Then he
said to her, "Please give me a little
water to drink, for I am thirsty." So
she opened a [1]bottle of milk and gave
him a drink; then she covered him.
**20** And he said to her, "Stand in the
doorway of the tent, and it shall be
if anyone comes and asks of you and
says, 'Is there a man here?' that you
shall say, 'No.'" **21** Then Jael, Heber's
wife, [a]took a tent peg and placed a
hammer in her hand and went se-
cretly to him and drove the peg into
his temple, and it went through into
the ground; for he was sound asleep
and exhausted. So he died. **22** Now

**4:6** [a]Heb 11:32 **4:7** [a]Ps 83:9 [1]Lit *multitude* **4:9** [a]Jdg 4:21 **4:10** [a]Jdg 5:18 [b]Jdg 4:14; 5:15 [1]Lit *at his feet* **4:11** [a]Jdg 1:16 [b]Jos 19:33 [1]Or *terebinth* **4:13** [a]Jdg 4:3 [b]Jdg 4:2 **4:14** [a]Dt 9:3; 2Sa 5:24; Ps 68:7 **4:15** [a]Dt 7:23; Jos 10:10 **4:16** [a]Ex 14:28; Ps 83:9 **4:18** [1]Or *blanket* **4:19** [a]Jdg 5:24-27 [1]A leather container **4:21** [a]Jdg 5:26

behold, Barak was pursuing Sisera, and Jael came out to meet him and said to him, "Come, and I will show you the man whom you are seeking." And he entered [1]with her, and behold, Sisera was lying dead with the tent peg in his temple.

23 So [a]God subdued on that day
Jabin the king of Canaan before the
sons of Israel. 24 And the hand of
the sons of Israel went forth heavier and heavier against Jabin the king of Canaan, until they had cut off Jabin the king of Canaan.

### *The Song of Deborah and Barak*

5 [a]Then Deborah and Barak the son of Abinoam sang on that day, saying,

2 "[a]When [1]the leaders
led in Israel,
When [b]the people
volunteered,
Bless Yahweh!
3 "Hear, O kings; give ear,
O rulers!
[a]As for me, to Yahweh,
I will sing;
I will sing praise to Yahweh,
the God of Israel.
4 "[a]O Yahweh, when You
went out from Seir,
When You marched
from the field of Edom,
[b]The earth quaked, the
heavens also dripped,
Even the clouds
dripped water.
5 "[a]The mountains [1]flowed
at the presence of Yahweh,
[b]This Sinai, at the presence
of Yahweh, the God of Israel.
6 "In the days of [a]Shamgar
the son of Anath,
In the days of [b]Jael,
the paths had ceased,
So travelers [1]went
by [2]roundabout paths.
7 "The peasantry ceased;
they ceased in Israel,
Until I, Deborah, arose,
Until I arose,
a mother in Israel.
8 "[a,1]God chose new *leaders*;
Then war *was* in the gates.
Not a shield or a spear
was seen
Among forty thousand
in Israel.
9 "My heart *goes out*
to [a]the commanders of Israel,
The volunteers
among the people;
Bless Yahweh!
10 "[a]You who ride
on [1]white donkeys,
You who sit on *rich* carpets,
And you who travel
on the road—muse *aloud*!
11 "At the sound of those who
divide *flocks*
among [a]the watering places,
There they shall
[1]commemorate [b]the
righteous deeds of Yahweh,
The righteous deeds for His
[2]peasantry in Israel.
Then the people of Yahweh
went down [c]to the gates.

**4:22** [1]Lit *to* **4:23** [a]Ne 9:24; Ps 18:47 ◆ **5:1** [a]Ex 15:1 **5:2** [a]Jdg 5:9 [b]Ps 110:3 [1]Or *locks hung loose in* **5:3** [a]Ps 27:6 **5:4** [a]Dt 33:2; Ps 68:7 [b]Ps 68:8, 9 **5:5** [a]Ex 19:18 [b]Ps 68:8 [1]Or *trembled* **5:6** [a]Jdg 3:31 [b]Jdg 4:17 [1]Lit *walked* [2]Lit *twisted* **5:8** [a]Dt 32:17 [1]Or *New gods were chosen* **5:9** [a]Jdg 5:2 **5:10** [a]Jdg 10:4; 12:14 [1]Or *tawny* **5:11** [a]Ge 24:11; 29:2, 3 [b]1Sa 12:7; Mic 6:5 [c]Jdg 5:8 [1]Lit *give* [2]Or *rural dwellers*

12 "[a]Awake, awake, Deborah;
Awake, awake, [1]utter a song!
Arise, Barak, and [b]take
away your captives,
O son of Abinoam.
13 "Then survivors came
down to the mighty ones;
The people of Yahweh came
down to me as warriors.
14 "From Ephraim those
whose root is
[a]in Amalek *came down*,
Following you, Benjamin,
with your peoples;
From Machir commanders
came down,
And from Zebulun those who
wield the staff of a scribe.
15 "And [1]the princes of Issachar
*were* with Deborah;
As *was* Issachar, so *was* Barak;
Into the valley they
rushed [a]at his [2]heels;
Among the divisions
of Reuben
*There was* great persistence
of *the* heart.
16 "Why did you sit
among [a]the [1]sheepfolds,
To hear the whistling
for the flocks?
Among the divisions
of Reuben
*There were* great probings
of *the* heart.
17 "[a]Gilead dwelt
across the Jordan;
And why did Dan
stay in ships?
Asher sat at the seashore,
And dwelt by its landings.
18 "[a]Zebulun *was* a people
who despised their
lives *even* to death,
And Naphtali also, on the high
places of the field.

19 "[a]The kings came *and* fought;
Then fought the kings
of Canaan
[b]At Taanach near the
waters of Megiddo;
[c]They took no gain of silver.
20 "[a]The stars fought
from heaven;
From their courses they
fought against Sisera.
21 "The river of Kishon
swept them away,
The ancient river,
the river Kishon.
[a]O my soul, march
on with strength.
22 "[a]Then the horses' hoofs beat
From the dashing, the dashing
of his [1]valiant steeds.
23 'Curse Meroz,' said the
angel of Yahweh,
'Utterly curse its inhabitants,
[a]Because they did not come
to the help of Yahweh,
To the help of Yahweh
against the warriors.'

24 "[a]Most blessed
of women is Jael,
The wife of Heber
the Kenite;
Most blessed is she
of women in the tent.
25 "He asked for water, *and*
she gave him milk;

---

**5:12** [a]Ps 57:8 [b]Ps 68:18; Eph 4:8 [1]Lit *speak* **5:14** [a]Jdg 12:15 **5:15** [a]Jdg 4:10 [1]As in ancient versions; Heb *My princes* [2]Lit *feet* **5:16** [a]Nu 32:1, 2, 24, 36 [1]Or *saddlebags* **5:17** [a]Jos 22:9 **5:18** [a]Jdg 4:6, 10 **5:19** [a]Jos 11:1-5; Jdg 4:13 [b]Jdg 1:27 [c]Jdg 5:30 **5:20** [a]Jos 10:12-14 **5:21** [a]Ex 15:2; Ps 44:5 **5:22** [a]Job 39:19-25 [1]Lit *mighty ones* **5:23** [a]Jdg 5:13 **5:24** [a]Jdg 4:19-21

In a mighty bowl she
brought him curds.
**26** "She sent forth her hand
for the tent peg,
And her right hand
for the workmen's hammer.
Then she beat Sisera; she
smashed his head,
And she crushed and
pierced his temple.
**27** "Between her feet he
bowed, he fell, he lay;
Between her feet he
bowed, he fell;
Where he bowed,
there he fell *violently*
devastated.

**28** "Out of the window she
looked and lamented,
The mother of Sisera
through the [1]lattice,
'Why does his chariot
delay in coming?
Why do the [2]hoofbeats
of his chariots tarry?'
**29** "Her wise princesses
would answer her,
Indeed she repeats her
words to herself,
**30** '[a]Are they not finding, are
they not dividing the spoil?
A maiden, two maidens
for every mighty man;
*To Sisera a spoil* of dyed work,
A spoil of dyed work
embroidered,
Dyed work of double
embroidery on the [1]neck
of the spoil?'
**31** "[a]Thus let all Your enemies
perish, O Yahweh;
[b]But let those who love Him
be like the rising
of the sun in its might."
And the land was quiet for forty
years.

### *Midian Prevails Against Israel*

**6** Then the sons of Israel [a]did what
was evil in the eyes of Yahweh;
and Yahweh gave them into the hands
of [b]Midian seven years. **2** And the
[1]power of Midian prevailed against
Israel. Because of Midian the sons
of Israel made for themselves [a]the
dens which were in the mountains
and the caves and the strongholds.
**3** And it was when Israel had sown,
that the Midianites would go up with
the Amalekites and the sons of the
east and go up against them. **4** So
they would camp against them and
[a]ruin the produce of the earth [1]as
far as Gaza and [b]leave no sustenance
in Israel as well as no sheep, ox,
or donkey. **5** For they would go up
with their livestock and their tents;
they would come in [a]like locusts for
number, both they and their camels
were innumerable; and they came
into the land to make it a ruin. **6** So
Israel was brought [a]very low because
of Midian, and the sons of Israel cried
out to Yahweh.
**7** Now it happened when the sons
of Israel cried out to Yahweh on account of Midian, **8** that Yahweh sent a
prophet to the sons of Israel, and [a]he
said to them, "Thus says Yahweh, the
God of Israel, 'It was I who brought
you up from Egypt and brought you
out from the house of slavery. **9** I
delivered you from the hands of the

**5:28** [1]Or *window* [2]Lit *steps* **5:30** [a]Ex 15:9 [1]Lit *necks* **5:31** [a]Ps 68:2; 92:9 [b]Ps 19:4-6; 89:36, 37
◆ **6:1** [a]Jdg 2:11 [b]Nu 22:4; 25:15-18; 31:1-3 **6:2** [a]1Sa 13:6; Heb 11:38 [1]Lit *hand* **6:4** [a]Lv 26:16 [b]Dt 28:31 [1]Lit *until your coming to* **6:5** [a]Jdg 7:12; 8:10 **6:6** [a]Dt 28:43 **6:8** [a]Jdg 2:1, 2

Egyptians and from the hands of all
your oppressors and drove them out
before you and gave you their land,
**10** and I said to you, "I am Yahweh
your God; you [a]shall not fear the
gods of the Amorites in whose land
you live. But you have not listened to
My voice."'"

### *Yahweh Sends Gideon to Save Israel*

**11** Then [a]the angel of Yahweh came
and sat under the [1]oak that was in
Ophrah, which belonged to Joash
the [b]Abiezrite as his son [c]Gideon
was beating out wheat in the wine
press in order to [2]preserve *it* from
the Midianites. **12** And the angel of
Yahweh appeared to him and said to
him, "Yahweh is with you, O mighty
man of valor." **13** Then Gideon said
to him, "O my lord, if Yahweh is with
us, why then has all this happened to
us? And where are all His wondrous
deeds which our fathers recounted
to us, saying, 'Did not Yahweh bring
us up from Egypt?' But [a]now Yahweh
has abandoned us and given us into
the hand of Midian." **14** Then Yahweh
turned to him and said, "[a]Go in this
strength of yours and save Israel from
the hand of Midian. Have I not sent
you?" **15** [a]But he said to Him, "O Lord,
with what shall I save Israel? Behold,
my clan is the least in [b]Manasseh,
and I am the youngest in my father's
house." **16** [a]But Yahweh said to him,
"Surely I will be with you, and you
shall strike down Midian as one
man." **17** So [1]Gideon said to Him, "If
now I have found favor in Your eyes,
then do [a]a sign for me that it is You
who speak with me. **18** Please do not
depart from here until I come *back* to
You, and I bring out my offering and
lay it before You." And He said, "I will
remain until you return."

**19** So Gideon went in and [a]prepared
a young goat and unleavened bread
from an [1]ephah of flour; he put the
meat in a basket [2]and the broth in
a pot and brought *them* out to him
under the [3]oak and presented *them*.
**20** And the angel of God said to him,
"Take the meat and the unleavened
bread and lay them on this rock and
pour out the broth." And he did so.
**21** Then the angel of Yahweh put out
the end of the staff that was in his
hand and touched the meat and the
unleavened bread; and [a]fire sprang
up from the rock and consumed
the meat and the unleavened bread.
Then the angel of Yahweh went away
from *before* his eyes. **22** [a]And Gideon
saw that he was the angel of Yahweh,
so [1]he said, "Alas, O Lord Yahweh! For
now I have seen the angel of Yahweh
face to face." **23** And Yahweh said to
him, "Peace to you. Do not fear; you
shall not die." **24** So Gideon built an
altar there to Yahweh and named it
[1]Yahweh is Peace. To this day it is still
[a]in Ophrah of the Abiezrites.

**25** Now it happened on the same
night that Yahweh said to him, "Take
your father's bull [1]and a second bull
seven years old, and pull down the
altar of Baal which belongs to your
father, and cut down the [a,2]Asherah
that is beside it, **26** and build an altar

**6:10** [a]2Ki 17:35; Jer 10:2 **6:11** [a]Jdg 2:1; 6:14; 13:3 [b]Jos 17:2; Jdg 6:15 [c]Heb 11:32 [1]Or *terebinth* [2]Lit *cause to escape* **6:13** [a]Jdg 6:1; Ps 44:9 **6:14** [a]Heb 11:32-34 **6:15** [a]Ex 3:11 [b]Jdg 6:11 **6:16** [a]Ex 3:12; Jos 1:5 **6:17** [a]Jdg 6:37; Is 38:7, 8 [1]Lit *he* **6:19** [a]Ge 18:6-8 [1]An ephah was approx. 21 qt. or 23 l [2]Lit *and he put* [3]Or *terebinth* **6:21** [a]Lv 9:24 **6:22** [a]Ge 32:30; Ex 33:20; Jdg 13:21, 22 [1]Lit *Gideon* **6:24** [a]Jdg 8:32 [1]Heb *Yahweh-shalom* **6:25** [a]Ex 34:13 [1]Or *even* [2]A wooden symbol of a female deity, also vv 26, 28, 30

to Yahweh your God on the top of
this stronghold in an orderly manner,
and take the second bull and offer
a burnt offering with the wood of
the Asherah which you shall cut
down." **27** So Gideon took ten men
of his servants and did as Yahweh had
spoken to him; and now it happened
that because he was too afraid of his
father's household and the men of the
city to do it by day, he did it by night.

***Gideon Tears Down the Altar of Baal***

**28** Then the men of the city arose
early in the morning, and behold,
the altar of Baal was torn down,
and the Asherah which was beside
it was cut down, and the second
bull was offered on the altar which
had been built. **29** And they said to
one another, "Who did this thing?"
And when they searched about and
inquired, they said, "Gideon the son
of Joash did this thing." **30** Then the
men of the city said to Joash, "Bring
out your son, that he may die, for he
has torn down the altar of Baal, and
indeed, he has cut down the Asherah
which was beside it." **31** But Joash said
to all who stood against him, "Will
you contend for Baal, or will you save
him? Whoever will contend for him
shall be put to death by morning.
If he is a god, let him contend for
*himself,* because someone has torn
down his altar." **32** Therefore on that
day he named him [a]Jerubbaal, that
is to say, "Let Baal contend against
him," because he had torn down his
altar.

**33** Now all the Midianites and the
Amalekites and the sons of the east
assembled themselves; and they
crossed over and camped in [a]the
valley of Jezreel. **34** But [a]the Spirit
of Yahweh clothed Gideon; and he
[b]blew a trumpet, and the Abiezrites
were called together to follow him.
**35** And he sent messengers through-
out Manasseh, and they also were
called together to follow him; and he
sent messengers to Asher, [a]Zebulun,
and Naphtali, and [b]they came up to
meet them.

***The Test of the Fleece***

**36** Then Gideon said to God, "[a]If You
will save Israel by my hand, as You
have spoken, **37** behold, I will put a
fleece of wool on the threshing floor.
If there is dew on the fleece only,
and it is dry on all the ground, then
I will know that You will save Israel
by my hand, as You have spoken."
**38** And it was so. Indeed he arose
early the next morning and squeezed
the fleece. And he drained the dew
from the fleece, a bowl full of water.
**39** Then Gideon said to God, "[a]Do
not let Your anger burn against me
that I may speak once more; please
let me make a test once more with
the fleece; let it now be dry only on
the fleece, and let there be dew on
all the ground." **40** And God did so
that night. So it was dry only on the
fleece, but dew was on all the ground.

***Gideon's 300 Men***

**7** Then [a]Jerubbaal (that is, Gideon)
and all the people who were with
him rose early and camped beside
[1]the spring of Harod; and the camp
of Midian was on the north side of
[2]them by the hill of [b]Moreh in the
valley.

---

**6:32** [a]Jdg 7:1 **6:33** [a]Jos 17:16 **6:34** [a]Jdg 3:10 [b]Jdg 3:27 **6:35** [a]Jdg 4:6, 10; 5:18 [b]Jdg 7:3
**6:36** [a]Jdg 6:14, 16, 17 **6:39** [a]Ge 18:32 ◆ **7:1** [a]Jdg 6:32 [b]Ge 12:6; Dt 11:30 [1]Or *En-Harod* [2]Lit *him*

**2** And Yahweh said to Gideon, "The people who are with you are too many for Me to give Midian into their hands, [a]lest Israel honor themselves, saying, 'My own hand has saved me.' **3** So now, [1]come, call out in the hearing of the people, saying, '[a]Whoever is afraid and trembling, let him return and depart from Mount Gilead.'" So 22,000 people returned, but 10,000 remained.

**4** [a]Then Yahweh said to Gideon, "The people are still too many; bring them down to the water, and I will test them for you there. And it will be that he of whom I say to you, 'This one shall go with you,' he shall go with you; but everyone of whom I say to you, 'This one shall not go with you,' he shall not go." **5** So he brought the people down to the water. And Yahweh said to Gideon, "Everyone who laps the water with his tongue as a dog laps, you shall set him aside by himself, and *so also* everyone who kneels to drink." **6** Now the number of those who lapped, putting their hand to their mouth, was 300 men; but all the rest of the people kneeled to drink water. **7** And Yahweh said to Gideon, "I will save you [a]with the 300 men who lapped and will give the Midianites into your hands; so let all the *other* people go, each man to his place." **8** So [1]the 300 men took the people's provisions and their trumpets into their hands. And [2]Gideon sent all the *other* men of Israel, each to his tent, but retained the 300 men; and the camp of Midian was below him in the valley.

**9** Now it happened the same night that Yahweh said to him, "Arise, go down against the camp, [a]for I have given it into your hands. **10** But if you are afraid to go down, *then both* you and Purah your young man, go down to the camp, **11** and you will hear what they say; and [a]afterward your hands will be strengthened, that you may go down against the camp." So he went with Purah his young man down to the [1]outskirts of the armed men that were in the camp. **12** Now the Midianites and the Amalekites and all the sons of the east were lying in the valley [a]as numerous as locusts; and their camels were without number, [b]as numerous as the sand on the seashore. **13** Then Gideon came, and behold, a man was recounting a dream to his friend. And he said, "Behold, I [1]had a dream; [2]a loaf of barley bread was tumbling into the camp of Midian, and it came to the tent and struck it so that it fell and turned it [3]upside down so that the tent lay flat." **14** And his friend answered and said, "This is nothing less than the sword of Gideon the son of Joash, a man of Israel; God has given Midian and all the camp [a]into his hand."

**15** Now it happened that when Gideon heard the account of the dream and its interpretation, he bowed in worship. Then he returned to the camp of Israel and said, "Arise, for Yahweh has given the camp of Midian into your hands." **16** And he divided the 300 men into three [1]companies, and he put trumpets

**7:2** [a]Dt 8:17, 18 **7:3** [a]Dt 20:8 [1]Or *please* **7:4** [a]1Sa 14:6 **7:7** [a]1Sa 14:6 **7:8** [1]Lit *they* [2]Lit *he*
**7:9** [a]Jos 2:24; 10:8; 11:6 **7:11** [a]Jdg 7:15; 1Sa 14:9, 10 [1]Lit *extremity of the battle array* **7:12** [a]Jdg 6:5; 8:10 [b]Jos 11:4 **7:13** [1]Lit *dreamed* [2]Lit *and behold, a loaf* [3]Lit *upwards* **7:14** [a]Jos 2:9 **7:16** [1]Lit *heads*

and empty pitchers into the hands
of all of them, with torches inside
the pitchers. **17** Then he said to them,
"Look at me and do likewise. And
behold, I will come to the outskirts
of the camp, and it will be that just
as I do so you do likewise. **18** And I
and all who are with me will blow
the trumpet. Then you also shall
blow the trumpets all around the
camp and say, 'For Yahweh and for
Gideon.'"

### *Gideon Kills the Princes of Midian*

**19** So Gideon and the hundred men
who were with him came to the out-
skirts of the camp at the beginning of
the middle watch, when they had just
set up the watch; and they blew the
trumpets and smashed the pitchers
that were in their hands. **20** Then the
three [1]companies blew the trumpets
and broke the pitchers, and they held
the torches in their left hands and
the trumpets in their right hands
for blowing and called out, "A sword
for Yahweh and for Gideon!" **21** And
each stood in his place around the
camp. Then [a]all of the camp ran,
and they made a loud shout and
fled. **22** So they blew 300 trumpets.
And [a]Yahweh set the sword of one
against another even throughout the
whole camp. And the camp fled as
*far as Beth-shittah toward* Zererah,
as far as the edge of [b]Abel-meholah,
by Tabbath. **23** And the men of Israel
were summoned from [a]Naphtali and
Asher and all Manasseh, and they
pursued Midian.

**24** Now Gideon had sent messen-
gers throughout all the hill country
of Ephraim, saying, "Come down to
meet Midian and [a]capture the waters
before them, as far as Beth-barah
and the Jordan." So all the men of
Ephraim were summoned, and they
captured the waters as far as Beth-
barah and the Jordan. **25** Then they
captured the two princes of Midian,
[a]Oreb and Zeeb, and they killed Oreb
at the rock of Oreb, and they killed
Zeeb at the wine press of Zeeb. Then
they pursued Midian and brought the
heads of Oreb and Zeeb to Gideon
[b]from across the Jordan.

### *Gideon Pursues Zebah and Zalmunna*

**8** Then the men of Ephraim said
to him, "[a]What is this thing you
have done to us, not calling us when
you went to fight against Midian?"
And they strongly contended with
him. **2** But he said to them, "What
have I done now in comparison
with you? Is not the gleaning *of the
grapes* of Ephraim better than the
grape harvest of Abiezer? **3** God has
given the princes of Midian, Oreb
and Zeeb, into your hands; and what
was I able to do in comparison with
you?" Then their [1]anger toward him
subsided when he spoke this word.

**4** Then Gideon and the 300 men
who were with him came [a]to the
Jordan *and* crossed over, weary yet
pursuing. **5** And he said to the men of
[a]Succoth, "Please give loaves of bread
to the people who are following me,
for they are weary, and I am pursuing
Zebah and Zalmunna, the kings of
Midian." **6** But the princes of Succoth
said, "[a,1]Are the hands of Zebah and

---

**7:20** [1]Lit *heads* **7:21** [a]2Ki 7:7 **7:22** [a]1Sa 14:20 [b]1Ki 4:12; 19:16 **7:23** [a]Jdg 6:35 **7:24** [a]Jdg 3:28
**7:25** [a]Ps 83:11; Is 10:26 [b]Jdg 8:4 ◆ **8:1** [a]Jdg 12:1 **8:3** [1]Lit *spirit* **8:4** [a]Jdg 7:25 **8:5** [a]Ge 33:17
**8:6** [a]Jdg 8:15 [1]Lit *Is the palm*

Zalmunna already in your hands, that
we should give bread to your army?"
7 And Gideon said, "Thus, [a]when Yah-
weh has given Zebah and Zalmunna
into my hand, then I will [1]thrash
your [2]bodies with the thorns of the
wilderness and with briers." 8 So he
went up from there to [a,1]Penuel and
spoke similarly to them; and the men
of Penuel answered him just as the
men of Succoth had answered. 9 So
he spoke also to the men of Penuel,
saying, "When I return safely, [a]I will
tear down this tower."

10 Now Zebah and Zalmunna were
in Karkor, and their camps with them,
about 15,000 men, all who were left
of the entire camp of the sons of the
east; [a]for the fallen were 120,000 men
who drew the sword. 11 And Gideon
went up by the way of those who
dwelt in tents on the east of Nobah
and Jogbehah and struck the camp
when the camp was [1]unsuspecting.
12 Then Zebah and Zalmunna fled.
And he pursued them and captured
the two kings of Midian, Zebah and
Zalmunna, and he threw the whole
camp into *utter* fright.

13 Then Gideon the son of Joash re-
turned from the battle [1]by the ascent
of Heres. 14 And he captured a youth
from the men of Succoth and ques-
tioned him. So *the youth* wrote down
for him the princes of Succoth and its
elders, seventy-seven men. 15 Then
he came to the men of Succoth and
said, "Behold Zebah and Zalmunna,
about whom you reproached me,
*saying,* '[a,1]Are the hands of Zebah
and Zalmunna already in your hand,
that we should give bread to your
men who are weary?'" 16 Then he
took the elders of the city as well as
thorns of the wilderness and briers,
and with them he [1]taught the men
of Succoth a lesson. 17 [a]And he tore
down the tower of Penuel and killed
the men of the city.

18 Then he said to Zebah and Zal-
munna, "What kind of men *were* they
whom you killed at Tabor?" And they
said, "They were like you, each one
[1]resembling the son of a king." 19 And
he said, "They *were* my brothers, the
sons of my mother. *As* Yahweh lives,
if only you had let them live, I would
not kill you." 20 So he said to Jether
his firstborn, "Rise, kill them." But
the youth did not draw his sword, for
he was afraid because he was still a
youth. 21 Then Zebah and Zalmunna
said, "Rise up yourself, and smite us;
for as the man, so is his might." [a]So
Gideon arose and killed Zebah and
Zalmunna and [b]took the crescent
ornaments which were on their
camels' necks.

### *Gideon Makes an Ephod*

22 Then the men of Israel said to
Gideon, "Rule over us, both you and
your son, also your son's son, for
you have saved us from the hand of
Midian." 23 But Gideon said to them,
"I will not rule over you, nor shall
my son rule over you; [a]Yahweh shall
rule over you." 24 Yet Gideon said to
them, "I would [1]make one request
of you, that each of you give me [2]an
earring from his spoil." (For they
had gold earrings because they were

---

**8:7** [a]Jdg 7:15 [1]Or *trample* [2]Lit *flesh* **8:8** [a]Ge 32:31 [1]In Ge 32:30, *Peniel* **8:9** [a]Jdg 8:17
**8:10** [a]Jdg 6:5; 7:12; Is 9:4 **8:11** [1]Or *secure* **8:13** [1]Or *from* **8:15** [a]Jdg 8:6 [1]Lit *Is the palm* **8:16** [1]Lit *made the men...to know* **8:17** [a]Jdg 8:9 **8:18** [1]Lit *like the form of the sons* **8:21** [a]Ps 83:11 [b]Jdg 8:26
**8:23** [a]1Sa 8:7; 10:19; 12:12; Ps 10:16 **8:24** [1]Lit *request a request* [2]Or *a nose ring*

[a]Ishmaelites.) **25** And they said, "We will surely give *them.*" So they spread out a garment, and every one of them threw an earring there from his spoil. **26** And the weight of the gold earrings that he requested was 1,700 *shekels* of gold, besides the crescent ornaments and the pendants and the purple robes which *were* on the kings of Midian, and besides the neck bands that *were* on their camels' necks. **27** Then Gideon made it into [a]an ephod and placed it in his city, Ophrah, and all Israel played the harlot with it there, so that it became a snare to Gideon and his household. **28** So Midian was subdued before the sons of Israel, and they did not lift up their heads anymore. And the land was quiet for forty years in the days of Gideon.

### *The Death and Burial of Gideon*

**29** Then [a]Jerubbaal the son of Joash went and lived in his own house. **30** Now Gideon had [a]seventy sons who [1]were his direct descendants, for he had many wives. **31** And his concubine who was in Shechem also bore him a son, and he [1]named him Abimelech. **32** Then Gideon the son of Joash died at a good old age and was buried in the tomb of his father Joash, in Ophrah of the Abiezrites.

**33** Then it happened, as soon as Gideon was dead, [a]that the sons of Israel turned back and played the harlot with the Baals and made [b]Baal-berith their god. **34** Thus the sons of Israel [a]did not remember Yahweh their God, who had delivered them from the hands of all their enemies on every side; **35** [a]nor did they show lovingkindness to the household of Jerubbaal (*that is,* Gideon) in accord with all the good that he had done to Israel.

### *Abimelech Kills His Brothers*

**9** And [a]Abimelech the son of Jerubbaal went to Shechem to his mother's [1]relatives and spoke to them and to the whole family of the household of his mother's father, saying, **2** "Speak, now, in the hearing of all the lords of Shechem, 'Which is better for you, that [a]seventy men, all the sons of Jerubbaal, rule over you, or that one man rule over you?' Also, remember that I am [b]your bone and your flesh." **3** And his mother's [1]relatives spoke all these words on his behalf in the hearing of all the lords of Shechem; and [2]they were inclined to follow Abimelech, for they said, "He is [a]our [3]relative." **4** So they gave him seventy *pieces* of silver from the house of [a]Baal-berith with which Abimelech hired worthless and reckless fellows, and they followed him. **5** Then he came to his father's house at Ophrah and [a]killed his brothers the sons of Jerubbaal, [b]seventy men, on one stone. But Jotham the youngest son of Jerubbaal was left, for he hid himself. **6** Then all the lords of Shechem and all [1]Beth-millo assembled together, and they went and made Abimelech king, by the [2]oak of the pillar which was in Shechem.

---

**8:24** [a]Ge 25:13-16 **8:27** [a]Ex 28:6-35; Jdg 17:5; 18:14-20 **8:29** [a]Jdg 7:1 **8:30** [a]Jdg 9:2, 5 [1]Lit *came from his loins* **8:31** [1]Lit *appointed his name* **8:33** [a]Jdg 2:11, 12 [b]Jdg 9:4, 27, 46 **8:34** [a]Dt 4:9; Jdg 3:7 **8:35** [a]Jdg 9:16-18 ◆ **9:1** [a]Jdg 8:31, 35 [1]Lit *brothers* **9:2** [a]Jdg 8:30; 9:5, 18 [b]Ge 29:14 **9:3** [a]Ge 29:15 [1]Lit *brothers* [2]Lit *their hearts inclined after* [3]Lit *brother* **9:4** [a]Jdg 8:33 **9:5** [a]2Ki 11:1, 2 [b]Jdg 8:30; 9:2, 18 **9:6** [1]Or *the house of Millo* [2]Or *terebinth*

7 Then they told Jotham, so he
went and stood on the top of [a]Mount
Gerizim and lifted his voice and
called out. Thus he said to them,
"Listen to me, O lords of Shechem,
that God may listen to you. 8 The
trees surely went forth to anoint
a king over them, and they said to
the olive tree, 'Reign over us!' 9 But
the olive tree said to them, 'Shall I
leave my fatness, with [1]which God
and men are honored, and go to wave
over the trees?' 10 Then the trees said
to the fig tree, 'You come, reign over
us!' 11 But the fig tree said to them,
'Shall I leave my sweetness and my
good produce and go to wave over the
trees?' 12 Then the trees said to the
vine, 'You come, reign over us!' 13 But
the vine said to them, 'Shall I leave
my new wine, which makes God and
men glad, and go to wave over the
trees?' 14 Then all the trees said to
the bramble, 'You come, reign over
us!' 15 And the bramble said to the
trees, 'If in [1]truth you are anointing
me as king over you, come and take
refuge in my shade; but if not, may
fire come out from the bramble and
consume the cedars of Lebanon.'

16 "So now, if you have dealt in
[1]truth and integrity and made Abim-
elech king, and if you have dealt well
with [a]Jerubbaal and his house and
[2]have dealt with him according to
the bountiful works of his hands—
17 for my father fought for you and
[1]risked his life and delivered you
from the hand of Midian; 18 but
*you have risen* against my father's
house today and have killed [a]his
sons, seventy men, on one stone,
and have made Abimelech, [b]the son
of his maidservant, king over the
lords of Shechem, because he is your
[1]relative— 19 if then you have dealt
in [1]truth and integrity with Jerubbaal
and his house this day, be glad in
Abimelech, and let him also be glad
in you. 20 But if not, let fire come out
from Abimelech and consume the
lords of Shechem and [1]Beth-millo;
and let fire come out from the lords
of Shechem and from [1]Beth-millo
and consume Abimelech." 21 Then
Jotham escaped and fled and went
to Beer and remained there because
of Abimelech his brother.

### *Zebul Deceives Abimelech*

22 And Abimelech governed over
Israel three years. 23 [a] Then God sent
an evil spirit between Abimelech and
the lords of Shechem; and the lords
of Shechem [b]dealt treacherously with
Abimelech, 24 [a]so that the violence
[1]done to the seventy sons of Jerub-
baal might come, and [b]their blood
might be laid on Abimelech their
brother, who killed them, and on the
lords of Shechem, who strengthened
his hands to kill his brothers. 25 And
the lords of Shechem set [1]men in
ambush against him on the tops of
the mountains, and they robbed all
who might pass by them along the
road; and it was told to Abimelech.

26 Then Gaal the son of Ebed
came with his [1]relatives, and they
crossed over into Shechem; and the
lords of Shechem put their trust
in him. 27 And they went out into

**9:7** [a]Dt 11:29, 30 **9:9** [1]Lit *which by me* **9:15** [1]Or *sincerity* **9:16** [a]Jdg 8:35 [1]Or *sincerity* [2]Lit *if you have* **9:17** [1]Lit *cast his soul in front* **9:18** [a]Jdg 8:30; 9:2, 5 [b]Jdg 8:31 [1]Lit *brother* **9:19** [1]Or *sincerity* **9:20** [1]Or *the house of Millo* **9:23** [a]1Sa 16:14; Is 19:2, 14 [b]Is 33:1 **9:24** [a]Dt 27:25; Jdg 9:56, 57 [b]Nu 35:33 [1]Lit *of the seventy* **9:25** [1]Lit *liers-in-wait for* **9:26** [1]Lit *brothers*

the field and gathered *the grapes*
*of* their vineyards and trod *them*
and celebrated a [1]festival; and they
came into the house of [a]their god
and ate and drank and cursed Abim-
elech. **28** Then Gaal the son of Ebed
said, "Who is Abimelech, and who
is Shechem, that we should serve
him? Is he not the son of Jerubbaal,
and *is* Zebul *not* his [1]officer? Serve
the men of [a]Hamor the father of
Shechem; but why should we serve
him? **29** [a,1]Would, therefore, that this
people were under my hand! Then I
would remove Abimelech." And he
said to Abimelech, "Increase your
army and come out."

**30** Then Zebul the ruler of the
city heard the words of Gaal the
son of Ebed, and his anger burned.
**31** And he sent messengers to Abim-
elech [1]deceitfully, saying, "Behold,
Gaal the son of Ebed and his [2]rela-
tives have come to Shechem; and
behold, they are [3]stirring up the
city against you. **32** So now, arise
by night, you and the people who
are with you, and lie in wait in the
field. **33** And it will be in the morn-
ing, as soon as the sun is up, that
you shall rise early and rush upon
the city; and behold, he and the
people who are with him will come
out against you, and you shall [a]do
*to them* [1]*whatever your hand finds*
*pleasing*."

**34** So Abimelech and all the people
who *were* with him arose by night
and lay in wait against Shechem in
four [1]companies. **35** And Gaal the
son of Ebed went out and stood in
the entrance of the city gate; and
Abimelech and the people who *were*
with him arose from the ambush.
**36** Then Gaal saw the people and
said to Zebul, "Behold, people are
coming down from the tops of the
mountains." But Zebul said to him,
"You are seeing the shadow of the
mountains as *if they were* men."
**37** Yet Gaal spoke again and said,
"Behold, people are coming down
from [a]the [1]highest part of the land,
and one [2]company comes by the way
of [3]the soothsayers' [4]oak." **38** Then
Zebul said to him, "Where is your
[1]boasting now with which you said,
'Who is Abimelech that we should
serve him?' Is this not the people
whom you rejected? Go out now and
fight with them!" **39** So Gaal went
out before the lords of Shechem
and fought with Abimelech. **40** And
Abimelech pursued him, and he fled
before him; and many fell slain up
to the entrance of the gate. **41** Then
Abimelech remained at Arumah,
but Zebul drove out Gaal and his
[1]relatives so that they could not
remain in Shechem.

**42** Now it happened the next day,
that the people went out to the field,
and it was told to Abimelech. **43** So
he took [1]his people and divided
them into three [2]companies and lay
in wait in the field; then he looked,
and behold, the people were coming
out from the city. So he arose against
them and struck them down. **44** Then
Abimelech and the [1]company who
was with him rushed forward and
stood in the entrance of the city gate;

---

**9:27** [a]Jdg 8:33; 9:46 [1]Lit *rejoicing* **9:28** [a]Ge 34:2 [1]Lit *overseer* **9:29** [a]2Sa 15:4 [1]Lit *And who will give this people into my hand* **9:31** [1]Or *in Tormah* [2]Lit *brothers* [3]Lit *besieging* **9:33** [a]1Sa 10:7 [1]Lit *as your hand can find* **9:34** [1]Lit *heads* **9:37** [a]Eze 38:12 [1]Or *center* [2]Lit *head* [3]Heb *Elommeonenim* [4]Or *terebinth* **9:38** [1]Lit *mouth* **9:41** [1]Lit *brothers* **9:43** [1]Lit *the* [2]Lit *heads* **9:44** [1]Singular with Gr; Heb plural, *heads*

but the other two [2]companies rushed
upon all who *were* in the field and
struck them down. **45** So Abimelech
fought against the city all that day,
and he captured the city and killed
the people who *were* in it; then he
[a]tore the city down and sowed it with
salt.

**46** Then all the lords of the tower
of Shechem heard of *it*, and they
entered the inner chamber of the
[1]temple of [a]El-berith. **47** And it was
told to Abimelech that all the lords of
the tower of Shechem were gathered
together. **48** So Abimelech went up
to Mount [a]Zalmon, he and all the
people who *were* with him; and
Abimelech took [1]an axe in his hand
and cut down a branch from the
trees and lifted it and laid *it* on his
shoulder. Then he said to the people
who *were* with him, "What you have
seen me do, hurry *and* do [2]likewise."
**49** And all the people also cut down
each one his branch and followed
Abimelech and put *them* on the inner
chamber and set the inner chamber
on fire over those *inside*, so that all
the men of the tower of Shechem
also died, about one thousand men
and women.

**50** Then Abimelech went to The-
bez, and he camped against Thebez
and captured it. **51** But there was a
strong tower in the center of the city,
and all the men and women with all
the lords of the city fled there and
shut themselves in; and they went
up on the roof of the tower. **52** So
Abimelech came to the tower and
fought against it and approached the
entrance of the tower to burn it with
fire. **53** But [a]a certain woman threw
an upper millstone on Abimelech's
head, and she smashed his skull.
**54** Then [a]he called quickly to the
young man, his armor bearer, and
said to him, "Draw your sword and
put me to death, lest they say of me,
'A woman killed him.'" So [1]the young
man pierced him through, and he
died. **55** Then the men of Israel saw
that Abimelech was dead, so each
went *away* to his [1]home. **56** Thus
[a]God returned the evil of Abimelech,
which he had done to his father in
killing his seventy brothers. **57** God
also returned all the evil of the men
of Shechem on their own heads,
and the curse of Jotham the son of
Jerubbaal came [1]upon them.

### *Tola and Jair Judge Israel*

**10** Then after Abimelech died,
Tola the son of Puah, the son
of Dodo, a man of Issachar, [a]arose
to save Israel; and he lived in Shamir
in the hill country of Ephraim. **2** And
he judged Israel twenty-three years.
Then he died and was buried in
Shamir.

**3** After him, Jair the Gileadite arose
and judged Israel twenty-two years.
**4** And he had thirty sons who rode on
thirty donkeys, and they had thirty
cities [1]in the land of Gilead [a]that are
called [2]Havvoth-jair to this day. **5** And
Jair died and was buried in Kamon.

### *Israel Forsakes Yahweh Again*

**6** Then the sons of Israel again did
what was evil in the eyes of Yah-
weh and [a]served *the Baals and the*
Ashtaroth, the gods of Aram, the gods

**9:44** [2]Lit *heads* **9:45** [a]2Ki 3:25 **9:46** [a]Jdg 8:33 [1]Lit *house* **9:48** [a]Ps 68:14 [1]Lit *the axes* [2]Lit *like me* **9:53** [a]2Sa 11:21 **9:54** [a]1Sa 31:4 [1]Lit *his* **9:55** [1]Lit *place* **9:56** [a]Ge 9:5, 6; Ps 94:23 **9:57** [1]Lit *to* ◆ **10:1** [a]Jdg 2:16 **10:4** [a]Nu 32:41 [1]Lit *which are in* [2]Lit *the towns of Jair* **10:6** [a]Jdg 2:13

of Sidon, the gods of Moab, [b]the gods
of the sons of Ammon, and the gods
of the Philistines; thus [c]they forsook
Yahweh and did not serve Him. **7** So
the anger of Yahweh burned against
Israel, and He [a]sold them into the
hands of the Philistines and into the
hands of the sons of Ammon. **8** And
they shattered and smashed the sons
of Israel [1]that year; for eighteen years
they *did this to* all the sons of Israel
who were beyond the Jordan [2]in
Gilead in the land of the Amorites.
**9** Then the sons of Ammon crossed
the Jordan to fight also against Judah,
Benjamin, and the house of Ephraim,
so that Israel was greatly distressed.

### *Israel Cries Out to Yahweh*

**10** And the [a]sons of Israel cried out
to Yahweh, saying, "We have sinned
against You, for indeed, we have for-
saken our God and served the Baals."
**11** Then Yahweh said to the sons of
Israel, "*Did I* not *save you* [a]from the
Egyptians, [b]the Amorites, [c]the sons
of Ammon, and the Philistines?
**12** Also the Sidonians, the Amalek-
ites, and the Maonites [a]oppressed
you. And you cried out to Me, and
I saved you from their hand. **13** Yet
[a]you have forsaken Me and served
other gods; therefore I will no longer
save you. **14** [a]Go and cry out to the
gods which you have chosen; let
them save you in the time of your
distress." **15** Then the sons of Israel
said to Yahweh, "We have sinned, so
You, [a]do to us whatever seems good
in Your eyes; only please deliver us
this day." **16** [a]So they removed the
foreign gods from among them and
served Yahweh; and [b,1]He could bear
the trouble of Israel no longer.
**17** Then the sons of Ammon were
summoned, and they camped in Gil-
ead. And the sons of Israel gathered
together and camped in [a]Mizpah.
**18** And the people, the princes of
Gilead, said to one another, "Who
is the man who will begin to fight
against the sons of Ammon? He shall
become head over all the inhabitants
of Gilead."

### *Jephthah Delivers Israel*

**11** Now [a]Jephthah the Gileadite
was a mighty man of valor, but
he was the son of a harlot. And Gil-
ead [1]became the father of Jephthah.
**2** And Gilead's wife bore him sons;
and when his wife's sons grew up,
they drove Jephthah out and said to
him, "You shall not have an inheri-
tance in our father's house, for you
are the son of another woman." **3** So
Jephthah fled from his brothers and
lived in the land of [a]Tob; and worth-
less fellows gathered themselves
[1]about Jephthah, and they went out
with him.
**4** Now it happened after a while
that [a]the sons of Ammon fought
against Israel. **5** So it happened
that as the sons of Ammon fought
against Israel, the elders of Gilead
went to get Jephthah from the land
of Tob; **6** and they said to Jephthah,
"Come and be our chief that we may
fight against the sons of Ammon."
**7** Then Jephthah said to the elders
of Gilead, "[a]Did you not hate me

---

**10:6** [b]Jdg 11:24 [c]Dt 31:16, 17; 32:15 **10:7** [a]1Sa 12:9 **10:8** [1]Lit *in that* [2]Lit *which is in* **10:10** [a]1Sa 12:10
**10:11** [a]Jdg 2:12 [b]Nu 21:21-25 [c]Jdg 3:13 **10:12** [a]Ps 106:42 **10:13** [a]Jer 2:13 **10:14** [a]Dt 32:37
**10:15** [a]1Sa 3:18 **10:16** [a]Jos 24:23 [b]Dt 32:36 [1]Lit *His soul was short with the trouble* **10:17** [a]Jdg 11:29
◆ **11:1** [a]Heb 11:32 [1]Lit *begat* **11:3** [a]2Sa 10:6, 8 [1]Lit *to* **11:4** [a]Jdg 10:9, 17 **11:7** [a]Ge 26:27

and drive me from my father's house? So why have you come to me now when you are in distress?" **8** And the elders of Gilead said to Jephthah, "For this reason we have now returned to you, that you may go with us and fight with the sons of Ammon and [a]become head over all the inhabitants of Gilead." **9** So Jephthah said to the elders of Gilead, "If you take me back to fight against the sons of Ammon and Yahweh gives them up [1]to me, will I become your head?" **10** And the elders of Gilead said to Jephthah, "[a]Yahweh is [1]witness between us; surely we will do [2]as you have said." **11** Then Jephthah went with the elders of Gilead, and the people made him head and chief over them; and Jephthah spoke all his words before Yahweh at [a]Mizpah.

**12** And Jephthah sent messengers to the king of the sons of Ammon, saying, "What is between you and me, that you have come to me to fight against my land?" **13** Then the king of the sons of Ammon said to the messengers of Jephthah, "Because Israel [a]took away my land when they came up from Egypt, from the Arnon as far as the [b]Jabbok and the Jordan; so now, return them peaceably." **14** But Jephthah sent messengers again to the king of the sons of Ammon, **15** and they said to him, "Thus says Jephthah, 'Israel did not take away the land of Moab nor the land of the sons of Ammon. **16** For when they came up from Egypt, and Israel [a]went through the wilderness to the [1]Red Sea and [b]came to Kadesh, **17** then Israel [a]sent messengers to the king of Edom, saying, "Please let us pass through your land," but the king of Edom would not listen. [b]And they also sent to the king of Moab, but he was not willing. So Israel remained at Kadesh. **18** Then they went through the wilderness and [a]around the land of Edom and the land of Moab and came to the *east* toward the sunrise of the land of Moab, and they camped beyond the Arnon; but they [b]did not enter the territory of Moab, for the Arnon *was* the border of Moab. **19** And Israel sent [a]messengers to Sihon king of the Amorites, the king of Heshbon, and Israel said to him, "Please let us pass through your land to our place." **20** But Sihon did not believe Israel *to allow* them to pass through his territory; so Sihon gathered all his people and camped in Jahaz and fought with Israel. **21** Then Yahweh, the God of Israel, gave Sihon and all his people into the hand of Israel, and they [a]struck them down; so Israel possessed all the land of the Amorites, the inhabitants of that country. **22** [a]So they possessed all the territory of the Amorites, from the Arnon as far as the Jabbok, and from the wilderness as far as the Jordan. **23** So now Yahweh, the God of Israel, dispossessed the Amorites from before His people Israel. Are you then to possess it? **24** Do you not possess what [a]Chemosh your god gives you to possess? So whatever Yahweh our God has

**11:8** [a]Jdg 10:18 **11:9** [1]Lit *before* **11:10** [a]Ge 31:50; Jer 29:23; 42:5; Mic 1:2 [1]Lit *hearer* [2]Lit *according to your word* **11:11** [a]Jdg 10:17; 11:29; 20:1; 1Sa 10:17 **11:13** [a]Nu 21:24 [b]Ge 32:22 **11:16** [a]Nu 14:25; Dt 1:40 [b]Nu 20:1, 4-21 [1]Lit *Sea of Reeds* **11:17** [a]Nu 20:14-21 [b]Jos 24:9 **11:18** [a]Nu 21:4; Dt 2:8 [b]Dt 2:9, 18, 19 **11:19** [a]Nu 21:21-32; Dt 2:26-36 **11:21** [a]Nu 21:24; Dt 2:32-34 **11:22** [a]Dt 2:36, 37 **11:24** [a]Nu 21:29; 1Ki 11:7

taken possession of before us, we
will possess it. **25** So now are you
any better than [a]Balak the son of
Zippor, king of Moab? Did he ever
strive with Israel, or did he ever fight
against them? **26** [a]While Israel lived
in Heshbon and its towns and in
Aroer and its towns and in all the
cities that are on the banks of the
Arnon, 300 years, why did you not
deliver them *for yourself* within that
time? **27** I therefore have not sinned
against you, but you are doing me
evil by making war against me; [a]may
Yahweh, the Judge, judge today
between the sons of Israel and the
sons of Ammon.'" **28** But the king of
the sons of Ammon did not listen to
the words which Jephthah sent him.

### *Jephthah Vows a Burnt Offering*

**29** Now [a]the Spirit of Yahweh came
upon Jephthah, so that he passed
through Gilead and Manasseh; then
he passed through Mizpah of Gilead,
and from Mizpah of Gilead he went
on to the sons of Ammon. **30** Then
Jephthah made a vow to Yahweh and
said, "If You will indeed give the sons
of Ammon into my hand, **31** then it
shall be that whatever comes out of
the doors of my house to meet me
when I return in peace from the sons
of Ammon, it shall be Yahweh's, and
I will offer it up as a burnt offering."
**32** So Jephthah crossed over to the
sons of Ammon to fight against them;
and Yahweh gave them into his hand.
**33** And he struck them with a very
great slaughter from Aroer [1]to the
entrance of [a]Minnith, twenty cities,
and as far as Abel-keramim. So the
sons of Ammon were subdued before
the sons of Israel.
**34** Then Jephthah came to his
house at [a]Mizpah. And behold, his
daughter was coming out to meet
him [b]with tambourines and with
dancing. Now she was his one *and*
only child; besides her he had no
son or daughter. **35** So it happened
that when he saw her, he tore his
clothes and said, "Alas, my daughter!
You have brought me very low, and
you are among those who trouble
me. But I have opened my mouth
*to vow* to Yahweh, and [a]I cannot
take *it* back." **36** So she said to him,
"My father, you have opened your
mouth *to vow* to Yahweh; [a]do to
me according to what has gone out
from your mouth, since Yahweh has
avenged you of your enemies, the
sons of Ammon." **37** Then she said
to her father, "Let this thing be done
for me; let me alone two months, that
I may [1]go to the mountains and weep
because of [a]my virginity, I and my
companions." **38** Then he said, "Go."
So he sent her away for two months;
and she went with her companions
and wept on the mountains because
of her virginity. **39** And it happened
at the end of two months that she
returned to her father, and he did to
her according to the vow which he
had made; and she did not know a
man. Thus it became a [1]custom in
Israel, **40** that the daughters of Israel
went yearly to [1]commemorate the
daughter of Jephthah the Gileadite
four days in the year.

---

**11:25** [a]Nu 22:2; Jos 24:9; Mic 6:5 **11:26** [a]Nu 21:25, 26; Dt 2:36 **11:27** [a]Ge 16:5; 18:25; 31:53; 1Sa 24:12, 15 **11:29** [a]Jdg 3:10 **11:33** [a]Eze 27:17 [1]Lit *even until you are coming to* **11:34** [a]Jdg 10:17; 11:11 [b]Ex 15:20; 1Sa 18:6; Jer 31:4 **11:35** [a]Nu 30:2; Ecc 5:4, 5 **11:36** [a]Nu 30:2 **11:37** [a]Ge 30:23; Lk 1:25 [1]Lit *go and go down on* **11:39** [1]Lit *statute* **11:40** [1]Lit *recount*; ancient versions *lament*

### *Jephthah Fights Ephraim*

**12** Then the men of Ephraim were summoned, and they crossed [1]to Zaphon and [a]said to Jephthah, "Why did you cross over to fight against the sons of Ammon, but did not call us to go with you? We will burn your house down on you." **2** Then Jephthah said to them, "I and my people were at great strife with the sons of Ammon. And I cried out to you, but you did not save me from their hand. **3** And I saw that you would not save *me*, so I [a,1]took my life in my hands and crossed over against the sons of Ammon, and Yahweh gave them into my hand. Why then have you come up to me this day to fight against me?" **4** Then Jephthah gathered all the men of Gilead and fought Ephraim; and the men of Gilead struck Ephraim down because they said, "You are fugitives of Ephraim, O Gileadites, in the midst of Ephraim *and* in the midst of Manasseh." **5** And the Gileadites [a]captured the fords of the Jordan opposite Ephraim. And it happened when *any of* the fugitives of Ephraim said, "Let me cross over," the men of Gilead would say to him, "Are you an Ephraimite?" If he said, "No," **6** then they would say to him, "Say now, 'Shibboleth.'" But he said, "Sibboleth," for he could not [1]pronounce it correctly. Then they seized him and slaughtered him at the fords of the Jordan. Thus there fell at that time 42,000 of Ephraim.

**7** And Jephthah judged Israel six years. Then Jephthah the Gileadite died and was buried in *one of* the cities of Gilead.

### *Ibzan, Elon, and Abdon Judge Israel*

**8** Then Ibzan of Bethlehem judged Israel after him. **9** And he had thirty sons, and thirty daughters *whom* he [1]gave in marriage outside *the family*, and he brought in thirty daughters from outside for his sons. And he judged Israel seven years. **10** Then Ibzan died and was buried in Bethlehem.

**11** Then Elon the Zebulunite judged Israel after him; and he judged Israel ten years. **12** And Elon the Zebulunite died and was buried at Aijalon in the land of Zebulun.

**13** Then Abdon the son of Hillel the Pirathonite judged Israel after him. **14** And he had forty sons and thirty grandsons who rode on seventy donkeys; and he judged Israel eight years. **15** Then Abdon the son of Hillel the Pirathonite died and was buried at Pirathon in the land of Ephraim, in the hill country of the Amalekites.

### *The Birth of Samson*

**13** Then the sons of Israel [a]again did what was evil in the eyes of Yahweh, so that Yahweh gave them into the hand of the Philistines forty years.

**2** And there was a certain man of [a]Zorah, of the family of the Danites, whose name was Manoah; and his wife was barren and had borne no *children*. **3** [a]Then the angel of Yahweh appeared to the woman and said to her, "Behold now, you are barren and have borne no *children*, but you [1]shall be with child and give birth to a son. **4** So now, be careful [a]not to

---

◆ **12:1** [a]Jdg 8:1 [1]Or *northward* **12:3** [a]1Sa 19:5; 28:21; Job 13:14 [1]Lit *put my soul in my palm* **12:5** [a]Jdg 3:28 **12:6** [1]Lit *speak so* **12:9** [1]Lit *sent outside* ◆ **13:1** [a]Jdg 2:11 **13:2** [a]Jos 19:41 **13:3** [a]Jdg 6:11, 14; 13:6, 8, 10, 11; Lk 1:11-13 [1]Lit *shall conceive*, cf. Ge 3:16; 21:2; 25:21; Ex 2:2; 1Sa 1:20; Lk 1:31, 36 **13:4** [a]Nu 6:2, 3; Lk 1:15

drink wine or strong drink, nor eat
any unclean thing. **5** [a]For behold, you
[1]shall be with child and give birth
to a son, and no razor shall come
upon his head, for the boy shall be
a [b]Nazirite to God from the womb;
and he shall begin to save Israel from
the hand of the Philistines." **6** Then
the woman came and told her hus-
band, saying, "[a]A man of God came
to me, and his appearance was like
the appearance of the angel of God,
very awesome. And I did not ask
him where he *came* from, nor did
he tell me his name. **7** And he said to
me, 'Behold, you [1]shall be with child
and give birth to a son, so now you
shall not drink wine or strong drink,
and you shall not eat any unclean
thing, for the boy shall be a Nazirite
to God from the womb to the day of
his death.'"

**8** Then Manoah entreated Yahweh
and said, "O Lord, please let [a]the man
of God whom You have sent come
to us again that he may instruct us
what to do for the boy who is to be
born." **9** And God listened to the
voice of Manoah; and [a]the angel
of God came again to the woman
as she was sitting in the field, but
Manoah her husband was not with
her. **10** So the woman ran quickly and
told her husband, and she said to
him, "Behold, [a]the man who came
the *other* day to me has appeared
to me." **11** Then Manoah arose and
followed his wife, and when he came
to the man he said to him, "Are you
[a]the man who spoke to the woman?"
And he said, "I am." **12** So Manoah
said, "Now your words will come *to
pass*. What shall be the judgment
*governing* the boy and his work?"
**13** So [a]the angel of Yahweh said to
Manoah, "[b]Let the woman be careful
in all that I said. **14** She should not eat
anything that comes from the [a]vine,
nor drink wine or strong drink, nor
eat any unclean thing; let her keep
all that I commanded."

**15** Then Manoah said to [a]the angel
of Yahweh, "Please let us delay you
so that we may prepare a young goat
for you." **16** And the angel of Yahweh
said to Manoah, "Though you delay
me, [a]I will not eat your [1]food, but if
you prepare a burnt offering, *then*
offer it to Yahweh." For Manoah did
not know that he was the angel of
Yahweh. **17** Then Manoah said to the
angel of Yahweh, "[a]What is your
name, so that when your words come
*to pass*, we may honor you?" **18** But
the angel of Yahweh said to him,
"Why do you ask my name, seeing
it is [a,1]wonderful?" **19** So [a]Manoah
took the young goat with the grain
offering and offered it on the rock
to Yahweh, and He did a wondrous
thing while Manoah and his wife
looked on. **20** Indeed, it happened
when the flame went up from the
altar toward heaven, that the angel
of Yahweh went up in the flame of
the altar. And Manoah and his wife
saw *this*, so they [a]fell on their faces
to the ground.

**21** Now the angel of Yahweh did not
appear to Manoah or his wife again.
[a]Then Manoah knew that he was the
angel of Yahweh. **22** So Manoah said

**13:5** [a]Lk 1:15 [b]Nu 6:2-5 [1]Or *shall conceive*, cf. Ge 3:16; 21:2; 25:21; Ex 2:2; 1Sa 1:20; Lk 1:31, 36
**13:6** [a]Jdg 6:11; 13:8, 10, 11 **13:7** [1]Or *shall conceive*, cf. Ge 3:16; 21:2; 25:21; Ex 2:2; 1Sa 1:20; Lk 1:31, 36
**13:8** [a]Jdg 13:3, 7 **13:9** [a]Jdg 13:8 **13:10** [a]Jdg 13:9 **13:11** [a]Jdg 13:8 **13:13** [a]Jdg 13:11 [b]Jdg 13:4
**13:14** [a]Nu 6:4 **13:15** [a]Jdg 13:3 **13:16** [a]Jdg 6:20 [1]Lit *bread* **13:17** [a]Ge 32:29 **13:18** [a]Is 9:6 [1]Or *incomprehensible* **13:19** [a]Jdg 6:20, 21 **13:20** [a]Lv 9:24; 1Chr 21:16; Eze 1:28; Mt 17:6 **13:21** [a]Jdg 13:16

to his wife, "[a]We will surely die, for
we have seen God." **23** But his wife
said to him, "If Yahweh had desired
to put us to death, He would not have
accepted a burnt offering and a grain
offering from our hands, nor would
He have [a]shown us all these things,
nor would He have let us hear *things*
like this at this time."

**24** Then the woman gave birth to a
son and named him Samson; and the
[a]child grew up, and Yahweh blessed
him. **25** And [a]the Spirit of Yahweh
began to stir him in [b,1]Mahaneh-dan,
between Zorah and Eshtaol.

### *Samson Takes a Philistine as His Wife*

**14** Then Samson went down to
Timnah and saw a woman in
Timnah, *one* of the daughters of the
Philistines. **2** So he came *back* up and
told his father and [1]mother, "I saw a
woman in Timnah, *one* of the daugh-
ters of the Philistines; so now, take
her for me as a wife." **3** But his father
and his mother said to him, "Is there
no woman among the daughters of
your [a,1]relatives, or among all [2]our
people, that you go to [b]take a wife
from the uncircumcised Philistines?"
But Samson said to his father, "Take
her for me, for she is right in my eyes."
**4** However, his father and mother did
not know that [a]it was of Yahweh, for
He was seeking an occasion against
the Philistines. Now at that time the
Philistines were ruling over Israel.

**5** Then Samson went down to
Timnah with his father and mother,
and they came as far as the vineyards
of Timnah; and behold, a young lion
*came* roaring toward him. **6** [a]And the
Spirit of Yahweh [1]came upon him
mightily, so that [b]he tore it as one
tears a young goat, though he had
nothing in his hand; but he did not
tell his father or mother what he had
done. **7** So he went down and spoke to
the woman; and she was right in the
eyes of Samson. **8** Then he returned
later to take her, and he turned aside
to see the carcass of the lion; and
behold, a swarm of bees and honey
were in the body of the lion. **9** So he
scraped [1]the honey into his [2]hands
and went on, eating as he went. Then
he went to his father and mother, and
he gave *some* to them, and they ate *it*;
but he did not tell them that he had
scraped the honey out of the body
of the lion.

**10** Then his father went down to
the woman; and Samson made a feast
there, for the young men customar-
ily did this. **11** Now it happened that
when they saw him, they took thirty
companions to be with him. **12** Then
Samson said to them, "Let me now
[a]propound a riddle to you; if you will
indeed tell it to me within the seven
days of the feast and find it out, then
I will give you thirty linen wraps and
thirty [b]changes of clothes. **13** But if
you are unable to tell me, then you
shall give me thirty linen wraps and
thirty changes of clothes." And they
said to him, "Propound your riddle,
that we may hear it." **14** So he said to
them,

"Out of the eater came
something to eat,

---

**13:22** [a]Ge 32:30; Dt 5:26; Jdg 6:22 **13:23** [a]Ps 25:14 **13:24** [a]1Sa 3:19; Lk 1:80 **13:25** [a]Jdg 3:10 [b]Jdg 18:11, 12 [1]Lit *the camp of Dan* ◆ **14:2** [1]Lit *mother, saying,* **14:3** [a]Ge 24:3, 4 [b]Ex 34:16; Dt 7:3 [1]Lit *brothers* [2]Lit *my* **14:4** [a]Jos 11:20 **14:6** [a]Jdg 3:10 [b]1Sa 17:34-36 [1]Lit *succeeded, rushed upon* **14:9** [1]Lit *it* [2]Lit *palms* **14:12** [a]Eze 17:2 [b]Ge 45:22; 2Ki 5:22

And out of the strong came
something sweet."
But they could not tell the riddle in
three days.
**15** Then it happened on the [1]fourth
day that they said to Samson's wife,
"[a]Entice your husband, so that he
will tell us the riddle, [b]or we will
burn you and your father's house
with fire. Have you invited us to
impoverish us? Is this not *so*?" **16** So
Samson's wife wept before him and
said, "[a]You only hate me, and you do
not love me; you have propounded a
riddle to the sons of my people and
have not told *it* to me." And he said
to her, "Behold, I have not told *it* to
my father or mother; so should I tell
you?" **17** However she wept before
him seven days while their feast
lasted. And on the seventh day he
told her because she pressed him so
hard. She then told the riddle to the
sons of her people. **18** So the men of
the city said to him on the seventh
day before the sun went down,
"What is sweeter than honey?
And what is stronger
than a lion?"
And he said to them,
"If you had not plowed
with my heifer,
You would not have found
out my riddle."
**19** Then [a]the Spirit of Yahweh [1]came
upon him mightily, and he went
down to Ashkelon and struck down
thirty of them and took their spoil
and gave the changes *of clothes* to
those who told the riddle. And his
anger burned, and he went up to his
father's house. **20** But Samson's wife
was [a]*given* to his companion who
had been his [1]friend.

### *Samson Strikes Down the Philistines*

**15** Now it happened that after a
while, in the time of the wheat
harvest, Samson visited his wife
[a]with a young goat and said, "I will
go in to my wife in *her* room." But her
father did not let him enter. **2** And her
father said, "I really thought that you
hated her intensely; so I [a]gave her to
your companion. Is not her younger
sister better than she? Please let her
be yours [1]instead." **3** Samson then
said to them, "This time I shall be
innocent in regard to the Philistines
when I do them harm." **4** So Samson
went and caught 300 foxes and took
torches and turned *the foxes* tail to
tail and put one torch in the middle
between two tails. **5** Then he set fire
to the torches and sent [1]the foxes
into the standing grain of the Philis-
tines. So he caused both the shocks
and the standing grain, along with
the vineyards *and* groves, to burn.
**6** Then the Philistines said, "Who did
this?" And they said, "Samson, the
son-in-law of the Timnite, because
[1]he took his wife and gave her to
his companion." So the Philistines
came up and [a]burned her and her
father with fire. **7** Then Samson said
to them, "If you act like this, then
I will surely take revenge on you,
but after that I will cease." **8** And he
struck them [1]ruthlessly with a great
slaughter; and he went down and
lived in the cleft of the rock of Etam.

**14:15** [a]Jdg 16:5 [b]Jdg 15:6 [1]As in some ancient versions; M.T. *seventh* **14:16** [a]Jdg 16:15
**14:19** [a]Jdg 3:10; 13:25 [1]Lit *succeeded, rushed upon* **14:20** [a]Jdg 15:2 [1]Or *best man* ◆ **15:1** [a]Ge 38:17
**15:2** [a]Jdg 14:20 [1]Lit *instead of her* **15:5** [1]Lit *them* **15:6** [a]Jdg 14:15 [1]The Timnite **15:8** [1]Lit *leg on thigh*

**9** Then the Philistines went up and camped in Judah and spread out in Lehi. **10** So the men of Judah said, "Why have you come up against us?" And they said, "We have come up to bind Samson in order to do to him as he did to us." **11** Then 3,000 men of Judah went down to the cleft of the rock of Etam and said to Samson, "Do you not know [a]that the Philistines are rulers over us? What then is this that you have done to us?" And he said to them, "As they did to me, so I have done to them." **12** And they said to him, "We have come down to bind you so that we may give you into the hand of the Philistines." And Samson said to them, "Swear to me that you yourselves will not [1]kill me." **13** So they said to [1]him, "No, but we will bind you fast and give you into their hands; yet surely we will not put you to death." Then they bound him with two new ropes and brought him up from the rock.

**14** *When* he came to Lehi, the Philistines shouted as they met him. And [a]the Spirit of Yahweh [1]came upon him mightily so that the ropes that were on his arms were as flax that is burned with fire, and his bonds [2]dropped from his hands. **15** And he found a fresh jawbone of a donkey, so he sent forth his hand and took it and struck down [a]1,000 men with it. **16** Then Samson said,

"With the jawbone of a donkey,
[1]Heaps upon heaps,
With the jawbone of a donkey
I have struck down
1,000 men."

**17** Now it happened that when he had finished speaking, he threw the jawbone from his hand; and he named that place [1]Ramath-lehi. **18** Then he became very thirsty, and he [a]called to Yahweh and said, "You have given this great salvation by the hand of Your slave, but now [1]shall I die of thirst [2]and fall into the hands of the uncircumcised?" **19** So God split the hollow place that is in Lehi and water came out of it. Then he drank, [a]and his spirit returned, and he revived. Therefore he named it [1]En-hakkore, which is in Lehi to this day. **20** And [a]he judged Israel twenty years in [b]the days of the Philistines.

### *Samson and Delilah*

**16** Then Samson went to [a]Gaza and saw a harlot there and went in to her. **2** *And it was told* to the Gazites, saying, "Samson has come here," so they [a]surrounded *the place* and lay in wait for him all night at the gate of the city. And they kept silent all night, saying, "*Let us wait* until the morning light; then we will kill him." **3** But Samson lay until midnight, and at midnight he arose and seized the doors of the city gate and the two posts and pulled them up along with the bars; then he put them on his shoulders and brought them up to the top of the mountain which is opposite Hebron.

**4** Now it happened afterwards that he loved a woman in the valley of Sorek, and her name was Delilah. **5** And the [a]lords of the Philistines

**15:11** [a]Lv 26:25; Dt 28:43f; Jdg 13:1; 14:4; Ps 106:40-42 **15:12** [1]Lit *fall upon me* **15:13** [1]Lit *him, saying* **15:14** [a]Jdg 14:19; 1Sa 11:6 [1]Lit *succeeded, rushed upon* [2]Lit *were melted* **15:15** [a]Lv 26:8; Jos 23:10 **15:16** [1]Lit *Heap, two heaps*; Heb is same root as donkey **15:17** [1]Lit *the high place of the jawbone* **15:18** [a]Jdg 16:28 [1]Or *I shall...uncircumcised* [2]Or *or* **15:19** [a]Is 40:29 [1]Lit *the spring of him who called* **15:20** [a]Jdg 16:31; Heb 11:32 [b]Jdg 13:1 ◆ **16:1** [a]Jos 15:47 **16:2** [a]1Sa 23:26; Ps 118:10-12 **16:5** [a]Jos 13:3

came up to her and said to her,
"[b]Entice him, and see where his
great strength *lies* and [1]how we may
overpower him that we may bind him
to afflict him. Then we will each give
you 1,100 *pieces* of silver." **6** So Delilah
said to Samson, "Please tell me where
your great strength is and [1]how you
may be bound to afflict you." **7** Sam-
son said to her, "If they bind me with
seven fresh cords that have not been
dried, then I will become weak and
be like any *other* man." **8** Then the
lords of the Philistines brought up
to her seven fresh cords that had not
been dried, and she bound him with
them. **9** Now she had *men* lying in
wait, sitting in an inner room. And
she said to him, "The Philistines are
upon you, Samson!" But he snapped
the cords as a string of tinder snaps
when it [1]touches fire. So his strength
was *still* not known.

**10** Then Delilah said to Samson,
"Behold, you have deceived me and
told me lies; now please tell me [1]how
you may be bound." **11** And he said
to her, "If they bind me tightly with
new ropes [1]which have not been
used for work, then I will become
weak and be like any *other* man."
**12** So Delilah took new ropes and
bound him with them and said to
him, "The Philistines are upon you,
Samson!" Now the *men* lying in wait
were sitting in the inner room. But
he snapped [1]the ropes from his arms
like a thread.

**13** Then Delilah said to Samson,
"Up to now you have deceived me
and told me lies; tell me [1]how you
may be bound." And he said to her,
"If you weave the seven locks of my
head with the web [2][and fasten it with
a pin, then I will become weak and
be like any other man." **14** So while
he slept, Delilah took the seven locks
of his [1]hair and wove them into the
web]. And she fastened *it* with the
pin and said to him, "The Philistines
are upon you, Samson!" But he awoke
from his sleep and pulled out the pin
of the loom and the web.

**15** Then she said to him, "[a]How can
you say, 'I love you,' when your heart
is not with me? You have deceived
me these three times and have not
told me where your great strength
is." **16** Now it happened when she
pressed him daily with her words
and urged him, that his soul was
[1]annoyed to death. **17** So he told her
all *that was* in his heart and said to
her, "A razor has never come on my
head, for I have been a [a]Nazirite to
God from my mother's womb. If I am
shaved, then my strength will leave
me and I will become weak and be
like every *other* man."

**18** And Delilah saw that he had
told her all *that was* in his heart, so
she sent and called the lords of the
Philistines, saying, "Come up once
more, for he has told me all *that is* in
his heart." Then the lords of the Phi-
listines came up to her and brought
up the silver in their hands. **19** Then
she made him sleep on her knees
and called for a man and had him
shave off the seven locks of his head.
Then she began to afflict him, and his
strength left him. **20** And she said,

---

**16:5** [b]Jdg 14:15 [1]Lit *by what* **16:6** [1]Lit *by what* **16:9** [1]Lit *smells* **16:10** [1]Lit *by what* **16:11** [1]Lit *with which work has not been done* **16:12** [1]Lit *them* **16:13** [1]Lit *by what* [2]The passage in brackets is found in Gr but not in any Heb mss **16:14** [1]Lit *head* **16:15** [a]Jdg 14:16 **16:16** [1]Lit *impatient to the point of, short to the point of*; cf. 10:16 **16:17** [a]Nu 6:2, 5; Jdg 13:5

"The Philistines are upon you, Sam-
son!" And he awoke from his sleep
and said, "I will go out as at other
times and shake myself free." But he
did not know that [a]Yahweh had left
him. **21** Then the Philistines seized
him and gouged out his eyes; and
they brought him down to Gaza
and bound him with bronze chains,
and he was a grinder in the prison.
**22** However, the hair of his head be-
gan to grow again after it was shaved
off.

**23** Now the lords of the Philistines
assembled to offer a great sacrifice to
[a]Dagon their god and to be glad; and
they said,

"Our god has given Samson
our enemy into our hands."

**24** Then the people saw him and
[a]praised their god, for they said,

"Our god has given our
enemy into our hands,
Even the destroyer
of our country,
Who has slain many of us."

**25** So it happened when their hearts
were merry, that they said, "Call for
Samson, that he may amuse us."
So they called for Samson from the
prison, and he [1]entertained them.
And they made him stand between
the pillars. **26** Then Samson said to
the boy who was holding his hand,
"Let me feel the pillars on which the
house is established, that I may lean
against them." **27** Now the house was
full of men and women, and all the
lords of the Philistines were there.
And about 3,000 men and women
were on the roof looking on while
Samson was amusing *them.*

### *Samson's Revenge*

**28** [a]Then Samson called to Yahweh
and said, "O Lord Yahweh, please
remember me and please strengthen
me just this time, O God, that I may
at once [b]be avenged of the Philistines
for my two eyes." **29** Samson grasped
the two middle pillars on which the
house was established and supported
himself against them, the one with
his right hand and the other with his
left. **30** And Samson said, "Let me die
with the Philistines!" And he bent
with his strength so that the house
fell on the lords and all the people
who were in it. So the dead whom
he put to death by his death were
more than those whom he put to
death in his life. **31** Then his brothers
and all his father's household came
down, carried him, brought him up,
and buried him between Zorah and
Eshtaol, in the tomb of Manoah his
father. [a]Thus he had judged Israel
twenty years.

### *Micah's Idolatry*

**17** Now there was a man of the
hill country of Ephraim whose
name was Micah. **2** He said to his
mother, "The 1,100 *pieces* of silver
which were taken from you, about
which you uttered a curse and spoke
*of it* [1]in my hearing, behold, the silver
is with me; it was I who took it." And
his mother said, "Blessed be my son
by Yahweh." **3** And he then returned
the 1,100 *pieces* of silver to his moth-
er, and his mother said, "I wholly
set apart the silver from my hand
as holy to Yahweh for my son [a]to
make a graven image and a molten

**16:20** [a]Nu 14:42, 43; Jos 7:12; 1Sa 16:14 **16:23** [a]1Sa 5:2 **16:24** [a]1Sa 31:9; 1Chr 10:9; Ps 97:7 **16:25** [1]Lit *made sport before them* **16:28** [a]Jdg 15:18 [b]Jer 15:15 **16:31** [a]Jdg 15:20 ◆ **17:2** [1]Lit *in my ears*
**17:3** [a]Ex 20:4, 23; 34:17

image; so now I will return [1]them
to you." **4** So he returned the silver
to his mother, and his mother took
200 *pieces* of silver and gave them to
the silversmith. And he made [1]them
into a graven image and a molten
image, and [2]they were in the house
of Micah. **5** And the man Micah had
a [a,1]shrine, and he made an [b]ephod
and [c,2]household idols and [3]ordained
one of his sons, [d]and he became his
priest. **6** In those days [a]there was no
king in Israel; [b]every man did what
was right in his own eyes.

**7** And there was a young man
from [a]Bethlehem in Judah, of the
family of Judah, who was a Levite;
and he was sojourning there. **8** Then
the man went from the city, from
Bethlehem in Judah, to sojourn
wherever he might find *a place*; and
as he made his journey, he came to
the [a]hill country of Ephraim to the
house of Micah. **9** And Micah said
to him, "Where do you come from?"
And he said to him, "I am a Levite
from Bethlehem in Judah, and I am
going to sojourn wherever I may find
*a place*." **10** Micah then said to him,
"Remain with me and be [a]a father
and a priest to me, and I will give you
ten *pieces* of silver a year, a suit of
clothes, and your sustenance." So
the Levite went *in*. **11** And the Levite
*was willing to remain* with the man,
and the young man became to him
like one of his sons. **12** So Micah
[1]ordained the Levite, and the young
man [a]became his priest and [2]lived in
the house of Micah. **13** Then Micah
said, "Now I know that Yahweh will
prosper me because I have a Levite
as priest."

### *Danites Seek an Inheritance*

**18** [a]In those days there was no king
of Israel; and [b]in those days the
tribe of the Danites was seeking an
inheritance for themselves to live in,
for until that day *the land* among the
tribes of Israel had not fallen to them
as an inheritance. **2** So the sons of
Dan sent from their family five men
out of their whole number, [1]men of
valor from [a]Zorah and Eshtaol, to
spy out the land and to search it;
and they said to them, "Go, search
the land." And they came to [b]the hill
country of Ephraim, to the house of
Micah, and lodged there. **3** They were
near the house of Micah, and they
recognized the voice of the young
man, the Levite. So they turned aside
there and said to him, "Who brought
you here? And what are you doing
in this *place*? And what do you have
here?" **4** And he said to them, "Thus
and so has Micah done to me, and he
has hired me, and [a]I have become his
priest." **5** And they said to him, "Ask
of God, please, that we may know
whether our way on which we are
going will be successful." **6** So the
priest said to them, "Go in peace;
your way in which you are going is
before Yahweh."

**7** Then the five men went *forth* and
came to [a]Laish and saw the people
who were in it living in security, after
the [1]manner of the Sidonians, quiet
and secure; for there was no [2]oppres-
sive conqueror dishonoring *them* for

---

**17:3** [1]Lit *it* **17:4** [1]Lit *it* [2]Lit *it was* **17:5** [a]Jdg 18:24 [b]Jdg 8:27; 18:14 [c]Ge 31:19 [d]Nu 3:10 [1]Lit *house of gods* [2]Heb *teraphim* [3]Lit *filled the hand of* **17:6** [a]Jdg 18:1; 19:1 [b]Dt 12:8; Jdg 21:25 **17:7** [a]Jdg 19:1; Ru 1:1, 2; Mic 5:2; Mt 2:1 **17:8** [a]Jos 24:33 **17:10** [a]Jdg 18:19 **17:12** [a]Nu 16:10; 18:1-7 [1]Lit *filled the hand of* [2]Lit *was* ◆ **18:1** [a]Jdg 17:6; 19:1 [b]Jos 19:40-48 **18:2** [a]Jdg 13:25 [b]Jdg 17:1 [1]Lit *men, sons of valor* **18:4** [a]Jdg 17:12 **18:7** [a]Jos 19:47; Jdg 18:29 [1]Lit *judgment* [2]Lit *the one who possesses oppression*

anything in the land, and they were
far from the Sidonians and had no
dealings with anyone. **8** So they came
back to their brothers at Zorah and
Eshtaol, and their brothers said to
them, "What *do* you *report*?" **9** And
they said, "Arise, and let us go up
against them; for we have seen the
land, and behold, it is very good. And
will you be silent? Do not delay to go,
to enter, to possess the land. **10** When
you enter, you will come to a secure
people and a spacious land; for God
has given it into your hand, [a]a place
where there is no lack of anything
that is on the earth."

**11** Then from the family of the
Danites, from Zorah and from Esh-
taol, 600 men armed with weapons
of war set out. **12** And they went up
and camped at Kiriath-jearim in
Judah. Therefore they called that
place [a,1]Mahaneh-dan to this day;
behold, it is [2]west of Kiriath-jearim.
**13** Then they passed from there to the
hill country of Ephraim and came to
the house of Micah.

### *Danites Take Micah's Idols*

**14** And the five men who went to spy
out the country of Laish answered
and said to their relatives, "Do you
know that there are in these houses
[a]an ephod and [1]household idols and
a graven image and a molten image?
So now, know what you should do."
**15** Then they turned aside there and
came to the house of the young man,
the Levite, to the house of Micah, and
*asked him of* his welfare. **16** Now the
600 men armed with their weapons
of war, who were of the sons of Dan,
were standing by the entrance of
the gate. **17** Then the five men who
went to spy out the land went up *and*
entered there, *and* took [a]the graven
image and the ephod and household
idols and the molten image. And the
priest was standing by the entrance
of the gate with the 600 men armed
with weapons of war. **18** Now these
had entered into Micah's house and
took the graven image, the ephod
and household idols and the molten
image. Then the priest said to them,
"What are you doing?" **19** And they
said to him, "Be silent; [a]put your
hand over your mouth and come
with us and be to us [b]a father and
a priest. Is it better for you to be a
priest to the house of one man or
to be priest to a tribe and a family
in Israel?" **20** And the priest's heart
was merry, and he took the ephod
and household idols and the graven
image and entered among the people.

**21** Then they turned and went
*away* and put the little ones and the
livestock and the valuables in front
of them. **22** They had gone some
distance from the house of Micah,
and the men who *were* in the houses
near Micah's house were summoned
and then overtook the sons of Dan.
**23** And they called out to the sons of
Dan, who turned [1]around and said to
Micah, "What is *the matter* with you,
that you were summoned together?"
**24** And he said, "You have taken away
my gods which I made, and the priest,
and have gone away, and what do I
have besides? So how can you say to
me, 'What is *the matter* with you?'"
**25** Then the sons of Dan said to him,

---

**18:10** [a]Dt 8:9 **18:12** [a]Jdg 13:25 [1]Lit *the camp of Dan* [2]Or *behind* **18:14** [a]Jdg 17:5 [1]Heb *teraphim,* so through v 20 **18:17** [a]Ge 31:19, 30; Is 41:29; Mic 5:13 **18:19** [a]Job 21:5; 29:9; 40:4 [b]Jdg 17:10 **18:23** [1]Lit *their faces*

"Do not let your voice be heard
among us, lest men, bitter of soul,
fall upon you and you [1]lose your life,
with the lives of your household."
**26** So the sons of Dan went on their
way; and when Micah saw that they
were too strong for him, he turned
and went back to his house.
**27** Now they took what Micah
had made and the priest who had
belonged to him, and they came to
[a]Laish, to a people quiet and secure,
and struck them with the edge of
the sword; and they burned the city
with fire. **28** And there was no one to
deliver *them* because it was far from
Sidon and they had no dealings with
anyone, and it was in the valley which
is near [a]Beth-rehob. And they rebuilt
the city and lived in it. **29** [a]And they
called the name of the city Dan, after
the name of Dan their father who was
born in Israel; however, the name of
the city formerly was Laish. **30** Then
the sons of Dan set up for themselves
[a]the graven image; and Jonathan, the
son of [b]Gershom, the son of [1]Moses,
[a]he and his sons were priests to the
tribe of the Danites until the day of
the exile of the land. **31** So they set up
for themselves Micah's graven image
which he had made, all the time that
the [a]house of God was at Shiloh.

### *Benjamites Violate a Levite's Concubine*

**19** Now it happened in those
days, when [a]there was no
king in Israel, that there was a cer-
tain Levite sojourning in the remote
part of the hill country of Ephraim,
who took a concubine for himself
from Bethlehem in Judah. **2** But his
concubine played the harlot against
him, and she went away from him
to her father's house in Bethlehem
in Judah and was there for a period
of four months. **3** Then her husband
arose and went after her to [a]speak to
her heart in order to bring her back,
and his young man was with him
as well as a pair of donkeys. So she
brought him into her father's house,
and the girl's father saw him and was
glad to meet him. **4** And his father-in-
law, the girl's father, prevailed upon
him; and he remained with him three
days. So they ate and drank and spent
the night there. **5** Now it happened
on the fourth day that they got up
early in the morning, and he arose
to go; and the girl's father said to his
son-in-law, "[a]Sustain [1]yourself with
a piece of bread, and afterward you
may go." **6** So both of them sat down
and ate and drank together; and the
girl's father said to the man, "Please
be willing to spend the night, and
[a]let your heart be merry." **7** Then the
man arose to go, but his father-in-law
pressed him so that he turned back
and spent the night there. **8** And on
the fifth day he arose to go early in
the morning, and the girl's father
said, "Please sustain [1]yourself and
wait until [2]afternoon"; so both of
them ate. **9** Then the man arose to
go along with his concubine and
young man, and his father-in-law,
the girl's father, said to him, "Behold
now, the day has drawn [1]to a close;
please spend the night. Behold, the

---

**18:25** [1]Lit *gather* **18:27** [a]Jos 19:47; Jdg 18:7 **18:28** [a]2Sa 10:6 **18:29** [a]Jos 19:47 **18:30** [a]Jdg 17:3, 5 [b]Ex 2:22; 18:3 [1]As in some Heb mss, LXX, and Vg.; M.T. *Manasseh* **18:31** [a]Jos 18:1 ◆ **19:1** [a]Jdg 18:1 **19:3** [a]Ge 34:3; 50:21 **19:5** [a]Ge 18:5; Jdg 19:8 [1]Lit *your heart* **19:6** [a]Jdg 16:25; 19:9, 22; Ru 3:7; 1Ki 21:7; Es 1:10 **19:8** [1]Lit *your heart* [2]Lit *the day declines* **19:9** [1]Lit *toward evening*

day is [2]coming to an end; spend the
night here that your heart may be
merry. Then tomorrow you may arise
early for your journey so that you
may go to your tent."

**10** But the man was not willing
to spend the night, so he arose and
went and came to *a place* before
[a]Jebus (that is, Jerusalem). And there
were with him a pair of saddled don-
keys; his concubine also was with
him. **11** They *were* alongside of Jebus,
and the day was almost gone. And
[a]the young man said to his master,
"Come, please, and let us turn aside
into this city of the Jebusites and
spend the night in it." **12** However,
his master said to him, "We will not
turn aside into the city of foreigners
who are not of the sons of Israel; but
we will pass on by until Gibeah."
**13** Then he said to his young man,
"Come and let us draw near to one
of these places; and we will spend
the night in Gibeah or Ramah." **14** So
they passed along and went their
way, and the sun set on them near
Gibeah which belongs to Benjamin.
**15** Then they turned aside there in
order to enter *and* to spend the night
in Gibeah. So [1]they entered and sat
down in the open square of the city.
Now no one was taking them into *his*
house to spend the night.

**16** But behold, an old man was
coming from his work, from the
field, at evening. Now the man was
from [a]the hill country of Ephraim,
and he was sojourning in Gibeah,
but the men of the place [b]were
Benjamites. **17** And he lifted up his
eyes and saw the traveler in the open
square of the city; and the old man
said, "Where are you going, and
where do you come from?" **18** And
he said to him, "We are passing from
Bethlehem in Judah to the remote
part of the hill country of Ephraim.
I am from there, and I went to
Bethlehem in Judah. But I am *now*
going to [1]the house of Yahweh, and
no man is taking me into his house.
**19** Yet there is both straw and fodder
for our donkeys, and also bread and
wine for me, [1]your maidservant, and
[a]the young man who is with your
servants; there is no lack of any-
thing." **20** Then the old man said,
"[a]Peace be to you. Only let me *take
care of* all that you lack; however,
do not spend the night in the open
square." **21** [a]So he brought him into
his house and gave the donkeys
fodder, and they washed their feet
and ate and drank.

**22** They were making their hearts
merry, and behold, [a]the men of
the city, certain [b,1]vile fellows, sur-
rounded the house, pounding the
door; and they spoke to the owner
of the house, the old man, saying,
"Bring out the man who came into
your house that we may [2]know him."
**23** Then the man, the owner of the
house, went out to them and said
to them, "No, my brothers, please
do not do evil. Since this man has
come into my house, [a]do not commit
this disgraceful act. **24** [a]Behold, my
daughter who is a virgin, and his
concubine—please let me bring
*them out* that you may violate them

---

**19:9** [2]Lit *declining* **19:10** [a]1Chr 11:4, 5 **19:11** [a]Jdg 19:19 **19:15** [1]As in Gr; M.T. *he* **19:16** [a]Jdg 19:1 [b]Jdg 19:14 **19:18** [1]Or *my house*, cf. 19:29 **19:19** [a]Jdg 19:11 [1]My concubine **19:20** [a]Ge 43:23; Jdg 6:23 **19:21** [a]Ge 24:32, 33 **19:22** [a]Ge 19:4, 5; Eze 16:46-48 [b]Dt 13:13; 1Sa 2:12; 1Ki 21:10; 2Co 6:15 [1]Lit *sons of Belial*, cf. 2Co 6:15 [2]Or *have relations with* **19:23** [a]Ge 34:7; Dt 22:21; Jdg 20:6; 2Sa 13:12 **19:24** [a]Ge 19:8

and do to them whatever is good in
your eyes. But do not commit such
a disgraceful act against this man."
**25** But the men were not willing to
listen to him. So the man took hold
of his concubine and brought *her*
out to them; and they knew her and
abused her all night until morning,
and they let her go at the [1]breaking of
dawn. **26** [1]As the day began to dawn,
the woman came and fell down at the
doorway of the man's house where
her master was, until *full* daylight.

**27** Then her master arose in the
morning and opened the doors of
the house and went out to go on his
way, and behold, the woman, his
concubine, was lying at the doorway
of the house with her hands on the
threshold. **28** And he said to her, "Get
up and let us go," [a]but there was no
answer. Then he took her on the
donkey; and the man arose and went
to his [1]home. **29** Then he entered his
house and took a knife and took
hold of his concubine and [a]cut her
in twelve pieces, limb by limb, and
sent her throughout the territory
of Israel. **30** And all who saw *it* said,
"Nothing like this has *ever* happened
or been seen from the day when the
sons of Israel came up from the land
of Egypt to this day. Consider it; [a]take
counsel and speak up!"

### *A Battle Between Israel and Benjamin*

**20** Then all the sons of Israel
from Dan to Beersheba,
including the land of Gilead, came
out, and the congregation assembled
as one man to Yahweh at [a]Mizpah.
**2** And the [1]chiefs of all the people,
*even* of all the tribes of Israel, took
their stand in the assembly of the
people of God, 400,000 foot [2]soldiers
[a]who draw the sword. **3** (Then the
sons of Benjamin heard that the sons
of Israel had gone up to Mizpah.) And
the sons of Israel said, "Tell *us*, how
did this evil take place?" **4** So the
Levite, the husband of the woman
who was murdered, answered and
said, "I came with my concubine
to spend the night at Gibeah which
belongs to Benjamin. **5** Then the
[a]men of Gibeah rose up against me
and surrounded the house at night
because of me. They intended to
kill me; instead, they [b]violated my
concubine, and she died. **6** And I
[a]seized my concubine and cut her
in pieces and sent her throughout
the land of Israel's inheritance; for
[b]they have committed a lewd and
disgraceful act in Israel. **7** Behold, all
you sons of Israel, [a]give your advice
and counsel here."

**8** Then all the people arose as one
man, saying, "Not one of us will go
to his tent, nor will any of us turn
aside to his house. **9** But now this
is the thing which we will do to
Gibeah; *we will go up* against it by
lot. **10** And we will take 10 men out
of 100 throughout the tribes of Israel,
and 100 out of 1,000, and 1,000 out
of 10,000 in order to take up provi-
sions for the people, that when they
come to [1]Gibeah of Benjamin, they
may do to *them* according to all the
disgraceful acts that they have done
in Israel." **11** Thus all the men of Israel

---

**19:25** [1]Lit *rising* **19:26** [1]Lit *At the turning of the morning* **19:28** [a]Jdg 20:5 [1]Lit *place*
**19:29** [a]1Sa 11:7 **19:30** [a]Jdg 20:7; Pr 13:10 ◆ **20:1** [a]1Sa 7:5 **20:2** [a]Jdg 8:10 [1]Lit *cornerstones*
[2]Lit *men* **20:5** [a]Jdg 19:22 [b]Jdg 19:25f **20:6** [a]Jdg 19:29 [b]Ge 34:7; Jos 7:15 **20:7** [a]Jdg 19:30
**20:10** [1]Heb *Geba*

were gathered against the city, united as one man.

**12** Then the tribes of Israel sent men through the entire [1]tribe of Benjamin, saying, "What is this evil that has taken place among you? **13** So now, give up the men, the [a,1]vile fellows in Gibeah, that we may put them to death and [b]purge *this* evil from Israel." But the sons of Benjamin were not willing to listen to the voice of their brothers, the sons of Israel. **14** Then the sons of Benjamin gathered from the cities to Gibeah, to go out to battle against the sons of Israel. **15** And from the cities on that day the [a]sons of Benjamin were [1]numbered, 26,000 men who draw the sword, besides the inhabitants of Gibeah who were [1]numbered, 700 choice men. **16** Out of all these people 700 [a]choice men were left-handed; each one could sling a stone at a hair and not miss.

**17** And the men of Israel besides Benjamin were [1]numbered, 400,000 men who draw the sword; all these were men of war.

**18** Then the sons of Israel arose, went up to Bethel, and [a]asked of God and said, "Who shall go up for us to begin the battle against the sons of Benjamin?" Then Yahweh said, "Judah shall begin *it*."

**19** So the sons of Israel arose in the morning and camped against Gibeah. **20** And the men of Israel went out to battle against Benjamin, and the men of Israel arranged *themselves* for battle against them at Gibeah. **21** Then the sons of Benjamin came out of Gibeah and [a]destroyed to the ground on that day 22,000 men of Israel. **22** But the people, the men of Israel, strengthened themselves and arranged themselves for battle again in the place where they had arranged *themselves* the first day. **23** [a]And the sons of Israel went up and wept before Yahweh until evening and [b]asked of Yahweh, saying, "Shall we again approach for battle against the sons of my brother Benjamin?" And Yahweh said, "Go up against him."

**24** Then the sons of Israel drew near to the sons of Benjamin the second day. **25** And Benjamin went out to meet them from Gibeah the second day and destroyed to the ground again 18,000 men of the sons of Israel; all these drew the sword. **26** Then [a]all the sons of Israel and all the people went up and came to Bethel and wept; thus they remained there before Yahweh and fasted that day until evening. And they offered burnt offerings and peace offerings before Yahweh. **27** Then the sons of Israel [a]asked of Yahweh (now the ark of the covenant of God *was* there in those days, **28** and Phinehas the son of Eleazar, Aaron's son, stood before it *to minister* in those days), saying, "Shall I yet again go out to battle against the sons of my brother Benjamin, or shall I cease?" And Yahweh said, "Go up, [a]for tomorrow I will give them into your hand."

**29** [a]So Israel set men in ambush around Gibeah. **30** And the sons of Israel went up against the sons of Benjamin on the third day and

**20:12** [1]Lit *tribes* **20:13** [a]2Co 6:15 [b]Dt 13:5; 17:12; 1Co 5:13 [1]Lit *sons of Belial*, cf. 2Co 6:15
**20:15** [a]Nu 1:36, 37; 2:23; 26:41 [1]Or *mustered* **20:16** [a]Jdg 3:15; 1Chr 12:2 **20:17** [1]Or *mustered*
**20:18** [a]Nu 27:21; Jdg 20:23, 27 **20:21** [a]Jdg 20:25 **20:23** [a]Jos 7:6, 7 [b]Jdg 20:18 **20:26** [a]Jdg 20:23; 21:2 **20:27** [a]Jdg 20:18 **20:28** [a]Jdg 7:9 **20:29** [a]Jos 8:4

arrayed themselves against Gibeah
as at other times. **31** [a]So the sons
of Benjamin went out to meet the
people and were drawn away from
the city, and they began to strike
[1]and slay some of the people as at
other times, on the highways, one
of which goes up to Bethel and the
other to Gibeah, *and* in the field,
about thirty men of Israel. **32** The
sons of Benjamin said, "They are
[1]defeated before us, as at the first."
But the sons of Israel said, "Let us
flee that we may draw them away
from the city to the highways."
**33** Then all the men of Israel arose
from their place and arrayed them-
selves at Baal-tamar; [a]and the men
of Israel in ambush burst forth of
their place, even out of Maareh-
geba. **34** Then 10,000 choice men
from all Israel came against Gibe-
ah, and the battle became heavy;
[a]but [1]Benjamin did not know that
[2]calamity was [3]about to reach
them. **35** Then Yahweh [1]defeated
Benjamin before Israel, so that the
sons of Israel destroyed 25,100 men
of Benjamin that day, all [2]who drew
the sword.

**36** So the sons of Benjamin saw
that they were [1]defeated. [a]Now the
men of Israel had given [2]ground to
Benjamin because they relied on the
men in ambush whom they had set
against Gibeah. **37** [a]So the men in
ambush hurried and rushed against
Gibeah. Then the men in ambush
deployed and struck all the city with
the edge of the sword. **38** Now the
appointed sign between the men of
Israel and the men in ambush was
[a]that they would make a great cloud
of smoke rise from the city. **39** So the
men of Israel *had* turned around in
the battle, and Benjamin *had* begun
to strike [1]and slay about thirty men
of Israel, [a]for they said, "Surely they
are [2]defeated before us, as in the first
battle." **40** But the cloud began to rise
from the city in a column of smoke,
and Benjamin turned [a]behind them;
and behold, the whole city was going
up *in smoke* to heaven. **41** Then the
men of Israel turned around *again*,
and the men of Benjamin were dis-
mayed; for they saw that [a,1]calamity
had [2]reached them. **42** Therefore,
they turned their backs before the
men of Israel [a]toward the direction
of the wilderness, but the battle
overtook them, and those who came
out of the cities destroyed them in
the midst of them. **43** [a]They sur-
rounded Benjamin, pursued them
without rest, *and* trod them down
opposite Gibeah to the *east* toward
the sunrise. **44** Thus 18,000 men of
Benjamin fell; all these were valiant
men. **45** [1]And the rest turned and
fled toward the wilderness to the
rock of [a]Rimmon, but they [2]caught
5,000 of them on the highways
and overtook them [3]at Gidom and
struck down 2,000 of them. **46** So all
of Benjamin who fell that day were
25,000 men who drew the sword;
all these were valiant men. **47** But
600 men turned and fled toward the
wilderness to the rock of Rimmon,
and they remained at the rock
of Rimmon four months. **48** Now

---

**20:31** [a]Jos 8:16 [1]Lit *slain ones* **20:32** [1]Lit *smitten* **20:33** [a]Jos 8:19 **20:34** [a]Jos 8:14; Job 21:13 [1]Lit *they* [2]Lit *evil* [3]Lit *touching* **20:35** [1]Lit *smote* [2]Lit *these* **20:36** [a]Jos 8:15 [1]Lit *smitten* [2]Lit *place* **20:37** [a]Jos 8:19 **20:38** [a]Jos 8:20 **20:39** [a]Jdg 20:32 [1]Lit *slain ones* [2]Lit *smitten* **20:40** [a]Jos 8:20 **20:41** [a]Pr 5:22; 11:5, 6; 29:6 [1]Lit *evil* [2]Lit *touched* **20:42** [a]Jos 8:15, 24 **20:43** [a]Hos 9:9; 10:9 **20:45** [a]Jdg 21:13 [1]As in Gr; Heb *And they* [2]Lit *gleaned* [3]Lit *as far as*

the men of Israel returned to the
sons of Benjamin and struck them
with the edge of the sword, both the
entire city with the cattle and all that
they found; they also set on fire all
the cities which they found.

### *A Tribe Is Cut Off*

**21** Now the men of Israel [a]had
sworn in Mizpah, saying,
"None of us shall give his daughter to
Benjamin as a wife." **2** [a]So the people
came to Bethel and sat there before
God until evening and lifted up their
voices and wept [1]bitterly. **3** And they
said, "Why, O Yahweh, God of Israel,
has this come about in Israel, so that
one tribe should be missing today
from Israel?" **4** Now it happened the
next day that the people arose early
and built [a]an altar there and offered
burnt offerings and peace offerings.
**5** Then the sons of Israel said,
"Who is there among all the tribes
of Israel who did not come up in the
assembly to Yahweh?" For [1]they had
taken a great oath concerning him
[a]who did not come up to Yahweh
at Mizpah, saying, "He shall surely
be put to death." **6** And the sons of
Israel were sorry for their brother
Benjamin and said, "One tribe is cut
off from Israel today. **7** What shall we
do for wives for those who are left?
But we have [a]sworn by Yahweh not
to give them any of our daughters in
marriage."

### *Sons of Benjamin Steal the Daughters of Shiloh*

**8** So they said, "What one is there
of the tribes of Israel who did not
come up to Yahweh at Mizpah?"
And behold, no one had come to
the camp from Jabesh-gilead to the
assembly. **9** Indeed the people were
[1]numbered, but behold, not one of
the inhabitants of Jabesh-gilead was
there. **10** And the congregation sent
12,000 of the men of valor there and
commanded them, saying, "Go and
[a]strike the inhabitants of Jabesh-
gilead with the edge of the sword,
with the women and the little ones.
**11** Now this is the thing that you shall
do: you [a]shall devote to destruction
every man and every woman who
has known, *that is* lain with, a man."
**12** And they found among the inhab-
itants of Jabesh-gilead 400 young
virgins who had not known a man
by lying with [1]him; and they brought
them to the camp at Shiloh, which is
in the land of Canaan.
**13** Then the whole congregation
sent *word* and spoke to the sons of
Benjamin who were [a]at the rock of
Rimmon and [b]called out peace to
them. **14** Then Benjamin returned at
that time, and they gave them the
women whom they had kept alive
from the women of Jabesh-gilead;
yet they did not find [1]enough for
them. **15** And the people were sorry
for Benjamin because Yahweh had
made a breach in the tribes of Israel.
**16** Then the elders of the congre-
gation said, "What shall we do for
wives for those who are left, since
the women are destroyed out of
Benjamin?" **17** And they said, "*There
must be* a possession for the survi-
vors of Benjamin, so that a tribe will
not be blotted out from Israel. **18** But

---

◆ **21:1** [a]Jdg 21:7, 18 **21:2** [a]Jdg 20:26 [1]Lit *with great weeping* **21:4** [a]Dt 12:5; 2Sa 24:25
**21:5** [a]Jdg 5:23 [1]Lit *there was a great oath* **21:7** [a]Jdg 21:1 **21:9** [1]Or *mustered* **21:10** [a]Nu 31:17; Jdg 5:23; 1Sa 11:7 **21:11** [a]Nu 31:17 **21:12** [1]Lit *a male* **21:13** [a]Jdg 20:47 [b]Dt 20:10 **21:14** [1]Lit *it so*

we cannot give them wives of our
daughters." For the sons of Israel
[a]had sworn, saying, "Cursed is he
who gives a wife to Benjamin."
**19** So they said, "Behold, there is a
feast of Yahweh from year to year in
[a]Shiloh, which is on the north side
of Bethel, on [1]the east side of the
highway that goes up from Bethel to
Shechem, and on the south side of
Lebonah." **20** And they commanded
the sons of Benjamin, saying, "Go and
lie in wait in the vineyards, **21** and
watch; and behold, if the daughters
of Shiloh come out to [a,1]take part
in the dances, then you shall come
out of the vineyards, and each of
you shall catch his wife from the
daughters of Shiloh and go to the
land of Benjamin. **22** And it will be
when their fathers or their brothers
come to contend with us, that we
shall say to them, 'Be gracious to us
concerning them because we did not
take for each man *of Benjamin* [1]a wife
in the battle, [a,2]and you did not give
*your daughters* to them; *otherwise*
you would now be guilty.'" **23** And the
sons of Benjamin did so and carried
away wives according to their num-
ber from those who danced, whom
they stole away. And they went and
returned to their inheritance and
[a]rebuilt the cities and lived in them.
**24** Then the sons of Israel went *away*
from there at that time, every man
to his tribe and family, and each one
of them went out from there to his
inheritance.
**25** [a]In those days there was no king
in Israel; everyone did what was right
in his own eyes.

# *The Book of* RUTH

### *Naomi's Husband and Sons Die*

**1** Now it happened in the days
[a]when the judges judged, that
there was [b]a famine in the land. And
a certain man [c]of Bethlehem in Judah
went to sojourn in the fields of Moab
[1]with his wife and his two sons. **2** The
*name of the man was* Elimelech, and
the name of his wife, Naomi; and the
names of his two sons *were* Mahlon
and Chilion, Ephrathites of Bethle-
hem in Judah. Now they [a]came to the
fields of Moab and remained there.
**3** Then Elimelech, Naomi's husband,
died; and she was left with her two
sons. **4** They took for themselves
Moabite women *as* wives; the name
of the one was Orpah and the name
of the other Ruth. And they lived
there about ten years. **5** Then [1]both
Mahlon and Chilion also died, and
the woman was left without her two
children and her husband.

### *Ruth Is Determined to Go with Naomi*

**6** Then she arose with her daughters-
in-law and returned from the fields
of Moab, for she had heard in the

**21:18** [a]Jdg 21:1 **21:19** [a]Jos 18:1; Jdg 18:31; 1Sa 1:3 [1]Lit *to the sunrise* **21:21** [a]Ex 15:20; Jdg 11:34 [1]Lit *dance* **21:22** [a]Jdg 21:1, 18 [1]Lit *his* [2]Lit *because* **21:23** [a]Jdg 20:48 **21:25** [a]Jdg 17:6; 18:1; 19:1
◆ **1:1** [a]Jdg 2:16-18 [b]Ge 12:10; 26:1; 2Ki 8:1 [c]Jdg 17:8; Mic 5:2 [1]Lit *he, and* **1:2** [a]Jdg 3:30 **1:5** [1]Lit *both of them*

fields of Moab that [1]Yahweh had
[a]visited His people to [b]give them
[2]food. **7** So she went forth from the
place where she was, and her two
daughters-in-law with her; and they
went on the way to return to the land
of Judah. **8** And Naomi said to her two
daughters-in-law, "Go, return each
of you to her mother's house. [a]May
Yahweh [1]show lovingkindness with
you as you have [2]shown with the
dead and with me. **9** May Yahweh
grant that you may find rest, each
in the house of her husband." Then
she kissed them, and they lifted up
their voices and wept. **10** And they
said to her, "*No*, but we will return
with you to your people." **11** But
Naomi said, "Return, my daughters.
Why should you go with me? Have
I yet sons in my womb, that [a]they
may be your husbands? **12** Return,
my daughters! Go, for I am too old
to have a husband. If I said I have
hope, if I should even have a husband
tonight and also bear sons, **13** would
you therefore wait until they were
grown? Would you therefore refrain
from marrying? No, my daughters;
for it is more bitter for me than for
you, for [a]the hand of Yahweh has
gone forth against me." **14** And they
lifted up their voices and wept again;
and Orpah kissed her mother-in-law,
but Ruth clung to her.

**15** Then she said, "Behold, your
sister-in-law has returned to her
people and her [a]gods; return after
your sister-in-law." **16** But Ruth said,
"Do not press me to forsake you in
turning back from following you; for
where you go, I will go, and where
you lodge, I will lodge. Your people
*shall be* my people, and your God,
my God. **17** Where you die, I will
die, and there I will be buried. Thus
may [a]Yahweh do to me, and more,
if *anything but* death separates you
and me." **18** So [a]she saw that she was
determined to go with her, and she
[1]said no more to her.

**19** Then they both went until
they came to Bethlehem. Now it
happened, when they had come to
Bethlehem, [a]all the city was stirred
because of them, and [1]the women
said, "Is this Naomi?" **20** She said to
them, "Do not call me [1]Naomi; call
me [2]Mara, for [a,3]the Almighty has
dealt very bitterly with me. **21** I went
out full, but [a]Yahweh has caused me
to return empty. Why do you call
me Naomi? Yahweh has answered
against me, and [1]the Almighty has
brought calamity against me."

**22** So Naomi returned, and with her
Ruth the Moabitess, her daughter-in-
law, who returned from the fields of
Moab. Now they came to Bethlehem
at [a]the beginning of barley harvest.

### *Ruth Gleans in Boaz' Field*

**2** Now Naomi had [1]a kinsman of
her husband, a [2]mighty man of
excellence, of the family of [a]Elim-
elech, whose name was Boaz. **2** And
Ruth the Moabitess said to Naomi,
"Please let me go to the field and

**1:6** [a]Ex 4:31; Jer 29:10; Zep 2:7 [b]Ps 132:15; Mt 6:11 [1]The personal covenant name of God, a form of I AM WHO I AM, cf. Ex 3:14-15 [2]Lit *bread*, cf. Bethlehem (house of bread), Ru 1:19 **1:8** [a]2Ti 1:16 [1]Lit *do*, cf. 1:17; 2:11, 19 [2]Lit *done*, cf. 1:17; 2:11, 19 **1:11** [a]Ge 38:11; Dt 25:5 **1:13** [a]Jdg 2:15; Job 19:21; Ps 32:4 **1:15** [a]Jos 24:15; Jdg 11:24 **1:17** [a]1Sa 3:17; 2Ki 6:31 **1:18** [a]Ac 21:14 [1]Lit *ceased to speak* **1:19** [a]Mt 21:10 [1]Lit *they* **1:20** [a]Ex 6:3; Job 6:4 [1]Lit *pleasant* [2]Lit *bitter* [3]Heb *Shaddai* **1:21** [a]Job 1:21 [1]Heb *Shaddai* **1:22** [a]Ex 9:31; Lv 23:10, 11 ◆ **2:1** [a]Ru 1:2 [1]Or *an acquaintance* [2]Or *mighty man of valor*, cf. Jdg 6:12; 11:1

[a]glean among the ears of grain after
one whom I may find favor in his
eyes." And she said to her, "Go, my
daughter." **3** So she went. And she
came and gleaned in the field after
the reapers. And [1]it so happened that
she happened *to come* to the portion
of the field belonging to Boaz, who
was of the family of Elimelech. **4** Now
behold, Boaz came from Bethlehem
and said to the reapers, "[a]May Yahweh
be with you." And they said to him,
"May Yahweh bless you." **5** Then Boaz
said to his young man who was [1]in
charge of the reapers, "Whose young
woman is this?" **6** The young man [1]in
charge of the reapers replied, "She
is the young Moabite woman who
returned with Naomi from the fields
of Moab. **7** And she said, 'Please let
me glean and gather after the reapers
among the sheaves.' Thus she came
and has remained from the morning
until now; she has been sitting in the
house for a little while."

**8** Then Boaz said to Ruth, "Have
you not heard, my daughter? Do
not go to glean in another field;
furthermore, do not go on from this
one, but [1]stay here with my young
women. **9** Let your eyes be on the
field which they reap, and go after
them. Indeed, I have commanded the
young men not to touch you. And *if*
you are thirsty, go to the [1]water jars
and drink from what the young men
draw." **10** Then she [a]fell on her face,
bowing to the ground and said to
him, "Why have I found favor in your
sight that you should take notice
of me, though I am a foreigner?"
**11** Boaz replied to her, "All that you
have done for your mother-in-law
after the death of your husband has
been fully told to me, and how you
forsook your father and your moth-
er and the land of your birth, and
came to a people that you did not
previously know. **12** [a]May Yahweh
fully repay your work, and may your
wages be full from Yahweh, the God
of Israel, [b]under whose wings you
have come to seek refuge." **13** Then
she said, "May I find favor in your
eyes, my lord, for you have comfort-
ed me and indeed have spoken to
the heart of your servant-woman,
though I am not like one of your
servant-women."

**14** At mealtime Boaz said to her,
"[1]Come here, that you may eat of
the bread and dip your piece of bread
in the vinegar." So she sat beside the
reapers; and he [2]served her roasted
grain, and she ate and was satisfied
[a]and had some left. **15** Then she rose
to glean, and Boaz commanded his
young men, saying, "Let her glean
even among the sheaves, and do
not dishonor her. **16** Also you shall
purposely pull out for her *some grain*
from the bundles and [1]leave *it* that
she may glean, and do not rebuke
her."

**17** So she gleaned in the field until
evening. Then she beat out what
she had gleaned, and it was about
an [1]ephah of barley. **18** She took *it*
up and went into the city, and her
mother-in-law saw what she had
gleaned. She also took *it* out and
[a]gave [1]Naomi what she had left after

**2:2** [a]Lv 19:9, 10; 23:22; Dt 24:19; Ru 2:7 **2:3** [1]Lit *her chance chanced upon* **2:4** [a]Jdg 6:12; Ps 129:8; Lk 1:28; 2Th 3:16 **2:5** [1]Lit *appointed over* **2:6** [1]Lit *who was appointed over* **2:8** [1]Lit *cling*, cf. 1:14 **2:9** [1]Lit *vessels* **2:10** [a]1Sa 25:23 **2:12** [a]1Sa 24:19 [b]Ru 1:16; Ps 17:8; 36:7; 57:1; 61:4; 63:7; 91:4 **2:14** [a]Ru 2:18 [1]Lit *Draw near* [2]Lit *held out to* **2:16** [1]Or *forsake*, cf. 1:16; 2:11, 20 **2:17** [1]An ephah was approx. 21 qt. or 23 l **2:18** [a]Ru 2:14 [1]Lit *her*

[2]she was satisfied. **19** Her mother-in-
law then said to her, "Where did
you glean today and where did you
[1]work? May he who [a]took notice
of you be blessed." So she told her
mother-in-law with whom she
had [2]worked and said, "The name
of the man with whom I worked
today is Boaz." **20** Naomi said to her
daughter-in-law, "[a]May he be blessed
of Yahweh who has not forsaken his
lovingkindness to the living and to
the dead." Then Naomi said to her,
"The man is [1]our relative; he is one
of our *kinsman* redeemers." **21** Then
Ruth the Moabitess said, "[1]Further-
more, he said to me, 'You should
[2]stay close to my young men until
they have finished all my harvest.'"
**22** Naomi said to Ruth her daughter-
in-law, "It is good, my daughter, that
you go out with his young women,
so that *others* do not oppress you in
another field." **23** So she [1]stayed close
by the young women of Boaz in order
to glean until [a]the end of the barley
harvest and the wheat harvest. And
she lived with her mother-in-law.

### *Boaz Will Redeem Ruth*

**3** Then Naomi her mother-in-law
said to her, "My daughter, shall I
not seek *a state of* rest for you, that it
may be well with you? **2** And now, is
not Boaz [a]our [1]kinsman, with whose
young women you were? Behold, he
is winnowing barley at the threshing
floor tonight. **3** So you shall wash
yourself and anoint yourself and put
on your *best* clothes, and you shall
go down to the threshing floor; *but*
do not make yourself known to the
man until he has finished eating and
drinking. **4** Let it be that when he
lies down, you shall know the place
where he lies, and you shall go and
uncover his feet and lie down; then
he will tell you what you shall do."
**5** She said to her, "[a]All that you say
I will do."

**6** So she went down to the threshing
floor and did according to all that her
mother-in-law had commanded her.
**7** And Boaz ate and drank and [a]his
heart was merry, and he went to lie
down at the end of the heap of grain;
and she came secretly and uncov-
ered his feet and lay down. **8** Then it
happened in the middle of the night
that the man was startled and [1]bent
forward; and behold, a woman was
lying at his feet. **9** And he said, "Who
are you?" And she answered, "I am
Ruth your maidservant. So spread
your [a]wing over your maidservant,
for you are a *kinsman* redeemer."
**10** Then he said, "[a]May you be blessed
of Yahweh, my daughter. You have
shown your last lovingkindness to
be better than the first by not going
after young men, whether poor or
rich. **11** So now, my daughter, do not
fear. All that you say, I will do for you;
for all my people within the gates *of
the city* know that you are [a]a woman
of excellence. **12** But now it is true I am
a *kinsman* redeemer; however, there
is a *kinsman* redeemer closer than I.
**13** Stay this night, and it will be in the
morning that, [a]if he will [1]redeem you,
good; let him redeem you. But if he
does not desire to [1]redeem you, then

**2:18** [2]Lit *her satiety* **2:19** [a]Ps 41:1 [1]Lit *do*, cf. 1:8, 17; 2:11 [2]Lit *done*, cf. 1:8, 17; 2:11 **2:20** [a]2Sa 2:5 [1]Lit *near to us* **2:21** [1]Lit *Also that* [2]Lit *cling*, cf. 1:14; 2:8 **2:23** [a]Dt 16:9 [1]Lit *clung*, cf. 1:14; 2:8, 21 ◆ **3:2** [a]Dt 25:5-10 [1]Or *acquaintance* **3:5** [a]Eph 6:1; Col 3:20 **3:7** [a]Jdg 19:6, 9; 2Sa 13:28; 1Ki 21:7; Es 1:10 **3:8** [1]Lit *twisted himself* **3:9** [a]Ru 2:12 **3:10** [a]Ru 2:20 **3:11** [a]Pr 12:4; 31:10 **3:13** [a]Dt 25:5; Mt 22:24 [1]Or *act as close relative to*

I will redeem you, [b]as Yahweh lives. Lie down until morning."

**14** So she lay at his feet until morning and rose before one could recognize another; and he said, "[a]Let it not be known that the woman came to the threshing floor." **15** And he said, "Give me the cloak that is on you and hold it." So she held it, and he measured six *measures* of barley and placed *it* on her. Then [1]she went into the city. **16** Then she came to her mother-in-law, and she said, "[1]How did it go, my daughter?" And she told her all that the man had done for her. **17** She said, "These six *measures* of barley he gave to me, for he said, 'Do not go to your mother-in-law empty.'" **18** Then she said, "Sit, *then*, my daughter, until you know how the matter falls *into place*; for the man will not remain quiet until he has finished the matter today."

### *Ruth Becomes Boaz' Wife*

**4** Now Boaz went up to the gate and sat down there, and behold, [a]the *kinsman* redeemer of whom Boaz spoke was passing by, so he said, "Turn aside, [1]my fellow, sit down here." And he turned aside and sat down. **2** Then he took ten men of the [a]elders of the city and said, "Sit down here." So they sat down. **3** Then he said to the *kinsman* redeemer, "Naomi, who has come back from the fields of Moab, has to sell the portion of the field [a]which belonged to our brother Elimelech. **4** So I thought to uncover *this matter* in your hearing, saying, '[a]Acquire *it* before those who are sitting *here* and before the elders of my people. If you will redeem *it*, redeem *it*; but if no one redeems *it*, tell me that I may know; for [b]there is no one but you to redeem *it*, and I am after you.'" And he said, "I will redeem *it*." **5** Then Boaz said, "On the day you acquire the field from the hand of Naomi, you must also [1]acquire Ruth the Moabitess, the widow of the one who had died, in order [a]to raise up the name of the one who had died, on behalf of his inheritance." **6** [a]So the *kinsman* redeemer said, "I cannot redeem *it* for myself, lest I ruin my own inheritance. You redeem my right of redemption for yourself, for I cannot redeem *it*."

**7** Now this was [a]*the custom* in former times in Israel concerning the right of redemption and the exchange *of land* to establish any matter: a man removed his sandal and gave it to another; and this was the *manner of* attestation in Israel. **8** So the *kinsman* redeemer said to Boaz, "Acquire *this* for yourself." And he removed his sandal. **9** Then Boaz said to the elders and all the people, "You are witnesses today that I have acquired all that belonged to Elimelech and all that belonged to Chilion and Mahlon from the hand of Naomi. **10** And also, I have acquired Ruth the Moabitess, the widow of Mahlon, to be my wife in order to raise up the name of the one who had died, on behalf of his inheritance, so [a]that the name of the one who had died will not be cut off from his brothers or from the gate of his *birth* place;

**3:13** [b]Jdg 8:19; Jer 4:2; 12:16 **3:14** [a]Ro 14:16; 2Co 8:21 **3:15** [1]As in many mss; M.T. *he* **3:16** [1]Lit *Who are you?* ◆ **4:1** [a]Ru 3:12 [1]Lit *a certain one* **4:2** [a]1Ki 21:8; Pr 31:23 **4:3** [a]Lv 25:25 **4:4** [a]Jer 32:7f [b]Lv 25:25 **4:5** [a]Ge 38:8; Dt 25:5f; Mt 22:24 [1]Or *acquire it from Ruth* **4:6** [a]Lv 25:25 **4:7** [a]Dt 25:8-10 **4:10** [a]Dt 25:6

you are witnesses today." **11** And all
the people who were in the gate, and
the elders, said, "*We are* witnesses.
May Yahweh grant the woman who
is coming into your home *to be* [a]like
Rachel and Leah, both of whom built
the house of Israel, and so you shall
[1]achieve [2]excellence in Ephrathah
and shall [3]proclaim *your* name in
Bethlehem. **12** Moreover, may your
house be like the house of [a]Perez
whom Tamar bore to Judah, through
the seed which Yahweh will grant you
by this young woman."

**13** So Boaz took Ruth, and she
became his wife, and he went in
to her. And [a]Yahweh granted her
conception, and she gave birth to
a son. **14** Then the [a]women said to
Naomi, "Blessed is Yahweh who has
not left you without a [1]*kinsman*
redeemer today, and may his name
[2]be proclaimed in Israel. **15** May he
also be to you a restorer of *your* soul
and a sustainer of your [1]old age; for
your daughter-in-law, who loves you
[a,2]and is better to you than seven
sons, has given birth to him."

### *The Generations of David*

**16** Then Naomi took the child [1]and
put him on her bosom and became
his nurse. **17** The neighbor women
gave him a name, saying, "A son has
been born to Naomi!" So they named
him Obed. He is the father of Jesse,
the father of David.

**18** Now these are the generations
of Perez:

[a]Perez became the father of
Hezron,
**19** and Hezron became the father
of Ram,
and Ram became the father of
Amminadab,
**20** and Amminadab became the
father of Nahshon,
and Nahshon became the
father of [1]Salmah,
**21** and Salmon became the father
of Boaz,
and Boaz became the father of
Obed,
**22** and Obed became the father
of Jesse,
and Jesse became the father of
David.

**4:11** [a]Ge 29:25-30 [1]Lit *do* [2]Or *wealth, valor* [3]Or *have your name called out* **4:12** [a]Ge 38:29; 46:12; Ru 4:18 **4:13** [a]Ge 29:31; 33:5 **4:14** [a]Lk 1:58 [1]Or *closest relative* [2]Lit *be called in* **4:15** [a]Ru 1:16, 17; 2:11, 12 [1]Or *gray hair* [2]Lit *who* **4:16** [1]As her own **4:18** [a]Mt 1:3-6 **4:20** [1]A variant spelling of Salmon, cf. 4:21

*The First Book of*

# SAMUEL

### *Elkanah and His Wives*

**1** Now there was a certain man from [a]Ramathaim-zophim from the [b]hill country of Ephraim, and his name was [c]Elkanah the son of Jeroham, the son of Elihu, the son of Tohu, the son of Zuph, an Ephraimite. **2** Now he had [a]two wives: the name of one was [b]Hannah and the name of the other Peninnah; and Peninnah had children, but Hannah had no children.

**3** Now that man would go up from his city [a]yearly [b]to worship and to sacrifice to [1]Yahweh of hosts in [c]Shiloh. And the two sons of Eli, Hophni and Phinehas, were priests to Yahweh there. **4** And the day came that Elkanah sacrificed, and he [a]would give portions to Peninnah his wife and to all her sons and her daughters; **5** but to Hannah he would give a double portion, for he loved Hannah, [a]but Yahweh had closed her womb. **6** Her rival, however, [a]would provoke her bitterly to irritate her because Yahweh had closed her womb. **7** And so it would happen year after year, as often as she went up to the house of Yahweh, she would provoke her; so she wept and would not eat. **8** Then Elkanah her husband said to her, "Hannah, why do you weep and why do you not eat and why is your heart sad? [a]Am I not better to you than ten sons?"

**9** Then Hannah rose after eating and drinking in Shiloh. Now Eli the priest was sitting on the seat by the doorpost of [a]the temple of Yahweh. **10** And she, bitter of soul, prayed to Yahweh and wept despondently. **11** And she [a]made a vow and said, "O Yahweh of hosts, if You will indeed [b]look on the affliction of Your maidservant and remember me and not forget Your maidservant, but will give Your maidservant a seed amongst men, then I will give him to Yahweh all the days of his life, and [c]a razor shall never come on his head."

**12** Now it happened, as she multiplied her praying before Yahweh, that Eli was watching her mouth. **13** As for Hannah, [a]she was speaking in her heart; only her lips were moving, but her voice was not heard. So Eli thought she was drunk. **14** Then Eli said to her, "[a]How long will you make yourself drunk? Put away your wine from you." **15** But Hannah answered and said, "No, my lord, I am a woman [1]oppressed in spirit; I have drunk neither wine nor strong drink, but I [a]have poured out my soul before Yahweh. **16** Do not [1]consider your maidservant as a vile woman, for *I have spoken* until now out of my great complaint and [2]provocation." **17** Then Eli answered and said, "[a]Go in peace; and may the God of Israel [b]grant your petition that you have

---

◆ **1:1** [a]1Sa 1:19 [b]Jos 17:17, 18; 24:33 [c]1Chr 6:22-28, 33-38 **1:2** [a]Dt 21:15-17 [b]Lk 2:36 **1:3** [a]Ex 34:23; 1Sa 1:21; Lk 2:41 [b]Ex 23:14; Dt 12:5-7; 16:16 [c]Jos 18:1 [1]The personal covenant name of God, a form of I AM WHO I AM, cf. Ex 3:14-15 **1:4** [a]Dt 12:17, 18 **1:5** [a]Ge 16:1; 30:1 **1:6** [a]Job 24:21 **1:8** [a]Ru 4:15 **1:9** [a]1Sa 3:3 **1:11** [a]Nu 30:6-11 [b]Ge 29:32 [c]Nu 6:5; Jdg 13:5 **1:13** [a]Ge 24:42-45 **1:14** [a]Ac 2:4, 13 **1:15** [a]Job 30:16; Ps 42:4; 62:8; Lam 2:19 [1]Lit *severe* **1:16** [1]Lit *give* [2]Lit *my provocation* **1:17** [a]Jdg 18:6; 1Sa 25:35; 2Ki 5:19; Mk 5:34; Lk 7:50 [b]Ps 20:3-5

asked of Him." **18** And she said, "[a]Let
your servant-woman find favor in
your sight." So the woman went her
way and ate, and [b]her face was no
longer *sad.*

### *The Birth of Samuel*

**19** Then they arose early in the morn-
ing and worshiped before Yahweh
and turned back and came to their
house in [a]Ramah. And Elkanah knew
Hannah his wife, and [b]Yahweh re-
membered her. **20** Now it happened
[1]in due time that Hannah conceived
and gave birth to a son; and she named
him Samuel, *saying,* "[a]Because I have
asked him of Yahweh."
**21** Then the man Elkanah [a]went
up with all his household to offer to
Yahweh the yearly sacrifice and *pay*
his vow. **22** But Hannah did not go
up, for she said to her husband, "*I
will not go up* until the young boy is
weaned; then I will [a]bring him, that
he may appear before Yahweh and
[b]stay there forever." **23** [a]And Elkanah
her husband said to her, "Do what
is good in your eyes. Remain until
you have weaned him; only [b]may
Yahweh establish His word." So the
woman remained and nursed her son
until she weaned him. **24** Now when
she had weaned him, [a]she took him
up with her, with a three-year-old
bull and one [1]ephah of flour and a
jug of wine and brought him to [b]the
house of Yahweh in Shiloh, although
the boy was young. **25** Then [a]they
slaughtered the bull and [b]brought
the young boy to Eli. **26** And she said,
"Oh, my lord! [a]As your soul lives, my
lord, I am the woman who stood
here beside you, praying to Yahweh.
**27** [a]For this young boy I prayed, and
Yahweh has given me my petition
which I asked of Him. **28** [a]So I have
also [1]dedicated him to Yahweh; as
long as he lives, he is [1]dedicated to
Yahweh." So [b]he worshiped Yahweh
there.

### *Hannah's Prayer*

**2** Then Hannah [a]prayed and said,
"My heart exults in Yahweh;
[b]My [1]horn is exalted
in Yahweh;
My mouth [2]speaks boldly
against my enemies,
Because [c]I am glad
in Your salvation.
**2** "[a]There is no one holy
like Yahweh;
Indeed, [b]there is no
one besides You,
[c]Nor is there any rock
like our God.
**3** "Do not multiply speaking
so very proudly;
[a]Let arrogance not come
out of your mouth;
[b]For Yahweh is a God
of knowledge,
[c]And with Him actions
are weighed.
**4** "[a]The bows of the mighty
are shattered,

**1:18** [a]Ge 33:15; Ru 2:13 [b]Ro 15:13 **1:19** [a]1Sa 1:1; 2:11 [b]Ge 21:1; 30:22 **1:20** [a]Ge 41:51, 52; Ex 2:10, 22; *Mt 1:21* [1]*Lit at the circuit of the days* **1:21** [a]Dt 12:11; 1Sa 1:3 **1:22** [a]Lk 2:22 [b]1Sa 1:11, 28 **1:23** [a]Nu 30:7, 10, 11 [b]1Sa 1:17 **1:24** [a]Nu 15:9, 10; Dt 12:5, 6 [b]Jos 18:1; 1Sa 4:3, 4 [1]An ephah was approx. 21 qt. or 23 l **1:25** [a]Lv 1:5 [b]Lk 2:22 **1:26** [a]2Ki 2:2, 4, 6; 4:30 **1:27** [a]1Sa 1:11-13; Ps 6:9; 66:19, 20 **1:28** [a]1Sa 1:11, 22 [b]Ge 24:26, 52 [1]Lit *lent*; Heb sounds like root for Samuel ◆ **2:1** [a]1Sa 2:1-10; Lk 1:46-55 [b]Dt 33:17; Job 16:15; Ps 75:10; 89:17, 24; 92:10; 112:9 [c]Ps 9:14; 13:5; 35:9; Is 12:2, 3 [1]A symbol of strength and power [2]Lit *is enlarged* **2:2** [a]Ex 15:11; Lv 19:2; Ps 86:8 [b]2Sa 22:32 [c]Dt 32:30, 31 **2:3** [a]Pr 8:13 [b]1Sa 16:7; 1Ki 8:39 [c]Pr 16:2; 24:12 **2:4** [a]Ps 37:15; 46:9

[b]But those who stumble
gird on strength.
5 "Those who were full hire
themselves out for bread,
But those who were hungry
cease *to hunger*.
[a]Even the barren gives
birth to seven,
But [b]she who has many
children languishes.
6 "[a]Yahweh puts to death
and makes alive;
[b]He brings down
to Sheol and raises up.
7 "[a]Yahweh makes poor and rich;
[b]He brings low; He also exalts.
8 "[a]He raises the poor
from the dust;
[b]He exalts the needy
from the ash heap
[c]To make them sit with nobles,
And inherit a seat of glory;
[d]For the pillars of the
earth are Yahweh's,
And He set the world on them.
9 "[a]He keeps the feet
of His holy ones,
[b]But the wicked ones are
silenced in darkness,
[c]For not by power shall
a man prevail.
10 "[a]Those who contend with
Yahweh will be dismayed;
[b]Against them He will
thunder in the heavens;
[c]Yahweh will render justice
to the ends of the earth,
[d]And He will give
strength to His king,
[e]And He will exalt the
[1]horn of His anointed."

11 Then Elkanah went to his home
at [a]Ramah. [b]But the young boy min-
istered to Yahweh before Eli the priest.

### *The Sin of Eli's Sons*

12 Now the sons of Eli were [a,1]vile
men; they did not know Yahweh.
13 [a]And *this was* the *legal* judgment
for the priests with the people: when
any man was offering a sacrifice, the
priest's young man would come while
the meat was boiling, with a three-
pronged fork in his hand. 14 Then he
would thrust it into the pan or kettle
or caldron or pot; all that the fork
would bring up the priest would take
for himself. Thus they would do in
Shiloh to all the Israelites who came
there. 15 Also, before [a]they offered up
the fat in smoke, the priest's young
man would come and say to the man
who was sacrificing, "Give the priest
meat for roasting; he will not take
boiled meat from you, only raw."
16 Then the man *would* say to him,
"They must surely offer up the fat in
smoke [1]first, and then take as much
as your soul desires," then he would
say, "No, you shall give *it* now; and if
not, I will take it by force." 17 Thus the
sin of the young men was very great
before Yahweh, for the men [a]spurned
the offering of Yahweh.

### *Samuel Before Yahweh as a Boy*

18 Now [a]Samuel was ministering be-
fore Yahweh, *as* a [1]young boy [b]girded

---

**2:4** [b]Ps 18:39; Heb 11:32-34 **2:5** [a]Ru 4:15; Ps 113:9 [b]Jer 15:9 **2:6** [a]Dt 32:39; 2Ki 5:7; Rev 1:18 [b]Is 26:19 **2:7** [a]Dt 8:17, 18 [b]Job 5:11; Ps 75:7; Jas 4:10 **2:8** [a]Job 42:10-12; Ps 75:7; 113:7 [b]2Sa 7:8; Da 2:48; Jas 2:5 [c]Job 36:7; Ps 113:8 [d]Job 38:4-6; Ps 75:3; 104:5 **2:9** [a]Ps 91:11, 12; 121:3; Pr 3:26; 1Pe 1:5 [b]Mt 8:12 [c]Ps 33:16, 17 **2:10** [a]Ex 15:6; Ps 2:9 [b]1Sa 7:10; 2Sa 22:14; Ps 18:13, 14 [c]Ps 96:13; 98:9; Mt 25:31, 32 [d]Ps 21:1, 7 [e]Ps 89:24 [1]A symbol of strength and power **2:11** [a]1Sa 1:1, 19 [b]1Sa 1:28; 2:18; 3:1 **2:12** [a]Jer 2:8; 9:3, 6; 2Co 6:15 [1]Lit *sons of Belial*, cf. 2Co 6:15 **2:13** [a]Lv 7:29-34 **2:15** [a]Lv 3:3-5, 16 **2:16** [1]Lit *like the day* **2:17** [a]Mal 2:7-9 **2:18** [a]1Sa 2:11; 3:1 [b]1Sa 2:28; 22:18; 2Sa 6:14; 1Chr 15:27 [1]Or *young man*, cf. 2:17

with a linen ephod. **19** And his mother
would make him a little [a]robe and
bring it to him from year to year
when she would come up with her
husband to offer [b]the yearly sacrifice.
**20** Then Eli would [a]bless Elkanah and
his wife and say, "May Yahweh estab-
lish for you a seed from this woman
in place of [1]the one she [b]dedicated
to Yahweh." And they went to their
own [2]home.

**21** [a]Yahweh indeed visited Hannah;
and she conceived and gave birth to
three sons and two daughters. And
[b]the young boy Samuel grew before
Yahweh.

### *Eli Hears About His Sons' Evils*

**22** Now Eli was very old; and he heard
[a]all that his sons were doing to all
Israel, and how they lay with [b]the
women who served at the doorway
of the tent of meeting. **23** So he said
to them, "Why do you do such things,
the evil things that I hear from all
these people? **24** No, my sons; for the
report is not good [a]which I hear the
people of Yahweh [1]passing about.
**25** If one man sins against another,
[a]God will mediate for him; but [b]if a
man sins against Yahweh, who can
pray for him?" But they would not
listen to the voice of their father,
for [c]Yahweh desired to put them to
death.

**26** Now the young boy [a]Samuel
[1]was growing in stature and in favor
both with Yahweh and with men.

### *Eli Honors His Sons Above Yahweh*

**27** Then [a]a man of God came to Eli
and said to him, "Thus says Yahweh,
'[b]Did I *not* indeed reveal Myself to
the house of your father when they
were in Egypt, *enslaved* to Pharaoh's
house? **28** [a]And did I *not* choose them
from all the tribes of Israel to be My
priests, to go up to My altar, to burn
incense, to carry an ephod before Me;
and did I *not* [b]give to the house of
your father all the fire *offerings* of the
sons of Israel? **29** Why do you [a]kick
at My sacrifice and at My offering
[b]which I have commanded *in My*
[c]habitation, and [d]honor your sons
above Me, by making yourselves fat
with the [1]choicest of every offering of
My people Israel?' **30** Therefore Yah-
weh, the God of Israel, declares, '[a]I
did indeed say that your house and
the house of your father should walk
before Me forever'; but now Yahweh
declares, 'Far be it from Me—for
[b]those who honor Me I will honor,
and those [c]who despise Me will be
cursed. **31** Behold, [a]the days are com-
ing, and I will break your [1]strength
and the [1]strength of your father's
house so that there will not be an old
man in your house. **32** And you will
look upon [a]the distress of *My* habita-
tion, in *spite of* all the good that [1]I do
for Israel; and an [b]old man will not be
in your house all the days. **33** Yet I will
not cut off every man of yours from
My altar [1]so that your eyes will fail
*from weeping* and your soul grieve,

---

**2:19** [a]Ex 28:31 [b]1Sa 1:3, 21 **2:20** [a]Lk 2:34 [b]1Sa 1:11, 27, 28 [1]Lit *the one asked for which was lent*; *Heb sounds like root* for Samuel [2]Lit *place* **2:21** [a]Ge 21:1 [b]Jdg 13:24; 1Sa 2:26; 3:19-21; Lk 1:80; 2:40 **2:22** [a]1Sa 2:13-17 [b]Ex 38:8 **2:24** [a]1Ki 15:26 [1]Or *making Yahweh's people transgress* **2:25** [a]Dt 1:17 [b]Nu 15:30; 1Sa 3:14; Heb 10:26, 27 [c]Jos 11:20 **2:26** [a]1Sa 2:21; Lk 2:52 [1]Lit *was going on both great and good* **2:27** [a]Dt 33:1; Jdg 13:6 [b]Ex 4:14-16; 12:1, 43 **2:28** [a]Ex 28:1-4; 30:7, 8; Lv 8:7, 8 [b]Lv 7:35, 36 **2:29** [a]1Sa 2:13-17 [b]Dt 12:5-9 [c]Ps 26:8 [d]Mt 10:37 [1]Or *first* **2:30** [a]Ex 29:9; Nu 25:13 [b]Ps 50:23 [c]Mal 2:9 **2:31** [a]1Sa 4:11-18; 22:17-20 [1]Or *arm* **2:32** [a]1Ki 2:26, 27 [b]Zec 8:4 [1]Lit *He does* **2:33** [1]Lit *to waste away your eyes and to grieve your soul*

and all the increase of your house
will be put to death [2]in the prime
of life. **34** Now this will be [a]the sign
to you which will come concerning
your two sons, Hophni and Phinehas:
[b]on the same day both of them will
be put to death. **35** But [a]I will raise
up for Myself a faithful priest who
will do according to what is in My
heart and in My soul; and [b]I will build
him a faithful house, and he will walk
before [c]My anointed always. **36** And
it will be that everyone who is left in
your house will come and bow down
to him for a [1]piece of silver or a loaf
of bread and say, "Please [2]assign me
to one of the priest's offices so that I
may eat a piece of bread."'"

### *Yahweh Calls Samuel*

**3** Now [a]the young boy Samuel was
ministering to Yahweh before Eli.
And [b]word from Yahweh was rare in
those days; [1]visions were infrequent.
**2** And it happened at that time as
Eli was lying down in his place (now
[a]his eyesight had begun to fade, *and*
he could not see *well*), **3** and [a]the
lamp of God had not yet gone out,
and Samuel was lying down in the
temple of Yahweh where the ark of
God *was*, **4** that Yahweh called Sam-
uel; and he said, "[a]Here I am." **5** Then
he ran to Eli and said, "Here I am, for
you called me." But he said, "I did not
call; go back, lie down." So he went
and lay down. **6** Then Yahweh called
yet again, "Samuel!" So Samuel arose
and went to Eli and said, "Here I am,
for you called me." But he [1]answered,
"I did not call, my son; go back, lie
down." **7** [a]Now Samuel did not yet
know Yahweh, nor had the word of
Yahweh yet been revealed to him. **8** So
Yahweh called Samuel again for the
third time. And he arose and went to
Eli and said, "Here I am, for you called
me." Then Eli discerned that Yahweh
was calling the young boy. **9** And Eli
said to Samuel, "Go lie down, and it
shall be if He calls you, that you shall
say, 'Speak, Yahweh, for Your slave is
listening.'" So Samuel went and lay
down in his place.
**10** Then Yahweh came and stood
and called as at other times, "Samuel!
Samuel!" And Samuel said, "Speak,
for Your slave is listening." **11** And
Yahweh said to Samuel, "Behold, [a]I
am about to do a thing in Israel at
which both ears of everyone who
hears it will tingle. **12** In that day [a]I
will establish against Eli all that I
have spoken concerning his house,
from beginning to end. **13** And [a]I have
told him that I am about to judge his
house forever for [b]the iniquity which
he knew because [c]his sons have been
bringing a curse on themselves, but
[d]he did not rebuke them. **14** Now
therefore I have sworn to the house
of Eli that [a]the iniquity of Eli's house
shall not be atoned for by sacrifice or
offering forever."
**15** So Samuel lay down until morn-
ing. Then he [a]opened the doors of
the house of Yahweh. But Samuel
was afraid to tell [b]the vision to Eli.
**16** Then Eli called Samuel and said,
"Samuel, my son." And he said, "Here

**2:33** [2]Lit *as men* **2:34** [a]1Sa 10:7-9; 1Ki 13:3 [b]1Sa 4:11, 17 **2:35** [a]1Sa 3:1; 7:9; 9:12, 13 [b]1Sa 8:3-5; 25:28; 2Sa 7:11, 27; 1Ki 11:38 [c]1Sa 10:9, 10; 12:3; 16:13 **2:36** [1]Or *payment* [2]Lit *attach* ◆ **3:1** [a]1Sa 2:11, 18 [b]Ps 74:9; Eze 7:26; Am 8:11, 12 [1]Lit *no vision spread abroad* **3:2** [a]Ge 27:1; 48:10; 1Sa 4:15 **3:3** [a]Ex 25:31-37; Lv 24:2, 3 **3:4** [a]Is 6:8 **3:6** [1]Lit *said* **3:7** [a]Ac 19:2; 1Co 13:11 **3:11** [a]2Ki 21:12; Jer 19:3 **3:12** [a]1Sa 2:27-36 **3:13** [a]1Sa 2:29-31 [b]1Sa 2:22 [c]1Sa 2:12, 17, 22 [d]Dt 17:12; 21:18 **3:14** [a]Lv 15:31; Is 22:14 **3:15** [a]1Chr 15:23 [b]1Sa 3:10

I am." 17 And he said, "What is the
word that He spoke to you? Please
do not hide it from me. [a]May God
do so to you, and more also, if you
hide anything from me of all the
words that He spoke to you." 18 So
Samuel told him everything and hid
nothing from him. And he said, "[a]It
is Yahweh; let Him do what seems
good in His eyes."

19 Thus [a]Samuel grew, and [b]Yah-
weh was with him and [c]let none of
his words fall to the ground. 20 So all
Israel [a]from Dan even to Beersheba
knew that Samuel was confirmed as
a prophet of Yahweh. 21 And [a]Yahweh
appeared again at Shiloh, [b]because
Yahweh revealed Himself to Samuel
at Shiloh by the word of Yahweh.

### *The Philistines Take the Ark*

4 Thus the word of Samuel came
to all Israel. Now Israel went out
to meet the Philistines in battle and
camped beside [a]Ebenezer, and the
Philistines camped in [b]Aphek. 2 And
the Philistines arranged *themselves* to
meet Israel. Then the battle spread,
and Israel was [1]defeated before the
Philistines who struck down about
4,000 men on the battlefield. 3 Then
the people came into the camp, and
the elders of Israel said, "[a]Why has
Yahweh [1]defeated us today before the
Philistines? [b]Let us take to ourselves
from Shiloh the ark of the covenant
of Yahweh, that [2]it may come among
us and save us from the power of our
enemies." 4 So the people sent to
Shiloh, and from there they carried
the ark of the covenant of Yahweh of
hosts [a]who sits *above* the cherubim;
and the two sons of Eli, Hophni and
Phinehas, *were* there with the ark of
the covenant of God.

5 And it happened that as the ark
of the covenant of Yahweh came into
the camp, [a]all Israel shouted with
a great shout, so that the earth was
thrown into confusion. 6 Then the
Philistines heard the noise of the
shout and said, "What *does* the noise
of this great shout in the camp of the
Hebrews *mean*?" Then they knew
that the ark of Yahweh had come
into the camp. 7 And the Philistines
were afraid, for they said, "God has
come into the camp." And they said,
"[a]Woe to us! For nothing like this has
happened before. 8 Woe to us! Who
shall deliver us from the hand of these
mighty gods? These are the gods who
struck the Egyptians with all *kinds of*
plagues in the wilderness. 9 [a]Be strong
and become men, O Philistines, lest
you become slaves to the Hebrews,
[b]as they have been slaves to you;
therefore, become men and fight."

10 So the Philistines fought, and
[a]Israel was [1]defeated, and [b]every
man fled to his tent; and the slaughter
was very great, for there fell of Israel
30,000 foot soldiers. 11 And the ark
of God was taken; and [a]the two sons
of Eli, Hophni and Phinehas, died.

### *The Death of Eli*

12 Now a man of Benjamin ran from
the battle line and came to Shiloh the
same day with [a]his robes torn and

**3:17** [a]2Sa 3:35 **3:18** [a]Ex 34:5-7; Lv 10:3; Job 2:10; Is 39:8 **3:19** [a]1Sa 2:21 [b]Ge 21:22; 28:15; 39:2 [c]1Sa 9:6 **3:20** [a]Jdg 20:1 **3:21** [a]Ge 12:7 [b]1Sa 3:10 ◆ **4:1** [a]1Sa 7:12 [b]Jos 12:18; 1Sa 29:1 **4:2** [1]Lit *smitten* **4:3** [a]Jos 7:7, 8 [b]Nu 10:35; Jos 6:6 [1]Lit *smitten* [2]Or *he* **4:4** [a]Ex 25:22; 2Sa 6:2; Ps 80:1 **4:5** [a]Jos 6:5, 20 **4:7** [a]Ex 15:14 **4:9** [a]1Co 16:13 [b]Jdg 13:1; 1Sa 14:21 **4:10** [a]Dt 28:15, 25; 1Sa 4:2 [b]2Sa 18:17; 19:8; 2Ki 14:12; 2Chr 25:22 [1]Lit *smitten* **4:11** [a]1Sa 2:34; Ps 78:56-64 **4:12** [a]Jos 7:6; 2Sa 1:2; 15:32; Ne 9:1; Job 2:12

[1]dust on his head. **13** And he came,
and behold, [a]Eli was sitting on *his*
seat [1]by the road eagerly watching
because his heart was trembling for
the ark of God. Now the man came
to tell *it* in the city, and all the city
cried out. **14** Then Eli heard the noise
of the outcry, and he said, "What *does*
the noise of this commotion *mean*?"
So the man came hurriedly and told
Eli. **15** Now Eli was ninety-eight years
old, and [a]his eyes had set so that he
could not see. **16** And the man said
to Eli, "I am the one who came from
the battle line. Indeed, I fled from the
battle line today." And he said, "[a]How
did things go, my son?" **17** Then the
one who brought the news answered
and said, "Israel has fled before the
Philistines, and there has also been
a great slaughter among the people,
and your two sons also, Hophni
and Phinehas, are dead, and the ark
of God has been taken." **18** And it
happened that when he mentioned
the ark of God, [a,1]Eli fell off the seat
backward beside the gate, and his
neck was broken, and he died, for
the man was old and heavy. Thus he
judged Israel forty years.

**19** Now his daughter-in-law,
Phinehas's wife, was with child and
about to give birth. And she heard
the report that the ark of God was
taken and that her *father-in-law and*
her husband had died, so she kneeled
down and gave birth, for her pains
came upon her. **20** And about the
time of her death the women who
stood by her said to her, "[a]Do not
be afraid, for you have given birth
to a son." But she did not answer or
pay attention. **21** And she called the
boy [1]Ichabod, saying, "[a]The glory
has departed from Israel," because
[b]the ark of God was taken and be-
cause of her father-in-law and her
husband. **22** And she said, "The glory
has departed from Israel, for the ark
of God was taken."

### *Yahweh's Hand Against the Philistines*

**5** Now the Philistines took the
ark of God and [a]brought it from
Ebenezer to [b]Ashdod. **2** Then the
Philistines took the ark of God and
brought it to [a]the house of Dagon
and set it by Dagon. **3** Then the Ash-
dodites arose early the next morning,
and behold, [a]Dagon had fallen on
his face to the ground before the ark
of Yahweh. So they took Dagon and
[b]set him in his place again. **4** But they
arose early the next morning, and
behold, [a]Dagon had fallen on his
face to the ground before the ark of
Yahweh. And the head of Dagon and
both the palms of his hands *were* cut
off on the threshold; [1]only the trunk
of Dagon was left to him. **5** Therefore
neither the priests of Dagon nor all
who enter Dagon's house [a]tread on
the threshold of Dagon in Ashdod
to this day.

**6** Now [a]the hand of Yahweh was
glorious against the Ashdodites, and
[b]He made them desolate and struck
them with [c]tumors, both Ashdod
and its territories. **7** Thus the men
of Ashdod saw that it was so and said,
"The ark of the God of Israel must

---

**4:12** [1]Lit *ground* **4:13** [a]1Sa 1:9; 4:18 [1]Gr *beside the gate watching the road* **4:15** [a]1Sa 3:2; 1Ki 14:4 **4:16** [a]2Sa 1:4 **4:18** [a]1Sa 4:13 [1]Lit *he* **4:20** [a]Ge 35:16-19 **4:21** [a]Ps 26:8; Jer 2:11 [b]1Sa 4:11 [1]Lit *no glory* ◆ **5:1** [a]1Sa 4:1; 7:12 [b]Jos 13:3 **5:2** [a]Jdg 16:23-30; 1Chr 10:8-10 **5:3** [a]Is 19:1; 46:1, 2 [b]Is 46:7 **5:4** [a]Eze 6:4, 6; Mic 1:7 [1]As in ancient versions; Heb *only Dagon* **5:5** [a]Zep 1:9 **5:6** [a]Ex 9:3; 1Sa 5:7, 11; Ps 32:4; 145:20; 147:6; Ac 13:11 [b]1Sa 6:5 [c]Dt 28:27; Ps 78:66

not remain with us, for His hand is
severe on us and on Dagon our god."
**8** So they sent and [a]gathered all the
lords of the Philistines to them and
said, "What shall we do with the ark
of the God of Israel?" And they said,
"Let the ark of the God of Israel be
brought around to Gath." And they
brought the ark of the God of Israel
*around.* **9** Now it happened after they
had brought it around, that [a]the hand
of Yahweh was against the city with
very great confusion; and He struck
the men of the city, both young
and old, so that [b]tumors broke out
on them. **10** So they sent the ark of
God to Ekron. And as the ark of God
came to Ekron the Ekronites cried
out, saying, "They have brought the
ark of the God of Israel around to [1]us,
to put [1]us and [2]our people to death."
**11** They [a]sent therefore and gathered
all the lords of the Philistines and
said, "Send away the ark of the God
of Israel, and let it return to its own
place, so that it will not put [1]us and
[2]our people to death." For there was
a deadly confusion throughout the
city; [b]the hand of God was very
glorious there. **12** Now the men who
did not die were struck with tumors
and [a]the cry of the city went up to
heaven.

### *The Ark Returned to Israel*

**6** Now the ark of Yahweh had been
in the [1]fields of the Philistines
seven months. **2** And [a]the Philistines
called for the priests and the divin-
ers, saying, "What shall we do with
the ark of Yahweh? Make us know
[1]how we shall send it to its place."
**3** So they said, "If you send away the
ark of the God of Israel, [a]do not send
it empty; but you shall surely [b]return
to Him a guilt offering. Then you will
be healed, and it will be known to
you why His hand is not turned away
from you." **4** Then they said, "What
shall be the guilt offering which we
shall return to Him?" And they said,
"Five golden [a]tumors and five golden
mice [b]*according to* the number of
the lords of the Philistines, for one
plague was on all of [1]you and on your
lords. **5** So you shall make likenesses
of your tumors and likenesses of
your mice that bring the land to ruin,
and [a]you shall give glory to the God
of Israel; perhaps [b]He will ease His
hand from you, [c]your gods, and your
land. **6** Why then do you [1]harden
your hearts [a]as the Egyptians and
Pharaoh [1]hardened their hearts?
When He had abused them, [b]did
they not allow [2]the people to go, and
they went? **7** So now, take and [a]make
a new cart and two milch cows on
which there [b]has never been a yoke;
and hitch the cows to the cart and
take their calves home, away from
them. **8** And take the ark of Yahweh
and place it on the cart; and put [a]the
articles of gold which you return to
Him as [b]a guilt offering in a box by
its side. Then send it away that it may
go. **9** See, if it goes up by the way of
its own territory to [a]Beth-shemesh,
then He has done us this great evil.
But if not, then [b]we will know that

---

**5:8** [a]1Sa 5:11; 29:6-11 **5:9** [a]Dt 2:15; 1Sa 5:11; 7:13; 12:15 [b]1Sa 5:6 **5:10** [1]Lit *me* [2]Lit *my* **5:11** [a]1Sa 5:8 [b]1Sa 5:6, 9 [1]Lit *me* [2]Lit *my* **5:12** [a]Ex 12:30; Is 15:3 ◆ **6:1** [1]Or *country* **6:2** [a]Ge 41:8; Ex 7:11; Is 2:6 [1]Or *with what* **6:3** [a]Ex 23:15; Dt 16:16 [b]Lv 5:15, 16 **6:4** [a]1Sa 5:6, 9, 12; 6:17 [b]Jos 13:3; Jdg 3:3; 1Sa 6:17, 18 [1]Lit *them* **6:5** [a]Jos 7:19; 1Chr 16:28, 29; Is 42:12; Jer 13:16; Jn 9:24; Rev 14:7 [b]1Sa 5:6, 11 [c]1Sa 5:3, 4, 7 **6:6** [a]Ex 7:13; 8:15, 32; 9:34; 14:17 [b]Ex 12:31 [1]Or *glory*, cf. 5:6, 11; 6:5 [2]Lit *them* **6:7** [a]2Sa 6:3 [b]Nu 19:2; Dt 21:3, 4 **6:8** [a]1Sa 6:4, 5 [b]1Sa 6:3 **6:9** [a]Jos 15:10; 21:16 [b]1Sa 6:3

it was not His hand that smote us; it
happened to us by chance."
**10** Then the men did so and took
two milch cows and hitched them
to the cart and shut up their calves
at home. **11** And they put the ark of
Yahweh on the cart, as well as the
box with the golden mice and the
likenesses of their tumors. **12** And
the cows took the straight way in the
[1]direction of [a]Beth-shemesh; they
went along [b]the highway, lowing as
they went, and did not turn aside to
the right or to the left. And the lords
of the Philistines went after them to
the border of Beth-shemesh.
**13** Now *the people of* Beth-shemesh
were reaping their wheat harvest
in the valley, and they raised their
eyes and saw the ark and were glad
to see *it*. **14** And the cart came into
the field of Joshua the Beth-shemite
and stood there, and a large stone
*was* there; and they split the wood
of the cart and [a]offered the cows as
a burnt offering to Yahweh. **15** [a]And
the Levites took down the ark of Yah-
weh and the box that was with it, in
which were the articles of gold, and
put them on the large stone; and the
men of Beth-shemesh offered burnt
offerings and sacrificed sacrifices
that day to Yahweh. **16** So the [a]five
lords of the Philistines saw it and
returned to Ekron that day.
**17** [a]*Now these* are the golden tu-
mors which the Philistines returned
for a guilt offering to Yahweh: one for
Ashdod, one for Gaza, one for Ash-
kelon, one for Gath, one for Ekron;
**18** and the golden mice, *according*
to the number of all the cities of
the Philistines belonging to the five
lords, [a]both of fortified cities and of
country villages. [b]The large [1]stone
on which they set the ark of Yahweh
*is a witness* to this day in the field of
Joshua the Beth-shemite.
**19** [a]Then He struck down some of
the men of Beth-shemesh because
they had looked into the ark of
Yahweh. He struck down of all the
people, 50,070 men, and the people
mourned because Yahweh had struck
the people with a great slaughter.
**20** And the men of Beth-shemesh
said, "[a]Who is able to stand before
Yahweh, this holy God? And to whom
shall He go up from us?" **21** So they
sent messengers to the inhabitants
of [a]Kiriath-jearim, saying, "The Phi-
listines have brought back the ark
of Yahweh; come down and take it
up to you."

**7** And the men of Kiriath-jearim
came and brought the ark of
Yahweh up and [a]brought it into the
house of Abinadab on the hill and set
apart Eleazar his son as holy in order
to keep the ark of Yahweh. **2** Now it
happened from the day when the ark
remained at Kiriath-jearim, that the
time was long; it was twenty years.
And all the house of Israel lamented
after Yahweh.

### *Samuel Judges Israel*

**3** Then Samuel spoke to all the house
of Israel, saying, "[a]If you are to return
to Yahweh with all your heart, *then*
[b]remove the foreign gods and the
[c]Ashtaroth from among you and

**6:12** [a]1Sa 6:9 [b]Nu 20:19 [1]Lit *way* **6:14** [a]2Sa 24:22; 1Ki 19:21 **6:15** [a]Jos 3:3 **6:16** [a]Jos 13:3; Jdg 3:3 **6:17** [a]1Sa 6:4 **6:18** [a]Dt 3:5 [b]1Sa 6:14, 15 [1]As in some mss and versions; Heb *abel* **6:19** [a]Ex 19:21; Nu 4:5, 15, 20; 2Sa 6:7 **6:20** [a]Lv 11:44, 45; 2Sa 6:9; Mal 3:2; Rev 6:17 **6:21** [a]Jos 9:17; 15:9, 60; 1Chr 13:5, 6 ◆ **7:1** [a]2Sa 6:3, 4 **7:3** [a]1Ki 8:48; Is 55:7; Hos 6:1; Joel 2:12-14 [b]Ge 35:2; Jos 24:14, 23; Jdg 10:16 [c]Jdg 2:13; 1Sa 31:10

[d]set your hearts toward Yahweh and
[e]serve Him alone; and He will deliver
you from the hand of the Philistines."
**4** So the sons of Israel removed the
Baals and the Ashtaroth and served
Yahweh alone.

**5** Then Samuel said, "Gather all
Israel to [a]Mizpah, and [b]I will pray
to Yahweh for you." **6** And they gath-
ered to Mizpah and drew water and
[a]poured it out before Yahweh and
[b]fasted on that day and said there,
"[c]We have sinned against Yahweh."
And Samuel judged the sons of Israel
at Mizpah.

**7** Then the Philistines heard that
the sons of Israel had gathered to Miz-
pah. And the lords of the Philistines
went up against Israel. Then the sons
of Israel heard it and [a]were afraid of
the Philistines. **8** So the sons of Israel
said to Samuel, "[a]Do not cease to cry
out to Yahweh our God for us, that
He may save us from the hand of
the Philistines." **9** And Samuel took
[a]a suckling lamb and offered it for a
whole burnt offering to Yahweh; and
Samuel cried out to Yahweh for Israel,
and [b]Yahweh answered him. **10** Now
Samuel was offering up the burnt of-
fering, and the Philistines drew near
to battle against Israel. But [a]Yahweh
thundered with a great [1]thunder on
that day against the Philistines and
[b]confused them, so that they were
[2]defeated before Israel. **11** So the men
of Israel went out of Mizpah and
pursued the Philistines and struck
them down as far as below Beth-car.

**12** Then Samuel [a]took a stone and
set it between Mizpah and Shen, and
he named it [1]Ebenezer. And he said,
"Thus far Yahweh has helped us."
**13** [a]So the Philistines were subdued,
and [b]they did not come anymore
within the border of Israel. And the
hand of Yahweh was against the Phi-
listines all the days of Samuel. **14** And
the cities which the Philistines had
taken from Israel were restored to
Israel, from Ekron even to Gath; and
Israel delivered their territory from
the hand of the Philistines. So there
was peace between Israel and [a]the
Amorites.

**15** Thus Samuel [a]judged Israel all
the days of his life. **16** And he used to
go annually on circuit to [a]Bethel and
[b]Gilgal and [c]Mizpah, and he judged
Israel in all these places. **17** But his
return *would be* to [a]Ramah, for his
house *was* there, and there he judged
Israel; and he [b]built there an altar to
Yahweh.

### *Israel Tells Samuel to Appoint a King*

**8** And it happened when Samuel
was old that [a]he appointed his
sons judges over Israel. **2** The name of
his firstborn was Joel, and the name
of his second, Abijah; *they* were judg-
ing in [a]Beersheba. **3** But his sons did
not walk in his ways, but turned aside
after greedy gain and [a]took bribes
and caused justice to turn aside.

**4** Then all the elders of Israel gath-
ered together and came to Samuel
at [a]Ramah; **5** and they said to him,

**7:3** [d]Dt 13:4; 2Chr 19:3 [e]Dt 6:13; 10:20; 13:4; Jos 24:14; Mt 4:10; Lk 4:8 **7:5** [a]Jdg 10:17; 20:1 [b]1Sa 8:6; 12:17-19 **7:6** [a]1Sa 1:15; Ps 62:8; Lam 2:19 [b]Lv 16:29; Ne 9:1 [c]Jdg 10:10; 1Ki 8:47; Ps 106:6 **7:7** [a]1Sa 13:6; 17:11 **7:8** [a]1Sa 12:19-24; Is 37:4 **7:9** [a]Lv 22:27 [b]Ps 99:6; Jer 15:1 **7:10** [a]1Sa 2:10; 2Sa 22:14, 15; Ps 29:3, 4 [b]Jos 10:10; Ps 18:14 [1]Lit *voice* [2]Lit *smitten* **7:12** [a]Ge 35:14; Jos 4:9; 24:26 [1]Lit *the stone of help*
**7:13** [a]Jdg 13:1-15 [b]1Sa 13:5 **7:14** [a]Nu 13:29; Jos 10:5-10 **7:15** [a]1Sa 7:6 **7:16** [a]Ge 28:19; 35:6 [b]Jos 5:9, 10 [c]1Sa 7:5 **7:17** [a]1Sa 1:1, 19; 2:11 [b]Jdg 21:4 ◆ **8:1** [a]Dt 16:18, 19 **8:2** [a]Ge 22:19; 1Ki 19:3; Am 5:5
**8:3** [a]Ex 23:6, 8; Dt 16:19 **8:4** [a]1Sa 7:17

"Behold, you have grown old, and
your sons do not walk in your ways.
Now [a]appoint a king for us to judge
us like all the nations." **6** But the thing
was [a]evil in the sight of Samuel when
they said, "Give us a king to judge
us." And [b]Samuel prayed to Yahweh.
**7** Then Yahweh said to Samuel,
"Listen to the voice of the people
in regard to all that they say to you,
for [a]they have not rejected you, but
they have rejected Me from being
king over them. **8** Like all the deeds
which they have done since the day
that I brought them up from Egypt
even to this day—in that they have
forsaken Me and served other gods—
so they are doing to you also. **9** So
now, listen to their voice; [a]however,
you shall solemnly [1]testify to them
and tell them of [b]the [2]custom of the
king who will reign over them."

### *The People Refuse Samuel's Words*

**10** So Samuel spoke all the words
of Yahweh to [a]the people who had
asked of him a king. **11** And he said,
"[a]This will be the [1]custom of the
king who will reign over you: [b]he
will take your sons and appoint
*them* for himself in his chariots and
among his horsemen, and [c]they will
run before his chariots. **12** [a]And he
will appoint for himself commanders
of thousands and of fifties, and *some*
*to* [1]*do his* plowing and to reap his
harvest and to make his weapons of
war and equipment for his chariots.
**13** He will also take your daughters
for perfumers and cooks and bakers.
**14** [a]He will take the best of your fields
and your vineyards and your olive
groves and give *them* to his [1]servants.
**15** He will take a tenth of your seed
and of your vineyards and give *it*
to his officers and to his servants.
**16** He will also take your male slaves
and your female slaves and your best
young men and your donkeys and
[1]use *them* for his work. **17** He will
take a tenth of your flocks, and you
yourselves will become his slaves.
**18** Then [a]you will cry out in that day
because of your king whom you have
chosen for yourselves, but [b]Yahweh
will not answer you in that day."

**19** Nevertheless, the people [a]re-
fused to listen to the voice of Samuel,
and they said, "No, but there shall be
a king over us, **20** [a]that we also may
be like all the nations, that our king
may judge us and go out before us
and fight our battles." **21** So Samuel
heard all the words of the people, and
[a]he repeated them in the hearing of
Yahweh. **22** Then Yahweh said to
Samuel, "[a]Listen to their voice and
[1]appoint them a king." So Samuel
said to the men of Israel, "Go every
man to his city."

### *Saul to Be Anointed over Israel*

**9** Now there was a man of Benjamin
whose name was [a]Kish the son of
Abiel, the son of Zeror, the son of Be-
corath, the son of Aphiah, the son of
a Benjamite, a mighty man of [1]valor.
**2** Now he had a son whose name was
Saul, a [a]choice and handsome *man*,
and there was not a more handsome

**8:5** [a]Dt 17:14, 15 **8:6** [a]1Sa 12:17 [b]1Sa 15:11 **8:7** [a]Ex 16:8; 1Sa 10:19 **8:9** [a]Eze 3:18 [b]1Sa 8:11-18; 10:25 [1]Or *warn* [2]Lit *judgment* **8:10** [a]1Sa 8:4 **8:11** [a]Dt 17:14-20; 1Sa 10:25 [b]1Sa 14:52 [c]2Sa 15:1 [1]Lit *judgment* **8:12** [a]Nu 31:14; 1Sa 22:7 [1]Lit *plow his plowing* **8:14** [a]1Ki 21:7; Eze 46:18 [1]Or *slave*, cf. 8:16; see Foreword, "The Terminology of Slave" **8:16** [1]Lit *make* **8:18** [a]Is 8:21 [b]Pr 1:25-28; Is 1:15; Mic 3:4 **8:19** [a]Is 66:4; Jer 44:16 **8:20** [a]1Sa 8:5 **8:21** [a]Jdg 11:11 **8:22** [a]1Sa 8:7 [1]Lit *cause a king to reign for them* ◆ **9:1** [a]1Sa 14:51; 1Chr 8:33; 9:36-39 [1]Or *wealth, influence* **9:2** [a]1Sa 10:24

person than he among the sons of Israel; [b]from his shoulders and up he was taller than any of the people.

**3** Now the donkeys of Kish, Saul's father, were lost. So Kish said to his son Saul, "Take now with you one of the young men, and arise, go search for the donkeys." **4** Thus he passed through [a]the hill country of Ephraim and passed through the land of [b]Shalishah, but they did not find *them*. Then they passed through the land of [c]Shaalim, but *they were* not *there*. Then he passed through the land of the Benjamites, but they did not find *them*.

**5** They came to the land of [a]Zuph. And Saul said to his young man who was with him, "Come, and let us return, [b]lest my father cease *to be concerned* about the donkeys and become anxious for us." **6** But he said to him, "Behold now, there is [a]a man of God in this city, and the man is held in honor; [b]all that he says surely comes true. Now let us go there, [c]perhaps he can tell us about our journey on which we have gone." **7** Then Saul said to his young man, "But behold, if we go, what shall we bring the man? For the bread is gone from our sack, and there is [a]no present to bring to the man of God. What do we have?" **8** And the young man answered Saul again and said, "Behold, I have in my hand a fourth of a [1]shekel of silver; I will give *it* to the man of God, and he will [a]tell us our way." **9** (Formerly in Israel, when a man went to inquire of God, he used to say, "Come, and let us go to the seer"; for *he who is called* a prophet now was formerly called [a]a seer.) **10** Then Saul said to his young man, "Your word is good; come, let us go." So they went to the city where the man of God was.

**11** *As* they were going up the slope to the city, [a]they found young women going out to draw water and said to them, "Is the seer here?" **12** And they answered them and said, "He is! Behold, *he is* ahead of you. Hurry now, for he has come into the city today, for [a]the people have a sacrifice on [b]the high place today. **13** As soon as you enter the city you will find him before he goes up to the high place to eat, for the people will not eat until he comes because [a]he must bless the sacrifice; afterward those who are invited will eat. So now, go up for you will find him at once." **14** So they went up to the city. As they came into the city, behold, Samuel was coming out to meet them to go up to the high place.

**15** Now a day before Saul's coming, [a]Yahweh had revealed *this* in Samuel's hearing, saying, **16** "About this time tomorrow I will send you a man from the land of Benjamin, and [a]you shall anoint him to be ruler over My people Israel; and he will save My people from the hand of the Philistines. For [b]I have regarded My people because their cry has come to Me." **17** Now Samuel saw Saul, and Yahweh answered him, "[a]Behold, the man of whom I spoke to you! This one shall restrict My people." **18** Then Saul approached Samuel in the gate

**9:2** [b]1Sa 10:23 **9:4** [a]Jos 24:33 [b]2Ki 4:42 [c]Jos 19:42 **9:5** [a]1Sa 1:1 [b]1Sa 10:2 **9:6** [a]Dt 33:1; 1Ki 13:1; 2Ki 5:8 [b]1Sa 3:19 [c]Ge 24:42 **9:7** [a]1Ki 14:3; 2Ki 5:15; 8:8, 9; Eze 13:19 **9:8** [a]1Sa 9:6 [1]A shekel was approx. 0.4 oz. or 11 gm **9:9** [a]2Sa 24:11; 2Ki 17:13; 1Chr 9:22; 26:28; 29:29; Is 30:10; Am 7:12 **9:11** [a]Ge 24:11, 15; 29:8, 9; Ex 2:16 **9:12** [a]Ge 31:54; Nu 28:11-15; 1Ki 3:2 [b]1Sa 7:17; 10:5 **9:13** [a]Lk 9:16; Jn 6:11 **9:15** [a]1Sa 15:1; Ac 13:21 **9:16** [a]1Sa 10:1 [b]Ex 3:7, 9 **9:17** [a]1Sa 16:12

and said, "Please tell me where the
seer's house is." **19** And Samuel an-
swered Saul and said, "I am the seer.
Go up before me to the high place,
for you shall eat with me today; and
in the morning I will let you go and
will tell you all that is on your heart.
**20** [a]As for your donkeys which were
lost three days ago, do not set your
heart on them, for they have been
found. And [b]for whom is all that is
desirable in Israel? Is it not for you
and for all your father's household?"
**21** And Saul answered and said, "[a]Am
I not a Benjamite, of [b]the smallest of
the tribes of Israel, and my family the
least of all the families of the [1]tribe
of Benjamin? Why then do you speak
to me in this way?"
**22** Then Samuel took Saul and his
young man and brought them into
the chamber and gave them a place at
the head of those who were invited,
who were about thirty men. **23** And
Samuel said to the cook, "[1]Bring the
portion that I gave you, concerning
which I said to you, 'Set it [2]aside.'"
**24** Then the cook [a]took up the leg
with what was on it and set *it* before
Saul. And *Samuel* said, "Here is what
has been reserved! Set *it* before you
*and* eat, because it has been kept for
you until the appointed time, [1]since
I said I have invited the people." So
Saul ate with Samuel that day.
**25** *Then they* came down from the
high place into the city, and *Samuel*
spoke with Saul [a]on the [1]roof. **26** And
they arose early; and at the [1]breaking
of dawn Samuel called to Saul on the
roof, saying, "Get up, that I may send
you away." So Saul arose, and both he
and Samuel went out into the street.
**27** *As* they were going down to the
edge of the city, Samuel said to Saul,
"Say to the young man that he might
pass before us and pass onwards, but
you remain standing now, that I may
cause you to hear the word of God."

### *Saul Among the Prophets*

**10** Then [a]Samuel took the flask
of oil, poured it on his head,
[b]kissed him, and said, "Has not
[c]Yahweh anointed you a ruler over
[d]His inheritance? **2** When you go
from me today, then you will find two
men close to [a]Rachel's tomb in the
territory of Benjamin at Zelzah; and
they will say to you, '[b]The donkeys
which you went to search for have
been found. Now behold, your father
has [1]ceased to be concerned about
the donkeys and is anxious for you,
saying, "What shall I do about my
son?"' **3** Then you will go on further
from there, and you will come as far
as the [a,1]oak of Tabor, and there three
men going up [b]to God at Bethel will
meet you, one carrying three young
goats, another carrying three loaves
of bread, and another carrying a jug
of wine; **4** and they will greet you and
give you two *loaves* of bread. And you
will take *them* from their hand. **5** Af-
terward you will come to [a,1]the hill of
God where the Philistine garrison is;
and it shall be as soon as you have
come there to the city, that you will
meet [b]a group of prophets coming

**9:20** [a]1Sa 9:3 [b]1Sa 8:5; 12:13 **9:21** [a]1Sa 15:17 [b]Jdg 20:46-48 [1]As in some ancient versions; Heb *tribes*
**9:23** [1]Lit *Give* [2]Lit *with you* **9:24** [a]Ex 29:22, 27; Lv 7:32, 33; Nu 18:18 [1]Lit *saying* **9:25** [a]Dt 22:8;
Lk 5:19; Ac 10:9 [1]Gr adds *and they spread a bed for Saul on the roof and he slept* **9:26** [1]Lit *rising*
◆**10:1** [a]Ex 30:23-33; 1Sa 16:13; 2Ki 9:3, 6 [b]Ps 2:12 [c]1Sa 16:13; 26:9; 2Sa 1:14 [d]Dt 32:9; Ps 78:71
**10:2** [a]Ge 35:16-20; 48:7 [b]1Sa 9:3-5 [1]Lit *abandoned the matter of* **10:3** [a]Ge 35:8 [b]Ge 28:19; 35:1, 3, 7
[1]Or *terebinth* **10:5** [a]1Sa 13:2, 3 [b]1Sa 19:20; 2Ki 2:3, 5, 15 [1]Or *Gibeath-haelohim*

down from the high place with harp,
tambourine, flute, and a lyre before
them, and [c]they will be prophesy-
ing. **6** Then [a]the Spirit of Yahweh
will [1]come upon you mightily, and
[b]you shall prophesy with them and
be changed into another man. **7** Now
it will be when these signs come to
you, [a]do for yourself whatever your
hand finds *to do,* for [b]God is with
you. **8** And [a]you shall go down before
me to Gilgal; and behold, I will come
down to you to offer burnt offerings
and [b]sacrifice peace offerings. [c]You
shall wait seven days until I come to
you and make you know what you
should do."

**9** Then it happened when he
turned his back to leave Samuel, God
[a]changed [1]his heart; and all those
signs came about on that day. **10** [a]And
they came to [1]the hill there, and be-
hold, a group of prophets met him;
and the Spirit of God [2]came upon
him mightily, so that he prophesied
among them. **11** Now it happened that
all who knew him previously saw,
and behold, he was prophesying with
the prophets, so the people said to
one another, "What has happened to
the son of Kish? [a]Is Saul also among
the prophets?" **12** And a man there
answered and said, "Now, who is
their father?" Therefore it became
a proverb: "[a]Is Saul also among
the prophets?" **13** Then he finished
prophesying and came to the high
place.

**14** Now [a]Saul's uncle said to him
and his young man, "Where did
you go?" And he said, "[b]To look for
the donkeys. And we saw that they
were not *anywhere,* so we went to
Samuel." **15** And Saul's uncle said,
"Please tell me what Samuel said
to you." **16** So Saul said to his uncle,
"[a]He told us plainly that the donkeys
had been found." But he did not tell
him about the matter of the kingdom
which Samuel had said.

### *Saul the King*

**17** Then Samuel called the [a]people
together to Yahweh at Mizpah; **18** and
he said to the sons of Israel, "[a]Thus
says Yahweh, the God of Israel, 'I
brought Israel up from Egypt, and I
delivered you from the hand of the
Egyptians and from the hand of all
the kingdoms that were oppressing
you.' **19** But you [a]have today rejected
your God, who saves you from all
your calamities and your distresses;
yet you have [1]said, 'No, but set a king
over us!' So now, [b]take your stand
before Yahweh by your tribes and by
your clans."

**20** Thus Samuel brought all the
tribes of Israel near, and the tribe of
Benjamin was taken *by lot.* **21** Then
he brought the tribe of Benjamin
near by its families, and the Matrite
family was taken. And Saul the son
of Kish was taken; but they looked
for him, and he could not be found.
**22** Therefore [a]they inquired further
of Yahweh, "Has the man come here
yet?" So Yahweh said, "Behold, he is
hiding himself by the baggage." **23** So
they ran and took him from there,

**10:5** [c]2Ki 3:15; 1Chr 25:1-6; 1Co 14:1 **10:6** [a]Nu 11:25, 29; Jdg 14:6 [b]1Sa 10:10; 19:23, 24 [1]Lit *succeeded, rushed upon* **10:7** [a]Ecc 9:10 [b]Jos 1:5; Jdg 6:12; Heb 13:5 **10:8** [a]1Sa 11:14; 13:8 [b]1Sa 11:15 [c]1Sa 13:8 **10:9** [a]1Sa 10:6 [1]Lit *for him another heart* **10:10** [a]1Sa 10:5, 6; 19:20 [1]Or *Gibeath* [2]Lit *succeeded, rushed upon* **10:11** [a]1Sa 19:24; Am 7:14, 15; Mt 13:54-57; Jn 7:15 **10:12** [a]1Sa 19:23, 24 **10:14** [a]1Sa 14:50 [b]1Sa 9:3-6 **10:16** [a]1Sa 9:20 **10:17** [a]Jdg 20:1; 1Sa 7:5 **10:18** [a]Jdg 6:8, 9 **10:19** [a]1Sa 8:6, 7; 12:12 [b]Jos 7:14-18; 24:1; Pr 16:33 [1]As in several mss and versions; M.T. *said to Him* **10:22** [a]1Sa 23:2, 4

and he stood among the people.
And [a]he was taller than any of the
people from his shoulders upward.
**24** And Samuel said to all the people,
"Do you see him [a]whom Yahweh has
chosen? Surely there is no one like
him among all the people." So all the
people shouted and said, "[b,1]*Long* live
the king!"
**25** Then Samuel spoke with the
people about [a]the *legal* judgments of
the kingdom and wrote *them* in the
book and [b]placed *it* before Yahweh.
And Samuel sent all the people away,
each one to his house. **26** Saul also
went [a]to his house at Gibeah; and the
valiant *men* whose hearts God had
touched went with him. **27** But cer-
tain [a,1]vile men said, "How can this
one save us?" And they despised him
and [b]did not bring him any present.
But he kept silent.

### *Saul Strikes Down the Ammonites*

**11** And [a]Nahash the Ammonite
came up and [1]besieged [b]Jabesh-
gilead; and all the men of Jabesh said
to Nahash, "Cut [c]a covenant with us,
and we will serve you." **2** But Nahash
the Ammonite said to them, "I will
cut *it* with you on this condition,
[a]that I will gouge out the right eye
of every one of you, thus I will make
it [b]a reproach on all Israel." **3** [a]Then
the elders of Jabesh said to him, "Let
*us alone for* seven days, that we may
send messengers throughout the
territory of Israel. Then, if there is
no one to save us, we will come out
to you." **4** Then the messengers came
[a]to Gibeah of Saul and spoke these
words in the hearing of the people,
and all the people [b]lifted up their
voices and wept.
**5** Now behold, Saul was coming
from the field [a]behind the oxen, and
[1]he said, "What is *the matter* with the
people that they weep?" So they re-
counted to him the words of the men
of Jabesh. **6** Then [a]the Spirit of God
[1]came upon Saul mightily when he
heard these words, and [2]he burned
with anger exceedingly. **7** Then he
took a pair of oxen and [a]cut them in
pieces and sent *them* throughout the
territory of Israel by the hand of mes-
sengers, saying, "[b]Whoever does not
come out after Saul and after Samuel,
so shall it be done to his oxen." Then
the dread of Yahweh fell on the peo-
ple, and they came out [c]as one man.
**8** And he [1]numbered them in [a]Bezek;
and the [b]sons of Israel were 300,000,
and the men of Judah 30,000. **9** And
they said to the messengers who had
come, "Thus you shall say to the men
of Jabesh-gilead, 'Tomorrow, by the
time the sun is hot, you will have
salvation.'" So the messengers went
and told the men of Jabesh; and they
were glad. **10** Then the men of Jabesh
said, "[a]Tomorrow we will come out to
you, and you may do to us whatever
seems good in your eyes." **11** Then the
next morning Saul put the people
[a]in three companies; and they came
into the midst of the camp at the
morning watch and struck down the

**10:23** [a]1Sa 9:2 **10:24** [a]Dt 17:15; 2Sa 21:6 [b]1Ki 1:25, 34, 39 [1]Lit *May the king live* **10:25** [a]Dt 17:14-20; 1Sa 8:11-18 [b]Dt 31:26 **10:26** [a]1Sa 11:4; 15:34 **10:27** [a]Dt 13:13; 1Sa 25:17 [b]1Ki 10:25; 2Chr 17:5 [1]Lit *sons of Belial*, cf. 2Co 6:15 ◆ **11:1** [a]1Sa 12:12 [b]Jdg 21:8; 1Sa 31:11 [c]Ge 26:28; 1Ki 20:34; Job 41:4; Eze 17:13 [1]Lit *camped against* **11:2** [a]Nu 16:14 [b]1Sa 17:26; Ps 44:13 **11:3** [a]1Sa 8:4 **11:4** [a]1Sa 10:26; 15:34 [b]Ge 27:38; Jdg 2:4; 20:23, 26; 21:2; 1Sa 30:4 **11:5** [a]1Ki 19:19 [1]Lit *Saul* **11:6** [a]Jdg 3:10; 6:34; 11:29; 13:25; 14:6; 1Sa 10:10; 16:13 [1]Lit *succeeded, rushed upon* [2]Lit *his anger burned exceedingly* **11:7** [a]Jdg 19:29 [b]Jdg 21:5, 8 [c]Jdg 20:1 **11:8** [a]Jdg 1:5 [b]Jdg 20:2 [1]Lit *mustered* **11:10** [a]1Sa 11:3 **11:11** [a]Jdg 7:16, 20

Ammonites until the heat of the day. Those who survived were scattered, so that no two of them were left together.

**12** Then the people said to Samuel, "[a]Who is he that said, 'Shall Saul reign over us?' [b,1]Bring the men, that we may put them to death." **13** But Saul said, "[a]Not a man shall be put to death this day, for today [b]Yahweh has accomplished salvation in Israel."

**14** Then Samuel said to the people, "Come and let us go to [a]Gilgal and [b]renew the kingdom there." **15** So all the people went to Gilgal, and there they made Saul king [a]before Yahweh in Gilgal. There they also [b]offered sacrifices of peace offerings before Yahweh; and there Saul and all the men of Israel were exceedingly glad.

### *Samuel Speaks to Israel*

**12** Then Samuel said to all Israel, "Behold, [a]I have listened to your voice in all that you said to me, and I [b]have [1]appointed a king over you. **2** So now, [a]here is the king walking before you, but [b]I am old and gray, and behold, [c]my sons are with you. And [d]I have walked before you from my youth even to this day. **3** Here I am; bear witness against me before Yahweh and [a]His anointed. [b]Whose ox have I taken, or whose donkey have I taken, or whom have I defrauded? Whom have I oppressed, or [c]from whose hand have I taken a bribe to blind my eyes with it? I will restore *it* to you." **4** And they said, "You have not extorted us or oppressed us or taken anything from any man's hand." **5** So he said to them, "Yahweh is witness against you, and His anointed is witness this day that [a]you have found nothing [b]in my hand." And they said, "*He is* witness."

**6** Then Samuel said to the people, "It is Yahweh who [a,1]appointed Moses and Aaron and who brought your fathers up from the land of Egypt. **7** So now, take your stand, [a]that I may judge you before Yahweh concerning all the righteous acts of Yahweh which He did for you and your fathers. **8** [a]When Jacob went into Egypt and [b]your fathers cried out to Yahweh, then [c]Yahweh sent Moses and Aaron [d,1]who brought your fathers out of Egypt and settled them in this place. **9** But [a]they forgot Yahweh their God, so [b]He sold them into the hand of Sisera, commander of the army of Hazor, and [c]into the hand of the Philistines and [d]into the hand of the king of Moab, and they fought against them. **10** [a]And they cried out to Yahweh and said, 'We have sinned because we have forsaken Yahweh and have served [b]the Baals and the Ashtaroth; but [c]now deliver us from the hands of our enemies, and we will serve You.' **11** Then Yahweh sent [a]Jerubbaal and [b,1]Bedan and [c]Jephthah and [d]Samuel, and He delivered you from the hands of your enemies all around, so that you lived in security. **12** But you saw

**11:12** [a]1Sa 10:27 [b]Lk 19:27 [1]Lit *Give* **11:13** [a]1Sa 10:27; 2Sa 19:22 [b]Ex 14:13, 30; 1Sa 19:5 **11:14** [a]1Sa 7:16; 10:8 [b]1Sa 10:25 **11:15** [a]1Sa 10:17 [b]1Sa 10:8 ◆ **12:1** [a]1Sa 8:7, 9, 22 [b]1Sa 10:24; 11:14, 15 [1]Lit *made* **12:2** [a]1Sa 8:20 [b]1Sa 8:1, 5 [c]1Sa 8:3, 5 [d]1Sa 3:10, 19, 20 **12:3** [a]1Sa 10:1; 24:6; 2Sa 1:14 [b]Ex 20:17; Nu 16:15; Ac 20:33 [c]Ex 23:8; Dt 16:19 **12:5** [a]Ac 23:9; 24:20 [b]Ex 22:4 **12:6** [a]Ex 6:26; Mic 6:4 [1]Lit *made* **12:7** [a]Eze 20:35; Mic 6:1-5 **12:8** [a]Ge 46:5, 6 [b]Ex 2:23-25 [c]Ex 3:10; 4:14-16 [d]1Sa 10:18 [1]Lit *and they brought* **12:9** [a]Dt 32:18; Jdg 3:7 [b]Jdg 4:2 [c]Jdg 3:31; 10:7; 13:1 [d]Jdg 3:12-30 **12:10** [a]Jdg 10:10 [b]Jdg 2:13; 3:7 [c]Jdg 10:15, 16 **12:11** [a]Jdg 6:31, 32; 7:1 [b]Jdg 4:6; 11:1 [c]Jdg 11:29 [d]1Sa 3:20 [1]Gr and Syr *Barak*

[a]that Nahash the king of the sons of
Ammon came against you, and you
said to me, '[b]No, but a king shall reign
over us,' [c]although Yahweh your God
*was* your king. **13** So now, [a]behold,
the king whom you have chosen,
[b]whom you have asked for, and
behold, Yahweh has set a king over
you. **14** [a]If you will fear Yahweh and
serve Him and listen to His voice and
not rebel against the [1]command of
Yahweh, then both you and also the
king who reigns over you will follow
Yahweh your God. **15** [a]But if you will
not listen to the voice of Yahweh,
but rebel against the [1]command of
Yahweh, then [b]the hand of Yahweh
will be against you, [c]*as it was* against
your fathers. **16** Even now, [a]take
your stand and see this great thing
which Yahweh will do before your
eyes. **17** [a]Is it not the wheat harvest
today? [b]I will call to Yahweh, that He
may send [1]thunder and rain. Then
you will know and see that [c]your
wickedness is great which you have
done in the eyes of Yahweh by asking
for yourselves a king." **18** So Samuel
called to Yahweh, and Yahweh sent
[1]thunder and rain that day; and [a]all
the people greatly feared Yahweh and
Samuel.

**19** Then all the people said to
Samuel, "[a]Pray for your servants
to Yahweh your God, so that we
*may not die*, for we have added to
all our sins [b]*this* evil by asking for
ourselves a king." **20** And Samuel said
to the people, "Do not fear. You have
committed all this evil, yet [a]do not
turn aside from following Yahweh,
but serve Yahweh with all your heart.
**21** And you must not turn aside, for
*then you would go* after [a]meaning-
less things which cannot profit and
cannot deliver, because they are
meaningless. **22** For [a]Yahweh will not
abandon His people [b]on account of
His great name, because Yahweh [c]has
been pleased to make you a people
for Himself. **23** Moreover, as for me,
[a]far be it from me that I should sin
against Yahweh by ceasing to pray
for you; but [b]I will instruct you in the
good and upright way. **24** [a]Only [1]fear
Yahweh and serve Him in truth with
all your heart; for see [b]what great
things He has done for you. **25** [a]But
if you still do wickedly, [b]both you and
your king [c]will be swept away."

### *Saul Strikes Down the Philistines*

**13** [1]Saul was [2]*thirty* years old
when he began to reign, and he
reigned [3]*forty*-two years over Israel.
**2** And Saul chose for himself 3,000
men of Israel, of which 2,000 were
with Saul in [a]Michmash and in the
hill country of Bethel, while 1,000
were with Jonathan at [b]Gibeah of
Benjamin. But he sent away the rest
of the people, each to his tent. **3** And

---

**12:12** [a]1Sa 11:1, 2 [b]1Sa 8:6, 19 [c]Jdg 8:23; 1Sa 8:7 **12:13** [a]1Sa 10:24 [b]1Sa 8:5; 12:17, 19; Hos 13:11 **12:14** [a]Jos 24:14 [1]Lit *mouth* **12:15** [a]Lv 26:14, 15; Jos 24:20; Is 1:20 [b]1Sa 5:9 [c]1Sa 12:9 [1]Lit *mouth* **12:16** [a]Ex 14:13, 31 **12:17** [a]Pr 26:1 [b]1Sa 7:9, 10; Jas 5:16ff [c]1Sa 8:7 [1]Lit *sounds* **12:18** [a]Ex 14:31 [1]Lit *sounds* **12:19** [a]Ex 9:28; 1Sa 12:23; Jer 15:1; 1Jn 5:16 [b]1Sa 12:17, 20 **12:20** [a]Dt 11:16 **12:21** [a]Dt 11:16; Is 41:29; Hab 2:18 **12:22** [a]Dt 31:6; 1Ki 6:13 [b]Ex 32:12; Nu 14:13; Jos 7:9; Ps 106:8; Jer 14:21 [c]Dt 7:6-11; 1Pe 2:9 **12:23** [a]Ro 1:9; 1Co 9:16; Col 1:9; 1Th 3:10; 2Ti 1:3 [b]1Ki 8:36; Ps 34:11; Pr 4:11 **12:24** [a]Ecc 12:13 [b]Dt 10:21; Is 5:12 [1]Or *reverence* **12:25** [a]Is 1:20; 3:11 [b]Jos 24:20 [c]1Sa 31:1-5; Hos 10:3 ◆ **13:1** [1]The Heb is difficult; lit *Saul was one year old when he began to reign. Now he reigned for two years over Israel* [2]As in some mss of the LXX; M.T. omits *thirty* [3]See Ac 13:21; M.T. omits *forty* **13:2** [a]1Sa 13:5; 14:31 [b]1Sa 10:26

Jonathan struck [a]the garrison of the
Philistines that was in [b]Geba, and
the Philistines heard of *it*. Then Saul
[c]blew the trumpet throughout the
land, saying, "Let the Hebrews hear."
**4** Then all Israel heard [1]the news that
Saul had struck the garrison of the
Philistines, and also that Israel [a]had
become odious to the Philistines. The
people were then summoned [2]to Saul
at Gilgal.
**5** Now the Philistines assembled to
fight with Israel, 30,000 chariots and
6,000 horsemen and [a]people like
the sand which is on the seashore
in abundance; and they came up
and camped in Michmash, east of
[b]Beth-aven. **6** Now the men of Israel
saw that they were in a strait (for the
people were hard-pressed). Then
[a]the people hid themselves in caves,
in thickets, in cliffs, in cellars, and
in pits. **7** Also *some of* the Hebrews
crossed the Jordan into the land of
[a]Gad and Gilead. But as for Saul, he
*was* still in Gilgal, and all the people
followed him trembling.

### *Saul Doesn't Keep Yahweh's Commandment*

**8** So [a]he waited seven days, according
to the appointed time set by Samuel,
but Samuel did not come to Gilgal; and
the people were scattering from him.
**9** So Saul said, "Bring near to me the
burnt offering and the peace offerings."
And [a]he offered the burnt offering.
**10** And as soon as he finished offering
the burnt offering, behold, Samuel
came; and [a]Saul went out to meet
him *and* to [1]greet him. **11** But Samuel
said, "What have you done?" And
Saul said, "Because I saw that the
people were scattering from me,
and that you did not come within the
appointed days, and that [a]the Philis-
tines were assembling at Michmash,
**12** therefore I said, 'Now the Philis-
tines will come down against me at
Gilgal, and I have not entreated the
favor of Yahweh.' So I forced myself
and offered the burnt offering." **13** And
Samuel said to Saul, "[a]You have act-
ed foolishly; [b]you have not kept the
commandment of Yahweh your God,
which He commanded you, for now
Yahweh would have established your
kingdom [1]over Israel [c]forever. **14** But
[a]now your kingdom shall not endure.
[b]Yahweh has sought out for Himself a
man after His own heart, and Yahweh
has appointed him as ruler over His
people because you have not kept
what Yahweh commanded you."
**15** Then Samuel arose and went up
from Gilgal to [a]Gibeah of Benjamin.
And Saul [1]numbered the people who
were present with him, [b]about six
hundred men. **16** Now Saul and his
son Jonathan and the people who
were present with them were staying
in [a]Geba of Benjamin, and the Philis-
tines camped at Michmash. **17** And
[a]the [1]raiders came from the camp
of the Philistines in three [2]compa-
nies: one [3]company turned [4]toward
[b]Ophrah, to the land of Shual, **18** and
another [1]company turned to the
way of [a]Beth-horon, and another
[1]company turned to the way of the

---

**13:3** [a]1Sa 10:5 [b]1Sa 13:16; 14:5 [c]Jdg 3:27; 6:34 **13:4** [a]Ge 34:30; Ex 5:21; 2Sa 10:6 [1]Lit *saying* [2]Lit *after* **13:5** [a]Jos 11:4 [b]Jos 18:12; 1Sa 14:23 **13:6** [a]Jdg 6:2 **13:7** [a]Nu 32:33 **13:8** [a]1Sa 10:8 **13:9** [a]Dt 12:5-14; 2Sa 24:25; 1Ki 3:4 **13:10** [a]1Sa 15:13 [1]Lit *bless* **13:11** [a]1Sa 13:2, 5, 16, 23 **13:13** [a]2Chr 16:9 [b]1Sa 15:11, 22, 28 [c]1Sa 1:22 [1]Lit *to* **13:14** [a]1Sa 15:28 [b]Ac 7:46; 13:22 **13:15** [a]1Sa 13:2 [b]1Sa 13:2, 6, 7; 14:2 [1]Lit *mustered* **13:16** [a]1Sa 13:2, 3 **13:17** [a]1Sa 14:15 [b]Jos 18:23 [1]Lit *destroyers* [2]Lit *heads* [3]Lit *head* [4]Lit *toward the direction of* **13:18** [a]Jos 16:3; 18:13, 14 [1]Lit *head*

border which overlooks the valley
of [b]Zeboim toward the wilderness.
**19** Now [a]no blacksmith could be
found in all the land of Israel, for the
Philistines said, "Lest the Hebrews
make [b,1]swords or spears." **20** So all
Israel went down to the Philistines,
each to sharpen his plowshare, his
mattock, his axe, and his [1]goad.
**21** And the charge was [1]two-thirds of
a shekel for the plowshares, the mat-
tocks, the forks, and the axes, and to
fix the goad. **22** So it happened on the
day of battle that [a]neither sword nor
spear was found in the hands of any
of the people who *were* with Saul and
Jonathan, but they were found with
Saul and his son Jonathan. **23** And
[a]the garrison of the Philistines went
out to [b]the pass of Michmash.

### *Jonathan Slaughters the Philistines*

**14** Now the day came that Jona-
than, the son of Saul, said to
the young man who was carrying his
armor, "Come and let us cross over
to the Philistines' garrison that is on
the other side." But he did not tell his
father. **2** And Saul was staying in the
outskirts of [a]Gibeah under the pome-
granate tree which is in [b]Migron. And
the people who *were* with him *were*
[c]about six hundred men, **3** and Ahi-
jah, the [a]son of Ahitub, [b]Ichabod's
brother, the son of Phinehas, the son
of Eli, the priest of Yahweh at [c]Shiloh,
[d]was [1]wearing an ephod. And the
people did not know that Jonathan
had gone. **4** [a]Now between the passes
by which Jonathan sought to cross
over to the Philistines' garrison, there
was a sharp crag on the one side and
a sharp crag on the other side, and the
name of the one was Bozez, and
the name of the other Seneh. **5** The
one crag rose on the north opposite
Michmash, and the other on the
south opposite Geba.
**6** Then Jonathan said to the young
man who was carrying his armor,
"Come and let us cross over to the
garrison of [a]these uncircumcised;
perhaps Yahweh will work for us,
for [b]Yahweh is not restrained to
save by many or by few." **7** And his
armor bearer said to him, "Do all
that is in your heart; turn yourself,
*and* here I am with you according to
your heart." **8** Then Jonathan said,
"[a]Behold, we will cross over to the
men and reveal ourselves to them. **9** If
they [1]say to us, 'Wait until we come to
you,' then we will stand in our place
and not go up to them. **10** But if they
[1]say, 'Come up to us,' then we will
go up, for Yahweh has given them
into our hands; and [a]this shall be
the sign to us." **11** So both of them
revealed themselves to the garrison
of the Philistines, and the Philistines
said, "Behold, [a]Hebrews are coming
out of the holes where they have
hidden themselves." **12** So the men
of the garrison [1]hailed Jonathan and
his armor bearer and said, "Come up
to us, and [a]we will make you know
something." And Jonathan said to his
armor bearer, "Come up after me, for
[b]Yahweh has given them into the
hands of Israel." **13** Then Jonathan

**13:18** [b]Ne 11:34 **13:19** [a]Jdg 5:8; 2Ki 24:14; Jer 24:1; 29:2 [b]Jdg 5:8 [1]Lit *sword or spear* **13:20** [1]Heb *plowshares* **13:21** [1]Heb *pim* **13:22** [a]Jdg 5:8 **13:23** [a]1Sa 14:1; 2Sa 23:14 [b]1Sa 14:4, 5; Is 10:28
◆ **14:2** [a]1Sa 13:15, 16 [b]Is 10:28 [c]1Sa 13:15 **14:3** [a]1Sa 22:9-12, 20 [b]1Sa 4:21 [c]1Sa 1:3 [d]1Sa 2:28 [1]Lit *carrying* **14:4** [a]1Sa 13:23 **14:6** [a]1Sa 17:26, 36; Jer 9:25, 26 [b]Jdg 7:4, 7; 1Sa 17:46, 47; Ps 115:3; 135:6; Zec 4:6; Mt 19:26 **14:8** [a]Jdg 7:9-14 **14:9** [1]Lit *say thus* **14:10** [a]Ge 24:14; Jdg 6:36 [1]Lit *say thus*
**14:11** [a]1Sa 13:6; 14:22 **14:12** [a]1Sa 17:43, 44 [b]2Sa 5:24 [1]Lit *answered*

climbed up on his hands and feet, with his armor bearer behind him; and they fell before Jonathan, and his armor bearer put some to death after him. **14** And that first slaughter which Jonathan and his armor bearer made was about twenty men within about half a furrow in an [1]acre of land. **15** And there was a trembling in the camp, in the field, and among all the people. Even the garrison and [a]the raiders trembled, and [b]the earth quaked so [c]that it became a [1]great trembling.

**16** Then Saul's watchmen in Gibeah of Benjamin looked, and behold, the multitude melted away; and they went here and *there.* **17** So Saul said to the people who *were* with him, "[1]Number now and see who has gone from us." And when they had [2]numbered, behold, Jonathan and his armor bearer were not *there.* **18** Then Saul said to Ahijah, "[a]Bring the ark of God here." For the ark of God was at that time with the sons of Israel. **19** [a]And it happened that while Saul talked to the priest, the commotion in the camp of the Philistines continued and increased; so Saul said to the priest, "Withdraw your hand." **20** Then Saul and all the people who *were* with him rallied and came to the battle; and behold, [a]every man's sword was against his fellow, *and there was* very great confusion. **21** Now the Hebrews *who* were with the Philistines previously, who went up with them all around in the camp, even [a]they also *turned* to be with the Israelites who *were* with Saul and Jonathan. **22** Now all the [a]men of Israel who had hidden themselves in the hill country of Ephraim heard that the Philistines had fled, and they pursued them closely in the battle. **23** So [a]Yahweh saved Israel that day, and the battle [1]spread beyond [b]Beth-aven.

### *Saul's Oath Makes the People Weary*

**24** Now the men of Israel were hard-pressed on that day. And Saul had [a]put the people under oath, saying, "Cursed be the man who eats food [1]before evening and until I have avenged myself on my enemies." So none of the people tasted food. **25** Now all *the people of* the land entered the forest, and there was honey on the ground. **26** So the people entered the forest, and behold, [a]*there was* a flow of honey; but no man put his hand to his mouth, for the people feared the sworn oath. **27** But Jonathan had not heard when his father put the people under a sworn oath; therefore, [a]he put out the end of the staff that *was* in his hand and dipped it in the honeycomb and put his hand to his mouth, and [b]his eyes brightened. **28** Then one of the people answered and said, "Your father strictly put the people under a sworn oath, saying, 'Cursed be the man who eats food today.'" And the people were weary. **29** Then Jonathan said, "[a]My father has troubled the land. See now, how my eyes have brightened because I tasted a little of this honey. **30** How much more, if only the people had eaten freely

**14:14** [1]Lit *oxen of field*; what oxen could plow in a day **14:15** [a]1Sa 13:17, 18 [b]1Sa 7:10 [c]Ge 35:5; 2Ki 7:6 [1]Lit *trembling of God* **14:17** [1]Lit *Muster(ed)* [2]Lit *muster(ed)* **14:18** [a]1Sa 23:9; 30:7 **14:19** [a]Nu 27:21 **14:20** [a]Jdg 7:22; 2Chr 20:23 **14:21** [a]1Sa 29:4 **14:22** [a]1Sa 13:6 **14:23** [a]Ex 14:30; 1Sa 10:19; 14:23; 1Chr 11:14; 2Chr 32:22; Ps 44:7 [b]1Sa 13:5 [1]Lit *passed over* **14:24** [a]Jos 6:26 [1]Lit *until* **14:26** [a]Mt 3:4 **14:27** [a]1Sa 14:43 [b]1Sa 30:12 **14:29** [a]Jos 7:25; 1Ki 18:18

today of the spoil of their enemies
which they found! For now the
slaughter among the Philistines has
not been great."

**31** Then they struck among the Phi-
listines that day from [a]Michmash to
[b]Aijalon. And the people were very
weary. **32** [a]So the people [1]rushed
greedily upon the spoil, and they
took sheep and oxen and calves and
slaughtered *them* on the ground; and
the people ate *them* [b]with the blood.
**33** Then they told Saul, saying, "Be-
hold, the people are [a]sinning against
Yahweh by eating with the blood." And
he said, "You have acted treacherously;
roll a great stone to me today." **34** And
Saul said, "Scatter yourselves among
the people and say to them, 'Each one
of you bring me his ox or his sheep,
and slaughter *it* here and eat; and do
not sin against Yahweh by eating with
the blood.'" So all the people that night
brought each one his ox [1]with him and
slaughtered *it* there. **35** And [a]Saul built
an altar to Yahweh; it was the first altar
that he built to Yahweh.

**36** Then Saul said, "Let us go down
after the Philistines by night and take
spoil among them until the morning
light, and let us not leave a man of
them." And they said, "Do whatever
seems good in your eyes." So [a]the
priest said, "Let us draw near to God
here." **37** And Saul [a]asked of God,
"Shall I *go down after* the Philistines?
Will You give them into the hand
of Israel?" But [b]He did not answer
him on that day. **38** And Saul said,
"[a]Draw near here, all you [1]chiefs of
the people, and know and see how
this sin has happened today. **39** For
[a]as Yahweh lives, who saves Israel,
though it is in Jonathan my son, he
shall surely die." But not one of all
the people answered him. **40** Then
he said to all Israel, "You shall be on
one side, and I and Jonathan my son
will be on the other side." And the
people said to Saul, "Do what seems
good in your eyes." **41** Therefore, Saul
said to Yahweh, the God of Israel,
"[a]Give a perfect *lot*." And Jonathan
and Saul were taken, but the people
escaped. **42** And Saul said, "Cast *lots*
between me and Jonathan my son."
And Jonathan was taken.

**43** Then Saul said to Jonathan,
"[a]Tell me what you have done."
So Jonathan told him and said, "[b]I
indeed tasted a little honey with the
end of the staff that was in my hand.
Here I am; I must die!" **44** And Saul
said, "[a]May God do [1]this *to me* and
more also, for [b]you shall surely die,
Jonathan." **45** But the people said to
Saul, "Must Jonathan die, who has
[1]brought about this great salvation
in Israel? Far from it! As Yahweh lives,
[a]not one hair of his head shall fall
to the ground, for [b]he has worked
with God this day." So the people
[2]redeemed Jonathan, and he did
not die. **46** Then Saul went up from
[1]pursuing the Philistines, and the
Philistines went to their own place.

### *Saul Fights Against His Enemies*

**47** Now Saul had taken the kingdom
over Israel, and he fought against all

---

**14:31** [a]1Sa 14:5 [b]Jos 10:12 **14:32** [a]1Sa 15:19 [b]Ge 9:4; Lv 3:17; 17:10-14; 19:26; Dt 12:16, 23; Ac 15:20 [1]Lit *did with regard to the spoil* **14:33** [a]Lv 7:26, 27; 19:26; Dt 12:16, 23-25; 15:23 **14:34** [1]Lit *in his hand* **14:35** [a]1Sa 7:12, 17; 2Sa 24:25; Jas 4:8 **14:36** [a]1Sa 14:3, 18, 19 **14:37** [a]1Sa 10:22 [b]1Sa 28:6 **14:38** [a]Jos 7:11, 12; 1Sa 10:19, 20 [1]Lit *corners* **14:39** [a]1Sa 14:24, 44; 2Sa 12:5 **14:41** [a]Ac 1:24 **14:43** [a]Jos 7:19 [b]1Sa 14:27 **14:44** [a]Ru 1:17; 1Sa 25:22 [b]1Sa 14:39 [1]Lit *thus* **14:45** [a]2Sa 14:11; 1Ki 1:52; Lk 21:18; Ac 27:34 [b]2Co 6:1 [1]Lit *worked* [2]Lit *ransomed* **14:46** [1]Lit *after*

his enemies on every side, against
Moab, [a]the sons of Ammon, Edom,
[b]the kings of Zobah, and [c]the Phi-
listines; and wherever he turned,
he [1]inflicted punishment. 48 And he
acted valiantly and [a]struck down the
Amalekites and delivered Israel from
the hands of [1]those who plundered
them.

49 Now [a]the sons of Saul were
Jonathan and Ishvi and Malchi-shua;
and the names of his two daughters
*were these*: the name of the firstborn
[b]Merab and the name of the younger
[c]Michal. 50 And the name of Saul's
wife was Ahinoam the daughter
of Ahimaaz. And [a]the name of the
commander of his army was Abner
the son of Ner, Saul's uncle. 51 [a]And
Kish *was* the father of Saul, and Ner
the father of Abner *was* the son of
Abiel.

52 Now the war against the Phi-
listines was severe all the days of
Saul; and Saul would see any mighty
man or any man of valor and would
[a]gather him to [1]his staff.

### *Saul's Disobedience*

15 Then Samuel said to Saul,
"[a]Yahweh sent me to anoint
you as king over His people, over
Israel; so now, [1]obey the voice of the
words of Yahweh. 2 Thus says Yahweh
of hosts, 'I will [1]punish Amalek [a]*for*
what he did to Israel, how he set
himself against him on the way while
he was coming up from Egypt. 3 Now
go and strike Amalek and [a]devote
to destruction all that he has, and
do not spare him; but [b]put to death
both man and woman, infant and
nursing baby, ox and sheep, camel
and donkey.'"

4 Then Saul summoned the peo-
ple and [1]numbered them in [a]Telaim,
200,000 foot soldiers and 10,000 men
of Judah. 5 And Saul came to the city
of Amalek and set an ambush in the
valley. 6 And Saul said to [a]the Kenites,
"Go, depart; go down from among the
Amalekites, lest I destroy you with
them; [b]you showed lovingkindness
to all the sons of Israel when they
came up from Egypt." So the Kenites
departed from among the Amalekites.
7 So [a]Saul struck the Amalekites, from
[b]Havilah as you go to [c]Shur, which is
[1]east of Egypt. 8 And he seized [a]Agag
the king of the Amalekites alive and
[b]devoted to destruction all the peo-
ple with the edge of the sword. 9 But
Saul and the people [a]spared Agag
and the best of the sheep, the oxen,
the fatlings, the lambs, and all that
was good, and they were not willing
to devote them to destruction; but
everything despised and worthless,
that they utterly destroyed.

### *Yahweh Regrets He Made Saul King*

10 Then the word of Yahweh came
to Samuel, saying, 11 "[a]I regret that
I have made Saul king, for [b]he has
turned back from [1]following Me and
has not established My words." And

**14:47** [a]1Sa 11:1-13 [b]2Sa 8:3-10 [c]1Sa 14:52 [1]Or *condemned* **14:48** [a]1Sa 15:3, 7 [1]Lit *its plunderers* **14:49** [a]1Sa 31:2; 1Chr 8:33; 10:2 [b]1Sa 18:17-19 [c]1Sa 18:20, 27; 19:12; 2Sa 6:20-23 **14:50** [a]2Sa 2:8 **14:51** [a]1Sa 9:1, 21 **14:52** [a]1Sa 8:11 [1]Lit *himself* ◆ **15:1** [a]1Sa 9:16; 10:1 [1]Or *listen to*, cf. 15:14, 19, 20, 24 **15:2** [a]Ex 17:8-16; Nu 24:20; Dt 25:17-19 [1]Or *visit* **15:3** [a]Nu 24:20; Dt 20:16-18; Jos 6:17-21 [b]1Sa 22:19 **15:4** [a]Jos 15:24 [1]Lit *mustered* **15:6** [a]Nu 24:21; Jdg 1:16; 4:11 [b]Ex 18:9, 10; Nu 10:29-32 **15:7** [a]1Sa 14:48 [b]Ge 25:18 [c]Ge 16:7; Ex 15:22; 1Sa 27:8 [1]Lit *before* **15:8** [a]Nu 24:7; 1Sa 15:20; Es 3:1 [b]1Sa 27:8, 9; 30:1; 2Sa 8:12 **15:9** [a]1Sa 15:3, 15, 19 **15:11** [a]Ge 6:6, 7; Ex 32:14; 1Sa 15:35; 2Sa 24:16 [b]Jos 22:16; 1Sa 13:13; 1Ki 9:6, 7 [1]Lit *after*

Samuel became angry and [c]cried out
to Yahweh all night. 12 Then Samuel
rose early in the morning to meet
Saul; and it was told to Samuel,
saying, "Saul came to [a]Carmel, and
behold, he set up a monument for
himself, then turned and proceeded
on [1]down to [b]Gilgal." 13 And Samuel
came to Saul, and Saul said to him,
"[a]Blessed are you of Yahweh! I have
established the word of Yahweh."
14 But Samuel said, "[a]What then is
this sound of the sheep in my ears
and the sound of the oxen which
I am hearing?" 15 And Saul said,
"They have brought them from the
Amalekites, for [a]the people spared
the best of the sheep and oxen, to
sacrifice to Yahweh your God; but the
rest we have devoted to destruction."
16 Then Samuel said to Saul, "Wait,
and let me tell you what Yahweh
spoke to me last night." And he said
to him, "Speak!"

17 And Samuel said, "Is it not true,
[a]though you were little in your own
eyes, you were *made* the head of
the tribes of Israel? And Yahweh
anointed you king over Israel, 18 and
Yahweh sent you on a [1]mission and
said, '[a]Go and devote to destruction
the sinners, the Amalekites, and
fight against them until they are
consumed.' 19 Why then did you
not [1]obey the voice of Yahweh, [a]but
*rushed upon the spoil* and did what
was evil in the eyes of Yahweh?"

20 Then Saul said to Samuel, "[a]I
did [1]obey the voice of Yahweh and
went on the way on which Yahweh
sent me and have brought back Agag
the king of Amalek and have devoted
the Amalekites to destruction. 21 But
[a]the people took *some* of the spoil,
sheep and oxen, the choicest of
the things devoted to destruction,
to sacrifice to Yahweh your God at
Gilgal." 22 And Samuel said,

"[a]Has Yahweh as much
delight in burnt offerings
and sacrifices
As in obeying the voice
of Yahweh?
Behold, [b]to obey is better
than sacrifice,
*And* to heed
than the fat of rams.
23 "For rebellion is as the
sin of [a]divination,
And insubordination is
as [b]wickedness and idolatry.
Because you have rejected
the word of Yahweh,
[c]He has also rejected you
from *being* king."

24 Then Saul said to Samuel, "[a]I
have sinned; [b]I have indeed tres-
passed against the [1]command of
Yahweh and your words because I
feared the people and obeyed their
voice. 25 So now, [a]please forgive my
sin and return with me, that I may
worship Yahweh." 26 But Samuel said
to Saul, "I will not return with you;
for [a]you have rejected the word of
Yahweh, and Yahweh has rejected you
from being king over Israel." 27 Then
Samuel turned to go, but [a]*Saul* seized

**15:11** [c]Ex 32:11-13; Lk 6:12 **15:12** [a]Jos 15:55; 1Sa 25:2 [b]1Sa 13:12, 15 [1]Lit *and went down* **15:13** [a]Ge 14:19; Jdg 17:2; Ru 3:10; 2Sa 2:5 **15:14** [a]Ex 32:21-24 **15:15** [a]Ge 3:12, 13; Ex 32:22, 23; 1Sa 15:9, 21 **15:17** [a]1Sa 9:21; 10:22 **15:18** [a]1Sa 15:3 [1]Lit *way* **15:19** [a]1Sa 14:32 [1]Or *listen to*, cf. 15:14 **15:20** [a]1Sa 15:13 [1]Or *listen to*, cf. 15:14 **15:21** [a]Ex 32:22, 23; 1Sa 15:15 **15:22** [a]Ps 40:6-8; 51:16, 17; Is 1:11-15; Mic 6:6-8; Heb 10:6-9 [b]Jer 7:22, 23; Hos 6:6; Mt 12:7; Mk 12:33 **15:23** [a]Dt 18:10 [b]Ge 31:19, 34 [c]1Sa 13:14 **15:24** [a]Nu 22:34; 2Sa 12:13; Ps 51:4 [b]Pr 29:25; Is 51:12, 13 [1]Lit *mouth* **15:25** [a]Ex 10:17 **15:26** [a]1Sa 13:14; 16:1 **15:27** [a]1Ki 11:30, 31

the edge of his robe, and it tore. **28** So
Samuel said to him, “[a]Yahweh has
torn the kingdom of Israel from you
today and has given it to your neigh-
bor, who is better than you. **29** Also
the [a]Eternal One of Israel [b]will not
lie or have regret; for He is not a man
that He should have regret.” **30** Then
he said, “I have sinned; [a]*but* please
honor me now before the elders of
my people and before Israel, and
return with me, [b]that I may worship
Yahweh your God.” **31** So Samuel
returned, following after Saul, and
Saul worshiped Yahweh.

**32** Then Samuel said, “Bring Agag
near to me, the king of the Amalek-
ites.” And Agag came to him [1]in
chains. And Agag said, “Surely the
bitterness of death has departed.”
**33** But Samuel said, “[a]As your sword
has made women childless, so shall
your mother be childless among
women.” And Samuel hacked Agag
to pieces before Yahweh at Gilgal.

**34** Then Samuel went to [a]Ramah,
but Saul went up to his house at
[b]Gibeah of Saul. **35** [a]So Samuel did
not see Saul again until the day of
his death; for Samuel [b]grieved over
Saul. And Yahweh regretted that He
had made Saul king over Israel.

### *David Anointed King*

**16** Then Yahweh said to Samuel,
“[a]How long will you be griev-
ing over Saul? [b]I have rejected him
from being king over Israel. [c]Fill
your horn with oil and go; I will send
you to [d]Jesse the Bethlehemite, for I
[e]see among his sons a king for Me.”
**2** But Samuel said, “How can I go?
Saul will hear *of it* and will kill me.”
Then Yahweh said, “[a]Take a heifer
with you and say, ‘I have come to
sacrifice to Yahweh.’ **3** And you shall
invite Jesse to the sacrifice, and [a]I
will make you know what you shall
do; and [b]you shall anoint for Me the
one whom I say to you.” **4** So Samuel
did what Yahweh said and came to
[a]Bethlehem. And the elders of the
city came trembling to meet him and
said, “[b]Do you come in peace?” **5** And
he said, “In peace; I have come to
sacrifice to Yahweh. [a]Set yourselves
apart as holy and come with me to
the sacrifice.” He also set apart Jesse
and his sons as holy and invited them
to the sacrifice.

**6** Now it happened, when they
entered, he looked at [a]Eliab and
thought, “Surely the anointed of
Yahweh is before Him.” **7** But Yahweh
said to Samuel, “Do not look at his
appearance or at the height of his
stature, because I have rejected
him; for [1]God *sees* not as man sees,
for man looks at the outward ap-
pearance, [a]but Yahweh looks at the
heart.” **8** Then Jesse called [a]Abinadab
and made him pass before Samuel.
And he said, “Yahweh has not chosen
this one either.” **9** Next Jesse made
[a,1]Shammah pass by. And he said,
“Yahweh has not chosen this one
either.” **10** Thus Jesse made seven
of his sons pass before Samuel. But

---

**15:28** [a]*1Sa 28:17, 18; 1Ki 11:31* **15:29** [a]1Chr 29:11 [b]Nu 23:19; Eze 24:14; Tit 1:2 **15:30** [a]Jn 5:44; 12:43 [b]Is 29:13 **15:32** [1]Or *cheerfully* **15:33** [a]Ge 9:6; Jdg 1:7; Mt 7:2 **15:34** [a]1Sa 7:17 [b]1Sa 11:4 **15:35** [a]1Sa 19:24 [b]1Sa 16:1 ◆ **16:1** [a]1Sa 15:35 [b]1Sa 13:13, 14; 15:23 [c]1Sa 9:16; 10:1; 2Ki 9:1 [d]Ru 4:17-22 [e]Ps 78:70, 71; Ac 13:22 **16:2** [a]1Sa 20:29 **16:3** [a]Ex 4:15; Ac 9:6 [b]Dt 17:14, 15; 1Sa 9:16 **16:4** [a]Ge 48:7; Lk 2:4 [b]1Ki 2:13; 2Ki 9:22; 1Chr 12:17, 18 **16:5** [a]Ge 35:2; Ex 19:10 **16:6** [a]1Sa 17:13 **16:7** [a]1Sa 2:3; 1Ki 8:39; 1Chr 28:9; Lk 16:15 [1]As in Gr; Heb He does *not* see *what man sees* **16:8** [a]1Sa 17:13 **16:9** [a]1Sa 17:13 [1]In 2Sa 13:3, *Shimeah*; in 1Chr 2:13, *Shimea*

Samuel said to Jesse, "Yahweh has not chosen these." **11** And Samuel said to Jesse, "Are these all the young men?" And he said, "[a]There remains yet the youngest, and behold, he is shepherding the sheep." Then Samuel said to Jesse, "Send and [1]bring him, for we will not turn around until he comes here." **12** So he sent and brought him in. Now he was ruddy, with [a]beautiful eyes and a handsome appearance. And Yahweh said, "[b]Arise, anoint him, for this is he." **13** Then Samuel took the horn of oil and [a]anointed him in the midst of his brothers; and [b]the Spirit of Yahweh [1]came mightily upon David from that day forward. And Samuel arose and went to Ramah.

### *David Becomes Saul's Armor Bearer*

**14** [a]Now the Spirit of Yahweh departed from Saul, and [b]an evil spirit from Yahweh terrorized him. **15** Saul's servants then said to him, "Behold now, an evil spirit from God is terrorizing you. **16** Let our lord now speak to your servants who are before you. Let them seek a man who is a skillful musician on the harp; and it shall be that when the evil spirit from God is on you, [a]he shall play *the harp* with his hand, and you will be well." **17** So Saul said to his servants, "Provide for me now a man who can play well and bring *him* to *me.*" **18** Then one of the young men answered and said, "Behold, I have seen a son of Jesse the Bethlehemite who is a skillful musician, [a]a mighty man of valor, a warrior, one who is understanding in speech, and man of fine form; and [b]Yahweh is with him." **19** So Saul sent messengers to Jesse and said, "Send me your son David who is with the flock." **20** And Jesse [a]took a donkey *loaded with* bread and a wineskin of wine and a young goat and sent *them* to Saul by David his son. **21** Then David came to Saul and [a]stood before him; and [1]Saul loved him greatly, and he became his armor bearer. **22** So Saul sent to Jesse, saying, "Let David now stand before me, for he has found favor in my sight." **23** Thus it happened that whenever [a]the *evil* spirit from God came to Saul, David would take the harp and play *it* with his hand; and Saul would be refreshed and be well, and the evil spirit would depart from him.

### *David and Goliath*

**17** Now [a]the Philistines gathered their camps for battle; and they were gathered at Socoh which belongs to Judah, and they camped between [b]Socoh and [c]Azekah, in [d]Ephes-dammim. **2** But Saul and the men of Israel were gathered and camped in [a]the valley of Elah and arranged *themselves* for battle to meet the Philistines. **3** Now the Philistines stood on the mountain on one side while Israel stood on the mountain on the other side, with the valley between them. **4** Then a champion came out from the camps of the Philistines named [a]Goliath, from [b]Gath, whose height was [1]six cubits and a [2]span. **5** *And he had* a

**16:11** [a]1Sa 17:12; 2Sa 13:3 [1]Lit *take* **16:12** [a]Ge 39:6; Ex 2:2; Ac 7:20 [b]1Sa 9:17 **16:13** [a]1Sa 10:1 [b]Nu 27:18; 1Sa 10:6, 9, 10 [1]Lit *succeeded, rushed upon* **16:14** [a]Jdg 16:20; 1Sa 11:6; 18:12; 28:15 [b]Jdg 9:23; 1Sa 16:15, 16; 18:10; 19:9; 1Ki 22:19-22 **16:16** [a]1Sa 18:10; 19:9; 2Ki 3:15 **16:18** [a]1Sa 17:32-36 [b]1Sa 3:19 **16:20** [a]1Sa 10:4, 27; Pr 18:16 **16:21** [a]Ge 41:46; Pr 22:29 [1]Lit *he* **16:23** [a]1Sa 16:14-16 ◆**17:1** [a]1Sa 13:5 [b]Jos 15:35; 2Chr 28:18 [c]Jos 10:10 [d]1Chr 11:13 **17:2** [a]1Sa 21:9 **17:4** [a]2Sa 21:19 [b]Jos 11:22 [1]Approx. 9 ft. or 2.7 m, a cubit was approx. 18 in. or 45 cm [2]A span was approx. 9 in. or 23 cm

bronze helmet on his head, and he
was clothed with scale-armor, and
the weight of that scale-armor was
five thousand [1]shekels of bronze.
**6** *He* also *had* bronze [1]greaves on his
legs and a [a]bronze [2]javelin *slung* be-
tween his shoulders. **7** [a]And the shaft
of his spear was like a weaver's beam,
and the head of his spear *weighed*
six hundred shekels of iron; [b]his
shield-carrier also walked before
him. **8** And he stood and called out
to the [1]battle lines of Israel and said
to them, "Why do you come out to
arrange *yourselves* for battle? Am I
not the Philistine and you [a]slaves of
Saul? Choose a man for yourselves
and let him come down to me. **9** [a]If
he is able to fight with me and strike
me down, then we will become
your slaves; but if I prevail against
him and strike him down, then you
shall become our slaves and serve
us." **10** Again the Philistine said, "[a]I
*openly* [1]reproach the battle lines of
Israel this day; give me a man that
we may fight together." **11** When Saul
and all Israel heard these words of
the Philistine, they were dismayed
and greatly afraid.

**12** Now David was [a]the son of
[1]the [b]Ephrathite of Bethlehem in
Judah, whose name was Jesse, and
[c]he had eight sons. And [2]Jesse was
old in the days of Saul, advanced *in*
*years* among men. **13** And the three
older sons of Jesse had gone. They
had gone after Saul to the battle.
And [a]the names of his three sons
who went to the battle were Eliab
the firstborn, and the second to him
Abinadab, and the third Shammah.
**14** [a]But David was the youngest. Now
the three oldest had gone after Saul,
**15** [a]but David went back and forth
from Saul [b]to shepherd his father's
flock at Bethlehem.

**16** Then the Philistine approached,
morning and evening, for forty days
and took his stand.

**17** Then Jesse said to David his
son, "[a]Take now for your brothers
an ephah of this roasted grain and
these ten loaves and run to the camp
to your brothers. **18** [a]You shall also
bring these ten cuts of cheese to
the commander of *their* thousand,
[b]and look into the welfare of your
brothers, and bring back [1]a token
from them. **19** And Saul and they and
all the men of Israel are in the valley
of Elah, fighting with the Philistines."

**20** So David arose early in the
morning and left the flock with a
keeper and carried *the supplies* and
went as Jesse had commanded him.
And he came to the [a]circle of the
camp while the military force was
going out in battle lines shouting
the war cry. **21** And Israel and the
Philistines arranged themselves in
battle lines, battle line [1]against battle
line. **22** Then David left his [a]baggage
in the [1]care of the baggage keeper and
ran to the battle line and entered in
order to greet his brothers. **23** As he
was speaking with them, behold, the
champion, the Philistine from Gath
named Goliath, was coming up from
the battle lines of the Philistines, and

---

**17:5** [1]A shekel was approx. 0.4 oz. or 11 gm **17:6** [a]1Sa 17:45 [1]Or *shin guards* [2]Or *scimitar*
**17:7** [a]2Sa 21:19; 1Chr 11:23 [b]1Sa 17:41 **17:8** [a]1Sa 8:17 [1]Lit *lines*, so in ch **17:9** [a]2Sa 2:12-16
**17:10** [a]1Sa 17:26, 36, 45; 2Sa 21:21 [1]Or *defy* **17:12** [a]Ru 4:22; 1Sa 16:18 [b]Ge 35:19 [c]1Sa 16:10, 11;
1Chr 2:13-15 [1]Lit *this* [2]Lit *the man* **17:13** [a]1Sa 16:6, 8, 9 **17:14** [a]1Sa 16:11 **17:15** [a]1Sa 16:21-23
[b]1Sa 16:11, 19 **17:17** [a]1Sa 25:18 **17:18** [a]1Sa 16:20 [b]Ge 37:13, 14 [1]Lit *their pledge* **17:20** [a]1Sa 26:5, 7
**17:21** [1]Lit *to meet* **17:22** [a]Jdg 18:21; Is 10:28 [1]Lit *hand*

he spoke [a]these same words; and
David heard *them.*

**24** Now all the men of Israel saw
the man, and they fled from him and
were greatly afraid. **25** And the men
of Israel said, "Have you seen this
man who is coming up? Surely he is
coming up to [1]reproach Israel. And
it will be that the king will enrich
the man who strikes him down with
great riches and [a]will give him his
daughter and make his father's house
[2]free in Israel."

**26** Then David spoke to the men
who were standing by him, saying,
"What will be done for the man who
strikes down this Philistine and takes
away [a]the reproach from Israel? For
who is this [b]uncircumcised Philis-
tine, that he should [c,1]reproach the
battle lines of [d]the living God?"
**27** And the people spoke to him in ac-
cord with this word, saying, "[a]Thus it
will be done for the man who strikes
him down."

**28** Then Eliab his oldest brother
heard when he spoke to the men;
and [a]Eliab's anger burned against
David, and he said, "Why have you
come down? And with whom have
you left those few sheep in the
wilderness? I myself know your
arrogance and the wickedness of
your heart, for you have come down
in order to see the battle." **29** But
David said, "What have I done now?
Was it not just a word?" **30** Then he
turned [1]away from him to another
and [a]said the same word; and the
people responded to him *with* the
same word as [2]before.

### *David Puts Goliath to Death*

**31** Then the words which David spoke
were heard. And they told *them* [1]to
Saul, and he sent for him. **32** And Da-
vid said to Saul, "[a]Let no man's heart
fail on account of him; [b]your servant
will go and fight with this Philistine."
**33** Then Saul said to David, "[a]You are
not able to go against this Philistine
to fight with him; for you are *but* a
youth while he has been a warrior
from his youth." **34** But David said to
Saul, "Your servant was shepherding
his father's sheep. And a lion and a
bear would come and take a lamb
from the flock, **35** and I would go out
after it and strike it and [a]rescue *the*
*lamb* from its mouth. Then it rose up
against me, and I would seize *it* by its
beard and strike it down and put it
to death. **36** Your servant has struck
down both the lion and the bear;
and this uncircumcised Philistine
will be like one of them, since he
has [1]reproached the battle lines of
the living God." **37** And David said,
"[a]Yahweh, who delivered me from
the hand of the lion and from the
hand of the bear, He will deliver me
from the hand of this Philistine."
And Saul said to David, "[b]Go, and
may Yahweh be with you." **38** Then
Saul clothed David with his robes and
put a bronze helmet on his head, and
he clothed him with armor. **39** And
David girded his sword over his ar-
mor and tried to walk, for he had not
tested *them.* So David said to Saul,
"I cannot go with these, for I have
not tested *them.*" And David took
them [1]off. **40** Then he took his stick

---

**17:23** [a]1Sa 17:8-10 **17:25** [a]Jos 15:16 [1]Or *defy* [2]Free from taxes and public service **17:26** [a]1Sa 11:2 [b]1Sa 14:6; 17:36; Jer 9:25, 26 [c]1Sa 17:10 [d]Dt 5:26; 2Ki 19:4; Jer 10:10 [1]Or *defy* **17:27** [a]1Sa 17:25 **17:28** [a]Ge 37:4, 8-36; Pr 18:19; Mt 10:36 **17:30** [a]1Sa 17:26, 27 [1]Lit *from beside him* [2]Lit *the former word* **17:31** [1]Lit *before* **17:32** [a]Dt 20:1-4 [b]1Sa 16:18 **17:33** [a]Nu 13:31 **17:35** [a]Am 3:12 **17:36** [1]Or *defied* **17:37** [a]2Co 1:10; 2Ti 4:17, 18 [b]1Sa 20:13; 1Chr 22:11, 16 **17:39** [1]Lit *off from himself*

in his hand and chose for himself
five smooth stones from the brook
and put them in the shepherd's bag
which he had, even in *his* pouch, and
[a]his sling was in his hand; and he
approached the Philistine.
**41** Then the Philistine came on
and drew near to David, with the
shield-bearer in front of him. **42** And
the Philistine looked and saw David.
And [a]he despised him; for he was
*but* a youth and [b]ruddy, with a
handsome appearance. **43** And the
Philistine said to David, "[a]Am I a dog,
that you come to me with sticks?"
And [b]the Philistine cursed David by
his gods. **44** The Philistine also said
to David, "Come to me, and I will give
your flesh [a]to the birds of the sky and
the beasts of the field." **45** Then David
said to the Philistine, "You come to
me with a sword, a spear, and a jav-
elin, [a]but I come to you in the name
of Yahweh of hosts, the God of the
battle lines of Israel, whom you have
[1]reproached. **46** This day Yahweh will
deliver you up into my hands, and
I will strike you down and remove
your head from you. And I will give
the [a]dead bodies of the camp of the
Philistines this day to the birds of the
sky and the beasts of the earth, [b]that
all the earth may know that there is
a God in Israel, **47** and that all this
assembly may know that [a]Yahweh
does not save by sword or by spear;
[b]for the battle is Yahweh's, and He
will give you into our hands."
**48** Then it happened when the
Philistine rose and came and drew
near to *meet* David, that [a]David ran
quickly toward the battle line to meet
the Philistine. **49** And David sent his
hand down into his bag and took from
it a stone and slung *it* and struck the
Philistine on his forehead. And the
stone sank into his forehead, so that
he fell on his face to the ground.
**50** Thus David prevailed over the
Philistine with a sling and a stone,
and he struck the Philistine and put
him to death; but there was no sword
in David's hand. **51** Then David ran
and stood over the Philistine and
[a]took his sword and drew it out of
its sheath and put him to death and
cut off his head with it. [b]Then the
Philistines saw that their champion
was dead, so they fled. **52** But the men
of Israel and Judah arose and shouted
and pursued the Philistines [1]as far as
the valley and to the gates of [a]Ekron.
And the slain Philistines *lay* fallen
along the way to [b]Shaaraim, even to
Gath and Ekron. **53** Then the sons
of Israel returned from hotly pur-
suing the Philistines and plundered
their camps. **54** And David took the
Philistine's head and brought it to
Jerusalem, but he put his weapons
in his tent.
**55** Now when Saul saw David going
out to meet the Philistine, he said
to Abner the commander of the
army, "Abner, whose son is [a]this
young man?" And Abner said, "By
your life, O king, I do not know."
**56** And the king said, "You inquire
whose son the youth is." **57** So when
David returned from striking down
the Philistine, Abner took him and
[a]brought him before Saul with the

**17:40** [a]Jdg 20:16 **17:42** [a]Ps 123:4; Pr 16:18 [b]1Sa 16:12 **17:43** [a]1Sa 24:14; 2Sa 3:8; 2Ki 8:13 [b]1Ki 20:10 **17:44** [a]1Sa 17:46 **17:45** [a]2Sa 22:35; 2Chr 32:8; Ps 124:8; Heb 11:32-34 [1]Or *defied* **17:46** [a]Dt 28:26 [b]Jos 4:24; 1Ki 8:43; 18:36; 2Ki 19:19; Is 37:20 **17:47** [a]1Sa 14:6; 2Chr 14:11; 20:15; Ps 44:6; Hos 1:7; Zec 4:6 [b]2Chr 20:15 **17:48** [a]Ps 27:3 **17:51** [a]1Sa 21:9; 2Sa 23:21 [b]Heb 11:34 **17:52** [a]Jos 15:11 [b]Jos 15:36 [1]Lit *until your coming to* **17:55** [a]1Sa 16:12, 21, 22 **17:57** [a]1Sa 17:54

Philistine's head in his hand. **58** And
Saul said to him, "Whose son are you,
young man?" And David answered,
"[a]*I am* the son of your servant Jesse
the Bethlehemite."

### *Jonathan Cuts a Covenant with David*

**18** Now it happened when he
had finished speaking to Saul,
that [a]the soul of Jonathan was knit
to the soul of David, and [b]Jonathan
loved him as his own soul. **2** And
Saul took him that day and [a]did not
let him return to his father's house.
**3** Then [a]Jonathan cut a covenant with
David because he loved him as his
own soul. **4** [a]And Jonathan stripped
himself of the robe that was on him
and gave it to David, with his armor,
even his sword and his bow and his
belt. **5** So David went out wherever
Saul sent him *and* [1]prospered; and
Saul set him over the men of war.
And it was pleasing in the eyes of all
the people and also in the eyes of
Saul's servants.

### *Saul Looks at David with Suspicion*

**6** And it happened as they were
coming, when David returned from
striking down the Philistine, that
[a]the women came out of all the
cities of Israel, singing and dancing,
to meet King Saul, with tambourines,
*with gladness*, and with [1]musical in-
struments. **7** And the women [a]sang as
they [1]were merry and said,

"[b]Saul has struck his
thousands,
[c]And David his ten
thousands."

**8** Then Saul became very angry, for
this saying was [1]displeasing in his
eyes; and he said, "They have as-
cribed to David ten thousands, but
to me they have ascribed thousands.
Now [a]what more can he have but the
kingdom?" **9** So Saul looked at David
with suspicion from that day on.

**10** Now it happened on the next
day that [a]an evil spirit from God
[1]came mightily upon Saul, and [b]he
raved in the midst of the house. Now
David was playing *the harp* with his
hand, [c,2]as usual; and [d,3]a spear *was*
in Saul's hand. **11** [a]Then Saul hurled
the spear for he thought, "I will [1]pin
David to the wall." But David [2]escaped
from his presence twice.

**12** And [a]Saul was afraid of David,
[b]for Yahweh was with him but [c]had
turned away from Saul. **13** Therefore
Saul turned him away from [1]his
presence and appointed him as his
commander of one thousand; and
[a]he went out and came in before the
people. **14** And David was [1]prospering
in all his ways, and [a]Yahweh *was* with
him. **15** Then Saul saw that he was
[1]prospering greatly, so he dreaded
him. **16** But [a]all Israel and Judah loved
David, for he went out and came in
before them.

**17** Then Saul said to David, "[a]Here
is my older daughter Merab; I will

---

**17:58** [a]1Sa 17:12 ◆ **18:1** [a]Ge 44:30 [b]Dt 13:6; 1Sa 20:17; 2Sa 1:26 **18:2** [a]1Sa 17:15 **18:3** [a]1Sa 20:8-17
**18:4** [a]Ge 41:42; 1Sa 17:38; Es 6:8 **18:5** [1]Or *acted wisely* **18:6** [a]Ex 15:20, 21; Jdg 11:34; Ps 68:25; 149:3 [1]Possibly three-stringed lutes **18:7** [a]Ex 15:21; 1Sa 21:11; 29:5 [b]1Sa 21:11 [c]2Sa 18:3 [1]Or *danced*
**18:8** [a]1Sa 15:28 [1]Lit *evil* **18:10** [a]1Sa 16:14 [b]1Sa 19:23, 24 [c]1Sa 16:23 [d]1Sa 19:9 [1]Lit *succeeded, rushed upon* [2]Lit *day by day* [3]Lit *the* **18:11** [a]1Sa 19:10; 20:33 [1]Lit *strike David and the wall* [2]Lit *turned about* **18:12** [a]1Sa 18:15, 29 [b]1Sa 16:13, 18 [c]1Sa 16:14; 28:15 **18:13** [a]Nu 27:17; 1Sa 18:16; 2Sa 5:2 [1]Lit *with him* **18:14** [a]Ge 39:2, 3, 23; Jos 6:27; 1Sa 16:18 [1]Or *acting wisely* **18:15** [1]Or *acting very wisely*
**18:16** [a]1Sa 18:5 **18:17** [a]1Sa 17:25

give her to you as a wife; only be
a man of valor for me and fight
[b]Yahweh's battles." For Saul thought,
"My hand shall not be against him,
but [c]let the hand of the Philistines
be against him." **18** But David said to
Saul, "[a]Who am I, and what is my life
*or* my father's family in Israel, that
I should be the king's son-in-law?"
**19** So it happened at the time when
Merab, Saul's daughter, should have
been given to David, that she was
given to [a]Adriel [b]the Meholathite
as a wife.

### *Saul's Daughter Given to David*

**20** And [a]Michal, Saul's daughter,
loved David. So they told Saul, and
the thing was right in his eyes. **21** And
Saul said, "I will give her to him that
she may become a snare to him,
and [a]that the hand of the Philis-
tines may be against him." Therefore
Saul said to David, "[b]For a second
time you may be my son-in-law to-
day." **22** Then Saul commanded his
servants, "Speak to David secretly,
saying, 'Behold, the king delights in
you, and all his servants love you;
so now, become the king's son-in-
law.'" **23** So Saul's servants spoke
these words in [1]David's hearing. But
David said, "Is it trivial in your eyes
to become the king's son-in-law,
[a]since I am a poor man and lightly
esteemed?" **24** And the servants of
Saul told to him [1]according to these
words *which* David spoke. **25** Saul
then said, "Thus you shall say to
David, 'The king does not desire any
[a]dowry except one hundred foreskins
of the Philistines, [b]to take vengeance
on the king's enemies.'" Now [c]Saul
planned to make David fall by the
hand of the Philistines. **26** Then his
servants told David these words, and
it was right in the eyes of David to
become the king's son-in-law. [a,1]So
before the days had expired, **27** David
rose up and went, [a]he and his men,
and struck down two hundred men
among the Philistines. Then [b]David
brought their foreskins, and they
gave them in full number to the king,
that he might become the king's son-
in-law. So Saul gave him Michal his
daughter as a wife. **28** Then Saul saw
and knew that Yahweh was with Da-
vid, and *that* Michal, Saul's daughter,
loved him, **29** so Saul was even more
afraid of David. So Saul was David's
enemy continually.

**30** Then the commanders of the
Philistines [a]went out *to battle*, and it
happened as often as they went out,
that David [b]behaved himself more
insightfully than all the servants
of Saul. So his name was highly
esteemed.

### *David Escapes from Saul*

**19** Then Saul spoke with Jonathan
his son and all his servants
[a]to put David to death. But [b]Jona-
than, Saul's son, greatly delighted
in David. **2** So Jonathan told David
saying, "Saul my father is seeking
to put you to death. So now, please
be careful in the morning, and stay
in a secret place and hide yourself.
**3** And I will go out and stand beside
my father in the field where you

---

**18:17** [b]Nu 21:14; 1Sa 17:36, 47; 25:28 [c]1Sa 18:21, 25 **18:18** [a]1Sa 9:21; 18:23; 2Sa 7:18 **18:19** [a]2Sa 21:8 [b]Jdg 7:22; 1Ki 19:16 **18:20** [a]1Sa 18:28 **18:21** [a]1Sa 18:17 [b]1Sa 18:26 **18:23** [a]Ge 29:20; 34:12 [1]Lit *the ears of David* **18:24** [1]Lit *by saying according* **18:25** [a]Ge 34:12; Ex 22:17 [b]1Sa 14:24 [c]1Sa 18:17 **18:26** [a]1Sa 18:21 [1]Lit *And the days had not expired* **18:27** [a]1Sa 18:17 [b]2Sa 3:14 **18:30** [a]2Sa 11:1 [b]1Sa 18:5 ◆ **19:1** [a]1Sa 18:8, 9 [b]1Sa 18:1-3

are, and I will speak with my father
about you; [a]what I [1]perceive, I will
tell you." **4** Then Jonathan [a]spoke
well of David to Saul his father and
said to him, "[b]Do not let the king
sin against his servant David, since
he has not sinned against you, and
since his works *have been* very good
for you. **5** For [a] he took his life in his
hand and struck the Philistine, and
[b]Yahweh brought about a great salva-
tion for all Israel; you saw *it* and were
glad. [c]Why then will you sin against
innocent blood by putting David to
death without a cause?" **6** And Saul
listened to the voice of Jonathan, and
Saul swore, "As Yahweh lives, he shall
not be put to death." **7** Then Jonathan
called David, and Jonathan told
him all these words. And Jonathan
brought David to Saul, and he was in
his presence as [a]formerly.

**8** Then there was war again. And
David went out and fought with the
Philistines and struck them with
a great slaughter, so that they fled
before him. **9** Now there was [a]an evil
spirit from Yahweh on Saul as he was
sitting in his house [b]with his spear
in his hand, [c]and David was playing
*the harp* with *his* hand. **10** [a]And Saul
tried to [1]pin David to the wall with
the spear, but he slipped away out of
Saul's presence, so that he [2]stuck the
spear into the wall. And David fled
and escaped that night.

**11** Then [a]Saul sent messengers to
David's house to keep watch over
him, in order to put him to death
in the morning. But Michal, David's
wife, told him, saying, "If you do not
make an escape for your life tonight,
tomorrow you will be put to death."
**12** [a]So Michal let David down through
a window, and he went out and fled
and escaped. **13** Then Michal took
[a]the [1]household idol and laid *it* on
the bed and put a quilt of goats'
*hair* at its head and covered *it* with
clothes. **14** Then Saul sent messen-
gers to take David, but she said, "[a]He
is sick." **15** So Saul sent messengers to
see David, saying, "Bring him up to
me on [1]his bed, that I may put him
to death." **16** The messengers came,
and behold, the [1]household idol *was*
on the bed with the quilt of goats'
*hair* at its head. **17** So Saul said to
Michal, "Why have you deceived me
like this and let my enemy go, so that
he has escaped?" And Michal said
to Saul, "He said to me, 'Let me go!
[a]Why should I put you to death?'"

**18** Now David fled and escaped
and came [a]to Samuel at Ramah and
told him all that Saul had done to
him. And he and Samuel went and
stayed in [b]Naioth. **19** And it was told
to Saul, saying, "Behold, David is at
Naioth in Ramah." **20** Then [a]Saul sent
messengers to take David, but they
saw [b]the company of the prophets
prophesying, with Samuel standing
*and* presiding over them. And the
Spirit of God came upon the messen-
gers of Saul; and [c]they also proph-
esied. **21** This was told to Saul, and he
sent other messengers, and they also

---

**19:3** [a]1Sa 20:9, 13 [1]Lit *see* **19:4** [a]1Sa 20:32; Pr 31:8, 9 [b]Ge 42:22; Pr 17:13; Jer 18:20 **19:5** [a]Jdg 9:17; 1Sa 17:49, 50; 28:21; Ps 119:109 [b]1Sa 11:13; 1Chr 11:14 [c]Dt 19:10-13; 1Sa 20:32; Ps 94:21; Mt 27:4 **19:7** [a]1Sa 16:21; 18:2, 10, 13 **19:9** [a]1Sa 16:14; 18:10, 11 [b]1Sa 18:10 [c]1Sa 16:16 **19:10** [a]1Sa 18:11; 20:33; Pr 1:16 [1]Lit *strike David and the wall* [2]Lit *struck* **19:11** [a]Jdg 16:2; Ps 59: title **19:12** [a]Jos 2:15; Ac 9:25; 2Co 11:33 **19:13** [a]Ge 31:19; Jdg 18:14, 17 [1]Heb *teraphim* **19:14** [a]Jos 2:5 **19:15** [1]Lit *the* **19:16** [1]Heb *teraphim* **19:17** [a]2Sa 2:22 **19:18** [a]1Sa 7:17 [b]1Sa 19:22, 23 **19:20** [a]1Sa 19:11, 14; Jn 7:32 [b]1Sa 10:5, 6, 10 [c]Nu 11:25; Joel 2:28

prophesied. So Saul sent messengers
again the third time, and they also
prophesied. **22** Then he himself went
to Ramah and came as far as the large
well that is in Secu; and he asked and
said, "Where are Samuel and David?"
And *someone* said, "Behold, they are
at Naioth in Ramah." **23** So he went
there, to Naioth in Ramah; and [a]the
Spirit of God came upon him also,
so that he went along prophesying
continually until he came to Naioth
in Ramah. **24** He also stripped off
his clothes, and he too prophesied
before Samuel and [1]lay down [a,2]naked
all that day and all that night. There-
fore they say, "[b]Is Saul also among
the prophets?"

### *David and Jonathan's Covenant*

**20** Then David fled from Naioth
in Ramah and came and [a]said
before Jonathan, "What have I done?
What is my iniquity? And what is my
sin before your father, that he is seek-
ing my life?" **2** And he said to him,
"Far from it, you shall not die. Behold,
my father does nothing either great
or small without revealing it in my
ear. So why should my father hide
this thing from me? It is not so!"
**3** Yet David [a]swore again, [1]saying,
"Your father knows well that I have
found favor in your sight, and he
has said, 'Do not let Jonathan know
this, lest he be grieved.' But truly [b]as
Yahweh lives and as your soul lives,
there is [2]hardly a step between me
and death." **4** Then Jonathan said to
David, "Whatever your soul says, I
will do for you." **5** So David said to
Jonathan, "Behold, tomorrow is [a]the
new moon, and I ought [b]to sit down
to eat with the king. But let me go,
[c]that I may hide myself in the field
until the third evening. **6** If your
father misses me at all, then say,
'David earnestly asked *leave* of me
to run to [a]Bethlehem his city because
it is [b]the yearly sacrifice there for the
whole family.' **7** If he [1]says, 'It is good,'
your servant will have peace; but if
he is very angry, [a]know that he has
decided on evil. **8** Therefore show
lovingkindness to your servant, for
[a]you have brought your servant into
a covenant of Yahweh with you. But
[b]if there is iniquity in me, put me to
death yourself; for why then should
you bring me to your father?" **9** And
Jonathan said, "Far be it from you! For
if I should indeed come to know that
evil has been decided by my father to
come upon you, then would I not tell
you about it?" **10** Then David said to
Jonathan, "Who will tell me [1]if your
father answers you harshly?" **11** And
Jonathan said to David, "Come, and
let us go out into the field." So both
of them went out to the field.
**12** Then Jonathan said to David,
"Yahweh, the God of Israel, *be
witness*! When I have examined my
father about this time tomorrow,
*or* the third day, behold, if there is
good *feeling* toward David, shall I
not then send to you and reveal it
in your ear? **13** If it please my father
*to do* you harm, [a]may Yahweh do so
to Jonathan and more also, if I do
not reveal it in your ear and send
*you away*, that you may go in peace.

---

**19:23** [a]1Sa 10:10 **19:24** [a]2Sa 6:20; Is 20:2; Mic 1:8 [b]1Sa 10:10-12 [1]Lit *fell* [2]Without outward garments ◆ **20:1** [a]1Sa 24:9 **20:3** [a]Dt 6:13 [b]1Sa 25:26; 2Ki 2:6 [1]Lit *and said* [2]Lit *about* **20:5** [a]Nu 10:10; 28:11-15; Am 8:5 [b]1Sa 20:24, 27 [c]1Sa 19:2 **20:6** [a]1Sa 17:58 [b]Dt 12:5; 1Sa 9:12 **20:7** [a]1Sa 25:17 [1]Lit *says thus* **20:8** [a]1Sa 18:3; 23:18 [b]2Sa 14:32 **20:10** [1]Lit *or what* **20:13** [a]Ru 1:17; 1Sa 3:17

And [b]may Yahweh be with you as He
has been with my father. **14** And if I
am still alive, will you not show me
the lovingkindness of Yahweh, that I
may not die? **15** [a]You shall not cut off
your lovingkindness from my house
forever, not even when Yahweh cuts
off every one of the enemies of David
from the face of the earth." **16** So Jona-
than cut a *covenant* with the house of
David, *saying*, "[a]May Yahweh require
*it* at the hands of David's enemies."
**17** And Jonathan made David swear
again because of his love for him,
because [a]he loved him as he loved
his own soul.

**18** Then Jonathan said to him,
"[a]Tomorrow is the new moon, and
you will be missed because your seat
will be missing. **19** When you have
stayed for three days, you shall go
down quickly and come to the place
[1]where you hid yourself on that event-
ful day, and you shall remain by the
stone Ezel. **20** And I will shoot three
arrows to the side, as though I sent
them towards a target. **21** And behold,
I will send the young man, *saying*,
'Go, find the arrows.' If I specifically
say to the young man, 'Behold, the
arrows are on this side of you, get
them,' then come, for there is peace
for you and [1]no harm, as Yahweh lives.
**22** But if I [1]say to the youth, '[a]Behold,
the arrows are beyond you,' go, for
Yahweh has sent you away. **23** [a]As for
the [1]agreement of which you and I
have spoken, behold, [b]Yahweh is
between you and me forever."

**24** So David hid in the field; and
when the new moon came, the king
sat down to eat food. **25** And the king
sat on his seat as usual, the seat by
the wall; then Jonathan rose up,
and Abner sat down by Saul's side,
but [a]David's place was missing.
**26** Nevertheless Saul did not speak
anything that day, for he said, "It is
an accident; [a]he is not clean; surely
*he is* not clean." **27** Now it happened
the next day, the second *day* of the
new moon, that David's place was
missing; so Saul said to Jonathan his
son, "Why has the son of Jesse not
come to the meal, either yesterday or
today?" **28** Jonathan then answered
Saul, "[a]David earnestly asked leave
of me *to go* to Bethlehem, **29** and he
said, 'Please send me *on my way*,
since our family has a sacrifice in the
city, and my brother has commanded
me to attend. So now, if I have found
favor in your sight, please let me get
away that I may see my brothers.' For
this reason he has not come to the
king's table."

### *Saul Is Angry with Jonathan*

**30** Then Saul's anger burned against
Jonathan, and he said to him, "You
son of a perverse, rebellious woman!
Do I not know that you are choosing
the son of Jesse to your own shame
and to the shame of your mother's
nakedness? **31** For [1]as long as the son
of Jesse lives on the earth, neither
you nor your kingdom will be estab-
lished. So now, send and bring him to
me, for [a]he [2]must surely die." **32** But
Jonathan answered Saul his father
and said to him, "[a]Why should he
be put to death? What has he done?"

---

**20:13** [b]Jos 1:5; 1Sa 17:37; 18:12; 1Chr 22:11, 16 **20:15** [a]2Sa 9:1, 3 **20:16** [a]Dt 23:21; 1Sa 25:22 **20:17** [a]1Sa 18:1 **20:18** [a]1Sa 20:5, 25 **20:19** [1]Or *on the* next *working day, to the place where you will hide yourself* **20:21** [1]Lit *there is nothing* **20:22** [a]1Sa 20:37 [1]Lit *say thus* **20:23** [a]1Sa 20:14, 15 [b]Ge 31:49, 53; 1Sa 20:42 [1]Lit *word* **20:25** [a]1Sa 20:18 **20:26** [a]Lv 7:20, 21; 15:5; 1Sa 16:5 **20:28** [a]1Sa 20:6 **20:31** [a]2Sa 12:5 [1]Lit *all the days which* [2]Lit *is a son of death* **20:32** [a]Ge 31:36; 1Sa 19:5; Pr 31:9; Mt 27:23

**33** Then [a]Saul hurled his spear at him
to strike him down; [b]so Jonathan
knew that his father had decided to
put David to death. **34** Then Jonathan
arose from the table in burning anger
and did not eat food on the second
day of the new moon, for he was
grieved over David because his father
had dishonored him.

**35** Now it happened in the
morning that Jonathan went out
into the field for the appointment
with David, and a very young man
*was* with him. **36** And he said to his
young man, "[a]Run, find now the
arrows which I am about to shoot."
As the young man was running, he
shot [1]an arrow past him. **37** When
the young man reached the place
of the arrow which Jonathan had
shot, Jonathan called after the lad
and said, "[a]Is not the arrow beyond
you?" **38** And Jonathan called after
the young man, "Hurry, be quick, do
not stay!" And Jonathan's young man
gathered up the arrow and came to
his master. **39** But the young man did
not know of anything; only Jonathan
and David knew about the matter.
**40** Then Jonathan gave his weapons
to his young man and said to him,
"Go, bring *them* to the city." **41** When
the young man was gone, David rose
from the south side and fell on his
[1]face to the ground and [a]bowed three
times. And they kissed each other
and wept together, but [b]David *wept*
more. **42** And Jonathan said to David,
"[a]Go in peace, inasmuch as we have
sworn to each other in the name of
Yahweh, saying, '[b]Yahweh will be
between me and you, and between
my seed and your seed forever.'"
[1]Then he rose and departed, while
Jonathan went into the city.

### *David Takes Consecrated Bread*

**21** Then David came to [a]Nob to
Ahimelech the priest; and
Ahimelech [b]came trembling to meet
David and said to him, "Why are you
alone, and no one is with you?" **2** And
David said to Ahimelech the priest,
"The king has commanded me with
a matter and has said to me, '[a]Let no
one know anything about the matter
on which I am sending you and with
which I have commanded you; and
I have directed the young men to a
certain place.' **3** So now, what [1]do you
have on hand? Give five loaves of
bread into my hand, or whatever can
be found." **4** And the priest answered
David and said, "There is no ordinary
bread [1]on hand, but there is [a]conse-
crated bread; if only the young men
have [b]kept themselves from women."
**5** And David answered the priest and
said to him, "[a]Surely women have
been kept from us as previously
when I set out and the [b]vessels of the
young men were holy, though it was
an ordinary journey; how much more
then today will [1]their vessels be holy?"
**6** So [a]the priest gave him consecrated
*bread*; for there was no bread there
but the [b]bread of the Presence which
was removed from before Yahweh,
in order to put hot bread *in its place*
when it was taken away.

**7** Now one of the servants of Saul
was there that day, detained before

**20:33** [a]1Sa 18:11; 19:10 [b]1Sa 20:7 **20:36** [a]1Sa 20:20, 21 [1]Lit *the* **20:37** [a]1Sa 20:22 **20:41** [a]Ge 42:6 [b]1Sa 18:3 [1]Lit *nose* **20:42** [a]1Sa 20:22 [b]1Sa 20:15, 16, 23 [1]Ch 21:1 in Heb ♦ **21:1** [a]1Sa 22:19; Ne 11:32; Is 10:32 [b]1Sa 16:4 **21:2** [a]Ps 141:3 **21:3** [1]Lit *is under your hand?* **21:4** [a]Ex 25:30; Lv 24:5-9; Mt 12:4 [b]Ex 19:15 [1]Lit *under my hand* **21:5** [a]Ex 19:14, 15 [b]1Th 4:4 [1]Lit *it* be holy *in the vessel* **21:6** [a]Mt 12:3, 4; Lk 6:3, 4 [b]Lv 24:5-9

Yahweh; and his name was [a]Doeg
the Edomite, the [b]chief of Saul's
shepherds.
**8** And David said to Ahimelech,
"Now is there not a spear or a sword
[1]on hand? For I brought neither
my sword nor my weapons in my
hand because the king's matter
was urgent." **9** Then the priest said,
"[a]The sword of Goliath the Philis-
tine, whom you struck down [b]in the
valley of Elah, behold, it is wrapped
in a cloth behind the ephod; if you
would take it for yourself, take *it*. For
there is no other except it here." And
David said, "There is none like it; give
it to me."

### *David Flees to Gath*

**10** Then David arose and fled that day
from Saul and went to [a]Achish king
of Gath. **11** But the [a]servants of Achish
said to him, "Is this not David the
king of the land? [b]Did they not sing
of this one as they danced, saying,
'Saul has struck his thousands,
And David his ten
thousands'?"
**12** And David [a]took these words [1]to
heart and greatly feared Achish king
of Gath. **13** So he [a]disguised his sanity
in their sight and acted insanely in
their hands and scribbled on the
doors of the gate and let his saliva run
down into his beard. **14** Then Achish
said to his servants, "Behold, you see
the man behaving as a madman. Why
do you bring him to me? **15** Do I lack
madmen, that you have brought this
one to act the madman before me?
Shall this one come into my house?"

### *David at the Cave of Adullam*

**22** So David departed from there
and [a]escaped to [b]the cave of
Adullam; and his brothers and all his
father's household heard *of it* and
went down there to him. **2** Then every-
one who was in distress, and everyone
who [1]was in debt, and everyone who
was bitter of soul, gathered to him;
and he became a commander over
them. Now there were [a]about four
hundred men with him.
**3** And David went from there to
Mizpah of Moab; and he said to the
king of Moab, "Please let my father
and my mother come *and stay* with
you until I know what God will do
for me." **4** Then he left them with the
king of Moab; and they stayed with
him all the time that David was in the
fortress. **5** [a]And the prophet Gad said
to David, "Do not stay in the fortress;
go, and enter into the land of Judah."
So David went and entered into the
forest of Hereth.

### *Saul Puts the Priests at Nob to Death*

**6** Then Saul heard that David
and the men who were with him
had been discovered. Now [a]Saul
was sitting in Gibeah, under the
tamarisk tree on the height with
his spear in his hand, and all his
servants were standing around him.
**7** And Saul said to his servants who
were standing around him, "Hear
now, O Benjamites! Will the son of
Jesse also give to all of you fields
and vineyards? [a]Will he make you
all commanders of thousands and
commanders of hundreds? **8** For all

**21:7** [a]1Sa 14:47; 22:9; Ps 52: title [b]1Chr 27:29, 31 **21:8** [1]Lit *under your hand* **21:9** [a]1Sa 17:51, 54 [b]1Sa 17:2 **21:10** [a]Ps 34: title **21:11** [a]Ps 56: title [b]1Sa 18:7; 29:5 **21:12** [a]Lk 2:19 [1]Lit *in his* **21:13** [a]Ps 34: title ◆ **22:1** [a]Ps 57: title [b]Jos 12:15; 15:35; 2Sa 23:13; Ps 142: title **22:2** [a]1Sa 23:13; 25:13 [1]Lit *had a creditor* **22:5** [a]2Sa 24:11; 1Chr 21:9; 29:29; 2Chr 29:25 **22:6** [a]Jdg 4:5; 1Sa 14:2 **22:7** [a]1Sa 8:12; 1Chr 12:16-18

of you have conspired against me
so that there is no one who reveals
in my ear [a]when my son cuts *a
covenant* with the son of Jesse, and
there is none of you [b]who is sorry
for me or reveals in my ear that my
son has caused my servant to rise
up against me to lie in ambush, as
*it is* this day." **9** Then [a]Doeg the
Edomite, who was [1]standing by
the servants of Saul, said, "[b]I saw
the son of Jesse coming to Nob,
to [c]Ahimelech the son of Ahitub.
**10** [a]And he asked of Yahweh for him,
[b]gave him provisions, and [c]gave him
the sword of Goliath the Philistine."

**11** Then the king sent someone to
summon Ahimelech the priest, the
son of Ahitub, and all his father's
household, the priests who were
in Nob; and all of them came to the
king. **12** And Saul said, "Listen now,
son of Ahitub." And he [1]answered,
"Here I am, my lord." **13** Saul then
said to him, "Why have you and the
son of Jesse conspired against me, in
that you have given him bread and
a sword and have asked of God on
his behalf, so that he would rise up
against me [a]by lying in ambush as *it
is* this day?"

**14** [a]Then Ahimelech answered
the king and said, "And who among
all your servants is as faithful as
David, even the king's son-in-law,
who [1]is captain over your guard,
and is honored in your house?
**15** Did I *just* begin [a]to ask of God
on his behalf today? Far be it from
*me!* [b]Do not let the king impute
anything to his servant *or* to any
of the household of my father, for
your servant knows nothing small
or great of this whole affair." **16** But
the king said, "You shall surely die,
Ahimelech, you and all your father's
household!" **17** And [a]the king said
to the [1]guards who were standing
by him, "Turn around and put the
priests of Yahweh to death because
their hand also is with David and
because they knew that he was
fleeing and did not reveal it in my
ears." But the [b]servants of the king
were not willing to send forth their
hands to fall upon the priests of
Yahweh. **18** Then the king said to
Doeg, "You turn around and [1]attack
the priests." And Doeg the Edomite
turned around and [2]attacked the
priests, and [a]he put to death that
day eighty-five men [b]who wore
the linen ephod. **19** So [a]he struck
Nob the city of the priests with the
edge of the sword, both men and
women, infants and nursing babies;
also oxen, donkeys, and sheep *he
struck* with the edge of the sword.

**20** But [a]one son of Ahimelech
the son of Ahitub, named Abiathar,
[b]escaped and fled after David. **21** And
Abiathar told David that Saul had
killed the priests of Yahweh. **22** Then
David said to Abiathar, "I knew on
that day, when [a]Doeg the Edomite
was there, that he would surely
tell Saul. It is I who have turned
against every person in your father's
household. **23** Stay with me; do not
be afraid, for [a]he who seeks my life
seeks your life, for you are [1]safe
with me."

---

**22:8** [a]1Sa 18:3; 20:16 [b]1Sa 23:21 **22:9** [a]Ps 52: title [b]1Sa 21:1 [c]1Sa 14:3; 21:1 [1]Or *set over* **22:10** [a]Nu 27:21; 1Sa 10:22 [b]1Sa 21:6 [c]1Sa 21:9 **22:12** [1]Lit *said* **22:13** [a]1Sa 22:8 **22:14** [a]1Sa 19:4, 5; 20:32 [1]As in Gr; Heb *turns aside to* **22:15** [a]2Sa 5:19, 23 [b]2Sa 19:18, 19 **22:17** [a]2Ki 10:25 [b]Ex 1:17 [1]Lit *runners* **22:18** [a]1Sa 2:31 [b]1Sa 2:18 [1]Lit *smite* [2]Lit *smote* **22:19** [a]1Sa 15:3 **22:20** [a]1Sa 23:6, 9; 30:7; 1Ki 2:26, 27 [b]1Sa 23:6 **22:22** [a]1Sa 21:7 **22:23** [a]1Ki 2:26 [1]Lit *a charge*

### David Saves Keilah

23 Then they told David, saying, "Behold, the Philistines are fighting against [a]Keilah and are pillaging the threshing floors." 2 So David [a]asked of Yahweh, saying, "Shall I go and strike these Philistines?" And Yahweh said to David, "Go and strike the Philistines and save Keilah." 3 But David's men said to him, "Behold, we are afraid here in Judah. How much more then if we go to Keilah against the battle lines of the Philistines?" 4 Then David asked of Yahweh once more. And Yahweh answered him and said, "Arise, go down to Keilah, for [a]I will give the Philistines into your hand." 5 So David and his men went to Keilah and fought with the Philistines; and he led away their livestock and struck them with a great slaughter. Thus David saved the inhabitants of Keilah.

6 Now it happened when Abiathar the son of Ahimelech [a]fled to David at Keilah, *that* he came down *with* an ephod in his hand. 7 Then it was told to Saul that David had come to Keilah, so Saul said, "God has [1]delivered him into my hand, for he shut himself in by entering a city with double gates and bars." 8 Then Saul summoned all the people for battle, to go down to Keilah to besiege David and his men. 9 But David *knew that* Saul *was* plotting evil against him; so he said to [a]Abiathar the priest, "[b]Bring the ephod here." 10 Then David said, "O Yahweh, the God of Israel, Your slave has heard for certain that Saul is seeking to come to Keilah to make the city a ruin on my account. 11 Will the men of Keilah surrender me into his hand? Will Saul come down just as Your slave has heard? O Yahweh, the God of Israel, I pray, tell Your slave." And Yahweh said, "He will come down." 12 Then David said, "Will the men of Keilah surrender me and my men into the hand of Saul?" And Yahweh said, "[a]They will surrender you." 13 Then David and his men, [a]about six hundred, arose and departed from Keilah, and they went [b]wherever they could go. Now it was told to Saul that David had escaped from Keilah, so he ceased going out *in pursuit*. 14 And David stayed in the wilderness in the strongholds and remained in the hill country in the wilderness of [a]Ziph. And Saul sought him every day, but [b]God did not give him into his hand.

### Saul Pursues David

15 Then David saw that Saul had come out to seek his life. Now David was in the wilderness of Ziph at Horesh. 16 So Jonathan, Saul's son, arose and went to David at Horesh and [a]strengthened his hand in God. 17 And he said to him, "[a]Do not be afraid, because the hand of Saul my father will not find you, and you will be king over Israel, and I will be second to you; and [b]Saul my father knows that also." 18 So [a]the two of them cut a covenant before Yahweh; and David stayed at Horesh while Jonathan went to his house.

19 Then [a]Ziphites came up to Saul at Gibeah, saying, "Is David not

◆ **23:1** [a]Jos 15:44; Ne 3:17, 18 **23:2** [a]1Sa 23:4, 6, 9-12; 2Sa 5:19, 23 **23:4** [a]Jos 8:7; Jdg 7:7
**23:6** [a]1Sa 22:20 **23:7** [1]Lit *alienated* **23:9** [a]1Sa 22:20 [b]1Sa 23:6; 30:7 **23:12** [a]Jdg 15:10-13; 1Sa 23:20
**23:13** [a]1Sa 22:2; 25:13 [b]2Sa 15:20 **23:14** [a]Jos 15:55; 2Chr 11:8 [b]Ps 32:7 **23:16** [a]1Sa 30:6; Ne 2:18
**23:17** [a]Ps 27:1, 3; 118:6; Is 54:17; Heb 13:6 [b]1Sa 20:31; 24:20 **23:18** [a]1Sa 18:3; 20:12-17, 42; 2Sa 9:1; 21:7
**23:19** [a]1Sa 26:1; Ps 54: title

hiding with us in the strongholds
at Horesh, on [b]the hill of Hachilah,
which is on the [1]south of [2]Jeshimon?
**20** So now, O king, according to all the
desire of your soul to come down,
come down *here*; and [a]our part *shall*
*be* to surrender him into the king's
hand." **21** And Saul said, "May you
be blessed of Yahweh, [a]for you have
had compassion on me. **22** Go now,
make more sure, and know and see
his place—where his *very* foot is—
*and* who has seen him there; for I
am told that he is very crafty. **23** So
see and know about all the hiding
places where he hides himself and
return to me with certainty, and I will
go with you; and if he is in the land,
I will search him out among all the
thousands of Judah."

**24** Then they arose and went to
Ziph before Saul. Now David and
his men were in the wilderness of
[a]Maon, in the Arabah to the [1]south
of [2]Jeshimon. **25** So Saul and his men
went to seek *him*, and they told
David, and he came down to the
rock and stayed in the wilderness of
Maon. And Saul heard *it* and pursued
David in the wilderness of Maon.
**26** And Saul went on one side of the
mountain, and David and his men on
the other side of the mountain; and
David was hurrying to get away from
Saul, but Saul and his men [a]were
surrounding David and his men to
seize them. **27** But a messenger came
to Saul, saying, "Hurry and come, for
the Philistines have made a raid on
the land." **28** So Saul returned from
pursuing David and went to meet the
Philistines; therefore they called that
place [1]the Rock of Escape. **29** [1]Then
David went up from there and stayed
in the strongholds of [a]Engedi.

### *David Does Not Kill Saul*

**24** Now [a]when Saul returned
from pursuing the Philistines,
[b]he was told, saying, "Behold, David
is in the wilderness of Engedi." **2** Then
[a]Saul took three thousand chosen
men from all Israel and went to seek
David and his men in front of the
Rocks of the Wild Goats. **3** And he
came to the sheepfolds on the way,
where there *was* a cave; and Saul
[a]went in to [1]relieve himself. Now
[b]David and his men were sitting in the
inner recesses of the cave. **4** Then the
men of David said to him, "Behold,
[a]*this is* the day of which Yahweh said
to you, 'Behold, [b]I am about to give
your enemy into your hand, and you
shall do to him as it seems good in
your eyes.'" Then David arose and cut
off the edge of Saul's robe secretly.
**5** And it happened afterward that
[a]David's heart struck him because
he had cut off the edge of Saul's *robe*.
**6** So he said to his men, "[a]Far be it
from me because of Yahweh that I
should do this thing to my lord, the
anointed of Yahweh, to send forth
my hand against him, since he is the
anointed of Yahweh." **7** And David
tore his men to pieces with *these*
words and did not allow them to rise
up against Saul. And Saul arose, [1]left
the cave, and went on *his* way.

**8** Now afterward David arose and
went out of the cave and called after

**23:19** [b]1Sa 26:3 [1]Lit *right side* [2]Or *the desert* **23:20** [a]1Sa 23:12 **23:21** [a]1Sa 22:8 **23:24** [a]Jos 15:55; 1Sa 25:2 [1]Lit *right side* [2]Or *the desert* **23:26** [a]Ps 17:9 **23:28** [1]Heb *Sela-hammahlekoth* **23:29** [a]Jos 15:62; 2Chr 20:2 [1]Ch 24:1 in Heb ◆ **24:1** [a]1Sa 23:28, 29 [b]1Sa 23:19 **24:2** [a]1Sa 26:2 **24:3** [a]Jdg 3:24 [b]Ps 57: title; Ps 142: title [1]Lit *cover his feet* **24:4** [a]1Sa 23:17; 25:28-30 [b]1Sa 26:8, 11 **24:5** [a]2Sa 24:10 **24:6** [a]1Sa 26:11 **24:7** [1]Lit *from*

Saul, saying, "My lord the king!" And when Saul looked behind him, [a]David bowed with his [1]face to the ground and prostrated himself. **9** And David said to Saul, "Why do you listen to the words of men, saying, 'Behold, David seeks [1]to do you evil'? **10** [a]Behold, this day your eyes have seen that Yahweh had given you today into my hand in the cave, and [b]some said to kill you, but *my eye* had pity on you; and I said, 'I will not send forth my hand against my lord, for he is the anointed of Yahweh.' **11** Now, [a]my father, see! Indeed, see the edge of your robe in my hand! For in that I cut off the edge of your robe and did not kill you, know and see that there is no evil or transgression in my hand, and I have not sinned against you, though you [b]are lying in wait for my life to take it. **12** [a]May Yahweh judge between [1]you and me, and may Yahweh avenge me on you; but my hand shall not be against you. **13** As the proverb of the ancients says, '[a]Out of the wicked comes forth wickedness'; but my hand shall not be against you. **14** After whom has the king of Israel come out? Whom are you pursuing? [a]After a dead dog, after [b]a single flea? **15** [a]Therefore Yahweh be judge and execute justice between [1]you and me; and may He see and [b]plead my cause and execute justice for me *to escape* from your hand."

**16** Now it happened that when David had finished speaking these words to Saul, Saul said, "[a]Is this your voice, my son David?" Then Saul lifted up his voice and wept. **17** [a]And he said to David, "You are more righteous than I; for [b]you have dealt well with me, while I have dealt evil with you. **18** And you have declared today that you have done good to me, that [a]Yahweh surrendered me into your hand, and *yet* you did not kill me. **19** For if a man [a]finds his enemy, will he let him go away [1]safely? May Yahweh therefore reward you with good in return for what you have done to me this day. **20** So now, behold, [a]I know that you will surely be king, and that [b]the kingdom of Israel will be established in your hand. **21** So now [a]swear to me by Yahweh that you will not cut off my seed after me and that you will not destroy my name from my father's household." **22** So David swore to Saul. And Saul went to his home, but David and his men went up to [a]the fortress.

### *The Death of Samuel*

**25** [a]Then Samuel died; and all Israel gathered together and [b]lamented for him and [c]buried him at his house in Ramah. And David arose and went down to the [d]wilderness of Paran.

### *David and Abigail*

**2** Now *there was* a man in [a]Maon whose work was in [b]Carmel; and the man was very great, and he had three thousand sheep and one thousand

**24:8** [a]1Sa 25:23, 24; 1Ki 1:31 [1]Lit *nose* **24:9** [1]Or *your harm* **24:10** [a]Ps 7:3, 4 [b]1Sa 24:4 **24:11** [a]2Ki 5:13 [b]1Sa 23:14, 23; 26:20 **24:12** [a]Ge 16:5; 31:53; Jdg 11:27; 1Sa 26:10, 23 [1]Lit *me and you* **24:13** [a]Mt 7:16-20 **24:14** [a]2Sa 9:8 [b]1Sa 26:20 **24:15** [a]1Sa 24:12 [b]Ps 35:1; 43:1; 119:154; Mic 7:9 [1]Lit *me and you* **24:16** [a]1Sa 26:17 **24:17** [a]1Sa 26:21 [b]Mt 5:44 **24:18** [a]1Sa 26:23 **24:19** [a]1Sa 23:17 [1]Lit *on a good road* **24:20** [a]1Sa 23:17 [b]1Sa 13:14 **24:21** [a]Ge 21:23; 1Sa 20:14-17; 2Sa 21:6-8 **24:22** [a]1Sa 23:29 ◆ **25:1** [a]1Sa 28:3 [b]Nu 20:29; Dt 34:8 [c]2Ki 21:18; 2Chr 33:20 [d]Ge 21:21; Nu 10:12; 13:3 **25:2** [a]1Sa 23:24 [b]Jos 15:55

goats. And it happened, while [c]he
was shearing his sheep in Carmel
**3** (now the man's name was Nabal,
and his [a]wife's name was Abigail.
And the woman was good in insight
and beautiful in appearance, but
the man was harsh and evil in *his*
dealings, and he was [b]a Calebite),
**4** that David heard in the wilderness
that Nabal was shearing his sheep.
**5** So David sent ten young men; and
David said to the young men, "Go up
to Carmel, come to Nabal, and greet
him in my name; **6** and thus you shall
say, '[1]Have a long life; [a]peace be to
you, and peace be to your house, and
peace be to all that you have. **7** So now
I have heard [a]that you have shearers;
now your shepherds have been with
us; and we have not dishonored them,
[b]nor have they missed anything all
the days they were in Carmel. **8** Ask
your young men, and they will tell
you. Therefore let *my* young men
find favor in your eyes, for we have
come on [a]a [1]festive day. Please give
whatever you find at hand to your
servants and to your son, to David.'"

**9** Then David's young men came
and spoke to Nabal according to all
these words in David's name. Then
they waited. **10** But Nabal answered
David's servants and said, "[a]Who is
David? And who is the son of Jesse?
There are many servants today
who are each breaking away from
his master. **11** Shall I then [a]take my
bread and my water and my meat that
I have slaughtered for my shearers,
and give it to men [1]whose origin I do
not know?" **12** So David's young men
went back on their way and returned;
and they came and told him according
to all these words. **13** Then David said
to his men, "Each *of you* gird on his
sword." So each man girded on his
sword. And David also girded on
his sword, and about [a]four hundred
men went up behind David, and two
hundred [b]stayed with the baggage.

**14** But one of the young men told
Abigail, Nabal's wife, saying, "Behold,
David sent messengers from the wil-
derness to [a,1]greet our master, and
he rushed at them *angrily*. **15** Yet the
men were very good to us, and we
were not [a]dishonored, nor did we
miss anything [1]as long as we went
about with them, while we were in
the field. **16** [a]They were a wall to us
both by night and by day, all the time
we were with them shepherding the
sheep. **17** So now, know and see what
you should do, for evil is decided
against our master and against all
his household; and he is such a [1]vile
man that no one can speak to him."

### *Abigail's Discernment*

**18** Then Abigail hurried and [a]took
two hundred *loaves* of bread and two
[1]jugs of wine and five sheep already
prepared and [2]five seahs of roasted
grain and one hundred clusters of
raisins and two hundred cakes of
figs, and loaded *them* on donkeys.
**19** Then she said to her young men,
"[a]Go on before me; behold, I am
coming after you." But she did not
tell her husband Nabal. **20** So it was

---

**25:2** [c]Ge 38:13; 2Sa 13:23 **25:3** [a]Pr 31:10 [b]Jos 15:13; 1Sa 30:14 **25:6** [a]1Chr 12:18; Ps 122:7; Lk 10:5 [1]Lit *To life* **25:7** [a]2Sa 13:23, 24 [b]1Sa 25:15, 21 **25:8** [a]Ne 8:10-12; Es 9:19, 22 [1]Lit *good* **25:10** [a]Jdg 9:28 **25:11** [a]Jdg 8:6, 15 [1]Lit *from where they are* **25:13** [a]1Sa 23:13 [b]1Sa 30:24 **25:14** [a]1Sa 13:10; 15:13 [1]Lit *bless* **25:15** [a]1Sa 25:7, 21 [1]Lit *all the days* **25:16** [a]Ex 14:22; Job 1:10 **25:17** [1]Lit *son of Belial* **25:18** [a]2Sa 16:1; 1Chr 12:40 [1]Heb is similar to Nabal [2]Approx. 35 qt. or 38.5 l, a seah was approx. 7 qt. or 7.7 l **25:19** [a]Ge 32:16, 20

happening, as she was riding on her
donkey and coming down by the
hidden part of the mountain, that be-
hold, David and his men were coming
down toward her; and she met them.
**21** Now David had said, "Surely for a
lie I have guarded all that this *man*
has in the wilderness, so that nothing
was missed of all that belonged to
him; and he has [a]returned me evil
for good. **22** [a]May God do so to the
enemies of David, and more also, [b]if
by morning I leave *as much as* one
[1]male of any who belong to him."

**23** Then Abigail saw David; so she
hurried and dismounted from her
donkey and fell on her face [1]before Da-
vid [a]and bowed herself to the ground.
**24** And she fell at his feet and said, "On
me [1]alone, my lord, be the blame. And
please let your maidservant speak in
your ears, and listen to the words of
your maidservant. **25** Please do not
let my lord [1]pay attention to this [2]vile
man, Nabal, for as his name is, so is
he. [3]Nabal is his name, and wicked
foolishness is with him; but I your
maidservant did not see the young
men of my lord whom you sent.

**26** "So now, my lord, as Yahweh lives
and as your soul lives, since Yahweh
has restrained you from [1]shedding
blood, and [a]from saving yourself by
your own hand, so now, [b]let your en-
emies and those who seek evil against
my lord, be as Nabal. **27** So now let
[a]this [1]gift which your servant-woman
has brought to my lord be given to the
young men who [2]went about with my
lord. **28** Please forgive [a]the transgres-
sion of your maidservant; for [b]Yahweh
will certainly make for my lord an
enduring house because my lord is
[c]fighting the battles of Yahweh, and
[d]evil will not be found in you all your
days. **29** And should anyone rise up to
pursue you and to seek your [1]life, then
the [1]life of my lord shall be bound in
the bundle of the living with Yahweh
your God; but the [1]lives of your ene-
mies [a]He will sling out [2]as from the
hollow of a sling. **30** And it will be that
when Yahweh does for my lord accord-
ing to all the good that He has spoken
concerning you, and [a]appoints you
ruler over Israel, **31** then this will not
[1]cause stumbling or a troubled heart
to my lord, both by having shed blood
without cause and by my lord having
saved himself. [a]When Yahweh deals
well with my lord, then remember
your maidservant."

**32** Then David said to Abigail,
"[a]Blessed be Yahweh, the God of Isra-
el, who sent you this day to meet me,
**33** and blessed be your discernment,
and blessed be you, [a]who have kept
me this day from [1]bloodshed and
from saving myself by my own hand.
**34** Nevertheless, as Yahweh, the God
of Israel, lives, [a]who has restrained
me from harming you, unless you
had hurried and come to meet me,
surely there would not have been
left to Nabal until the morning light
*as much as* one [1]male." **35** So David

---

**25:21** [a]Ps 109:5; Pr 17:13 **25:22** [a]1Sa 3:17; 20:13 [b]1Ki 14:10 [1]Lit *who urinates against the wall,* cf. 25:34; 1Ki 14:10; 16:11; 21:21; 2Ki 9:8 **25:23** [a]1Sa 20:41 [1]Lit *with her nose to* **25:24** [1]Lit *even me* **25:25** [1]Lit *set his heart to* [2]Lit *man of Belial* [3]Lit *Wicked fool* **25:26** [a]Heb 10:30 [b]2Sa 18:32 [1]Lit *coming in with blood* **25:27** [a]Ge 33:11; 1Sa 30:26 [1]Lit *blessing* [2]Lit *walk at the feet of* **25:28** [a]1Sa 25:24 [b]1Sa 22:14; 2Sa 7:11, 16 [c]1Sa 18:17 [d]1Sa 24:11; Ps 7:3 **25:29** [a]Jer 10:18 [1]Lit *soul* [2]Lit *in the midst* **25:30** [a]1Sa 13:14 **25:31** [a]Ge 40:14; 1Sa 25:30 [1]Lit *become staggering to you or a stumbling of the heart* **25:32** [a]Ex 18:10; 1Ki 1:48; Ps 41:13; 72:18; 106:48; Lk 1:68 **25:33** [a]1Sa 25:26 [1]Lit *coming in with blood* **25:34** [a]1Sa 25:26 [1]Lit *who urinates against the wall,* cf. 25:22; 1Ki 14:10; 16:11; 21:21; 2Ki 9:8

received from her hand what she had
brought him and said to her, "[a]Go up
to your house in peace. See, I have
listened to your voice and [b,1]granted
your request."

36 Then Abigail came to Nabal, and
behold, he was holding [a]a feast in his
house, like the feast of a king. And
Nabal's heart was merry within him,
[b]for he was very drunk; so [c]she did
not tell him anything small or great
until the morning light. 37 But in the
morning, when the wine had gone
out of Nabal, his wife told him these
things, and his heart died within him
so that he became *as* a stone. 38 Now
it happened that about ten days later,
[a]Yahweh smote Nabal, and he died.

### Abigail Becomes David's Wife

39 Then David heard that Nabal was
dead, so he said, "Blessed be Yahweh,
who has [a]pleaded the cause of my
reproach from the hand of Nabal and
[b]has kept back His servant from evil.
Yahweh has also returned the evil of
Nabal on his own head." Then David
sent [c,1]a proposal to Abigail, to take
her as his wife. 40 Then the servants
of David came to Abigail at Carmel
and spoke to her, saying, "David
has sent us to you to take you as his
wife." 41 And she arose [a]and bowed
with her [1]face to the ground and
said, "Behold, your maidservant is a
servant-woman [b]to wash the feet of
my lord's servants." 42 Then [a]Abigail
hurried and arose, and she rode on a
donkey, with her five young women
who [1]went about with her; and she
went after the messengers of David
and became his wife.

43 David had also taken Ahinoam
of [a]Jezreel, and [b]they both became
his wives.

44 Now Saul had given [a]Michal his
daughter, David's wife, to Palti the
son of Laish, who was from [b]Gallim.

### David Takes Saul's Spear

26 Then the Ziphites came to
Saul at Gibeah, saying, "[a]Is
not David hiding on the hill of Hachi-
lah, *which is* before [1]Jeshimon?" 2 So
Saul arose and went down to the
wilderness of Ziph, having with
him [a]three thousand chosen men
of Israel, to search for David in
the wilderness of Ziph. 3 And Saul
camped in the hill of Hachilah,
which is before [1]Jeshimon, [a]beside
the road. Now David was staying in
the wilderness, and [b]he saw that Saul
came after him into the wilderness.
4 So David sent out spies and knew
that Saul was certainly coming.
5 David then arose and came to the
place where Saul had camped. And
David saw the place where Saul lay,
as well as [a]Abner the son of Ner, the
commander of his army; and Saul
was lying in the circle of the camp,
and the people were camped around
him.

6 Then David answered and said
to Ahimelech [a]the Hittite and to
[b]Abishai the son of Zeruiah, Joab's
brother, saying, "Who [c]will go down
with me to Saul in the camp?" And
Abishai said, "I will go down with

---

**25:35** [a]1Sa 20:42; 2Ki 5:19 [b]Ge 19:21 [1]Lit *lifted up your face* **25:36** [a]2Sa 13:28 [b]Pr 20:1; Is 5:11; Hos 4:11 [c]1Sa 25:19 **25:38** [a]1Sa 26:10; 2Sa 6:7; Ps 104:29 **25:39** [a]1Sa 24:15; Pr 22:23 [b]1Sa 25:26, 34 [c]SS 8:8 [1]Lit *and spoke* **25:41** [a]1Sa 25:23 [b]Mk 1:7 [1]Lit *nose* **25:42** [a]Ge 24:61-67 [1]Lit *walked at her feet* **25:43** [a]Jos 15:56 [b]1Sa 27:3; 30:5 **25:44** [a]1Sa 18:27; 2Sa 3:14 [b]Is 10:30 ◆**26:1** [a]1Sa 23:19; Ps 54: title [1]Or *the desert* **26:2** [a]1Sa 13:2; 24:2 **26:3** [a]1Sa 24:3 [b]1Sa 23:15 [1]Or *the desert* **26:5** [a]1Sa 14:50, 51; 17:55 **26:6** [a]Ge 23:3; 26:34; Jos 3:10; 1Ki 10:29; 2Ki 7:6 [b]1Chr 2:16 [c]Jdg 7:10, 11

you." **7** So David and Abishai came
to the people by night, and behold,
Saul lay sleeping inside the circle of
the camp with his spear stuck in the
ground at his head; and Abner and
the people were lying around him.
**8** Then Abishai said to David, "Today
God has surrendered your enemy
into your hand; so now, please let
me strike him with the spear [1]to the
ground with one stroke, and I will
not [2]strike him the second time."
**9** But David said to Abishai, "Do
not destroy him, for [a]who can send
forth his hand against the anointed
of Yahweh and be without guilt?"
**10** David also said, "As Yahweh lives,
[a]surely Yahweh will smite him, or
[b]his day will come that he dies, or
[c]he will go down into battle and be
swept away. **11** [a]Yahweh forbid that
I should send forth my hand against
the anointed of Yahweh; but now
please take the spear that is at his
head and the jug of water, and let
us go." **12** So David took the spear
and the jug of water from *beside*
Saul's head, and they went away,
but no one saw or knew *it*, nor did
any awake, for they were all asleep,
because [a]a [1]sound sleep from Yah-
weh had fallen on them.

**13** Then David crossed over to the
other side and stood on top of the
mountain at a distance *with* a large
*area between them*. **14** And David
called to the people and to Abner
the son of Ner, saying, "Will you
not answer, Abner?" Then Abner
answered and said, "Who are you
who calls to the king?" **15** So David
said to Abner, "Are you not a man?
And who is like you in Israel? Why
then have you not guarded your lord
the king? For one of the people came
to destroy the king your lord. **16** This
thing that you have done is not good.
As Yahweh lives, *all* of you [a,1]must
surely die because you did not keep
watch over your lord, the anointed of
Yahweh. So now, see where the king's
spear is and the jug of water that was
at his head."

**17** Then Saul recognized David's
voice and said, "[a]Is this your voice,
my son David?" And David said,
"It is my voice, my lord the king."
**18** He also said, "[a]Why then is my
lord pursuing his servant? For what
have I done? Or what evil is in my
hand? **19** So now, please let my lord
the king listen to the words of his
servant. If [a]Yahweh has incited you
up against me, [b]let Him [1]accept an
offering; but [c]if it is [2]men, cursed
are they before Yahweh, for [d]they
have driven me out today so that I
would have no attachment with the
inheritance of Yahweh, saying, 'Go,
serve other gods.' **20** So now, do not
let my blood fall to the ground away
from the presence of Yahweh; for the
king of Israel has come out to search
for [a]a single flea, just as one pursues
a partridge in the mountains."

**21** Then Saul said, "[a]I have sinned.
Return, my son David, for I will not
harm you again because my life was
precious in your sight this day. Behold,
I have played the fool and have com-
mitted a serious error." **22** And David
replied, "Behold the spear of the king!

---

**26:8** [1]Lit *even into* [2]Lit *repeat with respect to him* **26:9** [a]1Sa 24:6, 7; 2Sa 1:14, 16 **26:10** [a]Dt 32:35; 1Sa 25:26, 38; Ro 12:19; Heb 10:30 [b]Ge 47:29; Dt 31:14; Ps 37:13 [c]1Sa 31:6 **26:11** [a]1Sa 24:6, 12; Ro 12:17, 19; 1Pe 3:9 **26:12** [a]Ge 2:21; 15:12; Is 29:10 [1]Or *deep sleep*, cf. Ge 2:21; 15:12 **26:16** [a]1Sa 20:31 [1]Lit *are surely sons of death* **26:17** [a]1Sa 24:16 **26:18** [a]1Sa 24:9, 11-14 **26:19** [a]2Sa 16:11 [b]Ge 8:21 [c]1Sa 24:9 [d]Jos 22:25-27 [1]Lit *smell* [2]Lit *sons of men* **26:20** [a]1Sa 24:14 **26:21** [a]Ex 9:27; 1Sa 15:24, 30; 24:17

Now let one of the young men come
over and take it. **23** [a]Now Yahweh will
repay each man *for* his righteousness
and his faithfulness; for Yahweh gave
you into *my* hand today, but [b]I was not
willing to send forth my hand against
the anointed of Yahweh. **24** Now behold,
as your life was [a]highly valued
in my sight this day, so may my life be
highly valued in the sight of Yahweh,
and may He [b]deliver me from all
distress." **25** Then Saul said to David,
"[a]Blessed are you, my son David; you
will both accomplish much and surely
prevail." So [b]David went on his way,
and Saul returned to his place.

### *David Escapes to the Philistines*

**27** Then David said in his heart,
"Now I will be swept away
one day by the hand of Saul. [a]There
is nothing better for me than that I
should utterly escape into the land
of the Philistines. Saul then will
despair of searching for me anymore
in all the territory of Israel, and I will
escape from his hand." **2** So David
arose and crossed over, he and [a]the
six hundred men who were with him,
to [b]Achish the son of Maoch, king of
Gath. **3** And David lived with Achish
at Gath, he and his men, [a]each with
his household, *even* David with [b]his
two wives, Ahinoam the Jezreelitess,
and Abigail the Carmelitess, Nabal's
wife. **4** And it was told to Saul that
David had fled to Gath, so he no
longer searched for him.

**5** Then David said to Achish, "If
now I have found favor in your sight,
let them give me a *place in one of the*
cities in the country, that I may live
there; for why should your servant
live in the royal city with you?" **6** So
Achish gave him Ziklag that day;
therefore [a]Ziklag has belonged to
the kings of Judah to this day. **7** And
the number of days that David lived
in the country of the Philistines was
[a]a year and four months.

**8** Now David and his men went
up and raided [a]the Geshurites and
the Girzites and [b]the Amalekites;
for they were the inhabitants of the
land from ancient times, as you come
to [c]Shur even as far as the land of
Egypt. **9** And David struck the land
and did not leave a man or a woman
alive, and he [a]took away the sheep,
the cattle, the donkeys, the camels,
and the clothing. Then he returned
and came to Achish. **10** And Achish
said, "Where have you [a]made a raid
today?" And David said, "Against
the [1]Negev of Judah and against the
[1]Negev of [b]the Jerahmeelites and
against the [1]Negev of [c]the Kenites."
**11** And David did not leave a man or a
woman alive to bring to Gath, saying,
"Lest they tell about us, saying, 'So
has David done and so *has been* his
custom all the time he has lived
in the country of the Philistines.'"
**12** So Achish believed David, saying,
"He has surely made himself odious
among his people Israel; therefore
he will become my servant forever."

### *Saul and the Woman of En-dor*

**28** Now it happened in those days
that [a]the Philistines gathered
their armed camps for war, to fight

**26:23** [a]1Sa 24:19; Ps 7:8; 18:20; 62:12 [b]1Sa 24:12 **26:24** [a]1Sa 18:30 [b]Ps 54:7 **26:25** [a]1Sa 24:19 [b]1Sa 24:22 ◆ **27:1** [a]1Sa 26:19 **27:2** [a]1Sa 25:13 [b]1Sa 21:10; 1Ki 2:39 **27:3** [a]1Sa 30:3; 2Sa 2:3 [b]1Sa 25:42, 43 **27:6** [a]Jos 15:31; 19:5; Ne 11:28 **27:7** [a]1Sa 29:3 **27:8** [a]Jos 13:2, 13 [b]Ex 17:8; 1Sa 15:7, 8 [c]Ex 15:22 **27:9** [a]1Sa 15:3; Job 1:3 **27:10** [a]1Sa 23:27 [b]1Sa 30:29; 1Chr 2:9, 25 [c]Jdg 1:16; 4:11 [1]South country ◆ **28:1** [a]1Sa 29:1

against Israel. And Achish said to
David, "Know assuredly that you
will go out with me in the camp, you
and your men." **2** And David said to
Achish, "Very well, you shall know
what your servant can do." So Achish
said to David, "Very well, I will make
you [1]my bodyguard [a]for life."

**3** Now [a]Samuel was dead, and
all Israel had lamented for him and
buried him [b]in Ramah, his own city.
And Saul had removed from the
land those who [c]were mediums and
spiritists. **4** So the Philistines gath-
ered together and came and camped
[a]in Shunem; and Saul gathered all
Israel together, and they camped in
[b]Gilboa. **5** Saul saw the camp of the
Philistines and was afraid and his
heart trembled greatly. **6** [a]So Saul
asked of Yahweh, but [b]Yahweh did
not answer him, either by [c]dreams
or by [d]Urim or by prophets. **7** So Saul
said to his servants, "Seek for me a
woman who is a medium, that I may
go to her and inquire of her." And
his servants said to him, "Behold,
[a]there is a woman who is a medium
at [b]En-dor."

**8** Then Saul [a]disguised himself
and put on other clothes, and he
went, he and two men with him, and
they came to the woman by night;
and he said, "[b]Divine for me, please,
and [c]bring up for me whom I shall
say to you." **9** But the woman said to
him, "Behold, you know [a]what Saul
has done, how he has cut off those
who are mediums and spiritists from
the land. Why are you then laying a
snare for my life to bring about my
death?" **10** Then Saul swore to her by
Yahweh, saying, "As Yahweh lives, no
punishment shall come upon you for
this thing." **11** Then the woman said,
"Whom shall I bring up for you?"
And he said, "Bring up Samuel for
me." **12** And the woman saw Samuel
and cried out with a loud voice; and
the woman spoke to Saul, saying,
"Why have you deceived me? For you
are Saul." **13** And the king said to her,
"Do not be afraid; but what do you
see?" And the woman said to Saul,
"I see a [1]divine being coming up out
of the earth." **14** And he said to her,
"What is his form?" And she said,
"An old man is coming up, and [a]he
is wrapped with a robe." And Saul
knew that it was Samuel, and [b]he
bowed with his [1]face to the ground
and prostrated himself.

**15** Then Samuel said to Saul, "Why
have you disturbed me by bringing
me up?" And Saul answered, "I am
greatly distressed, for the Philistines
are waging war against me, and [a]God
has turned away from me and [b]no lon-
ger answers me, either by the hand of
the prophets or by dreams; therefore
I have called you, that you may make
known to me what I should do." **16** And
Samuel said, "Why then do you ask me,
since Yahweh has turned away from
you and has become your adversary?
**17** So Yahweh has done [1]accordingly
[a]as He spoke by my hand, for Yahweh
has torn the kingdom out of your hand
and given it to your neighbor, to David.
**18** As [a]you did not listen to the voice
of Yahweh and did not execute His
burning anger on Amalek, so Yahweh

**28:2** [a]1Sa 1:22, 28 [1]Lit *keeper of my head* **28:3** [a]1Sa 25:1 [b]1Sa 7:17 [c]Lv 19:31; 20:27; Dt 18:10; 1Sa 15:23 **28:4** [a]Jos 19:18; 1Sa 28:4; 1Ki 1:3; 2Ki 4:8 [b]1Sa 31:1 **28:6** [a]1Chr 10:13, 14 [b]1Sa 14:37; Pr 1:24-31 [c]Nu 12:6; Joel 2:28 [d]Ex 28:30; Nu 27:21 **28:7** [a]Ac 16:16 [b]Jos 17:11; Ps 83:10 **28:8** [a]2Chr 18:29; 35:22 [b]1Chr 10:13; Is 8:19 [c]Dt 18:10, 11 **28:9** [a]1Sa 28:3 **28:13** [1]Or *god* **28:14** [a]1Sa 15:27 [b]1Sa 24:8 [1]Lit *nose* **28:15** [a]1Sa 16:14; 18:12 [b]1Sa 28:6 **28:17** [a]1Sa 15:28 [1]Lit *for himself* **28:18** [a]1Sa 15:20, 26; 1Ki 20:42

has done this thing to you this day. **19** Moreover Yahweh will also give over Israel along with you into the hands of the Philistines, therefore tomorrow [a]you and your sons will be with me. Indeed Yahweh will give over the camp of Israel into the hands of the Philistines!"

**20** Then Saul quickly fell full length upon the ground and was very afraid because of the words of Samuel; also there was no strength in him, for he had eaten no ˈfood all day and all night. **21** And the woman came to Saul and saw that he was terrified and said to him, "Behold, your servant-woman has listened to your voice, and [a]I have ˈtaken my life in my hand and have listened to your words which you spoke to me. **22** So now also, please listen to the voice of your servant-woman, and let me set a piece of bread before you that *you may* eat and have strength when you go on *your* way." **23** But he refused and said, "[a]I will not eat." [b]However, his servants together with the woman urged him, and he listened to ˈthem. So he arose from the ground and sat on [c]the bed. **24** And the woman had a [a]fattened calf in the house, and she quickly sacrificed it; and she [b]took flour, kneaded it, and baked unleavened bread from it. **25** And she brought *it* before Saul and his servants, and they ate. Then they arose and went away that night.

### *Achish Makes David Leave the Battle*

**29** Then [a]the Philistines gathered together all their camps to [b]Aphek, while the Israelites were camping by the spring which is in [c]Jezreel. **2** And the lords of the Philistines were proceeding on by hundreds and by thousands, and [a]David and his men were proceeding on in the rear with Achish. **3** Then the commanders of the Philistines said, "What *are* these Hebrews *doing here*?" And Achish said to the commanders of the Philistines, "Is this not David, the servant of Saul the king of Israel, [a]who has been with me these days, or *rather* these years, and [b]I have found no fault in him from the day he ˈdeserted *to me* to this day?" **4** But the commanders of the Philistines were angry with him, and the commanders of the Philistines said to him, "Make the man return, that he may return [a]to his place where you have assigned him, and do not let him go down to battle with us, [b]or in the battle he may become an adversary to us. For with what could this *man* make himself acceptable to his lord? *Would it* not *be* with the heads of ˈthese men? **5** Is this not David, [a]of whom they sing in the dances, saying,

> 'Saul has struck his thousands,
> And David his
> ten thousands'?"

**6** Then Achish called David and said to him, "*As* Yahweh lives, you *have been* upright, and [a]your going out and your coming in with me in the camp are pleasing in my sight; [b]for I have not found evil in you from the day of your coming to me to this day. Nevertheless, you are not pleasing in the sight of the lords. **7** So now,

**28:19** [a]1Sa 31:2; Job 3:17-19 **28:20** ˈLit *bread* **28:21** [a]Jdg 12:3; 1Sa 19:5; Job 13:14 ˈLit *put* **28:23** [a]1Ki 21:4 [b]2Ki 5:13 [c]Es 1:6; Eze 23:41 ˈLit *their voices* **28:24** [a]Ge 18:7; Lk 15:23, 27, 30 [b]Ge 18:6 ◆ **29:1** [a]1Sa 28:1 [b]Jos 12:18; 19:30; 1Sa 4:1; 1Ki 20:30 [c]1Ki 21:1; 2Ki 9:30 **29:2** [a]1Sa 28:1, 2 **29:3** [a]1Sa 27:7 [b]1Sa 27:1-6; 1Chr 12:19, 20; Da 6:5 ˈLit *fell* **29:4** [a]1Sa 27:6 [b]1Sa 14:21 ˈLit *those* **29:5** [a]1Sa 18:7; 21:11 **29:6** [a]2Sa 3:25; 2Ki 19:27; Is 37:28 [b]1Sa 27:8-12; 29:3

return and go in peace, that you may not do evil in the sight of the lords of the Philistines." **8** And David said to Achish, "[a]But what have I done? And what have you found in your servant from the day when I came before you to this day, that I may not go and fight against the enemies of my lord the king?" **9** But Achish answered and said to David, "I know that you are pleasing in my sight, [a]like an angel of God; nevertheless [b]the commanders of the Philistines have said, 'He must not go up with us to the battle.' **10** So now, arise early in the morning [a]with the servants of your lord who have come with you, and as soon as you have arisen early in the morning and have light, go." **11** So David arose early, he and his men, to go in the morning to return to the land of the Philistines. And the Philistines went up to Jezreel.

### *David Strikes Down the Amalekites*

**30** Then it happened when David and his men came to [a]Ziklag on the third day, that [b]the Amalekites had made a raid on the [1]Negev and on [c]Ziklag and had struck Ziklag and burned it with fire; **2** and they took captive the women *and all* who were in it, both small and great—[a]they did not put anyone to death—and carried *them* off and went their way. **3** Then David and his men came to the city, and behold, it was burned with fire, and their wives and their sons and their daughters had been taken captive. **4** So David and the people who were with him [a]lifted their voices and wept until there was no strength in them to weep. **5** Now [a]David's two wives had been taken captive, Ahinoam the Jezreelitess and Abigail the [1]widow of Nabal the Carmelite. **6** Moreover David was greatly distressed because [a]the people said to stone him, for all the people were [1]embittered, each one because of his sons and his daughters. But [b]David strengthened himself in Yahweh his God.

**7** Then [a]David said to [b]Abiathar the priest, the son of Ahimelech, "Please bring the ephod near to me." So Abiathar brought the ephod near to David. **8** [a]And David asked of Yahweh, saying, "[b]Shall I pursue this band? Shall I overtake them?" And He said to him, "Pursue, for you will surely overtake them, [c]and you will surely deliver *all.*" **9** So David went, [a]he and the six hundred men who were with him, and they came to the brook Besor, *where* those left behind remained. **10** But David pursued, he and four hundred men, for [a]two hundred who were too exhausted to cross the brook Besor remained *behind.*

**11** Then they found an Egyptian in the field and brought him to David and gave him bread, and he ate, and they provided him water to drink. **12** And they gave him a piece of fig cake and two clusters of raisins, and he ate; [a]then his spirit [1]revived. For he had not eaten bread or drunk water for three days and three nights. **13** And David said to him, "To whom do you belong? And where are you from?"

**29:8** [a]1Sa 27:10-12 **29:9** [a]2Sa 14:17, 20; 19:27 [b]1Sa 29:4 **29:10** [a]1Chr 12:19, 22 ◆**30:1** [a]1Sa 29:4, 11 [b]1Sa 15:7; 27:8-10 [c]1Sa 27:6, 8 [1]South country **30:2** [a]1Sa 27:11 **30:4** [a]Nu 14:1 **30:5** [a]1Sa 25:42, 43; 2Sa 2:2 [1]Lit *wife* **30:6** [a]Ex 17:4; Jn 8:59 [b]1Sa 23:16; Ps 18:2; 27:14; 31:24; 71:4, 5; Ro 4:20 [1]Lit *bitter in soul* **30:7** [a]1Sa 23:6, 9 [b]1Sa 22:20-23 **30:8** [a]1Sa 23:2, 4; Ps 50:15; 91:15 [b]Ex 15:9 [c]1Sa 30:18 **30:9** [a]1Sa 27:2 **30:10** [a]1Sa 30:9, 21 **30:12** [a]Jdg 15:19 [1]Lit *returned to him*

And he said, "I am a young man of
Egypt, a slave of an Amalekite; and
my master forsook me when I fell sick
three days ago. **14** We made a raid on
[a]the [1]Negev of the Cherethites and
on that which belongs to Judah and
on [b]the [1]Negev of Caleb, and [c]we
burned Ziklag with fire." **15** Then
David said to him, "Will you bring
me down to this band?" And he said,
"Swear to me by God that you will
not put me to death or surrender me
into the hands of my master, and I will
bring you down to this band."

**16** So he brought him down, and
behold, they were [1]spread over all
the land, [a]eating and drinking and
[2]celebrating because of [b]all the great
spoil that they had taken from the
land of the Philistines and from the
land of Judah. **17** Then David struck
them [a]down from the twilight [1]until
the evening of [2]the next day; and not
a man of them escaped, except four
hundred young men who rode on
[b]camels and fled. **18** So David [a]deliv-
ered all that the Amalekites had taken
and [1]delivered his two wives. **19** Indeed
nothing of theirs was missing, wheth-
er small or great, sons or daughters,
spoil or anything that they had taken
for themselves; [a]David brought *it* all
back. **20** And David took all the sheep
and the cattle *which the people* drove
ahead of [1]the *other* livestock, and they
said, "[a]This is David's spoil."

### *David Apportions the Spoils*

**21** Then [a]David came to the two hun-
*dred* men who were too exhausted to
follow David, who had also remained
at the brook Besor, and they went
out to meet David and to meet the
people who were with him, and
David approached the people and
greeted them. **22** Then all the evil
and vile men among those who went
with David said, "Because they did
not go with [1]us, we will not give
them any of the spoil that we have
delivered, except to every man his
wife and his children, that they may
lead *them* away and depart." **23** Then
David said, "You must not do so, my
brothers, with what Yahweh has
given us, who has kept us and given
into our hand the band that came
against us. **24** And who will listen
to you in this matter? For [a]as is the
portion of the one who goes down
to the battle, so shall the portion
be of the one who remains by the
baggage; they shall be apportioned
together." **25** So it has been from that
day forward, that he made it a statute
and a judgment for Israel to this day.

**26** Then David came to Ziklag and
sent *some* of the spoil to the elders
of Judah, to his friends, saying, "Be-
hold, [a]a [1]gift for you from the spoil of
[b]the enemies of Yahweh: **27** to those
who were in [a]Bethel, and to those
who were in [b]Ramoth of the [1]Negev,
and to those who were in [c]Jattir,
**28** and to those who were in [a]Aroer,
and to those who were in Siphmoth,
and to those who were in [b]Esh-
temoa, **29** and to those who were
in Racal, and to those who were in
the cities of [a]the Jerahmeelites, and

**30:14** [a]1Sa 30:1, 16; 2Sa 8:18; 1Ki 1:38, 44; Eze 25:16; Zep 2:5 [b]Jos 14:13; 15:13; 21:12 [c]1Sa 30:1 [1]South country **30:16** [a]Lk 12:19; 17:27f [b]1Sa 30:14 [1]Lit *left* [2]Lit *keeping a pilgrim-feast* **30:17** [a]1Sa 11:11 [b]Jdg 7:12; 1Sa 15:3 [1]Lit *even until* [2]Lit *their* **30:18** [a]Ge 14:16 [1]Or *David rescued* **30:19** [a]1Sa 30:8 **30:20** [a]1Sa 30:26-31 [1]Lit *those livestock* **30:21** [a]1Sa 30:10 **30:22** [1]Lit *me* **30:24** [a]Nu 31:27; Jos 22:8 **30:26** [a]1Sa 25:27 [b]1Sa 18:17; 25:28 [1]Lit *blessing* **30:27** [a]Ge 12:8; Jos 7:2; 8:9; 16:1 [b]Jos 19:8 [c]Jos 15:48; 21:14 [1]South country **30:28** [a]Jos 13:16; 1Chr 11:44 [b]Jos 15:50 **30:29** [a]1Sa 27:10

to those who were in the cities of [b]the Kenites, **30** and to those who were in [a]Hormah, and to those who were in [b]Bor-ashan, and to those who were in Athach, **31** and to those who were in [a]Hebron, and to all the places where David himself and his men [b]went about."

### *The Death of Saul and His Sons*

**31** [a]Now the Philistines were fighting against Israel, and the men of Israel fled from before the Philistines and fell slain [b]on Mount Gilboa. **2** And the Philistines closely pursued Saul and his sons; and the Philistines struck down [a]Jonathan and Abinadab and Malchi-shua, the sons of Saul. **3** [a]And the battle became heavy against Saul, and the archers [1]hit him; and he was badly wounded by the archers. **4** [a]Then Saul said to his armor bearer, "Draw your sword and pierce me through with it, lest [b]these uncircumcised come and pierce me through and abuse me." But his armor bearer was not willing, for he was greatly afraid. [c]So Saul took his sword and fell on it. **5** Then his armor bearer saw that Saul was dead, so he also fell on his sword and died with him. **6** Thus Saul died with his three sons, his armor bearer, and all his men on that day together.

**7** Then the men of Israel who were on the other side of the valley, with those who were beyond the Jordan, saw that the men of Israel had fled and that Saul and his sons were dead. So they forsook the cities and fled; and the Philistines came and lived in them.

**8** Now it happened on the [1]next day, that the Philistines came to strip the slain, and they found Saul and his three sons fallen on Mount Gilboa. **9** Then they cut off his head and stripped off his weapons and sent *them* all around the land of the Philistines, [a]to proclaim the good news [b]to the house of their idols and to the people. **10** And they placed his weapons in the [1]house of [a]Ashtaroth and [b]fastened his body to the wall of [c]Beth-shan. **11** Then [a]the inhabitants of Jabesh-gilead heard [1]what the Philistines had done to Saul, **12** [a]so all the valiant men arose and walked all night, and took the body of Saul and the bodies of his sons from the wall of Beth-shan, and they came to Jabesh and [b]burned them there. **13** And they took their bones and [a]buried them under [b]the tamarisk tree at Jabesh, and [c]fasted seven days.

---

**30:29** [b]Jdg 1:16; 1Sa 15:6 **30:30** [a]Nu 14:45; 21:3; Jos 12:14; 15:30; 19:4; Jdg 1:17 [b]Jos 15:42; 19:7
***30:31*** *[a]Nu 13:22; Jos 14:13-15; 21:11-13;* 2Sa 2:1 [b]1Sa 23:22 ◆ **31:1** [a]1Chr 10:1-12 [b]1Sa 28:4
**31:2** [a]1Chr 8:33f **31:3** [a]2Sa 1:6 [1]Lit *found* **31:4** [a]Jdg 9:54; 1Chr 10:4 [b]Jdg 14:3; 1Sa 14:6; 17:26, 36 [c]2Sa 1:6, 10 **31:8** [1]Lit *morrow* **31:9** [a]2Sa 1:20 [b]Jdg 16:23, 24 **31:10** [a]Jdg 2:13; 1Sa 7:3 [b]1Sa 31:12; 2Sa 21:12 [c]Jos 17:11 [1]Or *temple* **31:11** [a]1Sa 11:1-13 [1]Lit *about him what* **31:12** [a]2Sa 2:4-7 [b]2Chr 16:14
**31:13** [a]2Sa 21:12-14 [b]1Sa 22:6 [c]2Sa 1:12

*The Second Book of*

# SAMUEL

### *Saul and Jonathan Are Dead*

1 Now it happened after [a]the death
of Saul, that David returned from
[b]striking down the Amalekites. Then
David remained two days in Ziklag.
**2** Now it happened that on the third
day, behold, [a]a man came out of the
camp from Saul. And [b]his clothes
were torn and [1]dust was on his head.
And it happened when he came to
David, that [c]he fell to the ground and
prostrated himself. **3** Then David said
to him, "From where do you come?"
And he said to him, "I have escaped
from the camp of Israel." **4** And David
said to him, "[a]How did things go? Tell
me now." And he said, "The people
have fled from the battle, and also
many of the people have fallen and
are dead; and Saul and Jonathan his
son are dead also." **5** So David said to
the young man who told him, "How
do you know that Saul and his son
Jonathan are dead?" **6** And the young
man who told him said, "By chance
I happened to be on [a]Mount Gilboa,
and behold, [b]Saul was leaning on his
spear. And behold, the chariots and
the horsemen pursued him closely.
**7** Then he turned *to look* behind him,
and he saw me and called to me. And I
said, 'Here I am.' **8** And he said to me,
'Who are you?' And I [1]answered him,
'[a]I am an Amalekite.' **9** Then he said
to me, 'Please stand beside me and
put me to death, for agony has seized
me because my [1]life still lingers in
me.' **10** So I stood beside him [a]and
put him to death, because I knew that
he could not live after he had fallen.
And [b]I took the crown which *was* on
his head and the bracelet which *was*
on his arm, and I have brought them
here to my lord."

**11** Then [a]David took hold of his
clothes and tore them, and *so* also
*did* all the men who *were* with him.
**12** And they lamented and wept and
[a]fasted until evening for Saul and
his son Jonathan and for the people
of [1]Yahweh and the house of Israel,
because they had fallen by the sword.
**13** And David said to the young man
who told him, "Where are you from?"
And he [1]answered, "[a]I am the son of
a sojourner, an Amalekite." **14** Then
David said to him, "How is it you were
not afraid [a]to send forth your hand
to destroy the anointed of Yahweh?"
**15** And David called one of the young
men and said, "Approach *and* fall
upon him." [a]So he struck him and
he died. **16** And David said to him,
"[a]Your blood is on your head, for
[b]your mouth has answered against
you, saying, 'I have put the anointed
of Yahweh to death.'"

### *David's Lament for Saul and Jonathan*

**17** Then David [a]chanted with this *fu-*
*neral* lament over Saul and Jonathan

◆ **1:1** [a]1Sa 31:6 [b]1Sa 30:1, 17, 26 **1:2** [a]2Sa 4:10 [b]1Sa 4:12 [c]1Sa 25:23 [1]Lit *ground* **1:4** [a]1Sa 4:16 **1:6** [a]1Sa 28:4; 31:1-6; 1Chr 10:4-10 [b]1Sa 31:2-4 **1:8** [a]1Sa 15:3; 30:1, 13, 17 [1]Lit *said to* **1:9** [1]Lit *whole life is still in me* **1:10** [a]Jdg 9:54 [b]2Ki 11:12 **1:11** [a]Ge 37:29, 34; Jos 7:6; 2Chr 34:27; Ezr 9:3 **1:12** [a]2Sa 3:35 [1]The personal covenant name of God, a form of I AM WHO I AM, cf. Ex 3:14-15 **1:13** [a]2Sa 1:8 [1]Lit *said* **1:14** [a]1Sa 24:6; 26:9, 11, 16 **1:15** [a]2Sa 4:10, 12 **1:16** [a]1Sa 26:9; 2Sa 3:28, 29; 1Ki 2:32 [b]2Sa 1:10; Lk 19:22 **1:17** [a]2Chr 35:25

his son, **18** and he told *them* to teach
the sons of Judah *the song of* the bow;
behold, it is written in [a]the book of
Jashar.

**19** “[1]Your beauty, O Israel, is
slain on your high places!
[a]How have the mighty fallen!
**20** “[a]Tell *it* not in Gath,
Proclaim it not in the streets
of Ashkelon,
Lest [b]the daughters
of the Philistines be glad,
Lest the daughters of [c]the
uncircumcised exult.
**21** “[a]O mountains of Gilboa,
[b]Let not dew or rain be on
you, nor fields of offerings;
For there the shield
of the mighty was defiled,
The shield of Saul, not
[c]anointed with oil.
**22** “[a]From the blood of the slain,
from the fat of the mighty,
[b]The bow of Jonathan
did not turn back,
And the sword of Saul did
not return empty.
**23** “Saul and Jonathan, beloved
and pleasant in their life,
And in their death they
were not separated;
[a]They were swifter
than eagles,
[b]They were mightier
than lions.
**24** “O daughters of Israel,
weep over Saul,
Who clothed you
luxuriously in scarlet,
Who put ornaments
of gold on your clothing.
**25** “[a]How have the mighty fallen
in the midst of the battle!
Jonathan is slain
on your high places.
**26** “I am distressed for you,
my brother Jonathan;
You have been very
pleasant to me.
[a]Your love to me was
more wonderful
Than the love of women.
**27** “[a]How have the mighty fallen,
And [b]the weapons
of war perished!”

### *David Anointed King of Judah*

**2** Now it happened afterwards that
[a]David asked of Yahweh, saying,
“Shall I go up to one of the cities of
Judah?” And Yahweh said to him, “Go
up.” So David said, “Where shall I go
up?” And He said, “[b]To Hebron.” **2** So
David went up there, and [a]his two
wives also, Ahinoam the Jezreelitess
and Abigail the wife of Nabal the
Carmelite. **3** And [a]David brought up
his men who *were* with him, each
with his household; and they lived in
the cities of Hebron. **4** Then the men
of Judah came and there [a]anointed
David king over the house of Judah.
And they told David, saying, “It
was [b]the men of Jabesh-gilead who
buried Saul.” **5** And David sent mes-
sengers to the men of Jabesh-gilead,
and said to them, “[a]May you be
blessed of Yahweh because you have
[1]shown this lovingkindness with
your lord, with Saul, and have buried
him. **6** So now, [a]may Yahweh [1]show
lovingkindness and truth to you; and

**1:18** [a]Jos 10:13 **1:19** [a]2Sa 1:25, 27 [1]Lit *The* **1:20** [a]1Sa 31:8-13; Mic 1:10 [b]Ex 15:20, 21; 1Sa 18:6 [c]1Sa 14:6
**1:21** [a]1Sa 31:1 [b]Eze 31:15 [c]Is 21:5 **1:22** [a]Dt 32:42; Is 34:6 [b]1Sa 18:4 **1:23** [a]Jer 4:13 [b]Jdg 14:18
**1:25** [a]2Sa 1:19, 27 **1:26** [a]1Sa 18:1-4 **1:27** [a]2Sa 1:19, 25 [b]Is 13:5 ◆ **2:1** [a]1Sa 23:2, 4, 9-12 [b]Jos 14:13;
1Sa 30:31 **2:2** [a]1Sa 25:42, 43 **2:3** [a]1Sa 30:9; 1Chr 12:1 **2:4** [a]1Sa 16:13; 2Sa 5:3, 5 [b]1Sa 31:11-13
**2:5** [a]1Sa 23:21; Ps 115:15 [1]Lit *done* **2:6** [a]Ex 34:6; 2Ti 1:16 [1]Lit *do*

I also will [1]show this goodness to you,
because you have done this thing.
**7** So now, let your hands be strong
and be [1]valiant; for Saul your lord is
dead, and also the house of Judah has
anointed me king over them."

### *Ish-bosheth Made King over Israel*

**8** Now [a]Abner the son of Ner, com-
mander of Saul's army, had taken
[1]Ish-bosheth the son of Saul and
brought him over to [b]Mahanaim.
**9** And he made him king over [a]Gile-
ad, over the [b]Ashurites, over [c]Jezreel,
over Ephraim, and over Benjamin,
even over all Israel. **10** Ish-bosheth,
Saul's son, was forty years old when
he became king over Israel, and he
was king for two years. The house
of Judah, however, followed David.
**11** [a]And the [1]time that David was king
in Hebron over the house of Judah
was seven years and six months.

### *Abner Defeated Before David*

**12** Now Abner the son of Ner, went out
from Mahanaim to [a]Gibeon with the
servants of Ish-bosheth the son of Saul.
**13** And [a]Joab the son of Zeruiah and
the servants of David went out and
met [1]them by the pool of Gibeon;
and they sat down, [2]one on the one
side of the pool and [2]the other on the
other side of the pool. **14** Then Abner
said to Joab, "Now let the young men
arise and [a,1]hold a contest before us."
And Joab said, "Let them arise." **15** So
they arose and went over by count,
twelve for Benjamin and Ish-bosheth
the son of Saul, and twelve of the
servants of David. **16** And each one
of them seized his [1]opponent by
the head and *thrust* his sword in his
[2]opponent's side; so they fell down
together. Therefore that place was
called [3]Helkath-hazzurim, which is
in Gibeon. **17** And that day the battle
was very severe, and [a]Abner and the
men of Israel were [1]defeated before
the servants of David.

**18** Now [a]the three sons of Zeruiah
were there, Joab and Abishai and
Asahel; and Asahel *was* [b]*as* [1]swift-
footed as one of the gazelles which
is in the field. **19** And Asahel pursued
Abner and did not [1]turn to the right
or to the left from following Abner.
**20** Then Abner turned *to look* behind
him and said, "Is that you, Asahel?"
And he answered, "It is I." **21** So Abner
said to him, "[1]Turn to your right or to
your left, and seize one of the young
men for yourself, and take for your-
self his spoil." But Asahel was not
willing to turn aside from following
him. **22** And Abner repeated again to
Asahel, "Turn [1]aside from following
me. Why should I strike you to the
ground? [a]How then could I lift up my
face to your brother Joab?" **23** Howev-
er, he refused to turn aside; therefore
Abner struck him in the belly with
the butt end of the spear, so that the
spear came out at his back. And he
fell there and died on the spot. And
it happened that all who came to the
place where [a]Asahel had fallen and
died, stood still.

**24** But Joab and Abishai pursued
Abner. Now the sun was going down,

---

**2:6** [1]Lit *do* **2:7** [1]Lit *sons of valor* **2:8** [a]1Sa 14:50 [b]Ge 32:2; 2Sa 17:24 [1]Lit *man of shame*, also known as *Eshbaal*, cf. 1Chr 8:33 **2:9** [a]Jos 22:9 [b]Jdg 1:32 [c]1Sa 29:1 **2:11** [a]2Sa 5:5 [1]Lit *number of days* **2:12** [a]Jos 10:12; 18:25 **2:13** [a]2Sa 8:16; 1Chr 2:16; 11:6 [1]Lit *them together* [2]Lit *these* **2:14** [a]2Sa 2:16, 17 [1]Lit *make sport* **2:16** [1]Lit *fellow* [2]Lit *fellow's* [3]Lit *the field of sword-edges* **2:17** [a]2Sa 3:1 [1]Lit *smitten* **2:18** [a]1Chr 2:16 [b]1Chr 12:8; Hab 3:19 [1]Lit *light in his feet* **2:19** [1]Lit *turn to go to* **2:21** [1]Lit *Turn for yourself* **2:22** [a]2Sa 3:27 [1]Lit *aside for yourself* **2:23** [a]2Sa 20:12

and they came to the hill of Ammah,
which is in front of Giah by the way of
the wilderness of Gibeon. **25** And the
sons of Benjamin gathered together
behind Abner and became one band,
and they stood on the top of a certain
hill. **26** Then Abner called to Joab and
said, "Shall the sword devour forever?
Do you not know that it will be bitter
in the end? How long will you [1]refrain
from telling the people to turn back
from following their brothers?"
**27** And Joab said, "As God lives, if
you had not spoken, surely then the
people would have *only* gone away
in the morning, each from following
his brother." **28** So Joab blew the
trumpet; and all the people stood still
and pursued Israel no longer, [a]nor
did they continue to fight anymore.
**29** But Abner and his men then went
through the Arabah all that night; so
they crossed the Jordan, walked all
morning, and came to [a]Mahanaim.
**30** Now Joab returned from follow-
ing Abner. And he had gathered all
the people together, and [1]nineteen of
David's servants besides Asahel were
missing. **31** But the servants of David
had struck down many of Benjamin
and Abner's men, *so that* 360 men
died. **32** And they took up Asahel
and buried him [a]in his father's tomb
which was in Bethlehem. Then Joab
and his men went all night until the
day [1]dawned at Hebron.

### *The House of David Strengthened*

**3** Now [a]the war between the house
of Saul and the house of David
was long; and David grew steadily
stronger, but the house of Saul grew
weaker continually.
**2** [a]And sons were born to David at
Hebron: his firstborn was Amnon, by
[b]Ahinoam the Jezreelitess; **3** and his
second, Chileab, by Abigail the wife
of Nabal the Carmelite; and the third,
Absalom the son of [a]Maacah, the
daughter of Talmai king of [b]Geshur;
**4** and the fourth, [a]Adonijah the son
of Haggith; and the fifth, Shephatiah
the son of Abital; **5** and the sixth,
Ithream, by David's wife Eglah. These
were born to David at Hebron.

### *Abner Cuts a Covenant with David*

**6** Now it happened, while there was
war between the house of Saul and
the house of David that [a]Abner was
making himself strong in the house
of Saul. **7** Now Saul had a concubine
whose name was [a]Rizpah, the daugh-
ter of Aiah; and [1]Ish-bosheth said to
Abner, "Why have you gone in to my
father's concubine?" **8** Then Abner
was very angry over the words of Ish-
bosheth and said, "[a]Am I a dog's head
that belongs to Judah? Today I show
lovingkindness to the house of Saul
your father, to his brothers and to
his friends, and have not delivered
you into the hands of David; and yet
today you charge me with a guilt
concerning the woman. **9** [a]May God
*do so* to Abner, and more also, if [b]as
Yahweh has sworn to David, I do not
do this for him, **10** [a]to transfer the
kingdom from the house of Saul and
to establish the throne of David over
Israel and over Judah, [b]from Dan
even to Beersheba." **11** And he could

**2:26** [1]Lit *not tell the people* **2:28** [a]2Sa 3:1 **2:29** [a]2Sa 2:8 **2:30** [1]Lit *nineteen men*
**2:32** [a]Ge 47:29, 30; Jdg 8:32 [1]Lit *lighted on them* ◆ **3:1** [a]1Ki 14:30; Ps 46:9 **3:2** [a]1Chr 3:1-3
[b]1Sa 25:42, 43 **3:3** [a]1Sa 27:8; 1Chr 3:2 [b]2Sa 14:32; 15:8 **3:4** [a]1Ki 1:5 **3:6** [a]2Sa 2:8, 9 **3:7** [a]2Sa 21:8-11
[1]As in some ancient mss and versions; M.T. *he* **3:8** [a]1Sa 24:14; 2Sa 9:8 **3:9** [a]1Ki 19:2 [b]1Sa 15:28
**3:10** [a]1Sa 15:28 [b]1Sa 3:20

no longer respond a word to Abner,
because he was afraid of him.
**12** Then Abner sent messengers to
David in his place, saying, "Whose
is the land? Cut your covenant with
me, and behold, my hand shall be
with you to turn all Israel over to
you." **13** And he said, "Good! I will cut
a covenant with you, but I ask one
thing of you, [1]namely, [a]you shall not
see my face unless you [b]first bring
Michal, Saul's daughter, when you
come to see my face." **14** So David sent
messengers to Ish-bosheth, Saul's
son, saying, "Give me my wife Michal,
to whom I was betrothed [a]for one
hundred foreskins of the Philistines."
**15** And Ish-bosheth sent and took
her from *her* husband, from [1]Paltiel
the son of Laish. **16** But her husband
went with her, weeping as he went,
and followed her as far as [a]Bahurim.
Then Abner said to him, "Go, return."
So he returned.
**17** Now Abner had [1]consultation
with [a]the elders of Israel, saying, "In
times past you were seeking for David
to be king over you. **18** So now, do *it*!
For Yahweh has spoken of David,
saying, '[a]By the hand of My servant
David [1]I will save My people Israel
from the hand of the Philistines and
from the hand of all their enemies.'"
**19** Abner also spoke in the hearing
of Benjamin; and in addition Abner
went to speak in the hearing of David
in Hebron all that was good in the
sight of Israel and in the sight of [a]the
whole house of Benjamin.
**20** Then Abner and twenty men
with him came to David at Hebron.
And David made a feast for Abner
and the men who were with him.
**21** And Abner said to David, "Let me
arise and go and [a]gather all Israel to
my lord the king, that they may cut
a covenant with you, and that [b]you
may be king over all that your soul
desires." So David sent Abner away,
and he went in peace.
**22** And behold, [a]the servants of
David and Joab came from a raid and
brought much spoil with them; but
Abner was not with David in Hebron,
for he had sent him away, and he had
gone in peace. **23** Now Joab and all
the army that was with him arrived,
and they told Joab, saying, "Abner the
son of Ner came to the king, and he
has sent him away, and he has gone
in peace." **24** Then Joab came to the
king and said, "What have you done?
Behold, Abner came to you; why then
have you sent him away and he is
already gone? **25** You know Abner the
son of Ner, that he came to deceive
you and to know of [a]your going out
and your coming in and to know all
that you are doing."

### *Joab Strikes Abner*

**26** Then Joab came out from David
and sent messengers after Abner,
and they brought him back from
the well of Sirah; but David did not
know *it*. **27** So when Abner returned
to Hebron, Joab took him aside into
the middle of the gate to speak with
him privately, and there [a]he struck
him in the belly so that he died on
account of the blood of Asahel his
brother. **28** Afterward David heard it,

---

**3:13** [a]Ge 43:3 [b]1Sa 18:20; 19:11 [1]Lit *saying* **3:14** [a]1Sa 18:25, 27 **3:15** [1]In 1Sa 25:44, *Palti*
**3:16** [a]2Sa 16:5; 19:16 **3:17** [a]1Sa 8:4 [1]Lit *a word* **3:18** [a]1Sa 9:16; 15:28 [1]As in many ancient mss and versions; M.T. *he* **3:19** [a]1Sa 10:20, 21; 1Chr 12:29 **3:21** [a]2Sa 3:10, 12 [b]1Ki 11:37 **3:22** [a]1Sa 27:8
**3:25** [a]Dt 28:6; 1Sa 29:6; Is 37:28 **3:27** [a]2Sa 2:23; 20:9, 10; 1Ki 2:5

so he said, "I and my kingdom are
innocent before Yahweh forever of
the blood of Abner the son of Ner.
**29** [a]May it whirl on the head of Joab
and on all his father's house; and may
[b]one who has a discharge, or who is a
leper, or who takes hold of a spindle,
or who falls by the sword, or who
lacks bread not be cut off from the
house of Joab." **30** So Joab and Abishai
his brother killed Abner [a]because he
had put their brother Asahel to death
in the battle at Gibeon.

### *David's Lament for Abner*

**31** Then David said to Joab and to
all the people who were with him,
"[a]Tear your clothes and gird on
sackcloth and lament before Abner."
And King David walked behind the
bier. **32** Thus they buried Abner in
Hebron; and the king lifted up his
voice and wept at [a]the grave of Ab-
ner, and all the people wept. **33** [a]And
the king chanted a *lament* for Abner
and said,

"Should Abner die as a
wicked fool dies?
**34** "Your hands were not bound,
nor your feet put in fetters;
As one falls before the
[1]unrighteous, you
have fallen."

And all the people continued to weep
over him. **35** Then all the people came
[a]*to* [1]*persuade* David to eat bread
while it was still day; but David swore
*an oath*, saying, "[b]May God do so to
me, and more also, if I taste bread or
anything else [c]before the sun goes
down." **36** Now all the people took
note *of it*, and it was good in their
sight, just as everything the king
did was good in the sight of all the
people. **37** So all the people and all
Israel knew that day that it had not
been *the will* of the king to put Abner
the son of Ner to death. **38** Then the
king said to his servants, "Do you
not know that a prince and a great
man has fallen this day in Israel?
**39** Thus I am [a]weak today, though
anointed king; and these men [b]the
sons of Zeruiah are too difficult for
me. [c]May Yahweh repay the evildoer
according to his evil."

### *Ish-bosheth Put to Death*

**4** Then [1]Ish-bosheth, Saul's son
heard that [a]Abner had died in He-
bron. And [b,2]he lost courage, and all
Israel was dismayed. **2** Now Saul's son
*had* two men who were command-
ers of bands: the name of the one
was Baanah and the name of the
other Rechab, sons of Rimmon the
Beerothite, of the sons of Benjamin
(for [a]Beeroth is also considered [b]*part*
of Benjamin, **3** and the Beerothites
fled to [a]Gittaim and have been so-
journers there until this day).
**4** Now [a]Jonathan, Saul's son, had a
son crippled in his feet. He was five
years old when the [b]report of Saul
and Jonathan came from Jezreel, and
his nurse took him up and fled. And it
happened that in her hurry to flee, he
fell and became lame. And his name
was [c,1]Mephibosheth.
**5** So the sons of Rimmon the Bee-
rothite, Rechab and Baanah, went forth
and came to the house of [a]Ish-bosheth

---

**3:29** [a]Dt 21:6-9; 1Ki 2:31-33 [b]Lv 13:46 **3:30** [a]2Sa 2:23 **3:31** [a]Ge 37:34; Jdg 11:35 **3:32** [a]Job 31:28, 29; Pr 24:17 **3:33** [a]2Sa 1:17; 2Chr 35:25 **3:34** [1]Lit *sons of unrighteousness* **3:35** [a]2Sa 12:17 [b]1Sa 3:17 [c]2Sa 1:12 [1]Lit *cause* **3:39** [a]1Chr 29:1; 2Chr 13:7 [b]2Sa 19:5-7 [c]1Ki 2:32-34 ◆**4:1** [a]2Sa 3:27 [b]Ezr 4:4 [1]As in some ancient mss; M.T. *he* [2]Lit *his hands dropped* **4:2** [a]Jos 9:17 [b]Jos 18:25 **4:3** [a]Ne 11:33 **4:4** [a]2Sa 9:3, 6 [b]1Sa 31:1-4 [c]1Chr 8:34; 9:40 [1]Merib-baal **4:5** [a]2Sa 2:8

in the heat of the day while he was
taking his midday rest. **6** [1]They came
to the middle of the house as [2]if to
get wheat, and [a]they struck him in
the belly; and Rechab and Baanah his
brother escaped. **7** Thus they came
into the house, as he was lying on his
bed in his bedroom, and they struck
him and put him to death and be-
headed him. And they took his head
and [a]went on the way *leading* to the
Arabah all night. **8** Then they brought
the head of Ish-bosheth to David at
Hebron and said to the king, "Behold,
the head of Ish-bosheth [a]the son of
Saul, your enemy, who sought your
life; thus Yahweh has given my lord
the king vengeance this day on Saul
and his seed."

**9** And David answered Rechab and
Baanah his brother, sons of Rimmon
the Beerothite, and said to them, "As
Yahweh lives, [a]who has redeemed
my life from all distress, **10** [a]when
one told me, saying, 'Behold, Saul is
dead,' and [1]thought he was bringing
good news, I seized him and killed
him in Ziklag, which was the reward
I gave him for *his* news. **11** How much
more, when wicked men have killed
a righteous man in his own house on
his bed, shall I not now [a]require his
blood from your hand and purge you
from the earth?" **12** Then [a]David com-
manded the young men, and they
killed them and cut off their hands
and feet and hung them up beside
the pool in Hebron. But they took the
head of Ish-bosheth [b]and buried it in
the grave of Abner in Hebron.

### *David Anointed King over All Israel*

**5** [a]Then all the tribes of Israel came
to David at Hebron and [1]said,
"Behold, we are [b]your bone and
your flesh. **2** Previously, when Saul
was king over us, [a]you were the one
who led out and brought in Israel;
and Yahweh said to you, '[b]You will
shepherd My people Israel, and you
will be [c]a ruler over Israel.'" **3** So all
the elders of Israel came to the king
at Hebron, and King David [a]cut a cov-
enant with them in Hebron before
Yahweh; then [b]they anointed David
king over Israel. **4** Now David was
[a]thirty years old when he became
king, *and* [b]he reigned forty years.
**5** At Hebron [a]he reigned over Judah
seven years and six months, and in
Jerusalem he reigned thirty-three
years over all Israel and Judah.

**6** [a]Then the king and his men went
to [b]Jerusalem against the Jebusites,
the inhabitants of the land, and they
said to [1]David, "You shall not come
in here, but the blind and lame will
turn you away"; [2]thinking, "David
cannot enter here." **7** Nevertheless,
David captured the fortress of Zion,
that is [a]the city of David. **8** And David
said on that day, "Whoever would
strike down the Jebusites, let him
reach the lame and the blind, who
are hated by David's soul, through the
water tunnel." Therefore they say,
"The blind or the lame shall not come
into the house." **9** Then David lived
in the fortress and called it [a]the city
of David. And David built all around
from the [b,1]Millo and inward. **10** [a]And

**4:6** [a]2Sa 2:23 [1]Lit *And here* [2]Lit *takers of wheat* **4:7** [a]2Sa 2:29 **4:8** [a]1Sa 24:4; 25:29 **4:9** [a]Ge 48:16; 1Ki 1:29; Ps 31:7 **4:10** [a]2Sa 1:2, 4, 15 [1]Lit *he was as a bearer of good news in his own eyes* **4:11** [a]Ge 9:5; Ps 9:12 **4:12** [a]2Sa 1:15 [b]2Sa 3:32 ◆ **5:1** [a]1Chr 11:1-3 [b]2Sa 19:13 [1]Lit *said, saying* **5:2** [a]1Sa 18:5, 13, 16 [b]Ge 49:24; 2Sa 7:7 [c]1Sa 25:30 **5:3** [a]2Sa 3:21 [b]1Sa 16:13; 2Sa 2:4 **5:4** [a]Ge 41:46; Nu 4:3; Lk 3:23 [b]1Ki 2:11; 1Chr 26:31 **5:5** [a]2Sa 2:11; 1Chr 3:4; 29:27 **5:6** [a]1Chr 11:4-9 [b]Jos 15:63; 18:28; Jdg 1:21 [1]Lit *David, saying* [2]Lit *saying* **5:7** [a]2Sa 6:12, 16; 1Ki 2:10; 9:24 **5:9** [a]2Sa 5:7 [b]1Ki 9:15, 24 [1]Citadel **5:10** [a]2Sa 3:1

David became greater and greater,
and Yahweh, the God of hosts, was
with him.
11 [a]Then Hiram king of Tyre sent
messengers to David with cedar
trees and craftsmen of wood and
craftsmen of stone walls; and [b]they
built a house for David. 12 Thus David
knew that Yahweh had established
him as king over Israel, and that He
had lifted up his kingdom for the
sake of His people Israel.

### *David Takes More Wives*

13 And [a]David took more concubines
and wives from Jerusalem, after he
came from Hebron; and more sons
and daughters were born to David.
14 Now [a]these are the names of those
who were born to him in Jerusalem:
Shammua, Shobab, Nathan, Solomon,
15 Ibhar, Elishua, Nepheg, Japhia,
16 Elishama, Eliada and Eliphelet.

### *David Goes Up Against the Philistines*

17 Then the Philistines heard that
they had anointed David king over
Israel, so [a]all the Philistines went up
to seek out David. And David heard
*of it* and went down to the [b]fortress.
18 Now the Philistines had come and
spread themselves out in [a]the valley
of Rephaim. 19 Then [a]David asked of
Yahweh, saying, "Shall I go up against
the Philistines? Will You give them
into my hand?" And [b]Yahweh said to
David, "Go up, for I will certainly give
the Philistines into your hand." 20 So
David came to [a]Baal-perazim, and
there David struck them down; and
he said, "Yahweh has broken through
my enemies before me, like the
breakthrough of waters." Therefore
he named that place [1]Baal-perazim.
21 And they forsook their idols there;
so [a]David and his men carried them
away.
22 Then [a]the Philistines yet again
came up and spread themselves out
in the valley of Rephaim. 23 So [a]David
asked of Yahweh, and He said, "You
shall not go *directly* up; circle around
behind them and come at them in
front of the [1]balsam trees. 24 And
it will be that when [a]you hear the
sound of marching in the tops of
the [1]balsam trees, then you shall
act promptly, for then [b]Yahweh will
have gone out before you to strike
the camp of the Philistines." 25 Then
David did so, just as Yahweh had
commanded him, and struck down
the Philistines from [a,1]Geba [2]as far
as [b]Gezer.

### *The Ark Is Brought to Jerusalem*

6 [a]Then David again gathered all
the chosen men of Israel, thirty
thousand. 2 And David arose and
went with all the people who were
with him [1]from [a,2]Baale-judah, to
bring up from there the ark of God
which is called by the [b]Name, the
very name of Yahweh of hosts who
[c]is [3]enthroned *above* the cherubim.
3 And they [1]drove the ark of God on
[a]a new cart that they might bring it
from the house of Abinadab which
was on the hill; and [2]Uzzah and Ahio,
the sons of Abinadab, were leading

**5:11** [a]1Ki 5:1, 10, 18; 1Chr 14:1 [b]Ps 30: title **5:13** [a]Dt 17:17; 1Chr 3:9 **5:14** [a]1Chr 3:5-8 **5:17** [a]1Sa 29:1 [b]2Sa 23:14; 1Chr 11:16 **5:18** [a]Ge 14:5; Jos 15:8; 17:15; 18:16 **5:19** [a]1Sa 23:2 [b]2Sa 2:1 **5:20** [a]1Chr 14:11; Is 28:21 [1]Lit *the master of breakthrough* **5:21** [a]1Chr 14:12 **5:22** [a]2Sa 5:18 **5:23** [a]2Sa 5:19 [1]Or *baka-shrubs* **5:24** [a]2Ki 7:6 [b]Jdg 4:14 [1]Or *baka-shrubs* **5:25** [a]Is 28:21 [b]Jos 12:12; 21:21 [1]In 1Chr 14:16, *Gibeon* [2]Lit *until you are coming to* ◆**6:1** [a]1Chr 13:5-14 **6:2** [a]Jos 15:9, 10; 1Sa 7:1 [b]Lv 24:16 [c]Ex 25:22 [1]Or *to* [2]Kiriath-jearim, cf. Jos 15:9 [3]Lit *sitting* **6:3** [a]Nu 7:4-9; 1Sa 6:7 [1]Lit *caused to ride* [2]Or *Uzza*, cf. 1Chr 13:7

the new cart. 4 So [a]they brought it
with the ark of God from the house
of Abinadab, which was on the hill;
and Ahio was walking ahead of the
ark. 5 Now David and all the house of
Israel [a]were celebrating before Yah-
weh [b]with all kinds of *instruments
made of* [1]fir wood, and with lyres,
harps, tambourines, castanets, and
cymbals.

6 Then they came to the [a]threshing
floor of Nacon. And [1]Uzzah [b]reached
out toward the ark of God and took
hold of it, because the oxen nearly
upset *it*. 7 And the anger of Yahweh
burned against Uzzah, and [a]God
struck him down there for [1]his
irreverence; and he died there by
the ark of God. 8 And David became
angry because [1]of Yahweh's breaking
out against Uzzah; and that place is
called [2]Perez-uzzah to this day. 9 So
[a]David was afraid of Yahweh that
day; and he said, "How can the ark of
Yahweh come to me?" 10 And David
was unwilling to move the ark of Yah-
weh into the city of David with him;
but David took it aside to the house
of [a]Obed-edom the Gittite. 11 Thus
the ark of Yahweh remained in the
house of Obed-edom the Gittite
three months, and Yahweh [a]blessed
Obed-edom and all his household.

12 Then it was told to King David,
saying, "Yahweh has blessed the
house of Obed-edom and all that
belongs to him, on account of the
ark of God." So [a]David went and
brought up the ark of God from the
house of Obed-edom into [b]the city
of David with gladness. 13 And so it
happened, that when those [a]who
were carrying the ark of Yahweh
had gone six paces, he sacrificed an
[b]ox and a fatling. 14 And [a]David was
dancing before Yahweh with all *his*
strength, and David was [b]girded with
a linen ephod. 15 So David and all the
house of Israel were bringing up the
ark of Yahweh with shouting and
the sound of the trumpet.

### *David Dances Before Yahweh*

16 Then it happened *as* the ark of
Yahweh came into the city of David,
that [a]Michal the daughter of Saul
looked out of the window and saw
King David leaping and dancing be-
fore Yahweh; and she despised him
in her heart.

17 And they brought in the ark of
Yahweh and placed it [a]in its place in-
side the tent which David had pitched
for it; and [b]David offered burnt
offerings and peace offerings before
Yahweh. 18 Then David completed
offering the burnt offerings and the
peace offerings. And [a]he blessed
the people in the name of Yahweh
of hosts. 19 And he apportioned to
all the people, to all the multitude
of Israel, both to men and women, a
cake of bread and one of dates and
one of raisins to each one. Then all
the people went each to his house.

20 But David returned to bless his
household, and Michal the daughter of
Saul came out to meet David and said,
"How the king of Israel has glorified
himself today! [a]He uncovered himself

---

**6:4** [a]1Sa 7:1; 1Chr 13:7 **6:5** [a]1Sa 18:6, 7 [b]1Chr 13:8 [1]Or *cypress* **6:6** [a]1Chr 13:9 [b]Nu 4:15, 19, 20 [1]Or *Uzza*, cf. 1Chr 13:7 **6:7** [a]1Sa 6:19 [1]Lit *the* **6:8** [1]Lit *Yahweh broke through a breakthrough* [2]Lit *the breakthrough of Uzzah* **6:9** [a]Ps 119:120; Lk 5:8 **6:10** [a]1Chr 26:4-8 **6:11** [a]Ge 30:27; 39:5 **6:12** [a]1Chr 15:25-16:3 [b]1Ki 8:1 **6:13** [a]Nu 4:15; Jos 3:3; 1Chr 15:2, 15 [b]1Ki 8:5 **6:14** [a]Ex 15:20, 21; Jdg 11:34 [b]Ex 19:6; 1Sa 2:18, 28 **6:16** [a]2Sa 3:14 **6:17** [a]1Chr 15:1; 2Chr 1:4 [b]1Ki 8:62-65 **6:18** [a]1Ki 8:14, 15 **6:20** [a]2Sa 6:14, 16; Ecc 7:17

today in the eyes of his servants' maids
as one of the [b]worthless ones shame-
lessly uncovers himself!" 21 So David
said to Michal, "[a]*It was* before Yahweh,
who chose me above your father and
above all his house, to appoint me
ruler over the people of Yahweh, over
Israel; therefore I will celebrate before
Yahweh. 22 And I will be esteemed
even more lightly than this and will
be humble in my own eyes, but with
the maids of whom you have spoken,
with them I will be glorified." 23 And
Michal the daughter of Saul had no
child to the day of her death.

### *The Ark of God Inhabits a Tent*

7 [a]Now it happened when the king
inhabited his house, and Yahweh
had given him rest on every side from
all his enemies, 2 that the king said
to [a]Nathan the prophet, "See now,
I inhabit [b]a house of cedar, but the
ark of God [c]inhabits *tent* curtains."
3 So Nathan said to the king, "[a]Go, do
all that is in your heart, for Yahweh
is with you."

4 Now it happened in the same
night, that the word of Yahweh came
to Nathan, saying, 5 "Go and say to
My servant David, 'Thus says Yahweh,
"[a]Are you the one who would build
Me a house to inhabit? 6 For [a]I have
not inhabited a house since the day
I brought up the sons of Israel from
Egypt, even to this day; but I have been
going about [b]in a tent, even in a [1]taber-
nacle. 7 [a]Wherever I have gone about
with all the sons of Israel, did I speak
a word with one of the tribes of Israel,
[b]which I commanded to shepherd My
people Israel, saying, 'Why have you
not built Me a house of cedar?'"'

### *David's House Will Be Established Forever*

8 "So now, thus you shall say to My
servant David, 'Thus says Yahweh of
hosts, "[a]I Myself took you from the
pasture, from following the sheep,
[b]to be ruler over My people Israel.
9 [a]And I have been with you wher-
ever you have gone and [b]have cut
off all your enemies from before you;
and I will make you a great name, like
the name of the great men who are
on the earth. 10 And I will appoint a
place for My people Israel and [a]will
plant them, that they may dwell in
their own place and not be disturbed
again; [b]and the [1]unrighteous will not
afflict them any more as formerly,
11 even [a]from the day that I com-
manded judges *to be* over My people
Israel; and [b]I will give you rest from
all your enemies. Yahweh also de-
clares to you that [c]Yahweh will make
a house for you. 12 [a]When your days
are fulfilled and you [b]lie down with
your fathers, [c]I will raise up *one of*
your seed after you, who will come
forth from [1]your own body, and I
will establish his kingdom. 13 [a]He
shall build a house for My name,
and [b]I will establish the throne of
his kingdom forever. 14 [a]I will be a
father to him and he will be a son
to Me; [b]when he commits iniquity, I

**6:20** [b]Jdg 9:4 **6:21** [a]1Sa 13:14; 15:28 ◆ **7:1** [a]1Chr 17:1-27 **7:2** [a]2Sa 7:17; 12:1; 1Ki 1:22; 1Chr 29:29; 2Chr 9:29 [b]2Sa 5:11 [c]Ex 26:1 **7:3** [a]1Ki 8:17, 18; 1Chr 22:7 **7:5** [a]1Ki 5:3, 4; 8:19 **7:6** [a]Jos 18:1; 1Ki 8:16 [b]Ex 40:18, 34 [1]Lit *dwelling place* **7:7** [a]Lv 26:11, 12 [b]2Sa 5:2 **7:8** [a]1Sa 16:11, 12; Ps 78:70, 71 [b]2Sa 6:21 **7:9** [a]1Sa 5:10 [b]Ps 18:37-42 **7:10** [a]Ex 15:17; Is 5:2, 7 [b]Ps 89:22, 23; Is 60:18 [1]Lit *sons of unrighteousness* **7:11** [a]Jdg 2:14-16; 1Sa 12:9-11 [b]2Sa 7:1 [c]1Sa 25:28; 2Sa 7:27 **7:12** [a]1Ki 2:1 [b]Dt 31:16; Ac 13:36 [c]1Ki 8:20; Ps 132:11 [1]Lit *your bowels* **7:13** [a]1Ki 6:12; 8:19 [b]Is 9:7; 49:8 **7:14** [a]Ps 89:26, 27; 2Co 6:18; Heb 1:5 [b]1Ki 11:34; Ps 89:30-33

will reprove him with the rod of men
and the strikes from the sons of men,
**15** but My lovingkindness shall not
be removed from him, [a]as I removed
*it* from Saul, whom I removed from
before you. **16** [a]And your house and
your kingdom shall [1]endure before
[2]Me forever; your throne shall be
established forever."'" **17** According
to all these words and according to all
this vision, so Nathan spoke to David.

### *David Magnifies Yahweh's Name*

**18** Then David the king went in and sat
before Yahweh, and he said, "[a]Who
am I, O Lord Yahweh, and what is my
house, that You have brought me this
far? **19** And yet this was a small thing
in Your eyes, O Lord Yahweh, [a]for You
have spoken also of the house of Your
slave concerning the distant future.
And [b]this is the law of man, O Lord
Yahweh. **20** And again what more can
David say to You? And [a]You know
Your slave, O Lord Yahweh! **21** [a]For
the sake of Your word, and according
to Your own heart, You have done all
this greatness to let Your slave know.
**22** For this reason [a]You are great,
O Lord Yahweh; for [b]there is none
like You, and there is no God besides
You, [c]according to all that we have
heard with our ears. **23** And [a]what
one nation on the earth is like Your
people Israel, whom God went to
redeem for Himself as a people and
to make a name for Himself, and [b]to
do a great thing for You and awesome
things for Your land, before [c]Your
people whom [d]You have redeemed
for Yourself from Egypt, *from* nations
and their gods? **24** Yet [a]You have es-
tablished for Yourself Your people
Israel as Your own people forever,
and [b]You, O Yahweh, have become
their God. **25** So now, O Yahweh God,
the word that You have spoken con-
cerning Your slave and concerning
his house, establish *it* forever, and
do as You have spoken, **26** [a]that Your
name may be magnified forever,
by saying, 'Yahweh of hosts is God
over Israel'; and the house of Your
[1]servant David shall be established
before You. **27** For You, O Yahweh of
hosts, the God of Israel, have revealed
in the hearing of Your slave, saying,
'[a]I will build you a house'; therefore
Your slave has found *courage* in his
heart to pray this prayer to You. **28** So
now, O Lord Yahweh, You are God,
and [a]Your words are truth, and You
have [1]promised this good thing to
Your slave. **29** So now, be pleased and
bless the house of Your slave, that it
may be forever before You. For You,
O Lord Yahweh, have spoken; and
[a]with Your blessing may the house
of Your slave be blessed forever."

### *David Strikes Down Nations*

**8** [a]Now it happened afterwards,
that David struck the Philistines
and subdued them; and David took
[1]control of the chief city from the
hand of the Philistines.
**2** [a]He also struck [b]Moab, and mea-
sured them with the line, making

**7:15** [a]1Sa 15:23; 16:14 **7:16** [a]2Sa 7:13; Ps 89:36, 37 [1]Or *remain true* [2]As in Gr and some ancient mss; M.T. *you* **7:18** [a]Ex 3:11; 1Sa 18:18 **7:19** [a]2Sa 7:11-16; 1Chr 17:17 [b]Is 55:8, 9 **7:20** [a]1Sa 16:7; Jn 21:17 **7:21** [a]1Chr 17:19; Eph 4:32 **7:22** [a]Dt 3:24; Ps 48:1; 86:10 [b]Ex 15:11; 1Sa 2:2 [c]Ex 10:2; Ps 44:1 **7:23** [a]Dt 4:32-38 [b]Dt 10:21 [c]Dt 15:15 [d]Dt 9:26 **7:24** [a]Dt 32:6 [b]Ge 17:7, 8; Ex 6:7 **7:26** [a]Ps 72:18, 19; Mt 6:9 [1]Or *slave*, cf. 7:25; see Foreword, "The Terminology of Slave" **7:27** [a]2Sa 7:13 **7:28** [a]Ex 34:6; Jn 17:17 [1]Or *spoken* **7:29** [a]Nu 6:24-26 ◆ **8:1** [a]1Chr 18 [1]Lit *the bridle of the mother city* **8:2** [a]Nu 24:17 [b]1Sa 22:3, 4

them lie down on the ground; and
he measured two lines to put to death
and one full line to keep alive. And
[c]the Moabites became servants to
David, [d]bringing tribute.
**3** Then David struck [a]Hadadezer,
the son of Rehob king of Zobah, as
[b]he went to restore his [1]power at the
[2]River. **4** And David captured from
him 1,700 horsemen and 20,000 foot
soldiers; and David [a]hamstrung all
the chariot horses, but left *enough*
of them for 100 chariots. **5** Then [a]the
Arameans of Damascus came to help
Hadadezer, king of Zobah. And Da-
vid struck down 22,000 Arameans.
**6** Then David placed garrisons among
the Arameans of Damascus; and
[a]the Arameans became servants to
David, bringing tribute. And [b]Yahweh
granted salvation to David wherever
he went. **7** And David took the small
shields of gold which were [1]carried
by the servants of Hadadezer and
brought them to Jerusalem. **8** Also
from [1]Betah and from [a]Berothai,
cities of Hadadezer, King David took
a very large amount of bronze.
**9** Then Toi king of [a]Hamath heard
that David had struck down all the
military force of Hadadezer, **10** so Toi
sent [1]Joram his son to King David to
[2]greet him and to bless him, because
he had fought against Hadadezer and
struck him down; for Hadadezer
[3]had been at war with Toi. And in
[4]Joram's hand were articles of silver,
of gold, and of bronze. **11** King Da-
vid also [a]set these apart as holy to
Yahweh, with the silver and the gold
that he had set apart as holy from all
the nations which he had subdued:
**12** from [1]Aram, [a]Moab, [b]the sons of
Ammon, [c]the Philistines, [d]Amalek,
and from the spoil of Hadadezer, son
of Rehob, king of Zobah.
**13** So [a]David made a name *for
himself* when he returned from
striking down 18,000 [1]Arameans in
[b]the Valley of Salt. **14** Then he placed
garrisons in Edom. In all Edom
he placed garrisons, and [a]all the
Edomites became servants to David.
And [b]Yahweh granted salvation to
David wherever he went.
**15** So David reigned over all Israel;
and David was doing justice and righ-
teousness for all his people. **16** [a]Now
Joab the son of Zeruiah *was* over the
army, and [b]Jehoshaphat the son of
Ahilud *was* [c]recorder; **17** [a]and Zadok
the son of Ahitub and Ahimelech the
son of Abiathar *were* [b]priests, and
Seraiah *was* [c]scribe; **18** [a]and Bena-
iah the son of Jehoiada [1]was over
the [b]Cherethites and the Pelethites;
and the sons of David were [c,2]priests.

### *David's Lovingkindness to Mephibosheth*

**9** Then David said, "Is there yet
[1]anyone left of the house of Saul,
[a]that I may show him lovingkindness
for Jonathan's sake?" **2** Now there was

**8:2** [c]2Sa 8:6; 1Ki 4:21 [d]2Ki 3:4; 17:3 **8:3** [a]1Sa 14:47; 2Sa 10:16, 19 [b]2Sa 10:15-19 [1]Or *monument*; lit *hand* [2]The Euphrates River **8:4** [a]Jos 11:6, 9 **8:5** [a]1Ki 11:23-25 **8:6** [a]2Sa 8:2 [b]2Sa 3:18 **8:7** [1]Lit *on* **8:8** [a]Eze 47:16 [1]In 1Chr 18:8, *Tibhath* **8:9** [a]1Ki 8:65; 2Chr 8:4 **8:10** [1]In 1Chr 18:10, *Hadoram* [2]Lit *ask him of his welfare* [3]Lit *was a man of wars* [4]Lit *his* **8:11** [a]1Ki 7:51 **8:12** [a]2Sa 8:2 [b]2Sa 10:14 [c]2Sa 5:17-25 [d]1Sa 27:8; 30:17-20 [1]Some mss *Edom* **8:13** [a]2Sa 7:9 [b]2Ki 14:7 [1]Some mss *Edom* **8:14** [a]Ge 27:37-40; Nu 24:17, 18 [b]2Sa 3:18; 8:6 **8:16** [a]1Chr 11:6 [b]1Ki 4:3 [c]2Ki 18:18, 37 **8:17** [a]1Chr 6:4-8 [b]1Chr 16:39, 40 [c]2Ki 18:18 **8:18** [a]1Ki 4:4 [b]1Sa 30:14; 2Sa 15:18; 20:7, 23; 1Ki 1:38, 44 [c]1Chr 18:17 [1]Lit *and the Cherethites* [2]Or chiefs over the *priests*; possibly a special office associated with the priests, cf. 1Chr 18:17 ◆ **9:1** [a]1Sa 20:14-17, 42 [1]Lit *he who is*

a servant of the house of Saul whose
name was Ziba, and they called him
to David; and the king said to him,
"Are you [a]Ziba?" And he said, "*I*
*am* your servant." **3** And the king
said, "Is there not yet anyone of the
house of Saul to whom I may show
the [a]lovingkindness of God?" And
Ziba said to the king, "[b]There is still
a son of Jonathan who is crippled
in both feet." **4** So the king said to
him, "Where is he?" And Ziba said
to the king, "Behold, he is [a]in the
house of Machir the son of Ammiel
in Lo-debar." **5** Then King David
sent and took him from the house
of Machir the son of Ammiel, from
Lo-debar. **6** [a]So Mephibosheth, the
son of Jonathan the son of Saul,
came to David and [b]fell on his face
and prostrated himself. And David
said, "Mephibosheth." And he said,
"Here is your servant!" **7** And David
said to him, "Do not fear, for [a]I will
surely show lovingkindness to you
for the sake of your father Jonathan,
and [b]will restore to you all the [1]land
of your [2]grandfather Saul; and [c]you
shall [3]eat at my table continually."
**8** So he prostrated himself and said,
"What is your servant, that you
should regard [a]a dead dog like me?"
**9** Then the king called Saul's young
man Ziba and said to him, "[a]All
that belonged to Saul and to all his
house I have given to your master's
[1]grandson. **10** And you and your sons
and your servants shall cultivate the
land for him, and you shall bring in
*the produce* so that your master's
grandson may have food and eat
of it; nevertheless [a]Mephibosheth
your master's grandson [b]shall [1]eat
at my table continually." Now Ziba
had fifteen sons and twenty ser-
vants. **11** Then Ziba said to the king,
"According [a]to all that my lord the
king commands his servant so your
servant will do." So Mephibosheth
ate at [1]David's table as one of the
king's sons. **12** Now Mephibosheth
had a young son whose name was
Mica. And all who lived in the house
of Ziba were servants to Mephib-
osheth. **13** So Mephibosheth lived in
Jerusalem, for [a]he ate at the king's
table continually. Now [b]he was lame
in both feet.

### *The Ammonites Dishonor David's Men*

**10** [a]Now it happened afterwards,
that [b]the king of the sons of
Ammon died, and Hanun his son
became king in his place. **2** So David
said, "I will show lovingkindness to
Hanun the son of [a]Nahash, just as
his father showed lovingkindness to
me." So David sent to comfort him
concerning his father by the hand
of his servants. And David's servants
came to the land of the sons of Am-
mon. **3** But the princes of the sons
of Ammon said to Hanun their lord,
"In your eyes, is David honoring your
father because he has sent comfort-
ers to you? [a]Has David not sent his
servants to you in order to search the
city, to spy it out and overthrow it?"
**4** So Hanun took David's servants and
[a]shaved off half of their beards, and
[b]cut off their garments in the middle

**9:2** [a]2Sa 16:1-4; 19:17, 29 **9:3** [a]1Sa 20:14 [b]2Sa 4:4 **9:4** [a]2Sa 17:27-29 **9:6** [a]2Sa 16:4; 19:24-30 [b]1Sa 25:23 **9:7** [a]2Sa 9:1, 3 [b]2Sa 12:8 [c]2Sa 19:28; 1Ki 2:7; 2Ki 25:29 [1]Lit *field* [2]Lit *father* [3]Lit *eat bread* **9:8** [a]2Sa 16:9; 1Sa 24:14 **9:9** [a]2Sa 16:4; 19:29 [1]Lit *son* **9:10** [a]2Sa 9:7, 11, 13 [b]2Sa 19:28; 1Ki 2:7 [1]Lit *eat bread* **9:11** [a]2Sa 16:1-4; 19:24-30 [1]Lit *my* **9:13** [a]2Sa 9:7, 11 [b]2Sa 9:3 ◆**10:1** [a]1Chr 19:1-19 [b]1Sa 11:1 **10:2** [a]1Sa 11:1 **10:3** [a]Ge 42:9, 16 **10:4** [a]Is 15:2; Jer 41:5 [b]Is 20:4

as far as their hips, and sent them away. **5** Then they told *it* to David. And he sent to meet them, for the men were greatly dishonored. And the king said, "[1]Stay at Jericho until your beards grow, and *then* return."

**6** Then the sons of Ammon saw that [a]they had become odious to David. So the sons of Ammon sent and [b]hired the Arameans of [c]Beth-rehob and the [d]Arameans of Zobah, 20,000 foot soldiers, and the king of [e]Maacah with 1,000 men, and the men of Tob with 12,000 men. **7** Then David heard *of it* and sent Joab and all the army, the mighty men. **8** And the sons of Ammon came out and arranged *themselves* for battle [a]at the entrance of the gate *of the city*. But the Arameans of Zobah and of Rehob and the men of [b]Tob and Maacah were by themselves in the field.

### *David Defeats Ammon and Aram*

**9** Then Joab saw that [1]the battle was set against him from *the* front and from *the* rear. So he chose from all the choice men of Israel, and they arranged *themselves* to meet the Arameans. **10** But the remainder of the people he put in the hand of Abishai his brother; and he arranged them to meet the sons of Ammon. **11** And he said, "If the Arameans are too strong for me, then you shall save me, but if the sons of Ammon are too strong for you, then I will come to save you. **12** [a]Be strong, and let us show strength for the sake of our people and for the cities of our God; and [b]may Yahweh do what is good in His sight." **13** So Joab and the people who were with him drew near for the battle against the Arameans, and [a]they fled before him. **14** Now the sons of Ammon saw that the Arameans fled. So they *also* fled before Abishai and came into the city. [a]Then Joab returned from *fighting* against the sons of Ammon and came to Jerusalem.

**15** Then the Arameans saw that they had been [1]defeated by Israel. So they gathered themselves together. **16** [a]And Hadadezer sent and brought out the Arameans who were beyond the [1]River, and they came to Helam; and [b]Shobach the commander of the army of Hadadezer [2]led them. **17** And it was told to David, so he gathered all Israel together and crossed the Jordan, and came to Helam. And the Arameans arranged themselves to meet David and fought against him. **18** But the Arameans fled before Israel, and David killed of the Arameans [a]700 charioteers and 40,000 horsemen and struck down Shobach the commander of their army, and he died there. **19** Then all the kings, the servants of Hadadezer, saw that they were [1]defeated by Israel. So [a]they made peace with Israel and served them. And the Arameans were afraid to save the sons of Ammon anymore.

### *David and Bathsheba*

**11** [a]Now it happened [b,1]in the spring, at the time when [2]kings go out *to battle*, that David sent Joab and his servants with him and all

**10:5** [1]Lit *Return to* **10:6** [a]Ge 34:30; 1Sa 27:12 [b]2Sa 8:3, 5; 2Ki 7:6 [c]Jdg 18:28 [d]2Sa 8:3 [e]Dt 3:14 **10:8** [a]1Chr 19:9 [b]Jdg 11:3, 5 **10:9** [1]Lit *the faces of the battle were against* **10:12** [a]Dt 31:6; Jos 1:6; 1Co 16:13 [b]1Sa 3:18 **10:13** [a]1Ki 20:13-21 **10:14** [a]2Sa 11:1 **10:15** [1]Lit *smitten before* **10:16** [a]2Sa 8:3-8 [b]1Chr 19:16 [1]The Euphrates River [2]Lit *before* **10:18** [a]1Chr 19:18 **10:19** [a]2Sa 8:6 [1]Lit *smitten before* ◆ **11:1** [a]1Chr 20:1 [b]2Sa 10:14; 1Ki 20:22, 26 [1]Lit *at the return of the year* [2]As in mss and versions; M.T. *messengers*

Israel, and they destroyed the sons
of Ammon and [c]besieged Rabbah.
But David stayed at Jerusalem.
**2** Now when evening came David
arose from his bed and walked
around on [a]the roof of the king's
house, and from the roof he saw a
woman bathing; and the woman was
very beautiful in appearance. **3** So
David sent and [1]inquired about the
woman. And one said, "Is this not
[a]Bathsheba, the daughter of Eliam,
the wife of [b]Uriah the Hittite?"
**4** Then David sent messengers and
took her, and she came to him, and
[a]he lay with her; [b]and when she had
purified herself from her unclean-
ness, she returned to her house.
**5** And the woman became pregnant;
and she sent and told David, and said,
"[a]I am pregnant."
**6** Then David sent to Joab, *saying,*
"Send me Uriah the Hittite." So Joab
sent Uriah to David. **7** When Uriah
came to him, [a]David asked concerning
the [1]state of Joab and the [1]state of the
people and the [1]state of the war. **8** Then
David said to Uriah, "Go down to your
house, and [a]wash your feet." And Uri-
ah went out of the king's house, and a
present from the king went out after
him. **9** But Uriah lay down [a]at the door
of the king's house with all the servants
of his lord, and did not go down to his
house. **10** Then they told David, saying,
"Uriah did not go down to his house."
And David said to Uriah, "Have you
not come from a journey? Why did you
not go down to your house?" **11** And
Uriah said to David, "[a]The ark and
Israel and Judah are staying in [1]booths,
and my lord Joab and [b]the servants
of my lord are camping in the open
field. Shall I then go to my house to eat
and to drink and to lie with my wife?
By your life and the life of your soul, I
will not do this thing." **12** Then David
said to Uriah, "[a]Stay here today also,
and tomorrow I will send you out."
So Uriah remained in Jerusalem that
day and the [1]next. **13** Now David called
him, and he ate and drank before him,
and he [a]made him drunk; and in the
evening he went out to lie on his bed
[b]with his lord's servants, but he did
not go down to his house.
**14** Now it happened in the morning
that David [a]wrote a letter to Joab and
sent *it* by the hand of Uriah. **15** [a]And
he had written in the letter, saying,
"[1]Place Uriah in the front line of the
[2]fiercest battle and withdraw from
him, [b]so that he may be struck down
and die." **16** So it was as Joab kept
watch on the city, that he put Uriah
at the place where he knew there
*were* valiant men. **17** And the men of
the city went out and fought against
Joab, and some of the people among
David's servants fell; and [a]Uriah the
Hittite also died. **18** Then Joab sent
and told David all the events of the
war. **19** And he commanded the mes-
senger, saying, "When you have fin-
ished telling all the events of the war
to the king, **20** and if it happens that
the king's wrath rises and he says to
you, 'Why did you approach the city
to fight? Did you not know that they
would shoot from the wall? **21** Who
[a]struck down Abimelech the son of
Jerubbesheth? Did not a woman cast

**11:1** [c]2Sa 12:26-29; Jer 49:2, 3; Am 1:14 **11:2** [a]Dt 22:8; 1Sa 9:25; Mt 24:17; Ac 10:9 **11:3** [a]1Chr 3:5 [b]2Sa 23:39 [1]Or *sought out* **11:4** [a]Ps 51: title; Jas 1:14, 15 [b]Lv 12:2-5; 15:18-28; 18:19 **11:5** [a]Lv 20:10; Dt 22:22 **11:7** [a]Ge 37:14; 1Sa 17:22 [1]Lit *peace* **11:8** [a]Ge 43:24; Lk 7:44 **11:9** [a]1Ki 14:27, 28 **11:11** [a]2Sa 7:2, 6 [b]2Sa 20:6 [1]Temporary shelters **11:12** [a]Job 20:12-14 [1]Lit *morrow* **11:13** [a]Pr 20:1; 23:29-35 [b]2Sa 11:9 **11:14** [a]1Ki 21:8-10 **11:15** [a]Ecc 8:11; Jer 17:9 [b]2Sa 12:9 [1]Lit *Give* [2]Lit *strong* **11:17** [a]2Sa 11:21 **11:21** [a]Jdg 9:50-54

an upper millstone on him from the
wall so he died at Thebez? Why did
you approach the wall?'—then you
shall say, 'Your servant Uriah the
Hittite is dead also.'"
**22** So the messenger went and came
and told David all that Joab had sent
him *to tell.* **23** And the messenger said
to David, "The men prevailed against
us and came out against us in the
field, but we [1]pressed them as far as
the entrance of the gate. **24** And the
archers shot at your servants from the
wall; so some of the king's servants
died, and your servant Uriah the
Hittite also died." **25** Then David said
to the messenger, "Thus you shall say
to Joab, 'Do not let this thing be evil in
your sight, for the sword devours one
as well as another; make your battle
against the city stronger and [1]tear it
down'; and *so* strengthen him."
**26** Then the wife of Uriah heard
that Uriah her husband had died,
so [a]she lamented over her husband.
**27** Then the *time of* mourning passed
by, and David sent and gathered her
to his house and [a]she became his
wife; then she bore him a son. But
[b]the thing that David had done was
evil in the sight of Yahweh.

### *Yahweh Sends Nathan to David*

**12** Then Yahweh sent [a]Nathan to
David. And [b]he came to him
and [1]said,

"There were two men
 in one city, the one rich
 and the other poor.
**2** "The rich man had a great
 many flocks and herds.
**3** "But the poor man had nothing
 except [a]one little ewe lamb
Which he bought
 and nourished;
And it grew up together
 with him and his children.
It would eat his morsel
 *of bread* and drink of his
 cup and lie in his bosom,
And was like a daughter
 to him.
**4** "Now a visitor came
 to the rich man,
And he [1]was unwilling
 to take from his own
 flock or his own herd,
To prepare for the traveler
 who had come to him;
Rather he took the poor
 man's ewe lamb and
 prepared it for the man
 who had come to him."

**5** Then David's anger burned greatly
against the man, and he said to
Nathan, "As Yahweh lives, surely the
man who has done this [a,1]deserves to
die. **6** And he must make restitution
for the lamb [a]fourfold, because he did
this thing and had no compassion."
**7** Nathan then said to David, "[a]You
are the man! Thus says Yahweh, the
God of Israel, '[b]It is I who anointed
you king over Israel and it is I who
delivered you from the hand of Saul.
**8** I also gave you [a]your master's house
and your master's wives into your
[1]care, and I gave you the house of
Israel and Judah; and if *that had
been* too little, I would have added
to you many more things like these!
**9** Why [a]have you despised the word

---

**11:23** [1]Lit *were upon* **11:25** [1]Lit *pull* **11:26** [a]Ge 50:10; Dt 34:8; 1Sa 31:13 **11:27** [a]2Sa 12:9 [b]Ps 51:4, 5
◆ **12:1** [a]2Sa 7:2, 4, 17 [b]Ps 51: title [1]Lit *said to him* **12:3** [a]2Sa 11:3 **12:4** [1]Lit *spared* **12:5** [a]1Sa 26:16
[1]Lit *is a son of death* **12:6** [a]Ex 22:1; Lk 19:8 **12:7** [a]1Ki 20:42 [b]1Sa 16:13 **12:8** [a]2Sa 9:7 [1]Lit *bosom*
**12:9** [a]1Sa 15:23, 26

of Yahweh by doing evil in His sight?
[b]You have struck down Uriah the
Hittite with the sword, [c]have taken
his wife to be your wife, and have
killed him with the sword of the
sons of Ammon. **10** So now, [a]the
sword shall never depart from your
house, because you have despised
Me and have taken the wife of Uriah
the Hittite to be your wife.' **11** Thus
says Yahweh, 'Behold, I will raise
up evil against you from your own
household; [a]I will even take your
wives from before your sight and give
*them* to your companion, and he will
lie with your wives in the sight of this
sun. **12** Indeed [a]you did it secretly,
but [b]I will do this thing before all
Israel, and before the sun.'" **13** Then
David said to Nathan, "[a]I have sinned
against Yahweh." And Nathan said
to David, "Yahweh also has [b,1]taken
away your sin; you shall not die.
**14** However, because by this deed you
have [a]given occasion to the enemies
of Yahweh to blaspheme, the son also
that is born to you shall surely die."
**15** And Nathan went to his house.

### *David's Child Dies*

Then Yahweh smote the child that
Uriah's wife bore to David, so that
he was *very* sick. **16** David therefore
sought God about the boy; and Da-
vid [a]fasted and went and [b]spent the
night lying on the ground. **17** [a]And
the elders of his household stood
beside him in order to raise him up
from the ground, but he was un-
willing and would not eat food with
*them*. **18** Then it happened on the
seventh day that the child died. And
the servants of David were afraid to
tell him that the child was dead, for
they said, "Behold, while the child
was *still* alive, we spoke to him and
he did not listen to our voice. How
then can we tell him that the child
has died? He might do *himself* harm!"
**19** And David saw that his servants
were whispering together, so David
discerned that the child had died;
so David said to his servants, "Has
the child died?" And they said, "He
has died." **20** So David arose from the
ground, [a]washed, anointed *himself*,
and changed his clothes; and he
came into the house of Yahweh and
[b]worshiped. Then he came to his
own house, and he asked, and they
set food before him, and he ate.

**21** Then his servants said to him,
"What is this thing that you have
done? [1]While the child was alive,
you fasted and wept; but when the
child died, you arose and ate food."
**22** Then he said, "While the child was
*still* alive, [a]I fasted and wept; for I
said, '[b]Who knows, Yahweh may be
gracious to me, that the child may
live.' **23** But now he has died; why
should I fast? Can I bring him back
again? [a]I will go to him, but [b]he will
not return to me."

### *Solomon Is Born*

**24** Then David comforted his wife
Bathsheba, and went in to her and lay
with her; and she gave birth to a son,
and [a,1]he named him Solomon. Now
Yahweh loved him **25** and sent *word*
by the hand of Nathan the prophet,

---

**12:9** [b]2Sa 11:14-17 [c]2Sa 11:27 **12:10** [a]2Sa 13:28; 18:14; 1Ki 2:25 **12:11** [a]Dt 28:30; 2Sa 16:21, 22
**12:12** [a]2Sa 11:4-15 [b]2Sa 16:22 **12:13** [a]1Sa 15:24, 30; 2Sa 24:10; Lk 18:13 [b]Lv 20:10; 24:17; Pr 28:13; Mic 7:18
[1]Lit *caused your sin to pass away* **12:14** [a]Is 52:5; Ro 2:24 **12:16** [a]Ne 1:4 [b]2Sa 13:31 **12:17** [a]Ge 24:2
**12:20** [a]Ru 3:3; Mt 6:17 [b]Ps 95:6-8; 103:1, 8-17; Pr 3:7 **12:21** [1]Lit *On account of* **12:22** [a]Is 38:1-3
[b]Jon 3:9 **12:23** [a]Ge 37:35 [b]Job 7:8-10 **12:24** [a]1Chr 22:9; Mt 1:6 [1]Some mss *she*

and he named him [1]Jedidiah for the
sake of Yahweh.

### *Joab Fights Ammon*

**26** [a]Then Joab fought against [b]Rabbah
of the sons of Ammon and captured
the royal city. **27** And Joab sent mes-
sengers to David and said, "I have
fought against Rabbah, I have even
captured the city of waters. **28** So
now, gather the rest of the people
together and camp against the city
and capture it, lest I capture the city
myself and it be named after me."
**29** So David gathered all the people
and went to Rabbah, fought against it
and captured it. **30** Then [a]he took the
crown of [1]their king from his head;
and its weight *was* a [2]talent of gold,
and *in it* [3]*was* a precious stone; and
it was *placed* on David's head. And he
brought out the spoil of the city *in* a
very great amount. **31** He also brought
out the people who were in it and
[a]set *them* up with saws, sharp iron
instruments, and iron axes, and made
them pass through the brickkiln. And
thus he used to do to all the cities of
the sons of Ammon. Then David and
all the people returned *to* Jerusalem.

### *Amnon Violates Tamar*

**13** Now it happened afterwards
that [a]Absalom the son of David
had a beautiful sister whose name
was [b]Tamar, and [c]Amnon the son of
David loved her. **2** And Amnon was so
distressed because of his sister Tamar
that he made himself ill, for she was
a virgin. So it was hard in Amnon's
sight to do anything to her. **3** But
Amnon had a friend whose name
was Jonadab, the son of [a,1]Shimeah,
David's brother; and Jonadab was a
very [2]shrewd man. **4** And he said to
him, "O son of the king, why are you
so depressed morning after morning?
Will you not tell me?" Then Amnon
said to him, "I am in love with Tamar,
the sister of my brother Absalom."
**5** Jonadab then said to him, "Lie down
on your bed and pretend to be ill; and
your father will come to see you, and
you will say to him, 'Please let my
sister Tamar come and give me *some*
food to eat, and let her prepare the
food in my sight, that I may see *it* and
eat from her hand.'" **6** So Amnon lay
down and pretended to be ill; and the
king came to see him, and Amnon
said to the king, "Please let my sister
Tamar come and [a]make me a couple
of cakes in my sight, that I may eat
from her hand."

**7** Then David sent to the house
for Tamar, saying, "Go now to your
brother Amnon's house, and prepare
food for him." **8** So Tamar went to her
brother Amnon's house, and he was
lying down. And she took dough,
kneaded *it*, made cakes in his sight,
and baked the cakes. **9** And she took
the pan and [1]dished *them* out before
him, but he refused to eat. And Am-
non said, "[a]Have everyone go out
from me." So everyone went out from
him. **10** Then Amnon said to Tamar,
"Bring the food into the [1]bedroom,
that I may eat from your hand." So
Tamar took the cakes which she
had made and brought them into
the bedroom to her brother Amnon.

---

**12:25** [1]Lit *beloved of Yahweh* **12:26** [a]1Chr 20:1-3 [b]Dt 3:11 **12:30** [a]1Chr 20:2 [1]Or *Malcam*, cf. Zep 1:5 [2]A talent was approx. 75 lb. or 34 kg [3]Or were *precious stones* **12:31** [a]1Chr 20:3; Heb 11:37
◆**13:1** [a]2Sa 3:2, 3; 1Chr 3:2 [b]1Chr 3:9 [c]2Sa 3:2 **13:3** [a]1Sa 16:9 [1]In 1Sa 16:9, *Shammah*; in 1Chr 2:13, *Shimea* [2]Lit *wise* **13:6** [a]Ge 18:6 **13:9** [a]Ge 45:1 [1]Lit *poured* **13:10** [1]Or *inner room*

**11** Then she brought *them* near to him
to eat, but he [a]took hold of her and
said to her, "Come, lie with me, my
sister." **12** But she said to him, "No, my
brother, do not violate me, for [a]such
a thing is not done in Israel; do not do
this [b]disgraceful thing! **13** As for me,
where could I [1]get rid of my reproach?
And as for you, you will be like one
of the wicked fools in Israel. So now,
please speak to the king, for [a]he will
not withhold me from you." **14** But he
was not willing to listen to her voice.
Now he was stronger than she, so he
[a]violated her and lay with her.

**15** Then Amnon hated her with a
very great hatred; for the hatred with
which he hated her was greater than
the love with which he had loved her.
And Amnon said to her, "Get up, go
away!" **16** But she said to him, "No,
because this wrong in sending me
away is greater than the other that
you have done to me!" But he was
not willing to listen to her. **17** Then he
called his young man who attended
him and said, "Now cast this woman
out of my *presence*, and lock the door
behind her." **18** Now she had on [a]a
[1]long-sleeved garment; for in this
manner the virgin daughters of the
king dressed themselves in robes.
Then his attendant took her out and
locked the door behind her. **19** [a]Then
Tamar put [1]ashes on her head and
[b]tore her [2]long-sleeved garment
which *was* on her; and [c]she put her
hand on her head and went away,
crying aloud as she went.

**20** *So Absalom* her brother said
to her, "Has Amnon your brother
been with you? But now keep silent,
my sister, he is your brother; do not
take this matter to heart." So Tamar
remained and was desolate in her
brother Absalom's house. **21** Now
when King David heard of all these
matters, he was very angry. **22** But
Absalom did not speak to Amnon
[a]either good or bad; for [b]Absalom
hated Amnon because he had violated his sister Tamar.

**23** Now it happened after two full
years that Absalom [a]had sheepshearers in Baal-hazor, which is near
Ephraim, and Absalom invited all
the king's sons.

### *Absalom Strikes Down Amnon*

**24** And Absalom came to the king
and said, "Behold now, your servant
has sheepshearers; please let the
king and his servants go with your
servant." **25** But the king said to Absalom, "No, my son, we should not
all go, for we will be burdensome to
you." Although he [1]urged him, he
was not willing to go, but blessed
him. **26** Then [a]Absalom said, "If not,
please let my brother Amnon go with
us." And the king said to him, "Why
should he go with you?" **27** But Absalom [1]urged him, so he sent Amnon
and all the king's sons with him.

**28** Then Absalom commanded his
young men, saying, "See now, [a]when
Amnon's heart is merry with wine,
and when I say to you, 'Strike Amnon,' then put him to death. Do not
fear; have not I myself commanded
you? Be strong and be [1]valiant."
**29** Thus the young men of Absalom

**13:11** [a]Ge 39:12 **13:12** [a]Lv 20:17 [b]Jdg 19:23; 20:6 **13:13** [a]Ge 20:12 [1]Lit *cause to go* **13:14** [a]Lv 18:9; Dt 22:25; 27:22; 2Sa 12:11 **13:18** [a]Ge 37:3, 23 [1]Lit *a varicolored tunic* **13:19** [a]1Sa 4:12; Es 4:1 [b]Ge 37:29; 2Sa 1:11 [c]Jer 2:37 [1]Or *dust* [2]Lit *varicolored tunic* **13:22** [a]Ge 31:24 [b]Lv 19:17; 1Jn 2:9, 11; 3:10, 12, 15 **13:23** [a]1Sa 25:7 **13:25** [1]Lit *broke through* **13:26** [a]2Sa 3:27; 11:13-15 **13:27** [1]Lit *broke through* **13:28** [a]Jdg 19:6, 9, 22; 1Sa 25:36-38 [1]Lit *sons of valor*

did to Amnon just as Absalom had
commanded. Then all the king's sons
arose and each mounted [a]his mule
and fled.

**30** Now it was while they were
on the way that the report came to
David, saying, "Absalom has struck
down all the king's sons, and not
one of them is left." **31** Then the king
arose, [a]tore his clothes and [b]lay on
the ground; and all his servants were
standing by with clothes torn. **32** [a]But
Jonadab, the son of Shimeah, David's
brother, answered and said, "Do not
let my lord [1]suppose they have put to
death all the young men, the king's
sons, for Amnon alone has died;
because by the [2]intent of Absalom
this has been set since the day that he
violated his sister Tamar. **33** So now,
do not let my lord the king [a]take the
report to [1]heart, saying, 'all the king's
sons have died,' for only Amnon has
died."

**34** Then [a]Absalom fled. And [b]the
young man who was the watchman
raised his eyes and looked, and
behold, many people were coming
from the road behind him by the
side of the mountain. **35** And Jonadab
said to the king, "Behold, the king's
sons have come; according to your
servant's word, so it happened." **36** As
soon as he had finished speaking,
behold, the king's sons came and
lifted their voices and wept; and also
the king and all his servants wept
[1]very bitterly.

**37** Now [a]Absalom had fled and
went to [b]Talmai the son of Ammi-
hud, the king of [c]Geshur. And *David*
mourned for his son every day. **38** [a]So
Absalom had fled and gone to Geshur,
and was there three years. **39** *And the
heart of* King David was consumed
with going out to Absalom; for [a]he
was comforted concerning Amnon,
since he had died.

### *The Woman of Tekoa*

**14** Now Joab the son of Zeruiah
knew that [a]the king's heart
*was inclined* toward Absalom. **2** So
Joab sent to [a]Tekoa and [1]brought a
wise woman from there and said to
her, "Please pretend to be a mourner,
and put on mourning garments now,
and do not [b]anoint yourself with oil,
but be like a woman who has been
mourning for the dead many days;
**3** then you shall go to the king and
speak to him in this manner." So Joab
put [a]the words in her mouth.

**4** So the woman of Tekoa [1]spoke to
the king, and she fell on her [2]face to
the ground and [a]prostrated herself
and said, "[b]Save, O king." **5** And
the king said to her, "What is your
trouble?" And she [1]answered, "Truly
I am a widow; my husband has died.
**6** And your servant-woman had two
sons, but the two of them struggled
together in the field, and there was
no one to deliver between them, so
one struck the other and put him
to death. **7** And behold, [a]the whole
family has risen against your servant-
woman, and they say, 'Hand over the
one who struck his brother, that we
may put him to death for the life of
his brother whom he killed, [b]and
destroy the heir also.' Thus they will

---

**13:29** [a]2Sa 18:9; 1Ki 1:33, 38 **13:31** [a]2Sa 1:11 [b]2Sa 12:16 **13:32** [a]2Sa 13:3-5 [1]Lit *say* [2]Lit *mouth*
**13:33** [a]2Sa 19:19 [1]Lit *his heart* **13:34** [a]2Sa 13:37, 38 [b]2Sa 18:24 **13:36** [1]Lit *with a very great weeping*
**13:37** [a]2Sa 13:34 [b]2Sa 3:3 [c]2Sa 14:23, 32 **13:38** [a]2Sa 13:34 **13:39** [a]2Sa 12:19-23 ◆**14:1** [a]2Sa 13:39
**14:2** [a]2Sa 23:26; 2Chr 11:6; Am 1:1 [b]2Sa 12:20 [1]Lit *took* **14:3** [a]2Sa 14:19 **14:4** [a]1Sa 25:23 [b]2Ki 6:26-28
[1]Many mss and ancient versions *came* [2]Lit *nose* **14:5** [1]Lit *said* **14:7** [a]Nu 35:19; Dt 19:12, 13 [b]Mt 21:38

extinguish my coal which remains,
so as to [1]leave my husband neither
name nor remnant on the face of the
earth."

**8** Then the king said to the woman,
"Go to your house, and I will give a
command concerning you." **9** And
the woman of Tekoa said to the king,
"O my lord, the king, [a]the iniquity
is on me and my father's house, but
[b]the king and his throne are guilt-
less." **10** So the king said, "Whoever
speaks to you, bring him to me, and
he will not touch you anymore."
**11** Then she said, "Please let the king
remember Yahweh your God, [a]*so that*
the avenger of blood will not contin-
ue to bring about ruin, so that they
would not destroy my son." And he
said, "[b]As Yahweh lives, not one hair
of your son shall fall to the ground."

**12** Then the woman said, "Please
let your servant-woman speak a word
to my lord the king." And he said,
"Speak." **13** Then the woman said,
"[a]Why then have you thought up
such a thing against the people of
God? For in speaking this word the
king is as one who is guilty, *in that*
the king does not bring back [b]his
banished one. **14** For [a]we will surely
die and are [b]like water spilled on the
ground which cannot be gathered up
again. Yet God does not take away
life, but thinks up [1]ways so that [c]the
banished one will not be cast out
from him. **15** So now, [1]the reason I
have come to speak this word to my
lord the king is that the people have
made me afraid; so your servant-
woman said, 'Let me now speak to the
king, perhaps the king will perform
the word of his maidservant. **16** For
the king will listen [1]and deliver his
maidservant from the [2]hand of the
man who would destroy [3]both me
and my son from [a]the inheritance
of God.' **17** Then your servant-woman
said, 'Please let the word of my lord
the king be a resting place, for as [a]the
angel of God, so is my lord the king
to listen *with discernment* through
the good and evil. And may Yahweh
your God be with you.'"

**18** Then the king answered and
said to the woman, "Please do not
hide anything from me that I am
about to ask you." And the woman
said, "Let my lord the king please
speak." **19** So the king said, "Is the
hand of Joab with you in all this?"
And the woman answered and said,
"As your soul lives, my lord the king,
no one can turn to the right or to the
left from anything that my lord the
king has spoken. Indeed, it was [a]your
servant Joab who commanded me,
and it was he who put all these words
in the mouth of your servant-woman;
**20** in order to change the appearance
of things your servant Joab has done
this thing. But my lord is wise, [a]like
the wisdom of the angel of God, to
know all that is in the earth."

### *David Brings Back Absalom*

**21** Then the king said to Joab, "Be-
hold now, [a]I have done this thing;
go therefore, bring back the young
man Absalom." **22** And Joab fell on his
face to the ground, prostrated him-
self and blessed the king; then Joab

**14:7** [1]Lit *set* **14:9** [a]Ge 43:9; 1Sa 25:24 [b]1Ki 2:33 **14:11** [a]Nu 35:19, 21; Dt 19:4-10 [b]1Sa 14:45; 1Ki 1:52; Mt 10:30 **14:13** [a]2Sa 12:7; 1Ki 20:40-42 [b]2Sa 13:37, 38 **14:14** [a]Job 30:23; 34:15; Heb 9:27 [b]Ps 58:7 [c]Nu 35:15, 25, 28 [1]Lit *devices* **14:15** [1]Lit *that* **14:16** [a]Dt 32:9; 1Sa 26:19 [1]Lit *to* [2]Lit *palm* [3]Lit *together* **14:17** [a]1Sa 29:9; 2Sa 14:20; 19:27 **14:19** [a]2Sa 14:3 **14:20** [a]2Sa 14:17; 19:27 **14:21** [a]2Sa 14:11

said, "Today your servant knows that
I have found favor in your sight, O my
lord, the king, in that the king has
performed the word of his servant."
**23** So Joab arose and went to [a]Geshur
and brought Absalom to Jerusalem.
**24** However the king said, "Let him
turn to [a]his own house, and let him
not see my face." So Absalom turned
to his own house and did not see the
king's face.

**25** Now in all Israel was no one
as handsome as Absalom, so highly
praised; [a]from the sole of his foot
to the top of his head there was no
defect in him. **26** When he [a]shaved
the hair of his head (and it was at the
end of every year that he shaved *it*,
for it was heavy on him so he shaved
it), he weighed the hair of his head
at [1]200 shekels by the king's weight.
**27** [a]And to Absalom there were born
three sons, and one daughter whose
name was [b]Tamar; she was a woman
of beautiful appearance.

**28** Now Absalom lived two full
years in Jerusalem, [a]and did not see
the king's face. **29** Then Absalom sent
for Joab, to send him to the king, but
he was not willing to come to him. So
he sent again a second time, but he
was not willing to come. **30** Therefore
he said to his servants, "See, [a]Joab's
portion *of land* is next to mine, and
he has barley there; go and set it
on fire." So Absalom's servants set
the portion *of land* on fire. **31** Then
Joab arose, came to Absalom at his
house and said to him, "Why have
your servants set my portion *of land*
on fire?" **32** And Absalom [1]answered
Joab, "Behold, I sent for you, saying,
'Come here, that I may send you to
the king, to say, "Why have I come
from Geshur? It would be better
for me still to be there."' So now,
let me see the king's face, [a]and if
there is iniquity in me, let him put
me to death." **33** So Joab came to the
king and told him, and he called for
Absalom. Thus he came to the king
and prostrated himself on his [1]face to
the ground before the king, and [a]the
king kissed Absalom.

### *Absalom's Conspiracy*

**15** Now it happened afterwards,
that [a]Absalom prepared for
himself a chariot and horses and fifty
men as runners before him. **2** And Ab-
salom used to rise early and [a]stand
beside the way to the gate; and when
any man had a case to come to the king
for judgment, Absalom would call to
him and say, "From what city are you?"
And he would say, "Your servant is
from one of the tribes of Israel." **3** Then
Absalom would say to him, "See, [a]your
words are good and right, but no man
listens to you on the part of the king."
**4** Then Absalom would say, "[a]Oh that
one would appoint me judge in the
land, then every man who has any
case or judgment could come to me
and I would justify him." **5** And when
a man came near to prostrate himself
before him, he would send forth his
hand and take hold of him and [a]kiss
him. **6** In this manner Absalom dealt
with all Israel who came to the king for
judgment; [a]so Absalom stole away the
hearts of the men of Israel.

---

**14:23** [a]Dt 3:14; 2Sa 13:37, 38 **14:24** [a]2Sa 13:20 **14:25** [a]Dt 28:35; Job 2:7; Is 1:6 **14:26** [a]Eze 44:20 [1]Approx. 5 lb. or 2.2 kg, a shekel was approx. 0.4 oz. or 11 gm **14:27** [a]2Sa 18:18 [b]2Sa 13:1 **14:28** [a]2Sa 14:24 **14:30** [a]Jdg 15:3-5 **14:32** [a]1Sa 20:8; Pr 28:13 [1]Lit *said to* **14:33** [a]Ge 33:4; Lk 15:20 [1]Lit *nose* ◆ **15:1** [a]1Ki 1:5 **15:2** [a]Ru 4:1; 2Sa 19:8 **15:3** [a]Pr 12:2 **15:4** [a]Jdg 9:29 **15:5** [a]2Sa 14:33; 20:9 **15:6** [a]Ro 16:18

**7** Now it happened at the end
of [1]forty years that Absalom said
to the king, "Please let me go and
pay my vow which I have vowed
to Yahweh, in [a]Hebron. **8** For your
servant [a]vowed a vow while I was
living at Geshur in Aram, saying,
'[b]If Yahweh shall indeed bring me
back to Jerusalem, then I will serve
Yahweh.'" **9** And the king said to him,
"Go in peace." So he arose and went
to Hebron. **10** Then Absalom sent
spies throughout all the tribes of Is-
rael, saying, "As soon as you hear the
sound of the trumpet, then you shall
say, '[a]Absalom is king in Hebron.'"
**11** Now two hundred men went with
Absalom from Jerusalem, [a]who were
invited and [b]went [1]innocently, and
they did not know anything. **12** And
Absalom sent for [a]Ahithophel the
Gilonite, David's counselor, from his
city [b]Giloh, while he was offering the
sacrifices. And the conspiracy was
strong, for [c]the people increased
continually with Absalom.

### *David Flees Jerusalem*

**13** Then an informant came to David,
saying, "[a]The hearts of the men of
Israel [1]have followed Absalom." **14** So
David said to all his servants who
were with him at Jerusalem, "[a]Arise
and let us flee, for *otherwise* there will
be no escape for us from Absalom. Go
in haste, lest he overtake us hastily
and drive calamity on us and strike
the city with the edge of the sword."
**15** Then the king's servants said to
the king, "Behold, your servants *are*
*ready to do* whatever my lord the king
chooses." **16** So the king went out and
all his household [1]with him. But [a]the
king left ten concubines to keep the
house. **17** And the king went out and
all the people [1]with him, and they
stopped at the last house. **18** Now all
his servants passed on beside him,
[a]all the Cherethites, all the Pelethites,
and all the Gittites, [b]six hundred men
who had come [1]with him from Gath,
passed on before the king.

**19** Then the king said to [a]Ittai the
Gittite, "Why will you also go with
us? Return and remain with the
king, for you are a foreigner and also
an exile; *return* to your own place.
**20** You came *only* yesterday, and shall
I today make you wander with us,
going about, while [a]I go where I go?
Return and cause your brothers to
return; [b]lovingkindness and [1]truth
be with you." **21** But Ittai answered
the king and said, "As Yahweh lives,
and as my lord the king lives, surely
[a]wherever my lord the king may be,
whether for death or for life, there
also your servant will be." **22** So David
said to Ittai, "Go and pass over." So
Ittai the Gittite passed over with all
his men and all the little ones who
*were* with him. **23** While all the coun-
try was weeping with a loud voice,
all the people passed over. The king
also passed over [a]the brook Kidron,
and all the people passed over toward
[b]the way of the wilderness.

**24** Now behold, [a]Zadok also *came*,
and all the Levites with him [b]carry-
ing the ark of the covenant of God.

---

**15:7** [a]2Sa 3:2, 3 [1]Some ancient versions *four* **15:8** [a]2Sa 13:37, 38 [b]Ge 28:20, 21 **15:10** [a]1Ki 1:34; 2Ki 9:13 **15:11** [a]1Sa 9:13 [b]1Sa 22:15 [1]Lit *in their integrity* **15:12** [a]2Sa 15:31 [b]Jos 15:51 [c]Ps 3:1 **15:13** [a]Jdg 9:3; 2Sa 15:6 [1]Lit *are after* **15:14** [a]2Sa 12:11; Ps 3: title **15:16** [a]2Sa 16:21, 22 [1]Lit *at his feet* **15:17** [1]Lit *at his feet* **15:18** [a]2Sa 8:18 [b]1Sa 23:13; 25:13; 30:1, 9 [1]Lit *at his feet* **15:19** [a]2Sa 18:2 **15:20** [a]1Sa 23:13 [b]2Sa 2:6 [1]Or *faithfulness* **15:21** [a]Ru 1:16, 17; Pr 17:17 **15:23** [a]1Ki 15:13; 2Chr 29:16 [b]2Sa 15:28; 16:2 **15:24** [a]2Sa 8:17; 20:25 [b]Nu 4:15; 1Sa 4:4, 5

And they set down the ark of God, and [c]Abiathar came up until all the people had finished passing from the city. **25** Then the king said to Zadok, "Return the ark of God to the city. If I find favor in the sight of Yahweh, then [a]He will cause me to return and show me both it and [b]His habitation. **26** But if He should say thus, '[a]I have no delight in you,' behold, here I am, [b]let Him do to me as seems good in His sight." **27** The king said also to Zadok the priest, "Are you *not* [a]a seer? Return to the city in peace and your [b]two sons with you, your son Ahimaaz and Jonathan the son of Abiathar. **28** See, I am going to wait [a]at the fords of the wilderness until word comes from you to inform me." **29** So Zadok and Abiathar returned the ark of God to Jerusalem and remained there.

**30** But David went up the ascent of the *Mount of* Olives, and wept as he went, and [a]his head was covered and he was walking [b]barefoot. And all the people who were with him each covered his head and went up weeping as they went. **31** Now David informed *them*, saying, "[a]Ahithophel is among the conspirators with Absalom." And David said, "O Yahweh, I pray, [b]make the counsel of Ahithophel foolishness."

**32** Then it happened that as David was coming to the summit, where he used to worship God, that behold, Hushai the [a]Archite met him with his [1]coat torn and [2]dust on his head. **33** And David said to him, "If you pass over with me, then you will be [a]a burden to me. **34** But if you return to the city, and [a]say to Absalom, 'I will be your servant, O king; as I have been your father's servant in time past, so I will now be your servant,' then you can thwart the counsel of Ahithophel for me. **35** Are not Zadok and Abiathar the priests with you there? So it shall be that [a]whatever you hear from the king's house, you shall inform Zadok and Abiathar the priests. **36** Behold, [a]their two sons are with them there, Ahimaaz, Zadok's son and Jonathan, Abiathar's son; and [b]by their hand you shall send me everything that you hear." **37** So Hushai, [a]David's friend, came into the city, and [b]Absalom came into Jerusalem.

### *Ziba Meets David*

**16** Now David had passed [a]a little beyond the summit, and behold, [b]Ziba the young man of Mephibosheth met him [c]with a couple of saddled donkeys, and on them *were* two hundred loaves of bread, one hundred clusters of raisins, one hundred summer fruits, and a jug of wine. **2** And the king said to Ziba, "Why do you have these?" And Ziba said, "[a]The donkeys are for the king's household to ride, and the bread and summer fruit for the young men to eat, and the wine, [b]for whoever is faint in the wilderness to drink." **3** Then the king said, "And where is [a]your master's son?" And [b]Ziba said to the king, "Behold, he is staying

**15:24** [c]1Sa 22:20 **15:25** [a]Ps 43:3 [b]Ex 15:13; Jer 25:30 **15:26** [a]2Sa 11:27; 1Chr 21:7 [b]1Sa 3:18
**15:27** [a]1Sa 9:6-9 [b]2Sa 17:17 **15:28** [a]Jos 5:10; 2Sa 17:16 **15:30** [a]Es 6:12; Eze 24:17, 23 [b]Is 20:2-4
**15:31** [a]2Sa 15:12 [b]2Sa 16:23; 17:14, 23 **15:32** [a]Jos 16:2 [1]Or *tunic* [2]Lit *ground* **15:33** [a]2Sa 19:35
**15:34** [a]2Sa 16:19 **15:35** [a]2Sa 17:15, 16 **15:36** [a]2Sa 15:27 [b]2Sa 17:17 **15:37** [a]2Sa 16:16; 1Chr 27:33
[b]2Sa 16:15 ◆ **16:1** [a]2Sa 15:32 [b]2Sa 9:2-13 [c]1Sa 25:18 **16:2** [a]Jdg 10:4 [b]2Sa 17:29 **16:3** [a]2Sa 9:9, 10
[b]2Sa 19:26, 27

in Jerusalem, for he said, 'Today
the house of Israel will return the
kingdom of my father to me.'" 4 So
the king said to Ziba, "Behold, all that
belongs to Mephibosheth is yours."
And Ziba said, "I prostrate myself;
let me find favor in your sight, O my
lord, the king!"

### *Shimei Curses David*

5 And King David came to [a]Bahurim,
and behold, there came out from
there a man of the family of the
house of Saul [b]whose name was
Shimei, the son of Gera; he came out
[c]cursing continually as he came. 6 He
also threw stones at David and at all
the servants of King David; and all
the people and all the mighty men
were at his right hand and at his
left. 7 And thus Shimei said when
he cursed, "Get out, get out, [a]you
man of bloodshed, and vile fellow!
8 [a]Yahweh has returned upon you all
[b]the bloodshed of the house of Saul,
in whose place you have reigned; and
Yahweh has given the kingdom into
the hand of your son Absalom. And
behold, you are *taken* in your own
evil, for you are a man of bloodshed!"
9 Then [a]Abishai the son of Zeruiah
said to the king, "Why should [b]this
dead dog [c]curse my lord the king?
Let me pass over now and remove his
head." 10 But the king said, "[a]What
have I to do with you, O sons of
Zeruiah? [b]If he curses, and if Yahweh
has told him, 'Curse David,' [c]then
who shall say, 'Why have you done
so?'" 11 Then David said to Abishai
and to all his servants, "Behold, [a]my
son who came forth from my body
seeks my life; how much more now
this Benjamite? Let him alone and
let him curse, [b]for Yahweh has told
him. 12 Perhaps Yahweh will look on
my affliction and [a,1]return good to
me instead of his cursing this day."
13 So David and his men went on the
way; and Shimei went along on the
hillside parallel with him and as he
went he cursed and cast stones and
threw dust at him. 14 Then the king
and all the people who were with
him arrived weary and he refreshed
himself there.

### *Absalom Enters Jerusalem*

15 [a]Now Absalom and all the peo-
ple, the men of Israel, had entered
Jerusalem, and Ahithophel with
him. 16 And it happened that when
[a]Hushai the Archite, David's friend,
came to Absalom, that [b]Hushai said
to Absalom, "[c]*Long* live the king!
*Long* live the king!" 17 And Absalom
said to Hushai, "Is this your loving-
kindness to your friend? [a]Why did
you not go with your friend?" 18 Then
Hushai said to Absalom, "No! For
whom Yahweh, this people, and all
the men of Israel have chosen, his I
will be, and with him I will remain.
19 Besides, [a]whom should I serve?
*Should I* not *serve* in the presence
of his son? As I have served in your
father's presence, so I will be in your
presence."
20 Then Absalom said to Ahitho-
phel, "Give your advice. What shall
we do?" 21 And Ahithophel said to
Absalom, "[a]Go in to your father's

**16:5** [a]2Sa 3:16; 17:18 [b]2Sa 19:16-23; 1Ki 2:8, 9, 44 [c]Ex 22:28; 1Sa 17:43 **16:7** [a]2Sa 12:9 **16:8** [a]2Sa 21:1-9 [b]2Sa 1:16; 3:28, 29; 4:11, 12 **16:9** [a]1Sa 26:8; 2Sa 19:21; Lk 9:54 [b]2Sa 9:8 [c]Ex 22:28 **16:10** [a]2Sa 3:39; 19:22 [b]Jn 18:11 [c]Ro 9:20 **16:11** [a]2Sa 12:11 [b]Ge 45:5; 1Sa 26:19 **16:12** [a]Dt 23:5; Ro 8:28 [1]Lit *Yahweh will return* **16:15** [a]2Sa 15:12, 37 **16:16** [a]2Sa 15:37 [b]2Sa 15:34 [c]1Sa 10:24; 2Ki 11:12 **16:17** [a]2Sa 19:25 **16:19** [a]2Sa 15:34 **16:21** [a]2Sa 15:16; 20:3

concubines, whom he has left to keep
the house; then all Israel will hear
that you have made yourself odious
to your father. The hands of all who
are with you will also be strength-
ened." **22** So they pitched a tent for
Absalom on the roof, [a]and Absalom
went in to his father's concubines
[b]in the sight of all Israel. **23** [a]Now
the counsel of Ahithophel, which he
counseled in those days, *was* as if one
asked of the word of God; [b]so was all
the counsel of Ahithophel *regarded*
by both David and Absalom.

### *Absalom Calls for Hushai's Counsel*

**17** Then Ahithophel said to Ab-
salom, "Please let me choose
12,000 men that I may arise and
pursue David tonight. **2** [a]And I will
come upon him while he is weary
with *his* hands falling limp and
throw him into *utter* fright, so that
all the people who are with him will
flee. Then [b]I will strike down the
king alone, **3** and I will cause all the
people to return to you. [1]The return
of everyone depends on the man you
seek; *then* all the people will be at
[a]peace." **4** And the word was right
in the eyes of Absalom and all the
elders of Israel.

**5** Then Absalom said, "Call now
[a]Hushai the Archite also, and let
us hear what is also in his mouth."
**6** Then Hushai came to Absalom.
And Absalom spoke to him, saying,
"Ahithophel has spoken [1]thus. Shall
we [2]carry out his word? If not,
you speak." **7** And Hushai said to
Absalom, "[a]This time the counsel
that Ahithophel has counseled is
not good." **8** Then Hushai said, "You
know your father and his men, that
they are mighty men and they are
bitter of soul, [a]like a bear robbed of
her cubs in the field. And your father
is a man of war, and will not spend
the night with the people. **9** Behold,
he has now hidden himself in one of
the [1]caves or in another place; and
it will be [2]when he falls on them at
the first *attack*, that whoever hears *it*
will say, 'There has been a slaughter
among the people who follow Absa-
lom.' **10** And even the one who is a
man of valor, whose heart is like the
heart of a lion, [a]will utterly melt; for
all Israel knows that your father is a
mighty man and those who are with
him are men of valor. **11** But I counsel
that all Israel be utterly gathered to
you, [a]from Dan even to Beersheba,
[b]as the sand that is by the sea in
abundance, and that [1]you personally
go into battle. **12** So we shall come to
him in one of the places where he can
be found, and we will set down on
him [a]as the dew falls on the ground;
and of him and of all the men who are
with him, not even one will be left.
**13** If he withdraws into a city, then all
Israel shall carry ropes to that city,
and we will [a]drag it into the [1]valley
until not even a small stone is found
there." **14** Then Absalom and all the
men of Israel said, "The counsel of
Hushai the Archite is better than
the counsel of Ahithophel." For
[a]Yahweh had [1]ordained to thwart

---

**16:22** [a]2Sa 15:16; 20:3 [b]2Sa 12:11, 12 **16:23** [a]2Sa 17:14, 23 [b]2Sa 15:12 ◆ **17:2** [a]2Sa 16:14 [b]1Ki 22:31
**17:3** [a]Jer 6:14 [1]Lit *Like the return of the whole is the man whom you seek* **17:5** [a]2Sa 15:32-34
**17:6** [1]Lit *according to this word* [2]Lit *do* **17:7** [a]2Sa 16:21 **17:8** [a]Hos 13:8 **17:9** [1]Lit *pits* [2]Lit
*according to a falling among them* **17:10** [a]Jos 2:9-11 **17:11** [a]1Sa 3:20 [b]Ge 22:17; 1Sa 13:5 [1]Lit *your
face go* **17:12** [a]Ps 110:3; Mic 5:7 **17:13** [a]Mic 1:6 [1]Or *wadi* **17:14** [a]2Sa 15:31, 34; Ps 9:15, 16 [1]Lit
*commanded*

the good counsel of Ahithophel, so
that Yahweh might bring calamity
on Absalom.

### *Hushai Informs David*

**15** Then [a]Hushai said to Zadok and to
Abiathar the priests, "[1]This is what
Ahithophel counseled Absalom and
the elders of Israel, and [1]this is what
I have counseled. **16** So now, send
quickly and inform David, saying,
'[a]Do not spend the night at the fords
of the wilderness, but by all means
cross over, lest the king and all the
people who are with him be swal-
lowed up.'" **17** [a]Now Jonathan and
Ahimaaz were staying at [b]En-rogel,
and a servant-woman would go and
inform them, and they would go and
inform King David, for they could
not be seen entering the city. **18** But
a boy did see them and informed
Absalom; so the two of them went
quickly and came to the house of a
man [a]in Bahurim, who had a well in
his courtyard, and they went down
[1]into it. **19** And [a]the woman [1]took a
covering and spread it over the well's
mouth and scattered crushed grain
on it, so that nothing was known.
**20** Then Absalom's servants came
to the woman at the house and said,
"Where are Ahimaaz and Jonathan?"
And [a]the woman said to them, "They
have crossed the brook of water." And
when they searched and could not
find *them*, they returned to Jerusalem.

**21** Now it happened after they
went away, that they came up out of
the well and went and informed King
David; and they said to David, "[a]Arise
and cross over the water quickly
for thus Ahithophel has counseled
against you." **22** Then David and all
the people who *were* with him arose
and crossed the Jordan; and by [1]dawn
not even one remained who had not
crossed the Jordan.

**23** Now Ahithophel saw that
his counsel was not [1]followed. So
he [2]saddled *his* donkey and arose
and went to his home, to [a]his city,
and [b,3]set his house in order, and
[c]strangled himself; thus he died and
was buried in the grave of his father.
**24** Now David came to [a]Mahanaim.
And Absalom crossed the Jordan, he
and all the men of Israel with him.
**25** And Absalom set [a]Amasa over the
army in place of Joab. Now Amasa
was the son of a man whose name
was [1]Ithra the Israelite, who went in
to Abigail the daughter of [b]Nahash,
sister of Zeruiah, Joab's mother.
**26** And Israel and Absalom camped
in the land of Gilead.

**27** Now it happened that when
David had come to Mahanaim, Shobi
[a]the son of Nahash from [b]Rabbah
of the sons of Ammon, [c]Machir
the son of Ammiel from Lo-debar,
and [d]Barzillai the Gileadite from
Rogelim, **28** brought [a]beds, basins,
pottery, wheat, barley, flour, roasted
*grain*, beans, lentils, roasted *seeds*,
**29** honey, curds, sheep, and cheese of
the herd, for David and for the people
who *were* with him, [a]to eat; for they

---

**17:15** [a]2Sa 15:35, 36 [1]Lit *Thus and thus* **17:16** [a]2Sa 15:28 **17:17** [a]2Sa 15:27, 36 [b]Jos 15:7; 18:16 **17:18** [a]2Sa 3:16; 16:5 [1]Lit *there* **17:19** [a]Jos 2:4-6 [1]Lit *took and spread the covering* **17:20** [a]Lv 19:11; Jos 2:3-5; 1Sa 19:12-17 **17:21** [a]2Sa 17:15, 16 **17:22** [1]Lit *the light of the morning* **17:23** [a]2Sa 15:12 [b]2Ki 20:1 [c]Mt 27:5 [1]Lit *done* [2]Lit *bound* [3]Lit *gave charge to* **17:24** [a]Ge 32:2, 10; 2Sa 2:8 **17:25** [a]2Sa 19:13; 20:9-12; 1Ki 2:5, 32 [b]1Chr 2:16 [1]In 1Chr 2:17, *Jether the Ishmaelite* **17:27** [a]1Sa 11:1; 2Sa 10:1, 2 [b]2Sa 12:26, 29 [c]2Sa 9:4 [d]2Sa 19:31-39; 1Ki 2:7 **17:28** [a]Pr 11:25; Mt 5:7 **17:29** [a]2Sa 16:2, 14; Pr 21:26; Ecc 11:1; Ro 12:13

said, "The people are hungry and weary and thirsty in the wilderness."

### *Joab Puts Absalom to Death*

**18** Then David [1]numbered the people who were with him and [a]set over them commanders of thousands and commanders of hundreds. **2** And David sent the people out, [a]one-third under the hand of Joab, one-third under the hand of Abishai the son of Zeruiah, Joab's brother, and one-third under the hand of [b]Ittai the Gittite. And the king said to the people, "I myself will surely go out with you also." **3** But the people said, "[a]You should not go out; for if we indeed flee, they will not set their heart on us; even if half of us die, they will not set their heart on us. But now [1]you are worth ten thousand of us; so now it is better that you *be ready* to help us from the city." **4** Then the king said to them, "Whatever is good in your sight I will do." So [a]the king stood beside the gate, and all the people went out by hundreds and thousands. **5** Then the king commanded Joab and Abishai and Ittai, saying, "*Deal* gently for my sake with the young man Absalom." And [a]all the people heard when the king commanded all the commanders concerning Absalom.

**6** Then the people went out into the field to meet Israel, and the battle took place in [a]the forest of Ephraim. **7** And the people of Israel were [1]defeated there before the servants of David, and the slaughter there that day was great, 20,000 men. **8** And the battle there was scattered over the whole countryside, and the forest devoured more people that day than the sword devoured.

**9** Then Absalom happened to meet the servants of David. Now Absalom was riding on *his* mule, and the mule went under the thick branches of a great oak. And [a]his head caught fast in the oak, so he was [1]left hanging between heaven and earth, while the mule that was under him passed onward. **10** Then a certain man saw *it*, he told Joab and said, "Behold, I saw Absalom hanging in an oak." **11** Then Joab said to the man who had told him, "Now behold, you saw *him*! Why then did you not strike him there to the ground? And I would have given you ten *pieces* of silver and a belt." **12** So the man said to Joab, "Even if I should receive one thousand *pieces of* silver in my hand, I would not send forth my hand against the king's son; for [a]in our hearing the king commanded you and Abishai and Ittai, saying, '[1]Keep for me the young man Absalom!' **13** Otherwise, if I had dealt treacherously against his life (and [a]there is nothing hidden from the king), then you yourself would have stood aloof." **14** Then Joab said, "I will not wait around here before you." [a]So he took three [1]spears in his hand and thrust them through the heart of Absalom while he was yet alive in the [2]midst of the oak. **15** And ten young men who carried Joab's armor gathered around and struck Absalom and put him to death.

◆ **18:1** [a]Ex 18:25; Nu 31:14; 1Sa 22:7 [1]Lit *mustered* **18:2** [a]Jdg 7:16; 1Sa 11:11 [b]2Sa 15:19-22
**18:3** [a]2Sa 21:17 [1]As in some ancient versions; M.T. *for now there are ten thousand like us*
**18:4** [a]2Sa 18:24 **18:5** [a]2Sa 18:12 **18:6** [a]Jos 17:15, 18; 2Sa 17:26 **18:7** [1]Lit *smitten* **18:9** [a]2Sa 14:26 [1]Lit *placed* **18:12** [a]2Sa 18:5 [1]As in some mss and the ancient versions; M.T. *Take care whoever* you are *of* **18:13** [a]2Sa 14:19, 20 **18:14** [a]2Sa 14:30 [1]Or *rods* [2]Lit *heart*

**16** Then [a]Joab blew the trumpet,
and the people returned from pur-
suing Israel, for Joab restrained the
people. **17** And they took Absalom
and cast him into [1]a deep pit in the
forest and [a]set over him a very great
heap of stones. And [b]all Israel fled,
each to his tent. **18** Now Absalom in
his lifetime had taken and [a]set up
for himself a pillar which is in [b]the
King's Valley, for he had said, "[c]I have
no son [1]to preserve my name." So he
named the pillar after his own name,
and it is called Absalom's Monument
to this day.

### *David Weeps over Absalom*

**19** Then [a]Ahimaaz the son of Zadok
said, "Please let me run and proclaim
the good news to the king [b]that
Yahweh has judged *to save* him from
the hand of his enemies." **20** But Joab
said to him, "You are not the man for
the good news this day, but you shall
proclaim the good news another day;
however, you shall not proclaim the
good news today because the king's
son has died." **21** Then Joab said to the
Cushite, "Go, tell the king what you
have seen." So the Cushite bowed
to Joab and ran. **22** Now Ahimaaz
the son of Zadok said once more to
Joab, "But whatever happens, please
let me also run after the Cushite."
And Joab said, "Why would you run,
my son, since [a]you will have no re-
ward for going?" **23** "But whatever
happens," *he said,* "I will run." So he
said to him, "Run." Then Ahimaaz
ran by way of the plain and passed
the Cushite.

**24** Now [a]David was sitting between
the two gates; and [b]the watchman
went up to the roof of the gate by the
wall, and raised his eyes and looked,
and behold, a man running by him-
self. **25** And the watchman called and
told the king. And the king said, "If
he is by himself there is good news
in his mouth." And he came nearer
and nearer. **26** Then the watchman
saw another man running; and the
watchman called to the gatekeeper
and said, "Behold, *another* man
running by himself." And the king
said, "This one also is bringing good
news." **27** And the watchman said,
"I see that the running of the first
one [a]is like the running of Ahimaaz
the son of Zadok." And the king said,
"[b]This is a good man and comes with
good news."

**28** And Ahimaaz called and said
to the king, "Peace!" And [a]he pros-
trated himself before the king with
his [1]face to the ground. And he said,
"[b]Blessed is Yahweh your God, who
has delivered up the men who lifted
their hands against my lord the king."
**29** Then the king said, "[a]Is there peace
with the young man Absalom?" And
Ahimaaz said, "When Joab sent the
king's servant, and your servant, I
saw a great tumult, but [b]I did not
know what *it was.*" **30** Then the king
said, "Turn aside and stand here." So
he turned aside and stood still.

**31** Behold, the Cushite arrived, and
the Cushite said, "Let my lord the
king receive good news, for [a]Yahweh
has judged *to save* you this day from
the hand of all those who rose up

**18:16** [a]2Sa 2:28; 20:22 **18:17** [a]Dt 21:20, 21; Jos 7:26; 8:29 [b]2Sa 19:8; 20:1, 22 [1]Lit *the great*
**18:18** [a]1Sa 15:12 [b]Ge 14:17 [c]2Sa 14:27 [1]Lit *for the sake of remembering* **18:19** [a]2Sa 15:36
[b]2Sa 18:31 **18:22** [a]2Sa 18:29 **18:24** [a]2Sa 19:8 [b]2Sa 13:34; 2Ki 9:17 **18:27** [a]2Ki 9:20
[b]1Ki 1:42 **18:28** [a]1Sa 25:23; 2Sa 14:4 [b]1Sa 17:46 [1]Lit *nose* **18:29** [a]2Sa 20:9; 2Ki 4:26 [b]2Sa 18:22
**18:31** [a]Jdg 5:31; 2Sa 18:19

against you." 32 Then the king said
to the Cushite, "[a]Is there peace with
the young man Absalom?" And the
Cushite answered, "[b]Let the enemies
of my lord the king, and all who rise
up against you for evil, be as that
young man!"

33 [1]Then the king trembled and went
up to the chamber over the gate and
wept. And thus he said as he walked,
"[a]O my son Absalom, my son, my son
Absalom! [b]Would I had died instead
of you, O Absalom, my son, my son!"

### *Joab Tells David to Speak to His Servants*

19 Then it was told to Joab,
"Behold, [a]the king is weeping
and mourns for Absalom." 2 And
the salvation that day was turned to
mourning for all the people, for the
people heard *it* said that day, "The
king is grieved for his son." 3 So
the people stole away to enter into
the city that day, as people who are
dishonored steal away when they
flee in battle. 4 But as for the king, he
[a]wrapped his face up. Then the king
cried out with a loud voice, "[b]O my
son Absalom, O Absalom, my son,
my son!" 5 Then Joab came into the
house to the king and said, "Today
you have shamed the faces of all your
servants, who today have provided
escape for your life and the lives of
your sons and daughters, the lives
of your wives, and the lives of your
concubines, 6 by loving those who
hate you, and by hating those who
love you. For you have informed *all
of us* today that [1]princes and servants
are nothing to you; for I know this
day that if Absalom were alive and all
of us were dead today, surely then it
would be right in your eyes. 7 So now,
arise, go out and speak to the heart of
your servants, for I swear by Yahweh,
if you do not go out, surely [a]not a
man will pass the night with you,
and this will be of greater evil for you
than all the evil that has come upon
you from your youth until now."

### *David Returns to Jerusalem*

8 So the king arose and sat in the
gate. And they told all the people,
saying, "Behold, the king is [a]sitting
in the gate." Then all the people came
before the king.

Now [b]Israel had fled, each to his
tent. 9 And it happened that all the
people were disputing throughout
all the tribes of Israel, saying, "[a]The
king delivered us from the [1]hand of
our enemies and [b]provided us escape
from the [1]hand of the Philistines,
but now [c]he has fled out of the land
from Absalom. 10 However, Absalom,
whom we anointed over us, has died
in battle. So now, why are you silent
about having the king return?"

11 Now King David had sent to
[a]Zadok and Abiathar the priests,
saying, "Speak to the elders of Judah,
saying, 'Why are you the last to have
the king return to his house, while
the word of all Israel has come to the
king, *even* to his house? 12 You are
my brothers; [a]you are my bone and
my flesh. Why then should you be
the last to have the king return?'
13 And say to [a]Amasa, 'Are you not

---

**18:32** [a]2Sa 18:29 [b]1Sa 25:26 **18:33** [a]2Sa 19:4 [b]Ex 32:32; Ro 9:3 [1]Ch 19:1 in Heb ◆ **19:1** [a]2Sa 18:5, 14 **19:4** [a]2Sa 15:30 [b]2Sa 18:33 **19:6** [1]Or *commanders* **19:7** [a]Pr 14:28 **19:8** [a]2Sa 15:2; 18:24 [b]2Sa 18:17 **19:9** [a]2Sa 8:1-14 [b]2Sa 5:20; 8:1 [c]2Sa 15:14 [1]Lit *palm* **19:11** [a]2Sa 15:29 **19:12** [a]2Sa 5:1 **19:13** [a]2Sa 17:25

my bone and my flesh? [b]May God
do so to me, and more also, if you
will not be [c]commander of the army
before me continually [d]in place of
Joab.'" **14** Thus he inclined the hearts
of all the men of Judah [a]as one man,
so they sent *word* to the king, *saying*,
"Return, you and all your servants."
**15** The king then returned and came
as far as the Jordan. And Judah came
to [a]Gilgal in order to go to meet the
king, to cause the king to pass over
across the Jordan.

**16** Then [a]Shimei the son of Gera,
the Benjamite who was from Ba-
hurim, hurried and came down with
the men of Judah to meet King David.
**17** Now there were one thousand men
of Benjamin with him, with [a]Ziba the
young man of the house of Saul,
and his fifteen sons and his twenty
servants with him; and they rushed
to the Jordan before the king. **18** Then
they kept passing over the ford to
cause the king's household to pass
over, and to do what was good in his
sight. And Shimei the son of Gera
fell down before the king as he was
about to pass over the Jordan. **19** So
he said to the king, "[a]Let not my lord
consider me guilty, nor remember
what your servant did wrong on the
day when my lord the king went out
from Jerusalem, so that the king
would [1]take *it* to heart. **20** For your
servant knows that I have sinned;
therefore behold, I have come today,
[a]the first of all the house of Joseph to
go down to meet my lord the king."
**21** But Abishai the son of Zeruiah
said, "[a]Should not Shimei be put to
death for this, [b]because he cursed the
anointed of Yahweh?" **22** David then
said, "[a]What have I to do with you,
O sons of Zeruiah, that you should
this day be an adversary to me?
[b]Should any man be put to death in
Israel today? For do I not know that
I am king over Israel today?" **23** And
the king said to Shimei, "[a]You shall
not die." Thus the king swore to him.

**24** Now [a]Mephibosheth the [1]son
of Saul had come down to meet the
king; and [b]he had not done *anything*
for his feet, nor done *anything* for his
mustache, nor [c]washed his clothes,
from the day the king departed un-
til the day he came *home* in peace.
**25** Now it happened when he came
from Jerusalem to meet the king,
that the king said to him, "[a]Why did
you not go with me, Mephibosheth?"
**26** So he answered, "O my lord, the
king, my servant deceived me; for
your servant said, 'I will saddle a
donkey for myself that I may ride
on it and go with the king,' [a]because
your servant is lame. **27** Moreover,
[a]he has slandered your servant to my
lord the king; but my lord the king is
[b]like the angel of God, therefore do
what is good in your sight. **28** For [a]all
my father's household was nothing
but men *worthy of* death before
my lord the king; [b]yet you set your
servant among those who ate at your
own table. What right do I have yet
that I should [1]complain anymore
to the king?" **29** So the king said to
him, "Why do you still speak of your
affairs? I have [1]decided, 'You and
Ziba shall divide the land.'" **30** And

**19:13** [b]1Ki 19:2 [c]2Sa 8:16 [d]2Sa 3:27-39; 19:5-7 **19:14** [a]Jdg 20:1 **19:15** [a]Jos 5:9; 1Sa 11:14, 15
**19:16** [a]2Sa 16:5-13; 1Ki 2:8 **19:17** [a]2Sa 16:1-4; 19:26, 27 **19:19** [a]1Sa 22:15; 2Sa 16:6-8 [1]Lit *set*
**19:20** [a]2Sa 16:5 **19:21** [a]2Sa 16:7, 8 [b]Ex 22:28 **19:22** [a]2Sa 3:39; 16:9, 10 [b]1Sa 11:13 **19:23** [a]1Ki 2:8
**19:24** [a]2Sa 9:6-10 [b]2Sa 12:20 [c]Ex 19:10 [1]Or *grandson* **19:25** [a]2Sa 16:17 **19:26** [a]2Sa 9:3
**19:27** [a]2Sa 16:3, 4 [b]2Sa 14:17, 20 **19:28** [a]2Sa 21:6-9 [b]2Sa 9:7, 10, 13 [1]Lit *cry out* **19:29** [1]Lit *said*

Mephibosheth said to the king, "Let
him even take it all, since my lord the
king has come in peace to his own
house."

**31** Now [a]Barzillai the Gileadite
had come down from Rogelim; and
he passed over the Jordan with the
king in order to send him off over
the Jordan. **32** Now Barzillai was very
old, being eighty years old; and he
had [a,1]sustained the king while he
stayed at Mahanaim, for he was a
very great man. **33** And the king said
to Barzillai, "You pass over with me
and I will [1]sustain you in Jerusalem
with me." **34** But Barzillai said to the
king, "[a]How long [1]have I yet to live,
that I should go up with the king
to Jerusalem? **35** I am [1]now [a]eighty
years old. Can I know between good
and bad? Or can your servant taste
what I eat or what I drink? Or can I
hear anymore [b]the voice of singing
men and women? [c]Why then should
your servant be an added burden to
my lord the king? **36** Your servant
would merely pass over the Jordan
with the king. Why should the king
compensate me *with* this reward?
**37** Please let your servant return, that
I may die in my own city near the
grave of my father and my mother.
However, here is your servant
[a]Chimham, let him pass over with
my lord the king, and do for him what
is good in your sight." **38** So the king
answered, "Chimham shall pass over
with me, and I will do for him what
is good in your sight; and whatever
you [1]require of me, I will do for you."
**39** Then all the people passed over
the Jordan and the king passed over
too. The king then [a]kissed Barzillai
and blessed him, and he returned to
his place.

**40** Now the king went on to Gilgal,
and Chimham went on with him; and
all the people of Judah and also [a]half
the people of Israel [1]accompanied the
king. **41** And behold, all the men of
Israel came to the king and said to the
king, "[a]Why had our brothers [b]the
men of Judah stolen you away, and
caused the king and his household
and all David's men with him to pass
over the Jordan?" **42** Then all the men
of Judah answered the men of Israel,
"Because [a]the king is a close relative
to [1]us. Why then [2]are you angry about
this matter? Have we eaten at all at
the king's *expense*, or has [3]anything
been taken for us?" **43** But the men
of Israel answered the men of Judah
and said, "[a,1]We have ten parts in the
king, therefore [1]we also have more
*claim* on David than you. Why then
did you treat us with contempt? Was
it not [1]our word first to have [1]our king
return?" Yet the words of the men of
Judah were harsher than the words
of the men of Israel.

### *Sheba Goes Up Against David*

**20** Now [a]a vile fellow happened
to be there whose name was
Sheba, the son of [b]Bichri, a Benjamite;
and he blew the trumpet and said,

"[c]We have no portion in David,
Nor do we have inheritance
in [d]the son of Jesse;

---

**19:31** [a]2Sa 17:27-29; 1Ki 2:7 **19:32** [a]2Sa 17:27-29 [1]Or *provided food for* **19:33** [1]Or *provide food for* **19:34** [a]Ge 47:8 [1]Lit *are the days of the years of my life* **19:35** [a]Ps 90:10 [b]Ecc 2:8; Is 5:11, 12 [c]2Sa 15:33 [1]Lit *today* **19:37** [a]2Sa 19:40; 1Ki 2:7; Jer 41:17 **19:38** [1]Lit *choose* **19:39** [a]Ge 31:55; Ru 1:14; 2Sa 14:33 **19:40** [a]2Sa 19:9, 10 [1]Lit *crossed over with* **19:41** [a]Jdg 8:1; 12:1 [b]2Sa 19:11, 12 **19:42** [a]2Sa 19:12 [1]Lit *me* [2]Lit *is it hot to you* [3]Or *a gift* **19:43** [a]2Sa 5:1; 1Ki 11:30, 31 [1]Singular in Heb ◆ **20:1** [a]2Sa 16:7 [b]Ge 46:21 [c]2Sa 19:43; 1Ki 12:16 [d]1Sa 22:7-9

[e]Every man to his
tents, O Israel!"
**2** So all the men of Israel went up
from following David *and* followed
Sheba the son of Bichri; but the men
of Judah clung to their king, from the
Jordan even to Jerusalem.
**3** Then David came to his house
at Jerusalem, and [a]the king took the
ten women, the concubines whom
he had left to keep the house, and
placed them under guard and pro-
vided them with sustenance, but did
not go in to them. So they were shut
up until the day of their death, living
as widows.
**4** Then the king said to [a]Amasa,
"Call out the men of Judah for me
within three days, and you yourself
stand here." **5** So Amasa went to call
out *the men of* Judah, but he [a]delayed
longer than the set time which he
had appointed him. **6** And David said
to [a]Abishai, "Now Sheba the son of
Bichri will do us more harm than
Absalom; [b]take your lord's servants
and pursue him, lest he find for
himself fortified cities and deliver
*himself* from our sight." **7** So Joab's
men pursued him, [a]along with the
Cherethites and the Pelethites and all
the mighty men; and they went out
from Jerusalem to pursue Sheba the
son of Bichri. **8** They were at the large
stone which is in [a]Gibeon, and Ama-
sa came [1]to meet them. Now Joab
was [2]dressed in his military attire,
and over it was a belt with a sword
in its sheath fastened at his [3]waist;
and as he came out, it fell out. **9** Then
Joab said to Amasa, "Is it well with
you, my brother?" And [a]Joab took
Amasa by the beard with his right
hand to kiss him.

### *Joab Strikes Amasa*

**10** But Amasa was not on guard
against the sword which was in Joab's
hand so [a]he struck him in the belly
with it and poured out his inward
parts on the ground, and did not
*strike* him again, and he died. Then
Joab and Abishai his brother pursued
Sheba the son of Bichri. **11** Now there
stood by him one of Joab's young
men, and said, "Whoever delights
in Joab and whoever is for David, [a]*let*
*him* follow Joab." **12** But Amasa lay
wallowing in *his* blood in the middle
of the highway. And the man saw
that all the people stood still. So he
[1]removed Amasa from the highway
into the field and threw a garment
over him when he saw that everyone
who came by him stood still.

### *The Beheading of Sheba*

**13** As soon as he was removed from
the highway, all the men passed on
after Joab to pursue Sheba the son
of Bichri.
**14** Now he went through all the
tribes of Israel to Abel, even Beth-
maacah, and all the Berites; and they
were assembled and also came after
him. **15** So they came and besieged
him in [a]Abel Beth-maacah, and [b]they
[1]cast up a siege ramp against the city,
and it stood by the rampart; and all
the people who were with Joab were
wreaking destruction in order to
cause the wall to fall. **16** Then [a]a wise

---

**20:1** [e]1Sa 13:2; 2Sa 18:17; 2Chr 10:16 **20:3** [a]2Sa 15:16; 16:21, 22 **20:4** [a]2Sa 17:25; 19:13 **20:5** [a]1Sa 13:8 **20:6** [a]2Sa 21:17 [b]2Sa 11:11; 1Ki 1:33 **20:7** [a]2Sa 8:18; 1Ki 1:38 **20:8** [a]2Sa 2:13; 3:30 [1]Lit *before* [2]Lit *girded with military garment as clothing* [3]Lit *loins* **20:9** [a]Mt 26:49 **20:10** [a]2Sa 2:23; 3:27; 1Ki 2:5 **20:11** [a]2Sa 20:13 **20:12** [1]Lit *caused to turn* **20:15** [a]1Ki 15:20; 2Ki 15:29 [b]2Ki 19:32; Eze 4:2 [1]Lit *poured out* **20:16** [a]2Sa 14:2

woman called from the city, "Hear,
hear! Please tell Joab, 'Draw near that
I may speak with you.'" **17** So he drew
near to her, and the woman said, "Are
you Joab?" And he answered, "I am."
Then she said to him, "Listen to the
words of your maidservant." And he
answered, "I am listening." **18** Then
she spoke, saying, "Formerly they
used to speak *in this way*, saying,
'They will surely ask *advice* at Abel,'
and thus they ended *the dispute*. **19** I
am of those who are peaceable *and*
faithful in Israel. [a]You are seeking to
put to death a city, even a mother in
Israel. Why would you swallow up
[b]the inheritance of Yahweh?" **20** And
Joab answered and said, "Far be it, far
be it from me that I should swallow
up or destroy! **21** Such is not the case.
But a man from [a]the hill country of
Ephraim, [b]Sheba the son of Bichri by
name, has lifted up his hand against
King David. Give him over alone,
and I will go from the city." And the
woman said to Joab, "Behold, his
head will be thrown to you over the
wall." **22** Then the woman came to
all the people in her [a]wisdom. And
they cut off the head of Sheba the
son of Bichri and threw it to Joab. So
[b]he blew the trumpet, and they were
scattered from the city, each to his
tent. Joab also returned to the king
at Jerusalem.

**23** [a]Now Joab *was* over the whole
army of Israel, and Benaiah the son
of Jehoiada *was* over the Cherethites
and the Pelethites; **24** and Adoram
*was* over the forced labor, and
[a]Jehoshaphat the son of Ahilud
was the recorder; **25** and Sheva *was*
scribe, and Zadok and [a]Abiathar
*were* priests; **26** and Ira the Jairite was
also a priest to David.

### *David Gives Saul's Sons to the Gibeonites*

**21** And there was [a]a famine in the
days of David for three years,
year after year; and [b]David sought
the presence of Yahweh. And Yahweh
said, "It is for Saul and his bloody
house, because he put the Gibeonites
to death." **2** So the king called the
Gibeonites and spoke to them (now
the Gibeonites were not of the sons of
Israel but of the remnant of the Am-
orites, and [a]the sons of Israel [1]made
a covenant with them, but Saul had
sought to strike them down in his
zeal for the sons of Israel and Judah).
**3** Thus David said to the Gibeonites,
"What should I do for you? And how
can I make atonement that you may
bless [a]the inheritance of Yahweh?"
**4** Then the Gibeonites said to him,
"[a]We have no *concern* of silver or
gold with Saul or his house, nor is
it for us to put any man to death in
Israel." And he said, "I will do for you
whatever you say." **5** So they said to
the king, "[a]The man who consumed
us and who planned [1]to eradicate us
from standing within any border of
Israel, **6** let seven men from his sons
be given to us, and we will [1]hang
them [a]before Yahweh in Gibeah of
Saul, [b]the chosen of Yahweh." And
the king said, "I will give *them*."

**7** But the king spared [a]Mephib-
osheth, the son of Jonathan the son of

**20:19** [a]Dt 20:10 [b]1Sa 26:19; 2Sa 14:16; 21:3 **20:21** [a]Jos 24:33 [b]2Sa 20:2 **20:22** [a]2Sa 20:16; Ecc 9:13-16 [b]2Sa 20:1 **20:23** [a]2Sa 8:16-18; 1Ki 4:3-6 **20:24** [a]1Ki 4:3 **20:25** [a]1Ki 4:4 ◆ **21:1** [a]Ge 12:10; 26:1; 42:5 [b]Nu 27:21 **21:2** [a]Jos 9:3, 15-20 [1]Lit *had sworn to* **21:3** [a]1Sa 26:19; 2Sa 20:19 **21:4** [a]Nu 35:31, 32 **21:5** [a]2Sa 21:1 [1]Lit *against us that we should be eradicated* **21:6** [a]Nu 25:4 [b]1Sa 10:24 [1]Lit *expose them* **21:7** [a]2Sa 4:4; 9:10

Saul, [b]because of the oath of Yahweh
which was between them, between
David and Saul's son Jonathan. **8** So
the king took the two sons of [a]Rizpah
the daughter of Aiah, Armoni and
Mephibosheth whom she had borne
to Saul, and the five sons of [b,1]Merab
the daughter of Saul, whom she had
borne to Adriel the son of Barzillai
the [c]Meholathite. **9** Then he gave
them into the hand of the Gibeon-
ites, and they [1]hanged them in the
mountain before Yahweh, so that the
seven of them fell together; and they
were put to death in the first days of
harvest at [a]the beginning of barley
harvest.

**10** [a]And Rizpah the daughter of
Aiah took sackcloth and spread it
for herself on the rock, from the be-
ginning of harvest until [1]it rained on
them from the sky; and [b]she [2]allowed
neither the birds of the sky to rest
on them by day nor the beasts of the
field by night. **11** Then it was told to
David what Rizpah the daughter of
Aiah, the concubine of Saul, had
done. **12** So David went and took
[a]the bones of Saul and the bones of
Jonathan his son from the men of
Jabesh-gilead, who had stolen them
from the open square of [b]Beth-shan,
[c]where the Philistines had hanged
them on the day [d]the Philistines
struck down Saul in Gilboa. **13** And
he brought up the bones of Saul and
the bones of Jonathan his son from
there, and they gathered the bones of
those who had been [1]hanged. **14** Then
they buried the bones of Saul and
Jonathan his son in the land of Ben-
jamin in [a]Zela, in the grave of Kish
his father; thus they did all that the
king commanded, and afterwards
[b]God was moved by the entreaty for
the land.

### *War with the Philistines*

**15** And [a]the Philistines were at war
again with Israel, so David went
down and his servants with him; and
as they fought against the Philistines,
David became weary. **16** Then Ishbi-
benob, who was [a]among those born
to the [1]giants, the weight of whose
spear was [2]three hundred *shekels* of
bronze in weight, [3]was girded with
a new *sword*, and he [4]intended to
strike down David. **17** But [a]Abishai
the son of Zeruiah helped him, and
struck the Philistine and put him to
death. Then the men of David swore
to him, saying, "[b]You shall not go out
again with us to battle, so that you do
not extinguish [c]the lamp of Israel."

**18** [a]Now it happened afterwards
that there was war again with the
Philistines at Gob; then [b]Sibbecai the
Hushathite struck down Saph, who
was among those born to the [1]giants.
**19** There was war with the Philistines
again at Gob, and Elhanan the son of
Jaare-oregim the Bethlehemite struck
down [1]Goliath the Gittite, [a]the shaft
of whose spear was like a weaver's
beam. **20** Then there was war at
Gath again, and there was a man of
*great* stature who had six fingers on

---

**21:7** [b]1Sa 18:3; 20:12-17; 23:18; 2Sa 9:1-7 **21:8** [a]2Sa 3:7 [b]1Sa 18:19 [c]1Ki 19:16 [1]As in Gr and Heb mss; M.T. *Michal* **21:9** [a]Ex 9:31, 32 [1]Lit *exposed them* **21:10** [a]Dt 21:23 [b]1Sa 17:44, 46 [1]Lit *water was poured* [2]Lit *gave* **21:12** [a]1Sa 31:11-13 [b]Jos 17:11 [c]1Sa 31:10 [d]1Sa 31:3, 4 **21:13** [1]Lit *exposed* **21:14** [a]Jos 18:28 [b]Jos 7:26; 2Sa 24:25 **21:15** [a]2Sa 5:17-25 **21:16** [a]Nu 13:22, 28; Jos 15:14; 2Sa 21:18-22 [1]Lit *giant*; Heb *Raphah* [2]Approx. 7.5 lb. or 3.3 kg, a shekel was approx. 0.4 oz. or 11 gm [3]Lit *and he was* [4]Lit *said* **21:17** [a]2Sa 20:6-10 [b]2Sa 18:3 [c]2Sa 22:29; 1Ki 11:36 **21:18** [a]1Chr 20:4-8 [b]1Chr 11:29; 27:11 [1]Lit *giant*; Heb *Raphah* **21:19** [a]1Sa 17:7 [1]In 1Chr 20:5, *Lahmi, the brother of Goliath*

each hand and six toes on each foot,
twenty-four in number; and he also
had been born [a]to the [1]giants. **21** And
he [1]reproached Israel, so Jonathan
the son of Shimei, David's brother,
struck him down. **22** [a]These four
were born to the [1]giants in Gath, and
they fell by the hand of David and by
the hand of his servants.

### *David's Song of Deliverance*

**22** [a]And David spoke to Yahweh
[b]the words of this song in the
day that Yahweh delivered him from
the [1]hand of all his enemies and from
the [1]hand of Saul. **2** He said,

"[a]Yahweh is my [1]rock and my
fortress and my deliverer;
**3** [a,1]My God, my rock,
in whom I take refuge,
My [b]shield and [c]the horn
of my salvation, my
stronghold and [d]my refuge;
My savior, You save me
from violence.
**4** "I call upon Yahweh, [a]who
is worthy to be praised,
And I am saved
from my enemies.
**5** "For [a]the waves of death
encompassed me;
[b]The torrents of [1]vileness
terrorized me;
**6** [a]The cords of Sheol
surrounded me;
The snares of death
confronted me.
**7** "[a]In my distress I called
upon Yahweh,
And I called to my God;
And out of His temple
He heard my voice,
And my cry for help
*came* into His ears.
**8** "Then [a]the earth shook
and quaked;
[b]The foundations
of heaven were trembling
And were shaken, because
He was angry.
**9** "Smoke went up
[1]out of His nostrils,
[a]And fire from His
mouth devoured;
[b]Coals were kindled by it.
**10** "He bowed the heavens
and came down
With [a]thick darkness
under His feet.
**11** "[a]He rode on a cherub
and flew;
And He [1]appeared
upon [b]the wings of the wind.
**12** "[a]And He made darkness
[1]canopies around Him,
A mass of waters, thick
clouds of the skies.
**13** "From the brightness
before Him
[a]Coals of fire were kindled.
**14** "[a]Yahweh thundered
from heaven,
And the Most High gave
forth His voice.
**15** "[a]And He sent out arrows,
and scattered them,
Lightning, and [1]threw
them into confusion.

**21:20** [a]2Sa 21:16, 18 [1]Lit *giant*; Heb *Raphah* **21:21** [1]Or *defied* **21:22** [a]1Chr 20:8 [1]Lit *giant*; Heb *Raphah* ◆ **22:1** [a]Ps 18:2-50 [b]Ex 15:1; Dt 31:30 [1]Lit *palm* **22:2** [a]1Sa 23:25; 24:2; Ps 31:3; 71:3 [1]Lit *crag* **22:3** [a]Dt 32:4, 37; 1Sa 2:2 [b]Ge 15:1; Dt 33:29 [c]Lk 1:69 [d]Ps 9:9 [1]Lit *God of my rock* **22:4** [a]Ps 48:1; 96:4 **22:5** [a]Ps 93:4; Jon 2:3 [b]Ps 69:14, 15 [1]Heb *Belial* **22:6** [a]Ps 116:3 **22:7** [a]Ps 116:4; 120:1 **22:8** [a]Jdg 5:4; Ps 97:4 [b]Job 26:11 **22:9** [a]Ps 97:3; Heb 12:29 [b]2Sa 22:13 [1]Or *in His wrath* **22:10** [a]Ex 19:16; 1Ki 8:12; Ps 97:2; Na 1:3 **22:11** [a]2Sa 6:2 [b]Ps 104:3 [1]Many mss *sped* **22:12** [a]Job 36:29 [1]Or *pavilions* **22:13** [a]2Sa 22:9 **22:14** [a]Job 37:2-5; Ps 29:3 **22:15** [a]Dt 32:23; Jos 10:10; 1Sa 7:10 [1]Or *routed them*

16 “Then the channels
of the sea appeared,
The foundations
of the world were [1]laid bare
By the rebuke of Yahweh,
[a]At the blast of the breath
of His nostrils.
17 “[a]He sent from on high,
He took me;
[b]He drew me out
of many waters.
18 “He delivered me
from my strong enemy,
From those who hated me, for
they were too mighty for me.
19 “They confronted me
in the day of my disaster,
[a]But Yahweh was my support.
20 “[a]He brought me forth also
into a broad place;
He rescued me, [b]because
He delighted in me.
21 “[a]Yahweh has rewarded
me according
to my righteousness;
[b]According to the cleanness
of my hands He has
recompensed me.
22 “[a]For I have kept the
ways of Yahweh,
And have not wickedly
departed from my God.
23 “[a]For all His [1]judgments
were before me,
And *as for* His statutes, I did
not depart from [2]them.
24 “[a]I was also [1]blameless
toward Him,
And I kept myself
from my iniquity.
25 “[a]Therefore Yahweh has
recompensed me according
to my righteousness,
According to my cleanness
before His eyes.
26 “[a]With the [1]kind You
show Yourself [1]kind,
With the [2]blameless You
show Yourself [2]blameless;
27 [a]With the pure You
show Yourself pure,
[b]And with the crooked You
show Yourself [1]astute.
28 “[a]And You save an
afflicted people;
[b]But Your eyes are
on the haughty *whom*
You bring down.
29 “[a]For You are my lamp,
O Yahweh;
And Yahweh illumines
my darkness.
30 “[a]For by You I can [1]run
upon a troop;
By my God I can leap
over a wall.
31 “[a]As for God, His way
is [1]blameless;
[b]The word of Yahweh
is [2]tried;
[c]He is a shield to all who
take refuge in Him.
32 “[a]For who is God, but Yahweh?
[b]And who is a rock,
but our God?
33 “[a]God is my strong fortress;

**22:16** [a]Ex 15:8; Na 1:4 [1]Or *uncovered* **22:17** [a]Ps 144:7 [b]Ex 2:10 **22:19** [a]Ps 23:4 **22:20** [a]Ps 31:8; 118:5 [b]2Sa 15:26 **22:21** [a]1Sa 26:23; 1Ki 8:32 [b]Ps 24:4 **22:22** [a]Ge 18:19; Ps 128:1; Pr 8:32 **22:23** [a]Dt 6:6-9; Ps 119:30, 102 [1]Or *judgment* [2]Lit *it* **22:24** [a]Ge 6:9; 7:1; Eph 1:4; Col 1:21, 22 [1]Or *complete, having integrity* **22:25** [a]2Sa 22:21 **22:26** [a]Mt 5:7 [1]Or *holy* [2]Or *having integrity*; lit *mighty* **22:27** [a]Mt 5:8; 1Jn 3:3 [b]Lv 26:23, 24; Ro 1:28 [1]Lit *twisted* **22:28** [a]Ex 3:7, 8; Ps 72:12, 13 [b]Is 2:11, 12, 17; 5:15 **22:29** [a]2Sa 21:17; 1Ki 11:36; Ps 27:1 **22:30** [a]2Sa 5:6-8 [1]Or *crush a troop* **22:31** [a]Dt 32:4; Mt 5:48 [b]Ps 12:6; 119:140; Pr 30:5 [c]2Sa 22:3; Ps 84:9 [1]Or *having integrity*; lit *complete, perfect* [2]Or *tested*, cf. Pr 30:5 **22:32** [a]1Sa 2:2 [b]2Sa 22:2 **22:33** [a]2Sa 22:2; Ps 31:3, 4

And He [1]sets the [2]blameless
in [3]His way.
34 “[a]He makes [1]my feet
like hinds’ *feet*,
[b]And sets me on my high places.
35 “[a]He trains my hands for battle,
[b]So that my arms can
bend a bow of bronze.
36 “You have also given me [a]the
shield of Your salvation,
And Your answer *to me*
makes me great.
37 “[a]You enlarge my steps
under me,
And my ankles have
not given way.
38 “I pursued my enemies
and [a]destroyed them,
And I did not turn back
until they were consumed.
39 “And I have consumed them
and crushed them,
so that they did not rise;
And [a]they fell under my feet.
40 “For You have girded me
with strength for battle;
You have [1]subdued
under me [a]those who rose
up against me.
41 “[1]You have also [a]made
my enemies turn
their backs to me,
And I [2]destroyed those
who hated me.
42 “[a]They looked, but there
was none to save;
[b]*Even* to Yahweh, but He
did not answer them.
43 “[a]Then I beat them fine
as the dust of the earth;
[b]I pulverized *and*
stamped them as the
mire of the streets.
44 “[a]You have also delivered
me from the contentions
of my people;
[b]You have kept me
as head of the nations;
[c]A people whom I have
not known serve me.
45 “[a]Foreigners cower
before me;
As soon as they hear,
they obey me.
46 “Foreigners fade away,
[a]And [1]come trembling
out of their [2]fortresses.
47 “Yahweh lives, and
blessed be my rock;
And let [a,1]God, the rock of my
salvation, be lifted high,
48 [a]The God who executes
vengeance for me,
[b]And brings down
peoples under me,
49 Who also brings me out
from my enemies;
You even lift me above [a]those
who rise up against me;
[b]You rescue me
from the violent man.
50 “[a]Therefore I will give
thanks to You, O Yahweh,
among the nations,
And I will sing praises
to Your name.

**22:33** [1]Or *sets free* [2]Or *having integrity*; lit *complete, perfect* [3]Or *my* **22:34** [a]2Sa 2:18; Hab 3:19 [b]Dt 32:13 [1]Or *His* **22:35** [a]Ps 144:1 [b]Job 20:24 **22:36** [a]Eph 6:16, 17 **22:37** [a]2Sa 22:20; Pr 4:12 **22:38** [a]Ex 15:9 **22:39** [a]Mal 4:3 **22:40** [a]Ps 44:5 [1]Lit *caused to bow down* **22:41** [a]Ex 23:27; Jos 10:24 [1]Lit *And as for my enemies, You have given me their necks* [2]Or *silenced* **22:42** [a]Is 17:7, 8 [b]1Sa 28:6; Is 1:15 **22:43** [a]2Ki 13:7 [b]Is 10:6; Mic 7:10 **22:44** [a]2Sa 3:1; 19:9, 14 [b]2Sa 8:1-14 [c]Is 55:5 **22:45** [a]Ps 66:3; 81:15 **22:46** [a]1Sa 14:11; Mic 7:17 [1]Lit *gird themselves*; the Heb is difficult [2]Lit *fastnesses* **22:47** [a]2Sa 22:3; Ps 89:26 [1]Lit *the God of the rock* **22:48** [a]1Sa 24:12; 25:39; 2Sa 4:8; Ps 94:1 [b]Ps 144:2 **22:49** [a]Ps 44:5 [b]Ps 140:1, 4, 11 **22:50** [a]Ro 15:9

51 “[a]*He* [1]gives great salvation
to His king,
And [b]shows lovingkindness
to His anointed,
[c]To David and his
seed forever.”

### *David’s Last Words*

23 Now these are the last words
of David.
David the son of Jesse declares,
[a]The man who was raised
on high declares,
[b]The anointed of the
God of Jacob,
And the sweet psalmist
of Israel,
2 “[a]The Spirit of Yahweh
spoke by me,
And His word was
on my tongue.
3 “The God of Israel said,
[a]The Rock of Israel
spoke to me,
‘[b]He who rules over men
*as* a righteous one,
[c]Who rules in the fear of God,
4 [a]Is as the light of the morning
*when* the sun rises,
A morning without clouds,
From brightness
*of the sun* after rain.’
*With* the tender grass
*springing* from the earth,
5 [1]Truly is not my house
so with God?
For [a]He has made
an everlasting
covenant with me,
Ordered in all things,
and secured;
For all my salvation
and all *my* desire,
Will He not indeed
make *it* grow?
6 “[a]But the vile *men,* every
one of them will be thrust
away like thorns,
Because they cannot
be taken in hand;
7 But the man who
touches them
Must be [1]armed with iron
and the shaft of a spear,
And [a]they will be
completely burned
with fire where *they* sit.”

### *David’s Mighty Men*

8 [a]These are the names of the mighty
men whom David had: Josheb-
basshebeth a Tahchemonite, chief
of the [1]captains, he was *called* Adino
the Eznite, because of eight hundred
slain *by him* at one time; 9 and after
him was Eleazar the son of [a]Dodo
the [b]son of Ahohi, one of the three
mighty men with David when they
[1]reproached the Philistines who were
gathered together there to battle and
the men of Israel had gone up *to
retreat.* 10 [a]He arose and struck the
Philistines until his hand was weary
and [1]clung to the sword, and [b]Yahweh
brought about a great salvation that
day; and the people returned after
him only to strip *the slain.*
11 Now after him was Shammah
the son of Agee a [a]Hararite. And
the Philistines were gathered [1]into
a troop where there was a portion
of the field full of lentils; and the

---

**22:51** [a]Ps 144:10 [b]Ps 89:24 [c]2Sa 7:12-16 [1]Or *is a tower* ◆ **23:1** [a]2Sa 7:8, 9; Ps 78:70, 71 [b]1Sa 16:12, 13; Ps 89:20 **23:2** [a]Mt 22:43; 2Pe 1:21 **23:3** [a]2Sa 22:2, 3, 32 [b]Ps 72:1-3; Is 11:1-5 [c]2Chr 19:7, 9 **23:4** [a]Jdg 5:31; Ps 72:6 **23:5** [a]2Sa 7:12-16; Ps 89:29; Is 55:3 [1]Or *But my house is not so with God* **23:6** [a]Mt 13:41 **23:7** [a]Mt 3:10; 13:30; Heb 6:8 [1]Lit *filled* **23:8** [a]1Chr 11:11-47 [1]Or *3* **23:9** [a]1Chr 27:4 [b]1Chr 8:4 [1]Or *defied* **23:10** [a]1Chr 11:13 [b]1Sa 11:13; 19:5 [1]Lit *his hand clung* **23:11** [a]2Sa 23:33 [1]Possibly, at Lehi

people fled from before the Philis-
tines. **12** But he took his stand in the
midst of that portion and delivered
it and struck down the Philistines.
So [a]Yahweh brought about a great
salvation.

**13** Then three of the thirty chief
men went down and came to David
in the harvest time to the [a]cave of
Adullam, while the troop of the Phi-
listines was camping in [b]the valley of
Rephaim. **14** And David was then [a]in
the fortress, while the garrison of the
Philistines was then in Bethlehem.
**15** [a]Then David had a craving and
said, "Oh that someone would give
me water to drink from the well of
Bethlehem, which is by the gate!"
**16** [a]So the three mighty men broke
through the camp of the Philis-
tines and drew water from the well
of Bethlehem which was by the
gate, and carried *it* and brought *it*
to David. Nevertheless, he was not
willing to drink it, but [b]poured it out
to Yahweh; **17** and he said, "Be it far
from me, O Yahweh, that I should do
this. [a]*Shall I drink* the blood of the
men who went [1]at the risk of their
lives?" Therefore he was not willing
to drink it. These things the three
mighty men did.

**18** [a]Now Abishai, the brother of
Joab, the son of Zeruiah, was [b]chief
of the [1]thirty. And he swung his
spear against three hundred [2]*who
were* slain *by him*; and he had a name
as well as the three. **19** Of the thirty
he was most honored and became
their commander; however, he did
not attain to the three.

**20** Then [a]Benaiah the son of
Jehoiada, the son of a valiant man
of [b]Kabzeel, mighty in deeds, struck
down the [1]two *sons of* Ariel of Moab.
He also went down and struck down
a lion in the midst of a pit on a snowy
day. **21** He had also struck down an
Egyptian, [1]an impressive man. Now
in the Egyptian's hand was a spear,
but he went down to him with a club
and snatched the spear from the
Egyptian's hand and killed him with
his own spear. **22** These *things* [a]Bena-
iah the son of Jehoiada did, and had
a name as well as the three mighty
men. **23** He was honored among the
thirty, but he did not attain to the
three. And David appointed him over
his guard.

**24** [a]Asahel the brother of Joab was
among the thirty; Elhanan the son of
Dodo of Bethlehem, **25** [a]Shammah
the [b]Harodite, Elika the Harodite,
**26** Helez the Paltite, Ira the son
of Ikkesh the [a]Tekoite, **27** Abiezer
the [a]Anathothite, Mebunnai the
Hushathite, **28** Zalmon the Ahohite,
Maharai the [a]Netophathite, **29** [a]Heleb
the son of Baanah the Netophathite,
Ittai the son of Ribai of [b]Gibeah of
the sons of Benjamin, **30** Benaiah a
[a]Pirathonite, Hiddai of the brooks of
[b]Gaash, **31** Abi-albon the Arbathite,
Azmaveth the [a]Barhumite, **32** Eliahba
the [a]Shaalbonite, the sons of Jashen,
Jonathan, **33** [a]Shammah the Hararite,
Ahiam the son of Sharar the Ararite,

---

**23:12** [a]2Sa 23:10 **23:13** [a]1Sa 22:1 [b]2Sa 5:18 **23:14** [a]1Sa 22:4, 5 **23:15** [a]1Chr 11:17
**23:16** [a]1Chr 11:18 [b]Ge 35:14 **23:17** [a]Lv 17:10 [1]Lit *with their souls* **23:18** [a]2Sa 10:10, 14; 18:2
[b]1Chr 11:20, 21 [1]As in two Heb mss and Syr; M.T. *3* [2]Lit *slain ones* **23:20** [a]2Sa 8:18; 20:23 [b]Jos 15:21
[1]Or *two lion-like heroes* **23:21** [1]Lit *a man of appearance* **23:22** [a]2Sa 23:20 **23:24** [a]2Sa 2:18;
1Chr 27:7 **23:25** [a]1Chr 11:27 [b]Jdg 7:1 **23:26** [a]2Sa 14:2 **23:27** [a]Jos 21:18 **23:28** [a]2Ki 25:23
**23:29** [a]1Chr 11:30 [b]Jos 18:28 **23:30** [a]Jdg 12:13, 15 [b]Jos 24:30 **23:31** [a]2Sa 3:16 **23:32** [a]Jos 19:42
**23:33** [a]2Sa 23:11

34 Eliphelet the son of Ahasbai, the
son of [a]the Maacathite, [b]Eliam the
son of [c]Ahithophel the Gilonite,
35 [a]Hezro the [b]Carmelite, Paarai the
Arbite, 36 Igal the son of Nathan of
[a]Zobah, Bani the Gadite, 37 Zelek the
Ammonite, Naharai the [a]Beerothite,
armor bearers of Joab the son of
Zeruiah, 38 Ira the [a]Ithrite, Gareb
the Ithrite, 39 [a]Uriah the Hittite;
thirty-seven in all.

### *David Sins in Taking a Census*

24 [a]And [b]again the anger of
Yahweh burned against Israel,
and it incited David against them to
say, "[c]Go, number Israel and Judah."
2 So the king said to Joab the com-
mander of the military force who was
with him, "Go about now through
all the tribes of Israel, [a]from Dan
to Beersheba, and [1]take a census of
the people, that I may know the *total*
count of the people." 3 But Joab said
to the king, "[a]Now may Yahweh your
God add to the people a hundred
times as many as they are, while the
eyes of my lord the king *still* see; but
why does my lord the king delight
in this thing?" 4 Nevertheless, the
king's word *stood* strong against Joab
and against the commanders of the
military force. So Joab and the com-
manders of the military force went
out from the presence of the king to
[1]take a census of the people of Israel.
5 And they crossed the Jordan and
camped in [a]Aroer, on the right side
of the city that is in the middle of
the valley of Gad and toward [b]Jazer.
6 Then they came to Gilead and to
[1]the land of Tahtim-hodshi, and they
came to Dan-jaan and around to
[a]Sidon, 7 and came to the [a]fortified
*city* of Tyre and to all the cities of
the [b]Hivites and of the Canaanites,
and they went out to the south of
Judah, *to* [c]Beersheba. 8 So they had
gone about through the whole land,
and they came to Jerusalem at the
end of nine months and twenty days.
9 And Joab gave [a]the *total* count of
the [1]census of the people to the king;
and there were in Israel [b]800,000
valiant men who drew the sword, and
the men of Judah were 500,000 men.
10 Then [a]David's heart struck him
after he had counted the people. So
David said to Yahweh, "[b]I have sinned
greatly in what I have done. But
now, O Yahweh, please [1]take away
the iniquity of Your slave, for [c]I have
acted very foolishly." 11 Then David
arose in the morning, and the word
of Yahweh came to [a]the prophet
Gad, David's [b]seer, saying, 12 "Go and
speak to David, 'Thus says Yahweh, "I
am offering you three things; choose
for yourself one of them, and I will
do *that* to you."'" 13 So Gad came to
David and told him, and said to him,
"Shall [a]seven years of famine come
to you in your land? Or will you flee
three months before your adversar-
ies while they pursue you? Or shall
there be three days' pestilence in
your land? Now, know and see what
word I should return to Him who

***23:34*** [a]*2Sa 10:6, 8; 20:14* [b]2Sa 11:3 [c]2Sa 15:12 **23:35** [a]1Chr 11:37 [b]Jos 15:55 **23:36** [a]2Sa 8:3 **23:37** [a]2Sa 4:2 **23:38** [a]1Chr 2:53 **23:39** [a]2Sa 11:3, 6 ◆ **24:1** [a]1Chr 21:1 [b]2Sa 21:1, 2 [c]1Chr 27:23, 24 **24:2** [a]Jdg 20:1; 2Sa 3:10 [1]Lit *muster* **24:3** [a]Dt 1:11 **24:4** [1]Lit *muster* **24:5** [a]Dt 2:36; Jos 13:9, 16 [b]Nu 21:32; 32:35 **24:6** [a]Jos 19:28; Jdg 1:31 [1]Or *Kadesh in the land of the Hittite* **24:7** [a]Jos 19:29 [b]Jos 11:3; Jdg 3:3 [c]Ge 21:22-33 **24:9** [a]Nu 1:44-46 [b]1Chr 21:5 [1]Lit *muster* **24:10** [a]1Sa 24:5 [b]2Sa 12:13 [c]1Sa 13:13; 2Chr 16:9 [1]Lit *cause to pass away* **24:11** [a]1Sa 22:5; 1Chr 29:29 [b]1Sa 9:9 **24:13** [a]1Chr 21:12; Eze 14:21

sent me." **14** Then David said to Gad, "I am in great distress. Let us now fall into the hand of Yahweh, [a]for His compassions are abundant. But do not let me fall into the hand of man."

**15** So [a]Yahweh [1]sent a pestilence against Israel from the morning until the appointed time, and 70,000 men of the people [b]from Dan to Beersheba died. **16** [a]Then the angel sent forth his hand toward Jerusalem to destroy it, and [b]Yahweh [1]relented of the calamity and said to the angel who destroyed the people, "It is enough! Now relax your hand!" And the angel of Yahweh was by the threshing floor of Araunah the Jebusite. **17** Then David spoke to Yahweh when he saw the angel who was striking down the people, and said, "Behold, [a]it is I who have sinned, and it is I who have done unrighteousness; but [b]these sheep, what have they done? Please let Your hand be against me and my father's house."

### *David Erects an Altar*

**18** So Gad came to David that day and said to him, "[a]Go up, erect an altar to Yahweh on the threshing floor of [1]Araunah the Jebusite." **19** So David went up according to the word of Gad, just as Yahweh had commanded. **20** And Araunah looked down and saw the king and his servants crossing over toward him; and Araunah went out and bowed his face to the ground before the king. **21** Then Araunah said, "Why has my lord the king come to his servant?" And David said, "To buy the threshing floor from you, in order to build an altar to Yahweh, [a]that the plague may be checked from *being* upon the people." **22** And Araunah said to David, "Let my lord the king take and offer up what is good in his sight. Look, [a]the oxen for the burnt offering, the threshing sledges and the yokes of the oxen for the wood. **23** Everything, O king, Araunah gives to the king." And Araunah said to the king, "May Yahweh your God [a]accept you." **24** However, the king said to Araunah, "No, but I will surely buy *it* from you for a price, for [a]I will not offer burnt offerings to Yahweh my God [1]which cost me nothing." So [b]David bought the threshing floor and the oxen for fifty [2]shekels of silver. **25** Then David built there an altar to Yahweh and offered burnt offerings and peace offerings. [a]Thus Yahweh was moved by the entreaty for the land, and the plague was checked from *being* upon Israel.

---

**24:14** [a]Ps 51:1; 130:4, 7 **24:15** [a]1Chr 21:14; 27:24 [b]2Sa 24:2 [1]Lit *gave* **24:16** [a]Ex 12:23; 2Ki 19:35; Ac 12:23 [b]Ex 32:14; 1Sa 15:11 [1]Or *regretted*, cf. 15:11, 29, 35 **24:17** [a]2Sa 24:10 [b]2Sa 7:8; Ps 74:1 **24:18** [a]1Chr 21:18 [1]In 2Chr 3:1, *Ornan* **24:21** [a]Nu 16:44-50 **24:22** [a]1Sa 6:14; 1Ki 19:21 **24:23** [a]Eze 20:40, 41 **24:24** [a]Mal 1:13, 14 [b]1Chr 21:24, 25 [1]Lit *gratuitously* [2]A shekel was approx. 0.4 oz. or 11 gm **24:25** [a]2Sa 21:14

# The First Book of the
# KINGS

### David in Old Age

1 Now King David was old, ad-
vanced in age; and they covered
him with clothes, but he could not
keep warm. 2 So his servants said to
him, "Let them seek a young virgin
for my lord the king, and let her
stand before the king and become
his nurse; and let her lie in your
bosom, that my lord the king may
keep warm." 3 So they sought for a
beautiful young woman throughout
all the territory of Israel, and found
Abishag the [a]Shunammite, and
brought her to the king. 4 Now the
young woman was very beautiful;
and she became the king's nurse and
attended him, but the king did not
[1]know her.
5 Now [a]Adonijah the son of Hag-
gith exalted himself, saying, "I will
be king." So [b]he prepared for himself
a chariot and horsemen and fifty
men as runners before him. 6 But
his father had never [1]grieved him at
any time by asking, "Why have you
done so?" And he was also a very
handsome man in form, and [a,2]he
was born after Absalom. 7 [1]And he
had conferred with [a]Joab the son
of Zeruiah and with [b]Abiathar the
priest; and following [c]Adonijah,
they helped him. 8 But [a]Zadok the
priest, [b]Benaiah the son of Jehoiada,
[c]Nathan the prophet, [d]Shimei, Rei,
and [e]the mighty men who belonged
to *David*, were not with Adonijah.
9 And Adonijah sacrificed sheep
and oxen and fatlings by the [1]stone of
Zoheleth, which is beside [a]En-rogel;
and he invited all his brothers, the
king's sons, and all the men of Judah,
the king's servants. 10 But he did not
invite Nathan the prophet, Benaiah,
the mighty men, and [a]Solomon his
brother.

### Nathan Speaks to Bathsheba

11 Then Nathan spoke to [a]Bathshe-
ba the mother of Solomon, saying,
"Have you not heard that Adonijah
the son of Haggith has become king,
and David our lord does not know *it*?
12 So now come, please let me [a]give
you counsel and provide escape for
your life and the life of your son Solo-
mon. 13 Go [1]at once to King David and
say to him, 'Have you not, my lord,
O king, sworn to your maidservant,
saying, "[a]Surely Solomon your son
shall be king after me, and he shall
sit on my throne"? Why then has
Adonijah become king?' 14 Behold,
while you are still there speaking
with the king, I will come in after
you and fully confirm your words."
15 So Bathsheba went in to the king
in the bedroom. Now [a]the king was
very old, and Abishag the Shunam-
mite was ministering to the king.
16 Then Bathsheba bowed and pros-
trated herself [1]before the king. And
the king said, "What [2]do you wish?"
17 And she said to him, "My lord,

---

◆ **1:3** [a]Jos 19:18; 1Sa 28:4 **1:4** [1]Or *have relations with* **1:5** [a]2Sa 3:4 [b]2Sa 15:1 **1:6** [a]2Sa 3:3, 4 [1]Lit *pained him* [2]Lit *she gave him birth* **1:7** [a]1Chr 11:6 [b]1Sa 22:20, 23; 2Sa 20:25 [c]1Ki 2:22 [1]Lit *His words were* **1:8** [a]2Sa 20:25; 1Chr 16:39 [b]2Sa 8:18 [c]2Sa 12:1 [d]1Ki 4:18 [e]2Sa 23:8-39 **1:9** [a]Jos 15:7; 18:16; 2Sa 17:17 [1]Lit *Gliding, Serpent Stone* **1:10** [a]2Sa 12:24 **1:11** [a]2Sa 12:24 **1:12** [a]Pr 15:22 **1:13** [a]1Ki 1:30; 1Chr 22:9-13 [1]Lit *and enter* **1:15** [a]1Ki 1:1 **1:16** [1]Lit *to* [2]Lit *to you*

you swore to your maidservant by
[1]Yahweh your God, *saying*, '[a]Surely
your son Solomon shall be king after
me and he shall sit on my throne.'
**18** But now, behold, Adonijah is king;
and now, my lord the king, you do
not know *it*. **19** [a]And he has sacrificed
oxen and fatlings and sheep in abun-
dance, and has invited all the sons
of the king and Abiathar the priest
and Joab the commander of the army,
but he has not invited Solomon your
servant. **20** As for you now, my lord
the king, the eyes of all Israel are on
you, to tell them who shall sit on the
throne of my lord the king after him.
**21** Otherwise it will be, [a]as soon as my
lord the king sleeps with his fathers,
that I and my son Solomon will be
considered [1]offenders."

**22** Behold, while she was still
speaking with the king, Nathan the
prophet came in. **23** Then they told
the king, saying, "Here is Nathan
the prophet." And then he came
in before the king and prostrated
himself [1]before the king with his
[2]face to the ground. **24** Then Nathan
said, "My lord the king, have you said,
'Adonijah shall be king after me, and
he shall sit on my throne'? **25** [a]For he
has gone down today and has sacri-
ficed oxen and fatlings and sheep in
abundance, and has invited all the
king's sons and the commanders of
the army and Abiathar the priest, and
behold, they are eating and drinking
before him; and they say, '[b]*Long* live
King Adonijah!' **26** [a]But me, *even* me
your servant, and Zadok the priest
and Benaiah the son of Jehoiada and
your servant Solomon, he has not
invited. **27** Has this thing happened
by my lord the king, and you have
not made known to your [1]servants
who should sit on the throne of my
lord the king after him?"

**28** Then King David answered and
said, "Call Bathsheba to me." And she
came into the king's presence and
stood before the king. **29** And the king
swore and said, "[a]As Yahweh lives,
who has redeemed my life from all
distress, **30** surely as [a]I swore to you
by Yahweh, the God of Israel, saying,
'Surely your son Solomon shall be
king after me, and he shall sit on my
throne in my place'; I will surely do so
this day." **31** Then Bathsheba bowed
with her [1]face to the ground, and
prostrated herself [2]before the king
and said, "[a]May my lord King David
live forever."

**32** Then King David said, "Call to
me [a]Zadok the priest, Nathan the
prophet, and Benaiah the son of
Jehoiada." And they came into the
king's presence. **33** And the king
said to them, "Take with you [a]the
servants of your lord, and have my
son Solomon ride on my own mule,
and bring him down to [b]Gihon.
**34** And Zadok the priest and Nathan
the prophet shall [a]anoint him there
as king over Israel and [b]blow the
trumpet and say, '[c]*Long* live King
Solomon!' **35** Then you shall come up
after him, and he shall come and sit
on my throne. And he shall be king in
my place; for I have commanded him
to be ruler over Israel and Judah."
**36** Then Benaiah the son of Jehoiada

---

**1:17** [a]1Ki 1:13 [1]The personal covenant name of God, a form of I AM WHO I AM, cf. Ex 3:14-15
**1:19** [a]1Ki 1:9 **1:21** [a]Dt 31:16; 2Sa 7:12; 1Ki 2:10 [1]Lit *sinners* **1:23** [1]Lit *to* [2]Lit *nose* **1:25** [a]1Ki 1:9
[b]1Sa 10:24 **1:26** [a]1Ki 1:8, 10 **1:27** [1]Some mss *servant* **1:29** [a]2Sa 4:9 **1:30** [a]1Ki 1:13, 17
**1:31** [a]Da 2:4; 3:9 [1]Lit *nose* [2]Lit *to* **1:32** [a]1Ki 1:8 **1:33** [a]2Sa 20:6, 7 [b]2Chr 32:30; 33:14
**1:34** [a]1Sa 10:1; 16:3, 12; 2Sa 5:3; 1Ki 19:16; 2Ki 9:3 [b]2Sa 15:10 [c]1Ki 1:25

answered the king and said, "Amen!
Thus may Yahweh, the God of my
lord the king, say. **37** [a]As Yahweh has
been with my lord the king, so may
He be with Solomon, and [b]make his
throne greater than the throne of my
lord King David!"

### *Solomon Anointed King*

**38** So [a]Zadok the priest, Nathan the
prophet, Benaiah the son of Jehoiada,
[b]the Cherethites, and the Pelethites
went down and had Solomon ride on
King David's mule, and brought him
to [c]Gihon. **39** Zadok the priest then
[a]took the horn of oil from the tent
and [b]anointed Solomon. Then they
[c]blew the trumpet, and all the peo-
ple said, "[d]*Long* live King Solomon!"
**40** And all the people went up after
him, and the people [1]were playing
on flutes and were glad with great
gladness, so that the earth [2]shook
at their sound.

**41** And Adonijah and all the guests
who *were* with him heard *it* as they
finished eating. Then Joab heard
the sound of the trumpet and said,
"Why is the sound of the city such
an uproar?" **42** While he was still
speaking, behold, [a]Jonathan the son
of Abiathar the priest came. Then
Adonijah said, "Come in, for [b]you are
a valiant man and bring good news."
**43** But Jonathan answered and said to
Adonijah, "No! Our lord King David
has made Solomon king. **44** The king
has also sent with him Zadok the
priest, Nathan the prophet, Benaiah
the son of Jehoiada, the Cherethites,
*and the Pelethites*; and they have
made him ride on the king's mule.
**45** And Zadok the priest and Nathan
the prophet have anointed him king
in Gihon, and they have come up
from there with gladness, [a]so that
the city is in an uproar. This is the
sound which you have heard. **46** And
also, [a]Solomon has even taken his
seat on the throne of the kingdom.
**47** And also, the king's servants came
to bless our lord King David, saying,
'May [a]your God make the name of
Solomon better than your name and
his throne greater than your throne!'
And [b]the king bowed himself on the
bed. **48** And also, the king said thus,
'Blessed be Yahweh, the God of Israel,
who [a]has granted one to sit on my
throne today while my own eyes see
*it*.'"

**49** Then all the guests of Adonijah
trembled; and they arose and each
went on his way. **50** And Adonijah
was afraid of Solomon, and he arose,
went, and [a]took hold of the horns
of the altar. **51** Then it was told to
Solomon, saying, "Behold, Adoni-
jah is afraid of King Solomon, and
behold, he has taken hold of the
horns of the altar, saying, 'Let King
Solomon swear to me today that he
will not put his servant to death with
the sword.'" **52** And Solomon said,
"If he is a worthy man, [a]not one of
his hairs will fall to the ground; but
if evil is found in him, he will die."
**53** So King Solomon sent, and they
brought him down from the altar.
And he came and prostrated himself
[1]before King Solomon, and Solomon
said to him, "Go to your house."

---

**1:37** [a]Jos 1:5, 17; 1Sa 20:13 [b]1Ki 1:47 **1:38** [a]1Ki 1:8 [b]2Sa 8:18 [c]1Ki 1:33 **1:39** [a]Ex 30:23-32; Ps 89:20 [b]1Chr 29:22 [c]1Ki 1:34 [d]1Sa 10:24 **1:40** [1]Lit *fluting* [2]Lit *was split* **1:42** [a]2Sa 15:27, 36; 17:17 [b]2Sa 18:27 **1:45** [a]1Ki 1:40 **1:46** [a]1Chr 29:23 **1:47** [a]1Ki 1:37 [b]Ge 47:31 **1:48** [a]2Sa 7:12; 1Ki 3:6 **1:50** [a]Ex 27:2; 30:10; 1Ki 2:28 **1:52** [a]1Sa 14:45; 2Sa 14:11; Ac 27:34 **1:53** [1]Lit *to*

### *David's Command to Solomon*

**2** Then David's [a,1]time to die drew near, so he commanded Solomon his son, saying, **2** "[a]I am going the way of all the earth. [b]So you shall be strong, and be a man. **3** And you shall keep the responsibility *given by* Yahweh your God, to walk in His ways, to keep His statutes, His commandments, His judgments, and His testimonies, [a]according to what is written in the Law of Moses, that [b]you may be prosperous in all that you do and wherever you turn, **4** so that [a]Yahweh may establish His promise which He spoke concerning me, saying, '[b]If your sons keep their way, [c]to walk before Me in [1]truth with all their heart and with all their soul, He said, [d,2]you shall not have a man cut off from the throne of Israel.'

**5** "Now you also know what Joab the [a]son of Zeruiah did to me, what he did to the two commanders of the armies of Israel, to [b]Abner the son of Ner, and to [c]Amasa the son of Jether, whom he killed; he also [1]shed the blood of war in peace. And he put the blood of war on his belt [2]about his [3]waist, and on his sandals [4]on his feet. **6** [a]So act according to your wisdom, and do not let his gray hair go down to Sheol in peace. **7** But [a]show lovingkindness to the sons of Barzillai the Gileadite, and [b]let them be among those who eat at your table; [c]for they [1]assisted me when I fled from Absalom your brother. **8** Behold, [a]there is with you Shimei the son of Gera the Benjamite, of Bahurim; now it was he who cursed me with a [1]violent curse on the day I went to Mahanaim. But when [b]he came down to me at the Jordan, I swore to him by Yahweh, saying, 'I will not put you to death with the sword.' **9** So now, do not let him go unpunished, [a]for you are a wise man; and you will know what you ought to do to him, and you will bring his gray hair down to Sheol with blood."

### *The Death of David*

**10** Then [a]David slept with his fathers and was buried in [b]the city of David. **11** [a]And the [1]time which David reigned over Israel *was* forty years; in Hebron he reigned [b]seven years and in Jerusalem he reigned thirty-three years. **12** And [a]Solomon sat on the throne of David his father, and his kingdom was firmly established.

### *Adonijah's Request*

**13** Then Adonijah the son of Haggith came to Bathsheba the mother of Solomon. And she said, "[a]Do you come peacefully?" And he said, "Peacefully." **14** Then he said, "I have something *to say* to you." And she said, "Speak." **15** So he said, "You know that [a]the kingdom was mine and [b]that all Israel [1]expected me to be king; [c]however, the kingdom has turned about and become my brother's, [d]for it was his from Yahweh. **16** So now, I

◆ **2:1** [a]Ge 47:29; Dt 31:14 [1]Lit *days* **2:2** [a]Jos 23:14 [b]Dt 31:7, 23; Jos 1:6, 7 **2:3** [a]Dt 17:18-20 [b]1Chr 22:12, 13 **2:4** [a]2Sa 7:25 [b]Ps 132:12 [c]2Ki 20:3 [d]2Sa 7:12, 13; 1Ki 8:25; 9:5 [1]Or *faithfulness* [2]Lit *there shall not be cast off to you a man from before Me* **2:5** [a]2Sa 2:13, 18 [b]2Sa 3:27; 1Ki 2:32 [c]2Sa 20:10 [1]Lit *made* [2]Lit *that was about* [3]Lit *loins* [4]Lit *that were on* **2:6** [a]1Ki 2:9 **2:7** [a]2Sa 19:31-38 [b]2Sa 9:7, 10 [c]2Sa 17:27-29 [1]Lit *came near to* **2:8** [a]2Sa 16:5-8 [b]2Sa 19:18-23 [1]Or *grievous* **2:9** [a]1Ki 2:6 **2:10** [a]Ac 2:29; 13:36 [b]2Sa 5:7; 1Ki 3:1 **2:11** [a]2Sa 5:4, 5; 1Chr 3:4; 29:26, 27 [b]2Sa 5:5 [1]Lit *days* **2:12** [a]1Chr 29:23; 2Chr 1:1 **2:13** [a]1Sa 16:4 **2:15** [a]2Sa 3:3, 4; 1Ki 2:22 [b]1Ki 1:5-25 [c]1Ki 1:38-50 [d]1Chr 22:9, 10; 28:5-7 [1]Lit *set their faces on me*

am making one request of you; do
not [1]turn me away." And she said to
him, "Speak." **17** Then he said, "Please
speak to Solomon the king, for he will
not [1]turn you away, that he may give
me [a]Abishag the Shunammite as a
wife." **18** And Bathsheba said, "Very
well; I will speak to the king for you."

### *Adonijah Put to Death*

**19** So Bathsheba went to King Solo-
mon to speak to him for Adonijah.
And the king arose to meet her,
bowed before her, and sat on his
throne; then he [a]had a throne set
for the king's mother, and [b]she sat
on his right. **20** Then she said, "I am
making one small request of you; [a]do
not turn [1]me away." And the king said
to her, "Ask, my mother, for I will not
turn [2]you away." **21** So she said, "[a]Let
Abishag the Shunammite be given
to Adonijah your brother as a wife."
**22** Then King Solomon answered and
said to his mother, "And why are you
asking Abishag the Shunammite
for Adonijah? [a]Ask for him also
the kingdom—[b]for he is my older
brother—even for him, for [c]Abiathar
the priest, and for Joab the son of
Zeruiah!" **23** Then King Solomon
swore by Yahweh, saying, "May God
do so to me and more also, if Adoni-
jah has [a]not spoken this word against
his own [1]life. **24** So now, as Yahweh
lives, who has established me and set
me on the throne of David my father
and [a]who has made me a house as
He promised, surely Adonijah shall
be put to death today." **25** So King
Solomon [a]sent Benaiah the son of
Jehoiada; and he fell upon him so
that he died.

**26** Then to Abiathar the priest the
king said, "[a]Go to Anathoth to your
own field, [b]for you [1]deserve to die;
but I will not put you to death at this
time, because [c]you carried the ark of
Lord Yahweh before my father David,
and because [d]you were afflicted in
everything with which my father
was afflicted." **27** So Solomon drove
Abiathar away from being priest to
Yahweh, in order to fulfill [a]the word
of Yahweh, which He had spoken
concerning the house of Eli in Shiloh.

### *Joab Put to Death*

**28** Now the news came to Joab, [a]for
Joab had followed Adonijah, [b]although
he had not followed Absalom. And
Joab fled to the tent of Yahweh and
[c]took hold of the horns of the altar.
**29** And it was told to King Solomon
that Joab had fled to the tent of
Yahweh, and behold, he is beside the
altar. Then Solomon [a]sent Benaiah
the son of Jehoiada, saying, "[b]Go, fall
upon him." **30** So Benaiah came to
the tent of Yahweh and said to him,
"Thus the king has said, 'Come out.'"
But he said, "No, for I will die here."
And Benaiah brought the king word
again, saying, "Thus spoke Joab, and
thus he answered me." **31** And the king
said to him, "[a]Do as he has spoken
and fall upon him and bury him, [b]that
you may remove from me and from
my father's house the blood which
Joab shed without cause. **32** [a]And

---

**2:16** [1]Lit *turn away my face* **2:17** [a]1Ki 1:3, 4 [1]Lit *turn away your face* **2:19** [a]1Ki 15:13 [b]Ps 45:9 **2:20** [a]1Ki 2:16 [1]Lit *my face* [2]Lit *your face* **2:21** [a]1Ki 1:3, 4 **2:22** [a]2Sa 12:8 [b]1Ki 1:6; 2:15; 1Chr 3:2, 5 [c]1Ki 1:7 **2:23** [a]Ru 1:17 [1]Lit *soul* **2:24** [a]2Sa 7:11, 13; 1Chr 22:10 **2:25** [a]2Sa 8:18 **2:26** [a]Jos 21:18; Jer 1:1 [b]1Sa 26:16 [c]1Sa 23:6; 2Sa 15:24-29 [d]1Sa 22:20-23; 23:8, 9 [1]Lit *are a man of death* **2:27** [a]1Sa 2:27-36 **2:28** [a]1Ki 1:7 [b]2Sa 17:25; 18:2 [c]1Ki 1:50 **2:29** [a]1Ki 2:25 [b]Ex 21:14 **2:31** [a]Ex 21:14 [b]Nu 35:33; Dt 19:13; 21:8, 9 **2:32** [a]Ge 9:6; Jdg 9:24, 57; Ps 7:16

Yahweh will return his blood on his own head, [b]because he fell upon two men more righteous and better than he and killed them with the sword, but my father David did not know *it*: [c]Abner the son of Ner, commander of the army of Israel, and [d]Amasa the son of Jether, commander of the army of Judah. **33** [a]So shall their blood return on the head of Joab and on the head of his seed forever; but to David and his seed and his house and his throne, may there be peace from Yahweh forever." **34** Then [a]Benaiah the son of Jehoiada went up and fell upon him and put him to death, and he was buried at his own house [b]in the wilderness. **35** [a]And the king appointed Benaiah the son of Jehoiada over the army in his place, and the king appointed [b]Zadok the priest [c]in the place of Abiathar.

### *Shimei Put to Death*

**36** Then the king sent and called for [a]Shimei and said to him, "Build for yourself a house in Jerusalem and live there, and do not go out from there to any place. **37** Now it will be on the day you go out and [a]cross over the [1]brook Kidron, that you will know for certain that you shall surely die; [b]your blood shall be on your own head." **38** Shimei then said to the king, "The word is good. As my lord the king has said, so your servant will do." So Shimei lived in Jerusalem many days.

**39** But it happened at the end of three years, that two of the slaves of Shimei ran away [a]to Achish son of Maacah, king of Gath. And they told Shimei, saying, "Behold, your slaves are in Gath." **40** Then Shimei arose and saddled his donkey, and went to Gath to Achish to search for his slaves. And Shimei went and brought his slaves from Gath. **41** And it was told to Solomon that Shimei had gone from Jerusalem to Gath, and had returned. **42** So the king sent and called for Shimei and said to him, "Did I not make you swear by Yahweh and solemnly warn you, saying, 'You will know for certain that on the day you go out and go anywhere, you shall surely die'? And you said to me, 'The word which I have heard is good.' **43** Why then have you not kept the oath of Yahweh, and the command which I have commanded you?" **44** The king also said to Shimei, "[a]You know all the evil which [1]you acknowledge in your heart, which you did to my father David; therefore [b]Yahweh shall return your evil on your own head. **45** But King Solomon shall be blessed, and [a]the throne of David shall be established before Yahweh forever." **46** [a]So the king commanded Benaiah the son of Jehoiada, and he went out and fell upon him so that he died.

[b]Thus the kingdom was established in the hands of Solomon.

### *Solomon's Marriage and Sacrifices*

**3** Then [a]Solomon [1]formed a marriage alliance with Pharaoh king of Egypt, and took Pharaoh's daughter [b]and brought her to the city of David [c]until he had completed building his own house and the house of Yahweh and [d]the wall around Jerusalem.

**2:32** [b]2Chr 21:13, 14 [c]2Sa 3:27 [d]2Sa 20:9, 10 **2:33** [a]2Sa 3:29 **2:34** [a]1Ki 2:25 [b]Jos 15:61; Mt 3:1 **2:35** [a]1Ki 4:4 [b]1Chr 6:53; 24:3; 29:22 [c]1Ki 2:27 **2:36** [a]2Sa 16:5; 1Ki 2:8 **2:37** [a]2Sa 15:23; 2Ki 23:6; Jn 18:1 [b]Jos 2:19; 2Sa 1:16; Eze 18:13 [1]Or *wadi* **2:39** [a]1Sa 27:2 **2:44** [a]2Sa 16:5-13 [b]1Sa 25:39; 2Ki 11:1, 12-16; Ps 7:16 [1]Lit *your heart acknowledges* **2:45** [a]2Sa 7:13; Pr 25:5 **2:46** [a]1Ki 2:25, 34 [b]1Ki 2:12; 2Chr 1:1
◆**3:1** [a]1Ki 7:8; 9:16, 24; 2Chr 8:11 [b]1Ki 9:24 [c]1Ki 7:1; 9:10 [d]1Ki 9:15 [1]Lit *made himself a son-in-law of Pharaoh*

2 [a]The people were still sacrificing
on the high places because there
was no house built for the name of
Yahweh until those days.
3 And [a]Solomon loved Yahweh,
[b]walking in the statutes of his fa-
ther David, except he sacrificed and
burned incense on the high places.
4 [a]And the king went to [b]Gibeon to
sacrifice there, [c]for that was the great
high place; Solomon offered one thou-
sand burnt offerings on that altar. 5 [a]In
Gibeon, Yahweh appeared to Solomon
[b]in a dream at night; and God said,
"[c]Ask what I should give to you."

### *God Gives Wisdom to Solomon*

6 Then Solomon said, "[a]You have
shown great lovingkindness to Your
slave David my father, [b]according to
how he walked before You in [1]truth
and righteousness and uprightness
of heart toward You; and [c]You have
kept for him this great lovingkind-
ness, that You have given him a son
to sit on his throne, as *it is* this day.
7 So now, O Yahweh my God, [a]You
have made Your slave king in place of
my father David, yet [b]I am but a little
child; [c]I do not know how to go out
or come in. 8 [a]And Your slave is in
the midst of Your people which You
have chosen, [b]a numerous people
who are too many to be numbered
or counted. 9 So [a]give Your slave a
listening heart to judge Your people
[b]to discern between good and evil.
For who is able to [1]judge this glorious
people of Yours?"
10 [1]And it was pleasing in the sight
of the Lord that Solomon had asked
this thing. 11 And God said to him,
"Because you have asked this thing
and have [a]not asked for yourself
[1]long life, nor have asked riches for
yourself, nor have you asked for the
life of your enemies, but have asked
for yourself discernment to listen
to justice, 12 behold, [a]I have done
according to your words. Behold, [b]I
have given you a wise and discerning
heart, so that there has been no one
like you before you, nor shall one like
you arise after you. 13 [a]I have also
given you what you have not asked,
both [b]riches and honor, so that there
will not be any among the kings like
you all your days. 14 [a]Now if you walk
in My ways, keeping My statutes
and commandments, as your father
David walked, then I will [b]prolong
your days."
15 Then [a]Solomon awoke, and
behold, it was a dream. And he came
to Jerusalem and stood before the
ark of the covenant of the Lord, and
offered burnt offerings and made
peace offerings, and [b]made a feast
for all his servants.

### *Solomon Wisely Judges*

16 Then two women who were harlots
came to the king and stood before
him. 17 And the one woman said,
"Oh, my lord, [1]this woman and I live
in the same house; and I gave birth
to a child while she *was* in the house.
18 And it happened on the third day

---

**3:2** [a]Lv 17:3-5; Dt 12:2, 13, 14; 1Ki 22:43 **3:3** [a]Dt 6:5; 10:12, 13; 11:13; 30:16; Ps 31:23; 145:20; 1Co 8:3 [b]1Ki 2:3; 9:4; 11:4, 6, 38 **3:4** [a]2Chr 1:3 [b]Jos 18:21-25 [c]1Chr 16:39; 21:29 **3:5** [a]1Ki 9:2; 11:9 [b]Nu 12:6; Mt 1:20; 2:13 [c]Jn 15:7 **3:6** [a]2Sa 7:8-17; 2Chr 1:8 [b]1Ki 9:4 [c]1Ki 1:48 [1]Or *faithfulness* **3:7** [a]1Chr 22:9-13 [b]1Chr 29:1; Jer 1:6, 7 [c]Nu 27:17 **3:8** [a]Ex 19:6; Dt 7:6 [b]Ge 15:5; 22:17 **3:9** [a]2Chr 1:10; Ps 72:1, 2; Pr 2:3-9; Jas 1:5 [b]2Sa 14:17; Heb 5:14 [1]Or *do justice for* **3:10** [1]Lit *the thing* **3:11** [a]Jas 4:3 [1]Lit *many days* **3:12** [a]1Jn 5:14, 15 [b]1Ki 4:29-31; 5:12; 10:23, 24; Ecc 1:16 **3:13** [a]1Ki 4:21-24; 10:23, 27; Mt 6:33; Eph 3:20 [b]Pr 3:16 **3:14** [a]1Ki 3:6 [b]Ps 91:16; Pr 3:2 **3:15** [a]Ge 41:7 [b]1Ki 8:65 **3:17** [1]Lit *I and this woman*

after I gave birth, that this woman
also gave birth to a child, and we were
together. There was no stranger with
us in the house, only the two of us in
the house. **19** And this woman's son
died in the night because she lay on
him. **20** So she arose in the middle
of the night and took my son from
beside me while your maidservant
slept, and laid him in her bosom,
and laid her dead son in my bosom.
**21** When I rose in the morning to
nurse my son, behold, he was dead;
but when I looked at him carefully in
the morning, behold, he was not my
son, whom I had borne." **22** Then the
other woman said, "No! For the living
one is my son, and the dead one is
your son." But [1]the first woman said,
"No! For the dead one is your son,
and the living one is my son." Thus
they spoke before the king.
**23** Then the king said, "[1]The one
says, 'This is my son who is living,
and your son is the dead one'; and
[1]the other says, 'No! For your son is
the dead one, and my son is the living
one.'" **24** And the king said, "Get me a
sword." So they brought a sword be-
fore the king. **25** Then the king said,
"Divide the living child in two, and
give half to the one and half to the
other." **26** Then the woman whose
son *was* the living one spoke to the
king, for [a,1]she was deeply stirred
with compassion over her son and
said, "Oh, my lord, give her the living
child, and by no means put him to
death." But the other said, "He shall
be neither mine nor yours; divide
*him!*" **27** Then the king said, "Give
[1]the first woman the living child, and
by no means put him to death. She is
his mother." **28** Then all Israel heard
of the judgment which the king had
[1]handed down, and they feared the
king, for [a]they saw that the wisdom
of God was in him to do justice.

### *Solomon's Officials*

**4** So King Solomon was king over
all Israel. **2** These were his offi-
cials:
Azariah the son of Zadok *was*
[a]the priest;
3 Elihoreph and Ahijah, the
sons of Shisha *were* scribes;
[a]Jehoshaphat the son of
Ahilud *was* the recorder;
4 and [a]Benaiah the son of
Jehoiada *was* over the army;
and Zadok and [b]Abiathar *were*
priests;
5 and Azariah the son of Nathan
*was* over [a]the deputies;
and Zabud the son of Nathan,
a priest, *was* the king's friend;
6 and Ahishar *was* over the
household;
and Adoniram the son of Abda
*was* over the men subject to
forced labor.
**7** Now Solomon had twelve deputies
over all Israel, who sustained the king
and his household; each man had to
sustain *them* for a month in the year.
**8** These are their names:
Ben-hur, in the [a]hill country
of Ephraim;
9 Ben-deker in Makaz and
[a]Shaalbim and [b]Beth-shemesh
and Elonbeth-hanan;

---

**3:22** [1]Lit *this one was saying* **3:23** [1]Lit *this one* **3:26** [a]Ge 43:30; Is 49:15; Jer 31:20; Hos 11:8 [1]Lit *her compassion grew warm* **3:27** [1]Lit *her the living child* **3:28** [a]1Ki 3:9, 11, 12; Da 1:17; Col 2:2, 3 [1]Lit *judged* ◆ **4:2** [a]1Chr 6:10 **4:3** [a]2Sa 8:16 **4:4** [a]1Ki 2:35 [b]1Ki 2:27 **4:5** [a]1Ki 4:7 **4:8** [a]Jos 24:33 **4:9** [a]Jdg 1:35 [b]Jos 21:16

10 Ben-hesed, in Arubboth
([a]Socoh *was* his and all the
land of [b]Hepher);
11 Ben-abinadab, *in* all
[1]the [a]height of Dor (Taphath
the daughter of Solomon was
his wife);
12 Baana the son of Ahilud,
*in* [a]Taanach and Megiddo,
and all [b]Beth-shean which
is beside [c]Zarethan below
Jezreel, from Beth-shean to
[d]Abel-meholah as far as the
other side of [e]Jokmeam;
13 Ben-geber, in [a]Ramoth-gilead
(*now* [b,1]Havvoth-Jair—*Jair being*
the son of Manasseh—which is
in Gilead was his: [c]the region
of Argob, which is in Bashan,
sixty great cities with walls
and bronze bars *were* his);
14 Ahinadab the son of Iddo,
*in* [a]Mahanaim;
15 [a]Ahimaaz, in Naphtali
(he also married Basemath
the daughter of Solomon);
16 Baana the son of [a]Hushai,
in Asher and [1]Bealoth;
17 Jehoshaphat the son of
Paruah, in Issachar;
18 [a]Shimei the son of Ela,
in Benjamin;
19 Geber the son of Uri, in the
land of Gilead, [a]the country
of Sihon king of the Amorites
and of Og king of Bashan; and
*he was* the only deputy who
*was* in the land.

### *Judah's and Israel's Abundance and Security*

20 [a]Judah and Israel *were* as nu-
merous as the sand that is on the
[1]seashore in abundance; *they* were
eating and drinking and being glad.
21 [a,1]Now Solomon ruled over all
the kingdoms [b]from the [2]River *to*
the land of the Philistines and to the
border of Egypt; [c]*they* brought tribute
and served Solomon all the days of
his life.
22 And Solomon's [1]provision for
one day was [2]thirty kors of fine
flour and [3]sixty kors of meal, 23 ten
fat oxen, twenty [1]pasture-fed oxen,
one hundred sheep besides deer,
gazelles, roebucks, and fattened
fowl. 24 For he had dominion over
everything [1]west of the [2]River, from
Tiphsah even to [a]Gaza, [b]over all the
kings [1]west of the [2]River; and [c]he
had peace on all sides around about
him. 25 [a]So Judah and Israel lived in
security, every man under his vine
and his fig tree, [b]from Dan even to
Beersheba, all the days of Solomon.
26 [a]Solomon had [1]40,000 stalls of
horses for his chariots, and 12,000
horsemen. 27 And these deputies
sustained King Solomon and all
who came to King Solomon's table,
each in his month; they left nothing
lacking. 28 They also brought barley
and straw for the horses and [a]swift
steeds to the place where it should
be, each according to the *legal* judg-
ment for him.

**4:10** [a]Jos 15:35 [b]Jos 12:17 **4:11** [a]Jos 11:1, 2 [1]Or *Naphoth-dor* **4:12** [a]Jdg 5:19 [b]Jos 17:11 [c]Jos 3:16 [d]1Ki 19:16 [e]1Chr 6:68 **4:13** [a]1Ki 22:3-15 [b]Nu 32:41 [c]Dt 3:4 [1]Or *the towns of Jair* **4:14** [a]Jos 13:26 **4:15** [a]2Sa 15:27 **4:16** [a]2Sa 15:32 [1]Or *in Aloth* **4:18** [a]1Ki 1:8 **4:19** [a]Dt 3:8-10 **4:20** [a]Ge 22:17; 32:12; 1Ki 3:8 [1]Lit *sea* **4:21** [a]2Chr 9:26 [b]Ge 15:18; Jos 1:4 [c]2Sa 8:2, 6 [1]Ch 5:1 in Heb [2]The Euphrates River **4:22** [1]Lit *bread* [2]Approx. 195 bu. or 6.9 metric tons, a kor was approx. 6.5 bu. or 230 l [3]Approx. 390 bu. or 13.8 metric tons **4:23** [1]Lit *oxen of the pasture* **4:24** [a]Jdg 1:18 [b]Ps 72:11 [c]1Chr 22:9 [1]Lit *beyond* [2]The Euphrates River **4:25** [a]Jer 23:6; Mic 4:4; Zec 3:10 [b]1Sa 3:20 **4:26** [a]1Ki 10:26; 2Chr 1:14 [1]One ms *4,000*, cf. 2Chr 9:25 **4:28** [a]Es 8:10, 14; Mic 1:13

**29** And [a]God gave Solomon wis-
dom and very great discernment
and breadth of *understanding* in *his*
heart, [b]like the sand that is on the
seashore. **30** And Solomon's wisdom
surpassed the wisdom of all [a]the
sons of the east and [b]all the wisdom
of Egypt. **31** And [a]he was wiser than
all men, than [b]Ethan the Ezrahite,
Heman, [c]Calcol, and [1]Darda, the sons
of Mahol; and *the renown of* his name
was in all the surrounding nations.
**32** [a]He also spoke 3,000 proverbs,
and his songs were 1,005. **33** And he
spoke of trees, from the cedar that is
in Lebanon even to the hyssop that
grows on the wall; he spoke also
of animals and birds and creeping
things and fish. **34** [1]And men [a]came
from all peoples to hear the wisdom
of Solomon, from all the kings of the
earth who had heard of his wisdom.

### *Covenant with Hiram King of Tyre*

**5** [a,1]Then Hiram king of Tyre sent
his servants to Solomon, when
he heard that they had anointed
him king in place of his father, for
[b]Hiram had [2]always been one who
loved David. **2** And [a]Solomon sent
*word* to Hiram, saying, **3** "You know
that [a]David my father was unable to
build a house for the name of Yahweh
his God because of the wars which
surrounded him, until Yahweh put
them under the soles of his feet. **4** But
now [a]Yahweh my God has given me
rest on every side; there is neither
adversary nor [1]calamity. **5** So behold,
[a]I [1]intend to build a house for the
name of Yahweh my God, as Yahweh
spoke to David my father, saying,
'Your son, whom I will set on your
throne in your place, he will build the
house for My name.' **6** So now, com-
mand that they cut for me [a]cedars
from Lebanon, and my servants will
be with your servants; and I will
give you wages for your servants
according to all that you say, for you
know that there is no one among us
who knows how to cut timber like
the Sidonians."

**7** Now it happened, when Hiram
heard the words of Solomon, he was
very glad and said, "Blessed be Yah-
weh today, who has given to David a
wise son over this great people." **8** So
Hiram sent *word* to Solomon, saying,
"I have heard *the message* which you
have sent me; I will do [1]what you de-
sire concerning the cedar and cypress
timber. **9** My servants will bring *them*
down from Lebanon to the sea; and I
will make them into rafts *to go* by sea
[a]to the place where you [1]direct me,
and I will have them broken up there,
and you shall carry *them* away. Then
[b]you shall accomplish my desire by
giving food to my household." **10** So
[1]Hiram [2]gave Solomon [3]as much as
he desired of the cedar and cypress
timber. **11** [a]Solomon then gave Hiram
[1]20,000 kors of wheat as food for his
household, and [2]20 kors of beaten oil;
thus Solomon would give Hiram year
by year. **12** [a]Now Yahweh gave wisdom
to Solomon, just as He [1]promised him;

---

**4:29** [a]1Ki 3:12 [b]1Ki 4:20 **4:30** [a]Ge 29:1; Jdg 6:33 [b]Is 19:11; Ac 7:22 **4:31** [a]1Ki 3:12 [b]1Chr 15:19; Ps 89: title [c]1Chr 2:6 [1]In 1Chr 2:6, *Dara* **4:32** [a]Pr 1:1; 10:1; 25:1; Ecc 12:9; SS 1:1 **4:34** [a]1Ki 10:1; 2Chr 9:23 [1]Lit *they* ◆ **5:1** [a]2Chr 2:3 [b]2Sa 5:11; 1Chr 14:1 [1]Ch 5:15 in Heb [2]Lit *all the day* **5:2** [a]2Chr 2:3 **5:3** [a]2Sa 7:5; 1Chr 28:2, 3 **5:4** [a]1Ki 4:24; 1Chr 22:9 [1]Lit *evil occurrence* **5:5** [a]2Sa 7:12, 13; 1Chr 17:12; 22:10; 28:6; 2Chr 2:4 [1]Lit *say* **5:6** [a]2Chr 2:8 **5:8** [1]Lit *all your pleasure* **5:9** [a]2Chr 2:16 [b]Ezr 3:7; Eze 27:17 [1]Lit *send* **5:10** [1]Heb *Hirom* [2]Lit *was giving* [3]Lit *all his desire* **5:11** [a]2Chr 2:10 [1]Approx. 130,000 bu. or 4,600 metric tons [2]Approx. 130 bu. or 4,600 l **5:12** [a]1Ki 3:12 [1]Lit *spoke to*

and there was peace between Hiram
and Solomon, and the two of them
cut a covenant.
**13** And [a]King Solomon raised
up forced laborers from all Israel;
and the forced laborers [1]numbered
30,000 men. **14** And he sent them to
Lebanon, 10,000 a month in [1]shifts;
they were in Lebanon a month *and*
two months at home. And [a]Adoni-
ram *was* over the forced laborers.
**15** And [a]Solomon had 70,000 [1]who
carried loads, and 80,000 hewers *of*
*stone* in the mountains, **16** [a]besides
Solomon's 3,300 chief deputies who
*were* over the [1]project *and* who ruled
over the people who were doing the
work. **17** Then [a]the king commanded,
and they quarried great stones, pre-
cious stones, to lay the foundation
of the house with cut stones. **18** So
Solomon's builders and [1]Hiram's
builders and [a]the Gebalites [2]carved
them out, and prepared the timbers
and the stones to build the house.

### *The House Solomon Built for Yahweh*

**6** [a]Now it happened in the four
hundred and eightieth year after
the sons of Israel came out of the
land of Egypt, in the fourth year of
Solomon's reign over Israel, in the
month of Ziv which is the second
month, that he [1]began to build the
house of Yahweh. **2** As for the house
which King Solomon built for Yah-
weh, its length *was* [1]sixty cubits and
its width twenty *cubits* and its height
thirty cubits. **3** And the porch in front
of the nave of the house *was* twenty
cubits [1]in length, [2]corresponding to
the width of the house, *and* its [3]depth
along the front of the house *was* ten
cubits. **4** Also for the house [a]he made
windows with *artistic* frames. **5** [a]And
he built, against the wall of the house,
stories encompassing the walls of the
house around both the nave and the
[b]inner sanctuary; thus he made [c]side
chambers all around. **6** The lowest
story *was* five cubits wide, and the
middle *was* six cubits wide, and
the third *was* seven cubits wide; for
on the outside he [1]made offsets *in*
*the wall* of the house all around in
order that *the beams* would not [2]be
inserted in the walls of the house.
**7** [a]The house, while it was being
built, was built of stone [1]prepared
at the quarry, and there was neither
hammer nor axe nor any iron tool
heard in the house while it was being
built.
**8** The doorway for the [1]lowest
side chamber *was* on the right side
of the house; and they would go up
by winding stairs to the middle *story*,
and from the middle to the third. **9** So
[a]he built the house and completed it;
and he paneled the house with beams
and [1]planks of cedar. **10** He also built
the stories against the whole house,
each five [1]cubits high; and they [2]were
fastened to the house with timbers
of cedar.
**11** And the word of Yahweh came
to Solomon saying, **12** "*Concerning*
this house which you are building,

**5:13** [a]1Ki 4:6; 9:15 [1]Lit *was* **5:14** [a]1Ki 4:6; 12:18 [1]Lit *changes* **5:15** [a]1Ki 9:20-22; 2Chr 2:17, 18 [1]Or *burden bearers* **5:16** [a]1Ki 9:23 [1]Lit *work* **5:17** [a]1Ki 6:7; 1Chr 22:2 **5:18** [a]Jos 13:5; Eze 27:9 [1]Heb *Hirom's* [2]Or *chiseled* ◆ **6:1** [a]2Chr 3:1, 2 [1]Lit *built* **6:2** [1]Approx. 90 ft. long, 30 ft. wide, and 45 ft. high or 27 m, 9 m, and 14 m; a cubit was approx. 18 in. or 45 cm **6:3** [1]Lit *in its length* [2]Lit *on the face of* [3]Lit *width* **6:4** [a]Eze 40:16; 41:16 **6:5** [a]Eze 41:6 [b]1Ki 6:16, 19, 20 [c]Eze 41:5 **6:6** [1]Lit *gave* [2]Lit *take hold* **6:7** [a]Ex 20:25; Dt 27:5, 6 [1]Lit *finished* **6:8** [1]As in Gr and versions; M.T. *middle* **6:9** [a]1Ki 6:14, 38 [1]Lit *rows* **6:10** [1]A cubit was approx. 18 in. or 45 cm [2]Lit *took hold*

[a]if you will walk in My statutes and
do My judgments and keep all My
commandments by walking in them,
then I will establish My word with
you which I spoke to David your fa-
ther. **13** [a]And I will dwell among the
sons of Israel, and [b]will not forsake
My people Israel."

**14** [a]So Solomon built the house
and completed it. **15** Then he [a]built
the walls of the house on the inside
with boards of cedar; from the floor of
the house to the [1]ceiling he overlaid
*the walls* on the inside with wood,
and he overlaid the floor of the house
with boards of cypress. **16** [a]And he
built twenty cubits on the rear part
of the house with boards of cedar
from the floor to the [1]ceiling; he built
*them* for it on the inside as an inner
sanctuary, as [b]the Holy of Holies.
**17** And the house, that is, the nave
in front of *the inner sanctuary*, was
[1]forty cubits *long*. **18** And there was
cedar on the house within, carved
*in the shape* of [a]gourds and open
flowers; all was cedar, there was no
stone seen. **19** Then he prepared an
inner sanctuary within the house in
order to place there the ark of the
covenant of Yahweh. **20** Now [1]the
inner sanctuary *was* twenty cubits
in length, twenty cubits in width,
and twenty cubits in height, and he
overlaid it with pure gold. He also
overlaid the altar with cedar. **21** So
Solomon overlaid the inside of the
house with pure gold. And he drew
chains of gold across the front of the
inner sanctuary, and he overlaid it
with gold. **22** So he overlaid the whole
house with gold, until all the house
was finished. Also [a]the whole altar
which was by the inner sanctuary
he overlaid with gold.

**23** [a]Also in the inner sanctuary he
made two cherubim of olive wood,
each ten cubits high. **24** And five cu-
bits *was* the one wing of the cherub
and five cubits the other wing of the
cherub; from the end of one wing to
the end of the other wing *were* ten
cubits. **25** The other cherub *was* also
ten cubits; both the cherubim were
of the same measure and the same
form. **26** The height of the one cherub
*was* ten cubits, and so *was* the other
cherub. **27** And he put the cherubim
in the midst of the inner house, and
[a]the wings of the cherubim were
spread out, so that the wing of the
one was touching the *one* wall, and
the wing of the other cherub was
touching the other wall. And their
wings were touching each other in
the center of the house. **28** He also
overlaid the cherubim with gold.

**29** Then he carved all the walls of
the house round about with carved
engravings of cherubim, palm trees,
and open flowers, from *within* the
inner and outer *sanctuaries*. **30** And
he overlaid the floor of the house
with gold, in the inner and outer
*sanctuaries*.

**31** For the entrance of the inner
sanctuary he made doors of olive
wood, the lintel, *and* five-sided
doorposts. **32** So *he made* two doors
of olive wood, and he carved on them
carvings of cherubim, palm trees,
and open flowers, and overlaid them

**6:12** [a]2Sa 7:5-16; 1Ki 9:4 **6:13** [a]Ex 25:8; 29:45; Lv 26:11 [b]Dt 31:6; Jos 1:5; Heb 13:5 **6:14** [a]1Ki 6:9, 38 **6:15** [a]1Ki 7:7 [1]Lit *walls of ceiling* **6:16** [a]2Chr 3:8 [b]Ex 26:33, 34; Lv 16:2; 1Ki 8:6; Heb 9:3 [1]Lit *walls* **6:17** [1]Approx. 60 ft. or 18 m **6:18** [a]1Ki 7:24 **6:20** [1]Lit *before* **6:22** [a]Ex 30:1, 3, 6 **6:23** [a]Ex 37:7-9; 2Chr 3:10-12 **6:27** [a]Ex 25:20; 37:9; 1Ki 8:7

with gold; and he spread the gold on the cherubim and on the palm trees.

**33** So also he made for the entrance of the nave four-sided doorposts of olive wood **34** and [a]two doors of cypress wood; the two leaves of the one door turned on pivots, and the two [1]leaves of the other door turned on pivots. **35** And he carved *on it* cherubim, palm trees, and open flowers; and he overlaid *them* with gold evenly applied on the engraved work. **36** [a]And he built the inner court with three rows of cut stone and a row of cedar beams.

**37** [a]In the fourth year the foundation of the house of Yahweh was laid, in the month of Ziv. **38** Now in the eleventh year, in the month of Bul, which is the eighth month, the house was completed throughout all its parts and according to all its [1]plans. So he built it in seven years.

### *Solomon Builds His Own House*

**7** Now [a]Solomon built his own house thirteen years, and he completed all his house. **2** [a]And he built the house of the forest of Lebanon; its length was [1]100 cubits and its width 50 cubits and its height 30 cubits, on four rows of cedar pillars with cedar beams on the pillars. **3** And it was paneled with cedar above the side chambers which were on the 45 pillars, 15 in each row. **4** *Now there were artistic window* frames in three rows, and window was opposite window in three ranks. **5** And all the doorways and doorposts *had* squared *artistic frames,* and window was opposite window in three ranks.

**6** Then he made [a]the hall of pillars; its length was 50 cubits and its width 30 cubits, and a porch *was* in front of them and pillars and a [b]threshold in front of them.

**7** And he made the hall of the [a]throne where he was to judge, the hall of judgment, and [b]it was paneled with cedar from floor to floor.

**8** Now his house where he was to live, the other court inward from the hall, was of the same workmanship. [a]He also made a house like this hall for Pharaoh's daughter, [b]whom Solomon had married.

**9** All these were of precious stones, of stone cut according to measure, sawed with saws, inside and outside; even from the foundation to the coping, and so on the outside to the great court.

**10** And the foundation was of precious stones, *even* large stones, stones of ten cubits and stones of eight cubits. **11** And above were precious stones, stone cut according to measure, and cedar. **12** So [a]the great court all around *had* three rows of cut stone and a row of cedar beams even as the inner court of the house of Yahweh, and [b]the porch of the house.

### *Hiram's Work in the House of Yahweh*

**13** Then [a]King Solomon sent and brought Hiram from Tyre. **14** [a]He was a widow's son from the tribe of Naphtali, and his father was a man of Tyre, a worker in bronze; and [b]he was filled with wisdom and discernment and knowledge to do

---

**6:34** [a]Eze 41:23-25 [1]As in Gr; M.T. *curtains* **6:36** [a]1Ki 7:12; Jer 36:10 **6:37** [a]1Ki 6:1 **6:38** [1]Lit *judgments* ◆ **7:1** [a]1Ki 3:1; 9:10; 2Chr 8:1 **7:2** [a]1Ki 10:17, 21; 2Chr 9:16 [1]Approx. 150 ft. long, 75 ft. wide, and 45 ft. tall or 45 m, 22.5 m, and 13.5 m **7:6** [a]1Ki 7:12 [b]Eze 41:25, 26 **7:7** [a]Ps 122:5; Pr 20:8 [b]1Ki 6:15, 16 **7:8** [a]1Ki 9:24; 2Chr 8:11 [b]1Ki 3:1 **7:12** [a]1Ki 6:36 [b]1Ki 7:6 **7:13** [a]2Chr 2:13, 14; 4:11 **7:14** [a]2Chr 2:14 [b]Ex 28:3; 31:3-5; 35:31; 36:1

any work in bronze. So he came to
King Solomon and [c]did all his work.
**15** And he fashioned [a]the two
pillars of bronze; [b]eighteen cubits
was the height of one pillar, and a
line of twelve cubits [1]measured the
circumference of both. **16** He also
made two capitals of molten bronze
to set on the tops of the pillars; the
height of the one capital was five
[1]cubits and the height of the other
capital was five cubits. **17** *There were*
nets of network and twisted threads
of chainwork for the capitals which
were on the top of the pillars; seven
for the one capital and seven for
the other capital. **18** So he made
the pillars, and two rows around
on the one network to cover the
capitals which were on the top of
the pomegranates; and so he did for
the other capital. **19** Now the capitals
which *were* on the top of the pillars
in the porch were of lily design, four
cubits. **20** *And there were* capitals on
the two pillars, even right above the
[1]rounded projection which was on
the one side of the network; and [a]the
pomegranates *numbered* two hun-
dred in rows around [2]both capitals.
**21** [a]Thus he set up the pillars at the
[b]porch of the nave; and he set up the
right pillar and named it [1]Jachin, and
he set up the left pillar and named it
[2]Boaz. **22** And on the top of the pillars
was lily design. So the work of the
pillars was finished.
**23** [a]And he made the sea of [b]cast
*metal* ten cubits from brim to brim,
circular in form, and its height was
five cubits, and [1]thirty cubits in its
circumference. **24** Now under its brim
[a]gourds went around encircling it ten
to a cubit, [b]entirely encircling the
sea; the gourds were in two rows, cast
*with the Sea* when it was cast. **25** [a]It
stood on twelve oxen, three facing
north, three facing west, three facing
south, and three facing east; and the
sea *was set* on top of them, and all
their rear parts *turned* inward. **26** And
it was a [1]handbreadth thick, and its
brim was made like the brim of a cup,
*as* a lily blossom; it could hold [2]two
thousand baths.
**27** Then [a]he made the ten stands
of bronze; the length of each stand
was four cubits and its width four
cubits and its height three cubits.
**28** Now this was the workmanship
of the stands: they had borders, even
borders between the [1]frames, **29** and
on the borders which were between
the [1]frames *were* lions, oxen, and
cherubim; and on the [1]frames there
*was* a pedestal above, and beneath
the lions and oxen *were* wreaths of
hanging work. **30** Now each stand
had four bronze wheels with bronze
axles, and its four feet had supports;
beneath the laver *were* cast supports
with wreaths at each side. **31** And its
opening inside the capital at the
top *was* a cubit, and its opening
*was* round like the workmanship
of a pedestal, a cubit and a half;
and also on its opening *there were*
engravings, and their borders were
square, not round. **32** And the four
wheels *were* underneath the borders,

---

**7:14** [c]2Chr 4:11-16 **7:15** [a]2Ki 25:17; 2Chr 3:15; 4:12; Jer 52:21 [b]1Ki 7:41 [1]Lit *went around the other pillar* **7:16** [1]A cubit was approx. 18 in. or 45 cm **7:20** [a]1Ki 7:42; 2Chr 3:16; 4:13; Jer 52:23 [1]Lit *belly* [2]Lit *on the other capital* **7:21** [a]2Chr 3:17 [b]1Ki 6:3 [1]Lit *he shall establish* [2]Lit *in it is strength* **7:23** [a]2Chr 4:2 [b]2Ki 16:17; 25:13 [1]Lit *a line of thirty cubits went around it* **7:24** [a]1Ki 6:18 [b]2Chr 4:3 **7:25** [a]2Chr 4:4, 5; Jer 52:20 **7:26** [1]A handbreadth was approx. 3 in. or 7.6 cm [2]Approx. 12,000 gal. or 45,424 l, a bath was approx. 6 gal. or 23 l **7:27** [a]1Ki 7:38; 2Ki 25:13; 2Chr 4:14 **7:28** [1]Or *crossbars* **7:29** [1]Or *crossbars*

and the axles of the wheels *were* on
the stand. And the height of a wheel
*was* a cubit and a half. **33** Now the
workmanship of the wheels *was* like
the workmanship of a chariot wheel.
Their axles, their rims, their spokes,
and their hubs *were* all cast. **34** Now
*there were* four supports at the four
corners of each stand; its supports
*were* part of the stand itself. **35** And
on the top of the stand *there was* a
circular form half a [1]cubit high, and
on the top of the stand its [2]stays and
its borders *were* part of it. **36** And he
engraved on the plates of its stays
and on its borders, cherubim, lions,
and palm trees, according to the
clear space on each, with wreaths *all*
around. **37** [a]He made the ten stands
like this: all of them had one casting,
one measure and one form.

**38** [a]He also made ten lavers of
bronze, one laver held forty baths; each
laver *was* four cubits, *and* on each of
the ten stands *was* one laver. **39** Then
he set the stands, five on the right
side of the house and five on the left
side of the house; and he set the sea
*of cast metal* on the right side of the
house eastward toward the south.

**40** And Hiram made the lavers and
the shovels and the bowls. So Hiram
completed doing all the work that he
did for King Solomon *in* the house of
Yahweh: **41** the two pillars and the *two*
bowls of the capitals which *were* on
the top of the [a]two pillars, and the two
networks to cover the two bowls of
the capitals which were on the top of
*the pillars,* **42** *and the* [a]*four* hundred
pomegranates for the two networks,
two rows of pomegranates for each
network to cover the two bowls of
the capitals which were on the tops
of the pillars; **43** and the ten stands
with the ten lavers on the stands;
**44** and [a]the one sea and the twelve
oxen under the sea; **45** and [a]the pots
and the shovels and the bowls; and all
these utensils which Hiram made for
King Solomon *in* the house of Yahweh
*were* of polished bronze. **46** [a]On the
plain of the Jordan the king cast them,
in the clay ground between [b]Succoth
and [c]Zarethan. **47** And Solomon left
all the utensils *unweighed,* because
*they were* too many; [a]the weight of
the bronze could not be found out.

**48** Solomon also made all the
furniture which *was in* the house
of Yahweh: [a]the golden altar and
the golden table on which *was* the
[b]bread of the Presence; **49** and the
lampstands, five on the right side
and five on the left, in front of the
inner sanctuary, of pure gold; and
[a]the flowers and the lamps and the
tongs, of gold; **50** and the cups and
the snuffers and the bowls and the
spoons and the [a]firepans, of pure
gold; and the hinges both for the
doors of the inner house, the Holy
of Holies, *and* for the doors of the
house, *that is,* of the nave, of gold.

**51** [a]Thus all the work that King
Solomon did *in* the house of Yahweh
was finished. And [b]Solomon brought
in the things set apart as holy by his
father David, the silver and the gold
and the utensils, *and* he put *them*
in the treasuries of the house of
Yahweh.

---

**7:35** [1]A cubit was approx. 18 in. or 45 cm [2]Lit *hands* **7:37** [a]2Chr 4:14 **7:38** [a]Ex 30:18; 2Chr 4:6
**7:41** [a]1Ki 7:17, 18 **7:42** [a]1Ki 7:20 **7:44** [a]1Ki 7:23, 25 **7:45** [a]Ex 27:3; 2Chr 4:16 **7:46** [a]2Chr 4:17
[b]Ge 33:17; Jos 13:27 [c]Jos 3:16 **7:47** [a]1Chr 22:3, 14 **7:48** [a]Ex 30:1-3; 37:10-29; 2Chr 4:8 [b]Ex 25:30
**7:49** [a]Ex 25:31-38 **7:50** [a]Ex 27:3; 2Ki 25:15 **7:51** [a]2Chr 5:1 [b]2Sa 8:11; 1Chr 18:11; 2Chr 5:1

### *The Ark Brought into the House of Yahweh*

**8** [a]Then Solomon assembled the el-
ders of Israel and all [b]the heads of
the tribes, the leaders of the fathers'
*households* of the sons of Israel, to
King Solomon in Jerusalem, [c]to bring
up the ark of the covenant of Yahweh
from [d]the city of David, which is Zion.
**2** And all the men of Israel assembled
themselves to King Solomon at [a]the
feast, in the month Ethanim, which
is the seventh month. **3** Then all
the elders of Israel came, and [a]the
priests carried the ark. **4** And they
brought up the ark of Yahweh and
[a]the tent of meeting and all the holy
utensils, which were in the tent, and
the priests and the Levites brought
them up. **5** And King Solomon and
all the congregation of Israel, who
congregated to him being [a]with him
before the ark, were sacrificing [1]so
many sheep and oxen that they could
not be counted or numbered. **6** Then
[a]the priests brought the ark of the
covenant of Yahweh [b]to its place, into
the inner sanctuary of the house, to
the Holy of Holies, [c]under the wings
of the cherubim. **7** For the cherubim
spread *their* wings over the place of
the ark, and the cherubim made a
covering over the ark and its poles
from above. **8** But [a]the poles were
so long that the ends of the poles
could be seen from the holy place
before the inner sanctuary, but they
could not be seen outside; and they
are there to this day. **9** [a]There was
nothing in the ark except the two
tablets of stone which Moses laid
there at Horeb, where [b]Yahweh cut
a covenant with the sons of Israel,
when they came out of the land of
Egypt. **10** Now it happened that when
the priests came out of the holy
place, [a]the cloud filled the house of
Yahweh, **11** so that the priests could
not stand to minister because of the
cloud, for the glory of Yahweh filled
the house of Yahweh.

### *Solomon Blesses the People*

**12** [a]Then Solomon said,
"Yahweh has said that
[b]He would dwell in the
*cloud of* dense gloom.
**13** "[a]I have surely built You
a lofty house,
[b]A place for Your
dwelling forever."
**14** Then the king turned his face
around and [a]blessed all the assembly
of Israel, while all the assembly of
Israel was standing. **15** And he said,
"[a]Blessed be Yahweh, the God of
Israel, [b]who spoke with His mouth
to my father David and has fulfilled
*it* by His hand, saying, **16** '[a]Since the
day that I brought My people Israel
from Egypt, I did not choose a city
out of all the tribes of Israel *in which*
to build a house that [b]My name might
be there, but [c]I have chosen David to
be over My people Israel.' **17** [a]And it
was [1]in the heart of my father David
to build a house for the name of Yah-
weh, the God of Israel. **18** But Yahweh

---

◆ **8:1** [a]2Chr 5:2-10 [b]Nu 1:4; 7:2 [c]2Sa 6:12-17; 1Chr 15:25-29 [d]2Sa 5:7 **8:2** [a]Lv 23:34; 1Ki 8:65; 2Chr 7:8-10 **8:3** [a]Nu 7:9; Dt 31:9; Jos 3:3, 6 **8:4** [a]1Ki 3:4; 2Chr 1:3 **8:5** [a]2Sa 6:13; 2Chr 1:6 [1]Lit *sheep and oxen...numbered for multitude* **8:6** [a]1Ki 8:3 [b]1Ki 6:19 [c]1Ki 6:27 **8:8** [a]Ex 25:13-15; 37:4, 5 **8:9** [a]Ex 25:16, 21; Dt 10:2-5; Heb 9:4 [b]Ex 24:7, 8; 40:20; Dt 4:13 **8:10** [a]Ex 40:34, 35; 2Chr 7:1, 2 **8:12** [a]2Chr 6:1 [b]Lv 16:2; Ps 18:11; 97:2 **8:13** [a]2Sa 7:13 [b]Ex 15:17; Ps 132:14 **8:14** [a]2Sa 6:18; 1Ki 8:55 **8:15** [a]1Chr 29:10, 20; Ne 9:5; Lk 1:68 [b]2Sa 7:12, 13; 1Chr 22:10 **8:16** [a]2Sa 7:4, 5; 1Chr 17:3-10; 2Chr 6:5 [b]Dt 12:5, 11 [c]1Sa 16:1; 2Sa 7:8 **8:17** [a]2Sa 7:2, 3; 1Chr 17:1, 2 [1]Lit *with*

said to my father David, 'Because it
was [1]in your heart to build a house
for My name, you did well that it was
[1]in your heart. **19** [a]Nevertheless you
shall not build the house, but your
son who will [b]come forth from your
loins, he shall build the house for
My name.' **20** And Yahweh has estab-
lished His word which He spoke; and
[a]I have been established in place of
my father David and sit on the throne
of Israel, as Yahweh [1]promised, and
have built the house for the name
of Yahweh, the God of Israel. **21** And
there I have set a place for the ark,
[a]in which is the covenant of Yahweh,
which He cut with our fathers when
He brought them from the land of
Egypt."

### *Solomon's Prayer for Israel*

**22** Then [a]Solomon stood before the
altar of Yahweh before all the as-
sembly of Israel and [b]spread out his
hands toward heaven. **23** And he said,
"O Yahweh, the God of Israel, [a]there
is no god like You in heaven above
or upon earth beneath, [b]keeping
covenant and lovingkindness to Your
slaves who walk before You with all
their heart, **24** who have kept with
Your [1]servant, my father David, that
which You have [2]promised him;
indeed, You have [2]promised with
Your mouth and have fulfilled it by
Your hand as it is this day. **25** So now,
O Yahweh, the God of Israel, keep
with Your [1]servant David my father
that which You have [2]promised him,
saying, '[a]You shall not have a man
cut off from before Me who is to sit
on the throne of Israel, if only your
sons keep their way to walk as you
have walked before Me.' **26** So now,
O God of Israel, let Your word truly
[1]endure [a]which You have spoken to
Your [2]servant, my father David.

**27** "But will God truly dwell on the
earth? Behold, [a]heaven and the [1]high-
est heaven cannot [2]contain You; how
much less this house which I have
built! **28** Yet have regard to the [a]prayer
of Your slave and to his supplication,
O Yahweh my God, to listen to the cry
and to the prayer which Your slave
prays before You today; **29** [a]that Your
eyes may be open toward this house
night and day, toward [b]the place of
which You have said, 'My name shall
be there,' to listen to the prayer which
Your slave shall pray toward this place.
**30** [a]And listen to the supplication of
Your slave and of Your people Israel,
[b]when they pray toward this place;
listen in heaven Your dwelling place;
listen and [c]forgive.

**31** "[a]If a man sins against his
neighbor and is made to take an oath,
and he comes *and* takes an oath be-
fore Your altar in this house, **32** then
listen in heaven and act and judge
Your slaves, [a]condemning the wick-
ed by [1]bringing his way on his own
head and justifying the righteous by
[1]bringing him *reward* according to
his righteousness.

---

***8:18*** [1]Lit *with* **8:19** [a]2Sa 7:5, 12, 13; 1Ki 5:3, 5; 1Chr 17:11, 12; 22:8-10 [b]Ge 35:11 **8:20** [a]1Chr 28:5, 6 [1]Lit *spoke* **8:21** [a]Dt 31:26; 1Ki 8:9 **8:22** [a]1Ki 8:54; 2Chr 6:12 [b]Ex 9:33; Ezr 9:5 **8:23** [a]1Sa 2:2; 2Sa 7:22 [b]Dt 7:9; Ne 1:5; 9:32; Da 9:4 **8:24** [1]Or *slave*, cf. 8:23; see Foreword, "The Terminology of Slave" [2]Lit *spoken to* **8:25** [a]1Ki 2:4 [1]Or *slave*, cf. 8:23; see Foreword, "The Terminology of Slave" [2]Lit *spoken to* **8:26** [a]2Sa 7:25 [1]Or *be true* [2]Or *slave*, cf. 8:23; see Foreword, "The Terminology of Slave" **8:27** [a]2Chr 2:6; Ps 139:7-16; Is 66:1; Jer 23:24; Ac 7:49 [1]Lit *heaven of heavens* [2]Or *uphold*; lit *sustain* **8:28** [a]Php 4:6 **8:29** [a]2Chr 7:15; Ne 1:6 [b]Dt 12:11 **8:30** [a]Ne 1:6 [b]Da 6:10 [c]Ex 34:6, 7; Ps 85:2; Da 9:9; 1Jn 1:9 **8:31** [a]Ex 22:8-11 **8:32** [a]Dt 25:1 [1]Lit *giving*

**33** “[a]When Your people Israel are
[1]defeated before an enemy, because
they have sinned against You, [b]if they
turn to You again and confess Your
name and pray and make suppli-
cation to You in this house, **34** then
listen in heaven, and forgive the sin
of Your people Israel, and bring them
back to the land which You gave to
their fathers.

**35** “[a]When the heavens are shut
up and there is no rain, because they
have sinned against You, and they
pray toward this place and confess
Your name and turn from their sin
when You afflict them, **36** then listen
in heaven and forgive the sin of Your
slaves and of Your people Israel;
[a]indeed, teach them the good way in
which they should walk. And [b]give
rain on Your land, which You have giv-
en to Your people for an inheritance.

**37** “[a]If there is famine in the land, if
there is pestilence, if there is scorch-
ing wind *or* mildew, locust *or* grass-
hopper, if their enemy besieges them
in the land of their [1]cities, whatever
plague, whatever sickness *there is*,
**38** whatever prayer or supplication
is made by any man *or* by all Your
people Israel, each of whom knows
the [1]affliction of his own heart,
and spreads his [2]hands toward this
house; **39** then listen in heaven Your
dwelling place, and forgive and act
and give to each according to all his
ways, [a]whose heart You know, for
[b]You alone know the hearts of all the
sons of men, **40** that they may [1]fear
You all the days that they live upon
the face of the land which You have
given to our fathers.

**41** “Also concerning the foreigner
who is not of Your people Israel, if
he comes from a far country for Your
name's sake **42** (for they will hear of
Your great name [a]and Your strong
hand, and of Your outstretched arm);
so if he comes and prays toward
this house, **43** listen in heaven Your
dwelling place, and do according to
all for which the foreigner calls to
You, in order [a]that all the peoples of
the earth may know Your name to
[1]fear You, as *do* Your people Israel,
and to know that Your name is called
upon this house which I have built.

**44** “When Your people go out
to battle against [1]their enemy, by
whatever way You shall send them,
and [a]they pray to Yahweh [2]toward
the city which You have chosen and
the house which I have built for Your
name, **45** then listen in heaven to
their prayer and their supplication,
and do justice.

**46** “When they sin against You (for
[a]there is no man who does not sin)
and You are angry with them and give
them over to an enemy, so that [1]they
take them away captive [b]to the land
of the enemy, far off or near; **47** [a]and
if they cause *these things* to return
to their heart in the land where they
have been taken captive, and [1]return
and make supplication to You in the
land of those who have taken them
captive, saying, '[b]We have sinned and

---

**8:33** [a]Lv 26:17, 25; Dt 28:25, 48 [b]Lv 26:40-42 [1]Lit *smitten* **8:35** [a]Lv 26:19; Dt 11:16, 17; 2Sa 24:10-13 **8:36** [a]1Sa 12:23; Ps 5:8; 25:4, 5; 27:11; 86:11; 119:133; Jer 6:16 [b]1Ki 18:1, 41-45; Jer 14:22 **8:37** [a]Lv 26:16, 25, 26; Dt 28:21-23, 38-42 [1]Lit *gates* **8:38** [1]Lit *plague* [2]Lit *palms* **8:39** [a]1Sa 2:3; 16:7 [b]1Chr 28:9; Ps 11:4; Jer 17:10; Jn 2:24, 25; Ac 1:24 **8:40** [1]Or *reverence* **8:42** [a]Ex 13:3; Dt 3:24 **8:43** [a]Jos 4:23, 24; 1Sa 17:46; Ps 67:2 [1]Or *reverence* **8:44** [a]2Chr 14:11 [1]Lit *his* [2]Lit in *the way of* **8:46** [a]Ps 130:3, 4; 143:2; Pr 20:9; Ecc 7:20; Ro 3:23; 1Jn 1:8-10 [b]Lv 26:34-39; 2Ki 17:6, 18; 25:21 [1]Lit *their captors take them captive* **8:47** [a]Lv 26:40-42; Dt 30:1; Ne 9:2 [b]Ezr 9:6, 7; Ne 1:6; Ps 106:6; Da 9:5 [1]Or *repent*

have committed iniquity, we have
acted wickedly'; **48** [a]and if they return
to You with all their heart and with all
their soul in the land of their enemies
who have taken them captive, and
[b]pray to You toward their land which
You have given to their fathers, the
city which You have chosen, and the
house which I have built for Your
name; **49** then listen in heaven Your
dwelling place to their prayer and
their supplication, and do justice
for them, **50** and forgive Your people
who have sinned against You and all
their transgressions which they have
transgressed against You, and [a]give
them over as *objects of* compassion
before those who have taken them
captive, that they may have compas-
sion on them **51** ([a]for they are Your
people and Your inheritance which
You have brought forth from Egypt,
[b]from the midst of the iron furnace),
**52** [a]that Your eyes may be open to the
supplication of Your slave and to the
supplication of Your people Israel, to
listen to them whenever they call to
You. **53** For You have separated them
from all the peoples of the earth as
Your inheritance, [a]as You spoke by
the hand of Moses Your [1]servant,
when You brought our fathers forth
from Egypt, O Lord Yahweh."

### *Solomon Blesses Yahweh*

**54** [a]Now it happened that when
Solomon had [1]finished praying this
entire prayer and supplication to
Yahweh, [b]he arose from before the
altar of Yahweh, from kneeling on his
knees with his [2]hands spread toward
heaven. **55** And he stood and [a]blessed
all the assembly of Israel with a loud
voice, saying:

**56** "Blessed be Yahweh, who
has given rest to His people Israel,
[a]according to all that He [1]promised;
[b]not one promise has [2]failed of all His
good [3]promises, which He [1]promised
by the hand of Moses His [4]servant.
**57** May Yahweh our God be with us, as
He was with our fathers; [a]may He not
forsake us or abandon us, **58** that [a]He
may incline our hearts to Himself, to
walk in all His ways and to keep His
commandments and His statutes and
His judgments, which He command-
ed our fathers. **59** And may these
words of mine, with which I have
made supplication before Yahweh,
be near to Yahweh our God day and
night, that He may do justice for His
slave and justice for His people Israel,
[1]as each day requires, **60** so [a]that all
the peoples of the earth may know
that [b]Yahweh is God; there is no one
else. **61** [a]Let your heart therefore be
[1]wholly devoted to Yahweh our God,
to walk in His statutes and to keep
His commandments, as at this day."

### *The Offering for the House of Yahweh*

**62** [a]Now the king and all Israel with
him were [b]offering sacrifices before
Yahweh. **63** And Solomon offered for

---

***8:48*** [a]Dt 4:29; 1Sa 7:3, 4; Ne 1:9 [b]Da 6:10; Jon 2:4 **8:50** [a]2Chr 30:9; Ps 106:46; Ac 7:10 **8:51** [a]Ex 32:11, 12; Dt 9:26-29 [b]Dt 4:20; Jer 11:4 **8:52** [a]1Ki 8:29 **8:53** [a]Ex 19:5, 6; Dt 9:26-29 [1]Or *slave*, cf. 8:52; see Foreword, "The Terminology of Slave" **8:54** [a]2Chr 7:1 [b]2Chr 6:13 [1]Or *completed*, cf. 9:1; 2Chr 7:11; 8:16 [2]Lit *palms* **8:55** [a]Nu 6:23-26; 2Sa 6:18; 1Ki 8:14 **8:56** [a]Dt 12:10 [b]Jos 21:45; 23:14, 15 [1]Lit *spoke* [2]Lit *fallen* [3]Lit *word* [4]Or *slave*, cf. 8:52; see Foreword, "The Terminology of Slave" **8:57** [a]Dt 31:6, 17; Jos 1:5; 1Sa 12:22; Ro 8:31; Heb 13:5 **8:58** [a]Ps 119:36; Jer 31:33 **8:59** [1]Lit *the thing of a day in its day* **8:60** [a]Jos 4:24; 1Sa 17:46; 1Ki 8:43; 2Ki 19:19 [b]Dt 4:35; 1Ki 18:39; Jer 10:10-12 **8:61** [a]Dt 18:13; 1Ki 11:4; 2Ki 20:3 [1]Lit *complete with* **8:62** [a]2Chr 7:4-10 [b]2Sa 6:17-19; Ezr 6:16, 17

the sacrifice of peace offerings, which
he offered to Yahweh, 22,000 oxen
and 120,000 sheep. [a]So the king and
all the sons of Israel dedicated the
house of Yahweh. **64** On the same
day the king set apart as holy the
middle of the court that *was* before
the house of Yahweh, because there
he [1]offered the burnt offering and the
grain offering and the fat of the peace
offerings; for [a]the bronze altar that
*was* before Yahweh *was* too small
to hold the burnt offering and the
grain offering and the fat of the peace
offerings.

**65** So [a]Solomon celebrated the
feast at that time, and all Israel with
him, a great assembly [b]from [1]Lebo-
hamath [c]to the brook of Egypt, be-
fore Yahweh our God, for seven days
and seven *more* days, *even* fourteen
days. **66** On the eighth day he sent
the people away and they blessed
the king. Then they went to their
tents with gladness and goodness
of heart because of all the goodness
that Yahweh had shown to David His
[1]servant and to Israel His people.

### *Yahweh Appears to Solomon*

**9** [a]Now it happened when Solo-
mon had completed building the
house of Yahweh, and [b]the king's
house, and [c]all [1]that Solomon de-
sired to do, **2** that [a]Yahweh appeared
to Solomon a second time, as He had
appeared to him at Gibeon. **3** And Yah-
weh said to him, "[a]I have heard your
prayer and your supplication, which
you have made before Me; I have
set apart as holy this house which
you have built [b]by putting My name
there forever, and [c]My eyes and My
heart will be there perpetually. **4** As
for you, [a]if you will walk before
Me as your father David walked, in
integrity of heart and uprightness,
to do according to all that I have
commanded you *and* will keep My
statutes and My judgments, **5** then
[a]I will establish the throne of your
kingdom over Israel forever, just as
I [1]promised to your father David,
saying, 'You shall not have a man cut
off from the throne of Israel.'

**6** "[a]But if you or your sons indeed
turn away from following Me, and do
not keep My commandments *and* My
statutes which I have given before
you, and go and serve other gods
and worship them, **7** [a]then I will cut
off Israel from the land which I have
given them, and [b]the house which I
have set apart as holy for My name,
I will [1]cast out of My presence. So
[c]Israel will become a proverb and
a byword among all peoples. **8** And
this house will become [a,1]a heap of
ruins; everyone who passes by will
*feel* desolate and hiss and say, '[b]Why
has Yahweh done thus to this land
and to this house?' **9** And they will
say, '[a]Because they forsook Yahweh
their God, who brought their fathers
out of the land of Egypt, and took
hold of other gods and worshiped

---

**8:63** [a]Ezr 6:15-18; Ne 12:27 **8:64** [a]2Chr 4:1 [1]Lit *made* **8:65** [a]Lv 23:34-42; 1Ki 8:2 [b]Nu 34:8; Jos 13:5; Jdg 3:3; 2Ki 14:25 [c]Ge 15:18; Ex 23:31; Nu 34:5; Jos 13:3 [1]Or *the entrance of Hamath* **8:66** [1]Or *slave*, cf. 8:52; see Foreword, "The Terminology of Slave" ◆ **9:1** [a]2Chr 7:11 [b]1Ki 7:1, 2 [c]2Chr 8:6 [1]Lit *Solomon's desire which he was pleased to do* **9:2** [a]1Ki 3:5; 11:9; 2Chr 1:7 **9:3** [a]2Ki 20:5; Ps 10:17; 34:17 [b]1Ki 8:29 [c]Dt 11:12; 2Chr 6:40 **9:4** [a]1Ki 3:6, 14; 11:4, 6, 8; 2Ki 20:3; Ps 128:1 **9:5** [a]2Sa 7:12, 16; 1Ki 2:4; 6:12; 1Chr 22:10 [1]Lit *spoke* **9:6** [a]2Sa 7:14-16; 1Chr 28:9; Ps 89:30ff **9:7** [a]Lv 18:24-29; Dt 4:26; 2Ki 17:23 [b]Jer 7:4-14 [c]Dt 28:37; Ps 44:14; Jer 24:9 [1]Lit *send* **9:8** [a]2Ki 25:9; 2Chr 36:19 [b]Dt 29:24-26; 2Chr 7:21; Jer 22:8, 9, 28 [1]Heb *high* **9:9** [a]Dt 29:25-28; Jer 2:10-13

them and served them, therefore
Yahweh has brought all this calamity
on them.'"

### *Cities Given to Hiram*

**10** [a]Now it happened that [b]at the end
of twenty years in which Solomon
had built the two houses, the house
of Yahweh and the king's house
**11** (Hiram king of Tyre had supplied
Solomon with cedar and cypress
timber and gold according to all
his desire), that King Solomon then
gave Hiram twenty cities in the land
of Galilee. **12** So Hiram came out
from Tyre to see the cities which
Solomon had given him, and they
were not right in his eyes. **13** And he
said, "What are these cities which
you have given me, my brother?" So
[1]they were called the land of [a,2]Cabul
to this day. **14** [a]And Hiram sent to the
king [1]120 talents of gold.

### *Solomon Builds Cities and Ships*

**15** Now this is the account of the
forced labor which King Solomon
[a]raised up to build the house of Yah-
weh, his own house, the [b,1]Millo, the
wall of Jerusalem, [c]Hazor, [d]Megiddo,
and [e]Gezer. **16** *For* Pharaoh king of
Egypt had gone up and captured
Gezer and burned it with fire, and
killed the [a]Canaanites who lived in
the city, and had [b]given it *as* a dowry
to his daughter, Solomon's wife. **17** So
Solomon rebuilt Gezer and the low-
er [a]Beth-horon **18** and [a]Baalath and
Tamar in the wilderness, in the land
*of Judah*, **19** and all the storage cities
which Solomon had, and [a]the cities
for [1]his chariots, and the cities for
[b,1]his horsemen, and [c,2]all that Solo-
mon desired to build in Jerusalem, in
Lebanon, and in all the land [3]under
his rule. **20** *As for* all the people who
were left of the Amorites, the Hit-
tites, the Perizzites, the Hivites and
the Jebusites, who were not of the
sons of Israel, **21** [a]*namely*, their sons
who were left after them in the land
[b]whom the sons of Israel were unable
to devote to destruction, *from* [c]them
Solomon raised up [d]forced laborers
to this day. **22** But Solomon [a]did not
make slaves of the sons of Israel; for
they were men of war, his servants,
his princes, his captains, his chariot
commanders, and his horsemen.

**23** These *were* the [a,1]chief deputies
who *were* over Solomon's work, 550,
[b]who had dominion over the people
doing the work.

**24** As soon as [a]Pharaoh's daughter
came up from the city of David to her
house which *Solomon* had built for
her, [b]then he built the Millo.

**25** And [a]three times in a year
Solomon offered burnt offerings and
peace offerings on the altar which
he built to Yahweh, burning incense
with them *on the altar* which *was*
before Yahweh. So he finished the
house.

**26** King Solomon also made a [a]fleet
of ships in [b]Ezion-geber, which is

**9:10** [a]2Chr 8:1 [b]1Ki 6:37, 38; 7:1; 9:1 **9:13** [a]Jos 19:27 [1]Lit *he called them* [2]Lit *as good as nothing*
**9:14** [a]1Ki 9:11 [1]Approx. 4.5 tons or 4 metric tons, a talent was approx. 75 lb. or 34 kg **9:15** [a]1Ki 5:13
[b]2Sa 5:9; 1Ki 9:24 [c]Jos 11:1; 19:36 [d]Jos 17:11 [e]Jdg 1:29 [1]Citadel **9:16** [a]Jos 16:10 [b]1Ki 3:1; 7:8
**9:17** [a]Jos 10:10; 16:3; 21:22; 2Chr 8:5 **9:18** [a]Jos 19:44 **9:19** [a]1Ki 10:26; 2Chr 1:14 [b]1Ki 4:26 [c]1Ki 9:1
[1]Lit *the* [2]Lit *the desire of Solomon which he desired to build in Jerusalem* [3]Lit *of* **9:21** [a]Jdg 1:21-29; 3:1
[b]Jos 15:63; 17:12, 13 [c]Jdg 1:28, 35 [d]Ge 9:25, 26; Ezr 2:55, 58 **9:22** [a]Lv 25:39 **9:23** [a]2Chr 8:10 [b]1Ki 5:16
[1]Or *officers of the deputies* **9:24** [a]1Ki 3:1; 7:8 [b]2Sa 5:9; 1Ki 9:15; 11:27; 2Chr 32:5 **9:25** [a]Ex 23:14-17;
Dt 16:16 **9:26** [a]1Ki 22:48 [b]Nu 33:35; Dt 2:8; 1Ki 22:48

near Eloth on the shore of the [1]Red
Sea, in the land of Edom. **27** [a]And
Hiram sent his servants with the fleet
of ships, sailors who knew the sea,
along with the servants of Solomon.
**28** And they went to [a]Ophir and took
from there 420 talents of gold and
brought *it* to King Solomon.

### *The Queen of Sheba*

**10** [a]Now the [a]queen of [b]Sheba
heard the report about Solo-
mon concerning the name of Yah-
weh. So she came [c]to test him with
riddles. **2** She came to Jerusalem with
a very glorious retinue, with camels
[a]carrying spices and very much gold
and precious stones. And she came to
Solomon and spoke to him about all
that was in her heart. **3** And Solomon
declared to her *the answer* to all her
matters; there was not a matter which
was hidden from the king which he
did not declare to her. **4** Then the
queen of Sheba saw all the wisdom
of Solomon, the house that he had
built, **5** the food of his table, the seat-
ing of his servants, the disposition
of his attendants and their attire,
his cupbearers, and [1]his stairway by
which he went up to the house of
Yahweh, so that there was no more
spirit in her. **6** Then she said to the
king, "The word is true which I heard
in my own land about your words
and your wisdom. **7** Nevertheless I
did not believe *those* words, until I
came and my eyes had seen it. And
behold, the half was not declared
to me. You exceed, *in* wisdom and
prosperity, the report which I heard.
**8** How [a]blessed are your men, how
blessed are these your servants who
stand before you continually *and*
hear your wisdom. **9** [a]Blessed be
Yahweh your God who delighted in
you, to set you on the throne of Israel;
[b]because Yahweh loved Israel forever,
therefore He made you king, [c]to do
justice and righteousness." **10** [a]Then
she gave the king [1]120 talents of gold
and a very great *amount of* spices and
precious stones. Never again did such
abundance of spices come in as that
which the queen of Sheba gave King
Solomon.

**11** [a]Also, the ships of Hiram, which
carried gold from Ophir, brought in
from Ophir a very great *number of*
almug trees and precious stones.
**12** [a]And the king made of the almug
trees supports for the house of Yah-
weh and for the king's house, also
lyres and harps for the singers; such
almug trees have not come in *again*
nor have they been seen to this day.

**13** Thus King Solomon gave to the
queen of Sheba all her desire which
she asked, besides what he gave her
according to [1]his royal bounty. Then
she turned and went to her own land,
she and her servants.

### *Solomon's Riches and Wisdom*

**14** [a]Now the weight of gold which came
to Solomon in one year was 666 talents
of gold, **15** besides *that* from the traders
and the [1]wares of the merchants and
all the kings of the [a]Arabs and the
governors of the country. **16** [a]And King

---

**9:26** [1]Lit *Sea of Reeds* **9:27** [a]1Ki 5:6, 9; 10:11 **9:28** [a]1Chr 29:4; 2Chr 8:18 ◆ **10:1** [a]2Chr 9:1; Mt 12:42; Lk 11:31 [b]Ge 10:7, 28; Ps 72:10, 15 [c]Jdg 14:12-14; Ps 49:4 **10:2** [a]1Ki 10:10 **10:5** [1]Or *his burnt offering which he offered* **10:8** [a]Pr 8:34 **10:9** [a]1Ki 5:7 [b]1Chr 17:22; 2Chr 2:11 [c]2Sa 8:15; 23:3; Ps 72:2 **10:10** [a]1Ki 10:2 [1]Approx. 4.5 tons or 4.08 metric tons, a talent was approx. 75 lb. or 34 kg **10:11** [a]1Ki 9:27, 28; Job 22:24 **10:12** [a]2Chr 9:11 **10:13** [1]Lit *the hand of King Solomon* **10:14** [a]2Chr 9:13-28 **10:15** [a]2Chr 9:14 [1]Or *traffic* **10:16** [a]1Ki 14:26-28; 2Chr 12:9, 10

Solomon made 200 large shields of
beaten gold, [1]using 600 *shekels of* gold
on each large shield. **17** And *he made*
[a]300 shields of beaten gold, [1]using
[2]three minas of gold on each shield,
and [b]the king put them in the house
of the forest of Lebanon. **18** Moreover,
the king made a great throne of [a]ivory
and overlaid it with refined gold.
**19** *There were* six steps to the throne
and a round top to the throne at its
rear, and [1]arms [2]on each side of the
seat, and two lions standing beside
the [1]arms. **20** Twelve lions were also
standing there on the six steps on the
one side and on the other; nothing like
*it* was made for all the *other* kingdoms.
**21** Now all King Solomon's drinking
vessels *were* of gold, and all the vessels
of the house of the forest of Lebanon
*were* of pure gold. None was of silver;
it was not considered [1]valuable in the
days of Solomon. **22** For [a]the king had
at sea the ships of Tarshish with the
ships of Hiram; once every three years
the ships of Tarshish came carrying
gold and silver, ivory and apes and
peacocks.

**23** [a]So King Solomon became
greater than all the kings of the earth
in riches and in wisdom. **24** And all
the earth was seeking the presence of
Solomon, [a]to hear his wisdom which
God had put in his heart. **25** [a]And
they brought every man his present,
articles of silver and gold, garments,
weapons, spices, horses, and mules,
a set amount year by year.

**26** [a]And Solomon gathered chariots
and horsemen. And he had 1,400
chariots and 12,000 horsemen and
[1]stationed them in the [b]chariot cities
and with the king in Jerusalem. **27** [a]The
king also made silver *as plentiful* as
stones in Jerusalem, and he made ce-
dars as plentiful as sycamore trees that
are in the [1]Shephelah. **28** [a]Solomon's
import of horses was from Egypt and
Kue; the king's merchants procured
*them* from Kue for a price. **29** And a
chariot [1]was imported from Egypt
for 600 *shekels* of silver, and a horse
for 150; and [2]by the same means they
exported them [a]to all the kings of the
Hittites and to the kings of Aram.

### *Solomon Turns from Yahweh*

**11** Now [a]King Solomon loved many
foreign women along with
the daughter of Pharaoh: Moabite,
Ammonite, Edomite, Sidonian, and
Hittite women, **2** from the nations
concerning which Yahweh had said
to the sons of Israel, "[a]You shall not
[1]go along with them, nor shall they
[1]go along with you, *for* they will
surely turn your heart away after
their gods." Solomon clung to these
in love. **3** [a]And he had 700 wives—
princesses—and 300 concubines,
and his wives turned his heart away.
**4** Now it happened at the time that
Solomon was old, his wives turned
his heart away after other gods; and
[a]his heart was not [1]wholly devoted to
Yahweh his God, as the heart of David

**10:16** [1]Lit *he brought up* **10:17** [a]1Ki 14:26 [b]1Ki 7:2 [1]Lit *he brought up* [2]Approx. 3.8 lb. or 1.7 kg, a mina was approx. 1.25 lb. or 0.6 kg **10:18** [a]1Ki 10:22; 2Chr 9:17; Ps 45:8 **10:19** [1]Lit *hands* [2]Lit *on this side and on this at the place of the seat* **10:21** [1]Lit *anything* **10:22** [a]1Ki 9:26-28; 22:48; 2Chr 20:36 **10:23** [a]1Ki 3:12, 13; 4:30 **10:24** [a]1Ki 3:9, 12, 28 **10:25** [a]Ps 68:29 **10:26** [a]1Ki 4:26; 2Chr 1:14-17; 9:25 [b]1Ki 9:19 [1]As in ancient versions; Heb *led* **10:27** [a]Dt 17:17; 2Chr 1:15 [1]Or *lowland* **10:28** [a]Dt 17:16; 2Chr 1:16; 9:28 **10:29** [a]2Ki 7:6, 7 [1]Lit *came up and went out from* [2]Lit *in like manner by their hand*
◆ **11:1** [a]Dt 17:17; Ne 13:23-27 **11:2** [a]Ex 23:31-33; 34:12-16; Dt 7:3 [1]Lit *go among* **11:3** [a]2Sa 5:13-16
**11:4** [a]1Ki 9:4 [1]Lit *complete with*

his father *had been.* **5** For Solomon
went after [a]Ashtoreth the goddess of
the Sidonians and after [b,1]Milcom the
detestable idol of the Ammonites.
**6** And Solomon did what was evil in
the sight of Yahweh, and did not fol-
low Yahweh fully, as David his father
*had done.* **7** Then Solomon built a
high place for [a]Chemosh the detest-
able idol of Moab, on the mountain
which is [1]east of Jerusalem, and for
[b]Molech the detestable idol of the
sons of Ammon. **8** Thus also he did
for all his foreign wives, who burned
incense and sacrificed to their gods.

**9** Now [a]Yahweh was angry with
Solomon [b]because his heart was
turned away from Yahweh, the God
of Israel, [c]who had appeared to him
twice, **10** and [a]had commanded him
concerning this thing, that he should
not walk after other gods; but he did
not keep what Yahweh had command-
ed. **11** So Yahweh said to Solomon,
"Because this has happened with you:
you have not kept My covenant and
My statutes, which I have commanded
you, *so* [a]I will surely tear the kingdom
from you, and will give it to your ser-
vant. **12** Nevertheless I will not do it in
your days for the sake of your father
David, *but* I will tear it out of the hand
of your son. **13** However, [a]I will not
tear away all the kingdom, *but* [b]I will
give one tribe to your son for the sake
*of My servant David* and [c]for the sake
of Jerusalem which I have chosen."

### *Yahweh Raises Up Adversaries*

**14** Then Yahweh raised up an adver-
sary to Solomon, Hadad the Edomite;
he was of the seed of the king in
Edom.

**15** Now it happened that [a]when
David was in Edom, and Joab the
commander of the army had gone
up to bury the slain, and had [b]struck
down every male in Edom **16** (for Joab
and all Israel stayed there six months,
until he had cut off every male in
Edom), **17** that Hadad fled [1]to Egypt,
he and certain Edomites of his father's
servants with him, while Hadad *was*
a young boy. **18** Then they arose from
Midian and came to [a]Paran; and they
took men with them from Paran and
came to Egypt, to Pharaoh king of
Egypt. And he gave him a house and
assigned him food and gave him land.
**19** And Hadad found great favor in
the sight of Pharaoh. So he gave him
as a wife the sister of his own wife,
the sister of Tahpenes the queen.
**20** And the sister of Tahpenes bore
his son Genubath. And Tahpenes
weaned him in Pharaoh's house; and
Genubath was in Pharaoh's house
among the sons of Pharaoh.

**21** But [a]Hadad heard in Egypt that
David slept with his fathers and that
Joab the commander of the army
had died. So Hadad said to Pharaoh,
"Send me away, that I may go to my
own country." **22** Then Pharaoh said
to him, "But what have you lacked
with me, that behold, you are seeking
to go to your own country?" And he
answered, "Nothing; nevertheless
you must surely [1]let me go."

**23** [a]And God raised up *another*
adversary to him, Rezon the son of
Eliada, who had fled from his lord

**11:5** [a]Jdg 2:13; 10:6; 1Sa 7:3, 4 [b]1Ki 11:7 [1]In Jer 49:1, 3, *Malcam* **11:7** [a]Nu 21:29; Jdg 11:24; 2Ki 23:13 [b]Lv 20:2-5; 2Ki 23:10; Ac 7:43 [1]Lit *before* **11:9** [a]Ps 90:7 [b]1Ki 11:2, 4 [c]1Ki 3:5; 9:2 **11:10** [a]1Ki 6:12; 9:6, 7 **11:11** [a]1Sa 2:30; 1Ki 11:29-31; 12:15, 16, 20; 2Ki 17:15, 21 **11:13** [a]2Sa 7:15; 1Chr 17:13; Ps 89:33 [b]1Ki 11:32, 36; 12:20 [c]1Ki 8:29 **11:15** [a]2Sa 8:14; 1Chr 18:12, 13 [b]Dt 20:13 **11:17** [1]Lit *to go into* **11:18** [a]Nu 10:12; Dt 1:1 **11:21** [a]1Ki 2:10 **11:22** [1]Lit *send me away* **11:23** [a]1Ki 11:14

[b]Hadadezer king of Zobah. **24** And he
gathered men to himself and became
commander of a marauding band,
[a]after David killed *some of* [1]them; and
they went to Damascus and stayed
[2]there, and reigned in Damascus.
**25** So he was an adversary to Israel all
the days of Solomon, along with the
evil that Hadad *did*; and he abhorred
Israel and reigned over Aram.

**26** Now [a]Jeroboam the son of
Nebat, an Ephraimite of Zeredah,
Solomon's servant, whose mother's
name was Zeruah, a widow, [b]also
[1]raised his hand against the king.
**27** Now this was the reason why he
[1]raised his hand against the king:
[a]Solomon built the [2]Millo, *and*
closed up the breach of the city of
his father David. **28** Now the man
Jeroboam was a mighty man of valor.
And [a]Solomon saw that the young
man was [1]industrious and appointed
him over all the load-bearers of the
house of Joseph. **29** Now it happened
at that time, that Jeroboam went out
of Jerusalem, and [a]that the prophet
Ahijah the Shilonite found him
on the road. Now [1]he had covered
himself with a new cloak; and both
of them were alone in the field.
**30** Then [a]Ahijah took hold of the
new cloak which was on him and
tore it into twelve pieces. **31** And he
said to Jeroboam, "Take for yourself
ten pieces; for thus says Yahweh, the
God of Israel, 'Behold, [a]I will tear the
kingdom out of the hand of Solomon
and give you ten tribes, **32** [a]but he
will have one tribe, for the sake of
My servant David and for the sake
of Jerusalem, [b]the city which I have
chosen from all the tribes of Israel,
**33** because they have forsaken Me,
and [a]have worshiped Ashtoreth the
goddess of the Sidonians, [b]Chemosh
the god of Moab, and Milcom the god
of the sons of Ammon; and they have
not walked in My ways to do what
is right in My sight and *to keep* My
statutes and My judgments, as his
father David *did*. **34** Nevertheless I
will not take the whole kingdom out
of his hand, but I will make him [1]ruler
all the days of his life, for the sake
of My servant David whom I chose,
who kept My commandments and
My statutes; **35** but [a]I will take the
kingdom from his son's hand and
give it to you—the ten tribes. **36** But
[a]to his son I will give one tribe, [b]that
My servant David may have a lamp
always before Me in Jerusalem,
[a]the city where I have chosen for
Myself to put My name. **37** And I will
take you, and you shall reign over
whatever your soul desires, and you
shall be king over Israel. **38** Then it
will be, that if you listen to all that I
command you and walk in My ways,
and do what is right in My sight to
keep My statutes and My command-
ments, as My servant David did, then
[a]I will be with you and [b]build you an
enduring house as I built for David,
and I will give Israel to you. **39** Thus I
will afflict the seed of David for this,
but not always.'" **40** Solomon sought
therefore to put Jeroboam to death;
but Jeroboam arose and fled to Egypt

---

**11:23** [b]2Sa 8:3; 10:16 **11:24** [a]2Sa 10:8, 18 [1]Some of them from Zobah [2]Lit *in it* **11:26** [a]1Ki 11:11, 28; 12:2, 20; 2Chr 13:6 [b]2Sa 20:21 [1]Or *rebelled* **11:27** [a]1Ki 9:15, 24 [1]Or *rebelled* [2]Citadel **11:28** [a]Pr 22:29 [1]Lit *a doer of work* **11:29** [a]1Ki 12:15; 14:2; 2Chr 9:29 [1]Ahijah **11:30** [a]1Sa 15:27, 28 **11:31** [a]1Ki 11:11, 12 **11:32** [a]1Ki 11:13; 12:21 [b]1Ki 11:13; 14:21 **11:33** [a]1Sa 7:3; 1Ki 11:5-8 [b]Nu 21:29; Jer 48:7, 13 **11:34** [1]Or *prince* **11:35** [a]1Ki 11:12; 12:16, 17 **11:36** [a]1Ki 11:13 [b]1Ki 15:4; 2Ki 8:19; Ps 132:17 **11:38** [a]Dt 31:8; Jos 1:5 [b]2Sa 7:11, 27

to [a]Shishak king of Egypt, and he was
in Egypt until the death of Solomon.

### *The Death of Solomon*

**41** [a]Now the rest of the acts of Sol-
omon and whatever he did, and his
wisdom, are they not written in the
book of the acts of Solomon? **42** Thus
[a]the time that Solomon reigned in
Jerusalem over all Israel was forty
years. **43** And Solomon [a]slept with
his fathers and was buried in the
city of his father David, and his son
[b]Rehoboam became king in his place.

### *Rehoboam Forsakes the Elders' Counsel*

**12** [a]Then Rehoboam went to
Shechem, for all Israel had
come to [b]Shechem to make him king.
**2** And it happened, [a]when Jeroboam
the son of Nebat heard *of it,* [1]he was
living in Egypt (for he was yet in
Egypt, where he had fled from the
presence of King Solomon). **3** Then
they sent and called for him. And
Jeroboam and all the assembly of
Israel came and spoke to Rehoboam,
saying, **4** "[a]Your father made our yoke
harsh; but you, now, lighten the harsh
service of your father and his heavy
yoke which he put on us, and we will
serve you." **5** Then he said to them,
"[a]Go [1]for three days, then return to
me." So the people went away.
**6** Then King Rehoboam [a]took
counsel with the elders who had
stood before his father Solomon
while he was still alive, saying, "How
do you counsel *me* to respond to this
people?" **7** And they spoke to him,
saying, "[a]If you will be a servant to
this people today, and will serve them
and [1]grant them their petition, and
speak good words to them, then they
will be your servants forever." **8** But
he forsook the counsel of the elders
which they had counseled him, and
took counsel with the young men
who grew up with him and stood
before him. **9** So he said to them,
"What counsel do you give that we
may respond to this people who have
spoken to me, saying, 'Lighten the
yoke which your father put on us'?"
**10** Then the young men who grew up
with him spoke to him, saying, "Thus
you shall say to this people who
spoke to you, saying, 'Your father
made our yoke heavy, now you make
it lighter for us!' Thus you shall speak
to them, 'My little finger is thicker
than my father's loins! **11** So now, my
father loaded you with a heavy yoke,
but I will add to your yoke; my father
disciplined you with whips, but I will
discipline you with scorpions.'"
**12** So Jeroboam and all the people
came to Rehoboam on the third
day as the king had spoken, saying,
"[a]Return to me on the third day."
**13** And the king answered the people
harshly, and he forsook the counsel
of the elders which they had [1]given
him, **14** and he spoke to them accord-
ing to the counsel of the young men,
saying, "[a]My father made your yoke
heavy, but I will add to your yoke; my
father disciplined you with whips,
but I will discipline you with scor-
pions." **15** So the king did not listen
to the people; [a]for it was a turn *of*

**11:40** [a]1Ki 14:25; 2Chr 12:2-9 **11:41** [a]2Chr 9:29 **11:42** [a]2Chr 9:30 **11:43** [a]1Ki 2:10; 2Chr 9:31 [b]1Ki 14:21; Mt 1:7 ◆ **12:1** [a]2Chr 10:1 [b]Jdg 9:6 **12:2** [a]1Ki 11:26, 40 [1]Lit *Jeroboam* **12:4** [a]1Sa 8:11-18; 1Ki 4:7, 21-25; 9:15 **12:5** [a]1Ki 12:12 [1]Lit *yet 3* **12:6** [a]1Ki 4:1-6; Job 12:12; 32:7 **12:7** [a]2Chr 10:7; Pr 15:1 [1]Lit *answer them* **12:12** [a]1Ki 12:5 **12:13** [1]Lit *advised* **12:14** [a]Ex 1:13, 14; 5:5-9, 16-18 **12:15** [a]Dt 2:30; Jdg 14:4; 1Ki 12:24; 2Chr 10:15

*events* from Yahweh, [b]that He might
establish His word, which Yahweh
spoke through Ahijah the Shilonite
to Jeroboam the son of Nebat.

### *Israel Rebels Against Judah*

16 Then all Israel saw that the king
did not listen to them. So the people
responded to the king *with this* word,
saying,

"What portion do we
have in David?
*We have* no inheritance
in the son of Jesse;
[a]To your tents, O Israel!
Now see to your own
house, David!"

So Israel went to their tents. 17 But
[a]as for the sons of Israel who lived
in the cities of Judah, Rehoboam
reigned over them. 18 Then King
Rehoboam sent [a]Adoram, who *was*
over the forced labor, and all Israel
[1]stoned him and he died. And King
Rehoboam made haste to mount his
chariot to flee to Jerusalem. 19 [a]So
Israel has been in rebellion against
the house of David to this day.

20 Now it happened when all Israel
heard that Jeroboam had returned,
that they sent and called him to the
congregation and made him king
over all Israel. [a]None but the tribe
of Judah followed the house of David.

21 [a]Then Rehoboam came to Jeru-
salem and assembled all the house
of Judah and the tribe of Benjamin,
180,000 chosen men who could
wage war, to fight against the house
of Israel to return the kingdom to
Rehoboam the son of Solomon. 22 But
the word of God came to [a]Shemaiah
the man of God, saying, 23 "Speak
to Rehoboam the son of Solomon,
king of Judah, and to all the house
of Judah and Benjamin and to the
[a]rest of the people, saying, 24 'Thus
says Yahweh, "You shall not go up
and fight against your brothers, the
sons of Israel; return every man to
his house, [a]for this thing is from
Me."'" So they listened to the word of
Yahweh, and returned to go *their way*
according to the word of Yahweh.

### *Jeroboam Makes Golden Calves*

25 Then [a]Jeroboam built Shechem
in the hill country of Ephraim, and
lived [1]there. And he went out from
there and built [b]Penuel. 26 And Jer-
oboam said in his heart, "Now the
kingdom will return to the house of
David. 27 [a]If this people go up to offer
sacrifices in the house of Yahweh
at Jerusalem, then the heart of this
people will return to their lord, *even*
to Rehoboam king of Judah; and they
will kill me and return to Rehoboam
king of Judah." 28 So the king took
counsel, and [a]made two golden
[b]calves, and he said to them, "It is
too much for you to go up to Jeru-
salem; [c]behold your gods, O Israel,
that brought you up from the land of
Egypt." 29 And he set [a]one in [b]Bethel,
and one he put in [c]Dan. 30 Now [a]this
thing became a sin, for the people
went *to worship* before the one as far
as Dan. 31 And [a]he made houses on
high places, and [b]made priests from

**12:15** [b]1Ki 11:11, 31 **12:16** [a]2Sa 20:1 **12:17** [a]1Ki 11:13, 36 **12:18** [a]2Sa 20:24; 1Ki 4:6; 5:14 [1]Lit *stoned with stones* **12:19** [a]2Ki 17:21 **12:20** [a]1Ki 11:13, 32, 36 **12:21** [a]2Chr 11:1 **12:22** [a]2Chr 11:2; 12:5-7 **12:23** [a]1Ki 12:17 **12:24** [a]1Ki 12:15 **12:25** [a]Ge 12:6; Jdg 9:45-49 [b]Ge 32:30, 31; Jdg 8:8, 17 [1]Lit *in it* **12:27** [a]Dt 12:5-7, 14 **12:28** [a]2Ki 10:29; 17:16; Hos 8:4-7 [b]Hos 10:5 [c]Ex 32:4, 8 **12:29** [a]Hos 10:5 [b]Ge 28:19 [c]Jdg 18:26-31 **12:30** [a]1Ki 13:34; 2Ki 17:21 **12:31** [a]1Ki 13:32 [b]1Ki 13:33; 2Ki 17:32; 2Chr 11:15; 13:9

among [1]all the people who were not of the sons of Levi. **32** And Jeroboam made a feast in the eighth month on the fifteenth day of the month, [a]like the feast which is in Judah, and he [1]went up to the altar; thus he did in Bethel, to sacrifice to the calves which he had made. And he had [b]the priests of the high places, which he had made, stand in Bethel. **33** Then he [1]went up to the altar which he had made in Bethel on the fifteenth day in the eighth month, even in the month which he had [a,2]devised [3]in his own heart; and he made a feast for the sons of Israel and [1]went up to the altar [b]to burn [4]incense.

### *The Altar Shall Be Torn Apart*

**13** Now behold, there came [a]a man of God from Judah to Bethel by the word of Yahweh, while Jeroboam was standing by the altar [b]to burn incense. **2** [a]And he cried against the altar by the word of Yahweh, and said, "O altar, altar, thus says Yahweh, 'Behold, a son shall be born to the house of David, [b]Josiah is his name; and on you he shall sacrifice the priests of the high places who burn incense on you, and human bones shall be burned on you.'" **3** Then he gave a miraculous sign the same day, saying, "[a]This is the miraculous sign which Yahweh has spoken, 'Behold, the altar shall be torn apart and the [1]ashes which are on it shall be poured out.'" **4** Now it happened that when the king heard the word of the man of God, which he cried against the altar in Bethel, Jeroboam stretched out his hand from the altar, saying, "Seize him." But his hand which he stretched out against him dried up, so that he could not draw it back to himself. **5** The altar also was torn apart and the [1]ashes were poured out from the altar, according to the miraculous sign which the man of God had given by the word of Yahweh. **6** Then the king answered and said to the man of God, "Please [a,1]entreat Yahweh your God, and pray for me, that my hand may be restored to me." So [b]the man of God [2]entreated Yahweh, and the king's hand was restored to him, and it became as it was before. **7** Then the king said to the man of God, "Come home with me and refresh yourself, and [a]I will give you a gift." **8** But the man of God said to the king, "[a]If you were to give me half your house, I would not go with you, nor would I eat bread or drink water in this place. **9** For so [1]it was commanded me by the word of Yahweh, saying, 'You shall eat no bread, nor drink water, nor return by the way which you came.'" **10** So he went another way and did not return by the way which he came to Bethel.

### *The Prophet Rebels Against Yahweh*

**11** Now [a]an old prophet was living in Bethel; and his [1]sons came and recounted to him all the work which the man of God had done that day in Bethel; the words which he had spoken to the king, these also they recounted to their father. **12** And their

**12:31** [1]Or *the extremities of* **12:32** [a]Lv 23:33, 34; Nu 29:12; 1Ki 8:2, 5 [b]Am 7:10-13 [1]Or *offered upon* **12:33** [a]Nu 15:39 [b]1Ki 13:1 [1]Or *offered upon* [2]Lit *made* [3]Lit *from* [4]Or *sacrifices* ◆ **13:1** [a]1Ki 12:22; 2Ki 23:17 [b]1Ki 12:33 **13:2** [a]1Ki 13:32 [b]2Ki 23:15, 16 **13:3** [a]Ex 4:1-5; Jdg 6:17; Is 38:7; Jn 2:18; 1Co 1:22 [1]Lit *ashes of fat* **13:5** [1]Lit *ashes of fat* **13:6** [a]Ex 8:8, 28; 9:28; 10:17; Ac 8:24; Jas 5:16 [b]Lk 6:27, 28 [1]Lit *soften the face of* [2]Lit *softened the face of* **13:7** [a]1Sa 9:7, 8; 2Ki 5:15 **13:8** [a]Nu 22:18; 24:13; 1Ki 13:16, 17 **13:9** [1]Lit *he commanded me* **13:11** [a]1Ki 13:25; 2Ki 23:18 [1]Lit *son*

father said to them, "[1]Which way did
he go?" And his sons [2]had seen the
way which the man of God who came
from Judah had gone. **13** Then he said
to his sons, "Saddle the donkey for
me." So they saddled the donkey for
him and he rode away on it. **14** So
he went after the man of God and
found him sitting under [1]an oak; and
he said to him, "Are you the man of
God who came from Judah?" And he
said, "I am." **15** Then he said to him,
"Come home with me and eat bread."
**16** And he said, "[a]I cannot return with
you, nor go with you, nor will I eat
bread or drink water with you in this
place. **17** For a word *came* to me [a]by
the word of Yahweh, 'You shall eat
no bread, nor drink water there; do
not return by going the way which
you came.'" **18** And he said to him,
"[a]I also am a prophet like you, and
[b]an angel spoke to me by the word
of Yahweh, saying, 'Bring him back
with you to your house, that he may
eat bread and drink water.'" *But* [c]he
dealt falsely with him. **19** So he went
back with him, and ate bread in his
house and drank water.

**20** Now it happened as they were
sitting down at the table, that the
word of Yahweh came to the prophet
who had brought him back; **21** and
he called out to the man of God who
came from Judah, saying, "Thus says
Yahweh, 'Because you have rebelled
against the [1]word of Yahweh, and
have not kept the commandment
which Yahweh your God commanded
you, **22** but have returned and eaten
bread and drunk water in the place of
which He said to you, "Eat no bread
and drink no water"; your body
shall not come to the grave of your
fathers.'" **23** Now it happened after
he had eaten bread and after he had
drunk, that he saddled the donkey
for him, for the prophet whom he
had brought back. **24** Then he went
and on the way [a]a lion met him and
put him to death, and his body was
thrown on the road, with the donkey
standing beside it; the lion also was
standing beside the body. **25** And
behold, men passed by and saw the
body thrown on the road, and the
lion standing beside the body; so
they came and spoke *about it* in the
city where [a]the old prophet lived.

**26** Then the prophet, who brought
him back from the way, heard *it* and
said, "It is the man of God, who re-
belled against the [1]command of Yah-
weh; therefore Yahweh has given him
to the lion, which has mauled him
and put him to death, according to
the word of Yahweh which He spoke
to him." **27** Then he spoke to his sons,
saying, "Saddle the donkey for me."
And they saddled *it*. **28** And he went
and found his body thrown on the
road with the donkey and the lion
standing beside the body; the lion
had not eaten the body nor mauled
the donkey. **29** So the prophet took
up the body of the man of God and
laid it on the donkey and brought it
back, and he came to the city of the
old prophet to mourn and to bury
him. **30** He laid his body in his own
grave, and they mourned over him,
*saying*, "[a]Alas, my brother!" **31** Now

---

**13:12** [1]Lit *Where is the way he went* [2]Some ancient versions *showed him* **13:14** [1]Or a *terebinth*
**13:16** [a]1Ki 13:8, 9 **13:17** [a]1Ki 20:35 **13:18** [a]Mt 7:15; 1Jn 4:1 [b]Ga 1:8 [c]Pr 12:19, 22; 19:5; Jer 29:31, 32;
Eze 13:8, 9; 1Ti 4:1, 2 **13:21** [1]Lit *mouth* **13:24** [a]1Ki 20:36 **13:25** [a]1Ki 13:11 **13:26** [1]Lit *mouth*
**13:30** [a]Jer 22:18

it happened after he had buried him, that he spoke to his sons, saying, "When I die, you shall bury me in the grave in which the man of God is buried; [a]lay my bones beside his bones. **32** [a]For the word shall surely happen which he cried by the word of Yahweh against the altar in Bethel and [b]against all the houses of the high places which are in the cities of [c]Samaria."

**33** After this event Jeroboam did not return from his evil way, but [a]he returned and made priests of the high places from among [1]all the people; [b]any who delighted *to be so,* he ordained. So [2]they became priests of the high places. **34** [a,1]And this event became sin to the house of Jeroboam, [b]even to blot *it* out and destroy *it* from off the face of the earth.

### *The House of Jeroboam Is Cut Off*

**14** At that time Abijah the son of Jeroboam became sick. **2** And Jeroboam said to his wife, "Arise now, and [a]disguise yourself so that they will not know that you are the wife of Jeroboam, and go to [b]Shiloh; behold, Ahijah the prophet is there, who [c]spoke concerning me *that I would be* king over this people. **3** [a]And take ten loaves with you, *some* cakes, and a jar of honey, and go to him. He will tell you what will happen to the boy."

**4** Then Jeroboam's wife did so, and arose and went to [a]Shiloh, and came to the house of [b]Ahijah. Now Ahijah could not see, [c]for his eyes had [1]set because of his old age. **5** Now Yahweh had said to Ahijah, "Behold, the wife of Jeroboam is coming to [1]inquire of you concerning her son, for he is sick. You shall say thus and thus to her, for it will be when she arrives that [a]she will pretend to be another woman."

**6** Now it happened as Ahijah heard the sound of her feet coming in the doorway, that he said, "Come in, wife of Jeroboam, why do you pretend to be another woman? For I am sent to you *with* a harsh *message.* **7** Go, say to Jeroboam, 'Thus says Yahweh, the God of Israel, "[a]Because I exalted you from among the people and made you ruler over My people Israel, **8** and [a]tore the kingdom away from the house of David and gave it to you—[b]yet you have not been like My servant David, who kept My commandments and who walked after Me with all his heart, [c]to do only that which was right in My sight; **9** you also have done more evil than all who were before you, and [a]have gone and made for yourself other gods and [b]molten images to provoke Me to anger, and have [c]cast Me behind your back— **10** therefore behold, I am bringing evil on the house of Jeroboam: I [a]will cut off from Jeroboam [1]every male person, [b]both bond and free in Israel, and I [c]will make a clean sweep of the house of Jeroboam, as one sweeps away dung until it is all gone. **11** [a]Anyone

**13:31** [a]Ru 1:17; 2Ki 23:17, 18 **13:32** [a]1Ki 13:2 [b]Lv 26:30; 1Ki 12:31 [c]1Ki 16:24; Jn 4:5; Ac 8:14 **13:33** [a]1Ki 12:31, 32 [b]Jdg 17:5 [1]Or *the extremities of* [2]Lit *he* **13:34** [a]1Ki 12:30; 2Ki 17:21 [b]1Ki 14:10; 15:29, 30 [1]Lit *by this thing he became* ◆ **14:2** [a]1Sa 28:8; 2Sa 14:2; 2Chr 18:29 [b]Jos 18:1 [c]1Ki 11:29-31 **14:3** [a]1Sa 9:7, 8; 1Ki 13:7; 2Ki 4:42 **14:4** [a]1Ki 14:2 [b]1Ki 11:29 [c]1Sa 3:2; 4:15 [1]Became dim **14:5** [a]2Sa 14:2 [1]Lit *seek a word from* **14:7** [a]2Sa 12:7; 1Ki 11:28-31; 16:2 **14:8** [a]1Ki 11:31 [b]1Ki 11:33, 38 [c]1Ki 15:5 **14:9** [a]1Ki 12:28; 2Chr 11:15 [b]Ex 34:17 [c]Ne 9:26; Ps 50:17; Eze 23:35 **14:10** [a]1Ki 21:21; 2Ki 9:8 [b]Dt 32:36; 2Ki 14:26 [c]1Ki 15:29 [1]Lit *him who urinates against the wall*, cf. 1Sa 25:22, 34; 1Ki 16:11; 21:21; 2Ki 9:8 **14:11** [a]1Ki 16:4; 21:24

belonging to Jeroboam who dies in the
city the dogs will eat. And he who dies
in the field the birds of the sky will
eat; for Yahweh has spoken *it*."' **12** But
you, arise, go to your house. [a]When
your feet enter the city the child will
die. **13** And all Israel shall mourn for
him and bury him, for [1]he alone of
Jeroboam's *family* will come to the
grave, because in him [a]something
good was found toward Yahweh,
the God of Israel, in the house of
Jeroboam. **14** Moreover, [a]Yahweh will
raise up for Himself a king over Israel
who will cut off the house of Jeroboam
this day [1]and from now on.

**15** "So Yahweh will strike Israel, as
a reed is shaken in the water; and [a]He
will uproot Israel from [b]this good
land which He gave to their fathers,
and [c]will scatter them beyond the
[1]River, [d]because they have made
their [2]Asherim, provoking Yahweh to
anger. **16** And He will give Israel over
[a]on account of the sins of Jeroboam,
which he sinned and with which he
made Israel to sin."

**17** Then Jeroboam's wife arose and
went away and came to [a]Tirzah. [b]As
she was entering the threshold of
the house, the child died. **18** [a]And
all Israel buried him and mourned
for him, according to the word of
Yahweh which He spoke through His
servant Ahijah the prophet.

### *The Death of Jeroboam*

**19** Now the rest of the acts of Jer-
oboam, [a]how he made war and how
he reigned, behold, they are written
in the Book of the Chronicles of the
Kings of Israel. **20** Now the time that
Jeroboam reigned *was* twenty-two
years; and he slept with his fathers,
and Nadab his son became king in
his place.

### *Rehoboam Reigns over Judah*

**21** [a]Now Rehoboam the son of
Solomon became king in Judah.
Rehoboam was forty-one years old
when he became king, and he reigned
seventeen years in Jerusalem, [b]the
city which Yahweh had chosen from
all the tribes of Israel to put His name
there. And his mother's name was
Naamah the Ammonitess. **22** [a]And
Judah did what was evil in the sight of
Yahweh, and they [b]provoked Him to
jealousy more than all that their fa-
thers had done, with [1]the sins which
they sinned. **23** They also built for
themselves [a]high places and *sacred*
[b]pillars and [c,1]Asherim on every high
hill and [d]beneath every green tree.
**24** There were also [a]male cult prosti-
tutes in the land. They did according
to all the abominations of the nations
which Yahweh dispossessed before
the sons of Israel.

**25** [a]Now it happened in the fifth
year of King Rehoboam, that Shishak
king of Egypt came up against Jeru-
salem. **26** And he took the treasures
of the house of Yahweh and the
treasures of the king's house. And
[a]he took everything; he [b]even took
all the shields of gold which Solomon

**14:12** [a]1Ki 14:17 **14:13** [a]2Chr 19:3 [1]Lit *the one* **14:14** [a]1Ki 15:27-29 [1]Lit *and what even now?*
**14:15** [a]Dt 29:28; 2Ki 17:6; Ps 52:5 [b]Jos 23:15, 16 [c]2Ki 15:29 [d]Ex 34:13, 14; Dt 12:3, 4 [1]The Euphrates River
[2]Wooden symbols of a female deity **14:16** [a]1Ki 12:30; 13:34; 15:30, 34; 16:2 **14:17** [a]1Ki 15:21, 33; 16:6-9,
15, 23; SS 6:4 [b]1Ki 14:12 **14:18** [a]1Ki 14:13 **14:19** [a]1Ki 14:30; 2Chr 13:2-20 **14:21** [a]2Chr 12:13 [b]1Ki 11:32,
36 **14:22** [a]2Chr 12:1, 14 [b]Dt 32:21; Ps 78:58; 1Co 10:22 [1]Lit *their* **14:23** [a]Dt 12:2; Eze 16:24 [b]Dt 16:22
[c]1Ki 14:15 [d]2Ki 17:10; Is 57:5; Jer 2:20 [1]Wooden symbols of a female deity **14:24** [a]Ge 19:5; Dt 23:17;
1Ki 15:12; 22:46; 2Ki 23:7 **14:25** [a]1Ki 11:40; 2Chr 12:2, 9 **14:26** [a]1Ki 15:18; 2Chr 12:9 [b]1Ki 10:17; 2Chr 9:15, 16

had made. **27** Then King Rehoboam
made shields of bronze in their place
and [a]committed them into the hand
of the commanders of the [1]guard who
kept the door of the king's house.
**28** Now it happened as often as the
king entered the house of Yahweh,
that the [1]guards would carry them
and would bring them back into the
[1]guards' room.

### *The Death of Rehoboam*

**29** [a]Now the rest of the acts of Re-
hoboam and all that he did, are they
not written in the Book of the Chron-
icles of the Kings of Judah? **30** [a]Now
there was war between Rehoboam
and Jeroboam all *their* days. **31** And
Rehoboam slept with his fathers and
was buried with his fathers in the city
of David; and [a]his mother's name was
Naamah the Ammonitess. And Abi-
jam his son became king in his place.

### *Abijam Reigns over Judah*

**15** [a]Now in the eighteenth year of
King Jeroboam, the son of Ne-
bat, Abijam became king over Judah.
**2** He reigned three years in Jerusalem;
and his mother's name was [a,1]Maacah
the daughter of [b,2]Abishalom. **3** And
he walked in all the sins of his father
which he had committed before him;
and [a]his heart was not [1]wholly devot-
ed to Yahweh his God, like the heart of
*his father* David. **4** But for David's sake
Yahweh his God gave him a [a]lamp in
Jerusalem, to raise up his son after him
and to establish Jerusalem; **5** [a]because
David did what was right in the sight
of Yahweh, and had not turned aside
from anything that He commanded
him all the days of his life, [b]except in
the case of Uriah the Hittite. **6** [a]Now
there was war between Rehoboam
and Jeroboam all the days of his life.
**7** Now [a]the rest of the acts of Abi-
jam and all that he did, are they not
written in the Book of the Chronicles
of the Kings of Judah? [b]And there was
war between Abijam and Jeroboam.
**8** [a]And Abijam slept with his fathers,
and they buried him in the city of
David; and Asa his son became king
in his place.

### *Asa Reigns over Judah*

**9** Now in the twentieth year of Jer-
oboam the king of Israel, Asa began
to reign as king of Judah. **10** And he
reigned forty-one years in Jerusalem;
and [a]his mother's name was Maacah
the daughter of Abishalom. **11** [a]And
Asa did what was right in the sight of
Yahweh, like David his father. **12** [a]He
also put away the male cult prosti-
tutes from the land and [b]removed
all the idols which his fathers had
made. **13** [a,1]He also removed Maacah
his mother from *being* queen mother,
because she had made a horrid image
[2]for Asherah; and Asa cut down her
horrid image and [b]burned *it* at the
brook Kidron. **14** [a]But the high places
were not removed; nevertheless [b]the
heart of Asa was [1]wholly devoted

---

**14:27** [a]1Sa 8:11; 22:17 [1]Lit *runner* **14:28** [1]Lit *runners* **14:29** [a]2Chr 12:15, 16 **14:30** [a]1Ki 12:21; 15:6 **14:31** [a]1Ki 14:21 ◆ **15:1** [a]2Chr 13:1 **15:2** [a]2Chr 13:2 [b]2Chr 11:21 [1]In 2Chr 13:2, *Micaiah, the daughter of Uriel* [2]In 2Chr 11:20, *Absalom* **15:3** [a]1Ki 11:4; Ps 119:80 [1]Lit *complete with* **15:4** [a]2Sa 21:17; 1Ki 11:36; 2Chr 21:7 **15:5** [a]1Ki 9:4; 14:8; Lk 1:6 [b]2Sa 11:3f, 15-17; 12:9, 10 **15:6** [a]1Ki 14:30; 2Chr 12:15-13:20 **15:7** [a]2Chr 13:2, 21, 22 [b]2Chr 13:3-20 **15:8** [a]2Chr 14:1 **15:10** [a]1Ki 15:2 **15:11** [a]2Chr 14:2 **15:12** [a]Dt 23:17; 1Ki 14:24; 22:46 [b]1Ki 11:7, 8; 14:23; 2Chr 14:2-5 **15:13** [a]2Chr 15:16-18 [b]Ex 32:20 [1]Lit *Also Maacah his mother and he removed her* [2]Or *as an Asherah* **15:14** [a]1Ki 22:43; 2Ki 12:3 [b]1Ki 8:61; 15:3 [1]Lit *complete with*

to Yahweh all his days. **15** [a]And he
brought into the house of Yahweh
the holy things of his father and his
own holy things: silver and gold and
utensils.

### *Asa Wars Against Baasha*

**16** [a]Now there was war between Asa
and Baasha king of Israel all their
days. **17** [a]And Baasha king of Israel
went up against Judah and [b]built up
Ramah [c]in order to prevent *anyone*
from going out or coming in to Asa
king of Judah. **18** Then [a]Asa took all
the silver and the gold which were
left in the treasuries of the house
of Yahweh and the treasuries of the
king's house, and delivered them
into the hand of his servants. And
[b]King Asa sent them to Ben-hadad
the son of Tabrimmon, the son of
Hezion, king of Aram, who lived in
[c]Damascus, saying, **19** "*Let there be* a
[a]covenant between [1]you and me, *as*
between my father and your father.
Behold, I have sent you a gift of silver
and gold; go, break your covenant
with Baasha king of Israel so that
he will withdraw from me." **20** So
Ben-hadad listened to King Asa and
sent the commanders of his military
force against the cities of Israel, and
struck down [a]Ijon, [b]Dan, [c]Abel-beth-
maacah and all [d]Chinneroth, besides
all the land of Naphtali. **21** Now it
happened that when Baasha heard *of
it,* [a]he ceased building up Ramah and
remained in [b]Tirzah. **22** Then King
Asa caused *an announcement* to be
heard throughout all Judah—none
was exempt—and they carried away
the stones of Ramah and its timber
with which Baasha had been build-
ing. And King Asa built with them
[a]Geba of Benjamin and Mizpah.

**23** [a]Now the rest of all the acts of
Asa and all his might and all that he
did and the cities which he built, are
they not written in the Book of the
Chronicles of the Kings of Judah?
But in the time of his old age he was
diseased in his feet. **24** And Asa slept
with his fathers and was buried with
his fathers in the city of David his
father; and [a]Jehoshaphat his son
reigned in his place.

### *Nadab Reigns over Israel*

**25** Now [a]Nadab the son of Jeroboam
became king over Israel in the second
year of Asa king of Judah, and he
reigned over Israel two years. **26** And
he did what was evil in the sight of
Yahweh, and [a]walked in the way of
his father and [b]in his sin which he
made Israel sin. **27** Then [a]Baasha the
son of Ahijah of the house of Issachar
conspired against him, and Baasha
struck him down at [b]Gibbethon,
which belonged to the Philistines,
while Nadab and all Israel were
laying siege to Gibbethon.

**28** So Baasha put him to death
in the third year of Asa king of Ju-
dah and became king in his place.
**29** Now it happened that as soon as
he was king, he struck down all the
household of Jeroboam. He did not
leave to Jeroboam anyone *who drew*
breath, until he had destroyed them,

---

**15:15** [a]1Ki 7:51 **15:16** [a]1Ki 15:32 **15:17** [a]2Chr 16:1-6 [b]Jos 18:25; 1Ki 15:21, 22 [c]1Ki 12:26-29
**15:18** [a]1Ki 14:26; 15:15 [b]2Ki 12:17, 18; 2Chr 16:2 [c]Ge 14:15; 1Ki 11:23, 24 **15:19** [a]2Chr 16:7 [1]Lit *me and you* **15:20** [a]2Ki 15:29 [b]Jdg 18:29; 1Ki 12:29 [c]2Sa 20:15; 2Ki 15:29 [d]Jos 11:2; 12:3 **15:21** [a]1Ki 15:17 [b]1Ki 14:17; 16:15-18 **15:22** [a]Jos 18:24; 21:17 **15:23** [a]2Chr 16:11-14 **15:24** [a]1Ki 22:41-44; 2Chr 17:1; Mt 1:8
**15:25** [a]1Ki 14:20 **15:26** [a]1Ki 12:28-33; 13:33, 34 [b]1Ki 14:16; 15:30, 34 **15:27** [a]1Ki 14:14 [b]Jos 19:44; 21:23; 1Ki 16:15

[a]according to the word of Yahweh,
which He spoke by the hand of His
servant Ahijah the Shilonite, **30** *and*
because of the sins of Jeroboam which
he sinned, and [a]which he made Israel
sin, because of his provocation with
which he provoked Yahweh, the God
of Israel, to anger.
**31** [a]Now the rest of the acts of Na-
dab and all that he did, are they not
written in the Book of the Chronicles
of the Kings of Israel? **32** [a]Now there
was war between Asa and Baasha
king of Israel all their days.

### *Baasha Reigns over Israel*

**33** In the third year of Asa king of
Judah, Baasha the son of Ahijah
became king over all Israel at Tir-
zah, *and reigned* twenty-four years.
**34** And he did what was evil in the
sight of Yahweh, and [a]walked in the
way of Jeroboam and in his sin which
he made Israel sin.

**16** Now the word of Yahweh came
to [a]Jehu the son of [b]Hanani
against Baasha, saying, **2** "Inasmuch
as I [a]exalted you from the dust and
made you ruler over My people
Israel, and [b]you have walked in the
way of Jeroboam and have made My
people Israel sin, provoking Me to
anger with their sins, **3** behold, [a]I am
going to sweep away [b]Baasha and his
house, and [c]I will make your house
*like the house* of Jeroboam the son
of Nebat. **4** [a]Anyone of Baasha who
dies in the city the dogs will eat, and
anyone of his who dies in the field
the birds of the sky will eat."
**5** [a]Now the rest of the acts of
Baasha and what he did and his
might, are they not written in the
Book of the Chronicles of the Kings
of Israel? **6** And Baasha slept with his
fathers and was buried in [a]Tirzah,
and Elah his son became king in
his place. **7** Moreover, the word of
Yahweh through the hand of [a]the
prophet Jehu the son of Hanani also
came about against Baasha and his
household, both because of all the
evil which he did in the sight of Yah-
weh, provoking Him to anger with
[b]the work of his hands, in being like
the house of Jeroboam, and because
[c]he struck [1]it.

### *Elah Reigns over Israel*

**8** In the twenty-sixth year of Asa
king of Judah, Elah the son of Baasha
became king over Israel at Tirzah,
*and reigned* two years. **9** And his ser-
vant [a]Zimri, commander of half his
chariots, conspired against him. Now
he *was* at Tirzah drinking himself
drunk in the house of Arza, [b]who
*was* over the household at Tirzah.
**10** Then Zimri went in and struck him
and put him to death in the twenty-
seventh year of Asa king of Judah,
and became king in his place. **11** Now
it happened when he became king,
as soon as he sat on his throne, that
[a]he struck down all the household
of Baasha; he did not leave [1]a single
male—not *even any of* his kinsman
redeemers or his friends.
**12** Thus Zimri destroyed all the
household of Baasha, [a]according to

**15:29** [a]1Ki 14:9-16 **15:30** [a]1Ki 15:26 **15:31** [a]1Ki 14:19 **15:32** [a]1Ki 15:16 **15:34** [a]1Ki 15:26
◆ **16:1** [a]1Ki 16:7; 2Chr 19:2; 20:34 [b]2Chr 16:7-10 **16:2** [a]1Sa 2:8; 1Ki 14:7 [b]1Ki 15:34 **16:3** [a]1Ki 14:10; 21:21 [b]1Ki 16:11 [c]1Ki 15:29 **16:4** [a]1Ki 14:11; 21:24 **16:5** [a]1Ki 14:19; 15:31 **16:6** [a]1Ki 14:17; 15:21
**16:7** [a]1Ki 16:1 [b]Ps 115:4; Is 2:8 [c]1Ki 14:14; 15:27, 29 [1]Or *him* **16:9** [a]2Ki 9:30-33 [b]Ge 24:2; 39:4; 1Ki 18:3
**16:11** [a]1Ki 15:29; 16:3 [1]Lit *him who urinates against the wall*, cf. 1Sa 25:22, 34; 1Ki 14:10; 21:21; 2Ki 9:8
**16:12** [a]1Ki 16:3

the word of Yahweh, which He spoke
against Baasha by the hand of [b]Jehu
the prophet, **13** for all the sins of
Baasha and the sins of Elah his son,
which they sinned and which they
made Israel sin, [a]provoking Yahweh,
the God of Israel, to anger with their
[1]idols. **14** [a]Now the rest of the acts of
Elah and all that he did, are they not
written in the Book of the Chronicles
of the Kings of Israel?

### *Zimri Reigns over Israel*

**15** In the twenty-seventh year of Asa
king of Judah, Zimri reigned seven
days at Tirzah. Now the people were
camped against [a]Gibbethon, which
belonged to the Philistines. **16** And
the people who were camped heard
[1]it said, “Zimri has conspired and
has also struck down the king.”
Therefore all Israel made Omri, the
commander of the army, king over
Israel that day in the camp. **17** Then
Omri and all Israel with him went
up from Gibbethon and besieged
Tirzah. **18** Now it happened that
when Zimri saw that the city was
captured, he went into the citadel
of the king’s house and burned the
king’s house over him with fire, and
[a]died, **19** because of his sins which
he sinned, doing what is evil in
the sight of Yahweh, [a]walking in
the way of Jeroboam, and in his
sin which he did, making Israel
sin. **20** [a]Now the rest of the acts of
Zimri and his conspiracy which he
[1]carried out, are they not written in
the Book of the Chronicles of the
Kings of Israel?

### *Omri Reigns over Israel*

**21** Then the people of Israel were
divided into two parts: half of the
people followed Tibni the son of
Ginath, to make him king; the *other*
half followed Omri. **22** But the people
who followed Omri prevailed over
the people who followed Tibni the
son of Ginath. And Tibni died and
Omri became king. **23** In the thirty-
first year of Asa king of Judah, Omri
became king over Israel *and reigned*
twelve years; he reigned six years
at [a]Tirzah. **24** And he bought the
hill [1]Samaria from Shemer for two
[2]talents of silver; and he built on
the hill, and named the city which
he built [a,1]Samaria, after the name
of Shemer, the owner of the hill.

**25** [a]And Omri did what was evil in
the sight of Yahweh, and [b]acted more
wickedly than all who *were* before
him. **26** For he [a]walked in all the way
of Jeroboam the son of Nebat and
in his sins which he made Israel sin,
provoking Yahweh, the God of Israel,
to anger with their [1]idols. **27** Now the
rest of the acts of Omri which he did
and his might which he [1]showed, are
they not written in the Book of the
Chronicles of the Kings of Israel?
**28** So Omri slept with his fathers and
was buried in Samaria; and Ahab his
son became king in his place.

### *Ahab Reigns over Israel*

**29** Now Ahab the son of Omri became
king over Israel in the thirty-eighth
year of Asa king of Judah, and Ahab
the son of Omri reigned over Israel
in Samaria twenty-two years. **30** And

---

**16:12** [b]2Chr 19:2; 20:34 **16:13** [a]Dt 32:21; 1Ki 15:30 [1]Lit *vanities* **16:14** [a]1Ki 16:5 **16:15** [a]1Ki 15:27 **16:16** [1]Lit *saying* **16:18** [a]1Sa 31:4, 5; 2Sa 17:23 **16:19** [a]1Ki 12:28; 14:16; 15:26 **16:20** [a]1Ki 16:5, 14, 27 [1]Lit *conspired* **16:23** [a]1Ki 15:21 **16:24** [a]1Ki 16:28, 29, 32 [1]Heb *Shomeron* [2]A talent was approx. 75 lb. or 34 kg **16:25** [a]Mic 6:16 [b]1Ki 14:9; 16:30-33 **16:26** [a]1Ki 16:19 [1]Lit *vanities* **16:27** [1]Lit *did*

Ahab the son of Omri did what was
evil in the sight of Yahweh [a]more
than all who were before him.
**31** Now it happened, as though
it had been a trivial thing for him
to walk in the sins of Jeroboam the
son of Nebat, that [a]he took Jezebel
the daughter of Ethbaal king of the
[b]Sidonians as a wife, and went and
served Baal and worshiped him.
**32** So he erected an altar for Baal in
[a]the house of Baal which he built
in Samaria. **33** Ahab also made [a]the
[1]Asherah. Thus [b]Ahab did more to
provoke Yahweh, the God of Israel,
to anger than all the kings of Israel
who were before him. **34** [a]In his days
Hiel the Bethelite built Jericho; he
laid its foundations with the *loss of*
Abiram his firstborn, and set up its
gates with the *loss of* his youngest
son Segub, according to the word of
Yahweh, which He spoke by the hand
of Joshua the son of Nun.

### *A Widow Sustains Elijah*

**17** Now Elijah the Tishbite, who
was of [a,1]the settlers of Gilead,
said to Ahab, "[b]As Yahweh, the God
of Israel, lives, before whom I stand,
surely [c]there shall be neither dew
nor rain these years, except by my
word." **2** Then the word of Yahweh
came to him, saying, **3** "Go away
from here and turn eastward, and
*hide yourself* by the brook Cherith,
which is [1]east of the Jordan. **4** And
it will be that you will drink of the
brook, and [a]I have commanded the
ravens to sustain you there." **5** So he
went and did according to the word
of Yahweh, for he went and lived by
the brook Cherith, which is [1]east of
the Jordan. **6** And the ravens were
bringing him bread and meat in the
morning and bread and meat in the
evening, and he would drink from
the brook. **7** Now it happened after
a while that the brook dried up,
because there was no rain in the land.
**8** Then the word of Yahweh
came to him, saying, **9** "Arise, go
to [a]Zarephath, which belongs to
Sidon, and remain there; behold, [b]I
have commanded a widow there to
sustain you." **10** So he arose and went
to Zarephath, and when he came to
the gate of the city, behold, a widow
was there gathering sticks; and [a]he
called to her and said, "Please get
me a little water in a [1]jar, that I may
drink." **11** So she went to get *it*, and
he called to her and said, "Please get
me a piece of bread in your hand."
**12** But she said, "[a]As Yahweh your
God lives, [b]I have no [1]bread, only a
handful of flour in the [2]bowl and a
little oil in the jar; and behold, I am
gathering [3]a few sticks that I may go
in and prepare for me and my son,
that we may eat it and [c]die." **13** Then
Elijah said to her, "Do not fear; go,
do as you have said, but make me
a little bread cake from [1]it first and
bring *it* out to me, and afterward you
may make *one* for yourself and for
your son. **14** For thus says Yahweh,
the God of Israel, 'The [1]bowl of flour
shall not be exhausted, nor shall the
jar of oil [2]be empty, until the day that

**16:30** [a]1Ki 14:9; 16:25 **16:31** [a]Dt 7:1-5 [b]Jdg 18:7; 1Ki 11:1-5; 2Ki 10:18; 17:16 **16:32** [a]2Ki 10:21, 26, 27 **16:33** [a]2Ki 13:6 [b]1Ki 14:9; 16:29, 30; 21:25 [1]A wooden symbol of a female deity **16:34** [a]Jos 6:26 ◆ **17:1** [a]Jdg 12:4 [b]1Ki 18:10; 22:14; 2Ki 3:14; 5:20 [c]1Ki 18:1; Lk 4:25; Jas 5:17 [1]Or *Tishbe in Gilead* **17:3** [1]Lit *before* **17:4** [a]1Ki 17:9 **17:5** [1]Lit *before* **17:9** [a]Ob 20; Lk 4:26 [b]1Ki 17:4 **17:10** [a]Ge 24:17; Jn 4:7 [1]Or *vessel* **17:12** [a]1Ki 17:1 [b]2Ki 4:2-7 [c]Ge 21:15, 16 [1]Lit *cake* [2]Lit *pitcher* [3]Lit *two* **17:13** [1]Lit *there* **17:14** [1]Lit *pitcher* [2]Lit *lack*

Yahweh sends rain on the face of
the earth.'" **15** So she went and did
according to the word of Elijah, and
she and he and her household ate
for *many* days. **16** The [1]bowl of flour
was not exhausted nor did the jar of
oil [2]become empty, according to the
word of Yahweh which He spoke by
the hand of Elijah.

### Yahweh Returns Life to the Widow's Son

**17** Now it happened after these things
that the son of the woman, the mis-
tress of the house, became sick; and
his sickness was so severe that there
was no breath left in him. **18** So she
said to Elijah, "[a]What do I have to do
with you, O [b]man of God? [1]You have
come to me to bring my iniquity to
remembrance and to put my son to
death!" **19** And he said to her, "Give
me your son." Then he took him from
her bosom and carried him up to the
upper room where he was living, and
laid him on his own bed. **20** Then he
called to Yahweh and said, "O Yah-
weh my God, have You also brought
calamity to the widow with whom I
am sojourning, by causing her son to
die?" **21** [a]Then he stretched himself
upon the child three times, and called
to Yahweh and said, "O Yahweh my
God, I pray You, let this child's life re-
turn [1]to him." **22** And Yahweh heard
the voice of Elijah, [a]and the life of
the child returned [1]to him and he
became alive. **23** Then Elijah took the
child and brought him down from
the upper room into the house and
gave him to his mother; and Elijah
said, "See, your son is alive." **24** Then
the woman said to Elijah, "[a]Now I
know this: that you are a man of God
and that the word of Yahweh in your
mouth is truth."

### Obadiah Meets Elijah

**18** Now it happened [a]*after* many
days that the word of Yahweh
came to Elijah in the third year,
saying, "Go, show yourself to Ahab,
and [b]I will send rain on the face of
the earth." **2** So Elijah went to show
himself to Ahab. Now the famine
*was* severe in Samaria. **3** And Ahab
called Obadiah [a]who *was* over the
household. (Now Obadiah [b,1]feared
Yahweh greatly. **4** And it happened
that [a]when Jezebel was cutting down
the prophets of Yahweh, Obadiah
took one hundred prophets and hid
them by fifties in a cave, and [b]sus-
tained them with bread and water.)
**5** Then Ahab said to Obadiah, "Go
through the land to all the springs of
water and to all the valleys; perhaps
we will find grass and keep the horses
and mules alive, and not have to cut
down some of the cattle." **6** So they
divided the land between them to
pass through it; Ahab went one
way by himself and Obadiah went
another way by himself.

**7** Now it happened that as Obadiah
was on the way, behold, Elijah [1]met
him, [a]and he recognized him and
fell on his face and said, "Is this you,
Elijah my master?" **8** And he said to
him, "It is I. Go, say to your master,
'Behold, Elijah *is here.*'" **9** And he
said, "What [1]sin have I committed,

**17:16** [1]Lit *pitcher* [2]Lit *lack* **17:18** [a]2Sa 16:10; 2Ki 3:13; Lk 4:34; Jn 2:4 [b]1Ki 12:22 [1]Or *Have you come...death?* **17:21** [a]2Ki 4:34, 35; Ac 20:10 [1]Lit *upon his inward part* **17:22** [a]Lk 7:14; Heb 11:35 [1]Lit *upon his inward part* **17:24** [a]Jn 2:11; 3:2; 16:30 ◆ **18:1** [a]1Ki 17:1; Lk 4:25; Jas 5:17 [b]Dt 28:12 **18:3** [a]1Ki 16:9 [b]Ne 7:2; Job 28:28 [1]Or *reverenced* **18:4** [a]1Ki 18:13 [b]Mt 10:40-42 **18:7** [a]2Ki 1:6-8 [1]Lit *to meet* **18:9** [1]Lit *have I sinned*

that you are giving your servant
into the hand of Ahab to put me
to death? **10** [a]As Yahweh your God
lives, there is no nation or kingdom
where my master has not sent to
search for you; and if they said, 'He
is not *here,*' he made the kingdom or
nation swear that they could not find
you. **11** And now you are saying, 'Go,
say to your master, "Behold, Elijah
*is here.*"' **12** And it will be that *when*
I leave you, [a]the Spirit of Yahweh
will carry you where I do not know;
and I will come and tell Ahab, and he
will not find you, and he will kill me,
although *I* your servant have [1]feared
Yahweh from my youth. **13** [a]Has it
not been told to my master what I
did when Jezebel killed the prophets
of Yahweh, that I hid [1]one hundred
prophets of Yahweh by fifties in a
cave, and sustained them with bread
and water? **14** So now you are saying,
'Go, say to your master, "Behold,
Elijah *is here*"'; he will then kill me."
**15** And Elijah said, "[a]As Yahweh of
hosts lives, before whom I stand,
I will surely show myself to him
today." **16** So Obadiah went to meet
Ahab and told him; and Ahab went
to meet Elijah.

**17** Now it happened when Ahab
saw Elijah, that [a]Ahab said to him,
"Is this you, you troubler of Israel?"
**18** And he said, "I have not troubled
*Israel, but* you and your father's
house *have,* because [a]you have for-
saken the commandments of Yahweh
and [b]you have followed the Baals.
**19** So now then send *and* gather to me
all Israel at [a]Mount Carmel, [b]*together*
with 450 prophets of Baal and 400
prophets of [c]the Asherah, who eat
at Jezebel's table."

### *Yahweh or Baal on Mount Carmel*

**20** So Ahab sent *a message* among all
the sons of Israel and gathered the
prophets together at Mount Carmel.
**21** And Elijah came near to all the
people and said, "[a]How long *will* you
be limping between two opinions?
[b]If Yahweh is God, follow Him; but
if Baal, follow him." But the people
did not answer him a word. **22** Then
Elijah said to the people, "I [a]alone am
left a prophet of Yahweh, but Baal's
prophets are [b]450 men. **23** Now let
them give us two oxen; and let them
choose one ox for themselves and
cut it up, and place it on the wood,
but place no fire *under it*; and I will
prepare the other ox and put it on the
wood, and I will not place fire *under*
*it.* **24** Then you call on the name
of your god, and I will call on the
name of Yahweh, and [a]the God who
answers by fire, He is God." And all
the people answered and said, "[1]That
is a good word."

**25** So Elijah said to the prophets of
Baal, "Choose one ox for yourselves
and prepare it first for you are many,
and call on the name of your god, but
place no fire *under it.*" **26** Then they
took the ox which [1]was given them
and they prepared it and called on
the name of Baal from morning until
noon saying, "O Baal, answer us." But
there was [a]no voice and no one an-
swered. And they [2]limped about the
altar which [3]they had made. **27** Now

**18:10** [a]1Ki 17:1 **18:12** [a]2Ki 2:16; Eze 3:12, 14; Ac 8:39 [1]Or *reverenced* **18:13** [a]1Ki 18:4 [1]Lit *a hundred men of the prophets* **18:15** [a]1Ki 17:1 **18:17** [a]Jos 7:25; 1Ki 21:20 **18:18** [a]1Ki 9:9; 2Chr 15:2 [b]1Ki 16:31; 21:25, 26 **18:19** [a]Jos 19:26; 2Ki 2:25 [b]1Ki 18:22 [c]1Ki 16:33 **18:21** [a]2Ki 17:41; Mt 6:24 [b]Jos 24:15 **18:22** [a]1Ki 19:10, 14 [b]1Ki 18:19 **18:24** [a]1Ki 18:38 [1]Lit *The matter is good* **18:26** [a]Ps 115:4, 5; Jer 10:5 [1]Lit *he gave* [2]A type of ceremonial dance [3]As in some mss and the ancient versions; M.T. *he*

it happened at noon, that Elijah
mocked them and said, "Call out with
a loud voice, for he is a god; either
he is occupied or relieving himself,
or is on a journey, or perhaps he is
asleep and needs to be awakened."
**28** So they cried with a loud voice
and [a]gashed themselves according to
their custom with swords and lances
until the blood gushed out on them.
**29** Now it happened when noon had
passed, that they prophesied [a]until
the time of the offering of the *eve-
ning* sacrifice; but there was no voice,
no one answered, and no [1]one paid
attention.

**30** Then Elijah said to all the peo-
ple, "Come near to me." So all the
people came near to him. And [a]he
repaired the altar of Yahweh which
had been pulled down. **31** Then Elijah
took twelve stones according to the
number of the tribes of the sons of
Jacob, to whom the word of Yahweh
had come, saying, "[a]Israel shall be
your name." **32** And with the stones
he built an altar in [a]the name of Yah-
weh, and he made a trench around
the altar, large enough to hold two
[1]seahs of seed. **33** [a]Then he arranged
the wood and cut the ox in pieces
and placed *it* on the wood. **34** And
he said, "Fill four pitchers with water
and pour *it* on the burnt offering
and on the wood." And he said, "Do
it a second time," and they did it a
second time. And he said, "Do it a
third time," and they did it a third
time. **35** And the water flowed around
the altar and he also filled the trench
with water.

### *Yahweh, He Is God*

**36** [a]Now it happened at the time of
the offering of the *evening* sacrifice,
that Elijah the prophet came near
and said, "[b]O Yahweh, the God of
Abraham, Isaac and Israel, today let it
be known that [c]You are God in Israel
and that I am Your slave and [d]I have
done all these things at Your word.
**37** Answer me, O Yahweh, answer
me, that this people may know that
You, O Yahweh, are God, and *that* You
have turned their heart back again."
**38** Then the [a]fire of Yahweh fell and
consumed the burnt offering and the
wood and the stones and the dust,
and licked up the water that was in
the trench. **39** And all the people saw
it and fell on their faces and said,
"[a]Yahweh, He is God; Yahweh, He is
God." **40** Then Elijah said to them,
"Seize the prophets of Baal; do not let
one of them escape." So they seized
them; and Elijah brought them down
to [a]the brook Kishon, [b]and slaugh-
tered them there.

### *Yahweh Sends Rain*

**41** Now Elijah said to Ahab, "Go up,
eat and drink; for there is the sound
of the tumult of rain." **42** So Ahab
went up to eat and drink. But Elijah
went up to the top of [a]Carmel; and
he [b]stretched himself down toward
the ground and put his face between
his knees. **43** And he said to his young
man, "Go up now, look toward the
sea." So he went up and looked and
said, "There is nothing." And he
said, "Go back" seven times. **44** Now
it happened at the seventh time, that

---

**18:28** [a]Lv 19:28; Dt 14:1 **18:29** [a]Ex 29:39, 41 [1]Lit *attentiveness* **18:30** [a]1Ki 19:10, 14; 2Chr 33:16 **18:31** [a]Ge 32:28; 35:10; 2Ki 17:34 **18:32** [a]Col 3:17 [1]A seah was approx. 7 qt. or 7.7 l **18:33** [a]Ge 22:9; Lv 1:7, 8 **18:36** [a]1Ki 18:29 [b]Ge 28:13; Ex 3:6; 4:5; Mt 22:32 [c]1Ki 8:43 [d]Nu 16:28-32 **18:38** [a]Ge 15:17; Lv 9:24; 10:1, 2; Jdg 6:21; 2Ki 1:12; 1Chr 21:26; 2Chr 7:1; Job 1:16 **18:39** [a]1Ki 18:21, 24 **18:40** [a]Jdg 4:7; 5:21 [b]Dt 13:5; 18:20; 2Ki 10:24, 25 **18:42** [a]1Ki 18:19, 20 [b]Jas 5:18

he said, "Behold, [a]a cloud as small as a man's hand is coming up from the sea." And he said, "Go up, say to Ahab, '[1]Prepare *your chariot* and go down, so that the rain does not stop you.'" **45** Now it happened that in a little while the sky grew dark with clouds and wind, and there was a heavy rain. And Ahab rode and went to [a]Jezreel. **46** But [a]the hand of Yahweh was on Elijah, and [b]he girded up his loins and [1]outran Ahab unto *where* you enter Jezreel.

### *Elijah Runs from Jezebel*

**19** Now Ahab told Jezebel all that Elijah had done, and [a,1]how he had killed all the prophets with the sword. **2** Then Jezebel sent a messenger to Elijah, saying, "[a]So may the gods do to me and even more, if I do not make your [1]life as the [1]life of one of them by about this time tomorrow." **3** And he [1]was afraid and arose and [2]ran for his [3]life and came to [a]Beersheba, which belongs to Judah, and left his young man there. **4** But he himself went a day's journey into the wilderness, and came and sat down under a broom tree; and [a]he asked for himself that he might die, and said, "It is enough; now, O Yahweh, take my [1]life, for I am not better than my fathers." **5** Then he lay down *and slept* under a broom tree; and behold, there was [a]an angel touching him, and he said to him, "Arise, eat." **6** Then he looked and behold, there was at his head a bread cake *baked on* hot stones, and a jar of water. So he ate and drank and lay down again. **7** And the angel of Yahweh came again a second time and touched him and said, "Arise, eat, because the journey is too great for you." **8** So he arose and ate and drank, and went in the strength of that food [a]forty days and forty nights to [b]Horeb, the mountain of God.

### *Elijah at Horeb*

**9** Then he came there to a cave and lodged there; and behold, [a]the word of Yahweh *came* to him, and He said to him, "What are you doing here, Elijah?" **10** And he said, "[a]I have been very zealous for Yahweh, the God of hosts; for the sons of Israel have forsaken Your covenant, [b]pulled down Your altars and killed Your prophets with the sword. And [c]I alone am left; and they seek my life, to take it away."

**11** So He said, "[a]Go forth and stand on the mountain before Yahweh." And behold, Yahweh was passing by! And [b]a great and strong wind was tearing up the mountains and breaking in pieces the rocks before Yahweh; *but* Yahweh *was* not in the wind. And after the wind an earthquake, *but* Yahweh *was* not in the earthquake. **12** Then after the earthquake a fire, *but* Yahweh *was* not in the fire; and after the fire [a]a sound of a thin [1]gentle whisper. **13** Now it happened that when Elijah heard *it*, [a]he wrapped his face in his mantle and went out and stood in the entrance of the cave. And behold, [b]a voice *came* to him and said, "What

**18:44** [a]Lk 12:54 [1]Lit *Tie, Harness* **18:45** [a]Jos 17:16; Jdg 6:33 **18:46** [a]2Ki 3:15; Is 8:11; Eze 3:14 [b]2Ki 4:29; Jer 1:17; 1Pe 1:13 [1]Lit *ran before* ◆ **19:1** [a]1Ki 18:40 [1]Lit *all* about *how* **19:2** [a]Ru 1:17; 1Ki 20:10; 2Ki 6:31 [1]Lit *soul* **19:3** [a]Ge 21:31 [1]As in many mss; Heb possibly *saw* [2]Lit *he went* [3]Lit *soul* **19:4** [a]Nu 11:15; Jer 20:14-18; Jon 4:3, 8 [1]Lit *soul* **19:5** [a]Ge 28:12 **19:8** [a]Ex 24:18; 34:28; Dt 9:9-11, 18; Mt 4:2 [b]Ex 3:1; 4:27 **19:9** [a]Ex 33:21, 22 **19:10** [a]Ex 20:5; 34:14 [b]Ro 11:3, 4 [c]1Ki 18:22 **19:11** [a]Ex 19:20; 24:12, 18 [b]Eze 1:4 **19:12** [a]Job 4:16; Zec 4:6 [1]Lit *silence* **19:13** [a]Ex 3:6 [b]1Ki 19:9

are you doing here, Elijah?" **14** Then
he said, "[a]I have been very zealous
for Yahweh, the God of hosts; for the
sons of Israel have forsaken Your cov-
enant, pulled down Your altars and
killed Your prophets with the sword.
And I alone am left; and they seek my
life, to take it away."
**15** And Yahweh said to him, "Go,
return on your way to the wilderness
of Damascus, and you will arrive
and [a]anoint Hazael king over Aram;
**16** and [a]Jehu the son of Nimshi you
shall anoint king over Israel; and
[b]Elisha the son of Shaphat of Abel-
meholah you shall anoint as prophet
in your place. **17** And it will be that the
[a]one who escapes from the sword of
Hazael, Jehu [b]shall put to death, and
the one who escapes from the sword
of Jehu, Elisha shall put to death.
**18** [a]Yet I will leave 7,000 in Israel, all
the knees that have not bowed to
Baal and every mouth that has not
[b]kissed him."

### *Elijah Puts the Mantle on Elisha*

**19** So he went from there and found
Elisha the son of Shaphat, while he
was plowing with twelve pairs *of
oxen* before him, and he with the
twelfth. And Elijah passed over to
him and threw [a]his mantle on him.
**20** So he forsook the oxen and ran
after Elijah and said, "Please [a]let me
kiss my father and my mother, then
I will follow you." And he said to
him, "Go back again, for what have I
done to you?" **21** So he returned from
*following* him, and took the pair of
oxen and sacrificed them and [a]boiled
their flesh with the implements of
the oxen, and gave *it* to the people
and they ate. Then he arose and fol-
lowed Elijah and ministered to him.

### *Ahab Wars with Aram*

**20** Now [a]Ben-hadad king of Aram
gathered all his military force,
[b]and there *were* thirty-two kings with
him, and horses and chariots. And
he went up and [c]besieged Samaria
and fought against it. **2** Then he sent
messengers to the city to Ahab king
of Israel and said to him, "Thus says
Ben-hadad, **3** 'Your silver and your
gold are mine; your most beautiful
wives and children are also mine.'"
**4** Then the king of Israel answered
and said, "It is according to your
word, my lord, O king; I am yours,
and all that I have." **5** Then the mes-
sengers returned and said, "Thus
says [1]Ben-hadad, 'Surely, I sent to you
saying, "You shall give me your silver
and your gold and your wives and
your children," **6** but about this time
tomorrow I will send my servants to
you, and they will search your house
and the houses of your servants; and
[1]whatever is desirable in your eyes,
they will put in their hand and carry
away.'"
**7** Then the king of Israel called
all the elders of the land and said,
"Please know and [a]see how this man
is looking for trouble; for he sent to
me for my wives and my children and
my silver and my gold, and I withheld
nothing from him." **8** And all the el-
ders and all the people said to him,
"Do not listen or consent." **9** So he

---

**19:14** [a]1Ki 19:10 **19:15** [a]2Ki 8:8-15 **19:16** [a]2Ki 9:1-10 [b]1Ki 19:19-21; 2Ki 2:9, 15 **19:17** [a]2Ki 8:12; 13:3, 22 [b]2Ki 9:14-10:25 **19:18** [a]Ro 11:4 [b]Hos 13:2 **19:19** [a]1Sa 28:14; 2Ki 2:8, 13, 14 **19:20** [a]Mt 8:21, 22; Lk 9:61, 62; Ac 20:37 **19:21** [a]2Sa 24:22 ◆ **20:1** [a]1Ki 15:18, 20; 2Ki 6:24 [b]1Ki 22:31 [c]1Ki 16:24; 2Ki 6:24
**20:5** [1]Lit *Ben-hadad, saying* **20:6** [1]Lit *all the desire of your eyes* **20:7** [a]2Ki 5:7

said to the messengers of Ben-hadad,
"Say to my lord the king, 'All that you
sent for to your servant at the first I
will do, but this thing I cannot do.'"
And the messengers departed and
brought him word again. **10** Then
Ben-hadad sent to him and said, "May
[a]the gods do so to me and more also,
if the dust of Samaria will be suffi-
cient for [1]a handful for all the people
who [2]follow me." **11** Then the king of
Israel answered and said, "Speak *to*
*him*, '[a]Let not him who girds on *his*
*armor* boast like him who takes *it*
off.'" **12** Now it happened that when
*Ben-hadad* heard this message, as [a]he
was drinking [1]with the kings in the
booths, he said to his servants, "Sta-
tion *yourselves*." So they stationed
*themselves* against the city.

**13** Now behold, a prophet ap-
proached Ahab king of Israel and said,
"Thus says Yahweh, 'Have you seen all
this great multitude? Behold, [a]I will
deliver them into your hand today,
and [b]you shall know that I am Yah-
weh.'" **14** And Ahab said, "By whom?"
So he said, "Thus says Yahweh, 'By
the young men of the rulers of the
provinces.'" Then he said, "Who
shall [1]begin the battle?" And he said,
"You." **15** Then he mustered the young
men of the rulers of the provinces,
and there were 232; and after them
he mustered all the people, *even* all
*the sons of* Israel, 7,000.

**16** And they went out at noon,
while [a]Ben-hadad was drinking
himself drunk in the booths [1]with
the thirty-two kings who helped him.
**17** And the young men of the rulers
of the provinces went out first; and
Ben-hadad sent out and they told
him, saying, "Men have come out
from Samaria." **18** [a]Then he said, "If
they have come out for peace, take
them alive; or if they have come out
for war, take them alive."

**19** So these went out from the
city, the young men of the rulers
of the provinces, and the military
force which followed them. **20** And
they each struck his man; and the
Arameans fled and Israel pursued
them, and Ben-hadad king of Aram
escaped on a horse with horsemen.
**21** And the king of Israel went out and
struck down the horses and chariots,
and struck the Arameans with a great
slaughter.

**22** Then [a]the prophet came near
to the king of Israel and said to him,
"Go, strengthen yourself and know
and see what you have to do; for [b]at
the turn of the year the king of Aram
will come up against you."

**23** Now the servants of the king
of Aram said to him, "[a]Their gods
are gods of the mountains, therefore
they were stronger than we; but
rather let us fight against them in the
plain, *and* surely we will be stronger
than they. **24** Do this thing: remove
the kings, each from his place, and
put captains in their place, **25** and
you shall number a military force
like the military force that you have
lost, horse for horse, and chariot for
chariot. Then we will fight against
them in the plain, and surely we
will be stronger than they." And he
listened to their voice and did so.

---

**20:10** [a]1Ki 19:2; 2Ki 6:31 [1]Lit *handfuls* [2]Lit *are at my feet* **20:11** [a]Pr 27:1 **20:12** [a]1Ki 16:9; Pr 31:4, 5 [1]Lit *he and* **20:13** [a]1Ki 20:28 [b]1Ki 18:36 **20:14** [1]Lit *bind* **20:16** [a]1Ki 16:9; 20:12; Pr 20:1 [1]Lit *he and the thirty-two kings* **20:18** [a]2Ki 14:8-12 **20:22** [a]1Ki 20:13 [b]2Sa 11:1; 1Ki 20:26 **20:23** [a]1Ki 14:23; Jer 16:19-21; Ro 1:21-23

### *Israel Fights the Arameans*

26 [a]Now it happened at the turn of
the year, that Ben-hadad mustered
the Arameans and went up to [b]Aphek
to fight against Israel. 27 Now the sons
of Israel were mustered and were
provided for and went to meet them;
and the sons of Israel camped before
them like two little flocks of goats,
[a]but the Arameans filled the land.
28 Then [a]a man of God came near
and spoke to the king of Israel and
said, "Thus says Yahweh, 'Because
the Arameans have said, "[b]Yahweh
is a god of *the* mountains, but He is
not a god of *the* valleys," therefore [c]I
will give all this great multitude into
your hand, and you shall know that I
am Yahweh.'" 29 So they camped one
opposite the other seven days. Now
it happened that on the seventh day
the battle was joined, and the sons of
Israel struck down *of* the Arameans
100,000 foot soldiers in one day.
30 But the rest fled to [a]Aphek into
the city, and the wall fell on 27,000
men who were left. And Ben-hadad
fled and came into the city [b]into an
inner chamber.

31 [a]Then his servants said to him,
"Behold now, we have heard that the
kings of the house of Israel are kings
of lovingkindness, please let us [b]put
sackcloth on our loins and ropes on
our heads, and go out to the king of
Israel; perhaps he will preserve your
[1]life." 32 So [a]they girded sackcloth
on their loins and *put* ropes on their
heads, and came to the king of Israel
and said, "[b]Your servant Ben-hadad
says, 'Please let me live.'" And he said,
"Is he still alive? He is my brother."
33 Now the men interpreted this as
an omen, and hastily [1]catching his
word said, "Your brother Ben-hadad."
Then he said, "Go, bring him." Then
Ben-hadad came out to him, and he
[2]took him up into the chariot. 34 And
*Ben-hadad* said to him, "[a]The cities
which my father took from your fa-
ther I will return, and you shall make
streets for yourself in Damascus, as
my father made in Samaria." *Ahab
said*, "And I will let you go with this
covenant." So he cut a covenant with
him and let him go.

### *A Prophecy Enrages Ahab*

35 Now a certain man of [a]the sons
of the prophets said to [1]another [b]by
the word of Yahweh, "Please strike
me." But the man refused to strike
him. 36 Then he said to him, "Because
you have not listened to the voice
of Yahweh, behold, as soon as you
walk away from me, [a]a lion will
strike you down." And as soon as he
had walked away from him, a lion
found him and struck him down.
37 Then he found another man and
said, "Please [1]strike me." And the
man [2]struck him, [3]wounding him.
38 So the prophet walked away and
stood by, for the king, by the way, and
[a]disguised himself with a bandage
over his eyes. 39 Now it happened
that as the king was passing by, he
cried out to the king and said, "Your
servant went out into the midst of
the battle; and behold, a man turned
aside and brought a man to me and
said, 'Guard this man; if for any

**20:26** [a]1Ki 20:22 [b]2Ki 13:17 **20:27** [a]Jdg 6:3-5; 1Sa 13:5-8 **20:28** [a]1Ki 17:18 [b]1Ki 20:23 [c]1Ki 20:13 **20:30** [a]1Ki 20:26 [b]1Ki 22:25; 2Chr 18:24 **20:31** [a]1Ki 20:23-26 [b]Ge 37:34; 2Sa 3:31 [1]Lit *soul* **20:32** [a]1Ki 20:31 [b]1Ki 20:3-6 **20:33** [1]Lit *caught from him* [2]Lit *caused him to come up* **20:34** [a]1Ki 15:20 **20:35** [a]2Ki 2:3-7 [b]1Ki 13:17, 18 [1]Lit *his neighbor* **20:36** [a]1Ki 13:24 **20:37** [1]Lit *smite* [2]Lit *smote* [3]Lit *striking and wounding* **20:38** [a]1Ki 14:2

reason he is missing, [a]then your life
shall be for his life, or else you shall
pay a [1]talent of silver.' **40** Now it hap-
pened that while your servant was
busy here and there, he was gone."
And the king of Israel said to him, "So
shall your judgment be; you yourself
have decided *it*." **41** Then he hastily
took the bandage away from his eyes,
and the king of Israel recognized him,
that he was of the prophets. **42** And
he said to him, "Thus says Yahweh,
'Because you have let go out of *your*
hand the man whom I had devoted
to destruction, therefore [a]your [1]life
shall go for his [1]life, and your people
for his people.'" **43** So [a]the king of
Israel went to his house sullen and
enraged, and came to Samaria.

### *Ahab Takes Possession of Naboth's Vineyard*

**21** Now it happened after these
things that Naboth the Jez-
reelite had a vineyard which *was* in
[a]Jezreel beside the palace of Ahab
king of Samaria. **2** And Ahab spoke
to Naboth, saying, "[a]Give me your
vineyard, that I may have it for a
vegetable garden because it is close
beside my house, and I will give you
a better vineyard than it in its place;
if it is good in your sight, I will give
you the price of [1]it in money." **3** But
Naboth said to Ahab, "Yahweh *for-
bid me* [a]that I should give you the
inheritance of my fathers." **4** [a]So
Ahab came into his house sullen and
enraged because of the word which
Naboth the Jezreelite had spoken to
him; for he said, "I will not give you
the inheritance of my fathers." And
he lay down on his bed and turned
away his face and ate no [1]food.

**5** But Jezebel his wife came to
him and said to him, "How is it that
your spirit is so sullen that you are
not eating [1]food?" **6** So he said to
her, "Because I spoke to Naboth the
Jezreelite and said to him, 'Give me
your vineyard for money; or else,
if it pleases you, I will give you a
vineyard in its place.' But he said, 'I
will not give you my vineyard.'" **7** And
Jezebel his wife said to him, "[a]Do you
now exercise kingship over Israel?
Arise, eat bread, and let your heart
be merry; I will give you the vineyard
of Naboth the Jezreelite."

**8** [a]So she wrote letters in Ahab's
name and sealed them with his seal,
and sent letters to [b]the elders and
to the nobles who were living with
Naboth in his city. **9** And she wrote
in the letters, saying, "Call for a fast
and seat Naboth at the head of the
people; **10** and seat two [a]vile men
before him, and let them testify
against him, saying, '[b]You [1]cursed
God and the king.' Then take him out
and [c]stone him so that he will die."

**11** So the men of his city, the elders
and the nobles who lived in his city,
did as Jezebel had sent *word* to them,
just as it was written in the letters
which she had sent them. **12** They
[a]called for a fast and seated Naboth
at the head of the people. **13** Then
the two vile men came in and sat
before him; and the vile men testified
against him, against Naboth, before
the people, saying, "Naboth cursed

**20:39** [a]2Ki 10:24 [1]A talent was approx. 75 lb. or 34 kg **20:42** [a]1Ki 20:39 [1]Lit *soul* **20:43** [a]1Ki 21:4
◆ **21:1** [a]Jdg 6:33; 1Ki 18:45, 46 **21:2** [a]1Sa 8:14 [1]Lit *this* **21:3** [a]Lv 25:23; Nu 36:7; Eze 46:18
**21:4** [a]1Ki 20:43 [1]Lit *bread* **21:5** [1]Lit *bread* **21:7** [a]1Sa 8:14 **21:8** [a]Es 3:12; 8:8, 10 [b]1Ki 20:7
**21:10** [a]1Sa 2:12; 2Sa 20:1 [b]Ex 22:28; Lv 24:15, 16; Ac 6:11 [c]Lv 24:14 [1]Heb *bless*; used euphemistically for curse, cf. 21:13; Job 1:5, 11; 2:5, 9 **21:12** [a]Is 58:4

God and the king." [a]So they took him
outside the city and stoned him with
stones and he died. **14** Then they sent
*word* to Jezebel, saying, "Naboth has
been stoned and is dead."

**15** Now it happened that when
Jezebel heard that Naboth had been
stoned and was dead, Jezebel said to
Ahab, "Arise, take possession of the
vineyard of Naboth the Jezreelite,
which he refused to give you for
money; for Naboth is not alive,
but dead." **16** Now it happened that
when Ahab heard that Naboth was
dead, Ahab arose to go down to the
vineyard of Naboth the Jezreelite, to
take possession of it.

### *Yahweh Speaks Against Ahab*

**17** Then the word of Yahweh came to
Elijah the Tishbite, saying, **18** "Arise,
go down to meet Ahab king of Israel,
[a]who is in Samaria; behold, he is in
the vineyard of Naboth where he has
gone down to take possession of it.
**19** And you shall speak to him, saying,
'Thus says Yahweh, "[a]Have you murdered and also taken possession?"'
And you shall speak to him, saying,
'Thus says Yahweh, "[b]In the place
where the dogs licked up the blood
of Naboth the dogs will lick up your
blood, even yours."'"

**20** And Ahab said to Elijah, "[a]Have
you found me, O my enemy?" And
he [1]answered, "I have found *you*,
[b]because you have sold yourself
to do what is evil in the sight of
Yahweh. **21** Behold, I will bring evil
*upon* you, and [a]will utterly sweep
you away, and will cut off from Ahab
every [1]male, both bond and free in
Israel; **22** and [a]I will make your house
[b]like the house of Jeroboam the son
of Nebat, and like the house of Baasha the son of Ahijah, because of the
provocation with which you have
provoked *Me* to anger, and *because*
you [c]have made Israel sin. **23** Of
Jezebel also has Yahweh spoken,
saying, '[a]The dogs will eat Jezebel
in the [1]district of Jezreel.' **24** [a]The
one belonging to Ahab, who dies in
the city, the dogs will eat, and the
one who dies in the field the birds
of the sky will eat."

### *Ahab Humbles Himself*

**25** [a]Surely there was no one who
sold himself to do what is evil in the
sight of Yahweh like Ahab, whom
Jezebel his wife incited. **26** [a]And he
acted very abominably in following idols, [b]according to all that the
Amorites had done, whom Yahweh
dispossessed before the sons of
Israel.

**27** Now it happened when Ahab
heard these words, that [a]he tore his
clothes and put [1]on sackcloth and
fasted, and he lay in sackcloth and
went about [2]despondently. **28** Then
the word of Yahweh came to Elijah
the Tishbite, saying, **29** "Do you see
how Ahab has humbled himself
before Me? Because he has humbled
himself before Me, I will not bring
the evil in his days, *but* I will bring
the evil upon his house [a]in his son's
days."

---

**21:13** [a]2Ki 9:26; 2Chr 24:21; Ac 7:58, 59; Heb 11:37 **21:18** [a]1Ki 16:29 **21:19** [a]2Sa 12:9 [b]1Ki 22:38; 2Ki 9:26 **21:20** [a]1Ki 18:17 [b]1Ki 21:25; 2Ki 17:17; Ro 7:14 [1]Lit *said* **21:21** [a]1Ki 14:10; 2Ki 9:8 [1]Lit *him who urinates against the wall*, cf. 1Sa 25:22, 34; 1Ki 14:10; 16:11; 2Ki 9:8 **21:22** [a]1Ki 15:29 [b]1Ki 16:3, 11 [c]1Ki 12:30; 13:34; 14:16 **21:23** [a]2Ki 9:10, 30-37 [1]Lit *portion*; some mss *rampart* **21:24** [a]1Ki 14:11; 16:4 **21:25** [a]1Ki 16:30-33; 21:20 **21:26** [a]1Ki 15:12; 2Ki 17:12 [b]Ge 15:16; Lv 18:25-30; 2Ki 21:11 **21:27** [a]Ge 37:34; 2Sa 3:31; 2Ki 6:30 [1]Lit *sackcloth on his flesh* [2]Or *softly* **21:29** [a]2Ki 9:25-37

### *Ahab Battles Against Aram*

22 So [1]they lived for three years without war between Aram and Israel. **2** [a]Now it happened in the third year, that [b]Jehoshaphat the king of Judah came down to the king of Israel. **3** Then the king of Israel said to his servants, "Do you know that [a]Ramoth-gilead belongs to us, but we are *sitting* still so as not to take it out of the hand of the king of Aram?" **4** So he said to Jehoshaphat, "Will you go with me to battle at Ramoth-gilead?" And Jehoshaphat said to the king of Israel, "[a]I am as you are, my people as your people, my horses as your horses."

### *Ahab Hates Micaiah*

**5** Moreover, Jehoshaphat said to the king of Israel, "Please inquire [1]first for the word of Yahweh." **6** Then [a]the king of Israel gathered the prophets together, about four hundred men, and said to them, "Shall I go against Ramoth-gilead to battle or shall I refrain?" And they said, "Go up, for the Lord will give *it* into the hand of the king." **7** But [a]Jehoshaphat said, "Is there not yet a prophet of Yahweh here that we may inquire of him?" **8** And the king of Israel said to Jehoshaphat, "There is yet one man by whom we may inquire of Yahweh, but I hate him, because he does not prophesy good concerning me, but evil. *He is* Micaiah son of Imlah." But Jehoshaphat said, "Let not the king say so." **9** Then the king of Israel called an officer and said, "Hasten *to bring* Micaiah son of Imlah." **10** Now the king of Israel and Jehoshaphat king of Judah were sitting each on his throne, clothed in *their royal* garments, at the threshing floor at the entrance of the gate of Samaria; and [a]all the prophets were prophesying before them. **11** And Zedekiah the son of Chenaanah made [a]horns of iron for himself and said, "Thus says Yahweh, '[b]With these you will gore the Arameans until they are consumed.'" **12** All the prophets were also prophesying thus, saying, "Go up to Ramoth-gilead and succeed, and Yahweh will give *it* into the hand of the king."

### *Micaiah Prophesies Against Ahab*

**13** Now the messenger who went to summon Micaiah spoke to him saying, "Behold now, the words of the prophets, *as if* from one mouth, are good towards the king. Please let your word be like the word of one of them, and speak *that which is* good." **14** But Micaiah said, "[a]As Yahweh lives, what [b]Yahweh says to me, that I shall speak."

**15** Then he came to the king, and the king said to him, "Micaiah, shall we go to Ramoth-gilead to battle, or shall we refrain?" And he said to him, "[a]Go up and succeed, and Yahweh will give *it* into the hand of the king." **16** Then the king said to him, "How many times must I make you swear that you will speak to me nothing but the truth in the name of Yahweh?" **17** So he said,

"I saw all Israel
Scattered on the mountains,
[a]Like sheep which have
no shepherd.

---

◆ **22:1** [1]Lit the Israelites *sat for 3 years* **22:2** [a]2Chr 18:2 [b]1Ki 15:24 **22:3** [a]Dt 4:43; Jos 21:38; 1Ki 4:13 **22:4** [a]2Ki 3:7 **22:5** [1]Lit *as the day* **22:6** [a]1Ki 18:19 **22:7** [a]2Ki 3:11 **22:10** [a]1Ki 22:6 **22:11** [a]Zec 1:18-21 [b]Dt 33:17 **22:14** [a]1Ki 18:10, 15 [b]Nu 22:18; 24:13 **22:15** [a]1Ki 22:12 **22:17** [a]Nu 27:17; 1Ki 22:34-36; 2Chr 18:16; Mt 9:36; Mk 6:34

And Yahweh said,
'These have no master.
Let each of them return
to his house in peace.'"
**18** Then the king of Israel said to
Jehoshaphat, "[a]Did I not say to you
that he would not prophesy good
concerning me, but evil?"
**19** Then [1]Micaiah said, "Therefore,
hear the word of Yahweh. [a]I saw
Yahweh sitting on His throne, and
[b]all the host of heaven standing by
Him on His right and on His left.
**20** And Yahweh said, 'Who will entice
Ahab so that he will go up and fall at
Ramoth-gilead?' And one said this
while another said that. **21** Then a
spirit came forward and stood before
Yahweh and said, 'I will entice him.'
**22** And Yahweh said to him, 'How?'
And he said, 'I will go out and [a]be
a lying spirit in the mouth of all his
prophets.' Then He said, 'You shall
entice *him* and also prevail. Go
out and do so.' **23** So now, behold,
[a]Yahweh has put a lying spirit in the
mouth of all these your prophets; but
Yahweh has spoken calamity against
you."
**24** Then [a]Zedekiah the son of
Chenaanah came near and struck Mi-
caiah on the cheek and said, "[b]How
did the Spirit of Yahweh pass from
me to speak to you?" **25** And Micaiah
said, "Behold, you will see on that
day when you [a]enter an inner room
to hide." **26** Then the king of Israel
said, "Take Micaiah and return him
to Amon the commander of the city
and to Joash the king's son; **27** and say,
'Thus says the king, "[a]Put this *man* in
prison and feed him [1]sparingly with
bread and water until I come *back*
safely."'" **28** And Micaiah said, "[a]If
you indeed return safely, Yahweh
has not spoken by me." And he said,
"[b]Listen, all you people."

### *The Death of Ahab*

**29** So [a]the king of Israel and Je-
hoshaphat king of Judah went up
*against* Ramoth-gilead. **30** And the
king of Israel said to Jehoshaphat,
"[a]I will disguise myself and go into
the battle, but you put on your
garments." So the king of Israel
disguised himself and went into the
battle. **31** Now [a]the king of Aram had
commanded the thirty-two com-
manders of his chariots, saying, "Do
not fight with small or great, but with
the king of Israel alone." **32** Now it
happened that when the command-
ers of the chariots saw Jehoshaphat,
they said, "Surely it is the king of
Israel," and they turned aside to fight
against him, and Jehoshaphat cried
out. **33** So it happened that when the
commanders of the chariots saw that
it was not the king of Israel, they
turned back from pursuing him.
**34** Now a certain man drew his
bow at random and struck the king
of Israel [1]in a joint of the armor. So
he said to the driver of his chariot,
"Turn [2]around and take me out of
the [3]fight, [a]for I am severely wound-
ed." **35** Now the battle [1]raged that day,
and the king was propped up in his
chariot in front of the Arameans, and

**22:18** [a]1Ki 22:8 **22:19** [a]Is 6:1; Eze 1:26-28; Da 7:9, 10 [b]Job 1:6; 2:1; Ps 103:20, 21; Da 7:10; Mt 18:10; Heb 1:7, 14 [1]Lit *he* **22:22** [a]Jdg 9:23; 1Sa 16:14; 18:10; 19:9; Eze 14:9; 2Th 2:11 **22:23** [a]Eze 14:9 **22:24** [a]1Ki 22:11; Mt 5:39; Ac 23:2, 3 [b]2Chr 18:23 **22:25** [a]1Ki 20:30 **22:27** [a]2Chr 16:10; 18:25-27 [1]Lit *with bread of affliction and water of affliction* **22:28** [a]Dt 18:22 [b]Mic 1:2 **22:29** [a]1Ki 22:3, 4 **22:30** [a]2Chr 35:22 **22:31** [a]1Ki 20:1, 16, 24; 2Chr 18:30 **22:34** [a]2Chr 35:23 [1]Lit *between the scale-armor and the breastplate* [2]Lit *your hand* [3]Lit *camp* **22:35** [1]Lit *went up*

died at evening, and the blood from the wound ran into the bottom of the chariot. 36 [a]Then a shout of lament passed throughout the camp close to sunset, saying, "Every man to his city and every man to his land."

37 So the king died and was brought to Samaria, and they buried the king in Samaria. 38 And they washed the chariot by the pool of Samaria, and the dogs licked up his blood (now the harlots bathed themselves *there*), [a]according to the word of Yahweh which He spoke. 39 Now the rest of the acts of Ahab and all that he did and [a]the ivory house which he built and all the cities which he built, are they not written in the Book of the Chronicles of the Kings of Israel? 40 So Ahab slept with his fathers, and Ahaziah his son became king in his place.

### *Jehoshaphat Reigns over Judah*

41 [a]Now Jehoshaphat the son of Asa became king over Judah in the fourth year of Ahab king of Israel. 42 Jehoshaphat was thirty-five years old when he became king, and he reigned twenty-five years in Jerusalem. And his mother's name was Azubah the daughter of Shilhi. 43 [a]And he walked in all the way of Asa his father; he did not turn away from it, doing what is right in the sight of Yahweh. [b]However, the high places were not *taken away;* the people still sacrificed and burnt incense on the high places. 44 [a]Jehoshaphat also made peace with the king of Israel.

45 Now the rest of the acts of Jehoshaphat, and his might which he showed and how he warred, are they not written [a]in the Book of the Chronicles of the Kings of Judah? 46 And the remnant of [a]the male cult prostitutes who remained in the days of his father Asa, he purged from the land.

47 Now [a]there was no king in Edom; a deputy was king. 48 Jehoshaphat made [a]ships of Tarshish to go to [b]Ophir for gold, but [c]they did not go for the ships were broken at [d]Ezion-geber. 49 Then Ahaziah the son of Ahab said to Jehoshaphat, "Let my servants go with your servants in the ships." But Jehoshaphat was not willing. 50 [a]And Jehoshaphat slept with his fathers and was buried with his fathers in the city of his father David, and Jehoram his son became king in his place.

### *Ahaziah Reigns over Israel*

51 Ahaziah the son of Ahab [a]became king over Israel in Samaria in the seventeenth year of Jehoshaphat king of Judah, and he reigned two years over Israel. 52 And he did what was evil in the sight of Yahweh and [a]walked in the way of his father and in the way of his mother and in the way of Jeroboam the son of Nebat, who caused Israel to sin. 53 [a]So he served Baal and worshiped him and provoked Yahweh, the God of Israel, to anger, according to all that his father had done.

---

**22:36** [a]2Ki 14:12 **22:38** [a]1Ki 21:19 **22:39** [a]Am 3:15 **22:41** [a]2Chr 20:31 **22:43** [a]2Chr 17:3 [b]1Ki 15:14; 2Ki 12:3 **22:44** [a]1Ki 22:2; 2Ki 8:16, 18; 2Chr 19:2 **22:45** [a]2Chr 20:34 **22:46** [a]Ge 19:5; Dt 23:17; 1Ki 14:24; 15:12; Jd 7 **22:47** [a]2Sa 8:14; 2Ki 3:9 **22:48** [a]1Ki 10:22; 2Chr 20:36 [b]1Ki 9:28 [c]2Chr 20:37 [d]1Ki 9:26 **22:50** [a]2Chr 21:1 **22:51** [a]1Ki 22:40 **22:52** [a]1Ki 15:26; 21:25 **22:53** [a]Jdg 2:11; 1Ki 16:30-32

*The Second Book of the*

# KINGS

### *Ahaziah's Messengers Meet Elijah*

**1** Now [a]Moab revolted against Israel
after the death of Ahab. **2** And
Ahaziah fell through the lattice in
his upper chamber, which *was* in
Samaria, and became ill. So he sent
messengers and said to them, "Go,
[a]inquire of Baal-zebub, the god of
Ekron, [b]whether I will live from this
sickness." **3** But the angel of [1]Yahweh
said to [a]Elijah the Tishbite, "Arise,
go up to meet the messengers of the
king of Samaria and say to them,
'Is it because there is no God in
Israel *that* you are going to inquire
of [b]Baal-zebub, the god of Ekron?'
**4** Now therefore thus says Yahweh,
'[a,1]You shall not come down from
the bed where you have gone up,
but you shall surely die.'" Then Elijah
departed.

**5** So the messengers returned to
him, and he said to them, "[1]Why
have you returned?" **6** And they said
to him, "A man came up to meet us
and said to us, 'Go, return to the king
who sent you and say to him, "Thus
says Yahweh, 'Is it because there is
no God in Israel *that* you are sending
[a]to inquire of Baal-zebub, the god
of Ekron? Therefore [1]you shall not
come down from the bed where
you have gone up, but shall surely
die.'"'" **7** And he said to them, "What
[1]kind of man was he who came up to
meet you and spoke these words to
you?" **8** And they said to him, "[a]*He*
*was* a hairy man with a leather girdle
girded about his loins." And he said,
"It is Elijah the Tishbite."

**9** Then *the king* [a]sent to him a
commander of fifty with his fifty.
And he went up to him, and behold,
he was sitting on the top of the hill.
And he said to him, "O man of God,
the king says, 'Come down.'" **10** And
Elijah answered and spoke to the
commander of fifty, "If I am a man
of God, [a]let fire come down from
heaven and consume you and your
fifty." [b]Then fire came down from
heaven and consumed him and his
fifty.

**11** So he again sent to him another
commander of fifty with his fifty.
And he answered and spoke to him,
"O man of God, thus says the king,
'Come down quickly.'" **12** And Elijah
answered and spoke to them, "If I
am a man of God, let fire come down
from heaven and consume you and
your fifty." Then the fire of God came
down from heaven and consumed
him and his fifty.

**13** So he [a]again sent the command-
er of a third fifty with his fifty. Then
the third commander of fifty went
up and came and bowed down on his
knees before Elijah, and he begged
him and said to him, "O man of God,
please let my life and the lives of these
fifty servants of yours be precious in
your sight. **14** Behold, fire came down
from heaven and consumed the

---

◆ **1:1** [a]2Sa 8:2; 2Ki 3:5 **1:2** [a]2Ki 1:3, 6, 16; Mt 10:25; Mk 3:22 [b]2Ki 8:7-10 **1:3** [a]1Ki 17:1; 21:17 [b]2Ki 1:2 [1]The personal covenant name of God, a form of I AM WHO I AM, cf. Ex 3:14-15 **1:4** [a]2Ki 1:6, 16 [1]Lit *The bed where you went up, you shall not come down from it* **1:5** [1]Lit *What is this that you have returned?* **1:6** [a]2Ki 1:2 [1]v 4, note 1 **1:7** [1]Lit *judgment* **1:8** [a]Zec 13:4; Mt 3:4; Mk 1:6 **1:9** [a]2Ki 6:13, 14 **1:10** [a]1Ki 18:36-38; Lk 9:54 [b]Job 1:16 **1:13** [a]Is 1:5; Jer 5:3

first two commanders of fifty with
their fifties; but now let my [1]life be
precious in your sight." **15** [a]Then the
angel of Yahweh spoke to Elijah, "Go
down with him; [b]do not be afraid of
him." So he arose and went down
with him to the king. **16** Then he
spoke to him, "Thus says Yahweh,
'Because you have sent messengers
[a]to inquire of Baal-zebub, the god of
Ekron—is it because there is no God
in Israel to inquire of His word?—
therefore [1]you shall not come down
from the bed where you have gone
up, but shall surely die.'"

### *Jehoram Reigns over Israel*

**17** So Ahaziah died according to the
word of Yahweh which Elijah had
spoken. And because he had no son,
Jehoram became king in his place [a]in
the second year of Jehoram the son
of Jehoshaphat, king of Judah. **18** Now
the rest of the acts of Ahaziah which
he did, are they not written in the
Book of the Chronicles of the Kings
of Israel?

### *Elijah Taken to Heaven*

**2** Now it happened when Yahweh
was about to [a]take up Elijah by
a [1]whirlwind to heaven, that Elijah
went with [b]Elisha from [c]Gilgal. **2** And
Elijah said to Elisha, "[a]Stay here
please, for Yahweh has sent me as
*far as* [b]*Bethel." But* Elisha said, "[c]As
Yahweh lives and as your soul lives,
I will not forsake you." So they went
down to Bethel. **3** Then [a]the sons of
the prophets who *were at* Bethel
came out to Elisha and said to him,
"Do you know that Yahweh will take
away your master from over [1]you
today?" And he said, "Yes, I know;
be silent."

**4** And Elijah said to him, "Elisha,
please [a]stay here, for Yahweh has
sent me to [b]Jericho." But he said,
"[a]As Yahweh lives and as your soul
lives, I will not forsake you." So they
came to Jericho. **5** [a]Then the sons of
the prophets who *were* at Jericho
approached Elisha and said to him,
"[b]Do you know that Yahweh will take
away your master from over [1]you
today?" And he [2]answered, "Yes, I
know; be silent." **6** Then Elijah said to
him, "Please [a]stay here, for Yahweh
has sent me to [b]the Jordan." And he
said, "As Yahweh lives and as your
soul lives, I will not forsake you." So
the two of them went on.

**7** Now [a]fifty men of the sons of the
prophets went and stood opposite
*them* at a distance, but the two of
them stood by the Jordan. **8** And
Elijah [a]took his mantle and folded it
together and [b]struck the waters, and
they were divided here and there, so
that the two of them crossed over on
dry ground.

**9** Now it happened when they
crossed over, that Elijah said to
Elisha, "Ask what I shall do for you
before I am taken from you." And
*Elisha* said, "Please, let a [a]double
portion of your spirit be upon me."
**10** And he said, "You have asked a
hard thing. *Nevertheless,* if you [a]see
me when I am taken from you, it shall
be so for you; but if not, it shall not
be *so.*" **11** As they were going along

**1:14** [1]Lit *soul* **1:15** [a]2Ki 1:3 [b]Is 51:12; Jer 1:17; Eze 2:6 **1:16** [a]2Ki 1:3 [1]v 4, note 1 **1:17** [a]2Ki 3:1; 8:16
◆ **2:1** [a]Ge 5:24; Heb 11:5 [b]1Ki 19:16-21 [c]Jos 4:19 [1]Or *windstorm* **2:2** [a]Ru 1:15 [b]1Ki 12:28, 29 [c]1Sa 1:26; 2Ki 2:4, 6 **2:3** [a]2Ki 4:1, 38; 5:22 [1]Lit *your head* **2:4** [a]2Ki 2:2 [b]Jos 6:26 **2:5** [a]2Ki 2:3 [b]2Ki 2:3 [1]Lit *your head* [2]Lit *said* **2:6** [a]2Ki 2:2 [b]Jos 3:8, 15-17 **2:7** [a]2Ki 2:15, 16 **2:8** [a]1Ki 19:13, 19 [b]Ex 14:21, 22; 2Ki 2:14 **2:9** [a]Nu 11:17-25; Dt 21:17 **2:10** [a]Ac 1:10

and talking, behold, *there appeared*
[a]a chariot of fire and horses of fire,
and it separated the two of them. And
Elijah went up by a [1]whirlwind to
heaven. **12** And Elisha was seeing *this*
and he was crying out, "[a]My father,
my father, the [1]chariots of Israel and
its horsemen!" And he saw [2]Elijah
no more. Then [b]he took hold of his
own clothes and tore them in two
pieces. **13** He also took up the mantle
of Elijah that fell from him and re-
turned and stood by the bank of the
Jordan. **14** And he took the mantle of
Elijah that fell from him and struck
the waters and said, "Where is Yah-
weh, the God of Elijah?" Indeed, he
himself also [a]struck the waters, and
they were divided here and there!
And Elisha crossed over.

### *Elisha Has the Spirit of Elijah*

**15** Then [a]the sons of the prophets
who *were* at Jericho opposite *him*
saw him and said, "The spirit of Elijah
rests on Elisha." And they came to
meet him and bowed themselves to
the ground before him. **16** Then they
said to him, "Behold now, there are
with your servants fifty excellent
men, please let them go and search
for your master, lest [a]the Spirit of
Yahweh has taken him up and cast
him on some mountain or into
some valley." And he said, "You
shall not send." **17** But when [a]they
urged him until he was ashamed,
he said, "Send." They sent therefore
fifty men; and they searched three
days but did not find him. **18** So they
returned to him while he was staying
at Jericho; and he said to them, "Did
I not say to you, 'Do not go'?"
**19** Then the men of the city said
to Elisha, "Behold now, the habitat
of this city is pleasant, as my lord
sees; but the water is bad and the
land [1]is unfruitful." **20** And he said,
"Bring me a new jar, and put salt [1]in
it." So they brought *it* to him. **21** And
he went out to the spring of water
and [a]threw salt [1]in it and said, "Thus
says Yahweh, 'I have [2]purified these
waters; there shall not be from there
death or barrenness any longer.'"
**22** So the waters have been [1]purified
to this day, according to the word of
Elisha which he spoke.
**23** Then he went up from there to
Bethel; and as he was going up by
the way, young boys came out from
the city and [a]mocked him and said
to him, "Go up, you baldhead; go up,
you baldhead!" **24** Then he looked
behind him and saw them. And he
[a]cursed them in the name of Yahweh.
Then two female bears came out of
the woods and tore up forty-two lads
of [1]their number. **25** And he went
from there to [a]Mount Carmel, and
from there he returned to Samaria.

### *Moab Rebels Against Israel*

**3** Now Jehoram the son of Ahab
became king over Israel at Sa-
maria [a]in the eighteenth year of Je-
hoshaphat king of Judah, and reigned
twelve years. **2** And he did what was
evil in the sight of Yahweh, though
not like his father and his mother;
and [a]he took away the *sacred* pillar
of Baal [b]which his father had made.

**2:11** [a]2Ki 6:17 [1]Or *windstorm* **2:12** [a]2Ki 13:14 [b]Ge 37:34; Job 1:20 [1]Lit *chariot* [2]Lit *him* **2:14** [a]2Ki 2:8 **2:15** [a]2Ki 2:7 **2:16** [a]1Ki 18:12; Ac 8:39 **2:17** [a]2Ki 8:11 **2:19** [1]Lit *causes barrenness* **2:20** [1]Lit *there* **2:21** [a]Ex 15:25, 26; 2Ki 4:41; 6:6 [1]Lit *there* [2]Lit *healed* **2:22** [1]Lit *healed* **2:23** [a]2Chr 36:16; Ps 31:17, 18 **2:24** [a]Ne 13:25-27 [1]Lit *them* **2:25** [a]1Ki 18:19, 20; 2Ki 4:25 ◆ **3:1** [a]2Ki 1:17 **3:2** [a]Ex 23:24; 2Ki 10:18, 26-28 [b]1Ki 16:31, 32

3 Nevertheless, [a]he clung to the sins
of Jeroboam the son of Nebat, [b]which
he made Israel sin; he did not turn
away from them.
4 Now Mesha king of Moab was a
sheep breeder and [a]used to pay the
king of Israel 100,000 lambs and
the wool of 100,000 rams. 5 But it
happened that [a]when Ahab died,
the king of Moab rebelled against the
king of Israel. 6 And King Jehoram
went out of Samaria [1]at that time
and mustered all Israel. 7 Then he
went and sent *word* to Jehoshaphat
the king of Judah, saying, "The king
of Moab has rebelled against me.
Will you go with me to fight against
Moab?" And he said, "I will go up;
[a]I am as you are, my people as your
people, my horses as your horses."
8 And he said, "Which way shall we
go up?" And he [1]answered, "The way
of the wilderness of Edom."
9 So [a]the king of Israel went with
[b]the king of Judah and [c]the king of
Edom; and they went around on a
seven days' journey, and there was no
water for the camp or for the cattle
that [1]followed them. 10 Then the
king of Israel said, "Alas! For Yahweh
has called these three kings to give
them into the hand of Moab." 11 But
Jehoshaphat said, "[a]Is there not a
prophet of Yahweh here, that we
may inquire of Yahweh by him?" And
*one of the king of Israel's* servants
answered and said, "[b]Elisha the son
of Shaphat is here, [c]who used to
pour water on the hands of Elijah."
12 And Jehoshaphat said, "The word
of Yahweh is with him." So the king of
Israel and Jehoshaphat and the king
of Edom went down to him.
13 Now Elisha said to the king of Is-
rael, "What do I have to do with you?
[a]Go to the prophets of your father and
to the prophets of your mother." And
the king of Israel said to him, "No, for
Yahweh has called these three kings
*together* to give them into the hand
of Moab." 14 And Elisha said, "[a]As
Yahweh of hosts lives, before whom
I stand, were it not that I regard the
presence of Jehoshaphat the king
of Judah, I would not look at you
nor see you. 15 So now [a]bring me a
musician." And it came about, when
the musician played, that [b]the hand
of Yahweh came upon him. 16 And
he said, "Thus says Yahweh, 'Make
this valley full of trenches.' 17 For
thus says Yahweh, 'You shall not see
wind nor shall you see rain; yet that
valley [a]shall be filled with water, so
that you shall drink, both you and
your livestock and your cattle. 18 And
this is but a [a]light thing in the sight
of Yahweh; He will also give the
Moabites into your hand. 19 [a]Then
you shall strike every fortified city
and every choice city, and fell every
good tree and stop all springs of wa-
ter, and mar every good piece of land
with stones.'" 20 Then it happened
in the morning [a]about the time of
offering the sacrifice, that behold,
water came by the way of Edom, and
the country was filled with water.
21 Now all the Moabites heard that
the kings had come up to fight against
them. And they summoned all who
were able to [1]put on armor and older,

**3:3** [a]1Ki 12:28-32 [b]1Ki 14:9, 16 **3:4** [a]2Sa 8:2; Is 16:1, 2 **3:5** [a]2Ki 1:1 **3:6** [1]Lit *in that day*
**3:7** [a]1Ki 22:4 **3:8** [1]Lit *said* **3:9** [a]2Ki 3:1 [b]2Ki 3:7 [c]1Ki 22:47 [1]Lit *was at their feet* **3:11** [a]1Ki 22:7
[b]2Ki 2:25 [c]1Ki 19:21; Jn 13:4, 5, 13, 14 **3:13** [a]1Ki 18:19; 22:6-11, 22-25 **3:14** [a]1Ki 17:1; 2Ki 5:16
**3:15** [a]1Sa 16:23; 1Chr 25:1 [b]1Ki 18:46; Eze 1:3 **3:17** [a]Ps 107:35 **3:18** [a]Jer 32:17, 27; Mk 10:27; Lk 1:37
**3:19** [a]2Ki 3:25 **3:20** [a]Ex 29:39, 40 **3:21** [1]Lit *gird themselves with a belt*

and they stood on the border. 22 Then
they rose early in the morning, and
the sun shone on the water, and the
Moabites saw the water opposite
*them* as red as blood. 23 Then they
said, "This is blood; the kings have
surely fought together, and they have
struck down one another. So now,
Moab, to the spoil!" 24 So they came
to the camp of Israel. And the Isra-
elites arose and struck the Moabites.
So they fled before them; and they
went forward [1]into the land, striking
down the Moabites. 25 [a]Thus they
[1]tore down the cities; and each one
threw a stone on every piece of good
land and filled it. And they stopped
all the springs of water and felled all
the good trees, until in [b]Kir-hareseth
they let its stones remain; however,
the slingers went about *it* and struck
it. 26 Then the king of Moab saw that
the battle was too strong for him, so
he took with him 700 men who drew
swords, to break through to the king
of Edom; but they could not. 27 So he
took his oldest son, who was to reign
in his place, and [a]offered him as a
burnt offering on the wall. And there
came great wrath against Israel, and
they set out from him and returned
to their own land.

### *The Widow's Oil*

4 Now a certain woman of the
wives of [a]the sons of the prophets
cried out to [1]Elisha, "Your servant my
husband is dead, and you know that
your servant feared Yahweh; and
[b]the creditor has come to take my
*two children to be his* slaves." 2 And
Elisha said to her, "What shall I do
for you? Tell me, what do you have
in the house?" And she said, "Your
servant-woman has nothing in the
house except [a]a jar of oil." 3 Then he
said, "Go, ask for vessels for yourself,
from *those* outside, from all your
neighbors, *even* empty vessels; do
not get a few. 4 And you shall go in
and shut the door behind you and
your sons, and pour out into all these
vessels, and you shall set aside what
is full." 5 So she went from him and
shut the door behind her and her
sons; they were bringing *the vessels*
to her and she poured. 6 Now it hap-
pened that when [a]the vessels were
full, she said to her son, "Bring me
another vessel." And he said to her,
"There is not one vessel more." And
the oil stopped. 7 Then she came and
told [a]the man of God. And he said,
"Go, sell the oil and pay your debt,
and you *and* your sons can live on
the rest."

### *The Shunammite Woman Will Bear a Son*

8 Now there came a day when Elisha
passed over to [a]Shunem, where there
was a [1]prominent woman, and she
prevailed upon him to eat [2]food.
Now it happened, as often as he
passed by, that he turned in there
to eat [2]food. 9 And she said to her
husband, "Behold now, I know that
this is a holy [a]man of God passing by
us continually. 10 Please, let us [a]make
a little walled upper chamber and let
us set a bed for him there, and a table
and a chair and a lampstand; and it
will be, when he comes to us, *that* he
can turn in there."

**3:24** [1]Lit *into it* **3:25** [a]2Ki 3:19 [b]Is 16:7; Jer 48:31, 36 [1]Lit *pulled* **3:27** [a]Am 2:1; Mic 6:7
◆ **4:1** [a]2Ki 2:3 [b]Lv 25:39-41, 48; 1Sa 22:2; Ne 5:2-5 [1]Lit *Elisha, saying* **4:2** [a]1Ki 17:12 **4:6** [a]Mt 14:20
**4:7** [a]1Ki 12:22 **4:8** [a]Jos 19:18 [1]Lit *great* [2]Lit *bread* **4:9** [a]2Ki 4:7 **4:10** [a]Mt 10:41, 42; 25:40; Ro 12:13

11 Now it happened that one day he
came there and turned in to the up-
per chamber, and there he [1]lay down.
12 Then he said to [a]Gehazi his young
man, "Call this Shunammite." So he
called her, and she stood before him.
13 And he said to him, "Say now to
her, 'Behold, you have been [1]careful
for us with all this [2]care; what can
I do for you? Would you be spoken
for to the king or to the commander
of the army?'" And she [3]answered,
"I live among my own people." 14 So
he said, "What then is to be done for
her?" And Gehazi [1]answered, "Truly
she has no son, and her husband is
old." 15 And he said, "Call her." So
he called her, and she stood in the
doorway. 16 Then he said, "[a]At this
season [1]next year you will embrace
a son." And she said, "No, my lord,
O man of God, [b]do not lie to your
servant-woman."

17 Then the woman conceived and
bore a son at that season [1]the next
year, as Elisha had said to her.

### *A Dead Boy Opens His Eyes*

18 Then the child was grown. And
the day came that he went out to his
father to the reapers. 19 And he said
to his father, "My head, my head."
And he said to [1]his young man,
"Carry him to his mother." 20 Then
he carried him and brought him to
his mother, and he sat on her knees
*until* noon, and *then* died. 21 Then
she went up and [a]laid him on the
bed of [b]the man of God and shut
*the door* behind him and went out.
22 And she called to her husband
and said, "Please send me one of the
young men and one of the donkeys,
that I may run to the man of God and
return." 23 And he said, "Why will
you go to him today? It is neither
[a]new moon nor sabbath." And she
said, "*It is* well." 24 Then she saddled
a donkey and said to her young man,
"Drive and go; do not hold back *the*
*pace of* the ride for me unless I tell
you." 25 So she went and came to the
man of God to [a]Mount Carmel.

Now it happened that when the
man of God saw her at a distance,
he said to Gehazi his young man,
"Behold, [1]there is the Shunammite.
26 Please run now to meet her and
say to her, 'Is it well with you? Is it
well with your husband? Is it well
with the child?'" And she [1]answered,
"It is well." 27 Then she came to the
man of God [a]to the hill and took hold
of his feet. And Gehazi came near to
push her away; but the man of God
said, "Let her alone, for her soul is
bitter within her; and Yahweh has
hidden it from me and has not told
me." 28 Then she said, "Did I ask for a
son from my lord? Did I not say, '[a]Do
not deceive me'?"

29 Then he said to Gehazi, "[a]Gird
up your loins and [b]take my staff
in your hand, and go; if you meet
anyone, do not [c,1]greet him, and if
anyone [1]greets you, do not answer
him; and [d]lay my staff on the boy's
face." 30 But the mother of the boy
said, "[a]As Yahweh lives and as your
soul lives, I will not forsake you." And
he arose and followed her. 31 Now
Gehazi passed on before them and

---

**4:11** [1]Lit *lay there* **4:12** [a]2Ki 4:29-31; 5:20-27; 8:4, 5 **4:13** [1]Lit *fearful* [2]Lit *fear* [3]Lit *said* **4:14** [1]Lit *said* **4:16** [a]Ge 18:14 [b]2Ki 4:28 [1]Lit *when the time revives* **4:17** [1]Lit *when the time revived* **4:19** [1]Lit *the* **4:21** [a]2Ki 4:32 [b]2Ki 4:7 **4:23** [a]Nu 10:10; 28:11; 1Chr 23:31 **4:25** [a]2Ki 2:25 [1]Lit *this Shunammite* **4:26** [1]Lit *said* **4:27** [a]2Ki 4:25 **4:28** [a]2Ki 4:16 **4:29** [a]1Ki 18:46; 2Ki 9:1 [b]Ex 4:17; 2Ki 2:14 [c]Lk 10:4 [d]Ex 7:19, 20; 14:16 [1]Lit *bless* **4:30** [a]2Ki 2:2, 4

laid the staff on the boy's face, but
there was no sound or [1]response.
So he returned to meet him and
told him, saying, "The boy [a]has not
awakened."
**32** Then Elisha came into the house,
and behold, the boy was dead and
laid on his bed. **33** So he entered and
[a]shut the door behind them both
and prayed to Yahweh. **34** And [a]he
went up and lay on the child and put
his mouth on his mouth and his eyes
on his eyes and his hands on his hands,
and he stretched himself on him; and
the flesh of the child became warm.
**35** Then he returned and walked in
the house once back and forth, and
went up and [a]stretched himself on
him; and the boy sneezed seven times
and the boy opened his eyes. **36** Then
he called Gehazi and said, "Call this
Shunammite." So he called her. Then
she came in to him, and he said, "Take
up your son." **37** Then she came in and
fell at his feet and bowed herself to
the ground, and [a]she took up her son
and went out.

### *The Death in the Stew*

**38** Now Elisha returned to [a]Gilgal,
and *there was* [b]a famine in the
land. [1]As [c]the sons of the prophets
[d]were sitting before him, he said to
his young man, "[e]Put on the large
pot and boil stew for the sons of the
prophets." **39** Then one went out into
the field to gather herbs and found a
wild vine and gathered from it wild
gourds filling his cloak and came and
sliced them into the pot of stew, for
they *did not* know *what they were.*
**40** So they poured *it* out for the men
to eat. And it happened that as they
were eating of the stew, they cried
out and said, "O man of God, there
is [a]death in the pot." And they were
unable to eat. **41** But he said, "Now
bring flour." [a]He threw it into the pot
and said, "Pour *it* out for the people
that they may eat." Then there was
no harm in the pot.
**42** Now a man came from Baal-
shalishah, and brought the man of
God bread of the first fruits, twenty
loaves of barley and fresh ears
of grain in his sack. And he said,
"[a]Give *them* to the people that they
may eat." **43** And his attendant said,
"What, [a]will I give this before one
hundred men?" But he said, "Give
*them* to the people that they may eat,
for thus says Yahweh, 'They shall eat
and have *some* left over.'" **44** So he
gave *it* before them, and they ate and
[a]had *some* left over, according to the
word of Yahweh.

### *Naaman Cleaned from Leprosy*

**5** Now [a]Naaman, commander of
the army of the king of Aram,
was a great man [1]with his master,
and [2]highly respected, because by
him Yahweh had given salvation to
Aram. The man was also a mighty
man of valor, *but he was* a leper.
**2** Now the Arameans had gone out
[a]in marauding bands and had taken
captive a little girl from the land of
Israel; and she [1]waited on Naaman's
wife. **3** And she said to her mistress,
"I wish that my master were before
the prophet who is in Samaria! Then

**4:31** [a]Jn 11:11 [1]Lit *attentiveness* **4:33** [a]2Ki 4:4; Mt 6:6; Lk 8:51 **4:34** [a]1Ki 17:21-23 **4:35** [a]1Ki 17:21
**4:37** [a]Heb 11:35 **4:38** [a]2Ki 2:1 [b]2Ki 8:1 [c]2Ki 2:3 [d]Lk 10:39; Ac 22:3 [e]Eze 11:3, 7, 11; 24:3 [1]Lit *And*
**4:40** [a]Ex 10:17 **4:41** [a]Ex 15:25; 2Ki 2:21 **4:42** [a]Mt 14:16-21; 15:32-38 **4:43** [a]Lk 9:13; Jn 6:9
**4:44** [a]Mt 14:20; 15:37; Jn 6:13 ◆ **5:1** [a]Lk 4:27 [1]Lit *before* [2]Lit *the one whose face is lifted up*
**5:2** [a]2Ki 6:23; 13:20 [1]Lit *was before*

he would cure him of his leprosy."
**4** Then [1]Naaman went in and told
his master, saying, "Thus and thus
spoke the girl who is from the land of
Israel." **5** Then the king of Aram said,
"Go [1]now, and I will send a letter to
the king of Israel." So he went and
[a]took in his hand [2]ten talents of
silver and [3]six thousand *shekels* of
gold and ten [b]changes of clothes.

**6** And he brought the letter to the
king of Israel, saying,

"So now as this letter comes to
you, behold, I have sent Naaman
my servant to you, that you
may cure him of his leprosy."

**7** Now it happened that when the king
of Israel read the letter, [a]he tore his
clothes and said, "[b]Am I God, to put
to death and to make alive, that this
man is sending *word* to me to cure a
man of his leprosy? But [c]know now,
and see how he is seeking [1]a quarrel
against me."

**8** Now it happened when Elisha
[a]the man of God heard that the king
of Israel had torn his clothes, that
he sent *word* to the king, saying,
"Why have you torn your clothes?
Now let him come to me, and he
shall know that there is a prophet in
Israel." **9** So Naaman came with his
horses and his chariots and stood at
the doorway of the house of Elisha.
**10** And Elisha sent a messenger to
*him, saying*, "[a]Go and wash in the
Jordan seven times, and your flesh
will be restored to you and *you will*
be clean." **11** But Naaman was furious
and went away and said, "Behold, I
said *to myself*, 'He will surely come
out to me and stand and call on the
name of Yahweh his God, and wave
his hand over the place and cure the
leper.' **12** Are not [1]Abanah and Phar-
par, the rivers of Damascus, better
than all the waters of Israel? Could I
not wash in them and be clean?" So
he turned and [a]went away in wrath.
**13** [a]Then his servants approached
and spoke to him and said, "[b]My
father, had the prophet spoken with
you *to do some* great thing, would you
not have done *it*? How much more
*then*, when he says to you, 'Wash,
and be clean'?" **14** So he went down
and dipped *himself* seven times in
the Jordan, according to the word of
the man of God; and [a]his flesh was
restored like the flesh of a young boy
and [b]he was clean.

### *Gehazi's Leprosy*

**15** Then he returned to the man of
God [1]with all his camp, and came
and stood before him, and said,
"Behold now, [a]I know that there is
no God in all the earth, but in Israel;
so now please [b]take a blessing from
your servant." **16** But he said, "[a]As
Yahweh lives, before whom I stand,
[b]I will take nothing." And he urged
him to take *it*, but he refused. **17** So
Naaman said, "If not, please let your
servant *at least* be given two mules'
load of [a]earth; for your servant will
no longer offer burnt offering nor
will he sacrifice to other gods, but to
Yahweh. **18** In this matter may Yahweh
pardon your servant: when my master

---

**5:4** [1]Lit *He* **5:5** [a]1Sa 9:7; 2Ki 4:42 [b]Jdg 14:12; 2Ki 5:22, 23 [1]Lit *enter* [2]Approx. 750 lb. or 340 kg, a talent was approx. 75 lb. or 34 kg [3]Approx. 150 lb. or 66 kg, a shekel was approx. 0.4 oz. or 11 gm **5:7** [a]Ge 37:29 [b]Ge 30:2; 1Sa 2:6 [c]1Ki 20:7; Lk 11:54 [1]Lit *an occasion* **5:8** [a]1Ki 12:22 **5:10** [a]Jn 9:7 **5:12** [a]Pr 14:17; 16:32; 19:11 [1]Or *Amanah* **5:13** [a]1Sa 28:23 [b]2Ki 2:12; 6:21; 8:9 **5:14** [a]2Ki 5:10; Job 33:25 [b]Lk 4:27; 5:13 **5:15** [a]Jos 2:11; 1Sa 17:46, 47; 2Ki 5:8 [b]1Sa 25:27 [1]Lit *he and* **5:16** [a]2Ki 3:14 [b]Ge 14:22, 23; 2Ki 5:20, 26 **5:17** [a]Ex 20:24

goes into the house of Rimmon to
worship there, and [a]he leans on my
hand and I bow myself in the house
of Rimmon, when I bow myself in the
house of Rimmon, Yahweh pardon
your servant in this matter." **19** And
he said to him, "[a]Go in peace." So he
went from him some distance.

**20** Then [a]Gehazi, the young man
of Elisha the man of God, said *to him-*
*self*, "Behold, my master has spared
this Naaman the Aramean, [1]by not
receiving from his hands what he
brought. [b]As Yahweh lives, I will run
after him and take something from
him." **21** So Gehazi pursued Naaman.
And Naaman saw one running after
him, so he came down from the
chariot to meet him and said, "Is
*all* at peace?" **22** And he said, "[a]*All*
is at peace. My master has sent me,
saying, 'Behold, just now two young
men of the sons of the prophets have
come to me from [b]the hill country of
Ephraim. Please give them a talent of
silver and [c]two changes of clothes.'"
**23** Then Naaman said, "[a]Be pleased
to take two talents." And he urged
him and bound two talents of silver
in two bags with two changes of
clothes and gave *them* to two of his
young men; and they carried *them*
before him. **24** So he came to the
[1]hill, and he took them from their
hand and [a]deposited them in the
house. Then he sent the men away,
and they departed. **25** But he came
in and stood before his master. And
Elisha said to him, "Where have you
been, Gehazi?" And he said, "[a]Your
servant went nowhere."
**26** Then he said to him, "Did not
my heart go *with you*, when the man
turned from his chariot to meet you?
[a]Is it a time to receive money and
to receive clothes and olive groves
and vineyards and sheep and oxen
and male and female slaves? **27** Thus
the leprosy of Naaman shall cling to
you and to your seed forever." So he
went out from his presence [a]a leper
*as white* as snow.

### *The Axe Head Floats*

**6** And [a]the sons of the prophets
said to Elisha, "Behold now, the
place before you where we are living
is too limited for us. **2** Please let us
go to the Jordan and each of us take
from there a beam, and let us make
a place there for ourselves where we
may live." So he said, "Go." **3** Then
one said, "Please be willing to go with
your servants." And he [1]answered, "I
shall go." **4** So he went with them;
and they came to the Jordan and cut
down trees. **5** Now it happened that
as one was felling a beam, [1]the axe
head fell into the water; and he cried
out and said, "Alas, my master! For
it was borrowed." **6** Then the man of
God said, "Where did it fall?" And
when he showed him the place, [a]he
cut off a stick and threw *it* in there
and made the iron float. **7** And he
said, "Take it up for yourself." So he
sent forth his hand and took it.

### *Horses and Chariots of Fire Around Elisha*

**8** Now the king of Aram was warring
against Israel; and he [1]counseled

**5:18** [a]2Ki 7:2, 17 **5:19** [a]Ex 4:18; 1Sa 1:17; Mk 5:34 **5:20** [a]2Ki 4:12, 31, 36 [b]Ex 20:7; 2Ki 6:31 [1]Lit *from* **5:22** [a]2Ki 4:26 [b]Jos 24:33 [c]2Ki 5:5 **5:23** [a]2Ki 6:3 **5:24** [a]Jos 7:1, 11, 12, 21; 1Ki 21:16 [1]Heb *ophel* **5:25** [a]2Ki 5:22 **5:26** [a]2Ki 5:16 **5:27** [a]Ex 4:6; Nu 12:10 ◆ **6:1** [a]2Ki 2:3 **6:3** [1]Lit *said* **6:5** [1]Lit *as for the iron, it fell* **6:6** [a]Ex 15:25; 2Ki 2:21; 4:41 **6:8** [1]Lit *took counsel*

with his servants saying, "In such
and such a place shall be my camp."
**9** [a]And the man of God sent *word* to
the king of Israel saying, "Beware that
you do not pass this place, for the
Arameans are coming down there."
**10** And the king of Israel sent to the
place about which the man of God
had told him; thus he warned him, so
that he guarded himself there, [1]more
than once or twice.

**11** Then the heart of the king of
Aram was enraged over this thing;
and he called his servants and said
to them, "Will you not tell me which
of us is for the king of Israel?" **12** And
one of his servants said, "No, my lord,
O king; but Elisha, the prophet who
is in Israel, tells the king of Israel
the words that you speak in your
bedroom." **13** So he said, "Go and see
where he is, that I may send and take
him." And it was told to him, saying,
"Behold, he is in [a]Dothan." **14** So he
sent horses and chariots and a heavy
military force there, and they came
by night and surrounded the city.

**15** Then the attendant of the man
of God arose early and went out, and
behold, a military force with horses
and chariots was all around the city.
And his young man said to him,
"Alas, my master! [1]What shall we
do?" **16** So he said, "[a]Do not fear, for
[b]those who are with us are more than
*those who* are with them." **17** Then
Elisha prayed and said, "[a]O Yahweh, I
pray, open his eyes that he may see."
And Yahweh opened the eyes of the
young man and he saw; and behold,
the mountain was full of [b]horses and
chariots of fire all around Elisha.
**18** And they came down to him, and
Elisha prayed to Yahweh and said,
"Strike this [1]people with blindness,
I pray." So He [a]struck them with
blindness according to the word of
Elisha. **19** Then Elisha said to them,
"This is not the way, and this is not
the city; walk after me and I will walk
you over to the man whom you seek."
And he walked them over to Samaria.

**20** Now it happened that when
they had come into Samaria, Elisha
said, "O [a]Yahweh, open the eyes of
these *men*, that they may see." So
Yahweh opened their eyes and they
saw; and behold, they were in the
midst of Samaria. **21** Then the king
of Israel when he saw them, said
to Elisha, "[a]My father, shall I strike
*them* down? Shall I strike *them*
down?" **22** And he said, "You shall not
strike *them* down. Would you [a]strike
down those you have taken captive
with your sword and with your bow?
[b]Set bread and water before them,
that they may eat and drink and
walk *back* to their master." **23** So he
prepared a great feast for them; and
when they had eaten and drunk, he
sent them away, and they went to
their master. And [a]the marauding
bands of Arameans did not come
again into the land of Israel.

### *Aram's Siege of Samaria*

**24** Now it happened afterwards, that
[a]Ben-hadad king of Aram gathered
all his *military* camp and went up
and besieged Samaria. **25** Now there
was a great [a]famine in Samaria.

**6:9** [a]2Ki 4:1, 7; 6:12 **6:10** [1]Lit *not once or twice* **6:13** [a]Ge 37:17 **6:15** [1]Lit *How* **6:16** [a]Ex 14:13 [b]2Chr 32:7, 8; Ro 8:31 **6:17** [a]2Ki 6:20 [b]2Ki 2:11; Ps 68:17; Zec 6:1-7 **6:18** [a]Ge 19:11 [1]Lit *nation* **6:20** [a]2Ki 6:17 **6:21** [a]2Ki 2:12; 5:13; 8:9 **6:22** [a]Dt 20:11-16; 2Chr 28:8-15 [b]Ro 12:20 **6:23** [a]2Ki 5:2; 24:2 **6:24** [a]1Ki 20:1 **6:25** [a]Lv 26:26

And behold, they besieged it, until a donkey's head was sold for [1]eighty *shekels* of silver, and a fourth of a [2]kab of dove's dung for five *shekels* of silver. **26** As the king of Israel was passing by on the wall, a woman cried out to him, saying, "Save, my lord, O king!" **27** He said, "[1]If Yahweh does not save you, from where shall I save you? From the threshing floor, or from the wine press?" **28** And the king said to her, "[a]What [1]is the matter with you?" And she said, "This woman said to me, 'Give your son that we may eat him today, and we will eat my son tomorrow.' **29** [a]So we boiled my son and ate him; and I said to her on the next day, 'Give your son, that we may eat him'; but she has hidden her son." **30** Now it happened that when the king heard the words of the woman, [a]he tore his clothes—now he was passing by on the wall—and the people looked, and behold, he had sackcloth [1]beneath on his [2]body. **31** Then he said, "May [a]God do so to me and more also, if the head of Elisha the son of Shaphat [1]remains on him today."

### *Flour and Barley in Samaria*

**32** Now Elisha was sitting in his house, and [a]the elders were sitting with him. And *the king* sent a man from his presence; but before the messenger came to him, he said to the elders, "Do you [b]see how this son of a murderer has sent to take away my head? Look, when the messenger comes, shut the door and [1]hold the door shut against him. Is not the sound of his master's feet behind him?" **33** While he was still speaking with them, behold, the messenger came down to him and he said, "[a]Behold, this evil is from Yahweh; why should I wait for Yahweh any longer?"

**7** Then Elisha said, "Listen to the word of Yahweh; thus says Yahweh, '[a]About this time tomorrow a [1]seah of fine flour will be *sold* for a [2]shekel, and two [1]seahs of barley for a [2]shekel, in the gate of Samaria.'" **2** [a]And the royal officer on whose hand the king was leaning answered the man of God and said, "Behold, [b]if Yahweh should make windows in heaven, could this thing be?" Then he said, "Behold, you will see it with your own eyes, but you will not eat [1]of it."

### *Lepers Report the Arameans' Flight*

**3** Now there were four [a]leprous men at the entrance of the gate; and they said to one another, "Why do we sit here until we die? **4** If we say, 'We will enter the city,' then the famine is in the city and we will die there; and if we sit here, we die also. So now come, and let us [1]go over to [a]the camp of the Arameans. If they spare us, we will live; and if they put us to death, we will die." **5** So they arose at twilight to go to the camp of the Arameans. Then they came to the outskirts of the camp of the Arameans, but behold, there was no one there. **6** Now [a]the Lord had

**6:25** [1]Approx. 2 lb. or 0.8 kg, a shekel was approx. 0.4 oz. or 11 gm [2]A kab was approx. 2 qt. or 1.9 l **6:27** [1]Lit *No, let Yahweh help you* **6:28** [a]Jdg 18:23 [1]Lit *to you* **6:29** [a]Lv 26:27-29; Dt 28:52, 53, 57; Lam 4:10 **6:30** [a]1Ki 21:27 [1]Lit *within* [2]Lit *flesh* **6:31** [a]Ru 1:17; 1Ki 19:2 [1]Lit *stands* **6:32** [a]Eze 8:1; 14:1; 20:1 [b]1Ki 18:4, 13, 14; 21:10, 13 [1]Lit *press him with the door* **6:33** [a]Is 8:21 ◆ **7:1** [a]2Ki 7:18 [1]A seah was approx. 7 qt. or 7.7 l [2]A shekel was approx. 0.4 oz. or 11 gm **7:2** [a]2Ki 5:18; 7:17, 19 [b]Ge 7:11; Mal 3:10 [1]Lit *from there* **7:3** [a]Lv 13:45, 46; Nu 5:2-4; 12:10-14 **7:4** [a]2Ki 6:24 [1]Lit *fall* **7:6** [a]2Sa 5:24

caused the camp of the Arameans
to hear a sound of chariots and a
sound of horses, *even* the sound of a
great military force, so that they said
to one another, "Behold, the king
of Israel has hired against us [b]the
kings of the Hittites and [c]the kings
of the Egyptians, to come upon us."
**7** Therefore they [a]arose and fled in
the twilight, and forsook their tents
and their horses and their donkeys,
*even* the camp just as it was, and fled
for their life. **8** So these lepers came to
the outskirts of the camp and entered
one tent and ate and drank. Then
they [a]carried from there silver and
gold and clothes, and they went and
hid *them*; and they returned and en-
tered another tent and carried from
there *also* and went and hid *them*.

**9** Then they said to one another,
"We are not doing right. This day is
a day of good news, but we are keep-
ing silent; if we wait until morning
light, punishment will [1]overtake us.
So now, come, let us go and tell the
king's household." **10** So they came
and called to the gatekeepers of the
city, and they told them, saying, "We
came to the camp of the Arameans,
and behold, there was no one there,
nor the voice of man, only the horses
tied and the donkeys tied, and the
tents just as they were." **11** And the
gatekeepers called and told *it* within
the king's household. **12** Then the
king arose in the night and said to
his servants, "I will now tell you what
the Arameans have done to us. They
know that [a]we are hungry; therefore
they have gone from the camp [b]to
hide themselves in the field, saying,
'When they come out of the city, we
will capture them alive and get into
the city.'" **13** And one of his servants
answered and said, "Please, let some
*men* take five of the remaining horses,
which remain [1]in the city. Behold,
they *will be in any case* like all the
multitude of Israel who remain in it;
behold, they *will be in any case* like
all the multitude of Israel who have
already come to an end, so let us send
and see." **14** They took therefore two
chariots with horses, and the king
sent after the camp of the Arameans,
saying, "Go and see."

### *Plundering the Arameans*

**15** Then they went after them to the
Jordan, and behold, all the way was
full of clothes and equipment which
the Arameans had thrown away in
their haste. Then the messengers
returned and told the king.

**16** So the people went out and
plundered the camp of the Arameans.
Then a [1]seah of fine flour *was sold* for
a shekel and two [1]seahs of barley for
a shekel, [a]according to the word of
Yahweh. **17** Now the king appointed
[a]the royal officer on whose hand he
leaned [1]to have charge of the gate;
but the people trampled on him
at the gate, and he died just as the
man of God had spoken, [b]who spoke
when the king came down to him.
**18** So it happened just as the man of
God had spoken to the king, saying,
"[a]Two [1]seahs of barley for a shekel
and a [1]seah of fine flour for a shekel
will be *sold* tomorrow about this time
at the gate of Samaria." **19** And the
royal officer had answered the man

**7:6** [b]1Ki 10:29 [c]2Chr 12:2, 3; Is 31:1; 36:9 **7:7** [a]Ps 48:4-6; Pr 28:1 **7:8** [a]Jos 7:21 **7:9** [1]Lit *find*
**7:12** [a]2Ki 6:25-29 [b]Jos 8:4-12 **7:13** [1]Lit *in it* **7:16** [a]2Ki 7:1 [1]A seah was approx. 7 qt. or 7.7 l
**7:17** [a]2Ki 7:2 [b]2Ki 6:32 [1]Lit *over the gate* **7:18** [a]2Ki 7:1 [1]A seah was approx. 7 qt. or 7.7 l

of God and said, “Now behold, [a]if Yahweh should make windows in heaven, could such a thing be?” And he had said, “Behold, you will see it with your own eyes, but you will not eat [1]of it.” **20** And so it happened to him, for the people trampled on him at the gate and he died.

### *Jehoram Restores the Shunammite's Land*

**8** Now [a]Elisha spoke to the woman whose son he had restored to life, saying, “Arise and go [1]with your household, and sojourn wherever you can sojourn; for [b]Yahweh has called for a famine, and [c]it will even come on the land for seven years.” **2** So the woman arose and did according to the word of the man of God, and she went with her household and sojourned in the land of the Philistines seven years. **3** Now it happened at the end of seven years, that the woman returned from the land of the Philistines; and she went out to cry out to the king for her house and for her field. **4** Now the king was speaking with [a]Gehazi, the young man of the man of God, saying, “Please recount to me all the great things that Elisha has done.” **5** Now it happened as he was recounting to the king [a]how he had restored to life the one who was dead, that behold, the woman whose son he had restored to life was crying out to the king for her house and for her field. And Gehazi said, “My lord, O king, this is the woman, and this is her son, whom Elisha restored to life.” **6** Then the king asked the woman, and she recounted *it* to him. So the king appointed for her a certain officer, saying, “Restore all that was hers and all the produce of the field from the day that she left the land even until now.”

### *Elisha Weeps over Hazael's Evil*

**7** Then Elisha came to [a]Damascus. Now [b]Ben-hadad king of Aram was sick, and it was told to him, saying, “[c]The man of God has come here.” **8** And the king said to [a]Hazael, “[b]Take a present in your hand and go to meet the man of God, and [c]inquire of Yahweh by him, saying, ‘Will I be restored to life from this sickness?’” **9** So Hazael went to meet him and took a present in his hand, even every kind of good thing of Damascus, forty camels' loads; and he came and stood before him and said, “[a]Your son Ben-hadad king of Aram has sent me to you, saying, ‘Will I be restored to life from this sickness?’” **10** Then Elisha said to him, “[a]Go, say to him, ‘You will surely be restored to life,’ but [b]Yahweh has shown me that he will certainly die.” **11** And he [1]fixed his gaze steadily *on him* [a]until he was ashamed, and [b]the man of God wept. **12** Then Hazael said, “Why does my lord weep?” Then he said, “Because [a]I know the evil that you will do to the sons of Israel: their fortifications you will set on fire, and their young men you will kill with the sword, and their infants you [b]will dash in pieces, and their pregnant women you will rip up.” **13** Then Hazael said, “But what is your servant, [a]*who is but* a dog,

**7:19** [a]2Ki 7:2 [1]Lit *from there* ◆ **8:1** [a]2Ki 4:18, 31-35 [b]Ps 105:16; Hag 1:11 [c]Ge 41:27, 54 [1]Lit *you and your* **8:4** [a]2Ki 4:12; 5:20-27 **8:5** [a]2Ki 4:35 **8:7** [a]1Ki 11:24 [b]2Ki 6:24 [c]2Ki 5:20 **8:8** [a]1Ki 19:15, 17 [b]1Ki 14:3 [c]2Ki 1:2 **8:9** [a]2Ki 5:13 **8:10** [a]2Ki 8:14 [b]2Ki 8:15 **8:11** [a]2Ki 2:17 [b]Lk 19:41 [1]Lit *made his face stand fast and he set* **8:12** [a]2Ki 10:32, 33; 12:17; 13:3, 7 [b]2Ki 15:16; Na 3:10 **8:13** [a]1Sa 17:43; 2Sa 9:8

that he should do this great thing?"
And Elisha [1]answered, "[b]Yahweh has
shown me that you will be king over
Aram." **14** So he went from Elisha
and came to his master. And he
said to him, "What did Elisha say to
you?" And he said, "He said to me
that [a]you would surely be restored
to life." **15** Now it happened that on
the following day, he took the cover
and dipped it in water and spread it
on his face; [a]so he died. And Hazael
became king in his place.

### *Jehoram Reigns over Judah*

**16** Now in the fifth year of [a]Joram
the son of Ahab king of Israel,
Jehoshaphat being then the king
of Judah, Jehoram the son of Je-
hoshaphat king of Judah became
king. **17** He was [a]thirty-two years
old when he became king, and he
reigned eight years in Jerusalem.
**18** And he walked in the way of the
kings of Israel, just as the house of
Ahab had done, for [a]the daughter
of Ahab became his wife; and he did
what was evil in the sight of Yahweh.
**19** However, Yahweh was not willing
to make Judah a ruin, for the sake
of David His servant, [a]since He had
[1]promised him to give a [2]lamp to him
through his sons always.
**20** In his days [a]Edom revolted
from under the hand of Judah and
made a king over themselves. **21** Then
Joram crossed over to Zair, and all
his chariots with him. And he arose
by night and struck the Edomites
who were surrounding him and the
commanders of the chariots; [a]but
[1]*his* army fled to their tents. **22** [a]So
Edom revolted [1]against Judah to
this day. Then [b]Libnah revolted at
the same time. **23** Now the rest of the
acts of Joram and all that he did, are
they not written in the Book of the
Chronicles of the Kings of Judah?

### *Ahaziah Reigns over Judah*

**24** So Joram slept with his fathers and
[a]was buried with his fathers in the
city of David; and [b]Ahaziah his son
became king in his place.
**25** [a]In the twelfth year of Joram the
son of Ahab king of Israel, Ahaziah
the son of Jehoram king of Judah be-
came king. **26** [a]Ahaziah *was* twenty-
two years old when he became king,
and he reigned one year in Jerusalem.
And his mother's name was Athaliah
the granddaughter of Omri king of
Israel. **27** [a]He also walked in the way
of the house of Ahab and did what
was evil in the sight of Yahweh, like
the house of Ahab *had done*, because
he was a son-in-law of the house of
Ahab.
**28** Then he went with Joram the
son of Ahab to war with [a]Hazael king
of Aram at [b]Ramoth-gilead, and the
Arameans struck Joram. **29** So [a]King
Joram returned to be healed in Jezreel
of the wounds which the Arameans
had caused *by* striking him at [b]Ramah
when he fought against Hazael king
of Aram. Then [c]Ahaziah the son of
Jehoram king of Judah went down to
see Joram the son of Ahab in Jezreel
because he was sick.

---

**8:13** [b]1Ki 19:15 [1]Lit *said* **8:14** [a]2Ki 8:10 **8:15** [a]2Ki 8:10 **8:16** [a]2Ki 1:17; 3:1 **8:17** [a]2Chr 21:5-10
**8:18** [a]2Ki 8:27 **8:19** [a]2Sa 7:12-15; 1Ki 11:36 [1]Lit *said* [2]Descendant on the throne
**8:20** [a]1Ki 22:47; 2Ki 3:9, 26, 27; 8:22 **8:21** [a]2Sa 18:17; 19:8 [1]Lit *the people* **8:22** [a]Ge 27:40
[b]Jos 21:13; 2Ki 19:8 [1]Lit *from under the hand of* **8:24** [a]2Chr 21:20 [b]2Chr 21:1, 7 **8:25** [a]2Chr 22:1-6
**8:26** [a]2Chr 22:2 **8:27** [a]2Chr 22:3 **8:28** [a]2Ki 8:15 [b]1Ki 22:3, 29 **8:29** [a]2Ki 9:15 [b]2Ki 8:28;
2Chr 22:5, 6 [c]2Ki 9:16

### *Jehu Anointed King over Israel*

**9** Now Elisha the prophet called
one of [a]the sons of the prophets
and said to him, "[b]Gird up your loins,
and [c]take this flask of oil in your
hand and go to [d]Ramoth-gilead. **2** And
you will come there and look there
for [a]Jehu the son of Jehoshaphat the
son of Nimshi. And you will come
in and [b,1]bid him arise from among
his brothers. And you will cause him
to come in to an inner room. **3** Then
you will take the flask of oil and pour
it on his head and say, 'Thus says
Yahweh, "[a]I have anointed you king
over Israel."' Then open the door and
flee and do not wait."

**4** So [a]the young man—the young
man of the prophet—went to Ramoth-
gilead. **5** Then he came, and behold,
the commanders of the military were
sitting, and he said, "I have a word for
you, O commander." And Jehu said,
"[1]For which *one* of us?" And he said,
"For you, O commander." **6** And he
arose and came into the house, and
he poured the oil on his head and
said to him, "Thus says Yahweh, the
God of Israel, '[a]I have anointed you
king over the people of Yahweh, *even*
over Israel. **7** And you shall strike the
house of Ahab your master, [a]that I
may avenge [b]the blood of My slaves
the prophets, and the blood of all
the slaves of Yahweh, [c]at the hand
of Jezebel. **8** For the whole house of
Ahab shall perish, and [a]I will cut
off from Ahab [b]every [1]male person
[c]both bond and free in Israel. **9** [a]And
I will make the house of Ahab like the
house of Jeroboam the son of Nebat,
and [b]like the house of Baasha the son
of Ahijah. **10** [a]And the dogs shall eat
Jezebel in the [1]property of Jezreel,
and none shall bury *her*.'" Then he
opened the door and fled.

**11** Now Jehu came out to the ser-
vants of his master, and one said to
him, "[a]Is all well? Why did this [b]mad
fellow come to you?" And he said to
them, "You know the man and his
talk." **12** And they said, "It is a lie,
declare *it* to us now." And he said,
"Thus and thus he said to me, 'Thus
says Yahweh, "I have anointed you
king over Israel."'" **13** Then [a]they hur-
ried and each man took his garment
and placed it under him on the bare
steps, and [b]blew the trumpet, saying,
"Jehu is king!"

### *Jehu Deceives Joram*

**14** So Jehu the son of Jehoshaphat
the son of Nimshi conspired against
Joram. [a]Now Joram [1]with all Israel
was [2]guarding Ramoth-gilead against
Hazael king of Aram, **15** but [a]King
[1]Joram had returned to be healed in
Jezreel of the wounds which the Ar-
ameans had struck him with when he
fought with Hazael king of Aram. So
Jehu said, "If this is your mind, *then*
let no one escape *or* [2]leave the city to
go declare *it* in Jezreel." **16** Then Jehu
rode in a chariot and went to Jezreel,
for Joram was lying there. [a]Ahaziah

---

◆ **9:1** [a]2Ki 2:3 [b]2Ki 4:29 [c]1Sa 10:1; 16:1; 1Ki 1:39 [d]2Ki 8:28, 29 **9:2** [a]1Ki 19:16, 17; 2Ki 9:14, 20 [b]2Ki 9:5, 11 [1]Lit *cause him to* **9:3** [a]2Chr 22:7 **9:4** [a]2Ki 9:1 **9:5** [1]Lit *To whom of us all?* **9:6** [a]1Sa 2:7, 8; 1Ki 19:16; 2Ki 9:3; 2Chr 22:7 **9:7** [a]Dt 32:35, 43 [b]1Ki 18:4; 21:15, 21, 25 [c]2Ki 9:32-37 **9:8** [a]1Ki 21:21; 2Ki 10:17 [b]1Sa 25:22 [c]Dt 32:36; 2Ki 14:26 [1]Lit *him who urinates against the wall*, cf. 1Sa 25:22, 34; 1Ki 14:10, 21:21; 2Ki 9:8 **9:9** [a]1Ki 14:10, 11; 15:29 [b]1Ki 16:3-5, 11, 12 **9:10** [a]1Ki 21:23; 2Ki 9:35, 36 [1]Lit *portion* **9:11** [a]2Ki 9:17, 19, 22 [b]Jer 29:26; Hos 9:7; Mk 3:21 **9:13** [a]Mt 21:7, 8; Mk 11:7, 8 [b]2Sa 15:10; 1Ki 1:34, 39 **9:14** [a]1Ki 22:3; 2Ki 8:28 [1]Lit *he and* [2]Lit *keeping* **9:15** [a]2Ki 8:29 [1]Heb *Jehoram* [2]Lit *go out from* **9:16** [a]2Ki 8:29

king of Judah had come down to see
Joram.
**17** Now the watchman was stand-
ing on the tower in Jezreel and he saw
the [1]company of Jehu as he came, and
said, "I see a [1]company." And Joram
said, "Take a horseman and send him
to meet them and let him say, 'Is it
peace?'" **18** So a horseman went to
meet him and said, "Thus says the
king, 'Is it peace?'" And Jehu said,
"[a]What have you to do with peace?
Turn behind me." And the watchman
declared saying, "The messenger
came to them, but he did not return."
**19** Then he sent out a second horse-
man. And he came to them and said,
"Thus says the king, 'Is it peace?'"
And Jehu [1]answered, "What have
you to do with peace? Turn behind
me." **20** And the watchman declared
saying, "He came up to them, but he
did not return; and [a]the driving is
like the driving of [b]Jehu the son of
Nimshi, for he drives in madness."
**21** Then [1]Joram said, "[2]Get ready."
And they made his chariot ready.
[a,1]Joram king of Israel and Ahaziah
king of Judah went out, each in his
chariot, and they went out to meet
Jehu and found him in the [b,3]property
of Naboth the Jezreelite. **22** Now it
happened that when [1]Joram saw Jehu,
he said, "Is it peace, Jehu?" And he
[2]answered, "What peace, [a]so long as
the harlotries of your mother Jezebel
and her sorceries are so many?" **23** So
[1]Joram [2]turned about and fled and
said to Ahaziah, "[a]*There is* deception,
O Ahaziah!" **24** And [a]Jehu [1]drew his
bow with his full strength and struck
[2]Joram between his arms; and the
arrow went [3]through his heart and
he crouched down in his chariot.
**25** Then *Jehu* said to Bidkar his offi-
cer, "Lift *him* up and [a]cast him into
the [1]property of the field of Naboth
the Jezreelite, for I remember when
[2]you and I were riding together after
Ahab his father, that [b]Yahweh lifted
up this [c]oracle against him: **26** 'Surely
[a]I have seen yesterday the blood of
Naboth and the blood of his sons,'
says Yahweh, 'and [b]I will repay you
in this [1]property,' says Yahweh. So
now, lift *him* up and cast him into
the [1]property, according to the word
of Yahweh."

### *Jehu Strikes Down Ahaziah*

**27** [a]And Ahaziah the king of Judah
saw *this* and fled by the way of the
garden house. And Jehu pursued
him and said, "Strike him down too,
in the chariot." *So they struck him
down* at the ascent of Gur, which is
at [b]Ibleam. But he fled to Megiddo
and died there. **28** [a]Then his servants
carried him in a chariot to Jerusalem
and buried him in his grave with his
fathers in the city of David.
**29** Now in [a]the eleventh year of
Joram, the son of Ahab, Ahaziah
became king over Judah.

### *Jezebel Is Eaten by Dogs*

**30** Then Jehu came to Jezreel, and
Jezebel heard *of it* and [a]she painted
her eyes and adorned her head and
looked out the window. **31** As Jehu

**9:17** [1]Lit *multitude* **9:18** [a]2Ki 9:19, 22 **9:19** [1]Lit *said* **9:20** [a]2Sa 18:27 [b]1Ki 19:17 **9:21** [a]2Chr 22:7 [b]1Ki 21:1-7, 15-19; 2Ki 9:26 [1]Heb *Jehoram* [2]Lit *Yoke the chariot* [3]Lit *portion* **9:22** [a]1Ki 16:30-33; 18:19; 2Chr 21:13 [1]Heb *Jehoram* [2]Lit *said* **9:23** [a]2Ki 11:14 [1]Heb *Jehoram* [2]Lit *turned his hands* **9:24** [a]1Ki 22:34 [1]Lit *filled his hand with the bow* [2]Heb *Jehoram* [3]Lit *out at* **9:25** [a]1Ki 21:1 [b]1Ki 21:19, 24-29 [c]Is 13:1 [1]Lit *portion* [2]Lit *I and you* **9:26** [a]1Ki 21:13, 19 [b]2Ki 9:21, 25 [1]Lit *portion* **9:27** [a]2Chr 22:7, 9 [b]Jos 17:11; Jdg 1:27 **9:28** [a]2Ki 23:30 **9:29** [a]2Ki 8:25 **9:30** [a]Jer 4:30; Eze 23:40

entered the gate, she said, "[a]Is it [1]peace, Zimri, [2]your master's killer?" **32** Then he lifted up his face to the window and said, "Who is on my side? Who?" And two or three officials looked down at him. **33** And he said, "Throw her down." So they threw her down, and some of her blood was sprinkled on the wall and on the horses, and he trampled her under foot. **34** Then he came in and ate and drank. And he said, "Take care now of [a]this cursed woman and bury her, for [b]she is a king's daughter." **35** They went to bury her, but they found nothing more of her than the skull and the feet and the palms of her hands. **36** Therefore they returned and declared *it* to him. And he said, "This is the word of Yahweh, which He spoke by His servant Elijah the Tishbite, saying, '[a]In the [1]property of Jezreel the dogs shall eat the flesh of Jezebel; **37** and [a]the corpse of Jezebel will be as dung on the face of the field in the [1]property of Jezreel, so they cannot say, "This is Jezebel."'"

### *The Heads of Ahab's Sons Sent to Jehu*

**10** Now Ahab had seventy sons in [a]Samaria. And Jehu wrote letters and sent *them* to Samaria, to the rulers of Jezreel, the elders, and to the guardians of *the children of* Ahab, saying, **2** "So now, [a]when this letter comes to you, [1]since your master's sons are with you, [2]as well as the chariots and horses and a fortified city and the weapons, **3** look for the best and [1]fittest of your master's sons, and set *him* on his father's throne, and fight for your master's house." **4** But they feared exceedingly greatly and said, "Behold, [a]the two kings did not stand before him; how then can we stand?" **5** And the one who *was* over the household, and he who *was* over the city, the elders, and the guardians of *the children*, sent *word* to Jehu, saying, "[a]We are your servants, all that you say to us we will do, we will not make any man king; do what is good in your sight." **6** Then he wrote a letter to them a second time saying, "If you are on my side, and you will listen to my voice, take the heads of the men, your master's sons, and come to me about this time tomorrow at Jezreel." Now the king's sons, seventy persons, *were* with the great men of the city, *who* were rearing them. **7** Now it happened that when the letter came to them, they took the king's sons and [a]slaughtered *them*, seventy persons, and put their heads in baskets, and sent *them* to him at Jezreel. **8** Then the messenger came and told him, saying, "They have brought the heads of the king's sons." So he said, "Put them in two heaps at the entrance of the gate until morning." **9** Now it happened in the morning that he went out and stood and said to all the people, "You are righteous; behold, [a]I conspired against my master and killed him, but [b]who struck down all these? **10** Know then that [a]nothing from the word of Yahweh, which Yahweh spoke concerning the house of Ahab, shall fall to the earth. Indeed, Yahweh has done [b]what He spoke by the hand of

**9:31** [a]1Ki 16:9-20; 2Ki 9:18-22 [1]Or *well* [2]Lit *his* **9:34** [a]1Ki 21:25 [b]1Ki 16:31 **9:36** [a]1Ki 21:23 [1]Lit *portion* **9:37** [a]Jer 8:1-3 [1]Lit *portion* ◆ **10:1** [a]1Ki 16:24-29 **10:2** [a]2Ki 5:6 [1]Lit *and* [2]Lit *and with you the* **10:3** [1]Lit *most upright* **10:4** [a]2Ki 9:24, 27 **10:5** [a]Jos 9:8, 11; 1Ki 20:4, 32; 2Ki 18:14 **10:7** [a]Jdg 9:5; 2Ki 11:1 **10:9** [a]2Ki 9:14-24 [b]2Ki 10:6 **10:10** [a]2Ki 9:7-10 [b]1Ki 21:19-29

His servant Elijah." **11** So Jehu struck
down all who remained of the house
of Ahab in [a]Jezreel, and all his great
men and his acquaintances and his
priests, until [1]there was no survivor
remaining for him.

**12** Then he arose and came out and
went to Samaria. On the way, *while* he
was at [1]Beth-eked of the shepherds,
**13** [a]Jehu found the [1]relatives of Aha-
ziah king of Judah and said, "Who are
you?" And they said, "We are the [1]rela-
tives of Ahaziah; and we have come
down [2]to greet the sons of the king
and the sons of the queen mother."
**14** Then he said, "Take them alive." So
they took them alive and slaughtered
them at the pit of Beth-eked, forty-two
men; and he left none of them.

**15** Then he went from there and
found [a]Jehonadab the son of [b]Rechab
*coming* to meet him; and he [1]blessed
him and said to him, "Is your heart
right, as my heart is with your heart?"
And Jehonadab [2]answered, "It is." *Jehu
said,* "If it is, [c]give *me* your hand." And
he gave him his hand, and he took him
up to him into the chariot. **16** Then
he said, "Come with me and [a]see my
zeal for Yahweh." So [1]he made him
ride in his chariot. **17** And he came to
Samaria [a]and struck down all who
were left to Ahab in Samaria, until
he had destroyed him, [b]according to
the word of Yahweh which He spoke
to Elijah.

### *Jehu Destroys the Slaves of Baal*

**18** Then Jehu gathered all the people
and said to them, "[a]Ahab served Baal
a little; Jehu will serve him much.
**19** So now, [a]summon to me all the
prophets of Baal, all his slaves and
all his priests; let no one be missing,
for I have a great sacrifice for Baal;
whoever is missing shall not live."
But Jehu did it in [1]cunning, so that
he might cause the slaves of Baal to
perish. **20** And Jehu said, "[a]Sanctify
a solemn assembly for Baal." And
[b]they summoned *them.* **21** Then Jehu
sent [1]throughout Israel, and all the
slaves of Baal came, so that there was
not a man left who did not come. So
they came into [a]the house of Baal,
and the house of Baal was filled from
one end to the other. **22** Then he said
to the one who *was* [1]in charge of the
wardrobe, "Bring out garments for
all the slaves of Baal." So he brought
out garments for them. **23** And Jehu
came into the house of Baal with
Jehonadab the son of Rechab; and he
said to the slaves of Baal, "Search and
see lest there be here with you *any*
of the slaves of Yahweh, but only the
slaves of Baal." **24** Then they came in
to offer sacrifices and burnt offerings.

Now Jehu had placed for himself
eighty men outside, and he had said,
"[a]The one who permits *any* of the
men whom I cause to come into your
hands to escape, [1]shall give up his life
in exchange."

**25** Now it happened that as soon
as he had finished offering the burnt
offering, Jehu said to the [a,1]guard and
to the royal officers, "[b]Come in, strike
them down; let none come out." And
they struck them down with the edge

**10:11** [a]Hos 1:4 [1]Lit *he had no survivor* **10:12** [1]Lit *house of binding* **10:13** [a]2Ki 8:24, 29; 2Chr 21:17; 22:8 [1]Lit *brothers* [2]Lit *about the peace of* **10:15** [a]Jer 35:6-19 [b]1Chr 2:55 [c]Ezr 10:19; Eze 17:18 [1]Or *greeted* [2]Lit *said* **10:16** [a]1Ki 19:10 [1]Lit *they* **10:17** [a]2Ki 9:8 [b]2Ki 10:10 **10:18** [a]1Ki 16:31, 32 **10:19** [a]1Ki 18:19; 22:6 [1]Lit *insidiousness* **10:20** [a]Joel 1:14 [b]Ex 32:4-6 **10:21** [a]1Ki 16:32; 2Ki 11:18 [1]Lit *in all* **10:22** [1]Lit *over the* **10:24** [a]1Ki 20:30-42 [1]Lit *his soul for his soul* **10:25** [a]1Sa 22:17 [b]1Ki 18:40 [1]Lit *runners*

of the sword; and the [1]guard and the
royal officers threw *them* out and
went to the [2]inner room of the house
of Baal. **26** And they brought out the
*sacred* [a]pillars of the house of Baal
and burned them. **27** They also broke
down the *sacred* pillar of Baal and
broke down the house of Baal and
[a]made it a latrine to this day.

**28** Thus Jehu destroyed Baal out of
Israel. **29** However, [a]*as for* the sins of
Jeroboam the son of Nebat, which he
made Israel sin, from these Jehu did
not depart, *even* the [b]golden calves
that *were* at Bethel and that *were* at
Dan. **30** And Yahweh said to Jehu,
"Because you have done well in doing
what is right in My eyes, *and* have
done to the house of Ahab according
to all that *was* in My heart, [a]your
sons of the fourth generation shall sit
on the throne of Israel." **31** But Jehu
[a,1]was not careful to walk in the law
of Yahweh, the God of Israel, with all
his heart; [b]he did not depart from
the sins of Jeroboam, which he made
Israel sin.

**32** In those days [a]Yahweh began
to cut off *portions* [1]from Israel; and
[b]Hazael struck them throughout the
territory of Israel: **33** from the Jordan
*to the east* toward the sunrise, all the
land of Gilead, the Gadites and the
Reubenites and the Manassites, from
[a]Aroer, which is by the valley of the
Arnon, even [b]Gilead and Bashan.

### *Jehoahaz Reigns over Israel*

**34** Now the rest of the acts of Jehu
and all that he did and all his might,
*are they not written in the Book of*
the Chronicles of the Kings of Israel?
**35** And Jehu slept with his fathers,
and they buried him in Samaria. And
Jehoahaz his son became king in his
place. **36** Now the [1]time which Jehu
reigned over Israel in Samaria *was*
twenty-eight years.

### *Athaliah Reigns over Judah*

**11** [a]Now Athaliah the mother of
Ahaziah saw that her son had
died. So she rose and caused all the
royal seed to perish. **2** But Jehosheba,
the daughter of King Joram, sister
of Ahaziah, [a]took Joash the son of
Ahaziah and stole him from among
the king's sons who were being put
to death, *and put* him and his nurse
in the bedroom. So they hid him
from Athaliah, and he was not put
to death. **3** So he was hidden away
with her in the house of Yahweh six
years, while Athaliah was reigning
over the land.

**4** [a]Now in the seventh year Jehoia-
da sent for and took the commanders
of hundreds of [b]the Carites and of
the [1]guard, and brought them to
him in the house of Yahweh. Then
he cut a covenant with them and had
them swear in the house of Yahweh,
and showed them the king's son.
**5** And he commanded them, saying,
"This is the thing that you shall do:
[a]one-third of you, who come in on
the sabbath and keep watch over the
king's house **6** (one-third also *shall be*
at the gate Sur, and one-third at the
gate behind the [1]guards), [2]shall keep
watch over the house for defense.
**7** And two parts of you, *even* all who

---

**10:25** [1]Lit *runners* [2]Lit *city* **10:26** [a]1Ki 14:23; 2Ki 3:2 **10:27** [a]Ezr 6:11; Da 2:5; 3:29
**10:29** [a]1Ki 12:28-30; 13:33, 34 [b]1Ki 12:29 **10:30** [a]2Ki 15:12 **10:31** [a]Pr 4:23 [b]2Ki 10:29 [1]Lit *did not watch* **10:32** [a]2Ki 13:25; 14:25 [b]1Ki 19:17; 2Ki 8:12; 13:22 [1]Lit *in* **10:33** [a]Dt 2:36 [b]Am 1:3-5
**10:36** [1]Lit *days* ◆**11:1** [a]2Chr 22:10-12 **11:2** [a]2Ki 11:21; 12:1 **11:4** [a]2Chr 23:1-21 [b]2Sa 20:23; 2Ki 11:19
[1]Lit *runners* **11:5** [a]1Chr 9:25 **11:6** [1]Lit *runners* [2]Lit *and shall*

go out on the sabbath, shall also keep watch over the house of Yahweh for the king. **8** And you shall surround the king, each with his weapons in his hand; and whoever comes within the ranks shall be put to death. And [a]be with the king when he goes out and when he comes in."

**9** So the commanders of hundreds [a]did according to all that Jehoiada the priest commanded. And each one of them took his men who were to come in on the sabbath, with those who were to go out on the sabbath, and came to Jehoiada the priest. **10** [a]Then the priest gave to the commanders of hundreds the spears and small shields that *had been* King David's, which *were* in the house of Yahweh. **11** And the [1]guards stood each with his weapons in his hand, from the right [2]side of the house to the left [2]side of the house, by the altar and by the house, around the king. **12** Then he brought the king's son out and [a]put the crown on him and *gave him* [b]the testimony; and they made him king and anointed him, and they clapped their hands and said, "[c]*Long* live the king!"

**13** [a]Then Athaliah heard the noise of the guard *and of* the people, and she came to the people in the house of Yahweh. **14** And she looked, and behold, the king was standing [a]by the pillar, according to the custom, with the commanders and the [1]trumpeters beside the king; and [b]all the people of the land were glad and blew trumpets. Then Athaliah [c]tore her clothes and cried, "[d]Treason! Treason!" **15** And Jehoiada the priest commanded the commanders of hundreds who were appointed over the military force and said to them, "Bring her out [1]between the ranks, and whoever follows her put to death with the sword." For the priest said, "Let her not be put to death in the house of Yahweh." **16** So they [1]laid hands on her, and she arrived at the horses' entrance of the king's house and was [a]put to death there.

**17** Then [a]Jehoiada cut a covenant between Yahweh and the king and the people, that they would be the people of Yahweh, also [b]between the king and the people. **18** And all the people of the land came to [a]the house of Baal and tore it down; [b]his altars and his images they broke in pieces thoroughly, and they [c]killed Mattan the priest of Baal before the altars. And the priest appointed [1]overseers over the house of Yahweh. **19** And he took the commanders of hundreds and the [a]Carites and the [1]guards and all the people of the land; and they brought the king down from the house of Yahweh, and came by the way of [b]the gate of the [1]guards to the king's house. And he sat on the throne of the kings. **20** So [a]all the people of the land were glad, and the city was quiet. For they had put Athaliah to death with the sword at the king's house.

**21** [a,1]Jehoash was seven years old when he became king.

---

**11:8** [a]Nu 27:16, 17 **11:9** [a]2Chr 23:8 **11:10** [a]2Sa 8:7; 1Chr 18:7 **11:11** [1]Lit *runners* [2]Lit *shoulder* **11:12** [a]2Sa 1:10 [b]Ex 25:16; 31:18 [c]1Sa 10:24 **11:13** [a]2Chr 23:12 **11:14** [a]2Ki 23:3; 2Chr 34:31 [b]1Ki 1:39, 40 [c]Ge 37:29; 44:13 [d]2Ki 9:23 [1]Lit *trumpets* **11:15** [1]Lit *from within* **11:16** [a]Ge 9:6; Lv 24:17 [1]Lit *placed hands to her* **11:17** [a]Jos 24:25; 2Chr 15:12-14; 34:31 [b]1Sa 10:25; 2Sa 5:3 **11:18** [a]2Ki 10:26, 27 [b]Dt 12:2, 3 [c]1Ki 18:40 [1]Lit *oversight* **11:19** [a]2Ki 11:4 [b]2Ki 11:6 [1]Lit *runners* **11:20** [a]Pr 11:10 **11:21** [a]2Chr 24:1-14 [1]Ch 12:1 in Heb

### *Jehoash Reigns over Judah*

**12** In the seventh year of Jehu, [a]Jehoash became king, and he reigned forty years in Jerusalem; and his mother's name was Zibiah of Beersheba. **2** And Jehoash did what was right in the sight of Yahweh all his days in which Jehoiada the priest instructed him. **3** Only [a]the high places were not taken away; the people still sacrificed and burned incense on the high places.

### *Jehoash Repairs the House of Yahweh*

**4** Then Jehoash said to the priests, "All the money of the sacred things [a]which is brought into the house of Yahweh, *both* [b]the money for each [1]numbered man—the money from each person's assessment *in the census—and* all the money which any man's heart prompts him to bring into the house of Yahweh, **5** let the priests take it for themselves, each from his acquaintance; and they shall repair the [1]damages of the house wherever any damage may be found."

**6** Now it happened that in the twenty-third year of King Jehoash [a]the priests had not repaired the damages of the house. **7** Then King Jehoash called for Jehoiada the priest, and for the *other* priests and said to them, "Why do you not repair the damages of the house? So now, take no *more* money from your acquaintances, but give it over *to pay* for the damages of the house." **8** So the priests agreed that they would take no *more* money from the people, nor *repair the* damages of the house.

**9** But [a]Jehoiada the priest took a chest and bored a hole in its lid and put it beside the altar, on the right side as one comes into the house of Yahweh; and the priests who kept watch over the threshold put in it all the money which was brought into the house of Yahweh. **10** Now it happened that when they saw that there was much money in the chest, [a]the king's scribe and the high priest came up and tied *it* in bags and counted the money which was found in the house of Yahweh. **11** And they gave the money, which was weighed out, into the hands of those who did the work, who had the oversight of the house of Yahweh; and they [1]paid it out to the craftsmen of wood and the builders who worked on the house of Yahweh; **12** and [a]to the masons and the hewers of stone, and for buying timber and hewn stone to repair the damages to the house of Yahweh, and for all that [1]was laid out for the house to repair it. **13** But [a]there were not made for the house of Yahweh [b]silver cups, snuffers, bowls, trumpets, any vessels of gold, or vessels of silver from the money which was brought into the house of Yahweh; **14** for they gave that to those who did the work, and with it they repaired the house of Yahweh. **15** Moreover, [a]they did not require an accounting from the men into whose hand they paid the money in order to pay those who did the work, for they were doing it faithfully. **16** The [a]money from the guilt offerings and [b]the money from the sin offerings was not brought into

◆ **12:1** [a]2Chr 24:1 **12:3** [a]2Ki 14:4; 15:35 **12:4** [a]2Ki 22:4 [b]Ex 30:13-16; 35:5, 22, 29; 1Chr 29:3-9 [1]Lit *passed over*, cf. Ex 30:14 **12:5** [1]Lit *breaches*, so through v 12 **12:6** [a]2Chr 24:5 **12:9** [a]Mk 12:41; Lk 21:1 **12:10** [a]2Sa 8:17; 2Ki 19:2; 22:3, 4, 12 **12:11** [1]Lit *brought* **12:12** [a]2Ki 22:5, 6 [1]Lit *went out* **12:13** [a]2Chr 24:14 [b]1Ki 7:48, 50 **12:15** [a]2Ki 22:7; 1Co 4:2; 2Co 8:20 **12:16** [a]Lv 5:15-18 [b]Lv 4:24, 29

the house of Yahweh; [c]it was for the
priests.
**17** Then [a]Hazael king of Aram went
up and fought against Gath and cap-
tured it, and [b]Hazael set his face to
go up to Jerusalem. **18** [a]And Jehoash
king of Judah took all the holy things
that Jehoshaphat and Jehoram and
Ahaziah, his fathers, kings of Judah,
had set apart as holy, and [b]his own
holy things and all the gold that was
found among the treasuries of the
house of Yahweh and of the king's
house, and sent *them* to Hazael king
of Aram. Then he went away from
Jerusalem.

### *Amaziah Reigns over Judah*

**19** Now the rest of the acts of Joash and
all that he did, are they not written
in the Book of the Chronicles of the
Kings of Judah? **20** [a]And his servants
arose and made a conspiracy and
[b]struck down Joash at [c]the house of
Millo *as he was* going down to Silla.
**21** Now Jozacar the son of Shimeath
and Jehozabad the son of [a]Shomer,
his servants, struck *him* and he died;
and they buried him with his fathers
in the city of David, and [b]Amaziah
his son became king in his place.

### *Jehoahaz Reigns over Israel*

**13** In the twenty-third year of
Joash the son of Ahaziah, king
of Judah, Jehoahaz the son of Jehu
became king over Israel at Samaria,
*and he reigned* seventeen years.
**2** And he did what was evil in the
sight of Yahweh and followed the sins
of Jeroboam the son of Nebat, [a]with
which he made Israel sin; he did not
depart from them. **3** [a]So the anger
of Yahweh burned against Israel,
and He gave them continually into
the hand of [b]Hazael king of Aram,
and into the hand of [c]Ben-hadad
the son of Hazael. **4** Then [a]Jehoahaz
entreated the face of Yahweh, and
Yahweh listened to him; for [b]He
saw the oppression of Israel, how
the king of Aram oppressed them.
**5** And Yahweh gave Israel a [a]savior,
so that they came out from under
the hand of the Arameans; and the
sons of Israel lived in their tents as
formerly. **6** Nevertheless they did not
depart from the sins of the house
of Jeroboam, [a]with which he made
Israel sin, but walked in [1]them; and
[b]the Asherah also remained standing
in Samaria. **7** For he did not leave to
Jehoahaz *any* people *for the army*
except 50 horsemen and 10 chariots
and 10,000 foot soldiers, for the king
of Aram had caused them to perish
and [a]made them like the dust at
threshing. **8** Now the rest of the acts
of Jehoahaz, and all that he did and
his might, are they not written in the
Book of the Chronicles of the Kings
of Israel? **9** And Jehoahaz slept with
his fathers, and they buried him in
Samaria; and Joash his son became
king in his place.

### *Jehoash Reigns over Israel*

**10** In the thirty-seventh year of Joash
king of Judah, Jehoash the son of
Jehoahaz became king over Israel in
Samaria *and reigned* sixteen years.
**11** And he did what was evil in the

---

**12:16** [c]Lv 7:7; Nu 18:19 **12:17** [a]1Ki 19:17; 2Ki 8:12; 10:32, 33 [b]2Chr 24:23, 24 **12:18** [a]1Ki 14:26; 15:18; 2Ki 16:8; 18:15, 16 [b]2Ki 12:4 **12:20** [a]2Chr 24:25-27 [b]2Ki 14:5 [c]Jdg 9:6; 2Sa 5:9; 1Ki 11:27 **12:21** [a]2Chr 24:26 [b]2Ki 14:1 ◆ **13:2** [a]1Ki 12:26-33 **13:3** [a]Jdg 2:14 [b]2Ki 12:17 [c]2Ki 13:24, 25 **13:4** [a]Nu 21:7-9 [b]Ex 3:7, 9; 2Ki 14:26 **13:5** [a]2Ki 13:25; 14:25, 27; Ne 9:27 **13:6** [a]2Ki 13:2 [b]1Ki 16:33 [1]Lit *it* **13:7** [a]Am 1:3

sight of Yahweh; he did not depart
from all the sins of Jeroboam the
son of Nebat, with which he made
Israel sin, but he walked in [1]them.
**12** [a]Now the rest of the acts of Joash
and all that he did and his might with
which he fought against Amaziah
king of Judah, are they not written
in the Book of the Chronicles of
the Kings of Israel? **13** So Joash slept
with his fathers, and Jeroboam sat
on his throne; and Joash was buried
in Samaria with the kings of Israel.

### *The Death of Elisha*

**14** Now Elisha [1]became sick with the
illness of which he was to die. So
Joash the king of Israel came down
to him and wept over [2]him and said,
"[a]My father, my father, the chariots
of Israel and its horsemen!" **15** And
Elisha said to him, "Take a bow and
arrows." So he [1]took a bow and ar-
rows. **16** Then he said to the king of
Israel, "Put your hand on the bow."
And he put his hand *on it*, then Elisha
placed his hands on the king's hands.
**17** And he said, "Open the window
toward the east," and he opened *it*.
Then Elisha said, "Shoot!" And he
shot. And he said, "Yahweh's arrow of
salvation, even the arrow of salvation
over Aram; for you will strike the
Arameans at [a]Aphek until you have
consumed *them*." **18** Then he said,
"Take the arrows," and he took them.
And he said to the king of Israel,
"Strike the ground," and he struck
*it* three times and stood *still*. **19** So
[a]the man of God was angry with him
*and said*, "You should have struck
five or six times, then you would have
struck Aram until you would have
consumed *it*. But now you shall strike
Aram [b]*only* three times."

**20** And Elisha died, and they
buried him. Now [a]the marauding
bands of the Moabites would enter
into the land in the spring of the year.
**21** Now it happened that they were
burying a man, and behold, they saw
a marauding band; and they cast the
man into the grave of Elisha. And
when the man [1]touched the bones
of Elisha he [a]became alive and stood
up on his feet.

**22** Now [a]Hazael king of Aram had
oppressed Israel all the days of Jeho-
ahaz. **23** But [a]Yahweh was gracious to
them and [b]had compassion on them
and turned to them because of [c]His
covenant with Abraham, Isaac, and
Jacob, and would not bring them to
ruin or cast them from His presence
until now.

**24** Then Hazael king of Aram died,
and Ben-hadad his son became king
in his place. **25** Then [a]Jehoash the
son of Jehoahaz took again from the
hand of Ben-hadad the son of Hazael
the cities which he had taken in war
from the hand of Jehoahaz his father.
[b]Three times Joash struck him and
recovered the cities of Israel.

### *Amaziah Reigns over Judah*

**14** [a]In the second year of Joash
son of Joahaz king of Israel,
[b]Amaziah the son of Joash king of
Judah became king. **2** He was twenty-
five years old when he became king,
and he reigned twenty-nine years in

**13:11** [1]Lit *it* **13:12** [a]2Ki 13:14-19; 14:8-15 **13:14** [a]2Ki 2:12 [1]Lit *was sick with his sickness* [2]Lit *his face*
**13:15** [1]Lit *took to himself* **13:17** [a]1Ki 20:26 **13:19** [a]2Ki 5:20 [b]2Ki 13:25 **13:20** [a]2Ki 3:7; 24:2
**13:21** [a]Mt 27:52 [1]Lit *went and touched* **13:22** [a]2Ki 8:12, 13 **13:23** [a]2Ki 14:27 [b]1Ki 8:28 [c]Ge 13:16, 17; 17:2-5 **13:25** [a]2Ki 10:32, 33; 14:25 [b]2Ki 13:18, 19 ◆ **14:1** [a]2Chr 25:1 [b]2Ki 13:10

Jerusalem. And his mother's name was Jehoaddin of Jerusalem. **3** And he did what was right in the sight of Yahweh, yet not like David his father; he did according to all that Joash his father had done. **4** Only [a]the high places were not taken away; [b]the people still sacrificed and burned incense on the high places. **5** Now it happened as soon as the kingdom was strong in his hand, that he [a]struck down his servants who had struck down the king his father. **6** But the sons of those who struck *him* down he did not put to death, according to what is written in the book of the Law of Moses, which Yahweh commanded, saying, "[a]Fathers shall not be put to death for *their* sons, nor sons be put to death for *their* fathers; but [b]each shall be put to death for his own sin."

**7** He struck down 10,000 *of* Edom in [a]the Valley of Salt and seized [b]Sela by war and named it [c]Joktheel to this day.

**8** [a]Then Amaziah sent messengers to Jehoash, the son of Jehoahaz son of Jehu, king of Israel, saying, "[b]Come, let us face each other." **9** And Jehoash king of Israel sent to Amaziah king of Judah, saying, "[a]The thorn bush which was in Lebanon sent to the cedar which was in Lebanon, saying, 'Give your daughter to my son as a wife.' But a beast of the field that was in Lebanon passed by and trampled the thorn bush. **10** [a]You have indeed struck down Edom, and [b]your heart has lifted you up. Enjoy your glory and stay at home; for why should you provoke calamity so that you, even you, would fall, and Judah with you?"

**11** But Amaziah would not listen. So Jehoash king of Israel went up; and he and Amaziah king of Judah faced each other at [a]Beth-shemesh, which belongs to Judah. **12** And Judah was [1]defeated by Israel, and [a]they fled each to his tent. **13** Then Jehoash king of Israel seized Amaziah king of Judah, the son of Jehoash the son of Ahaziah, at Beth-shemesh, and came to Jerusalem and broke down the wall of Jerusalem from [a]the Gate of Ephraim to [b]the Corner Gate, [1]400 cubits. **14** [a]And he took all the gold and silver and all the utensils which were found in the house of Yahweh, and in the treasuries of the king's house, the hostages also, and returned to Samaria.

**15** [a]Now the rest of the acts of Jehoash which he did, and his might and how he fought with Amaziah king of Judah, are they not written in the Book of the Chronicles of the Kings of Israel? **16** So Jehoash slept with his fathers and was buried in Samaria with the kings of Israel; and Jeroboam his son became king in his place.

**17** [a]And Amaziah the son of Joash king of Judah lived fifteen years after the death of Jehoash son of Jehoahaz king of Israel. **18** Now the rest of the acts of Amaziah, are they not written in the Book of the Chronicles of the Kings of Judah? **19** And they conspired against him in Jerusalem, and he fled to [a]Lachish; but they sent after him to Lachish and put him to

**14:4** [a]2Ki 12:3 [b]2Ki 16:4 **14:5** [a]2Ki 12:20 **14:6** [a]Dt 24:16 [b]Jer 31:30; Eze 18:4, 20 **14:7** [a]2Sa 8:13; 1Chr 18:12; 2Chr 25:11 [b]Is 16:1 [c]Jos 15:38 **14:8** [a]2Chr 25:17-24 [b]2Sa 2:14-17 **14:9** [a]Jdg 9:8-15 **14:10** [a]2Ki 14:7 [b]Dt 8:14; 2Chr 26:16 **14:11** [a]Jos 19:38 **14:12** [a]2Sa 18:17 [1]Lit *smitten before* **14:13** [a]Ne 8:16; 12:39 [b]2Chr 25:23 [1]Approx. 600 ft. or 183 m, a cubit was approx. 18 in. or 45 cm **14:14** [a]1Ki 14:26; 2Ki 12:18 **14:15** [a]2Ki 13:12, 13 **14:17** [a]2Chr 25:25-28 **14:19** [a]Jos 10:31; 2Ki 18:14, 17

death there. **20** Then they carried him
on horses, and he was buried at Jeru-
salem with his fathers in the city of
David. **21** And all the people of Judah
took [1]Azariah, who *was* sixteen years
old, and made him king in the place
of his father Amaziah. **22** [a]He built
Elath and restored it to Judah after
the king slept with his fathers.

### *Jeroboam II Reigns over Israel*

**23** In the fifteenth year of Amaziah
the son of Joash king of Judah, Jer-
oboam the son of Joash king of Israel
became king in Samaria *and reigned*
forty-one years. **24** And he did what
was evil in the sight of Yahweh; he
did not depart from all the sins of
Jeroboam the son of Nebat, which he
made Israel sin. **25** [a]He restored the
border of Israel from [b,1]Lebo-hamath
as far as [c]the Sea of the Arabah,
according to the word of Yahweh,
the God of Israel, which He spoke
[2]through His servant [d]Jonah the son
of Amittai, the prophet, who was of
[e]Gath-hepher. **26** For [a]Yahweh saw
the affliction of Israel, *which was*
very bitter; for [b]there was neither
bond nor free, nor was there any
helper for Israel. **27** [a]But Yahweh did
not say that He would blot out the
name of Israel from under heaven,
so He saved them by the hand of
Jeroboam the son of Joash.

### *Zechariah Reigns over Israel*

**28** Now the rest of the acts of Jer-
oboam and all that he did and his
might, how he fought and how he
*restored* [a]*Damascus* and [b]Hamath to
Judah in Israel, are they not written
in the Book of the Chronicles of the
Kings of Israel? **29** And Jeroboam
slept with his fathers, even with the
kings of Israel, and Zechariah his son
became king in his place.

### *Azariah Reigns over Judah*

**15** [a]In the twenty-seventh year of
Jeroboam king of Israel, Aza-
riah son of Amaziah king of Judah
became king. **2** He was [a]sixteen years
old when he became king, and he
reigned fifty-two years in Jerusalem;
and his mother's name was [1]Jecoliah
of Jerusalem. **3** And he did what was
right in the sight of Yahweh, accord-
ing to all that his father Amaziah
had done. **4** Only [a]the high places
were not taken away; the people still
sacrificed and burned incense on the
high places. **5** [a]Then Yahweh smote
the king, so that he was a leper to
the day of his death. And he [b]lived
in a separate house, [1]while Jotham
the king's son *was* over the house,
judging the people of the land. **6** Now
the rest of the acts of Azariah and
all that he did, are they not written
in the Book of the Chronicles of the
Kings of Judah? **7** And Azariah slept
with his fathers, and they buried him
with his fathers in the city of David,
and Jotham his son became king in
his place.

### *Zechariah Reigns over Israel*

**8** [a]In the thirty-eighth year of Azariah
king of Judah, Zechariah the son of
Jeroboam became king over Israel in
Samaria *for* six months. **9** And he did

**14:21** [1]In 2Chr 26:1, *Uzziah* **14:22** [a]1Ki 9:26; 2Ki 16:6; 2Chr 8:17 **14:25** [a]2Ki 10:32; 13:25 [b]1Ki 8:65 [c]Dt 3:17 [d]Jon 1:1; Mt 12:39, 40 [e]Jos 19:13 [1]Or *the entrance of Hamath* [2]Lit *by* **14:26** [a]2Ki 13:4 [b]Dt 32:36 **14:27** [a]2Ki 13:23 **14:28** [a]1Ki 11:24 [b]2Chr 8:3 ◆ **15:1** [a]2Ki 14:17 **15:2** [a]2Chr 26:3, 4 [1]In 2Chr 26:3, *Jechiliah* **15:4** [a]2Ki 12:3 **15:5** [a]2Chr 26:21-23 [b]Lv 13:46; Nu 12:14 [1]Lit *and* **15:8** [a]2Ki 15:1

what was evil in the sight of Yahweh,
as his fathers had done; he did not
depart from the sins of Jeroboam
the son of Nebat, which he made
Israel sin. **10** Then Shallum the son
of Jabesh conspired against him and
[a]struck him before the people and
put him to death and became king
in his place. **11** Now the rest of the
acts of Zechariah, behold, they are
written in the Book of the Chronicles
of the Kings of Israel. **12** This is [a]the
word of Yahweh which He spoke to
Jehu, saying, "Your sons to the fourth
generation shall sit on the throne of
Israel." And so it was.

### *Shallum Reigns over Israel*

**13** Shallum son of Jabesh became king
in the [a]thirty-ninth year of Uzziah
king of Judah, and he reigned one
month in [b]Samaria. **14** Then Mena-
hem son of Gadi went up from
[a]Tirzah and came to Samaria, and
struck Shallum son of Jabesh in
Samaria, and put him to death and
became king in his place. **15** Now the
rest of the acts of Shallum and his
conspiracy which he made, behold,
they are written in the Book of the
Chronicles of the Kings of Israel.
**16** Then Menahem struck Tiphsah
and all who were in it and its borders
from Tirzah, because they did not
open *to him*; therefore he struck
*it* and ripped up [a]all its pregnant
women.

### *Menahem Reigns over Israel*

**17** In the [a]thirty-ninth year of Azariah
king of Judah, Menahem son of Gadi
became king over Israel *and reigned*
ten years in Samaria. **18** And he did
what was evil in the sight of Yahweh;
he did not depart all his days from the
sins of Jeroboam the son of Nebat,
which he made Israel sin.

**19** [a]Pul, king of Assyria, came
against the land, and Menahem gave
Pul one thousand [1]talents of silver
so that his hand might be with him
to [b]strengthen the kingdom in his
hand. **20** Then Menahem exacted
the money from Israel, even from
all the mighty men of valor, from
each man fifty [1]shekels of silver to
pay the king of Assyria. So the king
of Assyria returned and did not stay
there in the land. **21** Now the rest of
the acts of Menahem and all that he
did, are they not written in the Book
of the Chronicles of the Kings of Is-
rael? **22** And Menahem slept with his
fathers, and Pekahiah his son became
king in his place.

### *Pekahiah Reigns over Israel*

**23** In [a]the fiftieth year of Azariah king
of Judah, Pekahiah son of Menahem
became king over Israel in Samaria
*and reigned* two years. **24** And he
did what was evil in the sight of
Yahweh; he did not depart from
the sins of Jeroboam son of Nebat,
which he made Israel sin. **25** Then
Pekah son of Remaliah, his officer,
conspired against him and struck
him in Samaria, in [a]the castle of the
king's house with Argob and Arieh;
and with him were fifty men of the
Gileadites, and he put him to death
and became king in his place. **26** Now
the rest of the acts of Pekahiah and all
that he did, behold, they are written

---

**15:10** [a]Am 7:9 **15:12** [a]2Ki 10:30 **15:13** [a]2Ki 15:1, 8 [b]1Ki 16:24 **15:14** [a]1Ki 14:17 **15:16** [a]2Ki 8:12; Hos 13:16 **15:17** [a]2Ki 15:1, 8, 13 **15:19** [a]1Chr 5:25, 26 [b]2Ki 14:5 [1]A talent was approx. 75 lb. or 34 kg **15:20** [1]A shekel was approx. 0.4 oz. or 11 gm **15:23** [a]2Ki 15:1, 8, 13, 17 **15:25** [a]1Ki 16:18

in the Book of the Chronicles of the
Kings of Israel.

### *Pekah Reigns over Israel*

**27** In [a]the fifty-second year of Aza-
riah king of Judah, [b]Pekah son of
Remaliah became king over Israel in
Samaria *and reigned* twenty years.
**28** And he did what was evil in the
sight of Yahweh; he did not depart
from the sins of Jeroboam son of
Nebat, which he made Israel sin.
**29** In the days of Pekah king of
Israel, [a,1]Tiglath-pileser king of
Assyria came and took Ijon and Abel-
beth-maacah and Janoah and Kedesh
and Hazor and Gilead and Galilee, all
the land of Naphtali; and [b]he took
them away into exile to Assyria.
**30** And Hoshea the son of Elah made
a conspiracy against Pekah the son
of Remaliah and struck him and put
him to death and became king in his
place, in the twentieth year of Jotham
the son of Uzziah. **31** Now the rest
of the acts of Pekah and all that he
did, behold, they are written in the
Book of the Chronicles of the Kings
of Israel.

### *Jotham Reigns over Judah*

**32** In the second year of Pekah the son
of Remaliah king of Israel, Jotham the
son of [1]Uzziah king of Judah became
king. **33** [a]He was twenty-five years
old when he became king, and he
reigned sixteen years in Jerusalem.
And his mother's name was Jerusha
the daughter of Zadok. **34** [a]And he
did what was right in the sight of
*Yahweh; he did* according to all that
his father Uzziah had done. **35** Only
[a]the high places were not taken
away; the people still sacrificed and
burned incense on the high places.
[b]He built the upper gate of the house
of Yahweh. **36** Now the rest of the
acts of Jotham and all that he did,
are they not written in the Book of
the Chronicles of the Kings of Judah?
**37** In those days [a]Yahweh began to
send Rezin king of Aram and Pekah
the son of Remaliah against Judah.
**38** And Jotham slept with his fathers,
and he was buried with his fathers in
the city of David his father; and Ahaz
his son became king in his place.

### *Ahaz Reigns over Judah*

**16**
In the seventeenth year of
Pekah the son of Remaliah,
[a]Ahaz the son of Jotham, king of
Judah, became king. **2** [a]Ahaz *was*
twenty years old when he became
king, and he reigned sixteen years
in Jerusalem; and he did not do what
was right in the sight of Yahweh his
God, as David his father *had done.*
**3** But he walked in the way of the
kings of Israel, [a]and even made his
son pass through the fire, [b]according
to the abominations of the nations
whom Yahweh had dispossessed
from before the sons of Israel. **4** He
also [a]sacrificed and burned incense
on the high places and on the hills
and under every green tree.
**5** Then [a]Rezin king of Aram and
Pekah son of Remaliah, king of Israel,
went up to Jerusalem to *wage* war;
and they besieged Ahaz, [b]but could
not [1]overcome him. **6** At that time

---

**15:27** [a]2Ki 15:23 [b]2Chr 28:6; Is 7:1 **15:29** [a]2Ki 15:19 [b]2Ki 17:6 [1]In 1Chr 5:6, 26, *Tilgath-pilneser*
**15:32** [1]Azariah **15:33** [a]2Chr 27:1 **15:34** [a]2Ki 15:3, 4; 2Chr 26:4, 5 **15:35** [a]2Ki 12:3 [b]2Chr 23:20; 27:3
**15:37** [a]2Ki 16:5; Is 7:1 ◆ **16:1** [a]2Chr 28:1 **16:2** [a]2Chr 28:1-4 **16:3** [a]Lv 18:21; 2Ki 17:17; 21:6 [b]Dt 12:31;
2Ki 21:2, 11 **16:4** [a]Dt 12:2; 2Ki 14:4 **16:5** [a]2Ki 15:37; Is 7:1 [b]2Chr 28:5, 6 [1]Lit *fight*

Rezin king of Aram restored [a]Elath
for Aram and cleared the Judeans out
of [1]Elath entirely; and the [2]Arameans
came to Elath and have lived there
to this day.

### *Ahaz Sends for Help from Assyria*

**7** [a]So Ahaz sent messengers to
[b]Tiglath-pileser king of Assyria,
saying, "I am your servant and your
son; come up and save me from the
[1]hand of the king of Aram and from
the [1]hand of the king of Israel, who
are rising up against me." **8** [a]Ahaz
also took the silver and gold that was
found in the house of Yahweh and
in the treasuries of the king's house,
and sent a gift to the king of Assyria.
**9** [a]So the king of Assyria listened to
him; and the king of Assyria went up
against Damascus and [b]seized it and
took *the people of* it away into exile to
[c]Kir, and put Rezin to death.

### *Ahaz Has Urijah Build an Altar*

**10** Now King Ahaz went to Damas-
cus to meet [a]Tiglath-pileser king of
Assyria and saw the altar which *was*
at Damascus; and King Ahaz sent to
[b]Urijah the priest the likeness of
the altar and its pattern, according
to all its workmanship. **11** So Urijah
the priest built an altar; according to
all that King Ahaz had sent from Da-
mascus, thus Urijah the priest made
*it*, [1]before the coming of King Ahaz
from Damascus. **12** So the king came
from Damascus, and the king saw
the altar; then [a]the king drew near
the altar and [1]made offerings on
it, **13** and offered his burnt offering
and his meal offering up in smoke,
and poured his drink offering and
splashed the blood of his peace of-
ferings on the altar. **14** [a]Now *as for*
the bronze altar, which *was* before
Yahweh, [1]he drew *it* away from the
front of the house, from between
[b]*his* altar and the house of Yahweh,
and he put it on the north side of *his*
altar. **15** Then King Ahaz [1]command-
ed Urijah the priest, saying, "Upon
the great altar offer up in smoke
[a]the morning burnt offering and
the evening grain offering and the
king's burnt offering and his grain
offering, with the burnt offering of all
the people of the land and their grain
offering and their drink offerings;
and splash on it all the blood of the
burnt offering and all the blood of
the sacrifice. But [b]the bronze altar
shall be for me to inquire *by*." **16** So
Urijah the priest did according to all
that King Ahaz commanded.

**17** Then King Ahaz [a]cut off the
borders of the stands and removed
the laver from them; he also [b]took
down the sea from the bronze oxen
which were under it and put it on
a pavement of stone. **18** And the
covered way for the sabbath which
they had built in the house, and the
outer entry of the king, he removed
from the house of Yahweh because
of the king of Assyria.

### *Hezekiah Reigns over Judah*

**19** Now the rest of the acts of Ahaz
which he did, are they not written
[a]in the Book of the Chronicles of the
Kings of Judah? **20** So [a]Ahaz slept

**16:6** [a]2Ki 14:22; 2Chr 26:2 [1]Heb *Eloth* [2]As in some ancient versions; Heb *Edomites* **16:7** [a]2Chr 28:16 [b]2Ki 15:29 [1]Lit *palm* **16:8** [a]2Ki 12:17, 18; 18:15 **16:9** [a]2Chr 28:21 [b]Am 1:3-5 [c]Is 22:6; Am 9:7 **16:10** [a]2Ki 15:29 [b]Is 8:2 **16:11** [1]Lit *until* **16:12** [a]2Chr 26:16, 19 [1]Or *went up on it* **16:14** [a]Ex 27:1, 2; 40:6, 29; 2Chr 4:1 [b]2Ki 16:11 [1]Lit *he also* **16:15** [a]Ex 29:39-41 [b]2Ki 16:14 [1]Lit *commanded him, Urijah* **16:17** [a]1Ki 7:27, 28, 38 [b]1Ki 7:23, 25 **16:19** [a]2Chr 28:26 **16:20** [a]Is 14:28

with his fathers and [b]was buried
with his fathers in the city of David;
and Hezekiah his son became king
in his place.

### *Hoshea Reigns over Israel*

**17** In the twelfth year of Ahaz
king of Judah, [a]Hoshea the
son of Elah became king over Israel
in Samaria *and reigned* nine years.
**2** And he did what was evil in the
sight of Yahweh, only not as the
kings of Israel who were before him.
**3** [a]Shalmaneser king of Assyria went
up [b]against him, and Hoshea became
his servant and paid him tribute. **4** But
the king of Assyria found conspiracy
in Hoshea, who had sent messengers
to So king of Egypt and had offered
no tribute to the king of Assyria, as
*he had done* year by year; therefore
the king of Assyria shut him up and
bound him in prison.

**5** Then the king of Assyria went up
against the whole land and he went
up to [a]Samaria and besieged it three
years.

### *Israel Exiled to Assyria*

**6** In the ninth year of Hoshea, [a]the
king of Assyria captured Samaria
and [b]took Israel away into exile to
Assyria, and [c]settled them in Halah
and Habor, *on* the river of [d]Gozan,
and [e]in the cities of the Medes.

### *Israel Rejects Yahweh*

**7** Now [a]*this* happened because the
sons of Israel had sinned against Yah-
weh their God—[b]who had brought
them up from the land of Egypt from
under the hand of Pharaoh, king of
Egypt—[c]and they had [1]feared other
gods **8** and [a]walked in the statutes
of the nations whom Yahweh had
dispossessed from before the sons
of Israel, and *in the statutes* [b]of the
kings of Israel which they had made.
**9** And the sons of Israel [1]did things
secretly which were not right against
Yahweh their God. Moreover, they
built for themselves high places in
all their cities, from [a]watchtower
to fortified city. **10** [a]And they set
for themselves *sacred* pillars and
[b,1]Asherim on every high hill and
under every green tree, **11** and there
they burned incense on all the high
places as the nations *did* which
Yahweh had taken away into exile
before them; and they did evil things
provoking Yahweh to anger. **12** And
they served idols, [a]concerning which
Yahweh had said to them, "You shall
not do this thing." **13** Yet [a]Yahweh
warned Israel and Judah [b]by the
hand of all His prophets *and* [c]every
seer, saying, "[d]Turn from your evil
ways and keep My commandments,
My statutes according to all the law
which I commanded your fathers,
and which I sent to you by the hand
of My slaves the prophets." **14** Howev-
er, they did not listen, but [a]stiffened
their neck [1]like their fathers, who
did not believe in Yahweh their God.
**15** [a]They also rejected His statutes
and [b]His covenant which He cut with
their fathers and His warnings with
which He warned them. And [c]they

**16:20** [b]2Chr 28:27 ◆**17:1** [a]2Ki 15:30 **17:3** [a]Hos 10:14 [b]2Ki 18:9-12 **17:5** [a]Hos 13:16
**17:6** [a]Hos 13:16 [b]Dt 28:64; 29:27, 28 [c]2Ki 18:11; 1Chr 5:26 [d]Is 37:12 [e]Is 13:17; 21:2 **17:7** [a]Jos 23:16
[b]Ex 14:15-30 [c]Jdg 6:10 [1]Or *reverenced*, so in ch **17:8** [a]Lv 18:3; Dt 18:9 [b]2Ki 16:3; 17:19 **17:9** [a]2Ki 18:8
[1]Or *uttered words which* **17:10** [a]Ex 34:12-14 [b]1Ki 14:23; Mic 5:14 [1]Wooden symbols of a female deity
**17:12** [a]Ex 20:4 **17:13** [a]Ne 9:29, 30 [b]2Ki 17:23 [c]1Sa 9:9 [d]Jer 7:3-7; 18:11; Eze 18:31 **17:14** [a]Ex 32:9;
33:3; Ac 7:51 [1]Lit *like the neck of* **17:15** [a]Jer 8:9 [b]Ex 24:6-8; Dt 29:25 [c]Dt 32:21

followed vanity and [d]became vain,
and *went* after the nations which
surrounded them, concerning which
[e]Yahweh had commanded them not
to do like them. **16** And they forsook
all the commandments of Yahweh
their God and made for themselves
molten images, *even* [a]two calves, and
[b]made an [1]Asherah and [c]worshiped
all the host of heaven and [d]served
Baal. **17** Then [a]they made their sons
and their daughters pass through
the fire, and [b]practiced divination
and omens, and [c]sold themselves to
do what is evil in the sight of Yah-
weh, provoking Him to anger. **18** So
Yahweh was very angry with Israel
and [a]caused them to depart from His
[1]presence; [b]none was left except the
tribe of Judah alone.

**19** Also [a]Judah did not keep the
commandments of Yahweh their
God, but [b]walked in the statutes
[1]which Israel had made. **20** So Yah-
weh rejected all the seed of Israel and
afflicted them and [a]gave them into
the hand of plunderers, until He had
cast them [1]from His presence.

**21** When [a]He had torn Israel from
the house of David, [b]they made Jer-
oboam the son of Nebat king. Then
[c]Jeroboam drove Israel away from
following Yahweh and made them sin
a great sin. **22** And the sons of Israel
walked *in* all the sins of Jeroboam
which he did; they did not depart
from them **23** [a]until Yahweh caused
Israel to depart from His presence,
[b]as He spoke through all His slaves
the prophets. [a]So Israel went into
exile from their own land to Assyria
until this day.

### *Exiled Men in the Cities of Samaria*

**24** [a]And the king of Assyria brought
*men* from Babylon and from Cuthah
and from [b,1]Avva and from [c]Hamath
and Sepharvaim, and settled *them*
in the cities of Samaria in place of
the sons of Israel. So they possessed
Samaria and lived in its cities. **25** Now
it happened at the beginning of their
settlement there, that they [a]did not
fear Yahweh; therefore Yahweh sent
lions among them which were killing
them. **26** So they spoke to the king of
Assyria, saying, "The nations whom
you have taken away into exile and
settled in the cities of Samaria do
not know the custom of the god of
the land; so he has sent lions among
them, and behold, they are putting
them to death because they do not
know the custom of the god of the
land."

**27** Then the king of Assyria com-
manded, saying, "Take there one of
the priests whom you took away into
[1]exile and let [2]him go and live there;
and let him instruct them the custom
of the god of the land." **28** So one of
the priests whom they had taken
away into exile from Samaria came
and settled at Bethel, and instructed
them how they should fear Yahweh.

**29** But each nation was still making
gods of its own and put them [a]in the
houses of the high places which the
people of Samaria had made, each
nation in their cities in which they

**17:15** [d]Jer 2:5; Ro 1:21-23 [e]Dt 12:30, 31 **17:16** [a]1Ki 12:28 [b]1Ki 14:15, 23 [c]Dt 4:19; 2Ki 21:3 [d]1Ki 16:31 [1]A wooden symbol of a female deity **17:17** [a]2Ki 16:3 [b]Lv 19:26; Dt 18:10-12 [c]1Ki 21:20 **17:18** [a]2Ki 17:6 [b]1Ki 11:13, 32, 36 [1]Lit *face* **17:19** [a]1Ki 14:22, 23 [b]2Ki 16:3 [1]Lit *of Israel which they* **17:20** [a]2Ki 15:29 [1]Lit *from His face* **17:21** [a]1Ki 11:11, 31 [b]1Ki 12:20 [c]1Ki 12:28-33 **17:23** [a]2Ki 17:6 [b]2Ki 17:13 **17:24** [a]Ezr 4:2, 10 [b]2Ki 18:34 [c]1Ki 8:65 [1]In 2Ki 18:34, *Ivvah* **17:25** [a]2Ki 17:32-41 **17:27** [1]Lit *exile from there* [2]Lit *them* **17:29** [a]1Ki 12:31; 13:32

lived. **30** [a]And the men of Babylon made Succoth-benoth, the men of Cuth made Nergal, the men of Hamath made Ashima, **31** and the Avvites made Nibhaz and Tartak; and [a]the Sepharvites burned their children in the fire to [b]Adrammelech and Anammelech, the gods of *the* [c]Sepharvaim. **32** [a]They were also fearing Yahweh and [b,1]appointed from among all of themselves priests of the high places, and they were acting for them in the houses of the high places. **33** They were fearing Yahweh and serving their own gods according to the custom of the nations from among whom they had been taken away into exile.

**34** To this day they are acting according to the earlier customs: they are not fearing Yahweh; they are not acting according to their statutes or their judgments or the law, or the commandment which Yahweh commanded the sons of Jacob, [a]whom He named Israel; **35** with whom Yahweh cut a covenant and commanded them, saying, "[a]You shall not fear other gods, nor [b]worship them nor [c]serve them nor sacrifice to them. **36** But Yahweh, [a]who brought you up from the land of Egypt with great power and with [b]an outstretched arm, [c]Him you shall fear, and to Him you shall worship, and to Him you shall sacrifice. **37** And the statutes and the judgments and the law and the commandment which He wrote for you, [a]you shall be careful to do forever; and you shall not fear other gods. **38** And the covenant that I have cut with you, [a]you shall not forget, nor shall you fear other gods. **39** But Yahweh your God you shall fear; and He will deliver you from the hand of all your enemies." **40** However, they did not listen, but they were acting according to their earlier custom. **41** [a]So while these nations were fearing Yahweh, they also were serving their graven images; their children likewise and their grandchildren, as their fathers acted, so they are acting *this way* to this day.

### *Hezekiah Reigns over Judah*

**18** Now it happened [a]in the third year of Hoshea, the son of Elah king of Israel, that [b]Hezekiah the son of Ahaz king of Judah became king. **2** He was [a]twenty-five years old when he became king; and he reigned twenty-nine years in Jerusalem. And his mother's name was Abi, the daughter of Zechariah. **3** [a]And he did what was right in the sight of Yahweh, according to all that David his father had done. **4** [a]He took away the high places and shattered the *sacred* pillars and cut down the [1]Asherah. And he broke in pieces [b]the bronze serpent that Moses had made, for until those days the sons of Israel were burning incense to it; and it was called [2]Nehushtan. **5** [a]He trusted in Yahweh, the God of Israel; [b]so that after him there was none like him among all the kings of Judah, nor *among those* who were before him. **6** So he [a]clung to Yahweh; he did

---

**17:30** [a]2Ki 17:24 **17:31** [a]2Ki 17:17 [b]2Ki 19:37 [c]2Ki 17:24 **17:32** [a]Zep 1:5 [b]1Ki 12:31 [1]Lit *appointed from one extremity of themselves* **17:34** [a]Ge 32:28; 35:10 **17:35** [a]Jdg 6:10 [b]Ex 20:5 [c]Dt 5:9 **17:36** [a]Ex 14:15-30 [b]Ex 6:6; 9:15 [c]Lv 19:32; Dt 6:13 **17:37** [a]Dt 5:32 **17:38** [a]Dt 4:23; 6:12 **17:41** [a]Zep 1:5; Mt 6:24 ◆ **18:1** [a]2Ki 16:2; 17:1 [b]2Chr 28:27 **18:2** [a]2Chr 29:1, 2 **18:3** [a]2Ki 20:3; 2Chr 31:20 **18:4** [a]2Ki 18:22; 2Chr 31:1 [b]Nu 21:8, 9 [1]A wooden symbol of a female deity [2]Lit *a piece of bronze* **18:5** [a]2Ki 19:10 [b]2Ki 23:25 **18:6** [a]Dt 10:20; Jos 23:8

not turn away from following Him,
but kept His commandments, which
Yahweh had commanded Moses.

### *Hezekiah Prospers*

**7** [a]And Yahweh was with him; wher-
ever he went he prospered. And [b]he
rebelled against the king of Assyria
and did not serve him. **8** [a]He struck
the Philistines as far as Gaza and
its territory, from [b]watchtower to
fortified city.

**9** Now in the fourth year of King
Hezekiah, which was the seventh year
of Hoshea son of Elah king of Israel,
[a]Shalmaneser king of Assyria came
up against Samaria and besieged
it. **10** And at the end of three years
they captured it; in the sixth year of
Hezekiah, which was [a]the ninth year
of Hoshea king of Israel, Samaria was
captured. **11** Then the king of Assyria
took Israel away into exile to Assyria,
and put them in [a]Halah and on the
Habor, the river of Gozan, and in the
cities of the Medes, **12** because they
[a]did not listen to the voice of Yahweh
their God, but trespassed against His
covenant, *even* all that Moses the
servant of Yahweh commanded; they
would neither listen nor do *it.*

### *Sennacherib Comes Up Against Judah*

**13** [a]Now in the fourteenth year of
King Hezekiah, Sennacherib king of
Assyria came up against all the forti-
fied cities of Judah and seized them.
**14** Then Hezekiah king of Judah sent
to the king of Assyria at Lachish,
saying, "[a]I have done wrong. Turn
away from me; whatever *penalty* you
give to me I will bear." So the king of
Assyria set *a penalty* on Hezekiah
king of Judah [1]three hundred talents
of silver and [2]thirty talents of gold.
**15** [a]Thus Hezekiah gave *him* all the
silver which was found in the house
of Yahweh and in the treasuries of
the king's house. **16** At that time
Hezekiah cut off *the gold from* the
doors of the temple of Yahweh and
*from* the doorposts, which Hezekiah
king of Judah had overlaid, and gave
it to the king of Assyria.

**17** Then the king of Assyria
sent [a]Tartan and Rab-saris and
Rabshakeh from Lachish to King
Hezekiah with a heavy military
force to Jerusalem. So they went
up and came to Jerusalem. And
when they went up, they came and
stood by the [b]conduit of the upper
pool, which is on the highway of the
[1]fuller's field. **18** Then they called to
the king, and [a]Eliakim the son of
Hilkiah, who *was* over the house-
hold, and [b]Shebnah the scribe and
Joah the son of Asaph the recorder,
came out to them.

**19** Then Rabshakeh said to them,
"Say now to Hezekiah, 'Thus says
the great king, the king of Assyria,
"[a]What is this trust that you have?
**20** You say (but *they are* [1]only empty
words), '*I have* counsel and might
for the war.' Now on whom do you
trust, [a]that you have rebelled against
me? **21** Now behold, you [a,1]trust in
the staff of this crushed reed, *even*
on Egypt; on which if a man leans,

---

**18:7** [a]Ge 39:2, 3; 1Sa 18:14 [b]2Ki 16:7 **18:8** [a]2Chr 28:18; Is 14:29 [b]2Ki 17:9 **18:9** [a]2Ki 17:3-7
**18:10** [a]2Ki 17:6 **18:11** [a]1Chr 5:26 **18:12** [a]1Ki 9:6; Da 9:6, 10 **18:13** [a]2Chr 32:1; Is 36:1-39:8
**18:14** [a]2Ki 18:7 [1]Approx. 11.25 tons or 10.2 metric tons, a talent was approx. 75 lb. or 34 kg [2]Approx.
1.13 tons or 1 metric ton **18:15** [a]1Ki 15:18, 19; 2Ki 12:18; 16:8 **18:17** [a]Is 20:1 [b]2Ki 20:20; Is 7:3 [1]Or
*launderer's* **18:18** [a]2Ki 19:2; Is 22:20 [b]Is 22:15 **18:19** [a]2Chr 32:10 **18:20** [a]2Ki 18:7 [1]Lit *a word of
the lips* **18:21** [a]Is 30:2, 3, 7; Eze 29:6, 7 [1]Lit *rely for yourself*

it will go into his [2]hand and pierce
it. So is Pharaoh king of Egypt to all
who trust in him. **22** But if you say to
me, 'We trust in Yahweh our God,'
is it not He whose high places and
[a]whose altars Hezekiah has taken
away, and has said to Judah and to
Jerusalem, 'You shall worship before
this altar in Jerusalem'? **23** So now,
[1]come, make a bargain with my
master the king of Assyria, and I
will give you two thousand horses,
if you are able on your part to give
riders for them. **24** How then can
you [1]turn away one [2]official of the
least of my master's servants, and
trust in Egypt for chariots and for
horsemen? **25** So now, have I come
up [1]without the approval of Yahweh
against this place to make it a ruin?
Yahweh said to me, 'Go up against
this land and make it a ruin.'"'"

**26** Then Eliakim the son of Hilkiah,
and Shebnah and Joah, said to Rab-
shakeh, "Speak now to your servants
in Aramaic, for we [1]understand *it*; and
do not speak with us in [a,2]Judean in
the hearing of the people who are on
the wall." **27** But Rabshakeh said to
them, "Has my master sent me only to
your master and to you to speak these
words, *and* not to the men who sit on
the wall, *doomed* to eat their own dung
and drink their own urine with you?"

**28** Then Rabshakeh stood and
cried with a loud voice in Judean,
[1]saying, "Hear the word of the great
king, the king of Assyria. **29** Thus
says the king, '[a]Do not let Hezekiah
deceive *you*, for he will not be able
to deliver you from [1]his hand; **30** and
do not let Hezekiah make you trust
in Yahweh, saying, "Yahweh will
surely deliver us, and this city will
not be given into the hand of the
king of Assyria." **31** Do not listen to
Hezekiah, for thus says the king of
Assyria, "[1]Make your peace with me
and come out to me, and eat [a]each
of his vine and each of his fig tree
and drink each of the waters of his
own cistern, **32** until I come and take
you away [a]to a land like your own
land, a land of grain and new wine,
a land of bread and vineyards, a land
of olive oil and honey, that you may
live and not die." But do not listen to
Hezekiah when he misleads you, say-
ing, "Yahweh will deliver us." **33** [a]Has
any one of the gods of the nations
delivered his land from the hand of
the king of Assyria? **34** [a]Where are
the gods of Hamath and [b]Arpad?
Where are the gods of Sepharvaim,
Hena, and [c,1]Ivvah? When have they
delivered Samaria from my hand?
**35** Who among all the gods of the
lands [1]have delivered their land from
my hand, [a]that Yahweh would deliver
Jerusalem from my hand?'"

**36** But the people were silent and
answered him not a word, for the
king's commandment was, "Do not
answer him." **37** Then [a]Eliakim the
son of Hilkiah, who *was* over the
household, and Shebna the scribe
and Joah the son of Asaph, the re-
corder, came to Hezekiah [b]with their
clothes torn and told him the words
of Rabshakeh.

---

**18:21** [2]Lit *palm* **18:22** [a]2Ki 18:4; 2Chr 31:1 **18:23** [1]Lit *please exchange pledges* **18:24** [1]Lit *turn away the face of* [2]Or *governor* **18:25** [1]Lit *without Yahweh* **18:26** [a]Ezr 4:7; Da 2:4 [1]Lit *hear* [2]Hebrew **18:28** [1]Lit *and spoke, saying,* **18:29** [a]2Chr 32:15 [1]Ancient versions *my* **18:31** [a]1Ki 4:20, 25 [1]Lit *Make with me a blessing* **18:32** [a]Dt 8:7-9; 11:12 **18:33** [a]2Ki 19:12; Is 10:10, 11 **18:34** [a]2Ki 19:13 [b]Is 10:9 [c]2Ki 17:24 [1]In 2Ki 17:24, *Avva* **18:35** [a]Ps 2:1-3; 59:7 [1]Lit *who have* **18:37** [a]2Ki 18:26 [b]2Ki 6:30

### *Isaiah Tells Hezekiah Not to Be Afraid*

19 [a]Now it happened that when
King Hezekiah heard *it*, he
[b]tore his clothes, [c]covered himself
with sackcloth, and entered the
house of Yahweh. **2** Then he sent
Eliakim who *was* over the household
with Shebna the scribe and the
elders of the priests, [a]covered with
sackcloth, to [b]Isaiah the prophet the
son of Amoz. **3** And they said to him,
"Thus says Hezekiah, 'This day is a
day of distress, reproof, and rejec-
tion; for children have come to the
point of breaking forth, but there is
no strength to give birth. **4** [a]Perhaps
Yahweh your God will hear all the
words of Rabshakeh, whom his
master the king of Assyria has sent
[b]to [1]reproach the living God, and will
reprove the words which Yahweh
your God has heard. Therefore, lift
up a prayer for [c]the remnant that is
left.'" **5** So the servants of King Heze-
kiah came to Isaiah. **6** And Isaiah
said to them, "Thus you shall say to
your master, 'Thus says Yahweh, "Do
not be afraid because of the words
that you have heard, with which the
[a]young men of the king of Assyria
[b]have blasphemed Me. **7** Behold, I
will put a spirit in him so that [a]he
will hear a report and return to his
own land. And [b]I will make him fall
by the sword in his own land."'"

### *Sennacherib Deceives Hezekiah*

**8** Then Rabshakeh returned and
found the king of Assyria fighting
against [a]Libnah, for he had heard that
[1]the king had set out from [b]Lachish.
**9** Then he heard *them* say concerning
Tirhakah king of [1]Ethiopia, "Behold,
he has come out to fight against
you." So he sent messengers again to
Hezekiah saying, **10** "Thus you shall
say to Hezekiah king of [1]Judah, 'Do
not [a]let your God in whom you trust
deceive you, saying, "[b]Jerusalem
will not be given into the hand of
the king of Assyria." **11** Behold, you
have heard what the kings of Assyria
have done to all the lands, devoting
them to destruction. So will you be
delivered? **12** [a]Did the gods of [1]those
nations which my fathers brought
to ruin deliver them, *even* [b]Gozan
and [c]Haran and Rezeph and [d]the
sons of Eden who *were* in Telassar?
**13** [a]Where is the king of Hamath, the
king of Arpad, the king of the city
of Sepharvaim, and *of* Hena and
Ivvah?'"

### *Hezekiah's Prayer*

**14** Then [a]Hezekiah took the [1]letter
from the hand of the messengers
and read it, and he went up to the
house of Yahweh and [2]spread it out
before Yahweh. **15** And Hezekiah
prayed before Yahweh and said,
"O Yahweh, the God of Israel, [a]who
is [1]enthroned *above* the cherubim,
[b]You are the God, You alone, of all
the kingdoms of the earth. You have
made heaven and earth. **16** [a]Incline
Your ear, O Yahweh, and hear; [b]open
Your eyes, O Yahweh, and see; and
listen to the words of Sennacherib,

---

◆ **19:1** [a]2Chr 32:20-22; Is 37:1 [b]2Ki 18:37 [c]1Ki 21:27 **19:2** [a]2Sa 3:31 [b]Is 1:1; 2:1 **19:4** [a]Jos 14:12; 2Sa 16:12 [b]2Ki 18:35 [c]Is 1:9 [1]Or *defy*, cf. 1Sa 17:26 **19:6** [a]2Ki 18:17 [b]2Ki 18:22-25, 30, 35 **19:7** [a]2Ki 7:6 [b]2Ki 19:37 **19:8** [a]Jos 10:29 [b]2Ki 18:14 [1]Lit *he* **19:9** [1]Or *Cush*, cf. Ge 10:6 **19:10** [a]2Ki 18:5 [b]2Ki 18:30 [1]Lit *Judah, saying,* **19:12** [a]2Ki 18:33 [b]2Ki 17:6 [c]Ge 11:31 [d]Is 37:12 [1]Lit *the* **19:13** [a]2Ki 18:34 **19:14** [a]Is 37:14 [1]Lit *letters...read them* [2]Lit *Hezekiah spread* **19:15** [a]Ex 25:22; Is 37:14 [b]2Ki 5:15 [1]Lit *seated* **19:16** [a]Ps 31:2; Is 37:17 [b]1Ki 8:29; 2Chr 6:40

who sent them [c]to [1]reproach the
living God. 17 Truly, O Yahweh, the
kings of Assyria have laid waste
the nations and their lands 18 and
have put their gods into the fire, [a]for
they were not gods but the work of
men's hands, wood and stone. So
they have destroyed them. 19 But
now, O Yahweh our God, I pray, save
us from his hand [a]that all the king-
doms of the earth may know that You
alone, O [b]Yahweh, are God."

### *Isaiah Speaks of Sennacherib's Fall*

20 Then Isaiah the son of Amoz sent
*word* to Hezekiah saying, "Thus says
Yahweh, the God of Israel, 'Because
you have prayed to Me about Sen-
nacherib king of Assyria, [a]I have
heard *you.*' 21 This is the word that
Yahweh has spoken against him:

'She has despised you
and mocked you,
[a]The virgin daughter of Zion;
She [b]has shaken *her*
head behind you,
The daughter of Jerusalem!
22 'Whom have you [a,1]reproached
and [b]blasphemed?
And against whom have you
heightened *your* voice,
And [2]haughtily lifted
up your eyes?
Against the [c]Holy
One of Israel!
23 '[a]Through your
messengers you have
[1]reproached the Lord,
And you have said,
"With my many chariots
I came up to the heights
of the mountains,
To the remotest parts
of Lebanon;
And I [2]cut down its tall cedars
*and* its choice cypresses.
And I [2]entered its farthest
lodging place, its
[b]thickest forest.
24 "I dug *wells* and drank
foreign waters,
And with the sole of my
feet I [a,1]dried up
All the rivers of [2]Egypt."
25 '[a]Have you not heard?
Long ago I did it;
From days of old I formed it.
[b]Now I have brought it to pass,
That you should devastate
fortified cities
into ruinous heaps.
26 'So their inhabitants were
short of power,
They were dismayed
and put to shame;
They were [a]as the plant
of the field and
as the green herb,
As grass on the rooftops is
scorched before it rises.
27 'But [a]I know your sitting down,
And your going out and
your coming in,
And your raging against Me.
28 'Because of your raging
against Me,
And because your
[1]presumptuousness has
come up to My ears,

**19:16** [c]2Ki 19:4 [1]Or *defy*, cf. 1Sa 17:26 **19:18** [a]Is 44:9-20; Ac 17:29 **19:19** [a]1Ki 8:42, 43 [b]2Ki 19:15
**19:20** [a]2Ki 20:5 **19:21** [a]Jer 14:17; Lam 2:13 [b]Ps 109:25; Mt 27:39 **19:22** [a]2Ki 19:4 [b]2Ki 19:6 [c]Is 5:24; 30:11-15 [1]Or *defied*, cf. 1Sa 17:26 [2]Lit *on high* **19:23** [a]2Ki 18:17 [b]2Chr 26:10; Is 10:18 [1]Or *defied*, cf. 1Sa 17:26 [2]As in some ancient versions; M.T. *will cut...will enter* **19:24** [a]Is 19:6 [1]As in some ancient versions; M.T. *will dry up* [2]Lit *the besieged place* **19:25** [a]Is 45:7 [b]Is 10:5 **19:26** [a]Ps 129:6
**19:27** [a]Ps 139:1 **19:28** [1]Or *complacency*

Therefore I [a]will put My
hook in your nose,
And My bridle in your lips,
And [b]I will turn you back
by the way which you came.
**29** 'Then this shall be [a]the sign
for you: [1]you will eat this year what
grows of its own accord, in the
second year what springs from the
same, and in the third year sow, reap,
plant vineyards, and eat their fruit.
**30** [a]And the surviving remnant of the
house of Judah will again take root
downward and bear fruit upward.
**31** For out of Jerusalem will go forth
a remnant, and [a]out of Mount Zion
[1]survivors. [b]The zeal of [2]Yahweh will
do this.
**32** 'Therefore thus says Yahweh
concerning the king of Assyria, "[a]He
will not come to this city or shoot an
arrow there; and he will not come
before it with a shield or throw up a
siege ramp against it. **33** [a]By the way
that he came, by the same he will
return, and he shall not come to this
city,"' declares Yahweh. **34** '[a]Indeed I
will defend this city to save it for My
own sake and [b]for My servant David's
sake.'"
**35** [a]Now it happened that night,
that the angel of Yahweh went out
and struck 185,000 in the camp of
the Assyrians. And the [1]men arose
early in the morning, and behold,
all of [2]them were dead bodies. **36** So
[a]Sennacherib king of Assyria set out
and went away and returned *home*
and lived at [b]Nineveh. **37** Now it
happened that as he was worship-
ing in the house of Nisroch his god,
[a,1]Adrammelech and Sharezer struck
him down with the sword; and they
escaped into [b]the land of Ararat. And
[c]Esarhaddon his son became king in
his place.

### *Hezekiah's Illness and Restoration*

**20** [a]In those days Hezekiah be-
came ill to the point of death.
And Isaiah the prophet the son of
Amoz came to him and said to him,
"Thus says Yahweh, '[b]Set your house
in order, for you shall die and not
live.'" **2** Then he turned his face to
the wall and prayed to Yahweh, say-
ing, **3** "[a]Remember now, O Yahweh,
I beseech You, [b]how I have walked
before You in truth and with a whole
heart and have done what is good
in Your sight." And [c]Hezekiah wept
[1]greatly. **4** Now it happened that
Isaiah had not gone out of the mid-
dle court, and the word of Yahweh
came to him, saying, **5** "Return and
say to [a]Hezekiah the ruler of My
people, 'Thus says Yahweh, the God
of your father David, "[b]I have heard
your prayer, [c]I have seen your tears;
behold, I will heal you. On the third
day you shall go up to the house of
Yahweh. **6** And I will add fifteen years
to your [1]life, and I will deliver you
and this city from the hand of the
king of Assyria; and [a]I will defend
this city for My own sake and for My
servant David's sake."'" **7** Then Isaiah
said, "Take a cake of figs." And they

---

**19:28** [a]Eze 19:9; 29:4 [b]2Ki 19:33, 36 **19:29** [a]Ex 3:12; 2Ki 20:8, 9 [1]Lit *eating* **19:30** [a]2Ki 19:4; 2Chr 32:22, 23 **19:31** [a]Is 10:20 [b]Is 9:7 [1]Lit *those who escape* [2]Some ancient mss *Yahweh of hosts* **19:32** [a]Is 8:7-10 **19:33** [a]2Ki 19:28 **19:34** [a]2Ki 20:6; Is 31:5 [b]1Ki 11:12, 13 **19:35** [a]2Sa 24:16; 2Chr 32:21 [1]Lit *they* [2]Assyrians **19:36** [a]2Ki 19:7, 28, 33 [b]Jon 1:2 **19:37** [a]2Ki 19:17, 31 [b]Ge 8:4; Jer 51:27 [c]Ezr 4:2 [1]Some ancient mss *Adrammelech and Sharezer his sons struck him down*
◆ **20:1** [a]2Chr 32:24; Is 38:1-22 [b]2Sa 17:23 **20:3** [a]Ne 5:19; 13:14, 22, 31 [b]2Ki 18:3-6 [c]2Sa 12:21, 22 [1]Lit *great weeping* **20:5** [a]1Sa 9:16; 10:1 [b]2Ki 19:20 [c]Ps 39:12 **20:6** [a]2Ki 19:34 [1]Lit *days*

took and laid *it* on the boil, and he
was restored to life.
8 Now Hezekiah said to Isaiah,
"What will be the sign that Yahweh
will heal me, and that I shall go up
to the house of Yahweh the third
day?" 9 And Isaiah said, "[a]This shall
be the sign to you from Yahweh,
that Yahweh will do the thing that
He has spoken: shall the shadow go
forward ten steps or turn back ten
steps?" 10 So [1]Hezekiah [2]answered,
"It is easy for the shadow to stretch
forward ten steps; no, but let the
shadow turn backward ten steps."
11 Isaiah the prophet cried to Yahweh,
and [a]He turned the shadow on the
[1]stairway back ten steps by which it
had gone down on the [1]stairway of
Ahaz.

### *Hezekiah Shows Babylon His Treasures*

12 [a]At that time [1]Berodach-baladan a
son of Baladan, king of Babylon, sent
letters and a present to Hezekiah, for
he heard that Hezekiah had been sick.
13 And Hezekiah listened to them,
and showed them [a]all his treasure
house, the silver and the gold and the
spices and the good oil and the house
of his armor and all that was found
in his treasuries. There was nothing
in his house nor in all his dominion
that Hezekiah did not show them.
14 Then Isaiah the prophet came
to King Hezekiah and said to him,
"What did these men say, and from
where have they come to you?" And
Hezekiah said, "They have come from
*a far country*, from Babylon." 15 And
he said, "What have they seen in your
house?" So Hezekiah said, "They have
seen all that is in my house; there is
nothing among my treasuries that I
have not shown them."
16 Then Isaiah said to Hezekiah,
"Hear the word of Yahweh. 17 'Behold,
the days are coming when [a]all that
is in your house, and all that your
fathers have treasured up to this day
will be carried to Babylon; nothing
shall be left,' says Yahweh. 18 'And
some [a]of your sons who will issue
from you, whom you will beget, will
be taken away; and they will become
[b]officials in the palace of the king of
Babylon.'" 19 Then Hezekiah said to
Isaiah, "The word of Yahweh which
you have spoken is [a]good." For he
said, "Will it not be *good*, if there will
be peace and truth in my days?"
20 [a]Now the rest of the acts of
Hezekiah and all his might, and how
he [b]made the pool and the conduit
and brought water into the city, are
they not written in the Book of the
Chronicles of the Kings of Judah?
21 [a]So Hezekiah slept with his fa-
thers, and Manasseh his son became
king in his place.

### *Manasseh Reigns over Judah*

21 [a]Manasseh was twelve years old
when he became king, and he
reigned fifty-five years in Jerusalem;
and his mother's name was Heph-
zibah. 2 [a]And he did what was evil
in the sight of Yahweh, [b]according
to the abominations of the nations
whom Yahweh dispossessed before
the sons of Israel. 3 Indeed, [a]he rebuilt

**20:9** [a]Is 38:7 **20:10** [1]Heb *Yehezekiah*; lit *Yahweh will strengthen* [2]Lit *said* **20:11** [a]Jos 10:12-14; Is 38:8 [1]Lit *steps* **20:12** [a]2Chr 32:31; Is 39:1-8 [1]Many mss and ancient versions *Merodach-baladan*, cf. Is 39:1 **20:13** [a]2Chr 32:27 **20:17** [a]2Ki 24:13; 25:13-15; 2Chr 36:10; Jer 52:17-19 **20:18** [a]2Ki 24:12; 2Chr 33:11 [b]Da 1:3-7 **20:19** [a]1Sa 3:18 **20:20** [a]2Chr 32:32 [b]Ne 3:16 **20:21** [a]2Chr 32:33
◆ **21:1** [a]2Chr 33:1-9 **21:2** [a]Jer 15:4 [b]2Ki 16:3 **21:3** [a]2Ki 18:4

the high places which Hezekiah his
father had destroyed; and [b]he erected
altars for Baal and made an [1]Asherah,
as Ahab king of Israel had done, and
[c]worshiped all the host of heaven and
served them. **4** [a]And he built altars in
the house of Yahweh, of which Yahweh
had said, "[b]In Jerusalem I will put My
name." **5** Indeed, he built altars for [a]all
the host of heaven in [b]the two courts
of the house of Yahweh. **6** [a]He even
made his son pass through the fire,
[b]practiced soothsaying and interpret-
ed omens, and dealt with mediums
and spiritists. He did much that was
evil in the sight of Yahweh provoking
*Him to anger*. **7** Then [a]he put the grav-
en image of Asherah, which he had
made, in the house of which Yahweh
had said to David and to Solomon his
son, "[b]In this house and in Jerusalem,
which I have chosen from all the tribes
of Israel, I will put My name forever.
**8** And I [a]will not make the foot of
Israel wander anymore from the land
which I gave their fathers, if only they
will be careful to do according to all
that I have commanded them, and
according to all the law that My ser-
vant Moses commanded them." **9** But
they did not listen, and Manasseh
[a]led them astray in order to do more
evil than the nations whom Yahweh
destroyed before the sons of Israel.

### *Yahweh Brings Calamity on Israel*

**10** Then Yahweh spoke by the hand
of His slaves the prophets, saying,
**11** "[a]Because Manasseh king of Judah
has done these abominations—[b]he
has done evil more than all the Am-
orites did who *were* before him—and
[c]has also made Judah sin [d]with his
idols, **12** therefore thus says Yahweh,
the God of Israel, 'Behold, I am
bringing *such* calamity on Jerusalem
and Judah, that whoever hears of it,
[a]both his ears will tingle. **13** [a]And I
will stretch over Jerusalem the line of
Samaria and the level of the house of
Ahab, and I will wipe Jerusalem as one
wipes a dish—he wipes it and turns
it upside down. **14** And I will abandon
the remnant of My inheritance and
give them into the hand of their
enemies, and they will become as
plunder and spoil to all their enemies;
**15** because they have done what is evil
in My sight, and have been provoking
Me to anger since the day their fathers
came out of Egypt, even to this day.'"

**16** [a]Moreover, Manasseh shed very
much innocent blood until he had
filled Jerusalem from one end to an-
other; besides his sin [b]with which
he made Judah sin, in doing what is
evil in the sight of Yahweh. **17** [a]Now
the rest of the acts of Manasseh and
all that he did and his sin which he
sinned, are they not written in the
Book of the Chronicles of the Kings
of Judah? **18** [a]And Manasseh slept
with his fathers and was buried in
the garden of his own house, [b]in the
garden of Uzza. And Amon his son
became king in his place.

### *Amon Reigns over Judah*

**19** [a]Amon was twenty-two years old
when he became king, and he reigned

**21:3** [b]1Ki 16:31-33 [c]Dt 17:2-5; 2Ki 17:16; 23:5 [1]A wooden symbol of a female deity **21:4** [a]2Ki 16:10-16 [b]2Sa 7:13; 1Ki 8:29 **21:5** [a]2Ki 23:4, 5 [b]1Ki 7:12; 2Ki 23:12 **21:6** [a]Lv 18:21; 2Ki 16:3; 17:17 [b]Lv 19:26, 31; Dt 18:10-14 **21:7** [a]Dt 16:21; 2Ki 23:6 [b]1Ki 8:29; 9:3; 2Chr 7:12, 16 **21:8** [a]2Sa 7:10; 2Ki 18:11, 12 **21:9** [a]Pr 29:12 **21:11** [a]2Ki 21:2; 24:3, 4 [b]Ge 15:16; 1Ki 21:26 [c]2Ki 21:16 [d]2Ki 21:21 **21:12** [a]1Sa 3:11; Jer 19:3 **21:13** [a]Is 34:11; Am 7:7, 8 **21:16** [a]2Ki 24:4 [b]2Ki 21:11 **21:17** [a]2Chr 33:11-19 **21:18** [a]2Chr 33:20 [b]2Ki 21:26 **21:19** [a]2Chr 33:21-23

two years in Jerusalem; and his
mother's name was Meshullemeth
the daughter of Haruz of Jotbah.
20 And he did what was evil in the
sight of Yahweh, [a]as Manasseh his
father had done. 21 And he walked in
all the way that his father had walked
and served the idols that his father
had served and worshiped them.
22 So [a]he forsook Yahweh, the God
of his fathers, and did not walk in the
way of Yahweh. 23 [a]Then the servants
of Amon conspired against him and
put the king to death in his own
house. 24 Then [a]the people of the
land struck down all those who had
conspired against King Amon, and
the people of the land made Josiah
his son king in his place. 25 Now the
rest of the acts of Amon which he did,
are they not written in the Book of
the Chronicles of the Kings of Judah?
26 And he was buried in his grave [a]in
the garden of Uzza, and Josiah his
son became king in his place.

### *Josiah Reigns over Judah*

22 [a]Josiah was eight years old
when he became king, and he
reigned thirty-one years in Jerusalem;
and his mother's name was Jedidah
the daughter of Adaiah of [b]Bozkath.
2 And he did what was right in the
sight of Yahweh and walked in all the
way of his father David and did not
[a]turn aside to the right or to the left.

3 Now it happened [a]in the eigh-
teenth year of King Josiah, that the
king sent Shaphan, the son of Azaliah
the son of Meshullam the scribe, to
*the house of* Yahweh saying, 4 "[a]Go
up to Hilkiah the high priest that
he may [1]count the money brought
into the house of Yahweh which the
doorkeepers have gathered from
the people. 5 [a]And let them give it
into the hand of those who do the
work, who have the oversight of
the house of Yahweh, and let them
give it to those who do the work,
who are in the house of Yahweh, to
repair the [1]damages of the house, 6 to
the craftsmen and the builders and
the masons and for buying timber
and hewn stone to repair the house.
7 Only [a]no accounting shall be made
with them for the money given into
their hands, for they deal faithfully."

### *Hilkiah Finds the Book of the Law*

8 Then Hilkiah the high priest said to
Shaphan the scribe, "[a]I have found
the book of the law in the house
of Yahweh." And Hilkiah gave the
book to Shaphan and he read it.
9 Then Shaphan the scribe came to
the king and responded to the king
with a word and said, "Your servants
have poured out the money that was
found in the house and have given
it into the hand of those who do
the work, who have the oversight of
the house of Yahweh." 10 Moreover,
Shaphan the scribe told the king
saying, "Hilkiah the priest has given
me a book." And Shaphan read it in
the presence of the king.

11 Now it happened that when the
king heard the words of the book of
the law, [a]he tore his clothes. 12 Then
the king commanded Hilkiah the
priest, [a]Ahikam the son of Shaphan,

---

**21:20** [a]2Ki 21:2-6, 11, 16 **21:22** [a]2Ki 22:17; 1Chr 28:9 **21:23** [a]2Ki 12:20; 14:19 **21:24** [a]2Ki 14:5
**21:26** [a]2Ki 21:18 ◆ **22:1** [a]2Chr 34:1 [b]Jos 15:39 **22:2** [a]Dt 5:32; Jos 1:7 **22:3** [a]2Chr 34:8
**22:4** [a]2Ki 12:4, 9, 10 [1]Or *total* **22:5** [a]2Ki 12:11-14 [1]Lit *breach* **22:7** [a]2Ki 12:15; 1Co 4:2
**22:8** [a]Dt 31:24-26; 2Chr 34:14, 15 **22:11** [a]Ge 37:34; Jos 7:6 **22:12** [a]2Ki 25:22; Jer 26:24

[b,1]Achbor the son of Micaiah, Sha-
phan the scribe, and Asaiah the
king's servant, saying, 13 "Go, inquire
of Yahweh for me and the people and
all Judah, concerning the words of
this book that has been found, for
[a]great is the wrath of Yahweh which
is set aflame against us, because our
fathers have not listened to the words
of this book, to do according to all
that is written concerning us."

### *Huldah Says Yahweh Is Bringing Evil*

14 So Hilkiah the priest, Ahikam,
Achbor, Shaphan, and Asaiah went
to Huldah the prophetess, the wife of
Shallum the son of [a,1]Tikvah, the son
of Harhas, keeper of the wardrobe
(now she lived in Jerusalem in the
[b]Second Quarter); and they spoke to
her. 15 And she said to them, "Thus
says Yahweh, the God of Israel, 'Say
to the man who sent you to me,
16 thus says Yahweh, "Behold, I [a]am
bringing evil on this place and on
its inhabitants, *even* all the words of
the book which the king of Judah has
read. 17 [a]Because they have forsaken
Me and have burned incense to
other gods that they might provoke
Me to anger with all the work of
their hands, therefore My wrath is
set aflame against this place, and it
shall not be quenched."' 18 But to
[a]the king of Judah who sent you to
inquire of Yahweh thus you shall say
to him, 'Thus says Yahweh, the God
of Israel, "*Regarding* the words which
you have heard, 19 [a]because your
heart was soft and [b]you humbled
yourself before Yahweh when you
heard what I spoke against this place
and against its inhabitants that they
should become [c]an object of horror,
and a [d]curse, and you have [e]torn your
clothes and wept before Me, I truly
have heard you," declares Yahweh.
20 "Therefore, behold, I will gather
you to your fathers, and [a]you will
be gathered to your grave in peace,
so your eyes will not see all the evil
which I will bring on this place."'" So
they brought back word to the king.

### *Josiah Reads the Book of the Covenant*

23 [a]Then the king sent, and they
gathered to him all the elders
of Judah and Jerusalem. 2 And the
king went up to the house of Yahweh
and all the men of Judah and all the
inhabitants of Jerusalem with him,
and the priests and the prophets and
all the people, both small and great;
and [a]he read in their hearing all the
words of the book of the covenant
[b]which was found in the house of
Yahweh. 3 [a]Then the king stood by
the pillar and cut a covenant before
Yahweh, [b]to walk after Yahweh, and
to keep His commandments and His
testimonies and His statutes with all
*his* heart and all *his* soul, to establish
the words of this covenant that were
written in this book. And all the
people [1]entered into the covenant.
4 Then the king commanded Hilki-
ah the high priest and [a]the priests of
the second order and the [1]doorkeep-
ers, [b]to bring out of the temple of

**22:12** [b]2Chr 34:20 [1]In 2Chr 34:20, *Abdon, son of Micah* **22:13** [a]Dt 29:23-28; 31:17, 18
**22:14** [a]2Chr 34:22 [b]Zep 1:10 [1]In 2Chr 34:22, *Tokhath, son of Hasrah* **22:16** [a]Dt 29:27; Da 9:11-14
**22:17** [a]Dt 29:25, 26; 2Ki 21:22 **22:18** [a]2Chr 34:26 **22:19** [a]1Sa 24:5; Ps 51:17 [b]Ex 10:3; 1Ki 21:29
[c]Lv 26:31 [d]Jer 26:6 [e]2Ki 22:11 **22:20** [a]2Ki 23:30 ◆ **23:1** [a]2Chr 34:29-32 **23:2** [a]Dt 31:10-13
[b]2Ki 22:8 **23:3** [a]2Ki 11:14, 17 [b]Dt 13:4 [1]Lit *took a stand in* **23:4** [a]2Ki 25:18; Jer 52:24 [b]2Ki 21:3, 7;
2Chr 33:3 [1]Lit *keepers of the threshold*

Yahweh all the vessels that were made
for Baal, for [2]Asherah, and for all the
host of heaven; and [c]he burned them
outside Jerusalem in the fields of the
Kidron, and carried their ashes to
Bethel. **5** And he did away with the
idolatrous priests whom the kings of
Judah had appointed and who burn
incense in the high places in the cities
of Judah and in the surrounding area
of Jerusalem, as well as those who
burned incense to Baal, to the sun and
to the moon and to the constellations
and to all the [a]host of heaven. **6** And
he brought out the Asherah from the
house of Yahweh outside Jerusalem to
the brook Kidron, and burned it at the
brook Kidron, and [a]ground *it* to dust,
and [b]threw its dust on the graves of
the [1]common people. **7** He also tore
down the houses of the [a]*male* cult
prostitutes which *were* in the house
of Yahweh, where [b]the women were
weaving [1]hangings for the Asherah.
**8** Then he brought all the priests
from the cities of Judah and defiled
the high places where the priests
had burned incense, from [a]Geba to
Beersheba; and he tore down the high
places of the gates which *were* at the
entrance of the gate of Joshua the
ruler of the city, which *were* on one's
left at the city gate. **9** Nevertheless
[a]the priests of the high places did
not go up to the altar of Yahweh in
Jerusalem, but they ate unleavened
bread among their brothers. **10** [a]He
also defiled [1]Topheth, which is in the
valley of the son of Hinnom, [b]that
no man might make his son or his
daughter pass through the fire for
[c]Molech. **11** And he did away with the
horses which the kings of Judah had
given to the [a]sun, at the entrance of
the house of Yahweh, by the chamber
of Nathan-melech the official, which
*was* in the precincts; and he burned
the chariots of the sun with fire.
**12** [a]Also, the altars which *were* on
the roof, the upper chamber of Ahaz,
which the kings of Judah had made,
and [b]the altars which Manasseh had
made in the two courts of the house
of Yahweh, the king tore down; and he
[1]crushed them there and [c]threw their
dust into the brook Kidron. **13** And
the high places which *were* before
Jerusalem, which *were* on the right
of [a]the mount of destruction which
Solomon the king of Israel had built
for [b]Ashtoreth the detestable idol of
the Sidonians, and for [c]Chemosh
the detestable idol of Moab, and for
Milcom the abomination of the sons
of Ammon, the king defiled. **14** [a]And
he broke in pieces the *sacred* pillars
and cut down the Asherim and [b]filled
their places with human bones.

**15** Furthermore, [a]the altar that
*was* at Bethel *and* the [b]high place
which Jeroboam the son of Nebat,
who made Israel sin, had made, even
that altar and the high place he tore
down. Then he [c,1]demolished its
stones, ground them to dust, and
burned the Asherah. **16** Then Josiah
turned, and he saw the graves that
*were* there on the mountain, and he
sent and took the bones from the
graves and burned *them* on the altar

**23:4** [c]2Ki 23:15 [2]A wooden symbol of a female deity, so in ch **23:5** [a]2Ki 21:3 **23:6** [a]2Ki 23:15 [b]2Chr 34:4 [1]Lit *sons of the people* **23:7** [a]1Ki 14:24; 15:12 [b]Ex 35:25, 26; Eze 16:16 [1]Or *tents*; lit *houses* **23:8** [a]Jos 21:17; 1Ki 15:22 **23:9** [a]Eze 44:10-14 **23:10** [a]Is 30:33; Jer 7:31, 32; 19:4-6 [b]Lv 18:21 [c]1Ki 11:7 [1]Lit *place of burning* **23:11** [a]Dt 4:19; Job 31:26; Eze 8:16 **23:12** [a]Jer 19:13; Zep 1:5 [b]2Ki 21:5; 2Chr 33:5 [c]2Ki 23:4, 6 [1]Or *ran from there* **23:13** [a]1Ki 11:7 [b]1Ki 11:5 [c]Nu 21:29 **23:14** [a]Dt 7:5, 25 [b]2Ki 23:16 **23:15** [a]1Ki 13:1 [b]1Ki 12:28-33 [c]2Ki 23:6 [1]As in Gr; Heb *burned the high place*

and defiled it [a]according to the word of Yahweh which the man of God proclaimed, who proclaimed these things. **17** Then he said, "What is this monument that I see?" And the men of the city told him, "[a]It is the grave of the man of God who came from Judah and proclaimed these things which you have done against the altar of Bethel." **18** And he said, "Let him alone; let no one move his bones." So they [1]left his bones undisturbed [a]with the bones of the prophet who came from Samaria. **19** And also all the houses of the high places which *were* [a]in the cities of Samaria, which the kings of Israel had made provoking [1]Yahweh to anger, Josiah removed; and he did to them [2]just as he had done in Bethel. **20** And all the priests of the high places who *were* there [a]he [1]slaughtered on the altars and burned human bones on them. Then he returned to Jerusalem.

### *Josiah Celebrates the Passover*

**21** Then the king commanded all the people saying, "[a]Celebrate the Passover to Yahweh your God [b]as it is written in this book of the covenant." **22** [a]For such a Passover had not been celebrated from the days of the judges who judged Israel, nor in all the days of the kings of Israel and of the kings of Judah. **23** But in the eighteenth year of King Josiah, this Passover was celebrated to Yahweh in Jerusalem.

**24** Moreover, [a]the mediums and the spiritists and the [b]teraphim and [c]the idols and all the detestable things that were seen in the land of Judah and in Jerusalem, Josiah purged in order [d]that he might [1]establish the words of the law which were written [e]in the book that Hilkiah the priest found in the house of Yahweh. **25** And before him there was no king [a]like him who turned to Yahweh with all his heart and with all his soul and with all his might, according to all the law of Moses; nor did any like him arise after him.

**26** However, Yahweh did not turn from His great burning anger, His anger which burned against Judah, [a]because of all the provocations with which Manasseh had provoked Him to anger. **27** And Yahweh said, "I will remove Judah also from My presence, [a]as I have removed Israel. And [b]I will reject Jerusalem, this city which I have chosen, and the [1]house of which I said, 'My name shall be there.'"

### *Jehoahaz Reigns over Judah*

**28** Now the rest of the acts of Josiah and all that he did, are they not written in the Book of the Chronicles of the Kings of Judah? **29** [a]In his days [b]Pharaoh Neco king of Egypt went up to the king of Assyria to the river Euphrates. And King Josiah went to meet him, and when *Pharaoh Neco* saw him he put him to death at [c]Megiddo. **30** [a]And his servants drove [1]his body in a chariot from Megiddo and brought him to Jerusalem and buried him in his own tomb. [b]Then

**23:16** [a]1Ki 13:2 **23:17** [a]1Ki 13:1, 30, 31 **23:18** [a]1Ki 13:11, 31 [1]Lit *let his bones escape* **23:19** [a]2Chr 34:6, 7 [1]As in ancient versions [2]Lit *according to all the acts* **23:20** [a]2Ki 10:25; 11:18 [1]Lit *sacrificed* **23:21** [a]2Chr 35:1-17 [b]Nu 9:2-4; Dt 16:2-8 **23:22** [a]2Chr 35:18, 19 **23:24** [a]Lv 19:31; 2Ki 21:6 [b]Ge 31:19 mg [c]2Ki 21:11, 21 [d]Dt 18:10-22 [e]2Ki 22:8 [1]Or *perform* **23:25** [a]2Ki 18:5 **23:26** [a]2Ki 21:11-13; Jer 15:4 **23:27** [a]2Ki 18:11 [b]2Ki 21:13, 14 [1]Or *temple* **23:29** [a]2Chr 35:20-24 [b]Jer 46:2 [c]Jdg 5:19 **23:30** [a]2Ki 9:28 [b]2Chr 36:1-4 [1]Lit *him, dead*

the people of the land took Jehoahaz the son of Josiah and anointed him and made him king in place of his father.

### *Jehoahaz's Reign and Imprisonment*

**31** [a]Jehoahaz was twenty-three years old when he became king, and he reigned three months in Jerusalem; and his mother's name was [b]Hamutal the daughter of Jeremiah of Libnah. **32** And he did what was evil in the sight of Yahweh, [a]according to all that his fathers had done. **33** [a]And Pharaoh Neco imprisoned him at [b]Riblah in the land of [c]Hamath, that he might not reign in Jerusalem; and he imposed on the land a fine of one hundred [1]talents of silver and one talent of gold.

### *Jehoiakim Made King by Pharaoh*

**34** Then Pharaoh Neco made [a]Eliakim the son of Josiah king in the place of Josiah his father and [b]changed his name to Jehoiakim. But he took Jehoahaz and [c,1]brought *him* to Egypt, and he died there. **35** So Jehoiakim [a]gave the silver and gold to Pharaoh, but he taxed the land in order to give the money at the [1]command of Pharaoh. He exacted the silver and gold from the people of the land, each according to his valuation, to give it to Pharaoh Neco.

**36** [a]Jehoiakim was twenty-five years old when he became king, and he reigned eleven years in Jerusalem; and his mother's name was Zebidah the daughter of Pedaiah of Rumah. **37** And he did what was evil in the sight of Yahweh, [a]according to all that his fathers had done.

### *Jehoiakim Rebels Against Nebuchadnezzar*

**24** [a]In his days Nebuchadnezzar king of Babylon came up, and Jehoiakim became his servant *for* three years; then he turned and rebelled against him. **2** And Yahweh sent against him [a]marauding bands of Chaldeans, [b]marauding bands of Arameans, [c]marauding bands of Moabites, and marauding bands of Ammonites. So He sent them against Judah to destroy it, [d]according to the word of Yahweh which He had spoken by the hand of His slaves the prophets. **3** [a]Surely at the [1]command of Yahweh it came upon Judah, to remove *them* from His presence [b]because of the sins of Manasseh, according to all that he had done, **4** and [a]also for the innocent blood which he shed, for he filled Jerusalem with innocent blood; and Yahweh was not willing to pardon. **5** Now the rest of the acts of Jehoiakim and all that he did, are they not written in the Book of the Chronicles of the Kings of Judah?

### *Jehoiachin Reigns over Judah*

**6** So [a]Jehoiakim slept with his fathers, and Jehoiachin his son became king in his place. **7** [a]And the king of Egypt did not go out of his land again, [b]for the king of Babylon had taken all that belonged to the king of Egypt

**23:31** [a]1Chr 3:15; Jer 22:11 [b]2Ki 24:18 **23:32** [a]2Ki 21:2-7 **23:33** [a]2Ki 23:29 [b]2Ki 25:6 [c]1Ki 8:65 [1]A talent was approx. 75 lb. or 34 kg **23:34** [a]1Chr 3:15 [b]2Ki 24:17; 2Chr 36:4 [c]Jer 22:11, 12; Eze 19:3, 4 [1]As in Gr; Heb *he came* **23:35** [a]2Ki 23:33 [1]Lit *mouth* **23:36** [a]2Chr 36:5; Jer 22:18, 19; 26:1 **23:37** [a]2Ki 23:32 ◆ **24:1** [a]2Chr 36:6; Jer 25:1; Da 1:1, 2 **24:2** [a]Jer 35:11f [b]2Ki 6:23 [c]2Ki 13:20 [d]2Ki 23:27 **24:3** [a]2Ki 18:25 [b]2Ki 23:26 [1]Lit *mouth* **24:4** [a]2Ki 21:16 **24:6** [a]Jer 22:18, 19 **24:7** [a]Jer 37:5-7 [b]Jer 46:2

from [c]the brook of Egypt to the river
Euphrates.
**8** [a]Jehoiachin was [b]eighteen years
old when he became king, and he
reigned three months in Jerusalem;
and his mother's name was Nehushta
the daughter of Elnathan of Jerusa-
lem. **9** And he did what was evil in
the sight of Yahweh, [a]according to
all that his father had done.

### *Judah Exiled to Babylon*

**10** At that time the servants of Neb-
uchadnezzar king of Babylon went
up to Jerusalem, and the city came
under siege. **11** And Nebuchadnezzar
the king of Babylon came to the city,
while his servants were besieging it.
**12** [a]Then Jehoiachin the king of Judah
went out to the king of Babylon, he
and his mother and his servants and
his commanders and his officials.
So [b]the king of Babylon took him
captive in the eighth year of his reign.
**13** [a]And he brought out from there all
the treasures of the house of Yahweh,
and the treasures of the king's house,
and [b]cut in pieces all the vessels of
gold [c]which Solomon king of Israel
had made in the temple of Yahweh,
just as Yahweh had spoken. **14** Then
[a]he took away into exile all Jerusalem
and all the commanders and all the
mighty men of valor, [b]10,000 cap-
*tives,* and [c]all the craftsmen and the
smiths. None was left [d]except the
poorest people of the land.
**15** So [a]he took Jehoiachin away
into exile to Babylon; also the king's
mother and the king's wives and his
officials and the leading men of the
land, he led away into exile from
Jerusalem to Babylon. **16** Now all the
valiant men, [a]seven thousand, and
the craftsmen and the smiths, one
thousand, all mighty men who could
wage war, and these the king of Bab-
ylon brought into exile to Babylon.

### *Zedekiah Reigns over Judah*

**17** [a]Then the king of Babylon made
[1]his uncle Mattaniah king in his place
and changed his name to Zedekiah.
**18** [a]Zedekiah was twenty-one
years old when he became king, and
he reigned eleven years in Jerusalem;
and his mother's name was [b]Hamutal
the daughter of Jeremiah of Libnah.
**19** And he did what was evil in the
sight of Yahweh, [a]according to all
that Jehoiakim had done. **20** For
[a]through the anger of Yahweh *this*
came about in Jerusalem and Judah
until He cast them out from His
presence. And [b]Zedekiah rebelled
against the king of Babylon.

### *Nebuchadnezzar Besieges Jerusalem*

**25** [a]Now in the ninth year of
his reign, on the tenth day of
the tenth month, [b]Nebuchadnezzar
king of Babylon came, he and all his
military force, against Jerusalem, and
he camped against it and [c]built a siege
wall all around [1]it. **2** So the city came
under siege until the eleventh year
of King Zedekiah. **3** On the ninth day
of the *fourth* month [a]the famine was
so strong in the city that there was
no food for the people of the land.

**24:7** [c]Ge 15:18 **24:8** [a]1Chr 3:16 [b]2Chr 36:9 **24:9** [a]2Ki 21:2-7 **24:12** [a]Jer 22:24-30; 24:1; 29:1, 2 [b]2Chr 36:10 **24:13** [a]2Ki 20:17; Is 39:6 [b]2Ki 25:13-15 [c]1Ki 7:48-50 **24:14** [a]Jer 24:1 [b]2Ki 24:16; Jer 52:28 [c]Jer 24:1; 29:2 [d]2Ki 25:12 **24:15** [a]2Chr 36:10; Jer 22:24-28; Eze 17:12 **24:16** [a]2Ki 24:14 **24:17** [a]2Chr 36:10-13; Jer 37:1 [1]Jehoiachin's uncle **24:18** [a]Jer 27:1; 28:1; 52:1 [b]2Ki 23:31 **24:19** [a]2Ki 23:37 **24:20** [a]Dt 4:24; 29:27; 2Ki 23:26 [b]2Chr 36:13; Eze 17:15 ◆ **25:1** [a]2Chr 36:17-20; Jer 39:1-7 [b]Jer 21:2; 34:1, 2; Eze 24:2 [c]Eze 21:22 [1]Lit *against it* **25:3** [a]2Ki 6:24, 25; Lam 4:9, 10

**4** [a]Then the city was broken into, and
all the men of war *fled* by night by
way of the gate between the two walls
beside [b]the king's garden, though the
Chaldeans were all around the city.
And [1]they went by way of the Arabah.
**5** But the military force of the Chal-
deans pursued the king and overtook
him in the plains of Jericho and all
his military force was scattered from
him. **6** Then [a]they seized the king
and [b]brought him up to the king of
Babylon at [c]Riblah, and they spoke
*their* judgment on him. **7** [a]And they
slaughtered the sons of Zedekiah
before his eyes; then he [b]blinded
the eyes of Zedekiah and bound him
with bronze fetters and brought him
to Babylon.

### *Jerusalem Burned*

**8** [a]Now on the seventh day of the
[b]fifth month, which was the nine-
teenth year of King Nebuchadnezzar,
king of Babylon, Nebuzaradan the
captain of the guard, a servant of the
king of Babylon, came to Jerusalem.
**9** [a]And he burned the house of Yah-
weh, [b]the king's house, and all the
houses of Jerusalem; even every great
house he burned with fire. **10** So all
the military force of the Chaldeans
who *were with* the captain of the
guard [a]tore down the walls around
Jerusalem. **11** Then [a]the rest of the
people who were left in the city and
the defectors who had defected to the
king of Babylon and the rest of the
multitude, Nebuzaradan the captain
of the guard took away into exile.
**12** But the captain of the guard left
some of [a]the poorest of the land to
be vinedressers and plowmen.

**13** [a]Now the bronze pillars which
were in the house of Yahweh, and
the stands and [b]the bronze sea
which were in the house of Yahweh,
the Chaldeans shattered and carried
the [1]bronze to Babylon. **14** [a]They
also took away the pots, the shovels,
the snuffers, the spoons, and all the
bronze vessels which were used to
minister. **15** The captain of the guard
also took away the firepans and the
bowls, what was fine gold and what
was fine silver. **16** The two pillars,
the one sea, and the stands which
Solomon had made for the house of
Yahweh—[a]the bronze of all these
vessels was beyond weight. **17** [a]The
height of the one pillar was eigh-
teen [1]cubits, and a bronze capital
was on it; the height of the capital
was three [1]cubits, with a network
and pomegranates on the capital
all around, all of bronze. And the
second pillar was like these with
network.

**18** Then the captain of the guard
took [a]Seraiah the chief priest and
[b]Zephaniah the second priest,
with the three [1]doorkeepers of the
temple. **19** And from the city he took
one official who was overseer of the
men of war, and [a]five [1]of the king's
advisers who were found in the city;
and the [2]scribe of the commander of
the army who mustered the people

---

***25:4*** *[a]Eze 33:21* *[b]Ne 3:15* [1]As in some ancient mss and versions; M.T. *he* **25:6** [a]Jer 34:21, 22 [b]Jer 32:4 [c]2Ki 23:33 **25:7** [a]Jer 39:6, 7 [b]Eze 12:13 **25:8** [a]Jer 52:12 [b]Jer 39:8-12 **25:9** [a]1Ki 9:8; 2Chr 36:19; Ps 74:3-7 [b]Am 2:5 **25:10** [a]2Ki 14:13; Ne 1:3 **25:11** [a]2Chr 36:20 **25:12** [a]2Ki 24:14; Jer 40:7 **25:13** [a]1Ki 7:15-22; 2Ki 20:17; 2Chr 3:15-17; 36:18 [b]1Ki 7:23-26; 2Chr 4:2-4 [1]Lit *bronze of them* **25:14** [a]Ex 27:3; 1Ki 7:47-50; 2Chr 4:16 **25:16** [a]1Ki 7:47 **25:17** [a]1Ki 7:15-22 [1]A cubit was approx. 18 in. or 45 cm **25:18** [a]1Chr 6:14; Ezr 7:1 [b]Jer 21:1; 29:25, 29 [1]Lit *keepers of the door* **25:19** [a]Es 1:14 [1]Lit *men of those seeing the king's face* [2]Or *scribe, a captain*

of the land; and sixty men of the
people of the land who were found
in the city. **20** And Nebuzaradan the
captain of the guard took them and
led them to the king of Babylon at
[a]Riblah. **21** Then the king of Babylon
struck them down and put them
to death at Riblah in the land of
Hamath. [a]So Judah went into exile
from its land.

### *Gedaliah Appointed Judah's Governor*

**22** Now *as for* the people who were
left in the land of Judah, whom Neb-
uchadnezzar king of Babylon had
left, he appointed [a]Gedaliah the son
of Ahikam, the son of Shaphan over
them. **23** [a]Then all the commanders
of the military forces, they and *their*
men, heard that the king of Babylon
had appointed Gedaliah *governor*. So
they came to Gedaliah to [b]Mizpah,
namely, Ishmael the son of Nethani-
ah, and Johanan the son of Kareah,
and Seraiah the son of Tanhumeth
the Netophathite, and Jaazaniah the
son of the Maacathite, they and their
men. **24** Then Gedaliah swore to them
and their men and said to them, "Do
not be afraid of the servants of the
Chaldeans; live in the land and serve
the king of Babylon, and it will be
well with you."

**25** [a]But it happened in the seventh
month, that Ishmael the son of
Nethaniah, the son of Elishama, of
the royal seed, came [1]with ten men
and struck Gedaliah down so that
he died, along with the Jews and the
Chaldeans who were with him at
Mizpah. **26** [a]Then all the people, both
small and great, and the command-
ers of the military forces arose and
went to Egypt; for they were afraid
of the Chaldeans.

**27** [a]Now it happened in the thirty-
seventh year of [b]the exile of Jehoia-
chin king of Judah, in the twelfth
month, on the twenty-seventh *day* of
the month, that Evil-merodach king
of Babylon, in the year that he became
king, [c]lifted up the head of Jehoiachin
king of Judah from prison; **28** and he
[a]spoke to him good *words*, and he
set his throne above the throne of
the kings who *were* with him in Bab-
ylon. **29** So [1]Jehoiachin changed his
prison clothes and [a,2]had his meals
in [3]the king's presence continually
all the days of his life; **30** and for his
[a]allowance, a continual allowance
was given him by the king, a portion
for each day, all the days of his life.

---

**25:20** [a]2Ki 23:33 **25:21** [a]Dt 28:64; 2Ki 23:27 **25:22** [a]Jer 39:14; 40:7-9 **25:23** [a]Jer 40:7-9 [b]Jos 18:26 **25:25** [a]Jer 41:1, 2 [1]Lit *and ten men with him* **25:26** [a]Jer 43:4-7 **25:27** [a]Jer 52:31-34 [b]2Ki 24:12, 15 [c]Ge 40:13, 20 **25:28** [a]Da 2:37; 5:18, 19 **25:29** [a]2Sa 9:7 [1]Lit *he* [2]Lit *ate bread* [3]Lit *his presence* **25:30** [a]Ne 11:23; 12:47

The First Book of the

# CHRONICLES

### Generations from Adam to Abraham

1 [a]Adam, Seth, Enosh,
2 Kenan, Mahalalel, Jared,
3 Enoch, Methuselah, Lamech,
4 Noah, Shem, Ham, and
Japheth.

5 [a]The sons of Japheth *were*
Gomer, Magog, Madai, Javan,
Tubal, Meshech, and Tiras.
6 The sons of Gomer *were*
Ashkenaz, [1]Diphath,
and Togarmah.
7 The sons of Javan *were*
Elishah, Tarshish, Kittim,
and [1]Rodanim.

8 The sons of Ham *were* Cush,
Mizraim, Put, and Canaan.
9 The sons of Cush *were* Seba,
Havilah, Sabta, Raama, and
Sabteca;
and the sons of Raama *were*
Sheba and Dedan.
10 Cush [1]was the father of
Nimrod; he began to be
a mighty one on the earth.

11 [a]Mizraim was the father of the
people of [1]Lud, Anam, Lehab,
Naphtuh,
12 Pathrus, Casluh (from which
came the [1]Philistines),
and Caphtor.

13 Canaan was the father of
*Sidon, his firstborn*, Heth,
14 and the [a,1]Jebusites, the Am-
orites, the Girgashites,
15 the Hivites, the Arkites, the
Sinites,
16 the Arvadites, the Zemarites,
and the Hamathites.

17 [a]The sons of Shem *were* Elam,
Asshur, Arpachshad, Lud,
Aram, Uz, Hul, Gether, and
[1]Meshech.
18 Arpachshad was the father of
Shelah,
and Shelah was the father of
Eber.
19 Two sons were born to Eber,
the name of the one was
Peleg, for in his days the earth
was divided, and his brother's
name was Joktan.
20 Joktan was the father
of Almodad, Sheleph,
Hazarmaveth, Jerah,
21 Hadoram, Uzal, Diklah,
22 [1]Ebal, Abimael, Sheba,
23 Ophir, Havilah, and Jobab; all
these *were* the sons of Joktan.

24 [a]Shem, Arpachshad, Shelah,
25 Eber, Peleg, Reu,
26 Serug, Nahor, Terah,
27 Abram, that is Abraham.

### From Abraham to Jacob

28 The sons of Abraham *were* Isaac
and Ishmael. 29 [a]These are their
generations:

---

◆ **1:1** [a]Ge 4:25-5:32 **1:5** [a]Ge 10:2-4 **1:6** [1]In Ge 10:3, *Riphath* **1:7** [1]In Ge 10:4, *Dodanim* **1:10** [1]Lit *begot*, so in ch **1:11** [a]Ge 10:13-18 [1]Or *Ludim*, so for list of names in vv 11-12 **1:12** [1]Or *people of Pelisht* **1:14** [a]Ge 10:13-18 [1]Or *the Jebusite*, so for list of names in vv 14-16 **1:17** [a]Ge 10:22-29 [1]In Ge 10:23, *Mash* **1:22** [1]In Ge 10:28, *Obal* **1:24** [a]Ge 11:10-26; Lk 3:34-36 **1:29** [a]Ge 25:13-16

the firstborn of Ishmael *was*
Nebaioth, then Kedar, Adbeel,
Mibsam,
30 Mishma, Dumah, Massa,
Hadad, Tema,
31 Jetur, Naphish, and Kedemah;
these *were* the sons of
Ishmael.
32 [a]The sons of Keturah,
Abraham's concubine, *whom*
she bore, *were* Zimran,
Jokshan, Medan, Midian,
Ishbak, and Shuah.
And the sons of Jokshan *were*
Sheba and Dedan.
33 The sons of Midian were
Ephah, Epher, Hanoch, Abida,
and Eldaah. All these were the
sons of Keturah.
34 [a]Abraham became the father
of Isaac.
The sons of Isaac *were* [b]Esau
and Israel.
35 [a]The sons of Esau *were*
Eliphaz, Reuel, Jeush, Jalam,
and Korah.
36 The sons of Eliphaz *were*
Teman, Omar, [1]Zephi, Gatam,
Kenaz, Timna, and Amalek.
37 The sons of Reuel *were*
Nahath, Zerah, Shammah, and
Mizzah.
38 [a]The sons of Seir *were* Lotan,
Shobal, Zibeon, Anah, Dishon,
Ezer, and Dishan.
39 The sons of Lotan *were* Hori
and [1]Homam; and Lotan's
sister *was* Timna.
40 The sons of Shobal *were*
[1]Alian, Manahath, Ebal,
[2]Shephi, and Onam.
And the sons of Zibeon *were*
Aiah and Anah.
41 The [1]son of Anah *was* Dishon.
And the sons of Dishon *were*
[2]Hamran, Eshban, Ithran, and
Cheran.
42 The sons of Ezer *were* Bilhan,
Zaavan, and [1]Jaakan.
The sons of Dishon *were* Uz
and Aran.

43 [a]Now these are the kings who
reigned in the land of Edom
before *any* king of the sons of
Israel reigned. Bela was the
son of Beor, and the name of
his city was Dinhabah.
44 Then Bela died, and Jobab
the son of Zerah of [a]Bozrah
became king in his place.
45 Then Jobab died, and Husham
of the land of [a]the Temanites
became king in his place.
46 Then Husham died, and
Hadad the son of Bedad, who
struck down Midian in the
field of Moab, became king in
his place; and the name of his
city *was* Avith.
47 Then Hadad died, and Samlah
of Masrekah became king in
his place.
48 Then Samlah died, and Shaul
of Rehoboth by [1]the River
became king in his place.
49 Then Shaul died, and Baal-
hanan the son of Achbor
became king in his place.
50 Then Baal-hanan died, and
[1]Hadad became king in his
place; and the name of his

**1:32** [a]Ge 25:1-4 **1:34** [a]1Chr 1:28 [b]Ge 25:25, 26; 32:28 **1:35** [a]Ge 36:4-10 **1:36** [1]In Ge 36:11, *Zepho*
**1:38** [a]Ge 36:20-28 **1:39** [1]In Ge 36:22, *Hemam* **1:40** [1]In Ge 36:23, *Alvan* [2]In Ge 36:23, *Shepho*
**1:41** [1]Lit *sons* [2]In Ge 36:26, *Hemdan* **1:42** [1]In Ge 36:27, *Akan* **1:43** [a]Ge 36:31-43 **1:44** [a]Is 34:6
**1:45** [a]Job 2:11 **1:48** [1]The Euphrates River **1:50** [1]In Ge 36:39, *Hadar*

city was [2]Pai, and his wife's name was Mehetabel, the daughter of Matred, daughter of Mezahab.
51 Then Hadad died.
Now the chiefs of Edom were: chief Timna, chief [1]Aliah, chief Jetheth,
52 chief Oholibamah, chief Elah, chief Pinon,
53 chief Kenaz, chief Teman, chief Mibzar,
54 chief Magdiel, chief Iram. These *were* the chiefs of Edom.

### *Generations of David*

2 [a]These are the sons of Israel: Reuben, Simeon, Levi, Judah, Issachar, Zebulun,
2 Dan, Joseph, Benjamin, Naphtali, Gad, and Asher.

3 [a]The sons of Judah *were* Er, Onan, and Shelah; *these* three were born to him by Bath-shua the Canaanitess. And Er, Judah's firstborn, was evil in the sight of [1]Yahweh, so He put him to death.
4 [a]Tamar his daughter-in-law bore him Perez and Zerah. Judah had five sons in all.
5 The sons of Perez *were* Hezron and Hamul.
6 The sons of Zerah *were* [1]Zimri, Ethan, Heman, Calcol, and [2]Dara; five of them in all.
7 The [1]son of Carmi *was* [a2]Achar, the troubler of Israel, who violated what was devoted to destruction.
8 The [1]son of Ethan *was* Azariah.
9 Now the sons of Hezron, who were born to him *were* Jerahmeel, Ram, and Chelubai.
10 Ram [1]became the father of Amminadab, and Amminadab became the father of Nahshon, leader of the sons of Judah;
11 Nahshon became the father of Salma, Salma became the father of Boaz,
12 Boaz became the father of Obed, and Obed became the father of Jesse;
13 and Jesse became the father of Eliab his firstborn, then Abinadab the second, [1]Shimea the third,
14 Nethanel the fourth, Raddai the fifth,
15 Ozem the sixth, David the seventh;
16 and their sisters *were* Zeruiah and Abigail. And the three sons of Zeruiah *were* [1]Abshai, Joab, and Asahel.
17 Abigail bore Amasa, and the father of Amasa was [1]Jether the Ishmaelite.

18 Now Caleb the son of Hezron became a father by Azubah *his* wife, and by Jerioth; and these were her sons: Jesher, Shobab, and Ardon.

---

**1:50** [2]In Ge 36:39, *Pau* **1:51** [1]In Ge 36:40, *Alvah* ◆ **2:1** [a]Ge 35:22-26; 46:8-25 **2:3** [a]Ge 38:2-10 [1]The personal covenant name of God, a form of I AM WHO I AM, cf. Ex 3:14-15 **2:4** [a]Ge 38:13-30 **2:6** [1]In Jos 7:1, *Zabdi* [2]In 1Ki 4:31, *Darda* **2:7** [a]Jos 7:1 [1]Lit *sons* [2]In Jos 7:18, *Achan* **2:8** [1]Lit *sons* **2:10** [1]Lit *begot*, so in ch **2:13** [1]In 1Sa 16:9, *Shammah*; in 2Sa 13:3, *Shimeah* **2:16** [1]In 2Sa 2:18, *Abishai* **2:17** [1]In 2Sa 17:25, *Ithra the Israelite*

19 Then Azubah died, and Caleb took for himself Ephrath *as a wife*, and she bore him Hur.
20 Hur became the father of Uri, and Uri became the father of Bezalel.
21 Afterward Hezron went in to the daughter of Machir the father of Gilead, whom he took *as a wife* when he was sixty years old; and she bore him Segub.
22 Segub became the father of Jair, and he had twenty-three cities in the land of Gilead.
23 But Geshur and Aram took [1]Havvoth-jair from them, with Kenath and its villages, *even* sixty cities. All these were the sons of Machir, the father of Gilead.
24 After the death of Hezron in Caleb-ephrathah, Abijah, Hezron's wife, bore him Ashhur the father of Tekoa.

25 And the sons of Jerahmeel the firstborn of Hezron *were* Ram the firstborn, then Bunah, Oren, Ozem, *and* Ahijah.
26 Jerahmeel had another wife, whose name was Atarah; she was the mother of Onam.
27 The sons of Ram, the firstborn of Jerahmeel, were Maaz, Jamin, and Eker.
28 The sons of Onam were Shammai and Jada.
And the sons of Shammai *were* Nadab and Abishur.
29 The name of Abishur's wife *was* Abihail, and she bore him Ahban and Molid.
30 The sons of Nadab *were* Seled and Appaim, and Seled died without sons.
31 The [1]son of Appaim *was* Ishi.
And the [1]son of Ishi *was* Sheshan.
And the [1]son of Sheshan *was* Ahlai.
32 The sons of Jada the brother of Shammai *were* Jether and Jonathan, and Jether died without sons.
33 The sons of Jonathan *were* Peleth and Zaza.
These were the sons of Jerahmeel.
34 Now Sheshan had no sons, only daughters. And Sheshan had an Egyptian slave whose name was Jarha.
35 Sheshan gave his daughter to Jarha his servant as a wife, and she bore him Attai.
36 Attai became the father of Nathan,
and Nathan became the father of Zabad,
37 and Zabad became the father of Ephlal,
and Ephlal became the father of Obed,
38 and Obed became the father of Jehu,
and Jehu became the father of Azariah,
39 and Azariah became the father of Helez,
and Helez became the father of Eleasah,
40 and Eleasah became the father of Sismai,
and Sismai became the father of Shallum,

**2:23** [1]Or *the towns of Jair* **2:31** [1]Lit *sons*

41 and Shallum became the
father of Jekamiah,
and Jekamiah became the
father of Elishama.
42 Now the sons of Caleb, the
brother of Jerahmeel, *were*
Mesha his firstborn, who was
the father of Ziph; and [1]his
son was Mareshah, the father
of Hebron.
43 The sons of Hebron *were*
Korah and Tappuah and
Rekem and Shema.
44 Shema became the father of
Raham, the father of Jorkeam;
and Rekem became the father
of Shammai.
45 The son of Shammai was
Maon,
and Maon *was* the father of
Bethzur.
46 Ephah, Caleb's concubine,
bore Haran, Moza, and Gazez;
and Haran became the father
of Gazez.
47 The sons of Jahdai *were*
Regem, Jotham, Geshan, Pelet,
Ephah, and Shaaph.
48 Maacah, Caleb's concubine,
bore Sheber and Tirhanah.
49 She also bore Shaaph the
father of Madmannah, Sheva
the father of Machbena and
the father of Gibea; and
the daughter of Caleb *was*
Achsah.
50 These were the sons of Caleb.

The [1]sons of Hur, the firstborn
of Ephrathah, *were* Shobal the
*father of* Kiriath-jearim,
51 Salma the father of Bethlehem
*and* Hareph the father of
Beth-gader.
52 Shobal the father of Kiriath-
jearim had sons:
Haroeh, half of the
Manahathites,
53 and the families of Kiriath-
jearim:
the Ithrites, the Puthites,
the Shumathites, and the
Mishraites; from these
came the Zorathites and the
Eshtaolites.
54 The sons of Salma *were*
Bethlehem and the
Netophathites, Atroth-
beth-joab and half of the
Manahathites, the Zorites.
55 The families of scribes
who lived at Jabez *were* the
Tirathites, the Shimeathites,
*and* the Sucathites. Those are
the Kenites who came from
Hammath, the father of the
house of Rechab.

### *Sons of David*

3 [a]Now these were the sons of
David who were born to him in
Hebron:
the firstborn *was* Amnon, by
Ahinoam the Jezreelitess;
the second *was* Daniel, by
Abigail the Carmelitess;
2 the third *was* Absalom the son
of Maacah, the daughter of
Talmai king of Geshur;
the fourth *was* Adonijah the
son of Haggith;
3 the fifth *was* Shephatiah, by
Abital;
the sixth *was* Ithream, by his
wife Eglah.
4 Six were born to him in
Hebron, and [a]there he reigned
seven years and six months.

**2:42** [1]Lit *the sons of* **2:50** [1]Lit *son* ◆ **3:1** [a]2Sa 3:2-5 **3:4** [a]2Sa 2:11; 5:4, 5; 1Ki 2:11; 1Chr 29:27

And in Jerusalem he reigned
thirty-three years.
5 [a]These were born to him in
Jerusalem:
Shimea, Shobab, Nathan, and
[b]Solomon, four, by [c]Bath-shua
the daughter of Ammiel;
6 and Ibhar, Elishama, Eliphelet,
7 Nogah, Nepheg, and Japhia,
8 Elishama, Eliada, and
Eliphelet, nine.
9 All *these were* the sons of
David, besides the sons of the
concubines; and [a]Tamar *was*
their sister.

10 Now Solomon's son *was*
Rehoboam, Abijah *was* his
son, Asa his son, Jehoshaphat
his son,
11 Joram his son, Ahaziah his
son, Joash his son,
12 Amaziah his son, Azariah his
son, Jotham his son,
13 Ahaz his son, Hezekiah his
son, Manasseh his son,
14 Amon his son, Josiah his son.
15 The sons of Josiah *were*
Johanan the firstborn, and
the second *was* Jehoiakim,
the third Zedekiah, the fourth
Shallum.
16 The sons of Jehoiakim *were*
Jeconiah his son, Zedekiah his
son.
17 The sons of Jeconiah, the
prisoner, *were* Shealtiel his
son,
18 and Malchiram, Pedaiah,
Shenazzar, Jekamiah,
Hoshama, and Nedabiah.
19 The sons of Pedaiah *were*
Zerubbabel and Shimei.
And the [1]sons of Zerubbabel
*were* Meshullam and
Hananiah, and Shelomith *was*
their sister;
20 and Hashubah, Ohel,
Berechiah, Hasadiah, and
Jushab-hesed, five.
21 The [1]sons of Hananiah *were*
Pelatiah and Jeshaiah, the
sons of Rephaiah, the sons of
Arnan, the sons of Obadiah,
the sons of Shecaniah.
22 The sons of Shecaniah *were*
Shemaiah,
and the sons of Shemaiah:
Hattush, Igal, Bariah, Neariah,
and Shaphat, six.
23 The [1]sons of Neariah *were* Eli-
oenai, Hizkiah, and Azrikam,
three.
24 The sons of Elioenai *were*
Hodaviah, Eliashib, Pelaiah,
Akkub, Johanan, Delaiah, and
Anani, seven.

### *Sons of Judah*

4 [a]The sons of Judah *were* Perez,
Hezron, Carmi, Hur, and
Shobal.
2 Reaiah the son of Shobal
[1]became the father of Jahath,
and Jahath became the father
of Ahumai and Lahad. These
*were* the families of the
Zorathites.
3 These *were* the [1]sons of Etam:
Jezreel, Ishma, and Idbash;
and the name of their sister
*was* Hazzelelponi.
4 Penuel *was* the father of
Gedor, and Ezer the father
of Hushah. These *were* the
sons of Hur, the firstborn

**3:5** [a]2Sa 5:14-16; 1Chr 14:4-7 [b]2Sa 12:24, 25 [c]2Sa 11:3 **3:9** [a]2Sa 13:1 **3:19** [1]Lit *son* **3:21** [1]Lit *son*
**3:23** [1]Lit *son* ◆ **4:1** [a]1Chr 2:3 **4:2** [1]Lit *begot*, so in ch **4:3** [1]As in some ancient versions; Heb *father*

of Ephrathah, the father of
Bethlehem.
5 Ashhur, the father of Tekoa,
had two wives, Helah and
Naarah.
6 Naarah bore him Ahuzzam,
Hepher, Temeni, and
Haahashtari. These were the
sons of Naarah.
7 The sons of Helah *were*
Zereth, [1]Izhar, and Ethnan.
8 Koz became the father of
Anub and Zobebah, and the
families of Aharhel the son of
Harum.
9 Now Jabez was more
honorable than his brothers,
and his mother named him
Jabez saying, "Because I bore
*him* with pain."
10 Then Jabez called on the God
of Israel, saying, "Oh that You
would bless me indeed and
enlarge my border, and that
Your hand might be with me,
and that You would keep *me*
from harm that *it* may not
pain me!" And God brought
about what he asked.

11 Chelub the brother of Shuhah
became the father of Mehir,
who was the father of Eshton.
12 Eshton became the father
of Beth-rapha and Paseah,
and Tehinnah the father of
[1]Ir-nahash.
These are the men of Recah.

13 Now the sons of Kenaz *were*
*Othniel and Seraiah*.
And the sons of Othniel *were*
Hathath and Meonothai.
14 Meonothai became the father
of Ophrah,
and Seraiah became the
father of Joab the father of
[1]Ge-harashim, for they were
craftsmen.
15 The sons of Caleb the son of
Jephunneh *were* Iru, Elah, and
Naam;
and the [1]son of Elah *was*
[2]Kenaz.
16 The sons of Jehallelel *were*
Ziph and Ziphah, Tiria and
Asarel.
17 The [1]sons of Ezrah *were*
Jether, Mered, Epher, and
Jalon. ([2]And these are the
sons of Bithia the daughter of
Pharaoh, whom Mered took)
and she conceived *and bore*
Miriam, Shammai, and Ishbah
the father of Eshtemoa.
18 His Jewish wife bore Jered the
father of Gedor, and Heber the
father of Soco, and Jekuthiel
the father of Zanoah.
19 The sons of the wife of Hodiah,
the sister of Naham, *were* the
[1]fathers of Keilah the Garmite
and Eshtemoa the Maacathite.
20 The sons of Shimon *were*
Amnon and Rinnah,
Benhanan and Tilon.
And the sons of Ishi *were*
Zoheth and Ben-zoheth.
21 The sons of Shelah the son
of Judah *were* Er the father of
Lecah and Laadah the father
of Mareshah, and the families
of the house of the fine linen
workers at Beth-ashbea;
22 and Jokim, the men of Cozeba,
Joash, Saraph, who ruled in

---

**4:7** [1]Or *Zohar* **4:12** [1]Or *the city of Nahash* **4:14** [1]Lit *valley of craftsmen* **4:15** [1]Lit *sons* [2]Lit *and Kenaz* **4:17** [1]Lit *son* [2]In the Heb the words in ( ) are at the end of v 18 **4:19** [1]Lit *father*

Moab, and Jashubi-lehem.
And the [1]records are ancient.
23 These were the potters and the inhabitants of Netaim and Gederah; they lived there with the king for his work.

### *Sons of Simeon*

24 The sons of Simeon *were* [1]Nemuel and Jamin, [2]Jarib, [3]Zerah, Shaul;
25 Shallum his son, Mibsam his son, Mishma his son.
26 The sons of Mishma *were* Hammuel his son, Zaccur his son, Shimei his son.
27 Now Shimei had sixteen sons and
six daughters; but his brothers did
not have many sons, nor did all their
family multiply like the sons of Judah.
28 They lived at Beersheba, Moladah,
and Hazar-shual, 29 at Bilhah, Ezem,
Tolad, 30 Bethuel, Hormah, Ziklag,
31 Beth-marcaboth, Hazar-susim,
Beth-biri, and Shaaraim. These *were*
their cities until the reign of David.
32 Their villages *were* Etam, Ain,
Rimmon, Tochen, and Ashan, five
cities; 33 and all their villages that
*were* all around these cities as far as
[1]Baal. These *were* their settlements,
and they have their genealogy.
34 Meshobab and Jamlech and Joshah the son of Amaziah,
35 and Joel and Jehu the son of Joshibiah, the son of Seraiah, the son of Asiel,
36 and Elioenai, Jaakobah, Jeshohaiah, Asaiah, Adiel, Jesimiel, Benaiah,
37 Ziza the son of Shiphi, the son of Allon, the son of Jedaiah, the son of Shimri, the son of Shemaiah;
38 these, who came *into the record* by name, *were* leaders in their families; and their fathers' houses increased greatly.
39 They went to the entrance of Gedor,
even to the east side of the valley, to
seek pasture for their flocks. 40 They
found rich and good pasture, and
[a]the land was broad and quiet and
peaceful; for those who lived there
formerly *were* Hamites. 41 [a]And these,
recorded by name, came in the days
of Hezekiah king of Judah, and struck
down their tents and the Meunites
who were found there, and devoted
them to destruction to this day, and
lived in their place, because there was
pasture there for their flocks. 42 From
them, from the sons of Simeon, five
hundred men went to [a]Mount Seir,
with Pelatiah, Neariah, Rephaiah, and
Uzziel, the sons of Ishi, as their chiefs.
43 [a]They struck down the remnant
of the Amalekites who escaped, and
have lived there to this day.

### *Sons of Reuben*

5 Now the sons of Reuben the
firstborn of Israel (for [a]he was the
firstborn, but because [b]he profaned
his father's bed, [c]his birthright was
given to the sons of Joseph the son
of Israel; so that he is not recorded in
the genealogy according to the birth-
right. 2 [a]Though Judah prevailed over
his brothers, and [b]from him *came* the

**4:22** [1]Lit *words* **4:24** [1]In Ge 46:10 and Ex 6:15, *Jemuel* [2]In Nu 26:12, *Jachin* [3]In Ge 46:10 and Ex 6:15, *Zohar* **4:33** [1]In Jos 19:8, *Baalath* **4:40** [a]Jdg 18:7-10 **4:41** [a]1Chr 4:33-38 **4:42** [a]Ge 36:8, 9 **4:43** [a]1Sa 15:7, 8; 30:17 ◆ **5:1** [a]Ge 29:32; 1Chr 2:1 [b]Ge 35:22; 49:4 [c]Ge 48:15-22 **5:2** [a]Ge 49:8-10; Ps 60:7; 108:8 [b]Mic 5:2; Mt 2:6

ruler, yet the birthright belonged to
Joseph),

3 [a]the sons of Reuben the
firstborn of Israel *were*
Hanoch and Pallu, Hezron and
Carmi.
4 The sons of Joel *were* Shemaiah his son, Gog his son,
[a]Shimei his son,
5 Micah his son, Reaiah his son,
Baal his son,
6 Beerah his son, whom
[l]Tilgath-pilneser king of
Assyria took away into
exile; he was leader of the
Reubenites.

7 His [l]relatives by their families, [a]in
the genealogy of their generations,
*were* Jeiel the chief, then Zechariah,
8 and Bela the son of Azaz, the son
of Shema, the son of Joel, who lived
in [a]Aroer, even to Nebo and Baal-
meon. 9 To the east he lived as far as
the entrance of the wilderness from
the river Euphrates, [a]because their
cattle had increased in the land of
Gilead. 10 In the days of Saul [a]they
made war with the Hagrites, and they
fell by their hand. So they lived in
their tents throughout [l]all the land
east of Gilead.

### *Sons of Gad*

11 Now the sons of Gad lived opposite
them in the land of [a]Bashan as far as
[b]Salecah. 12 Joel *was* the chief and
Shapham the second, then Janai and
Shaphat in Bashan. 13 Their [l]relatives
of their fathers' households *were*
Michael, Meshullam, Sheba, Jorai,
Jacan, Zia, and Eber, seven. 14 These
*were* the sons of Abihail, the son of
Huri,

the son of Jaroah, the son of
Gilead,
the son of Michael, the son of
Jeshishai,
the son of Jahdo, the son of
Buz;

15 Ahi the son of Abdiel, the son
of Guni, *was* head of their fathers'
households. 16 They lived in Gilead,
in Bashan and in its towns, and in
all the pasture lands of [a]Sharon, as
far as their [l]borders. 17 All of these
were recorded in the genealogies in
the days of [a]Jotham king of Judah
and in the days of [b]Jeroboam king
of Israel.

18 The sons of Reuben and the Gad-
ites and the half-tribe of Manasseh,
*consisting* of men of valor, men who
bore shield and sword and shot with
bow and *were* learned in *the ways
of* battle, *were* 44,760, who [a]went
out for *military* duty. 19 They made
war against [a]the Hagrites, [b]Jetur,
Naphish, and Nodab. 20 They were
helped against them, and the Hag-
rites and all who *were* with them
were given into their hand; for [a]they
cried out to God in the battle, and He
was moved by their entreaty because
[b]they trusted in Him. 21 They took
captive their cattle: their 50,000
camels, 250,000 sheep, 2,000 don-
keys; and 100,000 [l]men. 22 For many
fell slain, because [a]the war *was* of
God. And [b]they lived in their place
until the [c]exile.

---

**5:3** [a]Ge 46:9; Ex 6:14; Nu 26:5-9 **5:4** [a]1Chr 5:8 **5:6** [l]In 2Ki 15:29, *Tiglath-pileser* **5:7** [a]1Chr 5:17 [l]Lit *brothers* **5:8** [a]Nu 32:34; Jos 12:2 **5:9** [a]Jos 22:8, 9 **5:10** [a]1Chr 5:18-21 [l]Lit *all the face of the east* **5:11** [a]Jos 13:11 [b]Dt 3:10 **5:13** [l]Lit *brothers* **5:16** [a]1Chr 27:29; SS 2:1; Is 35:2; 65:10 [l]Lit *goings out* **5:17** [a]2Ki 15:5, 32 [b]2Ki 14:16, 28 **5:18** [a]Nu 1:3 **5:19** [a]1Chr 5:10 [b]Ge 25:15; 1Chr 1:31 **5:20** [a]2Chr 14:11-13 [b]Ps 9:10; 20:7, 8; 22:4, 5 **5:21** [l]Lit *souls of men* **5:22** [a]Jos 23:10; 2Chr 32:8; Ro 8:31 [b]1Chr 4:41 [c]2Ki 15:29; 17:6

### *Sons of the Half-Tribe of Manasseh*

23 Now the sons of the half-tribe of
Manasseh lived in the land; from
Bashan to Baal-hermon and [a]Senir
and Mount Hermon they were nu-
merous. 24 These were the heads
of their fathers' households, even
Epher, Ishi, Eliel, Azriel, Jeremiah,
Hodaviah, and Jahdiel, mighty men
of valor, men of renown, heads of
their fathers' households.
25 But they [a]acted unfaithfully
against the God of their fathers and
[b]played the harlot [c]after the gods of
the peoples of the land, whom God
had destroyed before them. 26 So
the God of Israel stirred up the spirit
of [a]Pul, king of Assyria, even the
spirit of [1]Tilgath-pilneser, king of
Assyria, and he [b]took them away
into exile, namely the Reubenites,
the Gadites, and the half-tribe of
Manasseh, and brought them to
Halah, Habor, Hara, and to the river
of Gozan, to this day.

### *Sons of Levi*

6 [a,1]The sons of Levi *were*
[2]Gershon, Kohath, and Merari.
2 The sons of Kohath *were*
Amram, Izhar, Hebron, and
Uzziel.
3 The children of Amram *were*
Aaron, Moses, and Miriam.
And the sons of Aaron *were*
Nadab, Abihu, Eleazar, and
Ithamar.
4 Eleazar [1]became the father of
Phinehas,
*and* Phinehas became the
father of Abishua,
5 and Abishua became the
father of Bukki,
and Bukki became the father
of Uzzi,
6 and Uzzi became the father of
Zerahiah,
and Zerahiah became the
father of Meraioth,
7 Meraioth became the father of
Amariah,
and Amariah became the
father of Ahitub,
8 and [a]Ahitub became the
father of Zadok,
and Zadok [b]became the father
of Ahimaaz,
9 and Ahimaaz became the
father of Azariah,
and Azariah became the
father of Johanan,
10 and Johanan became the
father of Azariah ([a]it was he
who ministered as the priest
in the house [b]which Solomon
built in Jerusalem),
11 and [a]Azariah became the
father of Amariah,
and Amariah became the
father of Ahitub,
12 and Ahitub became the father
of Zadok,
and Zadok became the father
of [1]Shallum,
13 and Shallum became the
father of Hilkiah,
and Hilkiah became the father
of Azariah,
14 and Azariah became the
father of [a]Seraiah,
and Seraiah became the father
of Jehozadak;

**5:23** [a]Dt 3:9 **5:25** [a]Dt 32:15-18 [b]Ex 34:15 [c]2Ki 17:7 **5:26** [a]2Ki 15:19, 29; 2Chr 28:20 [b]2Ki 17:6 [1]In 2Ki 15:29, *Tiglath-pileser* ◆ **6:1** [a]Ge 46:11; Ex 6:16-25 [1]Ch 5:27 in Heb [2]In v 16, *Gershom* **6:4** [1]Lit *begot*, so in ch **6:8** [a]2Sa 8:17 [b]2Sa 15:27 **6:10** [a]2Chr 26:17 [b]1Ki 6:1; 2Chr 3:1 **6:11** [a]Ezr 7:3 **6:12** [1]In ch 9:11, *Meshullam* **6:14** [a]Ne 11:11

15 and Jehozadak went *along*
when Yahweh took Judah and
Jerusalem away into exile by
the hand of Nebuchadnezzar.

16 [a,1]The sons of Levi *were*
[2]Gershom, Kohath, and
Merari.
17 These are the names of the
sons of Gershom: Libni and
Shimei.
18 The sons of Kohath *were*
Amram, Izhar, Hebron, and
Uzziel.
19 The sons of [a]Merari *were*
Mahli and Mushi.
And these are the families of
the Levites according to their
fathers' *households*.
20 Of Gershom: Libni his son,
Jahath his son, Zimmah his
son,
21 Joah his son, Iddo his son,
Zerah his son, Jeatherai his
son.
22 The sons of Kohath *were*
Amminadab his son, Korah his
son, Assir his son,
23 Elkanah his son, Ebiasaph his
son, and Assir his son,
24 Tahath his son, Uriel his son,
Uzziah his son, and Shaul his
son.
25 The sons of Elkanah *were*
Amasai and Ahimoth.
26 *As for* Elkanah, the sons of
Elkanah *were* Zophai his son
and Nahath his son,
27 Eliab his son, Jeroham his son,
Elkanah his son.
28 *The sons* of Samuel *were* [a]Joel
the firstborn, and Abijah the
second.
29 The sons of Merari *were*
Mahli, Libni his son, Shimei
his son, Uzzah his son,
30 Shimea his son, Haggiah his
son, Asaiah his son.

31 [a]Now these are those whom
David caused to stand over the ser-
vice of song in the house of Yahweh,
[b]after the ark rested *there*. 32 And
they ministered with song before
the tabernacle of the tent of meeting,
until Solomon had built the house of
Yahweh in Jerusalem; and they stood
for their service according to their
custom. 33 These are those who stood
*for service* with their sons:

From the sons of the Kohath-
ites *were* Heman the singer, the
son of Joel, the son of Samuel,
34 the son of Elkanah, the son of
Jeroham, the son of Eliel, the
son of Toah,
35 the son of Zuph, the son of
Elkanah, the son of Mahath,
the son of Amasai,
36 the son of Elkanah, the son of
Joel, the son of Azariah, the
son of Zephaniah,
37 the son of Tahath, the son of
Assir, the son of Ebiasaph, the
son of Korah,
38 the son of Izhar, the son of
Kohath, the son of Levi, the
son of Israel.
39 *Heman's* brother Asaph stood
at his right hand, even Asaph
the son of Berechiah, the son
of Shimea,
40 the son of Michael, the
son of Baaseiah, the son of
Malchijah,
41 the son of Ethni, the son of
Zerah, the son of Adaiah,

**6:16** [a]Ge 46:11; Ex 6:16 [1]Ch 6:1 in Heb [2]In v 1, *Gershon* **6:19** [a]Nu 3:33; 1Chr 23:21 **6:28** [a]1Sa 8:2; 1Chr 6:33 **6:31** [a]1Chr 15:16-22, 27; 16:4-6 [b]2Sa 6:17; 1Ki 8:4; 1Chr 15:25-16:1

42 the son of Ethan, the son of
Zimmah, the son of Shimei,
43 the son of Jahath, the son of
Gershom, the son of Levi.
44 On the left hand *were* their
[1]relatives the sons of Merari:
Ethan the son of Kishi, the son
of Abdi, the son of Malluch,
45 the son of Hashabiah, the
son of Amaziah, the son of
Hilkiah,
46 the son of Amzi, the son of
Bani, the son of Shemer,
47 the son of Mahli, the son of
Mushi, the son of Merari, the
son of Levi.
48 Their [1]relatives the Levites were
given over unto all the service of the
tabernacle of the house of God.
49 But Aaron and his sons [a]offered
*offerings* up in smoke on the altar of
burnt offering and [b]on the altar of
incense, for all the work of the Holy
of Holies, and [c]to make atonement
for Israel, according to all that Moses
the servant of God had commanded.
50 [a]These are the sons of Aaron:
Eleazar his son, Phinehas his
son, Abishua his son,
51 Bukki his son, Uzzi his son,
Zerahiah his son,
52 Meraioth his son, Amariah his
son, Ahitub his son,
53 Zadok his son, Ahimaaz his
son.
54 Now these are their settlements
according to their camps within their
borders. To the sons of Aaron of the
families of the Kohathites (for the
[a]lot was theirs *first*), 55 to them they
gave [a]Hebron in the land of Judah,
with its pasture lands all around it;
56 [a]but the fields of the city and its
villages, they gave to Caleb the son
of Jephunneh. 57 [a]To the sons of
Aaron they gave the *following* cities
of refuge:
Hebron, Libnah also with its
pasture lands, Jattir, Eshtemoa
with its pasture lands,
58 [1]Hilen with its pasture lands,
Debir with its pasture lands,
59 [1]Ashan with its pasture lands,
and Beth-shemesh with its
pasture lands;
60 from the tribe of Benjamin:
Geba with its pasture lands,
[1]Allemeth with its pasture
lands, and Anathoth with its
pasture lands.
All their cities throughout
their families were thirteen
cities.

61 [a]Now to the rest of the sons
of Kohath *were given* by lot,
from the family of the tribe,
from the half-tribe, the half of
Manasseh, ten cities.
62 And to the sons of Gershom,
according to their families,
*were given* from the tribe of
Issachar and from the tribe of
Asher, the tribe of Naphtali,
and the tribe of Manasseh,
thirteen cities in Bashan.
63 [a]To the sons of Merari *were*
*given* by lot, according to their
families, from the tribe of
Reuben, the tribe of Gad, and
the tribe of Zebulun, twelve
cities.

**6:44** [1]Lit *brothers* **6:48** [1]Lit *brothers* **6:49** [a]Ex 27:1-8 [b]Ex 30:1-7 [c]Ex 30:10-16 **6:50** [a]1Chr 6:4-8; Ezr 7:5 **6:54** [a]Jos 21:4, 10 **6:55** [a]Jos 14:13; 21:11f **6:56** [a]Jos 15:13 **6:57** [a]Jos 21:13, 19 **6:58** [1]In Jos 21:15, *Holon* **6:59** [1]In Jos 21:16, *Ain* **6:60** [1]In Jos 21:18, *Almon* **6:61** [a]Jos 21:5; 1Chr 6:66-70 **6:63** [a]Jos 21:7, 34-40

64 [a]So the sons of Israel gave to the
Levites the cities with their pasture
lands. 65 They also gave by lot from
the tribe of the sons of Judah, the tribe
of the sons of Simeon, and the tribe
of the sons of Benjamin, [a]these cities
which are mentioned *here* by name.
66 [a]Now some of the families of
the sons of Kohath had cities of their
territory from the tribe of Ephraim.
67 And they gave to them the *following* cities of refuge:

Shechem, with its pasture lands, in the hill country of Ephraim, and Gezer with its pasture lands,
68 Jokmeam with its pasture lands, Beth-horon with its pasture lands,
69 Aijalon with its pasture lands, and Gath-rimmon with its pasture lands;
70 and from the half-tribe of Manasseh:
Aner with its pasture lands and Bileam with its pasture lands, for the family of the rest of the sons of Kohath.

71 To the sons of Gershom *were given*, from the family of the half-tribe of Manasseh:

Golan in Bashan with its pasture lands and Ashtaroth with its pasture lands;
72 and from the tribe of Issachar:
Kedesh with its pasture lands, Daberath with its pasture lands,
73 and Ramoth with its pasture lands, Anem with its pasture lands;
74 *and from the* tribe of Asher:
Mashal with its pasture lands, Abdon with its pasture lands,
75 Hukok with its pasture lands, and Rehob with its pasture lands;
76 and from the tribe of Naphtali:
Kedesh in Galilee with its pasture lands, Hammon with its pasture lands, and Kiriathaim with its pasture lands.

77 To the sons of Merari, the rest *of the Levites, were given*, from the tribe of Zebulun:

Rimmono with its pasture lands, Tabor with its pasture lands;
78 and beyond the Jordan at Jericho, on the east side of the Jordan, *were given them*, from the tribe of Reuben:
Bezer in the wilderness with its pasture lands, Jahzah with its pasture lands,
79 Kedemoth with its pasture lands, and Mephaath with its pasture lands;
80 and from the tribe of Gad:
Ramoth in Gilead with its pasture lands, Mahanaim with its pasture lands,
81 Heshbon with its pasture lands, and Jazer with its pasture lands.

### *Sons of Issachar*

7 Now the sons of Issachar: Tola, [1]Puah, [2]Jashub, and Shimron, four.
2 The sons of Tola *were* Uzzi, Rephaiah, Jeriel, Jahmai, Ibsam, and Samuel, heads of their fathers' households. *The sons* of Tola *were* mighty men of valor in their generations;

**6:64** [a]Nu 35:1-8; Jos 21:3, 41, 42 **6:65** [a]1Chr 6:57-60 **6:66** [a]Jos 21:20-26 ◆ **7:1** [1]In Ge 46:13, *Puvvah*; in Nu 26:23, *Puvah* [2]In Ge 46:13, *Iob*

[a]their number in the days of
David was 22,600.
3 The [1]son of Uzzi *was* Izrahiah.
And the sons of Izrahiah
*were* Michael, Obadiah, Joel,
Isshiah; all five of them *were*
[a]chief men.
**4** With them by their generations ac-
cording to their fathers' households
were 36,000 [1]troops of the army for
war, for they had many wives and
sons. **5** Their [1]relatives among all the
families of Issachar *were* mighty men
of valor, recorded by genealogy, in
all 87,000.

### *Sons of Benjamin*

6 [a]*The sons of* Benjamin: Bela
and Becher and Jediael, three.
7 The sons of Bela: Ezbon,
Uzzi, Uzziel, Jerimoth, and
Iri, five. They *were* heads of
fathers' households, mighty
men of valor, and were 22,034
recorded by genealogy.
8 The sons of Becher *were*
Zemirah, Joash, Eliezer, Eli-
oenai, Omri, Jeremoth, Abijah,
Anathoth, and Alemeth. All
these *were* the sons of Becher.
**9** They were recorded by genealogy,
according to their generations, heads
of their fathers' households, 20,200
mighty men of valor.
10 The [1]son of Jediael *was* Bilhan.
And the sons of Bilhan *were*
Jeush, Benjamin, Ehud,
Chenaanah, Zethan, Tarshish,
and Ahishahar.
**11** All these *were* sons of Jediael, ac-
cording to the heads of their fathers'
*households*, 17,200 mighty men of
valor, who went out with the army to
war. **12** [1]Shuppim and [2]Huppim *were*
the sons of [3]Ir; Hushim *was* the [4]son
of [5]Aher.

### *Sons of Naphtali*

**13** The sons of Naphtali *were* [1]Jahziel,
Guni, Jezer, and [2]Shallum, the sons
of Bilhah.

### *Sons of Manasseh*

**14** The sons of Manasseh *were* Asriel,
whom his Aramean concubine bore;
she bore Machir the father of Gilead.
**15** Now Machir took a wife for Hup-
pim and Shuppim, [1]whose sister's
name was Maacah. And the name
of the second was Zelophehad, and
Zelophehad had daughters. **16** And
Maacah the wife of Machir bore a
son, and she named him Peresh; and
the name of his brother *was* Sheresh,
and his sons *were* Ulam and Rakem.
**17** The [1]son of Ulam *was* Bedan.
These *were* the sons of Gilead the
son of Machir, the son of Manasseh.
**18** And his sister Hammolecheth bore
Ishhod and [1]Abiezer and Mahlah.
**19** The sons of Shemida were Ahian
and Shechem and Likhi and Aniam.

### *Sons of Ephraim*

**20** [a]The sons of Ephraim *were*
Shuthelah and [1]Bered his son, Tahath
his son, Eleadah his son, Tahath his
son, **21** Zabad his son, Shuthelah
his son, and Ezer and Elead whom
the men of Gath who were born in
the land killed, because they came
down to take their livestock. **22** And

---

**7:2** [a]2Sa 24:1-9 **7:3** [a]1Chr 5:24 [1]Lit *sons* **7:4** [1]Or *bands* **7:5** [1]Lit *brothers*, so in ch **7:6** [a]1Chr 8:1-40
**7:10** [1]Lit *sons* **7:12** [1]In Nu 26:39, *Shephupham* [2]In Nu 26:39, *Hupham* [3]In v 7, *Iri* [4]Lit *sons* [5]In
Nu 26:38, *Ahiram* **7:13** [1]In Ge 46:24, *Jahzeel* [2]In Ge 46:24 and Nu 26:49, *Shillem* **7:15** [1]Lit *and his*
**7:17** [1]Lit *sons* **7:18** [1]In Nu 26:30, *Iezer* **7:20** [a]Nu 26:35, 36 [1]In Nu 26:35, *Becher*

their father Ephraim [a]mourned
many days, and his relatives [b]came
to comfort him. **23** Then he went
in to his wife, and she conceived
and bore a son, and he named him
[1]Beriah, because calamity had come
upon his house. **24** And his daughter
was Sheerah, and [a]she built lower
and upper Beth-horon, also Uzzen-
sheerah. **25** Rephah was his son *along*
with Resheph, Telah his son, Tahan
his son, **26** Ladan his son, Ammihud
his son, Elishama his son, **27** [1]Non his
son and [a]Joshua his son.

**28** [a]Now their possessions and
settlements *were* Bethel with its
towns, and to the east [1]Naaran, and
to the west Gezer with its towns, and
Shechem with its towns as far as
[2]Ayyah with its towns, **29** and along
the [1]borders of the sons of Manasseh,
Beth-shean with its towns, Taanach
with its towns, Megiddo with its
towns, Dor with its towns. In these
lived the [a]sons of Joseph the son of
Israel.

### *Sons of Asher*

**30** [a]The sons of Asher *were*
Imnah, Ishvah, Ishvi, and
Beriah, and Serah their sister.
**31** The sons of Beriah *were* Heber
and Malchiel, who was the
father of Birzaith.
**32** Heber [1]became the father
of Japhlet, [2]Shomer, and
Hotham, and Shua their sister.
**33** The sons of Japhlet *were*
Pasach, Bimhal, and Ashvath.
These were the sons of
Japhlet.
**34** The sons of [1]Shemer *were* Ahi
and Rohgah, Jehubbah and
Aram.
**35** The [1]sons of his brother
Helem *were* Zophah, Imna,
Shelesh, and Amal.
**36** The sons of Zophah *were*
Suah, Harnepher, Shual, Beri,
and Imrah,
**37** Bezer, Hod, Shamma,
Shilshah, Ithran, and Beera.
**38** The sons of Jether *were*
Jephunneh, Pispa, and Ara.
**39** The sons of Ulla *were* Arah,
Hanniel, and Rizia.
**40** All these *were* the sons of
Asher, heads of the fathers'
houses, choice and mighty
men of valor, heads of the
princes. And the number of
them recorded by genealogy
for the army in war was
26,000 men.

### *Generations of Saul*

**8** And [a]Benjamin [1]became the
father of Bela his firstborn,
Ashbel the second, [b]Aharah
the third,
**2** Nohah the fourth, and Rapha
the fifth.
**3** Bela had sons: [1]Addar, Gera,
Abihud,
**4** Abishua, Naaman, Ahoah,
**5** Gera, Shephuphan, and
Huram.
**6** These are the sons of Ehud:
these are the heads of fathers'
*households* of the inhabitants
of Geba, and they took them
away into exile to Manahath,

**7:22** [a]Ge 37:34 [b]Job 2:11; Jn 11:19 **7:23** [1]Lit *on misfortune* **7:24** [a]Jos 16:3, 5; 2Chr 8:5 **7:27** [a]Ex 17:9-14; 24:13 [1]In Ex 33:11, *Nun* **7:28** [a]Jos 16:2 [1]In Jos 16:7, *Naarah* [2]Many mss *Azzah* **7:29** [a]Jdg 1:22-29 [1]Lit *hands* **7:30** [a]Ge 46:17; Nu 26:44-46 **7:32** [1]Lit *begot* [2]In v 34, *Shemer* **7:34** [1]In v 32, *Shomer* **7:35** [1]Lit *son* ◆ **8:1** [a]Ge 46:21; 1Chr 7:6-12 [b]1Chr 7:12 [1]Lit *begot*, so in ch **8:3** [1]In Ge 46:21 and Nu 26:40, *Ard*

7 namely, Naaman, Ahijah, and
Gera—he took them away
into exile; and he became the
father of Uzza and Ahihud.
8 Shaharaim became the father
of children in the [1]country of
Moab after he had [2]sent away
Hushim and Baara his wives.
9 By Hodesh his wife he became
the father of Jobab, Zibia,
Mesha, Malcam,
10 Jeuz, Sachia, Mirmah. These
were his sons, heads of
fathers' *households*.
11 By Hushim he became the
father of Abitub and Elpaal.
12 The sons of Elpaal *were* Eber,
Misham, and Shemed, who
built Ono and Lod, with its
towns;
13 and Beriah and Shema,
who were heads of fathers'
*households* of the inhabitants
of Aijalon, who made the
inhabitants of Gath flee;
14 and [1]Ahio, Shashak, and
Jeremoth.
15 Zebadiah, Arad, Eder,
16 Michael, Ishpah, and Joha
*were* the sons of Beriah.
17 Zebadiah, Meshullam, Hizki,
Heber,
18 Ishmerai, Izliah, and Jobab
*were* the sons of Elpaal.
19 Jakim, Zichri, Zabdi,
20 Elienai, Zillethai, Eliel,
21 Adaiah, Beraiah, and Shimrath
*were* the sons of [1]Shimei.
22 Ishpan, Eber, Eliel,
23 Abdon, Zichri, Hanan,
24 Hananiah, Elam, Anthothijah,
25 Iphdeiah and Penuel *were* the
sons of Shashak.
26 Shamsherai, Shehariah,
Athaliah,
27 Jaareshiah, Elijah, and Zichri
*were* the sons of Jeroham.
28 These were heads of the
fathers' *households* according
to their generations, *the* heads
[1]who lived in Jerusalem.

29 [a]Now in Gibeon, *Jeiel* the
father of Gibeon lived, and his
wife's name was Maacah;
30 and his firstborn son *was*
Abdon, then Zur, Kish, Baal,
Nadab,
31 Gedor, Ahio, and [1]Zecher.
32 Mikloth became the father
of [1]Shimeah. And they also
lived with their [2]relatives in
Jerusalem opposite their *other*
[2]relatives.
33 [a]Ner became the father of Kish,
and Kish became the father of
Saul,
and Saul became the father
of Jonathan, Malchi-shua,
[1]Abinadab, and [2]Eshbaal.
34 The son of Jonathan *was*
[1]Merib-baal,
and Merib-baal became the
father of Micah.
35 The sons of Micah *were*
Pithon, Melech, [1]Tarea, and
Ahaz.
36 Ahaz became the father of
[1]Jehoaddah,
and Jehoaddah became the
father of Alemeth, Azmaveth,
and Zimri;

**8:8** [1]Lit *field* [2]Lit *sent them away* **8:14** [1]Or *his brothers* **8:21** [1]In v 13, *Shema* **8:28** [1]Lit *these*
**8:29** [a]1Chr 9:35-38 **8:31** [1]In ch 9:37, *Zechariah* **8:32** [1]In 9:38, *Shimeam* [2]Lit *brothers*
**8:33** [a]1Chr 9:39-44 [1]In 1Sa 14:49, *Ishvi* [2]In 2Sa 2:8, *Ish-bosheth* **8:34** [1]In 2Sa 4:4, *Mephibosheth*
**8:35** [1]In 9:41, *Tahrea* **8:36** [1]In 9:42, *Jarah*

and Zimri became the father
of Moza.
37 Moza became the father of
Binea; [1]Raphah *was* his son,
Eleasah his son, Azel his son.
38 Azel had six sons, and these
*were* their names: Azrikam,
Bocheru, Ishmael, Sheariah,
Obadiah, and Hanan.
All these *were* the sons of Azel.
39 The sons of Eshek his brother
*were* Ulam his firstborn, Jeush
the second, and Eliphelet the
third.
40 The sons of Ulam were mighty
men of valor, archers, and had
many sons and grandsons, 150
*of them.*
All these *were* of the sons of
Benjamin.

### *Generations of Returned Exiles*

9 So all Israel was recorded by
genealogies; and behold, they
are written in the Book of the Kings
of Israel. And [a]Judah was taken
away into exile to Babylon for their
unfaithfulness.
2 [a]Now the first who lived in their
possessions in their cities *were*
Israel, the priests, the Levites, and
[b]the [1]temple servants. 3 And some
of the sons of Judah, of the sons of
Benjamin and of the sons of Ephraim
and Manasseh lived in [a]Jerusalem:
4 Uthai the son of Ammihud, the
son of Omri, the son of Imri,
the son of Bani, from the sons
of Perez the [a]son of Judah.
5 From *the Shilonites were*
Asaiah the firstborn and his
sons.
6 From the sons of Zerah *were*
Jeuel and their [1]relatives, 690
*of them.*
7 From the sons of Benjamin
*were* Sallu the son of
Meshullam, the son of
Hodaviah, the son of
Hassenuah,
8 and Ibneiah the son of
Jeroham, and Elah the son of
Uzzi, the son of Michri, and
Meshullam the son of Sheph-
atiah, the son of Reuel, the
son of Ibnijah;
9 and their relatives according
to their generations, [a]956.
All these *were* heads of
fathers' *households* according
to their fathers' houses.

10 [a]From the priests *were*
Jedaiah, Jehoiarib, Jachin,
11 and [1]Azariah the son of Hilkiah,
the son of Meshullam, the son
of Zadok, the son of Meraioth,
the son of Ahitub, [a]the leader
of the house of God;
12 and Adaiah the son of Jeroham,
the son of Pashhur, the son of
Malchijah, and Maasai the son
of Adiel, the son of Jahzerah,
the son of Meshullam, the son
of Meshillemith, the son of
Immer;
13 and their relatives, heads of
their fathers' households,
1,760 mighty men of valor for
the work of the service of the
house of God.

14 [a]Of the Levites *were* Shema-
iah the son of Hasshub, the

---

**8:37** [1]In 9:43, *Rephaiah* ◆ **9:1** [a]1Chr 5:25, 26 **9:2** [a]Ezr 2:70; Ne 7:73; 11:3-22 [b]Ezr 2:43, 58; 8:20
[1]Heb *Nethinim* **9:3** [a]Ne 11:1 **9:4** [a]Ge 46:12; Nu 26:20 **9:6** [1]Lit *brothers*, so in ch **9:9** [a]Ne 11:8
**9:10** [a]Ne 11:10-14 **9:11** [a]Jer 20:1 [1]In Ne 11:11, *Seraiah* **9:14** [a]Ne 11:15-19

son of Azrikam, the son of
Hashabiah, of the sons of
Merari;
15 and Bakbakkar, Heresh, and
Galal and Mattaniah the son
of Mica, the son of [1]Zichri, the
son of Asaph,
16 and [1]Obadiah the son of
[2]Shemaiah, the son of Galal,
the son of Jeduthun, and
Berechiah the son of Asa,
the son of Elkanah, who
lived in the villages of the
Netophathites.

17 Now the gatekeepers *were*
[1]Shallum and Akkub and
Talmon and Ahiman and their
relatives (Shallum the chief
18 *being stationed* until now at
[a]the king's gate to the east).
These *were* the gatekeepers
for the camp of the sons of
Levi.
**19** Shallum the son of Kore, the son
of [1]Ebiasaph, the son of Korah, and
his relatives of his father's house, the
Korahites, *were* over the work of the
service, keepers of the thresholds of
the tent; and their fathers had been
over the camp of Yahweh, keepers
of the entrance. **20** [a]And Phinehas
the son of Eleazar was ruler over
them previously, *and* Yahweh was
*with him.* **21** [a]Zechariah the son of
Meshelemiah was gatekeeper of the
entrance of the tent of meeting. **22** All
these who were chosen to be gate-
keepers at the thresholds were 212.
These were recorded by genealogy
in their villages, [a]whom David and
Samuel the seer established [b]in their
office of trust. **23** So they and their
sons were over the gates of the house
of Yahweh, *even* the house of the
tent, as those who kept watch. **24** The
gatekeepers were [1]on the four sides,
to the east, west, north, and south.
**25** And their relatives in their villages
[a]*were* to come in every seven days
from time to time *to be* with [1]them;
**26** for the four chief gatekeepers
who *were* Levites, were in an office
of trust, and were over the cham-
bers and over the treasuries in the
house of God. **27** And they spent the
night all around the house of God,
[a]because the watch was [1]committed
to them; and they *were* over opening
*it* morning by morning.
**28** Now some of them were over the
utensils of service, for [1]they counted
them when they brought them in and
when they took them out. **29** Some of
them also were appointed over the
furniture and over all the utensils
of the sanctuary and [a]over the fine
flour and the wine and the oil and the
frankincense and the spices. **30** Some
of [a]the sons of the priests prepared
the mixing of the spices. **31** And Mat-
tithiah, one of the Levites, who was
the firstborn of Shallum the Korahite,
had [a]the office of trust over the things
which were baked in pans. **32** Some
of their relatives of the sons of the
Kohathites [a]*were* over the showbread
to prepare it every sabbath.
**33** Now these are [a]the singers,
heads of fathers' *households* of the

**9:15** [1]In Ne 11:17, *Zabdi* **9:16** [1]In Ne 11:17, *Abda* [2]In Ne 11:17, *Shammua* **9:17** [1]In v 21, *Meshelemiah*; in 26:14, *Shelemiah*; in Ne 12:25, *Meshullam* **9:18** [a]Eze 44:1; 46:1, 2 **9:19** [1]In Ex 6:24, *Abiasaph* **9:20** [a]Nu 25:7-13 **9:21** [a]1Chr 26:2, 14 **9:22** [a]1Chr 26:1 [b]2Chr 31:15, 18 **9:24** [1]Lit *to the four winds* **9:25** [a]2Ki 11:5, 7; 2Chr 23:8 [1]Lit *these* **9:27** [a]1Chr 23:30-32 [1]Lit *on them* **9:28** [1]Lit *by count they brought them in and by count they took them out* **9:29** [a]1Chr 23:29 **9:30** [a]Ex 30:23-25 **9:31** [a]1Chr 9:22 **9:32** [a]Lv 24:5-8 **9:33** [a]1Chr 6:31-47; 25:1

Levites, *who lived* in the chambers *of*
*the temple* free *from other service*; for
they were over them [b]in their work
day and night. **34** These were heads
of fathers' *households* of the Levites
according to their generations, the
heads [1]who lived in Jerusalem.

### *Generations of Saul*

**35** [a]Now in Gibeon, Jeiel the
father of Gibeon lived, and his
wife's name was Maacah,
**36** and his firstborn son *was*
Abdon, then Zur, Kish, Baal,
Ner, Nadab,
**37** Gedor, Ahio, Zechariah,
and Mikloth.
**38** Mikloth became the father
of Shimeam. And they also
lived with their relatives in
Jerusalem opposite their *other*
relatives.
**39** [a]Ner became the father
of Kish,
and Kish became the father
of Saul,
and Saul became the father
of Jonathan, Malchi-shua,
Abinadab, and Eshbaal.
**40** The son of Jonathan *was*
Merib-baal,
and Merib-baal became the
father of Micah.
**41** The sons of Micah *were*
Pithon, Melech, Tahrea,
[a]*and Ahaz*.
**42** Ahaz became the father of
Jarah,
and Jarah became the father of
*Alemeth, Azmaveth, and Zimri*;
and Zimri became the father
of Moza.
**43** Moza became the father of
Binea and Rephaiah his son,
Eleasah his son, Azel his son.
**44** Azel had six sons, and these
*were* their names: Azrikam,
Bocheru, Ishmael, Sheariah,
Obadiah, and Hanan.
These *were* the sons of Azel.

### *The Death of Saul and His Sons*

**10** [a]Now the Philistines fought
against Israel; and the men
of Israel fled from before the Phi-
listines and fell slain on Mount
Gilboa. **2** And the Philistines closely
pursued Saul and his sons, and the
Philistines struck down Jonathan and
[a,1]Abinadab and Malchi-shua, the
sons of Saul. **3** And the battle became
heavy against Saul, and the archers
[1]hit him; and he was wounded by
the archers. **4** Then Saul said to his
armor bearer, "Draw your sword and
pierce me through with it, lest these
uncircumcised come and abuse me."
But his armor bearer was not willing,
for he was greatly afraid. [a]So Saul
took his sword and fell on it. **5** Then
his armor bearer saw that Saul was
dead, so he also fell on his sword and
died. **6** [a]Thus Saul died with his three
sons, and all *those* of his house died
together.
**7** Then all the men of Israel who
were in the valley saw that they had
fled, and that Saul and his sons were
dead. So they forsook their cities and
fled; and the Philistines came and
lived in them.
**8** Now it happened on the next day,
that the Philistines came to strip the
slain, and they found Saul and his

---

**9:33** [b]Ps 134:1 **9:34** [1]Lit *these* **9:35** [a]1Chr 8:29-32 **9:39** [a]1Chr 8:33-38 **9:41** [a]1Chr 8:35-37
◆ **10:1** [a]1Sa 31:1-13 **10:2** [a]1Sa 31:2 [1]In 1Sa 14:49, *Ishvi* **10:3** [1]Lit *found him* **10:4** [a]1Sa 31:4
**10:6** [a]1Sa 31:6

sons fallen on Mount Gilboa. **9** [a]So
they stripped him and took his head
and his weapons and sent *them* all
around the land of the Philistines,
to proclaim the good news to their
idols and to the people. **10** And they
placed his weapons in the house of
their gods and fastened his head in
the house of Dagon.

### *Jabesh-gilead Buries Saul*

**11** Then all Jabesh-gilead heard all
that the Philistines had done to
Saul, **12** [a]so all the valiant men arose
and took away the body of Saul and
the bodies of his sons and brought
them to Jabesh, and they buried their
bones under the oak in Jabesh and
fasted seven days.

**13** [a]Thus Saul died for his unfaith-
fulness, which he committed against
Yahweh, because of the word of
Yahweh which he did not keep; and
also [b]because he asked counsel of a
medium, making inquiry *of it*, **14** and
did not inquire of Yahweh. Therefore
He put him to death and [a]turned the
kingdom to David the son of Jesse.

### *David Anointed King over All Israel*

**11** [a]Then all Israel gathered to
David at Hebron [1]and said,
"Behold, we are your bone and your
flesh. **2** Previously, even when Saul
was king, you *were* the one who
led out and brought in Israel; and
Yahweh your God said to you, '[a]You
will shepherd My people Israel, and
you will be a ruler over My people
Israel.'" **3** So all the elders of Israel
came to the king at Hebron, and
David cut a covenant with them in
Hebron before Yahweh; then [a]they
anointed David king over Israel,
[b]according to the word of Yahweh
through Samuel.

### *David Captures Jerusalem*

**4** Then David and all Israel went to
Jerusalem ([a]that is, Jebus); and the
Jebusites, the inhabitants of the land,
*were* there. **5** Then the inhabitants of
Jebus said to David, "You shall not
come in here." Nevertheless, David
captured the fortress of Zion, that is,
the city of David. **6** And David said,
"Whoever strikes down a Jebusite
first shall be chief and commander."
[a]Joab the son of Zeruiah went up first,
so he became chief. **7** Then David
lived in the stronghold; therefore it
was called the city of David. **8** And
he [1]built the city all around, from
the [2]Millo even to the surrounding
area; and Joab [3]repaired the rest of
the city. **9** [a]And David became greater
and greater, and Yahweh of hosts *was*
with him.

### *David's Mighty Men*

**10** [a]Now these are the heads of the
mighty men whom David had, who
gave him strong support in his king-
dom, together with all Israel, to make
him king, [b]according to the word of
Yahweh concerning Israel. **11** These
*constitute* the list of the mighty men
whom David had: [a]Jashobeam, the
son of a Hachmonite, [b]the chief
of the thirty; he lifted up his spear
against three hundred [1]slain *by him*
at one time.

---

**10:9** [a]1Sa 31:9 **10:12** [a]1Sa 31:12f **10:13** [a]1Sa 13:13, 14; 15:23 [b]Lv 19:31; 20:6; 1Sa 28:7
**10:14** [a]1Sa 15:28; 1Chr 12:23 ◆ **11:1** [a]2Sa 5:1, 3, 6-10 [1]Lit *saying* **11:2** [a]2Sa 5:2; 7:7 **11:3** [a]2Sa 2:4;
5:3, 5 [b]1Sa 16:1, 3, 12, 13 **11:4** [a]Jos 15:8, 63; Jdg 1:21 **11:6** [a]2Sa 8:16 **11:8** [1]Or *fortified* [2]Citadel [3]Lit
*revived* **11:9** [a]2Sa 3:1 **11:10** [a]2Sa 23:8-39 [b]1Chr 11:3 **11:11** [a]2Sa 23:8 [b]1Chr 12:18 [1]Lit *slain ones*

**12** And after him was Eleazar the
son of [a]Dodo, the Ahohite, who *was*
[1]one of the three mighty men. **13** He
was with David at [1]Pasdammim.
[a]Now the Philistines had gathered
together there to battle, and there
was a portion of the field full of bar-
ley; and the people fled from before
the Philistines. **14** But they took their
stand in the midst of that portion and
delivered it, and struck down the Phi-
listines. So Yahweh saved them by a
great salvation.

**15** Then three of the thirty chief
men went down to the rock to David,
to the cave of Adullam, while [a]the
camp of the Philistines was camping
in the valley of Rephaim. **16** And Da-
vid was then in the fortress, while
[a]the garrison of the Philistines was
then in Bethlehem. **17** Then David
had a craving and said, "Oh that
someone would give me water to
drink from the well of Bethlehem,
which is by the gate!" **18** So the three
broke through the camp of the Phi-
listines and drew water from the well
of Bethlehem which was by the gate,
and carried *it* and brought *it* to David.
Nevertheless, David was not willing
to drink it, but poured it out to Yah-
weh; **19** and he said, "Be it far from
me before my God that I should do
this. Shall I drink the blood of these
men *who went* [1]at the risk of their
lives? For at the risk of their lives
they brought it." Therefore he was
not willing to drink it. These things
the three mighty men did.

**20** Now [1]Abshai, the brother of
Joab, was chief of the [2]thirty. And
he swung his spear against three
hundred [3]*who were* slain *by him*; and
he had a name as well as the [2]thirty.
**21** Of the three in the second *rank* he
was the most honored and became
their commander; however, he did
not attain to the *first* three.

**22** [a]Benaiah the son of Jehoiada,
the son of a valiant man of Kabzeel,
mighty in deeds, struck down the [1]two
*sons of* Ariel of Moab. He also went
down and struck down a lion in the
midst of a pit on a snowy day. **23** He
had also struck down an Egyptian, [1]an
impressive man, [2]five cubits tall. Now
in the Egyptian's hand was [a]a spear
like a weaver's beam, but he went
down to him with a club and snatched
the spear from the Egyptian's hand
and killed him with his own spear.
**24** These *things* Benaiah the son of
Jehoiada did, and had a name as well
as the three mighty men. **25** Behold, he
was honored among the thirty, but he
did not attain to the three. And David
appointed him over his guard.

**26** Now the mighty men of the
military forces *were*

Asahel the brother of Joab,
Elhanan the son of Dodo of
Bethlehem,
**27** [1]Shammoth the Harorite,
Helez the [2]Pelonite,
**28** Ira the son of Ikkesh the
Tekoite,
Abiezer the Anathothite,
**29** [1]Sibbecai the Hushathite,
[2]Ilai the Ahohite,
**30** Maharai the Netophathite,
[1]Heled the son of Baanah the
Netophathite,

---

**11:12** [a]1Chr 27:4 [1]Lit *among* **11:13** [a]2Sa 23:11, 12 [1]In 1Sa 17:1, *Ephes-dammim* **11:15** [a]1Chr 14:9
**11:16** [a]1Sa 10:5 **11:19** [1]Lit *with their souls* **11:20** [1]In 2Sa 23:18, *Abishai* [2]So Syr; M.T. *3* [3]Lit *slain ones*
**11:22** [a]2Sa 8:18 [1]Or *two lion-like heroes* of **11:23** [a]1Sa 17:7 [1]Lit *a man of appearance* [2]Approx. 7.5 ft.
or 2.3 m, a cubit was approx. 18 in. or 45 cm **11:27** [1]In 2Sa 23:25, *Shammah the Harodite* [2]In 2Sa 23:26,
*Paltite* **11:29** [1]In 2Sa 23:27, *Mebunnai* [2]In 2Sa 23:28, *Zalmon* **11:30** [1]In 2Sa 23:29, *Heleb*

31 Ithai the son of Ribai of
Gibeah of the sons of
Benjamin,
Benaiah the Pirathonite,
32 [1]Hurai of the brooks of Gaash,
[2]Abiel the Arbathite,
33 Azmaveth the Baharumite,
Eliahba the Shaalbonite,
34 the sons of [1]Hashem the
Gizonite,
Jonathan the son of Shagee
the Hararite,
35 Ahiam the son of [1]Sacar the
Hararite,
[2]Eliphal the son of Ur,
36 Hepher the Mecherathite,
Ahijah the Pelonite,
37 Hezro the Carmelite,
[1]Naarai the son of Ezbai,
38 Joel the brother of Nathan,
Mibhar the son of Hagri,
39 Zelek the Ammonite,
Naharai the Berothite, the
armor bearer of Joab the son
of Zeruiah,
40 Ira the Ithrite,
Gareb the Ithrite,
41 Uriah the Hittite,
Zabad the son of Ahlai,
42 Adina the son of Shiza the
Reubenite, a chief of the
Reubenites, and thirty with
him,
43 Hanan the son of Maacah
and Joshaphat the Mithnite,
44 Uzzia the Ashterathite,
Shama and Jeiel the sons of
Hotham the Aroerite,
45 Jediael the son of Shimri
and Joha his brother, the
Tizite,
46 Eliel the Mahavite
and Jeribai and Joshaviah, the
sons of Elnaam,
and Ithmah the Moabite,
47 Eliel and Obed and Jaasiel the
Mezobaite.

### *David's Mighty Men*

12 [a]Now these are the ones who
came to David at Ziklag, while
he was still restricted because of Saul
the son of Kish; and they were among
the mighty men who helped *him*
in war. 2 They were equipped with
bows, [a]using both the right hand and
the left *to sling* stones and *to shoot*
arrows from the bow; [b]*they were*
Saul's relatives from Benjamin.
3 The chief was Ahiezer, then
Joash, the sons of Shemaah
the Gibeathite; and Jeziel and
Pelet, the sons of Azmaveth,
and Beracah and Jehu the
Anathothite,
4 and Ishmaiah the Gibeonite, a
mighty man among the thirty,
and over the thirty. [1]Then
Jeremiah, Jahaziel, Johanan,
Jozabad the Gederathite,
5 [1]Eluzai, Jerimoth, Bealiah,
Shemariah, Shephatiah the
Haruphite,
6 Elkanah, Isshiah, Azarel,
Joezer, Jashobeam, the
Korahites,
7 and Joelah and Zebadiah, the
sons of Jeroham of Gedor.
8 From the Gadites, mighty men
of valor separated themselves
to David in the stronghold in
the wilderness, men of war

**11:32** [1]In 2Sa 23:30, *Hiddai* [2]In 2Sa 23:31, *Abi-albon* **11:34** [1]In 2Sa 23:32, *Jashen* **11:35** [1]In 2Sa 23:33, *Sharar* [2]In 2Sa 23:34, *Eliphelet the son of Ahasbai* **11:37** [1]In 2Sa 23:35, *Paarai the Arbite*
◆ **12:1** [a]1Sa 27:2-6 **12:2** [a]Jdg 3:15; 20:16 [b]1Chr 12:29 **12:4** [1]In Heb the beginning of v 5, making 41 vv in ch **12:5** [1]v 6 in Heb

*who had gone out for military*
duty, who could [1]handle large
shield and spear, and whose
faces were like the faces
of lions, and [a]*they were* as
swift as the gazelles on the
mountains.
9 Ezer *was* the first, Obadiah the
second, Eliab the third,
10 Mishmannah the fourth,
Jeremiah the fifth,
11 Attai the sixth, Eliel the
seventh,
12 Johanan the eighth, Elzabad
the ninth,
13 Jeremiah the tenth,
Machbannai the eleventh.
14 These of the sons of Gad were
chiefs of the army; [a]he who was least
was equal to one hundred and the
greatest to one thousand. 15 [a]These
are the ones who crossed the Jordan
in the first month when it was over-
flowing all its banks and they made
all those in the valleys flee, both to
the east and to the west.
16 Then some of the sons of Ben-
jamin and Judah came to the strong-
hold to David. 17 David went out
before them, and he answered and
said to them, "If you come peacefully
to me to help me, my heart shall be
united with you; but if to betray me
to my adversaries, since there is no
violence in my hands, may the God
of our fathers look on *it* and reprove."
18 And [a]the Spirit clothed [b]Amasai,
who was the chief of the thirty, *and*
*he said,*
"*We* are yours, O David,
And with you, O son of Jesse!
[c]Peace, peace to you,
And peace to him
who helps you;
Indeed, your God helps you!"
Then David received them and made
them chiefs of the band.
19 [a]Now from Manasseh also some
defected to David when he was about
to go to battle with the Philistines
against Saul. But they did not help
them, for the lords of the Philistines
after counsel sent him away, saying,
"At *the cost of* our heads he may de-
fect to his master Saul." 20 As he went
to Ziklag there defected to him from
Manasseh: Adnah, Jozabad, Jediael,
Michael, Jozabad, Elihu and Zillethai,
chiefs of thousands who belonged
to Manasseh. 21 They helped David
against [a]the marauding band, for
they were all mighty men of valor,
and were commanders in the army.
22 For day by day *men* came to David
to help him, until there was a great
camp [a]like the camp of God.

### *David's Military Companies in Hebron*

23 Now these are the numbers of the
[1]companies equipped for *military*
duty, [a]who came to David at He-
bron, [b]to turn the kingdom of Saul
to him, [c]according to the [2]command
of Yahweh.
24 The sons of Judah who bore
shield and spear *were* 6,800,
equipped for *military* duty.
25 Of the sons of Simeon, mighty
men of valor for *military* duty,
7,100.
26 Of the sons of Levi 4,600.
27 Now Jehoiada was the leader
of *the house of* Aaron, and
with him were 3,700,

**12:8** [a]2Sa 2:18 [1]Lit *arrange* **12:14** [a]Dt 32:30 **12:15** [a]Jos 3:15; 4:18 **12:18** [a]Jdg 3:10; 6:34 [b]1Chr 2:17 [c]1Sa 25:5, 6 **12:19** [a]1Sa 29:2-9 **12:21** [a]1Sa 30:1 **12:22** [a]Ge 32:2; Jos 5:13-15 **12:23** [a]2Sa 2:3, 4 [b]1Chr 10:14 [c]1Chr 11:10 [1]Lit *heads* [2]Lit *mouth*

28 also [a]Zadok, a young man
mighty of valor, and of his
father's house 22 commanders.
29 Of the sons of Benjamin,
[a]Saul's relatives, 3,000; for
until now [b]the greatest part of
them had kept their allegiance
to the house of Saul.
30 Of the sons of Ephraim
20,800, mighty men of valor,
men [1]who had a name in their
fathers' households.
31 Of the half-tribe of Manasseh
18,000, who were designated
by name to come and make
David king.
32 Of the sons of Issachar, [a]men
who knew *how to* discern the
times, to know what Israel
should do, their chiefs *were* two
hundred; and all their relatives
*were* at their command.
33 Of Zebulun, there were
50,000 who went out in the
army, who could arrange
*themselves* for battle with
all kinds of weapons of war
and helped *David* [1]with [a]an
undivided heart.
34 Of Naphtali *there were* 1,000
commanders, and with them
37,000 with large shield and
spear.
35 Of the Danites who could
arrange *themselves* for battle,
*there were* 28,600.
36 Of Asher *there were* 40,000
who went out in the army to
arrange *themselves* for battle.
37 From the other side of the
Jordan, of the Reubenites
and the Gadites and of the
half-tribe of Manasseh, *there
were* 120,000 with all *kinds*
of weapons for the army for
battle.

38 All these, being men of war who
could draw up in battle [1]lines, came
to Hebron with [a]*their* whole heart
to make David king over all Israel;
and all the rest also of Israel were
of one heart to make David king.
39 They were there with David three
days, eating and drinking, for their
relatives had prepared for them.
40 Moreover those who were near
to them, *even* as far as Issachar and
Zebulun and Naphtali, [a]brought food
on donkeys, camels, mules, and on
oxen, great provisions *of* flour, fig
cakes and bunches of raisins, wine,
oil, oxen, and sheep. There was
gladness indeed in Israel.

### *Uzza Dies from Touching the Ark*

13 Then David took counsel with
the commanders of the thousands and the hundreds, even with
every leader. 2 And David said to all
the assembly of Israel, "If it seems
good to you, and if it is from Yahweh
our God, let us send everywhere to
our relatives who remain in all the
lands of Israel, also to the priests and
Levites who are with them in their
cities with pasture lands, that they
may gather with us; 3 and let us bring
back the ark of our God to us, [a]for we
did not seek it in the days of Saul."
4 Then all the assembly said that they
would do so, for the thing was right
in the eyes of all the people.
5 [a]So David assembled all Israel
together, from the Shihor of Egypt

**12:28** [a]2Sa 8:17; 1Chr 6:8, 53 **12:29** [a]1Chr 12:2 [b]2Sa 2:8, 9 **12:30** [1]Or *of renown* **12:32** [a]Es 1:13
**12:33** [a]Ps 12:2 [1]Lit *not of double heart* **12:38** [a]2Sa 5:1-3; 1Chr 12:33 [1]Lit *line, array*; cf. 12:35, 36
**12:40** [a]1Sa 25:18 ◆ **13:3** [a]1Sa 7:1, 2 **13:5** [a]2Sa 6:1; 1Ki 8:65; 1Chr 15:3

even to [1]Lebo-hamath, [b]to bring
the ark of God from Kiriath-jearim.
6 [a]And David and all Israel went up
to [b]Baalah, *that is,* to Kiriath-jearim,
which belongs to Judah, to bring up
from there the ark of God, Yahweh,
[c]who is enthroned *above* the cheru-
bim, where His name is called.
7 And they drove the ark of God
on a new cart from [a]the house of
Abinadab, and Uzza and Ahio were
leading the cart. 8 Now David and
all Israel were celebrating before
God with all *their* strength, [a]even
with songs and with lyres, harps,
tambourines, cymbals, and with
trumpets.
9 Then they came to [a]the thresh-
ing floor of Chidon. And Uzza
reached out with his hand to take
hold of the ark, because the oxen
nearly upset *it.* 10 And the anger of
Yahweh burned against Uzza, and
He struck him down [a]because he
reached out with his hand to the
ark; [b]and he died there before God.
11 And David became angry because
[1]of Yahweh's breaking out against
Uzza; and that place is called [2]Perez-
uzza to this day. 12 So David was
afraid of God that day, saying, "How
can I bring the ark of God *back* to
me?" 13 And David did not move the
ark with him to the city of David, but
took it aside [a]to the house of Obed-
edom the Gittite. 14 Thus the ark of
God remained with the household
of Obed-edom in his house three
months; and [a]Yahweh blessed the
household of Obed-edom with all
that he had.

### *David Takes More Wives*

14 [a]Then Hiram king of Tyre sent
messengers to David with ce-
dar trees and craftsmen of walls and
craftsmen of wood, to build a house
for him. 2 Thus David knew that
Yahweh had established him as king
over Israel, *and* that his kingdom was
lifted up, for the sake of His people
Israel.
3 Then David took more wives at
Jerusalem, and David [1]became the
father of more sons and daughters.
4 [a]These are the names of the chil-
dren [1]born to him in Jerusalem:
Shammua, Shobab, Nathan,
Solomon,
5 Ibhar, Elishua, Elpelet,
6 Nogah, Nepheg, Japhia,
7 Elishama, Beeliada, and
Eliphelet.

### *David Strikes Down the Philistines*

8 Then the Philistines heard that Da-
vid had been anointed king over all
Israel, so all the Philistines went up
to seek out David. And David heard *of*
*it* and went out against them. 9 Now
the Philistines had come and [a]made a
raid in the valley of Rephaim. 10 Then
David asked of God, saying, "Shall I
go up against the Philistines? And
will You give them into my hand?"
And Yahweh said to him, "Go up, for
I will give them into your hand." 11 So
they came up to [1]Baal-perazim, and
there David struck them down; and
David said, "God has broken through
my enemies by my hand, like the
breakthrough of waters." Therefore
they named that place [1]Baal-perazim.

**13:5** [b]1Sa 6:21; 7:1 [1]Or *the entrance of Hamath* **13:6** [a]2Sa 6:2-11 [b]Jos 15:9 [c]Ex 25:22; 2Ki 19:15
**13:7** [a]1Sa 7:1 **13:8** [a]1Chr 15:16 **13:9** [a]2Sa 6:6 **13:10** [a]1Chr 15:13, 15 [b]Lv 10:2 **13:11** [1]Lit *Yahweh had broken through a breakthrough* [2]Lit *the breakthrough of Uzza* **13:13** [a]1Chr 15:25 **13:14** [a]1Chr 26:4, 5
◆ **14:1** [a]2Sa 5:11 **14:3** [1]Lit *begot* **14:4** [a]1Chr 3:5-8 [1]Lit *who were to him* **14:9** [a]1Chr 11:15; 14:13
**14:11** [1]Lit *the master of breakthroughs*

12 And they forsook their gods there;
so David said *the word*, and they were
burned with fire.
13 Then the Philistines [a]yet again
made a raid in the valley. 14 So David
again asked of God, and God said to
him, "You shall not go *directly* up af-
ter them; circle around from [1]behind
them and come at them in front of the
[2]balsam trees. 15 And it will be that
when you hear the sound of marching
in the tops of the [1]balsam trees, then
you shall go out to battle, for God will
have gone out before you to strike the
camp of the Philistines." 16 Then Da-
vid did just as God had commanded
him, and they struck down the camp
of the Philistines from [1]Gibeon even
as far as Gezer. 17 Then the name of
David went out into all the lands; and
[a]Yahweh brought the dread of him on
all the nations.

### *The Ark Is Brought to Jerusalem*

15 Then *David* made houses for
himself in the city of David;
and he prepared a place for the
ark of God and [a]pitched a tent for
it. 2 And David said, "[a]No one is to
carry the ark of God but the Levites;
for Yahweh chose them to carry the
ark of [1]God and to minister to Him
forever." 3 Then [a]David assembled all
Israel at Jerusalem to bring up the ark
of Yahweh [b]to its place which he had
prepared for it. 4 And David gathered
together the sons of Aaron and [a]the
Levites:

5 of the sons of Kohath, Uriel
the chief, and 120 of his
[1]relatives;
6 of the sons of Merari, Asaiah
the chief, and 220 of his
relatives;
7 of the sons of Gershom,
Joel the chief, and 130 of his
relatives;
8 of the sons of Elizaphan,
Shemaiah the chief, and 200
of his relatives;
9 of the sons of Hebron, Eliel
the chief, and 80 of his
relatives;
10 of the sons of Uzziel,
Amminadab the chief, and 112
of his relatives.

11 Then David called for [a]Zadok
and [b]Abiathar the priests, and for the
Levites, for Uriel, Asaiah, Joel, She-
maiah, Eliel and Amminadab, 12 and
said to them, "You are the heads of
the fathers' *households* of the Levites;
[a]set yourselves apart as holy, both
you and your relatives, that you may
bring up the ark of Yahweh, the God
of Israel, [b]to *the place* that I have
prepared for it. 13 [a]Because you did
not *carry it* at the first, Yahweh our
God broke out against us, for we did
not seek Him according to the *legal*
judgment." 14 [a]So the priests and
the Levites set themselves apart as
holy to bring up the ark of Yahweh,
the God of Israel. 15 And the sons of
[a]the Levites carried the ark of God
on their shoulders with the poles
thereon, as Moses had commanded
according to the word of Yahweh.
16 Then David said to the chiefs of
the Levites [a]to appoint their relatives
the singers, with instruments of
music, harps, lyres, loud-sounding

---

**14:13** [a]1Chr 14:9 **14:14** [1]Lit *from upon* [2]Or *baka-shrubs* **14:15** [1]Or *baka-shrubs* **14:16** [1]In 2Sa 5:25, *Geba* **14:17** [a]Ex 15:14-16; Dt 2:25 ◆ **15:1** [a]1Chr 15:3; 16:1; 17:1-5 **15:2** [a]Nu 4:15; Dt 10:8 [1]Some mss *Yahweh* **15:3** [a]1Ki 8:1; 1Chr 13:5 [b]Ex 40:20f; 2Sa 6:12, 17; 1Chr 15:1, 12 **15:4** [a]1Chr 6:16-30; 12:26 **15:5** [1]Lit *brothers*, so in ch **15:11** [a]1Chr 12:28 [b]1Sa 22:20-23; 1Ki 2:26, 35 **15:12** [a]Ex 19:14, 15; 2Chr 35:6 [b]1Chr 15:1, 3 **15:13** [a]2Sa 6:3; 1Chr 13:7 **15:14** [a]1Chr 15:12 **15:15** [a]Ex 25:14; Nu 4:5f **15:16** [a]1Chr 13:8; 25:1

cymbals, to raise a sound of gladness.
17 So [a]the Levites appointed Heman
the son of Joel, and from his relatives,
Asaph the son of Berechiah; and from
the sons of Merari their relatives,
Ethan the son of Kushaiah, 18 and
with them their relatives of the sec-
ond rank, Zechariah, [1]Ben, Jaaziel,
Shemiramoth, Jehiel, Unni, Eliab,
Benaiah, Maaseiah, Mattithiah, Eliph-
elehu, Mikneiah, Obed-edom, and
Jeiel, the gatekeepers. 19 So the sing-
ers, Heman, Asaph and Ethan *were*
*appointed* to sound aloud cymbals
of bronze; 20 and Zechariah, Aziel,
Shemiramoth, Jehiel, Unni, Eliab,
Maaseiah, and Benaiah, with [1]harps
*set* according to [a]alamoth; 21 and
Mattithiah, Eliphelehu, Mikneiah,
Obed-edom, Jeiel, and Azaziah, to
lead with [1]lyres *set* according to [a]the
sheminith. 22 Chenaniah, chief of the
Levites, was *in charge of* the [1]singing;
he gave instruction in singing because
he had understanding. 23 Berechiah
and Elkanah were gatekeepers for
the ark. 24 Shebaniah, Joshaphat,
Nethanel, Amasai, Zechariah, Bena-
iah, and Eliezer, the priests, [a]blew
the trumpets before the ark of God.
Obed-edom and Jehiah also *were*
gatekeepers for the ark.
25 [a]So *it was* David, with the elders
of Israel and the commanders over
thousands, who went to bring up the
ark of the covenant of Yahweh from
[b]the house of Obed-edom with glad-
ness. 26 Now this happened because
God was helping the Levites who were
carrying the ark of the covenant of
Yahweh. *And they sacrificed* [a]seven
bulls and seven rams. 27 Now David
was clothed with a robe of fine linen
with all the Levites who were carry-
ing the ark, as well as the singers and
Chenaniah the leader of the singing
*with* the singers. [a]David also wore a
linen ephod. 28 Thus all Israel was
bringing up the ark of the covenant
of Yahweh with shouting, and with
sound of the [1]horn, with trumpets,
with loud-sounding cymbals, with
harps, and lyres.
29 Now it happened *as* the ark
of the covenant of Yahweh came to
the city of David, that [a]Michal the
daughter of Saul looked out of the
window and saw King David leaping
and celebrating; and she despised
him in her heart.

### *A Tent for the Ark*

16 And they brought in the ark
of God and [a]placed it inside
the tent which David had pitched
for it, and they brought burnt
offerings and peace offerings near
before God. 2 Then David completed
offering the burnt offerings and the
peace offerings. And he blessed the
people in the name of Yahweh. 3 And
he apportioned to everyone of Israel,
both men and women, to everyone
a loaf of bread and a portion *of meat*
and a raisin cake.
4 And he made some of the Levites
ministers before the ark of Yahweh,
even to bring remembrance and to
thank and praise Yahweh, the God of
Israel: 5 Asaph the chief, and second
to him Zechariah, *then* [1]Jeiel, She-
miramoth, Jehiel, Mattithiah, Eliab,

---

**15:17** [a]1Chr 25:1 **15:18** [1]Omitted in Gr and many mss **15:20** [a]Ps 46: title [1]Or *harps of maiden-like tone* **15:21** [a]Ps 6: title [1]Or *octave harps* **15:22** [1]Lit *bearing up* **15:24** [a]1Chr 15:28; 16:6 **15:25** [a]2Sa 6:12, 15 [b]1Chr 13:13 **15:26** [a]Nu 23:1-4, 29 **15:27** [a]2Sa 6:14 **15:28** [1]Or *trumpet* **15:29** [a]2Sa 3:13f; 6:16 ◆ **16:1** [a]1Chr 15:1 **16:5** [1]In 1Chr 15:18, *Jaaziel*

Benaiah, Obed-edom, and Jeiel, with
musical instruments, harps, lyres;
also Asaph *played* loud-sounding
cymbals, 6 and Benaiah and Jahaziel
the priests *blew* trumpets continually
before the ark of the covenant of God.
7 Then on that day David [a]first
assigned [1]Asaph and his [2]relatives
to give thanks to Yahweh.

### *Song of Thanksgiving*

8 [a]Oh give thanks to Yahweh,
call upon His name;
[b]Make known His acts
among the peoples.
9 Sing to Him, sing
praises to Him;
Muse on all His
wondrous deeds.
10 Boast in His holy name;
Let the heart of those who
seek Yahweh be glad.
11 [a]Inquire of Yahweh
and His strength;
Seek His face continually.
12 [a]Remember His wondrous
deeds which He has done,
[b]His miraculous signs
and the judgments
uttered by His mouth,
13 O seed of Israel His servant,
O sons of Jacob, His
chosen ones!
14 He is Yahweh our God;
[a]His judgments are
in all the earth.
15 Remember His
covenant forever,
The word which He
commanded for
a thousand generations,
16 [a]Which He cut with Abraham,
And His oath to Isaac.
17 [a]Then He also confirmed
it to Jacob for a statute,
To Israel as an everlasting
covenant,
18 Saying, "[a]To you I will give
the land of Canaan,
As the portion of your
inheritance,"
19 [a]When you were only a
few men in number,
Of little account, and
sojourners in it,
20 And they wandered about
from nation to nation,
And from *one* kingdom
to another people,
21 He permitted no man
to oppress them,
And [a]He reproved kings
for their sakes,
22 "Do not touch My
anointed ones,
And [a]against My prophets
do no evil."
23 [a]Sing to Yahweh, all the earth;
Proclaim good news of His
salvation from day to day.
24 Recount His glory
among the nations,
His wondrous deeds
among all the peoples.
25 For [a]great is Yahweh, and
greatly to be praised;
And He is [b,1]more [2]fearsome
than all gods.
26 For all the gods of the
peoples are [a,1]idols,
[b]But Yahweh made
the heavens.

---

**16:7** [a]2Sa 22:1; 23:1 [1]Lit *by the hand of Asaph* [2]Lit *brothers* **16:8** [a]1Chr 16:8-36; Ps 105:1-15 [b]1Ki 8:43; 2Ki 19:19 **16:11** [a]Ps 24:6 **16:12** [a]Ps 103:2 [b]Ps 78:43-68 **16:14** [a]Ps 48:10 **16:16** [a]Ge 12:7; 17:2; 22:16-18; 26:3 **16:17** [a]Ge 35:11, 12 **16:18** [a]Ge 13:15 **16:19** [a]Ge 34:30; Dt 7:7 **16:21** [a]Ge 12:17; 20:3; Ex 7:15-18 **16:22** [a]Ge 20:7 **16:23** [a]Ps 96:1-13 **16:25** [a]Ps 144:3-6 [b]Ps 89:7 [1]Or *to be feared above all gods* [2]Or *awesome* **16:26** [a]Lv 19:4 [b]Ps 102:25 [1]Or *non-existent things*

27 Splendor and majesty
are before Him,
Strength and joy are
in His place.
28 Ascribe to Yahweh, O families
of the peoples,
Ascribe to Yahweh glory
and strength.
29 Ascribe to Yahweh the
glory of His name;
Lift up [1]an offering, and
come before Him;
[a]Worship Yahweh in the
splendor of holiness.
30 Tremble before Him,
all the earth;
Indeed, the world is
established, it will
not be shaken.
31 [a]Let the heavens be glad,
and let the earth rejoice;
And let them say
among the nations,
"[b]Yahweh reigns."
32 [a]Let the sea [1]roar,
as well as its fullness;
Let the field exult, and
all that is in it.
33 Then the trees of the forest will
sing for joy before Yahweh;
For He is coming
to judge the earth.
34 [a]Oh give thanks to Yahweh,
for He is good,
For His lovingkindness
endures forever.
35 [a]Then say, "Save us, O God
of our salvation,
And gather us and deliver us
from among the nations,
To give thanks
to Your holy name
And revel in Your praise."
36 [a]Blessed be Yahweh,
the God of Israel,
From everlasting to everlasting.
Then all the people [b]said, "Amen,"
and praised Yahweh.

### *Ministering Before the Ark*

37 So he left behind Asaph and his
[1]relatives there [a]before the ark of the
covenant of Yahweh to minister before
the ark continually, [b]as every day's
work required; 38 and [a]Obed-edom
with [1]his 68 relatives; Obed-edom,
also the son of Jeduthun, and [b]Hosah
as gatekeepers. 39 Now *he left behind*
[a]Zadok the priest and his [1]relatives
the priests [b]before the [2]tabernacle
of Yahweh in the high place, which
*was* at Gibeon, 40 to offer burnt offer-
ings to Yahweh on the altar of burnt
offering continually morning and
evening, [a]even according to all that is
written in the law of Yahweh, which
He commanded Israel. 41 And with
them *were* [a]Heman and Jeduthun,
and [b]the rest who were chosen, who
were designated by name, to [c]give
thanks to Yahweh, because His lov-
ingkindness endures forever. 42 And
with them *were* Heman and Jeduthun
*with* trumpets and cymbals for those
who should sound aloud, and *with*
instruments *for* [a]the songs of God,
and the sons of Jeduthun for the gate.
43 [a]Then all the people went each
to his house, and David returned to
bless his household.

**16:29** [a]Ps 29:2 [1]Or *a grain offering* **16:31** [a]Is 44:23; 49:13 [b]Ps 93:1; 96:10 **16:32** [a]Ps 98:7 [1]Or *thunder* **16:34** [a]2Chr 5:13; 7:3; Ezr 3:11; Ps 106:1; 136:1; Jer 33:11 **16:35** [a]Ps 106:47, 48 **16:36** [a]1Ki 8:15, 56; Ps 72:18 [b]Dt 27:15; Ne 8:6 **16:37** [a]1Chr 16:4, 5 [b]2Chr 8:14; Ezr 3:4 [1]Lit *brothers* **16:38** [a]1Chr 13:14 [b]1Chr 26:10 [1]Lit *their brothers, 68* **16:39** [a]1Chr 15:11 [b]1Ki 3:4 [1]Lit *brothers* [2]Lit *dwelling place* **16:40** [a]Ex 29:38-42; Nu 28:3, 4 **16:41** [a]1Chr 6:33 [b]1Chr 25:1-6 [c]2Chr 5:13 **16:42** [a]1Chr 25:7; 2Chr 7:6; 29:27 **16:43** [a]2Sa 6:19

### *The Ark of God Inhabits a Tent*

**17** [a]Now it happened when David
inhabited his house, that David
said to Nathan the prophet, "Behold,
I inhabit a house of cedar, but the ark
of the covenant of Yahweh is under
*tent* curtains." **2** So Nathan said to
David, "Do all that is in your heart,
for God is with you."
**3** Now it happened in the same
night, that the word of God came
to Nathan, saying, **4** "Go and say
to David My servant, 'Thus says
Yahweh, "[a]You shall not build Me
a house to inhabit; **5** for I have not
inhabited a house since the day that
I brought up Israel to this day, [a]but
I have been from tent to tent and
from *one* [1]dwelling place *to another*.
**6** Wherever I have gone about with all
Israel, did I speak a word [a]with *even*
one of the judges of Israel, whom I
commanded to shepherd My people,
saying, 'Why have you not built Me a
house of cedar?'"'

### *David's House Will Be Established Forever*

**7** "So now, thus shall you say to My
servant David, 'Thus says Yahweh of
hosts, "I Myself took you from the
pasture, from following the sheep, to
be ruler over My people Israel. **8** And
I have been with you wherever you
have gone, and have cut off all your
enemies from before you; and I will
make you a name like the name of
the great men who are on the earth.
**9** And I will appoint a place for My
people Israel and will plant them,
that they may dwell in their own
place and not be disturbed again; and
the [1]unrighteous will not waste them
anymore as formerly, **10** even from
the day that I commanded judges *to
be* over My people Israel. And I will
subdue all your enemies.
And I tell you that Yahweh will
build a house for you. **11** And it will be
that when your days are fulfilled to go
*to be* with your fathers, I will raise up
*one of* your seed after you, who will
be of your sons; and I will establish
his kingdom. **12** He shall build for
Me a house, and I will establish his
throne forever. **13** [a]I will be a father
to him and he will be a son to Me;
and I will not remove My loving-
kindness from him, [b]as I removed *it*
from him who was before you. **14** But
I will cause him to stand in My house
and in My kingdom forever, and his
throne shall be established forever."'"
**15** According to all these words and
according to all this vision, so Nathan
spoke to David.

### *David Magnifies Yahweh's Name*

**16** Then David the king went in and
sat before Yahweh and said, "[a]Who
am I, O Yahweh God, and what is
my house that You have brought me
this far? **17** And this was a small thing
in Your eyes, O God; but You have
spoken of the house of Your slave
concerning the distant future, and
have regarded me according to the
standard of a man of high degree,
O Yahweh God. **18** Again what more
can David *say* to You concerning the
glory *bestowed* on Your slave? You
know Your slave. **19** O Yahweh, [a]for
the sake of Your slave, and according
to Your own heart, You have done

---

◆ **17:1** [a]2Sa 7:1-29 **17:4** [a]1Chr 28:2, 3 **17:5** [a]Ex 40:2, 3; 2Sa 7:6 [1]Or *tabernacle*, cf. 2Sa 7:6
**17:6** [a]2Sa 7:7 **17:9** [1]Lit *sons of wickedness* **17:13** [a]2Co 6:18; Heb 1:5 [b]1Chr 10:14 **17:16** [a]2Sa 7:18
**17:19** [a]2Sa 7:21; Is 37:35

all this greatness, to make known
all these great things. **20** O Yahweh,
there is none like You, and there is
no God besides You, according to all
that we have heard with our ears.
**21** And what one nation in the earth
is like Your people Israel, whom God
went to redeem for Himself *as* a
people, to make You a name by great
and awesome things, in driving out
nations from before Your people,
whom You redeemed out of Egypt?
**22** [a]Yet You gave Your people Israel *to
be* Your own people forever, and You,
O Yahweh, have become their God.

**23** "So now, O Yahweh, let the word
that You have spoken concerning
Your slave and concerning his house
[1]endure forever, and do as You have
spoken, **24** that Your name [1]endure
and be magnified forever, by saying,
'Yahweh of hosts is the God of Israel,
*even* a God to Israel; and the house
of David Your [2]servant is established
before You.' **25** For You, O my God,
have revealed in the hearing of Your
slave that You will build for him a
house; therefore Your slave has
found *courage* to pray before You.
**26** So now, O Yahweh, You are God,
and You have [1]promised this good
thing to Your slave. **27** So now, You
have been pleased to bless the house
of Your slave, that it may be forever
before You. For You, O Yahweh, have
blessed, and it is blessed forever."

### *David Strikes Down Nations*

**18** Now [a]it happened afterwards,
that David struck the Philis-
tines and subdued them and took
Gath and its towns from the hand
of the Philistines. **2** He also struck
Moab, and the Moabites became
servants to David, bringing tribute.

**3** Then David struck Hadadezer
king of Zobah *as far as* Hamath, as he
went to set up his [1]power at the Eu-
phrates River. **4** And David captured
from him 1,000 chariots and 7,000
horsemen and 20,000 foot soldiers,
and David hamstrung all the chariot
horses, but left *enough* of them for
100 chariots.

**5** Then the Arameans of [1]Damas-
cus came to help Hadadezer king
[a]of Zobah. And David struck down
22,000 men of the Arameans. **6** Then
David placed *garrisons* among the
Arameans of [1]Damascus; and the
Arameans became servants to Da-
vid, bringing tribute. And Yahweh
granted salvation to David wherever
he went. **7** And David took the small
shields of gold which were [1]carried
by the servants of Hadadezer and
brought them to Jerusalem. **8** Also
from [1]Tibhath and from Cun, cities
of Hadadezer, David took a very
large amount of bronze, with which
[a]Solomon made the bronze sea and
the pillars and the bronze utensils.

**9** Then [1]Tou king of Hamath heard
that David had struck down all the
military force of Hadadezer king of
Zobah, **10** so he sent [1]Hadoram his
son to King David to [2]greet him and
to bless him, because he had fought
against Hadadezer and struck him
down; for Hadadezer had been at war
with Tou. And *Hadoram brought* all
kinds of articles of gold and silver

**17:22** [a]Ex 19:5, 6 **17:23** [1]Or *be true* **17:24** [1]Or *be true* [2]Or *slave*, cf. 17:23; see Foreword, "The Terminology of Slave" **17:26** [1]Lit *spoken* ◆ **18:1** [a]2Sa 8:1-18 **18:3** [1]Or *monument*; lit *hand* **18:5** [a]1Chr 19:6 [1]Heb *Darmeseq* **18:6** [1]Heb *Darmeseq* **18:7** [1]Lit *on* **18:8** [a]1Ki 7:40-47; 2Chr 4:11-18 [1]In 2Sa 8:8, *Betah* **18:9** [1]In 2Sa 8:9, *Toi* **18:10** [1]In 2Sa 8:10, *Joram* [2]Lit *ask him of his welfare*

and bronze. **11** King David also set
these apart as holy to Yahweh with
the silver and the gold which he had
carried away from all the nations:
from Edom, Moab, the sons of
Ammon, the Philistines, and from
Amalek.

**12** Moreover, Abishai the son of
Zeruiah [1]smote 18,000 of Edom in
the Valley of Salt. **13** Then he placed
garrisons in Edom, and all the
Edomites became servants to David.
And Yahweh granted salvation to
David wherever he went.

**14** So David reigned over all Israel;
and he was doing justice and righ-
teousness for all his people. **15** [a]Now
Joab the son of Zeruiah *was* over the
army, and Jehoshaphat the son of
Ahilud *was* recorder; **16** and Zadok the
son of Ahitub and Abimelech the son
of Abiathar *were* priests, and Shavsha
*was* scribe; **17** and Benaiah the son of
Jehoiada *was* over the Cherethites
and the Pelethites, and the sons of
David *were* chiefs at the king's side.

### *The Ammonites Dishonor David's Men*

**19** [a]Now it happened afterwards,
that Nahash the king of the
sons of Ammon died, and his son
became king in his place. **2** So David
said, "I will show lovingkindness to
Hanun the son of Nahash, because
his father showed lovingkindness
to me." So David sent messengers to
comfort him concerning his father.
And David's servants came into the
land of the sons of Ammon to Hanun
to comfort him. **3** But the princes of
the sons of Ammon said to Hanun,
"In your eyes, is David honoring your
father because he has sent comforters
to you? Have not his servants come to
you to search and to overthrow and
to spy out the land?" **4** So Hanun took
David's servants and shaved them
and cut off their garments in the
middle as far as their hips, and sent
them away. **5** Then *certain persons*
went and told David about the men.
And he sent to meet them, for the
men were greatly dishonored. And
the king said, "[1]Stay at Jericho until
your beards grow, and *then* return."

**6** Then the sons of Ammon saw
that they had made themselves
odious to David. So Hanun and the
sons of Ammon sent [1]1,000 talents of
silver to hire for themselves chariots
and horsemen from Mesopotamia,
from Aram-maacah, and [a]from Zo-
bah. **7** So they hired for themselves
32,000 chariots, and the king of Maa-
cah and his people, who came and
camped before [a]Medeba. And the
sons of Ammon gathered together
from their cities and came to battle.
**8** Then David heard *of it*, and he sent
Joab and all the army, the mighty
men. **9** And the sons of Ammon
came out and arranged *themselves*
for battle at the entrance of the city.
But the kings who had come were by
themselves in the field.

### *David Defeats Ammon and Aram*

**10** Then Joab saw that the [1]battle was
set against him in front and in the
rear. So he chose from all the choice
men of Israel and [2]they arranged
*themselves* to meet the Arameans.
**11** But the remainder of the people he

**18:12** [1]Or *struck down* **18:15** [a]1Chr 11:6 ◆**19:1** [a]2Sa 10:1-19 **19:5** [1]Lit *Return to* **19:6** [a]1Chr 18:5, 9 [1]Approx. 38 tons or 34 metric tons, a talent was approx. 75 lb. or 34 kg **19:7** [a]Nu 21:30; Jos 13:9, 16 **19:10** [1]Lit *the face of the battle* [2]Lit *he*...himself

put in the hand of [1]Abshai his brother; and they arranged themselves to meet the sons of Ammon. **12** And he said, "If the Arameans are too strong for me, then you shall save me; but if the sons of Ammon are too strong for you, then I will save you. **13** Be strong, and let us show strength for the sake of our people and for the cities of our God; and may Yahweh do what is good in His sight." **14** So Joab and the people who were with him drew near before the Arameans for the battle, and they fled before him. **15** Now the sons of Ammon saw that the Arameans fled. So they themselves also fled before Abshai his brother and came into the city. Then Joab came to Jerusalem.

**16** Then the Arameans saw that they had been [1]defeated by Israel. So they sent messengers and brought out the Arameans who were beyond the [2]River, and Shophach the commander of the army of Hadadezer [3]led them. **17** And it was told to David, so he gathered all Israel together and crossed the Jordan, and came upon them and arranged for battle against them. So David arranged *them* in battle to meet the Arameans. And they fought against him. **18** But the Arameans fled before Israel, and David killed of the Arameans 7,000 charioteers and 40,000 foot soldiers, and put to death Shophach the commander of the army. **19** Then the servants of Hadadezer saw that they were [1]defeated by Israel. So they made peace with David and served him. And the Arameans were not willing to save the sons of Ammon anymore.

### *War with Philistine Giants*

**20** [a]Now it happened [1]in the spring, at the time when kings go out *to battle*, that Joab led out the force of the military and brought the land of the sons of Ammon to ruin, and came and besieged Rabbah. But David stayed at Jerusalem. And [b]Joab struck Rabbah and [2]tore it down. **2** [a]Then David took the crown of [1]their king from his head; and he found it to weigh a [2]talent of gold, and in it *was* a precious stone; and it was *placed* on David's head. And he brought out the spoil of the city *in* a very great amount. **3** He also brought out the people who were in it [a]and [1]made *them* work with saws and with sharp iron instruments and with axes. And thus David used to do to all the cities of the sons of Ammon. Then David and all the people returned *to* Jerusalem.

**4** [a]Now it happened afterwards, that war [1]broke out at [2]Gezer with the Philistines; then Sibbecai the Hushathite struck down Sippai, *one* among those born of the [3]giants, and they were subdued. **5** And there was war with the Philistines again, and Elhanan the son of [a]Jair struck down Lahmi the brother of Goliath the Gittite, the [b]shaft of whose spear was like a weaver's beam. **6** Then there was war at Gath again, and there was a man of *great* stature

**19:11** [1]In 2Sa 10:10, *Abishai* **19:16** [1]Lit *smitten before* [2]The Euphrates River [3]Lit *before* **19:19** [1]Lit *smitten before* ◆ **20:1** [a]2Sa 11:1 [b]2Sa 12:26 [1]Lit *at the time of the return of the year* [2]Lit *pulled* **20:2** [a]2Sa 12:30, 31 [1]In Zep 1:5, *Malcam* [2]A talent was approx. 75 lb. or 34 kg **20:3** [a]2Sa 12:31 [1]Or *made them cut with saws, cut them with saws;* Heb vowels can indicate causative or simple active **20:4** [a]2Sa 21:18-22 [1]Lit *stood up* [2]In 2Sa 21:18, *Gob* [3]Heb *Raphah*, so in vv 6, 8 **20:5** [a]2Sa 21:19 [b]1Sa 17:7; 1Chr 11:23

who had twenty-four fingers and
toes, six *fingers on each hand* and
six *toes on each foot*; and he also
had been born to the giants. **7** And
he [1]reproached Israel, so Jonathan
the son of Shimea, David's brother,
struck him down. **8** These were born
to the giants in Gath, and they fell by
the hand of David and by the hand
of his servants.

### *David Sins by Numbering Israel*

**21** [a]Then Satan stood up against
Israel and incited David to
number Israel. **2** So David said to
Joab and to the princes of the people,
"[a]Go, count Israel from Beersheba
even to Dan, and bring me *word* that
I may know their *total* count." **3** But
Joab said, "[a]May Yahweh add to His
people a hundred times as many
as they are! But, my lord the king,
are they not all my lord's servants?
Why does my lord seek this thing?
Why should he be a cause of guilt
to Israel?" **4** Nevertheless, the king's
word *stood* strong against Joab. So,
Joab went out and went throughout
all Israel, and came to Jerusalem.
**5** And Joab gave the *total* count of
the [1]census of the people to David.
And [a]all Israel were 1,100,000 men
who drew the sword; and Judah *was*
470,000 men who drew the sword.
**6** [a]But he did not [1]number Levi and
Benjamin among them, for the king's
[2]command was abominable to Joab.
**7** And this thing was displeasing in
the sight of God, so He struck Israel.
**8** Then David said to God, "I have
sinned greatly, in that I have done
this thing. [a]But now, please take away
the iniquity of Your slave, for I have
acted very foolishly."
**9** And Yahweh spoke to [a]Gad, Da-
vid's [b]seer, saying, **10** "Go and speak to
David, saying, 'Thus says Yahweh, "I
[1]am offering you three things; choose
for yourself one of them, and I will
do *that* to you."'" **11** So Gad came to
David and said to him, "Thus says
Yahweh, 'Take for yourself **12** [a]either
three years of famine, or three
months to be swept away before your
adversaries, while the sword of your
enemies overtakes *you*, or else three
days of the sword of Yahweh, even
pestilence in the land, and the angel
of Yahweh destroying throughout all
the territory of Israel.' So now, see
what word I should return to Him
who sent me." **13** Then David said to
Gad, "I am in great distress. Let me
now fall into the hand of Yahweh,
[a]for His compassions are exceedingly
abundant. But do not let me fall into
the hand of man."
**14** [a]So Yahweh [1]sent a pestilence
against Israel; and 70,000 men of
Israel fell. **15** And God sent an angel
to Jerusalem to destroy it; but as
he was about to destroy *it*, Yahweh
saw and [a,1]relented concerning the
calamity, and said to the destroying
angel, "It is enough! Now relax your
hand." And the angel of Yahweh was
standing by the threshing floor of
[2]Ornan the Jebusite. **16** Then David
lifted up his eyes and saw the angel of
Yahweh standing between earth and
heaven, with his drawn sword in his
hand stretched out over Jerusalem.

**20:7** [1]Or *defied* ◆ **21:1** [a]2Sa 24:1-25 **21:2** [a]1Chr 27:23, 24 **21:3** [a]Dt 1:11 **21:5** [a]2Sa 24:9 [1]Lit *muster* **21:6** [a]1Chr 27:24 [1]Lit *muster* [2]Lit *word* **21:8** [a]2Sa 12:13 **21:9** [a]2Sa 24:11; 1Chr 29:29 [b]1Sa 9:9 **21:10** [1]Lit *stretch out to* **21:12** [a]2Sa 24:13 **21:13** [a]Ps 51:1; 130:4, 7 **21:14** [a]1Chr 27:24 [1]Lit *gave* **21:15** [a]Ex 32:14; 1Sa 15:11; Jon 3:10 [1]Or *regretted*, cf. 1Sa 15:11, 29, 3 [2]In 2Sa 24:16, *Araunah*

Then David and the elders, [a]covered
with sackcloth, fell on their faces.
17 And David said to God, "Is it not
I who [1]commanded to number the
people? Indeed, I am the one who
has sinned and done a great evil; [a]but
these sheep, what have they done?
O Yahweh my God, please let Your
hand be against me and my father's
household, but not against Your
people that they should be plagued."

### *David Erects an Altar*

18 [a]Then the angel of Yahweh said to
Gad to say to David, that David should
go up and erect an altar to Yahweh
on the threshing floor of Ornan the
Jebusite. 19 So David went up at the
word of Gad, which he spoke in
the name of Yahweh. 20 Now Ornan
turned back and saw the angel, and
his four sons *who were* with him hid
themselves. And Ornan was thresh-
ing wheat. 21 Then David came to
Ornan, and Ornan looked and saw
David, and went out from the thresh-
ing floor and bowed his [1]face to the
ground [2]before David. 22 Then David
said to Ornan, "Give me the [1]site of
*this* threshing floor, that I may build
on it an altar to Yahweh; for the full
price you shall give it to me, that the
plague may be checked from *being*
upon the people." 23 And Ornan said
to David, "Take *it* for yourself; and let
my lord the king do what is good in
his sight. See, I will give the oxen for
the burnt offerings and the threshing
sledges for the wood and the wheat
for the grain offering; I will give ev-
*erything.*" 24 However, King David
said to Ornan, "No, but I will surely
buy *it* for the full price; for I will not
lift up what is yours to Yahweh, or
offer a burnt offering [1]which costs me
nothing." 25 So [a]David gave Ornan
[1]600 shekels of gold by weight for
the [2]site. 26 Then David built there
an altar to Yahweh and offered burnt
offerings and peace offerings. And he
called to Yahweh and [a]He answered
him with fire from heaven on the al-
tar of burnt offering. 27 Then Yahweh
spoke to the angel, and he returned
his sword to its sheath.
28 At that time, when David saw
that Yahweh had answered him on
the threshing floor of Ornan the Jeb-
usite, he sacrificed there. 29 [a]Now the
tabernacle of Yahweh, which Moses
had made in the wilderness, and the
altar of burnt offering *were* in the
high place at Gibeon at that time.
30 But David could not go before it
to inquire of God, for he was terrified
by the sword of the angel of Yahweh.

### *Preparation to Build Yahweh's House*

22 Then David said, "[a]This is the
house of Yahweh God, and
this is the altar of burnt offering for
Israel."
2 So David said to gather [a]the
sojourners who were in the land of
Israel, and [b]he [1]appointed [2]stonecut-
ters to hew out stones to build the
house of God. 3 And David [a]prepared
large quantities of iron [1]to make the
nails for the doors of the gates and for
the clamps, and more [b]bronze than
could be weighed; 4 and timbers of
cedar logs beyond number, for [a]the

**21:16** [a]1Ki 21:27 **21:17** [a]2Sa 7:8; Ps 74:1 [1]Lit *said* **21:18** [a]2Chr 3:1 **21:21** [1]Lit *nose* [2]Lit *to*
**21:22** [1]Lit *place* **21:24** [1]Lit *gratuitously* **21:25** [a]2Sa 24:24 [1]Approx. 15 lb. or 6.6 kg, a shekel was approx. 0.4 oz. or 11 gm [2]Lit *place* **21:26** [a]Lv 9:24; Jdg 6:21 **21:29** [a]1Ki 3:4; 1Chr 16:39
◆ **22:1** [a]1Chr 21:18-28; 2Chr 3:1 **22:2** [a]1Ki 9:20, 21; 2Chr 2:17 [b]1Ki 5:17, 18 [1]Lit *caused to stand* [2]Lit *hewers* of stone **22:3** [a]1Chr 29:2, 7 [b]1Chr 22:14 [1]Lit *for* **22:4** [a]1Ki 5:6-10

Sidonians and Tyrians brought large
quantities of cedar timber to David.
**5** And David said, "My son [a]Solomon
is young and inexperienced, and the
house that is to be built for Yahweh
shall be highly exalted, for a name
and beauty throughout all lands.
*Therefore* now I will make prepa-
ration for it." So David made ample
preparations before his death.

### *Solomon to Build Yahweh's House*

**6** Then [a]he called for his son Solo-
mon, and commanded him to build a
house for Yahweh, the God of Israel.
**7** And David said to Solomon, "[a]My
son, [1]I had it within my heart to build
a house to the name of Yahweh my
God. **8** But the word of Yahweh came
to me, saying, '[a]You have shed much
blood and have [1]waged great wars;
you shall not build a house for My
name, because you have shed *so*
much blood on the earth before Me.
**9** Behold, a son will be born to you,
who shall be a man of rest; and [a]I will
give him rest from all his enemies
on every side; for [b]his name shall
be [1]Solomon, and I will give peace
and quiet to Israel in his days. **10** [a]He
shall build a house for My name, and
he shall be a son to Me and I will be
a father to him; and I will establish
the throne of his kingdom over Israel
forever.' **11** Now, my son, [a]Yahweh be
with you that you may be successful,
and build the house of Yahweh your
God just as He has spoken concern-
ing you. **12** [a]Only Yahweh give you
insight and understanding, and give
you command over Israel, so that
you may [b]keep the law of Yahweh
your God. **13** [a]Then you will succeed,
if you are careful to do the statutes
and the judgments which Yahweh
commanded Moses concerning Isra-
el. [b]Be strong and courageous, do not
fear nor be dismayed. **14** Now behold,
[1]with great pains I have prepared
for the house of Yahweh [a]100,000
[2]talents of gold and 1,000,000
talents of silver, and [b]bronze and
iron beyond weight, for [3]they are
in great quantity; also timber and
stone I have prepared, and you may
add to them. **15** Moreover, there are
many of those who do the work with
you, hewers *of stone* and craftsmen
of stone and wood, and all men who
are [1]wise in every kind of work. **16** Of
the gold, the silver and the bronze
and the iron there is no number.
Arise and work, and may [a]Yahweh
be with you."

**17** [a]David also commanded all
the officials of Israel to help his son
Solomon, *saying*, **18** "Is not Yahweh
your God with you? And [a]has He
not given you rest on every side? For
He has given the inhabitants of the
land into my hand, and the land is
subdued before Yahweh and before
His people. **19** Now [a]give your heart
and your soul to seek Yahweh your
God; arise, therefore, and build the
sanctuary of Yahweh God, [b]so that
you may bring the ark of the cov-
enant of Yahweh and the holy vessels
of God into the house that is to be
built [c]for the name of Yahweh."

---

**22:5** [a]1Ki 3:7; 1Chr 29:1 **22:6** [a]1Ki 2:1 **22:7** [a]2Sa 7:2, 3; 1Chr 17:1 [1]Lit *as for me, it was in my heart*
**22:8** [a]1Chr 28:3 [1]Lit *made* **22:9** [a]1Ki 4:20, 25 [b]2Sa 12:24, 25 [1]Lit *peaceful* **22:10** [a]2Sa 7:13, 14; 1Chr 17:12 **22:11** [a]1Chr 22:16 **22:12** [a]1Ki 3:9-12; 2Chr 1:10 [b]1Ki 2:3 **22:13** [a]1Chr 28:7 [b]Jos 1:6-9
**22:14** [a]1Chr 29:4 [b]1Chr 22:3 [1]Lit *in my affliction* [2]A talent was approx. 75 lb. or 34 kg [3]Lit *it is*
**22:15** [1]Or *skillful* **22:16** [a]1Chr 22:11 **22:17** [a]1Chr 28:1-6 **22:18** [a]1Chr 22:9; 23:25 **22:19** [a]1Chr 28:9 [b]1Ki 8:6, 21; 2Chr 5:7 [c]1Chr 22:7

### *Solomon Made King over Israel*

**23** [a]Now David became old and full of days, [b]and he made his son Solomon king over Israel. **2** And he gathered together all the leaders of Israel with the priests and the Levites.

### *The Work of the Levites*

**3** [a]And the Levites were numbered from thirty years old and upward, and [b]their number by [1]census of men was 38,000. **4** Of these, 24,000 were [a]to direct the work of the house of Yahweh; and 6,000 *were* [b]officers and judges, **5** and 4,000 *were* gatekeepers, and [a]4,000 *were* praising Yahweh with the instruments which [1]David made for giving praise. **6** And David divided them into divisions [a]according to the sons of Levi: Gershon, Kohath, and Merari.

### *The Sons of Gershon*

**7** Of the Gershonites *were*
[1]Ladan and Shimei.
**8** The sons of Ladan *were* Jehiel
the first and Zetham and Joel,
three.
**9** The sons of Shimei *were*
Shelomoth and Haziel and
Haran, three.
These were the heads of the
fathers' *households* of Ladan.
**10** The sons of Shimei *were*
Jahath, [1]Zina, Jeush, and
Beriah.
These four *were* the sons of
Shimei.
**11** Jahath was the first and Zizah
the second; but Jeush and
Beriah did not have many
sons, so they became a
father's household, one [1]unit.

### *The Sons of Kohath*

**12** The sons of Kohath: Amram,
Izhar, Hebron, and Uzziel, four.
**13** [a]The sons of Amram were
Aaron and Moses. And [b]Aaron
was separated in order to
sanctify him as most holy, he
and his sons forever, [c]to offer
*offerings* up in smoke before
Yahweh, to minister to Him and
to bless in His name forever.
**14** But *as for* [a]Moses the man
of God, his sons were named
among the tribe of Levi.
**15** The sons of Moses *were*
Gershom and Eliezer.
**16** The [1]son of Gershom *was*
[2]Shebuel the chief.
**17** The [1]son of Eliezer was
Rehabiah the chief; and
Eliezer had no other sons, but
the sons of Rehabiah were
very many.
**18** The [1]son of Izhar was [2]Shelomith the chief.
**19** The sons of Hebron *were*
Jeriah the first, Amariah the
second, Jahaziel the third and
Jekameam the fourth.
**20** The sons of Uzziel *were* Micah
the first and Isshiah the
second.

### *The Sons of Merari*

**21** The sons of Merari were Mahli
and Mushi. The sons of Mahli
*were* Eleazar and Kish.

---

◆ **23:1** [a]1Chr 29:28 [b]1Ki 1:1-40; 2:12; 1Chr 28:5; 29:22 **23:3** [a]Nu 4:3-49 [b]Nu 4:48; 1Chr 23:24 [1]Lit *their heads* **23:4** [a]Ezr 3:8, 9 [b]1Chr 26:29 **23:5** [a]1Chr 15:16 [1]Lit *I made* **23:6** [a]1Chr 6:1 **23:7** [1]In Ex 6:17, *Libni* **23:10** [1]In v 11, *Zizah* **23:11** [1]Lit *mustering* **23:13** [a]Ex 6:20 [b]Ex 28:1 [c]Ex 30:6-10 **23:14** [a]Dt 33:1; Ps 90: title **23:16** [1]Lit *sons* [2]In 24:20, *Shubael* **23:17** [1]Lit *sons...were* **23:18** [1]Lit *sons* [2]In 24:22, *Shelomoth*

22 And Eleazar died and had no
sons, but daughters only, so
their brothers, the sons of
Kish, took them up *as wives*.
23 The sons of Mushi: Mahli,
Eder, and Jeremoth, three.

### *The Service of the Levites*

24 [a]These were the sons of Levi ac-
cording to their fathers' households,
*even* the heads of the fathers' *house-
holds* of those of them who were
[1]counted, in the number of names
by their [2]census, doing the work for
the service of the house of Yahweh,
[b]from twenty years old and upward.
25 For David said, "Yahweh, the God of
Israel, [a]has given rest to His people,
and He dwells in Jerusalem forever.
26 Also, [a]the Levites will no longer
need to carry the tabernacle and all
its furnishings for its service." 27 For
by the last words of David the sons
of Levi *were* numbered from twenty
years old and upward. 28 For their
station is to be on hand for the sons of
Aaron with the service of the house
of Yahweh, in the courts and in the
chambers and in the cleansing of all
holy things, even the work of the ser-
vice of the house of God, 29 [a]and with
the showbread, and [b]the fine flour
for a grain offering, and unleavened
wafers, or [c]*what is made on* the grid-
dle, or [d]what is *well* stirred, and [e]all
measures of volume and size. 30 And
they are to stand every morning to
thank and to praise Yahweh, and
likewise at evening, 31 and to offer
all burnt offerings to Yahweh, [a]on the
sabbaths, the new moons and [b]the
appointed times in the number *set*
by the judgments concerning them,
continually before Yahweh. 32 Thus
[a]they shall keep responsibility of the
tent of meeting, and responsibility of
the holy place, and [b]responsibility
of the sons of Aaron their [1]relatives,
for the service of the house of Yah-
weh.

### *Divisions of Levites*

24 Now the divisions of the sons
of Aaron *were these*: [a]the sons
of Aaron *were* Nadab, Abihu, Eleazar,
and Ithamar. 2 [a]But Nadab and Abihu
died before their father and had no
[1]sons. So Eleazar and Ithamar min-
istered as priests. 3 And David, with
[a]Zadok of the sons of Eleazar and
Ahimelech of the sons of Ithamar,
divided them according to their
assignments for their service. 4 And
more chief men were found from the
[1]sons of Eleazar than the [1]sons of
Ithamar, so they divided them thus:
*there were* sixteen heads of fathers'
households of the [1]sons of Eleazar
and eight of the [1]sons of Ithamar,
according to their fathers' house-
holds. 5 [a]Thus they were divided
by lot, the one as the other; for they
were leaders for the sanctuary and
leaders for God, both from the sons
of Eleazar and the sons of Ithamar.
6 Shemaiah, the son of Nethanel
the scribe, from the Levites, wrote
them down in the presence of the
king, the princes, Zadok the priest,
[a]Ahimelech the son of Abiathar, and
the heads of the fathers' *households*
of the priests and of the Levites; one

**23:24** [a]Nu 10:17, 21 [b]1Chr 23:3 [1]Lit *mustered* [2]Lit *heads* **23:25** [a]1Chr 22:18 **23:26** [a]Nu 4:5, 15; 7:9; Dt 10:8 **23:29** [a]Lv 24:5-9 [b]Lv 6:20 [c]1Chr 9:31 [d]Lv 6:21 [e]Lv 19:35, 36 **23:31** [a]Is 1:13, 14 [b]Lv 23:2-4 **23:32** [a]Nu 1:53; 1Chr 9:27 [b]Nu 3:6-9, 38 [1]Lit *brothers* ◆ **24:1** [a]Ex 6:23 **24:2** [a]Lv 10:2 [1]Or *children* **24:3** [a]1Chr 6:8 **24:4** [1]Or *descendants* **24:5** [a]1Chr 24:31 **24:6** [a]1Chr 18:16

father's household taken for Eleazar
and one taken for Ithamar.
7 Now the first lot came out for
Jehoiarib,
the second for Jedaiah,
8 the third for Harim,
the fourth for Seorim,
9 the fifth for Malchijah,
the sixth for Mijamin,
10 the seventh for Hakkoz,
the eighth for [a]Abijah,
11 the ninth for Jeshua,
the tenth for Shecaniah,
12 the eleventh for Eliashib,
the twelfth for Jakim,
13 the thirteenth for Huppah,
the fourteenth for Jeshebeab,
14 the fifteenth for Bilgah,
the sixteenth for Immer,
15 the seventeenth for Hezir,
the eighteenth for Happizzez,
16 the nineteenth for Pethahiah,
the twentieth for Jehezkel,
17 the twenty-first for Jachin,
the twenty-second for Gamul,
18 the twenty-third for Delaiah,
the twenty-fourth for
Maaziah.
19 [a]These were their assignments for
their service when *they* came in to
the house of Yahweh according to
the *legal* judgment *rendered* to them
by the hand of Aaron their father,
just as Yahweh, the God of Israel, had
commanded him.
20 Now for the rest of the sons of
Levi:
of the sons of Amram,
[1]Shubael;
of the sons of Shubael,
Jehdeiah.
21 Of Rehabiah: of the sons of
Rehabiah, Isshiah the first.
22 Of the Izharites, [1]Shelomoth;
of the sons of Shelomoth,
Jahath.
23 The sons [a]*of Hebron:* Jeriah
*the first,* Amariah the second,
Jahaziel the third, Jekameam
the fourth.
24 The sons of Uzziel, Micah; of
the sons of Micah, Shamir.
25 The brother of Micah,
Isshiah; of the sons of Isshiah,
Zechariah.
26 The sons of Merari, Mahli and
Mushi; the sons of Jaaziah,
Beno.
27 The sons of Merari: by Jaaziah
*were* Beno, Shoham, Zaccur,
and Ibri.
28 By Mahli: Eleazar, who had no
sons.
29 By Kish: the sons of Kish,
Jerahmeel.
30 The sons of Mushi: Mahli,
Eder and Jerimoth.
These *were* the sons of the
Levites according to their
fathers' households.
31 [a]These also cast lots alongside
their [1]relatives the sons of Aaron
in the presence of David the king,
[b]Zadok, Ahimelech, and the heads of
the fathers' *households* of the priests
and of the Levites—the head of fa-
thers' *households* alongside those of
his younger brother.

### *Number and Services of Musicians*

25 Moreover, David and the
commanders of the army
separated for the service *some* of the
sons of [a]Asaph and of Heman and
of Jeduthun, who *were* to [b]prophesy
with lyres, [c]harps, and cymbals; and

**24:10** [a]Ne 12:4; Lk 1:5 **24:19** [a]1Chr 9:25 **24:20** [1]In 23:16, *Shebuel* **24:22** [1]In 23:18, *Shelomith*
**24:23** [a]1Chr 23:19 **24:31** [a]1Chr 24:5, 6 [b]1Chr 24:6 [1]Lit *brothers* ◆ **25:1** [a]1Chr 6:33, 39 [b]2Ki 3:15 [c]1Chr 15:16

the number of [1]those who performed
their service was:

2 Of the sons of Asaph:
Zaccur, Joseph, Nethaniah,
and [1]Asharelah; the sons
of Asaph *were* under the
[2]direction of Asaph, who
prophesied under the
[2]direction of the king.

3 [a]Of Jeduthun, the sons of
Jeduthun:
Gedaliah, [1]Zeri, Jeshaiah,
[2]Shimei, Hashabiah, and
Mattithiah, six, under the
[3]direction of their father
Jeduthun with the harp, who
prophesied in giving thanks
and praising Yahweh.

4 Of Heman, the sons of
Heman:
Bukkiah, Mattaniah, [1]Uzziel,
[2]Shebuel and Jerimoth,
Hananiah, Hanani, Eliathah,
Giddalti and Romamti-ezer,
Joshbekashah, Mallothi,
Hothir, Mahazioth.

5 All these *were* the sons of Heman
[a]the king's seer to [1]exalt him according
to the words of God. So God gave
fourteen sons and three daughters
to Heman. 6 All these were under
the [1]direction of their father to
sing in the house of Yahweh, [a]with
cymbals, harps, and lyres, for the
*service of the house* of God. [b]Asaph,
Jeduthun, and Heman *were* under
the [1]direction of the king. 7 And
their number who were trained
in singing to Yahweh, with their
[1]relatives, all who were skillful,
*was* [a]288.

### *Responsibilities of the Musicians*

8 [a]They cast lots for their responsibilities,
*each* alongside *the other*, the
small as well as the great, the teacher
*as well* as the pupil.

9 Now the first lot came out for
Asaph to Joseph,
the second for Gedaliah, he
with his relatives and sons
*were* twelve;

10 the third to Zaccur, his sons
and his relatives, twelve;

11 the fourth to [1]Izri, his sons
and his relatives, twelve;

12 the fifth to Nethaniah, his
sons and his relatives, twelve;

13 the sixth to Bukkiah, his sons
and his relatives, twelve;

14 the seventh to [1]Jesharelah, his
sons and his relatives, twelve;

15 the eighth to Jeshaiah, his
sons and his relatives, twelve;

16 the ninth to Mattaniah, his
sons and his relatives, twelve;

17 the tenth to Shimei, his sons
and his relatives, twelve;

18 the eleventh to Azarel, his
sons and his relatives, twelve;

19 the twelfth to Hashabiah, his
sons and his relatives, twelve;

20 for the thirteenth, Shubael, his
sons and his relatives, twelve;

21 for the fourteenth, Mattithiah,
his sons and his relatives,
twelve;

22 for the fifteenth to Jeremoth,
his sons and his relatives,
twelve;

23 for the sixteenth to Hananiah,
his sons and his relatives,
twelve;

---

**25:1** [1]Lit *workmen according to their service* **25:2** [1]In v 14, *Jesharelah* [2]Lit *hand(s)* **25:3** [a]1Chr 16:41, 42 [1]In v 11, *Izri* [2]As in mss and ancient versions, cf. 25:17 [3]Lit *hands* **25:4** [1]In v 18, *Azarel* [2]In v 20, *Shubael* **25:5** [a]2Sa 24:11; 1Chr 21:9 [1]Lit *lift up the horn* **25:6** [a]1Chr 15:16 [b]1Chr 15:19 [1]Lit *hands* **25:7** [a]1Chr 23:5 [1]Lit *brothers*, so in ch **25:8** [a]1Chr 26:13 **25:11** [1]In v 3, *Zeri* **25:14** [1]In v 2, *Asherelah*

24 for the seventeenth to Joshbekashah, his sons and his relatives, twelve;
25 for the eighteenth to Hanani, his sons and his relatives, twelve;
26 for the nineteenth to Mallothi, his sons and his relatives, twelve;
27 for the twentieth to Eliathah, his sons and his relatives, twelve;
28 for the twenty-first to Hothir, his sons and his relatives, twelve;
29 for the twenty-second to Giddalti, his sons and his relatives, twelve;
30 for the twenty-third to Mahazioth, his sons and his relatives, twelve;
31 for the twenty-fourth to Romamti-ezer, his sons and his relatives, twelve.

### *Divisions of the Gatekeepers*

26 For the divisions of the gatekeepers *there were* of the Korahites, [1]Meshelemiah the son of Kore, of the sons of [2]Asaph.
2 Meshelemiah had sons: Zechariah the firstborn, Jediael the second, Zebadiah the third, Jathniel the fourth,
3 Elam the fifth, Johanan the sixth, Eliehoenai the seventh.
4 [a]Obed-edom had sons: Shemaiah the firstborn, Jehozabad the second, Joah the third, Sacar the fourth, Nethanel the fifth,
5 Ammiel the sixth, Issachar the seventh *and* Peullethai the eighth; God had indeed blessed him.
6 Also to his son Shemaiah sons were born who ruled over the house of their father, for they were mighty men of valor.
7 The sons of Shemaiah *were* Othni, Rephael, Obed, and Elzabad, whose brothers, Elihu and Semachiah, were men of valor.
8 All these *were* of the sons of Obed-edom; they and their sons and their [1]relatives *were* valiant men with strength for the service, sixty-two from Obed-edom.
9 Meshelemiah had sons and relatives, eighteen men of valor.
10 Also [a]Hosah, *one* of the sons of Merari had sons: Shimri the first (although he was not the firstborn, his father made him first),
11 Hilkiah the second, Tebaliah the third, Zechariah the fourth; all the sons and relatives of Hosah *were* thirteen.

12 To these divisions of the gate-
keepers, the chief men, *were given*
responsibilities like their relatives
to minister in the house of Yahweh.
13 [a]And they cast lots, the small
and the great alike, according to
their fathers' households, for every
gate. 14 And the lot to the east fell
to [1]Shelemiah. Then they cast lots
*for* his son Zechariah, a counselor
with insight, and his lot came out to

◆ **26:1** [1]In v 14, *Shelemiah* [2]In 9:19, *Ebiasaph* **26:4** [a]2Sa 6:11; 1Chr 13:14 **26:8** [1]Lit *brothers*, so in ch **26:10** [a]1Chr 16:38 **26:13** [a]1Chr 24:5, 31; 25:8 **26:14** [1]In 9:17, *Shallum*

the north. **15** For Obed-edom *it fell* to the south, and to his sons went the house of storerooms. **16** For Shuppim and Hosah *it was* to the west, by the gate of Shallecheth, on the ascending highway. Guard corresponded to guard. **17** On the east there were six Levites, on the north four daily, on the south four daily, and at the storerooms two by two. **18** At the [a,1]Parbar on the west *there were* four at the highway and two at the Parbar. **19** These were the divisions of the gatekeepers of the sons of Korah and of the sons of Merari.

### *Caring for the Holy Treasure*

**20** [1]As for the Levites, Ahijhah was [a]over the treasures of the house of God and of the treasures of the holy gifts. **21** The sons of Ladan, the sons of the Gershonites belonging to Ladan, *namely*, the Jehielites, *were* the heads of the fathers' *households*, belonging to Ladan the Gershonite.

**22** The sons of Jehieli, Zetham, and Joel his brother, were over the treasures of the house of Yahweh. **23** As for the Amramites, the Izharites, the Hebronites and the Uzzielites, **24** Shebuel the son of Gershom, the son of Moses, was officer over the treasures. **25** And his relatives by Eliezer *were* Rehabiah his son, Jeshaiah his son, Joram his *son*, Zichri *his son*, and Shelomoth his son. **26** This Shelomoth and his relatives were over all the treasures of the holy gifts [a]which King David and the heads of the fathers' *households*, the commanders of thousands and hundreds, and the commanders of the army, had set apart as holy. **27** They set apart as holy part of what was won in battles and part of the spoil to repair the house of Yahweh. **28** And all that Samuel the seer had set apart as holy and Saul the son of Kish, Abner the son of Ner, and Joab the son of Zeruiah, everyone who had set apart *anything* as holy, *all of this* was [1]in the care of [2]Shelomoth and his relatives.

### *Outside Work*

**29** As for the Izharites, Chenaniah and his sons [a]were *assigned* to the outside work for Israel, as [b]officers and judges. **30** As for the Hebronites, [a]Hashabiah and his relatives, 1,700 men of valor, were over the administration of Israel across the Jordan to the west, for all the work of Yahweh and the service of the king. **31** As for the Hebronites, [a]Jerijah the chief [1](these Hebronites were investigated according to their generations and fathers' *households*, in the fortieth year of David's reign, and mighty men of valor were found among them at [b]Jazer of Gilead) **32** and his relatives, men of valor, *were* 2,700 in number, heads of fathers' *households*. And King David made them overseers of the Reubenites, the Gadites and the half-tribe of the Manassites [a]concerning [1]all the affairs of God and of the king.

### *Commanders of the Divisions*

**27** Now *this is* the *total* count of the sons of Israel, the heads of fathers' *households*, the commanders of thousands and of hundreds, and

**26:18** [a]2Ki 23:11 [1]Possibly *court, colonnade* **26:20** [a]1Chr 26:22, 24, 26; 28:12; Ezr 2:69 [1]Gr *The Levites, their relatives,* **26:26** [a]2Sa 8:11 **26:28** [1]Lit *under the hand* [2]Heb *Shelomith* **26:29** [a]Ne 11:16 [b]1Chr 23:4 **26:30** [a]1Chr 27:17 **26:31** [a]1Chr 23:19 [b]1Chr 6:81 [1]Heb *according to the Hebronites...father's households* **26:32** [a]2Chr 19:11 [1]Lit *every matter of God and matter of the king*

their officers who ministered to the king in each matter of the divisions which came in and went out month by month throughout all the months of the year, each division *numbering* 24,000:

**2** Jashobeam the son of Zabdiel *was* [a]over the first division for the first month; and in his division *were* 24,000.

**3** *He was* from the sons of Perez, *and was* chief of all the commanders of the army for the first month.

**4** Dodai the Ahohite and his division *were* over the division for the second month, Mikloth *being* the chief officer; and in his division *were* 24,000.

**5** The third commander of the army for the third month *was* Benaiah, the son of Jehoiada the priest, *as* chief; and in his division *were* 24,000.

**6** This Benaiah *was* the mighty man of the thirty, and *was* over thirty; and over his division was Ammizabad his son.

**7** The fourth for the fourth month *was* Asahel the brother of Joab, and Zebadiah his son after him; and in his division *were* 24,000.

**8** The fifth for the fifth month *was* the commander Shamhuth the Izrahite; and in his division *were* 24,000.

**9** The sixth for the sixth month *was* Ira *the son of* Ikkesh the Tekoite; and in his division *were* 24,000.

**10** The seventh for the seventh month *was* Helez the Pelonite of the sons of Ephraim; and in his division *were* 24,000.

**11** The eighth for the eighth month *was* Sibbecai the Hushathite of the Zerahites; and in his division *were* 24,000.

**12** The ninth for the ninth month *was* Abiezer the Anathothite of the Benjamites; and in his division *were* 24,000.

**13** The tenth for the tenth month *was* Maharai the Netophathite of the Zerahites; and in his division *were* 24,000.

**14** The eleventh for the eleventh month *was* Benaiah the Pirathonite of the sons of Ephraim; and in his division *were* 24,000.

**15** The twelfth for the twelfth month *was* Heldai the Netophathite of Othniel; and in his division *were* 24,000.

### *Chief Officers of the Tribes*

**16** Now *those* over the tribes of Israel: chief officer for the Reubenites was Eliezer the son of Zichri;
for the Simeonites, Shephatiah the son of Maacah;

**17** for Levi, Hashabiah the son of Kemuel;
for Aaron, Zadok;

**18** for Judah, Elihu, *one* of David's brothers;
for Issachar, Omri the son of Michael;

**19** for Zebulun, Ishmaiah the son of Obadiah;
for Naphtali, Jeremoth the son of Azriel;

**20** for the sons of Ephraim, Hoshea the son of Azaziah;

---

♦ **27:2** [a]2Sa 23:8-30; 1Chr 11:11-31

for the half-tribe of Manasseh,
Joel the son of Pedaiah;
**21** for the half-tribe of Manasseh
in Gilead, Iddo the son of
Zechariah;
for Benjamin, Jaasiel the son
of Abner;
**22** for Dan, Azarel the son of
Jeroham.
[a]These *were* the princes of the
tribes of Israel.

**23** But David did not take up a count
of those twenty years of age and
under, [a]because Yahweh had said
He would multiply Israel [b]as the
stars of heaven. **24** Joab the son of
Zeruiah had begun to number *them*,
but did not finish; and because of
[a]this, wrath came upon Israel, and
[1]this count was not included in the
*total* count of the chronicles of King
David.

### *Officials over David's Possessions*

**25** Now Azmaveth the son of
Adiel *was* over the king's
storehouses.
And Jonathan the son
of Uzziah *was* over the
storehouses in the country, in
the cities, in the villages and
in the towers.
**26** Ezri the son of Chelub *was*
over the [1]workers of the field
who cultivated the soil.
**27** Shimei the Ramathite *was*
over the vineyards;
and Zabdi the Shiphmite
*was* over the [1]produce of the
vineyards *stored* in the wine
cellars.
**28** Baal-hanan the Gederite *was*
over the olive and [a]sycamore
trees in the [1]Shephelah;
and Joash had charge of the
stores of oil.
**29** Shitrai the Sharonite *was* over
the cattle which were grazing
in [a]Sharon;
and Shaphat the son of Adlai
*was* over the cattle in the
valleys.
**30** Obil the Ishmaelite *was* over
the camels;
and Jehdeiah the Meronothite
*was* over the donkeys.
**31** Jaziz the [a]Hagrite *was* over the
flocks.
All these were officials
over the possessions which
belonged to King David.

### *Counselors*

**32** Also Jonathan, David's uncle,
*was* a counselor, a man of
understanding, and a scribe;
and Jehiel the son of Hachmoni
was with the king's sons.
**33** [a]Ahithophel *was* counselor to
the king;
and [b]Hushai the Archite *was*
the king's friend.
**34** Jehoiada the son of [a]Benaiah,
and [b]Abiathar [1]succeeded
Ahithophel;
and Joab was the [c]commander
of the king's army.

### *David Assembles His Commanders*

**28** And [a]David assembled at Jerusalem all the commanders of
Israel, the commanders of the tribes,

**27:22** [a]1Chr 28:1 **27:23** [a]1Chr 21:2-5 [b]Ge 15:5; 22:17; 26:4 **27:24** [a]2Sa 24:12-15; 1Chr 21:1-7 [1]Lit *the*
**27:26** [1]Lit *doers of the work of the field for the serving of...* **27:27** [1]Lit *what was in the vineyards of the storehouses of wine* **27:28** [a]1Ki 10:27; 2Chr 1:15 [1]Or *lowland* **27:29** [a]1Chr 5:16 **27:31** [a]1Chr 5:10
**27:33** [a]2Sa 15:12 [b]2Sa 15:32, 37 **27:34** [a]1Chr 27:5 [b]1Ki 1:7 [c]1Chr 11:6 [1]Lit *after* ◆ **28:1** [a]1Chr 23:2; 27:1-31

and the commanders of the divisions
that ministered to the king, and
the commanders of thousands, and
the commanders of hundreds, and
the commanders over all the proper-
ty and livestock belonging to the king
and his sons, with the officials and
[b]the mighty men, even all the mighty
men of valor. **2** Then King David rose
to his feet and said, "Listen to me,
my brothers and my people; I [a]*had
it* within my heart to build a house
of rest for the ark of the covenant
of Yahweh and for [b]the footstool of
the feet of our God. So I had made
preparations to build *it.* **3** But God
said to me, '[a]You shall not build a
house for My name because you are
a man of war and have shed blood.'
**4** Yet, Yahweh, the God of Israel,
[a]chose me from all the house of my
father to be king over Israel [b]forev-
er. For [c]He has chosen Judah to be
a ruler; and [d]in the house of Judah,
my father's house, and among the
sons of my father He took pleasure
in me to make *me* king over all Israel.
**5** [a]Now of all my sons (for Yahweh
has given me many sons), [b]He has
chosen my son Solomon to sit on the
throne of the kingdom of Yahweh
over Israel. **6** And He said to me, 'Your
son [a]Solomon is the one who shall
build My house and My courts; for I
have chosen him to be a son to Me,
and I will be a father to him. **7** And I
will establish his kingdom forever
[a]if he will be strong to do My com-
mandments and My judgments, as [1]is
done now.' **8** So now, in the sight of all
Israel, the assembly of Yahweh, and
in the hearing of our God, keep and
seek after all the commandments of
Yahweh your God so that you may
possess the good land and cause your
sons after you to inherit *it* forever.

**9** "As for you, my son Solomon,
know the God of your father, and
[a]serve Him with [1]a whole heart
and a delighted soul; [b]for Yahweh
searches all hearts, and understands
every intent of the thoughts. [c]If you
seek Him, He will be found; but if
you forsake Him, He will reject you
forever. **10** See now, for Yahweh has
chosen you to build a house for the
sanctuary; [a]be strong and act."

**11** Then David gave to his son Solo-
mon [a]the pattern of [b]the porch *of the
temple,* its buildings, its storehouses,
its upper rooms, its inner rooms, and
[c]the room for the mercy seat; **12** and
the pattern of all that he had in [1]mind,
for the courts of the house of Yahweh,
and for all the surrounding chambers,
for [a]the treasuries of the house of
God, and for the treasuries of the holy
things; **13** also for [a]the divisions of the
priests and [b]the Levites and for all
the work of the service of the house
of Yahweh and for all the utensils of
service in the house of Yahweh; **14** for
the golden *utensils,* the weight of gold
for all utensils for every kind of ser-
vice; for the silver utensils, the weight
*of silver* for all utensils for every kind
of service; **15** and the weight *of gold*
for the [a]golden lampstands and
their golden lamps, with the weight
of each lampstand and its lamps;
and *the weight of silver* for the silver
lampstands, with the weight of each

**28:1** [b]1Chr 11:10-47 **28:2** [a]1Chr 17:1, 2 [b]Ps 132:7; Is 66:1 **28:3** [a]1Chr 22:8 **28:4** [a]1Sa 16:6-13 [b]1Chr 17:23, 27 [c]Ge 49:8-10; 1Chr 5:2 [d]1Sa 16:1 **28:5** [a]1Chr 3:1-9; 14:3-7 [b]1Chr 22:9, 10 **28:6** [a]2Sa 7:13, 14 **28:7** [a]1Chr 22:13 [1]Lit *at this day* **28:9** [a]1Ki 8:61; 1Chr 29:17-19 [b]1Sa 16:7 [c]2Chr 15:2; Jer 29:13 [1]Or *the same* **28:10** [a]1Chr 22:13 **28:11** [a]Ex 25:40; 1Chr 28:12, 19 [b]1Ki 6:3 [c]Ex 25:17-22 **28:12** [a]1Chr 26:20, 28 [1]Lit *the spirit with him* **28:13** [a]1Chr 24:1 [b]1Chr 23:6 **28:15** [a]Ex 25:31-39

lampstand and its lamps according to
the service of each lampstand; **16** and
the gold by weight for the tables of
showbread, for each table; and silver
for the silver tables; **17** and the flesh
hooks, the bowls, and the jars of pure
gold; and for the golden bowls with
the weight for each bowl; and for the
silver bowls with the weight for each
bowl; **18** and for [a]the altar of incense
refined gold by weight; and gold for
the pattern of the chariot, *even* [b]the
cherubim that spread out *their wings*
and covered the ark of the covenant
of Yahweh.
**19** "All *this*," *said David*, "has been
granted to me as insight in writing by
the hand of Yahweh, [a]all the [1]details
of this pattern."
**20** Then David said to his son Sol-
omon, "[a]Be strong and courageous,
and act; do not fear nor be dismayed,
for Yahweh God, my God, is with you.
[b]He will not fail you nor forsake you
until all the work for the service of the
house of Yahweh is completed. **21** Now
behold, [a]*there are* the divisions of the
priests and the Levites for all the ser-
vice of the house of God, and [b]every
willing man with wisdom will be with
you in all the work for all the service.
The officials also and all the people
will be entirely at your command."

### *Offerings for the Temple*

**29** Then King David said to the
entire assembly, "My son Solo-
mon, whom alone God has chosen, [a]is
still young and inexperienced and the
work is great; for [b]the [1]temple is not
for man, but for Yahweh God. **2** Now
[a]with all my power I have prepared
for the house of my God the gold for
the *things of* gold, and the silver for the
*things of* silver, and the bronze for
the *things of* bronze, the iron for the
*things of* iron, and wood for the *things*
*of* wood, onyx stones and inlaid *stones*,
stones of antimony and stones of var-
ious colors, and all kinds of precious
stones and alabaster in abundance.
**3** Moreover, in my pleasure in the
house of my God, the treasure I have
of gold and silver, I give to the house
of my God, over and above all that I
have already prepared for the holy
[1]house, **4** *namely*, [a,1]3,000 talents of
gold, of [b]the gold of Ophir, and [2]7,000
talents of refined silver, to overlay the
walls of the [3]buildings; **5** of gold for
the *things of* gold and of silver for the
*things of* silver, that is, for all the work
*done* by the hand of craftsmen. Who
then would offer willingly [1]to ordain
himself this day to Yahweh?"
**6** Then [a]the commanders of the
fathers' *households*, and the com-
manders of the tribes of Israel, and
the commanders of thousands and
of hundreds, with [b]the commanders
of the king's work, offered willingly;
**7** and for the service for the house
of God they gave 5,000 talents and
10,000 [a,1]darics of gold, and 10,000
talents of silver, and 18,000 talents
of brass, and 100,000 talents of iron.
**8** [1]And whoever possessed *precious*
stones gave them to the treasury of
the house of Yahweh, [2]in the care of
[a]Jehiel the Gershonite. **9** Then the

---

**28:18** [a]Ex 30:1-10 [b]Ex 25:18-22 **28:19** [a]1Chr 28:11, 12 [1]Lit *works* **28:20** [a]1Chr 22:13 [b]Jos 1:5; Heb 13:5 **28:21** [a]1Chr 28:13 [b]Ex 35:25-35; 36:1, 2 ◆ **29:1** [a]1Chr 22:5 [b]1Chr 29:19 [1]Lit *palace*
**29:2** [a]1Chr 22:3-5 **29:3** [1]Or *temple* **29:4** [a]1Chr 22:14 [b]1Ki 9:28 [1]Approx. 112.5 tons or 102 metric tons [2]Approx. 262.5 tons or 238 metric tons [3]Lit *houses* **29:5** [1]Lit *to fill his hand* **29:6** [a]1Chr 27:1; 28:1 [b]1Chr 27:25-31 **29:7** [a]Ezr 2:69; Ne 7:70 [1]A Persian gold coin weighing approx. 0.3 oz. or 8 gm
**29:8** [a]1Chr 23:8 [1]Lit *Those with whom were found* [2]Lit *under the hand of*

people were glad because they had
offered so willingly, for they made
their freewill offering to Yahweh
[a]with a whole heart, and King David
also was exceedingly glad.

### *David Blesses Yahweh*

**10** So David blessed Yahweh in the
sight of all the assembly; and David
said, "Blessed are You, O Yahweh,
the God of Israel our father, from
everlasting to everlasting. **11** [a]Yours,
O Yahweh, is the greatness and the
[1]power and the glory and the [2]victory
and the majesty, indeed everything
that is in the heavens and the earth;
Yours is the kingdom, O Yahweh, and
You exalt Yourself as head over all.
**12** [a]Both riches and honor *come* from
You, and You rule over all, and [b]in
Your hand is power and might; and
it lies in Your hand to make great and
to strengthen everyone. **13** So now,
our God, we are thanking You and
praising Your glorious name.

**14** "But who am I and who are my
people that we should [1]be able to of-
fer as willingly as this? For all things
come from You, and from Your hand
we have given You. **15** For [a]we are
sojourners before You, and foreign
residents, like all our fathers were;
[b]our days on the earth are like a shad-
ow, and there is no hope. **16** O Yahweh
our God, all this abundance that we
have prepared to build You a house
for Your holy name, it is from Your
hand, and all is Yours. **17** And I know,
O my God, that [a]You try the heart
and [b]*delight in uprightness. I, in*
the uprightness of my heart, have
willingly offered all these *things*.
So now with gladness I have seen
Your people, who are present here,
make *their* offerings willingly to You.
**18** O Yahweh, the God of Abraham,
Isaac, and Israel, our fathers, keep
this forever in the [1]intentions of the
heart of Your people, and prepare
their heart to You; **19** and [a]give to
my son Solomon a whole heart to
keep Your commandments, Your tes-
timonies and Your statutes, and to do
*them* all, and [b]to build the [1]temple,
for which I have made preparation."

**20** Then David said to all the
assembly, "Now bless Yahweh your
God." And [a]all the assembly blessed
Yahweh, the God of their fathers,
and [b]bowed low and prostrated
themselves to Yahweh and to the king.

### *Sacrifices to Yahweh*

**21** And on the next day [a]they [1]made
sacrifices to Yahweh and offered
burnt offerings to Yahweh, 1,000
bulls, 1,000 rams, *and* 1,000 lambs,
with their drink offerings and sacri-
fices in abundance for all Israel. **22** So
they ate and drank that day before
Yahweh with great gladness.

### *David's Officials and Sons Pledge Allegiance*

And they made Solomon the son of
David king [a]a second time, and they
[b]anointed *him* as ruler for Yahweh
and Zadok as priest. **23** Then [a]Sol-
omon sat on the throne of Yahweh
as king instead of David his father;
and he succeeded, and all Israel
obeyed him. **24** And all the officials,

**29:9** [a]1Ki 8:61; 2Co 9:7 **29:11** [a]Mt 6:13; Rev 5:13 [1]Or *might*, cf. 29:12, 30 [2]Or *eternity*
**29:12** [a]2Chr 1:12 [b]2Chr 20:6 **29:14** [1]Lit *retain strength* **29:15** [a]Lv 25:23 [b]Job 14:2, 10-12
**29:17** [a]1Chr 28:9 [b]Ps 15:2 **29:18** [1]Lit *intent of the thoughts of the heart* **29:19** [a]1Chr 28:9; Ps 72:1 [b]1Chr 29:1, 2 [1]Lit *palace* **29:20** [a]Jos 22:33 [b]Ex 4:31 **29:21** [a]1Ki 8:62, 63 [1]Lit *sacrificed*
**29:22** [a]1Chr 23:1 [b]1Ki 1:33-39 **29:23** [a]1Ki 2:12

the mighty men, and also all the sons
of King David [1]pledged allegiance
to King Solomon. **25** [a]And Yahweh
highly exalted Solomon in the sight
of all Israel, and [b]granted to him royal
majesty which had not been on any
king before him in Israel.

**26** Now [a]David the son of Jesse
reigned over all Israel. **27** [a]And the
[1]time which he reigned over Israel
*was* forty years; in Hebron he reigned
seven years and [2]in Jerusalem thirty-
three *years*.

### *Death of David*

**28** Then he died in [a]a good old age,
[b]full of days, riches and glory; and
his son Solomon became king in his
place. **29** Now the acts of King David,
from first to last, behold, they are
written in the chronicles of [a]Samuel
the seer, in the chronicles of [b]Nathan
the prophet and in the chronicles of
[c]Gad the seer, **30** with all his reign, his
might, and the circumstances which
came on him, on Israel, and on all the
kingdoms of the lands.

# *The Second Book of the* CHRONICLES

### *Solomon Goes Before Yahweh*

**1** Now [a]Solomon the son of David
strengthened himself over his
kingdom, and [1]Yahweh his God *was*
with him and highly [b]exalted him.

**2** And Solomon spoke to all Israel,
[a]to the commanders of thousands
and of hundreds and to the judges
and to every leader in all Israel, the
heads of the fathers' *households*.
**3** Then Solomon and all the assem-
bly with him went to [a]the high place
which was at Gibeon, [b]for God's tent
of meeting was there, which Moses
the servant of Yahweh had made in
the wilderness. **4** However, David
had brought up [a]the ark of God from
Kiriath-jearim [1]to [b]the place he had
prepared for it, for he had pitched a
tent for it in Jerusalem. **5** Now [a]the
bronze altar, which Bezalel the son
of Uri, the son of Hur, had made,
[1]was there before the tabernacle of
Yahweh, and Solomon and the as-
sembly sought it out. **6** And Solomon
went up there before Yahweh to the
bronze altar which *was* at the tent of
meeting, and [a]offered one thousand
burnt offerings on it.

**7** [a]In that night God appeared to
Solomon and said to him, "Ask what
I should give to you."

### *God Gives Wisdom to Solomon*

**8** Then Solomon said to God, "You
have shown great lovingkindness to
my father David, and [a]have made me
king in his place. **9** Now, O Yahweh
God, [a]let Your [1]promise to my father
David [2]endure, for You have made
me king over [b]a people as numerous
as the dust of the earth. **10** [a]Give me

---

**29:24** [1]Lit *put a hand under King Solomon* **29:25** [a]2Chr 1:1 [b]1Ki 3:13; 2Chr 1:12 **29:26** [a]1Chr 18:14 **29:27** [a]2Sa 5:4, 5; 1Ki 2:11; 1Chr 3:4 [1]Lit *days* [2]Lit *he reigned in* **29:28** [a]Ge 15:15; Ac 13:36 [b]1Chr 23:1 **29:29** [a]1Sa 9:9 [b]2Sa 7:2-4; 12:1-7 [c]1Sa 22:5 ◆ **1:1** [a]1Ki 2:12, 46 [b]1Chr 29:25 [1]The personal covenant name of God, a form of I AM WHO I AM, cf. Ex 3:14-15 **1:2** [a]1Chr 28:1 **1:3** [a]1Ki 3:4 [b]Ex 36:8 **1:4** [a]1Chr 15:25-28 [b]2Chr 6:2 [1]Lit *where David had prepared for it* **1:5** [a]Ex 31:9; 38:1-7 [1]Lit *he put* **1:6** [a]1Ki 3:4 **1:7** [a]1Ki 3:5-14 **1:8** [a]1Chr 28:5 **1:9** [a]2Sa 7:12-16 [b]Ge 13:16; 22:17; 28:14 [1]Lit *word* [2]Or *be true* **1:10** [a]1Ki 3:9

now wisdom and knowledge, [b]that I
may go out and come in before this
people, for who can do justice for
this great people of Yours?" **11** [a]And
God said to Solomon, "Because [1]you
had this in your heart, and did not
ask for riches, wealth, or glory, or
the life of those who hate you, nor
have you even asked for long life, but
you have asked for yourself wisdom
and knowledge that you may do
justice for My people over whom
I have made you king, **12** wisdom
and knowledge have been given to
you. And [a]I will give you riches and
wealth and glory, [1]such as none of
the kings who were before you had
nor those who will [2]come after you."
**13** [a]So Solomon went [1]from the high
place which was at Gibeon, from the
tent of meeting, to Jerusalem, and he
reigned over Israel.

### Solomon's Chariots and Horsemen

**14** [a]And Solomon gathered chariots
and horsemen. [b]And he had 1,400
chariots and 12,000 horsemen, and
he stationed them in [c]the chariot
cities and with the king in Jerusa-
lem. **15** [a]The king also made [b]silver
and gold *as plentiful* as stones in
Jerusalem, and he made cedars as
plentiful as sycamore trees that are
in the [1]Shephelah. **16** Solomon's
import of [a]horses was from Egypt
and from Kue; the king's merchants
procured *them* from Kue for a price.
**17** And they [1]imported a chariot from
Egypt for [2]600 *shekels* of silver and
a horse for [3]150; and [4]by the same
means they [5]exported them to all the
kings of the Hittites and the kings of
Aram.

### Yahweh's House Will Be Great

**2** [a,1]Then Solomon [2]decided to build
a house for the name of Yahweh
and a [3]royal palace for himself. **2** [1]So
[a]Solomon numbered 70,000 men to
carry loads and 80,000 men to hew
*stone* in the mountains and 3,600 to
direct them.

**3** [a]Then Solomon sent *word* to
[1]Huram the king of Tyre, saying, "[b]As
you dealt with David my father and
sent him cedars to build him a house
to live in, *so do for me.* **4** Behold, I am
about to build a house for the name
of Yahweh my God, setting it apart
to Him as holy, [a]to burn fragrant
incense before Him and *to set out*
[b]the showbread continually, and to
offer [c]burnt offerings morning and
evening, [d]on sabbaths and on new
moons and on the appointed feasts of
Yahweh our God, this *being required*
forever in Israel. **5** Now the house
which I am about to build *will be*
great, for [a]greater is our God than all
the gods. **6** But [a]who is able to build a
house for Him, for the heavens and
the highest heavens cannot contain
Him? So who am I, that I should
build a house for Him, except to
[1]burn *incense* before Him? **7** So now,
[a]send me a wise man to work in gold,

---

**1:10** [b]Nu 27:17; 2Sa 5:2 **1:11** [a]1Ki 3:11 [1]Lit *this was in your heart* **1:12** [a]1Chr 29:25; 2Chr 9:22 [1]Lit *which was not so to the kings who were before you* [2]Lit *be* **1:13** [a]2Chr 1:3 [1]Lit *to* **1:14** [a]1Ki 10:26-29 [b]1Ki 4:26 [c]1Ki 9:19 **1:15** [a]1Ki 10:27 [b]Dt 17:17 [1]Or *lowland* **1:16** [a]Dt 17:16 **1:17** [1]Lit *brought up and brought out* [2]Approx. 15 lb. or 6.6 kg [3]Approx. 3.7 lb. or 1.6 kg [4]Lit *and in like manner by their hand* [5]Lit *brought out* ◆ **2:1** [a]1Ki 5:5 [1]Ch 1:18 in Heb [2]Lit *said* [3]Lit *house for his royalty* **2:2** [a]1Ki 5:15, 16; 2Chr 2:18 [1]Ch 2:1 in Heb **2:3** [a]1Ki 5:2-11 [b]1Chr 14:1 [1]In 1Ki 5:18, *Hiram* **2:4** [a]Ex 30:7 [b]Ex 25:30 [c]Ex 29:38-42 [d]Nu 28:9, 10 **2:5** [a]Ex 15:11; 1Chr 16:25 **2:6** [a]1Ki 8:27; 2Chr 6:18 [1]Lit *offer up in smoke* **2:7** [a]Ex 31:3-5; 2Chr 2:13, 14

silver, brass, and iron, and in purple,
crimson, and blue *fabrics*, and who
knows how to make engravings, to
*work* with the wise men [b,1]whom I
have in Judah and Jerusalem, whom
David my father prepared. **8** [a]Send me
also cedar, cypress and algum timber
from Lebanon, for I know that your
servants know how to cut timber of
Lebanon; and behold, [b]my servants
*will work* with your servants, **9** to pre-
pare timber in abundance for me, for
the house which I am about to build
*will be* great and wonderful. **10** And
behold, [a]I will give to your servants,
the woodsmen who cut the timber,
[1]20,000 kors of crushed wheat and
20,000 kors of barley, and [2]20,000
baths of wine and 20,000 baths of
oil."

### *Covenant with Huram King of Tyre*

**11** Then Huram king of Tyre said in
a letter [1]sent to Solomon: "[a]Because
Yahweh loves His people, He has giv-
en you *to be* king over them." **12** Then
Huram said, "Blessed be [a]Yahweh, the
God of Israel, who has made heaven
and earth, who has given King David
a wise son, knowledgeable in insight
and understanding, [b]who will build a
house for Yahweh and a [1]royal palace
for himself.

**13** "So now, I am sending Huram-
abi, a wise man, who is knowledge-
able in understanding, **14** [a]the son
of a [1]Danite woman and [2]a Tyrian
father, who knows how to work in
gold, silver, bronze, iron, stone, and
wood, *and* in purple, blue, linen, and
crimson fabrics, and *who knows how*
to make all kinds of engravings and
to devise any design which may be
given to him, *to work* with your wise
men and with the wise men of my
lord David your father. **15** So now, let
my lord send to his servants wheat
and barley, oil and wine, of [a]which
he has spoken. **16** [a]And we will cut
whatever timber you need from
Lebanon and bring it to you on rafts
by sea to Joppa, so that you may carry
it up to Jerusalem."

**17** Then Solomon numbered all the
sojourners who *were* in the land of Is-
rael, [a]following the [1]census which his
father David had [2]taken; and 153,600
were found. **18** [a]And he made 70,000
of them to carry loads and 80,000 as
hewers *of stone* in the mountains and
3,600 directors to make the people
work.

### *Solomon Builds Yahweh's House*

**3** [a]Then Solomon began to build
the house of Yahweh in Jerusalem
on Mount Moriah, where *Yahweh* had
appeared to his father David, at the
place that David had prepared [b]on
the threshing floor of [1]Ornan the
Jebusite. **2** Then he began to build on
the second *day* in the second month
[1]of the fourth year of his reign. **3** Now
these are the [1]foundations which
[a]Solomon laid for building the
house of God. The length in cubits,
according to the old standard *was*
[2]sixty cubits, and the width twenty

**2:7** [b]1Chr 22:15 [1]Lit *who are with me* **2:8** [a]1Ki 5:6 [b]2Chr 9:10, 11 **2:10** [a]1Ki 5:11 [1]Approx. 130,000 bu. or 4,600 metric tons, a kor was approx. 6.5 bu. or 230 l [2]Approx. 120,000 gal. or 454,249 l, a bath was approx. 6 gal. or 23 l **2:11** [a]1Ki 10:9; 2Chr 9:8 [1]Lit *and sent* **2:12** [a]Ps 33:6; 102:25 [b]2Chr 2:1 [1]Lit *house for his royalty* **2:14** [a]1Ki 7:14 [1]Lit *a woman of the daughters of Dan* [2]Lit *whose father is a Tyrian man* **2:15** [a]2Chr 2:10 **2:16** [a]1Ki 5:8, 9 **2:17** [a]1Chr 22:2 [1]Lit *numbering* [2]Lit *numbered of them* **2:18** [a]2Chr 2:2 ◆ **3:1** [a]1Ki 6:1 [b]1Chr 21:18 [1]In 2Sa 24:18, *Araunah* **3:2** [1]Lit *in* **3:3** [a]1Ki 6:2 [1]Lit *founding of Solomon to build* [2]Approx. 90 ft. long and 30 ft. wide or 27 m and 9 m, a cubit was approx. 18 in. or 45 cm

cubits. **4** And the porch which was in
front of the house [a]was as long as the
width of the house, [1]20 cubits, and
the height 120; and inside he overlaid
it with pure gold. **5** Now he overlaid
[a]the [1]main room with cypress wood
and overlaid it with fine gold, and
[2]ornamented it with palm trees
and chains. **6** Further, he overlaid
the house with precious stones
for beauty; and the gold was gold
from [1]Parvaim. **7** [a]He also covered
the house with gold—the beams,
the thresholds and its walls and its
doors; and he [b]carved cherubim on
the walls.

**8** And he made [a]the [1]room of the
Holy of Holies: its length across
the width of the house *was* twenty
cubits, and its width *was* twenty cu-
bits; and he covered it with fine gold,
*amounting* to [2]600 talents. **9** Now the
weight of the nails was [1]fifty shekels
of gold. He also covered [a]the upper
rooms with gold.

**10** [a]Then in the room of the Holy
of Holies he made two cherubim of
fashioned work and overlaid them
with gold. **11** Now the wingspan of
the cherubim *was* twenty cubits; the
wing of one, of five cubits, touched
the wall of the house, and *its* other
wing, of five cubits, touched the wing
of the other cherub. **12** And the wing
of the other cherub, of five cubits,
touched the wall of the house; and *its*
other wing of five cubits was attached
to the wing of the [1]first cherub. **13** The
wings of these cherubim extended
twenty cubits, and they stood on
their feet [1]facing the *main* room.
**14** [a]And he made the veil of blue,
purple, crimson, and fine linen, and
he ornamented cherubim on it.

**15** [a]He also made two pillars for the
front of the house, [1]thirty-five cubits
[2]high, and the capital on the top of
each *was* five cubits. **16** And he made
chains in the inner sanctuary and put
*them* on the top of the pillars; and
he made one hundred pomegranates
and put *them* on the chains. **17** [a]Thus
he set up the pillars in front of the
temple, one on the right and one on
the left, and named the one on the
right Jachin and the one on the left
Boaz.

### The Furnishings of the House of Yahweh

**4** Then [a]he made a bronze altar,
[1]twenty cubits in length and
twenty cubits in width and ten cubits
in height. **2** [a]And he made the sea of
cast *metal* ten cubits from brim to
brim, circular in form, and its height
was five cubits, and [1]thirty cubits in
[2]its circumference. **3** Now figures like
oxen *were* under it *and* encircling it,
ten cubits, entirely encircling the
sea. The oxen *were* in two rows, cast
[1]in one piece. **4** It stood on twelve
oxen, three facing the north, three
facing west, three facing south, and
three facing east; and the sea *was*
*set* on top of them, and all their rear

**3:4** [a]1Ki 6:3 [1]*Approx. 30 ft. long, 30 ft. wide, and 180 ft. tall or 9 m, 9 m, and 54 m* **3:5** [a]1Ki 6:17 [1]*Lit great house* [2]*Lit put on it palm trees* **3:6** [1]*Or country of gold* **3:7** [a]1Ki 6:20-22 [b]1Ki 6:29-35 **3:8** [a]Ex 26:33; 1Ki 6:16 [1]Lit *house* [2]Approx. 23 tons or 21 metric tons, a talent was approx. 75 lb. or 34 kg **3:9** [a]1Chr 28:11 [1]Approx. 1.25 lb. or 550 gm, a shekel was approx. 0.4 oz. or 11 gm **3:10** [a]Ex 25:18-20; 1Ki 6:23-28 **3:12** [1]Lit *other* **3:13** [1]Lit *and their faces to* **3:14** [a]Ex 26:31 **3:15** [a]1Ki 7:15-20 [1]Approx. 52.5 ft. or 15.75 m [2]Lit *long* **3:17** [a]1Ki 7:21 ◆ **4:1** [a]Ex 27:1, 2; 2Ki 16:14 [1]Approx. 30 ft. long, 30 ft. wide, and 10 ft. tall or 9 m, 9 m, and 4.5 m; a cubit was approx. 18 in. or 45 cm **4:2** [a]1Ki 7:23-26 [1]Approx. 45 ft. or 13.5 m [2]Lit *a line of 30 cubits encircling it round about* **4:3** [1]Lit *in its casting* parts *turned* inward. **5** And it was a [1]handbreadth thick, and its brim was made like the brim of a cup, *as* a lily blossom; it [a]could hold 3,000 baths. **6** [a]He also made ten lavers and set five on the right side and five on the left, in which to wash *things, that is,* in which they would rinse things for the burnt offering; but the sea *was* for the priests to wash in.

**7** Then [a]he made the ten golden lampstands [1]in the way prescribed for them and he put them in the temple, five on the right side and five on the left. **8** He also made [a]ten tables and placed them in the temple, five on the right side and five on the left. And he made one hundred golden bowls. **9** Then he made [a]the court of the priests and [b]the great court and doors for the court, and overlaid their doors with bronze. **10** [a]And he put the sea on the right [1]side *of the house* toward the southeast.

**11** [a]And Huram made the pots and the shovels and the bowls. So Huram completed doing the work which he did for King Solomon in the house of God: **12** the two pillars and the *two* bowls and the two capitals on top of the pillars, and the two networks to cover the two bowls of the capitals which were on top of the pillars, **13** and [a]the four hundred pomegranates for the two networks, two rows of pomegranates for each network to cover the two bowls of the capitals which were on the pillars. **14** [a]He also made the stands and he made the lavers on the stands, **15** *and* the one sea with the twelve oxen under it. **16** And the pots and the shovels and the flesh hooks and all its utensils, [a]Huram-abi made of polished bronze for King Solomon for the house of Yahweh. **17** On the plain of the Jordan the king cast them, in the clay ground between Succoth and Zeredah. **18** [a]Thus Solomon made all these utensils in great quantities, for the weight of the bronze could not be found out.

**19** Solomon also made all the furniture which *was in* the house of God: even the golden altar and [a]the tables with the bread of the Presence on them, **20** and the lampstands with their lamps of pure gold, [a]to burn in front of the inner sanctuary [1]in the way prescribed; **21** and the flowers and the lamps and the tongs of gold, of purest gold; **22** and the snuffers and the bowls and the spoons and the firepans, of pure gold; and the entrance of the house, its inner doors for the Holy of Holies and the doors of the house, *that is,* of the nave, of gold.

### *The Ark Brought into the House of Yahweh*

**5** [a]Thus all the work that Solomon did for the house of Yahweh was finished. And Solomon brought in the [b,1]things set apart as holy by his father David, even the silver and the gold and all the utensils, *and* he put *them* in the treasuries of the house of God.

**2** [a]Then Solomon assembled the elders of Israel and all the heads of the tribes, the leaders of the fathers' *households* of the sons of Israel to

**4:5** [a]1Ki 7:26 [1]A handbreadth was approx. 3 in. or 7.6 cm **4:6** [a]Ex 30:17-21; 1Ki 7:38, 40
**4:7** [a]Ex 25:31-40; 1Ki 7:49 [1]Lit *according to their judgment* **4:8** [a]1Ki 7:48 **4:9** [a]1Ki 6:36 [b]2Ki 21:5
**4:10** [a]1Ki 7:39 [1]Lit *shoulder* **4:11** [a]1Ki 7:40-51 **4:13** [a]1Ki 7:20 **4:14** [a]1Ki 7:27-43 **4:16** [a]1Ki 7:14; 2Chr 2:13 **4:18** [a]1Ki 7:47 **4:19** [a]2Chr 4:8 **4:20** [a]Ex 25:31-37; 2Chr 5:7 [1]Lit *according to the judgment*
◆ **5:1** [a]1Ki 7:51 [b]2Sa 8:11; 1Chr 18:11 [1]Lit *dedicated things of David his father,* **5:2** [a]1Ki 8:1-9

Jerusalem, [b]to bring up the ark of the covenant of Yahweh from the city of David, which is Zion. **3** [a]And all the men of Israel assembled themselves to the king at [b]the feast, that is *in* the seventh month. **4** Then all the elders of Israel came, and [a]the Levites carried the ark. **5** And they brought up the ark and the tent of meeting and all the holy utensils which were in the tent; the Levitical priests brought them up. **6** And King Solomon and all the congregation of Israel who congregated with him before the ark, were sacrificing [1]so many sheep and oxen that they could not be counted or numbered. **7** Then the priests brought the ark of the covenant of Yahweh to its place, into the inner sanctuary of the house, to the Holy of Holies, under the wings of the cherubim. **8** And the cherubim spread *their* wings over the place of the ark, and the cherubim made a covering over the ark and its poles from above. **9** But the poles were so long that [a]the ends of the poles of the ark could be seen before the inner sanctuary, but they could not be seen outside; and [1]they are there to this day. **10** [a]There was nothing in the ark except the two tablets which Moses put *there* at Horeb, where Yahweh cut a covenant with the sons of Israel, when they came out of Egypt.

### *The Glory of Yahweh Fills His House*

**11** Now it happened that when the priests came out of the holy place (for all the priests who *were present* had sanctified themselves, without regard [a]to divisions), **12** and all the Levitical singers, [a]Asaph, Heman, Jeduthun, and their sons and relatives, clothed in fine linen, [b]with cymbals, harps, and lyres, standing east of the altar, and with them 120 priests [c]blowing trumpets **13** in unison when the trumpeters and the singers were to make themselves heard with one voice to praise and to give thanks to Yahweh, and when they lifted up their voice [a]accompanied by trumpets and cymbals and instruments of music, and when they praised Yahweh *saying,* "[b]*He* indeed is good for His lovingkindness endures forever," then the house, the house of Yahweh, was filled with a cloud, **14** so that the priests could not stand to minister because of the cloud, for [a]the glory of Yahweh filled the house of God.

### *Solomon Blesses the People*

**6** [a]Then Solomon said,
"Yahweh has said that
He would dwell in the *cloud of* dense gloom.
**2** "Now I have built You
a lofty house,
And a place for Your
dwelling forever."

**3** Then the king turned his face around and blessed all the assembly of Israel, while all the assembly of Israel was standing. **4** And he said, "Blessed be Yahweh, the God of Israel, who spoke with His mouth to my father David and has fulfilled *it by His* hands, saying, **5** 'Since the day that I brought My people from

**5:2** [b]2Sa 6:12-15; 1Chr 15:25-28; 2Chr 1:4 **5:3** [a]1Ki 8:2 [b]2Chr 7:8-10 **5:4** [a]Jos 3:6; 2Chr 5:7 **5:6** [1]Lit *sheep...numbered for multitude* **5:9** [a]1Ki 8:8, 9 [1]Lit *it is* **5:10** [a]Dt 10:2-5; Heb 9:4 **5:11** [a]1Chr 24:1-5 **5:12** [a]1Chr 25:1-4 [b]1Chr 13:8; 15:16, 24 [c]2Chr 7:6 **5:13** [a]1Chr 16:42 [b]1Chr 16:34; 2Chr 7:3; Ezr 3:11; Ps 100:5; Jer 33:11 **5:14** [a]Ex 40:35; 1Ki 8:11 ◆ **6:1** [a]1Ki 8:12-50

the land of Egypt, I did not choose
a city out of all the tribes of Israel *in*
*which* to build a house that My name
might be there, nor did I choose any
man for a ruler over My people Is-
rael; **6** but [a]I have chosen Jerusalem
that My name might be there, and I
[b]have chosen David to be over My
people Israel.' **7** [a]And it was [1]in the
heart of my father David to build a
house for the name of Yahweh, the
God of Israel. **8** But Yahweh said to
my father David, 'Because it was [1]in
your heart to build a house for My
name, you did well that it was [1]in your
heart. **9** Nevertheless you shall not
build the house, but your son who
will [a]come forth from your loins, he
shall build the house for My name.'
**10** And Yahweh has established His
word which He spoke; and I have
been established in place of my father
David and sit on the throne of Israel,
as Yahweh [1]promised, and have built
the house for the name of Yahweh,
the God of Israel. **11** And there I have
set the ark [a]in which is the covenant
of Yahweh, which He cut with the
sons of Israel."

### *Solomon's Prayer for Israel*

**12** Then he stood before the altar
of Yahweh before all the assembly
of Israel and spread out his hands.
**13** [a]Now Solomon had made a bronze
platform, five cubits long, five cubits
wide and three cubits high, and had
put it in the midst of the court; and
he stood on it, [b]knelt on his knees in
the presence of all the assembly of Is-
rael, and spread out his hands toward
heaven. **14** And he said, "O Yahweh,
the God of Israel, [a]there is no god like
You in heaven or on earth, [b]keeping
covenant and lovingkindness to Your
slaves who walk before You with all
their heart; **15** [a]who have kept with
Your [1]servant David, my father, that
which You have [2]promised him;
indeed You have promised with
Your mouth and have fulfilled it by
Your hand, as it is this day. **16** So now,
O Yahweh, the God of Israel, keep
with Your servant David my father,
that which You have promised him,
saying, '[a]You shall not have a man
cut off from before Me who is to sit
on the throne of Israel, if only your
sons keep their way to walk in My law
as you have walked before Me.' **17** So
now, O Yahweh, the God of Israel, let
Your word *truly* [1]endure which You
have spoken to Your servant David.

**18** "But [a]will God truly dwell with
mankind on the earth? Behold,
[b]heaven and the [1]highest heaven
cannot contain You; how much
less this house which I have built.
**19** Yet have regard to the prayer of
Your slave and to his supplication,
O Yahweh my God, to listen to the
cry and to the prayer which Your
slave prays before You; **20** that Your
[a]eyes may be open toward this house
day and night, toward [b]the place of
which You have said that *You would*
place Your name there, to listen to
the prayer which Your slave shall
pray toward this place. **21** And listen
to the supplications of Your slave and
of Your people Israel, when they pray
toward this place; listen from Your

---

**6:6** [a]2Chr 12:13 [b]1Chr 28:4 **6:7** [a]1Ki 5:3; 1Chr 28:2 [1]Lit *with* **6:8** [1]Lit *with* **6:9** [a]Ge 35:11; 1Ki 8:19 **6:10** [1]Lit *spoke* **6:11** [a]2Chr 5:7, 10 **6:13** [a]Ne 8:4 [b]1Ki 8:54 **6:14** [a]Ex 15:11; Dt 3:24 [b]Dt 7:9 **6:15** [a]1Chr 22:9, 10 [1]Or *slave*, so in ch, cf. 6:14; see Foreword, "The Terminology of Slave" [2]Lit *spoken to*, so in ch **6:16** [a]1Ki 2:4; 2Chr 7:18 **6:17** [1]Or *be true* **6:18** [a]Ps 113:5, 6 [b]2Chr 2:6; Is 66:1; Ac 7:49 [1]Lit *heaven of heavens* **6:20** [a]Ps 33:18; 34:15 [b]Dt 12:11

dwelling place, from heaven; [a]listen
and forgive.
**22** "If a man sins against his neigh-
bor and is made to take an oath, and
he comes *and* takes an oath before
Your altar in this house, **23** then listen
from heaven and act and judge Your
slaves, [a,1]punishing the wicked by
[2]bringing his way on his own head
and justifying the righteous by
[2]bringing him *reward* according to
his righteousness.
**24** "And if Your people Israel are
[1]defeated before an enemy because
[a]they have sinned against You, and
they turn *to You* and confess Your
name, and pray and make supplica-
tion before You in this house, **25** then
listen from heaven and forgive the
sin of Your people Israel, and bring
them back to the land which You have
given to them and to their fathers.
**26** "When the [a]heavens are shut
up and there is no rain because they
have sinned against You, and they
pray toward this place and confess
Your name, *and* turn from their sin
when You afflict them; **27** then listen
in heaven and forgive the sin of Your
slaves and of Your people Israel;
indeed, [a]teach them the good way
in which they should walk. And give
rain on Your land, which You have
given to Your people for an inheri-
tance.
**28** "If there is [a]famine in the land,
if there is pestilence, if there is
scorching wind or mildew, if there
is locust or grasshopper, if their ene-
mies besiege them in the land of their
[1]*cities, whatever plague or whatever*
sickness *there is,* **29** whatever prayer
or supplication is made by any man
or by all Your people Israel, who
know his own affliction and his own
pain, and spread his hands toward
this house, **30** then listen from heav-
en Your dwelling place, and forgive,
and give to each according to all his
ways, whose heart You know, [a]for
You alone know the hearts of the
sons of men, **31** that they may [1]fear
You, to walk in Your ways all the days
they live upon the face of the land
which You have given to our fathers.
**32** "Also concerning [a]the foreigner
who is not of Your people Israel, if he
comes from a far country for Your
great name's sake and Your strong
hand and Your outstretched arm, so
if they come and pray toward this
house, **33** then listen from heaven,
from Your dwelling place, and do
according to all for which the for-
eigner calls to You, in order that all
the peoples of the earth may know
Your name even to [1]fear You, as
*do* Your people Israel, and to know
that Your name is [a]called upon this
house which I have built.
**34** "When Your people go out
to battle against their enemies, by
whatever way You shall send them,
and they pray to You toward this
city which You have chosen and the
house which I have built for Your
name, **35** then listen from heaven to
their prayer and their supplication,
and do justice.
**36** "When they sin against You
([a]for there is no man who does not
sin) and You are angry with them

**6:21** [a]Is 43:25; 44:22; Mic 7:18 **6:23** [a]Is 3:11; Ro 2:8, 9 [1]Lit *returning* [2]Lit *giving* **6:24** [a]Ps 51:4 [1]Lit *smitten* **6:26** [a]1Ki 17:1 **6:27** [a]Ps 94:12 **6:28** [a]2Chr 20:9 [1]Lit *gates* **6:30** [a]1Sa 16:7; 1Chr 28:9 **6:31** [1]Or *reverence* **6:32** [a]Is 56:3-8 **6:33** [a]2Chr 7:14 [1]Or *reverence* **6:36** [a]Job 15:14-16; Jas 3:2; 1Jn 1:8-10

and give them over to an enemy, so
that [1]they take them away captive to
a land far off or near, **37** and if they
[a]cause *these things* to return to their
heart in the land where they have
been taken captive, and [1]return and
make supplication to You in the land
of their captivity, saying, 'We have
sinned, we have committed iniquity
and have acted wickedly'; **38** [a]and if
they return to You with all their heart
and with all their soul in the land
of their captivity, where they have
been taken captive, and pray toward
their land which You have given to
their fathers and the city which You
have chosen, and toward the house
which I have built for Your name,
**39** then listen from heaven, from
Your dwelling place, to their prayer
and supplications, and do justice for
them and forgive Your people who
have sinned against You.

**40** "Now, O my God, I pray, [a]let Your
eyes be open and [b]Your ears attentive
to the prayer *offered* in this place.

**41** "[a]So now, arise, O Yahweh God,
to Your resting place, You and the ark
of Your strength; let Your priests,
O Yahweh God, be clothed with sal-
vation and let Your holy ones be glad
in what is good.

**42** "O Yahweh God, do not turn
away the face of Your anointed;
[a]remember *Your* lovingkindness to
Your servant David."

### *The Glory of Yahweh Fills His House*

**7** [a]Now when Solomon had [1]finished
praying, [b]fire came down from
heaven and consumed the burnt
offering and the sacrifices, and the glo-
ry of Yahweh filled the house. **2** [a]And
the priests could not enter into the
house of Yahweh because the glory
of Yahweh filled the house of Yahweh.
**3** And all the sons of Israel, seeing the
fire come down and the glory of Yah-
weh upon the house, bowed down on
the pavement with their faces to the
ground, and they worshiped and gave
praise to Yahweh, *saying*, "[a]For He is
good, for His lovingkindness endures
forever."

### *Offerings for the House of Yahweh*

**4** [a]Now the king and all the people
were offering sacrifices before Yah-
weh. **5** And King Solomon offered a
sacrifice of 22,000 oxen and 120,000
sheep. So the king and all the people
dedicated the house of God. **6** And the
priests stood at their posts, and [a]the
Levites also, with the instruments
of music to Yahweh, which King
David had made for giving thanks
to Yahweh—"for His lovingkind-
ness endures forever"—whenever
[1]he gave praise by their hand, while
[b]the priests on the other side blew
trumpets; and all Israel was standing.

**7** [a]Then Solomon set apart as holy
the middle of the court that *was* be-
fore the house of Yahweh, because
there he offered the burnt offerings
and the fat of the peace offerings; for
the bronze altar which Solomon had
made was not able to hold the burnt
offering and the grain offering and
the fat.

**8** So [a]Solomon celebrated the feast
at that time for seven days, and all

---

**6:36** [1]Lit *their captors take them captive* **6:37** [a]Dt 30:1 [1]Or *repent* **6:38** [a]Jer 29:12, 13
**6:40** [a]2Chr 7:15; Ne 1:6, 11 [b]Ps 17:1 **6:41** [a]Ps 132:8, 9 **6:42** [a]Ps 89:24, 28; 132:10-12; Is 55:3
◆ **7:1** [a]1Ki 8:54 [b]Lv 9:23f; 1Ki 18:24, 38 [1]Or *completed*, cf. 2Chr 7:11; 8:16 **7:2** [a]2Chr 5:14 **7:3** [a]2Chr 5:13; 20:21 **7:4** [a]1Ki 8:62, 63 **7:6** [a]1Chr 15:16-21 [b]2Chr 5:12 [1]Lit *David* **7:7** [a]1Ki 8:64-66 **7:8** [a]1Ki 8:65

Israel with him, a very great assembly
from [1]Lebo-hamath to the [b]brook of
Egypt. **9** And on the eighth day they
celebrated [a]a solemn assembly; for
the dedication of the altar they cele-
brated seven days and the feast seven
days. **10** And on the twenty-third day
of the seventh month he sent the
people to their tents, with gladness
and goodness of heart because of the
goodness that Yahweh had shown to
David and to Solomon and to Israel
His people.

### *Yahweh Appears to Solomon*

**11** [a]Thus Solomon completed the
house of Yahweh and the king's
house; and all that had come into
Solomon's heart to do in the house
of Yahweh and in his house, he did
successfully.
**12** Then Yahweh appeared to Solo-
mon at night and said to him, "I have
heard your prayer and [a]have chosen
this place for Myself as a house of
sacrifice. **13** [a]If I shut up the heavens
so that there is no rain, or if I com-
mand the grasshopper to devour the
land, or if I send pestilence among
My people, **14** [a]and My people [1]who
are called by My name humble
themselves and pray and seek My
face and turn from their evil ways,
then I will listen from heaven, I will
forgive their sin, and I will heal their
land. **15** [a]Now My eyes will be open
and My ears attentive to the [1]prayer
*offered* in this place. **16** So [a]now
I have chosen and set this house
apart as holy that My name may be
*there forever*, and My eyes and My
heart will be there perpetually. **17** As
for you, if you will walk before Me
as your father David walked, even
to do according to all that I have
commanded you, and will keep My
statutes and My judgments, **18** then
I will establish your royal throne as
I cut *a covenant* with your father
David, saying, '[a,1]You shall not have
a man cut off as ruler in Israel.'
**19** "[a]But if you turn away and
forsake My statutes and My com-
mandments which I have set before
you, and go and serve other gods and
worship them, **20** [a]then I will uproot
you from My land which I have given
[1]you, and this house which I have set
apart as holy for My name I will cast
out of My presence and I will make it
[b]a proverb and a byword among all
peoples. **21** As for this house, which
was exalted, everyone who passes by
it will *feel* desolate and say, '[a]Why has
Yahweh done thus to this land and to
this house?' **22** And they will say, 'Be-
cause [a]they forsook Yahweh, the God
of their fathers, who brought them
out of the land of Egypt and took
hold of other gods and worshiped
them and served them, therefore
He has brought all this calamity on
them.'"

### *Solomon Builds Cities*

**8** [a]Now it happened at the end of
the twenty years in which Solo-
mon had built the house of Yahweh
and his own house **2** that he built
the cities which Huram had given
to [1]him, and settled the sons of Israel
there.

**7:8** [b]Ge 15:18 [1]Or *the entrance of Hamath* **7:9** [a]Lv 23:36 **7:11** [a]1Ki 9:1-9 **7:12** [a]Dt 12:5, 11 **7:13** [a]2Chr 6:26-28 **7:14** [a]2Chr 6:37-39; Jas 4:10 [1]Lit *over whom My name is called* **7:15** [a]2Chr 6:20, 40 [1]Lit *prayer of this place* **7:16** [a]2Chr 7:12 **7:18** [a]1Ki 2:4; 2Chr 6:16 [1]Lit *There shall not be cut off to you a man* **7:19** [a]Lv 26:14, 33; Dt 28:15 **7:20** [a]Dt 29:28; 1Ki 14:15 [b]Dt 28:37 [1]Ancient versions and Heb *them* **7:21** [a]Dt 29:24-27 **7:22** [a]Jdg 2:13 ◆ **8:1** [a]1Ki 9:10-28 **8:2** [1]Lit *Solomon*

**3** Then Solomon went to Hamath-
zobah and overpowered it. **4** And he
built Tadmor in the wilderness and
all the storage cities which he had
built in Hamath. **5** He also built upper
[a]Beth-horon and lower Beth-horon,
[b]fortified cities *with* walls, gates and
bars; **6** and Baalath and all the storage
cities which Solomon had, and all
the cities for [1]his chariots, and the
cities for [1]his horsemen, and all that
Solomon desired to build in Jerusa-
lem, in Lebanon, and in all the land
[2]under his rule.
**7** [a]*As for* all the people who were
left of the Hittites, the Amorites,
the Perizzites, the Hivites, and the
Jebusites, who were not of Israel,
**8** *namely*, from their sons who were
left after them in the land whom the
sons of Israel had not consumed,
[a]*from* them Solomon raised up
forced laborers to this day. **9** But
Solomon did not make slaves for his
work from the sons of Israel; for they
were men of war, his chief captains
and his chariot commanders and his
horsemen. **10** These were the chief
[1]deputies of King Solomon, 250 who
ruled over the people.
**11** [a]Then Solomon brought Phar-
aoh's daughter up from the city of
David to the house which he had
built for her, for he said, "My wife
shall not live in the house of David
king of Israel, because [1]*the places are*
holy where the ark of Yahweh has
entered."
**12** Then Solomon offered burnt
offerings to Yahweh on [a]the altar of
Yahweh which he had built before
the porch; **13** and [a]*did so* according
to the daily rule, offering *them* up
[b]according to the commandment
of Moses, for [c]the sabbaths, [d]the
new moons and the [e]three annual
feasts—the Feast of Unleavened
Bread, the Feast of Weeks and the
Feast of Booths.
**14** And according to the judgment
of his father David, he caused [a]the
divisions of the priests to stand for
their service, and [b]the Levites for
their responsibilities to praise and
minister before the priests according
to the daily rule, and [c]the gatekeep-
ers by their divisions at every gate;
for [d]David the man of God had so
commanded. **15** And they did not
turn away from the commandment
of the king to the priests and Levites
in any manner or concerning the
treasuries.
**16** Thus all the work of Solomon
was carried out [1]from the day of the
foundation of the house of Yahweh,
and until it was completed. So the
house of Yahweh was finished.
**17** Then Solomon went to [a]Ezion-
geber and to [b]Eloth on the shore of
the sea in the land of Edom. **18** And
Huram by the hand of his servants
sent him ships and servants who
knew the sea; and they went with
Solomon's servants to Ophir, and
[a]took from there [1]450 talents of gold
and brought *them* to King Solomon.

### *The Queen of Sheba*

**9** [a]Now the queen of Sheba heard
the report about Solomon. So she
came to Jerusalem to test Solomon

**8:5** [a]1Chr 7:24 [b]2Chr 14:7 **8:6** [1]Lit *the* [2]Lit *of* **8:7** [a]Ge 15:18-21; 1Ki 9:20 **8:8** [a]1Ki 4:6; 9:21 **8:10** [1]Or *officers* **8:11** [a]1Ki 3:1; 7:8 [1]Lit *they are* **8:12** [a]2Chr 4:1 **8:13** [a]Ex 29:38-42 [b]Nu 28:3 [c]Nu 28:9, 10 [d]Nu 28:11 [e]Ex 23:14-17; 34:22, 23; Dt 16:16 **8:14** [a]1Chr 24:1 [b]1Chr 25:1 [c]1Chr 26:1 [d]Ne 12:24, 36 **8:16** [1]As in ancient versions; M.T. *as far as* **8:17** [a]1Ki 9:26 [b]2Ki 14:22 **8:18** [a]2Chr 9:10, 13 [1]Approx. 16.87 tons or 15.3 metric tons, a talent was approx. 75 lb. or 34 kg ◆ **9:1** [a]1Ki 10:1-13; Mt 12:42; Lk 11:31

with riddles. She had a very glorious retinue, with camels carrying spices and a large amount of gold and precious stones. And she came to Solomon and spoke with him about all that was in her heart. **2** And Solomon declared to her *the answer* to all her matters; and not a matter was hidden from Solomon which he did not declare to her. **3** Then the queen of Sheba saw the wisdom of Solomon, the house which he had built, **4** the food at his table, the seating of his servants, the disposition of his attendants and their attire, his cupbearers and their attire, and [1]his stairway by which he went up to the house of Yahweh, so that there was no more spirit in her. **5** Then she said to the king, "The word is true which I heard in my own land about your words and your wisdom. **6** Nevertheless I did not believe their words until I came and my eyes had seen it. And behold, the half of the greatness of your wisdom was not declared to me. You exceed the report which I heard. **7** How [1]blessed are your men, how [1]blessed are these your servants who stand before you continually and hear your wisdom. **8** Blessed be Yahweh your God who delighted in you, [a]to set you on His throne as king for Yahweh your God; [b]because your God loved Israel to cause them to stand forever, therefore He gave you as king over them, to do justice and righteousness." **9** Then she gave the king [1]120 talents of gold and a very great *amount of* spices and precious stones. There had never been spice like that which the queen of Sheba gave to King Solomon.

**10** Also, the servants of Huram and the servants of Solomon, [a]who brought gold from Ophir, brought algum trees and precious stones. **11** And the king made of the algum trees steps for the house of Yahweh and for the king's house, and lyres and harps for the singers; and none like that was seen before in the land of Judah.

**12** Thus King Solomon gave to the queen of Sheba all her desire which she asked, besides *a return for* what she had brought to the king. Then she turned around and went to her own land together with her servants.

### *Solomon's Riches and Wisdom*

**13** [a]Now the weight of gold which came to Solomon in one year was 666 talents of gold, **14** besides that which the traders and merchants brought; and all [a]the kings of Arabia and the governors of the country brought gold and silver to Solomon. **15** And King Solomon made 200 large shields of beaten gold, [1]using [2]600 *shekels of* beaten gold on each large shield. **16** And *he made* 300 shields of beaten gold, [1]using [2]300 shekels of gold on each shield, and the king put them in the house of the forest of Lebanon.

**17** Moreover, the king made a great throne of ivory and overlaid it with pure gold. **18** *And there were* six steps to the throne and a footstool in gold attached to the throne, and [1]arms [2]on each side of the seat, and two lions standing beside the [1]arms. **19** Twelve lions were also standing there on the

---

**9:4** [1]Or *his burnt offering which he offered* **9:7** [1]Or *happy* **9:8** [a]1Chr 28:5; 29:23 [b]Dt 7:8; 2Chr 2:11 **9:9** [1]Approx. 4.5 tons or 4.08 metric tons, a talent was approx. 75 lb. or 34 kg **9:10** [a]1Ki 10:11; 2Chr 8:18 **9:13** [a]1Ki 10:14-28 **9:14** [a]Ps 68:29; 72:10 **9:15** [1]Lit *he brought up* [2]Approx. 15 lb. or 8.4 kg **9:16** [1]Lit *he brought up* [2]Approx. 7.5 lb. or 4.2 kg **9:18** [1]Lit *hands* [2]Lit *on this side and on this at the place of the seat*

six steps on the one side and on the
other; nothing like *it* was made for any
*other* kingdom. **20** Now all King Solo-
mon's drinking vessels *were* of gold,
and all the vessels of the house of the
forest of Lebanon *were* of pure gold;
silver was not considered [1]valuable in
the days of Solomon. **21** [a]For the king
had ships which went to Tarshish with
the servants of Huram; once every
three years the ships of Tarshish came
carrying gold and silver, ivory and
apes and peacocks.
**22** [a]So King Solomon became
greater than all the kings of the earth
in riches and wisdom. **23** And all the
kings of the earth were seeking the
presence of Solomon, to hear his wis-
dom which God had put in his heart.
**24** [a]And they brought every man his
present, articles of silver and gold,
garments, weapons, spices, horses
and mules, a set amount year by year.
**25** And Solomon had [a]4,000 stalls
for horses and chariots and 12,000
horsemen, and he stationed them in
the chariot cities and with the king in
Jerusalem. **26** [a]And he was the ruler
over all the kings from the [1]River even
to the land of the Philistines, and to
the border of Egypt. **27** [a]The king also
made silver *as plentiful* as stones in
Jerusalem, and he made cedars as
plentiful as sycamore trees that are
in the [1]Shephelah. **28** [a]And they were
importing horses for Solomon from
Egypt and from all countries.

### *The Death of Solomon*

**29** [a]Now the rest of the acts of Solo-
mon, from first to last, [b]are they not
written in the [1]chronicles of Nathan
the prophet, and in the prophecy
of Ahijah the Shilonite, and in the
visions of [2]Iddo the seer concerning
Jeroboam the son of Nebat? **30** [a]Thus
Solomon reigned forty years in Jeru-
salem over all Israel. **31** And Solomon
slept with his fathers and was buried
in [a]the city of his father David; and
his son Rehoboam became king in
his place.

### *Rehoboam's Foolish Reign*

**10** [a]Then Rehoboam went to
Shechem, for all Israel had
come to Shechem to make him king.
**2** And it happened, when Jeroboam
the son of Nebat heard *of it* (for [a]he
was in Egypt where he had fled from
the presence of King Solomon), Jer-
oboam returned from Egypt. **3** Then
they sent and called for him. And
Jeroboam and all Israel came and
spoke to Rehoboam, saying, **4** "Your
father made our [a]yoke harsh; but
now, lighten the harsh service of
your father and his heavy yoke which
he put on us, and we will serve you."
**5** Then he said to them, "Return to me
again in three days." So the people
went away.
**6** Then King Rehoboam [a]took
counsel with the elders who had
[1]stood before his father Solomon
while he was still alive, saying, "How
do you counsel *me* to respond to this
people?" **7** And they spoke to him,
saying, "If you will be good to this
people and please them and [a]speak
good words to them, then they will
be your servants forever." **8** But he

**9:20** [1]Lit *anything* **9:21** [a]2Chr 20:36, 37 **9:22** [a]1Ki 3:13; 2Chr 1:12 **9:24** [a]Ps 72:10 **9:25** [a]Dt 17:16; 1Ki 4:26; 10:26; 2Chr 1:14 **9:26** [a]Ge 15:18; 1Ki 4:21, 24 [1]The Euphrates River **9:27** [a]2Chr 1:15-17 [1]Or *lowland* **9:28** [a]2Chr 1:16 **9:29** [a]1Ki 11:41-43 [b]1Chr 29:29 [1]Lit *words* [2]Heb *Jedo* **9:30** [a]1Ki 11:42, 43 **9:31** [a]1Ki 2:10 ◆ **10:1** [a]1Ki 12:1-20 **10:2** [a]1Ki 11:40 **10:4** [a]1Ki 5:13-16 **10:6** [a]Job 8:8, 9; 32:7 [1]Or *served* **10:7** [a]Pr 15:1

[a]forsook the counsel of the elders which they had counseled him, and took counsel with the young men who grew up with him and [1]stood before him. **9** So he said to them, "What counsel do you give that we may respond to this people, who have spoken to me, saying, 'Lighten the yoke which your father put on us'?" **10** Then the young men who grew up with him spoke with him, saying, "Thus you shall say to the people who spoke to you, saying, 'Your father made our yoke heavy, but you make it lighter for us.' Thus you shall say to them, 'My little finger is thicker than my father's loins! **11** So now my father loaded you with a heavy yoke, but I will add to your yoke; my father disciplined you with whips, but I *will discipline you* with scorpions.'"

**12** So Jeroboam and all the people came to Rehoboam on the third day as the king had spoken, saying, "Return to me on the third day." **13** And the king answered them harshly, and King Rehoboam forsook the counsel of the elders, **14** and he spoke to them according to the counsel of the young men, saying, "[1]My father made your yoke heavy, but I will add to it; my father disciplined you with whips, but I *will discipline you* with scorpions." **15** So the king did not listen to the people, [a]for it was a turn *of events* from God, [b]that Yahweh might establish His word, which He spoke through Ahijah the Shilonite to Jeroboam the son of Nebat.

**16** Now all Israel *saw* that the king *did not listen to them. So the people* responded to the king, saying,

"[a]What portion do we
have in David?
*We have* no inheritance
in the son of Jesse.
Every man to your
tents, O Israel;
Now see to your own
house, David."

[b]So all Israel went to their tents. **17** But as for the sons of Israel who lived in the cities of Judah, Rehoboam reigned over them. **18** Then King Rehoboam sent Hadoram, who was [a]over the forced labor, and the sons of Israel [1]stoned him and he died. And King Rehoboam made haste to mount his chariot to flee to Jerusalem. **19** So [a]Israel has been in rebellion against the house of David to this day.

### *Rehoboam Builds Fortification Cities*

**11** [a]Then Rehoboam came to Jerusalem and assembled the house of Judah and Benjamin, 180,000 chosen men who could wage war, to fight against Israel to return the kingdom to Rehoboam. **2** But the word of Yahweh came to [a]Shemaiah the man of God, saying, **3** "Speak to Rehoboam the son of Solomon, king of Judah, and to all Israel in Judah and Benjamin, saying, **4** 'Thus says Yahweh, "You shall not go up and fight against [a]your brothers; return every man to his house, [b]for this thing is from Me."'" So they listened to the words of Yahweh and returned from going against Jeroboam.

**5** Rehoboam lived in Jerusalem and [a]built cities for fortifications in Judah. **6** Thus he built Bethlehem, Etam, Tekoa, **7** Beth-zur, Soco, Adullam,

**10:8** [a]2Sa 17:14; Pr 13:20 [1]Or *served* **10:14** [1]Many mss *I have made* **10:15** [a]2Chr 25:16-20 [b]1Ki 11:29-39
**10:16** [a]2Sa 20:1 [b]2Chr 10:19 **10:18** [a]1Ki 4:6; 5:14 [1]Lit *stoned with stones* **10:19** [a]1Ki 12:19
◆ **11:1** [a]1Ki 12:21-24 **11:2** [a]2Chr 12:5-7, 15 **11:4** [a]2Chr 28:8-11 [b]2Chr 10:15 **11:5** [a]2Chr 8:2-6; 11:23

**8** Gath, Mareshah, Ziph, **9** Adoraim,
Lachish, Azekah, **10** Zorah, Aijalon
and Hebron, which are fortified cities
in Judah and in Benjamin. **11** He also
strengthened the fortresses and put
officers in them and stores of food,
oil and wine. **12** And *he put* large
shields and spears in every city and
strengthened them greatly. So he
held Judah and Benjamin.

**13** Moreover, the priests and the
Levites who were in all Israel took
their stand with him from all their
territories.

### *Jeroboam Sets Up His Own Priests*

**14** For [a]the Levites left their pasture
lands and their possession *of land*
and went to Judah and Jerusalem, for
[b]Jeroboam and his sons had rejected
them from ministering as priests to
Yahweh— **15** [a]And he set up priests
of his own for the high places, for the
goat demons and for the calves which
he had made— **16** [a]Now those from
all the tribes of Israel who gave their
hearts to seek Yahweh, the God of Is-
rael, [1]followed them to Jerusalem, to
sacrifice to Yahweh, the God of their
fathers. **17** [a]They strengthened the
kingdom of Judah and gave courage
to Rehoboam the son of Solomon for
three years, for they walked in the
way of David and Solomon for three
years.

### *Rehoboam's Family*

**18** Then Rehoboam took as a wife
Mahalath the daughter of Jerimoth
the son of David *and of* Abihail the
daughter of [a]Eliab the son of Jesse,
**19** and she bore him sons: Jeush,
Shemariah, and Zaham. **20** And after
her he took [a]Maacah the daughter
of [1]Absalom, and she bore him
Abijah, Attai, Ziza, and Shelomith.
**21** And Rehoboam loved Maacah the
daughter of Absalom more than all
his *other* wives and concubines. For
[a]he had taken eighteen wives and
sixty concubines and became the
father of twenty-eight sons and sixty
daughters. **22** [a]And Rehoboam set up
Abijah the son of Maacah *to be* head
and ruler among his brothers, for he
*intended* to make him king. **23** And
he acted with discernment and dis-
tributed [1]some of his sons through
all the lands of Judah and Benjamin
to all the fortified cities, and he gave
them sustenance in abundance. And
he sought a multitude of wives *for
them.*

### *Shishak of Egypt Comes Against Judah*

**12** [a]Now it happened that when
the kingdom of Rehoboam was
established and strong, [b]he and all
Israel with him forsook the law of
Yahweh. **2** [a]Now it happened in the
fifth year of King Rehoboam, because
they had been unfaithful to Yahweh,
that [b]Shishak king of Egypt came
up against Jerusalem **3** with 1,200
chariots and 60,000 horsemen.
And the people who came with him
from Egypt were without number:
[a]the Lubim, the Sukkiim and the
Ethiopians. **4** And he captured [a]the
fortified cities of Judah and came as
far as Jerusalem. **5** Now [a]Shemaiah

**11:14** [a]Nu 35:2-5 [b]1Ki 12:28-33; 2Chr 13:9 **11:15** [a]1Ki 12:31; 13:33 **11:16** [a]2Chr 15:9 [1]Lit *came after* **11:17** [a]2Chr 12:1 **11:18** [a]1Sa 16:6 **11:20** [a]1Ki 15:2; 2Chr 13:2 [1]In 1Ki 15:2, *Abishalom* **11:21** [a]Dt 17:17 **11:22** [a]Dt 21:15-17 **11:23** [1]Lit *from all* ◆ **12:1** [a]2Chr 11:17; 12:13 [b]2Chr 26:13-16 **12:2** [a]1Ki 14:25 [b]1Ki 11:40 **12:3** [a]2Chr 16:8; Na 3:9 **12:4** [a]2Chr 11:5-12 **12:5** [a]2Chr 11:2

the prophet came to Rehoboam and the princes of Judah who had gathered at Jerusalem because of Shishak, and he said to them, "Thus says Yahweh, '[b]You have forsaken Me, so I also have forsaken you [1]to Shishak.'" **6** So the princes of Israel and the king humbled themselves and said, "[a]Yahweh is righteous."

**7** When Yahweh saw that they humbled themselves, the word of Yahweh came to Shemaiah, saying, "[a]They have humbled themselves *so* I will not bring them to ruin, but I will grant them some *measure* of escape, and [b]My wrath shall not be poured out on Jerusalem by the hand of Shishak. **8** But they will become his slaves so [a]that they may know *the difference between* My slavery and the slavery of the kingdoms of the countries."

### *Shishak Takes from Yahweh's House*

**9** [a]So Shishak king of Egypt came up against Jerusalem, and took the treasures of the house of Yahweh and the treasures of the king's house. He took everything; [b]he even took the shields of gold which Solomon had made. **10** Then King Rehoboam made shields of bronze in their place and committed them to the hand of the commanders of the [1]guard who kept the door of the king's house. **11** Now it happened that as often as the king entered the house of Yahweh, the [1]guards would come and carry them and *then* bring them back into the [1]guards' room. **12** And [a]when *he humbled himself*, the anger of Yahweh turned away from him, so as not to ruin *him* completely; and also conditions [b]were good in Judah.

**13** [a]So King Rehoboam strengthened himself in Jerusalem and reigned. Now Rehoboam was forty-one years old when he became king, and he reigned seventeen years in Jerusalem, the city which Yahweh had chosen from all the tribes of Israel to put His name there. And his mother's name was Naamah the Ammonitess. **14** And he did evil [a]because he did not set his heart to seek Yahweh.

**15** [a]Now the acts of Rehoboam, from first to last, are they not written in the [1]records of [b]Shemaiah the prophet and of [c]Iddo the seer, according to genealogical record? Now *there were* wars between Rehoboam and Jeroboam all *their* days. **16** And Rehoboam slept with his fathers and was buried in the city of David; and [a]Abijah his son became king in his place.

### *Abijah Reigns over Judah*

**13** [a]In the eighteenth year of King Jeroboam, Abijah became king over Judah. **2** He reigned three years in Jerusalem; and his mother's name was Micaiah the daughter of Uriel of Gibeah.

[a]Now there was war between Abijah and Jeroboam. **3** And Abijah began the battle with a military force of mighty men, 400,000 chosen men, while Jeroboam arranged *them* all for battle against him with 800,000 chosen men *who were* mighty men of valor.

---

**12:5** [b]Dt 28:15; 2Chr 15:2 [1]Lit *in the hand of* **12:6** [a]Ex 9:27; Da 9:14 **12:7** [a]1Ki 21:29 [b]2Chr 34:25-27; Ps 78:38 **12:8** [a]Dt 28:47, 48 **12:9** [a]1Ki 14:26-28 [b]1Ki 10:16, 17; 2Chr 9:15, 16 **12:10** [1]Lit *runners* **12:11** [1]Lit *runners* **12:12** [a]2Chr 12:6, 7 [b]2Chr 19:3 **12:13** [a]1Ki 14:21 **12:14** [a]2Chr 19:3 **12:15** [a]1Ki 14:29 [b]2Chr 12:5 [c]2Chr 9:29 [1]Lit *words* **12:16** [a]2Chr 11:20 ◆ **13:1** [a]1Ki 15:1, 2 **13:2** [a]1Ki 15:7

### *God Smites Israel Before Judah*

**4** Then Abijah rose up on Mount
[a]Zemaraim, which is in the hill
country of Ephraim, and said, "Listen
to me, Jeroboam and all Israel: **5** Do
you not know that [a]Yahweh, the God
of Israel, gave the rule over Israel
forever to David [1]and his sons by [b]a
covenant of salt? **6** Yet [a]Jeroboam the
son of Nebat, the servant of Solo-
mon the son of David, rose up and
rebelled against his [1]master, **7** and
worthless men gathered about him,
vile men, who proved too strong for
Rehoboam, the son of Solomon; [a,1]he
was young and timid and could not
exert his strength before them.
**8** "So now you [1]intend to exert
your strength before the kingdom
of Yahweh by the hand of the sons
of David, [2]being a great multitude
and *having* with you [a]the golden
calves which Jeroboam made for gods
for you. **9** [a]Have you not driven out
the priests of Yahweh, the sons of
Aaron and the Levites, and made for
yourselves priests like the peoples
of *other* lands? Whoever comes [b]to
ordain himself with a bull from the
herd and seven rams, even he may
become a priest of *what are* [c]no gods.
**10** But as for us, Yahweh is our God,
and we have not forsaken Him; and
the sons of Aaron are ministering to
Yahweh as priests, and the Levites
are in their work. **11** And every
morning and evening [a]they [1]burn to
Yahweh burnt offerings and fragrant
incense, and [b]the showbread is *set*
on the clean table, and the golden
lampstand with its lamps is *ready*
to light every evening; for we keep
the responsibility *given by* Yahweh
our God, but you have forsaken Him.
**12** And behold, God is with us at *our*
head and [a]His priests with the signal
trumpets to raise the shout *of war*
against you. O sons of Israel, do not
fight against Yahweh, the God of your
fathers, for you will not succeed."
**13** But Jeroboam [a]had encircled an
ambush to come from the rear, so that
*Israel* was in front of Judah and the
ambush was behind them. **14** So Judah
turned around, and behold, [1]they were
attacked both front and rear; so [a]they
cried to Yahweh, and the priests blew
the trumpets. **15** Then the men of
Judah raised a shout *of war*, and when
the men of Judah raised the shout
*of war*, then it was that God [a]smote
Jeroboam and all Israel before Abijah
and Judah. **16** So the sons of Israel fled
before Judah, and [a]God gave them
into their hand. **17** And Abijah and his
people struck them down with a great
slaughter, and 500,000 chosen men
of Israel fell slain. **18** Thus the sons
of Israel were subdued at that time,
and the sons of Judah were strong
[a]because they leaned upon Yahweh,
the God of their fathers. **19** And Abijah
pursued Jeroboam and captured from
him *several* cities, Bethel with its
towns, Jeshanah with its towns, and
[1]Ephron with its towns.

### *Death of Jeroboam*

**20** Now Jeroboam did not again
recover power in the days of Abijah;

---

**13:4** [a]Jos 18:22 **13:5** [a]2Sa 7:12-16 [b]Lv 2:13; Nu 18:19 [1]Lit *to him and to his sons* **13:6** [a]1Ki 11:26 [1]Or *lord* **13:7** [a]2Chr 12:13 [1]Lit *Rehoboam* **13:8** [a]1Ki 12:28; 2Chr 11:15 [1]Lit *say* [2]Lit *and you are a* **13:9** [a]2Chr 11:14, 15 [b]Ex 29:29-33 [c]Jer 2:11; 5:7 **13:11** [a]Ex 29:38; 2Chr 2:4 [b]Ex 25:30-39; Lv 24:5-9 [1]Lit *offer up in smoke* **13:12** [a]Nu 10:8, 9 **13:13** [a]Jos 8:4-9 **13:14** [a]2Chr 14:11 [1]Lit *the battle was before and behind them* **13:15** [a]2Chr 14:12 **13:16** [a]2Chr 16:8 **13:18** [a]2Chr 14:11 **13:19** [1]Or *Ephrain*

and [a]Yahweh smote him and [b]he
died.
**21** But Abijah became stronger; and
he took fourteen wives to himself,
and became the father of twenty-two
sons and sixteen daughters. **22** Now
the rest of the acts of Abijah, and
his ways and his words are written
in [a]the [1]treatise of [b]the prophet Iddo.

### *Asa Reigns over Judah*

**14** [a,1]So Abijah slept with his
fathers, and they buried him
in the city of David; and Asa his son
became king in his place. The land was
quiet for ten years during his days.
**2** [1]And Asa did what was good
and right in the sight of Yahweh his
God, **3** for he removed [a]the foreign
altars and [b]high places, shattered the
*sacred* pillars, cut the [c,1]Asherim in
pieces, **4** and said for Judah to seek
Yahweh, the God of their fathers, and
to do the law and the commandment.
**5** He also [1]removed the high places
and the [a]incense altars from all the
cities of Judah. And the kingdom
was quiet before him. **6** [a]And he
built fortified cities in Judah, since
the land was quiet, and [1]there was
no one at war with him during those
years, [b]because Yahweh had given
him rest. **7** And he said to Judah, "[a]Let
us build these cities and surround
*them* with walls and towers, gates
and bars. The land is still [1]ours
because we have sought Yahweh
our God; we have sought Him, and
He has given us rest on every side."
So they built and succeeded. **8** Now
Asa had a military force of [a]300,000
from Judah, bearing large shields and
spears, and 280,000 from Benjamin,
bearing shields and wielding bows;
all of them were mighty men of valor.
**9** Then Zerah the Ethiopian [a]went
out against them with a military force
of one million men and 300 chariots,
and he came to [b]Mareshah. **10** So Asa
went out [1]to meet him, and they ar-
ranged *themselves* for battle in the
valley of Zephathah at Mareshah.
**11** Then Asa [a]called to Yahweh his
God and said, "Yahweh, there is no
one besides You to help *in the battle*
between those of abundant *power*
and those who have no power; so
help us, O Yahweh our God, [b]for
we lean on You, and in Your name
have come against this multitude.
O Yahweh, You are our God; let not
mortal man prevail against You."
**12** So [a]Yahweh smote the Ethiopians
before Asa and before Judah, and the
Ethiopians fled. **13** And Asa and the
people who *were* with him pursued
them as far as [a]Gerar; and so many
Ethiopians fell that [1]they could not
recover, for they were shattered be-
fore Yahweh and before His [2]army.
And they carried away very much
spoil. **14** And they struck down all the
cities around Gerar, [a]for the dread
of Yahweh had fallen on them; and
they plundered all the cities, for there
was much plunder in them. **15** They
also struck down [1]those who owned
livestock, and they carried away large
numbers of sheep and camels. Then
they returned to Jerusalem.

---

**13:20** [a]1Sa 25:38 [b]1Ki 14:20 **13:22** [a]2Chr 24:27 [b]2Chr 9:29 [1]Heb *midrash* ◆ **14:1** [a]1Ki 15:8 [1]Ch 13:23 in Heb **14:2** [1]Ch 14:1 in Heb **14:3** [a]Dt 7:5 [b]1Ki 15:12-14 [c]Ex 34:13 [1]Wooden symbols of a female deity **14:5** [a]2Chr 34:4, 7 [1]Or *took away*, cf. 2Ki 15:35; 18:4; 2Chr 17:6 **14:6** [a]2Chr 11:5 [b]2Chr 15:15 [1]Lit *there was not with him war* **14:7** [a]2Chr 8:5 [1]Lit *before us* **14:8** [a]2Chr 13:3 **14:9** [a]2Chr 12:2, 3; 16:8 [b]2Chr 11:8 **14:10** [1]Lit *before him* **14:11** [a]2Chr 13:14 [b]2Chr 13:18 **14:12** [a]2Chr 13:15 **14:13** [a]Ge 10:19 [1]Or *there was none left alive* [2]Lit *camp* **14:14** [a]2Chr 17:10 **14:15** [1]Lit *tents of livestock*

### *The Spirit of God Comes on Azariah*

**15** Now [a]the Spirit of God came
on Azariah the son of Oded,
**2** and he went out [1]to meet Asa and
said to him, "Listen to me, Asa, and
all Judah and Benjamin: [a]Yahweh is
with you when you are with Him.
And [b]if you seek Him, He will be
found; but if you forsake Him, He
will forsake you. **3** [a]Now for many
days Israel was without the true God
and without [b]a teaching priest and
without law. **4** But [a]in their distress
they turned to Yahweh, the God of
Israel, and they searched for Him,
and He was found *by them.* **5** [a]Now
in those times there was no peace
to him who went out or to him who
came in, for much confusion was
upon all the inhabitants of the lands.
**6** [a]And nation was crushed by nation,
and city by city, for God threw them
into confusion with every kind of
distress. **7** But you, [a]be strong and
do not let your hands fall limp, for
there is [b]reward for your work."

### *Asa Takes Away Detestable Idols*

**8** Now when Asa heard these words
and the [1]prophecy which Azariah the
son of Oded the prophet spoke, he
strengthened himself and took away
the detestable idols from all the land
of Judah and Benjamin and from [a]the
cities which he had captured in the
hill country of Ephraim. [b]He then re-
newed the altar of Yahweh which was
in front of the porch of Yahweh. **9** And
he gathered all Judah and Benjamin
and those from Ephraim, Manasseh
and Simeon [a]who sojourned with
them, for many defected to him
from Israel when they saw that
Yahweh his God was with him. **10** So
they assembled at Jerusalem in the
third month of the fifteenth year of
Asa's reign. **11** [a]And they sacrificed
to Yahweh that day 700 oxen and
7,000 sheep from the spoil they had
brought. **12** [a]They entered into the
covenant to seek Yahweh, the God of
their fathers, with all their heart and
soul; **13** and whoever would not seek
Yahweh, the God of Israel, [a]should be
put to death, whether small or great,
man or woman. **14** Moreover, they
swore *an oath* to Yahweh with a loud
voice, with shouting, with trumpets
and with horns. **15** All Judah was glad
concerning the oath, for they had
sworn with their whole heart and
had searched for Him with all their
desire, and He was found *by them.*
So [a]Yahweh gave them rest on every
side.

**16** [a]He also removed Maacah,
the mother of King Asa, from *being*
queen mother, because she had made
a horrid image [1]as [b]an Asherah; and
[c]Asa cut down her horrid image,
crushed *it* and burned *it* at the brook
Kidron. **17** But the high places were
not [1]removed from Israel; neverthe-
less Asa's heart was wholly devoted
all his days. **18** And he brought into
the house of God the holy things of
his father and his own holy things:
silver and gold and utensils. **19** And
there was no more war until the
thirty-fifth year of Asa's reign.

◆ **15:1** [a]2Chr 20:14; 24:20 **15:2** [a]2Chr 20:17 [b]2Chr 15:4, 15 [1]Lit *before Asa* **15:3** [a]1Ki 12:28-33 [b]Lv 10:8-11; 2Chr 17:9 **15:4** [a]Dt 4:29 **15:5** [a]Jdg 5:6 **15:6** [a]Mt 24:7 **15:7** [a]Jos 1:7, 9 [b]Ps 58:11 **15:8** [a]2Chr 13:19 [b]2Chr 4:1; 8:12 [1]As in several ancient versions; Heb *the prophecy, Oded the prophet* **15:9** [a]2Chr 11:16 **15:11** [a]2Chr 14:13-15 **15:12** [a]2Chr 23:16 **15:13** [a]Ex 22:20; Dt 13:6-9 **15:15** [a]2Chr 14:7 **15:16** [a]1Ki 15:13-15 [b]Ex 34:13 [c]2Chr 14:2-5 [1]Or for *Asherah* **15:17** [1]Or *taken away*, cf. 2Ki 15:35; 18:4; 2Chr 17:6

### *Asa Wars Against Baasha*

**16** In the thirty-sixth year of Asa's
reign [a]Baasha king of Israel
went up against Judah and built up
Ramah in order to prevent *anyone*
from going out or coming in to Asa
king of Judah. **2** Then Asa brought
out silver and gold from the trea-
suries of the house of Yahweh and
the king's house, and sent them to
Ben-hadad king of Aram, who lived
in Damascus, saying, **3** "*Let there be*
a covenant between [1]you and me, *as*
between my father and your father.
Behold, I have sent you silver and
gold; go, break your covenant with
Baasha king of Israel so that he will
withdraw from me." **4** So Ben-hadad
listened to King Asa and sent the
commanders of his military forces
against the cities of Israel, and they
struck down Ijon, Dan, Abel-maim,
and all [a]the [1]store cities of Naphtali.
**5** Now it happened that when Baasha
heard *of it*, he ceased building up
Ramah and stopped his work. **6** Then
King Asa brought all Judah, and they
carried away the stones of Ramah
and its timber with which Baasha
had been building, and with them
he built Geba and Mizpah.

### *Asa Imprisons a Seer*

**7** Now at that time [a]Hanani the seer
came to Asa king of Judah and said
to him, "[b]Because you have leaned
on the king of Aram and have not
leaned on Yahweh your God, there-
fore the military force of the king of
Aram has escaped out of your hand.
**8** Were not [a]the Ethiopians and the
Lubim [b]a vast military force with an
exceedingly vast *number* of chariots
and horsemen? Yet [c]because you
leaned on Yahweh, He gave them into
your hand. **9** For [a]the eyes of Yahweh
move to and fro throughout the earth
that He may strongly support those
[b]whose heart is wholly devoted to
Him. You have acted foolishly in
this. Indeed, from now on you will
surely have wars." **10** Then Asa was
vexed with the seer and put him in
[1]prison, for he was enraged at him for
this. And Asa oppressed some of the
people at the same time.
**11** [a]Now behold, the acts of Asa
from first to last, behold, they are
written in the Book of the Kings of
Judah and Israel. **12** And Asa became
diseased in his feet in the thirty-ninth
year of his reign. His disease was se-
vere, yet even in his disease he [a]did
not seek Yahweh, but the physicians.
**13** So Asa slept with his fathers. And
he died in the forty-first year of his
reign. **14** And they buried him in his
own tomb which he had [1]cut out for
himself in the city of David, and they
laid him in the resting place which
he had filled [a]with spices of various
kinds blended by the perfumers' art;
and [b]they made a very great fire for
him.

### *Jehoshaphat Reigns over Judah*

**17** [a]Jehoshaphat his son then
became king in his place, and
strengthened himself over Israel.
**2** And he put military forces in all
[a]the fortified cities of Judah, and put
garrisons in the land of Judah and in

◆ **16:1** [a]1Ki 15:17-22 **16:3** [1]Lit *me and you* **16:4** [a]Ex 1:11 [1]Lit *storage places of the cities*
**16:7** [a]1Ki 16:1; 2Chr 19:2 [b]2Chr 14:11; 32:7, 8 **16:8** [a]2Chr 14:9 [b]2Chr 12:3 [c]2Chr 13:16, 18 **16:9** [a]Pr 15:3; Jer 16:17; Zec 4:10 [b]2Chr 15:17 **16:10** [1]Lit *the house of the stocks* **16:11** [a]1Ki 15:23, 24 **16:12** [a]Jer 17:5
**16:14** [a]Ge 50:2; Jn 19:39, 40 [b]2Chr 21:19 [1]Lit *dug out* ◆ **17:1** [a]1Ki 15:24 **17:2** [a]2Chr 11:5

the cities of Ephraim [b]which Asa his
father had captured.

### *Jehoshaphat's Kingdom Established*

**3** And Yahweh was with Jehoshaphat
because he walked in the ways of
his father David's earlier days and
did not seek the Baals, **4** but sought
the God of his father, walked in His
commandments, [a]and did not act as
Israel did. **5** So Yahweh established
the kingdom in his hand, and all Ju-
dah brought presents to Jehoshaphat,
and [a]he had great riches and honor.
**6** And [1]his heart took great pride in
the ways of Yahweh, and again he
[a]took away the high places and the
[2]Asherim from Judah.
**7** Then in the third year of his
reign he sent his officials, Ben-hail,
Obadiah, Zechariah, Nethanel and
Micaiah, [a]to teach in the cities of
Judah; **8** and with them [a]the Levites,
Shemaiah, Nethaniah, Zebadiah,
Asahel, Shemiramoth, Jehonathan,
Adonijah, Tobijah, and Tobadonijah,
the Levites; and with them Elishama
and Jehoram, the priests. **9** And they
taught in Judah, *having* [a]the book of
the law of Yahweh with them; and
they went throughout all the cities of
Judah and taught among the people.
**10** Now [a]the dread of Yahweh
was on all the kingdoms of the
lands which *were* around Judah, so
that they did not make war against
Jehoshaphat. **11** Indeed, some of
the Philistines [a]brought presents
and silver as *their tax* burden to
Jehoshaphat; the Arabians also
brought him flocks, 7,700 rams and
7,700 male goats. **12** So Jehoshaphat
grew greater and greater, and he built
fortresses and store cities in Judah.
**13** And he had large supplies in the
cities of Judah, and men of war,
mighty men of valor, in Jerusalem.
**14** This was their muster according
to their fathers' households:

of Judah, commanders of
thousands, Adnah *was* the
commander, and with him
300,000 mighty men of valor;
**15** and next to him *was* Johanan
the commander, and with him
280,000;
**16** and next to him Amasiah
the son of Zichri, [a]who
volunteered for Yahweh, and
with him 200,000 mighty
men of valor;
**17** and of Benjamin, Eliada a
mighty man of valor, and with
him 200,000 equipped with
bow and shield;
**18** and next to him Jehozabad,
and with him 180,000 armed
for *military* duty.

**19** These are they who attended on
the king, apart from [a]those whom
the king put in the fortified cities
through all Judah.

### *Jehoshaphat Allies with Ahab*

**18** Now [a]Jehoshaphat had riches
and honor in abundance; and
he allied himself by marriage with
Ahab. **2** [a]And some years later he
went down to Ahab at Samaria. And
Ahab sacrificed sheep and oxen in
abundance for him and the people
who were with him, and incited

---

**17:2** [b]2Chr 15:8 **17:4** [a]1Ki 12:28 **17:5** [a]2Chr 18:1 **17:6** [a]2Chr 15:17 [1]Lit *his heart was high* [2]Wooden symbols of a female deity **17:7** [a]2Chr 15:3; 35:3 **17:8** [a]2Chr 19:8 **17:9** [a]Dt 6:4-9
**17:10** [a]2Chr 14:14 **17:11** [a]2Chr 9:14; 26:8 **17:16** [a]Jdg 5:2, 9; 1Chr 29:9 **17:19** [a]2Chr 17:2
◆ **18:1** [a]2Chr 17:5 **18:2** [a]1Ki 22:2-35

him to go up against Ramoth-gilead.
**3** And Ahab king of Israel said to Je-
hoshaphat king of Judah, "Will you
go with me *against* Ramoth-gilead?"
And he said to him, "I am as you are,
and my people as your people, and
*we will be* with you in the battle."

**4** Moreover, Jehoshaphat said to
the king of Israel, "Please inquire [1]first
for the word of Yahweh." **5** Then the
king of Israel gathered the prophets,
four hundred men, and said to them,
"Shall we go against Ramoth-gilead
to battle, or shall I refrain?" And
they said, "Go up, for God will give
*it* into the hand of the king." **6** But
Jehoshaphat said, "Is there not yet a
prophet of Yahweh here that we may
inquire of him?" **7** And the king of Is-
rael said to Jehoshaphat, "There is yet
one man by whom we may inquire of
Yahweh, but I hate him, because he
never prophesies good concerning
me but always evil. He is Micaiah,
son of Imla." But Jehoshaphat said,
"Let not the king say so."

### *Micaiah Prophesies Against Ahab*

**8** Then the king of Israel called an
officer and said, "Hasten to bring
Micaiah son of Imla." **9** Now the king
of Israel and Jehoshaphat the king of
Judah were sitting each on his throne,
clothed in *their royal* garments, and
*they* were sitting [a]at the threshing
floor at the entrance of the gate of
Samaria; and all the prophets were
prophesying before them. **10** And
Zedekiah the son of Chenaanah
made horns of iron for himself and
*said*, "Thus says Yahweh, 'With
these you shall gore the Arameans
until they are consumed.'" **11** All the
prophets were also prophesying thus,
saying, "Go up to Ramoth-gilead and
succeed, and Yahweh will give *it* into
the hand of the king."

**12** Now the messenger who went
to summon Micaiah spoke to him
saying, "Behold, the words of the
prophets, *as if* from one mouth, are
good to the king. So please let your
word be like one of them and speak
*that which is* good." **13** But Micaiah
said, "As Yahweh lives, [a]what my God
says, that I shall speak."

**14** Then he came to the king, and
the king said to him, "Micaiah, shall
we go to Ramoth-gilead to battle, or
shall I refrain?" And he said, "Go up
and succeed, and they will be given
into your hand." **15** Then the king
said to him, "How many times must
I make you swear to speak to me
nothing but the truth in the name
of Yahweh?" **16** So he said,

"I saw all Israel
Scattered on the mountains,
[a]Like sheep which have
no shepherd;
And Yahweh said,
'These have no master.
Let each of them return
to his house in peace.'"

**17** So the king of Israel said to
Jehoshaphat, "Did I not say to you
that he would not prophesy good
concerning me, but evil?"

**18** Then Micaiah said, "Therefore,
hear the word of Yahweh. [a]I saw
Yahweh sitting on His throne, and
all the host of heaven standing on
His right and on His left. **19** And
Yahweh said, 'Who will entice Ahab
king of Israel so that he will go up
and fall at Ramoth-gilead?' And one

**18:4** [1]Lit *as the day* **18:9** [a]Ru 4:1 **18:13** [a]Nu 22:18-20, 35 **18:16** [a]Nu 27:17; 1Ki 22:17; Eze 34:5; 35:4-8; Mt 9:36; Mk 6:34 **18:18** [a]Is 6:1-5; Da 7:9, 10

said this while another said that. **20** Then a [a]spirit came forward and stood before Yahweh and said, 'I will entice him.' And Yahweh said to him, 'How?' **21** And he said, 'I will go out and be [a]a lying spirit in the mouth of all his prophets.' Then He said, 'You shall entice *him* and also prevail. Go out and do so.' **22** So now, behold, [a]Yahweh has put a lying spirit in the mouth of these your prophets, but Yahweh has spoken calamity against you."

**23** Then Zedekiah the son of Chenaanah approached and [a]struck Micaiah on the cheek and said, "[1]How did the Spirit of Yahweh pass from me to speak to you?" **24** And Micaiah said, "Behold, you will see on that day when you enter an inner room to hide." **25** Then the king of Israel said, "[a]Take Micaiah and return him to Amon [b]the ruler of the city and to Joash the king's son; **26** and say, 'Thus says the king, "[a]Put this *man* in prison and feed him [1]sparingly with bread and water until I return safely."'" **27** And Micaiah said, "If you indeed return safely, Yahweh has not spoken by me." And he said, "[a]Listen, all you people."

### *The Death of Ahab*

**28** So the king of Israel and Jehoshaphat king of Judah went up against Ramoth-gilead. **29** And the king of Israel said to Jehoshaphat, "I will disguise myself and go into battle, but you put on your garments." So the king of Israel disguised himself, and they went into battle. **30** Now the king of Aram had commanded the commanders of his chariots, saying, "Do not fight with small or great, but with the king of Israel alone." **31** Now it happened that when the commanders of the chariots saw Jehoshaphat, they said, "It is the king of Israel," and they turned to fight against him. But Jehoshaphat [a]cried out, and Yahweh helped him, and God incited them away from him. **32** So it happened that when the commanders of the chariots saw that it was not the king of Israel, they turned back from pursuing him. **33** Now a certain man drew his bow at random and struck the king of Israel [1]in a joint of the armor. So he said to the driver of the chariot, "Turn [2]around and take me out of the [3]fight, for I am severely wounded." **34** Now the battle raged that day, and the king of Israel propped himself up in his chariot in front of the Arameans until the evening; and at sunset he died.

### *Jehoshaphat Returns to Jerusalem*

**19** Then Jehoshaphat the king of Judah returned in peace to his house in Jerusalem. **2** [a]And Jehu the son of Hanani the seer went out *to meet him* to his face and said to King Jehoshaphat, "[b]Should you help the wicked and love those who hate Yahweh and [c,1]so *bring* wrath on yourself from Yahweh? **3** But [a]*some* good has been found in you, for [b]you have purged the [1]Asheroth from the land and you [c]have set your heart to seek God."

---

**18:20** [a]Job 1:6; 2Th 2:9 **18:21** [a]Jn 8:44 **18:22** [a]Is 19:14; Eze 14:9 **18:23** [a]Jer 20:2; Mk 14:65; Ac 23:2 [1]Lit *Which way* **18:25** [a]2Chr 18:8 [b]2Chr 34:8 **18:26** [a]2Chr 16:10 [1]Lit *with bread of oppression and water of oppression* **18:27** [a]Mic 1:2 **18:31** [a]2Chr 13:14, 15 **18:33** [1]Lit *between the scale-armor and the breastplate* [2]Lit *your hand* [3]Lit *camp* ◆ **19:2** [a]1Ki 16:1; 2Chr 20:34 [b]2Chr 18:1, 3 [c]2Chr 24:18 [1]Lit *by this* **19:3** [a]2Chr 12:12 [b]2Chr 17:6 [c]2Chr 12:14 [1]Wooden pillars

**4** So Jehoshaphat lived in Jerusa-
lem. Indeed, he returned and went
out among the people from Beer-
sheba to the hill country of Ephraim
and [a]caused them to return back to
Yahweh, the God of their fathers.

### *Jehoshaphat Appoints Judges*

**5** And he appointed [a]judges in the
land in all the fortified cities of
Judah, in each city. **6** And he said to
the judges, "Consider what you are
doing, for [a]you do not judge for
man but for Yahweh who is with you
[1]when you render judgment. **7** So now
then let the dread of Yahweh be upon
you; [1]be careful what you do, because
[2]with Yahweh our God [a]there is no
unrighteousness [b]or partiality or the
taking of a bribe."
**8** In Jerusalem also Jehoshaphat
appointed some [a]of the Levites
and priests, and some of the heads
of the fathers' *households* of Israel,
for the judgment of Yahweh and to
judge [1]disputes. So they returned to
Jerusalem. **9** Then he commanded
them saying, "Thus you shall do in
the fear of Yahweh, faithfully and
wholeheartedly. **10** [a]Whenever any
dispute comes to you from your
brothers who live in their cities,
between blood and blood, between
law and commandment, statutes and
judgments, you shall warn them so
that they may not be guilty before
Yahweh and [b]wrath may *not* come
on you and your brothers. Thus you
shall do, and you will not be guilty.
**11** And behold, Amariah the chief
priest will be over you in [a,1]all that
pertains to Yahweh, and Zebadiah
the son of Ishmael, the ruler of the
house of Judah, in [1]all that pertains
to the king. Also the Levites shall be
officers before you. [b]Be strong and
act, and Yahweh be with the one who
is good."

### *War Against Judah*

**20** Now it happened after this,
that the sons of Moab and the
sons of Ammon, together with some
of the [a,1]Ammonites, came to make
war against Jehoshaphat. **2** Then
some came and told Jehoshaphat,
saying, "A great multitude is coming
against you from beyond the sea,
out of [1]Aram and behold, they are
in [a]Hazazon-tamar (that is Enge-
di)." **3** And Jehoshaphat was afraid
and [a,1]set his face to seek Yahweh,
and [b]called for a fast throughout all
Judah. **4** So Judah gathered together
to [a]seek *help* from Yahweh; they even
came from all the cities of Judah to
seek Yahweh.

### *Jehoshaphat Before the Assembly*

**5** Then Jehoshaphat stood in the
assembly of Judah and Jerusalem,
in the house of Yahweh before the
new court, **6** and he said, "O Yahweh,
the God of our fathers, [a]are You not
God in the heavens? And [b]are You
not ruler over all the kingdoms of
the nations? Power and might are
in Your hand so that no one can
take their stand against You. **7** Did
*You not*, O our God, dispossess the

---

**19:4** [a]2Chr 15:8-13 **19:5** [a]Dt 16:18-20 **19:6** [a]Lv 19:15; Dt 1:17 [1]Lit *in the word of judgment*
**19:7** [a]Ge 18:25; Dt 32:4 [b]Dt 10:17, 18 [1]Lit *be careful and do* [2]Lit *there is not with Yahweh our God*
**19:8** [a]2Chr 17:8, 9 [1]As in M.T.; or *And they lived in Jerusalem*; LXX and Vg. *disputes and they returned to Jerusalem* **19:10** [a]Dt 17:8 [b]2Chr 19:2 **19:11** [a]2Chr 19:8 [b]1Chr 28:20 [1]Lit *every matter of*
◆ **20:1** [a]1Chr 4:41; 2Chr 26:7 [1]Gr *Meunites* **20:2** [a]Ge 14:7 [1]Or *Edom* **20:3** [a]2Chr 19:3 [b]1Sa 7:6; Ezr 8:21 [1]Lit *gave* **20:4** [a]Joel 1:14 **20:6** [a]Dt 4:39 [b]1Chr 29:11

inhabitants of this land before Your
people Israel and [a]give it to the seed
of [b]Abraham Your friend forever?
**8** And they have lived in it, and have
built You a sanctuary there for Your
name, saying, **9** '[a]Should evil come
upon us, the sword, *or* judgment, or
pestilence, or famine, we will stand
before this house and before You (for
[b]Your name is in this house) and cry
to You in our distress, and You will
hear and save *us*.' **10** So now, behold,
[a]the sons of Ammon and Moab and
[1]Mount Seir, [b]whom You did not let
Israel invade when they came out of
the land of Egypt (they turned aside
from them and did not destroy them),
**11** and behold, they are rewarding us
by [a]coming to drive us out from Your
possession which You have caused
us to possess. **12** O our God, [a]will You
not judge them? For we are powerless
before this great multitude who are
coming against us; and we do not
know what we should do, but [b]our
eyes are on You."

**13** Now all Judah was standing
before Yahweh, with their little ones,
their wives, and their children.

### *Yahweh's Spirit Comes Upon Jahaziel*

**14** Then in the midst of the assembly
[a]the Spirit of Yahweh came upon Ja-
haziel the son of Zechariah, the son
*of* Benaiah, the son of Jeiel, the son of
Mattaniah, the Levite of the sons of
Asaph; **15** and he said, "Pay atten-
tion, all Judah and the inhabitants
of Jerusalem and King Jehoshaphat:
thus says Yahweh to you, '[a]Do not
fear or be dismayed because of this
great multitude, for [b]the battle is
not yours but God's. **16** Tomorrow
go down against them. Behold, they
will come up by the ascent of Ziz,
and you will find them at the end of
the valley in front of the wilderness
of Jeruel. **17** You *need* not fight in this
*battle*; take your stand—[a]stand and
see the salvation of Yahweh on your
behalf, O Judah and Jerusalem.' Do
not fear or be dismayed; tomorrow
go out to face them, [b]for Yahweh is
with you."

**18** So Jehoshaphat [a]bowed his head
with *his* face to the ground, and all Ju-
dah and the inhabitants of Jerusalem
fell down before Yahweh, worshiping
Yahweh. **19** Then the Levites, from
the sons of the Kohathites and of
the sons of the Korahites, rose up to
praise Yahweh, the God of Israel, with
a very loud voice.

### *Yahweh Eradicates the Multitude*

**20** And they rose early in the morning
and went out to the wilderness of
Tekoa; and when they went out,
Jehoshaphat stood and said, "Listen
to me, O Judah and inhabitants of
Jerusalem, [a]establish your faith in
Yahweh your God and you will be es-
tablished. Establish your faith in His
prophets and succeed." **21** When he
had taken counsel with the people,
he caused those who sang to Yahweh
and those who [a]praised Him to stand
in holy attire, as they went out before
the army, saying, "[b]Give thanks to
Yahweh, for His lovingkindness en-
dures forever." **22** When they began
singing for joy and praising, Yahweh

**20:7** [a]Is 41:8 [b]Jas 2:23 **20:9** [a]2Chr 6:28-30 [b]2Chr 6:20 **20:10** [a]2Chr 20:1, 22 [b]Nu 20:17-21 [1]Edom
**20:11** [a]Ps 83:12 **20:12** [a]Jdg 11:27 [b]Ps 25:15; 121:1, 2 **20:14** [a]2Chr 15:1; 24:20 **20:15** [a]Ex 14:13;
Dt 20:1-4; 2Chr 32:7, 8 [b]1Sa 17:47 **20:17** [a]Ex 14:13 [b]2Chr 15:2 **20:18** [a]Ex 4:31 **20:20** [a]Is 7:9
**20:21** [a]1Chr 16:29; Ps 29:2 [b]1Chr 16:34

[a]set ambushes against the sons of
[b]Ammon, Moab, and Mount Seir,
who had come against Judah; so they
were [1]defeated. **23** Indeed, the sons of
Ammon and Moab stood against the
inhabitants of Mount Seir to devote
*them* to destruction and to utterly
eradicate *them*; and when they had
finished with the inhabitants of Seir,
[a]they helped to bring one another to
ruin.

**24** Now Judah came to the lookout
of the wilderness, and they turned
toward the multitude, and behold,
they *were* corpses fallen on the
ground, and no one had escaped.
**25** So Jehoshaphat and his people
came to take their spoil and found
much among them, *including* goods,
[1]garments, and valuable things which
they took for themselves, more than
they could carry. And they were three
days taking the spoil because there
was so much.

### *Jehoshaphat Returns to Jerusalem*

**26** Then on the fourth day they assem-
bled in the valley of [1]Beracah, for there
they blessed Yahweh. Therefore they
have named that place "The Valley
of [1]Beracah" until today. **27** And every
man of Judah and Jerusalem returned
with Jehoshaphat at their head, re-
turning to Jerusalem with gladness,
[a]for Yahweh had made them glad
over their enemies. **28** And they came
to Jerusalem with harps, lyres, and
trumpets to the house of Yahweh.
**29** And [a]the dread of God was on
all the kingdoms of the lands when
*they heard that* Yahweh had fought
against the enemies of Israel. **30** So the
kingdom of Jehoshaphat was quiet,
[a]for his God gave him rest all around.

**31** [a]Thus Jehoshaphat reigned over
Judah. He *was* thirty-five years old
when he became king, and he reigned
in Jerusalem twenty-five years. And
his mother's name was Azubah the
daughter of Shilhi. **32** And he walked
in the way of his father Asa and did
not turn away from it, doing what is
right in the sight of Yahweh. **33** [a]The
high places, however, were not taken
away; [b]the people had not yet set their
hearts to the God of their fathers.

**34** Now the rest of the acts of Je-
hoshaphat, first [1]to last, behold, they
are written in the chronicles of [a]Jehu
the son of Hanani, which is [2]recorded
in the Book of the Kings of Israel.

### *Jehoshaphat Allies with Ahaziah*

**35** [a]Afterwards, Jehoshaphat king of
Judah allied himself with Ahaziah
king of Israel. He acted wickedly [1]in
so doing. **36** So he allied himself with
him to make ships to go [a]to Tarshish,
and they made the ships in Ezion-
geber. **37** Then Eliezer the son of
Dodavahu of Mareshah prophesied
against Jehoshaphat saying, "Be-
cause you have allied yourself with
Ahaziah, Yahweh has destroyed your
works." So the ships were broken and
could not go to Tarshish.

### *Jehoram Reigns over Judah*

**21** [a]And Jehoshaphat slept with
his fathers and was buried with
*his fathers* in the city of David, and
Jehoram his son became king in his

---

**20:22** [a]2Chr 13:13 [b]2Chr 20:10 [1]Lit *smitten* **20:23** [a]Jdg 7:22; 1Sa 14:20 **20:25** [1]As in several ancient mss; others *corpses* **20:26** [1]Lit *blessing* **20:27** [a]Ne 12:43 **20:29** [a]2Chr 14:14; 17:10 **20:30** [a]2Chr 14:6, 7; 15:15 **20:31** [a]1Ki 22:41-43 **20:33** [a]2Chr 17:6 [b]2Chr 19:3 **20:34** [a]2Chr 19:2 [1]Lit *and* [2]Lit *taken up* **20:35** [a]1Ki 22:48, 49 [1]Lit *to do* **20:36** [a]2Chr 9:21 ◆ **21:1** [a]1Ki 22:50

place. **2** Now he had brothers, the
sons of Jehoshaphat: Azariah, Jehiel,
Zechariah, [1]Azaryahu, Michael, and
Shephatiah. All these *were* the sons
of Jehoshaphat king [a]of Israel. **3** And
their father gave them many gifts
of silver, gold, and precious things,
[a]with fortified cities in Judah, but
he gave the kingdom to Jehoram
because he was the firstborn.

**4** So Jehoram arose over the
kingdom of his father and strength-
ened himself, and he [a]killed all his
brothers with the sword, and some
of the commanders of Israel also.
**5** [a]Jehoram *was* thirty-two years old
when he became king, and he reigned
eight years in Jerusalem. **6** [a]And he
walked in the way of the kings of
Israel, just as the house of Ahab had
done, [b]for Ahab's daughter was his
wife; and he did what was evil in the
sight of Yahweh. **7** However, Yahweh
was not willing to make the house of
David a ruin because of the covenant
which He had cut with David, [a]and
since He had promised to give a lamp
to him and his sons forever.

### *Revolt Against Judah*

**8** In his days [a]Edom revolted from
under the hand of Judah and made a
king over themselves. **9** Then Jehoram
crossed over with his commanders
and all his chariots with him. And
he arose by night and struck down
the Edomites who were surrounding
him and the commanders of the
chariots. **10** So Edom revolted from
under the hand of Judah to this day.
Then Libnah revolted at the same
time from under his hand, because
he had forsaken Yahweh, the God of
his fathers. **11** Moreover, [a]he made
high places in the mountains of
Judah, and caused the inhabitants
of Jerusalem [b]to play the harlot and
drove Judah astray.

**12** Then a letter came to him from
Elijah the prophet saying, "Thus says
Yahweh, the God of your father David,
'Because [a]you have not walked in the
ways of Jehoshaphat your father [b]and
the ways of Asa king of Judah, **13** but
[a]have walked in the way of the kings
of Israel, and have caused Judah and
the inhabitants of Jerusalem to play
the harlot [b]as the house of Ahab
played the harlot, and you [c]have
also killed your brothers, [1]your own
family, who were better than you,
**14** behold, Yahweh is going to smite
your people, your sons, your wives,
and all your possessions with a great
[1]calamity; **15** and [a]you will suffer
[1]severe sickness, a disease of your
bowels, until your bowels come out
because of the sickness, day by day.'"

**16** Then [a]Yahweh stirred up against
Jehoram the spirit of the Philistines
and [b]the Arabs who [1]bordered the
Ethiopians; **17** and they went up
against Judah and invaded it, and car-
ried away all the possessions found
in the king's house together with his
sons and his wives, so that no son
was left to him except [a,1]Jehoahaz,
the youngest of his sons.

**18** So after all this Yahweh smote
him [a]in his bowels with an incurable

**21:2** [a]2Chr 12:6; 23:2 [1]Or *Azariah* **21:3** [a]2Chr 11:5 **21:4** [a]Ge 4:8; Jdg 9:5 **21:5** [a]2Ki 8:17-22
**21:6** [a]1Ki 12:28-30 [b]2Chr 18:1 **21:7** [a]2Sa 7:12-17; 1Ki 11:13, 36 **21:8** [a]2Chr 20:22, 23; 21:10
**21:11** [a]1Ki 11:7 [b]Lv 20:5 **21:12** [a]2Chr 17:3, 4 [b]2Chr 14:2-5 **21:13** [a]2Chr 21:6 [b]1Ki 16:31-33
[c]2Chr 21:4 [1]Lit *your father's house* **21:14** [1]Lit *blow* **21:15** [a]2Chr 21:18, 19 [1]Lit *in many sicknesses*
**21:16** [a]2Chr 33:11 [b]2Chr 17:11; 22:1 [1]Lit *were at the hand of* **21:17** [a]2Chr 25:23 [1]In 2Chr 22:1, *Ahaziah*
**21:18** [a]2Chr 21:15

sickness. **19** Now it happened in the
course of time, at the end of two
years, that his bowels came out
because of his sickness and he died
with *this* greatly painful disease. And
his people made no fire for him like
[a]the fire for his fathers. **20** He was
thirty-two years old when he became
king, and he reigned in Jerusalem
eight years; and he departed [a,1]with
no one's regret, and they buried him
in the city of David, [b]but not in the
tombs of the kings.

### *Ahaziah Reigns over Judah*

**22** [a]Then the inhabitants of
Jerusalem made [1]Ahaziah,
his youngest son, king in his place,
for the band of men who came with
[b]the Arabs to the camp had killed all
the older *sons*. So Ahaziah the son of
Jehoram king of Judah became king.
**2** Ahaziah *was* [1]twenty-two years
old when he became king, and he
reigned one year in Jerusalem. And
his mother's name was Athaliah, the
[2]granddaughter of Omri. **3** He also
walked in the ways of the house of
Ahab, for his mother was his coun-
selor to do wickedly. **4** And he did
what was evil in the sight of Yahweh
like the house of Ahab, for they were
his counselors after the death of his
father, to [a]his destruction.

### *Ahaziah Goes with Jehoram of Israel*

**5** He also walked according to their
counsel, and went with Jehoram the
son of Ahab king of Israel to wage
war against Hazael king of Aram at
Ramoth-gilead. But the [a,1]Arameans
struck [2]Joram. **6** So he returned to
be healed in Jezreel of the wounds
which they caused by striking him
at Ramah, when he fought against
Hazael king of Aram. And [1]Ahaziah,
the son of Jehoram king of Judah,
went down to see Jehoram the son of
Ahab in Jezreel, because he was sick.
**7** Now [a]the downfall of Ahaziah
was from God, in that [1]he went to
Joram. And when he came, [b]he went
out with Jehoram against Jehu the
son of Nimshi, [c]whom Yahweh had
anointed to cut off the house of Ahab.

### *Jehu Kills the Princes of Judah*

**8** [a]Now it happened when Jehu was
executing judgment on the house of
Ahab, he found the princes of Judah
and the sons of Ahaziah's brothers
attending to Ahaziah, and killed
them. **9** [a]And he sought Ahaziah, and
they caught him while he was hiding
himself in Samaria; they brought him
to Jehu, put him to death, [b]and buried
him. For they said, "He is the son of
Jehoshaphat, [c]who sought Yahweh
with all his heart." So there was no
one of the house of Ahaziah to retain
the power of the kingdom.
**10** [a]Now Athaliah the mother of
Ahaziah saw that her son had died.
So she rose and destroyed all the roy-
al seed of the house of Judah. **11** But
Jehoshabeath the king's daughter
took Joash the son of Ahaziah, and
stole him from among the king's sons
who were being put to death, and put
him and his nurse in the bedroom.
So Jehoshabeath, the daughter of
King Jehoram, the wife of Jehoiada

---

**21:19** [a]2Chr 16:14 **21:20** [a]Jer 22:18, 28 [b]2Chr 24:25; 28:27 [1]Lit *without desire* ◆ **22:1** [a]2Ki 8:24-29 [b]2Chr 21:16 [1]In 2Chr 21:17, *Jehoahaz* **22:2** [1]As in some versions and 2Ki 8:26; Heb *42 years* [2]Lit *daughter* **22:4** [a]Pr 13:20 **22:5** [a]2Ki 8:28 [1]Heb *archers* [2]Jehoram **22:6** [1]As in 2Ki 8:29; Heb *Azariah* **22:7** [a]2Chr 10:15 [b]2Ki 9:21 [c]2Ki 9:6, 7 [1]Lit *to go* **22:8** [a]2Ki 10:11-14 **22:9** [a]2Ki 9:27 [b]2Ki 9:28 [c]2Chr 17:4 **22:10** [a]2Ki 11:1-3

the priest (for she was the sister of
Ahaziah), hid him from Athaliah, so
she did not put him to death. **12** So he
was hidden with them in the house
of God six years while Athaliah was
reigning over the land.

### *Jehoiada Makes Joash King*

**23** [a]Now in the seventh year Je-
hoiada strengthened himself,
and took commanders of hundreds:
Azariah the son of Jeroham, Ishmael
the son of Johanan, Azariah the son
of Obed, Maaseiah the son of Adaiah,
and Elishaphat the son of Zichri,
*and they entered* into a covenant
with him. **2** And they went around
Judah and gathered the Levites from
all the cities of Judah, and the heads
of the fathers' *households* of [a]Israel,
and they came to Jerusalem. **3** Then
all the assembly cut a covenant with
the king in the house of God. And
[1]Jehoiada said to them, "Behold, the
king's son shall reign, [a]as Yahweh has
spoken concerning the sons of David.
**4** This is the thing which you shall
do: one-third of you, of the priests
and Levites [a]who come in on the
sabbath, *shall be* gatekeepers at the
thresholds, **5** and one-third *shall be*
at the king's house, and a third at the
Gate of the Foundation; and all
the people *shall be* in the courts of
the house of Yahweh. **6** But let no one
enter the house of Yahweh except the
priests and [a]the ministering Levites;
they may enter, for they are holy. And
let all the people keep the charge of
Yahweh. **7** And the Levites will sur-
round the king, each man with his
weapons in his hand; and whoever
enters the house, let him be put to
death. And be with the king when
he comes in and when he goes out."
**8** So the Levites and all Judah did
according to all that Jehoiada the
priest commanded. And each one
of them took his men who were to
come in on the sabbath, with those
who were to go out on the sabbath,
for Jehoiada the priest did not dis-
miss *any of* [a]the divisions. **9** Then
Jehoiada the priest gave to the com-
manders of hundreds the spears and
the shields and small shields which
had been King David's, which were in
the house of God. **10** And he caused
all the people to stand, each man
with his weapon in his hand, from
the right [1]side of the house to the left
[1]side of the house, by the altar and by
the house, around the king. **11** Then
they brought out the king's son and
put the crown on him, and *gave him*
[a]the testimony and made him king.
And Jehoiada and his sons anointed
him and said, "[b]*Long* live the king!"

### *Athaliah Put to Death*

**12** Then Athaliah heard the noise of
the people running and praising the
king, so she came into the house
of Yahweh to the people. **13** And
she looked, and behold, the king
was standing by his pillar at the
entrance, and the commanders and
the [1]trumpeters *were* beside the king.
And all the people of the land were
glad and blew trumpets, the singers
with *their* musical instruments
[2]leading the praise. Then Athaliah
tore her clothes and said, "Treason!
Treason!" **14** Then Jehoiada the priest

◆ **23:1** [a]2Ki 11:4-20 **23:2** [a]2Chr 11:13-17; 21:2 **23:3** [a]2Sa 7:12; 2Chr 21:7 [1]Lit *he* **23:4** [a]1Chr 9:25
**23:6** [a]1Chr 23:28-32 **23:8** [a]1Chr 24:1 **23:10** [1]Lit *shoulder* **23:11** [a]Ex 25:16, 21 [b]1Sa 10:24
**23:13** [1]Lit *trumpets* [2]Lit *and leading for praising*

brought out the commanders of
hundreds who were appointed over
the military force and said to them,
"Bring her out [1]between the ranks;
and whoever follows her, let him be
put to death with the sword." For the
priest said, "You shall not put her to
death in the house of Yahweh." **15** So
they laid hands on her, and when she
arrived at the entrance of [a]the Horse
Gate of the king's house, they [b]put
her to death there.

### *Jehoiada Cuts a Covenant*

**16** Then [a]Jehoiada cut a covenant
between himself and all the people
and the king, that they would be
the people of Yahweh. **17** And all the
people came to the house of Baal
and tore it down, and his altars and
his images they broke in pieces, and
they [a]killed Mattan the priest of Baal
before the altars. **18** And Jehoiada
placed the assignments concerning
the house of Yahweh in the hand of
[a]the Levitical priests, [b]whom David
had divided *by lot to be* over the
house of Yahweh, to offer the burnt
offerings of Yahweh, as it is written
in the law of Moses—[c]with gladness
and singing according to the [1]order
of David. **19** And he caused [a]the
gatekeepers of the house of Yah-
weh to stand, so that no one would
enter *who was* in any way unclean.
**20** [a]And he took the commanders of
hundreds, the nobles, the rulers
of the people, and all the people
of the land, and brought the king
*down from the house of Yahweh,*
and they came through the upper
gate to the king's house. And they
sat the king upon the royal throne.
**21** So [a]all of the people of the land
were glad, and the city was quiet.
For they had put Athaliah to death
with the sword.

### *Joash Reigns over Judah*

**24** [a]Joash was seven years old
when he became king, and he
reigned forty years in Jerusalem; and
his mother's name was Zibiah from
Beersheba. **2** [a]And Joash did what
was right in the sight of Yahweh all
the days of Jehoiada the priest. **3** And
Jehoiada took up two wives for him,
and he became the father of sons and
daughters.

### *The Levites Did Not Act Quickly*

**4** Now it happened afterwards, that
Joash [1]had in *his* heart [a]to restore the
house of Yahweh. **5** And he gathered
the priests and Levites and said to
them, "Go out to the cities of Judah
and gather money from all [a]Israel
to [1]repair the house of your God
[2]annually, and you shall do the
matter quickly." But the Levites did
not act quickly. **6** So the king called
for Jehoiada the chief *priest* and said
to him, "Why have you not required
the Levites to bring in from Judah
and from Jerusalem [a]the levy *fixed by*
Moses the servant of Yahweh on the
congregation of Israel [b]for the tent
of the testimony?" **7** For [a]the sons of
the wicked Athaliah had broken into
the house of God and even [1]used the
*holy* things of the house of Yahweh
for the Baals.

**23:14** [1]Lit *from within* **23:15** [a]Ne 3:28; Jer 31:40 [b]2Chr 22:10 **23:16** [a]2Ki 11:17 **23:17** [a]Dt 13:6-9; 1Ki 18:40 **23:18** [a]2Chr 5:5 [b]1Chr 23:6, 25-31 [c]1Chr 25:1 [1]Lit *hands of* **23:19** [a]1Chr 9:22 **23:20** [a]2Ki 11:19 **23:21** [a]2Ki 11:20 ◆ **24:1** [a]2Ki 11:21; 12:1-15 **24:2** [a]2Chr 26:4, 5 **24:4** [a]2Chr 24:7 [1]Lit *was with a heart* **24:5** [a]2Chr 21:2 [1]Lit *to strengthen* [2]Lit *from year to year* **24:6** [a]Ex 30:12-16 [b]Nu 1:50 **24:7** [a]2Chr 21:17 [1]Lit *made*

### *The House of Yahweh Restored*

**8** So the king said *the word,* and [a]they
made a chest and put it outside by
the gate of the house of Yahweh.
**9** [a]And they [1]made a proclamation
in Judah and Jerusalem to bring to
Yahweh [b]the levy *fixed by* Moses the
servant of God on Israel in the wil-
derness. **10** And all the officials and
all the people were glad and brought
*in their levies* and [1]dropped *them* into
the chest until they had [2]finished.
**11** Now it happened that whenever
the chest was brought in to the king's
officer by the hand of the Levites,
and when [a]they saw that there was
much money, then the king's scribe
and the chief priest's officer would
come, empty the chest, take it, and
return it to its place. Thus they did
daily and collected much money.
**12** And the king and Jehoiada gave
it to those who did the work of the
service of the house of Yahweh; and
they hired masons and [1]carpenters
to restore the house of Yahweh, and
also craftsmen in iron and bronze to
[2]repair the house of Yahweh. **13** So
those who did the work labored,
and the repair work progressed in
their hands, and they [1]restored
the house of God [2]according to its
specifications and strengthened it.
**14** When they had completed, they
brought the rest of the money before
the king and Jehoiada; and it was
made into utensils for the house of
Yahweh, utensils for the ministry
and the burnt offering, and pans and
utensils of gold and silver. And they
were offering burnt offerings in the
house of Yahweh continually all the
days of Jehoiada.

**15** Then Jehoiada became old and
full of days, and he died; he was 130
years old at his death. **16** They buried
him [a]in the city of David among the
kings, because he had done what is
good in [b]Israel and [1]to God and His
house.

**17** But after the death of Jehoiada
the officials of Judah came and
bowed down to the king, and the king
listened to them. **18** And they forsook
[a]the house of Yahweh, the God of
their fathers, and [b]served the [1]Ashe-
rim and the idols; so [c]wrath came
upon Judah and Jerusalem for this
their guilt. **19** Yet [a]He sent prophets to
them to bring them back to Yahweh;
though they testified against them,
they did not give ear.

### *People Conspire Against Zechariah*

**20** [a]Now the Spirit of God clothed
Zechariah the son of Jehoiada the
priest; and he stood above the people
and said to them, "Thus says God,
'[b]Why do you trespass against the
commandments of Yahweh and do
not succeed? [c]Because you have
forsaken Yahweh, He has also for-
saken you.'" **21** So [a]they conspired
against him and at the command
of the king they stoned him [1]to
death in the court of the house of
Yahweh. **22** Thus Joash the king did
not remember the lovingkindness
which his father Jehoiada had shown
him, but he killed his son. And as he
died he said, "May [a]Yahweh see and
[1]avenge!"

---

**24:8** [a]2Ki 12:9 **24:9** [a]2Chr 36:22 [b]2Chr 24:6 [1]Lit *gave a voice* **24:10** [1]Lit *threw* [2]Lit *completed* **24:11** [a]2Ki 12:10 **24:12** [1]Or *craftsmen* of wood, cf. 2Sa 5:11; 2Chr 24:12b [2]Lit *strengthen* **24:13** [1]Lit *caused to stand* [2]Lit *upon its proportion* **24:16** [a]2Chr 21:20 [b]2Chr 21:2 [1]Lit *with* **24:18** [a]2Chr 24:4 [b]Ex 34:12-14 [c]Jos 22:20 [1]Wooden symbols of a female deity **24:19** [a]Jer 7:25 **24:20** [a]2Chr 20:14 [b]Nu 14:41 [c]2Chr 15:2 **24:21** [a]Ne 9:26; Mt 23:34, 35 [1]Lit *with stones* **24:22** [a]Ge 9:5 [1]Or *require*; lit *seek*

### *Aram Comes Up Against Judah*

**23** Now it happened at the turn of the
year that [a]the military force of the
Arameans came up against him; and
they came to Judah and Jerusalem,
destroyed all the officials of the
people from among the people, and
sent all their spoil to the king of Da-
mascus. **24** Indeed the military force
of the Arameans came with a small
number of men; yet [a]Yahweh gave a
very great military force into their
hands, [b]because they had forsaken
Yahweh, the God of their fathers.
Thus they executed judgment on
Joash.
**25** [a]When they had gone from him
(for they left him very sick), his ser-
vants conspired against him because
of the blood of the [1]son of Jehoiada
the priest, and killed him on his bed.
So he died, and they buried him in the
city of David, but they did not bury
him in the tombs of the kings. **26** Now
these are those who conspired against
him: Zabad the son of Shimeath the
Ammonitess, and Jehozabad the son
of Shimrith the Moabitess. **27** Now
as to his sons and the many [1]oracles
against him and [a]the [2]rebuilding of
the house of God, behold, they are
written in the [b,3]treatise of the Book
of the Kings. Then Amaziah his son
became king in his place.

### *Amaziah Reigns over Judah*

**25** [a]Amaziah was twenty-five
years old when he became
king, and he reigned twenty-nine
years in Jerusalem. And his *mother's
name was* Jehoaddan of Jerusalem.
**2** And he did what was right in the
sight of Yahweh, [a]yet not with a
whole heart. **3** Now [a]it happened as
soon as the kingdom was [1]strong in
his grasp, that he killed his servants
who had struck down the king his
father. **4** But he did not put their sons
to death, but *did* as it is written in the
law in the book of Moses, which Yah-
weh commanded, saying, "[a]Fathers
shall not be put to death for *their*
sons, nor sons be put to death for
*their* fathers, but each shall be put
to death for his own sin."

### *Amaziah Is Strong in Battle*

**5** Moreover, Amaziah assembled
Judah and appointed them according
to *their* fathers' households under
commanders of thousands and com-
manders of hundreds throughout
Judah and Benjamin; and he [1]took a
census of those [a]from twenty years
old and upward and found them to
be [b]300,000 choice men, *able* to go
out for *military* duty, *able to* handle
spear and large shield. **6** And he hired
also 100,000 mighty men of valor
out of Israel for one hundred [1]talents
of silver. **7** But [a]a man of God came
to him saying, "O king, do not let
the army of Israel go with you, for
Yahweh is not with Israel *nor with*
any of the sons of Ephraim. **8** But if
you do go, do *it*, be strong for the
battle; *yet* God will cause you to
stumble before the enemy, [a]for God
has power to help and to cause to
stumble." **9** Then Amaziah said to the
*man of God*, "But what *shall we* do
for the hundred talents which I have

**24:23** [a]2Ki 12:17 **24:24** [a]2Chr 16:7, 8 [b]2Chr 24:20 **24:25** [a]2Ki 12:20, 21 [1]As in some ancient versions; Heb *sons* **24:27** [a]2Chr 24:12 [b]2Chr 13:22 [1]Or *burdens upon* [2]Lit *founding* [3]Heb *midrash* ◆ **25:1** [a]2Ki 14:1-6 **25:2** [a]2Chr 25:14 **25:3** [a]2Ki 14:5 [1]Lit *firm upon him* **25:4** [a]Dt 24:16 **25:5** [a]Nu 1:3 [b]2Chr 26:13 [1]Lit *mustered* **25:6** [1]A talent was approx. 75 lb. or 34 kg **25:7** [a]2Ki 4:9 **25:8** [a]2Chr 14:11; 20:6

given to the troops of Israel?" And
the man of God answered, "[a]Yahweh
has much more to give you than
this." **10** Then Amaziah [1]dismissed
them, the troops which came to him
from Ephraim, to go [2]home; so their
anger burned against Judah and they
returned [2]home in burning anger.
**11** Now Amaziah strengthened
himself and led his people forth, and
went to [a]the Valley of Salt and struck
down 10,000 of the sons of Seir.
**12** The sons of Judah also captured
10,000 alive and brought them to the
top of the cliff and threw them down
from the top of the cliff, so that they
were all split open. **13** But the [1]troops
whom Amaziah sent back from going
with him to battle, raided the cities of
Judah, from Samaria to Beth-horon,
and struck down 3,000 of them and
plundered much plunder.

### *Amaziah Worships the Edomites' Gods*

**14** Now it happened that after Ama-
ziah came from striking down the
Edomites, [a]he brought the gods of
the sons of Seir, set them up as his
gods, worshiped them, and burned
incense to them. **15** Then the anger
of Yahweh burned against Amaziah,
and He sent him a prophet who said
to him, "Why have you sought the
gods of the people [a]who have not
delivered their own people from your
hand?" **16** Now it happened that as he
was talking with him, [1]the king said
to him, "Have we given you *to be* a
royal counselor? Stop! Why should
you be struck down?" Then the
prophet stopped and said, "I know
that God has counseled to destroy
you, because you have done this and
have not listened to my counsel."

### *Amaziah Defeated by Joash of Israel*

**17** [a]Then Amaziah king of Judah took
counsel and sent to Joash the son of
Jehoahaz the son of Jehu, the king
of Israel, saying, "Come, let us face
each other." **18** And Joash the king of
Israel sent to Amaziah king of Judah,
saying, "[a]The thorn bush which was
in Lebanon sent to the cedar which
was in Lebanon, saying, 'Give your
daughter to my son as a wife.' But a
beast of the field that was in Lebanon
passed by and trampled the thorn
bush. **19** You said, 'Behold, you have
struck down Edom.' And [a]your heart
has lifted you up to boast. Now stay
at home; for why should you provoke
calamity so that you, even you, would
fall and Judah with you?"
**20** But Amaziah would not listen,
for it was from God, that He might
give them into the hand *of Joash*
because they had sought the gods
of Edom. **21** So Joash king of Israel
went up, and he and Amaziah king
of Judah faced each other at Beth-
shemesh, which belonged to Judah.
**22** And Judah was [1]defeated by Israel,
and they fled each to his tent. **23** Then
Joash king of Israel seized Amaziah
king of Judah, the son of Joash the
son of [a]Jehoahaz, at Beth-shemesh,
and brought him to Jerusalem and
broke down the wall of Jerusalem
from the Gate of Ephraim to the
Corner Gate, [1]400 cubits. **24** And *he*

**25:9** [a]Dt 8:18; Pr 10:22 **25:10** [1]Lit *separated* [2]Lit *to their own place* **25:11** [a]2Ki 14:7 **25:13** [1]Lit *sons of the troops* **25:14** [a]2Chr 28:23 **25:15** [a]2Chr 25:11, 12 **25:16** [1]Lit *he* **25:17** [a]2Ki 14:8-14 **25:18** [a]Jdg 9:8-15 **25:19** [a]2Chr 26:16; 32:25 **25:22** [1]Lit *smitten before* **25:23** [a]2Chr 21:17; 22:1 [1]Approx. 200 yd. or 180 m

*took* all the gold and silver and all
the utensils which were found in the
house of God with [a]Obed-edom, and
the treasures of the king's house,
the hostages also, and returned to
Samaria.
25 [a]And Amaziah the son of Joash
king of Judah lived fifteen years after
the death of Joash son of Jehoahaz
king of Israel. 26 Now the rest of the
acts of Amaziah, from first to last,
behold, are they not written in the
Book of the Kings of Judah and Israel?
27 Now from the time that Amaziah
turned away from following Yahweh
they conspired against him in Jerusa-
lem, and he fled to Lachish; but they
sent after him to Lachish and put him
to death there. 28 Then they carried
him on horses and buried him with
his fathers in the city of Judah.

### *Uzziah Reigns over Judah*

26 And all the people of Judah
took [1]Uzziah, who *was* sixteen
years old, and made him king in the
place of his father Amaziah. 2 He
built Eloth and restored it to Judah
after the king slept with his fathers.
3 Uzziah was [a]sixteen years old when
he became king, and he reigned
fifty-two years in Jerusalem; and his
mother's name was [1]Jechiliah of Je-
rusalem. 4 And he did what was right
in the sight of Yahweh, according to
all that his father Amaziah had done.
5 [a]And he continued to seek God in
the days of Zechariah, [b]who had
understanding [1]through the vision
of God; and [c,2]as long as he sought
*Yahweh, God made* him succeed.

### *Uzziah's Fame Spreads Afar*

6 Then he went out and [a]fought
against the Philistines, and broke
down the wall of Gath and the wall of
Jabneh and the wall of Ashdod; and
he built cities in *the area of* Ashdod
and among the Philistines. 7 [a]And
God helped him against the Philis-
tines, and against the Arabians who
lived in Gur-baal, and the Meunites.
8 The Ammonites also gave [a]tribute
to Uzziah, and his [1]fame extended to
the border of Egypt, for he became
very strong. 9 Moreover, Uzziah built
towers in Jerusalem at [a]the Corner
Gate and at the [b]Valley Gate and at
the corner buttress and strength-
ened them. 10 He also built towers
in the wilderness and [a]hewed many
cisterns, for he had much livestock,
both in the [1]Shephelah and in the
plain. *He also had* plowmen and
vinedressers in the hill country
and the fertile fields, for he loved
the soil. 11 Moreover, Uzziah had a
military force which could wage war,
which went out for *military* duty by
divisions according to the number of
their muster, *prepared* by the hand
of Jeiel the scribe and Maaseiah the
officer, under the hand of Hananiah,
one of the king's officials. 12 The total
number of the heads of the [1]house-
holds, of mighty men of valor, was
2,600. 13 And under their hand was
a [1]mighty army of [a]307,500, who
could wage war with mighty power,
to help the king against the enemy.
14 Moreover, Uzziah prepared [1]for all
the army shields, spears, helmets,
body armor, bows, and stones for

---

**25:24** [a]1Chr 26:15 **25:25** [a]2Ki 14:17-22 ◆ **26:1** [1]In 2Ki 14:21, *Azariah* **26:3** [a]2Ki 15:2, 3 [1]In 2Ki 15:2, *Jecoliah* **26:5** [a]2Chr 24:2 [b]Da 1:17 [c]2Chr 15:2 [1]Many mss *in the fear of God* [2]Lit *in the days of his seeking* **26:6** [a]Is 14:29 **26:7** [a]2Chr 21:16 **26:8** [a]2Chr 17:11 [1]Lit *name went to the entering of Egypt* **26:9** [a]2Chr 25:23 [b]Ne 2:13, 15; 3:13 **26:10** [a]Ge 26:18-21 [1]Or *lowland* **26:12** [1]Lit *fathers* **26:13** [a]2Chr 25:5 [1]Lit *powerful* **26:14** [1]Lit *for them, for all*

sling. **15** In Jerusalem he also made
devices *of war* devised by skillful
designers to be on the towers and
on the corners for the purpose of
shooting arrows and great stones.
Hence his [1]fame spread afar, for he
was marvelously helped until he *was*
strong.

### *Uzziah's Pride*

**16** But [a]when he became strong, his
heart was so [1]proud that he acted
corruptly, and he was unfaithful to
Yahweh his God. And [b]he entered the
temple of Yahweh to burn incense on
the altar of incense. **17** Then [a]Azariah
the priest entered after him and with
him eighty priests of Yahweh, men
of valor. **18** [a]And they stood against
Uzziah the king and said to him,
"[b]It is not for you, Uzziah, to burn
incense to Yahweh, [c]but for the
priests, the sons of Aaron who are
set apart as holy to burn incense.
Get out of the sanctuary, for you
have been unfaithful and will have
no honor from Yahweh God." **19** But
Uzziah, with a censer in his hand
for burning incense, was enraged;
and while he was enraged with the
priests, [a]the leprosy broke out on
his forehead before the priests in the
house of Yahweh, beside the altar of
incense. **20** And Azariah the chief
priest and all the priests looked at
him, and behold, he *was* leprous on
his forehead; and they hurried him
out of there, and he himself also
hastened to get out because Yahweh
had smitten him. **21** [a]So King Uzziah
was a leper to the day of his death;
and he lived in [b]a separate house,
being a leper, for he was cut off from
the house of Yahweh. And Jotham
his son *was* over the king's house,
judging the people of the land.
**22** Now the rest of the acts of
Uzziah, first to last, the prophet
[a]Isaiah, the son of Amoz, has
written. **23** So Uzziah slept with his
fathers, and they buried him with
his fathers [a]in the field of the grave
which belonged to the kings, for they
said, "He is a leper." And Jotham his
son became king in his place.

### *Jotham Reigns over Judah*

**27** [a]Jotham was twenty-five years
old when he became king, and
he reigned sixteen years in Jerusalem.
And his mother's name was Jerushah
the daughter of Zadok. **2** And he did
what was right in the sight of Yahweh,
according to all that his father Uzziah
had done; [a]however he did not enter
the temple of Yahweh. But the people
continued acting corruptly. **3** He
built the upper gate of the house of
Yahweh, and he built extensively the
wall of [a]Ophel. **4** Moreover, he built
[a]cities in the hill country of Judah,
and he built fortresses and towers
on the wooded *hills*. **5** He fought also
with the king of the sons of Ammon
and prevailed over them. So the sons
of Ammon gave him during that
year [1]100 talents of silver, [2]10,000
kors of wheat, and 10,000 of barley.
The sons of Ammon also brought
back to him this *amount* in the
second and in the third year. **6** [a]So
Jotham became strong because he

**26:15** [1]Lit *name* **26:16** [a]Dt 32:15; 2Chr 25:19 [b]1Ki 13:1-4 [1]Lit *lifted up* **26:17** [a]1Chr 6:10
**26:18** [a]2Chr 19:2 [b]Nu 3:10; 16:39, 40 [c]Ex 30:7, 8 **26:19** [a]2Ki 5:25-27 **26:21** [a]2Ki 15:5-7 [b]Lv 13:46
**26:22** [a]Is 1:1 **26:23** [a]2Chr 21:20; 28:27; Is 6:1 ♦ **27:1** [a]2Ki 15:33-35 **27:2** [a]2Chr 26:16 **27:3** [a]2Chr 33:14;
Ne 3:26 **27:4** [a]2Chr 11:5 **27:5** [1]Approx. 3.75 tons or 3.4 metric tons, a talent was approx. 75 lb. or 34
kg [2]Approx. 65,000 bu. or 2,300 metric tons, a kor was approx. 6.5 bu. or 230 l **27:6** [a]2Chr 26:5

established his ways before Yahweh
his God. **7** [a]Now the rest of the acts
of Jotham, even all his wars and his
ways, behold, they are written in
the Book of the Kings of Israel and
Judah. **8** He was [a]twenty-five years
old when he became king, and he
reigned sixteen years in Jerusalem.
**9** And Jotham slept with his fathers,
and they buried him in the city of
David; and Ahaz his son became king
in his place.

### *Ahaz Reigns over Judah*

**28** [a]Ahaz *was* twenty years old
when he became king, and he
reigned sixteen years in Jerusalem;
and [b]he did not do what was right
in the sight of Yahweh, as David his
father *had done.* **2** [a]But he walked in
the ways of the kings of Israel; he also
[b]made molten images for the Baals.
**3** Moreover, [a]he offered *offerings* in
smoke in the valley of Ben-hinnom
and [b]burned his sons in the fire,
[c]according to the abominations
of the nations whom Yahweh had
dispossessed from before the sons
of Israel. **4** He also sacrificed and
[a]offered *offerings* in smoke on the
high places and on the hills and
under every green tree.

### *Judah Carried Away by Aram*

**5** So, [a]Yahweh his God gave him into
the hand of the king of Aram; and
they struck him and carried away
from him a great number of captives
and brought *them* to Damascus. And
he was also given into the hand of the
king of Israel, who struck him with
a great slaughter. **6** Indeed, [a]Pekah
the son of Remaliah killed in Judah
120,000 in one day, all men of valor,
because they had forsaken Yahweh,
the God of their fathers. **7** And Zichri,
a mighty man of Ephraim, killed
Maaseiah the king's son and Azrikam
the ruler of the house and Elkanah
the second to the king.

**8** [a]Then the sons of Israel carried
away captive of [b]their brothers
200,000 women, sons, and daugh-
ters; and they plundered also a great
deal of spoil from them and brought
the spoil to Samaria. **9** But a prophet
of Yahweh was there, whose name
*was* Oded; and [a]he went out before
the army which came to Samaria and
said to them, "Behold, because of the
[b]wrath of Yahweh, the God of your
fathers, against Judah, He has given
them into your hand, and you have
killed them in a rage [c]*which* has even
reached heaven. **10** So now you are
[1]intending to [a]subdue for yourselves
the people of Judah and Jerusalem
for male and female slaves. Surely,
*do* you not *have* your own *matters
of* guilt against Yahweh your God?
**11** So now, listen to me and return
the captives [a]whom you carried
away from your brothers, [b]for the
burning anger of Yahweh is against
you." **12** Then some of the heads of
the sons of Ephraim—Azariah the
son of Johanan, Berechiah the son
of Meshillemoth, Jehizkiah the son
of Shallum, and Amasa the son of
Hadlai—arose against those who
*were coming* from the *engagement
of* the army, **13** and said to them, "You

**27:7** [a]2Ki 15:36 **27:8** [a]2Chr 27:1 ◆ **28:1** [a]2Ki 16:2-4 [b]2Chr 27:2 **28:2** [a]2Chr 22:3 [b]Ex 34:17
**28:3** [a]Jos 15:8 [b]Lv 18:21; 2Chr 33:6 [c]2Chr 33:2 **28:4** [a]2Chr 28:25 **28:5** [a]2Ki 16:5; 2Chr 24:24;
Is 7:1 **28:6** [a]2Ki 16:5 **28:8** [a]Dt 28:25, 41 [b]2Chr 11:4 **28:9** [a]2Chr 25:15 [b]Is 47:6 [c]Ezr 9:6; Rev 18:5
**28:10** [a]Lv 25:39 [1]Lit *saying* **28:11** [a]2Chr 28:8 [b]Jas 2:13

must not bring the captives in here,
for you are [1]intending *to bring* upon
us guilt against Yahweh adding to
our sins and our guilt; for our guilt
is great so that *His* burning anger is
against Israel." **14** So the armed men
left the captives and the plunder
before the commanders and all the
assembly. **15** Then [a]the men who
were designated by name arose,
took hold of the captives, and they
clothed all their naked ones from the
spoil; and they gave them clothes and
sandals, fed them and [b]gave them
drink, anointed them *with oil*, led all
their feeble ones on donkeys, and
brought them to Jericho, [c]the city of
palm trees, to their brothers; then
they returned to Samaria.

### *Ahaz Sends to Assyria for Help*

**16** [a]At that time King Ahaz sent to the
[1]kings of Assyria for help. **17** [a]Indeed,
again the Edomites had come and
struck Judah and carried away cap-
tives. **18** [a]And the Philistines also had
raided the cities of the [1]Shephelah
and of the [2]Negev of Judah, and had
captured Beth-shemesh, Aijalon,
Gederoth, and Soco with its towns,
Timnah with its towns, and Gimzo
with its towns, and they settled
there. **19** For Yahweh humbled Judah
because of Ahaz king of [a]Israel, for
he had caused *it* to be out of control
in Judah and was very unfaithful
to Yahweh. **20** So [a]Tilgath-pilneser
king of Assyria came against him and
distressed him instead of strength-
ening him. **21** [a]Although Ahaz took
a portion out of the house of Yahweh
and out of the house of the king and
of the princes, and gave *it* to the king
of Assyria, it did not help him.
**22** Now in the time of his distress
this same King Ahaz [a]became yet
more unfaithful to Yahweh. **23** [a]Indeed,
he sacrificed to the gods of Damas-
cus which had struck him, and said,
"[b]Because the gods of the kings of
Aram helped them, I will sacrifice to
them that they may help me." But they
became the stumbling of him and all
Israel. **24** Ahaz gathered together the
utensils of the house of God. Then he
[a]cut the utensils of the house of God in
pieces; and he [b]closed the doors of the
house of Yahweh and [c]made altars for
himself in every corner of Jerusalem.
**25** Now in each and every city of Judah
he made high places to offer *offerings*
in smoke to other gods, and provoked
Yahweh, the God of his fathers, to an-
ger. **26** [a]Now the rest of his acts and all
his ways, from first to last, behold, they
are written in the Book of the Kings
of Judah and Israel. **27** [a]So Ahaz slept
with his fathers, and they buried him
in the city, in Jerusalem, for they did
not bring him into the tombs of the
kings of [b]Israel; and Hezekiah his son
became king in his place.

### *Hezekiah Reigns over Judah*

**29** [a]Hezekiah became king *when*
*he was* twenty-five years old;
and he reigned twenty-nine years in
Jerusalem. And his mother's name
was Abijah, the daughter of Zecha-
riah. **2** [a]And he did what was right in
the sight of Yahweh, according to all
that David his father had done.

---

**28:13** [1]Lit *saying* **28:15** [a]2Chr 28:12 [b]2Ki 6:22; Pr 25:21, 22 [c]Dt 34:3 **28:16** [a]2Ki 16:7 [1]Ancient versions *king* **28:17** [a]Ob 10, 14 **28:18** [a]Eze 16:57 [1]Or *lowland* [2]South country **28:19** [a]2Chr 21:2 **28:20** [a]1Chr 5:26 **28:21** [a]2Ki 16:8, 9 **28:22** [a]Is 1:5; Jer 5:3; Rev 16:11 **28:23** [a]2Chr 25:14 [b]Jer 44:17, 18 **28:24** [a]2Ki 16:17 [b]2Chr 29:7 [c]2Chr 30:14; 33:3-5 **28:26** [a]2Ki 16:19, 20 **28:27** [a]2Ki 16:20; 2Chr 24:25; Is 14:28 [b]2Chr 21:2 ◆ **29:1** [a]2Ki 18:1-3 **29:2** [a]2Chr 28:1; 34:2

3 In the first year of his reign, in the
first month, he [a]opened the doors of
the house of Yahweh and repaired
them. 4 And he brought in the priests
and the Levites and gathered them
into the square on the east.

### *Hezekiah Sets the House of God as Holy*

5 Then he said to them, "Listen to
me, O Levites. [a]Set yourselves apart
now as holy, and set apart as holy the
house of Yahweh, the God of your
fathers, and bring out the impurity
from the holy place. 6 For our fathers
have been unfaithful and have done
what is evil in the sight of Yahweh
our God, and have forsaken Him and
[a]turned their faces away from the
dwelling place of Yahweh, and have
[1]turned *their* backs. 7 They have also
[a]shut the doors of the porch and put
out the lamps, and have not burned
incense or offered burnt offerings in
the holy place to the God of Israel.
8 Therefore [a]the wrath of Yahweh was
against Judah and Jerusalem, and He
has made them an object of terror,
of horror, and of [b]hissing, as you see
with your own eyes. 9 And behold,
[a]our fathers have fallen by the sword,
and our sons and our daughters and
our wives are in captivity for this.
10 Now it is in my heart [a]to cut a
covenant with Yahweh, the God of Is-
rael, that His burning anger may turn
away from us. 11 My sons, do not be
at ease now, for [a]Yahweh has chosen
you to stand before Him, to minister
to Him, and to be His ministers *and
offer offerings up in* smoke."

12 Then the Levites arose:
[a]Mahath, the son of Amasai
and Joel the son of Azariah,
from the sons of [b]the
Kohathites;
and from the sons of Merari,
Kish the son of Abdi and
Azariah the son of Jehallelel;
and from the Gershonites,
Joah the son of Zimmah and
Eden the son of Joah;
13 and from the sons of
Elizaphan, Shimri and [1]Jeiel;
and from the sons of Asaph,
Zechariah and Mattaniah;
14 and from the sons of Heman,
[1]Jehiel and Shimei;
and from the sons of
Jeduthun, Shemaiah and
Uzziel.

15 And they gathered their brothers,
[a]set themselves apart as holy, and
went in [b]to cleanse the house of
Yahweh, according to the command-
ment of the king [c]by the words of
Yahweh. 16 So the priests went in to
the inner part of the house of Yahweh
to cleanse *it,* and every unclean thing
which they found in the temple of
Yahweh they brought out to the court
of the house of Yahweh. Then the
Levites received *it* to bring out to
[a]the Kidron [1]valley, to an outer area.
17 Then they began [1]to set *it* apart
as holy [a]on the first *day* of the first
month, and on the eighth day of the
month they entered the porch of Yah-
weh. Then they set apart the house
of Yahweh as holy in eight days, and
*completed* it on the sixteenth day of
the first month. 18 Then they went

**29:3** [a]2Chr 28:24; 29:7 **29:5** [a]2Chr 29:15, 34; 35:6 **29:6** [a]Eze 8:16 [1]Lit *given* **29:7** [a]2Chr 28:24
**29:8** [a]2Chr 24:20 [b]Jer 25:9, 18 **29:9** [a]2Chr 28:5-8, 17 **29:10** [a]2Chr 23:16 **29:11** [a]Nu 3:6; 8:6
**29:12** [a]2Chr 31:13 [b]Nu 3:19, 20 **29:13** [1]Or *Jeuel* **29:14** [1]Or *Jehuel,* 1Chr 15:18, 20 **29:15** [a]2Chr 29:5
[b]1Chr 23:28 [c]2Chr 30:12 **29:16** [a]2Chr 15:16 [1]Or *wadi* **29:17** [a]2Chr 29:3 [1]Or *to consecrate*

in to King Hezekiah and said, "We
have cleansed the whole house of
Yahweh, the altar of burnt offering
with all of its utensils, and the table
of showbread with all of its utensils.
19 Moreover, [a]all the utensils which
King Ahaz had rejected during his
reign in his unfaithfulness, we have
prepared and set apart as holy; and
behold, they are before the altar of
Yahweh."

### *Hezekiah Brings an Offering*

20 Then King Hezekiah arose early
and gathered the princes of the city
and went up to the house of Yahweh.
21 And they brought seven bulls,
seven rams, seven lambs, and seven
male goats [a]for a sin offering for the
kingdom, the sanctuary, and Judah.
And he ordered the priests, the sons
of Aaron, to offer *them* on the altar
of Yahweh. 22 So they slaughtered
the bulls, and the priests took the
blood and splashed it on the altar.
They also slaughtered the rams and
splashed the blood on the altar;
they slaughtered the lambs also and
[a]splashed the blood on the altar.
23 Then they had the male goats of
the sin offering approach before the
king and the assembly, and [a]they
laid their hands on them. 24 And the
priests slaughtered them and purged
the altar with their blood [a]to atone
for all Israel, for the king ordered the
burnt offering and the sin offering
for all Israel.

25 [a]He then caused the Levites to
stand in the house of Yahweh with
cymbals, with harps, and with lyres,
[b]according to the command of David
and of [c]Gad the king's seer, and of
[d]Nathan the prophet; for the com-
mand was from Yahweh by the hand
of His prophets. 26 And the Levites
stood with [a]the *musical* instruments
of David, and [b]the priests with the
trumpets. 27 Then Hezekiah said to
offer the burnt offering on the altar.
When the burnt offering began,
[a]the song to Yahweh also began
with the trumpets, [1]*accompanied*
by the instruments of David, king of
Israel. 28 While the whole assembly
worshiped, the singers also sang
and the trumpets sounded; all this
*continued* until the burnt offering
was completed.

29 Now at the completion of the
burnt offerings, [a]the king and all who
were present with him bowed down
and worshiped. 30 Moreover, King
Hezekiah and the officials ordered
the Levites to sing praises to Yahweh
with the words of David and Asaph
the seer. [a]So they sang praises with
gladness, and bowed down and
worshiped.

31 Then Hezekiah answered and
said, "[a]Now *that* you have [1]become
ordained to Yahweh, approach and
bring sacrifices and thank offerings
to the house of Yahweh." And the
assembly brought sacrifices and
thank offerings, and [b]all those who
were willing of heart brought burnt
offerings. 32 And the number of the
burnt offerings which the assembly
brought was 70 bulls, 100 rams, and
200 lambs; all these were for a burnt
offering to Yahweh. 33 And the holy

---

**29:19** [a]2Chr 28:24 **29:21** [a]Lv 4:3-14 **29:22** [a]Lv 4:18 **29:23** [a]Lv 4:15 **29:24** [a]Lv 4:26
**29:25** [a]1Chr 25:6 [b]2Chr 8:14 [c]2Sa 24:11 [d]2Sa 7:2 **29:26** [a]1Chr 23:5 [b]2Chr 5:12 **29:27** [a]2Chr 23:18
[1]Lit *and according to the authority of the instruments* **29:29** [a]2Chr 20:18 **29:30** [a]Ps 100:1; 106:12
**29:31** [a]2Chr 13:9 [b]Ex 35:5, 22 [1]Lit *filled your hands*

things were 600 bulls and 3,000 sheep. **34** But the priests were too few, so that they were unable to skin all the burnt offerings; [a]therefore their brothers the Levites helped them until the work was completed and until the *other* priests had set themselves apart as holy. For [b]the Levites were more upright of heart to set themselves apart as holy than the priests. **35** There *were* also [a,1]many burnt offerings with [b]the fat of the peace offerings and with [c]the drink offerings for the burnt offerings. Thus the service of the house of Yahweh was established *again.* **36** Then Hezekiah and all the people were glad over what God had prepared for the people, because the thing came about suddenly.

### *Hezekiah Celebrates the Passover*

**30** And Hezekiah sent to all Israel and Judah and wrote letters also to Ephraim and Manasseh, that they should come to the house of Yahweh at Jerusalem to [1]celebrate the Passover to Yahweh, the God of Israel. **2** And the king and his princes and all the assembly in Jerusalem had taken counsel [a]to celebrate the Passover in the second month, **3** since they could not celebrate it [a]at that time, because the priests had not set themselves apart as holy in sufficient numbers, nor had the people been gathered to Jerusalem. **4** Thus the thing was right in the eyes of the king and in the eyes of all the assembly. **5** So they established a decree to make a [1]*proclamation pass* throughout all Israel [a]from Beersheba even to Dan, that they should come to celebrate the Passover to Yahweh, the God of Israel, at Jerusalem. For they had not celebrated *it* in great numbers as it was written. **6** [a]And the [1]couriers went throughout all Israel and Judah with the letters from the hand of the king and his princes, even according to the commandment of the king, saying, "O sons of Israel, return to Yahweh, the God of Abraham, Isaac, and Israel, that He may return to those of you who escaped *and* remain from [b]the [2]hand of the kings of Assyria. **7** [a]Now do not be like your fathers and your brothers, who were unfaithful to Yahweh, the God of their fathers, so that [b]He made them an object of horror, as you see. **8** Now do not [a]stiffen your neck like your fathers, but give your hand to Yahweh and enter His sanctuary which He has set apart as holy forever, and serve Yahweh your God, [b]that His burning anger may turn away from you. **9** For [a]when you return to Yahweh, your brothers and your sons *will find* compassion before those who led them captive and will return to this land. [b]For Yahweh your God is gracious and compassionate, and will not turn *His* face away from you if you return to Him."

**10** So the [1]couriers passed from city to city through the country of Ephraim and Manasseh, and as far as Zebulun, but [a]they were laughing at them to scorn and mocking them. **11** Nevertheless [a]some men of Asher, Manasseh and Zebulun

**29:34** [a]2Chr 35:11 [b]2Chr 30:3 **29:35** [a]2Chr 29:32 [b]Lv 3:16 [c]Nu 15:5-10 [1]Lit *the burnt offerings to an abundance* ◆ **30:1** [1]Lit *do*, so in ch **30:2** [a]Nu 9:10, 11; 2Chr 30:13, 15 **30:3** [a]2Chr 29:17, 34 **30:5** [a]Jdg 20:1 [1]Lit *voice* **30:6** [a]Es 8:14; Job 9:25; Jer 51:31 [b]2Chr 28:20 [1]Lit *runners* [2]Lit *palm* **30:7** [a]Eze 20:13 [b]2Chr 29:8 **30:8** [a]Ex 32:9 [b]2Chr 29:10 **30:9** [a]Dt 30:2 [b]Ex 34:6, 7; Mic 7:18 **30:10** [a]2Chr 36:16 [1]Lit *runners* **30:11** [a]2Chr 30:18, 21, 25

humbled themselves and came to
Jerusalem. **12** The [a]hand of God was
also on Judah to give them one heart
to do what the king and the princes
commanded by the word of Yahweh.

**13** Now many people were gathered
at Jerusalem to celebrate the Feast of
Unleavened Bread [a]in the second
month, a very large assembly. **14** And
they arose and took away the altars
which *were* in Jerusalem; they also
[a]took away all the incense altars and
[b]cast *them* into the brook Kidron.
**15** Then [a]they slaughtered the Pass-
over *lambs* on the fourteenth of the
second month. And [b]the priests and
Levites were ashamed of themselves,
and set themselves apart as holy and
brought burnt offerings to the house
of Yahweh. **16** [a]And they stood at their
stations according to the *legal* judg-
ment for them, according to the law
of Moses the man of God; the priests
splashed the blood *which they received*
from the hand of the Levites. **17** For
*there were* many in the assembly who
had not set themselves apart as holy;
therefore, [a]the Levites *were* over the
slaughter of the Passover *lambs* for
everyone who *was* unclean, in order
to set *them* apart as holy to Yahweh.
**18** For a multitude of the people, [a]*even*
many from Ephraim and Manasseh,
Issachar, and Zebulun, had not
cleansed themselves, [b]yet they ate
the Passover [c]otherwise than what
was written. For Hezekiah prayed
for them, saying, "May Yahweh, *who
is* good, atone **19** [a]for everyone who
prepares his heart to seek God, Yah-
weh, the God of his fathers, though
not according to the *rules* of cleansing
of the sanctuary." **20** So Yahweh heard
Hezekiah and [a]healed the people.
**21** And the sons of Israel present in
Jerusalem [a]celebrated the Feast of
Unleavened Bread *for* seven days with
great gladness, and the Levites and
the priests praised Yahweh day after
day with loud instruments to Yahweh.
**22** Then Hezekiah [a]spoke to the hearts
of all the Levites who showed good
insight *in the things* of Yahweh. So
they ate for the appointed seven days,
sacrificing peace offerings and [b]giving
thanks to Yahweh, the God of their
fathers.

**23** Then the whole assembly [a]took
counsel *to determine* to celebrate
*the feast* another seven days, so
they celebrated the seven days with
gladness. **24** For [a]Hezekiah king of
Judah had contributed to the assem-
bly 1,000 bulls and 7,000 sheep, and
the princes had contributed to the
assembly 1,000 bulls and 10,000
sheep; and [b]a large number of priests
set themselves apart as holy. **25** And
all the assembly of Judah were glad,
with the priests and the Levites and
[a]all the assembly that came from
Israel, both the sojourners who came
from the land of Israel and those
living in Judah. **26** So there was great
gladness in Jerusalem, because there
was nothing like this in Jerusalem
[a]since the days of Solomon the son
of David, king of Israel. **27** Then [a]the
Levitical priests arose and [b]blessed
the people; and their voice was heard
and their prayer came to [c]His holy
habitation, to heaven.

**30:12** [a]2Co 3:5; Php 2:13; Heb 13:20, 21 **30:13** [a]2Chr 30:2 **30:14** [a]2Chr 28:24 [b]2Chr 29:16
**30:15** [a]2Chr 30:2, 3 [b]2Chr 29:34 **30:16** [a]2Chr 35:10, 15 **30:17** [a]2Chr 29:34 **30:18** [a]2Chr 30:11, 25
[b]Nu 9:10 [c]Ex 12:43-49 **30:19** [a]2Chr 19:3 **30:20** [a]Jas 5:16 **30:21** [a]Ex 12:15; 13:6 **30:22** [a]2Chr 32:6
[b]Ezr 10:11 **30:23** [a]1Ki 8:65 **30:24** [a]2Chr 35:7, 8 [b]2Chr 29:34; 30:3 **30:25** [a]2Chr 30:11, 18
**30:26** [a]2Chr 7:8-10 **30:27** [a]2Chr 23:18 [b]Nu 6:23 [c]Dt 26:15; Ps 68:5

31 Now when all this was completed, all Israel who were present went out to the cities of Judah, [a]shattered the pillars, cut the [1]Asherim in pieces, and tore down the high places and the altars throughout all Judah and Benjamin, as well as in Ephraim and Manasseh, until *the destruction* was completed. Then all the sons of Israel returned to their cities, each to his possession.

### Hezekiah Sets Up Priests for Service

**2** And Hezekiah set up [a]the divisions of the priests and the Levites by their divisions, each according to his service, *both* the priests and the Levites, [b]for burnt offerings and for peace offerings, to minister and to give thanks and to praise in the gates of the camp of Yahweh. **3** *He* also *appointed* [a]the king's portion of his goods for the burnt offerings, *namely*, for the morning and evening burnt offerings, and the burnt offerings for the sabbaths and for the new moons and for the appointed times, [b]as it is written in the law of Yahweh. **4** Also he said to the people who lived in Jerusalem to give [a]the portion due to the priests and the Levites, that they might be strong in [b]the law of Yahweh. **5** As soon as the word spread forth, the sons of Israel provided in abundance the first fruits of grain, new wine, oil, honey, and of all the produce of the field; and they brought in abundantly [a]the tithe of all. **6** Now the sons of Israel *and Judah who lived in* the cities of Judah also brought in the tithe of oxen and sheep, and [a]the tithe of the holy gifts which were made holy to Yahweh their God, and put *them* in heaps. **7** In the third month they began to [1]make the heaps, and completed *them* by the seventh month. **8** Then Hezekiah and the rulers came and saw the heaps, and they blessed Yahweh and [a]His people Israel. **9** Then Hezekiah inquired of the priests and the Levites concerning the heaps. **10** And Azariah the chief priest [a]of the house of Zadok said to [1]him, "[b]Since the contributions began to be brought into the house of Yahweh, *there has been* much to eat and be satisfied with and have left over, for Yahweh has blessed His people, and this great quantity is left over."

**11** Then Hezekiah ordered *them* to prepare [a]rooms in the house of Yahweh, and they prepared *them*. **12** And they faithfully brought in the contribution and the tithe and the holy things; and Conaniah the Levite *was* the officer over [a]them and his brother Shimei *was* second. **13** Now Jehiel, Azaziah, Nahath, Asahel, Jerimoth, Jozabad, Eliel, Ismachiah, Mahath, and Benaiah *were* overseers [1]*assisting* at the hand of Conaniah and Shimei his brother by the appointment of King Hezekiah, and [a]Azariah *was* the *chief* officer of the house of God. **14** And Kore the son of Imnah the Levite, the keeper of the eastern *gate, was* over the freewill *offerings* of God, to distribute the contributions for Yahweh and the

◆ **31:1** [a]2Ki 18:4 [1]Wooden symbols of a female deity **31:2** [a]1Chr 24:1 [b]1Chr 23:28-31 **31:3** [a]2Chr 35:7 [b]Nu 28:1-29:40 **31:4** [a]Nu 18:8 [b]Mal 2:7 **31:5** [a]Ne 13:12 **31:6** [a]Lv 27:30; Dt 14:28 **31:7** [1]Lit *found* **31:8** [a]Dt 33:29; Ps 33:12; 144:15 **31:10** [a]1Chr 6:8, 9 [b]Mal 3:10 [1]Lit *him, and he said* **31:11** [a]1Ki 6:5, 8 **31:12** [a]2Chr 35:9 **31:13** [a]2Chr 31:10 [1]Lit *from the hand of*

most holy things. **15** Now *assisting*
[1]by his hand *were* [a]Eden, Miniamin,
Jeshua, Shemaiah, Amariah, and
Shecaniah in [b]the cities of the priests,
to distribute faithfully *their portions*
to their brothers by divisions, whether
great or small, **16** without regard to
their genealogical record, to the males
from [a,1]thirty years old and upward—
everyone who entered the house of
Yahweh [b]for his daily obligations—for
their service in their responsibilities
according to their divisions; **17** as well
as the priests who were recorded
genealogically according to their
fathers' households, and the Levites
[a]from twenty years old and upwards,
by their responsibilities *and* their
divisions. **18** The genealogical record
*included* [1]all their little ones, their
wives, their sons, and their daughters,
for the whole assembly, for they
set themselves apart [2]faithfully
in holiness. **19** Also for the sons of
Aaron the priests *who were* in [a]the
pasture lands of their cities, or in
each and every city, [b]*there were*
men who were designated by name
to distribute portions to every male
among the priests and to everyone
genealogically recorded among the
Levites.

**20** Thus Hezekiah did throughout
all Judah; and [a]he did what *was* good,
right, and true before Yahweh his
God. **21** And every work which he
began in the service of the house of
God in law and in commandment—
to seek his God—he did with all his
heart and [a]succeeded.

### *Sennacherib Invades Judah*

**32** After these [1]acts of faithful-
ness [a]Sennacherib king of
Assyria came and invaded Judah and
encamped against the fortified cities,
and [2]thought to break into them for
himself. **2** Then Hezekiah saw that
Sennacherib had come and that
*he had set* his face to make war on
Jerusalem, **3** and he took counsel with
his commanders and his warriors
to stop up the *supply of* water from
the springs which *were* outside the
city, and they helped him. **4** So many
people gathered [a]and stopped up all
the springs and [b]the stream which
flowed in the midst of the land, say-
ing, "Why should the kings of Assyria
come and find abundant water?"
**5** And he strengthened himself and
[a]rebuilt all the wall that had been
broken down and [1]erected towers on
it, and *built* [b]another outside wall
and strengthened the [c,2]Millo *in* the
city of David, and made weapons
and shields in great number. **6** He
also put military commanders over
the people and gathered them to him
in the square at the city gate, and
[a]spoke to their hearts, saying, **7** "[a]Be
strong and courageous. Do not fear
or be dismayed because of the king
of Assyria nor because of all the mul-
titude that is with him; [b]for the one
with us is greater than the one with
him. **8** With him is *only* [a]an arm of
flesh, but [b]with us is Yahweh our God
to help us and to fight our battles."
And the people were sustained by
the words of Hezekiah king of Judah.

**31:15** [a]2Chr 29:12 [b]Jos 21:9-19 [1]Lit *under his hand* **31:16** [a]1Chr 23:3 [b]Ezr 3:4 [1]Heb *3*
**31:17** [a]1Chr 23:24 **31:18** [1]Lit *with all* [2]Lit *in their faithfulness* **31:19** [a]Lv 25:34; Nu 35:2-5
[b]2Chr 31:12-15 **31:20** [a]2Ki 20:3; 22:2 **31:21** [a]Dt 29:9; Pr 3:9, 10 ◆ **32:1** [a]2Ki 18:13-19, 37; Is 36:1-37:38
[1]Lit *things and this truth* [2]Lit *said* **32:4** [a]2Ki 20:20 [b]2Chr 32:30 **32:5** [a]2Chr 25:23 [b]2Ki 25:4
[c]1Ki 9:24 [1]Lit *raised on the towers* [2]Citadel **32:6** [a]2Chr 30:22 **32:7** [a]1Chr 22:13 [b]2Ki 6:16
**32:8** [a]Jer 17:5 [b]2Chr 20:17

### *Sennacherib Reproaches Yahweh*

**9** After this [a]Sennacherib king of
Assyria sent his servants to Jerusa-
lem while he *was* [1]besieging Lachish
with all his forces with him, against
Hezekiah king of Judah and against
all Judah who *were* at Jerusalem, say-
ing, **10** "Thus says Sennacherib king
of Assyria, 'On what are you trusting
that you are remaining in Jerusalem
under siege? **11** Is not Hezekiah incit-
ing you to give yourselves over to die
by hunger and by thirst, saying, "Yah-
weh our God will deliver us from the
[1]hand of the king of Assyria"? **12** [a]Has
not the same Hezekiah taken away
His high places and His altars, and
said to Judah and [1]Jerusalem, "You
shall worship before one altar, and
on it you shall offer *offerings* up in
smoke"? **13** Do you not know what I
and my fathers have done to all the
peoples of the lands? [a]Were the gods
of the nations of the lands able at all
to deliver their land from my hand?
**14** [a]Who *was there* among all the gods
of these nations which my fathers
devoted to destruction, who could
deliver his people from my hand, that
your God should be able to deliver
you from my hand? **15** So now, do not
let Hezekiah deceive you or incite you
like this, and do not believe him, for
[a]no god of any nation or kingdom
was able to deliver his people from
my hand or from the hand of my
fathers. How much less will your God
deliver you from my hand?'"

**16** His servants spoke further
against Yahweh God and against *His
servant Hezekiah.* **17** He also wrote
letters to [1]reproach Yahweh, the God
of Israel, and to speak against Him,
saying, "[a]As the gods of the nations
of the lands [2]have not delivered their
people from my hand, so the God of
Hezekiah will not deliver His people
from my hand." **18** [a]And they called
this out with a loud voice in the
language of Judah to the people of
Jerusalem who were on the wall, to
instill fear and terrify them, so that
they might capture the city. **19** And
they spoke [1]of the God of Jerusalem
as of [a]the gods of the peoples of the
earth, the work of men's hands.

### *Yahweh Wipes Out the Men of Assyria*

**20** But King Hezekiah and Isaiah the
prophet, the son of Amoz, prayed
about this and cried out to heaven.
**21** And Yahweh sent an angel who
wiped out every mighty man of valor,
ruler, and commander in the camp of
the king of Assyria. So he returned
[1]in shame to his own land. And he
entered the house of his god, and
some of [2]his own children caused
him to fall there by the sword. **22** So
Yahweh [a]saved Hezekiah and the
inhabitants of Jerusalem from the
hand of Sennacherib the king of As-
syria and from the hand of all *others,*
and He [1]guided them on every side.
**23** And [a]many were bringing presents
to Yahweh at Jerusalem and precious
things to Hezekiah king of Judah, so
that [b]he was lifted up in the sight of
all nations thereafter.

**24** [a]*In* those days Hezekiah be-
came sick to the point of death; and

---

**32:9** [a]2Ki 18:17 [1]Lit *against* **32:11** [1]Lit *palm* **32:12** [a]2Chr 31:1 [1]Lit *Jerusalem, saying,* **32:13** [a]2Ki 18:33-35 **32:14** [a]Is 10:9-11 **32:15** [a]Ex 5:2; Is 36:18-20; Da 3:15 **32:17** [a]2Chr 32:14 [1]Or *defy,* cf. 1Sa 17:26 [2]Lit *who have* **32:18** [a]2Ki 18:28 **32:19** [a]Ps 115:4-8 [1]Lit *to* **32:21** [1]Lit *in shame of face* [2]Lit *those who come from his loins* **32:22** [a]Is 31:5 [1]Or *gave them rest* **32:23** [a]2Sa 8:10 [b]2Chr 1:1 **32:24** [a]2Ki 20:1-11; Is 38:1-8

he prayed to Yahweh, and [1]Yahweh
spoke to him and gave him a mirac-
ulous sign. **25** But Hezekiah gave no
return for the benefit [1]he received,
[a]because his heart was [2]proud;
[b]therefore wrath came on him and
on Judah and Jerusalem. **26** However,
[a]Hezekiah [1]humbled the pride of his
heart, both he and the inhabitants
of Jerusalem, so that the wrath of
Yahweh did not come on them in the
days of Hezekiah.

**27** Now Hezekiah had abundant
riches and honor; and he made for
himself treasuries for silver, gold,
precious stones, spices, shields,
and all kinds of desirable articles,
**28** storehouses also for the produce
of grain, wine, and oil, stalls for all
kinds of cattle, and [1]sheepfolds for
the flocks. **29** He also made cities
for himself and acquired flocks and
herds in abundance, for [a]God had
given him exceedingly abundant
[1]wealth. **30** And it was Hezekiah
who [a]stopped the upper outlet of
the waters of [b]Gihon and directed
them to the west side of the city of
David. And Hezekiah succeeded in all
that he did. **31** Even *in the matter of*
[a]the envoys of the rulers of Babylon,
who sent to him to inquire of [b]the
miraculous sign that had happened
in the land, God left him *alone only*
[c]to test him, that He might know all
that was in his heart.

**32** Now the rest of the acts of
Hezekiah and his deeds of loving-
kindness, behold, they are written
in the vision of Isaiah the prophet,
the son of Amoz, in the Book of
the Kings of Judah and Israel. **33** So
Hezekiah slept with his fathers, and
they buried him in the [1]upper section
of the tombs of the sons of David;
and all Judah and the inhabitants of
Jerusalem [a]honored him at his death.
And Manasseh his son became king
in his place.

### *Manasseh Reigns over Judah*

**33** [a]Manasseh was twelve years
old when he became king,
and he reigned fifty-five years in
Jerusalem. **2** [a]And he did what was
evil in the sight of Yahweh, according
to the abominations of the nations
whom Yahweh dispossessed before
the sons of Israel. **3** Indeed, [a]he
rebuilt the high places which Heze-
kiah his father had torn down; and
[b]he erected altars for the Baals and
made [1]Asherim, and worshiped all
the host of heaven and served them.
**4** [a]And he built altars in the house
of Yahweh, of which Yahweh had
said, "[b]In Jerusalem My name shall
be forever." **5** Indeed, he built altars
for all the host of heaven in [a]the two
courts of the house of Yahweh. **6** [a]He
even made his sons pass through the
fire in the valley of Ben-hinnom; and
he practiced soothsaying, interpreted
omens, practiced sorcery, and [b]dealt
with mediums and spiritists. He did
much that was evil in the sight of
Yahweh, provoking Him *to anger*.
**7** Then he put [a]the graven image of
the [1]idol, which he had made, in the
house of God, of which God had said

---

**32:24** [1]Lit *He* **32:25** [a]2Chr 26:16; 32:31 [b]2Chr 24:18 [1]Lit *to him* [2]Lit *high* **32:26** [a]Jer 26:18, 19 [1]Lit *humbled himself in* **32:28** [1]As in ancient versions; Heb *flocks for the sheepfolds* **32:29** [a]1Chr 29:12 [1]Lit *possessions* **32:30** [a]2Ki 20:20 [b]1Ki 1:33 **32:31** [a]2Ki 20:12; Is 39:1 [b]2Chr 32:24; Is 38:7, 8 [c]Dt 8:16 **32:33** [a]Ps 112:6; Pr 10:7 [1]Or *ascent to* ◆ **33:1** [a]2Ki 21:1-9 **33:2** [a]2Chr 28:3; Jer 15:4 **33:3** [a]2Chr 31:1 [b]Dt 16:21; 2Ki 23:5, 6 [1]Wooden symbols of a female deity **33:4** [a]2Chr 28:24 [b]2Sa 7:13; 2Chr 7:16 **33:5** [a]2Chr 4:9 **33:6** [a]2Chr 28:3 [b]Lv 19:31; 20:27 **33:7** [a]2Chr 33:15 [1]Or *figure*

to David and to Solomon his son, “[b]In
this house and in Jerusalem, which
I have chosen from all the tribes of
Israel, I will put My name forever.
**8** And I will not again remove the
foot of Israel from the land [a]which
I have set up for your fathers, if only
they will be careful to do all that I
have commanded them according
to all the law, the statutes and the
judgments *given* by the hand of
Moses.” **9** Thus Manasseh led Judah
and the inhabitants of Jerusalem
astray in order to do more evil than
the nations whom Yahweh destroyed
before the sons of Israel.

### *Manasseh Removes Foreign Idols*

**10** Then Yahweh spoke to Manasseh
and his people, but [a]they paid no
attention. **11** [a]Therefore Yahweh
brought the commanders of the army
of the king of Assyria against them,
and they captured Manasseh with
[1]hooks, [b]bound him with bronze
*chains*, and took him to Babylon.
**12** And when [a]he was in distress,
he entreated Yahweh his God and
[b]humbled himself greatly before the
God of his fathers. **13** Then he prayed
to Him, and [a]He was moved by his
entreaty and heard his supplication,
and returned him back to Jerusalem
to his kingdom. Then Manasseh
[b]knew that Yahweh *was* God.

**14** Afterwards, he built the outer
wall of the city of David on the west
side of [a]Gihon, in the valley, even to
the entrance of the [b]Fish Gate; and he
encircled the [c]Ophel *with it* and made
it very high. *Then he put military*
commanders in all the fortified
cities of Judah. **15** He also [a]removed
the foreign gods and the [1]idol from
the house of Yahweh, as well as all the
altars which he had built on the
mountain of the house of Yahweh
and in Jerusalem, and he threw
*them* outside the city. **16** And he set
up the altar of Yahweh and sacrificed
[a]peace offerings and thank offerings
on it; and he said for Judah to serve
Yahweh, the God of Israel. **17** Never-
theless [a]the people still sacrificed
in the high places, *although* only to
Yahweh their God.

**18** Now the rest of the acts of
Manasseh, even [a]his prayer to his
God, and the words of [b]the seers who
spoke to him in the name of Yahweh,
the God of Israel, behold, they are
among the chronicles of the kings of
[c]Israel. **19** His prayer also and [a]*how*
*God* was entreated by him, and all
his sin, his unfaithfulness, and [b]the
sites on which he built high places
and erected the [1]Asherim and the
graven images, before he humbled
himself, behold, they are written in
the chronicles of the [2]Hozai. **20** And
Manasseh slept with his fathers, and
they buried him in his own house.
And Amon his son became king in
his place.

### *Amon Reigns over Judah*

**21** [a]Amon *was* twenty-two years
old when he became king, and he
reigned two years in Jerusalem.
**22** And he did what was evil in the
*sight of* Yahweh, as Manasseh his fa-
ther [a]had done, and Amon sacrificed

**33:7** [b]1Ki 9:3-5; 2Chr 7:16; 33:4 **33:8** [a]2Sa 7:10 **33:10** [a]Ne 9:29; Jer 25:4 **33:11** [a]Dt 28:36 [b]2Chr 36:6 [1]Hooks put through the nose, cf. 2Ki 19:28 **33:12** [a]Ps 118:5; 120:1; 130:1, 2 [b]2Chr 32:26 **33:13** [a]1Chr 5:20; Ezr 8:23 [b]Da 4:32 **33:14** [a]1Ki 1:33 [b]Ne 3:3 [c]2Chr 27:3 **33:15** [a]2Chr 33:3-7 [1]Or *figure* **33:16** [a]Lv 7:11-18 **33:17** [a]2Chr 32:12 **33:18** [a]2Chr 33:12, 13 [b]2Chr 33:10 [c]2Chr 21:2 **33:19** [a]2Chr 33:13 [b]2Chr 33:3 [1]Wooden symbols of a female deity [2]Gr *seers* **33:21** [a]2Ki 21:19-24 **33:22** [a]2Chr 33:2-7

to all [b]the graven images which his
father Manasseh had made, and he
served them. **23** Moreover, he did not
humble himself before Yahweh [a]as
his father Manasseh had humbled
himself, but Amon multiplied guilt.
**24** Then [a]his servants conspired
against him and put him to death in
his own house. **25** Then the people of
the land struck down all those who
had conspired against King Amon,
and the people of the land made
Josiah his son king in his place.

### *Josiah Reigns over Judah*

**34** [a]Josiah was eight years old
when he became king, and
he reigned thirty-one years in Jeru-
salem. **2** [a]And he did what was right
in the sight of Yahweh and walked in
the ways of his father David and did
not turn aside to the right or to the
left. **3** Now in the eighth year of his
reign while he was still a youth, he
began to [a]seek the God of his father
David; and in the twelfth year he
began [b]to cleanse Judah and Jerusa-
lem of the high places, the Asherim,
the graven images, and the molten
images. **4** And they tore down the
altars of the Baals in his presence,
and [a]the incense altars that were
high above them he cut in pieces;
also the Asherim, the graven images,
and the molten images he broke in
pieces and [b]ground to powder and
scattered *it* on the graves of those
who had sacrificed to them. **5** Then
[a]he burned the bones of the priests
on their altars and cleansed Judah
and Jerusalem. **6** [a]And in the cities
of Manasseh, Ephraim, Simeon, even
as far as Naphtali, in their surround-
ing [1]ruins, **7** he also tore down the
altars and [a]beat the Asherim and
the graven images into powder, and
cut in pieces all the incense altars
throughout the land of Israel. Then
he returned to Jerusalem.

### *Josiah Repairs the House of Yahweh*

**8** [a]Now in the eighteenth year of his
reign, when he had cleansed the land
and the house, he sent Shaphan the
son of Azaliah, and Maaseiah [b]an
official of the city, and Joah the son
of Joahaz the recorder, to repair the
house of Yahweh his God. **9** And they
came to [a]Hilkiah the high priest and
gave him the money that was brought
into the house of God, which the
Levites, the [1]doorkeepers, had gath-
ered from the hand of [b]Manasseh
and Ephraim, and from all the rem-
nant of Israel, and from all Judah
and Benjamin and the inhabitants
of Jerusalem. **10** Then they gave *it*
into the hand of [1]those who did the
work, who had the oversight of the
house of Yahweh; and those who did
the work, who were doing *this* in the
house of Yahweh, [2]used it to restore
and repair the house. **11** They in turn
gave *it* to the craftsmen and to the
builders to buy hewn stone and tim-
ber for clamps and to make beams
for the houses [a]which the kings of
Judah had let go to ruin. **12** [a]And the
men did the work faithfully with
foremen over them to direct: Jahath
and Obadiah, the Levites of the sons
of Merari, Zechariah and Meshullam

**33:22** [b]2Chr 34:3, 4 **33:23** [a]2Chr 33:12, 19 **33:24** [a]2Chr 25:27 ◆ **34:1** [a]2Ki 22:1, 2; Jer 1:2; 3:6 **34:2** [a]2Chr 29:2 **34:3** [a]2Chr 15:2; Pr 8:17 [b]1Ki 13:2; 2Chr 33:22 **34:4** [a]2Ki 23:4, 5, 11 [b]Ex 32:20 **34:5** [a]1Ki 13:2; 2Ki 23:20 **34:6** [a]2Ki 23:15, 19 [1]Or *waste places* **34:7** [a]2Chr 31:1 **34:8** [a]2Ki 22:3-20 [b]2Chr 18:25 **34:9** [a]2Chr 35:8 [b]2Chr 30:10, 18 [1]Lit *guardians of the threshold* **34:10** [1]Lit *the one who did* [2]Lit *gave* **34:11** [a]2Chr 33:4-7 **34:12** [a]2Ki 12:15

of the sons of the Kohathites, and
[b]the Levites, all who were skillful
with musical instruments. **13** *They
were* also over [a]those who carried
loads, and directed all those who did
the work from service to service; and
*some* of the Levites *were* scribes and
officials and gatekeepers.

### *Hilkiah Finds the Book of the Law*

**14** When they were taking out the
money which had been brought into
the house of Yahweh, [a]Hilkiah the
priest found the book of the law of
Yahweh *given* by the hand of Moses.
**15** So Hilkiah answered and said to
Shaphan the scribe, "I have found the
book of the law in the house of Yah-
weh." And Hilkiah gave the book to
Shaphan. **16** Then Shaphan brought
the book to the king and furthermore
[1]responded to the king with a word,
saying, "Everything that was given
to the hand of your servants they
are doing. **17** They have also poured
out the money that was found in the
house of Yahweh, and have given it
into the hand of the supervisors and
those who did the work." **18** More-
over, Shaphan the scribe told the
king saying, "Hilkiah the priest gave
me a book." And Shaphan read from
it in the presence of the king.

**19** Now it happened that when the
king heard [a]the words of the law, [b]he
tore his clothes. **20** Then the king
commanded Hilkiah, Ahikam the
son of Shaphan, [1]Abdon the son of
Micah, Shaphan the scribe, and Asa-
iah the king's servant, saying, **21** "Go,
*inquire of Yahweh* for me and those
who are left in Israel and in Judah,
concerning the words of the book
which has been found, for [a]great is
the wrath of Yahweh which is poured
out against us, because our fathers
have not kept the word of Yahweh,
to do according to all that is written
in this book."

### *Josiah Will Not See Yahweh's Wrath*

**22** So Hilkiah and *those* whom the king
[1]had told went to Huldah the prophet-
ess, the wife of Shallum the son
of [2]Tokhath, the son of Hasrah, keep-
er of the wardrobe (now she lived in
Jerusalem in the Second Quarter);
and they spoke to her regarding this.
**23** And she said to them, "Thus says
Yahweh, the God of Israel, 'Say to
the man who sent you to Me, **24** thus
says Yahweh, "Behold, [a]I am bringing
evil on this place and on its inhab-
itants, *even* all [b]the curses written
in the book which they have read in
the presence of the king of Judah.
**25** [a]Because they have forsaken Me
and have burned incense to other
gods that they might provoke Me
to anger with all the works of their
hands, therefore My wrath will be
poured out against this place, and
it shall not be quenched."' **26** But to
the king of Judah who sent you to
inquire of Yahweh, thus you shall
say to him, 'Thus says Yahweh, the
God of Israel, "*Regarding* the words
which you have heard, **27** [a]because
your heart was soft and you humbled
yourself before God when you heard
*His words* against this place and
against its inhabitants, and *because*

**34:12** [b]1Chr 25:1 **34:13** [a]Ne 4:10 **34:14** [a]2Chr 34:9 **34:16** [1]Lit *returned* **34:19** [a]Dt 28:3-68 [b]Jos 7:6 **34:20** [1]In 2Ki 22:12, *Achbor, son of Micaiah* **34:21** [a]2Chr 29:8 **34:22** [1]As in Gr [2]In 2Ki 22:14 *Tikvah, son of Harhas* **34:24** [a]2Chr 36:14-20 [b]Dt 28:15-68 **34:25** [a]2Chr 33:3 **34:27** [a]2Ki 22:19; 2Chr 12:7; 32:26

you humbled yourself before Me,
tore your clothes and wept before
Me, I truly have heard you," declares
Yahweh. **28** "Behold, I will gather you
to your fathers, and you will be gath-
ered to your grave in peace, so your
eyes will not see all the evil which
I will bring on this place and on its
inhabitants."'" So they brought back
word to the king.
**29** [a]Then the king sent and
gathered all the elders of Judah and
Jerusalem. **30** And the king went up
to the house of Yahweh and [a]all the
men of Judah, and the inhabitants
of Jerusalem, and the priests and
the Levites and all the people, from
the greatest to the least; and he read
in their hearing all the words of the
book of the covenant which was
found in the house of Yahweh.

### *Josiah Cuts a Covenant with Yahweh*

**31** Then the king [a]stood in his place
and [b]cut a covenant before Yahweh,
to walk after Yahweh, and to keep His
commandments and His testimonies
and His statutes with all his heart
and with all his soul, to do the words
of the covenant that were written in
this book. **32** Moreover, he made all
who were present in Jerusalem and
Benjamin to stand *with him.* So the
inhabitants of Jerusalem did accord-
ing to the covenant of God, the God
of their fathers. **33** And Josiah [a]took
away all the abominations from all
the lands belonging to the sons of
Israel, and made all who were present
in Israel to serve Yahweh their God.
Throughout his [1]lifetime they did not
turn away from following Yahweh,
the God of their fathers.

### *Josiah Celebrates the Passover*

**35** Then Josiah [a]celebrated the
Passover to Yahweh in Jeru-
salem, and [b]they slaughtered the
Passover *animals* on the fourteenth
*day* of the first month. **2** And he
caused the priests to stand in their
responsibilities and [a]strengthened
them in the service of the house of
Yahweh. **3** He also said to [a]the Levites
who provided understanding to all
Israel *and* who were holy to Yahweh,
"Put the holy ark in the house which
Solomon the son of David king of
Israel built; [b]it will be a burden on
*your* shoulders no longer. Now serve
Yahweh your God and His people
Israel. **4** [a]So prepare *yourselves* by your
fathers' households in your divisions,
according to the writing of David king
of Israel and [b]according to the writing
of his son Solomon. **5** Moreover,
[a]stand in the holy place according to
the sections of the fathers' households
of your brothers the [1]lay people, and
according to the Levites, by division
of a father's household. **6** Now
[a]slaughter the Passover *animals*,
[b]sanctify yourselves and prepare
for your brothers to do according to
the word of Yahweh by the hand of
Moses."
**7** And Josiah contributed to the
lay people, to all who were present,
flocks of lambs and young goats, all
for the Passover offerings, number-
ing 30,000 plus 3,000 bulls; these
were from the king's possessions.

---

**34:29** [a]2Ki 23:1-3 **34:30** [a]Ne 8:1-3 **34:31** [a]2Ki 11:14; 23:3; 2Chr 30:16 [b]2Chr 23:16; 29:10 **34:33** [a]2Chr 34:3-7 [1]Lit *days* ◆**35:1** [a]2Ki 23:21 [b]Ex 12:6; Nu 9:3 **35:2** [a]2Chr 29:11 **35:3** [a]2Chr 17:8, 9; Ne 8:7 [b]1Chr 23:26 **35:4** [a]1Chr 9:10-13 [b]2Chr 8:14 **35:5** [a]Ezr 6:18 [1]Lit *sons of the people*, so in ch **35:6** [a]2Chr 35:1 [b]2Chr 29:5

**8** His officials also contributed a
freewill offering to the people, the
priests, and the Levites. Hilkiah and
Zechariah and Jehiel, [a]the officers of
the house of God, gave to the priests
for the Passover offerings 2,600 *from
the flocks* and 300 bulls. **9** [a]Conaniah
also, and Shemaiah and Nethanel,
his brothers, and Hashabiah and
Jeiel and Jozabad, the [1]officials of the
Levites, contributed to the Levites for
the Passover offerings 5,000 *from the
flocks* and 500 bulls.

**10** So the service was prepared, and
[a]the priests stood at their stations
and the Levites by their divisions
according to the king's command-
ment. **11** [a]And [1]they slaughtered the
Passover *animals*, and while [b]the
priests splashed [2]the blood *received*
from their hand, [c]the Levites skinned
*them*. **12** Then they took away *the
portions for* the burnt offerings that
*they* might give them to the sections
of the fathers' households of the lay
people to bring near to Yahweh, as
it is written in the book of Moses.
*They did* this also with the bulls.
**13** So [a]they roasted the Passover
*animals* on the fire according to
the *legal* judgment, and they boiled
[b]the holy things in pots, in kettles,
in pans, and carried *them* speedily
to all the lay people. **14** Afterwards
they prepared for themselves and
for the priests, because the priests,
the sons of Aaron, *were* offering
the burnt offerings and the fat until
night; therefore the Levites prepared
for themselves and for the priests,
the *sons of Aaron*. **15** The singers,
the sons of Asaph, *were* also at their
stations [a]according to the command-
ment of David, Asaph, Heman, and
Jeduthun the king's seer; and [b]the
gatekeepers at each gate did not
have to turn aside from their service,
because the Levites their brothers
prepared for them.

**16** So all the service of Yahweh was
prepared on that day to celebrate the
Passover, and to offer burnt offerings
on the altar of Yahweh according to
the commandment of King Josiah.
**17** Thus [a]the sons of Israel who were
present celebrated the Passover at
that time, and the Feast of Unleav-
ened Bread seven days. **18** [a]And there
had not been celebrated a Passover
like it in Israel from the days of
Samuel the prophet; nor had any of
the kings of Israel celebrated such a
Passover as Josiah celebrated with
the priests, the Levites, all Judah
and Israel who were present, and the
inhabitants of Jerusalem. **19** In the
eighteenth year of Josiah's reign, this
Passover was celebrated.

### *Josiah Dies in War*

**20** [a]After all this, when Josiah had
set the [1]house in order, Neco king
of Egypt went up to make war at
[b]Carchemish on the Euphrates,
and Josiah went out to meet him.
**21** But [1]Neco sent messengers to
him, saying, "[a]What have I to do
with you, O King of Judah? *I am*
not *coming* against you today but
against the house with which I am
at war, and God has said for me to
*hurry*. Stop for your own sake from
*interfering with* God who is with
me, so that He will not bring you to

---

**35:8** [a]2Chr 31:13 **35:9** [a]2Chr 31:12 [1]Or *leaders* **35:10** [a]2Chr 35:5 **35:11** [a]2Chr 35:1, 6 [b]2Chr 29:22 [c]2Chr 29:34 [1]The Levites [2]As in Gr **35:13** [a]Ex 12:8, 9 [b]Lv 6:28 **35:15** [a]1Chr 25:1 [b]1Chr 26:12-19 **35:17** [a]Ex 12:1-20; 2Chr 30:21 **35:18** [a]2Ki 23:21; 2Chr 30:5 **35:20** [a]2Ki 23:29, 30 [b]Is 10:9; Jer 46:2 [1]Or *temple* **35:21** [a]2Chr 25:19 [1]Lit *he*

ruin." **22** However, Josiah would not
turn [1]away from him, but [a]disguised
himself in order to make war
with him; nor did he listen to the
words of Neco [b]from the mouth
of God, but came to make war on
the plain of [c]Megiddo. **23** Then the
archers shot King Josiah, and the
king said to his servants, "Take me
away, for I am badly wounded."
**24** So his servants took him out of
the chariot and drove him in the
second chariot which he had, and
brought him to Jerusalem [1]where
he died, and he was buried in the
tombs of his fathers. [a]And all Judah
and Jerusalem mourned for Josiah.
**25** Then [a]Jeremiah chanted a *lament*
for Josiah. And all the male and
female singers speak about Josiah
in their lamentations to this day.
And they made them a statute in
Israel; behold, they are also written
in the lamentations. **26** Now the rest
of the acts of Josiah and his deeds
of lovingkindness according to what
was written in the law of Yahweh,
**27** and his acts, first to last, behold,
they are written in the Book of the
Kings of Israel and Judah.

### *Joahaz Reigns over Judah*

**36** [a]Then the people of the land
took [b,1]Joahaz the son of
Josiah, and made him king in place
of his father in Jerusalem. **2** [1]Joahaz
was twenty-three years old when he
became king, and he reigned three
months in Jerusalem. **3** Then the king
of Egypt had him removed in Jerusa-
lem and imposed on the land a fine
of one hundred [1]talents of silver and
one talent of gold. **4** Then the king
of Egypt made Eliakim his brother
king over Judah and Jerusalem, and
changed his name to Jehoiakim. But
[a]Neco took Joahaz his brother and
brought him to Egypt.

### *Jehoiakim Reigns over Judah*

**5** [a]Jehoiakim was twenty-five years
old when he became king, and he
reigned eleven years in Jerusalem;
and he did what was evil in the sight
of Yahweh his God. **6** Nebuchadnez-
zar king of Babylon came up [a]against
him and [b]bound him with bronze
*chains* to lead him off to Babylon.
**7** [a]Nebuchadnezzar also brought
*some* of the articles of the house of
Yahweh to Babylon and put them in
his temple at Babylon. **8** [a]Now the
rest of the acts of Jehoiakim and
[1]the abominations which he did,
and what was found against him,
behold, they are written in the Book
of the Kings of Israel and Judah. And
Jehoiachin his son became king in
his place.

### *Jehoiachin Reigns over Judah*

**9** [a]Jehoiachin was eight years old
when he became king, and he
reigned three months and ten days
in Jerusalem, and he did what was
evil in the sight of Yahweh. **10** [a]And
at the turn of the year King Nebu-
chadnezzar sent and brought him to
Babylon with the valuable articles of
the house of Yahweh, and he made
his relative [b]Zedekiah king over
Judah and Jerusalem.

**35:22** [a]2Chr 18:29 [b]2Chr 35:21 [c]Jdg 5:19 [1]Lit *his face* **35:24** [a]Zec 12:11 [1]Lit *and* **35:25** [a]Jer 22:10; Lam 4:20 ◆ **36:1** [a]2Ki 23:30-34 [b]Jer 22:11 [1]Lit *Jehoahaz*, cf. 36:2; 2Ki 23:30 **36:2** [1]Shortened form of Jehoahaz, cf. 36:1; 2Ki 23:30 **36:3** [1]A talent was approx. 75 lb. or 34 kg **36:4** [a]Jer 22:10-12 **36:5** [a]2Ki 23:36, 37; Jer 22:13-19; 26:1; 35:1 **36:6** [a]2Ki 24:1; Jer 25:1-9 [b]2Chr 33:11 **36:7** [a]2Ki 24:13 **36:8** [a]2Ki 24:5 [1]Lit *his* **36:9** [a]2Ki 24:8-17 **36:10** [a]2Sa 11:1; Jer 22:25; 24:1; 29:1; Eze 17:12 [b]Jer 37:1

### *Zedekiah Reigns over Judah*

**11** [a]Zedekiah was twenty-one years old when he became king, and he reigned eleven years in Jerusalem. **12** And he did what was evil in the sight of Yahweh his God; [a]he did not humble himself [b]before Jeremiah the prophet *who spoke* from the mouth of Yahweh. **13** [a]He also rebelled against King Nebuchadnezzar who had made him swear *allegiance* by God. But [b]he stiffened his neck and hardened his heart against turning to Yahweh, the God of Israel. **14** Furthermore, all the leaders of the priests and the people were very unfaithful *following* all the abominations of the nations; and they defiled the house of Yahweh which He had set apart as holy in Jerusalem.

### *The Chaldeans Destroy Jerusalem*

**15** And Yahweh, the God of their fathers, [a]sent *word* to them [1]again and again by the hand of His messengers, because He had compassion on His people and on His habitation; **16** but they *continually* [a]mocked the messengers of God, [b]despised His words and scoffed at His prophets, [c]until the wrath of Yahweh arose against His people, until there was no remedy. **17** [a]Therefore He brought up against them the king of the Chaldeans who killed their choice men with the sword in the house of their sanctuary, and had no compassion on choice man or virgin, old man or infirm; He gave *them* all into his hand. **18** [a]And all the articles of the house of God, great and small, and the treasures of the house of Yahweh, and the treasures of the king and of his officials, he brought *them* all to Babylon. **19** Then [a]they burned the house of God and tore down the wall of Jerusalem, and burned all its palaces with fire and destroyed all its valuable articles. **20** And those who had escaped from the sword he [a]took away into exile to Babylon; and [b]they were slaves to him and to his sons until the rule of the kingdom of Persia, **21** [a]to fulfill the word of Yahweh by the mouth of Jeremiah, until [b]the land had made up for its sabbaths. [c]All the days of its desolation it kept sabbath [d,1]until seventy years were fulfilled.

### *The Proclamation of Cyrus*

**22** [a]Now in the first year of Cyrus king of Persia—in order to complete the word of Yahweh [b]by the mouth of Jeremiah—Yahweh [c]stirred up the spirit of Cyrus king of Persia, so that he had a proclamation pass throughout all his kingdom, and also *put it* in writing, saying, **23** "Thus says Cyrus king of Persia,

'Yahweh, the God of heaven,
has given me all the kingdoms
of the earth, and He has
appointed me to build Him
a house in Jerusalem, which
is in Judah. Whoever there is
among you of all His people,
may Yahweh his God be with
him, and let him go up!'"

---

**36:11** [a]*2Ki 24:18-20; Jer 27:1; 28:1; 52:1* **36:12** [a]2Chr 33:23 [b]Jer 21:3-7 **36:13** [a]Jer 52:3; Eze 17:15 [b]*2Chr 30:8* **36:15** [a]Jer 7:13; 25:3 [1]Lit *rising up early and sending* them *out* **36:16** [a]2Chr 30:10; Jer 5:12, 13 [b]Pr 1:24-32 [c]Ezr 5:12 **36:17** [a]2Ki 25:1-7; Jer 21:1-10 **36:18** [a]2Chr 36:7, 10 **36:19** [a]1Ki 9:8; 2Ki 25:9; Jer 52:13 **36:20** [a]2Ki 25:11 [b]Jer 27:7 **36:21** [a]Jer 29:10 [b]Lv 26:34 [c]Lv 25:4 [d]Jer 25:11 [1]Lit *to fulfill seventy years* **36:22** [a]Ezr 1:1-3 [b]Jer 25:12; 29:10 [c]Is 44:28

*The Book of*

# EZRA

### *The Proclamation of Cyrus*

1 [a]Now in the first year of Cyrus
king of Persia—in order to com-
plete the word of [1]Yahweh from the
mouth of Jeremiah—Yahweh stirred
up the spirit of Cyrus king of Persia,
so that he [b]had a proclamation pass
throughout all his kingdom, and also
*put it* in writing, saying:
2 "Thus says Cyrus king of Persia,
'Yahweh, the God of heaven,
has given me all the kingdoms
of the earth, and [a]He has
appointed me to build Him a
house in Jerusalem, which is
in Judah. **3** Whoever there is
among you of all His people,
may his God be with him!
Let him go up to Jerusalem
which is in Judah and rebuild
the house of Yahweh, the
God of Israel; [a]He is the
God who is in Jerusalem.
**4** So everyone who remains,
at whatever place he may
sojourn, let the men of [1]that
place support him with silver
and gold, with goods and
cattle, together with a freewill
offering for the house of God
which is in Jerusalem.'"

### *Articles from Yahweh's House Brought to Jerusalem*

**5** Then the heads of fathers' *house-
holds* of Judah and Benjamin and the
priests and the Levites arose, [a]*that
is* of everyone whose spirit God had
stirred to go up to rebuild the house
of Yahweh which is in Jerusalem. **6** All
those around them [a,1]strengthened
them with articles of silver, with
gold, with possessions, with cattle,
and with precious things, aside
from all that was given as a freewill
offering. **7** [a]Also King Cyrus brought
out the articles of the house of Yah-
weh, [b]which Nebuchadnezzar had
brought out from Jerusalem and put
in the house of his gods; **8** and Cyrus,
king of Persia, had them brought
out by the hand of Mithredath the
treasurer, and he counted them
out to [a]Sheshbazzar, the prince of
Judah. **9** Now this *was* their number:
30 [a]gold dishes, 1,000 silver dishes,
29 [1]duplicates; **10** 30 gold bowls, 410
silver bowls of a second *kind and*
1,000 other articles. **11** All the articles
of gold and silver *numbered* 5,400.
Sheshbazzar brought them all up
with the exiles who went up from
Babylon to Jerusalem.

### *The Exiles Who Returned*

2 [a]Now these are the [1]people of
the province who came up out
of the captivity of the exiles whom
Nebuchadnezzar the king of Babylon
had taken away into exile to Babylon,
and who returned to Jerusalem and
Judah, each to his city. **2** [1]These came
with Zerubbabel, Jeshua, Nehemi-
ah, [2]Seraiah, [3]Reelaiah, Mordecai,

---

◆ **1:1** [a]2Chr 36:22; Jer 25:12; 29:10 [b]Ezr 5:13 [1]The personal covenant name of God, a form of I AM WHO I AM, cf. Ex 3:14-15 **1:2** [a]Is 44:28; 45:1, 12, 13 **1:3** [a]1Ki 8:23; 18:39; Is 37:16; Da 6:26 **1:4** [1]Lit *his* **1:5** [a]Ezr 1:1, 2 **1:6** [a]Ne 6:9; Is 35:3 [1]Lit *strengthened their hands* **1:7** [a]Ezr 5:14; 6:5 [b]2Ki 24:13; 2Chr 36:7 **1:8** [a]Ezr 5:14 **1:9** [a]Ezr 8:27 [1]Heb obscure; other possible meanings are *knives, censers* ◆ **2:1** [a]2Ki 24:14-16; 25:11; 2Chr 36:20; Ne 7:6-73 [1]Lit *sons* **2:2** [1]Lit *Who* [2]In Ne 7:7, *Azariah* [3]In Ne 7:7, *Raamiah*

Bilshan, [4]Mispar, Bigvai, [5]Rehum, *and* Baanah.
The number of the men of the people of Israel:
3 the sons of Parosh, 2,172;
4 the sons of Shephatiah, 372;
5 the sons of [a]Arah, 775;
6 the sons of [a]Pahath-moab of the sons of Jeshua *and* Joab, 2,812;
7 the sons of Elam, 1,254;
8 the sons of Zattu, 945;
9 the sons of Zaccai, 760;
10 the sons of [1]Bani, 642;
11 the sons of Bebai, 623;
12 the sons of Azgad, 1,222;
13 the sons of [a]Adonikam, 666;
14 the sons of Bigvai, 2,056;
15 the sons of Adin, 454;
16 the sons of Ater of Hezekiah, 98;
17 the sons of Bezai, 323;
18 the sons of [1]Jorah, 112;
19 the sons of Hashum, 223;
20 the sons of [1]Gibbar, 95;
21 the sons of [a]Bethlehem, 123;
22 the men of Netophah, 56;
23 the men of Anathoth, 128;
24 the sons of [1]Azmaveth, 42;
25 the sons of [1]Kiriath-arim, Chephirah and Beeroth, 743;
26 the sons of [a]Ramah and Geba, 621;
27 the men of Michmas, 122;
28 the men of Bethel and Ai, 223;
29 the sons of Nebo, 52;
30 the sons of Magbish, 156;
31 the sons of the other Elam, 1,254;
32 the *sons of Harim, 320;*
33 the sons of Lod, Hadid and Ono, 725;
34 the [1]men of [a]Jericho, 345;
35 the sons of Senaah, 3,630.
36 [a]The priests:
the sons of Jedaiah of the house of Jeshua, 973;
37 the sons of [a]Immer, 1,052;
38 [a]the sons of Pashhur, 1,247;
39 the sons of [a]Harim, 1,017.
40 The Levites:
the sons of Jeshua and Kadmiel, of the sons of [1]Hodaviah, 74.
41 The singers:
the sons of Asaph, 128.
42 The sons of the gatekeepers:
the sons of Shallum, the sons of Ater, the sons of Talmon, the sons of Akkub, the sons of Hatita, the sons of Shobai, in all 139.
43 The [a]temple servants:
the sons of Ziha, the sons of Hasupha, the sons of Tabbaoth,
44 the sons of Keros, the sons of [1]Siaha, the sons of Padon,
45 the sons of Lebanah, the sons of Hagabah, the sons of Akkub,
46 the sons of Hagab, the sons of Shalmai, the sons of Hanan,
47 the sons of Giddel, the sons of Gahar, the sons of Reaiah,
48 the sons of Rezin, the sons of Nekoda, the sons of Gazzam,
49 the sons of Uzza, the sons of Paseah, the sons of Besai,

**2:2** [4]In Ne 7:7, *Mispereth* [5]In Ne 7:7, *Nehum* **2:5** [a]Ne 7:10 **2:6** [a]Ne 7:11 **2:10** [1]In Ne 7:15, *Binnui* **2:13** [a]Ezr 8:13 **2:18** [1]In Ne 7:24, *Hariph* **2:20** [1]In Ne 7:25, *Gibeon* **2:21** [a]Ge 35:19; Mt 2:6 **2:24** [1]In Ne 7:28, *Beth-azmaveth* **2:25** [1]In Ne 7:29, *Kiriath-jearim* **2:26** [a]Jos 18:25 **2:34** [a]1Ki 16:34; 2Chr 28:15 [1]Lit *sons* **2:36** [a]1Chr 24:7-18 **2:37** [a]1Chr 24:14 **2:38** [a]1Chr 9:12 **2:39** [a]1Chr 24:8 **2:40** [1]In Ezr 3:9, *Judah*; in Ne 7:43, *Hodevah* **2:43** [a]1Chr 9:2 **2:44** [1]In Ne 7:47, *Sia*

50 the sons of Asnah, the sons
of Meunim, the sons of
[1]Nephisim,
51 the sons of Bakbuk, the sons
of Hakupha, the sons of
Harhur,
52 the sons of [1]Bazluth, the sons
of Mehida, the sons of Harsha,
53 the sons of Barkos, the sons of
Sisera, the sons of Temah,
54 the sons of Neziah, the sons of
Hatipha.
55 The sons of [a]Solomon's servants:
the sons of Sotai, the sons of
[1]Hassophereth, the sons of
[2]Peruda,
56 the sons of Jaalah, the sons of
Darkon, the sons of Giddel,
57 the sons of Shephatiah, the
sons of Hattil, the sons of
Pochereth-hazzebaim, the
sons of [1]Ami.
58 All the [a]temple servants and
the sons of [b]Solomon's servants were
392.
59 Now these are those who came
up from Tel-melah, Tel-harsha,
Cherub, [1]Addan, *and* Immer, but
they were not able to declare their
fathers' households and their *fathers'*
seed, whether they were of Israel:
60 the sons of Delaiah, the sons of
Tobiah, the sons of Nekoda, 652.
61 Of the sons of the priests: the sons
of Hobaiah, the sons of Hakkoz, the
sons of [a]Barzillai, who took a wife
from the daughters of Barzillai the
Gileadite, and he was called by their
name. 62 These searched *in* their
genealogical records, but they could
not be found; [a]therefore they were
considered unclean *and excluded*
from the priesthood. 63 The [1]gover-
nor said to them [a]that they should
not eat from the most holy things
until a priest stood with [b]Urim and
Thummim.
64 The whole assembly together
*was* 42,360,
65 besides their male and female
slaves of whom *there were*
7,337;
and they had 200 [a]male and
female singers.
66 Their horses were 736; their
mules, 245;
67 their camels, 435; *their*
donkeys, 6,720.
68 Some of the heads of fathers'
*households*, when they arrived at
the house of Yahweh which is in
Jerusalem, gave a freewill offering for
the house of God to [1]restore it on its
foundation. 69 According to their
ability, they gave [a]to the treasury for
the work 61,000 gold [1]drachmas and
5,000 silver [2]minas and 100 priestly
tunics.
70 [a]So the priests and the Levites,
some of the people, the singers, the
gatekeepers, and the temple servants
lived in their cities, and all Israel in
their cities.

### *The Altar Is Built and Daily Offerings Begin*

3 Then the seventh month came,
and [a]the sons of Israel *were* in
the cities. And the people gathered
together as one man to Jerusalem.

**2:50** [1]In Ne 7:52, *Nephushesim* **2:52** [1]In Ne 7:54, *Bazlith* **2:55** [a]1Ki 9:21 [1]In Ne 7:57, *Sophereth* [2]In Ne 7:57, *Perida* **2:57** [1]In Ne 7:59, *Amon* **2:58** [a]1Chr 9:2 [b]1Ki 9:21 **2:59** [1]In Ne 7:61, *Addon* **2:61** [a]2Sa 17:27; 1Ki 2:7 **2:62** [a]Nu 16:39, 40 **2:63** [a]Lv 2:3, 10 [b]Ex 28:30; Nu 27:21 [1]Heb *Tirshatha*, a Persian title **2:65** [a]2Chr 35:25 **2:68** [1]Lit *establish* **2:69** [a]Ezr 8:25-34 [1]A Greek silver coin, approx. a laborer's daily wage [2]A mina was approx. 1.25 lb. or 0.6 kg **2:70** [a]1Chr 9:2; Ne 11:3
◆ **3:1** [a]Ne 7:73; 8:1

**2** Then [a]Jeshua the son of Jozadak
and his brothers the priests, and
[b]Zerubbabel the son [c]of Shealtiel
and his brothers arose and [d]built
the altar of the God of Israel to offer
burnt offerings on it, [e]as it is written
in the law of Moses, the man of
God. **3** So they set up the altar on its
foundation, for [a,1]they were terrified
because of the peoples of the lands;
and they [b]offered burnt offerings on
it to Yahweh, burnt offerings morning
and evening. **4** They celebrated the
[a]Feast of [1]Booths, [b]as it is written,
and *offered* [2]the fixed number of
burnt offerings daily, [c]according
to the *legal* judgment, as each day
required; **5** and afterward *there was*
a [a]continual burnt offering, also [b]for
the new moons and [c]for all the ap-
pointed times of Yahweh that were set
apart as holy, and from everyone who
offered a freewill offering to Yahweh.
**6** From the first day of the seventh
month they began to offer burnt of-
ferings to Yahweh, but the foundation
of the temple of Yahweh had not been
laid. **7** Then they gave money to the
masons and [1]carpenters, and [a]food,
drink, and oil to the Sidonians and
to the Tyrians, [b]to bring cedar wood
from Lebanon to the sea at [c]Joppa,
according to the permission they had
[2]from [d]Cyrus king of Persia.

### *The Foundation of the Temple of Yahweh*

**8** Now in the second year of their com-
ing to the house of God at Jerusalem
in the second month, [a]Zerubbabel
the son of Shealtiel and Jeshua the
son of Jozadak and the rest of their
brothers the priests and the Levites,
and all who came from the captivity
to Jerusalem, began *the work* and
[b]appointed the Levites from twenty
years and older to direct the work of
the house of Yahweh. **9** Then [a]Jeshua
*with* his sons and brothers stood
united *with* Kadmiel and his sons,
the sons of [1]Judah *and* the sons of
Henadad *with* their sons and broth-
ers the Levites, to direct those who do
the work in the house of God.

**10** So the builders [a]laid the
foundation of the temple of
Yahweh. Then [1]the priests stood in
their apparel with trumpets, and
the Levites, the sons of Asaph, with
cymbals, to praise Yahweh [b]according
to the [2]directions of King David of
Israel. **11** [a]And they sang, praising
and giving thanks to Yahweh,
*saying*, "[b]For He is good, for His
lovingkindness endures forever upon
Israel." And all the people shouted
with a great shout when they praised
Yahweh because the foundation of
the house of Yahweh was laid. **12** Yet
many of the priests and Levites and
heads of fathers' *households*, [a]the old
men who had seen the first house *of*
*Yahweh*, were weeping with a loud
voice when the foundation of this
house was laid before their eyes, while
many in loud shouts with gladness
*were* raising *their* voice, **13** so that
the people could not distinguish the

---

**3:2** [a]Ne 12:1, 8 [b]Ezr 2:2; Hag 1:1; 2:2 [c]1Chr 3:17 [d]Ex 27:1 [e]Dt 12:5, 6 **3:3** [a]Ezr 4:4 [b]Nu 28:2 [1]Lit *terror* was *upon them* **3:4** [a]Ne 8:14; Zec 14:16 [b]Ex 23:16 [c]Nu 29:12 [1]Or *Tabernacles* [2]Lit *by number* **3:5** [a]Ex 29:38; Nu 28:3 [b]Nu 28:11 [c]Nu 29:39 **3:7** [a]2Chr 2:10; Ac 12:20 [b]2Chr 2:16 [c]Ac 9:36 [d]Ezr 1:2; 6:3 [1]Or *craftsmen* of wood, cf. 2Sa 5:11 [2]Lit *of* **3:8** [a]Ezr 3:2; 4:3 [b]1Chr 23:4, 24 **3:9** [a]Ezr 2:40 [1]In Ezr 2:40, *Hodaviah* **3:10** [a]Zec 4:6-10 [b]1Chr 6:31; 25:1 [1]As in Gr and some mss; M.T. *they set the priests* [2]Lit *hands* **3:11** [a]2Chr 7:3; Ne 12:24, 40 [b]1Chr 16:34; 2Chr 5:13; Ps 100:5; 106:1; 107:1; 118:1; 131:1; Jer 33:11 **3:12** [a]Hag 2:3

[1]voices of the shouting of gladness
from the [1]voices of the weeping of the
people, for the people were shouting
with a loud shout, and those [1]voices
were heard far away.

### *Adversaries Discourage the Work*

4 Then [a]the adversaries of Judah
and Benjamin heard that [b]the
people of the exile were building a
temple to Yahweh, the God of Israel,
**2** so they approached Zerubbabel and
the heads of fathers' *households* and
said to them, "Let us build with you,
for we, like you, seek your God; [a]and
we have been sacrificing to Him since
the days of [b]Esarhaddon king of As-
syria, who brought us up here." **3** But
Zerubbabel and Jeshua and the rest
of the heads of fathers' *households* of
Israel said to them, "[a]You have noth-
ing in common with us in building a
house to our God; but we ourselves
will together build to Yahweh, the
God of Israel, [b]as King Cyrus, the
king of Persia has commanded us."
**4** So [a]the people of the land
[1]discouraged the people of Judah
and dismayed them from building,
**5** and hired counselors against them
to frustrate their counsel all the days
of Cyrus king of Persia, even until the
reign of Darius king of Persia.
**6** Now in the reign of [a,1]Ahasuerus,
in the beginning of his reign, they
wrote an accusation against the
inhabitants of Judah and Jerusalem.
**7** And in the days of [1]Artaxerxes,
Bishlam, Mithredath, Tabeel, and the
rest of his colleagues wrote to Arta-
xerxes king of Persia; and the [2]text of
the letter was written in Aramaic and
translated [a]*from* Aramaic.

### *The Letter to King Artaxerxes*

**8** [1]Rehum the commander and
Shimshai the scribe wrote a letter
against Jerusalem to King Artaxerxes,
as follows—
**9** then *wrote* Rehum the
commander and Shimshai
the scribe and [a]the rest of
their colleagues, the judges
and [b]the lesser governors, the
officials, the secretaries, the
men of Erech, the Babylonians,
the men of Susa, that is, the
Elamites, **10** and the rest of the
nations, which the great and
honorable [1]Osnappar took
away into exile and settled
in the city of Samaria and in
the rest of the region beyond
the [2]River. [a]And now—
**11** this is the copy of the letter which
they sent to him:
"To King Artaxerxes: Your
servants, the men in the region
beyond the River, and now—
**12** let it be known to the king
that the Jews who came up
from you have come to us at
Jerusalem; they are rebuilding
[a]the rebellious and evil city
and [b]are completing the walls
and repairing the foundations.
**13** Now let it be known to the
king, that if that city is rebuilt
and the walls are completed,
[a]they will not give tribute,
custom, or toll, and it will
damage the revenue of the

**3:13** [1]Lit *voice* ◆ **4:1** [a]Ezr 4:7-10 [b]Ezr 1:11 **4:2** [a]2Ki 17:32 [b]2Ki 19:37 **4:3** [a]Ne 2:20 [b]Ezr 1:1, 2
**4:4** [a]Ezr 3:3 [1]Lit *made the hands limp* **4:6** [a]Es 1:1; Da 9:1 [1]Or *Xerxes*; Heb *Ahash-verosh*
**4:7** [a]2Ki 18:26; Da 2:4 [1]Heb *Artah-shashta* [2]Lit *writing* **4:8** [1]Ch 4:8-6:18 is in Aram **4:9** [a]2Ki 17:24
[b]Ezr 5:6; 6:6 **4:10** [a]Ezr 4:11, 17; 7:12 [1]Probably Ashurbanipal [2]The Euphrates River, so in ch
**4:12** [a]2Chr 36:13 [b]Ezr 5:3, 9 **4:13** [a]Ezr 4:20; 7:24

kings. **14** Now because we [1]are
in the service of the palace,
and it is not fitting for us to see
the king's [2]dishonor, therefore
we have sent and made known
to the king, **15** that a search
be made in the record books
of your fathers. And you will
find in the record books and
come to know that that city is
a rebellious city and damaging
to kings and provinces, and
that they have incited revolt
within it in past days; therefore
that city was laid waste. **16** We
make known to the king that
if that city is rebuilt and the
walls completed, as a result
you will have no portion in *the
province* beyond the River."

### *A Decree Makes the Men Stop Rebuilding*

**17** *Then* the king sent an edict to
Rehum the commander, to Shimshai
the scribe, and to the rest of their
colleagues who live in Samaria and
in the rest of *the provinces* beyond
the River: "Peace. And now— **18** the
document which you sent to us has
been [a]plainly read before me.
**19** "So a decree has been [1]issued
by me, and a search has been
made and it has been found
that that city has lifted itself up
against the kings in past days,
that rebellion and revolt have
been perpetrated in it, **20** [a]that
strong kings have been over
Jerusalem, even rulers in all *the
provinces* [b]*beyond the River*,
and that [c]tribute, custom, and
toll were given to them. **21** Now
issue a decree to make those
men stop, that this city may
not be rebuilt until a decree is
issued by me. **22** And beware
of being negligent in doing
this *matter*; why should harm
increase to damage the kings?"
**23** Then as soon as the copy of
King Artaxerxes' document was
read before Rehum and Shimshai
the scribe and their colleagues,
they went in haste to Jerusalem to
the Jews and stopped them by force
and military.
**24** Then the work on the house of
God in Jerusalem stopped, and it was
stopped until the second year of the
reign of Darius king of Persia.

### *Rebuilding the House of God Begins Again*

**5** And the prophets, [a]Haggai the
prophet and [b]Zechariah the
son of Iddo, prophesied to the Jews
who were in Judah and Jerusalem in
the name of the God of Israel, who
was over them. **2** Then [a]Zerubbabel
the son of Shealtiel and Jeshua the
son of Jozadak arose and began to
rebuild the house of God which is
in Jerusalem; and [b]the prophets of
God were with them supporting
them.
**3** At that time [a]Tattenai, the governor
of *the province* beyond the
[1]River, and Shethar-bozenai and
their colleagues came to them and
spoke to them thus, "[b]Who issued
you a decree to rebuild this house
and to complete this structure?"
**4** [a]Then we told them accordingly

---

**4:14** [1]Lit *eat the salt* [2]Lit *nakedness* **4:18** [a]Ne 8:8 **4:19** [1]Lit *put* forth **4:20** [a]1Ki 4:21; 1Chr 18:3 [b]Ge 15:18; Jos 1:4 [c]Ezr 4:13; 7:24 ◆ **5:1** [a]Hag 1:1 [b]Zec 1:1 **5:2** [a]Ezr 3:2; Hag 1:12; Zec 4:6-9 [b]Ezr 6:14; Hag 2:4; Zec 3:1 **5:3** [a]Ezr 6:6, 13 [b]Ezr 1:3; 5:9 [1]The Euphrates River, so in ch **5:4** [a]Ezr 5:10

what the names of the men were
who were rebuilding this building.
5 But [a]the eye of their God was on the
elders of the Jews, and they did not
stop them until a report could come
to Darius, and then a document be
returned concerning this.

### *Tattenai and Others Write to King Darius*

6 *This is* the copy of the letter
which [a]Tattenai, the governor of
*the province* beyond the River, and
Shethar-bozenai and his colleagues
[b]the officials, who were beyond the
River, sent to Darius the king. 7 They
sent word to him in which it was
written thus:
"To Darius the king, all peace.
8 Let it be known to the king
that we have gone to the
province of Judah, to the house
of the great God, and it is being
built with huge stones, and
timber is being put within the
walls; and that work is going
on with all diligence and is
succeeding in their hands.
9 Then we asked those elders
and said to them thus, 'Who
issued you a decree to rebuild
this house and to complete
this structure?' 10 And we
also asked them their names
in order to make known to
you, *and* that we might write
down the names of the men
who were at their head.
11 "Thus they responded with a word
to us, saying,
'We are the servants of the God
of heaven and earth, and are
rebuilding the house that was
built many years ago, [a]which
a great king of Israel built and
completed. 12 But [a]because our
fathers had provoked the God
of heaven to wrath, [b]He gave
them into the hand of Nebu-
chadnezzar king of Babylon, the
Chaldean, *who* destroyed this
house and took the people away
into exile in Babylon. 13 However,
[a]in the first year of Cyrus king
of Babylon, King Cyrus [b]issued
a decree to rebuild this house
of God. 14 Also [a]the gold and
silver utensils of the house of
God, which Nebuchadnezzar
had taken from the temple [1]in
Jerusalem and brought them to
the temple of Babylon, these
King Cyrus took out from the
temple of Babylon, and they
were given to one [b]whose
name was Sheshbazzar, whom
he had appointed governor.
15 He said to him, "Take these
articles, go *and* deposit them
in the temple [1]in Jerusalem,
and let the house of God be
rebuilt in its place." 16 Then that
Sheshbazzar came *and* [a]laid
the foundations of the house
of God [1]in Jerusalem; and from
then until now it is being rebuilt,
and it is [b]not *yet* finished.'
17 So now if it seems good to
the king, [a]let a search be made
in the king's treasure house,
which is there in Babylon, if
it be that a decree was issued
by King Cyrus to rebuild that
house of God in Jerusalem;

---

**5:5** [a]Ezr 7:6, 28 **5:6** [a]Ezr 5:3 [b]Ezr 4:9 **5:11** [a]1Ki 6:1, 38 **5:12** [a]2Chr 36:16, 17 [b]2Ki 25:8-11; Jer 52:12-15 **5:13** [a]Ezr 1:1 [b]Ezr 1:1-4 **5:14** [a]Ezr 1:7; 6:5; Da 5:2 [b]Ezr 1:8; 5:16 [1]Lit *that was in* **5:15** [1]Lit *that is in* **5:16** [a]Ezr 3:8, 10 [b]Ezr 6:15 [1]Lit *that is in* **5:17** [a]Ezr 6:1, 2

and let the king send to us his
will concerning this *matter*."

### *The Scroll with Cyrus' Decree Is Found*

6 Then King Darius issued a decree,
and a [a]search was made in the
[1]archives, where the treasures were
deposited in Babylon. **2** And in
[1]Ecbatana in the fortress, which is
[a]in the province of Media, a scroll
was found and there was written in
it as follows:
"Memorandum— **3** [a]In the
first year of King Cyrus, Cyrus
the king issued a decree:
'*Concerning* the house of God
in Jerusalem, let that house,
the place where sacrifices are
offered, be rebuilt and let its
foundations be [1]retained, its
height being [2]60 cubits and
its width 60 cubits; **4** [a]with
three layers of huge stones
and [1]one layer of timbers. And
let the cost be given from the
[2]royal treasury. **5** And also let
[a]the gold and silver articles of
the house of God, which Neb-
uchadnezzar took out from
the temple in Jerusalem and
brought to Babylon, be returned
and [1]brought to their places
in the temple in Jerusalem;
and you shall deposit *them*
in the house of God.'

**6** "Now [a]Tattenai, governor of *the
province* beyond the [1]River,
Shethar-bozenai and their
colleagues, *the officials* of *the
provinces* beyond the River,
[2]keep away from there. **7** Leave
that work on the house of God
alone; let the governor of the
Jews and the elders of the Jews
rebuild that house of God in its
*designated* place. **8** Moreover, [a]I
issue a decree concerning what
you shall do for those elders
of Judah in the rebuilding of
that house of God: the full cost
is to be given to those people
from the royal treasury out
of the tribute of *the provinces*
beyond the River, and that
without negligence. **9** Whatever
is needed, both young bulls,
rams, and lambs for a burnt
offering to the God of heaven,
and wheat, salt, wine, and
anointing oil, according to what
the priests in Jerusalem say,
*it* is to be given to them daily
without negligence, **10** that
they may bring sweet-smelling
sacrifices near to the God of
heaven and [a]pray for the life of
the king and his sons. **11** And
I issued a decree that [a]any
man who violates this edict,
a timber shall be pulled out
from his house and he shall be
impaled on it and [b]his house
shall be made a refuse heap
on account of this. **12** May the
God who [a]has caused His name
to dwell there overthrow any
king or people who [1]stretches
out his hand to change *it*, so
as to destroy that house of
God in Jerusalem. I, Darius,

◆ **6:1** [a]Ezr 5:17 [1]Lit *house of the books* **6:2** [a]2Ki 17:6 [1]Aram *Achmetha* **6:3** [a]Ezr 1:1; 5:13 [1]Or *fixed, laid* [2]Approx. 90 ft. or 27 m, a cubit was approx. 18 in. or 45 cm **6:4** [a]1Ki 6:36 [1]As in Gr; Aram *a layer of new timber* [2]Lit *king's house* **6:5** [a]Ezr 1:7; 5:14 [1]Lit *go* **6:6** [a]Ezr 5:3; 6:13 [1]The Euphrates River, so in ch [2]Lit *be distant* **6:8** [a]Ezr 6:4; 7:14-22 **6:10** [a]Ezr 7:23; Jer 29:7; 1Ti 2:1, 2 **6:11** [a]Ezr 7:26 [b]Da 2:5; 3:29 **6:12** [a]Dt 12:5, 11; 1Ki 9:3 [1]Lit *sends his hand*

have issued *this* decree, let *it*
be done with all diligence!"

### *The Dedication of the House of God*

**13** Then [a]Tattenai, the governor of *the*
*province* beyond the River, Shethar-
bozenai and their colleagues carried
out *the decree* with all diligence, just
as King Darius had sent. **14** And [a]the
elders of the Jews were building and
succeeding through the prophesying
of Haggai the prophet and Zechariah
the son of Iddo. So they built and
completed *it* according to the decree
of the God of Israel and the decree
[b]of Cyrus, [c]Darius, and [d]Artaxerxes
king of Persia. **15** And this house was
brought to completion [1]on the third
day of the [a]month Adar; it was the
sixth year of the reign of King Darius.

**16** And the sons of Israel, the
priests, the Levites and the rest of
the [1]exiles, [a]celebrated the dedi-
cation of this house of God with
joy. **17** They brought near for the
dedication of this house of God 100
bulls, 200 rams, 400 lambs, and as
a sin offering for all Israel [a]12 male
goats, corresponding to the number
of the tribes of Israel. **18** Then they
appointed the priests to [a] their
sections and the Levites in [b] their
divisions for the service of God [1] in
Jerusalem, [c] as it is written in the
book of Moses.

### *Passover Celebrated*

**19** [a]And the exiles celebrated the
Passover on [b]the fourteenth of the
first month. **20** [a]For the priests and
the Levites had cleansed themselves
together; all of them were clean.
Then [b]they slaughtered the Passover
*lamb* for all the exiles, both for their
brothers the priests and for them-
selves. **21** Then the sons of Israel who
returned from exile and [a]all those
who had separated themselves from
[b]the uncleanness of the nations of
the land to *join* them, to seek Yahweh,
the God of Israel, ate *the Passover*.
**22** And [a]they celebrated the Feast of
Unleavened Bread seven days with
gladness, for Yahweh had caused
them to be glad and [b]had turned
the heart of [c]the king of Assyria
toward them to [1]strengthen them in
the work of the house of God, the
God of Israel.

### *Ezra Goes Up from Babylon to Jerusalem*

**7** [a]Now after these things, in
the reign of [b]Artaxerxes king
of Persia, *there went up* Ezra son
of Seraiah, son of Azariah, son of
Hilkiah, **2** son of Shallum, son
of Zadok, son of Ahitub, **3** son
of Amariah, son of Azariah, son of
Meraioth, **4** son of Zerahiah, son of
Uzzi, son of Bukki, **5** son of Abishua,
son of Phinehas, son of Eleazar, son
of Aaron the chief priest. **6** This Ezra
went up from Babylon, and he was a
[a]scribe skilled in the law of Moses,
which Yahweh, the God of Israel had
given; and the king granted him all
[1]he requested [b]because the hand
of Yahweh his God *was* upon him.
**7** [a]And some of the sons of Israel

**6:13** [a]Ezr 6:6 **6:14** [a]Ezr 5:1, 2 [b]Ezr 1:1; 5:13 [c]Ezr 4:24; 6:12 [d]Ezr 7:1 **6:15** [a]Es 3:7 [1]Lit *until*
**6:16** [a]1Ki 8:63; 2Chr 7:5 [1]Lit *sons of the captivity* **6:17** [a]Ezr 8:35 **6:18** [a]1Chr 24:1; 2Chr 35:5
[b]1Chr 23:6 [c]Nu 3:6; 8:9 [1]Lit *which is in* **6:19** [a]Ezr 1:11 [b]Ex 12:6 **6:20** [a]2Chr 29:34; 30:15 [b]2Chr 35:11
**6:21** [a]Ne 9:2; 10:28 [b]Ezr 9:11 **6:22** [a]Ex 12:15 [b]Ezr 7:27; Pr 21:1 [c]Ezr 1:1; 6:1 [1]Lit *strengthen their hands* ◆**7:1** [a]1Chr 6:4-14 [b]Ezr 7:12, 21; Ne 2:1 **7:6** [a]Ezr 7:11, 12, 21 [b]Ezr 7:9, 28; 8:22 [1]Lit *his request*
**7:7** [a]Ezr 8:1-20

and some of the priests, the Levites,
the singers, the gatekeepers, and
the temple servants went up to Je-
rusalem in the seventh year of King
Artaxerxes.
**8** He came to Jerusalem in the
fifth month, which was in the sev-
enth year of the king. **9** For on the
first of the first month [1]he began
to go up from Babylon; and on the
first of the fifth month he came to
Jerusalem, [a]because the good hand
of his God *was* upon him. **10** For Ezra
had set his heart to [1]study the law
of Yahweh and to practice *it*, and
[a]to teach *His* statute and judgment
in Israel.

### *The King's Decree on Behalf of Ezra*

**11** Now this is the copy of the letter
which King Artaxerxes gave to Ezra
the priest, the scribe, [1]learned in
the words of the commandments
of Yahweh and His statutes to Israel:
**12** "[1]Artaxerxes, [a]king of kings,
to Ezra the priest, the scribe of
the law of the God of heaven,
perfect *peace*. And now— **13** [a]I
have issued a decree that any
of the people of Israel and
their priests and the Levites
in my kingdom who freely
offer to go to Jerusalem, may
go with you. **14** Forasmuch as
you are sent from before the
king and his [a]seven counselors
to inquire concerning Judah
and Jerusalem according to
the law of your God which is
in your hand, **15** and to bring
*the silver* and gold, which the
king and his counselors have
freely offered to the God of
Israel, [a]whose dwelling is in
Jerusalem, **16** and [a]all the silver
and gold which you find in the
whole province of Babylon,
along [b]with the freewill offering
of the people and of the priests,
who [c]offered willingly for
the house of their God which
is in Jerusalem; **17** with this
money, therefore, you shall
with all diligence buy bulls,
rams, and lambs, [a]with their
grain offerings and their drink
offerings, and [b]bring them near
to the altar of the house of
your God which is in Jerusalem.
**18** And whatever seems good to
you and to your brothers to do
with the rest of the silver and
gold, you may do according to
the will of your God. **19** Also the
utensils which are given to you
for the service of the house of
your God, deliver in full before
the God of Jerusalem. **20** The
rest of the needs for the house
of your God, which may fall
upon you to provide, [a]provide
*for it* from the royal treasury.

**21** "So I, even I, King Artaxerxes,
issue a decree to all the
treasurers who are *in the
provinces* beyond the [1]River,
that whatever Ezra the priest,
[a]the scribe of the law of the
God of heaven, may ask of
*you*, *it* shall be done with
all diligence, **22** *even* up to

---

**7:9** [a]Ezr 7:6; Ne 2:8 [1]Lit *was the foundation* **7:10** [a]Dt 33:10; Ezr 7:25; Ne 8:1 [1]Lit *seek* **7:11** [1]Lit *the scribe of* **7:12** [a]Eze 26:7; Da 2:37 [1]Ch 7:12-26 is in Aram **7:13** [a]Ezr 6:1 **7:14** [a]Ezr 7:15, 28; 8:25 **7:15** [a]2Chr 6:2; Ezr 6:12; Ps 135:21 **7:16** [a]Ezr 8:25 [b]Ezr 1:4, 6 [c]1Chr 29:6 **7:17** [a]Nu 15:4-13 [b]Dt 12:5-11 **7:20** [a]Ezr 6:4 **7:21** [a]Ezr 7:6 [1]The Euphrates River, so in ch

[1]100 talents of silver, [2]100
kors of wheat, [3]100 baths of
wine, [3]100 baths of oil, and
salt without written order.
**23** Whatever is [1]decreed by the
God of heaven, let it be done
with zeal for the house of the
God of heaven, [a]so that there
will not be wrath against the
kingdom of the king and his
sons. **24** We also make known
to you that [a]it is not allowed
to [1]impose tribute, custom,
or toll [b]*on* any of the priests,
Levites, singers, doorkeepers,
temple servants, or *other*
servants of this house of God.

**25** "And you, Ezra, according to
the wisdom of your God which
is in your hand, [a]appoint
magistrates and judges that
they may judge all the people
who are in *the province* beyond
the River, *even* all those who
know the laws of your God;
and to anyone who does not
know *the laws*, you shall [b]make
*them* known. **26** [a]Whoever
will not do the law of your
God and the law of the king,
let judgment be done to him
with all diligence, whether
for death or for [1]banishment
*or for* confiscation of goods
or for imprisonment."

### *Yahweh Put This in the King's Heart*

**27** Blessed be Yahweh, the God of
our fathers, [a]who has put *such a
thing* as this in the king's heart, to
beautify the house of Yahweh which
is in Jerusalem, **28** and [a]has extended
lovingkindness to me before the
king and his counselors and before
all the king's mighty princes. Thus I
was strengthened according to [b]the
hand of Yahweh my God upon me,
and I gathered [1]chief men from Israel
to go up with me.

### *Genealogical Records*

**8** Now these are the heads of their
fathers' *households* and the gene-
alogical records of those who went
up with me from Babylon in the reign
of King Artaxerxes:

**2** of the sons of Phinehas,
Gershom;
of the sons of Ithamar, Daniel;
of the sons of David,
[a]Hattush;

**3** of the sons of Shecaniah *who
was* of the sons of [a]Parosh,
Zechariah and with him
150 males *who were in* the
genealogical records;

**4** of the sons of Pahath-moab,
Eliehoenai the son of Zerahiah
and 200 males with him;

**5** of the sons of Zattu,
Shecaniah, the son of Jahaziel
and 300 males with him;

**6** and of the sons of [a]Adin, Ebed
the son of Jonathan and 50
males with him;

**7** and of the sons of Elam,
Jeshaiah the son of Athaliah
and 70 males with him;

**8** and of the sons of Shephatiah,
Zebadiah the son of Michael
and 80 males with him;

---

**7:22** [1]Approx. 3.75 tons or 3.4 metric tons, a talent was approx. 75 lb. or 34 kg [2]Approx. 650 bu. or 23 metric tons, a kor was approx. 6.5 bu. or 230 l [3]Approx. 600 gal. or 2.3 metric tons, a bath was approx. 6 gal. or 23 l **7:23** [a]Ezr 6:10 [1]Lit *from the decree of* **7:24** [a]Ezr 4:13, 20 [b]Ezr 7:7 [1]Lit *throw on them* **7:25** [a]Ex 18:21; Dt 16:18 [b]Ezr 7:10; Mal 2:7; Col 1:28 **7:26** [a]Ezr 6:11, 12 [1]Lit *rooting out* **7:27** [a]Ezr 6:22 **7:28** [a]Ezr 9:9 [b]Ezr 5:5 [1]Lit *heads* ◆ **8:2** [a]1Chr 3:22 **8:3** [a]Ezr 2:3 **8:6** [a]Ezr 2:15; Ne 7:20; 10:16

9 of the sons of Joab, Obadiah
the son of Jehiel and 218 males
with him;
10 and of the sons of Bani,
Shelomith, the son of
Josiphiah and 160 males with
him;
11 and of the sons of Bebai,
Zechariah the son of Bebai
and 28 males with him;
12 and of the sons of Azgad,
Johanan the son of Hakkatan
and 110 males with him;
13 and of the sons of Adonikam,
the last ones, these being their
names, Eliphelet, [1]Jeiel, and
Shemaiah, and 60 males with
them;
14 and of the sons of Bigvai,
Uthai, and [1]Zabbud, and 70
males with [2]them.

### *Ezra Sends for Levites*

**15** Now I gathered them at [a]the river
that runs to Ahava, where we camped
for three days. And I [1]observed the
people and the priests, but I [b]did not
find any Levites there. **16** So I sent for
Eliezer, Ariel, Shemaiah, Elnathan,
Jarib, Elnathan, Nathan, Zechariah,
and Meshullam, [1]chief men, and for
Joiarib and Elnathan, teachers. **17** I
sent them out to Iddo the [1]chief man
at the place Casiphia; and I put words
in their mouths to say to [2]Iddo *and*
his brothers, [a]the temple servants
at the place Casiphia, *that is,* to
bring ministers to us for the house
of our God. **18** [a]So, according to the
good hand of our God upon us, they
brought us a [b]man of insight of the
sons of Mahli, the son of Levi, the
son of Israel, namely Sherebiah, and
his sons and brothers, 18 men; **19** and
Hashabiah and [1]Jeshaiah of the sons
of Merari, with his brothers and their
sons, 20 men; **20** and 220 of [a]the
temple servants, whom David and
the princes had given for the service
of the Levites, all of them designated
by name.

### *God's Protection Sought*

**21** Then I called for [a]a fast there at
[b]the river of Ahava, that we might
[c]humble ourselves before our God
to seek from Him a [1]direct journey
for us, our little ones, and all our
possessions. **22** For I was ashamed to
ask from the king for a military force
and horsemen to help us against the
enemy on the way, because we had
said to the king, "[a]The hand of our
God is upon all those who seek Him,
for *their* good, but [b]His strength and
His anger are against all those who
[c]forsake Him." **23** So we fasted and
sought our God concerning this
*matter,* and He [a,1]was moved by our
entreaty.

**24** Then I [1]set apart twelve of the
leading priests, [a]Sherebiah, Hash-
abiah, and with them ten of their
brothers; **25** and I [a]weighed out to
them [b]the silver, the gold, and the
utensils, the contribution for the
house of our God which the king and
[c]his counselors and his princes and
all Israel present *there* had offered.
**26** [a]*Thus* I weighed into their hands

---

**8:13** [1]Or *Jeuel* **8:14** [1]Or *Zakkur* [2]Or *him* **8:15** [a]Ezr 8:21, 31 [b]Ezr 7:7; 8:2 [1]Lit *understood, discerned* **8:16** [1]Lit *heads* **8:17** [a]Ezr 2:43 [1]Lit *head* [2]As in Gr; Heb *Iddo his brother* **8:18** [a]Ezr 7:6, 28 [b]2Chr 30:22 **8:19** [1]As in Gr; Heb *with him Jeshaiah* **8:20** [a]Ezr 2:43; 7:7 **8:21** [a]1Sa 7:6; 2Chr 20:3 [b]Ezr 8:15, 31 [c]Lv 16:29; 23:29; Is 58:3, 5 [1]Lit *straight way* **8:22** [a]Ezr 7:6, 9, 28 [b]Jos 22:16 [c]2Chr 15:2 **8:23** [a]1Chr 5:20; 2Chr 33:13 [1]Lit *was entreated by us* **8:24** [a]Ezr 8:18, 19 [1]Lit *separated* **8:25** [a]Ezr 8:33 [b]Ezr 7:15, 16 [c]Ezr 7:14 **8:26** [a]Ezr 1:9-11

[1]650 talents of silver, and silver uten-
sils *worth* 100 talents, *and* 100 gold
talents, **27** and 20 gold bowls *worth*
1,000 [1]darics, and two utensils of
fine shiny bronze, precious as gold.
**28** Then I said to them, "[a]You are
holy to Yahweh, and the [b]utensils
are holy; and the silver and the
gold are a freewill offering to Yahweh,
the God of your fathers. **29** Watch and
keep *them* [a]until you weigh *them*
before the officials of the priests,
the Levites and the officials of the
fathers' *households* of Israel at Jeru-
salem, *in* the chambers of the house
of Yahweh." **30** So the priests and the
Levites [a]accepted the weighed out
silver and gold and the utensils, to
bring *them* to Jerusalem to the house
of our God.

**31** Then we set out from [a]the river
Ahava on [b]the twelfth of the first
month to go to Jerusalem; and [c]the
hand of our God was upon us, and
He delivered us from the hand of the
enemy and the ambushes by the way.
**32** [a]Thus we came to Jerusalem and
remained there three days.

### *Silver, Gold, and Utensils Weighed*

**33** On the fourth day the silver and
the gold and the utensils [a]were
weighed out in the house of our God
into the hand of [b]Meremoth the son
of Uriah the priest, and with him
*was* Eleazar the son of Phinehas; and
with them *were* the Levites, Jozabad
the son of Jeshua and Noadiah the
son of Binnui. **34** Everything *was*
numbered *and* weighed, and all the
weight was written down at that
time.

**35** [a]The exiles who had come from
the captivity brought burnt offerings
near to the God of Israel: [b]12 bulls
for all Israel, 96 rams, 77 lambs, 12
male goats for a sin offering, all as
a burnt offering to Yahweh. **36** Then
[a]they gave the king's edicts to [b]the
king's satraps and to the governors
*in the provinces* beyond the [1]River,
and they supported the people and
the house of God.

### *The Unfaithfulness of the Exiles*

**9** Now when these things had
been completed, the princes ap-
proached me, saying, "The people of
Israel and the priests and the Levites
have not [a]separated themselves from
the peoples of the lands, [b]according
to their abominations, *those* of the
Canaanites, the Hittites, the Periz-
zites, the Jebusites, the Ammonites,
the Moabites, the Egyptians and the
Amorites. **2** For [a]they have taken
some of their daughters *as wives* for
themselves and for their sons, so
that [b]the holy seed has [c]intermin-
gled with the peoples of the lands;
indeed, the hands of the princes and
the officials have been foremost in
this unfaithfulness." **3** When I heard
about this matter, I [a]tore my garment
and my robe, and pulled some of the
hair from my head and my beard, and
[b]sat down in consternation. **4** Then
[a]everyone who trembled at the
words of the God of Israel on account
of the unfaithfulness of the exiles

---

**8:26** [1]Approx. 24 tons or 22 metric tons, a talent was approx. 75 lb. or 34 kg **8:27** [1]A Persian gold coin weighing approx. 0.3 oz. or 8 gm **8:28** [a]Lv 21:6-8 [b]Lv 22:2, 3 **8:29** [a]Ezr 8:33, 34 **8:30** [a]Ezr 1:9 **8:31** [a]Ezr 8:15, 21 [b]Ezr 7:9 [c]Ezr 8:22 **8:32** [a]Ne 2:11 **8:33** [a]Ezr 8:30 [b]Ne 3:4, 21 **8:35** [a]Ezr 2:1 [b]Ezr 6:17 **8:36** [a]Ezr 7:21-24 [b]Ezr 4:7; 5:6 [1]The Euphrates River ◆ **9:1** [a]Ezr 6:21; Ne 9:2 [b]Lv 18:24-30 **9:2** [a]Dt 7:3; Ezr 10:2, 18 [b]Ex 22:31; Dt 14:2; 2Co 6:14 [c]Ne 13:3 **9:3** [a]2Ki 18:37 [b]Ne 1:4 **9:4** [a]Ezr 10:3; Is 66:2

gathered to me, and I sat appalled
until [b]the evening offering.

### *Ezra's Confession*

**5** But at the evening offering I arose
from my [1]affliction, even with my
garment and my robe torn, and I fell
on my knees and [a]stretched out my
[2]hands to Yahweh my God; **6** and I
said, "O my God, I am ashamed
and humiliated to lift up my face to
You, my God, for our iniquities have
multiplied above our heads and our
[a]guilt has become great even to the
heavens. **7** [a]Since the days of our fa-
thers to this day we *have been* in great
guilt, and on account of our iniquities
we, our kings *and* our priests have
been given into the hand of the kings
of the lands, to the sword, to cap-
tivity, and to plunder and to [b,1]open
shame, as *it is* this day. **8** But now for
a brief moment grace has been *shown*
from Yahweh our God, [a]to leave us
an escaped remnant and to give us a
[b]peg in His holy place, that our God
may [c]enlighten our eyes and give us
a little reviving in our slavery. **9** [a]For
we are slaves; yet in our slavery our
God has not forsaken us, but [b]has
extended lovingkindness to us before
the kings of Persia, to give us reviving
to raise up the house of our God, to
restore its waste places, and to give
us a wall in Judah and Jerusalem.
**10** "So now, our God, what shall we
say after this? For we have forsaken
Your commandments, **11** which You
have commanded by the hand of
Your slaves the prophets, saying,
'*The land which* you are entering to
possess is an impure land with the
impurity of the peoples of the lands,
with their abominations which have
filled it from end to end, *and* [a]with
their uncleanness. **12** So now do not
[a]give your daughters to their sons
nor take their daughters to your
sons, and [b]never seek their peace
or their prosperity, that you may be
strong and eat the good *things* of the
land and [c]leave *it* as a possession to
your sons forever.' **13** After all that
has come upon us for our evil deeds
and [a]our great guilt, since You our
God have requited *us* less than our
iniquities *deserve*, and have given us
[b]an escaped remnant as this, **14** [a]shall
we again break Your commandments
and intermarry with the peoples
[1]who commit these abominations?
[b]Would You not be angry with us [2]to
the point of destruction, until there
is no remnant nor any who escape?
**15** O Yahweh, the God of Israel, [a]You
are righteous, for we have been left
an escaped remnant, as *it is* this day;
behold, we are before You in [b]our
guilt, for [c]no one can stand before
You because of this."

### *Ezra Makes Israel Swear an Oath*

**10** Now [a]while Ezra was pray-
ing and making confession,
weeping and prostrating himself
[b]before the house of God, a very
large assembly, men, women, and
children, gathered to him from Israel;
for the people wept bitterly. **2** And
Shecaniah the son of Jehiel, one of
*the sons of* Elam, answered and said
to Ezra, "[a]We have been unfaithful to

**9:4** [b]Ex 29:39 **9:5** [a]Ex 9:29 [1]Or *fasting* [2]Lit *palms* **9:6** [a]2Chr 28:9; Ezr 9:13, 15; Rev 18:5
**9:7** [a]2Chr 29:6; Ps 106:6 [b]Da 9:7 [1]Lit *shame of faces* **9:8** [a]Ezr 9:13-15 [b]Is 22:23 [c]Ps 13:3 **9:9** [a]Ne 9:36
[b]Ezr 7:28 **9:11** [a]Ezr 6:21 **9:12** [a]Ex 34:15, 16; Dt 7:3; Ezr 9:2 [b]Dt 23:6 [c]Pr 13:22 **9:13** [a]Ezr 9:6, 7
[b]Ezr 9:8 **9:14** [a]Ezr 9:2 [b]Dt 9:8, 14 [1]Lit *of these abominations* [2]Lit *to destroy* **9:15** [a]Ne 9:33; Da 9:7
[b]Ezr 9:6 [c]Job 9:2; Ps 130:3 ◆ **10:1** [a]Da 9:4, 20 [b]2Chr 20:9 **10:2** [a]Ezr 9:2; Ne 13:27

our God and have [1]married foreign
women from the peoples of the land;
yet now there is hope for Israel in
spite of this. **3** So now [a]let us cut a
covenant with our God to put away
all the wives and [b,1]their children,
according to the counsel of [2]my
lord and of [c]those who tremble at
the commandment of our God; and
let it be done [d]according to the law.
**4** Arise! For *this* matter is [1]your re-
sponsibility, but we will be with you;
[a]be strong and act."

**5** Then Ezra arose and [a]made the
leading priests, the Levites and all Is-
rael, swear *an oath* that they would do
according to this word; so they swore
*an oath.* **6** Then Ezra [a]arose from be-
fore the house of God and went into
the chamber of Jehohanan the son of
Eliashib. He went there, *but* [b]he did
not eat bread nor drink water, for he
was mourning over the unfaithful-
ness of the exiles. **7** And they made
a proclamation throughout Judah
and Jerusalem to all the exiles, that
they should gather at Jerusalem, **8** and
that whoever would not come within
three days, according to the counsel
of the prince and the elders, all his
possessions should be devoted to
destruction and he himself separated
from the assembly of the exiles.

**9** So all the men of Judah and
Benjamin gathered at Jerusalem within
the three days. *It was the ninth month*
on the twentieth of the month, and
all the people sat in the open square
*before* the house of God, [a]trembling
because of this matter and the heavy
rain. **10** Then Ezra the priest arose
and said to them, "You have been
unfaithful and have married foreign
wives adding to the guilt of Israel. **11** So
now, [a]make confession to Yahweh,
the God of your fathers, and [b]do His
will; and [c]separate yourselves from
the peoples of the land and from the
foreign wives." **12** Then all the assembly
answered and said with a loud voice,
"This is so! As you have said, so it is
[1]our duty to do. **13** But there are many
people; it is the rainy season, and we
are not able to stand outside. Nor *can*
the task *be done* in one or two days, for
we have transgressed greatly in this
matter. **14** Let our princes stand in for
the whole assembly, and let all those
in our cities who have married foreign
wives come at set times, together with
the elders and judges of each city,
until the [a]burning anger of our God
on account of this matter is turned
away from us." **15** However, Jonathan
the son of Asahel and Jahzeiah the
son of Tikvah stood against this, with
Meshullam and Shabbethai the Levite
helping them.

**16** But the exiles did so. And [1]Ezra
the priest separated out men *who
were* heads of fathers' *households* for
*each of* their father's households, all
of them by name. So they [2]convened
on the first day of the tenth month
to investigate the matter. **17** And they
completed *investigating* all the men
who had married foreign wives by
the first day of the first month.

### *Those Who Married Foreign Wives*

**18** Among the sons of the priests
who had married foreign wives were

**10:2** [1]Lit *given dwelling to* **10:3** [a]2Chr 34:31 [b]Ezr 10:44 [c]Ezr 9:4 [d]Dt 7:2, 3 [1]Lit *that which is born of them* [2]Or *the Lord* **10:4** [a]1Chr 28:10 [1]Lit *upon you* **10:5** [a]Ne 5:12; 13:25 **10:6** [a]Ezr 10:1 [b]Dt 9:18 **10:9** [a]1Sa 12:18; Ezr 9:4; 10:3 **10:11** [a]Lv 26:40; Pr 28:13 [b]Ro 12:2 [c]Ezr 10:3 **10:12** [1]Lit *upon us* **10:14** [a]2Ki 23:26; 2Chr 28:11-13; 29:10; 30:8 **10:16** [1]Heb *there were set apart Ezra the priest, men...* [2]Lit *sat*

found of the sons of [a]Jeshua the son
of Jozadak, and his brothers: Maa-
seiah, Eliezer, Jarib and Gedaliah.
19 They gave their hand *in pledge*
to put away their wives, and being
guilty, [a]*they offered* a ram of the flock
for their guilt.

20 Of the sons of Immer *there were* Hanani and Zebadiah;
21 and of the sons of Harim: Maaseiah, Elijah, Shemaiah, Jehiel and Uzziah;
22 and of the sons of Pashhur: Elioenai, Maaseiah, Ishmael, Nethanel, Jozabad and Elasah.

23 Of Levites *there were* Jozabad, Shimei, Kelaiah (that is, Kelita), Pethahiah, Judah and Eliezer.

24 Of the singers *there was* Eliashib; and of the gatekeepers: Shallum, Telem and Uri.

25 Of Israel, of the sons of [a]Parosh *there were* Ramiah, Izziah, Malchijah, Mijamin, Eleazar, Malchijah and Benaiah;
26 and of the sons of Elam: Mattaniah, Zechariah, Jehiel, Abdi, Jeremoth and Elijah;
27 and of the sons of [a]Zattu: Elioenai, Eliashib, Mattaniah, Jeremoth, Zabad and Aziza;
28 and of the sons of Bebai: Jehohanan, Hananiah, Zabbai *and* Athlai;
29 and of the sons of Bani: Meshullam, Malluch and Adaiah, Jashub, Sheal *and* Jeremoth;
30 and of the sons of Pahath-moab: Adna, Chelal, Benaiah, Maaseiah, Mattaniah, Bezalel, Binnui and Manasseh;
31 and *of* the sons of Harim: Eliezer, Isshijah, [a]Malchijah, Shemaiah, Shimeon,
32 Benjamin, Malluch *and* Shemariah;
33 of the sons of Hashum: Mattenai, Mattattah, Zabad, Eliphelet, Jeremai, Manasseh *and* Shimei;
34 of the sons of Bani: Maadai, Amram, Uel,
35 Benaiah, Bedeiah, Cheluhi,
36 Vaniah, Meremoth, Eliashib,
37 Mattaniah, Mattenai, Jaasu,
38 Bani, Binnui, Shimei,
39 Shelemiah, Nathan, Adaiah,
40 Machnadebai, Shashai, Sharai,
41 Azarel, Shelemiah, Shemariah,
42 Shallum, Amariah *and* Joseph.
43 Of the sons of [a]Nebo *there were* Jeiel, Mattithiah, Zabad, Zebina, Jaddai, Joel *and* Benaiah.
44 All these had taken up [a]foreign
women *as wives*, and some of them
had wives *by whom* they had chil-
dren.

---

**10:18** [a]Ezr 5:2; Hag 1:1, 12; 2:4; Zec 3:1; 6:11 **10:19** [a]Lv 5:15; 6:6 **10:25** [a]Ezr 2:3; 8:3; Ne 7:8 **10:27** [a]Ezr 2:8; Ne 7:13 **10:31** [a]Ne 3:11 **10:43** [a]Nu 32:38; Ezr 2:29 **10:44** [a]1Ki 11:1-3; Ezr 10:3

## The Book of
# NEHEMIAH

### *Nehemiah Prays for the Sons of Israel*

1 The words of [a]Nehemiah the son
of Hacaliah.
Now it happened in [b]the month
Chisley, [c]*in* the twentieth year—and
I was in [d]Susa the [1]capitol— **2** that
[a]Hanani, one of my brothers, and
[1]some men from Judah came; and
I asked them concerning the Jews
who had escaped and remain from
the captivity, and about Jerusalem.
**3** They said to me, "The remnant
there in the [a]province who remain
from the captivity are in great calam-
ity and [b]reproach, and [b]the wall of
Jerusalem is broken down and [c]its
gates are burned with fire."
**4** Now it happened that when I
heard these words, [a]I sat down and
wept and mourned for days; and I was
fasting and praying before [b]the God
of heaven. **5** I said, "I beseech You,
O [1]Yahweh, the God of heaven, [a]the
great and fearsome God, [b]who keeps
the covenant and lovingkindness for
those who love Him and keep His
commandments, **6** [a]let Your ear now
be attentive and Your eyes open to
hear the prayer of Your slave which
I am praying before You today, day
and night, on behalf of the sons of
Israel Your slaves, [b]confessing the
sins of the sons of Israel which we
have sinned against You; [c]I and my
father's house have sinned. **7** [a]We
have worked *in* utter destruction
against You and have not kept the
commandments, nor the statutes,
nor the judgments [b]which You
commanded Your [1]servant Moses.
**8** Remember the word which You
commanded Your [1]servant Moses,
saying, '[a]*If* you are unfaithful, I
will scatter you among the peoples;
**9** [a]but *if* you return to Me and keep
My commandments and do them,
though those of you who have been
banished were at the ends of the sky,
I [b]will gather them from there and
will bring them [c]to the place where
I have chosen to cause My name to
dwell.' **10** [a]They are Your slaves and
Your people whom You redeemed by
Your great power and by Your strong
hand. **11** O Lord, I beseech You, [a]may
Your ear be attentive to the prayer
of Your slave and the prayer of Your
slaves who delight to fear Your name,
and make Your slave successful today
and grant him compassion before
this man."
Now I was the [b]cupbearer to the
king.

### *God's Hand Was on Nehemiah*

2 Now it happened in the month
Nisan, [a]in the twentieth year
of King [b]Artaxerxes, that wine *was*
before him, and [c]I took up the wine
and gave it to the king. Now I had

---

◆ **1:1** [a]Ne 10:1 [b]Zec 7:1 [c]Ne 2:1 [d]Es 1:2; Da 8:2 [1]Or *palace, citadel* **1:2** [a]Ne 7:2 [1]Lit *he and some* **1:3** [a]Ne 7:6 [b]Ne 2:17 [c]Ne 2:3 **1:4** [a]Ezr 9:3; 10:1 [b]Ne 2:4 **1:5** [a]Ne 4:14; 9:32; Da 9:4 [b]Ex 20:6; Ps 89:2, 3 [1]The personal covenant name of God, a form of I AM WHO I AM, cf. Ex 3:14-15 **1:6** [a]Da 9:17 [b]Ezr 10:1; Da 9:20 [c]2Chr 29:6 **1:7** [a]Da 9:5 [b]Dt 28:14 [1]Or *slave*, cf. 1:6; see Foreword, "The Terminology of Slave" **1:8** [a]Lv 26:33 [1]Or *slave*, cf. 1:6; see Foreword, "The Terminology of Slave" **1:9** [a]Dt 30:2, 3 [b]Dt 30:4 [c]Dt 12:5 **1:10** [a]Ex 32:11; Dt 9:29 **1:11** [a]Ne 1:6 [b]Ge 40:21; Ne 2:1 ◆ **2:1** [a]Ne 1:1 [b]Ezr 7:1 [c]Ne 1:11

not been sad in his presence. **2** So the king said to me, "Why is your face sad though you are not sick? [a]This is nothing but sadness of heart." Then I was very much afraid. **3** I said to the king, "[a]Let the king live forever. Why should my face not be sad [b]when the city, the place of my fathers' tombs, lies waste and its gates have been consumed by fire?" **4** Then the king said to me, "What would you request?" [a]So I prayed to the God of heaven. **5** I said to the king, "If it is good for the king, and if your servant is good before you, send me to Judah, to the city of my fathers' tombs, that I may rebuild it." **6** Then the king said to me, the queen sitting beside him, "How long will your journey be, and when will you return?" So it was good to the king to send me, and [a]I gave him a set time. **7** And I said to the king, "If it is good to the king, let letters be given me [a]for the governors *of the provinces* beyond the [1]River, that they may allow me to pass through until I come to Judah, **8** and a letter to Asaph the keeper of the king's [a]forest, that he may give me timber to make beams for the gates of [b]the fortress which is by the house *of God*, for the wall of the city and for the house to which I will go." And the king granted *them* to me because [c]the good hand of my God *was* on me.

**9** Then I came to [a]the governors *of the provinces* beyond the River and gave them the king's letters. Now [b]the king had sent with me commanders *of the* military force and horsemen. **10** Then [a]Sanballat the Horonite and Tobiah the Ammonite [1]official heard *about it*, and it was a very great evil to them that someone had come to seek the good of the sons of Israel.

### *Nehemiah Inspects Jerusalem's Walls*

**11** So I [a]came to Jerusalem and was there three days. **12** And I arose in the night, I and a few men with me. I did not tell anyone what my God was putting into my heart to do for Jerusalem; and there was no animal with me except the animal on which I was riding. **13** So I went out at night by [a]the Valley Gate in the direction of the Dragon's Spring and *on* to the [1]Dung Gate, inspecting the walls of Jerusalem [b]which were broken down and its [c]gates which were consumed by fire. **14** Then I passed on to [a]the Spring Gate and [b]the King's Pool, but there was no place for [1]my animal to pass. **15** So I went up at night by the [a]ravine and inspected the wall. Then I turned and entered the Valley Gate and turned around. **16** Now the officials did not know where I had gone or what I was doing; nor had I as yet told the Jews, the priests, the nobles, the officials, or the rest who were doing the work.

**17** Then I said to them, "You see the calamity we are in, that [a]Jerusalem lies waste and its gates burned by fire. Come, let us rebuild the wall of Jerusalem so that we will no longer be a reproach." **18** And I told them how the hand of my God had been good to me and also about the king's words which he had said to me. Then they

**2:2** [a]Pr 15:13 **2:3** [a]Da 2:4 [b]2Ki 25:8-10; 2Chr 36:19; Ne 1:3; Jer 52:12-14 **2:4** [a]Ne 1:4 **2:6** [a]Ne 13:6 **2:7** [a]Ezr 7:21; 8:36 [1]The Euphrates River, so in ch **2:8** [a]Ecc 2:5, 6 [b]Ne 7:2 [c]Ezr 7:6; Ne 2:18 **2:9** [a]Ne 2:7 [b]Ezr 8:22 **2:10** [a]Ne 2:19; 4:1 [1]Lit *servant* **2:11** [a]Ezr 8:32 **2:13** [a]Ne 3:13 [b]Ne 1:3 [c]Ne 2:3, 17 [1]Lit *Gate of Ash-heaps* **2:14** [a]Ne 3:15 [b]2Ki 20:20 [1]Lit *the animal under me* **2:15** [a]Jn 18:1 **2:17** [a]Ne 1:3

said, "Let us arise and build." [a]So
they strengthened their hands for
the good *work.* **19** But Sanballat the
Horonite and Tobiah the Ammonite
[1]official and [a]Geshem the Arab heard
*it.* And [b]they mocked us and despised
us and said, "What is this thing you
are doing? [a]Are you rebelling against
the king?" **20** So I responded to them
with a word and said to them, "[a]The
God of heaven will give us success;
therefore we His slaves will arise and
build, [b]but you have no portion, right,
or remembrance in Jerusalem."

### *Building and Repairing the Wall*

**3** Then [a]Eliashib the high priest
arose with his brothers the priests
and built [b]the Sheep Gate; they set
it apart as holy and [c]made its doors
stand. And they set apart as holy [1]the
wall to [d]the Tower of the Hundred
*and* [e]the Tower of Hananel. **2** Next
to him [a]the men of Jericho built, and
next to [1]them Zaccur the son of Imri
built.

**3** Now the sons of Hassenaah built
[a]the Fish Gate; they laid its beams and
made its doors stand with its bolts
and bars. **4** Next to them Meremoth
the son of Uriah the son of Hakkoz
made repairs. And next to them
Meshullam the son of Berechiah the
son of Meshezabel made repairs. And
next to them Zadok the son of Baana
*also* made repairs. **5** Moreover, next
to them the Tekoites made repairs,
but their nobles did not [1]support the
service of their masters.

**6** Joiada the son of Paseah and
Meshullam the son of Besodeiah
repaired [a]the Old Gate; they laid its
beams and made its doors stand with
its bolts and its bars. **7** Next to them
Melatiah the Gibeonite and Jadon
the Meronothite, the men of Gibeon
and of Mizpah, [1]also made repairs for
the official seat of the [a]governor *of*
*the province* beyond the River. **8** Next
to him Uzziel the son of Harhaiah of
the [a]goldsmiths made repairs. And
next to him Hananiah, one of the
perfumers, made repairs, and they
restored Jerusalem as far as [b]the
Broad Wall. **9** Next to them Rephaiah
the son of Hur, [a]the official of half the
district of Jerusalem, made repairs.
**10** Next to them Jedaiah the son of
Harumaph made repairs opposite his
house. And next to him Hattush the
son of Hashabneiah made repairs.
**11** Malchijah the son of Harim and
Hasshub the son of Pahath-moab
repaired [1]another section and [a]the
Tower of Furnaces. **12** Next to him
Shallum the son of Hallohesh,
[a]the official of half the district of
Jerusalem, made repairs, he and his
daughters.

**13** Hanun and the inhabitants of
Zanoah repaired [a]the Valley Gate.
They built it and made its doors
stand with its bolts and its bars, and
[1]one thousand cubits of the wall to
the [2]Dung Gate.

**14** Malchijah the son of Rechab,
the official of the district of [a]Beth-
haccherem, repaired the [b,1]Dung

**2:18** [a]2Sa 2:7 **2:19** [a]Ne 6:6 [b]Ne 4:1 [1]Lit *servant* **2:20** [a]Ezr 4:3 [b]Ne 2:4; Ac 8:21 ◆ **3:1** [a]Ne 3:20; 13:28 [b]Ne 3:32; 12:39 [c]Ne 6:1; 7:1 [d]Ne 12:39 [e]Jer 31:38 [1]Lit *it* **3:2** [a]Ne 7:36 [1]Lit *him* **3:3** [a]Ne 12:39 **3:5** [1]Lit *bring their neck to* **3:6** [a]Ne 12:39 **3:7** [a]Ne 2:7 [1]Or *which was under the jurisdiction of the governor* of the province *beyond the River, also made repairs* **3:8** [a]Ne 3:31, 32 [b]Ne 12:38 **3:9** [a]Ne 3:12, 17 **3:11** [a]Ne 12:38 [1]Lit *a second measure,* so in ch **3:12** [a]Ne 3:9 **3:13** [a]Ne 2:13 [1]Approx. 500 yd. or 457 m, a cubit was approx. 18 in. or 45 cm [2]Lit *Gate of Ash-heaps* **3:14** [a]Jer 6:1 [b]Ne 2:13 [1]Lit *Gate of Ash-heaps*

Gate. He built it and made its doors
stand with its bolts and its bars.
15 Shallum the son of Col-hozeh,
the official of the district of Mizpah,
[a]repaired the Spring Gate. He built it,
covered it and made its doors stand
with its bolts and its bars, and the
wall of the Pool of Shelah at [b]the
king's garden as far as [c]the steps
that descend from the city of David.
16 After him Nehemiah the son of
Azbuk, [a]official of half the district
of Beth-zur, made repairs as far as *a*
*point* opposite the tombs of David,
and as far as [b]the artificial pool and
the house of the mighty men. 17 After
him the Levites made repairs *under*
Rehum the son of Bani. Next to him
Hashabiah, the official of half the
district of Keilah, made repairs for his
district. 18 After him their brothers
made repairs *under* Bavvai the son
of Henadad, the official of *the other*
half of the district of Keilah. 19 Next
to him Ezer the son of Jeshua, [a]the
official of Mizpah, repaired another
section in front of the ascent of the
armory [b]at the Angle. 20 After him
Baruch the son of Zabbai zealously
repaired another section, from the
Angle to the doorway of the house of
[a]Eliashib the high priest. 21 After him
Meremoth the son of Uriah the son
of Hakkoz repaired another section,
from the doorway of Eliashib's house
even as far as the end of Eliashib's
house. 22 After him the priests, [a]the
men of the [1]valley, made repairs.
23 After [1]them Benjamin and Has-
shub made repairs in front of their
*house. After* [1]*them* Azariah the son
of Maaseiah, son of Ananiah, made
repairs beside his house. 24 After him
Binnui the son of Henadad repaired
another section, from the house of
Azariah as far as [a]the Angle and as
far as the corner. 25 Palal the son of
Uzai *made repairs* in front of the
Angle and the tower projecting from
the upper house of the king, which
is by [a]the court of the guard. After
him Pedaiah the son of Parosh *made*
*repairs.* 26 [a]The temple servants
living in [b]Ophel *made repairs* as
far as the front of [c]the Water Gate
toward the east and the projecting
tower. 27 After [1]them [a]the Tekoites
repaired another section in front of
the great projecting tower and as far
as the wall of Ophel.
28 Above [a]the Horse Gate the
priests made repairs, each in front
of his house. 29 After [1]them Zadok
the son of Immer made repairs in
front of his house. And after him
Shemaiah the son of Shecaniah,
the keeper of the East Gate, made
repairs. 30 After him Hananiah the
son of Shelemiah, and Hanun the
sixth son of Zalaph, repaired another
section. After him Meshullam the
son of Berechiah made repairs in
front of his own [1]quarters. 31 After
him Malchijah, [1]one of [a]the gold-
smiths, made repairs as far as the
house of the temple servants and
of the merchants, in front of the
[2]Inspection Gate, and as far as the
upper room of the corner. 32 Between
the upper room of the corner and
[a]the *Sheep* Gate, the goldsmiths and
the merchants made repairs.

---

**3:15** [a]Ne 2:17 [b]2Ki 25:4 [c]Ne 12:37 **3:16** [a]Ne 3:9, 12, 17 [b]2Ki 20:20; Is 7:3 **3:19** [a]Ne 3:15 [b]2Chr 26:9
**3:20** [a]Ne 3:1 **3:22** [a]Ne 12:28 [1]Lower Jordan valley; lit *circle* **3:23** [1]Lit *him* **3:24** [a]Ne 3:19
**3:25** [a]Jer 32:2 **3:26** [a]Ne 7:46 [b]Ne 11:21 [c]Ne 8:1 **3:27** [a]Ne 3:5 [1]Lit *him* **3:28** [a]2Ki 11:16; 2Chr 23:15;
Jer 31:40 **3:29** [1]Lit *him* **3:30** [1]Or *cell* **3:31** [a]Ne 3:8, 32 [1]Lit *son of* [2]Or *Mustering* **3:32** [a]Ne 3:1;
12:39

### *Sanballat and Tobiah Mock the Jews' Work*

4 [1]Now it happened that when
[a]Sanballat heard that we were
rebuilding the wall, he became an-
gry and very vexed and mocked the
Jews. **2** He spoke in the presence of
his brothers and [a]the [1]wealthy *men*
of Samaria and said, "What are these
feeble Jews doing? Are they going to
restore *it* for themselves? Can they
offer sacrifices? Can they complete *it*
in a day? Can they bring the stones to
life from the [b,2]dusty rubble, though
they are burned?" **3** Now Tobiah the
Ammonite *was* near him and he said,
"Even what they are building—[a]if
a fox should [1]jump on *it*, he would
break their stone wall down!"

**4** [a]Hear, O our God, for we are
despised! [b]Return their reproach
on their own heads and give them
up for plunder in a land of captivity.
**5** Do not [a,1]forgive their iniquity
and let not their sin be blotted out
before You, for they have [2]vexed the
builders.

**6** So we built the wall and the
whole wall was joined together to
half its *height*, and the people had a
heart to work.

**7** [1]Now it happened that when
Sanballat, Tobiah, the Arabs, the
Ammonites, and the Ashdodites
heard that the [2]repair of the walls
of Jerusalem went on, *and* that the
*places* broken down began to be
closed, they were very angry. **8** All of
them [a]joined together to come *and*
fight against Jerusalem and to cause
a disturbance in it. **9** But we prayed
to our God, and because of them we
[a]stood a guard against them day and
night.

**10** Then Judah said,

"The [1]strength of the burden
bearers is failing,
Yet there is much [2]rubbish;
And we ourselves are unable
To rebuild the wall."

**11** Our adversaries said, "They will not
know or see until we come among
them, kill them, and put a stop to
the work." **12** Now it happened when
the Jews who lived near them came
and said to us ten times, "[1]They will
come up against us from every place
where you may turn," **13** that I had
*men* stand in the lowest parts of the
space behind the wall, the [1]exposed
places, and I [a]had the people stand
by families with their swords, spears,
and bows. **14** Then I saw *their fear*.
And I arose and said to the nobles,
the officials, and the rest of the peo-
ple: "[a]Do not fear them; remember
the Lord who is great and fearsome,
and [b]fight for your brothers, your
sons, your daughters, your wives,
and your houses."

### *Doing the Work and Holding a Weapon*

**15** Now it happened that when our
enemies heard that it was known to
us, and that [a]God had thwarted their
counsel, then all of us returned to
the wall, each one to his work. **16** And
it happened that from that day on,
half of my young men carried on the
work while half of them took hold of
the spears, the shields, the bows, and

◆ **4:1** [a]Ne 2:10 [1]Ch 3:33 in Heb **4:2** [a]Ezr 4:9, 10 [b]Ne 4:10 [1]Or *army* [2]Lit *heaps of dust* **4:3** [a]Lam 5:18 [1]Lit *go up* **4:4** [a]Ps 123:3, 4 [b]Ps 79:12 **4:5** [a]Ps 69:27, 28; Jer 18:23 [1]Lit *cover* [2]Or *offended against* **4:7** [1]Ch 4:1 in Heb [2]Lit *healing* **4:8** [a]Ps 83:3 **4:9** [a]Ne 4:11 **4:10** [1]Lit *power* [2]Lit *dust* **4:12** [1]As in Gr; Heb omits *They...up* **4:13** [a]Ne 4:17, 18 [1]Lit *bare* **4:14** [a]Nu 14:9; Dt 1:29, 30 [b]2Sa 10:12 **4:15** [a]2Sa 17:14

the breastplates; and the command-
ers *were* behind the whole house of
Judah. **17** Those who were rebuilding
the wall and those who carried bur-
dens took *their* load with one hand
doing the work and the other holding
a weapon. **18** As for the builders, each
*wore* his sword girded at his side as
he built, while [1]the trumpeter *stood*
near me. **19** I said to the nobles, the
officials and the rest of the people,
"The work is great and extensive, and
we are separated on the wall far from
one another. **20** At whatever place
you hear the sound of the trumpet,
there gather together to us. [a]Our God
will fight for us."

**21** So we kept doing the work with
half of them holding spears from
[1]dawn until the stars came out. **22** At
that time I also said to the people,
"Let each man with his young man
spend the night within Jerusalem
so that they may be a guard for us
by night and a worker by day." **23** So
neither I, my brothers, my young
men, nor the men of the guard who
followed me, none of us removed our
clothes, each *took* his weapon *even*
*to* the water.

### *Each Usury Is Forsaken*

**5** Then [a]there was a great outcry
of the people and of their wives
against their [b]Jewish brothers.
**2** Now there were those who were
saying, "We, *with* our sons and our
daughters, are many; therefore let
us [a]get grain that we may eat and
live." **3** There were others who were
*saying*, "We are mortgaging our
fields, our vineyards, and our houses,
that we might get grain because
of the famine." **4** Also there were
those who were saying, "We have
borrowed money [a]for the king's
tax *on* our fields and our vineyards.
**5** But now [a]our flesh is like the flesh
of our brothers, our children like
their children. Yet behold, [b]we are
forcing our sons and our daughters to
be slaves, and some of our daughters
are forced into subjugation, and we
have no power in our hands *to help*,
and our fields and vineyards belong
to others."

**6** Then I was very [a]angry when
I had heard their outcry and these
words. **7** I consulted within my
own heart and contended with the
nobles and the officials and said
to them, "[a]You are exacting usury,
each from his brother!" Therefore, I
held a great assembly against them.
**8** I said to them, "We, according to
our ability, [a]have bought *back* our
Jewish brothers who were sold to the
nations; and now would you also sell
your brothers that they may be sold
to us?" Then they were silent and
could not find a word *to say*. **9** And
I said, "The thing which you are
doing is not good; should you not
walk in the fear of our God because
of [a]the reproach of the nations, our
enemies? **10** And likewise I, my broth-
ers, and my young men are lending
them money and grain. Please, let us
forsake this usury. **11** Please, give back
to them this very day their fields,
their vineyards, their olive groves
and *their* houses, also the hundredth
*part* of the money and of the grain,
the new wine and the oil that you are

**4:18** [1]Lit *he who sounded the trumpet* **4:20** [a]Ex 14:14; Dt 1:30 **4:21** [1]Lit *rising of the dawn*
◆ **5:1** [a]Lv 25:35 [b]Dt 15:7 **5:2** [a]Hag 1:6 **5:4** [a]Ezr 4:13; 7:24 **5:5** [a]Ge 37:27 [b]Lv 25:39 **5:6** [a]Ex 11:8
**5:7** [a]Ex 22:25; Lv 25:36; Dt 23:19, 20 **5:8** [a]Lv 25:48 **5:9** [a]Ne 4:4

exacting from them." **12** Then they
said, "We [a]will give *it* back and [b]will
require nothing from them; we will
do exactly as you are saying." So I
called the priests and [c]made them
swear that they would do according
to this word. **13** I [a]also shook out the
[1]front of my garment and said, "Thus
may God shake out every man from
his house and from his possessions
who does not establish this word;
even thus may he be shaken out and
emptied." And [b]all the assembly said,
"Amen!" And they praised Yahweh.
Then the people did according to this
word.

### *Nehemiah as Governor*

**14** Moreover, from the day that I was
put in command to be their gover-
nor in the land of Judah, from [a]the
twentieth year to the [b]thirty-second
year of King Artaxerxes, *for* twelve
years, neither I nor my [1]relatives have
eaten the governor's food *allowance.*
**15** But the former governors who
were before me [1]laid heavy bur-
dens on the people and took from
them bread and wine besides forty
[2]shekels of silver; even their young
men exerted *their* power over the
people. But I did not do so [a]because
of the fear of God. **16** I also took hold
of the work on this wall; we did not
buy any land, and all my young men
were gathered there for the work.
**17** Moreover, [a]*there were* at my table
150 Jews and officials, besides those
who came to us from the nations that
were around us. **18** Now [a]that which
was prepared for each day was one
ox *and* six choice sheep, also birds
were prepared for me; and once in
ten days all sorts of wine *were fur-
nished* in abundance. Yet for all this
[b]I did not require the governor's food
*allowance,* because the slavery was
heavy on this people. **19** [a]Remember
me, O my God, for good, *according to*
all that I have done for this people.

### *Enemies Try to Make Nehemiah Fearful*

**6** Now it happened when it was
heard by Sanballat, Tobiah, Ge-
shem the Arab, and the rest of our
enemies that I had rebuilt the wall,
and *that* no breach remained in it,
[a]although at that time I had not
made the doors to stand in the gates,
**2** that Sanballat and Geshem sent *a
message* to me, saying, "Come, let
us meet together at [1]Chephirim in
the plain of [a]Ono." But they were
planning to [2]do me harm. **3** So I sent
messengers to them, saying, "I am
doing a great work and I cannot
come down. Why should the work
stop while I leave it and come down
to you?" **4** And they sent *messages* to
me four times in this manner, and I
responded to them in the same man-
ner. **5** Then Sanballat sent his young
man to me in the same manner a fifth
time with an open letter in his hand.
**6** In it was written,

"It is heard among the nations,
and [1]Gashmu says, that [a]you
and the Jews are planning
to rebel; therefore you are
rebuilding the wall. And you
are to be their king, according

---

**5:12** [a]2Chr 28:15 [b]Ne 10:31 [c]Ezr 10:5 **5:13** [a]Ac 18:6 [b]Ne 8:6 [1]Lit *bosom* **5:14** [a]Ne 1:1 [b]Ne 13:6 [1]Lit *brothers* **5:15** [a]Ne 5:9; Job 31:23 [1]Lit *made heavy* [2]A shekel was approx. 0.4 oz. or 11 gm **5:17** [a]1Ki 18:19 **5:18** [a]1Ki 4:22, 23 [b]2Th 3:8 **5:19** [a]Ne 13:14, 22, 31 ◆ **6:1** [a]Ne 3:1, 3 **6:2** [a]1Chr 8:12 [1]Or one of *the villages* [2]Lit *do evil to me* **6:6** [a]Ne 2:19 [1]In v 1 and elsewhere, *Geshem*

to these words. 7 You have also
[1]set up prophets to call out in
Jerusalem concerning [2]you, 'A
king is in Judah!' So now it will
be heard by the king according
to these words. So now, come,
let us take counsel together."
8 Then I sent *a message* to him,
saying,

"Such words as you are
saying have not been done,
but you are [a]devising them
in your own heart."

9 For all of them were *trying* to fright-
en us, [1]thinking, "Their hands will
[2]become limp in *doing* the work, and
it will not be done." But now, [a]*O God*,
strengthen my hands.
10 Now I entered the house of
Shemaiah the son of Delaiah, son
of Mehetabel, [a]who was [1]confined
at home, and he said, "Let us meet
together in the house of God, within
the temple, and let us close the doors
of the temple, for they are coming to
kill you, and they are coming to kill
you at night." 11 But I said, "[a]Should a
man like me flee? And could one such
as I go into the temple *just* to live? I
will not go in." 12 Then I recognized
[1]that surely God had not sent him,
but he spoke *his* prophecy against me
because Tobiah and Sanballat had
hired him. 13 He was hired for this
reason, [a]that I might become afraid
and act accordingly and sin, so that
they could give *me* a bad name in
order that they could reproach me.
14 [a]Remember, O my God, Tobiah
and Sanballat according to these
works of theirs, and also Noadiah
[b]the prophetess and the rest of the
prophets who were *trying* to make
me afraid.

### *The Wall Is Finished*

15 So [a]the wall was finished on the
twenty-fifth of *the month* Elul, in
fifty-two days. 16 [a]Now it happened
that when all our enemies heard *of
it*, and all the nations surrounding
us saw *it*, [1]their confidence fell.
And [b]they knew that it was from
our God that this work had been
accomplished. 17 Also in those days
many letters went from the nobles of
Judah to Tobiah, and Tobiah's *letters*
came to them. 18 For many in Judah
were sworn by oath to him because
he was the son-in-law of Shecaniah
the son of Arah, and his son Jeho-
hanan had taken the daughter of
Meshullam the son of Berechiah *as a
wife*. 19 Moreover, they were speaking
about his good deeds in my presence
and bringing my words to him. Then
Tobiah sent letters to make me afraid.

### *Census of First Returned Exiles*

7 Now it happened when [a]the wall
was rebuilt and I had made the
doors to stand, and the gatekeepers
and the singers and the Levites were
appointed, 2 that I commanded [a]Ha-
nani my brother and [b]Hananiah the
commander of [c]the fortress, *to be*
over Jerusalem, for he was [d]a faithful
man and feared God more than many.
3 Then I said to them, "The gates of
Jerusalem must not be opened until
the sun is hot; and until they are
*there* standing *guard*, they must shut

**6:7** [1]Lit *made prophets stand*, cf. 4:13; 6:1; 7:3 [2]Lit *you, saying* **6:8** [a]Job 13:4; Ps 52:2
**6:9** [a]Ps 138:3 [1]Lit *saying,* [2]Lit *drop from* **6:10** [a]Jer 36:5 [1]Lit *shut up* **6:11** [a]Pr 28:1 **6:12** [1]Lit *and behold, God* **6:13** [a]Ne 6:6 **6:14** [a]Ne 13:29 [b]Eze 13:17 **6:15** [a]Ne 4:1, 2 **6:16** [a]Ne 2:10; 4:1, 7 [b]Ex 14:25 [1]Lit *they fell exceedingly in their own eyes* ◆ **7:1** [a]Ne 6:1, 15 **7:2** [a]Ne 1:2 [b]Ne 10:23 [c]Ne 2:8 [d]Ne 13:13

and bolt the doors. Also have guards
from the inhabitants of Jerusalem
stand, each at his post, and each in
front of his own house." **4** Now the
city was large and spacious, but the
people in it were few and the houses
were not rebuilt.

**5** [a]Then my God put it into my
heart, and I gathered the nobles,
the officials, and the people to be
recorded by genealogies. Then I
found the book of the genealogy of
those who came up first, and in it I
found written:

**6** [a]These are the [1]people of the
province who came up out of the cap-
tivity of the exiles whom Nebuchad-
nezzar the king of Babylon had taken
away into exile, and who returned
to Jerusalem and Judah, each to his
city, **7** who came with Zerubbabel,
Jeshua, Nehemiah, [1]Azariah, [2]Raami-
ah, Nahamani, Mordecai, Bilshan,
[3]Mispereth, Bigvai, [4]Nehum, Baanah.

The number of men of the people of Israel:

**8** the sons of Parosh, 2,172;
**9** the sons of Shephatiah, 372;
**10** the sons of Arah, 652;
**11** the sons of Pahath-moab of the sons of Jeshua and Joab, 2,818;
**12** the sons of Elam, 1,254;
**13** the sons of Zattu, 845;
**14** the sons of Zaccai, 760;
**15** the sons of [1]Binnui, 648;
**16** the sons of Bebai, 628;
**17** the sons of Azgad, 2,322;
**18** the sons of Adonikam, 667;
**19** the sons of Bigvai, 2,067;
**20** the sons of Adin, 655;
**21** the sons of Ater, of Hezekiah, 98;
**22** the sons of Hashum, 328;
**23** the sons of Bezai, 324;
**24** the sons of [1]Hariph, 112;
**25** the sons of [1]Gibeon, 95;
**26** the men of Bethlehem and Netophah, 188;
**27** the men of Anathoth, 128;
**28** the men of [1]Beth-azmaveth, 42;
**29** the men of [1]Kiriath-jearim, Chephirah, and Beeroth, 743;
**30** the men of Ramah and Geba, 621;
**31** the men of Michmas, 122;
**32** the men of Bethel and Ai, 123;
**33** the men of the other Nebo, 52;
**34** the sons of the other Elam, 1,254;
**35** the sons of Harim, 320;
**36** the [1]men of Jericho, 345;
**37** the sons of Lod, Hadid and Ono, 721;
**38** the sons of Senaah, 3,930.

**39** The priests:
the sons of Jedaiah of the house of Jeshua, 973;
**40** the sons of Immer, 1,052;
**41** the sons of Pashhur, 1,247;
**42** the sons of Harim, 1,017.

**43** The Levites:
the sons of Jeshua, of Kadmiel, of the sons of [1]Hodevah, 74.

**44** The singers:
the sons of Asaph, 148.

**45** The gatekeepers:
the sons of Shallum, the sons of Ater, the sons of Talmon, the sons of Akkub, the sons of Hatita, the sons of Shobai, 138.

---

**7:5** [a]Pr 2:6; 3:6 **7:6** [a]Ezr 2:1-70 [1]Lit *sons* **7:7** [1]In Ezr 2:2, *Seraiah* [2]In Ezr 2:2, *Reelaiah* [3]In Ezr 2:2, *Mispar* [4]In Ezr 2:2, *Rehum* **7:15** [1]In Ezr 2:10, *Bani* **7:24** [1]In Ezr 2:18, *Jorah* **7:25** [1]In Ezr 2:20, *Gibbar* **7:28** [1]In Ezr 2:24, *Azmaveth* **7:29** [1]In Ezr 2:25, *Kiriath-arim* **7:36** [1]Lit *sons* **7:43** [1]In Ezr 2:40, *Hodaviah*

46 The temple servants:
the sons of Ziha, the sons of Hasupha, the sons of Tabbaoth,
47 the sons of Keros, the sons of [1]Sia, the sons of Padon,
48 the sons of Lebana, the sons of Hagaba, the sons of Shalmai,
49 the sons of Hanan, the sons of Giddel, the sons of Gahar,
50 the sons of Reaiah, the sons of Rezin, the sons of Nekoda,
51 the sons of Gazzam, the sons of Uzza, the sons of Paseah,
52 the sons of Besai, the sons of Meunim, the sons of [1]Nephushesim,
53 the sons of Bakbuk, the sons of Hakupha, the sons of Harhur,
54 the sons of [1]Bazlith, the sons of Mehida, the sons of Harsha,
55 the sons of Barkos, the sons of Sisera, the sons of Temah,
56 the sons of Neziah, the sons of Hatipha.
57 The sons of Solomon's servants:
the sons of Sotai, the sons of [1]Sophereth, the sons of [2]Perida,
58 the sons of Jaala, the sons of Darkon, the sons of Giddel,
59 the sons of Shephatiah, the sons of Hattil, the sons of Pochereth-hazzebaim, the sons of [1]Amon.
60 All the temple servants and the
sons of Solomon's servants *were* 392.
61 Now these *were* those who
came up from Tel-melah, Tel-harsha,
Cherub, [1]Addon, and Immer; but
they were not able to declare their
fathers' houses or their *fathers'* seed,
whether they were of Israel:
62 the sons of Delaiah, the sons of Tobiah, the sons of Nekoda, 642.
63 Of the priests:
the sons of [1]Hobaiah, the sons of Hakkoz, the sons of Barzillai, who took a wife of the daughters of Barzillai, the Gileadite, and he was called by their name.
64 These searched *in* their genealogi-
cal records, but it could not be found;
therefore they were considered un-
clean *and excluded* from the priest-
hood. 65 [a]And the [1]governor said to
them that they should not eat from
the most holy things until a priest
stood with [b,2]Urim and Thummim.

### *The Assembly and Their Gifts*

66 The whole assembly together *was* 42,360,
67 besides their male and their female slaves, [1]of whom *there were* 7,337;
and they had 245 male and female singers.
68 [a,1]Their horses were 736; their mules, 245;
69 *their* camels, 435; *their* donkeys, 6,720.
70 Some from among the heads of
fathers' *households* gave to the work.
The [a,1]governor gave to the treasury
1,000 gold [2]drachmas, 50 bowls, 530
priests' tunics. 71 Some of the heads
of fathers' *households* gave into the

**7:47** [1]In Ezr 2:44, *Siaha* **7:52** [1]In Ezr 2:50, *Nephisim* **7:54** [1]In Ezr 2:52, *Bazluth* **7:57** [1]In Ezr 2:55, *Hassophereth* [2]In Ezr 2:55, *Peruda* **7:59** [1]In Ezr 2:57, *Ami* **7:61** [1]In Ezr 2:59, *Addan* **7:63** [1]In Ezr 2:61, *Habaiah* **7:65** [a]Ne 8:9; 10:1 [b]Ex 28:30; Dt 33:8 [1]Heb *Tirshatha*, a Persian title [2]Lit *the lights and perfections* **7:67** [1]Lit *these* **7:68** [a]Ezr 2:66 [1]As in some ancient mss and Gr **7:70** [a]Ne 7:65; 8:9 [1]Heb *Tirshatha*, a Persian title [2]A Greek silver coin, approx. a laborer's daily wage

treasury of the work 20,000 gold
drachmas and 2,200 silver [1]minas.
**72** That which the rest of the people
gave was 20,000 gold drachmas and
2,000 silver minas and 67 priests'
tunics.

**73** So [a]the priests, the Levites, the
gatekeepers, the singers, some of the
people, the temple servants, and all
Israel lived in their cities.

[b]Then the seventh month came,
and the sons of Israel *were* in their
cities.

### *Ezra Reads the Book of the Law*

**8** And all the people gathered as
one man at the square which
was in front of [a]the Water Gate, and
they said to [b]Ezra the scribe to bring
[c]the book of the law of Moses which
Yahweh had commanded to Israel.
**2** Then [a]Ezra the priest brought the
law before the assembly of men,
women, and all who *could* under-
stand when listening, on [b]the first
day of the seventh month. **3** And he
read from it before the square which
was in front of [a]the Water Gate from
[1]early morning until midday, in the
presence of men and women, those
who could understand; and all the
ears of the people were attentive to
the book of the law. **4** Ezra the scribe
stood on a wooden podium which
they had made for the purpose. And
beside him stood Mattithiah, Shema,
Anaiah, Uriah, Hilkiah, and Maa-
seiah on his right hand; and Peda-
iah, Mishael, Malchijah, Hashum,
Hashbaddanah, Zechariah, *and*
Meshullam on his left hand. **5** And
Ezra opened [a]the book in the sight
of all the people for he was above all
the people; and when he opened it,
all the people [b]stood up. **6** Then Ezra
blessed Yahweh the great God. And
all the people answered, "[a]Amen,
Amen!" while lifting up their hands;
then [b]they bowed low and worshiped
Yahweh with *their* [1]faces to the
ground. **7** Also Jeshua, Bani, Sher-
ebiah, Jamin, Akkub, Shabbethai,
Hodiah, Maaseiah, Kelita, Azariah,
Jozabad, Hanan, Pelaiah, the Levites,
were providing understanding of the
law to the people while the people
*stood* in their place. **8** They read
from the book, from the law of God,
[1]explaining and [2]giving insight, and
they provided understanding of the
reading.

### *This Day Is Holy*

**9** Then Nehemiah, who was the
[a,1]governor, and Ezra [b]the priest *and*
scribe, and the Levites, who provided
the people with understanding, said
to all the people, "[c]This day is holy
to Yahweh your God; [d]do not mourn
or weep." For all the people were
weeping when they heard the words
of the law. **10** Then he said to them,
"Go, eat of the fat, drink of the sweet,
and [a]send portions to him who has
nothing prepared; for this day is holy
to our Lord. Do not be grieved, for the
joy of Yahweh is your strength." **11** So
the Levites quieted all the people,
saying, "Be still, for the day is holy;
do not be grieved." **12** Then all the
people went away to eat, to drink,
[a]to send portions, and to celebrate

---

**7:71** [1]A mina was approx. 1.25 lb. or 0.6 kg **7:73** [a]1Chr 9:2 [b]Ezr 3:1 ◆ **8:1** [a]Ne 3:26 [b]Ezr 7:6 [c]2Chr 34:15 **8:2** [a]Dt 31:9-11; Ne 8:9 [b]Lv 23:24 **8:3** [a]Ne 8:1 [1]Lit *the light* **8:5** [a]Ne 8:3 [b]Jdg 3:20; 1Ki 8:12-14 **8:6** [a]Ne 5:13 [b]Ex 4:31 [1]Lit *noses* **8:8** [1]Or *translating* [2]Or *giving the sense* **8:9** [a]Ne 7:65, 70 [b]Ne 12:26 [c]Ne 8:2 [d]Dt 12:7, 12 [1]Heb *Tirshatha*, a Persian title **8:10** [a]Dt 26:11-13 **8:12** [a]Ne 8:10

with great gladness, [b]because they
understood the words which had
been made known to them.

### *Feast of Booths Restored*

**13** Then on the second day the heads
of fathers' *households* of all the peo-
ple, the priests and the Levites were
gathered to Ezra the scribe that they
might gain insight into the words of
the law. **14** They found written in the
law how Yahweh had commanded by
the hand of Moses that the sons of
Israel [a]should live in booths during
the feast of the seventh month,
**15** [a]and that they should make the
report heard and make a proclama-
tion *of it* pass throughout all their
cities and [b]in Jerusalem, saying,
"[c]Go out to the hills, and bring olive
branches and [1]wild olive branches,
myrtle branches, palm branches, and
branches of *other* leafy trees, to make
booths, as it is written." **16** So the peo-
ple went out and brought *them* and
made booths for themselves, each
[a]on his roof, and in their courts and in
the courts of the house of God, and in
the square at [b]the Water Gate and in
the square at [c]the Gate of Ephraim.
**17** The entire assembly of those who
had returned from the captivity made
booths and lived in the booths. The
sons of Israel [a]had indeed not done
so from the days of Joshua the son
of Nun to that day. And [b]there was
exceedingly great gladness. **18** [a]And
he read from the book of the law of
God daily, from the first day to the
last day. And they [b]celebrated the
*feast seven* days, and on [c]the eighth
day *there was* a solemn assembly
according to the *legal* judgment.

### *Israel Confesses Their Sins*

**9** Now on the twenty-fourth day
of [a]this month the sons of Israel
gathered [b]with fasting, in sackcloth
and with [c]dirt upon them. **2** The
[a]seed of Israel separated themselves
from all foreigners, and stood and
[b]confessed their sins and the iniq-
uities of their fathers. **3** And [a]they
rose up in their place and read from
the book of the law of Yahweh their
God for a fourth of the day; and for
*another* fourth they were confessing
and worshiping Yahweh their God.
**4** [a]Then Jeshua rose up on the Levites'
platform, *along* with Bani, Kadmiel,
Shebaniah, Bunni, Sherebiah, Bani,
*and* Chenani, and they cried out with
a loud voice to Yahweh their God.
**5** And the Levites, Jeshua, Kadmiel,
Bani, Hashabneiah, Sherebiah,
Hodiah, Shebaniah, *and* Pethahiah,
said, "Rise up, bless Yahweh your God
from everlasting to everlasting!

O may Your glorious
  name be blessed
And exalted above all
  blessing and praise!
**6** "[a]You alone are Yahweh.
[b]You have made the heavens,
The heaven of heavens
  with all their host,
The earth and all that is on it,
The seas and all that
  is in them.
[c]You give life to all of them
And the heavenly host
  bows down to You.

---

**8:12** [b]Ne 8:7, 8 **8:14** [a]Lv 23:34, 40, 42 **8:15** [a]Lv 23:4 [b]Dt 16:16 [c]Lv 23:40 [1]Lit *oil tree*, species unknown **8:16** [a]Jer 32:29 [b]Ne 8:1 [c]2Ki 14:13; Ne 12:39 **8:17** [a]2Chr 7:8; 8:13 [b]2Chr 30:21 **8:18** [a]Dt 31:11 [b]Lv 23:36 [c]Nu 29:35 ◆ **9:1** [a]Ne 8:2 [b]Ezr 8:23 [c]1Sa 4:12 **9:2** [a]Ezr 10:11; Ne 13:3 [b]Pr 28:13; Jer 3:13 **9:3** [a]Ne 8:4 **9:4** [a]Ne 8:7 **9:6** [a]Dt 6:4; 2Ki 19:15 [b]Ge 1:1 [c]Col 1:16f

7 "You are Yahweh God,
[a]Who chose Abram
And brought him out
from [b]Ur of the Chaldees,
And [c]gave him the name
Abraham.
8 "You found [a]his heart
faithful before You,
And cut a covenant with him
To give *him* the land
of the Canaanite,
Of the Hittite and the Amorite,
Of the Perizzite, the Jebusite,
and the Girgashite—
To give *it* to his seed.
And You [b]have established
Your promise,
For You are righteous.

9 "[a]You saw the affliction
of our fathers in Egypt,
And [b]heard their cry
by the [1]Red Sea.
10 "Then You performed
[a]signs and wonders
against Pharaoh,
Against all his servants and
all the people of his land;
For You knew that [b]they
acted presumptuously
toward them,
And [c]made a name
for Yourself as *it is* this day.
11 "[a]You split the sea before them,
So they passed
through the midst
of the sea on dry land;
And [b]their pursuers You
cast into the depths,
Like a stone
into mighty waters.
12 "And with a pillar of cloud
[a]You led them by day,
And with a pillar
of fire by night
To light for them the way
In which they were to go.
13 "Then [a]You came down
on Mount Sinai,
And [b]spoke with them
from heaven;
You gave them [c]upright
judgments and true laws,
Good statutes
and commandments.
14 "So You made known to them
[a]Your holy sabbath,
And commanded
to them commandments,
statutes and law,
By the hand of Your
servant Moses.
15 "You [a]gave bread
from heaven for them
for their hunger,
You [b]brought forth water
from a rock for them
for their thirst,
And You [c]said to them
to enter in order to possess
The land which You
[1]swore to give them.

16 "But they, our fathers, [a]acted
presumptuously;
They [b,1]became stiff-necked
and would not listen
to Your commandments.
17 "They refused to listen,
And [a]did not remember Your
wondrous deeds
which You did among them;

**9:7** [a]Ge 12:1 [b]Ge 11:31 [c]Ge 17:5 **9:8** [a]Ge 15:6, 18-21 [b]Jos 21:43-45 **9:9** [a]Ex 3:7 [b]Ex 14:10-14, 31 [1]Lit *Sea of Reeds* **9:10** [a]Ex 7:8-12:32 [b]Ex 5:2 [c]Ex 9:16 **9:11** [a]Ex 14:21 [b]Ex 15:1, 5, 10 **9:12** [a]Ex 13:21, 22 **9:13** [a]Ex 19:11, 18-20 [b]Ex 20:1 [c]Ps 19:7-9 **9:14** [a]Ex 16:23; 20:8 **9:15** [a]Ex 16:4, 14, 15 [b]Ex 17:6; Nu 20:7-13 [c]Dt 1:8, 21 [1]Lit *lifted up Your hand* **9:16** [a]Ne 9:10 [b]Dt 1:26-33; 31:27; Ne 9:29 [1]Lit *stiffened their neck, so also v 17* **9:17** [a]Ps 78:11, 42-55

So they became stiff-necked
and [b]gave *themselves*
a chief to return to their
slavery [1]in Egypt.
But You are a God
[c]of lavish forgiveness,
Gracious and compassionate,
Slow to anger and abounding
in lovingkindness;
And You did not
forsake them.
18 "Even when they [a]made
for themselves
A molten calf
And said, 'This is your God
Who brought you up
from Egypt,'
And [1]committed great
[2]blasphemies,
19 [a]But You, in Your abundant
compassion,
Did not forsake them
in the wilderness;
[b]The pillar of cloud did not
depart from them by day,
To lead them on their way,
Nor the pillar of fire by night,
To light for them the way
in which they were to go.
20 '[a]You gave Your good Spirit
to give them insight,
Your manna You did not
withhold from their mouth,
And You gave them water
for their thirst.
21 "Indeed, [a]forty years
You sustained them
in the wilderness, *and*
they did not lack;
Their clothes did not wear
out, nor did their feet swell.
22 "You also gave them
kingdoms and peoples,
And apportioned *them*
to them as a [1]boundary.
[a]They took possession
of the land of Sihon
[2]the king of Heshbon
And the land of Og
the king of Bashan.
23 "You made their sons
numerous as [a]the
stars of heaven,
And You brought them
into the land
Which You had said for their
fathers to enter and possess.
24 "[a]So their sons entered and
possessed the land.
And [b]You subdued
before them the inhabitants
of the land, the Canaanites,
And You gave them into their
hand, with their kings and
the peoples of the land,
To do with them
according to their desire.
25 "[a]They captured fortified
cities and a [b,1]rich [2]land.
They took possession
of [c] houses full
of every good thing,
Hewn cisterns, vineyards,
olive groves,
Trees for food in abundance.
So they ate, were filled,
and [d]grew fat,
And [e]reveled in Your
great goodness.

26 "[a]But they became disobedient
and rebelled against You,

**9:17** [b]Nu 14:4 [c]Ex 34:6, 7; Nu 14:18 [1]As in Gr and some Heb mss; Heb *in their rebellion* **9:18** [a]Ex 32:4-8, 31 [1]Lit *did* [2]Lit *acts of contempt* **9:19** [a]Dt 8:2-4; Ne 9:27, 31 [b]Ne 9:12 **9:20** [a]Nu 11:17; Ne 9:30; Is 63:11-14 **9:21** [a]Dt 2:7 **9:22** [a]Nu 21:21-35 [1]Lit *side, corner* [2]As in Gr and Lat; Heb *and the land of the king of Heshbon* **9:23** [a]Ge 15:5; 22:17 **9:24** [a]Jos 11:23; 21:43 [b]Jos 18:1 **9:25** [a]Dt 3:5 [b]Nu 13:27 [c]Dt 6:11 [d]Dt 32:15 [e]1Ki 8:66 [1]Lit *fat* [2]Or *ground* **9:26** [a]Jdg 2:11

And [b]cast Your law
behind their backs
And [c]killed Your prophets
who had [d]testified to them
So that they might
return to You,
And [e]they [1]committed
great [2]blasphemies.
27 "Therefore You [a]gave them
into the hand of the
ones who distressed
them, and they afflicted
them with distress,
But [b]at the time of their
distress they cried to You,
And You listened from heaven,
and according to Your
abundant compassion
You [c]gave them saviors and
they saved them
from the hand of the ones
that distressed them.
28 "But [a]as soon as they had
rest, they returned to
do evil before You;
Therefore You forsook
them in the hand of their
enemies, so they had
dominion over them.
Then they returned and
cried to You. And You
listened from heaven,
And [b]many times You
delivered them according
to Your compassion,
29 And [a]testified to them
in order to turn them
back to Your law.
Yet [b]they acted
presumptuously and
did not listen to Your
commandments but sinned
against Your judgments,
By [c]which if a man does
them, he shall live.
And they [d]gave a stubborn
shoulder and stiffened
their neck, and
would not listen.
30 "[a]However, You bore
with them for many years,
And [b]testified to them
by [c]Your Spirit by the hand
of Your prophets,
Yet they would not give ear.
So You gave them
into the hand of
the peoples of the lands.
31 "Nevertheless, in Your
abundant compassion
You [a]did not make a
complete destruction
of them or forsake them,
For You are [b]a gracious and
compassionate God.

32 "So now, our God, [a]the
great, the mighty, and
the awesome God, who
keeps covenant and
lovingkindness,
Do not let all the hardship
seem insignificant
before You,
Which has found us, our
kings, our princes, our
priests, our prophets, our
fathers, and all Your people,
[b]From the days of the kings
of Assyria to this day.
33 "However, [a]You are righteous
in all that has come upon us;

**9:26** [b]1Ki 14:9 [c]2Chr 36:16 [d]Ne 9:30 [e]Ne 9:18 [1]Lit *did* [2]Lit *acts of contempt* **9:27** [a]Jdg 2:14 [b]Dt 4:29 [c]Jdg 2:16 **9:28** [a]Jdg 3:11 [b]Ps 106:43 **9:29** [a]Ne 9:26, 30 [b]Ne 9:10, 16 [c]Lv 18:5 [d]Zec 7:11 **9:30** [a]Ps 95:10; Ac 13:18 [b]2Ki 17:13-18; 2Chr 36:15, 16; Ne 9:26, 29 [c]Ne 9:20 **9:31** [a]Jer 4:27 [b]Ne 9:17 **9:32** [a]Ne 1:5 [b]2Ki 15:19, 29; 2Ki 17:3-6; Ezr 4:2, 10 **9:33** [a]Ge 18:25; Jer 12:1

For You have dealt in truth,
but we have acted wickedly.
34 "Now our kings, our princes,
our priests, and our fathers
did not do Your law
Or pay attention to Your
commandments and Your
testimonies with which
You testified against them.
35 "But [a]they, in their
own kingdom,
[b]With Your abundant
goodness which
You gave them,
With the broad and rich
land which You set
before them,
Did not serve You or turn
from their evil deeds.
36 "Behold, [a]we are slaves today,
And as to the land which
You gave to our fathers
to eat of its fruit and
its goodness,
Behold, we are slaves in it.
37 "[a]Its abundant produce
is for the kings
Whom You have put over us
because of our sins;
They also rule over our
bodies
And over our cattle
according to their desire,
So we are in great distress.

### *An Agreement Is Cut*

38 "[1]Now because of all this
[a]We are cutting an
agreement in writing;
And on the [b]sealed document
*are the names of* our
princes, our Levites,
*and* our priests."

### *Signers of the Document*

10 [1]Now on the [a]sealed document
*were the following names*:
Nehemiah the [2]governor,
the son of Hacaliah, and
Zedekiah,
2 Seraiah, Azariah, Jeremiah,
3 Pashhur, Amariah, Malchijah,
4 Hattush, Shebaniah,
Malluch,
5 Harim, Meremoth, Obadiah,
6 Daniel, Ginnethon, Baruch,
7 Meshullam, Abijah, Mijamin,
8 Maaziah, Bilgai, Shemaiah.
These *were* the priests.
9 And the Levites:
Jeshua the son of Azaniah,
Binnui of the sons of
Henadad, Kadmiel;
10 also their brothers Shebaniah,
Hodiah, Kelita, Pelaiah,
Hanan,
11 Mica, Rehob, Hashabiah,
12 Zaccur, Sherebiah,
Shebaniah,
13 Hodiah, Bani, Beninu.
14 The heads of the people:
Parosh, Pahath-moab, Elam,
Zattu, Bani,
15 Bunni, Azgad, Bebai,
16 Adonijah, Bigvai, Adin,
17 Ater, Hezekiah, Azzur,
18 Hodiah, Hashum, Bezai,
19 Hariph, Anathoth, Nebai,
20 Magpiash, Meshullam, Hezir,
21 Meshezabel, Zadok, Jaddua,
22 Pelatiah, Hanan, Anaiah,
23 Hoshea, Hananiah, Hasshub,
24 Hallohesh, Pilha, Shobek,
25 Rehum, Hashabnah,
Maaseiah,
26 Ahiah, Hanan, Anan,
27 Malluch, Harim, Baanah.

**9:35** [a]Dt 28:47 [b]Ne 9:25 **9:36** [a]Dt 28:48 **9:37** [a]Dt 28:33 **9:38** [a]Ne 10:29 [b]Ne 10:1 [1]Ch 10:1 in Heb ◆ **10:1** [a]Ne 9:38 [1]Ch 10:2 in Heb [2]Heb *Tirshatha*, a Persian title

### *The People Enter into an Oath*

**28** Now [a]the rest of the people—the
priests, the Levites, the gatekeepers,
the singers, the temple servants,
and [b]all those who had separated
themselves from the peoples of the
lands to the law of God, their wives,
their sons and their daughters—
all those who had knowledge *and*
understanding, **29** are [1]joining with
their [2]relatives, their nobles, and
are [a]entering into a curse and an
oath to walk in God's law, which was
given by the hand of Moses, God's
servant, and to keep and to do all
the commandments of Yahweh our
Lord and His judgments and His
statutes; **30** and [a]that we will not
give our daughters to the peoples
of the land or take their daughters
for our sons. **31** As [a]for the peoples
of the land who bring wares or any
grain on the sabbath day to sell, we
will not receive from them on the
sabbath or a holy day; and we will
forego *the crops* the [b]seventh year
and the [c]exaction of every debt.

**32** We also [1]set ourselves under
*the* commandments to give yearly
[a]one-third of a [2]shekel for the service
of the house of our God: **33** for the
[a]showbread, for the continual grain
offering, for the continual burnt offering, the sabbaths, the new moon,
for the appointed times, for the holy
things and for the sin offerings to
make atonement for Israel, and all
the work of the house of our God.

**34** Likewise [a]we cast lots [b]for the
supply of wood *among* the priests,
the Levites, and the people, in
order to bring it to the house of
our God, according to our fathers'
households, at fixed times annually,
to burn on the altar of Yahweh our
God, as it is written in the law;
**35** and to bring the first fruits of
our ground and [a]the first fruits
of all the fruit of every tree to the
house of Yahweh annually, **36** and
to [a]bring to the house of our God
the firstborn of our sons and of
our cattle, and the firstborn of our
herds and our flocks as it is written
in the law, for the priests who are
ministering in the house of our
God. **37** [a]We will also bring the first
of our [1]dough, our contributions,
the fruit of every tree, the new
wine and the oil [b]to the priests at
the chambers of the house of our
God, and the [c]tithe of our ground
to the Levites, for the Levites are
they who receive the tithes in all
the towns *where we* serve. **38** [a]And
the priest, the son of Aaron, shall be
with the Levites when the Levites
receive tithes, and the Levites shall
bring up the tenth of the tithes
to the house of our God, to the
chambers of [b]the storehouse. **39** For
the sons of Israel and the sons of
Levi shall bring the [a]contribution of
the grain, the new wine and the oil
to the chambers; the utensils of the
sanctuary are there, as well as the
priests who are ministering and
the gatekeepers and the singers.
Thus [b]we will not forsake the house
of our God.

---

**10:28** [a]Ezr 2:36-58 [b]Ne 9:2 **10:29** [a]Ne 5:12 [1]Lit *taking hold of* [2]Lit *brothers* **10:30** [a]Ex 34:16; Dt 7:3 **10:31** [a]Ne 13:15-22 [b]Ex 23:10, 11; Lv 25:1-7 [c]Dt 15:1, 2 **10:32** [a]Ex 30:11-16; Mt 17:24 [1]Lit *caused commands to stand on us,* cf. Ne 4:13; 7:3; 9:2 [2]A shekel was approx. 0.4 oz. or 11 gm **10:33** [a]Lv 24:5, 6; 2Chr 2:4 **10:34** [a]Ne 11:1 [b]Ne 13:31 **10:35** [a]Ex 23:19; 34:26; Dt 26:2 **10:36** [a]Ex 13:2 **10:37** [a]Lv 23:17 [b]Ne 13:5, 9 [c]Lv 27:30; Nu 18:21 [1]Or *coarse meal* **10:38** [a]Nu 18:26 [b]Ne 13:12, 13 **10:39** [a]Dt 12:6 [b]Ne 13:10, 11

### *The Heads of the Provinces in Jerusalem*

11 And [a]the officials of the people
lived in Jerusalem, but the rest
of the people [b]cast lots to bring one
out of ten to live in Jerusalem, [c]the
holy city, while nine-tenths *remained*
in the *other* cities. 2 And the people
blessed all the men who [a]freely
offered to live in Jerusalem.

3 [a]Now these are the heads of the
provinces who lived in Jerusalem,
but in the cities of Judah [b]each
lived in his own possession in their
cities—[1]the Israelites, the priests,
the Levites, the [c,2]temple servants,
and the [d]sons of Solomon's servants.
4 And some of the sons of Judah
and some of the sons of Benjamin
lived in Jerusalem. From the sons
of Judah:

Athaiah the son of Uzziah,
the son of Zechariah, the
son of Amariah, the son
of Shephatiah, the son of
Mahalalel, from the sons
of Perez;
5 and Maaseiah the son of
Baruch, the son of Col-hozeh,
the son of Hazaiah, the son of
Adaiah, the son of Joiarib, the
son of Zechariah, the son of
the Shilonite.
6 All the sons of Perez who lived
in Jerusalem were 468 valiant
men.

7 Now these are the sons of Benjamin:
Sallu the son of Meshullam,
the son of Joed, the son of
Pedaiah, the son of Kolaiah,
*the son of* Maaseiah, the son
of Ithiel, the son of Jeshaiah;
8 and after him Gabbai *and*
Sallai, 928.
9 Joel the son of Zichri was their
overseer,
and Judah the son of
Hassenuah was second [1]in
command of the city.

10 From the priests:
Jedaiah the son of Joiarib,
Jachin,
11 Seraiah the son of Hilkiah, the
son of Meshullam, the son of
Zadok, the son of Meraioth,
the son of Ahitub, the leader
of the house of God,
12 and their [1]relatives who did
the work of the [2]house, 822;
and Adaiah the son of
Jeroham, the son of Pelaliah,
the son of Amzi, the son of
Zechariah, the son of Pashhur,
the son of Malchijah,
13 and his relatives, heads of
fathers' *households*, 242; and
Amashsai the son of Azarel,
the son of Ahzai, the son of
Meshillemoth, the son of
Immer,
14 and their relatives, mighty
men of valor, 128.
And their overseer
was Zabdiel, the son of
[1]Haggedolim.

15 Now from the Levites:
Shemaiah the son of
Hasshub, the son of Azrikam,
the son of Hashabiah, the son
of Bunni;
16 and Shabbethai and Jozabad,
from the [1]chiefs of the Levites,
who were over [a]the outside
work of the house of God;

◆ **11:1** [a]Ne 7:4 [b]Ne 10:34 [c]Ne 11:18; Is 48:2 **11:2** [a]Jdg 5:9 **11:3** [a]1Chr 9:2-34 [b]Ne 7:73; 11:20 [c]Ezr 2:43 [d]Ne 7:57 [1]Lit *Israel* [2]Heb *Nethinim* **11:9** [1]Lit *over* **11:12** [1]Lit *brothers*, so in ch [2]Or *temple* **11:14** [1]Or *the great ones* **11:16** [a]1Chr 26:29 [1]Lit *heads*

17 and Mattaniah the son of
Mica, the son of [1]Zabdi,
the son of Asaph, who was
the [2]chief in beginning the
thanksgiving in prayer,
and Bakbukiah, the second
among his relatives;
and [3]Abda the son of
[4]Shammua, the son of Galal,
the son of Jeduthun.
18 All the Levites in [a]the holy city
*were* 284.
19 Now the gatekeepers, Akkub,
Talmon, and their relatives who kept
watch at the gates, *were* 172.

### *Villages Outside Jerusalem*

20 The rest of Israel, of the priests *and*
of the Levites, *were* in all the cities of
Judah, each [a]on his own inheritance.
21 But [a]the temple servants were liv-
ing in Ophel, and Ziha and Gishpa
were over the temple servants.
22 Now [a]the overseer of the Levites
in Jerusalem was Uzzi the son of Bani,
the son of Hashabiah, the son of
Mattaniah, the son of Mica, from the
sons of Asaph, who were the singers
[1]over the work of the house of God.
23 [a]For *there was* a commandment
from the king concerning them
and a firm regulation for the song
leaders [b]day by day. 24 Pethahiah
the son of Meshezabel, of the sons
[a]of Zerah the son of Judah, was the
[b]king's [1]representative in all matters
concerning the people.
25 Now as for the villages with
their fields,
some of the sons of Judah
lived in [a]Kiriath-arba and
its [1]towns, in [b]Dibon and its
towns, and in Jekabzeel and
its villages,
26 and in Jeshua, in Moladah and
Beth-pelet,
27 and in Hazar-shual, in
Beersheba and its towns,
28 and in Ziklag, in Meconah and
in its towns,
29 and in En-rimmon, in Zorah
and in Jarmuth,
30 Zanoah, Adullam, and their
villages, Lachish and its fields,
Azekah and its towns. So they
encamped from Beersheba as
far as the valley of Hinnom.
31 The sons of Benjamin also
*lived* from Geba *onward,* at
Michmash and Aija, at Bethel
and its towns,
32 at Anathoth, Nob, Ananiah,
33 Hazor, Ramah, Gittaim,
34 Hadid, Zeboim, Neballat,
35 Lod and Ono, the valley of
craftsmen.
36 From the Levites, *some*
divisions in Judah belonged to
Benjamin.

### *Priests and Levites Come Up with Zerubbabel*

12 Now these are [a]the priests and
the Levites who came up with
Zerubbabel the son of Shealtiel, and
Jeshua:
Seraiah, Jeremiah, Ezra,
2 Amariah, Malluch, Hattush,
3 Shecaniah, Rehum,
Meremoth,
4 Iddo, Ginnethoi, Abijah,
5 Mijamin, Maadiah, Bilgah,

**11:17** [1]In 1Chr 9:15, *Zichri* [2]Lit *head* [3]In 1Chr 9:16, *Obadiah* [4]In 1Chr 9:16, *Shemaiah* **11:18** [a]Ne 11:1
**11:20** [a]Ne 11:3 **11:21** [a]Ne 3:26 **11:22** [a]Ne 11:9, 14 [1]Lit *in front of* **11:23** [a]Ezr 6:8; 7:20 [b]Ne 12:47
**11:24** [a]Ge 38:30 [b]1Chr 18:17 [1]Lit *hand* **11:25** [a]Jos 14:15 [b]Jos 13:9, 17 [1]Lit *daughters*, so in ch
◆ **12:1** [a]Ezr 2:1; 7:7

6 Shemaiah and Joiarib, Jedaiah,
7 Sallu, Amok, Hilkiah, and
Jedaiah.
These were the heads of the
priests and their [1]relatives in
the days of Jeshua.
8 The Levites *were*
Jeshua, Binnui, Kadmiel,
Sherebiah, Judah, *and*
Mattaniah *who was* over of
the songs of thanksgiving, he
and his brothers.
9 Also Bakbukiah and Unni,
their brothers, stood opposite
them [a]in *keeping their*
responsibilities.
10 Jeshua [1]became the father of
Joiakim,
and Joiakim became the father
of Eliashib,
and Eliashib became the
father of Joiada,
11 and Joiada became the father
of Jonathan,
and Jonathan became the
father of Jaddua.
12 Now in the days of Joiakim, the
priests, the heads of fathers' *house-*
*holds* were:
of Seraiah, Meraiah; of
Jeremiah, Hananiah;
13 of Ezra, Meshullam; of Ama-
riah, Jehohanan;
14 of [1]Malluchi, Jonathan; of
Shebaniah, Joseph;
15 of Harim, Adna; of Meraioth,
Helkai;
16 of Iddo, Zechariah; of
Ginnethon, Meshullam;
17 of Abijah, Zichri; of Miniamin,
*of Moadiah*, Piltai;
18 of Bilgah, Shammua; of She-
maiah, Jehonathan;
19 of Joiarib, Mattenai; of Jedaiah,
Uzzi;
20 of Sallai, Kallai; of Amok,
Eber;
21 of Hilkiah, Hashabiah; of
Jedaiah, Nethanel.

### *The Heads of the Levites*

22 As for the Levites, in the days of
Eliashib, Joiada, and Johanan and
Jaddua, the heads of fathers' *house-*
*holds* were written down; the priests
*were* also in the reign of Darius the
Persian. 23 The sons of Levi, the heads
of fathers' *households*, were written
down in the Book of the Chronicles
up to the days of Johanan the son of
Eliashib.
24 The heads of the Levites *were*
Hashabiah, Sherebiah, and
Jeshua the son of Kadmiel,
with their brothers opposite
them, [a]to praise *and* give
thanks, by the commandment
of David the man of God,
[b]watch by watch.
25 Mattaniah, Bakbukiah,
Obadiah, Meshullam, Talmon,
*and* Akkub *were* gatekeepers
keeping watch at [a]the
storerooms of the gates.
26 These *served* in the days of Joiakim
the son of Jeshua, the son of Jozadak,
and in the days of [a]Nehemiah the
governor and of Ezra the priest *and*
scribe.

### *Dedication of the Wall*

27 Now at the dedication of the
wall of Jerusalem they sought out
the Levites from all their places,
to bring them to Jerusalem so that
they might celebrate the dedication

**12:7** [1]Lit *brothers* **12:9** [a]Ne 12:24 **12:10** [1]Lit *begot*, so through v 12 **12:14** [1]In Ne 12:2, *Malluch*
**12:24** [a]Ne 11:17 [b]Ne 12:9 **12:25** [a]1Chr 26:15 **12:26** [a]Ne 8:9

with gladness, with hymns of
thanksgiving and with songs [a]*to
the accompaniment* of cymbals,
harps and lyres. **28** So the sons of
the singers were gathered from the
district around Jerusalem and from
[a]the villages of the Netophathites,
**29** from Beth-gilgal and from *their*
fields in Geba and Azmaveth, for the
singers had built themselves villages
around Jerusalem. **30** The priests and
the Levites [a]cleansed themselves;
they also cleansed the people, the
gates, and the wall.

### *The Choirs in the House of God*

**31** Then I had the leaders of Judah
come up on top of the wall, and I
had two great choirs of thanksgiving
stand, [a,1]the first proceeding to the
right on top of the wall toward [b]the
Dung Gate.

**32** Hoshaiah and half of the
leaders of Judah followed
them,
**33** with Azariah, Ezra,
Meshullam,
**34** Judah, Benjamin, Shemaiah,
Jeremiah,
**35** and some of the sons of
the priests with trumpets;
*and* Zechariah the son of
Jonathan, the son of Shema-
iah, the son of Mattaniah,
the son of Micaiah, the son of
Zaccur, the son of Asaph,
**36** and his [1]relatives, Shemaiah,
Azarel, Milalai, Gilalai, Maai,
Nethanel, Judah, *and* Hanani,
[a]with the musical instruments
of David the man of God. And
Ezra the scribe *went* before
them.

**37** At [a]the Spring Gate they went
directly up [b]the steps of the city of
David by the stairway of the wall
above the house of David to [c]the
Water Gate on the east.

**38** [a]The second [1]choir proceeded
to the [2]left, while I followed them
with half of the people on the wall,
[b]above the Tower of Furnaces, to [c]the
Broad Wall, **39** and above [a]the Gate
of Ephraim, by [b]the Old Gate, by the
[c]Fish Gate, [d]the Tower of Hananel,
and the Tower of the Hundred, as far
as the Sheep Gate; and they stood
at [e]the Gate of the Guard. **40** Then
the two choirs took their stand in the
house of God. So did I and half of the
officials with me; **41** and the priests:

Eliakim, Maaseiah, Miniamin,
Micaiah, Elioenai, Zechariah
and Hananiah, with the
trumpets;
**42** and Maaseiah, Shemaiah,
Eleazar, Uzzi, Jehohanan,
Malchijah, Elam, and Ezer.

And the singers made *their voices*
heard, with Jezrahiah *their* overseer,
**43** and on that day they offered great
sacrifices and were glad because [a]God
had given them great gladness, even
the women and children were glad,
so that the gladness of Jerusalem was
heard from afar.

**44** On that day [a]men were also
appointed over the chambers for
the stores, the contributions, the
first fruits, and the tithes, to gather
into them from the fields of the
cities the portions required by the

---

**12:27** [a]1Chr 15:16, 28 **12:28** [a]1Chr 9:16 **12:30** [a]Ne 13:22, 30 **12:31** [a]Ne 12:38 [b]Ne 2:13 [1]Heb *and processions to the right* **12:36** [a]Ne 12:24 [1]Lit *brothers* **12:37** [a]Ne 2:14 [b]Ne 3:15 [c]Ne 3:26 **12:38** [a]Ne 12:31 [b]Ne 3:11 [c]Ne 3:8 [1]Lit *thanksgiving choir* [2]Lit *front* **12:39** [a]Ne 8:16 [b]Ne 3:6 [c]Ne 3:3 [d]Ne 3:1 [e]Ne 3:25 **12:43** [a]Ps 9:2; 92:4 **12:44** [a]Ne 13:4, 5, 12, 13

law for the priests and Levites; for
Judah was glad over the priests and
Levites who stood *to minister.* **45** And
they kept *their* responsibility *given*
*by* their God and the responsibility of
cleansing, together with the singers
and the gatekeepers, [a]according to
the commandment of David *and*
his son Solomon. **46** For in the days
of David and [a]Asaph, in ancient
times, *there were* [b,1]chiefs of the
singers, songs of praise and hymns
of thanksgiving to God. **47** So all
Israel in the days of Zerubbabel and
Nehemiah were giving the portions
due the singers and the gatekeepers
[a]as each day required, and [b]set apart
the holy *portion* for the Levites, and
the Levites set apart the holy *portion*
for the sons of Aaron.

### *Foreigners Are Separated from Israel*

**13** On that day [a]they read from the
book of Moses in the hearing
of the people; and there was found
written in it that [b]no Ammonite
or Moabite should ever enter the
assembly of God, **2** because they did
not meet the sons of Israel with bread
and water, but [a]hired Balaam against
them to curse them. However, [b]our
God turned the curse into a blessing.
**3** So when they heard the law, [a]they
separated [b]all foreigners from Israel.

### *Tobiah's Goods Removed from God's House*

**4** Now prior to this, Eliashib the
priest, [a]who was put in *charge* over
the chambers of the house of our
*God, being* [1]related to [b]Tobiah, **5** had
prepared a large [1]room for him, where
formerly they put the grain offerings,
the frankincense, the utensils, and
the tithes of grain, *also* new wine and
oil [a]commanded for the Levites, the
singers, and the gatekeepers, as well
as the [2]contributions for the priests.
**6** But during all this *time* I was not in
Jerusalem, for in [a]the thirty-second
year of [b]Artaxerxes king of Babylon
I had gone to the king. After some
time, however, I asked *leave* from
the king, **7** and I came to Jerusalem
and discerned the evil that Eliashib
had done for Tobiah, [a]by preparing a
chamber for him in the courts of the
house of God. **8** It was very evil to me,
so I [a]threw all of Tobiah's household
goods out of the chamber. **9** Then I
said *the word,* and [a]they cleansed the
chambers; and I returned there the
utensils of the house of God with the
grain offerings and the frankincense.

### *Why Is the House of God Forsaken?*

**10** I also came to know that [a]the
portions of the Levites had not
been given *them,* so the Levites and
the singers who did the work had
fled, [b]each to his own field. **11** So I
[a]contended against the officials
and said, "[b]Why is the house of
God forsaken?" Then I gathered
them together and had them stand
in their posts. **12** All Judah then
brought [a]the tithe of the grain, new
wine, and oil into the storehouses.
**13** In charge of the storehouses I
appointed Shelemiah the priest,
Zadok the scribe, and Pedaiah of the
Levites, and in addition to them was

---

**12:45** [a]1Chr 25:1 **12:46** [a]2Chr 29:30 [b]1Chr 9:33 [1]Lit *heads* **12:47** [a]Ne 11:23 [b]Nu 18:21
♦ **13:1** [a]Ne 9:3 [b]Dt 23:3-5; Ne 13:23 **13:2** [a]Nu 22:3-11 [b]Dt 23:5 **13:3** [a]Ne 9:2; 10:28 [b]Ex 12:38
**13:4** [a]Ne 12:44 [b]Ne 2:10; 6:1, 17, 18 [1]Lit *close to* **13:5** [a]Nu 18:21 [1]Or *chamber* [2]Lit *heave offerings*
**13:6** [a]Ne 5:14 [b]Ezr 6:22 **13:7** [a]Ne 13:5 **13:8** [a]Jn 2:13-16 **13:9** [a]2Chr 29:5, 15, 16 **13:10** [a]Dt 12:19;
Ne 10:37 [b]Ne 12:28, 29 **13:11** [a]Ne 13:17, 25 [b]Ne 10:39 **13:12** [a]Ne 10:37; 12:44; Mal 3:10

Hanan the son of Zaccur, the son of
Mattaniah; for [a]they were counted
as faithful, and it was [1]their task
to apportion *everything* to their
[2]relatives. **14** [a]Remember me for
this, O my God, and do not blot out
my lovingkindnesses which I have
shown for the house of my God and
its responsibilities.

### *Keep the Sabbath Day Holy*

**15** In those days I saw in Judah some
who were treading wine presses [a]on
the sabbath, and bringing in sacks of
grain and loading *them* on donkeys,
as well as wine, grapes, figs and all
kinds of loads, [b]and they brought
*them* into Jerusalem on the sabbath
day. So [c]I testified against *them* on
the day they sold food. **16** Also men of
Tyre were living [1]there *who* brought
in fish and all kinds of merchandise,
and sold *them* to the sons of Judah
on the sabbath, even in Jerusalem.
**17** Then [a]I contended with the nobles
of Judah and said to them, "What is
this evil thing you are doing, even
profaning the sabbath day? **18** [a]Did
not your fathers do the same, so our
God brought on us and on this city
all this calamity? Yet you are adding
to *His* anger on Israel by profaning
the sabbath."

**19** [a]Now it happened that just as it
grew dark at the gates of Jerusalem
before the sabbath, I said *the word*,
and the doors were shut. Then I said
that they should not open them until
after the sabbath. Then I had some
of my young men stand at the gates
*so that* no load would enter on the
sabbath day. **20** Once or twice the
traders and merchants of every kind
of merchandise spent the night out-
side Jerusalem. **21** Then [a]I [1] warned
them and said to them, "Why do you
spend the night in front of the wall?
If you do so again, I will send forth
*my* hand against you." From that time
on they did not come on the sabbath.
**22** And I said to the Levites that [a]they
should cleanse themselves and come
as gatekeepers to keep the sabbath
day holy. *For* this also [b]remember
me, O my God, and have compassion
on me according to the greatness of
Your lovingkindness.

### *You Shall Not Marry Foreigners*

**23** In those days I also saw that the
Jews had [a,1]married women from
[b]Ashdod, [c]Ammon, *and* Moab. **24** As
for their children, half spoke in the
language of Ashdod, and none of
them was able to speak the language
of Judah, but only [1]the tongue of his
own people. **25** So [a]I contended with
them and cursed them and [b]struck
some of them and pulled out their
hair and [c]made them swear by God,
"You shall not give your daughters to
their sons, nor take up their daugh-
ters for your sons or for yourselves.
**26** [a]Did not Solomon king of Israel
sin regarding these things? [b]Yet
among the many nations there was
no king like him, and [c]he was loved
by his God, and God gave him *to be*
king over all Israel; nevertheless the
foreign women caused even him to

---

**13:13** [a]Ne 7:2 [1]Lit *upon them* [2]Lit *brothers* **13:14** [a]Ne 5:19; 13:22, 31 **13:15** [a]Ex 20:8; 34:21; Dt 5:12-14; Jer 17:22 [b]Ne 10:31; Jer 17:21 [c]Ne 9:29; 13:21 **13:16** [1]Lit *in it* **13:17** [a]Ne 13:11, 25 **13:18** [a]Ezr 9:13; Jer 17:21 **13:19** [a]Lv 23:32 **13:21** [a]Ne 13:15 [1]Lit *witnessed against* **13:22** [a]1Chr 15:12; Ne 12:30 [b]Ne 13:14, 31 **13:23** [a]Ex 34:11-16; Dt 7:1-5; Ezr 9:2; Ne 10:30 [b]Ne 4:7 [c]Ezr 9:1; Ne 13:1 [1]Lit *given dwelling to* **13:24** [1]Lit *according to the tongue of people and people* **13:25** [a]Ne 13:11, 17 [b]Dt 25:2 [c]Ne 10:29, 30 **13:26** [a]1Ki 11:1 [b]1Ki 3:13; 2Chr 1:12 [c]2Sa 12:24, 25

sin. **27** [1]Do we then hear about you
that you have done all this great evil
[a]by acting unfaithfully against our
God by [2]marrying foreign women?"
**28** And even one of the sons of Joiada,
the son of Eliashib the high priest,
was a son-in-law of [a]Sanballat the
Horonite, so I made him flee away
from me. **29** [a]Remember them, O my
God, [1]because they have defiled the
priesthood and the [b]covenant of the
priesthood and the Levites.

**30** [a]Thus I cleansed them from
everything foreign and *ensured*
that the responsibilities stood for
the priests and the Levites, each in
his work, **31** and *I arranged* [a]for the
supply of wood at fixed times and for
the first fruits. [b]Remember me, O my
God, for good.

*The Book of*

# ESTHER

### *The Feasts of the King and Queen*

**1** Now it happened in the days of
[a]Ahasuerus, the Ahasuerus who
reigned [b]from India to [1]Ethiopia over
[c]127 provinces, **2** in those days as King
Ahasuerus [a]sat on his royal throne
which *was* at the citadel in [b]Susa, **3** in
the third year of his reign, [a]he held a
feast for all his princes and servants,
the military *officers* of Persia and
Media, the nobles and the princes of
his provinces being in his presence,
**4** [1]while he displayed the riches of
his royal glory and the splendor of
his great majesty for many days, 180
days.

**5** And when these days were ful-
filled, the king held a feast lasting
seven days for all the people who
were present at the citadel in Susa,
from the greatest to the least, in the
court of [a]the garden of the king's
palace. **6** *There were hangings of* fine
white and [1]blue linen held by cords of
*fine purple linen on silver* rings and
marble pillars, *and* [a]couches of gold
and silver on a mosaic pavement of
porphyry, marble, mother-of-pearl,
and precious stones. **7** And drinks
were served in golden vessels of
various kinds, and the royal wine
was plentiful [a]according to the
king's hand. **8** And the drinking was
*done* according to the law; there was
no compulsion, for so the king had
established *it* for each official of his
household—that he should do ac-
cording to what pleased each person.
**9** Queen Vashti also held a feast for
the women in the royal house which
belonged to King Ahasuerus.

### *Queen Vashti's Refusal*

**10** On the seventh day, when the heart
of the king was [a]merry with wine, he
said for Mehuman, Biztha, Harbona,
Bigtha, Abagtha, Zethar, and Carkas,
the seven eunuchs who attended to
the presence of King Ahasuerus, **11** to
bring Queen Vashti before the king

---

**13:27** [a]Ezr 10:2; Ne 13:23 [1]Or *Is it reported* [2]Lit *giving dwelling to* **13:28** [a]Ne 2:10, 19; 4:1
**13:29** [a]Ne 6:14 [b]Nu 25:13 [1]Lit *for the defilings of* **13:30** [a]Ne 10:30 **13:31** [a]Ne 10:34 [b]Ne 13:14, 22
◆ **1:1** [a]Ezr 4:6; Da 9:1 [b]Es 8:9 [c]Es 9:30 [1]Or *Cush*, cf. Ge 10:6 **1:2** [a]1Ki 1:46 [b]Ne 1:1; Da 8:2 **1:3** [a]Es 2:18
**1:4** [1]Lit *when* **1:5** [a]Es 7:7, 8 **1:6** [a]Eze 23:41; Am 6:4 [1]Or *violet* **1:7** [a]Es 2:18 **1:10** [a]Jdg 16:25

with *her* royal [a]crown in order to
display her beauty to the people and
the princes, for she was [1]beautiful
in appearance. **12** But Queen Vashti
refused to come at the word of the
king which *was delivered* by the
hand of the eunuchs. Then the king
became exceedingly furious, and his
wrath burned within him.

**13** Then the king said to [a]the wise
men [b]who knew the times—for it
was the custom of the king thus *to
speak* before all who knew law and
justice **14** and were close to him: Car-
shena, Shethar, Admatha, Tarshish,
Meres, Marsena, and Memucan, the
seven princes of Persia and Media
[a]who [1]had access to the king's pres-
ence and sat in the first place in the
kingdom— **15** "According to law, what
is to be done with Queen Vashti, be-
cause she did not do the declaration
of King Ahasuerus *delivered* by the
hand of the eunuchs?" **16** Then in the
presence of the king and the princes,
Memucan said, "Queen Vashti has
committed iniquity against not only
the king but *also* against all the
princes and all the peoples who are
in all the provinces of King Ahasue-
rus. **17** For the word about the queen
will get out to all the women causing
them to despise their husbands in
their eyes by saying, 'King Ahasuerus
said for Queen Vashti to be brought
in to his presence, but she did not
come.' **18** This day the ladies of Persia
and Media who have heard of the
word about the queen will speak in
*the same way* to all the king's princes,
and there will be plenty of spite and
indignation. **19** If it *seems* good to
the king, let a royal word go forth
from him, and let it be written in the
laws of Persia and Media so [a]that it
cannot [1]be repealed, that Vashti may
no longer come into the presence of
King Ahasuerus, and let the king give
her royal position to [2]another who
is better than she. **20** And the king's
sentence, which he will make, will be
heard throughout all his kingdom,
for it is [1]vast, and [a]all women will
give respect to their husbands, great
and small."

**21** And *this* word was good in the
eyes of the king and the princes, and
the king did according to the word
of Memucan. **22** So he sent letters
to all the king's provinces, [a]to each
province according to its script and
to every people according to their
tongue, that every man should [b]be
the ruler in his own house and the
one who speaks in the tongue of his
own people.

### *A Queen in Place of Vashti*

**2** After these things [a]when the
wrath of King Ahasuerus had
subsided, he remembered Vashti
and what she had done and [b]what
had been decided against her. **2** Then
the young men of the king, who
attended to him, said, "[a]Let young
virgins, beautiful in appearance,
be sought for the king. **3** And let
the king appoint overseers in [a]all
the provinces of his kingdom that
they may gather every young virgin,
beautiful in appearance, to the cit-
adel of Susa, to the harem, into the

**1:11** [a]Es 2:17; 6:8 [1]Lit *good,* so in Esth **1:13** [a]Jer 10:7; Da 2:2 [b]1Chr 12:32 **1:14** [a]2Ki 25:19; Mt 18:10 [1]Lit *saw the face of the king* **1:19** [a]Es 8:8; Da 6:8 [1]Lit *pass away* [2]Lit *her neighbor* **1:20** [a]Eph 5:22; Col 3:18 [1]Lit *great* **1:22** [a]Es 3:12; 8:9 [b]Eph 5:22-24 ◆ **2:1** [a]Es 7:10 [b]Es 1:19, 20 **2:2** [a]1Ki 1:2 **2:3** [a]Es 1:1, 2

hand of [b]Hegai, the king's eunuch,
who keeps *charge of* the women;
and [c]let their cosmetics be given
*to them.* **4** Then let the young lady
who is good in the eyes of the king
be queen in place of Vashti." And
the word was good in the eyes of the
king, and he did so.

**5** *Now* there was at the citadel
in Susa a Jew. And his name was
[a]Mordecai, the son of Jair, the son of
Shimei, the son of Kish, a Benjamite,
**6** [a]who had been taken away into exile
from Jerusalem with the exiles who
had been taken away into exile with
Jeconiah king of Judah, whom Nebu-
chadnezzar the king of Babylon had
taken away into exile. **7** And he was
bringing up Hadassah, that is [a]Esther,
his uncle's daughter, for she had no
father or mother. Now the young lady
was beautiful in form and beautiful
in appearance, and when her father
and her mother died, Mordecai took
her as his own daughter.

### *Esther Advances in Favor*

**8** Now it happened that when the word
and law of the king were heard and
[a]many young ladies were gathered to
the citadel of Susa into the hand of
[b]Hegai, that Esther was taken to the
king's [1]house into the hand of Hegai,
who kept *charge of* the women. **9** And
the young lady was good in his eyes,
and she advanced in lovingkindness
before him. So he hurried to give her
[a]cosmetics and portions *of food* to
her, *and* to give to her seven choice
young women from the king's [1]house.
And he transferred her and her young
women to the best place in the harem.

**10** [a]Esther did not tell *anyone* about
her people or her kinsmen, for Mor-
decai had commanded her that she
should not tell *anyone* about *them.*
**11** And every day Mordecai walked
back and forth in front of the court
of the harem to know the well-being
of Esther and [1]how she fared.

**12** Now when it reached the turn
of each young lady to go in to King
Ahasuerus, after the end of her
twelve months under the regulations
for the women—for the days of their
cosmetic treatment were fulfilled as
follows: six months with oil of myrrh
and six months with spices and the
cosmetics for women— **13** then the
young lady would go in to the king
in this way: anything that she said
*she desired* was given to her to come
with her from the harem to the king's
house. **14** In the evening she would
go in, and in the morning she would
return to the second harem, to the
hand of Shaashgaz, the king's eunuch
who kept *charge of* the concubines.
She would not again go in to the king
unless the king delighted in her and
she was summoned by name.

**15** Now when it reached the turn of
Esther, [a]the daughter of Abihail the
uncle of Mordecai who had taken her
as his daughter, to go in to the king,
she did not seek anything except
what [b]Hegai, the king's eunuch who
kept *charge of* the women, said. And
Esther advanced in favor in the eyes
of all who saw her. **16** So Esther was
taken to King Ahasuerus to his royal
house in the tenth month which is
the month Tebeth, in the seventh
year of his reign.

---

**2:3** [b]Es 2:8, 15 [c]Es 2:9, 12 **2:5** [a]Es 3:2 **2:6** [a]2Ki 24:14, 15; 2Chr 36:10 **2:7** [a]Es 2:15 **2:8** [a]Es 2:3 [b]Es 2:3, 15 [1]Or *palace* **2:9** [a]Es 2:3, 12 [1]Or *palace* **2:10** [a]Es 2:20 **2:11** [1]Lit *what was done to her* **2:15** [a]Es 2:7; 9:29 [b]Es 2:3, 8

### *Esther Is Made Queen*

**17** And the king loved Esther more
than all the women, and she ad-
vanced in favor and lovingkindness
before him more than all the virgins,
so that [a]he set the royal crown on her
head and made her queen in place
of Vashti. **18** Then [a]the king held a
great feast, Esther's feast, for all his
princes and his servants; he also held
a remission of taxes for the provinces
and gave gifts [b]according to the king's
hand.

**19** [a]And when the virgins were
gathered together the second time,
then Mordecai [b]was sitting at the
king's gate. **20** [a]Esther had not yet
told *anyone* about her kinsmen or
her people, just as Mordecai had
commanded her; indeed Esther was
doing [1]what Mordecai declared *that*
*she do*, just as she had done [b]when
she was being brought up by him.

### *Two of the King's Eunuchs Are Hanged*

**21** In those days, while Mordecai was
sitting at the king's gate, [a]Bigthan
and Teresh, two of the king's eunuchs
from those who were doorkeepers,
became furious and sought to send
forth *their* hand against King Ahas-
uerus. **22** But the matter became
known to Mordecai, and [a]he told *it*
to Queen Esther, and Esther said *it* to
the king in Mordecai's name. **23** Then
the matter was sought out and found
*to be true*, so they were both hanged
on a [1]gallows; and it was written in
[a]the book of the chronicles in the
king's presence.

### *Haman Seeks to Destroy the Jews*

**3** After these things, King Ahas-
uerus [a]magnified Haman, the
son of Hammedatha [b]the Agagite,
and [a]advanced him and set his seat
above all the princes who *were* with
him. **2** And all the king's servants who
were at the king's gate were bowing
down and prostrating themselves
before Haman, for so the king had
commanded concerning him. But
[a]Mordecai would not bow down
or prostrate himself. **3** So the king's
servants who were at [a]the king's gate
said to Mordecai, "[b]Why do you tres-
pass against the king's command?"
**4** Now it happened when they had
spoken daily to him and he would not
listen to them, that they told Haman
to see whether Mordecai's words
would stand; for he had told them
that he was a Jew. **5** Then Haman saw
that [a]Mordecai was not bowing down
or prostrating himself before him. So
Haman was filled with wrath. **6** But
he despised in his eyes to send forth
*his* hand against Mordecai alone, for
they had told him *who* the people
of Mordecai *were*; therefore Haman
[a]sought to destroy all the Jews,
the people of Mordecai, who *were*
throughout the whole kingdom of
Ahasuerus.

**7** In the first month, which is the
month Nisan, in the twelfth year of
King Ahasuerus, [1]Pur, that is the lot,
was [a]cast before Haman from day to
day and from month *to month*, [2]until
the twelfth month, that is [b]the month
Adar. **8** Then Haman said to King
Ahasuerus, "There is a certain people

---

**2:17** [a]Es 1:11 **2:18** [a]Es 1:3 [b]Es 1:7 **2:19** [a]Es 2:3, 4 [b]Es 2:21; 3:2 **2:20** [a]Es 2:10 [b]Es 2:7 [1]Lit *the declaration of Mordecai* **2:21** [a]Es 6:2 **2:22** [a]Es 6:1, 2 **2:23** [a]Es 10:2 [1]Lit *tree*, cf. Dt 21:22-23
◆ **3:1** [a]Es 5:11 [b]Es 3:10; 8:3 **3:2** [a]Es 2:19; 5:9 **3:3** [a]Es 2:19 [b]Es 3:2 **3:5** [a]Es 5:9 **3:6** [a]Ps 83:4
**3:7** [a]Es 9:24-26 [b]Ezr 6:15 [1]Lit *he cast Pur...before* [2]Gr *and the lot fell on the thirteenth day of*

scattered and separated among the
peoples in all the provinces of your
kingdom; [a]their laws are different
from *those* of all *other* people, and
they do not do the king's laws, so
it is not worth it for the king to let
them remain. **9** If it *seems* good to the
king, let it be written down that they
should perish, and I will pay [1]10,000
talents of silver into the hands of
those who do this work, to bring into
the king's treasuries." **10** Then [a]the
king removed his signet ring from
his hand and gave it to Haman, the
son of Hammedatha [b]the Agagite,
[c]the adversary of the Jews. **11** And
the king said to Haman, "The silver
is [1]yours, and the people *also*, to do
with them according to what is good
in your eyes."

**12** [a]Then the king's scribes were
summoned on the thirteenth day of
the first month, and it was written
just as Haman commanded to [b]the
king's satraps, to the governors who
were over each province, and to the
princes of each people, each province
according to its script, each people
according to its tongue, being written
[c]in the name of King Ahasuerus and
sealed with the king's signet ring.
**13** And letters were sent by the hand
of [a]couriers to all the king's provinces
[b]to destroy, to kill, and to cause all
the Jews to perish, both young and
old, little ones and women, [c]in one
day, the thirteenth *day* of the twelfth
month, which is the month Adar, and
to [d]plunder their spoil. **14** [a]A copy of
that which was written down to be
given as law in every province was
revealed to all the peoples so that
they should be ready for this day.
**15** The couriers went out, hastened
by the word of the king. And the
law was given at the citadel in Susa.
Now the king and Haman sat down
to drink, but [a]the city of Susa was in
confusion.

### *Esther Writhes in Anguish*

**4** Now Mordecai came to know of
[a]all that had been done. And [1]he
tore his clothes, put on sackcloth and
ashes, and went out into the midst
of the city and cried out loudly and
bitterly. **2** And he went as far as the
king's gate, for no one was to enter
the king's gate clothed in sackcloth.
**3** Now in each and every province
where the word and law of the king
reached, there was great mourning
among the Jews, with [a]fasting, weeping,
and wailing; and many made
their bed in sackcloth and ashes.

**4** Then Esther's young women and
her eunuchs came and told her, and
the queen writhed in great anguish.
And she sent garments to clothe
Mordecai and to remove his sackcloth
from upon him, but he did not accept
*them.* **5** Then Esther summoned Hathach
from the king's eunuchs, whom
[1]the king had appointed to attend
her, and commanded him *to go* to
Mordecai to know what this *was* and
why it *was.* **6** So Hathach went out to
Mordecai to the city square in front
of the king's gate. **7** And Mordecai told
him all that had happened to him,
and [a]the exact amount of silver that
Haman had promised to pay to the

**3:8** [a]Ezr 4:12-15; Ac 16:20, 21 **3:9** [1]Approx. 375 tons or 340 metric tons, a talent was approx. 75 lb. or 34 kg **3:10** [a]Ge 41:42; Es 8:2 [b]Es 3:1 [c]Es 7:6 **3:11** [1]Lit *given to you* **3:12** [a]Es 8:9 [b]Ezr 8:36 [c]1Ki 21:8; Es 8:8, 10 **3:13** [a]2Chr 30:6; Es 8:10, 14 [b]Es 7:4 [c]Es 8:12 [d]Es 8:11; 9:10 **3:14** [a]Es 8:13, 14 **3:15** [a]Es 8:15
◆ **4:1** [a]2Sa 1:11; Es 3:8-10; Jon 3:5, 6 [1]Lit *Mordecai* **4:3** [a]Es 4:16 **4:5** [1]Lit *he* **4:7** [a]Es 3:9

king's treasuries to cause the Jews to perish. **8** He also gave him [a]a copy of the written law which had been given in Susa for their destruction, in order to show Esther and to tell her and to command her to go in to the king to implore his favor and to seek him out for her people.

**9** Then Hathach came back and told Mordecai's words to Esther. **10** Then Esther spoke to Hathach and commanded him *to reply* to Mordecai: **11** "All the king's servants and the people of the king's provinces know that for any man or woman who [a]comes to the king to the inner court who is not summoned, [b]he has but one law, that he be put to death, unless the king holds out [c]to him the golden scepter so that he may live. And I have not been summoned to come to the king for these thirty days." **12** So they told Esther's words to Mordecai.

**13** Then Mordecai said *for them* to respond to Esther, "Do not imagine that you in the king's [1]house can escape any more than all the Jews. **14** For if you remain silent at this time, relief and [a]deliverance will arise for the Jews from another place, and you and your father's house will perish. And who knows whether you have not reached royalty for such a time as this?"

### *Esther and the Jews Fast*

**15** Then Esther said *for them* to respond to Mordecai, **16** "Go, gather all the Jews who are found in Susa, and fast for me; [a]do not eat or drink for [b]three days, night or day. I and my young women also will fast in the same way. And thus I will go in to the king, which is not according to the law; and if I perish, I perish." **17** So Mordecai went away and did just as Esther had commanded him.

### *Esther Prepares a Feast*

**5** Now it happened [a]on the third day, that Esther put on her royal robes and stood [b]in the inner court of the king's house in front of the king's [1]rooms, and the king was sitting on his royal throne in the [2]throne room, opposite the entrance to *his* house. **2** Now it happened that when the king saw Esther the queen standing in the court, [a]she advanced in favor in his eyes; and [b]the king extended to Esther the golden scepter which *was* in his hand. So Esther came near and [1]*reached out* and touched the top of the scepter. **3** Then the king said to her, "What is *troubling* you, Queen Esther? And what is [1]your request? [a]Even to half of the kingdom it shall be given to you." **4** And Esther said, "If it *seems* good to the king, may the king and Haman come this day to the feast that I have prepared for him."

**5** Then the king said, "[a]Bring Haman quickly that we may do the word of Esther." So the king and Haman came to the feast which Esther had prepared. **6** Then, [1]as they drank their wine at the feast, [a]the king said to Esther, "[b]What is [2]your petition? For it shall be given to you. And what is [3]your request? Even to half of the kingdom it shall be done."

---

**4:8** [a]Es 3:14 **4:11** [a]Es 5:1; 6:4 [b]Da 2:9 [c]Es 5:2; 8:4 **4:13** [1]Or *palace* **4:14** [a]Lv 26:42; 2Ki 13:5 **4:16** [a]Joel 1:14; 2:12 [b]Es 5:1 ◆ **5:1** [a]Es 4:16 [b]Es 4:11; 6:4 [1]Lit *house* [2]Lit *royal house* **5:2** [a]Es 2:9 [b]Es 4:11; 8:4 [1]The Heb root for *touched*, in a variant form, is translated as *reached* in Es 2:12, 15; 4:3, 14; 6:14; 8:17; 9:26 **5:3** [a]Es 7:2; Mk 6:23 [1]Or *that which you seek* **5:5** [a]Es 6:14 **5:6** [a]Es 7:2 [b]Es 5:3 [1]Lit *at the banquet of wine* [2]Or *that which you ask for* [3]Or *that which you seek*

7 So Esther answered and said, "[1]My
petition and [2]my request is: 8 [a]if I
have found favor in the eyes of the
king, and if it *seems* good to the king
to give *heed to* [1]my petition and to
do [2]my request, may the king and
Haman come to [b]the feast which I
will prepare for them, and tomorrow
I will do according to the word of the
king."

### *Haman Recounts His Glory*

9 Then Haman went out that day
glad and merry of heart; but when
Haman saw Mordecai [a]in the king's
gate and [b]that he did not stand up
or [1]tremble before him, Haman was
filled with wrath against Mordecai.
10 But Haman controlled himself,
went to his house, and sent for and
brought his friends and his wife
[a]Zeresh. 11 Then Haman recount-
ed to them the glory of his riches
and the [a,1]number of his sons and
every *instance* where the king had
magnified him and how he had
[b,2]advanced him above the princes
and servants of the king. 12 Haman
also said, "Even Esther the queen let
no one but me come with the king
to the feast which she had prepared;
and [a]tomorrow also I am called *to
come* to her with the king. 13 Yet all
of this is worth nothing to me every
time I see Mordecai the Jew sitting at
[a]the king's gate." 14 Then Zeresh his
wife and all his friends said to him,
"[a]Have a [1]gallows [2]fifty cubits high
made and in the morning say to the
king that Mordecai should be hanged
on it; then go gladly with the king to
the feast." And the word was good to
Haman, so he had the gallows made.

### *The Man Whom the King Honors*

6 During that night, sleep had
[a]fled from the king, so he said
*for them* to bring [b]the book of mem-
oranda, the chronicles, and they
were read before the king. 2 And it
was found written what [a]Mordecai
had told concerning Bigthana and
Teresh, two of the king's eunuchs
from those who were doorkeepers,
that they had sought to send forth
*their* hand against King Ahasu-
erus. 3 And the king said, "What
honor or greatness has been done
to Mordecai for this?" Then the
king's young men who attended
him said, "Nothing has been done
for him." 4 So the king said, "Who
is in the court?" Now Haman had
[a]entered the outer court of the
king's house in order to speak to the
king about [b]hanging Mordecai on
the gallows which he had set up for
him. 5 And the king's young men said
to him, "Behold, Haman is standing
in the court." And the king said, "Let
him come in." 6 So Haman came in,
and the king said to him, "What is to
be done for the man [a]whom the king
delights to honor?" And Haman said
in his heart, "Whom would the king
delight to honor more than me?"
7 Then Haman said to the king, "For
the man whom the king delights to
honor, 8 let them bring a royal robe
which the king clothes himself in,
and [a]the horse on which the king
has ridden, and on whose head [b]a

---

**5:7** [1]Or *What I ask for* [2]Or *what I seek* **5:8** [a]Es 7:3; 8:5 [b]Es 6:14 [1]Or *what I ask for* [2]Or *what I am seeking* **5:9** [a]Es 2:19 [b]Es 3:5 [1]Or *move for* **5:10** [a]Es 6:13 **5:11** [a]Es 9:7-10 [b]Es 3:1 [1]Lit *multitude* [2]Lit *lifted* **5:12** [a]Es 5:8 **5:13** [a]Es 5:9 **5:14** [a]Es 6:4; 7:9, 10 [1]Lit *tree*, cf. Dt 21:22-23 [2]Approx. 75 ft. or 23 m, a cubit was approx. 18 in. or 45 cm ◆ **6:1** [a]Da 6:18 [b]Es 2:23; 10:2 **6:2** [a]Es 2:21, 22 **6:4** [a]Es 4:11 [b]Es 5:14 **6:6** [a]Es 6:7, 9, 11 **6:8** [a]1Ki 1:33 [b]Es 1:11; 2:17

royal crown has been placed; **9** and
let the robe and the horse be given
over to the hand of one of the king's
most noble princes, and let them
clothe the man whom the king
delights to honor and lead him on
horseback through the city square
[a]and call out before him, 'Thus it
shall be done to the man whom the
king delights to honor.'"

### *Mordecai Is Honored*

**10** Then the king said to Haman, "Take
quickly the robes and the horse as
you have said, and do so for Mordecai
the Jew, who is sitting at the king's
gate; do not fall short in anything
of all that you have spoken." **11** So
Haman took the robe and the horse
and clothed Mordecai and led him
*on horseback* through the city square
and called out before him, "Thus it
shall be done to the man whom the
king delights to honor."

**12** Then Mordecai returned to the
king's gate. But Haman hastened
home, mourning, [a]with *his* head
covered. **13** And Haman recounted
[a]to Zeresh his wife and all his friends
everything that had happened to
him. Then his wise men and Zeresh
his wife said to him, "If Mordecai,
before whom you have begun to fall,
is of the seed of the Jews, you will
not overcome him, but will surely fall
*before him*."

**14** While they were still speaking
with him, the king's eunuchs reached
*Haman's home* and hastily [a]brought
Haman to the feast which Esther had
prepared.

### *Esther's Petition to the King*

**7** Then the king and Haman came to
drink *wine* with Esther the queen.
**2** And the king said to Esther on the
second day also [1]as they drank their
wine at the feast, "[a]What is [2]your
petition, Queen Esther? It shall be
given you. And what is [3]your request?
[b]Even to half of the kingdom it shall
be done." **3** Then Queen Esther an-
swered and said, "[a]If I have found
favor in your eyes, O king, and if it
*seems* good to the king, let my life
be given to me as [1]my petition, and
my people as [2]my request; **4** for [a]we
have been sold, I and my people, to
be destroyed, [b]to be killed, and to be
caused to perish. Now if we had only
been sold as slaves, men and women,
I would have remained silent, for
the [1]adversity would not be worth
the [2]annoyance to the king." **5** Then
King Ahasuerus said—he said to
Esther the Queen, "Who is this one,
and where is this one, who fills his
heart to do thus?" **6** So Esther said,
"[a]An adversary and an enemy is this
evil Haman!" Then Haman became
terrified before the king and queen.

### *Haman Is Hanged*

**7** And the king arose [a]in his wrath
from [1]drinking wine *and went* into
[b]the garden of *his* palace; but Haman
stayed to seek for his life from Queen
Esther, for he saw that calamity had
been determined against him by
the king. **8** Now the king returned
from the garden of *his* palace into
the [1]place where they were drinking
wine. And Haman was falling on

---

**6:9** [a]Ge 41:43 **6:12** [a]2Sa 15:30 **6:13** [a]Es 5:10 **6:14** [a]Es 5:8 ◆ **7:2** [a]Es 5:6; 9:12 [b]Es 5:3 [1]Lit *at the banquet of wine* [2]Or *that which you ask for* [3]Or *that which you seek*, cf. Es 7:7 **7:3** [a]Es 5:8; 8:5 [1]Or *that which I ask for* [2]Or *that which I seek*, cf. Es 7:7 **7:4** [a]Es 3:9 [b]Es 3:13 [1]Or *enemy could not compensate for the loss* [2]Or *damage* **7:6** [a]Es 3:10 **7:7** [a]Es 1:12 [b]Es 1:5 [1]Lit *the banquet of wine* **7:8** [1]Lit *house of the banquet of wine*

[a]the couch where Esther was. So the king said, "Will he even assault the queen with me in the house?" *As* the word went out of the king's mouth, they covered Haman's face. **9** Then Harbonah, one of the eunuchs who *were* before the king, said, "Behold indeed, [a]the gallows—which Haman made for Mordecai [b]who spoke good on behalf of the king—are standing at Haman's house fifty cubits high!" And the king said, "Hang him on it." **10** [a]So they hanged Haman on the [1]gallows which he had set up for Mordecai, [b]and the king's wrath subsided.

### *Esther Saves the Jews*

**8** On that day King Ahasuerus gave the house of Haman, [a]the adversary of the Jews, to Queen Esther; and Mordecai came before the king, for Esther had told [b]what he was to her. **2** [a]And the king removed his signet ring, which he had taken away from Haman, and gave it to Mordecai. And Esther set Mordecai over the house of Haman.

**3** Then Esther spoke again to the king, fell at his feet, wept, and implored him to [1]repeal the evil *scheme* of Haman the Agagite and his scheme which he had devised against the Jews. **4** [a]And the king extended the golden scepter to Esther. So Esther arose and stood before the king. **5** Then she said, "[a]If it *seems* good to the king, and if I have found favor before him and the matter *seems* proper to the king and I am good in his eyes, let it be written to turn back the [b]letters devised by Haman, the son of Hammedatha the Agagite, which he wrote to cause the Jews who are in all the king's provinces to perish. **6** For [a]how can I endure to see the calamity which will befall my people, and how can I endure to see the perishing of my kinsmen?"

### *The King's Decree Avenges the Jews*

**7** So King Ahasuerus said to Queen Esther and to Mordecai the Jew, "Behold, [a]I have given the house of Haman to Esther, and him they have hanged on the [1]gallows because he had sent forth his hand against the Jews. **8** Now you write to the Jews, according to what is good in your eyes, in the king's name, and [a]seal *it* with the king's signet ring; for a written *decree* which is written in the name of the king and sealed with the king's signet ring [b]may not be turned back."

**9** [a]So the king's scribes were called at that time in the third month (that is, the month Sivan), on the twenty-third [1]day; and it was written according to all that Mordecai commanded to the Jews, the satraps, the governors, and the princes of the provinces which *extended* [b]from India to [2]Ethiopia, 127 provinces, to [c]every province according to its script, and to every people according to their tongue as well as to the Jews according to their script and their tongue. **10** And he wrote in the name of King Ahasuerus and sealed it with the king's signet ring and sent letters by the hand of couriers on [a]horses, riding on steeds sired by the [1]royal stud. **11** [1]In them the king gave the Jews who were in each

**7:8** [a]Es 1:6 **7:9** [a]Es 5:14 [b]Es 2:22 **7:10** [a]Ps 7:16; 94:23 [b]Es 7:7, 8 [1]Lit *tree*, cf. Dt 21:22-23 ◆ **8:1** [a]Es 7:6 [b]Es 2:7, 15 **8:2** [a]Es 3:10 **8:3** [1]Or *take away*, cf. 8:2; lit *pass away* **8:4** [a]Es 4:11; 5:2 **8:5** [a]Es 5:8; 7:3 [b]Es 3:13 **8:6** [a]Es 7:4; 9:1 **8:7** [a]Es 8:1 [1]Lit *tree*, cf. Dt 21:22-23 **8:8** [a]Es 3:12; 8:10 [b]Es 1:19 **8:9** [a]Es 3:12 [b]Es 1:1 [c]Es 1:22; 3:12 [1]Lit *in it* [2]Or *Cush*, cf. Ge 10:6 **8:10** [a]1Ki 4:28 [1]Lit *offspring of swift mares* **8:11** [1]Lit *Which*

and every city *the right* [a]to assemble
and to make a stand for their lives, [b]to
destroy, to kill, and to cause to perish
the entire military force of any people
or province which would act as their
adversaries, including little ones and
women, and [c]to plunder their spoil,
**12** on [a]one day in all the provinces of
King Ahasuerus, the thirteenth *day* of
the twelfth month (that is, the month
Adar). **13** [a]A copy of that which was
written down to be given as law in
each and every province was revealed
to all the peoples, so that the Jews
would be ready for this day to avenge
themselves on their enemies. **14** The
couriers, hurried and hastened by the
king's word, went out, riding on the
royal steeds; and the law was given
out at the citadel in Susa.

**15** Then Mordecai went out from the
presence of the king [a]in royal robes
of [1]blue and fine white, with a large
crown of gold and [b]a garment of fine
linen and purple; and [c]the city of Susa
cried aloud and was glad. **16** For the
Jews there was [a]light and gladness
and joy and honor. **17** And in each and
every province and in each and every
city, wherever the king's word and his
law reached, there was gladness and
joy for the Jews, a feast and a [a,1]holiday.
And [b]many among the peoples of the
land became Jews, for the dread of the
Jews had fallen on them.

### *The Jews Strike Down Their Enemies*

**9** Now [a]in the twelfth month (that
is, the month Adar), on [b]the thir-
teenth [1]day [c]when the king's word
and law had reached *the point for*
*them* to be done, on the day when
the enemies of the Jews hoped to
gain power over them, it was turned
around so that the Jews themselves
gained power over those who hated
them. **2** [a]The Jews assembled in their
cities throughout all the provinces of
King Ahasuerus to send forth *their*
hand against those who sought their
calamity; and no one could stand
before them, [b]for the dread of them
had fallen on all the peoples. **3** Even
all the princes of the provinces,
[a]the satraps, the governors, and
those who were doing the king's
work [1]advanced the Jews, because
the dread of Mordecai had fallen on
them. **4** Indeed, Mordecai was great
in the king's house, and the report
about him went throughout all the
provinces; for the man Mordecai
[a]became greater and greater. **5** Thus
[a]the Jews struck all their enemies
with [1]the sword, killing and causing
*them* to perish; and they did what
they pleased to those who hated
them. **6** And at the citadel in Susa the
Jews killed and caused to perish 500
men, **7** and Parshandatha, Dalphon,
Aspatha, **8** Poratha, Adalia, Aridatha,
**9** Parmashta, Arisai, Aridai, and
Vaizatha, **10** [a]the 10 sons of Haman
the son of Hammedatha, the Jews'
adversary; but [b]they did not send
forth their hand for the plunder.

**11** On that day the number of
those who were killed at the citadel
in Susa came to the king. **12** So the
king said to Queen Esther, "The Jews
have killed and caused to perish 500
men and the 10 sons of Haman at

---

**8:11** [a]Es 9:2 [b]Es 3:13 [c]Es 9:10 **8:12** [a]Es 3:13; 9:1 **8:13** [a]Es 3:14 **8:15** [a]Es 5:11 [b]Ge 41:42 [c]Es 3:15 [1]Or *violet* **8:16** [a]Ps 97:11; 112:4 **8:17** [a]Es 9:19 [b]Es 9:27 [1]Lit *good day* ◆ **9:1** [a]Es 8:12 [b]Es 9:17 [c]Es 3:13 [1]Lit *day in it* **9:2** [a]Es 8:11; 9:15-18 [b]Es 8:17 **9:3** [a]Ezr 8:36 [1]Lit *lifted up* **9:4** [a]2Sa 3:1; 1Chr 11:9 **9:5** [a]Es 3:13 [1]Lit *stroke of sword* **9:10** [a]Es 5:11 [b]Es 8:11

the citadel in Susa. *Now* in the rest of
the king's provinces, what have they
done? [a]So what is [1]your petition? It
shall even be given to you. And what
is [2]your further request? It shall also
be done." **13** Then Esther said, "If it is
good to the king, [a]let tomorrow also
be given to the Jews who are in Susa
to do according to the law for today;
and let Haman's 10 sons be hanged
on the gallows." **14** So the king said
that it should be done so; and a law
was given in Susa, and Haman's 10
sons were hanged. **15** And the Jews
who were in Susa assembled also
on the fourteenth day of the month
Adar and killed [a]300 men in Susa,
but [b]they did not send forth their
hand for the plunder.

**16** Now [a]the rest of the Jews who
*were* in the king's provinces [b]assem-
bled, to make a stand for their lives
and obtain rest for themselves from
their enemies, and to kill 75,000 of
those who hated them; but they did
not send forth their hand for the
plunder. **17** *This was done* on [a]the
thirteenth day of the month Adar,
and [b]on the fourteenth [1]day they
rested and made it a day of feasting
and gladness.

**18** But the Jews who were in Susa
[a]assembled on the thirteenth and
[b]the fourteenth [1]of the same month,
and they rested on the fifteenth
[1]day and made it a day of feasting
and gladness. **19** Therefore the Jews
of the rural areas, who live in [a]the
rural towns, make the fourteenth day
of the month Adar *a* [b,1]holiday for
gladness and feasting and [c]sending
portions *of food* to one another.

### *The Feast of Purim Is Established*

**20** Then Mordecai wrote down these
events, and he sent letters to all the
Jews who were in all the provinces
of King Ahasuerus, both near and
far, **21** to establish among them to
celebrate the fourteenth day of
the month Adar, and the fifteenth
day [1]of the same month, annually,
**22** because on those days the Jews
obtained rest for themselves from
their enemies, and *it was a* month
which was [a]turned around for them
from sorrow into gladness and from
mourning into a [1]holiday; that they
should make them days of feasting
and gladness and [b]sending portions
*of food* to one another and gifts to
the poor.

**23** Thus the Jews *fully* accepted
what they had started to do and what
Mordecai had written to them. **24** For
Haman the son of Hammedatha,
the Agagite, the adversary of all the
Jews, had devised against the Jews to
cause them to perish and [a]had cast
Pur, that is the lot, to throw them into
confusion and cause them to perish.
**25** But [a]when it came before the king,
he said by letter [b]that his evil scheme,
which he had [1]devised against the
Jews, [c]should return on his own head
and that he and his sons should be
hanged on the [2]gallows. **26** Therefore
they called these days Purim after the
name of Pur. Therefore, [a]because of
the words in this letter, both what

---

**9:12** [a]Es 5:6; 7:2 [1]Or *that which you are asking for* [2]Or *that which you further seek*, cf. 9:2
**9:13** [a]Es 8:11; 9:15 **9:15** [a]Es 9:12 [b]Es 9:10 **9:16** [a]Es 9:2 [b]Lv 26:7, 8; Es 8:11 **9:17** [a]Es 9:1 [b]Es 9:21
[1]Lit *in it* **9:18** [a]Es 8:11; 9:2 [b]Es 9:21 [1]Lit *in it* **9:19** [a]Dt 3:5; Zec 2:4 [b]Es 9:22 [c]Ne 8:10 [1]Lit
*rejoicing and feasting and a good day and sending* **9:21** [1]Lit *in it* **9:22** [a]Ps 30:11 [b]Ne 8:12 [1]Lit
*good day* **9:24** [a]Es 3:7 **9:25** [a]Es 7:4-10 [b]Es 3:6-15 [c]Ps 7:16 [1]Lit *schemed* [2]Lit *tree*, cf. Dt 21:22-23
**9:26** [a]Es 9:20

they had seen in this regard and
what had reached them, **27** the Jews
established and accepted a custom
for themselves and for their seed and
for [a]all those who joined themselves
to them, so that [b,1]celebrating these
two days according to what was
written down and according to their
fixed time from year to year would
not pass away. **28** So these days were
to be remembered and celebrated
throughout every generation, every
family, every province, and every
city; thus these days of Purim were
not to pass away from among the
Jews, nor their memory come to an
end from their seed.
**29** Then Queen Esther, [a]daughter
of Abihail, with Mordecai the Jew,
wrote with full authority to establish
[b]this second letter about Purim.
**30** And he sent letters to all the Jews,
[a]to the 127 provinces of the kingdom
of Ahasuerus, *namely*, words of
peace and truth, **31** to establish these
days of Purim at their appointed
times, just as Mordecai the Jew and
Queen Esther had established for
them, and just as they had established
for themselves and for their
seed with words concerning [a]their
times of fasting and their crying
out. **32** And the declaration of Esther
established these words concerning
[a]Purim, and it was written in the
book.

### *Mordecai's Greatness*

**10** Then King Ahasuerus set
forced labor upon the land and
the [a]coastlands of the sea. **2** And the
entire work of his authority and his
might, and the full account of the
greatness of Mordecai, [a]whom the
king had made *so* great, are they not
written in [b]the book of the chronicles
of the kings of Media and Persia?
**3** For Mordecai the Jew was [a]second
*only* to King Ahasuerus and was great
among the Jews and pleasing to his
many *fellow* brothers, [b]one who
sought the good of his people and
one who spoke for the peace of all
his seed.

**9:27** [a]Es 8:17 [b]Es 9:20, 21 [1]Lit *to be celebrators* **9:29** [a]Es 2:15 [b]Es 9:20, 21 **9:30** [a]Es 1:1
**9:31** [a]Es 4:3 **9:32** [a]Es 9:26 ◆ **10:1** [a]Is 11:11; 24:15 **10:2** [a]Es 8:15; 9:4 [b]Es 2:23 **10:3** [a]Ge 41:43, 44
[b]Ne 2:10

*The Book of*

# JOB

### *Job Was Greatest of the Sons of the East*

**1** There was a man in the [a]land of Uz whose name was [b]Job; and that man was [c]blameless, upright, [d]fearing God, and [e]turning away from evil. **2** [a]Seven sons and three daughters were born to him. **3** [a]His possessions also were 7,000 sheep, 3,000 camels, 500 pairs of oxen, 500 female donkeys, and very many servants; and that man was [b]the greatest of all the sons of the east. **4** His sons used to go and hold a feast in the house of each one on his day, and they would send and invite their three sisters to eat and drink with them. **5** Now it happened when the days of feasting had completed their cycle, that Job would send and set them apart as holy. And he would rise up early in the morning and offer [a]burnt offerings *according to* the number of them all; for Job said, "[b]Perhaps my sons have sinned and [c,1]cursed God in their hearts." Thus Job did continually.

### *All Job Has Is in Satan's Hand*

**6** [a]Now it was the day that the [b]sons of God came to stand before [1]Yahweh, and [2]Satan also came among them. **7** And Yahweh said to Satan, "From where do you come?" Then Satan answered Yahweh and said, "[a]From roaming about on the earth and walking around on it." **8** Then Yahweh said to Satan, "Have you set your heart upon [a]My servant Job? For there is no one like him on the earth, [b]a blameless and upright man, [1]fearing God and turning away from evil." **9** And [a]Satan answered Yahweh and said, "Does Job [1]fear God without cause? **10** [a]Have You not made a hedge about him and his house and all that he has, on every side? [b]You have blessed the work of his hands, and his [c]possessions have increased in the land. **11** [a]But send forth Your hand now and [b]touch all that he has; he will surely curse You to Your face." **12** Then Yahweh said to Satan, "Behold, all that he has is in your hand, only do not send forth your hand toward him." So Satan went out from the presence of Yahweh.

### *Messengers Speak of the Fire of God*

**13** Now it happened that on the day when his sons and his daughters were eating and drinking wine in the house of their brother, the firstborn, **14** a messenger came to Job and said, "The oxen were plowing and the [1]donkeys feeding beside them, **15** and [1]the [a]Sabeans fell *upon them* and took them. They also struck down the young men with the edge of the sword, and [2]I alone have

---

◆ **1:1** [a]Jer 25:20; Lam 4:21 [b]Eze 14:14, 20; Jas 5:11 [c]Ge 6:9; 17:1; Dt 18:13 [d]Ge 22:12; 42:18; Ex 18:21; Pr 8:13 [e]Job 28:28 **1:2** [a]Job 42:13 **1:3** [a]Job 42:12 [b]Job 29:25 **1:5** [a]Ge 8:20; Job 42:8 [b]Job 8:4 [c]1Ki 21:10, 13 [1]Heb *blessed*; used euphemistically for cursed, cf. 1:11; 2:5, 9; 1Ki 21:10, 13 **1:6** [a]Job 2:1 [b]Job 38:7 [1]The personal covenant name of God, a form of I AM WHO I AM, cf. Ex 3:14-15 [2]Lit *the adversary*, so in chs 1 and 2 **1:7** [a]1Pe 5:8 **1:8** [a]Nu 12:7; Jos 1:2, 7; Job 42:7, 8 [b]Job 1:1 [1]Or *revering* **1:9** [a]Rev 12:9f [1]Or *reverence* **1:10** [a]Job 29:2-6; Ps 34:7 [b]Job 31:25 [c]Job 1:3; 31:25 **1:11** [a]Job 2:5 [b]Job 19:21 **1:14** [1]Lit *female donkeys* **1:15** [a]Ge 10:7; Job 6:19 [1]Lit *Sheba* [2]Lit *only I alone*, so in vv 16, 17, 19

escaped to tell you." **16** While this
one was still speaking, another also
came and said, "[a]The fire of God
fell from heaven and burned up
the sheep and the young men and
consumed them, and I alone have
escaped to tell you." **17** While this
one was still speaking, another also
came and said, "The [a]Chaldeans set
up three companies and made a raid
on the camels and took them and
struck down the young men with
the edge of the sword, and I alone
have escaped to tell you." **18** While
this one was still speaking, another
also came and said, "Your sons and
your daughters were eating and
drinking wine in the house of their
brother, the firstborn, **19** and behold,
a great wind came from across the
wilderness and touched the four
corners of the house, and it fell on
the young people, and they died, and
I alone have escaped to tell you."

**20** Then Job arose and [a]tore his robe
and shaved his head, and he fell to the
ground and worshiped. **21** And he said,

"[a]Naked I came from my
mother's womb,
And naked I shall return there.
[b]Yahweh gave, and Yahweh
has taken away.
Blessed be the name
of Yahweh."

**22** [a]Through all this Job did not sin,
*nor did he* give offense to God.

### *Satan Strikes Job's Flesh*

**2** [a]Again it was the day that the
sons of God came to stand be-
fore Yahweh, and Satan also came
among them to stand himself before
Yahweh. **2** And Yahweh said to Satan,
"Where do you come from?" Then
Satan answered Yahweh and said,
"From roaming about on the earth
and walking around on it." **3** And
Yahweh said to Satan, "Have you
set your heart upon My servant Job?
For there is no one like him on the
earth, a blameless and upright man,
[1]fearing God and turning away from
evil. And he still [a]holds fast his integ-
rity. So you incited Me against him
to swallow him up in vain." **4** Satan
answered Yahweh and said, "Skin
for skin! Yes, all that a man has he
will give for his life. **5** [a]However, send
forth Your hand now, and [b]touch his
bone and his flesh; he will curse You
in Your face." **6** So Yahweh said to
Satan, "Behold, he is in your hand,
only spare his life."

**7** Then Satan went out from the
presence of Yahweh and struck Job
with [a]terrible boils from the sole
of his foot to the top of his head.
**8** And he took a potsherd to scrape
himself while [a]he was sitting among
the ashes.

**9** Then his wife said to him, "Do
you still hold fast your integrity?
Curse God and die!" **10** But he said
to her, "You speak as one of the
wickedly foolish women speaks.
[a]Shall we indeed accept good from
God and not accept calamity?" [b]In
all this Job did not sin with his lips.

### *Job's Three Friends*

**11** Then Job's three friends heard of
all this calamity that had come upon

**1:16** [a]Ge 19:24; Lv 10:2; Nu 11:1-3 **1:17** [a]Ge 11:28, 31 **1:20** [a]Ge 37:29, 34; Jos 7:6 **1:21** [a]Ecc 5:15 [b]1Sa 2:7, 8; Job 2:10 **1:22** [a]Job 2:10 ◆ **2:1** [a]Job 1:6-8 **2:3** [a]Job 27:5, 6 [1]Or *revering* **2:5** [a]Job 1:11 [b]Job 19:20 **2:7** [a]Dt 28:35; Job 7:5; 13:28; 30:17, 18, 30 **2:8** [a]Job 42:6; Jer 6:26; Eze 27:30; Jon 3:6 **2:10** [a]Job 1:21 [b]Job 1:22; Ps 39:1; Jas 1:12

him. So they came each one from his
own place, Eliphaz the [a]Temanite,
Bildad the [b]Shuhite, and Zophar
the Naamathite; and they made
an appointment together to come
to [c]console him and comfort him.
**12** Then they lifted up their eyes at
a distance and did not recognize
him, and they lifted up their voices
and wept. And each of them [a]tore
his robe, and they [b]threw dust over
their heads toward the sky. **13** [a]Then
they sat down on the ground with
him for seven days and seven nights
with no one speaking a word to
him, for they saw that *his* pain was
very great.

### *Job Curses the Day of His Birth*

**3** Afterward Job opened his mouth
and cursed [1]the day of his *birth*.
**2** And Job answered and said,

**3** "[a]Let the day perish
on which I was to be born,
And the night *which* said,
'A man is conceived.'

**4** "May that day be darkness;
Let not God seek it
from above,
Nor light shine on it.

**5** "Let [a]darkness and shadow
of death redeem it;
Let a cloud dwell upon it;
Let the blackness
of the day terrify it.

**6** "*As for* that night,
let thick darkness take it;
Let it not rejoice
among the days of the year;
Let it not come into
the number of the months.

**7** "Behold, let that night
be barren;
Let no joyful shout enter it.

**8** "Let those curse it who
curse the day,
Who are [1]ready
to [a]rouse Leviathan.

**9** "Let the stars of its twilight
be darkened;
Let it hope for light
but have none,
And let it not see
the [1]breaking dawn,

**10** Because it did not shut
the opening of my
*mother's* [1]body,
Or hide trouble from my eyes.

**11** "[a]Why did I not die
from the womb,
Come forth from the womb
and breathe my last?

**12** "Why did the knees receive me,
And why the breasts,
that I should suck?

**13** "For now I [a]would have lain
down and been quiet;
I would have slept then; it
would have been rest to me,

**14** With [a]kings and *with*
[b]counselors of the earth,
Who rebuilt [c]waste places
for themselves,

**15** Or with [a]princes
[b]who had gold,
Who were filling their
houses *with* silver.

**16** "Or *why* was I not like a
miscarriage hidden away,
As infants that never
saw light?

---

**2:11** [a]Ge 36:11; Job 6:19; Jer 49:7 [b]Ge 25:2 [c]Job 42:11; Ro 12:15 **2:12** [a]Job 1:20 [b]Jos 7:6; Ne 9:1; Lam 2:10; Eze 27:30 **2:13** [a]Ge 50:10; Eze 3:15 ◆ **3:1** [1]Lit *his day* **3:3** [a]Jer 20:14-18 **3:5** [a]Jer 13:16 **3:8** [a]Job 41:1, 25 [1]Or *skillful* **3:9** [1]Lit *eyelids of* **3:10** [1]Lit *stomach* **3:11** [a]Job 10:18, 19 **3:13** [a]Job 3:13-19; 7:8-10, 21; 10:21, 22; 14:10-15, 20-22; 16:22; 17:13-16; 19:25-27; 21:13, 23-26; 24:19, 20; 26:5, 6; 34:22 **3:14** [a]Job 12:18 [b]Job 12:17 [c]Job 15:28; Is 58:12 **3:15** [a]Job 12:21 [b]Job 27:16, 17

17 “There the wicked cease
from raging,
And there the weary
of strength are at [a]rest.
18 “The prisoners are
at ease together;
They do not hear the voice
of the taskmaster.
19 “The small and the great
are there,
And the slave is free
from his master.

20 “Why is [a]light given
to him who is troubled,
And life to the bitter
of soul,
21 Who [a,1]long for death,
but there is none,
And dig for it more
than for [b]hidden treasures,
22 Who are glad with joy,
*And* rejoice when they
find the grave?
23 “*Why is light given* to a man
[a]whose way is hidden,
And whom [b]God has
hedged in?
24 “For [a]my groaning comes
at the sight of my food,
And [b]my roaring pours
out like water.
25 “For [a]the dread that I dread
comes upon me,
And what I am afraid
of befalls me.
26 “I [a]am not complacent,
nor am I quiet,
And I am not at rest,
and raging comes.”

### *Eliphaz Says the Innocent Do Not Suffer*

4 Then Eliphaz the Temanite answered and said,
2 “If one tries a word with you,
will you become weary?
But [a]who can hold back
[1]from speaking?
3 “Behold, [a]you have
disciplined many,
And you have strengthened
limp hands.
4 “Your words have [1]helped
the stumbling to stand,
And you have encouraged
[2]feeble knees.
5 “But now it has come to you,
and you [a]are impatient;
It [b]touches you, and
you are dismayed.
6 “Is not your [a,1]fear *of God*
[b]your confidence,
And the integrity of your
ways your hope?

7 “Remember now, [a]who *ever*
perished being innocent?
Or where were the upright
wiped out?
8 “According to what I
have seen, [a]those who
plow wickedness
And those who sow
trouble harvest it.
9 “By [a]the breath of God
they perish,
And [b]by the wind of His anger
they come to an end.
10 “The [a]roaring of the lion and
the voice of the *fierce* lion,

**3:17** [a]Job 17:16 **3:20** [a]Jer 20:18 **3:21** [a]Rev 9:6 [b]Pr 2:4 [1]Lit *wait* **3:23** [a]Job 19:6, 8, 12 [b]Job 19:8; Ps 88:8; Lam 3:7 **3:24** [a]Job 6:7; 33:20 [b]Job 30:16; Ps 42:4 **3:25** [a]Job 9:28; 30:15 **3:26** [a]Job 7:13, 14
◆ **4:2** [a]Job 32:18-20 [1]Lit *in words* **4:3** [a]Job 4:3, 4; 29:15, 16, 21, 25 **4:4** [1]Lit *caused* [2]Lit *bowing*
**4:5** [a]Job 6:14 [b]Job 19:21 **4:6** [a]Job 1:1 [b]Pr 3:26 [1]Or *reverence* **4:7** [a]Job 8:20; 36:6, 7; Ps 37:25
**4:8** [a]Job 15:31, 35; Pr 22:8; Hos 10:13; Ga 6:7 **4:9** [a]Job 15:30; Is 11:4; 30:33; 2Th 2:8 [b]Job 40:11-13
**4:10** [a]Job 5:15; Ps 58:6

And the teeth of the young
lions are broken.
11 "The [a]lion perishes
for lack of prey,
And the [b]whelps
of the lioness are scattered.

12 "Now a word [a]was brought
to me stealthily,
And my ear received
a [b]whisper of it.
13 "Amid disquieting [a]thoughts
from the visions
of the night,
When deep sleep falls on men,
14 Dread came upon me,
and trembling,
And made the multitude
of my bones shake in dread.
15 "Then a [1]spirit swept
by my face;
The hair of my flesh
bristled up.
16 "It stood still, but I could not
recognize its appearance;
A form *was* before my eyes;
*There was* silence,
then I heard a voice:
17 'Can [a]mankind be right
[1]before God?
Can a man be pure
[1]before his [b]Maker?
18 '[a]He puts no trust even
in His slaves;
And against His angels
He charges error.
19 'How much more those who
dwell in [a]houses of clay,
Whose [b]foundation
is in the dust,
Who are crushed
before the moth!
20 '[a]Between morning
and evening they are
broken in pieces;
[1]Unobserved, they
[b]perish forever.
21 'Is not their [a]tent-cord
pulled up within them?
They die,
yet [b]without wisdom.'

### *The Discipline of the Almighty*

5 "Call now, is there anyone
who will answer you?
And to which of the [a]holy
ones will you turn?
2 "For [a]vexation kills
the ignorant fool,
And jealousy puts
to death the simple.
3 "I have seen the [a]ignorant
fool taking root,
And I [b]cursed his
abode suddenly.
4 "His [a]sons are far
from salvation,
They are even crushed
in the gate,
And there is no deliverer.
5 "[1]His harvest the
hungry devour
And take it to a *place*
*of* thorns,
And the [a,2]schemer pants
after their wealth.
6 "For [a]wickedness does not
come out from the dust,
Nor does trouble sprout
from the ground,

**4:11** [a]Job 29:17; Ps 34:10 [b]Job 5:4; 20:10; 27:14 **4:12** [a]Job 4:12-17; 33:15-18 [b]Job 26:14 **4:13** [a]Job 33:15 **4:15** [1]Or *breath passed over* **4:17** [a]Job 9:2; 25:4 [b]Job 31:15; 32:22; 35:10; 36:3 [1]Lit *from* **4:18** [a]Job 15:15 **4:19** [a]Job 10:9; 33:6 [b]Ge 2:7; 3:19; Job 22:16 **4:20** [a]Job 14:2 [b]Job 14:20; 20:7 [1]Lit *Without establishing* **4:21** [a]Job 8:22 [b]Job 18:21; 36:12 ◆ **5:1** [a]Job 15:15 **5:2** [a]Pr 12:16; 27:3 **5:3** [a]Jer 12:2 [b]Job 24:18; 31:30 **5:4** [a]Job 4:11 **5:5** [a]Job 18:8-10; 22:10 [1]Lit *Whose* [2]Ancient versions *thirsty* **5:6** [a]Job 15:35

7 For [a]man is born for trouble,
As [1]sparks fly upward.

8 "But as for me, I would
[a]seek God,
And I would set my
cause before God,
9 Who [a]does great and
unsearchable things,
[1]Wonders without number.
10 "He [a]gives rain on the earth
And sends water
on the *fields* outside,
11 So that [a]He sets on high
those who are lowly,
And those who mourn
are lifted to salvation.
12 "He [a]frustrates the
thoughts of the crafty,
So that their hands
cannot attain *success*
of sound wisdom.
13 "He [a]catches the wise
by their own craftiness,
And the counsel
of the twisted
is quickly thwarted.
14 "By day they [a]meet
with darkness
And grope at noon
as in the night.
15 "But He saves from
[a]the sword of their mouth,
And [b]the needy
from the hand of the strong.
16 "So the poor has hope,
And [a]unrighteousness
must shut its mouth.

17 "Behold, how [a]blessed is the
man whom God reproves,
So do not reject the [b]discipline
of the [1]Almighty.
18 "For [a]He inflicts pain
and [1]gives relief;
He [2]wounds,
and His hands *also* heal.
19 "[1]From six distresses
[a]He will deliver you,
Even in seven [b]evil will
not touch you.
20 "In [a]famine He will redeem
you from death,
And [b]in war from hands
with swords.
21 "You will be [a]hidden
from the scourge of the tongue,
[b]And you will not be afraid
of devastation when it comes.
22 "You will [a]laugh at devastation
and starvation,
[b]And you will not be afraid
of the beasts of the earth.
23 "For your covenant will be
with the stones of the field,
And [a]the beasts of the field
will be at peace with you.
24 "You will know that your
[a]tent is at peace,
For you will visit your
abode and fear no loss.
25 "You will know also that
your [a]seed will be many,
And [b]your offspring
as the vegetation of the land.
26 "You will [a]come to the grave
in full vigor,

**5:7** [a]Job 14:1 [1]Or *sons of Reseph* **5:8** [a]Job 13:2, 3; Ps 50:15 **5:9** [a]Job 9:10; 37:14, 16; 42:3 [1]Or *Miracles* **5:10** [a]Job 36:27-29; 37:6-11; 38:26 **5:11** [a]Job 22:29; 36:7 **5:12** [a]Ps 33:10 **5:13** [a]Job 37:24; 1Co 3:19 **5:14** [a]Job 12:25; 15:30; 18:18; 20:26; 24:13 **5:15** [a]Job 4:10, 11; Ps 35:10 [b]Job 29:17; 34:28; 36:6, 15; 38:15 **5:16** [a]Ps 107:42 **5:17** [a]Ps 94:12 [b]Job 36:15, 16; Pr 3:11; Heb 12:5-11; Jas 1:12 [1]Heb *Shaddai*, so in Job **5:18** [a]Dt 32:39; 1Sa 2:6; Is 30:26; Hos 6:1 [1]Lit *binds* [2]Or *crushes* **5:19** [a]Ps 34:19 [b]Ps 91:10 [1]Lit *In* **5:20** [a]Ps 33:19; 37:19 [b]Ps 144:10 **5:21** [a]Job 5:15; Ps 31:20 [b]Ps 91:5, 6 **5:22** [a]Job 8:21 [b]Ps 91:13; Eze 34:25; Hos 2:18 **5:23** [a]Is 11:6-9; 65:25 **5:24** [a]Job 8:6 **5:25** [a]Ps 112:2 [b]Is 44:3, 4; 48:19 **5:26** [a]Job 42:17

Like the stacking
of grain in its season.
27 "Behold this; we have
investigated it, *and* so it is.
Hear it, and know
for yourself."

### *Job Answers Eliphaz*

6 Then Job answered and said,
2 "[a]Oh that my vexation
were actually weighed
And laid
in the balances together
with my destruction!
3 "For then it would be [a]heavier
than the sand of the seas;
Therefore my words
have been rash.
4 "For the [a]arrows of the
Almighty are within me,
[1]Their [b]poison my
spirit drinks;
The [c]horrors of God are
arranged against me.
5 "Does the [a]wild donkey
bray over *his* grass,
Or does the ox low
over his fodder?
6 "Can something tasteless
be eaten without salt,
Or is there any taste
in the slime of a [1]yolk?
7 "My soul [a]refuses to touch *them*;
They are like loathsome
food to me.
8 "Oh that my request
might come to pass,
And that God would
grant my hope!
9 "Would that God were
[a]willing to crush me,
That He would release His
hand and cut me off!
10 "But it is still my comfort,
And I rejoice
in unsparing pain,
That I [a]have not *at all*
hidden away the words
of the Holy One.
11 "What is my strength,
that I should wait?
And what is my end,
that I should [a,1]endure?
12 "Is my strength the
strength of stones,
Or is my flesh bronze?
13 "Is it that there is no
[a]help within me,
And that the [b,1]*success*
of sound wisdom is
driven from me?

14 "For the [a]despairing man
lovingkindness *should*
*be* from his friend;
But he [b]forsakes the [1]fear
of the Almighty.
15 "My brothers have [a]betrayed
*me* like a [1]wadi,
Like the torrents of [2]wadis
which pass away,
16 Which grow dark
because of ice
*And* upon which the snow
hides itself.
17 "When [a]they become
waterless, they [1]are silent;
When it is hot, they vanish
from their place.

◆ **6:2** [a]Job 31:6 **6:3** [a]Job 23:2 **6:4** [a]Job 16:13; Ps 38:2 [b]Job 20:16; 21:20 [c]Job 30:15 [1]Lit *Whose*
**6:5** [a]Job 39:5-8 **6:6** [1]Heb *hallamuth*, meaning uncertain; possibly the juice of a plant
**6:7** [a]Job 3:24; 33:20 **6:9** [a]Nu 11:15; 1Ki 19:4; Job 7:16; 9:21; 10:1 **6:10** [a]Job 22:22; 23:11, 12
**6:11** [a]Job 21:4 [1]Lit *prolong my soul* **6:13** [a]Job 26:2 [b]Job 26:3 [1]Ancient versions *deliverance*
**6:14** [a]Job 4:5 [b]Job 1:5; 15:4 [1]Or *reverence* **6:15** [a]Jer 15:18 [1]Or *brook* [2]Or *brooks* **6:17** [a]Job 24:19
[1]Or *cease*

18 “The [1]paths of their
course wind along;
They go up into a formless
*place* and perish.
19 “The caravans of [a]Tema looked;
The travelers of [b]Sheba
hoped for them.
20 “They [a]were ashamed
for they had trusted;
They came there and
were humiliated.
21 “Indeed, you have now
become such;
[a]You see a terror
and are afraid.
22 “Have I said,
‘Give me *something*,’
Or, ‘Offer a bribe for me
from your wealth,’
23 Or, ‘Give me escape from
the hand of the adversary,’
Or, ‘Redeem me from the hand
of the ruthless men’?

24 “Instruct me, and [a]I will
be silent;
And cause me to understand
how I have erred.
25 “How painful are
upright words!
But what does your
reproof prove?
26 “Do you think to reprove
*my* words,
Or *think* of the [a]words
of one in despair as wind?
27 “You would even [a]cast
*lots* for [b]the orphans
And [c]bargain
over your friend.
28 “So now be willing to face me,
And *see* if I [a]lie to your face.
29 “Now turn *from this*, let there
be no unrighteousness;
Even turn *from this*,
[a]my righteousness
is yet in it.
30 “Is there unrighteousness
on my tongue?
Cannot [a]my palate
discern [1]destruction?

7 “[1]Is not man [a]conscripted
to labor on earth,
And *are not* his days
like the days of [b]a hired man?
2 “As a slave who pants
for the shade,
And as a hired man who
eagerly hopes for his wages,
3 So am I apportioned months
of worthlessness,
And [a]nights of trouble
are appointed me.
4 “If I [a]lie down I say,
‘When shall I arise?’
But the twilight continues,
And I am saturated
with tossing until dawn.
5 “My [a]flesh is clothed with
worms and a crust of dirt;
My skin scabs over and
flows *out again*.
6 “My days are [a]swifter
than a weaver’s shuttle,
And come to an end
[b]without hope.

7 “Remember that my
life [a]is *but* wind;
My eye will [b]not again see good.

**6:18** [1]Or *caravans turn from their course* **6:19** [a]Ge 25:15; Is 21:14; Jer 25:23 [b]Job 1:15 **6:20** [a]Jer 14:3
**6:21** [a]Ps 38:11 **6:24** [a]Ps 39:1 **6:26** [a]Job 8:2; 15:2; 16:3 **6:27** [a]Joel 3:3; Na 3:10 [b]Job 22:9; 24:3, 9
[c]2Pe 2:3 **6:28** [a]Job 27:4; 33:3; 36:4 **6:29** [a]Job 13:18; 19:6; 23:10; 27:5, 6; 34:5; 42:1-6 **6:30** [a]Job 12:11
[1]Or *words* ◆ **7:1** [a]Job 5:7; 10:17; 14:1, 14 [b]Job 14:6 [1]Lit *Has not man compulsory labor* **7:3** [a]Job 16:7
**7:4** [a]Dt 28:67; Job 7:13, 14 **7:5** [a]Job 2:7; 17:14 **7:6** [a]Job 9:25 [b]Job 13:15; 14:19; 17:15, 16; 19:10
**7:7** [a]Job 7:16; Ps 78:39; Jas 4:14 [b]Job 9:25

8 “The [a]eye of him who sees me
will behold me no longer;
Your eyes *will be* on me,
but [b]I will not be.
9 “A [a]cloud vanishes,
and it is gone,
So [b]he who goes down
to [c]Sheol does not come up.
10 “He will not return again
to his house,
Nor will [a]his place recognize
him anymore.

11 “Indeed [a]I will not hold
back my mouth;
I will speak in the distress
of my spirit;
I will muse on the bitterness
of my soul.
12 “Am I the sea
or [a]the sea monster,
That You set a guard over me?
13 “If I say, ‘[a]My bed will
comfort me;
My couch will [1]ease my
*bitter* musing,’
14 Then You frighten me
with dreams
And terrify me by visions,
15 So that my soul would
choose suffocation,
Death rather than my [1]pains.
16 “I have [a]rejected *everything*;
I will not live forever.
Leave me alone, [b]for my
days are *but* a breath.
17 “[a]What is man that You
magnify him,
And that You set Your
heart on him,
18 That [a]You [1]examine him
every morning
And test him
every moment?
19 “[a,1]Will You never turn Your
gaze away from me,
Nor let me alone until I
swallow my spit?
20 “[a]Have I sinned?
What have I done to You,
O [b]watcher of men?
Why have You set me
as Your target,
So that I am a burden
to myself?
21 “Why then [a]do You not
forgive my transgression
And take away my iniquity?
For now I will [b]lie
down in the dust;
And You will seek me
earnestly, [c]but I will
not be.”

### *Bildad Claims God Rewards the Good*

8 Then Bildad the Shuhite answered and said,
2 “How long will you say
these things,
And the [a]words of your
mouth be a mighty wind?
3 “Does [a]God pervert justice?
Or does [1]the Almighty
pervert what is right?
4 “[a]If your sons sinned
against Him,
Then He sent them
into the [1]power
of their transgression.

**7:8** [a]Job 8:18; 20:9 [b]Job 7:21 **7:9** [a]Job 30:15 [b]Job 3:13-19 [c]2Sa 12:23; Job 11:8; 14:13; 17:13, 16 **7:10** [a]Job 8:18; 20:9; 27:21, 23 **7:11** [a]Job 10:1; 21:4; 23:2; Ps 40:9 **7:12** [a]Eze 32:2, 3 **7:13** [a]Job 7:4; Ps 6:6 [1]Lit *bear* **7:15** [1]Lit *bones* **7:16** [a]Job 6:9; 9:21; 10:1 [b]Job 7:7 **7:17** [a]Job 22:2; Ps 8:4; 144:3; Heb 2:6 **7:18** [a]Job 14:3 [1]Or *care for*, cf. Ps 8:4 **7:19** [a]Job 9:18; 10:20; 14:6 [1]Lit *How long will You not* **7:20** [a]Job 35:3, 6 [b]Ps 36:6 **7:21** [a]Job 9:28; 10:14 [b]Job 10:9 [c]Job 7:8 ◆**8:2** [a]Job 6:26 **8:3** [a]Ge 18:25; Dt 32:4; 2Chr 19:7; Job 34:10, 12; 36:23; 37:23; Ro 3:5 [1]Heb *Shaddai* **8:4** [a]Job 1:5, 18, 19 [1]Lit *hand*

5 “If you would [a]seek
God earnestly
And plead for the grace
of [1]the Almighty,
6 If you are pure and upright,
Indeed now [a]He would
rouse Himself for you
And make your
righteous [b]abode at peace.
7 “Though your beginning
was insignificant,
Yet your [a]end will
increase greatly.

8 “Please [a]ask
of past generations,
And establish the things
searched out
by their fathers.
9 “For we are *only* of yesterday
and know nothing,
Because [a]our days on earth
are *but* a shadow.
10 “Will they not instruct
you *and* tell you,
And bring forth words
from their hearts?

11 “Can the papyrus grow up
without a marsh?
Can the rushes grow
without water?
12 “While it is still green
*and* not cut down,
Yet it dries up
before any *other* [1]plant.
13 “So are the paths of [a]all
who forget God;
And the [b]hope
of the godless will perish,
14 Whose confidence is fragile,
And whose trust
a [a]spider’s [1]web.
15 “He relies on his [a]house,
but it does not stand;
He holds fast to it, but it
is not established.
16 “He [a,1]thrives before the sun,
And his [b]shoots go forth
over his garden.
17 “His roots wrap
around a rock pile;
He looks upon a house
of stones.
18 “If He swallows him up
from [a]his place,
Then it will deny him, *saying,*
‘[b]I never saw you.’
19 “Behold, [a]this is the
joy of [1]His way;
And out of the dust
others will spring.
20 “Behold, [a]God will not
reject a blameless *man,*
Nor [b]will He strengthen
the hand of the evildoers.
21 “He will yet fill [a]your
mouth with laughter
And your lips with shouting.
22 “Those who hate you will be
[a]clothed with shame,
And the [b]tent of the wicked
will be no longer.”

### *Job Replies There Is No Adjudicator*

9 Then Job answered and said,
2 “In truth I know
that this is so;
But how can a [a]man be
in the right [1]before God?

**8:5** [a]Job 5:17-27 [1]Heb *Shaddai* **8:6** [a]Job 22:27; 34:28; Ps 7:6 [b]Job 5:24 **8:7** [a]Job 42:12 **8:8** [a]Dt 4:32; 32:7; Job 15:18; 20:4 **8:9** [a]Job 14:2 **8:12** [1]Lit *reed* **8:13** [a]Ps 9:17 [b]Job 11:20; 13:16; 15:34; 20:5; 27:8 **8:14** [a]Is 59:5, 6 [1]Lit *house* **8:15** [a]Job 8:22; 27:18; Ps 49:11 **8:16** [a]Ps 37:35; Jer 11:16 [b]Ps 80:11 [1]Lit *is lush* **8:18** [a]Job 7:10 [b]Job 7:8 **8:19** [a]Job 20:5 [1]Or *his* **8:20** [a]Job 4:7 [b]Job 21:30 **8:21** [a]Job 5:22; Ps 126:1, 2 **8:22** [a]Ps 132:18 [b]Job 8:15; 15:34; 18:14; 21:28
◆ **9:2** [a]Job 4:17; 25:4 [1]Lit *with*

3 “If one desired
to [a]contend with Him,
He could not answer Him
once in a thousand *times.*
4 “[a]Wise in heart and
[b]mighty in power,
Who has [c]stiffened *his*
*neck* against Him and
been at peace?
5 “[a]*God* is the One who
removes the mountains,
they know not *how,*
When He overturns
them in His anger;
6 The One who [a]shakes
the earth out of its place,
And its [b]pillars tremble;
7 The One who says
for the [a]sun [1]not to shine,
And sets a seal upon the stars;
8 Who alone [a]stretches
out the heavens,
And [b,1]tramples down
the waves of the sea;
9 Who makes the [a]Bear,
Orion, and the Pleiades,
And the [b]chambers
of the south;
10 Who [a]does great things,
unsearchable,
And wondrous works,
innumerable.
11 “Were He to sweep by me,
[a]I would not see Him;
Were He to move past *me,*
I would not perceive Him.
12 “Were He to snatch away,
who could [a]turn Him back?
Who could say to Him,
‘[b]What are You doing?’

13 “God will not turn
back His anger;
Beneath Him crouch
the helpers of [a]Rahab.
14 “How then can [a]I [1]answer Him,
*And* choose my words
[2]before Him?
15 “For [a]though I were right,
I could not [1]answer;
I would have to [b]plead
for the grace of my judge.
16 “If I called and He
answered me,
I could not believe that He
was giving ear to my voice.
17 “For He [a]bruises me
with a tempest
And multiplies my wounds
without cause.
18 “He will [a]not allow me
to get my breath,
But saturates me
with [b]bitterness.
19 “If *it is a matter*
of power, [a]behold,
*He is* the mighty one!
And if *it is a matter* of justice,
who can make [1]Him testify?
20 “[a]Though I am righteous, my
mouth will [b]condemn me;
Though I am blameless,
He will declare me perverse.
21 “I am [a]blameless;
I do not know my soul;
I [b]reject my life.

---

**9:3** [a]Job 10:2; 13:19; 23:6; 40:2 **9:4** [a]Job 11:6; 12:13; 28:23; 38:36, 37 [b]Job 9:19; 23:6 [c]2Chr 13:12; Pr 29:1 **9:5** [a]Job 9:5-10; 26:6-14; 41:11 **9:6** [a]*Is 2:19, 21; 13:13; Hag 2:6* [b]Ps 75:3 **9:7** [a]Is 13:10; Eze 32:7, 8 [1]Lit *and it does not shine* **9:8** [a]Ge 1:1; Job 37:18; Ps 104:2; Is 40:22 [b]Job 38:16; Ps 77:19 [1]Lit *treads upon the heights of* **9:9** [a]Job 38:31, 32; Am 5:8 [b]Job 37:9 **9:10** [a]Job 5:9 **9:11** [a]Job 23:8, 9; 35:14 **9:12** [a]Job 10:7; 11:10 [b]Is 45:9 **9:13** [a]Job 26:12; Ps 89:10; Is 30:7; 51:9 **9:14** [a]Job 9:3, 32 [1]Or *plead my case before* [2]Lit *with* **9:15** [a]Job 9:20, 21; 10:15 [b]Job 8:5 [1]Or *plead my case* **9:17** [a]Job 16:12, 14; 30:22 **9:18** [a]Job 7:19; 10:20 [b]Job 13:26; 27:2 **9:19** [a]Job 9:4 [1]As in Gr; Heb *me* **9:20** [a]Job 9:15 [b]Job 9:29; 15:6 **9:21** [a]Job 1:1; 12:4; 13:18 [b]Job 7:16

22 “It is *all* one; therefore I say,
‘He [a]consumes the blameless
and the wicked.’
23 “If the scourge puts
to death suddenly,
He [a]mocks the despair
of the innocent.
24 “The earth [a]is given
into the hand of the wicked;
He [b]covers the faces
of its judges.
If *it is* not *He*, then who is it?

25 “Now [a]my days are swifter
than a runner;
They flee away; [b]they
do not see good.
26 “They sweep by
like [a]reed boats,
Like an [b]eagle that
swoops on its food.
27 “Though I say, ‘I will
forget [a]my musing,
I will forsake my *sad*
countenance and
be cheerful,’
28 I am [a]afraid of all my pains;
I know that [b]You will
not acquit me.
29 “I am accounted [a]wicked;
Why then should I
toil in vain?
30 “If I should [a]wash
myself with snow
And cleanse [b]my
hands with lye,
31 Yet You would plunge
me into the pit,
And my own clothes
would abhor me.
32 “For [a]*He is* not a man as I am
that [b]I may answer Him,
That we may go to court
*for judgment* together.
33 “There is no [a]adjudicator
between us,
Who may lay his hand
upon us both.
34 “Let Him [a]remove His
rod from me,
And let not dread
of Him terrify me.
35 “*Then* I [a]would speak
and not fear Him;
But I am not like that
in myself.

### *Job Cries Out to God*

10 “[a]My soul is loathed
by my life;
I will abandon *all restraint*
in myself to [b]my complaint;
I will speak in the bitterness
of my soul.
2 “I will say to God, ‘[a]Do not
account me as wicked;
Let me know why You
contend with me.
3 ‘Is it good to You that
You [a]oppress,
That You reject [b]the labor
of Your hands,
And [1]cause [c]the counsel
of the wicked to shine forth?
4 ‘Have You eyes of flesh?
Or do You [a]see
as a mortal man sees?
5 ‘Are Your days as the days
of a mortal man,
Or [a]Your years as man’s years,

**9:22** [a]Job 10:7, 8 **9:23** [a]Job 24:12 **9:24** [a]Job 10:3; 12:6; 16:11 [b]Job 12:17 **9:25** [a]Job 7:6 [b]Job 7:7 **9:26** [a]Is 18:2 [b]Job 39:29; Hab 1:8 **9:27** [a]Job 7:11 **9:28** [a]Job 3:25 [b]Job 7:21; 10:14 **9:29** [a]Job 10:2; Ps 37:33 **9:30** [a]Jer 2:22 [b]Job 31:7 **9:32** [a]Ecc 6:10 [b]Job 9:3; Ro 9:20 **9:33** [a]1Sa 2:25; Job 9:19; Is 1:18 **9:34** [a]Job 13:21 **9:35** [a]Job 13:22 ◆ **10:1** [a]Job 7:16 [b]Job 7:11 **10:2** [a]Job 9:29 **10:3** [a]Job 9:22-24; 16:11; 19:6; 27:2 [b]Job 10:8; 14:15; Ps 138:8; Is 64:8 [c]Job 21:16; 22:18 [1]Lit *You shine forth* **10:4** [a]1Sa 16:7; Job 28:24; 34:21 **10:5** [a]Job 36:26

6 That [a]You should seek
for my guilt
And search after my sin?
7 'According to Your knowledge
[a]I am indeed not wicked,
Yet there is [b]no [1]deliverer
from Your hand.

8 '[a]Your hands fashioned and
made me [1]altogether,
[b]And would You
swallow me up?
9 'Remember now, that You
have made me as [a]clay;
And would You [b]turn
me into dust again?
10 'Did You not pour me
out like milk
And curdle me like cheese,
11 Clothe me with skin
and flesh,
And knit me together
with bones and sinews?
12 'You have [a]made
alongside me life and
lovingkindness;
And Your care has
kept my spirit.
13 'Yet [a]these things You have
concealed in Your heart;
I know that this is within You:
14 If I sin, then You would
[a]take note of me
And [b]would not acquit
me of my guilt.
15 'If [a]I am wicked, woe to me!
And [b]if I am righteous,
I dare not lift up my head.
*I am* sated with disgrace—
so see my misery!
16 'Should *my head* be set
on high, [a]You would
hunt me like a lion;
And again You would show
Your [b]wonders against me.
17 'You renew [a]Your
witnesses against me
And increase Your
vexation toward me;
[b,1]Hardship after
hardship is with me.

18 '[a]Why then have You brought
me out of the womb?
Would that I had breathed my
last and no eye had seen me!
19 'I should have been as though
I had not been,
Carried from womb to tomb.'
20 "Would He not cease
[a]for a few of my days?
[b,1]Withdraw from me that I
may have a little cheer
21 Before I go—[a]and I
shall not return—
[b]To the land of darkness
and [c]shadow of death,
22 The land of utter gloom
as *the* thick darkness *itself*,
Of the shadow of death,
without order,
And which shines
as the thick darkness."

### *Zophar Asks, Can You Find the Depths of God?*

**11** Then Zophar the Naamathite
answered and said,
2 "Shall a multitude of words
go unanswered,

---

**10:6** [a]Job 14:16 **10:7** [a]Job 9:21; 13:18 [b]Job 9:12; 23:13; 27:22 [1]Or *deliverance* **10:8** [a]Job 10:3; Ps 119:73 [b]Job 9:22 [1]Lit *together round about* **10:9** [a]Job 4:19; 33:6 [b]Job 7:21 **10:12** [a]Job 33:4 **10:13** [a]Job 23:13 **10:14** [a]Job 7:20 [b]Job 7:21; 9:28 **10:15** [a]Job 10:7; Is 3:11 [b]Job 6:29 **10:16** [a]Is 38:13; Lam 3:10; Hos 13:7 [b]Job 5:9 **10:17** [a]Ru 1:21; Job 16:8 [b]Job 7:1 [1]Lit *Changes and warfare are with me* **10:18** [a]Job 3:11-13 **10:20** [a]Job 14:1 [b]Job 7:16, 19 [1]Lit *Put* **10:21** [a]2Sa 12:23; Job 3:13-19; 16:22 [b]Ps 88:12 [c]Job 10:22; 34:22; 38:17; Ps 23:4

And a [a]man of lips
be in the right?
3 "Shall your boasts
silence men?
And shall you [a]mock
and none rebuke?
4 "[a]You have said,
'My learning is pure,
And [b]I am innocent
in your eyes.'
5 "But would that God
might speak,
And open His lips
against you,
6 And tell you the secrets
of wisdom!
For sound wisdom
[a,1]has two sides.
Know then that God [2]forgets
a part of [b]your iniquity.

7 "[a]Can you find the
depths of God?
Can you find the limits
of the Almighty?
8 "*They are* [a]high as [1]the
heavens, what can you do?
Deeper than [b]Sheol,
what can you know?
9 "Its measure is longer
than the earth
And broader than the sea.
10 "If He sweeps by or shuts up,
Or calls an assembly, [a]who
can turn Him around?
11 "For [a]He knows worthless men,
And He [b]sees wickedness,
[1]so will He not carefully
consider *it*?
12 "[a,1]Yet an empty *headed*
man will obtain a
heart *of wisdom*,
And the [2]foal of a [b]wild
donkey is born a man.

13 "[a]If you would [b]set
your heart right
And [c]spread out your
hand to Him,
14 If wickedness is in your
hand, [a]put it far away,
And do not let
unrighteousness dwell
in your tents;
15 Then, indeed, you could
[a]lift up your face
without *moral* defect,
And you would be steadfast
and [b]not fear.
16 "For you would [a]forget
*your* trouble,
As [b]waters that pass by, so
you would remember *it*.
17 "And your lifetime
would [a]arise *brighter*
than noonday;
Darkness would be
like the morning.
18 "Then you would trust,
because there is hope;
And you would search
around and rest securely.
19 "You would [a]lie down and none
would make *you* tremble,
And many would
[b]entreat your [1]favor.
20 "But the [a]eyes of the wicked
will come to an end,

◆**11:2** [a]Job 8:2; 15:2; 18:2 **11:3** [a]Job 17:2; 21:3 **11:4** [a]Job 6:10 [b]Job 10:7 **11:6** [a]Job 9:4 [b]Job 15:5; 22:5 [1]Lit *is double* [2]Lit *causes to be forgotten for you* **11:7** [a]Job 33:12, 13; 36:26; 37:5, 23; Ro 11:33 **11:8** [a]Job 22:12; 35:5 [b]Job 26:6; 38:17 [1]Lit *the heights of heaven* **11:10** [a]Job 9:12 **11:11** [a]Job 34:21-23 [b]Job 24:23; 28:24; 31:4 [1]Or *even He does not consider* **11:12** [a]Ps 39:5, 11; 62:9; 144:4; Ecc 1:2; 11:10 [b]Job 39:5 [1]Lit *A hollow man* [2]Lit *donkey* **11:13** [a]Job 5:17-27; 11:13-20 [b]1Sa 7:3; Ps 78:8 [c]Job 22:27; Ps 88:9; 143:6 **11:14** [a]Job 22:23 **11:15** [a]Job 22:26 [b]Ps 27:3; 46:2 **11:16** [a]Is 65:16 [b]Job 22:11 **11:17** [a]Job 22:26 **11:19** [a]Lv 26:6; Is 17:2; Mic 4:4; Zep 3:13 [b]Is 45:14 [1]Lit *face* **11:20** [a]Dt 28:65; Job 17:5

And escape will [b]perish
from them;
And their [c]hope is
[d]the expiring of their soul."

### *Job Answers*

12 Then Job answered and said,
2 "Truly then [a]you
are the people,
And with you wisdom will die!
3 "But [a]I have a heart
*of wisdom* as well as you;
I do not fall *short* of you.
And [1]who does not know
such things as these?
4 "I am a [a]laughingstock
to [1]my friends,
The one who called on God
and He answered him;
The righteous *and* [b]blameless
*man* is a laughingstock.
5 "[1]As for upheaval, *there is*
*only* contempt by the
one who acts at ease,
*But* it is prepared
for those whose feet slip.
6 "The [a]tents of the destroyers
are complacent,
And those who provoke
God [b]are secure,
[1]Whom God brings
[c]into their power.

7 "But now ask the beasts,
and let them instruct you;
And the birds of the sky,
and let them tell you.
8 "Or muse to the earth,
and let it instruct you;
And let the fish of the sea
recount *it* to you.
9 "Who among all these
does not know
That [a]the hand of Yahweh
has done this,
10 [a]In whose hand is the life
of every living thing,
And [b]the breath of all
the flesh of man?
11 "Does not [a]the ear test words,
As the palate [1]tastes its food?
12 "Wisdom is with [a]aged men,
*With* [1]long life
is discernment.

### *Job Speaks of God's Strength*

13 "With Him are [a]wisdom
and [a]might;
To Him belong counsel
and [b]discernment.
14 "Behold, He [a]pulls down,
and it cannot be rebuilt;
He [b]closes a man in,
and it cannot be opened.
15 "Behold, He [a]restrains the
waters, and they dry up;
And He [b]sends them out, and
they overturn the earth.
16 "With Him are strength
and sound wisdom;
The [a]misled and the misleader
belong to Him.
17 "He makes [a]counselors
walk [1]barefoot
And makes fools of [b]judges.
18 "He [a]opens the [1]bond of kings
And binds their loins
with a belt.

***11:20*** [b]*Job 27:22; 34:22* [c]*Job 8:13* [d]*Job 6:9* ◆**12:2** [a]Job 17:10 **12:3** [a]Job 13:2 [1]Lit with whom is there *not like these?* **12:4** [a]Job 17:6; 30:1, 9, 10; 34:7 [b]Job 6:29 [1]Lit *his* **12:5** [1]Lit *Contempt for calamity is the thought of him who is at ease* **12:6** [a]Job 9:24; 21:7-9 [b]Job 24:23 [c]Job 22:18 [1]Or *He who brings God into his hand* **12:9** [a]Is 41:20 **12:10** [a]Ac 17:28 [b]Job 27:3; 33:4 **12:11** [a]Job 34:3 [1]Lit *tastes food for itself* **12:12** [a]Job 15:10; 32:7 [1]Lit *length of days* **12:13** [a]Job 9:4 [b]Job 11:6; 26:12; 32:8; 36:5; 38:36 **12:14** [a]Job 19:10; Is 25:2 [b]Job 37:7 **12:15** [a]Dt 11:17; 1Ki 8:35; 17:1 [b]Ge 7:11-24 **12:16** [a]Job 13:7, 9 **12:17** [a]Job 3:14 [b]Job 9:24 [1]Or *stripped* **12:18** [a]Ps 116:16 [1]Or *discipline*

19 "He makes priests
walk [1]barefoot
And subverts [a]the
enduring ones.
20 "He removes speech
from the faithful
And [a]takes away
the *discerning* taste
of the elders.
21 "He [a]pours contempt on nobles
And [b]loosens the belt
of the strong.
22 "He [a]reveals mysteries
from the darkness
And brings out the shadows
of death into light.
23 "He [a]makes the nations great,
then makes them perish;
He [1]enlarges the nations,
then leads them away.
24 "He [a]removes the heart
*of wisdom* from the heads
of the earth's people
And makes them wander
in a pathless [1]waste.
25 "They [a]grope in darkness
with no light,
And He makes them [b]wander
about like a drunken man.

### *I Will Be Declared Righteous*

13 "[a]Behold, my eye has
seen all *this*;
My ear has heard and
understood it.
2 "[a]What you know I also know;
I have not fallen *short* of you.

3 "But [a]I would speak
to [1]the Almighty,
And I desire to [b]argue
with God.
4 "But you [a]cover me
with lies;
You are all
[b]worthless physicians.
5 "O that you would [a]be
completely silent,
And that it would become
your wisdom!
6 "Please hear my argument
And give heed
to the contentions of my lips.
7 "Will you [a]speak what is
unrighteous for God,
And speak what is
deceitful for Him?
8 "Will you [a]show
partiality for Him?
Will you contend for God?
9 "Will it be well when He
examines you?
Or [a]will you deceive Him
as one deceives a man?
10 "He will surely reprove you
If you secretly
[a]show partiality.
11 "Will not [a]His exaltedness
terrify you,
And the dread of Him
fall on you?
12 "Your memorable sayings
are proverbs of ashes;
Your defenses are
defenses of clay.

13 "[a]Be silent before me
so that I may speak;
Then let come
on me what may.

**12:19** [a]Job 24:22; 34:24-28; 35:9 [1]Or *stripped* **12:20** [a]Job 17:4; 32:9 **12:21** [a]Job 34:19; Ps 107:40 [b]Job 12:18 **12:22** [a]Da 2:22; 1Co 4:5 **12:23** [a]Is 9:3; 26:15 [1]Or *spreads out* **12:24** [a]Job 12:20 [1]Or *formlessness* **12:25** [a]Job 5:14 [b]Is 24:20 ◆**13:1** [a]Job 12:9 **13:2** [a]Job 12:3 **13:3** [a]Job 13:22; 23:4 [b]Job 13:15 [1]Heb *Shaddai* **13:4** [a]Ps 119:69 [b]Jer 23:32 **13:5** [a]Job 13:13; 21:5; Pr 17:28 **13:7** [a]Job 27:4 **13:8** [a]Lv 19:15; Pr 24:23 **13:9** [a]Job 12:16 **13:10** [a]Job 13:8; 32:21; 34:19 **13:11** [a]Job 31:23 **13:13** [a]Job 13:5

14 "Why should I take my
flesh in my teeth
And [a]put my life in my [1]hands?
15 "[a,1]Though He slay me,
I will hope in Him.
Nevertheless I [b]will argue
my ways [2]before Him.
16 "This also will be
my [a]salvation,
For [b]a godless man may not
come before His presence.
17 "[1]Listen carefully to my words,
And let my declaration
*fill* your ears.
18 "Behold now, I have [a]arranged
my *case for* justice;
I know that [b]I will be
declared righteous.
19 "[a]Who will contend with me?
For now I am silent and
[b]will breathe my last.

20 "Only two things do
not do to me,
Then I will not hide
from Your face:
21 [a]Move Your [1]hand
far from me,
And let not the dread
of You terrify me.
22 "Then call, and [a]I will answer;
Or let me speak,
then respond to me.
23 "[a]How many are my
iniquities and sins?
Make known to me my
transgression and my sin.
24 "Why do You [a]hide Your face
And think of me
as [b]Your enemy?
25 "Will You cause a [a]driven
leaf to tremble?
Or will You pursue
the dry [b]chaff?
26 "For You write [a]bitter
things against me
And [b]make me to possess
the iniquities of my youth.
27 "You [a]put my feet
in the stocks
And kept watch
over all my paths;
You [1]set a limit
for the soles of my feet,
28 While [1]I am decaying
like a [a]rotten thing,
Like a garment that
is moth-eaten.

### *If a Man Dies, Will He Live Again?*

14 "[a]Man, who is born
of woman,
Is [1]short-lived and
[b]full of turmoil.
2 "[a]Like a flower he comes
forth and withers.
He also flees like [b]a shadow
and does not stand.
3 "You also [a]open Your
eyes on him
And [b]bring [1]me
into judgment with Yourself.
4 "[a]Who can make the clean
out of the unclean?
No one!

---

**13:14** [a]Ps 119:109 [1]Lit *palm* **13:15** [a]Job 7:6 [b]Job 27:5 [1]Or *He will slay me, I have no hope* [2]Lit *to His face* **13:16** [a]Job 23:7; Is 12:1, 2 [b]Job 34:21-23 **13:17** [1]Or *persist in listening* **13:18** [a]Job 23:4 [b]Job 9:21; 10:7; 12:4 **13:19** [a]Is 50:8 [b]Job 7:21; 10:8 **13:21** [a]Job 9:34; Ps 39:10 [1]Lit *palm* **13:22** [a]Job 9:16; 14:15 **13:23** [a]Job 7:21 **13:24** [a]Ps 13:1; 44:24; 88:14; Is 8:17 [b]Job 19:11; 33:10; Lam 2:5 **13:25** [a]Lv 26:36 [b]Job 21:18 **13:26** [a]Job 9:18 [b]Ps 25:7 **13:27** [a]Job 33:11 [1]Lit *carve for* **13:28** [a]Job 2:7 [1]Lit *he is* ◆ **14:1** [a]Job 5:7 [b]Ecc 2:23 [1]Lit *short of days* **14:2** [a]Ps 90:5, 6; 103:15; Is 40:6, 7; Jas 1:10; 1Pe 1:24 [b]Job 8:9 **14:3** [a]Ps 8:4; 144:3 [b]Ps 143:2 [1]Some ancient versions *him* **14:4** [a]Job 15:14; 25:4; Ps 51:5

5 "Since his days
are determined,
The [a]number of his
months is with You;
And his limits You have [1]set
so that he cannot pass.
6 "[a]Turn Your gaze from him
that he may cease *from toil,*
Until he accepts his day
like a hired man.

7 "For there is hope for a tree,
When it is cut down,
that it will change back
*sprouting* again,
And its shoots will not cease.
8 "Though its roots grow
old in the ground
And its stump dies
in the dry soil,
9 At the scent of water
it will flourish
And put forth sprigs
like a plant.
10 "But [a]man dies and
lies prostrate.
Man [b]breathes his last,
and where is he?
11 "*As* [a]water [1]evaporates
from the sea,
And a river becomes
parched and dried up,
12 So [a]man lies down and
does not rise.
Until the heavens
are no longer,
[1]He will not awake nor be
aroused out of [2]his sleep.

13 "Oh that You would
conceal me in Sheol,
That You would hide me [a]until
Your anger returns *to You,*
That You would set a limit
for me and remember me!
14 "If a man dies, will
he live *again?*
All the days of my
labor I will wait
Until my change comes.
15 "You will call, and I
will answer You;
You will long for [a]the
work of Your hands.
16 "For now You [a]number
my steps,
You do not [b]keep watch
over my sin.
17 "My transgression is
[a]sealed up in a bag,
And You [1]cover up my iniquity.

18 "But the falling mountain
[1]crumbles away,
And the rock moves
from its place;
19 Water wears away stones;
Its torrents wash away
the dust of the earth;
So You [a]make man's
hope perish.
20 "You forever overpower him
and he [a]goes *away;*
*You* alter his appearance
and send him away.
21 "His sons achieve honor,
but [a]he does not know *it;*
Or they become insignificant,
but he does not perceive it.
22 "But his flesh pains him,
And he mourns only
for himself."

**14:5** [a]Job 21:21 [1]Lit *made* **14:6** [a]Job 7:19; Ps 39:13 **14:10** [a]Job 3:13; 14:10-15 [b]Job 13:9
**14:11** [a]Is 19:5 [1]Lit *disappears* **14:12** [a]Job 3:13 [1]Lit *They* [2]Lit *their* **14:13** [a]Is 26:20 **14:15** [a]Job 10:3
**14:16** [a]Job 31:4; 34:21; Ps 139:1-3; Pr 5:21 [b]Job 10:6 **14:17** [a]Dt 32:32-34 [1]Lit *smear,* cf. Job 13:14
**14:18** [1]Lit *withers* **14:19** [a]Job 7:6 **14:20** [a]Job 4:20; 20:7 **14:21** [a]Ecc 9:5

### *Eliphaz Says Job's Lips Answer Against Him*

15 Then Eliphaz the Temanite answered and said,
2 "Should a wise man answer with windy knowledge
[a]And fill his belly with the east wind?
3 "Should he argue with a word that cannot be used,
Or with speech which is not profitable?
4 "Indeed, you annul *reverent* fear
And cut off musing before God.
5 "For [a]your iniquity teaches your mouth,
And you choose the tongue of [b]the crafty.
6 "Your [a]own mouth condemns you, and not I;
And your own lips answer against you.

7 "Were you the first man to be born,
Or [a]were you brought forth before the hills?
8 "Do you hear the [a]secret counsel of God,
And cut down wisdom *only* unto yourself?
9 "[a]What do you know that we do not know?
*What* do you understand that is not with us?
10 "Both the [a]gray-haired and the aged are among us,
Older than your father.
11 "Are [a]the consolations of God too small for you,
Even the [b]word *spoken* gently with you?
12 "Why does your [a]heart take you away?
And why do your eyes flash,
13 That you should turn your spirit against God
And allow *such* words to go out of your mouth?
14 "What is man, that [a]he should be pure,
Or [b]he who is born of a woman, that he should be righteous?
15 "Behold, He puts no faith in His [a]holy ones,
And the [b]heavens are not pure in His sight;
16 How much less one who is [a]abominable and corrupt,
Man, who [b]drinks [1]unrighteousness like water!

17 "I will tell you, listen to me;
And what I have beheld I will also recount;
18 What wise men have told,
And have not concealed from [a]their fathers,
19 To whom alone the land was given,
And no stranger passed among them.
20 "The wicked man writhes [a]in pain all *his* days,
And [1]numbered are the years [b]stored up for the ruthless.
21 "[1]Sounds of [a]dread are in his ears;

◆ **15:2** [a]Job 6:26 **15:5** [a]Job 22:5 [b]Job 5:12, 13 **15:6** [a]Job 18:7 **15:7** [a]Job 38:4, 21; Pr 8:25 **15:8** [a]Job 29:4; Ro 11:34; 1Co 2:11 **15:9** [a]Job 12:3; 13:2 **15:10** [a]Job 12:12; 32:6, 7 **15:11** [a]Job 5:17-19; 36:15, 16 [b]Job 6:10; 23:12 **15:12** [a]Job 11:13; 36:13 **15:14** [a]Job 14:4; Pr 20:9; Ecc 7:20 [b]Job 25:4 **15:15** [a]Job 5:1 [b]Job 25:5 **15:16** [a]Ps 14:1 [b]Job 34:7; Pr 19:28 [1]Or *injustice* **15:18** [a]Job 8:8; 20:4 **15:20** [a]Job 15:24 [b]Job 24:1; 27:13 [1]Lit *the number of years are* **15:21** [a]Job 15:24; 18:11; 20:25; 24:17; 27:20 [1]Lit *A sound of dreads*

[b]While at peace the destroyer
comes upon him.
22 “He does not believe that he
will [a]return from darkness,
And he is destined
for [b]the sword.
23 “He wanders about for food,
saying, ‘Where is it?’
He knows that a day
of [a]darkness is ready
at his hand.
24 “Distress and anguish
terrify him;
They overpower him like a
king ready for the attack,
25 Because he has stretched
out his hand against God
And [a]magnifies himself
against [1]the Almighty.
26 “He rushes [1]headlong at Him
With [2]his massive shield.
27 “For he has [a]covered his
face with his fat
And made his thighs
heavy with flesh.
28 “He has [a]dwelt
in desolate cities,
In houses no one
would inhabit,
Which are destined
to become [1]ruins.
29 “He [a]will not become rich,
nor will his wealth endure;
And his grain will not stretch
out over the land.
30 “He will [a]not be able
to [1]depart from darkness;
The [b]flame will wither
his shoots,
And by [c]the breath of His
mouth he will depart.
31 “Let him not [a]believe in
emptiness, deceiving himself;
For emptiness will
be his [1]reward,
32 When [a]his days are
not *yet* fulfilled,
And his palm [b]branch
is not green.
33 “He will drop off his unripe
grape like the vine,
And will [a]cast off his flower
like the olive tree.
34 “For the company
of [a]the godless is barren,
And fire consumes
[b]the tents of [1]the corrupt.
35 “They [a]conceive [1]trouble and
give birth to wickedness,
And their [2]belly
prepares deception.”

### *Troublesome Comforters*

16 Then Job answered and said,
2 “I have heard many
such things;
[a,1]Troublesome comforters
are you all.
3 “Is there *no* end
to [a]windy words?
Or what pains you
that you answer?
4 “I too could speak like you,
If your soul were
in the place of my soul.
I could compose words
against you
And [a]shake my head at you.

**15:21** [b]Job 20:21; 1Th 5:3 **15:22** [a]Job 15:30 [b]Job 19:29; 27:14; 33:18; 36:12 **15:23** [a]Job 15:22, 30
**15:25** [a]Job 36:9 [1]Heb *Shaddai* **15:26** [1]Lit *with a stiff neck* [2]Lit *the thick-bossed shields*
**15:27** [a]Ps 73:7; 119:70 **15:28** [a]Job 3:14; Is 5:8, 9 [1]Or *heaps* **15:29** [a]Job 27:16, 17 **15:30** [a]Job 5:14; 15:22 [b]Job 15:34; 20:26; 22:20; 31:12 [c]Job 4:9 [1]Lit *turn aside* **15:31** [a]Job 35:13; Is 59:4 [1]Lit *exchange*
**15:32** [a]Job 22:16; Ecc 7:17 [b]Job 18:16 **15:33** [a]Job 14:2 **15:34** [a]Job 8:13 [b]Job 8:22 [1]Lit *a bribe*
**15:35** [a]Ps 7:14; Is 59:4 [1]Or *pain, mischief* [2]Or *mind* ◆**16:2** [a]Job 13:4; 21:34 [1]Lit *Comforters of trouble*
**16:3** [a]Job 6:26 **16:4** [a]Ps 22:7; 109:25; Zep 2:15; Mt 27:39

5 "I could encourage you
with my mouth,
And the solace of my lips
could lessen *your pain*.

6 "If I speak, [a]my pain
is not lessened,
And if I cease,
what will go forth from me?
7 "But now He has [a]exhausted me;
You have made [b]desolate
all my company.
8 "You have shriveled me up,
[a]It has become a witness;
And my [b]leanness rises
up against me,
It answers to my face.
9 "His anger has [a]torn me
and [1]hunted me down;
He has [b]gnashed at me
with His teeth;
My [c]adversary sharpens
his eyes *to look* at me.
10 "They have [a]opened their
mouth wide at me;
They have [b]struck me
on the cheek in reproach;
They have [c]massed
themselves against me.
11 "God hands me over to ruffians
And tosses me into the hands
of the wicked.
12 "I was at ease,
but [a]He shattered me,
And He has grasped
me by the neck and
shaken me to pieces;
He has also set me up
as His [b]target.
13 "His [a]arrows surround me.
Without mercy He splits
my kidneys open;
He pours out [b]my gall
on the ground.
14 "He [a]breaks through me
with breach after breach;
He [b]runs at me like a warrior.
15 "I have sewed [a]sackcloth
over my skin
And [b]thrust my horn
in the dust.
16 "My face is flushed
from [a]weeping,
[b]And the shadow of death
is on my eyelids,
17 *Why?*—because there is no
[a]violence in my hands,
And [b]my prayer is pure.

18 "O earth, do not cover my blood,
And let there be no *resting*
place for my cry.
19 "Even now, behold,
[a]my witness is in heaven,
And my [1]advocate is [b]on high.
20 "My friends are my scoffers;
[a]My eye [1]weeps to God.
21 "O that a man might
argue with God
As a man with his neighbor!
22 "For when a few years are past,
I shall go the way
[a]of no return.

### *Job Seeks Hope*

17 "My spirit is broken; my
days are extinguished;
The [a,1]grave is *ready* for me.

---

**16:6** [a]Job 9:27, 28 **16:7** [a]Job 7:3 [b]Job 16:20; 19:13-15 **16:8** [a]Job 10:17 [b]Job 19:20; Ps 109:24
**16:9** [a]Job 19:11; Hos 6:1 [b]Ps 35:16; Lam 2:16; Ac 7:54 [c]Job 13:24; 33:10 [1]Lit *borne a grudge against me*
**16:10** [a]Ps 22:13 [b]Is 50:6; Lam 3:30; Ac 23:2 [c]Job 30:12; Ps 35:15 **16:12** [a]Job 9:17 [b]Job 7:20; Lam 3:12
**16:13** [a]Job 6:4; 19:12; 25:3 [b]Job 20:25 **16:14** [a]Job 9:17 [b]Joel 2:7 **16:15** [a]Ge 37:34; Ps 69:11 [b]Ps 7:5
**16:16** [a]Job 16:20 [b]Job 24:17 **16:17** [a]Is 59:6; Jon 3:8 [b]Job 27:4 **16:19** [a]Ge 31:50; Job 19:25-27; Ro 1:9; Php 1:8; 1Th 2:5 [b]Job 31:2 [1]Or *witness* **16:20** [a]Job 17:7 [1]Or *drips* **16:22** [a]Job 3:13 ◆ **17:1** [a]Ps 88:3, 4 [1]Lit *graves*

2 "[a]Surely mockers are with me,
And my eye [1]gazes
on their provocation.
3 "Establish, now, a pledge
[a]for me with Yourself;
Who is there that will clap
my hand *in pledge*?
4 "For You have [a]hidden their
heart from insight,
Therefore You will
not exalt *them*.
5 "He who [a]informs
against friends
for a share *of the spoil*,
The [b]eyes of his children
also will come to an end.

6 "But He has made me a
[a]byword of the people,
And I am [1]one
at whom men [b]spit.
7 "My eye has also grown
[a]dim because of grief,
And all my [b]members
are as a shadow.
8 "The upright will be
appalled at this,
And the [a]innocent will stir up
himself against the godless.
9 "Nevertheless [a]the righteous
will hold to his way,
And [b]he who has clean
hands will grow mightier
and mightier.
10 "But come again all
of [1]you now,
For I [a]do not find a wise
man among you.
11 "My [a]days are past; my
plans are torn apart,
*Even* the wishes of my heart.
12 "They make night
into day, *saying*,
'The light is near,'
in the presence of darkness.
13 "If I hope for [a]Sheol
as my home,
I [1]make my bed
in the darkness;
14 If I call to the [a]pit,
'You are my father';
To the [b]worm,
'my mother and my sister';
15 Where now is [a]my hope?
And who beholds my hope?
16 "[1]Will it go down with me
to Sheol?
Shall we together [a]go
down into the dust?"

### *Bildad Speaks of the Downfall of the Wicked*

18 Then Bildad the Shuhite answered and said,
2 "How long until you put an
end to *your* words?
Show understanding and
then we can talk.
3 "Why are we [a]regarded
as beasts,
As dense in your eyes?
4 "O [1]you who tear yourself
in your anger—
For your sake is the earth
to be forsaken,
Or the rock to be moved
from its place?

**17:2** [a]Job 12:4; 17:6 [1]Lit *lodges* **17:3** [a]Ps 119:122; Is 38:14 **17:4** [a]Job 12:20 **17:5** [a]Lv 19:13, 16 [b]Job 11:20 **17:6** [a]Job 17:2 [b]Job 30:10 [1]Lit *a spitting to the faces* **17:7** [a]Job 16:16 [b]Job 16:8 **17:8** [a]Job 22:19 **17:9** [a]Pr 4:18 [b]Job 22:30; 31:7 **17:10** [a]Job 12:2 [1]As in some ancient mss and versions; M.T. *them* **17:11** [a]Job 7:6 **17:13** [a]Job 3:13 [1]Lit *spread out* **17:14** [a]Job 7:5; 13:28; 30:30 [b]Job 21:26; 25:6 **17:15** [a]Job 7:6 **17:16** [a]Job 3:17; 21:33 [1]As in Gr; Heb possibly *Let my* limbs *sink down to Sheol, since there is rest in the dust for all* ◆ **18:3** [a]Ps 73:22 **18:4** [1]Lit *he...tears himself...his*

5 “Indeed, the [a]light
of the wicked goes out,
And the [1]flame of his
fire gives no light.
6 “The light in his tent
is [a]darkened,
And his lamp goes
out above him.
7 “His [1]vigorous stride
is shortened,
And his [a]own counsel
brings him down.
8 “For he is [a]thrown into the net
by his own feet,
And he steps on the netting.
9 “A snare seizes *him* by the heel,
*And* a device snaps
shut on him.
10 “A rope for him is hidden
in the ground,
And a trap for him on the path.
11 “All around [a]terrors
frighten him,
And [b]harass him at every step.
12 “His vigor is [a]famished,
And disaster is ready
at his side.
13 “The firstborn of death
eats parts of his skin;
It [a]eats parts of him.
14 “He is [a]torn from [1]the
security of his tent,
And [2]they march him in step
before the king of [b]terrors.
15 “[1]There dwells in his tent
nothing of his;
[a]Brimstone is scattered
on his abode.
16 “His [a]roots are dried below,
And his [b]branch is
cut off above.
17 “[a]Memory of him perishes
from the earth,
And he has no name abroad.
18 “[1]He is driven from light
[a]into darkness,
And [b]chased
from the inhabited world.
19 “He has neither [a]offspring
nor posterity
among his people,
Nor any survivor
where he sojourned.
20 “Those [1]in the west are
appalled at [a]his [2]fate,
And those [3]in the east are
seized with horror.
21 “Surely such are the
[a]dwellings of the unjust,
And this is the place of him
who does not know God.”

### *My Redeemer Lives*

19 Then Job answered and said,
2 “How long will you
torment my soul
And crush me with words?
3 “These ten times you have
dishonored me;
You are not ashamed
*that* you wrong me.
4 “[1]Even if I have truly erred,
My error lodges with me.
5 “If truly you [a]magnify
yourselves against me
And argue my disgrace to me,

**18:5** [a]Job 21:17; Pr 13:9; 20:20; 24:20 [1]Lit *spark* **18:6** [a]Job 12:25 **18:7** [a]Job 15:6 [1]Lit *steps of his strength* **18:8** [a]*Job 22:10; Ps 9:15; 35:8; Is 24:17, 18* **18:11** [a]Job 15:21 [b]Job 18:18; 20:8 **18:12** [a]Is 8:21 **18:13** [a]Zec 14:12 **18:14** [a]Job 8:22; 18:6 [b]Job 15:21 [1]Lit *his tent his trust* [2]Or *you or she shall march* **18:15** [a]Ps 11:6 [1]Or *Fire dwells in his tent* **18:16** [a]Is 5:24; Hos 9:16; Am 2:9; Mal 4:1 [b]Job 15:30, 32 **18:17** [a]Job 24:20; Ps 34:16; Pr 10:7 **18:18** [a]Job 5:14; Is 8:22 [b]Job 20:8; 27:21-23 [1]Lit *They drive him...And chase him* **18:19** [a]Job 27:14, 15; Is 14:22 **18:20** [a]Ps 37:13; Jer 50:27; Ob 12 [1]Lit *who come after* [2]Lit *day* [3]Lit *who have gone before* **18:21** [a]Job 21:28 ◆**19:4** [1]Or *Indeed, I have truly erred* **19:5** [a]Ps 35:26; 38:16; 55:12, 13

6 Know then that [a]God
has wronged me
And has closed [b]His
net around me.
7 "Behold, [a]I cry, 'Violence!'
but I get no answer;
I shout for help, but
there is no justice.
8 "He has [a]walled up my way
so that I cannot pass,
And He has put [b]darkness
on my paths.
9 "He has [a]stripped my
honor from me
And removed the [b]crown
from my head.
10 "He [a]breaks me down
on every side,
and I am gone;
And He has uprooted my
[b]hope [c]like a tree.
11 "He has also [a]kindled His
anger against me
And [b]counted me
as His adversary.
12 "His [a]troops
come together,
And [b]build up their
[1]way against me
And camp around my tent.

13 "He has [a]removed my
brothers far from me,
And my [b]acquaintances
are completely
estranged from me.
14 "My relatives have failed,
And my [a]familiar friends
have forgotten me.
15 "Those who sojourn
in my house and my
maidservants count
me a stranger.
I am a foreigner in their sight.
16 "I call to my servant,
but he does not answer;
I have to implore him
with my mouth.
17 "My breath is [1]offensive
to my wife,
And I am loathsome
to my own brothers.
18 "Even young children
reject me;
I rise up, and they
speak against me.
19 "All the men of my
[a]counsel abhor me,
And those I love have
turned against me.
20 "My [a]bone clings to my
skin and my flesh,
And I have escaped *only*
by the skin of my teeth.
21 "Pity me, pity me,
O you my friends,
For the [a]hand of God
has smitten me.
22 "Why do you [a]persecute
me as God *does*,
And are not satisfied
with my flesh?

23 "*Oh that* my words
were written!
Oh that they were
[a]inscribed in a book!
24 "That with an iron
stylus and lead

**19:6** [a]Job 16:11; 27:2 [b]Job 18:8-10; Ps 66:11; Lam 1:13 **19:7** [a]Job 9:24; 30:20, 24; Hab 1:2
**19:8** [a]Job 3:23; Lam 3:7, 9 [b]Job 30:26 **19:9** [a]Job 12:17, 19; Ps 89:44 [b]Job 16:15; Ps 89:39; Lam 5:16
**19:10** [a]Job 12:14 [b]Job 7:6 [c]Job 24:20 **19:11** [a]Job 16:9 [b]Job 13:24; 33:10 **19:12** [a]Job 16:13 [b]Job 30:12
[1]Siegework **19:13** [a]Job 16:7; Ps 69:8 [b]Job 16:20; Ps 88:8, 18 **19:14** [a]Job 19:19 **19:17** [1]Lit
*strange* **19:19** [a]Ps 38:11; 55:12, 13 **19:20** [a]Job 16:8; 33:21; Ps 102:5; Lam 4:8 **19:21** [a]Job 1:11; Ps 38:2
**19:22** [a]Job 13:24, 25; 16:11; 19:6; Ps 69:26 **19:23** [a]Is 30:8; Jer 36:2

They were engraved
in the rock forever!
25 "As for me, I know
that [a]my [1]Redeemer lives,
And [2]at the last He will rise up
over the dust *of this world*.
26 "Even after my skin
[1]is destroyed,
Yet from my flesh I shall
[a]behold God,
27 Whom I [1]myself shall behold,
And whom my eyes will
see and not another.
My [2]heart [a]faints [3]within me!
28 "If you say, 'How shall we
[a]persecute him?'
'And the root of the matter
is found in [1]him?'
29 "*Then* be afraid of [a]the
sword for yourselves,
For wrath *brings*
the punishment
of the sword,
So that you may know
[b]there is judgment."

### *Zophar Says the Joy of the Wicked Is Short*

20 Then Zophar the Naamathite
answered and said,
2 "Therefore my disquieting
thoughts make me [1]respond,
Even because of my
haste within me.
3 "I listened to [a]the discipline
which dishonors me,
And the spirit of my
understanding makes
me answer.
4 "Do you know this from [a]of old,
From the establishment
of man on earth,
5 That the [a]shouts of joy
of the wicked are short,
And [b]the gladness
of the godless momentary?
6 "Though his loftiness [a]goes
up to the heavens,
And his head touches
the clouds,
7 He [a]perishes forever
like his refuse;
Those who have seen him
[b]will say, 'Where is he?'
8 "He flies away like a [a]dream,
and they cannot find him;
Even like a vision of the night
he is [b]chased away.
9 "The [a]eye which saw him
sees him no longer,
And [b]his place no longer
beholds him.
10 "His [a]sons seek the
favor of the poor,
And his hands [b]give
back his wealth.
11 "His [a]bones are full
of his youthful vigor,
But it lies down with him
[1]in the dust.

12 "Though [a]evil is sweet
in his mouth
*And* he hides it
under his tongue,
13 *Though* he [1]desires it and
will not forsake it,
And holds it [a]to his palate,

**19:25** [a]Job 16:19; Ps 78:35; Pr 23:11; Is 43:14; Jer 50:34 [1]Or *Vindicator, Defender,* lit kinsman [2]Lit after, cf. Job 19:26 **19:26** [a]Ps 17:15; Mt 5:8; 1Co 13:12; 1Jn 3:2 [1]Lit *which they have cut off* **19:27** [a]Ps 73:26 [1]Or *on my side* [2]Lit *kidneys* [3]Lit *in my loins* **19:28** [a]Job 19:22 [1]Lit *me* **19:29** [a]Job 15:22 [b]Job 22:4; Ps 1:5; 9:7; Ecc 12:14 ◆ **20:2** [1]Lit *return* **20:3** [a]Job 19:3 **20:4** [a]Job 8:8 **20:5** [a]Job 8:12, 13; Ps 37:35, 36 [b]Job 8:13 **20:6** [a]Is 14:13, 14; Ob 3, 4 **20:7** [a]Job 4:20; 14:20 [b]Job 7:10; 8:18 **20:8** [a]Ps 73:20; 90:5 [b]Job 18:18; 27:21-23 **20:9** [a]Job 7:8; 8:18 [b]Job 7:10 **20:10** [a]Job 5:4; 27:14 [b]Job 20:18; 27:16, 17 **20:11** [a]Job 21:23, 24 [1]Lit *on* **20:12** [a]Job 15:16 **20:13** [a]Nu 11:18-20, 33; Job 20:23 [1]Lit *has compassion on*

14 *Yet* his food in his
stomach is changed
To the [1]venom of cobras
within him.
15 "He swallows up wealth,
But will [a]vomit it up;
God will expel it from his belly.
16 "He sucks [a]the poison of cobras;
The viper's tongue kills him.
17 "He does not look
at [a]the streams,
The rivers flowing
with honey and curds.
18 "He [a]returns what he
has attained
And cannot swallow *it*;
As to the wealth of his trading,
He cannot even enjoy *it*.
19 "For he has [a]crushed *and*
forsaken the poor;
He has seized a house
which he has not built.

20 "Because he knew no ease
within his belly,
In his covetousness, he does
[a]not let *anything* escape.
21 "Nothing remains
[1]for him to devour;
Therefore [a]his prosperity
does not endure.
22 "In the fullness of his plenty
he will be confined;
The [a]hand of everyone
who is troubled will
come *against* him.
23 "So it will be that he
[a]fills his belly,
*And God* will send His
burning anger on him
And will [b]rain *it* on him
[1]while he is eating.
24 "He may [a]flee from the
iron weapon,
*But* the bronze bow
will pierce him.
25 "It is drawn forth and
comes out of his back,
Even the glittering point
from [a]his gall;
[b]Bouts of dread come
upon him.
26 Complete [a]darkness is held
in reserve for his treasures;
A [b]fire unfanned will
devour him;
It will consume the survivor
in his tent.
27 "The [a]heavens will
reveal his iniquity,
And the earth will rise
up against him.
28 "The [a]increase of his
house will depart;
*His possessions* will flow away
[b]in the day of His anger.
29 "This is the wicked man's
[a]portion from God,
Even the inheritance
decreed to him by God."

### *God Does Not Punish the Wicked*

21 Then Job answered and said,
2 "Listen carefully
to my speech,
And let this be your *way*
*of* consolation.
3 "Bear with me that I may speak;
Then after I have spoken,
you may [a]mock.

**20:14** [1]Lit *gall* **20:15** [a]Job 20:10, 20, 21 **20:16** [a]Dt 32:24, 33 **20:17** [a]Dt 32:13, 14; Job 29:6 **20:18** [a]Job 20:10, 15 **20:19** [a]Job 24:2-4; 35:9 **20:20** [a]Ecc 5:13-15 **20:21** [a]Job 15:29 [1]Or *of what he devours* **20:22** [a]Job 5:5 **20:23** [a]Job 20:13, 14 [b]Nu 11:18-20, 33; Ps 78:30, 31 [1]Or *as his food* **20:24** [a]Is 24:18; Am 5:19 **20:25** [a]Job 16:13 [b]Job 18:11, 14 **20:26** [a]Job 18:18 [b]Job 15:30; Ps 21:9 **20:27** [a]Dt 31:28; Is 26:21 **20:28** [a]Dt 28:31 [b]Job 20:15; 21:30 **20:29** [a]Job 27:13; 31:2, 3 ◆ **21:3** [a]Job 11:3; 17:2

4 "As for me, is [a]my
musing [1]to man?
And [b]why should
[2]I not be impatient?
5 "Look at me, and be appalled,
And [a]put *your* hand
over *your* mouth.
6 "Even when I remember,
I am dismayed,
And [a]horror seizes my flesh.
7 "Why [a]do the wicked *still* live,
Continue on, also become
very [b]powerful?
8 "Their [a]seed is established
with them in their presence,
And their offspring
before their eyes,
9 Their houses [a]are
safe from dread,
And the rod of God
is not on them.
10 "His ox mates and does not fail;
His cow calves and
does not miscarry.
11 "They send forth their little
ones like the flock,
And their children skip about.
12 "They lift up the
tambourine and harp
And are glad at the sound
of the pipe.
13 "They [a]spend their days
in prosperity,
And [1]suddenly they go
down to Sheol.
14 "They say to God,
'[a]Depart from us!
We do not even desire
the knowledge of Your ways.
15 '[1]Who is [2]the Almighty,
that we should serve Him,
And [a]what would we profit
if we entreat Him?'
16 "Behold, their prosperity
is not in their hand;
The [a]counsel of the wicked
is far from me.
17 "How often is [a]the lamp
of the wicked put out,
Or does their [b]disaster
fall on them?
Does [1]God apportion
destruction in His anger?
18 "Are they as [a]straw
before the wind,
And like [b]chaff
which the storm steals away?
19 "*You say*, '[a]God stores away
[1]a man's wickedness
for his sons.'
Let [2]God repay him
so that he may know *it*.
20 "Let his [a]own eyes
see his decay,
And let him [b]drink of the wrath
of [1]the Almighty.
21 "For what desire does he have
for his household [1]after him,
When the number of his
months is cut off?
22 "Can anyone [a]teach
God knowledge,
In that He [b]judges
those on high?
23 "One [a]dies in his full strength,
Being wholly carefree
and at ease;

---

**21:4** [a]Job 7:11 [b]Job 6:11 [1]Or *against* [2]Lit *my spirit* **21:5** [a]Jdg 18:19; Job 13:5; 29:9; 40:4 **21:6** [a]Ps 55:5 **21:7** [a]Job 9:24; Ps 73:3; Jer 12:1; Hab 1:13 [b]Job 12:19 **21:8** [a]Ps 17:14 **21:9** [a]Job 12:6 **21:13** [a]Job 21:23; 36:11 [1]As in most versions; M.T. *are shattered by Sheol* **21:14** [a]Job 22:17 **21:15** [a]Job 22:17; 34:9 [1]Lit *What* [2]Heb *Shaddai* **21:16** [a]Job 22:18 **21:17** [a]Job 18:5, 6 [b]Job 31:2, 3 [1]Lit *He* **21:18** [a]Job 13:25; Ps 83:13 [b]Ps 1:4; 35:5; Is 17:13; Hos 13:3 **21:19** [a]Ex 20:5; Jer 31:29; Eze 18:2 [1]Lit *his* [2]Lit *Him* **21:20** [a]Nu 14:28-32; Jer 31:30; Eze 18:4 [b]Ps 60:3; Is 51:17; Jer 25:15; Rev 14:10 [1]Heb *Shaddai* **21:21** [1]After he dies **21:22** [a]Job 35:11; 36:22; Is 40:14; Ro 11:34 [b]Job 4:18; 15:15; Ps 82:1 **21:23** [a]Job 20:11; 21:13

24 His [1]sides are filled out with fat,
And the [a]marrow of his
bones is moist,
25 But another dies
with a bitter soul,
Never even eats
*anything* good.
26 "Together they [a]lie
down in the dust,
And [b]worms cover them.

27 "Behold, I know your thoughts,
And the plans by which you
do violence against me.
28 "For you say, 'Where is the
house of [a]the nobleman,
And where is the [b]tent,
the dwelling places
of the wicked?'
29 "Have you not asked those
who pass by along the way,
And do you not recognize
their [1]witness?
30 "That the [a]wicked is reserved
for the day of disaster;
They will be led forth
at [b]the day of fury.
31 "Who will declare to his
face about his actions,
And who will repay him
for what he has done?
32 "While he is led forth
to the grave,
*Men* will keep watch
over *his* tomb.
33 "The [a]clods of the valley
will [1]gently cover him;
Moreover, [b]all men will
draw up after him,
While countless ones
*go* before him.
34 "How then will you vainly
[a]comfort me,
Indeed *when* your answers
remain *full of* [1]falsehood?"

### Eliphaz Says Job Must Repent

22 Then Eliphaz the Temanite
answered and said,
2 "Can a mighty [a]man be
of use to God,
Or an insightful man be
useful to himself?
3 "Is there any pleasure
to [1]the Almighty
if you are righteous,
Or profit if you make
your ways perfect?
4 "Is it because of your *reverent*
fear that He reproves you,
That He [a]enters
into judgment against you?
5 "Is not [a]your evil great,
And your iniquities
without end?
6 "For you have [a]taken
pledges of your brothers
without cause,
And [b]stripped the clothing
of the naked.
7 "To the weary you have
[a]given no water to drink,
And from the hungry you
have [b]withheld bread.
8 "But the earth [a]belongs
to the [b]mighty man,
And [c]the [1]highly respected
man inhabits it.

**21:24** [a]Pr 3:8 [1]As in Syr; Heb uncertain; some Heb mss render as *his pails are full of milk* **21:26** [a]Job 3:13; 20:11; Ecc 9:2 [b]Job 24:20; Is 14:11 **21:28** [a]Job 1:3; 31:37 [b]Job 8:22; 18:21 **21:29** [1]Lit *signs* **21:30** [a]Job 20:29; Pr 16:4; 2Pe 2:9 [b]Job 21:17, 20; 40:11 **21:33** [a]Job 3:22; 17:16 [b]Job 3:19; 24:24 [1]Lit *be sweet to him* **21:34** [a]Job 16:2 [1]Or *faithlessness* ◆ **22:2** [a]Job 35:7; Lk 17:10 **22:3** [1]Heb *Shaddai* **22:4** [a]Job 14:3; 19:29 **22:5** [a]Job 11:6; 15:5 **22:6** [a]Ex 22:26; Dt 24:6, 17; Job 24:3, 9; Eze 18:16 [b]Job 31:19, 20 **22:7** [a]Job 31:16, 17 [b]Job 31:31 **22:8** [a]Job 9:24 [b]Job 12:19 [c]Is 3:3; 9:15 [1]Lit *the one whose face is lifted up*

9 "You have sent [a]widows
away empty,
And the [1]might
of the [b]orphans
has been crushed.
10 "Therefore [a]snares
surround you,
And sudden [b]dread
terrifies you,
11 Or [a]darkness, so that
you cannot see,
And an [b]abundance
of water covers you.

12 "Is not God [a]*in* the height
of heaven?
Look also at the [1]distant
stars, how high they are!
13 "You say, '[a]What does
God know?
Can He judge
through the dense gloom?
14 '[a]Clouds are a hiding place for
Him, so that He cannot see;
And He walks on the [1]vault
of heaven.'
15 "Will you keep to the
ancient path
Which [a]wicked men have trod,
16 Who were snatched away
[a]before their time,
Whose [b]foundations were
[1]washed away by a river?
17 "They [a]said to God,
'Depart from us!'
And 'What can [1]the
Almighty do to them?'
18 "Yet He [a]filled their houses
with good *things*,
But [b]the counsel of the wicked
is far from me.
19 "The [a]righteous see
and are glad,
And the innocent
mock them,
20 *Saying*, 'Truly those who rise
against us are wiped out,
And their [1]abundance [a]the
fire has consumed.'

21 "[a,1]Yield now and be
at peace with Him;
Thereby good will
come to you.
22 "Please receive [a,1]instruction
from His mouth
And set His words
in your heart.
23 "If you [a]return to [1]the Almighty,
you will be [2]restored;
If you [b]remove
unrighteousness far
from your tent,
24 And [a]put *your* [1]gold
in the dust,
And *the gold of* Ophir
among the stones
of the brooks,
25 Then [1]the Almighty
will be your [2]gold
And choice silver to you.
26 "For then you will [a]delight
in [1]the Almighty
And lift up your face to God.

**22:9** [a]Job 24:3, 21; 29:13; 31:16, 18 [b]Job 6:27 [1]Lit *arms* **22:10** [a]Job 18:8 [b]Job 15:21
**22:11** [a]Job 5:14 [b]Job 38:34; Ps 69:2; 124:5; Lam 3:54 **22:12** [a]Job 11:7-9 [1]Lit *head, top-most*
**22:13** [a]Ps 10:11; 59:7; 64:5; 94:7; Is 29:15; Eze 8:12 **22:14** [a]Job 26:9 [1]Lit circle **22:15** [a]Job 34:36
**22:16** [a]Job 15:32; 21:13, 18 [b]Job 14:19; Ps 90:5; Is 28:2; Mt 7:26, 27 [1]Lit *poured out* **22:17** [a]Job 21:14, 15 [1]Heb *Shaddai* **22:18** [a]Job 12:6 [b]Job 21:16 **22:19** [a]Ps 52:6; 58:10; 107:42 **22:20** [a]Job 15:30 [1]Or *excess* **22:21** [a]Ps 34:10 [1]Or *Make yourself useful*, cf. Job 22:2 **22:22** [a]Job 6:10; 23:12; Pr 2:6 [1]Or *law* **22:23** [a]Job 8:5; 11:13; Is 19:22; 31:6; Zec 1:3 [b]Job 11:14 [1]Heb *Shaddai* [2]Lit *built up*
**22:24** [a]Job 31:24, 25 [1]Lit *ore* **22:25** [1]Heb *Shaddai* [2]Lit *ore* **22:26** [a]Job 27:10; Ps 37:4; Is 58:14 [1]Heb *Shaddai*

27 "You will [a]entreat Him,
and [b]He will hear you;
And you will pay your vows.
28 "You will also decree a
thing, and it will be
established for you;
And [a]light will shine
on your ways.
29 "When [1]some are cast
down, you will speak
with [2]confidence,
And the [a,3]humble
person He will save.
30 "He will provide escape
for one who is not innocent,
And he will [a]escape
through the cleanness
of your hands."

### *Where Is God?*

23 Then Job answered and said,
2 "Even today my
[a]musing is rebellion;
[1]His hand is [b]heavy
despite my groaning.
3 "Oh that I knew
where I might find Him,
That I might come
to His seat!
4 "I would [a]arrange *my case*
*for* justice before Him
And fill my mouth
with arguments.
5 "I would know the words
*which* He would [1]answer,
And discern what He
would say to me.
6 "Would He contend
with me by [a]the greatness
of *His* power?
No, surely He would pay
attention to me.
7 "There the upright would
[a]argue with Him;
And I [1]would have [b]escaped
forever from my Judge.

8 "Behold, I go forward
but He is not *there*,
And backward, but I
[a]cannot discern Him;
9 When He acts on the left,
I cannot behold *Him*;
He turns on the right,
I cannot see Him.
10 "But He knows the
[1]way I take;
*When* He has [a]tested me,
I shall come forth as gold.
11 "My foot has [a]held
fast to His path;
I have kept His way and
not turned aside.
12 "I have not departed
from the command of His lips;
I have treasured the [a]words
of His mouth [1]more
than my [2]portion *of food*.
13 "But He is unique and
who can turn Him?
And *what* His soul
desires, that He does.
14 "For He performs what is
apportioned for me,
And many such *decrees*
are with Him.
15 "Therefore, I would be
dismayed at His presence;
I carefully consider, and
I am in dread of Him.

**22:27** [a]Job 11:13; 33:26; Is 58:9 [b]Job 34:28 **22:28** [a]Job 11:17; Ps 112:4 **22:29** [a]Job 5:11; 36:7; Mt 23:12; Jas 4:6; 1Pe 5:5 [1]Lit *they cast* you *down* [2]Lit *pride* [3]Lit *lowly of eyes* **22:30** [a]Job 42:7, 8; Ps 18:20; 24:3, 4 ◆ **23:2** [a]Job 7:11 [b]Job 6:2, 3; Ps 32:4 [1]As in Gr and Syr; M.T. *My* **23:4** [a]Job 13:18 **23:5** [1]Lit *answer me* **23:6** [a]Job 9:4 **23:7** [a]Job 13:3 [b]Job 13:16; 23:10 [1]Or *bring forth my justice forever* **23:8** [a]Job 9:11; 35:14 **23:10** [a]Job 7:18; Ps 7:9; 11:5; 66:10; Zec 13:9; 1Pe 1:7 [1]Lit *way with me* **23:11** [a]Job 31:7; Ps 17:5; 44:18 **23:12** [a]Job 6:10; 22:22 [1]Some versions *in my breast* [2]Lit *statute*

16 "*It is* God *who* has made
my [a]heart faint,
And the Almighty *who*
has dismayed me,
17 But I [a]am not silenced
by the darkness,
Nor [b]thick darkness
*which* covers me.

### *Who Can Prove Me a Liar?*

24 "[a]Why are [1]times not stored
up by the Almighty,
And why do those who know
Him not behold [b]His days?
2 "[1]Some [a]move the boundaries;
They seize and [2]devour flocks.
3 "They drive away the donkeys
of the [a]orphans;
They take the [b]widow's
ox for a pledge.
4 "They push [a]the needy
aside from the road;
The [b]afflicted of the land
are made to hide
themselves altogether.
5 "Behold, as [a]wild donkeys
in the wilderness
They [b]go forth seeking food
earnestly in their work,
The desert becomes [1]for him
a *place of* bread for
*his* young ones.
6 "They harvest their
fodder in the field
And glean the vineyard
of the wicked.
7 "[a]They spend the night
naked, without clothing,
And have no covering
against the cold.
8 "They are wet
with the mountain rains
And hug the rock
for want of a shelter.
9 "[1]Others snatch the [a]orphan
from the breast,
And against the afflicted
they take a pledge.
10 "Those *poor* ones walk about
naked without clothing,
And hungry ones carry
the sheaves.
11 "Within the walls they
produce oil;
They tread wine
presses but thirst.
12 "From the city men groan,
And the souls of the wounded
cry out;
Yet God [a]does not pay
attention to *such* offense.

13 "[1]Others have been with those
who rebel against the light;
They do not want to recognize
its ways
Nor abide in its paths.
14 "The murderer [a]arises at dawn;
He [b]kills the afflicted
and the needy,
And at night he is as a thief.
15 "The eye of the [a]adulterer
keeps watch for the twilight,
Saying, 'No eye will see me.'
And he [1]keeps his face hidden.
16 "In the dark they [a]dig
into houses;
They [b]shut themselves
up by day;
They do not know the light.

**23:16** [a]Dt 20:3; Job 27:2; Jer 51:46 **23:17** [a]Job 10:18, 19 [b]Job 19:8 ◆ **24:1** [a]Ac 1:7 [b]Is 2:12; Jer 46:10; Ob 15; Zep 1:7 [1]Times of judgment **24:2** [a]Dt 19:14; 27:17; Pr 23:10 [1]Lit *They* [2]Or *pasture* **24:3** [a]Job 6:27 [b]Dt 24:17; Job 22:9 **24:4** [a]Job 24:14; 29:16; 30:25; 31:19 [b]Job 29:12; Ps 41:1; Pr 14:31; 28:28; Am 8:4 **24:5** [a]Job 39:5-8 [b]Ps 104:23 [1]Lit *his bread* **24:7** [a]Ex 22:26; Job 22:6 **24:9** [a]Job 6:27 [1]Lit *They* **24:12** [a]Job 9:23, 24 **24:13** [1]Lit *They* **24:14** [a]Mic 2:1 [b]Ps 10:8 **24:15** [a]Pr 7:9 [1]Lit *sets* **24:16** [a]Ex 22:2; Mt 6:19 [b]Jn 3:20

17 "For the morning is the same to
him as the shadow of death,
For he recognizes the [a]terrors
of the shadow of death.

18 "[1]They are [a,2]insignificant
on the surface of the water;
Their portion is [b]cursed
on the earth.
They do not turn
[3]toward the [c]vineyards.
19 "Drought and heat [a]seize
the snow waters,
*So does* [b]Sheol *those
who* have sinned.
20 "A [a,1]mother will forget him;
The [b]worm feasts
sweetly till he is
[c]no longer remembered.
And unrighteousness will
be broken [d]like a tree.
21 "He feeds on the barren woman
who does not give birth
And does no good
for [a]the widow.

22 "But He drags off the mighty
by [a]His power;
He rises, but [b]no one
believes in his life.
23 "He provides them
[a]with security, and
they are supported;
And His [b]eyes are on their ways.
24 "They are exalted a [a]little
*while,* then they are gone;
Moreover, they are
[b]brought low and like
everything gathered up;
Even like the heads of grain
they are cut off.
25 "Now if it is not so,
[a]who can prove me a liar,
And make my
speech worthless?"

### *Bildad Says Can Man Be Right with God?*

25 Then Bildad the Shuhite answered and said,
2 "[a]Rule and dread
[1]belong to Him
Who makes peace
in [b]His heights.
3 "Is there any number
to [a]His troops?
And upon whom does
His light not rise?
4 "How then can mortal man
be [a]right with God?
Or how can he be [b]pure
who is born of woman?
5 "Behold even [a]the moon
has no brightness,
And the [b]stars are not
pure in His sight;
6 How much less [a]mortal
man, *that* [b]maggot,
And the son of man,
*that* worm!"

### *Who Can Understand God?*

26 Then Job answered and said,
2 "What a help you
are to [a]the one
without power!
How you have saved the arm
[b]without strength!

**24:17** [a]Job 15:21 **24:18** [a]Job 22:11, 16; 27:20 [b]Job 5:3 [c]Job 24:6, 11 [1]Implied, *they* (Job's friends) *say*; Job 24:18-21 [2]Or *light, swift* [3]Lit *to the path of* **24:19** [a]Job 6:16, 17 [b]Job 21:13 **24:20** [a]Is 49:15 [b]Job 21:26 [c]Job 18:17; Ps 34:16; Pr 10:7 [d]Job 19:10; Da 4:14 [1]Lit *womb* **24:21** [a]Job 22:9 **24:22** [a]Job 9:4 [b]Job 18:20 **24:23** [a]Job 12:6 [b]Job 10:4; 11:11 **24:24** [a]Ps 37:10 [b]Job 14:21 **24:25** [a]Job 6:28; 27:4 ◆ **25:2** [a]Job 9:4; 36:5, 22; 37:23; 42:2 [b]Job 16:19; 31:2 [1]Lit *are with Him* **25:3** [a]Job 16:13 **25:4** [a]Job 4:17; 9:2 [b]Job 14:4 **25:5** [a]Job 31:26 [b]Job 15:15 **25:6** [a]Job 7:17 [b]Job 17:14 ◆ **26:2** [a]Job 6:11, 12 [b]Ps 71:9

3 "What counsel you have given
to *one* without wisdom!
What sound wisdom you have
abundantly made known!
4 "To whom have you
declared words?
And whose breath comes
out from you?

5 "The [a,1]departed spirits tremble
Under the waters and
their inhabitants.
6 "Naked is [a]Sheol before Him,
And [b,1]Abaddon has no covering.
7 "He [a]stretches out the north
over what is formless
And hangs the earth on nothing.
8 "He [a]wraps up the waters
in His clouds,
And the cloud does not
break out under them.
9 "He [a,1]obscures the face
of *His* [2]throne
And spreads His cloud over it.
10 "He has marked a [a]circle
on the surface of the waters
At the [b]boundary
of light and darkness.
11 "The pillars of heaven tremble
And are astonished
at His rebuke.
12 "He [a]quieted the sea
with His power,
And by His [b]understanding
He crushed [c]Rahab.
13 "By His breath the [a]heavens
are *made* beautiful;
His hand has pierced
[b]the fleeing serpent.
14 "Behold, these are the
fringes of His ways;
And how *only*
*with* a whisper of [a]a word
do we hear of Him!
But His mighty [b]thunder,
who can understand?"

### *I Hold Fast My Righteousness*

27 Then Job continued to lift up
his [a,1]discourse and said,
2 "As God lives, [a]who has
removed my justice,
And the Almighty, [b]who
has embittered my soul,
3 For as long as breath is in me,
And the [a]spirit from God
is in my nostrils,
4 My lips certainly will not
speak unrighteousness,
Nor will [a]my tongue
utter deceit.
5 "Far be it from me that I
should declare you right;
Till I breathe my last [a]I will
not remove my
integrity from me.
6 "I [a]hold fast my righteousness
and will not let it go.
My heart does not reproach
any of my days.

7 "May my enemy be
as the wicked
And the one who rises
against me as the unjust.
8 "For what is [a]the hope of the
godless [1]when he is cut off,
When God requires [b]his [2]soul?

**26:5** [a]*Job 3:13; Ps 88:10* [1]*Or shades;* Heb *Rephaim* **26:6** [a]Job 9:5-10; 26:6-14; 38:17; 41:11 [b]Job 28:22; 31:12 [1]Lit the realm of *destruction* **26:7** [a]Job 9:8 **26:8** [a]Job 37:11; Pr 30:4 **26:9** [a]Job 22:14; Ps 97:2; 105:39 [1]Lit *covers* [2]Or *full moon* **26:10** [a]Job 38:1-11; Pr 8:29 [b]Job 38:19, 20, 24 **26:12** [a]Is 51:15; Jer 31:35 [b]Job 12:13 [c]Job 9:13 **26:13** [a]Job 9:8 [b]Is 27:1 **26:14** [a]Job 4:12 [b]Job 36:29; 37:4, 5
◆ **27:1** [a]Job 13:12; 29:1 [1]Lit *proverb* **27:2** [a]Job 16:11; 34:5 [b]Job 9:18 **27:3** [a]Job 32:8; 33:4
**27:4** [a]Job 6:28; 33:3 **27:5** [a]Job 6:29 **27:6** [a]Job 2:3; 13:18 **27:8** [a]Job 8:13; 11:20 [b]Job 12:10
[1]Or *though he gains* [2]Or *life*

9 "Will God [a]hear his cry
When [b]distress comes
upon him?
10 "Will he take [a]delight
in the Almighty?
Will he call on God
at all times?
11 "I will instruct you
in the [1]power of God;
What is with the Almighty
I will not conceal.
12 "Behold, all of you have seen *it*;
Why then do you speak
with utter vanity?

13 "This is [a]the portion of a
wicked man from God,
And the inheritance
*which* the [b]ruthless receive
from the Almighty.
14 "Though his sons are
many, [1]they are destined
[a]for the sword;
And his [b]offspring will not
be satisfied with bread.
15 "His survivors will be buried
because of the plague,
And [1]their [a]widows will
not be able to weep.
16 "Though he piles up
silver like dust
And prepares garments
as *plentiful as* the clay,
17 He may prepare *it*, [a]but the
righteous will wear *it*,
*And the innocent will*
divide the silver.
18 "He has built his [a]house
like the [1]moth,
Or as a hut *which*
the watchman has made.
19 "He lies down rich,
but never [1]again;
He opens his eyes,
and [a]it is no longer.
20 "[a]Terrors overtake him
like *many* waters;
A tempest steals him
away [b]in the night.
21 "The east [a]wind carries
him away, and he goes,
And it whirls him [b]away
from his place.
22 "For it will hurl at him
[a]without sparing;
He will surely try to [b]flee
from its [1]power.
23 "*Men* will clap their
hands at him
And will [a]hiss him
from his place.

### *Where Can Wisdom Be Found?*

28 "[1]Surely there is a
[2]mine for silver,
And a place [3]where they
refine for gold.
2 "Iron is taken from the dust,
And copper is smelted
from rock.
3 "*Man* puts an end to darkness,
And [a]to the farthest limit
he searches out
The rock in thick darkness
and shadow of death.
4 "He [1]sinks a shaft far
from [2]habitation,
Forgotten by the foot;

**27:9** [a]Job 35:12, 13; Ps 18:41; Pr 1:28; Is 1:15; Jer 14:12; Mic 3:4 [b]Pr 1:27 **27:10** [a]Job 22:26, 27; Ps 37:4; Is 58:14 **27:11** [1]Lit *hand* **27:13** [a]Job 20:29 [b]Job 15:20 **27:14** [a]Job 15:22; 18:19 [b]Job 20:10 [1]Lit *the sword is for them* **27:15** [a]Ps 78:64 [1]As in ancient versions; Heb *his* **27:17** [a]Job 20:18-21 **27:18** [a]Job 8:15; 18:14 [1]Ancient versions *spider's web* **27:19** [a]Job 7:8, 21; 20:7 [1]As in ancient versions; Heb *will be gathered* **27:20** [a]Job 15:21 [b]Job 20:8; 34:20 **27:21** [a]Job 21:18 [b]Job 7:10 **27:22** [a]Jer 13:14; Eze 5:11; 24:14 [b]Job 11:20 [1]Lit *hand* **27:23** [a]Job 18:18; 20:8 ◆ **28:1** [1]Or *For* [2]Or *source* [3]Lit *for gold they refine* **28:3** [a]Ecc 1:13 **28:4** [1]Lit *breaks open* [2]Lit *sojourning*

They hang and swing
to and fro far from men.
5 "The earth, from it comes food,
And underneath it is
overturned as fire.
6 "Its rocks are the [1]source
of sapphires,
And its dust *contains* gold.
7 "The path no bird
of prey knows,
Nor has the falcon's eye
caught sight of it.
8 "The [1]proud beasts have
not trodden it,
Nor has the *fierce* lion
passed over it.
9 "He sends his hand
forth to the flint;
He overturns the mountains
at the [1]base.
10 "He breaks out channels
through the rocks,
And his eye sees
anything precious.
11 "He dams up the streams
from [1]flowing,
And what is hidden he
brings out to the light.

12 "But [a]where can wisdom
be found?
And where is the place
of understanding?
13 "[a]Man does not know its worth,
And it is not found
in the land of the living.
14 "The deep says, 'It is not in me';
And the sea says, 'It
is not with me.'
15 "[a]Pure gold cannot be
given in place of it,
Nor can silver be
weighed as its price.
16 "It cannot be valued
in the gold of Ophir,
In precious onyx
or sapphire.
17 "[a]Gold or glass cannot
meet its worth,
Nor can it be exchanged
for articles of fine gold.
18 "Coral and crystal are not
to be mentioned;
And the acquisition
of [a]wisdom is above
*that of* pearls.
19 "The topaz of [1]Ethiopia
cannot meet its worth,
Nor can it be valued
in [a]pure gold.
20 "[a]Where then does
wisdom come from?
And where is the place
of understanding?
21 "Thus it is hidden
from the eyes of all living
And concealed
from the birds of the sky.
22 "[a,1]Abaddon and Death say,
'With our ears we have
heard a report of it.'

23 "[a]God understands its way,
And He knows its place.
24 "For He [a]looks to the
ends of the earth
And sees everything
under the heavens.
25 "When He set [a]weight
to the wind
And [b]meted out the waters
by measure,

**28:6** [1]Or *place* **28:8** [1]Lit *sons of pride* **28:9** [1]Lit *roots* **28:11** [1]Lit *weeping* **28:12** [a]Job 28:23, 28; Ecc 7:24 **28:13** [a]Mt 13:44-46 **28:15** [a]Pr 3:13, 14; 8:10, 11; 16:16 **28:17** [a]Pr 8:10; 16:16 **28:18** [a]Pr 8:11 **28:19** [a]Pr 8:19 [1]Or *Cush*, cf. Ge 10:6 **28:20** [a]Job 28:23, 28 **28:22** [a]Job 26:6; Pr 8:32-36 [1]Lit The realm of *destruction* **28:23** [a]Job 9:4; Pr 8:22-36 **28:24** [a]Ps 11:4; 33:13, 14; 66:7; Pr 15:3 **28:25** [a]Ps 135:7 [b]Job 12:15; 38:8-11

26 When He set a [a]limit
for the rain
And a course
for the [b]thunderbolt,
27 Then He saw it and
recounted it;
He established it and
also searched it out.
28 "So He said to man,
'Behold, the [a]fear
of the Lord, that is wisdom;
And to turn away from evil
is understanding.'"

### *Job Continues His Discourse*

29 And Job continued to lift up
his [a,1]discourse and said,
2 "Oh that I were as in months
gone by,
As in the days
when God [a]kept me,
3 When [a]His lamp shone
over my head,
*And* [b]by His light I walked
through darkness,
4 As I was in [1]the prime
of my days,
When the [a]*intimate* counsel
with God *was* over my tent,
5 When [1]the Almighty
was yet with me,
*And* my children were
around me,
6 When my steps were
bathed in [a]butter,
And the [b]rock poured out
for me streams of oil!
7 "When I went out to [a]the gate
of the city,
When I [1]took my seat
in the square,
8 The young men saw
me and hid,
And the old men arose
*and* stood.
9 "The princes [a]stopped talking
And [b]put *their* hands
on their mouths;
10 The voice of the nobles
was [a]hidden *away*,
And their [b]tongue clung
to their palate.
11 "For [a]the ear heard, and
it called me blessed,
And the eye saw, and it
gave witness of me,
12 Because I provided escape
for [a]the afflicted who
cried for help,
And the [b]orphan who
had no helper.
13 "The blessing of the
one [a]ready to perish
came upon me,
And I made the [b]widow's
heart sing for joy.
14 "I [a]clothed *myself*
with righteousness,
and it clothed me;
My justice was like a robe
and a turban.
15 "I was [a]eyes to the blind
And feet to the lame.
16 "I was a father to [a]the needy,
And I searched out the case
which I did not know.
17 "I [a]broke the fangs
of the unjust

**28:26** [a]Job 37:6, 11, 12; 38:26-28 [b]Job 37:3; 38:25 **28:28** [a]Ps 111:10; Pr 1:7; 9:10; Ecc 12:13
◆ **29:1** [a]Nu 23:7; 24:3; Job 13:12; 27:1 [1]Lit *proverb* **29:2** [a]Jer 31:28 **29:3** [a]Job 18:6 [b]Job 11:17
**29:4** [a]Job 15:8; Ps 25:14; Pr 3:32 [1]Lit *the days of my autumn* **29:5** [1]Heb *Shaddai* **29:6** [a]Dt 32:14; Job 20:17 [b]Dt 32:13; Ps 81:16 **29:7** [a]Job 31:21 [1]Lit *set up* **29:9** [a]Job 29:21 [b]Job 21:5
**29:10** [a]Job 29:22 [b]Ps 137:6 **29:11** [a]Job 4:3, 4 **29:12** [a]Job 24:4, 9; 34:28; Ps 72:12; Pr 21:13 [b]Job 31:17, 21
**29:13** [a]Job 31:19 [b]Job 22:9 **29:14** [a]Job 27:5, 6; Ps 132:9; Is 59:17; 61:10; Eph 6:14 **29:15** [a]Nu 10:31
**29:16** [a]Job 24:4; Pr 29:7 **29:17** [a]Ps 3:7

And snatched the prey
from his teeth.
18 "Then I [1]said, 'I will breathe
my last [2]in my nest,
And I shall multiply *my*
days as the sand.
19 'My [a]root is spread out
to the waters,
And [b]dew lies all night
on my branch.
20 'My glory is *ever* new with me,
And my [a]bow is renewed
in my hand.'
21 "To me [a]they listened
and waited,
And kept silent
for my counsel.
22 "After my words they did
not [a]speak again,
And [b]my speech
dropped on them.
23 "They waited for me
as for the rain,
And opened their mouth
as for the [1]late rain.
24 "I laughed with them *as* they
could not believe *it*,
And the light of my face
they did not cast down.
25 "I chose a way for them
and sat as [a]chief,
And dwelt as *their* head
among the troops,
As one who [b]comforted
the mourners.

30 "But now those younger
than I [a]laugh at me,
Whose fathers I rejected
*even* to put with the dogs
of my flock.
2 "Indeed, what *good was*
the strength of their
hands to me?
Vigor had perished
from them.
3 "From want and famine
they are gaunt,
Who gnaw the dry ground
by night in destruction
and desolation,
4 Who pluck [1]mallow
by the bushes,
And whose food is the root
of the broom tree.
5 "They are driven
from the community;
They shout against them
as *against* a thief,
6 So that they dwell
in the slopes of the [1]valleys,
In holes of the dust
and of the rocks.
7 "Among the bushes
they [1]cry out;
Under the nettles they are
gathered together.
8 "[1]Wicked fools, even [2]those
without a name,
They were scourged
from the land.

9 "And now I have become
their *mocking* [a]song;
I have even become
a [b]*taunting* word
to them.
10 "They abhor me *and* keep
a distance from me,
And they do not [1]hold
back from [a]spitting
at my face.

**29:18** [1]Or *thought* [2]Lit *with* **29:19** [a]Jer 17:8 [b]Hos 14:5 **29:20** [a]Ge 49:24; Ps 18:34 **29:21** [a]Job 4:3; 29:9 **29:22** [a]Job 29:10 [b]Dt 32:2 **29:23** [1]Spring **29:25** [a]Job 1:3; 31:37 [b]Job 4:4; 16:5 ◆ **30:1** [a]Job 12:4 **30:4** [1]Plant of the salt marshes **30:6** [1]Or *wadis* **30:7** [1]Or *bray* **30:8** [1]Lit *Sons of fools* [2]Lit *sons* **30:9** [a]Job 12:4 [b]Job 17:6; Ps 69:11; Lam 3:14, 63 **30:10** [a]Nu 12:14; Dt 25:9; Job 17:6; Is 50:6; Mt 26:67 [1]Lit *withhold spit from my face*

11 “Because [1]He has loosed
[2]His [3]bowstring and
[a]afflicted me,
They have thrust aside
[b]*their* bridle before me.
12 “On the right hand their
[1]brood arises;
They [a]thrust aside my feet
[b]and build up against me
their ways to disaster.
13 “They [a]break up my path;
They profit [1]from my
destruction;
They have no helper.
14 “As *through* a wide
breach they come,
[1]Amid the storm they roll on.
15 “[a]Terrors are turned against me;
They pursue my nobility
as the wind,
And my *hope for* salvation has
passed away [b]like a cloud.

16 “And now [a]my soul is
poured out [1]within me;
Days of affliction
have seized me.
17 “At night it pierces [a]my
bones [1]within me,
And my gnawing *pains*
take no rest.
18 “By a great force my
garment is [a]distorted;
It seizes me about
as the collar of my tunic.
19 “*He has* cast me into the [a]mire,
And I have become
like dust and ashes.
20 “I [a]cry out to You for help,
but You do not answer me;
I stand up, and You
carefully consider *how
to be* against me.
21 “You have [1]become cruel to me;
With the might of Your hand
You [a]hunted me down.
22 “You [a]lift me up to the wind
*and* cause me to ride;
And You melt me
away in a storm.
23 “For I know that You [a]will
bring me to death
And to the [b]house
of meeting for all living.

24 “Yet does not one in a heap
of ruins stretch out *his* hand,
Or, in his upheaval, is
there a [a]cry for help
because of them?
25 “Have I not [a]wept for the
[1]one whose life is hard?
Was not my soul grieved
for [b]the needy?
26 “When I [a]hoped for good,
then evil came;
When I waited for light,
[b]then thick darkness came.
27 “[1]I am boiling [a]within and
cannot be silent;
Days of affliction
confront me.
28 “I go about [a]darkened
*but* not by the sun;
I stand up in the assembly
*and* [b]cry out for help.

**30:11** [a]Ru 1:21; Ps 88:7 [b]Ps 32:9 [1]Or *they* [2]Some mss *my* [3]Or *cord* **30:12** [a]Ps 140:4, 5 [b]Job 19:12 [1]Possibly *sprout, offspring* **30:13** [a]Is 3:12 [1]Lit *for* **30:14** [1]Lit *Under* **30:15** [a]Job 3:25; 31:23; Ps 55:3-5 [b]Job 7:9; Hos 13:3 **30:16** [a]1Sa 1:15; Job 3:24; Ps 22:14; 42:4; Is 53:12 [1]Lit *upon* **30:17** [a]Job 30:30 [1]Lit *from upon* **30:18** [a]Job 2:7 **30:19** [a]Ps 69:2, 14 **30:20** [a]Job 19:7 **30:21** [a]Job 10:3; 16:9, 14; 19:6, 22 [1]Lit *turned to be* **30:22** [a]Job 9:17; 27:21 **30:23** [a]Job 9:22; 10:8 [b]Job 3:19; Ecc 12:5 **30:24** [a]Job 19:7 **30:25** [a]Ps 35:13, 14; Ro 12:15 [b]Job 24:4 [1]Lit *hard of day* **30:26** [a]Job 3:25, 26; Jer 8:15 [b]Job 19:8 **30:27** [a]Lam 2:11 [1]Lit *My inward parts are boiling* **30:28** [a]Job 30:31; Ps 38:6; 42:9; 43:2 [b]Job 19:7

29 "I have become a brother
to [a]jackals
And a companion of ostriches.
30 "My [a]skin turns black [1]on me,
And my [b]bones burn
with [2]fever.
31 "Therefore my [a]harp [1]is
turned to mourning,
And my flute to the sound
of those who weep.

# 31

"I have cut a covenant
with my [a]eyes;
How then could I
gaze at a virgin?
2 "And what is [a]the portion
of God from above
Or the inheritance of
the Almighty from on high?
3 "Is it not [a]disaster to the unjust
And misfortune to [b]those
who work iniquity?
4 "Does He not [a]see my ways
And [b]number all my steps?

5 "If I have [a]walked
with worthlessness,
And my foot has hastened
after deceit,
6 Let Him [a]weigh me
with [1]just scales,
And let God know
[b]my integrity.
7 "If my step has [a]turned
from the way,
Or my heart [1]followed my eyes,
Or if any [b]spot has
stuck to my hands,
8 Let me [a]sow and another eat,
And let my [b,1]crops
be uprooted.

9 "If my heart has been
[a]enticed by a woman,
Or I have lain in wait at my
neighbor's doorway,
10 May my wife [a]grind
for another,
And let [b]others [1]kneel
down over her.
11 "For that would be [a]lewdness;
Moreover, it would be
[b]an iniquity *punishable*
*by* judges.
12 "For it would be [a]fire that
consumes to [b,1]Abaddon,
And would [c]uproot
all my [2]produce.

13 "If I have [a]rejected the
justice of my male
or female [1]slaves
When they filed a complaint
against me,
14 What then could I do
when God arises?
And when He calls me
to account, *with* what
will I respond to Him?
15 "Did not [a]He who made me
in the womb make him,
And the same one fashion
us in the womb?

16 "If I have held back [a]the
poor from *their* desire,

---

**30:29** [a]Ps 44:19; Mic 1:8 **30:30** [a]Job 2:7 [b]Ps 102:3 [1]Lit *from upon* [2]Lit *heat* **30:31** [a]Is 24:8 [1]Lit *becomes* ◆ **31:1** [a]Mt 5:28 **31:2** [a]Job 20:29 **31:3** [a]Job 18:12; 21:30 [b]Job 34:22 **31:4** [a]2Chr 16:9; Job 24:23; 28:24; 34:21; 36:7; Pr 5:21; 15:3 [b]Job 14:16; 31:37 **31:5** [a]Job 15:31; Mic 2:11 **31:6** [a]Job 6:2, 3 [b]Job 23:10; 27:5, 6 [1]Lit *righteous*; Job 8:3, 6; 29:14 **31:7** [a]Job 23:11 [b]Job 9:30 [1]Lit *walked after* **31:8** [a]Lv 26:16; Job 20:18; Mic 6:15 [b]Job 31:12 [1]Or *offspring* **31:9** [a]Job 24:15; 31:1 **31:10** [a]Is 47:2 [b]Dt 28:30; Jer 8:10 [1]Sexual relations **31:11** [a]Lv 20:10; Dt 22:24 [b]Job 31:28 **31:12** [a]Job 15:30 [b]Job 26:6 [c]Job 20:28; 31:8 [1]Lit the realm of *destruction* [2]Or *yield* **31:13** [a]Dt 24:14, 15 [1]Or *servants*, cf. Job 1:3 **31:15** [a]Job 10:3 **31:16** [a]Job 5:16; 20:19

Or have caused the eyes
of [b]the widow to fail,
17 Or have [a]eaten my
morsel alone,
And [b]the orphan has
not eaten from it
18 (But from my youth he grew
up with me as *with* a father,
And from the womb of my
mother I guided her),
19 If I have seen anyone perish
[a]for lack of clothing,
Or that [b]the needy
had no covering,
20 If his loins have not
blessed me,
And if he has not been
warmed with the fleece
of my sheep,
21 If I have waved my hand
against [a]the orphan
Because I saw my help
[b]in the gate,
22 Let my shoulder fall
from the [1]socket,
And my [a]arm be broken
off [2]at the elbow.
23 "For [a]disaster from God
is a dread to me,
And because of [b]His
exaltedness I can
do nothing.

24 "If I have put my
confidence *in* [a]gold,
*And called* fine gold my trust,
25 If I have [a]been glad because
my wealth was great,
And because my hand
had found *so* much,
26 If I have [a]looked at the
[1]sun when it shone
Or the moon going
in splendor,
27 And my heart became
secretly enticed,
And my hand [1]threw a kiss
from my mouth,
28 That too would have been
[a]an iniquity *calling
for* [1]judgment,
For I would have [b]denied
God above.

29 "If I [a]have been glad
at the upheaval
of the one who hated me,
Or [1]exulted when evil
found him—
30 "But [a]I have not given over
my [1]mouth to sin
By asking for his life
in [b]a curse—
31 "If the men of my tent
have not said,
'Who can [1]find one who
has not been [a]satisfied
with his meat'—
32 "The sojourner has not
lodged outside,
*For* I have opened my doors
to the [1]traveler—
33 "If I have [a]covered my
transgressions like [1]Adam,
By hiding my iniquity
in my bosom,
34 Because I [a]feared the
great multitude,
And the contempt
of families terrified me,

**31:16** [b]Ex 22:22-24; Job 22:9 **31:17** [a]Job 22:7 [b]Job 29:12 **31:19** [a]Job 22:6; 29:13 [b]Job 24:4 **31:21** [a]Job 29:12; 31:17 [b]Job 29:7 **31:22** [a]Job 38:15 [1]Or *back*; lit *shoulder* [2]Lit *from the bone of the upper arm* **31:23** [a]Job 31:3 [b]Job 13:11 **31:24** [a]Job 22:24; Mk 10:23-25 **31:25** [a]Job 1:3, 10; Ps 62:10 **31:26** [a]Dt 4:19; 17:3; Eze 8:16 [1]Lit *light* **31:27** [1]Lit *kissed my mouth* **31:28** [a]Dt 17:2-7; Job 31:11 [b]Jos 24:27; Is 59:13 [1]Lit *judges* **31:29** [a]Pr 17:5; 24:17; Ob 12 [1]Lit *lifted myself up* **31:30** [a]Ps 7:4 [b]Job 5:3 [1]Lit *palate* **31:31** [a]Job 22:7 [1]Lit *give* **31:32** [1]M.T. *way* **31:33** [a]Ge 3:10; Pr 28:13 [1]Or *mankind* **31:34** [a]Ex 23:2

And I kept silent and did
not go out of doors—
35 "Oh that I had one to hear me!
Behold, here is my [1]signature;
[a]Let the Almighty answer me!
And the indictment which
my [b]accuser has written,
36 Surely I would carry it
on my shoulder;
I would bind it to myself
like a crown.
37 "I would declare to Him
[a]the number of my steps;
Like [b]a prince I would
approach Him—

38 "If my [a]land cries out
against me,
And its furrows weep together,
39 If I have [a]eaten its [1]fruit
without money,
Or have [b]caused [2]its owners
to lose their lives,
40 Let [a]briars come out
instead of wheat,
And stinkweed
instead of barley."
The words of Job are ended.

### *Elihu Answers in Anger*

32 Then these three men ceased
answering Job because he was
[a]righteous in his own eyes. 2 But the
anger of Elihu the son of Barachel
the [a]Buzite, of the family of Ram,
burned; against Job his anger burned
[b]because he was proving himself
righteous [c,1]before God. 3 And his an-
ger burned against his three friends
because they had found no answer,
and *yet had* condemned Job. 4 Now
Elihu had waited with *his* words for
Job because they were years older
than he. 5 Then Elihu saw that there
was no answer in the mouth of the
three men, so his anger burned.
6 So Elihu the son of Barachel the
Buzite answered and said,
"I am young in years
and you are [a]old;
Therefore I was shy
and afraid to tell you
my knowledge.
7 "I [1]thought [a,2]age should speak,
And [3]increased years should
make wisdom known.
8 "But it is a spirit in man,
And the [a]breath
of the Almighty
gives them [b]understanding.
9 "The [1]abundant *in years*
may not be wise,
Nor may [a]elders
understand justice.
10 "So I [1]say, 'Listen to me,
I too will tell my knowledge.'

11 "Behold, I waited
for your words,
I gave ear to your reasonings,
While you searched
out what to say.
12 "I even carefully
considered you;
And behold, there was no
one who reproved Job,
Not one of you who
answered his words.
13 "Lest you say,
'[a]We have found wisdom;
God will drive him
away, not man.'

**31:35** [a]Job 19:7; 30:20, 24, 28; 35:14 [b]Job 27:7 [1]Lit *mark* **31:37** [a]Job 31:4 [b]Job 1:3; 29:25 **31:38** [a]Job 24:2 **31:39** [a]Job 24:6, 10-12; Jas 5:4 [b]1Ki 21:19 [1]Lit *strength* [2]Lit *the soul of its owners to expire* **31:40** [a]Job 32:13; Is 5:6 ◆**32:1** [a]Job 10:7; 13:18; 27:5, 6; 31:6 **32:2** [a]Ge 22:21 [b]Job 27:5, 6 [c]Job 30:21 [1]Or *more than*; lit *from* **32:6** [a]Job 15:10 **32:7** [a]Job 8:8, 9 [1]Lit *said* [2]Lit *days* [3]Lit *many* **32:8** [a]Job 33:4 [b]Job 38:36 **32:9** [a]Job 32:7 [1]Or *nobles* **32:10** [1]Or *said* **32:13** [a]Jer 9:23

14 "Now he has not arranged
*his* words against me,
Nor will I respond to him
with your words.
15 "They are dismayed; they
no longer answer;
Words have moved
away from them.
16 "Shall I wait, because
they do not speak,
Because they stand *still*
*and* no longer answer?
17 "I myself will also
answer my share;
I also will tell my knowledge.
18 "For I am full of words;
The spirit within my
belly presses me.
19 "Behold, my belly is like
*unvented* wine, not opened;
Like new wineskins it
is about to burst.
20 "Let me speak that I
may get relief;
Let me open my lips
and answer.
21 "Let me now [a]be partial
to no one,
Nor flatter *any* man.
22 "For I do not know
how to flatter,
*Else* my Maker would
soon carry me away.

### *Elihu Asks Job to Hear and Respond*

33 "However now, Job, please
[a]hear my speech,
And give ear to all my words.
2 "Behold now, I open my mouth;
My tongue in my [1]mouth speaks.
3 "My words are *from* the
uprightness of my heart,
And my lips speak
[a]knowledge sincerely.
4 "The [a]Spirit of God
has made me,
And the [b]breath of [1]the
Almighty gives me life.
5 "[a]Respond to me if you can;
Arrange yourselves before me,
take your stand.
6 "Behold, I belong to God
like you;
I too have been [1]formed
out of the [a]clay.
7 "Behold, [a]no dread of me
should terrify you,
Nor should my pressure
weigh heavily on you.

8 "Surely you have spoken
in my hearing,
And I have heard the sound
of *your* speech:
9 'I am [a]pure,
[b]without transgression;
I am innocent, and there
[c]is no guilt in me.
10 'Behold, He finds *reasons*
*for* opposition against me;
He [a]counts me as His enemy.
11 'He [a]puts my feet in the stocks;
He keeps watch
over all my paths.'
12 "Behold, let me answer you;
[a]you are not right in this,
For God is greater
than mortal man.

13 "Why do you [a]contend
against Him?

**32:21** [a]Lv 19:15; Job 13:8, 10; 34:19 ◆ **33:1** [a]Job 13:6 **33:2** [1]Lit *palate* **33:3** [a]Job 6:28; 27:4; 36:4 **33:4** [a]Ge 2:7; Job 10:3; 32:8 [b]Job 27:3 [1]Heb *Shaddai* **33:5** [a]Job 33:32 **33:6** [a]Job 4:19 [1]Lit *cut out of* **33:7** [a]Job 13:21 **33:9** [a]Job 9:21; 10:7; 13:18; 16:17 [b]Job 7:21; 13:23; 14:17 [c]Job 10:14 **33:10** [a]Job 13:24 **33:11** [a]Job 13:27 **33:12** [a]Ecc 7:20 **33:13** [a]Job 40:2; Is 45:9

For He does not give
an answer for all His doings.
14 "Indeed [a]God speaks once,
Or twice, *yet* no one
perceives it.
15 "In a [a]dream, a vision
of the night,
When deep sleep
falls on men,
While they slumber
in their beds,
16 Then [a]He opens the ears
of men,
And seals in their discipline,
17 That He may turn man
aside *from his* conduct,
And [1]keep man from pride;
18 He [a]holds back his
soul from the pit,
And his life from passing
over [1]*to death* [b]by a weapon.

19 "[1]Man is also reproved
with [a]pain on his bed,
And with unceasing
contention in his bones,
20 So that his life [a]loathes bread,
And his soul favorite food.
21 "His [a]flesh wastes
away from sight,
And his [b]bones which were
not seen stick out.
22 "Then [a]his soul draws
near to the pit,
And his life to those
who bring death.

23 "If there is an angel
*as* [a]mediator for him,
One out of a thousand,
To declare to a man
what is [1]right for him,
24 Then let him be gracious
to him, and say,
'Deliver him from [a]going
down to the pit;
I have found [b]atonement';
25 Let his flesh become
fresher than in youth,
Let him return to the days
of his youthful vigor;
26 Then he will [a]entreat God,
and He will accept him,
And [b]he will see His face
with joyful shouts,
And He may restore His
righteousness to man.
27 "He will sing to men and say,
'I [a]have sinned and
perverted what is right,
But He has not done
[b]what is due to me.
28 'He has redeemed my soul
from passing into the pit,
And my life shall
[a]see the light.'

29 "Behold, God does [a]all
these *things* twice, three
times with men,
30 To [a]bring back his soul
from the pit,
That he may be enlightened
with the light of life.
31 "Pay attention, O Job,
listen to me;
Keep silent,
and I will speak.
32 "*Then* if [1]you have any
speech, respond to me;

---

**33:14** [a]Job 33:29; 40:5; Ps 62:11 **33:15** [a]Job 4:12-17; 33:15-18 **33:16** [a]Job 36:10, 15 **33:17** [1]Lit *hide* **33:18** [a]Job 33:22, 24, 28, 30 [b]Job 15:22 [1]Or *Sheol* **33:19** [a]Job 30:17 [1]Lit *He* **33:20** [a]Job 3:24; 6:7; Ps 107:18 **33:21** [a]Job 16:8 [b]Job 19:20; Ps 22:17; 102:5 **33:22** [a]Job 33:18, 28 **33:23** [a]Ge 40:8 [1]Lit *his uprightness* **33:24** [a]Job 33:18, 28; Is 38:17 [b]Job 36:18; Ps 49:7 **33:26** [a]Job 22:27; 34:28; Ps 50:14, 15 [b]Job 22:26 **33:27** [a]2Sa 12:13; Lk 15:21 [b]Ro 6:21 **33:28** [a]Job 22:28 **33:29** [a]Eph 1:11; Php 2:13 **33:30** [a]Job 33:18; Zec 9:11 **33:32** [1]Lit *there are words*

Speak, for I desire
to prove you righteous.
33 "If not, [a]listen to me;
Keep silent, and I will
teach you wisdom."

### *Elihu Answers That God Will Be Just*

34 Then Elihu answered and said,
2 "Hear my speech,
you wise men,
And give ear to me,
you who know.
3 "For [a]the ear tests words
*As* the palate tastes food.
4 "Let us choose
for ourselves what is just;
Let us know among
ourselves what is good.
5 "For Job has said,
'[a]I am righteous,
But [b]God has removed
my justice;
6 [1]Should I lie
concerning my justice?
My [a,2]wound is incurable,
*though I am*
without transgression.'
7 "What man is like Job,
Who [a]drinks up
mocking like water,
8 But he travels [a]in company
with the workers of iniquity,
And walks with wicked men?
9 "For he has said, '[a]It is
of no use to a man
When he [1]is pleased with God.'

10 "Therefore, listen to me, you
men with a heart *of wisdom.*
Far be it from God
to [a]do injustice,
And from the Almighty
to do wrong.
11 "For He pays a man
according to [a]his work,
And makes [1]him find it
according to his way.
12 "Truly, [a]God will not
act wickedly,
And the Almighty will
not pervert justice.
13 "Who [a]appointed Him
with authority over the earth?
And who [b]has laid *on Him*
the whole world?
14 "If He should set His
heart on it,
If He should [a]gather
to Himself His spirit
and His breath,
15 All [a]flesh would breathe
its last together,
And man would
[b]return to dust.

16 "But if *you have*
understanding, hear this;
Give ear to the sound
of my speech.
17 "Shall [a]one who hates
justice [1]rule?
And [b]will you condemn
the righteous mighty One,
18 Who says to a king,
'Vile one,'
To nobles, 'Wicked ones';
19 Who shows no [a]partiality
to princes

**33:33** [a]Ps 34:11 ◆ **34:3** [a]Job 12:11 **34:5** [a]Job 13:18; 33:9 [b]Job 27:2 **34:6** [a]Job 6:4 [1]Or *Although I am right I am accounted a liar* [2]Lit *arrow* **34:7** [a]Job 15:16 **34:8** [a]Job 22:15 **34:9** [a]Job 21:15; 35:3; Ps 50:18 [1]Or *takes delight in God* **34:10** [a]Ge 18:25; Dt 32:4; Job 8:3; 34:12; Ro 9:14 **34:11** [a]Job 34:25; Ps 62:12; Pr 24:12; Jer 32:19; Eze 33:20; Mt 16:27; Ro 2:6; 2Co 5:10; Rev 22:12 [1]Lit *a man* **34:12** [a]Job 34:10 **34:13** [a]Job 38:4 [b]Job 38:5 **34:14** [a]Job 12:10; Ps 104:29; Ecc 12:7 **34:15** [a]Ge 7:21; Job 9:22 [b]Ge 3:19; Job 10:9 **34:17** [a]2Sa 23:3; Job 34:30 [b]Job 40:8 [1]Lit *bind* **34:19** [a]Lv 19:15; Dt 10:17; 2Chr 19:7; Ac 10:34; Ro 2:11; Ga 2:6; Eph 6:9; Col 3:25; 1Pe 1:17

Nor recognizes the rich
above the poor,
For they all are the [b]work
of His hands?
20 "In a moment they die,
and [a]at midnight
People are shaken
and pass away,
And [b]the mighty are taken
away without a hand.

21 "For [a]His eyes are
upon the ways of a man,
And He sees all his steps.
22 "There is [a]no darkness
or shadow of death
Where the workers of iniquity
may hide themselves.
23 "[1]For He does not [a]*need*
*to* consider a man further,
That he should go
before God in judgment.
24 "He breaks in pieces
[a]mighty men without
searching *anything* out,
And sets others in their place.
25 "Therefore He [a]recognizes
their labors,
And [b]He overthrows
*them* in the night,
And they are crushed.
26 "He [a]strikes them
like the wicked
[1]In a public place,
27 Because they [a]turned aside
from following Him,
And [b]had no insight
from any of His ways;
28 So that they caused [a]the cry
of the poor to come to Him,
And that He might [b]hear
the cry of the afflicted.
29 So *if* He keeps quiet, who
then can condemn?
So *if* He hides His face, who
then can perceive Him?
*He is* above both nation
and man altogether,
30 So that [a]godless men
would not rule
Nor be snares of the people.

31 "For has anyone said to God,
'I have borne *chastisement*;
I will not work destructively
*anymore*;
32 Instruct me what I
do not behold;
If I have [a]done injustice,
I will not do it again'?
33 "Shall He [a]repay on your terms,
because you have rejected *it*?
For you must choose, and not I;
Therefore say what you know.
34 "Men with a heart *of wisdom*
will say to me,
And a wise man who hears me,
35 'Job [a]speaks without knowledge,
And his words are
without insight.
36 'Job ought to be tested
[1]to the limit
Because he answers
[a]like wicked men.
37 'For he adds [a]transgression
to his sin;
He [b]strikes his hands
together among us,
And multiplies his words
against God.'"

**34:19** [b]Job 10:3 **34:20** [a]Ex 12:29; Job 34:25; 36:20 [b]Job 12:19 **34:21** [a]Job 24:23; 31:4; Pr 5:21; 15:3; Jer 16:17 **34:22** [a]Ps 139:11, 12; Am 9:2, 3 **34:23** [a]Job 11:11 [1]Or *For he does not set upon man the time to go to God in the judgment* **34:24** [a]Job 12:19 **34:25** [a]Job 34:11 [b]Job 34:20 **34:26** [a]Ps 9:5; 11:5 [1]Lit *In the place of the ones seeing* **34:27** [a]1Sa 15:11 [b]Job 21:14 **34:28** [a]Job 35:9; Jas 5:4 [b]Ex 22:23; Job 22:27 **34:30** [a]Job 5:15; 20:5; 34:17; Pr 29:2-12 **34:32** [a]Job 33:27 **34:33** [a]Job 41:11 **34:35** [a]Job 35:16; 38:2 **34:36** [a]Job 22:15 [1]Or *to the end* **34:37** [a]Job 23:2 [b]Job 27:23

### *Elihu Answers Job*

35 Then Elihu answered and said,
2 "Do you think this is
according to [a]justice?
Do you say, 'My righteousness
is more than God's'?
3 "For you say, '[a]What use
will it be to [1]You?
[b]What profit will I have, more
than if I had sinned?'
4 "I will respond to you,
And your friends with you.
5 "[a]Look at the heavens
and see;
And perceive [b]the clouds—
they are higher than you.
6 "If you have sinned,
[a]what do you accomplish
against Him?
And if your transgressions
are many, what do
you do to Him?
7 "If you are righteous,
[a]what do you give to Him,
Or what does He receive
from your hand?
8 "Your wickedness is for a
man like yourself,
And your righteousness
is for a son of man.

9 "Because of [a]many
oppressions they cry out;
They cry for help
because of the arm
[b]of many *oppressors.*
10 "But [a]no one says,
'Where is God my Maker,
Who [b]gives songs
of praise in the night,
11 Who [a]teaches us more
than the beasts of the earth
And makes us wiser than
the birds of the heavens?'
12 "There [a]they cry out,
but He does not answer
Because of the pride
of evil men.
13 "Surely [a]God will not listen
to [1]an empty *cry*,
Nor will the Almighty
perceive it.
14 "How much less when [a]you say
you do not perceive Him,
The [b]case is before Him, and
you must wait for Him!
15 "And now, because He has
not visited *in* His anger,
Nor has He acknowledged
[1]transgression well,
16 So Job opens his mouth vainly;
He multiplies words
[a]without knowledge."

### *Elihu Says God Gives the Afflicted Justice*

36 Then Elihu continued and
said,
2 "Wait for me a little, and
I will show you
That there [1]is yet more to
be said in God's behalf.
3 "I will take up my
knowledge from afar,
And I will ascribe
[a]righteousness to my Maker.
4 "For truly [a]my words
are not a lie;
One who is [b,1]perfect
in knowledge is with you.

---

◆**35:2** [a]Job 27:2 **35:3** [a]Job 34:9 [b]Job 9:30, 31 [1]Or *you* **35:5** [a]Ge 15:5; Ps 8:3 [b]Job 22:12 **35:6** [a]Job 7:20; Pr 8:36; Jer 7:19 **35:7** [a]Job 22:2, 3; Pr 9:12; Lk 17:10; Ro 11:35 **35:9** [a]Ex 2:23 [b]Job 12:19 **35:10** [a]Job 21:14; 27:10; 36:13; Is 51:13 [b]Job 8:21; Ps 42:8; 77:6; 149:5; Ac 16:25 **35:11** [a]Job 36:22; Ps 94:12; Jer 32:33 **35:12** [a]Pr 1:28 **35:13** [a]Job 27:9; Pr 15:29; Is 1:15; Jer 11:11; Mic 3:4 [1]Or *falsehood* **35:14** [a]Job 9:11; 23:8, 9 [b]Job 31:35 **35:15** [1]Or *arrogance* **35:16** [a]Job 34:35; 38:2 ◆**36:2** [1]Lit *are yet words for God* **36:3** [a]Job 8:3; 37:23 **36:4** [a]Job 33:3 [b]Job 37:16 [1]Or *blameless*

5 "Behold, God is mighty
but does not [a]reject;
*He is* [b]mighty in the power
of *His* heart.
6 "He does not [a]keep the
wicked alive,
But gives justice to [b]the afflicted.
7 "He does not [a]withdraw His
eyes from the righteous;
But [b]with kings on the throne
He has seated them forever,
and they are exalted.
8 "And if they are bound in fetters,
And are caught in the cords
of [a]affliction,
9 Then He declares to them
their work
And their transgressions,
that they
have [a]magnified themselves.
10 "[a]He opens their ear
to discipline,
And [b]says that they return
from wickedness.
11 "If they hear and serve *Him*,
They will [a]end their
days in prosperity
And their years in [b]pleasures.
12 "But if they do not hear, they
shall pass away [a]by a weapon
And they will [b]breathe their
last without knowledge.
13 "But the godless in heart
lay up anger;
They do not cry for help
when He binds them.
14 "[1]They die in youth,
And their life *perishes*
among the [a]cult prostitutes.
15 "He delivers the afflicted
in [1]their [a]affliction,
And [b]opens their ear
in [2]*time of* oppression.
16 "Then indeed, He [a]enticed you
from the mouth of distress,
Instead of it, a broad place
with no constraint;
And the comfort of your
table full of [1]fatness.

17 "But you were full
of [a]judgment on the wicked;
Judgment and justice
take hold *of you*.
18 "*Beware* lest [a]wrath entice
you to scoffing;
And do not let the greatness
of the [b]atonement
turn you aside.
19 "Will your [1]cries keep
you from distress,
Or all the forces
of *your* power?
20 "Do not long for [a]the night,
When people [1]vanish
in their place.
21 "Be careful, do [a]not turn
to wickedness,
For you have chosen
this to [b]affliction.
22 "Behold, God is exalted
in His power;
Who is a [a]teacher like Him?
23 "Who has appointed
Him His way,
And who has said,
'[a]You have worked
*out* [1]unrighteousness'?

**36:5** [a]Ps 22:24; 69:33; 102:17 [b]Job 12:13 **36:6** [a]Job 8:22; 34:26 [b]Job 5:15 **36:7** [a]Ps 33:18; 34:15 [b]Job 5:11; Ps 113:8 **36:8** [a]Job 36:15, 21 **36:9** [a]Job 15:25 **36:10** [a]Job 33:16; 36:15 [b]2Ki 17:13; Job 36:21; Jon 3:8 **36:11** [a]1Ti 4:8 [b]Ps 16:11 **36:12** [a]Job 15:22 [b]Job 4:21 **36:14** [a]Dt 23:17 [1]Or *Their soul dies* **36:15** [a]Job 36:8, 21 [b]Job 36:10 [1]Lit *his* [2]Or *adversity* **36:16** [a]Hos 2:14 [1]Or *rich food* **36:17** [a]Job 22:5, 10, 11 **36:18** [a]Jon 4:4, 9 [b]Job 33:24 **36:19** [1]Or *riches* **36:20** [a]Job 34:20, 25 [1]Lit *go up* **36:21** [a]Job 36:10; Ps 31:6; 66:18 [b]Job 36:8, 15; Heb 11:25 **36:22** [a]Job 35:11 **36:23** [a]Dt 32:4; Job 8:3 [1]Or *injustice*

24 “Remember that you should
[a]exalt His work,
Of which men have [b]sung.
25 “All men have beheld it;
Man looks from afar.
26 “Behold, God is [a]exalted,
and [b]we do not know *Him*;
The [c]number of His years
is unsearchable.
27 “For [a]He draws up the
drops of water,
They distill rain for His [1]stream,
28 Which the clouds pour down,
They drip
upon man abundantly.
29 “Can anyone discern the
[a]spreading of the clouds,
The [b]thundering
of His [1]pavilion?
30 “Behold, He spreads His
[1]lightning about Him,
And He covers the depths
of the sea.
31 “For by these He
[a]judges peoples;
He [b]gives food in abundance.
32 “He covers *His* hands
with the [1]lightning,
And [a]commands it
to strike the mark.
33 “Its [a]thundering declares
about Him;
The cattle also, concerning
what is coming up.

### *Elihu Speaks of God’s Voice*

37 “At this also my
heart trembles,
And leaps from its place.
2 “[1]Listen closely to the
[a]thunder of His voice,
And the rumbling
that goes out
from His mouth.
3 “Under the whole heaven
He lets it loose,
And His [1]lightning
to the [a]ends of the earth.
4 “After it, a voice roars;
He thunders with His
majestic voice,
And He does not restrain
[1]the lightnings
when His voice is heard.
5 “God [a]thunders with His
voice marvelously,
Doing [b]great things
which we do not know.
6 “For to [a]the snow He says,
‘Fall on the earth,’
And to the [b]downpour
of rain and the downpour
of rains, ‘Be strong.’
7 “He [a]seals the hand
of every man,
That [b]all men may
know His work.
8 “Then the beast goes
into its [a]lair
And dwells in its [1]den.
9 “Out of the [a,1]south
comes the storm,
And out of the [2]north
the cold.
10 “From the breath of God
[a]ice is made,
And the expanse
of the waters is frozen.

**36:24** [a]Ps 92:5; Rev 15:3 [b]Ex 15:1; Jdg 5:1; 1Chr 16:9; Ps 59:16; 138:5 **36:26** [a]Job 11:7-9; 37:23 [b]1Co 13:12 [c]Job 10:5; Ps 90:2; 102:24, 27; Heb 1:12 **36:27** [a]Job 5:10; 36:26-29; 37:6, 11; 38:28; Ps 147:8 [1]Or *mist* **36:29** [a]Job 37:11, 16 [b]Job 26:14 [1]Lit *booth* **36:30** [1]Lit *light* **36:31** [a]Job 37:13 [b]Ps 104:27; 136:25; Ac 14:17 **36:32** [a]Job 37:11, 12, 15 [1]Lit *light* **36:33** [a]Job 37:2 ◆ **37:2** [a]Job 36:33; 37:4, 5; Ps 29:3-9 [1]Or *Persist in listening* **37:3** [a]Job 28:24; 37:11, 12; 38:13 [1]Lit *light* **37:4** [1]Lit *them* **37:5** [a]Job 26:14 [b]Job 5:9; 37:14, 16, 23 **37:6** [a]Job 38:22 [b]Job 36:27 **37:7** [a]Job 12:14 [b]Ps 111:2 **37:8** [a]Job 38:40; Ps 104:21, 22 [1]Lit *dens* **37:9** [a]Job 9:9 [1]Lit *chamber* [2]Lit *scattering winds* **37:10** [a]Job 38:29; Ps 147:17

11 "Also with moisture He
[a]loads the thick cloud;
He [b]scatters [c]the cloud
of His [1]lightning.
12 "It changes direction, turning
around by His guidance,
That [1]it may do whatever
He [a]commands [2]it
On the [b]face
of the inhabited earth.
13 "Whether for [a,1]correction,
or for [b]His world,
Or for [c]lovingkindness,
He causes it to [2]happen.

14 "Give ear to this, O Job,
Stand and carefully consider
the wondrous deeds of God.
15 "Do you know how God
establishes them,
And makes the [1]lightning
of His cloud to shine?
16 "Do you know about the
layers of the thick clouds,
The [a]wonders of one
[b,1]perfect in knowledge,
17 You whose garments are hot,
When the land is quiet
because of the south wind?
18 "Can you, with Him,
[a]spread out the skies,
Strong as a molten mirror?
19 "Make us know what we
shall say to Him;
We [a]cannot arrange *our case*
because of darkness.
20 "Shall it be recounted
to Him that I would speak?
[1]If a man says *a word*, will He
indeed be swallowed up?

21 "So now [1]men do not
see the light which is
bright in the skies;
But the wind has passed
and cleared them.
22 "Out of the north comes
golden *splendor*;
Around God is
fearsome majesty.
23 "The Almighty—[a]we
cannot find Him;
He is [b]exalted in power
And [c]He will not afflict
[d]justice and
abundant righteousness.
24 "Therefore men [a]fear Him;
He does not [b]regard any
who are wise of heart."

### *Yahweh Answers Job*

38 Then Yahweh [a]answered Job
out of the [1]whirlwind and said,
2 "Who is this that
[a]darkens counsel
By words without knowledge?
3 "Now [a]gird up your
loins like a man,
And [b]I will ask you, and
you make Me know!
4 "Where were you [a]when I laid
the foundation of the earth?
Tell *Me*, if you
know understanding,
5 Who set its [a]measurements?
Since you know.

---

**37:11** [a]Job 36:27 [b]Job 36:29 [c]Job 37:15 [1]Lit *light* **37:12** [a]Job 36:32; Ps 148:8 [b]Is 14:21; 27:6 [1]Lit *they* [2]Lit *them* **37:13** [a]Ex 9:18, 23; 1Sa 12:18, 19 [b]Job 38:26, 27 [c]1Ki 18:41-46 [1]Lit the rod [2]Lit be found **37:15** [1]Lit *light* **37:16** [a]Job 37:5, 14, 23 [b]Job 36:4 [1]Or *blameless* **37:18** [a]Job 9:8; Ps 104:2; Is 44:24; 45:12; Jer 10:12; Zec 12:1 **37:19** [a]Job 9:14; Ro 8:26 **37:20** [1]Or *If a man speaks, surely he shall be swallowed up* **37:21** [1]Lit *they* **37:23** [a]Job 11:7, 8; Ro 11:33; 1Ti 6:16 [b]Job 9:4; 36:5 [c]Is 63:9; Lam 3:33; Eze 18:23, 32; 33:11 [d]Job 8:3 **37:24** [a]Mt 10:28 [b]Job 5:13; Mt 11:25; 1Co 1:26 ◆ **38:1** [a]Job 40:6 [1]Or *storm* **38:2** [a]Job 35:16; 42:3 **38:3** [a]Job 40:7 [b]Job 42:4 **38:4** [a]Job 15:7; Ps 104:5; Pr 8:29; 30:4 **38:5** [a]Pr 8:29; Is 40:12

Or who stretched
the line on it?
6 "On what [a]were its bases sunk?
Or who laid its cornerstone,
7 When the morning
stars sang together
And all the [a]sons of God
shouted for joy?

8 "Or *who* [a]enclosed the
sea with doors
When, bursting forth,
it went out from the womb,
9 When I made a cloud
its garment
And dense gloom its
swaddling band,
10 And I [a,1]placed
boundaries on it
And set a bolt and doors,
11 And I said, 'Thus far you shall
come, but no farther;
And here shall your
proud waves stop'?

***Yahweh Answers Job, "Have You?"***

12 "Have you [1]ever in your life
commanded the morning,
*And* caused the dawn
to know its place,
13 That it might seize
[a]the ends of the earth,
And [b]the wicked be
shaken out of it?
14 "It is changed like clay
*under* the seal;
And they stand forth
like clothing.
15 "[a]From the wicked their
light is withheld,
And the arm [b]raised
high is broken.

16 "Have you entered
into [a]the springs of the sea
Or walked [1]in the recesses
of the deep?
17 "Have the gates of death
been revealed to you,
Or have you seen the gates
of the [a]shadow of death?
18 "Have you carefully considered
the [1]expanse of [a]the earth?
Tell *Me*, if you know all this.

19 "Where is the way
to *where* the light dwells?
And darkness,
where is its place,
20 That you may take it
to [a]its territory
And that you may discern
the paths to its [1]home?
21 "You know, for [a]you
were born then,
And the number
of your days is great!

22 "Have you entered the
storehouses [a]of the snow,
Or have you seen
the storehouses
of the [b]hail,
23 Which I have reserved
for the time of distress,
For the day of war and battle?
24 "Where is the way
that [a]the light is divided,
*Or* the east wind scattered
on the earth?

**38:6** [a]Job 26:7 **38:7** [a]Job 1:6 **38:8** [a]Ge 1:9; Ps 104:6-9; Pr 8:29; Jer 5:22 **38:10** [a]Ge 1:9; Ps 33:7; 104:9; Pr 8:29; Jer 5:22 [1]Lit *broke My decree on it* **38:12** [1]Lit *from your days* **38:13** [a]Job 28:24; 37:3 [b]Job 34:25, 26; 36:6 **38:15** [a]Job 5:14 [b]Nu 15:30; Ps 10:15; 37:17 **38:16** [a]Ge 7:11; 8:2; Pr 8:24, 28 [1]Or *in search of* **38:17** [a]Job 10:21; 26:6; 34:22 **38:18** [a]Job 28:24 [1]Or *width* **38:20** [a]Job 26:10 [1]Lit *house* **38:21** [a]Job 15:7 **38:22** [a]Job 37:6 [b]Ex 9:18; Jos 10:11; Is 30:30; Eze 13:11, 13; Rev 16:21 **38:24** [a]Job 26:10

25 “Who has cleft a conduit
for the flood,
Or a way
for the thunderbolt,
26 To bring [a]rain on a land
without [1]people,
*On* a desert
without a man in it,
27 To [a]satisfy the waste
and desolate land
And to make the growth
of grass to sprout?
28 “Has [a]the rain a father?
Or who has begotten
the drops of dew?
29 “From whose womb has
come the [a]ice?
And the frost of heaven,
who has given it birth?
30 “Water [1]becomes hard
like stone,
And the surface of the deep
[2]is interlocked.

31 “Can you bind the chains
of the [a]Pleiades,
Or loose the cords of Orion?
32 “Can you lead forth a
[1]constellation in its season,
And guide the Bear
with her [2]satellites?
33 “Do you know the [a]statutes
of the heavens,
Or fix their rule
over the earth?

34 “Can you raise your voice
up to the clouds,
So that an [a]abundance
of water will cover you?
35 “Can you [a]send forth
lightnings that they may go
And say to you, ‘Here we are’?
36 “Who has [a]given wisdom
in the [1]innermost being
Or given [b]understanding
to the [2]mind?
37 “Who can count the clouds
by wisdom,
Or [a]tip the water jars
of the heavens,
38 When the dust hardens
into a mass
And the clods stick together?

### *Yahweh Answers Job, “Where Were You?”*

39 “Can you hunt the [a]prey
for the lion,
Or fulfill the appetite
of the young lions,
40 When they [a]crouch
in *their* dens
*And* lie in wait in *their* lair?
41 “Who prepares for [a]the raven
its provision
When its young cry
for help to God
And wander about
without food?

39 “Do you know the time the
[a,1]mountain goats
give birth?
Do you keep watch
over the calving of the [b]deer?
2 “Can you count the
months they fulfill,
Or do you know the time
they give birth?

**38:26** [a]Job 36:27 [1]Lit *man* **38:27** [a]Ps 104:13, 14; 107:35 **38:28** [a]Job 36:27, 28; Ps 147:8; Jer 14:22
**38:29** [a]Job 37:10; Ps 147:17 **38:30** [1]Lit *hides itself* [2]Or *is frozen* **38:31** [a]Job 9:9; Am 5:8
**38:32** [1]Heb *Mazzaroth* [2]Lit *sons* **38:33** [a]Ps 148:6; Jer 31:35, 36 **38:34** [a]Job 22:11; 36:27, 28; 38:37 **38:35** [a]Job 36:32; 37:3 **38:36** [a]Job 9:4; Ps 51:6; Ecc 2:26 [b]Job 32:8 [1]Or *ibis* [2]Or *rooster*
**38:37** [a]Job 38:34 **38:39** [a]Ps 104:21 **38:40** [a]Job 37:8 **38:41** [a]Ps 147:9; Mt 6:26; Lk 12:24
◆ **39:1** [a]Dt 14:5; 1Sa 24:2; Ps 104:18 [b]Ps 29:9 [1]Lit *goats of the rock*

3 "They kneel down; they
bring forth their young;
They send out their
labor pains.
4 "Their children become
strong; they grow up
in the open field;
They leave and do not
return to them.

5 "Who sent out the [a]wild
donkey free?
And who loosed the bonds
of the swift donkey,
6 For whom I have set
[a]the desert plain as a home
And the salt land as his
dwelling place?
7 "He laughs at the tumult
of the city;
The shoutings of the driver
he does not hear.
8 "He explores the mountains
for his pasture
And searches
after every green thing.
9 "Will the [a]wild ox consent
to serve you,
Or will he spend the night
at your manger?
10 "Can you bind the wild ox
in a furrow with [1]ropes,
Or will he harrow
the valleys after you?
11 "Will you trust him because
his power is great
And leave your labor to him?
12 "Will you believe him
that he will return
your seed *of grain*
And gather *it from* your
threshing floor?
13 "The ostriches' wings
flap joyously
*But* are they the pinion and
plumage of a [1]stork?
14 For she leaves her
eggs to the earth
And warms them
in the dust,
15 And she forgets that a foot
may crush [1]them,
Or that a beast of the field
may trample [1]them.
16 "She treats her children
[a]cruelly, as if *they*
were not hers;
Though her labor be empty,
*she* is without dread,
17 Because God has made
her forget wisdom,
And has not given her
a share of understanding.
18 "When she raises
herself up high,
She laughs at the horse
and his rider.

19 "Do you give the horse
*his* might?
Do you clothe his neck
with a mane?
20 "Do you make him [a]leap
like the locust?
His splendid [b]snorting
is terrible.
21 "[1]*He paws in the* valley and
rejoices in *his* power;
He [a]goes out to meet
the weapons.
22 "He laughs at dread and
is not dismayed;
And he does not turn
back from the sword.

**39:5** [a]Job 6:5; 11:12; 24:5; Ps 104:11 **39:6** [a]Job 24:5; Jer 2:24; Hos 8:9 **39:9** [a]Nu 23:22; Dt 33:17; Ps 22:21; 29:6; 92:10; Is 34:7 **39:10** [1]Lit *his rope* **39:13** [1]Or *love* **39:15** [1]Lit *it* **39:16** [a]Lam 4:3 **39:20** [a]Joel 2:5 [b]Jer 8:16 **39:21** [a]Jer 8:6 [1]Lit *They paw*

23 "The quiver rattles against him,
The flashing spear and javelin.
24 "With shaking and rage he
[1]races over the ground,
And he does not [2]stand still
at the sound of the trumpet.
25 "As often as the trumpet
*sounds* he says, 'Aha!'
And he scents the battle
from afar,
And the thunder
of the commanders
and the shout *of war*.

26 "Is it by your understanding
that the hawk soars,
Stretching his wings
toward the south?
27 "Is it at your [1]command
that the eagle goes on high
And raises [a]his nest high?
28 "On the cliff he dwells
and lodges,
Upon the rocky crag,
a fortress.
29 "From there he [a,1]spies
out food;
His eyes see *it* from afar.
30 "His young ones also
suck up blood;
And [a]where the slain
are, there is he."

### *Job Places His Hand over His Mouth*

40 Then Yahweh answered Job
and said,
2 "Will the faultfinder [a]contend
with the Almighty?
Let him who [b]reproves
God answer it."

3 Then Job answered Yahweh and
said,
4 "Behold, I am insignificant;
what can I respond to You?
I [a]place my hand
over my mouth.
5 "Once I have spoken, and
[a]I will not answer;
Even twice, and I will
add nothing more."

### *Yahweh Will Ask Job*

6 Then [a]Yahweh answered Job out of
the [1]whirlwind and said,
7 "Now [a]gird up your
loins like a man;
I will [b]ask you, and you
make Me know.
8 "Will you really [a]annul
My judgment?
Will you [b]condemn Me
[c]that you may be justified?
9 "Or do you have an
arm like God,
And can you [a]thunder
with a voice like His?
10 "[a]Adorn yourself
with exaltation and loftiness,
And clothe yourself
with splendor and majesty.
11 "Pour out [a]the overflowings
of your anger,
And look on everyone
who is [b]proud, and
make him low.
12 "Look on everyone who is
proud, *and* [a]humble him,
And [b]tread down the wicked
[1]in their place.

---

**39:24** [1]Or *swallows up* [2]Lit *believe* **39:27** [a]Jer 49:16; Ob 4 [1]Lit *mouth* **39:29** [a]Job 9:26 [1]Or *paws*, cf. Job 39:21; lit *digs* **39:30** [a]Mt 24:28; Lk 17:37 ◆**40:2** [a]Job 9:3; 10:2; 33:13; Is 45:9 [b]Job 13:3; 23:4; 31:35 **40:4** [a]Job 21:5; 29:9 **40:5** [a]Job 9:3, 15 **40:6** [a]Job 38:1 [1]Or *storm* **40:7** [a]Job 38:3 [b]Job 38:3; 42:4 **40:8** [a]Ro 3:4 [b]Job 10:3, 7; 16:11; 19:6; 27:2 [c]Job 13:18; 27:6 **40:9** [a]Job 37:5; Ps 29:3 **40:10** [a]Ps 93:1; 104:1 **40:11** [a]Is 42:25; Na 1:6, 8 [b]Is 2:12; Da 4:37 **40:12** [a]1Sa 2:7; Is 2:12; 13:11; Da 4:37 [b]Is 63:3 [1]Lit *under them*

13 "[a]Hide them in the
dust together;
Bind their faces in
the hidden *place*.
14 "Then I will also praise you,
That your own right
hand can save you.

### *Behold the Behemoth*

15 "Behold now, [1]Behemoth,
which [a]I made
along with you;
It eats grass like an ox.
16 "Behold now, its power
in its loins
And its vigor in the muscles
of its belly.
17 "It hangs its tail like a cedar;
The sinews of its thighs
are knit together.
18 "Its bones are tubes of bronze;
Its [1]limbs are like bars of iron.

19 "It is the [a]first of the
ways of God;
Let its [b]Maker bring
near its sword.
20 "Surely the mountains
[a]bring it food,
And all the beasts
of the field [b]play there.
21 "Under the lotus plants
it lies down,
In the hidden place
of the reeds and the marsh.
22 "The lotus plants cover
it with [1]shade;
The willows of the brook
surround it.
23 "If a river oppresses,
it is not alarmed;
It is secure, though
the [a]Jordan bursts
forth to its mouth.
24 "Can anyone capture it
before its eyes,
With snares can anyone
pierce *its* nose?

### *Can You Draw Out Leviathan?*

41 "[1]Can you draw out
[a,2]Leviathan with
a fishhook?
Or press down its tongue
with a cord?
2 "Can you [a]put a [1]rope
in its nose
Or pierce its jaw
with a [2]hook?
3 "Will it make many
supplications to you,
Or will he speak
to you soft words?
4 "Will it cut a covenant
with you?
Will you take it
for a slave forever?
5 "Will you play with it
as with a bird,
Or will you bind it
for your young women?
6 "Will the [1]traders
bargain over it?
Will they divide it
among the merchants?
7 "Can you fill its skin
with harpoons,
Or its head
with fishing spears?
8 "Place your hand on it;
Remember the battle; [1]you
will not do that again!

---

**40:13** [a]Is 2:10-12 **40:15** [a]Job 40:19 [1]Possibly the hippopotamus **40:18** [1]Lit *bones*
**40:19** [a]Job 41:33 [b]Job 40:15 **40:20** [a]Ps 104:14 [b]Ps 104:26 **40:22** [1]Lit *his shade* **40:23** [a]Ge 13:10
◆ **41:1** [a]Job 3:8; Ps 74:14; 104:26; Is 27:1 [1]Ch 40:25 in Heb [2]Possibly the crocodile **41:2** [a]2Ki 19:28; Is 37:29 [1]Lit *rope of rushes* [2]Or *thorn, ring* **41:6** [1]Lit *partners* **41:8** [1]Lit *do not add*

9 "[1]Behold, [2]his expectation
is a lie;
Will [3]he be laid low even
at the sight of it?
10 "No one is so fierce that he
dares to [a]arouse it;
Who then is he that can
stand before Me?
11 "Who has [a,1]given to Me
that I should repay *him*?
*Whatever* is [b]under the whole
heaven is Mine.

12 "I will not keep silence
concerning its limbs,
Or its mighty strength or
its graceful frame.
13 "Who can [1]strip off its
[2]outer armor?
Who can come with its
doubled [3]bridle?
14 "Who can open the
doors of its face?
Around its teeth there
is dreadful terror.
15 "*Its* [1]strong scales are *its* pride,
Shut up *as with* a tight seal.
16 "One is so near to another
That no air can come
between them.
17 "They cling one to another;
They are interlocked and
cannot be separated.
18 "Its sneezes flash forth light,
And its eyes are like
the [a]eyelids of the morning.
19 "Out of its mouth go
burning torches;
Sparks of fire [1]leap forth.
20 "Out of its nostrils
smoke goes forth
As *from* a boiling pot
and *burning* reeds.
21 "Its breath kindles coals,
And a flame goes forth
from its mouth.
22 "In its neck lodges strength,
And dismay leaps before it.
23 "The folds of its flesh
cling together,
Hardened upon it and
is not shaken.
24 "Its heart is as hard as a stone,
Even as hard
as a lower millstone.
25 "When it raises itself up,
the [1]mighty fear,
Because of the crashing
they are [2]bewildered.
26 "The sword that reaches
it cannot avail,
Nor the spear, the dart,
or the javelin.
27 "It regards iron as straw,
Bronze as rotten wood.
28 "The [1]arrow cannot
make it flee;
Slingstones are turned
into stubble for it.
29 "Clubs are regarded
as stubble;
It laughs at the rattling
of the javelin.
30 "Its underparts are
*like* sharp potsherds;
It [1]spreads out
*like* a threshing sledge
on the mire.
31 "It makes the depths
boil like a pot;
It makes the sea
like a jar of ointment.

**41:9** [1]Ch 41:1 in Heb [2]Job's [3]Job **41:10** [a]Job 3:8 **41:11** [a]Ro 11:35 [b]Ex 19:5; Dt 10:14; Job 9:5-10; 26:6-14; 28:24; Ps 24:1; 50:12; 1Co 10:26 [1]Lit *anticipated* **41:13** [1]Lit *uncover the face of its garment* [2]Lit *clothing* [3]Gr *mail* **41:15** [1]Lit *rows of shields* **41:18** [a]Job 3:9 **41:19** [1]Lit *escape* **41:25** [1]Or *gods* [2]Lit as if in *sin* **41:28** [1]Lit *son of the bow* **41:30** [1]Or *moves across*

32 "Behind it, it makes a
wake to shine;
One would think the deep
to be gray-haired.
33 "[a]There is nothing
upon the [1]dust like it,
One made without terror.
34 "[1]It looks on everything
that is high;
It is king over all
the [a]sons of pride."

### *Job Repents in Dust and Ashes*

42 Then Job answered Yahweh
and said,
2 "I know that [a]You can
do all things,
And that no purpose
of Yours can be thwarted.
3 'Who is this
that [a]hides counsel
without knowledge?'
Therefore I have declared that
which I did not understand,
Things [b]too marvelous
for me, which I did not know.
4 'Hear, now, and I will speak;
I will [a]ask You, and You
make me know.'
5 "I have [a]heard of You
by the hearing of the ear;
But now my [b]eye sees You;
6 Therefore I reject *myself*,
And I repent in dust
and ashes."

### *Yahweh's Anger Towards Job's Friends*

7 Now it happened after Yahweh
had spoken these words to Job, that
Yahweh said to Eliphaz the Temanite,
"My anger burns against you and
against your two friends because you
have not spoken of Me what is right
[a]as My servant Job has.
8 So now,
take for yourselves [a]seven bulls and
seven rams, and go to My servant
Job, and offer up a [b]burnt offering
for yourselves, and My servant Job
will [c]pray for you. [d]For I will [1]accept
him so that I may not do with you
*according to your* folly, because you
have not spoken of Me what is right,
as My servant Job has."
9 So Eliphaz
the Temanite and Bildad the Shuhite
*and* Zophar the Naamathite went
and did as Yahweh told them; and
Yahweh [1]accepted Job.

### *Yahweh Restores Job's Fortunes*

10 And Yahweh [a]restored the fortunes
of Job when he prayed for his friends,
and Yahweh increased all that Job had
twofold.
11 Then all his [a]brothers and
all his sisters and all who had known
him before came to him, and they
ate bread with him in his house; and
they [b]consoled him and comforted
him for all the calamity that Yahweh
had brought on him. And each one
gave him one [1]qesitah, and each a
ring of gold.
12 [a]And Yahweh blessed
the latter *days* of Job more than his
beginning; [b]and he had 14,000 sheep
and 6,000 camels and 1,000 pairs
of oxen and 1,000 female donkeys.
13 [a]He also had seven sons and three
daughters.
14 And he named the first
Jemimah and the second Keziah and
the third Keren-happuch.
15 Now in

**41:33** [a]Job 40:19 [1]Or *earth* **41:34** [a]Job 28:8 [1]Ch 41:26 in Heb ◆ **42:2** [a]Ge 18:14; Mt 19:26 **42:3** [a]Job 38:2 [b]Ps 40:5; 131:1; 139:6 **42:4** [a]Job 38:3; 40:7 **42:5** [a]Job 26:14; Ro 10:17 [b]Is 6:5; Eph 1:17, 18 **42:7** [a]Job 40:3-5; 42:1-6 **42:8** [a]Nu 23:1 [b]Job 1:5 [c]Ge 20:17; Jas 5:16; 1Jn 5:16 [d]Job 22:30 [1]Lit *lift up his face* **42:9** [1]Lit *lifted up the face of* **42:10** [a]Dt 30:3; Job 1:2, 3; Ps 14:7; 85:1-3; 126:1-6 **42:11** [a]Job 19:13 [b]Job 2:11 [1]Ancient currency, cf. Ge 33:19; Jos 24:32 **42:12** [a]Job 1:10; 8:7; Jas 5:11 [b]Job 1:3 **42:13** [a]Job 1:2

all the land no women were found so
beautiful as Job's daughters; and their
father gave them inheritance among
their brothers. 16 And after this, Job
lived 140 years and saw his sons and
his grandsons, four generations.
17 [a]Then Job died, an old man and
full of days.

42:17 [a]Ge 15:15; 25:8; Job 5:26

# THE PSALMS

The following expressions occur often in the Psalms:

**Selah** Possibly indicates *Pause, Crescendo*, or *Musical Interlude*
**Maskil** Possibly *Contemplative, Didactic*, or *Skillful Psalm*
**Mikhtam** Possibly *Epigrammatic Poem* or *Atonement Psalm*

## BOOK 1

### PSALM 1

***The Way of the Righteous and Wicked***

**1** How blessed is the man
who [a]does not walk
in the [b]counsel of the wicked,
Nor stand in the [c]way
of sinners,
Nor [d]sit in the seat
of scoffers!
**2** But his [a]delight is [b]in the law
of [1]Yahweh,
And in His law he meditates
[c]day and [d]night.
**3** And he will be like [a]a
tree *firmly* planted
by [1]streams of water,
Which yields its fruit
in its season
And its [2]leaf does not wither;
And [3]in whatever he does,
[b]he prospers.

**4** The wicked are not so,
*But they are like* [a]chaff
which the wind drives away.
**5** Therefore [a]the wicked will
not rise in the [b]judgment,
Nor sinners
in [c]the congregation
of the righteous.
**6** For Yahweh [a,1]knows the way
of the righteous,
But the way of [b]the wicked
will perish.

### PSALM 2

***The Reign of Yahweh's Anointed***

**1** Why do [a]the [1]nations rage
And the peoples [b]meditate
on a vain thing?
**2** The [a]kings of the earth
take their stand
And the rulers take
counsel together
[b]Against Yahweh and
against His [c,1]Anointed, *saying*,
**3** "Let us [a]tear their
fetters apart
And cast away their
cords from us!"

**4** He who [1]sits
in the heavens [a]laughs,
The Lord [b]mocks them.
**5** Then He speaks to them
in His [a]anger

---

◆ **1:1** [a]Pr 4:14 [b]Ps 5:9, 10; 10:2-11; 36:1-4 [c]Ps 17:4; 119:104 [d]Ps 26:4, 5; Jer 15:17 **1:2** [a]Ps 119:14, 16, 35 [b]Jos 1:8 [c]Ps 25:5 [d]Ps 63:5, 6 [1]The personal covenant name of God, a form of I AM WHO I AM, cf. Ex 3:14-15 **1:3** [a]Ps 92:12-14; Jer 17:8; Eze 19:10 [b]Ge 39:2, 3, 23; Ps 128:2 [1]Or *canals* [2]Or *foliage* [3]Or *all that he does prospers* **1:4** [a]Job 21:18; Ps 35:5; Is 17:13 **1:5** [a]Ps 5:5 [b]Ps 9:7, 8, 16 [c]Ps 89:5, 7 **1:6** [a]Ps 37:18; Na 1:7; Jn 10:14; 2Ti 2:19 [b]Ps 9:5, 6; 11:6 [1]Or *approves, has regard to* ◆ **2:1** [a]Ps 46:6; 83:2-5; Ac 4:25, 26 [b]Ps 21:11 [1]Or *Gentiles* **2:2** [a]Ps 48:4-6 [b]Ps 74:18, 23 [c]Jn 1:41 [1]Or *Messiah* **2:3** [a]Jer 5:5 **2:4** [a]Ps 37:13 [b]Ps 59:8 [1]Or *is enthroned* **2:5** [a]Ps 21:8, 9; 76:7

And [b]terrifies them
in His fury, *saying*,
6 "But as for Me,
I have [1]installed
[a]My King
Upon Zion,
[b]My holy mountain."

7 "I will surely tell
of the [1]decree of Yahweh:
He said to Me,
'You are [a]My Son,
Today I have begotten You.
8 'Ask of Me, and [a]I will
surely give [b]the [1]nations
as Your inheritance,
And the [c]ends of the earth
as Your possession.
9 'You shall [a,1]break them
with a [2]rod of iron,
You shall [b]shatter them
like a potter's vessel.'"

10 So now, O kings,
[a]show insight;
Take warning, O [1]judges
of the earth.
11 Serve Yahweh with [a]fear
And rejoice
with [b]trembling.
12 [1]Kiss [a]the Son, lest He
become angry, and you
perish *in* the way,
For [b]His [2]wrath may
[3]soon be kindled.
How blessed are all who
[c]take refuge in Him!

## PSALM 3

### *Yahweh, Save Me*

A Psalm of David. When [†]he fled from Absalom his son.

1 O Yahweh, how [a]my
adversaries have
become many!
Many are rising up against me.
2 Many are saying [1]of my soul,
"There is no [a]salvation
for him in God." [2]Selah.

3 But You, O Yahweh,
are [a]a shield about me,
My [b]glory, and the One
who [c]lifts my head.
4 I was calling to Yahweh
with my voice,
And He [a]answered me
from [b]His holy
[1]mountain. Selah.
5 [1]I [a]lay down and slept;
I awoke, for Yahweh
sustains me.
6 I will [a]not be afraid of ten
thousands of people
Who *all* around [b]have set
themselves against me.

7 [a]Arise, O Yahweh; [b]save me,
O my God!
For You have [c]struck all my
enemies on the [1]cheek;
You [2]have [d]shattered
the teeth of the wicked.
8 [a,1]Salvation belongs
to Yahweh;

---

**2:5** [b]Ps 78:49, 50 **2:6** [a]Ps 45:6 [b]Ps 48:1, 2 [1]Or *consecrated* **2:7** [a]Ac 13:33; Heb 1:5; 5:5 [1]Or *decree: Yahweh said to Me* **2:8** [a]Ps 21:1, 2 [b]Ps 22:27 [c]Ps 67:7 [1]Or *Gentiles* **2:9** [a]Ps 89:23; 110:5, 6; Rev 2:26, 27; 12:5; 19:15 [b]Ps 28:5; 52:5; 72:4 [1]Or *rule* [2]Or *scepter, staff* **2:10** [a]Pr 8:15; 27:11 [1]Or leaders **2:11** [a]Ps 5:7 [b]Ps 119:119, 120 **2:12** [a]Ps 2:7 [b]Rev 6:16, 17 [c]Ps 5:11; 34:22 [1]Some ancient versions *Do homage purely, Lay hold of instruction* [2]Or *anger*, cf. 2:5 [3]Or *quickly, easily* ◆ **3:TITLE** [†]2Sa 15:13-17, 29 **3:1** [a]2Sa 15:12; Ps 69:4 **3:2** [a]Ps 22:7, 8; 71:11 [1]Or *to* [2]*Selah* may mean *Pause, Crescendo, Musical Interlude* **3:3** [a]Ps 5:12; 28:7 [b]Ps 62:7 [c]Ps 9:13; 27:6 **3:4** [a]Ps 4:3; 34:4 [b]Ps 2:6; 15:1; 43:3 [1]Or *hill* **3:5** [a]Lv 26:6; Ps 4:8; Pr 3:24 [1]Or *As for me, I* **3:6** [a]Ps 23:4; 27:3 [b]Ps 118:10-13 **3:7** [a]Ps 7:6 [b]Ps 6:4; 22:21 [c]Job 16:10 [d]Ps 57:4; 58:6 [1]Or *jaw* [2]Or *shatter* **3:8** [a]Ps 28:8; 35:3; Is 43:11 [1]Or *Deliverance*

Your [b]blessing [2]*be*
upon Your people! Selah.

## PSALM 4

### *Yahweh Makes Me Abide in Safety*

[†]For the choir director. With stringed instruments. A Psalm of David.

1 [a]Answer me
when [b]I call, O God
[1]of my righteousness!
You have [c,2]relieved me
in *my* distress;
Be [d]gracious to me
and [e]hear my prayer.

2 O sons of men,
how long will [a]my glory
become [b]a reproach?
*How long* will you love
[c]what is worthless
and seek [d]falsehood? [1]Selah.
3 But know that Yahweh
has [a,1]set apart the [b]holy
one for Himself;
Yahweh [c]hears
when I call to Him.

4 [a,1]Tremble, [b,2]and do not sin;
[c,3]Ponder in your heart
upon your bed,
and be still. Selah.
5 Offer [1]the [a]sacrifices
of righteousness,
And [b]trust in Yahweh.

6 Many are saying, "[a]Who
will show us good?"
[b]Lift up the light of Your
face upon us, O Yahweh!
7 You have put [a]gladness
in my heart,
More than when their grain
and new wine abound.
8 In peace I will [1]both [a]lie
down and sleep,
For You alone, O Yahweh,
make me to [b]abide in safety.

## PSALM 5

### *Lead Me in Your Righteousness*

For the choir director. For [†]the flutes. A Psalm of David.

1 [a]Give ear to my words,
O Yahweh,
Consider my [b]meditation.
2 Give heed to [a]the sound
of my cry for help,
[b]my King and my God,
For to You I pray.
3 O Yahweh,
in the morning, [1]You
will hear my voice;
In the [a]morning I will
order *my* [2]*prayer* to You
and *eagerly* [b]watch.

4 For You are not a God [a]who
delights in wickedness;
[b]Evil does not sojourn
with You.
5 The [a]boastful shall not
[b]stand before Your eyes;
You [c]hate all workers
of iniquity.

---

**3:8** [b]Ps 29:11 [2]Or *is* ◆ **4:TITLE** [†]Belonging to the choir director's anthology **4:1** [a]Ps 3:4; 17:6 [b]Ps 18:6 [c]Ps 18:18, 19 [d]Ps 25:16 [e]Ps 17:6; 39:12 [1]Who maintains my right [2]Lit *made room for* **4:2** [a]Ps 3:3 [b]Ps 69:7-10, 19, 20 [c]Ps 12:2; 31:6 [d]Ps 31:18 [1]*Selah* may mean *Pause, Crescendo, Musical Interlude* **4:3** [a]Ps 135:4 [b]Ps 31:23; 50:5; 79:2 [c]Ps 6:8, 9; 17:6 [1]Or *dealt wonderfully with* **4:4** [a]Ps 99:1 [b]Ps 119:11; Eph 4:26 [c]Ps 77:6 [1]With anger or fear [2]Or *but* [3]Lit *Speak* **4:5** [a]Dt 33:19; Ps 51:19 [b]Ps 37:3, 5; 62:8 [1]Or *righteous sacrifices* **4:6** [a]Job 7:7; 9:25 [b]Nu 6:26; Ps 80:3, 7, 19 **4:7** [a]Ps 97:11, 12; Is 9:3; Ac 14:17 **4:8** [a]Job 11:19; Ps 3:5 [b]Lv 25:18; Dt 12:10; Ps 16:9 [1]Or *at the same time* ◆ **5:TITLE** [†]Heb *Nehiloth* **5:1** [a]Ps 54:2 [b]Ps 104:34 **5:2** [a]Ps 140:6 [b]Ps 84:3 **5:3** [a]Ps 88:13 [b]Ps 130:5 [1]Or *May You hear* [2]Or sacrifice **5:4** [a]Ps 11:5; 34:16 [b]Ps 92:15 **5:5** [a]Ps 73:3; 75:4 [b]Ps 1:5 [c]Ps 11:5; 45:7

6 You [a]destroy those
who speak falsehood;
Yahweh abhors [b]the man
of bloodshed and deceit.
7 But as for me,
[a]in the abundance of Your
lovingkindness I will
enter Your house,
[1]At Your holy temple I will
[b]worship in [c]fear of You.

8 O Yahweh, [a]lead me
[b]in Your righteousness
[c]because of [1]my foes;
Make Your way [2]straight
before me.
9 There is [a]nothing [1]reliable
in their mouth;
Their [b]inward part is
destruction *itself*.
Their [c]throat is
an open grave;
They [2]flatter
with their tongue.
10 Hold them guilty, O God;
[a]By their own devices
let them fall!
In the abundance
of their transgressions
[b]thrust them out,
For they are [c]rebellious
against You.

11 But let all who [a]take refuge
in You [b]be glad,
Let them ever sing for joy;
And [1]may You [c]shelter them,
That those who [d]love Your
name may exult in You.
12 For it is You who [a]blesses
the righteous one, O Yahweh,
You [b]surround him with favor
as with a large shield.

## PSALM 6

### *Yahweh, Rescue My Soul*

For the choir director. With stringed instruments. According to the [†]Sheminith. A Psalm of David.

1 O Yahweh, [a]do not reprove
me in Your anger,
Nor discipline me
in Your wrath.
2 Be gracious to me, O Yahweh,
for I *am* [a]pining away;
[b]Heal me, O Yahweh,
for [c]my bones are dismayed.
3 And my [a]soul
is greatly dismayed;
But You, O Yahweh—
[b]how long?

4 Return, O Yahweh,
[a]rescue my [1]soul;
Save me because
of Your lovingkindness.
5 For [a]there is no remembrance
of You in death;
In Sheol who will give
You thanks?

6 I am [a]weary with my sighing;
Every night I make
my bed swim,
I flood my couch
with [b]my tears.
7 My [a]eye has wasted
away with grief;

---

**5:6** [a]Ps 52:4, 5 [b]Ps 55:23 **5:7** [a]Ps 69:13 [b]Ps 138:2 [c]Ps 115:11, 13 [1]Or *Toward* **5:8** [a]Ps 31:3 [b]Ps 31:1 [c]Ps 27:11 [1]Or *those who lie in wait for me* [2]Or *smooth* **5:9** [a]Ps 52:3 [b]Ps 7:14 [c]Ro 3:13 [1]Or *true* [2]Or *make their tongue smooth* **5:10** [a]Ps 9:16 [b]Ps 36:12 [c]Ps 107:10, 11 **5:11** [a]Ps 2:12 [b]Ps 33:1; 64:10 [c]Ps 12:7 [d]Ps 69:36 [1]Or *You shelter* **5:12** [a]Ps 29:11 [b]Ps 32:7, 10 ◆ **6:TITLE** [†]Possibly an eight-string instrument or a title for a tune, cf. 1Chr 15:21 **6:1** [a]Ps 38:1; 118:18 **6:2** [a]Ps 102:4, 11 [b]Ps 41:4; 147:3; Hos 6:1 [c]Ps 22:14; 31:10 **6:3** [a]Ps 88:3; Jn 12:27 [b]Ps 90:13 **6:4** [a]Ps 17:13 [1]Or *life* **6:5** [a]Ps 30:9; 88:10-12; 115:17; Ecc 9:10; Is 38:18 **6:6** [a]Ps 69:3 [b]Ps 42:3 **6:7** [a]Job 17:7; Ps 31:9; 38:10

It has become old because
of all my adversaries.

8 [a]Depart from me, all you
workers of iniquity,
For Yahweh [b]has heard
the sound of my weeping.
9 Yahweh [a]has heard
my supplication,
Yahweh [b]receives my prayer.
10 All my enemies will
[a]be ashamed and
greatly dismayed;
They shall [1]turn back, they
will [b]suddenly be ashamed.

### PSALM 7

***In You I Have Taken Refuge***

A [†]Shiggaion of David, which he sang to Yahweh concerning the words of Cush, a Benjamite.

1 O Yahweh my God, [a]in You
I have taken refuge;
Save me from all those who
pursue me, and [b]deliver me,
2 Lest he tear [1]my soul
[a]like a lion,
Rending me in pieces, while
there is none to deliver.

3 O Yahweh my God,
if I have done this,
If there is [a]injustice
in my hands,
4 If I have [a]rewarded evil to him
who [1]is at peace with me,
Or have [b]plundered my
adversary without cause,
5 Let the enemy pursue [1]my
soul and overtake [2]*it*;
And let him trample my
life down to the ground
And cause my glory to dwell
in the dust. [3]Selah.

6 [a]Arise, O Yahweh,
in Your anger;
[b]Lift up Yourself against [c]the
fury of my adversaries,
And [d]arouse Yourself
[1]for me; You have
appointed judgment.
7 Let the congregation of
the [a]peoples encompass You,
And over [1]them return on high.
8 Yahweh [a]judges the peoples;
[b,1]Give justice to me,
O Yahweh, according
to my righteousness and my
integrity that is in me.
9 O let [a]the evil of the wicked
come to an end,
but [b]establish the righteous;
For the righteous God [c]tests
the hearts and [1]minds.
10 My [a]shield is [1]with God,
Who [b]saves the upright
in heart.
11 God is a [a]righteous judge,
And a God who has
[b]indignation every day.

12 If [1]a man [a]does not repent,
He will [b]sharpen His sword;
He has [c]bent His bow
and prepared it.

**6:8** [a]Ps 119:115; Mt 7:23; Lk 13:27 [b]Ps 3:4; 28:6 **6:9** [a]Ps 116:1 [b]Ps 66:19, 20 **6:10** [a]Ps 71:13, 24 [b]Ps 73:19 [1]Or *again be ashamed suddenly* ◆ **7:TITLE** [†]Possibly a wild, passionate, and animated song **7:1** [a]Ps 31:1; 71:1 [b]Ps 31:15 **7:2** [a]Ps 57:4; Is 38:13 [1]Or *me* **7:3** [a]1Sa 24:11 **7:4** [a]Ps 109:4, 5 [b]1Sa 24:7; 26:9 [1]Lit *was* **7:5** [1]Or *me* [2]Or me [3]*Selah* may mean *Pause, Crescendo, Musical Interlude* **7:6** [a]Ps 3:7 [b]Ps 94:2 [c]Ps 138:7 [d]Ps 35:23; 44:23 [1]One ancient version *O my God* **7:7** [a]Ps 22:27 [1]Lit *it* **7:8** [a]Ps 96:13; 98:9 [b]Ps 18:20; 26:1; 35:24; 43:1 [1]Lit *Judge* **7:9** [a]Ps 34:21; 94:23 [b]Ps 37:23; 40:2 [c]Ps 11:4, 5; Jer 11:20; Rev 2:23 [1]Lit *kidneys*, figurative for inner man **7:10** [a]Ps 18:2, 30 [b]Ps 97:10, 11; 125:4 [1]Lit *upon* **7:11** [a]Ps 50:6 [b]Ps 90:9 **7:12** [a]Ps 58:5 [b]Dt 32:41 [c]Ps 64:7 [1]Lit *he*

13 He has also prepared
[1]for Himself deadly weapons;
He makes His [a]arrows
fiery shafts.
14 Behold, he travails
with wickedness,
And he [a]conceives
mischief and gives
birth to falsehood.
15 He has dug a pit
and hollowed it out,
And has [a]fallen into the hole
which he made.
16 His [a]mischief will return
upon his own head,
And his [b]violence will descend
upon [1]his own skull.

17 I will give thanks
to Yahweh [a]according
to His righteousness
And will [b]sing praise to the
name of Yahweh Most High.

## PSALM 8

### *How Majestic Is Your Name*

For the choir director. According to the Gittith. A Psalm of David.

1 O Yahweh, our Lord,
How majestic is Your
name in all the earth,
Who [a,1]displays Your splendor
above the heavens!
2 [a]From the mouth of infants
and nursing babies You have
established [b,1]strength
Because of Your adversaries,
To make [c]the enemy and
the revengeful cease.
3 When I [a]see [b]Your heavens,
the work of Your fingers,
The [c]moon and the stars,
which You have established;
4 [a]What is man that You
remember him,
And the son of man
that You care for him?
5 Yet You have made
him a [a]little lower
than *the* [1]angels,
And [b]You crown him
with [c]glory and majesty!
6 You make him to [a]rule over
the works of Your hands;
You have [b]put all things
under his feet,
7 All sheep and oxen,
And also the animals
of the field,
8 The birds of the heavens
and the fish of the sea,
Whatever passes through
the paths of the seas.

9 [a]O Yahweh, our Lord,
How majestic is Your
name in all the earth!

## PSALM 9

### *Yahweh Will Judge the World in Righteousness*

For the choir director. [†]Almuth-labben. A Psalm of David.

א *Aleph*

1 [1]I will give thanks to Yahweh
with all [a]my heart;
I will [b]recount all Your
[2]wondrous deeds.

---

**7:13** [a]Ps 18:14; 45:5 [1]Or *His deadly weapons* **7:14** [a]Job 15:35; Is 59:4; Jas 1:15 **7:15** [a]Job 4:8; Ps 57:6
**7:16** [a]Es 9:25; Ps 140:9 [b]Ps 140:11 [1]The crown of his own head **7:17** [a]Ps 71:15, 16 [b]Ps 9:2; 66:1, 2, 4
◆ **8:1** [a]Ps 57:5, 11; 113:4; 148:13 [1]Or *set* **8:2** [a]Mt 21:16; 1Co 1:27 [b]Ps 29:1; 118:14 [c]Ps 44:16 [1]Or *a bulwark*
**8:3** [a]Ps 111:2 [b]Ps 89:11; 144:5 [c]Ps 136:9 **8:4** [a]Job 7:17; Ps 144:3; Heb 2:6-8 **8:5** [a]Ge 1:26; Ps 82:6
[b]Ps 103:4 [c]Ps 21:5 [1]Or *God*; Heb *Elohim* **8:6** [a]Ge 1:26, 28 [b]1Co 15:27; Eph 1:22; Heb 2:8 **8:9** [a]Ps 8:1
◆ **9:TITLE** [†]Or *According to the Death of the Son*; possibly a title for a tune **9:1** [a]Ps 86:12 [b]Ps 26:7
[1]This poem loosely follows an acrostic pattern [2]Or *miracles*

א *Aleph*

2 I will be glad and [a]exult in You;
I will [b]sing praise to Your
name, O [c]Most High.

ב *Beth*

3 When my enemies turn back,
They stumble and
[a]perish before You.
4 For You have [a]maintained
my [1]justice and my cause;
You have sat on the throne
[b,2]judging righteously.

ג *Gimel*

5 You have [a]rebuked
the nations, You have
made the wicked perish;
You have [b]blotted out their
name forever and ever.

ה *He*

6 [1]The enemy has come to
an end in perpetual [2]ruins,
And You have uprooted
the cities;
The very [a]memory
of them has perished.

ו *Vav*

7 But [a]Yahweh [1]abides forever;
He has established His
[b]throne for judgment,

ו *Vav*

8 And He will [a]judge the world
in righteousness;
He will render justice
for the peoples with equity.

ו *Vav*

9 [1]Yahweh also will be a
[a]stronghold for the oppressed,
A stronghold in times
of [2]distress;

ו *Vav*

10 And [1]those who [a]know
Your name will put
their trust in You,
For You, O Yahweh, have not
[b]forsaken those who seek You.

ז *Zayin*

11 Sing praises to Yahweh,
who [a]abides in Zion;
[b]Declare among
the peoples His acts.
12 For [a]He who [1]requires
blood remembers them;
He does not forget [b]the
cry of the afflicted.

ח *Heth*

13 Be gracious to me, O Yahweh;
See my affliction
from those [a]who hate me,
You who [b]lift me up
from the gates of death,
14 That I may recount
[a]all Your praises,
That in the gates
of the daughter of Zion
I may [b]rejoice
in Your [1]salvation.

ט *Teth*

15 The nations have sunk
down [a]in the pit
which they have made;
In the [b]net which they
hid, their own foot
has been caught.
16 Yahweh has [a]made
Himself known;

---

**9:2** [a]Ps 5:11; 104:34 [b]Ps 66:2, 4 [c]Ps 83:18; 92:1 **9:3** [a]Ps 27:2 **9:4** [a]Ps 140:12 [b]Ps 50:6 [1]Or *right* [2]Or *a righteous Judge* **9:5** [a]Ps 119:21 [b]Ps 69:28; Pr 10:7 **9:6** [a]Ps 34:16 [1]Or *O enemy, desolations are finished forever; And their cities You have plucked up* [2]Or *waste places* **9:7** [a]Ps 10:16 [b]Ps 89:14 [1]Or *sits* as king **9:8** [a]Ps 96:13; 98:9 **9:9** [a]Ps 32:7; 59:9, 16, 17 [1]Or *Let Yahweh also be* [2]Or *trouble* **9:10** [a]Ps 91:14 [b]Ps 37:28; 94:14 [1]Or *let those...name put* **9:11** [a]Ps 76:2 [b]Ps 105:1; 107:22 **9:12** [a]Ge 9:5; Ps 72:14 [b]Ps 9:18 [1]Avenges bloodshed **9:13** [a]Ps 38:19 [b]Ps 30:3; 86:13 **9:14** [a]Ps 106:2 [b]Ps 13:5; 20:5; 35:9; 51:12 [1]Or *deliverance* **9:15** [a]Ps 7:15, 16 [b]Ps 57:6 **9:16** [a]Ex 7:5

He has [b]executed judgment.
In the work of his own hands
the wicked is snared.
[1]Higgaion [2]Selah.

י *Yodh*

17 The wicked will
[a,1]return to Sheol,
*Even* all the nations
who [b]forget God.

כ *Kaph*

18 For the [a]needy will not
always be forgotten,
Nor the [b]hope of the afflicted
perish forever.
19 [a]Arise, O Yahweh, do
not let man prevail;
Let the nations be
[b]judged before You.
20 Put them [a]in fear, O Yahweh;
Let the nations know that they
are [b]but men. Selah.

## PSALM 10

### *Do Not Forget the Afflicted*

ל *Lamedh*

1 [1]Why [a]do You stand afar off,
O Yahweh?
Why [b]do You hide [2]*Yourself*
in times of distress?
2 In *his* [a]lofty pride the wicked
[1]hotly pursues the afflicted;
[2]Let them be [b]caught
in the thoughts
which they have devised.

3 For the wicked [a]boasts
of his [b]soul's desire,
And [1]the greedy man curses
*and* [c]spurns Yahweh.
4 The wicked,
in the haughtiness
of his countenance,
[a]does not seek *Him*.
All his [1]thoughts are,
"[b]There is no God."

5 His ways [a,1]prosper at all times;
Your judgments are on high,
[b]out of his sight;
As for all his adversaries,
he snorts at them.
6 He says in his heart,
"[a]I will not be shaken;
[1]From generation
to generation [b]I will not
be in adversity."

פ *Pe*

7 His [a]mouth is full of curses
and deceit and [b]oppression;
[c]Under his tongue is mischief
and wickedness.

ע *Ayin*

8 He sits in the [a,1]places
of the villages
*where one* lies in wait;
In the hiding places he
[b]kills the innocent;
His eyes [2]stealthily watch
for the [c,3]unfortunate.
9 He lies in wait in a hiding
place as [a]a lion in his [1]lair;
He [b]lies in wait to catch
[c]the afflicted;
He catches the afflicted when
he draws him into his [d]net.

---

**9:16** [b]Ps 9:4 [1]Possibly resounding music or meditation [2]*Selah* may mean *Pause, Crescendo, Musical Interlude* **9:17** [a]Ps 49:14 [b]Job 8:13; Ps 50:22 [1]Or *turn* **9:18** [a]Ps 9:12; 12:5 [b]Ps 62:5; 71:5; Pr 23:18 **9:19** [a]Nu 10:35 [b]Ps 9:5 **9:20** [a]Ps 14:5 [b]Ps 62:9 ◆**10:1** [a]Ps 22:1 [b]Ps 13:1; 55:1 [1]This poem continues acrostic pattern started in Ps 9 [2]Or Your eyes **10:2** [a]Ps 73:6, 8 [b]Ps 7:16; 9:16 [1]Lit *burn* [2]Or *They will be caught* **10:3** [a]Ps 49:6; 94:3, 4 [b]Ps 112:10 [c]Ps 10:13 [1]Or *blesses the greedy man* **10:4** [a]Ps 10:13; 36:2 [b]Ps 14:1; 36:1 [1]Or *plots* **10:5** [a]Ps 52:7 [b]Ps 28:5 [1]Lit *are strong* **10:6** [a]Ps 49:11; Ecc 8:11 [b]Rev 18:7 [1]Lit *To* **10:7** [a]Ro 3:14 [b]Ps 73:8 [c]Job 20:12; Ps 140:3 **10:8** [a]Ps 11:2 [b]Ps 94:6 [c]Ps 72:12 [1]Lit *place of lying in wait* [2]Lit *lie hidden* [3]Or *poor* **10:9** [a]Ps 17:12 [b]Ps 59:3; Mic 7:2 [c]Ps 10:2 [d]Ps 140:5 [1]Or *thicket*

10 He [1]crouches,
he [2]bows down,
And the [3]unfortunate fall
[4]by his mighty ones.
11 He [a]says in his heart,
"God has forgotten;
He has hidden His face;
He will never see it."

ק *Qoph*

12 Arise, O Yahweh; O God,
[a]lift up Your hand.
[b]Do not forget the afflicted.
13 Why has the wicked
[a]spurned God?
He has said in his heart,
"You will not require *it*."

ר *Resh*

14 You have seen *it*, for You
have beheld [a]mischief
and vexation to [1]take
it into Your hand.
The [b,2]unfortunate commits
*himself* to You;
You have been the [c]helper
of the orphan.

ש *Shin*

15 [a]Break the arm of the wicked
and the evildoer,
[b,1]Seek out his wickedness
until You find none.

16 Yahweh is [a]King
forever and ever;
[b]Nations have perished
from His land.

ת *Tav*

17 O Yahweh, You have heard
the [a]desire of the [1]humble;
You will [b]strengthen their
heart, [c]You will cause
Your ear to give heed
18 To give justice to the [a]orphan
and the [b]oppressed,
So that man who is
of the earth will no
longer cause [c]terror.

## PSALM 11

### *Yahweh Is in His Holy Temple*

For the choir director. Of David.

1 In Yahweh I [a]take refuge;
How can you say to my
soul, "Flee *as* a bird
to your [b]mountain;
2 For, behold, the wicked
[a]bend the bow,
They [b,1]make ready their
arrow upon the string
To [c]shoot in darkness
at the upright in heart.
3 "If the [a]foundations
are destroyed,
What can the righteous do?"

4 Yahweh is in His [a]holy
temple; [1]Yahweh's
[b]throne is in heaven;
His [c]eyes behold,
His eyelids test
the sons of men.
5 Yahweh [a]tests
the righteous,
But [b]the wicked and
the one who loves
violence His soul hates.
6 May He [a]rain [1]snares
upon the wicked;

**10:10** [1]Or *is crushed* [2]Or *is bowed down* [3]Or *poor* [4]Or *into his claws* **10:11** [a]Ps 10:4 **10:12** [a]Ps 17:7; Mic 5:9 [b]Ps 9:12 **10:13** [a]Ps 10:3 **10:14** [a]Ps 10:7 [b]Ps 22:11 [c]Ps 68:5 [1]Lit *give* [2]Or *poor* **10:15** [a]Ps 37:17 [b]Ps 140:11 [1]Or *May You seek* **10:16** [a]Ps 29:10 [b]Dt 8:20 **10:17** [a]Ps 9:18 [b]1Chr 29:18 [c]Ps 34:15 [1]Or *afflicted*, cf. Ps 10:12 **10:18** [a]Ps 146:9 [b]Ps 9:9; 74:21 [c]Is 29:20 ◆ **11:1** [a]Ps 2:12 [b]Ps 121:1 **11:2** [a]Ps 7:12; 37:14 [b]Ps 64:3 [c]Ps 64:4 [1]Or *fixed* **11:3** [a]Ps 82:5; 87:1; 119:152 **11:4** [a]Ps 18:6; Mic 1:2; Hab 2:20 [b]Ps 103:19; Is 66:1; Mt 5:34; Rev 4:2 [c]Ps 33:18; 34:15, 16 [1]Lit *Yahweh, His throne* **11:5** [a]Ge 22:1; Ps 34:19; Jas 1:12 [b]Ps 5:5 **11:6** [a]Ps 18:13, 14 [1]Or *coals of fire*

[b]Fire and brimstone and
[c]burning wind will be
the portion of [d]their cup.
7 For Yahweh is [a]righteous,
[b]He loves [1]righteousness;
The upright will
[c]behold His face.

## PSALM 12

### *Yahweh Will Set the Needy in Safety*

For the choir director. According to the [†]Sheminith. A Psalm of David.

1 Save, O Yahweh, for [a]the
holy man ceases to be,
For the faithful disappear from
among the sons of men.
2 They [a]speak worthlessness
to one another;
With a [b]flattering lip and with
a double heart they speak.
3 May Yahweh cut off all
flattering lips,
The tongue that [a]speaks
great things;
4 Who [a]have said, "With our
tongue we will prevail;
Our lips are [1]our own;
who is lord over us?"
5 "Because of the [a]devastation
of the afflicted, because
of the groaning of the needy,
Now [b]I will arise," says
Yahweh; "I will [c]set
him in the [1]safety
for which he [2]longs."

6 The [a]words of Yahweh
are pure words;
As silver [b]tried in a furnace
on the ground, refined
seven times.
7 You, O Yahweh,
will keep them;
You will [a]guard him
from this generation forever.
8 The [a]wicked strut about
on every side
When [b,1]vileness is exalted
among the sons of men.

## PSALM 13

### *How Long, O Yahweh?*

For the choir director. A Psalm of David.

1 How long, O Yahweh? Will
You [a]forget me forever?
How long [b]will You hide
Your face from me?
2 How long shall I [a]take
counsel in my soul,
*Having* [b]sorrow in my
heart all the day?
How long will my enemy
be exalted over me?

3 [a]Look *and* answer me,
O Yahweh my God;
[b]Give light to my eyes,
lest I [c]sleep the *sleep*
*of* death,
4 Lest my enemy [a]says,
"I have overcome him,"
*And* [b]my adversaries rejoice
that I am shaken.

5 But I have [a]trusted
in Your lovingkindness;

---

**11:6** [b]Ge 19:24; Eze 38:22 [c]Jer 4:11, 12 [d]Ps 75:8 **11:7** [a]Ps 7:9, 11 [b]Ps 33:5; 45:7 [c]Ps 16:11; 17:15 [1]Or *righteous deeds* ◆ **12:TITLE** [†]Possibly an eight-string instrument or a title for a tune, cf. 1Chr 15:21 **12:1** [a]Is 57:1; Mic 7:2 **12:2** [a]Ps 10:7; 41:6 [b]Ps 28:3; 55:21; Jer 9:8; Ro 16:18 **12:3** [a]Da 7:8; Rev 13:5 **12:4** [a]Ps 73:8, 9 [1]Lit *with us* **12:5** [a]Ps 9:9; 10:18 [b]Is 33:10 [c]Ps 34:6; 35:10 [1]Or *salvation,* cf. 12:1 [2]Lit *breathes* **12:6** [a]2Sa 22:31; Ps 18:30; 19:8, 10; 119:140 [b]Pr 30:5 **12:7** [a]Ps 37:28; 97:10 **12:8** [a]Ps 55:10, 11 [b]Is 32:5 [1]Or *worthlessness* ◆ **13:1** [a]Ps 44:24 [b]Job 13:24; Ps 89:46 **13:2** [a]Ps 42:4 [b]Ps 42:9 **13:3** [a]Ps 5:1 [b]1Sa 14:29; Ezr 9:8; Job 33:30; Ps 18:28 [c]Jer 51:39 **13:4** [a]Ps 12:4 [b]Ps 25:2; 38:16 **13:5** [a]Ps 52:8

My heart shall [b]rejoice
in Your salvation.
6 I will [a]sing to Yahweh,
Because He has [b]dealt
bountifully with me.

## PSALM 14

### *There Is No One Who Does Good*

For the choir director. Of David.

1 The [1]wicked fool [a]says in his
heart, "There is no God."
They act corruptly, they
commit abominable [2]deeds;
There is [b]no one who does good.
2 Yahweh [a]looks down
from heaven
upon the sons of men
To see if there is anyone
who [b,1]has insight,
Anyone who [c]seeks after God.
3 They have all [a]turned aside,
altogether they have
become [1]worthless;
There is [b]no one who does
good, not even one.

4 Do all the workers
of iniquity [a]not know,
Who [b]eat up my people
*as* they eat bread,
*And* [c]do not call
upon Yahweh?
5 There they are in great dread,
For God is with the
[a]righteous generation.
6 You would put to shame
the counsel of the afflicted,
But Yahweh is his [a]refuge.
7 Oh, that [a]the salvation
of Israel [1]would come
out of Zion!
When Yahweh [b,2]restores
His captive people,
May Jacob rejoice, may
Israel be glad.

## PSALM 15

### *Who May Dwell on Your Holy Mountain?*

A Psalm of David.

1 O Yahweh, who may
[1]sojourn [a]in Your tent?
Who may dwell on Your
[b]holy mountain?
2 He who [a]walks blamelessly,
and works righteousness,
And [b]speaks truth
in his heart.
3 He [a]does not slander
[1]with his tongue,
Nor [b]does evil
to his neighbor,
Nor [c]takes up a reproach
against his friend;
4 In [1]whose eyes a reprobate
is despised,
But [2]who [a]honors those
who fear Yahweh;
He [b]swears to his own hurt
and does not change;
5 He [a]does not put out his
money [1]at interest,
Nor [b]does he take a bribe
against the innocent.
[c]He who does these things
will never be shaken.

**13:5** [b]Ps 9:14 **13:6** [a]Ps 96:1, 2 [b]Ps 116:7; 119:17; 142:7 ◆ **14:1** [a]Ps 10:4; 53:1 [b]Ps 14:1-3; 130:3; Ro 3:10-12 [1]One who rejects wisdom in rebellion against God [2]Lit *doings* **14:2** [a]Ps 33:13, 14; 102:19 [b]Ps 92:6 [c]1Chr 22:19 [1]Or *acts wisely* **14:3** [a]Ps 58:3 [b]Ps 143:2 [1]Or *corrupt* **14:4** [a]Ps 82:5 [b]Ps 27:2; Jer 10:25; Mic 3:3 [c]Ps 79:6; Is 64:7 **14:5** [a]Ps 73:15; 112:2 **14:6** [a]Ps 9:9; 40:17; 46:1; 142:5 **14:7** [a]Ps 53:6 [b]Ps 85:1, 2 [1]Lit *would be* [2]Or *restores the fortunes of His people* ◆ **15:1** [a]Ps 27:5, 6; 61:4 [b]Ps 24:3 [1]Or *abide* **15:2** [a]Ps 24:4; Is 33:15 [b]Zec 8:16; Eph 4:25 **15:3** [a]Ps 50:20 [b]Ps 28:3 [c]Ex 23:1 [1]Lit *according to* **15:4** [a]Ac 28:10 [b]Jdg 11:35 [1]Lit *his* [2]Lit *he* **15:5** [a]Ex 22:25; Lv 25:36; Dt 23:20; Eze 18:8 [b]Ex 23:8; Dt 16:19 [c]2Pe 1:10 [1]To a fellow Israelite

## PSALM 16

### *You Will Not Forsake My Soul*

A [†]Mikhtam of David.

1 [a]Keep me, O God,
for [b]I take refuge in You.
2 *O my soul,* you have said to
Yahweh, "You are [1]my Lord;
I [a]have no good without You."
3 As for the [a,1]saints who
are in the earth,
They are the majestic
ones [b]in whom is
all my delight.
4 The [a,1]pains of those who
have [2]bartered for another
*god* will be multiplied;
I shall not pour out their
drink offerings of [b]blood,
Nor will I [c]take their
names upon my lips.

5 Yahweh is the [a]portion of my
inheritance and my [b]cup;
You support my [c]lot.
6 The [a]lines have fallen
to me in pleasant places;
Indeed, my inheritance
is [b]beautiful to me.

7 I will bless Yahweh who
has [a]counseled me;
Indeed, my [b,1]mind instructs
me in the night.
8 [a]I have [b]set Yahweh
continually before me;
Because He is [c]at my right
hand, [d]I will not be shaken.
9 Therefore [a]my heart is glad
and [b]my glory rejoices;
My flesh also will
[c]dwell securely.
10 For You [a]will not forsake
my soul to Sheol;
You will not [b]give Your [1]Holy
One over to see [2]corruption.
11 You will make known
to me [a]the path of life;
In [b]Your presence is
fullness of joy;
In Your right hand there
are [c]pleasures forever.

## PSALM 17

### *In the Shadow of Your Wings*

A Prayer of David.

1 Hear a [a]righteous cause,
O Yahweh, [b]give heed
to my cry of lamentation;
[c]Give ear to my prayer, which
is not from [d]deceitful lips.
2 May [a]my [1]judgment come
from Your presence;
May Your eyes behold
[b]what is upright.
3 You have [a]tested my heart;
You have visited *me* by night;
You have [b]tried me and
[c]You find [1]nothing;
I have [d]purposed that my
mouth will not [2]transgress.
4 As for the deeds of men,
[a]by the word of Your lips
I have kept from the [b]paths
of the violent.

---

◆ **16:TITLE** [†]Possibly *Epigrammatic Poem, Atonement Psalm* **16:1** [a]Ps 17:8 [b]Ps 7:1 **16:2** [a]Ps 73:25 [1]*Or the Lord* **16:3** [a]Ps 101:6 [b]Ps 119:63 [1]Lit *holy ones* **16:4** [a]Ps 32:10 [b]Ps 106:37, 38 [c]Ex 23:13; Jos 23:7 [1]Sorrows due to idolatry [2]Or *hastened to* **16:5** [a]Ps 73:26; 119:57; 142:5; Lam 3:24 [b]Ps 23:5 [c]Ps 125:3 mg **16:6** [a]Ps 78:55 [b]Jer 3:19 **16:7** [a]Ps 73:24 [b]Ps 77:6 [1]Lit *kidneys,* figurative for inner man **16:8** [a]Ps 16:8-11; Ac 2:25-28 [b]Ps 27:8; 123:1, 2 [c]Ps 73:23; 110:5; 121:5 [d]Ps 112:6 **16:9** [a]Ps 4:7; 13:5 [b]Ps 30:12; 57:8; 108:1 [c]Ps 4:8 **16:10** [a]Ps 49:15; 86:13 [b]Ac 13:35 [1]Or *godly one* [2]Or *the pit* **16:11** [a]Ps 139:24; Mt 7:14 [b]Ps 21:6; 43:4 [c]Job 36:11; Ps 36:7, 8; 46:4 ◆ **17:1** [a]Ps 9:4 [b]Ps 61:1; 142:6 [c]Ps 88:2 [d]Is 29:13 **17:2** [a]Ps 103:6 [b]Ps 98:9; 99:4 [1]Vindication **17:3** [a]Ps 26:1, 2 [b]Job 23:10; Ps 66:10; Zec 13:9; 1Pe 1:7 [c]Jer 50:20 [d]Ps 39:1 [1]Or *no evil device in me; My mouth* [2]Lit *trespass* **17:4** [a]Ps 119:9, 101 [b]Ps 10:5-11

5 My [a]steps have held
fast to Your [1]paths.
My [b]footsteps have
not stumbled.

6 I have [a]called upon You,
for You will answer
me, O God;
[b]Incline Your ear to me,
hear my speech.
7 [a]Marvelously show Your
lovingkindnesses,
O [b]Savior of those who
take refuge [1]at Your
right hand
From those who rise
up *against them.*
8 Keep me as [1]the [a]apple
of the eye;
Hide me [b]in the shadow
of Your wings
9 From the [a]wicked who
devastate me,
My [b]deadly enemies
who surround me.
10 They have [a]closed their
[1]unfeeling *heart,*
With their mouth they
[b]speak proudly.
11 They have now [a]surrounded
us in our steps;
They set their eyes [b]to cast
*us* down to the ground.
12 He is [a]like a lion
that is eager to tear,
*And* as a young lion [b]lurking
in hiding places.
13 [a]Arise, O Yahweh, confront
him, [b]bring him low;
[c]Protect my soul
from the wicked
with [d]Your sword,
14 From men with [a]Your hand,
O Yahweh,
From men [1]of the world,
[b]whose portion is in *this* life,
And whose belly You [c]fill
with Your treasure;
They are satisfied
with children,
And leave their excess
to their infants.
15 As for me, I shall [a]behold
Your face in righteousness;
[b]I will be satisfied [1]with Your
[c]likeness when I awake.

## PSALM 18

### *Yahweh Is My Rock and My Fortress*

For the choir director. Of the servant of Yahweh, of David, [†]who spoke to Yahweh the words of this song in the day that Yahweh delivered him from the hand of all his enemies and from the hand of Saul.

1 He said, "I love You,
O Yahweh, [a]my strength."
2 Yahweh is [a]my [1]rock and [b]my
fortress and my [c]deliverer,
My God, my rock,
in whom I take refuge;
My [d]shield and the [e]horn
of my salvation,
my [f]stronghold.

---

**17:5** [a]Job 23:11; Ps 44:18; 119:133 [b]Ps 18:36; 37:31 [1]Lit *tracks* **17:6** [a]Ps 86:7; 116:2 [b]Ps 88:2 **17:7** [a]Ps 31:21 [b]Ps 20:6 [1]Or *from those who rise up...at Your right hand* **17:8** [a]Dt 32:10; Zec 2:8 [b]Ru 2:12; Ps 36:7; 57:1; 61:4; 63:7; 91:1, 4 [1]Lit *the pupil, the daughter of the eye* **17:9** [a]Ps 31:20 [b]Ps 27:12 **17:10** [a]Job 15:27; Ps 73:7 [b]1Sa 2:3; Ps 31:18; 73:8 [1]Lit *fat* **17:11** [a]Ps 88:17 [b]Ps 37:14 **17:12** [a]Ps 7:2 [b]Ps 10:9 **17:13** [a]Ps 3:7 [b]Ps 55:23 [c]Ps 22:20 [d]Ps 7:12 **17:14** [a]Ps 17:7 [b]Ps 73:3-7; Lk 16:25 [c]Ps 49:6 [1]Or *whose portion in life is of the world* **17:15** [a]Ps 11:7; 16:11; 140:13; 1Jn 3:2 [b]Ps 4:6, 7 [c]Nu 12:8 [1]Or *with* beholding ◆**18:TITLE** [†]2Sa 22:1-51 **18:1** [a]Ps 59:17 **18:2** [a]Dt 32:18; 1Sa 2:2; Ps 18:31, 46; 28:1; 31:3; 42:9; 71:3; 78:15 [b]Ps 144:2 [c]Ps 19:14 [d]Ps 28:7; 33:20; 59:11; 84:9, 11; Pr 30:5 [e]Ps 75:10 [f]Ps 59:9 [1]Or *crag*

3 I call upon Yahweh,
who is [a]worthy
to be praised,
And I am [b]saved
from my enemies.

4 The [a]cords of death
encompassed me,
And the [b]torrents
of vileness [1]terrified me.
5 The [a]cords of Sheol
surrounded me;
The snares of death
confronted me.
6 In my [a]distress I called
upon Yahweh,
And cried to my God for help;
He heard my voice
[b]out of His temple,
And my [c]cry for help before
Him came into His ears.

7 Then the [a]earth shook
and quaked;
And the [b]foundations
of the mountains
were trembling
And were shaken, because
He was angry.
8 Smoke went up
[1]out of His nostrils,
And [a]fire from His
mouth devoured;
Coals were kindled by it.
9 He [a]bowed the heavens
and came down
With thick [b]darkness
under His feet.
10 He rode upon a [a]cherub
and flew;
And He sped
upon the [b]wings of the wind.
11 He made [a]darkness His
hiding place, [b]His
[1]canopy around Him,
Darkness of waters, thick
clouds of the skies.
12 From the [a]brightness before
Him passed His thick clouds,
Hailstones and [b]coals of fire.
13 Yahweh also [a]thundered
in the heavens,
And the Most High gave
forth His voice,
Hailstones and coals of fire.
14 He [a]sent out His arrows,
and scattered them,
And lightning flashes
in abundance, and [1]threw
them into confusion.
15 Then the [a]channels
of water appeared,
And the foundations
of the world were [1]laid bare
At Your [b]rebuke, O Yahweh,
At the blast of the [c]breath
of Your nostrils.

16 He [a]sent from on high,
He took me;
He drew me out
of [b]many waters.
17 He [a]delivered me from
my strong enemy,
And from those who
hated me, for they were
[b]too mighty for me.
18 They confronted me
in [a]the day of my disaster,
But [b]Yahweh was my support.

**18:3** [a]Ps 48:1; 96:4; 145:3 [b]Ps 34:6 **18:4** [a]Ps 116:3 [b]Ps 69:2; 124:3, 4 [1]Or *were assailing* **18:5** [a]Ps 116:3 **18:6** [a]Ps 50:15; 120:1 [b]Ps 3:4 [c]Ps 34:15 **18:7** [a]Jdg 5:4; Ps 68:7, 8; Is 13:13; Hag 2:6 [b]Ps 114:4, 6 **18:8** [a]Ps 50:3 [1]Or *in His wrath* **18:9** [a]Ps 144:5 [b]Ps 97:2 **18:10** [a]Ps 80:1; 99:1 [b]Ps 104:3 **18:11** [a]Dt 4:11 [b]Ps 97:2 [1]Or *pavilion* **18:12** [a]Ps 104:2 [b]Ps 97:3; 140:10; Hab 3:4 **18:13** [a]Ps 29:3; 104:7 **18:14** [a]Ps 144:6; Hab 3:11 [1]Or *routed them* **18:15** [a]Ps 106:9 [b]Ps 76:6 [c]Ps 18:8 [1]Or *uncovered* **18:16** [a]Ps 144:7 [b]Ps 32:6 **18:17** [a]Ps 59:1 [b]Ps 35:10; 142:6 **18:18** [a]Ps 59:16 [b]Ps 16:8

19 He brought me forth also
into a [a]broad place;
He rescued me, because
[b]He delighted in me.

20 Yahweh has [a]rewarded
me according to my
righteousness;
According to the [b]cleanness
of my hands He has
recompensed me.
21 For I have [a]kept the ways
of Yahweh,
And have [b]not wickedly
departed from my God.
22 For all [a]His judgments
were before me,
And I did not put away His
[b]statutes from me.
23 I was also [a,1]blameless with Him,
And I [b]kept myself
from my iniquity.
24 Therefore Yahweh has
[a]recompensed me according
to my righteousness,
According to the cleanness
of my hands before His eyes.

25 With [a]the [1]kind You
show Yourself kind;
With the blameless [b]You
show Yourself blameless;
26 With the pure You show
Yourself [a]pure,
And with the crooked [b]You
show Yourself [1]astute.
27 For You [a]save
an afflicted people,
But [b]eyes *which are* lifted
up, You bring down.
28 For You [a]light my lamp;
Yahweh my God [b]illumines
my darkness.
29 For by You I can [a,1]run
upon a troop;
And by my God I can
[b]leap over a wall.

30 As for God, His way
is [a,1]blameless;
The [b]word of Yahweh is [2]tried;
He is a [c]shield to all who
take refuge in Him.
31 For [a]who is God,
but Yahweh?
And who is a [b]rock,
except our God,
32 The God who [a]girds
me with strength
And [1]makes my
way [b,2]blameless?
33 He [a]makes my feet
like hinds' *feet*,
And [b]sets me
upon my high places.
34 He [a]trains my hands for battle,
So that my arms can [b]bend
a bow of bronze.
35 You have also given me [a]the
shield of Your salvation,
And Your [b]right hand
upholds me;

**18:19** [a]Ps 4:1; 31:8; 118:5 [b]Ps 37:23; 41:11 **18:20** [a]1Sa 24:19; Job 33:26; Ps 7:8 [b]Job 22:30; Ps 24:4 **18:21** [a]Ps 37:34; 119:33; Pr 8:32 [b]2Chr 34:33; Ps 119:102 **18:22** [a]Ps 119:30 [b]Ps 119:83 **18:23** [a]Ps 18:32 [b]Ps 19:12, 13; 25:11; 66:18 [1]Or *having integrity*; lit *complete, perfect* **18:24** [a]1Sa 26:23; Ps 18:20 **18:25** [a]1Ki 8:32; Ps 62:12; Mt 5:7 [b]Ps 18:30 [1]Or *holy one* **18:26** [a]Job 25:5; Hab 1:13 [b]Lv 26:23, 24, 27, 28; Pr 3:34 [1]Lit *twisted* **18:27** [a]Ps 72:12 [b]Ps 101:5; Pr 6:17 **18:28** [a]1Ki 15:4; Job 18:6; Ps 132:17 [b]Ps 27:1 **18:29** [a]Ps 118:10-12 [b]Ps 18:33; 40:2 [1]Or *crush a troop* **18:30** [a]Dt 32:4; Ps 19:7; 145:17; Rev 15:3 [b]Ps 12:6 [c]Ps 17:7; 91:4 [1]v 23, note 1 [2]Or *tested*, cf. Pr 30:5 **18:31** [a]Dt 32:39; 1Sa 2:2; Ps 86:8-10; Is 45:5 [b]Dt 32:31; Ps 18:2; 62:2 **18:32** [a]Ps 18:39; Is 45:5 [b]Ps 18:23 [1]Or *has made* [2]Or *having integrity*; lit *complete* **18:33** [a]Hab 3:19 [b]Dt 32:13 **18:34** [a]Ps 144:1 [b]Job 29:20 **18:35** [a]Ps 33:20 [b]Ps 63:8; 119:117

And [c]Your [1]gentleness
makes me great.
36 You [a]enlarge my steps
under me,
And my [b]ankles have
not given way.

37 I [a]pursued my enemies
and overtook them,
And I did not turn
back [b]until they
were consumed.
38 I crushed them,
so that they were
[a]not able to rise;
They fell [b]under my feet.
39 For You have [a]girded
me with strength
for battle;
You have [b,1]subdued
under me those who
rose up against me.
40 [1]You have also made
my enemies [a]turn
their backs to me,
And I [b,2]destroyed those
who hated me.
41 They cried for help,
but there was [a]none to save,
*Even* to Yahweh, but [b]He
did not answer them.
42 Then I beat them fine
as the [a]dust before the wind;
I emptied them out
as the mire of the streets.

43 You have delivered me
from the [a]contentions
of the people;
You have placed me
as [b]head of the nations;
A [c]people whom I have
not known serve me.
44 As soon as they hear,
they obey me;
Foreigners [a,1]cower
before me.
45 Foreigners [a]fade away,
And [b]come trembling
out of their [1]fortresses.

46 Yahweh [a]lives, and
blessed be [b]my rock;
And let [c]the God
of my salvation
be lifted high,
47 The God who [a]executes
vengeance for me,
And [b]subdues peoples
under me.
48 Who [a]delivers me
from my enemies;
Surely You [b]lift me
above those who rise
up against me;
You rescue me
from the [c]violent man.
49 Therefore I will [a]give
thanks to You among
the nations, O Yahweh,
And I will [b]sing praises
to Your name.
50 He gives great [a,1]salvation
to His king,
And shows lovingkindness
to [b]His anointed,
To David and [c]his
seed forever.

**18:35** [c]Ps 138:6 [1]Or *condescension* **18:36** [a]Ps 18:33 [b]Ps 66:9; Pr 4:12 **18:37** [a]Ps 44:5 [b]Ps 37:20 **18:38** [a]Ps 36:12 [b]Ps 47:3 **18:39** [a]Ps 18:32 [b]Ps 18:47 [1]Lit *caused to bow down* **18:40** [a]Ps 21:12 [b]Ps 94:23 [1]Lit *And as for my enemies, You have given me their necks* [2]Or *silenced* **18:41** [a]Ps 50:22 [b]Job 27:9; Pr 1:28 **18:42** [a]Ps 83:13 **18:43** [a]2Sa 3:1; 19:9; Ps 35:1 [b]2Sa 8:1-18; Ps 89:27 [c]Is 55:5 **18:44** [a]Ps 66:3 [1]Give feigned obedience; lit *deceive me* **18:45** [a]Ps 37:2 [b]Mic 7:17 [1]Lit *fastnesses* **18:46** [a]Job 19:25 [b]Ps 18:2 [c]Ps 51:14 **18:47** [a]Ps 94:1 [b]Ps 18:43; 47:3; 144:2 **18:48** [a]Ps 3:7 [b]Ps 27:6; 59:1 [c]Ps 11:5 **18:49** [a]Ro 15:9 [b]Ps 108:1 **18:50** [a]Ps 21:1; 144:10 [b]Ps 28:8 [c]Ps 89:4 [1]Lit *salvations*

## PSALM 19

### *The Law of Yahweh Is Perfect*

For the choir director. A Psalm of David.

1 The [a]heavens are telling
of the glory of God;
And the [b]expanse is declaring
the work of His hands.
2 Day to [a]day pours
forth [1]speech,
And [b]night to night
reveals knowledge.
3 There is no [1]speech,
nor are there words;
Their voice is not heard.
4 Their [a,1]line has gone out
through all the earth,
And their utterances
to the end of the world.
In them He has [b]placed
a tent for the sun,
5 Which is as a bridegroom
coming out of his chamber;
It rejoices as a strong man
to run his course.
6 Its [a]rising is from [1]one
end of the heavens,
And its circuit to the [2]other
end of them;
And there is nothing
hidden from its heat.

7 [a]The law of Yahweh is
[b,1]perfect, [c]restoring
the soul;
The testimony of Yahweh
is [d]sure, making
[e]wise the simple.
8 The precepts of Yahweh are
[a]right, [b]rejoicing the heart;
The commandment
of Yahweh is [c]pure,
[d]enlightening the eyes.
9 The fear of Yahweh is clean,
enduring forever;
The judgments of Yahweh
are [a]true; they are
[b]righteous altogether.
10 *They are* more desirable
than [a]gold, even more
than much fine gold;
[b]Sweeter also than honey
and the drippings
of the honeycomb.
11 Moreover, by them [a]Your
slave is warned;
In keeping them there
is great [b]reward.
12 Who can [a]discern *his*
errors? [b]Acquit me
of [c]hidden *faults.*
13 Also keep back Your slave
[a]from presumptuous *sins;*
Let them not [b]rule over me;
Then I will be [c,1]blameless,
And I shall be acquitted
of [d]great transgression.
14 Let the [1]words of my
mouth and [a]the
meditation of my heart
Be acceptable in Your sight,
O Yahweh, [b]my rock and
my [c]Redeemer.

## PSALM 20

### *We Will Boast in the Name of Yahweh*

For the choir director. A Psalm of David.

1 May Yahweh answer you
[a]in the day of distress!

---

◆ **19:1** [a]Ps 8:1; 50:6; Ro 1:19, 20 [b]Ge 1:6, 7 **19:2** [a]Ps 74:16 [b]Ps 139:12 [1]Lit *a saying* **19:3** [1]Lit *a saying* **19:4** [a]Ro 10:18 [b]Ps 104:2 [1]Or *sound* **19:6** [a]Ps 113:3; Ecc 1:5 [1]Lit *the* [2]Lit *their ends* (from the ends) **19:7** [a]Ps 111:7 [b]Ps 119:160 [c]Ps 23:3 [d]Ps 93:5 [e]Ps 119:98-100 [1]Lit *blameless* **19:8** [a]Ps 119:128 [b]Ps 119:14 [c]Ps 12:6 [d]Ps 36:9 **19:9** [a]Ps 119:142 [b]Ps 119:138 **19:10** [a]Ps 119:72, 127 [b]Ps 119:103 **19:11** [a]Ps 17:4 [b]Ps 24:5, 6; Pr 29:18 **19:12** [a]Ps 40:12; 139:6 [b]Ps 51:1, 2 [c]Ps 90:8; 139:23, 24 **19:13** [a]Nu 15:30 [b]Ps 119:133 [c]Ps 18:32 [d]Ps 25:11 [1]Lit *complete* **19:14** [a]Ps 104:34 [b]Ps 18:2 [c]Ps 31:5; Is 47:4 [1]Lit *sayings* ◆ **20:1** [a]Ps 50:15

May the [b]name
of the [c]God of Jacob set
you *securely* on high!
2 May He send you help
[a]from the sanctuary
And [b]uphold you from Zion!
3 May He [a]remember all
your meal offerings
And [b]find your burnt offering
[1]acceptable! [2]Selah.

4 May He grant you your
[a]heart's desire
And [b]fulfill all your [1]counsel!
5 [1]We will [a]sing for joy
over your salvation,
And in the name of our God
we will [b]set up our banners.
May Yahweh [c]fulfill all
your petitions.

6 Now [a]I know that Yahweh
saves His anointed;
He will [b]answer him
from His holy heaven
With the [c,1]saving might
of His right hand.
7 Some *boast* in chariots
and some in [a]horses,
But [b]we will [1]boast in the name
of Yahweh, our God.
8 They have [a]bowed
down and fallen,
But we have [b]risen and
stood upright.
9 [a,1]Save, O Yahweh;
May the [b]King answer us
in the day we call.

## PSALM 21

### *The King Trusts in Yahweh*

For the choir director. A Psalm of David.

1 O Yahweh, in Your strength
the king will [a]be glad,
And in Your [1]salvation how
greatly he will rejoice!
2 You have [a]given him
his heart's desire,
And You have not withheld
the request
of his lips. [1]Selah.
3 For You [a]meet him with
the blessings of good things;
You set a [b]crown of fine
gold on his head.
4 He asked life of You,
You [a]gave it to him,
[b]Length of days
forever and ever.
5 His [a]glory is great
through Your [1]salvation,
[b]Splendor and majesty
You bestow upon him.
6 For You make him [1]most
[a]blessed forever;
You make him joyful [b]with
gladness in Your presence.

7 For the king [a]trusts in Yahweh,
And through
the lovingkindness
of the Most High [b]he
will not be shaken.
8 Your hand will [a]find out
all your enemies;
Your right hand will find
out those who hate you.

---

**20:1** [b]Ps 91:14 [c]Ps 46:7, 11 **20:2** [a]Ps 3:4 [b]Ps 110:2 **20:3** [a]Ac 10:4 [b]Ps 51:19 [1]Lit *fat* [2]*Selah* may mean *Pause, Crescendo, Musical Interlude* **20:4** [a]Ps 21:2 [b]Ps 145:19 [1]Or purpose **20:5** [a]Ps 9:14 [b]Ps 60:4 [c]1Sa 1:17 [1]Or *Let us sing* **20:6** [a]Ps 41:11 [b]Is 58:9 [c]Ps 28:8 [1]Or *mighty deeds of the victory of His right hand* **20:7** [a]Ps 33:17 [b]2Chr 32:8 [1]Or *make mention of, praise* **20:8** [a]Is 2:11, 17 [b]Ps 37:24; Mic 7:8 **20:9** [a]Ps 3:7 [b]Ps 17:6 [1]Or *Yahweh, save the king; answer us* ◆ **21:1** [a]Ps 59:16, 17 [1]Or *victory* **21:2** [a]Ps 20:4; 37:4 [1]*Selah* may mean *Pause, Crescendo, Musical Interlude* **21:3** [a]Ps 59:10 [b]2Sa 12:30 **21:4** [a]Ps 61:6; 133:3 [b]Ps 91:16 **21:5** [a]Ps 9:14; 20:5 [b]Ps 8:5; 96:6 [1]Or *victory* **21:6** [a]1Chr 17:27 [b]Ps 43:4 [1]Lit *blessings* **21:7** [a]Ps 125:1 [b]Ps 112:6 **21:8** [a]Is 10:10

9 You will make them
[a]as a fiery oven in
the time of your [1]anger;
Yahweh will [b]swallow
them up in His wrath,
And [c]fire will devour them.
10 Their [1]offspring You will
destroy from the earth,
And their [a]seed from
among the sons of men.
11 Though they [a,1]intended
evil against You
*And* [b]devised a scheme,
They will not succeed.
12 For You will [a]make them
turn their back;
You will [1]aim [b]with Your
bowstrings at their faces.
13 Be exalted, O Yahweh,
in Your strength;
We will [a]sing and
praise Your might.

## PSALM 22

### *Why Have You Forsaken Me?*

For the choir director. According to [†]Aijeleth Hashshahar. A Psalm of David.

1 [a]My God, my God,
why have You forsaken me?
[b,1]Far from my salvation
are the words
of my [c,2]groaning.
2 O my God, I [a]call by day,
but You do not answer;
*And by night, but* [1]*I have*
no rest.
3 Yet [a]You are holy,
[1]Enthroned upon
[b]the praises of Israel.
4 In You our fathers [a]trusted;
They trusted and You
[b]rescued them.
5 To You they cried out and
were granted escape;
[a]In You they trusted and
were not [1]disappointed.

6 But I am a [a] worm and not a man,
A [b]reproach of men and
[c]despised by the people.
7 All who see me [a]mock me;
They [1]smack *their* lip, they
[b]wag *their* head, *saying*,
8 "[1]Commit *yourself* to Yahweh;
[a]let Him rescue him;
Let Him deliver him, because
He delights in him."

9 Yet You are He who [a]brought
me out of the womb;
You made me trust *when*
upon my mother's breasts.
10 Upon You I was cast
[a]from [1]birth;
You have been my God
from my mother's womb.

11 [a]Be not far from me,
for [1]distress is near;
For there is [b]none to help.
12 Many [a]bulls have
surrounded me;

**21:9** [a]Mal 4:1 [b]Lam 2:2 [c]Ps 50:3 [1]Or *presence* **21:10** [a]Ps 37:28 [1]Lit *fruit* **21:11** [a]Ps 2:1-3 [b]Ps 10:2 [1]Lit *stretched out* **21:12** [a]Ps 18:40 [b]Ps 7:12, 13 [1]Lit *make ready* **21:13** [a]Ps 59:16; 81:1 ◆ **22:TITLE** [†]Lit *The Doe of the Dawn*; possibly a title for a tune **22:1** [a]Mt 27:46; Mk 15:34 [b]Ps 10:1 [c]Job 3:24; Ps 6:6; 32:3; 38:8 [1]Or Why are You so *far from helping me*, and from *the words of my groaning?* [2]Lit *roaring* **22:2** [a]Ps 42:3; 88:1 [1]Lit *there is no silence for me* **22:3** [a]Ps 99:9 [b]Dt 10:21; Ps 148:14 [1]Or *Inhabit the praises* **22:4** [a]Ps 78:53 [b]Ps 107:6 **22:5** [a]Is 49:23 [1]Or *ashamed* **22:6** [a]Job 25:6; Is 41:14 [b]Ps 31:11 [c]Is 49:7; 53:3 **22:7** [a]Ps 79:4; Is 53:3; Lk 23:35 [b]Mt 27:39; Mk 15:29 [1]Make clicking sounds; lit *separate the lip* **22:8** [a]Ps 91:14; Mt 27:43 [1]Or *He committed* himself; lit *Roll* **22:9** [a]Ps 71:5, 6 **22:10** [a]Is 46:3; 49:1 [1]Lit a *womb* **22:11** [a]Ps 71:12 [b]2Ki 14:26; Ps 72:12; Is 63:5 [1]Or *trouble* **22:12** [a]Ps 22:21; 68:30

Strong *bulls* of [b]Bashan
have encircled me.
13 They [a]open wide their
mouth at me,
*As* a [b]lion that tears and roars.
14 I am [a]poured out like water,
And all my [b]bones
are out of joint;
My [c]heart is like wax;
It is melted within [1]me.
15 My [a]strength is dried
up like a potsherd,
And [b]my tongue cleaves
to my jaws;
And You [c]lay me
[1]in the dust of death.
16 For [a]dogs have surrounded me;
[1]A band of evildoers has
encompassed me;
[2]They [b]pierced my
hands and my feet.
17 I count all my bones.
[a]They look, they stare at me;
18 They [a]divide my garments
among them,
And for my clothing
they cast lots.

19 But You, O Yahweh,
[a]be not far off;
O my Strength,
[b]hasten to my help.
20 Deliver my [1]soul
from [a]the sword,
My [b]only *life*
from the [2]power of the dog.
21 Save me from the mouth
of the [a]lion;
From the horns
of the [b]wild oxen You
[c]have answered me.

22 I will *surely* [a]recount Your
name to my brothers;
In the midst of the assembly
I will praise You.
23 [a]You who fear Yahweh,
praise Him;
All you seed of Jacob,
[b]glorify Him,
And [c]stand in awe of Him,
all you seed of Israel.
24 For He has [a]not despised
and He has not
abhorred the affliction
of the afflicted;
And He has not [b]hidden
His face from him;
But [c]when he cried to Him
for help, He heard.

25 Of You *is* [a]my praise
in the great assembly;
I shall [b]pay my vows
before those who fear Him.
26 The [1]afflicted will eat
and [a]be satisfied;
Those who seek Him
will [b]praise Yahweh.
May your [c]heart live forever!
27 All the [a]ends of the earth
will remember and
turn to Yahweh,
And all the [b]families
of the nations will
worship before [1]You.

---

***22:12*** *[b]Dt 32:14; Am 4:1* **22:13** [a]Job 16:10; Ps 35:21; Lam 2:16; 3:46 [b]Ps 10:9; 17:12 **22:14** [a]Job 30:16 [b]Ps 31:10; Da 5:6 [c]Jos 7:5; Job 23:16; Ps 73:26; Na 2:10 [1]Lit *my inward parts* ***22:15*** *[a]Ps 38:10* [b]Jn 19:28 [c]Ps 104:29 [1]Lit *to* **22:16** [a]Ps 59:6, 7 [b]Mt 27:35; Jn 20:25 [1]Or *An assembly* [2]Or *Like a lion, my...* **22:17** [a]Lk 23:27, 35 **22:18** [a]Mt 27:35; Mk 15:24; Lk 23:34; Jn 19:24 **22:19** [a]Ps 22:11 [b]Ps 70:5 **22:20** [a]Ps 37:14 [b]Ps 35:17 [1]Or *life* [2]Lit *paw* **22:21** [a]Ps 22:13 [b]Ps 22:12 [c]Ps 34:4; 118:5; 120:1 **22:22** [a]Ps 40:10; Heb 2:12 **22:23** [a]Ps 135:19, 20 [b]Ps 86:12 [c]Ps 33:8 **22:24** [a]Ps 69:33 [b]Ps 27:9; 69:17; 102:2 [c]Ps 31:22; Heb 5:7 **22:25** [a]Ps 35:18; 40:9, 10 [b]Ps 61:8; Ecc 5:4 **22:26** [a]Ps 107:9 [b]Ps 40:16 [c]Ps 69:32 [1]Or *poor* **22:27** [a]Ps 2:8; 82:8 [b]Ps 86:9 [1]Some versions *Him*

28 For the [a]kingdom is Yahweh's
And He [b]rules
over the nations.
29 All the [a,1]prosperous
of the earth will eat
and worship,
All those who [b]go
down to the dust will
bow before Him,
Even he who [c,2]cannot
keep his soul alive.
30 [a]*Their* seed will serve Him;
It will be recounted
about the Lord
to [b]the *coming* generation.
31 They will come and [a]will
declare His righteousness
To a people [b]who will be
born, that He has done *it*.

## PSALM 23

### *Yahweh Is My Shepherd*

A Psalm of David.

1 Yahweh is my [a]shepherd,
I [1]shall [b]not want.
2 He makes me lie down
in [a]green pastures;
He [b]leads me
beside [c,1]quiet waters.
3 He [a]restores my soul;
He [b]guides me in the [c,1]paths
of righteousness
For His name's sake.

4 Even though I [a]walk
through the [1]valley
of the shadow of death,
I [b]fear no [2]evil,
for [c]You are with me;
Your [d]rod and Your staff,
they comfort me.
5 You [a]prepare a table
before me in the presence
of my enemies;
You [1]have [b]anointed
my head with oil;
My [c]cup overflows.
6 [1]Surely [a]goodness and
lovingkindness will [2]pursue
me all the days of my life,
And I will [b,3]dwell in the house
of Yahweh [4]forever.

## PSALM 24

### *The King of Glory*

Of David. A Psalm.

1 The [a]earth is Yahweh's,
as well as its fullness,
The [b]world, and those
who dwell in it.
2 For He has [a]founded
it upon the seas
And established it
upon the rivers.
3 Who may [a]ascend into
the [b]mountain of Yahweh?
And who may rise
in His holy [c]place?
4 He who has [a]innocent
hands and a [b]pure heart,
Who has not [c]lifted up his
soul [1]to worthlessness
And has not
[d]sworn deceitfully.

---

**22:28** [a]Ps 47:7; Ob 21; Zec 14:9; Mt 6:13 [b]Ps 47:8 **22:29** [a]Ps 17:10; 45:12; Hab 1:16 [b]Ps 28:1; Is 26:19 [c]Ps 89:48 [1]Lit *fat ones* [2]Or *did not* **22:30** [a]Ps 102:28 [b]Ps 102:18 **22:31** [a]Ps 40:9; 71:18 [b]Ps 78:6 ◆**23:1** [a]Ps 78:52; 80:1; Is 40:11; Jer 31:10; Eze 34:11-13; Jn 10:11; 1Pe 2:25 [b]Ps 34:9, 10; Php 4:19 [1]Or *do* **23:2** [a]Ps 65:11-13; Eze 34:14 [b]Rev 7:17 [c]Ps 36:8; 46:4 [1]Lit *waters of rest* **23:3** [a]Ps 19:7 [b]Ps 5:8; 31:3 [c]Ps 85:13; Pr 4:11; 8:20 [1]Lit *tracks* **23:4** [a]Job 10:21, 22; Ps 107:14 [b]Ps 3:6; 27:1 [c]Ps 16:8; Is 43:2 [d]Mic 7:14 [1]Or *valley of deep darkness* [2]Or *harm* **23:5** [a]Ps 78:19 [b]Ps 92:10; Lk 7:46 [c]Ps 16:5 [1]Or *anoint* **23:6** [a]Ps 25:7, 10 [b]Ps 27:4-6 [1]Or *Only* [2]Or *follow* [3]Or *return to* [4]Lit *for length of days* ◆**24:1** [a]1Co 10:26 [b]Ps 89:11 **24:2** [a]Ps 104:3, 5; 136:6 **24:3** [a]Ps 15:1 [b]Ps 2:6 [c]Ps 65:4 **24:4** [a]Job 17:9; Ps 22:30; 26:6 [b]Ps 51:10; 73:1; Mt 5:8 [c]Eze 18:15 [d]Ps 15:4 [1]Or *in vain*

5 He shall lift up a [a]blessing
from Yahweh
And [b,1]righteousness from
the God of his salvation.
6 [1]This is the generation
of those who [a]seek Him,
Who seek Your face—*pay heed*
O Jacob. [2]Selah.

7 [a]Lift up your heads,
O gates,
And be lifted up,
O [1]ancient doors,
That the King of [b]glory
may come in!
8 Who is this King of glory?
Yahweh [a]strong and mighty,
Yahweh [b]mighty in battle.
9 Lift up your heads,
O gates,
And lift *yourselves* up,
O [1]ancient doors,
That the King of [a]glory
may come in!
10 Who is He, this King of glory?
Yahweh of [a]hosts,
He is the King of glory. Selah.

## PSALM 25

### *Lead Me in Your Truth*

Of David.

א *Aleph*

1 To You, O Yahweh,
I [a]lift up my soul.

ב *Beth*

2 O my God, in You [a]I trust,
Do not let me [b]be ashamed;
Do not let my [c]enemies
exult over me.

ג *Gimel*

3 Indeed, let [a]none who hope
in You be ashamed;
Let those who [b]deal
treacherously without cause
be ashamed.

ד *Daleth*

4 [a]Make me know Your
ways, O Yahweh;
Teach me Your paths.

ה *He* / ו *Vav*

5 Lead me in [a]Your truth
and teach me,
For You are the [b]God
of my salvation;
In You I [c]hope all
the day.

ז *Zayin*

6 [a]Remember, O Yahweh,
Your compassion and
Your lovingkindnesses,
For they have been
[b,1]from of old.

ח *Heth*

7 Do not remember
the [a]sins of my youth
or my transgressions;
[b]According to Your
lovingkindness
remember me,
For the sake of Your
[c]goodness, O Yahweh.

ט *Teth*

8 [a]Good and [b]upright
is Yahweh;
Therefore He [c]instructs
sinners in the way.

---

**24:5** [a]Ps 115:13 [b]Ps 36:10 [1]As vindicated **24:6** [a]Ps 27:4, 8 [1]Or *Such* [2]*Selah* may mean Pause, *Crescendo, Musical Interlude* **24:7** [a]Ps 118:20; Is 26:2 [b]Ps 29:2, 9; 97:6; Ac 7:2; 1Co 2:8 [1]Lit *everlasting* **24:8** [a]Dt 4:34; Ps 96:7 [b]Ex 15:3, 6; Ps 76:3-6 **24:9** [a]Ps 26:8; 57:11 [1]Lit *everlasting* **24:10** [a]Ge 32:2; Jos 5:14; 2Sa 5:10; Ne 9:6 ◆ **25:1** [a]Ps 86:4; 143:8 **25:2** [a]Ps 31:1 [b]Ps 25:20; 31:1 [c]Ps 13:4; 41:11 **25:3** [a]Ps 37:9; 40:1; Is 49:23 [b]Ps 119:158; Is 21:2; Hab 1:13 **25:4** [a]Ex 33:13; Ps 27:11; 86:11 **25:5** [a]Ps 25:10; 43:3 [b]Ps 79:9 [c]Ps 40:1 **25:6** [a]Ps 98:3 [b]Ps 103:17 [1]Or *everlasting* **25:7** [a]Job 13:26; 20:11 [b]Ps 51:1 [c]Ps 31:19 **25:8** [a]Ps 86:5 [b]Ps 92:15 [c]Ps 32:8

י *Yodh*

9 May He [a]lead the
[1]humble in justice,
And may He [b]teach
the [1]humble His way.

כ *Kaph*

10 All the paths of Yahweh are
[a]lovingkindness and truth
To [b]those who guard His
covenant and His testimonies.

ל *Lamedh*

11 For [a]Your name's
sake, O Yahweh,
[b]Pardon my iniquity,
for it is great.

מ *Mem*

12 Who is the man who
[a]fears Yahweh?
He will [b]instruct him
in the way he should choose.

נ *Nun*

13 His soul will [a]abide in goodness,
And his seed will
[b]inherit the [1]land.

ס *Samekh*

14 The [a,1]secret of Yahweh is
for those who fear Him,
[2]And He will [b]make them
know His covenant.

ע *Ayin*

15 My [a]eyes are continually
toward Yahweh,
For He will [b]bring my
feet out of the net.

פ *Pe*

16 [a]Turn to me and be
gracious to me,
For I am [b]alone
and afflicted.

צ *Tsadhe*

17 [1]The [a]troubles of my
heart are enlarged;
Bring me [b]out
of my distresses.

ר *Resh*

18 [a]See my affliction
and my [1]trouble,
And [b]forgive all my sins.

ר *Resh*

19 See my enemies,
for they [a]are many,
And they [b]hate me
with violent hatred.

ש *Shin*

20 [a]Keep my soul and deliver me;
Do not let me [b]be ashamed,
for I take refuge in You.

ת *Tav*

21 Let [a]integrity and
uprightness guard me,
For [b]I hope in You.
22 [a]Redeem Israel, O God,
Out of all his troubles.

## PSALM 26

### *Give Justice to Me, O Yahweh*

Of David.

1 [a]Give justice to me,
O Yahweh, for I have
[b]walked in my integrity,
And I have [c]trusted
in Yahweh; [d]I will not waver.
2 [a]Test me, O Yahweh,
and try me;
[b]Refine my [1]mind
and my heart.

**25:9** [a]Ps 23:3 [b]Ps 27:11 [1]Or *afflicted* **25:10** [a]Ps 40:11 [b]Ps 103:18 **25:11** [a]Ps 31:3; 79:9 [b]Ex 34:9 **25:12** [a]Ps 31:19 [b]Ps 25:8; 37:23 **25:13** [a]Pr 1:33; Jer 23:6 [b]Ps 37:11; 69:36; Mt 5:5 [1]Or *earth* **25:14** [a]Pr 3:32; Jn 7:17 [b]Ge 17:1, 2 [1]Or *counsel, intimacy* [2]Or *And His covenant, to make them know it* **25:15** [a]Ps 123:2; 141:8 [b]Ps 31:4; 124:7 **25:16** [a]Ps 69:16 [b]Ps 143:4 **25:17** [a]Ps 40:12 [b]Ps 107:6 [1]Or *Relieve the troubles of my heart* **25:18** [a]2Sa 16:12; Ps 31:7 [b]Ps 103:3 [1]Lit *toil* **25:19** [a]Ps 3:1 [b]Ps 9:13 **25:20** [a]Ps 86:2 [b]Ps 25:2 **25:21** [a]Ps 41:12 [b]Ps 25:3 **25:22** [a]Ps 130:8 ◆ **26:1** [a]Ps 7:8 [b]2Ki 20:3; Pr 20:7 [c]Ps 13:5; 28:7 [d]Heb 10:23 **26:2** [a]Ps 17:3; 139:23 [b]Ps 7:9 [1]Lit *kidneys*, figurative for inner man

3 For Your [a]lovingkindness
is before my eyes,
And I have [b]walked
in Your [1]truth.
4 I do not [a]sit
with worthless men,
And I will not go
with [b,1]pretenders.
5 I [a]hate the assembly
of evildoers,
And I will not sit
with the wicked.
6 I shall [a]wash my hands
in innocence,
So I will go around [b]Your
altar, O Yahweh,
7 In order to proclaim with
the voice of [a]thanksgiving
And to recount all Your
[1]wondrous deeds.

8 O Yahweh, I [a]love
the habitation of Your house
And the place [1]where
Your [b]glory dwells.
9 [a]Do not [1]take my soul away
*along* with sinners,
Nor my life with [b]men
of bloodshed,
10 In whose hands is
a [a]*wicked* scheme,
And whose right hand
is full of [b]bribes.
11 But as for me, I shall
[a]walk in my integrity;
[b]Redeem me, and be
gracious to me.
12 [a]My foot stands
on [b]level ground;
In the [c]congregations I
shall bless Yahweh.

## PSALM 27

### *Yahweh Is My Light and My Salvation*

Of David.

1 Yahweh is my [a]light and
my [b]salvation;
Whom shall I fear?
Yahweh is the [c,1]strong
defense of my life;
[d]Whom shall I dread?
2 When evildoers came
upon me to [a]devour my flesh,
My adversaries and my enemies,
they [b]stumbled and fell.
3 Though a [a]host encamp
against me,
My heart will not fear;
Though war arise against me,
In this I [b]trust.

4 [a]One thing I have asked from
Yahweh, that I shall seek:
That I may [b]dwell
in the house of Yahweh
all the days of my life,
To behold [c]the [1]beauty
of Yahweh
And to [d]inquire in His temple.
5 For in the [a]day of calamity
He will [b]conceal me
in His shelter;
In the secret place of His
tent He will [c]hide me;
He will [d]lift me up on a rock.
6 And now [a]my head will
be lifted up above my
enemies around me,

**26:3** [a]Ps 48:9 [b]2Ki 20:3; Ps 86:11 [1]Or *faithfulness* **26:4** [a]Ps 1:1 [b]Ps 28:3 [1]Or *dissemblers, hypocrites* **26:5** [a]Ps 31:6; 139:21 **26:6** [a]Ps 73:13 [b]Ps 43:3, 4 **26:7** [a]Ps 9:1 [1]Or *miracles* **26:8** [a]Ps 27:4 [b]Ps 24:7 [1]Lit *of the tabernacle of Your glory* **26:9** [a]Ps 28:3 [b]Ps 139:19 [1]Lit *gather* **26:10** [a]Ps 37:7 [b]Ps 15:5 **26:11** [a]Ps 26:1 [b]Ps 44:26; 69:18 **26:12** [a]Ps 40:2 [b]Ps 27:11 [c]Ps 22:22 ◆ **27:1** [a]Ps 18:28; Is 60:20; Mic 7:8 [b]Ex 15:2; Ps 62:7; 118:14; Is 33:2; Jon 2:9 [c]Ps 28:8 [d]Ps 118:6 [1]Or *refuge* **27:2** [a]Ps 14:4 [b]Ps 9:3 **27:3** [a]Ps 3:6 [b]Job 4:6 **27:4** [a]Ps 26:8 [b]Ps 23:6 [c]Ps 90:17 [d]Ps 18:6 [1]Lit *delightfulness* **27:5** [a]Ps 50:15 [b]Ps 31:20 [c]Ps 17:8 [d]Ps 40:2 **27:6** [a]Ps 3:3

And I will offer in His
tent [b]sacrifices
with loud shouts of joy;
I will [c]sing, and I will sing
praises to Yahweh.

7 [a]Hear, O Yahweh,
when I call with my voice,
And be gracious to me
and [b]answer me.
8 On Your *behalf* my heart
says, "[a]Seek My face,"
"Your face, O Yahweh,
[b]I shall seek."
9 [a]Do not hide Your
face from me,
Do not turn Your slave
away in [b]anger;
You have been [c]my help;
[d]Do not abandon me and
do not [e]forsake me,
O God of my salvation!
10 [1]For my father and [a]my
mother have forsaken me,
But [b]Yahweh will
take me up.

11 [a]Instruct me in Your way,
O Yahweh,
And lead me in a [b]level path
Because of [1]my foes.
12 Do not give me over
to the [a,1]desire
of my adversaries,
For [b]false witnesses have
risen against me,
And such as [c]breathe
out violence.
13 [1]*I would have despaired* unless
I had believed that I would
see the [a]goodness of Yahweh
In the [b]land of the living.
14 [a]Hope in Yahweh;
Be [b]strong and let your
heart take courage;
Hope in Yahweh.

## PSALM 28

### *Yahweh Is My Strength and My Shield*

Of David.

1 To You, O Yahweh, I call;
My [a]rock, do not be
silent to me,
Lest if You [b]are hesitant
toward me,
I will become like those
who [c]go down to the pit.
2 Hear the [a]voice of my
supplications when I
cry to You for help,
When I [b]lift up my
hands [c]toward [1]Your
holy [d]sanctuary.
3 [a]Do not drag me away
with the wicked
And with workers of iniquity,
Who [b]speak peace
with their neighbors,
While evil is in their hearts.
4 Give to them [a]according
to their work and according
to the evil of their actions;
Give to them according
to the deeds of their hands;
Return their dealings
upon them.

**27:6** [b]Ps 107:22 [c]Ps 13:6 **27:7** [a]Ps 4:3; 61:1 [b]Ps 13:3 **27:8** [a]Ps 105:4; Am 5:6 [b]Ps 34:4 **27:9** [a]Ps 69:17 [b]Ps 6:1 [c]Ps 40:17 [d]Ps 94:14 [e]Ps 37:28 **27:10** [a]Is 49:15 [b]Is 40:11 [1]Or *If my father...forsake me, Then Yahweh* **27:11** [a]Ps 25:4; 86:11 [b]Ps 5:8; 26:12 [1]Or *those who lie in wait for me* **27:12** [a]Ps 41:2 [b]Dt 19:18; Ps 35:11; Mt 26:60 [c]Ac 9:1 [1]Lit *soul* **27:13** [a]Ps 31:19 [b]Job 28:13; Ps 52:5; 116:9; 142:5; Is 38:11; Jer 11:19; Eze 26:20 [1]Or *If I had not believed* **27:14** [a]Ps 25:3; 37:34; 40:1; 62:5; 130:5; Pr 20:22; Is 25:9 [b]Ps 31:24 ◆**28:1** [a]Ps 18:2 [b]Ps 35:22; 39:12; 83:1 [c]Ps 88:4; 143:7; Pr 1:12 **28:2** [a]Ps 140:6 [b]Ps 134:2; 141:2; Lam 2:19; 1Ti 2:8 [c]Ps 5:7; 138:2 [d]1Ki 6:5 [1]Lit *the innermost place of Your sanctuary* **28:3** [a]Ps 26:9 [b]Ps 12:2; 55:21; 62:4; Jer 9:8 **28:4** [a]Ps 62:12; 2Ti 4:14; Rev 18:6; 22:12

5 Because they [a]do not regard
the works of Yahweh
Nor the deeds
of His hands,
He will tear them down
and not build them up.

6 Blessed be Yahweh,
Because He [a]has heard
the voice
of my supplications.
7 Yahweh is my [a]strength
and my [b]shield;
My heart [c]trusts in Him,
and I am helped;
Therefore [d]my heart exults,
And with [e]my song I
shall thank Him.
8 Yahweh is [1]their [a]strength,
And He is a [b,2]strong
defense of salvation
to His anointed.
9 [a]Save Your people and bless
[b]Your inheritance;
Be their [c]shepherd also,
and [d]carry them forever.

## PSALM 29

### *The Voice of Yahweh*

A Psalm of David.

1 [a]Ascribe to Yahweh,
O [1]sons of the mighty,
Ascribe to Yahweh glory
and strength.
2 Ascribe to Yahweh
the glory of His name;
Worship Yahweh
[a]in the splendor of holiness.
3 The [a]voice of Yahweh is
upon the waters;
The God of glory [b]thunders,
Yahweh is
over [c,1]many waters.
4 The voice of Yahweh
is [a]powerful,
The voice of Yahweh is
*full of* splendor.
5 The voice of Yahweh
breaks the cedars;
Indeed, Yahweh breaks
in pieces [a]the cedars
of Lebanon.
6 He makes Lebanon
[a]skip like a calf,
And [b]Sirion
like a young wild ox.
7 The voice of Yahweh hews
out [1]flames of fire.
8 The voice of Yahweh causes
the wilderness to tremble;
Yahweh causes the wilderness
of [a]Kadesh to tremble.
9 The voice of Yahweh makes
[a]the deer to calve
And strips the forests bare;
And [b]in His temple
everything says, "Glory!"

10 Yahweh sat *enthroned*
*over* the [a]flood;
Indeed, Yahweh sits
as [b]King forever.
11 [1]Yahweh will give [a]strength
to His people;
[2]Yahweh will bless His
people with [b]peace.

**28:5** [a]Is 5:12 **28:6** [a]Ps 28:2 **28:7** [a]Ps 18:2; 59:17 [b]Ps 3:3 [c]Ps 13:5; 112:7 [d]Ps 16:9 [e]Ps 40:3; 69:30 ***28:8*** *[a]Ps 20:6; 89:17 [b]Ps 27:1; 140:7* [1]A few mss and ancient versions the strength of His people [2]Or *refuge of salvation* **28:9** [a]Ps 106:47 [b]Dt 9:29; 32:9; 1Ki 8:51; Ps 33:12; 106:40 [c]Ps 80:1 [d]Dt 1:31; Is 40:11; 46:3; 63:9 ◆ **29:1** [a]1Chr 16:28, 29; Ps 96:7-9 [1]Or *sons of gods* **29:2** [a]2Chr 20:21; Ps 110:3 **29:3** [a]Ps 104:7 [b]Job 37:4, 5; Ps 18:13 [c]Ps 18:16; 107:23 [1]Or *great* **29:4** [a]Ps 68:33 **29:5** [a]Jdg 9:15; 1Ki 5:6; Ps 104:16; Is 2:13; 14:8 **29:6** [a]Ps 114:4, 6 [b]Dt 3:9 **29:7** [1]Lightning **29:8** [a]Nu 13:26 **29:9** [a]Job 39:1 [b]Ps 26:8 **29:10** [a]Ge 6:17 [b]Ps 10:16 **29:11** [a]Ps 28:8; 68:35; Is 40:29 [b]Ps 37:11; 72:3 [1]Or *May Yahweh give* [2]Or *May Yahweh bless*

## PSALM 30

### *You Have Turned My Mourning into Dancing*

A Psalm. A Song at the Dedication of the House. Of David.

1 I will [a]exalt You,
O Yahweh, for You
have [b]lifted me up,
And have not let my [c]enemies
be glad over me.
2 O Yahweh my God,
I [a]cried to You for help,
and You [b]healed me.
3 O Yahweh, You have [a]brought
up my soul from Sheol;
You have kept me alive,
[1]that I would not [b]go
down to the pit.
4 [a]Sing praise to Yahweh,
you [b]His holy ones,
And [c]give thanks
for the [d]remembrance
of His holy *name*.
5 For [a]His anger is
but for a moment,
His [b]favor is for a lifetime;
Weeping may [c]last
for the night,
But a shout of joy *comes*
in the morning.

6 Now as for me, I said
in my prosperity,
"I will [a]never be shaken."
7 *O Yahweh, by Your favor* You
have made my mountain
to stand strong;
You [a]hid Your face,
I was dismayed.
8 To You, O Yahweh, I called,
And to the Lord
I made supplication:
9 "What profit is there
in my blood, if I [a]go
down to the pit?
Will the [b]dust praise You?
Will it declare Your truth?

10 "[a]Hear, O Yahweh, and
be gracious to me;
O Yahweh, be my [b]helper."
11 You have turned for me [a]my
mourning into dancing;
You have [b]loosed my
sackcloth and girded
me with [c]gladness,
12 That *my* [a,1]glory may
sing praise to You
and not be silent.
O Yahweh my God, I will [b]give
thanks to You forever.

## PSALM 31

### *Into Your Hand I Commit My Spirit*

For the choir director. A Psalm of David.

1 [a]In You, O Yahweh,
I have taken refuge;
Let me never [b]be ashamed;
[c]In Your righteousness
protect me.
2 [a]Incline Your ear to me,
deliver me quickly;
Be to me a [b]rock of [1]strength,
A fortress to save me.
3 For You are my [a,1]high
rock and my fortress;
For [b]Your name's sake You
will lead me and guide me.

---

◆ **30:1** [a]Ps 118:28; 145:1 [b]Ps 3:3 [c]Ps 25:2; 35:19, 24 **30:2** [a]Ps 88:13 [b]Ps 6:2; 103:3; Is 53:5 **30:3** [a]Ps 86:13 [b]Ps 28:1 [1]Some mss *from among those who go down* **30:4** [a]Ps 149:1 [b]Ps 50:5 [c]Ps 97:12 [d]Ex 3:15; Ps 135:13; Hos 12:5 **30:5** [a]Ps 103:9; Is 26:20; 54:7, 8 [b]Ps 118:1 [c]Ps 126:5; 2Co 4:17 **30:6** [a]Ps 10:6; 62:2, 6 **30:7** [a]Dt 31:17; Ps 104:29; 143:7 **30:9** [a]Ps 28:1 [b]Ps 6:5 **30:10** [a]Ps 4:1; 27:7 [b]Ps 27:9; 54:4 **30:11** [a]Ecc 3:4; Jer 31:4, 13 [b]Is 20:2 [c]Ps 4:7 **30:12** [a]Ps 16:9; 57:8; 108:1 [b]Ps 44:8 [1]Or *soul* ◆ **31:1** [a]Ps 31:1-3; 71:1-3 [b]Ps 25:2 [c]Ps 143:1 **31:2** [a]Ps 17:6; 71:2; 86:1; 102:2 [b]Ps 18:2; 71:3 [1]Or *refuge* **31:3** [a]Ps 18:2; 71:3; 2Sa 22:2 [b]Ps 23:3; 25:11 [1]Or *rock*, cf. Ps 18:2; 71:3

4 You will [a]bring me out
of the net which they have
secretly laid for me,
For You are my [b]strength.
5 [a]Into Your hand I
commit my spirit;
You have [b]ransomed me,
O Yahweh, [c]God of truth.

6 I hate those who [a]regard
worthless idols,
But I [b]trust in Yahweh.
7 I will [a]rejoice and be glad
in Your lovingkindness,
Because You have [b]seen
my affliction;
You have known
the troubles of my soul,
8 And You have not [a]given
me over into the hand
of the enemy;
You have set my feet
in a large place.

9 Be gracious to me,
O Yahweh,
for [a]I am in distress;
My [b]eye is wasted away
from grief, [c]my soul
and [1]my body *also*.
10 For my life is worn down
with [a]sorrow
And my years with sighing;
My [b]strength fails because
of my iniquity,
And [c]my bones waste away.
11 Among all my adversaries,
I have become a [a]reproach,
Especially to my [b]neighbors,
And an object of dread
to my acquaintances;
Those who see me
in the street flee from me.
12 I am [a]forgotten like a dead
man—out of [1]mind—
I am like a broken vessel.
13 For I have heard [a,1]the
bad report of many,
[b]Terror is on every side;
While they [c]took counsel
together against me,
They [d]schemed to take my life.

14 But as for me, I trust in You,
O Yahweh,
I say, "[a]You are my God."
15 My [a]times are in Your hand;
[b]Deliver me from the hand
of my enemies and
from those who pursue me.
16 Make Your [a]face to shine
upon Your slave;
[b]Save me
in Your lovingkindness.
17 O Yahweh, let me not be [a]put
to shame, for I call upon You;
Let the [b]wicked be put
to shame, let them
[c]be silent in Sheol.
18 Let the [a]lying lips be mute,
Which [b]speak arrogantly
against the righteous
With lofty pride
and contempt.

19 How great is Your [a]goodness,
Which You have stored up
for those who fear You,

**31:4** [a]Ps 25:15 [b]Ps 46:1 **31:5** [a]Lk 23:46; Ac 7:59 [b]Ps 55:18; 71:23 [c]Dt 32:4; Ps 71:22 **31:6** [a]Jon 2:8 [b]Ps 52:8 **31:7** [a]Ps 90:14 [b]Ps 10:14 **31:8** [a]Dt 32:30; Ps 37:33 **31:9** [a]Ps 66:14; 69:17 [b]Ps 6:7 [c]Ps 63:1 [1]Lit *womb, stomach* **31:10** [a]Ps 13:2 [b]Ps 39:11 [c]Ps 32:3; 38:3; 102:3 **31:11** [a]Ps 69:19 [b]Job 19:13; Ps 38:11; 88:8, 18 **31:12** [a]Ps 88:5 [1]Lit *heart* **31:13** [a]Ps 50:20; Jer 20:10 [b]Lam 2:22 [c]Ps 62:4; Mt 27:1 [d]Ps 41:7 [1]Lit *whispering* **31:14** [a]Ps 140:6 **31:15** [a]Job 14:5; 24:1 [b]Ps 143:9 **31:16** [a]Nu 6:25; Ps 4:6; 80:3 [b]Ps 6:4 **31:17** [a]Ps 25:2, 20 [b]Ps 25:3 [c]1Sa 2:9; Ps 94:17; 115:17 **31:18** [a]Ps 109:2; 120:2 [b]1Sa 2:3; Ps 94:4; Jd 15 **31:19** [a]Ps 65:4; 145:7; Is 64:4; Ro 2:4; 11:22

Which You have worked
for those who [b]take
refuge in You,
[c]Before the sons of men!

20 You hide them in the [a]secret
place of Your presence from
the [b]conspiracies of man;
You keep them secretly
in a [1]shelter
from the [c]strife of tongues.

21 [a]Blessed be Yahweh,
For He has made [b]marvelous
His lovingkindness
to me in a besieged [c]city.

22 As for me, [a]I said in my alarm,
"I am [b]cut off
from before Your eyes";
Nevertheless,
You [c]heard the voice
of my supplications
When I cried to You for help.

23 Oh, love Yahweh, all you
[a]His holy ones!
Yahweh [b]guards the faithful
But [c]repays fully the one
who acts in lofty pride.

24 [a]Be strong and let your
heart take courage,
All you who wait for Yahweh.

## PSALM 32

### *You Forgave the Iniquity of My Sin*

Of David. A [†]Maskil.

1 [a]How blessed is he whose
transgression is forgiven,
Whose sin is covered!

2 How blessed is the man
whose iniquity Yahweh
[a]will not take into account,
And in whose spirit
there is [b]no deceit!

3 When [a]I kept silent *about my
sin*, [b]my [1]bones wasted away
Through my [c,2]groaning
all day long.

4 For day and night [a]Your hand
was heavy upon me;
My [b,1]vitality was drained
away *as* with the heat
of summer. [2]Selah.

5 I [a]acknowledged my
sin to You,
And my iniquity I [b]did
not cover up;
I said, "[c]I will confess my
transgressions to Yahweh;"
And You [d]forgave the [1]iniquity
of my sin. Selah.

6 Therefore, let every holy
one pray to You [a,1]at a time
when *You* may be found;
Surely [b]in a flood
of great waters they will
not reach him.

7 You are [a]my hiding place; You
[b]guard me from trouble;
You surround me with [c,1]songs
of deliverance. Selah.

8 *I will* [a]give you insight and
teach you in the way
which you should go;

**31:19** [b]Ps 5:11 [c]Ps 23:5 **31:20** [a]Ps 27:5 [b]Ps 37:12 [c]Job 5:21; Ps 31:13 [1]Or *pavilion* **31:21** [a]Ps 28:6 [b]Ps 17:7 [c]1Sa 23:7; Ps 87:5 **31:22** [a]Ps 116:11 [b]Ps 88:5; Is 38:11, 12; Lam 3:54 [c]Ps 18:6; 66:19; 145:19 **31:23** [a]Ps 30:4; 37:28; 50:5 [b]Ps 145:20; Rev 2:10 [c]Dt 32:41; Ps 94:2 **31:24** [a]Ps 27:14 ◆ **32:TITLE** [†]Possibly *Contemplative, Didactic, Skillful Psalm* **32:1** [a]Ps 85:2; 103:3; Ro 4:7, 8 **32:2** [a]2Co 5:19 [b]Jn 1:47 **32:3** [a]Ps 39:2, 3 [b]Ps 31:10 [c]Ps 38:8 [1]Or *substance* [2]Lit *roaring* **32:4** [a]1Sa 5:6; Job 23:2; 33:7; Ps 38:2; 39:10 [b]Ps 22:15 [1]Lit *life juices were turned into the drought of summer* [2]*Selah* may mean *Pause, Crescendo, Musical Interlude* **32:5** [a]Lv 26:40 [b]Job 31:33 [c]Ps 38:18; Pr 28:13; 1Jn 1:9 [d]Ps 103:12 [1]Or *guilt* **32:6** [a]Ps 69:13; Is 55:6 [b]Ps 46:1-3; 69:1; 124:5; 144:7; Is 43:2 [1]Lit *in a time of finding out* **32:7** [a]Ps 9:9; 31:20; 91:1; 119:114 [b]Ps 121:7 [c]Ex 15:1; Jdg 5:1; Ps 40:3 [1]Or *shouts* **32:8** [a]Ps 25:8

I will counsel you
[b]with My eye upon you.
9 Do not be [a]as the horse or
as the mule which have
no understanding,
Whose harness are bit and
bridle to control them,
*Otherwise* they will not
come near you.
10 Many are the [a]sorrows
of the wicked,
But [b]he who trusts
in Yahweh, lovingkindness
shall surround him.
11 Be [a]glad in Yahweh
and rejoice, you
righteous ones;
And shout for joy, all you
who are [b]upright in heart.

## PSALM 33

### *Yahweh Is Our Help and Our Shield*

1 [a]Sing for joy in Yahweh,
O righteous ones;
Praise is [b]becoming
to the upright.
2 Give thanks to Yahweh
with the [a]lyre;
Sing praises to Him
with a [b]harp of ten strings.
3 Sing to Him a [a]new song;
Play skillfully
with [b]a loud shout.
4 For the word of Yahweh
[a]is upright,
And all His work is *done*
[b]in faithfulness.
5 He [a]loves righteousness
and justice;
The [b]earth is full
of the lovingkindness
of Yahweh.
6 By the [a]word of Yahweh
the heavens were made,
And [b]by the breath of His
mouth [c]all their host.
7 He gathers the [a]waters
of the sea [1]as a heap;
He lays up the deeps
in storehouses.
8 Let [a]all the earth fear Yahweh;
Let all the inhabitants
of the world [b]stand
in awe of Him.
9 For [a]He spoke, and it was;
He commanded, and it [1]stood.
10 Yahweh [a]nullifies the counsel
of the nations;
He frustrates the thoughts
of the peoples.
11 The [a]counsel of Yahweh
stands forever,
The [b]thoughts of His
heart from generation
to generation.
12 Blessed is the [a]nation
whose God is Yahweh,
The people whom He
has [b]chosen for His
own inheritance.

13 Yahweh [a]looks from heaven;
He [b]sees all the sons of men;
14 From [a]the place of His
habitation He gazes
On all the inhabitants
of the earth,

---

**32:8** [b]Ps 33:18 **32:9** [a]Pr 26:3 **32:10** [a]*Ps 16:4; Pr 13:21; Ro 2:9* [b]Ps 5:11, 12; Pr 16:20 **32:11** [a]Ps 64:10; 68:3; 97:12 [b]Ps 7:10; 64:10 ◆ **33:1** [a]Ps 32:11; Php 3:1; 4:4 [b]Ps 92:1; 147:1 **33:2** [a]Ps 71:22; 147:7 [b]Ps 144:9 **33:3** [a]Ps 40:3; 96:1; 98:1; 144:9; Is 42:10; Rev 5:9 [b]Ps 98:4 **33:4** [a]Ps 19:8 [b]Ps 119:90 **33:5** [a]Ps 11:7; 37:28 [b]Ps 119:64 **33:6** [a]Ge 1:6; Ps 148:5; Heb 11:3 [b]Ps 104:30 [c]Ge 2:1 **33:7** [a]Ex 15:8; Jos 3:16; Ps 78:13 [1]A container; some ancient versions *in a water skin* **33:8** [a]Ps 67:7 [b]Ps 96:9 **33:9** [a]Ge 1:3; Ps 148:5 [1]Or *stood forth* **33:10** [a]Ps 2:1-3; Is 8:10; 19:3 **33:11** [a]Job 23:12; Pr 19:21 [b]Ps 40:5; 92:5; 139:17; Is 55:8 **33:12** [a]Ps 144:15 [b]Ex 19:5; Dt 7:6; Ps 28:9 **33:13** [a]Job 28:24; Ps 14:2 [b]Ps 11:4 **33:14** [a]1Ki 8:39, 43; Ps 102:19

15 He who [a]forms [1]the
hearts of them all,
He who [b]understands
all their works.
16 [a]The king is not saved
by a mighty army;
A warrior is not delivered
by great strength.
17 A [a]horse is a false hope
for salvation;
Nor does it provide escape to
anyone by its great strength.

18 Behold, [a]the eye of Yahweh
is on those who fear Him,
On those who [b]wait
for His lovingkindness,
19 To [a]deliver their soul
from death
And to keep them
alive [b]in famine.
20 Our soul [a]is patient
for Yahweh;
He is our [b]help and our shield.
21 For our [a]heart is glad in Him,
Because we trust
in His holy name.
22 Let Your lovingkindness,
O Yahweh, be upon us,
As we wait for You.

## PSALM 34

### *Taste and See That Yahweh Is Good*

Of David. When he feigned madness *before* [†]Abimelech, so that he drove him away and he departed.

א *Aleph*

1 I will [a]bless Yahweh
at all times;
His [b]praise shall continually
be in my mouth.

ב *Beth*

2 My soul will [a]make its
boast in Yahweh;
The [b]humble will hear
it and rejoice.

ג *Gimel*

3 O [a]magnify Yahweh
with me,
And let us [b]exalt His
name together.

ד *Daleth*

4 I [a]inquired of Yahweh,
and He answered me,
And [b]delivered me
from all that I dread.

ה *He* / ו *Vav*

5 They [a]looked to Him
and were radiant,
And their faces will [b]never
be humiliated.

ז *Zayin*

6 This [1]poor man called out,
and [a]Yahweh heard him
And saved him out of all
his troubles.

ח *Heth*

7 The [a]angel of Yahweh
encamps around those
who fear Him,
And rescues them.

ט *Teth*

8 O [a]taste and see
that Yahweh is good;
How [b]blessed is the man
who takes refuge in Him!

---

**33:15** [a]Job 10:8; Ps 119:73 [b]2Chr 16:9; Job 34:21; Jer 32:19 [1]Or *their heart together* **33:16** [a]Ps 44:6; 60:11 **33:17** [a]Ps 20:7; 147:10; Pr 21:31 **33:18** [a]Job 36:7; Ps 32:8; 34:15; 1Pe 3:12 [b]Ps 32:10; 147:11 **33:19** [a]Ps 56:13; Ac 12:11 [b]Job 5:20; Ps 37:19 **33:20** [a]Ps 62:1; 130:6; Is 8:17 [b]Ps 115:9 **33:21** [a]Ps 13:5; 28:7; Zec 10:7; Jn 16:22 ◆ **34:TITLE** [†]Possibly a title of King Achish of Gath, cf. 1Sa 21:10-15 **34:1** [a]Eph 5:20; 1Th 5:18 [b]Ps 71:6 **34:2** [a]Ps 44:8; Jer 9:24; 1Co 1:31 [b]Ps 69:32 **34:3** [a]Ps 35:27; 69:30; Lk 1:46 [b]Ps 18:46 **34:4** [a]2Chr 15:2; Ps 9:10; Mt 7:7 [b]Ps 34:6, 17, 19; Pr 10:24; Is 66:4 **34:5** [a]Ps 36:9; Is 60:5 [b]Ps 25:3 **34:6** [a]Ps 34:4 [1]Or *afflicted* **34:7** [a]Ps 91:11; Da 6:22 **34:8** [a]Ps 119:103; Heb 6:5; 1Pe 2:3 [b]Ps 2:12

י *Yodh*

9 Oh, fear Yahweh,
you [a]His saints;
For there is [b]no want
to those who fear Him.

כ *Kaph*

10 The young lions do lack
and suffer hunger;
But they who inquire
of Yahweh shall [a]not be
in want of any good thing.

ל *Lamedh*

11 [a]Come, you children,
listen to me;
[b]I will teach you
[c]the fear of Yahweh.

מ *Mem*

12 [a]Who is the man who
delights in life
And loves *many* days
that he may [b]see good?

נ *Nun*

13 Guard [a]your tongue from evil
And your lips
from speaking [b]deceit.

ס *Samekh*

14 [a]Depart from evil and do good;
Seek peace and [b]pursue it.

ע *Ayin*

15 The [a]eyes of Yahweh are
toward the righteous
And His ears are *open*
to their cry for help.

פ *Pe*

16 The [a]face of Yahweh is
against evildoers,
To [b]cut off the memory
of them from the earth.

צ *Tsadhe*

17 *The righteous* [a]cry, and
Yahweh hears
And delivers them out
of all their troubles.

ק *Qoph*

18 Yahweh [a]is near
to the [b]brokenhearted
And saves those who are
[c,1]crushed in spirit.

ר *Resh*

19 [a]Many are the [b]evils
*against* the righteous,
But Yahweh [c]delivers
him out of them all.

ש *Shin*

20 He keeps all his bones,
[a]Not one of them
is broken.

ת *Tav*

21 [a]Evil shall slay the wicked,
And those who hate
the righteous will
be [1]condemned.

22 Yahweh [a]redeems the soul
of His slaves,
And all those who [b]take
refuge in Him will not
be [1]condemned.

## PSALM 35

### *Yahweh Be Magnified*

Of David.

1 Contend, O Yahweh,
with those who
[a]contend with me;
Fight against those who
[b]fight against me.

---

**34:9** [a]Ps 31:23 [b]Ps 23:1 **34:10** [a]Ps 84:11 **34:11** [a]Ps 66:16 [b]Ps 32:8 [c]Ps 111:10 **34:12** [a]Ps 34:12-16; 1Pe 3:10-12 [b]Ecc 3:13 **34:13** [a]Ps 141:3; Pr 13:3; Jas 1:26 [b]1Pe 2:22 **34:14** [a]Ps 37:27; Is 1:16, 17 [b]Ro 14:19; Heb 12:14 **34:15** [a]Job 36:7; Ps 33:18 **34:16** [a]Lv 17:10; Jer 44:11; Am 9:4 [b]Job 18:17; Ps 9:6; 109:15; Pr 10:7 **34:17** [a]Ps 34:6; 145:19 **34:18** [a]Ps 145:18 [b]Ps 147:3; Is 61:1 [c]Ps 51:17; Is 57:15 [1]Or *contrite* **34:19** [a]Pr 24:16 [b]Ps 71:20; 2Ti 3:11f [c]Ps 34:4, 6, 17 **34:20** [a]Jn 19:33, 36 **34:21** [a]Ps 94:23; 140:11; Pr 24:16 [1]Or *held guilty* **34:22** [a]1Ki 1:29; Ps 71:23 [b]Ps 37:40 [1]Or *held guilty* ◆ **35:1** [a]Ps 18:43; Is 49:25 [b]Ps 56:2

2 Take hold of [a,1]shield
and large shield
And rise up for [b]my help.
3 Draw also the spear and
[1]the battle-axe to meet
those who pursue me;
Say to my soul, "I am
[a]your salvation."
4 Let those be [a]ashamed
and dishonored who
seek my [1]life;
Let those who devise evil
against me be [b]turned
back and humiliated.
5 Let them be [a]like chaff
before the wind,
With the angel of Yahweh
driving *them* on.
6 Let their way be dark
and [a]slippery,
With the angel of Yahweh
pursuing them.
7 For [a]without cause they
[b]hid their net for me;
Without cause they dug
a [1]pit for my soul.
8 Let [a]destruction,
which he does not know,
come upon him,
And [b]let the net,
which he hid, catch him;
Let him fall into it
in [c]destruction.

9 And my soul shall
[a]rejoice in Yahweh;
It shall [b]be joyful
in His salvation.
10 All my [a]bones will say,
"Yahweh, [b]who is like You,
Who delivers the afflicted
from him [c]who is too
strong for him,
And [d]the afflicted and
the needy from him
who robs him?"
11 [a]Malicious witnesses rise up,
Who ask me of things
that I do not know.
12 They [a]repay me evil
for good,
It is bereavement to my soul.
13 But as for me, [a]when they
were sick, my [b]clothing
was sackcloth;
I [c]humbled my soul
with fasting,
And my [d]prayer kept
returning to my bosom.
14 I walked about as though it
were my friend or brother;
I [a]bowed down [1]mourning,
as one who sorrows
for a mother.
15 But [a]at my [1]stumbling they
were glad and gathered
themselves together;
The [b,2]smiters whom I
did not know gathered
together against me,
They [c]tore at me and
never were silent.
16 Amongst the godless
jesters at a feast,
They [a]gnashed at me
with their teeth.

**35:2** [a]Ps 91:4 [b]Ps 44:26 [1]Small shield **35:3** [a]Ps 62:2 [1]Or *close up the path against those* **35:4** [a]Ps 70:2 [b]Ps 40:14; 129:5 [1]Or *soul* **35:5** [a]Job 21:18; Ps 83:13; Is 29:5 **35:6** [a]Ps 73:18; Jer 23:12 **35:7** [a]Ps 69:4; 109:3; 140:5 [b]Ps 9:15 [1]*Pit* has been transposed from line above **35:8** [a]Ps 55:23; Is 47:11; 1Th 5:3 [b]Ps 9:15 [c]Ps 73:18 **35:9** [a]Is 61:10 [b]Ps 9:14; 13:5; Lk 1:47 **35:10** [a]Ps 51:8 [b]Ex 15:11; Ps 86:8; Mic 7:18 [c]Ps 18:17 [d]Ps 37:14; 109:16 **35:11** [a]Ps 27:12 **35:12** [a]Ps 38:20; 109:5; Jer 18:20; Jn 10:32 **35:13** [a]Job 30:25 [b]Ps 69:11 [c]Ps 69:10 [d]Mt 10:13; Lk 10:6 **35:14** [a]Ps 38:6 [1]Or *dressed in black* **35:15** [a]Ob 12 [b]Job 30:1, 8, 12 [c]Ps 7:2 [1]Or *limping* [2]Or *smitten ones* **35:16** [a]Job 16:9; Ps 37:12; Lam 2:16

17 Lord, [a]how long will
You look on?
Bring back my soul
[b]from their ravages,
My [c]only *life* from the lions.
18 I will [a]give You thanks
in the great assembly;
I will [b]praise You
among a mighty people.
19 [a]Let those who are
wrongfully [b]my enemies
not be glad over me;
Nor let those [c]who hate
me without cause
[d,1]wink maliciously.
20 For they do not speak peace,
But they devise [a]deceitful
words against those who
are quiet in the land.
21 They [a]opened their mouth
wide against me;
They said, "[b]Aha, aha,
our eyes have seen it!"

22 [a]You have seen it, O Yahweh,
[b]do not keep silent;
O Lord, [c]do not be
far from me.
23 [a]Stir up Yourself, and
awake to my justice
And to my cause, my
God and my Lord.
24 [a]Judge me, O Yahweh
my God, according
to Your righteousness,
And [b]do not let them
be glad over me.
25 Do not let them say in their
heart, "[a]Aha, our desire!"
Do not let them say, "We
have [b]swallowed him up!"
26 Let [a]those be ashamed
and humiliated
altogether who are glad
at the evil *done to* me;
Let those be [b]clothed
with shame and
dishonor who [c]magnify
themselves over me.

27 Let them [a]shout for joy
and be glad, who delight
in [b]my righteousness;
And [c]let them say continually,
"Yahweh be magnified,
Who [d]delights in the peace
of His slave."
28 And [a]my tongue shall utter
Your righteousness
*And* Your praise all day long.

## PSALM 36

### *In Your Light We See Light*

For the choir director. Of the servant of Yahweh, of David.

1 [1]Transgression declares
to the [2]ungodly
within [3]his heart;
There is [a]no dread
of God before his eyes.
2 For it [a]flatters him
in his eyes
For one to discover his
iniquity *and* hate *it*.
3 The [a]words of his mouth are
wickedness and deceit;
He has [b]ceased to consider
to do good.

---

**35:17** [a]Ps 13:1; Hab 1:13 [b]Ps 35:7 [c]Ps 22:20, 21 **35:18** [a]Ps 22:22 [b]Ps 22:25 **35:19** [a]Ps 13:4; 30:1; 38:16 [b]Ps 38:19; 69:4 [c]Jn 15:25 [d]Pr 6:13; 10:10 [1]Or *wink the eye* **35:20** [a]Ps 55:21; Jer 9:8; Mic 6:12 **35:21** [a]Job 16:10; Ps 22:13 [b]Ps 40:15; 70:3 **35:22** [a]Ex 3:7; Ps 10:14 [b]Ps 28:1 [c]Ps 10:1; 22:11; 38:21; 71:12 **35:23** [a]Ps 7:6; 44:23; 59:4; 80:2 **35:24** [a]Ps 9:4; 26:1; 43:1 [b]Ps 35:19 **35:25** [a]Ps 35:21 [b]Ps 56:1; 124:3; Pr 1:12; Lam 2:16 **35:26** [a]Ps 40:14 [b]Ps 109:29 [c]Job 19:5; Ps 38:16 **35:27** [a]Ps 32:11 [b]Ps 9:4 [c]Ps 40:16; 70:4 [d]Ps 147:11; 149:4 **35:28** [a]Ps 51:14; 71:15, 24 ◆ **36:1** [a]Ro 3:18 [1]Or *An oracle of transgression is* [2]Lit *wicked* [3]Or *my heart* **36:2** [a]Dt 29:19; Ps 10:11; 49:18 **36:3** [a]Ps 10:7; 12:2 [b]Ps 94:8; Jer 4:22

4 He [a]devises wickedness
upon his bed;
He sets himself on a [b]path
that is not good;
He [c]does not despise evil.

5 Your [a]lovingkindness,
O Yahweh,
is in the heavens,
Your faithfulness *reaches*
to the skies.
6 Your [a]righteousness is
like the [1]mountains of God;
Your [b]judgments are
*like* a great deep.
O Yahweh, You [c]save
man and beast.
7 How [a]precious is Your
lovingkindness, O God!
And the sons of men [b]take
refuge in the shadow
of Your wings.
8 They [1]are [a]satisfied from
the [2]richness of Your house;
And You give them to drink
of the [b]river of Your delights.
9 For with You is
the [a]fountain of life;
In Your light we see light.

10 Continue Your lovingkindness
to [a]those who know You,
And Your [b]righteousness
to the upright in heart.
11 Let not the foot of [1]pride
come upon me,
And let not the hand of
the [2]ungodly drive me away.
12 There the workers
of wickedness have fallen;
They have been thrust
down and [a]cannot rise.

## PSALM 37

### *Delight Yourself in Yahweh*

Of David.

א *Aleph*

1 [a]Do not fret because
of evildoers,
Be not [b]envious toward doers
of unrighteousness.
2 For they will [a]wither
quickly like the grass
And [b]fade like the green herb.

ב *Beth*

3 [a]Trust in Yahweh
and do good;
[b]Dwell in the land and
[c,1]cultivate faithfulness.
4 [a]Delight yourself in Yahweh;
And He will [b]give you
the desires of your heart.

ג *Gimel*

5 [a]Commit your way to Yahweh,
Trust in Him,
and He will do it.
6 He will bring forth [a]your
righteousness as the light
And your judgment
[b]as the noonday.

ד *Daleth*

7 Be still in Yahweh and [a]wait
[1]patiently for Him;
[b]Do not fret because of him
who [c]prospers in his way,

**36:4** [a]Pr 4:16; Mic 2:1 [b]Is 65:2 [c]Ps 52:3; Ro 12:9 **36:5** [a]Ps 57:10; 103:11; 108:4 **36:6** [a]Ps 71:19 [b]Job 11:8; Ps 77:19; Ro 11:33 [c]Ne 9:6; Ps 104:14, 15; 145:16 [1]Or *mighty mountains* **36:7** [a]Ps 40:5; 139:17 [b]Ru 2:12; Ps 17:8; 57:1; 91:4 **36:8** [a]Ps 63:5; 65:4; Is 25:6; Jer 31:12-14 [b]Job 20:17; Ps 46:4; Rev 22:1 [1]Or *drink their fill* [2]Lit *fatness* **36:9** [a]Jer 2:13 **36:10** [a]Jer 22:16 [b]Ps 24:5 **36:11** [1]Lit *lofty pride* [2]Lit *wicked* **36:12** [a]Ps 140:10; Is 26:14 ◆**37:1** [a]Pr 23:17; 24:19 [b]Ps 73:3; Pr 3:31 **37:2** [a]Job 14:2; Ps 90:6; 92:7; Jas 1:11 [b]Ps 129:6 **37:3** [a]Ps 62:8 [b]Dt 30:20 [c]Is 40:11; Eze 34:13, 14 [1]Or *feed securely, feed on His faithfulness* **37:4** [a]Job 22:26; Ps 94:19; Is 58:14 [b]Ps 21:2; 145:19; Mt 7:7, 8 **37:5** [a]Ps 55:22; Pr 16:3; 1Pe 5:7 **37:6** [a]Ps 97:11; Is 58:8, 10; Mic 7:9 [b]Job 11:17 **37:7** [a]Ps 40:1; 62:5; Lam 3:26 [b]Ps 37:1, 8 [c]Jer 12:1 [1]Or *longingly*

Because of the man who
carries out schemes
of wickedness.

ה *He*

8 Cease from anger and
[a]forsake wrath;
Do not fret; *it leads*
only to evildoing.
9 For [a]evildoers will be cut off,
But those who hope
for Yahweh, they will
[b]inherit the land.

ו *Vav*

10 Yet [a]a little while and
the wicked man will
be no more;
You will look carefully
at [b]his place, and he
will not be *there.*
11 But [a]the lowly will
inherit the land
And will delight themselves
in [b]abundant peace.

ז *Zayin*

12 The wicked [a]schemes
against the righteous
And [b]gnashes at him
with his teeth.
13 The Lord [a]laughs at him,
For He sees that [b]his
day is coming.

ח *Heth*

14 The wicked have
drawn the sword and
[a]bent their bow
To cast down the [b]afflicted
and the needy,
To [c]slay those who are
upright in conduct.
15 Their sword will enter
their own heart,
And their [a]bows will
be broken.

ט *Teth*

16 [a]Better is the little
of the righteous
Than the abundance
of many wicked.
17 For the [a]arms of the wicked
will be broken,
But Yahweh [b]sustains
the righteous.

י *Yodh*

18 Yahweh [a]knows the days
of the [1]blameless,
And their [b]inheritance
will be forever.
19 They will not be ashamed
in the time of evil,
And [a]in the days
of famine they
will be satisfied.

כ *Kaph*

20 But the [a]wicked will perish;
And the enemies of Yahweh
will be like the [1]glory
of the pastures,
They vanish—[b]in smoke
they vanish away.

ל *Lamedh*

21 The wicked borrows
and does not pay back,
But the righteous [a]is
gracious and gives.
22 For [a]those blessed by Him
will [b]inherit the land,
But those [c]cursed by Him
will be cut off.

---

**37:8** [a]Eph 4:31; Col 3:8 **37:9** [a]Ps 37:2, 22 [b]Ps 25:13; Pr 2:21; Is 57:13; 60:21; Mt 5:5 **37:10** [a]Job 24:24 [b]Job 7:10; Ps 37:35, 36 **37:11** [a]Mt 5:5 [b]Ps 72:7 **37:12** [a]Ps 31:13, 20 [b]Ps 35:16 **37:13** [a]Ps 2:4 [b]1Sa 26:10; Job 18:20 **37:14** [a]Ps 11:2; Lam 2:4 [b]Ps 35:10; 86:1 [c]Ps 11:2 **37:15** [a]1Sa 2:4; Ps 46:9 **37:16** [a]Pr 15:16; 16:8 **37:17** [a]Job 38:15; Ps 10:15; Eze 30:21 [b]Ps 71:6; 145:14 **37:18** [a]Ps 1:6; 31:7 [b]Ps 37:27, 29 [1]Lit *complete, perfect* **37:19** [a]Job 5:20; Ps 33:19 **37:20** [a]Ps 73:27 [b]Ps 68:2; 102:3 [1]Flowers **37:21** [a]Ps 112:5, 9 **37:22** [a]Pr 3:33 [b]Ps 37:9 [c]Job 5:3

מ *Mem*

23 [a]The footsteps of a man are
established by Yahweh,
And He [b]delights in his way.
24 When [a]he falls, he will not
be hurled headlong,
Because [b]Yahweh is the One
[1]who sustains his hand.

נ *Nun*

25 I was young and now I am old,
Yet [a]I have not seen
the righteous forsaken
Or [b]his seed begging bread.
26 All day long [a]he is
gracious and lends,
And [b]his seed is a blessing.

ס *Samekh*

27 [a]Depart from evil and do good,
So you will dwell [b]forever.

ע *Ayin*

28 For Yahweh [a]loves [1]justice
And [b]will not forsake
His holy ones;
They are [c]kept forever,
But the [d]seed of the wicked
will be cut off.
29 The righteous will
[a]inherit the land
And [b]dwell in it forever.

פ *Pe*

30 The mouth of the righteous
[a]utters wisdom,
And his tongue [b]speaks justice.
31 The [a]law of his God
*is in his* heart;
His [b]steps do not slip.

צ *Tsadhe*

32 The [a]wicked spies
upon the righteous
And [b]seeks to put
him to death.
33 Yahweh will [a]not forsake
him in his hand;
[b]He will not condemn him
when he is judged.

ק *Qoph*

34 [a]Hope for Yahweh and
keep His way,
And He will exalt you
to inherit the land;
When the [b]wicked are cut
off, you will see it.

ר *Resh*

35 I have [a]seen a wicked,
ruthless man
Spreading himself
like a [b]luxuriant [1]tree
in its native soil.
36 Then [1]he passed away, and
behold, he [a]was no more;
I sought for him, but he
could not be found.

ש *Shin*

37 Observe the [a,1]blameless
man, and behold
the [b]upright;
For the man of peace will
have [2]a [c]posterity.
38 But transgressors will be
altogether [a]destroyed;
The [1]posterity of the wicked
will be [b]cut off.

---

**37:23** [a]1Sa 2:9; Ps 40:2; 66:9; 119:5 [b]Ps 147:11 **37:24** [a]Ps 145:14; Pr 24:16; Mic 7:8 [b]Ps 147:6 [1]Or *who sustains him with His hand* **37:25** [a]Ps 37:28; Is 41:17; Heb 13:5 [b]Ps 109:10 **37:26** [a]Dt 15:8; Ps 37:21 [b]Ps 147:13 **37:27** [a]Ps 34:14 [b]Ps 37:18; 102:28 **37:28** [a]Ps 11:7; 33:5 [b]Ps 37:25 [c]Ps 31:23 [d]Ps 21:10; 37:9; Pr 2:22; Is 14:20 [1]Lit *judgment* **37:29** [a]Ps 37:9; Pr 2:21 [b]Ps 37:18 **37:30** [a]Ps 49:3; Pr 10:13 [b]Ps 101:1; 119:13 **37:31** [a]Dt 6:6; Ps 40:8; 119:11; Is 51:7; Jer 31:33 [b]Ps 26:1; 37:23 **37:32** [a]Ps 10:8; 17:11 [b]Ps 37:14 **37:33** [a]Ps 31:8; 2Pe 2:9 [b]Ps 34:22; 109:31 **37:34** [a]Ps 27:14; 37:9 [b]Ps 52:5, 6; 91:8 **37:35** [a]Job 5:3; Jer 12:2 [b]Job 8:16 [1]Native plant; lit *native* **37:36** [a]Job 20:5; Ps 37:10 [1]Ancient versions *I passed by* **37:37** [a]Ps 37:18 [b]Ps 7:10 [c]Is 57:1, 2 [1]Or *perfect*; lit *complete* [2]Lit *an end* **37:38** [a]Ps 1:4-6; 37:20, 28 [b]Ps 37:9; 73:17 [1]Lit *end*

ת Tav

39 But the [a]salvation
of the righteous is
from Yahweh;
He is their strength
[b]in time of distress.
40 [a]Yahweh helps them
and protects them;
He [b]protects them from
the wicked and saves them,
Because they [c]take
refuge in Him.

## PSALM 38

### *Do Not Forsake Me, O Yahweh*

A Psalm of David. To bring to remembrance.

1 O Yahweh, [a]reprove me
not in Your wrath,
And discipline me not
in Your burning anger.
2 For Your [a]arrows have
pressed deep into me,
And [b]Your hand has
pressed down upon me.
3 There is [a]no soundness
in my flesh [b]because
of Your indignation;
There is no health [c]in my
bones because of my sin.
4 For my [a]iniquities go
over my head;
As a heavy burden they
weigh too much for me.
5 My [1]wounds stink *and* rot
Because of [a]my [2]folly.
6 I am bent over and
[a]greatly bowed down;
I [b]go mourning all day long.
7 For my loins are filled
with [a]burning,
And there is [b]no soundness
in my flesh.
8 I am [a]faint and [1]badly crushed;
I [b,2]groan because of
the [3]agitation of my heart.

9 Lord, all [a]my desire
is [1]before You;
And my [b]sighing is not
hidden from You.
10 My heart throbs, [a]my
strength forsakes me;
And the [b]light of my
eyes, even [1]that [2]has
gone from me.
11 My [a,1]loved ones and my
friends stand aloof
from my plague;
And my kinsmen
[b]stand afar off.
12 Those who [a]search for my
life [b]lay snares *for me*;
And those who [c]seek
[1]*to do* me evil have
[2]threatened destruction,
And they [d]meditate
on deception all day long.

13 But I, like a deaf man,
do not hear;
And *I am* like a [a]mute
man who does not
open his mouth.
14 And I am like a man
who does not hear,

---

**37:39** [a]Ps 3:8; 62:1 [b]Ps 9:9; 37:19 **37:40** [a]Ps 54:4 [b]Ps 22:4; Is 31:5; Da 3:17; 6:23 [c]1Chr 5:20; Ps 34:22 ◆ **38:1** [a]Ps 6:1 **38:2** [a]Job 6:4 [b]Ps 32:4 **38:3** [a]Is 1:6 [b]Ps 102:10 [c]Job 33:19; Ps 6:2; 31:10 **38:4** [a]Ezr 9:6; Ps 40:12 **38:5** [a]Ps 69:5 [1]Or *stripes* [2]A lack of wisdom due to negligence or carelessness; the activity of an ignorant fool **38:6** [a]Ps 35:14 [b]Job 30:28; Ps 42:9; 43:2 **38:7** [a]Ps 102:3 [b]Ps 38:3 **38:8** [a]Lam 1:13, 20f; 2:11; 5:17 [b]Job 3:24; Ps 22:1; 32:3 [1]Or *greatly* [2]Lit *roar* [3]Lit *growling* **38:9** [a]Ps 10:17 [b]Ps 6:6; 102:5 [1]Or known *to You* **38:10** [a]Ps 31:10 [b]Ps 6:7; 69:3; 88:9 [1]Lit *they have* [2]Lit *is not with me* **38:11** [a]Ps 31:11; 88:18 [b]Lk 23:49 [1]Or *lovers* **38:12** [a]Ps 54:3 [b]Ps 140:5 [c]Ps 35:4 [d]Ps 35:20 [1]Or *my calamity* [2]Lit *spoken* **38:13** [a]Ps 39:2, 9

And in whose mouth
are no reproofs.
15 For [a]I [1]wait on You, O Yahweh;
You [b]will answer,
O Lord my God.
16 For I said, "*Save*, lest they
be glad over me,
*Who*, when my foot
stumbles, [a]magnify
themselves against me."
17 For I am [a]ready to fall,
And [b]my [1]sorrow is
continually before me.
18 For I [a,1]confess my iniquity;
I am full of [b]anxiety
because of my sin.
19 But my [a]enemies are
vigorous *and* [1]strong,
And those who wrongfully
[b]hate me abound.
20 And those who [a]repay
evil for good,
They [b]accuse me, for I
pursue what is good.
21 Do not forsake me, O Yahweh;
O my God, [a]do not
be far from me!
22 Make [a]haste to help me,
O Lord, [b]my salvation!

## PSALM 39

### *Yahweh, Make Me Know My End*

For the choir director. For [†]Jeduthun.
A Psalm of David.

1 I said, "I will [a]keep
watch over my ways
That I [b]may not sin
with my tongue;
I will keep watch *over* [c]my
mouth as with a muzzle
While the wicked are
in my presence."
2 I was [a]mute with silence,
I *even* kept silent
from *speaking* good,
And my anguish grew worse.
3 My [a]heart was hot within me,
While I meditated the fire
was burning;
*Then* I spoke with my tongue:
4 "Yahweh, cause me
to know [a]my end
And what is the extent
of my days;
Let me know how
[b]transient I am.
5 "Behold, You have made [a]my
days *as* [1]handbreadths,
And my [b]lifetime
as nothing before You;
Surely every man,
*even* standing firm,
is [2]altogether [c]vanity. [3]Selah.
6 "Surely every man [a]walks
about as [1]a shadow;
Surely they make
an [b]uproar in vain;
He [c]piles up *riches* and
does not know who
will gather them.

7 "And now, Lord,
what do I hope in?
My [a]expectation is in You.
8 "[a]Deliver me from all
my transgressions;

---

**38:15** [a]Ps 39:7 [b]Ps 17:6 [1]Or *hope for* **38:16** [a]Ps 35:26 **38:17** [a]Ps 35:15 [b]Ps 13:2 [1]Lit *pain* **38:18** [a]Ps 32:5 [b]2Co 7:9, 10 [1]Or *declare* **38:19** [a]Ps 18:17 [b]Ps 35:19 [1]Or *numerous* **38:20** [a]Ps 35:12 [b]Ps 109:5; 1Jn 3:12 **38:21** [a]Ps 22:19; 35:22 **38:22** [a]Ps 40:13, 17 [b]Ps 27:1 ◆ **39:TITLE** [†]1Chr 16:41 **39:1** [a]1Ki 2:4; 2Ki 10:31; Ps 119:9 [b]Job 2:10; Ps 34:13; Jas 3:5-12 [c]Ps 141:3; Jas 3:2 **39:2** [a]Ps 38:13 **39:3** [a]Ps 32:4; Jer 20:9; Lk 24:32 **39:4** [a]Job 6:11; Ps 90:12; 119:84 [b]Ps 78:39; 103:14 **39:5** [a]Ps 89:47 [b]Ps 144:4 [c]Job 14:2; Ps 62:9; Ecc 6:12 [1]A handbreadth was approx. 3 in. or 7.6 cm [2]Or *mere breath* [3]*Selah* may mean *Pause, Crescendo, Musical Interlude* **39:6** [a]1Co 7:31; Jas 1:10, 11; 1Pe 1:24 [b]Ps 127:2; Ecc 5:17 [c]Ps 49:10; Ecc 2:26; 5:14; Lk 12:20 [1]Lit *an image* **39:7** [a]Ps 38:15 **39:8** [a]Ps 51:9, 14; 79:9

Make me not the [b]reproach
of the wicked fool.
9 "I have become [a]mute,
I do not open my mouth,
Because it is [b]You who
have done *it*.
10 "[a]Remove Your plague from me;
Because of [b]the opposition
of Your hand I am
wasting away.
11 "With [a]reproofs You chasten
a man for iniquity;
You [b]consume as a moth
what is precious to him;
Surely [c]every man
is vanity. Selah.

12 "[a]Hear my prayer,
O Yahweh, and give ear
to my cry for help;
Do not be silent [b]at my tears;
For I am [c]a sojourner with You,
A [d]foreign resident
like all my fathers.
13 "[a]Turn Your gaze away from
me, that I may [1]smile *again*
Before I go and am no more."

## PSALM 40

### *The One Who Rescues Me*

For the choir director. Of David. A Psalm.

1 I [a]hoped [1]earnestly for Yahweh;
And He inclined to me and
[b]heard my cry for help.
2 He brought me up out of
the [a]pit of destruction,
out of the [1]miry clay,
And [b]He set my feet
upon a high rock, [c]He
established my steps.
3 He put a [a]new song
in my mouth, a song
of praise to our God;
Many will [b]see and fear
And will trust in Yahweh.

4 How [a]blessed is the man who
has made Yahweh his trust,
And [b]has not [1]turned
to the proud, nor to those
who [c]stray into falsehood.
5 Many, O Yahweh my God,
are [a]the wondrous
deeds You have done,
And Your [b]thoughts toward us;
There is none to compare
with You.
I would declare and
speak of them,
*But* they [c]are too
numerous to recount.

6 [a,1]Sacrifice and meal offering
[2]You have not desired;
My ears You have [3]opened;
Burnt offering and sin offering
You have not required.
7 Then I said, "Behold, I come;
In the scroll of the book
it is [1]written of me.
8 "[a]I desire to do Your
will, O my God;
[b]Your law is
within my inner being."

---

**39:8** [b]Ps 44:13; 79:4; 119:22 **39:9** [a]Ps 39:2 [b]2Sa 16:10; Job 2:10 **39:10** [a]Job 9:34; 13:21 [b]Ps 32:4 **39:11** [a]Eze 5:15; 2Pe 2:16 [b]Job 13:28; Ps 90:7; Is 50:9 [c]Ps 39:5 **39:12** [a]Ps 102:1; 143:1 [b]2Ki 20:5; Ps 56:8 [c]Lv 25:23; 1Chr 29:15; Ps 119:19; Heb 11:13; 1Pe 2:11 [d]Ge 47:9 **39:13** [a]Job 7:19; 10:20, 21; 14:6; Ps 102:24 [1]Or *become cheerful* ◆ **40:1** [a]Ps 25:5; 27:14; 37:7 [b]Ps 34:15 [1]Or *intently* **40:2** [a]Ps 69:2, 14; Jer 38:6 [b]Ps 27:5 [c]Ps 37:23 [1]Lit *mud of the mire* **40:3** [a]Ps 32:7; 33:3 [b]Ps 52:6; 64:9 **40:4** [a]Ps 34:8; 84:12 [b]Job 37:24 [c]Ps 125:5 [1]Lit *regarded* **40:5** [a]Job 5:9; Ps 136:4 [b]Ps 139:17; Is 55:8 [c]Ps 71:15; 139:18 **40:6** [a]1Sa 15:22; Ps 51:16; Is 1:11; Jer 6:20; 7:22, 23; Am 5:22; Mic 6:6-8; Heb 10:5-7 [1]Blood sacrifice [2]Or *You have not taken pleasure in* [3]Lit *dug*; or possibly *pierced* **40:7** [1]Or *prescribed for* **40:8** [a]Jn 4:34 [b]Ps 37:31; Jer 31:33; 2Co 3:3

9 I [a]proclaim good news
of righteousness
in the great assembly;
Behold, I do [b]not
restrain my lips,
O Yahweh, [c]You know.
10 I do [a]not conceal
Your righteousness
within my heart;
I [b]speak of Your faithfulness
and Your salvation;
I do not hide Your
lovingkindness and Your
truth from the great assembly.

11 You, O Yahweh, will
not withhold Your
compassion from me;
[1]Your [a]lovingkindness
and Your truth will
continually guard me.
12 For evils beyond number
have [a]surrounded me;
My [b]iniquities have
overtaken me, so that
I am not able to see;
They are [c]more numerous
than the hairs of my head,
And my [d]heart has [1]failed me.

13 [a]Be pleased, O Yahweh,
to deliver me;
Make [b]haste, O Yahweh,
to help me.
14 Let those be [a]ashamed and
*humiliated together*
Who [b]seek my [1]life
to sweep it away;
Let those be turned back
and dishonored
Who delight in [2]evil
*against* me.
15 Let those [a]be [1]appalled
because of their shame
Who [b]say to me, "Aha, aha!"
16 [a]Let all who seek You rejoice
and be glad in You;
Let those who love Your
salvation [b]say continually,
"Yahweh be magnified!"
17 As for me, [a]I am afflicted
and needy,
[b,1]May the Lord think of me.
You are my help and the One
who rescues me;
Do not delay, O my God.

## PSALM 41

### *O Yahweh, Be Gracious to Me*

For the choir director. A Psalm of David.

1 How blessed is he who
[a]considers the [1]poor;
Yahweh will provide him
escape [b]in a day
of [2]calamity.
2 Yahweh will [a]keep him
and keep him alive,
And he shall be [b]blessed
upon the earth;
And [c]do not give him over
to the desire of his enemies.
3 Yahweh will sustain him
upon his sickbed;
In his illness, You [1]restore
him to health.

4 As for me, I said, "O Yahweh,
be gracious to me;
[a]Heal my soul, for [b]I have
sinned against You."

---

**40:9** [a]Ps 22:22, 25 [b]Ps 119:13 [c]Jos 22:22; Ps 139:4 **40:10** [a]Ac 20:20, 27 [b]Ps 89:1 **40:11** [a]Ps 43:3; 57:3; 61:7; Pr 20:28 [1]Or *May...guard me* **40:12** [a]Ps 18:5; 116:3 [b]Ps 38:4; 65:3 [c]Ps 69:4 [d]Ps 73:26 [1]Lit *forsaken* **40:13** [a]Ps 70:1 [b]Ps 22:19; 71:12 **40:14** [a]Ps 35:4, 26; 70:2; 71:13 [b]Ps 63:9 [1]Or *soul* [2]Or *my calamity* **40:15** [a]Ps 70:3 [b]Ps 35:21; 70:3 [1]Or *desolated* **40:16** [a]Ps 70:4 [b]Ps 35:27 **40:17** [a]Ps 70:5; 86:1; 109:22 [b]Ps 40:5; 1Pe 5:7 [1]Or *The Lord is mindful* ◆**41:1** [a]Ps 82:3, 4; Pr 14:21 [b]Ps 27:5; 37:19 [1]Or *helpless* [2]Lit *evil* **41:2** [a]Ps 37:28 [b]Ps 37:22 [c]Ps 27:12 **41:3** [1]Lit *turn all his bed* **41:4** [a]Ps 6:2; 103:3; 147:3 [b]Ps 51:4

5 My enemies [a]speak
evil against me,
“When will he die, and
his name perish?”
6 And [1]when he comes
to see *me*, he [a]speaks
[2]worthlessness;
His heart gathers
wickedness to itself;
When he goes outside,
he speaks it.
7 All who hate me whisper
together against me;
Against me, they [a]devise
for me [1]calamity, *saying*,
8 “A vile thing is poured
out [1]upon him,
That when he lies down,
he will [a]not rise up again.”
9 Even my [a]close friend
in whom I trusted,
Who ate my bread,
Has lifted up his heel
against me.

10 But You, O Yahweh,
be gracious to me
and [a]raise me up,
That I may repay them.
11 By this I know that [a]You
delight in me,
Because [b]my enemy makes no
shout in triumph over me.
12 As for me, [a]You uphold
me in my integrity,
And You make me [b]stand firm
in Your presence forever.

13 [a]Blessed be Yahweh,
the God of Israel,
From everlasting
to everlasting.
Amen and Amen.

## BOOK 2

### PSALM 42

#### *My Soul Thirsts for God*

For the choir director. A [†]Maskil of the sons of Korah.

1 As the deer [1]pants
for the water brooks,
So my soul [a,1]pants
for You, O God.
2 My soul [a]thirsts for God,
for the [b]living God;
When shall I come and
[c,1]appear before God?
3 My [a]tears have been my
food day and night,
While *they* [b]say to me all day
long, “Where is your God?”
4 These things I remember
and I [a]pour out my
soul within me.
For I [b]used to go along
with the throng *and*
[1]lead them in procession
to the house of God,
With the sound of a [c]shout
of joy and thanksgiving,
a multitude keeping festival.

5 [a]Why are you [b,1]in despair,
O my soul?

**41:5** [a]Ps 38:12 **41:6** [a]Ps 12:2; 62:4; Pr 26:24-26 [1]Or *if he* [2]Or *emptiness* **41:7** [a]Ps 56:5 [1]Lit *evil* **41:8** [a]Ps 71:10, 11 [1]Or *within* **41:9** [a]2Sa 15:12; Job 19:13, 19; Ps 55:12, 13, 20; Jer 20:10; Mic 7:5; Mt 26:23; *Lk 22:21; Jn 13:18* **41:10** [a]Ps 3:3 **41:11** [a]Ps 37:23; 147:11 [b]Ps 25:2 **41:12** [a]Ps 18:32; 37:17; 63:8 [b]Job 36:7; Ps 21:6 **41:13** [a]Ps 72:18, 19; 89:52; 106:48; 150:6 ◆ **42:TITLE** [†]Possibly *Contemplative, Didactic, Skillful Psalm* **42:1** [a]Ps 119:131 [1]Lit *longs* **42:2** [a]Ps 63:1; 84:2; 143:6 [b]Jos 3:10; Ps 84:2; Jer 10:10; Da 6:26; Mt 26:63; Ro 9:26; 1Th 1:9 [c]Ex 23:17; Ps 43:4; 84:7 [1]Some mss *see the face of God* **42:3** [a]Ps 80:5; 102:9 [b]Ps 79:10; 115:2; Joel 2:17; Mic 7:10 **42:4** [a]1Sa 1:15; Job 30:16; Ps 62:8; Lam 2:19 [b]Ps 55:14; 122:1; Is 30:29 [c]Ps 100:4 [1]Or *move slowly with them* **42:5** [a]Ps 42:11; 43:5 [b]Ps 38:6; Mt 26:38 [1]Or *sunk down*

And *why* are you
[c]disturbed within me?
[d]Wait for God, for I shall
still praise Him,
[2]*For* the [e,3]salvation
of His presence.
6 O my God, my soul is
[1]in despair within me;
Therefore I [a]remember You
from [b]the land of the Jordan
And the [2]peaks of [c]Hermon,
from Mount Mizar.
7 Deep calls to deep at
the sound of Your waterfalls;
All Your [a]breakers and Your
waves have rolled over me.
8 By day, Yahweh
will [a]command
His lovingkindness;
And [b]by night, His song
will be with me,
A prayer to [c]the God of my life.

9 I say to God [a]my rock, "Why
have You forgotten me?
Why do I go [b]mourning
[1]because of the [c]oppression
of the enemy?"
10 As a shattering of my bones,
my adversaries reproach me,
While they [a]say to me all day
long, "Where is your God?"
11 [a]Why are you [1]in despair,
O my soul?
And why are you
disturbed within me?
Wait for God, for I shall
still praise Him,
The salvation of my
presence and my God.

## PSALM 43

### *Send Out Your Light and Your Truth*

1 [a]Give justice to me, O God,
and [b]plead my case
against an unholy nation;
[1]Oh protect me
from [c]the deceitful and
unrighteous man!
2 For You are the [a]God
of my strength; why have
You [b]rejected me?
Why do I go [c]mourning
[1]because of the oppression
of the enemy?

3 Oh send out Your [a]light
and Your truth,
let them lead me;
Let them bring me
to Your [b]holy mountain
And to Your [c]dwelling places.
4 Then I will go to [a]the altar
of God,
To God [1]my exceeding [b]joy;
And upon the [c]lyre I shall
praise You, O God, my God.

5 [a]Why are you [1]in despair,
O my soul?
And why are you
disturbed within me?
Wait for God, for I shall
still praise Him,
The salvation of my
presence and my God.

---

**42:5** [c]Ps 77:3 [d]Ps 71:14; Lam 3:24 [e]Ps 44:3 [2]Some ancient versions *The help of my countenance and my God* [3]Or *saving acts* **42:6** [a]Ps 61:2 [b]2Sa 17:22 [c]Dt 3:8 [1]Or *sunk down* [2]Lit *Hermons* **42:7** [a]Ps 69:1, 2; 88:7; Jon 2:3 **42:8** [a]Ps 57:3; 133:3 [b]Job 35:10; Ps 16:7; 63:6; 77:6; 149:5 [c]Ecc 5:18; 8:15 **42:9** [a]Ps 18:2 [b]Ps 38:6 [c]Ps 17:9 [1]Or *while the enemy oppresses* **42:10** [a]Ps 42:3; Joel 2:17 **42:11** [a]Ps 42:5; 43:5 [1]Or *sunk down* ◆ **43:1** [a]Ps 26:1; 35:24 [b]1Sa 24:15; Ps 35:1 [c]Ps 5:6; 38:12 [1]Or *May You* **43:2** [a]Ps 18:1; 28:7; 31:4 [b]Ps 44:9; 88:14 [c]Ps 42:9 [1]Or *while the enemy oppresses* **43:3** [a]Ps 36:9 [b]Ps 2:6; 3:4; 42:4; 46:4 [c]Ps 84:1 **43:4** [a]Ps 26:6 [b]Ps 21:6 [c]Ps 33:2; 49:4; 57:8; 71:22 [1]Lit *the gladness of my joy* **43:5** [a]Ps 42:5, 11 [1]Or *sunk down*

## PSALM 44

### *Rise Up, Be Our Help*

For the choir director. Of the sons of Korah. A [†]Maskil.

1 O God, we have heard
with our ears,
Our [a]fathers have
recounted to us
The [b]work that You
did in their days,
In the [c]days of old.
2 You with Your own hand
[a]dispossessed the nations;
Then You [b]planted them;
You [c]afflicted the peoples,
Then You [d]cast them out.
3 For by their own sword they
[a]did not possess the land,
And their own arm did
not save them,
But Your right hand and
Your [b]arm and the [c]light
of Your presence,
For You [d]favored them.

4 You are [a]my King, O God;
[b]Command [1]salvation
for Jacob.
5 Through You we will [a]push
back our adversaries;
Through Your name we
will [b]tread down those
who rise up against us.
6 For I will [a]not trust in my bow,
And my sword will
not save me.
7 But You [a]have saved us
from our adversaries,
And You have [b]put to shame
those who hate us.
8 In God we have [a]boasted
all day long,
And we will [b]give thanks
to Your name forever. [1]Selah.

9 Yet You [a]have rejected *us* and
brought us to [b]dishonor,
And [c]do not go out
with our armies.
10 You cause us to [a]turn back
from the adversary;
And those who hate us
[b]have plundered *us*
for themselves.
11 You give us as [a]sheep
[1]to be eaten
And have [b]scattered us
among the nations.
12 You [a]sell Your people
[1]for no amount,
And You have not [2]profited
from their price.
13 You make us a [a]reproach
to our neighbors,
A mockery and a [b]derision
to those around us.
14 You make us [a]a byword
among the nations,
A [b,1]laughingstock
among the peoples.
15 All day long my dishonor
is before me

◆ **44:TITLE** [†]Possibly *Contemplative, Didactic, Skillful Psalm* **44:1** [a]Ex 12:26, 27; Dt 6:20; Jdg 6:13; Ps 78:3 [b]Ps 78:12 [c]Dt 32:7; Ps 77:5; Is 51:9; 63:9 **44:2** [a]Jos 3:10; Ne 9:24; Ps 78:55; 80:8 [b]Ex 15:17; 2Sa 7:10; Jer 24:6; Am 9:15 [c]Ps 135:10-12 [d]Ps 80:9-11; Zec 2:6 **44:3** [a]Dt 8:17, 18; Jos 24:12 [b]Ps 77:15 [c]Ps 4:6; 89:15 [d]Dt 4:37; 7:7, 8; 10:15; Ps 106:4 **44:4** [a]Ps 74:12 [b]Ps 42:8 [1]Lit *salvations* **44:5** [a]Dt 33:17; Ps 60:12; Da 8:4 [b]Ps 108:13; Zec 10:5 **44:6** [a]1Sa 17:47; Ps 33:16; Hos 1:7 **44:7** [a]Ps 136:24 [b]Ps 53:5 **44:8** [a]Ps 34:2 [b]Ps 30:12 [1]*Selah* may mean *Pause, Crescendo, Musical Interlude* **44:9** [a]Ps 43:2; 60:1, 10; 74:1; 89:38; 108:11 [b]Ps 69:19 [c]Ps 60:10; 108:11 **44:10** [a]Lv 26:17; Jos 7:8, 12; Ps 89:43 [b]Ps 89:41 **44:11** [a]Ps 44:22; Ro 8:36 [b]Lv 26:33; Dt 4:27; 28:64; Ps 106:27; Eze 20:23 [1]Lit *for food* **44:12** [a]Dt 32:30; Jdg 2:14; 3:8; Is 52:3, 4; Jer 15:13 [1]Lit *for no wealth* [2]Or *set a high price on them* **44:13** [a]Dt 28:37; Ps 79:4; 89:41 [b]Ps 80:6; Eze 23:32 **44:14** [a]Job 17:6; Ps 69:11; Jer 24:9 [b]2Ki 19:21; Ps 109:25 [1]Lit *shaking of the head*

And [1]the [a]shame of my
face has covered me,
16 Because of the voice of him
who [a]reproaches and reviles,
Because of the presence of
the [b]enemy and the avenger.

17 All this has come upon us, but
we have [a]not forgotten You,
And we have not [b]dealt falsely
with Your covenant.
18 Our heart has not [a]turned back,
Nor have our steps [b]deviated
from Your path,
19 Yet You have [a]crushed us
in a place of [b]jackals
And covered us with [c]the
shadow of death.

20 If we had [a]forgotten
the name of our God
Or spread our [1]hands
to [b]a strange god,
21 Would not God [a]find this out?
For He knows the secrets
of the heart.
22 But [a]for Your sake we are
killed all day long;
We are counted as [b]sheep
for the slaughter.
23 [a]Arouse Yourself, why [b]do
You sleep, O Lord?
Awake, [c]do not reject
us forever.
24 Why do You [a]hide Your face
*And* [b]*forget our affliction*
and our oppression?
25 For our [a]soul has sunk
down into the dust;
Our [1]body cleaves
to the earth.
26 [a]Rise up, be our help,
And [b]redeem us for the sake
of Your lovingkindness.

## PSALM 45

### *Your Throne, O God, Is Forever*

For the choir director. According to
[†]Shoshannim. Of the sons of Korah.
A [˙]Maskil. A Song of Love.

1 My heart [1]overflows
with a good theme;
I [2]address my [3]verses
to the [4]King;
My tongue is the pen
of [a]a skillful scribe.
2 You are fairer
than the sons of men;
[a]Grace is poured
[1]upon Your lips;
Therefore God has
[b]blessed You forever.

3 Gird [a]Your sword on *Your*
thigh, O [b,1]Mighty One,
*In* Your splendor and
Your majesty!
4 And in Your majesty ride
on victoriously,
For the cause of truth
and [a]meekness
*and* righteousness;
Let Your [b]right hand teach
You [1]awesome things.

---

**44:15** [a]2Chr 32:21; Ps 69:7 [1]Or *humiliation* **44:16** [a]Ps 74:10 [b]Ps 8:2 **44:17** [a]Ps 78:7; 119:61, 83, 109, 141, 153, 176 [b]Ps 78:57 **44:18** [a]Ps 78:57 [b]Job 23:11; Ps 119:51, 157 **44:19** [a]Ps 51:8; 94:5 [b]Job 30:29; Is 13:22; Jer 9:11 [c]Job 3:5; Ps 23:4 **44:20** [a]Ps 78:11 [b]Dt 6:14; Ps 81:9 [1]Lit *palms* **44:21** [a]Ps 139:1, 2; Jer 17:10 **44:22** [a]Ro 8:36 [b]Is 53:7; Jer 12:3 **44:23** [a]Ps 7:6 [b]Ps 78:65 [c]Ps 77:7 **44:24** [a]Job 13:24; Ps 88:14 [b]Ps 42:9; Lam 5:20 **44:25** [a]Ps 119:25 [1]Lit *womb, stomach* **44:26** [a]Ps 35:2 [b]Ps 6:4; 25:22 ◆ **45:TITLE** [†]Or possibly *Lilies* [˙]Possibly *Contemplative, Didactic, Skillful Psalm* **45:1** [a]Ezr 7:6 [1]Lit *is astir* [2]Lit *am saying* [3]Lit *works* [4]Probably refers to Solomon as a type of Christ **45:2** [a]Lk 4:22 [b]Ps 21:6 [1]Or *through* **45:3** [a]Heb 4:12; Rev 1:16 [b]Is 9:6 [1]Or *warrior* **45:4** [a]Zep 2:3 [b]Ps 21:8 [1]Or *fearful*

5 Your [a]arrows are sharp;
The [b]peoples fall under You;
*Your arrows are* [c]in the heart
of the King's enemies.

6 [a]Your throne, O God,
is forever and ever;
A scepter of [b]uprightness is
the scepter of Your kingdom.
7 You have [a]loved righteousness
and hated wickedness;
Therefore God, Your God,
has [b]anointed You
With the oil of joy
above Your companions.
8 All Your garments are
*fragrant with* [a]myrrh
and aloes *and* cassia;
Out of ivory palaces
[b]stringed instruments
have made You glad.
9 Kings' daughters are
among [a]Your noble ladies;
At Your [b]right hand
stands the queen
in [c]gold from Ophir.

10 Listen, O daughter,
give attention and
incline your ear:
[a]Forget your people and
your father's house;
11 Then the King will
desire your beauty.
Because He is your [a]Lord,
[b]bow down to Him.
12 The daughter of [a]Tyre *will*
*come* with a present;
The [b]rich among the people
will seek your favor.
13 The King's daughter is all
glorious within *her chamber*;
Her clothing is [a]interwoven
with gold.
14 She will be [a]led to the King
[b]in embroidered work;
The [c]virgins, her companions
who follow her,
Will be brought to You.
15 They will be led forth
with gladness and rejoicing;
They will enter into
the King's palace.

16 In place of your fathers
will be your sons;
You shall set them up
as princes in all the earth.
17 I will cause [a]Your name
to be remembered
from generation
to every generation;
Therefore the peoples
[b]will give You thanks
forever and ever.

## PSALM 46

### *God Is Our Refuge and Strength*

For the choir director. Of the sons of Korah. [†]According to Alamoth. A Song.

1 God is our [a]refuge
and strength,
[1]A very [b]present help
[c]in [2]trouble.
2 Therefore we will [a]not
fear, though [b]the earth
should change
And though [c]the
mountains shake
into the heart of the [1]sea;

---

**45:5** [a]Ps 18:14; 120:4; Is 5:28; 7:13 [b]Ps 92:9 [c]2Sa 18:14 **45:6** [a]Ps 93:2; Heb 1:8, 9 [b]Ps 98:9 **45:7** [a]Ps 11:7; 33:5 [b]Ps 2:2 **45:8** [a]SS 4:14; Jn 19:39 [b]Ps 150:4 **45:9** [a]SS 6:8 [b]1Ki 2:19 [c]1Ki 9:28; Is 13:12 **45:10** [a]Dt 21:13; Ru 1:16, 17 **45:11** [a]Ge 18:12; 1Pe 3:6 [b]Eph 5:33 **45:12** [a]Ps 87:4 [b]Ps 22:29; 68:29; 72:10, 11; Is 49:23 **45:13** [a]Ex 39:2, 3 **45:14** [a]SS 1:4 [b]Jdg 5:30; Eze 16:10 [c]Ps 45:9 **45:17** [a]Mal 1:11 [b]Ps 138:4 ◆ **46:TITLE** [†]Possibly *For Soprano Voices* **46:1** [a]Ps 14:6; 62:7, 8 [b]Dt 4:7; Ps 145:18 [c]Ps 9:9 [1]Or *Abundantly available for help* [2]Or *tight places* **46:2** [a]Ps 23:4; 27:1 [b]Ps 82:5 [c]Ps 18:7 [1]Lit *seas*

3 Though its [a]waters
roar *and* foam,
Though the mountains quake
at its lofty pride. [1]Selah.

4 There is a [a]river whose streams
make glad the [b]city of God,
The holy [c]dwelling places
of the Most High.
5 God is [a]in the midst of her,
she will not be shaken;
God will [b]help her
[1]when morning dawns.
6 The [1]nations [a]roar,
the kingdoms shake;
He [b]gives His voice,
the earth [c]melts.
7 Yahweh of hosts [a]is with us;
The God of Jacob is [b]our
stronghold. Selah.

8 Come, [a]behold the works
of Yahweh,
[1]Who has appointed
[b]desolations in the earth.
9 He [a]makes wars to cease
to the end of the earth;
He [b]breaks the bow and
cuts up the spear;
He [c]burns the chariots
with fire.
10 "[1]Cease *striving* and
[a]know that I am God;
I will be [b]exalted among
the [2]nations, I will be
exalted in the earth."
11 Yahweh of hosts is with us;
The God of Jacob is our
stronghold. Selah.

## PSALM 47

### *God Is King of All the Earth*

For the choir director. Of the sons of Korah.
A Psalm.

1 O [a]clap your hands,
all peoples;
[b]Make a loud shout
to God with the sound
of a shout of [1]joy.
2 For Yahweh Most High
is [a,1]fearsome,
A [b]great King
over all the earth.
3 He [a]subdues peoples under us
And nations under our feet.
4 He chooses our
[a]inheritance for us,
The [b]pride of Jacob
whom He loves. [1]Selah.

5 God has [a]ascended
[1]with a loud shout,
Yahweh, [1]with the [b]sound
of a trumpet.
6 [a]Sing praises to God,
sing praises;
Sing praises to [b]our
King, sing praises.
7 For God is the [a]King
of all the earth;
Sing praises
[b]with a [1]skillful psalm.

---

**46:3** [a]Ps 93:3, 4; Jer 5:22 [1]*Selah* may mean *Pause, Crescendo, Musical Interlude* **46:4** [a]Ps 36:8; 65:9; Is 8:6; Rev 22:1 [b]Ps 48:1; 87:3; 101:8; Is 60:14; Rev 3:12 [c]Ps 43:3 **46:5** [a]Dt 23:14; Is 12:6; Eze 43:7, 9; Hos 11:9; Joel 2:27; Zec 2:5 [b]Ps 37:40; Is 41:14; Lk 1:54 [1]Lit *at the turning of the morning* **46:6** [a]Ps 2:1, 2 [b]Ps 18:13; 68:33; Jer 25:30; Joel 2:11; Am 1:2 [c]Am 9:5; Mic 1:4; Na 1:5 [1]Or *Gentiles* **46:7** [a]Nu 14:9; 2Chr 13:12 [b]Ps 9:9; 48:3 **46:8** [a]Ps 66:5 [b]Is 61:4; Jer 51:43 [1]Or *Which He has wrought as desolations* **46:9** [a]Is 2:4; Mic 4:3 [b]1Sa 2:4; Ps 76:3 [c]Is 9:5; Eze 39:9 **46:10** [a]Ps 100:3 [b]Is 2:11, 17 [1]Or *Let go, Relax* [2]Or *Gentiles* ◆ **47:1** [a]Ps 98:8 [b]Ps 106:47 [1]Or *a ringing cry* **47:2** [a]Dt 7:21; Ne 1:5; Ps 66:3, 5; 68:35 [b]Mal 1:14 [1]Or *awesome* **47:3** [a]Ps 18:47 **47:4** [a]1Pe 1:4 [b]Am 6:8; 8:7; Na 2:2 [1]*Selah* may mean *Pause, Crescendo, Musical Interlude* **47:5** [a]Ps 68:18 [b]Ps 98:6 [1]Or *amid* **47:6** [a]Ps 68:4 [b]Ps 89:18 **47:7** [a]Zec 14:9 [b]1Co 14:15 [1]Heb *Maskil*; possibly *Contemplative, Didactic, Skillful Psalm*

8 God [a]reigns over the nations,
God [1]sits on [b]His holy throne.
9 The [a]nobles of the peoples
have assembled themselves
*with* the [b]people
of the God of Abraham,
For the [c]shields of the earth
belong to God;
He [1]is [d]highly exalted.

## PSALM 48

### *The City of Our God*

A Song. A Psalm of the sons of Korah.

1 [a]Great is Yahweh, and
greatly to be praised,
In the [b]city of our God,
His [c]holy mountain.
2 [a]Beautiful in elevation,
[b]the joy of the whole earth,
Is Mount Zion *in* the far north,
The [c]city of the great King.
3 God, in her palaces,
Has made Himself known
as a [a]stronghold.

4 For, behold, the [a]kings
assembled themselves,
They passed by together.
5 They saw *it*, then they
were astonished;
They were [a]dismayed,
they [1]fled in alarm.
6 [1]Panic seized them there,
Anguish, as of [a]a woman
in childbirth.
7 With the [a]east wind
You [b]break the [c]ships
of Tarshish.
8 As we have heard,
so have we seen
In the city of Yahweh of hosts,
in the city of our God;
God will [a]establish her
forever. [1]Selah.

9 We have thought on [a]Your
lovingkindness, O God,
In the midst of Your temple.
10 As is Your [a]name, O God,
So is Your [b]praise
to the ends of the earth;
Your [c]right hand is full
of righteousness.
11 Let Mount [a]Zion be glad,
Let the [a]daughters
of Judah rejoice
Because of Your judgments.
12 Walk about Zion and
go around her;
Count her [a]towers;
13 Consider her [a]ramparts;
Go through her palaces,
That you may [b]recount *it*
to the next generation.
14 For this is God,
Our God forever and ever;
He will [a]guide us
[1]over death.

## PSALM 49

### *Why Should I Fear in Days of Evil?*

For the choir director. Of the sons of Korah.
A Psalm.

1 [a]Hear this, all peoples;
Give ear, all [b]inhabitants
of the world,

**47:8** [a]1Chr 16:31; Ps 22:28 [b]Ps 97:2 [1]Or *has taken His seat* **47:9** [a]Ps 72:11; 102:22; Is 49:7, 23 [b]Ro 4:11, 12 [c]Ps 89:18 [d]Ps 97:9 [1]Lit *has greatly exalted Himself* ◆ **48:1** [a]1Chr 16:25; Ps 96:4; 145:3 [b]Ps 46:4 [c]Ps 2:6; 87:1; Is 2:3; Mic 4:1; Zec 8:3 **48:2** [a]Ps 50:2 [b]Lam 2:15 [c]Mt 5:35 **48:3** [a]Ps 46:7 **48:4** [a]2Sa 10:6-19 **48:5** [a]Ex 15:15 [1]Lit *were hurried away* **48:6** [a]Is 13:8 [1]Lit *Trembling* **48:7** [a]Jer 18:17 [b]1Ki 22:48 [c]1Ki 10:22; Eze 27:25 **48:8** [a]Ps 87:5 [1]*Selah* may mean *Pause, Crescendo, Musical Interlude* **48:9** [a]Ps 26:3; 40:10 **48:10** [a]Dt 28:58; Jos 7:9; Mal 1:11 [b]Ps 65:1, 2; 100:1 [c]Is 41:10 **48:11** [a]Ps 97:8 **48:12** [a]Ne 3:1, 11, 25-27 **48:13** [a]Ps 122:7 [b]Ps 78:5-7 **48:14** [a]Ps 23:4; Is 58:11 [1]Lit *upon*; some mss and Gr *forever* ◆ **49:1** [a]Ps 78:1; Is 1:2; Mic 1:2 [b]Ps 33:8

2 Both [a,1]low and [2]high,
Rich and poor together.
3 My mouth will
[a]speak wisdom,
And the meditation of my
heart *will be* [b]discernment.
4 I will incline my ear
to [a]a proverb;
[b]I will [1]express my
[c]riddle on the harp.

5 Why should I [a]fear
in days of evil,
When the iniquity of my
[1]supplanters surrounds me,
6 Even those who [a]trust
in their wealth
And boast in the abundance
of their riches?
7 Truly, no man can
[a]redeem *his* brother;
He cannot give to God
a [b]ransom for him—
8 For [a]the redemption price
for their soul is costly,
And *it* ceases forever—
9 That he should [a]live
on eternally,
That he should not
[b]see [1]corruption.

10 For he sees *that even*
[a]wise men die;
The [b,1]fool and the senseless
alike perish
*And* [c]leave their
wealth to others.
11 Their [a,1]inner thought is *that*
their houses [b]are forever
*And* their dwelling places
[2]from generation
to generation;
They have [c]called *their* lands
after their own names.
12 But [a]man in *his* honor
will not endure;
He is like the animals
that [1]perish.

13 This is the [a]way of those
who are foolish,
And of those after them
who [b]are pleased
[1]with their words. [2]Selah.
14 As sheep they are
appointed [a]for Sheol;
Death will shepherd them;
And the [b]upright shall
have dominion
over them in the morning,
And their form shall be
for Sheol [c]to consume,
*Far* away from his habitation.
15 But God will [a]redeem
my soul
from the [1]power of Sheol,
For [b]He will receive me. Selah.

16 Do not be afraid
[a]when a man becomes rich,
When the [1]glory of his
house increases;
17 For when he dies he will
not [a]take any of it;

**49:2** [a]Ps 62:9 [1]Lit *sons of men* [2]Lit *sons of men of rank* **49:3** [a]Ps 37:30 [b]Ps 119:130 **49:4** [a]Ps 78:2 [b]2Ki 3:15 [c]Nu 12:8 [1]Lit *open up* **49:5** [a]Ps 23:4; 27:1 [1]One who grabs the heel; one who cheats **49:6** [a]Job 31:24; Ps 52:7; Pr 11:28; Mk 10:24 **49:7** [a]Mt 25:8, 9 [b]Job 36:18, 19 **49:8** [a]Mt 16:26 **49:9** [a]Ps 22:29 [b]Ps 16:10; 89:48 [1]Or *the pit* **49:10** [a]Ecc 2:16 [b]Ps 92:6; 94:8 [c]Ps 39:6; Ecc 2:18, 21; Lk 12:20 [1]One who fails in wisdom due to willful sin **49:11** [a]Ps 64:6 [b]Ps 10:6 [c]Ge 4:17; Dt 3:14 [1]Some versions *graves are their houses* [2]Lit *to* **49:12** [a]Ps 49:20 [1]Lit *are destroyed* **49:13** [a]Jer 17:11 [b]Ps 49:18 [1]Lit *in their mouths* [2]*Selah* may mean *Pause, Crescendo, Musical Interlude* **49:14** [a]Ps 9:17 [b]Da 7:18; Mal 4:3; 1Co 6:2; Rev 2:26 [c]Job 24:19 **49:15** [a]Ps 16:10; 56:13; Hos 13:14 [b]Ge 5:24; Ps 16:11; 73:24 [1]Lit *hand* **49:16** [a]Ps 37:7 [1]Or *wealth* **49:17** [a]Ps 17:14; 1Ti 6:7

His [1]glory will not
descend after him.
18 For while he lives he
[a]blesses his soul—
And *men* will praise you when
you do well for yourself—
19 *But his soul* shall [a]go to
the generation of his fathers;
They will eternally
not see [b]light.
20 [a]Man in *his* honor, but *who*
does not understand,
Is [b]like the animals that [1]perish.

## PSALM 50

### *God Himself Is Judge*

A Psalm of [†]Asaph.

1 [a]The Mighty One, God,
Yahweh, has spoken,
And called the earth
[b]from the rising
of the sun to its setting.
2 Out of Zion, [a]the perfection
of beauty,
God [b]has shone forth.
3 May our God [a]come
and not be silent;
[b]Fire devours before Him,
And [c]a *storm* whirls
around Him.
4 He [a]calls the heavens above,
And the earth, to render
justice to His people:
5 "Gather My [a]holy ones to Me,
Those who have cut
a [b]covenant with Me
by [c]sacrifice."
6 And the [a]heavens declare
His righteousness,
For [b]God Himself
is judge. [1]Selah.

7 "[a]Hear, O My people,
and I will speak;
O Israel, I will testify
[1]against you;
I am God, [b]your God.
8 "I do [a]not reprove you
for your sacrifices,
And your burnt offerings are
continually before Me.
9 "I shall take no [a]young bull
out of your house
Nor male goats out
of your folds.
10 "For [a]every beast
of the forest is Mine,
The cattle
on a thousand hills.
11 "I know every [a]bird
of the mountains,
And everything that moves
in the field is [1]Mine.
12 "If I were hungry I would
not tell you,
For the [a]world is Mine,
as well as its fullness.
13 "Shall I eat the flesh of [a,1]bulls
Or drink the blood
of male goats?
14 "Offer to God [a]a sacrifice
of thanksgiving
And [b]pay your vows
to the Most High;

**49:17** [1]Or *wealth* **49:18** [a]Dt 29:19; Ps 10:3, 6; Lk 12:19 **49:19** [a]Ge 15:15 [b]Job 33:30; Ps 56:13 **49:20** [a]Ps 49:12 [b]Ecc 3:19 [1]Lit *are destroyed* ◆ **50:TITLE** [†]1Chr 15:17; 2Chr 29:30 **50:1** [a]Jos 22:22 [b]*Ps 113:3* ***50:2*** [a]*Ps 48:2;* Lam 2:15 [b]Dt 33:2; Ps 80:1; 94:1 **50:3** [a]Ps 96:13 [b]Lv 10:2; Nu 16:35; Ps 97:3; Da 7:10 [c]Ps 18:12, 13 **50:4** [a]Dt 4:26; 31:28; 32:1; Is 1:2 **50:5** [a]Ps 30:4; 37:28; 52:9 [b]Ex 24:7; 2Chr 6:11; Ps 25:10 [c]Ps 50:8 **50:6** [a]Ps 89:5; 97:6 [b]Ps 75:7; 96:13 [1]*Selah* may mean *Pause, Crescendo, Musical Interlude* **50:7** [a]Ps 49:1; 81:8 [b]Ex 20:2; Ps 48:14 [1]Or *to* **50:8** [a]Ps 40:6; 51:16; Is 1:11; Hos 6:6 **50:9** [a]Ps 69:31 **50:10** [a]Ps 104:24 **50:11** [a]Mt 6:26 [1]Or *in My mind*; lit *with Me* **50:12** [a]Ex 19:5; Dt 10:14; Ps 24:1; 1Co 10:26 **50:13** [a]Ps 50:9 [1]Lit *strong ones* **50:14** [a]Ps 27:6; 69:30; 107:22; 116:17; Hos 14:2; Ro 12:1; Heb 13:15 [b]Nu 30:2; Dt 23:21; Ps 22:25; 56:12; 61:8; 65:1; 76:11

15 [a]Call upon Me
in the day of distress;
I shall [b]rescue you, and
you will [c]glorify Me."

16 But to the wicked God says,
"What right have you
to recount My statutes
And to take [a]My covenant
in your mouth?
17 "For you [a]hate discipline,
And you [b]cast My
words behind you.
18 "When you see a thief, you
[a,1]are pleased with him,
And [2]you [b]associate
with adulterers.
19 "You [a,1]let your mouth
loose in evil
And you harness your
[b]tongue for deceit.
20 "You sit and [a]speak
against your brother;
You slander your own
mother's son.
21 "These things you have
done and [a]I kept silent;
You thought that I was
just like you;
I will [b]reprove you and
state *the case* in order
before your eyes.

22 "Now consider this, you
who [a]forget God,
Lest I [b]tear *you* in pieces, and
there will be none to deliver.
23 "He who [a]offers a sacrifice
of thanksgiving glorifies Me;
And he who [b,1]orders *his* way,
I shall [c]show the salvation
of God."

## PSALM 51

### *Create in Me a Clean Heart, O God*

For the choir director. A Psalm of David. When [†]Nathan the prophet came to him, after he had gone in to Bathsheba.

1 [a]Be gracious to me,
O God, according
to Your lovingkindness;
According to the abundance
of [b]Your compassion [c]blot
out my transgressions.
2 [a]Wash me thoroughly
from my iniquity
And [b]cleanse me from my sin.
3 For [1]I [a]know
my transgressions,
And my sin is ever before me.
4 [a]Against You, You only,
I have sinned
*And* done what is [b]evil
in Your sight,
So that [c]You [1]are justified
[2]when You speak
And pure when You judge.

5 Behold, I was [a]brought
forth in iniquity,
And in sin my mother
conceived me.
6 Behold, You delight in [a]truth
in the [1]innermost being,

---

**50:15** [a]Ps 91:15; 107:6, 13; Zec 13:9 [b]Ps 81:7 [c]Ps 22:23 **50:16** [a]Is 29:13 **50:17** [a]Pr 5:12; 12:1; Ro 2:21, 22 [b]1Ki 14:9; Ne 9:26 **50:18** [a]Ro 1:32 [b]1Ti 5:22 [1]Some ancient versions *run together* [2]Lit *your part is with* **50:19** [a]Ps 10:7 [b]Ps 36:3; 52:2 [1]Lit *send* **50:20** [a]Job 19:18; Mt 10:21 **50:21** [a]Ecc 8:11; Is 42:14; 57:11 [b]Ps 90:8 **50:22** [a]Job 8:13; Ps 9:17 [b]Ps 7:2 **50:23** [a]Ps 50:14 [b]Ps 85:13 [c]Ps 91:16 [1]Lit *sets* ◆ **51:TITLE** [†]2Sa 12:1 **51:1** [a]Ps 4:1; 109:26 [b]Ps 69:16; 106:45 [c]Ps 51:9; Is 43:25; 44:22; Ac 3:19; Col 2:14 **51:2** [a]Ps 51:7; Is 1:16; 4:4; Jer 4:14; Ac 22:16; Rev 1:5 [b]Jer 33:8; Eze 36:33; Heb 9:14; 1Jn 1:7, 9 **51:3** [a]Is 59:12 [1]Or *I myself know* **51:4** [a]Ge 20:6; 39:9; 2Sa 12:13; Ps 41:4 [b]Lk 15:21 [c]Ro 3:4 [1]Or *may be in the right* [2]Many mss *in Your words* **51:5** [a]Job 14:4; 15:14; Ps 58:3; Eph 2:3 **51:6** [a]Job 38:36; Ps 15:2 [1]Or *inward parts*

And in the hidden part
You will [b]make me
know wisdom.
7 [1]Purify me [a]with hyssop,
and I shall be clean;
[2]Wash me, and I shall be
[b]whiter than snow.
8 [1]Make me to hear [a]joy
and gladness,
Let the [b]bones which You
have crushed rejoice.
9 [a]Hide Your face from my sins
And blot out all
my iniquities.

10 [a]Create [1]in me a [b]clean
heart, O God,
And renew [2]a [c]steadfast
spirit within me.
11 [a]Do not cast me away
from Your presence
And do not take Your
[b]Holy Spirit from me.
12 Restore to me the [a]joy
of Your salvation
And sustain me
with a [b]willing spirit.
13 *Then* I will [a]teach
transgressors Your ways,
And sinners will [1]be
[b]converted to You.

14 Deliver me from
[a]bloodguiltiness, O God,
[b]the God of my salvation;
*Then* my [c]tongue will joyfully
sing of Your righteousness.
15 O Lord, [a,1]open my lips,
That my mouth may
[b]declare Your praise.
16 For You [a]do not delight
in sacrifice, otherwise
I would give it;
You are not pleased
with burnt offering.
17 The sacrifices of God are
a [a]broken spirit;
A broken and a [1]contrite heart,
O God, You will not despise.

18 [a]By Your favor do
good to Zion;
[b,1]Build the walls of Jerusalem.
19 Then You will delight
in [a,1]righteous sacrifices,
In [b]burnt offering and
whole burnt offering;
Then [2]young bulls will be
offered on Your altar.

## PSALM 52

### *I Trust in the Lovingkindness of God*

For the choir director. A [†]Maskil of David.
[*]When Doeg the Edomite came and told
Saul and said to him, "David has come to
the house of Ahimelech."

1 Why do you [a]boast
in evil, O mighty man?
The [b]lovingkindness of God
*endures* all day long.
2 Your tongue
devises [a]destruction,
Like a [b]sharp razor,
[c]O worker of deceit.

**51:6** [b]Pr 2:6; Ecc 2:26; Jas 1:5 **51:7** [a]Ex 12:22; Lv 14:4; Nu 19:18; Heb 9:19 [b]Is 1:18 [1]Or *May You purify...that I may be clean* [2]Or *May You wash* **51:8** [a]Is 35:10; Joel 1:16 [b]Ps 35:10 [1]Or *May You make* **51:9** [a]Jer 16:17 **51:10** [a]Eze 18:31; Eph 2:10 [b]Ps 24:4; Mt 5:8; Ac 15:9 [c]Ps 78:37 [1]Lit *for* [2]Or *an upright* **51:11** [a]2Ki 13:23; 24:20; Jer 7:15 [b]Is 63:10, 11 **51:12** [a]Ps 13:5 [b]Ps 110:3 **51:13** [a]Ac 9:21, 22 [b]Ps 22:27 [1]Or *turn back* **51:14** [a]2Sa 12:9; Ps 26:9 [b]Ps 25:5 [c]Ps 35:28; 71:15 **51:15** [a]Ex 4:15 [b]Ps 9:14 [1]Or *may You open* **51:16** [a]1Sa 15:22; Ps 40:6 **51:17** [a]Ps 34:18 [1]Lit *crushed* **51:18** [a]Ps 69:35; Is 51:3 [b]Ps 102:16; 147:2 [1]Or *May You build* **51:19** [a]Ps 4:5 [b]Ps 66:13, 15 [1]Or *sacrifices of righteousness* [2]Lit *they will offer young bulls* ◆ **52:TITLE** [†]Possibly *Contemplative, Didactic, Skillful Psalm* [*]1Sa 22:9 **52:1** [a]Ps 94:4 [b]Ps 52:8 **52:2** [a]Ps 5:9 [b]Ps 57:4; 59:7 [c]Ps 101:7

3 You [a]love evil more than good,
[b]Falsehood more than
speaking what is right. [1]Selah.
4 You love all words that devour,
O [a]deceitful tongue.

5 [1]But God will break you
down forever;
He will snatch you up
and [a]tear you away
from *your* tent,
And [b]uproot you from
the [c]land of the living, Selah.
6 So that the righteous
will [a]see and fear,
And will [b]laugh at him, *saying*,
7 "Behold, the man who would
not set God as his strength,
But [a]trusted in the abundance
of his riches
*And* [b]was strong
in his destruction."

8 But as for me, I am like a [a]green
olive tree in the house of God;
I [b]trust in the lovingkindness
of God forever and ever.
9 I will [a]give You thanks forever,
because You have done *it*,
And I will hope on Your name,
[b]for *it is* good, in the presence
of Your holy ones.

## PSALM 53

### *There Is No One Who Does Good*

*For the choir director.* According to
[†]Mahalath. A [˙]Maskil of David.

1 [a]The wicked fool says in his
heart, "There is no God,"
They act corruptly,
and commit
abominable injustice;
[b]There is no one who
does good.
2 God looks down
from heaven
upon the sons of men
To see if there is [a]anyone
who has insight,
Anyone who [b]seeks
after God.
3 [a]Every one of them has
turned back; together they
have become [1]worthless;
There is no one who does
good, not even one.

4 Do the workers
of iniquity [a]not know,
Who eat up my people
*as* they eat bread
*And* do not call upon God?
5 There they were
in great dread [a]*where*
no dread had been;
For God [b]scattered
the bones of [1]him who
encamped against you;
You [c]put *them* to shame,
because [d]God had
rejected them.
6 Oh, that [a]the salvation
of Israel [1]would come
out of Zion!
When God [2]restores His
captive people,
[3]May Jacob rejoice,
may Israel be glad.

---

**52:3** [a]Ps 36:4 [b]Ps 58:3; Jer 9:5 [1]*Selah* may mean *Pause, Crescendo, Musical Interlude* **52:4** [a]Ps 120:3 **52:5** [a]Is 22:18, 19 [b]Pr 2:22 [c]Ps 27:13 [1]Or *Also* **52:6** [a]Ps 37:34; 40:3 [b]Job 22:19 **52:7** [a]Ps 49:6 [b]Ps 10:6 **52:8** [a]Ps 92:12; 128:3; Jer 11:16 [b]Ps 13:5 **52:9** [a]Ps 30:12 [b]Ps 54:6 ◆ **53:TITLE** [†]Sickness, a sad tone [˙]Possibly *Contemplative, Didactic, Skillful Psalm* **53:1** [a]Ps 10:4; 14:1-7; 53:1-6 [b]Ro 3:10 **53:2** [a]Ro 3:11 [b]2Chr 15:2 **53:3** [a]Ro 3:12 [1]Or *corrupt* **53:4** [a]Jer 4:22 **53:5** [a]Lv 26:17, 36; Pr 28:1 [b]Ps 141:7; Jer 8:1, 2; Eze 6:5 [c]Ps 44:7 [d]2Ki 17:20; Jer 6:30; Lam 5:22 [1]Or possibly *those* **53:6** [a]Ps 14:7 [1]Lit *would be* [2]Or *restores the fortunes of His people* [3]Or *Jacob will rejoice, Israel will be glad*

## PSALM 54

### *God Is My Helper*

For the choir director. With stringed instruments. A [†]Maskil of David. [*]When the Ziphites came and said to Saul, "Is not David hiding himself among us?"

1 O God, save me
by [a]Your name,
And render justice
to me by [b]Your might.
2 [a]O God, hear my prayer;
[b]Give ear to the words
of my mouth.
3 For strangers have
[a]risen against me
And [b]ruthless men have
[c]sought my [1]life;
They have [d]not set God
before them. [2]Selah.

4 Behold, [a]God is my helper;
The Lord is among those
who [b]sustain my soul.
5 He will [a]return the evil
to my foes;
[b]Destroy them [c]in Your truth.

6 [a]With a freewill offering
I will sacrifice to You;
I will give [b]thanks
to Your name, O Yahweh,
for it is good.
7 For [1]He has [a]delivered
me from all [2]distress,
And my eye has [b]looked *in*
*triumph* upon my enemies.

## PSALM 55

### *He Will Never Allow the Righteous to Be Shaken*

For the choir director. With stringed instruments. A [†]Maskil of David.

1 [a]Give ear to my prayer, O God;
And [b]do not hide Yourself
from my supplication.
2 Give [a]heed to me and
answer me;
I am restless in my [b]complaint
and [c,1]am surely distracted,
3 Because of the voice
of the enemy,
Because of the [a]pressure
of the wicked;
For they [b]shake wickedness
down upon me
And in anger they [c]bear
a grudge against me.

4 My [a]heart is in anguish
within me,
And the terrors of [b]death
have fallen upon me.
5 Fear and [a]trembling
come upon me,
And [b,1]horror has covered me.
6 I said, "Oh, that I had
wings like a dove!
I would fly away and
[a,1]be at rest.
7 "Behold, I would
wander far away,
I would [a]lodge
in the wilderness. [1]Selah.

◆ **54:TITLE** [†]Possibly *Contemplative, Didactic, Skillful Psalm* [*]1Sa 23:19; 26:1 **54:1** [a]Ps 20:1 [b]2Chr 20:6 **54:2** [a]Ps 17:6; 55:1 [b]Ps 5:1 **54:3** [a]Ps 86:14 [b]Ps 18:48; 86:14; 140:1, 4, 11 [c]1Sa 20:1; 25:29; Ps 40:14; 63:9; 70:2 [d]Ps 36:1 [1]Or *soul* [2]*Selah* may mean *Pause, Crescendo, Musical Interlude* **54:4** [a]Ps 30:10; 37:40; 118:7 [b]Ps 37:17, 24; 41:12; 51:12; 145:14; Is 41:10 **54:5** [a]Ps 94:23 [b]Ps 143:12 [c]Ps 89:49; 96:13; Is 42:3 **54:6** [a]Nu 15:3; Ps 116:17 [b]Ps 50:14 **54:7** [a]Ps 34:6 [b]Ps 59:10; 92:11; 112:8; 118:7 [1]His name; or *it* [2]Or *trouble* ◆ **55:TITLE** [†]Possibly *Contemplative, Didactic, Skillful Psalm* **55:1** [a]Ps 54:2; 61:1; 86:6 [b]Ps 27:9 **55:2** [a]Ps 66:19; 86:6, 7 [b]1Sa 1:16; Job 9:27; Ps 64:1; 77:3; 142:2 [c]Is 38:14; 59:11; Eze 7:16 [1]Or *I must moan* **55:3** [a]Ps 17:9 [b]2Sa 16:7, 8 [c]Ps 71:11; 143:3 **55:4** [a]Ps 38:8 [b]Ps 18:4, 5; 116:3 **55:5** [a]Ps 119:120 [b]Job 21:6; Is 21:4; Eze 7:18 [1]Lit *shuddering* **55:6** [a]Job 3:13 [1]Lit *settle down* **55:7** [a]1Sa 23:14 [1]*Selah* may mean *Pause, Crescendo, Musical Interlude*

8 "I would hasten to my
place of refuge
From the [a]stormy wind
*and* tempest."

9 [1]Confuse, O Lord, [a]divide
their tongues,
For I have seen [b]violence
and strife in the city.
10 Day and night they go
around her upon her walls,
And wickedness and
mischief are in her midst.
11 [a]Destruction is in her midst;
[b]Oppression and deceit do not
depart from her [1]streets.

12 For it is [a]not an enemy
who reproaches me,
Then I could bear *it*;
Nor is it one who hates
me who [b]has magnified
himself against me,
Then I could hide
myself from him.
13 But it is you, a man [1]my equal,
My [a]close companion and
my [b,2]familiar friend;
14 We who had sweet
counsel together
[a]Walked in the house
of God in the throng.
15 Let [1]death come [a]deceitfully
upon them;
Let them [b]go down
alive to Sheol,
For evil is in their dwelling,
in their midst.

16 As for me, I shall [a]call
upon God,
And Yahweh will save me.
17 [a]Evening and [b]morning and
at [c]noon, I will bring my
complaint and moan,
And He will hear my voice.
18 He will [a]redeem my soul
in peace [1]from the battle
*which is* against me,
For they are [b]many *who
strive* with me.
19 God will [a]hear and
[1]answer them—
Even the one [b]who
[2]sits enthroned
from of old— Selah.
Because they [3]do not change,
And [c]do not fear God.
20 [1]*My companion* has put
forth his hands
against [a]those who were
at peace with him;
He has [b,2]violated
his covenant.
21 His [1]speech was [a]smoother
than butter,
But his heart was war;
His words were
[a]softer than oil,
Yet they were
drawn [b]swords.

22 [a]Cast [1]your burden
upon Yahweh and He
will sustain you;
[b]He will never allow
the righteous to [c,2]be shaken.

**55:8** [a]Is 4:6; 25:4; 29:6 **55:9** [a]Ge 11:9 [b]Ps 11:5; Jer 6:7 [1]Lit *Swallow up* **55:11** [a]Ps 5:9 [b]Ps 10:7; 17:9 [1]Or *plaza* **55:12** [a]Ps 41:9 [b]Ps 35:26 **55:13** [a]2Sa 15:12 [b]Job 19:14; Ps 41:9 [1]Lit *according to my valuation* [2]Or *acquaintance* **55:14** [a]Ps 42:4 **55:15** [a]Ps 64:7; Pr 6:15; Is 47:11; 1Th 5:3 [b]Nu 16:30, 33 [1]Or *desolations be upon them* **55:16** [a]Ps 57:2, 3 **55:17** [a]Ps 141:2; Da 6:10; Ac 3:1; 10:3, 30 [b]Ps 5:3; 88:13; 92:2 [c]Ac 10:9 **55:18** [a]Ps 103:4 [b]Ps 56:2 [1]Or *so that none may approach me* **55:19** [a]Ps 78:59 [b]Dt 33:27; Ps 90:2; 93:2 [c]Ps 36:1 [1]Or *afflict* [2]Or *abides from* [3]Lit *are no changes* **55:20** [a]Ps 7:4; 120:7 [b]Nu 30:2; Ps 89:34 [1]Lit *He* [2]Lit *profaned* **55:21** [a]Ps 12:2; 28:3; Pr 5:3, 4 [b]Ps 57:4; 59:7 [1]Lit *mouth* **55:22** [a]Ps 37:5; 1Pe 5:7 [b]Ps 37:24 [c]Ps 15:5; 112:6 [1]Or *what He has given you* [2]Or *totter*

23 But You, O God, will bring
them down to the [a,1]pit
of corruption;
[b]Men of bloodshed and
deceit will [c]not live
out half their days.
But I will [d]trust in You.

## PSALM 56

### *In God I Trust, I Shall Not Be Afraid*

For the choir director. According to [†]Jonath Elem Rehokim. A [˙]Mikhtam of David. [^]When the Philistines seized him in Gath.

1 Be gracious to me,
O God, for man has
[a,1]trampled upon me;
All day long, an attacker
[b]oppresses me.
2 My foes have [a,1]trampled
upon me all day long,
For many [b]attack
me proudly.
3 [1]When I am [a]afraid,
[2]I will [b]trust in You.
4 [a]In God, whose word
I praise,
In God I trust;
I shall not be afraid.
[b]What can *mere* [1]man
do to me?
5 All day long they
[a,1]distort my words;
All their [b,2]thoughts are
against me for evil.
6 They [a,1]attack, they lurk,
They [b]watch my heels,
As they have [c]hoped
*to take* my [2]life.
7 On account of *their*
wickedness, [a]will they
have an escape?
In anger, [b]bring down
the peoples, O God!

8 You [a]have taken account
of my wanderings;
Put my [b]tears
in Your bottle.
Are *they* not in [c]Your book?
9 Then my enemies will
[a]turn back [b]in the day
when I call;
This I know,
[1]that [c]God is for me.
10 In God, *whose* word
I praise,
In Yahweh,
*whose* word I praise,
11 In God I [1]trust, I shall
not be afraid.
What can man do to me?
12 Your [a]vows are *binding*
upon me, O God;
I will [1]fulfill thank
offerings to You.
13 [1]For You have [a]delivered
my soul from death,
Indeed [b]my feet
from stumbling,
So that I may [c]walk
before God
In the [d]light of the [2]living.

---

**55:23** [a]Ps 73:18; Is 38:17; Eze 28:8 [b]Ps 5:6 [c]Job 15:32; Pr 10:27 [d]Ps 25:2; 56:3 [1]Or *lowest pit*
◆ **56:TITLE** [†]Or *The silent dove of those who are far off, The dove of the distant terebinths* [˙]Possibly *Epigrammatic Poem, Atonement Psalm* [^]1Sa 21:10, 11 **56:1** [a]Ps 57:3 [b]Ps 17:9 [1]Or *snapped at*
**56:2** [a]Ps 35:25; 57:3; 124:3 [b]Ps 35:1 [1]Or *snapped at* **56:3** [a]Ps 55:4, 5 [b]Ps [illegible] [1]Lit *In the day*
[2]Or *I am one who puts* **56:4** [a]Ps 56:10, 11 [b]Ps 118:6; Heb 13:6 [1]Lit *flesh* **56:5** [a]2Pe 3:16 [b]Ps 41:7
[1]Or *trouble my affairs* [2]Or *purposes* **56:6** [a]Ps 59:3; 140:2; Is 54:15 [b]Ps 17:11 [c]Ps 71:10 [1]Or *stir up strife* [2]Lit *soul* **56:7** [a]Ps 36:12; Pr 19:5; Eze 17:15; Ro 2:3 [b]Ps 55:23 **56:8** [a]Ps 139:3 [b]2Ki 20:5; Ps 39:12
[c]Mal 3:16 **56:9** [a]Ps 9:3 [b]Ps 102:2 [c]Ps 41:11; 118:6; Ro 8:31 [1]Or *because* **56:11** [1]Or *trust without fear*
**56:12** [a]Ps 50:14 [1]Lit *pay* **56:13** [a]Ps 33:19; 49:15; 86:13 [b]Ps 116:8 [c]Ps 116:9 [d]Job 33:30 [1]Or *Have You not delivered* [2]Or *life*

## PSALM 57

### *Let Your Glory Be Above All the Earth*

For the choir director. [†]Al-tashheth.
Of David. A [˙]Mikhtam. [^]When he fled from
Saul in the cave.

1 Be gracious to me, O God,
be gracious to me,
For my soul [a]takes
refuge in You;
And in the [b]shadow of Your
wings I will take refuge
Until destruction [c]passes by.
2 I will call to God Most High,
To God who [a]accomplishes
*all things* for me.
3 He will [a]send from
heaven and save me;
He reproaches him who
[b,1]tramples upon me. [2]Selah.
God will send His
[c]lovingkindness
and His [3]truth.

4 My soul is among [a]lions;
I am lying down among those
who breathe forth fire,
Sons of men whose [b]teeth
are spears and arrows
And their [c]tongue
a sharp sword.
5 [a]Be exalted above
the heavens, O God;
*Let* Your glory *be*
above all the earth.
6 They have [1]set a [a]net
*for my steps;*
My soul is [b]bowed down;
They [c]dug a pit before me;
They *themselves* have [d]fallen
into the midst of it. Selah.
7 [a]My [b]heart is set, O God,
my heart is set;
I will sing, yes,
I will sing praises!
8 Awake, [a]my glory!
Awake, [b]harp and lyre!
I will awaken the dawn.
9 [a]I will give thanks to You,
O Lord,
among the peoples;
I will sing praises to You
among the [1]nations.
10 For Your [a]lovingkindness
is great to the heavens
And Your [1]truth to the skies.
11 [a]Be exalted
above the heavens, O God;
*Let* Your glory *be*
above all the earth.

## PSALM 58

### *There Is a God Who Judges on Earth*

For the choir director. [†]Al-tashheth.
Of David. A [˙]Mikhtam.

1 Do you indeed [1]speak
righteousness, O [2]gods?
Do you [a]judge [3]with
equity, O sons of men?
2 No, in heart you [a]work
unrighteousness;
On earth you [b,1]prepare
a path for the violence
of your hands.

---

◆ **57:TITLE** [†]Lit *Do Not Destroy* [˙]Possibly *Epigrammatic Poem, Atonement Psalm* [^]1Sa 22:1; 24:3 **57:1** [a]Ps 2:12; 34:22 [b]Ru 2:12; Ps 17:8; 36:7; 63:7; 91:4 [c]Is 26:20 **57:2** [a]Ps 138:8 **57:3** [a]Ps 18:16; 144:5, 7 [b]Ps 56:2 [c]Ps 25:10; 40:11 [1]Or *snaps at* [2]*Selah* may mean *Pause, Crescendo, Musical Interlude* [3]Or *faithfulness* **57:4** [a]Ps 35:17; 58:6 [b]Pr 30:14 [c]Ps 55:21; 59:7; 64:3; Pr 12:18 **57:5** [a]Ps 57:11; 108:5 **57:6** [a]Ps 10:9; 31:4; 35:7; 140:5 [b]Ps 145:14 [c]Ps 7:15 [d]Pr 26:27; 28:10; Ecc 10:8 [1]Or *spread* **57:7** [a]Ps 57:7-11; 108:1-5 [b]Ps 112:7 **57:8** [a]Ps 16:9; 30:12 [b]Ps 150:3 **57:9** [a]Ps 108:3 [1]Lit *peoples* **57:10** [a]Ps 36:5; 103:11; 108:4 [1]Or *faithfulness* **57:11** [a]Ps 57:5; 108:5 ◆ **58:TITLE** [†]Lit *Do Not Destroy* [˙]Possibly *Epigrammatic Poem, Atonement Psalm* **58:1** [a]Ps 82:2 [1]Or *speak righteousness in silence* [2]Or *mighty ones, judges* [3]Or *uprightly the sons of men* **58:2** [a]Mal 3:15 [b]Ps 94:20; Is 10:1 [1]Lit *make level*

3 The wicked are estranged
[a]from the womb;
These who speak
falsehood [b]wander
in error from [1]birth.
4 They have venom
like the [a]venom
of a serpent;
Like a deaf cobra
that stops up its ear,
5 So that it [a]does not hear
the voice of [b,1]charmers,
*Or* a skillful caster
of spells.

6 O God, [a]shatter their
teeth in their mouth;
Break out the fangs
of the young lions,
O Yahweh.
7 Let them [a]flow away
like water that runs off;
*When* he [b,1]aims his arrows,
let them be
as [2]headless shafts.
8 *Let them be* as a snail
which [1]melts away
as it goes along,
*Like* the [a]miscarriages
of a woman which
never behold the sun.
9 Before your [a]pots can
feel *the fire of* thorns
He will [b]sweep them away
with a whirlwind,
the living and
the burning alike.
10 The [a]righteous will be
glad when he [b]beholds
the vengeance;
He will [c]wash his feet
in the blood of the wicked.
11 And men will say, "Surely there
is a [a,1]reward for the righteous;
Surely there is a God who
[b]judges [2]on earth!"

## PSALM 59

### *Deliver Me from My Enemies*

For the choir director. [†]Al-tashheth.
Of David. A [˙]Mikhtam.
[^]When Saul sent *men* and
they watched the house in order to put
him to death.

1 [a]Deliver me from my
enemies, O my God;
[b,1]Set me *securely* on high
away from those who
rise up against me.
2 Deliver me from
[a]workers of iniquity
And save me from [b]men
of bloodshed.
3 For behold, they [a]have lain
in wait for my soul;
[1]Fierce men [a,2]launch
an attack against me,
[b]Not for my transgression
nor for my sin, O Yahweh,
4 [a,1]For no guilt of *mine*,
they run and set
themselves against me.
[b]Arouse Yourself
to meet me, and see!

---

**58:3** [a]Ps 51:5; Is 48:8 [b]Ps 53:3 [1]Lit *stomach* **58:4** [a]Dt 32:33; Ps 140:3 **58:5** [a]Jer 8:17 [b]Ecc 10:11 [1]Or *whisperers* **58:6** [a]Job 4:10; Ps 3:7 **58:7** [a]Jos 2:11; 7:5; Ps 112:10; Is 13:7; Eze 21:7 [b]Ps 64:3 [1]Lit *bends* [2]*Lit though they were cut off* **58:8** [a]Job 3:16; Ecc 6:3 [1]Secretes slime **58:9** [a]Ps 118:12; Ecc 7:6 [b]Job 27:21; Ps 83:15; Pr 10:25 **58:10** [a]Job 22:19; Ps 32:11; 64:10; 107:42 [b]Dt 32:43; Ps 91:8; Jer 11:20; 20:12 [c]Ps 68:23 **58:11** [a]Ps 18:20; 19:11; Is 3:10; Lk 6:23, 35 [b]Ps 9:8; 67:4; 75:7; 94:2 [1]Lit *fruit* [2]Or *in* ◆ **59:TITLE** [†]Lit *Do Not Destroy* [˙]Possibly *Epigrammatic Poem, Atonement Psalm* [^]1Sa 19:11 **59:1** [a]Ps 143:9 [b]Ps 20:1; 69:29 [1]Or *May You put me in an inaccessibly high place* **59:2** [a]Ps 28:3; 36:12; 53:4; 92:7; 94:16 [b]Ps 26:9; 139:19; Pr 29:10 **59:3** [a]Ps 56:6 [b]1Sa 24:11; Ps 7:3, 4; 69:4 [1]Or *Strong* [2]Or *stir up strife* **59:4** [a]Ps 35:19 [b]Ps 7:6; 35:23 [1]Lit *Without guilt*

5 You, [a]O Yahweh God
of hosts, the God of Israel,
Awake to [b,1]punish
all the nations;
[c]Do not be gracious
to any *who are* treacherous
in [2]iniquity. [3]Selah.
6 They [a]return at evening,
they howl like a [b]dog,
And go around the city.
7 Behold, they [a]pour
forth *speech*
with their mouth;
[b]Swords are in their lips,
For, *they say,*
“ [c]Who hears?”
8 But You, O Yahweh,
[a]laugh at them;
You [b]mock all
the nations.

9 *Because of* [1]his [a]strength
I will watch for You,
For God is my [b]stronghold.
10 [1]My God [a]in His
lovingkindness will
approach me;
God will let me
[b]look *triumphantly*
upon [2]my foes.
11 Do not slay them,
[a]or my people
will forget;
[b]Make them wander about
*by Your power,* and
bring them down,
O Lord, [c]our shield.
12 [1]*On account of* the [a]sin
of their mouth *and*
the word of their lips,
Let them even be [b]caught
in their pride,
And on account
of [c]curses and [2]lies
which they utter.
13 [a,1]Destroy *them* in wrath,
[1]destroy *them* that they
may be no more;
That *men* may [b]know
that God [2]rules in Jacob
To the ends of
the earth. Selah.
14 They [a]return at evening,
they howl like a dog,
And go around the city.
15 They [a]wander about [1]for food
And [2]growl if they are
not satisfied.

16 But as for me,
I shall [a]sing
of Your strength;
And I shall [b]joyfully sing
of Your lovingkindness
in the [c]morning,
For You have been
my [d]stronghold
And a [e]refuge in the day
of my distress.
17 [a]O my strength, I will
sing praises to You;
For God is my [b]stronghold,
the [1]God who shows
me lovingkindness.

**59:5** [a]Ps 69:6; 80:4; 84:8 [b]Ps 9:5; Is 26:14 [c]Is 2:9; Jer 18:23 [1]Lit *visit* [2]Or *wickedness* [3]*Selah* may mean *Pause, Crescendo, Musical Interlude* **59:6** [a]Ps 59:14 [b]Ps 22:16 **59:7** [a]Ps 94:4; Pr 15:2, 28 [b]Ps 57:4; Pr 12:18 [c]Job 22:13; Ps 10:11; 73:11; 94:7 **59:8** [a]Ps 37:13; Pr 1:26 [b]Ps 2:4 **59:9** [a]Ps 18:17 [b]Ps 9:9; 62:2 [1]Many mss and some ancient versions *my strength* **59:10** [a]Ps 21:3 [b]Ps 54:7 [1]Many mss and some ancient versions *The God of my lovingkindness* [2]Lit *those who lie in wait for me* **59:11** [a]Dt 4:9; 6:12 [b]Ps 106:27; 144:6; Is 33:3 [c]Ps 84:9 **59:12** [a]Pr 12:13 [b]Zep 3:11 [c]Ps 10:7 [1]Or *The sin of their mouth is the word of their lips,* [2]Lit *lying* **59:13** [a]Ps 104:35 [b]Ps 83:18 [1]Lit *Bring to an end* [2]Or *is Ruler* **59:14** [a]Ps 59:6 **59:15** [a]Job 15:23 [1]Or *to devour* [2]Or *tarry all night* **59:16** [a]Ps 21:13 [b]Ps 101:1 [c]Ps 5:3; 88:13 [d]Ps 59:9 [e]2Sa 22:3; Ps 46:1 **59:17** [a]Ps 59:9 [b]Ps 59:10 [1]Lit *God of my lovingkindness*

## PSALM 60

### *Through God We Shall Do Valiantly*

For the choir director. According to †Shushan Eduth. A ˙Mikhtam of David. For teaching. ^When he struggled with Aram-naharaim and with Aram-zobah, and Joab returned, and smote twelve thousand of Edom in the Valley of Salt.

1 O God, [a]You have rejected
us. You have [b,1]broken us;
You have been [c]angry;
Oh, [d]restore us.
2 You have made the [a,1]land
quake, You have split it open;
[b]Heal its breaches,
for it shakes.
3 You have [a]caused Your
people to see hardship;
You have given us [1]wine
to [b]drink that causes reeling.
4 You have given a [a]banner
to those who fear You,
[1]In order to flee *to it*
from the bow. [2]Selah.
5 [a]That Your [b]beloved
may be rescued,
[c]Save with Your right
hand, and answer [1]us!

6 God has spoken
in His [a,1]holiness:
"I will exult, I will portion out
[b]Shechem and measure
out the valley of [c]Succoth.
7 "[a]Gilead is Mine, and
Manasseh is Mine;
[b]Ephraim also is the [1]helmet
of My head;
Judah is My [c,2]scepter.
8 "[a]Moab is My washbowl;
Over [b]Edom I shall
throw My shoe;
Make a loud shout,
O [c]Philistia, because of Me!"

9 Who will bring me
into the fortified city?
Who [1]will lead me to Edom?
10 Have You Yourself, O God,
not [a]rejected us?
And [b]will You, O God,
not go forth
with our armies?
11 Oh give us help
against the adversary,
For [a]salvation [1]by man
is worthless.
12 [1]Through God we shall
[a]do valiantly,
And it is He who will [b]tread
down our adversaries.

## PSALM 61

### *Lead Me to the Rock*

For the choir director. On a stringed instrument. Of David.

1 [a]Hear my cry of lamentation,
O God;
[b]Give heed to my prayer.
2 From the [a]end of the earth
I call to You when my
heart is [b]faint;

---

◆ **60:TITLE** †Lit *The lily of testimony* ˙Possibly *Epigrammatic Poem, Atonement Psalm* ^2Sa 8:3, 13; 1Chr 18:3, 12 **60:1** [a]Ps 44:9 [b]2Sa 5:20 [c]Ps 79:5 [d]Ps 80:3 [1]Or *broken out upon us* **60:2** [a]Ps 18:7 [b]2Chr 7:14; Is 30:26 [1]Or *earth* **60:3** [a]Ps 66:12; 71:20 [b]Ps 75:8; Is 51:17, 22; Jer 25:15 [1]Lit *wine of staggering* **60:4** [a]Ps 20:5; Is 5:26; 11:12; 13:2 [1]Or *That it may be displayed because of the truth* [2]*Selah* may mean *Pause, Crescendo, Musical Interlude* **60:5** [a]Ps 60:5-12; 108:6-13 [b]Dt 33:12; Ps 127:2; Is 5:1; Jer 11:15 [c]Ps 17:7 [1]Some mss *me* **60:6** [a]Ps 89:35 [b]Ge 12:6; 33:18; Jos 17:7 [c]Ge 33:17; Jos 13:27 [1]Or *sanctuary* **60:7** [a]Jos 13:31 [b]Dt 33:17 [c]Ge 49:10 [1]Lit *protection* [2]Or *lawgiver* **60:8** [a]2Sa 8:2 [b]2Sa 8:14 [c]2Sa 8:1 **60:9** [1]Or *has led* **60:10** [a]Ps 60:1; 108:11 [b]Jos 7:12; Ps 44:9 **60:11** [a]Ps 146:3 [1]Lit *of* **60:12** [a]Nu 24:18; Ps 118:16 [b]Ps 44:5; Is 63:3 [1]Or *In, With* ◆ **61:1** [a]Ps 64:1 [b]Ps 86:6 **61:2** [a]Ps 42:6 [b]Ps 77:3

Lead me to [c]the rock
that is higher than I.
3 For You have been
a [a]refuge for me,
A [b]tower of strength
before the enemy.
4 Let me [a]sojourn
in Your tent forever;
Let me [b]take refuge
in the shelter
of Your wings. [1]Selah.

5 For You, O God, have
heard my [a]vows;
You have given *me*
the inheritance of those
who [b]fear Your name.
6 You will [a]add days
to the king's [1]life;
His years will be
from generation
to generation.
7 He will sit enthroned
[a]before God forever;
Appoint [b]lovingkindness
and truth that they
may guard him.
8 So I will [a]sing praise
to Your name forever,
As I [b]pay my vows
day by day.

## PSALM 62

### *God Is a Refuge for Us*

For the choir director. According to [†]Jeduthun. A Psalm of David.

1 [a]Surely my soul *waits*
in silence for God;
From Him [b]is my salvation.
2 Surely He is my [a]rock
and my salvation,
My [b]stronghold;
I shall not be
greatly shaken.

3 How long will you
assail a man,
That you may murder
*him,* all of you,
Like a [a]leaning wall,
like a fence thrust down?
4 Surely they have
counseled to thrust
him down from his
high position;
They [a]find pleasure
in falsehood;
They [b]bless
with [1]their mouth,
But inwardly they
curse. [2]Selah.

5 Surely [a]wait in silence
for God, O my soul,
For my hope is from Him.
6 Surely He is [a]my rock
and my salvation,
My stronghold;
I shall not be shaken.
7 On God my [a]salvation
and my glory *rest;*
The rock of my strength,
my [b]refuge is in God.
8 [a]*Trust* in Him at all
times, O people;
[b]Pour out your heart
before Him;
God is a refuge for us. Selah.

---

**61:2** [c]Ps 18:2; 94:22 **61:3** [a]Ps 62:7 [b]Ps 59:9; Pr 18:10 **61:4** [a]Ps 23:6; 27:4 [b]Ps 17:8; 91:4 [1]*Selah* may mean *Pause, Crescendo, Musical Interlude* **61:5** [a]Job 22:27; Ps 56:12 [b]Dt 28:58; Ne 1:11; Ps 86:11; 102:15; Is 59:19; Mal 2:5; 4:2 **61:6** [a]Ps 21:4 [1]Lit *days* **61:7** [a]Ps 41:12 [b]Ps 40:11 **61:8** [a]Jdg 5:3; Ps 30:4; 33:2; 71:22 [b]Ps 65:1; Is 19:21 **62:TITLE** [†]Cf. 1Chr 16:41; 25:1; Ps 39 and 77 titles ◆ **62:1** [a]Ps 33:20 [b]Ps 37:39 **62:2** [a]Ps 89:26 [b]Ps 59:17; 62:6 **62:3** [a]Is 30:13 **62:4** [a]Ps 4:2 [b]Ps 28:3; 55:21 [1]Lit *his* [2]*Selah* may mean *Pause, Crescendo, Musical Interlude* **62:5** [a]Ps 62:1 **62:6** [a]Ps 62:2 **62:7** [a]Ps 85:9; Jer 3:23 [b]Ps 46:1 **62:8** [a]Ps 37:3, 5; 52:8; Is 26:4 [b]1Sa 1:15; Ps 42:4; Lam 2:19

9 Surely [1]men of [a]low degree
are *merely* [b]vanity and
[2]men of rank are a [c]lie;
In the [d]balances they go up;
They are together lighter
than *a breath* of vanity.
10 [a]Do not trust in oppression
And do not put vain
hope in [b]robbery;
If riches increase, [c]do not
set *your* heart *upon them.*

11 [1]Once God has [a]spoken;
[2]Twice I have heard this:
That [b]strength belongs to God;
12 And that [a]to You, O Lord,
belongs lovingkindness,
For You [b]repay a man
according to his work.

## PSALM 63

### *My Soul Thirsts for You*

A Psalm of David. [†]When he was in the wilderness of Judah.

1 O God, [a]You are my God; I
shall seek You [1]earnestly;
My soul [b]thirsts for You, my
flesh [2]yearns for You,
In a [c]dry and weary land
without water.
2 Thus I have [a]beheld You
in the sanctuary,
To see Your power
and Your glory.
3 Because Your [a]lovingkindness
is better than life,
My lips will laud You.
4 Thus I will bless You
[a]as long as I live;
I will [b]lift up my hands
in Your name.
5 My soul is [a]satisfied as
with fatness and richness,
And my mouth offers
[b]praises with lips
of joyful songs.

6 When I remember
You [a]on my bed,
I meditate on You
in the [b]night watches,
7 For [a]You have been my help,
And in the [b]shadow of Your
wings I sing for joy.
8 My soul [a]clings [1]to You;
Your [b]right hand upholds me.

9 But those who [a]seek my
[1]life to destroy it,
Will go into the [b,2]depths
of the earth.
10 [1]They will be [a]delivered over
to the power of the sword;
They will be a [b]portion
for foxes.
11 But the [a]king will be
glad in God;
Everyone who [b]swears
by Him will boast,
For the [c]mouths
of those who speak
lies will be closed.

---

**62:9** [a]Ps 49:2 [b]Job 7:16; Ps 39:5; Is 40:17 [c]Ps 116:11 [d]Is 40:15 [1]Lit *sons of men* [2]Lit *sons of men of rank* **62:10** [a]Is 30:12 [b]Is 61:8; Eze 22:29; Na 3:1 [c]Job 31:25; Ps 49:6; 52:7; Mk 10:24; Lk 12:15; 1Ti 6:10 **62:11** [a]Job 33:14; 40:5 [b]Ps 59:17; Rev 19:1 [1]Or *One thing* [2]Or *These two things I have heard* **62:12** [a]Ps 86:5; 103:8; 130:7 [b]Job 34:11; Ps 28:4; Jer 17:10; Mt 16:27; Ro 2:6; 1Co 3:8; Rev 2:23 ◆ **63:TITLE** [†]1Sa 22:5; 23:14 **63:1** [a]Ps 118:28 [b]Ps 42:2; 84:2; Mt 5:6 [c]Ps 143:6 [1]Lit *early* [2]Lit *faints* **63:2** [a]Ps 27:4 **63:3** [a]Ps 69:16 **63:4** [a]Ps 104:33; 146:2 [b]Ps 28:2; 143:6 **63:5** [a]Ps 36:8 [b]Ps 71:23 **63:6** [a]Ps 4:4 [b]Ps 16:7; 42:8; 119:55 **63:7** [a]Ps 27:9 [b]Ps 17:8 **63:8** [a]Nu 32:12; Dt 1:36; Hos 6:3 [b]Ps 18:35; 41:12 [1]Lit *after* **63:9** [a]Ps 40:14 [b]Ps 55:15 [1]Lit *soul* [2]Lit *lowest places* **63:10** [a]Jer 18:21; Eze 35:5 [b]Lam 5:18 [1]Lit *They will pour him out* **63:11** [a]Ps 21:1 [b]Dt 6:13; Is 45:23; 65:16 [c]Job 5:16; Ps 107:42; Ro 3:19

## PSALM 64
### *The Righteous Will Be Glad in Yahweh*

For the choir director. A Psalm of David.

1 Hear my voice, O God,
in [a]my [1]complaint;
[b]Guard my life
from dread of the enemy.
2 Hide me from the [a]secret
counsel of evildoers,
From the tumult
of the [b]workers of iniquity,
3 Who [a]have sharpened their
tongue like a sword.
They [b]aimed bitter speech
*as* their arrow,
4 To [a]shoot [1]from places
of hiding at the blameless;
Suddenly they shoot at him,
and [b]do not fear.
5 They [1]hold fast to themselves
an evil purpose;
They [2]talk of [a]laying
snares secretly;
They say, "[b]Who can see them?"
6 They searched out
unrighteousness, *saying,*
"We have completed
a diligent search";
For the [a,1]inward thought of
a man and *his* heart are [2]deep.

7 But [a]God [1]will shoot
them with an arrow;
Suddenly they will
be wounded.
8 So [1]they will [a]cause
their own tongue
[b]to turn against them;
All who see them will
[c]shake *their* head.
9 Then all men [1]will [a]fear,
And they [2]will [b]declare
the work of God,
And [3]will consider
[4]what He has done.
10 The righteous man will be
[a]glad in Yahweh and will
[b]take refuge in Him;
And all the upright
in heart will boast.

## PSALM 65
### *Blessed Is the One Whom You Choose*

For the choir director. A Psalm of David.
A Song.

1 To You, there will be silence
*and* praise in Zion, O God,
And to You the [a]vow
will be paid.
2 O You who hear prayer,
To You [a]all flesh comes.
3 [a]Words of iniquity
prevail against me;
As for our transgressions,
You [b]atone for them.
4 How [a]blessed is the one
whom You [b]choose and
bring near *to You*
That he would dwell
in Your courts.
We will be [c]satisfied with
the goodness of Your house,
Your holy temple.

5 By [a,1]fearsome *deeds* You
answer us in righteousness,
O [b]God of our salvation,

◆ **64:1** [a]Ps 55:2 [b]Ps 140:1 [1]Or *concern* **64:2** [a]Ps 56[b]Ps 59:2 **64:3** [a]Ps 140:3 [b]Ps 58:7 **64:4** [a]Ps 10:8; 11:2 [b]Ps 55:19 [1]Lit *in* **64:5** [a]Ps 140:5ob 22:13; Ps 10:11 [1]Lit *make firm* [2]Lit *recount* **64:6** [a]Ps 49:11 [1]Or *inward part* [2]Or *unsearchable* ( [a]Ps 7:12, 13 [1]Or *shot* **64:8** [a]Ps 9:3 [b]Pr 12:13; 18:7 [c]Ps 22:7; 44:14; Jer 18:16; 48:27; Lam 2:15 [1]Or *theyke their tongue a stumbling for themselves* **64:9** [a]Ps 40:3 [b]Jer 51:10 [1]Or *feared* [2]Or *declared* [3]*onsidered* [4]Lit *His work* **64:10** [a]Job 22:19; Ps 32:11 [b]Ps 11:1; 25:20 ◆ **65:1** [a]Ps 116:18 **65:2** [a]I:9; 145:21; Is 66:23 **65:3** [a]Ps 38:4; 40:12 [b]Ps 79:9 **65:4** [a]Ps 33:12; 84:4 [b]Ps 4:3 [c]Ps 36:8 6[a]Ps 45:4; 66:3 [b]Ps 85:4 [1]Or *awesome*

*You who are* the trust of all
the [c]ends of the earth and
of the farthest [d,2]sea;
6 Who [a]establishes
the mountains
by His strength,
Being [b]girded with might;
7 Who [a]stills the rumbling
of the seas,
The rumbling
of their waves,
And the [b]tumult
of the peoples.
8 They who inhabit the [a]ends
*of the earth* are in fear on
account of Your signs;
You make [1]the dawn and
the sunset shout for joy.

9 You visit the earth and
[a]cause it to overflow;
You greatly [b]enrich it;
The [c,1]stream of God
is full of water;
You establish their
[d]grain, for thus You
establish [2]the earth.
10 You water its
furrows abundantly,
You smooth its ridges,
You soften it [a]with showers,
You bless its growth.
11 You crown the year
[1]with Your [a]goodness,
And Your [2]paths [b]drip
*with* richness.
12 [a]The pastures
of the wilderness drip,
And the [b]hills gird themselves
with rejoicing.
13 The meadows are
[a]clothed with flocks
And the valleys are
[b]covered with grain;
They [c]make a loud shout,
indeed, they sing.

## PSALM 66

### *Come and See the Works of God*

For the choir director.
A Song. A Psalm.

1 [a]Make a loud shout to God,
all the earth;
2 Sing praise for the [a]glory
of His name;
Establish His [b]praise
as glorious.
3 Say to God, "How [a,1]fearsome
are Your works!
Because of the abundance
of Your strength Your
enemies will [b,2]cower
before You.
4 "[a]All the earth will
worship You,
And will [b]sing praises
to You;
They will sing praises
to Your name." [1]Selah.

5 [a]Come and see
the works of God,
*Who is* [b]fearsome in *His* deeds
toward the sons of men.
6 He [a]turned the sea
into dry land;

**65:5** [c]Ps 22:27; 48:10 [d]Ps 107:23 [2]Or *seas* **6** [a]Ps 95:4 [b]Ps 93:1 **65:7** [a]Ps 89:9; 93:3, 4; 107:29; Mt 8:26 [b]Ps 2:1; 74:23; Is 17:12, 13 **65:8** [a]Ps 2139:9; Is 24:16 [1]Lit *the outgoings of the morning and evening* **65:9** [a]Lv 26:4; Job 5:10; Ps 68:9; 104:117:8; Jer 5:24 [b]Ps 104:24 [c]Ps 46:4 [d]Ps 104:14; 147:14 [1]Or *channel* [2]Lit *it* **65:10** [a]Dt 32:2; Ps 72:6; 147:**65:11** [a]Ps 104:28 [b]Job 36:28; Ps 147:14 [1]Lit *of* [2]Wagon tracks **65:12** [a]Job 38:26, 27; Joel 2:22 [b]Ps 9Is 55:12 **65:13** [a]Ps 144:13; Is 30:23 [b]Ps 72:16 [c]Ps 98:8; Is 44:23; 55:12 ◆ **66:1** [a]Ps 81:1; 95:1; 98:4; 100**66:2** [a]Ps 79:9; Is 42:8 [b]Is 42:12 **66:3** [a]Ps 47:2; 65:5; 145:6 [b]Ps 18:44; 81:15 [1]Or *awesome* [2]Lit *deceiv***66:4** [a]Ps 22:27; 67:7; 86:9; 117:1; Zec 14:16 [b]Ps 67:4 [1]*Selah* may mean *Pause, Crescendo, Musical Interlud***66:5** [a]Ps 46:8 [b]Ps 106:22 **66:6** [a]Ex 14:21; Ps 106:9

They passed through
[b]the river on foot;
There let us [c]be glad in Him!
7 He [a]rules by His might forever;
His [b]eyes keep watch
on the nations;
Let not the rebellious
[c]exalt themselves. Selah.

8 Bless our God, O peoples,
And [a,1]make the sound
of His praise heard,
9 Who [a,1]establishes us
among the living
And [b]does not allow our
feet to stumble.
10 For You have [a]tested
us, O God;
You have [b]refined us
as silver is refined.
11 You [a]brought us into the net;
You established an oppressive
burden upon our loins.
12 You made men [a]ride
over our heads;
We went through [b]fire
and through water,
Yet You [c]brought us out
into *a place of* abundance.
13 I shall [a]come into Your house
with burnt offerings;
I shall [b]pay You my vows,
14 Which my lips uttered
And my mouth spoke
when I was [a]in distress.
15 *I shall* [a]offer to You burnt
offerings of fat beasts,
With the smoke of [b]rams;
I shall make *an offering
of* [1]bulls
with male goats. Selah.

16 [a]Come *and* hear, all
who [1]fear God,
And I will [b]recount what He
has done for my soul.
17 I called out to Him
with my mouth,
And [1]He was [a]exalted
with my tongue.
18 If I [a,1]see wickedness
in my heart,
The [b]Lord [2]will not [3]hear;
19 But certainly [a]God has heard;
He has given heed
to the voice of my prayer.
20 [a]Blessed be God,
Who [b]has not turned
away my prayer
Nor His lovingkindness
from me.

## PSALM 67

### *Cause Your Face to Shine upon Us*

For the choir director. With stringed instruments. A Psalm. A Song.

1 God be gracious to us
and [a]bless us,
*And* [b]cause His face
to shine [1]upon us— [2]Selah.
2 That [a]Your way may be
known on the earth,
[b]Your salvation
among all nations.

---

**66:6** [b]Jos 3:16; Ps 114:3 [c]Ps 105:43 **66:7** [a]Ps 145:13 [b]Ps 11:4 [c]Ps 140:8 **66:8** [a]Ps 98:4 [1]Lit *cause to hear the sound of His praise* **66:9** [a]Ps 30:3 [b]Ps 121:3 [1]Lit *puts our soul in life* **66:10** [a]Job 23:10; Ps 7:9; 17:3; 26:2 [b]Is 48:10; Zec 13:9; Mal 3:3; 1Pe 1:7 **66:11** [a]Lam 1:13; Eze 12:13 **66:12** [a]Is 51:23 [b]Ps 78:21; Is 43:2 [c]Ps 18:19 **66:13** [a]Ps 96:8; Jer 17:26 [b]Ps 22:25; 116:14; Ecc 5:4 **66:14** [a]Ps 18:6 **66:15** [a]Ps 51:19 [b]Nu 6:14 [1]Or *cattle* **66:16** [a]Ps 34:11 [b]Ps 71:15, 24 [1]Or *reverence* **66:17** [a]Ps 30:1 [1]Lit *praise was under* **66:18** [a]Job 36:21; Jn 9:31 [b]Job 27:9; Ps 18:41; Pr 1:28; 28:9; Is 1:15; Jas 4:3 [1]Or *had regarded* [2]Or *would* [3]Or *have heard* **66:19** [a]Ps 18:6; 116:1, 2 **66:20** [a]Ps 68:35 [b]Ps 22:24 ◆ **67:1** [a]Nu 6:25 [b]Ps 4:6; 31:16; 80:3, 7, 19; 119:135 [1]Lit *with* [2]*Selah* may mean *Pause, Crescendo, Musical Interlude* **67:2** [a]Ps 98:2; Ac 18:25; Tit 2:11 [b]Is 52:10

3 Let the [a]peoples praise
You, O God;
Let all the peoples praise You.
4 Let the [a]nations be glad
and sing for joy;
For You will [b]judge the peoples
with uprightness
And [c]lead the nations
on the earth. Selah.
5 Let the [a]peoples praise
You, O God;
Let all the peoples praise You.
6 The [a]earth has yielded
its produce;
God, our God, [b]blesses us.
7 God blesses us,
[1]That [a]all the ends
of the earth may fear Him.

## PSALM 68

### *Let God's Enemies Be Scattered*

For the choir director. A Psalm of David.
A Song.

1 [1]Let [a]God arise, [2]let His
enemies be scattered,
And [3]let those who hate
Him flee before Him.
2 As [a]smoke is driven away,
*so* drive *them* away;
As [b]wax melts before the fire,
*So* let the [c]wicked
perish before God.
3 But let the [a]righteous be glad;
let them exult before God;
And let them rejoice
with gladness.
4 Sing to God, [a]sing praises
to His name;
[b,1]Lift up *a song* for Him who
[c]rides through the deserts,
Whose [d]name is [2]Yah,
and exult before Him.
5 A [a]father of the fatherless and
a [b]judge [1]for the widows,
Is God in His [c]holy habitation.
6 God [a]causes the lonely
to inhabit a home;
He [b]leads out the prisoners
into prosperity,
Only [c]the rebellious dwell
in a parched land.
7 O God, when You [a]went
forth before Your people,
When You [b]marched through
the wasteland, [1]Selah.
8 The [a]earth quaked;
The [b]heavens also dripped
*rain* at the presence of God;
[c,1]Sinai itself *quaked*
at the presence of God,
the God of Israel.
9 You [a]caused abundant rain
to sprinkle down, O God;
You established Your
inheritance when it
was [1]parched.
10 Your creatures inhabited it;
You [a]established it
in Your goodness
for the poor, O God.

**67:3** [a]Ps 66:4 **67:4** [a]Ps 100:1, 2 [b]Ps 9:8; 96:10, 13; 98:9 [c]Ps 47:8 **67:5** [a]Ps 67:3 **67:6** [a]Lv 26:4; Ps 85:12; Eze 34:27; Zec 8:12 [b]Ps 29:11; 115:12 **67:7** [a]Ps 22:27; 33:8 [1]Or *And let all...earth fear Him*
◆ **68:1** [a]Nu 10:35; Ps 12:5; 132:8 [1]Or *God shall* [2]Or *His enemies shall* [3]Or *those who hate Him shall* **68:2** [a]Ps 37:20; Is 9:18; Hos 13:3 [b]Ps 22:14; 97:5; Mic 1:4 [c]Ps 9:3; 37:20; 80:16 **68:3** [a]Ps 32:11; 64:10; 97:12 **68:4** [a]Ps 66:2 [b]Is 57:14; 62:10 [c]Dt 33:26; Ps 18:10; 68:33; Is 40:3 [d]Ex 6:3; Ps 83:18 [1]Or *Cast up a highway* [2]The shortened form of Yahweh, found in poetry and praise (e.g. *Hallelujah*), and in names (e.g. Zechar*iah*) **68:5** [a]Ps 10:14; 146:9 [b]Dt 10:18 [c]Dt 26:15 [1]Lit *of* **68:6** [a]Ps 107:4-7; 113:9 [b]Ps 69:33; 102:20; 107:10, 14; 146:7; Ac 12:7; 16:26 [c]Ps 78:17; 107:34, 40 **68:7** [a]Ex 13:21; Ps 78:14; Hab 3:13 [b]Jdg 5:4; Ps 78:52 [1]*Selah* may mean *Pause, Crescendo, Musical Interlude* **68:8** [a]Ex 19:18; Jdg 5:4; 2Sa 22:8; Ps 77:18; Jer 10:10 [b]Jdg 5:4; Ps 18:9; Is 45:8 [c]Ex 19:18; Jdg 5:5 [1]Lit *This is Sinai* which **68:9** [a]Lv 26:4; Dt 11:11; Job 5:10; Eze 34:26 [1]Lit *weary* **68:10** [a]Ps 65:9; 74:19; 78:20; 107:9

11 The Lord gives the word;
The [a]women who
proclaim the *good* news
are a great host:
12 “ [a]Kings of armies retreat,
they retreat,
And she who remains at home
will [b]divide the spoil!”
13 If you *men* lie down
[a]among the [1]sheepfolds,
*You all would be like* the wings
of a dove covered with silver,
And its pinions
with glistening gold.
14 When the Almighty
[a]dispersed the kings [1]there,
It was snowing in [b]Zalmon.

15 A [a,1]mountain of God is
the mountain of Bashan;
A mountain *of many* peaks is
the mountain of Bashan.
16 Why do you look
with envy, O mountains
with *many* peaks,
At the mountain which God has
[a]prized for His habitation?
Surely [b]Yahweh will
dwell *there* forever.
17 The [a]chariots of God are
[1]myriads, [b]thousands
upon thousands;
[2]The Lord is among them
*as at* Sinai, in holiness.
18 You have [a]ascended
on high, You have [b]led
captive *Your* captives;
You have received gifts
among men,
Even *among* the rebellious
also, that Yah—God—
may dwell *there*.
19 Blessed be the Lord, who
daily [a]bears our burden,
[b]The God *who* is our
salvation. Selah.
20 God is to us a [a]God
of [1]salvation;
And [b]to Yahweh the Lord
belong escapes
[2]from death.
21 Surely God will [a]crush
the head of His enemies,
The hairy [1]skull of him who
goes on in his guilty deeds.
22 The Lord [1]said, “ [a]I will bring
*them* back from Bashan.
I will bring *them* back
from the depths of the sea;
23 That [a,1]your foot may
crush *them* in blood,
The tongue of your [b]dogs
*may have* its portion
from *your* enemies.”

24 They have seen [a]Your
[1]procession, O God,
The [1]procession of my God, my
King, [b,2]into the sanctuary.
25 The [a]singers went on,
the musicians after *them*,
[1]In the midst of the [b]maidens
beating tambourines.

**68:11** [a]Ex 15:20; 1Sa 18:6 **68:12** [a]Jos 10:16; Jdg 5:19; Ps 135:11 [b]Jdg 5:30; 1Sa 30:24 **68:13** [a]Ge 49:14; Jdg 5:16 [1]Or *cooking stones, saddle bags* **68:14** [a]Jos 10:10 [b]Jdg 9:48 [1]Lit *in it* **68:15** [a]Ps 36:6 [1]Or *mighty mountain is* **68:16** [a]Dt 12:5; Ps 87:1, 2; 132:13 [b]Ps 132:14 **68:17** [a]2Ki 6:17; Hab 3:8 [b]Dt 33:2; Da 7:10 [1]Lit *twice ten thousand* [2]Or *The Lord came from Sinai into the sanctuary* **68:18** [a]Ps 7:7; 47:5; Eph 4:8 [b]Jdg 5:12 **68:19** [a]Ps 55:22; Is 46:4 [b]Ps 65:5 **68:20** [a]Ps 106:43 [b]Dt 32:39; Ps 49:15; 56:13 [1]Lit *salvations* [2]In view of; lit *for* **68:21** [a]Ps 110:6; Hab 3:13 [1]Or *crown* **68:22** [a]Nu 21:33; Am 9:1-3 [1]Or *says* **68:23** [a]Ps 58:10 [b]1Ki 21:19; Jer 15:3 [1]Some versions render, you may *bathe your foot in blood* **68:24** [a]Ps 77:13 [b]Ps 63:2 [1]Lit *goings* [2]Lit *in the sanctuary*; or *in holiness* **68:25** [a]1Chr 13:8; 15:6; Ps 47:6 [b]Ex 15:20; Jdg 11:34 [1]Or *The maidens in the midst*

26 [a]Bless God
in the congregations,
Yahweh, the [b]fountain of Israel.
27 There is [a]Benjamin,
the [1]youngest, [2]having
dominion over them,
The princes of Judah
*in* their throng,
The princes of [b]Zebulun,
the princes of Naphtali.

28 [1]Your God has [a]commanded
your strength;
Show Yourself strong,
O God, [b]who has worked
[2]on our behalf.
29 [1]Because of Your temple
at Jerusalem
[a]Kings will bring gifts to You.
30 Rebuke the [a]beast [1]in the reeds,
The herd of [b]bulls with
the calves of the peoples,
Trampling under foot
the pieces of silver;
He has [c]cast out the peoples
who delight in war.
31 Envoys will come out of [a]Egypt;
[b,1]Ethiopia will quickly stretch
out her hands to God.

32 Sing to God, O [a]kingdoms
of the earth,
[b]Sing praises to the Lord, Selah.
33 To Him who [a]rides upon
the [b,1]highest heavens, which
are from ancient times;
Behold, [c]He gives forth His
voice, a [d]voice *that is* strong.
34 [a]Ascribe strength to God;
His majesty is over Israel
And [b]His strength is
in the [1]skies.
35 [1]O God, *You are* [a]awesome
from Your [2]sanctuary.
The God of Israel Himself
[b]gives strength and
might to the people.
[c]Blessed be God!

## PSALM 69

### *Save Me, O God*

For the choir director. According to [†]Shoshannim. Of David.

1 Save me, O God,
For the [a]waters have
[1]threatened my life.
2 I have sunk in deep [a]clay,
and there is no foothold;
I have come into deep waters,
and a [b,1]flood overflows me.
3 I am [a]weary with my calling
out; my throat is parched;
My [b]eyes fail while I
wait for my God.
4 Those [a]who hate me
without cause are more
than the hairs of my head;
Those who would [1]destroy
me [b]are powerful, being
wrongfully my enemies;
[c]What I did not steal,
I then have to restore.

---

**68:26** [a]Ps 22:22, 23; 26:12 [b]Dt 33:28; Is 48:1 **68:27** [a]Jdg 5:14; 1Sa 9:21 [b]Jdg 5:18 [1]Or *smallest* [2]Or *their ruler* **68:28** [a]Ps 29:11; 44:4 [b]Is 26:12 [1]Some mss *Command, God* [2]Lit *for us* **68:29** [a]1Ki 10:10, 25; 2Chr 32:23; Ps 45:12; 72:10; Is 18:7 [1]Or *From Your temple* **68:30** [a]Job 40:21; Eze 29:3 [b]Ps 22:12 [c]Ps 18:14; 89:10 [1]Lit *of* **68:31** [a]Is 19:19, 21 [b]Is 45:14; Zep 3:10 [1]Or *Cush*, cf. Ge 10:6 **68:32** [a]Ps 102:22 [b]Ps 67:4 **68:33** [a]Dt 33:26; Ps 18:10; 104:3 [b]Dt 10:14; 1Ki 8:27 [c]Ps 46:6 [d]Ps 29:4 [1]Lit *heaven of heavens of old* **68:34** [a]Ps 29:1 [b]Ps 150:1 [1]Lit *clouds* **68:35** [a]Dt 7:21; 10:17; Ps 47:2; 66:5 [b]Ps 29:11; Is 40:29 [c]Ps 66:20; 2Co 1:3 [1]Or *Awesome is God from your sanctuary* [2]Lit *holy places* ◆ **69:TITLE** [†]Or possibly *Lilies* **69:1** [a]Job 22:11; Ps 32:6; 42:7; 69:14, 15; Jon 2:5 [1]Lit *come to the soul* **69:2** [a]Ps 40:2 [b]Jon 2:3 [1]Lit *flowing stream* **69:3** [a]Ps 6:6 [b]Dt 28:32; Ps 38:10; 119:82, 123; Is 38:14 **69:4** [a]Ps 35:19; Jn 15:25 [b]Ps 35:19; 38:19; 59:3 [c]Ps 35:11; Jer 15:10 [1]Or *silence*

5 O God, it is You who
knows [a]my folly,
And [b,1]all my guilt is not
hidden from You.
6 May those who hope for You
not [a]be ashamed through
me, O Lord Yahweh of hosts;
May those who seek You not
be dishonored through me,
O God of Israel,
7 Because [a]for Your sake I
have borne reproach;
[b]Dishonor has covered
my face.
8 I have become [a]estranged
[1]from my brothers
And a foreigner to my
mother's sons.
9 For [a]zeal for Your house
has consumed me,
And [b]the reproaches
of those who reproach You
have fallen on me.
10 When I wept [a]in my
soul with fasting,
It became my reproach.
11 When I made [a]sackcloth
my clothing,
I became [b]a byword to them.
12 Those who [a]dwell
at the gate moan about me,
And I *am* [b]the
drunkards' songs.

13 But as for me, my prayer
is to You, O Yahweh,
[a]at an acceptable time;
O God, in the [b]abundance
of Your lovingkindness,
Answer me with the truth
of Your salvation.
14 Deliver me from the [a]mire
and do not let me sink;
May I be [b]delivered
from [1]my foes and
from the [a,2]deep waters.
15 May the [a,1]flood of water
not overflow me
Nor the deep swallow me up,
Nor the [b]pit shut its
mouth on me.

16 Answer me, O Yahweh,
for [a]Your lovingkindness
is good;
[b]According to the abundance
of Your compassion,
[c]turn to me,
17 And [a]do not hide Your
face from Your slave,
For I am [b]in distress;
answer me quickly.
18 Oh draw near to my soul
*and* [a]redeem it;
[b]Ransom me because
of my enemies!
19 You know my [a]reproach
and my shame and
my dishonor;
All my adversaries
are [1]before You.

20 Reproach has [a]broken my
heart and I am so sick.
And [b]I hoped for sympathy,
but there was none,
And for [c]comforters,
but I found none.

---

**69:5** [a]Ps 38:5 [b]Ps 44:21 [1]Lit *my guilts* **69:6** [a]2Sa 12:14 **69:7** [a]Jer 15:15 [b]Ps 44:15; Is 50:6; Jer 51:51 **69:8** [a]Job 19:13-15; Ps 31:11; 38:11 [1]Lit *to* **69:9** [a]Ps 119:139; Jn 2:17 [b]Ps 89:41, 50; Ro 15:3 **69:10** [a]Ps 35:13 **69:11** [a]1Ki 20:31; Ps 35:13 [b]1Ki 9:7; Job 17:6; Ps 44:14; Jer 24:9 **69:12** [a]Ge 19:1; Ru 4:1 [b]Job 30:9 **69:13** [a]Ps 32:6; Is 49:8; 2Co 6:2 [b]Ps 51:1 **69:14** [a]Ps 69:2 [b]Ps 144:7 [1]Lit *those who hate me* [2]Lit *deep places of water* **69:15** [a]Ps 124:4, 5 [b]Nu 16:33; Ps 28:1; 141:7 [1]Lit *stream* **69:16** [a]Ps 63:3; 109:21 [b]Ps 51:1; 106:45 [c]Ps 25:16; 86:16 **69:17** [a]Ps 27:9; 102:2; 143:7 [b]Ps 31:9; 66:14 **69:18** [a]2Sa 4:9; Ps 26:11; 49:15 [b]Ps 119:134 **69:19** [a]Ps 22:6; 31:11 [1]Or known *to You* **69:20** [a]Jer 23:9 [b]Ps 142:4; Is 63:5 [c]Job 16:2

21 They also gave *me* [a,1]gall
[2]for my food
And for my thirst they [b]gave
me vinegar to drink.

22 May [a]their table before them
become a snare;
And [b,1]when they are in peace,
*may it become* a trap.
23 May their [a]eyes darken so
that they cannot see,
And make their [b]loins
quake continually.
24 [a]Pour out Your
indignation on them,
And may Your burning
anger overtake them.
25 May their [a,1]camp be desolate;
May none dwell in their tents.
26 For they have [a]persecuted
him whom [b]You Yourself
have struck down,
And they recount the pain
of those whom [c]You
have [1]wounded.
27 Add [a]iniquity to their iniquity,
And [b]may they not come
into [c]Your righteousness.
28 May they be [a]blotted
out of the [b]book of life
And may they not be [c,1]recorded
with the righteous.

29 But I am [a]afflicted and in pain;
[1]May Your salvation, O God,
[b]set me *securely* on high.
30 I will [a]praise the name
of God with song
And [b]magnify Him
with [c]thanksgiving.
31 And this will [a]please Yahweh
better than an ox
*Or* a young bull
with horns and hoofs.
32 The [a]humble [1]see *it*
*and* are glad;
You who seek God,
[b]let your heart [2]revive.
33 For [a]Yahweh hears
the needy
And [b]does not despise His
*who are* prisoners.

34 Let [a]heaven and earth
praise Him,
The seas and [b]everything
that moves in them.
35 For God will [a]save Zion and
[b]build the cities of Judah,
That they may dwell
there and [c]possess it.
36 The [a]seed of His slaves
will inherit it,
And those who love His
name [b]will dwell in it.

## PSALM 70

### *O Yahweh, Do Not Delay*

For the choir director. Of David.
To bring to remembrance.

1 [a]O God, *hasten* to deliver me;
O Yahweh, hasten to my help!

---

**69:21** [a]Dt 29:18 [b]Mt 27:34, 48; Mk 15:23, 36; Lk 23:36; Jn 19:28-30 [1]Or *poison* [2]Or *in* **69:22** [a]Ro 11:9, 10 [b]1Th 5:3 [1]Lit *for those who are secure* **69:23** [a]Is 6:10 [b]Da 5:6 **69:24** [a]Ps 79:6; Jer 10:25; Eze 20:8; Hos 5:10 **69:25** [a]Mt 23:38; Lk 13:35; Ac 1:20 [1]Lit *encampment* **69:26** [a]2Chr 28:9; Zec 1:15 [b]Is 53:4 [c]Ps 109:22 [1]Lit *pierced* **69:27** [a]Ne 4:5; Ps 109:14; Ro 1:28 [b]Is 26:10 [c]Ps 103:17 **69:28** [a]Ex 32:32, 33; Rev 3:5 [b]Php 4:3; Rev 13:8; 17:8; 20:15 [c]Ps 87:6; Eze 13:9; Lk 10:20; Heb 12:23 [1]Lit *written* **69:29** [a]Ps 70:5 [b]Ps 20:1; 59:1 [1]Or *Your salvation, O God, will set...* **69:30** [a]Ps 28:7 [b]Ps 34:3 [c]Ps 50:14 **69:31** [a]Ps 50:13, 14; 51:16 **69:32** [a]Ps 34:2 [b]Ps 22:26 [1]Some mss and ancient versions *will see* [2]Or *live* **69:33** [a]Ps 12:5 [b]Ps 68:6 **69:34** [a]Ps 96:11; 98:7; 148:1-13; Is 44:23; 49:13 [b]Is 55:12 **69:35** [a]Ps 46:5; 51:18 [b]Ps 147:2; Is 44:26 [c]Ob 17 **69:36** [a]Ps 25:13; 102:28 [b]Ps 37:29
◆ **70:1** [a]Ps 40:13-17; 70:1-5

2 [a]Let those be ashamed
and humiliated
Who seek my [1]life;
Let those be turned back
and dishonored
Who delight in [2]evil
*against* me.
3 [a]Let those [1]turn back
because of their shame
Who say, "Aha, aha!"

4 Let those be joyful
and glad in You
All who seek You
And let them say continually,
"Let God be magnified,"
*Those* who love Your salvation.
5 But [a]I am afflicted and needy;
[b]Hasten to me, O God!
You are my help and
my protector;
O Yahweh, do not delay.

### PSALM 71

#### *O God, Do Not Forsake Me*

1 [a]In You, O Yahweh, I
have taken refuge;
Let me never be ashamed.
2 [a]In Your righteousness deliver
me and protect me;
[b]Incline Your ear
to me and save me.
3 [a]Be to me a rock
of [b]habitation to which I
may continually come;
You have given the [c]command
to save me,
For You are [d]my [1]rock
and my fortress.
4 [a]Protect me, O my God, out
of the hand of the wicked,
Out of the [1]grasp
of the unrighteous and
ruthless man,
5 For You are my [a]hope;
O Lord Yahweh, *You are* my
[b]trust from my youth.
6 [1]By You I have been
[a]sustained from *my* birth;
You are He who [b]took me
from my mother's womb;
My [c]praise is continually
[2]of You.

7 I have become a [a]marvel
to many,
For You are [b]my strong refuge.
8 My [a]mouth is filled
with Your praise
And with [b]Your beauty
all day long.
9 Do not cast me off
in the [a]time of old age;
Do not forsake me
when my strength fails.
10 For my enemies have
spoken [1]against me;
And those who [a]watch my [2]life
[b]have counseled together,
11 Saying, " [a]God has
forsaken him;
Pursue and seize him, for
there is [b]no one to deliver."

12 O God, [a]do not be far from me;
O my God, [b]hasten to my help!
13 Let those who accuse my soul
be [a]ashamed *and* consumed;

**70:2** [a]Ps 35:4, 26 [1]Or *soul* [2]Or *my calamity* **70:3** [a]Ps 40:15 [1]Some mss *be appalled* **70:5** [a]Ps 40:17 [b]Ps 141:1 ◆ **71:1** [a]Ps 25:2, 3; 31:1-3; 71:1-3 **71:2** [a]Ps 31:1 [b]Ps 17:6 **71:3** [a]Ps 31:2, 3 [b]Dt 33:27; Ps 90:1; 91:9 [c]Ps 7:6; 42:8 [d]Ps 18:2 [1]Or *crag* **71:4** [a]Ps 140:1, 4 [1]Lit *palm* **71:5** [a]Ps 39:7; Jer 14:8; 17:7, 13, 17; 50:7 [b]Ps 22:9 **71:6** [a]Ps 22:10; Is 46:3 [b]Job 10:18; Ps 22:9 [c]Ps 34:1 [1]Lit *Upon You I have been supported* [2]Lit *in* **71:7** [a]Is 8:18; 1Co 4:9 [b]Ps 61:3 **71:8** [a]Ps 35:28; 63:5 [b]Ps 96:6; 104:1 **71:9** [a]Ps 71:18; 92:14; Is 46:4 **71:10** [a]Ps 56:6 [b]Ps 31:13; 83:3; Mt 27:1 [1]Lit *with reference to* [2]Lit *soul* **71:11** [a]Ps 3:2 [b]Ps 7:2 **71:12** [a]Ps 10:1; 22:11; 35:22; 38:21 [b]Ps 38:22; 40:13; 70:1, 5 **71:13** [a]Ps 35:4, 26; 40:14

Let them be [b]wrapped up
with reproach and dishonor,
who [c]seek [1]*to do* me evil.
14 But as for me, I will
[a]wait continually,
And will [b,1]praise You
yet more and more.
15 My [a]mouth shall recount
Your righteousness
*And* [b]Your salvation all day long;
For I [c]do not know
the [1]sum *of them*.
16 I will come [a]with the mighty
deeds of Lord Yahweh;
I will [b]bring to remembrance
Your righteousness,
Yours alone.

17 O God, You [a]have taught
me from my youth,
And I still [b]declare Your
wondrous deeds.
18 And even when *I am*
[a]old and gray, O God,
do not forsake me,
Until I [b]declare Your [1]strength
to *this* generation,
Your might to all who
are to come.
19 [1]For Your [a]righteousness,
O God, *reaches*
to the [2]heavens,
You who have [b]done
great things;
O God, [c]who is like You?
20 You, who have [a]shown [1]me
many troubles and [2]evils,
Will [b]revive [1]me again,
And will bring [1]me up
again [c]from the depths
of the earth.
21 May You increase
my [a]greatness
And turn *to* [b]comfort me.

22 I will also praise You
with [a,1]a harp,
*Even* Your [2]truth, O my God;
To You I will sing praises
with the [b]lyre,
O [c]Holy One of Israel.
23 My lips will [a]sing for joy
when I sing praises to You;
And my [b]soul,
which You have redeemed.
24 My [a]tongue also will utter
Your righteousness
all day long;
For they are [b]ashamed,
for they are humiliated who
seek [1]*to do* me evil.

## PSALM 72

### *Give the King Your Judgments*

Of Solomon.

1 O God, give the king
[a]Your judgments,
And [b]Your righteousness
to the king's son.
2 [1]May [2]he [a]render judgment
to Your people
with righteousness
And [b]Your [3]afflicted
with justice.

**71:13** [b]Ps 109:29 [c]Es 9:2; Ps 71:24 [1]Or *my calamity* **71:14** [a]Ps 130:7 [b]Ps 71:8 [1]Lit *add upon all Your praise* **71:15** [a]Ps 35:28 [b]Ps 96:2 [c]Ps 40:5 [1]Lit *numbers* **71:16** [a]Ps 106:2 [b]Ps 51:14 **71:17** [a]Dt 4:5; 6:7 [b]Ps 26:7; 40:5; 119:27 **71:18** [a]Ps 71:9 [b]Ps 22:31; 78:4, 6 [1]Lit *arm* **71:19** [a]Ps 36:6; 57:10 [b]Ps 126:2; Lk 1:49 [c]Dt 3:24; Ps 35:10 [1]Or *And* [2]Lit *height* **71:20** [a]Ps 60:3; Dt 31:17 [b]Ps 80:18; 85:6; 119:25; 138:7; Hos 6:1, 2 [c]Ps 86:13 [1]Or *us* [2]Or *calamities* **71:21** [a]Ps 18:35 [b]Ps 23:4; 86:17; Is 12:1; 49:13 **71:22** [a]Ps 33:2; 81:2; 92:1-3; 144:9 [b]Ps 33:2; 147:7 [c]2Ki 19:22; Ps 78:41; 89:18; Is 1:4 [1]Lit *an instrument of a harp* [2]Or *faithfulness* **71:23** [a]Ps 5:11; 32:11; 132:9, 16 [b]Ps 34:22; 55:18; 103:4 **71:24** [a]Ps 35:28 [b]Ps 71:13 [1]Or *my calamity* ◆ **72:1** [a]1Ki 3:9; 1Chr 22:13 [b]Ps 24:5 **72:2** [a]Is 9:7; 11:2-5; 32:1 [b]Ps 82:3 [1]Or *He will judge* [2]Many of the pronouns in this Psalm may be rendered *He* since the ultimate reference is to the Messiah [3]Or *humble*

3 Let the mountains lift up
[a,1]peace to the people,
And the hills, in righteousness.
4 [1]May he [a]give justice to
the [2]afflicted of the people,
Save the children of the needy,
And crush the oppressor.

5 [1]Let them fear You
[a]while the sun *endures*,
And [2]as long as the moon, *from*
generation to *all* generations.
6 [1]May he come down [a]like
rain upon the mown grass,
Like [b]showers
that water the earth.
7 [1]May the [a]righteous
flourish in his days,
And [b]abundance of peace
until the moon is no more.

8 May he also have dominion
[a]from sea to sea
And from the River
to the ends of the earth.
9 [1]Let [a]the desert creatures
[b]kneel before him,
And his enemies [c]lick the dust.
10 [1]Let the kings of [a]Tarshish
and of the [b]coastlands
bring a present;
The kings of [c]Sheba and
[d]Seba [e]offer tribute.
11 [1]And let all [a]kings bow
down to him,
All [b]nations serve him.
12 For he will [a]deliver the needy
when he cries for help,
The [1]afflicted also, and him
who has no helper.
13 He will have [a]compassion
on the poor and needy,
And the [1]lives of the needy
he will save.
14 He will [a]redeem their
[1]life from oppression
and violence,
And their blood will be
[b]precious in his sight;
15 So may he live! And
may they give to him
the [a]gold of Sheba;
And let each pray
for him continually;
Let each bless him
all day long.

16 May there be abundance
of grain in the earth
on top of the mountains;
May its fruit wave
like *the cedars of* [a]Lebanon;
And may those
from the city blossom
like [b]vegetation of the earth.
17 May his [a]name endure forever;
May his name [1]increase
[b,2]as long as the sun *shines*;
Let *all nations* [c,3]be
blessed in him;
[d]Let all nations call
him blessed.

---

**72:3** [a]Is 2:4; 9:5, 6; Mic 4:3, 4; Zec 9:10 [1]Or *prosperity* **72:4** [a]Is 11:4 [1]Or *He will vindicate* [2]Or *humble* **72:5** [a]Ps 72:17; 89:36, 37 [1]Or *They will fear* [2]Lit *before the moon* **72:6** [a]Dt 32:2; 2Sa 23:4; Hos 6:3 [b]Ps 65:10 [1]Or *He will come down* **72:7** [a]Ps 92:12 [b]Is 2:4 [1]Or *The righteous will flourish* **72:8** [a]Ex 23:31; Zec 9:10 **72:9** [a]Ps 74:14; Is 23:13 [b]Ps 22:29 [c]Is 49:23; Mic 7:17 [1]Or *The nomads will kneel* **72:10** [a]2Chr 9:21; Ps 48:7 [b]Ps 97:1; Is 42:4, 10; Zep 2:11 [c]1Ki 10:1; Job 6:19; Is 60:6 [d]Ge 10:7; Is 43:3 [e]Ps 45:12; 68:29 [1]Or *The kings...will bring* **72:11** [a]Ps 138:4; Is 49:23 [b]Ps 86:9 [1]Or *All kings will bow down* **72:12** [a]Job 29:12; Ps 72:4 [1]Or *humble* **72:13** [a]Pr 19:17; 28:8 [1]Lit *souls* **72:14** [a]Ps 69:18 [b]1Sa 26:21; Ps 116:15 [1]Lit *soul* **72:15** [a]Is 60:6 **72:16** [a]Ps 104:16 [b]Job 5:25 **72:17** [a]Ex 3:15; Ps 135:13 [b]Ps 89:36 [c]Ge 12:3; 22:18 [d]Lk 1:48 [1]To obtain descendants; or *sprout forth* [2]Lit *before the sun* [3]Or *experience blessing repeatedly, bless themselves*

18 [a]Blessed be Yahweh God,
the God of Israel,
Who alone [b]works
wondrous deeds.
19 And blessed be His
[a]glorious name forever;
And may the whole [b]earth
be filled with His glory.
[c]Amen, and Amen.

20 [1]The prayers of David, the son
of Jesse, are completed.

## BOOK 3

## PSALM 73

### *The Nearness of God Is My Good*

A Psalm of Asaph.

1 Surely God is [a]good to Israel,
To those who are
[b]pure in heart!
2 But as for me, [a]my feet
had almost stumbled,
My steps [1]had almost slipped.
3 For I was [a]envious
of the boastful,
I saw the [b]peace of the wicked.
4 For there are no pains
in their death,
And their [1]body is fat.
5 They are [a]not [1]in trouble
*as other* [2]men,
And they are not
[b]stricken along
with *the rest of* mankind.
6 Therefore lofty pride is
[a]their necklace;
The [b]garment of violence
covers them.
7 Their eye [1]bulges
from [a]fatness;
The delusions of *their*
heart overflow.
8 They [a]scoff and [1]wickedly
speak of oppression;
They [b]speak from on high.
9 They have [a]set their mouth
[1]against the heavens,
And their tongue goes
through the earth.

10 Therefore [1]his people return
here, *to his place,*
And waters of [a]fullness
are [2]drunk by them.
11 They say, "[a]How does
God know?
And is there knowledge
with the Most High?"
12 Behold, [a]these are
the wicked;
And always [b]at ease, they
have increased *in* wealth.
13 Surely [a]in vain I have
[1]kept my heart pure
And [b]washed my hands
in innocence;
14 For I have been stricken
[a]all day long
And [b,1]reproved
every morning.

15 If I had said, "I will
recount thus,"

---

**72:18** [a]1Chr 29:10; Ps 41:13; 89:52; 106:48 [b]Ex 15:11; Job 5:9; Ps 77:14; 86:10; 136:4 **72:19** [a]Ne 9:5; Ps 96:8 [b]Nu 14:21 [c]Ps 41:13 **72:20** [1]Possibly one of the last prayers of David for Solomon, which Solomon incorporated into his psalm ◆ **73:1** [a]Ps 86:5 [b]Ps 24:4; 51:10; Mt 5:8 **73:2** [a]Ps 94:18 [1]Lit *were caused to slip* **73:3** [a]Ps 37:1; Pr 23:17 [b]Job 21:7; Ps 37:7; Jer 12:1 **73:4** [1]Or *belly* **73:5** [a]Job 21:9; Ps 73:12 [b]Ps 73:14 [1]Lit *in the trouble of men* [2]Or *mortals* **73:6** [a]Ge 41:42; Pr 1:9 [b]Ps 109:18 **73:7** [a]Job 15:27; Ps 17:10; Jer 5:28 [1]Lit *goes forth* **73:8** [a]Ps 1:1 [b]Ps 17:10; 2Pe 2:18; Jd 16 [1]Or *they speak in wickedness; From on high they speak of oppression* **73:9** [a]Rev 13:6 [1]Or *in* **73:10** [a]Ps 23:5 [1]Or *His* [2]Lit *drained out* **73:11** [a]Job 22:13 **73:12** [a]Ps 49:6; 52:7 [b]Jer 49:31; Eze 23:42 **73:13** [a]Job 21:15; 34:9; 35:3 [b]Ps 26:6 [1]Or *cleansed my heart* **73:14** [a]Ps 38:6 [b]Job 33:19; Ps 118:18 [1]Lit *my rebuking*

Behold, I would have
betrayed the [a]generation
of Your children.
16 When I [a]gave thought
to know this,
It was trouble in my sight
17 Until I came
into the [a,1]sanctuary of God;
*Then* I understood their [b]end.
18 Surely You set them
in [a]slippery places;
You cause them to fall
to [b,1]destruction.
19 How they become [a]desolate
in a moment!
They are completely swept
away by [b]terrors!
20 Like a [a]dream when one awakes,
O Lord, when [b]aroused, You
will [c]despise their [1]form.

21 When my [a]heart
was embittered
And I was [b]pierced [1]within,
22 Then I was [a]senseless
and ignorant;
I was *like* [1]an [b]animal
[2]before You.
23 Nevertheless [a]I am
continually with You;
You have taken hold
of my right hand.
24 With Your counsel You
will [a]lead me,
*And afterward* [b]take
me [1]in glory.
25 [a]Whom have I
in heaven *but You*?
And [1]besides You,
I desire nothing on earth.
26 My [a]flesh and my heart fail,
But God is the rock of my heart
and my [b]portion forever.
27 For, behold, [a]those who are
far from You will [b]perish;
You have [1]destroyed everyone
who [c,2]is unfaithful to You.
28 But as for me, [a]the nearness
of God is my good;
I have set Lord Yahweh
as my [b]refuge,
That I may [c]recount
all Your works.

## PSALM 74

### *Yet God Is My King*

A [†]Maskil of Asaph.

1 Why, O God? Have You
[a]rejected *us* forever?
Why does Your anger
[b]smoke against the [c]sheep
of Your [1]pasture?
2 Remember Your
congregation, which You
have [a]purchased of old,
Which You have [b]redeemed
to be the [c]tribe
of Your inheritance;
*And* this Mount [d]Zion,
where You have dwelt.
3 Lift up Your steps toward
the [a]perpetual ruins;

**73:15** [a]Ps 14:5 **73:16** [a]Ecc 8:17 **73:17** [a]Ps 27:4; 77:13 [b]Ps 37:38 [1]Lit *sanctuaries* **73:18** [a]Ps 35:6 [b]Ps 35:8; 36:12 [1]Lit *ruins* **73:19** [a]Nu 16:21; Is 47:11 [b]Job 18:11 **73:20** [a]Job 20:8 [b]Ps 78:65 [c]1Sa 2:30 [1]Or *image* **73:21** [a]Jdg 10:16 [b]Ac 2:37 [1]Lit *in my kidneys* **73:22** [a]Ps 49:10; 92:6 [b]Job 18:3; Ps 49:20; Ecc 3:18 [1]Lit *animals* [2]Lit *with You* **73:23** [a]Ps 16:8 **73:24** [a]Ps 32:8; 48:14; Is 58:11 [b]Ge 5:24; Ps 49:15 [1]Or *with honor* **73:25** [a]Ps 16:2; Php 3:8 [1]Or *with* **73:26** [a]Ps 38:10; 40:12; 84:2; 119:81 [b]Ps 16:5 **73:27** [a]Ps 119:155 [b]Ps 37:20 [c]Ex 34:15; Nu 15:39; Ps 106:39; Hos 4:12; 9:1 [1]Or *silenced* [2]Lit *goes to a whoring from* **73:28** [a]Ps 65:4; Heb 10:22; Jas 4:8 [b]Ps 14:6; 71:7 [c]Ps 40:5; 107:22; 118:17
◆ **74:TITLE** [†]Possibly *Contemplative, Didactic, Skillful Psalm* **74:1** [a]Ps 44:9; 77:7 [b]Dt 29:20; Ps 18:8; 89:46 [c]Ps 79:13; 95:7; 100:3 [1]Or *pasturing* **74:2** [a]Ex 15:16; Dt 32:6 [b]Ex 15:13; Ps 77:15; 106:10; Is 63:9 [c]Dt 32:9; Is 63:17; Jer 10:16; 51:19 [d]Ps 9:11; 68:16 **74:3** [a]Is 61:4

The enemy [b]has
damaged everything
within the sanctuary.
4 Your adversaries have
[a]roared in the midst
of Your meeting place;
They have set up their
[b]own signs [c]for signs.
5 Each seems like one
who lifts up
[1]An [a]axe
against the undergrowth
of trees.
6 And now its [a]carved
work altogether
They smash with hatchet
and [1]hammers.
7 They have [a]set Your
sanctuary on fire;
*By bringing it*
to the ground, they have
[b]defiled the dwelling
place of Your name.
8 They [a]said in their heart,
"Let us [1]completely
[2]subdue them."
They have burned all
the meeting places
of God in the land.
9 We do not see our [a]signs;
There is [b]no longer
any prophet,
Nor is there any among us
who knows [c]how long.
10 How long, O God, will
the adversary [a]reproach?
Will the enemy [b]spurn
Your name forever?
11 Why [a]do You turn back Your
hand, even Your right hand?
From within Your bosom,
[b]destroy *them*!

12 Yet God is [a]my King
from of old,
Who works deeds of [1]salvation
in the midst of the earth.
13 You [a]divided the sea
by Your strength;
You [b]broke the heads
of the [c]sea monsters
[1]in the waters.
14 You crushed the heads
of [a,1]Leviathan;
You gave him as food for
the [2]creatures [b]of the desert.
15 [1]You [a]split open
spring and river;
[1]You [b]dried up
ever-flowing rivers.
16 Yours is the day, Yours
also is the night;
[1]You have [a]established
the [2]light and the sun.
17 [1]You have [a]caused all
the boundaries
of the earth to stand firm;
[1]You have formed
[b]summer and winter.

18 Remember this, O Yahweh,
that the enemy has
[a]reproached,
And a [b]wickedly foolish
people has spurned
Your name.

**74:3** [b]Ps 79:1 **74:4** [a]Lam 2:7 [b]Nu 2:2 [c]Ps 74:9 **74:5** [a]Jer 46:22 [1]Lit *Axes* **74:6** [a]1Ki 6:18, 29, 32, 35 [1]Or *axes* **74:7** [a]2Ki 25:9 [b]Ps 89:39; Lam 2:2 **74:8** [a]Ps 83:4 [1]Lit *altogether* [2]Or *oppress* **74:9** [a]Ps 78:43 [b]1Sa 3:1; Lam 2:9; Eze 7:26; Am 8:11 [c]Ps 6:3; 79:5; 80:4 **74:10** [a]Ps 44:16; 79:12; 89:51 [b]Lv 24:16 **74:11** [a]Lam 2:3 [b]Ps 59:13 **74:12** [a]Ps 44:4 [1]Lit *salvations* **74:13** [a]Ex 14:21; Ps 78:13 [b]Is 51:9 [c]Ps 148:7; Jer 51:34 [1]Lit *on* **74:14** [a]Job 41:1; Ps 104:26; Is 27:1 [b]Ps 72:9 [1]Or *the sea monster* [2]Lit *people* **74:15** [a]Ex 17:5, 6; Nu 20:11; Ps 78:15; 105:41; 114:8; Is 48:21 [b]Ex 14:21, 22; Jos 2:10; 3:13; Ps 114:3 [1]Or *You Yourself* **74:16** [a]Ge 1:14-18; Ps 104:19; 136:7, 8 [1]Or *You Yourself* [2]Or *luminary* **74:17** [a]Dt 32:8; Ac 17:26 [b]Ge 8:22; Ps 147:16-18 [1]Or *You Yourself* **74:18** [a]Ps 74:10 [b]Dt 32:6; Ps 14:1; 39:8; 53:1

19 Do not deliver the soul
of Your [a]turtledove
to the wild beast;
[b]Do not forget the life
of Your afflicted forever.
20 Look to the [a]covenant;
For the [b]dark places
of the land are full
of the haunts of violence.
21 Let not the [a]oppressed
return dishonored;
Let the [b]afflicted and needy
praise Your name.

22 Arise, O God, *and* [a]plead
Your own cause;
Remember [1]how the [b]wicked
fool reproaches You
all day long.
23 Do not forget the voice
of Your [a]adversaries,
The [b]rumbling of those who
rise against You
which ascends continually.

## PSALM 75

### *God Judges with Equity*

For the choir director. [†]Al-tashheth.
A Psalm of Asaph. [˙]A Song.

1 We [a]give thanks to You,
O God, we give thanks,
For Your name is [b]near;
Men recount [c]Your
wondrous deeds.
2 "For I select
an [a]appointed time,
It is I who [b]judge
with equity.
3 "The [a]earth and all who
dwell in it [1]melt;
It is I who have firmly set its
[b]pillars. [2]Selah.
4 "I said to the boastful,
'Do not boast,'
And to the wicked,
'[a]Do not raise up the horn;
5 Do not raise up your
horn on high,
[a]Nor speak
with insolent [1]pride.'"

6 For *one's* rising up does
not *come* from the east,
nor from the west,
And not from the [a,1]desert;
7 But [a]God is the Judge;
He [b]puts down one and
raises up another.
8 For a [a]cup is in the hand
of Yahweh, and
the wine foams;
It is [b]full of *His* mixture,
and He pours from this;
Surely all the wicked
of the earth must drain *and*
[c]drink down its dregs.

9 But as for me, I will
[a]declare *it* forever;
I will sing praises
to the God of Jacob.
10 And all the [a]horns
of the wicked I will cut off,
*But* [b]the horns
of the righteous will
be raised up.

---

**74:19** [a]SS 2:14 [b]Ps 9:18 **74:20** [a]Ge 17:7; Ps 106:45 [b]Ps 88:6; 143:3 **74:21** [a]Ps 103:6 [b]Ps 35:10; Is 41:17 **74:22** [a]Ps 43:1; Is 3:13; 43:26; Eze 20:35 [b]Ps 14:1; 53:1; 74:18 [1]Lit *Your reproach from the wicked fool* **74:23** [a]Ps 74:10 [b]Ps 65:7 ◆ **75:TITLE** [†]Lit *Do Not Destroy* [˙]Possibly a title for a tune, cf. Dt 9:26; 1Sa 26:9; Is 65:8 **75:1** [a]Ps 79:13 [b]Ps 145:18 [c]Ps 26:7; 44:1; 71:17 **75:2** [a]Ps 102:13 [b]Ps 9:8; 67:4; Is 11:4 **75:3** [a]Ps 46:6; Is 24:19 [b]1Sa 2:8 [1]Or *totter* [2]*Selah* may mean *Pause, Crescendo, Musical Interlude* **75:4** [a]Zec 1:21 **75:5** [a]1Sa 2:3; Ps 94:4 [1]Lit *neck* **75:6** [a]Ps 3:3 [1]Or *mountainous desert* **75:7** [a]Ps 50:6 [b]1Sa 2:7; Ps 147:6; Da 2:21 **75:8** [a]Job 21:20; Ps 11:6; 60:3; Jer 25:15 [b]Pr 23:30 [c]Ob 16 **75:9** [a]Ps 22:22; 40:10 **75:10** [a]Ps 101:8; Jer 48:25 [b]1Sa 2:1; Ps 89:17; 92:10; 148:14

## PSALM 76

### *God's Name Is Great in Israel*

For the choir director. With stringed instruments. A Psalm of Asaph. A Song.

1 God is [a]known in Judah;
His name is [b]great in Israel.
2 So His [a,1]tabernacle
is in [b]Salem;
His [c]dwelling place is in Zion.
3 There He [a]broke
the [1]flaming arrows,
The shield and the sword and
the battle. [2]Selah.

4 You are shining,
Majestic from the mountains
of prey.
5 The [a]stouthearted
were plundered,
[1]They sank into sleep;
And none of the [2]warriors
could use his hands.
6 At Your [a]rebuke,
O God of Jacob,
Both [b]chariot rider and horse
slumbered *into* a deep sleep.
7 But You, You are [a,1]fearsome;
And [b]who can stand
in Your presence
when once [2]You are angry?

8 You made *Your* cause
to be heard from heaven;
The earth [a]feared
and was quiet
9 When God [a]arose
to judgment,
To save all the humble
of the earth. Selah.
10 For the [a,1]wrath of man
shall praise You;
With a remnant of wrath
You will gird Yourself.

11 [a]Make vows to Yahweh your
God and [b]pay *them*;
Let all who are
around Him [c]bring gifts
to the Fearsome One.
12 He will cut off the spirit
of princes;
He is [a,1]feared by the kings
of the earth.

## PSALM 77

### *In My Distress I Sought the Lord*

For the choir director. According to [†]Jeduthun. Of Asaph. A Psalm.

1 My voice *rises* to God, and
I must [a]cry aloud;
My voice *rises* to God,
and He will hear me.
2 In the [a]day of my distress
I sought the Lord;
[b]In the night my [c]hand
was stretched out
[1]without weariness;
My soul [d]refused
to be comforted.
3 I remember God and
I am [a]disturbed;
I [b]muse and [c]my
spirit faints. [1]Selah.

---

◆ **76:1** [a]Ps 48:3 [b]Ps 99:3 **76:2** [a]Ps 27:5; Lam 2:6 [b]Ge 14:18 [c]Ps 9:11; 132:13; 135:21 [1]Lit *shelter* **76:3** [a]Ps 46:9 [1]Lit *fiery shafts of the bow* [2]*Selah* may mean *Pause, Crescendo, Musical Interlude* **76:5** [a]Is 10:12; 46:12 [1]Lit *They slumbered their sleep* [2]Lit *valiant men have found their hands* **76:6** [a]Ps 80:16 [b]Ex 15:1, 21; Ps 78:53 **76:7** [a]1Chr 16:25; Ps 89:7; 96:4 [b]Ezr 9:15; Ps 130:3; Na 1:6; Mal 3:2; Rev 6:17 [1]Or *awesome* [2]Lit *Your anger is* **76:8** [a]1Chr 16:30; 2Chr 20:29, 30; Ps 33:8 **76:9** [a]Ps 9:7, 8; 74:22; 82:8 **76:10** [a]Ex 9:16; Ro 9:17 [1]Lit *wraths* **76:11** [a]Ecc 5:4-6 [b]Ps 50:14 [c]2Chr 32:23; Ps 68:29 **76:12** [a]Ps 47:2 [1]Lit *awesome to* ◆ **77:TITLE** [†]1Chr 16:41 **77:1** [a]Ps 3:4; 142:1 **77:2** [a]Ps 50:15; 86:7 [b]Ps 63:6; Is 26:9 [c]Job 11:13; Ps 88:9 [d]Ge 37:35 [1]Lit *and did not grow numb* **77:3** [a]Ps 42:5, 11; 43:5 [b]Ps 55:2; 142:2 [c]Ps 61:2; 143:4 [1]*Selah* may mean *Pause, Crescendo, Musical Interlude*

4 You have held my eyelids *open*;
I am so troubled
that I [a]cannot speak.
5 I give thought
to the [a]days of old,
The years of long ago.
6 I remember my [a]music
in the night;
I [b]am musing with my heart,
And my spirit is searching:

7 Will the Lord
[a]reject evermore?
And will He [b]not be
favorable again?
8 Has His [a]lovingkindness
ceased forever?
Has *His* [b,1]word ended [2]from
generation to generation?
9 Has God [a]forgotten
to be gracious,
Or has He in anger shut up
His [b]compassion? Selah.
10 Then I said, "[a]It is my [1]grief,
That the [b]right hand of
the Most High has changed."

11 I shall remember
the [a]deeds of Yah;
Surely I will [a]remember
Your wonders of old.
12 I will [a]meditate
on all Your work
And muse on Your deeds.
13 O *God, Your way is* [a]*holy;*
[b]What god is great like God?
14 You are the [a]God who
works wonders;
You have [b]made known Your
strength among the peoples.
15 You have by *Your* arm
[a]redeemed Your people,
The sons of Jacob
and [b]Joseph. Selah.

16 The [a]waters saw You, O God;
The waters saw You, they
were in anguish;
The deeps also trembled.
17 The [a]clouds poured out water;
The skies [b]gave forth a sound;
Your [c]arrows went
here and there.
18 The [a]sound of Your thunder
was in the whirlwind;
The [b]lightnings lit
up the world;
The [c]earth trembled and shook.
19 Your [a]way was in the sea
And Your paths
in the mighty waters,
But Your footprints
were not known.
20 You [a]led Your people
like a flock
By the hand of [b]Moses
and Aaron.

## PSALM 78

### *That the Generation to Come Might Know*

A [†]Maskil of Asaph.

1 [a]Give ear, O my people,
to my [1]instruction;
[b]Incline your ears
to the words of my mouth.

**77:4** [a]Ps 39:9 **77:5** [a]Dt 32:7; Ps 44:1; 143:5; Is 51:9 **77:6** [a]Ps 42:8; Lam 5:14 [b]Ps 4:4 **77:7** [a]Ps 44:9 [b]Ps 85:1, 5 **77:8** [a]Ps 89:49 [b]2Pe 3:9 [1]Promise [2]Lit *to* **77:9** [a]Is 49:15 [b]Ps 25:6; 40:11; 51:1 **77:10** [a]Ps 31:22; 73:14 [b]Ps 44:2, 3 [1]Or *infirmity, the years of the right hand of the Most High* **77:11** [a]Ps 105:5; 143:5 **77:12** [a]Ps 145:5 **77:13** [a]Ps 63:2; 73:17 [b]Ex 15:11; Ps 71:19; 86:8 **77:14** [a]Ps 72:18 [b]Ps 106:8 **77:15** [a]Ex 6:6; Dt 9:29; Ps 74:2; 78:42 [b]Ps 80:1 **77:16** [a]Ex 14:21; Ps 114:3; Hab 3:8, 10 **77:17** [a]Jdg 5:4 [b]Ps 68:33 [c]Ps 18:14 **77:18** [a]Ps 18:13; 104:7 [b]Ps 97:4 [c]Jdg 5:4; Ps 18:7 **77:19** [a]Is 51:10; Hab 3:15 **77:20** [a]Ex 13:21; 14:19; Ps 78:52; 80:1; Is 63:11-13 [b]Ex 6:26; Ps 105:26 ◆ **78:TITLE** [†]Possibly *Contemplative, Didactic, Skillful Psalm* **78:1** [a]Is 51:4 [b]Is 55:3 [1]Or *law*

2 I will [a]open my mouth
in a parable;
I will pour forth [b]dark
sayings of old,
3 Which we have heard
and known,
And [a]our fathers have
recounted to us.
4 We will [a]not conceal them
from their children,
But [b]recount to
the generation to come
the praises of Yahweh,
And His strength and
His [c]wondrous deeds
that He has done.

5 For He established
a [a]testimony in Jacob
And set a [b]law in Israel,
Which He [c]commanded
our fathers
That they should [d,1]teach
them to their children,
6 [a]That the generation
to come might know,
*even* [b]the children
*yet* to be born,
*That* they may arise
and [c]recount *them*
to their children,
7 That they should set their
confidence in God
And [a]not forget
the deeds of God,
But [b]observe
His commandments,
8 And [a]not be
like their fathers,
A [b]stubborn and
rebellious generation,
A generation that [c]did
not [1]prepare its heart
And whose spirit was
not [d]faithful to God.

9 The sons of Ephraim
[1]were [a]archers
equipped with bows,
*Yet* [b]they turned back
in the day of battle.
10 They [a]did not keep
the covenant of God
And refused to [b]walk
in His law;
11 So they [a]forgot His acts
And His [1]wondrous deeds
that He had shown them.
12 [a]He did wonders
before their fathers
In the land of Egypt,
in the [b]field of Zoan.
13 He [a]split the sea and caused
them to pass through,
And He made the waters
stand [b]up like a heap.
14 Then He led them
with the cloud by [a]day
And all the night
with a [b]light of fire.
15 He was [a]splitting the rocks
in the wilderness
And so gave *them* abundant
drink like the ocean depths.

**78:2** [a]Ps 49:4; Mt 13:35 [b]Pr 1:6 **78:3** [a]Ps 44:1 **78:4** [a]Ex 12:26; Dt 6:7; 11:19; Job 15:18; Ps 145:4; *Is 38:19; Joel 1:3* [b]*Ex 13:8, 14;* Ps 22:30 [c]Job 37:16; Ps 26:7; 71:17 **78:5** [a]Ps 19:7; 81:5; Is 8:20 [b]Ps 147:19 [c]Dt 6:4-9 [d]Dt 4:9 [1]Lit *make them known* **78:6** [a]Ps 102:18 [b]Ps 22:31 [c]*Dt 11:19* **78:7** [a]*Dt 4:9; 6:12;* 8:14 [b]Dt 4:2; 5:1, 29; 27:1; Jos 22:5 **78:8** [a]2Ki 17:14; 2Chr 30:7; Eze 20:18 [b]Ex 32:9; Dt 9:7, 24; 31:27; Jdg 2:19; Is 30:9 [c]Job 11:13; Ps 78:37 [d]Ps 51:10 [1]Or *put right* **78:9** [a]1Chr 12:2 [b]Jdg 20:39; Ps 78:57 [1]Or *being* **78:10** [a]Jdg 2:20; 1Ki 11:11; 2Ki 17:15; 18:12 [b]Ps 119:1; Jer 32:23; 44:10, 23 **78:11** [a]Ps 106:13 [1]Or *miracles* **78:12** [a]Ex chs 7-12; Ps 106:22 [b]Nu 13:22; Ps 78:43; Is 19:11; 30:4; Eze 30:14 **78:13** [a]Ex 14:21; Ps 74:13; 136:13 [b]Ex 15:8; Ps 33:7 **78:14** [a]Ex 13:21; Ps 105:39 [b]Ex 14:24 **78:15** [a]Ex 17:6; Nu 20:11; Ps 105:41; 114:8; Is 48:21; 1Co 10:4

16 He [a]brought forth streams
also from the cliff face
And caused waters
to run down like rivers.

17 Yet they still continued
to sin against Him,
To [a]rebel against the Most
High in the desert.
18 And in their heart they
[a]put God to the test
By asking for [b]food
according to their desire.
19 Then they spoke against God;
They said, "[a]Can God prepare
a table in the wilderness?
20 "Behold, He [a]struck the rock
so that waters gushed out,
And streams
were overflowing;
Can He give bread also?
Will He prepare [b,1]meat
for His people?"

21 Therefore Yahweh heard
and [1]was [a]full of wrath;
And a fire was kindled
against Jacob
And anger also mounted
against Israel,
22 Because they [a]did not
believe in God
And did not trust
in His salvation.
23 *Yet He commanded*
the skies above
And [a]opened the doors
of heaven;
24 He [a]rained down manna
upon them to eat
And gave them [b]grain
from heaven.
25 Man ate the bread of [1]angels;
He sent them provision
[a]to satisfy.
26 He [a]led forth the east
wind in the heavens
And by His strength He
guided the south wind.
27 Then He rained [1]meat
upon them like the dust,
Even [a]winged fowl
like the sand of the seas,
28 He caused *them* to fall
in the midst of His camp,
All around His dwelling places.
29 So they [a]ate and were
very satisfied,
And their desire He
brought to them.
30 [1]Before they had satisfied
their desire,
[a]While their food was
in their mouths,
31 The [a]anger of God rose
against them
And killed [1]some of their
[b]stoutest ones,
And [2]subdued the choice
men of Israel.
32 In spite of all this they
[a]still sinned
And [b]did not believe
in His wondrous deeds.
33 So He brought [a]their days
to an end in [1]futility

---

**78:16** [a]Nu 20:8, 10, 11 **78:17** [a]Dt 9:22; Is 63:10; Heb 3:16 **78:18** [a]Ex 17:6; Dt 6:16; Ps 78:41, 56; 95:9; 106:14; 1Co 10:9 [b]Nu 11:4 **78:19** [a]Ex 16:3; Nu 11:4; 20:3; 21:5; Ps 23:5 **78:20** [a]Nu 20:11; Ps 78:15, 16 [b]Nu 11:18 [1]Lit *flesh* **78:21** [a]Nu 11:1 [1]Or *became infuriated* **78:22** [a]Dt 1:32; 9:23; Heb 3:18 **78:23** [a]Ge 7:11; Mal 3:10 **78:24** [a]Ex 16:4 [b]Ps 105:40; Jn 6:31 **78:25** [a]Ex 16:3 [1]Lit *mighty ones* **78:26** [a]Nu 11:31 **78:27** [a]Ex 16:13; Ps 105:40 [1]Lit *flesh* **78:29** [a]Nu 11:19, 20 **78:30** [a]Nu 11:33 [1]Lit *They were not estranged from* **78:31** [a]Nu 11:33, 34; Job 20:23 [b]Is 10:16 [1]Lit *among their fat ones* [2]Lit *caused to bow down* **78:32** [a]Num chs 14, 16, 17 [b]Nu 14:11; Ps 78:11 **78:33** [a]Nu 14:29, 35 [1]Lit *vanity, a mere breath*

And their years
in sudden terror.

34 When He killed them,
then they [a]sought Him,
And returned and sought
[b]earnestly for God;
35 And they remembered
that God was their [a]rock,
And the Most High God
their [b]Redeemer.
36 But they [a]deceived Him
with their mouth
And [b]lied to Him
with their tongue.
37 For their heart was
not [a]prepared
*to remain* with Him,
Nor were they faithful
in His covenant.
38 But He, being
[a]compassionate, [b]atoned
for *their* iniquity and
did not destroy *them*;
And He abounded in
[c]turning back His anger
And did not arouse
all His wrath.
39 Thus [a]He remembered
that they were but [b]flesh,
A [c,1]wind that goes and
does not return.

40 How often they
[a]rebelled against Him
in the wilderness
And [b]grieved Him
in the [c]wasteland!
41 Again and again they
[a,1]tested God,
And pained the [b]Holy
One of Israel.
42 They [a]did not remember
[b]His [1]power,
The day when He [c]redeemed
them from the adversary,
43 When He performed
His [a]signs in Egypt
And His [b]miracles
in the field of Zoan,
44 And [a]turned their
rivers to blood,
And their streams,
they could not drink.
45 He sent among them
swarms of [a]flies
which devoured them,
And [b]frogs
which destroyed them.
46 He gave also their crops
to the [a]grasshopper
And the fruit of their
labor to the [b]locust.
47 He killed their vines
with [a]hailstones
And their sycamore
trees with frost.
48 He gave over their [a]cattle
also to the hailstones
And their herds
to bolts of lightning.
49 He [a]sent upon them
His burning anger,
Fury and indignation
and [1]distress,
[2]A band of destroying angels.

---

***78:34*** [a]*Nu 21:7; Hos 5:15* [b]Ps 63:1 **78:35** [a]Dt 32:4 [b]Ex 15:13; Dt 9:26; Ps 74:2; Is 41:14 **78:36** [a]Ex 24:7, 8; Eze 33:31 [b]Ex 32:7, 8; Is 57:11 **78:37** [a]Ps 51:10; 78:8; Ac 8:21 **78:38** [a]Ex 34:6 [b]Nu 14:18-20 [c]Is 48:9 **78:39** [a]Job 10:9; Ps 103:14 [b]Ge 6:3 [c]Job 7:7, 16; Ps 103:14; Jas 4:14 [1]Or *breath* **78:40** [a]Ps 95:8, 9; 106:43; 107:11; Heb 3:16 [b]Ps 95:10; Is 63:10; Eph 4:30 [c]Ps 106:14 **78:41** [a]Nu 14:22 [b]2Ki 19:22; Ps 89:18 [1]Or *put God to the test* **78:42** [a]Jdg 8:34 [b]Ps 44:3 [c]Ps 106:10 [1]Lit *hand* **78:43** [a]Ps 105:27 [b]Ex 4:21; 7:3 **78:44** [a]Ex 7:20; Ps 105:29 **78:45** [a]Ex 8:24; Ps 105:31 [b]Ex 8:6; Ps 105:30 **78:46** [a]1Ki 8:37; Ps 105:34 [b]Ex 10:14 **78:47** [a]Ex 9:23-25; Ps 105:32 **78:48** [a]Ex 9:19 **78:49** [a]Ex 15:7 [1]Or *trouble* [2]Lit *A deputation of angels of evil*

50 He leveled a path for His anger;
He did not hold back their
soul from death,
But [a]gave over their
life to the plague,
51 So He [a]struck all
the firstborn in Egypt,
The [b]first of their vigor
in the tents of [c]Ham.
52 But He [a]led forth His own
people like sheep
And guided them in
the wilderness [b]like a flock;
53 He led them [a]safely, so
that they did not fear;
But [b]the sea covered
their enemies.

54 So [a]He brought them
to His holy [1]land,
To this [b,2]hill country [c]which
His right hand had acquired.
55 He also [a]drove out
the nations before them
And [b]apportioned them for
an inheritance
by measurement,
And made the tribes of Israel
dwell in their tents.
56 Yet they [a,1]tested and [b]rebelled
against the Most High God
And did not keep
His testimonies,
57 But turned back and
[a]acted treacherously
like their fathers;
They [b]turned aside
like a treacherous bow.
58 For they [a]provoked Him
with their [b]high places
And [c]aroused His jealousy
with their [d]graven images.
59 God heard and [1]was
filled with [a]wrath
And greatly [b]rejected Israel;
60 So that He [a]abandoned
the [b]dwelling place
at Shiloh,
The tent
[1]which He caused
to dwell among men,
61 And gave up His [a]strength
to captivity
And His beauty [b]into
the hand of the adversary.
62 He also [a]gave over His
people to the sword,
And [1]was filled with wrath
at His inheritance.
63 [a]Fire devoured [1]His
choice men,
And [1]His [b]virgins had
no wedding songs.
64 [1]His [a]priests fell
by the sword,
And [2]His [b]widows
could not weep.

65 Then the Lord [a]awoke
as *if from* sleep,
As *if He were a* [b]warrior
[1]overcome by wine.

**78:50** [a]Ex 12:29, 30 **78:51** [a]Ex 12:29; Ps 105:36; 135:8; 136:10 [b]Ge 49:3 [c]Ps 105:23, 27; 106:22 **78:52** [a]Ex 15:22 [b]Ps 77:20 **78:53** [a]Ex 14:19, 20 [b]Ex 14:27, 28; Ps 106:11 **78:54** [a]Ex 15:17 [b]Ps 68:16; Is 11:9 [c]Ps 44:3 [1]Lit *border, territory* [2]Or *mountain* **78:55** [a]Jos 11:16-23; Ps 44:2 [b]Jos 13:7; 23:4; Ps 105:11; 135:12 **78:56** [a]Ps 78:18 [b]Jdg 2:11-13; Ps 78:40 [1]Or *put to the test* **78:57** [a]Eze 20:27, 28 [b]Hos 7:16 **78:58** [a]Dt 4:25; Jdg 2:12; 1Ki 14:9; Is 65:3 [b]Lv 26:30; 1Ki 3:2; 2Ki 16:4; Jer 17:3 [c]Dt 32:16, 21; 1Ki 14:22 [d]Ex 20:4; Lv 26:1; Dt 4:25 **78:59** [a]Dt 1:34; 9:19; Ps 106:40 [b]Lv 26:30; Dt 32:19; Am 6:8 [1]Or *became infuriated* **78:60** [a]1Sa 4:11; Ps 78:67; Jer 7:12, 14; 26:6 [b]Jos 18:1 [1]Some ancient versions *where He dwelt* **78:61** [a]Ps 63:2; 132:8 [b]1Sa 4:17 **78:62** [a]Jdg 20:21; 1Sa 4:10 [1]Or *became infuriated* **78:63** [a]Nu 11:1; 21:28; Is 26:11; Jer 48:45 [b]Jer 7:34; 16:9; Lam 2:21 [1]Or *their* **78:64** [a]1Sa 4:17; 22:18 [b]Job 27:15; Eze 24:23 [1]Or *Their* [2]Or *their* **78:65** [a]Ps 44:23; 73:20 [b]Is 42:13 [1]Or *sobered up from*

66 He [a]struck His
adversaries backward;
He put on them
an everlasting reproach.
67 He also [a]rejected
the tent of Joseph,
And did not choose
the tribe of Ephraim,
68 But chose the tribe of Judah,
Mount [a]Zion which He loved.
69 And He [a]built His sanctuary
like the heights,
Like the earth which He
has founded forever.
70 He also [a]chose David
His servant
And took him
from the sheepfolds;
71 From [a]following the [b,1]nursing
ewes He brought him
To [c]shepherd Jacob His people,
And Israel [d]His inheritance.
72 So he shepherded them
according to the [a]integrity
of his heart,
And led them with his
skillful hands.

## PSALM 79

### *How Long, O Yahweh?*

A Psalm of Asaph.

1 O God, the [a]nations
have come
into [b]Your inheritance;
They have defiled Your
[c]holy temple;
They have [d]laid
Jerusalem in ruins.
2 They have given the [a]dead
bodies of Your slaves
for food to the birds
of the heavens,
The flesh of Your holy ones
to the beasts of the earth.
3 They have poured out their
blood like water
round about Jerusalem;
And there was [a]no one
to bury them.
4 We have become a [a]reproach
to our neighbors,
A mockery and derision
to those around us.
5 [a]How long, O Yahweh?
Will You be angry forever?
Will Your [b]jealousy
[c]burn like fire?
6 [a]Pour out Your wrath
upon the nations
which [b]do not know You,
And upon the kingdoms which
[c]do not call upon Your name.
7 For they have [a]devoured Jacob
And [b]laid waste his [1]abode.

8 [a]Do not remember *our* former
iniquities against us;
Let Your compassion
quickly [b]approach us,
For we are [c]brought very low.
9 [a]Help us, O God of our
salvation, for the glory
of [b]Your name;
And deliver us and
[c]atone for our sins
[d]for Your name's sake.

---

**78:66** [a]1Sa 5:6 **78:67** [a]Ps 78:60 **78:68** [a]Ps 87:2; 132:13 **78:69** [a]1Ki 6:1-38 **78:70** [a]1Sa 16:11, 12 **78:71** [a]2Sa 7:8; Is 40:11 [b]Ge 33:13 [c]2Sa 5:2; 1Chr 11:2; Ps 28:9 [d]1Sa 10:1 [1]Lit *ewes which gave suck* **78:72** [a]1Ki 9:4 ◆ **79:1** [a]Lam 1:10 [b]Ps 74:2 [c]Ps 74:3, 7 [d]2Ki 25:9, 10; 2Chr 36:17-19; Jer 26:18; 52:12-14; Mic 3:12 **79:2** [a]Dt 28:26; Jer 7:33; 16:4; 19:7; 34:20 **79:3** [a]Jer 14:16; 16:4 **79:4** [a]Ps 44:13; 80:6; Da 9:16 **79:5** [a]Ps 13:1; 74:1, 9, 10; 85:5; 89:46 [b]Dt 29:20; Eze 36:5; 38:19 [c]Ps 89:46; Zep 3:8 **79:6** [a]Ps 69:24; Jer 10:25; Eze 21:31; Zep 3:8 [b]1Th 4:5; 2Th 1:8 [c]Ps 14:4; 53:4 **79:7** [a]Ps 53:4 [b]2Chr 36:19; Jer 39:8 [1]Lit *pasture* **79:8** [a]Ps 106:6; Is 64:9 [b]Ps 21:3 [c]Dt 28:43; Ps 116:6; 142:6; Is 26:5 **79:9** [a]2Chr 14:11 [b]Ps 31:3 [c]Ps 25:11; 65:3 [d]Jer 14:7

10 [a]Why should the nations say,
“Where is their God?”
Let it be known among
the nations before our eyes:
[b]Vengeance for the blood
of Your slaves
which has been poured out.
11 Let [a]the groaning of
the prisoner come before You;
According to the greatness of
Your [1]power preserve [2]those
who are [a]doomed to die.
12 And return to our neighbors
[a]sevenfold [b]into their bosom
[1]The [c]reproach
with which they have
reproached You, O Lord.
13 But as for us, as Your
people and the [a]sheep
of Your pasture,
We will [b]give thanks
to You forever;
From generation to generation
we will [c]recount Your praise.

## PSALM 80

### *O God, Restore Us*

For the choir director. [†]El Shoshannim.
[˙]Eduth. Of Asaph. A Psalm.

1 O [a]Shepherd of Israel, give ear,
You who guide [b]Joseph
like a flock;
You who [c]are enthroned *above*
the cherubim, shine forth!
2 Before [a]Ephraim and
Benjamin and Manasseh,
[b]stir up Your might
And come to save us!
3 O God, [a]restore us
And [b]cause Your face
to shine *upon us*,
that we would be saved.

4 O [a]Yahweh God *of* hosts,
[b]How long will You [1]smolder
against the prayer
of Your people?
5 You have fed them
with the [a]bread of tears,
And You have made
them to drink tears
in [1]large measure.
6 You set us as [1]an object
of strife [a]to our neighbors,
And our enemies mock *us*
among themselves.
7 O God *of* hosts, restore us
And cause Your face
to shine *upon us*,
that we might be saved.

8 You removed a [a]vine
from Egypt;
You [b]drove out
the [1]nations and then
You [c]planted it.
9 You [a]cleared *the ground*
before it,
And it [b]took deep root
and filled the land.
10 The mountains were
covered with its shadow,
And [1]the cedars of God
with its [a]boughs.

**79:10** [a]Ps 42:10; 115:2 [b]Ps 94:1, 2 **79:11** [a]Ps 102:20 [1]Lit *arm* [2]Lit *the children of death*
**79:12** [a]Ge 4:15; Lv 26:21, 28; Ps 12:6; 119:164; Pr 6:31; 24:16; Is 30:26 [b]Ps 35:13; Is 65:6, 7; Jer 32:18; Lk 6:38 [c]Ps 74:10, 18, 22 [1]Lit *Their* **79:13** [a]Ps 74:1; 95:7; 100:3 [b]Ps 44:8 [c]Ps 89:1; Is 43:21
◆ **80:TITLE** [†]Possibly, *To Lilies* [˙]Lit *A testimony* **80:1** [a]Ps 23:1 [b]Ps 77:15; 78:67; Am 5:15 [c]Ex 25:22; 1Sa 4:4; 2Sa 6:2; Ps 99:1 **80:2** [a]Nu 2:18-24 [b]Ps 35:23 **80:3** [a]Ps 60:1; 80:7, 19; 85:4; 126:1; Lam 5:21 [b]Nu 6:25; Ps 4:6; 31:16 **80:4** [a]Ps 59:5; 84:8 [b]Ps 79:5; 85:5 [1]Lit *smoke* **80:5** [a]Ps 42:3; 102:9; Is 30:20 [1]Lit *a third part of a* **80:6** [a]Ps 44:13; 79:4 [1]Lit *a strife to* **80:8** [a]Ps 80:15; Is 5:1, 2, 7; Jer 2:21; 12:10; Eze 17:6; 19:10 [b]Jos 13:6; 2Chr 20:7; Ps 44:2; Ac 7:45 [c]Jer 11:17; 32:41; Eze 17:23; Am 9:15 [1]Or *Gentiles*
**80:9** [a]Ex 23:28; Jos 24:12; Is 5:2 [b]Hos 14:5 **80:10** [a]Ge 49:22 [1]Or *its boughs are like the cedars of God*

11 It sent out its branches
[a]to the sea
And its shoots to the River.
12 Why have You [a]broken
down its [1]hedges,
So that all who pass
*that* way pick its *fruit*?
13 A boar from the forest
[a]devours it
And whatever moves
in the field feeds on it.

14 O God *of* hosts, [a]return
now, we beseech You;
[b]Look down from heaven and
see, and visit this vine,
15 Even the [a,1]sapling which Your
right hand has planted,
And on the [2]son whom
You have [3]strengthened
for Yourself.
16 It is [a]burned with fire,
it is cut down;
They perish at the [b]rebuke
of Your face.
17 Let [a]Your hand be upon
the man of Your right hand,
Upon the son of man
whom You [b]made
strong for Yourself.
18 Then we shall not [a]turn
back from You;
[b]Revive us, and we will
call upon Your name.
19 O Yahweh God of hosts,
[a]restore us;
Cause Your face to shine *upon*
*us*, that we might be saved.

## PSALM 81

### *Oh That My People Would Listen to Me*

For the choir director. According to the Gittith. Of Asaph.

1 [a]Sing for joy to God
our [b]strength;
Make a loud [c]shout
to the [d]God of Jacob.
2 Lift up a song of praise,
strike [a]the tambourine,
The sweet sounding
[b]lyre with the [c]harp.
3 Blow the trumpet
at the [a]new moon,
At the full moon,
on our [b]feast day.
4 For it is a statute
for Israel,
[a]A judgment
of the God of Jacob.
5 He established it
for a testimony in Joseph
When he [a]went forth
over the land of Egypt.
I heard a [b]language
that I did not know:

6 "I [a,1]relieved his shoulder
of the burden,
His hands were freed
from the [2]basket.
7 "You [a]called in distress
and I rescued you;
I [b]answered you in the hiding
place of thunder;
I tested you at the [c]waters
of Meribah. [1]Selah.

---

**80:11** [a]Ps 72:8 **80:12** [a]Ps 89:40; Is 5:5 [1]Or *walls, fences* **80:13** [a]Jer 5:6 **80:14** [a]Ps 90:13 [b]Ps 102:19; Is 63:15 **80:15** [a]Ps 80:8 [1]Or *root* [2]Or figuratively: *branch* [3]Or *secured* **80:16** [a]2Chr 36:19; Ps 74:8; Jer 52:13 [b]Ps 39:11; 76:6 **80:17** [a]Ps 89:21 [b]Ps 80:15 **80:18** [a]Is 50:5 [b]Ps 71:20 **80:19** [a]Ps 80:3 ◆ **81:1** [a]Ps 51:14; 59:16; 95:1 [b]Ps 46:1 [c]Ps 66:1; 95:2; 98:4 [d]Ps 84:8 **81:2** [a]Ex 15:20; Ps 149:3 [b]Ps 92:3; 98:5; 147:7 [c]Ps 108:2; 144:9 **81:3** [a]Nu 10:10 [b]Lv 23:24 **81:4** [a]Dt 4:1 **81:5** [a]Ge 41:45; Ex 11:4 [b]Dt 28:49; Ps 114:1; Jer 5:15 **81:6** [a]Is 9:4; 10:27 [1]Lit *removed his shoulder from* [2]Or *brick load* **81:7** [a]Ex 2:23; 14:10; Ps 50:15 [b]Ex 19:19; 20:18 [c]Ex 17:6, 7; Nu 20:13; Ps 95:8 [1]*Selah* may mean *Pause, Crescendo, Musical Interlude*

8 “ [a]Hear, O My people, and I
will testify against you;
O Israel, if you [b]would
listen to Me!
9 “Let there be no [a]strange
god among you;
And you shall not worship
a foreign god.
10 “ [a]I am Yahweh your God,
Who brought you up
from the land of Egypt;
[b]Open your mouth wide
and I will [c]fill it.

11 “But My people [a]did not
listen to My voice,
And Israel was not
willing *to obey* Me.
12 “So I [a]released [1]them
over to the stubbornness
of their heart,
That they would walk
in their own devices.
13 “Oh that My people
[a]would listen to Me,
That Israel would [b]walk
in My ways!
14 “I would quickly [a]subdue
their enemies
And I would [b]turn My hand
against their adversaries.
15 “ [a]Those who hate Yahweh
would [b]cower before Him,
And their time *of punishment*
would be forever.
16 “ [1]But I would feed you with
the [a,2]finest of the wheat,
And with [b]honey from
the rock I would satisfy you.”

## PSALM 82

### *God Stands in Judgment*

A Psalm of Asaph.

1 God takes His [a]stand
in the congregation of [1]God;
He [b]judges in the midst
of [c,2]gods.
2 How long will you
[a]judge unrighteously
And [b]show partiality
to the wicked? [1]Selah.
3 [a]Give justice to the poor
and the orphan;
Justify the afflicted
and destitute.
4 [a]Protect the poor and needy;
Deliver *them* out
of the hand of the wicked.
5 They [a]do not know and
do not understand;
They [b]walk about in darkness;
All the [c]foundations
of the earth are shaken.
6 [1]I [a]said, “You are gods,
And all of you are [b]sons
of the Most High.
7 “Nevertheless [a]you
will die like men
And you will fall like *any*
[b]one of the princes.”
8 [a]Arise, O God, [b]judge the earth!
For it is You who [c]will
inherit all the nations.

---

**81:8** [a]Ps 50:7 [b]Ps 95:7 **81:9** [a]Ex 20:3; Dt 5:7; 32:12; Ps 44:20; Is 43:12 **81:10** [a]Ex 20:2; Dt 5:6 [b]Job 29:23 [c]Ps 37:4; 78:25; 107:9 **81:11** [a]Dt 32:15; Ps 106:25; Is 1:19 **81:12** [a]Job 8:4; Ac 7:42; Ro 1:24, 26 [1]Lit *him* **81:13** [a]Dt 5:29; Ps 81:8; Is 48:18 [b]Ps 128:1; Is 42:24; Jer 7:23 **81:14** [a]Ps 18:47; 47:3 [b]Am 1:8 **81:15** [a]Ro 1:30 [b]Ps 18:44; 66:3 **81:16** [a]Dt 32:14; Ps 147:14 [b]Dt 32:13 [1]Lit *He would feed him* [2]Lit *fat* ◆ **82:1** [a]Is 3:13 [b]2Chr 19:6; Ps 58:11 [c]Ex 21:6; 22:8, 28 [1]Heb *El*; the one true God [2]Or *rulers* **82:2** [a]Ps 58:1 [b]Dt 1:17; Pr 18:5 [1]*Selah* may mean *Pause, Crescendo, Musical Interlude* **82:3** [a]Dt 24:17; Ps 10:18; Is 11:4; Jer 22:16 **82:4** [a]Job 29:12 **82:5** [a]Ps 14:4; Jer 4:22; Mic 3:1 [b]Pr 2:13; Is 59:9; Jer 23:12 [c]Ps 11:3 **82:6** [a]Ps 82:1; Jn 10:34 [b]Ps 89:26 [1]Lit *I, on my part* **82:7** [a]Job 21:32; Ps 49:12; Eze 31:14 [b]Ps 83:11 **82:8** [a]Ps 12:5 [b]Ps 58:11; 96:13 [c]Ps 2:8; Rev 11:15

## PSALM 83

### *O God, Do Not Be Quiet*

A Song. A Psalm of Asaph.

1 O God, [a]do not remain
at rest;
[b]Do not be silent and,
O God, do not be quiet.
2 For behold, Your
enemies [a]roar,
And [b]those who hate
You have [c]lifted up
their heads.
3 They [a]make shrewd plans
against Your people,
And [1]conspire together against
[b]Your [2]treasured ones.
4 They have said, "Come,
and [a]let us wipe them
out [1]as a nation,
That the [b]name of Israel be
remembered no more."
5 For they have [a,1]conspired
together with one heart;
Against You they cut
a covenant:
6 The tents of [a]Edom and
the [b]Ishmaelites,
[c]Moab and the [d]Hagrites;
7 [a]Gebal and [b]Ammon
and [c]Amalek,
[d]Philistia with the inhabitants
of [e]Tyre;
8 [a]Assyria also has
joined with them;
They have become
[1]the power of the [b]children
of Lot. [2]Selah.

9 Do to them [a]as to Midian,
As [b]to Sisera, *and* Jabin
at the river of Kishon,
10 Who were destroyed at En-dor,
Who [a]were as dung
for the ground.
11 Make their nobles
like [a]Oreb and Zeeb
And all their princes
like [b]Zebah and Zalmunna,
12 Who said, "[a]Let us
possess for ourselves
The [b]pastures of God."

13 O my God, make them
like the [a,1]whirling dust,
Like [b]chaff before the wind.
14 Like [a]fire that burns
the forest
And like a flame that [b]burns
up the mountains,
15 So pursue them
[a]with Your tempest
And dismay them
with Your storm.
16 [a]Fill their faces with disgrace,
That they may seek Your
name, O Yahweh.
17 Let them be [a]ashamed
and dismayed forever,
And let them be humiliated
and perish,
18 That they may [a]know
that [b]You alone—Your
name is Yahweh—
Are the [c]Most High
over all the earth.

---

◆ **83:1** [a]Ps 28:1; 35:22 [b]Ps 109:1 **83:2** [a]Ps 2:1; Is 17:12 [b]Ps 81:15 [c]Jdg 8:28; Zec 1:21 **83:3** [a]Ps 64:2; Js 29:15 [b]Ps 27:5; 31:20 [1]Or *consult* [2]Or *hidden ones* **83:4** [a]Es 3:6; Ps 74:8; Jer 48:2 [b]Ps 41:5; Jer 11:19 [1]Lit *from* **83:5** [a]Ps 2:2; Da 6:7 [1]Or *consulted* **83:6** [a]2Chr 20:10; Ps 137:7 [b]Ge 25:12-16 [c]2Chr 20:10 [d]1Chr 5:10 **83:7** [a]Jos 13:5; Eze 27:9 [b]2Chr 20:10 [c]1Sa 15:2 [d]1Sa 4:1; 29:1 [e]Eze 27:3; Am 1:9 **83:8** [a]2Ki 15:19 [b]Dt 2:9 [1]Lit *an arm* [2]*Selah* may mean *Pause, Crescendo, Musical Interlude* **83:9** [a]Jdg 7:1-24 [b]Jdg 4:7, 15, 21-24 **83:10** [a]Zep 1:17 **83:11** [a]Jdg 7:25 [b]Jdg 8:12, 21 **83:12** [a]2Chr 20:11 [b]Ps 132:13 **83:13** [a]Is 17:13 [b]Job 21:18; Ps 35:5; Is 40:24; Jer 13:24 [1]Or *tumbleweed* **83:14** [a]Is 9:18 [b]Ex 19:18; Dt 32:22 **83:15** [a]Job 9:17; Ps 58:9 **83:16** [a]Job 10:15; Ps 109:29; 132:18 **83:17** [a]Ps 35:4; 70:2 **83:18** [a]Ps 59:13 [b]Ps 86:10; Is 45:21 [c]Ps 9:2; 18:13; 97:9

## PSALM 84

***Blessed Is the Man Who Trusts in You***

For the choir director. According to the [†]Gittith. Of the sons of Korah. A Psalm.

1 How lovely are Your
[a]dwelling places,
O Yahweh of hosts!
2 My [a]soul has longed
and even [1]fainted
for the courts of Yahweh;
My heart and my flesh sing
for joy to the [b]living God.
3 Even the bird has found a home,
And the swallow a nest
for herself, where she
sets her young,
At Your [a]altars,
O Yahweh of hosts,
[b]My King and my God.
4 How [a]blessed are those who
dwell in Your house!
They are [b]ever praising
You. [1]Selah.

5 How blessed is the man
whose [a]strength is in You,
In [1]whose heart are
the [b]highways *to Zion*!
6 Passing through the valley of
[1]Baca they make it a [2]spring;
The [a]early rain also wraps
it up with blessings.
7 They [a]go from strength
to strength,
[1]*Each one of them* [b]appears
before God in Zion.
8 O [a]Yahweh God of hosts,
hear my prayer;
Give ear,
O [b]God of Jacob! Selah.
9 See our [a]shield, O God,
And look upon the face
of [b]Your anointed.
10 For [a]better is a day
in Your courts
than a thousand *elsewhere.*
I would choose to stand
at the threshold
of the house of my God
Than dwell in the tents
of wickedness.
11 For Yahweh God is
[a]a sun and [b]shield;
Yahweh gives grace and [c]glory;
[d]No good thing does He
withhold [1]from those
who walk blamelessly.
12 O Yahweh of hosts,
How [a]blessed is the man
who trusts in You!

## PSALM 85

***Turn Us Back, O God***

For the choir director. Of the sons of Korah. A Psalm.

1 O Yahweh, You showed
[a]favor to Your land;
You [b,1]returned
the fortunes of Jacob.
2 You [a]forgave the iniquity
of Your people;
You [b]covered all their sin. [1]Selah.

◆ **84:TITLE** [†]Possibly an instrument or a title for a tune. **84:1** [a]Ps 43:3; 132:5 **84:2** [a]Ps 42:1, 2; 63:1 [b]Ps 42:2 [1]Lit *failed* **84:3** [a]Ps 43:4 [b]Ps 5:2 **84:4** [a]Ps 65:4 [b]Ps 42:5, 11 [1]*Selah* may mean *Pause, Crescendo, Musical Interlude* **84:5** [a]Ps 81:1 [b]Ps 86:11; 122:1; Jer 31:6 [1]Lit *their* **84:6** [a]Ps 107:35; Joel 2:23 [1]Probably *Weeping*; or *Balsam trees* [2]Or *place of springs* **84:7** [a]Pr 4:18; Is 40:31; Jn 1:16; 2Co 3:18 [b]Ex 34:23; Dt 16:16; Ps 42:2 [1]Some ancient versions *The God of gods will be seen in Zion* **84:8** [a]Ps 59:5; 80:4; 84:1 [b]Ps 81:1 **84:9** [a]Ge 15:1; Ps 3:3; 28:7; 59:11; 115:9-11 [b]1Sa 16:6; 2Sa 19:21; Ps 2:2; 132:17 **84:10** [a]Ps 27:4 **84:11** [a]Is 60:19, 20; Mal 4:2; Rev 21:23 [b]Ge 15:1 [c]Ps 85:9 [d]Ps 34:9, 10 [1]Lit *with regard to* **84:12** [a]Ps 2:12; 40:4 ◆ **85:1** [a]Ps 77:7; 106:4 [b]Ezr 1:11; Ps 14:7; 126:1; Jer 30:18; Eze 39:25; Hos 6:11; Joel 3:1 [1]Or *restore the captivity* **85:2** [a]Nu 14:19; 1Ki 8:34; Ps 78:38; 103:3; Jer 31:34 [b]Ps 32:1 [1]*Selah* may mean *Pause, Crescendo, Musical Interlude*

3 You [a]withdrew all Your fury;
You [b]turned back
from Your burning anger.
4 [a]Turn us back,
O God of our salvation,
And [b]cause Your vexation
toward us to cease.
5 Will [a]You be angry
with us forever?
Will You prolong Your
anger from generation
to generation?
6 Will You not Yourself
[a]return to [1]revive us,
That Your people may
[b]be glad in You?
7 Show us, O Yahweh,
Your lovingkindness,
And [a]give us Your salvation.

8 Let me hear what the God,
Yahweh, will speak;
For He will [a]speak peace to His
people, [1]to His holy ones;
But let them not [b]turn
back to [2]folly.
9 Surely [a]His salvation is near
to those who [1]fear Him,
That [b]glory may dwell
in our land.
10 [a]Lovingkindness and [1]truth
have met together;
[b]Righteousness and peace
have kissed each other.
11 [1]Truth [a]springs up
from the earth,
And righteousness looks
down from heaven.
12 Indeed, [a]Yahweh will
give what is good,
And our [b]land will
yield its produce.
13 [a]Righteousness will
go before Him
And will establish
the way of His steps.

## PSALM 86

### *To You, O Lord, I Lift Up My Soul*

A Prayer of David.

1 [a]Incline Your ear, O Yahweh,
*and* answer me;
For I am [b]afflicted
and needy.
2 [a]Keep my [1]soul,
for I am a [b]holy one;
O You my God, save Your
slave who [c]trusts in You.
3 Be [a]gracious to me, O Lord,
For [b]to You I call all day long.
4 Make glad the soul
of Your slave,
For to You, O Lord,
[a]I lift up my soul.
5 For You, Lord, are [a]good,
and [b]by nature forgiving,
And [c]abundant
in lovingkindness to all
who call upon You.
6 [a]Give ear, O Yahweh,
to my prayer;
And give heed to the voice
of my supplications!

**85:3** [a]Ps 78:38; 106:23 [b]Ex 32:12; Dt 13:17; Ps 106:23; Jon 3:9 **85:4** [a]Ps 80:3, 7 [b]Da 9:16
**85:5** [a]Ps 74:1; 79:5; 80:4 **85:6** [a]Ps 71:20; 80:18 [b]Ps 33:1; 90:14; 149:2 [1]Or *bring us to life*
**85:7** [a]Ps 106:4 **85:8** [a]Ps 29:11; Hag 2:9; Zec 9:10 [b]Ps 78:57; 2Pe 2:21 [1]Lit *even to* [2]Or *stupidity*
**85:9** [a]Ps 34:18; Is 46:13 [b]Ps 84:11; Hag 2:7; Zec 2:5; Jn 1:14 [1]Or *reverence* **85:10** [a]Ps 25:10; 89:14;
Pr 3:3 [b]Ps 72:3; Is 32:17 [1]Or *faithfulness* **85:11** [a]Is 45:8 [1]Or *Faithfulness* **85:12** [a]Ps 84:11;
Jas 1:17 [b]Lv 26:4; Ps 67:6; Eze 34:27; Zec 8:12 **85:13** [a]Ps 89:14 ◆ **86:1** [a]Ps 17:6; 31:2; 71:2 [b]Ps 40:17;
70:5 **86:2** [a]Ps 25:20 [b]Ps 4:3; 50:5 [c]Ps 25:2; 31:14; 56:4 [1]Or *life* **86:3** [a]Ps 4:1; 57:1 [b]Ps 25:5; 88:9
**86:4** [a]Ps 25:1; 143:8 **86:5** [a]Ps 25:8 [b]Ps 130:4 [c]Ex 34:6; Ne 9:17; Ps 103:8; 145:8; Joel 2:13; Jon 4:2
**86:6** [a]Ps 55:1

7 In [a]the day of my distress
I shall call upon You,
For [b]You will answer me.
8 There is [a]no one like You
among the gods, O Lord,
Nor are there any
works [b]like Yours.
9 [a]All nations whom You
have made shall come
and worship
before You, O Lord,
And they shall glorify
Your name.
10 For You are [a]great and [b]do
[1]wondrous deeds;
You alone [c]are God.

11 [a]Teach me Your way,
O Yahweh;
I will walk in Your truth;
[b]Unite my heart
to fear Your name.
12 I will [a]give thanks
to You, O Lord my God,
with all my heart,
And will glorify Your
name forever.
13 For Your lovingkindness
toward me is great,
And You have [a]delivered my
soul from Sheol below.

14 O God, arrogant men have
[a]risen up against me,
And [1]a band of ruthless men
have sought my [2]life,
And they have not set
You before them.
15 But You, O Lord,
are a God [a]compassionate
and gracious,
Slow to anger and abundant
in lovingkindness
and [1]truth.
16 [a]Turn to me, and be
gracious to me;
Oh [b]grant Your strength
to Your slave,
And save the [c]son
of Your maidservant.
17 [a,1]Show me a sign for good,
That those who hate
me may [b]see *it* and
be ashamed,
Because You, O Yahweh,
[c]have helped me and
comforted me.

## PSALM 87

### *Yahweh Loves the Gates of Zion*

Of the sons of Korah. A Psalm. A Song.

1 His [a]foundation is
in the holy mountains.
2 Yahweh [a]loves
the gates of Zion
More than all the dwelling
places of Jacob.
3 [a]Glorious things are
spoken of you,
O [b]city of God. [1]Selah.
4 "I shall mention [a,1]Rahab
and Babylon
among those who know Me;
Behold, Philistia and [b]Tyre
with [c,2]Ethiopia:
'This one was born there.'"

---

**86:7** [a]Ps 50:15; 77:2 [b]Ps 17:6 **86:8** [a]Ex 15:11; 2Sa 7:22; 1Ki 8:23; Ps 89:6; Jer 10:6 [b]Dt 3:24 **86:9** [a]Ps 22:27; 66:4; Is 66:23; Rev 15:4 **86:10** [a]Ps 77:13 [b]Ex 15:11; Ps 72:18; 77:14; 136:4 [c]Dt 6:4; 32:39; Ps 83:18; Is 37:16; 44:6, 8; Mk 12:29; 1Co 8:4 [1]Or *miracles* **86:11** [a]Ps 25:5 [b]Jer 32:39 **86:12** [a]Ps 111:1 **86:13** [a]Ps 30:3 **86:14** [a]Ps 54:3 [1]Or *an assembly* [2]Lit *soul* **86:15** [a]Ex 34:6-8; Ps 86:5 [1]Or *faithfulness* **86:16** [a]Ps 25:16 [b]Ps 68:35 [c]Ps 116:16 **86:17** [a]Jdg 6:17; Ps 119:122 [b]Ps 112:10 [c]Ps 118:13 [1]Lit *Do with* ◆ **87:1** [a]Ps 78:69; Is 28:16 **87:2** [a]Ps 78:67, 68 **87:3** [a]Is 60:1 [b]Ps 46:4; 48:8 [1]*Selah* may mean *Pause, Crescendo, Musical Interlude* **87:4** [a]Job 9:13; Ps 89:10; Is 19:23-25 [b]Ps 45:12 [c]Ps 68:31 [1]Egypt [2]Or *Cush*, cf. Ge 10:6

5 But of Zion it shall be said,
"This one and that one
were born in her";
And the Most High Himself
will [a]establish her.
6 Yahweh will count when He
[a]registers the peoples,
"This one was born
there." Selah.
7 And [a]singers, just like
the [b]dancers, *will all say*,
"All my [c]springs are in you."

## PSALM 88

### *Incline Your Ear to My Cry*

A Song. A Psalm of the sons of Korah. For the choir director. According to Mahalath Leannoth. A [1]Maskil of Heman the Ezrahite.

1 O Yahweh, the [a]God
of my salvation,
I have [b]cried out by
day and throughout
the night before You.
2 Let my prayer [a]come
before You;
[b]Incline Your ear to my
cry of lamentation!
3 For my [a]soul has been
saturated with calamities,
And [b]my life has
reached Sheol.
4 I am counted among those
who [a]go down to the pit;
I am like a man
[b]without strength,
5 Released [a]among
the dead,
Like the slain who lie
in the grave,
Whom You remember
no more,
And they are [b]cut off
from Your hand.
6 You have put me
in [a]the pit far below,
In [b]dark places,
in the [c]depths.
7 Your wrath [a]lies upon me,
And You afflict me with [b]all
Your breaking waves. [1]Selah.
8 You have removed [a]my
acquaintances far from me;
You have set me as [1]an
[b]abomination to them;
I am [c]shut up and
cannot go out.
9 My [a]eye has wasted away
because of affliction;
I have [b]called upon You
every day, O Yahweh;
I have [c]spread out my
[1]hands to You.

10 Will You do wonders
for the dead?
Will [a]the [1]departed spirits rise
*and* praise You? Selah.
11 Will Your lovingkindness be
recounted in the grave,
Your faithfulness
in [1]Abaddon?
12 Will Your wonders be known
in the [a]darkness?
And Your righteousness
in the land of forgetfulness?

---

**87:5** [a]Ps 48:8 **87:6** [a]Ps 69:28; Is 4:3; Eze 13:9 **87:7** [a]Ps 68:25; 149:3 [b]2Sa 6:14; Ps 30:11 [c]Ps 36:9
**88:TITLE** [1]*Possibly Contemplative, Didactic, Skillful Psalm* 1Ki 4:31; 1Chr 2:6; Ps 89:title
**88:1** [a]Ps 24:5; 27:9 [b]Ps 22:2; 86:3; Lk 18:7 **88:2** [a]Ps 18:6 [b]Ps 31:2; 86:1 **88:3** [a]Ps 107:26 [b]Ps 107:18; 116:3 **88:4** [a]Ps 28:1; 143:7 [b]Job 29:12; Ps 22:11 **88:5** [a]Ps 31:12 [b]Ps 31:22; Is 53:8 **88:6** [a]Ps 86:13; Lam 3:55 [b]Ps 143:3 [c]Ps 69:15 **88:7** [a]Ps 32:4; 39:10 [b]Ps 42:7 [1]*Selah* may mean *Pause, Crescendo, Musical Interlude* **88:8** [a]Job 19:13, 19; Ps 31:11; 142:4 [b]Job 30:10 [c]Ps 142:7; Jer 32:2; 36:5 [1]Lit *abominations* **88:9** [a]Ps 6:7; 31:9 [b]Ps 22:2; 86:3 [c]Job 11:13; Ps 143:6 [1]Lit *palms* **88:10** [a]Ps 6:5; 30:9 [1]Or *ghosts, shades* **88:11** [1]Lit the realm of *destruction* **88:12** [a]Job 10:21; Ps 88:6

13 But as for me, O Yahweh, I have
cried out [a]to You for help,
And [b]in the morning my
prayer comes before You.
14 O Yahweh, why [a]do You
reject my soul?
*Why* do You [b]hide Your
face from me?
15 I *have been* afflicted and
[a]about to breathe my
last from *my* youth on;
I bear [b]Your terrors;
I am [1]overcome.
16 Your [a]burning anger has
passed over me;
Your horrors have
[b,1]destroyed me.
17 They have [a]surrounded me
[b]like water all day long;
They have [c]encompassed
me altogether.
18 You have removed [a]lover
and friend far from me;
My acquaintances are
*in* darkness.

## PSALM 89

### *Sing of the Lovingkindness of Yahweh Forever*

A [†]Maskil of [˙]Ethan [^]the Ezrahite.

1 I will [a]sing
of the lovingkindnesses
of Yahweh forever;
From generation
to generation I will [b]make
known Your [c]faithfulness
with my mouth.
2 For I have said,
“ [a]Lovingkindness will
be built up forever;
In the heavens You
will establish Your
[b]faithfulness.”
3 “I have cut a covenant
with [a]My chosen;
I have [b]sworn to David
My [1]servant,
4 I will establish your
[a]seed forever
And build up your [b]throne
from generation
to generation.” [1]Selah.

5 The [a]heavens will praise
Your wonders, O Yahweh;
Your faithfulness also
[b]in the assembly
of the [c]holy ones.
6 For [a]who in the sky is
comparable to Yahweh?
Who among the [b,1]sons
of the mighty is like Yahweh,
7 A God [a]greatly dreaded
in the council
of the [b]holy ones,
And [c,1]fearsome
above all those who
are around Him?
8 O Yahweh God of hosts, [a]who
is like You, O mighty Yah?
Your faithfulness also
surrounds You.
9 You rule the swelling
of the sea;

---

**88:13** [a]Ps 30:2 [b]Ps 5:3; 119:147 **88:14** [a]Ps 43:2; 44:9 [b]Job 13:24; Ps 13:1; 44:24 **88:15** [a]Pr 24:11 [b]Job 6:4; 31:23 [1]Or *embarrassed* **88:16** [a]2Chr 28:11; Is 13:13; Lam 1:12 [b]Lam 3:54; Eze 37:11 [1]Or *silenced* **88:17** [a]Ps 118:10-12 [b]Ps 124:4 [c]Ps 17:11; 22:12, 16 **88:18** [a]Job 19:13; Ps 88:8; 31:11; 38:11
◆ **89:TITLE** [†]Possibly *Contemplative, Didactic, Skillful Psalm* [˙]1Ki 4:31 [^]Ps 88: title **89:1** [a]Ps 59:16; 101:1 [b]Ps 40:10 [c]Ps 36:5; 88:11; 89:5, 8, 24, 33, 49; 92:2; 119:90; Is 25:1; Lam 3:23 **89:2** [a]Ps 103:17 [b]Ps 36:5; 119:90 **89:3** [a]1Ki 8:16 [b]Ps 132:11 [1]Or *slave*, cf. 89:39; see Foreword, "The Terminology of Slave" **89:4** [a]2Sa 7:16 [b]2Sa 7:13; Is 9:7; Lk 1:33 [1]*Selah* may mean *Pause*, *Crescendo*, *Musical Interlude* **89:5** [a]Ps 19:1; 97:6 [b]Ps 149:1 [c]Job 5:1 **89:6** [a]Ps 86:8; 113:5 [b]Ps 29:1; 82:1 [1]Or *sons of gods* **89:7** [a]Ps 47:2; 68:35; 76:7, 11 [b]Ps 89:5 [c]Ps 96:4 [1]Or *awesome* **89:8** [a]Ps 35:10; 71:19

When its waves rise,
You [a]still them.
10 You Yourself crushed [a,1]Rahab
like one who is slain;
You [b]scattered Your enemies
with Your strong arm.

11 The [a]heavens are Yours,
the earth also is Yours;
The [b]world and its fullness,
You have founded them.
12 The [a]north and the south,
You have created them;
[b]Tabor and [c]Hermon [d]sing
with joy at Your name.
13 You have a mighty arm;
Your hand is strong, Your
[a]right hand is exalted.
14 [a]Righteousness and justice
are the foundation
of Your throne;
[b]Lovingkindness and
[1]truth go before You.
15 How blessed are the people
who know the [a]loud
shout of joy!
O Yahweh, they walk
in the [b]light of Your face.
16 In [a]Your name they
rejoice all the day,
And by Your righteousness
they are exalted.
17 For You are the beauty
of [a]their strength,
And by Your favor [1]our
[b]horn is exalted.
18 For our [a]shield belongs
to Yahweh,
[1]And our king to the [b]Holy
One of Israel.

19 Formerly You spoke in vision
to Your [1]holy [2]ones,
And said, "I have bestowed
help to a [a]mighty one;
I have exalted one [b]chosen
from the people.
20 "I have [a]found David
My [1]servant;
With My holy [b]oil I have
anointed him,
21 With whom [a]My hand
will be established;
My arm also will
[b]strengthen him.
22 "The enemy will not
[1]deceive him,
Nor the [a,2]son of
unrighteousness afflict him.
23 "But I shall [a]crush his
adversaries before him,
And strike those
who hate him.
24 "My [a]faithfulness and
My lovingkindness
will be with him,
And in My name his
[b]horn will be exalted.
25 "I shall also set his
hand [a]on the sea
And his right hand
on the rivers.

**89:9** [a]Ps 65:7; 107:29 **89:10** [a]Ps 87:4; Is 30:7; 51:9 [b]Ps 18:14; 68:1; 144:6 [1]Egypt **89:11** [a]Ge 1:1; 1Chr 29:11; Ps 96:5 [b]Ps 24:1 **89:12** [a]Job 26:7 [b]Jos 19:22; Jdg 4:6; Jer 46:18 [c]Dt 3:8; Jos 11:17; 12:1; Ps 133:3; SS 4:8 [d]Ps 98:8 **89:13** [a]Ps 98:1; 118:16 **89:14** [a]Ps 97:2 [b]Ps 85:13 [1]Or *faithfulness* **89:15** [a]Lv 23:24; Nu 10:10; Ps 98:6 [b]Ps 4:6; 44:3; 67:1; 80:3; 90:8 **89:16** [a]Ps 105:3 **89:17** [a]Ps 28:8 [b]Ps 75:10; 92:10; 148:14 [1]Or *You exalt our horn* **89:18** [a]Ps 47:9 [b]Ps 71:22; 78:41 [1]Or *Even to the Holy One of Israel our King* **89:19** [a]2Sa 17:10 [b]1Ki 11:34; Ps 78:70 [1]Or *ones of lovingkindness* [2]Some mss *one*, cf. 16:10 **89:20** [a]1Sa 13:14; 16:1-12; Ac 13:22 [b]1Sa 16:13 [1]Or *slave*, cf. 89:39; see Foreword, "The Terminology of Slave" **89:21** [a]Ps 18:35; 80:17 [b]Ps 18:32 **89:22** [a]2Sa 7:10; Ps 125:3 [1]Or *exact usury from him* [2]Or *unrighteous man* **89:23** [a]2Sa 7:9; Ps 18:40 **89:24** [a]Ps 89:1 [b]Ps 132:17 **89:25** [a]Ps 72:8

26 “He will call to Me,
‘You are [a]my Father,
My God, and the [b]rock
of my salvation.’
27 “I also shall make him
*My* [a]firstborn,
The [b]highest of the kings
of the earth.
28 “My [a]lovingkindness I will
keep for him forever,
And My [b]covenant shall
be confirmed to him.
29 “So I will set up his [a]seed
*to endure* forever
And his [b]throne
[c]as the days of heaven.

30 “If his sons [a]forsake My law
And do not walk in
My judgments,
31 If they profane My statutes
And do not keep
My commandments,
32 Then I will punish their
transgression with the [a]rod
And their iniquity
with striking.
33 “But I will not break off [a]My
lovingkindness from him,
Nor deal falsely
in My faithfulness.
34 “My [a]covenant I will
not profane,
Nor will I [b]alter what comes
forth from My lips.
35 “ [1]Once I have [a]sworn
by My holiness;
I will not lie to David.
36 “His [a]seed shall endure forever
And his [b]throne [c]as the sun
before Me.
37 “It shall be established
forever [a]like the moon,
And the [b]witness in the sky is
faithful.” [1]Selah.

38 But You have [a]cast off
and [b]rejected,
You have been full of wrath
[1]against Your [c]anointed.
39 You have [a]spurned
the covenant of Your [1]slave;
You have [b]profaned [c]his
crown to the ground.
40 You have [a]broken down
all his walls;
You have [b]beset his
strongholds with ruin.
41 [a]All who pass
along the way plunder him;
He has become a [b]reproach
to his neighbors.
42 You have [a]exalted the right
hand of his adversaries;
You have [b]made all his
enemies be glad.
43 You also turn back
the edge of his sword
And have [a]not made
him arise in battle.
44 You have made his
[a,1]splendor to cease
And cast his throne
to the ground.

**89:26** [a]2Sa 7:14; 1Chr 22:10; Jer 3:19 [b]2Sa 22:47; Ps 95:1 **89:27** [a]Ex 4:22; Ps 2:7; Jer 31:9; Col 1:15, 18 [b]Nu 24:7; Ps 72:11; Rev 19:16 **89:28** [a]Ps 89:33 [b]Ps 89:3, 34 **89:29** [a]Ps 18:50; 89:4, 36 [b]1Ki 2:4; Ps 89:4; 132:12; Is 9:7; Jer 33:17 [c]Dt 11:21 **89:30** [a]2Sa 7:14; Ps 119:53 **89:32** [a]Job 9:34; 21:9 **89:33** [a]2Sa 7:15 **89:34** [a]Dt 7:9; Jer 33:20, 21 [b]Nu 23:19 **89:35** [a]Ps 60:6; Am 4:2 [1]Or *One thing* **89:36** [a]Ps 89:29; Lk 1:33 [b]Ps 72:5 [c]Ps 72:17 **89:37** [a]Ps 72:5 [b]Job 16:19 [1]*Selah* may mean *Pause, Crescendo, Musical Interlude* **89:38** [a]Ps 44:9 [b]Dt 32:19; 1Chr 28:9 [c]Ps 20:6; 89:20, 51 [1]Lit *with* **89:39** [a]Ps 78:59; Lam 2:7 [b]Ps 74:7 [c]Lam 5:16 [1]Or *servant*, cf. Ps 89:3, 20 **89:40** [a]Ps 80:12 [b]Lam 2:2, 5 **89:41** [a]Ps 80:12 [b]Ps 44:13; 69:9, 19; 79:4 **89:42** [a]Ps 13:2 [b]Ps 80:6 **89:43** [a]Ps 44:10 **89:44** [a]Eze 28:7 [1]Lit *clearness, luster*

45 You have [a]shortened
the days of his youth;
You have [b]wrapped him up
with shame. Selah.

46 [a]How long, O Yahweh?
Will You hide Yourself forever?
Will Your [b]wrath
burn like fire?
47 [a]Remember [1]what my
span of life is;
For what [b]vanity [2]You have
created all the sons of men!
48 What man can live and
not [a]see death?
Can he [b]provide his soul
escape from the [1]power
of Sheol? Selah.

49 Where are Your former
lovingkindnesses, O Lord,
Which You [a]swore to David
in Your faithfulness?
50 Remember, O Lord,
the [a]reproach
of Your [1]slaves;
[2]How I bear in my bosom
*the reproach of* all
the many peoples,
51 With which [a]Your enemies
have reproached, O Yahweh,
With which they have
reproached the footsteps
of [b]Your anointed.

52 [a]Blessed be Yahweh forever!
Amen and Amen.

## BOOK 4

## PSALM 90

### *From Everlasting to Everlasting, You Are God*

A Prayer of [†]Moses, the man of God.

1 Lord, You have been our
[a,1]dwelling place from
generation to generation.
2 Before [a]the mountains
were born
[1]Or You [b]brought forth
the earth and the world,
Even [c]from everlasting
to everlasting, You are God.

3 You [a]turn man back into dust
And say,
"Return, O sons of men."
4 For [a]a thousand years
in Your sight
Are like [b]yesterday
when it passes by,
[1]Or *as* a [c]watch in the night.
5 You [a]have [1]swept them
away like a flood,
they [b,2]fall asleep;
In the morning they are like
[c]grass which [3]sprouts anew.
6 In the morning it [a]blossoms
and [1]sprouts anew;
Toward evening it [b]withers
away and [c]dries up.

7 For we have been [a]consumed
by Your anger
And by Your wrath we
have been [1]dismayed.

**89:45** [a]Ps 102:23 [b]Ps 44:15; 71:13; 109:29 **89:46** [a]Ps 13:1; 44:24 [b]Ps 79:5; 80:4 **89:47** [a]Job 7:7; 10:9; 14:1 [b]Ps 39:5; 62:9; Ecc 1:2; 2:11 [1]Lit *of what duration I am* [2]Or *have You...men?* **89:48** [a]Ps 22:29; 49:9 [b]Ps 49:15 [1]Lit *hand* **89:49** [a]2Sa 7:15; Jer 30:9; Eze 34:23 **89:50** [a]Ps 69:9; 74:18, 22 [1]Or *servants*, cf. Ps 89:3, 20 [2]Lit *My bearing in my bosom* **89:51** [a]Ps 74:10, 18, 22 [b]Ps 89:38 **89:52** [a]Ps 41:13; 72:19; 106:48 ◆ **90:TITLE** [†]Dt 33:1 **90:1** [a]Dt 33:27; Ps 71:3; 91:1; Eze 11:16 [1]Or *hiding place, help*; some ancient mss *place of refuge* **90:2** [a]Job 15:7; Pr 8:25 [b]Ge 1:1; Ps 102:25; 104:5 [c]Ps 93:2; 102:24, 27; Jer 10:10 [1]Or *And* **90:3** [a]Ge 3:19; Job 34:14, 15; Ps 104:29 **90:4** [a]2Pe 3:8 [b]Ps 39:5 [c]Ex 14:24; Jdg 7:19 [1]Or *And* **90:5** [a]Job 22:16; 27:20 [b]Job 14:12; 20:8; Ps 76:5 [c]Ps 103:15; Is 40:6 [1]Or *flooded* [2]Lit *become asleep* [3]Or *passes away* **90:6** [a]Job 14:2 [b]Ps 92:7; Mt 6:30 [c]Jas 1:11 [1]Or *passes away* **90:7** [a]Ps 39:11 [1]Or *terrified*

8 You have [a]set our
iniquities before You,
Our [b]secret *sins* in the light
of Your presence.
9 For [a]all our days have
declined in Your fury;
We have finished our
years like a [1]sigh.
10 As for the days of our [1]life,
[2]they contain seventy years,
Or if due to might,
[a]eighty years,
Yet their pride is *but* [b]labor
and wickedness;
For soon it is gone and
we [c]fly away.
11 Who knows the [a]power
of Your anger
And Your fury, according to
the [b]fear [1]that is due You?
12 [1]So [a]teach us
to number our days,
That we may [b,2]present
*to You* a heart of wisdom.

13 [a]Return, O Yahweh;
[b]how long *will it be*?
And [1]be [c]sorry for Your slaves.
14 O [a]satisfy us in the morning
with Your lovingkindness,
That we may [b]sing for joy
and be glad all our days.
15 [a]Make us glad [1]according to
the days You have afflicted us,
*And* the [b]years we
have seen [2]evil.
16 Let Your [a]work appear
to Your slaves
And Your [b]majesty
[1]to their sons.
17 Let the [a]favor of the Lord
our God be upon us;
And [b]establish for us
the work of our hands;
Establish the work
of our hands.

## PSALM 91

### *In the Shadow of the Almighty*

1 He who abides
in the [a]shelter
of the Most High
Will abide in the [b]shadow
of the Almighty.
2 I will say to Yahweh, "My
[a]refuge and my [b]fortress,
My God, in whom I [c]trust!"
3 For it is He who delivers
you from the [a]snare
of the trapper
*And* from the
destructive [b]pestilence.
4 He will [a]cover you
with His pinions,
And [b]under His wings
you will take refuge;
His [c]truth is a [d]large
shield and bulwark.

5 You [a]will not be afraid
of [b]terror by night,
Or [c]arrow that flies by day;

**90:8** [a]Ps 50:21; Jer 16:17 [b]Ps 19:12; Ecc 12:14 **90:9** [a]Ps 78:33 [1]Or *whisper* **90:10** [a]2Ki 19:35 [b]Ecc 12:2-7; Jer 20:18 [c]Job 20:8; Ps 78:39 [1]Lit *years* [2]Lit *in them are* **90:11** [a]Ps 76:7 [b]Ne 5:9 [1]Lit *of You* **90:12** [a]Dt 32:29; Ps 39:4 [b]Pr 2:1-6 [1]Lit *Cause us to know how to number our days* [2]Or *gain, bring in* **90:13** [a]Ps 6:4; 80:14 [b]Ps 6:3; 74:10 [c]Ex 32:12; Dt 32:36; Ps 106:45; 135:14; Am 7:3, 6; Jon 3:9 [1]Or *repent in regard to* **90:14** [a]Ps 36:8; 65:4; 103:5; Jer 31:14 [b]Ps 31:7; 85:6 **90:15** [a]Ps 86:4 [b]Dt 2:14-16; Ps 31:10 [1]Or *as many days as* [2]Or *trouble* **90:16** [a]Dt 32:4; Ps 44:1; 77:12; 92:4; Hab 3:2 [b]1Ki 8:11; Is 6:3 [1]Or *upon* **90:17** [a]Ps 27:4 [b]Ps 37:23; Is 26:12; 1Co 3:7 ◆ **91:1** [a]Ps 27:5; 31:20; 32:7 [b]Ps 17:8; 121:5; Is 25:4; 32:2 **91:2** [a]Ps 14:6; 91:9; 94:22; 142:5 [b]Ps 18:2; 31:3; Jer 16:19 [c]Ps 25:2; 56:4 **91:3** [a]Ps 124:7; Pr 6:5 [b]1Ki 8:37; 2Chr 20:9; Ps 91:6 **91:4** [a]Is 51:16 [b]Ps 17:8; 36:7; 57:1; 63:7 [c]Ps 40:11 [d]Ps 35:2 **91:5** [a]Job 5:19-23; Ps 23:4; 27:1 [b]SS 3:8 [c]Ps 64:4

6 Of [a]pestilence
that moves in darkness,
Or of [b]destruction
that devastates at noon.
7 A thousand may fall at your side
And ten thousand
at your right hand,
*But* [a]it shall not approach you.
8 You will only look
on with your eyes
And [a]see the recompense
of the wicked.
9 [1]For you have made
Yahweh—[a]my refuge,
The Most High—[b]your
dwelling place.
10 [a]No evil will befall you,
And no plague will come
near your [1]tent.

11 For He will command [a]His
angels concerning you,
To guard you in all your ways.
12 On their hands they
will [a]bear you up,
Lest you strike your foot
against a stone.
13 You will [a]tread upon
the fierce lion and cobra,
The young lion and the [1]serpent
you will trample down.

14 "[a]Because he has loved Me,
therefore I will protect him;
I will [b]set him *securely*
on high, because he has
[c]known My name.
15 "He will [a]call upon Me,
and I will answer him;
I will be with him
in *his* [1]distress;
I will rescue him and
[b]honor him.
16 "With [1]a [a]long life I
will satisfy him
And [b]I will show him
My salvation."

## PSALM 92

### *How Great Are Your Works, O Yahweh*

A Psalm. A Song for the Sabbath day.

1 It is [a]good to give
thanks to Yahweh
And to [b]sing praises to Your
name, O Most High;
2 To [a]declare Your
lovingkindness in
the morning
And Your [b]faithfulness
[1]by night,
3 [1]With the [a]ten-stringed
lute and with the [a]harp,
[1]With resounding music
[2]upon the [a]lyre.
4 For You, O Yahweh, have
made me glad
by [1]what You [a]have done,
I will [b]sing for joy
at the [c]works of Your hands.

5 How [a]great are Your
works, O Yahweh!
Your [b,1]thoughts are
very [c]deep.

---

**91:6** [a]2Ki 19:35; Ps 91:10 [b]Job 5:22 **91:7** [a]Ge 7:23; Jos 14:10 **91:8** [a]Ps 37:34; 58:10 **91:9** [a]Ps 91:2 [b]Ps 90:1 [1]Or *For You O Yahweh are my Refuge; You have made the Most High your dwelling place* **91:10** [a]Pr 12:21 [1]Or *dwelling* **91:11** [a]Ps 34:7; Mt 4:6; Lk 4:10, 11; Heb 1:14 **91:12** [a]Mt 4:6; Lk 4:11 **91:13** [a]Jdg 14:6; Da 6:22; Lk 10:19 [1]Or *dragon, sea monster, supernatural foe* **91:14** [a]Ps 145:20 [b]Ps 59:1 [c]Ps 9:10 **91:15** [a]Job 12:4; Ps 50:15 [b]1Sa 2:30; Jn 12:26 [1]Or *trouble* **91:16** [a]Dt 6:2; Ps 21:4; Pr 3:1, 2 [b]Ps 50:23 [1]Lit *length of days* ◆ **92:1** [a]Ps 147:1 [b]Ps 135:3 **92:2** [a]Ps 59:16 [b]Ps 89:1 [1]Lit *nights* **92:3** [a]1Sa 10:5; 1Chr 13:8; Ne 12:27; Ps 33:2 [1]Lit *Upon* [2]Lit *by means of* **92:4** [a]Ps 40:5; 90:16 [b]Ps 106:47 [c]Ps 8:6; 111:7; 143:5 [1]Lit *Your working* **92:5** [a]Ps 40:5; 111:2; Rev 15:3 [b]Ps 33:11; 40:5; 139:17 [c]Ps 36:6; Ro 11:33 [1]Or *purposes*

6 A [a]senseless man
does not know,
And a [a]fool does not
understand this:
7 That when the wicked
[a]flourished like grass
And all [b]*the* workers
of iniquity blossomed,
It *was only* that they might be
[c]destroyed forevermore.
8 But You are [a]on high
forever, O Yahweh.
9 For, behold, Your
enemies, O Yahweh,
For, behold, [a]Your
enemies will perish;
All *the* workers of iniquity
will be [b]scattered.

10 But You have raised up
my [a]horn like *that*
*of* the wild ox;
I have [1]been [b]anointed
with fresh oil.
11 And my eye has [a]looked
*exultantly* upon [1]my foes,
My ears hear
of the evildoers who
rise up against me.
12 The [a]righteous man
will [1]flourish
like the palm tree,
He will grow like a [b]cedar
in Lebanon.
13 [a]Planted in the house
of Yahweh,
They will flourish
[b]in the courts of our God.
14 They will still [a,1]yield
fruit in old age;
They shall be [2]rich and fresh,
15 To [1]declare that [a]Yahweh
is upright;
*He is* my [b]rock, and there
is [c]no unrighteousness
in Him.

## PSALM 93

### *Yahweh Reigns Forevermore*

1 [a]Yahweh [1]reigns, He is
[b]clothed with majesty;
Yahweh has [c]clothed
and girded Himself
with strength;
Indeed, the [d]world is
established, it will
not be shaken.
2 Your [a]throne is established
from of old;
You [b]are from everlasting.

3 The [a]rivers have lifted
up, O Yahweh,
The rivers have lifted
up their voice,
The rivers lift up their
pounding waves.
4 More than the voices
of many waters,
*Than* the mighty
breakers of the sea,
Yahweh [a]on high is mighty.
5 Your [a]testimonies are
very faithful;
[b]Holiness befits Your house,
O Yahweh, [1]forevermore.

---

**92:6** [a]Ps 49:10; 73:22; 94:8 **92:7** [a]Job 12:6; Ps 90:5 [b]Ps 94:4 [c]Ps 37:38 **92:8** [a]Ps 83:18; 93:4; 113:5 **92:9** [a]Ps 37:20 [b]Ps 68:1; 89:10 **92:10** [a]Ps 75:10; 89:17; 112:9 [b]Ps 23:5; 45:7 [1]Or *become moist* **92:11** [a]Ps 54:7; 91:8 [1]Or *those who lie in wait for me* **92:12** [a]Nu 24:6; Ps 1:3; 52:8; 72:7; Jer 17:8; Hos 14:5, 6 [b]Ps 104:16; Eze 31:3 [1]Lit *sprout* **92:13** [a]Ps 80:15; Is 60:21 [b]Ps 100:4; 116:19 **92:14** [a]Pr 11:30; Is 37:31; Jn 15:2; Jas 3:18 [1]Or *thrive in* [2]Lit *fat* **92:15** [a]Job 34:10; Ps 25:8 [b]Dt 32:4; Ps 18:2; 94:22 [c]Ro 9:14 [1]Or *show forth* ◆ **93:1** [a]Ps 96:10; 97:1; 99:1 [b]Ps 104:1 [c]Ps 65:6; Is 51:9 [d]Ps 96:10 [1]Or *has assumed kingship* **93:2** [a]Ps 45:6; Lam 5:19 [b]Ps 90:2 **93:3** [a]Ps 96:11; 98:7, 8 **93:4** [a]Ps 65:7; 89:6, 9; 92:8 **93:5** [a]Ps 19:7 [b]Ps 29:2; 96:9; 1Co 3:17 [1]Lit *for length of days*

## PSALM 94

### *God of Vengeance, Shine Forth*

1 O Yahweh,
God of [a,1]vengeance,
God of [1]vengeance,
[b,2]shine forth!
2 [a]Be lifted up,
O [b]Judge of the earth,
Render recompense
[c]to the proud.
3 How long shall the wicked,
O Yahweh,
How long shall
the [a]wicked exult?
4 They pour forth *words*,
they [a]speak arrogantly;
All workers of iniquity
[b]vaunt themselves.
5 They [a]crush Your people,
O Yahweh,
And [b]afflict
Your inheritance.
6 They [a]slay the widow
and the sojourner
And murder the orphans.
7 [a]They have said,
"Yah does not see,
Nor does the God
of Jacob discern."

8 Discern, you [a]senseless
among the people;
And when will you have
insight, [a]*you* fools?
9 He who [a]planted the ear,
[1]does He not hear?
He who formed the eye,
[1]does He not see?
10 He who [a,1]disciplines
the nations, will
He not rebuke,
*Even* He who [b]teaches
man knowledge?
11 Yahweh [a]knows
the thoughts of man,
[1]That they are vanity.

12 Blessed is the man
whom [a]You discipline, O Yah,
And [b]whom You teach
out of Your law;
13 That You may grant him [a]calm
from the [b]days of calamity,
Until [c]a pit is dug
for the wicked.
14 For [a]Yahweh will not
abandon His people,
Nor will He [b]forsake
His inheritance.
15 For [a,1]judgment will
[2]again be righteous,
And all the upright
in heart will [3]follow it.
16 Who will [a]arise for me
against evildoers?
Who will take his stand for me
[b]against workers of iniquity?

17 If [a]Yahweh had not
been my help,
My soul would soon have
dwelt in *the abode of* silence.
18 If I should say,
"[a]My foot has stumbled,"
Your lovingkindness,
O Yahweh, will hold me up.

---

◆ **94:1** [a]Dt 32:35; Is 35:4; Na 1:2; Ro 12:19 [b]Ps 50:2; 80:1 [1]Or *avenging acts* [2]Or *has shone forth* **94:2** [a]Ps 7:6 [b]Ge 18:25 [c]Ps 31:23 **94:3** [a]Job 20:5 **94:4** [a]Ps 31:18; 75:5 [b]Ps 10:3; 52:1 **94:5** [a]Is 3:15 [b]Ps 79:1 **94:6** [a]Is 10:2 **94:7** [a]Job 22:13; Ps 10:11 **94:8** [a]Ps 92:6 **94:9** [a]Ex 4:11; Pr 20:12 [1]Or *can* **94:10** [a]Ps 44:2 [b]Job 35:11; Is 28:26 [1]Or *instructs* **94:11** [a]Job 11:11; 1Co 3:20 [1]Or *For* **94:12** [a]Dt 8:5; Job 5:17; Ps 119:71; Pr 3:11, 12; Heb 12:5, 6 [b]Ps 119:171 **94:13** [a]Job 34:29; Hab 3:16 [b]Ps 49:5 [c]Ps 9:15; 55:23 **94:14** [a]1Sa 12:22; Lam 3:31; Ro 11:2 [b]Ps 37:28 **94:15** [a]Ps 97:2; Is 42:3; Mic 7:9 [1]Administration of justice [2]Lit *return to righteousness* [3]Lit *be after it* **94:16** [a]Nu 10:35; Is 28:21; 33:10 [b]Ps 17:13; 59:2 **94:17** [a]Ps 124:1, 2 **94:18** [a]Ps 38:16; 73:2

19 When my anxious thoughts
[1]multiply within me,
Your [a]consolations
delight my soul.
20 Can a [a,1]throne of destruction
be allied with You,
One [b]which forms
[2]trouble by statute?
21 They [a]band themselves
together against the [1]life
of the righteous
And [b]condemn [2]the
innocent to death.
22 But Yahweh has been
my [a]stronghold,
And my God the [b]rock
of my refuge.
23 He has [a]brought back their
[1]iniquity upon them
And will [b,2]destroy
them in their evil;
Yahweh our God will
[2]destroy them.

## PSALM 95

### *Let Us Kneel Before Yahweh Our Maker*

1 Oh come, let us [a]sing
for joy to Yahweh,
Let us make a loud shout
to [b]the rock of our salvation.
2 Let us [a]come before His
presence [b]with [1]thanksgiving,
Let us make a loud shout
to Him [c]with songs of praise.
3 For Yahweh is a [a]great God
And a great King
[b]above all gods,
4 In whose hand are
the [a]depths of the earth,
The peaks of the mountains
are His also.
5 [1]The sea is His, for it was
He [a]who made it,
And His hands formed
the dry land.

6 Come, let us [a]worship
and bow down,
Let us [b]kneel
before Yahweh our [c]Maker.
7 For He is our God,
And [a]we are the people
of His [b]pasture and
the sheep of His hand.
[c]Today, [1]if you hear His voice,
8 Do not harden your hearts,
as at [a,1]Meribah,
As in the day of [b,2]Massah
in the wilderness,
9 "When your fathers
[a]tried Me,
They tested Me, though
they had seen My work.
10 "For [a]forty years I loathed
*that* generation,
And said they are a people
who wander
in their heart,
And they do not
know My ways.
11 "Therefore I [a]swore
in My anger,
They shall never enter
into My [b]rest."

**94:19** [a]Is 57:18; 66:13 [1]Or *are many* **94:20** [a]Am 6:3 [b]Ps 50:16; 58:2 [1]Or *tribunal* [2]Or *misfortune* **94:21** [a]Ps 56:6; 59:3 [b]Ex 23:7; Ps 106:38; Pr 17:15; Mt 27:4 [1]Or *soul* [2]Lit *innocent blood* **94:22** [a]Ps 9:9; 59:9 [b]Ps 18:2; 71:7 **94:23** [a]Ps 7:16; 140:9, 11 [b]Ge 19:15 [1]Or *wickedness* [2]Or *silence* ◆ **95:1** [a]Ps 66:1; 81:1 [b]Ps 89:26 **95:2** [a]Mic 6:6 [b]Ps 100:4; 147:7; Jon 2:9 [c]Ps 81:2; Eph 5:19; Jas 5:13 [1]Or *a song of thanksgiving* **95:3** [a]Ps 48:1; 135:5; 145:3 [b]Ps 96:4; 97:9 **95:4** [a]Ps 135:6 **95:5** [a]Ge 1:9, 10; Ps 146:6; Jon 1:9 [1]Lit *Who has the sea* **95:6** [a]Ps 96:9; 99:5, 9 [b]2Chr 6:13; Da 6:10; Php 2:10 [c]Ps 100:3; 149:2; Is 17:7; Hos 8:14 **95:7** [a]Ps 79:13 [b]Ps 74:1 [c]Heb 3:7-11, 15; 4:7 [1]Or *O that you would obey* **95:8** [a]Ex 17:2-7; Nu 20:13 [b]Ex 17:7; Dt 6:16 [1]Or *place of strife* [2]Or *temptation* **95:9** [a]Nu 14:22; Ps 78:18; 1Co 10:9 **95:10** [a]Ac 7:36; 13:18; Heb 3:10, 17 **95:11** [a]Nu 14:23, 28-30; Dt 1:35; Heb 4:3, 5 [b]Dt 12:9

## PSALM 96

### *Ascribe to Yahweh Glory and Strength*

1 [a]Sing to Yahweh a [b]new song;
Sing to Yahweh, all the earth.
2 Sing to Yahweh, bless
His name;
[a]Proclaim good news of His
salvation from day to day.
3 Recount [a]His glory
among the nations,
His wondrous deeds
among all the peoples.
4 For [a]great is Yahweh and
[b]greatly to be praised;
He is [1]more [c,2]fearsome
[d]than all gods.
5 For [a]all the gods
of the peoples are [1]idols,
But [b]Yahweh made
the heavens.
6 [a]Splendor and majesty
are before Him,
Strength and beauty are
in His sanctuary.

7 [1]Ascribe to Yahweh,
O [a]families of the peoples,
[b,1]Ascribe to Yahweh
glory and strength.
8 Ascribe to Yahweh
the [a]glory of His name;
Lift up [1]an [b]offering and
come into His courts.
9 [a]Worship Yahweh
in the splendor of holiness;
[b]Tremble before Him,
all the earth.
10 Say among the nations,
" [a]Yahweh [1]reigns;
Indeed, the [a]world is
established, it will
not be shaken;
He will [b]render justice
to the peoples
with [2]equity."
11 Let the [a]heavens be glad,
and let the [b]earth rejoice;
Let [c]the sea [1]roar,
as well as its fullness;
12 Let the [a]field exult, and
all that is in it.
Then all the [b]trees
of the forest will sing for joy
13 Before Yahweh,
[a]for He is coming,
For He is coming
to judge the earth.
[b]He will judge the world
in righteousness
And the peoples
in His faithfulness.

## PSALM 97

### *Remember His Holy Name*

1 [a]Yahweh [1]reigns, let
the [b]earth rejoice;
Let the many [c]coastlands
be glad.
2 [a]Clouds and thick
darkness are all
around Him;
[b]Righteousness and justice
are the foundation
of His throne.

---

◆ **96:1** [a]1Chr 16:23-33 [b]Ps 40:3 **96:2** [a]Ps 71:15 **96:3** [a]Ps 145:12 **96:4** [a]Ps 48:1; 145:3 [b]Ps 18:3 [c]Ps 89:7 [d]Ps 95:3 [1]Or *to be feared above* [2]Or *awesome* **96:5** [a]1Chr 16:26; Jer 10:11 [b]Ps 115:15; Is 42:5 [1]Or *non-existent things* **96:6** [a]Ps 104:1 **96:7** [a]Ps 22:27 [b]1Chr 16:28, 29; Ps 29:1, 2 [1]Lit *Give* **96:8** [a]Ps 79:9; 115:1 [b]Ps 45:12; 72:10 [1]Or *a meal offering* **96:9** [a]1Chr 16:29; 2Chr 20:21; Ps 29:2; 110:3 [b]Ps 33:8; 114:7 **96:10** [a]Ps 93:1; 97:1 [b]Ps 9:8; 58:11; 67:4; 98:9 [1]Or *has assumed Kingship* [2]Or *uprightness* **96:11** [a]Ps 69:34; Is 49:13 [b]Ps 97:1 [c]Ps 98:7 [1]Or *thunder* **96:12** [a]Ps 65:13; Is 35:1; 55:12, 13 [b]Is 44:23 **96:13** [a]Ps 98:9 [b]Rev 19:11 ◆ **97:1** [a]Ps 96:10 [b]Ps 96:11 [c]Is 42:10, 12 [1]Or *has assumed Kingship* **97:2** [a]Ex 19:9; Dt 4:11; 1Ki 8:12; Ps 18:11 [b]Ps 89:14

3 [a]Fire goes before Him
And [b]burns up His
adversaries all around.
4 His [a]lightnings light
up the world;
The earth sees and [b]trembles.
5 The mountains [a]melt like wax
at the presence of Yahweh,
At the presence of the [b]Lord
of all the earth.
6 The [a]heavens declare
His righteousness,
And [b]all the peoples
see His glory.

7 Let all those be ashamed who
serve [a]graven images,
Who boast of [b]idols;
[c,1]Worship Him, all you [2]gods!
8 Zion [1]heard *this* and [a]was glad,
And the daughters
of Judah have rejoiced
Because of Your judgments,
O Yahweh.
9 For You are Yahweh [a]Most
High over all the earth;
You are exalted
far [b]above all [1]gods.

10 [a]Hate evil, you who
love Yahweh,
Who [b]keeps the souls
of His holy ones;
He [c]delivers them
from the hand of the wicked.
11 [a]Light is sown
for the righteous
And [b]gladness
for the upright in heart.
12 Be [a]glad in Yahweh, you
righteous ones,
And [b]give thanks
for the remembrance
of [1]His holy *name*.

## PSALM 98

***Sing to Yahweh a New Song***

A Psalm.

1 Sing to Yahweh a [a]new song,
For He has done
[b]wondrous deeds,
His [c]right hand and His
[d]holy arm have [1]worked
out His salvation.
2 [a]Yahweh has made
known His salvation;
He has [b]revealed His
righteousness in the eyes
of the nations.
3 He has [a]remembered
His lovingkindness
and His faithfulness
to the house of Israel;
[b]All the ends of the earth have
seen the salvation of our God.

4 [a]Make a loud shout
to Yahweh, all the earth;
[b]Break forth and sing
for joy and sing praises.
5 Sing praises to Yahweh
with the [a]lyre,
With the lyre and
the [b]sound of singing.

---

**97:3** [a]Ps 18:8; 50:3; Da 7:10; Hab 3:5 [b]Mal 4:1; Heb 12:29 **97:4** [a]Ex 19:16; Ps 77:18 [b]Ps 96:9; 104:32 **97:5** [a]Ps 46:6; Am 9:5; Mic 1:4; Na 1:5 [b]Jos 3:11 **97:6** [a]Ps 19:1; 50:6 [b]Ps 98:2; Is 6:3; 40:5; 66:18 **97:7** [a]Ps 78:58; Is 42:17; 44:9, 11; Jer 10:14 [b]Ps 106:36; Jer 50:2; Hab 2:18 [c]Heb 1:6 [1]Or *All the gods have worshiped Him* [2]Or *supernatural powers* **97:8** [a]Ps 48:11; Zep 3:14 [1]Or possibly *hears and is glad* **97:9** [a]Ps 83:18 [b]Ex 18:11; Ps 95:3; 96:4; 135:5 [1]Or *supernatural powers* **97:10** [a]Ps 34:14; Pr 8:13; Am 5:15; Ro 12:9 [b]Ps 31:23; 145:20; Pr 2:8 [c]Ps 37:40; Jer 15:21; Da 3:28 **97:11** [a]Job 22:28; Ps 112:4; Pr 4:18 [b]Ps 64:10 **97:12** [a]Ps 32:11 [b]Ps 30:4 [1]Lit *His holiness* ◆ **98:1** [a]Ps 33:3 [b]Ps 40:5; 96:3 [c]Ex 15:6 [d]Is 52:10 [1]Or *accomplished salvation* **98:2** [a]Is 52:10 [b]Is 62:2; Ro 3:25 **98:3** [a]Lk 1:54, 72 [b]Ps 22:27 **98:4** [a]Ps 100:1 [b]Is 44:23 **98:5** [a]Ps 92:3 [b]Is 51:3

6 With [a]trumpets and
the sound of the horn
[b]Make a loud shout
before [c]King Yahweh.

7 Let the [a]sea roar,
as well as its fullness,
The [b]world and those
who dwell in it.
8 Let the [a]rivers clap
their hands,
Let the [b]mountains sing
together for joy
9 Before Yahweh, for He is
coming to [a]judge the earth;
He will judge the world
with righteousness
And [b]the peoples with [1]equity.

## PSALM 99

### *Holy Is Yahweh Our God*

1 [a]Yahweh reigns, let
the peoples tremble;
He [b]sits enthroned
*above* the cherubim,
let the earth quake!
2 Yahweh is [a]great in Zion,
And He is [b]exalted
above all the peoples.
3 Let them praise Your [a]great
and awesome name;
[b]Holy is [1]He.
4 [1]The strength of the King
[a]loves [2]justice;
You have established [b,3]equity;
You have [c]done [2]justice and
righteousness in Jacob.
5 [a]Exalt Yahweh our God
And [b]worship at the footstool
of His feet;
[c]Holy is He.

6 [a]Moses and Aaron were
among His [b]priests,
And [a]Samuel was
among those who
[c]called on His name;
They [d]would call
upon Yahweh and He
would answer them.
7 He [a]would speak to them
in the pillar of cloud;
They [b]kept His testimonies
And the statute
that He gave them.
8 O Yahweh our God,
You [a]answered them;
You were a [b]forgiving
God to them,
And *yet* an [c]avenger
of their *evil* deeds.
9 Exalt Yahweh our God
And worship at His
holy mountain,
For holy is Yahweh our God.

## PSALM 100

### *Serve Yahweh with Gladness*

A Psalm of [†]Thanksgiving.

1 [a]Make a loud shout
to Yahweh, all the earth.
2 [a]Serve Yahweh with gladness;
[b]Come before Him
with joyful songs.

**98:6** [a]Nu 10:10; 2Chr 15:14 [b]Ps 66:1 [c]Ps 47:7 **98:7** [a]Ps 96:11 [b]Ps 24:1 **98:8** [a]Ps 93:3; Is 55:12 [b]Ps 65:12; 89:12 **98:9** [a]Ps 96:13 [b]Ps 96:10 [1]Or *uprightness* ◆ **99:1** [a]Ps 97:1 [b]Ex 25:22; 1Sa 4:4; Ps 80:1 **99:2** [a]Ps 48:1; Is 12:6 [b]Ps 97:9; 113:4 **99:3** [a]Dt 28:58; Ps 76:1 [b]Lv 19:2; Jos 24:19; 1Sa 2:2; Ps 22:3; Is 6:3 [1]Or *it* **99:4** [a]Ps 11:7; 33:5 [b]Ps 17:2; 98:9 [c]Ps 103:6; 146:7; Jer 23:5 [1]Or *You have established in equity the strength of the King who loves justice* [2]Or *judgment* [3]Or *uprightness* **99:5** [a]Ps 34:3; 107:32; 118:28 [b]Ps 132:7 [c]Ps 99:3 **99:6** [a]Jer 15:1 [b]Ex 24:6-8; 29:26; 40:23-27; Lv 8:1-30 [c]1Sa 7:9; 12:18; Ps 22:4, 5 [d]Ex 15:25; 32:30-34 **99:7** [a]Ex 33:9; Nu 12:5 [b]Ps 105:28 **99:8** [a]Ps 106:44 [b]Nu 14:20; Ps 78:38 [c]Ex 32:28; Nu 20:12; Ps 95:11; 107:12 ◆ **100:TITLE** [†]Or *thank offering* **100:1** [a]Ps 95:1; 98:4, 6 **100:2** [a]Dt 12:11, 12; 28:47 [b]Ps 95:2

3 Know that [a]Yahweh,
He is God;
It is He who has [b]made us,
and [1]not we ourselves;
*We are* [c]His people and
the sheep of His pasture.

4 Enter His gates
[a]with [1]thanksgiving
*And* His courts with praise.
Give thanks to Him,
[b]bless His name.
5 For [a]Yahweh is good;
[b]His lovingkindness
endures forever
And His [c]faithfulness,
generation unto generation.

## PSALM 101

### *Consider the Way of the Blameless*

Of David. A Psalm.

1 I will [a]sing of lovingkindness
and [1]justice,
To You, O Yahweh, I
will sing praises.
2 I will [a,1]consider the way
of the blameless.
When will You come to me?
I will walk within my house in
the [b,2]integrity of my heart.
3 I will set no [a]vile thing
before my eyes;
I hate the [1]work of those
who [b]fall away;
It shall not cling to me.
4 A [a]crooked heart shall
depart from me;
I will know no evil.
5 Whoever secretly
[a]slanders his neighbor,
him I will [1]destroy;
Whoever has a [b]haughty
look and an arrogant
heart, I will not endure.

6 My eyes shall be
upon the faithful of the land,
that they may abide with me;
He who walks in the [a]way
of the blameless is the one
who will minister to me.
7 He who [a]practices deceit shall
not dwell within my house;
He who speaks lies [b]shall
not be established
before my eyes.
8 [a]Every morning I will
[b,1]destroy all the wicked
of the land,
To [c]cut off from the [d]city
of Yahweh all the workers
of iniquity.

## PSALM 102

### *Do Not Hide Your Face from Me*

A Prayer of the afflicted when he is faint and [†]pours out his complaint before Yahweh.

1 [a]O Yahweh, hear my prayer!
And let my cry for help
[b]come to You.
2 [a]Do not hide Your face from
me in the day of my distress;
[b]Incline Your ear to me;
In the day when I call
[a]answer me quickly.

---

**100:3** [a]Dt 4:35; 1Ki 18:39; Ps 46:10 [b]Job 10:3, 8; Ps 95:6; 119:73 [c]Ps 74:1, 2; 95:7; Is 40:11; Eze 34:30, 31 [1]Some mss *His we are* **100:4** [a]Ps 95:2; 116:17 [b]Ps 96:2 [1]Or *a thank offering* **100:5** [a]1Chr 16:34; 2Chr 5:13; 7:3; Ezr 3:11; Ps 25:8; 86:5; 106:1; 107:1; 118:1; Jer 33:11; Na 1:7 [b]Ps 136:1 [c]Ps 119:90
◆ **101:1** [a]Ps 51:14; 89:1; 145:7 [1]Or *judgment* **101:2** [a]1Sa 18:5, 14 [b]1Ki 9:4 [1]Or *behave prudently in* [2]Or *blamelessness* **101:3** [a]Dt 15:9 [b]Jos 23:6; Ps 40:4 [1]Or *practice of apostasy* **101:4** [a]Pr 11:20 **101:5** [a]Ps 50:20; Jer 9:4 [b]Ps 10:4; 18:27; Pr 6:17 [1]Or *silence* **101:6** [a]Ps 119:1 **101:7** [a]Ps 43:1; 52:2 [b]Ps 52:4, 5 **101:8** [a]Jer 21:12 [b]Ps 75:10 [c]Ps 118:10-12 [d]Ps 46:4; 48:2, 8 [1]Or *silence*
◆ **102:TITLE** [†]Ps 142:2 **102:1** [a]Ps 39:12; 61:1 [b]Ex 2:23; 1Sa 9:16 **102:2** [a]Ps 69:17 [b]Ps 31:2

3 For my days [a]have
[1]vanished in smoke,
And my [b]bones have been
scorched like a hearth.
4 My heart [a]has been
stricken like [1]grass and
it has [b]dried up,
Indeed, I [c]forget
to eat my bread.
5 Because of the sound
of my groaning
My [a]bones [1]cling to my flesh.
6 I resemble a [a]pelican
of the wilderness;
I have become like an owl
of the waste places.
7 I [a]lie awake,
I have become like a lonely
bird on a roof.

8 My enemies [a]have reproached
me all day long;
Those who [b,1]ridicule me
[c]swear against me.
9 For I have eaten ashes
like bread
And [a]mixed my drinks
with weeping
10 [a]Because of Your indignation
and Your wrath,
For You have [b]lifted me
up and cast me away.
11 My days are like
an [a]outstretched shadow,
And as for me,
I [b]dry up like [1]grass.
12 But You, O Yahweh,
[a,1]abide forever,
And the [b]remembrance
of Your *name* [2]from
generation to generation.
13 You will [a]arise *and* have
[b]compassion on Zion—
For [c]it is time to be gracious to it,
For the [d]appointed
time has come.
14 For Your slaves [1]find
pleasure in its stones
And show grace to its dust—
15 [1]So the [a,2]nations will fear
the name of Yahweh
And [b]all the kings
of the earth Your glory.
16 For Yahweh has [a]built up Zion;
He has [b]appeared in His glory.
17 He has [a]turned toward
the prayer of the [1]destitute
And has not despised
their prayer.

18 [1]This will be [a]written
for the [b]generation to come,
And [c]a people yet to be
created will praise Yah.
19 For He [a]looked down
from His holy height;
[b]From heaven Yahweh
gazed [1]upon the earth,
20 To hear the [a]groaning
of the prisoner,
To [b]set free [1]those who
were doomed to death,

**102:3** [a]Ps 37:20; Jas 4:14 [b]Job 30:30; Lam 1:13 [1]Or *finished* **102:4** [a]Ps 90:5, 6 [b]Ps 37:2; Is 40:7 [c]1Sa 1:7; 2Sa 12:17; Ezr 10:6; Job 33:20 [1]Lit *vegetation* **102:5** [a]Job 19:20; Lam 4:8 [1]Lit *have cleaved* **102:6** [a]Is 34:11; Zep 2:14 **102:7** [a]Ps 77:4 **102:8** [a]Ps 31:11 [b]Ac 26:11 [c]2Sa 16:5; Is 65:15; Jer 29:22 [1]Or *made a fool of* **102:9** [a]Ps 42:3; 80:5 **102:10** [a]Ps 38:3 [b]Job 27:21; 30:22 **102:11** [a]Job 14:2; Ps 109:23 [b]Ps 102:4 [1]Lit *vegetation* **102:12** [a]Ps 9:7; 10:16; Lam 5:19 [b]Ex 3:15; Ps 135:13 [1]Or *sit enthroned* [2]Lit *to* **102:13** [a]Ps 12:5; 44:26 [b]Is 60:10; Zec 1:12 [c]Ps 119:126 [d]Ps 75:2; Da 8:19 **102:14** [1]Or *have found* **102:15** [a]1Ki 8:43; Ps 67:7 [b]Ps 138:4 [1]Or *And* [2]Or *Gentiles* **102:16** [a]Ps 147:2 [b]Is 60:1, 2 **102:17** [a]Ne 1:6; Ps 22:24 [1]Or *naked* **102:18** [a]Dt 31:19; Ro 15:4; 1Co 10:11 [b]Ps 22:30; 48:13 [c]Ps 22:31; 78:6f [1]Or *Let this be written* **102:19** [a]Dt 26:15; Ps 14:2; 53:2 [b]Ps 33:13 [1]Lit *toward* **102:20** [a]Ps 79:11 [b]Ps 146:7 [1]Lit *the sons of death*

21 To [a]recount the name
of Yahweh in Zion
And His praise in Jerusalem,
22 When [a]the peoples are
gathered together,
And the kingdoms,
to serve Yahweh.

23 He has afflicted my
strength in the way;
He has [a]shortened
my days.
24 I say, "O my God,
[a]do not take me away
in the [1]midst of my days,
Your [b]years are
from generation to
*all* generations.
25 "Of old You [a]founded
the earth,
And the [b]heavens are
the work of Your hands.
26 "[1]Even they will [a]perish,
but You will remain;
And all of them will wear
out like a garment;
Like clothing You will
change them and they
will be changed.
27 "But You are [a,1]the same,
And Your years will not
come to an end.
28 "The [a]children
of Your slaves will
dwell *securely*,
And their [b]seed will be
established before You."

## PSALM 103

### *Bless Yahweh, O My Soul*

Of David.

1 [a]Bless Yahweh, O my soul,
And all that is within me,
*bless* His [b]holy name.
2 Bless Yahweh, O my soul,
And [a]forget none
of His benefits;
3 Who [a]pardons all
your iniquities,
Who [b]heals all your diseases;
4 Who [a]redeems your
life from the pit,
Who [b]crowns you
with lovingkindness
and compassion;
5 Who [a]satisfies your [1]years
with good things,
*So that* your youth is
[b]renewed like the eagle.

6 Yahweh [a]performs
righteous deeds
And judgments for all
who are [b]oppressed.
7 He [a]made known His
ways to Moses,
His [b]acts to the sons of Israel.
8 Yahweh is [a]compassionate
and gracious,
[b]Slow to anger and abounding
in lovingkindness.
9 He [a]will not always
contend *with us*,
And He will not [b]keep
*His anger* forever.

**102:21** [a]Ps 22:22 **102:22** [a]Ps 22:27; 86:9; Is 49:22, 23; 60:3; Zec 8:20-23 **102:23** [a]Ps 39:5 **102:24** [a]Ps 39:13; Is 38:10 [b]Job 36:26; Ps 90:2; 102:12; Hab 1:12 [1]Lit *half* **102:25** [a]Ge 1:1; Ne 9:6; Heb 1:10-12 [b]Ps 96:5 **102:26** [a]Is 34:4; 51:6; Mt 24:35; 2Pe 3:10; Rev 20:11 [1]Lit *They themselves* **102:27** [a]Is 41:4; 43:10; Mal 3:6; Jas 1:17 [1]Lit *He* **102:28** [a]Ps 69:36 [b]Ps 89:4 ◆ **103:1** [a]Ps 104:1, 35 [b]Ps 33:21; 105:3; 145:21; Eze 36:21; 39:7 **103:2** [a]Dt 6:12; 8:11 **103:3** [a]Ex 34:7; Ps 86:5; 130:8; Is 43:25 [b]Ex 15:26; Ps 30:2; Jer 30:17 **103:4** [a]Ps 49:15 [b]Ps 5:12 **103:5** [a]Ps 107:9; 145:16 [b]Is 40:31 [1]Or *desire* **103:6** [a]Ps 99:4; 146:7 [b]Ps 12:5 **103:7** [a]Ex 33:13; Ps 99:7; 147:19 [b]Ps 78:11; 106:22 **103:8** [a]Ex 34:6; Nu 14:18; Ne 9:17; Ps 86:15; Jon 4:2; Jas 5:11 [b]Ps 145:8; Joel 2:13; Na 1:3 **103:9** [a]Ps 30:5; Is 57:16 [b]Jer 3:5, 12; Mic 7:18

10 He has [a]not dealt with us
according to our sins,
And He has not rewarded
us according to
our iniquities.
11 For as high [a]as the heavens
are above the earth,
So great is His lovingkindness
toward those who [1]fear Him.
12 As far as the east is
from the west,
So far has He [a]removed our
transgressions from us.
13 [a]As a father has compassion
on *his* children,
So Yahweh has compassion
on those who [1]fear Him.
14 For [a]He Himself knows
[1]our form;
He [b]remembers
that we are *but* [c]dust.

15 As for man, his days
are [a]like grass;
As a [b]flower of the field,
so he flowers.
16 When the [a]wind has passed
over it, it is no more,
And its [b]place acknowledges
it no longer.
17 But the [a]lovingkindness
of Yahweh is from
everlasting to everlasting
on those who [1]fear Him,
And His [2]righteousness
[b]to children's children,
18 To [a]those who keep
His covenant
And remember His
precepts to do them.
19 Yahweh has established His
[a]throne in the heavens,
And His [b]kingdom
rules over [1]all.
20 Bless Yahweh, you [a]His angels,
[b]Mighty in strength, who
[c]perform His word,
[d]Obeying the voice
of His word!
21 Bless Yahweh, all *you* [a]His hosts,
*You* [b]who serve Him,
doing His will.
22 Bless Yahweh, [a]all you
works of His,
In all places of His rule;
Bless Yahweh, O my soul!

## PSALM 104

### *The Glory of Yahweh Endures Forever*

1 [a]Bless Yahweh, O my soul!
O Yahweh my God,
You are very great;
You are [b]clothed
with splendor and majesty,
2 Wrapping Yourself
with [a]light as with a cloak,
[b]Stretching out the heavens
like a *tent* curtain.
3 [1]He [a]lays the beams
of His upper chambers
in the waters;
[1]He sets up the [b]clouds
*to be* His chariot;
[1]He walks upon the [c]wings
of the wind;

---

**103:10** [a]Ezr 9:13; Lam 3:22 **103:11** [a]Ps 36:5; 57:10 [1]Or *reverence* **103:12** [a]2Sa 12:13; Is 38:17; 43:25; Zec 3:9; Heb 9:26 **103:13** [a]Mal 3:17 [1]Or *reverence* **103:14** [a]Is 29:16 [b]Ps 78:39 [c]Ge 3:19; Ecc 12:7 [1]Of what we are made **103:15** [a]Ps 90:5; Is 40:6; 1Pe 1:24 [b]Job 14:2; Jas 1:10, 11 **103:16** [a]Is 40:7 [b]Job 7:10; 8:18; 20:9 **103:17** [a]Ps 25:6 [b]Ex 20:6; Dt 5:10; Ps 105:8 [1]Or *reverence* [2]Faithfulness to His gracious promises **103:18** [a]Dt 7:9; Ps 25:10 **103:19** [a]Ps 11:4 [b]Ps 47:2, 8; Da 4:17, 25 [1]The universe **103:20** [a]Ps 148:2 [b]Ps 29:1; 78:25 [c]Mt 6:10 [d]Ps 91:11; Heb 1:14 **103:21** [a]1Ki 22:19; Ne 9:6; Ps 148:2; Lk 2:13 [b]Ps 104:4 **103:22** [a]Ps 145:10 ◆**104:1** [a]Ps 103:22 [b]Ps 93:1 **104:2** [a]Da 7:9 [b]Is 40:22 **104:3** [a]Am 9:6 [b]Is 19:1 [c]Ps 18:10 [1]Lit *The one who*

4 [1]He makes His [2]angels
[a]the winds,
His ministers flaming [b]fire.

5 He [a]founded the earth
upon its place,
So that it will not [1]shake
forever and ever.
6 You [a]covered it
with the deep
as with a garment;
The waters were standing
above the mountains.
7 At Your [a]rebuke they fled,
At the [b]sound of Your
thunder they hurried
away in alarm.
8 The mountains went up;
the valleys went down
To the [a]place which You
founded for them.
9 You set a [a]boundary
that they may not pass over,
So that they will not return
to cover the earth.

10 [1]He sends forth [a]springs
in the valleys;
They flow
between the mountains;
11 They [a]give water to every
beast of the field;
The [b]wild donkeys
quench their thirst.
12 Above them the birds
of the heavens [a]dwell;
They give forth *their* voices
among the branches.
13 [1]He [a]gives water
to the mountains
from His upper chambers;
[b]The earth is satisfied
with the fruit
of His works.

14 [1]He causes the [a]grass
to grow for the [2]cattle,
And [b]vegetation
for man's [3]cultivation,
To bring forth [4]food
[c]from the earth,
15 And [a]wine which makes
man's heart glad,
[b]To make *his* face glisten
more than oil,
And [1]food which [c]sustains
man's heart.
16 The trees of Yahweh
are satisfied,
The cedars of Lebanon
which He planted,
17 Where the [a]birds build
their nests,
The [b]stork's home is
in the [1]fir trees.

18 The high mountains are
for the [a]wild goats;
The [b]cliffs are a refuge
for the [c,1]shephanim.
19 He made the moon
[a]for the seasons;
The [b]sun knows the place
of its setting.
20 You [a]appoint darkness
so that it becomes night,

**104:4** [a]Ps 148:8; Heb 1:7 [b]2Ki 2:11; 6:17 [1]Lit *Who* [2]Or *messengers* **104:5** [a]Job 38:4; Ps 24:2 [1]Or *move out of place* **104:6** [a]Ge 1:2 **104:7** [a]Ps 18:15; 106:9; Is 50:2 [b]Ps 29:3; 77:18 **104:8** [a]Ps 33:7 **104:9** [a]Job 38:10, 11; Jer 5:22 **104:10** [a]Ps 107:35; Is 41:18 [1]Lit *The one who sends* **104:11** [a]Ps 104:13 [b]Job 39:5 **104:12** [a]Mt 8:20 **104:13** [a]Ps 65:9; 147:8 [b]Jer 10:13 [1]Lit *Who* **104:14** [a]Job 38:27; Ps 147:8 [b]Ge 1:29; Ge 2:5 [c]Job 28:5 [1]Lit *Who* [2]Or *beasts* [3]Or *labor* [4]Lit *bread* **104:15** [a]Jdg 9:13; Pr 31:6; Ecc 10:19 [b]Ps 23:5; 92:10; 141:5; Lk 7:46 [c]Ge 18:5; Jdg 19:5, 8 [1]Lit *bread* **104:17** [a]Ps 104:12 [b]Lv 11:19 [1]Or *cypress* **104:18** [a]Job 39:1 [b]Pr 30:26 [c]Lv 11:5 [1]Small, shy, furry animals *(Hyrax syriacus)* **104:19** [a]Ge 1:14 [b]Ps 19:6 **104:20** [a]Ps 74:16; Is 45:7

In which all the [b]beasts
of the forest [c]creep about.
21 The [a]young lions roar
*to go* after their prey
And to [b]seek their
food from God.
22 *When* the sun rises they
gather together
And lie down in their [a]dens.
23 Man goes forth to [a]his work
And to his labor until evening.

24 How [a]numerous are Your
works, O Yahweh!
[1]In [b]wisdom You have
made them all;
The [c]earth is full
of Your [2]possessions.
25 This is the [a]sea,
great and [1]broad,
There *the* creeping things
are without number,
Creatures both small and great.
26 There the [a]ships move along,
*And* [b,1]Leviathan, which You
have formed to play in it.

27 They all [a]wait for You
To [b]give them their food
in [1]due season.
28 You give to them, they
gather *it* up;
You [a]open Your hand, they
are satisfied with good.
29 You [a]hide Your face,
they are dismayed;
You [b]take away their [1]spirit,
they breathe their last
And [c]return to their dust.
30 You send forth Your [a,1]Spirit,
they are created;
And You renew the face
of the ground.

31 Let the [a]glory of Yahweh
endure forever;
Let Yahweh [b]be glad
in His works;
32 [1]He [a]looks at the earth,
and it [b]trembles;
He [c]touches the mountains,
and they smoke.
33 [1]I will sing to Yahweh
[a]throughout my life;
[1]I will [b]sing praise to my God
[2]while I have *my* being.
34 Let my [a]musing be
pleasing to Him;
As for me, I shall [b]be
glad in Yahweh.
35 Let sinners be [a]consumed
from the earth
And let the [b]wicked be no more.
[c]Bless Yahweh, O my soul.
[d,1]Praise Yah!

## PSALM 105

### *Remember His Wondrous Deeds*

1 Oh [a]give thanks to Yahweh,
[b]call upon His name;
[c]Make known His acts
among the peoples.

**104:20** [b]Ps 50:10; Is 56:9; Mic 5:8 [c]Ge 1:26 **104:21** [a]Job 38:39 [b]Ps 145:15; Joel 1:20 **104:22** [a]Job 37:8 **104:23** [a]Ge 3:19 **104:24** [a]Ps 40:5 [b]Ps 136:5; Pr 3:19; Jer 10:12; 51:15 [c]Ps 65:9 [1]Or *With* [2]Or *creatures* **104:25** [a]Ps 8:8; 69:34 [1]Or *broad of dimensions*; lit *broad of hands* **104:26** [a]Ps 107:23; Eze 27:9 [b]Job 41:1; Ps 74:14; Is 27:1 [1]Or *a sea monster* **104:27** [a]Ps 145:15 [b]Job 36:31; 38:41; Ps 136:25; 147:9 [1]Lit *its appointed time* **104:28** [a]Ps 145:16 **104:29** [a]Dt 31:17; Ps 30:7 [b]Job 34:14, 15; Ps 146:4; Ecc 12:7 [c]Ge 3:19; Job 10:9; Ps 90:3 [1]Or *breath* **104:30** [a]Job 33:4; Eze 37:9 [1]Or *breath* **104:31** [a]Ps 86:12; 111:10 [b]Ge 1:31 **104:32** [a]Jdg 5:5; Ps 97:4, 5; 114:7 [b]Hab 3:10 [c]Ex 19:18; Ps 144:5 [1]Lit *The one who* **104:33** [a]Ps 63:4 [b]Ps 146:2 [1]Or *Let me sing* [2]Lit *while I still am* **104:34** [a]Ps 19:14 [b]Ps 9:2 **104:35** [a]Ps 59:13 [b]Ps 37:10 [c]Ps 104:1 [d]Ps 105:45; 106:48 [1]Or *Hallelujah!*
◆ **105:1** [a]1Chr 16:8-22, 34; Ps 106:1; Is 12:4 [b]Ps 99:6 [c]Ps 145:12

2 Sing to Him, [a]sing
praises to Him;
[b]Muse on all His
wondrous deeds.
3 Boast in His holy name;
Let the [a]heart of those who
seek Yahweh be glad.
4 Inquire of Yahweh and
[a]His strength;
[b]Seek His face continually.
5 Remember His [a]wondrous
deeds which He has done,
His miracles and
the [b]judgments [1]uttered
by His mouth,
6 O seed of [a]Abraham,
His servant,
O sons of [b]Jacob, His
[c]chosen ones!
7 He is Yahweh our God;
His [a]judgments are
in all the earth.

8 He has [a]remembered His
covenant forever,
The word which He
commanded for
a [b]thousand generations,
9 [a]Which He cut with Abraham,
And His [b]oath to Isaac.
10 Then He [a]confirmed it
to Jacob for a statute,
To Israel as an
everlasting covenant,
11 *Saying*, "[a]To you I will give
the land of Canaan
As the [b,1]portion
of your inheritance,"
12 When they were only
a [a]few men in number,
Of little account, and
[b]sojourners in it.
13 And they wandered
about from nation to nation,
From *one* kingdom
to another people.
14 He [a]permitted no man
to oppress them,
And He [b]reproved kings
for their sakes:
15 "[a]Do not touch My
anointed ones,
And to My prophets do no evil."

16 And He [a]called for a famine
upon the land;
He [b]broke the whole
staff of bread.
17 He [a]sent a man before them,
Joseph, *who* was
[b]sold as a slave.
18 They afflicted his [a]feet
with fetters,
[1]He himself was laid in irons;
19 Until the time that his
[a]word came to pass,
The word of Yahweh
[b]refined him.
20 The [a]king sent and
released him,
The ruler of peoples *sent*
and set him free.
21 He [a]set him up as lord
of his house
And ruler
over all his possessions,

**105:2** [a]Ps 96:1; 98:5 [b]Ps 77:12; 119:27; 145:5 **105:3** [a]Ps 33:21 **105:4** [a]Ps 63:2 [b]Ps 27:8 **105:5** [a]Ps 40:5; 77:11 [b]Ps 119:13 [1]Lit *of His mouth* **105:6** [a]Ps 105:42 [b]Ps 135:4 [c]1Chr 16:13; Ps 106:5; 135:4 **105:7** [a]Is 26:9 **105:8** [a]Ps 105:42; 106:45; Lk 1:72 [b]Dt 7:9 **105:9** [a]Ge 12:7; 17:2, 8; 22:16-18; Ga 3:17 [b]Ge 26:3 **105:10** [a]Ge 28:13-15 **105:11** [a]Ge 13:15; 15:18 [b]Jos 23:4; Ps 78:55 [1]Lit *measuring line* **105:12** [a]Ge 34:30; Dt 7:7 [b]Ge 23:4; Heb 11:9 **105:14** [a]Ge 20:7; 35:5 [b]Ge 12:17; 20:3, 7 **105:15** [a]Ge 26:11 **105:16** [a]Ge 41:54 [b]Lv 26:26; Is 3:1; Eze 4:16 **105:17** [a]Ge 45:5 [b]Ge 37:28, 36; Ac 7:9 **105:18** [a]Ge 39:20; 40:15 [1]Lit *His soul came into* **105:19** [a]Ge 40:20, 21 [b]Ps 66:10 **105:20** [a]Ge 41:14 **105:21** [a]Ge 41:40-44

22 To [1]imprison his
princes [a,2]at will,
And that he might teach
his elders wisdom.
23 [a]Then Israel came to Egypt;
And Jacob [b]sojourned
in the land of Ham.
24 And He [a]caused His people
to be very fruitful,
And He caused them
to be stronger
than their adversaries.

25 He [a]turned their heart
to hate His people,
To [b]deal craftily
with His slaves.
26 He [a]sent Moses His servant,
*And* [b]Aaron,
whom He had chosen.
27 They [a]set forth the words
of His signs among them,
And miracles
in the land of Ham.
28 He [a]sent darkness and
made *it* dark;
And they did not [b]rebel
against His words.
29 He [a]turned their
waters into blood
And caused their
fish to die.
30 Their land swarmed
with [a]frogs
*Even* in the [b]chambers
of their kings.
31 He spoke, and there came
a [a]swarm of flies
*And* [b]gnats in all
their territory.
32 He [1]gave them [a]hail for rain,
*And* flaming fire in their land.
33 He also [a]struck down their
vines and their fig trees,
And He shattered the trees
of their territory.
34 He spoke, and [a]locusts came,
And creeping locusts,
without number,
35 And [1]they ate up all
vegetation in their land,
And [1]they ate up the fruit
of their ground.
36 He also [a]struck down all
the firstborn in their land,
The [b]first of all their vigor.

37 Then He brought them out
with [a]silver and gold,
And there was none among
His tribes who stumbled.
38 Egypt was [a]glad
when they went out,
For the [b]dread of them
had fallen upon them.
39 He spread a [a]cloud
for a [1]covering,
And [b]fire to give light by night.
40 [1]They [a]asked, and He
brought [b]quail,
And He satisfied them
with the [c,2]bread of heaven.
41 He opened the [1]rock and
[a]water flowed out;
[2]It ran in the dry places
*like* a river.

**105:22** [a]Ge 41:44 [1]Lit *bind* [2]Lit *at his* **105:23** [a]Ge 46:6; Ac 7:15 [b]Ac 13:17 **105:24** [a]Ex 1:7, 9
**105:25** [a]Ex 1:8; 4:21 [b]Ex 1:10; Ac 7:19 **105:26** [a]Ex 3:10; 4:12 [b]Ex 4:14; Nu 16:5; 17:5-8
**105:27** [a]Ps 78:43-51; 105:27-36 **105:28** [a]Ex 10:21, 22 [b]Ps 99:7 **105:29** [a]Ex 7:20, 21 **105:30** [a]Ex 8:6
[b]Ex 8:3 **105:31** [a]Ex 8:21 [b]Ex 8:16, 17 **105:32** [a]Ex 9:23-25 [1]Or *made their rain hail* **105:33** [a]Ps 78:47
**105:34** [a]Ex 10:12-15 **105:35** [1]Lit *it* **105:36** [a]Ex 12:29; 13:15; Ps 135:8; 136:10 [b]Ge 49:3
**105:37** [a]Ex 12:35, 36 **105:38** [a]Ex 12:33 [b]Ex 15:16 **105:39** [a]Ex 13:21; Ne 9:12; Ps 78:14; Is 4:5 [b]Ex 40:38
[1]Or *curtain* **105:40** [a]Ex 16:12; Ps 78:18 [b]Ex 16:13; Nu 11:31; Ps 78:27 [c]Ex 16:15; Ne 9:15; Ps 78:24; Jn 6:31
[1]Or *One* [2]Or *food* **105:41** [a]Ex 17:6; Nu 20:11; Ps 78:15; 114:8; Is 48:21; 1Co 10:4 [1]Or *boulder* [2]Lit *They went*

42 For He [a]remembered
His holy word
*With* Abraham His servant;
43 And He brought His
people out with joy,
His chosen ones
with a shout of [a]joy.
44 He [a]gave them also the lands
of the [1]nations,
That they [b]might take
possession of *the fruit*
*of* the peoples' labor,
45 So that they might
[a]keep His statutes
And observe His laws,
[1]Praise Yah!

### PSALM 106

#### *Remember Me, O Yahweh*

1 [1]Praise Yah!
Oh [a]give thanks to Yahweh,
for He [b]is good;
For [c]His lovingkindness
endures forever.
2 Who can speak of the [a]mighty
deeds of Yahweh,
Or can make all His
praise to be heard?
3 How blessed are those
who keep [1]justice,
[2]*And he* who [a]does
righteousness at all times!

4 Remember me, O Yahweh,
in *Your* [a]favor
[1]toward Your people;
Visit me with Your salvation,
5 That I may see the [a]goodness
of Your chosen ones,
That I may [b]rejoice in
the gladness of Your nation,
That I may [c]boast
with Your [1]inheritance.

6 [a]We have sinned
[b]with our fathers,
We have committed iniquity,
we have acted wickedly.
7 Our fathers in Egypt
did not consider Your
wondrous deeds;
They [a]did not remember Your
abundant lovingkindnesses,
But they [b]rebelled
by the sea, at the [1]Red Sea.
8 Yet He saved them
[a]for the sake of His name,
That He might [b]make
His might known.
9 Thus He [a]rebuked the [1]Red
Sea and it [b]dried up,
And He [c]led them
through the deeps,
as through the wilderness.
10 So He [a]saved them
from the [1]hand of the one
who hated *them*,
And [b]redeemed them
from the [1]hand of the enemy.
11 [a]The waters covered
their adversaries;
Not one of them was left.
12 Then they [a]believed His words;
They [b]sang His praise.

**105:42** [a]Ge 15:13, 14; Ps 105:8 **105:43** [a]Ex 15:1; Ps 106:12 **105:44** [a]Jos 11:16-23; 13:7; Ps 78:55 [b]Dt 6:10, 11 [1]Or *Gentiles* **105:45** [a]Dt 4:1, 40 [1]Or *Hallelujah!* ◆**106:1** [a]Ps 105:1; 107:1; 118:1; 136:1; Jer 33:11 [b]2Chr 5:13; 7:3; Ezr 3:11; Ps 100:5 [c]1Chr 16:34, 41 [1]Or *Hallelujah!* **106:2** [a]Ps 145:4, 12; 150:2 **106:3** [a]Ps 15:2 [1]Lit *judgment* [2]Many Heb mss *The one who performs* **106:4** [a]Ps 44:3; 119:132 [1]Lit *of* **106:5** [a]Ps 1:3 [b]Ps 118:15 [c]Ps 105:3 [1]People **106:6** [a]1Ki 8:47; Ezr 9:7; Ne 1:7; Jer 3:25; Da 9:5 [b]2Chr 30:7; Ne 9:2; Ps 78:8, 57; Zec 1:4 **106:7** [a]Jdg 3:7; Ps 78:11, 42 [b]Ex 14:11, 12; Ps 78:17 [1]Lit *Sea of Reeds* **106:8** [a]Eze 20:9 [b]Ex 9:16 **106:9** [a]Ps 18:15; 78:13; Is 50:2; Na 1:4 [b]Ex 14:21; Is 51:10 [c]Is 63:11-13 [1]Lit *Sea of Reeds* **106:10** [a]Ex 14:30 [b]Ps 78:42; 107:2 [1]Or *power* **106:11** [a]Ex 14:27, 28; 15:5; Ps 78:53 **106:12** [a]Ex 14:31 [b]Ex 15:1-21; Ps 105:43

13 They quickly [a]forgot His works;
They [b]did not wait
for His counsel,
14 But [a]craved intensely
in the wilderness,
And [b]put God to the test
in the wasteland.
15 So He [a]gave them
their request,
But [b]sent a [1]wasting disease
against their lives.

16 Then they became [a]envious
of Moses in the camp,
And of Aaron, the holy
one of Yahweh,
17 The [a]earth opened and
swallowed up Dathan,
And covered up
the [1]company of Abiram.
18 And a [a]fire burned up
in their company;
The flame consumed
the wicked.

19 They [a]made a calf in Horeb
And worshiped
a molten image.
20 Thus they [a]exchanged
their glory
For the image of an ox
that eats grass.
21 They [a]forgot God their Savior,
Who had done [b]great
things in Egypt,
22 [a]Wondrous deeds
in the land of Ham
*And* awesome things
by the [1]Red Sea.
23 Therefore [a]He said that He
would destroy them,
Had not [b]Moses His
chosen one stood
in the breach before Him,
To turn away His wrath
from [1]eradicating *them*.
24 Then they [a]despised
the [b]pleasant land;
They [c]did not believe
in His word,
25 But [a]grumbled
in their tents;
They did not listen
to the voice of Yahweh.
26 So He [a,1]swore to them
To make them fall
in the wilderness,
27 And to [a]make their seed
fall among the nations
And to [b]scatter them
in the lands.

28 They then [a]joined
themselves to [1]Baal-peor,
And ate [b]sacrifices
*offered to* the dead.
29 Thus they [a]provoked *Him*
to anger with their actions,
And the plague broke
out among them.
30 Then Phinehas [a]stood
up and interceded,
And so the [b]plague
was checked.

**106:13** [a]Ex 15:24; 16:2; 17:2 [b]Ps 107:11 **106:14** [a]Nu 11:4; Ps 78:18; 1Co 10:6 [b]Ex 17:2; 1Co 10:9 **106:15** [a]Nu 11:31; Ps 78:29 [b]Is 10:16 [1]Or *leanness into their soul* **106:16** [a]Nu 16:1-3 **106:17** [a]Nu 16:32; Dt 11:6 [1]Or *assembly, band* **106:18** [a]Nu 16:35 **106:19** [a]Ex 32:4; Dt 9:8; Ac 7:41 **106:20** [a]Jer 2:11; Ro 1:23 **106:21** [a]Ps 78:11; 106:7, 13 [b]Dt 10:21 **106:22** [a]Ps 105:27 [1]Lit *Sea of Reeds* **106:23** [a]Ex 32:10; Dt 9:14; Eze 20:8, 13 [b]Ex 32:11-14; Dt 9:25-29 [1]Or *bringing* them *to ruin* **106:24** [a]Nu 14:31 [b]Dt 8:7; Jer 3:19; Eze 20:6 [c]Dt 1:32; 9:23; Heb 3:19 **106:25** [a]Nu 14:2; Dt 1:27 **106:26** [a]Nu 14:28-35; Ps 95:11; Eze 20:15; Heb 3:11 [1]Or *swore against*; lit *lifted up His hand* **106:27** [a]Dt 4:27 [b]Lv 26:33; Ps 44:11 **106:28** [a]Nu 25:3; Dt 4:3; Hos 9:10 [b]Nu 25:2 [1]Or *Baal of Peor* **106:29** [a]Nu 25:4 **106:30** [a]Nu 25:7 [b]Nu 25:8

31 And it was [a]counted
to him for righteousness,
From generation
to generation forever.

32 They also [a]provoked *Him*
to wrath at the waters
of [1]Meribah,
So that it [b]went badly
with Moses
on their account;
33 Because they [a]were rebellious
against [1]His Spirit,
He spoke rashly with his lips.

34 They [a]did not destroy
the peoples,
As [b]Yahweh
commanded them,
35 But [a]they mingled
with the nations
And learned their works,
36 And [a]served their idols,
[b]Which became
a snare to them.
37 They [a]sacrificed their
sons and their daughters
to the [b]demons,
38 And they shed
[a]innocent blood,
The blood of their [b]sons
and their daughters,
Whom they sacrificed
to the idols of Canaan;
And the land was [c]polluted
with the blood.
39 Thus they became [a]unclean
in their works,
And [b]played the harlot
in their actions.

40 So the [a]anger of Yahweh
was kindled
against His people
And He [b]abhorred His
[c,1]inheritance.
41 Then [a]He gave them
into the hand
of the [1]nations,
And those who hated
them ruled over them.
42 Their enemies
[a]oppressed them,
And they were subdued
under their hand.
43 Many times
He would
[a]deliver them;
But they were rebellious
in their [b]counsel,
And *so* they [c]sank down
in their iniquity.

44 Nevertheless He looked
upon their distress
When He [a]heard their
cry of lamentation;
45 And He [a]remembered
for them His covenant,
And [b,1]relented [c]according
to the abundance
of His lovingkindness.
46 He also made them [a]*objects*
of compassion
In the presence of all
their captors.

**106:31** [a]Ge 15:6; Nu 25:11-13 **106:32** [a]Nu 20:2-13; Ps 81:7; 95:9 [b]Nu 20:12 [1]Lit *strife*
**106:33** [a]Nu 20:3, 10; Ps 78:40; 107:11 [1]Or *his spirit* **106:34** [a]Jdg 1:21, 27-36 [b]Dt 7:2, 16
**106:35** [a]Jdg 3:5, 6 **106:36** [a]Jdg 2:12 [b]Dt 7:16 **106:37** [a]Dt 12:31; 32:17; 2Ki 16:3; 17:17; Eze 16:20, 21; 1Co 10:20 [b]Lv 17:7 **106:38** [a]Ps 94:21 [b]Dt 18:10 [c]Nu 35:33; Is 24:5; Jer 3:1, 2 **106:39** [a]Lv 18:24; Eze 20:18 [b]Lv 17:7; Nu 15:39; Jdg 2:17; Hos 4:12 **106:40** [a]Jdg 2:14; Ps 78:59 [b]Lv 26:30; Dt 32:19 [c]Dt 9:29; 32:9 [1]People **106:41** [a]Jdg 2:14; Ne 9:27 [1]Or *Gentiles* **106:42** [a]Jdg 4:3; 10:12
**106:43** [a]Jdg 2:16-18 [b]Ps 81:12 [c]Jdg 6:6 **106:44** [a]Jdg 3:9; 6:7; 10:10 **106:45** [a]Lv 26:42, 45; Ps 105:8 [b]Jdg 2:18 [c]Ps 69:16 [1]Lit *was sorry* **106:46** [a]1Ki 8:50; 2Chr 30:9; Ezr 9:9; Ne 1:11; Jer 42:12

47 [a]Save us, O Yahweh our God,
And [b]gather us
from among the nations,
To give thanks
to Your holy name
And [c]revel in Your praise.
48 [a]Blessed be Yahweh,
the God of Israel,
From everlasting
to everlasting.
And let all the people
say, "Amen."
[1]Praise Yah!

## BOOK 5

## PSALM 107

### *Yahweh Saves in Times of Trouble*

1 Oh [a]give thanks to Yahweh,
for [b]He is good,
For His lovingkindness
endures forever.
2 Let [a]the redeemed
of Yahweh say *so*,
Whom He has [b]redeemed
from the hand
of the adversary
3 And [a]gathered from the lands,
From the east and
from the west,
From the north and
from the [1]south.

4 They [a]wandered
in the wilderness along
the way of the wasteland;
They did not find
an inhabited [b]city.
5 Hungry [1]and thirsty,
Their [a]soul fainted
within them.
6 Then they [a]cried out
to Yahweh in their trouble;
He delivered them out
of their distresses.
7 He led them
by a [a,1]straight way,
To go to [b]an inhabited city.
8 [a]Let them give thanks
to Yahweh
for His lovingkindness,
And for His wondrous deeds
to the sons of men!
9 For He has [a]satisfied
the [1]thirsty soul,
And the [b]hungry soul
He has filled
with what is good.

10 There were those who
[a]inhabited darkness and
the shadow of death,
[b]Prisoners in affliction
and irons,
11 Because they had [a]rebelled
against the words of God
And [b]spurned the [c]counsel
of the Most High.
12 So He subdued their
heart with labor;
They stumbled and there
was [a]none to help.
13 Then they [a]cried out
to Yahweh in their trouble;
He saved them out
of their distresses.

---

**106:47** [a]1Chr 16:35, 36 [b]Ps 147:2 [c]Ps 47:1 **106:48** [a]Ps 41:13; 72:18; 89:52 [1]Or *Hallelujah!*
**107:1** [a]1Chr 16:34; Ps 106:1; 118:1; 136:1; Jer 33:11 [b]2Chr 5:13; 7:3; Ezr 3:11; Ps 100:5 **107:2** [a]Is 35:9, 10; 62:12; 63:4 [b]Ps 78:42; 106:10 **107:3** [a]Dt 30:3; Ne 1:9; Ps 106:47; Is 11:12; 43:5; 56:8; Eze 11:17; 20:34 [1]Lit *sea* **107:4** [a]Nu 14:33; 32:13; Dt 2:7; 32:10; Jos 5:6; 14:10 [b]Ps 107:7, 36 **107:5** [a]Ps 77:3 [1]Lit *also* **107:6** [a]Ps 50:15; 107:13, 19, 28 **107:7** [a]Ezr 8:21; Ps 5:8; Jer 31:9 [b]Ps 107:4, 36 [1]Or *level*
**107:8** [a]Ps 107:15, 21, 31 **107:9** [a]Ps 22:26; 34:10; 63:5; 103:5 [b]Ps 146:7; Mt 5:6; Lk 1:53 [1]Or *parched*
**107:10** [a]Ps 143:3; Is 42:7; Mic 7:8; Lk 1:79 [b]Job 36:8; Ps 102:20 **107:11** [a]Ps 78:40; 106:7; Lam 3:42 [b]Nu 15:31; 2Chr 36:16; Pr 1:25; Is 5:24 [c]Ps 73:24 **107:12** [a]Ps 22:11; 72:12 **107:13** [a]Ps 107:6

14 He [a]brought them
out of darkness and
the shadow of death
And [b]broke their
bands apart.
15 [a]Let them give thanks
to Yahweh for His
lovingkindness,
And for His wondrous deeds
to the sons of men!
16 For He has [a]shattered
the doors of bronze
And cut through
the bars of iron.

17 [1]Ignorant fools, because
of their way of transgression,
And [a]because of their
iniquities, were afflicted.
18 Their [a]soul abhorred
all kinds of food,
And they [b]reached
the [c]gates of death.
19 Then they cried out
to Yahweh in their trouble;
He saved them
out of their distresses.
20 He [a]sent His word and
[b]healed them,
And [c]provided *them* escape
from their [1]destructions.
21 [a]Let them give thanks
to Yahweh for His
lovingkindness,
And for His wondrous deeds
to the sons of men!
22 Let them also offer [a]sacrifices
of thanksgiving,
And [b]recount His works
with joyful singing.

23 Those who [a]go down
to the sea in ships,
Who do business
on many waters;
24 They have seen the works
of Yahweh,
And His wondrous
deeds in the deep.
25 He [a]spoke and set up
a [b]stormy wind,
Which [c]raised up
the waves [1]of the sea.
26 They went up
to the heavens, they went
down to the depths;
Their soul [a]melted away
in *the* [1]calamity.
27 They staggered and [a]swayed
like a drunken man,
And all their wisdom
was swallowed up.
28 Then they cried to Yahweh
in their trouble,
And He brought them
out of their distresses.
29 He [a]caused the storm
to stand still,
So that its waves were hushed.
30 Then they were glad because
they were quiet,
So He led them to their
desired haven.
31 [a]Let them give thanks
to Yahweh
for His lovingkindness,

**107:14** [a]Ps 86:13; 107:10 [b]Ps 116:16; Jer 2:20; 30:8; Na 1:13; Lk 13:16; Ac 12:7 **107:15** [a]Ps 107:8, 21, 31 **107:16** [a]Is 45:1, 2 **107:17** [a]Is 65:6, 7; Jer 30:14, 15; Lam 3:39; Eze 24:23 [1]One who lacks wisdom due to negligence or carelessness **107:18** [a]Job 33:20; Ps 102:4 [b]Job 33:22; Ps 88:3 [c]Job 38:17; Ps 9:13 **107:20** [a]Ps 147:15, 18; Mt 8:8 [b]2Ki 20:5; Ps 30:2; 103:3; 147:3 [c]Job 33:28, 30; Ps 30:3; 49:15; 56:13; 103:4 [1]Or *pits* **107:21** [a]Ps 107:8, 15, 31 **107:22** [a]Lv 7:12; Ps 50:14; 116:17 [b]Ps 9:11; 73:28; 118:17 **107:23** [a]Is 42:10; Jon 1:3 **107:25** [a]Ps 105:31, 34 [b]Ps 148:8; Jon 1:4 [c]Ps 93:3, 4 [1]Lit *of it* **107:26** [a]Ps 22:14; 119:28 [1]Lit *evil* **107:27** [a]Job 12:25; Is 24:20 **107:29** [a]Ps 65:7; 89:9; Mt 8:26; Lk 8:24 **107:31** [a]Ps 107:8, 15, 21

And for His [b]wondrous
deeds to the sons of men!
32 Let them [a]exalt Him also [b]in
the assembly of the people,
And [c]praise Him
at the seat of the elders.

33 He [a,1]makes rivers
into a [2]wilderness
And springs of water
into a thirsty ground;
34 A [a]fruitful land
into a [b]salt waste,
Because of the evil of those
who inhabited it.
35 He [a]makes a wilderness
into a pool of water
And a dry land
into springs of water;
36 And there He causes
the hungry to inhabit,
So that they may establish
[a]an inhabited city,
37 And sow fields and
[a]plant vineyards,
And produce a
fruitful harvest.
38 Also He blesses them and
they [a]multiply greatly,
And He [b]does not let
their cattle decrease.

39 But when they [a]decrease
and are [b]bowed down
Through oppression,
evil, and sorrow,
40 He [a]pours contempt
upon nobles
And [b]makes them wander
[c]in a pathless void.
41 But He [a]sets the needy
[1]securely on high away
from affliction,
And [b]makes *his* families
like a flock.
42 The [a]upright see it
and are glad;
But all [b]unrighteousness
shuts its mouth.
43 Who is [a]wise? Let him
keep these things,
And carefully consider
the [b]lovingkindnesses
of Yahweh.

## PSALM 108

### *He Will Tread Down Our Adversaries*

A Song. A Psalm of David.

1 [a]My heart is set, O God;
I will sing, I will sing praises,
even with my glory.
2 Awake, harp and lyre;
I will awaken the dawn!
3 I will give thanks to You,
O Yahweh,
among the peoples,
And I will sing praises
to You among the nations.
4 For Your [a]lovingkindness is
great [b]above the heavens,
And Your truth *reaches*
to the skies.
5 [a]Be exalted
above the heavens, O God,
And Your glory
above all the earth.

**107:31** [b]Ps 78:4; 111:4 **107:32** [a]Ps 34:3; 99:5; Is 25:1 [b]Ps 22:22, 25 [c]Ps 35:18 **107:33** [a]1Ki 17:1, 7; *Ps 74:15; Is 42:15; 50:2* [1]*Or turns* [2]*Or desert* **107:34** [a]Ge 13:10; 14:3; 19:24, 25; Dt 29:23 [b]Job 39:6; Jer 17:6 **107:35** [a]Ps 105:41; 114:8; Is 35:6, 7; 41:18 **107:36** [a]Ps 107:4, 7 **107:37** [a]2Ki 19:29; Is 65:21; Am 9:14 **107:38** [a]Ge 12:2; 17:20; Ex 1:7; Dt 1:10 [b]Dt 7:14 **107:39** [a]2Ki 10:32; Eze 5:11; 29:15 [b]Ps 38:6; 44:25; 57:6 **107:40** [a]Job 12:21 [b]Job 12:24 [c]Dt 32:10 **107:41** [a]1Sa 2:8; Ps 59:1; 113:7, 8 [b]Job 21:11; Ps 78:52; 113:9 [1]Lit *in an inaccessibly high place* **107:42** [a]Job 22:19; Ps 52:6 [b]Job 5:16; Ps 63:11; Ro 3:19 **107:43** [a]Ps 64:9; Jer 9:12; Hos 14:9 [b]Ps 107:1 ◆**108:1** [a]Ps 57:7-11; 108:1-5 **108:4** [a]Nu 14:18; Dt 7:9; Ps 36:5; 100:5; Mic 7:18-20 [b]Ps 113:4 **108:5** [a]Ps 57:5

6 [a]That Your beloved
may be rescued,
Save with Your right hand,
and answer me!

7 God has spoken
in His [1]holiness:
"I will exult, I will portion
out Shechem
And measure out
the valley of Succoth.
8 "Gilead is Mine,
Manasseh is Mine;
Ephraim also is the [1]helmet
of My head;
[a]Judah is My [2]scepter.
9 "Moab is My washbowl;
Over Edom I shall
throw My shoe;
Over Philistia I will make
a loud shout."

10 [a]Who will bring me
into the well-defended city?
Who [1]will lead me
to Edom?
11 Have You, O God,
not [a]rejected us?
And will You, O God,
not go forth
with our armies?
12 Oh give us help
against the adversary,
For [a]salvation [1]by man
is worthless.
13 [1]Through God we shall
do valiantly,
And [a]it is He who will tread
down our adversaries.

## PSALM 109

### *O God, Do Not Be Silent*

For the choir director. Of David. A Psalm.

1 O [a]God of my praise,
[b]Do not be silent!
2 For they have opened
a wicked mouth and
a [a]deceitful mouth
against me;
They have spoken to me
with a [b]lying tongue.
3 They have also surrounded
me with words of hatred,
And fought against me
[a]without cause.
4 In return [a]for my love
they accuse me;
But [b]I am *in* prayer.
5 Thus they have [a]set upon me
evil for good
And [b]hatred for my love.

6 Appoint a wicked
man over him,
And let an [a,1]accuser stand
at his right hand.
7 When he is judged,
let him [a]come forth
a wicked man,
And let his [b]prayer
become sin.
8 Let [a]his days be few;
Let [b]another take his office.
9 Let his [a]sons be orphans
And his [b]wife a widow.
10 Let his [a]sons wander
aimlessly and beg;
And let them [b]search *for food*
[1]from their ruined homes.

---

**108:6** [a]Ps 60:5-12; 108:6-13 **108:7** [1]Or *sanctuary* **108:8** [a]Ge 49:10 [1]Lit *protection* [2]Or *lawgiver* **108:10** [a]Ps 60:9 [1]Or *has led* **108:11** [a]Ps 44:9 **108:12** [a]Is 30:3 [1]Lit *of* **108:13** [a]Is 60:12; 63:1-4 [1]Or *In, With* ◆ **109:1** [a]Dt 10:21 [b]Ps 28:1; 83:1 **109:2** [a]Ps 10:7; 52:4 [b]Ps 120:2 **109:3** [a]Ps 35:7; 69:4; Jn 15:25 **109:4** [a]Ps 38:20 [b]Ps 69:13; 141:5 **109:5** [a]Ps 35:12; 38:20 [b]Jn 7:7; 10:32 **109:6** [a]Zec 3:1 [1]Or *adversary, Satan* **109:7** [a]Ps 1:5 [b]Pr 28:9 **109:8** [a]Ps 55:23 [b]Ac 1:20 **109:9** [a]Ex 22:24 [b]Jer 18:21 **109:10** [a]Ge 4:12; Job 30:5-8; Ps 59:15 [b]Ps 37:25 [1]Or *out of their waste places*

11 Let [a]the creditor [1]seize
all that he has,
And let [b]strangers plunder
the fruit of his labor.
12 Let there be none to [a,1]extend
lovingkindness to him,
And [b]let there be none to be
gracious to his orphans.
13 Let *those who* [a]follow
him be [1]cut off;
In a following generation let
their [b]name be blotted out.

14 Let [a]the iniquity of his
fathers be remembered
[1]before Yahweh,
And let not the sin of his
mother be [b]blotted out.
15 Let [a]them be
before Yahweh continually,
That He may [b]cut off their
memory from the earth;
16 Because he did not remember
to show lovingkindness,
But persecuted the [a]afflicted,
the needy man,
And the [b]disheartened
to [c]put *them* to death.
17 He also loved cursing,
so [a]it came to him;
And he did not delight
in blessing, so it was
far from him.
18 But he [a]clothed himself
with cursing as his garment,
And it [b]came into his
inward parts like water
And like oil into his bones.
19 Let it be to him
as [a]a garment with which
he wraps himself,
And for a belt with which he
constantly [b]girds himself.
20 This is the [a]reward of my
accusers from Yahweh,
And of those who [b]speak
evil against my soul.

21 But as for You, O Yahweh,
O Lord, deal with me
[a]for Your name's sake;
Because [b]Your lovingkindness
is good, deliver me;
22 For [a]I am afflicted and needy,
And [1]my heart is
[b]pierced within me.
23 I am passing [a]like a shadow
when it is stretched out;
I am shaken off [b]like the locust.
24 My [a]knees are feeble
from [b]fasting,
And my flesh has grown
lean, without fatness.
25 As for me, I have become
a [a]reproach to them;
They see me, they
[b]wag their head.

26 [a]Help me, O Yahweh my God;
Save me according to
Your lovingkindness.
27 [1]And let them [a]know
that this is Your hand;
You, O Yahweh, have done it.

**109:11** [a]Ne 5:7; Job 5:5; 20:15 [b]Is 1:7; Lam 5:2; Eze 7:21 [1]Lit *ensnare, strike at* **109:12** [a]Ezr 7:28; 9:9 [b]Job 5:4; Is 9:17 [1]Lit *continue* **109:13** [a]*Job 18:19; Ps 21:10; 37:28* [b]Ps 9:5; Pr 10:7 [1]Lit *for cutting off* ***109:14*** [a]*Ex 20:5; Nu 14:18; Is 65:6, 7;* Jer 32:18 [b]Ne 4:5; Jer 18:23 [1]Lit *to* **109:15** [a]Ps 90:8; Jer 16:17 [b]Job 18:17; Ps 34:16 **109:16** [a]Ps 37:14 [b][illegible]34:18 [c]Ps 37:32; 94:6 **109:17** [a]Pr 14:14; Eze 35:9; Mt 7:2 **109:18** [a]Ps 73:6; 109:29; Eze 7:27 [b]Nu 5:22 **109:19** [a]Ps 73:6; 109:29; Eze 7:27 [b]2Sa 22:40; Ps 30:11; Is 11:5 **109:20** [a]Ps 54:5; 94:23; Is 3:11; 2Ti 4:14 [b]Ps 41:5; 71:10 **109:21** [a]Ps 23:3; 25:11; 79:9; 106:8; Eze 36:22 [b]Ps 69:16 **109:22** [a]Ps 40:17; 86:1 [b]Job 24:12; Ps 143:4; Pr 18:14 [1]Lit *one has pierced my heart within me* **109:23** [a]Ps 102:11 [b]Ex 10:19; Job 39:20 **109:24** [a]Heb 12:12 [b]Ps 35:13 **109:25** [a]Ps 22:6 [b]Ps 22:7; Jer 18:16; Lam 2:15; Mt 27:39; Mk 15:29 **109:26** [a]Ps 119:86 **109:27** [a]Job 37:7 [1]Or *That they may know*

28 [a]Let them curse, but You bless;
They arise and will be
put to shame,
But Your [b]slave shall be glad.
29 [1]Let [a]my accusers be
clothed with dishonor,
And [2]let them [b]wrap
themselves with their own
shame as with a robe.

30 With my mouth I will
give thanks abundantly
to Yahweh;
And in the midst of many
[a]I will praise Him.
31 For He stands [a]at the right
hand of the needy,
To save him from those
who [b]judge his soul.

## PSALM 110

### *You Are a Priest Forever*

Of David. A Psalm.

1 [a]Yahweh says to my Lord:
"[b]Sit at My right hand
Until I put [c]Your enemies
as a footstool for Your feet."
2 Yahweh will stretch forth
Your strong [a]scepter
from Zion, *saying,*
"[b]Have dominion in the midst
of Your enemies."
3 Your [a]people [1]will offer
themselves freely
in the day of Your [2]power;
[b]In the splendor of holiness,
from the womb of the dawn,
The [c]dew of Your youthfulness
will be Yours.

4 [a]Yahweh has sworn and will
[b]not [1]change His mind,
"You are a [c]priest forever
According to the order
of Melchizedek."
5 The Lord is [a]at Your right hand;
He [1]will [b]crush kings
in the [c]day of His anger.
6 He will [a]render justice
among the nations,
He [1]will fill *them* with [b]corpses,
He [2]will [c]crush the [3]head
*that is* over *the* wide earth.
7 He will [a]drink from the brook
by the wayside;
Therefore He will [b]lift
up *His* head.

## PSALM 111

### *Yahweh Is Gracious and Compassionate*

א *Aleph*

1 [1]Praise Yah!
I [a]will give thanks to Yahweh
with all *my* heart,

ב *Beth*

In the [b]council of the upright
and in the congregation.

ג *Gimel*

2 [a]Great are the works
of Yahweh;

ד *Daleth*

*They are* [b]sought by all
who delight in them.

**109:28** [a]2Sa 16:11, 12 [b]Is 65:14 **109:29** [a]Job 8:22; Ps 132:18 [b]Job 8:22; Ps 35:26 [1]Or *My accusers will be* [2]Or *they will cover* **109:30** [a]Ps 22:22; 35:18; 111:1 **109:31** [a]Ps 16:8; 73:23; 110:5; 121:5 [b]Ps 37:33
◆ **110:1** [a]Mt 22:44; Mk 12:36; Lk 20:42, 43; Ac 2:34, 35; Heb 1:13 [b]Mt 26:64; Eph 1:20; Col 3:1; Heb 1:3; 8:1; 10:12; 12:2 [c]1Co 15:25; Eph 1:22 **110:2** [a]Ps 45:6; Jer 48:17; Eze 19:14 [b]Ps 2:9; 72:8; Da 7:13, 14 **110:3** [a]Jdg 5:2; Ne 11:2 [b]1Chr 16:29; Ps 96:9 [c]2Sa 17:12; Mic 5:7 [1]Lit *will be freewill offerings* [2]Or *army* **110:4** [a]Heb 7:21 [b]Nu 23:19 [c]Zec 6:13; Heb 5:6, 10; 6:20; 7:17, 21 [1]Lit *be sorry* **110:5** [a]Ps 16:8; 109:31 [b]Ps 68:14; 76:12 [c]Ps 2:5, 12; Ro 2:5; Rev 6:17 [1]Or *has shattered* **110:6** [a]Is 2:4; Joel 3:12; Mic 4:3 [b]Is 66:24 [c]Ps 68:21 [1]Or *has filled* [2]Or *has shattered* [3]Or *chief men* that are **110:7** [a]Jdg 7:5, 6 [b]Ps 27:6
◆ **111:1** [a]Ps 35:18; 138:1 [b]Ps 89:7; 149:1 [1]Or *Hallelujah!* **111:2** [a]Ps 92:5 [b]Ps 143:5

ה *He*

3 [a,1]Splendid and majestic
is His work,

ו *Vav*

And [b]His righteousness
stands forever.

ז *Zayin*

4 He has made
His wondrous deeds
[1]to be remembered;

ח *Heth*

Yahweh is [a]gracious
and compassionate.

ט *Teth*

5 He has [a]given [1]food
to those who [2]fear Him;

י *Yodh*

He will [b]remember His
covenant forever.

כ *Kaph*

6 He has declared to His people
the power of His works,

ל *Lamedh*

In giving them an inheritance
of the nations.

מ *Mem*

7 The works of His hands
are [a,1]truth and justice;

נ *Nun*

All His precepts [b]are faithful.

ס *Samekh*

8 They are [a]upheld
forever and ever;

ע *Ayin*

They are done in [b,1]truth
and uprightness.

פ *Pe*

9 He has sent [a]redemption
to His people;

צ *Tsadhe*

He has commanded His
covenant forever;

ק *Qoph*

[b]Holy and [1]fearsome
is His name.

ר *Resh*

10 The [a,1]fear of Yahweh
is the beginning
of wisdom;

שׂ *Sin*

[b]Good insight belongs
to all those who do
[2]*His commandments*;

ת *Tav*

His [c]praise stands forever.

## PSALM 112

### *The Righteous Will Be Remembered Forever*

א *Aleph*

1 [1]Praise Yah!
How [a]blessed is the man
who [2]fears Yahweh,

ב *Beth*

Who greatly [b]delights
in His commandments.

ג *Gimel*

2 His [a]seed will be
mighty [1]on earth;

ד *Daleth*

The generation
of the [b]upright
will be blessed.

ה *He*

3 [a]Wealth and riches
are in his house,

ו *Vav*

And his righteousness
stands forever.

---

**111:3** [a]Ps 96:6; 145:5 [b]Ps 112:3, 9; 119:142 [1]Lit *Splendor and majesty* **111:4** [a]Ps 86:5, 15; 103:8; 145:8 [1]Lit *a memorial* **111:5** [a]Mt 6:31-33 [b]Ps 105:8 [1]Lit *prey* [2]Or *reverence* **111:7** [a]Rev 15:3 [b]Ps 19:7; 93:5 [1]Or *faithfulness* **111:8** [a]Ps 119:160; Is 40:8; Mt 5:18 [b]Ps 19:9 [1]Or *faithfulness* **111:9** [a]Lk 1:68 [b]Ps 99:3; Lk 1:49 [1]Or *awesome* **111:10** [a]Job 28:28; Pr 1:7; 9:10; Ecc 12:13 [b]Ps 119:98; Pr 3:4 [c]Ps 145:2 [1]Or *reverence for* [2]Lit *them* ◆**112:1** [a]Ps 128:1 [b]Ps 1:2; 119:14, 16 [1]Or *Hallelujah! Blessed* [2]Or *reverences* **112:2** [a]Ps 102:28; 127:4 [b]Ps 128:4 [1]Or *in the land* **112:3** [a]Pr 3:16; 8:18; Mt 6:33

ז *Zayin*

4 Light arises in the darkness
[a]for the upright;

ח *Heth*

*He is* [b]gracious and
compassionate and righteous.

ט *Teth*

5 It is well with the man who
[a]is gracious and lends;

י *Yodh*

*Who* sustains his [1]works
with justice.

כ *Kaph*

6 For he will [a]never be shaken;

ל *Lamedh*

The [b]righteous will be
[1]remembered forever.

מ *Mem*

7 He will not fear an [a]evil report;

נ *Nun*

His [b]heart is set, [c]trusting
in Yahweh.

ס *Samekh*

8 His [a]heart is upheld,
he [b]will not fear,

ע *Ayin*

Until he [c]looks *in triumph*
on his adversaries.

פ *Pe*

9 [1]He [a]has given freely
to the needy,

צ *Tsadhe*

His righteousness
stands forever;

ק *Qoph*

His [b]horn will be
raised in glory.

ר *Resh*

10 The [a]wicked will see
it and be [1]vexed,

ש *Shin*

He will [b]gnash his teeth
and [c]melt away;

ת *Tav*

The [d]desire of the wicked
will perish.

## PSALM 113

### *Who Is like Yahweh Our God?*

1 [1]Praise Yah!
[a]Praise, O [b]slaves of Yahweh,
Praise the name of Yahweh.
2 [a]May the name of
Yahweh be blessed
From now until forever.
3 [a]From the rising
of the sun to its setting
The [b]name of Yahweh
is to be praised.
4 Yahweh is [a]high
above all nations;
His [b]glory is
above the heavens.

5 [a]Who is like Yahweh
our God,
The One who [b]sits on high,
6 The One who [a,1]brings
Himself low to see
*The things* in heaven
and on the earth?
7 Who [a]raises the poor
from the dust
And lifts high the needy
from the ash heap,

**112:4** [a]Job 11:17; Ps 97:11 [b]Ps 37:26 **112:5** [a]Ps 37:21 [1]Lit *words* **112:6** [a]Ps 15:5; 55:22 [b]Pr 10:7 [1]Lit *for an eternal remembrance* **112:7** [a]Pr 1:33 [b]Ps 57:7; 108:1 [c]Ps 56:4 **112:8** [a]Heb 13:9 [b]Ps 27:1; 56:11; Pr 1:33; 3:24; Is 12:2 [c]Ps 54:7; 59:10 **112:9** [a]2Co 9:9 [b]Ps 75:10; 89:17; 92:10; 148:14 [1]Lit *He has scattered, he has given to...* **112:10** [a]Ps 86:17 [b]Ps 35:16; 37:12; Mt 8:12; 25:30; Lk 13:28 [c]Ps 58:7 [d]Job 8:13; Pr 10:28; 11:7 [1]Or *angry* ◆ **113:1** [a]Ps 135:1 [b]Ps 34:22; 69:36; 79:10; 90:13 [1]Or *Hallelujah!* **113:2** [a]Ps 145:21; Da 2:20 **113:3** [a]Ps 50:1; Is 59:19; Mal 1:11 [b]Ps 18:3; 48:1, 10 **113:4** [a]Ps 97:9; 99:2 [b]Ps 8:1; 57:11; 148:13 **113:5** [a]Ex 15:11; Ps 35:10; 89:6 [b]Ps 103:19 **113:6** [a]Ps 11:4; 138:6; Is 57:15 [1]Or *looks far below in the heavens and on the earth?* **113:7** [a]1Sa 2:8; Ps 107:41

8 To make *them* [a]sit
with [1]nobles,
With the [1]nobles
of His people.
9 He [a]makes the barren
woman of the house sit
*As* a glad mother of children.
[1]Praise Yah!

## PSALM 114
### *When Israel Went Out from Egypt*

1 When Israel went out
[a]from Egypt,
The house of Jacob
from a people
of [b]strange language,
2 Judah became [a]His sanctuary,
Israel, [b]His dominion.

3 The [a]sea looked and fled;
The [b]Jordan turned back.
4 The mountains [a]skipped
like rams,
The hills, like lambs.
5 What [a]disturbs you,
O sea, that you flee?
O Jordan, that you turn back?
6 O mountains, that you
skip like rams?
O hills, like lambs?

7 [a]Tremble, O earth,
before the Lord,
Before the God of Jacob,
8 Who [a]turned the rock
into a [b]pool of water,
The [c]flint into a spring
of water.

## PSALM 115
### *To Yahweh's Name Give Glory*

1 [a]Not to us, O Yahweh,
not to us,
But [b]to Your name give glory
Because of Your
lovingkindness, because
of Your [1]truth.
2 [a]Why should the nations say,
"[b]Where, now, is their God?"
3 But our [a]God is in the heavens;
He [b]does whatever He pleases.
4 Their [a]idols are silver and gold,
The [b]work of man's hands.
5 They have mouths,
but they [a]do not speak;
They have eyes,
but they do not see;
6 They have ears,
but they do not hear;
They have noses,
but they do not smell;
7 As for their hands,
they do not feel;
As for their feet,
they do not walk;
They do not make a sound
with their throat.
8 [a]Those who make them
[1]will become like them,
Everyone who trusts in them.

9 O [a]Israel, [b]trust in Yahweh;
He is their [c]help and
their shield.
10 O house of [a]Aaron,
trust in Yahweh;
He is their help and
their shield.

---

**113:8** [a]Job 36:7 [1]*Or princes* **113:9** [a]1Sa 2:5; Ps 68:6; Is 54:1 [1]*Or Hallelujah!* ◆ **114:1** [a]Ex 12:51; 13:3 [b]Ps 81:5 **114:2** [a]Ex 15:17; 29:45, 46; Ps 78:68, 69 [b]Ex 19:6 **114:3** [a]Ex 14:21; Ps 77:16 [b]Jos 3:13, 16 **114:4** [a]Ex 19:18; Jdg 5:5; Ps 18:7; 29:6; Hab 3:6 **114:5** [a]Hab 3:8 **114:7** [a]Ps 96:9 **114:8** [a]Ex 17:6; Nu 20:11; Ps 78:15; 105:41 [b]Ps 107:35 [c]Dt 8:15 ◆ **115:1** [a]Is 48:11; Eze 36:22 [b]Ps 29:2; 96:8 [1]*Or faithfulness* **115:2** [a]Ps 79:10 [b]Ps 42:3, 10 **115:3** [a]Ps 103:19 [b]Ps 135:6; Da 4:35 **115:4** [a]Ps 115:4-8; 135:15-18; Jer 10:4 [b]Dt 4:28; 2Ki 19:18; Is 37:19; 44:10, 20; Jer 10:3 **115:5** [a]Jer 10:5 **115:8** [a]Ps 135:18; Is 44:9-11 [1]*Or are like them* **115:9** [a]Ps 118:2; 135:19 [b]Ps 37:3; 62:8 [c]Ps 33:20 **115:10** [a]Ps 118:3; 135:19

11 You who [a,1]fear Yahweh,
trust in Yahweh;
He is their help and
their shield.
12 Yahweh [a]remembered
us; He will bless!
He will bless the house
of Israel.
He will bless the house
of Aaron.
13 He will [a]bless those
who [1]fear Yahweh,
[b]The small together
with the great.
14 May Yahweh [a]give you increase,
You and your children.
15 May you be blessed of Yahweh,
[a]Who made heaven and earth.

16 The heavens are
[a]the heavens of Yahweh,
But [b]the earth He has given
to the sons of men.
17 It is not the [a]dead
that praise Yah,
And it is none of those who
go down to [b]silence;
18 But as for us, we will [a]bless Yah
From now until forever.
[1]Praise Yah!

## PSALM 116

### *I Love Yahweh*

1 [a]I love Yahweh, because
He [b]hears
My voice *and* my
supplications.
2 Because He has [a]inclined
His ear to me,
So I shall call *upon Him*
in all my days.
3 The [a]cords of death
encompassed me
And the [1]distresses
of Sheol found me;
I found distress and sorrow.
4 Then [a]I called
upon the name of Yahweh:
"O Yahweh, I beseech You,
[b,1]provide my soul escape!"

5 [a]Gracious is Yahweh,
and [b]righteous;
And our God is [c]compassionate.
6 Yahweh keeps [a]the simple;
I was [b]brought low,
and He saved me.
7 Return to your [a]rest,
O my soul,
For Yahweh has [b]dealt
bountifully with you.
8 For You have [a]rescued
my soul from death,
My eyes from tears,
My feet from stumbling.
9 I shall walk before Yahweh
In the [a,1]land of the living.
10 I [a]believed when I said,
"I am [b]greatly afflicted."
11 I [a]said in my alarm,
"[b]All men are liars."

12 What shall I [a]give
to Yahweh in return

---

**115:11** [a]Ps 22:23; 103:11; 135:20 [1]Or *reverence* **115:12** [a]Ps 98:3 **115:13** [a]Ps 103:11; 112:1; 128:1 [b]Rev 11:18; 19:5 [1]Or *reverence* **115:14** [a]Dt 1:11 **115:15** [a]Ge 1:1; Ne 9:6; Ps 96:5; 102:25; 121:2; 124:8; 134:3; 146:6; Ac 14:15; Rev 14:7 **115:16** [a]Ps 89:11 [b]Ps 8:6 **115:17** [a]Ps 6:5; 88:10-12; Is 38:18 [b]Ps 31:17 **115:18** [a]Ps 113:2; Da 2:20 [1]Or *Hallelujah!* ◆ **116:1** [a]Ps 18:1 [b]Ps 6:8; 66:19; Is 37:17; Da 9:18 **116:2** [a]Ps 17:6; 31:2; 40:1 **116:3** [a]Ps 18:4, 5 [1]Lit *straits* **116:4** [a]Ps 18:6; 118:5 [b]Ps 17:13; 22:20 [1]Or *deliver my soul!* **116:5** [a]Ps 86:15; 103:8 [b]Ezr 9:15; Ne 9:8; Ps 119:137; 145:17; Jer 12:1; Da 9:14 [c]Ex 34:6 **116:6** [a]Ps 19:7; Pr 1:4 [b]Ps 79:8; 142:6 **116:7** [a]Jer 6:16; Mt 11:29 [b]Ps 13:6; 142:7 **116:8** [a]Ps 49:15; 56:13; 86:13 **116:9** [a]Ps 27:13 [1]Lit *lands* **116:10** [a]2Co 4:13 [b]Ps 88:7 **116:11** [a]Ps 31:22 [b]Ps 62:9; Ro 3:4 **116:12** [a]2Chr 32:25; 1Th 3:9

For all His [b]bountiful
dealings [1]with me?
13 I shall lift up the [a]cup
of [1]salvation
And [b]call upon the name
of Yahweh.
14 I shall [a]pay my vows
to Yahweh,
Oh *may it be* [b]in the presence
of all His people.
15 [a]Precious in the sight
of Yahweh
Is the death of His holy ones.
16 O Yahweh, [1]surely I
am [a]Your slave,
I am Your slave, the [b]son
of Your maidservant,
You have [c]loosed my bonds.
17 To You I shall offer [a]a
sacrifice of thanksgiving,
And [b]call upon the name
of Yahweh.
18 I shall [a]pay my vows
to Yahweh,
Oh *may it be* in the presence
of all His people,
19 In the [a]courts of
the house of Yahweh,
In the midst of you,
O [b]Jerusalem.
[1]Praise Yah!

## PSALM 117

### *Yahweh's Lovingkindness Prevails*

1 [a]Praise Yahweh, all nations;
Laud Him, all peoples!
2 For His [a]lovingkindness
prevails over us,
And the [b,1]truth of Yahweh
is everlasting.
[2]Praise Yah!

## PSALM 118

### *Yahweh's Lovingkindness Endures Forever*

1 [a]Give thanks to Yahweh,
for [b]He is good;
For His lovingkindness
endures forever.
2 Oh let [a]Israel say,
"His lovingkindness
endures forever."
3 Oh let the [a]house
of Aaron say,
"His lovingkindness
endures forever."
4 Oh let those [a]who
[1]fear Yahweh say,
"His lovingkindness
endures forever."

5 From *my* [a]distress I
called upon Yah;
Yah answered me *and* [b]*set
me* in a large place.
6 Yahweh is [a]for me;
I will [b]not fear;
[c]What can man do to me?
7 Yahweh is for me
[a]among those who help me;
Therefore I will [b]look
*in triumph* on those
who hate me.
8 It is [a]better to take
refuge in Yahweh
Than to trust in man.

---

**116:12** [b]Ps 103:2 [1]Lit *upon* **116:13** [a]Ps 16:5 [b]Ps 80:18; 105:1 [1]Lit *salvations* **116:14** [a]Ps 50:14; 116:18 [b]*Ps 22:25* **116:15** [a]Ps 72:14 **116:16** [a]Ps 86:16; 119:125; 143:12 [b]Ps 86:16 [c]Ps 107:14 [1]Or *because* **116:17** [a]Lv 7:12; Ps 50:14 [b]Ps 116:13 **116:18** [a]Ps 116:14 **116:19** [a]Ps 92:13; 96:8; 135:2 [b]Ps 102:21 [1]Or *Hallelujah!* ◆ **117:1** [a]Ro 15:11 **117:2** [a]Ps 103:11 [b]Ps 100:5; 146:6 [1]Or *faithfulness* [2]Or *Hallelujah!* ◆ **118:1** [a]1Chr 16:8, 34; Ps 106:1; 107:1; Jer 33:11 [b]2Chr 5:13; 7:3; Ezr 3:11; Ps 100:5; 136:1-26 **118:2** [a]Ps 115:9 **118:3** [a]Ps 115:10 **118:4** [a]Ps 115:11 [1]Or *reverence* **118:5** [a]Ps 18:6; 86:7; 120:1 [b]Ps 18:19 **118:6** [a]Job 19:27; Ps 56:9; Heb 13:6 [b]Ps 23:4; 27:1 [c]Ps 56:4, 11 **118:7** [a]Ps 54:4 [b]Ps 54:7; 59:10 **118:8** [a]2Chr 32:7, 8; Ps 40:4; 108:12; Is 31:1, 3; 57:13; Jer 17:5

9 It is [a]better to take
refuge in Yahweh
Than to trust in nobles.

10 All nations [a]surrounded me;
In the name of Yahweh I will
surely [b]cut them off.
11 They [a]surrounded me, indeed,
they surrounded me;
In the name of Yahweh I
will surely cut them off.
12 They surrounded
me [a]like bees;
They were extinguished
as a [b]fire of thorns;
In the name of Yahweh I
will surely cut them off.
13 You [a]pushed me down
violently to *make* me fall,
But Yahweh [b]helped me.
14 [a]Yah is my strength
and song,
And He has become
[b]my salvation.

15 The sound of [a]joyful
shouting and salvation is
in the tents of the righteous;
The [b]right hand of Yahweh
does valiantly.
16 The [a]right hand
of Yahweh is exalted;
The right hand of Yahweh
does valiantly.
17 I [a]will not die; indeed
I will live,
And [b]recount
the works of Yah.
18 Yah has [a]disciplined
me severely,
But He has [b]not given
me over to death.

19 [a]Open to me the gates
of righteousness;
I shall enter through them,
I shall give thanks to Yah.
20 This is the gate of Yahweh;
The [a]righteous will
enter through it.
21 I shall give thanks to You,
for You have [a]answered me,
And You have [b]become
my salvation.

22 The [a]stone
which the builders rejected
Has become the chief
corner *stone*.
23 This is from Yahweh;
It is marvelous in our eyes.
24 This is the day
which Yahweh has made;
Let us [a]rejoice and
be glad in it.
25 O Yahweh, [a]save!
O Yahweh, [b]succeed!
26 [a]Blessed is the one who comes
in the name of Yahweh;
We have [b]blessed you
from the house of Yahweh.
27 [a]Yahweh is God, and He
has given us [b]light;
*Bind the festival sacrifice*
with cords [1]to the [c]horns
of the altar.

**118:9** [a]Ps 146:3 **118:10** [a]Ps 3:6; 88:17 [b]Ps 18:40 **118:11** [a]Ps 88:17 **118:12** [a]Dt 1:44 [b]Ps 58:9; Na 1:10 **118:13** [a]Ps 140:4 [b]Ps 86:17 **118:14** [a]Ex 15:2; Is 12:2 [b]Ps 27:1 **118:15** [a]Ps 68:3 [b]Ex 15:6; Ps 89:13; Lk 1:51 **118:16** [a]Ex 15:6; Ps 89:13 **118:17** [a]Ps 6:5; 116:8, 9; Hab 1:12 [b]Ps 73:28; 107:22 **118:18** [a]Ps 73:14; Jer 31:18; 1Co 11:32; 2Co 6:9 [b]Ps 16:10; 86:13 **118:19** [a]Is 26:2 **118:20** [a]Ps 15:1, 2; 24:3-6; 140:13; Is 35:8; Rev 22:14 **118:21** [a]Ps 116:1; 118:5 [b]Ps 118:14 **118:22** [a]Mt 21:42; Mk 12:10, 11; Lk 20:17; Ac 4:11; Eph 2:20; 1Pe 2:7 **118:24** [a]Ps 31:7 **118:25** [a]Ps 106:47 [b]Ps 122:6, 7 **118:26** [a]Mt 21:9; 23:39; Mk 11:9; Lk 13:35; 19:38; Jn 12:13 [b]Ps 129:8 **118:27** [a]1Ki 18:39 [b]Es 8:16; Ps 18:28; 27:1; 1Pe 2:9 [c]Ex 27:2
[1]Lit *unto*

28 [a]You are my God, and I
give thanks to You;
*You are* my God, [b]I exalt You.
29 [a]Give thanks to Yahweh,
for He is good;
For His lovingkindness
endures forever.

## PSALM 119

### *I Love Your Law, O Yahweh*

א *Aleph*

1 How blessed are those
whose way is [a,1]blameless,
Who [b]walk in the law
of Yahweh.
2 How blessed are those who
[a]observe His testimonies,
They [b]seek Him
[c]with all *their* heart.
3 They also do not [a]work
unrighteousness;
They walk in His ways.
4 You have [a]commanded *us*,
To keep Your
precepts [1]diligently.
5 Oh may my [a]ways
be established
To [b]keep Your statutes!
6 Then I [a]shall not be ashamed
When I look [1]upon all
Your commandments.
7 I shall [a]give thanks to You
with uprightness of heart,
When I learn Your
righteous judgments.
8 I shall keep Your statutes;
Do not [a]forsake me utterly!

ב *Beth*

9 How can a young man
keep his way pure?
By [a]keeping *it* according
to Your word.
10 With [a]all my heart I
have sought You;
Do not let me [b]stray
from Your commandments.
11 Your word I have [a]treasured
in my heart,
That I may not sin
against You.
12 Blessed are You, O Yahweh;
[a]Teach me Your statutes.
13 With my lips I have [a]recounted
All the [b]judgments
of Your mouth.
14 I have [a]rejoiced in the way
of Your testimonies,
[1]As much as in all riches.
15 I will [a]muse
upon Your precepts
And look upon [b]Your ways.
16 I shall [a,1]delight
in Your statutes;
I shall [b]not forget Your word.

ג *Gimel*

17 [a]Deal bountifully
with Your slave,
That I may live and
keep Your word.
18 Open my eyes,
that I may behold
Wonderful things
from Your law.

---

**118:28** [a]Ps 63:1; 140:6 [b]Ex 15:2; Is 25:1 **118:29** [a]Ps 118:1 ◆**119:1** [a]Ps 101:2, 6; Pr 11:20; 13:6 [b]Ps 128:1; Eze 11:20; 18:17; Mic 4:2 [1]Or *having integrity;* lit *complete* **119:2** [a]Ps 25:10; 99:7; 119:22, 168 [b]Dt 4:29; Ps 119:10 [c]Dt 6:5; 10:12; 11:13; 13:3; 30:2 **119:3** [a]1Jn 3:9; 5:18 **119:4** [a]Dt 4:13; Ne 9:13 [1]Or *carefully*, cf. Dt 4:9, 15 **119:5** [a]Ps 40:2; Pr 4:26 [b]Dt 12:1; 2Chr 7:17 **119:6** [a]Job 22:26; Ps 119:80 [1]Lit *to* **119:7** [a]Ps 119:62 **119:8** [a]Ps 38:21; 71:9, 18 **119:9** [a]1Ki 2:4; 8:25; 2Chr 6:16 **119:10** [a]2Chr 15:15; Ps 119:2, 145 [b]Ps 119:21, 118 **119:11** [a]Ps 37:31; 40:8; Lk 2:19, 51 **119:12** [a]Ps 119:26, 64, 108, 124, 135, 171 **119:13** [a]Ps 40:9 [b]Ps 119:72 **119:14** [a]Ps 119:111, 162 [1]Lit *As over all* **119:15** [a]Ps 1:2; 119:23, 48, 78, 97, 148 [b]Ps 25:4; 27:11; Is 58:2 **119:16** [a]Ps 1:2; 119:24, 35, 47, 70, 77, 92, 143, 174 [b]Ps 119:93 [1]Lit *delight myself* **119:17** [a]Ps 13:6; 116:7

19 I am a [a]sojourner in the earth;
Do not hide Your
commandments from me.
20 My soul is crushed
[a,1]with longing
For Your judgments
at all times.
21 You [a]rebuke the arrogant,
[1]the [b]cursed,
Who [c]stray from
Your commandments.
22 [a]Take away reproach and
contempt from me,
For I [b]observe Your
testimonies.
23 Even though [a]princes sit
*and* talk against me,
Your slave [b]muses
on Your statutes.
24 Your testimonies also
are my [a]delight;
*They are* [1]my counselors.

ד *Daleth*

25 My [a]soul clings to the dust;
[b]Revive me [c]according
to Your word.
26 I have recounted my ways,
and You have answered me;
[a]Teach me Your statutes.
27 Make me understand
the way of Your precepts,
So I will [a]muse on Your
wondrous deeds.
28 My [a]soul [1]weeps
because of grief;
[b]Raise me up according
to Your word.
29 Remove the false way from me,
And graciously grant
me Your law.
30 I have chosen the faithful way;
I have [1]placed Your
judgments *before me.*
31 I [a]cling to Your testimonies;
O Yahweh, do not put
me to shame!
32 I shall run the way of Your
commandments,
For You will [a]enlarge my heart.

ה *He*

33 [a]Instruct me, O Yahweh,
in the way of Your statutes,
That I may observe it to the end.
34 [a]Cause me to understand,
that I may [b]observe Your law
And keep it [c]with all *my* heart.
35 Cause me to walk in the [a]path
of Your commandments,
For I [b]delight in it.
36 [a]Cause my heart to incline
to Your testimonies
And not to [b]*dishonest* gain.
37 Cause my [a]eyes to turn
away from looking
at worthlessness,
And [b]revive me in Your ways.
38 [a]Cause Your [1]word to be
established for Your slave,
[2]As that which produces
fear for You.

---

**119:19** [a]Ge 47:9; Lv 25:23; 1Chr 29:15; Ps 39:12; 119:54; Heb 11:13 **119:20** [a]Ps 42:1, 2; 63:1; 84:2; 119:40, 131 [1]Lit *for* **119:21** [a]Ps 68:30 [b]Dt 27:26; Ps 37:22 [c]Ps 119:10, 118 [1]Or *Cursed are those who wander...* **119:22** [a]Ps 39:8; 119:39 [b]Ps 119:2 **119:23** [a]Ps 119:161 [b]Ps 119:15 **119:24** [a]Ps 119:16 [1]Lit *the men of my counsel* **119:25** [a]Ps 44:25 [b]Ps 119:37, 40, 88, 93, 107, 149, 154, 156, 159; 143:11 [c]Ps 119:65 **119:26** [a]Ps 25:4; 27:11; 86:11; 119:12 **119:27** [a]Ps 105:2; 145:5 **119:28** [a]Ps 22:14; 107:26 [b]Ps 20:2; 1Pe 5:10 [1]Lit *drops* **119:30** [1]Or *accounted Your ordinances worthy* **119:31** [a]Dt 11:22 **119:32** [a]1Ki 4:29; Is 60:5; 2Co 6:11, 13 **119:33** [a]Ps 119:5, 12 **119:34** [a]Ps 119:27, 73, 125, 144, 169 [b]1Chr 22:12; Eze 44:24 [c]Ps 119:2, 69 **119:35** [a]Ps 25:4; Is 40:14 [b]Ps 112:1; 119:16 **119:36** [a]1Ki 8:58 [b]Eze 33:31; Mk 7:21, 22; Lk 12:15; Heb 13:5 **119:37** [a]Is 33:15 [b]Ps 71:20; 119:25 **119:38** [a]2Sa 7:25 [1]Or *promise* [2]Lit *Which is for the fear of You*

39 [a]Cause my reproach
which I dread to pass away,
For Your judgments are good.
40 Behold, I [a]long
for Your precepts;
Revive me
in Your righteousness.

ו *Vav*

41 May Your [a]lovingkindnesses
also come to me, O Yahweh,
Your salvation [b]according
to Your [1]word;
42 So I will have an [a]answer for
him who [b]reproaches me,
For I trust in Your word.
43 And do not take away
the word of truth utterly
from my mouth,
For I [a,1]wait for Your judgments.
44 So I will [a]keep Your
law continually,
Forever and ever.
45 And I will [a]walk
in a wide place,
For I [b]seek Your precepts.
46 I will also speak of Your
testimonies [a]before kings
And I shall not be ashamed.
47 I shall [a,1]delight
in Your commandments,
Which I [b]love.
48 And I shall lift up my hands
to Your commandments,
Which I [a]love;
And I will [b]muse
on Your statutes.

ז *Zayin*

49 Remember the word
to Your slave,
[1]In which You have
made me wait.
50 This is my [a]comfort
in my affliction,
That Your word has [1]revived me.
51 The arrogant [a]utterly
scoff at me,
*Yet* I do not [b]turn aside
from Your law.
52 I have [a]remembered
Your judgments
from [1]of old, O Yahweh,
And comfort myself.
53 Burning [a]indignation
has seized me because
of the wicked,
Who [b]forsake Your law.
54 Your statutes have
become my songs
In the house of my [a]sojourning.
55 I [a]remember [b]in the night
Your name, O Yahweh,
So I keep Your law.
56 This has become mine,
[1]That I [a]observe Your precepts.

ח *Heth*

57 Yahweh is my [a]portion;
I have [1]promised
to [b]keep Your words.
58 I have [a]sought to please Your
face [b]with all *my* heart;
[c]Be gracious to me [d]according
to Your [1]word.

---

**119:39** [a]Ps 119:22 **119:40** [a]Ps 119:20 **119:41** [a]Ps 119:77 [b]Ps 119:58, 76, 116, 170 [1]Or *promise* **119:42** [a]Pr 27:11 [b]Ps 102:8; 119:39 **119:43** [a]Ps 119:49, 74, 81, 114, 147 [1]Or *hope in* **119:44** [a]Ps 119:33 **119:45** [a]Pr 4:12 [b]Ps 119:94, 155 **119:46** [a]Mt 10:18; Ac 26:1, 2 **119:47** [a]Ps 119:16 [b]Ps 119:97, 127, 159 [1]Lit *delight myself* **119:48** [a]Ps 119:97, 127, 159 [b]Ps 119:15 **119:49** [1]Lit *On* **119:50** [a]Job 6:10; Ro 15:4 [1]Or *preserved me alive* **119:51** [a]Job 30:1; Jer 20:7 [b]Job 23:11; Ps 44:18; 119:157 **119:52** [a]Ps 103:18 [1]Or *everlasting* **119:53** [a]Ex 32:19; Ezr 9:3; Ne 13:25; Ps 119:158 [b]Ps 89:30 **119:54** [a]Ge 47:9; Ps 119:19 **119:55** [a]Ps 63:6 [b]Ps 42:8; 92:2; 119:62; Is 26:9; Ac 16:25 **119:56** [a]Ps 119:22, 69, 100 [1]Or *Because* **119:57** [a]Ps 16:5; Lam 3:24 [b]Dt 33:9 [1]Lit *said that I would keep* **119:58** [a]1Ki 13:6 [b]Ps 119:2 [c]Ps 41:4; 56:1; 57:1 [d]Ps 119:41 [1]Or *promise*

59 I [a]thought upon my ways
And I turned my feet
to Your testimonies.
60 I hastened and did not delay
To keep
Your commandments.
61 The [a]cords of the wicked
have encircled me,
*But* I have [b]not forgotten
Your law.
62 At [a]midnight I shall rise
to give thanks to You
Because of Your
[b]righteous judgments.
63 I am a [a]companion of all
those who [1]fear You,
And of those who keep
Your precepts.
64 [a]The earth, O Yahweh, is full
of Your lovingkindness;
[b]Teach me Your statutes.

ט *Teth*

65 You have dealt well
with Your slave,
O Yahweh, according
to Your word.
66 Teach me good [a,1]discernment
and knowledge,
For I believe
in Your commandments.
67 [a]Before I was afflicted
I went astray,
But now I keep Your word.
68 You are [a]good and [b]do good;
[c]Teach me Your statutes.
69 The arrogant have [a]smeared
me with lying;
With all *my* heart I will
[b]observe Your precepts.
70 Their heart is [a,1]covered
with fat,
*But* I [b]delight in Your law.
71 It is [a]good for me
that I was afflicted,
That I may learn Your statutes.
72 The [a]law of Your mouth
is better to me
Than thousands of gold
and silver *pieces.*

י *Yodh*

73 [a]Your hands made me
and established me;
[b]Give me understanding,
that I may learn Your
commandments.
74 May those who [1]fear You
[a]see me and be glad,
Because I [b,2]wait for Your word.
75 I know, O Yahweh, that Your
judgments are [a]righteous,
And that [b]in faithfulness
You have afflicted me.
76 Oh may Your lovingkindness
[1]comfort me,
According to Your [2]word
to Your slave.
77 May [a]Your compassion come
to me that I may live,
For Your law is my [b]delight.
78 May [a]the arrogant be
ashamed, for they wrong
me [b]with lying;
*But* I shall [c]muse
on Your precepts.

---

**119:59** [a]Mk 14:72; Lk 15:17 **119:61** [a]Job 36:8; Ps 140:5 [b]Ps 119:83, 141, 153, 176 **119:62** [a]Ps 119:55 [b]Ps 119:7 **119:63** [a]Ps 101:6 [1]Or *reverence* **119:64** [a]Ps 33:5 [b]Ps 119:12 **119:66** [a]Php 1:9 [1]Or *judgment* **119:67** [a]Ps 119:71, 75; Jer 31:18, 19; Heb 12:5-11 **119:68** [a]Ps 86:5; 100:5; 106:1; 107:1; Mt 19:17 [b]Dt 8:16; 28:63; 30:5; Ps 125:4 [c]Ps 119:12 **119:69** [a]Job 13:4; Ps 109:2 [b]Ps 119:56 **119:70** [a]Dt 32:15; Job 15:27; Ps 17:10; Is 6:10; Jer 5:28; Ac 28:27 [b]Ps 119:16 [1]Lit *gross like fat* **119:71** [a]Ps 119:67, 75 **119:72** [a]Ps 19:10; 119:127; Pr 8:10, 11, 19 **119:73** [a]Job 10:8; 31:15; Ps 100:3; 138:8; 139:15, 16 [b]Ps 119:34 **119:74** [a]Ps 34:2; 35:27; 107:42 [b]Ps 119:43 [1]Or *reverence* [2]Or *hope in* **119:75** [a]Ps 119:138 [b]Heb 12:10 **119:76** [1]Lit *be for my comfort* [2]Or *promise* **119:77** [a]Ps 119:41 [b]Ps 119:16 **119:78** [a]Jer 50:32 [b]Ps 119:86 [c]Ps 119:15

79 May those who [1]fear
You turn to me,
And those who know
Your testimonies.
80 May my heart be [a,1]blameless
in Your statutes,
So that I will not
[b]be ashamed.

כ *Kaph*

81 My [a]soul fails *with longing*
for Your salvation;
I [b,1]wait for Your word.
82 My [a]eyes fail *with longing*
for Your [1]word,
Saying, “When will You
comfort me?”
83 For I [a]am like a wineskin
in the smoke,
But I do [b]not forget
Your statutes.
84 How many are the [a]days
of Your slave?
When will You [b]execute
judgment on those
who persecute me?
85 The arrogant have
[a]dug pits for me,
*Men* who are not
[1]in accord with Your law.
86 All Your commandments
are [a]faithful;
They have [b]persecuted me
with lying; [c]help me!
87 They almost made
an end of me
on the earth,
But as for me, I [a]did not
forsake Your precepts.
88 Revive me according
to Your lovingkindness,
So that I may keep
the testimony
of Your mouth.

ל *Lamedh*

89 [a]Forever, O Yahweh,
Your word stands
firm in heaven.
90 Your [a]faithfulness *endures*
[1]from generation
to generation;
You [b]established the earth,
and it [c]stands.
91 They stand this day
according to Your
[a]judgments,
For [b]all things are
Your slaves.
92 If Your law had not
been my [a]delight,
Then I would have perished
[b]in my affliction.
93 I will [a]never forget
Your precepts,
For by them You have
[b,1]revived me.
94 I am Yours, [a]save me;
For I have [b]sought
Your precepts.
95 The wicked [a]hope
for me—to destroy me;
I shall perceive
Your testimonies.
96 I have seen [1]a limit
to all perfection;
Your commandment is
exceedingly broad.

**119:79** [1]Or *reverence* **119:80** [a]Ps 119:1 [b]Ps 119:46 [1]Or *having integrity*; lit *complete* **119:81** [a]Ps 84:2 [b]Ps 119:43 [1]Or *hope in* **119:82** [a]Ps 69:3; 119:123; Is 38:14; Lam 2:11 [1]Or *promise* **119:83** [a]Job 30:30 [b]Ps 119:61 **119:84** [a]Ps 39:4 [b]Rev 6:10 **119:85** [a]Ps 7:15; 35:7; 57:6; Jer 18:22 [1]Lit *according to Your law* **119:86** [a]Ps 119:138 [b]Ps 35:19; 119:78, 161 [c]Ps 109:26 **119:87** [a]Is 58:2 **119:89** [a]Ps 89:2; 119:160; Is 40:8; Mt 24:35; 1Pe 1:25 **119:90** [a]Ps 36:5; 89:1, 2 [b]Ps 148:6 [c]Ecc 1:4 [1]Lit *to* **119:91** [a]Jer 31:35; 33:25 [b]Ps 104:2-4 **119:92** [a]Ps 119:16 [b]Ps 119:50 **119:93** [a]Ps 119:16, 83 [b]Ps 119:25 [1]Or *kept me alive* **119:94** [a]Ps 119:146 [b]Ps 119:45 **119:95** [a]Ps 40:14; Is 32:7 **119:96** [1]Lit *an end of*

מ *Mem*

97 Oh how I [a]love Your law!
It is my [b]meditation
all the day.
98 Your [a]commandments
make me wiser
than my enemies,
For they are [1]mine forever.
99 I have more insight
than all my teachers,
For Your testimonies are
my [a]meditation.
100 I perceive [a]more
than the aged,
Because I have [b]observed
Your precepts.
101 I have [a]restrained my feet
from every evil way,
That I may keep Your word.
102 I have not [a]turned aside
from Your judgments,
For You Yourself have
taught me.
103 How [a]sweet is Your
[1]word to my [2]taste!
*Sweeter* than honey
to my mouth!
104 From Your precepts I
[a]get perception;
Therefore I [b]hate
every false way.

נ *Nun*

105 Your word is a [a]lamp
to my feet
And a light to my path.
106 I have [a]sworn and I
have confirmed,
To keep Your
righteous judgments.
107 I am exceedingly [a]afflicted;
O Yahweh, [b,1]revive me
according to Your word.
108 Oh be pleased
with the [a]freewill offerings
of my mouth, O Yahweh,
And [b]teach me
Your judgments.
109 My [a]soul is continually
[1]in my hand,
Yet I do not [b]forget
Your law.
110 The wicked have [a]laid
a snare for me,
Yet I have not [b]wandered
from Your precepts.
111 I have [a]inherited Your
testimonies forever,
For they are the [b]joy
of my heart.
112 I have [a]inclined my heart
to do Your statutes
Forever, [b]to the end.

ס *Samekh*

113 I hate those
who are [a]double-minded,
But I love Your [b]law.
114 You are my [a]hiding place
and my [b]shield;
I [c,1]wait for Your word.
115 [a]Depart from me,
evildoers,
That I may [b]observe
the commandments
of my God.

---

**119:97** [a]Ps 119:47, 48, 127, 163, 165 [b]Ps 1:2; 119:15 **119:98** [a]Dt 4:6; Ps 119:130 [1]Or *with me* **119:99** [a]Ps 119:15 **119:100** [a]Job 32:7-9 [b]Ps 119:22, 56 **119:101** [a]Pr 1:15 **119:102** [a]Dt 17:20; Jos 23:6; 1Ki 15:5 **119:103** [a]Ps 19:10; Pr 8:11; 24:13, 14 [1]Or *promise* [2]Lit *palate* **119:104** [a]Ps 119:130 [b]Ps 119:128 **119:105** [a]Pr 6:23 **119:106** [a]Ne 10:29 **119:107** [a]Ps 119:25, 50 [b]Ps 119:25 [1]Or *keep me alive* **119:108** [a]Hos 14:2; Heb 13:15 [b]Ps 119:12 **119:109** [a]Jdg 12:3; Job 13:14 [b]Ps 119:16 [1]In danger **119:110** [a]Ps 91:3; 140:5; 141:9 [b]Ps 119:10 **119:111** [a]Dt 33:4 [b]Ps 119:14, 162 **119:112** [a]Ps 119:36 [b]Ps 119:33 **119:113** [a]1Ki 18:21; Jas 1:8; 4:8 [b]Ps 119:47 **119:114** [a]Ps 31:20; 32:7; 61:4; 91:1 [b]Ps 84:9 [c]Ps 119:74 [1]Or *hope in* **119:115** [a]Ps 6:8; 139:19; Mt 7:23 [b]Ps 119:22

116 [a]Sustain me according
to Your [1]word,
that I may live;
And [b]do not put me to shame
because of my hope.
117 Uphold me that I
may be [a]saved,
That I may [b]have regard for
Your statutes continually.
118 You have [1]rejected all
those [a]who stray
from Your statutes,
For their deceitfulness is a lie.
119 You [1]remove all the wicked
of the earth *like* [a]dross;
Therefore I [b]love
Your testimonies.
120 My flesh [a,1]quakes
for dread of You,
And I am [b]afraid
of Your judgments.

ע *Ayin*

121 I have [a]done justice
and righteousness;
Do not leave me
to my oppressors.
122 Be for Your slave
a [a]guarantee for good;
Do not let the arrogant
[b]oppress me.
123 My [a]eyes fail *with longing*
for Your salvation
And for Your righteous [1]word.
124 Deal with Your slave
[a]according to Your
lovingkindness
And [b]teach me Your statutes.
125 [a]I am Your slave; [b]give
me understanding,
That I may know
Your testimonies.
126 It is time for Yahweh to [a]act,
*For* they have broken
Your law.
127 Therefore I [a]love
Your commandments
Above gold, even
above fine gold.
128 Therefore I deem all *Your*
[a]precepts concerning
everything to be right,
I [b]hate every false way.

פ *Pe*

129 Your testimonies
are [a]wonderful;
Therefore my soul
[b]observes them.
130 The [a]unfolding of Your
words gives light;
It gives [b]understanding
to the simple.
131 I [a]opened my mouth
wide and [b]panted,
For I [c]longed for Your
commandments.
132 [a]Turn to me and be
gracious to me,
According to *Your*
judgment [1]for those
who love Your name.
133 Establish my [a]steps
in Your [1]word,
And do not let any wickedness
[b]overpower me.

**119:116** [a]Ps 37:17, 24; 54:4 [b]Ps 25:2, 20; 31:1, 17; Ro 5:5; 9:33; Php 1:20 [1]Or *promise* **119:117** [a]Ps 12:5; Pr 29:25 [b]Ps 119:6, 15 **119:118** [a]Ps 119:10, 21 [1]Lit *made light of* **119:119** [a]Is 1:22, 25; Eze 22:18, 19 [b]Ps 119:47 [1]Lit *caused to cease* **119:120** [a]Job 4:14; Hab 3:16 [b]Ps 119:161 [1]Lit *bristles up from* **119:121** [a]2Sa 8:15; Job 29:14 **119:122** [a]Job 17:3; Heb 7:22 [b]Ps 119:134 **119:123** [a]Ps 119:82 [1]Or *promise* **119:124** [a]Ps 51:1; 106:45; 109:26; 119:88, 149, 159 [b]Ps 119:12 **119:125** [a]Ps 116:16 [b]Ps 119:27 **119:126** [a]Jer 18:23; Eze 31:11 **119:127** [a]Ps 19:10; 119:47 **119:128** [a]Ps 19:8 [b]Ps 119:104 **119:129** [a]Ps 119:18 [b]Ps 119:22 **119:130** [a]Pr 6:23 [b]Ps 19:7 **119:131** [a]Job 29:23; Ps 81:10 [b]Ps 42:1 [c]Ps 119:20 **119:132** [a]Ps 25:16; 106:4 [1]Lit *to* **119:133** [a]Ps 17:5 [b]Ps 19:13; Ro 6:12 [1]Or *promise*

134 [a]Redeem me
from the oppression of man,
That I may keep
Your precepts.
135 [a]Make Your face shine
upon Your slave,
And [b]teach me Your statutes.
136 My eyes [1]shed [a]streams
of water,
Because they [b]do not
keep Your law.

צ *Tsadhe*

137 [a]Righteous are You,
O Yahweh,
And upright are
Your judgments.
138 In [a]righteousness, You
have commanded
Your testimonies
And in exceeding
[b]faithfulness.
139 My [a]zeal has [1]consumed me,
Because my adversaries have
forgotten Your words.
140 Your [a,1]word is
exceedingly refined,
Therefore Your slave [b]loves it.
141 I am small and [a]despised,
*Yet* I do not [b]forget
Your precepts.
142 Your righteousness
is an everlasting
righteousness,
And [a]Your law is truth.
143 Trouble and anguish
have found me,
*Yet* Your commandments
are my [a]delight.
144 Righteous are Your
[a]testimonies forever;
[b]Give me understanding
that I may live.

ק *Qoph*

145 I called [a]with all my heart;
answer me, O Yahweh!
I will [b]observe Your statutes.
146 I called to You; [a]save me
And I shall keep
Your testimonies.
147 I [a,1]eagerly greet the dawn
and cry for help;
I [2]wait for Your words.
148 My eyes [1]eagerly greet
the [a]night watches,
That I may [b]muse
on Your [2]word.
149 Hear my voice [a]according
to Your lovingkindness;
[b]O Yahweh, revive
me, according to
Your judgments.
150 [1]Near are those who
pursue wickedness;
They are far
from Your law.
151 [a]Near are You, O Yahweh,
And all Your commandments
are [b]truth.
152 Of old I have [a]known
from Your testimonies
That You have founded
them [b]forever.

**119:134** [a]Ps 119:84; 142:6; Lk 1:74 **119:135** [a]Nu 6:25; Ps 4:6; 31:16; 67:1; 80:3, 7, 19 [b]Ps 119:12
**119:136** [a]Jer 9:1, 18; 14:17; Lam 3:48 [b]Ps 119:158 [1]Lit *run down* **119:137** [a]Ezr 9:15; Ne 9:33; Ps 116:5; 129:4; 145:17; Jer 12:1; Lam 1:18; Da 9:7, 14 **119:138** [a]Ps 19:7-9; 119:144, 172 [b]Ps 119:86, 90 **119:139** [a]Ps 69:9; Jn 2:17 [1]Lit *destroyed* **119:140** [a]Ps 12:6; 19:8 [b]Ps 119:47 [1]Or *promise*
**119:141** [a]Ps 22:6 [b]Ps 119:61 **119:142** [a]Ps 19:9; 119:151, 160 **119:143** [a]Ps 119:24 **119:144** [a]Ps 19:9 [b]Ps 119:27 **119:145** [a]Ps 119:10 [b]Ps 119:22, 55 **119:146** [a]Ps 3:7 **119:147** [a]Ps 5:3; 57:8; 108:2 [1]Lit *approach the dawn* [2]Or *hope in* **119:148** [a]Ps 63:6 [b]Ps 119:15 [1]Lit *approach the night watches* [2]Or *promise* **119:149** [a]Ps 119:124 [b]Ps 119:25 **119:150** [1]Lit *They draw near* **119:151** [a]Ps 34:18; 145:18; Is 50:8 [b]Ps 119:142 **119:152** [a]Ps 119:125 [b]Ps 119:89; Lk 21:33

*ר Resh*

153 [a]See my [b]affliction
and rescue me,
For I do not [c]forget Your law.
154 [a]Plead my cause and
[b]redeem me;
Revive me according
to Your [1]word.
155 Salvation is [a]far
from the wicked,
For they [b]do not seek
Your statutes.
156 [a]Many are Your
[1]compassions, O Yahweh;
Revive me according
to Your judgments.
157 Many are my [a]persecutors
and my adversaries,
*Yet* I do not [b]turn aside
from Your testimonies.
158 I see the [a]treacherous
and [b]loathe *them*,
Those who do not
keep Your [1]word.
159 See how I [a]love Your precepts;
[b]O Yahweh, revive me
according to Your
lovingkindness.
160 The [a]sum of Your
word is [b]truth,
And every one of Your
righteous judgments
[c]is everlasting.

*שׂ Sin / שׁ Shin*

161 [a]Princes persecute me
without cause,
But my heart [b]is in dread
of Your words.
162 I [a]rejoice at Your [1]word,
As one who [b]finds
much spoil.
163 I [a]hate and abhor lying,
*But* I [b]love Your law.
164 Seven times a day
I praise You,
Because of Your
[a]righteous judgments.
165 Those who love Your law
have [a]much peace,
And [b,1]nothing causes
them to stumble.
166 I [a]hope for Your salvation,
O Yahweh,
And I do
Your commandments.
167 My [a]soul keeps
Your testimonies,
And I [b]love them exceedingly.
168 I [a]keep Your precepts and
Your testimonies,
For all my [b]ways are
before You.

*ת Tav*

169 Let my [a]cry of lamentation
come near
before You, O Yahweh;
[b]Give me understanding
[c]according to Your word.
170 Let my [a]supplication
come before You;
[b]Deliver me according
to Your [1]word.

---

**119:153** [a]Lam 5:1 [b]Ps 119:50 [c]Ps 119:16; Pr 3:1; Hos 4:6 **119:154** [a]1Sa 24:15; Ps 35:1; Mic 7:9 [b]Ps 119:134 [1]Or *promise* **119:155** [a]Job 5:4 [b]Ps 119:45, 94 **119:156** [a]2Sa 24:14 [1]Or *mercies* **119:157** [a]Ps 7:1; 119:86, 161 [b]Ps 119:51 **119:158** [a]Is 21:2; 24:16 [b]Ps 139:21 [1]Or *promise* **119:159** [a]Ps 119:47 [b]Ps 119:25 **119:160** [a]Ps 139:17 [b]Ps 119:142 [c]Ps 119:89, 152 **119:161** [a]1Sa 24:11; 26:18; Ps 119:23 [b]Ps 119:120 **119:162** [a]Ps 119:14, 111 [b]1Sa 30:16; Is 9:3 [1]Or *promise* **119:163** [a]Ps 31:6; 119:104, 128; Pr 13:5 [b]Ps 119:47 **119:164** [a]Ps 119:7, 160 **119:165** [a]Ps 37:11; Pr 3:2; Is 26:3; 32:17 [b]Pr 3:23; Is 63:13; 1Jn 2:10 [1]Lit *they have no stumbling block* **119:166** [a]Ge 49:18; Ps 119:81, 174 **119:167** [a]Ps 119:129 [b]Ps 119:47 **119:168** [a]Ps 119:22 [b]Job 24:23; Ps 139:3; Pr 5:21 **119:169** [a]Job 16:18; Ps 18:6; 102:1 [b]Ps 119:27, 144 [c]Ps 119:65, 154 **119:170** [a]Ps 28:2; 130:2; 140:6; 143:1 [b]Ps 22:20; 31:2; 59:1 [1]Or *promise*

171 Let my [a]lips pour forth praise,
For You [b]teach me
Your statutes.
172 Let my [a]tongue answer
with Your [1]word,
For all Your [b]commandments
are righteous.
173 Let Your [a]hand be
[1]ready to help me,
For I have [b]chosen
Your precepts.
174 I [a]long for Your salvation,
O Yahweh,
And Your law is my [b]delight.
175 Let my [a]soul live
that it may praise You,
And let Your judgments
help me.
176 I have [a]wandered off
like a lost sheep;
search for Your slave,
For I have [b]not forgotten
Your commandments.

## PSALM 120

### *O Yahweh, Deliver My Soul*

A Song of [†]Ascents.

1 [a]In my distress I called
to Yahweh,
And He answered me.
2 O Yahweh, deliver my
soul from a [a]lying lip,
From a [b]deceitful tongue.
3 What shall He give to you, and
what shall He add to you,
O [a]deceitful tongue?
4 [a]Sharp arrows of the warrior,
With the *burning* [b]coals
of the broom tree.
5 Woe is me, for I sojourn
in [a]Meshech,
*For* I dwell
among the [b]tents of [c]Kedar!
6 Too long has my soul
had its dwelling
With those who [a]hate peace.
7 I [a]am *for* peace,
but when I speak,
They are [b]for war.

## PSALM 121

### *My Help Comes from Yahweh*

A Song of Ascents.

1 I will [a]lift up my eyes
to [b]the mountains;
From where shall my
help come?
2 My [a]help *comes* from Yahweh,
Who [b]made heaven and earth.
3 [1]He will not [a]allow your
foot to stumble;
[2]He who [b]keeps you
will not slumber.
4 Behold, He who keeps Israel
Will not slumber and
will not sleep.

5 Yahweh is your [a]keeper;
Yahweh is your [b]shade
on your right hand.
6 The [a]sun will not
strike you by day,
Nor the moon by night.

**119:171** [a]Ps 51:15; 63:3 [b]Ps 94:12; 119:12; Is 2:3; Mic 4:2 **119:172** [a]Ps 51:14 [b]Ps 119:138 [1]Or *promise* **119:173** [a]Ps 37:24; 73:23 [b]Jos 24:22; Lk 10:42 [1]Lit *to help me* **119:174** [a]Ps 119:166 [b]Ps 119:16, 24 **119:175** [a]Is 55:3 **119:176** [a]Is 53:6; Jer 50:6; Mt 18:12; Lk 15:4 [b]Ps 119:16 ◆ **120:TITLE** [†]Ex 34:24; 1Ki 12:27 **120:1** [a]Ps 18:6; 66:14; 102:2; Jon 2:2 **120:2** [a]Ps 109:2; Pr 12:22 [b]Ps 52:4; Zep 3:13 **120:3** [a]Ps 52:4; Zep 3:13 **120:4** [a]Ps 45:5; Pr 25:18; Is 5:28 [b]Ps 140:10 **120:5** [a]Ge 10:2; 1Chr 1:5; Eze 27:13; 38:2, 3; 39:1 [b]SS 1:5 [c]Ge 25:13; Is 21:16; 60:7; Jer 2:10; 49:28; Eze 27:21 **120:6** [a]Ps 35:20 **120:7** [a]Ps 109:4 [b]Ps 55:21 ◆ **121:1** [a]Ps 123:1; Is 40:26 [b]Ps 87:1 **121:2** [a]Ps 124:8 [b]Ps 115:15 **121:3** [a]1Sa 2:9; Ps 66:9 [b]Ps 41:2; 127:1; Is 27:3 [1]Lit *May He not allow...* [2]Or *May He who keeps you not slumber* **121:5** [a]Ps 91:4 [b]Ps 16:8; 91:1; Is 25:4 **121:6** [a]Ps 91:5; Is 49:10; Jon 4:8; Rev 7:16

7 Yahweh will [a]keep you
from all evil;
He will keep your soul.
8 Yahweh will [a]keep your
going out and your
coming in
[b]From now until forever.

## PSALM 122

***Go to the House of Yahweh***

A Song of Ascents. Of David.

1 I was glad when they
said to me,
"Let us [a]go to the house
of Yahweh."
2 Our feet are standing
Within your [a]gates,
O Jerusalem,
3 Jerusalem, which is [a]built
As a city [b]joined altogether;
4 To which the tribes, the tribes
of Yah, [a]go up—
A testimony for Israel—
To give thanks
to the name of Yahweh.
5 For there, [a]thrones sit
for judgment,
The thrones of the house
of David.

6 Pray for the [a]peace
of Jerusalem:
"May they prosper
who [b]love you.
7 "May peace be
within your [a]walls,
And tranquility
within your [b]palaces."
8 For the sake of my [a]brothers
and my friends,
I will now say, "[b]May
peace be within you."
9 For the sake of the house
of Yahweh our God,
I will [a]seek your good.

## PSALM 123

***To You I Lift Up My Eyes***

A Song of Ascents.

1 To You I [a]lift up my eyes,
The One [b]enthroned
in the heavens!
2 Behold, as the eyes
of [a]slaves *look* to the hand
of their master,
As the eyes of a servant-girl
to the hand of her mistress,
So our [b]eyes *look*
to Yahweh our God,
Until He is gracious to us.

3 [a]Be gracious to us, O Yahweh,
be gracious to us,
For we are greatly saturated
[b]with contempt.
4 Our soul is greatly saturated
With the [a]mockery
of [b]those who are at ease,
*And* with the [c]contempt
of the proud.

## PSALM 124

***Yahweh Was on Our Side***

A Song of Ascents. Of David.

1 "[a]Had it not been Yahweh
who was on our side,"
[b]Let Israel now say,
2 "Had it not been Yahweh
who was on our side
When men rose up against us,

---

**121:7** [a]Ps 41:2; 91:10-12 **121:8** [a]Dt 28:6 [b]Ps 113:2; 115:18 ◆ **122:1** [a]Ps 42:4; Is 2:3; Mic 4:2; Zec 8:21 **122:2** [a]Ps 9:14; 87:2; 116:19; Jer 7:2 **122:3** [a]Ps 48:13; 147:2 [b]2Sa 5:9; Ne 4:6 **122:4** [a]Ex 23:17; Dt 16:16; Ps 84:5 **122:5** [a]Dt 17:8; 2Chr 19:8; Ps 89:29 **122:6** [a]Ps 29:11; Jer 29:7 [b]Ps 102:14 **122:7** [a]Ps 51:18; Is 62:6 [b]Ps 48:3, 13; Jer 17:27 **122:8** [a]Ps 133:1 [b]1Sa 25:6; Jn 20:19 **122:9** [a]Ne 2:10; Es 10:3 ◆ **123:1** [a]Ps 121:1; 141:8 [b]Ps 2:4; 11:4 **123:2** [a]Pr 27:18; Mal 1:6 [b]Ps 25:15 **123:3** [a]Ps 4:1; 51:1 [b]Ne 4:4; Ps 119:22 **123:4** [a]Ne 2:19; Ps 79:4 [b]Job 12:5; Is 32:9, 11; Am 6:1 [c]Ne 4:4; Ps 119:22 ◆ **124:1** [a]Ps 94:17 [b]Ps 129:1

3 Then they would have
[a]swallowed us alive,
When their [b]anger was
kindled against us;
4 Then the [a]waters would
have flowed over us,
The stream would have
[1]swept over our soul;
5 Then the [a]raging waters would
have [1]swept over our soul."

6 Blessed be Yahweh,
Who has not given us to be
[a]prey for their teeth.
7 Our soul has [a]escaped
[b]as a bird out of the [c]snare
of the trapper;
The snare is broken and
we have escaped.
8 Our [a]help is in the name
of Yahweh,
Who [b]made heaven and earth.

## PSALM 125

### *Yahweh Surrounds His People*

A Song of Ascents.

1 Those who trust in Yahweh
Are as Mount Zion,
which [a]will not be shaken
but [b]will abide forever.
2 As the mountains
surround Jerusalem,
So [a]Yahweh surrounds
His people
[b]From now until forever.
3 For the [a]scepter of wickedness
shall not rest upon
the [1]land of the righteous,
So that the righteous [b]would
not send forth their hands
in unrighteousness.
4 [a]Do good, O Yahweh,
to those who are good
And to those who are
[b]upright in their hearts.
5 But as for those who
[a]turn aside to their
[b]crooked ways,
Yahweh will lead them away
with the [c]workers of iniquity.
[d]Peace be upon Israel.

## PSALM 126

### *Those Who Sow in Tears Shall Reap with Joy*

A Song of Ascents.

1 When Yahweh [a,1]returned
[2]the captive ones of Zion,
We were [b]like those
who dream.
2 Then our [a]mouth was
filled with laughter
And our [b]tongue
with shouts of joy;
Then they said
among the nations,
"Yahweh has [c]done great
things for them."
3 Yahweh has done great
things for us;
We are [a]glad.

4 Restore our captivity,
O Yahweh,
As the [a,1]streams in the Negev.

**124:3** [a]Nu 16:30; Ps 35:25; 56:1; 57:3; Pr 1:12 [b]Ge 39:19; Ps 138:7 **124:4** [a]Job 22:11; Ps 18:16; 32:6; 69:2; 144:7 [1]Or *passed over* **124:5** [a]Job 38:11 [1]Or *passed over* **124:6** [a]Ps 27:2; Pr 30:14 **124:7** [a]Ps 141:10; 2Co 11:33; Heb 11:34 [b]Pr 6:5 [c]Ps 91:3; Hos 9:8 **124:8** [a]Ps 121:2 [b]Ge 1:1; Ps 134:3 ◆ **125:1** [a]Ps 46:5 [b]Ps 61:7; Ecc 1:4 **125:2** [a]Zec 2:5 [b]Ps 121:8 **125:3** [a]Ps 89:22; Pr 22:8; Is 14:5 [b]1Sa 24:10; Ps 55:20; Ac 12:1 [1]Lit *lot* **125:4** [a]Ps 119:68 [b]Ps 7:10; 11:2; 32:11; 36:10; 94:15 **125:5** [a]Job 23:11; Ps 40:4; 101:3 [b]Pr 2:15; Is 59:8 [c]Ps 92:7; 94:4 [d]Ps 128:6; Ga 6:16 ◆ **126:1** [a]Ps 85:1; Jer 29:14; Hos 6:11 [b]Ac 12:9 [1]Or *restored*, cf. Ps 126:4 [2]Or *those who returned to* **126:2** [a]Job 8:21 [b]Ps 51:14; Is 35:6 [c]1Sa 12:24; Ps 71:19; Lk 1:49 **126:3** [a]Is 25:9; Zep 3:14 **126:4** [a]Is 35:6; 43:19 [1]Lit *stream-beds*

5 Those who sow in [a]tears shall
reap with [b]shouts of joy.
6 He who goes to and fro weeping,
carrying *his* bag of seed,
Shall indeed come again
with a shout of joy, carrying
his sheaves *with him.*

## PSALM 127

***Unless Yahweh Builds the House***

A Song of Ascents. Of Solomon.

1 Unless Yahweh [a]builds
the house,
They labor in vain who build it;
Unless Yahweh
[b]watches the city,
The watchman keeps
awake in vain.
2 It is in vain that you
rise up early,
That you sit out late,
O you who [a]eat the bread
of [1]painful labors;
*For* in this manner, He gives
[b]sleep to His [c]beloved.

3 Behold, [a]children are [1]an
inheritance of Yahweh,
The [b]fruit of the womb
is a reward.
4 Like arrows in the hand
of a [a]warrior,
So are the children
of one's youth.
5 How [a]blessed is the man who
fills his quiver with them;
[b]They will not be ashamed
When they [c]speak
with enemies [d]in the gate.

## PSALM 128

***Blessed Is Everyone Who Fears Yahweh***

A Song of Ascents.

1 [a]How blessed is everyone
who fears Yahweh,
Who [b]walks in His ways.
2 When you shall [a]eat
of the [b,1]fruit of the labor
of your hands,
How blessed will you be and
[c]how well will it be for you.
3 Your wife shall be
like a [a]fruitful vine
In the innermost parts
of your house,
Your children like [b]olive plants
All around your table.
4 Behold, for thus shall
the man be blessed
Who fears Yahweh.

5 [a]May Yahweh bless
you [b]from Zion,
That you may see
the prosperity of Jerusalem
all the days of your life.
6 Indeed, may you see your
[a]children's children.
[b]Peace be upon Israel!

## PSALM 129

***Yahweh Has Cut the Cords of the Wicked***

A Song of Ascents.

1 "[1]Many times they have
[a,2]assailed me
from my [b]youth up,"
[c]Let Israel now say,

---

**126:5** [a]Ps 80:5; Jer 31:9, 16; Lam 1:2 [b]Is 35:10; 51:11; 61:7; Ga 6:9 ◆**127:1** [a]Ps 78:69 [b]Ps 121:4 **127:2** [a]Ge 3:17, 19 [b]Job 11:18, 19; Pr 3:24; Ecc 5:12 [c]Ps 60:5 [1]Lit *toils* **127:3** [a]Ge 33:5; 48:4; Jos 24:3, 4; Ps 113:9 [b]Dt 7:13; 28:4; Is 13:18 [1]Or *a heritage* **127:4** [a]Ps 112:2; 120:4 **127:5** [a]Ps 128:2, 3 [b]Pr 27:11 [c]Is 29:21; Am 5:12 [d]Ge 34:20 ◆**128:1** [a]Ps 112:1; 119:1 [b]Ps 119:3 **128:2** [a]Is 3:10 [b]Ps 109:11; Hag 2:17 [c]Ecc 8:12; Eph 6:3 [1]Lit *labor* **128:3** [a]Eze 19:10 [b]Ps 52:8; 144:12 **128:5** [a]Ps 134:3 [b]Ps 20:2; 135:21 **128:6** [a]Ge 48:11; 50:23; Job 42:16; Ps 103:17; Pr 17:6 [b]Ps 125:5 ◆**129:1** [a]Ex 1:11; Jdg 3:8; Ps 88:15 [b]Is 47:12; Jer 2:2; 22:21; Eze 16:22; Hos 2:15; 11:1 [c]Ps 124:1 [1]Lit *Much* [2]Lit *showed hostility toward*

2 “ [1]Many times they have
[2]assailed me
from my youth up;
Yet they have [a]not
prevailed against me.
3 “The plowers plowed
upon my back;
They lengthened
their furrows.”
4 Yahweh [a]is righteous;
He has cut up the [b]cords
of the wicked.

5 Let all who [a]hate Zion
Be [b]put to shame and
turned backward;
6 Let them be like [a]grass
upon the rooftops,
Which dries up
before it [1]grows up;
7 With which the reaper
does not fill his [1]hand,
Nor the binder of sheaves
the [a]fold of his garment;
8 And those who pass
by will not say,
“The [a]blessing of Yahweh
be upon you;
We bless you in the name
of Yahweh.”

## PSALM 130

### *Yahweh Will Redeem Israel*

A Song of Ascents.

1 Out of the [a]depths I called
to You, O Yahweh.
2 O Lord, [a]hear my voice!
Let [b]Your ears be attentive
To the [c]voice
of my supplications.
3 If You should keep
iniquities, O Yah,
O Lord, who could [a]stand?
4 But with You
there is [a]forgiveness,
That You may be [b]feared.

5 I hope for Yahweh, my
[a]soul does hope,
And [b]for His word do
I wait.
6 My soul *waits*
for the Lord
More than the watchmen
[a]for the morning,
The watchmen
for the morning.
7 O Israel, [a]wait for Yahweh;
For with Yahweh there
is [b]lovingkindness,
And with Him is
[c]abundant redemption.
8 And it is He who will
[a]redeem Israel
From all his iniquities.

## PSALM 131

### *I Have Quieted My Soul*

A Song of Ascents. Of David.

1 O Yahweh, my heart is not
[a]exalted, and my eyes
are not [b]raised high;
And I do not [1]involve myself
in [c]great matters,
Or in matters [d]too
marvelous for me.

**129:2** [a]Jer 1:19; 15:20; 20:11; Mt 16:18; 2Co 4:8, 9 [1]Lit *Much* [2]Lit *showed hostility toward* **129:4** [a]Ps 119:137 [b]Ps 140:5 **129:5** [a]Mic 4:11 [b]Ps 70:3; 71:13 **129:6** [a]2Ki 19:26; Ps 37:2; Is 37:27 [1]Lit *draws out* **129:7** [a]Ps 79:12 [1]Lit *palm* **129:8** [a]Ru 2:4; Ps 118:26 ◆ **130:1** [a]Ps 42:7; 69:2; Lam 3:55 **130:2** [a]Ps 64:1; 119:149 [b]2Chr 6:40; Ne 1:6, 11 [c]Ps 28:2; 140:6 **130:3** [a]Ps 76:7; 143:2; Na 1:6; Mal 3:2; Rev 6:17 **130:4** [a]Ex 34:7; Ne 9:17; Ps 86:5; Is 55:7; Da 9:9 [b]1Ki 8:39, 40; Jer 33:8, 9 **130:5** [a]Ps 27:14; 33:20; 40:1; 62:1, 5; Is 8:17; 26:8 [b]Ps 119:74, 81 **130:6** [a]Ps 63:6; 119:147 **130:7** [a]Ps 131:3 [b]Ps 86:5; 103:4 [c]Ps 111:9; Ro 3:24; Eph 1:7 **130:8** [a]Ps 103:3, 4; Lk 1:68; Tit 2:14 ◆ **131:1** [a]2Sa 22:28; Ps 101:5; Is 2:12; 52:13; Zep 3:11 [b]Pr 30:13; Is 5:15; 52:13 [c]Jer 45:5; Ro 12:16 [d]Job 42:3; Ps 139:6 [1]Lit *go after, walk*

2 Surely I have [a]soothed
and quieted my soul,
Like a weaned [b]child
with his mother,
Like a weaned child is
my soul [1]within me.
3 O Israel, [a]wait for Yahweh
[b]From now until forever.

## PSALM 132

### *Yahweh Has Chosen Zion*

A Song of Ascents.

1 Remember, O Yahweh,
on David's behalf,
All [a]his affliction;
2 How he swore to Yahweh
And vowed to [a]the
Mighty One of Jacob,
3 "Surely I will not come
into [a,1]my house,
Nor [2]lie in the [3]comfort
of my bed;
4 I will not [a]give sleep to my eyes
Or slumber to my eyelids,
5 Until I find a [a]place for Yahweh,
[1]A dwelling place for [b]the
Mighty One of Jacob."

6 Behold, we heard of it
in [a]Ephrathah,
We found it
in the [b]fields of [1]Jaar.
7 Let us come into His
[a,1]dwelling place;
Let us [b]worship
at the [c]footstool of His feet.
8 [a]Arise, O Yahweh,
to Your [b]resting place,
You and the ark
of Your [c]strength.
9 Let Your priests be [a]clothed
with righteousness,
And let Your [b]holy
ones sing for joy.

10 For the sake of David
Your servant,
Do not turn away the face
of Your [a]anointed.
11 Yahweh has [a]sworn to David
A truth from which He
will not turn back:
"[b]Of the fruit of your [1]body I
will set upon your throne.
12 "If your sons keep
My covenant
And My testimony
which I will teach them,
Their sons also shall [a]sit
upon your throne forever."

13 For Yahweh has [a]chosen Zion;
He has [b]desired it
for His habitation.
14 "This is My [a]resting
place forever;
Here I will [b]inhabit,
for I have desired it.
15 "I will abundantly [a]bless
her provision;
I will [b]satisfy her needy
with bread.
16 "Her [a]priests also I will
clothe with salvation,
And her [a]holy ones will
sing loudly for joy.

---

**131:2** [a]Ps 62:1 [b]Mt 18:3; 1Co 14:20 [1]Or *upon* **131:3** [a]Ps 130:7 [b]Ps 113:2 ◆ **132:1** [a]Ge 49:24; 2Sa 16:12 **132:2** [a]Ge 49:24; Is 49:26; 60:16 **132:3** [a]Job 21:28 [1]Lit *tabernacle of my house* [2]Lit *go up into* [3]Lit *couch* **132:4** [a]Pr 6:4 **132:5** [a]1Ki 8:17; 1Chr 22:7; Ps 26:8; Ac 7:46 [b]Ps 132:2 [1]Lit *Dwelling places* **132:6** [a]Ge 35:19; 1Sa 17:12 [b]1Sa 7:1 [1]Or *the wood* **132:7** [a]Ps 43:3 [b]Ps 5:7; 99:5 [c]1Chr 28:2 [1]Lit *dwelling places* **132:8** [a]Nu 10:35; 2Chr 6:41; Ps 68:1 [b]Ps 132:14 [c]Ps 78:61 **132:9** [a]Job 29:14 [b]Ps 30:4; 132:16; 149:5 **132:10** [a]Ps 2:2; 132:17 **132:11** [a]Ps 89:3, 35 [b]2Sa 7:12-16; 1Chr 17:11-14; 2Chr 6:16; Ps 89:4; Ac 2:30 [1]Or *stomach*; lit *womb* **132:12** [a]Lk 1:32; Ac 2:30 **132:13** [a]Ps 48:1, 2; 78:68 [b]Ps 68:16 **132:14** [a]Ps 132:8 [b]Ps 68:16; Mt 23:21 **132:15** [a]Ps 147:14 [b]Ps 107:9 **132:16** [a]2Chr 6:41; Ps 132:9

17 "There I will cause the [a]horn
of David to spring up;
I have prepared a [b]lamp
for Mine anointed.
18 "His enemies I will
[a]clothe with shame,
But upon him, his [b]crown
shall blossom."

## PSALM 133

### *How Good and Pleasant Is Unity*

A Song of Ascents. Of David.

1 Behold, how good and
how pleasant it is
For [a]brothers to dwell
together in unity!
2 It is like the good [a]oil
upon the head,
Coming down upon the beard,
Aaron's beard,
Coming down
upon the [b]edge of his robes.
3 It is like the [a]dew of [b]Hermon
Coming down upon
the [c]mountains of Zion;
For there, Yahweh [d]commanded
the blessing—[e]life forever.

## PSALM 134

### *Behold, Bless Yahweh*

A Song of Ascents.

1 Behold, [a]bless Yahweh, all
*you* [b]slaves of Yahweh,
Who [c]stand in the house
*of Yahweh* [d]*by night!*
2 [a]Lift up your hands
to the [b]sanctuary
And bless Yahweh.
3 May Yahweh [a]bless
you from Zion,
Who [b]made heaven and earth.

## PSALM 135

### *O Yahweh, Your Name Is Everlasting*

1 [a,1]Praise Yah!
Praise the name of Yahweh;
Praise *Him,* O [b]slaves
of Yahweh,
2 You who stand
in the house of Yahweh,
In the [a]courts of the house
of our God!
3 [1]Praise Yah,
for [a]Yahweh is good;
[b]Sing praises to His name,
[c]for it is lovely.
4 For Yah has [a]chosen
Jacob for Himself,
Israel for His
[b,1]treasured possession.

5 For I know
that [a]Yahweh is great
And that our Lord is
*greater* [b]than all gods.
6 [a]Whatever Yahweh
pleases, He does,
In heaven and on earth,
in the seas and in all deeps.
7 The One who [a]causes
the clouds to ascend
from the end of the earth;
Who [b]makes lightnings
for the rain,
Who [a]brings forth the wind
from His storehouses.

**132:17** [a]Eze 29:21; Lk 1:69 [b]1Ki 11:36; 15:4; 2Ki 8:19; 2Chr 21:7; Ps 18:28 **132:18** [a]Job 8:22; Ps 35:26; 109:29 [b]Ps 21:3 ◆ **133:1** [a]Ge 13:8; Heb 13:1 **133:2** [a]Ex 29:7; 30:25, 30; Lv 8:12 [b]Ex 28:33; 39:24 **133:3** [a]Pr 19:12; Hos 14:5; Mic 5:7 [b]Dt 3:9; 4:48 [c]Ps 48:2; 74:2; 78:68 [d]Lv 25:21; Dt 28:8; Ps 42:8 [e]Ps 21:4 ◆ **134:1** [a]Ps 103:21 [b]Ps 135:1, 2 [c]Dt 10:8; 1Chr 23:30; 2Chr 29:11 [d]1Chr 9:33 **134:2** [a]Ps 28:2; 1Ti 2:8 [b]Ps 63:2 **134:3** [a]Ps 128:5 [b]Ps 124:8 ◆ **135:1** [a]Ps 113:1 [b]Ps 134:1 [1]Or *Hallelujah!* **135:2** [a]Ps 92:13; 116:19 **135:3** [a]Ps 100:5; 119:68 [b]Ps 68:4 [c]Ps 147:1 [1]Or *Hallelujah!* **135:4** [a]Dt 7:6; 10:15; Ps 105:6 [b]Ex 19:5; Mal 3:17; Tit 2:14; 1Pe 2:9 [1]Or *special treasure* **135:5** [a]Ps 48:1; 95:3; 145:3 [b]Ps 97:9 **135:6** [a]Ps 115:3 **135:7** [a]Jer 10:13; 51:16 [b]Job 28:25, 26; 38:25, 26; Zec 10:1

8 [1]He [a]struck the firstborn
of Egypt,
From man to beast.
9 [1]He sent [a]signs and wonders
into your midst, O Egypt,
Amongst [b]Pharaoh
and all his slaves.
10 [a,1]He [b]struck many nations
And slew mighty kings,
11 [a]Sihon, king
of the Amorites,
And [b]Og, king of Bashan,
And [c]all the kingdoms
of Canaan;
12 And He [a]gave their land
as an inheritance,
An inheritance
to Israel His people.
13 O Yahweh, Your [a]name
is everlasting,
O Yahweh, Your [1]remembrance
is [2]from generation
to generation.
14 For Yahweh will [a]render
justice for His people
And [b]will give comfort
to His slaves.
15 The [a]idols of the nations
are silver and gold,
The work of man's hands.
16 They have mouths,
but they do not speak;
They have eyes,
but they do not see;
17 They have ears,
but they do not hear,
Surely, there is not any
breath in their mouths.
18 Those who make them
will be like them,
All who trust in them.

19 O house of [a]Israel,
bless Yahweh;
O house of Aaron,
bless Yahweh;
20 O house of Levi, bless Yahweh;
You [a]who fear Yahweh,
bless Yahweh.
21 Blessed be Yahweh [a]from Zion,
Who [b]dwells in Jerusalem.
[1]Praise Yah!

## PSALM 136

### *His Lovingkindness Endures Forever*

1 [a]Give thanks to Yahweh,
for [b]He is good,
For [c]His lovingkindness
endures forever.
2 Give thanks to
the [a]God of gods,
For His lovingkindness
endures forever.
3 Give thanks to
the [a]Lord of lords,
For His lovingkindness
endures forever.

4 To Him who [a]alone does
great [1]wonders,
For His lovingkindness
endures forever;
5 To Him who [a]made
the heavens [b]with [1]skill,
For His lovingkindness
endures forever;

**135:8** [a]Ex 12:12; Ps 78:51; 105:36 [1]Lit *The One who* **135:9** [a]Ex 7:10; Dt 6:22; Ps 78:43 [b]Ps 136:15 [1]Lit *The One who* **135:10** [a]Nu 21:24; Ps 135:10-12; 136:17-21 [b]Ps 44:2 [1]Lit *The One who* **135:11** [a]Nu 21:21-26; Dt 29:7 [b]Nu 21:33-35 [c]Jos 12:7-24 **135:12** [a]Dt 29:8; Ps 78:55; 136:21, 22 **135:13** [a]Ex 3:15; Ps 102:12 [1]Or *memorial* [2]Lit *to* **135:14** [a]Dt 32:36; Ps 50:4 [b]Ps 90:13; 106:46 **135:15** [a]Ps 115:4-8; 135:15-18 **135:19** [a]Ps 115:9 **135:20** [a]Ps 118:4 **135:21** [a]Ps 128:5; 134:3 [b]Ps 132:14 [1]Or *Hallelujah!* ◆ **136:1** [a]1Chr 16:34; Ps 106:1; 107:1; 118:1; Jer 33:11 [b]2Chr 5:13; 7:3; Ezr 3:11; Ps 100:5 [c]1Chr 16:41; 2Chr 20:21; Ps 118:1-4 **136:2** [a]Dt 10:17 **136:3** [a]Dt 10:17 **136:4** [a]Dt 6:22; Job 9:10; Ps 72:18 [1]Wonderful acts **136:5** [a]Ge 1:1 [b]Ps 104:24; Pr 3:19; Jer 10:12; 51:15 [1]Lit *understanding*

6 To Him who [a]spread out
the earth above the waters,
For His lovingkindness
endures forever;
7 To Him who [a]made
*the* great lights,
For His lovingkindness
endures forever:
8 The [a]sun to rule [1]by day,
For His lovingkindness
endures forever,
9 The [a]moon and stars
to rule [1]by night,
For His lovingkindness
endures forever.

10 To Him who [a]struck [1]the
Egyptians through
their firstborn,
For His lovingkindness
endures forever,
11 Then [a]brought Israel out
from their midst,
For His lovingkindness
endures forever,
12 With a [a]strong hand and
an [b]outstretched arm,
For His lovingkindness
endures forever.

13 To Him who [a]divided
the [1]Red Sea in two,
For His lovingkindness
endures forever,
14 And [a]made Israel pass
through the midst of it,
For His lovingkindness
endures forever,
15 But [a]He [1]overthrew Pharaoh
and his army in the [2]Red Sea,
For His lovingkindness
endures forever.

16 To Him who [a]led His people
through the wilderness,
For His lovingkindness
endures forever;

17 To Him who [a]struck
great kings,
For His lovingkindness
endures forever,
18 And [a]killed [1]mighty kings,
For His lovingkindness
endures forever:
19 [a]Sihon, king of the Amorites,
For His lovingkindness
endures forever,
20 And [a]Og, king of Bashan,
For His lovingkindness
endures forever,
21 And [a]gave their land
as an inheritance,
For His lovingkindness
endures forever,
22 Even an inheritance
to Israel His [a]servant,
For His lovingkindness
endures forever.

23 Who [a]remembered us
in our low estate,
For His lovingkindness
endures forever,
24 And has [a]snatched us
from our adversaries,

**136:6** [a]Ge 1:2, 6, 9; Ps 24:2; Is 42:5; 44:24; Jer 10:12 **136:7** [a]Ge 1:14-18; Ps 74:16 **136:8** [a]Ge 1:16 [1]Or *over the* **136:9** [a]Ge 1:16 [1]Or *over the* **136:10** [a]Ex 12:29; Ps 78:51; 135:8 [1]Lit *Egypt* **136:11** [a]Ex 12:51; 13:3; Ps 105:43 **136:12** [a]Ex 6:1; 13:9; 1Ki 8:42; Ne 1:10; Ps 44:3; Jer 32:21 [b]Ex 6:6; Dt 4:34; 5:15; 7:19; 9:29; 11:2; 2Ki 17:36; 2Chr 6:32; Jer 32:17 **136:13** [a]Ex 14:21; Ps 66:6; 78:13 [1]Lit *Sea of Reeds* **136:14** [a]Ex 14:22; Ps 106:9 **136:15** [a]Ex 14:27; Ps 78:53; 106:11 [1]Lit *shook off* [2]Lit *Sea of Reeds* **136:16** [a]Ex 13:18; 15:22; Dt 8:15; Ps 78:52 **136:17** [a]Ps 135:10-12; 136:17-22 **136:18** [a]Dt 29:7 [1]Lit *majestic* **136:19** [a]Nu 21:21-24 **136:20** [a]Nu 21:33-35 **136:21** [a]Jos 12:1 **136:22** [a]Ps 105:6; Is 41:8; 44:1; 45:4 **136:23** [a]Ps 9:12; 103:14; 106:45 **136:24** [a]Jdg 6:9; Ne 9:28; Ps 107:2

For His lovingkindness
endures forever;
25 Who [a]gives food to all flesh,
For His lovingkindness
endures forever.
26 Give thanks to the [a]God
of heaven,
For His lovingkindness
endures forever.

## PSALM 137

***We Wept When We Remembered Zion***

1 By the [a]rivers of Babylon,
There we sat and also [b]wept,
When we remembered Zion.
2 Upon the [a,1]willows
in the midst of it
We [b]hung our lyres.
3 For there our captors
[a]asked us
about the words of a song,
And [b]our tormentors
*asked* joyfully, *saying*,
"Sing for us one
of the songs of Zion."

4 How can we sing a song
of [a]Yahweh
In a foreign land?
5 If I [a]forget you, O Jerusalem,
May my right hand
[1]forget *her skill*.
6 May my [a]tongue cling
to the roof of my mouth
If I do not remember you,
If I do not [b,1]exalt Jerusalem
Above my chief joy.
7 Remember, O Yahweh,
against the sons of [a]Edom
The day of Jerusalem,
Who said, "Tear it down!
Tear it down
[b]To its very foundation."
8 O daughter of Babylon,
you [a]devastated one,
How blessed will be the one
who [b]repays you
With [1]the recompense
with which you have
recompensed us.
9 How blessed will be
the one who seizes and
[a]dashes your infants
Against the cliff.

## PSALM 138

***I Will Give Thanks to Your Name***

Of David.

1 [a]I will give You thanks
with all my heart;
I will sing praises to You
before the [b]gods.
2 I will worship
[a]toward Your holy temple
And [b]give thanks
to Your name for Your
lovingkindness and
Your [1]truth;
For You have [c]magnified
Your [2]word [3]according
to all Your name.
3 On the day I [a]called,
You answered me;
You made me bold
with [b]strength in my soul.

**136:25** [a]Ps 104:27; 145:15 **136:26** [a]Ge 24:3, 7; 2Chr 36:23; Ezr 1:2; 5:11; Ne 1:4 ◆**137:1** [a]Eze 1:1, 3 [b]Ne 1:4 **137:2** [a]Lv 23:40; Is 44:4 [b]Job 30:31; Is 24:8; Eze 26:13 [1]Or *poplars* **137:3** [a]Ps 80:6 [b]Is 49:17 **137:4** [a]2Chr 29:27; Ne 12:46 **137:5** [a]Is 65:11 [1]Become lame **137:6** [a]Job 29:10; Ps 22:15; Eze 3:26 [b]Ne 2:3 [1]Lit *cause to ascend* **137:7** [a]Ps 83:4-8; Is 34:5, 6; Jer 49:7-22; Lam 4:21; Eze 25:12-14; 35:2; Am 1:11; Ob 10-14 [b]Ps 74:7; Hab 3:13 **137:8** [a]Is 13:1-22; 47:1-15; Jer 25:12; 50:1-46; 51:1-64 [b]Jer 50:15; 51:24, 35, 36, 49; Rev 18:6 [1]Lit *your* **137:9** [a]2Ki 8:12; Is 13:16; Hos 13:16; Na 3:10 ◆**138:1** [a]Ps 111:1 [b]Ps 95:3; 96:4; 97:7 **138:2** [a]1Ki 8:29; Ps 5:7; 28:2 [b]Ps 140:13 [c]Is 42:21 [1]Or *faithfulness* [2]Or *promise* [3]Or *together with* **138:3** [a]Ps 118:5 [b]Ps 28:7; 46:1

4 [a]All the kings of the earth,
O Yahweh, will give
You thanks,
When they hear the words
of Your mouth.
5 And they will [a]sing
of the ways of Yahweh,
For [b]great is the glory
of Yahweh.
6 For [a]Yahweh is high,
Yet He [b]sees the lowly,
But the [c]one who exalts
*himself* He knows from afar.

7 Though I [a]walk
in the midst of [1]distress,
You will [b,2]revive me;
You will [c]stretch forth Your
hand against the wrath
of my enemies,
And Your right hand
will [d]save me.
8 Yahweh will [a]accomplish
what concerns me;
O Yahweh,
Your [b]lovingkindness
endures forever;
[c]Do not fail the [d]works
of Your hands.

## PSALM 139

### *Where Can I Go from Your Spirit?*

For the choir director. Of David.
A Psalm.

1 O Yahweh, You have [a]searched
me and known *me*.
2 You [a]know [1]when I sit down
and [2]when I rise up;
You [b]understand my
thought from afar.
3 You [a,1]scrutinize my [2]path
and my lying down,
And are intimately acquainted
with all my ways.
4 [1]Even before there is
a word on my tongue,
Behold, O Yahweh,
You [a]know it all.
5 You have [a]enclosed me
behind and before,
And You have [b]put Your
hand upon me.
6 *Such* [a]knowledge is [b]too
wonderful for me;
It is *too* high, I cannot
attain to it.

7 [a]Where can I go
from Your Spirit?
Or where can I flee
from Your presence?
8 [a]If I ascend to heaven,
You are there;
If I make my bed
in Sheol, behold,
[b]You are there.
9 If I lift up the wings
of the dawn,
If I dwell in the remotest
part of the sea,
10 Even there Your hand
will [a]lead me,
And Your right hand
will lay hold of me.
11 If I say, "Surely the [a]darkness
will [b]bruise me,

**138:4** [a]Ps 72:11; 102:15 **138:5** [a]Ps 145:7 [b]Ps 21:5 **138:6** [a]Ps 113:4-7; Is 52:13 [b]Pr 3:34; Is 52:13; 57:15; Lk 1:48; Jas 4:6; 1Pe 5:5 [c]Ps 40:4; 101:5 **138:7** [a]Ps 23:4; 143:11 [b]Ezr 9:8, 9; Ps 71:20; Is 57:15 [c]Ex 7:5; 15:12; Is 5:25; Jer 51:25; Eze 6:14; 25:13 [d]Ps 20:6; 60:5 [1]Or *trouble* [2]Or *keep me alive* **138:8** [a]Ps 57:2; Php 1:6 [b]Ps 136:1 [c]Job 10:8; Ps 27:9; 71:9; 119:8 [d]Job 10:3; 14:15; Ps 100:3 ◆ **139:1** [a]Ps 17:3; 44:21; Jer 12:3 **139:2** [a]2Ki 19:27 [b]Ps 94:11; Is 66:18; Mt 9:4 [1]Lit *my sitting* [2]Lit *my rising* **139:3** [a]Job 14:16; 31:4 [1]Lit *winnow* [2]Or *journeying* **139:4** [a]Heb 4:13 [1]Lit *When there is not* **139:5** [a]Ps 34:7; 125:2 [b]Job 9:33 **139:6** [a]Ro 11:33 [b]Job 42:3 **139:7** [a]Jer 23:24 **139:8** [a]Am 9:2-4 [b]Job 26:6; Pr 15:11 **139:10** [a]Ps 23:2, 3 **139:11** [a]Job 22:13 [b]Ge 3:15

And the light around me
will be night,"
12 Even the [a]darkness is
not too dark for You,
And the night is as bright
as the day.
[b]Darkness and light
are alike *to You.*

13 For You [a]formed my
[1]inward parts;
You [b]wove me in my
mother's womb.
14 I will give thanks to You,
for [1]I am fearfully and
wonderfully made;
[a]Wonderful are Your works,
And my soul knows
it very well.
15 My [a,1]frame was not
hidden from You,
When I was made in secret,
*And* [b]intricately woven
in the [c]depths of the earth;
16 Your [a]eyes have seen my
unshaped substance;
And in [b]Your book all
of them were written
The [c]days that were
formed *for me,*
When as yet there was
not one of them.

17 How precious are Your
[a]thoughts to me, O God!
How vast is the sum of them!
18 If I should count them, they
would [a]outnumber the sand.
When [b]I awake, I am
still with You.

19 Oh that You would [a]slay
the wicked, O God!
[b]O [c]men of bloodshed,
depart from me.
20 For they [a]speak
[1]against You wickedly,
And Your enemies [b,2]take
*Your name* in vain.
21 Do I not [a]hate those who
hate You, O Yahweh?
And do I not [b]revile those
who rise up against You?
22 I hate them
with the utmost hatred;
They have become
my enemies.

23 [a]Search me, O God, and
know my heart;
[b]Try me and know my
anxious thoughts;
24 And see if there be any
[a,1]hurtful way in me,
And [b]lead me
in the [c]everlasting way.

## PSALM 140

### *Rescue Me, O Yahweh, from Evil Men*

For the choir director. A Psalm of David.

1 [a]Rescue me, O Yahweh,
from evil men;
Guard me from [b]violent men
2 Who [a]think up evil things
in *their* hearts;
They [b]continually stir up wars.

---

**139:12** [a]Job 34:22; Da 2:22 [b]1Jn 1:5 **139:13** [a]Ps 119:73; Is 44:24 [b]Job 10:11 [1]Lit *kidneys* **139:14** [a]Ps 40:5 [1]Some ancient versions *You are fearfully wonderful* **139:15** [a]Job 10:8-10; Ecc 11:5 [b]Ex 26:36 [c]Ps 63:9 [1]Lit *bones were* **139:16** [a]Job 10:8-10; Ecc 11:5 [b]Ps 56:8 [c]Job 14:5 **139:17** [a]Ps 40:5; 92:5 **139:18** [a]Ps 40:5 [b]Ps 3:5 **139:19** [a]Is 11:4 [b]Ps 6:8; 119:115 [c]Ps 5:6; 26:9 **139:20** [a]Jd 15 [b]Ex 20:7; Dt 5:11 [1]Or *of* [2]Some mss *lift themselves up* against You **139:21** [a]2Chr 19:2; Ps 26:5; 31:6 [b]Ps 119:158 **139:23** [a]Job 31:6; Ps 26:2 [b]Ps 7:9; Pr 17:3; Jer 11:20; 1Th 2:4 **139:24** [a]Ps 146:9; Pr 15:9; 28:10; Jer 25:5; 36:3 [b]Ps 5:8; 143:10 [c]Ps 16:11 [1]Lit *way of pain* ◆ **140:1** [a]Ps 17:13; 59:2; 71:4 [b]Ps 18:48; 86:14; 140:11 **140:2** [a]Ps 7:14; 36:4; 52:2; Pr 6:14; Is 59:4; Hos 7:15 [b]Ps 56:6

3 They [a]sharpen their
tongues as a serpent;
[b]Poison of an asp is
under their lips. [1]Selah.

4 [a]Keep me, O Yahweh,
from the hands
of the wicked;
[b]Guard me from violent men
Who [1]give thought
to [c,2]trip up my steps.
5 The proud have [a]hidden
a trap for me, and cords;
They have spread a [b]net
by the [1]wayside;
They have set [c]snares
for me. Selah.

6 I [a]said to Yahweh, "You
are my God;
[b]Give ear, O Yahweh,
to the [c]voice of my
supplications.
7 "O Yahweh, O Lord, [a]the
strength of my salvation,
You have [b]covered my head
in the day of [1]battle.
8 "Do not grant, O Yahweh,
the [a]desires of the wicked;
Do not promote [b]his *evil*
[1]scheme, *that* they *not*
be exalted. Selah.

9 "As for the head of those
who surround me,
May the [a]trouble
*from* their lips cover them.
10 "May [a]burning coals be
shaken out upon them;
May He [b]cause them
to fall into the fire,
Into [1]bottomless pits
from which they
[c]can never rise.
11 "May a [1]slanderer not be
established in the earth;
[a]May evil hunt the violent
man [2]speedily."

12 I know that Yahweh will
[a]maintain the cause
for the afflicted
And [b]judgment for the needy.
13 Surely the [a]righteous will
give thanks to Your name;
The [b]upright will abide
in Your presence.

## PSALM 141

### *My Prayer as Incense Before You*

A Psalm of David.

1 O Yahweh, I call
upon You; [a]hasten to me!
[b]Give ear to my voice
when I call to You!
2 May my prayer be established
as [a]incense before You;
The [b]lifting up of my hands
as the [c]evening offering.
3 Set a [a]guard, O Yahweh,
[1]over my mouth;
Keep watch
over the [b]door of my lips.

---

**140:3** [a]Ps 57:4; 64:3 [b]Ps 58:4; Ro 3:13; Jas 3:8 [1]*Selah* may mean *Pause, Crescendo, Musical Interlude* **140:4** [a]Ps 71:4 [b]Ps 140:1 [c]Ps 36:11 [1]Or *devised* [2]Lit *push violently my steps* **140:5** [a]Job 18:9; Ps 35:7; 141:9; 142:3 [b]Ps 31:4; 57:6; Lam 1:13 [c]Ps 141:9; Is 8:14; Am 3:5 [1]Lit *track* **140:6** [a]Ps 16:2; 31:14 [b]Ps 143:1 [c]Ps 116:1; 130:2 **140:7** [a]Ps 28:8; 118:14 [b]Ps 144:10 [1]Lit *weapons* **140:8** [a]Ps 112:10 [b]Es 9:25; Ps 10:2, 3 [1]Or *plan* **140:9** [a]Ps 7:16; Pr 18:7 **140:10** [a]Ps 11:6 [b]Ps 21:9; Mt 3:10 [c]Ps 36:12 [1]Lit *watery* **140:11** [a]Ps 34:21 [1]Lit *man of tongue* [2]Lit *thrust upon thrust* **140:12** [a]1Ki 8:45, 49; Ps 9:4; 18:27; 82:3 [b]Ps 12:5; 35:10 **140:13** [a]Ps 97:12 [b]Ps 11:7; 16:11; 17:15 ◆ **141:1** [a]Ps 22:19; 38:22; 70:5 [b]Ps 5:1; 143:1 **141:2** [a]Ex 30:8; Lk 1:10; Rev 5:8; 8:3, 4 [b]1Ti 2:8 [c]Ex 29:39, 41; 1Ki 18:29, 36; Da 9:21 **141:3** [a]Ps 34:13; 39:1; Pr 13:3; 21:23 [b]Mic 7:5 [1]Lit *to*

4 [a]Do not incline my heart
to any evil thing,
To practice deeds
in wickedness
With men who are
[b]workers of iniquity;
And [c]do not let me eat
of their delicacies.

5 Let the [a]righteous smite
me in lovingkindness
and reprove me;
It is [b]oil upon the head;
Let not my head refuse it,
[1]For still my prayer [c]is
[2]against their evil deeds.
6 Their judges are [a]thrown
down by the sides
of the cliff,
And they hear my words,
for they are pleasant.
7 As when one [a]plows and
splits open the earth,
Our [b]bones have
been scattered
at the [c]mouth of Sheol.

8 For my [a]eyes are toward You,
O Yahweh, O Lord;
In You I [b]take refuge; [c]do not
pour out my soul *to death.*
9 Keep me from the [a,1]jaws
of the trap which they
have set for me,
And from the [b]snares
of workers of iniquity.
10 Let the wicked [a]fall
into their own nets,
As for myself—meanwhile,
[b]I am passing by.

## PSALM 142

### *Give Heed to My Cry*

A [†]Maskil of David. When he was
[·]in the cave. A Prayer.

1 With my voice to Yahweh,
I [a]cry aloud;
With my voice to Yahweh,
I [b]make supplication.
2 I [a]pour out my complaint
before Him;
I declare my [b]distress
before Him.
3 When [a]my spirit [1]was
faint within me,
You knew my path.
In the way where I walk
They have [b]hidden a trap for me.
4 Look to the right and see;
That there is [a]no one
who regards me;
[b]A *way of* escape has been
destroyed from me;
[c]No one cares for my soul.

5 I cried out to You, O Yahweh;
I said, "You are [a]my refuge,
My [b]portion in the [c]land
of the living.
6 "[a]Give heed to my cry
of lamentation,
For I am [b]brought very low;
Deliver me
from my persecutors,
For they are too
[c]strong for me.

---

**141:4** [a]Ps 119:36 [b]Is 32:6; Hos 6:8; Mal 3:15 [c]Pr 23:6 **141:5** [a]Pr 9:8; 19:25; 25:12; 27:6; Ecc 7:5; Ga 6:1 [b]Ps 23:5; 133:2 [c]Ps 35:14 [1]Lit *And my prayer* [2]Or *in spite of their calamities* **141:6** [a]2Chr 25:12 **141:7** [a]Ps 129:3 [b]Ps 53:5 [c]Nu 16:32, 33; Ps 88:3-5 **141:8** [a]Ps 25:15; 123:2 [b]Ps 2:12; 11:1 [c]Ps 27:9; Is 53:12 **141:9** [a]Ps 38:12; 64:5; 91:3; 119:110 [b]Ps 140:5 [1]Lit *hands* **141:10** [a]Ps 7:15; 35:8; 57:6 [b]Ps 124:7 ◆ **142:TITLE** [†]Possibly *Contemplative, Didactic, Skillful Psalm* [·]1Sa 22:1; 24:3 **142:1** [a]Ps 77:1 [b]Ps 30:8 **142:2** [a]Ps 102: title [b]Ps 77:2 **142:3** [a]Ps 77:3; 143:4 [b]Ps 140:5 [1]Lit *fainted* **142:4** [a]Ps 31:11; 88:8, 18 [b]Job 11:20; Jer 25:35 [c]Jer 30:17 **142:5** [a]Ps 91:2, 9 [b]Ps 16:5; 73:26 [c]Ps 27:13 **142:6** [a]Ps 17:1 [b]Ps 79:8; 116:6 [c]Ps 18:17

7 “[a]Bring my soul out of prison,
To give thanks to Your name;
The righteous will encircle me,
For You will [b]deal
bountifully with me.”

## PSALM 143

### *My Soul Reaches for You*

A Psalm of David.

1 O Yahweh, hear my prayer,
[a]Give ear to my supplications!
Answer me in Your
[b]faithfulness, in Your
[c]righteousness!
2 And [a]do not enter into
judgment with Your slave,
For [b]no one living is
righteous in Your sight.
3 For the enemy has
pursued my soul;
He has crushed my life
[a]to the ground;
He [b]has made me inhabit
dark places, like those who
have long been dead.
4 Therefore [a]my spirit was
faint within me;
My heart was [b,1]appalled
within me.

5 I [a]remember the days of old;
I [b]meditate on all
You have done;
I [c]muse on the work
of Your hands.
6 I [a]stretch out my hands to You;
My [b]soul *reaches* for You
like a weary land. [1]Selah.

7 [a]Answer me quickly,
O Yahweh, my [b]spirit
wastes away;
[c]Do not hide Your
face from me,
Or I will become like [d]those
who go down to the pit.
8 Cause me to hear Your
[a]lovingkindness [b]in
the morning;
For I trust [c]in You;
Cause me to know the [d]way
in which I should walk;
For to You I [e]lift up my soul.
9 [a]Deliver me from my
enemies, O Yahweh,
I have concealed *myself* in You.

10 [a]Teach me to do Your will,
For You are my God;
Let [b]Your good Spirit [c]lead
me on level [1]ground.
11 [a]For the sake of Your name,
O Yahweh, [b]revive me.
[c]In Your righteousness bring
my soul out of distress.
12 And in Your lovingkindness,
[a,1]cut off my enemies
And cause all those who
assail my soul to [b]perish,
For [c]I am Your slave.

## PSALM 144

### *Blessed Be Yahweh, My Rock*

Of David.

1 Blessed be Yahweh, [a]my rock,
Who [b]trains my hands for war,
My fingers for battle;

**142:7** [a]Ps 143:11; 146:7 [b]Ps 13:6 ◆ **143:1** [a]Ps 140:6 [b]Ps 89:1, 2 [c]Ps 71:2 **143:2** [a]Job 14:3; 22:4 [b]1Ki 8:46; Job 4:17; 9:2; 25:4; Ps 130:3; Ecc 7:20; Ro 3:10, 20; Ga 2:16 **143:3** [a]Ps 44:25 [b]Ps 88:6; Lam 3:6 **143:4** [a]Ps 77:3; 142:3 [b]Lam 3:11 [1]Or *desolate* **143:5** [a]Ps 77:5, 10, 11 [b]Ps 77:12 [c]Ps 105:2 **143:6** [a]Job 11:13; Ps 88:9 [b]Ps 42:2; 63:1 [1]*Selah* may mean *Pause, Crescendo, Musical Interlude* **143:7** [a]Ps 69:17 [b]Ps 73:26; 84:2; Jer 8:18; Lam 1:22 [c]Ps 27:9; 69:17; 102:2 [d]Ps 28:1; 88:4 **143:8** [a]Ps 90:14 [b]Ps 46:5 [c]Ps 25:2 [d]Ps 27:11; 32:8; 86:11 [e]Ps 25:1; 86:4 **143:9** [a]Ps 31:15; 59:1 **143:10** [a]Ps 25:4, 5; 119:12 [b]Ne 9:20 [c]Ps 23:3 [1]Lit *land* **143:11** [a]Ps 25:11 [b]Ps 119:25 [c]Ps 31:1; 71:2 **143:12** [a]Ps 54:5 [b]Ps 52:5 [c]Ps 116:16 [1]Or *silence* ◆ **144:1** [a]Ps 18:2 [b]2Sa 22:35; Ps 18:34

2 My lovingkindness
and [a]my fortress,
My [b]stronghold and
my deliverer,
My [c]shield and He
in whom I take refuge,
Who [d]subdues [1]my
people under me.
3 O Yahweh, [a]what is man,
that You know him?
Or the son of man,
that You think of him?
4 [a]Man is like a breath;
His [b]days are
like a passing shadow.

5 O Yahweh, [a]bow Your
heavens, and [b]come down;
[c]Touch the mountains,
that they may smoke.
6 Flash forth [a]lightning
and scatter them;
Send out Your [b]arrows
and confuse them.
7 Send forth Your hand
[a]from on high;
Set me free and [b]deliver
me out of many waters,
Out of the hand of [c]foreigners
8 Whose mouth
[a]speaks worthlessness,
And whose [b]right hand is
a right hand of lying.

9 O God, I will sing a [a]new
song to You;
Upon a [b]harp of ten strings
I will sing praises to You,
10 Who [a]gives salvation
to kings,
Who [b]sets David His
servant free
from the evil sword.
11 Set me free and deliver
me out of the hand
of the sons of a [a]foreigner,
Whose mouth
[b]speaks worthlessness
And whose [c]right hand is
a right hand of lying.

12 That our sons would be
as [a]grown-up plants
in their youth,
And our daughters as
[b]corner pillars [1]fashioned
as for a palace;
13 *That* our [a]granaries would
be full, furnishing every
kind of produce,
*And* our flocks would
bring forth thousands
and ten thousands
in our *fields* outside;
14 That our [a]cattle
would [1]bear
Without [b,2]mishap and
without [c,3]loss,
And without [d]outcry
in our streets!
15 How blessed are
the people
for whom this is so;
How [a]blessed are
the people for whom
God is Yahweh!

---

**144:2** [a]Ps 18:2; 91:2 [b]Ps 59:9 [c]Ps 3:3; 28:7; 84:9 [d]Ps 18:39 [1]Or *peoples* **144:3** [a]Job 7:17; Ps 8:4; Heb 2:6 **144:4** [a]Ps 39:11 [b]Job 8:9; 14:2; Ps 102:11; 109:23 **144:5** [a]Ps 18:9 [b]Is 64:1 [c]Ps 104:32 **144:6** [a]Ps 18:14 [b]Ps 7:13; 58:7; Hab 3:11; Zec 9:14 **144:7** [a]Ps 18:16 [b]Ps 69:1, 14 [c]Ps 18:44; 54:3 **144:8** [a]Ps 12:2; 41:6 [b]Ge 14:22; Dt 32:40; Ps 106:26; Is 44:20 **144:9** [a]Ps 33:3; 40:3 [b]Ps 33:2 **144:10** [a]Ps 18:50 [b]2Sa 18:7; Ps 140:7 **144:11** [a]Ps 18:44; 54:3 [b]Ps 12:2; 41:6 [c]Ge 14:22; Dt 32:40; Ps 106:26; Is 44:20 **144:12** [a]Ps 92:12-14; 128:3 [b]SS 4:4; 7:4 [1]Lit *cut after the pattern of* **144:13** [a]Pr 3:9, 10 **144:14** [a]Pr 14:4 [b]2Ki 25:10, 11 [c]Am 5:3 [d]Is 24:11; Jer 14:2 [1]Lit *be laden* [2]Lit *bursting forth* [3]Lit *going out* **144:15** [a]Ps 33:12

## PSALM 145

### *Yahweh's Greatness Is Unsearchable*

A Praise of David.

א *Aleph*

1 I will [a]exalt You, [b]my
God, O King,
And I will [c]bless Your
name forever and ever.

ב *Beth*

2 Every day I will bless You,
And I will [a]praise Your
name forever and ever.

ג *Gimel*

3 [a]Great is Yahweh, and
highly to be praised,
And His [b]greatness
is unsearchable.

ד *Daleth*

4 One [a]generation shall laud
Your works to another,
And shall declare Your
mighty deeds.

ה *He*

5 On the [a]glorious [1]splendor
of Your majesty
And [b]on the words of Your
wondrous deeds, I will muse.

ו *Vav*

6 Men shall speak
of the strength of Your
[a,1]fearsome acts,
And I will [b]recount
Your greatness.

ז *Zayin*

7 They shall pour forth
the memory of Your
[a]abundant goodness
And will [b]shout joyfully
of Your righteousness.

ח *Heth*

8 Yahweh is [a]gracious
and compassionate;
Slow to anger and great
in lovingkindness.

ט *Teth*

9 Yahweh is [a]good to all,
And His [b]compassions are
over all His works.

י *Yodh*

10 [a]All Your works, O Yahweh,
shall give thanks to You,
And Your [b]holy ones
shall bless You.

כ *Kaph*

11 They shall speak of the [a]glory
of Your kingdom
And talk of Your might;

ל *Lamedh*

12 To [a]make known to the sons
of men His mighty deeds
And the [b]glory of the majesty
of His kingdom.

מ *Mem*

13 Your kingdom is [1]an
[a]everlasting kingdom,
And Your dominion
*endures* from generation
to every generation.

ס *Samekh*

14 Yahweh [a]sustains all
who fall
And [b]raises up all who
are bowed down.

ע *Ayin*

15 The eyes of all wait on You,
And You [a]give them their
food in due time.

---

◆ **145:1** [a]Ps 30:1; 66:17 [b]Ps 5:2 [c]Ps 34:1 **145:2** [a]Ps 71:6 **145:3** [a]Ps 48:1; 86:10; 147:5 [b]Job 5:9; 9:10; 11:7; Is 40:28; Ro 11:33 **145:4** [a]Ps 22:30, 31; Is 38:19 **145:5** [a]Ps 145:12 [b]Ps 119:27 [1]Or *majesty of Your splendor* **145:6** [a]Dt 10:21; Ps 66:3; 106:22 [b]Dt 32:3 [1]Or *awesome* **145:7** [a]Ps 31:19; Is 63:7 [b]Ps 51:14 **145:8** [a]Ex 34:6; Nu 14:18; Ps 86:5, 15; 103:8 **145:9** [a]Ps 100:5; 136:1; Jer 33:11; Na 1:7; Mt 19:17; Mk 10:18 [b]Ps 145:15 **145:10** [a]Ps 19:1; 103:22 [b]Ps 68:26 **145:11** [a]Jer 14:21 **145:12** [a]Ps 105:1 [b]Ps 145:5; Is 2:10, 19, 21 **145:13** [a]Ps 10:16; 29:10; 1Ti 1:17; 2Pe 1:11 [1]Lit *a kingdom of all ages* **145:14** [a]Ps 37:24 [b]Ps 146:8 **145:15** [a]Ps 104:27; 136:25

פ *Pe*

16 You [a]open Your hand
And satisfy the desire
of every living thing.

צ *Tsadhe*

17 Yahweh is [a]righteous
in all His ways
And holy in all His works.

ק *Qoph*

18 Yahweh is [a]near to all
who call upon Him,
To all who call
upon Him [b]in truth.

ר *Resh*

19 He will [a]work out the desire
of those who fear Him;
He will [b]hear their cry for
help and He will save them.

ש *Shin*

20 Yahweh [a]keeps all
who love Him,
But all the [b]wicked
He will destroy.

ת *Tav*

21 My [a]mouth will speak
the praise of Yahweh,
And [b]all flesh will [c]bless His
holy name forever and ever.

## PSALM 146

### *I Will Praise Yahweh Throughout My Life*

1 [1]Praise Yah!
[a]Praise Yahweh, O my soul!
2 I will praise Yahweh
[a]throughout my life;
I will [b]sing praises to my God
while I have my being.
3 [a]Do not trust in nobles,
In *merely* a son of [b]man,
in whom there is
[c]no salvation.
4 His [a]spirit departs,
he [b]returns to [1]the earth;
In that very day his
[c]plans perish.
5 How [a]blessed is he whose
help is the God of Jacob,
Whose [b]hope is
in Yahweh his God,
6 Who [a]made heaven
and earth,
The [b]sea and all
that is in them;
Who [c]keeps truth forever;
7 Who [a]does justice
for the oppressed;
Who [b]gives food
to the hungry.
Yahweh [c]sets
the prisoners free.

8 Yahweh [a]opens *the eyes of* the blind;
Yahweh [b]raises up those
who are bowed down;
Yahweh [c]loves the righteous;
9 Yahweh [a]keeps
the sojourners;
He [b,1]helps up the orphan
and the widow,
But He bends [c]the way
of the wicked.
10 Yahweh will [a]reign forever,
Your God, O Zion, [1]from
generation to generation.
[2]Praise Yah!

---

**145:16** [a]Ps 104:28 **145:17** [a]Ps 116:5 **145:18** [a]Dt 4:7; Ps 34:18; 119:151 [b]Jn 4:24 **145:19** [a]Ps 21:2; 37:4 [b]Ps 10:17; Pr 15:29; 1Jn 5:14 **145:20** [a]Ps 31:23; 91:14; 97:10 [b]Ps 9:5; 37:38 **145:21** [a]Ps 71:8 [b]Ps 65:2; 150:6 [c]Ps 145:1, 2 ◆**146:1** [a]Ps 103:1 [1]Or *Hallelujah!* **146:2** [a]Ps 63:4 [b]Ps 104:33 **146:3** [a]Ps 118:9 [b]Ps 118:8; Is 2:22 [c]Ps 60:11; 108:12 **146:4** [a]Ps 104:29 [b]Ecc 12:7 [c]Ps 33:10; 1Co 2:6 [1]Lit *his earth* **146:5** [a]Ps 144:15; Jer 17:7 [b]Ps 71:5 **146:6** [a]Ps 115:15; Rev 14:7 [b]Ac 14:15 [c]Ps 117:2 **146:7** [a]Ps 103:6 [b]Ps 107:9; 145:15 [c]Ps 68:6; Is 61:1 **146:8** [a]Mt 9:30; Jn 9:7 [b]Ps 145:14 [c]Ps 11:7 **146:9** [a]Ex 22:21; Lv 19:34 [b]Dt 10:18; Ps 68:5 [c]Ps 147:6 [1]Or *relieves* **146:10** [a]Ex 15:18; Ps 10:16 [1]Lit *to* [2]Or *Hallelujah!*

## PSALM 147

### *He Heals the Brokenhearted*

1 [1]Praise Yah!
For [a]it is good to sing
praises to our God;
For [2]it is pleasant *and*
praise is [b]becoming.
2 Yahweh [a]builds up Jerusalem;
He [b]gathers the [1]outcasts
of Israel.
3 *He is* the One who heals
the [a]brokenhearted
And who [b]binds up
their [1]wounds,
4 Who [a]counts the number
of the stars;
He [b,1]gives names to all of them.
5 [a]Great is our Lord and
abundant in power;
His [b]discernment is [1]infinite.
6 Yahweh [a,1]helps up
the afflicted;
He brings down the wicked
to the ground.

7 [a]Sing to Yahweh
with thanksgiving;
Sing praises to our
God on the lyre.
8 *He is* the One who [a]covers
the heavens with clouds,
The One who [b]provides
rain for the earth,
The One who [c]makes grass
*to* sprout on the mountains,
9 Who [a]gives to the animal
its food,
*And* to the [b]young ravens
which call out.
10 He does not delight
in the might of the [a]horse;
He [b]does not take pleasure
in the legs of a man.
11 Yahweh [a]is pleased
with those who fear Him,
[b]Those who wait
for His lovingkindness.

12 Laud Yahweh, O Jerusalem!
Praise your God, O Zion!
13 For He strengthened
the [a]bars of your gates;
He [b]blessed your sons
within you.
14 *He is* the One who [a]sets
[1]peace in your borders,
He [b]satisfies you with
[c]the [2]finest of the wheat,
15 The One who sends
forth His [a]command
to the earth;
His [b]word runs very swiftly,
16 The One who gives
[a]snow like wool;
He scatters the [b]frost
like ashes,
17 Who casts forth His
[a]ice as fragments;
Who can stand
before His [b]cold?
18 He [a]sends forth His word
and melts them;
He [b]causes His wind to blow
and so the waters flow,

◆ **147:1** [a]Ps 92:1; 135:3 [b]Ps 33:1 [1]Or *Hallelujah!* [2]Or *He is gracious* **147:2** [a]Ps 51:18; 102:16 [b]Dt 30:3; Ps 106:47; Is 11:12; 56:8; Eze 39:28 [1]Or *banished ones*, cf. Dt 30:1; Is 11:12; 56:8; Jer 23:3 **147:3** [a]Ps 34:18; 51:17; Is 61:1 [b]Job 5:18; Is 30:26; Eze 34:16 [1]Lit *sorrows* **147:4** [a]Ge 15:5 [b]Is 40:26 [1]Or *calls them all by* their *names* **147:5** [a]Ps 48:1; 145:3 [b]Is 40:28 [1]Lit *innumerable* **147:6** [a]Ps 37:24; 146:8, 9 [1]Or *relieves* **147:7** [a]Ps 33:2; 95:1, 2 **147:8** [a]Job 26:8 [b]Job 5:10; 38:26; Ps 104:13 [c]Job 38:27; Ps 104:14 **147:9** [a]Ps 104:27, 28; 145:15 [b]Job 38:41; Mt 6:26 **147:10** [a]Ps 33:17 [b]1Sa 16:7 **147:11** [a]Ps 149:4 [b]Ps 33:18 **147:13** [a]Ne 3:3; 7:3 [b]Ps 37:26 **147:14** [a]Ps 29:11; Is 54:13; 60:17, 18 [b]Ps 132:15 [c]Dt 32:14; Ps 81:16 [1]Lit *your borders peace* [2]Lit *fat* **147:15** [a]Job 37:12; Ps 148:5 [b]Ps 104:4 **147:16** [a]Job 37:6; Ps 148:8 [b]Job 38:29 **147:17** [a]Job 37:10 [b]Job 37:9 **147:18** [a]Ps 33:9; 107:20; 147:15 [b]Ps 107:25

19 Who [a]declares His
words to Jacob,
His [b]statutes and His
judgments to Israel.
20 He [a]has not done so
with any nation;
So as for His judgments,
they have [b]not known them.
[1]Praise Yah!

## PSALM 148
### *Praise Yahweh!*

1 [1]Praise Yah!
Praise Yahweh
[a]from the heavens;
Praise Him [b]in the heights!
2 Praise Him, [a]all His angels;
Praise Him, [b]all His hosts!
3 Praise Him, sun and moon;
Praise Him, all stars of light!
4 Praise Him, [a]heavens
of heavens,
And the [b]waters that are
above the heavens!
5 Let them praise the name
of Yahweh,
For [a]He commanded and
they were created.
6 He caused them to [a]stand
forever and ever;
He gave a [b]statute and it
will never pass away.

7 Praise Yahweh
from the earth,
[a]Sea monsters and all [b]deeps;
8 [a]Fire and hail, [b]snow
and [c]clouds;
[d]Stormy wind, [e]doing
His word;
9 [a]Mountains and all hills;
Fruit [b]trees and all cedars;
10 [a]Beasts and all cattle;
[b]Creeping things and
winged bird;
11 [a]Kings of the earth
and all peoples;
Princes and all [1]judges
of the earth;
12 Both choice men
as well as virgins;
The old with the young.

13 Let them praise the name
of Yahweh,
For His [a]name alone
is set on high;
His [b]splendor is
above earth and heaven.
14 And He has [a]raised up
a horn for His people,
[b]Praise for all His holy ones;
For the sons of Israel,
a people [c]near to Him.
[1]Praise Yah!

## PSALM 149
### *Yahweh Takes Pleasure in His People*

1 [1]Praise Yah!
Sing to Yahweh a [a]new song,
His praise [b]in the assembly
of the holy ones.
2 Let Israel be glad
in [a]his Maker;
Let the sons of Zion
rejoice in their [b]King.

---

**147:19** [a]Dt 33:3, 4 [b]Mal 4:4 **147:20** [a]Dt 4:7, 8, 32-34; Ro 3:1, 2 [b]Ps 79:6; Jer 10:25 [1]Or *Hallelujah!*
◆ **148:1** [a]Ps 69:34 [b]Job 16:19; Ps 102:19; Mt 21:9 [1]Or *Hallelujah!* **148:2** [a]Ps 103:20 [b]Ps 103:21
**148:4** [a]Dt 10:14; 1Ki 8:27; Ne 9:6; Ps 68:33 [b]Ge 1:7 **148:5** [a]Ge 1:1; Ps 33:6, 9 **148:6** [a]Ps 89:37;
Jer 31:35, 36; 33:20, 25 [b]Job 38:33 **148:7** [a]Ge 1:21; Ps 74:13 [b]Ge 1:2; Dt 33:13; Hab 3:10
**148:8** [a]Ps 18:12 [b]Ps 147:16 [c]Ps 135:7 [d]Ps 107:25 [e]Job 37:12; Ps 103:20 **148:9** [a]Is 44:23; 49:13
[b]Is 55:12 **148:10** [a]Is 43:20 [b]Hos 2:18 **148:11** [a]Ps 102:15 [1]Or *leaders* **148:13** [a]Is 12:4 [b]Ps 8:1;
113:4 **148:14** [a]1Sa 2:1; Ps 75:10 [b]Dt 10:21; Ps 109:1; Jer 17:14 [c]Lv 10:3; Eph 2:17 [1]Or *Hallelujah!*
◆ **149:1** [a]Ps 33:3 [b]Ps 35:18; 89:5 [1]Or *Hallelujah!* **149:2** [a]Ps 95:6 [b]Jdg 8:23; Ps 47:6; Zec 9:9

3 Let them praise His name
with [a]dancing;
With [b]tambourine and lyre let
them sing praises to Him.
4 For Yahweh [a]takes pleasure
in His people;
He will [b]beautify the afflicted
ones with salvation.

5 Let the [a]holy ones exult in glory;
Let them [b]sing for joy
on their beds.
6 *Let* the [a]exaltations of God
*be* in their throats,
And a [b]two-edged [c]sword
in their hand,
7 To [a]execute vengeance
on the nations
And punishments
on the peoples,
8 To bind their kings [a]with chains
And their [b]honored men
with fetters of iron,
9 To [a]execute on them
the judgment written;
This is the [b]majesty
of all His holy ones.
[1]Praise Yah!

## PSALM 150

***Praise Him, Praise Yah!***

1 [1]Praise Yah!
Praise God in His
[a]sanctuary;
Praise Him in His
mighty [b,2]expanse.
2 Praise Him for His
[a]mighty deeds;
Praise Him according
to the abundance
of His [b]greatness.

3 Praise Him
with [a]trumpet blast;
Praise Him
with [b]harp and lyre.
4 Praise Him with [a]tambourine
and dancing;
Praise Him with [b]stringed
instruments and [c]pipe.
5 Praise Him
with resounding [a]cymbals;
Praise Him
with clashing cymbals.
6 Let [a]everything that has
breath praise Yah.
[1]Praise Yah!

---

**149:3** [a]2Sa 6:14; Ps 150:4 [b]Ex 15:20; Ps 81:2 **149:4** [a]Job 36:11; Ps 16:11; 35:27; 147:11 [b]Ps 132:16; Is 61:3 **149:5** [a]Ps 132:16 [b]Job 35:10; Ps 42:8 **149:6** [a]Ps 66:17 [b]Heb 4:12 [c]Ne 4:17 **149:7** [a]Eze 25:17; Mic 5:15 **149:8** [a]Job 36:8 [b]Na 3:10 **149:9** [a]Dt 7:12; Eze 28:26 [b]Ps 112:9; 148:14 [1]Or *Hallelujah!* ◆**150:1** [a]Ps 73:17; 102:19 [b]Ps 19:1 [1]Or *Hallelujah!* [2]Or *firmament* **150:2** [a]Ps 145:12 [b]Dt 3:24; Ps 145:3 **150:3** [a]Ps 98:6 [b]Ps 33:2 **150:4** [a]Ps 149:3 [b]Ps 45:8; Is 38:20 [c]Ge 4:21; Job 21:12 **150:5** [a]2Sa 6:5; 1Chr 13:8; 15:16; Ezr 3:10; Ne 12:27 **150:6** [a]Ps 103:22; 145:21 [1]Or *Hallelujah!*

# PROVERBS

### *To Know Wisdom*

1 The [a]proverbs of Solomon [b]the son of David, king of Israel:
2 To know [a]wisdom
and discipline,
To understand the sayings
of [b]understanding,
3 To [a]receive discipline
[1]*that leads to* insight,
[b]Righteousness, justice,
and equity,
4 To give [a]prudence
to the [b,1]simple,
To the youth [c]knowledge
and discretion;
5 Let the wise man hear and
[a]increase in learning,
And a [b]man of understanding
will acquire guidance,
6 To understand a proverb
and an enigma,
The words of the wise
and their [a]riddles.

7 [a]The fear of [1]Yahweh is
the beginning of knowledge;
[2]Ignorant fools despise
wisdom and discipline.

### *The Enticement of Sinners*

8 [a]Hear, my son, your
father's discipline
And [b]do not abandon your
mother's [1]instruction;
9 For they are a [a]garland
of grace for your head
And [b,1]ornaments
about your neck.
10 My son, if sinners [a]entice you,
[b]Do not be willing.
11 If they say, "Come with us,
Let us [a]lie in wait for blood,
Let us [b]ambush the innocent
without cause;
12 Let us [a]swallow them
alive like Sheol,
And whole, as those who
[b]go down to the pit;
13 We will find all *kinds*
of precious wealth,
We will fill our houses
with spoil;
14 Cast in your lot [1]with us,
We shall all have one purse,"
15 My son, [a]do not walk
in the way with them.
[b]Withhold your feet
from their pathway,
16 For [a]their feet run to evil
And they hasten
to shed blood.
17 For it is [1]no use
that a net is spread
In the sight of any [2]bird;
18 But they [a]lie in wait
for their own blood;
They ambush their
own [1]lives.

---

◆ **1:1** [a]1Ki 4:32; Pr 10:1; 25:1; Ecc 12:9 [b]Ecc 1:1 **1:2** [a]Pr 15:33 [b]Pr 4:1 **1:3** [a]Pr 2:1; 19:20 [b]Pr 2:9 [1]Lit *of*
**1:4** [a]Pr 8:5, 12 [b]Ps 19:7; 119:130 [c]Pr 2:10, 11; 3:21 [1]Or *naive* **1:5** [a]Pr 9:9 [b]Pr 14:6; Ecc 9:11
**1:6** [a]Nu 12:8; Ps 49:4; 78:2; Da 8:23 **1:7** [a]Job 28:28; Ps 111:10; Pr 9:10; 15:33; Ecc 12:13 [1]The personal covenant name of God, a form of I AM WHO I AM, cf. Ex 3:14-15 [2]One who lacks wisdom due to negligence or carelessness; so in Prov **1:8** [a]Pr 4:1 [b]Pr 6:20 [1]Or *law* **1:9** [a]Pr 4:9 [b]Ge 41:42; Da 5:29 [1]Lit *necklaces* **1:10** [a]Pr 16:29 [b]Ge 39:7-10; Dt 13:8; Ps 50:18; Eph 5:11 **1:11** [a]Pr 12:6; Jer 5:26 [b]Ps 10:8; Pr 1:18 **1:12** [a]Ps 124:3 [b]Ps 28:1 **1:14** [1]Lit *in the midst of us* **1:15** [a]Ps 1:1; Pr 4:14 [b]Ps 119:101
**1:16** [a]Pr 6:17, 18; Is 59:7 **1:17** [1]Lit *in vain* [2]Lit *possessor of wing* **1:18** [a]Pr 11:19 [1]Lit *souls*

19 So are the paths of everyone
who is [a]greedy for gain;
It takes away the [1]life
of its possessors.

### *The Call of Wisdom*

20 [a]Wisdom shouts
in the street,
She gives forth her voice
in the square;
21 At the head of the noisy
*streets* she calls out;
At the entrance
of the gates in the city
she utters her sayings:
22 “How long, O [a]simple ones,
will you love simplicity?
And [b]scoffers delight
in scoffing
And [1]fools [c]hate knowledge?
23 “Turn to my reproof,
Behold, I will [a]pour out
my spirit on you;
I will make my words
known to you.
24 “Because [a]I called and
you [b]refused,
I [c]stretched out my hand and
no one paid attention;
25 And you [a]neglected
all my counsel
And were not [b]willing
to accept my reproof;
26 I will also [a]laugh
at your [b]disaster;
I will mock when your
[c]dread comes,
27 When your dread
comes like a storm
And your disaster comes
like a [a]whirlwind,
When distress and anguish
come upon you.
28 “Then they will [a]call on me,
but I will not answer;
They will [b]seek me earnestly
but they will not find me,
29 Because they
[a]hated knowledge
And did not choose
the fear of Yahweh.
30 “They [a]were not willing
to accept my counsel,
They spurned all my reproof.
31 “So they shall [a]eat
of the fruit of their way
And be [b]satisfied
with their own devices.
32 “For the [a]turning away
of the simple will kill them,
And the complacency
of fools will destroy them.
33 “But [a]he who listens to me
shall dwell securely
And will be at ease
from the dread of evil.”

### *Yahweh Gives Wisdom*

2 My son, if you will
[a]receive my words
And [b]treasure my
commandments within you,
2 [a]To make your ear pay
attention to wisdom,
Incline your heart
to discernment;
3 For if you call out
for understanding,

---

**1:19** [a]Pr 15:27 [1]Lit *soul* **1:20** [a]Pr 8:1-3; 9:3 **1:22** [a]Pr 1:4, 32; 8:5; 9:4; 22:3 [b]Ps 1:1 [c]Pr 1:29; 5:12 [1]One who fails in wisdom due to willful sin **1:23** [a]Is 32:15; Joel 2:28; Jn 7:39 **1:24** [a]Is 65:12; 66:4; Jer 7:13 [b]Zec 7:11 [c]Is 65:2; Ro 10:21 **1:25** [a]Ps 107:11; Lk 7:30 [b]Pr 15:10 **1:26** [a]Ps 2:4 [b]Pr 6:15 [c]Pr 10:24 **1:27** [a]Pr 10:25 **1:28** [a]1Sa 8:18; Job 27:9; 35:12; Ps 18:41; Is 1:15; Jer 11:11; 14:12; Eze 8:18; Mic 3:4; Zec 7:13; Jas 4:3 [b]Pr 8:17 **1:29** [a]Job 21:14; Pr 1:22 **1:30** [a]Ps 81:11; Pr 1:25 **1:31** [a]Job 4:8; Pr 5:22, 23; 22:8; Is 3:11; Jer 6:19 [b]Pr 14:14 **1:32** [a]Jer 2:19 **1:33** [a]Ps 25:12, 13; Pr 3:24-26 ◆ **2:1** [a]Pr 4:10 [b]Pr 3:1 **2:2** [a]Pr 22:17

Give your voice
for discernment;
4 If you seek her as [a]silver
And search for her
as for [b]hidden treasures;
5 Then you will understand
the [a]fear of Yahweh
And find the knowledge
of God.
6 For [a]Yahweh gives wisdom;
From His mouth
*come* knowledge
and discernment.
7 He stores up sound wisdom
for the upright,
A [a]shield to those who
walk in integrity,
8 To guard the paths of justice,
And He [a]keeps the way
of His holy ones.
9 Then you will understand
[a]righteousness and justice
And equity—every
[b]good track.
10 For [a]wisdom will
enter your heart
And [b]knowledge will be
pleasant to your soul;
11 Discretion will [a]keep you,
Discernment will
guard you,
12 To [a]deliver you
from the way of evil,
From the man who speaks
[b]perverse things;
13 From those who [a]forsake
the paths of uprightness
To walk in the [b]ways
of darkness;
14 Who are [a]glad to do evil
And they rejoice
in the perversity of evil;
15 Whose paths are [a]crooked,
And who are devious
in their tracks;
16 To deliver you
from the [a,1]strange woman,
From the [b,2]foreign woman
who flatters
with her words;
17 Who forsakes the close
[a]companion of her youth
And forgets the [b]covenant
of her God;
18 For [a]her house [1]sinks
down to death
And her tracks *descend*
to the [2]dead;
19 All [a]who go to her
will not return,
And they will not reach
the [b]paths of life.
20 So that you will [a]walk
in the way of good men
And keep to the [b]paths
of the righteous.
21 For [a]the upright will
dwell in the land
And [b]the blameless
will remain in it;
22 But [a]the wicked will be
cut off from the land
And [b]the treacherous will
be [c]torn away from it.

**2:4** [a]Pr 3:14 [b]Job 3:21; Mt 13:44 **2:5** [a]Pr 1:7 **2:6** [a]1Ki 3:12; Job 32:8; Jas 1:5 **2:7** [a]Ps 84:11; Pr 30:5 **2:8** [a]1Sa 2:9; Ps 66:9 **2:9** [a]Pr 8:20 [b]Pr 4:18 **2:10** [a]Pr 14:33 [b]Pr 22:18 **2:11** [a]Pr 4:6; 6:22 **2:12** [a]Pr 28:26 [b]Pr 6:12 **2:13** [a]Pr 21:16 [b]Ps 82:5; Pr 4:19; Jn 3:19, 20 **2:14** [a]Pr 10:23; Jer 11:15 **2:15** [a]Ps 125:5; Pr 21:8 **2:16** [a]Pr 5:3, 20; 7:5; 22:14 [b]Pr 5:20; 6:24; 7:5; 23:27; 27:13 [1]A forbidden woman, outside of the marriage covenant; an adulteress; parallel with *foreign woman*; so in Prov [2]An unfamiliar woman, alien to the marriage covenant; parallel with *strange woman* **2:17** [a]Mal 2:14, 15 [b]Ge 2:24 **2:18** [a]Pr 7:27 [1]Lit *bows down* [2]Lit *departed spirits* **2:19** [a]Ecc 7:26 [b]Ps 16:11; Pr 5:6 **2:20** [a]Heb 6:12 [b]Pr 4:18 **2:21** [a]Ps 37:9, 29; Pr 10:30 [b]Pr 28:10 **2:22** [a]Ps 37:38; Pr 10:30 [b]Pr 11:3 [c]Dt 28:63; Ps 52:5

### *Trust, Fear, and Honor Yahweh*

**3** My son, [a]do not forget my [1]law,
But let your heart [b]guard
my commandments;
2 For [a]length of days
and years of life
And peace they will
add to you.
3 Do not let [a]lovingkindness
and truth forsake you;
[b]Bind them around your neck,
[c]Write them on the tablet
of your heart.
4 So you will [a]find favor
and [b]good insight
In the eyes of God and man.
5 [a]Trust in Yahweh
with all your heart
And [b]do not lean on your
own understanding.
6 In all your ways
[a,1]acknowledge Him,
And He will [b]make your
paths straight.
7 [a]Do not be wise
in your own eyes;
[b]Fear Yahweh and turn
away from evil.
8 It will be [a]healing
to your [1]body
And [b]refreshment
to your bones.
9 [a]Honor Yahweh
from your wealth
And from the [b]first
of all your produce;
10 So your [a]barns will be
filled with plenty
And your [b]vats will burst
with new wine.
11 [a]My son, do not reject
the [1]discipline of Yahweh
Or loathe His reproof,
12 For [a]whom Yahweh
loves He reproves,
Even [b]as a father
*reproves* the son
in whom he delights.

13 [a]How blessed is the man
who finds wisdom
And the man
who obtains discernment.
14 For her [a]profit is better
than the profit of silver
And her produce better
than fine gold.
15 She is [a]more precious
than [1]pearls;
And nothing you desire
compares with her.
16 [a]Length of days is
in her right hand;
In her left hand are
[b]riches and glory.
17 Her [a]ways are pleasant ways
And all her pathways
are [b]peace.
18 She is a [a]tree of life
to those who seize her,
And all those who hold
her fast are blessed.
19 Yahweh [a]by wisdom
founded the earth,
By discernment He
[b]established the heavens.

---

◆ **3:1** [a]Ps 119:61; Pr 4:5 [b]Ex 20:6; Dt 30:16 [1]Or *instruction* **3:2** [a]Ps 91:16; Pr 3:16; 4:10; 9:11; 10:27 **3:3** [a]2Sa 15:20; Pr 14:22 [b]Dt 6:8; 11:18; Pr 1:9; 6:21 [c]Pr 7:3; Jer 17:1; 2Co 3:3 **3:4** [a]1Sa 2:26; Pr 8:35; Lk 2:52 [b]Ps 111:10 **3:5** [a]Ps 37:3, 5; Pr 22:19 [b]Pr 23:4; Jer 9:23 **3:6** [a]1Chr 28:9; Pr 16:3; Php 4:6; Jas 1:5 [b]Is 45:13; Jer 10:23 [1]Lit *know* **3:7** [a]Ro 12:16 [b]Job 1:1; 28:28; Pr 8:13; 16:6 **3:8** [a]Pr 4:22 [b]Job 21:24 [1]Lit *navel* **3:9** [a]Is 43:23 [b]Ex 23:19; Dt 26:2; Mal 3:10 **3:10** [a]Dt 28:8 [b]Joel 2:24 **3:11** [a]Job 5:17; Heb 12:5, 6 [1]Or *instruction* **3:12** [a]Rev 3:19 [b]Dt 8:5; Pr 13:24 **3:13** [a]Pr 8:32, 34 **3:14** [a]Job 28:15-19; Pr 8:10, 19; 16:16 **3:15** [a]Job 28:18; Pr 8:11 [1]Or *corals* **3:16** [a]Pr 3:2 [b]Pr 8:18; 22:4 **3:17** [a]Mt 11:29 [b]Ps 119:165; Pr 16:7 **3:18** [a]Ge 2:9; Pr 11:30; 13:12; 15:4; Rev 2:7 **3:19** [a]Ps 104:24; Pr 8:27 [b]Pr 8:27, 28

20 By His knowledge
the [a]deeps were split up
And the [b]skies drip with dew.
21 My son, [a]let them not
deviate from your eyes;
Guard sound wisdom
and discretion,
22 So they will be [a]life
for your soul
And [b]grace for your neck.
23 Then you will [a]walk
in your way securely
And your foot will
not [b]stumble.
24 When you [a]lie down, you
will not be in dread;
You will lie down, and your
sleep will be pleasant.
25 [a]Do not be afraid
of sudden dread
Nor of the [b]storm
of the wicked when it comes;
26 For Yahweh will be
[1]your confidence
And will [a]keep your foot
from being caught.

27 [a]Do not withhold good
from [1]those to whom it is due,
When it is in your hand to do *it*.
28 [a]Do not say to your neighbor,
"Go, and come back,
And tomorrow I will give *it*,"
When it is there with you.
29 [a]Do not devise [1]harm
against your neighbor,
While he lives securely
beside you.
30 [a]Do not contend
with a man without cause,
If he has dealt you no [1]harm.
31 [a]Do not envy a man
of violence
And do not choose
any of his ways.
32 For the [a]devious one is
an abomination to Yahweh;
But His [b]secret council
is with the upright.
33 The [a]curse of Yahweh is on
the house of the wicked one,
But He [b]blesses the abode
of the righteous.
34 Though [a]He scoffs
at the scoffers,
Yet [b]He gives grace
to the humble.
35 [a]The wise will inherit glory,
But [1]fools raise up disgrace.

### *A Father's Wise Instruction*

4 Hear, *O* sons, the [a]discipline
of a father,
And [b]pay attention that you
may know understanding,
2 For I give you
[1]sound [a]learning;
[b]Do not forsake
my [2]instruction.
3 When I was a son to my father,
[a]Tender and [b]the only son
before my mother,
4 Then he [a]instructed me
and said to me,
"Let your heart [b]hold
fast my words;

**3:20** [a]Ge 7:11 [b]Dt 33:28; Job 36:28 **3:21** [a]Pr 4:21 **3:22** [a]Dt 32:47; Pr 4:22; 8:35; 16:22; 21:21 [b]Pr 1:9 **3:23** [a]Pr 4:12; 10:9 [b]Ps 91:12; Is 5:27; 63:13 **3:24** [a]Job 11:19; Ps 3:5; Pr 1:33; 6:22 **3:25** [a]Ps 91:5; 1Pe 3:14 [b]Job 5:21 **3:26** [a]1Sa 2:9 [1]Or *at your side* **3:27** [a]Ro 13:7; Ga 6:10 [1]Lit *its owners* **3:28** [a]Lv 19:13; Dt 24:15 **3:29** [a]Pr 6:14; 14:22 [1]Lit *evil* **3:30** [a]Pr 26:17; Ro 12:18 [1]Lit *evil* **3:31** [a]Ps 37:1; Pr 24:1 **3:32** [a]Pr 11:20 [b]Job 29:4; Ps 25:14 **3:33** [a]Lv 26:14, 16; Dt 11:28; Zec 5:3, 4; Mal 2:2 [b]Job 8:6; Ps 1:3 **3:34** [a]Jas 4:6 [b]1Pe 5:5 **3:35** [a]Da 12:3 [1]Or *He raises fools up in dishonor* ◆ **4:1** [a]Ps 34:11; Pr 1:8 [b]Pr 1:2; 2:2 **4:2** [a]Dt 32:2; Job 11:4 [b]Ps 89:30; 119:87; Pr 3:1 [1]Lit *good* [2]Or *law* **4:3** [a]1Chr 22:5; 29:1 [b]Zec 12:10 **4:4** [a]Eph 6:4 [b]Ps 119:168

[c]Keep my commandments
and live;
5 [a]Acquire wisdom! [b]Acquire
understanding!
Do not forget and do
not turn away from
the sayings of my mouth.
6 "Do not forsake her, and
she will keep you;
[a]Love her, and she
will guard you.
7 "[a,1]The beginning of wisdom
*is*: [b]Acquire wisdom;
And with all your acquiring,
acquire understanding.
8 "[a]Prize her, and she
will exalt you;
She will honor you
if you embrace her.
9 "She will give [a]for your
head a garland of grace;
She will present you
with a crown of beauty."

10 Hear, my son, and
[a]receive my sayings
And the [b]years of your
life will be many.
11 I have [a]instructed you
in the way of wisdom;
I have led you in upright tracks.
12 When you walk, your [a]steps
will not be impeded;
And if you run, you
[b]will not stumble.
13 [a]Seize discipline; do not let go.
Guard her, for she is your [b]life.
14 [a]Do not enter the path
of wicked men
And do not step
into the way of evil men.
15 Avoid it, do not pass by it;
[a]Stray from it and pass on.
16 For they [a]do not sleep
unless they do evil;
And [1]they are robbed
of sleep unless they make
*someone* stumble.
17 For they [a]eat the bread
of wickedness
And drink the wine
of violence.
18 But the [a]path
of the righteous is
like the [b]light of dawn,
That [c]shines brighter
and brighter
until the [d]fullness of day.
19 The [a]way of the wicked is
like thick darkness;
They do not know
over what they [b,1]stumble.

20 My son, [a]pay attention
to my words;
[b]Incline your ear
to my sayings.
21 [a]Do not let them deviate
from your eyes;
[b]Keep them in the midst
of your heart.
22 For they are [a]life to those
who find them
And [b]healing to all his flesh.
23 Guard your heart
with all diligence,
For [a]from it *flow*
the springs of life.

**4:4** [c]Pr 7:2 **4:5** [a]Pr 4:7 [b]Pr 16:16 **4:6** [a]2Th 2:10 **4:7** [a]Pr 8:23 [b]Pr 23:23 [1]Or *The primary thing is wisdom* **4:8** [a]1Sa 2:30 **4:9** [a]Pr 1:9 **4:10** [a]Pr 2:1 [b]Pr 3:2 **4:11** [a]1Sa 12:23 **4:12** [a]Job 18:7; Ps 18:36 [b]Ps 91:11; Pr 3:23 **4:13** [a]Pr 3:18 [b]Pr 3:22; Jn 6:63 **4:14** [a]Ps 1:1; Pr 1:15 **4:15** [a]Nu 5:12 **4:16** [a]Ps 36:4; Mic 2:1 [1]Lit *their sleep is robbed* **4:17** [a]Pr 13:2 **4:18** [a]Is 26:7; Mt 5:14; Php 2:15 [b]2Sa 23:4 [c]Da 12:3 [d]Job 11:17 **4:19** [a]Job 18:5, 6; Pr 2:13; Is 59:9, 10; Jer 23:12; Jn 12:35 [b]Jn 11:10 [1]Or *may stumble* **4:20** [a]Pr 5:1 [b]Pr 2:2 **4:21** [a]Pr 3:21 [b]Pr 7:1, 2 **4:22** [a]Pr 3:22 [b]Pr 3:8; 12:18 **4:23** [a]Mt 12:34; 15:18, 19; Mk 7:21; Lk 6:45

24 Put away from you
a [a]perverse mouth
And [b]put devious lips
far from you.
25 Let your eyes look
directly ahead
And *even* let your eyelids be
fixed straight in front of you.
26 [a]Watch the track of your feet
And all your [b]ways will
be established.
27 [a]Do not turn to the right
nor to the left;
[b]Turn your foot from evil.

### *Warning Against Adultery*

5 My son, [a]pay attention
to my wisdom,
[b]Incline your ear to
my discernment;
2 That you may [a]keep discretion
And that your [b]lips may
guard knowledge.
3 For the lips of a [a]strange
woman [b]drip honey
And [c]smoother
than oil is her [1]speech;
4 But her end is [a]bitter
as wormwood,
[b]Sharp as a two-edged sword.
5 Her feet [a]go down to death,
Her steps take hold of Sheol,
6 Lest she watch
the [a]path of life;
Her tracks are [b]unstable,
she [c]does not know *it*.

7 [a]So now, *my* sons, listen to me
And [b]do not turn away
from the words of my mouth.
8 [a]Keep your way far from her
And do not go
near the [b]door of her house,
9 Lest you give your
splendor to others
And your years to the cruel one;
10 Lest strangers be satisfied
by your strength
And by your painful
labor, *those* in the house
of a foreigner;
11 And you groan at your [1]end,
When your flesh and your
body are consumed;
12 And you say, "How I have
[a]hated discipline!
And my heart
[b]spurned reproof!
13 "I have not listened to the voice
of my [a]instructors,
And I have not inclined
my ear to my teachers!
14 "I was almost in utter ruin
In the midst of the assembly
and congregation."

15 Drink water from your
own cistern
And [1]fresh water
from your own well.
16 Should your [a]springs be
dispersed abroad,
Streams of water
in the streets?
17 Let them be for you alone,
And not for strangers
with you.
18 Let your [a]fountain be blessed,
And [b]be glad in the [c]wife
of your youth.

**4:24** [a]Pr 6:12; 10:32 [b]Pr 19:1 **4:26** [a]Pr 5:21; Heb 12:13 [b]Ps 119:5 **4:27** [a]Dt 5:32; 28:14 [b]Pr 1:15; Is 1:16
◆ **5:1** [a]Pr 4:20 [b]Pr 22:17 **5:2** [a]Pr 3:21 [b]Mal 2:7 **5:3** [a]Pr 2:16; 5:20; 7:5; 22:14 [b]SS 4:11 [c]Ps 55:21 [1]Lit *palate* **5:4** [a]Ecc 7:26 [b]Ps 57:4; Heb 4:12 **5:5** [a]Pr 7:27 **5:6** [a]Pr 4:26; 5:21 [b]2Pe 2:14 [c]Pr 30:20
**5:7** [a]Pr 7:24 [b]Ps 119:102 **5:8** [a]Pr 7:25 [b]Pr 9:14 **5:11** [1]Or *latter* **5:12** [a]Pr 1:7, 22, 29 [b]Pr 1:25; 12:1
**5:13** [a]Pr 1:8 **5:15** [1]Lit *flowing* **5:16** [a]Pr 5:18; 9:17; SS 4:12, 15 **5:18** [a]Pr 9:17; SS 4:12, 15 [b]Ecc 9:9
[c]Mal 2:14

19 *As* a loving [a]hind and
a graceful doe,
Let her breasts satisfy
you at all times;
Be [1]intoxicated always
with her love.
20 So why should you, my
son, be intoxicated
with a [a]strange woman
And embrace the bosom
of a [b]foreign woman?
21 For the [a]ways of a man are
before the eyes of Yahweh,
And He [b]watches
all his tracks.
22 His [a]own iniquities will
capture him *who is*
the wicked one,
And with the cords of his
sin he will be held fast.
23 He will [a]die for lack
of discipline,
And in the abundance
of his [1]folly he will [2]stumble
in intoxication.

### Practical Warnings

6 My son, if you have
become a [a]guarantor
for your neighbor,
Have struck your [1]hands
*in pledge* for a stranger,
2 *If* you have been snared with
the words of your mouth,
Have been caught with
the words of your mouth,
3 Do this then, my son,
and deliver yourself;
Since you have come into
the [1]hand of your neighbor,
Go, humble yourself, and
badger your neighbor.
4 Give no [a]sleep to your eyes,
Nor slumber to your eyelids;
5 Deliver yourself like a gazelle
from *the hunter's* hand
And like a [a]bird
from the hand of the fowler.

6 Go to the [a]ant, O [b]sluggard,
Observe her ways
and be wise,
7 Which, having [a]no chief,
Officer or ruler,
8 Prepares her food
[a]in the summer
*And* gathers her provision
in the harvest.
9 How long will you lie
down, O sluggard?
When will you arise
from your sleep?
10 "[a]A little sleep, a little slumber,
A little folding
of the hands to [1]rest"—
11 [a]Your poverty will come
in like [1]a vagabond
And your want
like [2]an armed man.

12 A [a]vile person, a wicked man,
Is the one who walks
with a [b]perverse mouth,
13 Who [a]winks with his eyes,
who [1]signals with his feet,
Who [2]points with his fingers;

**5:19** [a]SS 2:9, 17; 4:5; 7:3 [1]Or *exhilarated* **5:20** [a]Pr 5:3 [b]Pr 2:16; 6:24; 7:5; 23:27 **5:21** [a]Job 14:16; 31:4; 34:21; Ps 119:168; Pr 15:3; Jer 16:17; 32:19; Hos 7:2; Heb 4:13 [b]Pr 4:26 **5:22** [a]Nu 32:23; Ps 7:15; 9:15; 40:12; Pr 1:31, 32 **5:23** [a]Job 4:21; 36:12 [1]A lack of wisdom due to negligence or carelessness; the activity of an ignorant fool [2]Or *go astray* ◆ **6:1** [a]Pr 11:15; 17:18; 20:16; 22:26; 27:13 [1]Lit *palms* **6:3** [1]Lit *palm* **6:4** [a]Ps 132:4 **6:5** [a]Ps 91:3; 124:7 **6:6** [a]Pr 30:24, 25 [b]Pr 6:9; 10:26; 13:4; 20:4; 26:16 **6:7** [a]Pr 30:27 **6:8** [a]Pr 10:5 **6:10** [a]Pr 24:33 [1]Lit *lie down* **6:11** [a]Pr 24:34 [1]Lit *one who walks* [2]Lit *a man with a shield* **6:12** [a]Pr 16:27 [b]Pr 4:24; 10:32 **6:13** [a]Job 15:12; Ps 35:19; Pr 10:10 [1]Lit *scrapes* [2]Lit *instructs*

14 Who *with* [a]perversity
in his heart continually
[b]devises evil,
Who [c,1]spreads contentions.
15 Therefore [a]his disaster
will come suddenly;
[b]Instantly he will be
broken and there will
be [c]no healing.

16 There are six things
which Yahweh hates,
Even seven which are
an abomination [1]to Him:
17 [a]Haughty eyes,
a [b]lying tongue,
And hands that [c]shed
innocent blood,
18 A heart that devises
[a]wicked thoughts,
[b]Feet that hasten
to run to evil,
19 A [a]false witness *who*
breathes out lies,
And one who [b,1]spreads
strife among brothers.

### *Warning Against Adultery*

20 [a]My son, observe
the commandment
of your father
And do not abandon
the [1]law of your mother;
21 [a]Bind them continually
on your heart;
Tie them around your neck.
22 When you [a]walk about,
[1]they will lead you;
When you sleep, [1]they will
keep watch over you;
And when you awake,
[1]they will speak to you.
23 For [a]the commandment is
a lamp and the [1]law is light;
And reproofs for discipline
are the way of life
24 To [a]keep you
from the evil woman,
From the smooth tongue
of the foreign woman.
25 [a]Do not desire her beauty
in your heart,
Nor let her capture you
with her [b]eyelids.
26 For [a]on account of [1]a
harlot *one is reduced*
to a loaf of bread,
And [2]an adulteress [b]hunts
for the precious [3]life.
27 Can a man [1]take fire
in his bosom
And his clothes not
be burned?
28 Or can a man walk
on hot coals
And his feet not be scorched?
29 So is the one who [a]goes in
to his neighbor's wife;
Whoever touches her [b]will
not [1]go unpunished.
30 [1]*Men* do not despise
a thief if he steals
To [a]fill [2]himself
when he is hungry;
31 But when he is found, he
must [a]repay sevenfold;

**6:14** [a]Pr 17:20 [b]Pr 3:29; Mic 2:1 [c]Pr 6:19; 16:28 [1]Lit *sends out* **6:15** [a]Pr 24:22 [b]Is 30:13, 14; Jer 19:11 [c]2Chr 36:16 **6:16** [1]Lit *of His soul* **6:17** [a]Ps 18:27; 101:5; Pr 21:4; 30:13 [b]Ps 31:18; 120:2; Pr 12:22; 17:7 [c]Dt 19:10; Pr 28:17; Is 1:15; 59:7 **6:18** [a]Ge 6:5; Pr 24:2 [b]Pr 1:16; Is 59:7; Ro 3:15 **6:19** [a]Ps 27:12; Pr 12:17; 19:5, 9; 21:28 [b]Pr 6:14 [1]Lit *sends out* **6:20** [a]Eph 6:1 [1]Or *instruction* **6:21** [a]Pr 3:3 **6:22** [a]Pr 3:23 [1]Lit *she* **6:23** [a]Ps 19:8; 119:105 [1]Or *instruction* **6:24** [a]Pr 5:3; 7:5, 21 **6:25** [a]Mt 5:28 [b]2Ki 9:30; Jer 4:30; Eze 23:40 **6:26** [a]Pr 5:9, 10; 29:3 [b]Pr 7:23; Eze 13:18 [1]Or *a woman who is a harlot* [2]Or *a woman of another man* [3]Lit *soul* **6:27** [1]Lit *snatch up* **6:29** [a]Eze 18:6; 33:26 [b]Pr 16:5 [1]Lit *be innocent* **6:30** [a]Job 38:39 [1]Or *Do not men...?*; lit *They do not* [2]Lit *his soul* **6:31** [a]Ex 22:1-4

He must give all
the [1]substance of his house.
32 The one who commits
adultery with a woman is
[a]lacking a heart *of wisdom*;
He who would [b]destroy
his soul does it.
33 Wounds and disgrace
he will find,
And his reproach will
not be blotted out.
34 For [a]jealousy [1]enrages a man,
And he will not spare
in the [b]day of vengeance.
35 He will not [1]accept any ransom,
He will not be willing though
you give many bribes.

### *The Adulteress' Trap*

7 My son, [a]keep my words
And treasure my
commandments within you.
2 [a]Keep my commandments
and live,
And my [1]law [b]as the [2]apple
of your eye.
3 [a]Bind them on your fingers;
[b]Write them on the tablet
of your heart.
4 Say to wisdom,
"You are my sister,"
And call understanding
*your* intimate friend;
5 In order to keep you
from the strange woman,
From the foreign woman who
[1]flatters with her words.

6 For [a]at the window
of my house
I looked out
[b]through my lattice,
7 And I saw
among the [a]simple,
*And* discerned
among the [1]sons
A young man [b]lacking
a heart *of wisdom*,
8 Passing through the street
near [a]her corner;
And he strides
along the way to [b]her house,
9 In the [a]twilight,
in the evening of *that* day,
In the [1]middle
of the night, and
*in* the thick darkness.
10 And behold, a woman
*comes* to meet him,
[a]Dressed as a harlot and
[1]cunning of heart.
11 She is [a]boisterous
and rebellious,
Her [b]feet do not
dwell at home;
12 Stepping in the streets,
stepping [a]in the squares,
And near every corner
she [b]lies in wait.
13 So she seizes him
and kisses him
[1]And with a [a]brazen face
she says to him:
14 "The sacrifices of [a]peace
offerings are with me;
Today I [b]paid my vows.
15 "Therefore I have come
out to meet you,
To seek your face earnestly,
and I have found you.

**6:31** [1]Or *wealth* **6:32** [a]Pr 7:7; 9:4, 16; 10:13, 21; 11:12; 12:11 [b]Pr 7:22, 23 **6:34** [a]Pr 27:4; SS 8:6 [b]Pr 11:4 [1]Lit *is the rage of* **6:35** [1]Lit *lift up the face of* ◆ **7:1** [a]Pr 2:1; 6:20 **7:2** [a]Pr 4:4 [b]Dt 32:10; Ps 17:8; Zec 2:8 [1]Or *instruction* [2]Lit *pupil* **7:3** [a]Dt 6:8; 11:18; Pr 6:21 [b]Pr 3:3 **7:5** [1]Lit *is smooth* **7:6** [a]Jdg 5:28 [b]SS 2:9 **7:7** [a]Pr 1:22 [b]Pr 6:32; 9:4 [1]Or *youths* **7:8** [a]Pr 7:12 [b]Pr 7:27 **7:9** [a]Job 24:15 [1]Lit *pupil* (of the eye) **7:10** [a]Ge 38:14, 15; 1Ti 2:9 [1]Lit *guarded* **7:11** [a]Pr 9:13 [b]1Ti 5:13; Tit 2:5 **7:12** [a]Pr 9:14 [b]Pr 23:28 **7:13** [a]Pr 21:29 [1]Lit *She makes bold her face and says* **7:14** [a]Lv 7:11 [b]Lv 7:16

16 "I have spread my couch
with [a]coverings,
With colored [b]linens of Egypt.
17 "I have sprinkled my bed
With [a]myrrh, aloes,
and [b]cinnamon.
18 "Come, then, let us drink our
fill as lovers until morning;
Let us delight ourselves
with the pleasures of love.
19 "For [1]my husband is
not at home,
He has gone
on a journey far away;
20 He took a [a]bag of silver
in his hand,
On the day of the full moon
he will come home."
21 With her abundant
[1]persuasions she
entices him;
With her [a]flattering lips she
drives him *to herself*.
22 He suddenly follows her
As an ox goes to the slaughter,
Or [1]as *one in* fetters
to the discipline
of an ignorant fool,
23 Until an arrow pierces
through his liver;
As a [a]bird hastens to the snare,
And he does not know
that it *will cost him* his [1]soul.

24 So now, *my* sons, [a]listen to me,
And pay attention
to the words of my mouth.
25 Do not let your heart [a]go
astray into her ways,
Do not wander
*into* her pathways.
26 For many are the slain
*whom* she has cast down,
And [a]numerous are all
those killed by her.
27 The ways to Sheol *are*
*in* her [a]house,
Descending to the chambers
of death.

### *The Blessing of Wisdom*

8 Does not [a]wisdom call,
And discernment give
forth her voice?
2 At the top of [a]the heights
upon the way,
Where the pathways meet,
she takes her stand;
3 Beside the [a]gates,
at the opening to the city,
At the entrance of
the doors, she
makes a shout:
4 "To you, O men, I call,
And my voice is
to the sons of men.
5 "O [a]simple ones,
understand prudence;
And, O [b]fools, understand
a heart *of wisdom*.
6 "Listen, for I will speak
[a]noble things;
And the opening of my lips
*will reveal* [b]upright things.
7 "For my [a]mouth will
utter truth;
And wickedness is
an abomination to my lips.
8 "All the words of my mouth
are in righteousness;
There is nothing [a]twisted
or crooked in them.

**7:16** [a]Pr 31:22 [b]Is 19:9; Eze 27:7 **7:17** [a]Ps 45:8 [b]Ex 30:23 **7:19** [1]Lit *the man* **7:20** [a]Ge 42:35
**7:21** [a]Pr 5:3; 6:24 [1]Lit *learning* **7:22** [1]Some ancient versions *as a stag goes into a trap* **7:23** [a]Ecc 9:12
[1]Or *life* **7:24** [a]Pr 5:7 **7:25** [a]Pr 5:8 **7:26** [a]Pr 9:18 **7:27** [a]Pr 2:18; 5:5; 9:18; 1Co 6:9, 10; Rev 22:15
◆ **8:1** [a]Pr 1:20, 21; 8:1-3; 9:3; 1Co 1:24 **8:2** [a]Pr 9:3, 14 **8:3** [a]Job 29:7 **8:5** [a]Pr 1:4 [b]Pr 1:22, 32; 3:35
**8:6** [a]Pr 22:20 [b]Pr 23:16 **8:7** [a]Ps 37:30; Jn 8:14; Ro 15:8 **8:8** [a]Dt 32:5; Pr 2:15; Php 2:15

9 “They are all [a]straightforward
to him who understands,
And right to those who
[b]find knowledge.
10 “Take my [a]discipline
and not silver,
And knowledge rather
than choicest fine gold.
11 “For wisdom is [a]better
than pearls;
And [b]all desirable things
cannot compare with her.

12 “I, wisdom, [a]dwell
with prudence,
And I find [b]knowledge
*and* discretion.
13 “The [a]fear of Yahweh
is to hate evil;
[b]Pride and arrogance
and [c]the evil way
And the mouth
of [d,1]perverted *words*, I hate.
14 “[a]Counsel is mine and
[b]sound wisdom;
I am understanding,
[c]might is mine.
15 “By me [a]kings reign,
And rulers
mark out righteousness.
16 “By me princes rule, and nobles,
All who judge rightly.
17 “I [a]love those who love me;
And [b]those who earnestly
seek me will find me.
18 “[a]Riches and glory
are with me,
Enduring [b]wealth
and righteousness.
19 “My fruit is [a]better than fine
gold, even pure gold,
And my produce *better*
than [b]choice silver.
20 “I walk in the path
of righteousness,
In the midst of the pathways
of justice,
21 To give those who love me
an inheritance of wealth,
That I may [a]fill
their treasuries.

22 “Yahweh possessed me
[a]at the beginning of His way,
Before His deeds [1]of old.
23 “From everlasting I
was [a,1]installed,
From the beginning,
[b]from the earliest
times of the earth.
24 “When there were no [a]depths
I was [1]brought forth,
When there were no springs
heavy with water.
25 “[a]Before the mountains
were settled,
Before the hills I was
[1]brought forth;
26 While He had not yet
made the earth and
the *fields* outside,
Nor the first dust of the world.
27 “When He [a]established
the heavens, I was there,
When [b]He marked out a circle
on the face of the deep,
28 When He made firm
the skies above,

**8:9** [a]Pr 14:6 [b]Pr 3:13 **8:10** [a]Pr 3:14, 15; 8:19 **8:11** [a]Job 28:15, 18; Ps 19:10 [b]Pr 3:15 **8:12** [a]Pr 8:5 [b]Pr 1:4 **8:13** [a]Pr 3:7; 16:6 [b]1Sa 2:3; Pr 16:18; Is 13:11 [c]Pr 15:9 [d]Pr 6:12 [1]Lit *perversities* **8:14** [a]Pr 1:25; 19:20; Is 28:29; Jer 32:19 [b]Pr 2:7; 3:21; 18:1 [c]Ecc 7:19; 9:16 **8:15** [a]2Chr 1:10; Pr 29:4; Da 2:21; Mt 28:18; Ro 13:1 **8:17** [a]1Sa 2:30; Pr 4:6; Jn 14:21 [b]Pr 2:4, 5; Jn 7:37; Jas 1:5 **8:18** [a]Pr 3:16 [b]Ps 112:3; Mt 6:33 **8:19** [a]Job 28:15; Pr 3:14 [b]Pr 10:20 **8:21** [a]Pr 24:4 **8:22** [a]Job 28:26-28; Ps 104:24; Pr 3:19 [1]Lit *from then* **8:23** [a]Ps 2:6; Jn 1:1-3 [b]Jn 17:5 [1]Or *consecrated* **8:24** [a]Ge 1:2; Ex 15:5; Job 38:16; Pr 3:20 [1]Or *born* **8:25** [a]Job 15:7; Ps 90:2 [1]Or *born* **8:27** [a]Pr 3:19 [b]Job 26:10

When the springs
of the deep became strong,
29 When [a]He set for the sea
its boundary
So that the water would not
pass over His [1]command,
When He marked out [b]the
foundations of the earth;
30 Then [a]I was beside Him,
*as* a master workman;
And I was a daily delight,
[1]Rejoicing always before Him,
31 [1]Rejoicing in the world,
His earth,
[a]My delight *is*
in the sons of men.

32 "So now, O sons, [a]listen to me,
For [b]blessed are they
who keep my ways.
33 "[a]Hear discipline and be wise,
And do not neglect *it*.
34 "[a]How blessed is the man
who hears me,
To watch daily at my doors,
To keep watch at my doorposts.
35 "For [a]he who finds me finds life
And [b]obtains favor
from Yahweh.
36 "But he who [1]sins
against me [a]does violence
to his own soul;
All those who [b]hate
me [c]love death."

### *Wisdom and Foolishness Call Out*

9 Wisdom has [a]built her house,
She has hewn out her
seven pillars;
2 She has [a,1]slaughtered her cattle,
she has [b]mixed her wine;
She has also [c]prepared
her table;
3 She has [a]sent out her
maidens, she [b]calls
From the [c]tops
of the heights of the city:
4 "[a]Whoever is simple, let
him turn in here!"
To him who [b]lacks a heart
*of wisdom* she says,
5 "Come, [a]eat of my bread
And drink of the wine
I have mixed.
6 "[1]Forsake *your* simplicity
and [a]live,
And [b]step into the way
of understanding."

7 He who [a]disciplines a scoffer
receives disgrace for himself,
And he who reproves
a wicked man *receives*
injury for himself.
8 [a]Do not reprove a scoffer,
lest he hate you,
[b]Reprove a wise man and
he will love you.
9 Give *knowledge* to a wise man
and he will be still wiser,
Make a righteous man
know *it* and he will
[a]increase *his* learning.
10 The [a]fear of Yahweh is
the beginning of wisdom,
And the knowledge of
the Holy One
is understanding.

***8:29*** [a]*Job 38:10; Ps 104:9* [b]Job 38:6; Ps 104:5 [1]Lit *mouth* **8:30** [a]Jn 1:2, 3 [1]Or *Playing* **8:31** [a]Ps 16:3; Jn 13:1 [1]Or *Playing* **8:32** [a]Pr 5:7; 7:24 [b]Ps 119:1, 2; 128:1; Pr 29:18; Lk 11:28 **8:33** [a]Pr 4:1 **8:34** [a]Pr 3:13, 18 **8:35** [a]Pr 4:22; Jn 17:3 [b]Pr 3:4; 12:2 **8:36** [a]Pr 1:31, 32; 15:32 [b]Pr 5:12; 12:1 [c]Pr 21:6 [1]Or *misses me* ◆ **9:1** [a]1Co 3:9, 10; Eph 2:20-22; 1Pe 2:5 **9:2** [a]Mt 22:4 [b]Ps 23:5; SS 8:2 [c]Lk 14:16, 17 [1]Lit *slaughtered her slaughter* **9:3** [a]Ps 68:11; Mt 22:3 [b]Pr 8:1, 2 [c]Pr 9:14 **9:4** [a]Pr 8:5; 9:16 [b]Pr 6:32 **9:5** [a]SS 5:1; Is 55:1; Jn 6:27 **9:6** [a]Pr 8:35; 9:11 [b]Eze 11:20; 37:24 [1]Or *Forsake the simple ones* **9:7** [a]Pr 23:9 **9:8** [a]Pr 15:12; Mt 7:6 [b]Ps 141:5; Pr 10:8 **9:9** [a]Pr 1:5 **9:10** [a]Job 28:28; Ps 111:10; Pr 1:7

11 For [a]by me your days
will become many,
And years of life will
be added to you.
12 If you are wise, you are
wise [a]for yourself,
And if you [b]scoff, you
alone will bear it.

13 The woman of [1]foolishness
is [a]boisterous,
*A woman of* simplicity,
and [b]does not
know anything.
14 She sits at the doorway
of her house,
On a seat by [a]the high
places of the city,
15 To call to those who
pass by *that* way,
Who are making their
paths straight:
16 "[a]Whoever is simple, let
him turn in here,"
And to him who lacks a heart
*of wisdom* she says,
17 "Stolen water is sweet;
And [a]bread *eaten*
in secret is pleasant."
18 But he does not know
that the [1]dead are there,
*That* those she called are
in the [a]depths of Sheol.

### *Contrast of the Righteous and the Wicked*

10 The [a]proverbs of Solomon.
[b]A wise son makes
a father glad,
But [c]a foolish son is
a grief to his mother.
2 [a]Treasures *gained*
by wickedness do not profit,
But righteousness
delivers from death.
3 Yahweh [a]will not allow
the soul of the righteous
to hunger,
But He [b]will push away
the craving of the wicked.
4 Poor is he who works
with a slack [1]hand,
But the [a]hand of the diligent
makes rich.
5 He who gathers in summer is
a son who acts insightfully,
*But* he who sleeps in harvest is
a son who acts shamefully.
6 [a]Blessings are on the head
of the righteous,
But [b]the mouth of the wicked
covers up violence.
7 The [a]remembrance
of the righteous is blessed,
But [b]the name
of the wicked will rot.
8 The [a]wise of heart will
receive commandments,
But an ignorant fool of *loose*
lips will be [1]ruined.
9 He [a]who walks in integrity
walks securely,
But [b]he who makes his ways
crooked will be found out.
10 He [a]who winks the eye
causes pain,
And [b]an ignorant fool
of *loose* lips will be [1]ruined.

**9:11** [a]Pr 3:16; 10:27 **9:12** [a]Job 22:2; Pr 14:14 [b]Pr 19:29 **9:13** [a]Pr 7:11 [b]Pr 5:6 [1]Insolent foolishness of one who fails in wisdom due to willful sin **9:14** [a]Pr 9:3 **9:16** [a]Pr 9:4 **9:17** [a]Pr 20:17 **9:18** [a]Pr 7:27 [1]Lit *departed spirits* ◆ **10:1** [a]Pr 1:1 [b]Pr 15:20; 29:3 [c]Pr 17:25; 29:15 **10:2** [a]Ps 49:7; Pr 11:4; 21:6; Eze 7:19; Lk 12:19, 20 **10:3** [a]Ps 34:9, 10; 37:25; Pr 28:25; Mt 6:33 [b]Ps 112:10; Pr 28:9 **10:4** [a]Pr 13:4; 21:5 [1]Lit *palm* **10:6** [a]Pr 28:20 [b]Pr 10:11; Ob 10 **10:7** [a]Ps 112:6 [b]Ps 9:5, 6; 109:13; Ecc 8:10 **10:8** [a]Pr 9:8; Mt 7:24 [1]Lit *thrust down* **10:9** [a]Ps 23:4; Pr 3:23; 28:18; Is 33:15, 16 [b]Pr 26:26; Mt 10:26; 1Ti 5:25 **10:10** [a]Ps 35:19; Pr 6:13 [b]Pr 10:8 [1]Lit *thrust down*

11 The [a]mouth of the righteous
is a fountain of life,
But [b]the mouth of the wicked
covers up violence.
12 Hatred stirs up strife,
But [a]love covers
all transgressions.
13 On [a]the lips of the one
who has understanding,
wisdom is found,
But [b]a rod is for the back
of him who lacks
a heart *of wisdom.*
14 Wise men
[a]store up knowledge,
But [b]the mouth
of the ignorant fool
draws ruin near.
15 The [a]rich man's wealth
is his strong city,
The [b]ruin of the poor
is their poverty.
16 The [a,1]wages
of the righteous is life,
The income
of the wicked, punishment.
17 He [a]is *on* the path of life
who keeps discipline,
But he who forsakes
reproof makes [1]himself
wander about.
18 He [a]who covers up
hatred *has* lying lips,
And he who spreads
a bad report is a fool.
19 When there are [a]many
words, transgression
is unavoidable,
But [b]he who holds back
his lips has insight.
20 The tongue of the righteous
is *as* [a]choice silver,
The heart of the wicked
is *worth* little.
21 The [a]lips of the righteous
feed many,
But ignorant fools [b]die
for lack of a heart *of wisdom.*
22 It is the [a]blessing of Yahweh
that makes rich,
And He adds no pain with it.
23 Doing wickedness is
like [a]laughing to a fool,
And *so is* wisdom to a man
of discernment.
24 What [a]the wicked dreads
will come upon him,
But the [b]desire of
the righteous will
be granted.
25 When the [a]whirlwind passes,
the wicked is no more,
But the [b]righteous *has*
an everlasting foundation.
26 Like vinegar to the teeth and
like smoke to the eyes,
So is the [a]sluggard
to those who send him.
27 The [a]fear of Yahweh
prolongs [1]life,
But the [b]years of the wicked
will be shortened.
28 The [a]expectation
of the righteous is gladness,
But the [b]hope
of the wicked will perish.

**10:11** [a]Ps 37:30; Pr 13:14; 18:4 [b]Pr 10:6 **10:12** [a]*Pr 17:9; 1Co 13:4-7; Jas 5:20;* 1Pe 4:8 **10:13** [a]Pr 10:31 [b]*Pr 19:29; 26:3* **10:14** [a]*Pr 9:9* [b]Pr 10:8, 10; 13:3; 18:7 **10:15** [a]Job 31:24; Ps 52:7; Pr 18:11 [b]Pr 19:7 **10:16** [a]Pr 11:18, 19 [1]Or *work* **10:17** [a]Pr 6:23; 12:26 [1]Or *others* **10:18** [a]Pr 26:24 **10:19** [a]Job 11:2; Pr 18:21; Ecc 5:3 [b]Pr 17:27; Jas 1:19; 3:2 **10:20** [a]Pr 8:19 **10:21** [a]Pr 10:11 [b]Pr 5:23; Hos 4:6 **10:22** [a]Ge 24:35; 26:12; Dt 8:18; Pr 8:21 **10:23** [a]Pr 2:14; 15:21 **10:24** [a]Job 15:21; Ps 34:4; Pr 1:27; Is 66:4 [b]Ps 145:19; Pr 15:8; Mt 5:6; 1Jn 5:14, 15 **10:25** [a]Job 21:18; Ps 58:9; Pr 12:7 [b]Ps 15:5; Pr 12:3; Mt 7:24, 25 **10:26** [a]Pr 26:6 **10:27** [a]Pr 3:2; 9:11; 14:27 [b]Job 15:32, 33; 22:16; Ps 55:23 [1]Lit *days* **10:28** [a]Pr 11:23 [b]Job 8:13; 11:20; Pr 11:7

29 The [a]way of Yahweh is
a stronghold to the one
with integrity,
But [b]ruin to the workers
of iniquity.
30 The [a]righteous will
never be shaken,
But [b]the wicked will not
dwell in the land.
31 The [a]mouth of the righteous
bears wisdom,
But the tongue of [b]perversions
will be cut out.
32 The lips of the righteous
know [a]what is acceptable,
But the [b]mouth of the wicked
[1]what is perverse.

11 A [a]deceptive balance is
an abomination to Yahweh,
But a [b]just weight is
His delight.
2 When [a]arrogance comes,
then comes disgrace,
But with the meek is wisdom.
3 The [a]integrity of the upright
will lead them,
But the [b]crookedness
of the treacherous
will destroy them.
4 [a]Wealth will not profit
in the day of wrath,
But [b]righteousness will
deliver from death.
5 The [a]righteousness
of the blameless will make
his way straight,
But [b]the wicked will fall
by his own wickedness.
6 The righteousness of
the upright will deliver them,
But the treacherous will [a]be
captured by *their own* desire.
7 When a wicked man dies,
*his* [a]hope will perish,
And the [b]expectation
of vigorous men perishes.
8 The righteous is rescued
from [1]distress,
But the wicked [2]takes
his place.
9 With *his* [a]mouth the godless
man corrupts his neighbor,
But through knowledge
the [b]righteous will
be rescued.
10 When it [a]goes well with
the righteous, the city exults,
And when the wicked perish,
there is joyful shouting.
11 By the blessing of the upright
a city is raised up,
But by the mouth
of the wicked it is torn down.
12 He who despises his neighbor
lacks a heart *of wisdom*,
But a man of discernment
keeps silent.
13 He [a]who goes about
as a slanderer reveals secrets,
But he who is faithful
in spirit [b]conceals a matter.
14 Where there is no [a]guidance
the people fall,
But in abundance of
counselors there is salvation.
15 If one becomes a [a]guarantor
for a stranger, he
will surely suffer,
But he who hates [1]striking
hands *in pledge* is secure.

**10:29** [a]Pr 13:6 [b]Pr 21:15 **10:30** [a]Ps 37:29; 125:1; Pr 2:21 [b]Pr 2:22 **10:31** [a]Ps 37:30; Pr 10:13 [b]Pr 17:20 **10:32** [a]Ecc 12:10 [b]Pr 2:12; 6:12 [1]Lit *perversions* ◆ **11:1** [a]Lv 19:35, 36; Dt 25:13-16; Pr 20:10, 23; Mic 6:11 [b]Pr 16:11 **11:2** [a]Pr 16:18; 18:12; 29:23 **11:3** [a]Pr 13:6 [b]Pr 19:3; 22:12 **11:4** [a]Pr 10:2; Eze 7:19; Zep 1:18 [b]Ge 7:1 **11:5** [a]Pr 3:6 [b]Pr 5:22 **11:6** [a]Ps 7:15, 16; 9:15; Ecc 10:8 **11:7** [a]Pr 10:28 [b]Job 8:13, 14 **11:8** [1]Or *trouble* [2]Lit *enters* **11:9** [a]Pr 16:29 [b]Pr 11:6 **11:10** [a]Pr 28:12 **11:13** [a]Lv 19:16; Pr 20:19; 1Ti 5:13 [b]Pr 19:11 **11:14** [a]Pr 15:22; 20:18; 24:6 **11:15** [a]Pr 6:1; 27:13 [1]Or *being a guarantor*

16 A [a]gracious woman
holds fast to glory,
But ruthless men hold
fast to riches.
17 The man of [a]lovingkindness
deals bountifully
with his soul,
But the cruel man brings
trouble on his flesh.
18 The wicked earns
deceptive wages,
But he who [a]sows
righteousness *gets*
a true reward.
19 He who is steadfast
in [a]righteousness *will*
*attain* to life,
And [b]he who pursues
evil *will bring about*
his own death.
20 Those with a crooked
heart are an abomination
to Yahweh,
But those of a [a]blameless
way are His [b]delight.
21 [1]Assuredly, the evil man
will not go unpunished,
But the seed of the righteous
will escape.
22 *As* a [a]ring of gold
in a swine's snout
*So is* a beautiful woman who
turns away from [1]discretion.
23 The desire of the righteous
is only good,
*But* the [a]hope
of the wicked is wrath.
24 There is one who scatters, and
*yet* increases all the more,
And there is one who holds
back what is rightly due,
*and yet results* only in want.
25 The soul [1]that [a]blesses
will be [2]enriched,
And he who [b]waters will
himself be watered.
26 He who withholds grain,
the [a]people will curse him,
But [b]blessing will be
on the head of him
who [c]sells *it*.
27 He who earnestly seeks
good seeks favor,
But [a]he who searches
for evil, *evil* will come to him.
28 He who [a]trusts in his
riches will fall,
But [b]the righteous will
flourish like the *green* leaf.
29 He who [a]troubles his own
house will [b]inherit wind,
And [c]the ignorant
fool will be a slave
to the wise of heart.
30 The fruit of the righteous
is [a]a tree of life,
And [b]he who is wise
[1]wins souls.
31 If [a]the righteous will be
repaid in the earth,
How much more the wicked
and the sinner!

12 Whoever loves [1]discipline
loves knowledge,
But he who hates reproof
is senseless.
2 A [a]good man will obtain
favor from Yahweh,

***11:16*** [a]*Pr 31:28, 30* ***11:17*** [a]Mt 5:7; 25:34-36 **11:18** [a]Hos 10:12; Ga 6:8, 9; Jas 3:18 **11:19** [a]Pr 10:16; 12:28; 19:23 [b]Pr 21:16; Ro 6:23; Jas 1:15 **11:20** [a]Ps 119:1; Pr 13:6 [b]1Chr 29:17 **11:21** [1]Lit *Hand to hand* **11:22** [a]Ge 24:47 [1]Lit *taste* **11:23** [a]Pr 10:28; Ro 2:8, 9 **11:25** [a]Pr 3:9, 10; 2Co 9:6, 7 [b]Mt 5:7 [1]Lit *of blessing* [2]Lit *made fat* **11:26** [a]Pr 24:24 [b]Job 29:13 [c]Ge 42:6 **11:27** [a]Es 7:10; Ps 7:15, 16; 57:6 **11:28** [a]Ps 49:6; Mk 10:25; 1Ti 6:17 [b]Ps 1:3; 92:12; Jer 17:8 **11:29** [a]Pr 15:27 [b]Ecc 5:16 [c]Pr 14:19 **11:30** [a]Pr 3:18 [b]Pr 14:25; Da 12:3; 1Co 9:19-22; Jas 5:20 [1]Lit *takes* **11:31** [a]2Sa 22:21, 25; Pr 13:21; 1Pe 4:18
◆ **12:1** [1]Or *instruction* **12:2** [a]Pr 3:4; 8:35

But a man of evil schemes
He will condemn.
3 A man will [a]not be established
by wickedness,
But the root of the [b]righteous
will not be shaken.
4 [1]An [a]excellent wife is
the crown of her husband,
But she who causes shame
is like [b]rottenness
in his bones.
5 The thoughts
of the righteous are just,
*But* the guidance
of the wicked is deceitful.
6 The [a]words of the wicked
lie in wait for blood,
But the [b]mouth of the upright
will deliver them.
7 The [a]wicked are overthrown
and are no more,
But the [b]house
of the righteous will stand.
8 A man will be praised
according to his insight,
But one of perverse heart
will be despised.
9 Better is he who is lightly
esteemed and has a servant
Than he who honors
himself and lacks bread.
10 A [a]righteous man knows
*the value of* the life
of his animal,
But *even* the compassion
of the wicked is cruel.
11 He [a]who cultivates his land
will be satisfied with bread,
But he who pursues
empty *things* lacks
a heart *of wisdom.*
12 The [a]wicked man desires
a stronghold of evil men,
But the root of the righteous
[b]gives *fruit.*
13 The snare of an evil man is
in the transgression of his lips,
But the [a]righteous *man* will
come out from distress.
14 A man will be [a]satisfied
with good by the fruit
of his mouth,
And the good [b]deed of a man's
hands will return to him.
15 The [a]way of an ignorant fool
is right in his own eyes,
But a wise man is he who
listens to counsel.
16 An [a]ignorant fool's [1]anger
is known at once,
But a prudent man
conceals disgrace.
17 He who breathes out truth
declares what is right,
But a false witness, deceit.
18 There is one who [a]speaks
rashly like the thrusts
of a sword,
But the [b]tongue of the wise
brings healing.
19 Truthful lips will be
established forever,
But a [a]lying tongue is
only for a moment.
20 Deceit is in the heart
of those who devise evil,
But counselors of peace
have gladness.
21 [a]No misfortune befalls
the righteous,
But the wicked are filled
with calamity.

**12:3** [a]Pr 11:5 [b]Pr 10:25 **12:4** [a]Pr 31:11; 1Co 11:7 [b]Pr 14:30; Hab 3:16 [1]Or *A virtuous* **12:6** [a]Pr 1:11, 16 [b]Pr 14:3 **12:7** [a]Job 34:25; Pr 10:25 [b]Mt 7:24-27 **12:10** [a]Dt 25:4 **12:11** [a]Pr 28:19 **12:12** [a]Pr 21:10 [b]Pr 11:30 **12:13** [a]Pr 11:8; 21:23; 2Pe 2:9 **12:14** [a]Pr 13:2; 15:23; 18:20 [b]Job 34:11; Pr 1:31; 24:12; Is 3:10, 11; Hos 4:9 **12:15** [a]Pr 14:12; 16:2; 21:2 **12:16** [a]Pr 14:33; 27:3; 29:11 [1]Or *vexation* **12:18** [a]Ps 57:4 [b]Pr 4:22; 15:4 **12:19** [a]Ps 52:4, 5; Pr 19:9 **12:21** [a]Ps 91:10; 121:7; Pr 1:33; 1Pe 3:13

22 [a]Lying lips are an abomination
to Yahweh,
But doers of faithfulness
are His delight.
23 A [a]prudent man
conceals knowledge,
But the heart of fools
proclaims folly.
24 The hand of the diligent
will rule,
But [1]the slack *hand* will be
[a]put to forced labor.
25 [a]Anxiety in a man's heart
weighs it down,
But a [b]good word
makes it glad.
26 The righteous is a guide
to his neighbor,
But the way of the wicked
makes them wander about.
27 A slack *handed* man does
not [1]roast his prey,
But the wealth of a man is
[a]precious for the diligent.
28 [a]In the path
of righteousness is life,
And in *its* pathway
there is no death.

# 13

A [a]wise son *accepts his*
father's discipline,
But a [b]scoffer does not
listen to rebuke.
2 From the fruit of a man's
mouth he [a]eats
what is good,
But the soul of the treacherous
*desires* [b]violence.
3 The one who [a]guards his
mouth keeps his soul;
The one who [b]opens wide
his lips [1]*comes* to ruin.
4 The soul of the sluggard
craves and *gets* nothing,
But the soul of the diligent
is enriched.
5 A righteous man [a]hates
a lying word,
But a wicked man [b,1]acts
odiously and is humiliated.
6 Righteousness [a]guards
the [1]one whose way
is blameless,
But wickedness subverts
the [2]sinner.
7 There is one who [a]pretends
to be rich, but has nothing;
*Another* [1]pretends
to be [b]poor, but has
great wealth.
8 The ransom of a man's
life is his wealth,
But the poor hears no rebuke.
9 The [a]light of the righteous
is glad,
But the [b]lamp
of the wicked goes out.
10 With arrogance [1]comes
only quarreling,
But with those who receive
counsel is wisdom.
11 Wealth *obtained*
from empty effort dwindles,
But the one who gathers
[1]with *his* hand abounds.
12 [1]Hope deferred makes
the heart sick,
But desire [2]fulfilled
is a tree of life.

---

***12:22*** [a]Rev 22:15 **12:23** [a]Pr 10:14; 11:13; 13:16; 15:2; 29:11 **12:24** [a]Ge 49:15; Jdg 1:28; 1Ki 9:21 [1]Lit *slackness* **12:25** [a]Pr 15:13 [b]Is 50:4 **12:27** [a]Pr 10:4; 13:4 [1]Or *catch* **12:28** [a]Dt 30:15f; 32:46f; Jer 21:8 ◆ **13:1** [a]Pr 10:1; 15:20 [b]Pr 9:7, 8; 15:12 **13:2** [a]Pr 12:14 [b]Pr 1:31; Hos 10:13 **13:3** [a]Pr 18:21; 21:23; Jas 3:2 [b]Pr 18:7; 20:19 [1]Lit *ruin is his* **13:5** [a]Col 3:9 [b]Pr 3:35 [1]Lit *causes a bad odor and causes shame* **13:6** [a]Pr 11:3 [1]Lit *blamelessness of way* [2]Lit *sin* **13:7** [a]Pr 11:24; Lk 12:20, 21 [b]Lk 12:33; 2Co 6:10; Jas 2:5 [1]Lit *impoverishes himself* **13:9** [a]Job 29:3; Pr 4:18 [b]Job 18:5; Pr 24:20 **13:10** [1]Lit *gives* **13:11** [1]Or *gradually* **13:12** [1]Lit *Expectation* [2]Lit *coming*

13 The one who [a]despises
the word will be [1]in debt to it,
But the one who fears
the commandment
will be [b]rewarded.
14 The [1]instruction of the wise
is a [a]fountain of life,
To turn aside
from the [b]snares of death.
15 [a]Good insight gives grace,
But the way of the treacherous
is [1]unrelenting.
16 Every [a]prudent man acts
with knowledge,
But a fool spreads out folly.
17 A wicked messenger
falls into evil,
But [a]a faithful envoy
*brings* healing.
18 Poverty and disgrace
*come* to him who
[a]neglects [1]discipline,
But he who keeps reproof
will be honored.
19 Desire realized is
pleasant to the soul,
But it is an abomination to
fools to turn away from evil.
20 [a]He who walks
with the wise will be wise,
But the friend of fools
will suffer harm.
21 [a]Evil pursues sinners,
But the [b]righteous are
repaid with good.
22 A good man [a]leaves
an inheritance to his
[1]children's children,
And the [b]wealth
of the sinner is stored
up for the righteous.
23 [a]Abundant food *is*
*in* the fallow ground
of the poor,
But [1]it is swept away
by injustice.
24 He who [a]holds back his
[1]rod hates his son,
But he who loves him
[b,2]disciplines him diligently.
25 The [a]righteous eats
to the satisfaction of his soul,
But the stomach
of the [b]wicked lacks.

14 The [a,1]wise woman
builds her house,
But the woman of folly
tears it down
with her own hands.
2 He who [a]walks in his
uprightness fears Yahweh,
But he who is [b]devious
in his ways despises Him.
3 In the mouth of the ignorant
fool is a rod of lofty pride,
But [a]the lips of the wise
will keep them.
4 Where no oxen are,
the manger is clean,
But much revenue *comes*
by the strength of the ox.
5 A [a]faithful witness will not lie,
But a [b]false witness
[c]breathes out lies.
6 A scoffer seeks wisdom
and *finds* none,

**13:13** [a]Nu 15:31; 2Chr 36:16 [b]Pr 13:21 [1]Lit *pledged to it* **13:14** [a]Pr 10:11; 14:27 [b]Ps 18:5 [1]Or *law* **13:15** [a]Ps 111:10; Pr 3:4 [1]Lit *constant* **13:16** [a]Pr 12:23 **13:17** [a]Pr 25:13 **13:18** [a]Pr 15:5, 32 [1]Or *instruction* **13:20** [a]Pr 2:20; 15:31 **13:21** [a]Ps 32:10; 54:5; Is 47:11 [b]Pr 11:31; 13:13; Is 3:10 **13:22** [a]Ezr 9:12; Ps 37:25 [b]Job 27:16, 17; Pr 28:8; Ecc 2:26 [1]Lit *sons' sons* **13:23** [a]Pr 12:11 [1]Lit *there is what is swept* **13:24** [a]Pr 19:18; 22:15; 23:13, 14; 29:15, 17 [b]Dt 8:5; Pr 3:12; Heb 12:7 [1]Correction, discipline [2]Lit *seeks him earnestly with discipline* **13:25** [a]Ps 34:10; 103:5; 132:15; Pr 10:3 [b]Pr 13:18; Lk 15:14 ◆ **14:1** [a]Ru 4:11; Pr 31:10-27 [1]Lit *wise women* **14:2** [a]Pr 19:1; 28:6 [b]Pr 2:15 **14:3** [a]Pr 12:6 **14:5** [a]Rev 1:5; 3:14 [b]Ex 23:1; Dt 19:16; Pr 6:19; 12:17 [c]Pr 19:5

But knowledge is easy to one
who has understanding.
7 Leave the [a]presence of a fool,
As you have not known lips
of knowledge *there.*
8 The wisdom of the prudent
is to understand his way,
But [a]the folly of fools is deceit.
9 Ignorant fools scoff at guilt,
But [a]among the upright
there is favor.
10 The heart knows its
own [a]bitterness,
And a stranger does not
share its gladness.
11 The [a]house of the wicked
will be destroyed,
But the tent of the upright
will flourish.
12 There [a]is a way *which
seems* right to a man,
But its [b]end is the way
of death.
13 Even in laughter the heart
may be in pain,
And the [a]end of joy
may be grief.
14 The one who turns back
in *his* heart will be
satisfied with his [a]ways,
But a good man will [b]*be
satisfied* [1]with his.
15 The simple
believes everything,
But the prudent one
discerns his steps.
16 A wise man fears and
[a]turns away from evil,
But a fool gets angry
and *feels* secure.
17 A quick-tempered
man acts in folly,
And a man of evil
schemes is hated.
18 The simple inherit folly,
But the prudent are [1]crowned
with knowledge.
19 The [a]evil will bow down
before the good,
And the wicked at the gates
of the righteous.
20 The [a]poor is hated even
by his neighbor,
But those who love
the rich are many.
21 He who [a]despises his
neighbor sins,
But how [b]blessed is
he who is gracious
to the [1]poor.
22 Will they not wander
in error who [a]devise evil?
But lovingkindness and
truth *will be to* those
who devise good.
23 In all painful labor
there is profit,
But *mere* words from the lips
*lead* only to want.
24 The [a]crown of the wise
is their riches,
*But* the folly of fools is folly.
25 A truthful witness
delivers souls,
But he who [a]breathes
out lies is deceitful.
26 In the [a,1]fear of Yahweh
there is strong security,
And [2]his children will
have refuge.

**14:7** [a]Pr 23:9 **14:8** [a]1Co 3:19 **14:9** [a]Pr 3:34; 11:20 **14:10** [a]1Sa 1:10; Job 21:25 **14:11** [a]Job 8:15 **14:12** [a]Pr 12:15; 16:25 [b]Ro 6:21 **14:13** [a]Ecc 2:1, 2 **14:14** [a]Pr 1:31; 12:21 [b]Pr 12:14; 18:20 [1]Lit *from himself* **14:16** [a]Job 28:28; Ps 34:14; Pr 3:7; 22:3 **14:18** [1]Lit *surrounded* **14:19** [a]1Sa 2:36; Pr 11:29 **14:20** [a]Pr 19:7 **14:21** [a]Pr 11:12 [b]Ps 41:1; Pr 19:17; 28:8 [1]Or *afflicted* **14:22** [a]Ps 36:4; Pr 3:29; 12:2; Mic 2:1 **14:24** [a]Pr 10:22; 13:8; 21:20 **14:25** [a]Pr 14:5 **14:26** [a]Pr 18:10; 19:23; Is 33:6 [1]Or *reverence* [2]Or *His*

27 The [1]fear of Yahweh is
a fountain of life,
To turn aside
from the snares of death.
28 In a multitude of people
is a king's splendor,
But in the dearth of people
is a prince's ruin.
29 He who is [a]slow to anger
has great discernment,
But he who is
[1]quick-tempered
raises up folly.
30 A [a,1]tranquil heart is
life to the body,
But jealousy is [b]rottenness
to the bones.
31 He [a]who oppresses the poor
reproaches [b]his Maker,
But he who is gracious
to the needy honors Him.
32 The wicked is [a]thrust
down by his own evil,
But the [b]righteous takes
refuge *even* in his death.
33 Wisdom rests
in the heart of one who
has understanding,
But in the midst of fools it
is *merely* made known.
34 Righteousness exalts
a nation,
But sin is a disgrace
to *any* people.
35 The king's favor is
toward a [a]servant who
acts insightfully,
But his fury is toward him
who acts shamefully.

15 A [a]gentle answer
turns away wrath,
But a [b,1]harsh word
stirs up anger.
2 The [a]tongue of the wise makes
knowledge *look* good,
But the [b]mouth of [1]fools
pours forth [2]folly.
3 The [a]eyes of Yahweh
are in every place,
Watching the evil
and the good.
4 A tongue that brings
healing is a tree of life,
But perversion in it
breaks the spirit.
5 An ignorant fool spurns
his father's discipline,
But he who keeps
reproof is prudent.
6 The house of the [a]righteous
has much treasure,
But in the income
of the wicked *there is* trouble.
7 The lips of the wise
disperse knowledge,
But the hearts of fools
are not so.
8 The [a]sacrifice of the wicked is
an abomination to Yahweh,
But [b]the prayer of the upright
is His delight.
9 The way of the wicked is
an abomination to Yahweh,
But He loves one who
[a]pursues righteousness.
10 Grievous discipline is for him
who forsakes the way;
He who hates reproof will die.

**14:27** [1]Or *reverence* **14:29** [a]Pr 16:32; 19:11; Ecc 7:9; Jas 1:19 [1]Lit *short of spirit* **14:30** [a]Pr 15:13 [b]Pr 12:4; Hab 3:16 [1]Lit *healing* **14:31** [a]Pr 17:5; Mt 25:40; 1Jn 3:17 [b]Job 31:15; Pr 22:2 **14:32** [a]Pr 6:15; 24:16 [b]Ge 49:18; Ps 16:11; 17:15; 37:37; 73:24; 2Co 1:9; 5:8; 2Ti 4:18 **14:35** [a]Mt 24:45, 47; 25:21, 23
◆ **15:1** [a]Jdg 8:1-3; Pr 15:18; 25:15 [b]1Sa 25:10-13 [1]Lit *painful* **15:2** [a]Pr 15:7 [b]Pr 12:23; 13:16; 15:28 [1]One who fails in wisdom due to willful sin [2]A lack of wisdom due to negligence or carelessness; the activity of an ignorant fool **15:3** [a]2Chr 16:9; Job 31:4; Jer 16:17; Zec 4:10; Heb 4:13 **15:6** [a]Pr 8:21 **15:8** [a]Pr 21:27; Ecc 5:1; Is 1:11; Jer 6:20; Mic 6:7 [b]Pr 15:29 **15:9** [a]1Ti 6:11

11 [a]Sheol and Abaddon *lie*
*open* before Yahweh,
How much more the [b]hearts
of the sons of men!
12 A [a]scoffer does not love
one who reproves him,
He will not go to the wise.
13 A [a]glad heart makes
a face *look* good,
But [1]when the heart is [b]pained,
the [c]spirit is broken.
14 The [a]heart of the one
who has understanding
seeks knowledge,
But the mouth of fools
feeds on folly.
15 All the days
of the afflicted are evil,
But a good heart *has*
a continual feast.
16 [a]Better is a little
with the [1]fear of Yahweh
Than great treasure and
turmoil with it.
17 [a]Better is a [1]dish of [2]vegetables
where there is love
Than a [b]fattened ox
and hatred in it.
18 A [a]hot-tempered man
stirs up strife,
But the [b]slow to anger
[c]quiets a dispute.
19 The way of the sluggard is
as a hedge of thorns,
But the path of the upright
is a highway.
20 A [a]wise son makes
a father glad,
But a foolish man
[b]despises his mother.
21 Folly is gladness to him who
lacks a heart *of wisdom*,
But a man of discernment
[a]walks straight.
22 Without consultation,
[1]plans are frustrated,
But with many counselors
they [2]succeed.
23 A [a]man has gladness
in an [1]apt answer,
And how good is
a timely [b]word!
24 The [a]path of life *leads* upward
for the one who has insight
That he may turn away
from Sheol below.
25 Yahweh will [a]tear down
the house of the proud,
But He will [b]cause
the boundary
of the [c]widow to stand.
26 Evil thoughts are
an abomination to Yahweh,
But pleasant words are pure.
27 He who is [a]greedy for gain
troubles his own house,
But he who [b]hates gifts
*of bribery* will live.
28 The heart of the righteous
[a]ponders how to answer,
But the [b]mouth of the wicked
pours forth evil things.
29 Yahweh is [a]far
from the wicked,
But He [b]hears the prayer
of the righteous.

**15:11** [a]Job 26:6; Ps 139:8 [b]1Sa 16:7; 2Chr 6:30; Ps 44:21; Ac 1:24 **15:12** [a]Pr 13:1; Am 5:10 **15:13** [a]Pr 17:22 [b]Pr 12:25 [c]Pr 17:22; 18:14 [1]Lit *in sadness of heart* **15:14** [a]Pr 18:15 **15:16** [a]Ps 37:16; Pr 16:8; Ecc 4:6; 1Ti 6:6 [1]Or *reverence* **15:17** [a]Pr 17:1 [b]Mt 22:4; Lk 15:23 [1]Or *portion* [2]Or *herbs* **15:18** [a]Pr 16:28; 26:21; 29:22 [b]Pr 14:29 [c]Ge 13:8; Pr 16:14; Ecc 10:4 **15:20** [a]Pr 10:1; 29:3 [b]Pr 30:17 **15:21** [a]Pr 14:8; Eph 5:15 **15:22** [1]Lit *thoughts* [2]Or *are established* **15:23** [a]Pr 12:14 [b]Pr 25:11; Is 50:4 [1]Lit *answer of his mouth* **15:24** [a]Pr 4:18 **15:25** [a]Pr 12:7; 14:11 [b]Dt 19:14; Pr 23:10 [c]Ps 68:5; 146:9 **15:27** [a]Pr 1:19; 28:25; 1Ti 6:10 [b]Ex 23:8; Dt 16:19; 1Sa 12:3; Is 33:15 **15:28** [a]1Pe 3:15 [b]Pr 10:32; 15:2 **15:29** [a]Ps 18:41; Pr 1:28 [b]Ps 145:18, 19

30 [1]Bright eyes gladden
the heart;
A good report puts fat
on the bones.
31 He whose ear listens
to the life-giving reproof
Will lodge among the wise.
32 He who [a]neglects discipline
[b]despises his soul,
But he who [c]listens
to reproof acquires
a heart *of wisdom.*
33 The [1]fear of Yahweh is
the discipline [2]leading
to wisdom,
And before glory
*comes* humility.

16 The [a,1]plans of the heart
belong to man,
But the answer of the tongue
is from Yahweh.
2 All the ways of a man are
pure in his own sight,
But [a]Yahweh weighs
the [1]motives.
3 [a,1]Commit your works
to Yahweh
And your [2]plans will
be established.
4 Yahweh [a]has made everything
for [1]its own purpose,
Even the [b]wicked
for the day of evil.
5 Everyone who is proud
in heart is an abomination
to Yahweh;
Assuredly, he will not
be unpunished.
6 By [a]lovingkindness and truth
iniquity is atoned for,
And by the [b,1]fear of Yahweh
one turns away from evil.
7 When a man's ways are
pleasing to Yahweh,
He [a]makes even his enemies
to be at peace with him.
8 Better is a little
with righteousness
Than great produce
with injustice.
9 The heart of [a]man
[1]plans his way,
But [b]Yahweh [2]directs his steps.
10 A divine [a]decision is
in the lips of the king;
His mouth should not
[1]err in judgment.
11 A [a]just balance and scales
belong to Yahweh;
All the [1]weights of the bag
are His [2]work.
12 It is an abomination for kings
to commit wickedness,
For in righteousness
a [a]throne is established.
13 Righteous lips are
the delight of kings,
And he who speaks
uprightly is loved.
14 The wrath of a king is
*like* messengers of death,
But a wise man will
atone for it.
15 In the light of a king's
face is life,
And his favor is like a cloud
with the [a,1]late rain.
16 How much [a]better it
is to acquire wisdom
than fine gold!

**15:30** [1]Lit *The light of the eyes gladdens* **15:32** [a]Pr 1:7; 8:33 [b]Pr 8:36 [c]Pr 15:5 **15:33** [1]Or *reverence* [2]Lit *of* ◆ **16:1** [a]Pr 16:9; 19:21 [1]Lit *preparations* **16:2** [a]1Sa 16:7; Da 5:27 [1]Lit *spirits* **16:3** [a]Ps 37:5; 55:22; Pr 3:6; 1Pe 5:7 [1]Lit *Roll* [2]Lit *thoughts* **16:4** [a]Ge 1:31; Ecc 3:11 [b]Ro 9:22 [1]Or *His* **16:6** [a]Da 4:27; Lk 11:41 [b]Pr 8:13; 14:16 [1]Or *reverence* **16:7** [a]Ge 33:4; 2Chr 17:10 **16:9** [a]Pr 16:1; 16:3; 19:21 [b]Ps 37:23; Pr 20:24; Jer 10:23 [1]Lit *thinks upon* [2]Lit *establishes* **16:10** [a]1Ki 3:28 [1]Lit *be unfaithful* **16:11** [a]Pr 11:1 [1]Lit *stones* [2]Or *concern* **16:12** [a]Pr 25:5 **16:15** [a]Job 29:23 [1]Spring **16:16** [a]Pr 8:10, 19

And to acquire understanding
is to be chosen above silver.
17 The [a]highway of the upright
is to turn away from evil;
He who guards his way
keeps his [1]soul.
18 [a]Pride *goes* before destruction,
And a haughty spirit
before stumbling.
19 It is better to be [a]humble
in spirit with the lowly
Than to [b]divide the spoil
with the proud.
20 He who considers the word
will [a]find good,
And how [b]blessed is he
who trusts in Yahweh.
21 The [a]wise in heart will be
called understanding,
And sweetness of [1]lips
[b]increases learning.
22 Insight is a fountain
of life to one who has it,
But the discipline
of ignorant fools is [1]folly.
23 The [a]heart of the wise gives
insight to his mouth
And increases learning
to his lips.
24 [a]Pleasant words are
a honeycomb,
Sweet to the soul and
[b]healing to the bones.
25 [a]There is a way
*which seems* right to a man,
But its end is the way of death.
26 A worker's appetite
works for him,
For his mouth urges him *on*.
27 A [a]vile man digs up evil,
And *the words* on his lips
are like [b]scorching fire.
28 A perverse man spreads strife,
And a whisperer separates
close companions.
29 A man of violence
[a]entices his neighbor
And leads him in a way
that is not good.
30 He who winks his eyes *does so*
to devise perverse things;
He who compresses his
lips brings evil to pass.
31 [a]Gray hair is a crown
of beauty;
It [b]is found in the way
of righteousness.
32 He who is slow to anger is
better than the mighty,
And he who rules his
own spirit, than he
who captures a city.
33 The [a]lot is cast into the lap,
But its every [b]judgment
is from Yahweh.

17 [a]Better is a dry morsel
and tranquility with it
Than a house full
of [1]feasting with strife.
2 A slave who acts insightfully
will rule over a son who
acts shamefully,
And will share
in the inheritance
among brothers.
3 The [a]refining pot is for silver
and the furnace for gold,
But [b]Yahweh tests hearts.

***16:17*** [a]*Is 35:8* [1]Or *life* **16:18** [a]Pr 11:2; 18:12; Jer 49:16; Ob 3, 4 **16:19** [a]Pr 3:34; 29:23; Is 57:15 [b]Ex 15:9; Jdg 5:30; Pr 1:13, 14 **16:20** [a]Pr 19:8 [b]Ps 2:12; 34:8; Jer 17:7 **16:21** [a]Hos 14:9 [b]Pr 16:23 [1]Or *speech* **16:22** [1]A lack of wisdom due to negligence or carelessness; the activity of an ignorant fool **16:23** [a]Ps 37:30; Pr 15:28; Mt 12:34 **16:24** [a]Ps 19:10; Pr 15:26; 24:13, 14 [b]Pr 4:22; 17:22 **16:25** [a]Pr 12:15; 14:12 **16:27** [a]Pr 6:12, 14, 18 [b]Jas 3:6 **16:29** [a]Pr 1:10; 12:26 **16:31** [a]Pr 20:29 [b]Pr 3:1, 2 **16:33** [a]Pr 18:18 [b]Pr 29:26 ◆**17:1** [a]Pr 15:17 [1]Lit *sacrifices of strife* **17:3** [a]Pr 27:21 [b]1Chr 29:17; Ps 26:2; Pr 15:11; Jer 17:10; Mal 3:3

4 An [a]evildoer gives heed
to lips of wickedness;
[1]A liar gives ear
to a destructive tongue.
5 He who mocks the [a]poor
reproaches his Maker;
He who is [b]glad at disaster
will not go unpunished.
6 [a,1]Grandchildren are
the crown of old men,
And the [b]beauty of sons
is their fathers.
7 [a]Excellent lips are not
fitting for a [1]wicked fool,
Even less are [b]lying lips
for a noble man.
8 A [a]bribe is a [1]charm
in the eyes of its owner;
Wherever he turns,
he prospers.
9 He who [a]covers
a transgression seeks love,
But he who repeats
a matter [b]separates
close companions.
10 A rebuke goes deeper
into one who understands
Than a hundred blows
into a fool.
11 A rebellious man
seeks only evil,
So a cruel messenger will
be sent against him.
12 Let a [a]man meet a [b]bear
robbed of her cubs,
Rather than a fool in his folly.
13 He who [a]returns evil for good,
[b]Evil will not depart
from his house.
14 The beginning of strife is
*like* letting out water,
So [a]abandon the dispute
before it breaks out.
15 He who [a]justifies the wicked
and he who condemns
the righteous,
Both of them alike are
an abomination to Yahweh.
16 Why is there a price
in the hand of a fool
to [a]acquire wisdom,
When [1]he has no heart
*of wisdom*?
17 A [a]friend loves at all times,
And a brother is born
for adversity.
18 A man lacking a heart
*of wisdom* [a]strikes his
[1]hands *in pledge*
And becomes guarantor
in the presence
of his neighbor.
19 He who [a]loves transgression
loves quarreling;
He who [b]makes his doorway
high seeks destruction.
20 He who has a crooked
heart [a]finds no good,
And he who is [b]perverted
in his tongue falls into evil.
21 He who [a]begets a fool
*does so* to his grief,
And the father of a wicked
fool is not glad.
22 A [a]glad heart [1]is
good medicine,
But a broken spirit [b]dries
up the bones.

**17:4** [a]Pr 14:15 [1]Lit *Falsehood* **17:5** [a]Pr 14:31 [b]Job 31:29; Pr 24:17; Ob 12 **17:6** [a]Ge 48:11; Pr 13:22 [b]Ex 20:12; Mal 1:6 [1]Lit *Sons' sons* **17:7** [a]Pr 24:7 [b]Ps 31:18; Pr 12:22 [1]One who rejects wisdom in rebellion against God **17:8** [a]Pr 21:14; Is 1:23; Am 5:12 [1]Lit *stone of grace* **17:9** [a]Pr 10:12; Jas 5:20; 1Pe 4:8 [b]Pr 16:28 **17:12** [a]Pr 29:9 [b]2Sa 17:8; Hos 13:8 **17:13** [a]Ps 35:12; 109:5; Jer 18:20 [b]2Sa 12:10; 1Ki 21:22; Pr 13:21 **17:14** [a]Pr 20:3; 25:8; 1Th 4:11 **17:15** [a]Ex 23:7; Pr 18:5; 24:24; Is 5:23 **17:16** [a]Pr 23:23 [1]Lit *there is no heart* **17:17** [a]Ru 1:16; Pr 18:24 **17:18** [a]Pr 6:1; 11:15; 22:26 [1]Lit *palms* **17:19** [a]Pr 29:22 [b]Pr 16:18; 29:23 **17:20** [a]Pr 24:20 [b]Jas 3:8 **17:21** [a]Pr 10:1; 17:25; 19:13 **17:22** [a]Pr 15:13 [b]Ps 22:15 [1]Lit *causes good healing*

23 A wicked man receives
a [a]bribe from the bosom
To [b]thrust aside
the paths of justice.
24 Wisdom is in the presence
of the one who understands,
But the [a]eyes of a fool are
on the ends of the earth.
25 A [a]foolish son is a vexation
to his father
And [b]bitterness to her
who gave birth to him.
26 It is also not good
to [a]punish the righteous,
*Nor* to strike the noble
for *their* uprightness.
27 He who [a]holds back his
words [1]has knowledge,
And he who has
a [b]cool spirit is a man
of discernment.
28 Even an ignorant fool,
when he [a]keeps silent,
is considered wise;
When he closes his lips,
he is *considered*
understanding.

## 18

He who separates himself
seeks *his own* desire,
He [a]breaks out *in dispute*
against all sound wisdom.
2 A fool does not delight
in discernment,
But only [a]in revealing
his own heart.
3 When a wicked man comes,
despising also comes,
And with disgrace
*comes* reproach.
4 The words of a man's mouth
are [a]deep waters;
[1]The fountain of wisdom
is a flowing brook.
5 To [a]show partiality
to the wicked is not good,
*Nor* to [b]thrust aside
the righteous in judgment.
6 A fool's lips come with strife,
And his mouth calls
for [a]beatings.
7 A [a]fool's mouth is his ruin,
And his lips are the snare
of his soul.
8 The words of a whisperer
are like dainty morsels,
And they go down
into the [1]innermost
parts of the stomach.
9 He also who is [a]slack
in his work
[b]Is brother to him
who destroys.
10 The [a]name of Yahweh
is a [b]strong tower;
The righteous runs
into it and is [c]set
securely on high.
11 A [a]rich man's wealth
is his strong city,
And like a high wall
in his own delusion.
12 [a]Before destruction the heart
of man is haughty,
But [b]humility *goes*
before glory.
13 He who [a]responds
with a word before he hears,
It is folly and shame to him.

***17:23*** [a]*Pr 17:8* [b]*Ex 23:8; Mic 3:11; 7:3* **17:24** [a]Ecc 2:14 **17:25** [a]Pr 19:13 [b]Pr 10:1 **17:26** [a]Pr 17:15; 18:5 **17:27** [a]Pr 10:19; Jas 1:19 [b]Pr 14:29 [1]Lit *knows* **17:28** [a]Job 13:5 ◆ **18:1** [a]Pr 3:21; 8:14 **18:2** [a]Pr 12:23; 13:16; Ecc 10:3 **18:4** [a]Pr 20:5 [1]Or *A bubbling brook, a fountain of wisdom* **18:5** [a]Lv 19:15; Dt 1:17; 16:19; Ps 82:2; Pr 17:15; 24:23; 28:21 [b]Ex 23:2, 6; Pr 17:26; 31:5; Mic 3:9 **18:6** [a]Pr 19:29 **18:7** [a]Ps 64:8; 140:9; Pr 10:14; 12:13; 13:3; Ecc 10:12 **18:8** [1]Lit *chambers of the belly* **18:9** [a]Pr 10:4 [b]Pr 28:24 **18:10** [a]Ex 3:15 [b]2Sa 22:2, 3, 33; Ps 18:2; 61:3; 91:2; 144:2 [c]Pr 29:25 **18:11** [a]Pr 10:15 **18:12** [a]Pr 11:2; 16:18; 29:23 [b]Pr 15:33 **18:13** [a]Pr 20:25; Jn 7:51

14 The [a]spirit of a man can
endure his sickness,
But *as for* a [b]broken spirit,
who can bear it?
15 The [a]heart of
the understanding
acquires knowledge,
And the [b]ear of the wise
seeks knowledge.
16 A man's [a]gift makes
room for him
And leads him into
the presence of great men.
17 The first [1]to plead his
case *seems* right,
*Until* [2]another comes
and examines him.
18 The *cast* [a]lot puts an end
to contentions
And [1]decides
between the mighty ones.
19 A brother offended *is*
*harder to win over*
than a strong city,
And contentions are
like the bars of a citadel.
20 From the [a,1]fruit of a man's
mouth his stomach
will be satisfied;
[b]*With* the produce of his
lips he will be satisfied.
21 [a]Death and life are
in the [1]power of the tongue,
And those who love it
will eat its [b]fruit.
22 He who finds a [a]wife
finds a good thing
And [b]obtains favor
from Yahweh.
23 The [a]poor man
speaks supplications,
But the [b]rich man [c]answers
with strong *words*.
24 A man of *too many* friends
*comes* to [1]ruin,
But there is [a]a [2]friend who
sticks closer than a brother.

### *The Counsel of Yahweh Will Stand*

19 [a]Better is a poor man who
[b]walks in his integrity
Than he who is crooked
in lips and is a fool.
2 Also it is not good
for a person to be
without knowledge,
And he who hurries
[a,1]his footsteps sins.
3 The [a]folly of man
subverts his way,
But his heart [b]rages
against Yahweh.
4 [a]Wealth adds many friends,
But a poor man is separated
from his friend.
5 A [a,1]false witness will
not go unpunished,
And he who [b]breathes out
lies will not escape.
6 [a]Many will seek the favor
of a noble man,
And everyone is a friend
to a man who [b]gives gifts.
7 All the brothers of a poor
man hate him;
How much more do
his [a]friends distance
*themselves* from him!

---

**18:14** [a]Pr 17:22 [b]Pr 15:13 **18:15** [a]Pr 15:14; Eph 1:17 [b]Pr 15:31 **18:16** [a]Ge 32:20; 1Sa 25:27 **18:17** [1]Lit *in his plea* [2]Lit *his neighbor* **18:18** [a]Pr 16:33 [1]Lit *makes a division* **18:20** [a]Pr 12:14 [b]Pr 14:14 [1]Speech **18:21** [a]Pr 12:13; 13:3; Mt 12:37 [b]Pr 13:2; Is 3:10; Hos 10:13 [1]Lit *hand* **18:22** [a]Ge 2:18; Pr 12:4; 19:14; 31:10-31 [b]Pr 8:35 **18:23** [a]Pr 19:7 [b]Jas 2:3, 6 [c]1Ki 12:13; 2Chr 10:13 **18:24** [a]Pr 17:17; Jn 15:14, 15 [1]Lit *be broken in pieces* [2]Or *lover* ◆ **19:1** [a]Pr 28:6 [b]Ps 26:11; Pr 14:2; 20:7 **19:2** [a]Pr 21:5; 28:20; 29:20 [1]Lit *with his feet* **19:3** [a]Pr 11:3 [b]Is 8:21 **19:4** [a]Pr 14:20 **19:5** [a]Ex 23:1; Dt 19:16-19; Pr 19:9; 21:28 [b]Pr 6:19 [1]Lit *witness of lies*, cf. Ex 20:16 **19:6** [a]Pr 29:26 [b]Pr 18:16; 21:14 **19:7** [a]Ps 38:11

He [b]pursues *them with* words,
*but* they are no more.
8 He who acquires a heart
*of wisdom* loves his own soul;
He who keeps discernment
will [a]find good.
9 A [a,1]false witness will
not go unpunished,
And he who breathes
out lies will perish.
10 Luxury is [a]not fitting
for a fool;
Much less for a [b]slave
to rule over princes.
11 A man's [a]insight makes
him slow to anger,
And it is his honor
[b]to overlook a transgression.
12 The [a]king's wrath is
like the roaring of a lion,
But his favor is
like [b]dew on the grass.
13 A [a]foolish son is destruction
to his father,
And the [b]contentions of a wife
are a constant dripping.
14 House and wealth
are an [a]inheritance
from fathers,
But a wife who has insight
is from Yahweh.
15 [a]Laziness casts
into a deep sleep,
And a slack-handed soul
will suffer hunger.
16 He who [a]keeps
the commandment
keeps his soul,
*But* he who despises
his way will die.
17 He who [a]is gracious to a poor
man lends to Yahweh,
And He will repay him
for his [b]bountiful deed.
18 [a]Discipline your son
while there is hope,
And do not [1]direct your soul
to put him to death.
19 *A man of* great wrath will
bear the penalty,
For if you deliver *him*, you will
only have to do it again.
20 [a]Listen to counsel and
receive discipline,
That you may be wise
in [1]the end of your *days*.
21 Many [a,1]thoughts are
in a man's heart,
But it is the [b]counsel
of Yahweh that will stand.
22 What is desirable in a man
is his lovingkindness,
And better is a poor man
than a man of falsehood.
23 The [a,1]fear of Yahweh
*leads* to life,
So that one may
sleep [b]satisfied,
not [c]visited by evil.
24 The [a]sluggard buries his
hand [b]in the dish,
*But* will not even bring it
back to his mouth.
25 [a]Strike a scoffer and
the simple may
become prudent,

**19:7** [b]Pr 18:23 **19:8** [a]Pr 16:20 **19:9** [a]Pr 19:5; Da 6:24 [1]Lit *witness of lies*, cf. Ex 20:16 **19:10** [a]Pr 17:7; 26:1; Ecc 10:6, 7 [b]Pr 30:22 **19:11** [a]Pr 14:29; 16:32 [b]Mt 5:44; Eph 4:32; Col 3:13 **19:12** [a]Pr 16:14 [b]Ge 27:28; Dt 33:28; Ps 133:3; Hos 14:5; Mic 5:7 **19:13** [a]Pr 17:25 [b]Pr 21:9, 19; 27:15 **19:14** [a]2Co 12:14 **19:15** [a]Pr 6:9, 10; 24:33 **19:16** [a]Pr 13:13; 16:17; Lk 10:28; 11:28 **19:17** [a]Dt 15:7, 8; Pr 14:31; 28:27; Ecc 11:1, 2; Mt 10:42; 25:40; 2Co 9:6-8; Heb 6:10 [b]Pr 12:14; Lk 6:38 **19:18** [a]Pr 13:24; 23:13; 29:15, 17 [1]Lit *lift up* **19:20** [a]Pr 4:1; 8:33; 12:15 [1]Lit *your latter end* **19:21** [a]Pr 16:1, 9 [b]Ps 33:10, 11; Is 14:26, 27 [1]Or *plans* **19:23** [a]Pr 14:27; 1Ti 4:8 [b]Ps 25:13 [c]Ps 91:10; Pr 12:21 [1]Or *reverence* **19:24** [a]Pr 26:15 [b]Mt 26:23; Mk 14:20 **19:25** [a]Pr 21:11

But [b]reprove one who has
understanding and he will
understand knowledge.
26 He [a]who assaults *his* father
*and* causes *his* mother to flee
Is a son who brings shame
and humiliation.
27 Cease listening, my
son, to discipline,
*And you will* stray from
the words of knowledge.
28 A vile witness scoffs at justice,
And the mouth of the wicked
[a]swallows up iniquity.
29 [1]Judgments are established
for [a]scoffers,
And [b]beatings
for the back of fools.

### *Hope in Yahweh and He Will Save You*

20 [a]Wine is a mocker,
[b]strong drink a brawler,
And whoever is led astray
by it is not wise.
2 The terror of a king is
like the roar of a lion;
He who provokes him to anger
[a]sins against his own soul.
3 It is a glory for a man
to [a]cease quarreling,
But any ignorant fool will
break out *in dispute*.
4 The [a]sluggard does not
plow from winter *on*,
So he [1]begs during the harvest
and has nothing.
5 Counsel in the heart
of a man is *like* deep water,
But a man of discernment
draws it out.
6 Many a man will [a]call out
his own lovingkindness,
But a [b]faithful man,
who can find?
7 A righteous man who
[a]walks in his integrity—
[b]How blessed are his
sons after him.
8 [a]A king who sits
on the throne of justice
[1]Disperses all evil
with his eyes.
9 [a]Who can say, "I have
kept my heart pure,
I am clean from my sin"?
10 [a,1]Differing weights and
differing measures,
Both of them are
an abomination to Yahweh.
11 It is by his deeds
that a young man [a]makes
himself known
If his conduct is pure
and right.
12 The hearing [a]ear and
the seeing eye,
Yahweh has made
both of them.
13 [a]Do not love sleep, lest
you become poor;
Open your eyes, *and* you will
be satisfied with [1]food.
14 "Bad, bad," says the buyer,
But when he goes his
way, then he boasts.
15 There is gold, and
an abundance of pearls;

**19:25** [b]Pr 9:8 **19:26** [a]Pr 28:24 **19:28** [a]Job 15:16; 20:12, 13; 34:7 **19:29** [a]Ps 1:1; Pr 9:12 [b]Pr 10:13; 18:6; 26:3 [1]Gr *Rods* ◆ **20:1** [a]Ge 9:21; Pr 23:29, 30; Is 28:7; Hos 4:11 [b]Pr 31:4; Is 5:22; 56:12 **20:2** [a]Nu 16:38; 1Ki 2:23; Pr 8:36; Hab 2:10 **20:3** [a]Ge 13:7f; Pr 17:14 **20:4** [a]Pr 13:4; 21:25 [1]Lit *asks* **20:6** [a]Pr 25:14; Mt 6:2; Lk 18:11 [b]Ps 12:1; Lk 18:8 **20:7** [a]Pr 19:1 [b]Ps 37:26; 112:2 **20:8** [a]Pr 20:26; 25:5 [1]Or *Sifts* **20:9** [a]1Ki 8:46; 2Chr 6:36; Job 14:4; Ecc 7:20; Ro 3:9; 1Jn 1:8 **20:10** [a]Pr 11:1; 20:23 [1]Lit *A stone and a stone, an ephah and an ephah* **20:11** [a]Mt 7:16 **20:12** [a]Ex 4:11; Ps 94:9 **20:13** [a]Pr 6:9, 10; 19:15; 24:33 [1]Lit *bread*

But the lips of knowledge are
a more precious vessel.
16 Take his garment when
he becomes a guarantor
for a stranger;
And for foreigners, hold
him in pledge.
17 [a]Bread obtained by lying
is sweet to a man,
But afterward his mouth
will be filled with gravel.
18 [a,1]Thoughts are established
by counsel,
So [b]make war by guidance.
19 He who [a]goes about as
a slanderer reveals secrets,
Therefore do not associate
with [b,1]one of loose lips.
20 He who [a]curses his father
or his mother,
His [b]lamp will go out
in the [1]midst of darkness.
21 An inheritance gained
hurriedly at the beginning
In the end will not be blessed.
22 [a]Do not say,
"I will repay evil";
[b]Hope in Yahweh, and
He will save you.
23 [a,1]Differing weights are
an abomination to Yahweh,
And a [b]deceitful balance
is not good.
24 [a]The steps of a man
are from Yahweh,
How then can man
understand his way?
25 It is a trap for a man to say
rashly, "It is holy!"
And [a]after the vows
to make inquiry.
26 A [a]wise king winnows
the wicked,
And turns the [b]*threshing*
wheel over them.
27 The [a,1]breath of man is
the lamp of Yahweh,
Searching all the [2]innermost
parts of his body.
28 Lovingkindness and [a]truth
will guard the king,
And he upholds his throne
by lovingkindness.
29 The honor of young men
is their strength,
And the [a,1]majesty of old
men is their gray hair.
30 [a]Stripes that wound
scour away evil,
And strokes *reach*
the [1]innermost parts
of the body.

### *Salvation Belongs to Yahweh*

21 The king's heart is
*like* channels of water
in the hand of Yahweh;
He [a]turns it wherever
He pleases.
2 [a]Every man's way is right
in his own eyes,
But Yahweh [b]weighs the hearts.
3 To do [a]righteousness
and justice
Is chosen by Yahweh
over sacrifice.
4 Haughty eyes and
a proud heart—

***20:17*** [a]*Pr 9:17* **20:18** [a]Pr 11:14; 15:22 [b]Pr 24:6; Lk 14:31 [1]Or *Plans* **20:19** [a]Pr 11:13 [b]Pr 13:3 [1]Lit *one who opens his lips* **20:20** [a]Ex 21:17; Lv 20:9; Pr 30:11; Mt 15:4 [b]Job 18:5; Pr 13:9; 24:20 [1]Lit *pupil* (of the eye) **20:22** [a]Pr 24:29; Mt 5:39; Ro 12:17, 19; 1Th 5:15; 1Pe 3:9 [b]Ps 27:14 **20:23** [a]Pr 20:10 [b]Pr 11:1 [1]Lit *A stone and a stone* **20:24** [a]Pr 16:9 **20:25** [a]Ecc 5:4, 5 **20:26** [a]Pr 20:8 [b]Is 28:27 **20:27** [a]1Co 2:11 [1]Or *what a man breathes out* [2]Lit *chambers of the stomach* **20:28** [a]Pr 29:14 **20:29** [a]Pr 16:31 [1]Or *splendor* **20:30** [a]Ps 89:32; Pr 22:15; Is 53:5; 1Pe 2:24 [1]Lit *chambers of the stomach* ◆ **21:1** [a]Ezr 6:22 **21:2** [a]Pr 16:2 [b]Pr 16:2; 24:12; Lk 16:15 **21:3** [a]1Sa 15:22; Pr 15:8; Is 1:11, 16, 17; Hos 6:6; Mic 6:7, 8

The [a]fallow ground
of the wicked—are sin.

5 The [1]thoughts of the [a]diligent
*lead* surely to profit,
But everyone [b]who is hasty
*comes* surely to poverty.

6 [a]Working for treasures
by a lying tongue
Is a fleeting breath, by those
who pursue [b]death.

7 The destruction of the wicked
will drag them away,
Because they [a]refuse
to do justice.

8 The way of a guilty
man is [a]perverse,
But as for the pure, his
work is upright.

9 It is better to live
in a corner of a roof
Than [1]in a house shared
with a contentious woman.

10 The soul of the wicked
craves evil;
His [a]neighbor finds no
favor in his eyes.

11 When the [a]scoffer is
punished, the simple
becomes wise;
And when one considers
wisdom, he
receives knowledge.

12 The righteous one considers
the house of the wicked,
Turning the [a]wicked to ruin.

13 He who [a]shuts his ear
to the outcry of the poor
Will himself also call and
not be [b]answered.

14 A [a]gift in secret
subdues anger,
And a bribe in the bosom,
strong wrath.

15 To do justice is [1]pleasure
for the righteous,
But is [a]ruin to the workers
of iniquity.

16 A man who wanders
from the way of insight
Will [a]rest in the assembly
of the [1]dead.

17 He who [a]loves [1]pleasure
*will become* a poor man;
He who loves wine and oil
will not become rich.

18 The wicked is a [a]ransom
for the righteous,
And the [b]treacherous is
in the place of the upright.

19 [a]It is better to live
in a desert land
Than with a contentious
and vexing woman.

20 There is desirable
[a]treasure and oil
in the abode of the wise,
But a foolish man
[b]swallows it up.

21 He who
[a]pursues righteousness
and lovingkindness
Finds life, righteousness,
and glory.

22 A [a]wise man goes up
to the city of the mighty
And brings down
the [1]stronghold
in which they trust.

---

**21:4** [a]Pr 24:20; Lk 11:34 **21:5** [a]Pr 10:4; 13:4 [b]Pr 28:22 [1]Or *plans* **21:6** [a]Pr 13:11; 20:21 [b]Pr 8:36 **21:7** [a]Am 5:7; Mic 3:9 **21:8** [a]Pr 2:15 **21:9** [1]Lit *with a woman of contentions and a house of association* **21:10** [a]Ps 52:3; Pr 2:14; 14:21 **21:11** [a]Pr 19:25 **21:12** [a]Pr 14:11 **21:13** [a]Mt 18:30-34; 1Jn 3:17 [b]Jas 2:13 **21:14** [a]Pr 18:16; 19:6 **21:15** [a]Pr 10:29 [1]Lit *gladness* **21:16** [a]Ps 49:14 [1]Lit *departed spirits* **21:17** [a]Pr 23:21 [1]Lit *gladness* **21:18** [a]Is 43:3 [b]Pr 11:8 **21:19** [a]Pr 21:9 **21:20** [a]Ps 112:3; Pr 8:21; 22:4 [b]Job 20:15, 18 **21:21** [a]Pr 15:9; Mt 5:6; 1Co 15:58 **21:22** [a]2Sa 5:6-9; Pr 24:5; Ecc 7:19; 9:15, 16 [1]Lit *strength of trust*

23 He who [a]keeps his mouth
and his tongue,
Keeps his soul from troubles.
24 "Arrogant," "Haughty,"
"[a]Scoffer," are his names,
Who acts with [b]arrogant fury.
25 The [a]desire of the sluggard
puts him to death,
For his hands refuse to work;
26 All day long he [1]is
insatiably craving,
While the righteous [a]gives
and does not hold back.
27 The [a]sacrifice of the wicked
is an abomination,
How much more when he brings
it with a wicked scheme!
28 A [a]false witness will perish,
But the man who listens
will speak forever.
29 A wicked man [a,1]displays
a brazen face,
But as for the [b]upright, he
establishes his way.
30 There is [a]no wisdom, there
is no discernment
And there is no counsel
against Yahweh.
31 The [a]horse is set
for the day of battle,
But [b]salvation belongs
to Yahweh.

### *Yahweh Is the Maker of All*

22 A [a]*good* name is to be
chosen over great wealth,
Favor is better
than silver and gold.
2 The rich and the poor meet
together *in this*—
Yahweh is the [a]Maker
of them all.
3 A [a]prudent man sees
evil and hides,
But the simple pass on,
and are punished.
4 The reward of humility—
the [1]fear of Yahweh—
Is riches, glory, and life.
5 [a]Thorns *and* snares are
in the way of the crooked;
He who keeps his soul
will be far from them.
6 [a,1]Train up a child
[2]according to his way,
Even when he is old he will
not [3]depart from it.
7 The [a]rich rules over the poor,
And the borrower is
the slave of the lender.
8 He who [a]sows
unrighteousness will
reap iniquity,
And the [b]rod of his
fury will end.
9 He who [1]is [a]generous
will be blessed,
For he [b]gives from his
food to the poor.
10 [a]Drive out the scoffer,
and strife will go out,
Even contention and
disgrace will cease.
11 He who loves [a]purity of heart
*And* [b]grace on his lips,
the king is his friend.

**21:23** [a]Pr 12:13; 13:3; 18:21; Jas 3:2 **21:24** [a]Ps 1:1; Pr 1:22; 3:34; 24:9; Is 29:20 [b]Is 16:6; Jer 48:29 ***21:25*** *[a]Pr 13:4* **21:26** [a]Ps 37:26; 112:5, 9; Mt 5:42; Eph 4:28 [1]Lit *desires desire* **21:27** [a]Pr 15:8; Is 66:3; Jer 6:20; Am 5:22 **21:28** [a]Pr 19:5, 9 **21:29** [a]Ecc 8:1 [b]Ps 119:5; Pr 11:5 [1]Lit *makes firm with his face* **21:30** [a]Jer 9:23; Ac 5:38, 39; 1Co 3:19, 20 **21:31** [a]Ps 20:7; 33:17; Is 31:1 [b]Ps 3:8; Jer 3:23; 1Co 15:57 ◆ **22:1** [a]Pr 10:7; Ecc 7:1 **22:2** [a]Job 31:15; Pr 14:31 **22:3** [a]Pr 14:16; 27:12; Is 26:20 **22:4** [1]Or *reverence* **22:5** [a]Pr 15:19 **22:6** [a]Eph 6:4 [1]Lit *Dedicate* [2]Or *in the way he should go, according to his own way* [3]Lit *turn away* **22:7** [a]Pr 18:23; Jas 2:6 **22:8** [a]Job 4:8 [b]Ps 125:3 **22:9** [a]Pr 19:17; 2Co 9:6 [b]Lk 14:13 [1]Lit *has a good eye* **22:10** [a]Ge 21:9, 10; Pr 18:6; 26:20 **22:11** [a]Ps 24:4; Mt 5:8 [b]Pr 14:35; 16:13

12 The eyes of Yahweh
guard knowledge,
But He subverts the words
of the treacherous one.
13 The [a]sluggard says, "There
is a lion outside;
I will be killed in the streets!"
14 The mouth of [a]strange
women is a deep pit;
He who is [b]cursed
of Yahweh will fall [1]into it.
15 Folly is bound up
in the heart of a child;
The [a]rod of discipline will
remove it far from him.
16 He [a]who oppresses the poor
to make [1]more for himself
Or who gives to the rich
[b]*will* only *come to* lack.

17 [a]Incline your ear and hear
the words of the wise,
And set your heart
on my knowledge;
18 For it will be [a]pleasant if you
keep them within you,
[1]That they may be
established on your lips.
19 So that your [a]trust may
be in Yahweh,
I have made you know
today, even you.
20 Have I not written to you
[a,1]excellent things
Of counsels and knowledge,
21 To make you [a]know the veracity
of the words of truth
That you may [b,1]respond
with the words of truth
to him who sent you?

22 [a]Do not rob the poor
because he is poor,
And do not [b]crush
the afflicted at the gate;
23 For Yahweh will [a]plead
their case
And rob the soul of those
who rob them.

24 Do not befriend a man of anger;
And do not come along
with a man of [a]great wrath,
25 Lest you [a]learn his ways
And take *on* a snare
against your soul.

26 Do not be among those who
[a]strike [1]hands *in pledge*,
Among those who become
guarantors for debts.
27 If you have nothing
with which to pay,
Why should he [a]take your
bed from under you?

28 [a]Do not move
the ancient boundary
Which your fathers made.

29 Do you see a man skilled
in his work?
He will [a]stand before kings;
He will not stand
before obscure men.

### *The Fear of Yahweh*

23 When you sit down
to dine with a ruler,
Understand well
[1]what is before you,

**22:13** [a]Pr 26:13 **22:14** [a]Pr 2:16; 5:3; 7:5; 23:27 [b]Ecc 7:26 [1]Lit *there* **22:15** [a]Pr 13:24; 23:14
**22:16** [a]Ecc 5:8; Jas 2:13 [b]Pr 28:22 [1]Lit *much* **22:17** [a]Pr 5:1 **22:18** [a]Pr 2:10 [1]Lit *They together*
**22:19** [a]Pr 3:5 **22:20** [a]Pr 8:6 [1]Lit *thirty* sayings **22:21** [a]Lk 1:3, 4 [b]Pr 25:13; 1Pe 3:15 [1]Lit *return*
**22:22** [a]Ex 23:6; Job 31:16; Pr 22:16 [b]Zec 7:10; Mal 3:5 **22:23** [a]1Sa 25:39; Ps 12:5; 35:10; 140:12; Pr 23:11; Jer 51:36 **22:24** [a]Pr 29:22 **22:25** [a]1Co 15:33 **22:26** [a]Pr 17:18 [1]Lit *palms* **22:27** [a]Ex 22:26; Pr 20:16
**22:28** [a]Dt 19:14; 27:17; Job 24:2; Pr 23:10 **22:29** [a]Ge 41:46; 1Ki 10:8 ◆ **23:1** [1]Or *who*

2 So you should put a knife
to your throat
If you are a [a]man of appetite.
3 Do not [a]desire his delicacies,
For it is bread of falsehood.

4 [a]Do not weary yourself
to gain wealth,
[b]Because of your
understanding, cease!
5 Do you make your eyes fly *up
to see it*? But it is not there!
Because [a]it certainly
makes itself wings
Like an eagle that flies
*toward* the heavens.

6 [a]Do not eat the bread
of [1]a [b]selfish man,
And do not desire his delicacies;
7 For as he [1]calculates
in his soul, so he is.
"Eat and drink!" he says to you,
But [a]his heart is not with you.
8 You will [a]vomit up [1]the
morsel you have eaten,
And you will corrupt
your pleasant words.

9 [a]Do not speak
in the [1]hearing of a fool,
For he will [b]despise
the insight of your speech.

10 Do not move
the ancient boundary
And do not [a]come into
the fields of the orphans,
11 For their [a]Redeemer is strong;
[b]He will plead their
case against you.
12 Bring your heart to discipline
And your ears to [1]words
of knowledge.

13 [a]Do not withhold discipline
from the child,
Although you [1]strike him
with the rod, he will not die.
14 You shall [1]strike him
with the rod
And [a]deliver his soul
from Sheol.

15 My son, if your heart is [a]wise,
My own heart also will be glad;
16 And my [1]inmost
being will exult
When your lips speak
[a]upright things.

17 [a]Do not let your heart be
jealous of sinners,
But *be zealous* in the [b,1]fear
of Yahweh [2]always.
18 Surely there is a [a,1]future,
And your [b]hope will
not be cut off.
19 You, my son, listen
and [a]be wise,
And [b]direct your
heart in the way.
20 Do not be with [a]heavy
drinkers of wine,
*Or* with [b]gluttonous
eaters of meat;

**23:2** [a]Pr 23:20 **23:3** [a]Ps 141:4; Pr 23:6; Da 1:5, 8, 13, 15, 16 **23:4** [a]Pr 15:27; 28:20; Mt 6:19; 1Ti 6:9; Heb 13:5 [b]Pr 3:5, 7 **23:5** [a]Pr 27:24; 1Ti 6:17 **23:6** [a]Ps 141:4 [b]Dt 15:9; Pr 28:22 [1]Lit *an evil eye* **23:7** [a]Pr 26:24, 25 [1]Lit *reckons in his soul* **23:8** [a]Pr 25:16 [1]Lit *your* **23:9** [a]Mt 7:6 [b]Pr 1:7 [1]Lit *ears* **23:10** [a]Jer 22:3; Zec 7:10 **23:11** [a]Job 19:25; Jer 50:34 [b]Pr 22:23 **23:12** [1]Lit *sayings* **23:13** [a]Pr 13:24; 19:18 [1]Lit *smite* **23:14** [a]1Co 5:5 [1]Lit *smite* **23:15** [a]Pr 23:24f; 27:11; 29:3 **23:16** [a]Pr 8:6 [1]Lit *kidneys* **23:17** [a]Ps 37:1; Pr 24:1, 19 [b]Pr 28:14 [1]Or *reverence* [2]Lit *all the day* **23:18** [a]Ps 19:11; 58:11; Pr 24:14 [b]Ps 9:18 [1]Lit *latter end* **23:19** [a]Pr 6:6 [b]Pr 4:23; 9:6 **23:20** [a]Pr 20:1; 23:29, 30; Is 5:22; Mt 24:49; Lk 21:34; Ro 13:13; Eph 5:18 [b]Dt 21:20; Pr 28:7

21 For the [a]heavy drinker
and the glutton will
come to poverty,
And [b]drowsiness will
clothe *them* with rags.

22 [a]Listen to your father
who begot you,
And [b]do not despise your
mother when she is old.
23 [a]Buy truth, and do not sell *it*,
*Get* wisdom and discipline
and understanding.

24 The father of the righteous
will greatly rejoice,
And [a]he who begets a wise
son will be glad in him.
25 Let your [a]father and your
mother be glad,
And let her rejoice who
gave birth to you.

26 [a]Give your heart
to me, my son,
And let your eyes
[b,1]delight in my ways.
27 For a harlot is a [a]deep pit
And [1]a [b]foreign woman
is a narrow well.
28 Surely she [a]lies
in wait as a robber,
And adds to the treacherous
among men.

29 Who has [a]woe? Who
has sorrow?
Who has contentions?
Who has complaining?
Who has wounds
without cause?
Who has redness of eyes?
30 Those who [a]linger
long over wine,
Those who go to search
out [b]mixed wine.
31 Do not look on the wine
when it glistens red,
When it [1]sparkles in the cup,
When it [a]goes down smoothly;
32 At the end—like a serpent
it [a]bites,
And like a [b]viper it stings.
33 Your eyes will see
strange things
And your heart will [a]speak
perverse things.
34 And you will be
like one who lies down
in the heart of the sea,
Or like one who lies down
on the top of a [1]mast.
35 "They [a]struck me, *but* I
did not become [1]ill;
They beat me, *but* I
did not know *it*.
When shall I awake?
I will [b]seek yet another."

### *My Son, Fear Yahweh*

24 Do not be [a]jealous
of evil men,
And do not desire
to [b]be with them;
2 For their heart meditates
on [a]destruction,
And their lips [b]talk
of mischief.

**23:21** [a]Pr 21:17 [b]Pr 6:10, 11 **23:22** [a]Pr 1:8; Eph 6:1 [b]Pr 15:20; 30:17 **23:23** [a]Pr 4:7; 18:15; Mt 13:44 **23:24** [a]Pr 10:1; 15:20; 29:3 **23:25** [a]Pr 27:11 **23:26** [a]Pr 3:1; 4:4 [b]Ps 1:2; 119:24 [1]Or *observe* **23:27** [a]Pr 22:14 [b]Pr 5:20 [1]Or *an adulterous*, cf. Pr 2:16 **23:28** [a]Pr 6:26; 7:12; Ecc 7:26 **23:29** [a]Is 5:11, 22 **23:30** [a]1Sa 25:36; Pr 20:1; Is 5:11; 28:7; Eph 5:18 [b]Ps 75:8 **23:31** [a]SS 7:9 [1]Lit *gives its eye* **23:32** [a]Job 20:16; Pr 20:1; Eph 5:18 [b]Ps 91:13; Is 11:8 **23:33** [a]Pr 2:12 **23:34** [1]Or *lookout* **23:35** [a]Pr 27:22; Jer 5:3 [b]Pr 26:11; Is 56:12 [1]From the effect of wounds ◆ **24:1** [a]Ps 37:1; Pr 3:31; 23:17; 24:19 [b]Ps 1:1; Pr 1:15 **24:2** [a]Is 30:12; Jer 22:17 [b]Job 15:35; Ps 10:7; 38:12

3 [a]By wisdom a house is built,
And by discernment it is
firmly established;
4 And by knowledge
the rooms are [a]filled
With all precious and
pleasant riches.

5 A [a]wise man is [1]strong,
And a man of knowledge
strengthens his power.
6 For [a]by guidance you
will make war,
And [b]in abundance of
counselors there is salvation.

7 Wisdom is [a]*too* exalted
for an ignorant fool,
He does not open his
mouth [b]in the gate.

8 One who [a]deliberately
thinks to do evil,
Men will call a [1]schemer.
9 The [a]scheming of folly is sin,
And the scoffer is
an abomination to men.

10 If you [a]are slack in the day
of trouble,
Your strength is in trouble.

11 [a]Deliver those who are being
taken away to death,
And those who are stumbling
to the slaughter,
Oh hold *them* back.
12 If you say, "Behold, we
did not know this,"
Does not He [a]who weighs
the hearts [b]understand?
And [c]*does not* He who
[d]guards your soul know?
And will not He [e,1]render
to man according to his work?

13 Eat [a]honey, my son,
for it is good,
Indeed, the [b]honey
from the comb is sweet
to your taste;
14 Know *that* [a]wisdom is
thus for your soul;
If you find *it*, then there
will be a [b,1]future,
And your hope will
not be cut off.

15 [a]Do not lie in wait, O wicked
man, against the abode
of the righteous;
Do not destroy his resting place;
16 For a [a]righteous man falls
seven times, and rises again,
But the [b]wicked will
stumble in [1]calamity.

17 When your enemy falls,
[a]do not be glad,
And when he stumbles,
do not let your heart rejoice;
18 Lest Yahweh see *it* and it
be evil in His eyes,
And turn His anger
away from him.

19 [a]Do not fret because
of evildoers

---

***24:3*** [a]*Pr 9:1; 14:1* **24:4** [a]Pr 8:21 **24:5** [a]Pr 21:22 [1]Lit *in strength* **24:6** [a]Pr 20:18 [b]Pr 11:14
**24:7** [a]Ps 10:5; Pr 14:6; 17:16 [b]Job 5:4; Ps 127:5 **24:8** [a]Pr 6:14; 14:22; Ro 1:30 [1]Or *deviser of evil*
**24:9** [a]Mt 15:19; Ac 8:22 **24:10** [a]Dt 20:8; Job 4:5; Jer 51:46; Heb 12:3 **24:11** [a]Ps 82:4; Is 58:6, 7
**24:12** [a]1Sa 16:7; Pr 21:2 [b]Ecc 5:8 [c]Ps 94:9-11 [d]Ps 121:3-8 [e]Job 34:11; Pr 12:14 [1]Lit *bring back*
**24:13** [a]Ps 19:10; 119:103; Pr 25:16; SS 5:1 [b]Pr 16:24; 27:7; SS 4:11 **24:14** [a]Pr 2:10 [b]Pr 23:18 [1]Lit *latter end* **24:15** [a]Ps 10:9, 10 **24:16** [a]Job 5:19; Ps 37:24; Mic 7:8 [b]Pr 6:15; 14:32; 24:22; Jer 18:17 [1]Lit *evil*
**24:17** [a]Job 31:29; Ps 35:15, 19; Pr 17:5; Ob 12 **24:19** [a]Ps 37:1

Do not be [b]jealous
of the wicked;
20 For [a]there will be no
[b,1]future for the evil one;
The [c]lamp of the wicked
will go out.

21 My son, [a,1]fear Yahweh
and the king;
Do not associate
with those who change,
22 For suddenly their
[a]disaster will rise,
And who knows
the upheaval *that comes*
from both of them?

23 These also are [a]*sayings*
of the wise.
To [b,1]show partiality
in judgment is not good.
24 He [a]who says to the wicked,
"You are righteous,"
[b]Peoples will curse
him, nations will be
indignant with him;
25 But [a]to those who
reprove the *wicked,*
it will be pleasant,
And a good blessing will
come upon them.
26 He kisses the lips
Who responds
with right words.

27 Establish your work outside
And [a]make it ready
for yourself in the field;
And afterwards, you shall
build your house.

28 Do not be a [a]witness
against your neighbor
without cause,
Nor [b]deceive with your lips.
29 [a]Do not say, "As he did
to me so I shall do to him;
I will [1]render to the man
according to his work."

30 I passed by the field
of the sluggard
And by the vineyard
of the man [a]lacking
a heart *of wisdom,*
31 And behold, it was completely
[a,1]overgrown with thistles;
[b,2]Nettles have covered
its surface,
And its stone [c]wall has
been torn down.
32 And I beheld, I set my
heart upon it;
I saw, I received discipline.
33 "[a]A little sleep,
a little slumber,
A little folding
of the hands to rest,"
34 Then your poverty will
come *as* [1]a robber
And your want
like [2]an armed man.

### *Analogies of Wisdom*

25 These also are [a]proverbs of
Solomon which the men of
Hezekiah, king of Judah, transcribed.
2 It is the glory of God
to [a]conceal a matter,
But the glory of [b]kings is
to search out a matter.

**24:19** [b]Pr 23:17; 24:1 **24:20** [a]Job 15:31 [b]Pr 23:18 [c]Job 18:5, 6; 21:17; Pr 13:9; 20:20 [1]Lit *latter end* **24:21** [a]Ro 13:1-7; 1Pe 2:17 [1]Or *reverence* **24:22** [a]Pr 24:16 **24:23** [a]Pr 1:6; 22:17 [b]Pr 18:5; 28:21 [1]Lit *recognize a face* **24:24** [a]Pr 17:15; Is 5:23 [b]Pr 11:26 **24:25** [a]Pr 28:23 **24:27** [a]Pr 27:23-27 **24:28** [a]Pr 25:18 [b]Lv 6:2, 3; 19:11; Eph 4:25 **24:29** [a]Pr 20:22; Mt 5:39; Ro 12:17 [1]Lit *bring back* **24:30** [a]Pr 6:32 **24:31** [a]Ge 3:18 [b]Job 30:7 [c]Is 5:5 [1]Lit *gone up* [2]A kind of weed **24:33** [a]Pr 6:10 **24:34** [1]Or *a vagabond*; lit *one who walks* [2]Lit *a man with a shield* ◆ **25:1** [a]Pr 1:1 **25:2** [a]Dt 29:29; Ro 11:33 [b]Ezr 6:1

3 *As* the heavens for height
and the earth for depth,
So the heart of kings
is unsearchable.
4 Take away the [a]dross
from the silver,
And there comes out
a vessel for the [b]smith;
5 Take away the [a]wicked
before the king,
And his [b]throne will be
established in righteousness.
6 Do not promote your majesty
in the presence of the king,
And in the place of great
men do not stand;
7 For [a]it is better that it be said
to you, "Come up here,"
Than for you to be placed
lower in the presence
of a noble,
Whom your eyes have seen.

8 Do not go out [a]hastily
to plead *your case*;
Lest, what will you
do in [1]the end,
When your neighbor
humiliates you?
9 [a]Plead your case
with your neighbor,
And [b]do not reveal
the secret of another,
10 Lest he who hears *it* bring
disgrace upon you,
And the bad report about you
will not turn away.

11 *Like* apples of gold
in settings of silver
Is a [a]word spoken
in [1]right circumstances.
12 *Like* [1]an [a]earring of gold and
an [b]ornament of [c]fine gold
Is a wise reprover
to a [d]listening ear.
13 Like the cold of snow
in the [1]time of harvest
Is a [a]faithful envoy
to those who send him,
For he refreshes the soul
of his masters.
14 *Like* [a]clouds and [b]wind
without rain
Is a man who boasts
[1]of his gifts falsely.
15 [a]When one is slow to anger,
a ruler may be persuaded,
And a soft tongue
breaks the bone.
16 Have you [a]found honey?
Eat *only* enough for you,
Lest you have more
than your fill and vomit it.
17 Let your foot rarely be
in your neighbor's house,
Lest he have more than his
fill of you and hate you.
18 *Like* a club and a [a]sword
and a sharp [b]arrow
Is a man who bears
[c,1]false witness
against his neighbor.
19 *Like* [1]an aching tooth
and a slipping foot
Is trust in a [a]treacherous
man in a day of distress.
20 *Like* one who takes off
a garment on a cold day,
*or like* vinegar on [1]soda,

---

**25:4** [a]Pr 26:23; Eze 22:18 [b]Mal 3:2, 3 **25:5** [a]Pr 20:8 [b]Pr 16:12 **25:7** [a]Lk 14:7-11 **25:8** [a]Pr 17:14; Mt 5:25 [1]Lit *its* **25:9** [a]Mt 18:15 [b]Pr 11:13 **25:11** [a]Pr 15:23 [1]Lit *its* **25:12** [a]Ex 32:2; 35:22; Eze 16:12 [b]2Sa 1:24 [c]Job 28:17 [d]Pr 15:31; 20:12 [1]Or *a nose ring* **25:13** [a]Pr 13:17 [1]Lit *day* **25:14** [a]Jd 12 [b]Jer 5:13; Mic 2:11 [1]Lit *in a gift of falsehood* **25:15** [a]Ge 32:4; 1Sa 25:24; Ecc 10:4 **25:16** [a]Jdg 14:8; 1Sa 14:25 **25:18** [a]Ps 57:4; Pr 12:18 [b]Jer 9:8 [c]Ex 20:16; Pr 24:28 [1]Or *lying witness*, cf. Ex 20:16 **25:19** [a]Job 6:15; Is 36:6 [1]Lit *a bad* **25:20** [1]Or *natron*

Is he who sings songs
to [2]an aching heart.
21 [a]If [1]your enemy is hungry,
give him food to eat;
And if he is thirsty, give
him water to drink;
22 For you will [1]heap burning
coals on his head,
And [a]Yahweh will
repay you.
23 The north wind brings
forth rain,
And a [a]tongue of secrets,
an indignant face.
24 It is [a]better to live
in a corner of the roof
Than [1]in a house shared
with a contentious woman.
25 *Like* cold water
to a weary soul,
So is a [a]good report
from a distant land.
26 *Like* a [a]muddied spring
and a corrupted well
Is a righteous man shaking
before the wicked.
27 To eat too much honey
is not good,
Nor is it glory to [a]search
out [1]one's own glory.
28 *Like* a [a]city that is broken
into *and* without a wall
Is a man [b]without restraint
over his spirit.

# 26

Like snow in summer and
like [a]rain in harvest,
So glory is not [b]fitting
for a fool.
2 Like a [a]sparrow in *its* [1]flitting,
like a swallow in flying,
So a [b]curse without cause
does not come *to pass.*
3 A [a]whip is for the horse,
a bridle for the donkey,
And a [b]rod for the back
of fools.
4 [a]Do not answer a fool
according to his folly,
Lest you yourself also
be like him.
5 [a]Answer a fool according
to his folly,
Lest he be [b]wise
in his own eyes.
6 He cuts off *his own* feet
*and* drinks violence
Who sends words
by the hand of a fool.
7 *Like* the legs *which* hang
limp on the lame,
So is a proverb
in the mouth of fools.
8 Like [1]one who binds
a stone in a sling,
So is he who gives
glory to a fool.
9 *Like* a thorn *which* goes up
into the hand of a drunkard,
So is a proverb
in the mouth of fools.
10 [1]*Like* an archer who
wounds everyone,
So is he who hires a fool or
who hires those who pass by.
11 Like [a]a dog that returns
to its vomit

**25:20** [2]Lit *an evil* **25:21** [a]Ex 23:4, 5; 2Ki 6:22; 2Chr 28:15; Mt 5:44; Ro 12:20 [1]Lit *one who hates you* **25:22** [a]2Sa 16:12; Mt 6:4, 6 [1]Lit *snatch up* **25:23** [a]Ps 101:5 **25:24** [a]Pr 21:9 [1]Lit *with a woman of contentions and a house of association* **25:25** [a]Pr 15:30 **25:26** [a]Eze 32:2; 34:18, 19 **25:27** [a]Pr 27:2; Lk 14:11 [1]Lit *their* **25:28** [a]Pr 16:32 [b]2Chr 32:5; Ne 1:3 ◆ **26:1** [a]1Sa 12:17 [b]Pr 17:7 **26:2** [a]Pr 27:8; Is 16:2 [b]Nu 23:8; Dt 23:5; 2Sa 16:12 [1]Lit *wandering* **26:3** [a]Ps 32:9 [b]Pr 10:13; 19:29 **26:4** [a]Pr 23:9; 29:9; Is 36:21; Mt 7:6 **26:5** [a]Mt 16:1-4; 21:24-27 [b]Pr 3:7; 28:11; Ro 12:16 **26:8** [1]Lit *the binding of* **26:10** [1]Or *A master* workman *produces all things, But he who hires a fool is* like *one who hires those who pass by* **26:11** [a]2Pe 2:22

Is a fool who [b]repeats
[1]his folly.
12 Do you see a man [a]wise
in his own eyes?
[b]There is more hope
for a fool than for him.
13 The [a]sluggard says, "There is
a fierce lion in the road!
A lion is [1]among the streets!"
14 *As* the door turns
on its hinges,
So *does* the [a]sluggard
on his bed.
15 The [a]sluggard buries his
hand in the dish;
He is *too* weary to return
it to his mouth.
16 The sluggard is [a]wiser
in his own eyes
Than seven men who
can respond
with a discreet answer.
17 *Like* one who seizes
a dog by the ears
Is he who passes by *and*
becomes passionate about
[a]strife not belonging to him.
18 Like a madman who shoots
[a]Firebrands, arrows,
and death,
19 So is the man who
[a]deceives his neighbor,
And says, "[b]Am I not joking?"
20 With no wood the fire
goes out,
And where there is no
[a]whisperer, [b]strife
quiets down.
21 *Like* charcoal to hot embers
and wood to fire,
So is a [a]contentious man
to kindle strife.
22 The [a]words of a whisperer
are like dainty morsels,
And they go down
into the innermost
parts of the stomach.
23 *Like* an earthen [a]vessel
overlaid with silver [b]dross
Are fiery lips and an evil heart.
24 He who [a]hates disguises
*it* with his lips,
But he sets up [b]deceit
within himself.
25 When he [a]makes his voice
gracious, do not believe him,
For there are seven
abominations in his heart.
26 *Though his* hatred [a]covers
itself with guile,
His evil will be [b]revealed
in the assembly.
27 He who [a]digs a pit
will fall into it,
And he who rolls a stone,
it will turn back on him.
28 A lying tongue hates
[1]those it crushes,
And a [a]flattering mouth
works ruin.

***Instructions and Warnings***

27 [a]Do not boast
about tomorrow,
For you [b]do not know
what a day may bring forth.
2 Let a [a]stranger praise you,
and not your own mouth;
A foreigner, and not
your own lips.

**26:11** [b]Ex 8:15 [1]Lit *with his* **26:12** [a]Pr 3:7; 26:5 [b]Pr 29:20 **26:13** [a]Pr 22:13 [1]Lit *within* **26:14** [a]Pr 6:9 **26:15** [a]Pr 19:24 **26:16** [a]Pr 27:11 **26:17** [a]Pr 3:30 **26:18** [a]Is 50:11 **26:19** [a]Pr 24:28 [b]Eph 5:4 **26:20** [a]Pr 16:28 [b]Pr 22:10 **26:21** [a]Pr 15:18; 29:22 **26:22** [a]Pr 18:8 **26:23** [a]Mt 23:27; Lk 11:39 [b]Pr 25:4 **26:24** [a]Ps 41:6; Pr 10:18 [b]Pr 12:20 **26:25** [a]Ps 28:3; Pr 26:23; Jer 9:8 **26:26** [a]Mt 23:28 [b]Lk 8:17 **26:27** [a]Es 7:10; Pr 28:10 **26:28** [a]Pr 29:5 [1]Lit *its crushed ones*
◆ **27:1** [a]Jas 4:13-16 [b]Lk 12:19, 20; Jas 4:14 **27:2** [a]Pr 25:27; 2Co 10:12, 18; 12:11

3 A stone is heavy and
the sand weighty,
But the provocation
of an ignorant fool is
heavier than both of them.
4 Wrath is cruelty and
anger is a flood,
But [a]who can stand
before jealousy?
5 Better is reproof
that is [a]revealed
Than love that is hidden.
6 Faithful are the [a]wounds
of a friend,
But [1]deceitful are the [b]kisses
of an enemy.
7 A satisfied soul tramples
the honeycomb,
But to a hungry soul any
bitter thing is sweet.
8 Like a [a]bird that wanders
from her nest,
So is a man who [b]wanders
from his place.
9 [a]Oil and incense make
the heart glad,
So counsel from the [1]soul
is sweet to his friend.
10 Do not forsake your [a]friend
or [b]your father's friend,
And do not come to your
brother's house in the day
of your disaster;
Better is one who dwells near
than a brother far away.
11 [a]Be wise, my son, and
make my heart glad,
That I may [b]respond
with a word to him
who reproaches me.
12 A prudent man sees
evil *and* hides,
The simple pass on *and*
are punished.
13 [a]Take his garment
when he becomes
a guarantor for a stranger;
And for [1]a foreign woman
seize it as a pledge.
14 [a]He who blesses his friend
with a loud voice early
in the morning,
It will be counted
as a curse to him.
15 A [a]constant dripping
on a day of steady rain
And a contentious
woman are alike;
16 He who would [1]restrain
her [1]restrains the wind,
And [2]grasps oil
with his right hand.
17 Iron sharpens iron,
So one man
sharpens another.
18 He who guards the [a]fig
tree will eat its fruit,
And he who [b]keeps *watch*
*for* his master will be honored.
19 As in water face *reflects* face,
So the heart of man
*reflects* man.
20 [a]Sheol and Abaddon are
[b]never satisfied,
So the [c]eyes of man are
never satisfied.
21 The [a]refining pot is for silver
and the furnace for gold,
And each [b]*is tested*
by the mouth that praises him.

---

**27:4** [a]Pr 6:34; 1Jn 3:12 **27:5** [a]Pr 28:23; Ga 2:14 **27:6** [a]Ps 141:5; Pr 20:30 [b]Mt 26:49 [1]Or *excessive* **27:8** [a]Pr 26:2; Is 16:2 [b]Ge 21:14 **27:9** [a]Ps 23:5; 141:5 [1]Lit *soul's counsel* **27:10** [a]Pr 18:24 [b]1Ki 12:6-8; 2Chr 10:6-8 **27:11** [a]Pr 10:1; 23:15; 29:3 [b]Ps 119:42 **27:13** [a]Pr 20:16 [1]Or *an adulterous*, cf. 2:16 **27:14** [a]Ps 12:2 **27:15** [a]Pr 19:13 **27:16** [1]Lit *hide(s)* [2]Lit *encounters* **27:18** [a]2Ki 18:31; SS 8:12; Is 36:16; 1Co 3:8; 9:7; 2Ti 2:6 [b]Lk 12:42-44; 19:17 **27:20** [a]Job 26:6; Pr 15:11 [b]Pr 30:15, 16; Hab 2:5 [c]Ecc 1:8; 4:8 **27:21** [a]Pr 17:3 [b]Lk 6:26

22 Though you [a]pound
an ignorant fool in a mortar
with a pestle in the midst
of crushed grain,
His [1]folly will not turn
aside from him.

23 [a]Know well the [1]condition
of your flocks,
*And* pay attention to your herds;
24 For wealth is not forever,
Neither is a [a]crown from
generation to generation.
25 *When* the grass disappears
and the vegetation appears,
And the herbs
of the mountains
are [a]gathered in,
26 The lambs *will be*
for your clothing,
And the goats *will bring*
the price of a field,
27 And *there will be enough*
goats' milk for your food,
For the food
of your household,
And sustenance
for your maidens.

28 The wicked [a]flee when
there is no one pursuing,
But the righteous are
[1]secure as a lion.
2 By the transgression
of a land [a]many
are its princes,
But [b]by a man who
understands, who
knows, so it endures.
3 A [a]poor man who
oppresses the lowly
Is a driving rain
[1]which leaves no food.
4 Those who forsake the law
[a]praise the wicked,
But those who keep the law
[b]strive with them.
5 Evil men [a]do not
understand justice,
But those who seek Yahweh
[b]understand all things.
6 [a]Better is the poor who
walks in his integrity
Than he who is
crooked—[1]double dealing—
though he be rich.
7 He who observes the law is
a son who understands,
But he who befriends
[a]gluttons humiliates
his father.
8 He who increases his wealth
by [a]interest and usury
Gathers it [b]for him who is
gracious to the lowly.
9 He who turns away his ear
from listening to the law,
Even his [a]prayer is
an abomination.
10 He who leads the upright
astray in an evil way
Will [a]himself fall
into his own pit,
But the [b]blameless
will inherit good.
11 The rich man is [a]wise
in his own eyes,

---

**27:22** [a]Pr 23:35; 26:11; Jer 5:3 [1]A lack of wisdom *due to negligence or* carelessness; the activity *of an ignorant fool* ***27:23*** [a]Jer 31:10; Eze 34:12; Jn 10:3 [1]Lit *face* **27:24** [a]Job 19:9; Ps 89:39; Jer 13:18; Lam 5:16; Eze 21:26 **27:25** [a]Is 17:5; Jer 40:10, 12 ◆ **28:1** [a]Lv 26:17, 36; Ps 53:5 [1]Lit *trusting* **28:2** [a]1Ki 16:8-28; 2Ki 15:8-15 [b]Pr 11:11 **28:3** [a]Mt 18:28 [1]Lit *and there is no bread* **28:4** [a]Ps 49:18; Ro 1:32 [b]1Ki 18:18; Ne 13:11, 15; Mt 3:7; 14:4; Eph 5:11 **28:5** [a]Ps 92:6; Is 6:9; 44:18 [b]Ps 119:100; Pr 2:9; Jn 7:17; 1Co 2:15; 1Jn 2:20, 27 **28:6** [a]Pr 19:1 [1]Lit *two ways* **28:7** [a]Pr 23:20 **28:8** [a]Ex 22:25; Lv 25:36 [b]Job 27:17; Pr 13:22; 14:31 **28:9** [a]Ps 66:18; 109:7; Pr 15:8; 21:27 **28:10** [a]Ps 7:15; Pr 26:27 [b]Mt 6:33; Heb 6:12; 1Pe 3:9 **28:11** [a]Pr 3:7; 26:5, 12

But the lowly who
understands [1]searches him.
12 When the [a]righteous exult,
there is great honor,
But [b]when the wicked rise,
man has to be sought out.
13 He who [a]conceals his
transgressions will
not prosper,
But he who [b]confesses
and forsakes *them* will
receive compassion.
14 How blessed is the man
who [a]is always in dread,
But he who [b]hardens his heart
will fall into calamity.
15 *Like* a [a]roaring lion and
a rushing bear
Is a [b]wicked ruler
over a poor people.
16 A [a]leader who lacks
discernment abounds
in oppressions,
*But* he who hates greedy gain
will prolong *his* days.
17 A man [a]oppressed
with [b]the bloodguilt of life
Will flee until [1]death; let
no one uphold him.
18 He who walks blamelessly
will be saved,
But he who is
[a]crooked—[1]double
dealing—will fall all at once.
19 [a]He who cultivates his ground
will be [b]satisfied with food,
But he who pursues
empty *things* will be
satisfied with poverty.
20 A [a]faithful man will
abound with blessings,
But he who [b]makes
haste to be rich will
not go unpunished.
21 To [a,1]show partiality
is not good,
[b]Even for a piece of bread
a man will transgress.
22 A man with an [a]evil eye
[b]hurries after wealth
And does not know that
want will come upon him.
23 He who [a]reproves a man will
afterward find *more* favor
Than he who [b]flatters
with the tongue.
24 He who [a]robs his father
or his mother
And says, "It is not
a transgression,"
Is the [b]companion
of a man who destroys.
25 An [1]arrogant man
[a]stirs up strife,
But he who [b]trusts in Yahweh
[c]will [2]be enriched.
26 He who [a]trusts in his
own heart is a fool,
But he who walks
wisely will escape.
27 He who [a]gives to the poor
will never want,
But he who [1]shuts his eyes
will have many curses.
28 When the wicked rise,
men hide themselves;
But when they perish,
the righteous increase.

---

**28:11** [1]Or *sees right through him* **28:12** [a]Pr 11:10; 29:2 [b]Pr 28:28; Ecc 10:5, 6 **28:13** [a]Job 31:33; Ps 32:3 [b]Ps 32:5; 1Jn 1:9 **28:14** [a]Pr 23:17 [b]Ps 95:8; Ro 2:5 **28:15** [a]Pr 19:12; 1Pe 5:8 [b]Ex 1:14; Pr 29:2; Mt 2:16 **28:16** [a]Ecc 10:16; Is 3:12 **28:17** [a]Ge 9:6; Ex 21:14 [b]Lv 17:11 [1]Lit *the pit* **28:18** [a]Pr 10:27 [1]Lit *two ways* **28:19** [a]Pr 12:11 [b]Pr 20:13 **28:20** [a]Pr 10:6; Mt 24:45; 25:21 [b]Pr 20:21; 28:22; 1Ti 6:9 **28:21** [a]Pr 24:23 [b]Eze 13:19 [1]Lit *regard the face* **28:22** [a]Pr 23:6 [b]Pr 21:5 **28:23** [a]Pr 27:5, 6 [b]Pr 29:5 **28:24** [a]Pr 19:26 [b]Pr 18:9 **28:25** [a]Pr 15:18 [b]Pr 29:25; 1Ti 6:6 [c]Pr 11:25 [1]Lit *broad soul* [2]Lit *be made fat* **28:26** [a]Pr 3:5 **28:27** [a]Pr 11:24; 19:17 [1]Lit *hides*

29 A man who hardens *his*
neck after [a]much reproof
Will [b]suddenly be broken
[1]beyond healing.
2 When the [a]righteous
[1]increase, the people
are glad,
But when a wicked man
rules, people groan.
3 A man who [a]loves wisdom
makes his father glad,
But he who [b]befriends harlots
destroys *his* wealth.
4 By justice the [a]king causes
the land to stand,
But a man of bribes
tears it down.
5 A man who [a]flatters
his neighbor
Is spreading a net for his steps.
6 By transgression an evil
man is [a]ensnared,
But the righteous [b]sings
with joy and is glad.
7 The [a]righteous knows
the cause of the poor,
The wicked does not
understand *that*
knowledge.
8 Scoffers [a,1]set a city aflame,
But [b]wise men turn
away anger.
9 When a wise man is brought
into judgment with a man
who is an ignorant fool,
[1]The *ignorant fool* both
rages and laughs, and
there is no rest.
10 Men of [a]bloodshed hate
the blameless,
But the upright seek
*the well-being of* his soul.
11 A [a]fool [1]lets out all
of his spirit,
But a [b]wise man holds it back.
12 *If* a [a]ruler pays attention
to a lying word,
All his ministers
*become* wicked.
13 The [a]poor man and
the oppressor meet
together *in this*—
Yahweh gives [b]light
to the eyes of both.
14 If a [a]king judges the poor
with truth,
His [b]throne will be
established forever.
15 The [a]rod and reproof
give wisdom,
But a child [1]left
*to himself* [b]brings
shame to his mother.
16 When the wicked [1]increase,
transgression increases;
But the [a]righteous will
see their fall.
17 [a]Discipline your son, and
he will give you rest;
And he will [b]give delight
to your soul.
18 Where there is [a]no
[1]vision, the people
[b]are out of control,
But how [c]blessed is he
who keeps the law.

◆ **29:1** [a]1Sa 2:25; 2Chr 36:16; Pr 1:24-31 [b]Pr 6:15 [1]Lit *and there is no healing* **29:2** [a]Es 8:15; Pr 11:10; 28:12 [1]Or *become great* **29:3** [a]Pr 10:1; 15:20; 27:11; 28:7 [b]Pr 5:10; 6:26; Lk 15:30 **29:4** [a]2Chr 9:8; Pr 8:15; 29:14 **29:5** [a]Ps 5:9 **29:6** [a]Pr 22:5; Ecc 9:12 [b]Ex 15:1 **29:7** [a]Job 29:16; Ps 41:1; Pr 31:8, 9 **29:8** [a]Pr 11:11 [b]Pr 16:14 [1]Lit *breathe out* **29:9** [1]Lit *He* **29:10** [a]Ge 4:5-8; 1Jn 3:12 **29:11** [a]Pr 12:16; 14:33 [b]Pr 19:11 [1]Lit *sends forth all his spirit* **29:12** [a]1Ki 12:14 **29:13** [a]Pr 22:2 [b]Ezr 9:8; Ps 13:3 **29:14** [a]Ps 72:4; Is 11:4 [b]Pr 16:12; 25:5 **29:15** [a]Pr 13:24; 22:15 [b]Pr 10:1; 17:25 [1]Lit *set loose* **29:16** [a]Ps 37:34, 36; 58:10; 91:8; 92:11; Pr 21:12 [1]Or *become great* **29:17** [a]Pr 13:24; 29:15 [b]Pr 10:1 **29:18** [a]1Sa 3:1; Ps 74:9; Am 8:11, 12 [b]Ex 32:25 [c]Ps 1:1, 2; 106:3; 119:2; Pr 8:32; Jn 13:17 [1]Or *revelation*

19 A slave will not be corrected
by words *alone*;
For though he understands,
there will be no answer.
20 Do you behold a man who
is [a]hasty in his words?
There is [b]more hope
for a fool than for him.
21 He who pampers his slave
from childhood
Will in the end find him
to be [1]arrogant.
22 An [a]angry man stirs
up strife,
And a hot-tempered man
abounds in transgression.
23 A man's [a]lofty pride
will bring him low,
But a [b]lowly spirit will
take hold of glory.
24 He who [1]divides *the spoil* with
a thief hates his own soul;
He [a]hears the oath
but declares nothing.
25 [a]Trembling before man
[1]brings a snare,
But he who [b]trusts
in Yahweh will be set
securely on high.
26 [a]Many seek the face of a ruler,
But [b]justice for man
*comes* from Yahweh.
27 An [a]unjust man is
an abomination
to the righteous,
And he who is [b]upright
in the way is an abomination
to the wicked.

### *Every Word of God Is Tested*

30 The words of Agur the son of Jakeh, the [1]oracle.
The man declares to Ithiel, to Ithiel and Ucal:
2 Surely I am more [a]senseless
than any man,
And I do not have
the understanding
of mankind.
3 Neither have I
learned wisdom,
Nor do I know the [a]knowledge
of the Holy One.
4 Who has [a]ascended
into heaven and descended?
Who has gathered
the [b]wind in His fists?
Who has [c]wrapped the waters
in [1]His garment?
Who has [d,2]established all
the ends of the earth?
What is His [e]name? And
what is His [f]Son's name?
Surely you know!

5 Every [a]word of God is [1]tested;
He is a [b]shield to those who
take refuge in Him.
6 [a]Do not add to His words
Lest He reprove you, and
you be proved a liar.

7 Two things I asked of You,
Do not withhold
from me before I die:
8 Keep worthlessness and *every*
false word far from me,

---

**29:20** [a]Jas 1:19 [b]Pr 26:12 **29:21** [1]Or *a son* **29:22** [a]Pr 15:18; 26:21 **29:23** [a]Pr 11:2; 16:18; Da 4:30, 31; Mt 23:12; Jas 4:6 [b]Pr 15:33; 18:12; 22:4; Is 66:2; Lk 14:11; 18:14; Jas 4:10 **29:24** [a]Lv 5:1 [1]Or *partners* **29:25** [a]Ge 12:12; 20:2; Lk 12:4; Jn 12:42, 43 [b]Ps 91:1-16; Pr 18:10; 28:25 [1]Lit *gives* **29:26** [a]Pr 19:6 [b]Is 49:4; 1Co 4:4 **29:27** [a]Ps 6:8; 139:21, 22; Pr 12:8 [b]Ps 69:4; Pr 29:10; Mt 10:22; 24:9; Jn 15:18; 17:14; 1Jn 3:13 ◆**30:1** [1]Or *burden* **30:2** [a]Ps 49:10; 73:22; Pr 12:1 **30:3** [a]Pr 9:10 **30:4** [a]Ps 68:18; Jn 3:13; Eph 4:8 [b]Ex 15:10; Ps 135:7 [c]Job 26:8; 38:8, 9 [d]Ps 24:2; Is 45:18 [e]Ex 3:13-15; Rev 19:12 [f]Ex 4:22-23; Ps 2:7, 12 [1]Lit *the* [2]Lit *raised up* **30:5** [a]Ps 12:6; 18:30 [b]Ps 3:3; 84:11; Pr 2:7 [1]Or *tried*, cf. 2Sa 22:31; Ps 18:30 **30:6** [a]Dt 4:2; 12:32; Rev 22:18

Give me neither poverty
nor riches;
Feed me with the [a]food
that is my portion,
9 Lest I be [a]full and deny [b]*You*
and say, "Who is Yahweh?"
Or lest I be [c]impoverished
and steal,
And [d,1]profane the name
of my God.

10 Do not slander a slave
to his master,
Lest he [a]curse you and
you be found guilty.

11 There is a generation that
[a]curses its father
And does not bless
its mother.
12 There is a generation that is
[a]clean in its own eyes,
Yet is not washed
from its filthiness.
13 There is a generation—oh
how [a]haughty are its eyes!
And its eyelids are lifted up.
14 There is a generation whose
[a]teeth are *like* swords
And its [b]fangs *like* knives,
To [c]devour the afflicted
from the earth
And the needy
from among men.

15 The leech has two daughters,
"Give," "Give."
There are three things
that will not be satisfied,
Four that will not
*say, "Enough":*
16 [a]Sheol, and the [b]barren womb,
Earth that is never
satisfied with water,
And fire that never
says, "Enough."
17 The eye that [a]mocks a father
And [b]despises obedience
to a mother,
The [c]ravens of the valley
will pick it out,
And the young [c]eagles
will eat it.

18 There are three things which
are too wonderful for me,
Four which I
do not understand:
19 The way of an [a]eagle in the sky,
The way of a serpent on a rock,
The way of a ship
in the heart of the sea,
And the way of a man
with a virgin.
20 This is the way
of an [a]adulterous woman:
She eats and wipes her mouth,
And says, "I have done
no wrong."

21 Under three things
the earth quakes,
And under four,
it cannot bear up:
22 Under a [a]slave
when he becomes king,
And a wicked fool when he
is satisfied with food,
23 Under [1]an unloved woman
when she gets a husband,
And a servant-girl when she
supplants her mistress.

**30:8** [a]Job 23:12; Mt 6:11 **30:9** [a]Dt 8:12; 31:20; Ne 9:25; Hos 13:6 [b]Jos 24:27; Job 31:28 [c]Pr 6:30 [d]Ex 20:7 [1]Lit *take hold of* **30:10** [a]Ecc 7:21 **30:11** [a]Ex 21:17; Pr 20:20 **30:12** [a]Pr 16:2; Is 65:5; Lk 18:11; Tit 1:15, 16 **30:13** [a]Pr 6:17; Is 2:11; 5:15 **30:14** [a]Ps 57:4 [b]Job 29:17 [c]Ps 14:4; Am 8:4 **30:16** [a]Pr 27:20 [b]Ge 30:1 **30:17** [a]Ge 9:22 [b]Pr 15:20 [c]Dt 28:26 **30:19** [a]Dt 28:49; Jer 48:40; 49:22 **30:20** [a]Pr 5:6 **30:22** [a]Pr 19:10; Ecc 10:7 **30:23** [1]Lit *a hated*

24 Four things are small
on the earth,
But they are exceedingly wise:
25 The [a]ants are not
a strong people,
But they prepare their
food in the summer;
26 The [a,1]shephanim are not
a mighty people,
Yet they make their
houses in the cliff;
27 The locusts have no king,
Yet all of them go
out in [a]rank;
28 The lizard you may grasp
with the hands,
Yet it is in kings' palaces.

29 There are three things which
are stately in *their* march,
Even four which are stately
when they walk:
30 The lion *which* is [a]mighty
among the animals
And does not [b]turn
back before any,
31 The [1]strutting rooster,
the male goat also,
And a king *when his*
army is with him.

32 If you have been wickedly
foolish in lifting yourself up,
Or if you have schemed
*evil,* [a]*put your* hand
on your mouth.
33 For pressing milk brings
forth butter,
And pressing the nose
brings forth blood;
And pressing [a]anger
brings forth strife.

### *A Mother's Oracle*

31 The words of King Lemuel,
the [1]oracle *unto* which his
mother disciplined him:
2 What, O my son?
And what, O [a]son
of my womb?
And what, O son of my [b]vows?
3 [a]Do not give your
excellence to women,
Or your ways to that
which [b]blots out kings.
4 It is not for [a]kings, O Lemuel,
It is not for kings
to [b]drink wine,
Or for rulers to desire
strong drink,
5 Lest he drink and forget
what is decreed,
And [a]pervert the justice
of all the [1]afflicted.
6 Give strong drink to him
who is [a]perishing,
And wine to those
[b]whose soul is bitter.
7 Let him drink and
forget his poverty
And he will not remember
his trouble any longer.
8 [a]Open your mouth
for the mute,
For the justice of all
those [1]passing away.
9 Open your mouth,
[a]judge righteously,
And render [b]justice
to the afflicted and needy.

**30:25** [a]Pr 6:6 **30:26** [a]Lv 11:5; Ps 104:18 [1]Small, shy, furry animals *(Hyrax syriacus)* **30:27** [a]Joel 2:7 **30:30** [a]Jdg 14:18; 2Sa 1:23 [b]Mic 5:8 **30:31** [1]Lit *girt in the loins* **30:32** [a]Job 21:5; 40:4; Mic 7:16 **30:33** [a]Pr 10:12; 29:22 ◆ **31:1** [1]Or *burden* **31:2** [a]Is 49:15 [b]1Sa 1:11 **31:3** [a]Pr 5:9 [b]Dt 17:17; 1Ki 11:1; Ne 13:26 **31:4** [a]Ecc 10:17 [b]Pr 20:1; Is 5:22; Hos 4:11 **31:5** [a]Ex 23:6; Dt 16:19; Pr 17:15 [1]Lit *sons of affliction* **31:6** [a]Job 29:13 [b]Job 3:20; Is 38:15 **31:8** [a]Job 29:12-17; Ps 82 [1]Lit *sons of passing away* **31:9** [a]Lv 19:15; Dt 1:16 [b]Is 1:17; Jer 22:16

### *A Woman Who Fears Yahweh*

א *Aleph*

10 [1]An [a]excellent wife,
who can find?
For her worth is far
[b]above pearls.

ב *Beth*

11 The heart of her husband
trusts in her,
And he will have no lack of gain.

ג *Gimel*

12 She deals bountifully with
him for good and not evil
All the days of her life.

ד *Daleth*

13 She searches for wool and flax
And works with her
[1]hands [2]in delight.

ה *He*

14 She is like [a]merchant ships;
She brings her food from afar.

ו *Vav*

15 And she [a]rises
while it is still night,
And [b]gives [1]food
to her household
And a [2]portion to her
young women.

ז *Zayin*

16 She makes plans
for a field and buys it;
From the fruit of her [1]hands
she plants a vineyard.

ח *Heth*

17 She [a]girds [1]herself with strength
And makes her arms strong.

ט *Teth*

18 She senses that her gain is good;
Her lamp does not
go out at night.

י *Yodh*

19 She stretches out her
hands to the distaff,
And her [1]hands hold
fast the spindle.

כ *Kaph*

20 She [a,1]extends her
hand to the poor,
And she stretches out her
hands to the needy.

ל *Lamedh*

21 She is not afraid of the snow
for her household,
For all her household are
[a]clothed with scarlet.

מ *Mem*

22 She makes [a]coverings
for herself;
Her clothing is [b]fine
linen and [c]purple.

נ *Nun*

23 Her husband is known
[a]in the gates,
When he sits
with the elders of the land.

ס *Samekh*

24 She makes [a]linen garments
and sells *them*,
And gives belts
to the [1]tradesmen.

ע *Ayin*

25 Strength and [a]majesty
are her clothing,
And she smiles at the [1]future.

פ *Pe*

26 She [a]opens her mouth
in wisdom,
And the [1]instruction
of lovingkindness is
on her tongue.

---

***31:10*** [a]Ru 3:11; Pr 12:4; 19:14 [b]Job 28:18; Pr 8:11 [1]Lit *a woman of excellence, a woman of strength* **31:13** [1]Lit *palms* [2]Or *willingly* **31:14** [a]Eze 27:25 **31:15** [a]Pr 20:13; Ro 12:11 [b]Ps 111:5; Lk 12:42 [1]Lit *prey* [2]Or *prescribed task* **31:16** [1]Lit *palms* **31:17** [a]1Ki 18:46; 2Ki 4:29; Job 38:3 [1]Lit *her loins* **31:19** [1]Lit *palms* **31:20** [a]Dt 15:11; Job 31:16-20; Pr 22:9; Ro 12:13; Eph 4:28 [1]Lit *spreads out her palm* **31:21** [a]2Sa 1:24 **31:22** [a]Pr 7:16 [b]Ge 41:42; Rev 19:8, 14 [c]Jdg 8:26; Lk 16:19 **31:23** [a]Dt 16:18; Ru 4:1, 11 **31:24** [a]Jdg 14:12 [1]Lit *Canaanite* **31:25** [a]1Ti 2:9, 10 [1]Lit *latter days* **31:26** [a]Pr 10:31 [1]Or *law*

*צ Tsadhe*

27 She watches over the ways
of her household,
And does not eat the [a]bread
of [1]idleness.

*ק Qoph*

28 Her children rise up
and bless her;
As for her husband, he also
praises her, *saying*:

*ר Resh*

29 "Many daughters have
done excellently,
But you have gone
above them all."

*ש Shin*

30 [1]Charm is deceitful and
beauty is vain,
*But* a woman who
[a,2]fears Yahweh,
she shall be praised.

*ת Tav*

31 Give to her from the fruit
of her hands,
And let her works praise
her in the gates.

*The Book of*

# ECCLESIASTES

### All Is Vanity

1 The words of the [a,1]Preacher,
the son of David, king in Jerusalem.
2 "[a,1]Vanity of vanities,"
says the Preacher,
"[1]Vanity of vanities!
All is [2]vanity."

3 [a]What advantage does man
have in all his labor
In which he labors
under the sun?
4 A generation goes and
a generation comes,
But the [a]earth stands forever.
5 Also, [a]the sun rises
and the sun sets;
And [1]hastening to its place
it rises there *again*.
6 [a]Going toward the south,
Then [1]circling
toward the north,
The wind goes [1]circling along;
And on its circular courses
the wind returns.
7 All the rivers go into the sea,
Yet the sea is not full.
To the place
where the rivers go,
There they [1]continually go.
8 All things are wearisome;
Man is not able to speak *of it*.
[a]The eye is not satisfied
with seeing,
Nor is the ear filled
with hearing.
9 [a]That which has been is
that which will be,
And that which has been done
is that which will be done.
So there is nothing new
under the sun.
10 Is there anything
of which one might say,

**31:27** [a]Pr 19:15 [1]Lit *being a sluggard* **31:30** [a]Ps 112:1; Pr 22:4 [1]Lit *Gracefulness* [2]Or *reverences*
◆ **1:1** [a]Ecc 1:12; 7:27; 12:8-10 [1]Or *speaker of an assembly, leader of an assembly*; or possibly *the one who gathers an assembly*; Heb *Qoheleth* **1:2** [a]Ps 39:5, 6; 62:9; 144:4; Ecc 12:8; Ro 8:20 [1]Or *Futility of futilities* [2]Or *futile* **1:3** [a]Ecc 2:11; 3:9; 5:16 **1:4** [a]Ps 104:5; 119:90 **1:5** [a]Ps 19:6 [1]Lit *panting* **1:6** [a]Ecc 11:5; Jn 3:8 [1]Lit *turning* **1:7** [1]Lit *turn to go* **1:8** [a]Pr 27:20; Ecc 4:8 **1:9** [a]Ecc 1:10; 2:12; 3:15; 6:10

"See this, it is new"?
Already it has been for ages
Which were before us.
11 There is [a]no remembrance
of [1]earlier things;
And also of the [2]later
things which will be,
There will be for them
no remembrance
Among those who will
come [2]later *still.*

### *The Vanity of Wisdom*

**12** I, the [a]Preacher, have been king
over Israel in Jerusalem. **13** And I
[a]gave my heart to seek and [b]explore
by wisdom concerning all that has
been done under heaven. *It* is [1]a griev-
ous [c]endeavor *which* God has given to
the sons of men with which to occupy
*themselves.* **14** I have seen all the works
which have been done under the sun,
and behold, all is [a,1]vanity and striving
after wind. **15** What is [a]bent cannot
be straightened, and what is lacking
cannot be counted.

**16** I spoke within my heart, say-
ing, "Behold, I have magnified and
increased [a]wisdom more than all
who were over Jerusalem before me;
and my heart has seen an abundance
of wisdom and knowledge." **17** And I
[a]gave my heart to know wisdom and
to [b]know madness and simplemind-
ed folly; I came to know that this also
is [c]striving after wind. **18** Because
[a]in much wisdom there is much
vexation, and *whoever* increases
knowledge increases pain.

### *The Vanity of Pleasure and Possessions*

**2** I said in my heart, "Come now, I
will test you with [a]gladness, so
that you shall see good things." And
behold, it too was vanity. **2** [a]I said of
laughter, "It is madness," and of glad-
ness, "What does it do?" **3** I explored
with my heart *how* to [a,1]stimulate my
[2]body with wine—while my heart
was guiding *me* wisely—and how
to seize [b]simpleminded folly, until
I could see [c]where is this good for
the sons of men *in* what they do
under heaven the few days of their
lives. **4** I made my works great: I
[a]built houses for myself; I planted
[b]vineyards for myself; **5** I made for
myself [a]gardens and [b]parks, and I
planted in them all kinds of fruit
trees; **6** I made for myself [a]pools of
water from which to water a forest
of growing trees. **7** I bought male and
female slaves, and I had [a,1]homeborn
slaves. Also I possessed flocks and
[b]herds larger than all who preceded
me in Jerusalem. **8** Also, I collected
for myself silver and [a]gold and the
treasure of kings and provinces.
I provided for myself [b]male and
female singers and the pleasures of
the sons of men—many concubines.

**9** Then I became [a]great and in-
creased more than all who preceded
me in Jerusalem. My wisdom also
stood by me. **10** [a]All that my eyes
asked for I did not refuse them. I
did not withhold my heart from
any gladness, for my heart was glad

**1:11** [a]*Ecc 2:16; 9:5* [1]*Lit first, former* [2]Lit *latter, after* **1:12** [a]Ecc 1:1; 7:27; 12:8-10 **1:13** [a]Ecc 1:17 [b]Ecc 3:10, 11; 7:25; 8:17 [c]Ecc 2:23, 26; 3:10; 4:8 [1]Lit *an evil* **1:14** [a]Ecc 2:11, 17; 4:4; 6:9 [1]Or *futility* **1:15** [a]Ecc 7:13 **1:16** [a]1Ki 3:12; 4:30; 10:23; Ecc 2:9 **1:17** [a]Ecc 1:13; 7:25 [b]Ecc 2:12; 7:25 [c]Ecc 1:14; 2:11, 17; 4:4, 6, 16; 6:9 **1:18** [a]Ecc 2:23; 12:12 ◆ **2:1** [a]Ecc 7:4; 8:15 **2:2** [a]Pr 14:13; Ecc 7:3, 6 **2:3** [a]Jdg 9:13; Ps 104:15; Ecc 10:19 [b]Ecc 7:25 [c]Ecc 2:24; 3:12, 13; 5:18; 6:12; 8:15; 12:13 [1]Lit *drag* [2]Lit *flesh* **2:4** [a]1Ki 7:1-12 [b]SS 8:11 **2:5** [a]SS 4:16; 5:1 [b]Ne 2:8 **2:6** [a]Ne 2:14; 3:15, 16 **2:7** [a]Ge 14:14; 15:3 [b]1Ki 4:23 [1]Lit *sons of the house* **2:8** [a]1Ki 9:28; 10:10, 14, 21 [b]2Sa 19:35 **2:9** [a]1Chr 29:25; Ecc 1:16 **2:10** [a]Ecc 6:2

because of all my labor, and this was
my [b]reward for all my labor. **11** Thus
I turned to all my works which my
hands had done and the labor which
I had labored to do, and behold, all
was [a,1]vanity and striving after wind,
and there was [b]no advantage under
the sun.

### *Wisdom Excels Folly*

**12** So I turned to [a]see wisdom, mad-
ness, and simpleminded folly. What
*will* the man *do* who will come after
the king *except* [b]what has already
been done? **13** And I saw that there
is an advantage in [a]wisdom over
simpleminded folly as light has
an advantage over darkness. **14** The
wise man's eyes are in his head, but
the [a]fool walks in darkness. And yet
I know that the [b]fate of one becomes
the fate of all of them. **15** Then I said
in my heart, "[a]As is the fate of the
fool, so will my fate be also. [b]Why
then have I been extremely wise?" So
I said in my heart, "This too is vanity."
**16** For there is [a]no remembrance of
the wise man along with the fool
forever, inasmuch as *in* the coming
days all will be forgotten. And [b]how
the wise man dies with the fool! **17** So
I [a]hated life, for the work which
had been done under the sun was
[1]grievous to me; because everything
is vanity and striving after wind.

### *The Vanity of Labor*

**18** Thus I hated [a]all the fruit of
my labor for which I had labored
under the sun, for I must [b]leave
it to the man who will come after
me. **19** And who knows whether
he will be a wise man or [a]a *man*
*of* simpleminded folly? Yet he will
have [1]power over all the fruit of
my labor for which I have labored
and for which I have acted wisely
under the sun. This too is [b]vanity.
**20** Therefore I turned my heart to
despair of all my labor for which I
had labored under the sun. **21** When
there is a man who has labored with
wisdom, knowledge, and [a]skill,
then he [b]gives his portion to one
who has not labored with them.
This too is vanity and a great evil.
**22** For what does a man get in [a]all
his labor and in the striving of his
heart with which he labors under
the sun? **23** Because all his days his
endeavor is painful and [a]vexing;
even at night his heart [b]does not
lie down. This too is vanity.

**24** [1]There is [a]nothing better for
a man *than* to eat and drink and
have his soul see good in his labor.
This also I have seen that it is [b]from
the hand of God. **25** For who can
eat and who can have enjoyment
outside of [1]Him? **26** For to a man
who is good before Him, [a]He has
given wisdom and knowledge and
gladness, while to the sinner He has
given the endeavor of gathering and
collecting so that he may [b]give to
one who is good before God. This
too is [c]vanity and striving after
wind.

---

**2:10** [b]Ecc 3:22; 5:18; 9:9 **2:11** [a]Ecc 1:14; 2:22, 23 [b]Ecc 1:3; 3:9; 5:16 [1]Or *futility*, so in ch **2:12** [a]Ecc 1:17 [b]Ecc 1:9, 10; 3:15 **2:13** [a]Ecc 7:11, 12, 19; 9:18; 10:10 **2:14** [a]1Jn 2:11 [b]Ps 49:10; Ecc 3:19; 6:6; 7:2; 9:2, 3 **2:15** [a]Ecc 2:16 [b]Ecc 6:8, 11 **2:16** [a]Ecc 1:11; 9:5 [b]Ecc 2:14 **2:17** [a]Ecc 4:2, 3 [1]Lit *evil* **2:18** [a]Ecc 1:3; 2:11 [b]Ps 39:6; 49:10 **2:19** [a]1Ki 12:13 [b]1Ti 6:10 [1]Lit *dominion* **2:21** [a]Ecc 4:4 [b]Ecc 2:18 **2:22** [a]Ecc 1:3; 2:11 **2:23** [a]Job 5:7; 14:1; Ecc 1:18; 5:17 [b]Ps 127:2 **2:24** [a]Ecc 2:3; 3:12, 13, 22; 5:18; 6:12; 8:15; 9:7; Is 56:12; Lk 12:19; 1Co 15:32; 1Ti 6:17 [b]Ecc 3:13 [1]Lit *There is nothing good in man, who should eat* **2:25** [1]As in Gr; Heb *me* **2:26** [a]Job 32:8; Pr 2:6 [b]Job 27:16, 17; Pr 13:22 [c]Ecc 1:14

### A Time for Everything

**3** There is an appointed time for everything. And there is a [a]time for every [1]matter under heaven—

2 A time to give birth and
a [a]time to die;
A time to plant and a time
to uproot what is planted.
3 A [a]time to kill and
a time to heal;
A time to tear down and
a time to build up.
4 A time to [a]weep and
a time to [b]laugh;
A time to mourn and
a time to [c]dance.
5 A time to throw stones and
a time to gather stones;
A time to embrace and a time
to shun embracing.
6 A time to search and
a time to lose;
A time to keep and a time
to throw away.
7 A time to tear apart and
a time to sew together;
A time to [a]be silent and
a time to speak.
8 A time to love and
a time to [a]hate;
A time for war and
a time for peace.

9 [a]What advantage is there to
the worker from that in which he
labors? 10 I have seen the [a]endeavor
which God has given the sons of
men with which to occupy them-
selves.

### God Set Eternity in the Heart of Man

11 He has [a]made everything [1]beautiful
in its time. He has also set eternity in
their heart, [2]yet so that man [b]will not
find out the work which God has done
from the beginning even to the end.
12 I know that [1]there is [a]nothing
better for them than to be glad and to
do good in one's lifetime; 13 moreover,
that every man who eats and drinks
and sees good in all his labor—it is
the [a]gift of God. 14 I know that every-
thing God does will be forever; there
is nothing to add to it and there is
nothing to take from it—God has *so*
worked that men should [a,1]fear Him.
15 That [a]which is has been already
and that which will be has already
been, yet God seeks what is pursued.
16 Furthermore, I have seen under
the sun *that* in the place of justice
there is [a]wickedness, and in the place
of righteousness there is wickedness.
17 I said in my heart, "[a]God will judge
both the righteous man and the
wicked man," for a [b]time for every
[1]matter and for every work is there.
18 I said in my heart concerning the
sons of men, "God is testing them in
order for them to see that they are
but [a]beasts." 19 [a]For the fate of the
sons of men and the fate of beasts
is the same fate for *each of* them. As
one dies so dies the other, and they
all have the same breath. So there
is no advantage for man over beast,
for all is [1]vanity. 20 All go to the same
place. All came from the [a]dust, and

---

◆ **3:1** [a]Ecc 3:17; 8:6 [1]Lit *delight* **3:2** [a]*Job 14:5; Heb 9:27* **3:3** [a]Ge 9:6; 1Sa 2:6; Hos 6:1, 2 **3:4** [a]*Ro 12:15* [b]*Ps 126:2* [c]*Ex 15:20* **3:7** [a]Am 5:13 **3:8** [a]Ps 101:3; Pr 13:5 **3:9** [a]Ecc 1:3; 2:11; 5:16 **3:10** [a]Ecc 1:13; 2:26 **3:11** [a]Ge 1:31 [b]Job 5:9; Ecc 7:23; 8:17; Ro 11:33 [1]Or *appropriate* [2]Or *without which man* **3:12** [a]Ecc 2:24 [1]Lit *there is nothing good in man except to be glad* **3:13** [a]Ecc 2:24; 5:19 **3:14** [a]Ecc 5:7; 7:18; 8:12, 13; 12:13 [1]Or *be in awe before Him* **3:15** [a]Ecc 1:9; 6:10 **3:16** [a]Ecc 4:1; 5:8; 8:9 **3:17** [a]Ge 18:25; Ps 96:13; 98:9; Ecc 11:9; Mt 16:27; Ro 2:6-10; 2Th 1:6-9 [b]Ecc 3:1; 8:6 [1]Or *delight* **3:18** [a]Ps 49:12, 20; 73:22 **3:19** [a]Ps 49:12; Ecc 9:12 [1]Or *futility* **3:20** [a]Ge 3:19; Ps 103:14; Ecc 12:7

all return to the dust. **21** Who knows
that the [a]breath of man ascends
upward and the breath of the beast
descends downward to the earth?
**22** I have seen that [a]nothing is better
than that man should be glad in his
works, for that is his portion. For who
will bring him to see [b]what will occur
after him?

### *The Tears of the Oppressed*

**4** Then I looked again at all the acts
of [a]oppression which were being
done under the sun. And behold, *I
saw* the tears of the oppressed and
*that* they had [b]no one to comfort
*them*; and on the side of their op-
pressors was power, but they had no
one to comfort *them.* **2** So [a]I lauded
the dead who are already dead more
than the living who are still living.
**3** But [a]better *off* than both of them
is the one who never has been, who
has never seen the evil work that is
done under the sun.
**4** I have seen that every labor and
every [a]success of the work is *the
result of* jealousy between a man and
his neighbor. This too is [b,1]vanity and
striving after wind. **5** The fool [a]folds
his hands in embrace and [b]consumes
his own flesh. **6** One hand full of rest
is [a]better than two fists full of labor
and striving after wind.
**7** Then I looked again at vanity
under the sun. **8** There was a certain
man without a second man, having
neither a son nor a brother, yet
there was no end to all his labor.
Indeed, [a]his eyes were not satisfied
with riches—"And [b]for whom am
I laboring and depriving myself of
good?" This too is vanity, and it is
a [c]grievous endeavor.
**9** Two are better than one because
they have good wages for their labor.
**10** For if [1]either of them falls, the one
will lift up his companion. But woe to
the one who falls when there is not
a second one to lift him up. **11** Fur-
thermore, if two lie down together
they [1]keep warm, but [a]how can one
be warm *alone*? **12** And if [1]one can
overpower him who is alone, two can
stand against him. A cord of three
*strands* is not quickly torn apart.
**13** A [a]poor yet wise lad is better
than an old and foolish king who
no longer knows *how* to receive
[1]warning. **14** For he has come [a]out of
prison to become king, even though
he was born poor in his kingdom.
**15** I have seen all the living who walk
about under the sun *go along* with
the second lad who stands in place
of him. **16** There is no end to all the
people, to all who were before them,
and even the ones who will come
later will not be glad with him, for
this too is [a]vanity and striving after
wind.

### *Fear God*

**5** [a,1]Guard your steps as you go
to the house of God and draw
near to listen rather than to offer
the [b]sacrifice of fools; for they do
not know they are doing evil. **2** [1]Do
not be [a]hasty with your mouth or
[2]impulsive in your heart to bring up

**3:21** [a]Ecc 12:7 **3:22** [a]Ecc 2:24 [b]Ecc 2:18; 6:12; 8:7; 10:14 ◆ **4:1** [a]Job 35:9; Ps 12:5; Ecc 3:16; 5:8; Is 5:7 [b]Jer 16:7; Lam 1:9 **4:2** [a]Job 3:11-26; Ecc 2:17; 7:1 **4:3** [a]Job 3:11-22; Ecc 6:3; Lk 23:29 **4:4** [a]Ecc 2:21 [b]Ecc 1:14 [1]Or *futility*, so in ch **4:5** [a]Pr 6:10; 24:33 [b]Is 9:20 **4:6** [a]Pr 15:16, 17; 16:8 **4:8** [a]Pr 27:20; Ecc 1:8; 5:10 [b]Ecc 2:21 [c]Ecc 1:13 **4:10** [1]Lit *they fall* **4:11** [a]1Ki 1:1-4 [1]Lit *have warmth* **4:12** [1]Lit *he* **4:13** [a]Ecc 7:19; 9:15 [1]Or *instruction* **4:14** [a]Ge 41:14, 41-43 **4:16** [a]Ecc 1:14 ◆ **5:1** [a]Ex 3:5; 30:18-20; Is 1:12 [b]1Sa 15:22; Pr 15:8; 21:27 [1]Ch 4:17 in Heb **5:2** [a]Pr 20:25 [1]Ch 5:1 in Heb [2]Lit *hurry your heart*

a matter in the presence of God. For
God is in heaven but you are on the
earth; therefore let your [b]words be
few. **3** For the dream comes through
abundant endeavor and the voice of
a [a]fool through abundant words.
**4** When you [a]make a vow to God,
do not be late in paying it; for *He
takes* no delight in fools. [b]Pay what
you vow! **5** It is [a]better that you
should not vow than that you should
vow and not pay. **6** Do not allow your
mouth to cause your flesh to sin, and
do not say in the presence of the mes-
senger *of God* that it was a [a]mistake.
Why should God be angry on account
of your voice and wreak destruction
on the work of your hands? **7** For in
many dreams and vanities are many
words. Rather, [a,1]fear God.

### The Vanity of Riches

**8** If you see [a]oppression of the poor
and [b]robbery of justice and righ-
teousness in the province, do not
be [c]astonished over the [1]matter; for
a lofty one keeps watch over another
lofty one, and there are loftier ones
over them. **9** But *the* advantage of the
land in everything is this—a king
*committed* to a cultivated field.
**10** [a]He who loves money will not
be satisfied with money, nor he who
loves abundance *with its* produce.
This too is [1]vanity. **11** [a]When good
things increase, those who consume
them increase. So what is the success
to their masters except to look on
*with* their eyes? **12** The sleep of the
laboring man is [a]sweet, *whether he*
eats little or much; but the satisfac-
tion of the rich man does not [1]allow
him to sleep.
**13** There is a sickening evil *which* I
have seen under the sun: [a]riches being
[1]hoarded by their master to his own
evil *demise.* **14** And those riches were
lost through a bad endeavor; and he
became the father of a son, but there
was nothing in his hand *for him.* **15** [a]As
he had come naked from his mother's
womb, so will he return as he came.
He will [b]carry nothing from the fruit
of his labor that he can bring in his
hand. **16** This also is a sickening evil—
exactly as a man came, so will he go.
So [a]what is the advantage to him who
[b]labors for the wind? **17** Also, all his
days [a]he eats in darkness with [b]much
vexation, and his sickness and anger.
**18** Here is what I have seen to be
[a]good, which is [1]beautiful: to eat, to
drink, and to see good in all one's
labor in which he labors under the
sun *during* the few days of his life
which God has given him; for this is his
[b]portion. **19** Furthermore, as for every
man to whom [a]God has given riches
and wealth, He has also [b]empowered
him to eat from them and to take up
his portion and be glad in his labor;
this is the [c]gift of God. **20** For he will
not remember much the days of his life
because [a]God allows [1]him to occupy
himself with the gladness of his heart.

### The Vanity of Life

**6** There is an [a]evil which I have
seen under the sun and it is
*prevalent* [1]among men— **2** a man to

**5:2** [b]Pr 10:19; Mt 6:7 **5:3** [a]Job 11:2; Pr 15:2; Ecc 10:14 **5:4** [a]Nu 30:2; Ps 50:14; 76:11 [b]Ps 66:13, 14
**5:5** [a]Pr 20:25; Ac 5:4 **5:6** [a]Lv 4:2, 22; Nu 15:25 **5:7** [a]Ecc 3:14; 7:18; 8:12, 13; 12:13 [1]Or *reverence*
**5:8** [a]Ecc 4:1 [b]Eze 18:18 [c]1Pe 4:12 [1]Lit *delight* **5:10** [a]Ecc 1:8; 2:10, 11; 4:8 [1]Or *futility* **5:11** [a]Ecc 2:9
**5:12** [a]Pr 3:24 [1]Or *grant him rest* **5:13** [a]Ecc 6:2 [1]Lit *guarded* **5:15** [a]Job 1:21 [b]Ps 49:17; 1Ti 6:7
**5:16** [a]Ecc 1:3; 2:11; 3:9 [b]Pr 11:29 **5:17** [a]Ps 127:2 [b]Ecc 2:23 **5:18** [a]Ecc 2:24 [b]Ecc 2:10 [1]Or *appropriate*
**5:19** [a]2Chr 1:12; Ecc 6:2 [b]Ecc 6:2 [c]Ecc 3:13 **5:20** [a]Ex 23:25 [1]As in Gr ◆ **6:1** [a]Ecc 5:13 [1]Lit *upon*

whom God [a]gives riches and wealth
and honor so that his soul [b]lacks
nothing of all that he desires; yet
God does not empower him to eat
from them, for a foreigner eats from
them. This is [1]vanity and a sickening
evil. **3** If a man becomes the father of
one hundred *children* and lives many
years, however many the days of his
years may be, but his soul is not sat-
isfied with good things, and he does
not even have a *proper* [a]burial, *then*
I say, "Better [b]the miscarriage than
he, **4** for *that* one comes in vanity and
goes into darkness; and *that* one's
name is covered in darkness. **5** In-
deed, *that* one never sees the sun and
never knows *anything*; [1]*that* one has
more rest than he. **6** Even if the *other*
man lives one thousand years twice
and does not see good things—[a]do
not all go to the same place?"

**7** [a]All a man's labor is for his mouth,
and yet the soul is not fulfilled. **8** For
[a]what advantage does the wise man
have over the fool? What *advantage*
does the afflicted man have, knowing
*how* to walk before the living? **9** What
the eyes [a]see is better than what the
soul goes after. This too is [b]vanity
and striving after wind.

**10** Whatever [a]exists has already
been named, and it is known what
man is; and he [b]cannot dispute with
him who is stronger than he is. **11** For
there are many words which increase
vanity. What *then* is the advantage to
a man? **12** For who knows what is good
for a man during *his* lifetime, *during*
the few days of his vain life? He will
make do with them like a [a]shadow.
For who can tell a man [b]what will be
after him under the sun?

### *Wisdom and Folly Contrasted*

**7** Better is a [a]good name
than good oil,
And better is the [b]day
of *one's* death than the
day of one's birth.

**2** Better to go to a house
of mourning
Than to go to a house
of feasting
Because [1]that is the [a]end
of all mankind,
And the living [b]puts
*this* in his heart.

**3** [a]Better is vexation
than laughter,
For [b]when a face is sad
a heart may be merry.

**4** The heart of the wise is
in the house of mourning,
While the heart of fools is
in the house of gladness.

**5** Better to [a]listen to the
rebuke of a wise man
Than for one to listen
to the song of fools.

**6** For as the *crackling* sound of
[a]thorn bushes under a pot,
So is the [b]laughter of the fool;
And this too is vanity.

**7** For [a]oppression gives a wise
man over to madness,
And a [b]bribe [1]destroys
the heart.

**8** Better is the [a]end of a matter
than its beginning;

---

**6:2** [a]1Ki 3:13 [b]Ps 17:14; 73:7; Ecc 2:10 [1]Or *futility* **6:3** [a]Is 14:20; Jer 8:2; 22:19 [b]Job 3:16; Ecc 4:3
**6:5** [1]Lit *more rest has this one than that* **6:6** [a]Ecc 2:14 **6:7** [a]Pr 16:26 **6:8** [a]Ecc 2:15 **6:9** [a]Ecc 11:9
[b]Ecc 1:14 **6:10** [a]Ecc 1:9; 3:15 [b]Job 9:32; 40:2; Pr 21:30; Is 45:9 **6:12** [a]Ecc 7:12; 8:13 [b]Ecc 3:22
◆ **7:1** [a]Pr 22:1 [b]Ecc 4:2; 7:8 **7:2** [a]Ecc 2:14, 16; 3:19, 20; 6:6; 9:2, 3 [b]Ps 90:12 [1]Death **7:3** [a]Ecc 2:2
[b]2Co 7:10 **7:5** [a]Ps 141:5; Pr 6:23; 13:18; 15:31, 32; 25:12; Ecc 9:17 **7:6** [a]Ps 58:9; 118:12 [b]Ecc 2:2
**7:7** [a]Ecc 4:1; 5:8 [b]Ex 23:8; Dt 16:19; Pr 17:8, 23 [1]Lit *perishes* **7:8** [a]Ecc 7:1

[b]Better is patience of spirit
than haughtiness of spirit.
9 Do not be [a,1]eager in your
spirit to be vexed,
For vexation rests in the
bosom of fools.
10 Do not say, "Why is it
that the former days were
better than these?"
For it is not from wisdom
that you ask about this.
11 Wisdom along
with an inheritance is good
And an [a]advantage
to those who see the sun.
12 For [a]wisdom is a [b]shadow
*of protection as* money is
a shadow *of protection,*
And the advantage
of knowledge is that
[c]wisdom preserves the
lives of its masters.
13 See the [a]work of God,
For who is [b]able to straighten
what He has bent?
14 [a]In the day *when there is*
good be of good cheer,
But [b]in the day
*when there is* evil see—
God has made the one
as well as the other
So that man will [c]not
find out anything
*that will be* after him.

15 I have seen everything during
my [a]days of vanity; there is [b]a righ-
teous man who perishes in his righ-
teousness, and there is [c]a wicked man
who prolongs *his life* in his evildoing.
16 Do not be excessively [a]righteous,
and do not [b]be overly wise. Why
should you make yourself desolate?
17 Do not be excessively wicked, and
do not be a simpleminded fool. Why
should you [a]die before your time?
18 It is good that you seize one thing
and also not [1]let go of the other; for
the one who [a]fears God comes forth
with [2]both of them.
19 [a]Wisdom strengthens a wise
man more than ten *men with* power
who are in a city. 20 Indeed, [a]there
is not a righteous man on earth who
*continually* does good and who never
sins. 21 Also, do not give your heart to
all words which are spoken, so that
you will not hear your slave [a]cursing
you. 22 For your heart also knows
that you likewise have many times
cursed others.
23 I tested all this with wisdom,
*and* I said, "I will be wise," [a]but it
was far from me. 24 What has been
is far away and [a]exceedingly deep.
[b]Who can find it? 25 I [a]turned my
heart to know, to explore, and to seek
wisdom and an explanation, and to
know the wickedness of foolishness
and the simpleminded folly of mad-
ness. 26 And I found more [a]bitter
than death the woman whose heart
is [b]snares and nets, whose hands are
chains. [c]One who is good before God
will escape from her, but [d]the sinner
will be captured by her.
27 "See, I have found this," says
the Preacher, "*adding* one thing
to another to find an explanation,

---

**7:8** [b]*Pr 14:29; 16:32; Ga 5:22; Eph 4:2* **7:9** [a]Pr 14:17; Jas 1:19 [1]Lit *hasty in your spirit* **7:11** [a]Pr 8:10, 11; *Ecc 2:13* **7:12** [a]Ecc 7:19; 9:18 [b]Ecc 6:12 [c]Pr 3:18; 8:35 **7:13** [a]Ecc 3:11; 8:17 [b]Ecc 1:15 **7:14** [a]Dt 26:11; Ecc 3:22; 9:7; 11:9 [b]Dt 8:5; Job 2:10 [c]Ecc 3:22 **7:15** [a]Ecc 6:12; 9:9 [b]Ecc 8:14 [c]Ecc 8:12, 13 **7:16** [a]Pr 25:16; Php 3:6 [b]Ro 12:3 **7:17** [a]Job 22:16; Ps 55:23; Pr 10:27 **7:18** [a]Ecc 3:14; 5:7; 8:12, 13; 12:13 [1]Lit *rest your hand* [2]Lit *all* **7:19** [a]Ecc 7:12; 9:13-18 **7:20** [a]1Ki 8:46; 2Chr 6:36; Ps 143:2; Pr 20:9; Ro 3:23 **7:21** [a]Pr 30:10 **7:23** [a]Ecc 3:11; 8:17 **7:24** [a]Ro 11:33 [b]Job 11:7; 37:23; Ecc 8:17 **7:25** [a]Ecc 1:15, 17; 10:13 **7:26** [a]Pr 5:4 [b]Pr 7:23 [c]Pr 6:23, 24 [d]Pr 22:14

**28** which my soul still seeks but has
not found. I have found one man out
of a thousand, but I have not found
a [a]woman among all these. **29** See, I
have found only this, that [a]God made
men upright, but they have sought
out many devices."

### *Keep the Command of the King*

**8** Who is like the wise man and
who knows the interpretation of
a matter? A man's wisdom [a]illumines
his face and causes his [b]stern face to
[1]beam.
**2** I *say*, "Keep the [1]command of
the king because of the [a]sworn oath
[2]before God. **3** Do not be in a hurry [a]to
go from his presence. Do not stand in
an evil matter, for he will do whatever
he pleases." **4** Since the word of the
king is powerful, [a]who will say to
him, "What are you doing?"
**5** He who [a]keeps a *royal* command
[b]experiences no evil thing, for a wise
heart knows the *proper* time and
custom. **6** For [a]there is a *proper*
time and custom for every [1]matter,
though a man's trouble is multiplied
upon him. **7** If no one [a]knows what
will happen, who can tell him when
it will happen? **8** [a]There is no man
who has power to restrain the wind
with the wind, and there is none *who
has* power over the day of death; and
there is no discharge in the time of
war, and [b]wickedness will not pro-
vide escape to its masters. **9** All this
I have seen and given my heart to
every work that has been done under
the sun wherein a man has [a]power
over *another* man to his calamity.
**10** So then, I have seen the
wicked buried, those who used to
go in and out from the holy place,
and they are [a]*soon* forgotten in the
city where they did thus. This too
is vanity. **11** Because the [a]sentence
against an evil work is not executed
quickly, therefore [b]the hearts of the
sons of men among them are given
fully to do evil. **12** Although a sinner
does evil a hundred *times* and may
[a]prolong his *life*, still I know that it
will be [b]well for those who fear God,
who fear [1]Him openly. **13** But it will
[a]not be well for the wicked man,
and he will not prolong his days like
a [b]shadow, because he does not fear
[1]God openly.
**14** There is vanity which is done on
the earth, that is, there are [a]righteous
men to whom it [1]happens according
to the works of the wicked. On the
other hand, there are [b]wicked men
to whom it [1]happens according to the
works of the righteous. I say that this
too is vanity. **15** So I laud gladness,
for there is nothing good for [a]a man
under the sun except to eat and to
drink and to [1]be merry, and this will
join with him in his labor *throughout*
the days of his life which God has
given him under the sun.
**16** When I [a]gave my heart to know
wisdom and to see the endeavor
which has been done on the earth
(even though one [b]never sees sleep
with his eyes day or night), **17** and I

---

**7:28** [a]1Ki 11:3 **7:29** [a]Ge 1:27 ◆ **8:1** [a]Ex 34:29, 30 [b]Dt 28:50 [1]Or *change* **8:2** [a]Ex 22:11; 2Sa 21:7; Eze 17:18 [1]Lit *mouth* [2]Lit *of* **8:3** [a]Ecc 10:4 **8:4** [a]Job 9:12; Da 4:35 **8:5** [a]Ecc 12:13 [b]Pr 12:21 **8:6** [a]Ecc 3:1, 17 [1]Lit *delight* **8:7** [a]Ecc 3:22; 6:12; 7:14; 9:12 **8:8** [a]Ps 49:7 [b]Ecc 8:13 **8:9** [a]Ecc 4:1; 5:8; 7:7 **8:10** [a]Ecc 1:11; 2:16; 9:5, 15 **8:11** [a]Ex 34:6; Ps 86:15; Ro 2:4; 2Pe 3:9 [b]Ecc 9:3 **8:12** [a]Ecc 7:15 [b]Dt 4:40; 12:25; Ps 37:11; Pr 1:33; Is 3:10 [1]Lit *before Him* **8:13** [a]Ecc 8:8; Is 3:11 [b]Job 14:2; Ecc 6:12 [1]Lit *before Him* **8:14** [a]Ps 73:14; Ecc 7:15 [b]Job 21:7; Ps 73:3, 12; Jer 12:1; Mal 3:15 [1]Lit *strikes* **8:15** [a]Ecc 2:24; 3:12, 13; 5:18; 9:7 [1]Or *be glad*, cf. 8:15a; 3:12, 22; 5:19; Lk 12:19 **8:16** [a]Ecc 1:13, 14 [b]Ecc 2:23

saw every work of God, *I concluded*
that [a]man cannot find out the work
which has been done under the
sun. Even though man should seek
laboriously, he will not find *it* out;
and [b]though the wise man should
say, "I know," he cannot find *it* out.

### *Mankind Is in the Hand of God*

9 For I have given all this to my
heart and explain [1]it that righ-
teous men, wise men, and their
service are [a]in the hand of God.
[b]Man does not know whether *it will*
*be* [c]love or hatred; anything may be
before him.
2 [a]It is the same for all. There is
[b]one fate for the righteous and for
the wicked; for the good, for the
clean and for the unclean; for the
man who offers a sacrifice and for
the one who does not sacrifice.
As the good man is, so is the sinner;
as the swearer is, so is the one who [1]is
afraid to swear. 3 This is an evil in all
that is done under the sun, that there
is [a]one fate for all. Furthermore, [b]the
hearts of the sons of men are full of
evil, and [c]madness is in their hearts
throughout their lives. Afterwards
they *go* to the dead. 4 For whoever
is joined with all the living, there is
confidence; surely a live dog is bet-
ter than a dead lion. 5 For the living
know they will die; but the dead [a]do
not know anything, nor have they
any longer a reward, for the [b]memory
of them is forgotten. 6 Indeed their
love, their hate, and their zeal have
already perished, and they will never
again have a [a]portion in all that is
done under the sun.
7 Go *then,* [a]eat your bread in
gladness and drink your wine with
a merry heart; for God has already
accepted your works. 8 Let your
[a]clothes be white all the time, and
let not [b]oil be lacking on your head.
9 See life with the woman whom you
love all the days of your [a]vain life,
which He has given to you under the
sun—all the days of your [a]vanity;
for this is your [b]portion in life and in
your labor in which you have labored
under the sun.

### *Whatever Your Hand Finds to Do*

10 Whatever your hand finds to do,
[a]do *it* with *all* your might; for there is
no [b]working or explaining or knowl-
edge or wisdom in [c]Sheol where you
are going.
11 I again saw under the sun that
the [a]race is not to the swift and the
[b]battle is not to the mighty, and nei-
ther is bread to the wise nor [c]riches
to the discerning nor favor to men
who know; for time and [d]misfortune
overtake them all. 12 Moreover,
man does not [a]know his time: like
fish seized in an evil net and [b]birds
seized in a trap, so the sons of men
are [c]ensnared at an evil time when it
[d]suddenly falls on them.
13 Also this I came to see as
wisdom under the sun, and [1]it was
great to me. 14 There [a]was a small
city with few men in it, and a great

***8:17*** *[a]Ecc 3:11 [b]Ps 73:16; Ecc 7:23; Ro 11:33* ◆ **9:1** [a]Dt 33:3; Job 12:10; Ps 119:109 [b]Ecc 10:14 [c]Ecc 9:6 [1]*Lit all this* **9:2** [a]Job 9:22; Ecc 9:11 [b]Ecc 2:14; 3:19; 6:6; 7:2 [1]Lit *fears an oath* **9:3** [a]Ecc 9:2; Jer 17:10 [b]Ecc 8:11 [c]Ecc 1:17 **9:5** [a]Job 14:21 [b]Ps 88:12; Ecc 1:11; 2:16; 8:10; Is 26:14 **9:6** [a]Ecc 2:10; 3:22 **9:7** [a]Ecc 2:24; 8:15 **9:8** [a]Rev 3:4 [b]Ps 23:5 **9:9** [a]Ecc 6:12; 7:15 [b]Ecc 2:10 **9:10** [a]Ecc 11:6; Ro 12:11; Col 3:23 [b]Ecc 9:5 [c]Ge 37:35; Job 21:13; Is 38:10 **9:11** [a]Am 2:14, 15 [b]2Chr 20:15; Ps 76:5; Zec 4:6 [c]Dt 8:17, 18 [d]1Sa 6:9 **9:12** [a]Ecc 8:7 [b]Pr 7:23 [c]Pr 29:6; Is 24:18; Hos 9:8 [d]Lk 21:34, 35 **9:13** [1]Lit *great it was to me* **9:14** [a]2Sa 20:16-22

king came to it, surrounded it, and
built large siegeworks against it.
**15** But there was found in it a [a]poor
wise man, and he provided *a way of*
escape for the city [b]by his wisdom.
Yet [c]no one remembered that poor
man. **16** So I said, "[a]Wisdom is better
than strength." But the wisdom of
the poor man is despised, and his
words are not heard. **17** The [a]words
of the wise heard in restfulness are
*better* than the shouting of a ruler
among fools. **18** [a]Wisdom is better
than weapons of war, but [b]one sinner
destroys much good.

### *The Folly of a Simpleminded Fool*

**10** Dead flies make a [a]perfumer's
oil stink, so a little simpleminded-
ed folly is weightier than wisdom *and*
honor. **2** A wise man's heart *directs*
*him* toward the right, but the foolish
[a]man's heart *directs him* toward the
left. **3** Even when the simpleminded
fool walks along the road, his heart
lacks *wisdom*, and he [a]says to all *that*
he is a simpleminded fool. **4** If the
ruler's [1]temper rises against you, [a]do
not abandon your position, because
[b]calmness causes great offenses to
be abandoned.

**5** There is an evil I have seen under
the sun, like a mistake which goes
forth from the one in power— **6** [a,1]folly
is set in many exalted places while rich
men sit in humble places. **7** I have seen
[a]slaves *riding* [b]on horses and princes
walking like slaves on the land.

**8** [a]He who digs a pit may fall into
it, and a [b]serpent may bite him who
breaks through a wall. **9** He who quar-
ries stones may be hurt by them, and
he who splits logs may be endangered
by them. **10** If the [1]axe is dull and he
does not sharpen *its* edge, then he
must [2]exert more strength. Wisdom
has the advantage of giving success.
**11** If the serpent bites [a,1]before being
charmed, there is no advantage for
the charmer. **12** [a]Words from the
mouth of a wise man are gracious,
but the lips of a [b]fool swallow him up;
**13** the beginning of the words of his
mouth is simpleminded folly, and the
end of *what comes from* his mouth
is evil [a]madness. **14** Yet the [a]simple-
minded fool multiplies words. No
man knows what will happen, and
who can tell him [b]what will come
after him? **15** The labor of [1]a fool *so*
wearies him that he does not *even*
know how to go to a city. **16** Woe to
you, O land, whose [a]king is a young
man and whose princes [1]eat in the
morning. **17** Blessed are you, O land,
whose king is of nobility and whose
princes eat at the appropriate time—
for might and not for [a]drinking.
**18** Through [a]indolence the beams
sag, and through slack hands the
house leaks. **19** *Men* prepare bread
for laughter, and [a]wine makes life
glad, and [b]money [1]is the answer to
everything. **20** Furthermore, [a]in your
bedchamber do not [b]curse a king,
and in your sleeping rooms do not

**9:15** [a]Ecc 4:13 [b]2Sa 20:22 [c]Ecc 2:16; 8:10 **9:16** [a]Pr 21:22; Ecc 7:12, 19 **9:17** [a]Ecc 7:5; 10:12
**9:18** [a]Ecc 9:16 [b]Jos 7:1-26; 2Ki 21:2-17 ◆ **10:1** [a]Ex 30:25 **10:2** [a]Mt 6:33; Col 3:1 **10:3** [a]Pr 13:16; 18:2
**10:4** [a]Ecc 8:3 [b]1Sa 25:24-33; Pr 25:15 [1]Lit *spirit* **10:6** [a]Es 3:1, 5f; Pr 28:12; 29:2 [1]Or *simpleminded folly*, cf. Ecc 1:17; 2:3, 12, 13; 10:1, 13 **10:7** [a]Pr 19:10 [b]Es 6:8-10 **10:8** [a]Ps 7:15; Pr 26:27 [b]Am 5:19
**10:10** [1]Lit *iron* [2]Lit *strengthen* **10:11** [a]Ps 58:4, 5; Jer 8:17 [1]Lit *without enchantment* **10:12** [a]Pr 10:32; 22:11; Lk 4:22 [b]Pr 10:14; 18:7; Ecc 4:5 **10:13** [a]Ecc 7:25 **10:14** [a]Pr 15:2; Ecc 5:3 [b]Ecc 3:22; 6:12; 7:14; 8:7 **10:15** [1]Lit *fools* **10:16** [a]Is 3:4, 12 [1]Or *feast* **10:17** [a]Pr 31:4; Is 5:11 **10:18** [a]Pr 24:30-34
**10:19** [a]Jdg 9:13; Ps 104:15; Ecc 2:3 [b]Ecc 7:12 [1]Lit *answers all* **10:20** [a]2Ki 6:12; Lk 12:3 [b]Ex 22:28; Ac 23:5

curse a rich man, for a bird of the sky will bring the sound and the winged creature will tell the matter.

### *Cast Your Bread on the Waters*

11 [a]Cast your bread on the surface of the waters, for you [a]will find it [1]after many days. **2** [a]Divide your portion to seven, or even to eight, for you do not know what [b]calamity may occur on the earth. **3** If the clouds are full, they empty *the* rain upon the earth; and whether a tree falls toward the south or toward the north, wherever the tree falls, there it [1]lies. **4** He who [1]watches the wind will not sow, and he who looks at the clouds will not reap. **5** Just as you do not [a]know [1]the path of the wind and [b]how bones *are formed* in the womb of the [2]pregnant woman, so you do not [c]know the work of God who works all things.

**6** Sow your seed [a]in the morning and do not put your hands down in the evening, for you do not know whether [1]morning or evening sowing will succeed, or whether both of them alike will be good.

**7** The light is sweet, and *it is* good for the eyes to [a]see the sun. **8** Indeed, if a man should live many years, let him [a]be glad in them all, and let him remember the [b]days of darkness, for they will be many. Everything that is to come *will be* vanity.

**9** Be glad, young man, during your childhood, and let your heart be merry during the days of young manhood. And walk in the ways of your heart and in the [a]sights of your eyes. Yet know that [b]God will bring you to judgment for all these things. **10** So, remove vexation from your heart and put away [a]evil from your flesh because childhood and the prime of life are vanity.

### *Remember Your Creator in Your Youth*

12 [a]Remember also your Creator in the days of your youth, before the [b]evil days happen and the years draw near in which you will say, "I have no delight in them"; **2** before the [a]sun and the light, the moon and the stars are darkened, and clouds return after the rain; **3** in the day that the watchmen of the house tremble, and valiant men [a]bend down, the grinding ones stand idle because they are few, and [b]those who look through [1]windows grow dark; **4** and the doors on the street are shut as the [a]sound of the grinding mill is low, and one will arise at the sound of the bird, and all the [b]daughters of song will [1]sing softly. **5** Furthermore, [1]men are afraid of a high place and of terrors on the road; the almond tree blooms, the grasshopper drags itself along, and the caperberry is ineffective. For man goes to his eternal [a]home, but the [b]mourners go about in the street. **6** *Remember Him* before the silver [1]cord is [2]snapped and the [a]golden bowl is crushed, the pitcher by

---

◆ **11:1** [a]Dt 15:10; Pr 19:17; Mt 10:42; Ga 6:9; Heb 6:10 [1]Lit *in, within* **11:2** [a]Ps 112:9; Mt 5:42; Lk 6:30; 1Ti 6:18, 19 [b]*Ecc 11:8; 12:1* ***11:3*** [1]*Lit is* **11:4** [1]Lit *keeps* **11:5** [a]Jn 3:8 [b]Ps 139:13-16 [c]Ecc 1:13; 3:10, 11; *8:17* [1]*Many mss how the spirit* enters *the bones in the womb* [2]Lit *full* **11:6** [a]Ecc 9:10 [1]Lit *this or that* **11:7** [a]Ecc 6:5; 7:11 **11:8** [a]Ecc 9:7 [b]Ecc 12:1 **11:9** [a]Nu 15:39; Job 31:7; Ecc 2:10 [b]Ecc 3:17; 12:14; Ro 14:10 **11:10** [a]2Co 7:1; 2Ti 2:22 ◆ **12:1** [a]Dt 8:18; Ne 4:14; Ps 63:6; 119:55 [b]Ecc 11:8 **12:2** [a]Is 5:30; 13:10; Eze 32:7, 8; Joel 3:15; Mt 24:29 **12:3** [a]Ps 35:14; 38:6 [b]Ge 27:1; 48:10; 1Sa 3:2 [1]Or *holes* **12:4** [a]Jer 25:10; Rev 18:22 [b]2Sa 19:35 [1]Lit *be brought low* **12:5** [a]Job 17:13; 30:23 [b]Ge 50:10; Jer 9:17 [1]Lit *they* **12:6** [a]Zec 4:2, 3 [1]Or *vanity* [2]As in Gr; Heb *removed*

the spring is broken and the wheel at
the cistern is crushed; **7** then the [a]dust
will return to the earth as it was, and
the [b,1]spirit will return to [c]God who
gave it. **8** "[a]Vanity of vanities," says
the Preacher, "all is vanity!"

### *Fear God and Keep His Commandments*

**9** In addition to being a wise man,
the Preacher also taught the peo-
ple knowledge; and he pondered,
searched out, and [1]arranged [a]many
proverbs. **10** The Preacher sought to
find [a]delightful words and [b]words of
truth written uprightly.

**11** The [a]words of wise men are like
[b]goads, and masters of *these* collec-
tions are like [1]well-driven [c]nails; they
are given by one Shepherd. **12** But in
addition to this, my son, be warned:
the making of [a]many books is end-
less, and much [b]devotion *to books* is
wearying to the flesh.

**13** The end of the matter, all *that*
has been heard: [a]fear God and
[b]keep His commandments, because
this is *the end of the matter for* [c]all
mankind. **14** For [a]God will bring
every work to judgment, everything
which is hidden, whether it is good
or evil.

*The*

# SONG OF SONGS

### *The Shulammite Bride's Desire*

**1** The [1]Song of [a]Songs, which is
Solomon's.

**2** "[1]May he kiss me with the
kisses of his mouth!
For your [a]love is better
than wine.

**3** "Your [a]oils have a pleasing
fragrance,
Your [b]name is *like* [1]purified oil;
Therefore the [c,2]maidens
love you.

**4** "Draw me after you *and*
let us run *together*!
The [a]king has brought me
into his chambers."
"[1]We will rejoice
in you and be glad;
We will [2]extol your [b]love
more than wine.
Rightly do they love you."

**5** "[1]I am black but [a]lovely,
O [b]daughters of Jerusalem,
Like the [c]tents of [d]Kedar,
Like the curtains
of Solomon.

**6** "Do not look at me because
I am [1]swarthy,
For the sun has burned me.
My [a]mother's sons were
angry with me;

**12:7** [a]Ge 3:19; Job 34:15; Ps 104:29; Ecc 3:20 [b]Job 34:14; Ecc 3:21; Lk 23:46; Ac 7:59 [c]Nu 16:22; 27:16; Is 57:16; Zec 12:1 [1]Or *breath* **12:8** [a]Ecc 1:2 **12:9** [a]1Ki 4:32 [1]Lit *set straight* **12:10** [a]Pr 10:32 [b]Pr 22:20, 21 **12:11** [a]Pr 1:6; 22:17; Ecc 7:5; 10:12 [b]Ac 2:37 [c]Ezr 9:8; Is 22:23 [1]Lit *planted* **12:12** [a]1Ki 4:32 [b]Ecc 1:18 **12:13** [a]Ecc 3:14; 5:7; 7:18; 8:12 [b]Dt 4:2; Ecc 8:5 [c]Dt 10:12; Mic 6:8 **12:14** [a]Ecc 3:17; 11:9; Mt 10:26; Ro 2:16; 1Co 4:5 ◆ **1:1** [a]1Ki 4:32 [1]Or *Best of the Songs* **1:2** [a]SS 1:4; 4:10 [1]BRIDE **1:3** [a]SS 4:10; Jn 12:3 [b]Ecc 7:1 [c]Ps 45:14 [1]Lit *oil which is emptied* (from one vessel to another) [2]Or *virgins* **1:4** [a]Ps 45:14, 15 [b]SS 1:4; 4:10 [1]CHORUS [2]Lit *make remembrance of* **1:5** [a]SS 2:14; 4:3; 6:4 [b]SS 2:7; 3:5, 10; 5:8, 16; 8:4 [c]Ps 120:5 [d]Is 60:7 [1]BRIDE **1:6** [a]Ps 69:8 [1]Or *black*

They made me [b]caretaker
of the vineyards,
*But* I have not taken care
of my own vineyard.
7 "Tell me, O you
[a]whom my soul loves,
Where do you [b]shepherd
*your flock*,
Where do you make *it*
[c]lie down at noon?
For why should I be like
one who [1]veils herself
Beside the flocks of your
[d]companions?"

### *Solomon and His Bride Extol Each Other*

8 "[1]If you yourself do not know,
[a]Most beautiful
among women,
Go forth on the trail of the flock
And pasture your young goats
By the dwellings
of the shepherds.

9 "To a [a]mare of mine among
the chariots of Pharaoh
I compare you, O [b]my darling.
10 "Your [a]cheeks are lovely
with ornaments,
Your neck with strings
of [b,1]beads."

11 "[1]We will make for you
ornaments of gold
With beads of silver."

12 "[1]While the king was at his
[2]banqueting table,
My [a,3]perfume gave
forth its fragrance.
13 "My beloved is to me
a pouch of [a]myrrh
Which lies all night
between my breasts.
14 "My beloved is to me a cluster
of [a]henna blossoms
In the vineyards of [b]Engedi."

15 "[a,1]Behold, you are
beautiful, my darling,
Behold, you are beautiful!
Your [b]eyes are *like* doves."

16 "[1]Behold, you are handsome,
[a]my beloved,
Indeed, *so* pleasant!
Indeed, our couch
is luxuriant!
17 "The beams of our
houses are [a]cedars,
Our rafters, [b,1]cypresses.

2 "[1]I am the [a,2]rose of [b]Sharon,
The [c]lily of the valleys."

2 "[1]Like a lily
among the thorns,
So is [a]my darling
among the daughters."

3 "[1]Like an [a,2]apple tree
among the trees of the forest,
So is my beloved
among the sons.
In his shade I had great
desire and sat down,
And his [b]fruit was
sweet to my [3]taste.

---

**1:6** [b]SS 8:11 **1:7** [a]SS 3:1-4 [b]SS 2:16; 6:3 [c]Is 13:20; Jer 33:12 [d]SS 8:13 [1]Some versions *wanders*
**1:8** [a]SS 5:9; 6:1 [1]BRIDEGROOM **1:9** [a]2Chr 1:16, 17 [b]SS 1:15; 2:2, 10, 13 **1:10** [a]SS 5:13 [b]Ge 24:53; Is 61:10 [1]Or *shells* **1:11** [1]CHORUS **1:12** [a]SS 4:14; Mk 14:3; Jn 12:3 [1]BRIDE [2]Or *couch* [3]Lit *nard* **1:13** [a]Ps 45:8; Jn 19:39 **1:14** [a]SS 4:13 [b]1Sa 23:29 **1:15** [a]SS 1:16; 2:10, 13; 4:1, 7; 6:4, 10 [b]SS 4:1; 5:12 [1]BRIDEGROOM
**1:16** [a]SS 2:3, 9, 17; 5:2, 5, 6, 8 [1]BRIDE **1:17** [a]1Ki 6:9, 10; Jer 22:14 [b]2Chr 3:5 [1]Or *junipers* ◆ **2:1** [a]Is 35:1 [b]Is 33:9; 35:2 [c]SS 5:13; 7:2; Hos 14:5 [1]BRIDE [2]Lit *crocus* **2:2** [a]SS 1:9 [1]BRIDEGROOM **2:3** [a]SS 8:5 [b]SS 4:13, 16; 8:11, 12 [1]BRIDE [2]Or *apricot* [3]Lit *palate*

4 “He has [a]brought me to *his*
[1]house of banqueting,
And his [b]banner
over me is love.
5 “Sustain me with [a]raisin cakes,
Refresh me with [b,1]apples,
Because [c]I am lovesick.
6 “Let [a]his left hand be
under my head
And [a]his right hand
[b]embrace me.”

7 “[1]I [a]call you to *solemnly* swear,
O [b]daughters of Jerusalem,
By the [c]gazelles or by the
[d]hinds of the field,
[a]That you do not arouse
or awaken *my* love
Until [2]she pleases.”

### *The Bride Delights in Her Beloved*

8 “[1]The voice of my beloved!
Behold, he is coming,
Leaping [a]on the mountains,
Jumping on the hills!
9 “My beloved is like a [a]gazelle
or a [b]young [1]stag.
Behold, he is standing
behind our wall;
He gazes
through the windows;
He is peering
[c]through the lattice.

10 “My beloved answered
and said to me,
‘[a]Arise, my darling, my
beautiful one,
And come along.
11 ‘For behold, the winter
is past,
The rain is over; it is gone.
12 ‘The flowers have
appeared in the land;
The time for [1]pruning
has arrived;
And the voice of the
[a]turtledove has been
heard in our land.
13 ‘The [a]fig tree has
ripened its figs,
And the [b]vines
in blossom have given
forth *their* fragrance.
Arise, my darling, my
beautiful one,
And come along!’”

14 “[1]O [a]my dove, [b]in the
clefts of the [2]rock,
In the secret place
of the steep [3]pathway,
Let me see your appearance,
[c]Let me hear your voice;
For your voice is sweet,
And your appearance
is [d]lovely.”

15 “[a,1]Seize the foxes for us,
The [2]little foxes that are
wreaking destruction
on the vineyards,
While our [b]vineyards
are in blossom.”

16 “[a,1]My beloved is mine,
and I am his,
He who [b]shepherds *his*
*flock* among the lilies.

**2:4** [a]SS 1:4 [b]Ps 20:5 [1]Lit *house of wine* **2:5** [a]2Sa 6:19; 1Chr 16:3; Hos 3:1 [b]SS 7:8 [c]SS 5:8 [1]Or *apricots* **2:6** [a]SS 8:3 [b]Pr 4:8 **2:7** [a]SS 3:5; 5:8, 9; 8:4 [b]SS 1:5 [c]Pr 6:5; SS 2:9, 17; 3:5; 8:14 [d]Ge 49:21; Ps 18:33; Hab 3:19 [1]BRIDEGROOM [2]Or *it* **2:8** [a]SS 2:17; Is 52:7 [1]BRIDE **2:9** [a]Pr 6:5; SS 2:17; 3:5; 8:14 [b]SS 2:17; 8:14 [c]Jdg 5:28 [1]Lit *of the stags* **2:10** [a]SS 2:13 **2:12** [a]Ge 15:9; Ps 74:19; Jer 8:7 [1]Or *singing* **2:13** [a]Mt 24:32 [b]SS 7:12 **2:14** [a]SS 5:2; 6:9 [b]Jer 48:28 [c]SS 8:13 [d]SS 1:5 [1]BRIDEGROOM [2]Or *crag* [3]Or *cliff* **2:15** [a]Eze 13:4; Lk 13:32 [b]SS 2:13 [1]CHORUS [2]Or *young* **2:16** [a]SS 6:3; 7:10 [b]SS 4:5; 6:2, 3 [1]BRIDE

17 "[a]Until the day breathes
and the shadows flee,
Turn, my beloved, and
be like a [b]gazelle
Or a young stag [c]on the
mountains of [1]Bether."

### *The Bride's Troubled Dream*

3 "[1]On my bed night
after night I sought him
[a]Whom my soul loves;
I [b]sought him but did
not find him.
2 '[1]I must arise now and
[2]go about the city;
In the [a]streets and
in the squares
[3]I must seek him
whom my soul loves.'
I sought him but did
not find him.
3 "[a]The watchmen who go
about the city found me,
*And I said,* 'Have you seen
him whom my soul loves?'
4 "[a]Scarcely had I
passed them by
When I found him
whom my soul loves;
I [b]seized him and would
not let him go
Until I had [c]brought him
to my mother's house,
And into the chamber
of her who conceived me."

5 "[1]I [a]call you to *solemnly*
swear, O daughters
of Jerusalem,
By the [b]gazelles or by the
*hinds of the field,*
That you do not arouse
or awaken *my* love
Until [2]she pleases."

### *Solomon Arrives on His Wedding Day*

6 "[a,1]Who is this coming up
from the wilderness
Like [b]columns of smoke,
As rising incense of [c]myrrh
and [d]frankincense,
With all scented powders
of the merchant?
7 "Behold, it is the *traveling*
couch of Solomon;
Sixty mighty men around it,
Of the mighty men of Israel.
8 "All of them are those who
seize the sword,
[a]Learned in war;
Each man has his
[b]sword at his side,
*Guarding* against the
[c,1]dreadful things
of the night.
9 "King Solomon has made
for himself a sedan chair
From the timber of Lebanon.
10 "He made its posts of silver,
Its [1]back of gold
*And* its seat of purple fabric,
*With* its interior
inlaid with love
By the [a]daughters
of Jerusalem.
11 "Go forth and see,
O [a]daughters of Zion,
King Solomon
with the [1]crown
With which his mother
has crowned him
On the [b]day of his wedding,

---

**2:17** [a]SS 4:6 [b]SS 2:9 [c]SS 2:8 [1]Or *ravines, a kind of spice* ◆ **3:1** [a]SS 1:7 [b]SS 5:6 [1]BRIDE **3:2** [a]Jer 5:1 [1]Or *Let me arise* [2]Or *Let me go about* [3]Or *Let me seek* **3:3** [a]SS 5:7; Is 21:6-8, 11, 12 **3:4** [a]Pr 8:17 [b]Pr 4:13; Ro 8:35, 39 [c]SS 8:2 **3:5** [a]SS 2:7; 5:8; 8:4 [b]SS 2:7 [1]BRIDEGROOM [2]Or *it* **3:6** [a]SS 8:5 [b]Ex 13:21; Joel 2:30 [c]SS 1:13; 4:6, 14; Mt 2:11 [d]Ex 30:34; Rev 18:13 [1]CHORUS **3:8** [a]Jer 50:9 [b]Ps 45:3 [c]Ps 91:5 [1]Lit *dreadful thing* **3:10** [a]SS 1:5 [1]Or *support* **3:11** [a]Is 3:16, 17; 4:4 [b]Is 62:5 [1]Or *wreath*

And on the day of his
gladness of heart."

### *Solomon Praises the Beauty of His Bride*

4 "[1]Behold, you are beautiful,
[a]my darling,
Behold, you are beautiful!
Your [b]eyes are *like* doves
[c]behind your veil;
Your [d]hair is like a flock
of goats
That have leapt down
from Mount [e]Gilead.
2 "Your [a]teeth are like a flock
of *newly* shorn ewes
Which have come up
from *their* washing,
All of which bear twins,
And not one among them
has [1]lost her young.
3 "Your lips are
like a [a]scarlet thread,
And your [b]mouth is lovely.
Your [c]temples are like
a slice of a pomegranate
Behind your veil.
4 "Your [a]neck is like the
tower of David,
Built [1]with rows of stones
On which are [b]hung one
thousand shields,
All the small [c]shields
of the mighty men.
5 "Your [a]two breasts are
like two fawns,
Twins of a gazelle
Which [b,1]feed among the lilies.
6 "[a]Until the day breathes
And the shadows flee,
I will go my way to the
mountain of [b]myrrh
And to the hill
of [b]frankincense.
7 "[a]You are altogether
beautiful, my darling,
And there is no
blemish in you.
8 "*Come* with me
from [a]Lebanon, *my* [b]bride,
May you come with me
from Lebanon.
[1]Journey down
from the top of [c]Amana,
From the top of [d]Senir
and Hermon,
From the dens of lions,
From the mountains
of leopards.
9 "You have made my heart beat
faster, [a]my sister, *my* bride;
You have made my heart
beat faster with a single
*glance* of your eyes,
With a single strand
of your [b]necklace.
10 "[a]How beautiful is your love,
my sister, *my* bride!
How much [b]better is
your love than wine,
And the [c]fragrance of your oils
Than all *kinds* of [1]spices!
11 "Your lips, *my* bride, [a]drip
[b]honey from the comb;
Honey and milk are
under your tongue,
And the fragrance of your
garments is like the
[c]fragrance of Lebanon.

---

◆ **4:1** [a]SS 1:15 [b]SS 1:15; 5:12 [c]SS 6:7 [d]SS 6:5 [e]Mic 7:14 [1]BRIDEGROOM **4:2** [a]SS 6:6 [1]Or *miscarried* **4:3** [a]Jos 2:18 [b]SS 5:16 [c]SS 6:7 **4:4** [a]SS 7:4 [b]Eze 27:10, 11 [c]2Sa 1:21 [1]Or *for an arsenal* **4:5** [a]SS 7:3 [b]SS 2:16; 6:2, 3 [1]Lit *shepherd*, cf. SS 1:7, 8; 2:16; 6:2 **4:6** [a]SS 2:17 [b]SS 4:14 **4:7** [a]SS 1:15; Eph 5:27 **4:8** [a]1Ki 4:33; Ps 72:16 [b]SS 5:1; Is 62:5 [c]2Ki 5:12 [d]Dt 3:9; 1Chr 5:23; Eze 27:5 [1]Or *Look* **4:9** [a]SS 4:10, 12; 5:1, 2 [b]Ge 41:42; Pr 1:9; Eze 16:11; Da 5:7 **4:10** [a]SS 7:6 [b]SS 1:2, 4 [c]SS 1:3 [1]Or *balsam odors* **4:11** [a]Pr 5:3 [b]Ps 19:10; Pr 24:13 [c]Ge 27:27; Hos 14:6

12 "A garden locked is my
sister, *my* bride,
A [1]rock garden locked,
a [a]spring [b]sealed up.
13 "Your shoots are [1]an [a]orchard
of [b]pomegranates
With [c]choice fruits, [d]henna
with nard plants,
14 [a]Nard and saffron, calamus
and [b]cinnamon,
With all the trees
of [c]frankincense,
[d]Myrrh and aloes, along
with all the finest [1]spices.
15 "*You are* a garden spring,
A well of [a,1]fresh water,
And streams *flowing*
from Lebanon."

16 "[1]Awake, O north *wind*,
And come, *wind of* the south;
Make my [a]garden breathe
out *fragrance*,
Let its [2]spices flow forth.
May [b]my beloved come
into his garden
And eat its [c]choice fruits!"

### *The Bride Searches for Her Beloved*

5 "[1]I have [a]come into my garden,
[b]my sister, *my* bride;
I have picked my [c]myrrh
along with my balsam.
I have eaten my honeycomb
with my [d]honey;
I have [e]drunk my wine
with my milk.
Eat, [f]friends;
Drink and [2]imbibe
deeply, O lovers."

2 "[1]I was asleep, but my
heart was awake.
A voice! My beloved
was knocking:
'Open to me, [a]my sister,
my darling,
[b]My dove, my perfect one!
For my head is full of dew,
My [c]locks with the
[2]damp of the night.'
3 "I have [a]taken off my
long-sleeved garment,
How can I put it on *again*?
I have [b]washed my feet,
How can I dirty them *again*?
4 "My beloved sent forth his
hand through the opening,
And my [a,1]feelings
moaned for him.
5 "I arose to open to my beloved;
And my hands [a]dripped
with myrrh,
And my fingers
with [1]liquid myrrh,
On the handles of the lock.
6 "I opened to my beloved,
But my beloved had [a]turned
away *and* passed by!
My soul went out
*to him* as he [b]spoke.
I [c]searched for him,
but I did not find him;
I [d]called him, but he did
not answer me.
7 "The [a]watchmen who go
about in the city found me,

***4:12*** [a]*Pr 5:15-18* [b]*Ge 29:3* [1]*Lit stone heap* **4:13** [a]Ecc 2:5 [b]SS 6:11; 7:12 [c]SS 2:3; 4:16; 7:13 [d]SS 1:14 [1]Or *a park, a paradise* **4:14** [a]SS 1:12 [b]Ex 30:23 [c]SS 4:6 [d]Ps 45:8; SS 3:6; Jn 19:39 [1]Or *balsam odors* **4:15** [a]Zec 14:8; Jn 4:10 [1]Lit *living* **4:16** [a]SS 5:1; 6:2 [b]SS 1:13; 2:3, 8; 6:2 [c]SS 4:13 [1]BRIDE [2]Or *balsam odors* ◆ **5:1** [a]SS 6:2 [b]SS 4:9 [c]SS 1:13; 4:14 [d]SS 4:11 [e]Pr 9:5; Is 55:1 [f]Jdg 14:11, 20; Jn 3:29 [1]BRIDEGROOM [2]Or *become drunk* **5:2** [a]SS 4:9 [b]SS 2:14; 6:9 [c]SS 5:11 [1]BRIDE [2]Lit *drops* **5:3** [a]Lk 11:7 [b]Ge 19:2 **5:4** [a]Jer 31:20 [1]Lit *bowels* **5:5** [a]SS 5:13 [1]Lit *passing* **5:6** [a]SS 6:1 [b]SS 5:2 [c]SS 3:1 [d]Pr 1:28 **5:7** [a]SS 3:3

They struck me *and*
wounded me;
The guardsmen of the
walls took away my
shawl from me.
8 "I [a]call you to *solemnly*
swear, O daughters
of Jerusalem,
If you find my beloved,
What will you tell him?
*Tell him* that [b]I am
sick with love."

9 "[1]What is your beloved
*that he is* more than
*any other* beloved,
O [a]most beautiful
among women?
What is your beloved
*that he is* more
than *any other* beloved,
That thus you call us
to *solemnly* swear?"

### *The Bride Extols Her Beloved*

10 "[1]My beloved is dazzling
and [a]ruddy,
[b]Lifted up as a banner
among ten thousand.
11 "His head is *like* gold,
fine gold;
His [a]locks are
*like* clusters of dates
*And* black as a raven.
12 "His [a]eyes are like doves
Beside streams of water,
Washed in milk,
*And* sitting in *their* [b]setting.
13 "His cheeks are
like a [a]bed of spices,
Towers of sweet-scented herbs;
His lips are [b]lilies
[c]Dripping with liquid myrrh.
14 "His hands are rods of gold
Set with [a]beryl;
His abdomen is a plate
of ivory
Inlaid with [b,1]sapphires.
15 "His legs are pillars of marble
Set on bases of fine gold;
His appearance is
like [a]Lebanon
Choice as the [b]cedars.
16 "His [a,1]mouth is *full
of* sweetness.
And he is wholly [b]desirable.
This is my beloved and
this is my friend,
O daughters of Jerusalem."

### *Solomon and His Bride Extol Each Other*

6 "[a,1]Where has your
beloved gone,
O [b]most beautiful
among women?
Where has your
beloved turned,
That we may seek
him with you?"

2 "[1]My beloved has gone
down to his [a]garden,
To the [b]beds of spices,
To [c]shepherd *his flock*
in the gardens
And gather [d]lilies.
3 "[a]I am my beloved's and
my beloved is mine,
He who [b]shepherds *his
flock* among the lilies."

**5:8** [a]SS 2:7; 3:5 [b]SS 2:5 **5:9** [a]SS 1:8; 6:1 [1]CHORUS **5:10** [a]1Sa 16:12 [b]Ps 45:2 [1]BRIDE **5:11** [a]SS 5:2 **5:12** [a]SS 1:15; 4:1 [b]Ex 25:7 **5:13** [a]SS 6:2 [b]SS 2:1 [c]SS 5:5 **5:14** [a]Ex 28:20; 39:13; Eze 1:16; Da 10:6 [b]Ex 24:10; 28:18; Job 28:16; Is 54:11 [1]Lit *lapis lazuli* **5:15** [a]SS 7:4 [b]1Ki 4:33; Ps 80:10; Eze 17:23; 31:8 **5:16** [a]SS 7:9 [b]2Sa 1:23 [1]Lit *palate* ◆ **6:1** [a]SS 5:6 [b]SS 1:8 [1]CHORUS **6:2** [a]SS 4:16; 5:1 [b]SS 5:13 [c]SS 1:7 [d]SS 2:1; 5:13 [1]BRIDE **6:3** [a]SS 2:16; 7:10 [b]SS 2:16; 4:5

4 “[a,1]You are as beautiful
as [b]Tirzah, my darling,
As [c]lovely as [d]Jerusalem,
As [e]majestic as [2]an army
with banners.
5 “Turn your eyes away from me,
For they have
overwhelmed me;
[a]Your hair is
like a flock of goats
That have leapt down
from Gilead.
6 “[a]Your teeth are
like a flock of ewes
Which have come up
from *their* washing,
All of which bear twins,
And not one among them
has [1]lost her young.
7 “[a]Your temples are like
a slice of a pomegranate
Behind your veil.
8 “There are sixty [a]queens
and eighty concubines,
And [b,1]maidens
without number;
9 She is the only one—[a]my
dove, my perfect one;
She is the only one
of her mother;
She is the pure one
of her who bore her.
The [b]daughters saw her
and called her blessed,
The [c]queens and the
concubines *also*, and they
praised her, *saying*,
10 ‘Who is this that looks
down like the dawn,
As beautiful as the full [a]moon,
As pure [b]as the sun,
As [c]majestic as [1]an army
with banners?’

11 “[1]I went down to the
garden of nut trees
To see the blossoms
of the valley,
To see whether [a]the
vine had flourished
*Or* the [b]pomegranates
had bloomed.
12 “I did not know *it*,
*but* my soul set me
*Among* the chariots
of [1]my noble people.”

13 “[1,2]Come back, come back,
O Shulammite;
Come back, come back,
that we may behold you!”

“[3]Why should you behold
the Shulammite,
As at the [a]dance
of [b,4]the two companies?

7 “[1]How beautiful are your
[2]feet in sandals,
O [a]noble’s daughter!
The curves of your thighs
are like ornaments,
The work of the hands
of an artist.
2 “Your navel is
*like* a round basin
Which never lacks
mixed wine;
Your belly is
like a heap of wheat
Encircled with lilies.

**6:4** [a]SS 1:15 [b]1Ki 14:17 [c]SS 1:5 [d]Ps 48:2; 50:2 [e]SS 6:10 [1]BRIDEGROOM [2]Lit *bannered ones* **6:5** [a]SS 4:1 **6:6** [a]SS 4:2 [1]Or *miscarried* **6:7** [a]SS 4:3 **6:8** [a]1Ki 11:3 [b]SS 1:3 [1]Or *virgins* **6:9** [a]SS 2:14; 5:2 [b]Ge 30:13 [c]1Ki 11:3 **6:10** [a]Job 31:26 [b]Mt 17:2; Rev 1:16 [c]SS 6:4 [1]Lit *bannered ones* **6:11** [a]SS 7:12 [b]SS 4:13 [1]Possibly BRIDE, cf. 6:2; 7:13 **6:12** [1]Or *Ammi-nadib* **6:13** [a]Jdg 21:21 [b]Ge 32:2; 2Sa 17:24 [1]CHORUS [2]Ch 7:1 in Heb [3]BRIDEGROOM [4]Heb *Mahanaim* ◆ **7:1** [a]Ps 45:13 [1]Ch 7:2 in Heb [2]Lit *footsteps*

3 "Your [a]two breasts are
like two fawns,
Twins of a gazelle.
4 "Your [a]neck is
like a tower of ivory,
Your eyes *like* the pools
in [b]Heshbon
By the gate of Bath-rabbim;
Your nose is like the tower
of Lebanon,
Which faces
toward Damascus.
5 "Your head [1]crowns you
like [a]Carmel,
And the flowing locks
of your head are
like purple threads;
*The* king is captivated
by *your* tresses.
6 "How [a]beautiful and how
pleasant you are,
[1]*My* love, with *all*
your pleasures!
7 "[1]Your stature is
like a palm tree,
And your breasts are
*like its* clusters.
8 "I said, 'I will climb
the palm tree;
I will seize its fruit stalks.'
Oh, may your breasts be
like clusters of the vine,
And the fragrance of your
[1]breath like [a,2]apples,
9 And your [a,1]mouth
like the best wine!"

"[2]It [b]goes *down* smoothly
for my beloved,
Flowing gently *through* the
lips of those who fall asleep.

### *The Union of Love*

10 "[a]I am my beloved's,
And his [b]desire is for me.
11 "Come, my beloved, let us
go out into the [1]fields,
Let us spend the night
in the villages.
12 "Let us rise early *and go*
to the vineyards;
Let us [a]see whether
the vine has flourished
*And its* blossoms
have opened,
*And whether*
the pomegranates
have bloomed.
There I will give you my love.
13 "The [a]mandrakes have
given forth fragrance;
And over our doors are
all [b]choice *fruits*,
Both new and old,
Which I have treasured up
for you, my beloved.

### *The Power and Preciousness of Love*

8 "Oh that you were like
a brother to me
Who nursed at my
mother's breasts.
*If* I found you outside,
I would kiss you;
No one would despise
me, either.
2 "I would lead you *and*
[a]bring you
Into the house of my mother,
who used to teach me;
I would give you spiced wine
to drink from the sweet
wine of my pomegranates.

---

**7:3** [a]SS 4:5 **7:4** [a]SS 4:4 [b]Nu 21:26 **7:5** [a]Is 35:2 [1]Lit *is upon* **7:6** [a]SS 1:15, 16; 4:10 [1]Or With *love among your delights* **7:7** [1]Lit *This stature of yours* **7:8** [a]SS 2:5 [1]Lit *nose* [2]Or *apricots* **7:9** [a]SS 5:16 [b]Pr 23:31 [1]Lit *palate* [2]BRIDE **7:10** [a]SS 2:16; 6:3 [b]Ps 45:11; Ga 2:20 **7:11** [1]Lit *field* **7:12** [a]SS 6:11 **7:13** [a]Ge 30:14 [b]SS 2:3; 4:13, 16; Mt 13:52 ◆ **8:2** [a]SS 3:4

3 “Let [a]his left hand be
under my head
And his right hand
embrace me.”

4 “[a,1]I call you to *solemnly* swear,
O daughters of Jerusalem,
[2]Why should you arouse
or awaken *my* love
Until [3]she pleases?”

5 “[a,1]Who is this coming up
from the wilderness
Leaning on her beloved?”

“[2]Beneath the [b,3]apple
tree I awakened you;
There your mother was
in labor with you;
There she was in labor
*and* gave you birth.
6 “Put me like a [1]seal
over your heart,
Like a [a]seal on your arm.
For love is as strong as death,
[b,2]Jealousy is as severe
as Sheol;
Its flashes are flashes of fire,
[3]The *very* flame of [4]Yah.
7 “Many waters cannot
quench love,
Nor will rivers overflow it;
[a]If a man were to give all the
riches of his house for love,
It would be utterly despised.”

8 “[1]We have a little sister,
And she [a]has no breasts;
What shall we do for our sister
On the day when she
is spoken for?
9 “If she is a wall,
We will build on her
a battlement of silver;
But if she is a door,
We will barricade her
with [a]planks of cedar.”

10 “[1]I was a wall, and [a]my
breasts were like towers;
Then I became in his eyes
as one who finds peace.
11 “Solomon had a [a]vineyard
at Baal-hamon;
He [b]gave the vineyard
to [c]caretakers.
Each one was to bring
[1]one [d]thousand *shekels*
of silver for its [e]fruit.
12 “My very own vineyard
is before me;
The thousand *shekels* are
for you, Solomon,
And two hundred are for those
who take care of its fruit.”

13 “[1]O you who sit
in the gardens,
*My* [a]companions are giving
heed to your voice—
[b]Let me hear it!”

14 “[1,2]Hurry, my beloved,
And be [a]like a gazelle
or a young [3]stag
On the [b]mountains of spices.”

**8:3** [a]SS 2:6 **8:4** [a]SS 2:7; 3:5 [1]BRIDEGROOM [2]Or *Do not arouse* [3]Or *it* **8:5** [a]SS 3:6 [b]SS 2:3 [1]CHORUS [2]BRIDE [3]*Or apricot* **8:6** [a]*Is 49:16; Jer 22:24;* Hag 2:23 [b]Pr 6:34 [1]Or signet [2]Or *Its ardor is as inflexible* [3]Or *A vehement flame* [4]The shortened form of Yahweh, found in poetry and praise (e.g. Hallelu*jah*), and in names (e.g. Zechar*iah*) **8:7** [a]Pr 6:35 **8:8** [a]Eze 16:7 [1]CHORUS **8:9** [a]1Ki 6:15 **8:10** [a]Eze 16:7 [1]BRIDE **8:11** [a]Ecc 2:4 [b]Mt 21:33 [c]SS 1:6 [d]Is 7:23 [e]SS 2:3; 8:12 [1]Approx. 25 lb. or 11.3 kg, a shekel was approx. 0.4 oz. or 11 gm **8:13** [a]SS 1:7 [b]SS 2:14 [1]BRIDEGROOM **8:14** [a]SS 2:7, 9, 17 [b]SS 4:6 [1]BRIDE [2]Lit *Flee* [3]Lit *of the stags*

*The Book of*

# ISAIAH

### *Judah, a Sinful Nation*

1 The vision of Isaiah the son of Amoz
concerning [a]Judah and Jerusalem,
which he beheld in the days of [b]Uzzi-
ah, [c]Jotham, [d]Ahaz, *and* [e]Hezekiah,
kings of Judah.

2 [a]Hear, O heavens, and
give ear, O [b]earth;
For [1]Yahweh speaks,
"[c]Sons I have reared
and raised up,
But they have [d]transgressed
against Me.

3 "An ox knows its owner,
And a donkey its
master's manger,
*But* Israel [a]does not know;
My people [b]do not perceive."

4 Alas, sinful nation,
People heavy with iniquity,
[a]Seed of evildoers,
Sons who [b]act corruptly!
They have [c]forsaken Yahweh;
They have [d]spurned the
Holy One of Israel;
They have [1]become
estranged [2]from Him.

5 Where will you be
stricken again,
*As* you [a]continue
in *your* rebellion?
The whole head is [b]sick,
And the whole heart is faint.

6 [a]From the sole of the foot
even to the head
There is [b]nothing sound in it,
*Only* bruises, wounds,
and raw wounds,
[c]Not pressed out,
not bandaged,
Not softened with oil.

7 Your [a]land is desolate;
Your cities are burned
with fire;
Your fields—strangers
are devouring them
in your presence;
It is desolate, as overthrown
by strangers.

8 The daughter of Zion is left
like a shelter in a vineyard,
Like a watchman's hut
in a cucumber field,
like a besieged city.

9 [a]Unless Yahweh of hosts
Had left us a few [b]survivors,
We would be like [c]Sodom,
We would be like Gomorrah.

10 Hear [a]the word of Yahweh,
You rulers of [b]Sodom;
Give ear to the law
of our God,
You people of Gomorrah.

11 "[a]What are your multiplied
sacrifices to Me?"
Says Yahweh.

---

◆ **1:1** [a]Is 2:1; 40:9 [b]2Ki 15:1-7, 13; 2Chr 26:1-23 [c]2Ki 15:32-38; 2Chr 27:1-9 [d]2Ki 16:1-20; 2Chr 28:1-27; Is 7:1 [e]2Ki 18:1-20:21; 2Chr 29:1-32:33 **1:2** [a]Dt 32:1 [b]Mic 1:2 [c]Jer 3:22 [d]Is 30:1, 9; 65:2 [1]The personal covenant name of God, a form of I AM WHO I AM, cf. Ex 3:14-15 **1:3** [a]Jer 9:3, 6 [b]Is 44:18 **1:4** [a]Is 14:20 [b]Ne 1:7 [c]Is 1:28 [d]Is 5:24 [1]Or *turned away* [2]Lit *backward* **1:5** [a]Is 31:6 [b]Is 33:24; Eze 34:4, 16 **1:6** [a]Job 2:7 [b]Ps 38:3 [c]Jer 8:22 **1:7** [a]Lv 26:33; Jer 44:6 **1:9** [a]Ro 9:29 [b]Is 10:20-22; 11:11, 16; 37:4, 31, 32; 46:3 [c]Ge 19:24 **1:10** [a]Is 8:20; 28:14 [b]Is 3:9; Eze 16:49; Ro 9:29; Rev 11:8 **1:11** [a]Ps 50:8; Jer 6:20; Am 5:21, 22; Mal 1:10

"I [1]have had enough
of burnt offerings of rams
And the fat of fed cattle;
And in the blood
of bulls, lambs, or goats
[2]I take no pleasure.
12 "When you come
[a]to appear before Me,
Who requires [1]of you this
trampling of My courts?
13 "Bring your worthless
offerings no longer,
[a]Incense is an
abomination to Me.
[b]New moon and sabbath,
the [c]calling
of convocation—
I cannot [d]endure wickedness
and the solemn assembly.
14 "My soul hates your new
moon *festivals* and your
[a]appointed times,
They have become a
burden to Me;
I am [b]weary of bearing *them*.
15 "So when you [a]spread out
your hands *in prayer*,
[b]I will hide My eyes from you;
Indeed, even though you
[c]multiply prayers,
I will not listen.
[d]Your hands are full of blood.

16 "[a]Wash yourselves,
[b]purify yourselves;
[c]Remove the evil of your
deeds from before My eyes.
[d]Cease to do evil,
17 Learn to do good;
[a]Seek justice,
Reprove the ruthless,
[b]Execute justice
for the [1]orphan,
Plead for the widow.

18 "Come now, and [a]let us
reason together,"
Says Yahweh,
"[b]Though your sins
are as scarlet,
They will be as white as snow;
Though they are red
like crimson,
They will be like wool.
19 "[a]If you are willing and obey,
You will [b]eat the best
of the land;
20 But if you refuse and rebel,
You will be [a]eaten
by the sword."
For [b]the mouth
of Yahweh has spoken.

### *Zion Will Be Redeemed with Justice*

21 How the faithful city has
become a [a]harlot,
She *who* was full of justice!
Righteousness once
lodged in her,
But now murderers.
22 Your silver has become dross,
Your drink diluted with water.
23 Your [a]rulers are rebels
And companions of thieves;
Everyone [b]loves a bribe
And pursues rewards.
They [c]do not execute
justice for the [1]orphan,
Nor does the widow's plea
come before them.

---

**1:11** [1]Or *am sated with* [2]Or *I do not desire,* cf. Ps 40:6 **1:12** [a]Ex 23:17 [1]Lit *of your hand* **1:13** [a]Is 66:3 [b]1Chr 23:31 [c]Ex 12:16 [d]Jer 7:9, 10 **1:14** [a]Is 29:1, 2 [b]Is 7:13; 43:24 **1:15** [a]1Ki 8:22; Lam 1:17 [b]Is 8:17; 59:2 [c]Mic 3:4 [d]Is 59:3 **1:16** [a]Ps 26:6 [b]Is 52:11 [c]Is 55:7 [d]Jer 25:5 **1:17** [a]Jer 22:3; Zep 2:3 [b]Ps 82:3 [1]Or *fatherless* **1:18** [a]Is 41:1, 21; 43:26; Mic 6:2 [b]Ps 51:7; Is 43:25; 44:22; Rev 7:14 **1:19** [a]Dt 28:1; 30:15, 16 [b]Is 55:2 **1:20** [a]Is 3:25; 65:12 [b]Is 40:5; 58:14; Mic 4:4; Tit 1:2 **1:21** [a]Is 57:3-9; Jer 2:20 **1:23** [a]Hos 5:10; Mic 7:3 [b]Ex 23:8; Mic 7:3 [c]Is 10:2; Jer 5:28; Eze 22:7; Zec 7:10 [1]Or *fatherless*

24 Therefore the Lord,
Yahweh of hosts,
The [a]Mighty One
of Israel, declares,
“Ah, I will be comforted
concerning My adversaries,
And I will [b]avenge Myself
on My enemies.
25 “I will also turn My
hand against you,
And will [a]smelt away your
dross as with lye
And will remove all
your alloy.
26 “Then I will have your [a]judges
return as at the first,
And your counselors
as at the beginning;
Afterwards you will be called
the [b]city of righteousness,
A faithful town.”

27 Zion will be [a]redeemed
with justice
And her [1]repentant ones
with righteousness.
28 But [1]transgressors and sinners
will be [a]broken together,
And those who forsake
Yahweh will come to an end.
29 For [1]you will be ashamed
of the [a,2]oaks
which you have desired,
And you will be humiliated
*because* of the [b]gardens
which you have chosen.
30 For you will be like [1]an oak
whose [a]leaf withers away
Or as a garden that
has no water.
31 And the strong man will
become tinder,
His work also a spark.
Thus they shall both
[a]burn together,
And there will be [b]none
to quench *them*.

### *Yahweh Will Judge the Nations*

2 The word which [a]Isaiah the
son of Amoz beheld concerning
Judah and Jerusalem.
2 Now it will be that
[a]In the last days
The [b]mountain of the
house of Yahweh
Will be established [1]as the
head of the mountains,
And will be lifted up
above the hills;
And [c]all the nations
will stream to it.
3 And many peoples will
come and say,
“Come, let us go up
to the mountain of Yahweh,
To the house of the
God of Jacob,
That He may instruct
us [1]from His ways
And that we may walk
in His paths.”
For [a]from Zion the
[2]law will go forth
And the word of Yahweh
from Jerusalem.
4 And He will judge
between the nations,
And will [1]render decisions
for many peoples;

**1:24** [a]Ps 132:2; Is 49:26; 60:16 [b]Dt 28:63; Is 35:4; 59:18; 61:2; 63:4 **1:25** [a]Eze 22:19-22; Mal 3:3 **1:26** [a]Is 60:17 [b]Is 33:5; 60:14; 62:1, 2; Zec 8:3 **1:27** [a]Is 35:9f; 62:12; 63:4 [1]Or *returnees* **1:28** [a]Ps 9:5; Is 66:24; 2Th 1:8, 9 [1]Lit *breaking of transgressors and sinners shall be together* **1:29** [a]Is 57:5 [b]Is 65:3; 66:17 [1]As in some mss; M.T. *they* [2]Or *terebinths* **1:30** [a]Is 64:6 [1]Or *a terebinth* **1:31** [a]Is 5:24; 9:19; 26:11; 33:11-14 [b]Is 66:24; Mt 3:12; Mk 9:43 ◆ **2:1** [a]Is 1:1 **2:2** [a]Mic 4:1-3 [b]Is 27:13; 66:20 [c]Is 56:7 [1]Lit *on* **2:3** [a]Is 51:4, 5; Lk 24:47 [1]Or *some of* [2]Or *instruction* **2:4** [1]Or *reprove many*

And [a]they will hammer their
swords into plowshares
and their spears
into pruning hooks.
[b]Nation will not lift up
sword against nation,
And never again will
they learn war.

### *Yahweh Will Have a Day of Reckoning*

5 Come, [a]house of Jacob,
and let us walk in the
[b]light of Yahweh.
6 For You have [a]abandoned Your
people, the house of Jacob,
Because they are filled *with*
*influences* from the east,
And *they are* soothsayers
[b]like the Philistines,
And they [c]strike *bargains* with
the children of foreigners.
7 Their land has also been
filled with silver and gold,
And there is no end
to their treasures;
Their land has also been
filled with [a]horses,
And there is no end
to their chariots.
8 Their land has also been
[a]filled with idols;
They worship the [b]work
of their hands,
That which their fingers
have made.
9 So [a]the *common* man has
been bowed down,
And the man *of importance*
has been made low,
But [b]do not forgive them.
10 [a]Enter the rock and
hide in the dust
[b]From the dread of Yahweh
and from the splendor
of His majesty.
11 The [a,1]lofty look of [2]man
will be made low,
And the [b,3]men made high
will be bowed down,
And Yahweh alone will be
exalted in that day.

12 For Yahweh of hosts will
have a day *of reckoning*
Against [a]everyone who
is proud and high
And against everyone
who is lifted up,
That he may be made low.
13 And *it will be* against all the
cedars of Lebanon that
are high and lifted up,
Against all the [a]oaks
of Bashan,
14 Against all the [a]high
mountains,
Against all the hills
that are lifted up,
15 Against every [a]lofty tower,
Against every fortified wall,
16 Against all the [a]ships
of Tarshish
And against all
the desirable craft.
17 The loftiness of [1]man
will be bowed down,
And the [2]men who are
high will be made low;

**2:4** [a]Is 32:17, 18; Joel 3:10 [b]Is 9:5, 7; 11:6-9; Hos 2:18; Zec 9:10 **2:5** [a]Is 58:1 [b]Is 60:1, 2, 19, 20; 1Jn 1:5 **2:6** [a]Dt 31:17 [b]2Ki 1:2 [c]2Ki 16:7, 8; Pr 6:1 **2:7** [a]Dt 17:16; Is 30:16; 31:1; Mic 5:10 **2:8** [a]Is 10:11 [b]Ps 115:4-8; Is 17:8; 37:19; 40:19; 44:17 **2:9** [a]Ps 49:2; 62:9; Is 5:15 [b]Ne 4:5 **2:10** [a]Is 2:19, 21; Rev 6:15, 16 [b]2Th 1:9 **2:11** [a]Is 5:15; 37:23 [b]Ps 18:27; Is 13:11; 23:9; 2Co 10:5 [1]Lit *eyes of the loftiness of man* [2]Or common *man*, cf. 2:9 [3]Or *men* of importance, cf. 2:9 **2:12** [a]Job 40:11, 12; Is 24:4, 21; Mal 4:1 **2:13** [a]Zec 11:2 **2:14** [a]Is 40:4 **2:15** [a]Is 25:12 **2:16** [a]1Ki 10:22; Is 23:1, 14; 60:9 **2:17** [1]Or common *man*, cf. 2:9 [2]Or *men* of importance, cf. 2:9

And Yahweh alone will be
exalted in that day,
18 But the [a]idols will
completely vanish.
19 *Men* will [a]go into caves
of the rocks
And into holes of the [1]ground
Before the dread of Yahweh
And the splendor
of His majesty,
When He arises [b]to make
the earth tremble.
20 In that day men will [a]cast away
to the moles and the [b]bats
Their idols of silver and
their idols of gold,
Which they made
for themselves to worship,
21 In order to [a]go into the
caverns of the rocks and
the clefts of the cliffs
Before the dread
of Yahweh and the
splendor of His majesty,
When He arises to make
the earth tremble.
22 [a,1]Stop regarding [2]man,
whose breath *of life*
is in his nostrils;
For [b,3]why should he
be esteemed?

### *Yahweh Will Judge Judah's Leaders*

3 For behold, the Lord, Yahweh
of hosts, [a]is going to remove
from Jerusalem and Judah
Both [1]supply and support,
the whole [1]supply of bread
And the whole [1]supply
of water,
2 [a]The mighty man and
the man of war,
The judge and the prophet,
The diviner and the elder,
3 The commander of fifty
and the [1]highly
respected man,
The counselor and
the wise craftsman,
And the experienced
enchanter.
4 And I will make [a]young
men their princes,
And [1]capricious children
will rule over them,
5 And the people will
be [a]oppressed,
Each one by another,
and each one
by his [b]neighbor;
The youth will overwhelm
the elder
And the dishonorable
against the honorable.
6 When a man [a]grasps his
brother in his father's
house, *saying*,
"You have a cloak, you
shall be our ruler,
And these ruins will be
under your hand,"
7 He will [1]protest
on that day, saying,
"I will not be *your* [a,2]healer,
For in my house there is
neither bread nor cloak;
You should not appoint me
ruler of the people."
8 For [a]Jerusalem has stumbled
and Judah has fallen,

**2:18** [a]Is 21:9; Mic 1:7 **2:19** [a]Is 2:10 [b]Ps 18:7; Is 2:21; 13:13; 24:1, 19, 20; Hag 2:6, 7; Heb 12:26 [1]Lit *dust* **2:20** [a]Is 30:22; 31:7 [b]Lv 11:19 **2:21** [a]Is 2:19 **2:22** [a]Ps 146:3; Jer 17:5 [b]Ps 8:4; 144:3, 4; Is 40:15, 17; Jas 4:14 [1]Lit *Cease from man* [2]Or common *man*, cf. 2:9 [3]Lit *in what* ◆ **3:1** [a]Lv 26:26; Is 5:13; 9:20; Eze 4:16 [1]Lit *staff* **3:2** [a]2Ki 24:14; Is 9:14, 15; Eze 17:12, 13 **3:3** [1]Lit *one whose face is lifted up* **3:4** [a]Ecc 10:16 [1]Lit *arbitrary power will rule* **3:5** [a]Mic 7:3-6 [b]Is 9:19; Jer 9:3-8 **3:6** [a]Is 4:1 **3:7** [a]Eze 34:4; Hos 5:13 [1]Lit *lift up his voice* [2]Lit *binder of wounds* **3:8** [a]Is 1:7; 6:11

Because their [b]tongue
and their deeds are
against Yahweh,
To [c]rebel against [1]His
glorious presence.
9 [1]The expression of their faces
answers against them,
And they declare their
sin like [a]Sodom;
They do not *even* conceal *it*.
Woe to their soul!
For they have [b]dealt out
evil on themselves.
10 Say to the [a]righteous that *it
will go* well *with them*,
For they will eat the
fruit of their deeds.
11 Woe to the wicked! *It will
go* badly *with him*,
For [a,1]what he has dealt out
will be done to him.
12 O My people! Their
taskmasters [1]are [a]infants,
And women rule over them.
O My people! [b]Those who
guide you lead *you* astray
And swallow up the
way of your paths.

13 [a]Yahweh takes His
stand to contend,
And stands to judge the peoples.
14 Yahweh [a]enters into judgment
with the elders of His
people and His princes,
"It is you who have
[b]consumed the vineyard;
The [c]*plunder* robbed of the
afflicted is in your houses.
15 "What do you mean
by [a]crushing My people
And grinding the face
of the afflicted?"
Declares Lord Yahweh of hosts.

### *Yahweh Will Judge Zion's Daughters*

**16** Moreover, Yahweh said,
"Because the [a]daughters
of Zion are haughty
And walk with outstretched
necks and seductive eyes,
And go along
with mincing steps
And tinkle the bangles
on their feet,
17 Therefore the Lord will smite
the skull of the daughters
of Zion with scabs,
And Yahweh will make
their foreheads bare."
**18** In that day the Lord will remove the
beauty of *their* anklets, headbands,
[a]crescent ornaments, **19** dangling
earrings, bracelets, veils, **20** [a]head-
dresses, ankle chains, sashes,
perfume boxes, enchanted charms,
**21** [1]finger rings, [a]nose rings, **22** festal
robes, outer tunics, cloaks, money
purses, **23** hand mirrors, undergar-
ments, turbans, and shawls.
24 Now it will be that instead
of [1]sweet [a]perfume there
will be *the smell of* rot;
Instead of a belt, a rope;
Instead of [b]well-set hair,
a [c]plucked-out scalp;
Instead of fine clothes, a
[d]donning of sackcloth;

**3:8** [b]Ps 73:9-11; Is 9:17; 59:3 [c]Is 65:3 [1]Lit *the eyes of His glory* **3:9** [a]Ge 13:13; Is 1:10-15 [b]Pr 8:36; 15:32; Ro 6:23 [1]Or *Their partiality* **3:10** [a]Dt 28:1-14; Ecc 8:12; Is 54:17 **3:11** [a]Dt 28:15-68; Is 65:6, 7 [1]Lit *the dealing of his hands* **3:12** [a]Is 3:4 [b]Is 9:16; 28:14, 15 [1]Or *deal severely* **3:13** [a]Is 66:16; Hos 4:1; Mic 6:2 **3:14** [a]Job 22:4; Ps 143:2; Eze 20:35, 36 [b]Ps 14:4; Mic 3:3 [c]Job 24:9, 14; Ps 10:9; Pr 30:14; Is 10:1, 2; Eze 18:12; Jas 2:6 **3:15** [a]Ps 94:5 **3:16** [a]SS 3:11; Is 3:16-4:1, 4; 32:9-15 **3:18** [a]Jdg 8:21, 26 **3:20** [a]Ex 39:28 **3:21** [a]Ge 24:47; Eze 16:12 [1]Or *signet rings* **3:24** [a]Es 2:12 [b]1Pe 3:3 [c]Is 22:12; Eze 27:31; Am 8:10 [d]Is 15:3; Lam 2:10 [1]Or *balsam oil*

And branding
instead of beauty.
25 Your men will [a]fall
by the sword
And your [1]mighty
ones in battle.
26 And her [a,1]gates will
lament and mourn,
And deserted she will
[b]sit on the ground.

4 And seven women will take hold
of [a]one man in that day, saying,
"We will eat our own bread and
wear our own clothes, only let us be
called by your name; [b]take away our
reproach!"

### *The Branch of Yahweh Glorified*

2 In that day the [a]Branch of Yahweh
will be beautiful and glorious, and
the [b]fruit of the earth *will be* the pride
and the [1]honor of [c]those of Israel
who escape. 3 It will be that he who
[a]remains in Zion and is left in Jeru-
salem will be called [b]holy—everyone
who is [c]written down for life in Jeru-
salem. 4 When the Lord has washed
away the filth of the [a]daughters of
Zion and rinsed away the [b]bloodshed
of Jerusalem from her midst, by the
[c]spirit of judgment and the [d]spirit of
burning, 5 then Yahweh will create
over the whole area of Mount Zion
and over her convocation [a]a cloud by
day, even smoke, and the brightness
of a flaming fire by night; for over
all the [b]glory will be a canopy. 6 And
there will be a [a]booth to *give* shade
from the heat by day, and refuge and
a hiding place from the storm and
the rain.

### *The Song of the Vineyard*

5 Let me sing now
for my well-beloved
A song of my beloved
concerning His vineyard.
My well-beloved had
a [a]vineyard on [1]a fertile hill.
2 He dug it all around,
removed its stones,
And planted it with
[1]the [a]choicest vine.
And He built a tower
in the middle of it
And also hewed out a
[2]wine vat in it;
Then He [b]hoped for *it*
to produce *good* grapes,
But it produced *only*
[3]worthless ones.

3 "So now, O inhabitants
of Jerusalem and
men of Judah,
[a]Please judge between
Me and My vineyard.
4 "[a]What more was there
to do for My vineyard [1]that
I have not done in it?
Why, *when* I hoped for *it*
to produce *good* grapes did
it produce [2]worthless ones?
5 "So now let Me tell you
what I am going to do
to My vineyard:

**3:25** [a]Is 1:20; 65:12 [1]Lit *strength* **3:26** [a]Jer 14:2; Lam 1:4 [b]Lam 2:10 [1]Lit *entrances* ◆ **4:1** [a]Is 13:12 [b]Ge 30:23; Is 54:4 **4:2** [a]Is 11:1; 53:2; Jer 23:5; 33:15; Zec 3:8; 6:12 [b]Ps 72:16 [c]Is 10:20; 37:31, 32; Joel 2:32; Ob 17 [1]Lit *beautiful glory* **4:3** [a]Is 28:5; 46:3; Ro 11:4, 5 [b]Is 52:1; 62:12 [c]Ex 32:32; Ps 69:28; Lk 10:20 **4:4** [a]Is 3:16 [b]Is 1:15 [c]Is 28:6 [d]Is 1:31; 9:19; Mt 3:11 **4:5** [a]Ex 13:21, 22; 24:16; Nu 9:15-23 [b]Is 60:1, 2 **4:6** [a]Ps 27:5; Is 25:4; 32:1, 2 ◆ **5:1** [a]Ps 80:8; Jer 12:10; Mt 21:33; Mk 12:1; Lk 20:9 [1]Lit *a horn, the son of fatness* **5:2** [a]Jer 2:21 [b]Mt 21:19; Mk 11:13; Lk 13:6 [1]Lit *a bright red grape* [2]Or *wine press* [3]Or *wild grapes* **5:3** [a]Mt 21:40 **5:4** [a]2Chr 36:16; Jer 2:5; 7:25, 26; Mic 6:3; Mt 23:37 [1]Lit *and I have not done* [2]Or *wild grapes*

I will [a]remove its hedge,
and it will be consumed;
I will [b]break down its
wall, and it will become
[c]trampled ground.
6 "I will [a]lay it waste;
It will not be pruned or hoed,
But briars and thorns
will come up.
I will also command the
clouds to [b]rain no
rain on it."

7 For the [a]vineyard of Yahweh
of hosts is the house
of Israel
And the men of Judah
His delightful plant.
Thus He hoped for justice,
but behold, [b]bloodshed;
For righteousness,
but behold, a cry of distress.

### *Woes to Those Who Call Evil Good*

8 Woe to those who [a]add
house to house *and*
join field to field,
Until there is no more room,
So that you have to live alone
in the midst of the land!
9 In my ears Yahweh
of hosts *has sworn*, "Surely,
[a]many houses shall
become [b]desolate,
*Even* great and good ones,
without inhabitants.
10 "For [a]ten [1]acres of vineyard
will yield *only* one
[2]bath *of wine*,
And a [b,3]homer of seed
will yield *but* an
[4]ephah *of grain*."

11 Woe to those who rise early
in the morning that they
may pursue [a]strong drink,
Who stay up late
in the evening that wine
may inflame them!
12 And their banquets are
*accompanied* by lyre and
[a]harp, by tambourine
and flute, and by wine;
But they [b]do not look
upon the deeds of Yahweh,
Nor do they see the
work of His hands.

13 Therefore My people
go into exile for their
[a]lack of knowledge;
And [1]their [b]honorable
men are famished,
And their multitude is
parched with thirst.
14 Therefore [a]Sheol has enlarged
its [1]throat and opened its
mouth without limit;
And [2]Jerusalem's majesty,
her multitude, her rumbling,
and the exultant
within her, descend *into it*.
15 So the *common* man will
be bowed down and
the man of *importance*
will be made low,
[a]The eyes of the lofty also
will be made low.

---

***5:5*** [a]*Ps 89:40* [b]*Ps 80:12* [c]Is 10:6; 28:18; Lam 1:15; Lk 21:24; Rev 11:2 **5:6** [a]2Chr 36:19-21; Is 7:19-25; 24:1, 3; Jer 25:11 [b]1Ki 8:35; 17:1; Jer 14:1-22 **5:7** [a]Ps 80:8-11 [b]Is 3:14, 15; 30:12; 59:13 **5:8** [a]Jer 22:13-17; Mic 2:2; Hab 2:9-12 **5:9** [a]Is 6:11, 12 [b]Mt 23:38 **5:10** [a]Lv 26:26; Is 7:23; Hag 1:6; 2:16 [b]Eze 45:11 [1]One acre is what oxen could plow in one day [2]A bath was approx. 6 gal. or 23 l [3]A homer was approx. 6.5 bu. or 230 l [4]An ephah was approx. 21 qt. or 23 l **5:11** [a]Pr 23:29, 30; Ecc 10:16, 17; Is 5:22; 22:13; 28:1, 3, 7, 8 **5:12** [a]Am 6:5, 6 [b]Job 34:27; Ps 28:5 **5:13** [a]Is 1:3; 27:11; Hos 4:6 [b]Is 3:3 [1]Lit *their glory are men of famine* **5:14** [a]Pr 30:16; Hab 2:5 [1]Or *appetite* [2]Lit *her* **5:15** [a]Is 2:11; 10:33

16 But [a]Yahweh of hosts will
be [b]lofty in judgment,
And the holy God will
show Himself [c]holy
in righteousness.
17 [a]Then the lambs will graze
as in their pasture,
And sojourners will eat in the
waste places of the [1]wealthy.

18 Woe to those who drag
[a]iniquity with the cords
of worthlessness,
And sin as if with cart ropes,
19 [a]Who say, "Let Him hurry,
let Him hasten His work,
that we may see *it*;
And let the counsel of the
Holy One of Israel draw near
And come to pass, that
we may know *it*!"

20 Woe to those who [a]call evil
good and good evil,
Who [b,1]substitute darkness for
light and light for darkness,
Who [1]substitute bitter for
sweet and sweet for bitter!
21 Woe to those who are
[a]wise in their own eyes
And understanding
in their own [1]sight!
22 [a]Woe to those who are mighty
men in drinking wine
And valiant men
in mixing strong drink,
23 [a]Who [1]declare the wicked
righteous for a bribe,
And [b]remove the [2]righteous
standing of the ones
who are [3]righteous!

24 Therefore, [a]as a tongue
of fire consumes stubble
And dry grass collapses
into the flame,
So their [b]root will become
[c]like rot and their blossom
[1]blow away as dust;
For they have [d]rejected
the law of Yahweh of hosts
And the word of the Holy One
of Israel they have spurned.
25 On this account, the [a]anger
of Yahweh has burned
against His people,
And He has stretched out
His hand against them
and struck them down.
And the [b]mountains
trembled, and their [c]corpses
[1]lay like refuse in the
middle of the streets.
[d]For all this His anger
is not turned back,
But His [e]hand is still
stretched out.

26 He will also lift up a [a]standard
to the [1]distant nations,
And will [b]whistle for it
[c]from the ends of the earth;
And behold, it will [d]come
with speed swiftly.
27 [a]No one in it is weary
or stumbles,

---

**5:16** [a]Is 28:17; 30:18; 61:8 [b]Is 2:11, 17; 33:5, 10 [c]Is 8:13; 29:23; 1Pe 3:15 **5:17** [a]Is 7:25; Mic 2:12; Zep 2:6 [1]Lit *fat* **5:18** [a]Is 59:4-8; Jer 23:10-14 **5:19** [a]Eze 12:22; 2Pe 3:4 **5:20** [a]Pr 17:15; Am 5:7 [b]Job 17:12; Mt 6:22, 23; Lk 11:34, 35 [1]Lit *set* **5:21** [a]Pr 3:7; Ro 12:16; 1Co 3:18-20 [1]Lit *face* **5:22** [a]Pr 23:20; Is 5:11; 56:12; Hab 2:15 **5:23** [a]Ex 23:8; Is 1:23; 10:1, 2; Mic 3:11; 7:3 [b]Ps 94:21; Jas 5:6 [1]Or *justify the wicked for a bribe*, cf. 53:11 [2]Or *justification* [3]Or *justified* **5:24** [a]Is 9:18, 19; Joel 2:5 [b]Job 18:16 [c]Hos 5:12 [d]Is 8:6; 30:9, 12; Ac 13:41 [1]Lit *ascend* **5:25** [a]2Ki 22:13, 17; Is 66:15 [b]Ps 18:7; Is 64:3; Jer 4:24; Na 1:5 [c]2Ki 9:37; Is 14:19; Jer 16:4 [d]Is 9:12, 17, 19, 21; 10:4; Jer 4:8; Da 9:16 [e]Ex 7:19; Is 23:11 [1]Lit *were* **5:26** [a]Is 13:2, 3 [b]Is 7:18; Zec 10:8 [c]Dt 28:49 [d]Is 13:4, 5 [1]Probably Assyria **5:27** [a]Joel 2:7, 8

None slumbers or sleeps;
Nor is the [b]belt at its
waist undone,
Nor its sandal strap broken.
28 [a,1]Its arrows are sharp and
all its bows are bent;
The hoofs of its horses [2]seem
like flint and its *chariot*
[b]wheels like a whirlwind.
29 Its [a]roaring is like a lioness,
and it roars like young lions;
It growls and [b]seizes the prey
And carries *it* off
with [c]no one to deliver *it*.
30 And it will [a]growl over it in that
day like the roaring of the sea.
If one [b]looks to the
land, behold, there is
darkness *and* distress;
Even the light is darkened
by its clouds.

### *Isaiah's Vision of Yahweh*

6 In the year of [a]King Uzziah's
death [b]I saw the Lord sitting on
a throne, high and lifted up, with the
train of His robe filling the temple.
2 Seraphim stood above Him, [a]each
having six wings: with two he covered
his face, and with two he covered his
feet, and with two he flew. 3 And one
called out to another and said,

"[a]Holy, Holy, Holy,
is Yahweh of hosts;
The [b,1]whole earth is
full of His glory."

4 And the [1]foundations of the
thresholds shook at the voice of him
who called out, while the [a]house *of*
*God* was filling with smoke. 5 Then
I said,

"[a]Woe is me, for I am ruined!
For I am a man
of [b]unclean lips,
And I live among a [c]people
of unclean lips;
For my eyes have seen
the [d]King, Yahweh of hosts."

6 Then one of the seraphim flew to
me with a burning coal in his hand,
which he had taken from the [a]altar
with tongs. 7 And he [a]touched my
mouth *with it* and said, "Behold, this
has touched your lips; and [b]your in-
iquity is taken away, and your sin is
atoned for."

### *Yahweh Sends Isaiah*

8 Then I heard the [a]voice of the Lord,
saying, "Whom shall I send, and who
will go for Us?" Then [b]I said, "Here
am I. Send me!" 9 He said, "Go, and
tell this people:

'Keep on [a]hearing,
but do not understand;
Keep on seeing,
but do not know.'
10 "[a]Render the hearts of this
people [b,1]insensitive,
Their ears [2]dull,
And their eyes [3]dim,
[c]Lest they see with their eyes,
And hear with their ears,
And understand
with their hearts,
And return and be healed."

**5:27** [b]Job 12:18 **5:28** [a]Ps 7:12, 13; 45:5; Is 13:18 [b]Is 21:1; Jer 4:13 [1]Lit *Which, its arrows* [2]Lit *are regarded as* **5:29** [a]Jer 51:38; Zep 3:3; Zec 11:3 [b]Is 10:6; 49:24, 25; Mic 5:8 [c]Is 42:22 **5:30** [a]Is 17:12; Jer 6:23; Lk 21:25 [b]Is 8:22; Jer 4:23-28; Joel 2:10; Lk 21:25, 26 ◆ **6:1** [a]2Ki 15:7; 2Chr 26:23; Is 1:1 [b]Jn 12:41; Rev 4:2, 3; 20:11 **6:2** [a]Rev 4:8 **6:3** [a]Rev 4:8 [b]Nu 14:21; Ps 72:19 [1]Lit *fullness of the whole earth is His glory* **6:4** [a]Rev 15:8 [1]Lit *door sockets* **6:5** [a]Ex 33:20; Lk 5:8 [b]Ex 6:12, 30 [c]Is 59:3; Jer 9:3-8 [d]Jer 51:57 **6:6** [a]Rev 8:3 **6:7** [a]Jer 1:9; Da 10:16 [b]Is 40:2; 53:5, 6, 11; 1Jn 1:7 **6:8** [a]Eze 10:5; Ac 9:4 [b]Ac 26:19 **6:9** [a]Is 43:8; Mt 13:14; Mk 4:12; Lk 8:10; Jn 12:40; Ac 28:26; Ro 11:8 **6:10** [a]Mt 13:15 [b]Dt 31:20; 32:15 [c]Jer 5:21 [1]Lit *fat* [2]Lit *heavy, hardened*; cf. Ex 8:15; 1Sa 6:6 [3]Lit *besmeared*

**11** Then I said, "Lord, [a]how long?"
And He said,
"Until [b]cities are devastated
*and* without inhabitant,
Houses are without people,
And the land is devastated
*to* desolation,
**12** And Yahweh has [a]removed
men far away,
And the [b,1]forsaken places are
many in the midst of the land.
**13** "Yet there will be a tenth
portion in it,
And it will again be
*subject* to burning,
Like a terebinth or like an [a]oak
Whose stump remains
when it is felled.
The [b]holy seed is its stump."

### *Isaiah Sent to King Ahaz*

**7** Now it happened in the days of
[a]Ahaz, the son of Jotham, the son
of Uzziah, king of Judah, that [b]Rezin
the king of Aram and [c]Pekah the son
of Remaliah, king of Israel, went up to
Jerusalem to *wage* war against it, but
[d]could not [1]conquer it. **2** When it was
told to the [a]house of David, saying,
"[1]The Arameans [b]have camped in
[c]Ephraim," his heart and the hearts
of his people shook as the trees of the
forest shake before the wind.
**3** Then Yahweh said to Isaiah,
"Go out now to meet Ahaz, you and
your son [1]Shear-jashub, at the end
of the [a]conduit of the upper pool,
to the highway of the [2]fuller's field,
**4** and say to him, 'Take care and stay
[a]quiet, have no [b]fear and [c]do not be
fainthearted because of these two
stubs of smoldering [d]firebrands, on
account of the burning anger of Rezin
and Aram and the [e]son of Remaliah.
**5** Because [a]Aram, *with* Ephraim and
the son of Remaliah, has counseled
evil against you, saying, **6** "Let us go
up against Judah and [1]terrorize it,
and make for ourselves a breach in
[2]its walls and set up the son of Tabeel
as king in the midst of it," **7** thus says
Lord Yahweh: "[a]It shall not stand,
nor shall it happen. **8** For the head
of Aram is [a]Damascus and the head
of Damascus is Rezin (now within
another sixty-five years Ephraim will
be shattered, *so that it is* no longer a
people), **9** and the head of Ephraim is
Samaria and the head of Samaria is
the son of Remaliah. [a]If you do not
[1]establish your faith *in Yahweh*, you
surely shall not [2]be established."'"

### *The Sign of Immanuel*

**10** Then Yahweh spoke again to Ahaz,
saying, **11** "Ask a [a]sign for yourself
from Yahweh your God; [1]make *it*
deep as Sheol or high as [2]heaven."
**12** But Ahaz said, "I will not ask,
and I will not test Yahweh!" **13** Then
he said, "[1]Listen now, O [a]house of
David! Is it too slight a thing for you
to try the patience of men, that you
will [b]try the patience of [c]my God as

**6:11** [a]Ps 79:5 [b]Lv 26:31; Is 1:7; 3:8, 26 **6:12** [a]Dt 28:64 [b]Jer 4:29 [1]Or *forsakenness will be great*
**6:13** [a]Job 14:7 [b]Dt 7:6; Ezr 9:2 ◆ **7:1** [a]2Ki 16:1; Is 1:1 [b]2Ki 15:37 [c]2Ki 15:25; 2Chr 28:6 [d]Is 7:6, 7
[1]Lit *fight against* **7:2** [a]Is 7:13; 22:22 [b]Is 8:12 [c]Is 9:9 [1]Lit *Aram has settled down on* **7:3** [a]2Ki 18:17;
Is 36:2 [1]Lit *a remnant shall return* [2]Or *launderer's* **7:4** [a]Ex 14:13; Is 30:15; Lam 3:26 [b]Is 10:24; Mt 24:6
[c]Dt 20:3; 1Sa 17:32; Is 35:4 [d]Am 4:11; Zec 3:2 [e]Is 7:1, 9 **7:5** [a]Is 7:2 **7:6** [1]Lit *cause it a sickening dread*
[2]Lit *it* **7:7** [a]Is 8:10; 28:18; Ac 4:25, 26 **7:8** [a]Ge 14:15; Is 17:1-3 **7:9** [a]2Chr 20:20; Is 5:24; 8:6-8; 30:12-14
[1]Lit *believe* [2]Lit *be believed* **7:11** [a]2Ki 19:29; Is 37:30; 38:7, 8; 55:13 [1]As in the versions; M.T. *make the
request deep or high* [2]Lit *heights* **7:13** [a]Is 7:2 [b]Is 1:14; 43:24 [c]Is 25:1 [1]The verb *listen* and the second
person pronouns are plural in vv 13-14

well? **14** Therefore the Lord Himself
will give you a sign: Behold, [a]the
[1]virgin [2]will be with child and bear
a son, and she will call His name
[b,3]Immanuel. **15** He will eat [a]curds
and honey [1]in order that He will
know to refuse evil and choose good.
**16** [a]For before the boy will know to
refuse evil and choose good, [b]the
land whose two kings you dread will
be forsaken. **17** Yahweh will bring on
you, on your people, and on your
father's house days which have never
come since the day that [a]Ephraim
separated from Judah—the [b]king of
Assyria!"

### *Trials to Come for Judah*

**18** And it will be in that day, *that*
Yahweh will [a]whistle for the fly that
is in the [b,1]remotest part of the rivers
of Egypt and for the bee that is in
the land of Assyria. **19** And they will
all come and rest upon the steep
[1]ravines, on the [a]crevices of the cliffs,
[b]on all the thorn bushes, and on all
the [2]watering places.

**20** In that day, the Lord will [a]shave
with a [b]razor—*one* [c]hired from re-
gions beyond [d]the [1]River (*that is,*
the king of Assyria)—the head and
the hair of the legs; and it will also
remove the beard.

**21** And it will be in that day, *that* a
man may keep alive a [a]heifer and a
pair of sheep; **22** and because of the
abundance of the milk produced, he
will eat curds, for everyone that is
left within the land will eat [a]curds
and honey.

**23** And it will be in that day, [a]*that*
every place where there used to be
one thousand vines, *valued* at [1]one
thousand *shekels* of silver, will be-
come [b]briars and thorns. **24** *People*
will come there with bows and
arrows because all the land will be
briars and thorns. **25** As for all the
hills which used to be cultivated with
the hoe, you will not go there for fear
of briars and thorns; but they will
become a place for [a,1]pasturing oxen
and for sheep to trample.

### *The Coming Assyrian Invasion*

**8** Then Yahweh said to me, "Take
for yourself a large tablet and
[a]write on it [1]in ordinary letters:
[b]Concerning [2]Maher-shalal-hash-
baz. **2** And [1]I will take to Myself
faithful witnesses for testimony,
[a]Uriah the priest and Zechariah
the son of Jeberechiah." **3** Then I
drew near to the prophetess, and
she conceived and bore a son.
Then Yahweh said to me, "Call his
name [a,1]Maher-shalal-hash-baz,
**4** for [a]before the boy knows how to
cry out 'My father' or 'My mother,'
the wealth of [b]Damascus and the
spoil of Samaria will be carried away
before the king of Assyria."

**5** Again Yahweh spoke to me fur-
ther, saying,

---

**7:14** [a]Mt 1:23 [b]Is 8:8, 10 [1]Or *maiden* [2]Or *will conceive*, cf. Ge 3:16; 21:2; 25:21; Ex 2:2; 1Sa 1:20; Lk 1:31, 36 [3]Lit *God is with us* **7:15** [a]Is 7:22; Heb 5:8 [1]Or *when* **7:16** [a]Is 8:4 [b]Is 8:14; 17:3; Jer 7:15; Hos 5:3, 9, 14; Am 1:3-5 **7:17** [a]1Ki 12:16 [b]2Chr 28:20; Is 8:7, 8; 10:5, 6 **7:18** [a]Is 5:26 [b]Is 13:5 [1]The Nile Delta; or *mouth of the rivers* **7:19** [a]Is 2:19; Jer 16:16 [b]Is 7:24, 25 [1]Or *wadis* [2]Or *pastures* **7:20** [a]2Ki 18:13-16; Is 24:1 [b]Eze 5:1-4 [c]Is 10:5, 15 [d]Is 8:7; 11:15; Jer 2:18 [1]The Euphrates River **7:21** [a]Is 14:30; 27:10; Jer 39:10 **7:22** [a]Is 8:15 **7:23** [a]Is 5:10; 32:13, 14 [b]Is 5:6 [1]Approx. 25 lb. or 11 kg, a shekel was approx. 0.4 oz. or 11 gm **7:25** [a]Is 5:17 [1]Lit *sending* ◆ **8:1** [a]Is 30:8; Hab 2:2 [b]Is 8:3 [1]Lit *with the stylus of man* [2]Lit *swift is the spoil, speedy is the plunder*, cf. 8:1 **8:2** [a]2Ki 16:10, 11, 15, 16 [1]Or *take for me* **8:3** [a]Is 8:1 [1]Lit *swift is the spoil, speedy is the plunder* **8:4** [a]Is 7:16 [b]Is 7:8, 9

6 "Inasmuch as these people
have [a]rejected the gently
flowing waters of Shiloah
And rejoice in [b]Rezin and
the son of Remaliah;
7 Now therefore, behold,
the Lord is about to bring
on them the [a]mighty
and abundant waters
of the [b,1]River—
The [c]king of Assyria
and all his glory;
And it will [d]rise up
over all its channels
and go over all its banks.
8 "Then [a]it will sweep on
into Judah; it will overflow
and pass through;
It will [b]reach even
to the neck;
And the spread of its wings
will [1]fill the breadth
of [2]Your land, O [c]Immanuel.

### *Yahweh, a Sanctuary and a Stumbling Stone*

9 "[a]Be broken, O peoples,
and be [b,1]shattered;
And give ear, all remote
places of the earth.
Gird yourselves,
yet be [1]shattered;
Gird yourselves,
yet be [1]shattered.
10 "[a]Devise counsel,
but it will be thwarted;
Speak a word, but [b]it
will not stand,
For [c,1]God is with us."

11 For thus Yahweh spoke to me
with a [a]strong hand and disciplined
me [b]not to walk in the way of this
people, saying,
12 "You are not to say,
'*It is* a [a]conspiracy!'
In regard to all that this
people call a conspiracy;
And [b]you are not to fear
[1]what they fear, and you
shall not tremble.
13 "It is [a]Yahweh of hosts
[b]whom you should
regard as holy.
And He shall be your fear,
And He shall be your
cause of trembling.
14 "Then He shall become
a [a]sanctuary;
But to both the houses
of Israel, a [b]stone to strike
and a rock to stumble over,
*And* a snare and a [c]trap for
the inhabitants of Jerusalem.
15 "And many [a]will stumble
over them;
Then they will fall
and be broken;
They will even be snared
and caught."
16 [a]Bind up the testimony, [b]seal
the [1]law among [c]my disciples. 17 And
I will [a]wait for Yahweh [b]who is hiding
His face from the house of Jacob;
and I will hope for Him. 18 [a]Behold,
I and the children whom Yahweh has
given me are for [b]signs and wonders
in Israel from Yahweh of hosts, who
[c]dwells on Mount Zion.

**8:6** [a]Is 1:20; 5:24; 7:9; 30:12 [b]Is 7:1 **8:7** [a]Is 17:12, 13 [b]Is 7:20; 11:15 [c]Is 7:17; 10:5 [d]Am 8:8; 9:5 [1]The Euphrates River **8:8** [a]Is 10:6 [b]Is 30:28 [c]Is 7:14 [1]Lit *be the fullness of* [2]Or *your* **8:9** [a]Is 17:12-14 [b]Da 2:34, 35 [1]Or *dismayed* **8:10** [a]Job 5:12; Is 28:18 [b]Is 7:7 [c]Is 8:8; Ro 8:31 [1]Heb *Immanuel* **8:11** [a]Eze 3:14 [b]Eze 2:8 **8:12** [a]Is 7:2; 30:1 [b]1Pe 3:14, 15 [1]Lit *their fear* **8:13** [a]Is 5:16; 29:23 [b]Nu 20:12 **8:14** [a]Is 4:6; 25:4; Eze 11:16 [b]Lk 2:34; Ro 9:33; 1Pe 2:8 [c]Is 24:17, 18 **8:15** [a]Is 28:13; 59:10; Lk 20:18; Ro 9:32 **8:16** [a]Is 8:1, 2; 29:11, 12 [b]Da 12:4 [c]Is 50:4 [1]Or *teaching* **8:17** [a]Is 25:9; 30:18; Hab 2:3 [b]Dt 31:17; Is 1:15; 45:15; 54:8 **8:18** [a]Heb 2:13 [b]Lk 2:34 [c]Ps 9:11; Zec 8:3

### *Darkness to Light Through the Prince of Peace*

**19** Now when they say to you,
“[a]Inquire of the mediums and the
spiritists who whisper and mutter,”
should not a people [b]inquire of their
God? *Should they* [c]*inquire of* the dead
on behalf of the living? **20** To the
[a,1]law and to the testimony! If they do
not speak according to this word, it is
because [b]they have no dawn. **21** And
they will pass through [1]the land
[a]hard-pressed and hungry, and it will
be that when they are hungry, they
will be angry and curse [2]their king
and their God as they face upward.
**22** Then they will [a]look to the earth,
and behold, distress and darkness,
the gloom of anguish; and *they will
be* [b]banished into thick darkness.

**9** [1]But there will be no *more* [a]gloom
for her who was in anguish; in
earlier times He [b]treated the [c]land
of Zebulun and the land of Naphtali
with contempt, but later on He shall
make *it* glorious, by the way of the
sea, on the other side of Jordan,
Galilee of the [2]Gentiles.

2 [a,1]The people who
walk in darkness
Will see a great light;
Those who live in the land
of the shadow of death,
The light will shine on them.
3 [a]You shall multiply
the nation,
You [b]shall [1]make great
[2]their gladness;
They will be glad
in Your presence
As with the gladness
[3]of harvest,
As [c,4]men rejoice
when they divide the spoil.
4 For [a]You shall shatter
the yoke of their burden and
the staff on their shoulders,
The rod of their [b]taskmaster,
as [1]at the battle of [c]Midian.
5 For every boot of the
booted warrior in the
rumbling *of battle,*
And cloak rolled in blood,
will be for burning,
fuel for the fire.
6 For a [a]child will be born to us,
a [b]son will be given to us;
And the [c]government will
[1]rest [d]on His shoulders;
And His name will be
called [e]Wonderful
Counselor, [f]Mighty God,
Eternal [g]Father, Prince
of [h]Peace.
7 There will be [a]no end
to the increase of *His*
government or of peace,
On the [b]throne of David
and over his kingdom,
To establish it and
to uphold it with [c]justice
and righteousness
From then on and
forevermore.
[d]The zeal of Yahweh of hosts
will accomplish this.

**8:19** [a]Lv 20:6; 2Ki 21:6; 23:24; Is 19:3; 29:4; 47:12, 13 [b]Is 30:2; 45:11 [c]1Sa 28:8-11 **8:20** [a]Is 1:10; 8:16; Lk 16:29 [b]Is 8:22; Mic 3:6 [1]Or *teaching* **8:21** [a]Is 9:20, 21 [1]Lit *it* [2]Or *by their king* **8:22** [a]Is 5:30; 59:9; Jer 13:16; Am 5:18, 20; Zep 1:14, 15 [b]Is 8:20 ◆ **9:1** [a]Is 8:22 [b]2Ki 15:29; 2Chr 16:4 [c]Mt 4:15, 16 [1]Ch 8:23 in Heb [2]Or *nations* **9:2** [a]Mt 4:16; Lk 1:79; Eph 5:8 [1]Ch 9:1 in Heb **9:3** [a]Is 26:15 [b]Is 35:10; 65:14, 18, 19; 66:10 [c]1Sa 30:16 [1]M.T. *not increase* [2]Lit *the* [3]Lit *in* [4]Lit *they* **9:4** [a]Is 10:27; 14:25 [b]Is 14:4; 49:26; 51:13; 54:14 [c]Jdg 7:25; Is 10:26 [1]Lit *in the day of Midian* **9:6** [a]Is 7:14; 11:1, 2; 53:2; Lk 2:11 [b]Jn 3:16 [c]Mt 28:18; 1Co 15:25 [d]Is 22:22 [e]Is 28:29 [f]Dt 10:17; Ne 9:32; Is 10:21 [g]Is 63:16; 64:8 [h]Is 26:3, 12; 54:10; 66:12 [1]Lit *be* **9:7** [a]Da 2:44; Lk 1:32, 33 [b]Is 16:5 [c]Is 11:4, 5; 32:1; 42:3, 4; 63:1 [d]Is 37:32; 59:17

### *Yahweh's Anger with Israel's Arrogance*

8 The Lord sends a [1]message
against Jacob,
And it falls on Israel.
9 And all the people know *it*,
*That is*, [a]Ephraim and
the inhabitants of Samaria,
Saying in lofty pride and
in [b]arrogance of heart:
10 "The bricks have fallen down,
But we will [a]rebuild
with cut stones;
The sycamores have
been cut in pieces,
But we will replace
*them* with cedars."
11 Therefore Yahweh exalts
against them adversaries
from [a]Rezin
And incites their enemies,
12 The Arameans on the east and
the [a]Philistines on the west;
And they [b]devour Israel
with [1]gaping jaws.
[c]In *spite of* all this, His anger
does not turn back,
And His hand is still
stretched out.

13 Yet the people [a]do not
turn back to Him
who struck them,
Nor do they [b]seek
Yahweh of hosts.
14 So Yahweh cuts off [a]head
and tail from Israel,
*Both* palm branch and
bulrush [b]in a single day.
15 The head is [a]the elder and
the [1]highly respected man,
And the prophet who teaches
[b]falsehood is the tail.
16 [a]For those who guide
this people are leading
*them* astray;
And those who are guided
by them are [1]brought
to confusion.
17 Therefore the Lord [a]is not
glad in their choice men,
[b]Nor does He have
compassion on their
[1]orphans or their widows;
For every one of them is
[c]godless and an [d]evildoer,
And every [e]mouth is speaking
wicked foolishness.
[f]In *spite of* all this, His anger
does not turn back,
And His hand is still
stretched out.

18 [a]For wickedness
burns like a fire;
It consumes briars and thorns;
It even sets the thickets
of the forest aflame,
And they roll upward
in a column of smoke.
19 By the [a]fury of Yahweh of
hosts the [b]land is burned up,
And the [c]people are
like fuel for the fire;
No [d]man spares his brother.
20 [1]They slice off *what is* on
the right hand
but *still* are [a]hungry,

---

**9:8** [1]Lit *word* **9:9** [a]Is 7:8, 9; 28:1, 3 [b]Is 46:12 **9:10** [a]Mal 1:4 **9:11** [a]Is 7:1, 8 **9:12** [a]2Chr 28:18 [b]Ps 79:7; Jer 10:25 [c]Is 5:25 [1]Lit *the whole mouth* **9:13** [a]Jer 5:3; Hos 7:10 [b]Is 31:1; Hos 3:5 **9:14** [a]Is 19:15 [b]Rev 18:8 **9:15** [a]Is 3:2, 3 [b]Is 28:15; 59:3, 4; Jer 23:14, 32; Mt 24:24 [1]Lit *the one whose face is lifted up* **9:16** [a]Is 3:12; Mt 15:14; 23:16, 24 [1]Or *swallowed up* **9:17** [a]Jer 18:21; Am 4:10; 8:13 [b]Is 27:11 [c]Is 10:6; 32:6 [d]Is 1:4; 14:20; 31:2 [e]Mt 12:34 [f]Is 5:25 [1]Or *fatherless* **9:18** [a]Ps 83:14; Is 1:7; Na 1:10; Mal 4:1 **9:19** [a]Is 10:6; 13:9, 13; 42:25 [b]Joel 2:3 [c]Is 1:31; 24:6 [d]Mic 7:2, 6 **9:20** [a]Is 8:21, 22 [1]Lit *he slices*

And [2]they eat *what is*
on the left hand
but they are not satisfied;
Each of them eats the
[b]flesh of his own arm.
21 Manasseh *devours* Ephraim,
and Ephraim Manasseh,
[a]*And* together they are
against Judah.
[b]In *spite of* all this, His anger
does not turn back,
And His hand is still
stretched out.

10 Woe to those who
[a]enact evil statutes
And to those who constantly
record [1]mischief,
2 So as [a]to turn the poor
away from *their* cause
And rob the afflicted of My
people of *their* justice,
So [b]that widows may
be their spoil
And that they may
plunder the [1]orphans.
3 Now [a]what will you do
in the [b]day of visitation,
And in the devastation
which will come [c]from afar?
[d]To whom will you
flee for help?
And where will you
leave your [1]glory?
4 Nothing *remains*
but to crouch
[1]among the [a]captives
Or fall [1]among those [b]killed.
[c]In *spite of* all this, His anger
does not turn back
And His hand is still
stretched out.

### *Yahweh's Anger with Assyria's Arrogance*

5 Woe to [a]Assyria, the
[b]rod of My anger
And the staff in whose hands
is [c]My indignation,
6 I send it against a [a]godless
nation
And command it against
the [b]people of My fury
To capture spoil and
[c]to seize plunder,
And to [1]trample them down
like [d]mud in the streets.
7 But it [a]does not intend
*to act* in this way,
And it does not think
in its heart in this way,
Rather, *what is* in its
heart is to destroy
And to cut off [1]many nations.
8 For it says, "Are not my
princes [1]all kings?
9 "Is not [a]Calno
like [b]Carchemish,
Or [c]Hamath like Arpad,
Or [d]Samaria like [e]Damascus?
10 "As my hand has reached to
the [a]kingdoms of the idols,
Whose graven images *were*
greater than those
of Jerusalem and Samaria,
11 Shall I not [1]do to Jerusalem
and her images
Just as I have done
to Samaria and [a]her idols?"

***9:20*** [b]*Is 49:26* [2]Lit *he eats* **9:21** [a]2Chr 28:6, 8; Is 11:13 [b]Is 5:25 ◆**10:1** [a]Ps 94:20; Is 29:21; 59:4, 13 [1]Or *trouble* **10:2** [a]Is 5:23 [b]Is 1:23; 3:14, 15 [1]Or *fatherless* **10:3** [a]Job 31:14 [b]Is 13:6; 26:14, 21; 29:6; Jer 9:9; Hos 9:7; Lk 19:44 [c]Is 5:26 [d]Is 20:6; 30:5, 7; 31:3 [1]Or *wealth* **10:4** [a]Is 24:22 [b]Is 22:2; 34:3; 66:16 [c]Is 5:25 [1]Lit *under* **10:5** [a]Is 7:17; 8:7; 14:24-27; Zep 2:13-15 [b]Jer 51:20 [c]Is 13:5; 30:30; 34:2; 66:14 **10:6** [a]Is 9:17 [b]Is 9:19 [c]Is 5:29 [d]Is 5:25 [1]Lit *make them a trampled place* **10:7** [a]Ge 50:20; Mic 4:11, 12; Ac 2:23, 24 [1]Lit *not a few* **10:8** [1]Lit *altogether* **10:9** [a]Ge 10:10; Am 6:2 [b]2Chr 35:20 [c]Nu 34:8 [d]2Ki 17:6 [e]2Ki 16:9 **10:10** [a]2Ki 19:17, 18 **10:11** [a]Is 2:8 [1]Lit *do thus*

12 So it will be that when the Lord
has completed all His [a]work on
Mount Zion and on Jerusalem, *He will*
*say*, "I will [1]punish the fruit of the
arrogant heart of the king of Assyria
and [b]the pomp of his eyes *which are*
raised high." 13 For [a]he has said,

"By the power of my hand and
by my wisdom I did *this*,
For I have understanding;
And I [b]removed the
boundaries of the peoples
And plundered their treasures,
And like a mighty man
I brought down [1]*their*
inhabitants,
14 And my hand reached
for the wealth
of the peoples like a [a]nest,
And as one gathers abandoned
eggs, I gathered all the earth;
And there was not one that
flapped its wing or opened
*its* beak or chirped."

15 Is the [a]axe to [b]boast itself over
the one who chops with it?
Is the saw to magnify itself
over the one who wields it?
*That would be* like [c]a rod
wielding those who lift it,
*Or* like [c]a staff lifting *him*
*who* is not wood.
16 Therefore the Lord, Yahweh
of hosts, will send a
[a]wasting disease
among his [b]stout warriors;
And under his [c]glory
a fire will be kindled
like a burning flame.
17 And the [a]light of Israel
will become a fire and
his [b]Holy One a flame,
And it will [c]burn and
devour his thorns and his
briars in a single day.
18 And He will [a]bring to an
end the glory of his forest
and of his fruitful orchard,
both soul and body,
And it will be as when
a sick man wastes away.
19 And the [a]rest of the trees
of his forest will be so
small in number
That a child could
write them down.

### *A Remnant Will Return*

20 Now it will be in that day, *that* the
[a]remnant of Israel and those of the
house of Jacob [b]who have escaped,
will never again rely on the one who
struck them, but will truly [c]rely on
Yahweh, the Holy One of Israel.
21 A [a]remnant will return,
the remnant of Jacob,
to the [b]mighty God.
22 For [a]though your people,
O Israel, may be
like the sand of the sea,
*Only* a remnant
within them will return;
A [b]*destructive* end is
decreed, overflowing
with righteousness.
23 For a complete destruction, one
that is decreed, [a]Lord Yahweh of
hosts will do in the midst of the
whole land.

---

**10:12** [a]2Ki 19:31; Is 28:21, 22; 29:14; 65:7 [b]Is 37:23 [1]Or *visit* **10:13** [a]2Ki 19:22-24; Is 37:24-27; Eze 28:4; Da 4:30 [b]Hab 2:6-11 [1]Or *those who sit* on thrones **10:14** [a]Jer 49:16; Ob 4 **10:15** [a]Jer 51:20 [b]Is 29:16; 45:9; Ro 9:20, 21 [c]Is 10:5 **10:16** [a]Ps 106:15 [b]Is 17:4 [c]Is 8:7; 10:18 **10:17** [a]Is 30:33; 31:9 [b]Is 37:23 [c]Nu 11:1-3; Is 27:4; 33:12; Jer 4:4; 7:20 **10:18** [a]Is 10:33, 34 **10:19** [a]Is 21:17 **10:20** [a]Is 1:9; 11:11, 16; 46:3 [b]Is 4:2; 37:31, 32 [c]2Chr 14:11; Is 17:7, 8; 50:10 **10:21** [a]Is 7:3 [b]Is 9:6 **10:22** [a]Ro 9:27, 28 [b]Is 28:22; Da 9:27; Ro 9:28 **10:23** [a]Is 28:22; Da 9:27; Ro 9:28

**24** Therefore thus says Lord Yah-
weh of hosts, "O My people who in-
habit [a]Zion, [b]do not fear the Assyrian
[1]who [c]strikes you with the rod and
lifts up his staff against you, the way
Egypt *did.* **25** For in a very [a]little while
[b]My indignation *against you* will end
and My anger *will be directed* to their
destruction." **26** And Yahweh of hosts
will [a]waken a scourge against him
like the slaughter of [b]Midian at the
rock of Oreb; and His [c]staff will be
over the sea and He will lift it up [d]the
way *He did* in Egypt. **27** So it will be
in that day, *that* [1]his [a]burden will be
removed from your shoulders and his
yoke from your neck, and the yoke
will be broken because [b]of fatness.

**28** He has come against Aiath,
He has passed
through [a]Migron;
At [b]Michmash he deposited
his [c]baggage.

**29** They have gone
through [a]the pass, *saying,*
"[b]Geba will be our
lodging place."
[c]Ramah trembles, and [d]Gibeah
of Saul has fled away.

**30** Cry aloud with your voice,
O daughter of [a]Gallim!
Pay attention, Laishah *and*
[1]afflicted [b]Anathoth!

**31** Madmenah has fled.
The inhabitants of Gebim
have sought refuge.

**32** Yet today he will
stand at [a]Nob;
He [b]shakes his fist at the
mountain of the [c,1]daughter
of Zion, the hill of Jerusalem.

**33** Behold, the Lord, Yahweh of
hosts, will lop off the boughs
with a terrible crash;
Those also who are [a]high in
stature will be cut in pieces
And those who are lofty
will be made low.

**34** He will cut down the
thickets of the forest
with an iron *axe,*
And [a]Lebanon will fall
[1]by the Mighty One.

### *The Judgments of the Branch*

**11** Then a [a]shoot will spring
from the [b]stem of Jesse,
And a [c]branch from [d]his
roots will bear fruit.

**2** The [a]Spirit of Yahweh
will rest on Him,
The spirit of [b]wisdom
and understanding,
The spirit of counsel
and [c]might,
The spirit of knowledge
and the fear of Yahweh.

**3** And He will delight
in the fear of Yahweh,
And He will not judge
by what His eyes [a]see,
Nor render a decision
by what His ears hear;

**4** But with [a]righteousness He
will judge the [b]poor,

---

**10:24** [a]Ps 87:5, 6 [b]Is 7:4; 12:2; 37:6 [c]Ex 5:14-16 [1]Lit *he* **10:25** [a]Is 17:14; Hag 2:6 [b]Is 10:5; 26:20; Da 11:36 **10:26** [a]Is 37:36-38 [b]Jdg 7:25; Is 9:4 [c]Ex 14:16 [d]Ex 14:27 **10:27** [a]Is 9:4; 14:25 [b]Is 30:23; 55:2 [1]The Assyrian **10:28** [a]1Sa 14:2 [b]1Sa 13:2, 5 [c]Jdg 18:21; 1Sa 17:22 **10:29** [a]1Sa 13:23 [b]Jos 21:17; 1Sa 13:16 [c]Jos 18:25; 1Sa 7:17 [d]1Sa 10:26 **10:30** [a]1Sa 25:44 [b]Jos 21:18; Jer 1:1 [1]One ancient version *Answer her, O Anathoth* **10:32** [a]1Sa 21:1; 22:9 [b]Is 19:16; Zec 2:9 [c]Is 1:8; Jer 6:23 [1]Or *house of* **10:33** [a]Is 37:24, 36-38; Eze 31:3; Am 2:9 **10:34** [a]Is 2:13; 33:9; 37:24 [1]Or *as a mighty one* ♦ **11:1** [a]Is 4:2; 53:2 [b]Is 9:7; 11:10; Ac 13:23 [c]Is 6:13; Jer 23:5; Zec 3:8 [d]Rev 5:5; 22:16 **11:2** [a]Is 42:1; 48:16; 61:1; Mt 3:16; Jn 1:32 [b]Jn 16:13; 1Co 1:30; Eph 1:17, 18 [c]2Ti 1:7 **11:3** [a]Jn 2:25; 7:24 **11:4** [a]Is 9:7; 16:5; 32:1 [b]Ps 72:2, 13, 14; Is 3:14

And decide with uprightness
for the [c]afflicted
of the earth;
And He will strike the earth
with the [d]rod of His mouth,
And with the [e]breath of His
lips He will put
the wicked to death.
5 Also [a]righteousness will be
the belt about His loins,
And [b]faithfulness the
belt about His waist.

6 And the [a]wolf will [1]dwell
with the lamb,
And the leopard will lie down
with the young goat,
And the calf and
the young lion [2]and
the fatling together;
And a young boy will
lead them.
7 Also the cow and
the bear will graze,
Their young will lie
down together,
And the [a]lion will eat
straw like the ox.
8 And the nursing baby
will play by the hole
of the cobra,
And the weaned child will put
his hand on the viper's den.
9 They will [a]do no evil
nor act corruptly in all
My holy mountain,
For the [b]earth will be full
of the knowledge of Yahweh
As the waters cover the sea.

### *A Remnant Remains*

10 Then it will be in that day,
*That* the [a]nations will
seek the [b]root of Jesse,
Who will stand as a [c,1]standard
for the peoples;
And His [d]resting place
will be [2]glorious.

11 Then it will be in that
day, *that* the Lord
Will again acquire the second
time with His hand
The [a]remnant of His people,
who will remain,
From [b]Assyria, [c]Egypt,
Pathros, [1]Ethiopia, [d]Elam,
Shinar, Hamath,
And from the [e]coastlands
of the sea.
12 And He will lift up
a [a]standard for the nations
And [b]assemble the
banished ones of Israel,
And will gather the
scattered of Judah
From the four corners
of the earth.
13 Then the [a]jealousy
of Ephraim will depart,
And those who assail
Judah will be cut off;
Ephraim will not be
jealous of Judah,
And Judah will not
assail Ephraim.
14 And they will [a]swoop
down on the slopes of the
Philistines on the [b]west;

**11:4** [c]Is 29:19; 32:7; 61:1 [d]Ps 2:9; Is 49:2; Mal 4:6 [e]Job 4:9; Is 30:28, 33; 2Th 2:8 **11:5** [a]Eph 6:14 [b]Is 25:1 **11:6** [a]Is 65:25 [1]Lit *sojourn* [2]Some versions *will feed together* **11:7** [a]Is 65:25 **11:9** [a]Job 5:23; Is 65:25; Eze 34:25; Hos 2:18 [b]Ps 98:2, 3; Is 45:6; 52:10; 66:18-23; Hab 2:14 **11:10** [a]Lk 2:32; Ac 11:18 [b]Is 11:1; Ro 15:12 [c]Is 11:12; 49:22; 62:10; Jn 3:14, 15; 12:32 [d]Is 14:3; 28:12; 32:17, 18 [1]Or *signal* [2]Lit *glory* **11:11** [a]Is 10:20-22; 37:4, 31, 32; 46:3 [b]Is 19:23-25; Hos 11:11; Zec 10:10 [c]Is 19:21, 22; Mic 7:12 [d]Ge 10:22; 14:1 [e]Is 24:15; 42:4, 10, 12; 49:1; 51:5; 60:9; 66:19 [1]Or *Cush*, cf. Ge 10:6 **11:12** [a]Is 11:10 [b]Is 56:8; Zep 3:10; Zec 10:6 **11:13** [a]Is 9:21; Jer 3:18; Eze 37:16, 17, 22; Hos 1:11 **11:14** [a]Jer 48:40; 49:22; Hab 1:8 [b]Is 9:12

Together they will [c]plunder
the sons of the east;
[1]They will stretch out
their hands
*over* [d]Edom and [e]Moab,
And the sons of Ammon
[2]will obey them.
15 And Yahweh will [a]devote
to destruction
The tongue of the
[1]Sea of Egypt;
And He will [b]wave His
hand over the [c,2]River
With His scorching wind;
And He will strike it
into seven streams
And make *men* walk
over [3]dry-shod.
16 And there will be a
[a]highway from Assyria
For the [b]remnant of His
people who will remain,
Just as there was for Israel
In [c]the day that they came up
out of the land of Egypt.

### *Yahweh Is My Strength and My Song*

12 Then you will say in that day,
"[a]I will give thanks
to You, O Yahweh;
For [b]although You were
angry with me,
Your anger is turned away,
And You comfort me.
2 "Behold, [a]God is my salvation,
I will [b]trust and not dread;
For [c,1]Yah—Yahweh *Himself*—
is my strength and song,
And He has become
my salvation."
3 Therefore you will
joyously [a]draw water
From the [b]springs
of salvation.
4 And in that day you will [a]say,
"[b]Give thanks to Yahweh,
call on His name.
[c]Make known His deeds
among the peoples;
[1]Make *them* remember that
His name is exalted."
5 [a]Praise Yahweh in song, for He
has done [1]majestic things;
Let this be known
throughout the earth.
6 [a]Cry aloud and shout for joy,
O inhabitant of Zion,
For [b]great in your midst is
the Holy One of Israel.

### *An Oracle Concerning Babylon*

13 The [a,1]oracle concerning [b]Babylon which [c]Isaiah the son of
Amoz beheld.
2 [a]Lift up a standard
on the [b,1]bare hill,
Heighten your voice at them,
[c]Wave the hand that
they may [d]enter the
doors of the nobles.
3 I have commanded My
set apart ones,

**11:14** [c]Jer 49:28 [d]Is 63:1; Da 11:41; Joel 3:19; Am 9:12 [e]Is 16:14; 25:10 [1]Lit *Edom and Moab will be the outstretching of their hand* [2]Lit *their obedience* **11:15** [a]Is 43:16; 44:27; 50:2; 51:10, 11 [b]Is 19:16 [c]Is 7:20; 8:7; Rev 16:12 [1]Possibly the Red Sea [2]The Euphrates River [3]Lit *in sandals* **11:16** [a]Is 19:23; 35:8; 40:3; *62:10* [b]*Is 11:11* [c]*Ex 14:26-29* ◆ **12:1** [a]Ps 9:1; Is 25:1 [b]Ps 30:5; Is 40:1, 2; 54:7-10 **12:2** [a]Is 32:2; 45:17; 62:11 [b]Is 26:3 [c]Ex 15:2; Ps 118:14 [1]The shortened form of Yahweh, found in poetry and praise (e.g. Hallelu*jah*), and in names (e.g. Zechar*iah*) **12:3** [a]Jn 4:10; 7:37, 38 [b]Is 41:18; Jer 2:13 **12:4** [a]Is 24:15; 42:12; 48:20 [b]Ps 105:1 [c]Ps 145:4 [1]Or *Proclaim* to them *that* **12:5** [a]Ex 15:1; Ps 98:1; Is 24:14; 42:10, 11; 44:23 [1]Or *gloriously* **12:6** [a]Is 52:9; 54:1; Zep 3:14 [b]Is 1:24; 49:26; 60:16; Zep 3:15-17; Zec 2:5, 10, 11 ◆ **13:1** [a]Is 14:28; 15:1 [b]Is 13:19; 14:4; 47:1-15; Jer 24:1; 50:1-51:64; Mt 1:11; Rev 14:8 [c]Is 1:1 [1]Or *burden of* **13:2** [a]Is 5:26; Jer 50:2 [b]Jer 51:25 [c]Is 10:32; 19:16 [d]Is 45:1-3; Jer 51:58 [1]Or *wind-swept mountain*

I have even called My
[a]mighty warriors,
My [1]proudly exulting ones,
To *execute* My anger.
4 A [a]sound of tumult
on the mountains,
Like that of many people!
A sound of the rumbling
of kingdoms,
Of nations
gathered together!
Yahweh of hosts is mustering
the host for battle.
5 They are coming
from a far country,
From the [a]end of the sky,
Yahweh and His instruments
of [b]indignation,
To [c]wreak destruction
*on* the whole land.
6 Wail, for the [a]day
of Yahweh is near!
It will come as [b]destruction
from [1]the Almighty.
7 Therefore [a]all hands
will fall limp,
And every man's
[b]heart will melt.
8 They will be [a]terrified,
Pains and labor pangs will
take hold of *them*;
They will [b]writhe
like a woman in labor,
They will look at one another
in astonishment,
Their faces aflame.
9 Behold, [a]the day
of Yahweh is coming,
Cruel, with fury and
burning anger,
To make the land a desolation;
And He will exterminate
its sinners from it.
10 For the [a]stars of heaven
and their constellations
Will not flash forth
their light;
The [b]sun will be dark
when it rises
And the moon will not
shed its light.
11 Thus I will [a]punish
the world for its evil
And the [b]wicked
for their iniquity;
I will also put an end
to the [c]pride of the arrogant
And bring low the [d]lofty
pride of the [e,1]ruthless.
12 I will make mortal man
[a,1]scarcer than fine gold
And mankind than the
[b]gold of Ophir.
13 Therefore I will make
the [a]heavens tremble,
And [b]the earth will be
shaken from its place
At the fury of Yahweh of hosts
In [c]the day of His
burning anger.
14 And it will be that
like a hunted gazelle,
Or like [a]sheep with none
to gather *them*,
They will each turn
to his own people,

---

**13:3** [a]Joel 3:11 [1]Lit *lofty pride*, cf. 13:11 **13:4** [a]Is 5:30; 17:12; Joel 3:14 **13:5** [a]Is 5:26; 7:18 [b]Is 10:5 [c]Is 24:1 **13:6** [a]Is 2:12; 10:3; 13:9; 34:2, 8; 61:2; Eze 30:3; Am 5:18; Zep 1:7 [b]Is 10:25; 14:23; Joel 1:15 [1]Heb *Shaddai* **13:7** [a]Eze 7:17 [b]Is 19:1; Eze 21:7; Na 2:10 **13:8** [a]2Ki 19:26; Is 21:3; Jer 46:5 [b]Is 26:17; Jer 4:31; Jn 16:21 **13:9** [a]Is 13:6 **13:10** [a]Is 5:30; Eze 32:7; Joel 2:10; Mt 24:29; Mk 13:24; Lk 21:25; Rev 6:13; 8:12 [b]Is 24:23; 50:3; Eze 32:7; Ac 2:20; Rev 6:12 **13:11** [a]Is 26:21 [b]Is 3:11; 11:4; 14:5 [c]Is 2:11; 23:9; Da 5:22, 23 [d]Jer 48:29 [e]Is 25:3; 29:5, 20 [1]Or *tyrants, despots* **13:12** [a]Is 4:1; 6:11, 12 [b]1Ki 9:28; Job 28:16; Ps 45:9 [1]Lit *more precious* **13:13** [a]Is 34:4; 51:6 [b]Ps 18:7; Is 2:19; 24:1, 19, 20; Hag 2:6 [c]Lam 1:12 **13:14** [a]1Ki 22:17; Mt 9:36; Mk 6:34; 1Pe 2:25

And each one flee
to his own land.
**15** Anyone who is found will
be [a]pierced through,
And anyone who is captured
will fall by the sword.
**16** Their [a]infants also will
be dashed to pieces
Before their eyes;
Their houses will be plundered
And their wives ravished.

**17** Behold, I am going to [a]awaken
the Medes against them,
Who will not think
about silver or [b]take
pleasure in gold.
**18** And *their* bows will dash
the [a]young men to pieces,
They will not even have
compassion on the
fruit of the womb,
*Nor* will their [b]eye
pity [1]children.
**19** And it will be that
[a]Babylon, the [b]beauty
of kingdoms, the [1]honor
of the Chaldeans' pride,
Will be as when God
[c]overthrew Sodom
and Gomorrah.
**20** It will [a]never be inhabited or
dwelt in from generation
to generation;
Nor will the [b,1]Arab
pitch *his* tent there,
Nor will shepherds make
*their flocks* lie down there.
**21** But [a]desert creatures
will lie down there,
And their houses will
be full of [1]owls;
Ostriches also will dwell
there, and [2]shaggy
goats will leap there.
**22** [1]And hyenas will howl
in their fortified towers
And jackals in their
luxurious [a]palaces.
Her *fateful* time also
[2]will soon come
And her days will not
be prolonged.

### *Israel's Restoration and Dominion*

**14** When Yahweh will [a]have com-
passion on Jacob and again
[b]choose Israel, and [1]put them in their
own land, then [c]sojourners will join
them and attach themselves to the
house of Jacob. **2** And the peoples will
take them along and bring them to
their place, and the [a]house of Israel
will possess them as an inheritance
in the land of Yahweh [b]for *their* male
and female slaves; and [1]they will take
their captors captive and will have
dominion over their taskmasters.
**3** And it will be in the day when
Yahweh gives you [a]rest from your
pain and turmoil and harsh slavery in
which you have been enslaved, **4** that
you will [a]take up this [1]taunt against
the king of Babylon, and say,
"How [b]the taskmaster
has ceased,

**13:15** [a]Is 14:19; Jer 50:25; 51:3, 4 **13:16** [a]Ps 137:8, 9; Is 13:18; 14:21; Hos 10:14; Na 3:10 **13:17** [a]Jer 51:11; *Da 5:28* [b]*Pr 6:34, 35* **13:18** [a]2Ki 8:12; 2Chr 36:17 [b]Eze 9:5, 10 [1]Lit *sons* **13:19** [a]Is 21:9; 48:14 [b]Da 4:30; Rev 18:11-16, 19, 21 [c]Ge 19:24; Dt 29:23; Jer 49:18; Am 4:11 [1]Lit *beautiful glory* **13:20** [a]Is 14:23; 34:10-15; Jer 51:37-43 [b]2Chr 17:11 [1]Or *nomad* **13:21** [a]Is 34:11-15; Zep 2:14; Rev 18:2 [1]Or *howling creatures* [2]Or *goat demons* **13:22** [a]Is 25:2; 32:14; 34:13 [1]Or *howling creatures* [2]Lit *is near to come* ◆ **14:1** [a]Ps 102:13; Is 49:13, 15; 54:7, 8 [b]Is 41:8, 9; 44:1; 49:7; Zec 1:17; 2:12 [c]Is 56:3, 6; Eph 2:12-19 [1]Or *give them rest*, cf. 14:3, 7 **14:2** [a]Is 45:14; 49:23; 54:3 [b]Is 60:10; 61:5; Da 7:18, 27 [1]Lit *the captors will become their captives* **14:3** [a]Ezr 9:8, 9; Is 11:10; 40:2; Jer 30:10; 46:27 **14:4** [a]Hab 2:6 [b]Is 9:4; 16:4; 49:26; 51:13; 54:14 [1]Or *proverb*

*And how* [2]fury has ceased!
5 "Yahweh has broken
the staff of the wicked,
The scepter of rulers
6 [a]Which used to strike
the peoples in fury
with unceasing strokes,
Which had dominion over
the nations in anger with
unrestrained persecution.
7 "The whole earth is
at rest *and* is quiet;
They [a]break forth
into shouts of joy.
8 "Even the [a]cypress trees are
glad over you, *and* the cedars
of Lebanon, *saying*,
'Since you were laid low,
no *tree* cutter comes
up against us.'
9 "[a]Sheol from beneath trembles
*excitedly* over you to meet
you when you come;
It wakens for you
the [1]spirits of the dead,
all the [2]leaders of the earth;
It raises all the kings of the
nations from their thrones.
10 "[a]They will all answer
and say to you,
'Even you have been
made weak as we,
You have become like us.
11 'Your [a]pride *and* the
music of your harps
Have been brought
down to Sheol;
Maggots are spread out
*as your bed* beneath you
And worms are your covering.'
12 "How you have [a]fallen
from heaven,
O [b,1]star of the morning,
son of the dawn!
You have been cut
down to the earth,
You who have weakened
the nations!
13 "But you said in your heart,
'I will [a]ascend to heaven;
I will [b]raise my throne
above the stars of God,
And I will sit on the
mount of assembly
In the recesses of the north.
14 'I will ascend above
the heights of the clouds;
[a]I will make myself
like the Most High.'
15 "Nevertheless you
[a]will be brought
down to Sheol,
To the recesses of the pit.
16 "Those who see you
will gaze at you,
They will [1]carefully
consider you, *saying*,
'Is this the man who made
the earth tremble,
Who caused kingdoms
to quake,
17 Who made the world
like a [a]wilderness
And pulled down
its cities,
Who [b]did not [1]allow his
prisoners to *go* home?'
18 "All the kings of the
nations lie in glory,
Each in his own [1]place.

**14:4** [2]Amended from the meaningless *medhebah* to *marhebah* **14:6** [a]Is 10:14; 47:6 **14:7** [a]Ps 47:1-3; 98:1-9; 126:1-3 **14:8** [a]Is 55:12; Eze 31:16 **14:9** [a]Is 5:14 [1]Or *shades* [2]Lit *male goats* **14:10** [a]Eze 32:21 **14:11** [a]Is 5:14 **14:12** [a]Is 34:4; Lk 10:18; Rev 8:10; 9:1 [b]2Pe 1:19; Rev 2:28; 22:16 [1]Heb *Helel*; lit *shining one* **14:13** [a]Eze 28:2 [b]Da 5:22, 23; 8:10; 2Th 2:4 **14:14** [a]Is 47:8; 2Th 2:4 **14:15** [a]Eze 28:8; Mt 11:23; Lk 10:15 **14:16** [1]Lit *show themselves attentive to* **14:17** [a]Joel 2:3 [b]Is 45:13 [1]Lit *open* **14:18** [1]Lit *house*

19 “But you have been [a]cast
out of your grave
Like an abhorred branch,
[1]Clothed with those killed who
are pierced with a sword,
Who go down to the stones
of the [b]pit
Like a [c]trampled corpse.
20 “You will not be united
with them in burial,
Because you have ruined
your country,
You have killed your people.
May the [a]seed of evildoers
not be called upon forever.
21 “Prepare for his sons
a place of slaughter
Because of the [a]iniquity
of their fathers.
They must not arise and take
possession of the earth
And fill the face of
the world with cities.”

22 “I will rise up against them,”
declares Yahweh of hosts, “and will
cut off from Babylon [a]name and
remnant, [b]offspring and posterity,”
declares Yahweh. 23 “I will also make
it a possession for the [a]hedgehog and
swamps of water, and I will sweep
it with the broom of [b,1]destruction,”
declares Yahweh of hosts.

### *Yahweh’s Plan to Break Assyrian Rule*

24 Yahweh of hosts has sworn saying,
“Surely, [a]just as I have intended so
it has happened, and just as I have
counseled so it will stand, 25 to [a]break
Assyria in My land, and I will trod
him down on My mountains. Then
his [b]yoke will be removed from them
and his burden removed from their
shoulder. 26 This is the [a]counsel that is
counseled against the whole earth; and
this is the [b]hand that is stretched out
against all the nations. 27 For [a]Yahweh
of hosts has counseled, and who can
thwart *it*? And as for His stretched-out
hand, who can turn it back?”

### *An Oracle Concerning Philistia*

28 In the [a]year that King Ahaz died
this [b,1]oracle came:
29 “Do not be glad, O [a]Philistia,
all of you,
Because the rod that
[b]struck you is broken;
For from the serpent’s root
a [c]viper will come out,
And its fruit will be a
[d]flying fiery serpent.
30 “[1]And the foremost
[a]of the poor will eat,
And the needy will lie
down in security;
I will put to death your
root with [b]famine,
And it will kill off
your remnant.
31 “Wail, O [a]gate; cry, O city;
[1]Melt away, O [b]Philistia,
all of you;
For smoke comes
from the [c]north,
And [d]there is no straggler
in his ranks.

**14:19** [a]Is 22:16-18 [b]Jer 41:7, 9 [c]Is 5:25 [1]Or *As the clothing of those who are slain* **14:20** [a]Job 18:16, 19; Ps 21:10; 37:28; Is 1:4; 31:2 **14:21** [a]Ex 20:5; Lv 26:39; Is 13:16; Mt 23:35 **14:22** [a]Pr 10:7 [b]Job 18:19; Is 47:9 **14:23** [a]Is 34:11; Zep 2:14 [b]1Ki 14:10; Is 13:6 [1]Or *extermination*, cf. 13:9 **14:24** [a]Job 23:13; Is 46:11; 55:8, 9; Ac 4:28 **14:25** [a]Is 10:12; 30:31; 31:8 [b]Is 9:4; 10:27; Na 1:13 **14:26** [a]Is 23:9; Zep 3:6, 8 [b]Ex 15:12 **14:27** [a]2Chr 20:6; Is 43:13; Da 4:31, 35 **14:28** [a]2Ki 16:20; 2Chr 28:27 [b]Is 13:1 [1]Or *burden* **14:29** [a]Is 2:6; 11:14; Jer 47:1-7; Eze 25:15-17; Joel 3:4-8; Am 1:6-8; Zep 2:4-7; Zec 9:5-7 [b]2Chr 26:6 [c]Is 11:8 [d]Is 30:6 **14:30** [a]Is 3:14, 15; 7:21, 22; 11:4 [b]Is 8:21; 9:20; 51:19 [1]Lit *The firstborn of the poor* **14:31** [a]Is 3:26; 24:12; 45:2 [b]Is 14:29 [c]Jer 1:14 [d]Is 34:16 [1]Or *Become demoralized*

32 "How then will one answer the
[a]messengers of the nation?
That [b]Yahweh has
founded Zion,
And [c]the afflicted of His
people will take refuge in it."

### *An Oracle Concerning Moab*

15 The [1]oracle concerning [a]Moab.
Surely in a night [b]Ar of Moab
is destroyed *and* ruined;
Surely in a night Kir of Moab
is destroyed *and* ruined.
2 They have gone up to the
[1]temple and *to* [a]Dibon, *even*
to the high places to weep.
Moab wails over Nebo
and Medeba;
Everyone's head is [b]bald *and*
every beard is cut off.
3 In their streets they have
girded themselves
with [a]sackcloth;
[b]On their rooftops and
in their squares
Everyone is wailing,
[c,1]dissolved in weeping.
4 [a]Heshbon and Elealeh
also cry out,
Their voice is heard all
the way to Jahaz;
Therefore [1]the armed men
of Moab make a loud shout;
His soul trembles within him.
5 My heart cries out for Moab;
Those who flee *from* her
are as far as [a]Zoar *and*
Eglath-shelishiyah,
For they go up the [b]ascent
of Luhith weeping;
Surely on the road to
Horonaim they keep awake
with crying in distress
[c]over *their* destruction.
6 For the [a]waters of Nimrim
are [1]desolate.
Surely the grass is dried
up, the tender grass has
[2]completely ceased,
There is [b]no green thing.
7 Therefore the [a]abundance they
have made and stored up
They carry off over the brook
of [1]Arabim.
8 For the cry has gone
around the territory of Moab,
Its wailing *goes* as far
as Eglaim and its wailing
even to Beer-elim.
9 For the waters of Dimon
are full of [1]blood;
Surely I will put added
*woes* upon Dimon,
A [a]lion upon those of Moab
who have escaped
and upon the remnant
of the land.

16 [a]Send the *tribute* lamb
to the ruler of the land,
From [b,1]Sela by way of the
wilderness to the [c]mountain
of the daughter of Zion.
2 Then, like [a,1]fleeing birds
*or* scattered [2]nestlings,
The daughters of [b]Moab will
be at the fords of the [c]Arnon.

**14:32** [a]Is 37:9 [b]Ps 87:1, 5; 102:16; Is 28:16; 44:28; 54:11 [c]Is 4:6; 25:4; 57:13; Zep 3:12; Heb 11:10; Jas 2:5
◆**15:1** [a]Is 11:14; 25:10; Jer 48:1; Eze 25:8-11; Am 2:1-3; Zep 2:8-11 [b]Nu 21:28 [1]Or *burden of*
**15:2** [a]Jer 48:18, 22 [b]Lv 21:5; Jer 48:37 [1]Lit *house* **15:3** [a]Jon 3:6-8 [b]Jer 48:38 [c]Is 22:4 [1]Lit *going down in weeping* **15:4** [a]Nu 21:28; 32:3; Jer 48:34 [1]Or *the loins of* **15:5** [a]Jer 48:34 [b]Jer 48:5 [c]Is 59:7; Jer 4:20 **15:6** [a]Is 19:5-7; Jer 48:34 [b]Joel 1:10-12; 2:3 [1]Lit *desolations* [2]Lit *come to an end*
**15:7** [a]Is 30:6; Jer 48:36 [1]Or *the poplars* **15:9** [a]2Ki 17:25; Jer 50:17 [1]Heb *dam* (a wordplay)
◆**16:1** [a]2Ki 3:4; Ezr 7:17 [b]2Ki 14:7; Is 42:11 [c]Is 10:32 [1]Petra in Edom **16:2** [a]Pr 27:8 [b]Jer 48:20, 46 [c]Nu 21:13, 14 [1]Or *fluttering* [2]Lit *nest*

3 "Bring *us* counsel,
make a decision;
[1]Cast your [a]shadow
like night [2]at high noon;
[b]Hide those banished,
do not reveal the one
who flees.
4 "Let the [1]banished of Moab
sojourn with you;
Be a hiding place to them
from the destroyer."
For the extortioner
has come to an end,
destruction has ceased,
[a]Oppressors have completely
*disappeared* from the land.
5 And a [a]throne will
be established
in lovingkindness,
And a judge will sit on it
in truth in the tent of [b]David;
Moreover, he will seek justice
And be prompt
in righteousness.

6 [a]We have heard of the pride
of Moab, an excessive pride;
*Even* of his lofty pride,
pride, and fury;
[b]His idle boasts are [1]false.
7 Therefore Moab will wail;
everyone of Moab will wail.
You will moan for the [a]raisin
cakes of [b]Kir-hareseth
As those who are
utterly stricken.
8 For the fields of [a]Heshbon
have languished, the vines
of [b]Sibmah *as well*;
The lords of the nations
have trampled down
its choice clusters
Which reached as far as Jazer
*and* wandered to the deserts;
[c]Its tendrils spread themselves
out *and* passed over the sea.
9 Therefore I will [a]weep
bitterly for Jazer,
for the vine of Sibmah;
I will drench you
with my tears, O [b]Heshbon
and Elealeh;
For the shouting over your
[c]summer fruits and your
harvest has fallen away.
10 [a]Gladness and joy are
taken away from
the fruitful orchard;
In the [b]vineyards also there
will be no cries of joy or
shouts of jubilation,
No [c]treader treads out
wine in the presses,
*For* I have made the
shouting to cease.
11 Therefore my [a,1]inner being
moans like a harp for Moab
And my [2]inward feelings
for Kir-hareseth.
12 So it will be
when Moab [a]appears,
When he [b]wearies himself
upon *his* [c]high place
And comes to his
sanctuary to pray,
That he will not prevail.
13 This is the word which Yahweh
spoke earlier concerning Moab. 14 But

***16:3*** [a]Is 25:4; 32:2 [b]1Ki 18:4 [1]Lit *Set* [2]Lit *in the midst of the noon* **16:4** [a]Is 9:4; 14:4; 49:26; 51:13; 54:14 [1]As in the versions; M.T. *My banished ones, as for Moab* **16:5** [a]Is 9:6, 7; 32:1; 55:4; Da 7:14; Mic 4:7; Lk 1:33 [b]Is 9:7 **16:6** [a]Jer 48:29; Am 2:1; Ob 3, 4; Zep 2:8, 10 [b]Jer 48:30 [1]Lit *not so* **16:7** [a]1Chr 16:3 [b]2Ki 3:25; Jer 48:31 **16:8** [a]Is 15:4 [b]Nu 32:38 [c]Jer 48:32 **16:9** [a]Jer 48:32 [b]Is 15:4 [c]Jer 40:10, 12; 48:32 **16:10** [a]Is 24:8; Jer 48:33 [b]Jdg 9:27; Is 24:7; Am 5:11, 17 [c]Job 24:11; Am 9:13 **16:11** [a]Is 15:5; 63:15; Jer 48:36; Hos 11:8; Php 2:1 [1]Lit *entrails murmur* [2]Lit *inward part* **16:12** [a]Nu 22:39-41; Jer 48:35 [b]1Ki 18:29 [c]Is 15:2

now Yahweh speaks, saying, "Within three years, as [a,1]a hired man would count them, the glory of [b]Moab will be dishonored along with all *his* great population, and *his* remnant will be very small *and* not mighty."

### *An Oracle Concerning Damascus*

**17** The [a,1]oracle concerning [b]Damascus.
"Behold, Damascus is
about to be [c]removed
from being a city
And will become a [d]fallen ruin.
2 "The cities [1]of [a]Aroer
are forsaken;
They will be for [b]flocks, and
they will lie down in *them*;
And there will be [c]no one
to cause *them* to tremble.
3 "And the [a,1]fortified city will
cease from Ephraim,
And [2]sovereignty
from Damascus
And the remnant of Aram;
They will be like the [b]glory
of the sons of Israel,"
Declares Yahweh of hosts.

4 Now it will be in that
day, *that* the [a]glory
of Jacob will [1]wane,
And [b]the fatness of his
flesh will become lean.
5 *And it* will be [a]even
like the [1]reaper gathering
the standing grain,
As his arm harvests
the ears of grain,
Or it will be like one
gleaning ears of grain
In the [b]valley of Rephaim.
6 Yet [a]gleanings will remain
in it like the [1]shaking
of an olive tree,
Two *or* three olives
on the topmost branch,
Four *or* five on the twigs
of a fruitful tree,
Declares Yahweh,
the God of Israel.
7 In that day man will [a]have
regard for his Maker
And his eyes will look
to the Holy One of Israel.
8 He will not have regard
for the [a]altars,
the work of his hands,
Nor will he look to that
which his [b]fingers have made,
Even the [c,1]Asherim and
[2]incense stands.
9 In that day [1]their strong
cities will be like [2]forsaken
places in the forest,
Or like [3]branches
which they forsook
before the sons of Israel;
And [4]the land will be
a desolation.
10 For [a]you have forgotten
the [b]God of your salvation
And have not remembered the
[c]rock of your strong defense.

**16:14** [a]Job 7:1; 14:6; Is 21:16 [b]Is 25:10; Jer 48:42 [1]Lit *the years of a hireling* ◆ **17:1** [a]Is 13:1 [b]Ge 14:15; 15:2; 2Ki 16:9; Jer 49:23; Am 1:3-5; Zec 9:1; Ac 9:2 [c]Is 7:16; 8:4; 10:9 [d]Is 25:2; Jer 49:2; Mic 1:6 [1]Or *burden of* **17:2** [a]Nu 32:34 [b]Is 7:21, 22; Eze 25:5; Zep 2:6 [c]Mic 4:4 [1]Gr *forever and ever* **17:3** [a]Is 7:8, 16; 8:4 [b]Is 17:4; Hos 9:11 [1]Or *fortification* [2]Or *royal power, kingdom* **17:4** [a]Is 10:3 [b]Is 10:16 [1]Lit *become thin* **17:5** [a]Is 17:11; Jer 51:33; Joel 3:13; Mt 13:30 [b]2Sa 5:18, 22 [1]Lit *gathering of the harvest, the standing grain* **17:6** [a]Dt 4:27; Is 24:13; 27:12; Ob 5 [1]Lit *striking* **17:7** [a]Is 10:20; Hos 3:5; 6:1; Mic 7:7 **17:8** [a]2Chr 34:7; Is 27:9 [b]Is 2:8, 20; 30:22; 31:7 [c]Ex 34:13; Dt 7:5; Mic 5:14 [1]Wooden symbols of a female deity [2]Or *sun pillars* **17:9** [1]Man's [2]Gr *the deserted places of the Amorites and the Hivites which they abandoned* [3]Or *the treetop* [4]Lit *it* **17:10** [a]Is 51:13 [b]Ps 68:19; Is 12:2; 33:2; 61:10; 62:11 [c]Dt 32:4, 18, 31; Is 26:4; 30:29; 44:8

Therefore you plant
delightful plants
And set them with vine
branches of a strange *god*.
11 In the day that you plant *it*
you carefully fence *it* in,
And in the [a]morning
you cause your seed
to flourish;
*But* the harvest will
[b]*be* a heap
In a day of sickliness
and incurable pain.

12 Alas, the uproar
of many peoples
[a]Who roar like the
roaring of the seas,
And the rumbling of nations
Who rumble on
like the [b]rumbling
of mighty waters!
13 The [a]nations rumble
on like the rumbling
of many waters,
But He will [b]rebuke them,
and they will flee far away,
And be pursued
[c]like chaff in the mountains
before the wind,
Or like whirling dust
before a whirlwind.
14 At evening time, behold,
*there is* terror!
Before morning [a]they
are no more.
[1]Such *will be* the portion
of those who pillage us
And the lot of those
who plunder us.

### *A Message to Ethiopia*

18 Alas, O land of
whirring wings
Which lies beyond the
rivers of [a,1]Ethiopia,
2 Which sends envoys
by the sea,
Even in [a]papyrus vessels
on the surface of the waters.
Go, swift messengers,
to a nation [b,1]tall and smooth,
To a people [c]feared
[2]far and wide,
A powerful and
oppressive nation
Whose land the rivers divide.
3 [a]All you inhabitants of the
world and dwellers on earth,
As soon as a standard is
raised on the mountains,
[b]you will see *it*,
And as soon as the trumpet
is blown, you will hear *it*.
4 For thus Yahweh has told me,
"I will look [1]from My
[a]dwelling place quietly
Like dazzling heat
in the [b,2]sunshine,
Like a cloud of [c]dew
in the heat of harvest."
5 For [a]before the harvest,
as soon as the bud [1]blossoms
And the flower becomes
a ripening grape,
Then He will cut off the
sprigs with pruning knives
And remove *and* cut away
the spreading branches.
6 They will be left together
for mountain birds [a]of prey,

---

**17:11** [a]Ps 90:6 [b]Job 4:8; Hos 8:7; 10:13 **17:12** [a]Is 5:30; Jer 6:23; Eze 43:2; Lk 21:25 [b]Ps 18:4 **17:13** [a]Is 33:3 [b]Ps 9:5; Is 41:11 [c]Job 21:18; Ps 1:4; 83:13; Is 29:5; 41:15, 16 **17:14** [a]2Ki 19:35; Is 41:12 [1]Lit *This* ◆ **18:1** [a]2Ki 19:9; Is 20:3-5; Eze 30:4, 5, 9; Zep 2:12; 3:10 [1]Or *Cush*, cf. Ge 10:6 **18:2** [a]Ex 2:3 [b]Is 18:7 [c]Ge 10:8, 9; 2Chr 12:2-4; 14:9; 16:8 [1]Lit *drawn out* [2]Lit *from it and beyond* **18:3** [a]Ps 49:1; Mic 1:2 [b]Is 26:11 **18:4** [a]Is 26:21; Hos 5:15 [b]2Sa 23:4 [c]Pr 19:12; Is 26:19; Hos 14:5 [1]Lit *in* [2]Lit *light* **18:5** [a]Is 17:10, 11; Eze 17:6-10 [1]Lit *is finished* **18:6** [a]Is 46:11; 56:9; Jer 7:33; Eze 32:4-6; 39:17-20

And for the beasts of the earth;
And the birds of prey
will spend the summer
*feeding* on them,
And all the beasts
of the earth will spend
harvest time on them.
7 At that time a gift
of homage will be brought
to Yahweh of hosts
[1]From a [a]people [2]tall
and smooth,
Even from a people
feared [3]far and wide,
A powerful and
oppressive nation,
Whose land the
rivers divide—
To the [b]place of the name
of Yahweh of hosts,
*even* Mount Zion.

### *An Oracle Concerning Egypt*

19 The [a,1]oracle concerning [b]Egypt.
Behold, Yahweh is [c]riding
on a swift cloud and is
about to come to Egypt;
The [d]idols of Egypt will
shake at His presence,
And the [e]heart of the
Egyptians will melt
within them.
2 "So I will incite Egyptians
against Egyptians;
And they will [a]each fight
against his brother and
each against his neighbor,
City against city *and* kingdom
against kingdom.
3 "Then the spirit
of the Egyptians will be
emptied to destruction
within them;
And I will confuse
their counsel,
So that [a]they will seek idols
and ghosts of the dead
And to [1]mediums
and spiritists.
4 "Moreover, I will deliver
the Egyptians into
the hand of a [a]cruel master,
And a [1]strong king will rule
over them," declares
the Lord, Yahweh of hosts.

5 [a]The waters
from the sea will dry up,
And the river will be
parched and dry.
6 The [a]rivers will emit
a stench,
The [b,1]streams of Egypt will
thin out and dry up;
[c]The reeds and rushes
will rot away.
7 The bulrushes by the [a]Nile,
by the [1]edge of the Nile
And all the sown fields
by the Nile
Will become dry, be driven
away, and be no more.
8 And the [a]fishermen
will lament,
And all those who cast a [1]line
into the Nile will mourn,
And those who spread nets
on the waters will [2]languish.

---

**18:7** [a]Ps 68:31; Is 45:14; Zep 3:10; Ac 8:27-38 [b]Zec 14:16, 17 [1]As in DSS and some ancient versions; M.T. implies *Consisting of a people* [2]Lit *drawn out* [3]Lit *from it and beyond* ◆ **19:1** [a]Is 13:1 [b]Joel 3:19 [c]Ps 18:9, 10; 104:3; Mt 26:64; Rev 1:7 [d]Ex 12:12; Jer 43:12; 44:8 [e]Jos 2:11; Is 13:7 [1]Or *burden of* **19:2** [a]Jdg 7:22; 1Sa 14:20; 2Chr 20:23; Mt 10:21, 36 **19:3** [a]1Chr 10:13; Is 8:19; Da 2:2 [1]Or *ghosts and spirits* **19:4** [a]Is 20:4; Jer 46:26; Eze 29:19 [1]Or *fierce* **19:5** [a]Is 50:2; Jer 51:36; Eze 30:12 **19:6** [a]Ex 7:18 [b]Is 37:25 [c]Ex 2:3; Job 8:11; Is 15:6 [1]The delta; or *Nile branches* **19:7** [a]Is 23:3, 10 [1]Or *mouth* **19:8** [a]Eze 47:10; Hab 1:15 [1]Lit *hook* [2]Or *pine away*

9 Moreover, the manufacturers
of linen made
from combed flax
And the weavers of white
[a]cloth will be ashamed.
10 And [1]the [a]pillars *of Egypt*
will be crushed;
All the hired laborers will
be grieved in soul.

11 The princes of [a,1]Zoan are
merely ignorant fools;
The counsel of Pharaoh's
wisest counselors has
become [2]senseless.
How can you *men*
say to Pharaoh,
"I am a son of the [b]wise,
a son of the kings of old"?
12 Well then, where are
your wise men?
Please let them tell you,
And let them [1]understand
what Yahweh of hosts
Has [a]counseled
against Egypt.
13 The princes of [1]Zoan have
acted as ignorant fools,
The princes of [a]Memphis
are deluded;
*Those who are* the
[b]cornerstone of her tribes
[2]Have led Egypt astray.
14 Yahweh has mixed within her
a spirit of [a]distortion;
[b]They have led Egypt astray
in all [1]that it does,
As a [c]drunken man [2]strays
into his vomit.
15 There will be no
work for Egypt
[a]Which *its* head or tail,
*its* palm branch or
bulrush, may do.

### *Yahweh Will Bless Egypt, Assyria, and Israel*

16 In that day the Egyptians will
become like women, and they will
tremble and be in [a]dread because of
the [b]waving of the hand of Yahweh of
hosts, which He is going to wave over
them. 17 And the land of Judah will
become a [1]terror to Egypt; everyone
[2]to whom it is mentioned will be in
dread of it because of the [a]counsel
of Yahweh of hosts which He is
counseling against them.
18 In that day five cities in the
land of Egypt will be speaking the
language of Canaan and [a]swearing
*allegiance* to Yahweh of hosts; one
will be called the City of [1]Destruction.
19 In that day there will be an [a]altar
to Yahweh in the midst of the land of
Egypt, and a [b]pillar to Yahweh near
its border. 20 And it will become
a sign and a witness to Yahweh of
hosts in the land of Egypt; for they
will cry to Yahweh because of op-
pressors, and He will send them a
[a]Savior and a [b,1]Champion, and He
will deliver them. 21 Thus Yahweh
will make Himself known to Egypt,
and the Egyptians will know Yahweh
in that day. They will even worship
with [a]sacrifice and offering, and they
will make a vow to Yahweh and pay

**19:9** [a]Pr 7:16; Eze 27:7 **19:10** [a]Ps 11:3 [1]Lit *her pillars* **19:11** [a]Nu 13:22; Ps 78:12, 43; Is 30:4 [b]Ge 41:38, 39; 1Ki 4:30; Ac 7:22 [1]Or *Tanis* [2]Or *brutish* **19:12** [a]Is 14:24; Ro 9:17 [1]Or *know* **19:13** [a]Jer 2:16; 46:14, 19; Eze 30:13 [b]Zec 10:4 [1]Or *Tanis* [2]Or *Have caused Egypt to stagger* **19:14** [a]Pr 12:8; Mt 17:17 [b]Is 3:12; 9:16 [c]Is 28:7 [1]Lit *its work* [2]Or *goes astray* **19:15** [a]Is 9:14, 15 **19:16** [a]2Co 5:11; Heb 10:31 [b]Is 11:15 **19:17** [a]Is 14:24; Da 4:35 [1]Or *cause of shame* [2]Lit *who mentions it will be in dread to it* **19:18** [a]Is 45:23; 65:16 [1]Some ancient mss and versions *the Sun* **19:19** [a]Is 56:7; 60:7 [b]Ge 28:18; Ex 24:4; Jos 22:10, 26, 27 **19:20** [a]Is 43:3, 11; 45:15, 21; 49:26; 60:16; 63:8 [b]Is 49:25 [1]Lit *Mighty One* **19:21** [a]Is 56:7; 60:7; Zec 14:16-18

it. **22** And Yahweh will smite Egypt, smiting but [a]healing; so they will [b]return to Yahweh, and He will be moved by their entreaty and will heal them.

**23** In that day there will be a [a]highway from Egypt to Assyria, and the Assyrians will come into Egypt and the Egyptians into Assyria, and the Egyptians will [b]worship with the Assyrians.

**24** In that day Israel will be the third *party* with Egypt and Assyria, a blessing in the midst of the earth, **25** whom Yahweh of hosts has blessed, saying, "Blessed is [a]Egypt My people, and Assyria [b]the work of My hands, and Israel My inheritance."

### *A Prophecy About Egypt and Ethiopia*

**20** In the year that the [a,1]commander came to [b]Ashdod, when Sargon the king of Assyria sent him and he fought against Ashdod and captured it, **2** at that time Yahweh spoke by the hand of [a]Isaiah the son of Amoz, saying, "Go and loosen the [b]sackcloth from your hips and take your [c]shoes off your feet." And he did so, going [d]naked and barefoot. **3** And Yahweh said, "Even as My servant Isaiah has gone naked and barefoot three years as a [a]sign and wonder against Egypt and [b,1]Ethiopia, **4** so the [a]king of Assyria will lead away the captives of Egypt and the exiles of Ethiopia, [b]young and old, naked and barefoot with buttocks uncovered, to the [1]shame of Egypt. **5** Then they will be [a]dismayed and ashamed because of Ethiopia their hope and Egypt their [b]boast. **6** So the inhabitants of this coastland will say in that day, 'Behold, such is our hope, where we fled [a]for help to be delivered from the king of Assyria; and we, [b]how shall we escape?'"

### *Fallen, Fallen Is Babylon*

**21** The [a,1]oracle concerning the [b,2]wilderness of the sea.
As [c]whirlwinds in the
[3]Negev sweep on,
It comes from the wilderness,
from a fearsome land.
2 A [a]harsh vision has been
declared to me;
The [b]treacherous one *still*
deals treacherously, and
the destroyer *still* destroys.
Go up, [c]Elam, lay siege, Media;
I have made an end of all [1]the
groaning she has caused.
3 For this reason my [a]loins
are full of anguish;
Pains have seized me like the
pains of a [b]woman in labor.
I am so bewildered I
cannot hear, so terrified
I cannot see.
4 My heart [1]reels; [2]horror
terrorizes me;
The twilight I longed
for has been [a]turned
for me into trembling.

---

**19:22** [a]Dt 32:39; Is 30:26; 57:18; Heb 12:11 [b]Is 27:13; 45:14; Hos 14:1 **19:23** [a]Is 11:16; 35:8; 49:11; 62:10 [b]Is 27:13 **19:25** [a]Is 45:14 [b]Ps 100:3; Is 29:23; 45:11; 60:21; 64:8; Eph 2:10 ◆ **20:1** [a]2Ki 18:17 [b]1Sa 5:1 [1]Heb *Tartan* **20:2** [a]Is 1:1; 13:1 [b]Zec 13:4; Mt 3:4 [c]Eze 24:17, 23 [d]1Sa 19:24; Mic 1:8 **20:3** [a]Is 8:18 [b]Is 37:9; 43:3 [1]Or *Cush*, so in vv 4, 5, cf. Ge 10:6 **20:4** [a]Is 19:4 [b]Is 47:2, 3 [1]Lit *nakedness* **20:5** [a]2Ki 18:21; Is 30:3-5; 31:1; Eze 29:6, 7 [b]Jer 9:23, 24; 17:5; 1Co 3:21 **20:6** [a]Is 10:3; 30:7; 31:3; Jer 30:1, 7, 15-17; 31:1-3 [b]Mt 23:33; 1Th 5:3; Heb 2:3 ◆ **21:1** [a]Is 13:1 [b]Is 13:20-22; 14:23; Jer 51:42 [c]Zec 9:14 [1]Or *burden of* [2]Or *sandy wastes, sea country* [3]South country **21:2** [a]Ps 60:3 [b]Is 24:16; 33:1 [c]Is 22:6; Jer 49:34 [1]Lit *her groaning* **21:3** [a]Is 13:8; 16:11 [b]Ps 48:6; Is 13:8; 26:17; 1Th 5:3 **21:4** [a]Dt 28:67 [1]Lit *wandered* [2]Lit *shuddering*

5 They [a]set the table, they
[1]spread out the cloth,
they eat, they drink;
"Rise up, commanders,
oil the shields,"
6 For thus the Lord says to me,
"Go, station the lookout, let
him [a]declare what he sees.
7 "Indeed, he shall see [a]riders,
horsemen in pairs,
Riders of donkeys,
riders of camels,
So let him pay close attention,
very close attention."
8 Then [1]the lookout called,
"[a]O Lord, I stand continually
by day on the watchtower,
And I am stationed every
night at my guard post.
9 "Now behold, here comes a troop
of riders, horsemen in pairs."
And one answered and said,
"[a]Fallen, fallen is Babylon;
And all the [b]graven images
of her gods [1]are shattered
on the ground."
10 O my [a]trampled *people* and my
[1]afflicted of the threshing floor!
What I have heard
from Yahweh of hosts,
The God of Israel,
I have declared to you.

### *Oracles Concerning Dumah and Arabia*

11 The [1]oracle concerning [a,2]Dumah.
One keeps calling
to me from [b]Seir,
"Watchman, [3]how far gone
is the night?
Watchman, [3]how far gone
is the night?"
12 The watchman says,
"Morning comes but also night.
If you would inquire, inquire;
Come back again."

13 The [1]oracle about [a,2]Arabia.
In the thickets of [2]Arabia you
[3]must spend the night,
O caravans of [b]Dedanites.
14 Bring water to meet the thirsty,
O inhabitants of the land
of [a]Tema,
Meet with bread the
one who has fled.
15 For they have [a]fled
from the swords,
From the drawn sword,
and from the bent bow
And from the heaviness of battle.
16 For thus the Lord said to me, "In
a [a]year, as [1]a hired man would count
it, all the glory of [b]Kedar will end;
17 and the [a]remainder of the number
of bowmen, the mighty men of the
sons of Kedar, will be few; for Yah-
weh, the God of Israel, [b]has spoken."

### *An Oracle Concerning the Valley of Vision*

22 The [1]oracle concerning the
[a]valley of vision.
What is the matter with you
now, that you have all gone
up to the [b]housetops?

**21:5** [a]Jer 51:39, 57; Da 5:1-4 [1]Or *spread out the rugs;* or possibly *they arranged the seating* **21:6** [a]2Ki 9:17-20 **21:7** [a]Is 21:9 **21:8** [a]Hab 2:1 [1]As in DSS; M.T. *he called* like *a lion* **21:9** [a]Is 13:19; 47:5, 9; 48:14; Jer 51:8; Rev 14:8; 18:2 [b]Is 46:1; Jer 50:2; 51:44 [1]Lit *he has shattered to the earth* **21:10** [a]Jer 51:33; Mic 4:13 [1]Lit *son* **21:11** [a]Ge 25:14 [b]Ge 32:3 [1]Or *burden of* [2]Lit *Silence*; Gr *Edom* [3]Lit *what* is the time *of the night?* **21:13** [a]Jer 25:23, 24; 49:28 [b]Ge 10:7; Eze 27:15 [1]Or *burden* [2]Or *the desert* [3]Or *will spend* **21:14** [a]Ge 25:15; Job 6:19 **21:15** [a]Is 13:14, 15; 17:13 **21:16** [a]Is 16:14 [b]Ps 120:5; SS 1:5; Is 42:11; 60:7; Eze 27:21 [1]Lit *the years of a hireling* **21:17** [a]Is 10:19 [b]Nu 23:19; Zec 1:6
◆ **22:1** [a]Ps 125:2; Jer 21:13; Joel 3:12, 14 [b]Is 15:3 [1]Or *burden of*

2 You who were full of noise,
You roaring city,
you [a]exultant town;
Your slain were [b]not slain
with the sword,
Nor [1]did they die in battle.
3 [a]All your rulers have
fled together,
*And* have been captured
[1]without the bow;
All of you who were found
were captured together,
[2]Though they had
fled far away.
4 Therefore I say, "Turn your
gaze away from me,
Let me [a]weep bitterly,
Do not insist on comforting me
concerning the destruction
of the daughter of my people."
5 [a]For Lord Yahweh of hosts
has a [b]day of confusion,
[c]oppression, and panic
[d]In the valley of vision,
A breaking down of walls
And a crying [1]to the mountain.
6 [a]Now Elam took up the quiver
With the chariots, [1]infantry,
*and* horsemen;
And [b]Kir uncovered the shield.
7 Then your choicest valleys
were full of chariots,
And the horsemen took up
fixed positions at the gate.
8 And He revealed the [1]defense
of Judah.
In that day you looked to
the weapons of the [a]house
of the forest,
9 And you saw that the breaches
In the *wall* of the city
of David were many;
And you [a]collected the
waters of the lower pool.
10 Then you counted
the houses of Jerusalem
And tore down houses
to fortify the wall.
11 And you made a reservoir
[a]between the two walls
For the waters of the [b]old pool.
But you did not look
to Him who made it,
Nor did you see Him who
formed it long ago.

12 Therefore in that day Lord
Yahweh of hosts called *you*
to [a]weeping, to wailing,
To [b]shaving the head, and
to wearing sackcloth.
13 Instead, behold,
*there is* [a]joy and gladness,
Killing of cattle and
slaughtering of sheep,
Eating of meat and
drinking of wine:
"[b]Let us eat and drink,
for tomorrow we may die."
14 But Yahweh of hosts revealed
Himself in my ears,
"Surely this [a]iniquity [b]shall
not be atoned for you
[c]Until you die," says Lord
Yahweh of hosts.

15 Thus says Lord Yahweh of hosts,
"Come, go to this steward,
To [a]Shebna, who is in charge
of the *royal* household,

---

**22:2** [a]Is 23:7; 32:13 [b]Jer 14:18; Lam 2:20 [1]Lit *dead in battle* **22:3** [a]Is 21:15 [1]Lit *from a bow* [2]As in ancient versions; Heb *They fled far away* **22:4** [a]Is 15:3; Jer 9:1; Lk 19:41 **22:5** [a]Lam 1:5; 2:2 [b]Is 37:3 [c]Is 10:6; 63:3 [d]Is 22:1 [1]Or *against* **22:6** [a]Is 21:2; Jer 49:35 [b]2Ki 16:9; Am 1:5; 9:7 [1]Lit *man* **22:8** [a]1Ki 7:2; 10:17 [1]Lit *screen, covering* **22:9** [a]2Ki 20:20; Ne 3:16 **22:11** [a]2Ki 25:4; Jer 39:4 [b]2Ki 20:20; 2Chr 32:3, 4 **22:12** [a]Is 32:11; Joel 1:13; 2:17 [b]Mic 1:16 **22:13** [a]Is 5:11, 22; 28:7, 8; Lk 17:26-29 [b]Is 56:12; 1Co 15:32 **22:14** [a]Is 13:11; 26:21; 30:13; 65:7 [b]1Sa 3:14; Eze 24:13 [c]Is 65:20 **22:15** [a]2Ki 18:18, 26, 37; Is 36:3, 11, 22; 37:2

16 'What right do you have here,
And whom do you have here,
That you have [a]hewn
a tomb for yourself here,
You who hew a tomb
on the height,
You who carve a dwelling
place for [1]yourself
in the cliff?
17 'Behold, Yahweh is about to
hurl you headlong, O man.
And He is about
to grasp you firmly
18 *And* He will surely roll
you tightly like a ball,
*To be* [a]*cast* into a vast country;
There you will die,
And there your glorious
chariots will be,
You disgrace of your
master's house.'
19 "I will [a]push you
out of your office,
And [1]I will pull you down
from your station.
20 "Then it will be in that day,
That I will summon My
servant [a]Eliakim the son
of Hilkiah,
21 And I will clothe him
with your tunic
And tie your sash
securely about him.
I will give your [1]authority
into his hand,
And he will become
a [a]father to the inhabitants
of Jerusalem and
to the house of Judah.
22 "Then I will set [a]the key
of the [b]house of David
on his shoulder,
When he opens no
one will shut,
When he shuts no
one will [c]open.
23 "I will drive him
*like* a [a]peg in a firm place,
And he will become a [b]throne
of glory to his father's house.
24 "So they will hang on him all the
glory of his father's house, offspring
and [1]issue, all the least of vessels,
from bowls to all the jars. 25 In that
day," declares Yahweh of hosts, "the
[a]peg driven in a firm place will give
way; it will even [b]break off and fall,
and the load hanging on it will be cut
off, for [c]Yahweh has spoken."

### *An Oracle Concerning Tyre*

23 The [1]oracle concerning [a]Tyre.
Wail, O [b]ships of [c]Tarshish,
For *Tyre* is destroyed,
without house *or* [d,2]harbor;
It is revealed to them
from the land of [e,3]Cyprus.
2 [a]Be silent, you inhabitants
of the coastland,
You merchants of Sidon;
[1]Your messengers
crossed the sea
3 And *were* on many waters.
[a]The [1]grain of [b,2]Shihor,
the harvest of the Nile
was her revenue;
And she was
the nations' [c]gain.

**22:16** [a]2Sa 18:18; 2Chr 16:14; Mt 27:60 [1]Lit *himself* **22:18** [a]Job 18:18; Is 17:13 **22:19** [a]Job 40:11, 12; Eze 17:24 [1]As in many ancient versions; Heb *He* **22:20** [a]2Ki 18:18; Is 36:3, 22; 37:2 **22:21** [a]Ge 45:8; Job 29:16 [1]Lit *rule* **22:22** [a]Rev 3:7 [b]Is 7:2, 13 [c]Job 12:14 **22:23** [a]Ezr 9:8; Zec 10:4 [b]1Sa 2:8; Job 36:7 **22:24** [1]Or possibly *leaf* **22:25** [a]Is 22:23 [b]Es 9:24, 25 [c]Is 46:11; Mic 4:4 ◆ **23:1** [a]Jos 19:29; 1Ki 5:1; Jer 25:22; 47:4; Eze 26:1-27:36; Joel 3:4-8; Am 1:9; Zec 9:2-4 [b]Is 2:16 [c]Ge 10:4; 1Ki 10:22 [d]Is 24:10 [e]Ge 10:4; Is 23:12; Eze 27:6 [1]Or *burden of* [2]Lit *entering* [3]Heb *Kittim* **23:2** [a]Is 47:5 [1]As in DSS; M.T. *Who passed over the sea, they replenished you* **23:3** [a]Is 19:7-9 [b]Jos 13:3; 1Chr 13:5; Jer 2:18 [c]Eze 27:3-23 [1]Lit *seed* [2]Part of the Nile

4 Be ashamed, O [a]Sidon;
For the sea speaks, the strong
defense of the sea, saying,
"I have neither travailed
nor given birth;
I have neither brought
up choice men *nor*
reared virgins."
5 When the report
*reaches* Egypt,
They will be in [a]travail
at the report of Tyre.
6 Pass over to [a]Tarshish;
Wail, O inhabitants
of the coastland.
7 Is this your [a]exultant *city*,
Whose origin is
from days of old,
Whose feet used to lead
her to sojourn
in distant places?

8 Who has counseled this
against Tyre, [a]the
bestower of crowns,
Whose merchants were
princes, whose traders were
the honored of the earth?
9 [a]Yahweh of hosts has
counseled it, to [b]defile
the pride of all beauty,
To make contemptuous all
the [c]honored of the earth.
10 [1]Overflow your land like the
Nile, O daughter of Tarshish;
There is no more [2]restraint.
11 He has [a]stretched His hand
out [b]over the sea;
He has [c]made
the kingdoms tremble;
Yahweh has given
a command concerning
Canaan to [d]demolish
its strong defenses.

12 So He said, "[a]You shall
exult no more, O crushed
virgin daughter of Sidon.
Arise, pass over
to [b,1]Cyprus; even there
you will find no rest."
13 Behold, the land of the
Chaldeans—this is the people *which*
was not; [a]Assyria established it for
[b]desert creatures—they erected
their siege towers, they stripped its
palaces, [c]they made it a ruin.
14 Wail, O [a]ships of Tarshish,
For your strong defense
is destroyed.
15 Now it will be in that day, that Tyre
will be forgotten for [a]seventy years
like the days of one king. At the end
of seventy years it will happen to
Tyre as *in* the song of the harlot:
16 Take *your* harp, walk
about the city,
O forgotten harlot;
Pluck the strings skillfully,
sing many songs,
That you may be remembered.
17 And it will be at [a]the end of seventy
years that Yahweh will visit Tyre.
Then she will go back to her harlot's
wages and will [b]play the harlot with
all the kingdoms [1]on the face of
the earth. 18 And her [a]gain and her
harlot's wages will be [b]set apart to
Yahweh; it will not be treasured up
or hoarded, but her gain will become

**23:4** [a]Ge 10:15, 19; Jos 11:8; Jdg 10:6; Jer 25:22; 27:3; 47:4; Eze 28:21, 22 **23:5** [a]Ex 15:14-16; Jos 2:9-11 **23:6** [a]Is 23:1 **23:7** [a]Is 22:2; 32:13 **23:8** [a]Eze 28:2 **23:9** [a]Is 2:11; 13:11 [b]Job 40:11, 12; Da 4:37 [c]Is 5:13; 9:15 **23:10** [1]Lit *Pass over* [2]Possibly *girdle, shipyard* **23:11** [a]Ex 14:21; Is 14:26 [b]Is 19:5; 50:2 [c]Is 13:13 [d]Is 25:2; Zec 9:3, 4 **23:12** [a]Eze 26:13, 14; Rev 18:22 [b]Is 23:1 [1]Heb *Kittim* **23:13** [a]Is 10:5 [b]Is 13:21; 18:6 [c]Is 10:7 **23:14** [a]Is 2:16; Eze 27:25, 26 **23:15** [a]Jer 25:11, 22 **23:17** [a]Is 23:15 [b]Eze 16:25-29; Na 3:4 [1]Lit *of the earth on the face of the land* **23:18** [a]Ps 72:10, 11; Is 60:5-9; Mic 4:13 [b]Ex 28:36; Zec 14:20

sufficient food and choice attire for
those who inhabit the presence of
Yahweh.

### *Yahweh Will Empty the Earth*

**24** Behold, Yahweh [a]empties
the earth to destruction,
eviscerates it, distorts its surface,
and scatters its inhabitants. **2** And the
people will be like the priest, the male
slave like his master, the female slave
like her mistress, the buyer like the
seller, the lender like the borrower,
the [a]creditor like the debtor. **3** The
earth will be completely emptied
to destruction and completely
plundered, for Yahweh has spoken
this word. **4** The [a]earth mourns *and*
withers; the world languishes *and*
withers; the [b]exalted of the people of
the earth languish. **5** The earth is also
[a]polluted [1]by its inhabitants, for they
trespassed laws, violated statutes,
[b]broke the everlasting covenant.
**6** Therefore, a [a]curse devours the
earth, and those who inhabit it are
held guilty. Therefore, the [b]inhab-
itants of the earth are burned, and
few men remain.

7 The [a]new wine mourns;
The vine languishes;
All the glad of heart sigh.
8 The [a]joy
of tambourines ceases;
The rumbling of those
exulting stops;
The joy of the harp ceases.
9 They do not drink
wine with song;
[a]Strong drink is [b]bitter
to those who drink it.
10 The [a]city of chaos is
broken down;
[b]Every house is shut up
so that none may enter.
11 There is an [a]outcry in the
streets concerning the wine;
[b]All gladness [1]turns to gloom.
The joy of the earth is
taken away into exile.
12 Desolation remains in the city,
And the [a]gate is struck
down to ruins.
13 For [a]thus it will be
in the midst of the earth
among the peoples,
As the [1]shaking of an olive tree,
As the gleanings when the
grape harvest is over.
14 [a]They lift up their voices,
they shout for joy;
They cry out from the
[1]west concerning the
majesty of Yahweh.
15 Therefore [a]glorify
Yahweh in the [1]east,
The [b]name of Yahweh,
the God of Israel,
In the [c,2]coastlands of the sea.
16 From the [a]ends of the earth
we hear songs, "[b]Glory
to the Righteous One,"
But I say, "[c,1]I waste away!
[1]I waste away! Woe is me!
The [d]treacherous deal
treacherously,
And the treacherous deal
very treacherously."

◆ **24:1** [a]Is 2:19; 13:13; 24:19, 20; 30:32; 33:9 **24:2** [a]Lv 25:36, 37; Dt 23:19, 20 **24:4** [a]Is 33:9 [b]Is 2:12; 24:21 **24:5** [a]Ge 3:17; Nu 35:33; Is 9:17; 10:6 [b]Is 33:8 [1]Lit *under* **24:6** [a]Jos 23:15; Is 34:5; 43:28; Zec 5:3, 4 [b]Is 1:31; 5:24; 9:19 **24:7** [a]Is 16:10; Joel 1:10, 12 **24:8** [a]Is 5:12, 14; Eze 26:13; Hos 2:11; Rev 18:22 **24:9** [a]Is 5:11, 22 [b]Is 5:20 **24:10** [a]Is 34:11 [b]Is 23:1 **24:11** [a]Jer 14:2; 46:12 [b]Is 16:10; 32:13 [1]Lit is *darkened* **24:12** [a]Is 14:31; 45:2 **24:13** [a]Is 17:6; 27:12 [1]Lit *striking* **24:14** [a]Is 12:6; 48:20; 52:8; 54:1 [1]Lit *sea* **24:15** [a]Is 25:3 [b]Mal 1:11 [c]Is 11:11; 42:4, 10, 12; 49:1; 51:5; 60:9; 66:19 [1]Lit *region of light* [2]Or *islands* **24:16** [a]Is 11:12; 42:10 [b]Is 28:5; 60:21 [c]Lv 26:39 [d]Is 21:2; 33:1; Jer 3:20; 5:11 [1]Lit *Wasting to me!*

17 [a]Panic and pit and pitfall
Are upon you, O inhabitant
of the earth.
18 Then it will be that he who
flees the sound of panic
will fall into the pit,
And he who [1]climbs
out of the pit will be
caught in the pitfall;
For the [a]windows
[2]above are opened,
and the [b]foundations
of the earth quake.
19 [a]The earth is
broken asunder;
The earth is [b]split through;
The earth is shaken violently.
20 The earth [a]reels to and
fro like a drunkard
And it totters like a [1]shack,
For its [b]transgression
is heavy upon it,
And it will fall, [c]never
to rise again.
21 So it will be in that day,
That Yahweh will [a]punish
the host of heights on high,
And the [b]kings of the
earth on earth.
22 They will be
gathered together
*Like* [a]prisoners in the [1]pit,
And will be confined
in prison;
And after many days they
*will* [b]*be* punished.
23 Then the [a]moon will
be humiliated and
the sun ashamed,
For [b]Yahweh of hosts will
reign on [c]Mount Zion
and in Jerusalem,
And *His* glory will be
before His elders.

### *Yahweh Will Swallow Up Death*

25 O Yahweh, You are [a]my God;
I will exalt You, I will give
thanks to Your name;
For You have
[b]worked wonders,
[c]Counsels *formed* long ago,
with perfect faithfulness.
2 For You have made a
city into a [a]heap,
A [b]fortified town into a ruin;
A [c]palace of strangers
is a city no more,
It will never be rebuilt.
3 Therefore a strong people
will [a]glorify You;
[b]Towns of ruthless
nations will fear You.
4 For You have been a [a]strong
defense for the poor,
A strong defense for the
needy in his distress,
A [b]refuge from the storm,
a shade from the heat;
For the breath of the [c]ruthless
Is like a *rain* storm
*against* a wall.
5 Like heat in a dry land,
You subdue the [a]rumbling
of strangers;
*Like* heat by the shadow
of a cloud, the song of the
ruthless is [1]silenced.

---

**24:17** [a]Jer 48:43; Am 5:19 **24:18** [a]Ge 7:11 [b]Ps 18:7; 46:2; Is 2:19, 21; 13:13 [1]Lit *goes up from the midst of* [2]Heaven; lit *from the height* **24:19** [a]Is 24:1 [b]Nu 16:31, 32; Dt 11:6 **24:20** [a]Is 19:14; 24:1; 28:7 [b]Is 1:28; 43:27; 66:24 [c]Da 11:19; Am 8:14 [1]Or *hut* **24:21** [a]Is 10:12; 13:11 [b]Ps 76:12 **24:22** [a]Is 10:4; 42:22 [b]Eze 38:8; Zec 9:11, 12 [1]Or *dungeon* **24:23** [a]Is 13:10 [b]Is 60:19, 20; Zec 14:6, 7; Rev 21:23; 22:5 [c]Mic 4:7; Heb 12:22 ◆**25:1** [a]Ex 15:2; Ps 118:28; Is 7:13; 49:4, 5; 61:10 [b]Ps 40:5; 98:1 [c]Eph 1:11 **25:2** [a]Is 17:1; 26:5; 27:10; 32:19 [b]Is 17:3; 25:12 [c]Is 13:22; 32:14; 34:13 **25:3** [a]Is 24:15 [b]Is 13:11 **25:4** [a]Is 14:32; 17:10; 27:5; 33:16 [b]Is 4:6; 32:2 [c]Is 29:5, 20; 49:25 **25:5** [a]Jer 51:54-56 [1]Lit *humbled*

6 [a]And Yahweh of hosts
will prepare a [1]lavish
banquet for [b]all peoples
on this mountain;
A banquet of [2]aged wine,
[3]choice pieces with marrow,
*And* [4]refined, aged wine.
7 And on this mountain
He will swallow up
the [a,1]covering
which is over all peoples,
Even the veil which is
[2]stretched over all nations.
8 He will [a]swallow up
death for all time,
And Lord Yahweh will [b]wipe
tears away from all faces,
And He will remove the
[c]reproach of His people
from all the earth;
For Yahweh has spoken.
9 And it will be said in that day,
"Behold, [a]this is our God
in whom we have [b]hoped
that [c]He would save us.
This is Yahweh
in whom we have hoped;
[d]Let us rejoice and be glad
in His salvation."
10 For the hand of Yahweh will
rest on this mountain,
And [a]Moab will be trodden
down in his place
As straw is trodden down in
the water of a manure pile.
11 And he will [a]spread out his
hands in the middle of it
As a swimmer spreads out
*his hands* to swim,
But *Yahweh* will [b]lay low his
lofty pride together with
the trickery of his hands.
12 The [a]unassailable
fortifications of your walls
He will bring down,
Lay low, *and* cast to the
ground, even to the dust.

### *Yahweh Will Establish Peace*

26 [a]In that day this song will be
sung in the land of Judah:
"We have a [b]strong city;
He sets up walls and
ramparts for [c]salvation.
2 "Open the [a]gates, that the
[b]righteous nation may enter,
The one
that keeps faithfulness.
3 "The steadfast of mind You
will keep in perfect [a]peace
Because he trusts in You.
4 "[a]Trust in Yahweh forever,
For in Yah—Yahweh
*Himself—we have* an
everlasting [b]Rock.
5 "For He has laid low those
who settle on high,
the [a,1]exalted city;
[b]He brings it low, He brings
it low to the ground,
He casts it to the dust.
6 "[a]The foot will trample it,
The feet of the [b]afflicted,
the steps of the poor."

**25:6** [a]Is 1:19 [b]Is 2:2-4; 56:7 [1]Abundance; lit *feast of fat things* [2]Lit *wine on the lees* [3]Lit *fat pieces* [4]Lit *wine refined on the lees* **25:7** [a]2Co 3:15, 16; Eph 4:18 [1]Lit *face of the covering* [2]Lit *woven* **25:8** [a]Hos 13:14; 1Co 15:54 [b]Is 30:19; 35:10; 51:11; 65:19; Rev 7:17; 21:4 [c]Ps 69:9; 89:50, 51; Is 51:7; 54:4; Mt 5:11; 1Pe 4:14 **25:9** [a]Is 35:2; 40:9; 52:10 [b]Is 8:17; 30:18; 33:2 [c]Is 33:22; 35:4; 49:25, 26; 60:16 [d]Ps 20:5; Is 35:1, 2, 10; 65:18; 66:10 **25:10** [a]Is 16:14; Jer 48:1-47; Eze 25:8-11; Am 2:1-3; Zep 2:9 **25:11** [a]Is 5:25; 14:26 [b]Job 40:11; Is 2:10-12, 15-17; 16:6, 14 **25:12** [a]Is 15:1; 25:2; 26:5 ◆ **26:1** [a]Is 4:2; 12:1 [b]Is 14:31; 31:5, 9; 33:5, 6, 20-24 [c]Is 60:18 **26:2** [a]Is 60:11, 18; 62:10 [b]Is 45:25; 54:14, 17; 58:8; 60:21; 61:3; 62:1, 2 **26:3** [a]Is 26:12; 27:5; 57:19; 66:12 **26:4** [a]Is 12:2; 50:10; 51:5 [b]Is 17:10; 30:29; 44:8 **26:5** [a]Is 25:12 [b]Job 40:11-13 [1]Or *unassailable* **26:6** [a]Is 28:3 [b]Is 3:14, 15; 11:4; 29:19

7 The [a]way of the righteous
is upright;
O Upright One, [b]make the path
of the righteous level.
8 Indeed, *while following*
the way of [a]Your
judgments, O Yahweh,
We have hoped
for You eagerly;
[b]Your name—the [c]memory
of You—is the desire
of *our* souls.
9 [a]At night [1]my soul
longs for You,
Indeed, [2]my spirit within me
[b]seeks You earnestly;
For when the earth
[3]experiences Your
judgments,
The inhabitants of the world
[c]learn righteousness.
10 *Though* the wicked
is shown favor,
He does not [a]learn
righteousness;
He [b]deals unjustly
in the land of uprightness,
And does not perceive
the majesty of Yahweh.

11 O Yahweh, Your hand is
raised up *high*, *yet* they
[a]do not behold it.
[1]They behold [b]*Your* zeal
for the people and
are put to shame;
Indeed, [c,2]fire will devour
Your adversaries.
12 Yahweh, You will establish
[a]peace for us,
Since You have also
performed for us
all our works.
13 O Yahweh our God,
[a]other masters besides You
have ruled us;
*But* through You alone
we [b]bring Your name
to remembrance.
14 [a]The dead will not live;
the [1]departed spirits
will not rise;
Therefore You have [b]visited
and destroyed them,
And You have made
all remembrance
of them perish.
15 [a]You have increased
the nation, O Yahweh;
You have increased the nation,
You are glorified;
You have [b]extended all
the borders of the land.
16 O Yahweh, they visited
You [a]in distress;
They [1]could only
whisper a prayer;
Your chastening was
upon them.
17 [a]As the [1]woman
with child draws near
to *the time* to give birth,
She writhes *and* cries out
*in her pangs of labor*,
Thus were we before You,
O Yahweh.

**26:7** [a]Is 57:2 [b]Ps 25:4, 5; 27:11; Is 42:16; 52:12 **26:8** [a]Is 51:4; 56:1 [b]Is 12:4; 24:15; 25:1; 26:13 [c]Ex 3:15 **26:9** [a]Ps 63:5, 6; 77:2; 119:62; Is 50:10; Lk 6:12 [b]Ps 63:1; 78:34; Mt 6:33 [c]Is 55:6; Hos 5:15 [1]Lit with *my soul I long* [2]Lit with *my spirit...I seek* [3]Lit *has* **26:10** [a]Is 22:12, 13; 32:6, 7 [b]Hos 11:7; Jn 5:37, 38 **26:11** [a]Is 44:9, 18 [b]Is 9:7; 37:32; 59:17 [c]Is 5:24; 9:18, 19; 10:17; 66:15, 24; Heb 10:27 [1]Or *Let them see...and be* [2]Or *let the fire for Your adversaries devour them* **26:12** [a]Is 26:3 **26:13** [a]Is 2:8; 10:11 [b]Is 63:7 **26:14** [a]Dt 4:28; Ps 135:17; Is 8:19; Hab 2:19 [b]Is 10:3 [1]Or *shades* **26:15** [a]Is 9:3 [b]Is 33:17; 54:2, 3 **26:16** [a]Is 37:3; Hos 5:15 [1]Lit *sound forth a whisper* **26:17** [a]Is 13:8; 21:3; Jn 16:21 [1]Or *pregnant woman*

18 We were [1]with child,
we writhed *in labor*;
We [a]gave birth, as it seems,
*only* to wind.
We could not accomplish
salvation for the earth,
And the [b]inhabitants
of the world [2]were not born.
19 Your [a]dead will live;
[1]Their corpses will rise.
You who dwell in the dust,
[b]awake and shout for joy,
For your dew *is as* the
dew of the [2]dawn,
And the earth will [3]give birth
to the [4]departed spirits.

20 Come, my people, [a]enter
into your rooms
And close your doors
behind you;
Hide for a little [b,1]while
Until [c]indignation
passes by.
21 For behold, Yahweh is about
to [a]come out from His place
To [b]visit the iniquity of
the inhabitants of the earth;
And the earth will [c]reveal
her bloodshed
And will no longer cover those
of hers who were killed.

### *Yahweh Will Deliver Israel*

27 In that day [a]Yahweh will
[1]punish [b,2]Leviathan
the fleeing serpent,
With His fierce and great
and [3]mighty sword,
Even [2]Leviathan
the twisted serpent;
And [c]He will kill the dragon
who *lives* in the sea.

2 In that day,
"A [a,1]vineyard of delight,
sing of it!
3 "I, Yahweh, am its keeper;
[a]I water it every moment.
Lest anyone [1]damage it,
I [b]keep it night and day.
4 "I have no wrath.
Who would *ever* give
Me [a]briars *and* thorns
in the battle?
I would step on them, [b]I would
burn them [1]completely.
5 "Or let him [a,1]rely on My
strong defense,
Let him make peace with Me,
Let him [b]make peace
with Me."
6 [1]In the days to come
Jacob [a]will take root,
Israel will [b]blossom and bud,
And they will fill the [2]whole
world with [c]produce.

7 Like the striking of Him
who has struck them,
has [a]He struck them?
Or like the slaughter of those
of His who were killed,
[1]have they been killed?

**26:18** [a]Is 33:11; 59:4 [b]Ps 17:14 [1]Or *pregnant* [2]Lit *had never fallen* **26:19** [a]Is 25:8; Eze 37:1-14; Da 12:2; Hos 13:14 [b]Eph 5:14 [1]As in some ancient versions; Heb *My* [2]Lit *lights* [3]Lit *cause to fall* [4]Or *shades* **26:20** [a]Ex 12:22, 23; Ps 91:1, 4 [b]Ps 30:5; Is 54:7, 8; 2Co 4:17 [c]Is 10:5, 25; 13:5; 34:2; 66:14 [1]Lit *moment* **26:21** [a]Mic 1:3; Jd 14 [b]Is 13:11; 30:12-14; 65:6, 7 [c]Job 16:18; Lk 11:50 ◆ **27:1** [a]Is 66:16 [b]Job 3:8; 41:1; Ps 74:14; 104:26 [c]Is 51:9 [1]Or *visit*, cf. 26:14, 16, 21 [2]Or *the sea monster* [3]Lit *strong* **27:2** [a]Ps 80:8; Is 5:7; Jer 2:21 [1]Some mss *vineyard of wine* **27:3** [a]Is 58:11 [b]1Sa 2:9; Is 31:5; Jn 10:28 [1]Lit *punish* **27:4** [a]2Sa 23:6; Is 10:17 [b]Is 33:12; Mt 3:12; Heb 6:8 [1]Lit *altogether* **27:5** [a]Is 12:2; 25:4 [b]Job 22:21; Is 26:3, 12; Ro 5:1; 2Co 5:20 [1]Lit *take hold of* **27:6** [a]Is 37:31 [b]Is 35:1, 2; Hos 14:5, 6 [c]Is 4:2 [1]Lit *Those coming* [2]Lit *face of* **27:7** [a]Is 10:12, 17; 30:31-33; 31:8, 9; 37:36-38 [1]Lit *he was slain*

8 You contended with them
[1]by driving them away,
by [a]making them forlorn.
With His fierce wind He
has expelled *them* on the
day of the [b]east wind.
9 Therefore through this, Jacob's
iniquity will be [a]atoned for;
And this will be the whole
fruit of the [b]turning
away of his sin:
When he makes all
the [c]altar stones like
pulverized chalk stones,
*When* [1]Asherim and incense
altars will not stand.
10 For the fortified city
is [a]isolated,
A [1]haunt [2]forlorn and
forsaken like the desert;
[b]There the calf will graze,
And there it will lie down
and [3]feed on its twigs.
11 When its [a]limbs are dry,
they are broken off;
Women come *and* light
a fire with them,
For they are not a people
of [b]discernment,
Therefore [c]their
Maker [d]will not have
compassion on them.
And their Creator will not
be gracious to them.

12 And it will be in that day, *that*
Yahweh [a]will start *His* threshing from
the flowing stream of the [b,1]River to
the brook of Egypt, and you will be
[c]gathered up one by one, O sons of
Israel. 13 And it will be in that day,
*that* a great [a]trumpet will be blown,
and those who were perishing in
the land of [b]Assyria and who were
banished in the land of Egypt will
come and [c]worship Yahweh in the
holy mountain at Jerusalem.

### *Woe to Ephraim*

28 Woe to the proud crown of
the [a]drunkards
of [b]Ephraim,
And to the fading flower
of its glorious beauty,
Which is at the head
of the [1]fertile valley
Of those who are
[2]overcome with wine!
2 Behold, the Lord has a strong
and [a]courageous *agent*;
As a storm of [b]hail,
a tempest of destruction,
Like a storm of [c]mighty
overflowing waters,
He has set *it* down
to the earth with *His* hand.
3 The proud crown
of the drunkards of Ephraim
is [a]trodden under foot.
4 And the fading flower
of its glorious beauty,
Which is at the head
of the [1]fertile valley,
Will be like the [a]first-ripe
fig prior to summer,
Which [2]one sees,
*And* [3]as soon as it is in his [4]hand,

**27:8** [a]Is 50:1; 54:7 [b]Jer 4:11; Eze 19:12; Hos 13:15 [1]Some ancient versions *by exact measure* **27:9** [a]Is 1:25; 48:10; Da 11:35 [b]Ro 11:27 [c]Ex 34:13; Dt 12:3; 2Ki 10:26; Is 17:8 [1]Wooden symbols of a female deity **27:10** [a]Is 32:13, 14 [b]Is 17:2 [1]Lit *pasture* [2]Lit *sent away* [3]Lit *consume* **27:11** [a]Is 18:5 [b]Dt 32:28; Is 1:3; 5:13; Jer 8:7 [c]Dt 32:18; Is 43:1, 7; 44:2, 21, 24 [d]Is 9:17 **27:12** [a]Is 11:11; 17:6; 24:13; 56:8 [b]Ge 15:18 [c]Dt 30:3, 4; Ne 1:9 [1]The Euphrates River **27:13** [a]Lv 25:9; 1Chr 15:24; Mt 24:31; Rev 11:15 [b]Is 19:24, 25 [c]Is 19:21, 23; 49:7; 66:23; Zec 14:16; Heb 12:22 ◆ **28:1** [a]Is 28:7; Hos 7:5 [b]Is 9:9 [1]Lit *valley of fatness* [2]Lit *smitten* **28:2** [a]Is 8:7; 40:10 [b]Is 28:17; 30:30; 32:19; Eze 13:11 [c]Is 8:6, 7; 30:28; Na 1:8 **28:3** [a]Is 26:6; 28:18 **28:4** [a]Hos 9:10; Mic 7:1; Na 3:12 [1]Lit *valley of fatness* [2]Lit *the one seeing sees* [3]Lit *while it is yet* [4]Lit *palm*

He swallows it.
5 In that day [a]Yahweh
of hosts will become
a beautiful [b]crown
And a glorious diadem to
the remnant of His people;
6 A [a]spirit of *just* judgment for
him who sits in judgment,
A [b]might to those who
turn back the [1]onslaught
at the gate.
7 And these also [a]reel
with wine and stagger
from strong drink:
[b]The priest and [c]the prophet
reel with strong drink;
They are swallowed up
by wine, they stagger
from [d]strong drink;
They reel while [1]having [e]visions;
They totter
*when rendering* a verdict.
8 For all the tables are full
of filthy [a]vomit,
without a *single clean* place.

9 "[a]Whom would He instruct
in knowledge,
And whom would He
provide understanding
about the report?
Those *just* [b]weaned from milk?
Those *just* taken
from the breast?
10 "For *He says,*
'[a,1]Order on order,
order on order,
Line on line, line on line,
A little here, a little there.'"
11 Indeed, He will speak
to this people
Through [a]stammering lips
and a foreign tongue,
12 He who said to them, "Here is
[a]rest, give rest to the weary,"
And, "Here is repose,"
but they would not listen.
13 So the word of Yahweh
to them will be,
"[1]Order on order, order on order,
Line on line, line on line,
A little here, a little there,"
That they may go and
[a]stumble backward,
be broken, snared,
and taken captive.

### *A Cornerstone in Zion*

14 Therefore, [a]hear the word
of Yahweh, O [b]scoffers,
Who rule this people who
are in Jerusalem,
15 Because you have said,
"We have cut
a [a]covenant with death,
And with Sheol we
have made a [1]pact.
[b]The overflowing [2]scourge
will not reach us
when it passes by,
For we have made
[c]falsehood our refuge
and we have [d]hidden
ourselves with lying."

---

**28:5** [a]Is 41:16; 45:25; 60:1, 19 [b]Is 62:3 **28:6** [a]1Ki 3:28; Is 11:2; 32:15, 16; Jn 5:30 [b]2Chr 32:6-8; Is 25:4 [1]Lit *battle* **28:7** [a]Is 5:11, 22; 22:13; 56:12; Hos 4:11 [b]Is 24:2 [c]Is 9:15 [d]Hab 2:15, 16 [e]Is 29:11 [1]Lit *seeing* **28:8** [a]Jer 48:26 **28:9** [a]Is 2:3; 28:26; 30:20; 48:17; 50:4; 54:13 [b]Ps 131:2 **28:10** [a]2Chr 36:15; Ne 9:30 [1]Heb *Sav lasav, sav lasav, Kav lakav, kav lakav, Ze' er sham, ze' er sham*; These Hebrew monosyllables, imitating the babbling of a child, mock the prophet's preaching **28:11** [a]Is 33:19; 1Co 14:21 **28:12** [a]Is 11:10; 30:15; 32:17, 18; Jer 6:16; Mt 11:28, 29 **28:13** [a]Is 8:15; Mt 21:44 [1]See v 10 note 1, Yahweh responds to their scoffing by imitating their mockery, to represent the unintelligible language of a conqueror **28:14** [a]Is 1:10; 28:22 [b]Is 29:20 **28:15** [a]Is 28:18 [b]Is 8:8; 28:2; 30:28; Da 11:22 [c]Is 9:15; 30:9; 44:20; 59:3, 4; Eze 13:22 [d]Is 29:15 [1]As in some ancient versions; Heb *seer* [2]Or *flood*

16 Therefore thus says Lord Yahweh,
“[a]Behold, I am laying in Zion
a stone, a tested [b]stone,
A costly cornerstone *for* the
foundation, [1]firmly placed.
He who believes *in it* will
not be [2]disturbed.
17 “I will make [a]justice the
measuring line
And righteousness the level;
Then [b]hail will sweep away
the refuge of falsehood,
And the waters will overflow
the secret place.
18 “Your [a]covenant with death
will be [b,1]canceled,
And your pact with Sheol
will not stand;
When the [a]overflowing
scourge passes through,
Then you will become
its [c]trampling *place*.
19 “As [a]often as it passes
through, it will take you;
For [b]morning after morning it
will pass through, *anytime*
during the day or night,
And it will be [1]sheer [c]terror
to understand the report.”
20 The bed is too short
on which to stretch out,
And the [a]blanket is too
narrow to wrap oneself in.
21 For Yahweh will rise up
as *at* Mount [a]Perazim;
He will be stirred up
as in the valley of [b]Gibeon,
To work His [c]work,
His [d,1]unusual work,
And to labor in His labor,
His [2]exceptional labor.
22 So now do not carry
on as [a]scoffers,
Lest your fetters be
made stronger;
For I have heard
from Lord Yahweh of hosts
Of complete [b]destruction,
one that is decreed,
on all the earth.

23 Give ear and hear my voice,
Pay attention and
hear my words.
24 Does the [1]farmer plow
[2]continually to plant seed?
Does he *continually* [3]turn
and harrow his ground?
25 Does he not level its surface
And sow dill and scatter [a]cumin
And [1]plant [b]wheat in rows,
Barley in its place and
rye within its [2]area?
26 For his God disciplines
and teaches him
*proper* judgment.
27 For dill is not threshed
with a [a]threshing sledge,
Nor is the wheel of a cart
[1]driven over cumin;
But dill is beaten out with a
staff, and cumin with a rod.
28 *Grain for* bread is crushed,
But he does not continue
to thresh it forever.
Because the wheel
of *his* cart and his horses
*eventually* [1]disturb *it*,

**28:16** [a]Ro 9:33; 10:11; 1Pe 2:6 [b]Ps 118:22; Is 8:14, 15; Mt 21:42; Mk 12:10; Lk 20:17; Ac 4:11; Eph 2:20 [1]Lit *well-laid* [2]Lit *in a hurry* **28:17** [a]2Ki 21:13; Is 5:16; 30:18; 61:8; Am 7:7-9 [b]Is 28:2 **28:18** [a]Is 28:15 [b]Is 7:7; 8:10 [c]Is 28:3; Da 8:13 [1]Lit *covered over* **28:19** [a]2Ki 24:2 [b]Is 50:4 [c]Job 6:4; 18:11; 24:17; Ps 55:4; 88:15; Lam 2:22 [1]Lit *only* **28:20** [a]Is 59:6 **28:21** [a]2Sa 5:20; 1Chr 14:11 [b]Jos 10:10, 12; 2Sa 5:25; 1Chr 14:16 [c]Is 10:12; 29:14; 65:7 [d]Lam 2:15; 3:33; Lk 19:41-44 [1]Lit *task is strange* [2]Lit *work is foreign* **28:22** [a]Is 28:14 [b]Is 10:22, 23 **28:24** [1]Lit *plowman* [2]Lit *all day* [3]Lit *open* **28:25** [a]Mt 23:23 [b]Ex 9:32 [1]Lit *put* [2]Lit *region* **28:27** [a]Am 1:3 [1]Lit *rolled* **28:28** [1]Lit *confuse*

He does not crush it longer.
29 This also comes
from Yahweh of hosts,
*Who* has made *His* counsel
[a]wonderful and *His*
wisdom [b]great.

### *Woe to Ariel*

29 Woe, O [1]Ariel, [1]Ariel the city
*where* David *once* [a]camped!
Add year to year, [b,2]observe
*your* feasts on schedule.
2 I will bring distress to [1]Ariel,
And she will be *a city*
*of* mourning and [a]moaning;
And she will be
like an Ariel to me.
3 And I will [a]camp
against you [1]encircling *you*,
And I will fortify siegeworks
against you,
And I will raise up
fortifications against you.
4 Then you will [a]be
brought low;
From the earth you will speak,
And from the dust
*where* you are prostrate
Your words *will come*.
Your voice will also be like that
of a [1]spirit from the ground,
And your speech will
whisper from the dust.

5 But it will be that the multitude
of your [1]enemies will
become like fine [a]dust,
And the multitude
of the [b]ruthless ones like
the chaff which [2]blows away;
And it will happen
[c]instantly, suddenly.
6 From Yahweh of hosts you
will be [a]punished with
[b]thunder and earthquake
and loud noise,
*With* whirlwind and
tempest and the flame
of a consuming fire.
7 And it will be that the
[a]multitude of all the nations
who wage war against [1]Ariel,
Even all who wage war against
her and her stronghold,
and who distress her,
Will be like a dream,
a [b]vision of the night.
8 And it will be as when
a hungry man dreams—
And behold, he is eating;
But he awakens, and
his soul is empty,
Or as when a thirsty
man dreams—
And behold, he is drinking,
But he awakens, and
behold, he is faint,
And his soul is not quenched.
[a]Thus the multitude
of all the nations will be
Who wage war
against Mount Zion.

9 [a]Astonish yourselves
and be astonished,
Blind yourselves and be blind;
They [b]become drunk,
but not with wine;
They stagger, but not
with strong drink.

**28:29** [a]Is 9:6 [b]Is 31:2; Ro 11:33 ◆ **29:1** [a]2Sa 5:9 [b]Is 1:14; 5:12; 22:12, 13; 29:9, 13 [1]Lion of God, lion of Jerusalem [2]Lit *let your feasts run their round* **29:2** [a]Is 3:26; Lam 2:5 [1]See v 1, note 1 **29:3** [a]Lk 19:43, 44 [1]Lit *like a circle* **29:4** [a]Is 8:19 [1]Or *ghost* **29:5** [a]Is 17:13; 41:15, 16 [b]Is 13:11; 25:3; 29:20 [c]Is 17:14; 30:13; 47:11; 1Th 5:3 [1]Lit *strangers* [2]Lit *passes away* **29:6** [a]Is 10:3; 26:14, 21 [b]1Sa 2:10; Mt 24:7; Mk 13:8; Lk 21:11; Rev 11:13, 19; 16:18 **29:7** [a]Mic 4:11, 12; Zec 12:9 [b]Job 20:8; Ps 73:20; Is 17:14 [1]v 1, note 1 **29:8** [a]Is 54:17 **29:9** [a]Is 29:1 [b]Is 51:17, 21, 22; 63:6

10 For Yahweh has poured over
you a spirit of deep [a]sleep;
He has [b]shut your eyes,
the prophets;
And He has covered your
heads, the seers.
11 The entire vision will be to you like
the words of a sealed [a,1]book, which
when they give it to the one who [2]is
literate, saying, "Please read this," he
will say, "I cannot, for it is sealed."
12 Then the [1]book will be given to
the one who [2]does not know *how
to read* a book, saying, "Please read
this." And he will say, "I [3]do not know
*how to read* a book."
13 Then the Lord said,
"Because [a]this people draw
near with their mouth
And honor Me with their lips,
But they remove their
hearts far from Me,
And their fear of Me is
*in the* command of men
learned *by rote*,
14 Therefore behold, I will once
again deal [a]marvelously
with this people,
wondrously marvelous;
And [b]the wisdom of their
wise men will perish,
And the discernment
of their discerning men
will be hidden."

15 *Woe to those* who deeply
[a]hide their counsel
from Yahweh,
And whose [b]deeds are
*done* in a dark place,
And they say, "[c]Who sees
us?" or "Who knows us?"
16 You turn *things* around!
Shall the potter be
considered [1]as equal
with the clay,
That [a]what is made
would say to its maker,
"He did not make me";
Or what is formed say
to him who formed it,
"He has no understanding"?

### *The Afflicted Will Rejoice*

17 Is it not yet just a little while
[1]Before Lebanon
will be turned
into a [a]fruitful orchard,
And the fruitful orchard will
be counted as a forest?
18 On that day the [a]deaf will
hear [b]words of a book,
And out of [1]darkness and
thick darkness the [c]eyes
of the blind will see.
19 The [a]afflicted also
will increase their
gladness in Yahweh,
And the [b]needy
of mankind will rejoice
in the Holy One of Israel.
20 For the [a]ruthless will
come to an end and the
[b]scoffer will be finished,
Indeed [c]all who are watching
out to do evil will be cut off;

**29:10** [a]Ps 69:23; Is 6:9, 10; Mic 3:6; Ro 11:8 [b]Is 44:18; 2Th 2:9-12 **29:11** [a]Is 8:16; Da 12:4, 9; Mt 13:11 [1]Or *scroll* [2]Lit *knows books* **29:12** [1]Or *scroll* [2]Lit *does not know books* [3]Lit *do not know books* **29:13** [a]Eze 33:31; Mt 15:8, 9; Mk 7:6, 7 **29:14** [a]Is 6:9, 10; 28:21; 65:7; Hab 1:5 [b]Is 44:25; Jer 8:9; 49:7; 1Co 1:19 **29:15** [a]Ps 10:11, 13; Is 28:15; 30:1 [b]Job 22:13; Is 57:12; Eze 8:12 [c]Ps 94:7; Is 47:10; Mal 2:17 **29:16** [a]Is 45:9; 64:8; Jer 18:1-6; Ro 9:19-21 [1]Lit *like* **29:17** [a]Ps 84:6; 107:33, 35; Is 32:15 [1]Lit *And* **29:18** [a]Is 35:5; 42:18, 19; 43:8; Mt 11:5; Mk 7:37 [b]Is 29:11 [c]Ps 119:18; Pr 20:12; Is 32:3 [1]Lit *thick darkness and darkness*, cf. 8:22; 9:2 **29:19** [a]Ps 25:9; 37:11; Is 11:4; 61:1; Mt 5:5; 11:29 [b]Is 3:14, 15; 11:4; 14:30, 32; 25:4; 26:6; Mt 11:5; Jas 1:9; 2:5 **29:20** [a]Is 29:5 [b]Is 28:14 [c]Is 59:4; Mic 2:1

**21** Who [1]cause a person
to sin by a word,
And [a]ensnare him who
reproves at the gate,
And [b,2]defraud the
one in the right with
[3]meaningless arguments.

**22** Therefore thus says Yahweh, who
redeemed [a]Abraham, concerning the
house of Jacob:
"Jacob [b]shall not now be
ashamed, and now his
face shall not turn pale;
**23** But when [1]he sees his
[a]children, the [b]work
of My hands, in his midst,
They will sanctify My name;
Indeed, they will [c]sanctify
the Holy One of Jacob
And will stand trembling
*before* the God of Israel.
**24** "Those who [a]err in spirit will
[b]know discernment,
And those who [1]criticize
will [c,2]gain learning.

### *Alliance with Egypt Condemned*

**30** "Woe to the [a]rebellious
children," declares Yahweh,
"Who [b]execute counsel,
but not Mine,
And [c,1]make an alliance,
but not of My Spirit,
In order to add sin to sin,
**2** Who [a]go down to Egypt—
But did not [b]ask [1]Me—
[c]To find strength in the
strong defense of Pharaoh
And to take refuge
in the shadow of Egypt!
**3** "Therefore the strong defense of
Pharaoh will be [a]your shame
And the refuge in the shadow
of Egypt, your dishonor.
**4** "For [a]their princes are at Zoan
And their messengers
reach Hanes.
**5** "Everyone will be [a]ashamed
because of a people who
cannot profit them,
*Who are* [b]not for help or
profit, but for shame and
also for reproach."

**6** The [1]oracle concerning the [a]beasts
of the [b]Negev.
Through a land of [c]distress
and anguish,
From [2]where *come* lioness
and lion, viper and
[d]flying fiery serpent,
They [e]carry their wealth on
the [3]backs of young donkeys
And their treasures
on [f]camels' humps,
To a people who cannot
profit *them*;
**7** Even Egypt, whose [a]help
is vain and empty.
Therefore, I have called [1]her
"[b,2]Rahab who has ceased."
**8** Now go, [a]write it on a
tablet before them

**29:21** [a]Am 5:10 [b]Is 32:7; Am 5:12 [1]Lit *bring a person under condemnation* [2]Lit *turn aside* [3]Lit *confusion*
**29:22** [a]Is 41:8; 51:2; 63:16 [b]Is 45:17; 49:23; 50:7; 54:4 **29:23** [a]Is 49:20-26 [b]Is 26:12; 45:11; Eph 2:10
[c]Is 5:16; 8:13 [1]Or *his children see* **29:24** [a]Is 30:21; Heb 5:2 [b]Is 41:20; 60:16 [c]Is 54:13 [1]Lit *murmur*
[2]Lit *learn* ◆ **30:1** [a]Is 1:2, 23; 30:9; 65:2 [b]Is 29:15 [c]Is 8:11, 12 [1]Lit *pour out a drink offering*
**30:2** [a]Is 31:1; Jer 43:7 [b]Is 8:19 [c]Is 36:9 [1]Lit *My mouth* **30:3** [a]Is 20:5, 6; 36:6; Jer 42:18, 22
**30:4** [a]Is 19:11 **30:5** [a]Jer 2:36 [b]Is 10:3; 30:7; 31:3 **30:6** [a]Is 46:1, 2 [b]Ge 12:9 [c]Ex 5:10, 21; Dt 4:20; 8:15;
Is 5:30; 8:22; Jer 11:4 [d]Dt 8:15; Is 14:29 [e]Is 15:7; 46:1, 2 [f]1Ki 10:2 [1]Or *burden of* [2]Lit *them* [3]Lit *shoulders*
**30:7** [a]Is 30:5 [b]Job 9:13; Ps 87:4; 89:10; Is 51:9 [1]Lit *this* one [2]M.T. *They are Rahab* (or *arrogance*), *to sit*
*still* **30:8** [a]Is 8:1

And inscribe it on a scroll,
That it may be in the time
to come
[1]As a witness forever.
9 For this is a [a]rebellious
people, [b]false sons,
Sons who are not
willing to [c]listen
To the law of Yahweh,
10 Who say to the [a]seers,
"You must not see,"
And to those who have
visions, "You must not
[b]behold visions
for us of what is right,
[c]Speak to us [1]pleasant words,
Behold visions of illusions.
11 "Get out of the way, [a]turn
aside from the path,
[b,1]Cease *speaking*
before us about the Holy
One of Israel."
12 Therefore thus says the Holy One
of Israel,
"[a]Since you have
rejected this word
And have put your trust
in [b]oppression and
deviousness and have
relied on them,
13 Therefore this [a]iniquity
will be to you
Like a [b]breach about to fall,
A bulge in a high wall,
Whose breaking comes
[c]suddenly in an instant,
14 Whose breaking is like the
breaking of a [a]potter's jar,
[1]So ruthlessly shattered
That a potsherd will
not be found
among its pieces
To [2]take fire from a hearth
Or to scoop water
from a cistern."
15 For thus Lord Yahweh, the Holy
One of Israel, has said,
"In [1]repentance and [a]rest
you will be saved,
In [b]quietness and trust
is your might."
But you were not willing,
16 And you said, "No, for we
will flee on [a]horses,"
Therefore you shall flee!
"And we will ride
on swift *horses*,"
Therefore those who pursue
you shall be swift.
17 [a]One thousand *will flee*
at the threat of one *man*;
You will flee at the
threat of five,
Until you are left as a [1]flag
on a mountain top
And as a [2]standard on a hill.

### *Yahweh Is Gracious and Just*

18 Therefore Yahweh [a]waits
*with longing* to be
gracious to you,
And therefore He is
on [b]high to have
compassion on you.
For Yahweh is a [c]God
of justice;
How blessed are all those
who [d]wait for Him.

**30:8** [1]As in the versions; Heb *Forever and ever* **30:9** [a]Is 30:1 [b]Is 28:15; 59:3, 4 [c]Is 1:10; 5:24; 24:5 **30:10** [a]Is 29:10 [b]Is 5:20; Jer 11:21; Am 2:12; 7:13 [c]1Ki 22:8, 13; Jer 6:14; 23:17, 26; Eze 13:7; Ro 16:18; 2Ti 4:3, 4 [1]Lit *smooth things* **30:11** [a]Ac 13:8 [b]Job 21:14 [1]Lit *Cause to cease from our presence* **30:12** [a]Is 5:24; 7:9; 8:6 [b]Is 3:14, 15; 5:7; 59:13 **30:13** [a]Is 26:21 [b]1Ki 20:30; Ps 62:4; Is 58:12 [c]Is 29:5; 47:11 **30:14** [a]Ps 2:9; Jer 19:10, 11 [1]Lit *Crushed, it will not be spared* [2]Lit *snatch up* **30:15** [a]Ps 116:7; Is 28:12 [b]Is 7:4; 32:17 [1]Lit *returning* **30:16** [a]Is 2:7; 31:1, 3 **30:17** [a]Lv 26:36; Dt 28:25; 32:30; Jos 23:10; Pr 28:1 [1]Lit *pole* [2]Or *signal* **30:18** [a]Is 42:14, 16; 48:9; Jon 3:4, 10; 2Pe 3:9, 15 [b]Is 2:11, 17; 33:5 [c]Is 5:16; 28:17; 61:8 [d]Is 8:17; 25:9; 26:8; 33:2

**19** [1]O people in Zion, [a]inhabitant
in Jerusalem, you will [b]weep no
longer. He will surely be gracious to
you at the sound of your cry; when
He hears it, He will [c]answer you.
**20** The Lord has given you [a]bread
of distress and water of oppression;
*He*, your Teacher will no longer [b]hide
Himself, but your eyes will see your
Teacher. **21** And your ears will hear a
word behind you, "[1]This is the [a]way,
walk in it," whenever you [b]turn to
the right or to the left. **22** And you will
defile your graven [a]images overlaid
with your silver, and your molten
[a]images plated with your gold. You
will scatter them as an impure thing
*and* say to [1]them, "[b]Be gone!"

**23** Then He will [a]give *you* rain for
[1]the seed which you will sow in the
ground, and bread *from* the produce
of the ground, and it will be [2]rich and
fat; on that day [b]your livestock will
graze in a roomy pasture. **24** Also the
oxen and the donkeys which work the
ground will eat salted fodder, which
[1]has been [a]winnowed with shovel
and fork. **25** And it will be that on
every lofty mountain and on [a]every
lifted up hill there will be [1]streams
running with water on the day of the
great [b]slaughter, when the towers fall.
**26** [a]And the light of the moon will be
as the light of the sun, and the light of
the sun will be seven times *brighter*,
like the light of seven days, on the
day [b]Yahweh binds up the [c]fracture
of His people and [d]heals the bruise
[1]He has inflicted.

**27** Behold, [a]the name of
Yahweh comes from afar;
[b]Burning is His anger and
heavy is *His* [1]smoke;
His lips are filled
with [c]indignation
And His tongue is
like a [d]consuming fire;
**28** His [a]breath is like an
overflowing torrent,
Which [b]reaches to the neck,
To [c]shake the nations back
and forth in a [1]sieve
of worthlessness,
And to *put* in the jaws
of the peoples [d]the bridle
which staggers one to ruin.
**29** You will have [1]songs as in the
night when you set yourself
apart as holy for the festival,
And gladness of heart
as when one marches
to *the sound of* the flute,
To go to the mountain
of Yahweh, to the
Rock of Israel.
**30** And Yahweh will cause [1]His
splendid voice to be heard,
And the [2]descending
of His arm to be seen
in raging anger,
And *in* the flame
of a consuming fire
In cloudburst, downpour,
and hailstones.

---

**30:19** [a]Is 65:9; Eze 37:25, 28 [b]Is 25:8; 60:20; 61:1-3 [c]Ps 50:15; Is 58:9; 65:24; Mt 7:7-11 [1]M.T. *A people will inhabit Zion, Jerusalem* **30:20** [a]1Ki 22:27; Ps 80:5 [b]Ps 74:9; Am 8:11 **30:21** [a]Ps 25:8, 9; Pr 3:6; Is 35:8, 9; 42:16 [b]Is 29:24 [1]Lit *saying, "This* **30:22** [a]Ex 32:2, 4; Jdg 17:3, 4; Is 46:6 [b]Mt 4:10 [1]Lit it, "Go out" **30:23** [a]Ps 65:9-13; 104:13, 14 [b]Ps 144:13; Is 32:20; Hos 4:16 [1]Lit *your* [2]Lit *fatness* **30:24** [a]Mt 3:12; Lk 3:17 [1]Lit *one winnows* **30:25** [a]Is 35:6, 7; 41:18; 43:19, 20 [b]Is 34:2 [1]Lit *canals, streams of water* **30:26** [a]Is 24:23; 60:19, 20; Rev 21:23; 22:5 [b]Is 61:1 [c]Is 1:6; 30:13, 14 [d]Dt 32:39; Job 5:18; Is 33:24; Jer 33:6; Hos 6:1, 2 [1]Lit *of His blow* **30:27** [a]Is 59:19 [b]Is 10:17 [c]Is 10:5; 13:5; 66:14 [d]Is 66:15 [1]Lit *uplifting* **30:28** [a]Is 11:4; 30:33; 2Th 2:8 [b]Is 8:8 [c]Am 9:9 [d]2Ki 19:28; Is 37:29 [1]Lit *sifting of the worthless* **30:29** [1]Lit *the song* **30:30** [1]Lit *the majesty of His voice* [2]Lit *descent*

31 For [a]at the voice of Yahweh
[b]Assyria will be dismayed,
*When* He strikes with the [c]rod.
32 And every [1]blow of the
[a,2]appointed staff,
Which Yahweh will cause
to rest upon him,
Will be with *the music*
*of* [b]tambourines and lyres;
And in battles, [c]waving
*weapons* He will fight them.
33 For [a,1]Topheth has
long been ready,
Indeed, it has been
prepared for the king.
He has made it deep
and large,
[2]A pyre of fire
with plenty of wood;
The [b]breath of Yahweh,
like a torrent
of [c]brimstone, sets it afire.

### *Woe to Those Who Go down to Egypt*

31 Woe to those who go down
to [a]Egypt for help
*And* [b]rely on horses,
And trust in chariots
because they are many
And in horsemen because
they are very mighty,
But they do not [c]regard
at the [d]Holy One of Israel,
nor seek Yahweh!
2 Yet He also is [a]wise and *will*
[b]bring about an evil *demise*
And does [c]not turn
His words aside,
But will arise against
the house of [d]evildoers
And against the help
of the [e]workers of iniquity.
3 Now the Egyptians are
[a]men and not God,
And their [b]horses are
flesh and not spirit;
So Yahweh will [c]stretch
out His hand,
And [d]he who helps
will stumble,
And he who is helped
will fall,
And all of them will come
to an end together.

4 For thus says Yahweh to me,
"As the [a]lion or the young
lion growls over its prey,
Against which a multitude
of shepherds is called out,
*And* it will not be dismayed
at their voice nor
afflicted at their noise,
So will Yahweh of hosts come
down to wage [b]war on
Mount Zion and on its hill."
5 Like [1]flying [a]birds so
Yahweh of hosts will
defend Jerusalem.
He will [b]defend and deliver *it*;
He will pass over and
provide a way of escape.
6 [a]Return to Him against whom
[1]you have [b]deeply rebelled, O sons
of Israel. 7 For in that day every man
will [a]reject his silver idols and his

**30:31** [a]Is 11:4 [b]Is 10:12; 14:25; 31:8 [c]Is 10:26; 11:4 **30:32** [a]Is 10:24 [b]1Sa 18:6; Jer 31:4 [c]Eze 32:10 [1]Lit *passing* [2]Lit *staff of foundation* **30:33** [a]2Ki 23:10; Jer 7:31; 19:6 [b]Is 11:4; 30:28 [c]Ge 19:24; Is 34:9 [1]The place of human sacrifice to Molech [2]Lit *Its pile* ◆ **31:1** [a]Is 30:2, 7; 36:6 [b]Dt 17:16; Ps 20:7; 33:17; Is 2:7; 30:16 [c]Is 9:13; Da 9:13; Am 5:4-8 [d]Is 10:17; 43:15; Hos 11:9; Hab 1:12; 3:3 **31:2** [a]Is 28:29; Ro 16:27 [b]Is 45:7 [c]Nu 23:19; Jer 44:29 [d]Is 1:4; 9:17; 14:20 [e]Is 22:14; 32:6 **31:3** [a]Eze 28:9; 2Th 2:4 [b]Is 36:9 [c]Is 9:17; Jer 15:6; Eze 20:33, 34 [d]Is 30:5, 7; Mt 15:14 **31:4** [a]Nu 24:9; Hos 11:10; Am 3:8 [b]Is 42:13; Zec 12:8 **31:5** [a]Dt 32:11; Ps 91:4 [b]Is 37:35; 38:6 [1]Or *hovering* **31:6** [a]Is 44:22; 55:7; Jer 3:10, 14, 22; Eze 18:31, 32 [b]Is 1:2, 5 [1]Lit *they* **31:7** [a]Is 2:20; 30:22

gold idols, which your [b]hands have made for you as [b]a sin.

8 And the [a]Assyrian will fall
by a sword not of man,
And a [b]sword not of man
will devour him.
So he will [c,1]flee
from the sword,
And his choice men will
become [d]forced laborers.
9 "His [a]rock will pass away
because of terror,
And his princes will be
dismayed at the [b]standard,"
Declares Yahweh, whose
[c]fire is in Zion and whose
furnace is in Jerusalem.

### *A King Will Reign Righteously*

32 Behold, a [a]king will
reign righteously
And princes will rule justly.
2 Each will be like a [a]refuge
from the wind
And a shelter from the storm,
Like [b,1]streams of water
in a dry country,
Like the [a]shade of a [2]huge
rock in [3]a weary land.
3 Then [a]the eyes of those who
see will not be [1]blinded,
And the ears of those who
hear will pay attention.
4 And the heart of the [a]hasty
will discern knowledge,
And the tongue of the
stammerers will hasten
to speak clearly.
5 No longer will the [a]wicked
fool be called noble,
Or the rogue be spoken
of *as* generous.
6 For a wicked fool speaks
wicked folly,
And his heart
[a]does wickedness:
To do [b]ungodliness and to
speak error against Yahweh,
In order to [c]make the
hungry person empty;
He even causes the thirsty
to lack a drink.
7 As for a rogue, his
weapons are evil;
He [a]counsels wicked schemes
To [b]wreak destruction *on the*
afflicted with lying words,
[c]Even though *the* needy
one speaks justly.
8 But [a]the noble man
counsels noble plans;
And by noble plans
he rises up.

9 Rise up, you [a]women
who are at ease,
*And* hear my voice;
[b]Give ear to my word,
You complacent daughters.
10 Within a year and *a few* days
You will quake,
O complacent *daughters*;
[a]For the grape harvest
is ended,
*And* the *fruit* gathering
will not come.
11 Tremble, you *women*
who are at ease;
[a]Quake, you
complacent *daughters*;

**31:7** [b]1Ki 12:30 **31:8** [a]Is 10:12; 14:25; 30:31-33; 37:7, 36-38 [b]Is 66:16 [c]Is 21:15 [d]Ge 49:15; Is 14:2 [1]Lit *flee for himself* **31:9** [a]Dt 32:31, 37 [b]Is 5:26; 13:2; 18:3 [c]Is 10:16, 17; 30:33; Zec 2:5 ◆ **32:1** [a]Ps 72:1-4; Is 9:6, 7; 11:4, 5; Jer 23:5; 33:15; Eze 37:24; Zec 9:9 **32:2** [a]Is 4:6; 25:4 [b]Is 35:6; 41:18; 43:19, 20 [1]Lit *canals* [2]Lit *heavy* [3]Lit *an exhausted* **32:3** [a]Is 29:18 [1]Or *turned away* **32:4** [a]Is 29:24 **32:5** [a]1Sa 25:25 **32:6** [a]Pr 19:3; 24:7-9; Is 59:7, 13 [b]Is 9:17; 10:6 [c]Is 3:15; 10:2 **32:7** [a]Jer 5:26-28; Mic 7:3 [b]Is 11:4; 61:1 [c]Is 5:23 **32:8** [a]Pr 11:25 **32:9** [a]Is 47:8; Am 6:1; Zep 2:15 [b]Is 28:23 **32:10** [a]Is 5:5, 6; 7:23; 24:7 **32:11** [a]Is 22:12

[b]Strip, undress, and put
*sackcloth* on *your* waist,
12 [a]Beat your breasts
for the desirable fields,
for the fruitful vine,
13 [a]For the land of my people
*in which* thorns *and*
briars shall come up,
Indeed, against all the
joyful houses *and*
the [b]exultant city.
14 Because [a]the palace has been
abandoned, the [1]populated
[b]city forsaken.
[2]Hill and watchtower have
become [c]caves forever,
A joy for [d]wild donkeys,
a pasture for flocks,
15 Until the [a]Spirit is poured
out upon us from on high,
And the wilderness becomes
a [b]fruitful orchard,
And the fruitful orchard
is counted as a forest.
16 Then [a]justice will dwell
in the wilderness,
And righteousness will live
in the fruitful orchard.
17 And the [a]work
of righteousness
will be peace,
And the service
of righteousness, [b]quietness
and security forever.
18 Then my people will live
in a [a]peaceful abode,
And in secure dwellings and in
undisturbed [b]resting places;
19 And it will [a]hail when
the [b]forest comes down,
And [c]the city will be
utterly laid low.
20 How [a]blessed will you be, you
who sow beside all waters,
Who [1]let out freely the
ox and the donkey.

### *The King in His Beauty*

33 Woe [a]to you, O destroyer,
While you were
not destroyed;
And he [b]who is treacherous,
while *others* did not deal
treacherously with him.
As soon as you finish
destroying, [c]you will
be destroyed;
As soon as you cease
to deal treacherously,
*others* will [d]deal
treacherously with you.
2 O Yahweh, [a]be gracious
to us; we have
[b]hoped in You.
Be [1]their [c,2]strength
every morning,
Our salvation also
in the [d]time of distress.
3 At the sound of the
tumult [a]peoples flee;
At the [b]lifting up of Yourself
nations scatter.
4 Your spoil is gathered
*as* the caterpillar gathers;
As locusts rushing about
men rush about on it.

---

**32:11** [b]Is 47:2 **32:12** [a]Na 2:7 **32:13** [a]Is 5:6, 10, 17; 27:10 [b]Is 22:2; 23:9 **32:14** [a]Is 13:22; 25:2; 34:13 [b]Is 6:11; 22:2; 24:10, 12 [c]Is 13:21; 34:13 [d]Ps 104:11; Jer 14:6 [1]Lit *multitude of the* [2]Or *Ophel* **32:15** [a]Is 11:2; 44:3; 59:21; Eze 39:29; Joel 2:28 [b]Ps 107:35; Is 29:17; 35:1, 2 **32:16** [a]Is 33:5; Zec 8:3 **32:17** [a]Ps 72:2, 3; 85:8; 119:165; Is 2:4; Ro 14:17; Jas 3:18 [b]Is 30:15 **32:18** [a]Is 26:3, 12 [b]Is 11:10; 14:3; 30:15; Hos 2:18-23; Zec 2:5; 3:10 **32:19** [a]Is 28:2, 17; 30:30 [b]Is 10:18, 19, 34 [c]Is 24:10, 12; 26:5; 27:10; 29:4 **32:20** [a]Ecc 11:1; Is 30:23, 24 [1]Lit *send out the foot of the ox* ◆ **33:1** [a]Is 10:6; 21:2 [b]Is 24:16; 48:8 [c]Is 10:12; 14:25; 31:8; Hab 2:8 [d]Jer 25:12-14; Mt 7:2 **33:2** [a]Is 30:18, 19 [b]Is 25:9 [c]Is 40:10; 51:5; 59:16 [d]Is 37:3 [1]Some versions *our* [2]Lit *arm* **33:3** [a]Is 17:13; 21:15 [b]Is 10:33; 17:13; 59:16-18; Jer 25:30, 31

5 Yahweh is [a]exalted,
for He dwells on high;
He has [b]filled Zion with
justice and righteousness.
6 And He will be the
[a,1]stability of your times,
A [b]wealth of salvation,
wisdom, and [c]knowledge;
The [d]fear of Yahweh
is his treasure.
7 Behold, their brave men
cry in [1]the streets;
The [a]messengers
of peace weep bitterly.
8 The highways are desolate,
[1]the [a]traveler has ceased;
He has [b]broken the covenant,
he has rejected the cities;
He has no regard for man.
9 [a]The land mourns
*and* languishes,
[b]Lebanon is humiliated
*and* withers;
[c]Sharon is like a desert plain,
And Bashan and Carmel
[1]lose *their foliage*.
10 "Now [a]I will be on high,"
says Yahweh,
"Now I will be lifted up,
now I will be lifted up.
11 "You have [a]conceived [1]chaff,
you will give birth to stubble;
[2]My [b]breath will consume
you like a fire.
12 "The peoples will be
burned to lime,
[a]Like cut thorns
which are burned in the fire.
13 "You who are far away, [a]hear
what I have done;
And you who are near,
[1]acknowledge My might."
14 [a]Sinners in Zion are in dread;
[b]Trembling has seized
the godless.
"Who among us can sojourn
with [c]the consuming fire?
Who among us can
sojourn with [1]continual
[d]burning?"
15 He who [a]walks righteously
and speaks uprightly;
He who rejects greedy
gain of [1]oppression,
And shakes his hands
so that they hold no bribe;
He who stops his ears from
hearing about bloodshed
And [b]shuts his eyes
from looking upon evil;
16 He will dwell on the heights,
[a]His refuge will be the
strongholds of the cliffs;
[b]His bread will be given *him*,
His water will be sure.

17 Your eyes will behold
[a]the King in His beauty;
They will see
[b]a far-distant land.
18 Your heart will meditate
on [a]terror:
"Where is [b]he who counts?
Where is he who weighs?
Where is he who counts
the towers?"

---

**33:5** [a]Ps 97:9 [b]Is 1:26; 28:6; 32:16 **33:6** [a]Is 33:20 [b]Is 45:17; 51:6 [c]Is 11:9 [d]2Ki 18:7; Ps 112:1-3; Is 11:3; *Mt 6:33* [1]*Or faithfulness* ***33:7*** [a]*2Ki 18:18, 37* [1]*Lit the outside* **33:8** [a]Is 35:8 [b]Is 24:5 [1]Lit *he who passes along the way* **33:9** [a]Is 3:26; 24:4; 29:2 [b]Is 2:13; 10:34 [c]Is 35:2; 65:10 [1]Lit *shake off* **33:10** [a]Ps 12:5; Is 2:19, 21 **33:11** [a]Ps 7:14; Is 26:18; 59:4; Jas 1:15 [b]Is 1:31 [1]Lit *dry grass* [2]As in one ancient version; M.T. *Your breath* **33:12** [a]2Sa 23:6, 7; Is 10:17; 27:4 **33:13** [a]Ps 48:10; Is 49:1 [1]Lit *know* **33:14** [a]Is 1:28 [b]Is 32:11 [c]Is 30:27, 30; Heb 12:29 [d]Is 9:18, 19; 10:16; 47:14 [1]Lit *everlasting* **33:15** [a]Ps 15:2; 24:4; Is 58:6-11 [b]Ps 119:37 [1]Lit *oppressions* **33:16** [a]Is 25:4 [b]Is 49:10 **33:17** [a]Is 6:5; 24:23; 33:21, 22 [b]Is 26:15 **33:18** [a]Is 17:14 [b]1Co 1:20

19 You will no longer see
a fierce people,
A people of [a,1]unintelligible
speech [2]which no one
comprehends,
Of a stammering tongue
[3]which no one
understands.
20 [a]Behold Zion, the city
of our appointed times;
Your eyes will see Jerusalem,
an [b]abode at ease,
[c]A tent which will
not be folded;
Its stakes will never
be pulled up,
Nor any of its cords
ever be torn apart.
21 But there the Mighty *One*,
Yahweh, will be for us
A place of [a]rivers *and*
wide canals
On which no boat
with oars will go,
And on which no mighty
ship will pass—
22 For Yahweh is our [a]judge,
Yahweh is [b]our lawgiver,
Yahweh is [c]our king;
[d]He will save us—
23 Your cords hang slack;
They cannot hold the base
of their mast firmly,
Nor spread out the sail.
Then the [a]prey of an abundant
*spoil* will be divided;
[b]The lame will take
the plunder.
24 And no one who dwells *there*
will say, "I am [a]sick";
The people who inhabit
[1]there will be [b]forgiven
*their* iniquity.

### Yahweh's Wrath Against the Nations

34 Draw near, [a]O nations,
to hear; and pay
attention, O peoples!
[b]Let the earth hear, as well as
its fullness, the world and
all that springs from it.
2 For the [a]indignation
of Yahweh is
against all the nations,
And *His* wrath
against all their [1]hosts;
He has [b,2]devoted them
to destruction;
He has given them over
to [c]slaughter.
3 So their slain will be
[a]cast out,
And their corpses [1]will
give off their [b]stench,
And the mountains will [2]be
drenched with their [c]blood.
4 And [a]all the host
of heaven will rot away,
And the [b]sky will be
rolled up like a scroll;
All their hosts will
also wither away
As a leaf withers
from the vine,
Or as *one* withers
from the fig tree.

**33:19** [a]Dt 28:49, 50; Is 28:11; Jer 5:15 [1]Lit *deepness of lip* [2]Lit *from hearing* [3]Lit *there is no understanding* **33:20** [a]Ps 48:12 [b]Ps 46:5; 125:1, 2; Is 32:18 [c]Is 54:2 **33:21** [a]Is 41:18; 43:19, 20; 48:18; 66:12 **33:22** [a]Is 2:4; 11:4; 16:5; 51:5 [b]Is 1:10; 51:4, 7; Jas 4:12 [c]Ps 89:18; Is 33:17; Zec 9:9 [d]Is 25:9; 35:4; 49:25, 26; 60:16 **33:23** [a]2Ki 7:16 [b]2Ki 7:8; Is 35:6 **33:24** [a]Is 30:26; 58:8; Jer 30:17 [b]Is 40:2; 44:22; Jer 50:20; Mic 7:18, 19; 1Jn 1:7-9 [1]Lit *in it* ◆ **34:1** [a]Ps 49:1; Is 41:1; 43:9 [b]Dt 32:1; Is 1:2 **34:2** [a]Is 26:20 [b]Is 13:5; 24:1 [c]Is 30:25; 63:6; 65:12 [1]Lit *host* [2]Or *put them under the ban* **34:3** [a]Is 14:19 [b]Joel 2:20; Am 4:10 [c]Eze 14:19; 35:6; 38:22 [1]Lit *their stench will go up* [2]Lit *dissolve* **34:4** [a]Is 13:13; 51:6; Eze 32:7, 8; Joel 2:31; Mt 24:29; 2Pe 3:10 [b]Rev 6:12-14

5 For [a]My sword is
satiated in heaven;
Behold, it shall descend
for judgment upon [b]Edom
And upon the people
whom I have [c]devoted
to destruction.
6 The sword of Yahweh is
filled with blood;
It is [1]sated with fat,
with the blood
of lambs and goats,
With the fat of the
kidneys of rams.
For Yahweh has a
sacrifice in [a]Bozrah
And a great slaughter
in the land of [b]Edom.
7 [a]And wild oxen will also
[1]fall with them,
And [b]young bulls
with strong ones;
Thus their land will be
[c]soaked with blood,
And their dust [2]become
greasy with fat.
8 For Yahweh has a day
of [a]vengeance,
A year of recompense
for the [1]cause of Zion.
9 [1]And its streams will be
turned into pitch,
And its dust into [a]brimstone,
And its land will become
burning pitch.
10 It will [a]not be quenched
night or day;
Its [b]smoke will go up forever.
From [c]generation
to generation it will
be laid waste;
[d]None will pass
through it forever and ever.
11 But [a,1]pelican and hedgehog
will possess it,
And [2]owl and raven
will dwell in it;
And He will stretch over it the
[b]line of *utter* formlessness
And the [3]plumb line
of *utter* void.
12 Its nobles—there is
[a]no one there
*Whom* they may
proclaim king—
And all its princes will
be [b]non-existent.
13 And thorns will come up
in its [a]fortified towers,
Weeds and thistles
in its fortified cities;
It will also be a haunt
of [b]jackals
*And* an abode of ostriches.
14 And the desert [a]creatures will
meet with the [1]wolves;
The [a,2]hairy goat also
will cry to its kind;
Surely, the [3]night creature
will obtain relief there
And will find itself a
resting place.
15 The [1]owl will make its nest
and find its escape there,
And it will hatch *its eggs* and
gather *them* in its shade.

---

**34:5** [a]Dt 32:41, 42; Jer 46:10; Eze 21:3-5 [b]Is 63:1; Jer 49:7, 8, 20; Eze 25:12-14; 35:1-15; Am 1:11, 12; Ob 1-14; Mal 1:4 [c]Is 24:6; 43:28 **34:6** [a]Is 63:1; Jer 49:13 [b]Is 63:1 [1]Lit *made fat* **34:7** [a]Nu 23:22; Ps 22:21 [b]Ps 68:30; Jer 50:27 [c]Is 63:6 [1]Lit *go down* [2]Lit *made fat* **34:8** [a]Is 13:6; 35:4; 47:3; 61:2; 63:4 [1]Or *controversy* **34:9** [a]Dt 29:23; Ps 11:6; Is 30:33 [1]Edom's **34:10** [a]Is 1:31; 66:24 [b]Rev 14:11; 19:3 [c]Is 13:20-22; 24:1; 34:10-15; Mal 1:3, 4 [d]Eze 29:11 **34:11** [a]Zep 2:14 [b]2Ki 21:13; Is 24:10; Lam 2:8 [1]Or *owl, jackdaw* [2]Or *great horned owl* [3]Lit *stones of void* **34:12** [a]Jer 27:20; 39:6 [b]Is 41:11, 12 **34:13** [a]Is 13:22; 25:2; 32:13 [b]Ps 44:19; Jer 9:11; 10:22 **34:14** [a]Is 13:21 [1]Or *howling creatures* [2]Or *goat demon* [3]Heb *Lilith* **34:15** [1]Or *tree snake*

Surely, [a]the [2]falcons will
be gathered there,
Every one with its kind.

16 Seek from the [a]book of Yahweh,
and read:
Not one of these will
be missing;
None will lack its mate.
For [b,1]His mouth
has commanded,
And His Spirit has
gathered them.
17 He has cast the [a]lot for them,
And His hand has divided
it to them by [b]line.
They shall possess it forever;
From [c]generation to generation
they will dwell in it.

### *The Joy of the Redeemed*

35 The [a]wilderness and the
desert will be delighted,
And the [b,1]Arabah will
rejoice and flourish;
Like the crocus
2 It will [a]flourish profusely
And [b]rejoice with rejoicing
and shout of joy.
The [c]glory of Lebanon
will be given to it,
The majesty of [d]Carmel
and Sharon.
They will see the [e]glory
*of Yahweh,*
The majesty of our God.
3 [a]Strengthen limp
hands, and give courage
to the knees
of the stumbling.
4 Say to those with an
[a]anxious heart,
"Be strong, fear not.
Behold, your God will
come *with* [b]vengeance;
The [c]recompense
of God will come,
But He will [d]save you."
5 Then the [a]eyes
of the blind will be opened,
And the ears of the deaf
will be unstopped.
6 Then the [a]lame will
leap like a deer,
And the [b]tongue of the
mute will shout for joy.
For waters will break forth
in the [c]wilderness
And streams in the [1]Arabah.
7 Then the [1]scorched land
will become a pool
And the thirsty ground
[a]springs of water;
In the [b]haunt of jackals,
its resting place,
Grass *becomes* reeds and rushes.
8 [a]And a [1]roadway will be
there, [b]a highway,
And it will be called the
Highway of [c]Holiness.
The unclean will not
pass by on it,
But it *will* be for him who
walks *in that* way,
And [d]ignorant fools will
not wander *on it.*

**34:15** [a]Dt 14:13 [2]Or *hawks* **34:16** [a]Is 30:8 [b]Is 1:20; 40:5; 58:14 [1]As in DSS; M.T. *My* **34:17** [a]Is 17:13, 14; Jer 13:25 [b]Is 34:11 [c]Is 34:10 ◆ **35:1** [a]Is 6:11; 7:21-25; 27:10; 41:18; 55:12, 13 [b]Is 41:19; 51:3 [1]Or *desert* **35:2** [a]Is 27:6; 32:15 [b]Is 25:9; 35:10; 55:12, 13; 66:10, 14 [c]Is 60:13 [d]SS 7:5 [e]Is 25:9 **35:3** [a]Job 4:3, 4; Heb 12:12 **35:4** [a]Is 32:4 [b]Is 1:24; 47:3; 61:2; 63:4 [c]Is 34:8; 59:18 [d]Ps 145:19; Is 33:22; 35:4 **35:5** [a]Is 29:18; 32:3, 4; 42:7, 16; 50:4; Mt 11:5; Jn 9:6, 7 **35:6** [a]Mt 15:30; Jn 5:8, 9; Ac 3:8 [b]Mt 9:32; Lk 11:14 [c]Is 35:1; 41:18; 43:19; 49:10; 51:3; Jn 7:38 [1]Or *desert* **35:7** [a]Is 49:10 [b]Is 13:22; 34:13 [1]Or *mirage* **35:8** [a]Is 11:16; 19:23; 40:3; 49:11; 62:10 [b]Is 30:21; 51:10 [c]Is 4:3; 52:1; Mt 7:13, 14; 1Pe 1:15, 16 [d]Is 33:8 [1]Or *highway*, cf. 36:2; 40:3; 49:11

9 No [a]lion will be there,
Nor will any vicious
beast go up on it;
[1]These will not be found there.
But [b]the redeemed
will walk *there*,
10 And [a]the ransomed
of Yahweh will return
And come with joyful
shouting to Zion,
With everlasting gladness
upon their heads.
They will [1]attain delight
and gladness,
And [b]sorrow and sighing
will flee away.

### *Sennacherib Invades Judah*

36 [a]Now it happened in the four-
teenth year of King Hezekiah,
*that* [b]Sennacherib king of Assyria
came up against all the fortified cities
of Judah and seized them. **2** And the
[a]king of Assyria sent Rabshakeh
from Lachish to Jerusalem to King
Hezekiah with a heavy military force.
And he stood by the [b]conduit of the
upper pool on the highway of the
[1]fuller's field. **3** Then [a]Eliakim the son
of Hilkiah, who was over the house-
hold, and [b]Shebna the scribe, and
Joah the son of Asaph, the recorder,
came out to him.
**4** Then [a]Rabshakeh said to them,
"Say now to Hezekiah, 'Thus says the
great king, the king of Assyria, "What
is this trust that you have? **5** I say,
'Your counsel and might for the war
are only [1]empty words.' Now in whom
do you trust, that [a]you have rebelled
against me? **6** Behold, you trust in the
[a]staff of this crushed reed, *even* on
Egypt, on which if a man leans, it will
go into his [1]hand and pierce it. [b]So
is Pharaoh king of Egypt to all who
trust in him. **7** But if you say to me,
'We trust in Yahweh our God,' is it not
He [a]whose high places and whose
altars Hezekiah has taken away and
has said to Judah and to Jerusalem,
'You shall worship before this altar'?
**8** So now, [1]come make a bargain with
my master the king of Assyria, and I
will give you two thousand horses,
if you are able on your part to give
riders for them. **9** How then can you
[1]turn away one [2]official of the least
of my master's servants and [a]trust in
Egypt for chariots and for horsemen?
**10** So now, have I come up [1]without
the approval of Yahweh against this
land to make it a ruin? [a]Yahweh said
to me, 'Go up against this land and
make it a ruin.'"'"
**11** Then Eliakim and Shebna and
Joah said to Rabshakeh, "Speak now
to your servants in [a]Aramaic, for we
[1]understand *it*; and do not speak with
us in [b,2]Judean in the hearing of the
people who are on the wall." **12** But
Rabshakeh said, "Has my master sent
me only to your master and to you
to speak these words, *and* not to the
men who sit on the wall, *doomed* to
eat their own dung and drink their
own urine with you?"
**13** Then Rabshakeh stood and [a]cried
with a loud voice in Judean and said,

**35:9** [a]Is 5:29; 30:6 [b]Is 51:10; 62:12; 63:4 [1]Lit *It* **35:10** [a]Is 1:27; 51:11 [b]Is 25:8; 30:19; 65:19; Rev 7:17; 21:4 [1]Lit *overtake* ◆ **36:1** [a]2Ki 18:13 [b]2Chr 32:1 **36:2** [a]2Ki 18:17-20:11; 2Chr 32:9-24; Is 36:2-38:8 [b]Is 7:3 [1]Or *launderer's* **36:3** [a]Is 22:20 [b]Is 22:15 **36:4** [a]2Ki 18:19 **36:5** [a]2Ki 18:7 [1]Lit *words of lips* **36:6** [a]Eze 29:6, 7 [b]Ps 146:3; Is 30:3, 5, 7 [1]Lit *palm* **36:7** [a]Dt 12:2-5; 2Ki 18:4, 5 **36:8** [1]Lit *please exchange pledges* **36:9** [a]Is 20:5; 30:2-5, 7; 31:3 [1]Lit *turn away the face of* [2]Or *governor* **36:10** [a]1Ki 13:18; 22:6, 12 [1]Lit *without Yahweh* **36:11** [a]Ezr 4:7; Da 2:4 [b]Is 36:13 [1]Lit *hear* [2]Hebrew **36:13** [a]2Chr 32:18

"Hear the words of the great king, the king of Assyria. **14** Thus says the king, 'Do not let Hezekiah [a]deceive you, for he will not be able to deliver you; **15** and do not let Hezekiah make you [a]trust in Yahweh, saying, "Yahweh will surely deliver us, this city will not be given into the hand of the king of Assyria." **16** Do not listen to Hezekiah,' for thus says the king of Assyria, '[1]Make your peace with me and come out to me, and eat each of his [a]vine and each of his fig tree, and drink each of the [b]waters of his own cistern, **17** until I come and take you away to a land like your own land, a land of grain and new wine, a land of bread and vineyards. **18** *Beware* lest Hezekiah mislead you, saying, "[a]Yahweh will deliver us." Has any one of the gods of the nations delivered his land from the hand of the king of Assyria? **19** Where are the gods of [a]Hamath and Arpad? Where are the gods of [a]Sepharvaim? And when have they [b]delivered Samaria from my hand? **20** Who among all the [a]gods of these lands [1]have delivered their land from my hand, that [b]Yahweh would deliver Jerusalem from my hand?'"

**21** But they were silent and [a]answered him not a word, for the king's commandment was, "Do not answer him." **22** Then [a]Eliakim the son of Hilkiah, who *was* over the household, and [b]Shebna the scribe, and Joah the son of Asaph, the recorder, came to Hezekiah with their clothes torn and told him the words of Rabshakeh.

### *Hezekiah Seeks Isaiah's Help*

**37** Now it happened that [a]when King Hezekiah heard *it*, he tore his clothes, covered himself with sackcloth, and entered the house of Yahweh. **2** Then he sent [a]Eliakim, who was over the household with [b]Shebna the scribe, and the elders of the priests, covered with sackcloth, to [c]Isaiah the prophet, the son of Amoz. **3** And they said to him, "Thus says Hezekiah, 'This day is a [a]day of distress, reproof, and rejection; for [b]children have come to the point of breaking forth, but there is no strength to give birth. **4** Perhaps Yahweh your God will hear the words of Rabshakeh, whom his master the king of Assyria has sent to [a,1]reproach the living God, and will reprove the words which Yahweh your God has heard. Therefore, lift up a prayer for [b]the remnant that is left.'"

**5** So the servants of King Hezekiah came to Isaiah. **6** And Isaiah said to them, "Thus you shall say to your master, 'Thus says Yahweh, "[a]Do not be afraid because of the words that you have heard, with which the young men of the king of Assyria have blasphemed Me. **7** Behold, I will put a spirit in him so that he will [a]hear a report and [b]return to his own land. And I will make him fall by the sword in his own land."'"

**8** Then Rabshakeh returned and found the king of Assyria fighting against [a]Libnah, for he had heard that [1]the king had set out from [b]Lachish. **9** Then he [a]heard *them*

**36:14** [a]Is 37:10 **36:15** [a]Is 36:18, 20; 37:10, 11 **36:16** [a]1Ki 4:25; Mic 4:4; Zec 3:10 [b]Pr 5:15 [1]Lit *Make with me a blessing* **36:18** [a]Is 36:15 **36:19** [a]Is 10:9-11; 37:11-13; Jer 49:23 [b]2Ki 17:6 **36:20** [a]1Ki 20:23, 28 [b]Is 36:15 [1]Lit *who have* **36:21** [a]Pr 9:7, 8; 26:4 **36:22** [a]Is 22:20; 36:3 [b]Is 22:15 ◆ **37:1** [a]2Ki 19:1-37; Is 37:1-38 **37:2** [a]Is 22:20 [b]Is 22:15 [c]Is 1:1; 20:2 **37:3** [a]Is 22:5; 26:16; 33:2 [b]Is 26:17, 18; 66:9; Hos 13:13 **37:4** [a]Is 36:13-15, 18, 20 [b]Is 1:9; 10:20-22; 37:31, 32; 46:3 [1]Or *defy*, cf. 1Sa 17:26 **37:6** [a]Is 7:4; 35:4 **37:7** [a]Is 37:9 [b]Is 37:37, 38 **37:8** [a]Nu 33:20; Jos 10:29 [b]Jos 10:31, 32 [1]Lit *he* **37:9** [a]Is 37:7

say concerning Tirhakah king of
[b,1]Ethiopia, "He has come out to
fight against you." So he heard *it* and
sent messengers to Hezekiah, saying,
**10** "Thus you shall say to Hezekiah
king of [1]Judah, '[a]Do not let your
God in whom you trust deceive you,
saying, "Jerusalem will not be given
into the hand of the king of Assyria."
**11** [a]Behold, you have heard what the
kings of Assyria have done to all the
lands, devoting them to destruction.
So will you be delivered? **12** Did the
gods of [1]those nations, which my
fathers have brought to ruin, deliver
them, *even* [a]Gozan and [b]Haran and
Rezeph and the sons of Eden who
*were* in Telassar? **13** Where is the king
of Hamath, the king of Arpad, the
king of the city of Sepharvaim, *and*
*of* Hena and Ivvah?'"

### *Hezekiah's Prayer in the Temple*

**14** Then Hezekiah took the [1]letter
from the hand of the messengers and
read it, and he went up to the house
of Yahweh and [2]spread it out before
Yahweh. **15** And Hezekiah prayed
to Yahweh saying, **16** "O Yahweh of
hosts, the God of Israel, [a]who is
enthroned *above* the cherubim, You
are the [b]God, You alone, of all the
kingdoms of the earth. [c]You have
made heaven and earth. **17** [a]Incline
Your ear, O Yahweh, and hear; open
Your eyes, O Yahweh, and see; and
[b]listen to all the words of Sennach-
erib, who sent *them* to [c,1]reproach
the living God. **18** Truly, O Yahweh,
the [a]kings of Assyria have laid waste
to all the countries and their lands
**19** and have cast their gods into the
fire, for they were not gods but the
[a]work of men's hands, wood and
stone. So they have [b]destroyed
them. **20** But now, O Yahweh our God,
[a]save us from his hand that [b]all the
kingdoms of the earth may know that
[1]You are Yahweh, You alone."

### *Yahweh's Answer Through Isaiah*

**21** Then [a]Isaiah the son of Amoz sent
*word* to Hezekiah, saying, "Thus says
Yahweh, the God of Israel, 'Because
you have prayed to Me about Sen-
nacherib king of Assyria, **22** this is
the word that Yahweh has spoken
against him:

"She has despised you
and mocked you,
The [a]virgin [b]daughter of Zion;
She has [c]shaken *her*
head behind you,
The daughter of Jerusalem!
**23** "Whom have you [a,1]reproached
and blasphemed?
And against whom have you
heightened *your* voice
And [2]haughtily [b]lifted
up your eyes?
Against the [c]Holy
One of Israel!
**24** "Through your servants you
have [1]reproached the Lord,
And you have said,
'With my many chariots

***37:9*** [b]*Is 18:1; 20:5* [1]Or *Cush*, cf. Ge 10:6 **37:10** [a]Is 36:15 [1]Lit *Judah, saying* **37:11** [a]Is 10:9-11; 36:18-20 **37:12** [a]2Ki 17:6; 18:11 [b]Ge 11:31; 12:1-4; Ac 7:2 [1]Lit *the* **37:14** [1]Lit *letters* [2]Lit *Hezekiah spread* **37:16** [a]Ex 25:22; 1Sa 4:4; Ps 80:1; 99:1 [b]Dt 10:17; Ps 86:10; 136:2, 3 [c]Is 42:5; 45:12; Jer 10:12 **37:17** [a]2Chr 6:40; Ps 17:6; Da 9:18 [b]Ps 74:22 [c]Is 37:4 [1]Or *defy* **37:18** [a]2Ki 15:29; 16:9; 17:6, 24; 1Chr 5:26 **37:19** [a]Is 2:8; 17:8; 41:24, 29 [b]Is 26:14 **37:20** [a]Is 25:9; 33:22; 35:4 [b]1Ki 18:36, 37; Ps 46:10; Is 37:16; Eze 36:23 [1]DSS and 2Ki 19:19 *You alone, O Yahweh, are God* **37:21** [a]Is 37:2 **37:22** [a]Jer 14:17; Lam 2:13 [b]Ps 9:14; Zep 3:14; Zec 2:10 [c]Job 16:4 **37:23** [a]Is 37:4 [b]Is 2:11; 5:15, 21 [c]Eze 39:7; Hab 1:12 [1]Or *defied* [2]Lit *on high* **37:24** [1]Or *defied*

I came up to the heights
of the mountains,
To the remotest parts
of [a]Lebanon;
And I cut down its tall [b]cedars
*and* its choice cypresses.
And I will go to its [2]highest
peak, its thickest [c]forest.
25 'I dug *wells* and drank waters,
And [a]with the sole
of my feet I dried up
All the rivers of [1]Egypt.'
26 "[a]Have you not heard?
Long ago I did it;
From days of old I [b]formed it.
Now [c]I have brought it to pass,
That [d]you should devastate
fortified cities
into [e]ruinous heaps.
27 "So their inhabitants were
short of power;
They were dismayed
and put to shame;
They were *as* the [a]plant of the
field and *as* the green herb,
*As* [b]grass on the rooftops [1]is
scorched before it rises.
28 "But I [a]know your sitting down
And your going out and
your coming in
And your raging against Me.
29 "Because of your raging
against Me
And because your
[a,1]*presumptuousness* has
come up to My ears,
Therefore I will put My
[b]hook in your nose
And My [c]bridle in your lips,
And I will turn you back [d]by
the way which you came.

30 "Then this shall be the sign
for you: [1]you will eat this year what
[a]grows of its own accord, in the
second year what springs from the
same, and in the third year sow, reap,
plant vineyards, and eat their fruit.
31 And the [a]surviving [b]remnant of
the house of Judah will again [c]take
root downward and bear fruit up-
ward. 32 For out of Jerusalem will go
forth a [a]remnant and out of Mount
Zion [1]survivors. The [b]zeal of Yahweh
of hosts will do this."'

33 "Therefore, thus says Yahweh
concerning the king of Assyria, 'He
will not come to this city or shoot an
arrow there; and he will not come
before it with a shield or throw up
a [a]siege ramp against it. 34 [a]By the
way that he came, by the same he
will return, and he will not come to
this city,' declares Yahweh. 35 'Indeed
I will [a]defend this city to save it [b]for
My own sake and for My servant
David's sake.'"

### *The Defeat and Death of Sennacherib*

36 Then the [a]angel of Yahweh went
out and struck 185,000 in the camp
of the Assyrians. And [1]the men arose
early in the morning, and behold,
all of them were dead bodies. 37 So
Sennacherib king of Assyria set out
and [1]returned *home* and lived at
[a]Nineveh. 38 Now it happened that

---

**37:24** [a]Is 10:33, 34 [b]Is 14:8 [c]Is 10:18 [2]Lit *farthest height* **37:25** [a]Dt 11:10; 1Ki 20:10 [1]Or *the besieged place* **37:26** [a]Is 40:21, 28 [b]Ac 2:23; 4:27, 28; 1Pe 2:8 [c]Is 46:11 [d]Is 10:6 [e]Is 17:1; 25:2 **37:27** [a]Is 40:7 [b]Ps 129:6 [1]As in DSS and 2Ki 19:26; M.T. as *a plowed field* **37:28** [a]Ps 139:1 **37:29** [a]Is 10:12 [b]Eze 29:4; 38:4 [c]Is 30:28 [d]Is 37:34 [1]Lit *complacency* **37:30** [a]Lv 25:5, 11 [1]Lit *eating* **37:31** [a]Is 4:2; 10:20 [b]Is 37:4 [c]Is 27:6 **37:32** [a]Is 37:4 [b]2Ki 19:31; Is 9:7; 59:17; Joel 2:18; Zec 1:14 [1]Lit *those who escape* **37:33** [a]Jer 6:6; 32:24 **37:34** [a]Is 37:29 **37:35** [a]2Ki 20:6; Is 31:5; 38:6 [b]Is 43:25; 48:9, 11 **37:36** [a]2Ki 19:35; Is 10:12, 33, 34 [1]Lit *they* **37:37** [a]Ge 10:11; Jon 1:2; 3:3; 4:11; Zep 2:13 [1]Lit *went and returned*

as he was worshiping in the house of
Nisroch his god, Adrammelech and
Sharezer his sons struck him down
with the sword; and they escaped
into the land of [a]Ararat. And [b]Esar-
haddon his son became king in his
place.

### *Hezekiah's Illness and Recovery*

**38** [a]In those days Hezekiah be-
came ill to the point of death.
And [b]Isaiah the prophet the son of
Amoz came to him and said to him,
"Thus says Yahweh, '[c]Set your house
in order, for you shall die and not
live.'" **2** Then Hezekiah turned his
face to the wall and prayed to Yah-
weh **3** and said, "[a]Remember now,
O Yahweh, I beseech You, how I have
[b]walked before You in truth and with
a [c]whole heart and [d]have done what
is good in Your sight." And Hezekiah
[e]wept [1]greatly.
**4** Then the word of Yahweh came
to Isaiah, saying, **5** "Go and say to
Hezekiah, 'Thus says Yahweh, the
God of your father David, "I have
heard your prayer; I have seen your
tears; behold, I will add [a]fifteen years
to your [1]life. **6** And I will [a]deliver you
and this city from the hand of the
king of Assyria; and I will defend this
city."'
**7** "Now this shall be the [a]sign to
you from Yahweh, that Yahweh will
do this word that He has spoken:
**8** Behold, I will [a]cause the shadow
on the stairway, which has gone
down with the sun on the stairway
of Ahaz, to go back ten steps." So the
[b]sun's *shadow* went back ten steps
on the stairway on which it had gone
down.
**9** A writing of Hezekiah king of
Judah after his illness and [1]recovery:

**10** I said, "[a]In the middle
of my [1]life
I am to enter the [b]gates
of Sheol;
I am to be [c]deprived
of the rest of my years."
**11** I said, "I will not see Yah,
Yah [a]in the land of the living;
I will look on man no more
among the inhabitants
of the world.
**12** "Like a shepherd's [a]tent
my dwelling is pulled up
and removed from me;
As a [b]weaver I [c]rolled
up my life.
He [d]cuts me off
from the loom;
From [e]day until night You
make an end of me.
**13** "I soothed *my soul*
until morning.
[a]Like a lion—so He
[b]shatters all my bones;
From [c]day until night You
make an end of me.
**14** "[a]Like a swallow,
*like* a crane, so I chirped;
I [b]moan like a dove;
My [c]eyes look wistfully
to the heights;
O Lord, I am oppressed,
be my [d]security.

***37:38*** [a]*Ge 8:4; Jer 51:27* [b]*Ezr 4:2* ◆ **38:1** [a]*2Ki 20:1-6, 9-11; 2Chr 32:24; Is 38:1-8* [b]*Is 1:1; 37:2* [c]2Sa 17:23 **38:3** [a]Ne 13:14 [b]2Ki 18:5, 6; Ps 26:3 [c]1Chr 28:9; 29:19 [d]Dt 6:18 [e]Ps 6:6-8 [1]Lit *great weeping* **38:5** [a]2Ki 18:2, 13 [1]Lit *days* **38:6** [a]Is 31:5; 37:35 **38:7** [a]Jdg 6:17, 21, 36-40; Is 7:11, 14; 37:30 **38:8** [a]2Ki 20:9-11 [b]Jos 10:12-14 **38:9** [1]Lit *he lived after his illness* **38:10** [a]Ps 102:24 [b]Ps 107:18 [c]Job 17:11, 15; 2Co 1:9 [1]Lit *days* **38:11** [a]Ps 27:13; 116:9 **38:12** [a]2Co 5:1, 4; 2Pe 1:13, 14 [b]Job 7:6 [c]Heb 1:12 [d]Job 6:9 [e]Job 4:20; Ps 73:14 **38:13** [a]Job 10:16 [b]Ps 51:8; Da 6:24 [c]Ps 32:4 **38:14** [a]Job 30:29; Ps 102:6 [b]Is 59:11; Eze 7:16; Na 2:7 [c]Ps 119:123 [d]Job 17:3; Ps 119:122

15 “[a]What shall I say?
[1]Indeed, He has spoken to me,
and He Himself has done it;
I will [b]wander about all
my years because of the
[c]bitterness of my soul.
16 “O Lord, [a]by *these*
things *men* live,
And in all these is the
life of my spirit;
[b,1]O restore me to health
and [c]let me live!

17 “Behold, for *my own* well-being
I had great bitterness;
But it is You who has [a,1]held
back my soul from the
pit of [2]nothingness,
For You have [b]cast all my
sins behind Your back.
18 “For [a]Sheol cannot thank You;
Death cannot praise You;
Those who go down
[b]to the pit cannot keep
watch for Your truth.
19 “It is the [a]living, the living
who give thanks to You,
as I do today;
A [b]father makes known
to his sons about Your truth.
20 “Yahweh *is here* to save me;
So we will [a]play my songs
on stringed instruments
[b]All *the* days of our life
[c]at the house of Yahweh.”
21 Now [a]Isaiah had said, “Let them
take up a cake of figs and apply it to
the boil, that he may live.” 22 Then
Hezekiah had said, “What is the
[a]sign that I shall go up to the house
of Yahweh?”

### *Hezekiah Shows His Treasures to Babylon*

39 [a]At that time Merodach-
baladan son of Baladan, king
of Babylon, sent letters and a present
to Hezekiah, for he heard that he had
been sick and was growing stronger.
2 And Hezekiah was [a]glad about
these things and showed them *all*
his treasure house, the [b]silver and
the gold and the spices and the good
oil and his whole armory and all that
was found in his treasuries. There
was nothing in his house nor in all
his dominion that Hezekiah did
not show them. 3 Then Isaiah the
[a]prophet came to King Hezekiah
and said to him, “What did these men
say, and from where have they come
to you?” And Hezekiah said, “They
have come to me from a far [b]country,
from Babylon.” 4 And he said, “What
have they seen in your house?” So
Hezekiah said, “They have seen all
that is in my house; there is nothing
among my treasuries that I have not
shown them.”

5 Then Isaiah said to Hezekiah,
“Hear the [a]word of Yahweh of hosts,
6 ‘Behold, the days are coming when
[a]all that is in your house and all that
*your fathers* have treasured up to
this day will be carried to Babylon;
nothing will be left,’ says Yahweh.
7 ‘And *some* of your sons who will
issue from you, whom you will beget,

---

**38:15** [a]Ps 39:9 [b]1Ki 21:27 [c]Job 7:11; 10:1; Is 38:17 [1]DSS and Targum *And what shall I say for He* **38:16** [a]Ps 119:71, 75 [b]Ps 39:13 [c]Ps 119:25 [1]Lit *You will* **38:17** [a]Ps 30:3; 86:13; Jon 2:6 [b]Is 43:25; Jer 31:34; Mic 7:19 [1]As in some versions; Heb *loved* [2]Or *destruction* **38:18** [a]Ps 6:5; 30:9; 88:11; Ecc 9:10 [b]Nu 16:33; Ps 28:1 **38:19** [a]Ps 118:17; 119:175 [b]Dt 6:7; 11:19; Ps 78:5-7 **38:20** [a]Ps 33:1-3; 68:24-26 [b]Ps 104:33; 116:2; 146:2 [c]Ps 116:17-19 **38:21** [a]2Ki 20:7, 8 **38:22** [a]Is 38:7 ◆ **39:1** [a]2Ki 20:12-19; 2Chr 32:31; Is 39:1-8 **39:2** [a]2Chr 32:25, 31; Job 31:25 [b]2Ki 18:15, 16 **39:3** [a]2Sa 12:1; 2Chr 16:7 [b]Dt 28:49; Jer 5:15 **39:5** [a]1Sa 13:13, 14; 15:16 **39:6** [a]2Ki 24:13; 25:13-15; Jer 20:5

[a]will be taken away, and [b]they will
become officials in the palace of the
king of Babylon.'" **8** [a]Then Hezekiah
said to Isaiah, "The word of Yahweh
which you have spoken is good." For
he said, "For there will be peace and
truth [b]in my days."

### *The Glory of Yahweh Will Be Revealed*

**40** "[a]Comfort, O comfort My
people," says your God.
**2** "[a]Speak to the heart
of Jerusalem;
And call out to her,
that her [b,1]warfare
has been fulfilled,
That her [c,2]iniquity has
been removed,
That she has received
from the hand of Yahweh
[d]Double for all her sins."

**3** [a]A voice [1]is calling,
"[b]Prepare the way for Yahweh
in the wilderness;
Make smooth in the desert
a highway for our God.
**4** "Let every valley be lifted up,
And every mountain and
hill be made low;
And let the rough ground
become a plain,
And the rugged terrain
a broad valley;
**5** [1]Then the [a]glory of Yahweh
will be revealed,
And [b]all flesh will
see *it* together;
For the [c]mouth of Yahweh
has spoken."
**6** A voice says, "Call out."
Then [1]he answered,
"What shall I call out?"
[a]All flesh is grass, and all
its lovingkindness is
like the flower of the field.
**7** The [a]grass [1]withers,
the flower fades,
[2]When the [b]breath
of Yahweh blows upon it;
Surely the people are grass.
**8** The grass [1]withers,
the flower fades,
But [a]the word of our
God stands forever.

**9** Get yourself up
on a [a]high mountain,
O Zion, bearer of [b]good news,
Raise up your
voice powerfully,
O Jerusalem, bearer
of good news;
Raise *it* up, do not fear.
Say to the [c]cities of Judah,
"[d]Behold your God!"
**10** Behold, Lord Yahweh will
come [a]with strength,
With His [b]arm ruling for Him.
Behold, His [c]reward
is with Him
And His recompense
before Him.

---

**39:7** [a]2Ki 24:10-16; 2Chr 36:10 [b]Da 1:1-7 **39:8** [a]2Chr 32:26 [b]2Chr 34:28 ◆ **40:1** [a]Is 12:1; 49:13; *51:3, 12; 52:9;* 61:2; 66:13; Jer 31:10-14; Zep 3:14-17; 2Co 1:4 **40:2** [a]Is 35:4; Zec 1:13 [b]Is 41:11-13; 49:25; 54:15, 17 [c]Is *33:24;* 53:5, 6, 11 [d]*Jer 16:18; Zec 9:12; Rev 18:6* [1]Or *hard service* [2]Or *penalty of iniquity has been accepted as paid off* **40:3** [a]Mt 3:3; Mk 1:3; Lk 3:4-6; Jn 1:23 [b]Mal 3:1; 4:5, 6 [1]Or *of one calling out* **40:5** [a]Is 6:3; Hab 2:14 [b]Is 52:10; Joel 2:28 [c]Is 1:20; 34:16; 58:14 [1]Or *In order that the* **40:6** [a]Job 14:2; Ps 102:11; 103:15; 1Pe 1:24, 25 [1]Or *I said* **40:7** [a]Ps 90:5, 6; Jas 1:10, 11 [b]Job 4:9; 41:21; Is 11:4; 40:24 [1]Or *dries up*, cf. 42:15; Ps 90:5-6 [2]Or *Because* **40:8** [a]Is 55:11; 59:21; Mt 5:18 [1]Or *dries up*, cf. 42:15; Ps 90:5-6 **40:9** [a]Is 52:7 [b]Is 61:1 [c]Is 44:26 [d]Is 25:9; 35:2 **40:10** [a]Is 9:6, 7 [b]Is 59:16, 18 [c]Is 62:11; Rev 22:12

11 Like a shepherd He will
[a]shepherd His flock;
In His arm He will
gather the lambs
And carry *them* in His bosom;
He will gently lead the
nursing *ewes.*

12 Who has [a]measured
the [1]waters in the
hollow of His hand,
And [2]encompassed
the heavens by the [3]span,
And [4]calculated the dust
of the earth by the measure,
And weighed the
mountains in a balance
And the hills in a pair of scales?
13 [a]Who has [1]encompassed
the Spirit of Yahweh,
Or as His [b]counselor
has informed Him?
14 [a]With whom did He take
counsel and *who* [b]gave
Him understanding?
And *who* taught Him
in the path of justice and
taught Him knowledge
And made Him know the
way of understanding?
15 Behold, the [a]nations are
like a drop from a bucket,
And are counted as a speck
of [b]dust on the scales;
Behold, He lifts up the
coastlands like fine dust.
16 Even Lebanon is not
enough to burn,
Nor its [a]beasts enough
for a burnt offering.
17 [a]All the nations are
as nothing before Him;
They are counted by Him
as non-existent and
*utterly* formless.

18 [a]To whom then will
you liken God?
Or what likeness will you
compare with Him?
19 *As for* the [a]graven images,
a craftsman casts it,
A goldsmith [b]plates
it with gold,
And a silversmith *fashions*
chains of silver.
20 He who is too impoverished
*to make such* a contribution
Chooses a [a]tree that
does not rot;
He seeks out for himself
a wise craftsman
To [1]prepare a graven image
that [b]will not be shaken.

21 [a]Do you not know? Have
you not heard?
Has it not been declared
to you from the beginning?
Have you not understood
[b]from the foundations
of the earth?
22 It is He who [1]inhabits above
the [a,2]circle of the earth,
And its inhabitants are
like [b]grasshoppers;

**40:11** [a]Jer 31:10; Eze 34:12-14, 23, 31; Mic 5:4; Jn 10:11, 14-16 **40:12** [a]Job 38:8-11; Ps 102:25, 26; Is 48:13; Heb 1:10-12 [1]DSS *waters of the sea* [2]Or *measured, marked off* [3]A span was approx. 9 in. or 23 cm [4]Lit *contained, comprehended* **40:13** [a]Ro 11:34; 1Co 2:16 [b]Is 41:28 [1]Or *measured, marked off* **40:14** [a]Job 38:4 [b]Job 21:22; Col 2:3 **40:15** [a]Jer 10:10 [b]Is 17:13; 29:5 **40:16** [a]Ps 50:9-11; Mic 6:6, 7; Heb 10:5-9 **40:17** [a]Is 29:7 **40:18** [a]Ex 8:10; 15:11; 1Sa 2:2; Is 40:25; 46:5; Mic 7:18; Ac 17:29 **40:19** [a]Ps 115:4-8; Is 41:7; 44:10; Hab 2:18, 19 [b]Is 2:20; 30:22 **40:20** [a]Is 44:14 [b]1Sa 5:3, 4; Is 41:7; 46:7 [1]Or *set up* **40:21** [a]Ps 19:1; 50:6; Is 37:26; Ac 14:17; Ro 1:19 [b]Is 48:13; 51:13 **40:22** [a]Job 22:14; Pr 8:27 [b]Nu 13:33 [1]Or *is enthroned* [2]Or *vault*

It is He who [c]stretches
out the heavens
like a [d]curtain
And spreads them out
like a [e]tent to inhabit.
23 It is He who reduces
[a]rulers to nothing,
Who [b]makes the [1]judges
of the earth *utterly* formless.
24 [1]Scarcely have they
been planted;
[1]Scarcely have they
been sown;
[1]Scarcely has their stem
taken root in the earth,
But He merely blows
on them, and they [2]wither,
And the [a]storm carries
them away like stubble.
25 "[a]To whom then will
you liken Me
That I would be *his* equal?"
says the Holy One.
26 [a]Lift up your eyes on high
And see [b]who has
created these *stars*,
The [c]One who leads forth
their host by number,
He calls them all by name;
Because of the [d]greatness
of His vigor and the
[1]strength of *His* power,
[e]Not one *of them* is missing.

27 [a]Why do you say, O Jacob,
and assert, O Israel,
"My way is [b]hidden
from Yahweh,
And the [c]justice due me
passes by [d]my God"?
28 [a]Do you not know?
Have you not heard?
The [b]Everlasting God,
Yahweh, the Creator
of the ends of the earth,
Does not become
weary or tired.
His understanding
is [c]unsearchable.
29 He gives power to the [a]weary,
And to *him who* lacks vigor
He [b]increases might.
30 Though [a]youths grow
weary and tired,
And choice [b]young men
stumble badly,
31 Yet those who hope in Yahweh
Will [a]gain new power;
They will [b,1]mount up
*with* [2]wings like eagles;
They will run and
not get tired;
They will walk and not
become weary.

### *Do Not Fear, for I Am with You*

41 "[a]Coastlands, listen
to Me [b]in silence,
And let the peoples
[c]gain new power;
[d]Let them come forward,
then let them speak;
[e]Let us draw near together
for judgment.
2 "[a]Who has awakened
one from the east

**40:22** [c]Job 9:8; Is 37:16; 42:5; 44:24 [d]Ps 104:2 [e]Job 36:29; Ps 18:11; 19:4 **40:23** [a]Job 12:21; Ps 107:40; Is 34:12 [b]Is 5:21; Jer 25:18-27 [1]Or *leaders* **40:24** [a]Is 17:13; 41:16 [1]Or *Not even* [2]Or *dry up*, cf. 42:15; Ps 90:5-6 **40:25** [a]Is 40:18 **40:26** [a]Is 51:6 [b]Is 42:5; 48:12, 13 [c]Ps 147:4 [d]Ps 89:11-13 [e]Is 34:16; 48:13 [1]As in DSS and ancient versions; M.T. *strong* **40:27** [a]Is 49:4, 14 [b]Is 54:8 [c]Job 27:2; 34:5; Lk 18:7, 8 [d]Is 25:1 **40:28** [a]Is 40:21 [b]Ge 21:33; Ps 90:2 [c]Ps 147:5; Ro 11:33 **40:29** [a]Is 50:4; Jer 31:25 [b]Is 41:10 **40:30** [a]Jer 6:11; 9:21 [b]Is 9:17 **40:31** [a]Job 17:9; Ps 103:5; 2Co 4:8-10, 16 [b]Ex 19:4; Dt 32:11; Lk 18:1; 2Co 4:1, 16; Ga 6:9; Heb 12:3 [1]Or *sprout wings* [2]Or *pinions* ◆ **41:1** [a]Is 11:11 [b]Hab 2:20; Zec 2:13 [c]Is 40:31 [d]Is 34:1; 48:16 [e]Is 1:18; 43:26; 50:8 **41:2** [a]Is 41:25; 45:1-3; 46:11

Whom He [b]calls
in righteousness to His [1]feet?
He [c]gives up nations
before him
And [2]has dominion over kings.
He makes them like [d]dust
with his sword,
As the wind-driven
[e]chaff with his bow.
3 "He pursues them,
passing on in peace,
By a way he had not
[1]come with his feet.
4 "[a]Who has worked and done *it*,
Calling forth the generations
from the beginning?
'[b]I, Yahweh, am the first; and
with the last, [c]I am He.'"

5 The [a]coastlands have
seen and are afraid;
The [b]ends of the
earth tremble;
They have drawn near
and have come.
6 Each one helps his neighbor
And says to his brother,
"Be strong!"
7 So the [a]craftsman
strengthens the [b]smelter,
*And* he who smooths
*metal* with the hammer
*strengthens* him who
beats the anvil,
Saying of the soldering,
*"It is* good";
And he strengthens
it with nails,
[c]*So that* it will not be shaken.
8 "But you, Israel, [a]My servant,
Jacob whom I have chosen,
Seed of [b]Abraham My [c]friend,
9 You whom I have [a,1]strongly
taken hold of from the
ends of the earth,
And called from its
[b]remotest parts
And said to you, 'You
are [c]My servant,
I have [d]chosen you and
not rejected you.
10 'Do not [a]fear, for I
am with you;
Do not anxiously look about
you, for I am your God.
I will make you mighty,
surely [b]I will help you;
Surely I will uphold you with
My righteous [c]right hand.'
11 "Behold, [a]all those who are
angered at you will be
shamed and dishonored;
[b]Those who contend
with you will be
as nothing and will perish.
12 "[a]You will seek those
who quarrel with you,
but will not find them,
Those who war
with you will be
as nothing and non-existent.
13 "For I am Yahweh your God,
[a]who [1]strongly takes hold
of your right hand,
Who says to you,
'[b]Do not fear, I will help you.'
14 "Do not fear, you [a]worm
Jacob, you men of Israel;

**41:2** [b]Is 42:6 [c]2Chr 36:23; Ezr 1:2 [d]2Sa 22:43 [e]Is 40:24 [1]Lit *foot* [2]Or *subdues* **41:3** [1]Lit *coming*
**41:4** [a]Is 41:26; 44:7; 46:10 [b]Is 43:10; 44:6; Rev 1:8, 17; 22:13 [c]Is 43:13; 46:4; 48:12 **41:5** [a]Is 41:1; Eze 26:15, 16 [b]Jos 5:1; Ps 67:7 **41:7** [a]Is 44:12, 13 [b]Is 40:19 [c]Is 40:20; 46:7 **41:8** [a]Is 42:19; 43:10; 44:1, 2, 21 [b]Is 29:22; 51:2; 63:16 [c]2Chr 20:7; Jas 2:23 **41:9** [a]Is 11:11 [b]Is 43:5-7 [c]Is 42:1; 44:1 [d]Dt 7:6; 14:2; Ps 135:4 [1]Normally *taken hold of*, but cf. 41:7 **41:10** [a]Dt 20:1; 31:6; Jos 1:9; Ps 27:1; Is 41:13, 14; 43:2, 5; Ro 8:31 [b]Is 41:14; 44:2; 49:8 [c]Ps 89:13, 14 **41:11** [a]Is 45:24 [b]Is 17:13; 29:5, 7, 8 **41:12** [a]Job 20:7-9; Ps 37:35, 36; Is 17:14 **41:13** [a]Is 42:6; 45:1 [b]Is 41:10 [1]Normally *takes hold of*, but cf. 41:7 **41:14** [a]Job 25:6; Ps 22:6

I will help you," declares
Yahweh, "[1]and [b]your
Redeemer is the Holy
One of Israel.

15 "Behold, I have made you
a new, sharp threshing
sledge with double edges;
[a]You will thresh the [b]mountains
and pulverize *them*,
And will make the
hills like chaff.

16 "You will [a]winnow them,
and the wind will
carry them away,
And the storm will
scatter them;
But you will [b]rejoice
in Yahweh;
You will boast
in the Holy One of Israel.

17 "The [1]afflicted and needy
are seeking [a]water,
but there is none,
And their tongue is
parched with thirst;
I, Yahweh, [b]will answer
them Myself,
*As* the God of Israel I [c]will
not forsake them.

18 "I will open [a]rivers
on the bare heights
And springs in the midst
of the valleys;
I will make [b]the wilderness
a pool of water
And the dry land
fountains of water.

19 "I will put the cedar
in the wilderness,
The acacia and the [a]myrtle
and the [1]olive tree;
I will place the [a]juniper
in the desert
Together with the box
tree and the cypress,

20 That [a]they may see
and know,
And establish and gain
insight as well,
That the [b]hand of Yahweh
has done this,
And the Holy One
of Israel has created it.

21 "Bring near your case,"
Yahweh says.
"Bring forward your
mighty *arguments*,"
The [a]King of Jacob says.

22 [a]Let them bring *it* forth
and declare to us what
is going to take place;
As for the [b]former *events*,
declare what they *were*,
That we may establish
our heart on them and
know their outcome.
Or cause us to hear
of what is coming;

23 [a]Declare the things that
are to come afterward,
That we may know
that you are gods;
Indeed, [b]do good or evil,
that we may anxiously look
about us and fear together.

24 Behold, [a]you are nothing,
And [b]your work
is non-existent;

---

**41:14** [b]Is 35:10; 43:14; 44:6, 22-24 [1]Or *even your Redeemer, the Holy One* **41:15** [a]Mic 4:13; Hab 3:12 [b]Is 42:15; 64:1; Jer 9:10; Eze 33:28 **41:16** [a]Jer 51:2 [b]Is 25:9; 35:10; 51:3; 61:10 **41:17** [a]Is 43:20; 44:3; 49:10; 55:1 [b]Is 30:19; 65:24 [c]Is 42:16; 62:12 [1]Or *poor* **41:18** [a]Is 30:25; 43:19 [b]Ps 107:35; Is 35:6, 7 **41:19** [a]Is 35:1; 55:13; 60:13 [1]Or *oleaster* **41:20** [a]Is 40:5; 43:10 [b]Job 12:9; Is 66:14 **41:21** [a]Is 44:6 **41:22** [a]Is 44:7; 45:21; 46:10 [b]Is 43:9 **41:23** [a]Is 42:9; 44:7, 8; 45:3; Jn 13:19 [b]Jer 10:5 **41:24** [a]Ps 115:8; Is 44:9; 1Co 8:4 [b]Is 37:19; 41:29

He who chooses you is
an [c]abomination.

25 "I have awakened [a]one
from the north, and
he has come;
From the rising of the sun
he will call on My name;
And he will come upon
officials as *upon* [b]mortar,
Even as the potter treads clay."
26 Who has [a]declared *this*
from the beginning,
that we might know?
Or from former times, that
we may say, "*He is* right!"?
Surely there was [b]no
one who declared;
Surely there was no
one who caused *those*
*words* to be heard;
Surely there was no one
who heard your words.
27 "[a]Formerly *I said* to Zion,
'Behold, here they are.'
And to Jerusalem, 'I will give a
[b]messenger of good news.'
28 "But [a]I look, and there
is no one,
And there is no [b]counselor
[1]among them
Who, if I ask, can [c]respond
*with* a word.
29 "Behold, all of them are [1]false;
Their [a]works are
[b]non-existent;
Their molten images are [c]wind
and *utter* formlessness.

### *Yahweh's Chosen Servant*

42 "[a]Behold, My [b]Servant,
whom I [1]uphold;
My [c]chosen one *in whom*
My [d]soul is well-pleased.
I have put My [e]Spirit
upon Him;
He will bring forth [f]justice
to the [2]nations.
2 "He will not cry out or
raise *His voice*,
Nor make His voice
heard in the street.
3 "A crushed reed He
will not break
And a faintly burning wick
He will not extinguish;
He will bring forth
[a]justice in truth.
4 "He will not be [a]faint
or crushed
Until He has established
justice in the earth;
And the [b]coastlands
will wait expectantly
for His [1]law."

5 Thus says the God, Yahweh,
Who [a]created the heavens
and [b]stretched them out,
Who spread out the [c]earth
and its [1]offspring,
Who [d]gives breath
to the people on it
And spirit to those
who walk in it,
6 "I am Yahweh, I have [a]called
You in righteousness;

**41:24** [c]Pr 3:32; 28:9 **41:25** [a]Is 41:2; Jer 50:3 [b]2Sa 22:43; Is 10:6; Mic 7:10; Zec 10:5 **41:26** [a]Is 41:22; 44:7; 45:21 [b]Hab 2:18, 19 **41:27** [a]Is 48:3-8 [b]Is 40:9; 44:28; 52:7; Na 1:15 **41:28** [a]Is 50:2; 59:16; 63:5 [b]Is 40:13, 14 [c]Is 46:7 [1]Lit *out of those* **41:29** [a]Is 2:8; 17:8; 41:24 [b]Is 44:9 [c]Jer 5:13 [1]Or *nothing*
◆ **42:1** [a]Mt 12:18-21 [b]Is 41:8; 43:10; 49:3-6; 52:13; 53:11; Mt 12:18-21; Php 2:7 [c]Lk 9:35; 1Pe 2:4, 6 [d]Mt 3:17; 17:5; Mk 1:11; Lk 3:22 [e]Is 11:2; 59:21; 61:1; Mt 3:16; Lk 4:18, 19, 21 [f]Is 2:4 [1]Or *hold fast* [2]Or *Gentiles*
**42:3** [a]Ps 72:2, 4; 96:13 **42:4** [a]Is 40:28 [b]Is 11:11; 24:15; 42:10, 12; 49:1; 51:5; 60:9; 66:19 [1]Or *instruction*
**42:5** [a]Ps 102:25, 26; Is 45:18 [b]Ps 104:2; Is 40:22 [c]Ps 24:1, 2; 136:6 [d]Job 12:10; 33:4; Is 57:16; Da 5:23; Ac 17:25 [1]Or *vegetation* **42:6** [a]Is 41:2; Jer 23:5, 6

I will also [b]take hold of You
by the hand and [c]guard You,
And I will give You as a
[d]covenant to the people,
As a [e]light to the nations,
7 To [a]open blind eyes,
To [b]bring out prisoners
from the dungeon
And those who inhabit
darkness from the prison.
8 “[a]I am Yahweh, that
is [b]My name;
I will not give My
[c]glory to another,
Nor My praise
to [1]graven images.
9 “Behold, the [a]former things
have come to pass;
Now I declare [b]new things;
Before they spring forth I
cause you to hear *them.*”

10 Sing to Yahweh a [a]new song,
*Sing* His praise from the
[b]end of the earth!
[c]You who go down to the sea,
[d]as well as its fullness.
You [e]coastlands, and those
who inhabit them.
11 Let the [a]wilderness and its
cities lift up *their voices,*
The villages
where [b]Kedar inhabits.
Let the inhabitants
of [c]Sela sing aloud,
Let them shout for joy from
the tops of the [d]mountains.
12 Let them [a]give glory
to Yahweh
And declare His praise
in the [b]coastlands.
13 [a]Yahweh will go forth
like a warrior;
He will awaken *His* [b]zeal
like a man of war.
He will make a loud shout,
indeed, He will raise
a war cry.
He will [c]prevail
against His enemies.

### *Israel’s Blindness and Deafness*

14 “[a]I have kept silent
for a long time;
I have kept still and
restrained Myself.
*Now* like a woman
in labor I will groan;
I will both gasp and pant.
15 “I will [a]lay waste the
mountains and hills
And dry up all their
vegetation;
I will [b]make the rivers
into coastlands
And dry up the pools
*of waters.*
16 “I will [a]lead the blind
by a way they do not know,
In paths they do not know
I will guide them.
I will [b]make darkness
into light before them
And [c]rugged places into plains.
These are the things I will do,
And I will [d]not forsake them.”
17 They will be turned back *and*
be [a]utterly put to shame,

**42:6** [b]Is 41:13; 45:1 [c]Is 26:3; 27:3 [d]Is 49:8 [e]Is 49:6; 51:4; 60:1, 3; Lk 2:32; Ac 13:47; 26:23 **42:7** [a]Is 29:18; 35:5 [b]Is 49:9; 61:1 **42:8** [a]Is 43:3, 11, 15 [b]Ex 3:15; Ps 83:18 [c]Ex 20:3-5; Is 48:11 [1]Or *idols* **42:9** [a]Is 48:3 [b]Is 43:19; 48:6 **42:10** [a]Ps 33:3; 40:3; 98:1 [b]Is 49:6; 62:11 [c]Ps 65:5; 107:23 [d]Ex 20:11; 1Chr 16:32; Ps 96:11 [e]Is 42:4 **42:11** [a]Is 32:16; 35:1, 6 [b]Is 21:16; 60:7 [c]Is 16:1 [d]Is 52:7; Na 1:15 **42:12** [a]Is 24:15 [b]Is 42:4 **42:13** [a]Ex 15:3 [b]Is 9:7; 26:11; 37:32; 59:17 [c]Is 66:14-16 **42:14** [a]Ps 50:21; Is 57:11 **42:15** [a]Is 2:12-16; Eze 38:19, 20 [b]Is 44:27; 50:2; Na 1:4-6 **42:16** [a]Is 29:18; 30:21; 32:3; Jer 31:8, 9; Lk 1:78, 79 [b]Is 29:18; Eph 5:8 [c]Is 40:4; Lk 3:5 [d]Jos 1:5; Ps 94:14; Is 41:17; Heb 13:5 **42:17** [a]Ps 97:7; Is 1:29; 44:9, 11; 45:16

Who trust in graven images,
Who say to molten images,
"You are our gods."

18 [a]Hear, you deaf!
And look, you blind,
that you may see.
19 Who is blind
but My [a]servant,
Or so deaf as My [b]messenger
whom I send?
Who is so blind as he that
is [c,1]at peace *with Me*,
Or so blind as the
servant of Yahweh?
20 [a]You have seen many things,
but you do not keep *them*;
*Your* ears are open,
but none hears.
21 Yahweh was pleased
for His righteousness' sake
That He make the law
[a]great and majestic.
22 But this is a people plundered
and *pillaged* as spoil;
All of them are [a]trapped
in [1]caves,
Or are [b]hidden away
in prisons;
They have become a plunder
with none to deliver *them*,
And a spoil, with none
to say, "Have *them* return!"

23 Who among you will
give ear to this?
Who will give heed and
hear hereafter?
24 Who gave Jacob up for spoil,
and Israel to plunderers?
Was it not Yahweh, against
whom we have sinned,
And in whose ways they
[a]were not willing to walk,
And whose law they
did not [b]obey?
25 So He poured out on him
the heat of His anger
And the [a]fierceness of battle;
And it set him aflame
all around,
Yet he did not know *it*;
And it burned him, but he did
not [b]set it upon his heart.

### *The Redemption of Israel*

43 But now, thus says Yahweh,
your [a]Creator, O Jacob,
And He who [b]formed
you, O Israel,
"Do not [c]fear, for I have
[d]redeemed you;
I have [e]called you
by name; you are [f]Mine!
2 "When you [a]pass
through the waters,
[b]I will be with you;
And through the rivers,
they will not overflow you.
When you [c]walk
through the fire,
you will not be scorched,
Nor will the flame burn you.
3 "For [a]I am Yahweh your God,
The Holy One of Israel,
your [b]Savior;
I have given Egypt
as your ransom,
[c,1]Ethiopia and Seba
in your place.

**42:18** [a]Is 29:18; 35:5 **42:19** [a]Is 41:8 [b]Is 44:26 [c]Is 26:3; 27:5 [1]Or *the devoted one* **42:20** [a]Ro 2:21 **42:21** [a]Is 42:4; 51:4 **42:22** [a]Is 24:18 [b]Is 24:22 [1]Or *holes* **42:24** [a]Is 30:15 [b]Is 48:18; 57:17 **42:25** [a]Is 5:25; 9:19 [b]Is 29:13; 47:7; 57:1; Hos 7:9 ◆ **43:1** [a]Is 43:15 [b]Is 43:7, 21; 44:2, 21, 24 [c]Is 43:5 [d]Is 44:22, 23; 48:20 [e]Ge 32:28; Is 43:7; 45:3, 4 [f]Is 43:21 **43:2** [a]Ps 66:12; Is 8:7, 8 [b]Dt 31:6, 8 [c]Is 29:6; 30:27-29; Da 3:25, 27 **43:3** [a]Ex 20:2 [b]Is 19:20; 43:11; 45:15, 21; 49:26; 60:16; 63:8 [c]Is 20:3-5 [1]Or *Cush*, cf. Ge 10:6

4 “Since you are [a]precious
in My sight,
*Since* you are [b]honored
and I [c]love you,
I will give *other* men
in your place and *other*
peoples in exchange
for your life.
5 “Do not fear,
for [a]I am with you;
I will bring [b]your seed
from the east,
And [c]gather you
from the west.
6 “I will say to the [a]north,
‘Give *them* up!’
And to the south,
‘Do not hold *them* back.’
Bring My [b]sons from afar
And My daughters
from the [c]ends of the earth,
7 Everyone who is [a]called
by My name,
And whom I have [b]created
for My [c]glory,
[d]Whom I have formed,
even whom I have made.”

### *Israel Is Yahweh’s Witness*

8 Bring out the people
who are [a]blind,
even though they have eyes,
And the deaf,
even though they have ears.
9 All the nations have
[a]gathered together
So that the peoples may
be assembled.
Who among them can
[b]declare this
And make us hear
the former things?
Let them present [c]their
witnesses [d]that they
may be justified,
Or let them hear and say,
“It is true.”
10 “You are [a]My witnesses,”
declares Yahweh,
“And [b]My servant
whom I have chosen,
So that you may know
and believe Me
And understand that
[c]I am He.
[d]Before Me there was
no god formed,
And there will be
none after Me.
11 “I, even I, am Yahweh,
And there is no [a]savior
[b]besides Me.
12 “It is I who have declared
and saved and caused
*it* to be heard,
And there was no [a]strange
*god* among you;
So you are My witnesses,”
declares Yahweh,
“And I am God.
13 “Even [a,1]from eternity [b]I am He,
And there is [c]none who can
deliver out of My hand;
[d]I act and who can reverse it?”

### *Rivers in the Wasteland*

14 Thus says Yahweh your [a]Redeem-
er, the Holy One of Israel,
“For your sake I have
sent to Babylon,

**43:4** [a]Ex 19:5, 6 [b]Is 49:5 [c]Is 63:9 **43:5** [a]Is 8:10; 43:2 [b]Is 41:8; 49:12; 61:9 [c]Is 49:12 **43:6** [a]Ps 107:3 [b]2Co 6:18 [c]Is 45:22 **43:7** [a]Is 56:5; 62:2; Jas 2:7 [b]Ps 100:3; Is 29:23; Eph 2:10 [c]Is 44:23; 46:13 [d]Is 43:1 **43:8** [a]Is 6:9; 42:19; Eze 12:2 **43:9** [a]Is 34:1; 41:1 [b]Is 41:22, 23, 26 [c]Is 44:9 [d]Is 43:26 **43:10** [a]Is 44:8 [b]Is 41:8 [c]Is 41:4 [d]Is 45:5, 6 **43:11** [a]Is 43:3; 45:21; Hos 13:4 [b]Is 44:6, 8 **43:12** [a]Dt 32:16; Ps 81:9 **43:13** [a]Ps 90:2; Is 48:16 [b]Is 41:4 [c]Ps 50:22 [d]Job 9:12; Is 14:27 [1]As in Gr; Heb *from the day* **43:14** [a]Is 41:14

And will bring down those
who fled—all of them,
[1]Even the [b]Chaldeans—
into the [c]ships [2]in which
they shouted for joy.
15 "I am Yahweh, your Holy One,
[a]The Creator of Israel,
your [b]King."
16 Thus says Yahweh,
Who [a]makes a way
through the sea
And a path
through the mighty waters,
17 Who brings forth
the [a]chariot and the horse,
The military force and
the mighty man;
They will lie down together
*and* not rise again;
They have been [b]extinguished
*and* quenched like a wick:
18 "[a]Do not remember
the former things,
Nor carefully consider
things of the past.
19 "Behold, I will do
something [a]new;
Now it will spring forth;
Will you not know it?
I will even [b]make a roadway
in the wilderness,
Rivers in the wasteland.
20 "The beasts of the field
will glorify Me,
The [a]jackals and the ostriches,
Because I have [b]given
waters in the wilderness
And rivers in the wasteland,
To give drink to My
chosen people.
21 "The people
whom [a]I formed for Myself
[b]Will recount My praise.

22 "Yet you have not called
on Me, O Jacob;
But you have become
[a]weary of Me, O Israel.
23 "You have [a]not brought
to Me the sheep of your
burnt offerings,
Nor have you [b]glorified Me
with your sacrifices.
I have not [c]burdened
you with [1]offerings,
Nor wearied you
with [d]frankincense.
24 "You have not bought Me
[a,1]sweet cane with money,
Nor have you satisfied
Me with the fat
of your sacrifices;
Rather you have burdened
Me with your sins;
You have [b]wearied Me
with your iniquities.

25 "I, even I, am the one
who [a]wipes out
your transgressions
[b]for My own sake,
And I will [c]not remember
your sins.
26 "[1]Bring Me to remembrance,
[a]let us enter
into judgment together;

**43:14** [b]Is 23:13 [c]Jer 51:13 [1]Or *As for the Chaldeans, their rejoicing* is turned *into lamentations* [2]Lit *of their rejoicing* **43:15** [a]Is 43:1 [b]Is 41:20; 44:6 **43:16** [a]Ex 14:21, 22; Ps 77:19; Is 11:15; 44:27; 50:2; 51:10; 63:11, 12 **43:17** [a]Ex 15:19 [b]Ps 118:12; Is 1:31 **43:18** [a]Is 65:17; Jer 23:7 **43:19** [a]Is 42:9; 48:6; 2Co 5:17 [b]Ex 17:6; Nu 20:11; Dt 8:15; Ps 78:16; Is 35:1, 6; 41:18, 19; 49:10; 51:3 **43:20** [a]Is 13:22; 35:7 [b]Is 41:17, 18; 48:21 **43:21** [a]Is 43:1 [b]Ps 102:18; Is 42:12; Lk 1:74, 75; 1Pe 2:9 **43:22** [a]Mic 6:3; Mal 1:13; 3:14 **43:23** [a]Am 5:25 [b]Zec 7:5, 6; Mal 1:6-8 [c]Jer 7:21-26 [d]Ex 30:34; Lv 2:1; 24:7 [1]Or *a meal offering* **43:24** [a]Ex 30:23; Jer 6:20 [b]Ps 95:10; Is 1:14; 7:13; Eze 6:9; Mal 2:17 [1]Or *calamus* **43:25** [a]Is 44:22; 55:7; Jer 50:20 [b]Is 37:35; 48:9, 11; Eze 36:22 [c]Is 38:17; Jer 31:34 **43:26** [a]Is 1:18; 41:1; 50:8 [1]Or *Report to Me*

Recount your *cause*, [b]that
you may be proved right.
27 "Your [a]first father sinned,
And your [b,1]spokesmen have
[2]transgressed against Me.
28 "So I will [1]profane the
[2]princes of the sanctuary,
And I will give Jacob to be
[a]devoted to destruction
and Israel to [b]revilement.

### *No God Besides Yahweh*

44 "But now hear, O Jacob,
My [a]servant,
And Israel, whom I
have chosen:
2 Thus says Yahweh
who made you
And [a]formed you from the
womb, who [b]will help you,
'[c]Do not fear, O Jacob
My servant,
And you [d]Jeshurun
whom I have chosen.
3 'For [a]I will pour out water
on [1]the thirsty *ground*
And streams
on the dry land;
I will [b]pour out My Spirit
on your [c]seed
And My blessing
on your offspring;
4 And they will spring up
[1]among the grass
Like [a]poplars
by streams of water.'
5 "This one will say,
'I am Yahweh's';
And this one [1]will call
on the name of Jacob;
And this one will [a]write
[2]*on* his hand, 'Belonging
to Yahweh,'
And will name Israel's
name with honor.

6 "Thus says Yahweh, the [a]King of
Israel and his [b]Redeemer, Yahweh
of hosts:
'I am the [c]first,
and I am the last,
And there is no God
[d]besides Me.
7 'Who is like Me? [a]Let him
call out and declare it;
And let him tell it
to Me in order,
[1]From the time that
I established the
ancient [2]people.
And let them declare
to them the things
that are to come
And the events that are
going to take place.
8 'Do not be in dread and
do not be afraid;
[a]Have I not long since
caused *it* to be heard
to you and declared *it*?
And [b]you are My witnesses.
Is there any God
[c]besides Me,
Or is there any
*other* [d]Rock?
I know of none.'"

**43:26** [b]Is 43:9 **43:27** [a]Is 51:2; Eze 16:3 [b]Is 9:15; 28:7; 29:10; Jer 5:31 [1]Or *interpreters* [2]Or *rebelled*
**43:28** [a]Is 24:6; 34:5; Jer 24:9; Da 9:11; Zec 8:13 [b]Ps 79:4; Eze 5:15 [1]Or *pierce through* [2]Or *holy princes*
◆ **44:1** [a]Is 41:8; Jer 30:10; 46:27, 28 **44:2** [a]Is 44:21, 24 [b]Is 41:10 [c]Is 43:5 [d]Dt 32:15; 33:5, 26
**44:3** [a]Is 41:17; Eze 34:26; Joel 3:18 [b]Is 32:15; Joel 2:28 [c]Is 61:9; 65:23 [1]Or *him who is thirsty*
**44:4** [a]Lv 23:40; Job 40:22 [1]Or *like grass among the waters* **44:5** [a]Ex 13:9; Ne 9:38 [1]Or *will be called by the name of Jacob* [2]Or *with* **44:6** [a]Is 41:21; 43:15 [b]Is 41:14; 43:1, 14 [c]Is 41:4; 43:10; 48:12; Rev 1:8, 17; 22:13 [d]Is 43:11; 44:8; 45:5, 6, 21 **44:7** [a]Is 41:22, 26 [1]Lit *From My establishing of* [2]Or *nation*
**44:8** [a]Is 42:9; 48:5 [b]Is 43:10 [c]Dt 4:35, 39; 1Sa 2:2; Is 45:5; Joel 2:27 [d]Is 17:10; 26:4; 30:29

### *The Futility of Idolatry*

**9** Those who form [1]a graven image are
all of them [2]futile, and their desirable
things are of no profit; even their own
witnesses fail to see or know, so that
they will be [a]put to shame. **10** Who has
formed a god or cast a graven image
to [a]no profit? **11** Behold, all his com-
panions will be [a]put to shame. The
craftsmen themselves are mere men.
Let them all assemble themselves, let
them stand up, let them be in dread,
let them together be put to shame.

**12** The [a]man crafts iron into a
cutting tool and does his work over
the coals, [1]forming it with hammers
and working it with his powerful
arm. He also gets hungry and has
no power; he drinks no water and
becomes weary. **13** [a]*Another* crafts
wood, he extends a measuring line;
he outlines it with [1]a stylus. He makes
it with planes and outlines it with a
compass and makes it like the form
of a man, like the glory of [b]man, so
that it may sit in a [c]house. **14** In order
to cut cedars for himself, he takes a
[1]cypress or an oak and [2]raises *it* for
himself among the trees of the forest.
He plants a fir, and the rain makes it
grow. **15** Then it becomes *something*
for a man to burn, so he takes one
of them and warms himself; he also
kindles a fire to bake bread. He also
[a]works *to produce* a god and wor-
ships it; he makes it a graven image
and [b]falls down before it. **16** Half of it
he burns in the fire; over *this* half he
eats meat as he roasts a roast and is
satisfied. He also warms himself and
says, "Aha! I am warm; I have seen the
fire." **17** But the rest of it he [a]makes
into a god, his graven image. He falls
down before it and worships; he also
[b]prays to it and says, "Deliver me, for
you are my god."

**18** They do not [a]know, nor do they
understand, for He has [b]smeared
over their eyes so that they cannot
see and their hearts so that they will
have no insight. **19** No one causes *this*
to return to his heart, nor is there
[a]knowledge or understanding to
say, "I have burned half of it in the
fire and also have baked bread over
its coals. I roast meat and eat *it*.
Then [1]I make the rest of it into an
[b]abomination; [2]I fall down before
a block of wood!" **20** He [a,1]feeds on
ashes; a [b]deceived heart has turned
him aside. And he cannot deliver his
soul, and he cannot say, "[c]Is there not
a lie in my right hand?"

### *Yahweh Forgives and Redeems*

**21** "[a]Remember these
things, O Jacob,
And Israel, for you are
[b]My servant;
I have formed you,
you are My servant;
O Israel, you will [c]not
be forgotten by Me.
**22** "I have [a]wiped out your
transgressions like
a thick cloud

**44:9** [a]Ps 97:7; Is 42:17; 44:11; 45:16 [1]Or *an idol* [2]Lit *formless* **44:10** [a]Is 41:29; Jer 10:5; Hab 2:18; Ac 19:26 **44:11** [a]Ps 97:7; Is 42:17; 44:9; 45:16 **44:12** [a]Is 40:19, 20; 41:6, 7; 46:6, 7; Jer 10:3-5; Hab 2:18 [1]Lit *and forms* **44:13** [a]Is 41:7 [b]Ps 115:5-7 [c]Jdg 17:4, 5; Eze 8:10, 11 [1]Or *red chalk* **44:14** [1]Or *holm-oak* [2]Lit *makes strong* **44:15** [a]Is 44:17 [b]2Chr 25:14 **44:17** [a]Is 44:15 [b]1Ki 18:26, 28; Is 45:20 **44:18** [a]Is 1:3; Jer 10:8, 14 [b]Ps 81:12; Is 6:9, 10; 29:10 **44:19** [a]Is 5:13; 44:18, 19; 45:20 [b]Dt 27:15; 1Ki 11:5, 7; 2Ki 23:13, 14 [1]Or *shall I make...?* [2]Or *shall I fall...?* **44:20** [a]Ps 102:9 [b]Job 15:31; Hos 4:12; Ro 1:21, 22; 2Th 2:11; 2Ti 3:13 [c]Is 57:11; 59:3, 4, 13; Ro 1:25 [1]Or *is a companion of ashes* **44:21** [a]Is 46:8; Zec 10:9 [b]Is 44:1, 2 [c]Is 49:15 **44:22** [a]Ps 51:1, 9; Is 43:25; Ac 3:19

And your sins like a cloud.
[b]Return to Me, for I have
[c]redeemed you."
23 [a]Shout for joy, O heavens,
for Yahweh has done *it*!
Make a loud shout,
you lower parts
of the earth;
[b]Break forth into a shout
of joy, you mountains,
O forest, and every tree in it;
For [c]Yahweh has
redeemed Jacob
And in Israel He [d]shows
forth His beautiful glory.

24 Thus says Yahweh, your [a]Redeem-
er, and the one who [b]formed you
from the womb,
"I, Yahweh, am the maker
of all things,
[c]Stretching out
the heavens by Myself
And spreading out
the earth [1]all alone,
25 [a]Causing the [1]omens
of boasters to be annulled,
And [2]making fools
out of diviners,
[b]Causing wise men
to turn back,
And [2]making foolishness
out of their knowledge,
26 [a]Confirming the word
of His servant—
And the counsel
of His messengers
He will complete—
*And being* the One who
says of Jerusalem,
'She shall be inhabited!'
And of the [b]cities of Judah,
'[c]They shall be built.'
And I will raise up her
waste places *again*.
27 "*It is I* who says to the depth
of the sea, 'Be dried up!'
And I will make your
rivers [a]dry.
28 "*It is I* who says of [a]Cyrus,
'*He is* My shepherd!
And all My good pleasure
he will complete.'
And saying of Jerusalem,
'[b]She will be built,'
And of the temple,
'[1]Your foundation
will be laid.'"

### *Cyrus, Yahweh's Anointed*

45 Thus says Yahweh to
[a]Cyrus His anointed,
Whom I have taken hold
of by his right [b]hand,
To [c]subdue nations before him
And [1]to [d]loose the
loins of kings,
To open doors before him
so that gates will not be shut:
2 "I will go before you and [a]make
the [1]rough places smooth;
I will [b]shatter the doors
of bronze and cut
through their iron [c]bars.
3 "I will give you the
[a,1]treasures of darkness

**44:22** [b]Is 31:6; 55:7 [c]Is 43:1; 48:20; 1Co 6:20; 1Pe 1:18, 19 **44:23** [a]Ps 69:34; 96:11, 12; Is 42:10; 49:13 [b]Ps 98:7, 8; 148:7, 9; Is 55:12 [c]Is 43:1 [d]Is 49:3; 61:3 **44:24** [a]Is 41:14; 43:14 [b]Is 44:2 [c]Is 40:22; 42:5; 45:12, 18; 51:13 [1]Or *who was with Me?* **44:25** [a]Is 47:13 [b]2Sa 15:31; Job 5:12-14; Ps 33:10; Is 29:14; Jer 51:57; 1Co 1:20, 27 [1]Lit *signs* [2]Lit *He makes* **44:26** [a]Zec 1:6; Mt 5:18 [b]Is 40:9 [c]Jer 32:15, 44 **44:27** [a]Is 42:15; 50:2; Jer 50:38; 51:36 **44:28** [a]Is 45:1 [b]2Chr 36:22, 23; Ezr 1:1; Is 14:32; 45:13; 54:11 [1]Lit *You will be founded* ◆ **45:1** [a]Is 44:28 [b]Ps 73:23; Is 41:13; 42:6 [c]Is 41:2, 25; Jer 50:3, 35; 51:11, 20, 24 [d]Job 12:21; Is 45:5 [1]Lit *I will open*, cf. 45:1b **45:2** [a]Is 40:4 [b]Ps 107:16 [c]Jer 51:30 [1]Or *mountains* **45:3** [a]Jer 41:8; 50:37 [1]Or *hoarded treasures*

And hidden wealth
of secret places,
So that you may know
that it is I,
Yahweh, the God of Israel,
who [b]calls you by your name.
4 "For the sake of [a]Jacob
My servant,
And Israel My chosen *one*,
I have also [b]called you
by your name;
I have given you
a title of honor
Though you have
[c]not known Me.
5 "I am Yahweh, and
[a]there is no other;
[b]Besides Me there is no God.
I will [c,1]gird you, though you
have not known Me,
6 That [a]they may know
from the rising
to the setting of the sun
That there is [b]no one
besides Me.
I am Yahweh, and
there is no other,
7 The One [a]forming light
and [b]creating darkness,
Producing peace and
[c]creating calamity;
I am Yahweh who
does all these.

### *Yahweh the Maker*

8 "[a]Drip down, O heavens,
from above,
And let the skies pour
down righteousness;
Let the [b]earth open up and
salvation bear fruit,
[c]And righteousness
[1]spring up with it.
I, Yahweh, have created it.

9 "Woe to *the one* who [a]contends
with his [1]Maker—
An earthenware vessel
[2]among the vessels
of earth!
Will the [b]clay say
to the [1]potter,
'What are you doing?'
Or the thing you are making
*say*, 'He has no hands'?
10 "Woe to him who says
to a father, 'What are
you begetting?'
Or to a woman, '*With* what
are you in labor pains?'"

11 Thus says [a]Yahweh, the Holy One
of Israel, and his [b,1]Maker:
"[c,2]Ask Me about the
things that are to come
[3]concerning My [d]sons,
And you shall [4]commit to Me
[e]the work of My hands.
12 "It is I who [a]made the earth
and created man upon it.
I [b]stretched out the heavens
with My hands,
And I commanded
[c]all their host.
13 "I have awakened him
in [a]righteousness,
And I will [b]make all
his ways smooth;

**45:3** [b]Ex 33:12, 17; Is 43:1; 49:1 **45:4** [a]Is 41:8, 9; 44:1 [b]Is 43:1 [c]Ac 17:23 **45:5** [a]Is 45:6, 14, 18, 21; 46:9 [b]Is 44:6, 8 [c]Ps 18:39 [1]Or *arm* **45:6** [a]Ps 102:15; Mal 1:11 [b]Is 45:5 **45:7** [a]Is 42:16 [b]Ps 104:20; 105:28 [c]Is 31:2; 47:11; Am 3:6 **45:8** [a]Ps 72:6; Hos 10:12; 14:5; Joel 3:18 [b]Ps 85:11 [c]Is 60:21; 61:11 [1]Or *branch forth*, cf. 61:11 **45:9** [a]Job 15:25; 40:8, 9; Ps 2:2, 3; Pr 21:30; Jer 50:24 [b]Is 29:16; 64:8; Jer 18:6; Ro 9:20, 21 [1]Lit *Fashioner* [2]Lit *with* **45:11** [a]Is 43:15; 48:17; Eze 39:7 [b]Is 44:2; 54:5 [c]Is 8:19 [d]Jer 31:9 [e]Is 19:25; 29:23; 60:21; 64:8 [1]Lit *Fashioner* [2]Or *Will you ask...?* [3]Or *upon* [4]Lit *command* **45:12** [a]Is 42:5; 45:18; Jer 27:5 [b]Ps 104:2; Is 42:5; 44:24 [c]Ge 2:1; Ne 9:6 **45:13** [a]Is 41:2 [b]Is 45:2

He will [c]build My city and
will [d]let My exiles go,
Without any payment
or reward," says
Yahweh of hosts.

14 Thus says Yahweh,
"The fruit of the labor
of [a]Egypt and
the profit of [b,1]Ethiopia
And the Sabeans,
men of stature,
Will [c]come over to you
and will be yours;
They will walk behind you;
they will come over
in [d]chains
And will [e]bow down to you;
They will make
supplication to you:
'[2]Surely, [f]God is [3]with you,
and [g]there is none else,
No other God.'"
15 Truly, You are a God who
[a]hides Himself,
O God of Israel, [b]Savior!
16 They will be [a]put to shame
and even dishonored,
all of them;
The [b]craftsmen of idols
will go away together
in dishonor.
17 Israel has been saved
by Yahweh
With an [a]everlasting
salvation;
You [b]will not be put
to shame or dishonored
To all eternity.

18 For thus says Yahweh, who [a]created the heavens (He is the God who [b]formed the earth and made it; He established it *and* did not create it [1]a [c]formless place, *but* formed it to be [d]inhabited),
"I am Yahweh, and [e]there
is none else.
19 "[a]I have not spoken in secret,
In [1]some dark land;
I did not say to the [b]seed
of Jacob,
'[c]Seek Me in [2]a formless place';
I, Yahweh,
[d]speak righteousness,
[e]Declaring things that
are upright.

20 "[a]Gather yourselves and come;
Draw near together,
you who have escaped
from the nations;
[b]They do not know,
Who [c]carry about their
graven image of wood
And [d]pray to a god
who cannot save.
21 "[a]Declare and draw near
*with your case*;
Indeed, let them
consult together.
[b]Who has made this
heard from of old?
Who has long since declared it?
Is it not I, Yahweh?
And there is [c]no other
God besides Me,
A righteous God and a [d]Savior;
There is none except Me.

***45:13*** [c]*2Chr 36:22, 23; Is 44:28* [d]*Is 52:3* **45:14** [a]Ps 68:31; Is 19:21 [b]Is 18:1; 43:3 [c]Is 14:1, 2; 49:23; 54:3 [d]Ps 149:8 [e]Is 49:23; 60:14 [f]Jer 16:19; Zec 8:20-23; 1Co 14:25 [g]Is 45:5 [1]Or *Cush*, cf. Ge 10:6 [2]Or *God is with you alone* [3]Or *in* **45:15** [a]Ps 44:24; Is 1:15; 8:17; 57:17 [b]Is 43:3 **45:16** [a]Is 42:17; 44:9 [b]Is 44:11 **45:17** [a]Is 26:4; 51:6; Ro 11:26 [b]Is 49:23; 50:7; 54:4 **45:18** [a]Is 42:5 [b]Is 45:12 [c]Ge 1:2 [d]Ge 1:26; Ps 115:16 [e]Is 45:5 [1]Or *in vain* **45:19** [a]Is 48:16 [b]Is 45:25; 65:9 [c]2Chr 15:2; Ps 78:34; Jer 29:13, 14 [d]Ps 19:8; Is 45:23; 63:1 [e]Is 43:12; 44:8 [1]Lit *a place of a land of darkness* [2]Or *vain* **45:20** [a]Is 43:9 [b]Is 44:18, 19; 48:5-7 [c]Is 46:1, 7; Jer 10:5 [d]Is 44:17; 46:6, 7 **45:21** [a]Is 41:23; 43:9 [b]Is 41:26; 44:7; 48:14 [c]Is 45:5 [d]Is 43:3, 11

22 “[a]Turn to Me and [b]be saved,
all the ends of the earth;
For I am God,
and there is no other.
23 “[a]I have sworn by Myself,
The [b]word has gone forth from
My mouth in righteousness
And will not turn back,
That to Me [c]every knee
will bow, every tongue
will [d]swear *allegiance*.
24 “They will say of Me,
‘Only [a]in Yahweh are
righteousness and strength.’
Men will come to Him,
And [b]all who were angry
at Him will be put to shame.
25 “In Yahweh all the seed of Israel
Will be [a]justified and
will [b]boast.”

### *Babylon’s Idols and the True God*

46 [a]Bel has bowed down,
Nebo stoops over;
Their images are on the
beasts and the cattle.
The things [1]that you carry
are burdensome,
A load for the weary *beast*.
2 They stooped over, they have
bowed down together;
They could not rescue
the load,
But [1]have themselves
[a]gone into captivity.

3 “[a]Hear Me, O house of Jacob,
And all [b]the remnant
of the house of Israel,
You who have been
[c]burdening Me from [1]birth
And have been carried
from the womb;
4 Even to *your* old age
[a,1]I will be the same,
And even to *your* [b,2]graying
years I will bear *you*!
I have [3]done *it*, and I
will carry *you*;
And I will bear *you*, and
I will rescue *you*.

5 “[a]To whom would you liken Me
And make Me equal
and compare Me,
That we would be alike?
6 “Those who [a]lavish gold
from the purse
And weigh silver on the scale,
They hire a goldsmith,
and he makes it *into* a god;
They [b]fall down, indeed
they worship it.
7 “They [a]carry it upon the
shoulder *and* bear it;
They set it in its place,
and it stands *there*.
[b]It does not move
from its place.
Though one may cry to it,
it [c]cannot answer;
It [d]cannot save him
from his distress.

8 “[a]Remember this,
and be [1]assured;
[b]Cause it to return to your
heart, you [c]transgressors.

**45:22** [a]Nu 21:8, 9; 2Chr 20:12; Mic 7:7; Zec 12:10 [b]Is 30:15; 49:6, 12; 52:10 **45:23** [a]Ge 22:16; Is 62:8; Heb 6:13 [b]Is 55:11 [c]Ro 14:11; Php 2:10 [d]Dt 6:13; Ps 63:11; Is 19:18; 65:16 **45:24** [a]Jer 33:16 [b]Is 41:11 **45:25** [a]1Ki 8:32; Is 53:11 [b]Is 41:16; 60:19 ◆**46:1** [a]Is 2:18; 21:9; Jer 50:2-4; 51:44 [1]Lit *carried by you* **46:2** [a]Jdg 18:17, 18, 24; 2Sa 5:21; Jer 43:12, 13; 48:7; Hos 10:5, 6 [1]Or *their soul has* **46:3** [a]Is 46:12 [b]Is 10:21, 22 [c]Ps 71:6; Is 49:1 [1]Lit *the belly* **46:4** [a]Is 41:4; 43:13; 48:12 [b]Ps 71:18 [1]Lit *I am He* [2]Lit *gray hairs* [3]Or *made* you **46:5** [a]Is 40:18, 25 **46:6** [a]Is 40:19; 41:7; 44:12-17; Jer 10:4 [b]Is 44:15, 17 **46:7** [a]Is 45:20; 46:1; Jer 10:5 [b]Is 40:20; 41:7 [c]Is 41:28 [d]Is 45:20 **46:8** [a]Is 44:21 [b]Is 44:19 [c]Is 50:1 [1]Lit *firm*

9 "Remember the [a]former
things long past,
For I am God, and there
is [b]no other;
*I am* God, and there is
[c]no one like Me,
10 Declaring the end
from the beginning,
And from ancient times things
which have not been done,
Saying, '[a]My counsel
will be established,
And I will accomplish all
My good pleasure',
11 Calling a [a]bird of prey
from the [b]east,
The man of [1]My counsel
from a far country.
Truly I have [c]spoken;
truly I will bring it to pass.
I have formed *it*, surely
I will do it.

12 "[a]Hear Me, you
[b]stubborn of heart,
Who are [c]far
from righteousness.
13 "I [a]bring near My righteousness,
it is not far off;
And My salvation
will not delay.
And I will grant
[b]salvation in Zion,
*And* My [c]glory for Israel.

### *Lament for Babylon*

47 "[a]Come down and
sit in the dust,
O [b]virgin [c]daughter of Babylon;
Sit on the ground
without a throne,
O daughter of the Chaldeans!
For you shall no longer be
called [d]tender and delicate.
2 "Take the [a]millstones
and [b]grind flour.
Uncover your [c]veil,
[d]strip off the skirt,
Uncover the leg,
cross the rivers.
3 "Your [a]nakedness will
be uncovered;
Your reproach also
will be seen;
I will [b]take vengeance and
will not [1]spare a man."
4 Our [a]Redeemer, Yahweh
of hosts is His name,
The Holy One of Israel.
5 "[a]Sit silently, and go
into [b]darkness,
O daughter of the Chaldeans,
For you will no longer
be called
The [c]queen of [d]kingdoms.
6 "I was furious with My people;
I profaned My inheritance
And gave them into your hand.
You did not show
compassion to them,
On the [a]aged you made
your yoke very heavy.
7 "Yet you said, 'I will be
a [a]queen forever.'
These things you did not
[b]put on your heart
Nor remember the
[c]outcome of [1]them.

***46:9*** [a]*Dt 32:7; Is 42:9; 65:17* [b]*Is 45:5, 21* [c]Is 41:26, 27 **46:10** [a]Ps 33:11; Pr 19:21; Is 14:24; 25:1; 40:8; Ac 5:39 **46:11** [a]Is 18:6 [b]Is 41:2 [c]Nu 23:19; Is 14:24; 37:26 [1]Lit *His* **46:12** [a]Is 46:3 [b]Ps 76:5; Is 48:4; Zec 7:11, 12; Mal 3:13 [c]Ps 119:150; Is 48:1; Jer 2:5 **46:13** [a]Is 51:5; 61:11; Ro 3:21 [b]Is 61:3; 62:11; Joel 3:17; 1Pe 2:6 [c]Is 43:7; 44:23 ◆ **47:1** [a]Is 3:26; Jer 48:18 [b]Is 23:12; 37:22; Jer 46:11 [c]Ps 137:8; Jer 50:42; 51:33; Zec 2:7 [d]Dt 28:56 **47:2** [a]Ex 11:5; Jer 25:10 [b]Job 31:10; Ecc 12:4; Mt 24:41 [c]Ge 24:65; Is 3:23; 1Co 11:5 [d]Is 32:11 **47:3** [a]Eze 16:37; Na 3:5 [b]Is 34:8; 63:4 [1]Lit *meet* **47:4** [a]Is 41:14 **47:5** [a]Is 23:2; Jer 8:14; Lam 2:10 [b]Is 13:10 [c]Is 47:7 [d]Is 13:19; Da 2:37 **47:6** [a]Dt 28:50 **47:7** [a]Is 47:5 [b]Is 42:25; 57:11 [c]Dt 32:29; Jer 5:31; Eze 7:2, 3 [1]Lit *it*

8 “So now, hear this,
you [a]sensual one,
Who [b]sits securely,
Who says in [1]your heart,
‘[c]I am, and there is no
one besides me.
I will [d]not sit as a widow,
Nor know loss of children.’
9 “But these [a]two things
will come on you
[b]suddenly in one day:
Loss of children
and widowhood.
They will come on you
in full measure
In spite of your
many [c]sorceries,
In spite of the great
might of your spells.
10 “You felt [a]secure in your
evil and said,
‘[b]No one sees me,’
Your [c]wisdom and your
knowledge [1]have
turned you *astray*;
So you have said in your heart,
‘[d]I am, and there is no
one besides me.’
11 “But [a]evil will come on you
Which you will not know
how to charm away;
And disaster will fall on you
For which you cannot atone;
And [b]destruction about
which you do not know
Will come on you [c]suddenly.

12 “Stand *fast* now in your [a]spells
And in your many sorceries
With which you have
labored from your youth;
Perhaps you will be
able to profit;
Perhaps you may
cause trembling.
13 “You are [a]wearied
with your many counsels;
Let now the [b]astrologers,
Those who behold
*visions* by the stars,
Those who predict
by the new moons,
Stand up and [c]save you from
what will come upon you.
14 “Behold, they have become
[a]like stubble,
[b]Fire burns them;
They cannot deliver themselves
from the power
of the flame;
There will be [c]no coal
to warm by
*Nor* a fire to sit before!
15 “Thus they have become
for you, those among
whom you have labored,
Who have [a]traded
with you from your youth;
Each has wandered
in his own [1]way;
There is [b]none to save you.

### *My Glory I Will Not Give to Another*

48 “[a]Hear this, O house
of Jacob, who are
called by the name Israel
And who came forth
from the [b,1]loins of Judah,

**47:8** [a]Is 22:13; 32:9; Jer 50:11 [b]Is 32:9, 11; Zep 2:15 [c]Is 45:5, 6, 18; 47:10; Zep 2:15 [d]Rev 18:7 [1]Lit *her* **47:9** [a]Is 13:16, 18; 14:22 [b]Ps 73:19; 1Th 5:3; Rev 18:8, 10 [c]Is 47:13; Na 3:4; Rev 18:23 **47:10** [a]Ps 52:7; 62:10; Is 59:4 [b]Is 29:15; Eze 8:12; 9:9 [c]Is 5:21; 44:20 [d]Is 47:8 [1]Lit *it has* **47:11** [a]Is 57:1 [b]Is 13:6; Jer 51:8, 43; Lk 17:27; 1Th 5:3 [c]Is 47:9 **47:12** [a]Is 47:9 **47:13** [a]Jer 51:58, 64 [b]Is 8:19; 44:25; 47:9; Da 2:2, 10 [c]Is 47:15 **47:14** [a]Is 5:24; Na 1:10; Mal 4:1 [b]Is 10:17; Jer 51:30, 32, 58 [c]Is 44:16 **47:15** [a]Rev 18:11 [b]Is 5:29; 43:13; 46:7 [1]Lit *side, region* ◆**48:1** [a]Is 46:12 [b]Nu 24:7; Dt 33:28; Ps 68:26 [1]Lit *waters*

Who [c]swear by the
name of Yahweh
And bring to remembrance
the God of Israel,
*But* not in truth or
in [d]righteousness.
2 "For they call themselves
after the [a]holy city
And [b]are supported
by the God of Israel;
Yahweh of hosts is His name.
3 "I [a]declared the former
things long ago,
And they went forth from
My mouth, and I caused
them to be heard.
[b]Suddenly I acted,
and they [c]came to pass.
4 "Because I know that
you are [a,1]stiff,
And your [b]neck is
an iron sinew
And your [c]forehead bronze,
5 Therefore I declared *them*
to you long ago,
Before [1]they happened
I caused *them* to be
heard by you,
Lest you say, 'My [a]idol
has done them,
And my graven image and
my molten image have
commanded them.'
6 "You have heard; look
at all this.
And you, will you
not declare it?
I caused you to hear [a]new
things from this time,
Even hidden things
which you have not known.
7 "They are created now
and not long ago;
And before today you
have not heard them,
Lest you say, 'Behold,
I knew them.'
8 "Indeed, you have not
[a]heard; indeed,
you have not known.
Indeed, even from long ago
your ear has not been open
Because I knew that you would
deal very treacherously;
And you have been
called a [b,1]transgressor
from the [2]womb.
9 "[a]For the sake of My name
I [b]delay My anger,
And *for* My praise I
restrain *it* for you,
In order not to cut you off.
10 "Behold, I have refined you,
but [a]not as silver;
I have tested you in the
[b]furnace of affliction.
11 "[a]For My own sake,
for My own sake, I will act;
For how can *My name*
be profaned?
And My [b]glory I will not
give to another.

### *Yahweh Redeems Jacob*

12 "Hear Me, O Jacob, even
Israel [1]whom I called;
[a]I am He, [b]I am the first,
I am also the last.

---

**48:1** [c]Dt 6:13; Is 45:23; 65:16 [d]Is 58:2; Jer 4:2 **48:2** [a]Is 52:1; 64:10 [b]Is 10:20; Jer 7:4; 21:2; Mic 3:11; Ro 2:17 **48:3** [a]Is 41:22; 42:9; 43:9; 44:7, 8; 45:21; 46:10 [b]Is 29:5; 30:13 [c]Jos 21:45; Is 42:9 **48:4** [a]Ex 32:9; Dt 31:27; Eze 2:4; 3:7 [b]2Chr 36:13; Pr 29:1; Ac 7:51 [c]Eze 3:7-9 [1]Or *harsh* **48:5** [a]Jer 44:15-18 [1]Lit *it* **48:6** [a]Is 42:9; 43:19 **48:8** [a]Is 42:25; 47:11; Hos 7:9 [b]Dt 9:7, 24; Ps 58:3; Is 46:8 [1]Or *rebel* [2]Lit *belly* **48:9** [a]Is 48:11 [b]Ne 9:30, 31; Ps 78:38; 103:8-10; Is 30:18; 65:8 **48:10** [a]Jer 9:7; Eze 22:18-22 [b]Dt 4:20; 1Ki 8:51; Jer 11:4 **48:11** [a]1Sa 12:22; Ps 25:11; 106:8; Is 37:35; 43:25; Jer 14:7; Eze 20:9, 14, 22, 44; Da 9:17-19 [b]Dt 32:26, 27; Is 42:8 **48:12** [a]Is 41:4; 43:10-13; 46:4 [b]Is 44:6; Rev 1:17; 22:13 [1]Lit *My called one*

13 “Also, My hand [a]founded
the earth,
And My right hand spread
out the heavens;
When I [b]call to them,
they stand together.
14 “[a]Assemble, all of you, and hear!
[b]Who among them has
declared these things?
Yahweh loves him; he
will [c]carry out His good
pleasure on [d]Babylon,
And His arm *will be*
*against* the Chaldeans.
15 “I, even I, have spoken;
indeed I have [a]called him,
I have brought him, and He will
make his ways successful.
16 “[a]Draw near to Me, hear this:
From the first I have [b]not
spoken in secret,
[c]From the time it took
place, I was there.
So now [d]Lord Yahweh has
sent Me, and His Spirit.”

17 Thus says Yahweh, your [a]Redeem-
er, the Holy One of Israel,
“I am Yahweh your God,
who teaches you to profit,
Who [b]leads you in the way
you should go.
18 “If only you had [a]paid attention
to My commandments!
Then your [b]peace would
have been like a river,
And your [c]righteousness
like the waves of the sea.
19 “Your [a]seed would have
been like the sand,
And the offspring from your
loins like its grains;
[b]Their name would never
be cut off or destroyed
from My presence.”

20 [a]Go forth from Babylon!
Flee from the Chaldeans!
Declare with the sound
of [b]joyful shouting,
cause this to be heard,
[c]Bring it forth to the
end of the earth;
Say, “[d]Yahweh has redeemed
His servant Jacob.”
21 And they did not [a]thirst
when He led them
through the waste places.
He [b]made the water flow
out of the rock for them;
He split the rock, and
[c]the water gushed forth.
22 “[a]There is no peace
for the wicked,” says Yahweh.

### *I Will Give You as a Light of the Nations*

49 Listen to Me,
O [a]coastlands,
And pay attention,
you peoples from afar.
[b]Yahweh called Me
from the womb;
From the [1]body of My
mother He made My name
to be remembered.

---

**48:13** [a]Ex 20:11; Ps 102:25; Is 42:5; 45:12, 18; Heb 1:10-12 [b]Is 40:26 **48:14** [a]Is 43:9; 45:20 [b]Is 45:21 [c]Is 46:10, 11 [d]Is 13:4, 5, 17-19; Jer 50:21-29; 51:24 **48:15** [a]Is 41:2; 45:1, 2 **48:16** [a]Is 34:1; 41:1; 57:3 [b]Is 45:19 [c]Is 43:13 [d]Zec 2:9, 11 **48:17** [a]Is 41:14; 43:14; 49:7, 26; 54:5, 8 [b]Ps 32:8; Is 30:21; 49:9, 10 **48:18** [a]Dt 5:29; 32:29; Ps 81:13-16 [b]Ps 119:165; Is 32:16-18; 66:12 [c]Is 45:8; 61:10, 11; 62:1; Hos 10:12; Am 5:24 **48:19** [a]Ge 22:17; Is 10:22; 44:3, 4; 54:3; Jer 33:22 [b]Is 56:5; 66:22 **48:20** [a]Jer 50:8; 51:6, 45; Zec 2:6, 7; Rev 18:4 [b]Is 42:10; 49:13; 52:9 [c]Is 62:11; Jer 31:10; 50:2 [d]Is 43:1; 52:9; 63:9 **48:21** [a]Is 30:25; 35:6, 7; 41:17, 18; 43:19, 20; 49:10 [b]Ex 17:6; Ps 78:15, 16 [c]Ps 78:20; 105:41 **48:22** [a]Is 57:21 ◆ **49:1** [a]Is 42:4 [b]Is 44:2, 24; 46:3; Jer 1:5 [1]Lit *inward parts*

2 He has set My [a]mouth
like a sharp sword;
In the [b]shadow of His hand
He has concealed Me;
And He has also set Me
as a [1]select [c]arrow;
He has hidden Me in His quiver.
3 He said to Me, "[a]You are
My Servant, Israel,
[b]In Whom I will [1]show forth
My beautiful glory."
4 But I said, "I have
[a]toiled in vain;
I have spent My might
for [1]nothing and vanity;
Yet surely the justice *due*
to Me is with Yahweh,
And My [b]reward
with My God."

5 So now says [a]Yahweh,
who formed Me from
the womb to be His Servant,
To return Jacob back
to Him, so that [b]Israel might
be gathered to Him
(For I am [c]glorified
in the sight of Yahweh,
And My God is My [d]strength),
6 He says, "It is too [1]small
a thing that You should
be My Servant
To raise up the tribes of Jacob
and to cause the [a]preserved
ones of Israel to return;
I will also give You
as a [b]light [2]of the nations
So that My salvation may
[3]reach to the [c]end
of the earth."
7 Thus says Yahweh,
the [a]Redeemer of Israel
*and* its Holy One,
To the [b]despised One,
To the One abhorred
by the nation,
To the Servant of rulers,
"[c]Kings will see and arise,
Princes will also [d]bow down,
Because of Yahweh who is
faithful, the Holy One of
Israel who has chosen You."

8 Thus says Yahweh,
"In an [a]acceptable time I
have answered You,
And in a day of salvation
I have helped You;
And I will [b]guard You and
[c]give You for a covenant
of the people,
To [d]establish the land,
to make *them* inherit the
desolate [1]inheritance;
9 Saying to those who are
[a]bound, 'Go forth,'
To those who are in darkness,
'[1]Show yourselves.'
Along the roads they
will [2]feed,
And their pasture *will be*
on all [b]bare heights.
10 "They will [a]not hunger
or thirst,
Nor will the scorching [b]heat
or sun strike them down;
For [c]He who has compassion
on them will [d]guide them
And will lead them
to [e]springs of water.

**49:2** [a]Is 11:4; Heb 4:12; Rev 1:16; 2:12, 16 [b]Is 51:16 [c]Hab 3:11 [1]Or *sharpened* **49:3** [a]Zec 3:8 [b]Is 44:23 [1]Or *glorify Myself* **49:4** [a]Is 65:23 [b]Is 35:4; 59:18 [1]Lit *formlessness* **49:5** [a]Is 44:2 [b]Is 11:12; 27:12 [c]Is 43:4 [d]Is 12:2 **49:6** [a]Ps 37:28; 97:10 [b]Is 42:6; 51:4; Lk 2:32; Ac 13:47; 26:23 [c]Is 48:20 [1]Lit *light* [2]Or *to* [3]Lit *be* **49:7** [a]Is 48:17 [b]Ps 22:6-8; 69:7-9; Is 53:3 [c]Is 52:15 [d]Is 19:21, 23; 27:13; 66:23 **49:8** [a]Ps 69:13; 2Co 6:2 [b]Is 26:3; 27:3; 42:6 [c]Is 42:6 [d]Is 44:26 [1]Lit *inheritances* **49:9** [a]Is 42:7; 61:1; Lk 4:18 [b]Is 41:18 [1]Lit *Reveal* [2]Or *be shepherded* **49:10** [a]Is 33:16; 48:21; Rev 7:16 [b]Ps 121:6 [c]Is 14:1 [d]Ps 23:2; Is 40:11 [e]Is 35:7; 41:17

11 “I will set all [a]My
mountains as a road,
And My [b]highways
will be raised up.
12 “Behold, these will
come [a]from afar;
And behold, these *will*
*come* from the [b]north
and from the west,
And these from the
land of Sinim.”
13 [a]Shout for joy, O heavens!
And rejoice, O earth!
Break forth into joyful
shouting, O mountains!
For [b]Yahweh has
comforted His people
And will [c]have compassion
on His afflicted.

### *Promise to Zion*

14 But Zion said, “Yahweh
has forsaken me,
And the Lord has
forgotten me.”
15 “Can a woman forget her infant
And have no compassion
on the son of her womb?
Even these may forget,
but [a]I will not forget you.
16 “Behold, I have [a]inscribed you
on the palms *of My hands*;
Your [b]walls are continually
before Me.
17 “Your [1]builders hurry;
Your [a]destroyers and
devastators
Will depart from you.
18 “[a]Lift up your eyes and
look around;
[b]All of them gather together;
[c]they come to you.
[d]As I live,” declares Yahweh,
“You will surely [e]put on all
of them as [1]jewels and
bind them on as a bride.
19 “For [a]your [1]devastated
and desolate places and
your destroyed land—
Surely now you will be [b]too
cramped for the inhabitants,
And those who [c]swallowed
you will be far away.
20 “The [a]children of
[1]whom you were bereaved
will yet say in your ears,
‘The place is too
cramped for me;
Make room for me that
I may live *here*.’
21 “Then you will [a]say
in your heart,
‘Who has borne these for me?
Indeed, I have been
bereaved of my children
And am [b]barren, an [c]exile
and a wanderer.
And who has reared these?
Behold, I [d]remained alone;
[e,1]From where did these come?’”

22 Thus says Lord Yahweh,
“Behold, I will lift up My
hand to the nations
And make high My [a]standard
to the peoples;
And they will [b]bring your
sons in *their* bosom,
And your daughters will be
lifted up on *their* shoulders.

**49:11** [a]Is 40:4 [b]Is 11:16; 19:23; 35:8; 62:10 **49:12** [a]Is 49:1; 60:4 [b]Is 43:5, 6 **49:13** [a]Is 44:23 [b]Is 40:1; 51:3, 12 [c]Is 54:7, 8, 10 **49:15** [a]Is 44:21 **49:16** [a]SS 8:6; Hag 2:23 [b]Ps 48:12, 13; Is 62:6, 7 **49:17** [a]Is 10:6; 37:18 [1]As in DSS and ancient versions; M.T. *sons* **49:18** [a]Is 60:4; Jn 4:35 [b]Is 43:5; 54:7; 60:4 [c]Is 49:12 [d]Is 45:23; 54:9 [e]Is 52:1; 61:10 [1]Lit *an ornament* **49:19** [a]Is 1:7; 3:8; 5:6; 51:3 [b]Is 54:1, 2; Zec 10:10 [c]Ps 56:1, 2 [1]Or *waste* **49:20** [a]Is 54:1-3 [1]Lit *your bereavement* **49:21** [a]Is 29:23; 54:6, 7 [b]Is 27:10; Lam 1:1 [c]Is 5:13 [d]Is 1:8 [e]Is 60:8 [1]Lit *These, where are they?* **49:22** [a]Is 11:10, 12; 18:3; 62:10 [b]Is 14:2; 43:6; 60:4

23 “[a]Kings will be your guardians,
And their princesses
your nurses.
They will [b]bow down to you
with their [1]faces to the earth
And [c]lick the dust of your feet;
And *you* will [d]know
that I am Yahweh;
Those who [e]hope in Me will
[f]not be put to shame.

24 “[a]Can the prey be taken
from the mighty man,
Or the captives of *the* [1]righteous
be granted escape?”
25 Surely, thus says Yahweh,
“Even the [a]captives of the mighty
man will be taken away,
And the prey of the tyrant
will be granted escape;
For I will contend with the one
who contends with you,
And I will [b]save your sons.
26 “I will feed [a]those who mistreat
you with their [b]own flesh,
And they will become drunk
with their own blood
as with sweet wine;
And [c]all flesh will know that
I, Yahweh, am your [d]Savior
And your [e]Redeemer, the
Mighty One of Jacob.”

### *Yahweh Helps His Servant*

50 Thus says Yahweh,
“Where is the
[a]certificate of divorce
By which I have [b]sent
your mother away?
Or to which of My creditors
did I [c]sell you?
Behold, you were sold
for your [d]iniquities,
And for your [e]transgressions
your mother [f]was
sent away.
2 “Why was there [a]no
man when I came?
When I called, why was
there none to answer?
Is My [b]hand so short that
it cannot ransom?
Or have I no power to deliver?
Behold, I [c]dry up the sea
with My rebuke;
I [d]make the rivers
a wilderness;
Their fish stink
for lack of water
And die of thirst.
3 “I [a]clothe the heavens
with blackness
And make sackcloth
their covering.”

4 Lord Yahweh has given Me
the tongue of [a]disciples,
That I may know how
to [b]sustain the weary
one with a word.
He awakens *Me* [c]morning
by morning;
He awakens My ear
to listen as a disciple.
5 Lord Yahweh has
[a]opened My ear;
And I did [b]not rebel
Nor did I turn back.

***49:23*** *[a]Is 14:1, 2; 60:3, 10, 11* [b]Is 45:14; 60:14 [c]Ps 72:9; Mic 7:17 [d]Is 41:20; 43:10; 60:16 [e]Ps 37:9; Is 25:9; 26:8 [f]Ps 25:3; Is 45:17; Joel 2:27 [1]Lit *noses* **49:24** [a]Mt 12:29; Lk 11:21 [1]DSS and ancient versions *tyrant*, cf. 49:25 **49:25** [a]Is 10:6; 14:1, 2; Jer 50:33, 34 [b]Is 25:9; 33:22; 35:4 **49:26** [a]Is 9:4; 14:4; 16:4; 51:13; 54:14 [b]Is 9:20 [c]Is 45:6; Eze 39:7 [d]Is 43:3 [e]Is 49:7 ◆**50:1** [a]Dt 24:1, 3; Jer 3:8 [b]Is 54:6, 7 [c]Dt 32:30; 2Ki 4:1; Ne 5:5 [d]Is 52:3; 59:2 [e]Is 1:28; 43:27 [f]Jer 3:8 **50:2** [a]Is 41:28; 59:16; 66:4 [b]Ge 18:14; Nu 11:23; Is 59:1 [c]Ex 14:21; Is 19:5; 43:16; 44:27 [d]Jos 3:16; Is 42:15 **50:3** [a]Is 13:10; Rev 6:12 **50:4** [a]Is 8:16; 54:13 [b]Is 57:19; Jer 31:25 [c]Ps 5:3; 88:13; 119:147; 143:8 **50:5** [a]Ps 40:6; Is 35:5 [b]Mt 26:39; Jn 8:29; 14:31; 15:10; Ac 26:19; Php 2:8; Heb 5:8; 10:7

6 I [a]gave My back to those
who strike *Me*,
And My cheeks to those
who pluck out the beard;
I did not hide My face
from dishonor and spitting.
7 Even *now* Lord Yahweh
[a]helps Me,
Therefore, I am
[b]not dishonored;
Therefore, I have set
My face like [c]flint,
And I know that I will
not be ashamed.
8 He who [a,1]vindicates Me is near;
Who will contend with Me?
Let us [b]stand up to each other;
Who has a judgment
against Me?
Let him approach Me.
9 Behold, [a]Lord Yahweh helps Me;
[b]Who is he who
condemns Me?
Behold, [c]they will all wear
out like a garment;
The moth will eat them.
10 Who is among you that
fears Yahweh,
That listens to the voice
of His [a]Servant,
That [b]walks in darkness
and has no light?
Let him [c]trust in the name of
Yahweh and rely on his God.
11 Behold, all you who
[a]*kindle* a fire,
Who gird yourselves
with firebrands,
Walk in the light of your fire
And among the brands
you have set ablaze.
This you will have
from My hand:
You will [b]lie down in torment.

### *Yahweh's Righteousness Is Forever*

51 "[a]Listen to Me, you who
[b]pursue righteousness,
Who seek Yahweh:
Look to the [c]rock
from which you were hewn
And to the [1]quarry
from which you were dug.
2 "Look to [a]Abraham
your father
And to Sarah who brought you
forth through labor pains;
When *he* [b]*was but* one
I called him,
Then I blessed him and
multiplied him."
3 Indeed, [a]Yahweh will
comfort Zion;
He will comfort all her
[b]waste places.
And her [c]wilderness He
will make like [d]Eden,
And her desert
like the [e]garden of Yahweh;
[f]Joy and gladness will
be found in her,
Thanksgiving and
sound of a melody.

4 "[a]Pay attention to Me,
O My people,
And give ear to Me,
O My [1]nation;

**50:6** [a]Mt 26:67; 27:30; Mk 14:65; 15:19; Lk 22:63 **50:7** [a]Is 42:1; 49:8 [b]Is 45:17; 54:4 [c]Eze 3:8, 9 **50:8** [a]Is 45:25; Ro 8:33, 34 [b]Is 1:18; 41:1; 43:26 [1]Or *justifies*, cf. 53:11 **50:9** [a]Is 41:10 [b]Is 54:17 [c]Job 13:28; Is 51:8 **50:10** [a]Is 49:2, 3; 50:4 [b]Is 9:2; 26:9; Eph 5:8 [c]Is 12:2; 26:4 **50:11** [a]Pr 26:18; Is 9:18; Jas 3:6 [b]Is 8:22; 65:13-15; Am 4:9, 10 ◆ **51:1** [a]Is 46:3; 48:12; 51:7 [b]Ps 94:15; Pr 15:9 [c]Ge 17:15-17 [1]Lit *excavation of a pit* **51:2** [a]Is 29:22; 41:8; 63:16 [b]Ge 12:1; 15:5; Dt 1:10; Eze 33:24 **51:3** [a]Is 40:1; 49:13 [b]Is 52:9 [c]Is 35:1; 41:19 [d]Ge 2:8; Joel 2:3 [e]Ge 13:10 [f]Is 25:9; 41:16; 65:18; 66:10 **51:4** [a]Ps 50:7; 78:1 [1]Or *people*

For a [b]law will go
forth from Me,
And I will [2]set My [c]justice
for a [d]light of the peoples.
5 "My [a]righteousness is near,
My salvation has gone forth,
And My [b]arms will
judge the peoples;
The [c]coastlands will
hope in Me,
And for My [d]arm they
will wait expectantly.
6 "[a]Lift up your eyes to the sky,
Then look to the
earth beneath;
For the [b]sky will vanish
like smoke,
And the [b]earth will wear
out like a garment,
And its inhabitants will
die [1]in like manner;
But My [c]salvation
will be forever,
And My righteousness
will not be dismayed.
7 "[a]Listen to Me, you who
know righteousness,
A people in whose [b]heart
is My law;
Do not fear the
[c]reproach of man,
Nor be dismayed
at their revilings.
8 "For the [a]moth will eat
them like a garment,
And the [b]grub will eat
them like wool.
But My [c]righteousness
will be forever,
And My salvation
to all generations."

9 [a]Awake, awake, put on
strength, O arm of Yahweh;
Awake as in the [b]days of old,
the generations of long ago.
[c]Was it not You who chopped
Rahab in pieces,
Who pierced the [d]dragon?
10 Was it not You who
[a]dried up the sea,
The waters of the great deep,
Who made the depths
of the sea a pathway
For the [b]redeemed
to cross over?
11 So the [a]ransomed
of Yahweh will return
And come with joyful
shouting to Zion,
And [b]everlasting gladness
*will be* on their heads.
They will obtain joy
and gladness,
And [c]sorrow and sighing
will flee away.

12 "I, even I, am He who
[a]comforts you.
Who are you that you are
afraid of [b]man who dies
And of the son of man who
is made [c]like grass,
13 That you have [a]forgotten
Yahweh your Maker,
Who [b]stretched out the heavens
And laid the foundations
of the earth,

**51:4** [b]*Dt 18:18; Is 2:3; Mic 4:2* [c]Is 1:27; 42:4 [d]Is 42:6; 49:6 [2]Lit *cause to rest* **51:5** [a]Is 46:13; 54:17 [b]Is 40:10 [c]Is 42:4; 60:9 [d]Is 59:16; 63:5 **51:6** [a]Is 40:26 [b]Ps 102:25, 26; Is 13:13; 34:4; Mt 24:35; Heb 1:10-12; 2Pe 3:10 [c]Is 45:17; 51:8 [1]Or *like gnats* **51:7** [a]Is 51:1 [b]Ps 37:31 [c]Is 25:8; 54:4; Mt 5:11; Ac 5:41 **51:8** [a]Is 50:9 [b]Is 14:11; 66:24 [c]Is 51:6 **51:9** [a]Is 51:17; 52:1 [b]Ex 6:6; Dt 4:34 [c]Job 26:12; Ps 89:10; Is 30:7 [d]Ps 74:13; Is 27:1 **51:10** [a]Is 11:15, 16; 50:2; 63:11, 12 [b]Ex 15:13; Ps 106:10; Is 63:9 **51:11** [a]Is 35:10; Jer 31:11, 12 [b]Is 60:19; 61:7 [c]Is 25:8; 60:20; 65:19; Rev 7:17; 21:1, 4; 22:3 **51:12** [a]Is 51:3 [b]Ps 118:6; Is 2:22 [c]Is 40:6, 7; 1Pe 1:24 **51:13** [a]Dt 6:12; 8:11; Is 17:10 [b]Job 9:8; Ps 104:2; Is 40:22; 45:12, 18; 48:13

That you [c]tremble in dread
continually all day long
because of the wrath of
the one who brings distress,
As he makes ready
to bring ruin?
But where is the wrath of the
[d]one who brings distress?
**14** "The [a]one in chains will soon be
set free and will not die in the pit,
[b]nor will his bread be lacking. **15** For
I am Yahweh your God, who [a]stirs up
the sea, and its waves roar—Yahweh
of hosts is His name. **16** I have [a]put
My words in your mouth and have
[b]covered you with the shadow of My
hand, to [c,1]establish the heavens, to
found the earth, and to say to Zion,
'You are My people.'"

**17** [a]Awaken yourself! Awaken
yourself! Arise, O Jerusalem,
You who have [b]drunk from
the hand of Yahweh the
cup of His wrath;
The [1]chalice of reeling you
have [2]drained to the dregs.

**18** There is [a]none to guide
her among all the sons
she has borne,
Nor is there one to take hold
of her by the hand among
all the sons she has reared.

**19** These two things have
befallen you;
*Who will console you?*
The [a]devastation and
destruction, famine
and sword;
How shall I comfort you?

**20** Your sons have fainted;
They [a]lie *helpless*
at the head of every street,
Like an [b]antelope in a net,
Full of the wrath of Yahweh,
The [c]rebuke of your God.

**21** Therefore, now, listen
to this, you [a]afflicted,
Who are [b]drunk,
but not with wine:

**22** Thus says your Lord,
Yahweh, even your God
Who [a]contends for His people,
"Behold, I have taken
out of your hand the
[b]cup of reeling,
The [1]chalice of My wrath;
You will never drink it again.

**23** "I will [a]set it into the hand of
those who cause you grief,
Who have said to [1]you,
'[b]Lie down that we
may walk over *you.*'
You have even set your back
*down* like the ground
And like the street for those
who walk over *it.*"

### *Hope for Captive Zion*

**52** [a]Awake, awake,
Clothe yourself in your
strength, O Zion;
Clothe yourself in your
[b]glorious garments,
O Jerusalem, the [c]holy city;
For the uncircumcised
and the [d]unclean
Will no longer come into you.

**51:13** [c]Is 7:4; 10:24 [d]Is 49:26; 54:14 **51:14** [a]Is 48:20; 52:2 [b]Is 33:6; 49:10 **51:15** [a]Ps 107:25; Jer 31:35 **51:16** [a]Dt 18:18; Is 59:21 [b]Ex 33:22; Is 49:2 [c]Is 66:22 [1]Lit *plant* **51:17** [a]Is 51:9; 52:1 [b]Job 21:20; Is 29:9; 63:6; Jer 25:15; Rev 14:10; 16:19 [1]Lit *bowl of the cup of* [2]Lit *drunk* **51:18** [a]Ps 88:18; 142:4; Is 49:21 **51:19** [a]Is 8:21; 9:20; 14:30 **51:20** [a]Is 5:25; Jer 14:16 [b]Dt 14:5 [c]Is 66:15 **51:21** [a]Is 54:11 [b]Is 29:9; 51:17; 63:6 **51:22** [a]Is 3:12, 13; 49:25; Jer 50:34 [b]Is 51:17 [1]Lit *bowl of the cup of* **51:23** [a]Is 49:26; Jer 25:15-17, 26, 28; Zec 12:2 [b]Jos 10:24 [1]Lit *your soul* ◆ **52:1** [a]Is 51:9, 17 [b]Ex 28:2, 40; 1Chr 16:29; Ps 110:3; Is 49:18; 61:3, 10; Zec 3:4 [c]Ne 11:1; Is 48:2; 64:10; Zec 14:20, 21; Mt 4:5; Rev 21:2-27 [d]Is 35:8

2 Shake yourself
[a]from the dust, [b]rise up,
O captive Jerusalem;
[c]Loose yourself from the
chains around your neck,
O captive daughter of Zion.
3 For thus says Yahweh, "You were
[a]sold for nothing, and you will be
[b]redeemed [c]without money." 4 For
thus says Lord Yahweh, "My people
[a]went down at the first into Egypt
to sojourn there; then the Assyrian
oppressed them without cause. 5 So
now, what do I have here," declares
Yahweh, "since My people have been
taken away for nothing?" Yahweh
declares, "Those who rule over them
howl, and My [a]name is continually
blasphemed all day long. 6 Therefore
My people shall [a]know My name;
therefore in that day I am the one
who is speaking, 'Here I am.'"

7 How lovely on the mountains
Are the feet of him who
proclaims [a]good news,
Who [1]announces [2]peace
And proclaims good
news of good things,
Who [1]announces salvation,
*And* says to Zion,
"Your [b]God [3]reigns!"
8 The voice of Your watchmen!
They lift up *their* [a]voices;
They shout joyfully together;
For they will see
[1]with their own eyes
When Yahweh returns to Zion.
9 [a]Break forth, shout
joyfully together,
You [b]waste places
of Jerusalem;
For Yahweh has comforted
His people;
He has [c]redeemed Jerusalem.
10 Yahweh has bared
His holy [a]arm
In the sight of all the nations,
[1]That [b]all the ends
of the earth may see
The salvation of our God.

11 [a]Depart, depart, go
out from there,
[b]Touch nothing unclean;
Go out of the midst of her,
[c]purify yourselves,
You who carry the
vessels of Yahweh.
12 But you will not go
out in [a]haste,
Nor will you go
as those who flee;
For [b]Yahweh will go
before you,
And [c]the God of Israel *will*
*be* your rear guard.

### *The Exalted Servant*

13 Behold, My [a]Servant
will prosper;
He will be high and lifted
up and [1]greatly [b]exalted.
14 Just as many were appalled
at you, *My people*,
So His [a]appearance was
marred more than any man
And His form more than
the sons of men.

**52:2** [a]Is 29:4 [b]Is 60:1 [c]Is 9:4; 10:27; 14:25; Zec 2:7 **52:3** [a]Ps 44:12; Jer 15:13 [b]Is 1:27; 62:12; 63:4 [c]Is 45:13 **52:4** [a]Ge 46:6 **52:5** [a]Eze 36:20, 23; Ro 2:24 **52:6** [a]Is 49:23 **52:7** [a]Is 40:9; 61:1; Na 1:15; Ro 10:15; Eph 6:15 [b]Ps 93:1; Is 24:23 [1]Or *causes peace to be heard* [2]Or *well-being* [3]Or *is King* **52:8** [a]Is 62:6 [1]Lit *eye to eye* **52:9** [a]Ps 98:4; Is 44:23 [b]Is 44:26; 51:3; 61:4 [c]Is 43:1; 48:20 **52:10** [a]Ps 98:1-3; Is 51:9; 66:18, 19 [b]Is 45:22; 48:20 [1]Lit *And...earth will see* **52:11** [a]Is 48:20; Jer 50:8; Zec 2:6, 7; 2Co 6:17 [b]Nu 19:11, 16 [c]Lv 22:2; Is 1:16 **52:12** [a]Ex 12:11, 33; Dt 16:3 [b]Is 26:7; 42:16; 49:10, 11 [c]Ex 14:19, 20; Is 58:8 **52:13** [a]Is 42:1; 49:1-7; 53:11 [b]Is 57:15; Php 2:9 [1]Or *very high, exceedingly lofty*; cf. 5:16; 7:11 **52:14** [a]Is 53:2, 3

15 Thus He will [a]sprinkle
many nations,
Kings will [b]shut their mouths
on account of Him;
For [c]what had not been
told them they will see,
And what they had not heard
they will understand.

### *The Suffering Servant*

53 [a]Who has believed
our report?
And to whom has the arm
of Yahweh been revealed?
2 For He grew up before Him
like a [a]tender [1]shoot,
And like a root
out of parched ground;
He has [b]no *stately*
form or majesty
That we should look upon Him,
Nor appearance that we
should desire Him.
3 He was [a]despised and
forsaken of men,
A man of [1]sorrows and
[b]acquainted with [2]grief;
And like one from whom
men hide their face
He was [c]despised, and we
did not [d]esteem Him.

4 Surely our [1]griefs He
Himself [a,2]bore,
And our [3]sorrows He [4]carried;
Yet we ourselves esteemed
Him stricken,
[5]Smitten of [b]God, and afflicted.
5 But He was [1]pierced through
for [a]our transgressions,
He was crushed
for [b]our iniquities;
The [c]chastening for our
peace *fell* upon Him,
And by [d]His [2]wounds
we are healed.
6 All of us like sheep
have gone astray,
Each of us has turned
to his own way;
But Yahweh has caused
the iniquity of us all
To [1]fall on Him.

7 He was oppressed and
He was afflicted,
Yet He did not [a]open
His mouth;
[b]Like a lamb that is
led to slaughter,
And like a sheep that is
silent before its shearers,
So He did not open His mouth.
8 By oppression and judgment
He was taken away;
And as for His generation,
who considered
That He was cut off out
of the land of [1]the living,
[a]*That* for the transgression
of my people, striking
*was due* to Him?
9 So His grave was assigned
with wicked men,
Yet He was with a [a]rich
man in His death,
[b]Because He had [c]done
no violence,
Nor was there any deceit
in His mouth.

**52:15** [a]Nu 19:18-21; Eze 36:25 [b]Job 21:5 [c]Ro 15:21; Eph 3:5 ◆ **53:1** [a]Jn 12:38; Ro 10:16 **53:2** [a]Is 11:1 [b]Is 52:14 [1]Lit *suckling* **53:3** [a]Ps 22:6; Is 49:7; Lk 18:31-33 [b]Is 53:10 [c]Mk 10:33, 34 [d]Jn 1:10, 11 [1]Or *pains* [2]Or *sickness* **53:4** [a]Mt 8:17 [b]Jn 19:7 [1]Or *sickness* [2]Or *carried* [3]Or *pains* [4]Or *bore* [5]Or *Struck down by* **53:5** [a]Is 53:8; Heb 9:28 [b]Is 53:10; Ro 4:25; 1Co 15:3 [c]Dt 11:2; Heb 5:8 [d]1Pe 2:24, 25 [1]Or *wounded* [2]Lit *wound* **53:6** [1]Lit *encounter Him* **53:7** [a]Mt 26:63; 27:12-14; Mk 14:61; 15:5; Lk 23:9; Jn 19:9 [b]Ac 8:32, 33; Rev 5:6 **53:8** [a]Is 53:5, 12 [1]Or *life* **53:9** [a]Mt 27:57-60 [b]Is 42:1-3 [c]1Pe 2:22

10 But [1]Yahweh was pleased
To [a]crush Him, [b,2]putting
*Him* to grief;
If You would place His soul
*as* a guilt [c]offering,
He will see [d]*His* seed,
He will prolong *His* days,
And the [3]good [e]pleasure
of Yahweh will succeed
in His hand.
11 As a result of the [1]anguish
of His soul,
He will [a]see [2]*it and*
be satisfied;
By His [b]knowledge the
Righteous One,
My Servant, will
[3]justify the many,
As He will [c]bear
their iniquities.
12 Therefore, I will divide for Him
a [a]portion with the many,
And He will divide the
spoil with the strong;
Because He poured out
[b]His soul to death,
And was [c]numbered
with the transgressors;
Yet He Himself [d,1]bore
the sin of many,
And interceded for the
transgressors.

### *The Inheritance of the Slaves of Yahweh*

54 "[a]Shout for joy, O barren
woman, who has
not given birth;
Break forth into joyful
shouting and cry aloud, *you*
who have not been in [1]labor;
For [b]more numerous are the
sons of the [c]desolate one
Than the sons of the married
woman," says Yahweh.
2 "[a]Enlarge the place of your tent;
[1]Stretch out the curtains
of your dwellings,
do not hold back;
Lengthen your [b]cords
And strengthen your [b]pegs.
3 "For you will [a]spread abroad
to the right and to the left.
And your seed will
[b]possess nations
And will [c]resettle the
desolate cities.

4 "Do not be afraid, for you will
[a]not be put to shame;
And do not feel dishonored,
for you will not be
humiliated;
But you will forget the [b]shame
of your virginity,
And the [c]reproach of your
widowhood you will
remember no more.
5 "For your [a]husband
is your Maker,
Whose name is
Yahweh of hosts;
And your [b]Redeemer is
the Holy One of Israel,
Who is called the [c]God
of all the earth.

**53:10** [a]Is 53:5 [b]Is 53:3, 4 [c]Is 53:6, 12; Jn 1:29 [d]Ps 22:30; Is 54:3; 61:9; 66:22 [e]Is 46:10 [1]Or *it was the desire of Yahweh*, cf. Ps 40:6 [2]Or *He put Him to grief*; lit *He made Him sick* [3]Or will of, desire of, cf. Ps 40:6 **53:11** [a]Jn 10:14-18 [b]Is 45:25; Ro 5:18, 19 [c]Is 53:5, 6 [1]Or *toilsome labor* [2]Or *light* [3]Or *declare the many righteous*, cf. 53:11a; 5:23 **53:12** [a]Is 52:13; Php 2:9-11 [b]Mt 26:38, 39, 42 [c]Mk 15:28; Lk 22:37 [d]Is 53:6, 11; 2Co 5:21 [1]Or *carried* ◆ **54:1** [a]Ga 4:27 [b]1Sa 2:5; Is 49:20 [c]Is 62:4 [1]Or *labor pains* **54:2** [a]Is 33:20; 49:19, 20 [b]Ex 35:18; 39:40 [1]Lit *Let them stretch out* **54:3** [a]Ge 28:14; Is 43:5, 6; 60:3 [b]Is 14:1, 2 [c]Is 49:19 **54:4** [a]Is 45:17 [b]Jer 31:19 [c]Is 4:1; 25:8; 51:7 **54:5** [a]Jer 3:14; Hos 2:19 [b]Is 43:14; 48:17 [c]Is 6:3; 11:9; 65:16

6 “For Yahweh has called you,
Like a wife [a]forsaken and
grieved in spirit,
Even like a wife of *one's* youth
when she is rejected,”
Says your God.
7 “[1]For a [a]brief moment
I forsook you,
But with great compassion
I will [b]gather you.
8 “In [1]a [a]flood of fury
I hid My face from you
for a moment,
But with everlasting
[b]lovingkindness I will [c]have
compassion on you,”
Says Yahweh your [d]Redeemer.

9 “For [1]this is like the days
of Noah to Me,
When I swore that the waters
of Noah
Would [a]not [2]overflow
the earth again;
So I have sworn that I will
[b]not be furious with you
Nor will I rebuke you.
10 “For the [a]mountains may
be removed and the
hills may shake,
But My lovingkindness will
not be removed from you,
And My [b]covenant of peace
will not be shaken,”
Says [c]Yahweh who has
compassion on you.

11 “O [a]afflicted one, storm-tossed,
*and* [b]not comforted,
Behold, I will lay your
stones in antimony,
And your foundations I
will [c]set in [d,1]sapphires.
12 “Moreover, I will make your
battlements of [1]rubies,
And your gates of [2]crystal,
And your entire [3]wall
of [4]precious stones.
13 “[a]All your sons will be
[1]taught of Yahweh;
And the peace of your
sons will be [b]great.
14 “In [a]righteousness you
will be established;
You will be far
from [b]oppression,
for you will [c]not fear,
And from [d]terror, for it will
not come near you.
15 “If anyone fiercely attacks *you*
it will not be from Me.
[a]Whoever attacks you will
fall because of you.
16 “Behold, I Myself have
created the craftsman who
blows the fire of coals
And brings out a weapon
for its work;
And I have created the
bringer of ruin
to wreak destruction.
17 “[a]No weapon that is formed
against you will succeed;
And [b]every tongue that
[1]accuses you in judgment
you will condemn.
This is the inheritance
of the [2]slaves of Yahweh,

---

**54:6** [a]Is 49:14-21; 50:1, 2; 62:4 **54:7** [a]Is 26:20 [b]Is 11:12; 43:5; 49:18 [1]Lit *In* **54:8** [a]Is 60:10 [b]Is 54:10; 63:7 [c]Is 49:10, 13 [d]Is 54:5 [1]Lit *an overflowing* **54:9** [a]Ge 9:11 [b]Is 12:1; Eze 39:29 [1]Some mss *the waters of Noah this is to Me* [2]Lit *cross over* **54:10** [a]Ps 102:26; Is 51:6 [b]2Sa 23:5; Ps 89:34; Is 55:3; 59:21; 61:8 [c]Is 54:8 **54:11** [a]Is 51:21 [b]Is 51:18, 19 [c]Is 14:32; 28:16; 44:28 [d]Job 28:16; Rev 21:19 [1]Or *lapis lazuli* **54:12** [1]Bright red [2]Or *carbuncles* [3]Lit *border, boundary* [4]Lit *desirable* **54:13** [a]Jn 6:45 [b]Is 48:18; 66:12 [1]Or *disciples* **54:14** [a]Is 1:26, 27; 9:7; 62:1 [b]Is 9:4; 14:4 [c]Is 54:4 [d]Is 33:18 **54:15** [a]Is 41:11-16 **54:17** [a]Is 17:12-14; 29:8 [b]Is 50:8, 9 [1]Lit *rises against* [2]Or *servants*

And their [c]righteousness is
from Me," declares Yahweh.

### Seek Yahweh While He May Be Found

55 "Ho! Every one who [a]thirsts,
come to the waters;
And you who have [b]no
[1]money come, buy and eat.
Come, buy [c]wine and milk
[d]Without money and
without cost.
2 "Why do you [1]spend money
for what is [a]not bread,
And your wages for what
does not satisfy?
Listen carefully to Me,
and [b]eat what is good,
And [c]delight your
soul in richness.
3 "[a]Incline your ear and
come to Me.
Listen, that your
soul may [b]live;
And I will cut [c]an everlasting
covenant with you,
*According to* the [d]faithful
lovingkindnesses of David.
4 "Behold, I have given [a]him
as a witness to the peoples,
A [b]ruler and commander
for the peoples.
5 "Behold, you will call
a [a]nation you do not know,
And a nation which knows
you not will [b]run to you,
Because of Yahweh your God,
even the Holy One of Israel;
For He has [c]adorned you
with beautiful glory."
6 [a]Seek Yahweh
while He may be found;
[b]Call upon Him
while He is near.
7 [a]Let the wicked
forsake his way
And the unrighteous
man his [b]thoughts;
And let him [c]return to Yahweh,
And He will have
[d]compassion on him,
And to our God,
For He will
[e]abundantly pardon.
8 "For My thoughts are not
[a]your thoughts,
Nor are [b]your ways My ways,"
declares Yahweh.
9 "For [a]*as* the heavens are
higher than the earth,
So are My ways higher
than your ways
And My thoughts
than your thoughts.
10 "For as the [a]rain and
the snow come down
from heaven,
And do not return there
without watering the earth
And making it bear
and sprout,
And giving [b]seed to the sower
and bread to the eater,
11 So will My [a]word be which
goes forth from My mouth;
It will [b]not return
to Me empty,
Without [c]accomplishing
what pleases Me,

---

**54:17** [c]Is 45:24; 46:13 ◆ **55:1** [a]Ps 42:1, 2; 63:1; 143:6; Is 41:17; 44:3; Jn 4:14; 7:37; Rev 21:6 [b]Lam 5:4 [c]SS 5:1; Joel 3:18 [d]Hos 14:4; Mt 10:8 [1]Lit *silver* **55:2** [a]Ecc 6:2; Hos 8:7 [b]Ps 22:26; Is 1:19; 62:8, 9 [c]Is 25:6; Jer 31:14 [1]Lit *weigh out silver* **55:3** [a]Is 51:4 [b]Lv 18:5; Ro 10:5 [c]Is 61:8 [d]Ac 13:34 **55:4** [a]Ps 18:43; Jer 30:9; Hos 3:5 [b]Eze 34:24; 37:24, 25; Da 9:25; Mic 5:2 **55:5** [a]Is 45:14, 22-24; 49:6, 12, 23 [b]Zec 8:22 [c]Is 60:9 **55:6** [a]Ps 32:6; Is 45:19, 22; 49:8; Am 5:6 [b]Is 58:9; 65:24 **55:7** [a]Is 1:16, 19; 58:6 [b]Is 32:7; 59:7 [c]Is 31:6; 44:22 [d]Is 14:1; 54:8, 10 [e]Is 1:18; 40:2; 43:25; 44:22 **55:8** [a]Is 65:2; 66:18 [b]Is 53:6 **55:9** [a]Ps 103:11 **55:10** [a]Is 30:23 [b]2Co 9:10 **55:11** [a]Is 45:23; Mt 24:35 [b]Is 44:26; 59:21 [c]Is 46:10; 53:10

And without succeeding
*in the matter*
for which I sent it.
12 "For you will go out
with [a]gladness
And be led forth with [b]peace;
The [c]mountains and the
hills will break forth into
shouts of joy before you,
And all the [d]trees of the field
will clap *their* hands.
13 "Instead of the [a]thorn bush
the [b]cypress will come up,
And instead of the [c]nettle
the myrtle will come up,
And [1]it will be to Yahweh
for *His* [d,2]renown,
For an everlasting [e]sign
which [f]will not be cut off."

### *Salvation for the Foreigner*

56 Thus says Yahweh,
"[a]Keep justice and
do righteousness,
For My [b]salvation is
about to come
And My righteousness
to be revealed.
2 "How [a]blessed is the man
who does this,
And the son of man who
[b]takes hold of it,
Who [c]keeps
from profaning the sabbath,
And keeps his hand
from doing any evil."
3 Let not the [a]foreigner
who has joined himself
to Yahweh say,
"Yahweh will surely separate
me from His people."
Nor let the [b]eunuch say,
"Behold, I am a dry tree."
4 For thus says Yahweh,
"To the eunuchs who
[a]keep My sabbaths,
And choose
what pleases Me,
And [b]hold fast My covenant,
5 To them I will give in My
[a]house and within My
[b]walls a [1]memorial,
And a name better than that
of sons and daughters;
I will give [2]them an
everlasting [c]name
which [d]will not be cut off.

6 "Also the [a]foreigners
who join themselves
to Yahweh,
To minister to Him, and
to love the name of Yahweh,
To be His [1]slaves, every one
who [b]keeps
from profaning the sabbath
And takes hold
of My covenant,
7 Even [a]those I will bring
to My [b]holy mountain
And [c]make them glad
in My house of prayer.
Their burnt offerings and
their sacrifices will be
acceptable on [d]My altar;
For [e]My house will be
called a house of prayer
for all the peoples."

---

**55:12** [a]Ps 105:43; Is 51:11; 52:9 [b]Is 54:10, 13; Jer 29:11 [c]Is 44:23; 49:13 [d]1Chr 16:33 **55:13** [a]Is 7:19 [b]Is 60:13 [c]Is 5:6; 7:24; 32:13 [d]Is 63:12, 14; Jer 33:9 [e]Is 19:20 [f]Is 56:5 [1]The transformation of the desert [2]Lit *name* ◆ **56:1** [a]Is 1:17; 33:5; 61:8 [b]Ps 85:9; Is 46:13; 51:5 **56:2** [a]Ps 112:1; 119:1, 2 [b]Is 56:4, 6 [c]Ex 20:8-11; 31:13-17; Is 56:6; 58:13; Jer 17:21, 22; Eze 20:12, 20 **56:3** [a]Is 14:1; 56:6 [b]Dt 23:1; Jer 38:7; Ac 8:27 **56:4** [a]Is 56:2, 6 [b]Is 56:6 **56:5** [a]Is 2:2, 3; 56:7; 66:20 [b]Is 26:1; 60:18 [c]Is 62:2 [d]Is 48:19; 55:13 [1]Lit *hand* [2]As in DSS; M.T. *him* **56:6** [a]Is 56:3; 60:10; 61:5 [b]Is 56:2, 4 [1]Or *servants* **56:7** [a]Is 2:2, 3; 60:11; Mic 4:1, 2 [b]Is 11:9; 65:25 [c]Is 61:10 [d]Is 60:7 [e]Mt 21:13; Mk 11:17; Lk 19:46

8 Lord Yahweh,
who [a]gathers the banished
of Israel, declares,
"Yet [b]*others* I will gather
to [1]them, to those
*already* gathered."

9 All you [a]beasts of the field,
All you beasts in the forest,
Come to eat.
10 His [a]watchmen are [b]blind;
All of them know nothing.
All of them are mute
dogs unable to bark,
[1]Dreamers lying down,
who love to slumber;
11 And the dogs *have* a [a]strong
[1]appetite; they do not
know satisfaction.
And they are shepherds
who [b]do not know
understanding;
They have all [c]turned
to their own way,
Each one to his greedy
gain, to the last one.
12 "Come," *they say*,
"let [1]us take [a]wine,
and let us drink heavily
of strong drink;
And [b]tomorrow will be
like today—
[2]beyond exceedingly great."

### *Evil Leaders Rebuked*

57 The righteous man
perishes, and no man
[a]puts it upon his heart;
And men of lovingkindness
are gathered away,
while no one understands.
For the righteous man is
gathered away from [b]evil,
2 He enters into peace;
They rest in their [1]beds,
*Each one* who [a]walked
in his upright way.
3 "But draw near, you sons
of a [a]soothsayer,
[b]Seed of an adulterer
and [1]a [c]prostitute.
4 "Against whom do you jest?
Against whom do you
open wide your mouth
And stick out your tongue?
Are you not children
of [a]transgression,
Seed of lying,
5 *Who* inflame yourselves
among the [a,1]oaks,
[b]Under every green tree,
Who [c]slaughter the children
in the [2]ravines,
Under the clefts of the cliffs?
6 "Among the [a,1]smooth
*stones* of the [2]ravine
Is your portion, [3]they are
your lot;
Even to them you have
[b]poured out a drink offering;
You have made
a grain offering.
Shall I [c,4]relent
concerning these things?
7 "Upon a mountain [a]lofty
and lifted up

**56:8** [a]Is 11:12 [b]Is 60:3-11; 66:18-21; Jn 10:16 [1]Lit *him* **56:9** [a]Is 18:6; 46:11 **56:10** [a]Eze 3:17 [b]Is 29:9-14; Jer 14:13, 14 [1]As in DSS; M.T. *Ravers* **56:11** [a]Is 28:7; Eze 13:19; Mic 3:5, 11 [b]Is 1:3 [c]Is 57:17; Jer 22:17 [1]Lit *soul* **56:12** [a]Is 5:11, 12, 22 [b]Ps 10:6; Lk 12:19, 20 [1]As in DSS and many versions; M.T. *me* [2]Lit *remainder* ◆ **57:1** [a]Is 42:25; 47:7 [b]2Ki 22:20; Is 47:11; Jer 18:11 **57:2** [a]Is 26:7 [1]Graves **57:3** [a]Mal 3:5 [b]Is 1:4; Mt 16:4 [c]Is 1:21; 57:7-9 [1]As in ancient versions; Heb *she prostitutes herself* **57:4** [a]Is 48:8 **57:5** [a]Is 1:29 [b]2Ki 16:4; Jer 2:20; 3:13 [c]2Ki 23:10; Ps 106:37, 38; Jer 7:31 [1]Or *terebinths* [2]Or *wadis* **57:6** [a]Jer 3:9; Hab 2:19 [b]Jer 7:18 [c]Jer 5:9, 29; 9:9 [1]Symbols of fertility gods [2]Or *wadi* [3]Lit *they, they* [4]Or *regret, be comforted*; cf. 40:1 **57:7** [a]Jer 3:6; Eze 16:16

You have [b]made your bed.
You also went up there
to offer sacrifice.
8 "Behind the door and
the doorpost
You have set up
your memorial;
Indeed, far removed
from Me, you have
[a]uncovered yourself,
And have gone up and
made your bed wide,
And you have cut *a covenant*
for yourself with them;
You have loved their [1]bed;
You have looked
on *their* [2]manhood.
9 "You have journeyed
to the king with oil
And increased your perfumes;
You have [a]sent your envoys
a great distance
And made *them* go
down to Sheol.
10 "You were tired out
by the length of your road,
*Yet* you did not say,
'[a]It is hopeless.'
You found [1]renewed strength;
Therefore you did not [2]faint.

11 "Of [a]whom were you
anxious and fearful
When you lied and did
[b]not remember Me,
Nor *even* [c]put *Me*
upon your heart?
Was I not silent even
for a long time
So you do not fear Me?
12 "I will [a]declare your
righteousness and
your [b]deeds,
But they will not profit you.
13 "When you cry out, [a]let your
collection *of idols*
deliver you.
But the wind will lift
all of them up,
*And* a breath will take
*them away.*
But he who [b]takes refuge
in Me will [c]inherit the land
And will [d]possess My
holy mountain."

### *Yahweh Revives the Spirit of the Lowly*

14 And it will be said,
"[a]Build up, build up,
prepare the way,
[1]Remove *every* stumbling
block out of the way
of My people."
15 For thus says the One
[a]high and lifted up
Who [b]dwells forever,
whose name is Holy,
"I [c]dwell *on* a high
and holy place,
And *also* with the [d]crushed
and lowly of spirit
In order to [e]revive the spirit
of the lowly
And to revive the heart
of the crushed.
16 "For I will [a]not contend forever,
[b]Nor will I always be angry;
For the spirit would grow
faint before Me,

**57:7** [b]Eze 23:41 **57:8** [a]Eze 23:18 [1]Or *lying down* [2]Lit *hand* **57:9** [a]Eze 23:16, 40 **57:10** [a]Jer 2:25; 18:12 [1]Lit *the life of your hand* [2]Or *become sick* **57:11** [a]Pr 29:25; Is 51:12, 13 [b]Jer 2:32; 3:21 [c]Ps 50:21; Is 42:14 **57:12** [a]Is 58:1, 2 [b]Is 29:15; 59:6; 65:7; 66:18; Mic 3:2-4 **57:13** [a]Jer 22:20; 30:14 [b]Ps 37:3, 9; Is 25:4 [c]Is 49:8; 60:21 [d]Is 65:9 **57:14** [a]Is 62:10; Jer 18:15 [1]Lit *Make high*, cf. 57:15; 6:1 **57:15** [a]Is 52:13 [b]Dt 33:27; Is 40:28 [c]Is 33:5; 66:1 [d]Ps 34:18; 51:17; Is 66:2 [e]Ps 147:3; Is 61:1-3 **57:16** [a]Ge 6:3 [b]Ps 85:5; 103:9; Mic 7:18

And the [c]breath *of those*
*whom* I have made.
17 "Because of the iniquity
of his [a]greedy gain I was
angry and struck him;
I hid *My face* and was angry,
And he went on [b]turning
away, in the way of his heart.
18 "I have seen his ways,
but I will [a]heal him;
I will [b]lead him and [c]pay
him and his mourners
in full *with* comfort,
19 Creating the [a,1]praise
of the lips.
[b]Peace, peace to him who is
[c]far and to him who is near,"
Says Yahweh,
"and I will heal him."
20 But the [a]wicked are
like the tossing sea,
For it cannot be quiet,
And its waters toss up
refuse and mud.
21 "[a]There is no peace," says [b]my
God, "for the wicked."

### *Fasting as Yahweh Chooses*

58 "[a]Call out from your
throat, do not hold back;
Raise your voice like a trumpet,
And declare to My people
their [b]transgression
And to the house
of Jacob their sins.
2 "Yet they [a]seek Me day
by day and find pleasure
in knowing My ways,
As a nation that has done
[b]righteousness
And [c]has not forsaken
the judgment of their God.
They ask Me *for* righteous
judgments;
They find pleasure
in [d]the nearness of God.
3 'Why have we [a]fasted
and You do not see?
*Why* have we afflicted our
souls and You do not know?'
Behold, on the [b]day of your
fast you find *your* desire,
And oppress all your workers.
4 "Behold, you fast
for contention and
[a]quarreling and to strike
with a wicked fist.
You do not fast like *you*
*do* today to [b]make your
voice heard on high.
5 "Is it a fast like this which I
choose, a day for a man
to afflict himself?
Is it for bowing [1]one's
head like a reed
And for spreading
out [a]sackcloth and
ashes as a bed?
Will you call this a fast,
even an [b]acceptable
day to Yahweh?
6 "Is this not the fast
which I choose,
To [a]loosen the bonds
of wickedness,
To release the bands
of [1]the yoke,
And to [b]let the
oppressed go free
And [c]break every [1]yoke?

**57:16** [c]Is 42:5 **57:17** [a]Is 2:7; 56:11; Jer 6:13 [b]Is 1:4; Jer 3:14, 22 **57:18** [a]Is 19:22; 30:26; 53:5 [b]Is 52:12 [c]Is 61:1-3 **57:19** [a]Is 6:7; 51:16; 59:21; Heb 13:15 [b]Is 26:12; 32:17 [c]Ac 2:39; Eph 2:17 [1]Lit *fruit of the lips* **57:20** [a]Job 18:5-14; Is 3:9, 11 **57:21** [a]Is 48:22; 59:8 [b]Is 49:4 ◆ **58:1** [a]Is 40:6 [b]Is 43:27; 50:1; 59:12 **58:2** [a]Is 1:11; Tit 1:16 [b]Is 48:1; Jer 7:9, 10 [c]Is 1:4, 28; 59:13 [d]Ps 119:151; Is 29:13; 57:3; Jas 4:8 **58:3** [a]Mal 3:14; Lk 18:12 [b]Is 22:12, 13; Zec 7:5, 6 **58:4** [a]Is 3:14, 15; 59:6 [b]Is 1:15; 59:2; Joel 2:12-14 **58:5** [a]1Ki 21:27 [b]Is 49:8; 61:2 [1]Lit *his* **58:6** [a]Ne 5:10-12; Jer 34:8 [b]Is 1:17 [c]Is 58:9 [1]Lit *the bar of the yoke*

7 “Is it not to [a]divide your
bread [1]with the hungry
And [b]bring the afflicted
homeless into the house;
When you see the [c]naked,
you cover him;
And not to [d]hide yourself
from your own flesh?
8 “Then your [a]light will break
out like the dawn,
And your [b]recovery will
speedily spring forth;
And your [c]righteousness
will go before you;
The glory of [d]Yahweh will
be your rear guard.
9 “Then you will [a]call, and
Yahweh will answer;
You will cry, and He will
say, ‘Here I am.’
If you [b]remove the [1]yoke
from your midst,
The [c,2]pointing
of the finger and [d]speaking
wickedness,
10 And if you [a,1]offer your
soul to the hungry
And satisfy the soul
of the afflicted,
Then your [b]light will
rise in darkness
And your thick darkness
*will become* like midday.
11 “And [a]Yahweh will
continually guide you,
*And* [b]satisfy your soul
in scorched places,
And [c]fortify your bones;
And you will be
like a [d]watered garden,
And like a [e]spring of water
whose waters do not [1]fail.
12 “Those from among you
will [a]rebuild the ancient
waste places;
You will [b]raise up the
foundations of *past*
generation upon generation;
And you will be called
the repairer of the [c]breach,
The restorer of the paths
*for one* to inhabit.

### *Keeping the Sabbath*

13 “If because of the sabbath,
you [a]turn your foot
From doing your *own*
desire on My holy day,
And call the sabbath a
[b]delight, the holy *day*
of Yahweh honorable,
And honor it, by not doing
your [c]*own* ways,
By not finding your
*own* desire
And [d]speaking *your*
*own* word,
14 Then you will take
[a]delight in Yahweh,
And I will make you ride
[b]on the heights of the earth;
And I will feed you
*with* the inheritance
of Jacob your father,
For the [c]mouth of Yahweh
has spoken.”

---

**58:7** [a]Job 31:19, 20; Is 58:10; Eze 18:7, 16 [b]Is 16:3, 4; Heb 13:2 [c]Mt 25:35, 36; Lk 3:11 [d]Dt 22:1-4; Lk 10:31, 32 [1]Lit *for* **58:8** [a]Is 58:10 [b]Is 30:26; 33:24; Jer 30:17; 33:6 [c]Ps 85:13; Is 62:1 [d]Ex 14:19; Is 52:12 **58:9** [a]Ps 50:15; Is 55:6; 65:24 [b]Is 58:6 [c]Pr 6:13 [d]Ps 12:2; Is 59:13 [1]Lit *bar of the yoke* [2]Lit *sending out* **58:10** [a]Dt 15:7; Is 58:7 [b]Job 11:17; Ps 37:6; Is 42:16; 58:8 [1]Lit *furnish* **58:11** [a]Is 49:10; 57:18 [b]Ps 107:9; Is 41:17 [c]Is 66:14 [d]SS 4:15; Is 27:3; Jer 31:12 [e]Jn 4:14; 7:38 [1]Or *deceive* **58:12** [a]Is 49:8; 61:4; Eze 36:10 [b]Is 44:28 [c]Is 30:13; Am 9:11 **58:13** [a]Ex 31:16, 17; 35:2, 3; Is 56:2, 4, 6; Jer 17:21-27 [b]Ps 27:4; 42:4; 84:2, 10 [c]Is 55:8 [d]Is 59:13 **58:14** [a]Job 22:26; Is 61:10 [b]Dt 32:13; 33:29; Is 33:16; Hab 3:19 [c]Is 1:20; 40:5

### *Separation from Yahweh*

59 Behold, [a]the hand
of Yahweh is not so short
That it cannot save;
[b]Nor is His ear so [1]dull
That it cannot hear.
2 But your [a]iniquities have
made a separation
between you and your God,
And your sins have hidden
*His* [1]face from you
so that He does [b]not hear.
3 For your [a]hands are
defiled with blood
And your fingers with iniquity;
Your lips have spoken a [b]lie;
Your tongue
mutters unrighteousness.
4 [a]No one calls
in righteousness, and [b]no
one seeks justice in truth.
They [c]trust in [1]confusion
and speak worthlessness;
They [d]conceive trouble and
give birth to wickedness.
5 They break open vipers' eggs
and [a]weave the spider's web;
He who eats of their eggs dies,
And *from* that which
is crushed a snake
breaks forth.
6 Their webs will not
become a garment,
Nor will they [a]cover
themselves with their works;
Their [b]works are works
of wickedness,
And a [c]deed of violence
is in their [1]hands.
7 [a]Their feet run to evil,
And they are quick
to shed innocent blood;
[b]Their thoughts are
thoughts of wickedness;
Devastation and destruction
are in their highways.
8 They do not know the
[a]way of peace,
And there is [b]no justice
in their tracks;
They have made their
paths crooked,
[c]Whoever treads on [1]them
does not know peace.

### *Trangressing and Denying Yahweh*

9 Therefore [a]justice is
far from us,
And righteousness does
not overtake us;
We [b]hope for light,
but behold, darkness,
For brightness, but we
walk in thick darkness.
10 We [a]grope along the wall
like blind men;
We grope like those
who have no eyes;
We [b]stumble at midday
as in the twilight,
Among those who are vigorous
*we are* [c]like dead men.
11 All of us growl like bears,
And [a]moan sadly like doves;
We hope for [b]justice,
but there is none,
For salvation,
*but* it is far from us.

◆ **59:1** [a]*Nu 11:23; Is 50:2; Jer 32:17* [b]Is 58:9; 65:24; Eze 8:18 [1]Lit *heavy*, hardened; cf. Ex 8:15; 1Sa 6:6
**59:2** [a]Is 1:15; 50:1 [b]Is 58:4 [1]As in versions; M.T. *faces* **59:3** [a]Is 1:15, 21; Jer 2:30, 34; Eze 7:23;
Hos 4:2 [b]Is 28:15; 30:9; 59:13 **59:4** [a]Is 5:7; 59:14 [b]Is 59:14, 15 [c]Is 30:12; Jer 7:4, 8 [d]Job 15:35; Ps 7:14;
Is 33:11 [1]Lit *formless* **59:5** [a]Job 8:14 **59:6** [a]Is 28:20 [b]Is 57:12; Jer 6:7 [c]Is 58:4; Eze 7:11 [1]Lit *palms*
**59:7** [a]Pr 1:16; 6:17; Ro 3:15-17 [b]Is 65:2; 66:18; Mk 7:21, 22 **59:8** [a]Lk 1:79 [b]Is 59:9, 11; Hos 4:1 [c]Is 57:20,
21 [1]Lit *it* **59:9** [a]Is 59:14 [b]Is 5:30; 8:21, 22 **59:10** [a]Dt 28:29; Job 5:14 [b]Is 8:14, 15; 28:13 [c]Lam 3:6
**59:11** [a]Is 38:14; Eze 7:16 [b]Is 59:9, 14

12 For our [a]transgressions are
multiplied before You,
And our [b]sins answer
against us;
For our transgressions
are with us,
And [1]we know our iniquities:
13 Transgressing and
[a]denying Yahweh,
And turning back from our God,
Speaking [b]oppression
and revolt,
Conceiving *in* and [c]uttering
from the heart lying words.
14 [a]Justice is turned back,
And [b]righteousness
stands far away;
For truth has stumbled
in the street,
And rightness cannot enter.
15 So it is that truth is missing;
And he who turns aside from
evil [a]makes himself plunder.

Then Yahweh saw,
And it was evil in His eyes
[b]that there was no justice.
16 And He saw that there
was [a]no man,
And was astonished that there
was no one to intercede;
Then His [b]own arm brought
salvation to Him,
And His righteousness
upheld Him.
17 He put on [a]righteousness
like a breastplate,
And a [b]helmet of salvation
on His head;
And He put on [c]garments
of vengeance for clothing
And wrapped Himself
with [d]zeal as a mantle.
18 [a]According to [1]what
they deserve, [2]so He
will pay in full,
Wrath to His adversaries,
[1]what is deserved
to His enemies;
To the coastlands He will
[1]pay what they deserve.
19 So they will fear the name
of Yahweh from the [a]west
And His glory from the
[b]rising of the sun,
For He will [c]come
like a [1]rushing stream
Which the wind
of Yahweh makes flee.
20 "A [a]Redeemer will
come to Zion,
And to those who [b]turn
from transgression
in Jacob," declares Yahweh.
21 "As for Me, this is My [a]covenant
with them," says Yahweh: "My [b]Spirit
which is upon you, and My [c]words
which I have put in your mouth,
shall not depart from your mouth,
nor from the mouth of your seed, nor
from the mouth of your seed's seed,"
says Yahweh, "from now and forever."

### *A Glorified Zion*

60 "[a]Arise, shine, for your
[b]light has come,
And the [c]glory of Yahweh
has risen upon you.

**59:12** [a]Ezr 9:6; Is 58:1 [b]Is 3:9; Jer 14:7; Hos 5:5 [1]Lit *our iniquities we know them* **59:13** [a]Jos 24:27; Pr 30:9; Mt 10:33; Tit 1:16 [b]Is 5:7; 30:12; Jer 9:3, 4 [c]Is 59:3, 4; Mk 7:21, 22 **59:14** [a]Is 1:21; 5:7 [b]Is 46:12; Hab 1:4 **59:15** [a]Is 5:23; 10:2; 29:21; 32:7 [b]Is 1:21-23 **59:16** [a]Is 41:28; 63:5; Eze 22:30 [b]Ps 98:1; Is 52:10; 63:5 **59:17** [a]Eph 6:14 [b]Eph 6:17; 1Th 5:8 [c]Is 63:2, 3 [d]Is 9:7; 37:32; Zec 1:14 **59:18** [a]Job 34:11; Is 65:6, 7; 66:6; Jer 17:10 [1]Lit *recompense* [2]Lit *accordingly* **59:19** [a]Is 49:12 [b]Ps 113:3 [c]Is 30:28; 66:12 [1]Lit *narrow* **59:20** [a]Ro 11:26 [b]Eze 18:30, 31; Ac 2:38, 39 **59:21** [a]Jer 31:31-34; Ro 11:27 [b]Is 11:2; 32:15; 44:3 [c]Is 55:11 ◆**60:1** [a]Is 52:2 [b]Is 60:19, 20 [c]Is 24:23; 35:2; 58:8

2 "For behold, [a]darkness
will cover the earth
And dense gloom
the peoples;
But Yahweh will rise upon you,
And His [b]glory will
appear upon you.
3 "[a]Nations will come
to your light,
And kings to the brightness
of your rising.

4 "[a]Lift up your eyes round
about and see;
They all gather together;
they [b]come to you.
Your sons will come from afar,
And your [c]daughters will be
[1]carried on the nurses' hip.
5 "Then you will see and
be [a]radiant,
And your heart will tremble
and be large *with joy*;
Because the [b]abundance of
the sea will be turned to you,
The [c]wealth of the nations
will come to you.
6 "A multitude of camels
will cover you,
The young camels
of Midian and [a]Ephah;
All those from [b]Sheba
will come;
They will bring [c]gold
and frankincense,
And will [d]bear good news
of the praises of Yahweh.
7 "All the flocks of [a]Kedar will be
gathered together to you;
The rams of Nebaioth
will minister to you;
They will go up
with acceptance on My [b]altar,
And I shall [c,1]adorn My
[2]glorious house
with beautiful glory.
8 "[a]Who are these who
fly like a cloud
And like the doves
to their [1]lattices?
9 "Surely the [a]coastlands
will hope in Me;
And the [b]ships of Tarshish
*will come* first,
To [c]bring your sons from afar,
Their silver and their
gold with them,
For the name of Yahweh
your God,
And for the Holy One of Israel
because He has [d,1]adorned
you with beautiful glory.

10 "[a]Foreigners will build
up your walls,
And their [b]kings will
minister to you;
For in My [c]wrath I struck you,
And in My favor I have had
compassion on you.
11 "Your [a]gates will be
open continually;
They will not be closed
day or night,
So that *men* may [b]bring to you
the wealth of the nations,
With [c]their kings led
in procession.

**60:2** [a]*Is 58:10; Jer 13:16; Col 1:13* [b]Is 4:5 **60:3** [a]Is 2:3; 45:14, 22-25; 49:23 **60:4** [a]Is 11:12; 49:18 [b]Is 49:20-22 [c]Is 43:6; 49:22 [1]Lit *nursed upon the side* **60:5** [a]Ps 34:5 [b]Is 23:18; 24:14 [c]Is 61:6 **60:6** [a]Ge 25:4 [b]Ge 25:3; Ps 72:10 [c]Is 60:9; Mt 2:11 [d]Is 42:10 **60:7** [a]Ge 25:13 [b]Is 19:19; 56:7 [c]Is 60:13; Hag 2:7, 9 [1]Or *beautify* [2]Or *beautiful* **60:8** [a]Is 49:21 [1]Or *dovecotes, windows* **60:9** [a]Is 11:11; 24:15; 42:4, 10, 12; 49:1; 51:5; 66:19 [b]Ps 48:7; Is 2:16 [c]Is 14:2; 43:6; 49:22 [d]Is 55:5 [1]Lit *beautified* **60:10** [a]Is 14:1, 2; 61:5; Zec 6:15 [b]Is 49:23; Rev 21:24 [c]Is 54:8 **60:11** [a]Is 26:2; 60:18; 62:10; Rev 21:25, 26 [b]Is 60:5 [c]Ps 149:8; Is 24:21

12 "For the [a]nation and the
kingdom which will not
serve you will perish,
And the nations will
surely be laid waste.
13 "The [a]glory of Lebanon
will come to you,
The [b]juniper, the box tree,
and the cypress together,
To adorn the place
of My sanctuary
with beautiful glory;
And I shall make the [c]place
of My feet glorious.
14 "The [a]sons of those who
afflicted you will come
bowing to you,
And all those who spurned
you will bow themselves
at the soles of your feet;
And they will call you
the [b]City of Yahweh,
The [c]Zion of the Holy
One of Israel.

15 "Instead of being [a]forsaken
and [b]hated
With no one passing through,
I will make you an
everlasting [c]pride,
A joy from generation
to generation.
16 "You will also [a]suck
the milk of nations
And suck the breast of kings;
*Then you will* know that I,
Yahweh, am your [b]Savior
And your [c]Redeemer, the
Mighty One of Jacob.
17 "Instead of bronze I
will bring gold,
And instead of iron I
will bring silver,
And instead of wood, bronze,
And instead of stones, iron.
And I will make peace
your overseers
And righteousness
your taskmasters.
18 "[a]Violence will not be heard
again in your land,
Nor [b]devastation or
destruction within
your borders;
But you will call your
[c]walls salvation, and
your [d]gates praise.
19 "No longer will you have
the [a]sun for light by day,
Nor for brightness will
the moon give you light;
But you will have [b]Yahweh
for an everlasting light,
And your [c]God for your [1]glory.
20 "Your [a]sun will no longer set,
Nor will your moon wane;
For you will have Yahweh
for an everlasting light,
And the days of your
[b]mourning will be finished.
21 "Then all your [a]people
*will be* righteous;
They will [b]possess
the land forever,
The branch of [1]My planting,
The [c]work of My hands,
That I may show forth
My [d]beautiful glory.

---

**60:12** [a]Is 14:2; Zec 14:17 **60:13** [a]Is 35:2 [b]Is 41:19 [c]1Chr 28:2; Ps 99:5; 132:7 **60:14** [a]Is 14:1, 2; 45:14, 23; 49:23; Rev 3:9 [b]Is 1:26 [c]Heb 12:22 **60:15** [a]Is 1:7-9; 6:11-13; Jer 30:17 [b]Is 66:5 [c]Is 4:2; 65:18 **60:16** [a]Is 66:11 [b]Is 19:20; 43:3, 11; 45:15, 21; 63:8 [c]Is 59:20; 63:16 **60:18** [a]Is 54:14 [b]Is 51:19 [c]Is 26:1 [d]Is 60:11 **60:19** [a]Rev 21:23; 22:5 [b]Is 2:5; 9:2 [c]Is 41:16; 45:25; Zec 2:5 [1]Or *beauty* **60:20** [a]Is 30:26 [b]Is 35:10; 65:19; Rev 21:4 **60:21** [a]Is 45:24, 25; 52:1 [b]Ps 37:11, 22; Is 57:13; 61:7 [c]Is 19:25; 29:23; 45:11; 64:8 [d]Is 61:3 [1]Lit *His*

22 "The [a]smallest one will
become a [1]clan,
And the miniscule one
a mighty nation.
I, Yahweh, will hasten
it in its time."

### *Exaltation of the Afflicted*

**61** The [a]Spirit of Lord
Yahweh is upon me
Because Yahweh has
anointed me
To [b]bring good news
to the [c,1]afflicted;
He has sent me to [d]bind
up the brokenhearted,
To [e]proclaim release
to captives
And [2]freedom to prisoners,
2 To [a]proclaim the favorable
year of Yahweh
And the [b]day of vengeance
of our God,
To [c]comfort all who mourn,
3 To [a]grant those who
mourn *in* Zion,
Giving them a headdress
instead of ashes,
The [b]oil of rejoicing
instead of mourning,
The mantle of praise instead
of a spirit of fainting.
So they will be called [c,1]oaks
of righteousness,
The planting of Yahweh,
that He may show forth
His beautiful glory.

4 Then they will [a]rebuild the
ancient waste places;
They will raise up
the former desolations;
And they will make new
the ruined cities,
The desolations from
generation to generation.
5 [a]Strangers will stand and
pasture your flocks,
And [1]foreigners will
be your farmers and
your vinedressers.
6 But you will be called
the [a]priests of Yahweh;
You will be spoken of *as*
[b]ministers of our God.
You will eat the [c]wealth
of nations,
And in their glories
you will boast.
7 Instead of your [a]shame *you
will have a* [b]double *portion*,
And *instead of* dishonor
they will shout for joy
over their portion.
Therefore they will
possess a double
*portion* in their land;
[c]Everlasting gladness
will be theirs.
8 For I, Yahweh, [a]love justice,
I hate robbery [1]in the
burnt offering;
And in truth I will give
them their recompense
And cut an [b]everlasting
covenant with them.
9 Then their seed will be known
among the nations,
And their offspring in the
midst of the peoples.

---

**60:22** [a]Is 10:22; 51:2 [1]Or *thousand* ◆ **61:1** [a]Is 11:2; 48:16; Lk 4:18 [b]Mt 11:5; Lk 7:22 [c]Is 11:4; 29:19; 32:7 [d]Is 57:15 [e]Is 42:7; 49:9 [1]Or *humble* [2]Lit *opening to those who are bound* **61:2** [a]Is 49:8; 60:10 [b]Is 2:12; 13:6; 34:2, 8 [c]Is 57:18; Jer 31:13; Mt 5:4 **61:3** [a]Is 60:20 [b]Ps 23:5; 45:7; 104:15 [c]Is 60:21; Jer 17:7, 8 [1]Or *terebinths* **61:4** [a]Is 49:8; 58:12; Eze 36:33; Am 9:14 **61:5** [a]Is 14:2; 60:10 [1]Lit *sons of the foreigner* **61:6** [a]Is 66:21 [b]Is 56:6 [c]Is 60:5, 11 **61:7** [a]Is 54:4 [b]Is 40:2; Zec 9:12 [c]Ps 16:11 **61:8** [a]Is 5:16; 28:17; 30:18 [b]Ge 17:7; Ps 105:10; Is 55:3; Jer 32:40 [1]Or *with iniquity*

All who see them will
recognize them
Because they are the [a]seed
*whom* Yahweh has blessed.

10 I will [a]rejoice greatly
in Yahweh;
My soul will rejoice in [b]my God,
For He has [c]clothed me
with garments of salvation,
He has wrapped me with
a robe of righteousness,
As a bridegroom decks
himself with a headdress,
And [d]as a bride adorns
herself with her jewels.
11 For as the [a]earth brings
forth its branches,
And as a garden causes
the things sown
in it to branch out,
So Lord Yahweh will [b]cause
[c]righteousness and praise
To branch out
before all the nations.

### *Zion's Glory and New Name*

62 For Zion's sake I will
not keep silent,
And for Jerusalem's sake
I will not keep quiet,
Until her [a]righteousness
goes forth like brightness,
And her [b]salvation
like a torch that is burning.
2 *The* [a]*nations will* see
your righteousness,
And all kings your glory;
And you will be called
by a new [b]name
Which the mouth
of Yahweh will designate.
3 You will also be a [a]crown
of glory in the hand
of Yahweh,
And a turban of royalty
in the hand of your God.
4 It will no longer be said
to you, "[a,1]Forsaken,"
Nor to your land will it any
longer be said, "[2]Desolate";
But you will be called,
"[3]My delight is in her,"
And your land, "[b,4]Married";
For [c]Yahweh takes
pleasure in you,
And *to Him* your land
will be married.
5 For *as* a young man
marries a virgin,
*So* your sons will marry you;
And *as* the [1]bridegroom
rejoices over the bride,
*So* your [a]God will
rejoice over you.

6 On your walls, O Jerusalem,
I have appointed
[a]watchmen;
All day and all night they
will never keep silent.
You who [b]remind Yahweh,
take no rest for yourselves;
7 And [a]give Him no rest
until He establishes
And sets [b]Jerusalem
as a praise in the earth.
8 [a]Yahweh has sworn
by His right hand and
by His strong arm,

---

**61:9** [a]Is 44:3 **61:10** [a]Is 12:1, 2; 25:9; 41:16; 51:3 [b]Is 49:4 [c]Is 49:18; 52:1 [d]Rev 21:2 **61:11** [a]Is 4:2; 55:10 [b]Is 45:23, 24; 60:18, 21 [c]Ps 72:3; 85:11 ◆ **62:1** [a]Is 1:26; 58:8; 61:11 [b]Is 46:13; 52:10 **62:2** [a]Is 60:3 [b]Is 56:5; 62:4, 12; 65:15 **62:3** [a]Is 28:5; Zec 9:16; 1Th 2:19 **62:4** [a]Is 54:6, 7; 60:15, 18 [b]Hos 2:19, 20 [c]Jer 32:41; Zep 3:17 [1]Heb *Azubah* [2]Heb *Shemamah* [3]Heb *Hephzibah* [4]Heb *Beulah* **62:5** [a]Is 65:19 [1]Lit *exultation of the bridegroom* **62:6** [a]Is 52:8; Jer 6:17; Eze 3:17; 33:7 [b]Ps 74:2; Jer 14:21; Lam 5:1, 20 **62:7** [a]Lk 18:1-8 [b]Is 60:18; Jer 33:9; Zep 3:19, 20 **62:8** [a]Is 45:23; 54:9

"I will [b]never again give
your grain *as* food
for your enemies;
Nor will [1]foreigners drink
your new wine for which
you have labored."
9 But those who [a]collect it will
eat it and praise Yahweh;
And those who gather it
will drink it in the courts
of My sanctuary.

10 Go through, [a]go
through the gates,
Clear the way [1]for the people;
[b]Build up, build up
the [c]highway,
Remove the stones, raise up a
[d]standard over the peoples.
11 Behold, Yahweh has
[1]announced to the
[a]end of the earth,
[b]Say to the daughter
of Zion, "Behold, your
[c]salvation comes;
[d]Behold, His reward is
with Him, and His
recompense before Him."
12 And they will call them,
"[a]The holy people,
The [b]redeemed of Yahweh";
And you will be called, "Sought
out, a city [c]not forsaken."

### *Vengeance of Yahweh*

63 Who is this who comes
from [a]Edom,
With [b]garments of [1]glowing
colors from [c]Bozrah,
This One who is majestic
in His clothing,
[2]Marching in the greatness
of His power?
"It is I who speak
in righteousness,
[d]mighty to save."
2 Why is Your clothing red,
And Your garments
like the one who [a]treads
in the wine press?
3 "[a]I have trodden the
wine trough alone,
And from the peoples there
was no man with Me.
I also [b]trod them in My anger
And [c]trampled them
in My wrath;
And [d]their [1]lifeblood is
sprinkled on My garments,
And I [2]stained all My clothes.
4 "For the [a]day of vengeance
was in My heart,
And My year of redemption
has come.
5 "I looked, and there was
[a]no one to help,
And I was astonished,
and there was no
one to uphold;
So My [b]own arm brought
salvation to Me,
And My wrath upheld Me.
6 "I [a]trod down the peoples
in My anger
And made them [b]drunk
in My wrath,
And I brought down their
lifeblood to the earth."

**62:8** [b]Lv 26:16; Dt 28:31, 33; Jdg 6:3-6; Is 1:7; Jer 5:17 [1]Lit *sons of foreigners* **62:9** [a]Is 65:13, 21-23
**62:10** [a]Is 26:1; 60:11, 18 [b]Is 57:14 [c]Is 11:16; 19:23; 35:8; 49:11 [d]Is 11:10, 12; 49:22 [1]Lit *of* **62:11** [a]Is 42:10; 49:6 [b]Mt 21:5; Zec 9:9 [c]Is 51:5 [d]Is 40:10; Rev 22:12 [1]Or *caused it to be heard* **62:12** [a]Dt 7:6; Is 4:3; 1Pe 2:9 [b]Is 35:9; 51:10 [c]Is 41:17; 42:16; 62:4 ◆ **63:1** [a]Ps 137:7; Is 34:5, 6; Eze 25:12-14; 35:1-15; Ob 1-14; Mal 1:2-5 [b]Is 63:2 [c]Is 34:6; Jer 49:13; Am 1:12 [d]Zep 3:17 [1]Or *crimson* [2]Lit *Inclining* **63:2** [a]Rev 19:13, 15
**63:3** [a]Rev 14:20; 19:15 [b]Is 22:5; 28:3 [c]Mic 7:10 [d]Rev 19:13 [1]Lit *juice* [2]Lit *defiled* **63:4** [a]Is 34:8; 35:4; 61:2; Jer 51:6 **63:5** [a]Is 59:16 [b]Ps 44:3; Is 40:10; 52:10 **63:6** [a]Is 22:5; 34:2; 65:12 [b]Is 29:9; 51:17, 21

### *Remember the Lovingkindness of Yahweh*

7 I shall bring to remembrance
the [a]lovingkindnesses
of Yahweh, the praises
of Yahweh,
According to all *the ways*
that Yahweh has dealt
bountifully with us,
And the abundant [b]goodness
toward the house of Israel,
Which He has dealt bountifully
to them according
to His [c]compassion
And according to the
abundance of His
lovingkindnesses.
8 And He said, "Surely,
they are [a]My people,
Sons who will not deal falsely."
So He became their [b]Savior.
9 In all their distress [a,1]He
was distressed,
And the [b]angel of His
presence saved them;
In His [c]love and in His mercy
He [d]redeemed them,
And He [e]lifted them and carried
them all the ancient days.
10 But they [a]rebelled
And grieved His [b]Holy Spirit;
Therefore He turned Himself
to become their enemy;
He fought against them.
11 Then [a]His people remembered
the ancient days, of Moses.
Where is [b]He who brought
them up out of the sea with
the [1]shepherds of His flock?
Where is He who [c]put
His Holy Spirit
in the midst of [2]them,
12 Who caused His [a]glorious
arm to go at the right
hand of Moses,
Who [b]split the waters before
them to make for Himself
an everlasting name,
13 Who led them
through the depths?
Like the horse in the
wilderness, they did
not [a]stumble;
14 As the cattle which go
down into the valley,
The Spirit of [a]Yahweh
gave [1]them rest.
So You [b]led Your people,
To make for Yourself
a glorious name.

### *Prayer for Mercy and Help*

15 [a]Look down from heaven
and see from Your holy
and glorious [b]habitation;
Where are Your [c]zeal and
Your mighty deeds?
The [d]tumults within You
and Your compassion are
restrained toward me.
16 For You are our [a]Father,
though [b]Abraham
does not know us
And Israel does not
recognize us.
You, O Yahweh, are our Father,
Our [c]Redeemer from
everlasting is Your name.

---

**63:7** [a]Ps 25:6; 92:2; Is 54:8, 10 [b]1Ki 8:66; Ne 9:25, 35 [c]Ps 51:1; 86:5, 15; Is 54:7, 8; Eph 2:4 **63:8** [a]Ex 6:7; Is 3:15; 51:4 [b]Is 60:16 **63:9** [a]Jdg 10:16 [b]Ex 23:20-23; 33:14, 15 [c]Dt 7:7, 8 [d]Is 43:1; 52:9 [e]Dt 1:31; 32:10-12; Is 46:3 [1]Or *He was not an adversary* **63:10** [a]Ps 78:40; 106:33; Ac 7:51; Eph 4:30 [b]Ps 51:11; Is 63:11 **63:11** [a]Ps 106:44, 45 [b]Is 51:10 [c]Nu 11:17, 25, 29; Hag 2:5 [1]Some mss *shepherd* [2]Lit *him* **63:12** [a]Ex 6:6; 15:16 [b]Ex 14:21, 22; Is 11:15; 51:10 **63:13** [a]Jer 31:9 **63:14** [a]Jos 21:44; 23:1 [b]Dt 32:12 [1]Lit *him* **63:15** [a]Dt 26:15; Ps 80:14 [b]Ps 68:5; 123:1 [c]Is 9:7; 26:11; 37:32; 42:13; 59:17 [d]Jer 31:20; Hos 11:8 **63:16** [a]Is 1:2; 64:8 [b]Is 29:22; 41:8; 51:2 [c]Is 41:14; 44:6; 60:16

17 Why, O Yahweh,
do You [a]cause us
to stray from Your ways
And [b]stiffen our heart
from fearing You?
[c]Return for the sake
of Your slaves, the tribes
of Your inheritance.
18 Your holy people possessed
Your sanctuary
for a little while;
Our adversaries have
[a]trodden *it* down.
19 We have become *like*
those over whom You
have never ruled,
*Like* those who were not
called by Your name.

64 [1]Oh, that You would
rend the heavens
*and* [a]come down,
That the mountains might
[b]quake at Your presence—
2 [1]As fire kindles
the brushwood, *as* fire
causes water to boil—
To make Your name known
to Your adversaries,
*That* the [a]nations may
tremble at Your presence!
3 When You did [a]awesome
things for which we
did not hope,
You came down;
the mountains quaked
at Your presence.
4 For from ancient *times* [a]they
have not heard or given ear,
Nor has the eye seen
a God besides You,
Who acts in behalf of the one
who [b]waits for Him.
5 You [a]meet him who rejoices
and [b]does righteousness,
Who [c]remembers You
in Your ways.
Behold, [d]You were angry;
indeed we have sinned—
*We continued* in them
a long time—
And shall we be saved?
6 For all of us have become
like one who is [a]unclean,
And all our [b]righteous deeds
are like a filthy garment;
And all of us [c]wither
like a leaf,
And our [d]iniquities,
like the wind, carry us away.
7 There is [a]no one who
calls on Your name,
Who awakens himself
to take hold of You,
For You have [b]hidden
Your face from us
And have [1]melted us
into the hand of our iniquities.
8 But now, O Yahweh,
[a]You are our Father;
We are the [b]clay,
and You our potter;
And all of us are
the [c]work of Your hand.
9 Do not be [a]angry
beyond measure, O Yahweh,
[b]Nor remember
iniquity forever;
Behold, look now, all of us
are [c]Your people.

**63:17** [a]Is 30:28; Eze 14:7-9 [b]Is 29:13, 14 [c]Nu 10:36 **63:18** [a]Ps 74:3-7; Is 64:11 ◆ **64:1** [a]Ex 19:18; Ps 18:9; 144:5; Mic 1:3, 4; Hab 3:13 [b]Jdg 5:5; Ps 68:8; Na 1:5 [1]Ch 63:19b in Heb **64:2** [a]Ps 99:1; Jer 5:22; 33:9 [1]Ch 64:1 in Heb **64:3** [a]Ps 65:5; 66:3, 5; 106:22 **64:4** [a]1Co 2:9 [b]Is 25:9; 30:18; 40:31 **64:5** [a]Ex 20:24 [b]Is 56:1 [c]Is 26:13; 63:7 [d]Is 12:1 **64:6** [a]Is 6:5 [b]Is 46:12; 48:1 [c]Ps 90:5, 6; Is 1:30 [d]Is 50:1 **64:7** [a]Is 59:4; Eze 22:30 [b]Dt 31:18; Is 1:15; 54:8 [1]DSS and versions *delivered* **64:8** [a]Is 63:16 [b]Is 29:16; 45:9 [c]Ps 100:3; Is 60:21 **64:9** [a]Is 57:17; 60:10 [b]Is 43:25; Mic 7:18 [c]Ps 79:13; Is 63:8

10 Your [a]holy cities have
become a [b]wilderness;
Zion has become a wilderness,
Jerusalem a desolation.
11 Our holy and glorious [a]house,
Where our fathers praised You,
Has been burned *by* fire;
And [b]all our precious things
have become a waste place.
12 Will You [a]restrain Yourself
at these things, O Yahweh?
Will You keep silent and
afflict us beyond measure?

### *Judgment and Salvation*

65 "I permitted Myself
to be sought by [a]those
who did not ask *for Me*;
I permitted Myself to be
found by those who
did not seek Me.
I said, 'Here am I, here am I,'
To a nation which [b]did
not call on My name.
2 "[a]I have spread out My
hands all day long to a
[b]rebellious people,
Who walk *in* the way which
is not good, [1]following
their own [c]thoughts,
3 A people who continually
[a]provoke Me to My face,
Offering sacrifices
in [b]gardens and [c]burning
incense on bricks,
4 *Who sit* among graves
and spend the night
in secret places,
Who [a]eat swine's flesh,
And the broth of offensive
meat is *in* their pots,
5 Who say, '[a]Keep to yourself,
do not come near me,
For I am holier than you!'
These are smoke
in My [1]nostrils,
A fire that burns all the day.
6 "Behold, it is written before Me:
I will [a]not keep silent,
but [b]I will repay;
I will even repay
into their bosom,
7 Both [1]their own [a]iniquities
and the iniquities
of their fathers together,"
says Yahweh.
"Because they have [b]burned
incense on the mountains
And [c]reproached Me
on the hills,
Therefore I will [d]measure
their former work
into their bosom."

8 Thus says Yahweh,
"As the new wine is found
in the cluster,
And one says,
'Do not make it a ruin,
for there is [1]benefit in it,'
So I will act on behalf
of My slaves
In order [a]not to make
[2]all of them a ruin.
9 "I will bring forth
a [a]seed from Jacob,
And a [b]possessor of My
mountains from Judah;

**64:10** [a]Is 48:2; 52:1 [b]Is 1:7; 6:11 **64:11** [a]2Ki 25:9; Ps 74:5-7; Is 63:18 [b]Lam 1:7, 10, 11 **64:12** [a]Ps 74:10, 11, 18, 19; Is 42:14; 63:15 ◆ **65:1** [a]Ro 9:24-26; 10:20 [b]Is 63:19; Hos 1:10 **65:2** [a]Ro 10:21 [b]Is 1:2, 23; 30:1, 9 [c]Ps 81:11, 12; Is 59:7; 66:18 [1]Lit *after* **65:3** [a]Job 1:11; 2:5; Is 3:8 [b]Is 1:29; 66:17 [c]Is 66:3 **65:4** [a]Lv 11:7; Is 66:3, 17 **65:5** [a]Mt 9:11; Lk 7:39; 18:9-12 [1]Lit *nose* **65:6** [a]Ps 50:3, 21; Is 42:14; 64:12 [b]Jer 16:18 **65:7** [a]Is 13:11; 22:14; 26:21; 30:13, 14 [b]Is 57:7; Hos 2:13 [c]Eze 20:27, 28 [d]Jer 5:29; 13:25 [1]Lit *your* **65:8** [a]Is 1:9; 10:21, 22; 48:9 [1]Lit *blessing* [2]Lit *the whole* **65:9** [a]Is 45:19, 25; Jer 31:36, 37 [b]Is 49:8; 60:21; Am 9:11-15

Even [c]My chosen ones
shall possess it,
And [d]My slaves will dwell there.
10 “[a]Sharon will be a pasture
land for flocks,
And the [b]valley of Achor
a resting place for herds,
For My people who [c]seek Me.
11 “But you who [a]forsake Yahweh,
Who forget My
[b]holy mountain,
Who set a table for [1]Fortune,
And who fill *cups* with
mixed wine for [2]Destiny,
12 I will destine you
for the [a]sword,
And all of you will bow
down to the [b]slaughter,
Because I called, but you
[c]did not answer;
I spoke, but you did not hear.
And you did what was
evil in My eyes
And chose that in which
I was not pleased.”

13 Therefore, thus says Lord Yahweh,
“Behold, My slaves will [a]eat,
but you will be [b]hungry.
Behold, My slaves will [c]drink,
but you will be [d]thirsty.
Behold, My slaves will
[e]be glad, but you will
be [f]put to shame.
14 “Behold, My slaves will [a]shout
joyfully with a merry heart,
But you will [b]cry out
with a pained heart,
And you will wail
with a broken spirit.
15 “You will leave your name for
a [a,1]curse to My chosen ones,
And Lord Yahweh will
put you to death.
But [2]My slaves will be called
by [b]another name,
16 Because he who [1]is
blessed in the earth
Will [1]be blessed by the
[a]God of truth,
And he who swears
in the earth
Will [b]swear by the God of truth;
Because the former
distresses are forgotten,
And because they are
hidden from My sight!

### *New Heavens and a New Earth*

17 “For behold, I am creating
a [a]new heavens and
a new earth;
And the [b]former things will
not be remembered or
come upon the heart.
18 “But be [a]joyful and rejoice
forever in what I create;
For behold, I create
Jerusalem *for* rejoicing
And her people *for* joy.
19 “I will also [a]rejoice in Jerusalem
and be joyful in My people;
And there will no longer
be heard in her
The voice of [b]weeping and
the voice of crying.

**65:9** [c]Is 57:13 [d]Is 32:18 **65:10** [a]Is 33:9; 35:2 [b]Jos 7:24, 26; Hos 2:15 [c]Is 51:1; 55:6 **65:11** [a]Dt 29:24, 25; Is 1:4, 28 [b]Is 2:2, 3; 66:20 [1]Heb *Gad* [2]Heb *Meni* **65:12** [a]Is 27:1; 34:5, 6; 66:16 [b]Is 63:6 [c]2Chr 36:15, 16; Pr 1:24; Is 41:28; 50:2; 66:4; Jer 7:13 **65:13** [a]Is 1:19 [b]Is 8:21 [c]Is 41:17, 18; 49:10 [d]Is 5:13 [e]Is 61:7; 66:14 [f]Is 42:17; 44:9, 11; 66:5 **65:14** [a]Ps 66:4; Is 51:11; Jas 5:13 [b]Is 13:6; Mt 8:12 **65:15** [a]Jer 24:9; 25:18; Zec 8:13 [b]Is 62:2 [1]Lit *oath* [2]As in Gr; Heb *He will call His slaves* **65:16** [a]Ex 34:6; Ps 31:5 [b]Is 19:18; 45:23 [1]Or *experience(s) blessing repeatedly, bless(es) himself* **65:17** [a]Is 66:22; 2Pe 3:13; Rev 21:1 [b]Is 43:18; Jer 3:16 **65:18** [a]Ps 98; Is 12:1, 2; 25:9; 35:10; 41:16; 51:3; 61:10 **65:19** [a]Is 62:4, 5; Jer 32:41 [b]Is 25:8; 30:19; 35:10; 51:11; Rev 7:17; 21:4

20 “No longer will there be
[1]in it an infant *who*
*lives but a few* days,
Or an old man who does
[a]not fulfill his days;
For the youth will die
at the age of one hundred,
And the [b,2]one who does
not reach the age
of one hundred
Will be *thought* accursed.
21 “They will [a]build houses
and inhabit *them;*
They will also [b]plant
vineyards and eat
their fruit.
22 “They will not build and
[a]another inhabit;
They will not plant
and another eat;
For [b]as the [1]lifetime
of a tree, *so will be* the
days of My people,
And My chosen ones will
[c]wear out the work
of their hands.
23 “They will [a]not labor in vain,
Or bear *children* for terror;
For they are the [b]seed
of those blessed by Yahweh,
And their offspring with them.
24 “And it will be that before they call,
I will [a]answer, and while they are still
speaking, I will hear. 25 The [a]wolf and
the lamb will graze together, and the
[b]*lion will eat straw like the ox;* and
[c]dust will be the serpent’s food. They
will [d]do no evil nor act corruptly in
all My [e]holy mountain,” says Yahweh.

### *Heaven Is Yahweh’s Throne*

66 Thus says Yahweh,
“[a]Heaven is My throne,
and the earth is the
footstool of My feet.
Where then is a [b]house you
could build for Me?
And where is a place
that [1]I may rest?
2 “For [a]My hand made
all these things,
Thus all these things
came into being,”
declares Yahweh.
“But to this one I will look,
To him who is humble and
[b]contrite of spirit, and who
[c]trembles at My word.

3 “*But* he who slaughters
an ox is the one who
strikes down a man;
He who sacrifices a lamb is the
one who breaks a dog’s neck;
He who offers a grain
offering *is the one who*
*offers* [a]swine’s blood;
He who [b]offers a memorial
offering of frankincense
is the one who blesses
wickedness.
As they have chosen
their [c]*own* ways,
And their soul takes pleasure
in their [d]detestable things,
4 So I will [a]choose their
[1]punishments
And will [b]bring on them
what they dread,

**65:20** [a]Dt 4:40; Job 5:26; Ps 34:12 [b]Ecc 8:12, 13; Is 3:11; 22:14 [1]Lit *from there* [2]Lit *one who misses the mark* **65:21** [a]Is 32:18; Am 9:14 [b]Is 30:23; 37:30; Jer 31:5 **65:22** [a]Is 62:8, 9 [b]Ps 92:12-14 [c]Ps 21:4; 91:16 [1]Lit *days* **65:23** [a]Dt 28:3-12; Is 55:2 [b]Is 61:9; Jer 32:38, 39; Ac 2:39 **65:24** [a]Ps 91:15; Is 55:6; 58:9; Da 9:20-23; 10:12 **65:25** [a]Is 11:6 [b]Is 11:7 [c]Ge 3:14; Mic 7:17 [d]Is 11:9; Mic 4:3 [e]Is 65:11 ◆ **66:1** [a]1Ki 8:27; Ps 11:4; Mt 5:34, 35; 23:22 [b]2Sa 7:5-7; Jer 7:4; Jn 4:20, 21; Ac 7:48-50 [1]Lit *is My resting place?* **66:2** [a]Is 40:26 [b]Ps 34:18; Is 57:15; Mt 5:3, 4; Lk 18:13, 14 [c]Ps 119:120; Is 66:5 **66:3** [a]Is 65:4 [b]Lv 2:2; Is 1:13 [c]Is 57:17; 65:2 [d]Is 44:19 **66:4** [a]Pr 1:31, 32; Is 65:7 [b]Pr 10:24 [1]Lit *ill treatments*

Because I called,
but [c]no one answered;
I spoke, but they did not listen.
And they did what was
[d]evil in My eyes
And chose that in which I
did not take pleasure."
5 Hear the word of Yahweh, you
who [a]tremble at His word:
"Your brothers who [b]hate
you, who [c]exclude you
for My name's sake,
Have said, 'Let Yahweh be
glorified, that we may
see your gladness.'
But [d]they will be put to shame.
6 "A voice of rumbling
from the city, a voice
from the temple,
The voice of Yahweh who
is [a]paying recompense
to His enemies.

7 "Before she was in labor
pains, [a]she gave birth;
Before her pangs came,
[b]she delivered a male *child*.
8 "[a]Who has heard such a thing?
Who has seen such things?
Can a land be [1]brought
forth through labor
pains in one day?
Can a nation be born
all at once?
As soon as Zion was
in labor pains, she also
gave birth to her sons.
9 "Shall I bring to the point
of breaking forth and [a]not
cause birth?" says Yahweh.
"Or shall I who causes
birth shut *the womb*?"
says your God.

### *Joy in Jerusalem's Future*

10 "Be [a]glad with Jerusalem
and rejoice for her,
all you who [b]love her;
Be exceedingly [c]joyful
with her, all you who
mourn over her,
11 That you may nurse and
[a]be satisfied with her
comforting breasts,
That you may suck and
be delighted with her
[b]bountiful bosom."
12 For thus says Yahweh,
"Behold, I stretch out
[a]peace to her like a river,
And the [b]glory of the nations
like an overflowing stream;
And you will [1]be nursed; you
will be [c]carried
on the [2]hip and played
with on the knees.
13 "As one whom his mother
comforts, so I will
[a]comfort you;
And you will be comforted
in Jerusalem."
14 Then you will [a]see *this*, and
your [b]heart will be joyful,
And your [c]bones will flourish
like the new grass;
And the [d]hand of Yahweh
will be made known
to His slaves,
But He will be [e]indignant
toward His enemies.

---

**66:4** [c]Pr 1:24; Is 65:12; Jer 7:13 [d]2Ki 21:2, 6; Is 59:7; 65:12; Jer 7:30 **66:5** [a]Is 66:2 [b]Ps 38:20; Is 60:15 [c]Mt 5:10-12; 10:22; Jn 9:34; 15:18-20 [d]Lk 13:17 **66:6** [a]Is 59:18; 65:6; Joel 3:7 **66:7** [a]Is 37:3; 54:1 [b]Rev 12:5 **66:8** [a]Is 64:4 [1]Lit *travailed with* **66:9** [a]Is 37:3 **66:10** [a]Dt 32:43; Is 65:18; Ro 15:10 [b]Ps 26:8; 122:6 [c]Ps 137:6 **66:11** [a]Is 49:23; 60:16; Joel 3:18 [b]Is 60:1, 2; 62:2 **66:12** [a]Ps 72:3, 7; Is 48:18 [b]Is 60:5; 61:6 [c]Is 60:4 [1]Lit *nurse* [2]Lit *side* **66:13** [a]Is 12:1; 40:1, 2; 49:13; 51:3; 2Co 1:3, 4 **66:14** [a]Is 33:20 [b]Zec 10:7 [c]Pr 3:8; Is 58:11 [d]Ezr 7:9; 8:31 [e]Is 10:5; 13:5; 34:2

15 For behold, Yahweh
will come in [a]fire
And His [b]chariots
like the whirlwind,
To return His anger
with wrath,
And His rebuke
with flames of fire.
16 For Yahweh will execute
judgment by [a]fire
And by His [b]sword on all flesh,
And those slain
by Yahweh will be many.
17 "Those who sanctify and
purify themselves
*to go* to the [a]gardens,
[1]Following one in the center,
Who eat [b]swine's flesh,
detestable things, and mice,
Will [c]come to an
end altogether,"
declares Yahweh.

18 "And I [1]know their works and
their [a]thoughts; [2]the time is coming
to [b]gather all nations and tongues.
And they shall come and see My
glory. 19 I will set a [a]sign among
them and will send those who have
escaped from them to the nations:
[b]Tarshish, [1]Put, [c]Lud, [2]Meshech,
[d]Tubal, and [3]Javan, to the distant
[e]coastlands that have neither heard
My report nor seen My glory. And
they will [f]declare My glory among
the nations. 20 Then they shall
[a]bring all your brothers from all the
nations as a grain offering to Yahweh,
on horses, in chariots, in litters, on
mules, and on camels, to My [b]holy
mountain Jerusalem," says Yahweh,
"just as the sons of Israel bring their
grain offering in a [c]clean vessel to
the house of Yahweh. 21 I will also
take some of them for [a]priests *and*
for Levites," says Yahweh.

22 "For just as the [a]new heavens
and the new earth
Which I make will
endure before Me,"
declares Yahweh,
"So your [b]seed and your
[c]name will endure.
23 "And it shall be from [a]new
moon to new moon
And from sabbath to sabbath,
All [1]mankind will come
to [b]worship
before Me," says Yahweh.
24 "Then they will go
forth and look
On the [a]corpses of the men
Who have [b,1]transgressed
against Me.
For their [c]worm will not die
[d]And their fire will not
be quenched;
And they will be an *object of*
[e]contempt to all [2]mankind."

**66:15** [a]Is 10:17; 30:27, 33; 31:9 [b]Ps 68:17; Is 5:28; Hab 3:8 **66:16** [a]Is 30:30; Eze 38:22 [b]Is 65:12; Eze 38:21 **66:17** [a]Is 1:29; 65:3 [b]Lv 11:7; Is 65:4 [c]Is 1:28, 31 [1]Lit *After* **66:18** [a]Is 59:7; 65:2 [b]Is 45:22-25; Jer 3:17 [1]As in Gr; Heb omits *know* [2]Lit *it is coming* **66:19** [a]Is 11:10, 12; 49:22; 62:10 [b]Is 2:16; 60:9 [c]Eze 27:10 [d]Ge 10:2 [e]Is 11:11; 24:15; 60:9 [f]1Chr 16:24; Is 42:12 [1]As in Gr; Heb *Pul* [2]As in Gr; Heb *those who draw the bow* [3]Greece **66:20** [a]Is 43:6; 49:22; 60:4 [b]Is 2:2, 3; 11:9; 56:7; 65:11, 25 [c]Is 52:11 **66:21** [a]Ex 19:6; Is 61:6; 1Pe 2:5, 9 **66:22** [a]Is 65:17; Heb 12:26, 27; 2Pe 3:13; Rev 21:1 [b]Is 61:8, 9; 65:22, 23; Jn 10:27-29; 1Pe 1:4, 5 [c]Is 56:5 **66:23** [a]Is 1:13, 14; Eze 46:1, 6 [b]Is 19:21, 23; 27:13; 49:7 [1]Lit *flesh* **66:24** [a]Is 5:25; 34:3 [b]Is 1:28; 24:20 [c]Is 14:11; Mk 9:48 [d]Is 1:31; Mt 3:12 [e]Da 12:2 [1]Or *rebelled* [2]Lit *flesh*

*The Book of*

# JEREMIAH

### *Yahweh Sends Jeremiah the Prophet*

**1** The words of [a]Jeremiah the son of
Hilkiah, of the priests who were in
[b]Anathoth in the land of Benjamin,
**2** to whom the word of [1]Yahweh
came in the days of [a]Josiah the son
of [b]Amon, king of Judah, in the
[c]thirteenth year of his reign. **3** And
it came in the days of [a]Jehoiakim
the son of Josiah, king of Judah,
until the end of the eleventh year of
[b]Zedekiah the son of Josiah, king of
Judah, until the exile of Jerusalem in
the fifth month.

**4** Now the word of Yahweh came
to me saying,

**5** "Before I [a]formed you in the
[1]innermost parts I knew you,
And [b]before you came out from
the womb I set you apart;
I have [c]given you as a
prophet to the nations."

**6** Then [a]I said, "Alas,
Lord Yahweh!
Behold, I do not know
how to speak
Because [b]I am a youth."

**7** But Yahweh said to me,
"Do not say, 'I am a youth,'
[a]Because everywhere I
send you, you shall go,
And [b]all that I command
you, you shall speak.

**8** "[a]Do not be afraid of them,
For [b]I am with you to deliver
you," declares Yahweh.

**9** Then Yahweh sent forth His hand
and [a]touched my mouth, and Yahweh
said to me,

"Behold, I have [b]put My
words in your mouth.

**10** "See, [a]I have appointed you
this day over the nations
and over the kingdoms,
[b]To uproot and to tear down,
To cause to perish and
to pull down,
[c]To build and to plant."

### *The Almond Rod and Boiling Pot*

**11** Now the word of Yahweh came to
me saying, "What do you see, [a]Jere-
miah?" And I said, "I see a rod of an
[1]almond tree." **12** Then Yahweh said
to me, "You have seen well, for [a]I am
[1]watching over My word to do it."

**13** The word of Yahweh came to me
a second time saying, "[a]What do you
see?" And I said, "I see a boiling [b]pot,
facing away from the north." **14** Then
Yahweh said to me, "[a]From the north
the evil [1]will break open on all the
inhabitants of the land. **15** For, behold,
I am calling [a]all the families of the
kingdoms of the north," declares Yah-
weh; "and they will come, and each

---

◆ **1:1** [a]2Chr 35:25; 36:12, 21, 22; Ezr 1:1; Da 9:2; Mt 2:17; 16:14; 27:9 [b]Jos 21:18; 1Ki 2:26; 1Chr 6:60; Is 10:30; Jer 11:21; 32:7 **1:2** [a]1Ki 13:2; 2Ki 21:24; 22:3; 2Chr 34:1; Jer 3:6; 36:2 [b]2Ki 21:18, 24 [c]Jer 25:3 [1]The personal *covenant name of God, a form of I AM WHO I AM,* cf. Ex 3:14-15 **1:3** [a]2Ki 23:34; 1Chr 3:15; 2Chr 36:5-8; Jer 25:1 [b]2Ki 24:17; 1Chr 3:15; 2Chr 36:11-13; Jer 39:2 **1:5** [a]Ps 139:15, 16 [b]Is 49:1, 5; Lk 1:15 [c]Jer 1:10; 25:15-26 [1]Lit *stomach* **1:6** [a]Ex 4:10 [b]1Ki 3:7 **1:7** [a]Eze 2:3, 4 [b]Nu 22:20; Jer 1:17 **1:8** [a]Ex 3:12; Dt 31:6; Jos 1:5; Jer 15:20 [b]Eze 2:6 **1:9** [a]Is 6:7; Mk 7:33-35 [b]Ex 4:11-16; Dt 18:18; Is 51:16 **1:10** [a]Rev 11:3-6 [b]Jer 18:7-10; Eze 32:18; 2Co 10:4 [c]Is 44:26-28; Jer 24:6; 31:28, 40 **1:11** [a]Jer 24:3; Am 7:8 [1]Heb *shaqed* **1:12** [a]Jer 31:28 [1]Heb *shoqed* **1:13** [a]Zec 4:2 [b]Eze 11:3, 7 **1:14** [a]Is 41:25; Jer 4:6; 10:22 [1]Lit *will be opened* **1:15** [a]Jer 25:9

one of them will [b]put his throne at
the opening of the gates of Jerusalem,
and against all its walls round about
and against all the [c]cities of Judah.
16 I will speak My judgments on them
concerning all their evil, whereby
they have [a]forsaken Me and have
[b]burned incense to other gods and
worshiped the [c]works of their own
hands. 17 Now, [a]gird up your loins and
arise and speak to them all which I
command you. [b]Do not be dismayed
before them, lest I dismay you before
them. 18 Now behold, I have given you
today as a fortified city and as a pillar
of iron and as walls of bronze against
the whole land, to the kings of Judah,
to its princes, to its priests, and to the
people of the land. 19 And they will
fight against you, but they will not
overcome you, for [a]I am with you to
deliver you," declares Yahweh.

### *Judah Transgresses Against Yahweh*

2 Now the word of Yahweh came to
me saying, 2 "Go and [a]call out in
the ears of Jerusalem, saying, 'Thus
says Yahweh,

"I remember concerning you
the [b]lovingkindness
of your youth,
The love of your betrothals,
[c]Your walking after Me
in the wilderness,
Through a land not sown.
3 "*Israel was* [a]holy to Yahweh,
The [b]first of His produce.
[c]All who ate of it
became guilty;
Evil came upon them,"
declares Yahweh.'"

4 Hear the word of Yahweh,
O house of Jacob and all the families
of the house of Israel. 5 Thus says
Yahweh,

"[a]What injustice did your
fathers find in Me,
That they went far from Me
And walked after [b]vanity
and became vain?
6 "They did not say,
'Where is Yahweh
Who [a]brought us up
out of the land of Egypt,
Who [b]led us
through the wilderness,
Through a land
of deserts and of pits,
Through a land of drought
and of the shadow of death,
Through a land that
no one crossed
And where no
man inhabited?'
7 "I brought you
into the [a]fruitful land
To eat its fruit and its
good things.
But you came and
[b]defiled My land,
And My inheritance you
made an abomination.
8 "The [a]priests did not say,
'Where is Yahweh?'
And those who handle
the law [b]did not know Me;
The [1]shepherds also
transgressed against Me,
And the [c]prophets
prophesied by Baal
And walked after [d]things
that did not profit.

**1:15** [b]Is 22:7; Jer 39:3 [c]Jer 4:16; 9:11 **1:16** [a]Dt 28:20 [b]Jer 7:9; 19:4; 44:17 [c]Is 2:8; 37:19; Jer 10:3-5 **1:17** [a]1Ki 18:46; Job 38:3 [b]Eze 2:6; 3:16-18 **1:19** [a]Nu 14:9; Jer 1:8; 20:11 ◆ **2:2** [a]Is 58:1; Jer 7:2; 11:6 [b]Eze 16:8; Hos 2:15 [c]Dt 2:7; Jer 2:6 **2:3** [a]Ex 19:5, 6; Dt 7:6; 14:2 [b]Jas 1:18; Rev 14:4 [c]Is 41:11; Jer 30:16; 50:7 **2:5** [a]Is 5:4; Mic 6:3 [b]2Ki 17:15; Jer 8:19; Ro 1:21 **2:6** [a]Ex 20:2; Is 63:11 [b]Dt 8:15; 32:10 **2:7** [a]Dt 8:7-9; 11:10-12 [b]Ps 106:38; Jer 3:2; 16:18 **2:8** [a]Jer 10:21 [b]Jer 4:22; Mal 2:7, 8 [c]Jer 23:13 [d]Jer 16:19; Hab 2:18 [1]Rulers

9 "Therefore I will yet [a]contend
with you," declares Yahweh,
"And with your sons'
sons I will contend.
10 "For [a]cross to the coastlands
of [1]Kittim and see,
And send to [b]Kedar and
perceive closely
And see if there has been
such *a thing* as this!
11 "Has a nation changed gods
Though [a]they were not gods?
But My people have
[b]changed their glory
For that which does not profit.
12 "Be appalled, [a]O heavens,
at this,
And be horribly afraid,
be very devastated,"
declares Yahweh.
13 "For My people have
done two evils:
They have forsaken Me,
The [a]fountain of living waters,
To hew for themselves [b]cisterns,
Broken cisterns
That can hold no water.

14 "Is Israel [a]a slave? Or is he
a homeborn *slave*?
Why has he become plunder?
15 "The young [a]lions have
roared at him;
They have given forth
their voice.
And they have [b]made his
land a desolation;
His cities have been
turned into ruin,
without inhabitant.
16 "Also the [1]men of [a]Memphis
and Tahpanhes
Have [2]shaved the [b]top
of your head.
17 "Have you not [a]done
this to yourself
By your forsaking
Yahweh your God
When He [a]led you in the way?
18 "But now what are you doing
[a]on the road to Egypt,
To drink the waters
of the [b,1]Nile?
Or what are you doing
on the road to Assyria,
To drink the waters
of the [2]River?
19 "[a]Your own evil will
chastise you,
And your [b]acts of faithlessness
will reprove you;
Know therefore and see
that it is evil and [c]bitter
For you to forsake
Yahweh your God,
And [d]the dread of Me is
not in you," declares
Lord Yahweh of hosts.

20 "For long ago [a,1]I broke
your yoke
*And* tore off your bonds;
But you said, 'I will not serve!'
For on every [b]high hill
And under every green tree
You have lain down
as a harlot.
21 "Yet I [a]planted you
a choice vine,
A completely true seed.

---

**2:9** [a]Jer 2:35; Eze 20:35, 36 **2:10** [a]Is 23:12 [b]Ps 120:5; Is 21:16; Jer 49:28 [1]Cyprus and other islands **2:11** [a]Is 37:19; Jer 5:7; 16:20 [b]Ps 106:20; Ro 1:23 **2:12** [a]Is 1:2; Jer 4:23 **2:13** [a]Ps 36:9; Jer 17:13; Jn 4:14 [b]Jer 14:3 **2:14** [a]Jer 5:19; 17:4 **2:15** [a]Jer 50:17 [b]Jer 4:7 **2:16** [a]Is 19:13; Jer 44:1; Hos 9:6 [b]Dt 33:20; Jer 48:45 [1]Or *sons* [2]Lit *grazed* **2:17** [a]Dt 32:10; Jer 4:18 **2:18** [a]Is 30:2 [b]Jos 13:3 [1]Heb *Shihor* [2]The Euphrates River **2:19** [a]Is 3:9; Jer 4:18; Hos 5:5 [b]Jer 3:6, 8, 11, 14; Hos 11:7 [c]Job 20:12-16; Am 8:10 [d]Ps 36:1; Jer 5:24 **2:20** [a]Lv 26:13 [b]Dt 12:2; Is 57:5, 7; Jer 3:2, 6; 17:2 [1]Or *you* **2:21** [a]Ex 15:17; Ps 44:2; 80:8; Is 5:2

How then have you turned
yourself before Me
Into the [b]degenerate shoots
of a foreign vine?
22 "Although you [a]wash
yourself with lye
And [1]use much soap,
The [b]stain of your iniquity
is before Me," declares
Lord Yahweh.
23 "[a]How can you say,
'I am not defiled;
I have not walked after
the [b]Baals'?
Look at your way
in the [c]valley!
Know what you have done!
You are a swift young camel
[d]entangling her ways,
24 A [a]wild donkey accustomed
to the wilderness,
That sniffs the wind
in her passion.
In *the time of* her [1]heat who
can turn her away?
All who seek her will
not become weary;
In her month they
will find her.
25 "Keep your feet
from being barefoot
And your throat from thirst;
But you said, '[a]It is [1]hopeless!
No! For I have
[b]loved strangers,
*And after them I will walk.*'

26 "As the [a]thief is shamed
when he is found,
So the house of Israel
is shamed;
They, their kings,
their princes,
And their priests and
their prophets,
27 Who say to a tree,
'You are my father,'
And to a stone,
'You gave me birth.'
For they have turned
*their* [a]back to Me
And not *their* face;
But in the [b]time *when* their
evil *comes* they will say,
'Arise and save us.'
28 "But where are your [a]gods
Which you made for yourself?
Let them arise, if they
can [b]save you
In the time *when* your
evil *comes*;
For [c]*according to*
the number of your cities
Are your gods, O Judah.

29 "Why do you contend with Me?
You have [a]all transgressed
against Me,"
declares Yahweh.
30 "[a]In vain I have struck
your sons;
They received no discipline.
Your [b]sword has devoured
your prophets
Like a destroying lion.
31 "O generation, [1]behold
the word of Yahweh.
Have I been a wilderness
to Israel
Or a [a]land of thick darkness?
Why do My people say,
'[b]We *are free to* roam;

**2:21** [b]Is 5:4 **2:22** [a]Jer 4:14 [b]Job 14:17; Hos 13:12 [1]Lit *cause to be great to you* **2:23** [a]Pr 30:12 [b]Jer 9:14 [c]Jer 7:31 [d]Jer 2:33, 36; 31:22 **2:24** [a]Jer 14:6 [1]Lit *occasion* **2:25** [a]Jer 18:12 [b]Dt 32:16; Jer 14:10 [1]Or *desperate* **2:26** [a]Jer 48:27 **2:27** [a]Jer 18:17; 32:33 [b]Jdg 10:10; Is 26:16 **2:28** [a]Dt 32:37; Jdg 10:14; Is 45:20; Jer 1:16 [b]Jer 11:12 [c]2Ki 17:30, 31; Jer 11:13 **2:29** [a]Jer 5:1; 6:13; Da 9:11 **2:30** [a]Is 1:5; Jer 5:3; 7:28 [b]Ne 9:26; Jer 26:20-24; Ac 7:52; 1Th 2:15 **2:31** [a]Is 45:19 [b]Dt 32:15; Jer 2:20, 25 [1]Lit *see*

We will no longer
come to You'?
32 "Can a virgin forget
her ornaments,
Or a bride her attire?
Yet My people have
[a]forgotten Me
Days without number.
33 "How well you prepare
your way
To seek love!
Therefore even
[1]the wicked women
You have taught your ways.
34 "Also on your skirts is found
The [a]lifeblood of
the innocent needy;
You did not find them
[b]breaking in.
But in spite of all these things,
35 Yet you said, 'I am innocent;
Surely His anger is turned
away from me.'
Behold, I will [a]enter
into judgment with you
Because you [b]say,
'I have not sinned.'
36 "Why do you [a]despise
*Him* so much
In changing your way?
Also, [b]you will be put
to shame by Egypt
As you were put
to shame by [c]Assyria.
37 "From this *place* also
you will go out
With [a]your hands
on your head;
For Yahweh has rejected
[b]those in whom you trust,
And you will not succeed
with them."

### The Polluted Land

3 God [1]says, "[a]If a husband
divorces his wife
And she goes from him
And belongs to another man,
Will he still return to her?
Will not that land be
completely [2]polluted?
But you [b]are a harlot
*with* many [3]lovers;
Yet you [c]turn to Me,"
declares Yahweh.
2 "Lift up your eyes to
the [a]bare heights and see;
Where have you not
been ravished?
By the roads you have
[b]sat for them
Like [1]an Arab
in the wilderness,
And you have [c]polluted a land
With your harlotry and
with your evil.
3 "Therefore the [a]showers
have been withheld,
And the [1]late rain
has not [2]come.
Yet you had
a [b]harlot's forehead;
You refused to feel dishonor.
4 "Have you not just now
called to Me,
'[a]My Father, You are the
[b,1]close companion
of my [c]youth?
5 '[a]Will He be angry forever?
Will He keep *it* to the end?'

**2:32** [a]Ps 106:21; Is 17:10; Jer 3:21; 13:25; Hos 8:14 **2:33** [1]Or *in wickedness* **2:34** [a]2Ki 21:16; 24:4; Ps 106:38; Jer 7:6; 19:4 [b]Ex 22:2 **2:35** [a]Jer 25:31 [b]Pr 28:13; 1Jn 1:8, 10 **2:36** [a]Jer 2:23; 31:22; Hos 12:1 [b]Is 30:3 [c]2Chr 28:16, 20, 21 **2:37** [a]2Sa 13:19; Jer 14:3, 4 [b]Jer 37:7-10 ◆ **3:1** [a]Dt 24:1-4 [b]Jer 2:20; Eze 16:26, 28, 29 [c]Jer 4:1; Zec 1:3 [1]Lit *saying* [2]Or *alienated* [3]Lit *companions* **3:2** [a]Dt 12:2; Jer 2:20; 3:21; 7:29 [b]Ge 38:14; Eze 16:25 [c]Jer 2:7 [1]Or *a nomad* **3:3** [a]Lv 26:19; Jer 14:3-6 [b]Jer 6:15; 8:12 [1]Spring [2]Lit *been* **3:4** [a]Jer 3:19; 31:9 [b]Ps 71:17; Pr 2:17 [c]Jer 2:2; Hos 2:15 [1]Lit *leader* **3:5** [a]Ps 103:9; Is 57:16; Jer 3:12

Behold, you have spoken
And have done evil things,
And you have [1]had your way."

### *Faithless Israel Called to Repentance*

**6** Then Yahweh said to me in the days
of Josiah the king, "Have you seen
what faithless Israel did? She [a]went
up on every high hill and under every
green tree, and she was a harlot there.
**7** [a]I said, 'After she has done all these
things, she will return to Me'; but she
did not return, and her [b]treacherous
sister Judah saw it. **8** And I saw that for
all the adulteries of faithless Israel, I
had sent her away and [a]given her a
certificate of divorce, yet her [b]treach-
erous sister Judah did not fear; but
she went and was a harlot also. **9** So
it was, because of the lightness of her
harlotry, that she [a]polluted the land
and committed adultery with [b]stones
and trees. **10** Yet in spite of all this,
her treacherous sister Judah did not
return to Me with all her heart, but
rather in [a]lying," declares Yahweh.
**11** And Yahweh said to me, "[a]Faith-
less Israel has proved herself more
righteous than treacherous Judah.
**12** Go and call out these words toward
the north and say,

'[a,1]Return, faithless Israel,'
declares Yahweh;
'[b]I will not [2]look
upon you in anger.
For I am [c]One
of lovingkindness,'
declares Yahweh;
'I will not be angry forever.
**13** 'Only [a,1]acknowledge
your iniquity,
That you have transgressed
against Yahweh your God
And have [b]scattered your ways
*of harlotry* to the strangers
[c]under every green tree,
And you have not listened to
My voice,' declares Yahweh.
**14** '[1]Return, O faithless sons,'
declares Yahweh;
'For I am a [a]master to you,
And I will take you one from a
city and two from a family,
And [b]I will bring you to Zion.'

**15** "Then I will give you [a]shepherds
after My own heart, who will
[b,1]shepherd you on knowledge and
understanding. **16** It shall be in those
days when you are multiplied and
fruitful in the land," declares Yah-
weh, "they will [a]no longer say, 'The
ark of the covenant of Yahweh.' And
it will not come upon the heart, nor
will they remember it, nor will they
miss *it*, nor will it be made again. **17** At
that time they will call Jerusalem
'The [a]Throne of Yahweh,' and [b]all
the nations will be gathered to it, to
Jerusalem, for the [c]name of Yahweh;
nor will they [d]walk anymore after
the stubbornness of their evil heart.
**18** [a]In those days the house of Judah
will walk with the house of Israel,
and they will come together [b]from
the land of the north to the [c]land that
I gave your fathers as an inheritance.

---

**3:5** [1]Lit *been able* **3:6** [a]Jer 17:2; Eze 23:4-10 **3:7** [a]2Ki 17:13 [b]Jer 3:11; Eze 16:47 **3:8** [a]Dt 24:1, 3; Is 50:1 [b]Eze 16:46, 47; 23:11 **3:9** [a]Jer 2:7; 3:2 [b]Is 57:6; Jer 2:27; 10:8 **3:10** [a]Jer 12:2; Hos 7:14 **3:11** [a]Eze 16:51, 52; 23:11 **3:12** [a]Jer 3:14, 22; Eze 33:11 [b]Jer 3:5 [c]Ps 86:15; Jer 12:15; 31:20; 33:26 [1]Or *Return, O Israel, who has turned away* [2]Lit *cause My countenance to fall upon you* **3:13** [a]Dt 30:1-3; Jer 3:25; 14:20; 1Jn 1:9 [b]Jer 2:20, 25; 3:2, 6 [c]Dt 12:2 [1]Lit *know* **3:14** [a]Jer 31:32; Hos 2:19 [b]Jer 31:6, 12 [1]Or *Return, O sons, who have turned away* **3:15** [a]Jer 23:4; 31:10; Eze 34:23; Eph 4:11 [b]Ac 20:28 [1]Or *feed* **3:16** [a]Is 65:17 **3:17** [a]Jer 17:12; Eze 43:7 [b]Jer 3:19; 4:2; 12:15, 16; 16:19 [c]Is 60:9 [d]Jer 11:8 **3:18** [a]Is 11:13; Jer 50:4, 5; Hos 1:11 [b]Jer 16:15; 31:8 [c]Am 9:15

19 "Then I said,
'How I would set you
among [1]My sons
And give you a pleasant land,
The most [a]beautiful
inheritance of the nations!'
And I said, 'You shall call
Me, "[b]My Father,"
And not turn away
from following Me.'
20 "Surely, as a woman
treacherously departs
from her [1]lover,
So you have [a]dealt
treacherously with Me,
O house of Israel,"
declares Yahweh.

21 A voice is heard
on the [a]bare heights,
The weeping *and*
the supplications
of the sons of Israel;
Because they have
perverted their way,
They have [b]forgotten
Yahweh their God.
22 [1]"Return, O faithless sons;
[a]I will heal your faithlessness."
"Behold, we come to You,
For You are Yahweh our God.
23 "Surely, [a]the hills are a lie,
A tumult *on* the mountains.
Surely in [b]Yahweh our God
Is the salvation of Israel.

24 "But [a]the shameful thing has
devoured the labor of our fathers
since our youth, their flocks and their
herds, their sons and their daughters.
25 Let us lie down in our [a]shame, and
let our dishonor cover us; for we have
sinned against Yahweh our God, we
and our fathers, [b]from our youth
even to this day. And we have not
listened to the voice of Yahweh our
God."

### *Yahweh Calls Israel to Return to Him*

4 "If you will [a]return, O Israel,"
declares Yahweh,
"*Then* you should return to Me.
And [b]if you will put away
your detested things
from My presence
And will not waver
2 And you will [a]swear,
'As Yahweh lives,'
[b]In truth, in justice, and
in righteousness;
Then the [c]nations will
[1]be blessed in Him,
And [d]in Him they will boast."

3 For thus says Yahweh to the men of
Judah and to Jerusalem,
"[a,1]Break up your
fallow ground,
And [b]do not sow
among thorns.
4 "[a]Circumcise yourselves
to Yahweh
And remove the foreskins
of your heart,
Men of Judah and inhabitants
of Jerusalem,
Lest My [b]wrath go
forth like fire

**3:19** [a]Ps 16:6 [b]Is 63:16; Jer 3:4 [1]Lit *the* **3:20** [a]Is 48:8 [1]Or *companion* **3:21** [a]Is 15:2; Jer 3:2; 7:29 [b]Is 17:10; Jer 2:32; 13:25 **3:22** [a]Jer 30:17; 33:6; Hos 6:1; 14:4 [1]Or *Return, O sons, who have turned away* **3:23** [a]Jer 17:2 [b]Ps 3:8; Jer 17:14; 31:7 **3:24** [a]Hos 9:10 **3:25** [a]Ezr 9:6, 7 [b]Jer 22:21 ◆**4:1** [a]Jer 3:22; 15:19; Joel 2:12 [b]Jer 7:3, 7; 35:15 **4:2** [a]Dt 10:20; Is 45:23; 65:16; Jer 12:16 [b]Is 48:1 [c]Ge 22:18; Jer 3:17; 12:15, 16; Ga 3:8 [d]Is 45:25; Jer 9:24; 1Co 1:31 [1]Or *experience blessing repeatedly, bless themselves* **4:3** [a]Hos 10:12 [b]Mt 13:7 [1]Lit *Plow for yourselves plowed ground* **4:4** [a]Dt 10:16; 30:6; Jer 9:25, 26; Ro 2:28, 29; Col 2:11 [b]Is 30:27, 33; Jer 21:12; Zep 2:2

And burn with [c]none
to quench it
Because of the evil
of your deeds."

### *Evil from the North*

5 Declare in Judah and make *it*
heard in Jerusalem and say,
"[a]Blow the trumpet in the land;
Call out, make *your*
*voice* full, and say,
'[b]Gather yourselves,
and let us go
Into the fortified cities.'
6 "Lift up a [a]standard
toward Zion!
Seek safety, do not stand *still,*
For I am bringing [b]evil
from the north,
And great destruction.
7 "A [a]lion has gone up
from his thicket,
And a [b]destroyer
of nations has set out;
He has gone out
from his place
To [c]make your land
a desolation.
Your cities will be
turned into ruins
Without inhabitant.
8 "For this, [a]I gird myself
with sackcloth,
Lament and wail;
*For the* [b]*burning*
anger of Yahweh
Has not turned back from us."

9 "It will be in that day," declares Yah-
weh, "*that* the [a]heart of the king and
the heart of the princes will perish;
and the priests will be appalled, and
the [b]prophets will be astonished."
10 Then I said, "Ah, Lord Yahweh!
Surely You have utterly [a]deceived
this people and Jerusalem, saying,
'[b]You will have peace'; whereas a
sword touches the [1]throat."
11 In that time it will be said to
this people and to Jerusalem, "A
[a,1]scorching wind from the bare
heights in the wilderness along the
way of the daughter of My people—
not to winnow and not to cleanse,
12 a wind too full for these things—
will come [1]for My *purpose*; now I will
also speak judgments against them.

13 "Behold, he [a]goes up
like clouds,
And his [b]chariots
like the whirlwind;
His horses are [c]swifter
than eagles.
Woe to us,
for [d]we are devastated!"
14 Wash your heart
from evil, O Jerusalem,
That you may be saved.
How long will your
[a]wicked thoughts
Lodge within you?
15 For a voice declares
from [a]Dan,
And makes wickedness heard
from Mount Ephraim.
16 "Make mention *of it* to the
nations, *saying,* 'Behold!'
Make *it* heard over Jerusalem,
'Besiegers come
from a [a]far country,

---

**4:4** [c]Am 5:6; Mk 9:43, 48 **4:5** [a]Jer 6:1; Hos 8:1 [b]Jos 10:20; Jer 8:14 **4:6** [a]Is 62:10; Jer 4:21; 50:2 [b]Jer 1:14, 15; 6:1, 22 **4:7** [a]Jer 5:6; 25:38; 50:17 [b]Jer 25:9; Eze 26:7-10 [c]Is 1:7; 6:11; Jer 2:15 **4:8** [a]Is 22:12; Jer 6:26 [b]Is 5:25; 10:4; Jer 30:24 **4:9** [a]Is 22:3-5; Jer 48:41 [b]Is 29:9, 10; Eze 13:9-16 **4:10** [a]Eze 14:9; 2Th 2:11 [b]Jer 5:12; 14:13 [1]Or *life* **4:11** [a]Jer 13:24; 51:1; Eze 17:10; Hos 13:15 [1]Lit *shimmering* **4:12** [1]Lit *for Me* **4:13** [a]Is 19:1; Na 1:3 [b]Is 5:28; 66:15 [c]Lam 4:19; Hab 1:8 [d]Is 3:8 **4:14** [a]Pr 1:22; Jer 6:19; 13:27; Jas 4:8 **4:15** [a]Jer 8:16 **4:16** [a]Is 39:3; Jer 5:15

And [b]give forth their voices
against the cities of Judah.
17 'Like watchmen of a field they
are [a]against her round about
Because she has
[b]rebelled against Me,'
declares Yahweh.
18 "Your [a]ways and your deeds
Have done these things to you.
This is your evil. How [b]bitter!
How it has touched
your heart!"

### *Anguish over Judah's Desolation*

19 [a]My [1]soul, my [1]soul! I am
in anguish! [2]Oh, my heart!
My [b]heart is pounding in me;
I cannot be silent
Because [3]you have
heard, O my soul,
The [c]sound of the trumpet,
The shout of war.
20 [a]Destruction upon
destruction is called out,
For the [b]whole land
is devastated;
Suddenly my [c]tents
are devastated,
My curtains in an instant.
21 How long must I see
the standard
And hear the sound
of the trumpet?
22 "[a]For My people are
ignorant fools,
They know Me not;
They are
simpleminded children
And have no understanding.
They are wise to [b]do evil,
But to do good they
do not know."

23 I saw on the earth,
and behold, *it was*
[a,1]formless and void;
And to the heavens,
and they had no light.
24 I saw on the mountains,
and behold, they
were [a]quaking,
And all the hills [1]moved
to and fro.
25 I saw, and behold,
there was no man,
And all the [a]birds
of the sky had fled.
26 I saw, and behold,
[1]the [a]fruitful orchard
was a wilderness,
And all its cities were
torn down
Before Yahweh,
before His burning anger.

27 For thus says Yahweh,
"The [a]whole land shall
be a desolation,
Yet I will [b]not execute
a complete destruction.
28 "For this the [a]earth
shall mourn
And the [b]heavens
above be dark
Because I have [c]spoken;
I have purposed,
And I will not [1]relent,
nor will I turn from it."

**4:16** [b]Eze 21:22 **4:17** [a]2Ki 25:1, 4 [b]Is 1:20, 23; Jer 5:23 **4:18** [a]Ps 107:17; Is 50:1; Jer 2:17, 19 [b]Jer 2:19 **4:19** [a]Is 15:5; 16:11; 21:3; 22:4; Jer 9:1, 10; 20:9 [b]Hab 3:16 [c]Nu 10:9 [1]Lit *inward parts* [2]Lit *The walls of my heart* [3]Or *I, my soul, heard* **4:20** [a]Ps 42:7; Eze 7:26 [b]Jer 4:27 [c]Jer 10:20 **4:22** [a]Jer 5:4, 21; 10:8; Ro 1:22 [b]Jer 9:3; 13:23; Ro 16:19; 1Co 14:20 **4:23** [a]Ge 1:2; Is 24:19 [1]Or *a waste and emptiness* **4:24** [a]Is 5:25; Jer 10:10; Eze 38:20 [1]Lit *moved lightly* **4:25** [a]Jer 9:10; 12:4; Zep 1:3 **4:26** [a]Jer 9:10 [1]Or *Carmel* **4:27** [a]Jer 12:11, 12; 25:11 [b]Jer 5:10, 18; 30:11; 46:28 **4:28** [a]Jer 12:4, 11; 14:2; Hos 4:3 [b]Is 5:30; 50:3; Joel 2:30, 31 [c]Nu 23:19; Jer 23:20; 30:24 [1]Or *regret*, cf. 1Sa 15:11, 29, 3

29 At the sound of the horseman
and bowman [a]every
city flees;
They [b]go into the thickets
and climb up
among the rocks;
[c]Every city is forsaken,
And no man inhabits them.
30 And you, O devastated one,
[a]what will you do?
Although you dress in scarlet,
Although you decorate
*yourself with* ornaments
of gold,
Although you [b]enlarge
your eyes with paint,
In vain you make
yourself beautiful.
*Your* [c,1]lovers despise you;
They seek your life.
31 For I heard a sound as
of a woman in labor pains,
The distress as of one giving
birth to her first child,
The sound of the daughter
of Zion [a]gasping for breath,
[b]Stretching out her
[1]hands, *saying*,
"Ah, woe is me, for my soul
faints before murderers."

### *Jerusalem Refuses to Repent*

5 "[a]Roam to and fro through
the streets of Jerusalem,
And see now and know,
And seek in her open squares,
If you can [b]find a man,
[c]If there is one who does justice,
who seeks faithfulness,
Then I will pardon her.
2 "And [a]if they say,
'As Yahweh lives,'
Then they swear to a lie."
3 O Yahweh, do not [a]Your eyes
*look* for faithfulness?
You have [b]struck them,
But they did not [1]weaken;
You have consumed them,
*But* they [c]refused
to receive discipline.
They have [d]made their faces
stronger than rock;
They have refused to [2]repent.

4 Then I said, "They are
only the poor;
They are foolish;
For they [a]do not know
the way of Yahweh
*Or* the *legal* judgment
of their God.
5 "Let me go to the great
And let me speak to them,
For [a]they know the
way of Yahweh
*And* the *legal* judgment
of their God."
But they too, altogether,
have [b]broken the yoke
*And* torn apart the bonds.
6 Therefore [a]a lion from the
forest will strike them down;
A [b]wolf of the deserts
will devastate them;
A [c]leopard is watching
their cities.
Everyone who goes out
of them will be torn in pieces
Because their [d]transgressions
are many;

**4:29** [a]2Ki 25:4 [b]Is 2:19-21; Jer 16:16 [c]Jer 4:7 **4:30** [a]Is 10:3; 20:6; Jer 13:21 [b]2Ki 9:30; Eze 23:40 [c]Jer 22:20, 22; Lam 1:2, 19; Eze 23:9, 10, 22 [1]Lit *paramours* **4:31** [a]Is 42:14 [b]Is 1:15; Lam 1:17 [1]Lit *palms* ◆ **5:1** [a]2Chr 16:9; Da 12:4 [b]Eze 22:30 [c]Ge 18:26, 32 **5:2** [a]Is 48:1; Tit 1:16 **5:3** [a]2Chr 16:9 [b]Is 1:5; 9:13; Jer 2:30 [c]Jer 7:28; 8:5; Zep 3:2 [d]Jer 7:26; 19:15; Eze 3:8 [1]Or *become sick* [2]Lit *return* **5:4** [a]Is 27:11; Jer 8:7; Hos 4:6 **5:5** [a]Mic 3:1 [b]Ex 32:25; Ps 2:3; Jer 2:20 **5:6** [a]Jer 4:7 [b]Eze 22:27; Hab 1:8; Zep 3:3 [c]Hos 13:7 [d]Jer 30:14, 15

Their acts of faithlessness
are mighty.

7 "Why should I pardon you?
Your sons have forsaken Me
And [a]sworn by those
who are [b]not gods.
I had satisfied them to the full,
Then they
[c]committed adultery
And trooped
to the harlot's house.
8 "They were well-fed
lusty horses,
Each one neighing
after his [a]neighbor's wife.
9 "Shall I not punish [1]these
*people*," declares Yahweh,
"And on a nation such as this
[a]Shall I not avenge Myself?

10 "Go up through her vine rows
and make them a ruin,
But do not make a
complete destruction;
Remove her branches,
For they are not Yahweh's.
11 "For the [a]house of Israel
and the house of Judah
Have dealt very treacherously
with Me," declares Yahweh.
12 They have [a]dealt falsely
about Yahweh
And said, "[b,1]Not He;
Calamity will [c]not come on us,
And we [d]will not see
sword or famine.
13 "The [a]prophets are *as* wind,
And the word is not in them.
Thus it will be done to them!"

### *A Stubborn and Rebellious People*

14 Therefore, thus says Yahweh, the
God of hosts,
"Because you have
spoken this word,
Behold, I am [a]making My
words in your mouth fire
And this people wood,
and it will devour them.
15 "Behold, I am [a]bringing
a nation against you
from afar, O house
of Israel," declares Yahweh.
"It is an enduring nation;
It is an ancient nation,
A nation whose [b]tongue
you do not know,
Nor can you [1]understand
what they say.
16 "Their [a]quiver is
like an [b]open grave;
All of them are mighty men.
17 "They will [a]devour your
harvest and your food;
They will devour your sons
and your daughters;
They will devour your
flocks and your herds;
They will devour your
[b]vines and your fig trees;
They will demolish with
the sword your [c]fortified
cities in which you trust.

18 "Yet even in those days," de-
clares Yahweh, "I will not make you
a complete destruction. 19 It shall
come about [a]when [1]they say, 'Why
has Yahweh our God done all these
things to us?' then you shall say to
them, 'As you have forsaken Me and

**5:7** [a]Jos 23:7; Jer 12:16; Zep 1:5 [b]Dt 32:21; Jer 2:11; Ga 4:8 [c]Jer 7:9 **5:8** [a]Jer 13:27; 29:23; Eze 22:11 **5:9** [a]Jer 9:9 [1]Or *for these things* **5:11** [a]Jer 3:6, 7, 20 **5:12** [a]2Chr 36:16 [b]Pr 30:9; Jer 14:22; 43:1-4 [c]Jer 23:17 [d]Jer 14:13 [1]Lit *He is not* **5:13** [a]Job 8:2; Jer 14:13, 15; 22:22 **5:14** [a]Is 24:6; Jer 1:9; 23:29; Hos 6:5; Zec 1:6 **5:15** [a]Dt 28:49; Is 5:26; Jer 4:16 [b]Is 28:11 [1]Lit *hear* **5:16** [a]Is 5:28; 13:18 [b]Ps 5:9 **5:17** [a]Lv 26:16; Dt 28:31, 33; Jer 8:16; 50:7, 17 [b]Jer 8:13 [c]Hos 8:14 **5:19** [a]Dt 29:24-26; 1Ki 9:8, 9; Jer 13:22; 16:10-13 [1]Or *you*

served foreign gods in your land, so
you will [b]serve strangers in a land
that is not yours.'
20 "Declare this
in the house of Jacob
And cause *it* to be heard
in Judah, saying,
21 'Now hear this, O people *who*
*are* simpleminded fools and
without a heart *of wisdom*,
Who have [a]eyes
but do not see,
Who have ears but do not hear.
22 'Do you not [a]fear Me?'
declares Yahweh.
'Do you not tremble
in My presence?
For I have [b]placed the sand
as a boundary for the sea,
A perpetual statute,
so it cannot cross over it.
Though the waves toss,
yet they cannot prevail;
Though they roar, yet they
cannot cross over it.
23 'But this people has
a [a]stubborn and
rebellious heart;
They have turned aside
and gone away.
24 'They do not say in their heart,
"Let us now fear
Yahweh our God,
Who [a]gives rain in its season,
Both [b]the [1]early rain
and the [2]late rain,
Who keeps for us
The [c]appointed weeks
of the harvest."
25 'Your [a]iniquities have
turned these away,
And your sins have withheld
good from you.
26 'For wicked men are found
among My people;
They [a]watch like fowlers
[1]lying in wait;
They set a [2]trap;
They catch men.
27 'Like a cage full of birds,
So their houses are
full of [a]deceit;
Therefore they have
become great and rich.
28 'They are [a]fat,
they are sleek;
They also [1]excel
in deeds of evil;
They do not plead the cause,
The cause of the [b,2]orphan,
that they may succeed;
And they do not [3]render
justice for the poor.
29 '[a]Shall I not punish [1]these
*people*?' declares Yahweh,
'On a nation such as this
Shall I not avenge Myself?'

30 "A horrible and
[a]appalling thing
Has happened in the land:
31 The [a]prophets prophesy
with lying,
And the priests have dominion
[1]by their *own* hand;
And My people [b]love it so!
But what will you do
at the end of it?

**5:19** [b]Dt 28:48; Jer 16:13 **5:21** [a]Is 6:9; 43:8; Eze 12:2; Mt 13:14; Mk 8:18; Jn 12:40; Ac 28:26; Ro 11:8 **5:22** [a]Dt 28:58; Ps 119:120; Jer 2:19; 10:7; Rev 15:4 [b]Job 38:8-11; Ps 104:9; Pr 8:29 **5:23** [a]Dt 21:18; Ps 78:8; Jer 4:17; 6:28 **5:24** [a]Ps 147:8; Jer 3:3; Mt 5:45; Ac 14:17 [b]Joel 2:23 [c]Ge 8:22 [1]Autumn [2]Spring **5:25** [a]Jer 2:17; 4:18 **5:26** [a]Ps 10:9; Pr 1:11; Jer 18:22; Hab 1:15 [1]Lit *subside* [2]Lit *destruction* **5:27** [a]Jer 9:6 **5:28** [a]Dt 32:15 [b]Is 1:23; Jer 7:6; 22:3; Zec 7:10 [1]Or *overlook deeds*; lit *pass over* [2]Or *fatherless* [3]Lit *judge* **5:29** [a]Jer 5:9; Mal 3:5 [1]Or *for these things* **5:30** [a]Jer 23:14; Hos 6:10 **5:31** [a]Eze 13:6 [b]Mic 2:11 [1]Lit *over their own hands*

### *Yahweh Disciplines Israel*

6 "Flee for safety, O sons
of [a]Benjamin,
From the midst of Jerusalem!
Now blow a trumpet in Tekoa
And raise a signal
over [b,1]Beth-haccerem,
For evil looks down
from the [c]north,
As well as great destruction.
2 "The comely and [a]delicate
one, [b]the daughter
of Zion, I will ruin.
3 "[a]Shepherds and their
flocks will come to her;
They will [b]pitch *their*
tents [1]around her;
They will pasture each
in his [2]place.
4 "[a]Set *yourselves* apart
for war against her;
Arise, and let us go
up at [b]noon.
Woe to us, for the
day declines,
For the shadows of the
evening stretch out!
5 "Arise, and let us go up by night
And [a,1]destroy her [2]palaces!"
6 For thus says Yahweh of hosts,
"[a]Cut down her trees
And cast up a [b]siege
against Jerusalem.
This is the city to be punished,
In whose midst there is
only [c]oppression.
7 "[a]Like a well [1]keeps its
waters fresh,
So she [1]keeps fresh her evil.
[b]Violence and devastation
are heard in her;
[c]Sickness and wounds are
continually before Me.
8 "[a]Heed discipline,
O Jerusalem,
Lest [b]My soul become
disgusted at you,
Lest I make you a desolation,
A land not inhabited."

9 Thus says Yahweh of hosts,
"They will [a]thoroughly
glean as the vine
the [b]remnant of Israel;
Pass your hand again
like a grape gatherer
Over the branches."
10 To whom shall I speak
and give warning
That they may hear?
Behold, their [a]ears
are uncircumcised,
And they cannot give heed.
Behold, [b]the word
of Yahweh has become
a reproach to them;
They have no delight in it.
11 But I am [a]full of the
wrath of Yahweh;
I am [b]weary of holding *it* in.
"[c]Pour *it* out on the
infants in the street
And on the [1]gathering
of choice men together;
For both husband and
wife shall be captured,
The aged with *the*
*one* full of days.

◆ **6:1** [a]Jos 18:28 [b]Ne 3:14 [c]Jer 1:14; 4:6; 6:22 [1]Lit *house of the vineyard* **6:2** [a]Dt 28:56 [b]Is 1:8; Jer 4:31 **6:3** [a]Jer 12:10 [b]2Ki 25:1; Jer 4:17; Lk 19:43 [1]Lit *against her round about* [2]Lit *hand* **6:4** [a]Jer 6:23; Joel 3:9 [b]Jer 15:8; Zep 2:4 **6:5** [a]Is 32:14; Jer 52:13 [1]Or *bring to corruption*, cf. 6:28 [2]Or *fortified towers* **6:6** [a]Dt 20:19, 20 [b]Jer 32:24; 33:4 [c]Jer 22:17 **6:7** [a]Jas 3:11f [b]Jer 20:8; Eze 7:11, 23 [c]Jer 30:12, 13 [1]Lit *keeps cold* **6:8** [a]Jer 7:28; 17:23 [b]Eze 23:18; Hos 9:12 **6:9** [a]Jer 16:16; 49:9; Ob 5, 6 [b]Jer 8:3; 11:23 **6:10** [a]Jer 5:21; 7:26; Ac 7:51 [b]Jer 20:8 **6:11** [a]Job 32:18, 19; Mic 3:8 [b]Jer 15:6; 20:9 [c]Jer 7:20; 9:21 [1]Lit *council*

12 "Their [a]houses shall be
turned over to others,
Their fields and their
wives together,
For I will [b]stretch out My hand
Against the inhabitants of
the land," declares Yahweh.
13 "For [a]from the least of them
even to the greatest
of them,
Everyone is [b]greedy for gain,
And from the prophet
even to the priest
Everyone practices lying.
14 "They have [a]healed
the brokenness of My
people superficially,
Saying, 'Peace, peace,'
But there is no peace.
15 "Were they [a]ashamed because
of the abomination
they have done?
They were not even
ashamed at all;
They did not even know
how to feel dishonor.
Therefore they shall fall
among those who fall;
At the time that I punish them,
They shall be cast down,"
says Yahweh.

16 Thus says Yahweh,
"Stand by the ways and see and
ask for the [a]ancient paths,
Where the good way
is, and walk in it;
And [b]you will find rest
for your souls.
But they said,
'We will not walk *in it*.'
17 "And I set [a]watchmen
over you, *saying*,
'Give heed to the sound
of the trumpet!'
But they said,
'We will not give heed.'
18 "Therefore hear, O nations,
And know, O congregation,
what is among them.
19 "[a]Hear, O earth: behold, I am
bringing evil on this people,
The [b]fruit of their [1]plans,
Because they have not given
heed to My words,
And as for My law, they
have [c]rejected it also.
20 "[a]For what purpose does
[b]frankincense come
to Me from Sheba
And the [c,1]sweet cane
from a distant land?
[d]Your burnt offerings
are not acceptable,
And your sacrifices are
not pleasing to Me."
21 Therefore, thus says Yahweh,
"Behold, [a]I am [1]laying stumbling
blocks before this people.
And they will stumble
against them,
[b]Fathers and sons together;
Neighbor and [2]friend
will perish."

### *Mourn the Coming Destroyer*

22 Thus says Yahweh,
"Behold, [a]a people is coming
from the land of the north,
And a great nation will be
aroused from the [b]remote
parts of the earth.

**6:12** [a]Dt 28:30; Jer 8:10; 38:22, 23 [b]Jer 15:6 **6:13** [a]Jer 8:10 [b]Is 56:11; 57:17; Jer 8:10; 22:17 **6:14** [a]Jer 8:11; Eze 13:10 **6:15** [a]Jer 3:3; 8:12 **6:16** [a]Is 8:20; Jer 12:16; 18:15; 31:21; Mal 4:4; Lk 16:29 [b]Mt 11:29 **6:17** [a]Is 21:11; 58:1; Jer 25:4; Eze 3:17; Hab 2:1 **6:19** [a]Is 1:2; Jer 19:3, 15; 22:29 [b]Pr 1:31 [c]Jer 8:9 [1]Or *devices* **6:20** [a]Ps 50:7-9; Is 1:11; 66:3; Mic 6:6 [b]Is 60:6 [c]Ex 30:23 [d]Ps 40:6; Am 5:22 [1]Lit *good* **6:21** [a]Is 8:14; Jer 13:16 [b]Is 9:14-17; Jer 9:21, 22 [1]Lit *giving* [2]Lit *his friend* **6:22** [a]Jer 1:15; 10:22; 50:41-43 [b]Ne 1:9

23 “They take hold
of [a]bow and spear;
They are [b]cruel and have
no compassion;
Their voice [c]roars like the sea,
And they ride on horses,
Arranged as a man
for the battle
Against you, O daughter
of Zion!”
24 We have [a]heard the
report of it;
Our hands are limp.
[b]Distress has taken hold of us,
Pain as of a woman
in childbirth.
25 [a]Do not go out into the field
And [b]do not walk on the road,
For the enemy has a sword;
[c]Terror is on every side.
26 O daughter of my people,
[a]gird yourself with sackcloth
And [b]roll in ashes;
[c,1]Mourn as for an only son,
A lamentation most bitter.
For suddenly the destroyer
Will come upon us.

27 “I have [a]made you a tester
*of metals and* [1]an assayer
among My people,
That you may know and
test their way.”
28 All of them are
rebelliously stubborn,
[a]Going about as a slanderer.
*They are* [b]bronze and iron;
They, all of them, are corrupt.
29 The bellows blow fiercely;
The lead [1]is consumed
by the fire;
In vain the refining goes on,
But the [a]evil ones are
not [2]separated.
30 [a]They call them rejected silver
Because [b]Yahweh has
rejected them.

### *Yahweh’s Warning from the Temple Gate*

7 The word that came to Jeremiah
from Yahweh, saying, 2 “[a]Stand
in the gate of the house of Yahweh,
and you shall call out there this word,
and you shall say, ‘Hear the word of
Yahweh, all you of Judah, who enter
by these gates to worship Yahweh!’”
3 Thus says Yahweh of hosts, the God
of Israel, “[a]Make your ways and your
deeds good, and I will let you dwell
in this place. 4 [a]Do not trust in lying
words, saying, ‘[1]This is the temple
of Yahweh, the temple of Yahweh,
the temple of Yahweh.’ 5 For [a]if
you truly make your ways and your
deeds good, if you truly [b]do justice
between a man and his neighbor, 6 *if*
you do not oppress the sojourner, the
[a,1]orphan, or the widow, and do not
shed [b]innocent blood in this place,
nor [c]walk after other gods to your
own evil *demise,* 7 then I will let you
[a]dwell in this place, in the [b]land that I
gave to your fathers forever and ever.
8 “Behold, you are trusting in [a]lying
words to no avail. 9 Will you steal,
murder, and commit adultery and
swear *while* lying, and [a]burn incense

**6:23** [a]Is 13:18; Jer 4:29 [b]Jer 50:42 [c]Is 5:30 **6:24** [a]Is 28:19; Jer 4:19-21 [b]Is 21:3; Jer 4:31; 13:21; 30:6; 49:24; 50:43 **6:25** [a]Jer 14:18 [b]Jdg 5:6 [c]Jer 20:10; 46:5; 49:29 **6:26** [a]Jer 4:8 [b]Jer 25:34; Mic 1:10 [c]Am 8:10; Zec 12:10 [1]Lit *Make for yourself mourning* **6:27** [a]Jer 1:18; 15:20 [1]Or *a fortification* **6:28** [a]Jer 9:4 [b]Eze 22:18 **6:29** [a]Jer 15:19 [1]Lit *comes to an end* [2]Or *drawn off* **6:30** [a]Ps 119:119; Is 1:22 [b]Jer 7:29; Hos 9:17; Zec 11:8 ◆**7:2** [a]Jer 17:19; 26:2 **7:3** [a]Jer 4:1; 7:5; 18:11; 26:13 **7:4** [a]Jer 7:8; Mic 3:11 [1]Lit *They are* **7:5** [a]Is 1:19; Jer 4:1, 2 [b]1Ki 6:12; Jer 21:12; 22:3 **7:6** [a]Ex 22:21-24; Jer 5:28 [b]Jer 2:34; 19:4 [c]Dt 6:14, 15; 8:19; 11:28; Jer 13:10 [1]Or *fatherless* **7:7** [a]Dt 4:40 [b]Jer 3:18 **7:8** [a]Jer 7:4; 28:15 **7:9** [a]Jer 11:13, 17

to Baal and walk after [b]other gods
that you have not known, 10 then
[a]come and stand before Me in [b]this
house, which is called by My name,
and say, 'We are delivered!'—that
you may do all these abominations?
11 Has [a]this house, which is called by
My name, become a [b]robbers' den in
your sight? Behold, [c]I, even I, have
seen *it*," declares Yahweh.

12 "But go now to My place which
was in [a]Shiloh, where I [b]made My
name dwell at the first, and [c]see what
I did to it because of the evil of My
people Israel. 13 And now, because
you have done all these works," de-
clares Yahweh, "and I spoke to you,
[a]rising up early and [b]speaking, but
you did not hear, and I [c]called you
but you did not answer, 14 therefore,
I will do to the [a]house which is called
by My name, [b]in which you trust, and
to the place which I gave you and
your fathers, as I [c]did to Shiloh. 15 I
will [a]cast you out of My presence, as
I have cast out all your brothers, all
the seed of [b]Ephraim.

16 "As for you, [a]do not pray for
this people and do not lift up a cry
of lamentation or prayer for them
and do not intercede with Me, for I
am not hearing you. 17 Are you not
seeing what they are doing in the
cities of Judah and in the streets of
*Jerusalem?* 18 The [1]children gather
wood, and the fathers make the fire
burn, and the women knead dough to
make cakes for the queen of heaven;
and *they* [a]pour out drink offerings to
other gods in order to [b]provoke Me.
19 [a]"Do they provoke Me?" declares
Yahweh. "Is it not themselves *they*
*provoke* to the [b]shame of their own
face?" 20 Therefore thus says Lord
Yahweh, "Behold, My [a]anger and
My wrath will be poured out on this
place, on man and on beast and on
the [b]trees of the field and on the fruit
of the ground; and it will burn and
not be quenched."

21 Thus says Yahweh of hosts,
the God of Israel, "Add your [a]burnt
offerings to your sacrifices and [b]eat
flesh. 22 For I did not [a]speak to your
fathers or command them in the day
that I brought them out of the land
of Egypt concerning burnt offerings
and sacrifices. 23 But this is [1]what I
commanded them, saying, '[a]Listen
to My voice, and [b]I will be your God,
and you will be My people; and you
will walk in the entire way which I
command you, that it may [c]be well
with you.' 24 Yet they [a]did not listen
or incline their ear, but walked in
*their own* counsels *and* in the
stubbornness of their evil heart and
[b,1]went backward and not forward.
25 Since the day that your fathers
came out of the land of Egypt until
this day, I have [a]sent you all My slaves
the prophets, daily rising up early
and sending *them*. 26 Yet they did not
listen to Me or incline their ear, but

**7:9** [b]Ex 20:3; Jer 7:6; 19:4 **7:10** [a]Eze 23:39 [b]Jer 7:11, 14, 30; 32:34 **7:11** [a]Is 56:7 [b]Mt 21:13; Mk 11:17; Lk 19:46 [c]Jer 29:23 **7:12** [a]Jdg 18:31; Jer 26:6 [b]Jos 18:1, 10 [c]1Sa 4:10, 11, 22; Ps 78:60-64 **7:13** [a]Jer 7:25 [b]Jer 35:17 [c]Pr 1:24; Is 65:12; 66:4 **7:14** [a]Dt 12:5; 1Ki 9:7 [b]Jer 7:4 [c]Jer 7:12 **7:15** [a]Jer 15:1; 52:3 [b]Ps 78:67; Hos 7:13; 9:13; 12:1 **7:16** [a]Ex 32:10; Dt 9:14; Jer 11:14 **7:18** [a]Jer 19:13 [b]Dt 32:16, 21; 1Ki 14:9; 16:2; Jer 11:17; Eze 8:17 [1]Lit *sons* **7:19** [a]Job 35:6; 1Co 10:22 [b]Jer 9:19; 15:9; 22:22 **7:20** [a]Is 42:25; Jer 6:11, 12; 42:18; Lam 2:3-5; 4:11 [b]Jer 8:13; 11:16 **7:21** [a]Is 1:11; Jer 6:20; 14:12; Am 5:22 [b]Eze 33:25; Hos 8:13 **7:22** [a]1Sa 15:22; Ps 51:16; Hos 6:6 **7:23** [a]Ex 15:26; 16:32; Dt 6:3 [b]Ex 19:5, 6; Lv 26:12; Jer 11:4; 13:11 [c]Is 3:10; Jer 38:20; 42:6 [1]Lit *the word which* **7:24** [a]Dt 29:19; Ps 81:11; Jer 11:8; Eze 20:8, 13, 16, 21 [b]Jer 15:6 [1]Lit *they were* **7:25** [a]2Chr 36:15; Jer 25:4; 29:19; Lk 11:49

[a]stiffened their neck; they [b]did more
evil than their fathers.
**27** "You shall [a]speak all these
words to them, but they will not
listen to you; and you shall call to
them, but they will [b]not answer you.
**28** You shall say to them, 'This is the
nation that [a]did not listen to the
voice of Yahweh their God or receive
discipline; [b,1]truth has perished and
has been cut off from their mouth.
**29** '[a]Cut off [1]your hair
    and cast *it* away,
  And [b]lift up a *funeral*
    lamentation on the
    bare heights;
  For Yahweh has [c]rejected
    and abandoned
  The generation of His wrath.'
**30** "For the sons of Judah have done
that which is evil in My sight,"
declares Yahweh, "they have [a]set
their detestable things in the house,
which is called by My name, to defile
it. **31** They have [a]built the high places
of Topheth, which is in the valley of
the son of Hinnom, to [b]burn their
sons and their daughters in the fire,
which I [c]did not command, and it did
not come upon My heart.
**32** "[a]Therefore, behold, days are
coming," declares Yahweh, "when
it will no longer be called Topheth
or the valley of the son of Hinnom,
but the valley of the Slaughter; for
they will [b]bury in Topheth [1]because
there is no *other* place. **33** The [a]dead
bodies of this people will be food for
the birds of the sky and for the beasts
of the earth; and no one will frighten
*them away*. **34** Then I will make to
[a]cease from the cities of Judah and
from the streets of Jerusalem the
voice of joy and the voice of gladness,
the voice of the bridegroom and the
voice of the bride, for the [b]land will
become a waste place.

### *The Faithlessness of Jerusalem*

**8** "At that time," declares Yahweh,
"they will [a]bring out the bones
of the kings of Judah and the bones
of its princes, and the bones of the
priests and the bones of the proph-
ets, and the bones of the inhabitants
of Jerusalem from their graves. **2** And
they will spread them out to the
sun, the moon, and to all the [a]host
of heaven, which they have loved and
which they have served, and which
they have walked after and which
they have sought, and which they
have worshiped. They will not be
gathered [b]or buried; [c]they will be as
dung on the face of the ground. **3** And
[a]death will be chosen rather than life
by all the remnant that remains of
this evil family, that remains in all
the [b]places to which I have banished
them," declares Yahweh of hosts.
**4** "You shall say to them, 'Thus says
Yahweh,
  "Do *men* [a]fall and not
    get up again?
  Does one turn away and
    not [1]turn back?

**7:26** [a]Ne 9:16; Jer 17:23; 19:15 [b]Jer 16:12; Mt 23:32 **7:27** [a]Jer 1:7; 26:2; Eze 2:7 [b]Is 50:2; 65:12; Zec 7:13 **7:28** [a]Jer 6:17; 11:10 [b]Is 59:14, 15; Jer 9:5 [1]Lit *faithfulness* **7:29** [a]Job 1:20; Is 15:2; 22:12; Jer 16:6; Mic 1:16 [b]Jer 3:21; 9:17, 18 [c]Jer 6:30; 14:19 [1]Lit *your crown* **7:30** [a]2Ki 21:3f; 2Chr 33:3-5, 7; Jer 32:34, 35; Eze 7:20; Da 9:27; 11:31 **7:31** [a]2Ki 23:10; Jer 19:5; 32:35 [b]Lv 18:21; 2Ki 17:17; Ps 106:38 [c]Dt 17:3 **7:32** [a]Jer 19:6, 11 [b]2Ki 23:10 [1]Or *until there is no place left* **7:33** [a]Dt 28:26; Ps 79:2; Jer 12:9; 19:7 **7:34** [a]Is 24:7, 8; Jer 16:9; 25:10; Eze 26:13; Hos 2:11; Rev 18:23 [b]Lv 26:33; Is 1:7; Jer 4:27 ◆ **8:1** [a]Eze 6:5 **8:2** [a]2Ki 23:5; Jer 19:13; Zep 1:5; Ac 7:42 [b]Jer 22:19; 36:30 [c]2Ki 9:37; Ps 83:10; Jer 9:22 **8:3** [a]Job 3:21, 22; 7:15, 16; Jon 4:3; Rev 9:6 [b]Dt 30:1, 4; Jer 23:3, 8; 29:14 **8:4** [a]Pr 24:16; Am 5:2; Mic 7:8 [1]Or *repent*

5 “Why then has this
people, Jerusalem,
[a,1]Turned away
in continual faithlessness?
They [b]hold fast to deceit;
They [c]refuse to return.
6 “I [a]have given heed and heard,
They have spoken
what is not right;
[b]No man regretted his evil,
Saying, ‘What have I done?’
Everyone turned to his course,
Like a [c]horse charging
into the battle.
7 “Even the stork in the sky
[a]Knows her seasons;
And the [b]turtledove and
the swift and the crane
Keep the time
of their [1]migration;
But [c]My people do not know
The *legal* judgment of Yahweh.

8 “[a]How can you say,
‘We are wise,
And the law of Yahweh
is with us’?
But behold, the lying
pen of the scribes
Has made *it* into a lie.
9 “The wise men are
[a]put to shame;
They are dismayed
and captured;
Behold, they have [b]rejected
the word of Yahweh,
And what kind of wisdom
do they have?
10 “Therefore I will [a]give
their wives to others,
Their fields
to [1]new possessors,
Because from the least
even to the greatest
Everyone is [b]greedy for gain;
From the prophet even
to the priest
Everyone practices lying.
11 “They [a]heal the brokenness
of the daughter of My
people superficially,
Saying, ‘Peace, peace,’
But there is no peace.
12 “Were they [a]ashamed because
of the abomination
they had done?
They certainly were
not ashamed,
And they did not know
how to feel dishonor;
Therefore they shall [b]fall
among those who fall;
At the [c]time of their
[1]punishment they shall
be brought down,”
Says Yahweh.

13 “I will [a]surely gather them
up,” declares Yahweh;
“There will be [b]no
grapes on the vine
And [c]no figs on the fig tree,
And the leaf will wither;
And what I have given
them will pass away.”’”
14 Why are we sitting still?
[a]Gather yourselves,
and let us [b]go
into the fortified cities
And let us be silent there

**8:5** [a]Jer 5:6; 7:24 [b]Jer 5:27; 9:6 [c]Jer 5:3 [1]Or *Turned away in continually turning* **8:6** [a]Ps 14:2; Mal 3:16 [b]Eze 22:30; Mic 7:2; Rev 9:20 [c]Job 39:21-25 **8:7** [a]Pr 6:6-8; Is 1:3 [b]SS 2:12 [c]Jer 5:4 [1]Lit *coming* **8:8** [a]Job 5:12, 13; Jer 4:22; Ro 1:22 **8:9** [a]Is 19:11; Jer 6:15; 1Co 1:27 [b]Jer 6:19 **8:10** [a]Dt 28:30; Jer 6:12, 13; 38:22f [b]Is 56:11; 57:17; Jer 6:13 [1]Lit *possessing ones* **8:11** [a]Jer 6:14; 14:13, 14; Lam 2:14; Eze 13:10 **8:12** [a]Ps 52:1, 7; Is 3:9; Jer 3:3; 6:15; Zep 3:5 [b]Is 9:14; Jer 6:21; Hos 4:5 [c]Dt 32:35; Jer 10:15 [1]Or *visitation*, so in Jer **8:13** [a]Jer 14:12; Eze 22:20, 21 [b]Jer 5:17; 7:20; Joel 1:7 [c]Mt 21:19; Lk 13:6 **8:14** [a]Jer 4:5 [b]2Sa 20:6; Jer 35:11

Because Yahweh our
God has silenced us
And given us [c,1]poisoned
water to drink,
For [d]we have sinned
against Yahweh.
15 *We* [a]waited for peace,
but there was no good;
For a time of healing,
but behold, terror!
16 From [a]Dan is heard
the snorting of his horses;
At the sound of the neighing
of his [b]valiant steeds
The whole land quakes;
And they come and
[c]devour the land
as well as its fullness,
The city and its inhabitants.
17 "For behold, I am [a]sending
serpents against you,
Vipers, for which there
is [b]no charm,
And they will bite you,"
declares Yahweh.

### *Sorrow over Zion*

18 [1]My [a]sorrow is
beyond healing;
My [b]heart is faint within me!
19 Behold, *the* sound!
The cry of the daughter
of my people
from a [a]distant land:
"Is Yahweh not in Zion?
Is her King not within her?"
"Why have they [b]provoked
Me to anger with their
graven images,
with foreign [c,1]idols?"
20 "Harvest is past,
summer is ended,
And we are not saved."
21 For the [a]brokenness
of the daughter of my
people I am broken;
I [b]mourn, desolation has
taken hold of me.
22 Is there no [a]balm in Gilead?
Is there no physician there?
[b]Why then has not
the [1]health of the daughter
of my people gone up?

9 [a,1]Oh that my head were waters
And my eyes a fountain
of tears,
That I might weep
day and night
For the slain of the
[b]daughter of my people!
2 [a,1]Oh that I had in the desert
A travelers' lodging place,
That I might leave my people
And go from them!
For all of them
are [b]adulterers,
A solemn assembly
of [c]treacherous men.
3 "They [a]bend their tongue
*like* their bow;
Lies and unfaithfulness
prevail in the land,
For they [b]go onward
from evil to evil,
And they [c]do not know
Me," declares Yahweh.

**8:14** [c]Dt 29:18; Ps 69:21; Jer 9:15; 23:15; Lam 3:19; Mt 27:34 [d]Jer 3:25; 14:20 [1]Or *gall* **8:15** [a]Jer 8:11; 14:19 **8:16** [a]Jdg 18:29; Jer 4:15 [b]Jdg 5:22 [c]Jer 3:24; 10:25 **8:17** [a]Nu 21:6; Dt 32:24 [b]Ps 58:4, 5 **8:18** [a]Is 22:4; Lam 1:16, 17 [b]Jer 23:9; Lam 5:17 [1]As in Gr and versions **8:19** [a]Is 13:5; 39:3; Jer 4:16; 9:16 [b]Dt 32:21; Jer 7:19 [c]Ps 31:6 [1]Lit *vanities* **8:21** [a]Jer 4:19; 9:1; 14:17 [b]Jer 14:2; Joel 2:6; Na 2:10 **8:22** [a]Ge 37:25; Jer 46:11 [b]Jer 14:19; 30:13 [1]Or *healing* ◆ **9:1** [a]Is 22:4; Jer 8:18; 13:17; Lam 2:18 [b]Jer 6:26; 8:21, 22 [1]Ch 8:23 in Heb **9:2** [a]Ps 55:6, 7; 120:5, 6 [b]Jer 5:7, 8; 23:10; Hos 4:2 [c]Jer 5:11; 12:1, 6 [1]Ch 9:1 in Heb **9:3** [a]Ps 64:3; Is 59:4; Jer 9:8 [b]Jer 4:22 [c]Jdg 2:10; 1Sa 2:12; Jer 4:22; 5:4, 5; Hos 4:1; 1Co 15:34

4 "Let everyone [a]beware
of his neighbor,
And [b]do not trust any brother,
Because every [c]brother
[1]surely supplants,
And every neighbor [d]goes
about as a slanderer.
5 "Everyone [a]deceives
his neighbor
And does not speak the truth;
They have taught their
tongue to speak lies;
They [b]weary themselves
committing iniquity.
6 "Your [a]habitation is
in the midst of deceit;
Through deceit they [b]refuse to
know Me," declares Yahweh.

7 Therefore thus says Yahweh of
hosts,
"Behold, I will refine them
and [a]test them;
For [b]what *else* can I do,
because of the daughter
of My people?
8 "Their [a]tongue is a
slaughtering arrow;
It speaks deceit;
With his mouth one [b]speaks
peace to his neighbor,
But inwardly he [c]sets an
ambush for him.
9 "[a]Shall I not punish them
*for these* things?"
declares Yahweh.
"On a nation such as this
Shall I not avenge Myself?

10 "For the [a]mountains I will take
up a weeping and wailing,
And for the pastures
of the [b]wilderness
a *funeral* lamentation,
Because they are [c]turned
into ruin so that no
one passes through,
And the lowing of the
cattle is not heard;
Both the [d]birds of the
sky and the beasts have
fled; they are gone.
11 "I will make Jerusalem
a [a]heap of ruins,
A haunt of [b]jackals;
And I will make the cities
of Judah a [c]desolation,
without inhabitant."

12 Who is the [a]wise man that
may understand this? And *who is*
he to whom [b]the mouth of Yahweh
has spoken, that he may declare it?
[c]Why has the land perished, turned
into ruin like a desert, so that no
one passes through? 13 Yahweh said,
"Because they have [a]forsaken My law,
which I set before them, and have
not listened to My voice nor walked
according to it, 14 but have [a]walked
after the stubbornness of their
heart and after the [b]Baals, as their
[c]fathers taught them," 15 therefore
thus says Yahweh of hosts, the
God of Israel, "behold, [a]I will feed
them, this people, with wormwood
and give them [b,1]poisoned water to
drink. 16 I will [a]scatter them among

**9:4** [a]Ps 12:2; Pr 26:24, 25; Jer 9:8; Mic 7:5, 6 [b]Jer 12:6 [c]Ge 27:35 [d]Ps 15:3; Pr 10:18; Jer 6:28 [1]Heb sounds like Jacob (a play on words) **9:5** [a]Mic 6:12 [b]Jer 12:13; 51:58, 64 **9:6** [a]Ps 120:5, 6; Jer 5:27; 8:5 [b]Job 21:14, 15; Pr 1:24; Jer 11:10; 13:10; Jn 3:19, 20 **9:7** [a]Is 1:25; Jer 6:27; Mal 3:3 [b]Hos 11:8 **9:8** [a]Jer 9:3 [b]Ps 28:3 [c]Jer 5:26 **9:9** [a]Is 1:24; Jer 5:9, 29 **9:10** [a]Jer 4:24; 7:29 [b]Jer 4:26; Hos 4:3 [c]Jer 12:4, 10; Eze 14:15; 29:11; 33:28 [d]Jer 4:25; 12:4; Hos 4:3 **9:11** [a]Is 25:2; Jer 51:37 [b]Is 13:22; 34:13 [c]Jer 4:27; 26:9 **9:12** [a]Ps 107:43; Is 42:23; Hos 14:9 [b]Jer 9:20; 23:16 [c]Ps 107:34; Jer 23:10 **9:13** [a]2Chr 7:19; Ps 89:30; Jer 5:19; 22:9 **9:14** [a]Jer 7:24; 11:8; Ro 1:21-24 [b]Jer 2:8, 23; 23:27 [c]Ga 1:14; 1Pe 1:18 **9:15** [a]Ps 80:5 [b]Dt 29:18; Jer 8:14; 23:15; Lam 3:15 [1]Or *gall* **9:16** [a]Lv 26:33; Dt 28:64; Jer 13:24

the nations, whom neither they nor
their fathers have known; and I will
send the [b]sword after them until I
have consumed them."

**17** Thus says Yahweh of hosts,
"Carefully consider and call
for the [a]mourning women,
that they may come;
And send for the [b,1]skillful
women, that they may come!
**18** "Let them make haste and
take up a wailing for us,
That our [a]eyes may shed tears
And our eyelids flow
with water.
**19** "For a voice of [a]wailing
is heard from Zion,
'[b]How we are destroyed!
We are put to great shame,
For we have [c]left the land
Because they have cast
down our dwellings.'"
**20** Indeed, hear the word
of Yahweh, O you [a]women,
And let your ear receive
the word of His mouth;
Teach your daughters wailing,
And everyone her neighbor
a *funeral* lamentation.
**21** For [a]death has come up
through our windows;
It has entered our palaces
To cut off the [b]infants
from the streets,
The choice men
from the open squares.
**22** Speak, "Thus declares Yahweh,
'The corpses of men will fall
[a]like dung on the open field
And like the sheaf
after the reaper,
But no one will gather *them*.'"

**23** Thus says Yahweh, "[a]Let not a
wise man boast in his wisdom, and
let not the [b]mighty man boast in his
might; let not a [c]rich man boast in
his riches, **24** but let him who boasts
[a]boast in this, that he [1]understands
and knows Me, that I am Yahweh who
[b]shows lovingkindness, justice, and
righteousness on earth; for I [c]delight
in these things," declares Yahweh.

**25** "Behold, the days are coming,"
declares Yahweh, "that I will punish
all who are circumcised and yet
[a]uncircumcised— **26** Egypt and
Judah, and Edom and the sons of
Ammon, and Moab and [a]all those
inhabiting the desert who clip the
hair on their temples; for all the nations are uncircumcised, and all the
house of Israel are [b]uncircumcised
of heart."

### *Yahweh Alone Is the Living God*

**10** Hear the word which Yahweh
speaks to you, O house of
Israel. **2** Thus says Yahweh,
"[a]Do not learn the way
of the nations,
And do not be terrified
by the signs of the heavens
Although the nations are
terrified by them;
**3** For the statutes of the
peoples are [a]vanity
Because [b]it is wood cut
from the forest,

**9:16** [a]Jer 44:27; Eze 5:2, 12 **9:17** [a]2Chr 35:25; Ecc 12:5 [b]Am 5:16 [1]Lit *wise* **9:18** [a]Is 22:4; Jer 9:1; 14:17
**9:19** [a]Jer 7:29; Eze 7:16-18 [b]Dt 28:29; Jer 4:13 [c]Jer 7:15; 15:1 **9:20** [a]Is 32:9 **9:21** [a]2Chr 36:17; Jer 15:7; 18:21; Eze 9:5, 6; Am 6:9, 10 [b]Jer 6:11 **9:22** [a]Ps 83:10; Is 5:25; Jer 8:2; 16:4; 25:33 **9:23** [a]Ecc 9:11; Is 47:10; Eze 28:3-7 [b]1Ki 20:10, 11; Is 10:8-12 [c]Job 31:24, 25; Ps 49:6-9 **9:24** [a]Ps 20:7; 44:8; Is 41:16; Jer 4:2; 1Co 1:31; 2Co 10:17; Ga 6:14 [b]Ex 34:6, 7; Ps 36:5, 7; 51:1 [c]Is 61:8; Mic 7:18 [1]Lit *has insight*
**9:25** [a]Jer 4:4; Ro 2:28, 29 **9:26** [a]Jer 25:23 [b]Lv 26:41; Jer 4:4; 6:10; Eze 44:7; Ro 2:28 ◆ **10:2** [a]Lv 18:3; 20:23; Dt 12:30 **10:3** [a]Jer 14:22 [b]Is 44:9-20

The work of the hands
of a craftsman
with a cutting tool.
4 "They [a]make *it* beautiful
with silver and with gold;
They [b]strengthen it with
nails and with hammers
So that it will not totter.
5 "Like a scarecrow in a
cucumber field are they,
And they [a]cannot speak;
They must be [b]carried
Because they cannot
take a step!
Do not fear them,
For they [c]can do no harm,
Nor can they do any good."

6 [a]There is none like You,
O Yahweh;
You are [b]great, and great
is Your name in might.
7 [a]Who would not fear You,
O [b]King of the nations?
Indeed it is Your due!
For among all the [c]wise
men of the nations
And in all their kingdoms,
There is none like You.
8 But they are altogether
[a]senseless and foolish;
*They are in* a discipline of
[1]vanities—it is *mere* wood!
9 Beaten [a]silver is brought
from [b]Tarshish,
And [c]gold from Uphaz,
The work of a craftsman
and of the hands
of a goldsmith;
Blue and purple are
their clothing;
They are all the [d]work
of wise *craftsmen*.
10 But Yahweh is the [a]true God;
He is the [b]living God and
the [c]everlasting King.
At His wrath the
[d]earth quakes,
And the nations cannot
[e]endure His indignation.
11 [1]Thus you shall say to them, "The
[a]gods that did not make the heavens
and the earth will [b]perish from the
earth and from under [2]the heavens."
12 *It is* [a]He who made the earth
by His power,
Who [b]established
the world by His wisdom;
And by His understanding
He has [c]stretched
out the heavens.
13 When He gives forth His
[a]voice, *there is* a tumult
of waters in the heavens,
And He causes the [b]clouds
to ascend from the end
of the earth;
He makes lightning
for the rain,
And brings out the [c]wind
from His storehouses.
14 Every man is [a]senseless,
devoid of knowledge;
Every goldsmith is put to
shame by his graven images;
For his molten images are a lie,
And there is no
breath in them.

**10:4** [a]Is 40:19 [b]Is 40:20; 41:7 **10:5** [a]Ps 115:5; Is 46:7; Jer 10:14; 1Co 12:2 [b]Ps 115:7; Is 46:1, 7 [c]Is 41:23, 24 **10:6** [a]Ex 15:11; Dt 33:26; Ps 86:8, 10; Jer 10:16 [b]Ps 48:1; 96:4; Is 12:6; Jer 32:18 **10:7** [a]Rev 15:4 [b]Ps 22:28 [c]Da 2:27, 28; 1Co 1:19, 20 **10:8** [a]Jer 4:22; 5:4; 10:14 [1]Or *idols* **10:9** [a]Is 40:19 [b]Ps 72:10; Is 23:6 [c]Da 10:5 [d]Ps 115:4 **10:10** [a]Is 65:16 [b]Jer 4:2 [c]Ps 10:16; 29:10 [d]Jer 4:24; 50:46 [e]Ps 76:7 **10:11** [a]Ps 96:5 [b]Is 2:18; Zep 2:11 [1]This verse is in Aram [2]Or *these* **10:12** [a]Ge 1:1, 6; Job 38:4-7; Ps 136:5; 148:4, 5; Jer 51:15, 19 [b]Ps 78:69; Is 45:18 [c]Job 9:8; Is 40:22 **10:13** [a]Ps 29:3-9 [b]Job 36:27-29 [c]Ps 135:7 **10:14** [a]Jer 10:8; 51:17, 18

15 They are [a]vanity,
a work of mockery;
In the [b]time of their
punishment they will perish.
16 The [a]portion of Jacob
is not like these;
For the [b,1]Maker of all is He,
And [c]Israel is the tribe
of His inheritance;
[d]Yahweh of hosts is His name.

17 [a]Gather up your bundle
from the ground,
You who inhabit
*a land* under siege!
18 For thus says Yahweh,
"Behold, I am [a]slinging
out the inhabitants
of the land
At this time,
And will cause them distress,
That they may find *it*."

19 [a]Woe is me, because
of my [1]injury!
My [b]wound is desperately sick.
But I said,
"Truly this is a sickness,
And I [c]must bear it."
20 My [a]tent is destroyed,
And all my ropes are torn out;
My [b]sons have gone
from me and are no more.
There is [c]no one to stretch
out my tent again
Or to set up my curtains.
21 For the shepherds have
become senseless
And [a]have not sought Yahweh;
Therefore they have
not prospered,
And [b]all their flock
is scattered.
22 The sound of a [a]report!
Behold, it comes—
A great quaking [b]out
of the land of the north—
To [c]make the cities of Judah
A desolation, a haunt
of jackals.

23 I know, O Yahweh, that [a]a man's
way is not in himself,
[b]Nor is it in a man who
walks to [1]direct his steps.
24 [a]Discipline me, O Yahweh,
but with justice;
Not with Your anger, lest You
[1]bring me to nothing.
25 [a]Pour out Your wrath
on the nations that
[b]do not know You
And on the families that
[c]do not call Your name,
For they have devoured Jacob;
They have [d]devoured him
and consumed him
And have made desolate
his [1]abode.

### *The Broken Covenant*

11 The word which came to Jeremi-
ah from Yahweh, saying, 2 "[a]Hear
the words of this [b]covenant, and you
shall speak to the men of Judah and
to the inhabitants of Jerusalem 3 and
say to them, 'Thus says Yahweh, the
God of Israel, "[a]Cursed is the man

**10:15** [a]Is 41:24; Jer 8:19; 14:22 [b]Jer 8:12; 51:18 **10:16** [a]Ps 16:5; 73:26; 119:57; Jer 51:19; Lam 3:24 [b]Is 45:7; Jer 10:12 [c]Dt 32:9; Ps 74:2 [d]Jer 31:35; 32:18 [1]Lit *Fashioner* **10:17** [a]Eze 12:3-12 **10:18** [a]1Sa 25:29 **10:19** [a]Jer 4:31 [b]Jer 14:17 [c]Mic 7:9 [1]Lit *breaking* **10:20** [a]Jer 4:20; Lam 2:4 [b]Jer 31:15; Lam 1:5 [c]Is 51:18 **10:21** [a]Jer 2:8 [b]Jer 23:2 **10:22** [a]Jer 4:15 [b]Jer 1:14; 25:9 [c]Jer 9:11; 49:33 **10:23** [a]Pr 16:1; 20:24 [b]Is 26:7 [1]Lit *establish* **10:24** [a]Ps 6:1; 38:1 [1]Lit *diminish me* **10:25** [a]Ps 79:6, 7; Zep 3:8 [b]Job 18:21; 1Th 4:5; 2Th 1:8 [c]Zep 1:6 [d]Jer 8:16; 50:7, 17 [1]Or *pasture* ◆ **11:2** [a]Jer 11:6 [b]Ex 19:5 **11:3** [a]Dt 27:26; Jer 17:5; Ga 3:10

who does not hear the words of this
covenant **4** which I commanded your
fathers in the [a]day that I brought them
out of the land of Egypt, from the
[b]iron furnace, saying, '[c]Listen to My
voice, and [1]do according to all which
I command you; so you shall be [d]My
people, and I will be your God,' **5** in
order to establish the [a]oath which I
swore to your fathers, to give them a
land flowing with milk and honey, as
*it is* this day."'" Then I answered and
said, "[b]Amen, O Yahweh."

**6** And Yahweh said to me, "[a]Call
out all these words in the cities of
Judah and in the streets of Jerusalem,
saying, '[b]Hear the words of this cov-
enant so that you will [c]do them. **7** For
I solemnly [a]warned your fathers in
the [b]day that I brought them up from
the land of Egypt, even to this day,
[c]rising up early and warning, saying,
"[d]Listen to My voice." **8** Yet they [a]did
not listen or incline their ear, but
walked, each one, in the stubborn-
ness of his evil heart; therefore I
brought on them all the [b]words of
this covenant, which I commanded
*them* to do, but they did not.'"

**9** Then Yahweh said to me, "A
[a]conspiracy has been found among
the men of Judah and among the in-
habitants of Jerusalem. **10** They have
[a]turned back to the iniquities of their
[1]ancestors who [b]refused to hear My
words, and they [c]have walked after
other gods to serve them; the house
of Israel and the house of Judah have
[d]broken My covenant which I cut
with their fathers." **11** Therefore thus
says Yahweh, "Behold, I am [a]bringing
calamity on them which they will
[b]not be able to get out of; and they
will [c]cry to Me, yet I will not listen
to them. **12** Then the cities of Judah
and the inhabitants of Jerusalem will
[a]go and cry to the gods to whom they
burn incense, but they surely will
not save them in the time of their
calamity. **13** For your gods are [a]the
number of your cities, O Judah; and
the number of the streets of Jerusa-
lem are the altars you have set up to
the [b]shameful thing, altars to [c]burn
incense to Baal.

**14** "But as for you, [a]do not pray
for this people, nor lift up a cry of
lamentation or prayer for them; for
I will [b]not listen when they call to
Me because of their calamity.

**15** "What *possession* has My
[a]beloved in My house
When [b]she has done many
schemes of wickedness?
Can the flesh, *which is* set
apart as holy, take away
from you your calamity,
[1]So *that* you can exult?"

**16** Yahweh called your name,
"A [a]green olive tree,
beautiful in fruit
and form";
With the [b]noise
of a great tumult

**11:4** [a]Ex 24:3-8; Jer 31:32 [b]Dt 4:20; 1Ki 8:51 [c]Lv 26:3; Dt 11:27; Jer 7:23; 26:13 [d]Jer 24:7; Zec 8:8 [1]Lit *do them* **11:5** [a]Ex 13:5; Dt 7:12; Ps 105:9; Jer 32:22 [b]Jer 28:6 **11:6** [a]Jer 3:12; 7:2 [b]Jer 11:2 [c]Jn 13:17; Ro 2:13; Jas 1:22 **11:7** [a]1Sa 8:9 [b]Jer 11:4 [c]Ex 15:26; 2Chr 36:15; Jer 7:25 [d]Jer 11:7 **11:8** [a]Jer 7:24; 9:14; 35:15; Eze 20:8 [b]Lv 26:14-43 **11:9** [a]Eze 22:25; Hos 6:9 **11:10** [a]1Sa 15:11; Jer 3:10, 11; Eze 20:18 [b]Dt 9:7; Ps 78:8-10; Jer 13:10 [c]Jdg 2:11-13 [d]Jer 3:6-11; Eze 16:59 [1]Lit *former fathers* **11:11** [a]2Ki 22:16; Jer 6:19; 11:17 [b]Is 24:17; Jer 25:35 [c]Ps 18:41; Pr 1:28; Is 1:15; Jer 11:14; 14:12; Eze 8:18; Mic 3:4; Zec 7:13 **11:12** [a]Dt 32:37; Jer 44:17 **11:13** [a]2Ki 23:13; Jer 2:28 [b]Jer 3:24 [c]Jer 7:9 **11:14** [a]Ex 32:10; Jer 7:16; 14:11; 1Jn 5:16 [b]Ps 66:18; Jer 11:11; Hos 5:6 **11:15** [a]Jer 13:27 [b]Eze 16:25 [1]Lit *Then* **11:16** [a]Ps 52:8; Ro 11:17 [b]Ps 83:2

He has [c]kindled fire on it,
And its foliage has
an evil *demise.*

**17** Yahweh of hosts, who [a]planted
you, has [b]spoken forth evil against
you because of the evil of the house
of Israel and of the house of Judah,
which they have [1]done to provoke
Me to anger by [c]burning incense to
Baal.

### *Men Seek Jeremiah's Life*

**18** Moreover, Yahweh [a]made it
known to me, and I knew it;
Then You showed me
their deeds.
**19** But I was like a gentle [a]lamb
led to the slaughter;
And I did not know that they
had [b]devised thoughts
against me, *saying,*
"Let us make the tree
with its [1]fruit a ruin,
And [c]let us cut him off
from the [d]land of the living,
That his [e]name be
remembered no more."
**20** But, O Yahweh of hosts, who
[a]judges righteously,
Who [b]tests the [1]insides
and the heart,
Let me see Your
vengeance on them,
For to You have I
revealed my case.

**21** Therefore thus says Yahweh
concerning the men of [a]Anathoth,
who [b]seek your life, saying, "[c]Do not
prophesy in the name of Yahweh, so
that you will not [d]die at our hand";
**22** therefore thus says Yahweh of
hosts, "Behold, I am about to [a]punish
them! The [b]choice men will die by
the sword; their sons and daughters
will die by famine; **23** and a remnant
[a]will not be left to them, for I will
[b]bring calamity on the men of
Anathoth—[c]the year of their pun-
ishment."

### *Jeremiah's Plea*

**12** [a]Righteous are You,
O Yahweh, when I would
plead *my* case with You;
Indeed I would [b]speak matters
of justice with You:
Why has the [c]way of the
wicked succeeded?
*Why* are all those who [d]deal
in treachery complacent?
**2** You have [a]planted them;
they have also taken root;
They grow; they have
even produced fruit.
You are [b]near [1]to their lips
But far from their
[2]inmost being.
**3** But You, O Yahweh,
You [a]know me;
You see me;
And You [b]test my heart's
*attitude* toward You.
Drag them off like sheep
for the slaughter
And [1]set them apart
for a [c]day of carnage!

---

**11:16** [c]Ps 80:16; Is 27:11; Jer 21:14 **11:17** [a]Is 5:2; Jer 2:21; 12:2 [b]Jer 1:14; 16:10; 19:15 [c]Jer 7:9; 11:13; 32:29 [1]Or *done for themselves* **11:18** [a]1Sa 23:11, 12; 2Ki 6:9, 10; Eze 8:6 **11:19** [a]Is 53:7 [b]Jer 18:18; 20:10 [c]Ps 83:4; Is 53:8 [d]Job 28:13; Ps 52:5 [e]Ps 109:13 [1]Lit *bread* **11:20** [a]Ge 18:25; Ps 7:8; Jer 20:12 [b]1Sa 16:7; Ps 7:9; Jer 17:10 [1]Lit *kidneys* **11:21** [a]Jer 1:1 [b]Jer 12:5, 6; 20:10 [c]Am 2:12 [d]Jer 26:8; 38:4 **11:22** [a]Jer 21:14 [b]2Chr 36:17; Jer 18:21 **11:23** [a]Jer 6:9 [b]Jer 23:12; Hos 9:7; Mic 7:4 [c]Lk 19:44
◆ **12:1** [a]Ezr 9:15; Ps 51:4; 129:4; Jer 11:20 [b]Job 13:3 [c]Job 12:6; Jer 5:27, 28; Hab 1:4; Mal 3:15 [d]Jer 3:7, 20; 5:11 **12:2** [a]Jer 11:17; 45:4; Eze 17:5-10 [b]Is 29:13; Jer 3:10; Eze 33:31; Tit 1:16 [1]Lit *in their mouth* [2]Lit *kidneys* **12:3** [a]Ps 139:1-4 [b]Ps 7:9; 11:5; Jer 11:20 [c]Jer 17:18; 50:27; Jas 5:5 [1]Lit *sanctify them*

4 How long is the [a]land
to mourn
And the [b]plants of every
field to dry up?
Because of the [c]evil
of those who inhabit it,
[d]Animals and birds have
been swept away,
Because *men* have said,
"He will not see our
latter [e]ending."

### *Yahweh Answers Jeremiah*

5 "If you have run with footmen
and they have tired
you out,
Then how can you
compete with horses?
If you fall down in a
land of peace,
How will you do in the
[a,1]thicket of the Jordan?
6 "For even your [a]brothers
and the household
of your father,
Even they have dealt
treacherously with you,
Even they have called
aloud after you.
Do not believe them,
although they may say
[b]nice things to you."

7 "I have [a]forsaken My house;
I have abandoned
My inheritance;
I have given the [b]beloved
of My soul
Into the hand of her enemies.
8 "My inheritance has
become to Me
Like a lion in the forest;
She has [a]given forth its
voice against Me;
Therefore I have come
to [b]hate her.
9 "Is My inheritance
like a speckled bird
of prey to Me?
Are the [a]birds of prey
against her on every side?
Go, gather all the [b]beasts
of the field,
Bring them to devour!
10 "Many [a]shepherds have
ruined My [b]vineyard;
They have [c]trampled
down My portion;
They have made My
[d]desired portion
A desolate wilderness.
11 "[1]It has been made
a desolation;
Desolate, it [a]mourns
[2]before Me;
The [b]whole land has
been made desolate
Because no man [c]sets
it upon his heart.
12 "On all the [a,1]bare heights
in the wilderness
Destroyers have come,
For a [b]sword of Yahweh
is devouring
From one end of the land
even to the [2]other;
There is [c]no peace
for any flesh.

**12:4** [a]Jer 4:28; 9:10; 23:10 [b]Joel 1:10-17 [c]Ps 107:34 [d]Jer 4:25; 7:20; 9:10; Hos 4:3; Hab 3:17 [e]Jer 5:31; Eze 7:2 **12:5** [a]Jer 49:19; 50:44 [1]Lit *pride* **12:6** [a]Ge 37:4-11; Job 6:15; Ps 69:8; Jer 9:4, 5 [b]Ps 12:2; Pr 26:25 **12:7** [a]Is 2:6; Jer 7:29; 23:39 [b]Jer 11:15; Hos 11:1-8 **12:8** [a]Is 59:13 [b]Hos 9:15; Am 6:8 **12:9** [a]2Ki 24:2; Eze 23:22-25 [b]Is 56:9; Jer 7:33; 15:3; 34:20 **12:10** [a]Jer 6:3; 23:1 [b]Ps 80:8-16; Is 5:1-7 [c]Is 63:18 [d]Jer 3:19 **12:11** [a]Jer 12:4; 14:2; 23:10 [b]Jer 4:20, 27; 25:11 [c]Is 42:25 [1]Lit *One has made it* [2]Or *upon* **12:12** [a]Jer 3:2, 21 [b]Is 34:6; Jer 47:6; Am 9:4 [c]Jer 16:5; 30:5 [1]Or *caravan trails* [2]Lit *other end of the land*

13 “They have [a]sown wheat
and have reaped thorns;
They have [b]strained
themselves [1]to no profit.
But be ashamed of
your [c]produce
Because of the [d]burning
anger of Yahweh.”

14 Thus says Yahweh concerning
all My [a]evil neighbors who [b]beat at
the inheritance with which I have
caused My people Israel to inherit,
“Behold, I am about to uproot them
from their land and will [c]uproot the
house of Judah from among them.
15 And it will come about that after
I have uprooted them, I will [a]return
and have compassion on them; and I
will [b]cause them to return, each one
to his inheritance and each one to his
land. 16 Then if they will really [a]learn
the ways of My people, to [b]swear by
My name, ‘As Yahweh lives,’ even as
they taught My people to [c]swear by
Baal, they will be [d]built up in the
midst of My people. 17 But if they will
not listen, then I will [a]uproot that
nation, uproot and make it perish,”
declares Yahweh.

### *The Ruined Belt*

13 Thus Yahweh said to me, “Go
and [a]buy yourself a linen belt
and put it around your loins, but do
not put it in water.” 2 So I bought the
belt in accordance with the [a]word of
Yahweh and put it around my loins.
3 Then the word of Yahweh came to
me a second time, saying, 4 “Take the
belt that you have bought, which is
around your loins, and arise, go to
[1]the [a]Euphrates and hide it there
in a crevice of the rock.” 5 So I went
and hid it by the Euphrates, [a]as
Yahweh had commanded me. 6 Now
it happened that after many days
Yahweh said to me, “Arise, go to the
Euphrates and take from there the
belt which I commanded you to hide
there.” 7 Then I went to the Euphrates
and dug, and I took the belt from
the place where I had hidden it; and
behold, the belt was ruined; it was
totally worthless.

8 Then the word of Yahweh came
to me, saying, 9 “Thus says Yahweh,
‘Just so will I ruin the [a]pride of Judah
and the great pride of Jerusalem.
10 This evil people, who [a]refuse to
listen to My words, who [b]walk in
the stubbornness of their hearts
and have walked after other gods to
serve them and to worship them, let
them be just like this belt which is
totally worthless. 11 For as the belt
clings to the loins of a man, so I
made the whole household of Israel
and the whole household of Judah
[a]cling to Me,’ declares Yahweh, ‘that
they might be for Me a people, for a
[b]name, for [c]praise, and for beauty;
but they [d]did not listen.’

### *The Magnitude of Israel’s Iniquity*

12 “Therefore you are to say this
word to them, ‘Thus says Yahweh,
the God of Israel, “Every jug is to
be filled with wine.”’ And they will

**12:13** [a]Lv 26:16; Dt 28:38; Mic 6:15; Hag 1:6 [b]Is 55:2; Jer 9:5 [c]Jer 17:10 [d]Jer 4:26; 25:37, 38 [1]Lit *they do not profit* **12:14** [a]Jer 49:1, 7; Zep 2:8-10 [b]Jer 2:3; 50:11, 12; Zec 2:8 [c]Dt 30:3; Ps 106:47; Is 11:11-16 **12:15** [a]Jer 48:47; 49:6, 39 [b]Am 9:14 **12:16** [a]Is 42:6; 49:6 [b]Jer 4:2; Zep 1:5 [c]Jos 23:7; Jer 5:7 [d]Jer 3:17; 4:2; 16:19 **12:17** [a]Ps 2:8-12; Is 60:12 ◆ **13:1** [a]Jer 13:11 **13:2** [a]Is 20:2; Eze 2:8 **13:4** [a]Jer 51:63 [1]Or *Parah*, cf. Jos 18:23; so through v 7 **13:5** [a]Ex 39:42, 43; 40:16 **13:9** [a]Lv 26:19; Is 2:10-17; 23:9; Jer 13:15-17; Zep 3:11 **13:10** [a]Nu 14:11; 2Chr 36:15, 16; Jer 11:10 [b]Jer 9:14; 11:8; 16:12 **13:11** [a]Ex 19:5, 6; Dt 32:10, 11 [b]Jer 32:20 [c]Is 43:21; Jer 33:9 [d]Ps 81:11; Jer 7:13, 24, 26

say to you, 'Do we not very well
know that every jug is to be filled
with wine?' 13 Then you shall say to
them, 'Thus says Yahweh, "Behold,
I am about to fill all the inhabitants
of this land—the kings that sit for
David on his throne, the priests, the
prophets, and all the inhabitants
of Jerusalem—with [a]drunkenness!
14 I will [a]shatter them against each
other, both the [b]fathers and the sons
together," declares Yahweh. "I will
[c]not spare nor show pity nor have
compassion so as not to ruin them."'"

15 Listen and give ear,
do not be [a]haughty,
For Yahweh has spoken.
16 [a]Give glory to Yahweh
your God,
Before He brings [b]darkness
And before your [c]feet [1]stumble
On the dusky mountains;
And while you are
hoping for light,
He makes it
into the [d]shadow of death
*And* turns *it* into dense gloom.
17 But [a]if you will not listen
to it,
My soul will [b]cry in secret
for *such* pride;
And my eyes will bitterly weep
And flow down with tears
Because the [c]flock of Yahweh
has been taken captive.
18 Say to the [a]king and
the queen mother,
"[b]Take a lowly seat,
For your beautiful [c]crown
Has come down
from your head."
19 The [a]cities of the Negev
have been closed up,
And there is no one
to open *them*;
All [b]Judah has been taken
away into exile,
Wholly taken away into exile.

20 "Lift up your eyes and see
Those coming
[a]from the north.
Where is the [b]flock that
was given you,
Your beautiful sheep?
21 "What will you say when He
appoints over you—
And you yourself had
taught them—
Former [a,1]companions
to be head over you?
Will not [b]pangs seize you
Like a woman in childbirth?
22 "If you [a]say in your heart,
'[b]Why have these things
happened to me?'
Because of the [c]magnitude
of your iniquity
[d]Your skirts have
been uncovered
And your heels have
suffered violence.
23 "[a]Can the Ethiopian
change his skin
Or the leopard his spots?
*Then* you also can [b]do good
Who are accustomed
to doing evil.

**13:13** [a]Ps 60:3; 75:8; Is 51:17; 63:6; Jer 25:27; 51:7, 57 **13:14** [a]Is 9:20, 21; Jer 19:9-11 [b]Jer 6:21; Eze 5:10 [c]Dt 29:20; Is 27:11; Jer 16:5; 21:7 **13:15** [a]Pr 16:5; Is 28:14-22 **13:16** [a]Jos 7:19; Ps 96:8 [b]Is 5:30; 8:22; 59:9; Am 5:18; 8:9 [c]Pr 4:19; Jer 23:12 [d]Ps 44:19; 107:10, 14; Jer 2:6 [1]Lit *smite* **13:17** [a]Mal 2:2 [b]Ps 119:136; Jer 9:1; 14:17; Lk 19:41, 42 [c]Ps 80:1; Jer 23:1, 2 **13:18** [a]2Ki 24:12, 15; Jer 22:26 [b]2Chr 33:12, 19 [c]Ex 39:28; Is 3:20; Eze 24:17, 23; 44:18 **13:19** [a]Jer 32:44 [b]Jer 20:4; 52:27-30 **13:20** [a]Jer 1:15; 6:22; Hab 1:6 [b]Jer 13:17; 23:2 **13:21** [a]Jer 2:25; 38:22 [b]Is 13:8; Jer 4:31 [1]Or *chieftains* **13:22** [a]Dt 7:17 [b]Jer 5:19; 16:10 [c]Jer 2:17-19; 9:2-9 [d]Is 47:2; Eze 16:37; Na 3:5 **13:23** [a]Pr 27:22; Is 1:5 [b]Jer 4:22; 9:5

24 “Therefore I will [a]scatter them
like chaff passing away
Into the wilderness [b]wind.
25 “This is your [a]lot, the portion
measured to you
From Me,” declares Yahweh,
“Because you have
[b]forgotten Me
And trusted in lies.
26 “So I Myself have also
[a]stripped your skirts
off over your face,
That your disgrace
may be seen.
27 “As for your [a]adulteries and
your *lustful* neighings,
The [b]lewdness
of your prostitution
On the [c]hills in the field,
I have seen your
detestable things.
Woe to you, O Jerusalem!
[d]How long will you not
cleanse yourself?”

### *Yahweh Will Not Listen to Their Cry*

14 That which came as the word of
Yahweh to Jeremiah in regard to
the [a]drought:
2 “Judah mourns,
And [a]her gates languish;
They sit on the ground
[b]in mourning,
And the [c]outcry
of Jerusalem has gone up.
3 “Their mighty ones have [a]sent
their [1]underlings for water;
They have come
to the [b]trenches and
found no water.
They have returned with
their vessels empty;
They have been [c]put
to shame and dishonored,
And they [d]cover their heads.
4 “Because the [a]ground
is [1]dismayed,
For there has been [b]no
rain on the land,
The [c]farmers have been
put to shame;
They have covered
their heads.
5 “For even the doe in the field
has given birth only
to forsake *her young*
Because there is [a]no grass.
6 “The [a]wild donkeys stand
on the bare heights;
They pant for air like jackals;
Their eyes fail
For there is [b]no vegetation.
7 “Although our [a]iniquities
answer against us,
O Yahweh, act
[b]for Your name’s sake!
Truly our [c]acts of faithlessness
have been many;
We have [d]sinned against You.
8 “O [a]Hope of Israel,
Its [b]Savior in [c]time of distress,
Why are You like a
sojourner in the land
Or like a traveler who
has pitched his *tent*
to lodge for the night?
9 “Why are You like a
man confused,
Like a mighty man who
[a]cannot save?

---

**13:24** [a]Lv 26:33; Jer 9:16; Eze 5:2, 12 [b]Jer 4:11; 18:17 **13:25** [a]Job 20:29; Ps 11:6; Mt 24:51 [b]Ps 9:17; Jer 2:32; 3:21 **13:26** [a]Lam 1:8; Eze 23:29; Hos 2:10 **13:27** [a]Jer 5:7, 8 [b]Jer 11:15 [c]Is 65:7; Jer 2:20; Eze 6:13 [d]Pr 1:22; Hos 8:5 ◆ **14:1** [a]Jer 17:8 **14:2** [a]Is 3:26 [b]Jer 8:21 [c]1Sa 5:12; Jer 11:11; 46:12; Zec 7:13 **14:3** [a]1Ki 18:5 [b]2Ki 18:31; Jer 2:13 [c]Job 6:20; Ps 40:14 [d]2Sa 15:30 [1]Lit *little ones* **14:4** [a]Joel 1:19, 20 [b]Jer 3:3 [c]Joel 1:11 [1]Cracked **14:5** [a]Is 15:6 **14:6** [a]Job 39:5, 6; Jer 2:24 [b]Joel 1:18 **14:7** [a]Is 59:12; Hos 5:5 [b]Ps 25:11; Jer 14:21 [c]Jer 5:6; 8:5 [d]Jer 3:25; 8:14; 14:20 **14:8** [a]Jer 17:13 [b]Is 43:3; 63:8 [c]Ps 9:9; 50:15 **14:9** [a]Nu 11:23; Is 50:2; 59:1

Yet [b]You are in our midst,
O Yahweh,
And we are [c]called
by Your name;
Do not leave us!"

10 Thus says Yahweh to this peo-
ple, "Even so they have [a]loved to
wander; they have not [b]kept their
feet in check. Therefore Yahweh
does [c]not accept them; now He will
[d]remember their iniquity and punish
their sins." 11 So Yahweh said to me,
"[a]Do not pray for the good of this
people. 12 When they fast, I am [a]not
going to listen to their cry; and when
they offer [b]burnt offering and grain
offering, I am not going to accept
them. Rather I am going to [c]make an
end of them by the [d]sword, famine,
and pestilence."

### *Lying Prophets*

13 But, "Ah, Lord Yahweh!" I said,
"Behold, the prophets are saying to
them, 'You [a]will not see the sword
nor will you have famine, but I will
give you true [b]peace in this place.'"
14 Then Yahweh said to me, "The
[a]prophets are prophesying lies in
My name. [b]I have neither sent them
nor commanded them nor spoken to
them; they are prophesying to you
a [c]vision of lies, divination, futility,
and the deception of their own
hearts. 15 Therefore thus says Yahweh
concerning the prophets who are
prophesying in My name, although
it was not I who sent them—yet they
keep saying, 'There will be no sword
or famine in this land'—[a]by that
sword and famine those prophets
shall [1]meet their end! 16 The people
also to whom they are prophesying
will be [a]thrown out into the streets
of Jerusalem because of the famine
and the sword; and there will be no
one to [b]bury them—*neither* them,
*nor* their wives, nor their sons, nor
their daughters—for I will [c]pour out
their *own* evil on them.

17 "And you will say this
word to them,
'[a]Let my eyes flow down
with tears night and day,
And let them not cease,
For the virgin [b]daughter
of my people has
been shattered
with a mighty shattering,
With a sorely [c]sick wound.
18 'If I [a]go out to the field,
Behold, those [1]slain
with the sword!
Or if I enter the city,
Behold, diseases of famine!
For [b]both prophet and priest
Have gone around
as merchants in the land
that they do not know.'"

19 Have You completely
[a]rejected Judah?
Or [1]have You loathed Zion?
Why have You stricken
us so that [b]there is
no healing for us?
*We* [c]hoped for peace,
but there was no good;

**14:9** [b]Ex 29:45; Ps 46:5; Jer 8:19 [c]Is 63:19; Jer 15:16 **14:10** [a]Jer 2:25; 3:13 [b]Ps 119:101 [c]Jer 6:20; Am 5:22 [d]Jer 44:21-23; Hos 8:13; 9:9 **14:11** [a]Ex 32:10; Jer 7:16; 11:14 **14:12** [a]Pr 1:28; Is 1:15; Jer 11:11; Eze 8:18; Mic 3:4; Zec 7:13 [b]Jer 6:20; 7:21 [c]Jer 8:13 [d]Jer 21:9 **14:13** [a]Jer 5:12; 23:17 [b]Jer 6:14; 8:11 **14:14** [a]Jer 5:31; 23:25 [b]Jer 23:21 [c]Jer 23:16, 26; 27:9, 10; Eze 12:24 **14:15** [a]Jer 23:15; Eze 14:10 [1]Lit *be finished* **14:16** [a]Ps 79:2, 3; Jer 7:33; 15:2, 3 [b]Jer 8:1, 2 [c]Pr 1:31; Jer 13:22-25 **14:17** [a]Jer 9:1; 13:17; Lam 1:16 [b]Is 37:22; Jer 8:21; Lam 1:15; 2:13 [c]Jer 10:19; 30:14 **14:18** [a]Jer 6:25; Lam 1:20; Eze 7:15 [b]Jer 6:13; 8:10 [1]Lit *pierced* **14:19** [a]Jer 6:30; 7:29; 12:7; Lam 5:22 [b]Jer 30:13 [c]Job 30:26; Jer 8:15; 1Th 5:3 [1]Lit *has Your soul*

And for a time of healing,
but behold, terror!
20 We [a]know our wickedness,
O Yahweh,
The iniquity of our fathers,
for [b]we have sinned
against You.
21 Do not [1]despise *us*,
[a]for Your own name's sake;
Do not disgrace the
[b]throne of Your glory;
Remember *and* do not break
Your covenant with us.
22 Are there any among
the [a,1]idols of the nations
who [b]give rain?
Or can the heavens
give showers?
Is it not You, O Yahweh
our God?
Therefore we [c,2]hope in You,
For You are the one who has
done all these things.

### *Yahweh Appoints Four Kinds of Doom*

15 Then Yahweh said to me, "Even
[a]though [b]Moses and [c]Samuel
were to [d]stand before Me, My soul
would not be [1]with this people; [e]send
them away from My presence and let
them go! 2 And it will be that when
they say to you, 'Where should we
go?' then you are to tell them, 'Thus
says Yahweh:
"Those *destined* [a]for death,
to death;
And those *destined*
for the sword, to the sword;
And those *destined*
for famine, to famine;
And those *destined*
for captivity, to captivity."'
3 "I will [a]appoint over them four
kinds *of doom*," declares Yahweh:
"the sword to kill, the [b]dogs to drag
off, and the [c]birds of the sky and the
beasts of the earth to devour and
bring to ruin. 4 I will [a]give them over
*to be* an example of terror among all
the kingdoms of the earth because
of [b]Manasseh, the son of Hezekiah,
the king of Judah, for what he did in
Jerusalem.
5 "Indeed, who will [a]spare
you, O Jerusalem,
Or who will [b]console you,
Or who will turn aside to ask
about your well-being?
6 "You who have [a]abandoned
Me," declares Yahweh,
"You keep [b]going backward.
So I will [c]stretch out My
hand against you and
bring you to ruin;
I am [d]tired of [1]relenting!
7 "And I will [a]winnow them
with a winnowing fork
At the gates of the land;
I will [b]bereave *them*
of children; I will make
My people perish;
[c]They did not [1]repent
of their ways.
8 "Their [a]widows will be more
numerous before Me
Than the sand of the seas;

**14:20** [a]Ne 9:2; Ps 32:5; Jer 3:25 [b]Jer 8:14; 14:7; Da 9:8 **14:21** [a]Ps 25:11; Jer 14:7 [b]Jer 3:17; 17:12 [1]Or *spurn* **14:22** [a]Is 41:29; Jer 10:3 [b]1Ki 17:1; Jer 5:24 [c]Lam 3:26 [1]Lit *vanities* [2]Or *wait for*
◆ **15:1** [a]Ps 99:6; Eze 14:14, 20 [b]Ex 32:11-14; Nu 14:13-20; Ps 99:6; 106:23 [c]1Sa 7:9; 12:23 [d]Jer 15:19; 18:20; 35:19 [e]2Ki 17:20; Jer 7:15; 10:18; 52:3 [1]Lit *toward* **15:2** [a]Jer 14:12; 24:10; 43:11; Eze 5:2, 12; Zec 11:9; Rev 13:10 **15:3** [a]Lv 26:16, 22, 25; Eze 14:21 [b]1Ki 21:23, 24 [c]Dt 28:26; Is 18:6; Jer 7:33 **15:4** [a]Lv 26:33; Jer 24:9; 29:18; Eze 23:46 [b]2Ki 21:1-18; 23:26, 27; 24:3, 4; 2Chr 33:1-9 **15:5** [a]Ps 69:20; Is 51:19; Jer 13:14; 21:7 [b]Na 3:7 **15:6** [a]Jer 6:19; 8:9 [b]Is 1:4; Jer 7:24 [c]Jer 6:12; Zep 1:4 [d]Jer 6:11; 7:16 [1]Or *regretting* **15:7** [a]Ps 1:4; Jer 51:2 [b]Jer 18:21; Hos 9:12-16 [c]Is 9:13 [1]Lit *turn back from* **15:8** [a]Is 3:25, 26; 4:1

I will bring against them,
against the mother
of a choice man,
A [b]destroyer at noonday;
I will suddenly bring
down on her
Anguish and terror.
9 "She who [a]bore seven
*sons* languishes;
[1]Her breathing is labored.
Her [b]sun has set
while it was yet day;
She has been [c]shamed
and humiliated.
So I will [d]give over their
survivors to the sword
Before their enemies,"
declares Yahweh.

### *Jeremiah Pleads for Vengeance*

10 [a]Woe to me, my mother,
that you have borne me
*As* a [b]man of strife and a man
of contention to all the land!
I have not [c]lent, nor have
men lent money to me,
*Yet* everyone curses me.
11 Yahweh said, "Surely I
will [a]set you free
for *purposes of* good;
Surely I will cause the [b]enemy
to intercede with you
In a time of disaster and
a time of distress.
12 "*Can anyone smash iron,*
[a]Iron from the north,
or bronze?
13 "Your [a]wealth and
your treasures
I will give for plunder
[b]without cost,
Even for all your sins
And within all your borders.
14 "Then I will cause your
enemies to pass [1]*it* over
Into a [a]land you do
not know,
For a [b]fire has been
kindled in My anger;
It will burn upon you."

15 [a]You who know, O Yahweh,
Remember me,
take notice of me,
And [b]take vengeance
for me on my persecutors.
Do not, in view of Your
patience, take me away;
Know that [c]for Your sake
I endure reproach.
16 Your words were found,
and I [a]ate them,
And Your [b]words became
for me joy and gladness
in my heart,
For I have been [c]called
by Your name,
O Yahweh God of hosts.
17 I [a]did not sit in the circle
of merrymakers,
Nor did I exult.
Because of Your hand
*upon me* I sat [b]alone,
For You [c]filled me
with indignation.
18 Why has my pain
been perpetual
And my [a]wound incurable,
refusing to be healed?

**15:8** [b]Jer 22:7 **15:9** [a]1Sa 2:5; Is 47:9 [b]Jer 6:4; Am 8:9 [c]Jer 50:12 [d]Jer 21:7 [1]Or *She has breathed out her soul* **15:10** [a]Job 3:1, 3; Jer 20:14 [b]Jer 1:18, 19; 15:20; 20:7, 8 [c]Ex 22:25; Lv 25:36, 37; Dt 23:19 **15:11** [a]Ps 138:3; Is 41:10 [b]Jer 21:2; 37:3; 38:14; 42:2 **15:12** [a]Jer 28:14 **15:13** [a]Jer 17:3; 20:5 [b]Ps 44:12; Is 52:3 **15:14** [a]Dt 28:36, 64; Jer 16:13 [b]Dt 32:22; Ps 21:9; Jer 17:4 [1]Your possessions **15:15** [a]Jer 12:3 [b]Jer 11:20 [c]Ps 44:22; 69:7-9; Jer 20:8 **15:16** [a]Eze 3:3 [b]Job 23:12; Ps 119:103 [c]Jer 14:9 **15:17** [a]Ps 1:1; Jer 16:8; 2Co 6:17 [b]Ps 102:7; Jer 13:17; Lam 3:28; Eze 3:24, 25 [c]Jer 6:11 **15:18** [a]Job 34:6; Jer 30:12, 15; Mic 1:9

Will You indeed be to me
[b]like a deceptive *stream*
With water that is unreliable?

### *Yahweh's Answer*

19 Therefore thus says Yahweh,
"[a]If you return, then I will
cause you to return—
[b]Before Me you will stand;
And [c]if you extract the
precious from the worthless,
You will become
[1]My mouthpiece.
They for their part
may turn to you,
But as for you, you must
not turn to them.
20 "Then I will [a]make you
to this people
A fortified wall of bronze;
And they will fight
against you,
But they will not prevail
against you,
For [b]I am with you to save you
And deliver you,"
declares Yahweh.
21 "So I will [a]deliver you from
the hand of the evil ones,
And I will [b]redeem you
from the [1]grasp
of the ruthless ones."

### *Yahweh Withdraws His Favor*

16 The word of Yahweh also came
to me saying, 2 "You shall not
take a wife for yourself nor have sons
or daughters in this place." 3 For thus
says Yahweh concerning the sons
and daughters born in this place and
concerning their [a]mothers who bear
them and their [b]fathers who beget
them in this land: 4 "They will [a]die
of deadly diseases; they [b]will not be
lamented or buried; they will be as
[c]dung on the surface of the ground
and come to an end by sword and
famine, and their carcasses will be-
come food for the [d]birds of the sky
and for the beasts of the earth."
5 For thus says Yahweh, "Do not
enter the house of the [a]funeral meal,
or go to lament or to console them;
for I have [b]withdrawn My peace from
this people," declares Yahweh, "*My*
[c]lovingkindness and compassion.
6 Both [a]great men and small will die
in this land; they will not be buried;
they will not be lamented, nor will
anyone [b]gash himself or [c]shave
his head for them. 7 Men will not
[a]break *bread* in mourning for them,
to comfort anyone for the dead, nor
give them a cup of comforting to
drink for anyone's father or mother.
8 Moreover you shall [a]not go into a
house of feasting to sit with them to
eat and drink." 9 For thus says Yahweh
of hosts, the God of Israel: "Behold,
I am going to [a]cause to cease from
this place, before your eyes and in
your days, the voice of rejoicing and
the voice of gladness, the voice of
the groom and the voice of the bride.
10 "Now when you tell this people
all these words, they will say to you,
'[a]For what reason has Yahweh de-
clared all this great calamity against

---

**15:18** [b]Job 6:15, 20; Jer 14:3 **15:19** [a]Jer 4:1; Zec 3:7 [b]1Ki 17:1; Jer 15:1; 35:19 [c]Jer 6:29; Eze 22:26; 44:23 [1]Lit *as My mouth* **15:20** [a]Jer 1:18, 19; Eze 3:9 [b]Ps 46:7; Is 41:10; Jer 1:8, 19; 15:15; 20:11 **15:21** [a]Ps 37:40; Is 49:25; Jer 20:13; 39:11, 12 [b]Ge 48:16; Is 49:26; 60:16; Jer 31:11; 50:34 [1]Lit *palm* ◆**16:3** [a]Jer 15:8 [b]Jer 6:21 **16:4** [a]Jer 15:2 [b]Jer 25:33 [c]Ps 83:10; Jer 9:22; 25:33 [d]Ps 79:2; Is 18:6; Jer 15:3; 34:20 **16:5** [a]Eze 24:16-23 [b]Jer 12:12; 15:1-4 [c]Ps 25:6; Is 27:11; Jer 13:14 **16:6** [a]2Chr 36:17; Eze 9:6 [b]Dt 14:1; Jer 41:5; 47:5 [c]Is 22:12 **16:7** [a]Dt 26:14; Eze 24:17; Hos 9:4 **16:8** [a]Ecc 7:2-4; Is 22:12-14; Jer 15:17; Am 6:4-6 **16:9** [a]Jer 7:34; 25:10; Eze 26:13; Hos 2:11; Rev 18:23 **16:10** [a]Dt 29:24; 1Ki 9:8; Jer 5:19; 13:22; 22:8

us? And what is our iniquity, or what
is our sin which we have committed
against Yahweh our God?' **11** Then
you are to say to them, '*It is* [a]because
your fathers have forsaken Me,'
declares Yahweh, 'and have walked
after [b]other gods and served them
and worshiped them; but Me they
have forsaken and have not kept My
law. **12** You too have done evil, *even*
[a]more than your fathers; for behold,
you are each one walking according
to the [b]stubbornness of his own
[c]evil heart, without listening to Me.
**13** So I will [a]hurl you out of this land
into the [b]land which you have not
known, neither you nor your fathers;
and there you will [c]serve other gods
day and night, for I will grant you no
favor.'

### *They Shall Know My Name Is Yahweh*

**14** "[a]Therefore behold, days are com-
ing," declares Yahweh, "when it will
no longer be said, 'As Yahweh lives,
who [b]brought up the sons of Israel
out of the land of Egypt,' **15** but, 'As
Yahweh lives, who brought up the
sons of Israel from the [a]land of the
north and from all the lands where
He had banished them.' For I will
return them to their own land which
I gave to their fathers.

**16** "Behold, I am going to send for
many [a]fishermen," declares Yah-
weh, "and they will fish for them;
and afterwards I will send for many
hunters, and they will [b]hunt them
[c]from every mountain and every
hill and from the crevices of the
rocks. **17** [a]For My eyes are on all
their ways; they are not hidden
from My face, [b]nor is their iniquity
concealed from My eyes. **18** I will
first [a]doubly repay their iniquity
and their sin because they have
[b]profaned My land; they have filled
My inheritance with the carcasses
of their [c]detestable idols and with
their abominations."

**19** O Yahweh, my [a]strength
and my strong defense,
And my [b]refuge in
the day of distress,
To You the [c]nations
will come
From the ends of the earth
and say,
"Our fathers have inherited
nothing but [d]lies,
Futility and [e,1]things
of no profit."

**20** Can man make gods
for himself?
Yet they are [a]not gods!

**21** "Therefore behold, I am going
to make them know—
This time I will [a]make
them know
My [1]power and My might;
And they shall [b]know that
My name is Yahweh."

**16:11** [a]Dt 29:25; 1Ki 9:9; 2Chr 7:22; Ne 9:26-29; Jer 22:9 [b]Dt 29:26; 1Ki 9:9; Ps 106:35-41; Jer 5:7-9; 8:2; Eze 11:21; 1Pe 4:3 **16:12** [a]Jer 7:26 [b]1Sa 15:23; Jer 7:24; 9:14; 13:10 [c]Ecc 9:3; Mk 7:21 **16:13** [a]Dt 4:26, 27; 2Chr 7:20; Jer 15:1 [b]Jer 15:14; 17:4 [c]Dt 4:28; 28:36; Jer 5:19 **16:14** [a]Is 43:18; Jer 23:7 [b]Ex 20:2; Dt 15:15 **16:15** [a]Ps 106:47; Is 11:11-16; 14:1; Jer 3:18; 23:8; 24:6 **16:16** [a]Am 4:2; Hab 1:14, 15 [b]1Sa 26:20; Mic 7:2 [c]Is 2:21; Am 9:3 **16:17** [a]2Chr 16:9; Job 34:21; Ps 90:8; Pr 5:21; 15:3; Jer 23:24; 32:19; Zec 4:10; Lk 12:2; 1Co 4:5; Heb 4:13 [b]Jer 2:22 **16:18** [a]Jer 17:18; Rev 18:6 [b]Nu 35:33, 34; Jer 2:7; 3:9 [c]Jer 7:30; Eze 11:18, 21 **16:19** [a]Ps 18:1, 2; Is 25:4 [b]Na 1:7 [c]Ps 22:27; Is 2:2; Jer 3:17; 4:2 [d]Is 44:20; Hab 2:18 [e]Is 44:10 [1]Lit *there is nothing profitable in them* **16:20** [a]Ps 115:4-8; Is 37:19; Jer 2:11; 5:7; Hos 8:4-6; Ga 4:8 **16:21** [a]Ps 9:16 [b]Ps 83:18; Is 43:3; Jer 33:2; Am 5:8 [1]Lit *hand*

### *The Deceitful Heart*

17 The [a]sin of Judah is written
down with an [b]iron stylus;
With a diamond point
it is [c]engraved upon
the tablet of their heart
And on the horns
of [1]their altars,
2 As they remember
their [a]children,
So they *remember* their altars
and their [b,1]Asherim
By [c]green trees
on the high hills.
3 O [a]mountain of Mine
in the countryside,
I will [b]give over your wealth and
all your treasures for plunder,
Your high places for sin
throughout your borders.
4 And you will, even of yourself,
[a]let go of your inheritance
That I gave you;
And I will make you
serve your [b]enemies
In the [c]land which you
do not know,
For you have [d]kindled
a fire in My anger
Which will burn forever.

5 Thus says Yahweh,
"[a]Cursed is the man who
trusts in mankind
And makes [b]flesh his [1]strength,
And whose heart turns
away from Yahweh.
6 "And he will be like a
[a]juniper in the desert
And will not see when
prosperity comes,
But will dwell in stony
wastes in the wilderness,
A [b]land of salt
[1]*which is* not inhabited.
7 "[a]Blessed is the man who
trusts in Yahweh
And whose [b]trust is Yahweh.
8 "And he will be like a [a]tree
planted by the water,
That sends forth its
roots by a stream
And will not fear
when the heat comes;
But its leaves will be green,
And it will not be anxious
in a year of [b]drought
Nor refrain
from yielding fruit.

9 "The [a]heart is more
[b]deceitful than all else
And is [1]desperately [c]sick;
Who can know it?
10 "I, Yahweh, [a]search the heart;
I test the [1]inmost being,
Even [b]to give to each man
according to his ways,
According to the fruit
of his deeds.
11 "*As* a partridge that hatches
eggs which it has not laid,
*So* is he who [a]makes a
fortune, but unjustly;

◆ **17:1** [a]Jer 2:22; 4:14 [b]Job 19:24 [c]Pr 3:3; 7:3; Is 49:16; 2Co 3:3 [1]As in ancient versions; M.T. *your*
**17:2** [a]Jer 7:18 [b]Ex 34:13; 2Chr 24:18; 33:3; Is 17:8 [c]Jer 3:6 [1]Wooden symbols of a female deity
**17:3** [a]*Jer 26:18; Mic 3:12* [b]2Ki 24:13; Is 39:4-6; Jer 15:13; 20:5 **17:4** [a]Jer 12:7; Lam 5:2 [b]Dt 28:48; Is 14:3; Jer 15:14; 27:12, 13 [c]Jer 16:13 [d]Is 5:25; Jer 7:20; 15:14 **17:5** [a]Ps 146:3; Is 2:22; 30:1; Eze 29:7 [b]2Chr 32:8; Is 31:3 [1]Lit *arm* **17:6** [a]Jer 48:6 [b]Dt 29:23; Job 39:6 [1]Lit *and is not inhabited* **17:7** [a]Ps 2:12; 34:8; 84:12; Pr 16:20 [b]Ps 40:4 **17:8** [a]Ps 1:3; 92:12-14; Eze 31:3-9 [b]Jer 14:1-6 **17:9** [a]Ecc 9:3; Mk 7:21, 22 [b]Ro 7:11; Eph 4:22 [c]Is 1:5, 6; 6:10; Mt 13:15; Mk 2:17; Ro 1:21 [1]Or *incurably* **17:10** [a]1Sa 16:7; 1Chr 28:9; Ps 139:23; Pr 17:3; Jer 11:20; 20:12; Ro 8:27; Rev 2:23 [b]Ps 62:12; Jer 32:19; Ro 2:6 [1]Lit *kidneys*
**17:11** [a]Jer 6:13; 8:10; 22:13, 17

In the midst of his days
it will forsake him,
And in [1]the end he will
be a [b]wicked fool."

12 [a]A glorious throne on high
from the beginning
Is the place of our sanctuary.
13 O Yahweh, the [a]hope of Israel,
All who [b]forsake You will
be put to shame.
Those who turn [1]away on
earth will be [c]written down
Because they have forsaken
the fountain of living
water, even Yahweh.
14 [a]Heal me, O Yahweh,
and I will be healed;
[b]Save me and I will be saved,
For You are my [c]praise.
15 Behold, they keep
[a]saying to me,
"Where is the word of Yahweh?
Let it come now!"
16 But as for me, I have not
hurried away from *being*
a shepherd after You,
Nor have I longed
for the [1]sickening day;
[a]You Yourself know that
the utterance of my lips
Was in Your presence.
17 Do not be a [a]terror to me;
You are my [b]refuge
in the day of calamity.
18 Let those who pursue me be
[a]put to shame, but as for me,
[b]let me not be put to shame;
Let them be dismayed,
but let me not be dismayed.
[c]Bring on them a day
of calamity,
And [1]crush them with
twofold [2]crushing!

### *Keep the Sabbath Day Holy*

19 Thus Yahweh said to me, "Go and
stand in the [1]public gate, through
which the kings of Judah come in
and go out, as well as in all the gates
of Jerusalem, 20 and say to them,
'[a]Listen to the word of Yahweh,
[b]kings of Judah and all Judah and all
inhabitants of Jerusalem who come
in through these gates: 21 Thus says
Yahweh, "[a]Take care of yourselves,
and [b]do not carry any load on the
sabbath day or bring anything in
through the gates of Jerusalem.
22 You shall not bring a load out of
your houses on the sabbath day [a]nor
do any work, but keep the sabbath
day holy, as I [b]commanded your
fathers. 23 Yet they [a]did not listen or
incline their ears, but [b]stiffened their
necks in order not to listen or receive
discipline.

24 "But it will be, if you [a]listen
carefully to Me," declares Yahweh,
"to [b]bring no load in through the
gates of this city on the sabbath day,
[c]but to keep the sabbath day holy by
doing no work on it, 25 [a]then there
will come in through the gates of
this city kings and princes [b,1]sitting
on the throne of David, riding in

**17:11** [b]Lk 12:20 [1]Lit *his* **17:12** [a]Jer 3:17; 14:21 **17:13** [a]Jer 14:8; 50:7 [b]Is 1:28 [c]Lk 10:20 [1]Lit *away from Me* **17:14** [a]Jer 30:17; 33:6 [b]Ps 54:1; 60:5 [c]Dt 10:21; Ps 109:1 **17:15** [a]Is 5:19; 2Pe 3:4 **17:16** [a]Jer 12:3 [1]Or *incurable* **17:17** [a]Ps 88:15 [b]Jer 16:19; Na 1:7 **17:18** [a]Ps 35:4, 26; Jer 17:13; 20:11 [b]Jer 1:17 [c]Ps 35:8 [1]Lit *break* [2]Lit *breaking, destruction* **17:19** [1]Lit *gate of the sons of the people* **17:20** [a]Eze 2:7 [b]Ps 49:1, 2; Jer 19:3, 4 **17:21** [a]Dt 4:9, 15, 23; Mk 4:24 [b]Nu 15:32-36; Ne 13:15-21; Jn 5:9-12 **17:22** [a]Ex 16:23-29; 20:8-10; Dt 5:12-14; Is 56:2-6; 58:13 [b]Ex 31:13-17; Eze 20:12; Zec 1:4 **17:23** [a]Jer 7:24, 28; 11:10 [b]Pr 29:1; Jer 7:26; 19:15 **17:24** [a]Ex 15:26; Dt 11:13; Is 21:7; 55:2 [b]Jer 17:21, 22 [c]Ex 20:8-11; Eze 20:20 **17:25** [a]Jer 22:4 [b]2Sa 7:16; Is 9:7; Jer 33:15, 17, 21; Lk 1:32 [1]Or *inhabiting*, cf. 17:25b

chariots and on horses, they and
their princes, the men of Judah and
the inhabitants of Jerusalem, and this
[c]city will be inhabited forever. **26** And
they will come in from the [a]cities of
Judah and from all around Jerusalem,
from the land of Benjamin, from the
[b,1]Shephelah, from the hill country,
and from the [c]Negev, bringing burnt
offerings, sacrifices, grain offerings,
and frankincense, and bringing sac-
rifices of thanksgiving to the house
of Yahweh. **27** But [a]if you do not listen
to Me to keep the sabbath day holy
by not carrying a load and coming
in through the gates of Jerusalem on
the sabbath day, then [b]I will kindle
a fire in its gates, and it will [c]devour
the palaces of Jerusalem and [d]not be
quenched."'"

### *The Potter and the Clay*

**18** The word which came to Jer-
emiah from Yahweh saying,
**2** "Arise and [a]go down to the potter's
house, and there I will make you hear
My words." **3** Then I went down to the
potter's house, and behold, he was
making something on the [1]wheel.
**4** But the vessel that he was making
of clay was ruined in the hand of
the potter, so he turned around and
made it into another vessel, accord-
ing to what was right in the eyes of
the potter to make.
**5** Then the word of Yahweh came
to me saying, **6** "Can I not, O house
of Israel, deal with you as this potter
*does*?" declares Yahweh. "Behold,
like the [a]clay in the potter's hand,
so are you in My hand, O house of Is-
rael. **7** At one moment I might speak
concerning a nation or concerning
a kingdom to [a]uproot, to tear down,
or to make *it* perish; **8** [a]but if that
nation against which I have spoken
turns from its evil, I will [b,1]relent
concerning the calamity I planned to
do against it. **9** Or at another moment
I might speak concerning a nation or
concerning a kingdom to [a]build up
or to plant *it*; **10** but if it does [a]evil
in My sight by not listening to My
voice, then I will [b,1]relent concerning
the good which I promised, to do
good to it. **11** So now then, speak to
the men of Judah and against the
inhabitants of Jerusalem saying,
'Thus says Yahweh, "Behold, I am
[a]forming calamity against you and
devising a plan against you. Oh [b]turn
back, each of you from his evil way,
and do good in your ways and your
deeds."' **12** But [a]they will say, 'It's
hopeless! For we are going to follow
our own plans, and each of us will
act according to the [b]stubbornness
of his evil heart.'

**13** "Therefore thus says Yahweh,
'[a]Ask now among the nations,
Who ever heard the like
of [1]this?
The [b]virgin of Israel
Has done a most
[c]appalling thing.
**14** 'Does the snow of Lebanon
forsake the rock
of the open country?

---

**17:25** [c]Ps 132:13, 14; Heb 12:22 **17:26** [a]Jer 32:44; 33:13 [b]Zec 7:7 [c]Ps 107:22; Jer 33:11 [1]Or *lowland*
**17:27** [a]Is 1:20; Jer 22:5; 26:4; Zec 7:11-14 [b]Lam 4:11 [c]2Ki 25:9; Jer 39:8; Am 2:5 [d]Jer 7:20; Eze 20:47
◆ **18:2** [a]Jer 19:1, 2 **18:3** [1]Lit *pair of stone discs* **18:6** [a]Is 45:9; 64:8; Mt 20:15; Ro 9:21 **18:7** [a]Jer 1:10
**18:8** [a]Jer 7:3-7; 12:16; Eze 18:21 [b]Ps 106:45; Jer 26:3, 13, 19; Hos 11:8; Joel 2:13, 14; Jon 3:10 [1]Or *regret*, cf.
1Sa 15:11, 29, 3 **18:9** [a]Jer 1:10; 31:28; Am 9:11-15 **18:10** [a]Ps 125:5; Jer 7:24-28; Eze 33:18 [b]1Sa 2:30; 13:13
[1]Lit *regret* **18:11** [a]Is 5:5; Jer 4:6; 11:11 [b]2Ki 17:13; Is 1:16-19; Jer 4:1; Ac 26:20 **18:12** [a]Is 57:10; Jer 2:25
[b]Dt 29:19; Jer 7:24; 16:12 **18:13** [a]Is 66:8; Jer 2:10, 11 [b]Jer 14:17; 31:4 [c]Jer 5:30; 23:14; Hos 6:10 [1]Lit *these*

Or is the cold flowing
water *from* a strange
*land* ever uprooted?
15 'For [a]My people have
forgotten Me;
[b]They burn incense [1]to
worthless gods,
And they [2]have stumbled
[3]from their ways,
[3]From the [c]ancient paths,
To walk in bypaths,
Not on a [d]highway,
16 To make their land an
[a]object of horror,
*An object of* perpetual [b]hissing;
Everyone who passes
by it will be [1]horrified
And [c]shake his head.
17 'Like an [a]east wind I
will [b]scatter them
Before the enemy;
I will [1]show them [c]My
back and not *My* face
[d]In the day of their disaster.'"

18 Then they said, "Come and let
us [a]devise plans against Jeremiah.
Surely the [b]law is not going to perish
from the priest, nor [c]counsel to the
wise man, nor the *divine* [d]word to the
prophet! Come on and let us [e]strike
at him with *our* tongue, and let us
[f]give no heed to any of his words."

19 Do give heed to me, O Yahweh,
And listen to the voice of those
who contend against me!
20 [a]*Should* good be
repaid with evil?
For they have [b]dug
a pit for [1]me.
Remember how I
[c]stood before You
To speak good on their behalf,
So as to turn away Your
wrath from them.
21 Therefore, [a]give their
children over to famine
And deliver them up
to the [1]power of the sword;
And let their wives become
[b]childless and [c]widowed.
Let their men also be
[2]smitten to death,
Their [d]young men struck
down by the sword
in battle.
22 May an [a]outcry be heard
from their houses,
When You suddenly bring
raiders upon them;
[b]For they have dug a pit
to capture me
And [c]hidden snares
for my feet.
23 Yet You, O Yahweh, know
All their [1]deadly counsel
against me;
[a]Do not atone
for their iniquity
Or blot out their sin
from before You.
But may they be [b,2]overthrown
before You;
Deal with them in the [c]time
of Your anger!

---

**18:15** [a]Jer 2:32; 3:21 [b]Is 65:7; Jer 7:9; 10:15; 44:17 [c]Jer 6:16 [d]Is 57:14; 62:10 [1]Lit *to worthlessness* [2]As in ancient versions; Heb *caused them to* [3]Or *in* **18:16** [a]Jer 25:9; 49:13; 50:13; Eze 33:28, 29 [b]1Ki 9:8; Lam 2:15; Mic 6:16 [c]Ps 22:7; Is 37:22; Jer 48:27 [1]Or *desolate*, cf. Lv 26:32 **18:17** [a]Ps 48:7 [b]Job 27:21; Jer 13:24 [c]Jer 2:27; 32:33 [d]Jer 46:21 [1]As in ancient versions; M.T. *look them in the back and not in the face* **18:18** [a]Jer 11:19; 18:11 [b]Jer 2:8; Mal 2:7 [c]Job 5:13; Jer 8:8 [d]Jer 5:13 [e]Ps 52:2; Jer 20:10 [f]Jer 43:2 **18:20** [a]Ps 109:4 [b]Ps 35:7; 57:6; Jer 5:26; 18:22 [c]Ps 106:23 [1]Lit *my soul* **18:21** [a]Ps 109:9-20; Jer 11:22; 14:16 [b]1Sa 15:33; Is 13:18 [c]Jer 15:8; Eze 22:25 [d]Jer 9:21; 11:22 [1]Lit *hands of* [2]Lit *killed* **18:22** [a]Jer 6:26; 25:34, 36 [b]Jer 18:20 [c]Ps 140:5 **18:23** [a]Ne 4:5; Ps 109:14; Is 2:9 [b]Jer 6:15, 21 [c]Jer 7:20; 17:4 [1]Lit *unto death* [2]Lit *ones made to stumble*

### *The Broken Jar*

**19** Thus says Yahweh, "Go and
buy a [a]potter's earthenware
[b]jar, and *take* some of the [c]elders of
the people and some of the [d]elders
of the priests. **2** Then go out to the
[a]valley of Ben-hinnom, which is by
the entrance of the potsherd gate,
and there [b]call out the words that
I tell you **3** and say, 'Hear the word
of Yahweh, O [a]kings of Judah and
inhabitants of Jerusalem: thus says
Yahweh of hosts, the God of Israel,
"Behold, I am about to bring a [b]ca-
lamity upon this place, at which the
[c]ears of everyone that hears of it will
tingle. **4** Because they have [a]forsaken
Me and have [b]made this a foreign
place and have burned incense in it
to [c]other gods, that neither they nor
their fathers nor the kings of Judah
had *ever* known, and *because* they
have filled this place with the [d]blood
of the innocent **5** and have built the
[a]high places of Baal to burn their
[b]sons in the fire as burnt offerings
to Baal, a thing which I never com-
manded or spoke of, nor did it *ever*
come upon My heart, **6** therefore,
behold, [a]days are coming," declares
Yahweh, "when this place will no lon-
ger be called [b]Topheth or [c]the valley
of Ben-hinnom, but rather the valley
of Slaughter. **7** I will [a]empty out the
counsel of Judah and Jerusalem to *the*
*point of* destruction in this place, and
[b]I will cause them to fall by the sword
before their enemies and by the hand
of those who seek their life; and I will
give over their [c]carcasses as food for
the birds of the sky and the beasts of
the earth. **8** I will also make this city
an [a]object of horror and of hissing;
[b]everyone who passes by it will be
[1]horrified and hiss because of all its
[2]slaughtering. **9** I will make them [a]eat
the flesh of their sons and the flesh
of their daughters, and they will eat
one another's flesh in the siege and in
the distress with which their enemies
and those who seek their life will
distress them."'

**10** "Then you are to break the [a]jar
in the sight of the men who accompa-
ny you, **11** and you shall say to them,
'Thus says Yahweh of hosts, "Just so
will I [a]break this people and this city,
even as one breaks a potter's vessel,
which cannot again be repaired; and
they will [b]bury in Topheth [1]because
there is no *other* place for burial.
**12** This is what I will do to this place
and its inhabitants," declares Yahweh,
"so as to make this city like Topheth.
**13** And the [a]houses of Jerusalem and
the houses of the kings of Judah will
be [b]defiled like the place Topheth
because of all the [c]houses on whose
rooftops they burned incense to [d]all
the heavenly host and [e]poured out
drink offerings to other gods."'"

**14** Then Jeremiah came from
Topheth, where Yahweh had sent
him to prophesy; and he stood in

---

◆**19:1** [a]Jer 18:2 [b]Jer 19:10 [c]Nu 11:16 [d]2Ki 19:2; Eze 8:11 **19:2** [a]Jos 15:8; 2Ki 23:10; Jer 7:31, 32; 32:35 [b]Pr 1:20 **19:3** [a]Jer 17:20 [b]Jer 6:19; 19:15 [c]1Sa 3:11 **19:4** [a]Dt 28:20; Is 65:11; Jer 2:13, 17, 19; 17:13 [b]Eze 7:22; Da 11:31 [c]Jer 7:9; 11:13 [d]2Ki 21:6, 16; Jer 2:34; 7:6 **19:5** [a]Nu 22:41; Jer 32:35 [b]Lv 18:21; 2Ki 17:17; Ps 106:37, 38 **19:6** [a]Jer 7:32 [b]Is 30:33 [c]Jos 15:8 **19:7** [a]Ps 33:10, 11; Is 28:17, 18; Jer 8:8, 9 [b]Lv 26:17; Dt 28:25; Jer 15:2, 9 [c]Ps 79:2; Jer 16:4 **19:8** [a]Jer 18:16; 49:13; 50:13 [b]1Ki 9:8; 2Chr 7:21 [1]Or *desolate*, cf. Lv 26:32 [2]Lit *striking* **19:9** [a]Lv 26:29; Dt 28:53, 55; Is 9:20; Lam 4:10; Eze 5:10 **19:10** [a]Jer 19:1 **19:11** [a]Ps 2:9; Is 30:14; Lam 4:2; Rev 2:27 [b]Jer 7:32 [1]Or *until there is no place* left *to bury* **19:13** [a]Jer 52:13 [b]2Ki 23:10; Ps 74:7; 79:1; Eze 7:21, 22 [c]Jer 32:29; Zep 1:5 [d]Dt 4:19; 2Ki 17:16; Jer 8:2 [e]Jer 7:18; 44:18; Eze 20:28

the [a]court of the house of Yahweh
and said to all the people: **15** "Thus
says Yahweh of hosts, the God of
Israel, 'Behold, I am about to bring on
this city and all its towns the entire
calamity that I have spoken against
it because they have [a]stiffened their
necks so [b]as not to hear My words.'"

### *Yahweh Speaks Against Pashhur*

**20** Then Pashhur the priest,
the son of [a]Immer, who was
[b]ruling overseer in the house of
Yahweh, heard Jeremiah prophesy-
ing these words; **2** and Pashhur had
Jeremiah the prophet [a]struck and put
him in the [b]stocks that were at the
upper [c]Benjamin Gate, which was by
the house of Yahweh. **3** Now it hap-
pened that on the next day, Pashhur
released Jeremiah from the stocks.
And Jeremiah said to him, "Pashhur
is not the name Yahweh has [a]called
you, but rather [b,1]Magor-missabib.
**4** For thus says Yahweh, 'Behold, I
am going to make you a [a]terror to
yourself and to all your friends; and
while [b]your eyes look on, they will
fall by the sword of their enemies.
So I will [c]give over all Judah to the
hand of the king of Babylon, and he
will take them away into [d]exile to
Babylon and will strike them down
with the sword. **5** I will also give over
all the [a]*wealth of this city, all the*
fruit of its labor, and all its precious
things; even all the treasures of the
kings of Judah I will give over to the
[b]hand of their enemies, and they will
plunder them, take them away, and
bring them to Babylon. **6** And you,
[a]Pashhur, and all who live in your
house will go into captivity; and you
will enter Babylon, and there you will
die, and there you will be buried, you
and all your [b]friends to whom you
have [c]prophesied lies.'"

### *Jeremiah Curses the Day He Was Born*

**7** O Yahweh, You have enticed
me, and I was enticed;
You were [a]stronger than
I, and You prevailed.
I have become
a [b]laughingstock all
day long;
Everyone [c]mocks me.
**8** For each time I speak,
I cry aloud;
I [a]call out violence
and devastation
Because for me the [b]word
of Yahweh has [1]resulted
In reproach and derision
all day long.
**9** But if I say, "I will not
[a]remember Him
Or speak anymore
in His name,"
Then in [b]my heart it becomes
like a burning fire
Shut up in my bones;
And I am weary
of holding *it* in,
And [c]I cannot prevail.

---

**19:14** [a]2Chr 20:5; Jer 26:2 **19:15** [a]Ne 9:17, 29; Jer 7:26; 17:23 [b]Ps 58:4 ◆ **20:1** [a]1Chr 24:14; Ezr 2:37, 38 [b]2Ki 25:18 **20:2** [a]1Ki 22:27; 2Chr 16:10; 24:21; Jer 1:19; Am 7:10-13 [b]Job 13:27; 33:11 [c]Jer 37:13; 38:7; Zec 14:10 **20:3** [a]Is 8:3; Hos 1:4, 9 [b]Jer 6:25; 20:10 [1]Lit *terror on every side* **20:4** [a]Job 18:11-21; Jer 6:25; 46:5; Eze 26:21 [b]Jer 29:21; 39:6, 7 [c]Jer 21:4-10; 25:9 [d]Jer 13:10; 52:27 **20:5** [a]Jer 15:13; 17:3 [b]2Ki 20:17, 18; 2Chr 36:10; Jer 27:21, 22 **20:6** [a]Jer 20:1 [b]Jer 20:4; 29:21 [c]Jer 14:14, 15; Lam 2:14 **20:7** [a]Eze 3:14 [b]Job 12:4; Lam 3:14 [c]Ps 22:7; Jer 38:19 **20:8** [a]Jer 6:7 [b]2Chr 36:16; Jer 6:10 [1]Lit *become* **20:9** [a]1Ki 19:3, 4; Jon 1:2, 3 [b]Job 32:18-20; Ps 39:3; Jer 4:19; 23:9; Eze 3:14; Ac 4:20 [c]Job 32:18-20

10 For [a]I have heard the bad
report of many,
“[b]Terror on every side!
[c]Denounce *him*; yes,
let us denounce him!”
[1]All my [d]trusted friends,
Keeping watch for my fall, say:
“Perhaps he will be
[2]deceived, so that we may
[e]prevail against him
And take our revenge on him.”
11 But [a]Yahweh is with me like
a ruthless mighty one;
Therefore my [b]persecutors
will stumble and not prevail.
They will be utterly
ashamed, because they
have not prospered,
With an [c]everlasting dishonor
that will not be forgotten.
12 Yet, O Yahweh of hosts,
You who [a]test the righteous,
Who see the [1]mind
and the heart;
Let me [b]see Your
vengeance on them,
For [c]to You I have
revealed my cause.
13 [a]Sing to Yahweh, praise Yahweh!
For He has [b]delivered the soul
of the needy one
From the hand of evildoers.

14 Cursed be the [a]day
when I was born;
Let the day not be blessed
when my mother bore me!
15 Cursed be the man who
brought the good news
To my father, saying,
“A [a,1]baby boy has been
born to you!”
*And* made him very glad.
16 But let that man be
like the cities
Which Yahweh [a]overthrew
without [1]relenting,
And let him hear an
[b]outcry in the morning
And a [2]shout of war at noon,
17 Because he did not [a]put me
to death from the womb,
So that my mother would
have been my grave,
And her womb ever pregnant.
18 Why did I ever come
forth from the womb
To [a]look on trouble
and sorrow,
So that my [b]days have
been spent in [c]shame?

### *Jeremiah’s Message for Zedekiah*

21 The word which came to Jeremiah from Yahweh when [a]King
Zedekiah sent to him [b]Pashhur, the
son of Malchijah, and [c]Zephaniah
the priest, the son of Maaseiah,
saying, 2 “Please [a]inquire of Yahweh
on our behalf, for [b,1]Nebuchadnezzar
king of [c]Babylon is warring against
us; perhaps Yahweh will deal with us
[d]according to all His [2]wonderful acts,
so that *the enemy* will go up from us.”

**20:10** [a]Ps 31:13 [b]Jer 6:25 [c]Ne 6:6-13; Is 29:21; Jer 18:18 [d]Ps 41:9 [e]1Ki 19:2 [1]Lit *Every man of my peace* [2]*Or persuaded* **20:11** [a]Jer 1:8; 15:20; Ro 8:31 [b]Dt 32:35, 36; Jer 15:15, 20; 17:18 [c]Jer 23:40
**20:12** [a]Ps 7:9; 11:5; 17:3; 139:23; Jer 11:20; 17:10 [b]Ps 54:7; 59:10; Jer 11:20 [c]Ps 62:8 [1]Lit kidneys
**20:13** [a]Jer 31:7 [b]Ps 34:6; 69:33; Jer 15:21 **20:14** [a]Job 3:3-6; Jer 15:10 **20:15** [a]Ge 21:6, 7 [1]Lit *male child* **20:16** [a]Ge 19:25 [b]Jer 18:22; 48:3, 4 [1]Or *regret* [2]Or *trumpet blast* **20:17** [a]Job 3:10, 11, 16; 10:18, 19
**20:18** [a]Job 3:20; 5:7; 14:1; Jer 15:10; Lam 3:1 [b]Ps 90:9; 102:3 [c]Ps 69:19; Jer 3:25; 1Co 4:9-13
◆ **21:1** [a]2Ki 24:17, 18; Jer 32:1-3; 37:1; 52:1-3 [b]1Chr 9:12; Jer 38:1 [c]2Ki 25:18; Jer 29:25, 29; 37:3; 52:24
**21:2** [a]Ex 9:28; Jer 37:3, 17; Eze 14:7; 20:1-3 [b]2Ki 25:1 [c]Ge 10:10; 2Ki 17:24 [d]Ps 44:1-3; Jer 32:17 [1]Heb *Nebuchadrezzar*, a variant spelling of Nebuchadnezzar in Jer and Ezek [2]Or *miracles*

3 Then Jeremiah said to them,
"Thus you shall say to Zedekiah,
4 'Thus says Yahweh, the God of
Israel, "Behold, I am about to [a]turn
back the weapons of war which are
in your hands, with which you are
warring against the king of Babylon
and the Chaldeans who are besieg-
ing you outside the wall; and I will
[b]gather them into the center of this
city. 5 I [a]Myself will war against you
with an [b]outstretched hand and a
strong arm, even in [c]anger and wrath
and great indignation. 6 I will also
strike down the inhabitants of this
city, both man and beast; they will
die of a great [a]pestilence. 7 Then
afterwards," declares Yahweh, "[a]I
will give over Zedekiah king of Judah
and his servants and the people, even
those who remain in this city from
the pestilence, the sword, and the
famine, into the hand of Nebuchad-
nezzar king of Babylon and into the
hand of their enemies and into the
hand of those who seek their lives;
and he will strike them down with
the edge of the sword. He [b]will not
show pity on them nor spare nor
have compassion."'

8 "You shall also say to this people,
'Thus says Yahweh, "Behold, I [a]set
before you the way of life and the way
of death. 9 He who [a]inhabits this city
will die by the [b]sword and by famine
*and by* pestilence; but he who goes
out and falls away to the Chaldeans
who are besieging you will live, and
he will have his own life as spoil.
10 For I have [a]set My face against
this city for [1]evil and not for good,"
declares Yahweh. "It will be [b]given
into the hand of the king of Babylon,
and he will [c]burn it with fire."'

11 "Then *say* to the household of
the [a]king of Judah, 'Hear the word
of Yahweh, 12 O [a]house of David, thus
says Yahweh:

"[b]Render justice
[1]every [c]morning;
And deliver the *person* who
has been robbed from
the [2]power of *his* oppressor,
[d]Lest My wrath go
forth like fire
And [e]burn with none
to extinguish *it*,
Because of the evil
of their deeds.

13 "Behold, [a]I am against you,
O [b]inhabitant of the valley,
O [1]rocky plain,"
declares Yahweh,
"You men who say, '[c]Who will
come down against us?
Or who will enter
into our dwelling places?'
14 "But I will punish you
[a]according to the
[1]results of your deeds,"
declares Yahweh,
"And I will [b]kindle a fire
in its forest
That it may devour all
its surroundings."'"

**21:4** [a]Jer 32:5; 33:5; 37:8-10; 38:2, 3, 17, 18 [b]Is 5:5; 13:4; Jer 39:3; Lam 2:5, 7; Zec 14:2 **21:5** [a]Is 63:10 [b]Ex 6:6; Dt 4:34; Jer 6:12 [c]Is 5:25; Jer 32:37 **21:6** [a]Jer 14:12; 32:24 **21:7** [a]2Ki 25:5-7, 18-21; Jer 37:17; 39:5-9; 52:9 [b]2Chr 36:17; Jer 13:14; Eze 7:9; Hab 1:6-10 **21:8** [a]Dt 30:15, 19; Is 1:19, 20 **21:9** [a]Jer 38:2, 17-23; 39:18; 45:5 [b]Jer 14:12; 24:10 **21:10** [a]Lv 17:10; Jer 44:11, 27; Am 9:4 [b]Jer 32:28, 29; 38:3 [c]2Chr 36:19; Jer 34:2; 37:10; 38:18; 39:8; 52:13 [1]Or *calamity* **21:11** [a]Jer 17:20 **21:12** [a]Is 7:2, 13 [b]Ps 72:1; Is 1:17; Jer 7:5; 22:3; Zec 7:9, 10 [c]Ps 101:8; Zep 3:5 [d]Jer 4:4; 17:4; Eze 20:47, 48; Na 1:6 [e]Is 1:31; Jer 7:20 [1]Or *in the* [2]Lit *hand* **21:13** [a]Jer 23:30-32; Eze 13:8 [b]Ps 125:2; Is 22:1 [c]2Sa 5:6, 7; Jer 49:4; Lam 4:12; Ob 3, 4 [1]Lit *rock of the level place* **21:14** [a]Is 3:10, 11; Jer 17:10; 32:19 [b]2Chr 36:19; Is 10:16, 18; Jer 11:16; 17:27; 52:13; Eze 20:47, 48 [1]Lit *fruit*

### *O Land, Hear Yahweh*

22 Thus says Yahweh, "Go down to
the house of the king of Judah,
and there you shall speak this word
2 and say, 'Hear the word of Yahweh,
O king of Judah, who [a]sits on David's
throne, you and your servants and
your people who enter these gates.
3 Thus says Yahweh, "[a]Do justice and
righteousness, and deliver the one
who has been robbed from the power
of *his* [b]oppressor. Also [c]do not mis-
treat *or* do violence to the sojourner,
the orphan, or the widow; and do not
[d]shed innocent blood in this place.
4 For if you men will indeed do this
thing, then [a]kings will enter the gates
of this house, sitting for David on
his throne, riding in chariots and on
horses, *even the king* himself and his
servants and his people. 5 [a]But if you
will not obey these words, I [b]swear by
Myself," declares Yahweh, "that this
house will become a waste place."'"
6 For thus says Yahweh concerning
the house of the king of Judah:

"You are *like* [a]Gilead to Me,
*Like* the summit of Lebanon;
Yet most assuredly I will make
you like a [b]wilderness,
*Like* cities which are
not inhabited.

7 "For I will set apart
[a]destroyers against you,
Each with his weapons;
And they will [b]cut down
your choicest cedars
And [c]throw *them* on the fire.

8 "Many nations will pass by this
city; and they will [a]say to one anoth-
er, 'Why has Yahweh done thus to
this great city?' 9 Then they will say,
'Because they [a]forsook the covenant
of Yahweh their God and worshiped
other gods and served them.'"

10 [a]Do not weep for the
dead or console him,
*But* weep continually for
the one who goes away,
For [b]he will never return
Or see the land of his birth.

11 For thus says Yahweh in regard
to [a,1]Shallum the son of Josiah, king
of Judah, who became king in the
place of Josiah his father, who went
forth from this place, "He will nev-
er return there; 12 but in the place
where they took him away into exile,
there he will [a]die and not see this
land again.

13 "Woe to him who builds
his house
[a]without righteousness
And his [1]upper rooms
without justice,
Who uses his neighbor's
services without pay
And [b]does not give
him his wages,
14 Who says, 'I will [a]build
myself a roomy house
With spacious
[1]upper rooms
And cut out its windows,
[2]Paneling *it* with [b]cedar and
painting *it* [3]bright red.'

◆ **22:2** [a]Is 9:7; Jer 17:25; 22:4, 30; Lk 1:32 **22:3** [a]Is 58:6, 7; Jer 7:5, 23; 21:12; Mic 6:8; Zec 7:9; 8:16; Mt 23:23 [b]Ps 72:4 [c]Ex 22:21-24 [d]Jer 7:6; 19:4; 22:17 **22:4** [a]Jer 17:25 **22:5** [a]Jer 17:27; 26:4 [b]Ge 22:16; Am 6:8; Heb 6:13 **22:6** [a]Ge 37:25; Nu 32:1; SS 4:1 [b]Ps 107:34; Is 6:11; Jer 7:34; Mic 3:12 **22:7** [a]Is 10:3-6; Jer 4:6, 7 [b]Is 10:33, 34; 37:24 [c]Jer 21:14 **22:8** [a]Dt 29:24-26; 1Ki 9:8, 9; 2Chr 7:20-22; Jer 16:10 **22:9** [a]2Ki 22:17; 2Chr 34:25; Jer 11:3 **22:10** [a]Ecc 4:2; Is 57:1; Jer 16:7; 22:18 [b]Jer 25:27; 44:14 **22:11** [a]2Ki 23:30-34; 1Chr 3:15; 2Chr 36:1-4 [1]Jehoahaz **22:12** [a]2Ki 23:34; Jer 22:18 **22:13** [a]Jer 17:11; Mic 3:10; Hab 2:9 [b]Lv 19:13; Jas 5:4 [1]Or *roof chambers* **22:14** [a]Is 5:8 [b]2Sa 7:2; Hag 1:4 [1]Or *roof chambers* [2]Or *Paneled* [3]Or *vermilion*

15 "Do you become a king
because you are
competing in cedar?
Did not your father
eat and drink
And [a]do justice
and righteousness?
Then it was [b]well with him.
16 "He pled the cause
of the [a]afflicted and needy;
Then it was well.
[b]Is not that what it means
to know Me?"
Declares Yahweh.
17 "But your eyes and your heart
Are *set* on nothing except
your own [a]greedy gain
And on [b]shedding
innocent blood
And on doing oppression
and extortion."

18 Therefore thus says Yahweh in regard to [a]Jehoiakim the son of Josiah, king of Judah,
"They will not [b]lament for him:
'[c]Alas, my brother!'
or, 'Alas, sister!'
They will not lament for him:
'Alas for the master!'
or, 'Alas for his splendor!'
19 "He will be [a]buried with
a donkey's burial,
Dragged off and thrown
out beyond the gates
*of Jerusalem.*
20 "Go up to Lebanon and cry out,
And lift up your voice
in Bashan;
Cry out also from [a]Abarim,
For all your [b]lovers
have been broken.
21 "I spoke to you
in your prosperity,
But [a]you said,
'I will not listen!'
[b]This has been your way
[c]from your youth,
That you have not
listened to My voice.
22 "The wind will sweep away
all your [a]shepherds,
And your [b]lovers will
go into captivity;
Then you will surely be
[c]ashamed and feel dishonor
Because of all your evil.
23 "You who inhabit Lebanon,
Nested in the cedars,
How you will groan
when pangs come upon you,
[a]Pain like a woman
in childbirth!

24 "As I live," declares Yahweh,
"even though [a,1]Coniah the son of Je-
hoiakim king of Judah were a [b]signet
*ring* on My right hand, yet I would
pull [1]you [2]off; 25 and I will [a]give you
over into the hand of those who are
seeking your life, indeed, into the
hand of those whom you dread, even
into the hand of Nebuchadnezzar
king of Babylon and into the hand
of the Chaldeans. 26 I will [a]hurl you
*and your* [b]mother who bore you into
another land—there you were not
born, but there you will die. 27 But
as for the land to which their soul
desires to return, they will not return
to it.

---

**22:15** [a]2Ki 23:25; Jer 7:5; 21:12 [b]Ps 128:2; Is 3:10; Jer 42:6 **22:16** [a]Ps 72:1-4, 12, 13 [b]1Chr 28:9; Jer 9:24 **22:17** [a]Jer 6:13; 8:10; Lk 12:15-20 [b]2Ki 24:4; Jer 22:3 **22:18** [a]2Ki 23:36-24:6; 2Chr 36:5 [b]Jer 22:10; 34:5 [c]1Ki 13:30 **22:19** [a]1Ki 21:23, 24; Jer 36:30 **22:20** [a]Nu 27:12; Dt 32:49 [b]Jer 2:25; 3:1 **22:21** [a]Jer 13:10; 19:15 [b]Jer 3:25 [c]Jer 3:24; 32:30 **22:22** [a]Jer 23:1 [b]Jer 30:14 [c]Is 65:13; Jer 20:11 **22:23** [a]Jer 4:31; 6:24 **22:24** [a]2Ki 24:6; 1Chr 3:16; 2Chr 36:9; Jer 37:1 [b]SS 8:6; Is 49:16; Hag 2:23 [1]Jehoiachin [2]Lit *off from there* **22:25** [a]2Ki 24:15, 16; Jer 21:7; 34:20, 21 **22:26** [a]2Ki 24:15; Jer 10:18; 16:13 [b]2Ki 24:8

28 "Is this man Coniah
a despised, shattered jar?
Or is he
an [a]undesirable vessel?
Why have he and his seed
been [b]hurled out
And cast into a [c]land that
they had not known?
29 "[a]O land, land, land,
Hear the word of Yahweh!
30 "Thus says Yahweh,
'Write this man
down [a]childless,
A man who will [b]not
succeed in his days;
For no man of his [c]seed
will succeed
Sitting on the throne of David
Or ruling again in Judah.'"

### *The Righteous Branch*

23 "[a]Woe to the shepherds who
are [b,1]destroying and scatter-
ing the [c]sheep of My pasture!" de-
clares Yahweh. 2 Therefore thus says
Yahweh, the God of Israel, concern-
ing the shepherds who are shepherd-
ing My people: "You have scattered
My flock and banished them and
have not attended to them; behold,
I am about to [a]attend to you for the
[b]evil of your deeds," declares Yah-
weh. 3 "Then I Myself will [a]gather the
remnant of My flock out of all the
land where I have banished them and
cause them to return to their pasture,
and they will be fruitful and multiply.
4 I will also raise up [a]shepherds over
them, and they will [1]shepherd them;
and they will [b]not be afraid any lon-
ger, nor be terrified, [c]nor will any be
left unattended," declares Yahweh.
5 "Behold, *the* [a]days are
coming," declares Yahweh,
"When I will raise up for David
a righteous [b,1]Branch;
And He will [c]reign
as king and [2]prosper
And [d]do justice and
righteousness in the land.
6 "In His days Judah
will be saved,
And [a]Israel
will dwell securely;
And this is His [b]name
by which He will be called,
'[c]Yahweh our righteousness.'
7 "[a]Therefore behold, *the* days are
coming," declares Yahweh, "when
they will no longer say, 'As Yahweh
lives, who brought up the sons of
Israel from the land of Egypt,' 8 [a]but,
'As Yahweh lives, who [b]brought up
and brought back the seed of the
household of Israel from *the* north
land and from all the lands where I
had banished them.' Then they will
live on their own soil."

### *Polluted Prophets and Priests*

9 As for the prophets:
My [a]heart is broken
within me;
All my bones tremble;
I have become
like a drunken man,

**22:28** [a]Ps 31:12; Jer 48:38; Hos 8:8 [b]Jer 15:1 [c]Jer 17:4 **22:29** [a]Dt 4:26; Jer 6:19; Mic 1:2 **22:30** [a]1Chr 3:17; Mt 1:12 [b]Jer 2:37; 10:21 [c]Ps 94:20; Jer 36:30 ◆ **23:1** [a]Eze 13:3; 34:2; Zec 11:17 [b]Is 56:9-12; Jer 10:21; 50:6 [c]Eze 34:31 [1]Lit *causing to perish* **23:2** [a]Ex 32:34 [b]Jer 21:12; 44:22 **23:3** [a]Is 11:11, 12, 16; Jer 31:7, 8; 32:37 **23:4** [a]Jer 3:15; 31:10; Eze 34:23 [b]Jer 30:10; 46:27, 28 [c]Jn 6:39; 10:28; 1Pe 1:5 [1]Or *feed* **23:5** [a]Jer 33:14 [b]Is 4:2; 11:1-5; 53:2; Jer 30:9; 33:15, 16; Zec 3:8; 6:12, 13 [c]Is 9:7; 52:13; Lk 1:32, 33 [d]Ps 72:2; Is 9:7; 32:1; Da 9:24 [1]Lit *Sprout* [2]Or *act with insight* **23:6** [a]Dt 33:28; Jer 30:10; Zec 14:11 [b]Is 7:14; 9:6; Mt 1:21-23 [c]Is 45:24; Jer 33:16; Da 9:24; Ro 3:22; 1Co 1:30 **23:7** [a]Is 43:18, 19; Jer 16:14, 15 **23:8** [a]Jer 16:15 [b]Is 43:5, 6; Eze 34:13; Am 9:14, 15 **23:9** [a]Jer 8:18; Hab 3:16

Even like a man overcome
with wine,
Because of Yahweh
And because of His
holy words.
10 For the land is full of [a]adulterers;
For the land [b]mourns
because of the curse.
The [c]pastures of the
wilderness have dried up.
Their course also is evil,
And their might is not right.
11 "For [a]both prophet and
priest are polluted;
Even in My house I have found
their evil," declares Yahweh.
12 "Therefore their way will be
like [a]slippery paths to them;
They will be driven away
into the [b]thick darkness
and fall down in it;
For I will bring *their*
[c]evil upon them,
The year of their [1]punishment,"
declares Yahweh.

13 "Moreover, among the
prophets of Samaria I saw
an [a]offensive thing:
They [b]prophesied by Baal and
[c]led My people Israel astray.
14 "Also among the prophets
of Jerusalem I have seen
an [a]appalling thing:
The committing of [b]adultery
*and walking in lying;*
And they strengthen
the hands of [c]evildoers,
So that no one has turned
back from his evil.
All of them have become
to Me like [d]Sodom,
And her inhabitants
like Gomorrah.
15 "Therefore thus says Yahweh of
hosts concerning the prophets,
'Behold, I am going to [a]feed
them wormwood
And make them drink
[1]poisoned water,
For from the prophets
of Jerusalem
Pollution has gone forth
into all the land.'"

16 Thus says Yahweh of hosts,
"[a]Do not listen to the words
of the prophets who are
prophesying to you.
They are [b]leading
you into vanity;
They speak a [c]vision
of their own heart,
Not [d]from the mouth
of Yahweh.
17 "They keep saying to those
who [a]spurn Me,
'Yahweh has said,
"[b]You will have peace"';
And as for everyone who
walks in the [c]stubbornness
of his own heart,
They say, '[d]Evil will not
come upon you.'
18 "But [a]who has stood
in the council of Yahweh,
That he should see and
hear His word?
Who has given [b]heed
to [1]His word and heard?

**23:10** [a]Jer 9:2; Hos 4:2, 3; Mal 3:5 [b]Jer 12:4 [c]Ps 107:34; Jer 9:10 **23:11** [a]Jer 6:13; Zep 3:4 **23:12** [a]Ps 35:6; Pr 4:19; Jer 13:16 [b]Is 8:22; Jn 12:35 [c]Jer 11:23 [1]Or *visitation* **23:13** [a]Hos 9:7, 8 [b]1Ki 18:18-21; Jer 2:8; 23:32 [c]Is 9:16 **23:14** [a]Jer 5:30 [b]Jer 29:23 [c]Jer 23:22; Eze 13:22, 23 [d]Ge 18:20; Dt 32:32; Is 1:9, 10; Jer 20:16; 49:18; Mt 11:24 **23:15** [a]Dt 29:18; Jer 8:14; 9:15 [1]Or *gall* **23:16** [a]Jer 27:9, 10, 14-17; 1Jn 4:1 [b]Mt 7:15; 2Co 11:13-15; Ga 1:8, 9 [c]Jer 14:14; Eze 13:3, 6 [d]Jer 9:12, 20 **23:17** [a]Mic 2:11 [b]Jer 8:11; Eze 13:10 [c]Jer 13:10; 18:12 [d]Jer 5:12; Am 9:10; Mic 3:11 **23:18** [a]Job 15:8, 9; Jer 23:22; 1Co 2:16 [b]Job 33:31 [1]Or *My*

19 “Behold, the [a]storm of Yahweh
has gone forth in wrath,
Even a whirling storm;
It will whirl down on the head
of the wicked.
20 “The [a]anger of Yahweh
will not turn back
Until He has [b]done
and established the
purposes of His heart;
[c]In the last days you will
clearly understand it.
21 “[a]I did not send *these* prophets,
But they ran.
I did not speak to them,
But they prophesied.
22 “But if they had [a]stood
in My council,
Then they would have
[b]caused My words to be
heard by My people
And would have turned them
back from their evil way
And from the evil of
their deeds.

23 “Am I a God who is [a]near,”
declares Yahweh,
“And not a God far off?
24 “Can a man [a]hide himself
in hiding places
So I do not see him?”
declares Yahweh.
“[b]Do I not fill the heavens and
the earth?” declares Yahweh.
25 “I have [a]heard what the proph-
ets have said who [b]prophesy a lie in
My name, saying, ‘I had a [c]dream,
I had a dream!’
26 How long? Is
there *anything* in the hearts of the
prophets who prophesy a lie, even
*these* prophets of the [a]deception of
their own heart,
27 who intend to
[a]make My people forget My name
by their dreams which they recount
to one another, just as their fathers
[b]forgot My name because of Baal?
28 The prophet who has a dream
may recount *his* dream, but let him
who has [a]My word speak My word
in truth. [b]What does straw have
*in common* with grain?” declares
Yahweh.
29 “Is not My word like
[a]fire?” declares Yahweh, “and like
a [b]hammer which shatters a rock?
30 Therefore behold, [a]I am against
the prophets,” declares Yahweh,
“who steal My words from each
other.
31 Behold, I am against the
prophets,” declares Yahweh, “who
take their tongues and declare, ‘*Yah-
weh* declares.’
32 Behold, I am against
those who have prophesied [a]lying
dreams,” declares Yahweh, “and who
recounted them and led My people
astray by their lying and [b]reckless
boasting; yet [c]I did not send them,
and I did not command them, and
they do not [d]furnish this people the
slightest benefit,” declares Yahweh.
33 “Now when this people or the
prophet or a priest asks you, saying,
‘What is the [a,1]oracle of Yahweh?’
then you shall say to them, ‘What
oracle?’ Yahweh declares, ‘I will
[b]abandon you.’
34 Then as for the

---

**23:19** [a]Jer 25:32; 30:23; Am 1:14 **23:20** [a]2Ki 23:26, 27; Jer 30:24 [b]Is 55:11; Zec 1:6 [c]Ge 49:1
**23:21** [a]Jer 14:14; 23:32; 27:15 **23:22** [a]Jer 9:12; 23:18 [b]Jer 35:15; Zec 1:4 **23:23** [a]Ps 139:1-10
**23:24** [a]Job 22:13, 14; 34:21, 22; Ps 139:7-12; Is 29:15; Jer 49:10; Heb 4:13 [b]1Ki 8:27; 2Chr 2:6; Is 66:1
**23:25** [a]Jer 8:6; 1Co 4:5 [b]Jer 14:14 [c]Nu 12:6; Jer 23:28, 32; 29:8; Joel 2:28 **23:26** [a]1Ti 4:1, 2
**23:27** [a]Dt 13:1-3; Jer 29:8 [b]Jdg 3:7; 8:33, 34 **23:28** [a]Jer 9:12, 20 [b]1Co 3:12, 13 **23:29** [a]Jer 5:14; 20:9
[b]2Co 10:4, 5 **23:30** [a]Dt 18:20; Ps 34:16; Jer 14:14, 15; Eze 13:8 **23:32** [a]Dt 13:1, 2; Jer 23:25 [b]Zep 3:4
[c]Jer 23:21; Lam 3:37 [d]Jer 7:8; Lam 2:14 **23:33** [a]Is 13:1; Na 1:1; Hab 1:1; Zec 9:1; Mal 1:1 [b]Jer 12:7; 23:39
[1]Or *burden*, so in ch

prophet or the priest or the people
who say, 'The [a]oracle of Yahweh,'
I will bring punishment upon that
man and his household. **35** Thus will
each of you say to his neighbor and
to his brother, '[a]What has Yahweh
answered?' or, 'What has Yahweh
spoken?' **36** For you will no longer
remember the oracle of Yahweh
because every man's own word will
become the oracle, and you have
[a]perverted the words of the [b]living
God, Yahweh of hosts, our God.
**37** Thus you will say to *that* prophet,
'What has Yahweh answered you?'
and, 'What has Yahweh spoken?'
**38** For if you *all* say, 'The oracle of
Yahweh!' surely thus says Yahweh,
'Because you said this word, "The
oracle of Yahweh!" I have also sent to
you, saying, "You shall not say, 'The
oracle of Yahweh!'"' **39** Therefore
behold, [a]I will surely forget you and
abandon you, along with the city
which I gave you and your fathers, *so
that you are* out of My presence. **40** I
will put an everlasting [a]reproach on
you and an everlasting humiliation
which will not be forgotten."

### *The Good and the Rotten Figs*

**24** After [a]Nebuchadnezzar king
of Babylon had taken away into
exile Jeconiah the son of Jehoiakim,
king of Judah, and the officials of
*Judah with* the craftsmen and smiths
from Jerusalem, and had brought
them to Babylon, Yahweh showed me:
behold, two [b]baskets of figs set before
the temple of Yahweh! **2** One basket
had very good figs, like [a]first-ripe figs,
and the other basket had [b]very rotten
figs which could not be eaten due to
rottenness. **3** Then Yahweh said to me,
"[a]What do you see, Jeremiah?" And I
said, "Figs, the good figs, very good;
and the rotten *figs*, very rotten, which
cannot be eaten due to rottenness."

**4** Then the word of Yahweh came to
me, saying, **5** "Thus says Yahweh, the
God of Israel, 'Like these good figs, so
I will recognize [a]as good the exiles of
Judah, whom I have sent out of this
place *into* the land of the Chaldeans.
**6** For I will set My eyes on them for
good, and I will [a]return them to this
land; and I will [b]build them up and not
pull them down, and I will [c]plant them
and not uproot them. **7** I will give them
a [a]heart to know Me, for I am Yahweh;
and they will be [b]My people, and I will
be their God, for they will [c]return to
Me with their whole heart.

**8** 'But like the [a]rotten figs which
cannot be eaten due to rottenness—
indeed, thus says Yahweh—so I will
give over [b]Zedekiah king of Judah
and his officials and the [c]remnant
of Jerusalem who remain in this land
and the ones who inhabit the land
of [d]Egypt. **9** I will [a]give them over
*to be* a terror *and an* evil for all the
kingdoms of the earth, as a [b]reproach
*and a proverb*, a byword and a [c]curse
in all places where I will banish them.
**10** I will send the [a]sword, the famine,
and the pestilence upon them until
they come to an end from *being* upon

---

**23:34** [a]Lam 2:14; Zec 13:3 **23:35** [a]Jer 33:3; 42:4 **23:36** [a]Ga 1:7, 8; 2Pe 3:16 [b]2Ki 19:4; Jer 10:10
**23:39** [a]Jer 7:14, 15; 23:33; Eze 8:18 **23:40** [a]Jer 20:11; 42:18; Eze 5:14, 15 ◆ **24:1** [a]2Ki 24:10-16; 2Chr 36:10;
Jer 27:20; 29:1, 2 [b]Am 8:1 **24:2** [a]Mic 7:1; Na 3:12 [b]Is 5:4, 7; Jer 29:17 **24:3** [a]Jer 1:11, 13; Am 8:2; Zec 4:2
**24:5** [a]Na 1:7; Zec 13:9 **24:6** [a]Jer 12:15; 29:10; 32:37; Eze 11:17 [b]Jer 31:4; 32:41; 33:7; 42:10 [c]Jer 32:41
**24:7** [a]Dt 30:6; Jer 31:33; 32:40; Eze 11:19; 36:26 [b]Is 51:16; Jer 7:23; 30:22; 31:33; 32:38; Eze 14:11; Zec 8:8;
Heb 8:10 [c]1Sa 7:3; Ps 119:2; Jer 29:13 **24:8** [a]Jer 29:17 [b]Jer 39:5; Eze 12:12, 13 [c]Jer 39:9 [d]Jer 44:1, 26-30
**24:9** [a]Jer 15:4; 29:18; 34:17 [b]1Ki 9:7; Ps 44:13, 14 [c]Is 65:15 **24:10** [a]Is 51:19; Jer 21:9; 27:8; Eze 5:12-17

the land which I gave to them and
their fathers.'"

### *Seventy Years of Captivity*

**25** The word that came to
Jeremiah concerning all the
people of Judah in the [a]fourth year
of [b]Jehoiakim the son of Josiah, king
of Judah (that was the [c]first year of
Nebuchadnezzar king of Babylon),
**2** which Jeremiah the prophet spoke
to all the [a]people of Judah and to all
the inhabitants of Jerusalem, saying,
**3** "From the [a]thirteenth year of [b]Josiah
the son of Amon, king of Judah, even
to this day, [1]these [c]twenty-three years
the word of Yahweh has come to me,
and I have spoken to you, [d,2]rising up
early and speaking, but you have not
listened. **4** And Yahweh has sent to
you all His [a]slaves the prophets, rising
up early and sending, but you have
not listened nor inclined your ear to
hear, **5** saying, '[a]Turn now everyone
from his evil way and from the evil
of your deeds, and live on the ground
which Yahweh has given to you and
your fathers [b]forever and ever; **6** and
[a]do not walk after other gods to [1]serve
them and to [2]worship them, and do
not provoke Me to anger with the
work of your hands, and I will bring
no evil against you.' **7** Yet you have not
listened to Me," declares Yahweh, "in
order that you might [a]provoke Me to
anger with the work of your hands to
your own evil *demise*.
**8** "Therefore thus says Yahweh
of hosts, 'Because you have not
listened to My words, **9** behold, I
will [a]send and take all the families
of the north,' declares Yahweh, 'and
*I will send* to Nebuchadnezzar king
of Babylon, [b]My servant, and will
bring them against this land and
against its inhabitants and against
all these surrounding nations; and I
will [1]devote them to destruction and
[c]make them an object of horror and
of hissing and an everlasting waste
place. **10** Moreover, I will [a,1]make the
voice of joy and the voice of gladness,
the voice of the bridegroom and the
voice of the bride, the [b]sound of the
millstones and the light of the lamp, to
perish from them. **11** [a]This whole land
will be a waste place and an object of
horror, and these nations will serve
the king of Babylon [b]seventy years.

### *Punishment Against Babylon*

**12** 'Then it will be [a]when seventy
years are fulfilled, *that* I will [b]punish
the king of Babylon and that nation,'
declares Yahweh, 'for their iniquity,
even the land of the Chaldeans; and
[c]I will make it an everlasting deso-
lation. **13** I will bring upon that land
all My words which I have spoken
against it, all that is written in [a]this
book which Jeremiah has prophesied
against [b]all the nations. **14**—[1]For
[a]many nations and great kings will
make slaves of them, even them; and

◆ **25:1** [a]Jer 36:1; 46:2 [b]2Ki 24:1, 2; 2Chr 36:4-6; Da 1:1, 2 [c]Jer 32:1 **25:2** [a]Jer 18:11 **25:3** [a]Jer 1:2 [b]2Chr 34:1-3, 8 [c]Jer 36:2 [d]Jer 7:25; 11:7; 26:5 [1]Lit *this* [2]Lit *I rise early* **25:4** [a]2Chr 36:15; Jer 26:5 **25:5** [a]2Ki 17:13; Is 55:6, 7; Jer 4:1; 35:15; Eze 18:30; Jon 3:8-10 [b]Ge 17:8; Jer 7:7; 17:25 **25:6** [a]Dt 6:14; 8:19; 2Ki 17:35; Jer 35:15 [1]Or *worship* [2]Or *bow down to* **25:7** [a]2Ki 17:17; 21:15; Jer 7:19; 32:30-33 **25:9** [a]Jer 1:15; 6:22, 23 [b]Is 13:3; Jer 27:6; 43:10 [c]1Ki 9:7, 8; Jer 18:16; 25:18 [1]Or *put them under the ban* **25:10** [a]Is 24:8-11; Jer 7:34; 16:9; Eze 26:13; Rev 18:23 [b]Ecc 12:4; Is 47:2 [1]Lit *cause to perish* **25:11** [a]Jer 4:27; 12:11, 12 [b]2Chr 36:21; Jer 29:10; Da 9:2; Zec 7:5 **25:12** [a]Ezr 1:1; Jer 29:10; Da 9:2 [b]Is 13:14; Jer ch 50, 51 [c]Is 13:19 **25:13** [a]Jer 36:4, 29, 32 [b]Jer 1:5, 10; 36:2 **25:14** [a]Jer 27:7; 50:9, 41; 51:27, 28 [1]Or *For they have served many nations and great kings*

I will [b]repay them according to their
deeds and according to the work of
their hands—'"

**15** For thus Yahweh, the God of
Israel, says to me, "Take this [a]cup of
the wine of wrath from My hand and
cause all the nations to whom I send
you to drink it. **16** They will [a]drink
and stagger and go mad because of
the sword that I will send among
them."

**17** Then I took the cup from the
hand of Yahweh and [a]made all
the nations to whom Yahweh sent
me drink it: **18** [a]Jerusalem and the
cities of Judah and its kings *and* its
princes, to make them a waste place,
an object of horror, an object of
hissing, and a curse, as it is this day;
**19** [a]Pharaoh king of Egypt, his ser-
vants, his princes, and all his people,
**20** and all the [a,1]foreign people, all
the kings of the [b]land of Uz, all the
kings of the land of the [c]Philistines
(even Ashkelon, Gaza, Ekron, and
the remnant of [d]Ashdod), **21** [a]Edom,
[b]Moab, and the sons of [c]Ammon,
**22** and all the kings of [a]Tyre, all the
kings of Sidon, and the kings of [b]the
coastlands which are beyond the sea,
**23** and [a]Dedan, Tema, [b]Buz, and all
who [c]cut [1]the corners *of their hair*,
**24** and all the kings of [a]Arabia and
all the kings of the [b,1]foreign people
who dwell in the desert, **25** and all
*the kings of* Zimri, all the kings of
[a]Elam, and all the kings of [b]Media,
**26** and all the kings of the north, near
and far, one with another; and [a]all
the kingdoms of the earth which are
upon the face of the ground, and the
king of [b,1]Sheshach shall drink after
them.

**27** "You shall say to them, 'Thus
says Yahweh of hosts, the God of
Israel, "[a]Drink, be drunk, vomit,
fall, and rise no more because of
the [b]sword which I will send among
you."' **28** And it will be, if they [a]refuse
to take the cup from your hand to
drink, then you will say to them,
'Thus says Yahweh of hosts: "[b]You
shall surely drink! **29** For behold, I
am [a]beginning to bring evil against
*this* city which is [b]called by My name.
But shall you be completely free from
punishment? You will not be free
from punishment, for [c]I am calling
for a sword against all the inhabitants
of the earth," declares Yahweh of
hosts.'

**30** "Therefore you shall prophesy
against them all these words, and you
shall say to them,

'[a]Yahweh will [b]roar
from on high
And give forth His voice
from His holy habitation;
He will roar mightily
against His [1]pasture.
He will bellow a shout like
those who tread *the grapes*,
Against all the inhabitants
of the earth.

**25:14** [b]Jer 51:6, 24, 56 **25:15** [a]Job 21:20; Ps 75:8; Is 51:17, 22; Jer 51:7 **25:16** [a]Na 3:11 **25:17** [a]Jer 1:10; 25:28 **25:18** [a]Ps 60:3; Is 51:17 **25:19** [a]Jer 46:2-28; Na 3:8-10 **25:20** [a]Jer 25:24; 50:37; Eze 30:5 [b]Job 1:1; Lam 4:21 [c]Jer 47:1-7 [d]Is 20:1 [1]Or *mixed multitude* **25:21** [a]Ps 137:7; Jer 49:7-22 [b]Jer 48:1-47; Am 2:1-3 [c]Jer 49:1-6; Am 1:13-15 **25:22** [a]Jer 47:4; Zec 9:2-4 [b]Jer 31:10 **25:23** [a]Is 21:13; Jer 49:7, 8 [b]Ge 22:21 [c]Jer 9:26; 49:32 [1]Or *fringes* of the desert **25:24** [a]2Chr 9:14 [b]Jer 25:20; 50:37; Eze 30:5 [1]Or *mixed multitude* **25:25** [a]Ge 10:22; Is 11:11; Jer 49:34 [b]Is 13:17; Jer 51:11, 28 **25:26** [a]Jer 25:9; 50:9 [b]Jer 51:41 [1]Cryptic name for Babylon **25:27** [a]Jer 25:16; Hab 2:16 [b]Eze 21:4, 5 **25:28** [a]Job 34:33 [b]Jer 49:12 **25:29** [a]Pr 11:31; Is 10:12; Jer 13:13; Eze 9:6; 1Pe 4:17 [b]1Ki 8:43 [c]Eze 38:21 **25:30** [a]Is 42:13; Jer 25:38 [b]Joel 2:11; 3:16; Am 1:2 [1]Or *habitation*

**31** 'A rumbling has come to
the end of the earth
Because Yahweh has
[a]a contention
against the nations.
He is entering into
[b]judgment with all flesh;
As for the wicked, He has
given them to the sword,'
declares Yahweh."

**32** Thus says Yahweh of hosts,
"Behold, evil is going forth
From [a]nation to nation,
And a great [b]storm is
being stirred up
From the remotest
parts of the earth.
**33** "Those [a]slain by Yahweh on
that day will be from one end of the
earth to the [1]other. They will [b]not be
lamented, gathered, or buried; they
will be like [c]dung on the face of the
ground.
**34** "Wail, you shepherds,
and cry out;
And [a]roll yourselves *in ashes*,
you masters of the flock;
For the days of your [b]slaughter
and your scatterings
are being fulfilled,
And you will fall
like a desirable vessel.
**35** "[a]Refuge will perish
from the shepherds
And escape from the mighty
ones of the flock.
**36** "*Hear* the sound of the cry
of the shepherds,
And the wailing of the mighty
ones of the flock!
For Yahweh is destroying
their pasture,
**37** And the peaceful [a]pastures
are made silent
Because of the [b]burning
anger of Yahweh.
**38** "He has forsaken His hiding
place [a]like the lion;
For their land has become
an object of horror
Because of the burning
*desire* of [1]the oppressor
And because of His
burning anger."

### The Words of Yahweh Against Judah

**26** In the beginning of the reign of
[a]Jehoiakim the son of Josiah,
king of Judah, this word came from
Yahweh, saying, **2** "Thus says Yahweh,
'[a]Stand in the court of the house of
Yahweh, and you shall speak to all
the cities of Judah who have [b]come to
worship *in* the house of Yahweh [c]all
the words that I have commanded you
to speak to them. [d]Do not take away a
word! **3** [a]Perhaps they will listen and
everyone will turn from his evil way,
that [b]I may [1]relent of the evil which I
am devising to [2]bring against them
because of the evil of their deeds.'
**4** And you will say to them, 'Thus says
Yahweh, "[a]If you will not listen to
Me, to [b]walk in My law which I have
given before you, **5** to listen to the
words of [a]My slaves the prophets,
whom I have been sending to you,

---

**25:31** [a]Hos 4:1; Mic 6:2 [b]Is 66:16; Eze 20:35, 36; Joel 3:2 **25:32** [a]2Chr 15:6; Is 34:2 [b]Is 30:30; Jer 23:19 **25:33** [a]Is 34:2, 3; 66:16 [b]Ps 79:3; Jer 16:4; Eze 39:4, 17 [c]Is 5:25 [1]Lit *other end of the earth* **25:34** [a]Jer 6:26; Eze 27:30 [b]Is 34:6, 7; Jer 50:27 **25:35** [a]Job 11:20; Jer 11:11; Am 2:14 **25:37** [a]Is 27:10, 11; Jer 5:17; 13:20 [b]Ps 97:1-3; Is 66:15; Heb 12:29 **25:38** [a]Jer 4:7; 5:6; Hos 5:14; 13:7, 8 [1]Lit *the one who mistreats*
◆ **26:1** [a]2Ki 23:36; 2Chr 36:4, 5 **26:2** [a]2Chr 24:20, 21; Jer 7:2; 19:14 [b]Dt 12:5 [c]Jer 1:17; 42:4; Mt 28:20; Ac 20:20, 27 [d]Dt 4:2 **26:3** [a]Is 1:16-19; Jer 36:3-7 [b]Jer 18:8; Jon 3:8 [1]Or *regret*, cf. 1Sa 15:11, 29, 3 [2]Lit *do*
**26:4** [a]Lv 26:14; 1Ki 9:6; Is 1:20; Jer 17:27; 22:5 [b]Jer 32:23; 44:10, 23 **26:5** [a]2Ki 9:7; Ezr 9:11; Jer 7:13; 25:3, 4

rising up early and sending, but you
have not listened, **6** then I will make
this house like [a]Shiloh, and this city
I will make a [b]curse to all the nations
of the earth."'"

### *Plot to Murder Jeremiah*

**7** The [a]priests and the prophets
and all the people heard Jeremiah
speaking these words in the house
of Yahweh. **8** Now it happened that
when Jeremiah finished speaking all
that Yahweh had commanded *him* to
speak to all the people, the priests
and the prophets and all the people
seized him, saying, "[a]You must surely
die! **9** Why have you prophesied in the
name of Yahweh saying, 'This house
will be like Shiloh, and this city will
be [a]laid waste, without inhabitant'?"
And [b]all the people gathered about
Jeremiah in the house of Yahweh.
**10** When the [a]officials of Judah
heard these things, they came up
from the king's house to the house
of Yahweh and sat in the [b]entrance of
the New Gate of *the house* of Yahweh.
**11** Then the priests and the prophets
[a]spoke to the officials and to all the
people, saying, "A [b]judgment of death
for this man! For he has prophesied
[c]against this city as you have heard
in your hearing."
**12** Then Jeremiah spoke to all the
officials and to all the people, saying,
"[a]*Yahweh* sent me to prophesy against
this house and against this city all the
words that you have heard. **13** So now,
[a]make good your ways and your deeds
and listen to the voice of Yahweh your
God; and Yahweh will [1]relent of the
evil *demise* which He has spoken
against you. **14** But as for me, behold,
[a]I am in your hands; do with me as is
good and right in your eyes. **15** Only
know for certain that if you put me to
death, you will bring [a]innocent blood
on yourselves and on this city and on
its inhabitants; for truly Yahweh has
sent me to you to speak all these words
in your hearing."

### *Jeremiah Spared from Death*

**16** Then the officials and all the people
[a]said to the priests and to the prophets,
"No [b]judgment of death for this man!
For he has spoken to us in the name
of Yahweh our God." **17** Then [a]some
of the elders of the land rose up and
spoke to all the assembly of the peo-
ple, saying, **18** "[a,1]Micah of Moresheth
prophesied in the days of Hezekiah
king of Judah; and he spoke to all the
people of Judah, saying, 'Thus Yahweh
of hosts has said,

"[b]Zion will be plowed *as* a field,
And Jerusalem will become
a heap of ruins,
And the [c]mountain of the
house *will become* [2]the high
places of a forest."'

**19** "Did Hezekiah king of Judah and
all Judah put him to death? Did
he not [a]fear Yahweh and entreat
the favor of Yahweh, and [b]Yahweh
[1]relented of the evil *demise* which

**26:6** [a]Jos 18:1; 1Sa 4:12; Ps 78:60, 61; Jer 7:12, 14 [b]2Ki 22:19; Is 65:15; Jer 24:9; 25:18 **26:7** [a]Jer 5:31; Mic 3:11 **26:8** [a]Jer 11:19; 18:23; Lam 4:13, 14; Mt 21:35, 36; 23:34, 35; 27:20 **26:9** [a]Jer 9:11; 33:10 [b]Ac 3:11; 5:12 **26:10** [a]Jer 26:21 [b]Jer 36:10 **26:11** [a]Jer 18:23 [b]Dt 18:20; Mt 26:66 [c]Jer 38:4; Ac 6:11-14 **26:12** [a]Jer 1:17, 18; 26:15; Am 7:15; Ac 4:19; 5:29 **26:13** [a]Jer 7:3, 5; 18:8, 11; 26:3; 35:15; Joel 2:14; Jon 3:9; 4:2 [1]Or *regret*, cf. 1Sa 15:11, 29, 35 **26:14** [a]Jer 38:5 **26:15** [a]Nu 35:33; Pr 6:16, 17; Jer 7:6 **26:16** [a]Jer 26:11; 36:19, 25; 38:7, 13 [b]Ac 5:34-39; 23:9, 29; 25:25; 26:31 **26:17** [a]Ac 5:34 **26:18** [a]Mic 1:1 [b]Ne 4:2; Ps 79:1; Jer 9:11; Mic 3:12 [c]Is 2:2, 3; Jer 17:3; Mic 4:1; Zec 8:3 [1]Lit *Micaiah the Morasthite* [2]Or *a wooded height*
**26:19** [a]2Chr 29:6-11; 32:26; Is 37:1, 4, 15-20 [b]Ex 32:14; 2Sa 24:16 [1]Or *regretted*

He had spoken against them? But we are [c]committing a great evil against ourselves."

**20** Indeed, there was also a man who prophesied in the name of Yahweh, Uriah the son of Shemaiah from [a]Kiriath-jearim; and he prophesied against this city and against this land words similar to all those of Jeremiah. **21** And King Jehoiakim and all his mighty men and all the officials heard his words. So the [a]king sought to put him to death; but Uriah heard *it*, and he was afraid and [b]fled and went to Egypt. **22** Then King Jehoiakim sent men to Egypt: [a]Elnathan the son of Achbor and *certain* men with him *went* into Egypt. **23** And they brought Uriah out from Egypt and led him to King Jehoiakim, who [a]struck him down with a sword and cast his dead body into the [1]burial place of the [2]common people.

**24** But the hand of [a]Ahikam the son of Shaphan was with Jeremiah, so that he was [b]not given into the hands of the people to put him to death.

### *The Yoke of Nebuchadnezzar*

**27** In the beginning of the reign of [a,1]Zedekiah the son of Josiah, king of Judah, this word came to Jeremiah from Yahweh, saying— **2** thus says Yahweh to me—"Make for yourself [a]bonds and the [b]bars of a yoke and put them on your neck, **3** and you shall send [1]word to the king of [a]Edom, to the king of [a]Moab, to the king of the sons of [a]Ammon, to the king of [a]Tyre, and to the king of [a]Sidon by the hand of messengers who come to Jerusalem to Zedekiah king of Judah. **4** And you shall command them *to go* to their masters, saying, 'Thus says Yahweh of hosts, the God of Israel, thus you shall say to your masters, **5** "[a]I have made the earth, the men, and the animals which are on the face of the earth [b]by My great power and by My outstretched arm, and I will [c]give it to the one who is right in My eyes. **6** So now, I [a]have given all these lands into the hand of Nebuchadnezzar king of Babylon, [b]My servant, and I have given him even the [c]wild beasts of the field to serve him. **7** [a]All the nations shall serve him and his son and his grandson [b]until the time of his own land comes; then [c]many nations and great kings will [1]make him their servant.

**8** "And it will be, *that* the nation or the kingdom which [a]will not serve him, Nebuchadnezzar king of Babylon, and which will not put its neck under the yoke of the king of Babylon, I will punish that nation with the [b]sword, with famine, and with pestilence," declares Yahweh, "until I have brought [1]it to an end by his hand. **9** But as for you, [a]do not listen to your prophets, your diviners, your [1]dreamers, your soothsayers, or your sorcerers who speak to you,

---

**26:19** [c]Jer 44:7; Hab 2:10 **26:20** [a]Jos 9:17; 1Sa 6:21; 7:2 **26:21** [a]2Chr 16:10; 24:21; Jer 36:26; Mt 14:5 [b]1Ki 19:2-4; Mt 10:23 **26:22** [a]Jer 36:12 **26:23** [a]Jer 2:30 [1]Lit *graves* [2]Lit sons of the people **26:24** [a]2Ki 22:12-14; Jer 39:14; 40:5-7 [b]1Ki 18:4; Jer 1:18, 19 ◆ **27:1** [a]2Ki 24:18-20; 2Chr 36:11-13 [1]Many mss *Jehoiakim* **27:2** [a]Jer 30:8 [b]Jer 28:10, 13 **27:3** [a]Jer 25:21, 22 [1]Lit *them* **27:5** [a]Ps 96:5; 146:5, 6; Is 42:5; 45:12; Jer 10:12; 51:15 [b]Dt 9:29; Jer 32:17; Da 4:17 [c]Ps 115:15, 16; Ac 17:26 **27:6** [a]Jer 21:7; 22:25; Eze 29:18-20 [b]Is 44:28; Jer 25:9; 43:10 [c]Jer 28:14; Da 2:38 **27:7** [a]2Chr 36:20; Jer 44:30; 46:13 [b]Da 5:26; Zec 2:8, 9 [c]Is 14:4-6; Jer 25:12 [1]Or *enslave him* **27:8** [a]Jer 38:17-19; 42:15, 16; Eze 17:19-21 [b]Jer 24:10; 27:13; 29:17, 18; Eze 14:21 [1]Lit *them* **27:9** [a]Ex 22:18; Dt 18:10; Pr 19:27; Is 8:19; Mal 3:5; Eph 5:6 [1]Lit *dreams*

saying, 'You will not serve the king
of Babylon.' **10** For they prophesy a
[a]lie to you in order to [b]remove you
far from your land; and I will banish
you, and you will perish. **11** But the
nation which will [a]bring its neck
under the yoke of the king of Babylon
and serve him, I will [b]leave *it* on its
land," declares Yahweh, "and they
will serve it and inhabit it."'"

**12** I spoke words like all these to
[a]Zedekiah king of Judah, saying,
"Bring your necks under the yoke of the
king of Babylon and serve him and his
people, and live! **13** Why will you [a]die,
you and your people, by the sword,
famine, and pestilence, as Yahweh has
spoken to that nation which will not
serve the king of Babylon? **14** So [a]do
not listen to the words of the prophets
who speak to you, saying, 'You will not
serve the king of Babylon,' for they
prophesy a [b]lie to you; **15** for [a]I have
not sent them," declares Yahweh, "but
they [b]prophesy a lie in My name, in
order that I may [c]banish you and that
you may perish, [d]you and the prophets
who prophesy to you."

**16** *Then* I spoke to the priests and
to all this people, saying, "Thus says
Yahweh: Do not listen to the words
of your prophets who prophesy to
you, saying, 'Behold, the [a]vessels of
the house of Yahweh will now shortly
be returned from Babylon'; for they
*are prophesying* a [b]lie to you. **17** Do
not listen to them; serve the king of
Babylon, and live! Why should this
city [a]become a waste place? **18** But [a]if
they are prophets, and if the word of
Yahweh is with them, let them now
[b]intercede with Yahweh of hosts
that the vessels which are left in the
house of Yahweh, in the house of
the king of Judah, and in Jerusalem
may not go to Babylon. **19** For thus
says Yahweh of hosts concerning the
[a]pillars, concerning the sea, concern-
ing the stands, and concerning the
rest of the vessels that are left in
this city, **20** which Nebuchadnezzar
king of Babylon did not take when
he [a]carried away into exile Jeconiah
the son of Jehoiakim, king of Judah,
from Jerusalem to Babylon, and all
the nobles of Judah and Jerusalem.
**21** Indeed, thus says Yahweh of hosts,
the God of Israel, concerning the
vessels that are left in the house of
Yahweh and in the house of the king
of Judah and in Jerusalem, **22** 'They
will be [a]brought to Babylon, and they
will be there until the [b]day I [1]visit
them,' declares Yahweh. 'Then I will
[c]bring them up and return them to
this place.'"

### *Hananiah's Rebellion Against Yahweh*

**28** Now it happened in the same
year, [a]in the beginning of
the reign of [b]Zedekiah king of Ju-
dah, in the fourth year, in the fifth
month, *that* [c]Hananiah the son of
Azzur, the prophet, who was from
[d]Gibeon, spoke to me in the house

**27:10** [a]Jer 23:25 [b]Jer 8:19; 32:31 **27:11** [a]Jer 27:2, 8, 12 [b]Jer 21:9; 38:2; 40:9-12; 42:10, 11
**27:12** [a]Jer 27:3; 28:1; 38:17 **27:13** [a]Pr 8:36; Jer 27:8; 38:23; Eze 18:31 **27:14** [a]Jer 27:9; 2Co 11:13-15
[b]Jer 14:14; 23:21; 27:10; 29:8, 9; Eze 13:22 **27:15** [a]Jer 23:21; 29:9 [b]Jer 23:25 [c]2Chr 25:16; Jer 27:10
[d]Jer 6:13-15; 14:15, 16 **27:16** [a]2Ki 24:13; 2Chr 36:7, 10; Jer 28:3; Da 1:2 [b]Jer 27:10 **27:17** [a]Jer 7:34
**27:18** [a]1Ki 18:24 [b]1Sa 7:8; 12:19, 23; Jer 18:20 **27:19** [a]1Ki 7:15; 2Ki 25:13, 17; Jer 52:17-23
**27:20** [a]2Ki 24:12, 14-16; 2Chr 36:10, 18; Jer 22:28; 24:1 **27:22** [a]Jer 34:2, 3 [b]Jer 25:11, 12; 27:7; 29:10; 32:5
[c]Ezr 1:7-11; 5:13-15; 7:19 [1]Same Heb root as "punish" in Jer, cf. 5:9; 9:8; 29:32; 30:20 ◆ **28:1** [a]Jer 27:1;
49:34 [b]2Ki 24:18-20; 2Chr 36:11-13; Jer 27:3, 12 [c]Jer 28:17 [d]Jos 9:3; 10:12; 1Ki 3:4

of Yahweh in the sight of the priests
and all the people, saying, 2 "[a]Thus
says Yahweh of hosts, the God of
Israel, 'I have broken the yoke of the
king of Babylon. 3 Within two years
I am going to return to this place [a]all
the vessels of the house of Yahweh,
which Nebuchadnezzar king of Bab-
ylon took away from this place and
carried to Babylon. 4 I am [a]also going
to return to this place [b]Jeconiah the
son of Jehoiakim, king of Judah, and
all the [c]exiles of Judah who went
to Babylon,' declares Yahweh, 'for I
will break the [d]yoke of the king of
Babylon.'"

5 Then the prophet Jeremiah
spoke to the prophet Hananiah in
the sight of the priests and in the
sight of all the people who were
standing in the [a]house of Yahweh,
6 and the prophet Jeremiah said,
"[a]Amen! May Yahweh do so; may
Yahweh establish your words which
you have prophesied to return the
vessels of the house of Yahweh
and all the exiles, from Babylon
to this place. 7 Yet [a]hear now this
word which I am about to speak in
your hearing and in the hearing of
all the people! 8 The prophets who
were before me and before you from
ancient times [a]prophesied against
many lands and against great king-
doms, of war and of calamity and
of pestilence. 9 The prophet who
prophesies of peace, [a]when the
word of the prophet comes to pass,
then that prophet will be known *as*
one whom Yahweh has truly sent."

10 Then Hananiah the prophet
took [a]the bar of the yoke from the
neck of Jeremiah the prophet and
broke it. 11 And Hananiah spoke in
the sight of all the people, saying,
"[a]Thus says Yahweh, 'Even so will I
break within two full years the yoke
of Nebuchadnezzar king of Babylon
from the neck of all the nations.'"
Then the prophet Jeremiah went his
way.

12 Then the [a]word of Yahweh
came to Jeremiah after Hananiah
the prophet had broken the bar of
the yoke from off the neck of the
prophet Jeremiah, saying, 13 "Go and
speak to Hananiah, saying, 'Thus
says Yahweh, "You have broken the
bars of a yoke *made* of wood, but you
have made in their place the [a]bars of
a yoke *made* of iron." 14 For thus says
Yahweh of hosts, the God of Israel, "I
have put a [a]yoke of iron on the neck
of all these nations, that they may
serve Nebuchadnezzar king of Bab-
ylon, and they will [b]serve him. And [c]I
have even given him the beasts of the
field."'" 15 Then Jeremiah the prophet
said to Hananiah the prophet, "Lis-
ten now, Hananiah, Yahweh has not
sent you, and [a]you have made this
people trust in a lie. 16 Therefore thus
says Yahweh, '[a]Behold, I am about
to [1]remove you from the face of the
earth. This year you are going to [b]die
because you have [c]spoken rebellion
against Yahweh.'"

17 So Hananiah the prophet died
in the same year in the seventh
month.

---

**28:2** [a]Jer 27:12; 28:11 **28:3** [a]2Ki 24:13; 2Chr 36:10; Jer 27:16; Da 1:2 **28:4** [a]Jer 22:26, 27 [b]2Ki 25:27; Jer 22:24; 24:1 [c]Jer 22:10 [d]Jer 27:8 **28:5** [a]Jer 28:1 **28:6** [a]1Ki 1:36; Ps 41:13; Jer 11:5 **28:7** [a]1Ki 22:28 **28:8** [a]Lv 26:14-39; 1Ki 14:15; 17:1; 22:17; Is 5:5-7; Joel 1:20; Am 1:2; Na 1:2 **28:9** [a]Dt 18:22 **28:10** [a]Jer 27:2 **28:11** [a]Jer 14:14; 27:10; 28:15 **28:12** [a]Jer 1:2 **28:13** [a]Ps 107:16; Is 45:2 **28:14** [a]Dt 28:48; Jer 27:8 [b]Jer 25:11 [c]Jer 27:6 **28:15** [a]Jer 20:6; 29:31; Lam 2:14; Eze 13:2, 3, 22; 22:28; Zec 13:3 **28:16** [a]Ge 7:4; Ex 32:12; Dt 6:15; 1Ki 13:34 [b]Jer 20:6 [c]Dt 13:5; Jer 29:32 [1]Lit *send you away*

### Jeremiah's Letter to the Exiles

29 Now these are the words of
the [a]letter which Jeremiah
the prophet sent from Jerusalem
to the rest of the elders of the exile,
the priests, the prophets, and all the
people whom Nebuchadnezzar had
taken away into exile from Jerusalem
to Babylon. **2** (This was after King
[a]Jeconiah and the [b]queen mother,
the court officials, the princes of
Judah and Jerusalem, the craftsmen,
and the smiths had gone out from Je-
rusalem.) **3** *The letter was sent* by the
hand of Elasah the son of Shaphan
and Gemariah the son of [a]Hilkiah,
whom Zedekiah king of Judah sent to
Babylon to Nebuchadnezzar king of
Babylon, saying, **4** "Thus says Yahweh
of hosts, the God of Israel, to all the
exiles whom I have [a]sent into exile
from Jerusalem to Babylon, **5** '[a]Build
houses and live *in them*; and plant
gardens and eat their fruit. **6** Take
[a]wives and [1]become the fathers of
sons and daughters, and take wives
for your sons and give your daughters
to husbands, that they may bear sons
and daughters; and multiply there
and do not decrease. **7** [a]Seek the
peace of the city where I have sent
you into exile, and [b]pray to Yahweh
on its behalf; for in its peace you will
have peace.' **8** For thus says Yahweh
of hosts, the God of Israel, 'Do not let
*your* [a]*prophets* who are in your midst
and your diviners [b]deceive you, and
do not listen to [c]your dreams which
you dream. **9** For they [a]prophesy a lie
to you in My name; [b]I have not sent
them,' declares Yahweh.

**10** "For thus says Yahweh, 'When
[a]seventy years have been fulfilled for
Babylon, I will [1]visit you and establish
My [b]good word to you, to return you
to this place. **11** For I know the [a]plans
that I [1]have for you,' declares Yahweh,
'plans for [b]peace and not for calami-
ty, to give you a future and a [c]hope.
**12** Then you will [a]call upon Me and
come and pray to Me, and I will [b]listen
to you. **13** You will [a]seek Me and find
*Me* when you [b]search for Me with all
your heart. **14** I will be [a]found by you,'
declares Yahweh, 'and I will [b,1]return
your [2]fortunes and will [c]gather you
from all the nations and from all the
places where I have banished you,'
declares Yahweh, 'and I will [d]cause
you to return to the place from where
I sent you into exile.'

**15** "Because you have said, 'Yahweh
has raised up [a]prophets for us in
Babylon'— **16** for thus says Yahweh
concerning the king who sits on the
throne of David and concerning all
the people who live in this city, your
brothers who did [a]not go with you
into exile— **17** thus says Yahweh of
hosts, 'Behold, I am sending upon
them the [a]sword, famine, and
pestilence, and I will make them
like [b]split-open figs that cannot be
eaten due to rottenness. **18** I will

---

◆ **29:1** [a]2Chr 30:1, 6; Es 9:20; Jer 29:25, 29 **29:2** [a]2Ki 24:12-16; 2Chr 36:9, 10; Jer 22:24-28; 24:1; 27:20 [b]2Ki 24:12, 15; Jer 13:18; 22:26 **29:3** [a]1Chr 6:13 **29:4** [a]Jer 24:5 **29:5** [a]Jer 29:28 **29:6** [a]Jer 16:2-4 [1]Lit *beget* **29:7** [a]Da 4:27; 6:4, 5 [b]Ezr 6:10; 7:23; Da 4:19; 1Ti 2:1, 2 **29:8** [a]Jer 27:9; 29:1 [b]Jer 14:14; 23:21; 27:14, 15; 28:15; Eph 5:6 [c]Jer 23:25, 27 **29:9** [a]Jer 27:15; 29:21 [b]Jer 29:31 **29:10** [a]2Chr 36:21-23; Jer 25:12; 27:22; Da 9:2; Zec 7:5 [b]Jer 24:6, 7; Zep 2:7 [1]Same Heb root as "punish" in Jer, cf. 5:9; 9:8; 29:32; 30:20 **29:11** [a]Ps 40:5; Jer 23:5, 6; 30:9, 10 [b]Is 40:9-11; Jer 30:18-22 [c]Jer 31:17; Hos 2:15 [1]Lit *am planning* **29:12** [a]Ps 50:15; Jer 33:3; Da 9:3 [b]Ps 145:19 **29:13** [a]Dt 4:29; Ps 32:6; Mt 7:7 [b]1Chr 22:19; 2Chr 22:9; Jer 24:7 **29:14** [a]Dt 30:1-10; Ps 32:6; Is 55:6 [b]Jer 30:3; 32:37-41 [c]Is 43:5, 6; Jer 23:8; 32:37 [d]Jer 3:14; 12:15; 16:15 [1]Or *restore* [2]Or *captivity* **29:15** [a]Jer 29:21, 24 **29:16** [a]Jer 38:2, 3, 17-23 **29:17** [a]Jer 27:8; 29:18; 32:24 [b]Jer 24:3, 8-10

pursue them with the sword, with
famine, and with pestilence; and I
will [a]give them over *to be* a terror
to all the kingdoms of the earth, to
be a [b]curse and an object of horror
and of [c]hissing, and a reproach
among all the nations where I have
banished them, **19** because they have
[a]not listened to My words,' declares
Yahweh, 'which I sent to them by [b]My
slaves the prophets, rising up early
and sending; but you did not listen,'
declares Yahweh. **20** You, therefore,
hear the word of Yahweh, all you
exiles, whom I have [a]sent away from
Jerusalem to Babylon.

**21** "Thus says Yahweh of hosts,
the God of Israel, concerning Ahab
the son of Kolaiah and concerning
Zedekiah the son of Maaseiah, who
are [a]prophesying to you falsely in My
name, 'Behold, I will give them into
the hand of Nebuchadnezzar king
of Babylon, and he will strike them
down before your eyes. **22** And be-
cause of them a [a]curse will be [1]used
by all the exiles from Judah who are in
Babylon, saying, "May Yahweh make
you like Zedekiah and like Ahab,
whom the king of Babylon [b]roasted
in the fire **23** because they have [a]acted
with wicked foolishness in Israel and
[b]have committed adultery with their
neighbors' wives and have [c]spoken
words in My name falsely, which I
did not command them; and I am
He who [d]knows and am a witness,"
declares Yahweh.'"

**24** And to [a]Shemaiah the Nehelamite
you shall speak, saying, **25** "Thus says
Yahweh of hosts, the God of Israel,
'Because you have sent [a]letters in
your own name to all the people who
are in Jerusalem and to [b]Zephaniah
the son of Maaseiah, the priest, and to
all the priests, saying, **26** "Yahweh has
given you *to be* a priest instead of Je-
hoiada the priest, to be the [a,1]overseer
in the house of Yahweh over every
[b]madman who [c]prophesies, to [d]put
him in the stocks and in the iron
collar, **27** so now, why have you not
rebuked Jeremiah of [a]Anathoth who
prophesies to you? **28** For he has [a]sent
to us in Babylon, saying, '*The exile*
will be [b]long; [c]build houses and live
*in them* and plant gardens and eat
their fruit.'"'"

**29** [a]So Zephaniah the priest read
this letter in the hearing of Jeremiah
the prophet. **30** Then came the word of
Yahweh to Jeremiah, saying, **31** "Send
to [a]all the exiles, saying, 'Thus says
Yahweh concerning [b]Shemaiah the
Nehelamite, "Because Shemaiah
has [c]prophesied to you, although I
did not send him, and he has [d]made
you trust in a lie," **32** therefore thus
says Yahweh, "Behold, I am about to
[a]punish Shemaiah the Nehelamite
and his seed; he will [b]not have any-
one living among this people, [c]and
he will not see the good that I am
about to do to My people," declares
Yahweh, "because he has [d]spoken
rebellion against Yahweh."'"

---

**29:18** [a]Dt 28:25; 2Chr 29:8; Jer 15:4; 24:9; 34:17; Eze 12:15 [b]Is 65:15; Jer 42:18 [c]Jer 25:9; Lam 2:15, 16 **29:19** [a]*Jer 6:19* [b]*Jer 25:4; 26:5;* 35:15 **29:20** [a]Jer 24:5; Eze 11:9; Mic 4:10 **29:21** [a]Jer 14:14, 15; 29:8, 9; Lam 2:14; 2Pe 2:1 **29:22** [a]Is 65:15 [b]Da 3:6, 21 [1]Lit *taken* **29:23** [a]Ge 34:7; 2Sa 13:12 [b]Jer 5:8; 23:14 [c]Jer 29:8, 9, 21 [d]Pr 5:21; Jer 7:11; 16:17; Mal 3:5; Heb 4:13 **29:24** [a]Jer 29:31, 32 **29:25** [a]Jer 29:1 [b]2Ki 25:18; Jer 21:1; 29:29; 37:3; 52:24 **29:26** [a]Jer 20:1 [b]2Ki 9:11; Hos 9:7; Mk 3:21; Jn 10:20; Ac 26:24, 25; 2Co 5:13 [c]Dt 13:1-5; Zec 13:1-5 [d]Jer 20:1, 2; Ac 16:24 [1]Lit *overseers* **29:27** [a]Jer 1:1 **29:28** [a]Jer 29:1 [b]Jer 29:10 [c]Jer 29:5 **29:29** [a]Jer 29:25 **29:31** [a]Jer 29:20 [b]Jer 29:24 [c]Jer 14:14, 15; 29:9, 23; Eze 13:8-16, 22, 23 [d]Jer 28:15 **29:32** [a]Jer 36:31 [b]1Sa 2:30-34; Jer 22:30 [c]2Ki 7:2, 19, 20; Jer 17:6; 29:10 [d]Dt 13:5; Jer 28:16

### *Yahweh Will Return the Fortunes of His People*

30 The word which came to Jer-
emiah from Yahweh, saying,
2 “Thus says Yahweh, the God of Isra-
el, ‘[a]Write all the words which I have
spoken to you in a book. 3 For behold,
[a]days are coming,’ declares Yahweh,
‘when I will [b,1]return the [2]fortunes of
My people [c]Israel and Judah.’ Yahweh
says, ‘I will also [d]cause them to return
to the land that I gave to their fathers,
and they shall possess it.’”
4 Now these are the words which
Yahweh spoke concerning Israel and
concerning Judah:

5 “For thus says Yahweh,
‘We have heard a sound
of [a]trembling,
Of dread, and there
is no peace.
6 ‘Ask now, and see
If a male can give birth.
Why do I see every man
*With* his hands on his loins,
[a]as a woman in childbirth?
And *why* have all faces
turned pale?
7 ‘Alas! For that [a]day is great,
There is [b]none like it;
And it is the time
of Jacob’s [c]distress,
But he will be [d]saved from it.
8 ‘And it will be in that day,’ de-
clares Yahweh of hosts, ‘*that* I will
[a]*break his yoke from* off your neck
and will tear off your [b]bonds; and
strangers will no longer [c]make [1]them
their slaves. 9 But they shall be a slave
to Yahweh their God and [a]David their
king, whom I will raise up for them.
10 ‘[a]Fear not, O Jacob My
[1]servant,’ declares Yahweh,
‘And do not be dismayed,
O Israel;
For behold, I will save
you [b]from afar
And your seed from the
land of their captivity.
And Jacob will return and
will be [c]quiet and at ease,
And [d]no one will make
him tremble.
11 ‘For [a]I am with you,’ declares
Yahweh, ‘to save you;
For I will [b]make a complete
destruction of all the nations
where I have scattered you,
Only I will [c]not make a
complete destruction of you.
But I will [d]chasten you justly
And will by no means leave
you unpunished.’

12 “For thus says Yahweh,
‘Your injury is incurable,
And your [a]wound is
desperately sick.
13 ‘There is no one
to plead your cause;
*No* healing for *your* sore,
[a]No recovery for you.
14 ‘All your [a]lovers have
forgotten you;

◆ **30:2** [a]Is 30:8; Jer 25:13; 36:4, 28, 32; Hab 2:2 **30:3** [a]Jer 29:10 [b]Ps 53:6; Jer 29:14; 30:18; 32:44; Eze 39:25; Am 9:14; Zep 3:20 [c]Jer 3:18 [d]Jer 16:15; 23:7, 8; Eze 20:42; 36:24 [1]Or *restore* [2]Or *captivity* **30:5** [a]Is 5:30; Jer 6:25; 8:16; Am 5:16-18 **30:6** [a]Jer 4:31; 6:24; 22:23 **30:7** [a]Is 2:12; Hos 1:11; Joel 2:11; Am 5:18; Zep 1:14 [b]Lam 1:12; Da 9:12; 12:1 [c]Jer 2:27, 28; 14:8 [d]Jer 30:10; 50:19 **30:8** [a]Is 9:4; Jer 2:20; Eze 34:27 [b]Jer 27:2 [c]Eze 34:27 [1]Lit *him their slave* **30:9** [a]Is 55:3-5; Eze 34:23, 24; 37:24, 25; Hos 3:5; Lk 1:69; Ac 2:30; 13:23, 34 **30:10** [a]Is 41:13; 43:5; 44:2; Jer 46:27, 28 [b]Is 60:4; Jer 23:3, 8; 29:14 [c]Is 35:9; Jer 33:16; Hos 2:18 [d]Mic 4:4 [1]Or *slave*, cf. 30:8, 9; see Foreword, “The Terminology of Slave” **30:11** [a]Jer 1:8, 19 [b]Jer 46:28; Am 9:8 [c]Jer 4:27; 5:10, 18 [d]Ps 6:1; Jer 10:24 **30:12** [a]2Chr 36:16; Jer 15:18; 30:15 **30:13** [a]Jer 14:19; 46:11 **30:14** [a]Jer 22:20, 22; Lam 1:2

They do not seek you;
For I have [b,1]wounded
you with the wound
of an enemy,
With the [c]punishment
of a [d]cruel one,
Because your [e]iniquity
is numerous
*And* your [f]sins are mighty.
15 'Why do you cry out
over your injury?
Your pain is incurable.
Because your iniquity
is numerous
*And* your sins are mighty,
I have done these
things to you.
16 'Therefore all who [a]devour
you will be devoured;
And all your adversaries,
every one of them,
[b]will go into captivity;
And those who take you
as spoil will be spoil,
And all who plunder you
I will give as plunder.
17 'For I will [1]restore you
to [a,2]health,
And I will heal you of your
wounds,' declares Yahweh,
'Because they have called you
a [b]banished one, saying:
"It is Zion; no one is
seeking her."'

18 "Thus says Yahweh,
'Behold, I will [a,1]return
the [2]fortunes of the tents
of Jacob
And [b]have compassion on
his dwelling places;
And the [c]city will be
rebuilt on its ruin,
And the [d]palace will sit
on its just place.
19 'From them will come
forth [a]thanksgiving
And the voice of those
who [b,1]celebrate;
And I will [c]multiply them,
and they will not decrease;
I will also [d]honor them,
and they will not
be insignificant.
20 '[1]Their children also
will be as formerly,
And [2]their congregation shall
be [a]established before Me;
And I will punish all
[2]their oppressors.
21 'And [1]their [a]mighty one
shall be one of them,
And [1]their ruler shall come
forth from [1]their midst;
And I will [b]bring Him near,
and He shall approach Me;
For who would *dare*
to give his heart as security
to [c]approach Me?'
declares Yahweh.
22 'You shall be [a]My people,
And I will be your God.'"

23 Behold, the [a]storm of Yahweh!
Wrath has gone forth,
A [1]sweeping storm;
It will burst on the head
of the wicked.

---

**30:14** [b]Lam 2:4, 5 [c]Job 30:21 [d]Jer 6:23; 50:42 [e]Jer 32:30-35; 44:22 [f]Jer 5:6 [1]Lit *struck* **30:16** [a]Jer 2:3; 8:16; 10:25 [b]Is 14:2; Joel 3:8 **30:17** [a]Ex 15:26; Ps 107:20; Is 30:26; Jer 8:22; 33:6 [b]Is 11:12; 56:8; Jer 33:24 [1]Lit *cause to go up* [2]Or *healing* **30:18** [a]Jer 30:3; 31:23 [b]Ps 102:13 [c]Jer 31:4, 38-40 [d]1Chr 29:1, 19; Ps 48:3, 13; 122:7 [1]Or *restore* [2]Or *captivity* **30:19** [a]Is 12:1; 35:10; 51:3; Jer 17:26; 33:11 [b]Ps 126:1, 2; Is 51:11; Jer 31:4; Zep 3:14 [c]Jer 33:22 [d]Is 55:5; 60:9 [1]Or *dance* **30:20** [a]Is 54:14 [1]Lit *His* [2]Lit *his* **30:21** [a]Jer 30:9; Eze 34:23, 24; 37:24 [b]Nu 16:5; Ps 65:4 [c]Ex 3:5; Jer 50:44 [1]Lit *his* **30:22** [a]Ex 6:7; Jer 32:38; Eze 36:28; Hos 2:23; Zec 13:9 **30:23** [a]Jer 23:19 [1]Or *raging*

24 The [a]burning anger of
Yahweh will not turn back
Until He has done and
until He has established
The intent of His heart;
In the [b]last days you will
understand this.

### *Israel's Mourning Turned to Joy*

31 "At that time," declares Yah-
weh, "I will be the [a]God of all
the [b]families of Israel, and they shall
be My people."

2 Thus says Yahweh,
"The people who
survived the sword
[a]Found grace
in the wilderness—
Israel, when it went
to [b]find its relief."
3 Yahweh appeared to [1]him
from afar, *saying*,
"I have [a]loved you
with an everlasting love;
Therefore I have drawn you
with [b]lovingkindness.
4 "[a]Again I will build you,
and you will be rebuilt,
O virgin of Israel!
Again you will [1]take up
your [b]tambourines
And go forth to the dances
of those [c]celebrating.
5 "Again you
will [a]plant vineyards
*On the* [1]*hills* of Samaria;
The planters will plant
And will [2]enjoy *them*.
6 "For there will be a day
when watchmen
On the hills of Ephraim
call out,
'Arise, and [a]let us go
up *to* Zion,
To Yahweh our God.'"

7 For thus says Yahweh,
"[a]Sing aloud
with gladness for Jacob,
And shout among the
[b]head of the nations;
Make *it* heard, give
praise, and say,
'O Yahweh, [c]save Your people,
The [d]remnant of Israel.'
8 "Behold, I am [a]bringing them
from the north country,
And I will [b]gather them
from the remote
parts of the earth,
Among them the [c]blind
and the [d]lame,
The woman with child
and she who is in labor
with child, together;
A great assembly, they
will return here.
9 "[a]With weeping they
will come,
And by supplication I
will lead them;
I will make them walk
by [b]streams of waters,
On a straight path in which
*they will* [c]not stumble;
For I am a [d]father to Israel,
And Ephraim is [e]My firstborn."

10 Hear the word
of Yahweh, O nations,

---

**30:24** [a]Jer 4:8 [b]Jer 23:20 ◆ **31:1** [a]Jer 30:22 [b]Ge 17:7, 8; Is 41:10; Ro 11:26-28 **31:2** [a]Nu 14:20 [b]Ex 33:14; Nu 10:33; Dt 1:33; Jos 1:13 **31:3** [a]Dt 4:37; 7:8; Mal 1:2 [b]Ps 25:6 [1]Lit *me* **31:4** [a]Jer 24:6; 33:7 [b]Is 30:32 [c]Jer 30:19 [1]Or *be adorned with* **31:5** [a]Ps 107:37; Is 65:21; Eze 28:26; Am 9:14 [1]Or *mountains* [2]Lit *defile* **31:6** [a]Is 2:3; Jer 31:12; 50:4, 5; Mic 4:2 **31:7** [a]Ps 14:7; Jer 20:13 [b]Dt 28:13; Is 61:9 [c]Ps 28:9 [d]Is 37:31; Jer 23:3 **31:8** [a]Jer 3:18; 23:8 [b]Dt 30:4; Is 43:6; Eze 34:13 [c]Is 42:16 [d]Is 40:11; Eze 34:16; Mic 4:6 **31:9** [a]Ps 126:5; Jer 50:4 [b]Is 43:20; 49:10 [c]Is 63:13 [d]Is 64:8; Jer 3:4, 19 [e]Ex 4:22

And declare in the [a]coastlands
far away,
And say, "He who dispersed
Israel will [b]gather him
And keep him as a [c]shepherd
keeps his flock."

11 For Yahweh has
[a]ransomed Jacob
And redeemed him
from the hand of him who
was [b]stronger than he.

12 "They will [a]come and sing
for joy on the [b]height
of Zion,
And they will be [c]radiant over
the goodness of Yahweh—
Over the [d]grain and the
new wine and the oil,
And over the young
of the [e]flock and the herd;
And their soul will be
like a [f]watered garden,
And they will [g]never
waste away again.

13 "Then the virgin will be
glad in the [a]dance,
And the young men and
the old, together,
For I will [b]turn their
mourning into joy
And will comfort them
and give them [c]gladness
for their sorrow.

14 "I will [1]fill the soul of
the priests with [2]richness,
And My people will be
[a]satisfied with My
goodness," declares Yahweh.

15 Thus says Yahweh,
"[a]A voice is heard in [b]Ramah,
Wailing *and* bitter weeping.
Rachel is weeping
for her children;
She [c]refuses to be comforted
for her children
Because [d]they are no more."

16 Thus says Yahweh,
"[a]Restrain your voice
from weeping
And your eyes from tears,
For your [b]work will be
rewarded," declares Yahweh,
"And they will [c]return
from the land of the enemy.

17 "And there is [a]hope for your
future," declares Yahweh,
"And *your* children will return
to their own territory.

18 "I have surely heard
Ephraim [a]grieving,
'You have [b]chastised me,
and I was chastised,
Like an untrained [c]calf;
[d]Cause me to return
that I may return,
For You are Yahweh my God.

19 'For after I turned away,
I [a]repented;
And after I was instructed,
I [b]slapped *my* thigh;
I was [c]ashamed and
also dishonored
Because I bore the reproach
of my youth.'

20 "Is [a]Ephraim My dear son?
Is he a delightful child?

**31:10** [a]Is 66:19; Jer 25:22 [b]Jer 50:19 [c]Is 40:11; Eze 34:12 **31:11** [a]Is 44:23; 48:20; Jer 15:21; 50:34 [b]Ps 142:6 **31:12** [a]*Jer 31:6, 7* [b]*Eze 17:23* [c]Is 2:2; Mic 4:1 [d]Hos 2:22; Joel 3:18 [e]Jer 31:24; 33:12, 13 [f]Is 58:11 [g]Is 35:10; 60:20; 65:19; Jn 16:22; Rev 21:4 **31:13** [a]Jdg 21:21; Ps 30:11; Zec 8:4, 5 [b]Is 61:3 [c]Is 51:11 **31:14** [a]Jer 50:19 [1]Lit *saturate* [2]Lit *fatness* **31:15** [a]Mt 2:18 [b]*Jos 18:25; Jdg 4:5;* Is 10:29; Jer 40:1 [c]Ge 37:35; Ps 77:2 [d]Ge 5:24; 42:13, 36; Jer 10:20 **31:16** [a]Is 25:8; 30:19 [b]Ru 2:12; Heb 6:10 [c]Jer 30:3; Eze 11:17 **31:17** [a]Jer 29:11 **31:18** [a]Jer 3:21 [b]Job 5:17; Ps 94:12 [c]Hos 4:16 [d]Ps 80:3, 7, 19; Jer 17:14; Lam 5:21; Ac 3:26 **31:19** [a]Eze 36:31; Zec 12:10 [b]Eze 21:12; Lk 18:13 [c]Jer 3:25 **31:20** [a]Hos 11:8

Indeed, as often as I have
spoken against him,
I certainly still remember him;
Therefore My [b,1]inmost
being yearns for him;
I will surely [c]have compassion
on him," declares Yahweh.

21 "Set up roadmarks for yourself,
Place for yourself guideposts;
[a]Set your heart to
the highway,
The way by which you went.
[b]Return, O virgin of Israel,
Return to these your cities.
22 "How long will you go
here and there,
O [a]faithless daughter?
For Yahweh has created
a new thing in the earth—
A [1]woman will
encompass a man."
23 Thus says Yahweh of hosts, the
God of Israel, "Once again they will
speak this word in the land of Judah
and in its cities when I [a,1]return their
[2]fortunes,
'Yahweh bless you,
O [b]abode of righteousness,
O [c]holy hill!'
24 "And Judah and all its cities will
[a]inhabit it together, the farmer
and they who go about with flocks.
25 [a]For I satisfy the weary soul and
fill up every soul who wastes away."
26 At *this* I [a]*awoke and looked*, and
my [b]sleep was pleasant to me.

### *The New Covenant*

27 "Behold, days are coming," declares
Yahweh, "when I will [a]sow the house
of Israel and the house of Judah with
the seed of man and with the seed of
beast. 28 And it will be that as I have
[a]watched over them to [b]uproot, to
tear down, to pull down, to destroy,
and to bring calamity, so I will watch
over them to [c]build and to plant,"
declares Yahweh.
29 "In those days they will
not say again,
'[a]The fathers have
eaten sour grapes,
And the children's teeth
are [1]set on edge.'
30 "But [a]everyone will die for his own
iniquity; each man who eats the sour
grapes, his teeth will be [1]set on edge.
31 "[a]Behold, days are coming,"
declares Yahweh, "when I will cut
a [b]new covenant with the house of
Israel and with the house of Judah,
32 not like the [a]covenant which I cut
with their fathers in the day I [b]took
them by the hand to bring them out
of the land of Egypt, My [c]covenant
which they broke, but I was a hus-
band to them," declares Yahweh.
33 "But [a]this is the covenant which I
will cut with the house of Israel after
those days," declares Yahweh: "[b]I will
put My law within them, and on
their heart I will write it; and [c]I will
be their God, and they shall be My
people. 34 And they will [a]not teach

---

**31:20** [b]Ge 43:30; Jdg 10:16; Is 63:15; Hos 11:8 [c]Is 55:7; 57:18; Hos 14:4; Mic 7:18 [1]Lit *inward parts*
**31:21** [a]Jer 50:5 [b]Is 48:20; 52:11 **31:22** [a]Jer 3:6; 49:4 [1]Lit *female* **31:23** [a]Jer 30:18; 32:44 [b]Is 1:26; Jer 50:7 [c]Ps 48:1; 87:1; Zec 8:3 [1]Or *restore* [2]Or *captivity* **31:24** [a]Jer 31:12; Eze 36:10; Zec 8:4-8
**31:25** [a]Ps 107:9; Jer 31:12, 14; Mt 5:6; Jn 4:14 **31:26** [a]Zec 4:1 [b]Pr 3:24 **31:27** [a]Eze 36:9, 11; Hos 2:23 **31:28** [a]Jer 44:27; Da 9:14 [b]Jer 1:10; 18:7 [c]Jer 24:6 **31:29** [a]Lam 5:7; Eze 18:2 [1]Or *dull* **31:30** [a]Dt 24:16; Is 3:11; Eze 18:4, 20 [1]Or *dull* **31:31** [a]Jer 31:31-34; Heb 8:8-12 [b]Jer 32:40; 33:14; Eze 37:26; Lk 22:20; 1Co 11:25; 2Co 3:6; Heb 8:8-12; 10:16, 17 **31:32** [a]Ex 19:5; 24:6-8; Dt 5:2, 3 [b]Dt 1:31; Is 63:12 [c]Jer 11:7, 8 **31:33** [a]Jer 32:40; Heb 10:16 [b]Ps 40:8; 2Co 3:3 [c]Jer 24:7; 30:22; 32:38
**31:34** [a]1Th 4:9; 1Jn 2:27

again, each man his neighbor and
each man his brother, saying, 'Know
Yahweh,' for they will all [b]know Me,
from the least of them to the greatest
of them," declares Yahweh, "for I will
[c]forgive their iniquity, and their [d]sin
I will remember no more."

35 Thus says Yahweh,
Who [a]gives the sun
for light by day
And the statutes for the moon
and the stars for light
by night,
Who [b]stirs up the sea so
that its waves roar;
[c]Yahweh of hosts is His name:
36 "[a]If these statutes are removed
From before Me,"
declares Yahweh,
"Then the seed of Israel
also will [b]cease
From being a nation
before Me [1]forever."
37 Thus says Yahweh,
"[a]If the heavens
above can be measured
And the foundations of the
earth searched out below,
Then I will also [b]reject
all the seed of Israel
For all that they have done,"
declares Yahweh.

38 "Behold, days are coming,"
declares Yahweh, "when the [a]city
will be rebuilt for Yahweh from the
[b]Tower of Hananel to the [c]Corner
Gate. 39 The [a]measuring line will
go out farther, straight ahead to the
hill Gareb; then it will turn to Goah.
40 And [a]the whole valley of the dead
bodies and of the ashes, and all the
fields as far as the brook [b]Kidron, to
the corner of the [c]Horse Gate toward
the east, shall be [d]holy to Yahweh; it
will not be uprooted or pulled down
anymore forever."

### *Jeremiah Imprisoned*

32 The word that came to Jeremiah
from Yahweh in the [a]tenth year
of Zedekiah king of Judah, which
was the eighteenth year of Nebu-
chadnezzar. 2 Now at that time the
military force of the king of Babylon
was besieging Jerusalem, and Jere-
miah the prophet was shut up in the
[a]court of the guard, which *was in* the
house of the king of Judah, 3 because
Zedekiah king of Judah had [a]shut him
up, saying, "Why do you [b]prophesy,
saying, '[c]Thus says Yahweh, "Behold,
I am about to [d]give this city into the
hand of the king of Babylon, and he
will capture it; 4 and Zedekiah king
of Judah will [a]not escape out of the
hand of the Chaldeans, but he will
surely be given into the hand of the
king of Babylon, and he will [b]speak
with him [1]face to face and see him eye
to eye; 5 and he will [a]lead Zedekiah to
Babylon, and he will be there until I
[1]visit him," declares Yahweh. "If you
fight against the Chaldeans, you will
[b]not succeed"'?"

**31:34** [b]Is 11:9; 54:13; Jer 24:7; Hab 2:14; Jn 6:45; 1Jn 2:20 [c]Jer 33:8; 50:20; Mic 7:18; Ro 11:27 [d]Is 43:25; Heb 10:17 **31:35** [a]Ge 1:14-18; Dt 4:19; Ps 19:1-6; 136:7-9 [b]Is 51:15 [c]Jer 10:16; 32:18; 50:34 **31:36** [a]*Ps 89*:36, 37; 148:6; Is 54:9, 10; Jer 33:20-26 [b]Am 9:8, 9 [1]Lit all the days **31:37** [a]Is 40:12; Jer 33:22 [b]Jer 33:24-26; Ro 11:2-5, 26, 27 **31:38** [a]Jer 30:18; 31:4 [b]Ne 3:1; 12:39; Zec 14:10 [c]2Ki 14:13; 2Chr 26:9 **31:39** [a]Zec 2:1 **31:40** [a]Jer 7:32; 8:2 [b]2Sa 15:23; 2Ki 23:6, 12; Jn 18:1 [c]2Ki 11:16; 2Chr 23:15; Ne 3:28 [d]Joel 3:17; Zec 14:20 ◆ **32:1** [a]2Ki 25:1, 2; Jer 39:1, 2 **32:2** [a]Ne 3:25; Jer 33:1; 37:21; 38:6; 39:14 **32:3** [a]2Ki 6:32 [b]Jer 26:8, 9 [c]Jer 21:3-7; 34:2, 3 [d]Jer 21:4-7; 32:28, 29; 34:2, 3 **32:4** [a]2Ki 25:4-7; Jer 37:17; 38:18, 23; 39:4-7 [b]Jer 39:5 [1]Lit *mouth to mouth* **32:5** [a]Jer 27:22; 39:7; Eze 12:12, 13 [b]Eze 17:9, 10, 15 [1]Same Heb root as "punish" in Jer, cf. 5:9; 9:8; 29:32; 30:20

6 And Jeremiah said, "The word of Yahweh came to me, saying, 7 'Behold, Hanamel the son of Shallum your uncle is coming to you, saying, "Buy for yourself my field which is at [a]Anathoth, for you have the [b]*legal* judgment for redemption to buy *it*."' 8 Then Hanamel my uncle's son came to me in the [a]court of the guard according to the word of Yahweh and said to me, 'Buy my field, please, that is at [b]Anathoth, which is in the land of Benjamin; for you have the *legal* judgment for possession, and the redemption is yours; buy *it* for yourself.' Then I knew that this was the [c]word of Yahweh.

9 "I bought the field which was at Anathoth from Hanamel my uncle's son, and I [a]weighed out the silver for him, seventeen [b,1]shekels of silver. 10 And I [a,1]signed and [b]sealed the deed and [c]called in witnesses and weighed out the silver on the scales. 11 Then I took the deeds of purchase, both the sealed *copy containing* the [a]commandment and statutes and the open *copy*, 12 and I gave the deed of purchase to [a]Baruch the son of [b]Neriah, the son of Mahseiah, in the sight of Hanamel my uncle's *son* and in the sight of the witnesses who signed the deed of purchase, in the sight of all the Jews who were sitting in the court of the guard. 13 And I commanded Baruch in their sight, saying, 14 'Thus says Yahweh of hosts, the God of Israel, "Take these deeds—this deed of purchase—that is the sealed one as well as this open deed, and put them in an earthenware jar, that they may [1]last a long time." 15 For thus says Yahweh of hosts, the God of Israel, "[a]Houses and fields and vineyards will again be bought in this land."'

### *Jeremiah Prays, Yahweh Responds*

16 "After I had given the deed of purchase to Baruch the son of Neriah, then I [a]prayed to Yahweh, saying, 17 '[a]Ah Lord Yahweh! Behold, You have [b]made the heavens and the earth by Your great power and by Your outstretched arm! [c]Nothing is too difficult for You, 18 who [a]shows lovingkindness to thousands, but [b]repays the iniquity of fathers into the bosom of their children after them, O [c]great *and* [d]mighty God. [e]Yahweh of hosts is His name, 19 [a]great in counsel and abundant in deeds, whose [b]eyes are open to all the ways of the sons of men, [c]giving to everyone according to his ways and according to the fruit of his deeds, 20 who has [a]set signs and wonders in the land of Egypt, *and* even to this day both in Israel and among mankind; and You have [b]made a name for Yourself, as at this day. 21 You [a]brought Your people Israel out of the land of Egypt

**32:7** [a]Jer 1:1; 11:21 [b]Lv 25:25; Ru 4:3, 4 **32:8** [a]Jer 32:2; 33:1 [b]Jer 1:1; 32:7 [c]1Sa 9:16, 17; 10:3-7; 1Ki 22:25; Jer 32:25 **32:9** [a]Ge 23:16; Zec 11:12 [b]Ge 24:22; Ex 21:32; Ne 5:15; Eze 4:10 [1]A shekel was approx. 0.4 oz. or 11 gm **32:10** [a]Is 44:5; Jer 32:44 [b]Dt 32:34; Job 14:17 [c]Ru 4:1, 9; Is 8:2 [1]Or *wrote...on the document* **32:11** [a]Lk 2:27 **32:12** [a]Jer 32:16; 36:4, 5, 32; 43:3; 45:1 [b]Jer 51:59 **32:14** [1]Lit *stand many days* **32:15** [a]Jer 30:18; 31:5, 12, 24; 32:37, 43, 44; 33:12, 13; Am 9:14, 15; Zec 3:10 **32:16** [a]Ge 32:9-12; Jer 12:1; Php 4:6, 7 **32:17** [a]Jer 1:6; 4:10 [b]2Ki 19:15; Ps 102:25; Is 40:26-29; Jer 27:5 [c]Ge 18:14; Jer 32:27; Zec 8:6; Mt 19:26; Mk 10:27; Lk 1:37; 18:27 **32:18** [a]Ex 20:6; 34:6, 7; Dt 5:9, 10; 7:9, 10 [b]1Ki 14:9, 10; 16:1-3; Mt 23:32-36 [c]Ps 145:3 [d]Ps 50:1; Is 9:6; Jer 20:11 [e]Jer 10:16; 31:35 **32:19** [a]Is 9:6; 28:29 [b]Job 34:21; Jer 23:24 [c]Ps 62:12; Jer 17:10; 21:14; Mt 16:27; Jn 5:29 **32:20** [a]Ps 78:43; 105:27 [b]Ex 9:16; Is 63:12, 14; Da 9:15 **32:21** [a]Ex 6:6; Dt 4:34; 7:19; 26:8; 2Sa 7:23; 1Chr 17:21; Ps 136:11

with signs and with wonders, and with a strong hand and with an outstretched arm and with great terror 22 and gave them this land, which You [a]swore to their fathers to give them, a land flowing with milk and honey. 23 They [a]came in and took possession of it, but they [b]did not listen to Your voice and did not [c]walk in Your law. They have not done anything that You commanded them to do; therefore You have made [d]all this *harmful* evil come upon them. 24 Behold, the [a]siege ramps have come to the city to capture it; and the city is [b]given into the hand of the Chaldeans, who fight against it, because of the [c]sword, the famine, and the pestilence; and what You have spoken has [d]happened; and behold, You see *it*. 25 And You have said to me, O Lord Yahweh, "Buy for yourself the field with money and call in witnesses"—but the city is given into the hand of the Chaldeans.'"

26 Then the word of Yahweh came to Jeremiah, saying, 27 "Behold, I am Yahweh, the [a]God of all flesh; is anything [b]too difficult for Me?" 28 Therefore thus says Yahweh, "Behold, I am about to [a]give this city into the hand of the Chaldeans and into the hand of Nebuchadnezzar king of Babylon, and he will capture it. 29 And the Chaldeans who are fighting against this city will enter and [a]set this city on fire and burn it, with the [b]houses where *people* have burned incense to Baal on their roofs and poured out drink offerings to other gods to provoke Me to anger. 30 Indeed the sons of Israel and the sons of Judah have been doing only [a]evil in My sight from their youth; for the sons of Israel have been only [b]provoking Me to anger by the work of their hands," declares Yahweh. 31 "Indeed this city has been to Me *a* [a]*provocation of* My anger and My wrath from the day that they built it, even to this day, so that it should be [b]removed from before My face 32 because of all the evil of the sons of Israel and the sons of Judah which they have done to provoke Me to anger—they, their [a]kings, their princes, their priests, their prophets, the men of Judah, and the inhabitants of Jerusalem. 33 And they have turned *their* back to Me and not *their* face; though *I* taught them, [a]rising up early and teaching, they would not listen [1]and receive discipline. 34 But they [a]put their detestable things in the house which is called by My name, to defile it. 35 And they built the [a]high places of Baal that are in the valley of Ben-hinnom to cause their sons and their daughters to pass through *the fire* to [b]Molech, which I had not commanded them, nor had it come upon My heart that they should do this abomination, to cause Judah to sin.

**32:22** [a]Ex 3:8, 17; 13:5; Dt 1:8; Ps 105:9-11; Jer 11:5 **32:23** [a]Ps 44:2, 3; 78:54, 55; Jer 2:7 [b]Ne 9:26; Jer 11:8; Da 9:10-14 [c]Ezr 9:7; Jer 26:4; 44:10 [d]Lam 1:18; Da 9:11, 12 **32:24** [a]Jer 33:4; Eze 21:22 [b]Jer 20:5; 21:4-7; 32:5 [c]*Jer 14:12; 29:17, 18; 32:36;* 34:17; Eze 14:21 [d]Dt 4:26; Jos 23:15, 16; Zec 1:6 **32:27** [a]Nu 16:22; 27:16 [b]Jer 32:17; Mt 19:26 **32:28** [a]2Ki 25:11; 2Chr 36:17-21; Jer 19:7-12; 32:3, 24, *36;* 34:2, 3 **32:29** [a]2Chr 36:19; Jer 21:10; 37:8, 10; 39:8 [b]Jer 19:13; 44:17-19, 25; 52:13 **32:30** [a]Dt 9:7-12; Is 63:10; Jer 2:7; 7:22-26 [b]Jer 8:19; 11:17; 25:7 **32:31** [a]1Ki 11:7, 8; 2Ki 21:4-7, 16; Jer 5:9-11; 6:6, 7; Mt 23:37 [b]2Ki 23:27; 24:3, 4; Jer 27:10 **32:32** [a]Ezr 9:7; Is 1:4-6, 23; Jer 2:26; 44:17, 21; Da 9:8 **32:33** [a]2Chr 36:15, 16; Jer 7:13; 25:3; 26:5; 35:15; Jn 8:2 [1]Lit *to* **32:34** [a]2Ki 21:1-7; Jer 7:30; 19:4-6; Eze 8:5 **32:35** [a]2Chr 28:2, 3; 33:6; Jer 7:31; 19:5 [b]Lv 18:21; 20:2-5; 1Ki 11:7; 2Ki 23:10; Ac 7:43

**36** "So now, therefore thus says
Yahweh, the God of Israel, concern-
ing this city of which you are saying,
'It is [a]given into the hand of the king
of Babylon by sword, by famine,
and by pestilence.' **37** Behold, I will
[a]gather them out of all the lands
to which I have banished them in
My anger, in My wrath, and in great
indignation; and I will cause them to
return to this place and [b]make them
inhabit *it* in safety. **38** And they shall
be [a]My people, and I will be their
God; **39** and I will [a]give them one
heart and one way, that they may
fear Me always, for their own [b]good
and for *the good of* their children
after them. **40** And I will cut an
[a]everlasting covenant with them
that I will [b]not turn away from them,
to do them good; and I will [c]put the
fear of Me in their hearts so that they
will not turn away from Me. **41** And
I will [a]rejoice over them to do them
good and will truly [b]plant them in
this land with [c]all My heart and with
all My soul. **42** For thus says Yahweh,
'[a]Just as I brought all this great evil
on this people, so I am going to
[b]bring on them all the good that I am
promising them. **43** [a]Thus fields will
be bought in this land of which you
*all* are saying, "[b]It is a desolation,
without man or beast; it is given
into the hand of the Chaldeans."
**44** Men will buy fields for money,
[a,1]sign and seal deeds, and call in
witnesses in the [b]land of Benjamin,
in the surroundings of Jerusalem,
in the cities of Judah, in the cities
of the hill country, in the cities of
the [2]Shephelah, and in the cities of
the [3]Negev; for I will [c,4]return their
[5]fortunes,' declares Yahweh."

### *Yahweh Will Pardon the People's Iniquity*

**33** Then the word of Yahweh came
to Jeremiah the second time,
while he was still [a,1]confined in the
court of the guard, saying, **2** "Thus
says [a]Yahweh who made [1]*the earth*,
Yahweh who formed it to establish
it; [b]Yahweh is His name, **3** '[a]Call to
Me and I will answer you, and I will
tell you [b]great and mighty things,
[c]which you do not know.' **4** For thus
says Yahweh, the God of Israel, con-
cerning the [a]houses of this city and
concerning the houses of the kings of
Judah which are torn down *to make a
defense* against the [b]siege ramps and
against the sword, **5** 'While *they* are
coming to [a]fight with the Chaldeans
and to fill them with the corpses of
men whom I have struck down in
My anger and in My wrath, and I
have [b]hidden My face from this city
because of all their evil: **6** Behold, I
will bring to it [a]health and healing,
and I will heal them; and I will reveal
to them an [b]abundance of peace and

---

**32:36** [a]Jer 32:24 **32:37** [a]Dt 30:3; Ps 106:47; Is 11:11-16; Jer 16:14, 15; 23:3, 8; Eze 11:17; Hos 1:11; Am 9:14, 15 [b]Jer 23:6; Eze 34:25, 28; Zec 14:11 **32:38** [a]Jer 24:7 **32:39** [a]2Chr 30:12; Jer 31:33; Eze 11:19; Jn 17:21; Ac 4:32 [b]Dt 11:18-21; Eze 37:25 **32:40** [a]Is 55:3; Jer 31:33, 34; 50:5; Eze 37:26 [b]Dt 31:6, 8; Eze 39:29 [c]Jer 24:7; 31:33 **32:41** [a]Dt 30:9; Is 62:5; 65:19 [b]Jer 24:6; 31:28; Am 9:15 [c]Hos 2:19, 20 **32:42** [a]Jer 31:28; Zec 8:14, 15 [b]Jer 33:14 **32:43** [a]Jer 32:15, 25; Eze 37:11-14 [b]Jer 33:10 **32:44** [a]Jer 32:10 [b]Jer 17:26; 33:13 [c]Jer 31:23; 33:7, 11, 26 [1]Lit *write on the document and seal* [2]Or *lowland* [3]South country [4]Or *restore* [5]Or *captivity* ◆ **33:1** [a]Jer 32:2, 8; 37:21; 38:28 [1]Lit *shut up* **33:2** [a]Jer 51:19 [b]Ex 3:15; 6:3; 15:3; Jer 10:16 [1]Lit *it* **33:3** [a]Ps 50:15; 91:15; Is 55:6, 7; Jer 29:12 [b]Jer 32:17, 27 [c]Is 48:6 **33:4** [a]Is 32:13, 14 [b]Jer 32:24; Eze 4:2; 21:22; Hab 1:10 **33:5** [a]Jer 21:4-7; 32:5 [b]Is 8:17; Jer 21:10; Mic 3:4 **33:6** [a]Jer 17:14; 30:17; Hos 6:1 [b]Is 66:12; Ga 5:22, 23

truth. **7** I will [a,1]return the [2]fortunes
of Judah and the [2]fortunes of Israel
and will [b]rebuild them as they were
at first. **8** And I will [a]cleanse them
from all their iniquity by which they
have sinned against Me, and I will
pardon all their iniquities by which
they have sinned against Me and by
which they have transgressed against
Me. **9** And [1]it will be to Me a [a]name
of joy, praise, and beauty before
[b]all the nations of the earth which
will hear of all the [c]good that I do
for them, and they will [d]be in dread
and tremble because of all the good
and all the peace that I make for it.'

**10** "Thus says Yahweh, 'Yet again
there will be heard in this place, of
which you say, "It is a [a]waste, without
man and without beast," *that is*, in
the cities of Judah and in the streets
of Jerusalem that are [b]desolate, with-
out man and without inhabitant and
without beast, **11** the voice of [a]joy and
the voice of gladness, the voice of
the bridegroom and the voice of the
bride, the voice of those who say,

"[b]Give thanks
to Yahweh of hosts,
For Yahweh is good,
For His lovingkindness
endures forever";

*and of those* who bring a [c]thank of-
fering into the house of Yahweh. For
I will [1]return the [2]fortunes of the land
as they were at first,' says Yahweh.

**12** "Thus says Yahweh of hosts,
'There will again be in this place
which is waste, [a]without man or
beast, and in all its cities, [1]an abode
of shepherds who cause their [b]flocks
to lie down. **13** In the [a]cities of the hill
country, in the cities of the [1]Sheph-
elah, in the cities of the Negev, in the
land of Benjamin, in the surround-
ings of Jerusalem, and in the cities
of Judah, the flocks will again [b]pass
under the hands of the one who
numbers them,' says Yahweh.

### *The Righteous Branch of David*

**14** 'Behold, [a]days are coming,' de-
clares Yahweh, 'when I will [b]establish
the good word which I have spoken
concerning the house of Israel and
the house of Judah. **15** In those
days and at that time I will cause a
[a]righteous Branch of David to branch
forth; and He shall do [b]justice and
righteousness on the earth. **16** In
those days [a]Judah will be saved, and
Jerusalem will dwell in security; and
this is *the name* by which she will be
called: [b]Yahweh is our righteousness.'
**17** For thus says Yahweh, '[1]David shall
[a]not have a man cut off from sitting
on the throne of the house of Israel;
**18** [1]and the [a]Levitical priests shall
not have a man cut off from before
Me who is to offer burnt offerings, to
offer up grain offerings in smoke, and
to [b]perform sacrifices [2]continually.'"

---

**33:7** [a]Ps 85:1; Jer 30:18; 32:44; 33:26; Am 9:14 [b]Is 1:26; Jer 30:18; 31:4, 38; Am 9:14, 15 [1]Or *restore* [2]Or *captivity* **33:8** [a]Ps 51:2; Is 44:22; Jer 50:20; Eze 36:25, 33; Mic 7:18, 19; Zec 13:1; Heb 9:11-14 **33:9** [a]Is 62:2, 4, 7; Jer 13:11 [b]Jer 3:17, 19; 4:2; 16:19 [c]Jer 24:6; 32:42 [d]Ne 6:16; Ps 40:3; Is 60:5; Hos 3:5 [1]This city **33:10** [a]Jer 32:43 [b]Jer 26:9; 34:22 **33:11** [a]Is 35:10; 51:3, 11 [b]1Chr 16:8, 34; 2Chr 5:13; 7:3; Ezr 3:11; Ps 100:4, 5; 106:1; 107:1; 118:1; 136:1 [c]Lv 7:12, 13; Ps 107:22; 116:17; Jer 17:26; Heb 13:15 [1]Or *restore* [2]Or *captivity* **33:12** [a]Jer 32:43; 36:29; 51:62 [b]Is 65:10; Jer 31:12; Eze 34:12-15; Zep 2:6, 7 [1]Or *a pasture* **33:13** [a]Jer 17:26; 32:44 [b]Lv 27:32; Lk 15:4 [1]Or *lowland* **33:14** [a]Jer 23:5 [b]Is 32:1, 2; Jer 29:10; 32:42; 33:9; Eze 34:23-25; Hag 2:6-9 **33:15** [a]Is 4:2; 11:1-5; Jer 23:5, 6; 30:9; Zec 3:8; 6:12, 13 [b]Ps 72:1-5 **33:16** [a]Is 45:17, 22; Jer 23:6 [b]Is 45:24, 25; Jer 23:6; 1Co 1:30; 2Co 5:21; Php 3:9 **33:17** [a]2Sa 7:16; 1Ki 2:4; 8:25; 1Chr 17:11-14; Ps 89:29-37 [1]Lit *There shall not be cut off for David* **33:18** [a]Nu 3:5-10; Dt 18:1; 24:8; Jos 3:3; Eze 44:15 [b]Ezr 3:5; Heb 13:15 [1]Lit *there shall not be cut off for the Levitical priests* [2]Lit *all the days*

**19** Then the word of Yahweh came
to Jeremiah, saying, **20** "Thus says
Yahweh, 'If you can [a]break My cov-
enant for the day and My covenant
for the night, so that day and night
will not be at their appointed time,
**21** then [a]My covenant may also be
broken with David My servant so
that he will not have a son to reign
on his throne, and with the Levitical
priests, My ministers. **22** As the [a]host
of heaven cannot be counted and the
[b]sand of the sea cannot be measured,
so I will [c]multiply the seed of David
My servant and the [d]Levites who
minister to Me.'"

**23** And the word of Yahweh came
to Jeremiah, saying, **24** "Have you not
seen what this people have spoken,
saying, 'The [a]two families which Yah-
weh chose, He has [b]rejected them'?
Thus they have [c]spurned My people
from being a nation any longer [1]in
their sight. **25** Thus says Yahweh, 'If
My [a]covenant *for* day and night *stand*
not, *and* the statutes for heaven and
earth I have [b]not established, **26** then
I would [a]reject the seed of Jacob and
David My servant, [1]not taking from
his seed [b]rulers over the seed of
Abraham, Isaac, and Jacob. But I will
[c,2]return their [3]fortunes and will have
[d]compassion on them.'"

### *A Prophecy Against Zedekiah*

**34** *The word which came to*
Jeremiah from Yahweh, when
[a]Nebuchadnezzar king of Babylon
and all his military force, with [b]all
the kingdoms of the earth that
were under his [1]dominion and all
the peoples, were fighting against
Jerusalem and against all its cities,
saying, **2** "Thus says Yahweh, the
God of Israel, '[a]Go and speak to
Zedekiah king of Judah and say to
him: "Thus says Yahweh, 'Behold,
[b]I am giving this city into the hand
of the king of Babylon, and [c]he will
burn it with fire. **3** [a]And you will not
escape from his hand, for you will
surely be seized and given into his
hand; and you will [b]see the king of
Babylon eye to eye, and he will speak
with you [1]face to face, and you will go
to Babylon.'"' **4** Yet hear the word of
Yahweh, O Zedekiah king of Judah!
Thus says Yahweh concerning you,
'You will not die by the sword. **5** You
will die in peace; and as *spices* were
burned for your fathers, the former
kings who were before you, so they
will [a]burn *spices* for you; and [b]they
will lament for you, "Alas, lord!"' For
I have spoken the word," declares
Yahweh.

**6** Then Jeremiah the prophet
spoke [a]all these words to Zedekiah
king of Judah in Jerusalem **7** when
the military force of the king of Bab-
ylon was fighting against Jerusalem
and against all the cities of Judah
that were left, *that is,* [a]Lachish and
[b]Azekah, for they *alone* remained as
[c]fortified cities among the cities of
Judah.

**33:20** [a]Ps 89:37; 104:19-23; Is 54:9, 10; Jer 31:35-37; 33:25 **33:21** [a]2Sa 23:5; 2Chr 7:18; 21:7 **33:22** [a]Ge 15:5; Jer 31:37 [b]Ge 22:17 [c]Eze 37:24-27 [d]Is 66:21; Jer 33:18 **33:24** [a]Is 7:17; 11:13; Jer 3:7, 8, 10, 18; 33:26; Eze 37:22 [b]Jer 30:17 [c]Ne 4:2-4; Es 3:6, 8, 9; Ps 44:13, 14; 83:4 [1]Lit *to their faces* **33:25** [a]Ge 8:22; Jer 31:35, 36; 33:20 [b]Ps 74:16, 17 **33:26** [a]Jer 31:37 [b]Ge 49:10 [c]Jer 33:7 [d]Is 14:1; 54:8; Jer 31:20; Eze 39:25; Hos 1:7; 2:23 [1]Lit *from taking* [2]Or *restore* [3]Or *captivity* ◆ **34:1** [a]2Ki 25:1; Jer 32:2; 39:1; 52:4 [b]Jer 1:15; 27:7; Da 2:37, 38 [1]Lit *dominion of his hand* **34:2** [a]2Chr 36:11, 12; Jer 22:1, 2; 37:1, 2 [b]Jer 21:10; 32:3; 34:22; 37:8-10 [c]Jer 32:29 **34:3** [a]2Ki 25:4, 5; Jer 21:7; 32:4; 34:21 [b]2Ki 25:6, 7; Jer 39:6, 7 [1]Lit *mouth to mouth* **34:5** [a]2Chr 16:14; 21:19 [b]Jer 22:18 **34:6** [a]1Sa 3:18; 15:16-24 **34:7** [a]Jos 10:3, 5; 2Ki 14:19; 18:14; Is 36:2 [b]Jos 10:10; 2Chr 11:9 [c]2Chr 11:5-10

8 The word which came to Jeremiah
from Yahweh after King Zedekiah had
[a]cut a covenant with all the people
who were in Jerusalem to [b]proclaim
[1]release to them: 9 that each man
should let his male slave go free and
each man his female slave, a [a]Hebrew
man or a Hebrew woman, so that
[b]no one should enslave them, each
*being* a Jew, his brother. 10 And all the
[a]officials and all the people obeyed
who had entered into the covenant
that each man should let his male
slave go free and each man his female
slave, so that no one should enslave
them any longer; they obeyed and
let *them* go *free.* 11 But afterwards
they turned around and returned *to*
*themselves* the male slaves and the
female slaves, whom they had let go
as free, and subdued them to be male
slaves and female slaves.

12 Then the word of Yahweh came
to Jeremiah from Yahweh, saying,
13 "Thus says Yahweh, the God of
Israel, 'I [a]cut a covenant with your
fathers in the day that I [b]brought
them out of the land of Egypt, from
the house of slavery, saying, 14 "[a]At
the end of seven years each of you
shall let his Hebrew brother go who
[1]has been sold to you and has served
you six years, and you shall let him go
*to be* free from you; but your fathers
[b]did not obey Me or incline their ear
to Me. 15 Although recently you *had*
turned and [a]done what is right in My
sight, each man proclaiming [1]release
to his neighbor, and you had [b]cut a
covenant before Me [c]in the house
which is called by My name. 16 Yet
you [a]turned and [b]profaned My
name, and each man [1]returned *to*
*themselves* his male slave and each
man his female slave whom you
had let go as free according to their
desire, and you subdued them to be
your male slaves and female slaves."'

17 "Therefore thus says Yahweh,
'You have not obeyed Me in proclaiming
[1]release each man to his
brother and each man to his neighbor.
Behold, I am [a]proclaiming a
[1]release to you,' declares Yahweh, 'to
the [b]sword, to the pestilence, and
to the famine; and I will make you
a [c]terror to all the kingdoms of the
earth. 18 And I will give the men who
have [a]trespassed against My covenant,
who have not established the
words of the covenant which they
cut before Me, *when* they [b]cut the
calf in two and passed between its
parts— 19 the [a]officials of Judah and
the officials of Jerusalem, the court
officers and the priests and all the
people of the land who passed between
the parts of the calf— 20 And I
will give them into the hand of their
enemies and into the hand of those
who [a]seek their life. And their [b]dead
bodies will be food for the birds of
the sky and the beasts of the earth.
21 [a]And as for Zedekiah king of Judah
and his officials, I will give *them* into
the hand of their enemies and into

**34:8** [a]2Ki 11:17; 23:2, 3 [b]Ex 21:2; Lv 25:10, 39-46; Ne 5:1-13; Is 58:6; Jer 34:14, 17 [1]Or *liberty* **34:9** [a]Ge 14:13; Ex 2:6 [b]Lv 25:39 **34:10** [a]Jer 26:10, 16 **34:13** [a]Ex 24:3, 7, 8; Dt 5:2, 3, 27; Jer 31:32 [b]Ex 20:2 **34:14** [a]Ex 21:2; Dt 15:12; 1Ki 9:22 [b]1Sa 8:7, 8; 2Ki 17:13, 14 [1]Or *has sold himself* **34:15** [a]Jer 34:8 [b]2Ki 23:3; Ne 10:29 [c]Jer 7:10f; 32:34 [1]Or *liberty* **34:16** [a]1Sa 15:11; Jer 34:11; Eze 3:20; 18:24 [b]Ex 20:7; Lv 19:12 [1]Lit *caused them to return* **34:17** [a]Lv 26:34, 35; Es 7:10; Da 6:24; Mt 7:2 [b]Jer 32:24; 38:2 [c]Dt 28:25; Jer 29:18 [1]Or *liberty* **34:18** [a]Dt 17:2; Hos 6:7; 8:1; Ro 2:8 [b]Ge 15:10 **34:19** [a]Jer 34:10; Eze 22:27; Zep 3:3, 4 **34:20** [a]Jer 11:21; 21:7; 22:25 [b]Dt 28:26; 1Sa 17:44, 46; 1Ki 14:11; 16:4; Ps 79:2; Jer 7:33; 16:4; 19:7 **34:21** [a]2Ki 25:18-21; Jer 32:3, 4; 39:6; 52:10, 24-27; Eze 17:16

the hand of those who seek their life
and into the hand of the military
force of the king of Babylon which
has [b]gone away from you. **22** Behold,
I am going to command,' declares
Yahweh, 'and I will cause them to
return to this city; and they will fight
against it and [a]capture it and burn it
with fire; and I will make the cities
of Judah a [b]desolation [c]without
inhabitant.'"

### *The Rechabites Listen to Jonadab*

**35** The word which came to
Jeremiah from Yahweh in
the days of [a]Jehoiakim the son of
Josiah, king of Judah, saying, **2** "Go
to the house of the [a]Rechabites and
speak to them and bring them into
the house of Yahweh, into one of the
[b]chambers, and give them wine to
drink." **3** Then I took Jaazaniah the
son of Jeremiah, son of Habazziniah,
and his brothers and all his sons and
the whole house of the Rechabites,
**4** and I brought them into the house
of Yahweh, into the chamber of the
sons of Hanan the son of Igdaliah,
the [a]man of God, which was beside
the chamber of the officials, which
was above the chamber of Maaseiah
the son of Shallum, [b]the doorkeeper.
**5** Then I put before the [1]men of the
house of the Rechabites pitchers
full of wine and cups; and I said
to them, "[a]Drink wine!" **6** But they
said, "We will not drink wine, for
[a]Jonadab the son of [b]Rechab, our
father, commanded us, saying, 'You
shall [c]not drink wine, you or your
sons, forever. **7** And you shall not
build a house, and you shall not
sow seed, and you shall not plant
a vineyard or own one; but [a]tents
you shall inhabit all your days, that
you may live [b]many days in the land
where you [c]sojourn.' **8** So we have
[a]listened to the voice of Jonadab the
son of Rechab, our father, in all that
he commanded us, not to drink wine
all our days, we, our wives, our sons,
or our daughters, **9** nor to build our-
selves houses to inhabit; and we [a]do
not have vineyard or field or seed.
**10** We have only [a]inhabited tents
and have listened and have done
according to all that [b]Jonadab our
father commanded us. **11** But it hap-
pened that when [a]Nebuchadnezzar
king of Babylon came up against the
land, we said, 'Come, let us [b]come to
Jerusalem before the military force
of the Chaldeans and before the
military force of the Arameans.' So
we have inhabited Jerusalem."

### *Yahweh Warns of Judah's Discipline*

**12** Then the word of Yahweh came to
Jeremiah, saying, **13** "Thus says Yah-
weh of hosts, the God of Israel, 'Go
and say to the men of Judah and the
inhabitants of Jerusalem, "[a]Will you
not receive discipline by listening to
My words?" declares Yahweh. **14** "The
[a]words of Jonadab the son of Rechab,
which he commanded his sons, not
to drink wine, are established. So
they do not drink *wine* to this day,

---

**34:21** [b]Jer 37:5-11 **34:22** [a]Jer 34:2; 39:1, 2, 8; 52:7, 13 [b]Jer 4:7; 9:11 [c]Jer 33:10; 44:22 ◆ **35:1** [a]2Ki 23:34-36; 24:1; 2Chr 36:5-7; Jer 1:3; 27:20; Da 1:1 **35:2** [a]2Ki 10:15; 1Chr 2:55 [b]1Ki 6:5, 8; 1Chr 9:26, 33 **35:4** [a]Dt 33:1; Jos 14:6; 1Ki 12:22; 2Ki 1:9-13 [b]1Chr 9:18f **35:5** [a]Am 2:12 [1]Lit *sons* **35:6** [a]2Ki 10:15, 23 [b]1Chr 2:55 [c]Lv 10:9; Nu 6:2-4; Jdg 13:7, 14; Lk 1:15 **35:7** [a]Ge 25:27; Heb 11:9 [b]Ex 20:12; Eph 6:2, 3 [c]Ge 36:7 **35:8** [a]Pr 1:8, 9; 4:1, 2, 10; 6:20; Eph 6:1; Col 3:20 **35:9** [a]Ps 37:16; Jer 35:7; 1Ti 6:6 **35:10** [a]Jer 35:7 [b]Jer 35:6 **35:11** [a]2Ki 24:1, 2; Da 1:1, 2 [b]Jer 4:5-7; 8:14 **35:13** [a]Is 28:9-12; Jer 5:3; 6:8-10; 32:33 **35:14** [a]Jer 35:6-10

for they have listened to their father's
command. But I have spoken to you,
[b]rising up early and speaking; yet you
have [c]not listened to Me. **15** Also I
have sent to you all My [a]slaves the
prophets, rising up early and send-
ing, saying: '[b]Turn now every man
from his evil way and make good
your deeds, and [c]do not walk after
other gods to [1]serve them. Then you
will [d]inhabit the land which I have
given to you and to your fathers; but
you have not [e]inclined your ear or
listened to Me. **16** Indeed, the sons
of Jonadab the son of Rechab have
[a]established the command of their
father which he commanded them,
but this people has not listened to
Me.'"' **17** Therefore thus says Yahweh,
the God of hosts, the God of Israel,
'Behold, [a]I am bringing on Judah and
on all the inhabitants of Jerusalem all
the *harmful* evil that I have spoken
against them because I [b]spoke to
them but they did not listen, and I
have called them but they did not
answer.'"

**18** Then Jeremiah said to the house
of the Rechabites, "Thus says Yahweh
of hosts, the God of Israel, 'Because
you have [a]listened to the command
of Jonadab your father, kept all his
commands, and done according to all
that he commanded you, **19** therefore
thus says Yahweh of hosts, the God
of Israel, "Jonadab the son of Rechab
[a]shall not have a man cut off from
[b]standing before Me [1]always."'"

### *Jeremiah's Scroll Read in the Temple*

**36** Now it happened that in the
[a]fourth year of Jehoiakim the
son of Josiah, king of Judah, this
word came to Jeremiah from Yahweh,
saying, **2** "Take a [a]scroll of a book and
write on it all the [b]words which I have
spoken to you concerning [c]Israel and
concerning Judah and concerning
all the [d]nations, from the [e]day I *first*
spoke to you, from the days of Josiah,
even to this day. **3** [a]Perhaps the house
of Judah will hear all the evil which
I devise [1]to bring on them, in order
that every man will [b]turn from his
evil way; then I will [c]forgive their
iniquity and their sin."

**4** Then Jeremiah called [a]Baruch the
son of Neriah, and Baruch wrote on a
[b,1]scroll [2]at the dictation of Jeremiah
all the words of Yahweh which He
had spoken to him. **5** And Jeremiah
commanded Baruch, saying, "I am
[a,1]confined; I cannot go into the
house of Yahweh. **6** So you shall go
and [a]read from the scroll, which you
have [b]written [1]at my dictation, the
words of Yahweh [2]in the hearing of
the people in the house of Yahweh
on a [c]fast day. And also you shall
read them in the hearing of all *the
people of* Judah who come from their
cities. **7** [a]Perhaps their supplication

---

**35:14** [b]2Chr 36:15; Jer 7:13, 25; 11:7; 25:3, 4 [c]Is 30:9; 50:2 **35:15** [a]Jer 7:25; 25:4; 26:5; 29:19; 32:33 [b]Is 1:16, 17; Jer 4:1; 18:11; 25:5f; Eze 18:30-32; Ac 26:20 [c]Dt 6:14; Jer 7:6; 13:10; 25:6 [d]Jer 7:7; 25:5, 6 [e]Jer 7:24, 26; 11:8; 17:23; 34:14 [1]Or *be a slave for* **35:16** [a]Jer 35:14; Mal 1:6 **35:17** [a]Jos 23:15; Jer 19:3, 15; 21:4-10; Mic 3:12 [b]Pr 1:24, 25; Is 65:12; 66:4; Jer 7:13, 26, 27; 26:5; Lk 13:34, 35; Ro 10:21 **35:18** [a]Ex 20:12; Eph 6:1-3 **35:19** [a]1Chr 2:55; Jer 33:17 [b]Jer 15:19; Lk 21:36 [1]Lit *all the days* ◆ **36:1** [a]2Ki 24:1; 2Chr 36:5-7; Jer 25:1, 3; 45:1; 46:2; Da 1:1 **36:2** [a]Ex 17:14; Is 8:1; Ps 40:7; Jer 36:4, 6, 23, 28; Eze 2:9; Zec 5:1, 2 [b]Jer 1:9, 10; 30:2; Hab 2:2 [c]Jer 3:3-10; 23:13, 14; 32:30-32 [d]Jer 1:5, 10; 25:9-29; chs 47-51 [e]Jer 1:2, 3; 25:3 **36:3** [a]Jer 26:3; 36:7; Eze 12:3 [b]Dt 30:2, 8; 1Sa 7:3; Is 55:7; Jer 18:8, 11; 35:15; Jon 3:8 [c]Jon 3:10; Mk 4:12; Ac 3:19 [1]Lit *to do* **36:4** [a]Jer 32:12; 36:18; 43:3; 45:1 [b]Jer 36:14; Eze 2:9 [1]Lit *scroll of a book* [2]Lit *from the mouth of* **36:5** [a]Jer 32:2; 33:1; 2Co 11:23 [1]Lit *shut up* **36:6** [a]Jer 36:8 [b]Jer 36:4 [c]Jer 36:9; Zec 8:19 [1]Lit *from my mouth* [2]Lit *in the ears of*, so in this context **36:7** [a]1Ki 8:33; 2Chr 33:12, 13; Jer 26:3; 36:3

will [1]come before Yahweh, and ev-
eryone will turn from his evil way, for
[b]great is the anger and the wrath that
Yahweh has spoken against this peo-
ple." **8** So Baruch the son of Neriah
did according to all that Jeremiah the
prophet commanded him, [a]reading
from the book the words of Yahweh
in the house of Yahweh.

**9** Now it happened in the [a]fifth
year of Jehoiakim the son of Josiah,
king of Judah, in the [b]ninth month,
that all the people in Jerusalem and
all the people who [c]came from the
cities of Judah to Jerusalem called
for a [d]fast before Yahweh. **10** Then
Baruch read from the book the words
of Jeremiah in the house of Yahweh
in the [a]chamber of [b]Gemariah the
son of Shaphan the [c]scribe, in the
upper court, at the [d]entry of the New
Gate of the house of Yahweh, in the
hearing of all the people.

**11** Then [a]Micaiah the son of
Gemariah, the son of Shaphan,
heard all the words of Yahweh from
the book. **12** And he went down to
the king's house, into the scribe's
chamber. And behold, all the offi-
cials were sitting there—[a]Elishama
the scribe, and [b]Delaiah the son of
Shemaiah, and [c]Elnathan the son
of Achbor, and Gemariah the son of
Shaphan, and Zedekiah the son of
Hananiah, and all the *other* officials.
**13** And Micaiah [a]declared to them all
the words that he had heard when
Baruch read from the book in the
hearing of the people. **14** Then all
the officials sent [a]Jehudi the son of
Nethaniah, the son of Shelemiah, the
son of Cushi, to Baruch, saying, "Take
in your hand the scroll from which
you have read in the hearing of the
people and come." So Baruch the son
of Neriah [b]took the scroll in his hand
and went to them. **15** And they said
to him, "Sit down, please, and read
it in our hearing." So Baruch [a]read it
in their hearing. **16** Now it happened
that when they heard all the words,
they turned in [a]dread one to another
and said to Baruch, "We will surely
[b]declare all these words to the king."
**17** And they asked Baruch, saying,
"Declare to us, please, [a]how did you
write all these words? *Was it* [1]at his
dictation?" **18** Then Baruch said to
them, "He [a]dictated all these words
to me, and I wrote them with ink on
the book." **19** Then the officials said
to Baruch, "Go, [a]hide yourself, you
and Jeremiah, and do not let anyone
know where you are."

### *The Scroll Is Burned*

**20** So they went to the [a]king in the
court, but they had deposited the
scroll in the chamber of [a]Elishama
the scribe, and they declared all the
words in the hearing of the king.
**21** Then the king sent Jehudi to get
the scroll, and he took it out of the
chamber of Elishama the scribe.
And Jehudi [a]read it in the hearing
of the king as well as in the hearing
of all the officials who stood beside
the king. **22** Now the king was sitting

---

**36:7** [b]Dt 28:15; 31:16, 17; 2Ki 22:13, 17; Jer 4:4; 21:5; Lam 4:11 [1]Lit *fall* **36:8** [a]Jer 1:17; 36:6 **36:9** [a]Jer 36:1 [b]Jer 36:22 [c]Jer 36:6 [d]Jdg 20:26; 1Sa 7:6; 2Chr 20:3; Es 4:16; Joel 1:14; 2:15; Jon 3:5 **36:10** [a]Jer 35:4 [b]Jer 36:11, 25 [c]2Sa 8:17; Jer 52:25 [d]Jer 26:10 **36:11** [a]Jer 36:13 **36:12** [a]Jer 36:20 [b]Jer 36:25 [c]Jer 26:22 **36:13** [a]2Ki 22:10 **36:14** [a]Jer 36:21 [b]Jer 36:2; Eze 2:7-10 **36:15** [a]Jer 36:21 **36:16** [a]Jer 36:24; Ac 24:25 [b]Jer 13:18; Am 7:10, 11 **36:17** [a]Jn 9:10, 15, 26 [1]Lit *from his mouth*, so in this context **36:18** [a]Jer 36:4 **36:19** [a]1Ki 17:3; 18:4, 10; Jer 26:20-24; 36:26 **36:20** [a]Jer 36:12 **36:21** [a]2Ki 22:10; 2Chr 34:18; Eze 2:4, 5

in the [a]winter house in the [b]ninth month, with *a fire* burning in the brazier before him. **23** And it happened that when Jehudi had read three or four columns, *the king* cut it with a scribe's knife and [a]threw *it* into the fire that was in the brazier, until all the scroll [1]was consumed in the fire that was in the brazier. **24** Yet the king and all his servants who heard all these words were [a]not in dread, nor did they [b]tear their garments. **25** Even though Elnathan and Delaiah and Gemariah [a]interceded with the king not to burn the scroll, he would not listen to them. **26** And the king commanded Jerahmeel the king's son, Seraiah the son of Azriel, and Shelemiah the son of Abdeel to [a]take Baruch the scribe and Jeremiah the prophet, but [b]Yahweh hid them.

### *The Scroll Is Replaced*

**27** Then the word of Yahweh came to Jeremiah after the king had [a]burned the scroll and the words which [b]Baruch had written at the dictation of Jeremiah, saying, **28** "[a]Take again another scroll and write on it all the former words that were [b]on the first scroll which Jehoiakim the king of Judah burned. **29** And concerning Jehoiakim king of Judah you shall say, 'Thus says Yahweh, "You have [a]burned this scroll, saying, '[b]Why have you written on it [1]that the [c]king of Babylon will certainly come and make this land a ruin and will make man and beast to cease from it?'" **30** Therefore thus says Yahweh concerning Jehoiakim king of Judah, "He shall have [a]no one to sit on the throne of David, and his [b]dead body shall be cast out to the heat of the day and the frost of the night. **31** And I will also [a]punish him and his seed and his servants for their iniquity, and I will [b]bring on them and the inhabitants of Jerusalem and the men of Judah all the evil that I have spoken about to them—but they did not listen."'"

**32** Then Jeremiah took another scroll and gave it to Baruch the son of Neriah, the scribe, and he [a]wrote on it at the dictation of Jeremiah all the words of the book which Jehoiakim king of Judah had burned in the fire; and many [1]similar words were added to them.

### *Jeremiah Warns Against Trust in Pharaoh*

**37** Now [a]Zedekiah the son of Josiah, whom Nebuchadnezzar king of Babylon had [b]made king in the land of Judah, reigned as king in place of [c]Coniah the son of Jehoiakim. **2** But [a]neither he nor his servants nor the people of the land listened to the words of Yahweh which He spoke through Jeremiah the prophet.

**3** Yet [a]King Zedekiah sent Jehucal the son of Shelemiah and [b]Zephaniah the son of Maaseiah, the priest, to Jeremiah the prophet, saying,

---

**36:22** [a]Jdg 3:20; Am 3:15 [b]Jer 36:9 **36:23** [a]1Ki 22:8, 27; Pr 1:30; Is 5:18, 19; 28:14, 22; Jer 36:29 [1]Lit *came to an end* **36:24** [a]*Ps 36:1; 64:5; Jer 36:16* [b]*Ge 37:29, 34; 2Sa 1:11;* 1Ki 21:27; 2Ki 19:1, 2; 22:11, 19; Is 36:22; 37:1; Jon 3:6 **36:25** [a]Ge 37:22, 26, 27; Ac 5:34-39 **36:26** [a]1Ki 19:1-3, 10, 14; Mt 23:34, 37 [b]Ps 91:1 **36:27** [a]Jer 36:23 [b]Jer 36:4, 18 **36:28** [a]Zec 1:5, 6 [b]Jer 36:4, 23 **36:29** [a]Dt 29:19; Job 15:24, 25; Is 45:9 [b]Is 29:21; 30:10; Jer 26:9; 32:3 [c]Jer 25:9-11 [1]Lit *saying* **36:30** [a]2Ki 24:12-15; Jer 22:30 [b]Jer 22:19 **36:31** [a]Jer 23:34 [b]Dt 28:15; Pr 29:1; Jer 19:15; 35:17 **36:32** [a]Ex 4:15, 16; 34:1; Jer 36:4, 18, 23 [1]Lit *like those* ◆ **37:1** [a]2Ki 24:17; 1Chr 3:15; 2Chr 36:10 [b]Eze 17:12-21 [c]2Ki 24:12; 1Chr 3:16; 2Chr 36:9, 10; Jer 22:24, 28; 24:1; 52:31 **37:2** [a]2Ki 24:19, 20; 2Chr 36:12-16; Pr 29:12 **37:3** [a]Jer 21:1, 2 [b]Jer 29:25; 52:24

"[c]Please pray to Yahweh our God on
our behalf." 4 Now Jeremiah was *still*
coming in and going out among the
people; they had not *yet* [a]put him in
the prison. 5 Meanwhile, [a]Pharaoh's
military force had come out from
Egypt; and the Chaldeans who had
been besieging Jerusalem heard the
report about them. So they [b]withdrew
from Jerusalem.

6 Then the word of Yahweh came
to Jeremiah the prophet, saying,
7 "Thus says Yahweh, the God of
Israel, '[a]Thus you are to say to the
king of Judah, who sent you to Me to
inquire of Me: "Behold, [b]the military
force of Pharaoh which has come
out for your assistance is going to
return to its own land of Egypt. 8 The
Chaldeans will also [a]return and fight
against this city, and they will capture
it and burn it with fire."' 9 Thus says
Yahweh, 'Do not [a]deceive yourselves,
saying, "The Chaldeans will surely
go away from us," for they will not
go. 10 For [a]even if you had struck
down the entire military force of the
Chaldeans who were fighting against
you, and there were *only* wounded
men remaining among them, each
man in his tent, they would rise up
and [b]burn this city with fire.'"

### *Jeremiah Imprisoned*

11 Now it happened when the military
force of the Chaldeans had with-
drawn from Jerusalem because of
the military force of Pharaoh, 12 that
Jeremiah went out from Jerusalem to
go to the land of Benjamin in order to
[a]obtain his portion of *some* property
there among the people. 13 Now it
happened that while he was at the
[a]Gate of Benjamin, the master of
the guard whose name was Irijah
the son of Shelemiah the son of
Hananiah was there; and he [b]seized
Jeremiah the prophet, saying, "You
are [1]going over to the Chaldeans!"
14 But Jeremiah said, "[a]A lie! I am not
[1]going over to the Chaldeans"; yet
he would not listen to him. So Irijah
seized Jeremiah and brought him
to the officials. 15 Then the officials
were [a]angry at Jeremiah and struck
him, and they [b]put him in jail in the
house of Jonathan the scribe because
they had made *that house* into the
prison. 16 For Jeremiah had come into
the [a,1]pit, that is, the vaulted cell; and
Jeremiah stayed there many days.

17 Then King Zedekiah sent and
took him *out*; and in his palace the
king [a]secretly asked him and said,
"Is there a [b]word from Yahweh?" And
Jeremiah said, "There is!" Then he
said, "You will be [c]given into the hand
of the king of Babylon!" 18 Moreover,
Jeremiah said to King Zedekiah, "[a]*In*
what *way* have I sinned against you
or against your servants or against
this people, that you have put me
in prison? 19 [a]Where then are your
prophets who prophesied to you,

---

**37:3** [c]1Ki 13:6; Jer 2:27; 15:11; 21:1, 2; 42:1-4, 20; Ac 8:24 **37:4** [a]Jer 32:2, 3; 37:15 **37:5** [a]2Ki 24:7; Jer 37:7; Eze 17:15 [b]Jer 37:11 **37:7** [a]2Ki 22:18; Jer 21:1, 2; 37:3 [b]Is 30:1-3; 31:1-3; Jer 2:18, 36; Lam 4:17; Eze 17:17 **37:8** [a]Jer 34:22; 38:23; 39:2-8 **37:9** [a]Jer 29:8; Ob 3; Mt 24:4, 5; Eph 5:6 **37:10** [a]Lv 26:36-38; Is 30:17; Jer 21:4, 5 [b]Jer 37:8 **37:12** [a]Jer 32:8 **37:13** [a]Jer 38:7; Zec 14:10 [b]Jer 18:18; 20:10; Lk 23:2; Ac 6:11; 24:5-9, 13 [1]Lit *falling* **37:14** [a]Ps 27:12; 52:1, 2; Jer 40:4-6; Mt 5:11, 12 [1]Lit *falling* **37:15** [a]Jer 18:23; 20:1-3; 26:16; Mt 21:35 [b]Ge 39:20; 2Chr 16:10; 18:26; Jer 38:26; Ac 5:18 **37:16** [a]Jer 38:6 [1]Lit *house of the pit* **37:17** [a]1Ki 14:1-4; Jer 38:5, 14-16, 24-27 [b]1Ki 22:15, 16; 2Ki 3:11, 12; Jer 15:11; 21:1, 2; 37:3 [c]Jer 21:7; 24:8; Eze 12:12, 13; 17:19, 20 **37:18** [a]1Sa 24:9; 26:18; Da 6:22; Jn 10:32; Ac 25:8, 11, 25 **37:19** [a]Dt 32:37, 38; 2Ki 3:13; Jer 2:28

saying, 'The [b]king of Babylon will
not come against you or against this
land'? **20** But now, please listen, O my
lord the king; please let my [a]suppli-
cation [1]come before you, and do not
make me return to the house of Jon-
athan the scribe, that I may not die
there." **21** Then King Zedekiah gave
commandment, and they committed
Jeremiah to the [a]court of the guard
and gave him a loaf of [b]bread daily
from the bakers' street, until all the
bread in the city had [c]come to an end.
So Jeremiah remained in the court of
the guard.

### *Jeremiah Brought Up from the Cistern*

**38** And Shephatiah the son of
Mattan, and Gedaliah the
son of Pashhur, and Jucal the [a]son
of Shelemiah, and [b]Pashhur the son
of Malchijah heard the words that
Jeremiah was speaking to all the
people, saying, **2** "Thus says Yahweh,
'He who [a]stays in this city will die
by the [b]sword and by the famine
and by the pestilence, but he who
goes out to the Chaldeans will live
and have his *own* [c]life as spoil and
stay alive.' **3** Thus says Yahweh, 'This
city will certainly be [a]given into the
hand of the military force of the king
of Babylon, and he will capture it.'"
**4** Then the [a]officials said to the king,
"Now let this man be put to death,
inasmuch as he is [b]making the hands
of the men of war who remain in this
city as well as the hands of all the
people limp, by speaking such words
to them; for this man [c]is not seeking
peace for this people but rather
calamity." **5** So King Zedekiah said,
"Behold, he is in your [1]hands; for the
king [a]can *do* nothing against you."
**6** Then they took Jeremiah and cast
him into the [a,1]cistern *of* Malchijah
the king's son, which was in the court
of the guard; and they let Jeremiah
down with ropes. Now in the cistern
there was no water but only [b]mire,
and Jeremiah sank into the mire.
**7** But [a]Ebed-melech the Ethiopian,
[1]a [b]eunuch, while he was in the
king's palace, heard that they had
put Jeremiah into the cistern. Now
the king was sitting in the [c]Gate of
Benjamin; **8** and Ebed-melech went
out from the king's house and spoke
to the king, saying, **9** "My lord the
king, these men have done evil in all
that they have done to Jeremiah the
prophet whom they have cast into
the cistern; and he [1]will die right
where he is because of the famine,
for there is [a]no more bread in the
city." **10** Then the king commanded
Ebed-melech the Ethiopian, saying,
"Take in your hand thirty men from
here and bring up Jeremiah the
prophet from the cistern before he
dies." **11** So Ebed-melech took the
men in his hand and went into the
king's palace to *a place* beneath
the storeroom and took from there
worn-out clothes and worn-out
rags and let them down by ropes
into the cistern to Jeremiah. **12** Then

**37:19** [b]Jer 27:14; 28:1-4, 10-17 **37:20** [a]Jer 36:7; 38:26 [1]Lit *fall* **37:21** [a]Jer 32:2; 38:13, 28 [b]1Ki 17:6; Job 5:20; Ps 33:18, 19; Is 33:16 [c]2Ki 25:3; Jer 38:9; 52:6 ◆ **38:1** [a]Jer 37:3 [b]Jer 21:1 **38:2** [a]Jer 21:9 [b]Jer 34:17; 42:17 [c]Jer 21:9; 39:18; 45:5 **38:3** [a]Jer 21:10; 32:3-5 **38:4** [a]Jer 18:23; 26:11, 21; 36:12 [b]Ex 5:4; 1Ki 18:17, 18; 21:20; Ne 6:9; Am 7:10; Ac 16:20 [c]Jer 29:7 **38:5** [a]2Sa 3:39 [1]Lit *hand* **38:6** [a]Jer 37:16, 21; Ac 16:24 [b]Ps 40:2; 69:2, 14, 15; Jer 38:22; Zec 9:11 [1]Or *pit*, so in ch, cf. Ge 37:24; Lam 3:53; Zec 9:11 **38:7** [a]Jer 39:16 [b]Jer 29:2; Ac 8:27 [c]Dt 21:19; Job 29:7; Jer 37:13; Am 5:10 [1]Or *an official* **38:9** [a]Jer 37:21; 52:6 [1]M.T. *has died*

Ebed-melech the Ethiopian said to
Jeremiah, "Now put these worn-out
clothes and rags under your armpits
under the ropes"; and Jeremiah did
so. **13** So they pulled Jeremiah up with
the ropes and brought him up from
the cistern, and Jeremiah stayed in
the [a]court of the guard.

### *Zedekiah Sends for Jeremiah*

**14** Then King Zedekiah [a]sent and
[1]had Jeremiah the prophet brought
to him at the third entrance that is
in the house of Yahweh; and the king
said to Jeremiah, "I am going to [b]ask
you something; do not hide anything
from me." **15** Then Jeremiah said to
Zedekiah, "[a]If I tell you, will you not
certainly put me to death? Besides, if
I give you counsel, you will not listen
to me." **16** But King Zedekiah swore
to Jeremiah in [a]secret saying, "As
Yahweh lives, who made this [b,1]life
for us, surely I will not put you to
death, nor will I give you over to the
hand of [c]these men who are seeking
your [1]life."

**17** Then Jeremiah said to Zedekiah,
"Thus says Yahweh [a]God of hosts,
the [b]God of Israel, 'If you will indeed
[c]go out to the [1]officers of the king of
Babylon, then [2]you will live, this city
will not be burned with fire, and you
and your household will live. **18** But
if you will [a]not go out to the [1]officers
of the king of Babylon, then this city
[b]will be given over to the hand of the
Chaldeans; and they will burn it
with fire, and [c]you yourself will not
escape from their hand.'" **19** Then
King Zedekiah said to Jeremiah, "I
[a]am anxious *because of* the Jews who
have [b,1]gone over to the Chaldeans,
lest they give me over into their hand
and they [c]deal severely with me."
**20** But Jeremiah said, "They will not
give you over. Please [a]listen to the
voice of Yahweh in what I am saying
to you, that it may go [b]well with you
and [c,1]you may live. **21** But if you keep
refusing to go out, this is the word
which Yahweh has shown me: **22** 'And
behold, all of the [a]women who have
remained in the house of the king of
Judah are going to be brought out to
the [1]officers of the king of Babylon;
and behold, those women will say,

"[2]Your close friends
Have misled and
overpowered you;
While your feet were
sunk in the mud,
They turned back."

**23** 'And they will also bring out all
your wives and your [a]sons to the
Chaldeans, and [b]you yourself will
not escape from their hand, but will
be seized by the hand of the king of
Babylon, and [b]this city will be burned
with fire.'"

**24** Then Zedekiah said to Jeremi-
ah, "Let no man know about these
words and you will not die. **25** But
if the [a]officials hear that I have

**38:13** [a]Ne 3:25; Jer 32:2; 37:21; 38:6; 39:14, 15; Ac 23:35; 24:27; 28:16, 30 **38:14** [a]Jer 21:1, 2; 37:17 [b]1Sa 3:17, 18; 1Ki 22:16; Jer 15:11; 42:2-5, 20 [1]Lit *took Jeremiah the prophet to him* **38:15** [a]Lk 22:67, 68 **38:16** [a]Jer 37:17; Jn 3:2 [b]Nu 16:22; 27:16; Is 42:5; 57:16; Zec 12:1; Ac 17:25, 28 [c]Jer 34:20; 38:4-6 [1]Lit *soul* **38:17** [a]Ps 80:7, 14; Am 5:27 [b]1Chr 17:24; Eze 8:4 [c]2Ki 24:12; 25:27-30; Jer 21:8-10; 27:12, 17; 38:2; 39:3 [1]Or *princes* [2]Lit *your soul* **38:18** [a]Jer 27:8 [b]2Ki 25:4-10; Jer 24:8-10; 32:3-5; 37:8; 38:3 [c]Jer 32:4; 34:3 [1]Or *princes* **38:19** [a]Is 51:12, 13; 57:11; Jn 12:42; 19:12, 13 [b]Jer 39:9 [c]2Chr 30:10; Ne 4:1; Jer 38:22 [1]Lit *fallen* **38:20** [a]2Chr 20:20; Jer 11:4, 8; 26:13; Da 4:27; Ac 26:29 [b]Jer 7:23 [c]Ge 19:20; Is 55:3 [1]Lit *your soul* **38:22** [a]Jer 6:12; 8:10; 43:6 [1]Or *princes* [2]Lit *The men of your peace* **38:23** [a]2Ki 25:7; Jer 39:6; 41:10 [b]Jer 38:18 **38:25** [a]Jer 38:4-6, 27

talked with you and come to you and say to you, 'Tell us now what you said to the king and what the king said to you; do not hide *it* from us, and we will not put you to death,' **26** then you are to say to them, 'I was [a]presenting my petition before the king, not to make me return to the house of Jonathan to die there.'" **27** Then all the officials came to Jeremiah and questioned him. So he told them in accordance with all these words which the king had commanded; and they ceased speaking with him since the [1]conversation had not been overheard. **28** So Jeremiah [a]stayed in the court of the guard until the day that Jerusalem was captured.

### *The Walls of Jerusalem Torn Down*

**39** [1]Now when Jerusalem was captured [a,2]in the ninth year of Zedekiah king of Judah, in the tenth month, Nebuchadnezzar king of Babylon and all his military force came to Jerusalem and laid siege to it; **2** in the eleventh year of Zedekiah, in the fourth month, in the ninth *day* of the month, the city was [a]breached. **3** Then all the [a]officials of the king of Babylon came in and sat down at the [b]Middle Gate: Nergal-sar-ezer, Samgar-nebu, Sar-sekim the [1]Rab-saris, Nergal-sar-ezer *the* [2]Rab-mag, and all the rest of the officials of the king of Babylon. **4** Now it happened that when Zedekiah the king of Judah and all the men of war saw them, they [a]fled and went out of the city at night by way of the king's garden through the gate [b]between the two walls; and he went out toward the [1]Arabah. **5** But the military force of the [a]Chaldeans pursued them and overtook Zedekiah in the [b,1]plains of Jericho; and they took him and brought him up to Nebuchadnezzar king of Babylon at [c]Riblah in the land of Hamath, and he spoke judgment on him. **6** Then the [a]king of Babylon slaughtered the sons of Zedekiah [b]before his eyes at Riblah; the king of Babylon also slaughtered all the [c]nobles of Judah. **7** He then [a]blinded Zedekiah's eyes and bound him in [b]fetters of bronze to bring him to [c]Babylon. **8** The Chaldeans also [a]burned with fire the house of the king and the houses of the people, and they [b]tore down the walls of Jerusalem. **9** And as for the rest of the people who remained in the city, the [a,1]defectors who had gone over to him and [b]the rest of the people who remained, [c]Nebuzaradan the [d]captain of the bodyguard took *them* away into exile in Babylon. **10** But some of the [a]poorest people who had nothing, [a]Nebuzaradan the captain of the bodyguard had *them* remain in the land of Judah and gave them vineyards and fields [1]at that time.

---

**38:26** [a]Jer 37:20 **38:27** [1]Lit *word* **38:28** [a]Ps 23:4; Jer 15:20, 21; 37:20, 21; 38:13; 39:13, 14
◆ **39:1** [a]*2Ki 25:1-12; Jer 52:4; Eze 24:1, 2* [1]*Ch 38:28b in Heb* [2]*Ch 39:1 in Heb* **39:2** [a]*2Ki 25:4; Jer 52:7*
**39:3** [a]Jer 38:17 [b]Jer 21:4 [1]Lit *chief official* [2]Title of a high official **39:4** [a]2Ki 25:4; Is 30:16; Jer 52:7; Am 2:14 [b]2Chr 32:5 [1]Jordan valley **39:5** [a]Jer 32:4, 5; 38:18, 23; 52:8 [b]Jos 4:13; 5:10 [c]2Ki 23:33; Jer 52:9, 26, 27 [1]Same Heb root as Arabah in 39:4 **39:6** [a]2Ki 25:7; Jer 52:10 [b]Dt 28:34 [c]Jer 21:7; 24:8-10; 34:19-21 **39:7** [a]2Ki 25:7; Jer 52:11; Eze 12:13 [b]Jdg 16:21 [c]Jer 32:5 **39:8** [a]2Ki 25:9; Jer 21:10; 38:18; 52:13 [b]2Ki 25:10; Ne 1:3; Jer 52:14 **39:9** [a]Jer 38:19; 52:15 [b]Jer 24:8 [c]2Ki 25:11, 20; Jer 39:13; 40:1; 52:12-16, 26 [d]Ge 37:36 [1]Lit *fallers who had fallen* **39:10** [a]2Ki 25:12; Jer 52:16 [1]Lit *on that day*

### *Jeremiah Delivered*

**11** Now Nebuchadnezzar king of
Babylon gave a command about
[a]Jeremiah through Nebuzaradan
the captain of the bodyguard, saying,
**12** "Take him and set your eyes *to look*
after him and [a]do nothing harmful to
him, but rather deal with him just as
he speaks to you." **13** So Nebuzaradan
the captain of the bodyguard sent
*word*, along with Nebushazban the
[1]Rab-saris and Nergal-sar-ezer the
[2]Rab-mag and all the leading officers
of the king of Babylon; **14** they even
sent and [a]took Jeremiah out of the
court of the guard and gave him over
to [b]Gedaliah, the son of [c]Ahikam, the
son of Shaphan, to take him home.
So he stayed among the people.

**15** Now the word of Yahweh had
come to Jeremiah while he was
[a]confined in the court of the guard,
saying, **16** "Go and speak to [a]Ebed-
melech the Ethiopian, saying, 'Thus
says Yahweh of hosts, the God of
Israel, "Behold, I am about to bring
My words on this city [b]for [1]calamity
and not for [2]prosperity; and they will
[c]take place before you on that day.
**17** But I will [a]deliver you on that day,"
declares Yahweh, "and you will not
be given into the hand of the men of
whom you are terrified. **18** For I will
certainly provide you escape, and
you will not fall by the sword; but
you will have your *own* [a]life as spoil
because you have [b]trusted in Me,"
declares Yahweh.'"

### *Jeremiah Stays in Judah*

**40** The word which came to
Jeremiah from Yahweh
after [a]Nebuzaradan captain of the
bodyguard had released him from
[b]Ramah, when he had taken him
bound in [c]chains among all the exiles
of Jerusalem and Judah who were
being exiled to Babylon. **2** And the
captain of the bodyguard had taken
Jeremiah and said to him, "[a]Yahweh
your God promised this calamity
against this place; **3** and Yahweh
has brought *it* on and done just as
He promised. Because you *people*
[a]sinned against Yahweh and did not
listen to His voice, therefore this
thing has happened to you. **4** So now,
behold, I am [a]freeing you today from
the chains which are on your hands.
If it is good in your eyes to come with
me to Babylon, come *along*, and I will
set my eyes *to look* after you; but if it
[1]is displeasing in your eyes to come
with me to Babylon, [2]never mind.
Look, the [b]whole land is before you;
go wherever it seems good and right
in your eyes to go." **5** But as [1]Jeremiah
had not yet *set out to* return, [2]*he said*,
"Return then to [a]Gedaliah the son of
Ahikam, the son of Shaphan, whom
the king of Babylon has [b]appointed
over the cities of Judah, and stay with
him among the people; or else go
anywhere that is right in your eyes to
go." So the captain of the bodyguard
gave him a [c]ration and a [d]gift and
let him go. **6** Then Jeremiah went

---

**39:11** [a]Job 5:15, 16; Jer 1:8; 15:20, 21; Ac 24:23 **39:12** [a]Ps 105:14, 15; Pr 16:7; 21:1; 1Pe 3:13 **39:13** [1]Lit *chief official* [2]Title of a high official **39:14** [a]Jer 38:28; 40:1-6 [b]Jer 40:5 [c]2Ki 22:12, 14; 2Chr 34:20; Jer 26:24 **39:15** [a]Jer 38:28 **39:16** [a]Jer 38:7 [b]Jer 21:10; Da 9:12; Zec 1:6 [c]Ps 91:8 [1]Lit *evil* [2]Lit *good* **39:17** [a]Ps 41:1, 2; 50:15 **39:18** [a]Jer 21:9; 38:2; 45:5 [b]Ps 34:22; Jer 17:7, 8 ◆ **40:1** [a]Jer 39:9, 11 [b]Jer 31:15 [c]Ac 12:6, 7; 21:13; 28:20; Eph 6:20 **40:2** [a]Lv 26:14-38; Dt 28:15-68; 29:24-28; 31:17; 32:19-25; Jer 22:8, 9 **40:3** [a]Jer 50:7; Da 9:11; Ro 2:5 **40:4** [a]Jer 39:11, 12 [b]Ge 13:9; 20:15; 47:6 [1]Lit *is evil in your eyes* [2]Lit *refrain!* **40:5** [a]Jer 39:14 [b]2Ki 25:23 [c]Jer 52:34 [d]2Ki 8:7-9 [1]Lit *he* [2]Nebuzaradan

to [a]Mizpah to [b]Gedaliah the son of
Ahikam and stayed with him among
the people who remained in the land.
7 [a]Then all the [1]commanders of
the military forces that were in the
field, they and their men, heard that
the king of Babylon had appointed
Gedaliah the son of Ahikam over
the land and that he had appointed
him over the men, women, little
ones, and those of the [b]poorest of
the land who had not been exiled to
Babylon. 8 So they came to Gedaliah
at Mizpah, along with [a]Ishmael the
son of Nethaniah, and [b]Johanan and
Jonathan the sons of Kareah, and Se-
raiah the son of Tanhumeth, and the
sons of Ephai the [c]Netophathite, and
[d]Jezaniah the son of the [e]Maacathite,
*both* they and their men. 9 Then
Gedaliah the son of Ahikam, the
son of Shaphan, [a]swore to them
and to their men, saying, "[b]Do not
be afraid of serving the Chaldeans;
stay in the land and serve the king
of Babylon, that it may go well with
you. 10 Now as for me, behold, I am
going to stay at Mizpah to [a]stand
*for you* before the Chaldeans who
come to us; but as for you, [b]gather
in wine and [c]summer fruit and oil
and put *them* in your *storage* vessels
and stay in your cities that you have
seized." 11 And also all the Jews, who
were in [a]Moab and among the sons
of [b]Ammon and in [c]Edom and who
were in all the *other* lands, heard
that the king of Babylon had left a
remnant for Judah and that he had
appointed over them Gedaliah the
son of Ahikam, the son of Shaphan.
12 Then all the Jews [a]returned from
all the places to which they had been
banished and came to the land of
Judah, to Gedaliah at Mizpah, and
gathered in wine and summer fruit
in great abundance.
13 Now Johanan the son of Kareah
and all the commanders of the
military forces that were in the field
came to Gedaliah at Mizpah 14 and
said to him, "Do you indeed know
that Baalis the king of the sons of
[a]Ammon has sent Ishmael the son of
Nethaniah to strike down your life?"
But Gedaliah the son of Ahikam did
not believe them. 15 Then Johanan
the son of Kareah spoke secretly to
Gedaliah in Mizpah, saying, "[a]Let
me go and strike down Ishmael the
son of Nethaniah, and not a man will
know! Why should he [b]strike down
your life, so that all the Jews who are
gathered to you would be scattered
and the [c]remnant of Judah would
perish?" 16 But Gedaliah the son of
Ahikam said to Johanan the son of
Kareah, "[a]Do not do this thing, for
you are telling a lie about Ishmael."

### *Ishmael Strikes Down Gedaliah*

41 [a]Now it happened in the sev-
enth month, that [b]Ishmael
the son of Nethaniah, the son of
Elishama, of the royal seed and *one*
of the chief officers of the king, along
with ten men, came to Mizpah to
[c]Gedaliah the son of Ahikam. And

**40:6** [a]Jdg 20:1; 21:1; 1Sa 7:5; 2Chr 16:6 [b]Jer 39:14 **40:7** [a]2Ki 25:23 [b]Jer 39:10; 52:16 [1]Or *princes*
**40:8** [a]Jer 40:14; 41:2 [b]Jer 40:13, 15; 42:1; 43:2 [c]2Sa 23:28, 29; Ezr 2:22; Ne 7:26 [d]Jer 42:1 [e]Dt 3:14; Jos 12:5; 2Sa 10:6, 8 **40:9** [a]1Sa 20:16, 17; 2Ki 25:24 [b]Jer 27:11; 38:17-20 **40:10** [a]Dt 1:38; 1Ki 10:8; Jer 35:19 [b]Dt 16:13; Jer 39:10 [c]Is 16:9; Jer 40:12; 48:32 **40:11** [a]Nu 22:1; 25:1, 2; Is 16:4; Jer 9:26 [b]1Sa 11:1; 12:12 [c]Ge 36:8; Is 11:14 **40:12** [a]Jer 43:5 **40:14** [a]1Sa 11:1-3; 2Sa 10:1-6; Jer 25:21; 41:10 **40:15** [a]1Sa 26:8 [b]2Sa 21:17 [c]Jer 42:2 **40:16** [a]Mt 10:16; 1Co 13:5 ◆ **41:1** [a]2Ki 25:25 [b]Jer 40:8, 14 [c]Jer 39:14; 40:5, 6

they [d]were eating bread together
there in Mizpah. **2** Then Ishmael the
son of Nethaniah and the ten men
who were with him arose and [a]struck
down Gedaliah the son of Ahikam,
the son of Shaphan, with the sword
and [b]put to death the one [c]whom the
king of Babylon had appointed over
the land. **3** Ishmael also struck down
all the Jews who were with him, *that
is* with Gedaliah at Mizpah, as well as
the Chaldeans who were found there,
the men of war.

**4** Now it happened on the [1]next
day after putting Gedaliah to death,
when no one knew about *it*, **5** that
eighty men [a]came from [b]Shechem,
from [c]Shiloh, and from [d]Samaria
with [e]their beards shaved off and
their clothes torn and [1]their bodies
[f]gashed, having grain offerings
and frankincense in their hands
to bring to the [g]house of Yahweh.
**6** Then Ishmael the son of Nethani-
ah went out from Mizpah to meet
them, [a]weeping as he went; and it
happened that as he encountered
them, he said to them, "Come to
Gedaliah the son of Ahikam!" **7** But it
happened that as soon as they came
inside the city, Ishmael the son of
Nethaniah and the men that were
with him [a]slaughtered them *and
cast them* into the cistern. **8** But ten
men who were found among them
said to Ishmael, "Do not put us to
death; for we have [a]stores of wheat,
barley, oil, and honey hidden in the
field." So he refrained and did not
put them to death along with their
[1]companions.

**9** Now as for the cistern where
Ishmael had cast all the corpses of
the men whom he had struck down
[1]because of Gedaliah, it was the [a]one
that King Asa had made on [b]account
of Baasha, king of Israel; Ishmael the
son of Nethaniah filled it with the
slain. **10** Then Ishmael took captive
all the [a]remnant of the people
who were in Mizpah, the [b]king's
daughters and all the people who
remained in Mizpah, over whom
Nebuzaradan the captain of the
bodyguard had appointed Gedaliah
the son of Ahikam; thus Ishmael the
son of Nethaniah took them captive
and went to cross over to the sons
of [c]Ammon.

### *Johanan Rescues the People*

**11** But Johanan the son of Kareah and
all the [a]commanders of the military
forces that were with him heard of
all the evil that Ishmael the son of
Nethaniah had done. **12** So they took
all the men and went to [a]fight with
Ishmael the son of Nethaniah, and
they found him by the [b]great [1]pool
that is in Gibeon. **13** Now it happened
as soon as all the people who were
with Ishmael saw Johanan the son
of Kareah and all the commanders
of the military forces that were with
him, they were glad. **14** So all the peo-
ple whom Ishmael had taken captive
from Mizpah turned around and
returned and went to Johanan the

**41:1** [d]Ps 41:9; Jer 40:13, 14 **41:2** [a]2Sa 3:27; 20:9, 10; 2Ki 25:25; Ps 41:9; 109:5; Jn 13:18 [b]2Ki 25:25 [c]Jer 40:5 **41:4** [1]Or *second* **41:5** [a]2Ki 10:13, 14 [b]Ge 33:18; 37:12; Jdg 9:1; 1Ki 12:1, 25 [c]Jos 18:1; Jdg 18:31; 1Sa 3:21; Ps 78:60 [d]1Ki 16:24, 29 [e]Lv 19:27; Dt 14:1 [f]Dt 14:1; Jer 16:6 [g]1Sa 1:7; 2Ki 25:9 [1]Lit *having cut themselves* **41:6** [a]2Sa 3:16; Jer 50:4 **41:7** [a]Ps 55:23; Is 59:7; Eze 22:27; 33:24, 26 **41:8** [a]Is 45:3 [1]Lit *brothers* **41:9** [a]1Ki 15:17-22; 2Chr 16:1-6 [b]Jdg 6:2; 1Sa 13:6; 2Sa 17:9; Heb 11:38 [1]Or *by the side of* **41:10** [a]Jer 40:11, 12 [b]Jer 43:6 [c]Ne 2:10, 19; 4:7; Jer 40:14 **41:11** [a]Jer 40:7, 8, 13-16 **41:12** [a]Ge 14:14-16; 1Sa 30:1-8, 18, 20 [b]2Sa 2:13 [1]Lit *waters*

son of Kareah. **15** But Ishmael the son
of Nethaniah [a]escaped from Johanan
with eight men and went to the sons
of Ammon. **16** Then Johanan the son
of Kareah and all the commanders of
the military forces that were with
him took from Mizpah [a]all the
remnant of the people whom he had
returned from Ishmael the son of
Nethaniah, after he had struck down
Gedaliah the son of Ahikam, *that is*,
the mighty men who were men of
war, *the* women, *the* little ones, and
*the* eunuchs, whom he had returned
from Gibeon. **17** And they went
and stayed in [a,1]Geruth Chimham,
which is beside Bethlehem, in order
to [b]proceed into Egypt **18** because
of the Chaldeans; for they were
[a]afraid of them, since Ishmael the
son of Nethaniah had struck down
Gedaliah the son of Ahikam, whom
[b]the king of Babylon had appointed
over the land.

### *The People Ask Jeremiah to Pray*

**42** Then all the [1]commanders of
the military forces, [a]Johanan
the son of Kareah, Jezaniah the son
of Hoshaiah, and all the people [b]both
small and great approached **2** and
said to Jeremiah the prophet, "Please
let our [a]supplication [1]come before
you, and [b]pray for us to Yahweh your
God, *that is* for all this remnant,
because we remain *but* a [c]few out of
many, as your own eyes *now* see us,
**3** that Yahweh your God may tell us
the [a]way in which we should walk
and the thing that we should do."
**4** Then Jeremiah the prophet said to
them, "I have heard *you*. Behold, I
am going to [a]pray to Yahweh your
God in accordance with your words;
and I will tell you the whole [1]message
which [b]Yahweh will answer you. I
will [c]not keep back a word from
you." **5** And they said to Jeremiah,
"May [a]Yahweh be a true and faithful
witness against us if we do not act in
accordance with the whole [1]message
with which Yahweh your God will
send you to us. **6** Whether *it* is good
or bad, we will [a]listen to the voice
of Yahweh our God to whom we are
sending you, so that good [b]may come
to us when we listen to the voice of
Yahweh our God."

**7** Now it happened that at the [a]end
of ten days the word of Yahweh came
to Jeremiah. **8** Then he called for Jo-
hanan the son of Kareah and all the
[1]commanders of the military forces
that were with him, and for all the
people both small and great, **9** and
said to them, "Thus [a]says Yahweh
the God of Israel, to whom you sent
me to present your supplication
before Him: **10** 'If you will indeed
stay in this land, then I will [a]build
you up and not pull you down, and
I will plant you and not uproot you;
for I have [b,1]relented of the calamity
that I have done against you. **11** [a]Do

---

**41:15** [a]1Sa 30:17; 1Ki 20:20; Job 21:30; Pr 28:17 **41:16** [a]Jer 42:8; 43:4-7 **41:17** [a]2Sa 19:37, 38, 40 [b]*Jer 42:14* [1]*Or the lodging place of Chimham* **41:18** [a]Is 51:12, 13; 57:11; Jer 42:11, 16; 43:2, 3; Lk 12:4, 5 [b]Jer 40:5 ◆ **42:1** [a]Jer 40:8, 13; 41:11, 18 [b]*Jer 6:13; 8:10; 42:8; 44:12; Ac 8:10* [1]*Or princes* **42:2** [a]Jer 36:7; 37:20 [b]Ex 8:28; 1Sa 7:8; 12:19; 1Ki 13:6; Is 37:4; Jer 37:3; 42:20; Ac 8:24; Jas 5:16 [c]Lv 26:22; Dt 28:62; Is 1:9; Lam 1:1 [1]Lit *fall* **42:3** [a]Ps 86:11; Pr 3:6; Jer 6:16; Mic 4:2 **42:4** [a]Ex 8:29; 1Sa 12:23 [b]1Ki 22:14; Jer 23:28 [c]1Sa 3:17, 18; Ps 40:10; Ac 20:20 [1]Lit *word* **42:5** [a]Ge 31:50; Jdg 11:10; Jer 43:2; Mic 1:2; Mal 2:14; 3:5 [1]Lit *word* **42:6** [a]Ex 24:7; Dt 5:27; Jos 24:24 [b]Dt 5:29, 33; 6:3; Jer 7:23 **42:7** [a]Ps 27:14; Is 30:18 **42:8** [1]Or *princes* **42:9** [a]2Ki 19:4, 6, 20; 22:15 **42:10** [a]Jer 24:6; 31:28; 33:7; Eze 36:36 [b]Jer 18:7, 8; Hos 11:8; Joel 2:13; Am 7:3, 6; Jon 3:10; 4:2 [1]Or *regret*, cf. 1Sa 15:11, 29, 35 **42:11** [a]Jer 1:8; 27:12, 17; 41:18

not be afraid of the king of Babylon,
whom you are *now* fearing; do not
be afraid of him,' declares Yahweh,
'for [b]I am with you to save you and
deliver you from his hand. **12** I will
also show you compassion, so that
[a]he will have compassion on you
and return you to your own soil.
**13** But if you are going to say, "We
will [a]not stay in this land," so as not
to listen to the voice of Yahweh your
God, **14** saying, "No, but we will [a]go
to the land of Egypt, where we will
not see war or [b]hear the sound of a
trumpet or hunger for bread, and we
will stay there," **15** then now, listen to
the word of Yahweh, O remnant of
Judah. Thus says Yahweh of hosts,
the God of Israel, "If you really set
your face to enter [a]Egypt, and you
will enter to sojourn there, **16** then
the [a]sword, which you are afraid of,
will overtake you there in the land of
Egypt; and the famine, about which
you are anxious, will [1]follow closely
after you there *in* Egypt, and you will
die there. **17** So all the men who set
their face to go to Egypt to sojourn
there will die by the [a]sword, by the
famine, and by the pestilence; and
they will [b]have no survivors or *any*
*who* escaped from the calamity that
I am going to bring on them."'"

**18** For thus says Yahweh of hosts,
the God of Israel, "As My [a]anger and
wrath have been poured out on the
inhabitants of Jerusalem, so My wrath
will be poured out on you when you
enter Egypt. And you will become a
[b]curse, an object of horror, an impre-
cation, and a reproach; and [c]you will
see this place no more." **19** Yahweh
has spoken to you, O remnant of
Judah, "Do not [a]go into Egypt!" You
should clearly [b]know that today I
have [c]testified against you. **20** For you
have *only* [a,1]led yourselves astray; for
it is you who sent me to Yahweh your
God, saying, "Pray for us to Yahweh
our God; and according to all that
Yahweh our God says, tell us so, and
we will do it." **21** So I have [a]told you
today, but you have [b]not listened to
the voice of Yahweh your God, even
according to all that He has sent me
to *tell* you. **22** So now, you should
clearly know that you will [a]die by the
sword, by famine, and by pestilence,
in the [b]place where you desire to go
to sojourn.

### *Jeremiah Taken to Egypt*

**43** But it happened that as soon
as Jeremiah, whom Yahweh
their God had sent, had [a]finished
speaking to all the people all the
words of Yahweh their God—that is,
all these words— **2** Azariah the [a]son
of Hoshaiah, and Johanan the son
of Kareah, and all the arrogant men
said to Jeremiah, "You are [b]speaking
a lie! Yahweh our God has not sent
you to say, 'You are not to enter Egypt
to sojourn there'; **3** but [a]Baruch the
son of Neriah is inciting you against
us to give us over into the hand of

---

**42:11** [b]Nu 14:9; 2Chr 32:7, 8; Ps 46:7, 11; 118:6; Is 8:9, 10; 43:2, 5; Jer 1:19; 15:20; Ro 8:31 **42:12** [a]Ne 1:11; Ps 106:46; Pr 16:7 **42:13** [a]Ex 5:2; Jer 44:16 **42:14** [a]Is 31:1; Jer 41:17 [b]Ex 16:3; Nu 11:4; Jer 4:19, 21 **42:15** [a]Dt 17:16; Jer 42:17; 44:12-14 **42:16** [a]Jer 44:13, 27; Eze 11:8; Am 9:1-4 [1]Lit *cling* **42:17** [a]Jer 24:10; 38:2; 42:22; 44:13 [b]Jer 44:14, 28 **42:18** [a]2Chr 36:16-19; Jer 7:20; 33:5; 39:1-9 [b]Dt 29:21; Is 65:15; Jer 18:16; 24:9; 29:18; 44:12 [c]Jer 22:10, 27 **42:19** [a]Dt 17:16; Is 30:1-7 [b]Eze 2:5 [c]Ne 9:26, 29, 30 **42:20** [a]Jer 43:2; Eze 14:3 [1]Or *acted errantly in your souls* **42:21** [a]Dt 11:26; Jer 43:1; Eze 2:7; Zec 7:11; Ac 20:26, 27 [b]Jer 43:4 **42:22** [a]Jer 43:11; Eze 6:11 [b]Hos 9:6 ◆ **43:1** [a]Jer 26:8; 51:63 **43:2** [a]Jer 42:1 [b]2Chr 36:13; Is 7:9; Jer 5:12, 13; 42:5 **43:3** [a]Jer 36:4, 10, 26, 32; 43:6; 45:1-3

the Chaldeans, so they will put us
to death or exile us to Babylon." **4** So
[a]Johanan the son of Kareah and all the
[1]commanders of the military forces
and all the people [b]did not listen to
the voice of Yahweh to [c]stay in the
land of Judah. **5** But Johanan the son
of Kareah and all the [1]commanders
of the military forces took the [a]entire
remnant of Judah, who had returned
from all the nations to which they
had been banished, in order to
sojourn in the land of Judah— **6** the
men, the women, the little ones, the
[a]king's daughters, and [b]every person
that Nebuzaradan the captain of the
bodyguard had left with Gedaliah
the son of Ahikam [1]and grandson of
Shaphan, together with [c]Jeremiah
the prophet and Baruch the son of
Neriah— **7** and they entered the land
of Egypt (for they did not listen to the
voice of Yahweh) and went in as far
as [a]Tahpanhes.
**8** Then the word of Yahweh came
to Jeremiah in [a]Tahpanhes, saying,
**9** "Take *some* large stones in your
[1]hands and hide them in the mortar
in the [2]brick *terrace* which is at
the entrance of Pharaoh's house in
Tahpanhes, in the sight of [3]some *of
the* Jews; **10** and you will say to them,
'Thus says Yahweh of hosts, the God
of Israel, "Behold, I am going to send
and get [a]Nebuchadnezzar the king of
Babylon, [b]My servant, and I am going
to set his throne *right* over these
stones that I have hidden; and he will
spread his [c]canopy over them. **11** He
will also come and [a]strike the land
of Egypt; those who are *meant* for
death *will be given over* to death, and
those for captivity to captivity, and
[b]those for the sword to the sword.
**12** And [1]I shall set fire to the houses
of the [a]gods of Egypt, and he will
burn them and take them captive.
So he will [b]wrap himself with the
land of Egypt as a shepherd wraps
himself with his garment, and he
will depart from there safely. **13** He
will also shatter the [1]*sacred* pillars
of [2]Heliopolis, which is in the land of
Egypt; and the houses of the gods of
Egypt he will burn with fire."'"

### *Wrath Against the Israelites in Egypt*

**44** The word that came to Jeremi-
ah for all the Jews living in the
land of Egypt, those who were living
in [a]Migdol, [b]Tahpanhes, [c]Memphis,
and the land of [d]Pathros, saying,
**2** "Thus says Yahweh of hosts, the
God of Israel, 'You yourselves have
seen all the evil that I have brought
on Jerusalem and all the cities of
Judah; and behold, this day they are
a [a]waste place and no one lives in
them **3** [a]because of their evil which
they did so as to [b]provoke Me to an-
ger by continuing to [c]burn incense
*and* to [d]serve other gods whom they
had not known, *neither* they, you,
nor your fathers. **4** Yet I [a]sent you

**43:4** [a]Jer 42:8 [b]2Chr 25:16; Jer 42:5, 6; 44:5 [c]Ps 37:3; Jer 42:10-12 [1]Or *princes* **43:5** [a]Jer 40:11 [1]Or *princes* **43:6** [a]Jer 41:10 [b]Jer 39:10; 40:7 [c]Ecc 9:1, 2; Lam 3:1 [1]Lit *the son* **43:7** [a]Jer 2:16; 44:1 **43:8** [a]Jer 2:16; 44:1; 46:14; Eze 30:18 **43:9** [1]Lit *hand* [2]Or *brickwork* [3]Lit *men* **43:10** [a]Jer 25:9, 11 [b]Is 44:28; 45:1; Jer 25:9; 27:6 [c]Ps 18:11; 27:5; 31:20 **43:11** [a]Is 19:1-25; Jer 25:15-19; 44:13; 46:1, 2, 13-26; Eze 29:19, 20 [b]Jer 15:2 **43:12** [a]Ex 12:12; Is 19:1; Jer 46:25; Eze 30:13 [b]Ps 104:2; 109:18, 19; Is 49:18 [1]Some ancient versions *He will set* **43:13** [1]Or *obelisks* [2]The house of the sun-god; Heb *Beth-shemesh* ◆ **44:1** [a]Ex 14:2; Jer 46:14 [b]Jer 43:7; Eze 30:18 [c]Is 19:13; Jer 2:16; 46:14; Eze 30:13, 16; Hos 9:6 [d]Is 11:11; Eze 29:14; 30:14 **44:2** [a]Is 6:11; Jer 4:7; 9:11; 34:22; Mic 3:12 **44:3** [a]Ne 9:33; Jer 2:17-19; 44:23; Eze 8:17, 18; Da 9:5 [b]Is 3:8; Jer 7:19; 32:30-32; 44:8 [c]Jer 19:4 [d]Dt 13:6; 29:26; 32:17 **44:4** [a]Jer 7:13, 25; 25:4; 26:5; 29:19; 35:15; Zec 7:7

all My slaves the prophets, rising up
early and sending, saying, "Oh, do
not do this [b]abominable thing which
I hate." 5 But [a]they did not listen or
incline their ears to turn from their
evil, so as not to burn incense to
other gods. 6 Therefore My [a]wrath
and My anger were poured out and
burned in the [b]cities of Judah and in
the streets of Jerusalem, so they have
become a waste place and a [c]desola-
tion as it is this day. 7 So now, thus
says Yahweh, the God of hosts, the
God of Israel, "Why are you [a]doing
great evil against yourselves, so as
to [b]cut off from you man and wom-
an, infant and nursing baby, from
among Judah, leaving yourselves
without remnant, 8 [a]provoking Me to
anger with the works of your hands,
[b]burning incense to other gods in the
land of Egypt, where you are enter-
ing to sojourn, so that you might be
cut off and become an [c]imprecation
and a reproach among all the nations
of the earth? 9 Have you forgotten
the [a]evil of your fathers, the evil of
the kings of Judah, and the evil of
their wives, your own evil, and the
evil of your wives, which they did in
the land of Judah and in the streets
of Jerusalem? 10 But they [a]have not
become [1]contrite even to this day,
nor have they feared nor [b]walked
in My law or My statutes, which I
have put before you and before your
fathers."'

11 "Therefore thus says Yahweh of
hosts, the God of Israel, 'Behold, I am
going to [a]set My face against you for
*your* evil *demise*, even to cut off all
Judah. 12 And I will [a]take away the
remnant of Judah who have set their
face on entering the land of Egypt
to sojourn there, and they will all
[b,1]meet their end in the land of Egypt;
they will fall by the sword *and* [1]meet
their end by famine. Both small and
great will die by the sword and fam-
ine; and they will become a [c]curse,
an object of horror, an imprecation,
and a reproach. 13 And I will [a]punish
those who live in the land of Egypt,
as I have punished Jerusalem, with
the sword, with famine, and with
pestilence. 14 So there will be [a]no
one who escapes or *any* survivors
for the remnant of Judah who have
entered the land of Egypt to sojourn
there and then to return to the land
of Judah, to which they are [b,1]longing
to return to live; for none will [c]return
except *a few* who escape.'"

15 Then [a]all the men who knew
that their wives were burning in-
cense to other gods, along with all
the women who were standing by,
*as* a large assembly, [1]including all
the people who were living in Path-
ros in the land of Egypt, answered
to Jeremiah, saying, 16 "As for the
[a,1]message that you have spoken to
us in the name of Yahweh, [b]we are
not going to listen to you! 17 But

**44:4** [b]Jer 16:18; 32:34, 35; Eze 8:10 **44:5** [a]Jer 11:8, 10; 13:10 **44:6** [a]Is 51:17-20; Jer 42:18; Eze 8:18 [b]Jer 7:17, 34 [c]Jer 4:27; 34:22 **44:7** [a]Nu 16:38; Jer 26:19; Eze 33:11; Hab 2:10 [b]Jer 3:24; 9:21; 51:22 **44:8** [a]2Ki 17:15-17; Jer 25:6, 7; 44:3; 1Co 10:21, 22 [b]Jer 7:9; 11:12, 17; 44:3; Hos 4:13; Hab 1:16 [c]1Ki 9:7, 8; 2Chr 7:20; Jer 42:18 **44:9** [a]Jer 7:9, 10, 17, 18; 44:17, 21 **44:10** [a]Jer 6:15; 8:12 [b]Jer 26:4; 32:23; 44:23 [1]Lit *crushed* **44:11** [a]Lv 17:10; 20:5, 6; 26:17; Jer 21:10; Am 9:4 **44:12** [a]Jer 42:15-18, 22 [b]Is 1:28; Jer 16:4; 44:7 [c]Is 65:15; Jer 18:16; 24:9; 26:6; 29:18; 42:18; Zec 8:13 [1]Lit *be finished* **44:13** [a]Jer 11:22; 44:27, 28 **44:14** [a]Jer 22:10; 44:27 [b]Jer 22:26, 27 [c]Is 4:2; 10:20; Jer 44:28; Ro 9:27 [1]Lit *lifting up their soul* **44:15** [a]Pr 11:21; Is 1:5; Jer 5:1-5 [1]Lit *and* **44:16** [a]Jer 43:2 [b]Pr 1:24-27; Jer 11:8, 10; 13:10 [1]Lit *word*

rather we will certainly [a]carry out
every word that has proceeded from
our mouths, [1]by burning incense to
the [b]queen of heaven and pouring
out drink offerings to her, just as [c]we
ourselves, our fathers, our kings, and
our princes did in the cities of Judah
and in the streets of Jerusalem; for
*then* we had [d]plenty of [2]food and
were well off and saw no evil. **18** But
since we stopped burning incense
to the queen of heaven and pouring
out drink offerings to her, we have
[a]lacked everything and have [1]met
our end by the sword and by famine."
**19** "And," *said the women*, "when we
were [a]burning incense to the queen
of heaven and [1]were pouring out
drink offerings to her, was it [b]without
our husbands that we made for her
*sacrificial* cakes [2]in her image and
poured out drink offerings to her?"

**20** Then Jeremiah said to all the
people, to the men and women—
even to all the people who were
answering him with *such* a word—
saying, **21** "As for the [a,1]smoking
sacrifices that you offered in the
cities of Judah and in the [b]streets
of Jerusalem, you and your fathers,
your kings and your princes, and the
people of the land, did not Yahweh
[c]remember them and did not *all
this* come upon His heart? **22** So
Yahweh was [a]no longer able to bear
*it*, [b]because of the evil of your deeds,
because of the abominations which
you have done; thus your land has
become a [c]waste place, an object of
horror, and an imprecation, with-
out an inhabitant, as *it is* this day.
**23** Because you have burned incense
and have sinned against Yahweh and
[a]not listened to the voice of Yahweh
or [b]walked in His law, His statutes, or
His testimonies, therefore this [c]evil
has befallen you, as *it has* this day."

**24** Then Jeremiah said to all the
people, including all the women,
"[a]Hear the word of Yahweh, all Judah
who are [b]in the land of Egypt, **25** thus
says Yahweh of hosts, the God of Isra-
el, saying: 'As for you and your wives,
you have spoken with your mouths
and fulfilled *it* with your hands,
saying, "We will [a]certainly perform
our vows that we have vowed, to
burn incense to the queen of heaven
and pour out drink offerings to her."
[b,1]Go ahead and establish your vows,
and certainly perform your vows!'
**26** [1]Nevertheless, hear the word of
Yahweh, all Judah who are living in
the land of Egypt, 'Behold, I have
[a]sworn by My great name,' says
Yahweh, '[b]never shall My name be
called upon again by the mouth of
any man of Judah in all the land of
Egypt, saying, "[c]As Lord Yahweh
lives." **27** Behold, I am watching over
them [a]for [1]evil and not for good, and
[b]all the men of Judah who are in the
land of Egypt will [2]meet their end
by the sword and by famine until

**44:17** [a]Nu 30:12; Dt 23:23 [b]2Ki 17:16; Jer 7:18 [c]Ne 9:34; Jer 32:32; 44:21 [d]Ex 16:3; Hos 2:5-9; Php 3:19 [1]Or *so as to burn* [2]Lit *bread* **44:18** [a]Nu 11:5, 6; Jer 40:12; Mal 3:13-15 [1]Lit *been finished*
**44:19** [a]Jer 7:18 [b]Nu 30:6, 7; Jer 44:15 [1]Lit *to pour* [2]Lit *to make an image of her* **44:21** [a]Eze 8:10, 11 [b]Jer 11:13; 44:9, 17 [c]Ps 79:8; Is 64:9; Jer 14:10; Hos 7:2; Am 8:7 [1]Heb sounds like root for incense
**44:22** [a]Is 7:13; 43:24; Mal 2:17 [b]Jer 4:4; 21:12; 30:14 [c]Ge 19:13; Ps 107:33, 34; Jer 25:11, 18, 38; 29:18; 42:18; 44:12 **44:23** [a]Jer 7:13-15; 40:3 [b]Jer 44:10; Ps 119:136, 150 [c]1Ki 9:9; Ne 13:18; Jer 44:2; Da 9:11, 12
**44:24** [a]Jer 42:15; 44:16 [b]Jer 43:7; 44:15, 26 **44:25** [a]Jer 44:17; Mt 14:9; Ac 23:12 [b]Eze 20:39 [1]Lit *Surely cause to stand* **44:26** [a]Ge 22:16; Dt 32:40, 41; Jer 22:5; Am 6:8; Heb 6:13 [b]Ps 50:16; Eze 20:39 [c]Is 48:1, 2; Jer 5:2 [1]Lit *Therefore* **44:27** [a]Jer 1:10; 31:28; 39:16 [b]2Ki 21:14; Jer 44:14 [1]Or *harm* [2]Lit *be finished*

they [3]are completely consumed.
**28** [a]Those who escape the sword will
return out of the land of Egypt to the
land of Judah [b,1]few in number. Then
all the remnant of Judah who have
gone to the land of Egypt to sojourn
there will know [c]whose word will be
established, Mine or theirs. **29** This
will be the [a]sign to you,' declares
Yahweh, 'that I am going to punish
you in this place, so that you may
know that [b]My words will surely be
established against you for [1]evil.'
**30** Thus says Yahweh, 'Behold, I
am going to give over [a]Pharaoh
Hophra king of Egypt to the hand
of his enemies, to the hand of those
who seek his life, just as I gave over
[b]Zedekiah king of Judah to the hand
of Nebuchadnezzar king of Babylon,
*who was* his enemy and was seeking
his life.'"

### *Word to Baruch*

**45** *This is* the message which
Jeremiah the prophet spoke
to [a]Baruch the son of Neriah, when
he had [b]written down these words
in a book [1]at Jeremiah's dictation,
in the [c]fourth year of Jehoiakim the
son of Josiah, king of Judah, saying:
**2** "Thus says Yahweh the God of Isra-
el to you, O Baruch: **3** 'You said, "Ah,
woe is me! For Yahweh has added
sorrow to my pain; I am [a]weary
with my sighing and have found no
rest."' **4** Thus you are to say to him,
'Thus says Yahweh, "Behold, [a]what
I have built I am about to pull down,
and what I have planted I am about
to uproot, that is, the whole land."
**5** But as for you, are you [a]seeking
great things for yourself? Do not
seek *them*; for behold, I am going
to [b]bring calamity on all flesh,' de-
clares Yahweh, 'but I will [c]give your
life to you as spoil in all the places
where you may go.'"

### *Word Against Egypt*

**46** That which came as the word
of Yahweh to Jeremiah the
prophet [a]concerning the nations.
**2** To [a]Egypt, concerning the mili-
tary force of [b]Pharaoh Neco king of
Egypt, which was by the Euphrates
River at [c]Carchemish, which Nebu-
chadnezzar king of Babylon struck
down in the [d]fourth year of Jehoiakim
the son of Josiah, king of Judah:

**3** "[a]Arrange the shield
and large shield,
And draw near for the battle!
**4** "Harness the horses,
And [1]mount the steeds,
And take your stand
with helmets *on*!
[a]Polish the spears,
Put on the [b]scale-armor!
**5** "Why have I seen *it*?
They are shattered;
They are [a]drawing back,
And their [b]mighty
men are crushed

**44:27** [3]Lit *come to an end* **44:28** [a]Jer 44:14 [b]Is 10:19; 27:12, 13 [c]Ps 33:11; Is 14:27; 46:10, 11; Zec 1:6 [1]Lit *men of number* **44:29** [a]Is 7:11, 14; 8:18; Jer 44:30; Mt 24:15, 16, 32 [b]Pr 19:21; Is 40:8 [1]Or *harm* **44:30** [a]Jer 43:9-13; 46:25; Eze 29:3; 30:21 [b]2Ki 25:4-7; Jer 34:21; 39:5-7 ◆ **45:1** [a]Jer 32:12, 16; 43:3, 6 [b]Jer 36:4, 18, 32 [c]2Ki 24:1; 2Chr 36:5-7; Jer 25:1; 36:1; 46:2; Da 1:1 [1]Lit *from the mouth of Jeremiah* **45:3** [a]Ps 6:6; 69:3; 2Co 4:1, 16; Ga 6:9 **45:4** [a]Is 5:5; Jer 1:10; 11:17; 18:7-10; 31:28 **45:5** [a]1Ki 3:9, 11; 2Ki 5:26; Mt 6:25, 32; Ro 12:16 [b]Is 66:16; Jer 25:31 [c]Jer 21:9; 38:2; 39:18 ◆ **46:1** [a]Jer 1:10; 25:15-38 **46:2** [a]Jer 46:14; Ezek chs 29-32 [b]2Ki 18:21; 23:29, 33-35; Jer 25:19 [c]2Chr 35:20; Is 10:9 [d]Jer 45:1 **46:3** [a]Is 21:5; Jer 51:11; Joel 3:9; Na 2:1; 3:14 **46:4** [a]Eze 21:9-11 [b]1Sa 17:5, 38; 2Chr 26:14; Ne 4:16; Jer 51:3 [1]Or *go up, you horsemen* **46:5** [a]Is 42:17; Jer 46:21 [b]Is 5:25; Eze 39:18

And have fled to refuge,
Without facing back;
[c,1]Terror is on every side!"
Declares Yahweh.
6 Let not the [a]swift man flee,
Nor the mighty man escape;
In the north
beside the river Euphrates
They have [b]stumbled
and fallen.
7 Who is this that [a]rises
like the Nile,
Like the rivers
whose waters toss about?
8 Egypt rises like the Nile,
Even like the rivers
whose waters toss about;
And He has said, "I will [a]rise
and cover *that* land;
I will surely [b]cause the city
to perish, as well as
its inhabitants."
9 Go up, you horses, and [a,1]drive
madly, you chariots,
That the mighty men
may go forth:
[2]Ethiopia and [b,3]Put,
who seize the shield,
And the [c,4]Lydians,
who seize *and* bend the bow.
10 Indeed, [a]that day belongs
to Lord Yahweh of hosts,
A day of [b]vengeance, so
as to avenge Himself
on His adversaries;
And the [c]sword will devour
and be satiated
And [1]drink its fill
of their blood;
For there will be a [d]sacrifice
to Lord Yahweh of hosts
In the land of the north by
the river Euphrates.
11 Go [a]up to Gilead and
obtain balm,
[b]O virgin daughter of Egypt!
In vain have you
multiplied [1]remedies;
There is [c]no healing for you.
12 The nations have heard
of your [a]disgrace,
And the earth is full
of your [b]outcry;
For one [c]warrior has
stumbled over [1]another,
And both of them have
fallen down together.

13 *This is* the [1]message which Yah-
weh spoke to Jeremiah the prophet
about the [a]coming of Nebuchadnez-
zar king of Babylon to [b]strike down
the land of Egypt:

14 "Declare in Egypt and cause
*it* to be heard in [a]Migdol;
Cause *it* to be heard also
in Memphis
and [b]Tahpanhes;
Say, 'Take your stand and
get yourself ready,
For the [c]sword has devoured
those around you.'
15 "Why are your [a]mighty
ones thrown down?
They do not stand
because Yahweh has
[b]thrust them down.
16 "They have
repeatedly [a]stumbled;

---

**46:5** [c]Jer 6:25; 20:3; 49:29 [1]Heb *Magor-missabib* **46:6** [a]Is 30:16 [b]Jer 46:12, 16; Da 11:19
**46:7** [a]Jer 47:2 **46:8** [a]Is 37:24 [b]Is 10:13 **46:9** [a]Jer 47:3; Na 2:4 [b]Na 3:9 [c]Is 66:19 [1]Lit *act like madmen* [2]Or *Cush*, cf. Ge 10:6 [3]Libya (or Somaliland) [4]Heb *Ludim* **46:10** [a]Joel 1:15 [b]Jer 50:15, 18 [c]Dt 32:42; Is 31:8; Jer 12:12 [d]Is 34:6; Zep 1:7 [1]Lit *be saturated with* **46:11** [a]Jer 8:22 [b]Is 47:1; Jer 31:4, 21 [c]Jer 30:13; Mic 1:9; Na 3:19 [1]Lit *healings* **46:12** [a]Jer 2:36; Na 3:8-10 [b]Jer 14:2 [c]Is 19:2 [1]Lit *warrior*
**46:13** [a]Jer 43:10-13 [b]Is 19:1 [1]Lit *word* **46:14** [a]Jer 44:1 [b]Jer 43:8 [c]Is 1:20; Jer 2:30; 46:10; Na 2:13
**46:15** [a]Is 66:15, 16; Jer 46:5 [b]Ps 18:14, 39; 68:1, 2 **46:16** [a]Lv 26:36, 37; Jer 46:6

Indeed, they have fallen
one against another.
Then they said, 'Rise up!
And [b]let us return
To our own people and
land of our birth
Away from the [c,1]sword
of the oppressor.'
17 "[1]They called out there,
'Pharaoh king of Egypt
*is but* [a]a rumbling;
He has let the appointed
time pass by!'
18 "As I live," declares the [a]King
Whose name is
Yahweh of hosts,
"Surely one shall come *who*
*looms up* like [b]Tabor
among the mountains,
Or like [c]Carmel by the sea.
19 "Make your baggage
ready for [a]exile,
O inhabitant of the [b]daughter
of Egypt,
For [c]Memphis will
become a desolation;
It will even be turned into ruin
*and* without inhabitants.
20 "Egypt is a pretty [a]heifer,
*But* a [1]horsefly is coming [b]from
the north—it is coming!
21 "Also her [a]mercenaries
in her midst
Are like [1]fattened [b]calves,
For even they have
turned back *and* have
fled away together;
They did not stand
*their ground.*
For the day of their disaster
has come upon them,
The time
of their [c]punishment.
22 "Its sound moves
along like a serpent;
For they move on
[1]like a military force
And come to her as
woodcutters with axes.
23 "They have cut down
her [a]forest,"
declares Yahweh;
"Surely it will no *longer*
be searched out,
Even though [1]they are
*now* more numerous
than [b]locusts
And are without number.
24 "The daughter of Egypt has
been put to shame,
Given over to the hand
of the [a]people of the north."

25 Yahweh of hosts, the God of
Israel, says, "Behold, I am going
to punish Amon of [a]Thebes, and
[b]Pharaoh, and Egypt along with her
[c]gods and her kings, even Pharaoh
and those who [d]trust in him. 26 I shall
give them into the hand of those who
are [a]seeking their lives, even into
the hand of Nebuchadnezzar king
of Babylon and into the hand of his
servants. [b]Afterwards, however, it
will be dwelt in like in the days of
old," declares Yahweh.

27 "But as for you, O Jacob My
servant, [a]do not fear,
Nor be dismayed, O Israel!

**46:16** [b]Jer 51:9 [c]Jer 50:16 [1]Lit *oppressing sword* **46:17** [a]Ex 15:9, 10; 1Ki 20:10, 11; Is 19:11-16 [1]Some ancient versions *Call the name of Pharaoh a rumbling* **46:18** [a]Jer 48:15; Mal 1:14 [b]Jos 19:22; Jdg 4:6; Ps 89:12 [c]Jos 12:22; 1Ki 18:42 **46:19** [a]Is 20:4 [b]Jer 48:18 [c]Jer 46:14; Eze 30:13 **46:20** [a]Hos 10:11 [b]Jer 1:14; 47:2 [1]Or possibly *mosquito* **46:21** [a]2Sa 10:6; 2Ki 7:6; Jer 46:5 [b]Is 34:7 [c]Jer 48:44; Hos 9:7; Ob 13; Mic 7:4 [1]Lit *of the stall* **46:22** [1]Or *in force* **46:23** [a]Jer 21:14 [b]Jdg 6:5; 7:12; Joel 2:25 [1]Trees of the forest, the Egyptians **46:24** [a]Jer 1:15 **46:25** [a]Eze 30:14-16; Na 3:8 [b]Jer 44:30 [c]Ex 12:12; Jer 43:12, 13; Eze 30:13; Zep 2:11 [d]Is 20:5 **46:26** [a]Jer 44:30; Eze 32:11 [b]Eze 29:8-14 **46:27** [a]Is 41:13, 14; Jer 30:10, 11

For behold, I am going to
[b]save you from afar,
And your seed from the
land of their captivity;
And Jacob will return
and have [c]quiet
And be at ease, with no one
making *him* tremble.
28 “O Jacob My servant, do not
fear,” declares Yahweh,
“For [a]I am with you.
For I will make a complete
destruction of all
the nations
Where I have banished you,
Yet I will [b]not make a
complete destruction of you;
But I will [c]discipline
you with justice
And by no means leave
you unpunished.”

### *Word Against Philistia*

**47** That which came as the word
of Yahweh to Jeremiah the
prophet concerning the [a]Philistines,
before Pharaoh struck down [b]Gaza.
2 Thus says Yahweh:
“Behold, waters are going
to rise from [a]the north
And become an
overflowing torrent,
And [b]overflow the land
as well as its fullness,
The city and those
who inhabit it;
And the men will [c]cry out,
And every inhabitant
of the land will wail.
3 “Because of the noise
of the [a,1]galloping hoofs
of his [2]valiant steeds,
The quaking of his
chariots, *and* the
tumult of his wheels,
The fathers have not
turned back
for *their* children,
Because of the limpness
of *their* hands,
4 On account of the day
that is coming
To [a]destroy all
the Philistines,
To cut off from [b]Tyre
and Sidon
Every ally that is left;
For Yahweh is going
to destroy the Philistines,
The remnant of the
coastland of [c]Caphtor.
5 “[a]Baldness has come
upon Gaza;
[b]Ashkelon has been ruined.
O remnant of their valley,
How long will you
[c]gash yourself?
6 “Ah, [a]sword of Yahweh,
How long will you
not be quiet?
Withdraw into your sheath;
[1]Be at rest and stay still.
7 “How can [1]it be quiet?
Yahweh has [a]given it
a command;
Against Ashkelon and
against the seacoast—
There He has [b]assigned it.”

**46:27** [b]*Is 11:11; Jer 23:3, 4; 29:14; Mic 7:12* [c]*Jer 23:6; 50:19* **46:28** [a]Ps 46:7, 11; Is 8:10; 43:2; Jer 1:19 [b]Jer 4:27; Am 9:8, 9 [c]Jer 10:24; Hab 3:2 ◆ **47:1** [a]Jer 25:20; Zec 9:6 [b]Ge 10:19; 1Ki 4:24; Jer 25:20; Am 1:6; Zep 2:4 **47:2** [a]Is 14:31; Jer 1:14; 6:22; 46:20, 24 [b]Is 8:7, 8 [c]Is 15:2-5; Jer 46:12 **47:3** [a]Jdg 5:22; Jer 8:16; Na 3:2 [1]Lit *stamping of the* [2]Lit *mighty ones* **47:4** [a]Is 14:31 [b]Is 23:5; Jer 25:22; Joel 3:4; Am 1:9, 10; Zec 9:2-4 [c]Ge 10:14; Dt 2:23; Am 9:7 **47:5** [a]Jer 48:37; Mic 1:16 [b]Jdg 1:18; Jer 25:20; Am 1:7, 8; Zep 2:4, 7; Zec 9:5 [c]Jer 16:6; 41:5 **47:6** [a]Jdg 7:20; Jer 12:12; Eze 21:3-5 [1]Lit *Have relief* **47:7** [a]Is 10:6; Eze 14:17 [b]Mic 6:9 [1]Lit *you*

### Word Against Moab

48 Concerning [a]Moab. Thus says Yahweh of hosts, the God of Israel,
"Woe to [b]Nebo, for it has
been destroyed;
[c]Kiriathaim has been put to
shame, it has been captured;
The lofty stronghold has been
put to shame and [1]shattered.
2 "There is praise for
Moab no longer;
In [a]Heshbon they have
devised calamity against her:
'Come and let us cut her off
from *being* a nation!'
You too, [1]Madmen,
will be silenced;
The sword will follow
after you.
3 "The sound of an outcry
from [a]Horonaim,
'[1]Devastation and
great destruction!'
4 "Moab is broken;
Her little ones have made
*their* cry *of distress* heard.
5 "For by the ascent of [a]Luhith
They will ascend with
continual weeping;
For at the descent
of Horonaim
They have heard the distressed
cry of destruction.
6 "[a]Flee, escape with your lives,
That you may be like a
juniper in the wilderness.
7 "For because of your
[a]trust in your own
works and treasures,
Even you yourself will
be captured;
And [b]Chemosh will
go off into exile
Together with his priests
and his princes.
8 "A destroyer will come
to every city,
So that no city will escape;
The valley also will perish,
And the [a]plateau will
be destroyed,
As Yahweh has said.
9 "Give [a,1]wings to Moab,
For she will [2]flee away;
And her cities will become
a [b]desolation,
Without inhabitants in them.
10 "[a]Cursed be the one who
does the work of Yahweh
[b]with a slack *hand*,
And cursed be the one
who restrains his
[c]sword from blood.

11 "Moab has been [a]at ease
since his youth;
He has also had [b]quiet,
*like wine* on [1]its dregs,
And he has not been [c]emptied
from vessel to vessel,
Nor has he gone into exile.
Therefore [2]he retains
his flavor,
And his aroma has
not changed.
12 "Therefore behold, the days are
coming," declares Yahweh, "when I
will send to him those who tip *vessels*,
and they will tip him over, and they

◆ **48:1** [a]Is 15:1; Eze 25:9 [b]Nu 32:3, 38; Jer 48:22 [c]Nu 32:37; Jer 48:23; Eze 25:9 [1]Or *dismayed*
**48:2** [a]Nu 21:25; Jer 48:34, 45; 49:3 [1]A city of Moab **48:3** [a]Is 15:5; Jer 48:5, 34 [1]Or *destruction*, cf. 48:1
**48:5** [a]Is 15:5 **48:6** [a]Jer 51:6 **48:7** [a]Ps 52:7; Is 59:4; Jer 9:23 [b]Nu 21:29; 1Ki 11:33; Jer 48:13, 46
**48:8** [a]Jos 13:9, 17, 21 **48:9** [a]Ps 11:1; Is 16:2; Jer 48:28 [b]Jer 44:22 [1]Or *salt* [2]Or *fall in ruins*
**48:10** [a]Jer 11:3 [b]1Ki 20:39, 40, 42; 2Ki 13:19 [c]Jer 47:6, 7 **48:11** [a]Jer 22:21; Eze 16:49; Zec 1:15 [b]Zep 1:12
[c]Na 2:2 [1]Lit *his* [2]Lit *his flavor has stayed in him*

will empty his vessels and shatter [1]his
jars. **13** And Moab will be [a]ashamed
of [b]Chemosh, as the house of Israel
was ashamed of [c]Bethel, their trust.

**14** "How can you say, 'We are
[a]mighty warriors,
And men valiant for battle'?

**15** "Moab has been destroyed,
and [1]men have gone
up to [2]his cities;
His choicest [a,3]young men
have also gone down
to the slaughter,"
Declares the [b]King, whose
name is Yahweh of hosts.

**16** "The disaster of Moab
will [a]soon come,
And his calamity has
quickly hastened.

**17** "Mourn for him, all you
who *live* around him,
Even all of you who
know his name;
Say, 'How has the strong
[a,1]scepter been broken,
A staff of beauty!'

**18** "[a]Come down from your glory
And inhabit
[1]the parched ground,
O inhabitant of the
[b]daughter of [c]Dibon;
For the destroyer of Moab
has come up against you,
He has ruined
your strongholds.

**19** "Stand by the road and
keep watch,
O inhabitant of [a]Aroer;
[b]Ask him who flees and
her who escapes
*And* say,
'What has happened?'

**20** "Moab has been put to shame,
for it has been [1]shattered.
Wail and cry out;
Declare by the [a]Arnon
That Moab
has been destroyed.

**21** "Judgment has also come
upon the plain, upon Holon, upon
[a]Jahzah, and against [b]Mephaath,
**22** and against Dibon, Nebo, and
Beth-diblathaim, **23** and against
Kiriathaim, Beth-gamul, and
[a]Beth-meon, **24** and against [a]Keri-
oth, Bozrah, and all the cities of the
land of Moab, far and near. **25** The
[a]horn of Moab has been cut in pieces
and his [b]arm broken," declares
Yahweh. **26** "[a]Make him drunk, for
he has [b]magnified *himself* against
Yahweh; so Moab will [1]wallow in
his vomit, and he also will become
a laughingstock. **27** Now was not
Israel a [a]laughingstock to you? Or
was he [b,1]caught among thieves? For
each time you speak about him you
[c]shake *your head in scorn.*

**28** "Leave the cities and dwell
among the [a]crags,
O inhabitants of Moab,
And be like a [b]dove that nests
Beyond the mouth
of the chasm.

**29** "[a]We have heard of the pride of
Moab—he *is* very proud—

---

**48:12** [1]Lit *their* **48:13** [a]Is 45:16; Jer 48:39 [b]Jdg 11:24 [c]1Ki 12:29; Hos 8:5, 6 **48:14** [a]Ps 33:16; Is 10:13-16 **48:15** [a]Is 40:30, 31; Jer 50:27 [b]Jer 46:18; 51:57; Mal 1:14 [1]Lit *one has* [2]Lit *her* [3]Warriors **48:16** [a]Is 13:22 **48:17** [a]Is 9:4; 14:5 [1]Or *rod* **48:18** [a]Is 47:1 [b]Jer 46:19 [c]Nu 21:30; Jos 13:9, 17; Is 15:2; Jer 48:22 [1]Lit *in thirst* **48:19** [a]Dt 2:36; Jos 12:2 [b]1Sa 4:13, 14, 16 **48:20** [a]Nu 21:13 [1]Or *dismayed* **48:21** [a]Nu 21:23; Is 15:4; Jer 48:34 [b]Jos 13:18 **48:23** [a]Jos 13:17 **48:24** [a]Jer 48:41; Am 2:2 **48:25** [a]Ps 75:10; Zec 1:19-21 [b]Job 22:9; Ps 10:15 **48:26** [a]Jer 25:15 [b]Ex 5:2; Jer 48:42; Da 5:23 [1]Or *splash into* **48:27** [a]Lam 2:15-17; Mic 7:8-10 [b]Jer 2:26 [c]Job 16:4; Jer 18:16 [1]Or *found* **48:28** [a]Jdg 6:2; Is 2:19; Jer 49:16; Ob 3 [b]Ps 55:6; SS 2:14 **48:29** [a]Is 16:6; Zep 2:8

Of his haughtiness, his [b]pride,
his arrogance, and the
exaltedness of his heart.
30 "I know his [a]fury,"
declares Yahweh,
"But it is nothing;
His idle boasts have
accomplished nothing.
31 "Therefore I will [a]wail
for Moab,
Even for all Moab
will I cry out;
[1]I will moan for the
men of [b]Kir-heres.
32 "More than the [a]weeping
for [b]Jazer
I will weep for you,
O vine of Sibmah!
Your branches stretched
across the sea,
They reached to the sea
of Jazer;
Upon your summer fruits
and your grape harvest
The destroyer has fallen.
33 "So [a]gladness and joy
are gathered up
From the fruitful orchard,
even from the land of Moab.
And I have made the
wine to [b]cease
from the wine presses;
No one will tread *them*
with shouting,
The shouting will not
be shouts *of joy*.
34 "[a]From the outcry at Heshbon even
to [b]Elealeh, even to Jahaz they have
given forth their voice, from [c]Zoar
even to Horonaim *and to* Eglath-
shelishiyah; for even the waters of
Nimrim will become desolate. 35 I will
make Moab cease," declares Yahweh,
"the one who offers *offerings* on the
[a]high place and the one who [b]offers
*offerings* in smoke to his gods.
36 "Therefore My [a]heart moans
for Moab like flutes; My heart also
moans like flutes for the men of
Kir-heres. Therefore they have [b]lost
the abundance it produced. 37 For
[a]every head is bald and every beard
cut short; there are gashes on all the
hands and [b]sackcloth on the loins.
38 On all the [a]rooftops of Moab and
in its open squares [1]there is lamen-
tation everywhere; for I have broken
Moab like an undesirable [b]vessel,"
declares Yahweh. 39 "How [1]shattered
it is! *How* they have wailed! How
Moab has turned his back—he is
ashamed! So Moab will become
a laughingstock and an [a]object of
terror to all around him."
40 For thus says Yahweh:
"Behold, one will [a]swoop
like an eagle
And [b]spread out his
wings against Moab.
41 "Kerioth has been captured,
And the strongholds
have been seized,
So the [a]hearts of the mighty
men of Moab in that day
Will be like the heart
of a [b]woman in labor.
42 "Moab will be [a]destroyed
from *being* a people

**48:29** [b]Job 40:11, 12; Ps 138:6 **48:30** [a]Is 37:28 **48:31** [a]Is 15:5; 16:7, 11 [b]2Ki 3:25; Is 16:7, 11; Jer 48:36 [1]Or *He* **48:32** [a]Is 16:8, 9 [b]Nu 21:32 **48:33** [a]Is 16:10; Jer 25:10; Joel 1:12 [b]Is 5:10; Hag 2:16 **48:34** [a]Is 15:4-6 [b]Nu 32:3, 37 [c]Ge 13:10; 14:2; Is 15:5, 6 **48:35** [a]Is 15:2; 16:12 [b]Jer 7:9; 11:13 **48:36** [a]Is 15:5; 16:11 [b]Is 15:7 **48:37** [a]Is 15:2; Jer 16:6; 41:5; 47:5 [b]Ge 37:34; Is 15:3; 20:2 **48:38** [a]Is 22:1 [b]Jer 19:10, 11; 22:28; 25:34 [1]Lit *all of it is lamentation* **48:39** [a]Eze 26:16 [1]Or *dismayed* **48:40** [a]Dt 28:49; Jer 49:22; Hos 8:1; Hab 1:8 [b]Is 8:8 **48:41** [a]Jer 49:22 [b]Is 13:8; 21:3; Jer 30:6; Mic 4:9, 10 **48:42** [a]Ps 83:4; Jer 48:2

Because he has [b]magnified
*himself* against Yahweh.
43 "[a]Panic and pit and pitfall
are *coming* upon you,
O inhabitant of Moab,"
declares Yahweh.
44 "The one who [a]flees
from the panic
Will fall into the pit,
And the one who climbs
up out of the pit
Will be caught in the pitfall;
For I shall bring upon her,
*even* upon Moab,
The year of their [b]punishment,"
declares Yahweh.

45 "In the shadow of Heshbon
Those who flee stand
without strength;
For a fire has gone forth
from Heshbon
And a [a]flame from the midst
of [b]Sihon,
And it has devoured the
[c]top of the head of Moab
And the scalps of [1]those
who rumble.
46 "[a]Woe to you, Moab!
The people of [b]Chemosh
have perished;
For your sons have been
taken away captive
And your daughters
into captivity.
47 "Yet I will [a,1]return
the [2]fortunes of Moab
In the last days,"
declares Yahweh.
Thus far the judgment on Moab.

### *Word Against Ammon*

49 Concerning the sons of
[a]Ammon. Thus says Yahweh:
"Does Israel have no sons?
Or has he no one who
can take possession?
Why then has [1]Malcam
taken possession of Gad
And his people settled
in its cities?
2 "Therefore behold,
the days are coming,"
declares Yahweh,
"That I will cause a [a,1]trumpet
blast of war to be heard
Against [b]Rabbah of the
sons of Ammon;
And it will become a
desolate heap,
And her [c]towns will
be set on fire.
Then Israel will take
[d]possession of
his possessors,"
Says Yahweh.
3 "Wail, O [a]Heshbon,
for [b]Ai has been destroyed!
Cry out, O daughters
of Rabbah,
[c]Gird yourselves
with sackcloth and lament,
And rush back and forth
inside the walls;
For [1]Malcam will [d]go into exile
Together with his priests
and his princes.
4 "How [a]boastful you are
about the valleys!
Your valley is flowing *away*,
O [b]faithless daughter

**48:42** [b]Is 37:23; Jer 48:26 **48:43** [a]Is 24:17, 18; Lam 3:47 **48:44** [a]1Ki 19:17; Is 24:18; Am 5:19 [b]Jer 46:21 **48:45** [a]Nu 21:28, 29 [b]Nu 21:21, 26; Ps 135:11 [c]Nu 24:17 [1]Lit *sons of tumult* **48:46** [a]Nu 21:29 [b]Jdg 11:24; 1Ki 11:7; Jer 48:7 **48:47** [a]Jer 12:14-17; 49:6, 39 [1]Or *restore* [2]Or *captivity* ◆ **49:1** [a]Dt 23:3, 4; 2Chr 20:1; Eze 21:28-32; 25:2-10; Am 1:13-15; Zep 2:8-11 [1]In 1Ki 11:5, 33 and Zep 1:5, *Milcom* **49:2** [a]Nu 10:9; Jer 4:19 [b]Dt 3:11; 2Sa 11:1; Eze 21:20 [c]Jos 17:11, 16 [d]Is 14:2 [1]Or *shout of* **49:3** [a]Jer 48:2 [b]Jos 7:2-5; 8:1-29; Ezr 2:28 [c]Is 32:11; Jer 48:37 [d]Jer 46:25; 48:7 [1]Cf. 49:1 **49:4** [a]Jer 9:23 [b]Jer 31:22

Who trusts in her
[c]treasures, *saying*,
'[d]Who will come against me?'
5 "Behold, I am going to bring
[a]dread upon you,"
Declares Lord Yahweh
of hosts,
"From all around you;
And each of you will be
[b]banished [1]headlong,
With no one to gather
the [c]one who flees.
6 "But afterward I will [a,1]return
The [2]fortunes
of the sons of Ammon,"
Declares Yahweh.

### *Word Against Edom*

7 Concerning [a]Edom.
Thus says Yahweh of hosts,
"Is there no longer any
[b]wisdom in [c]Teman?
Has counsel been lost
to the understanding?
Has their wisdom decayed?
8 "Flee away, turn back,
inhabit the depths,
O inhabitants of [a]Dedan,
For I [1]will bring the [b]disaster
of Esau upon him
At the time I [2]punish him.
9 "[a]If grape gatherers
came to you,
Would they not have
gleanings remain?
If thieves *came* by night,
They would ruin *only*
[1]until they had enough.
10 "But I have [a]stripped Esau bare;
I have uncovered his
hiding places,
So that he will not be able
to conceal himself;
His seed has been destroyed
along with his [1]relatives
And his neighbors, and
[b]he is no more.
11 "Leave your [a,1]orphans behind,
I will keep *them* alive;
And let your [b]widows
trust in Me."
12 For thus says Yahweh, "Behold,
those who are not *under* judgment
to drink the [a]cup will certainly drink
*it*, but are you the one who will go
[b]completely unpunished? You will
not go unpunished, but you will cer-
tainly drink *it*. 13 For I have [a]sworn
by Myself," declares Yahweh, "that
[b]Bozrah will become an [c]object of
horror, a reproach, a ruin, and an
imprecation; and all its cities will
become perpetual [1]ruins."
14 I have [a]heard a message
from Yahweh,
And an [b]envoy is sent
among the nations, *saying*,
"[c]Gather yourselves together
and come against her,
And rise up for battle!"
15 "For behold, I have made you
small among the nations,
Despised among men.
16 "As for the terror of you,
The arrogance of your
heart has deceived you,

**49:4** [c]Ps 62:10; Eze 28:4, 5; 1Ti 6:17 [d]Jer 21:13 **49:5** [a]Jer 48:43f; 49:29 [b]Jer 16:16; 46:5 [c]Lam 4:15 [1]Lit *before him* **49:6** [a]Jer 48:47; 49:39 [1]Or *restore* [2]Or *captivity* **49:7** [a]Ge 25:30; 32:3; Is 34:5, 6; Jer 25:21; Eze 25:12; Am 1:11; Ob 1-21 [b]Job 2:11; Jer 8:9 [c]Ge 36:11, 15, 34; Jer 49:20 **49:8** [a]Is 21:13; Jer 25:23 [b]Jer 46:21; Mal 1:3, 4 [1]Or *brought* [2]Or *punished* **49:9** [a]Ob 5 [1]Lit *their sufficiency* **49:10** [a]Jer 13:26 [b]Is 17:14 [1]Lit *brothers* **49:11** [a]Ps 68:5; Hos 14:3 [b]Ps 68:5; Zec 7:10 [1]Or *fatherless* **49:12** [a]Jer 25:15 [b]Jer 25:28, 29; 1Pe 4:17 **49:13** [a]Ge 22:16; Is 45:23; Jer 44:26; Am 6:8 [b]Ge 36:33; 1Chr 1:44; Is 34:6; 63:1; Am 1:12 [c]Is 34:9-15; Jer 18:16 [1]Or *waste places* **49:14** [a]Ob 1-4 [b]Is 18:2; 30:4 [c]Jer 50:14

O you who dwell in the
clefts of [1]the [a]rock,
Who seize the height
of the hill.
Though you make your nest
as [b]high as an eagle's,
I will [c]bring you down from
there," declares Yahweh.

**17** "Edom will become [1]an [a]object
of horror; everyone who passes by it
will [2]be horrified and will [b]hiss at all
its wounds. **18** Like the [a]overthrow
of Sodom and Gomorrah with its
neighbors," says Yahweh, "[b]no one
will live there, nor will a son of
man sojourn in it. **19** [a]Behold, one
will come up like a lion from the
[b,1]thickets of the Jordan against an
enduring pasture; for in an instant I
will make him run away from it, and
whoever is [c]chosen I shall appoint
over it. For who is [d]like Me, and who
will [2]summon Me *into court*? And
who then is the shepherd [e]who can
stand against Me?"

**20** Therefore hear the [a]counsel
of Yahweh which He has counseled
against Edom, and His purposes
which He has purposed against the
inhabitants of Teman: surely they
will drag them off, *even* the little
ones of the flock; surely He will make
their pasture [b]desolate because of
them. **21** The [a]earth has quaked at
the noise of their downfall. There is
an outcry! The noise of it has been
heard at the [1]Red Sea. **22** Behold,
[1]He will mount up and [a]swoop like
an eagle and spread out His wings
[2]against Bozrah; and the [b]hearts of
the mighty men of Edom in that day
will be like the heart of a woman in
labor.

### *Word Against Damascus*

**23** Concerning [a]Damascus.
"[b]Hamath and [c]Arpad
are put to shame,
For they have heard
a bad report;
They are [d]melting away.
There is anxiety by the sea,
It [e]cannot be quieted.

**24** "Damascus has become
limp *in their hands*;
She has turned away to flee,
And panic has taken
hold of her;
[a]Distress and pangs
have seized her
Like a woman in childbirth.

**25** "How [1]the [a]city of praise
has not been forsaken,
The town of My joy!

**26** "Therefore, her [a]young men
will fall in her open squares,
And all the men of war will
be [1]silenced in that day,"
declares Yahweh of hosts.

**27** "I will [a]set fire to the
wall of Damascus,
And it will devour
the [1]fortified towers
of [b]Ben-hadad."

**49:16** [a]2Ki 14:7; Jer 48:28 [b]Job 39:27; Is 14:13-15 [c]Am 9:2 [1]Or *Sela* **49:17** [a]Jer 18:16; 49:13; 50:13; Eze 35:7 [b]1Ki 9:8; Jer 51:37 [1]Or *a desolation* [2]Or *feel desolate* **49:18** [a]Ge 19:24, 25; Dt 29:23; Jer 50:40; *Am 4:11; Zep 2:9* [b]*Job 18:15-18*; Jer 49:33 **49:19** [a]Jer 50:44 [b]Jos 3:15; Jer 12:5 [c]Nu 16:5 [d]Ex 15:11; Is 46:9 [e]Job 41:10 [1]Lit *pride* [2]Or *cause Me to testify*, cf. Job 9:19 **49:20** [a]Is 14:24, 27; Jer 50:45 [b]Mal 1:3, 4 **49:21** [a]Jer 50:46; Eze 26:15, 18 [1]Lit *Sea of Reeds* **49:22** [a]Jer 4:13; 48:40; Hos 8:1 [b]Is 13:8; Jer 30:6; 48:41 [1]Or *one* [2]Or *over* **49:23** [a]Ge 14:15; 15:2; 2Ki 5:12; 2Chr 16:2; Is 7:8; 17:1; Am 1:3; Ac 9:2 [b]Nu 13:21; Is 10:9; Jer 39:5; Am 6:2 [c]2Ki 18:34; 19:13; Is 10:9 [d]Ex 15:15; Na 2:10 [e]Is 57:20 **49:24** [a]Is 13:8 **49:25** [a]Jer 33:9; 51:41 [1]Or *deserted is the city of praise* **49:26** [a]Jer 11:22; 50:30; Am 4:10 [1]Or *destroyed* **49:27** [a]Jer 43:12; Am 1:3-5 [b]1Ki 15:18-20; 2Ki 13:3 [1]Or *palaces*

### *Word Against Kedar and Hazor*

28 Concerning [a]Kedar and the king-
doms of Hazor, which Nebuchad-
nezzar king of Babylon struck down.
Thus says Yahweh,
"Arise, go up to Kedar
And destroy the [b,1]men
of the east.
29 "They will take away their
tents and their flocks;
They will carry off
for themselves
Their tent [a]curtains,
all their goods, and
their [b]camels,
And they will call out
to one another, '[c]Terror
on every side!'
30 "Run away, flee earnestly!
Inhabit the depths,
O inhabitants of Hazor,"
declares Yahweh;
"For [a]Nebuchadnezzar king
of Babylon has taken
counsel against you
And purposed a purpose
against you.
31 "Arise, go up against a nation
which is [a]at ease,
Which inhabits *its land*
securely," declares Yahweh.
"It has [b]no gates or bars;
They [c]dwell alone.
32 "Their camels will
become plunder,
And their many
cattle for spoil,
And I will [a]scatter to all
the winds those who [b]cut
the corners *of their hair*;
And I will bring their
[1]disaster from every
side," declares Yahweh.
33 "Hazor will become a
[a]haunt of jackals,
A desolation forever;
No one will inhabit there,
Nor will a son of man
sojourn in it."

### *Word Against Elam*

34 That which came as the word of
Yahweh to Jeremiah the prophet con-
cerning [a]Elam, [b]in the beginning of
the reign of Zedekiah king of Judah,
saying:
35 "Thus says Yahweh of hosts,
'Behold, I am going to
[a]break the bow of Elam,
The [1]finest of their might.
36 'I will bring upon Elam
the [a]four winds
From the four ends
of heaven,
And I will [b]scatter them
to all these winds;
And there will be no nation
To which the banished ones
of Elam will not go.
37 'So I will [1]shatter Elam
before their enemies
And before those who
seek their lives;
And I will [a]bring calamity
upon them,
Even My [b]burning anger,'
declares Yahweh,
'And I will [c]send out the
sword after them
Until I have consumed them.

**49:28** [a]Ge 25:13; Ps 120:5; Is 21:16, 17; Jer 2:10; Eze 27:21 [b]Job 1:3; Is 11:14 [1]Lit *sons* **49:29** [a]Hab 3:7 [b]1Chr 5:21 [c]Jer 46:5 **49:30** [a]Jer 25:9; 27:6 **49:31** [a]Jdg 18:7; Is 47:8 [b]Is 42:11 [c]Nu 23:9; Dt 33:28; Mic 7:14 **49:32** [a]Eze 5:10; 12:14, 15 [b]Jer 9:26; 25:23 [1]Heb root is similar to Edom **49:33** [a]Is 13:20-22; Jer 9:11; 10:22; 51:37; Zep 2:9, 13-15; Mal 1:3 **49:34** [a]Ge 10:22; 14:1, 9; Is 11:11; Jer 25:25; Eze 32:24; Da 8:2 [b]2Ki 24:17, 18; Jer 28:1 **49:35** [a]Ps 46:9; Is 22:6; Jer 51:56 [1]Lit *first* **49:36** [a]Da 7:2; 8:8; Rev 7:1 [b]Jer 49:32; Eze 5:10; Am 9:9 **49:37** [a]Jer 6:19 [b]Jer 30:24 [c]Jer 9:16; 48:2 [1]Or *dismay*

38 'Then I will set My
throne in Elam
And cause king and princes
from there to perish,'
Declares Yahweh.
39 'But it will be in the last days
That I will [a,1]return the
[2]fortunes of Elam,'"
Declares Yahweh.

### *Word Against Babylon*

50 The word which Yahweh
spoke concerning [a]Babylon,
the land of the Chaldeans, by the
hand of Jeremiah the prophet:
2 "[a]Declare and make *it* heard
among the nations.
Make *it* heard and [b]lift
up a standard.
Do not conceal *it but* say,
'[c]Babylon has been captured;
[d]Bel has been put
to shame; [1]Marduk has
been [2]shattered;
Her [e]images have been
put to shame; her idols
have been shattered.'
3 "For a nation has come up against
her out of the [a]north; it will make her
land [b]an object of horror, and there
will be [c]no inhabitant in it. Both man
and beast have wandered off; they
have gone away!
4 "In those days and at that time,"
declares Yahweh, "the sons of Israel
will come, *both* they and the sons
of Judah [a]as well; they will go along
[b]weeping as they go, and it will be
[c]Yahweh their God they will seek.
5 They will [a]ask for the way to Zion—
*turning* their faces [1]in its direction
*and saying*, '[2]Come!'—in order that
they may join themselves to Yahweh
*in* an [b]everlasting covenant that will
not be forgotten.
6 "My people have become
[a]lost sheep;
[b]Their shepherds have
led them astray.
They have made them turn
away *on* the [c]mountains;
They have gone
along from mountain to hill
And have forgotten their
[d]resting place.
7 "All who came out against
them have devoured them;
And their adversaries have
said, '[a]We are not guilty,
Inasmuch as they have sinned
against Yahweh, *who is* the
[b]abode of righteousness,
Even Yahweh, the [c]hope
of their fathers.'

8 "Wander away from the
[a]midst of Babylon
And [1]go forth from the
land of the Chaldeans;
Be also like male goats
[2]at the head of the flock.
9 "For behold, I am going
to [a]arouse and bring
up against Babylon
An assembly of great nations
from the land of the north,
And they will arrange *their*
battle lines against her;

---

**49:39** [a]Jer 48:47 [1]Or *restore* [2]Or *captivity* ◆ **50:1** [a]Ge 10:10; 11:9; 2Ki 17:24; Is 13:1; 47:1; Da 1:1; Rev 14:8 **50:2** [a]Jer 4:16 [b]Jer 51:27 [c]Jer 51:31 [d]Is 46:1 [e]Jer 51:47 [1]Heb *Merodach* [2]Or *dismayed* **50:3** [a]Is 13:17; Jer 50:9; 51:11, 27 [b]Is 14:22, 23; Jer 50:13 [c]Jer 9:10, 11; Zep 1:3 **50:4** [a]Is 11:12, 13; Jer 3:18; 31:31; 33:7; Hos 1:11 [b]Ezr 3:12, 13; Ps 126:5; Jer 31:9 [c]Hos 3:5 **50:5** [a]Is 35:8; Jer 6:16 [b]Is 55:3; Jer 32:40; Heb 8:6-10 [1]Lit *hither* [2]Gr *they will come and join themselves* **50:6** [a]Is 53:6; Eze 34:15, 16; Mt 9:36; 10:6 [b]Jer 23:11-14 [c]Jer 13:16; Eze 34:6 [d]Jer 33:12; 50:19 **50:7** [a]Jer 2:3; Zec 11:5 [b]Jer 31:23; 40:2, 3 [c]Ps 22:4; Jer 14:8; 17:13 **50:8** [a]Is 48:20; Jer 51:6; Rev 18:4 [1]Or *let them go forth* [2]Or *in front of* **50:9** [a]Jer 51:1

From there she will be
taken captive.
Their arrows will be
like [1]a warrior who
makes *one* childless
Who does not return
empty-handed.
10 "[a,1]Chaldea will become spoil;
All who take her spoil will have
enough," declares Yahweh.

11 "Because you are glad,
because you exult,
O you who [a]plunder
My inheritance,
Because you skip about
[1]like a threshing [b]heifer
And neigh like [2]valiant steeds,
12 Your [a]mother [1]will be
greatly ashamed;
She who gave you birth
[1]will be humiliated.
Behold, *she will be* the least
of the nations,
A [b]wilderness, a parched
land, and a desert.
13 "Because of the wrath
of Yahweh she will
[a]not be inhabited,
But she will be
[b]completely desolate;
Everyone who passes by
Babylon [c]will be in desolation
And will hiss because
of all her wounds.
14 "Arrange your battle
lines against Babylon
on every side,
All you who [1]bend the bow;
Shoot at her, do not be
sparing with *your* arrows,
For she has [a]sinned
against Yahweh.
15 "Raise a loud shout against
her on every side!
She has [a]given [1]herself up,
her pillars have fallen,
Her [b]walls have been
pulled down.
For this is the [c]vengeance
of Yahweh:
Take vengeance on her;
[d]As she has done
*to others, so* do to her.
16 "Cut off the [a]sower
from Babylon
And the one who seizes the
sickle at the time of harvest;
From before [1]the [b]sword
of the oppressor
[c]They will each turn back
to his own people,
And they will each flee
to his own land.

17 "Israel is a [a]scattered [1]flock; the
[b]lions have banished *them* away. The
first one *who* devoured him was the
[c]king of Assyria, and this last one *who*
has broken his bones is [d]Nebuchad-
nezzar king of Babylon. 18 Therefore
thus says Yahweh of hosts, the God of
Israel: 'Behold, I am going to punish
the king of Babylon and his land, just
as I [a]punished the king of Assyria.
19 And I will [a,1]return Israel back to
his pasture, and he will graze on
Carmel and Bashan, and his [2]desire
will be satisfied in the [b]hill country of

---

**50:9** [1]Some mss and versions *an expert warrior* **50:10** [a]Jer 51:24, 35; Eze 11:24 [1]Or *The Chaldeans* **50:11** [a]Jer 12:14 [b]Jer 46:20 [1]Or *in the grass* [2]Lit *mighty ones* **50:12** [a]Jer 15:9 [b]Jer 22:6; 51:43 [1]Or *has become* **50:13** [a]Jer 34:22 [b]Jer 51:26 [c]Jer 18:16; 49:17 **50:14** [a]Hab 2:8, 17 [1]Lit *tread* (in order to string) **50:15** [a]1Chr 29:24; 2Chr 30:8; Lam 5:6 [b]Jer 50:44; 51:58 [c]Jer 46:10 [d]Ps 137:8; Rev 18:6 [1]Lit *her hand* **50:16** [a]Joel 1:11 [b]Jer 25:38; 46:16 [c]Is 13:14 [1]Or *the oppressing sword* **50:17** [a]Joel 3:2 [b]Jer 2:15; 4:7 [c]2Ki 15:19; 17:6; 18:9-13 [d]2Ki 24:1, 10-12; 25:1-7 [1]Lit *sheep* **50:18** [a]Is 10:12; Eze 31:3, 11, 12; Na 3:7, 18, 19 **50:19** [a]Is 65:10; Jer 31:10; 33:12; Eze 34:13 [b]Jer 31:6 [1]Or *restore* [2]Lit *soul*

Ephraim and Gilead. **20** In those days
and at that time,' declares Yahweh,
'search will be made for the iniquity
of Israel, but [a]there will be none; and
for the sins of Judah, but they will
not be found; for I will pardon those
[b]whom I leave as a remnant.'

**21** "Against the land of
[1]Merathaim, go up against it,
And against the inhabitants
of [a,2]Pekod.
Put *them* to the sword
and [3]devote them
to destruction,"
declares Yahweh,
"And do according to all that
I have commanded you.

**22** "The [a]noise of battle
is in the land,
And great destruction.

**23** "How the [a]hammer
of the whole earth
Has been cut in pieces
and broken!
How Babylon has become
An object of horror
among the nations!

**24** "I [a]set a snare for you, and you
were also [b]caught,
O Babylon,
But you yourself did not know;
You have been found
and also seized
Because you have engaged
in [c]conflict with Yahweh."

**25** Yahweh has opened
His armory
And has brought forth
the [a]weapons
of His indignation,
For it is a [b]work of Lord
Yahweh of hosts
In the land of the Chaldeans.

**26** Come to her from the
[1]farthest border;
[a]Open up her barns;
Pile her up like heaps,
And [b,2]devote her
to destruction;
Let nothing of her remain.

**27** [a]Put all her young bulls
to the sword;
Let them [b]go down
to the slaughter!
Woe be upon them,
for their [c]day has come,
The time
of their punishment.

**28** There is a [a]sound of those
who flee and escape
from the land of Babylon,
To declare in Zion
the [b]vengeance
of Yahweh our God,
Vengeance for His [c]temple.

**29** "Summon [1]many
against Babylon,
All those who [2]bend the bow:
Encamp against her
on every side,
Let there be no escape[3].
Repay her
according to her work;
[a]According to all that she
has done, *so* do to her;
For she has become [b]arrogant
against Yahweh,
Against the Holy One of Israel.

---

**50:20** [a]Is 43:25; Jer 31:34; Mic 7:19 [b]Is 1:9 **50:21** [a]Eze 23:23 [1]Lit *double rebellion* [2]Lit *punishment* [3]Lit *put under the ban* **50:22** [a]Jer 4:19-21; 51:54-56 **50:23** [a]Jer 51:20-24 **50:24** [a]Jer 48:43, 44 [b]Jer 51:31; Da 5:30, 31 [c]Job 9:4; 40:2, 9 **50:25** [a]Is 13:5 [b]Jer 50:15; 51:12, 25, 55 **50:26** [a]Is 45:3; Jer 50:10 [b]Is 14:23 [1]Lit *end* [2]Or *put her under the ban* **50:27** [a]Is 34:7 [b]Jer 48:10 [c]Ps 37:13; Jer 46:21; 48:44; Eze 7:7 **50:28** [a]Is 48:20 [b]Ps 149:6-9; Jer 50:15; 51:10 [c]Lam 1:10; 2:6, 7 **50:29** [a]Ps 137:8; Jer 50:15; 51:56; 2Th 1:6 [b]Ex 10:3; Jer 49:16; Da 4:37 [1]Or *archers* [2]Lit *tread* (in order to string) [3]Some mss add *to her*

30 “Therefore her [a]young men
will fall in her open squares,
And all her men of war
will be [b,1]silenced in that
day,” declares Yahweh.
31 “Behold, [a]I am against you,
O [1]arrogant one,”
Declares Lord Yahweh
of hosts,
“For your day has come,
The time [2]when I will
punish you.
32 “The [a,1]arrogant one will
stumble and fall
With no one to raise him up;
And I will [b]set fire to his cities,
And it will devour him
on every side.”

33 Thus says Yahweh of hosts,
“The sons of Israel
are oppressed,
And the sons of Judah as well;
And [a]all who took them
captive have held them fast;
They have refused
to let them go.
34 “Their [a]Redeemer is strong,
[b]Yahweh of hosts is His name;
He will vigorously
[c]plead their case
So that He may [d]bring
relief to [1]the earth,
But turmoil to the
inhabitants of Babylon.
35 “A [a]sword
against the Chaldeans,”
declares Yahweh,
“And against the inhabitants
of Babylon
And against her [b]officials
and her [c]wise men!
36 “A sword against the
[a]oracle priests, and they
will become fools!
A sword against her
[b]mighty men, and they
will be [c,1]shattered!
37 “A sword against [1]their [a]horses
and against [1]their chariots
And against all the
[b,2]foreigners who are
in the midst of her,
And they will become [c]women!
A sword against her treasures,
and they will be plundered!
38 “A [a,1]drought on her waters,
and they will be dried up!
For it is a land
of [b]graven images,
And they are mad
over terrifying idols.

39 “Therefore the [a]desert
creatures will live *there*
along with the jackals;
The ostriches also will live in it,
And it will [b]never
again be lived in
Or dwelt in from generation
to generation.
40 “As when God
overthrew [a]Sodom
And Gomorrah
with its neighbors,”
declares Yahweh,

**50:30** [a]Is 13:17, 18; Jer 9:21; 18:21; 49:26; 51:4 [b]Jer 51:57 [1]Or *made lifeless, destroyed* **50:31** [a]Jer 21:13; Na 2:13 [1]Lit *arrogance* [2]Or *of your punishment* **50:32** [a]Is 10:12-15 [b]Jer 21:14; 49:27 [1]Lit *arrogance* **50:33** [a]Is 14:17; 58:6 **50:34** [a]Pr 23:11; Is 43:14; Jer 15:21; 31:11; Rev 18:8 [b]Is 47:4; Jer 32:18; 51:19 [c]Jer 51:36; Mic 7:9 [d]Is 14:3-7 [1]Or their *land* **50:35** [a]Jer 47:6; Hos 11:6 [b]Da 5:1, 2 [c]Da 5:7, 8 **50:36** [a]Is 44:25 [b]Jer 49:22 [c]Na 3:13 [1]Or *dismayed* **50:37** [a]Ps 20:7, 8; Jer 51:21, 22 [b]Jer 25:20; Eze 30:5 [c]Jer 48:41; 51:30; Na 3:13 [1]Lit *his* [2]Lit *mixed multitude* **50:38** [a]Is 44:27; Jer 51:32, 36; Rev 16:12 [b]Is 46:1, 6, 7 [1]Or *sword* **50:39** [a]Is 13:21; 34:14; Rev 18:2 [b]Is 13:20; Jer 25:12 **50:40** [a]Ge 19:24, 25; Is 13:19; Jer 49:18; Lk 17:28-30; 2Pe 2:6; Jd 7

"No man will live there,
Nor will *any* son of
man sojourn in it.

41 "Behold, a people is coming
[a]from the north,
And a great nation
and many kings
Will be aroused from the
remote parts of the earth.
42 "They [a]seize *their* bow
and [1]javelin;
They are [b]cruel and have
no compassion.
Their [c]voice roars like the sea;
And they ride on [d]horses,
[e]Arranged like a man
for the battle
Against you, O daughter
of Babylon.
43 "The [a]king of Babylon has
heard the report about them,
And his hands hang limp;
[b]Distress has taken
hold of him,
Agony like a woman
in childbirth.

44 "[a]Behold, one will come up
like a lion from the [1]thicket of the
Jordan to an enduring pasture; for in
an instant I will make them run away
from it, and whoever is [b]chosen I
will appoint over it. For who is [c]like
Me, and who will [2]summon Me *into*
*court*? And who then is the shep-
herd who can [d]stand before Me?"
45 Therefore hear the [a]counsel of
Yahweh which He has counseled
against Babylon, and His purposes
which He has purposed against the
land of the Chaldeans: [b]surely they
will drag them off, *even* the little
ones of the flock; surely He will make
their [1]pasture desolate because of
them. 46 At the sound, "Babylon has
been seized!" the [a]earth is shaken,
and an [b]outcry is heard among the
nations.

### *Yahweh Sends Calamity to Babylon*

51 Thus says Yahweh:
"Behold, I am going
to arouse against Babylon
And against the inhabitants
of [1]Leb-kamai
[2]The [a]spirit of a destroyer.
2 "I will send [1]strangers
to Babylon that they
may [a]winnow her
And may empty her land
to destruction;
For on every side they
will be against her
In the day of *her* calamity.
3 "[1]Let not [2]him who [a,3]bends
his bow [3]bend *it*,
[1]Nor let him rise up
in his [b]scale-armor;
So do not spare her
young men;
Devote all her army
to destruction.
4 "They will fall down [1]slain
in the land of the Chaldeans,
And [a]pierced through
in their streets."

---

**50:41** [a]Is 13:2-5; Jer 6:22; 50:3, 9; 51:27, 28 **50:42** [a]Jer 6:23 [b]Is 13:17, 18; 47:6 [c]Is 5:30 [d]Jer 8:16; 47:3; Hab 1:8 [e]Jer 50:9, 14; Joel 2:5 [1]Or *scimitar* **50:43** [a]Jer 51:31 [b]Jer 30:6; 49:24 **50:44** [a]Jer 49:19-21 [b]Nu 16:5 [c]Is 46:9 [d]Job 41:10; Jer 30:21 [1]Lit *pride* [2]Or *cause Me to testify*, cf. Job 9:19 **50:45** [a]Ps 33:11; Is 14:24; Jer 51:10, 11 [b]Jer 49:20 [1]Or *habitation* **50:46** [a]Jer 10:10; 49:21; Eze 26:18; 31:16 [b]Is 5:7; 15:5; Jer 46:12; 51:54; Eze 27:28 ◆ **51:1** [a]Jer 4:11, 12; 23:19; Hos 13:15 [1]Cryptic name for Chaldea; or *the heart of those who rise up against Me* [2]Or *A destroying wind* **51:2** [a]Is 41:16; Jer 15:7; Mt 3:12 [1]Some versions *winnowers* **51:3** [a]Jer 50:14, 29 [b]Jer 46:4 [1]M.T. *Against him who* [2]The Chaldean defender [3]Lit *tread(s)* (in order to string) **51:4** [a]Is 13:15; 14:19; Jer 49:26; 50:30, 37 [1]Or *wounded*

5 For [a]neither Israel nor Judah
has been widowed
By his God, by Yahweh
of hosts,
Although their land
is [b]full of guilt
[1]Before the Holy One of Israel.
6 [a]Flee from the midst
of Babylon,
And each of you escape
with his life!
Do not be [b,1]silenced
in her [2]iniquity,
For this is [c]Yahweh's
time of vengeance;
He is going to [d]render
recompense to her.
7 Babylon has been a golden
[a]cup in the hand of Yahweh,
Intoxicating all the earth.
The [b]nations have
drunk of her wine;
Therefore the nations
are [c]going mad.
8 Suddenly [a]Babylon has
fallen and been broken;
[b]Wail over her!
[c]Take [1]balm for her pain;
Perhaps she may be healed.
9 We applied healing to Babylon,
but she was not healed;
Forsake her and [a]let us each
go to his own country,
For her judgment has
[b]touched heaven
And lifts up to the very skies.
10 Yahweh has [a]brought [1]about
our righteousness;
Come and let us
[b]recount in Zion
The work of Yahweh our God!

11 [a]Sharpen the arrows,
fill the quivers!
Yahweh has aroused the spirit
of the kings of the Medes
Because His purpose is against
Babylon to destroy it;
For it is the [b]vengeance
of Yahweh, vengeance
for His temple.
12 [a]Lift up a standard
against the walls of Babylon;
Make strong the watch;
Raise up [1]watchmen;
Establish men in ambush!
For Yahweh has both
[b]purposed and performed
What He spoke concerning
the inhabitants of Babylon.
13 O you who [a]dwell
by abundant waters,
Abundant in [b]treasures,
Your end has come,
The [1]measure of your [c,2]end.
14 [a]Yahweh of hosts has
sworn by Himself:
"Surely I will fill you with
a [1]population like [b]locusts,
And they will cry out with
[2]shouts of victory over you."

15 *It is* [a]He who made
the earth by His power,
Who established
the world by His wisdom,

**51:5** [a]Is 54:7, 8; Jer 33:24-26 [b]Hos 4:1, 2 [1]Lit *From* **51:6** [a]Jer 50:8, 28; Rev 18:4 [b]Nu 16:26 [c]Jer 50:15 [d]Jer 25:14 [1]Or *made lifeless* [2]Or *penalty for iniquity* **51:7** [a]Jer 25:15; Hab 2:16; Rev 14:8; 17:4 [b]Rev 14:8; 18:3 [c]Jer 25:16 **51:8** [a]Is 21:9; Jer 50:2; Rev 14:8; 18:2 [b]Is 13:6; Rev 18:9 [c]Jer 46:11 [1]Or *balsam resin* **51:9** [a]Is 13:14; Jer 46:16; 50:16 [b]Ezr 9:6; Rev 18:5 **51:10** [a]Ps 37:6; Mic 7:9 [b]Is 40:2; Jer 50:28 [1]Lit *forth* **51:11** [a]Jer 46:4, 9; Joel 3:9, 10 [b]Jer 50:28 **51:12** [a]Is 13:2; Jer 50:2; 51:27 [b]Jer 4:28; 23:20; 51:29 [1]Or *sentries* **51:13** [a]Rev 17:1 [b]Is 45:3 [c]Is 57:17; Hab 2:9-11 [1]Lit *cubit* [2]Lit *being cut off* **51:14** [a]Jer 49:13 [b]Jer 51:27; Na 3:15 [1]Or *mankind* [2]Something like the song of grape treaders **51:15** [a]Ge 1:1; Jer 10:12-16; 51:15-19

And by His understanding
He [b]stretched out
the heavens.
16 When He gives forth His
[a]voice, *there is* a tumult
of waters in the heavens,
And He causes the [b]clouds
to ascend from the
end of the earth;
He makes lightning
for the rain
And brings forth the [c]wind
from His storehouses.
17 [a]All mankind is senseless,
devoid of knowledge;
Every goldsmith is put to
shame by his graven image,
For his molten images
are [b]a lie,
And there is no
breath in them.
18 They are [a]vanity,
a work of mockery;
In the time of their
punishment they will perish.
19 The [a]portion of Jacob
is not like these;
For the [1]Maker of all is He,
And of the [2]tribe
of His inheritance;
[b]Yahweh of hosts is His name.
20 *He says*, "You are My
[a]*instrument* of shattering,
*My* weapon of war;
And with you I
[b]shatter nations,
And with you
I destroy kingdoms.
21 "With you I [a]shatter
the horse and his rider,
And with you I shatter
the [b]chariot and its rider,
22 And with you I shatter
[a]man and woman,
And with you I shatter
old man and [b]youth,
And with you I shatter
choice man and virgin,
23 And with you I shatter
the shepherd and his flock,
And with you I shatter the
farmer and his pair *of oxen*,
And with you I shatter
governors and prefects.
24 "But I will repay Babylon and all
the inhabitants of [a]Chaldea for [b]all
their evil that they have done in Zion
before your eyes," declares Yahweh.
25 "Behold, [a]I am against you,
[b]O destroying mountain,
Who destroys the whole
earth," declares Yahweh,
"And I will stretch out My
hand against you
And roll you down
from the crags,
And I will make you
a [c]burnt out mountain.
26 "They will not take from you
*even* a stone for a corner
Nor a stone for foundations,
But you will be a
perpetual [a]desolation,"
declares Yahweh.

27 [a]Lift up a standard in the land,
Blow a trumpet
among the nations!
Set apart the nations
against her;

**51:15** [b]Job 9:8; Ps 146:5, 6; Jer 32:17; Ac 14:15; Ro 1:20 **51:16** [a]Job 37:2-6; Ps 18:13 [b]Ps 135:7; Jer 10:13 [c]Jon 1:4 **51:17** [a]Is 44:18-20; Jer 10:14 [b]Hab 2:18, 19 **51:18** [a]Jer 18:15 **51:19** [a]Ps 73:26; Jer 10:16 [b]Jer 50:34 [1]Lit *Fashioner* [2]Or *Scepter*, cf. Nu 24:17 **51:20** [a]Is 10:5; 41:15, 16; Jer 50:23 [b]Is 8:9; 41:15, 16; Mic 4:12, 13 **51:21** [a]Ex 15:1 [b]Ex 15:4; Is 43:17 **51:22** [a]2Chr 36:17; Is 13:15, 16 [b]Is 13:18 **51:24** [a]Jer 50:10 [b]Jer 50:15, 29 **51:25** [a]Jer 50:31 [b]Is 13:2; Zec 4:7 [c]Rev 8:8 **51:26** [a]Is 13:19-22; Jer 50:13; 51:29 **51:27** [a]Is 13:2-5; 18:3; Jer 50:2; 51:12

Summon against her
the [b]kingdoms of [c]Ararat,
Minni, and [d]Ashkenaz;
Appoint a marshal against her;
Bring up the [e]horses
like bristly locusts.
28 Set apart the nations
against her,
The kings of the Medes,
[1]Their governors and
all [1]their [2]prefects
And every land of [3]their rule.
29 So the [a]land quakes
and writhes,
For the purposes of Yahweh
against Babylon stand,
To make the land of Babylon
[1]A [b]desolation
without inhabitants.
30 The [a]mighty men of Babylon
have ceased fighting;
They inhabit the strongholds;
[b]Their might is dried up;
They are becoming
[b]*like* women;
Their dwelling places
are set on fire;
The [c]bars of her *gates*
are broken.
31 One [a]runner runs
to meet [1]another,
And one [b]messenger
to meet [2]another,
To give a message to the king
*of Babylon*
That his city has been
captured from end *to end*;
32 The fords also have
been seized,
And they have burned
the marshes with fire,
And the men of war
are terrified.
33 For thus says Yahweh of hosts, the
God of Israel:
"The daughter of Babylon is
like a [a]threshing floor
At the time [1]it is stamped firm;
Yet in a little while the time of
[b]harvest will come for her."

34 "Nebuchadnezzar king
of Babylon has [a]devoured
me *and* brought me
into confusion;
He has set me down
*like* an [b]empty vessel;
He has [c]swallowed me
like a sea monster;
He has filled his stomach
with my delicacies;
He has rinsed me away.
35 "May the [a]violence *done*
to me and to my flesh
be upon Babylon,"
The [1]inhabitant of Zion
will say;
And, "May my blood be upon
the inhabitants of Chaldea,"
Jerusalem will say.
36 Therefore thus says Yahweh,
"Behold, I am going
to [a]plead your case
And [b]exact full
vengeance for you;
And [c]I will dry up her [1]sea
And make her fountain dry.

**51:27** [b]Jer 50:3, 9 [c]Ge 8:4; 2Ki 19:37; Is 37:38 [d]Ge 10:3 [e]Jer 50:42 **51:28** [1]Lit *Her* [2]Lieutenant governors [3]Lit *his* **51:29** [a]Jer 8:16; 10:10; 50:46; Am 8:8 [b]Is 13:19, 20; 47:11; Jer 50:13; 51:26, 43 [1]Or *An object of horror* **51:30** [a]Ps 76:5; Jer 50:15, 36, 37 [b]Is 13:7, 8; Na 3:13 [c]Is 45:1, 2; Lam 2:9; Am 1:5; Na 3:13 **51:31** [a]2Chr 30:6 [b]2Sa 18:19-31 [1]Lit *runner* [2]Or *messenger*; lit *announcer* **51:33** [a]Is 21:10; 41:15, 16; Mic 4:13 [b]Is 17:5; Hos 6:11; Joel 3:13; Rev 14:15 [1]Lit *of treading it* **51:34** [a]Jer 50:17 [b]Is 24:1-3 [c]Job 20:15; Jer 51:44 **51:35** [a]Ps 137:8 [1]Lit *inhabitress* **51:36** [a]Ps 140:12 [b]Jer 51:6, 11; Ro 12:19 [c]Jer 50:38 [1]Or *broad river*

37 "[a]Babylon will become
a heap *of ruins*,
a haunt of jackals,
An [b]object of horror and
hissing, without inhabitants.
38 "They will roar together
like [a]young lions;
They will growl like
lions' cubs.
39 "When they become heated
up, I will set
*before them* their feast
And [a]make them drunk,
that they may exult
And may [b]sleep
a perpetual sleep
And not wake up,"
declares Yahweh.
40 "I will bring them down like
[1]lambs [a]to the slaughter,
Like rams together
with male goats.

41 "How [a,1]Sheshak has
been captured,
And [b]the praise of the whole
earth been seized!
How Babylon has become
an object of horror
among the nations!
42 "The [a,1]sea has come
up over Babylon;
She has been covered
with its tumultuous waves.
43 "Her cities have become
an [a]object of horror,
A parched land, and a desert,
A land in which [b]no man lives
And through which no
*son* of man passes.
44 "[a]I will punish Bel in Babylon,
And I will make what he
has swallowed [b]come
out of his mouth;
And the nations will no
longer [c]stream to him.
Even the [d]wall of Babylon
has fallen down!

45 "[a]Come forth from her
midst, My people,
And each of you [b]escape
with his life
From the burning
anger of Yahweh.
46 "Now [a]lest your heart grow faint,
And you fear the [b]report that
*will be* heard in the land—
For the report will
come [1]one year,
And after that [2]another
report in [2]another year,
And violence *will
be* in the land
With [c]ruler against ruler—
47 Therefore behold,
days are coming
When I will punish the
[a]graven images of Babylon;
And her whole land will
be [b]put to shame,
And all her slain will
fall in her midst.
48 "Then [a]heaven and earth
and all that is in them
Will shout for joy
over Babylon,
For [b]the destroyers will come
to her from the north,"
Declares Yahweh.

**51:37** [a]Rev 18:2 [b]Jer 25:9 **51:38** [a]Jer 2:15 **51:39** [a]Jer 25:27; 48:26; 51:57 [b]Ps 76:5
**51:40** [a]Jer 48:15; 50:27 [1]Or *young rams* **51:41** [a]Jer 25:26 [b]Jer 49:25 [1]Cryptic name for Babylon
**51:42** [a]Is 8:7, 8; Jer 51:55; Da 9:26 [1]Or *broad river* **51:43** [a]Jer 50:12 [b]Is 13:20; Jer 2:6 **51:44** [a]Is 46:1; Jer 50:2 [b]Ezr 1:7, 8 [c]Is 2:2 [d]Jer 50:15; 51:58 **51:45** [a]Is 48:20; Jer 50:8, 28; 51:6; Rev 18:4 [b]Ge 19:12-16; Ac 2:40 **51:46** [a]Is 43:5; Jer 46:27, 28 [b]2Ki 19:7; Is 13:3-5 [c]Is 19:2 [1]Lit *in the* [2]Lit *the* **51:47** [a]Is 21:9; 46:1, 2; Jer 50:2; 51:52 [b]Jer 50:12, 35-37 **51:48** [a]Is 44:23; 48:20; 49:13; Rev 18:20 [b]Jer 50:3

49 [a]Indeed Babylon is to fall
*for* the slain of Israel,
*As* also for Babylon [b]the slain
of all the earth have fallen.
50 You [a]who have escaped
the sword,
Go! Do not stand around!
[b]Remember Yahweh from afar,
And let Jerusalem come
upon your heart.
51 [a]We are ashamed because
we have heard reproach;
Dishonor has covered
our faces,
For [b]strangers have entered
The holy places of the
house of Yahweh.

52 "Therefore behold, the days
are coming,"
declares Yahweh,
"When I will punish her
[a]graven images,
And the mortally
wounded will groan
throughout her land.
53 "Though Babylon should
[a]ascend to the heavens,
And though she should fortify
[1]her lofty stronghold,
From [b]Me destroyers
will come to her,"
declares Yahweh.

54 The [a]sound of an outcry
from Babylon,
And of great destruction from
the land of the Chaldeans!
55 For Yahweh is going
to destroy Babylon,
And He will make *her* loud
[1]noise [2]vanish from her.
And their [a]waves will roar
like many waters;
The rumbling of their
voices [3]sounds forth.
56 For the [a]destroyer is
coming against her,
against Babylon,
And her mighty men
will be captured;
Their [b]bows are shattered;
For Yahweh is a God
of [c]recompense,
He will fully repay.
57 "I will [a]make her princes and
her wise men drunk,
Her governors, her prefects,
and her mighty men,
That they may sleep a
[b]perpetual sleep and
not wake up,"
[c]Declares the King, whose
name is Yahweh of hosts.
58 Thus says Yahweh of hosts,
"The broad [a]wall of Babylon
will be completely razed,
And her high [b]gates
will be set on fire;
So the peoples will
[c]toil for nothing,
And the nations become
[d]weary *only* for fire."

59 The [1]message which Jeremiah
the prophet commanded Seraiah
the son of [a]Neriah, the grandson
of Mahseiah, when he went with
[b]Zedekiah the king of Judah to Bab-
ylon in the fourth year of his reign.
(Now Seraiah was quartermaster.)

**51:49** [a]Ps 137:8; Jer 50:29 [b]Rev 18:24 **51:50** [a]Jer 44:28 [b]Dt 4:29-31; Ps 137:6 **51:51** [a]Ps 44:15 [b]Ps 74:3-8; Lam 1:10 **51:52** [a]Jer 50:38 **51:53** [a]Ge 11:4; Job 20:6; Ps 139:8-10; Is 14:12-14; Jer 49:16; Am 9:2; Ob 4 [b]Is 13:3 [1]Lit *the height of her strength* **51:54** [a]Jer 48:3-5; 50:22, 46 **51:55** [a]Ps 18:4; 69:2; 124:2, 4, 5; Jer 51:42 [1]Or *voice* [2]Lit *perish* [3]Lit *is given* **51:56** [a]Jer 51:48, 53; Hab 2:8 [b]Ps 46:9; 76:3 [c]Dt 32:35; Ps 94:1, 2; Jer 51:6, 24 **51:57** [a]Jer 25:27 [b]Ps 76:5, 6 [c]Jer 46:18; 48:15 **51:58** [a]Jer 50:15 [b]Is 45:1, 2 [c]Hab 2:13 [d]Jer 9:5; 51:64; Lam 5:5 **51:59** [a]Jer 32:12; 36:4; 45:1 [b]Jer 28:1; 52:1 [1]Lit *word*

**60** So Jeremiah [a]wrote in a single
[1]scroll all the calamity which would
come upon Babylon, *that is,* all these
words which have been written con-
cerning Babylon. **61** Then Jeremiah
said to Seraiah, "As soon as you come
to Babylon, then see that you read
all these words aloud, **62** and then
you will say, 'You, O Yahweh, have
[1]promised concerning this place
to [a]cut it off, so that there will be
[b]nothing inhabiting it, [2]whether man
or beast, but it will be a perpetual
desolation.' **63** And as soon as you
finish reading this [1]scroll, you will
tie a stone to it and [a]throw it into
the middle of the Euphrates, **64** and
then you will say, 'Just so shall Bab-
ylon sink down and [a]not rise again
because of the calamity that I am
going to bring upon her; and they
will become [b]*utterly* weary.'" [c]Thus
far are the words of Jeremiah.

### *The Anger of Yahweh Towards Judah*

**52** [a]Zedekiah was twenty-one
years old when he became
king, and he reigned eleven years in
Jerusalem; and his mother's name was
[b,1]Hamutal the daughter of Jeremiah
of [c]Libnah. **2** And he did [a]what was
evil in the sight of Yahweh, according
to all that [b]Jehoiakim had done. **3** For
through the [a]anger of Yahweh *this*
came about in Jerusalem and Judah
until He cast them out from His
presence. And Zedekiah [b]rebelled
against the king of Babylon. **4** [a]Now
it happened in the ninth year of his
reign, on the tenth *day* of the tenth
month, that Nebuchadnezzar king of
Babylon came, he and all his military
force, against Jerusalem, and they
camped against it and built a [b]siege
wall all around [1]it. **5** [a]So the city came
under siege until the eleventh year of
King Zedekiah. **6** On the ninth *day* of
the [a]fourth month, the [b]famine was
so strong in the city that there was
no food for the people of the land.
**7** Then the city was [a]breached, and
all the [b]men of war fled and went
forth from the city at night by way of
the gate between the two walls which
*was* by the king's garden, though
the Chaldeans were [c,1]all around the
city. And they went by way of the
Arabah. **8** But the military force of
the Chaldeans pursued the king and
[a]overtook Zedekiah in the [1]plains of
Jericho, and all his military force was
scattered from him. **9** Then they
seized the king and [a]brought him up
to the king of Babylon at [b]Riblah in
the land of [c]Hamath, and he [1]spoke
*his* judgment on him. **10** Then the
king of Babylon [a]slaughtered the
sons of Zedekiah before his eyes, and
he also slaughtered all the [1]princes of
Judah in Riblah. **11** Then he [a]blinded
the eyes of Zedekiah; and the king
of Babylon bound him with bronze

---

**51:60** [a]Is 30:8; Jer 30:2, 3; 36:2, 4, 32 [1]Or *book* **51:62** [a]Is 13:19-22; 14:22, 23; Jer 50:3, 13, 39, 40 [b]Jer 51:43; Eze 35:9 [1]Lit *spoken* [2]Lit *from man even to beast* **51:63** [a]Jer 19:10, 11; Rev 18:21 [1]Or *book* **51:64** [a]Na 1:8, 9 [b]Jer 51:58 [c]Job 31:40; Ps 72:20 ◆ **52:1** [a]2Ki 24:18; 2Chr 36:11 [b]2Ki 23:31; 24:18 [c]Jos 10:29; 2Ki 8:22; Is 37:8 [1]Or *Hamital* **52:2** [a]1Ki 14:22; 2Ki 24:19; 2Chr 36:12 [b]Jer 36:30, 31 **52:3** [a]2Ki 24:20; Is 3:1, 4, 5 [b]2Chr 36:13; Eze 17:12-16 **52:4** [a]2Ki 25:1; Jer 39:1; Eze 24:1, 2; Zec 8:19 [b]Jer 32:24 [1]Lit *against it* **52:5** [a]2Ki 25:2 **52:6** [a]Jer 39:2 [b]2Ki 25:3; Is 3:1; Jer 38:9; Eze 4:16; 5:16; 14:13 **52:7** [a]2Ki 25:4; Jer 39:2 [b]Jer 39:4-7; 51:32 [c]Eze 33:21 [1]Lit *against the city on every side* **52:8** [a]Jer 21:7; 32:4; 34:21; 37:17; 38:23 [1]Same root as Arabah in 52:7 **52:9** [a]2Ki 25:6; Jer 32:4; 39:5 [b]Nu 34:11; Jer 39:5 [c]Nu 13:21; Jos 13:5 [1]Lit *spoke judgments with* **52:10** [a]2Ki 25:7; Jer 22:30; 39:6 [1]Or *commanders* **52:11** [a]Jer 39:7; Eze 12:13

fetters and brought him to Babylon and put him in prison until the day of his death.

**12** [a]Now on the tenth *day* of the fifth month, which was the [b]nineteenth year of King Nebuchadnezzar, king of Babylon, [c]Nebuzaradan the captain of the bodyguard, who stood before the king of Babylon, came to Jerusalem. **13** And he [a]burned the house of Yahweh, the [b]king's house, and all the houses of Jerusalem; even every large house he burned with fire. **14** So all the military force of the Chaldeans who *were* with the captain of the guard [a]tore down all the walls around Jerusalem. **15** Then Nebuzaradan the captain of the guard [a]took away into exile some of the poorest of the people, the rest of the people who remained in the city, the [b,1]defectors who had defected to the king of Babylon, and the rest of the artisans. **16** But [a]Nebuzaradan the captain of the guard had some of the poorest of the land remain to be vinedressers and [1]plowmen.

**17** Now the bronze [a]pillars which belonged to the house of Yahweh and the [b]stands and the bronze [c]sea, which were in the house of Yahweh, the Chaldeans shattered and carried all their bronze to Babylon. **18** They also took away the [a]pots, the shovels, *the snuffers,* the bowls, the [1]pans, and all the bronze vessels which were used to minister. **19** And the captain of the guard also took away the [a]cups, the firepans, the bowls, the pots, the lampstands, the [1]pans, and the offering bowls, what was fine gold and what was fine silver. **20** The two pillars, the one sea, and the twelve bronze bulls that were under [1]the sea, *and* the stands, which King Solomon had made for the house of Yahweh—the bronze of all these vessels was [a]beyond weight. **21** As for the pillars, the [a]height of each pillar *was* [1]eighteen cubits, and [2]it *was* twelve cubits in [a]circumference and four fingers in thickness, *and* hollow. **22** Now a [a]capital of bronze was on it; and the height of each capital was five cubits, with network and [b]pomegranates upon the capital all around, all of bronze. And the second pillar was like these, including pomegranates. **23** There were ninety-six [1]exposed pomegranates; all [a]the pomegranates *numbered* one hundred on the network all around.

**24** Then the captain of the guard took [a]Seraiah the chief priest and [b]Zephaniah the second priest, with the three [c,1]doorkeepers of the temple. **25** And from the city he took one official who was overseer of the men of war, and seven [1]of the [a]king's advisers who were found in the city, and the scribe of the commander of the army who mustered the people of

**52:12** [a]2Ki 25:8-21; Zec 7:5; 8:19 [b]2Ki 24:12; 25:8; Jer 52:29 [c]Jer 39:9 **52:13** [a]1Ki 9:8; 2Ki 25:9; 2Chr 36:19; Ps 74:6-8; 79:1; Is 64:10, 11; Lam 2:7; Mic 3:12 [b]Jer 39:8 **52:14** [a]2Ki 25:10; Ne 1:3 **52:15** [a]2Ki 25:11 [b]Jer 39:9 [1]Lit *fallers who had fallen* **52:16** [a]2Ki 25:12; Jer 39:10; 40:2-6 [1]Or *unpaid laborers* **52:17** [a]1Ki 7:15-22; 2Ki 25:13; Jer 27:19-22; 52:20-23 [b]1Ki 7:27-37 [c]1Ki 7:23-26 **52:18** [a]Ex 27:3; 1Ki 7:40, 45; 2Ki 25:14 [1]Or *spoons* for incense **52:19** [a]1Ki 7:49, 50; 2Ki 25:15 [1]Or *spoons* for incense **52:20** [a]1Ki 7:47; 2Ki 25:16 [1]As in Gr and Syr; Heb omits *the sea* **52:21** [a]1Ki 7:15; 2Ki 25:17; 2Chr 3:15 [1]Approx. 27 ft. high and 18 ft. in circumference or 8 m and 5.4 m [2]Lit *a line of 12 cubits would encircle it* **52:22** [a]1Ki 7:16; 2Ki 25:17 [b]1Ki 7:20, 42 **52:23** [a]1Ki 7:20 [1]Lit *windward* **52:24** [a]2Ki 25:18; 1Chr 6:14; Ezr 7:1 [b]2Ki 25:18; Jer 21:1; 29:25, 29; 37:3 [c]1Chr 9:19; Jer 35:4 [1]Lit *keepers of the door* **52:25** [a]2Ki 25:19; Es 1:14 [1]Lit *men of those seeing the king's face*

the land, and sixty men of the people
of the land who were found in the
midst of the city. **26** And Nebuzara-
dan the captain of the guard took
them and [a]led them to the king of
Babylon at Riblah. **27** Then the king of
Babylon [a]struck them down and put
them to death at Riblah in the land
of Hamath. So Judah [b]went into exile
from its land.

**28** These are the people whom
[a]Nebuchadnezzar took away into
exile: in the [1]seventh year 3,023
Jews; **29** in the eighteenth year of
Nebuchadnezzar 832 persons from
Jerusalem; **30** in the twenty-third year
of Nebuchadnezzar, [a]Nebuzaradan
the captain of the guard took away
into exile 745 Jewish people; there
were 4,600 persons in all.

**31** [a]Now it happened in the
thirty-seventh year of the exile of
Jehoiachin king of Judah, in the
twelfth month, on the twenty-fifth
of the month, that [1]Evil-merodach
king of Babylon, in the *first* year
of his reign, [b]lifted up the head of
Jehoiachin king of Judah and brought
him out of prison; **32** [a]and he spoke
to him good *words*, and he set his
throne above the throne of the kings
who *were* with him in Babylon. **33** So
[1]Jehoiachin [a]changed his prison
clothes and [b,2]had his meals in [3]the
king's presence continually all the
days of his life. **34** For his allowance,
a [a]continual allowance was given
him by the king of Babylon, a daily
portion all the days of his life until
the day of his death.

# THE LAMENTATIONS
## *of Jeremiah*

### *Zion Lays Desolate*

*א Aleph*

**1** How [a]lonely sits the city
That was [b]great with people!
She has become like a [c]widow
Who was *once* [d]great
  among the nations!
She who was a princess
  among the [1]provinces
Has become a [e]forced laborer!

*ב Beth*

**2** She [a]weeps bitterly
  in the night,
And her tears are
  on her cheeks;
She has none to comfort her
Among all her [b]lovers.
All her friends have [c]dealt
  treacherously with her;
They have become her enemies.

*ג Gimel*

**3** [a]Judah has gone into exile
  because of affliction
And because of great slavery;
She sits [b]among the nations,
*But* she has found no rest;

---

**52:26** [a]2Ki 25:20 **52:27** [a]2Ki 25:21; Eze 8:11-18 [b]Is 6:11, 12; 27:10; 32:13, 14; Jer 13:19; 20:4; 25:9-11; 39:9; Eze 33:28; Mic 4:10 **52:28** [a]2Ki 24:2, 3, 12-16; 2Chr 36:20; Ezr 2:1; Ne 7:6; Da 1:1-3 [1]Or possibly *seventeenth* **52:30** [a]2Ki 25:11; Jer 39:9 **52:31** [a]2Ki 25:27 [b]Ge 40:13, 20; Ps 3:3; 27:6 [1]Or *Awil-Marduk* ("Man of Marduk") **52:32** [a]2Ki 25:28 **52:33** [a]Ge 41:14, 42; 2Ki 25:29 [b]2Sa 9:7, 13; 1Ki 2:7 [1]Lit *he* [2]Lit *ate* [3]Lit *his presence* **52:34** [a]2Sa 9:10; 2Ki 25:30 ◆ **1:1** [a]Is 3:26 [b]Is 22:2 [c]Is 54:4 [d]1Ki 4:21; Ezr 4:20; Jer 31:7 [e]2Ki 23:35; Jer 40:9 [1]Or *districts* **1:2** [a]Ps 6:6; 77:2-6; Lam 1:16 [b]Jer 2:25; 3:1; 22:20-22 [c]Job 19:13, 14; Ps 31:11; Mic 7:5 **1:3** [a]Jer 13:19 [b]Lv 26:39; Dt 28:64-67

All [c]her pursuers have
overtaken her
In the midst of [1]distress.

ד *Daleth*

4 The roads [1]of Zion are
in mourning
Because [a]no one comes
to the appointed times.
All her gates are [b]desolate;
Her priests are sighing,
Her [c]virgins are grieving,
And she herself [2]is [d]bitter.

ה *He*

5 Her adversaries have
become [1]her masters;
Her enemies are complacent;
For [2]Yahweh has
[a]caused her grief
Because of the greatness
of her transgressions;
Her infants have gone away
As captives
before the adversary.

ו *Vav*

6 So all her [a]majesty
Has gone out from the
daughter of Zion;
Her princes have
become like deer
That have found no pasture;
So they have [b,1]fled
without strength
Before the pursuer.

ז *Zayin*

7 In the days of her affliction
and homelessness
[a]Jerusalem remembers all
her precious things
That were from the
days of old,
When her people fell into
the hand of the adversary
And [b]no one helped her.
The adversaries saw her;
They [c]laughed at her [1]ruin.

ח *Heth*

8 Jerusalem sinned [a]greatly;
Therefore [b]she has become
an impure thing.
All who honored her
despise her
Because they have seen
her nakedness;
Even [c]she herself sighs
and turns away.

ט *Teth*

9 Her [a]uncleanness was
in her skirts;
She did not remember
her [b]future.
Therefore she has
[c]gone down astonishingly;
[d]She has no comforter.
"[e]See, O Yahweh,
my affliction,
For the enemy has
[f]magnified himself!"

י *Yodh*

10 The adversary has
stretched out his hand
Over all her desirable things,
For she has seen the [a]nations
enter her sanctuary,
The ones whom
You commanded
That they should [b]not enter
into Your assembly.

כ *Kaph*

11 All her people are sighing,
[a]seeking bread;

---

**1:3** [c]2Ki 25:4, 5 [1]Or *narrow places* **1:4** [a]Is 24:4-6; Lam 2:6, 7 [b]Jer 9:11; 10:22 [c]Lam 2:10, 21 [d]Joel 1:8-13 [1]Or *to* [2]Or *suffers bitterly* **1:5** [a]Ps 90:7, 8; Eze 8:17, 18; 9:9, 10 [1]Lit *head* [2]The personal covenant name of God, a form of I AM WHO I AM, cf. Ex 3:14-15 **1:6** [a]Jer 13:18 [b]2Ki 25:4, 5 [1]Lit *gone* **1:7** [a]Ps 42:4; 77:5-9 [b]Jer 37:7; Lam 4:17 [c]Ps 79:4; Jer 48:27 [1]Lit *cessation* **1:8** [a]Is 59:2-13; Lam 1:5, 20 [b]Lam 1:17 [c]Lam 1:11, 21, 22 **1:9** [a]Jer 2:34; Eze 24:13 [b]Dt 32:29; Is 47:7 [c]Is 3:8; Jer 13:17, 18 [d]Ecc 4:1; Jer 16:7 [e]Ps 25:18; 119:153 [f]Ps 74:23; Zep 2:10 **1:10** [a]Ps 74:4-8; Is 64:10, 11; Jer 51:51 [b]Dt 23:3 **1:11** [a]Jer 38:9; 52:6

They have given their
desirable things for food
To [b]restore *their* souls.
"See, O Yahweh, and look,
For I am [c]despised."

ל *Lamedh*

12 "Is [a]it nothing to all you
who pass this way?
Look and see if there is
any [1]pain like my [1]pain
Which was dealt
severely to me,
Which [b]Yahweh grieved
*me* with on the day
of His [c]burning anger.

מ *Mem*

13 "From on high He sent
fire into my [a]bones,
And it dominated *them*.
He has spread a [b]net
for my feet;
He has turned me back;
He has made me [c]desolate,
[1]Faint all day long.

נ *Nun*

14 "The [a]yoke of my
transgressions is bound;
By His hand they are
knit together.
They have [b]come
upon my neck;
He has made my
strength stumble.
The Lord [c]has given me
into the hands
Of *those against whom*
I am not able to stand.

ס *Samekh*

15 "The [a]Lord has rejected
all my mighty men
In my midst;
He has called an appointed
time against me
To break my [b]young men;
The Lord has [c]trodden
*as in* a wine press
The virgin daughter of Judah.

ע *Ayin*

16 "For these things
I [a]am weeping;
[1]My eyes run down with water;
Because far from me
is a [b]comforter,
One who restores my soul.
My children are desolate
Because the enemy
has prevailed."

פ *Pe*

17 Zion [a]stretches out her hands;
There is no one
to comfort her;
Yahweh has [b]commanded
concerning Jacob
That the ones round
about him should be
his adversaries;
[c]Jerusalem has become an
impure thing among them.

צ *Tsadhe*

18 "Yahweh is [a]righteous;
For I have [b]rebelled
against His [1]command;
Hear now, all peoples,
And [c]behold my [2]pain;
[d]My virgins and my
young men
Have gone into captivity.

ק *Qoph*

19 "I [a]called to my lovers,
*but* they deceived me;

**1:11** [b]1Sa 30:12 [c]Jer 15:19 **1:12** [a]Jer 18:16; 48:27 [b]Jer 30:23, 24 [c]Is 13:13; Jer 4:8 [1]Or *sorrow* **1:13** [a]Job 30:30; Ps 22:14; Hab 3:16 [b]Job 19:6; Ps 66:11 [c]Jer 44:6 [1]Or *Sick* **1:14** [a]Pr 5:22; Is 47:6 [b]Jer 28:13, 14 [c]Jer 32:3, 5; Eze 25:4, 7 **1:15** [a]Is 41:2; Jer 13:24; 37:10 [b]Jer 6:11; 18:21 [c]Mal 4:3 **1:16** [a]Jer 14:17; Lam 2:11, 18; 3:48, 49 [b]Ps 69:20; Ecc 4:1; Lam 1:2 [1]Lit *My eye, my eye* **1:17** [a]Is 1:15; Jer 4:31 [b]2Ki 24:2-4; Jer 12:9 [c]Lam 1:8 **1:18** [a]Ps 119:75; Jer 12:1 [b]1Sa 12:14, 15; Jer 4:17 [c]Lam 1:12 [d]Dt 28:32, 41 [1]Lit *mouth* [2]Or *sorrow* **1:19** [a]Job 19:13-19; Lam 1:2

My [b]priests and my elders
breathed their last
in the city
While they sought food
for themselves in order
to [c]restore their souls.

ר *Resh*

20 "See, O Yahweh,
for I am in distress;
My [a,1]inmost being is
greatly disturbed;
My heart is overturned
within me,
For I have been
very [b]rebellious.
In the street the
sword bereaves;
In the house it is like death.

ש *Shin*

21 "They have heard that
I [a]am sighing;
There is no one to comfort me;
All my enemies have heard
of the [1]evil *done to* me;
They [b]rejoice that You
have done *it.*
You have brought
the day which You
have proclaimed,
So that they will
become [c]like me.

ת *Tav*

22 "Let all their evil come
before You;
*And* [a]deal severely with
them as You have dealt
severely with me
For all my transgressions;
For my groans are great
and my heart is faint."

### *The Anger of Yahweh*

א *Aleph*

2 How the Lord has [a]covered
the daughter of Zion
With a cloud in His anger!
He has [b]cast
from heaven to earth
The [c]beauty of Israel,
And has not remembered
the [d]footstool of His feet
In the day of His anger.

ב *Beth*

2 The Lord has [a]swallowed
up; He has not spared
All the habitations of Jacob.
In His wrath He has
[b]pulled down
The strongholds of the
daughter of Judah;
He has [c]brought *them*
down to the ground;
He has [d]profaned the
kingdom and its princes.

ג *Gimel*

3 In [1]hot anger He has
cut in pieces
[2]All the [a]strength of Israel;
He has [b]turned back
His right hand
From before the enemy.
And He has [c]burned
in Jacob like a flaming fire
Devouring round about.

ד *Daleth*

4 He has bent His [a]bow
like an enemy;
He has set His right hand
like an adversary
And killed all that were
[b]desirable to the eye;

---

**1:19** [b]Jer 14:15; Lam 2:20 [c]Lam 1:11 **1:20** [a]Is 16:11; Lam 2:11 [b]Jer 14:20 [1]Lit *inward parts are in ferment* **1:21** [a]Lam 1:4, 8, 22 [b]Ps 35:15; Jer 50:11; Lam 2:15 [c]Is 14:5, 6; 47:6, 11; Jer 30:16 [1]Or *calamity* **1:22** [a]Ne 4:4, 5; Ps 137:7, 8 ◆ **2:1** [a]Eze 30:18 [b]Is 14:12-15; Eze 28:14-16 [c]Is 64:11 [d]Ps 99:5; 132:7 **2:2** [a]Ps 21:9; Lam 3:43 [b]Lam 2:5; Mic 5:11, 14 [c]Is 25:12; 26:5 [d]Ps 89:39, 40; Is 43:28 **2:3** [a]Ps 75:5, 10; Jer 48:25 [b]Ps 74:11; Jer 21:4, 5 [c]Is 42:25; Jer 21:14 [1]Lit *burning* [2]Lit *Every horn* **2:4** [a]Job 6:4; 16:13; Lam 3:12, 13 [b]Eze 24:25

In the tent of the
daughter of Zion
He has [c]poured out His
wrath like fire.

ה *He*

5 The Lord has become
like an [a]enemy.
He has [b]swallowed up Israel;
He has swallowed up
all its [c]palaces;
He has brought its
strongholds to ruin
And [d]multiplied in the
daughter of Judah
Mourning and moaning.

ו *Vav*

6 And He has violently
treated His [1]tabernacle
like a garden *booth*;
He has [a]brought His appointed
[2]meeting place to ruin.
Yahweh has [b]caused
to be forgotten
The appointed time and
sabbath in Zion,
And He has [c]spurned
king and priest
In the indignation
of His anger.

ז *Zayin*

7 The Lord has [a]rejected His altar;
He has abandoned
His sanctuary;
He [b]has delivered into the
hand of the enemy
The walls of her palaces.
They have made a [c]noise
in the house of Yahweh
As in the day of an
appointed time.

ח *Heth*

8 Yahweh [1]determined
to bring to ruin
The wall of the
daughter of Zion.
He has [a]stretched out a line;
He has not turned His hand
back from swallowing up,
And He has [b]caused rampart
and wall to mourn;
They have
languished together.

ט *Teth*

9 Her [a]gates have sunk
into the ground;
He has destroyed and
broken her bars.
Her king and her princes
are among the nations;
The [b]law is no more.
Also, her prophets find
[c]No vision from Yahweh.

י *Yodh*

10 The elders of the
daughter of Zion
[a]Sit on the ground;
they [b]are silent.
They have thrown [c]dust
up on their heads;
They have girded themselves
with [d]sackcloth.
The [e]virgins of Jerusalem
Have bowed their heads
down to the ground.

כ *Kaph*

11 My [a]eyes fail because of tears;
My [b,1]inmost being is
greatly disturbed;
My [c,2]heart is poured
out on the earth

**2:4** [c]Is 42:25; Jer 7:20 **2:5** [a]Jer 30:14 [b]Lam 2:2 [c]Jer 52:13; Lam 2:2 [d]Jer 9:17-20 **2:6** [a]Jer 52:13 [b]Jer 17:27; Lam 1:4; Zep 3:18 [c]Lam 4:16 [1]Lit *booth* [2]Or *time*, cf. 2:6b, 7 **2:7** [a]Ps 78:59-61; Is 64:11; Eze 7:20-22 [b]Jer 33:4, 5; 52:13 [c]Ps 74:3-8 **2:8** [a]2Ki 21:13; Is 34:11; Am 7:7-9 [b]Is 3:26; Jer 14:2 [1]Lit *thought* **2:9** [a]Ne 1:3 [b]Hos 3:4 [c]Jer 14:14; 23:16; Eze 7:26 **2:10** [a]Job 2:13; Is 3:26; 47:1 [b]Am 8:3 [c]Job 2:12; Eze 27:30 [d]Is 15:3; Jon 3:6-8 [e]Lam 1:4 **2:11** [a]Lam 1:16; 3:48, 51 [b]Jer 4:19 [c]Job 16:13 [1]Lit *inward parts are in ferment* [2]Lit *liver*

[d]Because of the [3]destruction of
the daughter of my people,
When [e]infants and
nursing babies faint
In the open squares of the city.

ל *Lamedh*

12 They say to their mothers,
"[a]Where is grain and wine?"
As they faint like a
wounded man
In the open squares of the city,
As their [b]life is poured out
On their mothers' bosom.

מ *Mem*

13 What shall I testify about you?
To what [a]shall I equate you,
O daughter of Jerusalem?
To what shall I liken you
as I comfort you,
O [b]virgin daughter of Zion?
For your [1]destruction is
as vast as the sea;
Who can [c]heal you?

נ *Nun*

14 Your [a]prophets have
beheld for you
Worthless and
ineffective *visions*;
And they have not
[b]uncovered your iniquity
So as to [1]return you
from captivity,
But they have [c]beheld
for you worthless and
misleading [2]oracles.

ס *Samekh*

15 All who pass along the way
[a]Clap their hands
*in derision* at you;
They [b]hiss and shake
their heads
At the daughter of Jerusalem,
"Is this the city
of which they said,
'[c]The perfection of beauty,
[d]The joy of the whole earth'?"

פ *Pe*

16 All [a]your enemies
Have opened their mouths
wide against you;
They hiss and [b]gnash
*their* teeth.
They say, "We have
[c]swallowed *her* up!
Surely this is the [d]day
for which we have hoped;
We have found *it*, we
have seen *it*."

ע *Ayin*

17 Yahweh has [a]done
what He purposed;
He has completed
His word
Which He commanded
from days of old.
He has pulled down
[b]without sparing,
And He has caused the enemy
to [c]be glad over you;
He has [d]exalted the [1]might
of your adversaries.

צ *Tsadhe*

18 Their [a]heart cried
out to the Lord,
"O [b]wall of the daughter
of Zion,
Let *your* [c]tears run down
like a river day and night;

---

**2:11** [d]Is 22:4; Lam 4:10 [e]Jer 44:7; Lam 2:19 [3]Lit *breaking* **2:12** [a]Jer 5:17 [b]Job 30:16; Ps 42:4; 62:8 **2:13** [a]Lam 1:12 [b]Is 37:22 [c]Jer 8:22; 30:12-15 [1]Lit *breaking* **2:14** [a]Jer 23:25-29; 29:8, 9 [b]Is 58:1; Eze 23:36; Mic 3:8 [c]Jer 23:36; Eze 22:25, 28 [1]Or *restore* [2]Lit *burdens* **2:15** [a]Job 27:23; Eze 25:6 [b]Ps 22:7; Is 37:22; Jer 18:16; 19:8; Zep 2:15 [c]Ps 50:2 [d]Ps 48:2 **2:16** [a]Job 16:10; Ps 22:13; Lam 3:46 [b]Job 16:9; Ps 35:16; 37:12 [c]Ps 56:2; 124:3; Jer 51:34 [d]Ob 12-15 **2:17** [a]Jer 4:28 [b]Lam 2:1, 2; Eze 5:11; 7:8, 9; 8:18 [c]Ps 35:24, 26; 89:42; Is 14:29 [d]Dt 28:43, 44; Lam 1:5 [1]Lit *horn* **2:18** [a]Ps 119:145; Hos 7:14 [b]Lam 2:8; Hab 2:11 [c]Ps 119:136; Jer 9:1; Lam 1:2, 16; 3:48, 49

Give yourself no relief;
Let [1]your eyes not be still.

ק *Qoph*

19 “Arise, cry aloud in the [a]night
At the head of the
night watches;
[b]Pour out your heart like water
Before the presence
of the Lord;
Lift up your hands to Him
For the [c]life of your infants
Who are [d]faint because
of hunger
At the head of every street.”

ר *Resh*

20 See, O Yahweh, and look!
With [a]whom have
You dealt thus?
Should women [b]eat
their [1]offspring,
The infants who were
[2]born healthy?
Should [c]priest and
prophet be killed
In the sanctuary of the Lord?

ש *Shin*

21 On the ground in the streets
Lie [a]young and old;
My [b]virgins and my
young men
Have fallen by the sword.
You have killed *them*
in the day of Your anger;
You have slaughtered,
[c]not sparing.

ת *Tav*

22 You called as in the day
of an appointed time
My [a]terrors on every side;
And there was [b]no one who
escaped or survived
In the day of Yahweh’s anger.
Those [c]whom I [1]gave
birth to and reared,
My enemy consumed them.

### *Jeremiah’s Heavy Chain*

א *Aleph*

**3** I am the man who has
[a]seen affliction
Because of the rod
of His wrath.
2 He has driven me and
made me walk
In [a]darkness and not
in light.
3 Surely against me He has
[a]turned His hand
Repeatedly all the day.

ב *Beth*

4 He has caused my [a]flesh and
my skin to waste away;
He has [b]broken my bones.
5 He has [a]besieged and
encompassed me
with [b]gall and hardship.
6 [a]Dark places He has
made me inhabit,
Like those who have
long been dead.

ג *Gimel*

7 He has [a]walled me in so
that I cannot go out;
He has made my
[b,1]chain heavy.
8 Even when I cry out
and call for help,
He [a]shuts out my prayer.

**2:18** [1]Lit *the daughter of your eye* **2:19** [a]Ps 42:3; Is 26:9 [b]1Sa 1:15; Ps 42:4; 62:8 [c]Lam 2:11 [d]Is 51:20 **2:20** [a]Ex 32:11; Dt 9:26 [b]Jer 19:9; Lam 4:10 [c]Ps 78:64; Jer 14:15; 23:11, 12 [1]Lit *fruit* [2]Or *tenderly cared for* **2:21** [a]2Chr 36:17; Jer 6:11 [b]Ps 78:62, 63 [c]Jer 13:14; Zec 11:6 **2:22** [a]Ps 31:13; Is 24:17; Jer 6:25 [b]Jer 11:11 [c]Jer 16:2-4; 44:7 [1]Lit *bore healthy, tenderly cared for* ◆ **3:1** [a]Ps 88:7, 15, 16 **3:2** [a]Job 30:26; Is 59:9; Jer 4:23 **3:3** [a]Ps 38:2; Is 5:25 **3:4** [a]Ps 31:9, 10; 38:2-8; 102:3-5 [b]Ps 51:8; Is 38:13 **3:5** [a]Job 19:8 [b]Jer 23:15; Lam 3:19 **3:6** [a]Ps 88:5, 6; 143:3 **3:7** [a]Job 3:23; 19:8 [b]Jer 40:4 [1]Lit *bronze piece* **3:8** [a]Job 30:20; Ps 22:2

9 He has [a]blocked my
ways with cut stone;
He has made my
paths crooked.

ד *Daleth*

10 He is to me like a bear
lying in wait,
*Like* a lion in secret places.
11 He has turned aside my ways
and [a]torn me to pieces;
He has made me desolate.
12 He [a]bent His bow
And [b]set me as a target
for the arrow.

ה *He*

13 He made the [1]arrows
of His [a]quiver
To enter into my [2]inward parts.
14 I have become
a [a]laughingstock
to all my people,
Their [b]music of *mockery*
all the day.
15 He has [a]saturated me
with bitterness;
He has sated me
with wormwood.

ו *Vav*

16 He has [a]broken my
teeth with [b]gravel;
He has made me cower
in the [c]dust.
17 My soul has been rejected
[a]from peace;
I have forgotten goodness.
18 So I say, "My strength
has perished,
As well as my [a]hopeful waiting
*which comes* from Yahweh."

### *The Lord Will Not Reject Forever*

ז *Zayin*

19 Remember my affliction and
my [1]homelessness, the
[a]wormwood and gall.
20 Surely [a]my soul remembers
And is [b]bowed down
within me.
21 This I will return to my heart;
Therefore I will [a]wait in hope.

ח *Heth*

22 The [a]lovingkindnesses of
Yahweh [1]indeed never cease,
[b]For His compassions
never fail.
23 *They* are new [a]every morning;
Great is [b]Your faithfulness.
24 "Yahweh is my [a]portion,"
says my soul,
"Therefore I [b]wait for Him."

ט *Teth*

25 Yahweh is good to those
who [a]hope in Him,
To the soul who [b]seeks Him.
26 *It is* good that he
[a]waits silently
For the salvation of Yahweh.
27 *It is* good for a man that
he should bear
The yoke in his youth.

י *Yodh*

28 Let him [a]sit alone
and be silent
Since He has laid *it* on him.
29 Let him [1]put his mouth
in the [a]dust;
Perhaps there is [b]hope.
30 Let him give his [a]cheek
to the one who strikes him;

**3:9** [a]Is 63:17; Hos 2:6 **3:11** [a]Job 16:12, 13; Jer 15:3; Hos 6:1 **3:12** [a]Ps 7:12; Lam 2:4 [b]Job 6:4; 7:20; Ps 38:2 **3:13** [a]Jer 5:16 [1]Lit *sons* [2]Lit *kidneys* **3:14** [a]Ps 22:6, 7; 123:4; Jer 20:7 [b]Job 30:9; Lam 3:63 **3:15** [a]Jer 9:15 **3:16** [a]Ps 3:7; 58:6 [b]Pr 20:17 [c]Jer 6:26 **3:17** [a]Is 59:11; Jer 12:12 **3:18** [a]Job 17:15; Eze 37:11 **3:19** [a]Jer 9:15; Lam 3:5, 15 [1]Or *bitterness* **3:20** [a]Job 21:6 [b]Ps 42:5, 6, 11; 43:5; 44:25 **3:21** [a]Ps 130:7 **3:22** [a]Ps 78:38; Jer 3:12; 30:11 [b]Mal 3:6 [1]Or *that we are not consumed* **3:23** [a]Is 33:2; Zep 3:5 [b]Heb 10:23 **3:24** [a]Ps 16:5; 73:26 [b]Ps 33:18 **3:25** [a]Ps 27:14; Is 25:9 [b]Is 26:9 **3:26** [a]Ps 37:7 **3:28** [a]Jer 15:17 **3:29** [a]Job 16:15; 40:4 [b]Jer 31:17 [1]Lit *give* **3:30** [a]Job 16:10; Is 50:6

Let him be saturated
with reproach.

כ *Kaph*

31 For the Lord will [a]not
reject forever,
32 For if He causes grief,
Then He will have [a]compassion
According to His
abundant lovingkindness.
33 For He [a]does not afflict
from His heart
Or grieve the sons of men.

ל *Lamedh*

34 To crush under His feet
All the prisoners of the [1]land,
35 To [1]deprive a man of [a]justice
In the presence of the Most High,
36 To [a,1]defraud a man
in his *legal* case—
These things the Lord does
not see *with approval.*

מ *Mem*

37 Who is [1]there who speaks
and it [a]happens,
Unless the Lord has
commanded *it*?
38 *Is it* not from the mouth
of the Most High
That [a]both calamities
and [1]good go forth?
39 Why should *any* living
[1]person or *any* man
[a]Complain because of his sins?

נ *Nun*

40 Let us [a]search out and
examine our ways,
And let us return to Yahweh.
41 We [a]lift up our heart
to *our* hands
Toward God in heaven;
42 We have [a]transgressed
and rebelled;
You have [b]not pardoned.

ס *Samekh*

43 You have covered *Yourself*
with [a]anger
And [b]pursued us;
You have killed *and*
[c]have not spared.
44 You have [a]covered
Yourself with a cloud
So that [b]no prayer can
pass through.
45 *You have made us mere*
[a]scum and refuse
In the midst of the peoples.

פ *Pe*

46 All our enemies have [a]opened
their mouths against us.
47 [a]Panic and pitfall have
befallen us,
Devastation and destruction;
48 My [a,1]eyes run down
with streams of water
Because of the destruction
of the daughter
of my people.

ע *Ayin*

49 My eyes pour
down [a]unceasingly,
Without stopping,
50 Until Yahweh [a]looks down
And sees from heaven.
51 My eyes deal severely
with my soul

**3:31** [a]Ps 77:7; 94:14; Is 54:7-10 **3:32** [a]Ps 78:38; 106:43-45; Hos 11:8 **3:33** [a]Ps 119:67, 71, 75; Eze 33:11; Heb 12:10 **3:34** [1]Or *earth* **3:35** [a]Ps 140:12; Pr 17:15 [1]Or *turn aside a man's case* **3:36** [a]Jer 22:3; Hab 1:13 [1]Lit *make crooked* **3:37** [a]Ps 33:9-11 [1]Lit *this* **3:38** [a]Job 2:10; Is 45:7; Jer 32:42 [1]Lit *the good* **3:39** [a]Jer 30:15; Mic 7:9; Heb 12:5, 6 [1]Or *human being* **3:40** [a]Ps 119:59; 139:23, 24; 2Co 13:5 **3:41** [a]Ps 25:1; 28:2; 141:2 **3:42** [a]Ne 9:26; Jer 14:20; Da 9:5 [b]2Ki 24:4; Jer 5:7, 9 **3:43** [a]Lam 2:21 [b]Ps 83:15; Lam 3:66 [c]Lam 2:2, 17, 21 **3:44** [a]Ps 97:2 [b]Lam 3:8; Zec 7:13 **3:45** [a]1Co 4:13 **3:46** [a]Job 30:9, 10; Ps 22:6-8; Lam 2:16 **3:47** [a]Is 24:17, 18; Jer 48:43, 44 **3:48** [a]Ps 119:136; Jer 9:1, 18; Lam 1:16; 2:11, 18 [1]Lit *eye brings* **3:49** [a]Ps 77:2; Jer 14:17 **3:50** [a]Ps 80:14; Is 63:15; Lam 5:1

Because of all the
daughters of my city.

צ *Tsadhe*

52 My enemies [a]without cause
Hunted me down [b]like a bird;
53 They have silenced my
life [a]in the pit
And have [b,1]placed a stone
on me.
54 Waters flowed [a]over my head;
I said, "I am cut off!"

ק *Qoph*

55 I [a]called on Your name,
O Yahweh,
Out of the lowest pit.
56 You have [a]heard my voice,
"[b]Do not hide Your ear
from my *prayer for* relief,
From my cry for help."
57 You [a]drew near
when I called on You;
You said, "[b]Do not fear!"

ר *Resh*

58 O Lord, You [a]have pleaded
my soul's cause;
You have [b]redeemed my life.
59 O Yahweh, You have [a]seen
my oppression;
[b]Judge my case.
60 You have seen
all their vengeance,
All their [a]purposes against me.

שׂ *Sin* / שׁ *Shin*

61 You have heard their
[a]reproach, O Yahweh,
All their purposes against me.
62 The [a]lips of those who
rise against me and
their whispering
*Are* against me all day long.
63 Look on their [a]sitting
and their rising;
[b]I am their mocking song.

ת *Tav*

64 You will [a]recompense
them, O Yahweh,
According to the work
of their hands.
65 You will give them
[a,1]dullness of heart;
Your curse will be on them.
66 You will [a]pursue them
in anger and destroy them
From under the [b]heavens
of Yahweh!

### *Yahweh's Wrath Spent*

א *Aleph*

4 How [a]dark the gold
has become,
*How* the pure gold
has changed!
The sacred stones
are poured out
At the head of every street.

ב *Beth*

2 The precious sons of Zion,
Weighed against fine gold,
How they are regarded
as [a]earthen jars,
The work of a potter's hands!

ג *Gimel*

3 Even [a]jackals offer the breast;
They nurse their young;
*But* the daughter of my
people has become [b]cruel
Like [c]ostriches
in the wilderness.

**3:52** [a]Ps 35:7, 19 [b]1Sa 26:20; Ps 11:1; 124:7 **3:53** [a]Jer 37:16; 38:6, 9 [b]Da 6:17 [1]Or *cast stones*
**3:54** [a]Ps 69:2; Jon 2:3-5 **3:55** [a]Ps 130:1; Jon 2:2 **3:56** [a]Job 34:28 [b]Ps 55:1 **3:57** [a]Ps 145:18
[b]Is 41:10, 14 **3:58** [a]Jer 50:34 [b]Ps 34:22 **3:59** [a]Jer 18:19, 20 [b]Ps 26:1; 43:1 **3:60** [a]Jer 11:19
**3:61** [a]Ps 74:18; 89:50; Lam 5:1; Zep 2:8 **3:62** [a]Ps 59:7, 12; 140:3; Eze 36:3 **3:63** [a]Ps 139:2
[b]Job 30:9; Lam 3:14 **3:64** [a]Ps 28:4; Jer 51:6, 24, 56 **3:65** [a]Ex 14:8; Dt 2:30; Is 6:10 [1]Or *insolence*
**3:66** [a]Lam 3:43 [b]Ps 8:3 ◆ **4:1** [a]Eze 7:19-22 **4:2** [a]Is 30:14; Jer 19:1, 11 **4:3** [a]Is 13:22; 34:13 [b]Is 49:15;
Eze 5:10 [c]Job 39:14-17

ד *Daleth*

4 The [a]tongue of the
nursing baby cleaves
To the roof of its mouth
because of [b]thirst;
The infants [c]ask for bread,
*But* no one breaks
*it* for them.

ה *He*

5 Those who ate [a]delicacies
Are desolate in the streets;
Those [1]reared in crimson
Embrace ash pits.

ו *Vav*

6 So the [1]iniquity of the
daughter of my people
Is greater than the
[a,2]sin of Sodom,
Which was [b]overthrown
as in a moment,
And no hands [3]whirled
toward her.

ז *Zayin*

7 Her [1]Nazirites were
[a]purer than snow;
They were whiter
than milk;
They were more ruddy
*in* [2]body than corals,
Their polishing *was*
*like* [b,3]lapis lazuli.

ח *Heth*

8 Their form is [a]blacker
than soot;
They are not recognized
in the streets;
Their [b]skin is shriveled
on their bones;
It is withered, it has
become like wood.

ט *Teth*

9 Better are those [a]pierced
through with the sword
Than those pierced
through with hunger;
For their *life* [b]flows away,
being stricken
For lack of the produce
of [1]the field.

י *Yodh*

10 The hands
of compassionate women
[a]Boiled their own children;
They became [b]food for them
Because of the destruction
of the daughter of my people.

כ *Kaph*

11 Yahweh has [a]spent His wrath;
He has poured out His
burning anger;
And He has [b]kindled
a fire in Zion
Which has devoured
its foundations.

ל *Lamedh*

12 The kings of the earth
did not believe,
Nor *did* any of [a]the
inhabitants of the world,
That the adversary
and the enemy
Could [b]enter the gates
of Jerusalem.

מ *Mem*

13 Because of the sins
of her [a]prophets
*And* the iniquities
of her priests,
Who have shed in her midst
The [b]blood of the righteous;

**4:4** [a]Ps 22:15 [b]Jer 14:3 [c]Lam 2:12 **4:5** [a]Jer 6:2; Am 6:3-7 [1]Lit *established in crimson* **4:6** [a]Ge 19:24 [b]Ge 19:25; Jer 20:16 [1]Or *punishment for iniquity* [2]Or *punishment for sin* [3]Or *wrung over her* **4:7** [a]Ps 51:7 [b]Ex 24:10; Job 28:16 [1]Or *dedicated ones* [2]Lit *bones* [3]Heb *sappir* **4:8** [a]Job 30:30; Lam 5:10 [b]Job 19:20; Ps 102:3-5 **4:9** [a]Jer 16:4 [b]Lv 26:39; Eze 24:23 [1]Lit *my fields* **4:10** [a]Lv 26:29; Dt 28:57; 2Ki 6:29; Jer 19:9; Lam 2:20; Eze 5:10 [b]Dt 28:53-55 **4:11** [a]Jer 7:20; Lam 2:17; Eze 22:31 [b]Dt 32:22; Jer 17:27 **4:12** [a]Dt 29:24 [b]Jer 21:13 **4:13** [a]Jer 5:31; 6:13; Lam 2:14; Eze 22:26-28 [b]Jer 2:30; 26:8, 9; Mt 23:31

*נ Nun*

14 They wandered, [a]blind,
in the streets;
They were defiled with [b]blood
So that no one could touch
their [c]garments.

*ס Samekh*

15 “Depart! [a]Unclean!”
[1]they cried of themselves.
“Depart, depart, do not touch!”
So they [b]fled and wandered;
*Men* among the nations said,
“They shall not continue
to sojourn *with us*.”

*פ Pe*

16 The presence of Yahweh
has eradicated them;
He will not continue
to look at them;
They did not [a,1]honor
the priests;
They did not favor
the elders.

*ע Ayin*

17 Yet our eyes were spent,
*Looking* for [1]help was [a]vanity;
In our watching we
have watched
For a [b]nation that
could not save.

*צ Tsadhe*

18 They [a]hunted our steps
So that we could not walk
in our open squares;
Our [b]end drew near,
Our days were [1]finished,
For our end had come.

*ק Qoph*

19 Our pursuers were [a]swifter
Than the eagles of the sky;
They hotly pursued us
on the mountains;
They waited in ambush
for us in the wilderness.

*ר Resh*

20 The [a]breath of our nostrils,
the [b]anointed of Yahweh,
Was [c]captured in their pits,
Of whom we had said,
“Under his [d]shadow
We shall live
among the nations.”

*שׂ Sin*

21 Rejoice and be glad,
O daughter of [a]Edom,
Who inhabits the land of Uz;
*But* the [b]cup will pass
on to you as well;
You will become drunk and
make yourself naked.

*ת Tav*

22 *The punishment* of your
iniquity has come [a]to an
end, O daughter of Zion;
He will exile you no longer.
*But* He [b]will punish your
iniquity, O daughter
of Edom;
He will expose your sins!

### *O Yahweh, Remember Us!*

5 Remember, O Yahweh,
what has happened to us;
Look, and see our [a]reproach!
2 Our inheritance has been
turned over to [a]strangers,
Our [b]houses to foreigners.
3 We have become orphans
[a]without a father;
Our mothers are like widows.

---

**4:14** [a]Dt 28:28, 29; Is 29:10; 56:10; 59:9, 10 [b]Is 1:15 [c]Jer 2:34 **4:15** [a]Lv 13:45, 46 [b]Jer 49:5 [1]Or *they* (men) *cried to them* **4:16** [a]Is 9:14-16; Jer 52:24-27 [1]Lit *lift up the faces of* **4:17** [a]Jer 37:7; Lam 1:7 [b]Eze 29:6, 7, 16 [1]Lit *our help* **4:18** [a]Jer 16:16 [b]Jer 5:31; Eze 7:2-12; Am 8:2 [1]Lit *full* **4:19** [a]Is 5:26-28; 30:16, 17; Jer 4:13; Hab 1:8 **4:20** [a]Ge 2:7 [b]2Sa 1:14; 19:21 [c]Jer 39:5; 52:9 [d]Da 4:12 **4:21** [a]Ps 137:7; Jer 25:21 [b]Ob 16 **4:22** [a]Is 40:2; Jer 33:7, 8 [b]Jer 49:10; Mal 1:3, 4 ◆ **5:1** [a]Ps 44:13-16 **5:2** [a]Is 1:7; Hos 8:7, 8 [b]Zep 1:13 **5:3** [a]Ex 22:24; Jer 15:8; 18:21

4 We drink our [a]water
by means of silver;
Our wood comes
*to us* at a price.
5 [1]Our pursuers are at our necks;
We are worn out; there
is [a]no rest for us.
6 We have given over *our* [1]hands
to [a]Egypt *and* Assyria
[2]to get enough bread.
7 Our [a]fathers sinned;
they are no more;
It is we who have borne
their iniquities.
8 [a]Slaves rule over us;
There is [b]no one to tear us
away from their hand.
9 We get our bread [1]at the
[a]risk of our lives
[2]Because of the sword
in the wilderness.
10 Our skin has become
as [a]hot as an oven
Because of [1]the burning
heat of famine.
11 They violated the
[a]women in Zion,
The virgins in the
cities of Judah.
12 Princes were hung
by their hands;
[a,1]Elders were not respected.
13 Young men [a]lifted up *the*
*stone* at the grinding mill,
And youths [b]stumbled down
under *loads* of wood.
14 Elders have ceased
from *being at* the gate,
Young men
from their [a]music.
15 The joy of our hearts
has [a]ceased;
Our dancing has been
turned into mourning.
16 The [a]crown has fallen
from our head;
[b]Woe to us, for we
have sinned!
17 Because of this our
[a]heart is faint;
Because of these things
our [b]eyes are dim;
18 Because of [a]Mount Zion
which lies desolate,
[b]Foxes walk about in it.

19 [a]You, O Yahweh, sit
enthroned forever;
Your [b]throne is from
generation to generation.
20 Why do You [a]forget
us forever?
Why do You forsake
us [1]so long?
21 [a]Cause us to return to You,
O Yahweh, that we
may be returned;
Renew [b]our days as of old,
22 Even if [a]You have
utterly rejected us
*And* are exceedingly
[b]angry with us.

---

**5:4** [a]Is 3:1 **5:5** [a]Ne 9:36, 37 [1]Lit *We have been pursued upon* **5:6** [a]Hos 9:3; 12:1 [1]Lit *hand* [2]Lit *to be satisfied with* **5:7** [a]Jer 14:20; 16:12 **5:8** [a]Ne 5:15 [b]Ps 7:2; Zec 11:6 **5:9** [a]Jer 40:9-12 [1]Lit *with our soul* [2]Or *In the face of* **5:10** [a]Job 30:30; Lam 4:8 [1]Or *the ravages of hunger* **5:11** [a]Is 13:16; Zec 14:2 **5:12** [a]Is 47:6; Lam 4:16 [1]Lit *The faces of elders* **5:13** [a]Jdg 16:21 [b]Jer 7:18 **5:14** [a]Is 24:8; Jer 7:34 **5:15** [a]Jer 25:10; Am 8:10 **5:16** [a]Job 19:9; Ps 89:39; Jer 13:18 [b]Is 3:9-11 **5:17** [a]Is 1:5 [b]Job 17:7; Lam 2:11 **5:18** [a]Mic 3:12 [b]Ne 4:3 **5:19** [a]Ps 102:12, 25-27 [b]Ps 45:6 **5:20** [a]Ps 13:1; 44:24 [1]Lit *to length of days* **5:21** [a]Ps 80:3; Jer 31:18 [b]Is 60:20-22 **5:22** [a]Ps 60:1, 2; Jer 7:29 [b]Is 64:9

*The Book of*

# EZEKIEL

### *The Vision of Four Living Creatures*

**1** Now it happened in the thirtieth
year, on the fifth *day* of the fourth
month, while I was by the [a]river
Chebar among the exiles, *that* the
[b]heavens were opened, and I saw
[c,1]visions of God. **2** (On the fifth of
the month [1]in the [a]fifth year of King
Jehoiachin's exile, **3** the [a]word of
[1]Yahweh came expressly to Ezekiel
the priest, son of Buzi, in the [b]land
of the Chaldeans by the river Chebar;
and there [c]the hand of Yahweh came
upon him.)
**4** Then I looked, and behold, a
[a]storm wind was coming from the
north, a great cloud with fire flashing
forth continually and a bright light all
around it, and in its midst something
like the gleam of [b]glowing metal in
the midst of the fire. **5** And within
it there were figures with the like-
ness of [a]four living creatures. And
this was their appearance: they had
the [b]likeness of a man. **6** And each
of them had [a]four faces and [b]four
wings. **7** And their legs were straight,
and [1]their feet were like a calf's hoof,
and they sparkled like the gleam of
[a]burnished bronze. **8** And under
their wings on their [a]four sides
*were* [b]hands of a man. As for the
faces and wings of the four of them,
**9** their wings touched one another;
*their faces* did [a]not turn as they
went; each [b]went straight forward.
**10** And as for the [a]likeness of their
faces, *each* had the [b]face of a man;
[1]all four had the face of a lion on the
right and the face of a bull on the left,
and [1]all four had the face of an eagle.
**11** And such were their faces. Their
wings were spread out above; each
had two touching another *being*,
and [a]two covering their bodies.
**12** And [a]each went straight forward;
[b]wherever the spirit was about to go,
they would go, without turning as
they went. **13** [1]As for the likeness of
the living creatures, their appearance
was like burning coals of [a]fire, [2]like
the appearance of torches going back
and forth among the living creatures.
The fire was bright, and lightning
was [2]flashing from the fire. **14** And
the living creatures [a]ran to and fro
with the appearance of [b]lightning.
**15** Then I looked at the living
creatures, and behold, there was one
[a]wheel on the earth beside the living
creatures, [1]for *each of* the four of them.
**16** The [a]appearance of the wheels and
their workmanship *was* like the gleam
of [b]beryl, and all four of them had the

---

◆ **1:1** [a]Eze 3:23; 10:15, 20 [b]Mt 3:16; Mk 1:10; Lk 3:21; Ac 7:56; 10:11; Rev 4:1; 19:11 [c]Ex 24:10; Nu 12:6; Is 1:1; 6:1; Eze 8:3; 11:24; 40:2; Da 8:1, 2 [1]Some ancient mss and versions *a vision* **1:2** [a]2Ki 24:12-15; Eze 8:1; 20:1 [1]Lit *it was* **1:3** [a]2Pe 1:21 [b]Eze 12:13 [c]1Ki 18:46; 2Ki 3:15; Eze 3:14, 22 [1]The personal covenant name of God, a form of I AM WHO I AM, cf. Ex 3:14-15 **1:4** [a]Is 21:1; Jer 23:19; Eze 13:11, 13 [b]Eze 1:27; 8:2 **1:5** [a]Eze 10:15, 17, 20; Rev 4:6-8 [b]Ge 1:26-28; Eze 1:26 **1:6** [a]Eze 1:10; 10:14, 21 [b]Eze 1:23 **1:7** [a]Da 10:6; Rev 1:15 [1]Lit *the soles of their feet* **1:8** [a]Eze 1:17; 10:11 [b]Eze 10:8, 21 **1:9** [a]Eze 1:17 [b]Eze 1:12; 10:22 **1:10** [a]Rev 4:7 [b]Eze 10:14 [1]Lit *the four of them* **1:11** [a]Is 6:2; Eze 1:23 **1:12** [a]Eze 1:9 [b]Eze 1:20 **1:13** [a]Ps 104:4; Rev 4:5 [1]Some ancient versions *And in the midst of the living* [2]Lit *coming out* **1:14** [a]Zec 4:10 [b]Mt 24:27; Lk 17:24 **1:15** [a]Eze 1:19-21; 10:9 [1]Lit *for his four faces* **1:16** [a]Eze 10:9-11 [b]Eze 10:9; Da 10:6

same likeness, their appearance and
workmanship *being* as if [1]one wheel
were within another. **17** Whenever
they went, they went in any of their
four [1]directions without [a]turning as
they went. **18** And as for their rims,
they were lofty and awesome, and the
rims of all four of them were [a]full of
eyes all around. **19** [a]And when the
living creatures went, the wheels
went beside them. And when the
living creatures [b]rose from the earth,
the wheels rose *also.* **20** [a]Wherever
the spirit was about to go, they would
go in that direction, [1]*where* the spirit
*was about* to go. And the wheels rose
alongside of them; for the spirit of the
living [2]creatures *was* in the wheels.
**21** [a]Whenever those went, these went;
and whenever those stood still, these
stood still. And whenever those rose
from the earth, the wheels rose close
beside them; for the spirit of the living
[1]creatures *was* in the wheels.

### *The Vision of the Glory of Yahweh*

**22** Now [a]over the heads of the living
[1]creatures *there was* something with
the likeness of an expanse, like the
awesome gleam of [2]crystal, spread
out over their heads above. **23** And
underneath the expanse their wings
*were stretched out* straight, one toward
the other; each one also had
[a]two wings covering its body on
the one side and on the other. **24** I
also heard the sound of their wings
like the [a]sound of many waters as
they went, like the [b,1]sound of [2]the
Almighty, a sound of tumult like the
[c]sound of an army camp; whenever
they stood still, they dropped their
wings. **25** And there came a sound
from above the [a]expanse that was
over their heads; whenever they
stood still, they dropped their wings.
**26** Now [a]above the expanse that
was over their heads there was something
in the [b]likeness of a throne, like
[c]sapphire stone in appearance; and
upon the likeness of the throne, high
up, *was* the likeness of one with the
appearance of a [d]man. **27** Then I saw
from the appearance of His loins and
upward something [a]like the gleam of
[1]glowing metal with the appearance of
fire all around within it, and from the
appearance of His loins and downward
I saw something with the appearance
of fire; and *there was* a radiance all
around Him. **28** As the appearance
of the [a]rainbow [1]in the clouds on a
rainy day, so *was* the appearance of
the radiance all around. Such *was*
the appearance of the likeness of the
[b]glory of Yahweh. And I saw *this,* and
I [c]fell on my face and heard a sound *of
a voice* speaking.

### *The Sending of Ezekiel*

**2** Then He said to me, "Son of man,
[a]stand on your feet that I may
speak with you!" **2** And as He spoke
to me, the [a]Spirit entered me and
caused me to stand on my feet; and
I heard *Him* speaking to me. **3** Then
He said to me, "Son of man, I am
sending you to the sons of Israel, to a

**1:16** [1]Lit *the wheel in the midst of the wheel* **1:17** [a]Eze 1:9, 12; 10:11 [1]Lit *sides* **1:18** [a]Eze 10:12; Rev 4:6, 8
**1:19** [a]Eze 10:16 [b]Eze 10:19 **1:20** [a]Eze 1:12 [1]Some ancient versions omit the final clause [2]M.T. *creature*
**1:21** [a]Eze 10:17 [1]M.T. *being* **1:22** [a]Eze 10:1 [1]As in some ancient mss and versions; M.T. *creature* [2]Or *ice*
**1:23** [a]Eze 1:6, 11 **1:24** [a]Eze 43:2; Rev 1:15; 19:6 [b]Eze 10:5 [c]2Ki 7:6; Da 10:6 [1]Or *voice* [2]Heb *Shaddai*
**1:25** [a]Eze 1:22; 10:1 **1:26** [a]Eze 1:22; 10:1 [b]Is 6:1; Eze 10:1; Da 7:9 [c]Ex 24:10; Is 54:11 [d]Eze 43:6, 7; Rev 1:13
**1:27** [a]Eze 1:4; 8:2 [1]Or *electrum* **1:28** [a]Ge 9:13; Rev 4:3; 10:1 [b]Ex 24:16; Eze 8:4; 11:22, 23; 43:4, 5
[c]Ge 17:3; Eze 3:23; Da 8:17; Rev 1:17 [1]Lit *which occurs in* ◆ **2:1** [a]Da 10:11; Ac 9:6 **2:2** [a]Eze 3:24; Da 8:18

rebellious people who have [a]rebelled
against Me; [b]they and their fathers
have transgressed against Me to this
very day. **4** I am sending you to them
who are [a,1]stiff-[2]faced and strong-
hearted children, and you shall say
to them, 'Thus says Lord Yahweh.'
**5** As for them, [a]whether they listen
or whether they refuse—for they are
a rebellious house—they will [b]know
that a prophet has been among them.
**6** Now as for you, son of man, [a]do
not fear them and do not fear their
words, though [b]thistles and briers
are with you and you sit on scorpi-
ons; neither fear their words nor be
dismayed at their presence, for they
are a rebellious house. **7** But you shall
[a]speak My words to them [b]whether
they listen or whether they refuse,
for they are rebellious.
**8** "Now as for you, son of man,
listen to what I am speaking to you;
do not be rebellious like that rebel-
lious house. Open your mouth and
[a]eat what I am giving you." **9** Then I
looked, and behold, a [a]hand was sent
forth to me; and behold, a [b,1]scroll
*was* in it. **10** Then He spread it out
before me, and it was written on the
front and back, and written on it were
lamentations, sighing, and [a]woe.

### *Ezekiel Sent to the House of Israel*

**3** Then He said to me, "Son of man,
eat what you find; [a]eat this scroll,
and go, speak to the house of Israel."
**2** So I [a]opened my mouth, and He [1]fed
me this scroll. **3** And He said to me,
"Son of man, [1]feed your stomach and
[a]fill your [2]body with this scroll which
I am giving you." Then I [b]ate it, and
it was sweet as [c]honey in my mouth.
**4** Then He said to me, "Son of man,
go *now*, come to the house of Israel,
and you shall speak with My words
to them. **5** For [a]you are not being sent
to a people of [b,1]unintelligible lips or
a difficult tongue, *but* to the house
of Israel, **6** nor to many peoples of
[1]unintelligible lips or a difficult
tongue, whose words you cannot
[2]understand. [3]But I have sent you
to them [4]who should listen to you;
**7** yet the house of Israel will not be
willing to listen to you, since they
are [a]not willing to listen to Me.
Surely the whole house of Israel is
[1]*stubborn with* a strong forehead and
stiff heart. **8** Behold, I have made your
face as strong as their faces and your
forehead as strong as their foreheads.
**9** Like [1]diamond stronger than flint I
have made your forehead. Do not be
afraid of them or be dismayed before
them, though they are a rebellious
house." **10** Moreover, He said to me,
"Son of man, take into your heart all
My [a]words which I will speak to you
and listen with your ears. **11** And go
*now*, come to the exiles, to the sons
of your people, and you shall speak

**2:3** [a]1Sa 8:7, 8; Jer 3:25 [b]Eze 20:18, 30 **2:4** [a]Ps 95:8; Is 48:4; Jer 5:3; 6:15; Eze 3:7 [1]Or *obstinate and stubborn* [2]Or *of presence*, cf. 2:6 **2:5** [a]Eze 2:7; 3:11, 27; Mt 10:12-15; Ac 13:46 [b]Eze 33:33; Lk 10:10, 11; Jn 15:22 **2:6** [a]Is 51:12; Jer 1:8, 17; Eze 3:9 [b]2Sa 23:6, 7; Eze 28:24; Mic 7:4 **2:7** [a]Jer 1:7, 17; Eze 3:10, 17 [b]Eze 2:5 **2:8** [a]Jer 15:16; Eze 3:3; Rev 10:9 **2:9** [a]Eze 8:3 [b]Jer 36:2; Eze 3:1; Rev 5:1-5; 10:8-11 [1]Lit *scroll of a book* **2:10** [a]Is 3:11; Rev 8:13 ◆ **3:1** [a]Eze 2:9 **3:2** [a]Jer 25:17 [1]Lit *made me eat*, cf. 3:1, 3b **3:3** [a]Jer 6:11; 20:9 [b]Jer 15:16 [c]Ps 19:10; 119:103; Rev 10:9, 10 [1]Lit *make your stomach eat*, cf. 3:3b [2]Lit *inward parts* **3:5** [a]Jon 1:2; Ac 14:11; 26:17 [b]Is 28:11; 33:19 [1]Lit *deepness of lip and heaviness of tongue, deepness of lip and hardness of tongue*, cf. Ex 4:10 **3:6** [1]Lit *deepness of lip and heaviness of tongue, deepness of lip and hardness of tongue*, cf. Ex 4:10 [2]Lit *hear* [3]Or *If I had sent you to them, they would listen to you* [4]Lit *they* **3:7** [a]1Sa 8:7 [1]Or *stubborn and obstinate* **3:9** [1]Lit *corundum* **3:10** [a]Job 22:22; Eze 2:8; 3:1-3

to them and say to them, whether
they listen or whether they refuse,
'Thus says Lord Yahweh.'"
12 Then the [a]Spirit lifted me up,
and I heard a great [b]rumbling sound
behind me, "Blessed be the glory of
Yahweh [1]in His place." 13 And I *heard*
the sound of the wings of the living
creatures touching one another and
the sound of the [a]wheels beside
them, even a great rumbling sound.
14 So the Spirit lifted me up and took
me away; and I went embittered in
the wrath of my spirit, and [a]the hand
of Yahweh was strong on me. 15 Then
I came to the exiles who lived beside
the river Chebar at Tel-abib, and I
sat there [a]seven days where they
were living, causing [1]consternation
among them.
16 [a]Now it happened at the end of
seven days, that the word of Yahweh
came to me, saying, 17 "Son of man,
I have given you as a [a]watchman
to the house of Israel; so you will
hear a word from My mouth, and
you shall [b]warn them from Me.
18 When I say to the wicked, 'You
will surely die,' and you do not
warn him or speak out to warn the
wicked from his wicked way that
he may live, that wicked man shall
die in his iniquity, but his [a]blood I
will require at your hand. 19 Yet if
you have [a]warned the wicked and
he does not turn from his wicked-
ness or from his wicked way, he
shall die in his iniquity; but you
have [b]delivered yourself. 20 Again,
[a]when a righteous man turns away
from his righteousness and does
evil, and I put a [b]stumbling block
before him, he will die; since you
have not warned him, he shall die
in his sin, and his righteous deeds
which he has done shall not be
remembered; but his blood I will
require at your hand. 21 However,
if you have [a]warned [1]the righteous
man that the righteous should not
sin and he does not sin, he shall
surely live because he took warning;
and you have delivered yourself."
22 And the hand of Yahweh was
on me there, and He said to me,
"Get up, go out to the plain, and
there I will [a]speak to you." 23 So I
got up and went out to the plain;
and behold, the [a]glory of Yahweh
was standing there, like the glory
which [b]I saw by the river Chebar,
and I fell on my face. 24 The [a]Spirit
then entered me and caused me
to stand on my feet, and He spoke
with me and said to me, "Go, shut
yourself up in your house. 25 Now
as for you, son of man, they will
[a]put ropes on you and bind you
with them so that you cannot go
out among them. 26 Moreover, [a]I
will make your tongue cling to [1]the
roof of your mouth so that you will
be mute and cannot be a man who
reproves them, for they are a rebel-
lious house. 27 But [a]when I speak
to you, I will open your mouth, and
you will say to them, 'Thus says Lord
Yahweh.' He who hears, let him hear;
and he who refuses, let him refuse;
[b]for they are a rebellious house.

**3:12** [a]Eze 3:14; 8:3; Ac 8:39 [b]Ac 2:2 [1]Or *from* **3:13** [a]Eze 1:15; 10:16, 17 **3:14** [a]2Ki 3:15 **3:15** [a]Job 2:13 [1]Or *horror, a sense of desolation* **3:16** [a]Jer 42:7 **3:17** [a]Is 52:8; 56:10; 62:6; Jer 6:17; Eze 33:7-9 [b]2Chr 19:10; Is 58:1; Hab 2:1 **3:18** [a]Eze 3:20; 33:6, 8 **3:19** [a]2Ki 17:13, 14; Eze 33:3, 9 [b]Eze 14:14, 20; Ac 18:6; 1Ti 4:16 **3:20** [a]Ps 125:5; Eze 18:24; 33:18; Zep 1:6 [b]Is 8:14; Jer 6:21; Eze 14:3, 7-9 **3:21** [a]Ac 20:31 [1]Lit *him, the righteous* **3:22** [a]Ac 9:6 **3:23** [a]Eze 1:28; Ac 7:55 [b]Eze 1:1 **3:24** [a]Eze 2:2 **3:25** [a]Eze 4:8 **3:26** [a]Lk 1:20, 22 [1]Lit *your palate* **3:27** [a]Eze 24:27; 33:22 [b]Eze 12:2, 3

### *Ezekiel Bears Israel's Iniquity*

4 "Now as for you, son of man, [a]get
yourself a brick, set it before you,
and inscribe a city on it, Jerusalem.
**2** Then [a]set a siege against it, build a
siege wall against it, [1]raise up a ramp
against it, set up camps against it,
and place battering rams against it all
around. **3** Now as for you, get yourself
an iron plate and set it up as an iron
wall between you and the city, and
establish your face toward it so that
[a]it is under siege, and besiege it. This
is a [b]sign to the house of Israel.
**4** "Now as for you, lie down on your
left side and lay the iniquity of the
house of Israel on it; you shall [a]bear
their iniquity for the number of days
that you lie on it. **5** Now I have set a
number of days for you corresponding
to the years of their iniquity, 390 days;
thus [a]you shall bear the iniquity of the
house of Israel. **6** And you shall com-
plete these, and you shall lie down a
second time, *but* on your right side
and bear the iniquity of the house of
Judah; I have set it for you for forty
days, a day for [a]each year. **7** Then you
shall establish your face toward the
siege of Jerusalem with your arm
bared and [a]prophesy against it. **8** Now
behold, I will [a]set ropes upon you so
that you cannot turn from one side to
the other until you have completed
the days of your siege.

### *Making Unclean Bread*

**9** "Now as for you, take wheat, barley,
beans, lentils, millet, and [a]spelt; set
them in one vessel and make them
into bread for yourself; you shall eat
it according to the number of the days
that you lie on your side, 390 days.
**10** And your food which you eat *shall
be* [a,1]twenty shekels a day by weight;
you shall eat it from time to time.
**11** The water you drink shall be the
sixth part of a [1]hin by measure; you
shall drink it from time to time. **12** You
shall eat it as a barley cake, having
baked *it* in their sight over human
[a]dung." **13** Then Yahweh said, "Thus
will the sons of Israel eat their bread
[a]unclean among the nations where I
will banish them." **14** But I said, "[a]Ah,
Lord Yahweh! Behold, I have [b]never
been defiled; for from my youth until
now I have never eaten what [c]died of
itself or was torn by beasts, nor has
any [d]offensive meat ever entered my
mouth." **15** Then He said to me, "See,
I will set for you cow's dung in place
of human dung over which you will
prepare your bread." **16** Moreover, He
said to me, "Son of man, behold, I am
going to [a]break the staff of bread in
Jerusalem, and they will eat bread by
[b]weight and with anxiety, and they
will drink water by [c]measure and
in desolation **17** because bread and
water will be lacking; and they will
be in desolation with one another
and [a]rot away in their iniquity.

### *The Siege of Jerusalem*

5 "Now as for you, son of man, take
a [a]sharp sword; take and [1]use it
*as* a barber's razor on your head and

◆ **4:1** [a]Is 20:2; Jer 13:1; 18:2; 19:1 **4:2** [a]Jer 6:6; Eze 21:22 [1]Lit *cast* **4:3** [a]Jer 39:1, 2; Eze 5:2 [b]Is 8:18; 20:3; Eze 12:6, 11; 24:24-27 **4:4** [a]Lv 10:17; 16:22; Nu 18:1 **4:5** [a]Nu 14:34 **4:6** [a]Nu 14:34; Da 9:24-26; 12:11, 12; Rev 11:2, 3 **4:7** [a]Eze 21:2 **4:8** [a]Eze 3:25 **4:9** [a]Ex 9:32; Is 28:25 **4:10** [a]Eze 45:12 [1]Approx. 8 oz. or 220 gm, a shekel was approx. 0.4 oz. or 11 gm **4:11** [1]A hin was approx. 1 gal. or 3.8 l **4:12** [a]Is 36:12 **4:13** [a]Da 1:8; Hos 9:3 **4:14** [a]Jer 1:6; Eze 9:8; 20:49 [b]Ac 10:14 [c]Lv 17:15; 22:8; Eze 44:31 [d]Dt 14:3; Is 65:4; 66:17 **4:16** [a]Lv 26:26; Is 3:1; Eze 5:16; 14:13 [b]Eze 4:10, 11; 12:19 [c]Lam 5:4; Eze 12:18, 19 **4:17** [a]Lv 26:39; Eze 24:23; 33:10 ◆ **5:1** [a]Lv 21:5; Is 7:20; Eze 44:20 [1]Lit *make it pass over your head*

beard. Then take [b]scales for weighing
and divide [2]the hair. **2** One-third you
shall burn in the fire at the center of
the city when the [a]days of the siege
are fulfilled. Then you shall take one-
third and strike *it* with the sword all
around [1]the city, and one-third you
shall scatter to the wind; and I will
[b]unsheathe a sword behind them.
**3** You shall also take a few in num-
ber from [1]them and bind them in
the edges of your *robes.* **4** Take again
some of them and throw them into
the fire and burn them in the fire;
from it a fire will [1]spread to all the
house of Israel.

**5** "Thus says Lord Yahweh, 'This
is [a]Jerusalem; I have set her at the
[b]center of the nations, with lands
all around her. **6** But she has rebelled
against My judgments more wickedly
than the nations and against My
statutes [a]more than the lands which
are all around her; for they have
[b]rejected My judgments and have not
walked [1]in My statutes.' **7** Therefore,
thus says Lord Yahweh, 'Because
you have [a]more turmoil than the
nations which are all around you
*and* have not walked in My statutes,
nor done My judgments, nor done
the judgments of the nations which
are all around you,' **8** therefore, thus
says Lord Yahweh, 'Behold, I, even I,
am [a]against you, and I will [b]execute
judgments among you in the sight of
the nations. **9** And I will do among
you what I have [a]not done and the
like of which I will never do again
because of all your abominations.
**10** Therefore, [a]fathers will eat *their*
sons among you, and sons will
eat their fathers; for I will execute
judgments on you and [b]scatter all
your remnant to every wind. **11** So as
I live,' declares Lord Yahweh, 'surely,
because you have [a]defiled My sanc-
tuary with all your [b]detestable idols
and with all your abominations,
therefore I will also withdraw, and
My eye will have no pity, and I will
not spare. **12** One-third of you will
die by the [a]plague or be consumed
by the famine among you, one-third
will fall by the sword around you,
and one-third I will [b]scatter to every
wind, and I will [c]unsheathe a sword
behind them.

**13** 'Thus My anger will be spent,
and I will cause My wrath against
them to be at rest, and I will be
[a,1]appeased; then they will know
that I, Yahweh, have [b]spoken in My
zeal when I have spent My wrath
upon them. **14** Moreover, I will make
you a [1]ruin and a [a]reproach among
the nations which are all around
you, in the sight of all who pass by.
**15** So [1]it will be a reproach, a reviling,
a [a]chastisement, and a desecration
to the nations who are all around
you when I [b]execute judgments
against you in anger, wrath, and
wrathful reproofs. I, Yahweh, have
spoken. **16** When I send against
them the [1]deadly arrows of famine

**5:1** [b]Da 5:27 [2]Lit *them* **5:2** [a]Jer 39:1, 2; Eze 4:2-8 [b]Lv 26:33 [1]Lit *it* **5:3** [1]Lit *there* **5:4** [1]Lit *go out*
**5:5** [a]Jer 6:6; Eze 4:1 [b]Dt 4:6; Lam 1:1; Eze 16:14 **5:6** [a]2Ki 17:8-20; Eze 16:47, 48, 51 [b]Ne 9:16, 17; Ps 78:10;
Jer 11:10; Zec 7:11 [1]Lit *in them, My statutes* **5:7** [a]2Ki 21:9-11; 2Chr 33:9; Jer 2:10, 11 **5:8** [a]Jer 21:5, 13;
Eze 15:7; 21:3; Zec 14:2 [b]Jer 24:9; Eze 5:15; 11:9 **5:9** [a]Da 9:12; Am 3:2; Mt 24:21 **5:10** [a]Lv 26:29; Jer 19:9;
Lam 4:10 [b]Ps 44:11; Eze 5:2, 12; 6:8; 12:14; Am 9:9; Zec 2:6; 7:14 **5:11** [a]Jer 7:9-11; Eze 8:5, 6, 16 [b]Jer 16:18;
Eze 7:20 **5:12** [a]Jer 15:2; 21:9; Eze 5:17; 6:11, 12 [b]Eze 5:2, 10; Am 9:9; Zec 2:6 [c]Jer 43:10, 11; 44:27; Eze 5:2; 12:14
**5:13** [a]Is 1:24 [b]Is 59:17; Eze 36:5, 6; 38:19 [1]Lit *comforted* **5:14** [a]Ps 74:3-10; 79:1-4; Eze 22:4 [1]Or *waste
place* **5:15** [a]Is 26:9; Jer 22:8, 9; 1Co 10:11 [b]Is 66:15, 16; Eze 5:8; 25:17 [1]Ancient versions *you* **5:16** [1]Lit *evil*

which [2]were for the destruction of
those whom I will send to destroy
you, then I will also intensify the
famine upon you and break the staff
of bread. **17** Moreover, [a]I will send
on you famine and wild beasts, and
they will bereave you of children;
[b]plague and bloodshed also will
pass through you, and I will bring
the sword on you. I, Yahweh, have
spoken.'"

### *Yahweh Will Destroy Israel's Pagan Altars*

**6** And the word of Yahweh came
to me saying, **2** "Son of man, set
your face toward the [a]mountains of
Israel, and prophesy against them
**3** and say, 'Mountains of Israel, hear
the word of Lord Yahweh! Thus says
Lord Yahweh to the mountains, the
hills, the ravines, and the valleys:
"Behold, I Myself am going to bring
a sword on you, and [a]I will destroy
your high places. **4** So your [a]altars
will become desolate, and your
incense altars will be broken; and I
will make your slain fall in front of
your idols. **5** I will also put the dead
bodies of the sons of Israel in front
of their idols; and I will scatter your
[a]bones all around your altars. **6** In al
your *places of* habitation, [a]cities wil
become waste, and the high place
will be desolate, that your altars may
become waste and [1]desolate, you
[b]idols may be broken and cease, you
incense altars may be cut in pieces
and your works may be blotted out

**7** The slain will fall among you, and
you will know that I am Yahweh.
**8** "However, I will leave a [a]remnant,
for you will have those who [b]escaped
the sword among the nations when
you are scattered among the lands.
**9** Then those of you who escape will
[a]remember Me among the nations
to which they will be carried captive,
how I have [b]been broken over their
adulterous hearts which turned away
from Me, and by their eyes which
played the harlot after their idols;
and they will [c]loathe themselves to
their own faces for the evils which
they have done, for all their abomi-
nations. **10** Then they will know that
I am Yahweh; I have not said in vain
that I would do this *calamitous* evil
against them."'
**11** "Thus says Lord Yahweh, 'Strike
your hands *together*, [a]stamp your
foot and say, "[b]Alas, because of all
the evil abominations of the house of
Israel, which will fall by the [c]sword,
by the famine, and by the plague!
**12** He who is [a]far off will die by the
plague, and he who is near will fall by
the sword, and he who remains and
is besieged will die by the famine.
Thus will I [b]spend My wrath on them.
**13** Then you will know that I am
Yahweh when their [a]slain are among
their idols all around their altars, on
[b]every high hill, on all the tops of
the mountains, under every green
tree, and under every leafy oak—the
places where they [1]offered a sooth-
ing aroma to all their idols. **14** So

---

**5:16** [2]Or *are for destruction, which I will send* **5:1**Lv 26:22; Rev 6:8 [b]Eze 38:22 ◆ **6:2** [a]Eze 36:1
**6:3** [a]Lv 26:30 **6:4** [a]Lv 26:30; 2Chr 14:5; Is 27:9; Ez6 **6:5** [a]2Ki 23:14, 16, 20; Jer 8:1, 2
**6:6** [a]Lv 26:31; Is 6:11; Eze 5:14 [b]Eze 6:4; Mic 1:7; Zec [1]As in some ancient versions; Heb *bear their guilt* **6:8** [a]Is 6:13; Jer 30:11 [b]Jer 44:14, 28; Ez16; 14:22 **6:9** [a]Dt 4:29; 30:2; Jer 51:50
[b]Ps 78:40; Is 7:13; 43:24; Hos 11:8 [c]Job 42:6; Eze 20:46:31 **6:11** [a]Eze 25:6 [b]Eze 9:4 [c]Eze 5:12; 7:15
**6:12** [a]Da 9:7 [b]Lam 4:11, 22; Eze 5:13 **6:13** [a]Eze 6:[b]1Ki 14:23; 2Ki 16:4; Is 57:5-7; Eze 20:28; Hos 4:13
[1]Lit *gave*

throughout all their habitations I will
[a]stretch out My hand against them
and make the land more desolate
and desecrated than the wilderness
toward Diblah; thus they will know
that I am Yahweh.""'"

### *The Pitiless Wrath of Yahweh*

7 Moreover, the word of Yahweh
came to me saying, 2 "Now as
for you, son of man, thus says Lord
Yahweh to the land of Israel, 'An
[a]end! The end is coming on the
four corners of the earth. 3 Now the
end is upon you, and I will send My
anger against you; I will judge you
according to your ways and put all
your abominations upon you. 4 For
My eye will have no pity on you, nor
will I spare *you*, but I will [a]put your
ways upon you, and your abomina-
tions will be among you; then you
will [b]know that I am Yahweh!'
5 "Thus says Lord Yahweh, 'A
[a]*calamitous* evil, a unique *calami-
tous* evil, behold, it is coming! 6 An
end has come; the end has come! It
has [a]awakened against you; behold,
it is coming! 7 Your doom has come
to you, O inhabitant of the land.
The [a]time has come; the [b]day is
near—confusion rather than joyful
shouting on the mountains. 8 Now
*it is* near *when* I will [a]pour out My
wrath on you and spend My anger
against you and [b]judge you according
to your ways and put on you all your
abominations. 9 My eye will show no
pity, nor will I spare. I will give to you
according to your ways, while your
abominations are among you; then
you will know that I, Yahweh, do the
striking.
10 'Behold, the day! Behold, it is
coming! *Your* doom has gone forth;
the [a]rod has blossomed; arrogance
has budded. 11 Violence [1]has grown
into a rod of [a]wickedness. None of
them *shall remain*, none of their
multitude, none of their [b]moaning,
nor anything eminent among them.
12 The [a]time has come; the day has
arrived. Let not the [b]buyer be glad
nor the seller mourn; for [c]wrath is
against all their multitude. 13 Indeed,
the seller will not [a]return *to himself*
[1]what he sold as long as [2]they *both*
live; for the vision regarding all their
multitude will not return *empty*, nor
will any of them strengthen his life
by his iniquity.
14 'They have [a]blown the trumpet
and made everything ready, but no
one is going to the battle, for My
wrath is against all [1]their multitude.
15 The [a]sword is outside, and the
plague and the famine are inside.
He who is in the field will die by the
sword; famine and the plague will
also devour those in the city. 16 Even
when their survivors [a]escape, they
will be on the mountains like [b]doves
of the valleys, all of them [c]moaning,
each over his own iniquity. 17 All
hands will hang limp, and all knees
will [1]become *like* water. 18 They will

**6:14** [a]Is 5:25; 9:12; Eze 14:13; 20:33, 34 ◆ **7:2** [a]Eze 7:5, 6; 11:13; Am 8:2, 10 **7:4** [a]Eze 11:21; 22:31; Hos 9:7 [b]Eze 6:7, 14; 7:27 **7:5** [a]2Ki 21:12, 13; Na 1:9 **7:6** [a]Zec 13:7 **7:7** [a]Eze 7:12; 12:23-25, 28 [b]Is 22:5 **7:8** [a]Is 42:25; Eze 9:8; 14:19; Na 1:6 [b]Eze 7:3; 33:20; 39 **7:10** [a]Ps 89:32; Is 10:5 **7:11** [a]Ps 73:8; 125:3; Is 59:6-8 [b]Zep 1:18 [1]Lit *has risen* **7:12** [a]Eze 7:5-7, 1Co 7:29-31; Jas 5:8, 9 [b]Pr 20:14; 1Co 7:30 [c]Is 5:13, 14; Eze 6:11, 12; 7:14 **7:13** [a]Lv 25:24-28, 31 [1]His inhed land; lit *thing sold* [2]Lit *their life among the living ones* **7:14** [a]Nu 10:9; Jer 4:5 [1]Lit *her* **7:15** [a]14:18; Eze 5:12; 6:11, 12; 12:16 **7:16** [a]Ezr 9:15; Is 37:31; Eze 6:8; 14:22 [b]Is 38:14 [c]Is 59:11; Na 2:7 **7:17** [a]Is 13:7; Eze 21:7; 22:14; Heb 12:12 [1]Lit *run with water*

[a]gird themselves with sackcloth, and
[b]horror will cover them; and shame
*will be* on all faces and [c]baldness on
all their heads. **19** They will [a]throw
their silver into the streets, and
their gold will become an impure
thing; their [b]silver and their gold
will not be able to deliver them in
the day of the fury of Yahweh. They
cannot satisfy their soul, nor can
they fill their stomachs, for their
iniquity has become an occasion
of stumbling.

### *The Temple Profaned*

**20** 'They [1]transformed the beauty of
His ornaments into pride, and [a]they
made the images of their abomina-
tions *and* their detestable things
with it; therefore I will make it an
impure thing to them. **21** I will give
it into the hands of the [a]foreigners
as plunder and to the wicked of the
earth as spoil, and they will profane
it. **22** I will also turn My [a]face from
them, and they will profane My
secret place; then robbers will enter
and profane it.

**23** '[a]Make the chain, for the land
is full of [b]judgments *that promote*
bloodshed, and the city is [c]full of
violence. **24** Therefore, I will bring the
*most* evil of the [a]nations, and they
will possess their houses. I will also
make the [b]pride of the strong ones
cease, and their [c]holy places will be
profaned. **25** Anguish has come, and
they will seek [a]peace, but there will
be none. **26** [a]Disaster will come upon
disaster, and [b]report will be *added* to
report; then they will seek a [c]vision
from a prophet, but the [d]law will be
lost from the priest and [e]counsel
from the elders. **27** The king will
mourn, the prince will be [a]clothed
with desolation, and the hands of the
people of the land will be dismayed.
According to their way I will deal
with them, and by their judgments I
will judge them. And they will know
that I am Yahweh.'"

### *Visions of Abominations in the Sanctuary*

**8** Now it happened in the sixth
year, on the fifth *day* of the sixth
month, as I was sitting in my house
with the elders of Judah sitting before
me, that the hand of Lord Yahweh fell
on me there. **2** Then I looked, and be-
hold, a likeness as the appearance of
[1]*one on* fire; from His loins and down-
ward *there was* the [a]appearance of
fire, and from His loins and upward
the appearance of brightness, like
[b]the gleam of [2]glowing metal. **3** He
sent forth the form of a hand and
took me by a lock of my head; and
the [a]Spirit lifted me up between
earth and heaven and brought me
in the visions of God to Jerusalem,
to the entrance of the [1]north gate of
the inner *court*, where the seat of the
figure of jealousy, which [b]provokes to
jealousy, was *located*. **4** And behold,
the [a]glory of the God of Israel *was*
there, like the appearance which I
saw in the plain.

---

**7:18** [a]Is 15:3; Eze 27:31; Am 8:10 [b]Job 21:6; Ps 55:5 [c]Eze 27:31 **7:19** [a]Is 2:20; 30:22 [b]Pr 11:4; Zep 1:18
**7:20** [a]Jer 7:30 [1]Lit *set* **7:21** [a]2Ki 24:13; Ps 74:2-8; Jer 52:13 **7:22** [a]Jer 18:17; Eze 39:23, 24
**7:23** [a]Jer 27:2 [b]Eze 9:9; Hos 4:2 [c]Eze 8:17 **7:24** [a]Eze 21:31; 28:7 [b]Eze 33:28 [c]2Chr 7:20; Eze 24:21
**7:25** [a]Eze 13:10, 16 **7:26** [a]Is 47:11; Jer 4:20 [b]Eze 21:7 [c]Jer 21:2; 37:17 [d]Ps 74:9; Eze 22:26; Mic 3:6
[e]Jer 18:18; Eze 11:2 **7:27** [a]Job 8:22; Ps 35:26; 109:18, 29; Eze 26:16 ◆ **8:2** [a]Eze 1:27 [b]Eze 1:4, 27 [1]Lit
*fire*; Gr *a man* [2]Or *electrum* **8:3** [a]Eze 3:12; 11:1 [b]Ex 20:4; Dt 32:16 [1]Lit *facing north* **8:4** [a]Eze 1:28;
3:22, 23

**5** Then He said to me, "Son of man,
[a]raise your eyes now toward the
north." So I raised my eyes toward
the north, and behold, to the north
of the altar gate *was* this [b]figure of
jealousy at the entrance. **6** And He
said to me, "Son of man, are you
seeing what they are doing, the great
[a]abominations which the house of
Israel is doing here, so that I would be
far from My sanctuary? But yet you
will see still greater abominations."
**7** Then He brought me to the
entrance of the court, and when I
looked, behold, a hole in the wall.
**8** He said to me, "Son of man, now
[a]dig through the wall." So I dug
through the wall, and behold, an
entrance. **9** And He said to me, "Go
in and see the evil abominations that
they are doing here." **10** So I entered
and looked, and behold, every form
of creeping things and beasts *and*
detestable things, with all the idols
of the house of Israel, were carved
on the wall all around. **11** Standing in
front of them were [a]seventy [b]elders
of the house of Israel, with Jaazaniah
the son of Shaphan standing among
them, each man with his [c]censer in
his hand and the fragrance of the
cloud of incense rising. **12** Then He
said to me, "Son of man, do you see
what the elders of the house of Israel
are doing in the dark, each man in
the room of his carved images? For
they say, '[a]Yahweh does not see us;
Yahweh has [b]forsaken the land.'"
**13** And He said to me, "Yet you will
see still greater abominations which
they are doing."
**14** Then He brought me to the
entrance of the [a]gate of the house
of Yahweh which *was* toward the
north; and behold, women were
sitting there weeping for Tammuz.
**15** He said to me, "Do you see *this,* son
of man? Yet you will see still greater
abominations than these."
**16** Then He brought me into the
inner court of the house of Yahweh.
And behold, at the entrance to the
temple of Yahweh, between the porch
and the altar, *were* about twenty-five
men with their [a]backs to the temple
of Yahweh and their faces toward
the east; and [b]they were [1]prostrat-
ing themselves eastward toward
the sun. **17** He said to me, "Do you
see *this,* son of man? Is it too light a
thing for the house of Judah to do the
abominations which they have done
here, that they have [a]filled the land
with violence and [b]provoked Me to
anger still more? For behold, they
are sending forth the twig to their
nose. **18** Therefore, I also will do *this*
in wrath: My eye will have no pity,
nor will I spare; and [a]they will cry in
My ears with a loud voice, yet I will
not listen to them."

### *The Vision of Yahweh's Wrath*

**9** Then He cried out in my hearing
with a loud [a]voice saying, "Draw
near, [1]O executioners of the city, each
with his destroying weapon in his
hand." **2** And behold, six men were
coming from the direction of the up-
per gate which faces north, each with
his shattering weapon in his hand;
and among them was [a]a certain man

**8:5** [a]Jer 3:2; Zec 5:5 [b]Ps 78:58; Jer 7:30; 32:34; Eze 8:3 **8:6** [a]2Ki 23:4, 5; Eze 5:11; 8:9, 17 **8:8** [a]Is 29:15 **8:11** [a]Nu 11:16, 25; Lk 10:1 [b]Jer 19:1 [c]Nu 16:17, 35 **8:12** [a]Ps 14:1; Is 29:15; Eze 9:9 [b]Ps 10:11 **8:14** [a]Eze 44:4; 46:9 **8:16** [a]2Chr 29:6; Jer 2:27; Eze 23:39 [b]Dt 4:19; 17:3; Job 31:26-28; Jer 44:17 [1]Or *worshiping* **8:17** [a]Eze 7:11, 23; 9:9; Am 3:10; Mic 2:2 [b]Jer 7:18, 19; Eze 16:26 **8:18** [a]Is 1:15; Jer 11:11; Mic 3:4; Zec 7:13 ◆ **9:1** [a]Is 6:8 [1]Lit *you who punish* **9:2** [a]Lv 16:4

clothed in linen with a [1]scribe's case
at his loins. And they went in and
stood beside the bronze altar.
**3** Then the [a]glory of the God of
Israel went up from the cherub on
which it had been, to the threshold
of the house *of Yahweh*. And He
called to the man clothed in linen at
whose loins was the [1]scribe's case.
**4** Yahweh said to him, "Go through
the midst of the city, *even* through
the midst of Jerusalem, and put a
[a]mark on the foreheads of the men
who [b]sigh and groan over all the
abominations which are being done
in its midst." **5** But to the others He
said in my hearing, "Go through the
city after him and strike; do not let
your eye have pity and do not spare.
**6** [a]Kill to *utter* destruction old men,
chosen men, virgins, little ones, and
women, but do not [b]touch any man
on whom is the mark; and you shall
[c]start from My sanctuary." So they
started with the [1]elders who *were*
before the house. **7** And He said to
them, "[a]Defile the house and fill the
courts with the slain. Go out!" Thus
they went out and struck down *the
people* in the city. **8** Now it happened
as they were striking *the people* and
I *alone* remained, that I [a]fell on my
face and cried out and said, "[b]Alas,
Lord Yahweh! Are You destroying the
whole remnant of Israel [1]by pouring
out Your wrath on Jerusalem?"
**9** Then He said to me, "The iniquity
of the house of Israel and Judah is
very, very great, and the land is [a]filled
with bloodshed, and the city is [b]full of
perversion; for [c]they say, 'Yahweh has
forsaken the land, and Yahweh does
not see!' **10** But as for Me, [a]My eye will
have no pity, nor will I spare, but [b]I
will put their way upon their heads."
**11** Then behold, the man clothed in
linen at whose loins was the *scribe's*
[1]case responded with a word, saying,
"I have done just as You have commanded me."

### *Vision of Yahweh's Glory Departing the Temple*

**10** Then I looked, and behold, in
the [a,1]expanse that was over
the heads of the cherubim something
like a [b]sapphire stone, in appearance
in the likeness of a [c]throne, appeared
above them. **2** And He spoke to the
man clothed in linen and said, "Enter
between the [a]whirling wheels under
the [1]cherubim and fill your hands
with [b]coals of fire from between the
cherubim and scatter *them* over the
city." And he entered in my sight.
**3** Now the cherubim were standing
on the right side of the house when
the man entered, and the cloud filled
the [a]inner court. **4** Then the [a]glory
of Yahweh rose up from the cherub
to the threshold of the house, and
the [b]house was filled with the cloud,
and the court was filled with the
[c]brightness of the glory of Yahweh.
**5** Moreover, the sound of the wings of
the cherubim was heard as far as the

---

**9:2** [1]Or *scribal inkhorn* **9:3** [a]Eze 10:4; 11:22, 23 [1]Or *scribal inkhorn* **9:4** [a]Ex 12:7, 13; Eze 9:6; 2Co 1:22; 2Ti 2:19; Rev 7:2, 3; 9:4; 14:1 [b]Ps 119:53, 136; Jer 13:17; Eze 6:11; 21:6 **9:6** [a]2Chr 36:17 [b]Ex 12:23; Rev 9:4 [c]Jer 25:29; Am 3:2; Lk 12:47 [1]Or *old men* **9:7** [a]2Chr 36:17; Eze 7:20-22 **9:8** [a]1Chr 21:16 [b]Eze 11:13; Am 7:2-6 [1]Lit *by Your pouring* **9:9** [a]2Ki 21:16; Jer 2:34; Eze 7:23; 22:2, 3 [b]Eze 22:29; Mic 3:1-3; 7:3 [c]Job 22:13; Ps 10:11; 94:7; Is 29:15; Eze 8:12 **9:10** [a]Is 65:6; Eze 8:18; 24:14 [b]Eze 7:4; 11:21; Hos 9:7 **9:11** [1]Or *inkhorn* ◆ **10:1** [a]Eze 1:22, 26 [b]Ex 24:10 [c]Rev 4:2, 3 [1]Or *firmament* **10:2** [a]Eze 1:15-21; 10:13 [b]Ps 18:10-13; Is 6:6; Eze 1:13; Rev 8:5 [1]As in Gr; Heb *cherub* **10:3** [a]Eze 8:3, 16 **10:4** [a]Eze 9:3; 11:22, 23 [b]Ex 40:34, 35; Is 6:1-4 [c]Eze 1:28

outer court, like the [a]voice of [1]God
Almighty when He speaks.
**6** Now it happened that when He
commanded the man clothed in lin-
en, saying, "Take fire from between
the whirling wheels, from between
the cherubim," he entered and stood
beside a wheel. **7** Then the cherub
sent forth his hand from between
the cherubim to the fire which was
between the cherubim, took *some*
up, and put *it* into the hands of the
one clothed in linen, who took *it*
and went out. **8** And the cherubim
appeared to have the form of a man's
hand under their wings.
**9** Then I looked, and behold, [a]four
wheels beside the cherubim, one
wheel beside each cherub; and the
appearance of the wheels *was* like
the gleam of a [b,1]Tarshish stone. **10** As
for their appearance, all four of them
had the same likeness, as if one wheel
were within another wheel. **11** As they
went, they went [a]in *any of* their four
[1]directions without turning as they
went; but they went in the direction
which [2]they faced, without turning as
they went. **12** And their [a]whole body,
their backs, their hands, their wings,
and the [b]wheels were full of eyes all
around, the wheels belonging to all
four of them. **13** The wheels were
called in my hearing, the whirling
wheels. **14** And [a]each one had four
faces. The first face *was* the face of a
cherub, the second face *was* the face
of a man, the third the face of a lion,
and the fourth the face of an eagle.
**15** Then the cherubim rose up. They
are the [a]living creatures that I saw by
the river Chebar. **16** Now as the cher-
ubim went, the wheels went beside
them; also when the cherubim lifted
up their wings to rise from the ground,
the wheels would not turn from beside
them. **17** When [1]the cherubim [a]stood
still, [1]the wheels would stand still; and
when they rose up, [1]the wheels would
rise with them, for the spirit of the
living creatures *was* in them.
**18** Then the glory of Yahweh
departed from the threshold of the
house and stood [a]over the cherubim.
**19** When [a]the cherubim departed,
they lifted their wings and rose up
from the earth in my sight with the
wheels beside them; and they stood
still at the entrance of the east gate of
the house of Yahweh, and the glory of
the God of Israel [1]hovered over them.
**20** These are the [a]living creatures
that I saw beneath the God of Israel
by [b]the river Chebar; so I knew that
they *were* cherubim. **21** [a]Each one had
four faces and each one four wings,
and beneath their wings *was* the
likeness of human hands. **22** As for
the likeness of their faces, they were
the same faces whose appearance I
had seen by the river Chebar. Each
one went straight ahead.

### *Judgment on Evil Counselors*

**11** Moreover, the [a]Spirit lifted me
up and brought me to the east
gate of the house of Yahweh which
faced eastward. And behold, at the
entrance of the gate, *there were*
twenty-five men, and I saw among
them Jaazaniah son of Azzur and
[b]Pelatiah son of Benaiah, officials

**10:5** [a]Job 40:9; Eze 1:24; Rev 10:3 [1]Heb *El Shaddai* **10:9** [a]Eze 1:15-17 [b]Da 10:6; Rev 21:20 [1]Possibly *beryl* **10:11** [a]Eze 1:17 [1]Lit *sides* [2]Lit *the head turned* **10:12** [a]Rev 4:6, 8 [b]Eze 1:18 **10:14** [a]1Ki 7:29, 36; Eze 1:6, 10; 10:21; Rev 4:7 **10:15** [a]Eze 1:3, 5 **10:17** [a]Eze 1:21 [1]Lit *they* **10:18** [a]Ps 18:10 **10:19** [a]Eze 11:22 [1]Lit *over them from above* **10:20** [a]Eze 1:5, 22, 26; 10:15 [b]Eze 1:1 **10:21** [a]Eze 1:6, 8; 10:14; 41:18, 19 ◆ **11:1** [a]Eze 3:12, 14; 8:3; 11:24; 43:5 [b]Eze 11:13

of the people. **2** He said to me, "Son of man, these are the men who devise wickedness and [a]give evil counsel in this city, **3** who say, '*The time* is not near to build houses. [1]This [a]*city* is the pot, and we are the flesh.' **4** Therefore, [a]prophesy against them, son of man, prophesy!"

**5** Then the Spirit of Yahweh fell upon me, and He said to me, "Say, 'Thus says Yahweh, "So you say, house of Israel, for [a]I know what comes up in your [b]spirit. **6** You have [a]multiplied your slain in this city, and you have filled its streets with [1]them." **7** Therefore, thus says Lord Yahweh, "Your [a]slain whom you have laid in the midst of [1]the city are the flesh, and this *city* is the pot; but [2]I will [b]bring you out of it. **8** You have [a]feared a sword; so a sword I will [b]bring upon you," Lord Yahweh declares. **9** "And I will bring you out of the midst of [1]the city and give you into the hands of [a]strangers and [b]execute judgments against you. **10** You will [a]fall by the sword. I will judge you to the [b]border of Israel; so you shall know that I am Yahweh. **11** This *city* will [a]not be a pot for you, nor will you be flesh in the midst of it, *but* I will judge you to the border of Israel. **12** Thus you will know that I am Yahweh; for you have not walked in My statutes, nor have you [a]*executed* My judgments, but have executed according to the judgments of the [b]nations around you."'"

**13** Now it happened as I prophesied, that [a]Pelatiah son of Benaiah died. Then I fell on my face and cried out with a loud voice and said, "[b]Alas, Lord Yahweh! Will You bring the remnant of Israel to complete destruction?"

### *Yahweh Will Gather the Exiles*

**14** Then the word of Yahweh came to me, saying, **15** "Son of man, your brothers, your [1]relatives, [2]your fellow exiles, and the whole house of Israel, all of them, *are those* to whom the inhabitants of Jerusalem have said, 'Go far from Yahweh; this land has been given to [a]us as a possession.' **16** Therefore say, 'Thus says Lord Yahweh, "Though I had removed them far away among the nations, and though I had scattered them among the countries, yet I was a [a]sanctuary for them a little while in the countries where they had gone."' **17** Therefore say, 'Thus says Lord Yahweh, "I will [a]gather you from the peoples and assemble you out of the countries among which you have been scattered, and I will give you the land of Israel."' **18** When they come there, they will [a]remove all its [b]detestable things and all its abominations from it. **19** And I will [a]give them one heart and give within [1]them a new spirit. And I will take the [b]heart of stone out of their flesh and give them a [c]heart of flesh, **20** that they may [a]walk in

**11:2** [a]Ps 2:1, 2; 52:2; Is 30:1; Jer 5:5; Mic 2:1 **11:3** [a]Jer 1:13; Eze 11:7, 11; 24:3, 6 [1]Or *This is* **11:4** [a]Eze 3:4, 17 **11:5** [a]Jer 11:20; 17:10 [b]Eze 38:10 **11:6** [a]Is 1:15; Eze 7:23; 22:2-6, 9, 12, 27 [1]Lit *the slain* **11:7** [a]Eze 24:3-13; Mic 3:2, 3 [b]2Ki 25:18-22; Jer 52:24-27; Eze 11:9 [1]Lit *it* [2]As in Gr; Heb *he will bring you out* **11:8** [a]Pr 10:24; Is 66:4 [b]Job 3:25; Is 24:17, 18 **11:9** [a]Dt 28:36, 49, 50; Ps 106:41 [b]Eze 5:8; 16:41 [1]Lit *it* **11:10** [a]Jer 52:9, 10 [b]2Ki 14:25 **11:11** [a]Eze 11:3, 7; 24:3, 6 **11:12** [a]Eze 18:8, 9 [b]Eze 8:10, 14, 16 **11:13** [a]Eze 11:1 [b]Eze 9:8 **11:15** [a]Eze 33:24 [1]Lit *brothers* [2]As in Gr and some ancient versions; Heb *the men of your redemption* **11:16** [a]Ps 31:20; 90:1; 91:9; Is 8:14; Jer 29:7, 11 **11:17** [a]Is 11:11-16; Jer 3:12, 18; 24:5; Eze 20:41, 42; 28:25 **11:18** [a]Eze 37:23 [b]Eze 5:11; 7:20 **11:19** [a]Jer 24:7; 32:39; Eze 18:31; 36:26 [b]Zec 7:12; Ro 2:4, 5 [c]2Co 3:3 [1]As in Gr and many mss; Heb *you* **11:20** [a]Ps 105:45; Eze 36:27

My statutes and keep My judgments
and do them. Then they will be [b]My
people, and I shall be their God.
**21** [1]But as for those whose hearts
walk after their [a]detestable things
and abominations, I will [b]give *what*
*is due* for their way on their heads,"
declares Lord Yahweh.

### *The Glory of Yahweh Leaves Jerusalem*

**22** Then the cherubim [a]lifted up
their wings with the wheels beside
them, and [b]the glory of the God of
Israel [1]hovered over them. **23** The
[a]glory of Yahweh went up from the
midst of the city and [b]stood over the
mountain which is east of the city.
**24** Now the [a]Spirit lifted me up and
brought me in a vision by the Spirit
of God to the exiles in [1]Chaldea. So
the vision that I had seen [b]went up
*and* away from me. **25** Then I [a]told
the exiles all the things that Yahweh
had shown me.

### *The Vision of Captivity*

**12** Then the word of Yahweh
came to me, saying, **2** "Son of
man, you live in the [a]midst of the
[b]rebellious house, who [c]have eyes
to see but do not see, ears to hear but
do not hear; for they are a rebellious
house. **3** Now as for you, son of man,
prepare for yourself baggage for exile
and go into exile by day in their sight;
even go into exile from your place to
another place in their sight. [a]Perhaps
they will see, though they are a re-
bellious house. **4** Bring your baggage
out by day in their sight, as baggage
for exile. Then you will go out [a]at
evening in their sight, as those going
into exile. **5** In their sight, dig a hole
through the wall and [1]go out through
it. **6** In their sight, carry *the baggage*
on *your* shoulder *and* bring *it* out in
the dark. You shall [a]cover your face
so that you cannot see the land, for I
have set you as a [b]wondrous sign to
the house of Israel."

**7** I [a]did so, as I had been com-
manded. By day I [b]brought out my
baggage like the baggage of an exile.
Then in the evening I dug through
the wall with my hands; I went out
in the dark *and* carried *the baggage*
on *my* shoulder in their sight.

**8** And in the morning the word of
Yahweh came to me, saying, **9** "Son of
man, has not the house of Israel, the
[a]rebellious house, said to you, '[b]What
are you doing?' **10** Say to them, 'Thus
says Lord Yahweh, "This [a,1]oracle
*concerns* the prince in Jerusalem as
well as all the house of Israel who
are [2]in it."' **11** Say, 'I am [1]a [a]wondrous
sign to you. As I have done, so it will
be done to them; they will [b]go into
exile, into captivity.' **12** The [a]prince
who is among them will carry *his*
*baggage* on *his* shoulder in the dark
and go out. [1]They will dig a hole
through the wall to bring *it* out. He

---

**11:20** [b]Eze 14:11 **11:21** [a]Jer 16:18; Eze 11:18 [b]Eze 9:10; 16:43 [1]Lit *And to the heart of their detestable things and their abomination their heart goes* **11:22** [a]Eze 10:19 [b]Eze 43:2 [1]Lit *over them from above* **11:23** [a]Eze 8:4 [b]Zec 14:4 **11:24** [a]Eze 8:3; 11:1; 37:1; 2Co 12:2-4 [b]Ac 10:16 [1]Babylonia **11:25** [a]Eze 2:7; 3:4, 17, 27 ◆**12:2** [a]Is 6:5 [b]Ps 78:40; Is 1:23; Eze 2:7, 8 [c]Is 6:9f; 43:8; Jer 5:21; Mt 13:13, 14; Mk 4:12; 8:18; Lk 8:10; Jn 9:39-41; 12:40; Ac 28:26f; Ro 11:8 **12:3** [a]Jer 26:3; 36:3, 7; Lk 20:13; 2Ti 2:25 **12:4** [a]2Ki 25:4; Jer 39:4; Eze 12:12 **12:5** [1]Lit *bring it out* **12:6** [a]1Sa 28:8; Eze 12:12, 13 [b]Is 8:18; 20:3; Eze 4:3; 12:11; 24:24 **12:7** [a]Eze 24:18; 37:7, 10 [b]Eze 12:3-6 **12:9** [a]Eze 2:5-8; 12:1-3 [b]Eze 17:12; 20:49; 24:19 **12:10** [a]2Ki 9:25; Is 13:1; Eze 12:3-8 [1]Or *burden, what is carried*; cf. 12:6-7, 12 [2]Lit *in their midst* **12:11** [a]Eze 12:6 [b]Jer 15:2; 52:15, 28-30; Eze 12:3 [1]Lit *your sign* **12:12** [a]2Ki 25:4; Jer 39:4; 52:7; Eze 12:6 [1]Possibly the king's attendants

will cover his face so that he cannot
see the land with *his* eyes. **13** I will
also spread My [a]net over him, and
he will be caught in My snare. And I
will bring him to Babylon in the land
of the Chaldeans; yet he will [b]not see
it, though he will die there. **14** And I
will [a]scatter to every wind all who are
around him, his helpers and all his
troops; and I will draw out a sword
after them. **15** So they will [a]know that
I am Yahweh when I scatter them
among the nations and spread them
among the countries. **16** But I will
[1]spare a few of them from [a]sword,
famine, and pestilence that they
may recount all their abominations
among the nations where they go,
and [2]may [b]know that I am Yahweh."

**17** Moreover, the word of Yahweh
came to me saying, **18** "Son of man,
[a]you shall eat your bread with trem-
bling and drink your water with quiv-
ering and anxiety. **19** Then you will
say to the people of the land, 'Thus
says Lord Yahweh concerning the
inhabitants of Jerusalem in the land of
Israel, "They will eat their bread with
anxiety and drink their water with
desolation because [1]their *very* soil
will be [a]made desolate of its fullness
on account of the violence of all who
inhabit it. **20** The inhabited [a]cities will
be laid waste, and the [b]land will be a
desolation. So you will know that I
am Yahweh."'"

**21** Then the word of Yahweh came
to me, saying, **22** "Son of man, what
is this [a]proverb you *people* have
concerning the land of Israel, saying,
'The [b]days are long, and every [c]vision
fails'? **23** Therefore say to them, 'Thus
says Lord Yahweh, "I will make this
proverb cease so that they will no
longer use it as a proverb in Israel."
But speak to them, "[a]The days draw
near as well as the [1]fulfillment of ev-
ery vision. **24** For there will no longer
be any [a]worthless vision or flattering
divination in the midst of the house
of Israel. **25** For I, Yahweh, will speak,
and whatever [a]word I speak will be
done. It will no longer be delayed, for
in [b]your days, O [c]rebellious house,
I will speak the word and do it,"
declares Lord Yahweh.'"

**26** Furthermore, the word of Yah-
weh came to me, saying, **27** "Son of
man, behold, the house of Israel is
saying, 'The vision that he beholds
is for [a]many [1]years *from now*, and
he prophesies of times far off.'
**28** Therefore say to them, 'Thus says
Lord Yahweh, "None of My words
will be delayed any longer. Whatever
word I speak will be done,"'" declares
Lord Yahweh.

### *Yahweh's Wrath Against Lying Prophets*

**13** Then the word of Yahweh
came to me saying, **2** "Son of
man, prophesy against the [a]prophets
of Israel who prophesy, and say to
those who prophesy from their own
heart, '[b]Hear the word of Yahweh!

**12:13** [a]Is 24:17, 18; Eze 17:20; 19:8; Hos 7:12 [b]Jer 39:7; 52:11 **12:14** [a]2Ki 25:4, 5; Eze 5:2; 17:21 **12:15** [a]Eze 6:7, 14; 12:16, 20 **12:16** [a]Eze 7:15; 14:21 [b]Jer 22:8, 9 [1]Lit *leave over from them men* few *in number* [2]Or *they will know* **12:18** [a]Lam 5:9; Eze 4:16 **12:19** [a]Jer 10:22; Eze 6:6, 7, 14; Mic 7:13; Zec 7:14 [1]Lit *her* **12:20** [a]Is 3:26; Jer 4:7; Eze 5:14 [b]Is 7:23, 24; Jer 25:9; Eze 36:3 **12:22** [a]Eze 16:44; 18:2, 3 [b]Jer 5:12; Eze 11:3; 12:27; Am 6:3; 2Pe 3:4 [c]Eze 7:26 **12:23** [a]Ps 37:13; Joel 2:1; Zep 1:14 [1]Lit *word* **12:24** [a]Jer 14:13-16; Eze 13:6, 23; Zec 13:2-4 **12:25** [a]Nu 14:28-34; Is 14:24; Eze 6:10; 12:28 [b]Jer 16:9; Hab 1:5 [c]Eze 12:2 **12:27** [a]Eze 12:22; Da 10:14 [1]Lit *days* ◆ **13:2** [a]Is 9:15; Jer 37:19; Eze 22:25, 28 [b]Is 1:10; Am 7:16

**3** Thus says Lord Yahweh, “Woe to
the [a]wickedly foolish prophets who
are walking after their own spirit
and have [b]seen nothing. **4** O Israel,
your prophets have been like foxes
among waste places. **5** You have not
[a]gone up into the [b]breaches, nor did
you build the wall around the house
of Israel to stand in the battle on
the [c]day of Yahweh. **6** They behold
[a]worthlessness and lying divination
who are saying, ‘Yahweh declares,’
when Yahweh has not sent them; [b]yet
they wait for the establishing of *their*
word. **7** [a]Did you not see a worthless
vision and speak a lying divination
when you said, ‘Yahweh declares,’
but it is not I who have spoken?”’”

**8** Therefore, thus says Lord Yah-
weh, “Because you have spoken
worthlessness and beheld a lie,
therefore behold, [a]I am against
you,” declares Lord Yahweh. **9** “So My
hand will be against the [a]prophets
who see worthless visions and utter
lying divinations. They will not be in
the council of My people, [b]nor will
they be written down in the register
of the house of Israel, nor will they
enter the land of Israel, [1]that you may
know that I am Lord Yahweh. **10** It is
definitely because they have [a]misled
My people by saying, ‘[b]Peace!’ when
there is [c]no peace. And when anyone
builds a wall, behold, they plaster it
over with whitewash; **11** *so* tell those
who plaster *it* over with whitewash
that it will fall. A [a]flooding rain will
come, and you, O hailstones, will
fall; and a stormy wind will break
out. **12** Now behold, the wall will
fall. Will it *then* not be said to you,
‘Where is the plaster with which you
plastered *it*?’” **13** Therefore, thus says
Lord Yahweh, “I will make a stormy
wind break out in My wrath. There
will also be in My anger a flooding
rain and [a]hailstones to consume *it*
in wrath. **14** So I will pull down the
wall which you plastered over with
whitewash and bring it down to the
ground, so that its [a]foundation is laid
bare; and it will fall, and you will be
[b]consumed in its midst. And you will
[c]know that I am Yahweh. **15** Thus I
will spend My wrath on the wall and
on those who have plastered it over
with whitewash; and I will say to you,
‘The wall [1]is gone, and its plasterers
are gone— **16** the prophets of Israel
who prophesy to Jerusalem and who
[a]see visions of peace for her when
there is [b]no peace,’ declares Lord
Yahweh.

**17** “Now as for you, son of man, set
your face against the daughters of
your people who are [a]prophesying
[b]from their own heart. Prophesy
against them **18** and say, ‘Thus says
Lord Yahweh, “Woe to the women
who sew *magic* bands on [1]all wrists
and make veils for the heads of
*persons* of every stature to [a]hunt
down [2]souls! Will you hunt down
My people’s souls, but preserve your
own souls? **19** [a]For handfuls of barley
and fragments of bread, you have
profaned Me to My people to put to

**13:3** [a]Lam 2:14; Hos 9:7; Zec 11:15 [b]Jer 23:28-32 **13:5** [a]Ps 106:23; Jer 23:22; Eze 22:30 [b]Is 58:12 [c]Is 13:6, 9; Eze 7:19 **13:6** [a]Jer 29:8; Eze 22:28 [b]Jer 28:15; 37:19 **13:7** [a]Eze 22:28 **13:8** [a]Eze 5:8; 21:3; Na 2:13 **13:9** [a]Jer 20:3-6; 28:15-17 [b]Ps 69:28; 87:6; Jer 17:13; Da 12:1 [1]Or *and you will know* **13:10** [a]Jer 23:32; 50:6 [b]Jer 6:14; 8:11; 14:13 [c]Eze 7:25; 13:16 **13:11** [a]Eze 38:22 **13:13** [a]Ex 9:24, 25; Ps 18:12, 13; Is 30:30; Rev 11:19; 16:21 **13:14** [a]Mic 1:6; Hab 3:13 [b]Jer 6:15; 14:15 [c]Eze 13:9 **13:15** [1]Lit *is not...are not* **13:16** [a]Jer 6:14; 8:11; Eze 13:10 [b]Is 57:21 **13:17** [a]Jdg 4:4; 2Ki 22:14; Lk 2:36; Ac 21:9 [b]Eze 13:2; Rev 2:20 **13:18** [a]2Pe 2:14 [1]Lit *all joints of the hand*; M.T. *of my hands* [2]Or *lives*, so in ch **13:19** [a]Pr 28:21; Mic 3:5

death souls who should not die and
to [b]keep *other* souls alive who should
not live, by your lying to My people
who listen to lies.”’”
**20** Therefore, thus says Lord
Yahweh, “Behold, I am against your
*magic* bands by which you hunt
souls there as [1]birds, and I will tear
them from your arms; and I will let
*their* souls go, *the very* souls whom
you hunt as [1]birds. **21** I will also
tear off your veils and [a]deliver My
people from your hands, and they
will no longer be in your hands to be
hunted; and you will know that I am
Yahweh. **22** Because you [a]disheart-
ened the righteous with falsehood
when I did not cause him grief, but
have [b]strengthened the hands of the
wicked not to [c]turn from his evil way
*and* preserve his life, **23** therefore, you
women will no longer see [a]worthless
visions or practice divination, and I
will [b]deliver My people out of your
hand. Thus you will [c]know that I am
Yahweh.”

### *Idolatrous Elders Punished*

**14** Then some [a]elders of Israel
came to me and [b]sat down
before me. **2** And the word of Yahweh
came to me, saying, **3** “Son of man,
these men have [a]set up their idols
in their hearts and have [b]put right
*before their faces* the stumbling
block of their iniquity. Should I be
[c]inquired by them at all? **4** Therefore
speak to them and tell them, ‘Thus
says Lord Yahweh, “Any man of the
house of Israel who sets up his idols
in his heart, puts right before his face
the stumbling block of his iniquity,
and *then* comes to the prophet, I
Yahweh will be brought to give him
an answer [1]in light of it, [1]in light of
the [a]multitude of his idols, **5** in order
to seize the house of Israel by [a]their
heart, *those* who are [b,1]estranged
from Me through all their idols.”’
**6** “Therefore say to the house
of Israel, ‘Thus says Lord Yahweh,
“[a,1]Turn back and turn away from
your idols and turn your faces away
from all your [b]abominations. **7** For
anyone of the house of Israel or of
the [a]sojourners who sojourn in Israel
who separates himself from Me, sets
up his idols in his heart, puts right
before his face the stumbling block
of his iniquity, and *then* comes to the
prophet to inquire of Me for himself,
[b]I, Yahweh, will be brought to answer
him in My own person. **8** I will [a]set
My face against that man and make
him a [b]sign and [1]a proverb, and I will
cut him off from among My people.
So you will know that I am Yahweh.
**9** “But if the prophet is enticed to
speak a word, it is I, Yahweh, who have
enticed that prophet, and I will stretch
out My hand against him and [a]destroy
him from among My people Israel.
**10** They will bear *the punishment of*
their iniquity; as the iniquity of the in-
quirer is, so the iniquity of the prophet
will be, **11** in order that the house of

---

**13:19** [b]Jer 23:14, 17 **13:20** [1]Or *flying ones* **13:21** [a]Ps 91:3; 124:7 **13:22** [a]Am 5:12 [b]Jer 23:14; 34:16, 22 [c]Eze 18:21, 27, 30-32; 33:14-16 **13:23** [a]Eze 12:24; 13:6; Mic 3:6; Zec 13:3 [b]Eze 13:21; 34:10 [c]Eze 13:9, 21 ◆ **14:1** [a]2Ki 6:32; Eze 8:1; 20:1 [b]Is 29:13; Eze 33:31, 32 **14:3** [a]Eze 20:16 [b]Eze 7:19; 14:4, 7; Zep 1:3 [c]Is 1:15; Jer 11:11; Eze 20:3, 31 **14:4** [a]1Ki 21:20-24; 2Ki 1:16; Is 66:4 [1]Or *when he comes with*; lit *by it* **14:5** [a]Jer 17:10; Zec 7:12 [b]Is 1:4; Jer 2:11; Zec 11:8 [1]Or *all estranged from Me through their idols* **14:6** [a]1Sa 7:3; Ne 1:9; Is 2:20; 30:22; 55:6, 7; Eze 18:30 [b]Eze 8:6; 14:4 [1]Or *Repent* **14:7** [a]Ex 12:48; 20:10 [b]Eze 14:4 **14:8** [a]Jer 44:11; Eze 15:7 [b]Is 65:15; Eze 5:15 [1]Lit *proverbs* **14:9** [a]Jer 6:14, 15; 14:15

Israel may no longer [a]wander from
Me and no longer [b]defile themselves
with all their transgressions. Thus
they will be [c]My people, and I shall be
their God,"' declares Lord Yahweh."

### *Calamitous Judgments of Jerusalem*

**12** Then the word of Yahweh came to
me saying, **13** "Son of man, if a coun-
try sins against Me by [a]committing
unfaithfulness, and I stretch out
My hand against it, break its [b]staff
of bread, send famine against it,
and cut off from it both man and
beast, **14** even [a]*though* these three
men, [b]Noah, [c]Daniel, and [d]Job
were in its midst, by their *own*
righteousness they could *only* de-
liver [e]themselves," declares Lord
Yahweh. **15** "If I were to cause [a]wild
beasts to pass through the land and
they bereaved it of children and
it became desolate so that no one
would pass through it because of
the beasts, **16** *though* these three
men were in its midst, as I live,"
declares Lord Yahweh, "they could
not deliver either *their* sons or *their*
daughters. [a]They alone would be
delivered, but the country would
become desolate. **17** Or *if* I should
[a]bring a sword on that country and
say, 'Let the sword pass through
the country and [b]cut off man
and beast from it,' **18** even *though*
these three men were in its midst,
as I live," declares Lord Yahweh,
"they could not deliver either *their*
sons or *their* daughters, but they
alone would be delivered. **19** Or *if* I
should send a [a]plague against that
country and pour out My wrath
in blood on it to cut off man and
beast from it, **20** even *though* Noah,
Daniel, and Job were in its midst,
as I live," declares Lord Yahweh,
"they could not deliver either *their*
son or *their* daughter. They would
deliver only themselves by their
righteousness."

**21** For thus says Lord Yahweh,
"How much more when [a]I send My
four calamitous judgments against
Jerusalem: sword, famine, wild
beasts, and plague to cut off man
and beast from it! **22** Yet, behold,
[1]survivors will be left in it who
will be brought out, *both* sons and
daughters. Behold, they are going to
come forth to you, and you will [a]see
their way and actions; then you will
be [b]comforted for the calamity which
I have brought against Jerusalem for
everything which I have brought
upon it. **23** Then they will comfort
you when you see their way and
actions, so you will know that I have
not done [a]in vain all that I did [1]to it,"
declares Lord Yahweh.

### *Is Jerusalem Useful for Anything?*

**15** Then the word of Yahweh
came to me, saying, **2** "Son of
man, how is the wood of the [a]vine
*better* than any wood of a branch
which is among the trees of the
forest? **3** Can wood be taken from
it to make [1]anything, or can *men*
take a peg from it on which to hang

---

**14:11** [a]Eze 44:10, 15; 48:11 [b]Eze 11:18; 37:23 [c]Eze 11:20; 34:30; 36:28 **14:13** [a]Eze 15:8; 20:27 [b]Lv 26:26; Is 3:1; Eze 4:16 **14:14** [a]Jer 15:1 [b]Ge 6:8; 7:1; Heb 11:7 [c]Eze 28:3; Da 1:6; 9:21; 10:11 [d]Job 1:1, 5; 42:8, 9 [e]Eze 16:18, 20; 18:20 **14:15** [a]Lv 26:22; Nu 21:6; Eze 5:17; 14:21 **14:16** [a]Ge 19:29; Eze 18:20 **14:17** [a]Lv 26:25; Eze 5:12; 21:3, 4 [b]Eze 25:13; Zep 1:3 **14:19** [a]Jer 14:12; Eze 5:12; 14:21 **14:21** [a]Eze 5:17; 33:27; Am 4:6-10; Rev 6:8 **14:22** [a]Eze 12:16; 36:20 [b]Eze 16:54; 31:16; 32:31 [1]Lit *escaped ones* **14:23** [a]Jer 22:8, 9 [1]Or *in* ◆ **15:2** [a]Ps 80:8-16; Is 5:1-7; Hos 10:1 **15:3** [1]Lit *a work*

any vessel? **4** [1]If it has been put into
the [a]fire for fuel, *and* the fire has
consumed both of its ends, and its
middle part has been charred, is it
*then* useful for [2]anything? **5** Behold,
while it is intact, it is not made into
[1]anything. How much less, when the
fire has consumed it and it is charred,
can it still be made into [1]anything!
**6** Therefore, thus says Lord Yahweh,
'As the wood of the vine among the
trees of the forest, which I have given
to the fire for fuel, so have I given up
the inhabitants of Jerusalem; **7** and
I will [a]give My face *to be* against
them. *Though* they have [b]come out
of the fire, yet the fire will consume
them. Then you will know that I am
Yahweh, when I set My face against
them. **8** Thus I will give over the land
*to* desolation because they have
[a]acted unfaithfully,'" declares Lord
Yahweh.

### *Jerusalem Plays the Harlot*

**16** Then the word of Yahweh
came to me, saying, **2** "Son of
man, [a]make known to Jerusalem her
abominations **3** and say, 'Thus says
Lord Yahweh to Jerusalem, "Your
origin and your birth are from the
land of the Canaanite; your father
was an Amorite and your mother a
Hittite. **4** As for your birth, [a]on the
day you were born your navel cord
was not cut, nor were you washed
with water for cleansing; you were
not rubbed with salt or even wrapped
in cloths. **5** No eye had pity on you
to do any of these things for you,
to have compassion on you. Rather
you were thrown out into the [a,1]open
field, for your soul was abhorred on
the day you were born.

**6** "Then I passed by you and saw
you squirming in your blood. So I
said to you *while you were* in your
blood, 'Live!' Indeed I said to you
*while you were* in your blood, 'Live!'
**7** I [a]made you [1]numerous like plants
of the field. Then you grew up, be-
came tall, and came into the age for
fine ornaments; *your* breasts were
formed, and your hair had grown.
Yet you were naked and bare.

**8** "Then I passed by you and saw
you, and behold, [1]you were at the time
for love; so I [a]spread My skirt over
you and covered your nakedness. I
also [b]swore to you and [c]entered
into a covenant with you so that
you [d]became Mine," declares Lord
Yahweh. **9** "Then I washed you with
water, rinsed your blood off from you,
and [a]anointed you with oil. **10** I also
clothed you with [a]embroidered cloth
and put sandals of porpoise skin on
your feet; and I wrapped you with
fine linen and covered you with silk.
**11** I also adorned you with ornaments
and put [a]bracelets on your hands and
a [b]necklace around your neck. **12** I
also put a [a]ring in your nose, earrings
in your ears, and a [b]splendid crown
on your head. **13** Thus you were
adorned with [a]gold and silver, and
your clothing was of fine linen, silk,
and embroidered cloth. You ate fine
flour, honey, and oil; so you were
exceedingly beautiful and advanced

---

**15:4** [a]Is 27:11; Eze 15:6; 19:14 [1]Or *Behold* [2]Lit *a work* **15:5** [1]Lit *a work* **15:7** [a]Lv 26:17; Ps 34:16; Jer 21:10; Eze 14:8 [b]1Ki 19:17; Is 24:18; Am 9:1-4 **15:8** [a]Eze 14:13; 17:20 ◆**16:2** [a]Is 58:1; Eze 20:4; 22:2 **16:4** [a]Hos 2:3 **16:5** [a]Dt 32:10 [1]Lit *surface* **16:7** [a]Ex 1:7; Dt 1:10 [1]Lit *a myriad* **16:8** [a]Ru 3:9; Jer 2:2 [b]Ge 22:16-18 [c]Ex 24:7, 8 [d]Ex 19:5; Eze 20:5; Hos 2:19, 20 [1]Lit *your time was* **16:9** [a]Ru 3:3 **16:10** [a]Ex 26:36; Eze 16:13, 18; 26:16; 27:7, 16 **16:11** [a]Ge 24:22, 47; Is 3:19; Eze 23:42 [b]Ge 41:42; Pr 1:9 **16:12** [a]Ge 24:47; Is 3:21 [b]Is 28:5; Jer 13:18; Eze 16:14 **16:13** [a]Ps 45:13, 14; Eze 16:17

to [b]royalty. **14** Then your [a]name went forth among the nations on account of your beauty, for it was [b]perfect because of My majesty which I set on you," declares Lord Yahweh.

**15** "But you [a]trusted in your beauty and [b]played the harlot because of your name, and you poured out your harlotries on every passer-by [1]who might be *willing.* **16** You took some of your clothes, made for yourself high places of various colors, and played the harlot on them, [1]which should never come about nor happen. **17** You also took your splendid [a,1]jewelry *made* of My gold and of My silver, which I had given you, and made for yourself male images that you might play the harlot with them. **18** Then you took your embroidered cloth and covered them and gave My oil and My incense before them. **19** Also [a]My bread which I gave you, fine flour, oil, and honey with which I had you eat, you gave before them for a soothing aroma; so it happened," declares Lord Yahweh. **20** "Moreover, you took your sons and daughters, whom you had borne to [a]Me, and [b]sacrificed them to [1]idols to be devoured. Were your harlotries so small a matter? **21** You slaughtered [a]My children and gave them up to [1]idols by [b]causing them to pass through *the fire.* **22** Besides all your abominations and harlotries you did not remember the days of [a]your youth, when you were naked and bare—you were squirming in your blood!

**23** "Now it happened after all your evil—'Woe, woe to you!' declares Lord Yahweh— **24** that you built yourself a [a]shrine and made yourself a [b]high place in every square. **25** You built yourself a high place at the head of [a]every street and made your beauty abominable, and you spread your legs to every passer-by to multiply your harlotry. **26** You also played the harlot with the Egyptians, your [1]lustful neighbors, and you multiplied your harlotry to [a]provoke Me to anger. **27** Behold now, I have stretched out My hand against you and cut off your rations. And I gave you up to the desire of those who hate you, the [a]daughters of the Philistines, who are ashamed of your lewd way. **28** Moreover, you played the harlot with the [a]Assyrians because you were not satisfied; you played the harlot with them and still were not satisfied. **29** You also multiplied your harlotry with the land of merchants, Chaldea, yet even with this you were not satisfied."'"

**30** "How [a]languishing is your heart," declares Lord Yahweh, "while you do all these things, the actions of a [b,1]bold-faced harlot. **31** When you built your shrine at the head of every way and made your high place in every square, in [a]disdaining *your* earnings, you were not like a harlot. **32** You adulteress wife, who takes strangers instead of her husband! **33** [1]Men give gifts to all harlots, but you [a]give your gifts to all your lovers

**16:13** [b]1Sa 10:1; 1Ki 4:21 **16:14** [a]1Ki 10:1, 24 [b]Ps 50:2; Lam 2:15 **16:15** [a]Eze 16:25; 27:3 [b]Is 57:8; Jer 2:20 [1]Lit *to whom it might be* **16:16** [1]Lit *things which had not happened nor will it be* **16:17** [a]Eze 16:11, 12 [1]Lit *articles* **16:19** [a]Hos 2:8 **16:20** [a]Ex 13:2, 12; Dt 29:11, 12 [b]Ps 106:37, 38; Jer 7:31; Eze 20:31; 23:37 [1]Lit *them* **16:21** [a]Ex 13:2 [b]2Ki 17:17; Jer 19:5 [1]Lit *them* **16:22** [a]Jer 2:2 **16:24** [a]Jer 11:13; Eze 16:31, 39; 20:28, 29 [b]Ps 78:58; Is 57:7 **16:25** [a]Pr 9:14 **16:26** [a]Jer 7:18, 19; Eze 8:17 [1]Lit *great of flesh* **16:27** [a]Is 9:12; Eze 16:57 **16:28** [a]2Ki 16:7, 10-18; 2Chr 28:16, 20-23; Jer 2:18, 36; Eze 23:12; Hos 10:6 **16:30** [a]Pr 9:13; Is 1:3; Jer 4:22 [b]Is 3:9; Jer 3:3 [1]Lit *domineering* **16:31** [a]Is 52:3 **16:33** [a]Is 57:9; Eze 16:41; Hos 8:9, 10 [1]Lit *They*

to bribe them to come to you from all
around for your harlotries. **34** Thus
you are the opposite of those women
in your harlotries, in that no one
plays the harlot [1]as you do, because
you give away *your* earnings and no
earnings are given to you; thus you
are the opposite."
**35** Therefore, O harlot, hear the
word of Yahweh. **36** Thus says Lord
Yahweh, "Because your lewdness
was poured out and your nakedness
uncovered through your harlotries
with your lovers and with all your
abominable [a]idols, and because of
the blood of your sons which you
gave to [1]idols, **37** therefore, behold,
I will [a]gather all your lovers with
whom you took pleasure, even all
those whom you loved *and* all those
whom you [b]hated. So I will gather
them against you from all around and
[c]uncover your nakedness to them
that they may see all your nakedness.
**38** Thus I will [a]judge you like women
who commit adultery or shed blood
are judged; and I will bring on you the
blood of [b]wrath and jealousy. **39** I will
also give you into [1]the hands of your
lovers, and they will pull down your
shrines, tear down your high places,
[a]strip you of your clothing, take away
your [2]splendid jewelry, and will leave
you naked and bare. **40** They will
*bring up an* [a]assembly against you,
and they will stone you and cut you
to pieces with their swords. **41** They
will [a]burn your houses with fire and
execute judgments on you in the
sight of many women. Then I will
[b]make you cease from playing the
harlot, and you will also no longer
give [1]*your* earnings *to your lovers.*
**42** So I [a]will [1]cause My wrath against
you to be at rest, and My jealousy
will depart from you, and I will be
quiet, and I will [b]not be provoked
anymore. **43** Because you have [a]not
remembered the days of your youth
but [1]have [b]enraged Me by all these
things, behold, I in turn will [c]bring
your way down on your own head,"
declares Lord Yahweh, "so that you
will not commit this lewdness on top
of all your *other* abominations.
**44** "Behold, everyone who quotes
[a]proverbs will quote *this* proverb
concerning you, saying, '[1]Like
mother, [1]like daughter.' **45** You are
the daughter of your mother, who
loathed her husband and children.
You are also the [a]sister of your sisters,
who [b]loathed their husbands and
children. Your mother was a Hittite
and your father an Amorite. **46** Now
your [a]older sister is Samaria, who
lives [1]north of you with her [2]daugh-
ters; and your younger sister, who
lives [3]south of you, is [b]Sodom with
her daughters. **47** Yet you have not
merely walked in their ways or done
according to their abominations; but,
as if that were [a]too little, you acted
[b]more corruptly in all your ways

---

**16:34** [1]Lit *after you* **16:36** [a]Jer 19:5; Eze 20:31; 23:37 [1]Lit *them* **16:37** [a]Jer 13:22, 26; Eze 23:9, 22; Hos 2:3, 10; Na 3:5, 6 [b]Eze 23:17, 28 [c]Is 47:3 **16:38** [a]Eze 23:45 [b]Ps 79:3, 5; Jer 18:21; Eze 23:25; Zep 1:17 **16:39** [a]Eze 23:26; Hos 2:3 [1]Lit *their hands, and they* [2]Lit *articles of beauty* **16:40** [a]Eze 23:47; Hab 1:6-10 **16:41** [a]2Ki 25:9; Jer 39:8; 52:13 [b]Eze 23:48 [1]Lit *a harlot's hire* **16:42** [a]2Sa 24:25; Eze 5:13; 21:17; Zec 6:8 [b]Is 40:1, 2; 54:9, 10; Eze 39:29 [1]Or *calm* **16:43** [a]Ps 78:42; 106:13; Eze 16:22 [b]Is 63:10; Eze 6:9 [c]Eze 11:21; 22:31 [1]As in ancient versions; Heb *are angry against* **16:44** [a]1Sa 24:13; Eze 12:22, 23; 18:2, 3 [1]Lit *Her* **16:45** [a]Eze 23:2 [b]Is 1:4; Eze 23:37-39; Zec 11:8 **16:46** [a]Jer 3:8-11; Eze 23:4 [b]Ge 13:10-13; 18:20; Eze 16:48, 49, 53-56, 61 [1]Lit *on your left* [2]Environs, so through v 55 [3]Lit *from your right* **16:47** [a]1Ki 16:31 [b]2Ki 21:9; Eze 5:6; 16:48, 51

than they. **48** As I live," declares Lord
Yahweh, "Sodom your sister and her
daughters have [a]not done as you and
your daughters have done. **49** Behold,
this was the iniquity of your sister
Sodom: she and her daughters had
[a]lofty pride, [b]abundant food, and
[c]quiet ease, but she did not strength-
en the hand of the [d]afflicted and
needy. **50** Then they were haughty
and committed [a]abominations before
Me. So I [b]removed them [1]when I saw
*it*. **51** Furthermore, Samaria did not
commit half of your sins, for you have
multiplied your abominations more
than they. Thus you have made your
sisters appear [a]righteous by all your
abominations which you have done.
**52** Also bear your dishonor in that you
have [1]made judgment favorable for
your sisters. Because of your sins in
which you acted [a]more abominably
than they, they are more in the right
than you. Yes, be also ashamed and
bear your dishonor, in that you made
your sisters appear righteous.

**53** "Nevertheless, I will [1]return their
captivity, the captivity of Sodom and
her daughters, the captivity of Samaria
and her daughters, and [2]along with
them [3]your own captivity, **54** in order
that you may bear your dishonor and
feel [a]dishonor for all that you have
done when you become [b]a comfort
to them. **55** Your sisters, Sodom with
her daughters and Samaria with her
daughters, [1]will return to their former
state, and you with your daughters
will *also* return to your former state.
**56** As *the name of* your sister Sodom
was not heard in your mouth in your
day of lofty pride, **57** before your
[a]wickedness was uncovered, [1]so
now you have become the [b]reproach
of the daughters of [2]Edom and of all
who are around her, of the daughters
of the Philistines—those all around
*you* who despise you. **58** You have
[a]borne *the penalty of* your lewdness
and abominations," declares Yahweh.
**59** For thus says Lord Yahweh, "I will
also do with you as you have done,
you who have [a]despised the oath by
breaking the covenant.

### *Yahweh's Everlasting Covenant*

**60** "Nevertheless, I Myself will re-
member My covenant with you in
the days of your youth, and I will
establish an [a]everlasting covenant
with you. **61** Then you will [a]remem-
ber your ways and feel dishonor
when you receive your sisters, *both*
your older and your younger; and I
will give them to you as daughters,
but not because of your covenant.
**62** Thus I will [a]establish My covenant
with you, and you shall [b]know that
I am Yahweh, **63** so that you may
[a]remember and be ashamed and
[b]never open your mouth anymore
because of your dishonor, when I
have [c]atoned for you for all that you
have done," declares Lord Yahweh.

---

**16:48** [a]Mt 10:15; 11:23, 24 **16:49** [a]Ge 19:9; Ps 138:6; Is 3:9; Eze 28:2, 9, 17 [b]Ge 13:10; Is 22:13; Am 6:4-6 [c]*Lk 12:16-20; 16:19* [d]Eze 18:7, 12, 16 **16:50** [a]Ge 13:13; 18:20; 19:5 [b]Ge 19:24, 25 [1]Many ancient mss and versions *as you have seen* **16:51** [a]Jer 3:8-11 **16:52** [a]Eze 16:47, 48, 51 [1]Lit *mediated for* **16:53** [1]Or *restore* [2]Lit *in their midst* [3]Lit *the captivity of your captivity* **16:54** [a]Jer 2:26 [b]Eze 14:22, 23 **16:55** [1]Heb also includes *will return...state* after Sodom **16:57** [a]Eze 16:36, 37 [b]2Ki 16:5-7; 2Chr 28:5, 6, 18-23; Eze 5:14, 15; 22:4 [1]Lit *as at the time of* [2]As in many mss and one version; M.T. *Aram* **16:58** [a]Eze 23:49 **16:59** [a]Is 24:5; Eze 17:19 **16:60** [a]Is 55:3; Jer 32:38-41; Eze 37:26 **16:61** [a]Jer 50:4, 5; Eze 6:9 **16:62** [a]Eze 20:37; 34:25; 37:26 [b]Jer 24:7; Eze 20:43, 44 **16:63** [a]Eze 36:31, 32; Da 9:7, 8 [b]Ps 39:9; Ro 3:19 [c]Ps 65:3; 78:38; 79:9

### *Parable of Two Eagles and a Vine*

**17** Now the word of Yahweh
came to me saying, **2** "Son of
man, propound a riddle and speak a
[a]parable to the house of Israel, **3** and
you will say, 'Thus says Lord Yahweh,
"A great [a]eagle with [b]great wings,
long pinions, and a full plumage
of [1]many colors came to [c]Lebanon
and took away the top of the cedar.
**4** He plucked off the topmost of its
young twigs and brought it to a land
of merchants; he set it in a city of
traders. **5** He also took some of the
seed of the land and planted it in a
[a]field *fit for* seed. He [1]placed *it* be-
side abundant waters; he set it *like*
a [b]willow. **6** Then it sprouted and
became a low, spreading vine with
its foliage turned toward him, but its
roots remained under it. So it became
a vine and yielded shoots and sent
out branches.
**7** "But there was [1]another great
eagle with great wings and much
plumage; and behold, this vine bent
its roots toward him and sent out its
foliage toward him from the beds
where it was [a]planted, that he might
water it. **8** It was planted in a good
field beside abundant waters, that it
might yield branches and bear fruit
*and* become a majestic vine."' **9** Say,
'Thus says Lord Yahweh, "Will it suc-
ceed? Will he not pull up its roots and
cut off its fruit, so that it dries up—so
that all its sprouting leaves dry up?
And neither by great [1]strength nor by
many people can it be raised from its
roots *again*. **10** And behold, though
it is planted, will it succeed? Will it
not [a]completely dry up as soon as
the east wind strikes it—dry up on
the beds where it sprouted?"'"

### *The King Shall Die in Babylon*

**11** Moreover, the word of Yahweh
came to me, saying, **12** "Say now to
the [a]rebellious house, 'Do you not
[b]know what these things *mean*?'
Say, 'Behold, the [c]king of Babylon
came to Jerusalem, took its king and
princes, and brought them to him in
Babylon. **13** He took one of the royal
[a]seed and cut a covenant with him
and brought him under [b]oath. He
also took away the [c]dominant one
of the land, **14** that the kingdom
might [a,1]become lowly, not lifting
itself up, *but* keeping his covenant
that it might continue. **15** But he
[a]rebelled against him by sending his
messengers to Egypt that they might
give him horses and many [1]troops.
Will he succeed? Will he who does
such things [b]escape? Can he indeed
break the covenant and escape? **16** As
I live,' declares Lord Yahweh, 'Surely
in the [1]country of the king who made
him king, whose oath he [a]despised
and whose covenant he broke, [b,2]in
Babylon he shall die. **17** [a]And Pharaoh
with *his* mighty military force and
great assembly will not [1]help him in
the war, when they cast up ramps
and build siege walls to cut off many
lives. **18** Now he despised the oath by
breaking the covenant, and behold,

---

◆ **17:2** [a]Eze 20:49; 24:3 **17:3** [a]Jer 48:40; Eze 17:12; Hos 8:1 [b]Da 4:22 [c]Jer 22:23 [1]Or *embroidery*, cf. 16:18 **17:5** [a]Dt 8:7-9 [b]Is 44:4 [1]Lit *took* **17:7** [a]Eze 31:4 [1]As in several ancient versions; M.T. *one* **17:9** [1]Lit *arm* **17:10** [a]Eze 19:14; Hos 13:15 **17:12** [a]Eze 2:3-5 [b]Eze 12:9-11; 24:19 [c]2Ki 24:11, 12, 15; Eze 1:2; 17:3 **17:13** [a]2Ki 24:17; Eze 17:5 [b]2Chr 36:13 [c]2Ki 24:15, 16 **17:14** [a]Eze 29:14 [1]Lit *low* **17:15** [a]2Ki 24:20; 2Chr 36:13; Jer 52:3; Eze 17:7 [b]Jer 34:3; 38:18, 23; Eze 17:18 [1]Lit *people* **17:16** [a]2Ki 24:17, 20; Eze 16:59; 17:13, 18, 19 [b]Jer 52:11; Eze 12:13 [1]Lit *place* [2]Lit *with him in Babylon* **17:17** [a]Is 36:6; Jer 37:5, 7; Eze 29:6, 7 [1]Lit *act with*

he [a,1]pledged his allegiance, yet did
all these things; he shall not escape.'"
19 Therefore, thus says Lord Yahweh,
"As I live, surely My oath which he
despised and My covenant which
he broke, I will [1]put on his head.
20 I will spread My [a]net over him,
and he will be [b]caught in My snare.
Then I will bring him to Babylon and
[c]enter into judgment with him there
*regarding* the unfaithful act which he
has committed against Me. 21 All the
[a,1]choice men in all his troops will fall
by the sword, and the remnant will be
scattered to every wind; and you will
know that I, Yahweh, have spoken."
22 Thus says Lord Yahweh, "I will
also take *a sprig* from the lofty top of
the cedar and set *it* out; I will pluck
from the topmost of its young twigs
a tender one, and I will plant *it* on an
[a]exalted and lofty mountain. 23 On
the high mountain of Israel I will
plant it, that it may lift up [1]boughs
and yield fruit and become a majestic
[a]cedar. And birds of every [2]kind will
dwell under it; they will dwell in
the shade of its [3]branches. 24 And
all the [a]trees of the field will know
that I am Yahweh; I bring down the
exalted tree, exalt the low tree, dry
up the green tree, and make the dry
tree [b]flourish. I am Yahweh; I have
spoken, and I will do *it*."

### *The Soul Who Sins Will Die*

**18** Then the word of Yahweh came
to me, saying, 2 "[a]What do you
mean by using this proverb concern-
ing the land of Israel, saying,

'[b]The fathers eat the
sour grapes,
But the children's teeth
[1]are set on edge'?

3 "As I live," declares Lord Yahweh,
"you are surely not going to use this
proverb in Israel anymore. 4 Behold,
[a]all [1]souls are Mine; the [2]soul of the
father as well as the [2]soul of the son
is Mine. The [3]soul who [b]sins will die.
5 "But if a man is righteous and
does justice and righteousness,
6 and does not [a]eat at the mountain
*shrines* or [b]lift up his eyes to the idols
of the house of Israel, or [c]defile his
neighbor's wife or approach a woman
during her menstrual period— 7 if a
man does not mistreat anyone, but
[a]returns to the debtor his pledge,
[b]does not commit robbery, *but*
[c]gives his bread to the hungry and
covers the naked with clothing, 8 if
he does not lend *money* on [a]interest
or take [b]increase, *if* he turns his hand
from injustice *and* [c]does true justice
between man and man, 9 *if* he walks
in [a]My statutes and My judgments
*and* is careful to do *the* truth—[b]he
is righteous *and* will surely [c]live,"
declares Lord Yahweh.
10 "Then he may [1]have a violent
son who sheds blood and who does
any of these things to a brother
11 (though he himself did not do any
of these things), that is, he even eats
at the mountain *shrines* and [a]defiles

**17:18** [a]1Chr 29:24 [1]Lit *gave his hand* **17:19** [1]Lit *give it* **17:20** [a]Eze 12:13; 32:3 [b]Jer 39:5-7 [c]Jer 2:35; Eze 20:35, 36 **17:21** [a]2Ki 25:5, 11; Eze 5:2, 10, 12-14 [1]As in many ancient mss and versions; M.T. *fugitives* **17:22** [a]Ps 72:16; Eze 20:40; 37:22 **17:23** [a]Ps 92:12 [1]Or *branches*, cf. 17:8 [2]Lit *wing* [3]Or *foliage*, cf. 17:7 **17:24** [a]Ps 96:12; Is 55:12 [b]Am 9:11 ◆**18:2** [a]Is 3:15 [b]Jer 31:29; Lam 5:7 [1]Lit *become dull* **18:4** [a]Nu 16:22; 27:16; Is 42:5; 57:16 [b]Eze 18:20; Ro 6:23 [1]Or *lives* [2]Or *life* [3]Or *person* **18:6** [a]Eze 6:13; 18:15; 22:9 [b]Dt 4:19; Eze 18:12, 15; 20:24; 33:25 [c]Eze 18:15; 22:11 **18:7** [a]Dt 24:13; Eze 33:15; Am 2:8 [b]Lv 19:13; Am 3:10 [c]Dt 15:11; Eze 18:16; Mt 25:35-40; Lk 3:11 **18:8** [a]Ex 22:25; Dt 23:19, 20 [b]Lv 25:36 [c]Zec 7:9; 8:16 **18:9** [a]Lv 18:5 [b]Ro 8:1 [c]Am 5:4; Hab 2:4; Ro 1:17 **18:10** [1]Lit *beget* **18:11** [a]1Co 6:9

his neighbor's wife; **12** he mistreats
the [a]afflicted and needy, [b]commits
robbery, does not return a pledge, but
lifts up his eyes to the idols *and* [c]does
abominations; **13** he [a]lends *money* on
interest and takes increase; will he
live? He will not live! He has done
all these abominations; he will surely
be put to death; his [b]blood will be on
himself.

**14** "Now behold, he [1]has a son who
has seen all his father's sins which he
has done. And he [a]saw *this* but does
not do likewise. **15** He does not eat at
the mountain *shrines* or lift up his
eyes to the idols of the house of Isra-
el, or defile his neighbor's wife **16** or
mistreat anyone, or retain a pledge
or commit robbery, *but* he [a]gives
his bread to the hungry and covers
the naked with clothing; **17** he turns
his hand away from [1]the afflicted,
does not take interest or increase,
*but* does My judgments *and* walks
in My statutes; [a]he will not die for
his father's iniquity; he will surely
live. **18** As for his father, because
he practiced extortion, robbed *his*
brother, and did what was not good
among his people, behold, he will die
for his iniquity.

**19** "Yet you say, '[a]Why should the
son not bear the punishment for
the father's iniquity?' But the son
has done [b]justice and righteousness
and has kept all My statutes and done
them. He shall surely live. **20** The soul
who [a]sins will die. The [b]son will not
bear the iniquity of the father, nor
will the father bear the iniquity of
the son; the [c]righteousness of the
righteous will be upon himself, and
the wickedness of the wicked will be
upon himself.

**21** "But if the [a]wicked man turns
from all his sins which he has done
and keeps all My statutes and does
justice and righteousness, he shall
surely live; he shall not die. **22** [a]All
his transgressions which he has done
will not be remembered against him;
because of his [b]righteousness which
he has done, he will live. **23** [a]Do I have
any pleasure in the death of the
wicked," declares Lord Yahweh, "is
it not that he should [b]turn from his
ways and live?

**24** "But when a righteous man
[a]turns away from his righteousness,
does injustice, and does according to
all the abominations that a wicked
man does, will he live? [b]All his righ-
teous deeds which he has done will
not be remembered for his [c]unfaith-
fulness which he has committed and
his sin which he has committed; for
them he will die. **25** Yet you say, '[a]The
way of the Lord is not right.' Hear
now, O house of Israel! Is [b]My way
not right? Is it not your ways that are
not right? **26** When a righteous man
turns away from his righteousness,
does injustice, and dies because of
it, for his injustice which he has
done he will die. **27** Again, when a
wicked man turns away [a]from his

**18:12** [a]Am 4:1; Zec 7:10 [b]Is 59:6, 7; Jer 22:3, 17; Eze 7:23; 18:7, 16, 18 [c]2Ki 21:11; Eze 8:6, 17
**18:13** [a]Ex 22:25 [b]Eze 33:4, 5 **18:14** [a]2Chr 29:6-10; 34:21 [1]Lit *begets* **18:16** [a]Job 31:16, 20; Ps 41:1; Is 58:7, 10; Eze 18:7 **18:17** [a]Ro 2:7 [1]Gr *iniquity*, as in 18:8 **18:19** [a]Ex 20:5; Jer 15:4; Eze 18:2 [b]Eze 18:9; 20:18-20; Zec 1:3-6 **18:20** [a]2Ki 14:6; 22:18-20; Eze 18:4 [b]Dt 24:16; Jer 31:30 [c]1Ki 8:32; Is 3:10, 11; Mt 16:27; Ro 2:6-9 **18:21** [a]Eze 18:27, 28; 33:12, 19 **18:22** [a]Is 43:25; Jer 50:20; Eze 18:24; 33:16; Mic 7:19 [b]Ps 18:20-24
**18:23** [a]Eze 18:32; 33:11 [b]Ps 147:11; Mic 7:18 **18:24** [a]1Sa 15:11; 2Chr 24:2, 17-22; Eze 3:20; 18:26; 33:18 [b]Eze 18:22; Ga 3:3, 4 [c]Pr 21:16; Eze 17:20; 20:27 **18:25** [a]Eze 18:29; 33:17, 20; Mal 2:17; 3:13-15 [b]Ge 18:25; Jer 12:1; Zep 3:5 **18:27** [a]Is 1:18; 55:7

wickedness which he has done and
does justice and righteousness, he
will preserve his life.
28 Again, he
considered and turned away from
all his transgressions which he had
done; he shall surely live; he shall not
die.
29 But the house of Israel says,
'The way of the Lord is not right.' Are
My ways not right, O house of Israel?
Is it not your ways that are not right?
30 "Therefore I will judge you,
O house of Israel, each according
to his way," declares Lord Yahweh.
"[a,1]Turn back and turn away from all
your transgressions, so that iniquity
may not become a stumbling block to
you.
31 [a]Cast away from yourselves all
your transgressions which you have
committed and [1]make yourselves a
[b]new heart and a new spirit! Now
why will you die, O house of Israel?
32 For I have [a]no pleasure in the
death of anyone who dies," declares
Lord Yahweh. "Therefore, [1]turn back
and live."

### *A Lament for the Princes of Israel*

19 "As for you, take up a [a]lamentation for the [b]princes of Israel
2 and say,
'[1]What was your mother?
A lioness among lions!
She lay down
among young lions;
She reared her cubs.
3 'So she brought up
one of her cubs;
He became a lion,
And he learned
to tear *his* prey;
He devoured men.
4 'Then nations heard
about him;
He was captured in their pit,
And they [a]brought
him with hooks
To the land of Egypt.
5 'Then she saw,
as she waited,
*That* her hope was lost,
So she took [1]another
of her cubs
And made him a young lion.
6 'And he [a]walked about
among the lions;
He became a young lion;
He learned to tear *his* prey;
He devoured men.
7 'He [1]knew *how to destroy*
their [2]fortified towers
And laid waste their cities;
And the land was
in desolation, as well as
its fullness
Because of the sound
of his roaring.
8 'Then [a]nations put
*themselves* against him
All around
from *their* provinces,
And they spread their
net over him;
He was captured
in their pit.
9 '[a]They put him
in a cage with hooks
And [b]brought him
to the king of Babylon;
They brought him
in hunting nets
So that his voice would
be heard no more

**18:30** [a]Eze 14:6; 33:11; Hos 12:6 [1]Or *Repent* **18:31** [a]Is 1:16, 17; 55:7 [b]Ps 51:10; Eze 11:19; 36:26 [1]Or *do*, cf. 18:24, 26, 27 **18:32** [a]Eze 18:23; 33:11 [1]Or *repent* ◆ **19:1** [a]Eze 2:10; 19:14 [b]2Ki 23:29, 30, 34; 24:6, 12; 25:5-7 **19:2** [1]Or *Why did your mother, a lioness, lie down among lions; among young lions rear her cubs?* **19:4** [a]2Ki 23:34; 2Chr 36:4, 6 **19:5** [1]Lit *one* **19:6** [a]2Ki 24:9; 2Chr 36:9 **19:7** [1]Targum *destroy* [2]Or *widows* **19:8** [a]2Ki 24:11 **19:9** [a]2Chr 36:6 [b]2Ki 24:15

On the mountains of Israel.
10 'Your mother was [a]like
a vine in your [1]vineyard,
Planted by the waters;
It was fruitful and
full of branches
Because of
abundant waters.
11 'And it had [a,1]strong
thick branches *fit*
for scepters of rulers,
And its [b]height was exalted
above the clouds
So that it was seen in its
exaltedness with
the mass of its foliage.
12 'But it was [a]uprooted
in wrath;
It was [b]cast down
to the ground;
And the [c]east wind
dried up its fruit.
Its [d,1]strong thick branch
[2]was torn off
So that [3]it dried up;
The fire consumed it.
13 'So now it is planted
in the [a]wilderness,
In a dry and thirsty land.
14 'And [a]fire has gone out
from *its* thick branch;
It has consumed its
shoots *and* fruit,
So that there is not in it
a [1]*strong* thick branch,
A scepter to rule.'"
This is a lamentation and has become
a lamentation.

### *The Abominations of the Fathers of Israel*

20 Now it happened in the sev-
enth year, in the fifth *month*,
on the tenth of the month, *that* [1]some
of the [a]elders of Israel came to inquire
of Yahweh and sat before me. 2 And
the word of Yahweh came to me
saying, 3 "Son of man, speak to the
elders of Israel and say to them, 'Thus
says Lord Yahweh, "Do you come to
inquire of Me? As I live," declares
Lord Yahweh, "[a]I will not be inquired
of by you."' 4 Will you judge them, will
you judge them, son of man? [a]Make
them know the abominations of their
fathers 5 and say to them, 'Thus says
Lord Yahweh, "On the day when
I [a]chose Israel and [1]swore to the
seed of the house of Jacob and made
Myself known to them in the land of
Egypt, when I swore to them, saying,
[b]I am Yahweh your God, 6 on that day
I swore to them, [a]to bring them out
from the land of Egypt into a land that
I had [1]selected for them, [b]flowing with
milk and honey, which is [c]the glory of
all lands. 7 I said to them, '[a]Cast away,
each of you, the detestable things of
his eyes, and [b]do not defile yourselves
with the idols of Egypt; [c]I am Yahweh
your God.' 8 But they [a]rebelled against
Me and were not willing to listen to
Me; each one did not cast away the
detestable things of their eyes, nor
did they forsake the [b]idols of Egypt.
Then I said I would [c]pour out My
wrath on them, to [1]spend My anger

**19:10** [a]Ps 80:8-11 [1]As in some ancient mss; M.T. *blood* **19:11** [a]Ps 80:15 [b]Eze 31:3 [1]Lit *rods of strength* **19:12** [a]Jer 31:28 [b]Lam 2:1; Eze 28:17 [c]Eze 17:10; Hos 13:15 [d]Is 27:11; Eze 19:11 [1]Lit *rods of her strength* [2]As in Gr; M.T. *they were* [3]As in Gr; M.T. *they* **19:13** [a]2Ki 24:12-16; Eze 19:10; 20:35; Hos 2:3 **19:14** [a]Eze 15:4; 20:47, 48 [1]Lit *rod of strength* ◆ **20:1** [a]Eze 8:1, 11, 12 [1]Lit *men* **20:3** [a]Eze 14:3 **20:4** [a]Eze 16:2; 22:2; Mt 23:32 **20:5** [a]Ex 6:6-8 [b]Ex 6:2, 3 [1]Lit *lifted up My hand*, so in ch **20:6** [a]Jer 32:22 [b]Ex 13:5; 33:3 [c]Ps 48:2 [1]Lit *spied out* **20:7** [a]Ex 20:4, 5; 22:20 [b]Lv 18:3; Dt 29:16-18 [c]Ex 20:2 **20:8** [a]Dt 9:7; Is 63:10 [b]Ex 32:1-9 [c]Eze 5:13; 7:8; 20:13, 21 [1]Or make a *complete destruction with*, so in ch, cf. 20:13, 17

against them in the midst of the land
of Egypt. **9** But I acted [a]for the sake
of My name, that it should [b]not be
profaned in the sight of the nations
among whom they *lived*, in whose
sight I made Myself known to them
by bringing them out of the land of
Egypt. **10** So I took them out of the
land of Egypt and brought them into
the [a]wilderness. **11** I gave them My
[a]statutes and made them know My
judgments, [b]which, if a man does
them, he will live by them. **12** And
I also gave them My sabbaths to be
a [a]sign between Me and them, that
they might know that I am Yahweh
who sanctifies them. **13** But the house
of Israel [a]rebelled against Me in the
wilderness. They did not walk in
My statutes, and they rejected My
judgments, [b]which, if a man does
them, he will live by them; and My
[c]sabbaths they greatly profaned.
Then I said *I would* [d]pour out My
wrath on them in the wilderness,
to completely destroy them. **14** But I
acted for the sake of My name, that
it should not be profaned in the sight
of the nations, before whose sight
I had brought them out. **15** Also [a]I
swore to them in the wilderness
that I would not bring them into the
land which I had given them, flowing
with milk and honey, which is the
glory of all lands, **16** because they
rejected My judgments, and as for My
statutes, they did not walk in them;
they even profaned My sabbaths,
for their [a]heart continually walked
after their idols. **17** Yet My eye had
pity on them rather than bringing
them to ruin, and I did not make *of*
them a [a]complete destruction in the
wilderness.

**18** "I said to their [a,1]children in
the wilderness, '[b]Do not walk in the
statutes of your fathers and do not
keep their judgments and do not
defile yourselves with their idols.
**19** [a]I am Yahweh your God; [b]walk in
My statutes and keep My judgments
and do them. **20** [a]Keep My sabbaths
holy; and they shall be a sign be-
tween Me and you, that you may
know that I am Yahweh your God.'
**21** But the [a]children rebelled against
Me; they did not walk in My statutes,
nor were they careful to do My judg-
ments, which, *if* a man does them,
he will live by them; they profaned
My sabbaths. So I said *I would* pour
out My wrath on them, to spend My
anger against them in the wilderness.
**22** But I [a]turned back My hand and
acted [b]for the sake of My name, that
it should not be profaned in the sight
of the nations in whose sight I had
brought them out. **23** Also I swore to
them in the wilderness that I would
[a]scatter them among the nations
and [1]disperse them among the lands
**24** because they had not done My
judgments, but had rejected My stat-
utes and had profaned My sabbaths,
and [a]their eyes were *going* after the
idols of their fathers. **25** And I also
gave them statutes that were [a]not
good and judgments by which they

---

**20:9** [a]Ex 32:11-14; Eze 20:14, 22; 36:21, 22 [b]Eze 39:7 **20:10** [a]Ex 19:1 **20:11** [a]Ex 20:1-23:33 [b]Lv 18:5; Eze 20:13 **20:12** [a]Ex 31:13, 17; Eze 20:20 **20:13** [a]Nu 14:11, 12, 22; Eze 20:8 [b]Lv 18:5 [c]Is 56:6; Eze 20:21 [d]Ex 32:10; Dt 9:8; Eze 20:8, 21 **20:15** [a]Nu 14:30; Ps 95:11; 106:26 **20:16** [a]Eze 11:21; 14:3-7; 20:8 **20:17** [a]Jer 4:27; 5:18; Eze 11:13 **20:18** [a]Nu 14:31; Dt 4:3-6 [b]Zec 1:4 [1]Lit *sons* **20:19** [a]Ex 6:7; 20:2 [b]Dt 5:32, 33; 6:1, 2; 8:1, 2; 11:1; 12:1 **20:20** [a]Jer 17:22 **20:21** [a]Nu 21:5; 25:1-3 **20:22** [a]Job 13:21; Ps 78:38; Eze 20:17 [b]Is 48:9-11; Jer 14:7, 21; Eze 20:9, 14 **20:23** [a]Lv 26:33; Dt 4:27; 28:64 [1]Or *scatter*, cf. Ps 44:11; 106:27 **20:24** [a]Eze 6:9 **20:25** [a]Ps 81:12; Is 66:4; Ro 1:21-25, 28

could not live; **26** and I pronounced
them [a]unclean because of their
gifts, in that they [b]caused all [1]their
firstborn to pass through *the fire* so
that I might make them desolate, in
order that they might [c]know that I
am Yahweh."'

**27** "Therefore, son of man, [a]speak
to the house of Israel and say to them,
'Thus says Lord Yahweh, "Yet in this
your fathers have [b]blasphemed Me
by [c]acting unfaithfully against Me.
**28** Indeed, I [a]brought them into the
land which I swore to give to them,
and they saw every [b]high hill and
every leafy tree, and they offered
there their sacrifices, and there
they gave the provocation of their
offering. There also they made their
soothing aroma, and there they
poured out their drink offerings.
**29** Then I said to them, 'What is the
high place to which you are going?'
So its name is called [1]Bamah to this
day."' **30** Therefore, say to the house
of Israel, 'Thus says Lord Yahweh,
"Will you defile yourselves in the way
of your [a]fathers and play the harlot
after their detestable things? **31** [1]And
when you offer your gifts, when you
[a]cause your sons to pass through the
fire, you are defiling yourselves with
all your idols to this day. And shall
I be inquired of by you, O house
of Israel? As I live," declares Lord
Yahweh, "I will not be inquired of by
you. **32** And what [a]comes upon your
spirit will not happen, when you say:
'We will be like the nations, like the
families of the lands, [b]to minister to
wood and stone.'

### *Yahweh Judges His People*

**33** "As I live," declares Lord Yahweh,
"surely with a strong hand and with
an [a]outstretched arm and with wrath
poured out, I shall be [b]king over you.
**34** And I will [a]bring you out from
the peoples and gather you from
the lands where you are scattered,
with a strong hand and with an
outstretched arm and with [b]wrath
poured out; **35** and I will bring you
into the [a]wilderness of the peoples,
and there I will enter into judgment
with you face to face. **36** As I [a]entered
into judgment with your fathers in
the [b]wilderness of the land of Egypt,
so I will enter into judgment with
you," declares Lord Yahweh. **37** "And
I will make you [a]pass under the rod,
and I will bring you into the bond
of the covenant; **38** and I will [a]purge
from you the rebels and those who
transgress against Me; I will bring
them out of the land where they
sojourn, but they will [b]not enter the
[1]land of Israel. Thus you will know
that I am Yahweh.

**39** "As for you, O house of Israel,"
thus says Lord Yahweh, "[a]Go, serve
everyone his idols; [1]but after *this* you
will surely listen to Me, and My holy
name you will [b]profane no longer

**20:26** [a]Lv 18:21; 20:2-5; Is 63:17; Eze 20:30; Ro 11:8 [b]Jer 7:31; 19:4-9 [c]Eze 6:7; 20:12, 20 [1]Lit *that which opens the womb* **20:27** [a]Eze 2:7; 3:4, 11, 27 [b]Nu 15:30; Ro 2:24 [c]Eze 18:24; 39:23, 26 **20:28** [a]Jos 23:3, 14; Ne 9:22-26; Ps 78:55; Jer 2:7 [b]1Ki 14:23; Ps 78:58; Is 57:5-7; Jer 3:6; Eze 6:13 **20:29** [1]Lit *high place* **20:30** [a]Jdg 2:19; Jer 7:26; 16:12 **20:31** [a]Ps 106:37-39; Jer 7:31; Eze 16:20; 20:26 [1]Lit *In your lifting up* **20:32** [a]Eze 11:5 [b]Jer 2:25; 44:17 **20:33** [a]Jer 21:5 [b]Jer 51:57 **20:34** [a]Is 27:12, 13; Eze 20:38; 34:16 [b]Jer 42:18; 44:6; Lam 2:4 **20:35** [a]Eze 19:13; 20:36; Hos 2:14 **20:36** [a]Nu 11:1-35; Ps 106:15; Eze 20:13, 21; 1Co 10:5-10 [b]Dt 32:10 **20:37** [a]Lv 27:32; Jer 33:13 **20:38** [a]Eze 34:17-22; Am 9:9, 10; Zec 13:8, 9; Mal 3:3; 4:1-3 [b]Nu 14:29, 30; Ps 95:11; Eze 13:9; 20:15, 16; Heb 4:3 [1]Lit *ground, soil* **20:39** [a]Jer 44:25, 26 [b]Is 1:13-15; Eze 23:38, 39; 43:7 [1]Or *and afterwards, if you will not listen to Me, but*

with your gifts and with your idols.
**40** For on My holy mountain, on the
high mountain of Israel," declares
Lord Yahweh, "there the whole house
of Israel, [a]all of them, will serve Me
in the land; there I will [b]accept
them, and there I will [1]seek your
contributions and the choicest of
your gifts, with all your holy things.
**41** [1]As a soothing aroma I will accept
you when I [a]bring you out from the
peoples and gather you from the
lands where you are scattered; and I
will prove Myself [b]holy among you in
the sight of the nations. **42** And [a]you
will know that I am Yahweh, [b]when I
bring you onto the ground of Israel,
into the [c]land which I swore to give
to your fathers. **43** And there you will
[a]remember your ways and all your
deeds with which you have defiled
yourselves; and you will [b]loathe
yourselves to your own faces for all
the evil things that you have done.
**44** Then [a]you will know that I am
Yahweh when I have dealt with you
[b]for My name's sake, not according to
your evil ways or according to your
corrupt deeds, O house of Israel,"
declares Lord Yahweh.'"

**45** [1]Now the word of Yahweh
came to me, saying, **46** "Son of man,
set your face toward [1]Teman and
speak, dripping out *words*, against
the [a]south and [b]prophesy against
the [c]forest [2]land of the Negev **47** and
say to the forest of the Negev, 'Hear
the word of Yahweh: thus says Lord
Yahweh, "Behold, I am about to [a]kindle
a fire in you, and it will consume
every [1]green tree in you, as well as
every dry tree; the blazing flame will
not be quenched, and [b,2]the whole
surface from south to north will be
scorched by it. **48** And all flesh will
see that I, Yahweh, have made it burn;
it shall [a]not be quenched."'" **49** Then
I said, "Ah Lord Yahweh! They are
saying of me, 'Is he not *just* speaking
[a]parables?'"

### *The Prophecy of Yahweh's Sword*

**21** [1]And the word of Yahweh came
to me, saying, **2** "Son of man,
[a]set your face toward Jerusalem and
[b]speak, dripping out *words* against
the sanctuaries and prophesy against
the land of Israel **3** and say to the land
of Israel, 'Thus says Yahweh, "Behold,
[a]I am against you; and I will bring
out My sword from its sheath and
cut off from you the [b]righteous and
the wicked. **4** Because I will cut off
from you the righteous and the
wicked, therefore My sword will
go out from its sheath against [a]all
flesh from south *to* north. **5** Thus
all flesh will know that I, Yahweh,
have brought out My sword from
its sheath. It will [a]not return *to its
sheath* again."' **6** Now as for you, son
of man, groan with breaking [1]heart
and bitter grief, groan in their sight.
**7** And it will be *that* when they say to
you, 'Why do you groan?' you shall
say, 'Because of the [a]report that is

**20:40** [a]Is 66:23; Eze 37:22, 24 [b]Is 56:7; 60:7; Eze 43:12, 27 [1]Or *require* **20:41** [a]Is 27:12, 13; Eze 11:17; 28:25 [b]Is 5:16; Eze 28:25; 36:23 [1]Lit *With* **20:42** [a]Eze 36:23; 38:23 [b]Eze 11:17; 34:13; 36:24 [c]Eze 20:6, 15 **20:43** [a]Eze 6:9; 16:61, 63; Hos 5:15 [b]Jer 31:18; Eze 36:31; Zec 12:10 **20:44** [a]Eze 24:24 [b]Eze 36:22 **20:45** [1]Ch 21:1 in Heb **20:46** [a]Jer 13:19; Eze 21:4 [b]Eze 21:2; Am 7:16 [c]Is 30:6-11 [1]Or *the South* [2]Lit *of the field* **20:47** [a]Is 9:18, 19; Jer 21:14 [b]Is 13:8 [1]Lit *moist* [2]Or *all the faces* **20:48** [a]Jer 7:20; 17:27 **20:49** [a]Eze 17:2; Mt 13:13; Jn 16:25 ◆ **21:1** [1]Ch 21:6 in Heb **21:2** [a]Eze 20:46; 25:2; 28:21 [b]Job 29:22; Eze 20:46 **21:3** [a]Jer 21:13; Eze 5:8; Na 2:13; 3:5 [b]Is 57:1 **21:4** [a]Jer 12:12; Eze 7:2; 20:47 **21:5** [a]1Sa 3:12; Jer 23:20; Eze 21:30; Na 1:9 **21:6** [1]Lit *loins* **21:7** [a]Eze 7:26

coming; and [b]every heart will melt,
all hands will fall limp, every spirit
will [1]faint, and all knees will [2]be weak
as water. Behold, it is coming, and it
will happen,' declares Lord Yahweh."
**8** Again the word of Yahweh came
to me, saying, **9** "Son of man, prophe-
sy and say, 'Thus says [1]the Lord.' Say,

'[a]A sword, a sword sharpened
And also polished!
**10** 'Sharpened to make
a [a]slaughter,
Polished [1]to flash
like lightning!'

Or shall we [2]rejoice *in* the [3]scepter of
My son? *The sword* [b]despises every
tree. **11** It is given to be polished, that
it may be seized by the [1]hand; the
sword is sharpened and polished,
to give it into the hand of the one
who kills. **12** [a]Cry out and wail, son of
man; for it is against My people; it is
against all the [b]princes of Israel. They
are delivered over to the sword with
My people; therefore slap *your* thigh.
**13** For *there is* a testing; and what if
even the [1]scepter [2]which *the sword*
despises will be no more?" declares
Lord Yahweh.
**14** "You therefore, son of man,
prophesy and strike *your* hands to-
gether; and let the sword be [a]doubled
the third time, the sword for the slain.
It is the sword for the great one slain,
which surrounds them, **15** that *their*
[a]hearts may melt, and many *will be*
[b]stumbling blocks at all their [c]gates.
I have given the glittering sword. Ah!
It is made *for striking* like lightning,
it is wrapped up *in readiness* for
slaughter. **16** [1]Show yourself sharp,
go to the right; set yourself; go to the
left, wherever your [2]edge is appoint-
ed. **17** And I will also strike My hands
together, and I will [a,1]cause My wrath
to be at rest; I, Yahweh, have spoken."

### *A Sword for Slaughter*

**18** And the word of Yahweh came to
me saying, **19** "Now as for you, son of
man, [a,1]make two ways for the sword
of the king of Babylon to come; both
of them will go out of one land. And
[2]make a signpost; [3]make it at the head
of the way to the city. **20** You shall
[1]mark a way for the sword to come to
[a]Rabbah of the sons of Ammon and
to Judah into [b]fortified Jerusalem.
**21** For the king of Babylon stands at
the [1]parting of the way, at the head
of the two ways, to use [a]divination;
he [b]shakes the arrows; he asks the
[c,2]household idols; he looks at the
liver. **22** Into his right hand came
the divination, 'Jerusalem,' to [a]set
battering rams, to open the mouth
[1]for killing, to lift up the voice with
a shout of war, to set battering rams
against the gates, to cast up ramps, to
build a siege wall. **23** And it will be to
them like a worthless divination in
their eyes; [a]they have *sworn* solemn
oaths. But he [b]brings iniquity to re-
membrance, that they may be seized.

---

**21:7** [b]Is 13:7; Na 2:10 [1]Lit *be dim* [2]Lit *flow* **21:9** [a]Dt 32:41 [1]Some mss and versions *Yahweh* **21:10** [a]Is 34:5, 6 [b]Ps 110:5, 6; Eze 20:47 [1]Lit *lightning to be to her* [2]Or *rejoice, the scepter of My son despising every tree?* [3]Or *rod* **21:11** [1]Lit *palm* **21:12** [a]Eze 21:6; Joel 1:13 [b]Eze 21:25; 22:6 **21:13** [1]Or *rod* [2]Or *which despises* **21:14** [a]Lv 26:21, 24; 2Ki 24:1, 10-16; 25:1 **21:15** [a]Jos 2:11; 2Sa 17:10; Ps 22:14; Eze 21:7 [b]Is 59:10; Jer 13:16; 18:15 [c]Jer 17:27; Eze 21:19 **21:16** [1]Or *Unite yourself* [2]Lit *face* **21:17** [a]Eze 5:13 [1]Or *appease* **21:19** [a]Jer 1:10; Eze 4:1-3 [1]Or *set for yourself* [2]Lit *cut out a hand* [3]Lit *cut it* **21:20** [a]Dt 3:11; Jer 49:2; Eze 25:5; Am 1:14 [b]Ps 48:12, 13; 125:1, 2 [1]Lit *set* **21:21** [a]Nu 22:7; 23:23 [b]Pr 16:33 [c]Ge 31:19, 30; Jdg 17:5; 18:17, 20 [1]Lit *mother* [2]Heb *teraphim* **21:22** [a]Eze 4:2; 26:9 [1]Lit *in* **21:23** [a]Eze 17:16, 18 [b]Nu 5:15; Eze 21:24; 29:16

**24** "Therefore, thus says Lord Yah-
weh, 'Because you have made your
iniquity to be remembered, in that
your transgressions are uncovered,
so that in all your deeds your sins
appear—because you have come to
remembrance, you will be seized with
the hand. **25** And you, O slain, wicked
one, the prince of Israel, whose [a]day
has come, in the time of the iniquity
of the end,' **26** thus says Lord Yahweh,
'Remove the turban and take off the
[a]crown; this *will* [1]no longer *be* the
same. [b]Make high that which is low
and make low that which is high.
**27** [a]A ruin, a ruin, a ruin, I will make
it. This also will be no more until [b]He
comes to whom the *legal* judgment
belongs, and I will give it *to Him.*'

**28** "Now as for you, son of man,
prophesy and say, 'Thus says Lord
Yahweh concerning the sons of Am-
mon and concerning their [a]reproach,'
and say: 'A sword, a sword is drawn,
polished for the slaughter, to cause
it [1]to [b]consume, that it may be like
lightning— **29** while they behold for
you [a]worthless visions, while they
divine lies for you—to place you on
the necks of the wicked who are slain,
whose day has come, in the [b]time of
the iniquity of the end. **30** [a]Return
*it* to its sheath. In the [b]place where
you were created, in the land of your
origin, I will judge you. **31** And I will
[a]pour out My indignation on you; I
will [b]blow on you with the fire of My
fury, and I will give you into the hand
of brutal men, [c]craftsmen of destruc-
tion. **32** You will be [a,1]fuel for the fire;
your blood will be in the midst of the
land. You will [b]not be remembered,
for I, Yahweh, have spoken.'"

### *The Abominations of Israel*

**22** Then the word of Yahweh
came to me, saying, **2** "Now as
for you, son of man, will you judge,
will you judge the city of blood?
Then you shall cause her to know
all her abominations. **3** And you shall
say, 'Thus says Lord Yahweh, "A city
[a]shedding blood in her midst, so that
her time will come; and she makes
idols against herself for defilement!
**4** You have become [a]guilty by [1]the
blood which you have shed, and
defiled by your idols which you have
made. Thus you have brought your
[2]day near and have come to your
years; therefore I have made you a
[b]reproach to the nations and a mock-
ing to all the lands. **5** Those who are
near and those who are far from you
will mock you, you of unclean name,
full of [a]turmoil.

**6** "Behold, the [a]princes of Israel,
each according to his [1]power, have
been in you for the purpose of shed-
ding blood. **7** They have [a]treated father
and mother with contempt within
you. The [b]sojourner they have op-
pressed in your midst; the [c]fatherless
and the widow they have mistreated
in you. **8** You have [a]despised My holy
things and [b]profaned My sabbaths.

---

**21:25** [a]Ps 37:13; Eze 7:2, 3, 7 **21:26** [a]Jer 13:18; Eze 16:12 [b]Ps 75:7; Eze 17:24 [1]Lit *not this*
**21:27** [a]Hag 2:21, 22 [b]Ps 2:6; 72:7, 10; Jer 23:5, 6; Eze 34:24; 37:24 **21:28** [a]Eze 36:15; Zep 2:8-10 [b]Is 31:8;
Jer 12:12; 46:10, 14 [1]Lit *to finish* **21:29** [a]Jer 27:9; Eze 13:6-9; 22:28 [b]Eze 21:25; 35:5 **21:30** [a]Jer 47:6, 7
[b]Eze 25:5 **21:31** [a]Eze 14:19; 25:7; Na 1:6 [b]Ps 18:15; Is 30:33; Eze 22:20, 21; Hag 1:9 [c]Jer 4:7; 6:22, 23;
51:20-23; Hab 1:6, 10 **21:32** [a]Eze 20:47, 48; Mal 4:1 [b]Eze 25:10 [1]Lit *food* ◆**22:3** [a]Eze 22:6, 27; 23:37,
45 **22:4** [a]2Ki 21:16; Eze 24:7, 8 [b]Ps 44:13, 14; Eze 5:14, 15; 16:57 [1]Lit *your* [2]Lit *days* **22:5** [a]Is 22:2
**22:6** [a]Is 1:23; Eze 22:27 [1]Lit *arm* **22:7** [a]Ex 20:12; Lv 20:9; Dt 5:16; 27:16 [b]Ex 22:21f; 23:9; Dt 24:17;
Jer 7:6; Zec 7:10 [c]Ex 22:22; Eze 22:25; Mal 3:5 **22:8** [a]Eze 22:26 [b]Eze 20:13, 21, 24; 23:38, 39

**9** Slanderous men have been in you
for the purpose of shedding blood,
and in you they have eaten at the
mountain *shrines*. In your midst they
have [a]done acts of lewdness. **10** In you
[1]they have [a]uncovered *their* fathers'
nakedness; in you they have hum-
bled her who was [b]unclean in her
menstrual impurity. **11** One has also
done what is an abomination with
his [a]neighbor's wife, and another has
lewdly defiled his [b]daughter-in-law.
And another in you has [c]violated
his sister, his father's daughter. **12** In
you they have [a]taken bribes for the
purpose of shedding blood; you have
taken [b]interest and profits, and you
have injured your neighbors for gain
by [c]oppression, and you have [d]forgot-
ten Me," declares Lord Yahweh.

**13** "Now behold, I have struck My
hand at your [a]greedy gain which you
have acquired and at [1]the bloodshed
which is among you. **14** Can [a]your
heart stand, or can your hands be
strong in the days that I will act
*against* you? [b]I, Yahweh, have spo-
ken and will act. **15** I will [a]scatter
you among the nations, and I will
disperse you through the lands, and I
will [b]put an end to your uncleanness
from you. **16** You will profane yourself
in the sight of the nations, and you
will [a]know that I am Yahweh."'"

**17** And the word of Yahweh came to
me, saying, **18** "Son of man, the house
of Israel has become [a]dross to Me; all
of them are [b]bronze and tin and iron
and lead in the [c]furnace; they are the
dross of silver. **19** Therefore, thus says
Lord Yahweh, 'Because all of you have
become dross, therefore, behold, I
am going to gather you into the midst
of Jerusalem. **20** As they gather silver
and bronze and iron and lead and tin
into the [a]furnace to blow fire on it in
order to melt *it*, so I will gather *you* in
My anger and in My wrath, and I will
lay you *there* and melt you. **21** And I
will collect you *together* and blow
on you with the fire of My fury, and
you will be melted in the midst of it.
**22** As silver is melted in the furnace,
so you will be melted in the midst of
it; and you will know that I, Yahweh,
have [a]poured out My wrath on you.'"

**23** And the word of Yahweh came
to me, saying, **24** "Son of man, say
to her, 'You are a land that is [a]not
cleansed *or* rained on in the day of
indignation.' **25** There is a [a]conspir-
acy of her prophets in her midst like
a roaring lion tearing the prey. They
have [b]devoured lives; they have
taken treasure and precious things;
they have made many [c]widows in
the midst of her. **26** Her [a]priests
have done violence to My law and
have [b]profaned My holy things;
they have made no [c]separation
between the holy and the profane,
and they have not made known the
difference between the [d]unclean
and the clean; and they hide their
eyes from My sabbaths, and I am
profaned among them. **27** Her

**22:9** [a]Eze 23:29; Hos 4:2, 10, 14 **22:10** [a]Lv 18:8 [b]Lv 18:19; Eze 18:6 [1]Lit *he has* **22:11** [a]Eze 18:11; 33:26 [b]Lv 18:15 [c]2Sa 13:11-14 **22:12** [a]Ex 23:8; Dt 16:19; 27:25; Mic 7:2, 3 [b]Lv 25:36; Dt 23:19 [c]Lv 19:13 [d]Ps 106:21; Eze 23:35 **22:13** [a]Is 33:15; Am 2:6-8; Mic 2:2 [1]Lit *your* **22:14** [a]Eze 21:7 [b]Eze 17:24 **22:15** [a]Dt 4:27; Ne 1:8; Eze 20:23; Zec 7:14 [b]Eze 23:27, 48 **22:16** [a]Ps 83:18; Eze 6:7 **22:18** [a]Ps 119:119; Is 1:22; Lam 4:1 [b]Jer 6:28-30 [c]Pr 17:3; Is 48:10 **22:20** [a]Is 1:25 **22:22** [a]Eze 20:8, 33; Hos 5:10 **22:24** [a]Is 9:13; Jer 2:30; Eze 24:13; Zep 3:2 **22:25** [a]Jer 11:9; Hos 6:9 [b]Jer 2:34; Eze 13:19; 22:27 [c]Jer 15:8; Eze 22:7 **22:26** [a]Jer 2:8, 26; Eze 7:26 [b]1Sa 2:12-17, 22; Eze 22:8 [c]Lv 10:10; Eze 44:23 [d]Hag 2:11-14

princes within her are like wolves
tearing the prey by shedding blood
*and* [a]destroying lives in order to get
[b]greedy gain. **28** And her prophets
have smeared whitewash for them,
beholding [a]worthless visions and
divining lies for them, saying, 'Thus
says Lord Yahweh,' when Yahweh
has not spoken. **29** The people of
the land have practiced [a]oppression
and committed robbery, and they
have mistreated the afflicted and
needy and have [b]oppressed the
sojourner without justice. **30** And
I [a]searched for a man among them
who would [b]build up the wall and
[c]stand in the breach before Me for
the land, so that I would not bring it
to ruin; but I found [1]no one. **31** Thus
I have poured out My [a]indignation
on them; I have consumed them
with the fire of My fury; [b]their way
I have brought upon their heads,"
declares Lord Yahweh.

### *The Harlotries of Oholah and Oholibah*

**23** The word of Yahweh came to
me again, saying, **2** "Son of
man, there were [a]two women, the
daughters of one mother; **3** and they
played the harlot in Egypt. They
[a]played the harlot in their youth;
there their breasts were pressed,
and there their virgin bosom was
handled. **4** Their names were Oholah
the elder and Oholibah her sister.
And they became Mine, and they
bore sons and daughters. And *as for*
their names, Samaria is Oholah and
Jerusalem is Oholibah.

**5** "Oholah played the harlot [1]while
she was Mine; and she lusted after
her lovers, after the [a]Assyrians, *her*
neighbors, **6** who were clothed in
purple, [a]governors and officials, all
of them desirable young men, horse-
men riding on horses. **7** She gave her
harlotries to them, all of them the
choicest [1]men of Assyria; and with all
whom she lusted after, with all their
idols she [a]defiled herself. **8** She did
not forsake her harlotries [a]from *the*
*time in* Egypt; for in her youth [1]men
had lain with her, and they handled
her virgin bosom and poured out
their harlotry on her. **9** Therefore, I
gave her into the hand of her [a]lovers,
into the hand of the [1]Assyrians, after
whom she lusted. **10** They [a]uncovered
her nakedness; they took her sons
and her daughters, but they killed
her with the sword. Thus she became
a *despised* name among women, and
they executed judgments on her.

**11** "Now her sister Oholibah saw
*this*, yet she was [a]more corrupt in
her lust than she, and her harlotries
were more than the harlotries of
her sister. **12** She lusted after the
[a,1]Assyrians, governors and officials,
the ones near, magnificently dressed,
horsemen riding on horses, all of
them desirable choice men. **13** And
I saw that she had defiled herself;
they both took [1]the same way. **14** So
she increased her harlotries. And
she saw men [a]portrayed on the wall,

---

**22:27** [a]Eze 22:25 [b]Eze 22:13 **22:28** [a]Jer 23:25-32; Eze 13:6 **22:29** [a]Is 5:7; Eze 9:9; 22:7; Am 3:10 [b]Ex 23:9 **22:30** [a]Is 59:16; 63:5; Jer 5:1 [b]Eze 13:5 [c]Ps 106:23; Jer 15:1 [1]Lit *not* **22:31** [a]Is 10:5; 13:5; 30:27; Eze 22:20 [b]Eze 7:3, 8, 9; 9:10; 16:43; Ro 2:8, 9 ◆ **23:2** [a]Eze 16:46 **23:3** [a]Lv 17:7; Jer 3:9 **23:5** [a]2Ki 15:19; 16:7; 17:3; Eze 16:28; Hos 5:13; 8:9, 10 [1]Lit *under Me* **23:6** [a]Eze 23:12, 13 **23:7** [a]Eze 20:7; 22:3, 4; Hos 5:3; 6:10 [1]Lit *sons of Asshur* **23:8** [a]Ex 32:4; 1Ki 12:28; 2Ki 10:29; 17:16; Eze 23:3, 19 [1]Lit *they* **23:9** [a]Eze 16:37; 23:22 [1]Lit *sons of Asshur* **23:10** [a]Eze 16:37, 41 **23:11** [a]Jer 3:8-11; Eze 16:51 **23:12** [a]2Ki 16:7 [1]Lit *sons of Asshur* **23:13** [1]Lit *one* **23:14** [a]Eze 8:10

images of the [b]Chaldeans portrayed
with vermilion, **15** girded with belts
on their loins, with flowing turbans
on their heads, all of them looking
like officers, in the likeness of the
[1]Babylonians *in* Chaldea, the land
of their birth. **16** [1]And she saw them
and [a]lusted after them and sent
messengers to them in Chaldea. **17** So
the [a,1]Babylonians came to her to the
bed of love and defiled her with their
harlotry. Then she became defiled by
them, and her soul became disgusted
with them. **18** And she [a]uncovered
her harlotries and uncovered her
nakedness; then My soul became
[b]disgusted with her, as My soul had
become disgusted with her [c]sister.
**19** Yet she multiplied her harlotries,
remembering the days of her youth,
when she played the harlot in the
land of Egypt. **20** She [a]lusted after
their paramours, whose flesh is *like*
the flesh of donkeys and whose issue
is *like* the issue of horses. **21** Thus
you [1]longed for the [a]lewdness of
your youth, when [2]the Egyptians
handled your bosom because of the
breasts of your youth.
**22** "Therefore, O Oholibah, thus
says Lord Yahweh, 'Behold, I will
arouse your lovers against you, *those*
with whom your soul was disgusted,
and I will bring them against you
*from every side:* **23** the [a,1]Babylonians
and all the [b]Chaldeans, [c]Pekod and
Shoa and Koa, *and* all the [d,2]Assyri-
ans with them; desirable choice men,
governors and officials, all of them,
officers and [3]men of renown, all of
them riding on horses. **24** They will
come against you with weapons,
[a]chariots and [1]wagons, and with an
assembly of peoples. They will set
themselves against you on every
side with large shield and shield and
helmet; and I will give the [b]judgment
to them, and they will judge you ac-
cording to their judgments. **25** And
I will set My [a]jealousy against you,
that they may deal with you in
wrath. They will remove your nose
and your ears; and your [1]survivors
will fall by the sword. They will take
your [b]sons and your daughters; and
your [1]survivors will be consumed
by the fire. **26** They will also [a]strip
you of your clothes and take away
your [b]beautiful jewelry. **27** Thus [a]I
will make your lewdness and your
harlotry *brought* from the land of
Egypt to cease from you, so that you
will not lift up your eyes to them or
remember Egypt anymore.' **28** For
thus says Lord Yahweh, 'Behold, I
will give you into the hand of those
whom you [a]hate, into the hand of
those with whom your soul was dis-
gusted. **29** They will [a]deal with you in
hatred, take all the fruit of your labor,
and leave you naked and bare. And
the nakedness of your harlotries will
be uncovered, both your lewdness
and your harlotries. **30** These things
will be done to you because you have
[a]played the harlot with the nations,

**23:14** [b]Eze 16:29 **23:15** [1]Lit *sons of Babel* **23:16** [a]Eze 23:20; Mt 5:28 [1]Lit *At the sight of her eyes* **23:17** [a]2Ki 24:17 [1]Lit *sons of Babel* **23:18** [a]Jer 8:12; Eze 21:24; 23:10 [b]Ps 78:59; 106:40; Jer 12:8 [c]Eze 23:9; Am 5:21 **23:20** [a]Eze 16:26; 17:15 **23:21** [a]Jer 3:9; Eze 23:3 [1]Lit *visited* [2]As in two mss; M.T. *from Egypt* **23:23** [a]2Ki 20:14-17; Eze 21:19; 23:14-17 [b]2Ki 24:2; Job 1:17; Is 23:13 [c]Jer 50:21 [d]Ge 2:14; 25:18; Ezr 6:22 [1]Lit *sons of Babylon* [2]Lit *sons of Assyria* [3]Lit *the called ones* **23:24** [a]Jer 47:3; Eze 26:10; Na 2:3, 4 [b]Jer 39:5, 6; Eze 16:38; 23:45 [1]Lit *wheels* **23:25** [a]Ex 34:14; Eze 5:13; 8:17, 18; Zep 1:18 [b]Eze 23:47; Hos 2:4 [1]Lit *remainder* **23:26** [a]Jer 13:22; Eze 16:39; 23:29 [b]Is 3:18-23 **23:27** [a]Eze 16:41 **23:28** [a]Jer 21:7-10; 34:20; Eze 16:37; 23:17, 22 **23:29** [a]Dt 28:48; Eze 23:25, 26, 45-47 **23:30** [a]Eze 6:9

because you have defiled yourself
with their idols. **31** You have walked
in the way of your sister; therefore
I will give [a]her cup into your hand.'
**32** Thus says Lord Yahweh,
'You will [a]drink your
sister's cup,
Which is deep and wide.
[1]You will be [b]laughed at
and held in derision;
It contains much.
**33** 'You will be filled with
[a]drunkenness and sorrow,
The cup of horror
and desolation,
The cup of your
sister Samaria.
**34** 'You will [a]drink it and drain it.
Then you will gnaw
its fragments
And tear your breasts;
for I have spoken,' declares Lord
Yahweh. **35** Therefore, thus says Lord
Yahweh, 'Because you have [a]forgot-
ten Me and [b]cast Me behind your
back, bear now the *punishment* of
your lewdness and your harlotries.'"
**36** Moreover, Yahweh said to me,
"Son of man, will you [a]judge Oholah
and Oholibah? Then [b]declare to them
their abominations. **37** For they have
committed adultery, and blood is on
their hands. Thus they have com-
mitted adultery with their idols and
even caused their sons, [a]whom they
bore to Me, to pass through *the fire*
to [1]them as food. **38** Again, they have
done this to Me: they have [a]defiled
My sanctuary on the same day and
have [b]profaned My sabbaths. **39** For
when they had slaughtered their
children for their idols, they entered
My [a]sanctuary on the same day to
profane it; and behold, thus they did
within My house.
**40** "Furthermore, [1]they have even
sent for men who come from afar,
to whom a messenger was sent; and
behold, they came—for whom you
bathed, [a]painted your eyes, and
[b]decorated yourselves with orna-
ments; **41** and you sat on a splendid
[a]couch with a [b]table arranged before
it on which you had set My [c]incense
and My [c]oil. **42** The sound of a mul-
titude [a]at ease was with her; and
[b]drunkards were brought from the
wilderness with men of the [1]common
sort. And they put [c]bracelets on [2]the
hands of the women and beautiful
crowns on their heads.
**43** "Then I said concerning her
who was [a]worn out by adulteries,
'[1]Will they now commit harlotry with
her when she is *thus*?' **44** [1]But they
went in to her as they would go in to
a harlot. Thus they went in to Oholah
and to Oholibah, the lewd women.
**45** But they, righteous men, will
[a]judge them with the judgment of
adulteresses and with the judgment
of women who shed blood, because
they are adulteresses and blood is on
their hands.

**23:31** [a]2Ki 21:13; Jer 7:14, 15; Eze 23:33 **23:32** [a]Ps 60:3; Is 51:17; Jer 25:15 [b]Eze 5:14, 15; 16:57; 22:4, 5 [1]*Or It will be for jesting and deriding because of its great size* **23:33** [a]Jer 25:15, 16, 27; Hab 2:16 **23:34** [a]Ps 75:8; Is 51:17 **23:35** [a]Is 17:10; Jer 3:21; Eze 22:12; Hos 8:14; 13:6 [b]1Ki 14:9; Jer 2:27; 32:33 **23:36** [a]Jer 1:10; Eze 20:4; 22:2 [b]Is 58:1; Eze 16:2; Mic 3:8 **23:37** [a]Eze 16:20; 20:26 [1]Idols **23:38** [a]2Ki 21:4, 7; Eze 5:11; 7:20 [b]Jer 17:27; Eze 20:13, 24 **23:39** [a]Jer 7:9-11 **23:40** [a]2Ki 9:30; Jer 4:30 [b]Is 3:18-23; Eze 16:13-16 [1]Or *you* (women) **23:41** [a]Es 1:6; Is 57:7; Am 6:4 [b]Is 65:11; Eze 44:16 [c]Jer 44:17; Hos 2:8 **23:42** [a]Eze 16:49; Am 6:3-6 [b]Jer 51:7 [c]Ge 24:30; Eze 16:11, 12 [1]Lit *multitude of mankind* [2]Lit *their hands* **23:43** [a]Eze 23:3 [1]Or *Now they will commit adultery with her, and she with them.* **23:44** [1]Or *And* **23:45** [a]Eze 16:38

46 "For thus says Lord Yahweh,
'Bring up an assembly against them
and give them over to [a]terror and
plunder. 47 The assembly will [a]stone
them with stones and cut them down
with their swords; they will kill their
sons and their daughters and [b]burn
their houses with fire. 48 Thus I will
make lewdness cease from the land,
that all women may be chastised
and not commit [1]lewdness as you
have done. 49 Your lewdness [1]will be
[a]requited upon you, and you will bear
the sin of *worshiping* your idols; thus
you will know that I am Lord Yahweh.'"

### *The Parable of the Boiling Pot*

24 And the word of Yahweh came
to me in the ninth year, in the
tenth month, on the tenth of the
month, saying, 2 "Son of man, write
the name of the day, this very day.
The king of Babylon [1]has [a]laid siege
to Jerusalem this very day. 3 Speak
a [a]parable to the [b]rebellious house,
and you shall say to them, 'Thus says
Lord Yahweh,

"Put on the [c]pot, put *it* on
and also pour water in it;
4 [a,1]Put in it the pieces,
Every good piece, the thigh
and the shoulder;
Fill *it* with choice bones.
5 "Take the [a]choicest
of the flock,
And also pile [1]wood
under [2]the pot.
Make it seethe vigorously.
Also boil its bones in it."

6 'Therefore, thus says Lord Yahweh,
"Woe to the [a]city of blood,
To the pot in which
there is rust
And whose rust has
not gone out of it!
Take out of it piece
after piece,
[1]Without making a choice.
7 "For her blood is in her midst;
She placed it on the bare rock;
She did not [a]pour it
on the ground
To cover it with dust.
8 "That it may [a]cause wrath
to come up to take vengeance,
I have put her blood
on the bare rock,
That it may not be covered."
9 'Therefore, thus says Lord Yahweh,
"[a]Woe to the city of blood!
I also will make the pile great.
10 "Heap on the wood,
kindle the fire,
Completely *cook* the flesh
And mix in the spices
And let the bones be burned.
11 "Then [a]stand it empty
on its coals
So that it may be hot
And its bronze may [1]glow
And its [b]uncleanness
may be melted in it,
Its rust brought to a
complete end.
12 "She has [a]wearied *Me* with toil,
Yet her great rust has
not gone from her;
*Let* her rust *be* in the fire!

**23:46** [a]Jer 15:4; 24:9; 29:18 **23:47** [a]Lv 20:10; Eze 16:40 [b]Jer 39:8 **23:48** [1]Lit *according to your lewdness* **23:49** [a]Is 59:18; Eze 7:4, 9; 9:10; 23:35 [1]Lit *they will give* ◆**24:2** [a]2Ki 25:1; Jer 39:1; 52:4 [1]Lit *leaned on* **24:3** [a]Ps 78:2; Eze 17:2; 20:49 [b]Is 1:2; 30:1, 9; Eze 2:3, 6, 8 [c]Jer 1:13, 14; Eze 11:3, 7, 11; 24:6 **24:4** [a]Mic 3:2, 3 [1]Lit *Gather her pieces* **24:5** [a]Jer 39:6; 52:10, 24-27 [1]Lit *bones* [2]Lit *it* **24:6** [a]2Ki 24:3, 4; Eze 22:2, 3, 27; Mic 7:2; Na 3:1 [1]Lit *No lot has fallen on it* **24:7** [a]Lv 17:13; Dt 12:16 **24:8** [a]Is 26:21 **24:9** [a]Eze 24:6; Hab 2:12 **24:11** [a]Jer 21:10; Mal 4:1 [b]Eze 22:15; 23:27 [1]Lit *become hot* **24:12** [a]Jer 9:5

**13** "In your uncleanness
is lewdness.
Because I *would* have
cleansed you,
Yet you are [a]not clean;
You will not be cleansed
from your uncleanness again
Until I have [b,1]caused My wrath
against you to be at rest.

**14** "I, Yahweh, have spoken; it is
[a]coming, and I will act. I will not
regret, and I will not [b]pity, and I will
not [1]relent; [c]according to your ways
and according to your deeds [2]I will
judge you," declares Lord Yahweh.'"

### *Ezekiel's Wife Dies as a Sign*

**15** And the word of Yahweh came to
me saying, **16** "Son of man, behold,
I am about to take from you the
[a]desire of your eyes with a [b]blow;
but you shall not [c]mourn, and you
shall not weep, and your [d]tears shall
not come. **17** Groan silently; make
[a]no mourning for the dead. Bind on
your headdress and put your shoes
on your feet and do not cover *your*
mustache and [b]do not eat the bread
of men." **18** So I spoke to the people
in the morning, and in the evening
my wife died. And in the morning
I did as I was commanded. **19** The
people said to me, "Will you not tell
us what these things that you are
doing mean for us?" **20** Then I said
to them, "The word of Yahweh came
to me saying, **21** 'Say to the house
of Israel, "Thus says Lord Yahweh,
'Behold, I am about to profane My
sanctuary, the pride of your strength,
the [a]desire of your eyes, and the de-
light of your soul; and your [b]sons and
your daughters whom you have left
behind will fall by the sword. **22** And
you will do as I have done; you will
not cover *your* mustache, and you
will not eat the bread of men. **23** And
your headdresses will be on your
heads and your shoes on your feet.
You [a]will not mourn, and you will
not weep, but [b]you will rot away in
your iniquities, and you will groan [1]to
one another. **24** Thus Ezekiel will be
a [a]wondrous sign to you; according
to all that he has done you will do;
when it comes, then you will know
that I am Lord Yahweh.'"

**25** 'Now as for you, son of man, will
*it* not be on the day when I take from
them their [a]strong defense, the joy of
their beauty, the desire of their eyes,
and what lifts up their soul, their
sons and their daughters, **26** that on
that day he who [a]escapes will come
to you with a report for *your* ears?
**27** On that day your [a]mouth will be
opened to him who escaped, and you
will speak and be mute no longer.
Thus you will be a wondrous sign to
them, and they will know that I am
Yahweh.'"

### *Prophesy Against Ammon*

**25** And the word of Yahweh came
to me saying, **2** "Son of man,
set your face toward the [a]sons of
Ammon and prophesy against them
**3** and say to the sons of Ammon,
'Hear the word of Lord Yahweh! Thus
says Lord Yahweh, "Because you said,

**24:13** [a]Jer 6:28-30; Eze 22:24 [b]Eze 5:13; 8:18 [1]Or *spent* **24:14** [a]Ps 33:9; Is 55:11 [b]Jer 13:14; Eze 9:10 [c]Is 3:11; Eze 18:30; 36:19 [1]Or *regret* [2]As in several ancient mss and versions; M.T. *they* **24:16** [a]SS 7:10; Eze 24:18 [b]Job 23:2 [c]Jer 16:5; 22:10 [d]Jer 13:17 **24:17** [a]Lv 21:10-12 [b]Jer 16:7; Hos 9:4 **24:21** [a]Ps 27:4; 84:1; Eze 24:16 [b]Jer 6:11; 16:3, 4; Eze 23:25, 47 **24:23** [a]Job 27:15; Ps 78:64 [b]Lv 26:39; Eze 33:10 [1]Lit *a man to his brother* **24:24** [a]Eze 4:3; Lk 11:29, 30 **24:25** [a]Ps 48:2; 50:2; Eze 24:21 **24:26** [a]1Sa 4:12; Job 1:15-19 **24:27** [a]Eze 3:26; 33:22 ◆**25:2** [a]Jer 49:1-6; Am 1:13-15; Zep 2:9

'[a]Aha!' against My sanctuary when it
was profaned, and against the land
of Israel when it was made desolate,
and against the house of Judah when
they went into exile, **4** therefore, be-
hold, I am going to give you to the
[a]sons of the east for a possession,
and they will set their encampments
among you and make their dwellings
among you; they will [b]eat your fruit
and drink your milk. **5** I will make
[a]Rabbah a pasture for camels and
the sons of Ammon a resting place
for flocks. Thus you will know that
I am Yahweh." **6** For thus says Lord
Yahweh, "Because you have [a]clapped
your hands and stamped your feet
and [b]were glad with all the scorn of
your soul against the land of Israel,
**7** therefore, behold, I have [a]stretched
out My hand against you, and I will
give you for [b]plunder to the nations.
And I will [c]cut you off from the peo-
ples and [d]make you perish from the
lands; I will destroy you. Thus you
will [e]know that I am Yahweh."

### *Prophesy Against Moab*

**8** 'Thus says Lord Yahweh, "Be-
cause [a]Moab and Seir say, 'Behold,
the house of Judah is like all the
nations,' **9** therefore, behold, I am
going to open the flank of Moab by
*its* cities, by its cities which are on
its [1]frontiers, the glory of the land,
[a]Beth-jeshimoth, [b]Baal-meon, and
[c]Kiriathaim, **10** and I will give it for
a possession along with the sons of
Ammon to the [a]sons of the east, so
that the sons of Ammon will not be
remembered among the nations.
**11** Thus I will execute judgments on
Moab, and they will know that I am
Yahweh."

### *Prophesy Against Edom*

**12** 'Thus says Lord Yahweh, "Because
[a]Edom has acted against the house of
Judah by taking vengeance and has
incurred grievous guilt and avenged
themselves upon them," **13** therefore
thus says Lord Yahweh, "I will also
[a]stretch out My hand against Edom
and [b]cut off man and beast from it.
And I will lay it waste; from [c]Teman
even to [d]Dedan they will fall by the
sword. **14** [a]I will lay My vengeance
on Edom by the hand of My people
Israel. Therefore, they will act in
Edom [b]according to My anger and
according to My wrath; thus they will
know My vengeance," declares Lord
Yahweh.

### *Prophesy Against Philistia*

**15** 'Thus says Lord Yahweh, "Because
the Philistines have acted in [a]revenge
and have taken vengeance with scorn
of soul to bring ruin with everlasting
enmity," **16** therefore thus says Lord
Yahweh, "Behold, I will [a]stretch out
My hand against the Philistines and
cut off the [b]Cherethites and cause
the remnant of the seacoast to perish.
**17** So I will execute great vengeance
on them with wrathful reproofs; and
they will [a]know that I am Yahweh
when I lay My vengeance on them."'"

---

**25:3** [a]Ps 70:2, 3; Eze 21:28; 25:6; 26:2; 36:2 **25:4** [a]Jdg 6:3, 33; 1Ki 4:30 [b]Dt 28:33, 51; Is 1:7
**25:5** [a]Dt 3:11; 2Sa 12:26; Jer 49:2; Eze 21:20 **25:6** [a]Job 27:23; Na 3:19 [b]Ob 12; Zep 2:8, 10
**25:7** [a]Eze 25:13, 16; Zep 1:4 [b]Is 33:4; Eze 26:5 [c]Eze 21:32 [d]Am 1:14, 15 [e]Eze 6:14 **25:8** [a]Is 15:1; Jer 48:1; Am 2:1, 2 **25:9** [a]Nu 33:49; Jos 12:3; 13:20 [b]Nu 32:3, 38; Jos 13:17; 1Chr 5:8; Jer 48:23 [c]Nu 32:37; Jos 13:19; Jer 48:1, 23 [1]Lit *end* **25:10** [a]Eze 25:4 **25:12** [a]2Chr 28:17; Ps 137:7; Jer 49:7-22 **25:13** [a]Jer 49:8, 13 [b]Eze 29:8; Mal 1:3, 4 [c]Ge 36:34; Jer 49:7; Am 1:12 [d]Jer 25:23; 49:8 **25:14** [a]Is 11:14 [b]Eze 35:11
**25:15** [a]Is 14:29-31; Eze 25:6, 12; Joel 3:4 **25:16** [a]Jer 25:20; 47:1-7 [b]1Sa 30:14; Zep 2:5 **25:17** [a]Ps 9:16

### *Prophesy Against Tyre*

26 Now it happened in the
eleventh year, on the first of
the month, *that* the word of Yahweh
came to me saying, 2 "Son of man,
because [a]Tyre has said concerning
Jerusalem, 'Aha, the [b]gateway of the
peoples is broken; it has [c,1]opened
to me. I shall be filled, *now that* she
is laid waste,' 3 therefore thus says
Lord Yahweh, 'Behold, I am against
you, O Tyre, and I will bring up
[a]many nations against you, as the
[b]sea brings up its waves. 4 They will
[a]make the walls of Tyre a ruin and
pull down her towers; and I will
scrape her dust from her and make
her a bare rock. 5 She will be a place
for the spreading of nets in the midst
of the sea, for I have spoken,' declares
Lord Yahweh, 'and she will become
[a]plunder for the nations. 6 Also her
[a]daughters who are [1]on the mainland
will be killed by the sword, and they
will know that I am Yahweh.'"

7 For thus says Lord Yahweh,
"Behold, I will bring upon Tyre from
the north Nebuchadnezzar king
of Babylon, [a]king of kings, with
horses, [b]chariots, horsemen, and an
assembly, a great *number of* people.
8 He will kill your daughters [1]on the
mainland with the sword; and he will
make [a]siege walls against you, cast
up a [b]ramp against you, and raise
up a large shield against you. 9 The
blow of his battering rams he will
direct against your walls, and with
his swords he will tear down your
towers. 10 Because of the abundance
of his [a]horses, the fine dust *raised*
*by* them will cover you; your walls
will [b]shake at the noise of horsemen
and [1]wagons and chariots when he
[c]enters your gates as men enter a city
that is breached. 11 With the hoofs of
his [a]horses he will trample all your
streets. He will kill your people with
the sword; and your strong pillars
will [b]come down to the ground.
12 Also they will make a spoil of
your wealth and a plunder of your
[a]merchandise, and [b]pull down your
walls and tear down your [c]desirable
houses, and [1]throw your stones and
your timbers and your debris [d]into
the water. 13 So I will cause the tu-
mult of your [a]songs to cease, and the
sound of your [b]harps will be heard no
more. 14 I will make you a bare rock;
you will be a place for the spreading
of nets. You will be [a]built no more,
for I [b]Yahweh have spoken," declares
Lord Yahweh.

15 Thus says Lord Yahweh to Tyre,
"Shall not the [a]coastlands [b]shake at
the sound of your downfall when
the wounded groan, when the killing
occurs in your midst? 16 Then all the
princes of the sea will [a]go down from
their thrones, remove their robes,
and strip off their embroidered gar-
ments. They will [b]clothe themselves
with [1]trembling; they will sit on the
ground, [c]tremble every moment, and
be appalled at you. 17 They will take

◆ **26:2** [a]2Sa 5:11; Is 23:1; Jer 25:22 [b]Is 62:10 [c]Eze 25:8; 35:10 [1]Lit *turned* **26:3** [a]Mic 4:11 [b]Is 5:30; Jer 50:42; 51:42 **26:4** [a]Is 23:11; Eze 26:9; Am 1:10 **26:5** [a]Eze 25:7; 29:19 **26:6** [a]Eze 16:46, 53; 26:8 [1]Lit *in the field* **26:7** [a]Ezr 7:12; Is 10:8; Jer 52:32; Da 2:37, 47 [b]Eze 23:24; Na 2:3, 4 **26:8** [a]Jer 52:4; Eze 21:22 [b]Jer 32:24 [1]Lit *in the field* **26:10** [a]Jer 4:13; 47:3 [b]Eze 26:15; 27:28 [c]Jer 39:3 [1]Lit *wheels* **26:11** [a]Is 5:28; Hab 1:8 [b]Is 26:5; Jer 43:13 **26:12** [a]Is 23:8, 18; Eze 27:3-27; Zec 9:3 [b]Jer 52:14 [c]2Chr 32:27; Am 5:11 [d]Eze 27:27, 32, 34; 28:8 [1]Lit *put* **26:13** [a]Is 23:16; 24:8, 9; Am 6:5 [b]Is 5:12; Rev 18:22 **26:14** [a]Dt 13:16; Job 12:14; Mal 1:4 [b]Is 14:27 **26:15** [a]Eze 26:18; 27:35 [b]Jer 49:21; Eze 31:16 **26:16** [a]Jon 3:6 [b]Job 8:22; Ps 35:26; Eze 7:27; 1Pe 5:5 [c]Eze 32:10; Hos 11:10 [1]Lit *tremblings*

up a [a]lamentation over you and say
to you,

'[b]How you have perished,
O inhabited one,
From the seas,
O city that was praised,
Which was [c]strong on the sea,
She and her inhabitants,
Who [1]imposed [2]her terror
On all her inhabitants!
18 'Now the [a]coastlands
will tremble
On the day of your downfall;
Yes, the coastlands which
are by the sea
Will be dismayed
at your [b]departure.'"

19 For thus says Lord Yahweh,
"When I make you a city laid waste,
like the cities which are not inhabit-
ed, when I [a]bring up the deep over
you and the great waters cover you,
20 then I will bring you down with
those who [a]go down to the pit, to
the people of old, and I will make you
inhabit the [b]lower parts of the earth,
like the ancient waste places, with
those who go down to the pit, so that
you will not [1]be inhabited; but I will
set [c]glory in the land of the living.
21 I will [1]bring [a]terrors on you, and
you will be no more; though you will
be sought, [b]you will never be found
again," declares Lord Yahweh.

### *Lament over Tyre*

27 Moreover, the word of Yahweh
came to me saying, 2 "Now
as for you, son of man, [a]take up a
lamentation over Tyre 3 and say to
Tyre, [a]who inhabits the [1]entrance
to the sea, a [b]trader of the peoples
to many coastlands, 'Thus says Lord
Yahweh,

"O Tyre, you have said,
'I am perfect in beauty.'
4 "Your borders are in the
heart of the seas;
Your builders have
perfected your beauty.
5 "They have [1]made all
*your* planks of fir
trees from [a]Senir;
They have taken a cedar
from Lebanon to make
a mast for you.
6 "Of [a]oaks from [b]Bashan they
have made your oars;
With ivory they have [1]inlaid
your deck of boxwood from
the coastlands of [c]Cyprus.
7 "Your [1]sail was of fine
embroidered linen from Egypt
So that it became
your [2]standard;
Your [3]awning was [a,4]blue
and purple from the
coastlands of [b]Elishah.
8 "The inhabitants of Sidon and
[a]Arvad were your rowers;
Your [b]wise men, O Tyre,
were [1]aboard; they
were your pilots.
9 "The elders of [a]Gebal and her
wise men were with you
repairing your seams;
All the ships of the sea and
their sailors were with you

---

**26:17** [a]Eze 19:1, 14; 27:2, 32; 32:2, 16 [b]Is 14:12; Jer 48:39; 50:23 [c]Eze 27:3, 10, 11; 28:2 [1]Lit *put* [2]Lit *their*
**26:18** [a]Is 41:5; Eze 26:15; 27:35 [b]Is 23:5-7, 10, 11 **26:19** [a]Is 8:7, 8; Eze 26:3 **26:20** [a]Is 14:9, 10; Eze 32:30
[b]Ps 88:6; Am 9:2; Jon 2:2, 6 [c]Jer 33:9; Zec 2:8 [1]Or *return* **26:21** [a]Eze 26:15, 16; 27:36 [b]Rev 18:21
[1]Lit *give you terrors* ◆ **27:2** [a]Jer 9:10, 17-20; Eze 28:12 **27:3** [a]Eze 28:2 [b]Is 23:3 [1]Lit *entrances*
**27:5** [a]Dt 3:9; 1Chr 5:23; SS 4:8 [1]Lit *built* **27:6** [a]Is 2:13; Zec 11:2 [b]Nu 21:33; Is 2:13; Jer 22:20 [c]Ge 10:4;
Is 23:1, 12; Jer 2:10 [1]Lit *made* **27:7** [a]Ex 25:4; Jer 10:9 [b]Ge 10:4 [1]Lit *spreading* [2]Or *banner* [3]Lit *covering*
[4]Or *violet* **27:8** [a]Ge 10:18; 1Chr 1:16; Eze 27:11 [b]1Ki 9:27 [1]Lit *in you* **27:9** [a]Jos 13:5; 1Ki 5:18

in order to deal
in your merchandise.

**10** "[a]Persia and [a]Lud and [a]Put were
in your military force, your men of
war. They hung shield and helmet
in you; they set forth your majesty.
**11** The sons of Arvad and your mil-
itary force were on your walls, *all*
around, and the [1]Gammadim were
in your towers. They hung their small
shields on your walls *all* around; they
perfected your beauty.

**12** "Tarshish was your customer
because of the abundance of all
*kinds* of wealth; with silver, iron, tin,
and lead they paid for your wares.
**13** [a]Javan, [a]Tubal, and [b]Meshech, they
were your traders; with the [c]lives of
men and vessels of bronze they paid
for your merchandise. **14** Those from
[a]Beth-togarmah gave horses and war
horses and mules for your wares.
**15** The sons of [a]Dedan were your
traders. Many coastlands were [1]cus-
tomers at your hand; [b]ivory tusks and
ebony they brought as your payment.
**16** [a]Aram was your customer because
of the abundance of your [1]goods; they
paid for your wares with [b]emeralds,
purple, [c]embroidered work, fine
linen, coral, and rubies. **17** Judah and
the land of Israel, they were your
traders; with the wheat of [a]Minnith,
[1]cakes, honey, oil, and balm they paid
for your merchandise. **18** [a]Damascus
was your customer because of the
abundance of your [1]goods, because of
the abundance of all *kinds* of wealth,
because of the wine of Helbon and
white wool. **19** Also Vedan and Javan
paid for your wares [1]from Uzal;
wrought iron, cassia, and [2]sweet
cane were among your merchan-
dise. **20** [a]Dedan traded with you in
saddlecloths for riding. **21** [a]Arabia and
all the princes of Kedar, they were
[1]customers at your hand for [b]lambs,
rams, and goats; for these, they were
your customers. **22** The traders of
[a]Sheba and Raamah, they traded
with you; they paid for your wares
with the best of all *kinds* of [b]spices
and with all *kinds* of precious stones
and gold. **23** Haran, Canneh, [a]Eden,
the traders of Sheba, Asshur, *and*
Chilmad traded with you. **24** They
traded with you in choice garments,
in clothes of [1]blue and embroidered
work, and in carpets of many colors
*and* tightly wound cords, *which were*
among your merchandise. **25** The
[a]ships of Tarshish were [1]the carriers
for your merchandise.

And you were filled and
were very [2]glorious
In the heart of the seas.

**26** "Your rowers have brought you
Into [a]great waters;
The [b]east wind has broken you
In the heart of the seas.
**27** "Your wealth, your wares,
your merchandise,
Your sailors and your pilots,
Your repairers of seams, your
dealers in merchandise,
And all your men of war
who are in you,

---

**27:10** [a]Eze 30:5; 38:5 **27:11** [1]Or *valorous ones* **27:13** [a]Ge 10:2; Is 66:19; Eze 27:19 [b]Ge 10:2; Eze 38:2; 39:1 [c]Joel 3:3; Rev 18:13 **27:14** [a]Ge 10:3; Eze 38:6 **27:15** [a]Jer 25:23; Eze 25:13; 27:20 [b]1Ki 10:22; Rev 18:12 [1]Or *market* **27:16** [a]Jdg 10:6; Is 7:1-8; Eze 16:57 [b]Eze 28:13 [c]Eze 16:13, 18 [1]Lit *works* **27:17** [a]Jdg 11:33 [1]Heb *pannag* **27:18** [a]Ge 14:15; Is 7:8; Jer 49:23; Eze 47:16-18 [1]Lit *works* **27:19** [1]Or *with yarn* [2]Or *calamus* **27:20** [a]Ge 25:3 **27:21** [a]Is 21:13 [b]Is 60:7 [1]Lit *markets* **27:22** [a]Ge 10:7; Is 60:6; Eze 38:13 [b]Ge 43:11; 1Ki 10:2 **27:23** [a]2Ki 19:12; Is 37:12; Am 1:5 **27:24** [1]Or *violet* **27:25** [a]Is 2:16 [1]Lit *your travelers* [2]Lit *honored* **27:26** [a]Eze 26:19 [b]Ps 48:7; Jer 18:17; Ac 27:14

With all your assembly
that is in your midst,
Will fall into the heart of the seas
On the day of your downfall.
28 "At the sound of the
cry of your pilots
The pasture lands will [a]shake.
29 "All who handle the oar,
The [a]sailors *and* all the
pilots of the sea,
Will come down from
their ships;
They will stand on the land,
30 And they will [a]make their
voice heard over you
And will cry bitterly.
They will [b]cast dust
on their heads;
They will [c]wallow in ashes.
31 "Also they will make
themselves [a]bald for you
And [b]gird themselves
with sackcloth;
And they will [c]weep for you
in bitterness of soul
With bitter mourning.
32 "Moreover, in their wailing
they will take up a
[a]lamentation for you
And lament over you:
'Who is like Tyre,
Like her who is silent in
the midst of the sea?
33 'When your wares went
out from the seas,
You satisfied a great
*number of* peoples;
With the [a]greatness
of your wealth and
your merchandise
You enriched
the kings of earth.
34 '[1]Now that you are
[a]broken by the seas
In the depths of
the waters,
Your [b]merchandise and
all your assembly
Have fallen in the
midst of you.
35 'All the [a]inhabitants of
the coastlands
Are appalled at you,
And their kings are
horribly horrified;
They are troubled
in countenance.
36 'The merchants among
the peoples [a]hiss at you;
You have become [1]terrified,
And you [b]will cease
to be forever.'"'"

### *Prophesy Against the King of Tyre*

28 The word of Yahweh came
again to me, saying, 2 "Son of
man, say to the ruler of Tyre, 'Thus
says Lord Yahweh,
"Because your heart is lofty
And you have said,
'[a]I am a god;
I sit enthroned in the seat
of [1]gods
In the heart of the seas';
Yet you are a [b]man
and not God,
Although you make your heart
like the heart of God—
3 Behold, you are wiser
than [a]Daniel;

**27:28** [a]Eze 26:10, 15, 18 **27:29** [a]Rev 18:17-19 **27:30** [a]Is 23:1-6; Eze 26:17 [b]1Sa 4:12; 2Sa 1:2; Lam 2:10; Rev 18:19 [c]Jer 6:26; Jon 3:6 **27:31** [a]Is 15:2; Eze 29:18 [b]Is 22:12; Eze 7:18 [c]Is 16:9; 22:4 **27:32** [a]Eze 26:17; 27:2; 28:12 **27:33** [a]Eze 27:12, 18; 28:4, 5 **27:34** [a]Eze 26:12; 27:26, 27 [b]Zec 9:3, 4 [1]Lit *The time* **27:35** [a]Is 23:6; Eze 26:16 **27:36** [a]Jer 18:16; 19:8; 49:17; 50:13; Zep 2:15 [b]Ps 37:10, 36 [1]Lit *terrors* ◆**28:2** [a]Is 14:14; 47:8; Eze 28:9; 2Th 2:4 [b]Ps 9:20; 82:6, 7; Is 31:3; Eze 28:9 [1]Or *God* **28:3** [a]Da 1:20; 2:20-23, 28; 5:11, 12

There is no secret that
is a match for you.
4 "By your wisdom
and understanding
You have acquired
[a]wealth for yourself
And have acquired gold and
silver for your treasuries.
5 "By your great wisdom,
by your [a]trade
You have increased
your wealth,
And your [b]heart is lofty
because of your wealth—
6 Therefore thus says Lord Yahweh,
'Because you have
[a]made your heart
Like the heart of God,
7 Therefore, behold, I will bring
[a]strangers upon you,
The [b]most ruthless
of the nations.
And they will draw
their swords
Against the beauty of
your wisdom
And defile your splendor.
8 'They will bring you
down to the pit,
And you will die the [a]death
of those who are slain
In the heart of the seas.
9 'Will you still say,
"I am a god,"
In the presence of the
one who kills you,
Though you are a man
and not God,
In the hands of those
who slay you?
10 'You will die the death of
the [a]uncircumcised
By the hand of strangers,
For I have spoken!' declares
Lord Yahweh!"'"

### *Lament over the King of Tyre*

11 Again the word of Yahweh came
to me saying, 12 "Son of man, [a]take
up a lamentation over the king of
Tyre and say to him, 'Thus says Lord
Yahweh,
"You [1]had the seal
of perfection,
Full of wisdom and
perfect in beauty.
13 "You were in [a]Eden,
the garden of God;
[b]Every precious stone
was your covering:
The [c]ruby, the topaz,
and the diamond;
The beryl, the onyx,
and the jasper;
The [1]lapis lazuli, the turquoise,
and the emerald;
And the gold, the
workmanship of your
[d,2]settings and [3]sockets,
Was in you.
On the day that you
were created
They were prepared.
14 "You were the [a]anointed
cherub who [1]covers,
And I placed you *there*.
You were on the holy
[b]mountain of God;
You walked in the midst
of the [c]stones of fire.

**28:4** [a]Eze 27:33; Zec 9:2, 3 **28:5** [a]Eze 27:12; Hos 12:7, 8 [b]Job 31:24, 25; Ps 52:7; Eze 28:2; Hos 13:6 **28:6** [a]Ex 9:17; Eze 28:2 **28:7** [a]Eze 26:7 [b]Eze 30:11; 31:12; 32:12; Hab 1:6-8 **28:8** [a]Eze 27:26, 27, 34 **28:10** [a]1Sa 17:26, 36; Eze 31:18; 32:30 **28:12** [a]Eze 19:1; 26:17; 27:2 [1]Lit were *the one sealing a pattern* **28:13** [a]Ge 2:8; Is 51:3; Eze 31:8, 9, 16; 36:35 [b]Eze 27:16, 22 [c]Ex 28:17-20 [d]Is 24:8; 30:32 [1]Heb *sappir* [2]Or *tambourines* [3]Or *flutes* **28:14** [a]Ex 25:17-20; 30:26; 40:9; Eze 28:16 [b]Eze 20:40; 28:16 [c]Eze 28:13, 16; Rev 18:16 [1]Or *guards*

15 "You were [a]blameless
in your ways
From the day you were created
Until [b]unrighteousness
was found in you.
16 "By the [a]abundance
of your trade
[1]You were internally
[b]filled with violence,
And you sinned;
Therefore I have cast
you as profane
From the mountain of God.
And I have destroyed you,
O [2]covering cherub,
From the midst of the
stones of fire.
17 "Your heart was lofty because
of your [a]beauty;
You [b]corrupted your wisdom
by reason of your splendor.
I cast you to the ground;
I put you before [c]kings,
That they may see you.
18 "By the abundance of
your iniquities,
In the unrighteousness
of your trade
You profaned
your sanctuaries.
Therefore I have brought out
[a]fire from the midst of you;
It has consumed you,
And I have turned you to
[b]ashes on the earth
In the eyes of all who see you.
19 "All who know you
among the peoples
Are appalled at you;
You have become [a,1]terrified,
And you will cease to
be [b]forever."'"

### *Prophesy Against Sidon*

20 And the word of Yahweh came to
me saying, 21 "Son of man, [a]set your
face toward [b]Sidon, prophesy against
her 22 and say, 'Thus says Lord Yahweh,
"Behold, I am against
you, O Sidon,
And I will [1]be glorified
in your midst.
Then they will know that I
am Yahweh when I [a]execute
judgments in her,
And I will manifest My
holiness in her.
23 "For [a]I will send
pestilence to her
And blood to her streets,
And the [b]wounded will
[1]fall in her midst
By the sword upon her
on every side;
Then they will know
that I am Yahweh.
24 "And there will be no more for the
house of Israel a [a]prickling brier or a
painful thorn from any round about
them who scorned them; then they
will know that I am Lord Yahweh."

### *Israel Regathered*

25 'Thus says Lord Yahweh, "When
I [a]gather the house of Israel from
the peoples, among whom they
are scattered, and will manifest My
holiness in them in the sight of the
nations, then they will [b]live in their
[1]land which I gave to My servant

**28:15** [a]Eze 27:3, 4; 28:3-6, 12 [b]Eze 28:17, 18 **28:16** [a]Eze 27:12 [b]Eze 8:17; Hab 2:8, 17 [1]Lit *They filled your midst* [2]Or *guardian* **28:17** [a]Eze 27:3, 4; 28:7 [b]Is 19:11 [c]Eze 26:16 **28:18** [a]Am 1:9, 10 [b]Mal 4:3 **28:19** [a]Eze 26:21; 27:36 [b]Jer 51:64 [1]Lit *terrors* **28:21** [a]Eze 6:2; 25:2 [b]Ge 10:15, 19; Is 23:2, 4; Eze 27:8 **28:22** [a]Eze 28:26; 30:19 [1]Or *glorify Myself* **28:23** [a]Eze 38:22 [b]Jer 51:52 [1]Or *be judged* **28:24** [a]Nu 33:55; Jos 23:13; Is 55:13; Eze 2:6 **28:25** [a]Ps 106:47; Is 11:12, 13; Jer 32:37; Eze 20:41; 34:13, 27 [b]Jer 23:8; 27:11 [1]Lit *ground*

Jacob. **26** They will [a]live in it securely;
and they will [b]build houses, plant
vineyards, and live securely when
I [c]execute judgments upon all who
scorn them all around them. Then
they will know that I am Yahweh
their God."'"

### *Prophesy Against Egypt*

**29** In the [a]tenth year, in the
tenth *month*, on the twelfth
of the month, the word of Yahweh
came to me saying, **2** "Son of man,
set your face against [a]Pharaoh king
of Egypt and prophesy against him
and against all [b]Egypt. **3** Speak and
say, 'Thus says Lord Yahweh,

"Behold, I am against you,
Pharaoh king of Egypt,
The great [a,1]monster that
lies in the midst of his
canals of the Nile,
That [b]has said, 'My Nile
is mine, and I myself
have made *it*.'

**4** "I will put [a]hooks in your jaws
And make the fish
of your canals of the Nile
cling to your scales.
And I will bring you up
out of the midst of your
canals of the Nile,
And all the fish of your
canals of the Nile will
cling to your scales.

**5** "I will [a]abandon you
to the wilderness, you and
all the fish of your
canals of the Nile;
You will fall on the [1]open field;
you will not be brought
together or [b,2]gathered.
I have given you for [c]food to
the beasts of the earth and
to the birds of the sky.

**6** "Then all the inhabitants
of Egypt will know
that I am Yahweh
Because they have been
*only* a [a]staff *made* of reed
to the house of Israel.

**7** "When they seized you
with the hand,
You [a]tore and split open
all their [1]shoulders;
And when they leaned on you,
You broke and made all
their loins [2]quake."

**8** 'Therefore thus says Lord Yah-
weh, "Behold, I will [a]bring upon
you a sword, and I will cut off from
you man and beast. **9** The [a]land of
Egypt will become a desolation and
waste. Then they will know that I am
Yahweh.

Because [1]you [b]said, 'The Nile is
mine, and I have made *it*,' **10** there-
fore, behold, I am [a]against you and
against your canals of the Nile, and I
will make the land of Egypt an utter
waste and desolation, from Migdol
*to* Syene and even to the border of
[1]Ethiopia. **11** A man's foot will [a]not
pass through it, and the foot of a
beast will not pass through it, and it
will not be inhabited for forty years.
**12** So I will make the land of Egypt a
desolation in the [a]midst of desolated

***28:26*** [a]*Jer 23:6; Eze 34:25-28; 38:8* [b]Jer 32:15, 43, 44; Am 9:13, 14 [c]Eze 25:11; 28:22 ◆ **29:1** [a]Eze 26:1; 29:17; 30:20 **29:2** [a]Jer 44:30 [b]Is 19:1-17; Jer 46:2-26; Eze 30:1-32:32 **29:3** [a]Is 27:1; Eze 32:2 [b]Eze 29:9; 30:12 [1]Lit *tannim* **29:4** [a]2Ki 19:28; Eze 38:4 **29:5** [a]Eze 32:4-6 [b]Jer 8:2; 25:33 [c]Jer 7:33; 34:20; Eze 39:4 [1]Lit *faces of the field* [2]Targum and several mss *buried* **29:6** [a]2Ki 18:21; Is 36:6 **29:7** [a]2Ki 18:21; Is 36:6; Eze 17:15-17 [1]Some ancient versions *hands* [2]Lit *stand* **29:8** [a]Jer 46:13; Eze 14:17 **29:9** [a]Eze 29:10-12; 30:7, 8, 13-19 [b]Pr 16:18; 18:12; Eze 29:3 [1]Lit *he* **29:10** [a]Eze 13:8; 21:3; 26:3; 29:3 [1]Or *Cush*, cf. Ge 10:6 **29:11** [a]Jer 43:11, 12; 46:19; Eze 32:13 **29:12** [a]Jer 25:15-19; 27:6-11; Eze 30:7

lands. And her cities, in the midst of cities that are laid waste, will be desolate forty years; and I will [b]scatter the Egyptians among the nations and disperse them among the lands."

**13** 'For thus says Lord Yahweh, "At the end of forty years I will [a]gather the Egyptians from the peoples [1]among whom they were scattered. **14** I will return the fortunes of Egypt and make them return to the land of [a]Pathros, to the land of their origin, and there they will be a lowly kingdom. **15** It will be the [a]lowest of the kingdoms, and it will never again lift itself up above the nations. And I will make them so small that they will not [b]have dominion over the nations. **16** And it will never again be the [a]security of the house of Israel, [b]bringing to remembrance the iniquity of their having turned *to go* after Egypt. Then they will know that I am Lord Yahweh."'"

**17** Now in the [a]twenty-seventh year, in the first *month*, on the first of the month, the word of Yahweh came to me saying, **18** "Son of man, [a]Nebuchadnezzar king of Babylon made his military force [1]labor hard against Tyre; every head was made [b]bald, and every shoulder was rubbed bare. But he and his military force had no wages from Tyre for the [2]labor that he had [3]labored against it." **19** Therefore thus says Lord Yahweh, "Behold, I [a]will give the land of Egypt to Nebuchadnezzar king of Babylon. And he will carry off her [b,1]abundance and capture her spoil and seize her plunder; and it will be wages for his military force. **20** I have given him the land of Egypt *for* his work which he [a,1]labored because they acted for Me," declares Lord Yahweh.

**21** "On that day I will make a [a]horn sprout for the house of Israel, and I will [b,1]open your mouth in their midst. Then they will know that I am Yahweh."

### *Those Who Support Egypt Will Fall*

**30** The word of Yahweh came again to me saying, **2** "Son of man, prophesy and say, 'Thus says Lord Yahweh,

"[a]Wail, 'Alas for the day!'
**3** "For the day is near,
Even [a]the day
of Yahweh is near;
It will be a day of [b]clouds,
A time *of doom* for the nations.
**4** "A sword will come upon Egypt,
And anguish will be
in [1]Ethiopia;
When the slain fall in Egypt,
They [a]take away
her multitude,
And her foundations
are pulled down.

**5** "[1]Ethiopia, Put, Lud, all [a,2]Arabia, [3]Libya, and the [4]people of the land [5]that is in covenant will fall with them by the sword."

**29:12** [b]Jer 46:19; Eze 30:23, 26 **29:13** [a]Is 19:22; Jer 46:26 [1]Lit *where* **29:14** [a]Is 11:11; Jer 44:1, 15; Eze 30:14 **29:15** [a]Eze 17:6, 14; 30:13; Zec 10:11 [b]Eze 31:2; 32:2; Na 3:8-10 **29:16** [a]Is 20:5; 30:1-3; 31:1; 36:6; Eze 17:15; 29:6, 7 [b]Is 64:9; Jer 14:10; Eze 21:23; Hos 8:13 **29:17** [a]Eze 24:1; 26:1; 29:1; 30:20; 40:1 **29:18** [a]Jer 25:9; 27:6; Eze 26:7-12 [b]Jer 48:37; Eze 27:31 [1]Or *a great slavery*; lit *a great service* [2]Or *slavery*; lit *service* [3]Or *slaved*; lit *served* **29:19** [a]Eze 30:10, 24, 25; 32:11 [b]Jer 43:10-13; Eze 30:14 [1]Or *multitude* **29:20** [a]Is 10:6, 7; 45:1-3; Jer 25:9 [1]Or *slaved*; lit *served* **29:21** [a]1Sa 2:10; Ps 92:10; 132:17 [b]Eze 3:27; 24:27; 33:22; Am 3:7, 8; Lk 21:15 [1]Lit *give you an opening of the mouth* ◆ **30:2** [a]Is 13:6; 15:2; Eze 21:12; Joel 1:5, 11, 13 **30:3** [a]Eze 7:19; 13:5; Joel 1:15; 2:1; Ob 15 [b]Eze 30:18; 32:7; 34:12 **30:4** [a]Eze 29:19 [1]Or *Cush*, cf. Ge 10:6 **30:5** [a]Jer 25:20, 24 [1]Or *Cush*, cf. Ge 10:6 [2]Or *the mixed people* [3]Or *Cub* [4]Lit *sons* [5]Lit *of*

6 'All the [a]birds of the sky
nested in its boughs,
And under its branches all the
beasts of the field gave birth,
And all great nations
lived under its shade.

7 'So it was beautiful
in its greatness, in the
length of its foliage;
For its [1]roots extended
to many waters.

8 'The [a]cedars in [b]God's garden
[1]could not match it;
The [2]cypresses [1]could
not liken *themselves*
with its boughs,
And the plane trees were
not like its branches.
No tree in [b]God's garden
[1]could liken *itself*
with it in its beauty.

9 'I made it beautiful with the
multitude of its foliage,
And all the trees of [a]Eden,
which were in the [a]garden
of God, were jealous of it.

10 'Therefore thus says Lord Yah-
weh, "Because [1]it is lofty in height and
has put its top among the [2]clouds, and
its [a]heart is high up in its loftiness,
11 therefore I will give it into the hand
of a [a,1]dominant one of the nations; he
will thoroughly deal with it. Accord-
ing to its wickedness I have [b]driven it
away. 12 [a]Strangers—[b]ruthless ones
of the nations have cut it down and
abandoned it; on the [c]mountains and
in all the valleys its foliage have fallen,
and its boughs have been broken in
all the ravines of the land. And all
the peoples of the earth have [d]gone
down from its shade and abandoned
it. 13 On its downfall all the [a]birds of
the sky will dwell, and all the beasts of
the field will be on its *fallen* branches
14 so that all the trees by the waters
may not be lofty in their height, nor
put their top among the [1]clouds,
nor their dominant ones—all the
[2]well-watered ones—stand in their
loftiness. For they have all been given
over to death, to the [a]earth beneath,
among the sons of men, with those
who go down to the pit."

15 'Thus says Lord Yahweh, "On the
day when it went down to Sheol I
[a]caused mourning; I covered it with
the [1]deep over it and held back its
rivers. And *its* many waters were
stopped up, and I made Lebanon
[2]mourn for it, and all the trees of
the field wilted away on account
of it. 16 I made the nations [a]quake
at the sound of its downfall when I
made it [b]go down to Sheol with those
who go down to the pit; and all the
trees of Eden, the choicest and best
of [c]Lebanon, all the [1]well-watered
ones, were [d]comforted in the earth
beneath. 17 They also [a]went down
with it to Sheol to those who were
[b]slain by the sword; and those who
were its [1]strength lived [c]under its
shade among the nations.

**31:6** [a]Eze 17:23; 31:13; Da 4:12, 21; Mt 13:32 **31:7** [1]Lit *root was* **31:8** [a]Ps 80:10; Eze 31:3 [b]Ge 2:8, 9; 13:10; Is 51:3; Eze 28:13; 31:16, 18 [1]Lit *did* [2]Or *Phoenician junipers* **31:9** [a]Ge 2:8, 9; 13:10; Is 51:3; Eze 28:13; 31:16, 18 **31:10** [a]2Chr 32:25; Is 10:12; 14:13, 14; Eze 28:17; Da 5:20 [1]Lit *you are* [2]Or *thick boughs* **31:11** [a]Eze 30:10, 11; 32:11, 12; Da 5:18, 19 [b]Dt 18:12; Na 3:18 [1]Lit *ram* **31:12** [a]Eze 7:21; 28:7; 30:12; Hab 1:6 [b]Eze 28:7; 30:11; 32:12 [c]Eze 32:5; 35:8 [d]Eze 31:17; Da 4:14; Na 3:17, 18 **31:13** [a]Is 18:6; Eze 29:5; 31:6; 32:4 **31:14** [a]Nu 16:30, 33; Ps 63:9; Eze 26:20; 31:18; 32:24; Am 9:2; Jon 2:2, 6; Eph 4:9 [1]Or *thick boughs* [2]Lit *drinkers of water* **31:15** [a]Eze 32:7; Na 2:10 [1]Subterranean waters [2]Lit *be darkened* **31:16** [a]Eze 26:15; 27:28; Hag 2:7 [b]Is 14:15; Eze 32:18 [c]Is 14:8; Hab 2:17 [d]Eze 14:22, 23; 32:31 [1]Lit *drinkers of water* **31:17** [a]Ps 9:17 [b]Eze 32:20f [c]Eze 31:3, 6; Da 4:12 [1]Lit *arm*

18 "To which among the trees of
Eden do you thus liken *yourself* in
glory and greatness? Yet you will be
brought down with the trees of Eden
to the earth beneath; you will lie in
the midst of the [a]uncircumcised,
with those who were slain by the
sword. [b]So is Pharaoh and all his
multitude!"' declares Lord Yahweh."

### *A Lament over Pharaoh and Egypt*

32 And it happened in the
[a]twelfth year, in the twelfth
*month*, on the first of the month,
*that* the word of Yahweh came to
me saying, 2 "Son of man, take up a
[a]lamentation over Pharaoh king of
Egypt and say to him,

'You liken yourself to a young
[b]lion of the nations,
Yet you are like the
[c]monster in the seas;
And you [d]burst forth
in your rivers
And muddied the waters
with your feet
And [1]fouled their rivers.'"

3 Thus says Lord Yahweh,
"So I will [a]spread My
net over you
With an assembly
of many peoples,
And they shall bring
*you up in My* net.
4 "I will abandon you
on the land;
I will hurl you on the
[1]open field.
And I will cause all the [a]birds
of the sky to dwell on you,
And I will satisfy the beasts
of the whole earth [2]with you.
5 "I will put your flesh
[a]on the mountains
And fill the valleys
with your refuse.
6 "I will also make the land drink
the discharge of your [a]blood
As far as the mountains,
And the ravines will
be full of you.
7 "And when *I* [a]extinguish you,
I will [b]cover the heavens
and darken their [c]stars;
I will cover the [d]sun
with a cloud,
And the moon will
not give its light.
8 "All the shining [a]lights
in the heavens
I will darken over you
And will give darkness
on your land,"
Declares Lord Yahweh.

9 "I will also [a]vex the hearts of many
peoples when I [b]bring your destruc-
tion among the nations, into lands
which you have not known. 10 I will
make many peoples [a,1]appalled at
you, and their kings will be horribly
afraid of you when I brandish My
sword before them; and [b]they will
tremble every moment, every man
for his own life, on the day of your
downfall."

11 For [a]thus says Lord Yahweh,
"The sword of the king of Babylon

**31:18** [a]Jer 9:25, 26; Eze 28:10; 32:19, 21 [b]Ps 52:7; Mt 13:19 ◆ **32:1** [a]Eze 30:20; 31:1; 32:17; 33:21
**32:2** [a]Eze 19:1; 27:2; 28:12; 32:16 [b]Jer 4:7; Eze 19:2-6; Na 2:11-13 [c]Is 27:1; Eze 29:3 [d]Jer 46:7, 8 [1]Lit *fouled by stamping* **32:3** [a]Eze 12:13 **32:4** [a]Is 18:6 [1]Lit *surface of the field* [2]Lit *from* **32:5** [a]Eze 31:12
**32:6** [a]Ex 7:17; Is 34:3, 7; Eze 35:6; Rev 14:20 **32:7** [a]Job 18:5, 6; Pr 13:9 [b]Ex 10:21-23; Is 34:4; Eze 30:3, 18; 34:12 [c]Is 13:10 [d]Joel 2:2, 31; 3:15; Am 8:9; Mt 24:29; Mk 13:24f; Lk 21:25; Rev 6:12; 8:12 **32:8** [a]Ge 1:14
**32:9** [a]Eze 27:29-32; 28:19; Rev 18:10-15 [b]Ex 15:14-16 **32:10** [a]Eze 27:35 [b]Eze 26:16 [1]Or *feel desolate*
**32:11** [a]Jer 46:26

will come upon you. 12 By the swords
of the mighty ones I will cause your
multitude to fall; all of them are
[a]ruthless ones of the nations,

And they will [b]devastate
the lofty pride of Egypt,
And all its multitude
will be destroyed.
13 "I will also make all its
cattle perish
from beside many waters;
And [a]the foot of man will not
muddy them anymore,
And the hoofs of beasts
will not muddy them.
14 "Then I will make their
waters settle
And will cause their rivers
to [1]run like oil,"
Declares Lord Yahweh.
15 "When I make the land
of Egypt a [a]desolation,
And the land is desolate
of its fullness,
When I strike all those
who inhabit it,
Then they shall [b]know
that I am Yahweh.

16 "This is a [a]lamentation, and they
shall [1]lament over it. The daughters
of the nations shall [1]lament over it.
Over Egypt and over all her multitude
they shall [1]lament over it," declares
Lord Yahweh.

17 Now it happened in the [a]twelfth
year, on the [a]fifteenth of the month,
*that* the word of Yahweh came to me
saying, 18 "Son of man, [a]wail for the
hordes of Egypt and [b]bring it down,
her and the daughters of the powerful nations, to the [c]nether world,
with those who go down to the pit;

19 'Whom do you surpass
in beauty?
Go down and make your bed
with the [a]uncircumcised.'

20 "They shall fall in the midst of
those who are slain by the sword.
[1]She is given over to the sword; they
have [a]drawn her and all her multitude away. 21 The [a,1]dominant among
the mighty ones shall speak of him
*and* his helpers from the midst of
Sheol, 'They have gone down, they
lie still, the uncircumcised, slain by
the sword.'

22 "[a]Assyria is there and all her assembly; [1]her graves are round about
[2]her. All of them are slain, fallen by
the sword, 23 whose [a]graves are put
in the remotest parts of the pit, and
her assembly is all round about her
grave. All of them are slain, fallen by
the sword, who put terror in the land
of the living.

24 "[a]Elam is there and all her
multitude all around her grave; all
of them slain, fallen by the sword,
who went down uncircumcised to
the [b]lower parts of the earth, who put
their terror in the [c]land of the living
and [d]bore their dishonor with those
who went down to the pit. 25 They
have put a [a]bed for her among the
slain with all her multitude. Her
graves are all around it; all of them

---

**32:12** [a]Eze 28:7 [b]Eze 28:19 **32:13** [a]Eze 29:11 **32:14** [1]Lit *go, walk* **32:15** [a]Ps 107:33, 34; Eze 29:12, 19, 20 [b]Ex 7:5; 14:4, 18; Ps 9:16; 83:17, 18; Eze 6:7; 30:19, 26 **32:16** [a]2Sa 1:17; 3:33, 34; 2Chr 35:25; Jer 9:17; Eze 26:17; 32:2 [1]Or *chant* **32:17** [a]Eze 31:1; 32:1; 33:21 **32:18** [a]Is 16:9; Eze 21:6; 32:2, 16; Mic 1:8 [b]Jer 1:10; Eze 43:3; Hos 6:5 [c]Eze 31:14, 16, 18; 32:24 **32:19** [a]Jer 9:25, 26; Eze 31:18; 32:21, 24, 29, 30 **32:20** [a]Ps 28:3 [1]Or *The sword is given* **32:21** [a]Is 14:9-12; Eze 32:27 [1]Lit *rams* **32:22** [a]Eze 27:23; 31:3, 16 [1]Lit *his* [2]Lit *him* **32:23** [a]Is 14:15 **32:24** [a]Ge 10:22; 14:1; Is 11:11; Jer 25:25; 49:34-39 [b]Eze 26:20; 31:14, 18; 32:18 [c]Job 28:13; Ps 27:13; 52:5; 142:5; Is 38:11; Jer 11:19 [d]Eze 16:52, 54; 32:25, 30 **32:25** [a]Ps 139:8

are uncircumcised, slain by the sword (although their terror was put in the land of the living), and they bore their dishonor with those who go down to the pit; [1]they were put in the midst of the slain.

**26** “[a]Meshech, [b]Tubal, and all their multitude are there; their graves are all around them. All of them were slain by the sword [c]uncircumcised, though they put their terror in the land of the living. **27** [a]Nor do they lie beside the fallen [b]mighty ones of the uncircumcised, who went down to Sheol with their weapons of war and whose swords were put under their heads; but the *punishment for* their [c]iniquity rested on their bones, though the terror of *these* mighty ones *was once* in the land of the living. **28** But as for you, in the midst of the uncircumcised you will be broken and lie with those slain by the sword.

**29** “There also is [a]Edom, its kings, and all its [1]princes, who [2]for *all* their might are put with those slain by the sword; they will lie with the uncircumcised and with those who go down to the pit.

**30** “There also are the [1]chiefs of the [a]north, all of them, and all the [b]Sidonians, who in spite of the terror resulting from their might, in shame went down with the slain. So they lay down uncircumcised with those slain by the sword and bore their dishonor with those who go down to the pit.

**31** “These Pharaoh will see, and he will be [a]comforted for all his multitude slain by the sword, *even* Pharaoh and all his military force,” declares Lord Yahweh. **32** “Though I put a terror of him in the land of the living, yet he will be made to lie down among *the* uncircumcised *along* with those slain by the sword, *even* Pharaoh and all his hordes,” declares Lord Yahweh.

### *Ezekiel, Israel’s Watchman*

**33** And the word of Yahweh came to me, saying, **2** “Son of man, speak to the [a]sons of your people and say to them, ‘If I bring a sword upon a land, and the people of the land take one man from among them and make him their watchman, **3** and he sees the sword coming upon the land and [a]blows on the trumpet and warns the people, **4** then [1]he who hears the sound of the trumpet and [a]does not take warning, and a sword comes and takes him away, his [b]blood will be on his *own* head. **5** He heard the sound of the trumpet but did not take warning; his blood will be on himself. But had he taken warning, he would have [a]escaped with his life. **6** But if the watchman sees the sword coming and does not blow the trumpet and the people are not warned, and a sword comes and takes a person from them, he is [a]taken away [1]in his iniquity; but his [b]blood I will require from the watchman’s hand.’

**32:25** [1]As in ancient versions; M.T. *he was* **32:26** [a]Ge 10:2; Eze 27:13; 38:2, 3; 39:1 [b]Ge 10:2; Is 66:19; Eze 27:13; 38:2, 3; 39:1 [c]Eze 32:19 **32:27** [a]Is 14:18, 19 [b]Job 3:13-15; Eze 32:21 [c]Job 20:11; Ps 109:18 **32:29** [a]Is 34:5-15; Jer 49:7-22; Eze 25:13; 35:9, 15 [1]Or *leaders* [2]Or *in* **32:30** [a]Jer 1:15; 25:26; Eze 38:6, 15; 39:2 [b]Jer 25:22; Eze 28:21-23 [1]Or *princes* **32:31** [a]Eze 14:22; 31:16 ◆ **33:2** [a]Eze 3:11; 33:12, 17, 30; 37:18 **33:3** [a]Ne 4:18-20; Is 58:1; Eze 33:9; Hos 8:1; Joel 2:1 **33:4** [a]2Chr 25:16; Jer 6:17; Zec 1:4 [b]Eze 18:13; 33:5, 9; Ac 18:6 [1]Lit *the hearer who hears* **33:5** [a]Ex 9:19-21; Heb 11:7 **33:6** [a]Eze 18:20, 24; 33:8, 9 [b]Eze 3:18, 20 [1]Or *for*, so in ch

7 “Now as for you, son of man, I
have [a]given you as a watchman for
the house of Israel; so you will hear a
word from My mouth and give them
[b]warning from Me. 8 When I say to
the wicked, ‘O wicked man, you will
[a]surely die,’ and you do not speak to
warn the wicked from his way, that
wicked man shall die in his iniquity,
but his blood I will require from your
hand. 9 But as for you, if you on your
part warn a wicked man to turn from
his way and he [a]does not turn from
his way, he will die in his iniquity, but
you have [b]delivered your life.

10 “Now as for you, son of man,
say to the house of Israel, ‘Thus
you have spoken, saying, “Surely
our transgressions and our sins are
upon us, and we are [a]rotting away
in them; [b]how then can we live?”’
11 Say to them, ‘[a]As I live!’ declares
Lord Yahweh, ‘I take [b]no pleasure in
the death of the wicked, but rather
that the wicked [c]turn from his way
and live. [d]Turn back, turn back from
your evil ways! Why then will you
die, O house of Israel?’ 12 Now as for
you, son of man, say to the sons of
your people, ‘The [a]righteousness of
a righteous man will not deliver him
in the day of his transgression, and
as for the wickedness of the wicked,
he will [b]not stumble because of it
in the day when he turns from his
wickedness; whereas a righteous
man will not be able to live [1]by his
righteousness on the day when he
commits sin.’ 13 When I say to the
righteous he will surely live, and he
*so* trusts in his righteousness that he
[a]does iniquity, none of his righteous
deeds will be remembered; but in
that same iniquity of his which he
has done he will die. 14 But when I
say to the wicked, ‘You will surely
die,’ and he [a]turns from his sin and
does [b]justice and righteousness,
15 *if a* wicked man restores a pledge,
[a]pays back what he has taken by
robbery, walks by the [b]statutes of
life without committing iniquity,
he shall surely live; he shall not die.
16 [a]None of his sins that he has done
will be remembered against him. He
has done justice and righteousness;
he shall surely live.

17 “Yet the sons of your people say,
‘The way of the Lord is not right,’ when
it is their own way that is not right.
18 When the righteous turns from
his righteousness and [a]does iniquity,
then he shall die in [1]it. 19 But when
the wicked turns from his wickedness
and does justice and righteousness,
he will live by them. 20 Yet you say,
‘[a]The way of the Lord is not right.’
O house of Israel, I will judge each of
you according to his ways.”

### *Jerusalem Has Been Struck Down*

21 Now [a]it happened in the [b]twelfth
year of our exile, on the fifth of the
tenth month, *that* those who escaped
from Jerusalem came to me, saying,
“[c]The city has been struck down.”

**33:7** [a]*Is 62:6; Eze 3:17-21* [b]*Jer 1:17; 26:2; Eze 2:7, 8; Ac 5:20* **33:8** [a]Is 3:11; Eze 18:4, 13, 18, 20; 33:14
**33:9** [a]Ac 13:40, 41, 46 [b]Eze 3:19, 21; Ac 20:26 **33:10** [a]Lv 26:39; Eze 4:17; 24:23 [b]Is 49:14; Eze 37:11
**33:11** [a]Is 49:18; Eze 5:11 [b]Eze 18:23, 32; Hos 11:8 [c]Jer 31:20; 1Ti 2:4; 2Pe 3:9 [d]Is 55:6, 7; Jer 3:22; Eze 18:30, 31; Hos 14:1; Ac 3:19 **33:12** [a]Eze 3:18; 18:24; 33:20 [b]2Chr 7:14; Eze 18:21; 33:19 [1]Lit *by it*
**33:13** [a]Eze 18:26; Heb 10:38; 2Pe 2:20, 21 **33:14** [a]Is 55:7; Jer 18:7, 8; Eze 18:27; 33:8, 19; Hos 14:1, 4 [b]Mic 6:8 **33:15** [a]Ex 22:1-4; Lv 6:4, 5; Lk 19:8 [b]Ps 119:59; 143:8; Eze 20:11 **33:16** [a]Is 1:18; 43:25; Eze 18:22
**33:18** [a]Eze 3:20; 18:24; 33:12, 13 [1]Lit *them* **33:20** [a]Eze 18:25 **33:21** [a]Eze 31:1; 32:1, 17 [b]Jer 39:1, 2; 40:1; 52:4-7; Eze 24:1, 2 [c]2Ki 25:10; Jer 39:8

22 Now the [a]hand of Yahweh had
been upon me in the evening, be-
fore those who escaped came. And
He [b]opened my mouth [1]at the time
*they* came to me in the morning; so
my mouth was [c]opened, and I was
no longer mute.
23 Then the word of Yahweh came
to me saying, 24 "Son of man, they
who [a]inhabit these waste places in
the land of Israel are saying, '[b]Abra-
ham was *only* one, yet he possessed
the land; so to [c]us who are many the
land has been given as a possession.'
25 Therefore say to them, 'Thus says
Lord Yahweh, "You eat *meat* with the
[a]blood *in it* and lift up your eyes to
your idols as you shed blood. [b]Should
you then possess the land? 26 You
[a]stand on account of your sword, you
do abominations, and each of you
defiles his neighbor's wife. Should
you then possess the land?"' 27 Thus
you shall say to them, 'Thus says Lord
Yahweh, "As I live, surely those who
are in the waste places will [a]fall by the
sword, and whoever is in the [1]open
field I will give to the beasts to be
devoured, and those who are in the
strongholds and in the [b]caves will die
of pestilence. 28 I will [a]make the land
a desolation and a desecration, and
the [b]lofty pride of her strength will
cease; and the mountains of Israel
*will be desolate so that* no one will
pass through. 29 Then they will know
that I am Yahweh, when I make the
land a desolation and a desecration
because of all their abominations
which they have done."'
30 "But as for you, son of man, the
sons of your people who talk about
you by the walls and in the doorways
of the houses, speak to one another,
each to his brother, saying, '[a]Come
now and hear what the word is
which comes forth from Yahweh.'
31 They come to you as people come
and sit before you *as* My people and
hear your words, but they do not do
them, for they do the lustful desires
*expressed* by their [a]mouth, *and*
their heart goes after their [b]greedy
gain. 32 Behold, you are to them
like a lustful song by one who has
a [a]beautiful voice and plays well on
an instrument; for they hear your
words but they do not do them. 33 So
when it [a]comes to pass—behold, it
is coming—then they will know that
a prophet has been in their midst."

### *Prophecy Against the Shepherds of Israel*

34 Then the word of Yahweh
came to me saying, 2 "Son
of man, prophesy against the
[a]shepherds of Israel. Prophesy and
say to [1]those shepherds, 'Thus says
Lord Yahweh, "Woe, shepherds of
Israel who have been [b,2]shepherding
themselves! Should not the shep-
herds [c]shepherd the flock? 3 You
[a]eat the fat and clothe yourselves
with the wool; you [b]sacrifice the fat
*sheep* without shepherding the flock.

**33:22** [a]Eze 1:3; 8:1; 37:1 [b]Eze 3:26, 27; 24:27 [c]Lk 1:64 [1]Lit *until he came* **33:24** [a]Jer 39:10; 40:7; Eze 33:27 [b]Is 51:2; Lk 3:8; Ac 7:5; Ro 4:12 [c]Eze 11:15 **33:25** [a]Lv 17:10, 12, 14; Dt 12:16, 23; 15:23 [b]Jer 7:9, 10 **33:26** [a]Mic 2:1, 2; Zep 3:3 **33:27** [a]Jer 15:2, 3; 42:22; Eze 5:12 [b]1Sa 13:6; Is 2:19 [1]Lit *surface of the field* **33:28** [a]Eze 5:14; 6:14; Mic 7:13 [b]Eze 7:24; 24:21; 30:6 **33:30** [a]Is 29:13; 58:2; Eze 14:3; 20:3, 31 **33:31** [a]Ps 78:36, 37; Is 29:13; 1Jn 3:18 [b]Eze 22:13, 27; Lk 12:15 **33:32** [a]Mk 6:20 **33:33** [a]Jer 28:9; Eze 33:29 ◆**34:2** [a]Jer 2:8; 3:15; 10:21; 12:10 [b]Jer 23:1; Eze 22:25; 34:8-10; Mic 3:1-3, 11 [c]Ps 78:71, 72; Is 40:11; Eze 34:14, 15; Jn 10:11; 21:15-17 [1]Lit *them, the shepherds* [2]Or *feeding*, so in ch **34:3** [a]Zec 11:16 [b]Eze 22:25, 27

4 Those who are sickly you have not
strengthened, and the [1]diseased you
have not healed, and [a]the broken
you have not bound up, and the scat-
tered you have not brought back, nor
have you [b]searched for the lost; but
with strength and with severity you
have dominated them. 5 They were
[a]scattered for lack of a shepherd,
and they became [b]food for every
beast of the field and were scattered.
6 My flock [a]wandered through all
the mountains and on every high
hill; [b]My flock was scattered over
all the surface of the earth, and there
was [c]no one to seek or search *for*
*them*."'"

7 Therefore, you shepherds, hear
the word of Yahweh: 8 "As I live," de-
clares Lord Yahweh, "surely because
My flock has become [a]plunder, My
flock has even become food for all
the beasts of the field for lack of a
shepherd, and My shepherds did
not seek for My flock, but *rather*
the shepherds shepherded them-
selves and did not shepherd My
flock; 9 therefore, you shepherds,
hear the word of Yahweh: 10 'Thus
says Lord Yahweh, "Behold, I am
[a]against the shepherds, and I will
seek My flock from their hand and
make them [b]cease from shepherding
the flock. So the shepherds will not
shepherd themselves anymore, but
I will [c]deliver My flock from their
mouth so that they will not be food
for them."'"

### *Yahweh Will Shepherd His Flock*

11 For thus says Lord Yahweh, "Be-
hold, I Myself will [a]seek My sheep
and care for them. 12 [a]As a shepherd
[1]cares for his herd in the day when he
is among his [2]sheep which are spread
out, so I will [b,1]care for My [2]sheep and
will deliver them from all the places
to which they were scattered on a
[c]cloudy and gloomy day. 13 I will bring
them out from the peoples and gath-
er them from the countries and bring
them to their own land; and I will
[a]shepherd them on the mountains of
Israel, by the [b]streams, and in all the
inhabited places of the land. 14 I will
shepherd them in a [a]good pasture,
and their grazing ground will be on
the mountain heights of Israel. There
they will lie down on good grazing
ground and *be* shepherded in [b,1]rich
pasture on the mountains of Israel.
15 I will [a]shepherd My flock, and I will
make them lie down," declares Lord
Yahweh. 16 "I will search for the lost,
bring back the scattered, bind up the
broken, and strengthen the sick; but
the [a]fat and the strong I will destroy.
I will [b]shepherd them with judgment.

17 "As for you, My flock, thus says
Lord Yahweh, 'Behold, I will [a]judge
between one [1]sheep and another,
between the rams and the male
goats. 18 Is it too [a]slight a thing for
you that you should *be* shepherded in
the good pasture, that you must tread
down with your feet the rest of your
pastures? Or that you should drink of

---

**34:4** [a]Zec 11:16 [b]Mt 9:36; 10:6; 18:12, 13; Lk 15:4 [1]Lit *sick* **34:5** [a]Nu 27:17; 2Chr 18:16; Jer 10:21; 23:2; 50:6, 7; Mt 9:36; Mk 6:34 [b]Eze 34:8, 28 **34:6** [a]Jer 40:11, 12; Eze 7:16; 1Pe 2:25 [b]Jn 10:16 [c]Ps 142:4 **34:8** [a]Ac 20:29 **34:10** [a]Jer 21:13; Eze 5:8; 13:8; 34:2; Zec 10:3 [b]1Sa 2:29, 30; Jer 52:24-27 [c]Ps 72:12-14; Eze 13:23 **34:11** [a]Eze 11:17; 20:41 **34:12** [a]Jer 31:10 [b]Is 40:11; 56:8; Jer 23:3; 31:8; Lk 19:10; Jn 10:16 [c]Jer 13:16; Eze 30:3; Joel 2:2 [1]Or *seek(s) out* [2]Or *flock* **34:13** [a]Eze 34:23; 36:29, 30; Mic 7:14 [b]Is 30:25 **34:14** [a]Ps 23:2; Jer 31:12-14, 25; Jn 10:9 [b]Eze 28:25, 26; 36:29, 30 [1]Lit *fat* **34:15** [a]Ps 23:1, 2; Eze 34:23 **34:16** [a]Is 10:16 [b]Is 49:26 **34:17** [a]Eze 20:38; 34:20-22; Mal 4:1; Mt 25:32 [1]Or *lamb* **34:18** [a]Nu 16:9, 13; 2Sa 7:19; Is 7:13

the clear waters, that you must [1]foul
the rest with your feet? **19** As for My
flock, they must *be* shepherded on
what you tread down with your feet
and drink what you [1]foul with your
feet!'"

**20** Therefore, thus says Lord Yah-
weh to them, "Behold, I, even I, will
judge between the fat sheep and the
lean sheep. **21** Because you push with
side and with shoulder, and [a]thrust
at all the sickly with your horns until
you have scattered them [1]abroad,
**22** therefore, I will [a]save My flock, and
they will no longer be plunder;
and I will judge between one sheep
and another.

**23** "Then I will [a]establish over them
one [b]shepherd, My servant [c]David,
and he will shepherd them; he will
shepherd them himself and be their
shepherd. **24** And I, Yahweh, will be
their God, and My servant [a]David will
be prince among them; I, Yahweh,
have spoken.

### *Yahweh's Covenant of Peace*

**25** "I will cut a [a]covenant of peace
with them and [b]cause harmful
beasts to cease from the land so
that they may [c]live securely in the
wilderness and sleep in the woods.
**26** I will make them and the places
all around My hill a [a]blessing. And I
*will cause* [b]showers to come down in
their season; they will be showers of
[c]blessing. **27** Also the tree of the field
will yield its fruit, and the earth will
yield its produce, and they will be
[a]secure on their land. Then they will
know that I am Yahweh, when I have
[b]broken the bars of their yoke and
have delivered them from the hand
of those who enslaved them. **28** They
will no longer be plunder to the
nations, and the beasts of the earth
will not devour them; but they will
[a]live securely, and no one will make
*them* tremble. **29** I will establish for
them a [a,1]renowned planting place,
and they will [b]not again be [2]victims
of famine in the land, and they will
not [c]bear the dishonor of the nations
anymore. **30** Then they will know that
[a]I, Yahweh their God, am with them,
and that they, the house of Israel, are
My people," declares Lord Yahweh.
**31** "As for you, My [a]sheep, the [b]sheep
of My pasture, you are men, and I am
your God," declares Lord Yahweh.

### *Prophecy Against Mount Seir*

**35** Moreover, the word of Yahweh
came to me saying, **2** "Son of
man, set your face against [a]Mount
Seir and prophesy against it **3** and say
to it, 'Thus says Lord Yahweh,

"Behold, I am against you,
Mount Seir,
And I will [a]stretch out
My hand against you
And make you a [b]desolation
and a desecration.
**4** "I will [a]lay waste your cities,
And you will become
a desolation.

---

**34:18** [1]Lit *foul by trampling* **34:19** [1]Lit *foul by trampling* **34:21** [a]Dt 33:17; Da 8:4; Lk 13:14-16 [1]Lit *to the outside* **34:22** [a]Ps 72:12-14; Jer 23:3; Eze 34:10 **34:23** [a]Rev 7:17 [b]Is 40:11; Jn 10:11 [c]Jer 30:9; Eze 37:24 **34:24** [a]Is 55:3; Jer 30:9; Eze 37:24, 25; Hos 3:5 **34:25** [a]Eze 16:60; 20:37; 37:26 [b]Job 5:22, 23; Is 11:6-9 [c]Jer 33:16; Eze 28:26; 34:27, 28 **34:26** [a]Ge 12:2; Eze 34:14 [b]Dt 11:13-15; 28:12 [c]Lv 25:21; Is 44:3 **34:27** [a]Eze 38:8, 11 [b]Lv 26:13; Is 52:2, 3; Jer 30:8 **34:28** [a]Jer 30:10; Eze 39:26 **34:29** [a]Is 4:2; 60:21; 61:3 [b]Eze 34:26, 27; 36:29 [c]Eze 36:6, 15 [1]Lit *name* [2]Lit *those gathered* **34:30** [a]Ps 46:7, 11; Eze 14:11; 36:28 **34:31** [a]Ps 78:52; 80:1; Eze 36:38 [b]Ps 100:3; Jer 23:1 ◆ **35:2** [a]Ge 36:8; Eze 25:12; 36:5 **35:3** [a]Jer 6:12; 15:6; Eze 25:13 [b]Jer 49:13, 17, 18; Eze 35:7 **35:4** [a]Eze 6:6; 35:9; Mal 1:3, 4

Then you will know
that I am Yahweh.
**5** "Because you have had everlasting
[a]enmity and have [1]delivered the sons
of Israel to the power of the sword
at the time of their disaster, at the
time of the [b,2]punishment of the
end, **6** therefore as I live," declares
Lord Yahweh, "I will [1]prepare you
for [a]bloodshed, and bloodshed will
pursue you; you surely have not
hated bloodshed, so bloodshed will
pursue you. **7** I will make Mount Seir
a waste and a desolation, and I will
cut off from it the one who passes
through and returns. **8** I will [a]fill its
mountains with its slain; on your
hills and in your valleys and in all
your ravines those slain by the sword
will [1]fall. **9** I will make you an ever-
lasting [a]desolation, and your cities
will not be inhabited. Then you will
know that I am Yahweh.

**10** "Because you have [a]said, 'These
two nations and these two lands will
be mine, and we will possess [1]them,'
although [b]Yahweh was there, **11** there-
fore as I live," declares Lord Yahweh,
"I will deal *with you* [a]according to
your anger and according to your
jealousy which you dealt *with them*
because of your hatred against them;
so I will [b]make Myself known among
them when I judge you. **12** Then you
will know [1]that I, Yahweh, have heard
all your [2]contempt which you have
spoken against the mountains of
Israel saying, 'They are laid desolate;
they are [a]given to us for food.' **13** And
you have [a]magnified *yourselves* with
your mouth against Me and have
multiplied your words against Me;
[b]I have heard *it*." **14** Thus says Lord
Yahweh, "As all the [a]earth delights,
I will make you a desolation. **15** As
you [a]delighted over the inheritance
of the house of Israel because it was
desolate, [b]so I will do to you. You
will be a [c]desolation, O Mount Seir,
and all Edom, all of it. Then they will
know that I am Yahweh."'

### *Mountains of Israel Will Bear Fruit*

**36** "Now as for you, son of man,
prophesy to the mountains of
Israel and say, 'O mountains of Israel,
hear the word of Yahweh. **2** Thus says
Lord Yahweh, "Because the enemy
has spoken against you, 'Aha!' and,
'The everlasting [a,1]heights have
become our possession,' **3** therefore
prophesy and say, 'Thus says Lord
Yahweh, "[1]For good reason they have
made you [a]desolate and bruised you
from every side, that you would
become a possession of the rest of
the nations, and you have been taken
up in the [b,2]speech of *their* tongue
and the rumors of the people."'"
**4** Therefore, O [a]mountains of Israel,
hear the word of Lord Yahweh. Thus
says Lord Yahweh to the mountains
and to the hills, to the ravines and
to the valleys, to the desolate wastes
and to the forsaken cities which
have become [b]plunder and *objects*

**35:5** [a]*Ps 137:7; Eze 25:12, 15; 36:5;* Am 1:11; Ob 10 [b]Eze 7:2; 21:25, 29 [1]Lit *poured* [2]Or *iniquity*
**35:6** [a]Is 63:2-6; Eze 16:38; 32:6 [1]Lit *do* **35:8** [a]Is 34:5, 6; Eze 31:12; 32:4, 5; 39:4, 5 [1]Lit *fall in them*
**35:9** [a]Jer 49:13; Eze 25:13 **35:10** [a]Ps 83:4-12; Eze 36:2, 5 [b]Ps 48:1-3; 132:13, 14; Is 12:6; Eze 48:35; Zep 3:15
[1]Lit *it* **35:11** [a]Ps 137:7; Eze 25:14; Am 1:11 [b]Ps 9:16; 73:17, 18 **35:12** [a]Jer 50:7; Eze 36:2 [1]Or *that I am Yahweh: I have heard* [2]Or *blasphemies*, cf. Ne 9:18, 26 **35:13** [a]Is 10:13, 14; 36:20; Jer 48:26, 42; Da 11:36
[b]Jer 7:11; 29:23 **35:14** [a]Is 44:23; 49:13; Jer 51:48 **35:15** [a]Jer 50:11; Lam 4:21 [b]Ob 15 [c]Is 34:5, 6; Eze 35:3, 4
◆ **36:2** [a]Dt 32:13; Ps 78:69; Is 58:14; Hab 3:19 [1]Heb *Bamoth* **36:3** [a]Jer 2:15 [b]Ps 44:13, 14; Jer 18:16; Eze 35:13 [1]Or *By the cause*; lit *Because* [2]Lit *lip of the tongue* **36:4** [a]Dt 11:11; Eze 36:1, 6, 8 [b]Eze 34:8, 28

*of* scoffing to the rest of the nations
which are round about, **5** therefore
thus says Lord Yahweh, "Surely in
the fire of My [a]jealousy I have spo-
ken against the [b]rest of the nations
and against all Edom, who gave My
land to themselves as a possession
with wholehearted [c]gladness *and*
with scorn of soul, to drive it out
for plunder." **6** Therefore prophesy
concerning the land of Israel and say
to the mountains and to the hills,
to the ravines and to the valleys,
"Thus says Lord Yahweh, 'Behold, I
have spoken in My jealousy and in
My wrath because you have [a]borne
the dishonor of the nations.' **7** There-
fore thus says Lord Yahweh, 'I have
[1]sworn that surely the nations which
are around you will themselves bear
their dishonor. **8** But you, O moun-
tains of Israel, you will [a]put forth
your branches and bear your fruit
for My people Israel; for they will
soon come. **9** For, behold, I am for
you, and I will [a]turn to you, and you
will be [b]cultivated and sown. **10** I will
multiply men on you, [a]all the house
of Israel, all of it; and the [b]cities will
be inhabited, and the waste places
will be rebuilt. **11** I will multiply on
you man and beast; and they will
multiply and be fruitful; and I will
cause you to be inhabited as you were
[a]formerly and will [1]treat you [b]better
than at the first. Thus you will know
that I am Yahweh. **12** And I will cause
[a]men—My people Israel—to walk on
you and possess you so that you will
become their [b]inheritance and never
again [c]bereave them of children.'
**13** "Thus says Lord Yahweh, 'Be-
cause they say to you, "You are a
[a]devourer of men and have bereaved
your [1]nation of children," **14** therefore
you will no longer devour men and
no longer bereave your nation of
children,' declares Lord Yahweh. **15** I
will not let you hear [a]dishonor from
the nations anymore, nor will you
bear [b]reproach from the peoples any
longer, nor will you cause your na-
tion to [c]stumble any longer," declares
Lord Yahweh.'"

### *Yahweh's Name Profaned Among the Nations*

**16** Then the word of Yahweh came to
me saying, **17** "Son of man, when the
house of Israel was living in their own
land, they [a]defiled it by their ways
and their deeds; their way before
Me was like [b]the uncleanness of a
woman in her impurity. **18** Therefore
I [a]poured out My wrath on them for
the blood which they had shed on
the land, because they had defiled it
with their idols. **19** Also I [a]scattered
them among the nations, and they
were dispersed throughout the lands.
[b]According to their ways and their
deeds I judged them. **20** Then they
came to the nations to which they
came. And they [a]profaned My holy
name because it was said of them,
'These are the [b]people of Yahweh;

**36:5** [a]Eze 5:13; 36:6; 38:19 [b]Jer 25:9, 15-29; Eze 36:3 [c]Jer 50:11; Eze 35:15; Mic 7:8 **36:6** [a]Ps 74:10; 123:3, 4; Eze 34:29 **36:7** [1]Lit *lifted up My hand, borne up my hand*; cf. 36:7b **36:8** [a]Is 4:2; 27:6; Eze 17:23; 34:26-29 **36:9** [a]Lv 26:9 [b]Eze 28:26; 34:14; 36:34 **36:10** [a]Is 27:6; 49:17-23; Eze 37:21, 22 [b]Jer 31:27, 28; 33:12; Eze 36:33 **36:11** [a]Jer 30:18; Eze 16:55; Mic 7:14 [b]Job 42:12; Is 51:3 [1]Lit *cause good* **36:12** [a]Eze 34:13, 14 [b]Eze 47:14 [c]Jer 15:7; Eze 22:12, 27 **36:13** [a]Nu 13:32 [1]Or *nations*, so in ch **36:15** [a]Is 60:14; Eze 34:29; 36:7 [b]Ps 89:50; Is 54:4; Eze 22:4 [c]Is 63:13; Jer 13:16; 18:15 **36:17** [a]Jer 2:7 [b]Lv 15:19 **36:18** [a]2Chr 34:21, 25; Lam 2:4; 4:11; Eze 22:20, 22 **36:19** [a]Dt 28:64; Eze 5:12; 22:15; Am 9:9 [b]Eze 24:14; 39:24; Ro 2:6 **36:20** [a]Is 52:5; Eze 12:16; Ro 2:24 [b]Jer 33:24

sons of Israel, his companions'; then
take another stick and write on it,
'For [c]Joseph, the stick of Ephraim and
all the house of Israel, his compan-
ions.' **17** Then [a]draw them together
for yourself one to another into one
stick, that they may become one in
your hand. **18** And when the sons
of your people speak to you saying,
'Will you not declare to us [a]what
you mean by these?' **19** say to them,
'Thus says Lord Yahweh, "Behold, I
will take the stick of Joseph, which
is in the hand of Ephraim, and the
tribes of Israel, his companions; and
I will put them with it, with the stick
of Judah, and make them one stick,
and they will be one in My hand."'
**20** And the sticks on which you write
will be in your hand before their eyes.
**21** And speak to them, 'Thus says
Lord Yahweh, "Behold, I will [a]take
the sons of Israel from among the
nations where they have gone, and
I will gather them from every side
and bring them into their own land;
**22** and I will make them [a]one nation
in the land, on the mountains of Isra-
el; and [b]one king will be king for all of
them; and they will no longer be two
nations and no longer be divided into
two kingdoms. **23** They also will [a]no
longer defile themselves with their
idols or with their detestable things
or with any of their transgressions;
but [b]I will save them from all their
[1]*places of* habitation in which they
have sinned, and I will cleanse them.
And they will be My people, and I will
be their God.

### *Yahweh Cuts a Covenant*

**24** "And My servant [a]David will be
king over them, and they will all
have [b]one shepherd; and they will
walk in My judgments and keep My
statutes and do them. **25** They will
inhabit the land that I gave to Jacob
My servant, which your fathers in-
habited; and they will inhabit it, they,
and their sons and their sons' sons,
forever; and [a]David My servant will
be their prince forever. **26** And I will
cut a [a]covenant of peace with them;
it will be an [b]everlasting covenant
with them. And I will give them *the
land* and [c]multiply them and will set
My [d]sanctuary in their midst forever.
**27** My [a,1]dwelling place also will be
with them; and [b]I will be their God,
and they will be My people. **28** And
the nations will know that I am Yah-
weh [a]who sanctifies Israel, when My
sanctuary is in their midst forever."'"

### *Prophecy Against Gog*

**38** And the word of Yahweh came
to me saying, **2** "Son of man,
set your face toward [a]Gog of the
land of [b]Magog, the [c,1]chief prince
of [d]Meshech and [d]Tubal, and proph-
esy against him **3** and say, 'Thus says
Lord Yahweh, "Behold, I am against
you, O Gog, [1]chief prince of Meshech
and Tubal. **4** I will turn you about and
put hooks into your jaws, and I will

---

**37:16** [c]1Ki 12:16-20; 2Chr 10:19 **37:17** [a]Is 11:13; Jer 50:4; Eze 37:22-24; Hos 1:11; Zep 3:9 **37:18** [a]Eze 12:9; 17:12; 20:49; 24:19 **37:21** [a]Is 43:5, 6; Jer 29:14; Eze 36:24; 39:27; Am 9:14, 15 **37:22** [a]Jer 3:18; 50:4, 5; Eze 36:10 [b]Eze 34:23, 24; 37:24 **37:23** [a]Eze 36:25 [b]Eze 36:28, 29 [1]Or *backslidings* **37:24** [a]Jer 30:9; Eze 34:24; 37:25; Hos 3:5 [b]Ps 78:71; Is 40:11; Eze 34:23 **37:25** [a]Is 11:1; Eze 37:24; Zec 6:12 **37:26** [a]Eze 16:62; 20:37; 34:25 [b]Ps 89:3, 4; Is 55:3; 59:21; Eze 16:60 [c]Jer 30:19; Eze 36:10, 11, 37 [d]Eze 20:40; 43:7 **37:27** [a]Jn 1:14; Rev 21:3 [b]Eze 37:23; 2Co 6:16 [1]Or *tabernacle* **37:28** [a]Ex 31:13; Eze 20:12 ◆ **38:2** [a]Eze 38:3, 14, 16, 18; 39:1, 11; Rev 20:8 [b]Ge 10:2; Eze 39:6; Rev 20:8 [c]Eze 38:3; 39:1 [d]Eze 27:13; 38:3; 39:1 [1]Or *prince of Rosh, Meshech, and Tubal* **38:3** [1]Or *prince of Rosh, Mesech, and Tubal*

[a]bring you out, and all your mili-
tary force, [b]horses and horsemen,
all of them [1]magnificently dressed,
a great assembly *with* large shield
and shield, all of them [2]wielding
swords; **5** [a]Persia, [b,1]Ethiopia, and
[c]Put with them, all of them *with*
shield and helmet; **6** [a]Gomer with
all its troops; [b]Beth-togarmah *from*
the remote parts of the north with all
its troops—many peoples with you.
**7** "[a]Be prepared, and prepare your-
self, you and all your assembly that
are assembled about you, and be a
guard for them. **8** [a]After many days
you will be mustered; in the last years
you will come into the land that is
[1]restored from the sword, *whose in-
habitants* have been [b]gathered from
many peoples to the [c]mountains of
Israel which had been a continual
waste; but [2]its people were brought
out from the peoples, and they are
[d]living securely, all of them. **9** And
you will go up; you will come [a]like
a storm; you will be like a [b]cloud
covering the land, you and all your
troops and many peoples with you."
**10** 'Thus says Lord Yahweh, "It will
be in that day, *that* [1]thoughts will
come into your heart, and you
will [a]devise an evil plan, **11** and you
will say, 'I will go up against the
land of [a,1]unwalled villages. I will
go against those who [b]*dwell* quietly,
that live securely, all of them living
without walls and having no bars or
gates, **12** to [a]capture spoil and to seize
plunder, to turn your hand against
the waste places, which are *now*
inhabited, and against the people
who are gathered from the nations,
who have acquired cattle and prop-
erty, who live at the [1]center of the
world.' **13** [a]Sheba and [b]Dedan and the
merchants of [c]Tarshish with all its
[1]young lions will say to you, 'Have
you come to capture spoil? Have you
assembled your assembly to seize
plunder, to carry away silver and
gold, to take away cattle and goods,
to capture great [d]spoil?'"'

**14** "Therefore prophesy, son of
man, and say to Gog, 'Thus says
Lord Yahweh, "On that day when My
people Israel are [a]living securely, will
you not know *it*? **15** [a]You will come
from your place out of the remote
parts of the north, you and numerous
peoples with you, all of them riding
on horses, a great assembly and a
numerous military force; **16** and you
will come up against My people Israel
like a cloud to cover the land. It will
be in the last days that I will bring you
against My land so that the nations
may [a]know Me when I [b]prove Myself
holy through you before their eyes,
O Gog."

**17** 'Thus says Lord Yahweh, "Are
you the one of whom I spoke in
former days by the hand of My
slaves the prophets of Israel, who
[a]prophesied in those days for *many*

**38:4** [a]Is 43:17 [b]Eze 38:15; Da 11:40 [1]Or *clothed in full armor* [2]Lit *seizing* **38:5** [a]2Chr 36:20; Ezr 1:1; Eze 27:10; Da 8:20 [b]Ge 10:6-8; Eze 30:4, 5 [c]Eze 27:10; 30:5 [1]Or *Cush*, cf. Ge 10:6 **38:6** [a]Ge 10:2, 3 [b]Ge 10:3; Eze 27:14 **38:7** [a]Is 8:9 **38:8** [a]Is 24:22 [b]Is 11:11; Eze 36:24; 37:21; 38:12; 39:27, 28 [c]Eze 34:13; 36:1-8 [d]Eze 38:11, 14; 39:26 [1]Lit *returned* [2]Lit *it was* **38:9** [a]Is 5:28; 21:1; 25:4; 28:2; Jer 4:13 [b]Eze 30:18; 38:16; Joel 2:2 **38:10** [a]Ps 36:4; Mic 2:1 [1]Lit *words* **38:11** [a]Zec 2:4 [b]Jer 49:31 [1]Or *open country* **38:12** [a]Is 10:6; Eze 29:19 [1]Lit *navel* **38:13** [a]Eze 27:22, 23 [b]Eze 25:13; 27:15, 20 [c]Eze 27:12 [d]Is 10:6; 33:23; Jer 15:13 [1]Or *villages* **38:14** [a]Jer 23:6; Eze 38:8, 11; Zec 2:5, 8 **38:15** [a]Eze 39:2 **38:16** [a]Ps 83:18; Eze 36:23; 38:23 [b]Is 5:16; 8:13; 29:23; Eze 28:22 **38:17** [a]Is 5:26-29; 34:1-6; 63:1-6; 66:15, 16; Joel 3:9-14

will [a,1]forget their dishonor and all
their unfaithfulness which they [2]per-
petrated against Me, when they [b]live
securely on their *own* land with [c]no
one to make *them* tremble. **27** When
I [a]return them from the peoples and
gather them from the lands of their
enemies, then I shall [b]prove Myself
holy [1]through them in the sight of
the many nations. **28** Then they will
know that I am Yahweh their God
because I made them go into exile
among the nations, and then collect-
ed them *again* to their own land; and
I will leave none of them there any
longer. **29** And I will not hide My face
from them any longer, for I will have
[a]poured out My Spirit on the house
of Israel," declares Lord Yahweh.

### *Visions of the House of Yahweh*

**40** In the [a]twenty-fifth year of
our exile, at the beginning of
the year, on the tenth of the month,
in the fourteenth year after the [b]city
was struck down, on that same day
the [c]hand of Yahweh was upon me,
and He brought me there. **2** In the
[a]visions of God He brought me into
the land of Israel and caused me to
rest on a very [b]high mountain, and on
it [c]to the south *there was* a [d]structure
like a city. **3** So He brought me there;
and behold, there was a man whose
appearance was like the appearance
of [a]bronze, with a [b]line of flax and a
[c]measuring [1]rod in his hand; and he
was standing in the gateway. **4** And
the man spoke to me, "[a]Son of man,
[b]see with your eyes, hear with your
ears, and set your heart on all that I
am going to show you; for you have
been brought here in order to show *it*
to you. [c]Declare to the house of Israel
all that you are seeing."

### *The East Gate*

**5** And behold, there was a [a]wall on
the outside of the house *of Yahweh*
all around, and in the man's hand
was a measuring rod of six cubits,
*each of which was* a [1]cubit and a
[2]handbreadth. So he measured the
thickness of the [3]wall, one rod; and
the height, one rod. **6** Then he went
to the gate which faced [a]east, went up
its steps, and measured the threshold
of the gate, one rod [1]in width; and the
other threshold *was* one rod [1]in width.
**7** The [a]guardroom *was* one rod long
and one rod wide; and *there were* five
cubits between the guardrooms. And
the threshold of the gate by the porch
of the gate [1]facing inward *was* one
rod. **8** Then he measured the porch
of the gate [1]facing inward, one rod.
**9** He measured the porch of the gate,
eight cubits; and its side pillars, two
cubits. And the porch of the gate was
[1]faced inward. **10** The guardrooms of
the gate toward the east *numbered*
three on each side; the three of
them had the same measurement.
The side pillars also had the same

**39:26** [a]Eze 16:63; 20:43; 36:31 [b]1Ki 4:25; Eze 34:25-28 [c]Is 17:2; Mic 4:4 [1]Or *bear* [2]Lit *acted unfaithfully*
**39:27** [a]Eze 36:24; 37:21 [b]Eze 36:23; 38:16, 23 [1]Lit *in* **39:29** [a]Is 32:15; Eze 36:27; 37:14; Joel 2:28
◆ **40:1** [a]Eze 32:1, 17; 33:21 [b]2Ki 25:1-7; Jer 39:1-9; 52:4-11; Eze 33:21 [c]Eze 1:3; 3:14, 22; 37:1 **40:2** [a]Eze 1:1; 8:3; Da 7:1, 7 [b]Is 2:2, 3; Eze 17:23; 20:40; 37:22; Mic 4:1; Rev 21:10 [c]Ps 48:2; Is 14:13 [d]1Chr 28:12, 19
**40:3** [a]Eze 1:7; Da 10:6; Rev 1:15 [b]Eze 47:3; Zec 2:1, 2 [c]Rev 11:1; 21:15 [1]Lit *reed*, so in ch **40:4** [a]Eze 2:1, 3, 6, 8; 44:5 [b]Eze 2:7, 8; 44:5 [c]Is 21:10; Jer 26:2; Ac 20:27 **40:5** [a]Is 26:1; Eze 42:20 [1]A cubit was approx. 18 in. or 45 cm [2]A handbreadth was approx. 3 in. or 7.5 cm [3]Lit *building* **40:6** [a]Eze 8:16; 11:1; 40:20; 43:1 [1]Or *in depth* **40:7** [a]Eze 40:10-16, 21, 29, 33, 36 [1]Lit *from the house* **40:8** [1]Lit *from the house*
**40:9** [1]Lit *from the house*

measurement on each side. **11** And he
measured the width of the entrance
of the gate, ten cubits, and the length
of the gate, thirteen cubits. **12** *There
was* a [1]barrier *wall* one cubit *wide* in
front of the guardrooms on each side;
and the guardrooms *were* six cubits
*square* on each side. **13** He measured
the gate from the roof of the one
guardroom to the roof of the other,
a width of twenty-five cubits from
*one* door to *the* door opposite. **14** He
made the side pillars sixty cubits
*high;* the gate *extended* round about
to the side pillar of the [a]courtyard.
**15** *From* the front of the entrance
gate to the front of the inner porch
of the gate *was* fifty cubits. **16** *There
were* [a,1]shuttered windows *looking*
toward the guardrooms and toward
their side pillars within the gate all
around, and likewise for the porches.
And *there were* windows all around
inside; and on *each* side pillar *were*
[b]palm tree ornaments.

### *The Outer Court Chambers*

**17** Then he brought me into the
[a]outer court, and behold, *there were*
[b]chambers and a pavement made for
the court all around; thirty chambers
[1]faced the pavement. **18** The pavement
(*that is,* the lower pavement) *was* by
the [1]side of the gates, corresponding
to the length of the gates. **19** Then he
measured the width from the front
of the [a]lower gate to the front of
the exterior of the inner court, [1]one
[b]hundred cubits on the east and on
the north.

### *The North Gate*

**20** *As for* the [a]gate of the outer court
which faced the north, he measured
its length and its width. **21** [1]It had
three [a]guardrooms on each side;
and its [b]side pillars and its porches
[2]had the same measurement as the
first gate. Its length *was* [c,3]fifty cubits
and the width [d]twenty-five cubits.
**22** Its [a]windows and its porches and
its palm tree ornaments *had* the
same measurements as the [b]gate
which faced toward the east; and [1]it
was reached by seven [c]steps, and its
[2]porch *was* in front of them. **23** The
inner court had a gate opposite the
gate on the north as well as *the gate*
on the east; and he measured one
[a]hundred cubits from gate to gate.

### *The South Gate*

**24** Then he led me toward the south,
and behold, there was a [a]gate toward
the south; and he measured its [b]side
pillars and its porches according to
[1]those same measurements. **25** [1]The
gate and its porches had [a]windows
all around like [2]those other windows;
the length *was* [b]fifty cubits and the
width twenty-five cubits. **26** *There
were* seven [a]steps going up to it,
and its porches *were* in front of them;
and it had [b]palm tree ornaments on

**40:12** [1]Lit *border* **40:14** [a]Ex 27:9; 1Chr 28:6; Ps 100:4; Is 62:9; Eze 8:7; 42:1 **40:16** [a]1Ki 6:4; Eze 41:16, 26 [b]1Ki 6:29, 32, 35; 2Chr 3:5; Eze 40:22, 26, 31, 34, 37; 41:18-20, 25, 26 [1]Or *beveled inwards* **40:17** [a]Eze 10:5; 42:1; 46:21; Rev 11:2 [b]2Ki 23:11; 1Chr 9:26; 23:28; 2Chr 31:11; Eze 40:38 [1]Lit *to* **40:18** [1]Lit *shoulder* **40:19** [a]Eze 40:23, 27; 46:1, 2 [b]Eze 40:23, 27 [1]Approx. 150 ft. or 45 m **40:20** [a]Eze 40:6 **40:21** [a]Eze 40:7 [b]Eze 40:16, 30 [c]Eze 40:15 [d]Eze 40:13 [1]Lit *Its guardrooms were 3* [2]Lit *were* [3]Approx. 75 ft. long and 37.5 ft. wide or 22.5 m and 11.25 m **40:22** [a]Eze 40:16 [b]Eze 40:6 [c]Eze 40:26, 31, 34, 37, 49 [1]Lit *they were going up into it* [2]Or *porches* **40:23** [a]Eze 40:19, 27 **40:24** [a]Eze 40:6, 20, 35; 46:9 [b]Eze 40:21 [1]Lit *these measurements*, so in ch **40:25** [a]Eze 40:16, 22, 29 [b]Eze 40:21, 33 [1]Lit *It* [2]Lit *these windows* **40:26** [a]Eze 40:6, 22 [b]Eze 40:16

went higher; and thus one went up from the lowest *story* to the highest by way of the [1]second *story.* **8** I saw also that the house had a raised [1]platform all around; the foundations of the side chambers were a full rod of [a,2]six [3]long cubits *in height.* **9** The [1]thickness of the outer wall of the side chambers *was* five cubits. But the [a]free space between the side chambers belonging to the house **10** and the *outer* [a]chambers *was* twenty cubits in width all around the house on every side. **11** The [1]doorways of the [2]side chambers toward the [a]free space *consisted of* one doorway toward the north and another doorway toward the south; and the width of the place of the [a]free space *was* five cubits all around.

**12** The [a]building that *was* in front of the [b]separate area at the side toward the west *was* [1]seventy cubits wide; and the wall of the building *was* five cubits [2]thick all around, and its length *was* [3]ninety cubits.

### *The Measurements of the Building*

**13** Then he measured the house, [1]one [a]hundred cubits long; the [b]separate area with the [c]building and its walls *were* also one [a]hundred cubits long. **14** Also the width of the front of the house and *that of* the separate [1]areas along the east *side totaled* one hundred cubits.

**15** He measured the length of the [a]building [1]along the front of the [b]separate area behind it, with a [c,2]gallery on each side, one hundred cubits, along with the inner nave and the porches of the court.

### *Carvings and Furnishings*

**16** The [a]thresholds, the [b,1]latticed windows, and the [c,2]galleries round about their [d]three stories, opposite the threshold, were [e]paneled with wood all around, and *from* the ground to the windows (but the windows were covered), **17** over the entrance, and to the inner house, and on the outside, and on all the wall all around inside and outside, by measurement. **18** It was [1]carved with [a]cherubim and [b]palm trees; and a palm tree was between cherub and cherub, and every cherub had two faces, **19** a [a]man's face toward the palm tree on one side and a young [a]lion's face toward the palm tree on the other side; they were [1]carved on all the house all around. **20** From the ground to above the entrance [a]cherubim and [a]palm trees were [1]carved, as well as *on* the wall of the nave.

**21** The [a]doorposts of the [b]nave were square; as for the front of the sanctuary, the appearance of one doorpost was like that of the other. **22** The [a]altar *was* of wood, three cubits high and its length two cubits; its corners, its [1]base, and its [2]sides *were*

**41:7** [1]Lit *middle* **41:8** [a]Eze 40:5 [1]Lit *height* [2]Approx. 10.25 ft. or 3.1 m, a long cubit was approx. 20.5 in. or 52 cm [3]Or *to the joint* **41:9** [a]Eze 41:11 [1]Lit *width* **41:10** [a]Eze 40:17 **41:11** [a]Eze 41:9 [1]Lit *doorway* [2]Lit *side chamber* **41:12** [a]Eze 41:13, 15; 42:1 [b]Eze 41:14; 42:10, 13 [1]Approx. 105 ft. or 31.5 m [2]Lit *wide* [3]Approx. 135 ft. or 40.5 m **41:13** [a]Eze 40:47 [b]Eze 41:13-15; 42:1, 10, 13 [c]Eze 41:12 [1]Approx. 150 ft. or 45 m **41:14** [1]Lit *area* **41:15** [a]Eze 41:12, 13; 42:1 [b]Eze 41:14; 42:1, 10, 13 [c]Eze 41:16; 42:3, 5 [1]Lit *to* [2]Or *passageway* **41:16** [a]Is 6:4; Eze 10:18; 40:6; 41:25 [b]1Ki 6:4; Eze 40:16, 25; 41:26 [c]Eze 41:15 [d]Eze 42:3 [e]1Ki 6:15 [1]Or *framed* [2]Or *passageways* **41:18** [a]1Ki 6:29, 32, 35; 7:36; Eze 41:20, 25 [b]2Chr 3:5; Eze 40:16 [1]Lit *made* **41:19** [a]Eze 1:10; 10:14 [1]Lit *made* **41:20** [a]Eze 41:18 [1]Lit *made* **41:21** [a]1Ki 6:33; Eze 40:9, 14, 16; 41:1 [b]Eze 41:1 **41:22** [a]Ex 30:1-3; 1Ki 6:20; Rev 8:3 [1]Lit *length* [2]Lit *walls*

of wood. And he said to me, "This
is the [b]table that is before Yahweh."
**23** The [a]nave and the [b]sanctuary each
had a double [c]door. **24** Each of the
doors had two leaves, two [a,1]swinging
leaves; two *leaves* for one door and
two leaves for the other. **25** Also there
were [1]carved on them, on the doors of
the nave, [a]cherubim and [a]palm trees
like those [1]carved on the walls; and
*there was* a [b]canopy of wood over the
front of the porch outside. **26** *There
were* [a,1]latticed windows and [b]palm
trees on one side and on the other,
on the sides of the [c]porch; thus *were*
the [d]side chambers of the house and
the canopies.

### *The Chambers*

**42** Then he [a]brought me out
into the [b]outer court, the
way [c]toward the north; and he
brought me to the [d]chamber which
*was* opposite the [e]separate area and
opposite the [f]building toward the
north. **2** Along the length, *which
was* [1]one [a]hundred cubits, *was* the
north door; the width *was* fifty cu-
bits. **3** Opposite the [a,1]twenty *cubits*
which belonged to the inner court,
and opposite the [b]pavement which
belonged to the outer court, *was*
[c,2]gallery corresponding to [2]gallery in
three stories. **4** Before the [a]chambers
*was* an inner walk ten cubits wide, a
way of [1]one *hundred* cubits; and their
openings *were* on the north. **5** Now
the upper chambers *were* [1]smaller
because the [a,2]galleries took more
*space* away from them than from the
lower and middle ones in the build-
ing. **6** For they *were* in [a]three stories
and had no pillars like the pillars of
the courts; therefore *the upper cham-
bers* were [1]set back from the ground
upward, more than the lower and
middle ones. **7** As for the [a]outer wall
by the side of the chambers, toward
the outer court facing the chambers,
its length *was* fifty cubits. **8** For the
length of the chambers which *were*
in the outer court *was* fifty cubits;
and behold, *the length of those* facing
the temple *was* one [a]hundred cubits.
**9** Below these chambers *was* the
[a]entrance on the east side, as one
enters them from the outer court.
**10** In the [1]thickness of the [a]wall of
the court toward the east, facing the
[b]separate area and facing the build-
ing, *there were* [c]chambers. **11** The
[a]way in front of them *was* like the
appearance of the chambers which
*were* on the north, according to their
length so was their width, and all
their exits *were* both according to
their [1]arrangements and openings.
**12** Corresponding to the openings of
the chambers which were toward the
south was an opening at the head of
the way, the way in front of the [a]wall
toward the east, as one enters them.
**13** Then he said to me, "The north
chambers *and* the south chambers,

**41:22** [b]Ex 25:23, 30; Lv 24:6; Eze 23:41; 44:16; Mal 1:7, 12 **41:23** [a]Eze 41:1 [b]Eze 41:4 [c]1Ki 6:31-35 **41:24** [a]1Ki 6:34 [1]Or *turning* **41:25** [a]Eze 41:18 [b]Eze 41:16 [1]Lit *made* **41:26** [a]Eze 41:16 [b]Eze 40:16 [c]Eze 40:9, 48 [d]Eze 41:5 [1]Or *framed* ◆ **42:1** [a]Eze 40:17, 28, 48; 41:1 [b]Eze 40:17, 20 [c]Eze 40:20 [d]Eze 40:17; 42:4 [e]Eze 41:12; 42:10, 13 [f]Eze 41:12 **42:2** [a]Eze 41:13 [1]Approx. 150 ft. long and 75 ft. wide or 45 m and 22.5 m **42:3** [a]Eze 41:10 [b]Eze 40:17 [c]Eze 41:15, 16; 42:5 [1]Approx. 30 ft. or 9 m [2]Or *passageway* **42:4** [a]Eze 46:19 [1]Or *one cubit* in width **42:5** [a]Eze 42:3 [1]Lit *shorter* [2]Or *passageways* **42:6** [a]Eze 41:6 [1]Or *reduced* **42:7** [a]Eze 42:10, 12 **42:8** [a]Eze 41:13, 14 **42:9** [a]Eze 44:5; 46:19 **42:10** [a]Eze 42:7 [b]Eze 42:1, 13 [c]Eze 40:17 [1]Lit *width* **42:11** [a]Eze 42:4 [1]Lit *judgments* **42:12** [a]Eze 42:7

them near before Yahweh, and the priests shall throw [a]salt on them, and they shall offer them up as a burnt offering to Yahweh. **25** [a]For seven days you shall offer daily a goat for a sin offering; also a bull from the herd and a ram from the flock, without blemish, shall be offered. **26** For seven days they shall make atonement for the altar and purify it; so shall they [1]ordain it. **27** So they will complete the days. And it shall be that on the [a]eighth day and onward, the priests shall [1]offer on the altar your burnt offerings and your [b]peace offerings; and I will [c]accept you,' declares Lord Yahweh."

### *The Gate of the Prince*

**44** Then He brought me back by the way of the [a]outer gate of the sanctuary, which faces the east; and it was shut. **2** Yahweh said to me, "This gate shall be shut; it shall not be opened, and no one shall enter by it, for [a]Yahweh, the God of Israel, has entered by it; therefore it shall be shut. **3** As for the [a]prince, he shall sit in it as prince to [b]eat bread before Yahweh; he shall [c]enter by way of the [d]porch of the gate and shall go out [1]by the same way."

**4** Then He brought me by way of the [a]north gate to the front of the house; and I looked, and behold, the [b]glory of Yahweh filled the house of Yahweh, and I [c]fell on my face. **5** Then Yahweh said to me, "Son of man, [a]set your heart on and see with your eyes and hear with your ears all that I say to you concerning all the [b]statutes of the house of Yahweh and concerning all its laws; and set your heart on the entrance of the house, with all exits of the sanctuary. **6** And you shall say to the [a,1]rebellious ones, to the house of Israel, 'Thus says Lord Yahweh, "[b]Enough of all your abominations, O house of Israel, **7** when you brought in [a]foreigners, [b]uncircumcised in heart and uncircumcised in flesh, to be in My sanctuary to profane it, *even* My house, when you [c]brought near My food, the fat and the blood. So they [d]made My covenant void—*this* in addition to all your abominations. **8** And you have not [a]kept the responsibility of My holy things yourselves, but you have set *foreigners* as keepers of the responsibility *given by* Me for My sanctuary."

**9** 'Thus says Lord Yahweh, "[a]No foreigner, uncircumcised in heart and uncircumcised in flesh, of all the foreigners who are among the sons of Israel, shall enter My sanctuary. **10** But the Levites who went far from Me when Israel went astray, who [a]went astray from Me after their idols, shall [b]bear the punishment for their iniquity. **11** Yet they shall be [a]ministers in My sanctuary, having [b]oversight at the gates of the house and [c]ministering in the house; they shall [d]slaughter the burnt offering and the sacrifice for the people,

---

**43:24** [a]Lv 2:13; Nu 18:19; Mk 9:49, 50; Col 4:6 **43:25** [a]Ex 29:35-37; Lv 8:33, 35 **43:26** [1]Lit *fill its hands* **43:27** [a]Lv 9:1 [b]Lv 3:1; 17:5 [c]Eze 20:40 [1]Lit *make* ◆**44:1** [a]Eze 40:6, 17; 42:14 **44:2** [a]Eze 43:2-4 **44:3** [a]Eze 34:24; 37:25 [b]Ge 31:54; Ex 24:9-11 [c]Eze 46:2, 8-10 [d]Eze 40:9 [1]Lit *by his way* **44:4** [a]Eze 40:20, 40 [b]Is 6:3, 4; Eze 1:28; 3:23; 43:4, 5; Hag 2:7 [c]Eze 1:28; 43:3 **44:5** [a]Dt 32:46; Eze 40:4 [b]Dt 12:32; Eze 43:10, 11 **44:6** [a]Eze 2:5-7; 3:9 [b]Eze 45:9; 1Pe 4:3 [1]Lit *rebellion* **44:7** [a]Ex 12:43-49 [b]Lv 26:41; Dt 10:16; Jer 4:4; 9:26 [c]Lv 22:25 [d]Ge 17:14 **44:8** [a]Lv 22:2; Nu 18:7 **44:9** [a]Eze 44:7; Joel 3:17; Zec 14:21 **44:10** [a]2Ki 23:8, 9; Eze 22:26; 44:12 [b]Nu 18:23 **44:11** [a]Nu 3:5-37; 4:1-33; 18:2-7 [b]1Chr 26:1-19 [c]Eze 40:45; 44:14 [d]2Chr 29:34; 30:17

and they shall [e]stand before them
to minister to them. **12** Because they
ministered to them [a]before their
idols and became a [b]stumbling
block of iniquity to the house of Is-
rael, therefore I have [c,1]sworn against
them," declares Lord Yahweh, "that
they shall [d]bear *the punishment for*
their iniquity. **13** And they shall [a]not
approach Me to minister as a priest
to Me, nor approach any of My holy
things, to the things that are most
holy; but they will [b]bear their dis-
honor and their abominations which
they have done. **14** Yet I will [1]appoint
them as [a]keepers of the responsibili-
ty for the house, of all its service and
of all that shall be done in it.

### *The Levitical Responsibilities*

**15** "But the [a]Levitical priests, the
sons of [b]Zadok, who [c]kept the re-
sponsibility of My sanctuary when
the sons of Israel [d]went astray from
Me, shall come near to Me to minister
to Me; and they shall [e]stand before
Me to bring near to Me the [f]fat and
the blood," declares Lord Yahweh.
**16** "They shall [a]enter My sanctuary;
they shall come near to My [b]table
to minister to Me and keep the re-
sponsibility *given by* Me. **17** And it
will be that when they enter at the
gates of the inner court, they shall
be clothed with [a]linen garments; and
wool shall not [1]be on them while they
are ministering in the gates of the
inner court and in the house. **18** Linen
[a]headdresses shall be on their heads,
and [b]linen undergarments shall be
on their loins; they shall not gird
themselves with *anything which*
*makes them* sweat. **19** And when they
go out into the outer court, into the
outer court to the people, they shall
[a]put off their garments in which they
have been ministering and lay them
in the holy chambers; then they shall
put on other garments so that they
will [b]not transmit holiness to the
people with their garments. **20** Also
they shall [a]not shave their heads, yet
they shall not [b]let their locks [1]grow
long; they shall only trim *the hair of*
their heads. **21** [a]Nor shall any of the
priests drink wine when they enter
the inner court. **22** And they shall not
[1]take a widow or a [a]divorced woman
as a wife but shall [b]take virgins from
the seed of the house of Israel or a
widow who is the widow of a priest.
**23** Moreover, they shall instruct My
people *about the* [a]*difference* between
the holy and the profane, and make
them know *the difference* between
the unclean and the clean. **24** And in
a dispute, [a]they shall take their stand
to judge; they shall judge it according
to My judgments. They shall also
keep My laws and My statutes in all
My [b]appointed times and [c]keep My
sabbaths holy. **25** But [a,1]they shall not
go to a dead person to make *them-*
*selves* unclean; however, for father,

---

**44:11** [e]Nu 16:9 **44:12** [a]2Ki 16:10-16 [b]Eze 14:3, 4 [c]Eze 20:15, 23 [d]Eze 44:10 [1]Lit *lifted up My hand, bore up my hand*; cf. 44:12b **44:13** [a]Nu 18:3 [b]Eze 16:61, 63; 39:26 **44:14** [a]Nu 18:4; 1Chr 23:28-32; Eze 44:11 [1]Lit *give* **44:15** [a]Jer 33:18-22 [b]Eze 40:46; 43:19; 48:11 [c]Nu 18:7; Eze 40:45 [d]Eze 44:10; 48:11 [e]Zec 3:1, 7 [f]Lv 3:16, 17; 17:5, 6; Eze 44:7 **44:16** [a]Nu 18:5, 7, 8 [b]Eze 41:22; Mal 1:7, 12 **44:17** [a]Ex 28:42, 43; 39:27-29; Rev 19:8 [1]Lit *come upon* **44:18** [a]Ex 28:40; Is 3:20; Eze 24:17, 23 [b]Ex 28:42; Lv 16:4 **44:19** [a]Lv 6:10; 16:4, 23, 24; Eze 42:14 [b]Lv 6:27; Eze 46:20 **44:20** [a]Lv 21:5 [b]Nu 6:5 [1]Or *hang loose* **44:21** [a]Lv 10:9 **44:22** [a]Lv 21:7, 14 [b]Lv 21:13 [1]Lit *take as wives for themselves* **44:23** [a]Lv 10:10; Eze 22:26; Hos 4:6; Mic 3:9-11; Zep 3:4; Hag 2:11-13; Mal 2:6-8 **44:24** [a]Dt 17:8, 9; 19:17; 21:5; 1Chr 23:4; 2Chr 19:8-10 [b]Lv 23:2, 4, 44 [c]Eze 20:12, 20 **44:25** [a]Lv 21:1-4 [1]Lit *he*

as a [b]burnt offering to Yahweh [c]seven
bulls and seven rams without blem-
ish on every day of the seven days,
and a male goat daily for a sin
offering. **24** And he shall provide as
a [a]grain offering an ephah [1]with a
bull, an ephah [1]with a ram, and a
[2]hin of oil [1]with an ephah. **25** In the
[a]seventh *month*, on the fifteenth day
of the month, at the feast, he shall
provide like this, seven days [1]for the
sin offering, the burnt offering, the
grain offering, and the oil."

### *The Prince, Feast, and Offerings*

**46** "Thus says Lord Yahweh, "The
[a]gate of the [b]inner court
facing east shall be [c]shut the six
[d]working days; but it shall be opened
on the [e]sabbath day and opened on
the day of the [f]new moon. **2** Then
the [a]prince shall enter by way of the
porch of the gate from outside and
stand by the [b]post of the gate. Then
the priests shall provide his burnt
offering and his peace offerings, and
he shall worship at the threshold of
the gate and then go out; but the gate
shall not be [c]shut until the evening.
**3** And the [a]people of the land shall
also worship at the entrance of that
gate before Yahweh on the sabbaths
and on the [b]new moons. **4** Now the
[a]burnt offering which the prince shall
bring near to Yahweh on the sabbath
day shall be [b]six lambs without
blemish and a ram without blemish;
**5** and the [a]grain offering shall be an
ephah [1]with the ram, and the grain
offering with the lambs shall be [b]a
gift from his hand, as well as a [2]hin
of oil with an ephah. **6** And on the
day of the [a]new moon *he shall offer*
a bull from the herd without blemish,
also six lambs and a ram, *which* shall
be without blemish. **7** And he shall
[1]provide a [a]grain offering, an ephah
with the bull and an ephah with the
ram, and with the lambs as [2]much
as he is [b]able, and a hin of oil with
an ephah. **8** And when the [a]prince
enters, he shall go in by way of the
porch of the gate and go out [1]by the
same way. **9** But when the people of
the land come [a]before Yahweh at the
appointed times, he who enters by
way of the north gate to worship shall
go out by way of the south gate. And
he who enters by way of the south
gate shall go out by way of the north
gate. [1]No one shall return by way of
the gate by which he entered but
shall go straight out. **10** So when they
go in, the prince shall go in [a]among
them; and when they go out, [1]he shall
go out.

**11** "Now at the [a]feasts and the
appointed times the [b]grain offering
shall be an [1]ephah with a bull and
an ephah with a ram, and with the
lambs shall be a gift from his hand,
as well as a hin of oil with an ephah.
**12** And when the prince provides a
[a]freewill offering, a burnt offering, or

**45:23** [b]Nu 28:16-25 [c]Nu 23:1, 2; Job 42:8 **45:24** [a]Nu 28:12-15; Eze 46:5-7 [1]Lit *for* [2]A hin was approx. 1 gal. or 3.8 l **45:25** [a]Lv 23:33-43; Nu 29:12-38; 2Chr 5:3; 7:8, 10 [1]Lit *according to* ◆ **46:1** [a]Eze 45:19 [b]Eze 8:16; 10:3 [c]Eze 44:1, 2 [d]Ex 20:9 [e]Is 66:23; Eze 45:17 [f]Eze 45:18; 46:3, 6 **46:2** [a]Eze 44:3; 46:8 [b]Eze 45:19 [c]Eze 46:12 **46:3** [a]Lk 1:10 [b]Eze 46:1 **46:4** [a]Eze 45:17 [b]Nu 28:9 **46:5** [a]Nu 28:12; Eze 45:24; 46:7, 11 [b]Eze 46:7 [1]Lit *for*, so through v 11 [2]A hin was approx. 1 gal. or 3.8 l **46:6** [a]Eze 46:1 **46:7** [a]Eze 46:5 [b]Lv 14:21; Dt 16:17; Eze 46:5 [1]Or *offer*, so in ch [2]Lit *his hand can reach* **46:8** [a]Eze 44:3; 46:2 [1]Lit *by its way* **46:9** [a]Ex 34:23; Ps 84:7; Mic 6:6 [1]Lit *He shall not* **46:10** [a]2Sa 6:14, 15; 1Chr 29:20, 22; 2Chr 6:3; 7:4; Ps 42:4 [1]As in many mss and the ancient versions; M.T. *they* **46:11** [a]Eze 45:17 [b]Eze 46:5, 7 [1]An ephah was approx. 21 qt. or 23 l **46:12** [a]Lv 23:38; 2Chr 29:31

peace offerings *as* a freewill offering
to Yahweh, the gate facing east shall
be [b]opened for him. And he shall pro-
vide his burnt offering and his peace
offerings as he does on the [c]sabbath
day. Then he shall go out, and the gate
shall be shut after he goes out.

**13** "And you shall provide a [a]lamb a
year old without blemish for a burnt
offering to Yahweh daily; [b]morning by
morning you shall provide it. **14** Also
you shall provide a grain offering with
it morning by morning—a [a]sixth of
an ephah as well as a third of a hin of
oil to moisten the fine flour—a grain
offering to Yahweh continually by a
perpetual statute. **15** Thus they shall
provide the lamb, the grain offering,
and the oil, morning by morning, for
a [a]continual burnt offering."

**16** 'Thus says Lord Yahweh, "If
the prince gives a [a]gift *out of* his
inheritance to any of his sons, it
shall belong to his sons; it is their
possession by inheritance. **17** But if
he gives a gift from his inheritance
to one of his servants, it shall be his
until the [a]year of liberty; then it shall
return to the prince. His inheritance
*shall be* only his sons'; it shall belong
to them. **18** Now the prince shall [a]not
take from the people's inheritance,
[b]mistreating them out of their pos-
session; he shall give his sons inher-
itance from his own possession so
that My people will not be scattered,
anyone from his possession."'"

### *The Boiling Places*

**19** Then he brought me through the
[a]entrance, which *was* at the side of
the gate, into the holy chambers
for the priests, which faced north;
and behold, there *was* a place at
the extreme rear toward the west.
**20** Then he said to me, "This is the
place where the priests shall boil the
[a]guilt offering and the sin offering
*and* where they shall [b]bake the grain
offering, in order that they may not
bring *them* out into the outer court
to transmit holiness to the people."

**21** Then he brought me out into the
outer court and had me pass through
to the four corners of the court; and
behold, in every corner of the court
*there was* a *small* court. **22** In the
four corners of the court *there were*
enclosed courts, [1]forty *cubits* long
and thirty wide; these four in the
corners *were* [2]the same size. **23** *Now*
*there was* a row *of masonry* round
about in them, around the four of
them, and boiling places were made
under the rows round about. **24** Then
he said to me, "These are the boiling
[1]places where the ministers of the
house shall boil the sacrifices of the
people."

### *The River of Yahweh's House*

**47** Then he brought me back to
the [a]door of the house; and
behold, [b]water was flowing from
under the threshold of the house
toward the east, for the house faced
east. And the water was flowing
down from under, from the right side
of the house, from south of the altar.
**2** He brought me out by way of the
north gate and led me around by way
of the outside to the outer gate by

**46:12** [b]Eze 44:3; 46:1, 2, 8 [c]Eze 45:17 **46:13** [a]Nu 28:3-5 [b]Is 50:4 **46:14** [a]Nu 28:5 **46:15** [a]Ex 29:42; Nu 28:6 **46:16** [a]2Chr 21:3 **46:17** [a]Lv 25:10 **46:18** [a]Eze 45:8 [b]1Ki 21:19; Eze 22:27; Mic 2:1, 2 **46:19** [a]Eze 42:9; 44:5 **46:20** [a]2Chr 35:13; Eze 44:29 [b]Lv 2:4-7 **46:22** [1]Approx. 60 ft. long and 30 ft. wide or 18 m and 13.5 m [2]Lit *one measure* **46:24** [1]Lit *houses* ◆ **47:1** [a]Eze 41:2, 23-25 [b]Ps 46:4; Is 30:25; 55:1; Jer 2:13; Joel 3:18; Zec 13:1; 14:8; Rev 22:1, 17

way of *the gate* that faces east. And
behold, water was trickling from the
south side.
**3** When the man went out toward
the east with a line in his hand, he
measured [1]one thousand cubits, and
he had me pass through the water,
water *reaching* the ankles. **4** Again
he measured one thousand and had
me pass through the water, water
*reaching* the knees. Again he mea-
sured one thousand and had me pass
through *the water*, water *reaching*
the loins. **5** Again he measured one
thousand; *and it was* a river that I
could not pass through, for the water
had become high—*enough* water to
swim in, a [a]river that could not be
passed through. **6** And he said to me,
"Son of man, have you [a]seen *this*?"
Then he led and returned me back
to the bank of the river. **7** When I had
returned, now behold, on the bank of
the river there *were* very many [a]trees
on the one side and on the other.
**8** Then he said to me, "These waters
go out toward the eastern region
and go down into the [a]Arabah; then
they go toward the sea, being made
to flow out to the [b]sea, and the wa-
ters *of the sea* [1]will be healed. **9** And
it will be that every living creature,
which swarms in every place where
the [1]river goes, will live. And there
will be very many fish, for these
waters go there and *the other waters*
[2]are healed; so [a]everything will live
where the river goes. **10** And it will be
that [a]fishermen will stand beside it;
from [b]Engedi to Eneglaim there will
be a place for the [c]spreading of nets.
Their fish will be according to their
kinds, like the fish of the [d]Great Sea,
[e]very many. **11** But its marshes and
swamps will not be [1]healed; they will
be [2]left for [a]salt. **12** [a]And by the river
on its bank, on one side and on the
other, will grow all *kinds of* [b]trees for
food. Their [c]leaves will not wither,
and their fruit will not [1]fail. They
will bear every month because their
water flows out from the sanctuary,
and their fruit will be for food and
their [d]leaves for healing."

### Apportionment of the Land

**13** Thus says Lord Yahweh, "This *shall
be* the [a]boundary by which you shall
apportion the land for an inheritance
among the twelve tribes of Israel;
Joseph *shall have* two [b]portions.
**14** You shall then apportion it for an
inheritance, each one [1]equally with
the other; for I [a,2]swore to give it to
your fathers, and this land shall fall
to you [3]as an inheritance.
**15** "This *shall be* the boundary of
the land: on the [a]north side, from
the Great Sea *by* the way of Hethlon,
to the entrance of [b,1]Zedad; **16** [a,1]Ha-
math, Berothah, Sibraim, which is
between the border of [b]Damascus
and the border of Hamath; Hazer-
hatticon, which is by the border of
Hauran. **17** And the boundary shall
be from the sea *to* [a]Hazar-enan *at*

---

**47:3** [1]*Approx. 500 yd. or 450 m* **47:5** [a]Is 11:9; Hab 2:14 **47:6** [a]Eze 8:6; 40:4; 44:5 **47:7** [a]Is 60:13, 21; 61:3; Eze 47:12 **47:8** [a]Dt 3:17; Is 35:6, 7; 41:17-19; 44:3 [b]Jos 3:16 [1]Fresh **47:9** [a]Is 12:3; 55:1; Jn 4:14; 7:37, 38 [1]Lit *two rivers* [2]Fresh **47:10** [a]Mt 4:19; 13:47; Lk 5:10 [b]Ge 14:7; Jos 15:62; 1Sa 23:29; 24:1; 2Chr 20:2 [c]Eze 26:5, 14 [d]Nu 34:6; Ps 104:25; Eze 47:15; 48:28 [e]Lk 5:5-9; Jn 21:6 **47:11** [a]Dt 29:23 [1]Fresh [2]Lit *given* **47:12** [a]Eze 47:7; Rev 22:2 [b]Ge 2:9 [c]Ps 1:3; Jer 17:8 [d]Rev 22:2 [1]Lit *come to an end* **47:13** [a]Nu 34:2-12 [b]Ge 48:5; Eze 48:4, 5 **47:14** [a]Dt 1:8; Eze 20:6 [1]Lit *like his brother* [2]Lit *lifted up My hand* [3]Lit *in* **47:15** [a]Nu 34:7-9 [b]Nu 34:8 [1]Or *Hamath* **47:16** [a]Nu 13:21; Is 10:9; Eze 47:17, 20; 48:1; Zec 9:2 [b]Ge 14:15; Eze 47:17, 18; 48:1 [1]Or *Zedad* **47:17** [a]Nu 34:9

the border of Damascus, and on the
north toward the north is the border
of Hamath. This is the north side.
18 "And the [a]east side, from be-
tween Hauran, Damascus, [b]Gilead,
and the land of Israel, *shall be* the
[c]Jordan; from the *north* border to the
eastern sea you shall measure. This
is the east side.
19 "And the [a]south side toward the
south *shall extend* from [b]Tamar as far
as the waters of [c]Meribath-kadesh, to
the [d]brook *of Egypt and* to the [e]Great
Sea. This is the south side toward the
south.
20 "And the [a]west side *shall be* the
Great Sea, from the *south* border to a
point opposite [b,1]Lebo-hamath. This
is the west side.
21 "So you shall divide this land
among yourselves according to the
tribes of Israel. 22 And it will be
that you shall divide it by [a]lot for
an inheritance among yourselves
and among the [b]sojourners who
sojourn in your midst, who bring
forth sons in your midst. And they
shall be to you as the native-born
among the sons of Israel. They shall
be allotted an [c]inheritance with you
among the tribes of Israel. 23 And it
will be that in the tribe with which
the sojourner sojourns, there you
shall give *him* his inheritance,"
declares Lord Yahweh.

48 "Now [a]these are the names of
the tribes: from the northern
extremity, [1]beside the way of Hethlon
to [2]Lebo-hamath, *as far as* Hazar-
enan *at* the border of Damascus,
toward the north [1]beside Hamath,
[3]running from east to west, [b]Dan,
one *portion.* 2 And beside the bor-
der of Dan, from the east side to the
west side, [a]Asher, one *portion.* 3 And
beside the border of Asher, from the
east side to the west side, [a]Naphtali,
one *portion.* 4 And beside the border
of Naphtali, from the east side to the
west side, [a]Manasseh, one *portion.*
5 And beside the border of Manasseh,
from the east side to the west side,
[a]Ephraim, one *portion.* 6 And beside
the border of Ephraim, from the east
side to the west side, [a]Reuben, one
*portion.* 7 And beside the border of
Reuben, from the east side to the
west side, [a]Judah, one *portion.*
8 "And beside the border of Judah,
from the east side to the west side,
shall be the contribution which you
shall contribute, 25,000 [1]*cubits* in
width, and in length like one of the
portions, from the east side to the
west side; and the [a]sanctuary shall be
in the middle of it. 9 The contribution
that you shall contribute to Yahweh
*shall be* [1]25,000 *cubits* in length
and 10,000 in width. 10 And the
holy contribution shall be for these,
*namely* for the [a]priests, toward the
north 25,000 *cubits in length,* toward
the west 10,000 in width, toward the
east 10,000 in width, and toward
the south 25,000 in length; and the
sanctuary of Yahweh shall be in its

**47:18** [a]Nu 34:10-12 [b]Ge 37:25; Jer 50:19 [c]Ge 13:10, 11 **47:19** [a]Nu 34:3-5 [b]Eze 48:28 [c]Dt 32:51 [d]Nu 34:5; 1Ki 8:65; Is 27:12 [e]Eze 47:10, 15 **47:20** [a]Nu 34:6 [b]Jdg 3:3; 2Chr 7:8; Eze 48:1; Am 6:14 [1]Or *the entrance of Hamath* **47:22** [a]Nu 26:55, 56 [b]Is 14:1; 56:6, 7 [c]Ac 11:18; 15:9; Eph 2:12-14; 3:6; Col 3:11 ◆ **48:1** [a]Ex 1:1 [b]Jos 19:40-48 [1]Lit *at the hand of* [2]Or *the entrance of Hamath* [3]Lit *and there shall be to it an east and west side* **48:2** [a]Jos 19:24-31 **48:3** [a]Jos 19:32-39 **48:4** [a]Jos 13:29-31; 17:1-11 **48:5** [a]Jos 16:5-9; 17:8-10, 14-18 **48:6** [a]Jos 13:15-21 **48:7** [a]Jos 15:1-63; 19:9 **48:8** [a]Is 12:6; 33:20-22; Eze 45:3, 4 [1]Or possibly *reeds*, so in ch **48:9** [1]Approx. 7.1 mi. long and 2.8 mi. wide or 11.25 km and 4.5 km **48:10** [a]Eze 44:28; 45:4

midst. **11** *It shall be* for the priests who are sanctified of the [a]sons of Zadok, who have kept the responsibility *given by* Me, who did not go astray when the sons of Israel went astray as the [b]Levites went astray. **12** And it shall be a contribution to them from the contribution of the land, a Holy of Holies, by the border of the Levites. **13** Now alongside the border of the priests, the Levites *shall have* 25,000 *cubits* in length and 10,000 in width. The whole length *shall be* 25,000 *cubits* and the width 10,000. **14** Moreover, they [a]shall not sell or exchange any of it, or let this [1]choice *portion* of land pass over *to another*; for it is holy to Yahweh.

**15** "And the remainder, [1]5,000 *cubits* in width and 25,000 [2]in length, shall be for [a]common use for the city, for *places of* habitation, and for [3]open spaces; and the city shall be in its midst. **16** And these *shall be* its measurements: the north side [1]4,500 *cubits*, the south side [a]4,500 *cubits*, the east side 4,500 *cubits*, and the west side 4,500 *cubits*. **17** And the city shall have [1]open spaces: on the north [2]250 *cubits*, on the south 250 *cubits*, on the east 250 *cubits*, and on the west 250 *cubits*. **18** And the remainder of the length alongside the holy contribution shall be 10,000 *cubits* toward the east and 10,000 toward the west; and it shall be [1]alongside the holy contribution. And its produce shall be food for the workers of the city. **19** The workers of the city, out of *all the tribes* of Israel, shall cultivate it. **20** The whole contribution *shall be* 25,000 by 25,000 *cubits*; you shall contribute the holy contribution, a [1]square, with the city's possession *of land*.

**21** "And the [a]remainder *shall be* for the prince, on the one side and on the other of the holy contribution and of the city's possession *of land*; in front of the 25,000 *cubits* of the contribution toward the east border and westward in front of the 25,000 toward the west border, alongside the portions, *it shall be* for the prince. And the holy contribution and the sanctuary of the house shall be in the middle of it. **22** And apart from the Levites' possession and the city's possession, *which* are in the middle of that which belongs to the prince, *everything* between the border of Judah and the border of Benjamin shall be for the prince.

**23** "Now as for the rest of the tribes: from the east side to the west side, [a]Benjamin, one *portion*. **24** And beside the border of Benjamin, from the east side to the west side, [a]Simeon, one *portion*. **25** And beside the border of Simeon, from the east side to the west side, [a]Issachar, one *portion*. **26** And beside the border of Issachar, from the east side to the west side, [a]Zebulun, one *portion*. **27** And beside the border of Zebulun, from the east side to the west side, [a]Gad, one *portion*. **28** And beside the border of Gad, at the south side toward the south, the border shall be from [a]Tamar to the waters of Meribath-kadesh, to

**48:11** [a]Eze 40:46; 44:15 [b]Eze 44:10, 12 **48:14** [a]Lv 25:32-34; 27:10, 28, 33 [1]Lit *first, first fruits* **48:15** [a]Eze 42:20; 45:6 [1]Approx. 1.4 mi. or 2.25 km [2]Lit *in front* [3]Or *pasture land* **48:16** [a]Rev 21:16 [1]Approx. 1.3 mi. or 2 km **48:17** [1]Or *pasture land* [2]Approx. 375 ft. or 112.5 m **48:18** [1]Or *exactly as* **48:20** [1]Lit *fourth* **48:21** [a]Eze 34:24; 45:7; 48:22 **48:23** [a]Jos 18:21-28 **48:24** [a]Jos 19:1-9 **48:25** [a]Jos 19:17-23 **48:26** [a]Jos 19:10-16 **48:27** [a]Jos 13:24-28 **48:28** [a]Ge 14:7; 2Chr 20:2; Eze 47:19

the brook *of Egypt*, to the [b]Great
Sea. **29** This is the [a]land which you
shall divide by lot to the tribes of
Israel for an inheritance, and these
are their *several* portions," declares
Lord Yahweh.

### *Yahweh Is There*

**30** "And these are the exits of the city:
on the [a]north side, 4,500 *cubits* by
measurement. **31** "And the gates of the
city *shall be* [a,1]named for the tribes of
Israel, three gates toward the north:
the gate of Reuben, one; the gate
of Judah, one; the gate of Levi,
one. **32** And on the east side, 4,500
*cubits*, [1]shall be three gates: the gate
of Joseph, one; the gate of Benjamin,
one; the gate of Dan, one. **33** And
on the south side, 4,500 *cubits* by
measurement, [1]shall be three gates:
the gate of Simeon, one; the gate of
Issachar, one; the gate of Zebulun,
one. **34** *On* the west side, 4,500 *cubits*,
*shall be* three gates: the gate of Gad,
one; the gate of Asher, one; the gate
of Naphtali, one. **35** *The city shall be*
[1]18,000 *cubits* round about; and the
[a]name of the city from *that* day *shall
be*, '[b,2]Yahweh is there.'"

*The Book of*

# DANIEL

### *Daniel Brought to Babylon*

**1** In the third year of the reign of
[a]Jehoiakim king of Judah, [b]Nebu-
chadnezzar king of Babylon came to
Jerusalem and besieged it. **2** And the
[a]Lord gave Jehoiakim king of Judah
into his hand, along with some of
the [b]vessels of the house of God;
and he brought them to the land
of [c]Shinar, to the house of his [1]god,
and he brought the vessels into the
treasury of his [d,1]god.
**3** Then the king said for Ashpenaz,
the chief of his [1]officials, to bring in
*some of the* sons of Israel, including
some of the royal [a]seed and of the
nobles, **4** youths in whom was [a]no
defect, who were good in appear-
ance, showing [b]insight in every
*branch of* wisdom, being thorough-
ly [1]knowledgeable and discerning
knowledge, and who had ability to
stand in the king's palace; and *he said
for him* to teach them the [2]literature
and [c]tongue of the [d]Chaldeans. **5** And
the king appointed for them a daily
ration from the [a]king's choice food
and from the wine which he drank,
and *appointed* that they should be
[1]educated three years, at the end of
which they were to [b]stand before the
king. **6** Now among them from the
sons of Judah were [a]Daniel, Hanani-
ah, Mishael, and Azariah. **7** Then the

**48:28** [b]Eze 47:10, 15, 19, 20 **48:29** [a]Eze 47:13-20 **48:30** [a]Eze 48:32-34 **48:31** [a]Rev 21:12, 13 [1]Lit *according to the names of* **48:32** [1]Lit *and* **48:33** [1]Lit *and* **48:35** [a]Jer 23:6; 33:16 [b]Is 12:6; 14:32; 24:23; Jer 3:17; 8:19; 14:9; Eze 35:10; Joel 3:21; Zec 2:10; Rev 21:3; 22:3 [1]Approx. 5.1 mi. or 8.1 km [2]Heb *Yahweh-shammah* ◆ **1:1** [a]2Ki 24:1; 2Chr 36:5, 6 [b]Jer 25:1; 52:12, 28-30 **1:2** [a]Is 42:24; Da 2:37, 38 [b]2Chr 36:7; Jer 27:19, 20; Da 5:2 [c]Ge 10:10; 11:2; Is 11:11; Zec 5:11 [d]Jer 50:2; 51:44 [1]Or *gods* **1:3** [a]2Ki 24:15; Is 39:7 [1]Or *eunuchs*, so in ch **1:4** [a]2Sa 14:25 [b]Da 1:17 [c]Is 36:11; Jer 5:15; Da 2:4 [d]Da 2:2, 4, 5, 10; 3:8; 4:7; 5:7, 11, 30; 9:1 [1]Lit *knowing knowledge* [2]Or *writing* **1:5** [a]Da 1:8 [b]1Sa 16:22; Da 1:19 [1]Or *reared* **1:6** [a]Eze 14:14, 20; 28:3; Mt 24:15

commander of the officials set names
for them; and for Daniel he set *the*
*name* [a]Belteshazzar, for Hananiah
[b]Shadrach, for Mishael [b]Meshach,
and for Azariah [b]Abed-nego.

### *Daniel's Heart*

**8** But Daniel set in his heart that
he would not [a]defile himself with
the [b]king's choice food or with the
[c]wine which he drank; so he sought
*permission* from the commander of
the officials that he might not defile
himself. **9** Now God granted Daniel
[a]lovingkindness and compassion be-
fore the commander of the officials,
**10** and the commander of the officials
said to Daniel, "I am afraid of my lord
the king, who has appointed your
food and your drink; for why should
he see your faces looking more hag-
gard than the youths who are your
own age? Then you would [1]make me
forfeit my head to the king." **11** But
Daniel said to the overseer whom
the commander of the officials had
appointed over Daniel, Hananiah,
Mishael, and Azariah, **12** "Please test
your servants for ten days, and let
us be [a]given some vegetables to eat
and water to drink. **13** Then let our
appearance be [1]observed before you
and the appearance of the youths
who are eating the king's choice
food; and deal with your servants
according to what you see."
**14** So he listened to them in this
matter and tested them for ten days.
**15** At the end of ten days it was seen
that their appearance was [a]better
and that [1]they were fatter than all
the youths who had been eating the
king's choice food. **16** So the overseer
continued to [1]withhold their choice
food and the wine they were to drink,
and kept [a]giving them vegetables.
**17** And as for these four youths,
[a]God gave them knowledge and in-
sight in every *branch of* [1]literature
and wisdom; Daniel even understood
all *kinds of* [b]visions and dreams.
**18** Then at the end of the days which
the king had spoken of for bringing
them in, the commander of the
officials brought them in before Neb-
uchadnezzar. **19** And the king talked
with them, and out of them all not
one was found like [a]Daniel, Hananiah,
Mishael, and Azariah; so they [b]stood
*in service* before the king. **20** And as
for every matter of [a]wisdom in un-
derstanding which the king sought
from them, he found them [b]ten times
[c]better than all the [d,1]magicians *and*
conjurers who *were* in all his kingdom.
**21** And Daniel [1]continued until the
[a]first year of Cyrus the king.

### *Nebuchadnezzar's Troubling Dream*

**2** Now in the second year of the
reign of Nebuchadnezzar, Nebu-
chadnezzar [a,1]had dreams; and his
spirit was troubled, and his [b]sleep
[2]left him. **2** Then the king said to call
in the [a,1]magicians, the conjurers, the
sorcerers, and the [2]Chaldeans to tell

---

**1:7** [a]Da 2:26; 4:8; 5:12 [b]Da 2:49; 3:12 **1:8** [a]Lv 11:47; Eze 4:13, 14; Hos 9:3, 4 [b]Ps 141:4; Da 1:5 [c]Dt 32:38; Da 5:4 **1:9** [a]*Ge 39:21; 1Ki 8:50;* Job 5:15, 16; Ps 106:46; Pr 16:7 **1:10** [1]Lit make my head guilty
**1:12** [a]Da 1:16 **1:13** [1]Lit *seen* **1:15** [a]Ex 23:25; Pr 10:22 [1]Lit *fat of flesh* **1:16** [a]Da 1:12 [1]Lit *take away*
**1:17** [a]1Ki 3:12, 28; Job 32:8; Da 1:20; 2:21, 23; Ac 7:22 [b]Da 2:19; 7:1; 8:1 [1]Or *writing* **1:19** [a]Da 1:6, 7 [b]Ge 41:46; Da 1:5 **1:20** [a]1Ki 4:30, 31; Da 1:17 [b]Ge 31:7; Nu 14:22; Ne 4:12; Job 19:3 [c]Da 2:27, 28, 46, 48 [d]Is 19:3; Da 2:2; 4:18; 5:7 [1]Or *soothsayer priests* **1:21** [a]Da 6:28; 10:1 [1]Lit *was* ◆ **2:1** [a]Ge 40:5-8; 41:1, 8; Job 33:15-17; Da 2:3; 4:5 [b]Es 6:1; Da 6:18 [1]Lit *dreamed dreams* [2]Lit *was gone upon him* **2:2** [a]Ge 41:8; Ex 7:11; Is 47:12, 13; Da 1:20; 2:10, 27; 4:6; 5:7 [1]Or *soothsayer priests* [2]Or *master astrologers*, so in ch

the king his dreams. So they came in
and stood before the king. **3** Then the
king said to them, "I [a,1]had a dream,
and my spirit is troubled to know the
dream."

**4** Then the Chaldeans spoke to the
king in [a,1]Aramaic: "[b]O king, live for-
ever! [c]Say the dream to your servants,
and we will declare the interpreta-
tion." **5** The king answered and said
to the Chaldeans, "The word from me
is firm: if you do not make known to
me the dream and its interpretation,
you will be [a,1]torn limb from limb,
and your houses will be made a
rubbish heap. **6** But if you declare the
dream and its interpretation, you will
receive from me [a]gifts and a reward
and great glory; therefore declare to
me the dream and its interpretation."
**7** They answered a second time and
said, "Let the king [a]say the dream to
his servants, and we will declare the
interpretation." **8** The king answered
and said, "I know for certain that you
are buying time, inasmuch as you
have seen that the word from me is
firm, **9** that if you do not make the
dream known to me, there is only
[a]one law for you. Indeed, you have
agreed together to speak lying and
corrupt [1]words before me until the
time is changed; therefore say the
dream to me, that I may [b]know that
you can declare to me its interpre-
tation." **10** The Chaldeans answered
[1]the king and said, "There is not a
man on earth who is able to declare
the matter [2]for the king, inasmuch
as no great king or powerful ruler
has *ever* asked *about* a matter like
this of any [a,3]magician, conjurer, or
Chaldean. **11** Moreover, the matter
which the king asks is [1]difficult,
and there is no one else who could
declare it [2]to the king except [a]gods,
whose [b]dwelling place is not with
flesh."

**12** Because of this the king became
[a]indignant and very furious and said
*for them* to destroy all the wise men
of Babylon. **13** So the law went forth
that the wise men were to be killed;
and they sought out [a]Daniel and his
friends to [1]kill *them.*

**14** Then Daniel replied with dis-
cretion and discernment to [a]Arioch,
the captain of the king's [1]bodyguard,
who had gone forth to kill the wise
men of Babylon; **15** he answered and
said to Arioch, a powerful [1]official
for the king, "For what reason is the
law from the king *so* [2]urgent?" Then
Arioch made the matter known to
Daniel. **16** So Daniel went in and
sought from the king that he would
[1]give him time, in order that he might
declare the interpretation to the king.

### *God Reveals Nebuchadnezzar's Dream*

**17** Then Daniel went to his house
and made the matter known to his
friends, to [a]Hananiah, Mishael, and
Azariah, **18** so that they might [a]seek
compassion from the God of heaven
concerning this mystery, so that
Daniel and his friends would not be
[b]destroyed with the rest of the wise

**2:3** [a]Ge 40:8; 41:15; Da 4:5 [1]Lit *dreamed* **2:4** [a]Ezr 4:7; Is 36:11 [b]Da 3:9; 5:10 [c]Da 2:7 [1]The text is in Aramaic from here through 7:28 **2:5** [a]Ezr 6:11; Da 2:12; 3:29 [1]Lit *made into limbs* **2:6** [a]Da 2:48; 5:7, 16, 29 **2:7** [a]Da 2:4 **2:9** [a]Es 4:11; Da 3:15 [b]Is 41:23 [1]Lit *word* **2:10** [a]Da 2:2, 27 [1]Lit *before the* [2]Lit *of* [3]Or *soothsayer priest* **2:11** [a]Ge 41:39; Da 5:11 [b]Ex 29:45; Is 57:15 [1]Or *rare* [2]Lit *before* **2:12** [a]Ps 76:10; Da 2:5; 3:13, 19 **2:13** [a]Da 1:19, 20 [1]Lit *be killed* **2:14** [a]Da 2:24 [1]Or *executioners* **2:15** [1]Or *ruler* [2]Or *harsh* **2:16** [1]Or *appoint a time for him* **2:17** [a]Da 1:6 **2:18** [a]Es 4:15, 16; Is 37:4; Jer 33:3; Eze 36:37; Da 2:23 [b]Ge 18:28; Mal 3:18

men of Babylon. 19 Then the mystery
was revealed to Daniel in a night
[a]vision. Then Daniel blessed the
God of heaven; 20 Daniel answered
and said,

"Let the name of God be
[a]blessed forever and ever,
For [b]wisdom and might
belong to Him.
21 "And He [a]changes the
times and the seasons;
He [b]removes kings and
[1]establishes kings;
He gives [c]wisdom to wise men
And knowledge to [2]men
of understanding.
22 "He [a]reveals the deep
and hidden things;
[b]He knows what is
in the darkness,
And the [c]light dwells
with Him.
23 "To You, O [a]God of my fathers,
I give thanks and praise,
For You have given me
[b]wisdom and might;
Even now You have made
known to me what we
[c]sought from You,
For You have made known
to us the king's matter."

24 Therefore, Daniel went in to
Arioch, whom the king had appointed
to destroy the wise men of Babylon;
he went and said thus to him: "[a]Do
not destroy the wise men of Babylon!
Bring me before the king, and I will
declare the interpretation to the king."

25 Then Arioch hurriedly [a]brought
Daniel before the king and said thus
to him: "I have found a man among
the [b,1]exiles from Judah who can
make the interpretation known to
the king!" 26 The king answered
and said to Daniel, whose name
was [a]Belteshazzar, "Are you able to
make known to me the dream which
I have seen and its interpretation?"
27 Daniel answered before the king
and said, "As for the mystery about
which the king is asking, neither
[a]wise men, conjurers, [1]magicians,
*nor* diviners are able to declare *it* to
the king. 28 However, there is a [a]God
in heaven who reveals mysteries, and
He has made known to King Nebu-
chadnezzar what will take place in
the [b,1]last days. This was your dream
and the [c]visions of your head *while*
on your bed. 29 As for you, O king,
*while* on your bed your thoughts
[1]turned to what would happen [2]in
the future; and [a]He who reveals
mysteries has made known to you
what will happen. 30 But as for me,
this mystery has not been revealed to
me by any [a]wisdom which is in me
more than *in* any *other* living man,
but for the purpose of making the in-
terpretation known to the king, and
that you may know the [b]thoughts of
your heart.

### *Daniel Interprets the Dream*

31 "You, O king, were looking, and be-
hold, there was a single great [1]image;

**2:19** [a]Nu 12:6; Job 33:15, 16; Da 1:17; 7:2, 7, 13 **2:20** [a]Ps 103:1, 2; 113:1, 2; 115:18; 145:1, 2, 21 [b]1Chr 29:11, 12; Job 12:13, 16-22; Da 2:21-23 **2:21** [a]Ps 31:15; Da 2:9; 7:25 [b]Job 12:18; Ps 75:6, 7; Da 4:17, 32 [c]1Ki 3:9, 10; 4:29; Jas 1:5 [1]Or *sets up* [2]Lit *knowers* **2:22** [a]Job 12:22; Ps 25:14; Da 2:19, 28 [b]Job 26:6; Ps 139:12; Is 45:7; Jer 23:24; Heb 4:13 [c]Ps 36:9; Da 5:11, 14; Jas 1:17; 1Jn 1:5 **2:23** [a]Ge 31:42; Ex 3:15 [b]Da 1:17; 2:21 [c]Ps 21:2, 4; Da 2:18, 29, 30 **2:24** [a]Da 2:12, 13; Ac 27:24 **2:25** [a]Ge 41:14 [b]Da 1:6; 5:13; 6:13 [1]Lit *sons of the exile of* **2:26** [a]Da 1:7; 4:8; 5:12 **2:27** [a]Da 2:2, 10, 11; 5:7, 8 [1]Or *soothsayer priests* **2:28** [a]Ge 40:8; 41:16; Da 2:22, 45 [b]Ge 49:1; Is 2:2; Da 10:14; Mic 4:1 [c]Da 4:5 [1]Lit *end of the days* **2:29** [a]Da 2:23, 47 [1]Lit *came up* [2]Lit *after this* **2:30** [a]Ge 41:16; Da 1:17 [b]Ps 139:2; Am 4:13 **2:31** [1]Or *statue*, so in ch

that image, which was large and [2]of extraordinary splendor, was rising up in front of you, and its appearance was [a,3]awesome. **32** The [a]head of that image *was made* of fine gold, its breast and its arms of silver, its belly and its thighs of bronze, **33** its legs of iron, its feet partly of iron and partly of clay. **34** You [1]continued looking until a [a]stone was cut out [b]without hands, and it struck the image on its feet of iron and clay and [c]crushed them. **35** Then the iron, the clay, the bronze, the silver, and the gold were crushed [1]all at the same time and became [a]like chaff from the summer threshing floors; and the wind carried them away so that [b]not a trace of them was found. But the stone that struck the image became a great [c]mountain and filled the whole earth.

**36** "This *was* the dream; now we will say [a]its interpretation before the king. **37** You, O king, are the [a]king of kings, to whom the God of heaven has given the [1]kingdom, the [b]power, the strength, and the glory; **38** and wherever the sons of men inhabit, *or* the [a]beasts of the field, or the birds of the sky, He has given *them* into your hand and has made you rule with power over them all. You are the head of gold. **39** But after you there will arise another kingdom inferior to you, then another third kingdom of bronze, which will rule with power over all the earth. **40** Then there will be a [a]fourth kingdom as strong as iron; inasmuch as iron crushes and shatters all things, so, like iron that breaks in pieces, it will crush and break all these in pieces. **41** Now in that you saw the feet and toes, partly of potter's clay and partly of iron; it will be a divided kingdom; but it will have in it the toughness of iron, inasmuch as you saw the iron mixed with [1]common clay. **42** *And as* the toes of the feet *were* partly of iron and partly of clay, *so* some of the kingdom will be strong and part of it will be brittle. **43** And in that you saw the iron mixed with [1]common clay; they will combine with one another [2]in the seed of men; but they will not cling to one another, even as iron does not combine with clay. **44** And in the days of those kings the [a]God of heaven will [b]cause a [c]kingdom to rise up which will never be destroyed, and *that* kingdom will not be [1]left for another people; it will [d]crush and put an end to all these kingdoms, but it will itself stand forever. **45** Inasmuch as you saw that a [a]stone was cut out of the mountain without hands and that it crushed the iron, the bronze, the clay, the silver, and the gold, the [b]great God has made known to the king what [c]will happen [1]in the future; so the dream is certain, and its interpretation is trustworthy."

### *Daniel and Friends Promoted*

**46** Then King Nebuchadnezzar fell on his face and did [a]homage to Daniel and said *for them* to present to him

**2:31** [a]Hab 1:7 [2]Lit *its splendor was surpassing* [3]Or *fearsome* **2:32** [a]Da 2:38 **2:34** [a]Da 2:45 [b]Da 8:25; Zec 4:6 [c]Ps 2:9; Is 60:12 [1]Lit *were* **2:35** [a]Ps 1:4; Is 17:13; 41:15, 16; Hos 13:3 [b]Ps 37:10, 36 [c]Is 2:2; Mic 4:1 [1]Lit *like one* **2:36** [a]Da 2:24 **2:37** [a]Is 47:5; Jer 27:6, 7; Eze 26:7 [b]Ps 62:11 [1]Or *sovereignty* **2:38** [a]Ps 50:10, 11; Da 4:21, 22 **2:40** [a]Da 7:23 **2:41** [1]Lit *clay of mud* **2:43** [1]Lit *clay of mud* [2]Or *with* **2:44** [a]Da 2:28, 37 [b]Is 9:6, 7 [c]Ps 145:13; Eze 37:25; Da 4:3, 34; 6:26; 7:14, 27; Mic 4:7; Lk 1:32, 33 [d]Ps 2:9; Is 60:12; Da 2:34, 35 [1]Or *passed on to* **2:45** [a]Da 2:34 [b]Dt 10:17; 2Sa 7:22; Ps 48:1; Jer 32:18, 19; Da 2:29; Mal 1:11 [c]Ge 41:28, 32 [1]Lit *after this* **2:46** [a]Da 3:5, 7; Ac 10:25; 14:13; Rev 19:10; 22:8

an offering and [b,1]fragrant incense.
**47** The king answered Daniel and
said, "Truly [a]your God is a [b]God
of gods and a Lord of kings and a
[c]revealer of mysteries since you have
been able to reveal this mystery."
**48** Then the king [a,1]promoted Daniel
and gave him many great gifts, and
he made him rule with power over
the whole [b]province of Babylon and
chief [2]prefect over all the wise men of
Babylon. **49** And Daniel sought of the
king, and he [a]appointed [b]Shadrach,
Meshach, and Abed-nego over the
administration of the province of
Babylon, while Daniel *was* at the
king's [c,1]court.

### *Nebuchadnezzar's Golden Image*

**3** Nebuchadnezzar the king made
an [a]image of gold, the height of
which *was* [1]sixty cubits *and* its width
six cubits; he set it up on the plain
of Dura in the [b]province of Babylon.
**2** Then Nebuchadnezzar the king
sent *word* to assemble the [a]satraps,
the prefects and the governors,
the counselors, the treasurers, the
judges, the magistrates and all the
rulers of the provinces to come to
the dedication of the image that
Nebuchadnezzar the king had set up.
**3** Then the satraps, the prefects and
the governors, the counselors, the
treasurers, the judges, the magistrates
and all the rulers of the provinces
were assembled for the dedication
of the image that Nebuchadnezzar
the king had set up; and they were
standing before the image that Neb-
uchadnezzar had set up. **4** Then the
herald loudly called out: "To you it is
said, [a]O peoples, nations, and *men of*
*every* tongue, **5** that at the time you
[a]hear the sound of the horn, flute,
[1]lyre, [2]trigon, [3]psaltery, bagpipe,
and all kinds of music, you are to
fall down and worship the golden
image that Nebuchadnezzar the king
has set up. **6** But whoever does not
fall down and worship shall [1]imme-
diately be [a]cast into the midst of a
[b]furnace of blazing fire." **7** Therefore
at that time, when all the peoples
heard the sound of the horn, flute,
[1]lyre, trigon, psaltery, bagpipe, and
all kinds of music, all the peoples,
nations, and *men of every* tongue
fell down *and* worshiped the golden
image that Nebuchadnezzar the king
had set up.

### *We Will Not Serve Your Gods*

**8** For this reason at that time certain
[a]Chaldeans came near and [b,1]brought
charges against the Jews. **9** They an-
swered and said to Nebuchadnezzar
the king: "[a]O king, live forever! **10** You,
O king, have [a]made a decree that every
man who hears the sound of the horn,
flute, [1]lyre, trigon, psaltery, and bag-
pipe and all kinds of music, is to [b]fall
down and worship the golden image.
**11** But whoever does not fall down and
worship shall be cast into the midst
of a furnace of blazing fire. **12** There

---

**2:46** [b]Lv 26:31; Ezr 6:10 [1]Lit *sweet odors* **2:47** [a]Da 3:15; 4:25 [b]Dt 10:17; Ps 136:2, 3; Da 11:36 [c]Da 2:22, 30; Am 3:7 **2:48** [a]Ge 41:39-43; Da 2:6; 5:16, 29 [b]Da 3:1, 12, 30 [1]Lit *made great* [2]Lit *of the prefects* **2:49** [a]Da 3:12 [b]Da 1:7 [c]Es 2:19, 21; Am 5:15 [1]Lit *gate* ◆ **3:1** [a]1Ki 12:28; Is 46:6; Jer 16:20; Da 2:31; Hos 2:8; 8:4; Hab 2:19 [b]Da 2:48; 3:30 [1]Approx. 90 ft. high and 9 ft. wide or 27 m and 2.7 m **3:2** [a]Da 3:3, 27; 6:1-7 **3:4** [a]Da 3:7; 4:1; 6:25 **3:5** [a]Da 3:7, 10, 15 [1]Or *zither* [2]A triangular lyre [3]A type of harp **3:6** [a]Da 3:11, 15, 21; 6:7 [b]Jer 29:22; Eze 22:18-22; Mt 13:42, 50; Rev 9:2; 14:11 [1]Or *in the same hour* **3:7** [1]v 5, notes 1, 2, 3 **3:8** [a]Da 2:2, 10; 4:7 [b]Ezr 4:12-16; Es 3:8, 9; Da 6:12, 13 [1]Lit *ate the pieces of* **3:9** [a]Da 2:4; 5:10; 6:6, 21 **3:10** [a]Es 3:12-14; Da 3:4-6; 6:12 [b]Da 3:5, 7, 15 [1]v 5, notes 1, 2, 3

are certain Jews whom you have
[a]appointed over the administration
of the province of Babylon, *namely*
Shadrach, Meshach, and Abed-nego.
These men, O king, do not pay atten-
tion to you; they do not serve your
gods and do not worship the golden
image which you have set up."

**13** Then Nebuchadnezzar in [a]rage
and wrath said to bring Shadrach,
Meshach, and Abed-nego; then these
men were brought before the king.
**14** Nebuchadnezzar answered and
said to them, "Is it true, Shadrach,
Meshach, and Abed-nego, that you
are not serving [a]my gods and do not
worship the golden image that I have
set up? **15** Now if you are ready, [a]at
the time you hear the sound of the
horn, flute, [1]lyre, trigon, psaltery, and
bagpipe and all kinds of music, then
you shall fall down and worship the
image that I have made. But if you do
not worship, you will [2]immediately
be [b]cast into the midst of a furnace
of blazing fire; and [c]what god is there
who can save you out of my hands?"

**16** [a]Shadrach, Meshach, and Abed-
nego answered and said to the king,
"O Nebuchadnezzar, we do not need
to respond to you *with* an answer
concerning this matter. **17** [1]If it be *so*,
our [a]God whom we serve is able to
save us from the furnace of blazing
fire; [2]and [b]He will save us out of your
*hand, O king*. **18** [a]But if not, [b]let it be
known to you, O king, that we are not
going to serve your gods, and we will
not worship the golden image that
you have set up."

### *Daniel's Friends Delivered*

**19** Then Nebuchadnezzar was filled
with [a]wrath, and the image of his
face changed toward Shadrach,
Meshach, and Abed-nego. He an-
swered and said to heat the furnace
seven times more than it was usually
heated. **20** And he said to certain
mighty men of valor who *were* in
his military [1]host to tie up Shadrach,
Meshach, and Abed-nego in order to
cast *them* into the furnace of blazing
fire. **21** Then these men were tied
up in their [a,1]trousers, their [2]coats,
their caps, and their *other* clothes
and were cast into the midst of the
furnace of blazing fire. **22** For this
reason, because the king's word *was*
[a,1]urgent and the furnace had been
heated to an extraordinary degree,
the flame of the fire killed those men
who carried up Shadrach, Meshach,
and Abed-nego. **23** But these three
men, Shadrach, Meshach, and
Abed-nego, [a]fell into the midst
of the furnace of blazing fire *still*
tied up.

**24** Then Nebuchadnezzar the
king was astounded and hurriedly
stood up; he answered and said to
his high officials, "Was it not three
men we cast tied up into the midst
of the fire?" They answered and said
to the king, "Certainly, O king." **25** He
answered and said, "Look! I see four
men loosed *and* [a]walking about in
the midst of the fire [1]without harm,
and the appearance of the fourth
is like a son of *the* [b]gods!" **26** Then
Nebuchadnezzar came near to the

---

**3:12** [a]Da 2:49 **3:13** [a]Da 2:12; 3:19 **3:14** [a]Is 46:1; Jer 50:2; Da 3:1; 4:8 **3:15** [a]Da 3:5 [b]Da 3:6 [c]Ex 5:2; Is 36:18-20; Da 2:47 [1]v 5, notes 1, 2, 3 [2]Or *in the same hour* **3:16** [a]Da 1:7; 3:12 **3:17** [a]Job 5:19; Ps 27:1, 2; Is 26:3, 4; Jer 1:8; 15:20, 21 [b]1Sa 17:37; Mic 7:7; 2Co 1:10 [1]Or *If our God...is able* [2]Or *then* **3:18** [a]Jos 24:15; 1Ki 19:14, 18; Is 51:12, 13; Da 3:28 [b]Heb 11:25 **3:19** [a]Es 7:7; Da 3:13 **3:20** [1]Or *force* **3:21** [a]Da 3:27 [1]Or *leggings* [2]Or *cloaks* **3:22** [a]Ex 12:33; Da 2:15 [1]Or *harsh* **3:23** [a]Is 43:2 **3:25** [a]Ps 91:3-9; Is 43:2 [b]Jer 1:8, 19; 15:21 [1]Lit *there is no injury in them*

door of the furnace of blazing fire;
he answered and said, "Shadrach,
Meshach, and Abed-nego, come out,
you servants of the [a]Most High God,
and come here!" Then Shadrach,
Meshach, and Abed-nego [b]came out
of the midst of the fire. **27** Then the
[a]satraps, the prefects, the governors,
and the king's high officials gathered
around *and* saw in regard to these
men that the [b]fire had no power
over [1]the bodies of these men, nor
was the hair of their head singed,
nor were their [c,2]trousers [3]damaged,
nor had the smell of fire *even* come
upon them.

**28** Nebuchadnezzar answered
and said, "Blessed be the [a]God of
Shadrach, Meshach, and Abed-
nego, who has [b]sent His angel and
saved His servants who put their
[c]trust in Him, [1]violating the king's
word, and gave up their bodies so
as [d]not to serve and not to worship
any god except their own God.
**29** Therefore I [a]make a decree that
any people, nation, or tongue that
says anything offensive against the
God of [b]Shadrach, Meshach, and
Abed-nego shall be torn limb from
limb and their [c]houses reduced
to a rubbish heap, inasmuch as
there is [d]no other god who is able
to deliver in this way." **30** Then the
king [a]caused Shadrach, Meshach,
and Abed-nego to succeed in the
province of Babylon.

### *Nebuchadnezzar Declares the Most High God*

**4** [1]Nebuchadnezzar the king to all
the peoples, nations, and *men*
*of every* tongue that inhabit all the
earth: "May your [a,2]peace abound! **2** It
has seemed good to me to declare the
signs and wonders which the [a]Most
High God has done for me.
**3** "How great are His [a]signs,
And how strong are
His wonders!
His [b]kingdom is an
everlasting kingdom,
And His [1]dominion is from
generation to generation.

### *Nebuchadnezzar's Dream of a Great Tree*

**4** "[1]I, Nebuchadnezzar, was at ease
in my house and [a]flourishing in my
palace. **5** I saw a [a]dream, and it made
me fearful; and *these* fantasies *as I*
*lay* on my bed and the [b]visions in my
head kept alarming me. **6** So I gave a
decree to [a]bring into my presence
all the wise men of Babylon, that
they might make known to me the
interpretation of the dream. **7** Then
the [a,1]magicians, the conjurers, the
[2]Chaldeans, and the diviners came
in, and I said the dream [3]to them,
but they could not make its [b]inter-
pretation known to me. **8** But at last
Daniel came in before me, whose
name is [a]Belteshazzar according to
the name of my god, and in whom is

**3:26** [a]Da 3:17; 4:2 [b]Dt 4:20; 1Ki 8:51; Jer 11:4 **3:27** [a]Da 3:2, 3 [b]Is 43:2; Heb 11:34 [c]Da 3:21 [1]Lit *their* [2]Or *cloaks* [3]Lit *changed* **3:28** [a]Da 2:47; 3:15-17 [b]Ps 34:7, 8; Is 37:36; Da 3:25; 6:22; Ac 5:19; 12:7 [c]Ps 22:4, 5; 40:4; 84:12; Is 12:2; 26:3, 4; 50:10; Jer 17:7 [d]Da 3:16-18 [1]Lit and changed the king's *word* **3:29** [a]Da 6:26 [b]Da 1:7, 19; 2:17, 49; 3:12 [c]Ezr 6:11; Da 2:5 [d]Da 2:47; 3:15 **3:30** [a]Da 2:49; 3:12
◆ **4:1** [a]Ezr 4:17; Da 6:25 [1]Ch 3:31 in Aram [2]Or *welfare, prosperity* **4:2** [a]Da 3:26; 4:17, 24, 25, 32, 34
**4:3** [a]Ps 77:19; 105:27; Is 25:1; Da 6:27 [b]Da 2:44; 4:34; 6:26 [1]Or *powerful reign*; or in Heb *powerful rule* **4:4** [a]Ps 30:6; Is 47:7, 8 [1]Ch 4:1 in Aram **4:5** [a]Da 2:3 [b]Da 2:1, 28; 4:10, 13 **4:6** [a]Ge 41:8; Da 2:2
**4:7** [a]Ge 41:8; Da 2:10, 27; 5:7 [b]Is 44:25; Jer 27:9, 10; Da 2:7 [1]Or *soothsayer priests*, so in ch [2]Or *master astrologers* [3]Lit *before* **4:8** [a]Da 1:7; 2:26; 5:12

[b,1]a spirit of the holy gods; and I said
the dream [2]to him: **9** 'O Belteshazzar,
[a]chief of the magicians, since I know
that [b]a spirit of the holy gods is in
you, and [c]no mystery is difficult for
you, [d]say to *me* the visions of my
dream which I have seen, along with
its interpretation.

**10** 'Now *these were* the [a]visions in
my head *as I lay* on my bed: I was
looking, and behold, *there was* a
[b]tree in the midst of the [1]earth, and
its height *was* great.

**11** 'The tree grew large and
became strong,
And its height [a]reached
to the sky,
And it *was* visible to the end
of the whole earth.

**12** 'Its foliage *was* [a]beautiful
and its fruit abundant,
And in it *was* food for all.
The [b]beasts of the field
found [c]shade under it,
And the [d]birds of the sky
inhabited its branches,
And all flesh fed itself from it.

**13** 'I was looking in the [a]visions in my
head *as I lay* on my bed, and behold,
[b]a [1]watcher, a [c]holy one, descended
from heaven.

**14** 'He called out loudly
and said thus:
"[a]Chop down the tree and
cut off its branches,
*Strip off* its foliage and
scatter its fruit;
Let the [b]beasts flee
from under it
And the birds
from its branches.

**15** "Yet [a]leave the stump
[1]with its roots in the earth,
But with a band of iron
and bronze *around it*
In the new grass of the field;
And let him be drenched
with the dew of heaven,
And let [2]him share with
the beasts in the grass
of the earth.

**16** "Let his heart be changed
from *that of* a man,
And let the heart of a
beast be given to him,
And let [a]seven [1]periods
of time pass over him.

**17** "This edict is by the resolution
of the watchers,
And the decision is a
command of the holy ones,
In order that the living
may [a]know
That the Most High is
the powerful ruler over
the kingdom of mankind
And [b]gives it
to whom He wishes
And sets up over it
the [c]lowliest of men."

**18** 'This is the dream *which* I, King
Nebuchadnezzar, have seen. Now
you, Belteshazzar, say to *me* its in-
terpretation, inasmuch as none of
the [a]wise men of my kingdom is able
to make known to me the interpre-
tation; but you are able, for a [b]spirit
of the holy gods is in you.'

---

**4:8** [b]Da 4:9, 18; 5:11, 14 [1]Or *the Spirit of the holy God*, so in ch [2]Lit *before* **4:9** [a]Da 1:20; 2:48; 5:11 [b]Ge 41:38; Da 4:8 [c]Eze 28:3; Da 2:47 [d]Ge 41:15; Da 2:4, 5 **4:10** [a]Da 4:5 [b]Eze 31:3, 6 [1]Or *land*, so in ch **4:11** [a]Dt 9:1; Da 4:21, 22 **4:12** [a]Eze 31:7 [b]Jer 27:6; Eze 31:6 [c]Lam 4:20 [d]Eze 17:23; Mt 13:32; Lk 13:19 **4:13** [a]Da 7:1 [b]Da 4:17, 23 [c]Dt 33:2; Ps 89:7; Da 8:13 [1]Angel, so in ch **4:14** [a]Eze 31:10-14; Da 4:23; Mt 3:10; 7:19; Lk 13:7-9 [b]Eze 31:12, 13; Da 4:12 **4:15** [a]Job 14:7-9 [1]Lit *of* [2]Lit *his portion be with* **4:16** [a]Da 4:23, 25, 32 [1]Years **4:17** [a]Ps 9:16; 83:18; Da 2:21; 5:21 [b]Jer 27:5-7; Da 4:25; 5:18, 19 [c]1Sa 2:8; Da 11:21 **4:18** [a]Ge 41:8, 15; Da 4:7; 5:8, 15 [b]Da 4:8, 9

### *Daniel Interprets the Dream*

**19** “Then Daniel, whose name is Belte-
shazzar, was appalled for a while as
his [a]thoughts were alarming him. The
king answered and said, ‘Belteshazzar,
do not [b]let the dream or its inter-
pretation alarm you.’ Belteshazzar
answered and said, ‘[c]My lord, *if only*
the dream applied to those who hate
you and its interpretation to [d]your
adversaries! **20** The [a]tree that you
saw, which became large and grew
strong, whose height reached to the
sky and was visible to all the earth,
**21** and whose foliage *was* beautiful
and its fruit abundant, and in which
*was* food for all, under which the
beasts of the field inhabited, and in
whose branches the birds of the sky
dwelt— **22** it is [a]you, O king; for you
have become great and grown strong,
and your greatness has become *even*
greater and reached to the sky and
your [b,1]dominion to the end of the
earth. **23** But in that the king saw a
watcher, a holy one, descending from
heaven and saying, “[a]Chop down the
tree and destroy it; yet leave the stump
[1]with its roots in the earth, but with a
band of iron and bronze *around it* in
the new grass of the field, and let him
be drenched with the dew of heaven,
and let [2]him share with the beasts
of the field until [b]seven [3]periods of
time pass over him,” **24** this is the
interpretation, O king, and this is the
resolution of the Most High, which
has [a]reached my lord the king: **25** that
you be [a]driven away from mankind
and your *place of* habitation be with
the beasts of the field, and you be
given grass to eat like cattle and be
drenched with the dew of heaven; and
seven [1]periods of time will pass over
you, until you know that the [b]Most
High is the powerful ruler over the
kingdom of mankind and [c]gives it to
whomever He wishes. **26** And in that
they said to [a]leave the stump [1]with the
roots of the tree, your kingdom will
endure for you after you know that
*it is* [b]Heaven *that* rules with power.
**27** Therefore, O king, may my [a]advice
seem good to you: [b,1]break away now
from your sins by *doing* righteousness
and from your iniquities by [c]showing
mercy to *the* poor, in case there may
be a [d]prolonging of your prosperity.’

### *The Dream Is Accomplished*

**28** “All *this* [a]reached Nebuchadnez-
zar the king. **29** [a]At the end of twelve
months he was walking on the
*roof of* the royal palace of Babylon.
**30** The king answered and said, ‘Is
this not Babylon the [a]great, which
I myself have built as a royal house
by the strength of my power and for
the glory of my majesty?’ **31** While
the word *was* in the king’s mouth,
a voice [1]came from heaven, *saying,*
‘King Nebuchadnezzar, to you it is
said: the kingdom has been removed
from you, **32** and [a]you will be driven
away from mankind, and your *place
of* habitation *will be* with the beasts
of the field. You will be given grass
to eat like cattle, and [b]seven [1]periods

**4:19** [a]Jer 4:19; Da 7:15, 28; 8:27; 10:16, 17 [b]1Sa 3:17; Da 4:4, 5 [c]2Sa 18:31; Da 4:24; 10:16 [d]2Sa 18:32 **4:20** [a]Da 4:10-12 **4:22** [a]2Sa 12:7; Da 2:37, 38 [b]Jer 27:6, 7 [1]Or *powerful reign*; or in Heb *powerful rule* **4:23** [a]Da 4:14, 15 [b]Da 4:16 [1]Lit *of* [2]Lit *his portion be with* [3]Years **4:24** [a]Job 40:11, 12; Ps 107:40 **4:25** [a]Da 4:33; 5:21 [b]Ps 83:18; Jer 27:5; Da 4:2, 17 [c]Da 2:37; 4:17; 5:21 [1]Years **4:26** [a]Da 4:15, 23 [b]Da 2:18, 19, 28, 37, 44; 4:31 [1]Lit *of* **4:27** [a]Ge 41:33-37 [b]Pr 28:13; Is 55:6, 7; Eze 18:7, 21, 22; Ac 8:22 [c]Ps 41:1-3; Is 58:6, 7, 10 [d]1Ki 21:29; Jon 3:9 [1]Or *redeem now your sins* **4:28** [a]Nu 23:19; Zec 1:6 **4:29** [a]2Pe 3:9 **4:30** [a]Hab 2:4 **4:31** [1]Lit *fell* **4:32** [a]Da 4:25 [b]Da 4:16 [1]Years

of time will pass over you until you
know that the [c]Most High is the
powerful ruler over the kingdom of
mankind and gives it to whomever
He wishes.' **33** Immediately the word
concerning Nebuchadnezzar was ac-
complished; and he was [a]driven away
from mankind and began eating grass
like cattle, and his body was drenched
with the dew of heaven until his hair
had grown like eagles' *feathers* and
his nails like birds' *claws.*

**34** "But at the end of *those* days, I,
Nebuchadnezzar, lifted up my eyes
toward heaven, and my knowledge
returned to me, and I blessed the
[a]Most High and praised and honored
[b]Him who lives forever;

For His [1]dominion is an
 [c]everlasting [1]dominion,
And His kingdom *endures* from
 generation to generation.

**35** "[a]And all the inhabitants
 of the earth are
 accounted as nothing,
But [b]He does according to His
 will in the host of heaven
And *among* the
 inhabitants of earth;
And [c]no one can strike
 against His hand
Or say to Him,
 '[d]What have You done?'

**36** "At that time my [a]knowledge
returned to me. And my majesty
and [b]splendor were returned to me
for the glory of my kingdom, and
my high officials and my nobles
began seeking me out; so I was
reestablished in my kingdom, and
extraordinary [c]greatness was added
to me. **37** Now I, Nebuchadnezzar,
praise, exalt, and honor the King of
[a]heaven, for [b]all His works are [1]true
and His ways [2]just, and He is able to
humble those who [c]walk in pride."

### *Belshazzar's Feast*

**5** Belshazzar the king [1]held a great
[a]feast for one thousand of his
nobles, and he was drinking wine in
the presence of the thousand. **2** When
Belshazzar tasted the wine, he said
to bring the gold and silver [a]vessels
which Nebuchadnezzar his [1]father
had taken out of the temple which *was*
in Jerusalem, so that the king and his
nobles, his wives and his concubines
might drink from them. **3** Then they
brought the gold vessels that had been
taken out of the temple, the house of
God which *was* in Jerusalem; and the
king and his nobles, his wives and his
concubines drank from them. **4** They
[a]drank the wine and praised the gods
of [b]gold and silver, of bronze, iron,
wood and stone.

**5** Suddenly the fingers of a man's
hand came out and began writing op-
posite the lampstand on the plaster of
the wall of the king's palace, and the
king saw the [1]back of the hand that
did the writing. **6** Then the [a,1]splendor
of the king's *face* changed, and his
thoughts alarmed him, and his [b]hip
joints [2]went slack, and his [c]knees

---

**4:32** [c]Da 4:17 **4:33** [a]Da 4:25; 5:21 **4:34** [a]Da 4:2; 5:18, 21 [b]Ps 102:24-27; Da 6:26; 12:7; Rev 4:10 [c]Ps 145:13; Jer 10:10; Da 4:3; Mic 4:7; Lk 1:33 [1]Or *powerful reign*; or in Heb *powerful rule* **4:35** [a]Ps 39:5; Is 40:15, 17 [b]Ps 33:11; 115:3; 135:6; Da 6:27 [c]Job 42:2; Is 43:13 [d]Job 9:12; Is 45:9; Ro 9:20
**4:36** [a]2Chr 33:12, 13; Da 4:34 [b]Da 2:31 [c]Pr 22:4; Da 4:22 **4:37** [a]Da 4:26; 5:23 [b]Dt 32:4; Ps 33:4, 5; Is 5:16 [c]Ex 18:11; Job 40:11, 12; Da 5:20 [1]Lit *truth* [2]Lit *justice* ◆ **5:1** [a]Es 1:3; Is 22:12-14 [1]Lit *made*
**5:2** [a]2Ki 24:13; 25:15; Ezr 1:7-11; Da 1:2 [1]Or *forefather*, so in ch **5:4** [a]Is 42:8; Da 5:23; Rev 9:20 [b]Ps 115:4; 135:15; Is 40:19, 20; Da 3:1; Hab 2:19 **5:5** [1]Or *palm* **5:6** [a]Da 5:9, 10; 7:28 [b]Ps 69:23 [c]Eze 7:17; 21:7; Na 2:10 [1]Lit *brightness changed for him* [2]Lit *became loosened*

were knocking against each other.
**7** The king called out loudly to bring
in the [a]conjurers, the [1]Chaldeans,
and the diviners. The king answered
and said to the wise men of Babylon,
"Any man who can read this writing
and declare its interpretation to me
shall be [b]clothed with purple and
*have* a [c]necklace of gold around his
neck and rule with power as [d,2]third
*ruler* in the kingdom." **8** Then all the
king's wise men came in, but [a]they
could not read the writing or make
known its interpretation to the king.
**9** Then King Belshazzar was greatly
[a]alarmed, and the [b,1]splendor of his
*face* changed *further*, and his nobles
were perplexed.

**10** The queen entered the banquet
[1]hall because of the words of the king
and his nobles; the queen answered
and said, "[a]O king, live forever! Do
not let your thoughts alarm you
or the [2]splendor of your *face* be
changed. **11** There is a [a]man in your
kingdom in whom is [1]a [b]spirit of the
holy gods; and in the days of your
father, illumination, insight, and
wisdom like the wisdom of the gods
were found in him. And King Nebu-
chadnezzar, your father, your father
[c,2]the king, set him as chief of the
[3]magicians, conjurers, [4]Chaldeans,
*and* diviners. **12** *This was* because
an [a]extraordinary spirit, knowledge
and insight, interpretation of dreams,
explanation of enigmas, and [1]solving
of difficult problems were found in
this Daniel, whom the king named
[b]Belteshazzar. Let Daniel now be
summoned, and he will declare the
interpretation."

### *Daniel Interprets the Writing on the Wall*

**13** Then Daniel was brought in before
the king. The king answered and said
to Daniel, "Are you that Daniel who is
one of the [a,1]exiles from Judah, whom
my father the king [b]brought from Ju-
dah? **14** Now I have heard about you
that [1]a spirit of the gods is in you,
and that illumination, insight, and
extraordinary wisdom have been
found in you. **15** Just now the [a]wise
men *and* the conjurers were brought
in before me that they might read this
writing and make its interpretation
known to me, but they [b]could not
declare the interpretation of the
[1]message. **16** But I personally have
heard about you, that you are able
to give interpretations and [1]solve
difficult problems. Now if you are
able to read the writing and make
its [a]interpretation known to me, you
will be [b]clothed with purple and *wear*
a necklace of gold around your neck,
and you will rule with power as the
[2]third *ruler* in the kingdom."

**17** Then Daniel answered and
said before the king, "Let your
[a]gifts *remain* with you or give your
rewards to someone else; however, I
will read the writing to the king and
make the interpretation known to

---

**5:7** [a]Is 44:25; 47:13; Da 4:6, 7; 5:11, 15 [b]Ge 41:42-44; Da 5:16, 29 [c]Eze 16:11 [d]Da 2:48; 5:16, 29; 6:2, 3 [1]Or *master astrologers* [2]Or *a triumvir* **5:8** [a]Ge 41:8; Da 2:27; 4:7; 5:15 **5:9** [a]Job 18:11; Is 21:2-4; Jer 6:24; Da 2:1; 5:6 [b]Is 13:6-8 [1]Lit *brightness was changing upon him* **5:10** [a]Da 3:9; 6:6 [1]Lit *house* [2]Lit *brightness be changed* **5:11** [a]Ge 41:11-15; Da 2:47 [b]Da 4:8, 9, 18; 5:14 [c]Da 2:48 [1]Or *the Spirit of the holy God* [2]Or *O king* [3]Or *soothsayer priests* [4]Or *master astrologers* **5:12** [a]Da 5:14; 6:3 [b]Da 1:7; 4:8 [1]Lit *loosening* **5:13** [a]Ezr 4:1; 6:16, 19, 20; Da 2:25; 6:13 [b]Da 1:1, 2 [1]Lit *sons of the exile* **5:14** [1]Or possibly *the Spirit of God* **5:15** [a]Da 5:7 [b]Is 47:12f; Da 5:8 [1]Lit *word* **5:16** [a]Ge 40:8 [b]Da 5:7, 29 [1]Lit *loosen* [2]Or *triumvir* **5:17** [a]2Ki 5:16

him. **18** [1]O king, the [a]Most High God
[b]granted the kingdom, [c]grandeur, glo-
ry, and majesty to Nebuchadnezzar
your father. **19** And because of the
grandeur which He bestowed on him,
all the peoples, nations, and *men of*
*every* tongue feared and were in dread
before him; [a]whomever he wished
he killed, and whomever he wished
he kept alive, and whomever he
wished he raised up, and whomever
he wished he made low. **20** But when
his heart was [a]raised up and his spirit
became so [b]strong that he behaved
arrogantly, he was [c]deposed from his
royal throne, and *his* glory was taken
away from him. **21** He was also [a]driven
away from the sons of [1]men, and his
heart was made like *that of* beasts,
and his *place* of habitation *was* with
the [b]wild donkeys. He was given grass
to eat like cattle, and his body was
drenched with the dew of the sky un-
til he knew that the [c]Most High God is
the powerful ruler over the kingdom
of mankind and *that* He sets up over
it whomever He wishes. **22** Yet you,
his [1]son, Belshazzar, have [a]not made
your heart lowly, [2]even though you
knew all this, **23** but you have [a]raised
yourself up against the [b]Lord of heav-
en; and they have brought the vessels
of His house before you, and you and
your nobles, your wives and your
concubines have been drinking wine
*from them; and* you have praised the
[c]gods of silver and gold, of bronze,
iron, wood and stone, which do not
see, hear, or know. But the God [d]in
whose hand are your life-breath and
all your [e]ways, you have not honored.
**24** Then the [a,1]hand was sent from
Him, and this writing was [2]inscribed.

**25** "Now this is the writing that was
[1]inscribed: '[2]MENĒ, [2]MENĒ, [3]TEKĒL,
[4]UPHARSIN.' **26** This is the interpre-
tation of the [1]message: 'MENĒ'—God
has numbered your kingdom and
[a]put an end to it. **27** 'TEKĒL'—you
have been [a]weighed on the scales
and found lacking. **28** 'PERĒS'—your
kingdom has been divided and given
over to the [a]Medes and [1]Persians."

**29** Then Belshazzar said *the word*,
and they [a]clothed Daniel with purple
and *put* a necklace of gold around his
neck and issued a proclamation con-
cerning him that he *now* would be the
[1]third powerful ruler in the kingdom.

**30** That same night [a]Belshazzar
the Chaldean king was [b]killed.

**31** [1]So [a]Darius the Mede received
the kingdom at about the age of
sixty-two.

### *Darius' Officials Seek to Accuse Daniel*

**6** [1]It seemed good to Darius that he
set 120 satraps over the kingdom,
that they would be in charge of the
whole kingdom, **2** and over them three
commissioners (of whom [a]Daniel was

**5:18** [a]Da 4:2; 5:21 [b]Da 2:37, 38; 4:17 [c]Jer 25:9; 27:5-7 [1]Lit *You, O king* **5:19** [a]Da 2:12, 13; 3:6; 11:3, 16, 36 **5:20** [a]Ex 9:17; Job 15:25; Is 14:13-15; Da 4:30, 31 [b]2Ki 17:14; 2Chr 36:13 [c]Job 40:11, 12; Jer 13:18 **5:21** [a]Job 30:3-7; Da 4:32, 33 [b]Job 39:5-8 [c]Ex 9:14-16; Ps 83:17, 18; Eze 17:24; Da 4:17, 34, 35 [1]Lit *man* **5:22** [a]Ex 10:3; 2Chr 33:23; 36:12 [1]Or *descendant* [2]Lit *inasmuch as you* **5:23** [a]2Ki 14:10; Is 2:12; 37:23; Jer 50:29; Da 5:3, 4 [b]Da 4:37 [c]Ps 115:4-8; Is 37:19; Hab 2:18, 19 [d]Job 12:10 [e]Job 31:4; Ps 139:3; Pr 20:24; Jer 10:23 **5:24** [a]Da 5:5 [1]Lit *palm of the hand* [2]Or *signed*, cf. 6:9-14 **5:25** [1]Or *signed*, cf. 6:9-14 [2]Or *a mina* (50 shekels), from verb "to number" [3]Or *a shekel*, from verb "to weigh" [4]Or *and half-shekels* (sing: *perēs*), from verb "to divide" **5:26** [a]Is 13:6, 17-19; Jer 50:41-43 [1]Lit *word* **5:27** [a]Job 31:6; Ps 62:9 **5:28** [a]Is 13:17; 21:2; 45:1, 2; Da 5:31; 6:8, 28; Ac 2:9 [1]Aram: *Pāras* **5:29** [a]Da 5:7, 16 [1]Or *triumvir* **5:30** [a]Da 5:1, 2 [b]Is 21:4-9; 47:9; Jer 51:11, 31, 39, 57 **5:31** [a]Da 6:1; 9:1 [1]Ch 6:1 in Aram ◆ **6:1** [1]Ch 6:2 in Aram **6:2** [a]Da 2:48, 49; 5:16, 29

one), that these satraps might be ac-
countable to them, and that the king
might not suffer [b]loss. **3** Then this
Daniel began distinguishing himself
[1]among the commissioners and sa-
traps because an [a]extraordinary spirit
was in him, and the king planned to
set him over the [b]entire kingdom.
**4** Then the commissioners and satraps
began [a]seeking to find a ground of
accusation against Daniel in regard
to *matters of* the kingdom; but they
were not able to find [b]any ground of
accusation or *evidence of* corruption,
inasmuch as he was faithful, and
no negligence or corruption was *to
be* found in him. **5** Then these men
said, "We will not find any ground of
accusation against this Daniel unless
we find *it* against him with regard to
the [a]law of his God."

**6** Then these commissioners and
satraps came [1]by agreement to the
king and said thus to him: "King Da-
rius, [a]live forever! **7** All the [a]commis-
sioners of the kingdom, the prefects
and the satraps, the high officials and
the governors have [b]counseled to-
gether that the king should establish
a statute and enforce an injunction
that anyone who seeks *to make* a
petition [1]to any god or man besides
you, O king, for thirty days, shall
[c]be cast into the lions' [2]den. **8** Now,
O king, [a]establish the injunction and
[1]sign the written *document* so that
it may not be changed, according to
the [b]law of the Medes and Persians,
which [2]may not be revoked." **9** There-
fore King Darius [a]signed the written
*document*, that is, the injunction.

**10** Now when Daniel knew that
the written *document* was signed,
he entered his house (now in his
roof chamber he had windows open
[a]toward Jerusalem); and he contin-
ued [b]kneeling on his knees three
times a day, [c]praying and [d]giving
thanks before his God, [1]as he had
been doing previously. **11** Then these
men came [a,1]by agreement and found
Daniel seeking *to make* a petition and
making supplication before his God.
**12** Then they came near and [a]said be-
fore the king concerning the king's
injunction, "Did you not sign an
injunction that any man who seeks
*to make* a petition [1]to any god or man
besides you, O king, for thirty days,
is to be cast into the lions' den?" The
king answered and said, "The word is
certain, according to the [b]law of the
Medes and Persians, which [2]may not
be revoked." **13** Then they answered
and said before the king, "[a]Daniel,
who is one of the [1]exiles from Judah,
pays [b]no attention to you, O king, or
to the injunction which you signed,
but keeps seeking *to make* his peti-
tion three times a day."

**14** Then, as soon as the king heard
this word, he was greatly [a]distressed
within himself and set *his* mind on
saving Daniel; and even until sunset
he kept exerting himself to deliver
him. **15** Then these men came [1]by

---

**6:2** [b]Ezr 4:22; Es 7:4 **6:3** [a]Da 5:12, 14; 9:23 [b]Ge 41:40; Es 10:3 [1]Lit *above* **6:4** [a]Ge 43:18; Jdg 14:4; *Jer 20:10; Da 3:8; Lk 20:20* [b]Da 6:22; Lk 20:26; 23:14, 15; Php 2:15; 1Pe 2:12; 3:16 **6:5** [a]Ac 24:13-16, 20, 21 **6:6** [a]Ne 2:3; Da 2:4; 5:10; 6:21 [1]Or *thronging* **6:7** [a]Da 3:2, 27 [b]Ps 59:3; 62:4; 64:2-6; *83:1-3* [c]*Ps 10:9;* Da 3:6; 6:16 [1]Lit *from* [2]Or *pit*, so in ch **6:8** [a]Es 3:12; 8:10; Is 10:1 [b]Es 1:19; 8:8; Da 6:12, 15 [1]Or *inscribed*, so in ch, cf. 5:24-25; 10:21 [2]Lit *does not pass away* **6:9** [a]Ps 118:9; 146:3 **6:10** [a]1Ki 8:44, 48, 49; Ps 5:7; Jon 2:4 [b]Ps 55:17; 95:6 [c]Da 9:4-19 [d]Ps 34:1; Php 4:6; 1Th 5:17, 18 [1]Or *because* **6:11** [a]Ps 37:32, 33; Da 6:6 [1]Or *thronging* **6:12** [a]Da 3:8-12; Ac 16:19-21 [b]Es 1:19; Da 6:8, 15 [1]Lit *from* [2]Lit *does not pass away* **6:13** [a]Da 2:25; 5:13 [b]Es 3:8; Da 3:12; Ac 5:29 [1]Lit *sons of the exile* **6:14** [a]Mk 6:26 **6:15** [1]Or *thronging*

agreement to the king and said to
the king, "Know, O king, that it is a
[a]law of the Medes and Persians that
no injunction or statute which the
king establishes may be changed."

### *Daniel in the Lions' Den*

**16** Then the king said *the word,* and
Daniel was brought in and [a]cast into
the lions' den. The king answered and
said to Daniel, "[b,1] Your God whom
you constantly serve will Himself save
you." **17** And a [a]stone was brought and
placed over the mouth of the den;
and the king sealed it with his own
signet ring and with the signet rings
of his nobles so that nothing would be
changed in regard to Daniel. **18** Then
the king went off to his palace and
spent the night [a]fasting, and no en-
tertainment was brought before him;
and his [b]sleep fled from him.

**19** Then the king arose at dawn,
at the break of day, and hurriedly
went to the lions' den. **20** When he
had come near the den to Daniel, he
cried out with a troubled voice. The
king answered and said to Daniel,
"Daniel, servant of the living God,
has [a]your God, whom you constantly
serve, been [b]able to save you from
the lions?" **21** Then Daniel spoke
[1]to the king, "[a]O king, live forever!
**22** My God [a]sent His angel and [b]shut
the lions' mouths, and they have
not harmed me, inasmuch as [1]I was
found innocent before Him; and also
[2]toward you, O king, I have done no
harm." **23** Then the king was greatly
pleased and said for Daniel to be taken
up out of the den. So Daniel was taken
up out of the den, and [a]no harm what-
soever was found on him because
he had [b]believed in his God. **24** The
king then said *the word,* and they
brought those men who had [1]brought
charges against Daniel, and they
[a]cast them, their [b]children, and their
wives into the lions' den; and they
had not reached the bottom of the
den before the lions overpowered
them and crushed all their bones.

**25** Then Darius the king wrote to
all the [a]peoples, nations, and *men of
every* tongue who were inhabiting all
the land: "[b]May your [1]peace abound!
**26** [1]I [a]make a decree that in all the
[2]dominion of my kingdom, men are
to fear and be in dread before the God
of Daniel;

For He is the [b]living God
and [c]enduring forever,
And [d]His kingdom is one
which will not be destroyed,
And His [2]dominion *will
be* unto the end.

**27** "He saves and delivers and
does [a]signs and wonders
In heaven and on earth,
Who has *also* saved
Daniel from the [1]power
of the lions."

---

**6:15** [a]Es 8:8; Ps 94:20, 21; Da 6:8, 12 **6:16** [a]2Sa 3:39; Jer 38:5; Da 6:7 [b]Job 5:19; Ps 37:39, 40; Is 41:10; Da 3:17, 28; 6:20; 2Co 1:10 [1]Or *May your God...Himself deliver you* **6:17** [a]Lam 3:53; Mt 27:66 **6:18** [a]2Sa 12:16, 17 [b]Es 6:1; Ps 77:4; Da 2:1 **6:20** [a]Da 6:16, 27 [b]Ge 18:14; Nu 11:23; Jer 32:17; Da 3:17 **6:21** [a]Da 2:4; 6:6 [1]Lit *with* **6:22** [a]Nu 20:16; Is 63:9; Da 3:28; Ac 12:11; Heb 1:14 [b]Ps 91:11-13; 2Ti 4:17; Heb 11:33 [1]Lit *innocence was found for me* [2]Lit *before* **6:23** [a]Da 3:25, 27 [b]1Chr 5:20; 2Chr 20:20; Ps 118:8, 9; Is 26:3; Da 3:17, 28 **6:24** [a]Dt 19:18, 19; Es 7:10 [b]Dt 24:16; 2Ki 14:6; Es 9:10 [1]Lit *eaten the pieces of Daniel* **6:25** [a]Ezr 1:1, 2; Es 3:12; 8:9; Da 4:1 [b]Ezr 4:17; 1Pe 1:2 [1]Or *welfare, prosperity* **6:26** [a]Ezr 6:8-12; 7:13, 21; Da 3:29 [b]Da 4:34; 6:20; Hos 1:10; Ro 9:26 [c]Ps 93:1, 2; Mal 3:6 [d]Da 2:44; 4:3; 7:14, 27; Lk 1:33 [1]Lit *From me a decree is made* [2]Or *powerful reign*; or in Heb *powerful rule* **6:27** [a]Da 4:2, 3 [1]Lit *hand*

28 So this [a]Daniel enjoyed success
in the kingdom of Darius and in the
kingdom of [b]Cyrus the Persian.

### *The Vision of the Four Beasts*

7 In the first year of Belshazzar king
of Babylon Daniel saw a [a]dream
and visions in his head *as he lay* on his
bed; then he [b]wrote the dream down
*and* said the [1]*following* summary of
the matter. 2 Daniel answered and
said, "I was [a]looking in my vision by
night, and behold, the [b]four winds
of heaven were stirring up the great
sea. 3 And four great [a]beasts were
coming up from the sea, different
from one another. 4 The first *was*
[a]like a lion and had *the* wings of an
eagle. I kept looking until its wings
were plucked, and it was lifted up
from the ground and made to stand
on two feet like a man; and a heart of
a man was given to it. 5 And behold,
another beast, a second one in the
likeness of a bear. And it was raised
up on one side, and three ribs *were* in
its mouth between its teeth; and thus
they said to it, 'Arise, devour much
meat!' 6 After this I kept looking, and
behold, another one, [a]like a leopard,
which had on its [1]back four wings
of a bird; the beast also had [b]four
heads, and [2]dominion was given to it.
7 After this I kept looking in the night
visions, and behold, a [a]fourth beast,
fearsome and terrifying and extraor-
dinarily strong; and it had large iron
teeth. It devoured and crushed and
trampled down the remainder with
its feet; and it was different from all
the beasts that were before it, and
it had [b]ten horns. 8 While I was
contemplating the horns, behold,
[a]another horn, a little one, came up
among them, and three of the first
horns were pulled out by the roots
before it; and behold, [1]this horn
possessed eyes like the eyes of a man
and [b]a mouth speaking great *boasts*.

### *The Ancient of Days*

9 "I kept looking
Until [a]thrones were set up,
And the Ancient
of Days was seated;
His [b]clothing *was*
like white snow
And the [c]hair of His
head like pure wool.
His [d]throne *was*
[1]ablaze with fire,
Its [e]wheels *were* a burning fire.
10 "A river of [a]fire was flowing
And coming out
from before Him;
[b]Thousands upon thousands
were attending Him,
And myriads upon myriads
were standing before Him;
The [c]court sat,
And [d]the books were opened.
11 "Then I kept looking because of
the sound of the great *boastful* words
which the horn was speaking; I kept
looking until the beast was killed,
and its body was destroyed and given
to the [a]burning [1]fire. 12 As for the rest
of the beasts, their [1]dominion was

**6:28** [a]Da 1:21 [b]2Chr 36:22, 23; Da 10:1 ◆ **7:1** [a]Job 33:14-16; Da 1:17; 2:1, 26-28; 4:5-9; Joel 2:28 [b]Jer 36:4, 32 [1]Or *beginning* **7:2** [a]Da 7:7, 13 [b]Rev 7:1 **7:3** [a]Da 7:17; Rev 13:1; 17:8 **7:4** [a]Jer 4:7 **7:6** [a]Rev 13:2 [b]Da 8:22 [1]Or *sides* [2]Or *powerful reign*; or in Heb *powerful rule* **7:7** [a]Da 7:19, 20, 23 [b]Rev 12:3; 13:1 **7:8** [a]Da 8:9 [b]Rev 13:5, 6 [1]Lit *in this horn* were *eyes* **7:9** [a]Rev 20:4 [b]Mk 9:3 [c]Rev 1:14 [d]Eze 1:13, 26 [e]Eze 10:2, 6 [1]Lit *flames of fire* **7:10** [a]Ps 18:8; 50:3; 97:3; Is 30:27, 33 [b]Dt 33:2; 1Ki 22:19; Rev 5:11 [c]Ps 96:11-13; Da 7:22, 26 [d]Da 12:1; Rev 20:11-15 **7:11** [a]Rev 19:20; 20:10 [1]Lit *of the fire* **7:12** [1]Or *powerful reign*; or in Heb *powerful rule*

taken away, but an extension of life
was given to them for an appointed
season of time.

### *The Son of Man*

13 "I kept looking
in the night visions,
And behold, with the clouds
of heaven
One like a [a]Son of Man
was coming,
And He came up
to the Ancient of Days
And came near before Him.
14 "And to Him was
given [a,1]dominion,
Glory, and [b]a kingdom,
[c]That all the peoples, nations,
and *men of every* tongue
Might serve Him.
[d]His [1]dominion is an
everlasting [1]dominion
Which will not be taken away;
[e]And His kingdom is one
Which will not be destroyed.

### *The Vision Interpreted*

15 "As for me, Daniel, my spirit was
distressed [1]within me, and the [a]vi-
sions of my head kept [b]alarming me.
16 I came near to one of those who
were [a]standing by and began seeking
out *from* him the [1]exact meaning of
all this. So he [b]said *it* to me and made
known to me the interpretation of
*these things:* 17 'These great beasts,
which are four *in number*, are four
kings *who* will arise from the earth.
18 But the [a,1]saints of the Highest
One will [b]receive the kingdom and
possess the kingdom forever, [2]for all
ages to come.'
19 "Then I desired to know the
[1]exact meaning of the [a]fourth beast,
which was different from all [2]the oth-
ers, extraordinarily fearsome, with its
teeth of iron and its claws of bronze,
*and which* devoured, crushed, and
trampled down the remainder with
its feet, 20 and *the meaning* of the
ten horns that *were* on its head and
the other *horn* which came up and
before which three *of them* fell,
namely, that horn which had eyes
and a mouth speaking great *boasts*
and [1]which was larger in appearance
than its associates. 21 I kept looking,
and that horn was [a]waging war with
the saints and overcoming them
22 until the Ancient of Days came and
[a]judgment was given in favor of the
saints of the Highest One, and the
season arrived when the saints took
possession of the kingdom.
23 "Thus he said: 'The fourth beast
will be a fourth kingdom on the earth,
which will be different from all the
*other* kingdoms and will devour the
whole earth and tread it down and
crush it. 24 As for the [a]ten horns, out
of this kingdom ten kings will arise;
and another will arise after them,
*and he will be different* from the pre-
vious ones and will make low three
kings. 25 He will [a]speak words against
the [b]Most High and [c]wear down the

---

**7:13** [a]Mt 24:30; 26:64; Mk 13:26; 14:62; Lk 21:27; Rev 1:7, 13; 14:14 **7:14** [a]Da 7:27; Jn 3:35; 1Co 15:27; Eph 1:20-22; Php 2:9-11; Rev 1:6; 11:15 [b]Da 2:37 [c]Ps 72:11; 102:22 [d]Mic 4:7; Lk 1:33 [e]Heb 12:28 [1]Or *powerful reign*; or in Heb *powerful rule* **7:15** [a]Da 7:1 [b]Da 4:19; 7:28 [1]Lit *in the midst of* its *sheath* **7:16** [a]Zec 1:9, 19; Rev 5:5; 7:13, 14 [b]Da 8:16, 17; 9:22 [1]Lit *truth concerning* **7:18** [a]Da 7:22, 25, 27 [b]Ps 149:5-9; Is 60:12-14; Da 7:14; Rev 2:26, 27; 20:4; 22:5 [1]Lit *holy ones*, so in ch [2]Lit *and unto the age of the ages* **7:19** [a]Da 7:7, 8 [1]Lit *truth concerning* [2]Lit *of them* **7:20** [1]Lit *its appearance was larger* **7:21** [a]Rev 11:7; 13:7 **7:22** [a]Da 7:10; 1Co 6:2, 3 **7:24** [a]Da 7:7; Rev 17:12 **7:25** [a]Da 11:36; Rev 13:6 [b]Da 3:26; 4:2, 17, 34 [c]Rev 13:7; 18:24

saints of the Highest One, and he will intend to make [d]changes in seasons and in law; and [1]they will be given into his hand for a [e,2]time, [2]times, and half a [2]time. **26** But the court will sit *for judgment*, and his dominion will be [a]taken away, [1]annihilated and destroyed [2]forever. **27** Then the [a,1]reign, the dominion, and the greatness of *all* the kingdoms under the whole heaven will be given to the people of the saints of the Highest One; His kingdom *will be* an [b]everlasting kingdom, and all the dominions will [c]serve and obey Him.'

**28** "[1]At this point the matter *of this revelation* ended. As for me, Daniel, my thoughts were [a]greatly alarming me, and the [2]splendor of my *face* changed, but I [b]kept the matter in my heart."

### *The Vision of the Ram and Goat*

**8** In the third year of the reign of Belshazzar the king, a vision appeared to me, [1]Daniel, after the one which appeared to me [2]previously. **2** And I [a]looked in the vision. And it happened that while I was looking, I was in the citadel of [b]Susa, which is in the province of [c]Elam; and I looked in the vision, and I myself was beside the Ulai [1]Canal. **3** Then I lifted my eyes and looked, and behold, a [a]ram which had two horns was standing in front of the [1]canal. Now the two horns *were* [2]long, but one *was* [2]longer than the other, with the [2]longer one coming up last. **4** I saw the ram [a]butting westward, northward, and southward, and no *other* beasts could stand before it, nor was there anyone to deliver from its [1]power, but [b]it did as it pleased and magnified *itself*.

**5** And while I was considering, behold, a male goat was coming from the west over the surface of the whole earth without touching the ground; and the [1]goat *had* a [a]conspicuous horn between its eyes. **6** Then it came up to the ram that had the two horns, which I had seen standing in front of the [1]canal, and ran at it in his strong wrath. **7** And I saw it reach the side of the ram, and it was enraged at it; and it struck the ram and broke its two horns in pieces, and the ram had no strength to stand in [1]opposition to it. So it threw it down to the ground and trampled on it, and there was none to deliver the ram from its [2]power. **8** Then the male goat magnified *itself* exceedingly. But as soon as [a]it was mighty, the [b]large horn was broken; and in its place there came up four conspicuous *horns* toward the [c]four winds of [1]heaven.

### *The Small Horn*

**9** And out of one of them came forth a rather [a]small horn. And it grew exceedingly great toward the south, toward the east, and toward the [b,1]Beautiful *Land*. **10** Then it grew up to the host of heaven and caused some of the host and some of

---

**7:25** [d]Da 2:21 [e]Da 12:7; Rev 12:14 [1]The saints [2]Year(s) **7:26** [a]Rev 17:14; 19:2 [1]Lit *to annihilate and to destroy* [2]Lit *to the end* **7:27** [a]Is 54:3; Da 7:14, 18, 22; Rev 20:4 [b]Ps 145:13; Is 9:7; Da 2:44; 4:34; 7:14; Lk 1:33; Rev 11:15; 22:5 [c]Ps 2:6-12; 22:27; 72:11; 86:9; Is 60:12; Rev 11:1 [1]Or *kingdom* **7:28** [a]Da 4:19 [b]Lk 2:19, 51 [1]Lit *To here the end of the word* [2]Lit *brightness was changing upon me* ◆ **8:1** [1]Lit *I, Daniel* [2]Lit *at the beginning* **8:2** [a]Nu 12:6; Da 7:2, 15; 8:3 [b]Ne 1:1; Es 1:2; 2:8 [c]Ge 10:22; 14:1; Is 11:11; Jer 25:25; Eze 32:24 [1]Or *River* **8:3** [a]Da 8:20 [1]Or *river* [2]Lit *high(er)* **8:4** [a]Dt 33:17; 1Ki 22:11; Eze 34:21 [b]Da 11:3 [1]Lit *hand* **8:5** [a]Da 8:8, 21; 11:3 [1]Lit *buck* **8:6** [1]Or *river* **8:7** [1]Lit *before* [2]Lit *hand* **8:8** [a]2Chr 26:16; Da 5:20 [b]Da 8:22 [c]Da 7:2; Rev 7:1 [1]Or the *sky* **8:9** [a]Da 8:23 [b]Ps 48:2; Da 11:16, 41 [1]Israel

the [a]stars to fall to the earth, and it
[b]trampled them down. **11** And it even
[a]magnified *itself* [1]to be equal with
the [2]Commander of the host; and it
removed the [b]regular sacrifice from
Him, and the place of His sanctuary
was thrown down. **12** And on account
of transgression the host will be giv-
en over *to the horn* along with the
regular sacrifice; and it will [a]throw
truth down to the ground and do
*its will* and succeed. **13** Then I heard
a [a]holy one speaking, and another
holy one said to that particular one
who was speaking, "[b]How long will
the vision *about* the regular sacri-
fice apply, [1]while the transgression
causes desolation, so as to allow
both the holy place and the host
[2]to be [c]trampled?" **14** He said to me,
"For [a]2,300 evenings *and* mornings;
then the holy place will be [1]made
righteous."

### *Daniel Seeks to Understand the Vision*

**15** Now it happened when [a]I, Daniel,
had seen the vision, that I sought [1]to
understand it; and behold, standing
before me was one [2]who had the ap-
pearance of a [b]man. **16** And I heard
the voice of a man between *the banks
of* Ulai, and he called out and said,
"[a]Gabriel, give this *man* an under-
standing of what has appeared."
**17** So he came near to where I was
standing, and when he came I was
terrified and [a]fell on my face; but he
said to me, "Son of man, understand
that the vision pertains to the [b]time
of the end."

**18** Now while he was talking with
me, I [a]sank into a deep sleep with my
face to the ground; but he [b]touched
me and made me stand [1]upright.
**19** Then he said, "Behold, I am going
to [a]let you know what will happen at
the final period of the indignation,
for *it* pertains to the appointed time
of the end. **20** The [a]ram which you
saw with the two horns is the kings of
Media and Persia. **21** Now the shaggy
[1]goat is the [2]king of Greece, and the
large horn that is between his eyes
is the first king. **22** And the [a]broken
*horn* and the four *horns that* stood
in its place *are* four kingdoms *which*
will *take their* stand from *his* nation,
although not with his power.

**23** "In the latter period
of their [1]reign,
When the transgressors
have [2]run *their course*,
A king will stand,
[3]Insolent and skilled
in [4]intrigue.
**24** "His power will be mighty,
but not by his *own* power,
And he will [a,1]destroy
to an [2]astonishing degree
And succeed and do *his will*;
He will [1]destroy mighty men
and [3]the holy people.

---

**8:10** [a]Is 14:13; Jer 48:26; Rev 12:4 [b]Da 7:7; 8:7 **8:11** [a]2Ki 19:22, 23; 2Chr 32:15-17; Is 37:23; Da 8:25; 11:36, 37 [b]Eze 46:14; Da 11:31; 12:11 [1]Lit *up to the* [2]Or *Prince* **8:12** [a]Is 59:14 **8:13** [a]Da 4:13, 23; 1Pe 1:12 [b]Ps 74:10; 79:5; Is 6:11; Da 12:6, 8; Rev 6:10 [c]Is 63:18; Jer 12:10; Lk 21:24; Heb 10:29; Rev 11:2 [1]Or possibly *and the transgression that horrifies* [2]Lit *as a trampling* **8:14** [a]Da 7:25; 12:7, 11; Rev 11:2, 3; 12:14; 13:5 [1]Or *properly restored* **8:15** [a]Da 8:1 [b]Da 7:13; 10:16, 18 [1]Lit *understanding* [2]Lit *like the appearance of a man* **8:16** [a]Da 9:21; Lk 1:19, 26 **8:17** [a]Eze 1:28; 44:4; Da 2:46; Rev 1:17 [b]Da 8:19; 11:35, 40 **8:18** [a]Da 10:9; Lk 9:32 [b]Eze 2:2; Da 10:10, 16, 18 [1]Lit *on my standing* **8:19** [a]Da 8:15-17 **8:20** [a]Da 8:3 **8:21** [1]Lit *buck* [2]Or *kingdom* **8:22** [a]Da 8:8 **8:23** [1]Or *kingdom* [2]Lit *finished* [3]Lit *Strong of face* [4]Or *ambiguous speech* **8:24** [a]Da 8:11-13; 11:36; 12:7 [1]Or *corrupt* [2]Or *wondrous*; lit *extraordinary* [3]Lit *people of the saints*, cf. 7:27

**25** "And through his insight
He will cause deceit
to succeed by his hand;
And he will magnify
*himself* in his heart,
And he will [1]destroy many
while *they are* [2]at ease.
He will even [a]stand against
the Prince of princes,
But he will be broken
[b]without hands.
**26** "And what had appeared about
the evenings and mornings
Which has been told is [a]true;
But as for you, [b]conceal
the vision,
For *it* pertains to many
[c]days *in the future*."
**27** Then I, Daniel, was [a,1]exhausted
and sick for days. Then I rose up
*again* and [b]did the king's work; but
I was appalled at what had appeared,
and there was none to make *me*
understand *it*.

### *Daniel's Prayer of Supplication*

**9** In the first year of [a]Darius the
son of Ahasuerus, from the seed
of the Medes, who was made king
over the kingdom of the Chaldeans—
**2** in the first year of his reign, I, Daniel,
discerned in the books the [a]number
of the years *concerning* which the
word of [1]Yahweh came to [b]Jeremiah
the prophet for the fulfillment of the
laying waste of Jerusalem, *namely*,
[b]seventy years. **3** So I gave my face to
the Lord God to seek *Him by* prayer and
supplications, with fasting, sackcloth,
and ashes. **4** And I prayed to Yahweh
my God and confessed and said, "Alas,
O Lord, the [a]great and awesome God,
who [b]keeps His covenant and loving-
kindness for those who love Him and
keep His commandments, **5** [a]we have
sinned and committed iniquity and
acted wickedly and [b]rebelled, even
[c]turning aside from Your command-
ments and judgments. **6** Moreover, we
have not [a]listened to Your slaves the
prophets, who spoke in Your name
to our kings, our princes, our fathers,
and all the people of the land.
**7** "[a]To You, O Lord, belongs righ-
teousness, but to us [b,1]open shame,
as it is this day—to the men of Judah,
the inhabitants of Jerusalem, and all
Israel, those who are nearby and those
who are far away in [c]all the countries
to which You have banished them,
because of their unfaithful deeds
which they have committed against
You. **8** O Yahweh, to us belongs [1]open
shame, to our kings, our princes, and
our fathers, because we have sinned
against You. **9** To the Lord our God *be-*
*long* [a]compassion and forgiveness, [1]for
we have [b]rebelled against Him; **10** nor
have we listened to the voice of Yahweh
our God, to walk in His [1]laws which He
[a]put before us through His slaves the
prophets. **11** Indeed [a]all Israel has tres-
passed against Your law, even turning
aside, not listening to Your voice; so
the [b]curse has been poured out on us,
along with the oath which is written

---

**8:25** [a]Da 8:11 [b]Job 34:20; Da 2:34, 45 [1]Or *corrupt* [2]Or *secure* **8:26** [a]Da 10:1 [b]Eze 12:27; Da 12:4, 9; Rev 22:10 [c]Da 10:14 **8:27** [a]Da 7:28; 8:17; Hab 3:16 [b]Da 2:48 [1]Or *done in* ◆ **9:1** [a]Da 5:31; 11:1 **9:2** [a]Lv 25:15, 16, 50 [b]2Chr 36:21; Ezr 1:1; Jer 25:11, 12; 29:10; Zec 7:5 [1]The personal covenant name of God, a form of I AM WHO I AM, cf. Ex 3:14-15 **9:4** [a]Dt 7:21; Ne 9:32 [b]Dt 7:9 **9:5** [a]1Ki 8:48; Ne 9:33; Ps 106:6; Is 64:5-7; Jer 14:7 [b]Lam 1:18, 20 [c]Ps 119:176; Is 53:6; Da 9:11 **9:6** [a]2Chr 36:16; Jer 44:4, 5 **9:7** [a]Jer 23:6; 33:16; Da 9:18 [b]Ps 44:15; Jer 2:26, 27; 3:25 [c]Dt 4:27 [1]Lit *the shame of face* **9:8** [1]Lit *the shame of face* **9:9** [a]Ne 9:17; Ps 130:4 [b]Ps 106:43; Jer 14:7; Da 9:5, 6 [1]Or *though* **9:10** [a]2Ki 17:13-15; 18:12 [1]Or *instructions*, cf. 9:11 **9:11** [a]Is 1:3, 4; Jer 8:5-10 [b]Dt 27:15-26

in the [1]law of Moses the [2]servant of
God, for we have sinned against Him.
**12** Thus He has [a]established His words
which He had spoken against us and
against our [b]judges who judged us, to
bring on us great calamity; for under
the whole heaven there has [c]not been
done *anything* like what was done to
Jerusalem. **13** As it is written in the [a,1]law
of Moses, all this calamity has come
on us; yet we have [b]not [2]entreated the
favor of Yahweh our God by [c]turning
from our iniquity and acting wisely
in Your truth. **14** Therefore Yahweh
has [a]watched over the calamity and
brought it on us; for Yahweh our God is
[b]righteous with respect to all His deeds
which He has done, but we have not
listened to His voice.

**15** "So now, O Lord our God, who
have [a]brought Your people out of the
land of Egypt with a strong hand and
have [b]made a name for Yourself, as it
is this day—we have sinned; we have
acted wickedly. **16** O Lord, in accor-
dance with all Your righteousness,
let now Your [a]anger and Your wrath
turn away from Your city Jerusalem,
Your [b]holy mountain; for because
of our sins and the iniquities of our
fathers, Jerusalem and Your people
*have become* a [c]reproach to all those
around us. **17** So now, our God, listen
to the prayer of Your slave and to his
supplications, and for [1]Your sake,
O Lord, [a]let Your face shine on Your
[b]desolate sanctuary. **18** O my God,
[a]incline Your ear and listen! Open
Your eyes and [b]see our desolations
and the city which is [c]called by Your
name; for we are not [d,1]presenting our
supplications before You on account
of *any* righteousness of our own,
but on account of Your abundant
compassion. **19** O Lord, listen! O Lord,
forgive! O Lord, give heed and take
action! For Your own sake, O my God,
[a]do not delay, because Your city and
Your people are called by Your name."

### Gabriel Brings Understanding

**20** Now while I was [a]speaking and
praying, and [b]confessing my sin
and the sin of my people Israel, and
[1]presenting my supplication before
Yahweh my God in behalf of the holy
mountain of my God, **21** and while
I was still speaking in prayer, then
the man [a]Gabriel, whom I had seen
in the vision [1]previously, [2]touched
me [3]in *my* extreme weariness about
the time of the [b]evening offering.
**22** Then he made *me* understand and
spoke with me and said, "O Daniel,
I have now come forth to give you
insight with [a]understanding. **23** At
the [a]beginning of your supplications
the word was issued, so I have come
to tell *you*, for you are [b,1]highly es-
teemed; so understand the message
*and gain* [c]understanding in what has
appeared.

**9:11** [1]Or *instruction*, cf. 9:10 [2]Or *slave*, cf. 9:10; see Foreword, "The Terminology of Slave"
**9:12** [a]Is 44:26; Jer 44:2-6; Lam 2:17; Zec 1:6 [b]Job 12:17; Ps 82:2-7; 148:11 [c]Lam 1:12; 2:13; Eze 5:9
**9:13** [a]Lv 26:14-45; Dt 28:15-68; Da 9:11 [b]Job 36:13; Is 9:13; Jer 2:30; 5:3 [c]Jer 31:18 [1]Or *instruction*, cf. 9:10-11 [2]Lit *softened the face of* **9:14** [a]Jer 31:28; 44:27 [b]Ps 51:14; Da 9:7 **9:15** [a]Dt 5:15 [b]Ne 9:10; Jer 32:20 **9:16** [a]Jer 32:31, 32 [b]Ps 87:1-3; Da 9:20; Joel 3:17; Zec 8:3 [c]Eze 5:14 **9:17** [a]Nu 6:24-26; Ps 80:3, 7, 19 [b]Lam 5:18 [1]Lit *the sake of the Lord* **9:18** [a]Is 37:17 [b]Ps 80:14 [c]Jer 7:10-12 [d]Jer 36:7 [1]Lit *causing to fall* **9:19** [a]Ps 44:23; 74:10, 11 **9:20** [a]Ps 145:18; Is 58:9; Da 9:3; 10:12 [b]Is 6:5 [1]Lit *causing to fall* **9:21** [a]Da 8:16; Lk 1:19, 26 [b]Ex 29:39; 1Ki 18:36; Ezr 9:4 [1]Lit *at the beginning* [2]Or *touching*; lit *was reaching* [3]Lit *wearied with weariness* **9:22** [a]Da 8:16; 10:21; Zec 1:9 **9:23** [a]Da 10:12 [b]Da 10:11, 19 [c]Mt 24:15 [1]Or *precious*; lit *desirable*

### *Seventy Weeks and the Messiah*

**24** "Seventy [a,1]weeks have been determined for your people and for your holy city, to [2]finish the transgression, to [3]make an end of sin, to [b]make atonement for iniquity, to bring in [c]everlasting righteousness, to seal up vision and [4]prophecy, and to anoint *the* Holy of Holies. **25** So you are to know and have insight *that* from the going out of a [a,1]word to restore and rebuild Jerusalem until [b,2]Messiah the [c]Prince, *there will be* seven weeks and sixty-two weeks; it will be restored and rebuilt, with [3]plaza and moat, even in times of distress. **26** Then after the sixty-two weeks the [1]Messiah will be [a]cut off and have [2]nothing, and the people of the prince who is to come will [b]destroy the city and the sanctuary. And [3]its end *will come* with a [c]flood; even to the end [4]there will be war; desolations are decreed. **27** And he will make a [1]firm covenant with the many for one week, but in the middle of the week he will make sacrifice and grain offering cease; and on the wing of [a,2]abominations *will come* one who [3]makes desolate, even until a [b]complete destruction, one that is decreed, is poured out on the one who [3]makes desolate."

### *Daniel's Terrifying Vision of a Man*

**10** In the third year of [a]Cyrus king of Persia, a word was revealed to [b]Daniel, who was named Belteshazzar; and the [c]word was true and *one of* great [1]conflict, but he understood the word and had an [d]understanding of what had appeared.

**2** In those days, I, Daniel, had been [a]mourning for three entire [1]weeks. **3** I [a]did not eat any [1]tasty food, nor did meat or wine enter my mouth, nor did I use any ointment at all until the entire three [2]weeks were fulfilled.

**4** And on the twenty-fourth day of the first month, while I was by the bank of the great [a]river, that is, the [1]Tigris, **5** I lifted my eyes and looked, and behold, there was a certain man [a]dressed in linen, whose loins were [b]girded with *a belt of* pure [c]fine gold of Uphaz. **6** His body also *was* like [1]beryl, his face [2]had the appearance of lightning, [a]his eyes were like flaming torches, his arms and feet like the gleam of burnished bronze, and the sound of his words like the sound of a multitude. **7** Now I, Daniel, [a]alone saw the *vision* that appeared, but the [b]men who were with me did not see the *vision* that appeared; nevertheless, a great [c]terror fell on them, and they ran away to hide themselves. **8** So I alone [a]remained and saw this great *vision* that appeared; yet [b]no might remained in me, for my *outward* splendor turned to [1]a deathly pallor, and I retained no might. **9** But I heard the sound of his words; and

**9:24** [a]Lv 25:8; Nu 14:34; Eze 4:5, 6 [b]2Chr 29:24; Is 53:10; Ro 5:10 [c]Is 51:6, 8; 56:1; Jer 23:5, 6; Ro 3:21, 22 [1]Or *units of seven*, so in ch [2]Or *restrain* [3]Or *seal up sins* [4]Lit *prophet* **9:25** [a]Ezr 4:24; 6:1-15; Ne 2:1-8; 3:1 [b]Jn 1:41; 4:25 [c]Is 9:6; Da 8:11, 25 [1]Or *decree* [2]Or *an anointed one* [3]Or *streets* **9:26** [a]Is 53:8; Mk 9:12; Lk 24:26 [b]Mt 24:2; Mk 13:2; Lk 19:43, 44 [c]Na 1:8 [1]Or *anointed one* [2]Or *no one* [3]Or *his* [4]Or *war will be decreed for desolations* **9:27** [a]Da 11:31; Mt 24:15; Mk 13:14; Lk 21:20 [b]Is 10:23; 28:22 [1]Or *covenant prevail* [2]Or *detestable things* [3]Or *causes horror* ◆ **10:1** [a]Da 1:21; 6:28 [b]Da 1:7 [c]Da 8:26 [d]Da 1:17; 2:21 [1]Or *warfare* **10:2** [a]Ezr 9:4, 5; Ne 1:4 [1]Lit *weeks of days* **10:3** [a]Da 6:18 [1]Lit *bread of desirability* [2]Lit *weeks of days* **10:4** [a]Eze 1:3; Da 8:2 [1]Heb *Hiddekel* **10:5** [a]Eze 9:2; Da 12:6, 7 [b]Rev 1:13; 15:6 [c]Jer 10:9 **10:6** [a]Rev 1:14; 2:18; 19:12 [1]Or *yellow serpentine* [2]Lit *like* **10:7** [a]2Ki 6:17-20 [b]Ac 9:7 [c]Eze 12:18 **10:8** [a]Ge 32:24 [b]Da 7:28; 8:27; Hab 3:16 [1]Lit *ruin*

as soon as I heard the sound of his
words, I [a]fell into a deep sleep on my
face, with my face to the ground.

### *Daniel Is Strengthened*

**10** Then behold, a hand [a]touched me
and set me shaking on my [1]hands and
knees. **11** And he said to me, "O [a]Dan-
iel, man of [1]high esteem, [b]understand
the words that I am about to speak to
you and [c]stand [2]upright, for I have
now been sent to you." And when he
had spoken this word to me, I stood
up [d]trembling. **12** Then he said to me,
"[a]Do not be afraid, Daniel, for from
the first day that you gave your heart
to understand *this* and to [b]humble
yourself before your God, your
words were heard, and I have come
*in response* [c]to your words. **13** But the
[1]prince of the kingdom of Persia was
[2]standing against me for twenty-one
days; then behold, [a]Michael, one of
the chief princes, came to help me.
Now I had been left there with the
kings of Persia. **14** Now I have come to
[a]give you an understanding of what
will happen to your people in the
[b,1]last days, for the vision pertains to
[c]the days yet *future*." **15** When he
had spoken to me according to these
words, I [1]turned my face toward the
ground and became [a]speechless.
**16** And behold, [a]one [1]in the likeness
of the sons of men was [b]touching
*my lips; then I* opened my mouth
and spoke and said to him who was
standing before me, "O my lord, as
a result of the *vision* that appeared,
[c]pains have come upon me, and I
have retained no might. **17** Now [a]how
can such a servant of my lord talk
with such as my lord? As for me, right
now [b]no might stands within me, nor
does any breath remain within me."
**18** Then *this* one with the appear-
ance of a man touched me again and
[a]strengthened me. **19** And he said,
"O man of [1]high esteem, [a]do not be
afraid. Peace [2]be with you; gather
[b]strength and be strong!" Now as soon
as he spoke to me, I received strength
and said, "May my lord speak, for you
have [c]strengthened me." **20** Then he
said, "Do you know why I came to
you? But I shall now return to fight
against the [1]prince of Persia; so I am
going forth, and behold, the [a,1]prince
of [2]Greece is about to come. **21** How-
ever, I will tell you what is [1]inscribed
in the writing of [a]truth. Now there is
no one who [2]exerts strength with me
against these *forces* except [b]Michael
your prince.

### *Kingdoms and Wars*

**11** "Now I, in the [a]first year of
Darius the Mede, [1]I stood to
strengthen and to be a fortress for
him. **2** So now I will tell you the
[a]truth. Behold, three more kings
are going to stand [1]in Persia. Then a

**10:9** [a]Ge 15:12; Job 4:13; Da 8:18 **10:10** [a]Jer 1:9; Da 8:18 [1]Lit *knees and the palms of my hands*
**10:11** [a]Da 10:19 [b]Da 8:16, 17 [c]Eze 2:1 [d]Job 4:14, 15 [1]Or *preciousness*; lit *desirability* [2]Lit *upon your standing* **10:12** [a]Is 41:10, 14; Da 10:19 [b]Da 9:20-23; 10:2, 3 [c]Ac 10:30, 31 **10:13** [a]Da 10:21; 12:1; Jd 9; Rev 12:7 [1]Satanic angel [2]Lit *standing opposite* **10:14** [a]Da 8:16; 9:22 [b]Dt 31:29; Da 2:28 [c]Da 8:26; 12:4, 9 [1]Lit *end of the days* **10:15** [a]Eze 3:26; 24:27; Lk 1:20 [1]Lit *gave* **10:16** [a]Da 8:15 [b]Is 6:7; Jer 1:9 [c]Da 7:15, 28; 8:17, 27; 10:8, 9 [1]Lit *as* **10:17** [a]Ex 24:10, 11; Is 6:1-5 [b]Da 10:8 **10:18** [a]Is 35:3, 4
**10:19** [a]Jdg 6:23; Is 43:1; Da 10:12 [b]Jos 1:6, 7, 9; Is 35:4 [c]Ps 138:3; 2Co 12:9 [1]Or *preciousness*; lit *desirability* [2]Lit *to you* **10:20** [a]Da 8:21; 11:2 [1]Satanic angel [2]Heb *Javan* **10:21** [a]Da 12:4 [b]Da 10:13; Rev 12:7 [1]Or *signed*, cf. 6:9-14 [2]Lit *shows himself strong* ◆ **11:1** [a]Da 5:31; 9:1 [1]Lit *my standing up* was
**11:2** [a]Da 8:26; 10:1, 21 [1]Lit *for*

fourth will gain far more riches than
all *of them*; as soon as he becomes
strong through his riches, [2]he will
arouse the whole *empire* against
the kingdom of [b,3]Greece. **3** And a
[a]mighty king will stand, and he will
[1]dominate with great [2]domination
and [b]do as he pleases. **4** But as soon
as he stands, his kingdom will be
broken up and parceled out [a]toward
the [b]four winds of [1]heaven, but not to
his *own* descendants, nor according
to his [2]domination with which he
[3]dominated, for his kingdom will
be [c]uprooted and *given* to others
besides [4]them.

**5** "Then the [a]king of the South will
grow strong, [1]along with *one* of his
princes [2]who will grow strong over
him and [3]obtain dominion; indeed,
his [4]domain *will be* a great [4]domin-
ion. **6** And [1]after some years they will
form an alliance, and the daughter of
the king of the South will come to the
[a]king of the North to carry out [2]an eq-
uitable arrangement. But she will not
retain her [3]position of power, nor will
he *continue to* stand with his [4]power,
but she will be given up, along with
those who brought her in and the
one who fathered her as well as he
who strengthened her in *those* times.
**7** But one of the [1]descendants of her
line will stand in his place, and he
will come against *their* military force
and enter the [a]fortress of the king of
the North, and he will deal with them
and display strength. **8** And also their
[a]gods with their [1]metal images *and*
their desirable vessels of silver and
gold he will bring into captivity to
Egypt, and he on his part will stand
*back* from *attacking* the king of the
North for *some* years. **9** Then [1]the lat-
ter will enter the kingdom of the king
of the South, but will return to his
*own* land.

**10** "And his sons will wage war. So
they will gather a multitude of great
forces; and one of them will keep
on coming and [a]overflow and pass
through, that he may [1]again wage
war up to his *very* fortress. **11** And the
[a]king of the South will be enraged
and go forth and fight [1]with the king
of the North. Then the latter will
cause a great multitude to stand,
but *that* multitude will be given into
[2]the hand of the *former*. **12** Then the
multitude will be carried away, his
heart will be lifted up, and he will
cause tens of thousands to fall; yet
he will not prevail. **13** And the king
of the North will again cause a much
*greater* multitude than the former to
stand, and at the [a]end of the times of
*those* years, he will keep on coming
with a great military force and much
equipment.

**14** "Now in those times many will
stand against the king of the South;
the violent ones among your people
will also lift themselves up in order
to cause the vision to stand, but
they will [1]fall down. **15** Then the
king of the North will come, cast

**11:2** [b]Da 8:21; 10:20 [2]Or they *all will stir up the realm of Greece* [3]Heb *Javan* **11:3** [a]Da 8:5, 21 [b]Da 5:19; 8:4; 11:16, 36 [1]Lit *rule* [2]Lit *rulership* **11:4** [a]Da 8:8, 22 [b]Jer 49:36; Eze 37:9; Da 7:2; 8:8; Zec 2:6; Rev 7:1 [c]Jer 12:15, 17; 18:7 [1]Or the *sky* [2]Lit *rulership* [3]Lit *ruled* [4]His descendants **11:5** [a]Da 11:9, 11, 14, 25, 40 [1]Lit *and* [2]Lit *and he* [3]Lit *and then rule* [4]Lit *rule* **11:6** [a]Da 11:7, 13, 15, 40 [1]Lit *at the end of* [2]Or *an upright agreement* [3]Lit *strength of arm* [4]Lit *arm* **11:7** [a]Da 11:19, 38, 39 [1]Lit *branch of her roots* **11:8** [a]Is 37:19; 46:1, 2; Jer 43:12, 13 [1]Lit *cast images* **11:9** [1]Lit *he will*, so in ch **11:10** [a]Is 8:8; Jer 46:7, 8; 51:42; Da 11:26, 40 [1]Or *return and wage* **11:11** [a]Da 11:5 [1]Lit *with him, with* [2]Lit *his hand* **11:13** [a]Da 4:16; 12:7 **11:14** [1]Lit *stumble*, so in ch

up a [a]siege ramp, and capture a
well-fortified city; and the might of
the South will not stand, not even
[1]their choicest troops, for there will
be no strength to make a stand. **16** But
he who comes against him will [a]do
as he pleases, and [b]no one will *be
able to* stand in [1]opposition to him;
he will also stand *for a time* in the
[c,2]Beautiful Land, with destruction
in his hand. **17** And he will [a]set his
face to come with the authority of his
whole kingdom, [1]bringing with him
[2]an equitable proposal which he will
[3]put into effect; he will also give him
the daughter of women to destroy
it. But she will not take a stand *for
him* or be [4]on his side. **18** Then he
will turn his face to the [a]coastlands
and capture many. But a ruler will
make his reproach against him cease;
moreover, he will [b]repay him for his
reproach. **19** So he will turn his face
toward the fortresses of his own land,
but he will [a]stumble and fall and be
[b]found no more.

**20** "Then in his place one will
stand who will [a]have an [1]oppres-
sor pass through the [2]Jewel of *his*
kingdom; yet within a few days he
will be broken, though not in anger
nor in battle. **21** And in his place a
despised person will stand, to whom
the splendor of the kingdom has
not been given, but he will come in
*a time of* ease and [a]take hold of the
kingdom by intrigue. **22** But the over-
flowing [a,1]might will be flooded away
before him and broken, and also the
prince of the covenant. **23** And after
an alliance is made with him, he will
[1]practice deception, and he will go up
and gain power with a small *force of*
people. **24** [1]In a time of ease he will
enter the [a]richest *parts* of the prov-
ince, and he will do what his fathers
never did, nor his fathers' fathers;
he will distribute plunder, spoil,
and possessions among them, and
he will devise his schemes against
strongholds, but *only* for a time.
**25** And he will stir up his strength
and heart against the [a]king of the
South with a great military force; so
the king of the South will wage war
with an extremely large and mighty
military force for war; but he will not
stand, for schemes will be devised
against him. **26** And those who eat
his choice food will break him, and
his military force will [a,1]overflow, but
many will fall down slain. **27** And as
for both kings, their hearts will be
*intent* on [a]evil, and they will [b]speak
falsehood at the same table; but it
will not succeed, for the [c]end is still *to
come* at the appointed time. **28** Then
he will return to his land with great
possessions; but his heart will be *set*
against the holy covenant, and he
will take action and *then* return to
his *own* land.

**29** "At the appointed time he will
return and come into the South, but
[1]this last time it will not happen the
way it did before. **30** Indeed, ships of

**11:15** [a]Jer 6:6; Eze 4:2; 17:17 [1]Lit *the people of its choice ones* **11:16** [a]Da 5:19; 11:3, 36 [b]Jos 1:5 [c]Da 8:9; 11:41 [1]Lit *before* [2]Israel **11:17** [a]2Ki 12:17; Eze 4:3, 7 [1]Lit *and* [2]Lit *upright things* [3]Lit *do* [4]For her father; lit *for him* **11:18** [a]Ge 10:5; Is 66:19; Jer 2:10; 31:10; Zep 2:11 [b]Hos 12:14 **11:19** [a]Ps 27:2; Jer 46:6 [b]Job 20:8; Ps 37:36; Eze 26:21 **11:20** [a]Is 60:17 [1]Or *exactor* of tribute [2]Lit *adornment* **11:21** [a]2Sa 15:6 **11:22** [a]Da 9:26; 11:10 [1]Or *power*, cf. 11:6; lit *arms* **11:23** [1]Lit *do* **11:24** [a]Nu 13:20; Ne 9:25; Eze 34:14 [1]Lit *Into tranquility and the richest...he will enter* **11:25** [a]Da 11:5 **11:26** [a]Da 11:10, 40 [1]Or *be swept away, and many* **11:27** [a]Ps 52:1; 64:6 [b]Ps 12:2; Jer 9:3-5; 41:1-3 [c]Da 8:19; 11:35, 40; Hab 2:3 **11:29** [1]Lit *it will not happen as the first and as the last*

[a,1]Kittim will come against him; there-
fore he will be disheartened and will
return and become indignant at the
holy covenant and take action; so he
will come back and show regard for
those who forsake the holy covenant.
**31** Mighty forces from him will stand,
[a]profane the sanctuary fortress, and
abolish the regular sacrifice. And
they will set up the [b]abomination
[1]of desolation. **32** And by [a]smooth
*words* he will [1]turn to godlessness
those who act wickedly toward the
covenant, but the people who know
their God will display [b]strength and
take action. **33** And [a,1]those who have
insight among the people will give
understanding to the many; yet they
will [b]fall by sword and by flame, by
captivity and by plunder for *many*
days. **34** Now when they fall, they will
be granted a little help, and many will
[a]join with them in [b,1]intrigue. **35** And
some of [1]those who have insight will
fall, in order to [a]refine, [b]purge, and
make them [c,2]pure until the time of
the [d]end, because *it is* still *to come* at
the appointed time.

**36** "Then the king will [a]do as
he pleases, and he will exalt and
[b]magnify himself above every god
and will [c]speak [1]astonishing things
against the [d]God of gods; and he
will succeed until the [e]indignation
is finished, for that which is [f]decreed
will be done. **37** He will show no
regard for the [1]gods of his fathers or
for the desire of women, nor will he
show regard for any *other* god; for
he will magnify himself above *them*
all. **38** But [1]instead he will honor a
god of fortresses, a god whom his
fathers did not know; he will honor
*him* with gold, silver, costly stones,
and desirable things. **39** And he will
take action against the strongest of
fortresses with *the help of* a foreign
god; he will give great honor to [1]those
who recognize *him* and will cause
them to rule over the many and will
apportion land for a price.

**40** "And at [a]the time of the end, the
[b]king of the South will collide with
him, and the [c]king of the North will
[d]storm against him with chariots,
with horsemen, and with many ships;
and he will enter lands, [e]overflow
*them*, and pass through. **41** And he
will also enter the [a,1]Beautiful Land,
and many *countries* will fall; but
these will be rescued out of his hand:
Edom, [b]Moab, and the foremost of
the sons of [c]Ammon. **42** Then he will
send forth his hand against *other*
countries, and the land of Egypt will
not escape. **43** But he will rule over the
hidden treasures of gold and silver
and over all the desirable things of
Egypt; and [a]Libyans and [b]Ethiopians
*will follow* at his [1]heels. **44** But reports
from the East and from the North will
dismay him, and he will go forth with

**11:30** [a]Ge 10:4; Nu 24:24; Is 23:1, 12; Jer 2:10 [1]Cyprus **11:31** [a]Da 8:11-13; 12:11 [b]Da 9:27; Mt 24:15; Mk 13:14 [1]Or *that causes horror*; lit *that makes desolate* **11:32** [a]Da 11:21, 34 [b]Mic 5:7-9; Zec 9:13-16; 10:3-6 [1]Or *pollute those* **11:33** [a]Mal 2:7 [b]Mt 24:9; Jn 16:2; Heb 11:36-38 [1]Or *instructors of the people* **11:34** [a]Mt 7:15; Ac 20:29, 30 [b]Da 11:21, 32; Ro 16:18 [1]Or *hypocrisy* **11:35** [a]Dt 8:16; Pr 17:3; Da 12:10; Zec 13:9; Mal 3:2, 3 [b]Jn 15:2 [c]Rev 7:14 [d]Da 11:27 [1]Or *the instructors* [2]Lit *white* **11:36** [a]Da 5:19; 11:3, 16 [b]Is 14:13; Da 5:20; 8:11, 25; 2Th 2:4 [c]Rev 13:5, 6 [d]Dt 10:17; Ps 136:2; Da 2:47 [e]Is 10:25; 26:20; Da 8:19 [f]Da 9:27 [1]Or *wondrous*; lit *extraordinary* **11:37** [1]Or *God* **11:38** [1]Lit *in his place* **11:39** [1]Lit *the one who acknowledges* **11:40** [a]Da 11:27, 35; 12:4, 9 [b]Da 11:11, 25 [c]Da 11:7, 13, 15 [d]Is 5:28; Jer 4:13 [e]Da 11:10, 26 **11:41** [a]Da 8:9; 11:16 [b]Jer 48:47 [c]Jer 49:6 [1]Israel **11:43** [a]2Chr 12:3; Na 3:9 [b]2Chr 12:3; Eze 30:4, 5; Na 3:9 [1]Lit *footsteps*

great wrath to destroy and [1]devote
many to destruction. **45** And he will
pitch the tents of his royal pavilion
between the seas and the beautiful
[a]Holy Mountain; yet he will come
to his end, and no one will help him.

### *The End of the Days*

**12** "Now at that time, [a]Michael,
the great prince who stands
*guard* over the sons of your people,
will stand. And there will be a [b]time
of distress [c]such as never happened
since there was a nation until that
time; and at that time your people,
everyone who is found written in the
[d]book, will be rescued. **2** [a]And many
of those who sleep in the dust of the
ground will awake, [b]these to everlast-
ing life, but the others to reproach
*and* everlasting [1]contempt. **3** [1]And
those who have [a]insight will [b]shine
brightly like the brightness of the
[2]expanse *of heaven*, and those who
[c]lead the many to righteousness, like
the stars forever and ever. **4** But as
for you, Daniel, [a]conceal these words
and [b]seal up the book until the [c]time
of the end; [d]many will go to and fro,
and knowledge will increase."

**5** Then I, Daniel, looked, and
behold, two others were standing,
one on this bank of the river and
the other on that bank of the river.
**6** And [a]one said to the man [b]dressed
in linen, who was above the waters of
the river, "[c]How long *will it be* until
the end of *these* wonders?" **7** And I
heard the man dressed in linen, who
was above the waters of the river, [1]as
he [a]raised his right hand and his left
toward heaven, and swore by [b]Him
who lives forever that it would be for
a [c,2]time, [2]times, and half *a* [2]*time*; and
as soon as [3]they complete [d]shatter-
ing the [4]power of the holy people,
all these *events* will be completed.
**8** As for me, I heard but could not
understand; so I said, "My lord, what
*will be* the [1]outcome of these *events*?"
**9** Then he said, "Go *your way*, Daniel,
for *these* words are concealed and
[a]sealed up until the time of the end.
**10** [a]Many will be purged, [1]purified,
and refined, but the [b]wicked will act
wickedly; and none of the wicked will
understand, but [2]those who [c]have
insight will understand. **11** But from
the time that the regular sacrifice is
abolished and the [a,1]abomination
of desolation is set up, *there will be*
1,290 days. **12** How [a]blessed is he
who keeps waiting and reaches the
[b]1,335 days! **13** But as for you, go *your*
*way* to the [1]end; then you will enter
into [a]rest and stand *again* for your
[b]allotted portion at the end of the
days."

---

**11:44** [1]Lit *devote to destruction* **11:45** [a]Is 11:9; 27:13; 65:25; 66:20; Da 9:16, 20 ◆ **12:1** [a]Da 10:13, 21; Rev 12:7 [b]Rev 7:14; 16:18 [c]Jer 30:7; Eze 5:9; Da 9:12; Mt 24:21; Mk 13:19 [d]Da 7:10; 10:21 **12:2** [a]Is 26:19; Eze 37:12-14 [b]Mt 25:46; Jn 5:28, 29 [1]Lit *abhorrence* **12:3** [a]Da 11:33, 35; 12:10 [b]Jn 5:35 [c]Is 53:11; Da 11:33 [1]Or *The instructors will* [2]Or *firmament* **12:4** [a]Da 8:26; 12:9 [b]Is 8:16; Da 12:9; Rev 22:10 [c]Da 8:17; 12:9, 13 [d]Is 11:9; 29:18, 19; Da 11:33 **12:6** [a]Da 8:16; Zec 1:12, 13 [b]Eze 9:2; Da 10:5 [c]Da 8:13; 12:8; Mt 24:3; Mk 13:4 **12:7** [a]Eze 20:5; Rev 10:5, 6 [b]Da 4:34 [c]Da 7:25; Rev 12:14 [d]Da 8:24; Lk 21:24 [1]Lit *and* [2]Year(s) [3]Lit *to finish* [4]Lit *hand* **12:8** [1]Or *final end* **12:9** [a]Da 12:4 **12:10** [a]Zec 13:9 [b]Is 32:6, 7; Rev 22:11 [c]Da 12:3; Hos 14:9; Jn 7:17; 8:47 [1]Lit *made white* [2]Or *the instructors will* **12:11** [a]Da 9:27; 11:31; Mt 24:15; Mk 13:14 [1]Or *horrible abomination* **12:12** [a]Is 30:18 [b]Da 8:14; Rev 11:2; 12:6; 13:5 **12:13** [a]Is 57:2; Rev 14:13 [b]Ps 16:5 [1]End of your life

The Book of
# HOSEA

### *Hosea's Wife and Children*

1 The word of [1]Yahweh which came
to [a]Hosea the son of Beeri, in the
days of [b]Uzziah, [c]Jotham, [d]Ahaz, *and*
[e]Hezekiah, kings of Judah, and in the
days of [f]Jeroboam the son of Joash,
king of Israel.

2 When Yahweh first spoke through
Hosea, Yahweh said to Hosea, "[a]Go,
take for yourself a wife of harlotry
and *have* children of harlotry; for
[b]the land commits flagrant harlotry,
[1]forsaking Yahweh." 3 So he went and
took Gomer the daughter of Diblaim,
and she conceived and [a]gave birth
to a son for him. 4 And Yahweh said
to him, "Name him [a]Jezreel; for yet
a little while, and [b]I will visit the
bloodshed of Jezreel upon the house
of Jehu, and [c]I will cause the kingdom
of the house of Israel to cease. 5 And
it will be in that day, that I will [a]break
the bow of Israel in the [b]valley of
Jezreel."

6 Then she conceived again
and gave birth to a daughter. And
[1]Yahweh said to him, "Name her
[2]Lo-ruhamah, for I will no longer
[a]have compassion on the house of
Israel, that I would ever forgive them.
7 But I will have [a]compassion on the
house of Judah and [b]save them by
Yahweh their God, and I will not save
them by [c]bow, sword, battle, horses,
or horsemen."

8 Then she weaned Lo-ruhamah.
And she conceived and gave birth
to a son. 9 And [1]Yahweh said, "Name
him [2]Lo-ammi, for you are not My
people, and I am not [3]your God."

10 [1]Yet the number of the sons
of Israel
Will be like the [a]sand
of the sea,
Which cannot be measured
or numbered;
And it will be that [b]in the place
Where it is said to them,
"You are [c]not My people,"
It will be said to them,
"*You are* the [d]sons
of the living God."

11 And the [a]sons of Judah and
the sons of Israel will be
[b]gathered together,
And they will set
for themselves [c]one head,
And they will go up
from the land,
For great will be the day
of Jezreel.

### *No Compassion for Children of Harlotry*

2 [1]Say to your brothers, "[2]Ammi,"
and to your sisters, "[3]Ruhamah."

---

◆**1:1** [a]Ro 9:25 [b]2Chr 26:1-23; Is 1:1; Am 1:1 [c]2Ki 15:5, 7, 32-38; 2Chr 27:1-9 [d]2Ki 16:1-20; 2Chr 28:1-27; Is 1:1; 7:1-17; Mic 1:1 [e]2Ki 18:1-20:21; 2Chr 29:1-32:33; Mic 1:1 [f]2Ki 13:13; 14:23-29; Am 1:1 [1]The personal *covenant name of God, a form of* I AM WHO I AM, cf. Ex 3:14-15 **1:2** [a]Hos 3:1 [b]Dt 31:16; Jer 3:1; Eze 23:3-21; Hos 2:5; 5:3 [1]Lit *from not following after* **1:3** [a]Eze 23:4 **1:4** [a]Hos 2:22 [b]2Ki 10:11 [c]2Ki 15:8-10 **1:5** [a]Jer 49:35; Eze 39:3 [b]Jos 17:16; Jdg 6:33 **1:6** [a]Hos 2:4 [1]Lit *He* [2]Lit *she has not obtained compassion* **1:7** [a]2Ki 19:29-35; Is 30:18 [b]Jer 25:5, 6; Zec 9:9, 10 [c]Ps 44:3-7; Zec 4:6 **1:9** [1]Lit *He* [2]Lit *not my people* [3]Lit *yours* **1:10** [a]Ge 22:17; 32:12; Jer 33:22 [b]Ro 9:26 [c]Is 65:1; Hos 1:9 [d]Is 63:16; 64:8; Jn 1:12; 1Pe 2:10 [1]Ch 2:1 in Heb **1:11** [a]Is 11:12 [b]Jer 23:5, 6; 50:4, 5; Eze 37:21-24 [c]Jer 30:21; Hos 3:5 ◆**2:1** [1]Ch 2:3 in Heb [2]Lit *my people* [3]Lit *she has obtained compassion*

2 "Contend with your
mother, [a]contend,
For she is [b]not my wife,
and I am not her husband;
And let her remove her
[c]harlotry from her face
And her adultery
from between her breasts,
3 Lest I strip her [a]naked
And set her forth as on
the [b]day when she was born
And [c]make her
like a wilderness
And [1]make her like dry land
And put her to death
with [d]thirst.
4 "Also, I will have
no compassion
on her children
Because they are
[a]children of harlotry.
5 "For their mother has
[a]played the harlot;
She who conceived them
has acted shamefully.
For she said, '[a]I will go
after my lovers,
Who [b]give *me* my bread
and my water,
My wool and my flax,
my [c]oil and my drink.'
6 "Therefore, behold, I
will [a]hedge up [1]her
way with [b]thorns,
And I will build [2]a wall
against her so that she
cannot find her [c]paths.
7 "So she will [a]pursue her
lovers, but she will
not overtake them;
And she will seek them,
but will not find *them*.
Then she will say, '[b]I will
go, and I will return
to my [c]first husband,
For it was [d]better for me
then than now!'
8 "Now she does [a]not know
that it was [b]I who gave
her the grain, the new
wine, and the oil,
And multiplied silver
and gold for her,
*Which* they [1]used for Baal.
9 "Therefore, I will [a]take back
My grain at [1]harvest time
And My new wine
in its season.
I will also deliver My wool
and My flax *from them*
*Given* to cover her nakedness.
10 "So now I will [a]uncover
her lewdness
In the sight of her lovers,
And no one will deliver
her out of My hand.
11 "I will also [a]cease all her joy,
Her [b]feasts, her [c]new
moons, her sabbaths,
And all her appointed times.
12 "And I will [a]make desolate
her vines and fig trees,
Of which she said,
'These are my wages
Which my lovers
have given me.'
And I will [b]make them a forest,
And the [c]beasts of the field
will devour them.

**2:2** [a]Eze 23:45; Hos 2:5; 4:5 [b]Is 50:1 [c]Jer 3:1, 9, 13 **2:3** [a]Jer 13:22; Eze 16:7, 22, 39 [b]Eze 16:4 [c]Is 32:13, 14; Hos 13:15 [d]Jer 14:3; Am 8:11-13 [1]Lit *set* **2:4** [a]Jer 13:14 **2:5** [a]Is 1:21; Jer 2:25; 3:1, 2; Hos 3:1 [b]Jer 44:17, 18; Hos 2:12 [c]Hos 2:8 **2:6** [a]Job 19:8; Lam 3:7, 9 [b]Hos 9:6; 10:8 [c]Jer 18:15 [1]As in some ancient versions; Heb *your* [2]Lit *her wall so that* **2:7** [a]Hos 5:13 [b]Lk 15:17, 18 [c]Jer 2:2; 3:1; Eze 16:8; 23:4 [d]Jer 14:22; Hos 13:6 **2:8** [a]Is 1:3 [b]Eze 16:19 [1]Or *made into the* **2:9** [a]Hos 8:7; 9:2 [1]Lit *its time* **2:10** [a]Eze 16:37 **2:11** [a]Jer 7:34; 16:9 [b]Hos 3:4; Am 5:21; 8:10 [c]Is 1:13, 14 **2:12** [a]Jer 5:17; 8:13 [b]Is 5:5; 7:23 [c]Hos 13:8

13 "So I will visit the [a]days
of the Baals upon her
When she used to [b,1]offer
*offerings* in smoke to them
And [c]adorn herself with her
[2]earrings and jewelry
And go after her lovers,
so that she [d]forgot Me,"
declares Yahweh.

### *Yahweh's Faithful Betrothal*

14 "Therefore, behold,
I will allure her
[a]And bring her
into the wilderness
And speak to her heart.
15 "Then I will give her her
[a]vineyards from there
And [b]the valley of Achor
as a door of hope.
And she will [c,1]sing there
as in the days of her youth,
As in the [d]day when she came
up from the land of Egypt.
16 "And it will be in that day,"
declares Yahweh,
"*That* you will call Me [a,1]Ishi
And will no longer
call Me [2]Baali.
17 "So [a]I will remove
the names of the Baals
from her mouth
So that they will be
remembered by their
names no more.
18 "And in that day I will cut
a covenant for them
With the [a]beasts of the field,
The birds of the sky,
And the creeping things
of the ground.
And I will [b]break the
bow, the sword, and
war from the land,
And I will make them [c]lie
down in security.
19 "And I will [a]betroth you
to Me forever;
Indeed, I will betroth you
to Me in [b]righteousness
and in justice,
In lovingkindness and
in compassion,
20 And I will betroth you
to Me in faithfulness.
Then you will
[a]know Yahweh.

21 "And it will be in that day,
*that* [a]I will answer,"
declares Yahweh.
"I will answer the heavens,
and they will answer
the earth,
22 And the [a]earth will answer
the grain, the new
wine, and the oil,
And they will answer [1]Jezreel.
23 "And I will [a]sow her
for Myself in the land.
[b]I will also have compassion
on [1]her who had not
obtained compassion,
And [c]I will say to [2]those who
were [d]not My people,
'You are My people!'
And [3]they will say,
'*You are* my God!'"

---

**2:13** [a]Hos 4:13; 11:2 [b]Jer 7:9 [c]Eze 16:12, 17; 23:40 [d]Hos 4:6; 8:14; 13:6 [1]Or *burn incense* [2]Or *nose rings* **2:14** [a]Eze 20:33-38 **2:15** [a]Eze 28:25, 26 [b]Jos 7:26 [c]Jer 2:1-3; Eze 16:8-14 [d]Hos 11:1; 12:9, 13; 13:4 [1]Or *give answer* **2:16** [a]Is 54:5; Hos 2:7 [1]Lit *my husband* [2]Lit *my master, my Baal* **2:17** [a]Ex 23:13; Jos 23:7; Ps 16:4 **2:18** [a]Job 5:23; Is 11:6-9; Eze 34:25 [b]Is 2:4; Eze 39:1-10 [c]Lv 26:5; Jer 23:6; Eze 34:25 **2:19** [a]Is 62:4, 5 [b]Is 1:27; 54:6-8 **2:20** [a]Jer 31:33, 34; Hos 6:6; 13:4 **2:21** [a]Is 55:10; Zec 8:12; Mal 3:10, 11 **2:22** [a]Jer 31:12; Joel 2:19 [1]Lit *God sows* **2:23** [a]Jer 31:27 [b]Hos 1:6 [c]Ro 9:25; 1Pe 2:10 [d]Hos 1:9 [1]Heb *Lo-ruhamah* [2]Heb *Lo-ammi* [3]Lit *he*

### *Hosea Marries Again*

**3** Then Yahweh said to me, "Go
again, love a [1]woman *who* is
loved by *her* companion and is an
adulteress, even [a]as Yahweh loves
the sons of Israel, though they turn
to other gods and love raisin [b]cakes."
**2** So I [a]bargained for her for myself
for fifteen [1]*shekels* of silver and a
[2]homer and a [3]half of barley. **3** Then
I said to her, "You shall [a]stay with
me for many days. You shall not play
the harlot, nor shall you have a [1]man;
so I will also be toward you." **4** For
the sons of Israel will remain for
many days [a]without king or prince,
[b]without sacrifice or *sacred* [c]pillar,
and without [d]ephod or [e,1]household
idols. **5** Afterward the sons of Israel
will [a]return and seek Yahweh their
God and [b]David their king; and [c]they
will come [1]in dread to Yahweh and to
His goodness in the last days.

### *Yahweh's Contention with Israel*

**4** [a]Listen to the word of Yahweh,
O sons of Israel,
For Yahweh has a [b]contention
against the inhabitants
of the land,
Because there is [c]no truth
or [1]lovingkindness
Or [d]knowledge
of God in the land.
**2** *There is* [a]swearing of oaths,
[b]deception, [c]murder,
[d]stealing, and [e]adultery.
They break forth *in violence*
so that [f]bloodshed
[1]follows bloodshed.
**3** Therefore the land [a]mourns,
And everyone who
inhabits it languishes
Along with the beasts of the
field and the birds of the sky,
And also the fish
of the sea [1]disappear.

**4** Yet let no man [a]contend,
and let no man offer reproof;
Indeed, your people are
like those who [b]contend
with the priest.
**5** So you will [a]stumble by day,
And the prophet also will
stumble with you by night;
And I will destroy
your [b]mother.
**6** [a]My people are destroyed
for lack of knowledge.
Because you have
[b]rejected knowledge,
I also will [c]reject you from
ministering as My priest.
Since you have [d]forgotten
the [e]law of your God,
I Myself also will forget
your children.

**7** The more they [a]multiplied,
the more they sinned
against Me;
I will [b]change their
glory into disgrace.

◆ **3:1** [a]Jer 3:20 [b]2Sa 6:19; 1Chr 16:3; SS 2:5 [1]Gomer **3:2** [a]Ru 4:10 [1]A shekel was approx. 0.4 oz. or 11 gm [2]A homer was approx. 6.5 bu. or 230 l [3]Heb *lethech* **3:3** [a]Dt 21:13 [1]Or *husband* **3:4** [a]Hos 10:3; 13:10, 11 [b]Da 9:27; 11:31; 12:11; Hos 2:11 [c]Hos 10:1, 2 [d]Ex 28:4-12; 1Sa 23:9-12 [e]Ge 31:19, 34; Jdg 17:5; 18:14, 17; 1Sa 15:23 [1]Heb *teraphim* **3:5** [a]Jer 50:4, 5 [b]Jer 30:9; Eze 34:24 [c]Is 2:2, 3; Jer 31:9 [1]Or *trembling*, cf. Is 19:16; Hos 11:10-11 ◆ **4:1** [a]Hos 5:1 [b]Hos 12:2; Mic 6:2 [c]Is 59:4; Jer 7:28 [d]Jer 4:22 [1]Or *loyalty* **4:2** [a]Dt 5:11; Hos 10:4 [b]Hos 7:3; 10:13; 11:12 [c]Ge 4:8; Hos 6:9 [d]Dt 5:19; Hos 7:1 [e]Dt 5:18; Hos 7:4 [f]Hos 6:8; 12:14 [1]Lit *touches* **4:3** [a]Is 24:4; 33:9; Am 5:16; Zep 1:3 [1]Lit *are gathered up* **4:4** [a]Eze 3:26; Am 5:10, 13 [b]Dt 17:12 **4:5** [a]Eze 14:3, 7; Hos 5:5 [b]Jer 15:8; Hos 2:2, 5 **4:6** [a]Is 5:13 [b]Hos 4:14; Mal 2:7, 8 [c]Zec 11:8, 9, 15-17 [d]Hos 2:13; 8:14; 13:6 [e]Hos 8:1, 12 **4:7** [a]Hos 10:1; 13:6 [b]Hab 2:16

8 They [a]eat the [1]sin of My people
And [b]lift up [2]their soul
toward their iniquity.
9 And it will be like people,
[a]like priest;
So I will [b]punish them
for their ways
And cause their deeds
to return to them.
10 [a]They will eat, but not
be satisfied;
They will [b]play the harlot, but
not break forth *in number*,
Because they have [c,1]forsaken
Yahweh to keep *harlotry*.

11 Harlotry, [a]wine, and new wine
take away a heart *of wisdom*.
12 My people [a]ask their wooden
idol, and their *diviner's*
wand declares to them;
For a spirit of harlotry
has led *them* astray,
And they have played
the harlot, *departing*
[1]from their God.
13 They offer sacrifices on the
[a]tops of the mountains
And [b,1]burn incense on the hills,
[c]Under oak, poplar,
and terebinth
Because their shade is good.
Therefore your daughters
play the harlot,
And your [2]brides
commit adultery.
14 I will not punish your
daughters when they
play the harlot
Or your [1]brides when they
commit adultery,
For *the men* themselves
go apart with harlots
And offer sacrifices with
[a]cult prostitutes;
So the people without
understanding are [2]ruined.

15 Though you, Israel,
play the harlot,
Do not let Judah
become guilty;
Also do not go to [a]Gilgal
Nor go up to Beth-aven
[b]And swear the oath:
"As Yahweh lives!"
16 Since Israel is [a]stubborn
Like a stubborn heifer,
[1]Can Yahweh now
[b]feed them
Like a lamb in a large field?
17 Ephraim is joined to [a]idols;
[b]Let him alone.
18 Their drink gone;
They play the harlot
continually;
[a]Their [1]rulers dearly
love disgrace.
19 [a]The wind binds them
up in its wings,
And they will be ashamed
because of their sacrifices.

### Yahweh Withdraws from Israel

5 Hear this, O priests!
Give heed, O house of Israel!
Give ear, O house of the king!
For the judgment is for you,

**4:8** [a]Hos 10:13 [b]Is 56:11; Mic 3:11 [1]Or *sin offering* [2]Lit *his* **4:9** [a]Is 24:2; Jer 5:31 [b]Hos 8:13; 9:9 **4:10** [a]Lv 26:26; Is 65:13; Mic 6:14 [b]Hos 7:4 [c]Hos 9:17 [1]Or *forsaken Yahweh to practice* (v 11) *harlotry*; lit *forsaken giving heed* **4:11** [a]Pr 20:1; Is 5:12; 28:7 **4:12** [a]Is 44:19; Jer 2:27 [1]Lit *from under* **4:13** [a]Jer 3:6 [b]Hos 2:13; 11:2 [c]Is 1:29; Jer 2:20 [1]Or *offer sacrifices* [2]Or *daughters-in-law* **4:14** [a]Dt 23:17 [1]Or *daughters-in-law* [2]Lit *thrust down* **4:15** [a]Hos 9:15; 12:11 [b]Jer 5:2; 44:26; Am 8:14 **4:16** [a]Ps 78:8 [b]Is 5:17; 7:25 [1]Or *Now Yahweh will pasture...field* **4:17** [a]Hos 13:2 [b]Ps 81:12; Hos 4:4 **4:18** [a]Mic 3:11 [1]Lit *shields* **4:19** [a]Hos 12:1; 13:15

For you have been a
[a]snare at Mizpah
And a net spread out on Tabor.
2 And the [a]revolters have [b]dug
deep into slaughtering,
But I will chastise all of them.
3 I [a]know Ephraim, and Israel
is not hidden from Me;
For now, O Ephraim, you
have played the harlot;
Israel has defiled itself.
4 Their deeds will not
allow them
To return to their God.
For a [a]spirit of harlotry
is within them,
And they [b]do not know Yahweh.
5 Moreover, the [a]pride of Israel
answers against him,
And Israel and Ephraim
stumble in their iniquity;
[b]Judah also has stumbled
with them.
6 They will [a]go with their
flocks and herds
To seek Yahweh, but they
will [b]not find *Him*;
He has [c]withdrawn from them.
7 They have [a]dealt
treacherously
against Yahweh,
For they have borne
[b]children of strangers.
Now the [c]new moon
will devour them
with their portions.

8 [a]Blow the horn in [b]Gibeah,
The trumpet in Ramah.
Make a loud shout
at Beth-aven:
"[c]Behind you, Benjamin!"
9 Ephraim will become
a [a]desolation in the [b]day
of reproof;
Among the tribes
of Israel I [c]will make
known what is true.
10 The princes of Judah have
become like those who
[a]move a boundary;
On them I will [b]pour out
My wrath [c]like water.
11 Ephraim is [a]oppressed,
crushed in judgment,
[b]Because he was
determined to [1]walk
after *man's* command.
12 Therefore I am
like a [a]moth to Ephraim
And like rottenness
to the house of Judah.
13 Then Ephraim saw
his sickness,
And Judah his sore,
So Ephraim went to [a]Assyria
And sent to [b,1]King Jareb.
But he is [c]unable
to heal you
Or to cure you of your sore.
14 For I *will be* [a]like a
lion to Ephraim
And like a young lion
to the house of Judah.
[b]I, even I, will tear
to pieces and go away;
I will carry away, and there
will be [c]none to deliver.

◆ **5:1** [a]Hos 9:8 **5:2** [a]Hos 9:15 [b]Is 29:15; Hos 4:2; 6:9 **5:3** [a]Am 3:2; 5:12 **5:4** [a]Hos 4:12 [b]Hos 4:6, 14 **5:5** [a]Hos 7:10 [b]Eze 23:31-35 **5:6** [a]Hos 8:13; Mic 6:6, 7 [b]Pr 1:28; Is 1:15; Jer 14:12 [c]Eze 8:6 **5:7** [a]Is 48:8; Jer 3:20; Hos 6:7 [b]Hos 2:4 [c]Is 1:14; Hos 2:11 **5:8** [a]Joel 2:1 [b]Hos 9:9; 10:9 [c]Jdg 5:14 **5:9** [a]Is 28:1-4; Hos 9:11-17 [b]Is 37:3 [c]Is 46:10; Zec 1:6 **5:10** [a]Dt 19:14; 27:17 [b]Eze 7:8 [c]Ps 32:6; 93:3, 4 **5:11** [a]Dt 28:33 [b]Mic 6:16 [1]Some ancient versions *follow nothingness* **5:12** [a]Ps 39:11; Is 51:8 **5:13** [a]Hos 7:11; 8:9; 12:1 [b]Hos 10:6 [c]Jer 30:12-15 [1]Or *the avenging king, the great king* **5:14** [a]Ps 7:2; Hos 13:7, 8; Am 3:4 [b]Ps 50:22 [c]Mic 5:8

15 I will go away *and*
return to My place
Until they [a,1]acknowledge
their guilt and seek
My face;
In their affliction they will
[b]seek Me earnestly.

### *Israel Chastised*

6 "[a]Come, let us return
to Yahweh.
For [b]He has torn *us*,
but [c]He will heal us;
He has struck *us*, but He
will [d]bandage us.
2 "He will [a]make us alive
after two days;
He will [b]raise us up
on the third day,
That we may live before Him.
3 "So let us [a]know, let us
pursue to know Yahweh.
His [b]going forth is
established as the dawn;
And He will come
to us like the [c]rain,
Like the [1]late rain
watering the earth."

4 What shall I do with you,
O [a]Ephraim?
What shall I do with you,
O Judah?
For your lovingkindness is
like a [b]morning cloud
And like the dew
which goes away early.
5 Therefore I have [a]hewn *them*
in pieces by the prophets;
I have killed them
by the [b]words of My mouth;
And the judgments on you are
*like* the light that goes forth.
6 For [a]I delight
in lovingkindness
[b]rather than sacrifice,
And in the knowledge of God
rather than burnt offerings.
7 But [a]like [1]Adam
they have [b]trespassed
against the covenant;
There they have [c]dealt
treacherously against Me.
8 [a]Gilead is a city
of workers of iniquity,
With a track of [b]blood.
9 And as [a]raiders wait for a man,
*So* a band of priests [b]murder
on the way to Shechem;
Surely they have
committed [c]lewdness.
10 In the house of Israel I have
seen an [a]appalling thing;
Ephraim's [b]harlotry is there;
Israel has defiled itself.
11 Also, O Judah, there is
a [a]harvest set for you
When I [b]restore the
fortunes of My people,
7 When I [a]would heal Israel,
Then the iniquity
of Ephraim is uncovered,
And the evil deeds of Samaria,
For they work [b]falsehood;
The thief enters in;
[c]Raiders [1]ransack outside,
2 And they do not say
to their hearts

---

**5:15** [a]Is 64:7-9; Jer 3:13, 14 [b]Ps 50:15; 78:34; Jer 2:27; Hos 3:5 [1]Or *bear their punishment*
◆ **6:1** [a]Jer 50:4, 5 [b]Dt 32:39; Hos 5:14 [c]Jer 30:17; Hos 14:4 [d]Is 30:26 **6:2** [a]Ps 30:5 [b]1Co 15:4
**6:3** [a]Is 2:3; Mic 4:2 [b]Ps 19:6; Mic 5:2 [c]Job 29:23; Ps 72:6; Joel 2:23 [1]Spring **6:4** [a]Hos 7:1; 11:8
[b]Ps 78:34-37; Hos 13:3 **6:5** [a]1Sa 15:32, 33; Jer 1:10; 5:14 [b]Jer 23:29 **6:6** [a]Mt 9:13; 12:7 [b]Is 1:11
**6:7** [a]Job 31:33 [b]Hos 8:1 [c]Hos 5:7 [1]Or *men* **6:8** [a]Hos 12:11 [b]Hos 4:2 **6:9** [a]Hos 7:1 [b]Jer 7:9, 10;
Hos 4:2 [c]Eze 22:9; 23:27; Hos 2:10 **6:10** [a]Jer 5:30, 31; 23:14 [b]Hos 5:3 **6:11** [a]Jer 51:33; Joel 3:13
[b]Zep 2:7 ◆ **7:1** [a]Eze 24:13; Hos 6:4; 7:13; 11:8 [b]Hos 4:2 [c]Hos 6:9 [1]Lit *strip*

*That* I [a]remember
all their evil.
Now their [b]deeds are
all around them;
They are before My face.
3 [a]With their evil they
make the [b]king glad,
And the princes
with their [c]deceptions.
4 They are [a]all adulterers,
Like an oven heated
by the baker
Who ceases to stir up *the fire*
From the kneading of the
dough until it is leavened.
5 On the [1]day of our king,
the princes [a]became sick
with the heat of wine;
He stretched out his
hand with [b]scoffers,
6 For their hearts are
like an [a]oven
*As* they draw near
in their [1]plotting;
Their [2]anger [3]smolders
all night;
In the morning it burns
like a flaming fire.
7 All of them are hot like an oven,
And they devour their [a]judges;
All their kings have fallen.
[b]None of them calls on Me.

8 Ephraim [a]mixes himself
with the peoples;
Ephraim has become a cake
not turned.
9 [a]Strangers devour his power,
Yet he [b]does not know *it*;
Gray hairs also are
sprinkled on him,
Yet he does not know *it*.
10 So the [a]pride of Israel
answers against him,
Yet [b]they have not returned
to Yahweh their God,
Nor have they sought
Him, for all this.
11 So [a]Ephraim has become
like a silly dove,
[b]without a heart *of wisdom*;
They call to [c]Egypt; they
go to [d]Assyria.
12 When they go, I will [a]spread
My net over them;
I will bring them down
like the birds of the sky.
I will [b]chastise them in
accordance with the report
to their congregation.
13 [a]Woe to them, for they
have [b]fled from Me!
Destruction is theirs, for
they have transgressed
against Me!
And I [c]would redeem
them, but they speak
lies against Me.
14 And [a]they do not cry out
to Me in their heart
When they wail
on their beds;
For the sake of grain and
new wine they [b,1]gather
together as sojourners;
They [c]depart from Me.
15 Although I disciplined *and*
strengthened their arms,

**7:2** [a]Ps 25:7; Jer 14:10; 17:1; Hos 8:13; 9:9; Am 8:7 [b]Jer 2:19; 4:18; Hos 4:9 **7:3** [a]Ro 1:32 [b]Jer 28:1-4; Hos 7:5; Mic 7:3 [c]Hos 4:2; 11:12 **7:4** [a]Jer 9:2; 23:10 **7:5** [a]Is 28:1, 7 [b]Is 28:14 [1]A festive occasion **7:6** [a]Ps 21:9 [1]Lit *ambush* [2]As in some ancient versions; M.T. *baker* [3]Lit *sleeps* **7:7** [a]Hos 13:10 [b]Is 64:7 **7:8** [a]Ps 106:35 **7:9** [a]Is 1:7; Hos 8:7 [b]Hos 4:6 **7:10** [a]Hos 5:5 [b]Is 9:13 **7:11** [a]Hos 11:11 [b]Hos 4:6, 11, 14; 5:4 [c]Hos 8:13; 9:3, 6 [d]Hos 5:13; 8:9; 12:1 **7:12** [a]Eze 12:13 [b]Lv 26:14-39; Dt 28:15 **7:13** [a]Hos 9:12 [b]Jer 14:10; Eze 34:6; Hos 9:17 [c]Jer 51:9; Hos 7:1; Mt 23:37 **7:14** [a]Job 35:9-11; Hos 8:2; Zec 7:5 [b]Jdg 9:27; Am 2:8; Mic 2:11 [c]Hos 13:16 [1]Gr and many ancient mss *gash themselves*

Yet they [a]devise evil
against Me.
16 They turn, *but* not [1]upward;
They are like a [a]deceitful bow;
Their princes will fall
by the sword
Because of the [b,2]indignation
of their tongue.
This *will be* their [c]scoffing
in the land of Egypt.

### *Israel Reaps the Whirlwind*

8 [a]*Put* the trumpet
to your [1]mouth!
[b]Like an eagle *the enemy*
*comes* [c]against the
house of Yahweh
Because they have [d]trespassed
against My covenant
And transgressed
against My [e]law.
2 [a]They cry out to Me,
"My God, [b]we of Israel
know You!"
3 Israel has rejected the good;
The enemy will pursue him.
4 [a]They have set up kings,
but not by Me;
They have appointed princes,
but I did not know *it*.
With their [b]silver and
gold they have made
idols for themselves,
That [1]they might be cut off.
5 [1]He has rejected your [a]calf,
O Samaria, *saying*,
"My anger burns against them!"
How long will they be
incapable of [b]innocence?
6 For from Israel is even this!
A [a]craftsman made it,
so it is not God;
Surely the calf of Samaria will
be smashed to splinters.
7 For [a]they sow the wind,
And they reap the [b]whirlwind.
The standing grain
has no growth;
It makes [c]no flour.
Should it make *anything*,
strangers would swallow it up.
8 Israel is [a]swallowed up;
They are now
among the nations
Like a [b]vessel in which
no one delights.
9 For they have gone
up to [a]Assyria
*Like* [b]a wild donkey all alone;
Ephraim has [c]hired [1]lovers.
10 Even though they hire *allies*
among the nations,
Now I will [a]gather them up;
And they will begin
[b]to [1]diminish
Because of the burden
of the [c]king of princes.
11 Since Ephraim has
[a]multiplied altars for sin,
They have become altars
of sinning for him.
12 Though [a]I wrote
for him ten thousand
*precepts* of My [b]law,
They are counted
as a strange thing.

**7:15** [a]Na 1:9 **7:16** [a]Ps 78:57 [b]Ps 12:3, 4; 17:10; 73:9; Da 7:25; Mal 3:13, 14 [c]Eze 23:32; Hos 9:3, 6 [1]Or possibly *to the Most High* [2]Or *cursing* ◆ **8:1** [a]Jer 4:13; Hos 5:8 [b]Hab 1:8 [c]Dt 28:49 [d]Hos 6:7 [e]Hos 4:6 [1]Lit *palate* **8:2** [a]Ps 78:34; Hos 7:14 [b]Tit 1:16 **8:4** [a]2Ki 15:13, 17, 25; Hos 13:10, 11 [b]Hos 2:8; 13:1, 2 [1]Lit *he* **8:5** [a]Hos 10:5; 13:2 [b]Ps 19:13; Jer 13:27 [1]Or *Your calf has rejected you* **8:6** [a]Hos 13:2 **8:7** [a]Pr 22:8 [b]Is 66:15; Na 1:3 [c]Hos 2:9 **8:8** [a]2Ki 17:6; Jer 51:34 [b]Jer 22:28; 25:34 **8:9** [a]Hos 7:11 [b]Jer 2:24 [c]Eze 16:33, 34 [1]Lit *loves* **8:10** [a]Eze 16:37; 22:20 [b]Jer 42:2 [c]Is 10:8 [1]Or *suffer for awhile* **8:11** [a]Hos 10:1 **8:12** [a]Dt 4:6, 8 [b]Hos 4:6

13 As for My [a]sacrificial gifts,
They [b]sacrifice
the flesh and eat *it*,
*But* Yahweh has not
accepted them.
Now He will [c]remember
their iniquity
And [d]punish *them*
for their sins;
They will return to [e]Egypt.
14 So Israel has [a]forgotten his
Maker and [b]built palaces;
And Judah has multiplied
fortified cities,
But I will send a [c]fire on its
cities that it may consume
its palatial dwellings.

### *Days of Punishment Have Come*

9 [a]Do not be glad, O Israel, [1]with
rejoicing like the peoples!
For you have [b]played the
harlot, [2]forsaking your God.
You have loved *harlots'*
earnings on [3]every
threshing floor.
2 Threshing floor and wine
press will [a]not feed them,
And the new wine will
deceive [1]them.
3 They will not remain
in [a]the land of Yahweh,
But Ephraim will
return to [b]Egypt,
And in [c]Assyria they will
eat [d]unclean *food*.
4 They will not pour out
drink offerings
of [a]wine to Yahweh;
[b]Their sacrifices will
not please Him.
*Their bread will* [1]*be*
like [2]mourners' bread;
All who eat of it will
be [c]defiled,
For their bread will be
for [3]themselves *alone*;
It will not enter the
house of Yahweh.
5 [a]What will you do on the day
of the appointed festival
And on the day of the [b]feast
of Yahweh?
6 For behold, they will go
because of destruction;
Egypt will gather them up;
[a]Memphis will bury them.
Weeds will possess their
desirable items of silver;
[b]Thorns *will be* in their tents.
7 The days of [a]punishment
have come;
The days of [b]recompense
have come;
[1]Let Israel know *this*!
The prophet is an
[c]ignorant fool,
The [2]inspired man
has [d]madness,
Because of the abundance
of your [e]iniquity
And *because* your hostility
has abounded.
8 Ephraim *was* a watchman
with my God, a prophet;
*Yet* the snare of a bird
catcher is in all his ways,

**8:13** [a]Hos 5:6 [b]Jer 6:20; 7:21 [c]Jer 14:10; Hos 7:2; Lk 12:2; 1Co 4:5 [d]Hos 4:9; 9:7 [e]Hos 9:3, 6
**8:14** [a]Dt 32:18; Hos 2:13; 4:6; 13:6 [b]Is 9:9, 10 [c]Jer 17:27 ◆**9:1** [a]Is 22:12, 13; Hos 10:5 [b]Hos 4:12 [1]Lit *to* [2]Lit *away from your God* [3]Lit *all threshing floors of grain* **9:2** [a]Hos 2:9 [1]Lit *her* **9:3** [a]Lv 25:23; Jer 2:7 [b]Hos 7:16; 8:13 [c]Hos 7:11 [d]Eze 4:13 **9:4** [a]Ex 29:40 [b]Jer 6:20; Hos 8:13 [c]Hag 2:13, 14 [1]Lit be *to them* [2]Or *bread of misfortune* [3]Lit *their appetite* **9:5** [a]Is 10:3; Jer 5:31 [b]Hos 2:11; Joel 1:13 **9:6** [a]Is 19:13; Jer 2:16; 44:1; 46:14, 19; Eze 30:13, 16 [b]Is 5:6; 7:23; Hos 10:8 **9:7** [a]Is 10:3; Jer 10:15; Mic 7:4; Lk 21:22 [b]Is 34:8; Jer 16:18; 25:14 [c]Lam 2:14; Eze 13:3, 10 [d]Is 44:25 [e]Eze 14:9, 10 [1]Or *Israel will know it* [2]Lit *man of the spirit*

*And* there is *only* hostility
in the house of his God.
9 They have dug [a]deep
[1]in corruption
As in the days of [b]Gibeah;
He will [c]remember
their iniquity;
He will punish their sins.

### *Grapes in the Wilderness*

10 I found Israel like [a]grapes
in the wilderness;
I saw your fathers as the
[b]earliest fruit on the fig
tree in its first *season.*
*But* they came to [c]Baal-peor
and devoted themselves
to [d,1]shame,
And they became
as [e]detestable as that
which they loved.
11 As for Ephraim, their [a]glory
will fly away like a bird—
No birth, no pregnancy,
and no conception!
12 Though they bring up
their children,
Yet I will bereave them
[1]until not a man is left.
Surely, [a]woe to them indeed
when I depart from them!
13 Ephraim, as I have seen,
Is planted in a pasture
like [a]Tyre;
But Ephraim will bring out
his children for killing.
14 Give them, O Yahweh—
what will You give?
Give them a [a,1]miscarrying
womb and dry breasts.
15 All their evil is at [a]Gilgal;
Indeed, I came to hate
them there!
Because of the [b]evil
of their deeds
I will drive them
out of My house!
I will love them no more;
All their princes are [c]rebels.
16 [a]Ephraim is stricken;
their root is dried up;
They will bear [b]no fruit.
Even though they
bear children,
I will put to death
the [c]desirable ones
of their womb.
17 My God will despise them
Because they have [a]not
listened to Him;
And they will be [b]those who
flee among the nations.

### *You Have Sinned, O Israel*

10 Israel is a [1]luxuriant [a]vine;
He produces fruit
for himself.
The more abundant his fruit,
The more altars
he [b]abounded;
The better his land,
The better [2]he made
the *sacred* [c]pillars.
2 Their heart is [a,1]faithless;
Now they must bear
their [b]guilt.
[2]Yahweh will [c]break
down their altars
*And* destroy their
*sacred* pillars.

**9:9** [a]Is 31:6 [b]Jdg 19:12, 16-30; Hos 10:9 [c]Hos 7:2; 8:13 [1]Lit *they have corrupted* **9:10** [a]Mic 7:1 [b]Jer 24:2 [c]Nu 25:1-5; Ps 106:28, 29 [d]Jer 11:13; Hos 4:18 [e]Ps 115:8; Eze 20:8 [1]Baal **9:11** [a]Hos 4:7; 10:5 **9:12** [a]Dt 31:17; Hos 7:13 [1]Lit *without a man* **9:13** [a]Eze 26:1-21 **9:14** [a]Hos 9:11 [1]Lit *bereaving* **9:15** [a]Hos 4:15; 12:11 [b]Hos 4:9; 7:2; 12:2 [c]Is 1:23; Hos 5:2 **9:16** [a]Hos 5:11 [b]Hos 8:7 [c]Eze 24:21 **9:17** [a]Hos 4:10 [b]Hos 7:13 ◆ **10:1** [a]Is 5:1-7; Eze 15:1-6 [b]Jer 2:28; Hos 8:11; 12:11 [c]1Ki 14:23; Hos 3:4 [1]Or *degenerate* [2]Lit *they* **10:2** [a]1Ki 18:21; Zep 1:5 [b]Hos 13:16 [c]Hos 10:8; Mic 5:13 [1]Lit *smooth* [2]Lit *He*

3 Surely now they will say,
"We have [a]no king,
For we do not fear Yahweh.
As for the king,
what can he do for us?"
4 They speak *mere* words;
[1]With [a]worthless oaths
they cut covenants;
And [b]judgment flourishes
like gall in the furrows
of the field.
5 The dweller of Samaria
will fear
For the [a,1]calf of [b]Beth-aven.
Indeed, its people will
mourn for it,
And its [c]idolatrous priests
[2]will cry out over it,
Over its [d]glory, since it has
gone into exile from them.
6 The thing itself will be
carried to [a]Assyria
As tribute to [b,1]King Jareb;
Ephraim will [c]receive shame,
And Israel will be ashamed
of its [d]own counsel.
7 Samaria will be [a]ruined
*with* her king
Like a stick on the
surface of the water.
8 Also the [a]high places
of Aven, the [b]sin of Israel,
will be [1]eradicated;
[c]Thorn and thistle will
grow on their altars;
Then they will [d]say
to the mountains,
"Cover us!" And to the
hills, "Fall on us!"
9 From the days of Gibeah you
have sinned, O Israel;
There they stand!
Will not the battle against
the sons of injustice
overtake them in Gibeah?
10 When it is My [a]desire,
I will [b,1]chastise them;
And [c]the peoples will be
gathered against them
When they are bound
for their double guilt.

### *The Trained Heifer*

11 And Ephraim is a trained
[a]heifer that loves to thresh,
But I will [b]come over her
fair neck *with a yoke*;
I will harness Ephraim;
Judah will plow; Jacob will
harrow for himself.
12 [a]Sow with a view
to righteousness,
Reap in accordance
with lovingkindness;
[b]Break up your fallow ground,
Indeed, it is time
to [c]seek Yahweh
Until He [d]comes and [e,1]rains
righteousness on you.
13 You have [a]plowed wickedness;
you have reaped injustice;
You have eaten the fruit
of [b]deception.
Because you have trusted
in your way, in your
[c]abundant warriors,
14 Therefore a rumbling will
arise among your people,

---

**10:3** [a]Ps 12:4; Is 5:19 **10:4** [a]Eze 17:13-19; Hos 4:2 [b]Dt 31:16, 17; 2Ki 17:3, 4; Am 5:7 [1]Or *Swearing falsely in cutting a covenant* **10:5** [a]Hos 8:5, 6 [b]Hos 4:15; 5:8 [c]2Ki 23:5 [d]Hos 9:11 [1]As in some ancient versions; Heb *heifers* [2]Or who *used to rejoice over* **10:6** [a]Hos 11:5 [b]Hos 5:13 [c]Hos 4:7 [d]Is 30:3; Jer 7:24 [1]Or *the avenging king, the great king* **10:7** [a]Hos 13:11 **10:8** [a]Hos 4:13 [b]1Ki 12:28-30; 13:34 [c]Is 32:13; Hos 9:6; 10:2 [d]Is 2:19; Lk 23:30; Rev 6:16 [1]Or *destroyed* **10:10** [a]Eze 5:13 [b]Hos 4:9 [c]Jer 16:16 [1]Or *bind* **10:11** [a]Jer 50:11; Hos 4:16; Mic 4:13 [b]Jer 28:14 **10:12** [a]Pr 11:18 [b]Jer 4:3 [c]Hos 12:6 [d]Hos 6:3 [e]Is 44:3; 45:8 [1]Or *teaches* **10:13** [a]Job 4:8; Pr 22:8; Ga 6:7, 8 [b]Hos 4:2; 7:3; 11:12 [c]Ps 33:16

And all your [a]fortifications
will be destroyed,
As Shalman destroyed
Beth-arbel on the day
of battle,
*When* [b]mothers were dashed
in pieces with *their* children.
15 Thus it will be done
to you at Bethel because
of your evil of evils.
At dawn the king of Israel
will be completely ruined.

### *The Beloved Son*

11 When Israel *was* a
youth I loved him,
And [a]out of Egypt I
[b]called My son.
2 The more [a,1]they called them,
The more they went
from [1]them;
They kept [b]sacrificing
to the Baals
And [c]burning incense
to graven images.
3 Yet it is I who taught
Ephraim to walk;
[1]I [a]took them in My arms;
But they did not know
that I [b]healed them.
4 I [a]led them with cords
of a man, with bonds of love,
And [b]I became to them
as one who lifts the yoke
from their jaws;
And I bent down *and*
[c]fed them.

5 [1]They will not return
to the land of Egypt;
But Assyria—he will
be [2]their king
Because they [a]refused
to return *to Me.*
6 And the [a]sword will whirl
against [1]their cities
And will consume
[1]their gate bars
And [b]devour *them* because
of their [c]counsels.
7 So My people are hung up
on [a]turning from Me.
Though [1]they call [2]them
to *the One* on high,
None at all exalts *Him.*

8 [a]How can I give you
up, O Ephraim?
How can I surrender
you, O Israel?
How can I give you over
*to be* like [b]Admah?
How can I make you
like [b]Zeboiim?
My heart is turned
over within Me;
[1]All My compassions
are stirred.
9 I will [a]not execute My
burning anger;
I will not make Ephraim
a ruin [b]again.
For [c]I am God and not man,
the [d]Holy One in your midst,
And I will not come in [1]wrath.
10 They will [a]walk after Yahweh;
He will [b]roar like a lion;
Indeed, He will roar,
And *His* sons will come
[c]trembling from the west.

---

**10:14** [a]Is 17:3 [b]Hos 13:16 ◆ **11:1** [a]Hos 2:15; 12:9, 13; 13:4 [b]Ex 4:22, 23; Mt 2:15 **11:2** [a]2Ki 17:13-15 [b]Hos 2:13; 4:13 [c]Is 65:7; Jer 18:15 [1]God's prophets **11:3** [a]Dt 1:31; 32:10, 11 [b]Ps 107:20; Jer 30:17 [1]As in ancient versions; Heb *He...His* **11:4** [a]Jer 31:2, 3 [b]Lv 26:13 [c]Ex 16:32; Ps 78:25 **11:5** [a]Hos 7:16 [1]Lit *He* [2]Lit *his* **11:6** [a]Hos 13:16 [b]Lam 2:9 [c]Hos 4:16, 17 [1]Lit *his* **11:7** [a]Jer 3:6, 7; 8:5 [1]God's prophets [2]Israel; lit *him* **11:8** [a]Hos 6:4; 7:1 [b]Ge 14:8; Dt 29:23 [1]Lit *Together* **11:9** [a]Dt 13:17 [b]Jer 26:3; 30:11 [c]Nu 23:19 [d]Is 5:24; 12:6; 41:14, 16 [1]Lit *excitement* **11:10** [a]Hos 3:5; 6:1-3 [b]Is 31:4; Joel 3:16; Am 1:2 [c]Is 66:2, 5

11 They will come trembling
like birds from [a]Egypt
And like [b]doves
from the land of [a]Assyria;
And I will [c]settle them
in their houses,
declares Yahweh.

12 [1]Ephraim surrounds
Me with [a,2]lies
And the house of Israel
with deceit;
And Judah is also unruly
against God,
Even against the Holy
One who is faithful.

12 [1]Ephraim feeds on [a]wind
And pursues the [b]east
wind continually;
He abounds in falsehood
and destruction.
Moreover, [2]he cuts a
covenant with Assyria,
And oil is carried to Egypt.

### *Yahweh's Contention with Judah*

2 And Yahweh has a
[a]contention with Judah
And will punish Jacob
[b]according to his ways;
He will cause *everything*
to return to him
according to his deeds.
3 In the womb he [a]took his
brother by the heel,
And in his maturity he
[b,1]wrestled with God.
4 Indeed, he [1]wrestled with
the angel and prevailed;
He wept and [a]sought His favor.
He found Him at [b]Bethel,
And there He spoke with us,
5 Even Yahweh,
the God of hosts,
Yahweh is His [a,1]*name*
of remembrance.
6 Therefore, [a]return
to your God,
[b]Keep lovingkindness
and justice,
And [c]hope in your
God continually.
7 A [1]merchant, in whose hands
are deceptive [a]balances,
He loves to oppress.
8 And Ephraim said, "Surely
I have become [a]rich;
I have found wealth for myself;
In all my labors they
will find in me
[b]No iniquity,
which *would be* sin."
9 But I *have been* Yahweh your
God since the land of Egypt;
I will make you [a]settle
in tents again,
As in the days of the
appointed festival.
10 And I have spoken
to the [a]prophets,
And I [1]made visions abound,
And by the hand of the
prophets I gave [b]parables.
11 Is there wickedness *in* Gilead?
Surely they are worthless.
In Gilgal they sacrifice bulls;
Yes, [a]their altars are
like the stone heaps
Beside the furrows of the field.

---

**11:11** [a]Is 11:11 [b]Is 60:8; Hos 7:11 [c]Eze 28:25, 26; 34:27, 28 **11:12** [a]Hos 4:2; 7:3 [1]Ch 12:1 in Heb [2]Lit *lie*
◆ **12:1** [a]Jer 22:22 [b]Ge 41:6; Eze 17:10 [1]Ch 12:2 in Heb [2]Lit *they cut* **12:2** [a]Hos 4:1; Mic 6:2 [b]Hos 4:9; 7:2
**12:3** [a]Ge 25:26 [b]Ge 32:28 [1]Or *strove*, cf. Ge 32:28 **12:4** [a]Ge 32:26 [b]Ge 28:13-19; 35:10-15 [1]Or *strove*, cf. Ge 32:28 **12:5** [a]Ex 3:15 [1]Lit *memorial* **12:6** [a]Hos 6:1-3; 10:12 [b]Mic 6:8 [c]Mic 7:7 **12:7** [a]Pr 11:1; Am 8:5; Mic 6:11 [1]Or *Canaanite* **12:8** [a]Ps 62:10; Hos 13:6; Rev 3:17 [b]Hos 4:8; 14:1 **12:9** [a]Lv 23:42
**12:10** [a]2Ki 17:13; Jer 7:25 [b]Eze 17:2; 20:49 [1]Lit *multiplied the vision* **12:11** [a]Hos 8:11; 10:1, 2

12 Now [a]Jacob fled to the field
of Aram,
And [b]Israel worked
for a wife,
And for a wife he kept *sheep.*
13 But by a [a]prophet
Yahweh brought Israel
up from Egypt,
And by a prophet he was kept.
14 [a]Ephraim has provoked
to bitter anger;
So his Lord will leave his
[b]bloodguilt on him
And cause his [c]reproach
to return to him.

### *Ephraim's Idolatry*

13 [a]When Ephraim [1]spoke,
*there was* trembling.
He [b]lifted himself up
in Israel,
But through [c]Baal he
became guilty and died.
2 And now they sin
more and more
And make for themselves
[a]molten images,
Idols [b]*made* from their
silver according to their
understanding,
All of them the [c]work
of craftsmen.
They are saying of them,
"Let the [1]men who sacrifice
kiss the [d]calves!"
3 Therefore they will be
like the [a]morning cloud
And like dew
which [1]soon disappears,
Like [b]chaff which is
blown away
from the threshing floor
And like [c]smoke
from a [2]chimney.

4 Yet I *have been* [a]Yahweh
your God
Since the land of Egypt;
And you were not to know
[b]any god except Me,
And there is no savior
[c]besides Me.
5 I Myself [a]knew you
in the wilderness,
[b]In the land of drought.
6 As *they had* their pasture, then
they became [a]satisfied,
Indeed, they were satisfied,
and their [b]heart
became raised up;
Therefore they [c]forgot Me.
7 So I will be [a]like a
lion to them;
Like a [b]leopard I will [1]lie
in wait by the wayside.
8 I will encounter them [a]like
a bear robbed of her cubs,
And I will tear open
[1]the chest *enclosing*
their heart;
There I will also [b]devour
them like a lioness,
*As* a beast of the field
would rip them open.

9 *It is* your ruin, O Israel,
[1]That *you are* [a]against Me,
against your [b]help.

**12:12** [a]Ge 28:5 [b]Ge 29:20 **12:13** [a]Ex 14:19-22; Is 63:11-14 **12:14** [a]2Ki 17:7-18 [b]Eze 18:10-13 [c]Da 11:18; Mic 6:16 ◆ **13:1** [a]Job 29:21, 22 [b]Jdg 8:1; 12:1 [c]Hos 2:8-17; 11:2 [1]Or *spoke with trembling* **13:2** [a]Is 46:6; Jer 10:4; Hos 2:8 [b]Is 44:17-20 [c]Hos 8:6 [d]Hos 8:5, 6; 10:5 [1]Lit *sacrificers of mankind* **13:3** [a]Hos 6:4 [b]Ps 1:4; Is 17:13; Da 2:35 [c]Ps 68:2 [1]Lit *goes away early* [2]Lit *window* **13:4** [a]Hos 12:9 [b]Ex 20:3; 2Ki 18:35 [c]Is 43:11; 45:21, 22 **13:5** [a]Dt 2:7; 32:10 [b]Dt 8:15 **13:6** [a]Dt 8:12, 14; 32:13-15; Jer 5:7 [b]Hos 7:14 [c]Hos 2:13; 4:6; 8:14 **13:7** [a]Lam 3:10; Hos 5:14 [b]Jer 5:6 [1]Or *watch* **13:8** [a]2Sa 17:8 [b]Ps 50:22 [1]Lit *the enclosure of their heart* **13:9** [a]Jer 2:17, 19; Mal 1:12, 13 [b]Dt 33:26, 29 [1]Or *But in Me is your help*

10 Where now is your [a]king,
That he may save you
in all your cities,
And your [b]judges
of whom you said,
"Give me a king and princes"?
11 I [a]gave you a king
in My anger
And [b]took him away
in My wrath.

12 The iniquity of Ephraim
is bound up;
His sin is [a]stored up.
13 The pains of [a]childbirth
come upon him;
He is [b]not a wise son,
For [1]it is not the time that
he should [c]delay at the
opening of the womb.
14 Shall I [a]ransom them
from the [1]power of Sheol?
Shall I redeem them
from death?
[b]O Death, where are
your thorns?
O Sheol, where is your sting?
[c]Compassion will be
hidden from My sight.

15 Though he [a]is fruitful
among the [1]reeds,
An [b]east wind will come,
The wind of Yahweh coming
up from the wilderness;
And his fountain will
[c]become dry,
And his spring will be dried up;
It will [d]plunder *his* treasury
of every desirable article.
16 [1]Samaria will be held [a]guilty,
For she has [b]rebelled
against her God.
[c]They will fall by the [d]sword;
Their infants will be
[e]dashed in pieces,
And their pregnant [f]women
will be ripped open.

### *Yahweh's Anger Turns Away from Israel*

14 [a,1]Return, O Israel,
to Yahweh your God,
For you have stumbled
in your [b]iniquity.
2 Take words with you and
return to Yahweh.
Say to Him, "[a]Forgive all iniquity
And [1]take *what is* good,
That we may [b]pay in full
[2]the fruit of our lips.
3 "Assyria will not save us;
We will [a]not ride on horses,
Nor will we say again,
'[b]Our god,'
To the [c]work of our hands;
For in [d]You the [1]orphan
finds compassion."

4 I will [a]heal their turning
away *from Me*;
I will [b]love them freely,
For My anger has [c]turned
away from them.

**13:10** [a]2Ki 17:4; Hos 8:4 [b]1Sa 8:5, 6 **13:11** [a]1Sa 8:7; 10:17-24 [b]1Sa 15:26; 1Ki 14:7-10; Hos 10:7 **13:12** [a]Dt 32:34, 35; Job 14:17; Ro 2:5 **13:13** [a]Is 13:8; Mic 4:9, 10 [b]Dt 32:6; Hos 5:4 [c]Is 37:3; 66:9 [1]Lit *it is the time that he should not tarry at the breaking forth of children* **13:14** [a]Ps 49:15; Eze 37:12, 13 [b]1Co 15:55 [c]Jer 20:16; 31:35-37 [1]Lit *hand* **13:15** [a]Ge 49:22; Hos 10:1 [b]Ge 41:6; Jer 4:11, 12; Eze 17:10; 19:12 [c]Jer 51:36 [d]Jer 20:5 [1]Or *brothers* **13:16** [a]Hos 10:2 [b]Hos 7:14 [c]2Ki 8:12 [d]Hos 11:6 [e]Hos 10:14 [f]2Ki 15:16 [1]Ch 14:1 in Heb ◆**14:1** [a]Hos 6:1; 10:12; 12:6; Joel 2:13 [b]Hos 4:8; 5:5; 9:7 [1]Ch 14:2 in Heb **14:2** [a]Mic 7:18, 19 [b]Ps 51:16, 17; Hos 6:6; Heb 13:15 [1]Or *accept that which is good* [2]As in ancient versions; M.T. *our lips as bulls* **14:3** [a]Ps 33:17; Is 31:1 [b]Hos 8:6; 13:2 [c]Hos 4:12 [d]Ps 10:14; 68:5 [1]Or *fatherless* **14:4** [a]Is 57:18; Hos 6:1 [b]Zep 3:17 [c]Is 12:1

5 I will be like the [a]dew
to Israel;
He will flourish like the [b]lily,
And he will [1]take root
like *the cedars of* [c]Lebanon.
6 His shoots will go forth,
And his splendor will be
like the [a]olive tree
And his fragrance like *the
cedars of* [b]Lebanon.
7 Those who [a]live
in his shadow
Will [1]again raise [b]grain,
And they will flourish
like the vine.
His *name of* remembrance *will
be* like the wine of Lebanon.
8 O Ephraim, what more have
I to do with [a]idols?
It is I who answer and
look after [1]you.
I am like a luxuriant [b]cypress;
From [c]Me [2]comes your fruit.

9 [a]Whoever is wise, so let him
discern these things;
*Whoever* is discerning,
let him know them.
For the [b]ways
of Yahweh are right,
And the [c]righteous will
walk in them,
But [d]transgressors will
stumble in them.

*The Book of*

# JOEL

### *The Locusts Bring Desolation*

1 The [a]word of [1]Yahweh that came
to [b]Joel, the son of Pethuel:
2 [a]Hear this, O [b]elders,
And give ear, all inhabitants
of the land.
[c]Has *anything like* this
happened in your days
Or in your fathers' days?
3 [a]Recount about it
to your sons,
And *let* your sons
*recount about it*
*to* their sons,
And their sons to the
next generation.
4 What the [a]gnawing locust
has left, the swarming
locust has consumed;
And what the [b]swarming
locust has left, the creeping
locust has consumed;
And what the creeping locust
has left, the [c]stripping
locust has consumed.
5 Awake, [a]drunkards, and weep;
And wail, all you wine drinkers,
On account of the sweet wine
That is [b]cut off
from your mouth.
6 For a [a]nation has come
up against my land,

**14:5** [a]Pr 19:12; Is 26:19 [b]SS 2:1; Mt 6:28 [c]Is 35:2 [1]Lit *strike his roots* **14:6** [a]Jer 11:16 [b]SS 4:11 **14:7** [a]Eze 17:23 [b]Hos 2:21, 22 [1]Or *return, they will raise grain* **14:8** [a]Job 34:32; Hos 14:3 [b]Is 41:19 [c]Eze 17:23 [1]Lit *him* [2]Lit *is found* **14:9** [a]Ps 107:43; Jer 9:12 [b]Ps 111:7, 8; Pr 10:29; Zep 3:5 [c]Is 26:7 [d]Is 1:28 ◆ **1:1** [a]Jer 1:2; Eze 1:3; Hos 1:1 [b]Ac 2:16 [1]The personal covenant name of God, a form of I AM WHO I AM, cf. Ex 3:14-15 **1:2** [a]Hos 4:1; 5:1 [b]Job 8:8; Joel 1:14 [c]Jer 30:7; Joel 2:2 **1:3** [a]Ex 10:2; Ps 78:4 **1:4** [a]Dt 28:38; Joel 2:25; Am 4:9 [b]Na 3:15, 16 [c]Is 33:4 **1:5** [a]Joel 3:3 [b]Is 32:10 **1:6** [a]Joel 2:2, 11, 25

Mighty and without number;
[b]Its teeth are the teeth
of a lion,
And it has the fangs
of a lionness.
7 It has [a]made my vine
a desolation
And my fig tree [1]splinters.
It has stripped them bare
and cast *them* away;
Their branches have
become white.
8 [a]Wail like a virgin [b]girded
with sackcloth
For the bridegroom
of her youth.
9 The [a]grain offering and
the drink offering are cut off
From the house of Yahweh.
The [b]priests mourn,
The ministers of Yahweh.
10 The field is [a]destroyed;
[b]The land mourns,
For the grain is destroyed,
The new wine dries up,
Fresh oil [1]fails.
11 [a,1]Be ashamed, O farmers,
Wail, O vinedressers,
For the wheat and the barley,
Because the [b]harvest
of the field perishes.
12 The [a]vine dries up,
And the fig tree [1]fails;
The [b]pomegranate, the [c]palm
also, and the [d,2]apple tree,
All the trees of the field dry up.
Indeed, [e]rejoicing dries up
From the sons of men.

### *The Day of Yahweh Is Near*

13 [a]Gird yourselves
*with sackcloth*
And lament, O priests;
[b]Wail, O ministers of the altar!
Come, [c]spend the night
in sackcloth,
O ministers of my God;
For the grain offering and
the drink offering
Are withheld from the
house of your God.
14 [a]Set apart a fast as holy,
Call for a [b]solemn assembly;
Gather the elders
*And* all the inhabitants
of the land
To the house of Yahweh
your God,
And [c]cry out to Yahweh.
15 [a]Alas for the day!
For the [b]day of Yahweh is near,
And it will come
as [c]destruction
from the [1]Almighty.
16 Has not [a]food been cut
off before our eyes,
Gladness and [b]joy
from the house of our God?
17 The [a,1]seeds shrivel
under their [2]clods;
The storehouses are desolate;
The barns are pulled down,
For the grain is dried up.
18 How [a]the beasts groan!
The herds of cattle
wander aimlessly
Because there is no
pasture for them;

---

**1:6** [b]Rev 9:8 **1:7** [a]Is 5:6; Am 4:9 [1]Or *a stump* **1:8** [a]Is 22:12 [b]Joel 1:13; Am 8:10 **1:9** [a]Hos 9:4; Joel 1:13; 2:14 [b]Joel 2:17 **1:10** [a]Is 24:4, 7 [b]Jer 12:11 [1]Lit *wastes away* **1:11** [a]Jer 14:4; Am 5:16 [b]Is 17:11; Jer 9:12 [1]Or *The farmers are ashamed, The vinedressers wail* **1:12** [a]Joel 1:10; Hab 3:17 [b]Hag 2:19 [c]SS 7:8 [d]SS 2:3 [e]Is 16:10; 24:11; Jer 48:33 [1]Lit *wastes away* [2]Or *apricot* **1:13** [a]Jer 4:8; Eze 7:18 [b]Jer 9:10 [c]1Ki 21:27 **1:14** [a]Joel 2:15, 16 [b]Lv 23:36 [c]Jon 3:8 **1:15** [a]Is 13:9; Jer 30:7; Am 5:16 [b]Joel 2:1, 11, 31 [c]Is 13:6; Eze 7:2-12 [1]Heb *Shaddai* **1:16** [a]Is 3:7; Am 4:6 [b]Dt 12:7; Ps 43:4 **1:17** [a]Is 17:10, 11 [1]Or *dried figs* [2]Or *shovels* **1:18** [a]1Ki 8:5; Jer 12:4; 14:5, 6; Hos 4:3

Even the flocks
of sheep [1]suffer.
19 [a]To You, O Yahweh, I cry;
For [b]fire has consumed the
pastures of the wilderness,
And the flame has burned up
all the trees of the field.
20 Even the beasts of the field
[a,1]pant for You;
For the [b]water brooks
are dried up,
And fire has consumed the
pastures of the wilderness.

2 [a]Blow a trumpet in Zion,
And make a loud shout
on My holy mountain!
Let all the inhabitants
of the land tremble,
For the [b]day of Yahweh
is coming;
Surely it is near,
2 A day of [a]darkness and
thick darkness,
A day of clouds and
dense gloom.
As the dawn is spread
over the mountains,
*So* there is a [b]numerous
and mighty people;
There has [c]never been
*anything* like it,
Nor will there be again after it
For the years from generation
to generation.
3 A [a]fire consumes before them,
And behind them
a flame burns.
The land is [b]like the garden
of Eden before them
But a [c]desolate wilderness
behind them,
And nothing at all
escapes them.
4 Their [a]appearance is like
the appearance of horses;
And like war horses,
so they run.
5 [1]With a [a]noise as of chariots
They leap on the tops
of the mountains,
Like the [2]crackling of a [b]flame
of fire consumes the stubble,
Like a mighty people
arranged for battle.
6 Before them the peoples
are [a]writhing;
All [b]faces [1]turn pale.
7 They run like mighty men;
They climb up the wall
like men of war;
And they each [a]march [1]in line,
And they do not deviate
from their paths.
8 They do not crowd each other;
They march everyone
in his path;
When they fall against the
*defending* weapons,
They do not break ranks.
9 They rush on the city;
They run on the wall;
They climb up
into the [a]houses;
They [b]enter through
the windows like a thief.
10 Before them
the earth [a]trembles;
The heavens quake;

***1:18*** [1]*Lit bear punishment* **1:19** [a]Ps 50:15; Mic 7:7 [b]Jer 9:10; Am 7:4 **1:20** [a]Ps 104:21; 147:9; Joel 1:18 [b]1Ki 17:7; 18:5 [1]Lit *long for* ◆**2:1** [a]Jer 4:5; Joel 2:15; Zep 1:16 [b]Joel 1:15; 2:11, 31; 3:14; Ob 15; Zep 1:14 **2:2** [a]Joel 2:10, 31; Am 5:18; Zep 1:15 [b]Joel 1:6; 2:11, 25 [c]Lam 1:12; Da 9:12; 12:1; Joel 1:2 **2:3** [a]Ps 97:3; Is 9:18, 19 [b]Is 51:3; Eze 36:35 [c]Ex 10:5, 15; Ps 105:34, 35; Zec 7:14 **2:4** [a]Rev 9:7 **2:5** [a]Rev 9:9 [b]Is 5:24; 30:30 [1]Lit *Like the noise of chariots* [2]Lit *noise* **2:6** [a]Is 13:8; Na 2:10 [b]Jer 30:6 [1]Lit *gather* their *radiance* **2:7** [a]Pr 30:27 [1]Lit *in his ways* **2:9** [a]Ex 10:6 [b]Jer 9:21; Jn 10:1 **2:10** [a]Ps 18:7; Joel 3:16; Na 1:5

The [b]sun and the moon
grow dark,
And the stars [1]lose
their brightness.
11 But Yahweh [a]gives forth
His voice before [b]His
military force;
Surely His camp is
very numerous,
For [c]mighty is he who
does His word.
The [d]day of Yahweh is indeed
great and very awesome,
And [e]who can endure it?

### *Return to Yahweh*

12 "Yet even now,"
declares Yahweh,
"[a]Return to Me
with all your heart
And with [b]fasting,
weeping, and [1]wailing;
13 And [a]tear your heart and
not [b]your garments."
Now return to Yahweh
your God,
For He is [c]gracious and
compassionate,
Slow to anger, abounding
in lovingkindness,
And [d]relenting concerning evil.
14 Who knows [a]whether He
will *not* turn and relent
And leave a [b]blessing
behind Him,
*Even* [c]a grain offering
and a drink offering
For Yahweh your God?

15 [a]Blow a trumpet in Zion,
[b]Set apart a fast as holy,
call for a solemn assembly,
16 Gather the people, [a]set apart
the congregation as holy,
Assemble the elders,
Gather the infants and
the nursing babies.
Let the [b]bridegroom
come out of his room
And the bride out of her
*bridal* chamber.
17 Let the priests,
the ministers of Yahweh,
Weep [a]between the
porch and the altar,
And let them say, "[b]Pity
Your people, O Yahweh,
And do not make Your
inheritance a [c]reproach,
A byword among the nations.
Why should they
among the peoples say,
'[d]Where is their God?'"

### *Yahweh Will Spare His People*

18 Then Yahweh [1]will be
[a]zealous for His land
And [2]will [b]spare His people.
19 Then Yahweh [1]will answer
and say to His people,
"Behold, I am going to [a]send
you grain, new wine, and oil,
And you will be satisfied
*in full* with [2]them;
And I will [b]never again
make you a reproach
among the nations.

---

**2:10** [b]Is 13:10; 34:4; Jer 4:23; Eze 32:7, 8; Joel 2:31; 3:15; Mt 24:29; Rev 8:12 [1]Lit *gather together* **2:11** [a]Ps 46:6; Is 13:4; Jer 25:30; Joel 3:16 [b]Joel 2:25 [c]Jer 50:34; Rev 18:8 [d]Jer 30:7; Joel 1:15; 2:1, 31; 3:14; Zep 1:14, 15; Rev 6:17 [e]Eze 22:14; Mal 3:2 **2:12** [a]Dt 4:29; Jer 4:1, 2; Eze 33:11; Hos 12:6 [b]Da 9:3 [1]Or *lamentation*, cf. 1:13 **2:13** [a]Ps 34:18; 51:17; Is 57:15 [b]Ge 37:34; 2Sa 1:11; Job 1:20; Jer 41:5 [c]Ex 34:6 [d]Jer 18:8; 42:10; Am 7:3, 6 **2:14** [a]Jer 26:3; Jon 3:9 [b]Hag 2:19 [c]Joel 1:9, 13 **2:15** [a]Nu 10:3; 2Ki 10:20 [b]Joel 1:14 **2:16** [a]1Sa 16:5; 2Chr 29:5 [b]Ps 19:5 **2:17** [a]2Chr 8:12; Eze 8:16 [b]Ex 32:11, 12; Is 37:20; Am 7:2, 5 [c]Ps 44:13; 74:10 [d]Ps 42:10; 79:10; 115:2 **2:18** [a]Zec 1:14; 8:2 [b]Is 60:10; 63:9, 15 [1]Or *was zealous* [2]Or *had spared* **2:19** [a]Jer 31:12; Hos 2:21, 22; Joel 1:10; Mal 3:10 [b]Eze 34:29; 36:15 [1]Or *answered and said* [2]Lit *it*

20 "But I will remove
the [a]northern *military*
*force* far from you,
And I will drive it into
a parched and desolate land,
And its vanguard
into the [b]eastern sea,
And its rear guard
into the [c]western sea.
And its [d]stench will
rise up, and its foul
smell will rise up,
For it has done great things."

21 [a]Do not fear, O land,
rejoice and be glad,
For Yahweh has done
[b]great things.
22 Do not fear, beasts of the field,
For the [a]pastures
of the wilderness
have turned green,
For the tree has
borne its fruit;
The fig tree and the vine have
yielded [1]their full force.
23 So rejoice, O [a]sons of Zion,
And [b]be glad in Yahweh
your God,
For He has [c]given you [1]the early
rain in righteousness.
And He has poured
down for you the rain,
The [2]early and [d,3]late
rains [4]as before.
24 The threshing floors
will be full of grain,
And the vats will [a]overflow
with the new wine and oil.
25 "Then I will pay back to you
in full for the years
That the swarming [a]locust
has consumed,
The creeping locust,
the stripping locust,
and the gnawing locust,
My great military force
which I sent among you.
26 "And you will have plenty to
[a]consume and be satisfied
And [b]praise the name
of Yahweh your God,
Who has [c]dealt
wondrously with you;
Then My people will [d]never
be put to shame.
27 "Thus you will [a]know that I
am in the midst of Israel,
And that I am Yahweh
your God,
And there is [b]no other;
And My people will never
be [c]put to shame.

### *Yahweh Will Pour Out His Spirit*

28 "[a,1]And it will be afterwards
That I will [b]pour out My
Spirit on all [c,2]mankind;
And your sons and your
daughters shall prophesy;
Your old men will
dream dreams;
Your young men will
see visions.
29 "Even on the [a]male slaves
and female slaves
I will in those days pour
out My Spirit.

***2:20*** [a]Jer 1:14, 15 [b]Zec 14:8 [c]Dt 11:24 [d]Is 34:3; Am 4:10 **2:21** [a]Is 54:4; Jer 30:10; Zep 3:16, 17 [b]Ps 126:3; Joel 2:26 **2:22** [a]Ps 65:12, 13 [1]Or *their excellence* **2:23** [a]Ps 149:2 [b]Is 12:2-6 [c]Dt 11:14; Is 41:16; Jer 5:24; Hab 3:18; Zec 10:7 [d]Lv 26:4; Hos 6:3; Zec 10:1 [1]Autumn; or possibly word play to mean *the teacher for righteousness*, cf. Is 30:20 [2]Autumn [3]Spring [4]As in ancient versions; Heb *in the first* **2:24** [a]Lv 26:10; Am 9:13; Mal 3:10 **2:25** [a]Joel 1:4-7; 2:2-11 **2:26** [a]Lv 26:5; Dt 11:15; Is 62:9 [b]Dt 12:7; Ps 67:5-7 [c]Ps 126:2, 3; Is 25:1 [d]Is 45:17 **2:27** [a]Lv 26:11, 12; Joel 3:17, 21 [b]Is 45:5, 6 [c]Is 49:23 **2:28** [a]Ac 2:17-21 [b]Is 32:15; 44:3; Eze 39:29; Zec 12:10 [c]Is 40:5; 49:26 [1]Ch 3:1 in Heb [2]Lit *flesh* **2:29** [a]1Co 12:13; Ga 3:28

### *Deliverance in the Day of Yahweh*

30 “And I will [a]put wonders
in the sky and on the earth,
Blood, fire, and columns
of smoke.
31 “The [a]sun will be turned
into darkness
And the moon into blood
Before the [b]great and
awesome day
of Yahweh comes.
32 “And it will be that
[a]everyone who calls
on the name of Yahweh
Will [1]be delivered;
For [b]on Mount Zion
and in Jerusalem
There will be those
who [c]escape,
As Yahweh has said,
Even among the [d]survivors
whom Yahweh calls.

### *Yahweh Will Judge the Nations*

3 “[1]For behold, [a]in those
days and at that time,
When I [b]restore the fortunes
of Judah and Jerusalem,
2 I will [a]gather all the nations
And bring them down to
the [b]valley of [1]Jehoshaphat.
Then I will [c]enter into
judgment with them there
On behalf of My people and
My inheritance, Israel,
Whom they have [d]scattered
among the nations;
And they have [e]divided
up My land.
3 “They have also [a]cast
lots for My people,
[b,1]Traded a boy for a harlot,
And sold a girl for wine
that they may drink.
4 “Moreover, what are you to Me,
O [a]Tyre, Sidon, and all the regions of
[b]Philistia? Are you rendering Me a rec-
ompense? But if you do recompense
Me, swiftly and speedily I will [c]return
your recompense on your head. 5 Since
you have [a]taken My silver and My
gold, brought My desirable [1]treasures
to your temples, 6 and sold the [a]sons
of Judah and the sons of Jerusalem
to the sons of the [1]Greeks in order to
remove them far from their borders,
7 behold, I am going to [a]rouse them
from the place where you have sold
them and return your recompense on
your head. 8 Also I will [a]sell your sons
and your daughters into the hand of
the sons of Judah, and they will sell
them to the [b]Sabeans, to a distant
nation,” for Yahweh has spoken.
9 [a]Call out this *message*
among the nations:
[b]Set *yourselves* apart for a war;
[c]rouse the mighty men!
Let all the men of war
approach, let them come up!
10 [a]Beat your plowshares
into swords
And your pruning
hooks into spears;

**2:30** [a]Mt 24:29; Mk 13:24, 25; Lk 21:11, 25, 26; Ac 2:19 **2:31** [a]Is 13:10; 34:4; Joel 2:10; 3:15; Mt 24:29; Mk 13:24; Lk 21:25; Ac 2:20; Rev 6:12, 13 [b]Is 13:9; Zep 1:14-16; Mal 4:1, 5 **2:32** [a]Jer 33:3; Ac 2:21; Ro 10:13 [b]Is 46:13; Ro 11:26 [c]Is 4:2; Ob 17 [d]Is 11:11; Jer 31:7; Mic 4:7; Ro 9:27 [1]Lit *escape* ◆ **3:1** [a]Jer 30:3; Eze 38:14 [b]Jer 16:15 [1]Ch 4:1 in Heb **3:2** [a]Is 66:18; Mic 4:12; Zec 14:2 [b]Joel 3:12, 14 [c]Is 66:16; Jer 25:31; Eze 38:22 [d]Jer 50:17; Eze 34:6 [e]Eze 35:10; 36:1-5 [1]Lit *Yahweh judges* **3:3** [a]Ob 11; Na 3:10 [b]Am 2:6 [1]Lit *Given* **3:4** [a]Is 23:1-18; Am 1:9, 10; Zec 9:2-4; Mt 11:21, 22; Lk 10:13, 14 [b]Is 14:29-31; Jer 47:1-7; Eze 25:15-17; Am 1:6-8; Zec 9:5-7 [c]Is 34:8; 59:18 **3:5** [a]2Ki 12:18; 2Chr 21:16, 17 [1]Lit *good things* **3:6** [a]Eze 27:13 [1]Lit *Javan* **3:7** [a]Is 43:5, 6; Jer 23:8; Zec 9:13 **3:8** [a]Is 14:2; 60:14 [b]Job 1:15; Ps 72:10; Eze 38:13 **3:9** [a]Jer 51:27 [b]Jer 6:4; Eze 38:7; Mic 3:5 [c]Is 8:9, 10; Jer 46:3, 4; Zec 14:2, 3 **3:10** [a]Is 2:4; Mic 4:3

[b]Let the weak say,
"I am a mighty man."
11 [a,1]Hasten and come, all you
surrounding nations,
And gather yourselves.
There, bring down, O Yahweh,
Your [b]mighty ones.
12 Let the nations be roused up
And come up to the [a]valley
of [1]Jehoshaphat,
For there I will sit to [b]judge
All the surrounding nations.
13 [a]Send in the sickle,
for the [b]harvest is ripe.
Come, [c,1]tread, for the
[d]wine press is full;
The vats overflow,
for their [e]evil is great.
14 [a]Multitudes, multitudes
in the [b]valley of [1]decision!
For the [c]day of Yahweh is near
in the valley of [1]decision.
15 The [a]sun and moon
grow dark,
And the stars lose
their brightness.
16 And Yahweh [a]roars from Zion
And [b]gives forth His voice
from Jerusalem,
And the [c]heavens and
the earth quake.
But Yahweh is a [d]refuge
for His people
And a [e]strong defense
to the sons of Israel.
17 Then you will [a]know that
I am Yahweh your God,
Dwelling in Zion,
My [b]holy mountain.
So Jerusalem will be [c]holy,
And [d]strangers will pass
through it no more.

### *Yahweh Dwells in Zion*

18 And it will be in that day,
*That* the [a]mountains will
drip with [1]sweet wine,
And the hills will
[b]flow with milk,
And all the [c]brooks of Judah
will flow with water;
And a [d]spring will go out
from the house of Yahweh
To water the valley of [2]Shittim.
19 Egypt will become
a desolation,
And Edom will become
a desolate wilderness,
Because of the [a]violence
[1]done to the sons of Judah,
In whose land they have
shed innocent blood.
20 But Judah will be
[a]inhabited forever
And Jerusalem from
generation to generation.
21 And I will [a]avenge their blood
which I have not avenged,
Indeed, Yahweh
dwells in Zion.

---

**3:10** [b]Zec 12:8 **3:11** [a]Eze 38:15, 16 [b]Is 13:3 [1]Or *Lend aid* **3:12** [a]Joel 3:2, 14 [b]Ps 7:6; 96:13; 98:9; Is 2:4; 3:13 [1]Lit *Yahweh judges* **3:13** [a]Rev 14:14-19 [b]Jer 51:33; Hos 6:11 [c]Rev 14:19, 20; 19:15 [d]Is 63:3; Lam 1:15 [e]Ge 18:20 [1]Or *dominate* **3:14** [a]Is 34:2-8 [b]Joel 3:2, 12 [c]Joel 1:15; 2:1, 11, 31 [1]God's verdict **3:15** [a]Joel 2:10, 31 **3:16** [a]Hos 11:10; Am 1:2 [b]Joel 2:11 [c]Eze 38:19; Joel 2:10; Hag 2:6 [d]Ps 61:3; Is 33:16; Jer 17:17 [e]Jer 16:19; Na 1:7 **3:17** [a]Joel 2:27 [b]Is 11:9; 56:7; Eze 20:40 [c]Is 4:3; Ob 17 [d]Is 52:1; Na 1:15 **3:18** [a]Am 9:13 [b]Ex 3:8 [c]Is 30:25; 35:6 [d]Eze 47:1-12 [1]Lit *freshly pressed out grape juice* [2]Or *acacias* **3:19** [a]Ob 10 [1]Lit *of the sons* **3:20** [a]Eze 37:25; Am 9:15 **3:21** [a]Is 4:4

# *The Book of*
# AMOS

### *Amos' Vision of Yahweh's Fire*

**1** The words of Amos, who was
among the [a]sheepherders from
[b]Tekoa, which he beheld *in visions*
concerning Israel in the days of [c]Uzzi-
ah king of Judah, and in the days of
[d]Jeroboam son of Joash, king of Israel,
two years before the [e]earthquake.
**2** And he said,
"[a,1]Yahweh roars from Zion
And from Jerusalem He
gives forth His voice;
And the shepherds' [b]pasture
grounds mourn,
And the [c,2]top
of Carmel dries up."

**3** Thus says Yahweh,
"For [a]three transgressions
of [b]Damascus and for four
I will not turn back
its *punishment*
Because they threshed
Gilead with *implements*
of sharp iron.
**4** "So I will send fire
upon the house of Hazael,
And it will consume
the citadels of [a]Ben-hadad.
**5** "I will also [a]break the *gate*
bar of Damascus
And cut off the inhabitant
from the [1]valley of Aven
And him who holds
the scepter from Beth-eden;
So the people of Aram will
go into exile to [b]Kir,"
Says Yahweh.

**6** Thus says Yahweh,
"For three transgressions
of [a]Gaza and for four
I will not turn back
its *punishment*
Because they took away
into exile the whole
*community* of exiles
To [b]deliver *it* up to Edom.
**7** "So I will send fire
upon the wall of Gaza,
And it will consume
her citadels.
**8** "I will also cut off the
inhabitant from [a]Ashdod
And him who holds the scepter
from [b]Ashkelon;
I will even turn My hand
against Ekron,
And the remnant of
the [c]Philistines will perish,"
Says Lord Yahweh.

**9** Thus says Yahweh,
"For three transgressions
of [a]Tyre and for four
I will not turn back
its *punishment*
Because they delivered up
the whole *community*
of exiles to Edom

◆**1:1** [a]Am 7:14 [b]2Sa 14:2; Jer 6:1 [c]2Chr 26:1-23; Is 1:1 [d]2Ki 14:23-29; Hos 1:1; Am 7:10, 11 [e]Zec 14:5
**1:2** [a]Is 42:13; Jer 25:30; Joel 3:16 [b]Jer 12:4; Joel 1:18, 19 [c]Am 9:3 [1]The personal covenant name of God, a form of I AM WHO I AM, cf. Ex 3:14-15 [2]Lit *head* **1:3** [a]Am 2:1, 4, 6 [b]Is 8:4; 17:1-3; Jer 49:23-27; Zec 9:1
**1:4** [a]1Ki 20:1; 2Ki 6:24 **1:5** [a]Jer 51:30; Lam 2:9 [b]2Ki 16:9; Am 9:7 [1]Possibly Baalbek **1:6** [a]1Sa 6:17; Jer 47:1, 5; Zep 2:4 [b]Eze 35:5; Ob 11 **1:8** [a]2Chr 26:6; Am 3:9; Zec 9:6 [b]Jer 47:5; Zep 2:4 [c]Is 14:29-31; Jer 47:1-7; Eze 25:16; Joel 3:4-8; Zep 2:4-7; Zec 9:5-7 **1:9** [a]Is 23:1-18; Jer 25:22; Eze 26:2-4; Joel 3:4-8; Zec 9:1-4; Mt 11:21, 22; Lk 10:13, 14

And did not remember *the*
covenant of [b,1]brotherhood.
10 "So I will [a]send fire
upon the wall of Tyre,
And it will consume
her citadels."

11 Thus says Yahweh,
"For three transgressions
of [a]Edom and for four
I will not turn back
its *punishment*
Because he [b]pursued his
brother with the sword
While he corrupted
his compassion;
And his anger also
[c]tore continually,
And he kept his wrath forever.
12 "So I will send fire upon [a]Teman,
And it will consume the
citadels of Bozrah."

13 Thus says Yahweh,
"For three transgressions
of the sons of [a]Ammon
and for four
I will not turn back
its *punishment*
Because they [b]ripped open the
pregnant women of Gilead
In order to [c]enlarge
their borders.
14 "So I will kindle a fire
on the wall of [a]Rabbah,
And it will consume
her citadels
Amid a [b]loud shout on
the day of battle
And a [c]storm on the day
of tempest.
15 "And their [a]king will go into exile,
He and his princes together,"
Says Yahweh.

2 Thus says Yahweh,
"For three transgressions
of [a]Moab and for four
I will not turn back
its *punishment*
Because he [b]burned the bones
of the king of Edom to lime.
2 "So I will send fire upon Moab,
And it will consume the
citadels of [a]Kerioth;
And Moab will die
amid *great* [b]rumbling,
Amid a loud shout and the
sound of a trumpet.
3 "I will also cut off the
[a,1]judge from her midst
And kill all her [b]princes
with him," says Yahweh.

### *Punishment of Judah and Israel*

4 Thus says Yahweh,
"For three transgressions
of [a]Judah and for four
I will not turn back
its *punishment*
Because they [b]rejected
the law of Yahweh
And have not kept
His statutes;
Their [c,1]falsehood also
has led them astray,
*That* which their [d]fathers
walked after.

***1:9*** [b]*1Ki 9:11-14* [1]*Lit brothers* **1:10** [a]Zec 9:4 **1:11** [a]Is 34:5, 6; 63:1-6; Jer 49:7-22; Eze 25:12-14; 35:1-15; Ob 1-14; Mal 1:2-5 [b]Nu 20:14-21; 2Chr 28:17; Ob 10-12 [c]Is 57:16; Mic 7:18 **1:12** [a]Jer 49:7, 20; Ob 9 **1:13** [a]Jer 49:1-6; Eze 21:28-32; 25:2-7; Zep 2:8, 9 [b]2Ki 15:16; Hos 13:16 [c]Is 5:8; Eze 35:10 **1:14** [a]Dt 3:11; 1Chr 20:1; Jer 49:2 [b]Eze 21:22; Am 2:2 [c]Is 29:6; 30:30 **1:15** [a]Jer 49:3 ◆ **2:1** [a]Is 15:1-16:14; 25:10-12; Jer 48:1-47; Eze 25:8-11; Zep 2:8, 9 [b]2Ki 3:26, 27 **2:2** [a]Jer 48:24, 41 [b]Jer 48:45 **2:3** [a]Ps 2:10; 141:6; Am 5:7, 12; 6:12 [b]Job 12:21; Is 40:23 [1]Or *executive officer* **2:4** [a]2Ki 17:19; Hos 12:2; Am 3:2 [b]Jdg 2:17-20; 2Ki 22:11-17; Jer 6:19; 8:9 [c]Is 9:15, 16; 28:15; Jer 16:19; Hab 2:18 [d]Jer 9:14; 16:11, 12; Eze 20:18, 24, 30 [1]Or *false gods*

5 “So I will [a]send fire
upon Judah,
And it will consume
the citadels of Jerusalem.”

6 Thus says Yahweh,
“For three transgressions
of [a]Israel and for four
I will not turn back
its *punishment*
Because they [b]sell the
righteous for money
And the needy for a
pair of sandals.
7 “These who [1]pant after
the *very* dust of the earth
on the head of the [a]poor
Also [b]turn aside the
way of the humble;
And a [c]man and his father go
to the same [2]young woman
In order to profane
My holy name.
8 “On garments [a]taken as
pledges they stretch out
beside [b]every altar,
And in the house of their
God they [c]drink the wine of
those who have been fined.

9 “Yet it was I who destroyed
the [a]Amorite before them,
[1]Though his [b]height *was*
like the height of cedars,
And he *was* strong as the oaks;
I even destroyed his [c]fruit
above and his root below.
10 “And it was I who [a]brought you
up from the land of Egypt,
And I led you in the
wilderness [b]forty years
[1]That you might take
possession of the land
of the [c]Amorite.
11 “Then I [a]raised up some of
your sons to be prophets
And some of your choice
men to be [b]Nazirites.
Is this not so, O sons of
Israel?” declares Yahweh.
12 “But you made the
Nazirites drink wine,
And you commanded
the prophets saying,
‘You [a]shall not prophesy!’
13 “Behold, I am [a,1]weighted
down beneath you
As a wagon [2]is weighted
down when filled
with sheaves.
14 “[a]So [1]flight will perish
from the swift,
And the strong will not
instill his power
with courage,
Nor will the [b]mighty man
make his [2]life escape.
15 “He who [a]grasps the bow will
not stand *his ground*,
The swift of foot will
not escape,
Nor will he who rides
the [b]horse make
his [1]life escape.
16 “Even the [1]most courageous
of heart among the mighty
men will [a]flee naked in that
day,” declares Yahweh.

**2:5** [a]Jer 17:27; 21:10; Hos 8:14 **2:6** [a]2Ki 18:11, 12 [b]Joel 3:3; Am 5:11, 12; 8:6 **2:7** [a]Am 8:4; Mic 2:2, 9 [b]Am 5:12 [c]Hos 4:14 [1]Or *trample upon the head of the helpless on the dust* [2]Possibly a harlot or a temple prostitute **2:8** [a]Ex 22:26 [b]Am 3:14 [c]Am 4:1; 6:6 **2:9** [a]Nu 21:23-25; Jos 10:12 [b]Nu 13:32 [c]Eze 17:9; Mal 4:1 [1]Lit *Whose height* **2:10** [a]Ex 12:51; 20:2; Am 3:1; 9:7 [b]Dt 2:7 [c]Ex 3:8 [1]Lit *To possess* **2:11** [a]Dt 18:18; Jer 7:25 [b]Nu 6:2, 3; Jdg 13:5 **2:12** [a]Is 30:10; Jer 11:21; Am 7:13, 16; Mic 2:6 **2:13** [a]Is 1:14 [1]Or *tottering* [2]Or *totters* **2:14** [a]Is 30:16, 17 [b]Ps 33:16; Jer 9:23 [1]Or *a place of refuge* [2]Lit *soul* **2:15** [a]Jer 51:56; Eze 39:3 [b]Is 31:3 [1]Lit *soul* **2:16** [a]Jdg 4:17 [1]Lit *stout of heart*

### Yahweh Speaks Against Israel

3 Hear this word which Yahweh has spoken against you, sons of Israel, against the entire [a,1]family which [2]He brought up from the land of Egypt, saying,

2 "[a]You only have I known
among all the families
of the earth;
Therefore I will [b,1]punish you
for all your iniquities."
3 Do two men walk together
unless they have made
an [1]appointment?
4 Does a [a]lion roar in the forest
when it has no prey?
Does a young lion give forth
its voice from its den unless
it has captured *something*?
5 Does a bird fall into a trap
on the ground when
there is no [1]bait in it?
Does a trap spring up
from the earth when it
captures nothing at all?
6 If a [a]trumpet is blown
in a city will not the
people tremble?
If a [b]calamity happens in a
city has not Yahweh done it?
7 [1]Surely Lord Yahweh
does nothing
Unless He [a]reveals His
secret counsel
To His slaves the prophets.
8 A [a]lion has roared!
Who will not fear?
[b]Lord Yahweh has spoken!
[c]Who can but prophesy?

9 Make it heard on the citadels
in [a]Ashdod and on the citadels in
the land of Egypt and say, "Gather
yourselves on the [b]mountains of Sa-
maria and see *the* great confusions
within her and *the* [c]oppressions in
her midst. 10 But they [a]do not know
how to do what is right," declares
Yahweh, "these who [b]hoard up
[1]violence and devastation in their
citadels."
11 Therefore, thus says Lord Yah-
weh,

"An [a]adversary, even one
surrounding the land,
Will pull down your
[1]strength from you,
And your [b]citadels will
be plundered."
12 Thus says Yahweh,
"Just as the shepherd
[a]delivers from the lion's
mouth a couple of legs
or a piece of an ear,
So will the sons of Israel
inhabiting Samaria
be delivered—
With *the* [b]corner of a bed and
*the* [c,1]cover of a couch!
13 "Hear and [a]testify
against the house of Jacob,"
Declares Lord Yahweh,
the God of hosts.
14 "For on the day that I punish
Israel's transgressions,
I will also punish the altars
of [a]Bethel;
The horns of the altar
will be cut in pieces,

◆ ***3:1*** [a]*Jer 8:3; 13:11* [1]Nation [2]Lit *I* **3:2** [a]Ge 18:19; Ex 19:5, 6; Dt 4:32-37; 7:6 [b]Jer 14:10; Eze 20:36; Da 9:12; Ro 2:9 [1]Lit *visit* **3:3** [1]Or *agreement* **3:4** [a]Ps 104:21; Hos 5:14; 11:10 **3:5** [1]Or *striker-bar set* **3:6** [a]Jer 4:5, 19, 21; 6:1; Hos 5:8; Zep 1:16 [b]Is 14:24-27; 45:7 **3:7** [a]Ge 6:13; 18:17; Jer 23:22; Da 9:22; Jn 15:15 [1]Or *For* **3:8** [a]Am 1:2 [b]Jon 1:1-3; 3:1-3 [c]Jer 20:9; Ac 4:20 **3:9** [a]1Sa 5:1 [b]Am 4:1; 6:1 [c]Am 5:11; 8:6 **3:10** [a]Ps 14:4; Jer 4:22; Am 5:7; 6:12 [b]Hab 2:8-10; Zep 1:9; Zec 5:3, 4 [1]The plunder from violence **3:11** [a]Am 6:14 [b]Am 2:5 [1]Or *stronghold* **3:12** [a]1Sa 17:34-37 [b]Ps 132:3 [c]Es 1:6; 7:8; Am 6:4 [1]Lit *damask* **3:13** [a]Eze 2:7 **3:14** [a]2Ki 23:15; Hos 10:5-8, 14, 15; Am 4:4; 5:5, 6; 7:10, 13

And they will fall
to the ground.
15 "I will also strike the [a,1]winter
house together
with the [b]summer house;
The houses of [c,2]ivory
will also perish,
And the [d]great houses
will come to an end,"
Declares Yahweh.

### *Yet You Have Not Returned to Me*

4 Hear this word, you cows
of [a]Bashan who are on the
[b]mountain of Samaria,
Who [c]oppress the poor,
who crush the needy,
Who say to their [1]husbands,
"Bring now, that we
may [d]drink!"
2 Lord Yahweh has [a]sworn
by His [b]holiness that,
"Behold, the days are
coming upon you,
And [1]they will take you
away with [c]meat hooks,
And the last of you
with [d]fish hooks.
3 "And you will [a]go out *through*
breaches *in the walls*,
Each one straight before her,
And you [1]will be cast to
Harmon," declares Yahweh.

4 "Enter Bethel and transgress;
In Gilgal
multiply transgression!
[a]Bring your sacrifices
every morning,
Your tithes every three days.
5 "[1]And offer a [a]thank
offering also from that
which is leavened,
And call for [b]freewill offerings;
cause *them* to be heard about.
For so you [c]love *to do*,
you sons of Israel,"
Declares Lord Yahweh.

6 "But I gave you also [a]cleanness
of teeth in all your cities
And lack of bread
in all your places,
Yet you have [b]not returned
to Me," declares Yahweh.
7 "And I also [a]withheld
the rain from you
While *there were* still three
months until harvest.
Then I would send
rain on one city,
And on [b]another city I
would not send rain;
One portion would
be rained on,
While the portion not
rained on would dry up.
8 "So two or three cities would
wander around to another
city to drink [a]water,
But would [b]not be satisfied;
Yet you have [c]not returned
to Me," declares Yahweh.
9 "I [a]struck you with scorching
*wind* and mildew;
And the [b]gnawing locust
was devouring
Your many gardens and
vineyards, fig trees,
and olive trees;

---

**3:15** [a]Jer 36:22 [b]Jdg 3:20 [c]1Ki 22:39; Ps 45:8 [d]Am 2:5; 6:11 [1]Or *autumn* [2]Ivory inlay ◆ **4:1** [a]Ps 22:12; Eze 39:18 [b]Am 3:9; 6:1 [c]Am 5:11; 8:6 [d]Am 2:8; 6:6 [1]Or *lords* **4:2** [a]Am 6:8; 8:7 [b]Ps 89:35 [c]Is 37:29; Eze 38:4 [d]Jer 16:16; Eze 29:4; Hab 1:15 [1]Lit *he* **4:3** [a]Jer 52:7 [1]As in Gr; M.T. *will cast* **4:4** [a]Nu 28:3; Am 5:21, 22 **4:5** [a]Lv 7:13 [b]Lv 22:18-21 [c]Jer 7:9, 10; Hos 9:1, 10 [1]Lit *Offer up incense* **4:6** [a]Is 3:1; Jer 14:18 [b]Is 9:13; Jer 5:3; Hag 2:17 **4:7** [a]Dt 11:17; 2Chr 7:13; Is 5:6 [b]Ex 9:4, 26; 10:22, 23 **4:8** [a]1Ki 18:5; Jer 14:4 [b]Eze 4:16, 17; Hag 1:6 [c]Jer 3:7 **4:9** [a]Dt 28:22; Hag 2:17 [b]Joel 1:4, 7; Am 7:1, 2

Yet you have [c]not returned
to Me," declares Yahweh.
10 "I sent a [a]pestilence
among you after the
manner of Egypt;
I [b]killed your choice men
by the sword along with
your [c]captured horses,
And I made the [d]stench
of your camp rise up
even in your nostrils;
Yet you have [e]not
returned to Me,"
declares Yahweh.
11 "I overthrew you as [a]God
overthrew Sodom
and Gomorrah,
And you were like
a [b]firebrand [1]delivered
from a blaze;
Yet you have [c]not returned
to Me," declares Yahweh.
12 "Therefore thus I will do
to you, O Israel;
Because I will do this to you,
Prepare to [a]meet your
God, O Israel."
13 For behold, He who
[a]forms mountains and
[b]creates the wind
And [c]declares to man
what are His thoughts,
He who [d]makes dawn
into gloom
And [e]treads on the high
places of the earth,
[f]Yahweh God of hosts
is His name.

### *Seek Me That You May Live*

5 Hear this word which I take
up for you as a *funeral*
[a]lament, O house of Israel:
2 She has fallen; she will
[a]not rise again—
The [b]virgin Israel.
She *lies* abandoned
on her land;
There is [c]none to raise her up.
3 For thus says Lord Yahweh,
"The city which goes forth
one thousand *strong*
Will have one [a]hundred left,
And the one which goes
forth one hundred *strong*
Will have [b]ten left
to the house of Israel."

4 For thus says Yahweh to the house
of Israel,
"[a]Seek Me [b]that you may live.
5 "But do not seek [a]Bethel,
And do not come to [b]Gilgal,
Nor cross over to [c]Beersheba;
For Gilgal will certainly
go into [1]exile,
And Bethel will become [2]evil.
6 "[a]Seek Yahweh that
you may live,
Lest He come mightily like a
[b]fire, [1]O house of Joseph,
And it will consume with none
to quench *it* for Bethel,
7 *For* those who overturn
[a]justice into wormwood
And put righteousness
down to the earth."

---

**4:9** [c]Jer 3:10 **4:10** [a]*Ex 9:3; Lv 26:25; Dt 28:27, 60; Ps 78:50* [b]Jer 11:22; 18:21; 48:15 [c]2Ki 13:3, 7 [d]*Joel 2:20* [e]Is 9:13 **4:11** [a]Ge 19:24, 25; Dt 29:23; Is 13:19 [b]Zec 3:2 [c]Jer 23:14 [1]Or *snatched*
**4:12** [a]Is 32:11; 64:2; Jer 5:22 **4:13** [a]Job 38:4-7; Ps 65:6; Is 40:12 [b]Ps 135:7; Jer 10:13 [c]Da 2:28, 30 [d]Jer 13:16; Joel 2:2; Am 5:8 [e]Mic 1:3 [f]Is 47:4; Jer 10:16; Am 5:8, 27; 9:6 ◆ **5:1** [a]Jer 7:29; 9:10, 17; Eze 19:1
**5:2** [a]Am 8:14 [b]Jer 14:17 [c]Is 51:18; Jer 50:32 **5:3** [a]Is 6:13 [b]Am 6:9 **5:4** [a]Dt 4:29; 32:46, 47; Jer 29:13 [b]Is 55:3 **5:5** [a]1Ki 12:28, 29; Am 3:14; 4:4; 7:10, 13 [b]1Sa 7:16; 11:14 [c]Ge 21:31-33; Am 8:14 [1]Gilgal sounds like Heb root *galah*, which means *to go into exile* [2]Or Beth *Aven*, cf. Hos 4:15; 5:8; 10:5 **5:6** [a]Is 55:3, 6, 7; Am 5:14 [b]Dt 4:24 [1]Or in *the house* **5:7** [a]Am 2:3; 5:12; 6:12

8 He who made the
[a]Pleiades and Orion
And [b]overturns the shadow
of death into morning,
[1]Who also [c]darkens
day *into* night,
Who [d]calls for the
waters of the sea
And pours them out
on the surface of the earth,
[e]Yahweh is His name.
9 It is He who [a]flashes
forth *with* devastation
upon the strong
So that [b]devastation comes
upon the fortification.

10 They hate him who
[a]reproves in the [1]gate,
And they [b]abhor him who
speaks *with* integrity.
11 Therefore because
you [1]impose heavy
rent on the poor
And take a tribute
of grain from them,
*Though* you have built
[a]houses of cut stone,
Yet you will not live in them;
You have planted desirable
vineyards, yet you will
[b]not drink their wine.
12 For I know your transgressions
are many and your
sins are mighty,
*You* who [a]distress the
righteous *and* take bribes
And [1]turn aside the
needy in the [2]gate.
13 Therefore at [1]such a time
the one with insight [a]keeps
silent, for it is an evil time.

14 Seek good and not evil,
in order that you may live;
And thus may Yahweh God
of hosts be with you,
[a]Just as you have said!
15 [a]Hate evil, love good,
And set justice at the [1]gate!
Perhaps Yahweh God of hosts
[b]May be gracious to the
[c]remnant of Joseph.

16 Therefore thus says Yahweh God
of hosts, the Lord,
"There is [a]wailing
in all the plazas,
And in all the streets
they say, 'Alas! Alas!'
They also call the [b]farmer
to mourning
And [c,1]professional
weepers to wailing.
17 "And in all the [a]vineyards
*there is* wailing
Because I will pass through the
midst of you," says Yahweh.

18 Woe, you who are longing
for the [a]day of Yahweh,
For what purpose *will* the
day of Yahweh *be* to you?
It *will be* [b]darkness
and not light;
19 As when a man [a]flees
from a lion
And a bear meets him;

**5:8** [a]Job 9:9; 38:31 [b]Job 12:22; 38:12; Is 42:16 [c]Ps 104:20 [d]Ps 104:6-9; Am 9:6 [e]Am 4:13 [1]Lit *And He darkened* **5:9** [a]Is 29:5; Am 2:14 [b]Mic 5:11 **5:10** [a]Is 29:21; Am 5:15 [b]1Ki 22:8; Is 59:15; Jer 17:16-18 [1]The place where court was held **5:11** [a]Am 3:15; 6:11 [b]Mic 6:15 [1]Or *trample upon* **5:12** [a]Is 1:23; 5:23; Am 2:6 [1]Lit *they turn* [2]The place where court was held **5:13** [a]Ecc 3:7; Hos 4:4 [1]Lit *that time* **5:14** [a]Mic 3:11 **5:15** [a]Ps 97:10; Ro 12:9 [b]Joel 2:14 [c]Mic 5:3, 7, 8 [1]The place where court was held **5:16** [a]Jer 9:10, 18-20; Am 8:3 [b]Joel 1:11 [c]2Chr 35:25; Jer 9:17 [1]Lit *those who know lamentation* **5:17** [a]Is 16:10; Jer 48:33 **5:18** [a]Is 5:19; Jer 30:7; Joel 1:15; 2:1, 11, 31 [b]Is 5:30; Joel 2:2 **5:19** [a]Job 20:24; Is 24:17, 18; Jer 15:2, 3; 48:44

[1]Or he goes home,
leans his hand
against the wall,
And a snake bites him.
20 *Will* not the day of Yahweh *be*
[a]darkness instead of light,
Even thick darkness
with no brightness in it?

21 "I hate, I [a]reject your feasts,
Nor do I [b,1]delight in your
solemn assemblies.
22 "Even though you [a]offer up
to Me burnt offerings and
your grain offerings,
I will not accept *them*;
And I will not *even* look
at the [b]peace offerings
of your fatlings.
23 "Remove from Me the
tumult of your songs;
I will not even listen
to the melody of your harps.
24 "But let [a]justice roll
down like waters
And righteousness like
an ever-flowing stream.

25 " [a,1]Did you present Me with
sacrifices and grain offerings in the
wilderness for forty years, O house
of Israel? 26 [a]You also carried along
[1]Sikkuth your king and [2]Kiyyun,
your images, [3]the star of your gods
which you made for yourselves.
27 Therefore, I will make you go
into exile beyond Damascus," says
Yahweh, whose name is the God of
hosts.

### *Woe to Those at Ease in Zion*

6 [a]Woe to those who are
at ease in Zion
And to those who *feel* secure
in the mountain of Samaria,
The [b]distinguished men
of the first of the nations,
To whom the house
of Israel comes.
2 Pass on over to [a]Calneh
and look,
And go from there
to [b]Hamath the great,
Then go down to [c]Gath
of the Philistines.
Are [1]they better
than these kingdoms,
Or are their borders greater
than your borders?
3 Do you [a]put off the
day of calamity,
And would you [b]cause the seat
of violence to approach?

4 Those who lay down
on beds of ivory
And sprawl on their [a]couches
And [b]eat lambs
from the flock
And calves from the
midst of the stall,
5 Who improvise to the
[1]sound of the harp,
*And* like David have
[2]composed [a]songs
for themselves,
6 Who [a]drink wine
from [1]*sacrificial* bowls

**5:19** [1]Or *Then* **5:20** [a]Is 13:10; Zep 1:15 **5:21** [a]Is 1:11-16; 66:3; Am 4:4, 5; 8:10 [b]Lv 26:31; Jer 14:12; Hos 5:6 [1]Lit *like to smell* **5:22** [a]Is 66:3; Mic 6:6, 7 [b]Lv 7:11-15; Am 4:5 **5:24** [a]Jer 22:3; Eze 45:9; Mic 6:8 **5:25** [a]Dt 32:17; Jos 24:14; Ne 9:18-21; Ac 7:42, 43 [1]Or *You presented Me with the sacrifices and a grain offering* **5:26** [a]Ac 7:43 [1]Or *Sakkuth (Saturn), shrine of your Moloch* [2]Or *Kaiwan (Saturn), stands of* [3]Or *your star gods* ◆ **6:1** [a]Is 32:9-11; Zep 1:12; Lk 6:24 [b]Ex 19:5; Am 3:2 **6:2** [a]Ge 10:10; Is 10:9 [b]1Ki 8:65; 2Ki 18:34; Is 10:9 [c]1Sa 5:8; 2Chr 26:6 [1]Or *you* **6:3** [a]Is 56:12; Am 9:10 [b]Am 3:10 **6:4** [a]Am 3:12 [b]Eze 34:2, 3 **6:5** [a]1Chr 15:16; 23:5; Is 5:12 [1]Lit *mouth* [2]Or *invented musical instruments* **6:6** [a]Am 2:8; 4:1 [1]Lit *sprinkling basins*

While they anoint themselves
with the first *pick* of the oils,
Yet they have not
[b]grieved over the
destruction of Joseph.
7 Therefore, they will now
[a]go into exile among
the first of the exiles,
And the [b]sprawlers'
[1]banqueting will turn aside.

8 Lord Yahweh has [a]sworn
by Himself, Yahweh God
of hosts has declared:
"I [b]abhor the lofty
pride of Jacob
And hate his [c]citadels;
Therefore I will [d]deliver up *the*
city as well as its fullness."
9 And it will be, if [a]ten men are left
in one house, they will die. 10 Then
one's [1]uncle, or the one who [a,2]burns
his *bones*, will lift him up to bring out
*his* bones from the house, and he will
say to the one who is in the innermost
part of the house, "Is anyone else
with you?" And that one will say, "No
one." Then he will [3]answer, "[b]Keep
quiet. For [4]the name of Yahweh is
[c]not to be mentioned." 11 For behold,
Yahweh is going to [a]command and
will strike the [b]great house to pieces
and the small house to fragments.
12 Do horses run on rocks?
Or does one plow
[1]them with oxen?
Yet you have overturned
[a]justice into gall
And the fruit of righteousness
into [2]wormwood,
13 You who are glad in [a,1]Lo-debar
[2]And say, "Have we not
[b]by our *own* strength taken
[3]Karnaim for ourselves?"
14 "For behold, [a]I am going to
raise up a nation against you,
O house of Israel," declares
Yahweh God of hosts,
"And they will press down
on you from [b,1]Lebo-hamath
To the [b]brook of the Arabah."

### Yahweh Will Rise Up Against Israel

7 Thus Lord Yahweh showed me,
and behold, He was forming a
[a]locust-swarm [1]when the spring
crop began to come up. And behold,
the spring crop *was* after the king's
[2]mowing. 2 And it happened [1]when it
had [a]completed eating the vegetation
of the land, that I said,
"[b]Lord Yahweh, please pardon!
[2]How can Jacob rise up,
For he is [c]small?"
3 Yahweh [a,1]relented
concerning this.
"It shall not be," said Yahweh.
4 Thus Lord Yahweh showed me,
and behold, Lord Yahweh was calling
to contend *with them* by [a]fire, and it
consumed the great deep and began to
consume the [1]farm land. 5 Then I said,

**6:6** [b]Eze 9:4 **6:7** [a]Am 7:11, 17 [b]1Ki 20:16-21; Da 5:4-6, 30 [1]Or *cultic feasts* **6:8** [a]Ge 22:16; Jer 22:5; 51:14; Am 4:2; 8:7 [b]Lv 26:30; Dt 32:19; Ps 106:40; Am 5:21 [c]Am 3:10, 11 [d]Hos 11:6 **6:9** [a]Am 5:3 **6:10** [a]1Sa 31:12 [b]Am 5:13; 8:3 [c]Jer 44:26; Eze 20:39 [1]Or *beloved one* [2]Lit *burns him* [3]Lit *say* [4]Lit *not to make mention of the name of* **6:11** [a]Is 55:11 [b]2Ki 25:9; Am 3:15; 5:11 **6:12** [a]1Ki 21:7-13; Is 59:13, 14; Hos 10:4; Am 5:7, 11, 12 [1]Or *the sea with oxen* [2]Or *bitterness* **6:13** [a]Job 8:14, 15; Ps 2:2-4; Lk 12:19, 20 [b]Ps 75:4, 5; Is 28:14, 15 [1]Lit *a thing of nothing* [2]Lit *Who* [3]Lit *a pair of horns* **6:14** [a]Jer 5:15 [b]Nu 34:7, 8; 1Ki 8:65; 2Ki 14:25 [1]Or *the entrance of Hamath* ◆ **7:1** [a]Joel 1:4; Am 4:9; Na 3:15 [1]Lit *at the beginning of the coming up of* [2]Or *shearings* **7:2** [a]Ex 10:15 [b]Jer 14:7, 20, 21; Eze 9:8; 11:13 [c]Is 37:4; Jer 42:2 [1]Lit *if* [2]Lit *As who* **7:3** [a]Dt 32:36; Jer 26:19; Hos 11:8; Am 5:15; Jon 3:10 [1]Or *regretted* **7:4** [a]Dt 32:22; Is 66:15, 16; Am 2:5 [1]Lit *portion*

"[a]Lord Yahweh, please stop!
[b,1]How can Jacob rise up,
for he is small?"
6 Yahweh [a,1]relented
concerning this.
"This too shall not be,"
said Lord Yahweh.

**7** Thus He showed me, and behold, the Lord was standing [1]by a wall *made with* a [2]plumb line, and in His hand was a [2]plumb line. **8** And Yahweh said to me, "[a]What do you see, Amos?" And I said, "A plumb line." Then the Lord said,

"Behold, I am about
to put a [b]plumb line
In the midst of My
people Israel.
I will [c]pass over them
no longer.
9 "The [a]high places of Isaac
will be desolated
And the [b]sanctuaries
of Israel laid waste.
Then I will [c]rise up against
the house of Jeroboam
with the sword."

### *Amos Accused*

**10** Then Amaziah, the [a]priest of Bethel, sent *word* to [b]Jeroboam king of Israel, saying, "Amos has [c]conspired against you in the midst of the house of Israel; the land is unable to endure all his words. **11** For thus Amos says, 'Jeroboam will die by the sword, and Israel will certainly go from its land into exile.'" **12** Then Amaziah said to Amos, "[a]Go, you seer, flee away to the land of Judah, and there eat bread, and there do your prophesying! **13** But [a]no longer prophesy at Bethel, for it is a [b]sanctuary of the king and a royal house."

**14** Then Amos answered and said to Amaziah, "I am not a prophet, nor am I the [a]son of a prophet; for I am a herdsman and a [1]grower of sycamore figs. **15** But Yahweh took me from [1]following the flock, and Yahweh said to me, 'Go [a]prophesy to My people Israel.' **16** So now, hear the word of Yahweh: you are saying, 'You [a]shall not prophesy against Israel, [b]nor shall you drip out *words* against the house of Isaac.' **17** Therefore, thus says Yahweh, 'Your [a]wife will play the harlot in the city, your [b]sons and your daughters will fall by the sword, your land will be divided up by a *measuring* line, and you yourself will die [1]upon [c]unclean land. Moreover, Israel will certainly go from its land into exile.'"

### *A Famine for Hearing the Words of Yahweh*

**8** Thus Lord Yahweh showed me, and behold, *there was* a basket of summer fruit. **2** And he said, "What do you see, Amos?" And [a]I said, "A basket of summer fruit." Then Yahweh said to me, "The [b]end has come for My people Israel. I will [c]pass over them no longer. **3** And they will [a]wail *with* the [b]songs of the palace in that

**7:5** [a]Ps 85:4; Joel 2:17 [b]Am 7:2 [1]Lit *Who* **7:6** [a]Ps 106:45; Am 7:3; Jon 3:10 [1]Or *regretted*, cf. 1Sa 15:11, 29, 35 **7:7** [1]*Or upon* [2]*Lit tin*; presumably the weight of a plumb line **7:8** [a]Jer 1:11; Am 8:2 [b]2Ki 21:13; Is 28:17; 34:11; Lam 2:8 [c]Jer 15:6; Eze 7:4-9; Am 8:2 **7:9** [a]Ge 46:1; Hos 10:8; Mic 1:5 [b]Lv 26:31; Is 63:18; Jer 51:51; Am 7:13 [c]2Ki 15:8-10; Am 7:11 **7:10** [a]1Ki 12:31, 32; 13:33 [b]2Ki 14:23, 24 [c]Jer 26:8-11; 38:4 **7:12** [a]Mt 8:34 **7:13** [a]Am 2:12; Ac 4:18 [b]1Ki 12:29, 32; Am 7:9 **7:14** [a]1Ki 20:35; 2Ki 2:3, 5; 4:38; 2Chr 19:2 [1]Or *nipper* **7:15** [a]Jer 1:7; Eze 2:3, 4 [1]Lit *behind* **7:16** [a]Am 2:12; 7:13 [b]Dt 32:2; Eze 20:46; 21:2 **7:17** [a]Hos 4:13, 14 [b]Jer 14:16 [c]2Ki 17:6; Eze 4:13; Hos 9:3 [1]Or *in an unclean land* ◆ **8:2** [a]Jer 24:3 [b]Eze 7:2, 3, 6 [c]Am 7:8 **8:3** [a]Am 5:16 [b]Am 5:23; 6:4, 5; 8:10

day," declares Lord Yahweh. "Many
*will be* the [c]corpses; in every place
[1]they will cast them forth [2]in silence."
4 Hear this, you who [a,1]trample the
needy, even to cause the humble of
the land to cease, 5 saying,
"When will the [a]new
moon pass over,
So that we may sell grain,
And the [b]sabbath, that we may
open the wheat *market*,
To make the [1]bushel smaller
and the [2]shekel bigger,
And to [c]cheat
with a deceptive balance,
6 So as to [a]buy the poor
for [1]money
And the needy for a
pair of sandals,
And *that* we may sell the
refuse of the wheat?"

7 Yahweh has [a]sworn by the
[b]lofty pride of Jacob,
"Indeed, I will [c]never forget
any of their works.
8 "Because of this will not
the land [a]tremble
And everyone who
inhabits it [b]mourn?
Indeed, all of it will [c]rise
up like the Nile,
And it will be tossed about
And subside like the
Nile of Egypt.
9 "And it will be in that day,"
declares Lord Yahweh,
"That I will make the [a]sun
go down at noon
And [b]make the earth dark
in [1]broad daylight.
10 "Then I will [a]overturn your
feasts into mourning
And all your songs
into [1]lamentation;
And I will bring up [b]sackcloth
on everyone's loins
And baldness on every head.
And I will make it [c]like *a time*
*of* mourning for an only son,
And the end of it will
be like a bitter day.

11 "Behold, days are coming,"
declares Lord Yahweh,
"When I will send a
famine on the land,
Not a famine for bread
or a thirst for water,
But rather [a]for hearing
the words of Yahweh.
12 "People will wander
from sea to sea
And from the north
even to the east;
They will go to and fro to
[a]seek the word of Yahweh,
But they will not find *it*.
13 "In that day the
beautiful [a]virgins
And the choice men will
[b]faint from thirst.
14 "*As for* those who swear
by the [a,1]guilt of Samaria,
Who say, 'As your god
lives, O [b]Dan,'
And, 'As the way
of [c]Beersheba lives,'

**8:3** [c]Am 6:8-10 [1]Lit *he has thrown* [2]Or *—hush!* **8:4** [a]Ps 14:4; Pr 30:14; Am 2:7; 5:11, 12 [1]Or *snap at* **8:5** [a]Nu 28:11; 2Ki 4:23 [b]Ex 31:13-17; Ne 13:15 [c]Hos 12:7; Mic 6:11 [1]Lit *ephah* [2]A shekel was approx. 0.4 oz. or 11 gm **8:6** [a]Am 2:6 [1]Lit *silver* **8:7** [a]Am 4:2 [b]Dt 33:26, 29; Ps 68:34; Am 6:8 [c]Ps 10:11; Hos 7:2; 8:13 **8:8** [a]Ps 18:7; 60:2; Is 5:25 [b]Hos 4:3 [c]Jer 46:7, 8; Am 9:5 **8:9** [a]Job 5:14; Is 13:10; Jer 15:9; Mic 3:6 [b]Is 59:9, 10; Am 4:13; 5:8 [1]Lit *a day of light* **8:10** [a]Job 20:23; Am 5:21 [b]Is 15:2, 3; Jer 48:37; Eze 7:18; 27:31 [c]Jer 6:26; Zec 12:10 [1]Or *a dirge* **8:11** [a]1Sa 3:1; 2Chr 15:3; Ps 74:9; Eze 7:26; Mic 3:6 **8:12** [a]Eze 20:3, 31 **8:13** [a]Lam 1:18; 2:21 [b]Is 41:17; Hos 2:3 **8:14** [a]Hos 8:5 [b]1Ki 12:28, 29 [c]Am 5:5 [1]Or *Ashimah*

They will fall and
[d]not rise again."

### *Sinful Israelites Will Die by the Sword*

9 I saw the Lord standing beside
the [a]altar, and He said,
"Strike the capitals so that the
[b]thresholds will quake,
And [c]break them on the
heads of them all!
Then I will [d]kill the rest
of them with the sword;
[e]Not one of them who
can flee will flee,
And not one of them who
can survive will escape.
2 "Though they dig into [a]Sheol,
From there will My
hand take them;
And though they
[b]ascend to heaven,
From there will I bring
them down.
3 "And though they hide
on the [1]top of Carmel,
From there I will [a]search
them out and take them;
And though they [b]conceal
themselves from My eyes
on the floor of the sea,
From there I will command
the [c]serpent, and it
will bite them.
4 "And though they go
into [a]captivity
before their enemies,
From there I will command
the sword that it
kill them,
And I will [b]set My eyes
against them for evil
and not for good."
5 Now Lord Yahweh of hosts,
The One who [a]touches the
land so that it melts,
And [b]all those who
inhabit it mourn,
And all of it rises up like the Nile
And subsides like the
Nile of Egypt;
6 The One who builds
His [a,1]upper chambers
in the heavens
And has founded His vaulted
dome over the earth;
The One who [b]calls
for the waters of the sea
And [c]pours them out
on the face of the earth;
[d]Yahweh is His name.

7 "Are you not as the sons
of [a]Ethiopia to Me,
O sons of Israel?"
declares Yahweh.
"Have I not brought up Israel
from the land of Egypt,
And the [b]Philistines
from Caphtor and
the [c]Arameans from [d]Kir?
8 "Behold, the [a]eyes
of Lord Yahweh are
on the sinful kingdom,
And I will [b]destroy it
from the face of the earth;
Nevertheless, I will [c]not totally
destroy the house of Jacob,"
Declares Yahweh.

**8:14** [d]Am 5:2 ◆ **9:1** [a]Am 3:14 [b]Zep 2:14 [c]Ps 68:21; Hab 3:13 [d]Am 7:17 [e]Jer 11:11 **9:2** [a]Ps 139:8 [b]Jer 51:53; Ob 4 **9:3** [a]Jer 16:16 [b]Job 34:22; Ps 139:9, 10 [c]Is 27:1 [1]Lit *head*, cf. 9:1 **9:4** [a]Lv 26:33 [b]Lv 17:10; Jer 21:10; 39:16; 44:11 **9:5** [a]Ps 104:32; 144:5; Is 64:1; Mic 1:4 [b]Am 8:8 **9:6** [a]Ps 104:3, 13 [b]Am 5:8 [c]Ps 104:6 [d]Am 4:13 [1]Or *stairs* **9:7** [a]2Chr 14:9, 12; Is 20:4; 43:3 [b]Dt 2:23; Jer 47:4 [c]Am 1:5 [d]2Ki 16:9; Is 22:6 **9:8** [a]Jer 44:27; Am 9:4 [b]Am 7:17; 9:10 [c]Jer 5:10; 30:11; 31:35, 36; Joel 2:32; Am 3:12; Ob 17

9 “For behold, I am commanding,
And I will [a]shake the house
of Israel among all nations
As *grain* is shaken in a sieve,
But not a [1]kernel will
fall to the ground.
10 “All the [a]sinners of My people
will die by the sword,
Those who say,
‘[b]The calamity will not
overtake or confront us.’

### *Yahweh Will Rebuild Israel*

11 “In that day I will [a]raise up the
fallen [b,1]booth of David
And wall up its [c]breaches;
I will also raise up its ruins
And rebuild it as
in the [d]ancient days,
12 [a]That they may possess
the remnant of [b]Edom
And all the [1]nations who
are [c]called by My name,”
Declares Yahweh who does this.
13 “Behold, days are coming,”
declares Yahweh,
“When the [a]plowman will
overtake the reaper
And the treader of grapes
him who sows seed;
When the [b]mountains
will drip [1]sweet [c]wine
And all the hills will melt.
14 “Also I will [a]restore the
[1]captivity of My people Israel,
And they will [b]rebuild
the desolated cities
and live *in them*;
They will also [c]plant vineyards
and drink their wine
And make gardens and
eat their fruit.
15 “I will also plant them
on their land,
And [a]they will not again be
uprooted from their land
Which I have given them,”
Says Yahweh your God.

*The Book of*

# OBADIAH

### *Edom Will Be Brought Down*

1 The vision of Obadiah.
Thus says Lord [1]Yahweh concerning
[a]Edom—
[b]We have heard a report
from Yahweh,
And an [c]envoy has been
sent among the
nations *saying*,
“[d]Arise! And let us arise
against her for battle”—
2 “Behold, I will make you
[a]small among the nations;
You are greatly despised.
3 “The [a]arrogance of your
heart has deceived you,
You who dwell in the
clefts of [1]the [b]cliff,

---

**9:9** [a]Is 30:28; Lk 22:31 [1]Or *pebble* **9:10** [a]Is 33:14; Zec 13:8 [b]Am 6:3 **9:11** [a]Ac 15:16-18 [b]Is 16:5 [c]Ps 80:12 [d]Is 63:11; Jer 46:26 [1]Or *shelter, tabernacle* **9:12** [a]Ob 19 [b]Nu 24:18; Is 11:14 [c]Is 43:7 [1]Or *Gentiles* **9:13** [a]Lv 26:5 [b]Joel 3:18 [c]Ge 49:11 [1]Lit *freshly pressed out grape juice* **9:14** [a]Ps 53:6; Is 60:4; Jer 30:3, 18 [b]Is 61:4; 65:21 [c]Jer 24:6; 31:28 [1]Or *fortunes* **9:15** [a]Is 60:21; Eze 34:28; 37:25 ◆**1** [a]Ps 137:7; Is 21:11, 12; 34:1-17; 63:1-6; Jer 49:7-22; Eze 25:12-14; 35:15; Joel 3:19; Am 1:11, 12; Mal 1:4 [b]Jer 49:14-16; Ob 1-4 [c]Is 18:2; 30:4 [d]Jer 6:4, 5 [1]The personal covenant name of God, a form of I AM WHO I AM, cf. Ex 3:14-15 **2** [a]Nu 24:18; Is 23:9 **3** [a]Is 16:6; Jer 49:16 [b]2Ki 14:7; 2Chr 25:11f [1]Or *Sela*

In the height
of your habitation,
Who says in his heart,
'[c]Who will bring me
down to earth?'

4 "Though you [a]build
loftily like the eagle,
Though you set your nest
among the [b]stars,
From there I will bring you
down," declares Yahweh.

5 "If [a]thieves came to you,
If [1]robbers by night—
Oh how you will be ruined!—
Would they not thieve *only*
[2]until they had enough?
If grape gatherers came to you,
[b]Would they not allow some
gleanings to remain?

6 "Oh how Esau will be
[a]searched out
*And* his hidden treasures
ransacked!

7 "All the [a]men *who have*
[1]a covenant with you
Will send you forth
to the border,
And the men at peace with you
Will deceive you and
overpower you.
*They who eat* your [b]bread
Will set an ambush for you.
(There is [c]no discernment
[2]in him.)

8 "Will I not on that day,"
declares Yahweh,
"[a]Cause the wise men
to perish from Edom
And discernment from
the mountain of Esau?

9 "Then your [a]mighty men will
be dismayed, O [b]Teman,
So that each one may be [c]cut
off from the mountain
of Esau by slaughter.

10 "Because of [a]violence
to your brother Jacob,
[1]You will be covered
*with* shame,
[b]And you will be cut
off forever.

11 "On the day that you
[a]stood aloof,
On the day that strangers
took his wealth captive
And foreigners
entered his gate
And [b]cast lots for Jerusalem—
[c]You too were as one of them.

12 "[a]Now do not look on your
brother's day *with triumph,*
The day of his misfortune.
And [b]do not be glad
over the sons of Judah
In the day *when* they perish;
And [c]do not [1]let your mouth
*speak* great things
In the day of *their* distress.

13 "Do not enter the gate
of My people
In the [a]day of their disaster.
Indeed, you, do not look
on their calamity
*with triumph*
In the day of their disaster.
And do not [b]send out
for their wealth
In the day of their disaster.

**3** [c]Is 14:13-15; Rev 18:7 **4** [a]Job 20:6, 7; Hab 2:9 [b]Is 14:12-15 **5** [a]Jer 49:9 [b]Dt 24:21 [1]Lit *devastators of the night* [2]Lit *their sufficiency* **6** [a]Jer 49:10 **7** [a]Jer 30:14 [b]Ps 41:9 [c]Is 19:11; Jer 49:7 [1]Lit *your covenant* [2]In Esau; or *of it* **8** [a]Job 5:12-14; Is 29:14 **9** [a]Jer 49:22 [b]Ge 36:11; 1Chr 1:45; Job 2:11; Jer 49:7; Eze 25:13; Am 1:12; Hab 3:3 [c]Is 34:5-8; 63:1-3; Ob 5 **10** [a]Ge 27:41; Eze 25:12; Joel 3:19; Am 1:11 [b]Eze 35:9 [1]Lit *Shame will cover you* **11** [a]Ps 83:5, 6; 137:7; Am 1:6, 9 [b]Joel 3:3; Na 3:10 [c]Eze 35:10 **12** [a]Mic 4:11; 7:10 [b]Pr 17:5; Eze 35:15; 36:5 [c]Ps 31:18; Eze 35:12 [1]Lit *make your mouth large* **13** [a]Eze 35:5 [b]Eze 35:10; 36:2, 3

14 "Do not [a]stand at the
fork of the road
To cut down those
among them who escape;
And do not deliver over
their survivors
In the day of their distress.

### *The Day of Yahweh Is Near*

15 "For the [a]day of Yahweh draws
near on all the nations.
[b]As you have done, it
will be done to you.
Your [c]dealings will return
on your own head.
16 "Because just as you *all* [a]drank
on [b]My holy mountain,
All the nations [c]will
drink continually.
They will drink and [1]swallow,
And they will be as if
they never were.
17 "But on Mount [a]Zion there
will be those who escape,
And it will be holy.
And the house of Jacob will
[b]possess their possessions.
18 "Then the house of Jacob
will be a [a]fire
And the house
of Joseph a flame;
But the house of Esau
*will be* as stubble.
And they will set [1]them
on fire and consume [1]them
So that there will be
[b]no survivor of the
house of Esau,"
For Yahweh has spoken.

### *The Kingdom of Yahweh*

19 Then *those of* the [1]Negev
will [a]possess the
mountain of Esau,
And *those of* the [2]Shephelah,
the [b]Philistine *plain*;
And they will [c]possess the
territory of Ephraim and
the territory of Samaria,
And Benjamin *will*
*possess* Gilead.
20 And the exiles of this
[1]military force
of the sons of Israel,
Who are *among* the Canaanites
as far as [a]Zarephath,
And the exiles of Jerusalem
who are in Sepharad,
Will possess the [b]cities
of the Negev.
21 And the [a]saviors will
ascend Mount Zion
To judge the mountain
of Esau,
And the [b]kingdom will
belong to Yahweh.

---

**14** [a]Is 16:3, 4 **15** [a]Eze 30:3; Joel 1:15; 2:1, 11, 31; Am 5:18, 20 [b]Jer 50:29; 51:56; Hab 2:8 [c]Eze 35:11
**16** [a]Jer 49:12 [b]Joel 3:17 [c]Is 51:22, 23; Jer 25:15, 16 [1]Or *stagger* **17** [a]Is 4:2, 3 [b]Is 14:1, 2; Am 9:11-15
**18** [a]Is 5:24; 9:18, 19; Zec 12:6 [b]Jer 11:23; Am 1:8 [1]The people of Esau **19** [a]Is 11:14; Am 9:12 [b]Is 11:14
[c]Jer 31:5; 32:44 [1]South country [2]Or *lowland* **20** [a]1Ki 17:9; Lk 4:26 [b]Jer 32:44; 33:13 [1]Or *rampart*
**21** [a]Ne 9:27 [b]Ps 22:28; 47:7-9; 67:4; Zec 14:9; Rev 11:15

*The Book of*

# JONAH

### *Jonah Flees from Yahweh's Presence*

**1** Now the word of [1]Yahweh came to [a]Jonah the son of Amittai saying, **2** "Arise, go to [a]Nineveh, the great city, and [b]call out against it, for their [c]evil has come up before Me." **3** Yet Jonah arose to flee to [a]Tarshish [b]from the presence of Yahweh. So he went down to [c]Joppa, found a ship which was going to Tarshish, and [1]paid its fare and went down into it to go with them to Tarshish from the presence of Yahweh.

**4** But [a]Yahweh hurled a great wind on the sea, and there was a great storm on the sea so that the ship gave thought to [1]breaking apart. **5** Then the sailors became fearful, and every man cried to [a]his god, and they [b]hurled the [1]cargo which was in the ship into the sea to lighten *it* [2]for them. But Jonah had gone down *below* into the innermost part of the vessel, lain down, and fallen deep asleep. **6** So the captain came near to him and said to him, "How is it that you are deeply sleeping? Arise, [a]call on your god. Perhaps *your* [b]god will be concerned about us so that we will not perish."

**7** Then each man said to the other, "Come, let us [a,1]have *the* lots fall so we may know on whose account this *calamitous* evil *has struck* us." So they [1]had *the* lots fall, and the [b]lot fell on Jonah. **8** Then they said to him, "[a]Tell us, now! On whose account *has* this *calamitous* evil *struck* us? What is your [b]occupation? And where do you come from? What is your country? From what people are you?" **9** And he said to them, "I am a [a]Hebrew, and I [b]fear Yahweh, the [c]God of heaven, who [d]made the sea and the dry land."

**10** Then the men became greatly fearful, and they said to him, "What is this you have done?" For the men knew that he was [a]fleeing from the presence of Yahweh because he had told them. **11** So they said to him, "What should we do to you that the sea may become quiet [1]for us?"—for the sea was becoming increasingly stormy. **12** So he said to them, "Lift me up and hurl me into the sea. Then the sea will become quiet [1]for you, for I know that [a]on account of me this great storm *has come* upon you." **13** However, the men [1]rowed *desperately* to return to dry land, but they could not, for the sea was becoming increasingly stormy against them. **14** Then they called on [a]Yahweh and said, "Ah! O Yahweh, we earnestly pray, do not let us perish on

---

◆**1:1** [a]2Ki 14:25; Mt 12:39-41; 16:4; Lk 11:29, 30, 32 [1]The personal covenant name of God, a form of I AM WHO I AM, cf. Ex 3:14-15 **1:2** [a]Ge 10:11; 2Ki 19:36; Is 37:37; Na 1:1; Zep 2:13 [b]Is 58:1 [c]Ge 18:20; Hos 7:2 **1:3** [a]Is 23:1, 6, 10; Jer 10:9 [b]Ge 4:16; Ps 139:7, 9, 10 [c]Jos 19:46; 2Chr 2:16; Ezr 3:7; Ac 9:36, 43 [1]Lit *gave its wages* **1:4** [a]Ps 107:23-28; 135:6, 7 [1]Lit *be broken* **1:5** [a]1Ki 18:26 [b]Ac 27:18, 19, 38 [1]Lit *vessels* [2]Lit *from upon them* **1:6** [a]Ps 107:28 [b]2Sa 12:22; Am 5:15; Jon 3:9 **1:7** [a]Jos 7:14-18; 1Sa 10:20, 21; 14:41, 42; Ac 1:23-26 [b]Nu 32:23; Pr 16:33 [1]Or *cast lots* **1:8** [a]Jos 7:19; 1Sa 14:43 [b]Ge 47:3; 1Sa 30:13 **1:9** [a]Ge 14:13; Ex 1:15; 2:13 [b]2Ki 17:25, 28, 32, 33 [c]Ezr 1:2; Ne 1:4; Ps 136:26; Da 2:18 [d]Ne 9:6; Ps 95:5; 146:6 **1:10** [a]Job 27:22; Jon 1:3 **1:11** [1]Lit *from upon us* **1:12** [a]2Sa 24:17; 1Chr 21:17 [1]Lit *from upon you* **1:13** [1]Lit *dug their oars into the water* **1:14** [a]Ps 107:28; Jon 1:16

account of this man's life, and do not
put innocent blood on us; for [b]You,
O Yahweh, as You have pleased You
have done."
15 So they lifted Jonah up and
hurled him into the sea, and the sea
[a]stood still from its raging. 16 Then
the men greatly feared Yahweh, and
they offered a sacrifice to Yahweh
and made [a]vows.
17 [1]And Yahweh appointed a great
fish to swallow Jonah, and Jonah was
in the [a]stomach of the fish three days
and three nights.

### *Jonah's Prayer*

2 [1]Then Jonah prayed to Yahweh
his God [a]from the stomach of the
fish, 2 and he said,

"I [a]called out of my
distress to Yahweh,
And He answered me.
I cried for help
from the belly of [b]Sheol;
You heard my voice.
3 "For You had [a]cast me
into the deep,
Into the heart of the seas,
And the current
surrounded me.
All Your [b]breakers and
waves passed over me.
4 "So I said, 'I have been [a]driven
away from [1]Your sight.
Nevertheless I will look again
[b]toward Your holy temple.'
5 "[a]Water encompassed
me to *my very* soul.
The great [b]deep
surrounded me,
Weeds were wrapped
around my head.
6 "I [a]went down to the [1]base
of the mountains.
The earth with its [b]bars
*closed* behind me forever,
But You have [c]brought up
my life from [2]the pit,
O Yahweh my God.
7 "While my soul was
[a]fainting within me,
I [b]remembered Yahweh,
And my [c]prayer came to You,
To [d]Your holy temple.
8 "Those who [a]regard
worthless idols
Forsake their lovingkindness,
9 But as for me, I will
[a]sacrifice to You
With the voice
of thanksgiving.
That which I have
vowed I will [b]pay.
[c]Salvation belongs to Yahweh."

10 Then Yahweh spoke to the [a]fish,
and it vomited Jonah up onto the dry
land.

### *Ninevites Turn from Their Evil Ways*

3 Now the word of Yahweh came
to Jonah the second time, saying,
2 "Arise, go to [a]Nineveh, the great
city, and [b]call out to it this *very* call
which I am going to speak to you."
3 So Jonah arose and went to Nineveh
according to the word of Yahweh.

**1:14** [b]Ps 115:3; 135:6; Da 4:34, 35 **1:15** [a]Ps 65:7; 93:3, 4; 107:29 **1:16** [a]Ps 50:14; 66:13, 14
**1:17** [a]Mt 12:40; 16:4 [1]Ch 2:1 in Heb ◆ **2:1** [a]Job 13:15; Ps 130:1, 2; Lam 3:53-56 [1]Ch 2:2 in Heb
**2:2** [a]1Sa 30:6; Ps 18:4-6; 22:24; 120:1 [b]Ps 18:5, 6; 86:13; 88:1-7 **2:3** [a]Ps 69:1, 2, 14, 15; Lam 3:54 [b]Ps 42:7
**2:4** [a]Ps 31:22; Jer 7:15 [b]1Ki 8:38; 2Chr 6:38; Ps 5:7 [1]Lit *before Your eyes* **2:5** [a]Lam 3:54 [b]Ps 69:1, 2
**2:6** [a]Ps 18:5; 116:3 [b]Is 38:10; Mt 16:18 [c]Job 33:28; Ps 16:10; 30:3; Is 38:17 [1]Lit *bases* [2]Or *corruption*
**2:7** [a]Ps 142:3 [b]Ps 77:10, 11; 143:5 [c]2Chr 30:27; Ps 18:6 [d]Ps 11:4; 65:4; Jon 2:4; Mic 1:2; Hab 2:20
**2:8** [a]2Ki 17:15; Ps 31:6; Jer 10:8 **2:9** [a]Ps 50:14, 23; Jer 33:11; Hos 14:2 [b]Job 22:27; Ecc 5:4, 5 [c]Ps 3:8;
Is 45:17 **2:10** [a]Jon 1:17 ◆ **3:2** [a]Zep 2:13 [b]Jer 1:17; Eze 2:7

Now Nineveh was [1]an [a]exceedingly
great city, a three days' walk. **4** Then
Jonah began to go into the city, one
day's walk; and he [a]called out and
said, "Yet forty days and Nineveh will
be overthrown."

**5** And the [1]people of Nineveh
believed in God; and they called a
[a]fast and put on sackcloth, from
the greatest to the least of them.
**6** Then the word reached the king
of Nineveh, and he arose from his
throne, laid aside his mantle from
him, [a]covered *himself* with sack-
cloth, and sat on the [1]ashes. **7** And
he [a]cried out and said,

> "In Nineveh by the [1]decree of
> the king and his nobles[2]: Do
> not let man, [3]animal, herd, or
> flock taste a thing. Do not let
> them eat, and do not let them
> drink water. **8** But both man
> and [1]animal must be covered
> with sackcloth; and let [2]men
> [a]call on God with *their*
> strength that each may [b]turn
> from his evil way and from
> the violence which is in [3]his
> hands. **9** [a]Who knows, God
> may turn and relent and turn
> away from His burning anger
> so that we will not perish."

**10** Then God saw their works, that
they [a]turned from their evil way, so
[b]God [1]relented concerning the evil
which He had spoken He would
[2]bring upon them. And He did not
[2]bring *it upon them.*

### *Jonah's Anger*

**4** But this was a great evil to Jonah,
and he became [a]angry. **2** And he
[a]prayed to Yahweh and said, "Ah!
O Yahweh, was not this my word *to*
*myself* while I was still in my *own*
land? Therefore I went ahead to
[b]flee to Tarshish, for I knew that You
are a [c]gracious and compassionate
God, slow to anger and abundant in
lovingkindness, and one who relents
concerning evil. **3** So now, O Yahweh,
please [a]take my [1]life from me, for
death is [b]better to me than life."
**4** And Yahweh said, "Do you have
good reason to be angry?"

**5** Then Jonah went out from the
city and sat east of the city. And there
he made a booth for himself and [a]sat
under it in the shade until he could
see what would happen in the city.
**6** So Yahweh God appointed a [1]plant,
and it came up over Jonah to be a
shade over his head to deliver him
from his *miserable* evil. And Jonah
was [2]extremely glad about the plant.
**7** But God appointed a worm at the
[1]breaking of dawn the next day, and
it struck the plant, and [2]it [a]dried up.
**8** Then it happened that as the sun
rose up, God appointed a scorching
[a]east wind, and the [b]sun struck down
on Jonah's head so that he became
faint and asked with *all* his soul to
die and said, "[c]Death is better to me
than life."

**9** Then God said to Jonah, "Do you
have good reason to be angry about

---

**3:3** [a]Jon 1:2; 4:11 [1]Lit *a great city to God* **3:4** [a]Mt 12:41; Lk 11:32 **3:5** [a]Da 9:3; Joel 1:14 [1]Lit *men* ***3:6*** *[a]Es 4:1-4; Jer 6:26; Eze 27:30, 31* [1]Or *dust* **3:7** [a]2Chr 20:3; Ezr 8:21; Jon 3:5 [1]Lit *taste*, cf. 3:7b [2]Lit *saying* [3]Lit *beast, cattle* **3:8** [a]Ps 130:1; Jon 1:6, 14 [b]Is 1:16-19; 55:6, 7; Jer 18:11 [1]Lit *beast, cattle* [2]Lit *them* [3]Lit *their* **3:9** [a]2Sa 12:22; Joel 2:14 **3:10** [a]1Ki 21:27-29; Jer 31:18 [b]Ex 32:14; Jer 18:8; Am 7:3, 6 [1]Or *regretted*, cf. 1Sa 15:11, 29, 35 [2]Lit *do* ◆ **4:1** [a]Jon 4:4, 9; Mt 20:15; Lk 15:28 **4:2** [a]Jer 20:7 [b]Jon 1:3 [c]Ex 34:6; Nu 14:18; Ps 86:5, 15; Joel 2:13 **4:3** [a]1Ki 19:4; Job 6:8, 9 [b]Job 7:15, 16; Ecc 7:1 [1]Lit *soul* **4:5** [a]1Ki 19:9, 13 **4:6** [1]Probably a castor oil plant, so through v 10 [2]Lit *greatly* **4:7** [a]Joel 1:12 [1]Lit *rising* [2]The plant **4:8** [a]Eze 19:12; Hos 13:15 [b]Ps 121:6; Is 49:10 [c]Jon 4:3

the plant?" And he said, "I have good
reason to be angry, even to death."
**10** Then Yahweh said, "You had pity
on the plant for which you did not
work and *which* you did not cause to
grow, which [1]came to be overnight
and perished [2]overnight. **11** So should
I not [a]have pity on Nineveh, the great
city, in which there are more than
120,000 persons who do not [b]know
*the difference* between their right and
left hand, as well as many [c,1]animals?"

*The Book of*

# MICAH

### *Calamity in Israel and Judah*

**1** The [a]word of [1]Yahweh which came
*to* [b]Micah of Moresheth in the days
of [c]Jotham, [d]Ahaz, *and* [e]Hezekiah,
kings of Judah, which he beheld
concerning Samaria and Jerusalem.

**2** Hear, O peoples, all of [1]you;
[a]Give heed, O earth,
as well as its fullness,
And let Lord Yahweh be
a [b]witness against you,
The Lord from His
holy temple.

**3** For behold, Yahweh is [a]going
forth from His place.
He will come down and
[b]tread on the high
places of the [1]earth.

**4** [a]The mountains will
melt under Him,
And the valleys will be split,
Like wax before the fire,
Like water poured
down a steep place.

**5** All this is for the transgression
of Jacob
And for the sins of the
house of Israel.
What is the [a]transgression
of Jacob?
Is it not [b]Samaria?
What is the [c]high
[1]place of Judah?
Is it not Jerusalem?

**6** So I will make Samaria
a [a]heap of ruins in the field,
[b]Planting places
for a vineyard.
And I will [c]pour her stones
down into the valley
And will [d]lay bare her
foundations.

**7** And all of her [a]graven
images will be smashed,
And all of her earnings will
be burned with fire
And all of her idols I
will make desolate,
For she collected *them*
from a [b]harlot's earnings,
And to the earnings
of a harlot they will return.

**8** Because of this I must
lament and wail;
I must go [a]barefoot and naked;

**4:10** [1]Lit *was a son of a night* [2]Lit *a son of a night* **4:11** [a]Jon 3:10 [b]Dt 1:39; Is 7:16 [c]Ps 36:6 [1]Lit *beasts, cattle*; cf. 3:7-8 ◆ **1:1** [a]2Pe 1:21 [b]Jer 26:18 [c]2Ki 15:5, 32-38; 2Chr 27:1-9; Is 1:1; Hos 1:1 [d]2Ki 16:1-20; 2Chr 28:1-27; Is 7:1-12 [e]2Ki 18:1-20; 2Chr 29:1-31 [1]The personal covenant name of God, a form of I AM WHO I AM, cf. Ex 3:14-15 **1:2** [a]Jer 6:19; 22:29 [b]Is 50:7 [1]Lit *them* **1:3** [a]Is 26:21 [b]Am 4:13 [1]Or *land* **1:4** [a]Ps 97:5; Is 64:1, 2; Na 1:5 **1:5** [a]Jer 2:19 [b]Is 7:9; Am 8:14 [c]2Chr 34:3, 4 [1]Lit *places* **1:6** [a]2Ki 19:25; Mic 3:12 [b]Jer 31:5; Am 5:11 [c]Lam 4:1 [d]Eze 13:14 **1:7** [a]Dt 9:21; 2Chr 34:7 [b]Dt 23:18; Is 23:17 **1:8** [a]Is 32:11

I must make a lament
like the [b]jackals
And a mourning
like the ostriches.
9 For her [a,1]wound is incurable,
For [b]it has come to Judah;
It has reached the [c]gate
of my people,
*Even* to Jerusalem.
10 [a]Tell it not in Gath,
Weep not at all.
At [1]Beth-le-aphrah roll
yourself in the dust.
11 [1]Pass on by, inhabitant
of [2]Shaphir,
in [a]shameful nakedness.
The inhabitant of [b,3]Zaanan
does not go out.
The lamentation of [4]Beth-ezel:
"He will take
from you its [5]support."
12 For the inhabitant of [1]Maroth
Writhes [a]*in waiting* for good
Because a [2]calamity has
come down from Yahweh
To the [b]gate of Jerusalem.
13 Harness the chariot
to the team of horses,
O inhabitant of [a]Lachish—
She was the beginning of sin
To the daughter of Zion—
Because in you were found
The [b]transgressions of Israel.
14 Therefore you will give
parting [a]gifts
On behalf of [1]Moresheth-gath;
The houses of [b,2]Achzib *will*
become a [c]deception
To the kings of Israel.
15 Moreover, I will bring on you
The one who takes possession,
O inhabitant of [a,1]Mareshah.
The glory of Israel will
enter [b]Adullam.
16 Make yourself [a]bald and
cut off your hair,
Because of the children
of your delight;
Extend your baldness
like the eagle,
For they will [b]go
from you into exile.

### *An Evil Time*

2 Woe to those who
[a]devise wickedness,
Who work out evil on their beds!
[b]When the light of the
morning *comes*, they do it,
For it is in the [c]power
of their hands.
2 And they [a]covet fields and
then [b]tear *them* away,
And houses, and take
*them* away.
And they [c]oppress
a man and his house,
A man and his inheritance.
3 Therefore thus says Yahweh,
"Behold, I am [a]devising against
this [b]family an evil *demise*
From which you [c]cannot
remove your necks;
And you will not
walk [d]haughtily,
For it will be an [e]evil time.

**1:8** [b]Is 13:21, 22 **1:9** [a]*Is 3:26; Jer 30:12, 15* [b]*2Ki 18:13; Is 8:7, 8* [c]Mic 1:12 [1]Lit *wounds are* ***1:10*** [a]*2Sa 1:20* [1]Lit *house of dust* **1:11** [a]Eze 23:29 [b]Jos 15:37 [1]Go into captivity [2]Lit *pleasantness* [3]Lit *going out* [4]Lit *house of removal* [5]Lit *standing place* **1:12** [a]Is 59:9-11; Jer 14:19 [b]Mic 1:9 [1]Lit *bitterness* [2]Lit *evil* **1:13** [a]Jos 10:3; 2Ki 14:19; Is 36:2 [b]Mic 1:5 **1:14** [a]2Ki 16:8 [b]Jos 15:44 [c]Jer 15:18 [1]Lit *possession of Gath* [2]Lit *deception* **1:15** [a]Jos 15:44 [b]Jos 12:15; 15:35; 2Sa 23:13 [1]Lit *to take possession* **1:16** [a]Is 22:12 [b]2Ki 17:6; Am 7:11, 17 ◆ **2:1** [a]Ps 36:4; Is 32:7; Na 1:11 [b]Hos 7:6, 7 [c]Ge 31:29; Dt 28:32; Pr 3:27 **2:2** [a]Jer 22:17; Am 8:4 [b]Is 5:8 [c]1Ki 21:1-15 **2:3** [a]Dt 28:48; Jer 18:11 [b]Jer 8:3; Am 3:1, 2 [c]Lam 1:14; 5:5 [d]Is 2:11, 12 [e]Am 5:13

4 "On that day they will [a]take
up against you a [1]taunt
And [b,2]utter a bitter
wailing *and* say,
'We are
completely [c]devastated!
He exchanges the portion
of my people;
How He removes it from me!
To the faithless one, He
[d]apportions our fields.'
5 "Therefore you will have
no one [a,1]stretching
a measuring line
For you by lot
in the assembly of Yahweh.

6 '[a]Do not speak, dripping
out *words*,' they say
*while* dripping out *words*.
*But if* [1]they do [b]not drip
out *words*
concerning these things,
[c]Dishonor will not be
turned back.
7 "Is it being said,
O house of Jacob:
'Is the Spirit
of Yahweh [a]impatient?
Are these His deeds?'
Do not My words [b]do good
To the one
[c]walking uprightly?
8 "[1]And recently My people have
arisen as an [a]enemy—
You [b]strip the [2]robe
off the garment
From [c]unsuspecting
passers-by,
*From* those returned from war.
9 "The women of My people
you [a]drive out,
Each *one* from her
pleasant house.
From her infants you take
My [b]splendor forever.
10 "Arise and go,
For this is no place [a]of rest
Because of the [b]uncleanness
that wreaks destruction,
A painful destruction.
11 "If a man walking
after wind and [a]lying
Had acted falsely
*and said*,
'I will speak, dripping out
*words* to you concerning
[b]wine and liquor,'
He would be one who drips
out *words as a* spokesman
to [c]this people.

12 "I will surely [a]assemble
all of you, Jacob;
I will surely gather the
[b]remnant of Israel.
I will put them together
like sheep in the fold;
Like a flock in the midst
of its pasture
They will be noisy
with men.
13 "The breaker goes up
before them;
They break out,
pass through the gate,
and go out by it.
So their king goes on
before them,
And Yahweh at their head."

**2:4** [a]Hab 2:6 [b]Jer 9:10, 17-21; Mic 1:8 [c]Is 6:11; 24:3; Jer 4:13 [d]Jer 6:12; 8:10 [1]Or *proverb* [2]Lit *lament*
**2:5** [a]Nu 34:13, 16-29; Dt 32:8; Jos 18:4, 10 [1]Lit *casting* **2:6** [a]Is 30:10; Am 2:12; 7:16 [b]Is 29:10; Mic 3:6
[c]Mic 6:16 [1]God's prophets **2:7** [a]Is 50:2; 59:1 [b]Ps 119:65, 68, 116; Jer 15:16 [c]Ps 15:2; 84:11 **2:8** [a]Jer 12:8
[b]Mic 3:2, 3; 7:2, 3 [c]Ps 120:6, 7 [1]Lit *And yesterday* [2]Or *ornaments* **2:9** [a]Jer 10:20 [b]Eze 39:21; Hab 2:14
**2:10** [a]Dt 12:9 [b]Ps 106:38 **2:11** [a]Jer 5:31 [b]Is 28:7 [c]Is 30:10, 11 **2:12** [a]Mic 4:6, 7 [b]Mic 5:7, 8; 7:18

### *Yahweh Will Not Answer*

3 And I said,
"[a]Hear now, heads of Jacob
And rulers of the
house of Israel.
Is it not for you
to [b]know justice?
2 "You who hate good
and love evil,
Who [a]tear off their
skin from them
And their flesh
from their bones,
3 And who [a]eat the flesh
of my people,
Strip off their skin from them,
Break their bones,
And [b]spread *them* out
as for the pot
And as meat in a caldron."
4 Then they will [a]cry
out to Yahweh,
But He will not answer them.
Instead, He will [b]hide His face
from them at that time
Because they have
[c]practiced evil deeds.

5 Thus says Yahweh concerning the
prophets who [a]lead my people astray;
When they have *something*
to bite with their teeth,
They [b]call out, "Peace,"
But against him who puts
nothing in their mouths,
They set *themselves*
apart for war.
6 Therefore *it will be* [a]night
for you—without vision,
And darkness for you—
*without divination.*
The [b]sun will go down
on the prophets,
And the day will grow
black over them.
7 The seers will be [a]ashamed,
And the [b]diviners will
be humiliated.
Indeed, they will all
[c]cover *their* [1]mouths
Because there is [d]no
answer from God.
8 On the other hand [a]I am
filled with power—
With the Spirit of Yahweh—
And with justice and might
To [b]declare to Jacob
his transgression,
Even to Israel his sin.
9 Now hear this, [a]heads
of the house of Jacob
And rulers of the
house of Israel,
Who [b]abhor justice
And twist everything
that is straight,
10 Who [a]build Zion
with bloodshed
And Jerusalem
with violent injustice.
11 Her heads pronounce
[a]judgment for a bribe,
And her [b]priests instruct
for a price,
And her prophets
divine for money.
Yet they lean
on Yahweh saying,
"[c]Is not Yahweh in our midst?
Evil will not come upon us."
12 *Therefore*, on account of you
[a]Zion will be plowed as a field;

◆ **3:1** [a]Is 1:10; Mic 3:9 [b]Ps 82:1-5; Jer 5:5 **3:2** [a]Ps 53:4; Eze 22:27; Mic 2:8; 7:2, 3 **3:3** [a]Ps 14:4; 27:2; Zep 3:3 [b]Eze 11:3, 6, 7 **3:4** [a]Ps 18:41; Pr 1:28; Is 1:15; Jer 11:11 [b]Dt 31:17; Is 59:2 [c]Is 3:11; Mic 7:13 **3:5** [a]Is 3:12; 9:15, 16; Jer 14:14, 15 [b]Jer 6:14 **3:6** [a]Is 8:20-22; 29:10-12 [b]Is 59:10 **3:7** [a]Zec 13:4 [b]Is 44:25; 47:12-14 [c]Mic 7:16 [d]1Sa 28:6; Mic 3:4 [1]Lit *mustache* **3:8** [a]Is 61:1, 2; Jer 1:18 [b]Is 58:1 **3:9** [a]Mic 1:1 [b]Ps 58:1, 2; Is 1:23 **3:10** [a]Jer 22:13, 17; Hab 2:12 **3:11** [a]Is 1:23; Mic 7:3 [b]Jer 6:13 [c]Is 48:2 **3:12** [a]Jer 26:18

[b]Jerusalem will become
a heap of ruins,
And the [c]mountain of
the house *of God will become*
high places of a forest.

### *The Law Will Go Forth from Zion*

4 Now it will be
that in the [a]last days
The [b]mountain of the house
of Yahweh
Will be established [1]as the
head of the mountains,
And will be lifted up
above the hills,
And the [c]peoples will
stream to it.
2 [a]And many nations
will come and say,
"[b]Come and let us go up
to the mountain of Yahweh
And to the house
of the God of Jacob,
That [c]He may instruct
us from His ways
And that we may walk
in His paths."
For [d]from Zion will
go forth the law,
And the word of Yahweh
from Jerusalem.
3 And He will [a]judge
between many peoples
And will render decisions
for mighty, [1]distant nations.
And they will hammer their
swords [b]into plowshares
And their spears
into pruning hooks;
Nation will not lift up
sword against nation,
And never again will
they learn war.
4 And each of them will
[a]sit under his vine
And under his fig tree,
With [b]no one to make
*them* tremble,
For the [c]mouth of Yahweh
of hosts has spoken.
5 Though all the peoples walk
Each in the [a]name of his god,
As for us, [b]we will walk
In the name of [c]Yahweh our
God forever and ever.

6 "In that day," declares Yahweh,
"I will assemble the [a]lame
And [b]gather the banished,
Even those *upon* whom I
have brought calamity.
7 "I will make the lame
a [a]remnant
And the outcasts
a mighty nation,
And [b]Yahweh will reign
over them in Mount Zion
From now on and forever.
8 "And as for you, [a,1]tower
of the flock,
[2]Hill of the daughter of Zion,
To you it will come—
Even the [b]former
dominion will come,
The kingdom of the
daughter of Jerusalem.

9 "Now, why do you [a]make
a loud shout?

**3:12** [b]Ps 79:1; Jer 9:11 [c]Mic 4:1 ◆ **4:1** [a]Is 2:2-4; Da 2:28; 10:14; Hos 3:5 [b]Eze 43:12; Mic 3:12; Zec 8:3 [c]Ps 22:27; 86:9; Jer 3:17 [1]Lit *on* **4:2** [a]Zec 2:11; 14:16 [b]Is 2:3; Jer 31:6 [c]Ps 25:8, 9, 12; Is 54:13 [d]Is 42:1-4; Zec 14:8, 9 **4:3** [a]Is 2:4; 11:3-5 [b]Joel 3:10 [1]Lit *at a distance* **4:4** [a]1Ki 4:25; Zec 3:10 [b]Lv 26:6; Jer 30:10 [c]Is 1:20; 40:5 **4:5** [a]2Ki 17:29 [b]Zec 10:12 [c]Jos 24:15; Is 26:8, 13 **4:6** [a]Zep 3:19 [b]Ps 147:2; Eze 34:13, 16; 37:21 **4:7** [a]Mic 5:7, 8; 7:18 [b]Is 24:23 **4:8** [a]Ps 48:3, 12; 61:3; Mic 2:12 [b]Is 1:26; Zec 9:10 [1]Heb *Migdal-eder* [2]Heb *Ophel* **4:9** [a]Jer 8:19

Is there no king among you,
Or has your
[b]counselor perished,
That writhing has taken
hold of you like a
woman in childbirth?
10 “[a]Writhe and labor
to give birth,
Daughter of Zion,
Like a woman in childbirth;
For now you will [b]go
out of the city,
Dwell in the field,
And go to Babylon.
[c]There you will be delivered;
[d]There Yahweh will
redeem you
From the hand
of your enemies.
11 “But now [a]many nations
have been assembled
against you
Who say, ‘Let her be polluted,
And let our eyes behold
Zion *in triumph*.’
12 “But they do not [a]know the
thoughts of Yahweh,
And they do not understand
His counsel;
For He has gathered
them like sheaves
to the threshing floor.
13 “Arise and [a]thresh,
daughter of Zion,
For your horn I will
make iron,
And your hoofs I will
make bronze,
That you may [b]pulverize
many peoples,
That you may [c]devote
to Yahweh their greedy
gain unto destruction
And their wealth to the
Lord of all the earth.

### *The Ruler Will Come from Bethlehem*

5 “[1]Now muster yourselves in
troops, daughter of troops;
[2]They have laid siege
against us;
With a rod they will [a]strike the
judge of Israel on the cheek.
2 “[1]But as for [a]you,
Bethlehem Ephrathah,
*Too* little to be
among the clans of Judah,
From [b]you One will go forth
for Me to be [c]ruler in Israel.
[2]His goings forth are
[d]from everlasting,
From the ancient days.”
3 Therefore He will [a]give
them *up* until the time
When she [b]who is
in childbirth has borne
a child.
Then the [c]remainder
of His brothers
Will return to the
sons of Israel.
4 And He will stand and
[a]shepherd *His flock*
In the strength of Yahweh,
In the majesty of the name
of Yahweh His God.
And they will [1]remain
Because [2]at that time
He will be great
To the [b]ends of the earth.

---

**4:9** [b]Is 3:1-3 **4:10** [a]Mic 5:3 [b]2Ki 20:18; Hos 2:14 [c]Is 43:14; 45:13; Mic 7:8-12 [d]Is 48:20; 52:9-12
**4:11** [a]Is 5:25-30; 17:12-14 **4:12** [a]Ps 147:19, 20 **4:13** [a]Is 41:15 [b]Jer 51:20-23 [c]Is 60:9 ◆ **5:1** [a]1Ki 22:24; Job 16:10; Lam 3:30 [1]Ch 4:14 in Heb [2]Lit *He has* **5:2** [a]Ge 35:19; 48:7; Ru 4:11; Mt 2:6 [b]Is 11:1; Lk 2:4; Jn 7:42 [c]Jer 30:21; Zec 9:9 [d]Ps 102:25; Pr 8:22, 23; Hab 1:12 [1]Ch 5:1 in Heb [2]Or *His appearances are from long ago, from days of old* **5:3** [a]Hos 11:8; Mic 4:10; 7:13 [b]Mic 4:9, 10 [c]Is 10:20-22; Mic 5:7, 8
**5:4** [a]Is 40:11; 49:9; Eze 34:13-15, 23, 24; Mic 7:14 [b]Is 45:22; 52:10 [1]Or *live* in safety [2]Lit *now*

5 And this One [a]will be peace.

When the [b]Assyrian
enters our land,
When he treads
on our [1]citadels,
Then we will raise
against him
Seven shepherds and
eight princes of men.
6 And they will [a]shepherd
the land of Assyria
with the sword,
The land of [b]Nimrod
at its entrances;
And He will [c]deliver *us*
from the Assyrian
When he enters our land
And when he treads
within our borders.

7 Then the [a]remnant of Jacob
Will be among many peoples
Like [b]dew from Yahweh,
Like [c]showers on vegetation
Which do not hope for man
Or wait for the sons of men.
8 Then the remnant of Jacob
Will be among the nations,
Among many peoples
[a]Like a lion among the
beasts of the forest,
Like a young lion
among flocks of sheep,
Which, if it passes through,
[b]Tramples down and [c]tears,
And there is [d]none to deliver.
9 Your hand will be [a]raised up
against your adversaries,
And all your enemies
will be cut off.

10 "And it will be in that day,"
declares Yahweh,
"[a]That I will cut off your
[b]horses from among you
And destroy your chariots.
11 "And I will cut off the
[a]cities of your land
And pull down
all your [b]fortifications.
12 "And I will cut off [a]sorceries
from your hand,
And you will have
soothsaying no more.
13 "[a]And I will cut off your
graven images
And your *sacred* pillars
from among you
So that you will no
longer worship
The work of your hands.
14 "And I will uproot your
[a,1]Asherim from
among you
And [2]eradicate your cities.
15 "And I will [a]execute vengeance
in anger and wrath
On the nations
which have not [1]listened."

### *Yahweh's Case Against His People*

6 [1]Listen now to what Yahweh is
saying,
"Arise, plead your case
[2]before the mountains,
And let the hills [1]listen
to your voice.

**5:5** [a]Is 9:6; Lk 2:14; Eph 2:14; Col 1:20 [b]Is 8:7, 8; 10:24-27 [1]Or *palaces* **5:6** [a]Na 2:11-13; Zep 2:13 [b]Ge 10:8-11 [c]Is 14:25; 37:36, 37 **5:7** [a]Mic 2:12; 4:7; 5:3; 7:18 [b]Dt 32:2; Ps 110:3; Hos 14:5 [c]Ps 72:6; Is 44:3 **5:8** [a]Ge 49:9; Nu 24:9 [b]Ps 44:5; Is 41:15, 16; Mic 4:13; Zec 10:5 [c]Hos 5:14 [d]Ps 50:22 **5:9** [a]Ps 10:12; 21:8; Is 26:11 **5:10** [a]Zec 9:10 [b]Dt 17:16; Is 2:7; Hos 14:3 **5:11** [a]Is 1:7; 6:11 [b]Is 2:12-17; Hos 10:14; Am 5:9 **5:12** [a]Dt 18:10-12; Is 2:6; 8:19 **5:13** [a]Is 2:18; 17:8; Eze 6:9 **5:14** [a]Ex 34:13; Is 17:8; 27:9 [1]Wooden symbols of a female deity [2]Or *destroy* **5:15** [a]Is 1:24; 65:12 [1]Or *heard*, cf. Mic 1:2; 3:1, 9; 6:9; 7:7
◆ **6:1** [1]Or *hear*, cf. Mic 1:2; 3:1, 9; 6:9; 7:7 [2]Lit *with*

2 “[1]Listen, you mountains,
to the case of Yahweh,
And you enduring
[a]foundations of the earth,
Because [b]Yahweh has a case
against His people;
Even with Israel He
will reprove.
3 “[a]My people, [b]what have
I done to you,
And [c]how have I wearied
you? Answer Me.
4 “Indeed, I [a]brought you
up from the land of Egypt
And [b]ransomed you
from the house of slavery,
And I sent before you [c]Moses,
Aaron, and [d]Miriam.
5 “My people, remember now
What [a]Balak king
of Moab counseled
And what Balaam son
of Beor answered him,
*And* from [b]Shittim
to [c]Gilgal,
So [1]that you might know
the [d]righteous acts
of Yahweh.”

### *What Yahweh Requires*

6 [a]With what shall I come
before Yahweh
*And* bow myself
before the God on high?
Shall I come before Him
with [b]burnt offerings,
With yearling calves?
7 Is Yahweh pleased
with [a]thousands of rams,
With ten thousand
rivers of oil?
Shall I give my [b]firstborn
*for* my transgression,
The fruit of my body
for the sin of my soul?
8 He has [a]told you, O man,
what is good;
And [b]what does Yahweh
require of you
But to [c]do justice, to [d]love
lovingkindness,
And to walk [e,1]humbly
with your God?

9 The voice of Yahweh will
call to the city—
And it is sound wisdom
to fear Your name:
“Hear, O tribe. Who even
has appointed [1]its time?
10 “Is there yet a man
in the wicked house,
*Along with* treasures
of [a]wickedness,
And a [b,1]short measure
*which is* cursed?
11 “Can I purify wicked [a]scales
And a bag of deceptive weights?
12 “For the rich men of [1]*the* city
are full of [a]violence,
And her inhabitants
speak [b]lies,
And their [c]tongue is
deceitful in their mouth.
13 “So also I will make *you*
[a]sick, striking you down,
[b]Desolating *you* because
of your sins.

**6:2** [a]*2Sa 22:16; Ps 104:5* [b]*Is 1:18;* Hos 4:1; 12:2 [1]Or *hear*, cf. Mic 1:2; 3:1, 9; 6:9; 7:7 **6:3** [a]Ps 50:7 [b]Jer 2:5 [c]Is 43:22, 23 **6:4** [a]Ex 12:51; 20:2 [b]Dt 7:8 [c]Ex 4:10-16; Ps 77:20 [d]Ex 15:20 **6:5** [a]Nu 22:5, 6 [b]Nu 25:1; Jos 2:1; 3:1 [c]Jos 4:19; 5:9, 10 [d]1Sa 12:7; Is 1:27 [1]Lit *to know* **6:6** [a]Ps 40:6-8 [b]Ps 51:16, 17 **6:7** [a]Ps 50:9; Is 1:1; 40:16 [b]Lv 18:21; 20:1-5; 2Ki 16:3; Jer 7:31 **6:8** [a]Dt 30:15 [b]Dt 10:12 [c]Is 56:1; Jer 22:3 [d]Hos 6:6 [e]Is 57:15; 66:2 [1]Or *circumspectly* **6:9** [1]Lit *it* **6:10** [a]Jer 5:26, 27; Am 3:10 [b]Eze 45:9, 10; Am 8:5 [1]Lit *shrunken ephah* **6:11** [a]Lv 19:36; Hos 12:7 **6:12** [a]Is 1:23; 5:7; Am 6:3, 4; Mic 2:1, 2 [b]Jer 9:2-6, 8; Hos 7:13; Am 2:4 [c]Is 3:8 [1]Lit *her* **6:13** [a]Mic 1:9 [b]Is 1:7; 6:11

14 "You will eat, but you will
[a]not be satisfied,
And your [1]vileness will
be in your midst.
And you will *try to* remove
*something for safekeeping,*
But you will [b]not cause
*anything* to escape,
And that which you do
have escape, I will
give to the sword.
15 "You will sow but you
will [a]not reap.
You will tread the olive but will
not anoint yourself with oil;
And the grapes, but you
will [b]not drink wine.
16 "The statutes of [a]Omri
And all the works of the
house of [b]Ahab are kept;
And in their counsels you [c]walk.
Therefore I will give you up
as [d]an object of horror
And [1]your inhabitants
as an [e]object of hissing,
And you will bear the
[f]reproach of My people."

### *There Is No Upright Person*

7 Woe is me! For I am
Like the fruit pickers,
like the [a]grape gatherers.
There is not a cluster
of grapes to eat,
*Or* a [b]first-ripe fig
*which* my soul desires.
2 The [1]holy one has [a]perished
from the land,
And there is no upright
*person* among men.
All of them lie in wait
for [b]bloodshed;
Each of them hunts the
other with a [c]net.
3 Concerning evil, both
hands do it [a]well.
The prince asks, also the
judge, for a [b]payment,
And a great man speaks
the craving of his soul;
So they weave it together.
4 The best of them is
like a [a]briar,
The most upright
like a [b]thorn hedge.
The day when you post
your watchmen,
Your [c]punishment will come.
[1]At that time their
[d]panic will happen.
5 Do not [a]believe
in a neighbor;
Do not have confidence
in a close companion.
From her who lies
in your bosom
Guard the openings
of your mouth.
6 For [a]son treats father
as a wicked fool;
Daughter rises up
against her mother,
Daughter-in-law
against her mother-in-law;
[b]A man's enemies are the men
of his own household.

### *Yahweh Is a Light for Me*

7 But as for me, I will [a]watch
expectantly for Yahweh;

---

**6:14** [a]Is 9:20 [b]Is 30:6 [1]Or possibly *garbage, excreta* **6:15** [a]Dt 28:38-40; Jer 12:13 [b]Am 5:11; Zep 1:13 **6:16** [a]1Ki 16:25, 26 [b]1Ki 16:29-33 [c]Jer 7:24 [d]Jer 18:16; Mic 6:13 [e]Jer 19:8; 25:9, 18; 29:18 [f]Ps 44:13; Jer 51:51; Hos 12:14 [1]Lit *her* ◆ **7:1** [a]Is 24:13 [b]Is 28:4; Hos 9:10 **7:2** [a]Is 57:1 [b]Is 59:7; Mic 3:10 [c]Jer 5:26; Hos 5:1 [1]Or *one of lovingkindness* **7:3** [a]Pr 4:16, 17 [b]Am 5:12; Mic 3:11 **7:4** [a]Eze 2:6; 28:24 [b]Na 1:10 [c]Is 10:3; Hos 9:7 [d]Is 22:5 [1]Lit *Now* **7:5** [a]Jer 9:4 **7:6** [a]Mt 10:21, 35; Lk 12:53 [b]Mt 10:36 **7:7** [a]Hab 2:1

I will [b]wait for the God
of my salvation.
My [c]God will hear me.

8 [a]Do not be glad over me,
O [b]my enemy.
Though I fall I will [c]rise;
Though I inhabit
the darkness, Yahweh
is a [d]light for me.

9 I will bear the rage of Yahweh
Because I have sinned
against Him,
Until He [a]pleads my case
and does justice for me.
He will bring me out
to the [b]light,
*And* I will see
His [c,1]righteousness.

10 Then my enemy will see,
And shame will cover
her who [a]said to me,
"Where is Yahweh your God?"
My eyes will look on her;
[1]At that time she will [2]be
[b]trampled down
Like mire of the streets.

11 *It will be* a day
for [a]building your walls.
On that day your boundary
will be extended.

12 It *will be* a day when [1]they
will [a]come to you
From Assyria and the
cities of Egypt,
From Egypt even
to the [2]River,
Even from sea to sea and
mountain to mountain.

13 And the earth will become
[a]desolate because of
her inhabitants,
On account of the [b]fruit
of their deeds.

14 [a]Shepherd Your people
with Your [b]scepter,
The flock of Your inheritance
Which dwells by itself
in the forest,
In the midst of [1]a
fruitful orchard.
Let them feed in [c]Bashan
and Gilead
[d]As in the ancient days.

15 "As in the days when you
came out from the
land of Egypt,
I will show [a,1]you
wondrous deeds."

16 Nations [a]will see and
be ashamed
Of all their might.
They will [b]put *their* hand
on *their* mouth;
Their ears will be deaf.

17 They will [a]lick the dust
like a serpent,
Like [b]crawling things
of the earth.
They will come [c]trembling
out of their [1]fortresses;
To Yahweh our God they
will come in [d]dread,
And they will be afraid
before You.

18 Who is a God like You,
who [a]forgives iniquity

***7:7*** [b]*Ps 130:5; Is 25:9* [c]*Ps 4:3* ***7:8*** [a]*Pr 24:17; Ob 12* [b]Mic 7:10 [c]Am 9:11 [d]Is 9:2 **7:9** [a]Jer 50:34 [b]Ps 37:6; Is 42:7, 16 [c]Is 46:13; 56:1 [1]Right dealing **7:10** [a]Joel 2:17 [b]Is 51:23; Zec 10:5 [1]Lit *Now* [2]Lit *become a trampled* place **7:11** [a]Is 54:11; Am 9:11 **7:12** [a]Is 19:23-25; 60:4, 9 [1]Lit *he* [2]The Euphrates River **7:13** [a]Jer 25:11; Mic 6:13 [b]Is 3:10, 11; Mic 3:4 **7:14** [a]Ps 95:7; Is 40:11; 49:10; Mic 5:4 [b]Lv 27:32; Ps 23:4 [c]Jer 50:19 [d]Am 9:11 [1]Or *Carmel* **7:15** [a]Ex 3:20; 34:10; Ps 78:12 [1]Lit *him* **7:16** [a]Is 26:11 [b]Mic 3:7 **7:17** [a]Ps 72:9; Is 49:23 [b]Dt 32:24 [c]Ps 18:45 [d]Is 25:3; 59:19 [1]Lit *fastnesses* **7:18** [a]Ex 34:7, 9; Is 43:25

And passes over the
transgression of the
[b]remnant of His
inheritance?
He does not [c]hold fast
to His anger forever
Because He [d]delights
in lovingkindness.
19 He will again have
compassion on us;
[a]He will subdue our iniquities.
And You will [b]cast
all [1]their sins
Into the depths of the sea.
20 You will give [a,1]truth to Jacob
*And* lovingkindness
to Abraham,
Which You [b]swore
to our fathers
From the days of old.

*The Book of*
# NAHUM

### *Yahweh's Wrath Against Nineveh*

1 The [a,1]oracle of [b]Nineveh. The
book of the vision of Nahum the
Elkoshite.

א *Aleph*

2 A [a]jealous and avenging
God is [1]Yahweh;
Yahweh is [b]avenging
and [2]wrathful.
Yahweh is [c]avenging
against His adversaries,
And He keeps *His anger*
for His enemies.
3 Yahweh is [a]slow to anger
and great in power,
And Yahweh will by no
means leave
*the guilty* unpunished.

ב *Beth*

In [b]whirlwind and
storm is His way,
And [c]clouds are the dust
beneath His feet.

ג *Gimel*

4 He [a]rebukes the sea
and makes it dry;
He dries up all the rivers.
[b]Bashan and Carmel
languish;
The blossoms
of Lebanon languish.

ה *He*

5 Mountains [a]quake
because of Him,

ו *Vav*

And the hills [b]melt;
Indeed the earth is [c]upheaved
by His presence,
The [d]world and all
the inhabitants in it.

ז *Zayin*

6 [a]Who can stand
before His indignation?
Who can endure
the [b]burning
of His anger?

---

**7:18** [b]Mic 2:12; 4:7; 5:7, 8 [c]Ps 103:8, 9, 13 [d]Jer 32:41 **7:19** [a]Jer 50:20 [b]Is 38:17; 43:25; Jer 31:34 [1]Several ancient versions *our* **7:20** [a]Ge 24:27; 32:10 [b]Dt 7:8, 12 [1]Or *faithfulness* ◆ **1:1** [a]Is 13:1; 19:1; Jer 23:33, 34; Hab 1:1; Zec 9:1; Mal 1:1 [b]2Ki 19:36; Jon 1:2; Na 2:8; Zep 2:13 [1]Or *burden* **1:2** [a]Ex 20:5; Jos 24:19 [b]Dt 32:35, 41 [c]Ps 94:1 [1]The personal covenant name of God, a form of I AM WHO I AM, cf. Ex 3:14-15 [2]Lit *a possessor of wrath* **1:3** [a]Ex 34:6, 7; Ne 9:17; Ps 103:8 [b]Ex 19:16; Is 29:6 [c]Ps 104:3; Is 19:1 **1:4** [a]Jos 3:15, 16; Ps 106:9; Is 50:2; Mt 8:26 [b]Is 33:9 **1:5** [a]Ex 19:18; 2Sa 22:8; Ps 18:7 [b]Mic 1:4 [c]Is 24:1, 20 [d]Ps 98:7 **1:6** [a]Jer 10:10; Mal 3:2 [b]Is 13:13

ח *Heth*
His [c]wrath is poured
out like fire,
And the [d]rocks are torn
down by Him.
ט *Teth*
7 Yahweh is [a]good,
A strong defense
in the day of distress,
י *Yodh*
And [b]He knows those who
take refuge in Him.
8 But with an [a]overflowing flood
כ *Kaph*
He will make a complete
destruction of [1]its place
And will pursue His
enemies into [b]darkness.

9 Whatever you [a]devise
against Yahweh,
He will make a [b]complete
destruction of it.
Distress will not rise up twice.
10 Like tangled [a]thorns,
And like those who are
[b]drunken with their drink,
They are [c]consumed
As stubble fully dried up.
11 From you has gone forth
One who [a]devised evil
against Yahweh,
A [b,1]vile counselor.
12 Thus says Yahweh,
"Though they are at full
*strength* and likewise many,
Even so, they will be [a]cut
off and pass away.
Though I have afflicted you,
I will afflict you [b]no longer.
13 "So now, I will [a]break his
yoke bar from upon you,
And I will break your
bands apart."

14 And Yahweh has commanded
concerning [1]you:
"[2]There will [a]no longer be
seed from your name.
From the house of your gods,
I will cut off [b]graven image
and molten image.
I will prepare your [c]grave,
For you are contemptible."

15 [1]Behold, [a]on the mountains
the feet of him who
proclaims good news,
Who [2]announces peace!
[b]Celebrate your feasts,
O Judah;
Pay your vows.
For [c]never again will the [3]vile
one pass through you;
He is [d]cut off completely.

### *Yahweh's Destruction of Nineveh*

2 [1]The one who [a]scatters has
come up against [2]you.
Guard the fortification,
watch the road;
Strengthen your loins,
[3]instill *your* power
with exceeding courage.
2 For Yahweh will restore
the [a]majesty of Jacob

**1:6** [c]Is 66:15 [d]1Ki 19:11 **1:7** [a]*Ps 25:8; 37:39, 40; Jer 33:11* [b]Ps 1:6; Jn 10:14; 2Ti 2:19 **1:8** [a]Is 28:2, 17f; *Am 8:8* [b]*Is 13:9, 10* [1]*Nineveh's* **1:9** [a]Ps 2:1; Na 1:11 [b]Is 28:22 **1:10** [a]2Sa 23:6; Mic 7:4 [b]Is 56:12; Na 3:11 [c]Is 5:24; 10:17; Mal 4:1 **1:11** [a]Is 10:7-11; Na 1:9 [b]Eze 11:2 [1]Or *worthless*; Heb *Belial* **1:12** [a]Is 10:16-19, 33, 34 [b]Lam 3:31, 32 **1:13** [a]Is 9:4; 10:27; Jer 2:20 **1:14** [a]Job 18:17; Ps 109:13; Is 14:22 [b]Is 46:1, 2; Mic 5:13, 14 [c]Eze 32:22, 23 [1]The king of Nineveh [2]Lit *No more of your name will be sown* **1:15** [a]Is 40:9; 52:7; Ro 10:15 [b]Lv 23:2, 4 [c]Is 52:1; Joel 3:17 [d]Is 29:7, 8 [1]Ch 2:1 in Heb [2]Or *causes peace to be heard* [3]Or *worthless*; Heb *Belial* ◆ **2:1** [a]Jer 51:20-23 [1]Ch 2:2 in Heb [2]Lit *your face* [3]Or *make your power courageous* **2:2** [a]Is 60:15

[b]Like the majesty of Israel,
Even though those who
empty *them* have emptied
them to destruction
And [c]ruined their
vine branches.

3 The shields of [1]his mighty
men are *colored* red,
The valiant men are
dressed in [a,2]scarlet,
The chariots are *enveloped*
in [3]flashing steel
[4]When he is set up *to march*,
And the cypress [b]*spears*
are brandished.
4 The [a]chariots race madly
in the streets;
They rush wildly
in the [1]squares;
Their appearance is
like torches;
They dash to and fro
like lightning flashes.
5 He remembers his
[a]mighty ones;
They [b]stumble
in their march;
They hurry to her wall,
And the [1]mantelet is set up.
6 The gates of the rivers
are opened,
And the palace is melted away.
7 So it stands fixed:
She is exiled, she is
carried away,
And her maidservants
are [a]moaning like the
sound of doves,
[b]Beating on their hearts.
8 Though Nineveh *was*
like a pool of water
throughout her days,
Now they are fleeing;
"Stand! Stand!"
But [a]no one [1]turns back.
9 Plunder the silver!
Plunder the [a]gold!
And there is no limit
to the treasure—
[1]Wealth from every kind
of desirable object.
10 She is [a]emptied! Yes, she is
emptied out and eviscerated!
[b]Hearts are melting and
knees knocking!
Also anguish is in all *their* loins,
And all their [c]faces [1]turn pale!
11 Where is the den of the lions
And the feeding place
of the [a]young lions,
Where the lion, lioness,
and lion's cub prowled,
With nothing to make
*them* tremble?
12 The lion tore enough
for its cubs
And strangled *enough*
for its lionesses
And filled its lairs
with torn up prey
And its dens
with torn up flesh.

13 "Behold, [a]I am against you,"
declares Yahweh of hosts. "And I will
[b]burn up her chariots in smoke, and
a sword will devour your young lions;
and I will [c]cut off your prey from the
land, and no longer will the voice of
your messengers be heard."

---

**2:2** [b]Eze 37:21-23 [c]Ps 80:12, 13 **2:3** [a]Eze 23:14, 15 [b]Job 39:23 [1]Those attacking Nineveh [2]Or *crimson*, cf. Lam 4:5 [3]Lit *fire of steel* [4]Lit *On the day of his preparation* **2:4** [a]Is 66:15; Jer 4:13; Eze 26:10; Na 3:2, 3 [1]Lit *broad places* **2:5** [a]Na 3:18 [b]Jer 46:12 [1]Lit *covering* (used in a siege) **2:7** [a]Is 38:14; 59:11 [b]Is 32:12 **2:8** [a]Jer 46:5; 47:3 [1]Lit *gathers* **2:9** [a]Rev 18:12, 16 [1]Lit *Glory* **2:10** [a]Is 24:1; 34:10-13; Na 2:2 [b]Ps 22:14; Is 13:7, 8; Eze 21:7 [c]Joel 2:6 [1]Lit *gather* their *radiance* **2:11** [a]Is 5:29 **2:13** [a]Jer 21:13; Eze 5:8; Na 3:5 [b]Jos 11:6, 9; Ps 46:9 [c]Is 49:24, 25; Na 3:1

### *Woe to Nineveh*

3 [a]Woe to the city of
[1]bloodshed, completely full
of deception *and* pillage;
*Her* prey never departs.
2 The [a]sound of the whip,
And the sound of the
rumbling of the wheel,
Galloping horses,
And [1]bounding chariots!
3 Horsemen charging,
And swords flaming, and
[a]spears flashing,
[b]Many slain, a mass
of corpses,
And [c]there is no end
to dead bodies—
They stumble
over [1]the dead bodies!
4 *All* because of the [a]many
harlotries of the harlot,
The charming one,
the [b]mistress of sorceries,
Who [c]sells nations
by her harlotries
And families by her sorceries.
5 "Behold, [a]I am against you,"
declares Yahweh of hosts;
"And I will [b]uncover your
skirts over your face
And [c]show to the nations
your nakedness
And to the kingdoms
your disgrace.
6 "I will [a]throw detestable
*filth* on you
And [b]display you
as a wicked fool
And set you up as a [c]spectacle.
7 "And it will be that all
who see you
Will flee from you and say,
'Nineveh is devastated!
[a]Who will console her?'
Where will I seek
comforters for you?"

8 Are you better
than [a,1]No-amon,
Which sits along the
[b]waters of the Nile,
With water surrounding her,
Whose rampart *was* [2]the sea,
Whose wall *consisted*
of [2]the sea?
9 [a,1]Ethiopia was *her* might,
And Egypt too, without end.
[b]Put and [c]Lubim were
among [2]her helpers.
10 Yet she [a]became an exile;
She went into captivity;
Also her [b]infants were
dashed to pieces
[c]At the head of every street;
They [d]cast lots for her
honorable men,
And all her great men were
bound with fetters.
11 You too will become [a]drunk;
You will be [b]hidden.
You too will search for a strong
defense from the enemy.
12 All your fortifications are [a]fig
trees with [b,1]ripe fruit—
When shaken, they fall
into the eater's mouth.

---

◆ **3:1** [a]Eze 24:6, 9 [1]Or *blood,* cf. Eze 22:2; 24:6 ***3:2*** [a]*Job 39:22-25;* Jer 47:3; Na 2:3, 4 [1]Lit *skipping* ***3:3*** [a]*Hab 3:11* [b]*Is 34:3; 66:16* [c]Is 37:36; Eze 39:4 [1]Lit *their* **3:4** [a]Is 23:17; Eze 16:25-29; Rev 17:1, 2 [b]Is 47:9, 12, 13 [c]Rev 18:3 **3:5** [a]Jer 50:31; Eze 26:3; Na 2:13 [b]Is 47:2, 3; Jer 13:26 [c]Eze 16:37 **3:6** [a]Job 9:31 [b]Job 30:8; Mal 2:9 [c]Is 14:16; Jer 51:37 **3:7** [a]Is 51:19; Jer 15:5 **3:8** [a]Jer 46:25; Eze 30:14-16 [b]Is 19:6-8 [1]The city of Amon: Thebes [2]The Nile **3:9** [a]Is 20:5 [b]Jer 46:9; Eze 27:10; 30:5; 38:5 [c]2Chr 12:3; 16:8 [1]Or *Cush*, cf. Ge 10:6 [2]Lit *your* **3:10** [a]Is 19:4; 20:4 [b]Ps 137:9; Is 13:16; Hos 13:16 [c]Lam 2:19 [d]Joel 3:3; Ob 11 **3:11** [a]Is 49:26; Jer 25:27; Na 1:10 [b]Is 2:10, 19; Hos 10:8 **3:12** [a]Rev 6:13 [b]Is 28:4 [1]Lit *first fruits*

13 Behold, your people are
[a]women in your midst!
The gates of your land
are [b]opened wide
to your enemies;
Fire consumes your
gate bars.
14 [a]Draw for yourself
water for the siege!
[b]Strengthen your
fortifications!
Go into the clay and
tread the mortar!
[1]Take hold of the brick mold!
15 There, [a]fire will consume you;
The sword will cut you down;
It will [b]consume you
as the locust *does*.

Multiply yourself
like the creeping locust,
Multiply yourself like the
swarming locust.
16 You have increased your
[a]traders more than the
stars of heaven—
The creeping locust
[1]strips and flies away.
17 Your [a,1]guardsmen are
like the swarming locust.
Your [b]marshals are
like a locust-swarm
Encamping in the stone
walls on a cold day.
The sun rises, and
they flee,
And the place where they
are is not known.
18 Your shepherds are [a]sleeping,
O [b]king of Assyria;
Your [c]mighty ones are
[1]lying down.
Your people are [d]scattered
on the mountains,
And there is no one
to regather *them*.
19 There is [a]no relief
for your breakdown,
Your [b]wound is incurable.
All who hear the
report about you
Will [c]clap *their* hands
over you,
For on whom has
not your evil
passed continually?

**3:13** [a]Is 19:16; Jer 50:37; 51:30 [b]Is 45:1, 2; Na 2:6 **3:14** [a]2Chr 32:3, 4 [b]Na 2:1 [1]Or *strengthen*, cf. 3:14a **3:15** [a]Is 66:15, 16; Na 2:13; 3:13 [b]Joel 1:4 **3:16** [a]Is 23:8 [1]Strips vegetation; or *molts* **3:17** [a]Rev 9:7 [b]Jer 51:27 [1]Or *officials* **3:18** [a]Ps 76:5, 6; Is 56:10; Jer 51:57 [b]Jer 50:18 [c]Na 2:5 [d]1Ki 22:17; Is 13:14 [1]Lit *dwelling* **3:19** [a]Jer 46:11; Mic 1:9 [b]Jer 30:12 [c]Job 27:23; Lam 2:15

*The Book of*

# HABAKKUK

### *Habakkuk Calls for Help*

1 The [a,1]oracle which Habakkuk the
prophet beheld.
2 [a]How long, O [1]Yahweh,
will I call for help,
And You will not hear?
I cry out to You, "Violence!"
Yet You do [b]not save.
3 Why do You make me
[a]see wickedness
And cause *me* to look
on trouble?
Indeed, [b]devastation and
violence are before me;
[c]And there is strife, and
contention is lifted up.
4 Therefore the [a]law is [1]ignored,
And justice never comes forth.
For the wicked [b]surround
the righteous;
Therefore justice comes
forth [c]perverted.

### *Yahweh Raises the Dreaded Chaldeans*

5 "[a]See among the
nations! And look!
Be also astonished!
[b]Be astounded!
Because *I am* doing
[c]something in your days—
You would not believe if it
was recounted *to you.*
6 "For behold, I am [a]raising
up the Chaldeans,
That bitter and hasty nation
Who walks on the
breadth of the land
To [b]possess dwelling places
which are not theirs.
7 "They are dreaded
and [a]feared;
Their [b]justice and exaltation
come forth from themselves.
8 "Their [a]horses are swifter
than leopards
And [1]sharper than [b]wolves
in the evening.
Their [2]horsemen
come galloping;
Their horsemen come
from afar;
They fly like an [c]eagle
swooping *down* to devour.
9 "All of them come for violence.
[1]Their horde of [a]faces
*moves* forward.
And they gather
captives like sand.
10 "And they [a]mock at kings,
And rulers are a laughing
matter to them.
They [b]laugh at every fortress
And [c]heap up dirt
and capture it.
11 "Then they will sweep through
*like* the [a]wind and pass on.
But they will be held [b]guilty,
They whose [c]power
is their god."

◆ ***1:1*** [a]*Is 13:1; Na 1:1* [1]*Or burden* **1:2** [a]Ps 13:1, 2; 22:1, 2 [b]Jer 14:9 [1]The personal covenant name of God, a form of I AM WHO I AM, cf. Ex 3:14-15 **1:3** [a]Ps 55:9-11; Jer 20:18 [b]Jer 20:8 [c]Jer 15:10 **1:4** [a]Ps 58:1, 2; 119:126; Is 59:12-14 [b]Ps 22:12; Is 1:21-23 [c]Is 5:20; Eze 9:9 [1]Or *ineffective*; lit *numbed* **1:5** [a]Ac 13:41 [b]Is 29:9 [c]Is 29:14; Eze 12:22-28 **1:6** [a]2Ki 24:2; Jer 4:11-13 [b]Jer 8:10 **1:7** [a]Is 18:2, 7 [b]Jer 39:5-9 **1:8** [a]Jer 4:13 [b]Zep 3:3 [c]Eze 17:3; Hos 8:1 [1]Or *more eager* to attack [2]Or *steeds paw* the ground **1:9** [a]2Ki 12:17; Da 11:17 [1]Or *The eagerness of their faces* **1:10** [a]2Chr 36:6, 10; Is 37:13 [b]Is 10:9; 14:16 [c]Jer 32:24; Eze 26:8 **1:11** [a]Jer 4:11, 12 [b]Jer 2:3 [c]Da 4:30; Hab 1:16

### *Yahweh Has Placed Them to Judge*

12 Are You not from [a]everlasting,
O Yahweh, my God,
my Holy One?
We will not die.
You, O Yahweh, have
[b]placed them to judge;
And You, O [c]Rock, have
established them
to reprove.
13 *Your* eyes are too
[a]pure to see evil,
And You cannot look
on trouble.
Why do You [b]look
On those
who deal [c]treacherously?
*Why* are You [d]silent when
the wicked [e]swallow up
Those more righteous
than they?
14 And You have made men
like the fish of the sea,
Like creeping things
without a ruler over them.
15 *The Chaldeans* [a]bring all
of them up with a hook,
[b]Drag them away
with their net,
And gather them together
in their fishing net.
Therefore they are
glad and rejoice.
16 Therefore they offer a
sacrifice to their net
And [1]burn incense
to their fishing net
Because through [a]these
things their portion is rich
And their food is fat.
17 Will they therefore
empty their [a]net
And continually [b]kill nations
without sparing?

### *The Righteous Will Live by His Faith*

2 I will [a]stand on my guard post
And station myself
on the fortification;
And I will [b]keep watch to see
[c]what He will speak to me
And how I may respond
[1]when I am reproved.
2 Then Yahweh answered
me and said,
"[a]Write down the vision
And write *it*
on tablets distinctly,
That [1]the one who
[2]reads it may run.
3 "For the vision is yet
for the [a]appointed time;
It pants toward its end,
and it will not [1]lie.
Though it tarries, [b]wait for it;
For it will certainly come;
it [c]will not delay.

4 "Behold, as for the [a]proud one,
His soul is not right
within him;
But the [b]righteous will
live by his [1]faith.
5 "And indeed, [a]wine betrays
the [b]haughty man
So that he does not
[c]stay at home.
He [d]enlarges his
appetite like Sheol,

---

**1:12** [a]Dt 33:27; Ps 90:2; Mal 3:6 [b]Is 10:5, 6; Mal 3:5 [c]Dt 32:4 **1:13** [a]Ps 11:4-6; 34:15, 16 [b]Jer 12:1, 2 [c]Is 24:16 [d]Ps 50:21 [e]Ps 35:25 **1:15** [a]Jer 16:16; Am 4:2 [b]Ps 10:9 **1:16** [a]Jer 44:17 [1]Or *sacrifice* **1:17** [a]Is 19:8 [b]Is 14:5, 6 ◆ **2:1** [a]Is 21:8 [b]Ps 5:3 [c]Ps 85:8 [1]Lit *upon my reproof* **2:2** [a]Dt 27:8; Ro 15:4; Rev 1:19 [1]Or *one may read it fluently* [2]Or *is to proclaim it* **2:3** [a]Da 8:17, 19; 10:14 [b]Ps 27:14 [c]Eze 12:25; Heb 10:37 [1]Or *fail* **2:4** [a]Ps 49:18; Is 13:11 [b]Ro 1:17; Ga 3:11; Heb 10:38 [1]Or *faithfulness* **2:5** [a]Pr 20:1 [b]Pr 21:24 [c]2Ki 14:10 [d]Pr 27:20; 30:16; Is 5:11-15

And he is like death,
never satisfied.
He also gathers
to himself all nations
And assembles
to himself all peoples.

6 "Will not all of these [a]lift up
a taunt-song against him,
Even satire *and* riddles
against him
And say, '[b]Woe to him who
increases what is not his—
For how long—
And makes himself
[1]rich with loans?'
7 "Will not [1]your creditors
[a]rise up suddenly,
And those who make you
tremble awaken?
Indeed, you will become
spoil for them.
8 "Because you have [a]taken
many nations as spoil,
All that is left of the peoples
will take you as spoil—
Because of human
bloodshed and violence
[1]done to the land,
To the town and all
its inhabitants.

9 "Woe to him who is greedy
for [a]evil gain for his house
To [b]put his nest on high,
To be delivered
from the hand of evil!
10 "You have counseled
a [a]shameful thing
for your house
*By cutting off many peoples;*
So you are [b]sinning
against your own soul.
11 "Surely the [a]stone will cry
out from the wall,
And the rafter will answer
it from the [1]framework.

12 "Woe to him who [a]builds
a city with bloodshed
And founds a town
with injustice!
13 "Is it not, behold,
from Yahweh of hosts
That peoples [a]toil for fire,
And nations grow weary
for nothing?
14 "For the earth will
be [a]filled
With the knowledge
of the glory of Yahweh,
As the waters cover the sea.

15 "Woe to you who make
[1]your neighbors drink,
Who mix in your venom
even to make *them* drunk
So as to look
on their nakedness!
16 "You will be filled
with disgrace rather
than glory.
Now you yourself [a]drink
and [1]expose your
*own* nakedness.
The [b]cup in Yahweh's
right hand will come
around to you,
And [c]utter disgrace *will*
*come* upon your glory.
17 "For the [a]violence [1]done
to Lebanon will cover you,

**2:6** [a]Is 14:4-10; Jer 50:13 [b]Job 20:15-29; Hab 2:12 [1]Lit *heavy* **2:7** [a]Pr 29:1 [1]Lit *those who bite you* **2:8** [a]Is 33:1; Jer 27:7; Zec 2:8 [1]Lit *of the land* **2:9** [a]Jer 22:13; Eze 22:27 [b]Jer 49:16 **2:10** [a]2Ki 9:26; Na 1:14; Hab 2:16 [b]Jer 26:19 **2:11** [a]Jos 24:27; Lk 19:40 [1]Lit *wood* **2:12** [a]Mic 3:10; Na 3:1 **2:13** [a]Is 50:11; Jer 51:58 **2:14** [a]Ps 22:27; Is 11:9; Zec 14:9 **2:15** [1]Lit *his neighbor* **2:16** [a]Lam 4:21 [b]Jer 25:15, 17 [c]Na 3:6 [1]As in DSS and ancient versions; or *stagger*; lit *show yourself uncircumcised* **2:17** [a]Joel 3:19; Zec 11:1 [1]Lit *of Lebanon*

And the devastation
of *its* beasts [2]by which
you terrified them,
[b]Because of human
bloodshed and [c]violence
[3]done to the land,
To the town and all
its inhabitants.

18 “What [a]profit is the graven
image when its maker
has engraved it,
*Or* a molten image, a
[b]teacher of [1]lies?
For *its* maker [c]trusts
in his *own* making
When he fashions
speechless idols.
19 “Woe to him who [a]says
to a *piece of* wood, ‘[b]Awake!’
To a mute stone, ‘Arise!’
*And* that is *your* teacher?
Behold, it is overlaid
with [c]gold and silver,
And there is [d]no breath
at all inside it.
20 “But [a]Yahweh is in His
holy temple.
[1]Let all the earth [b]be
silent before Him.”

### *Yet I Will Exalt in Yahweh*

3 A prayer of Habakkuk the prophet, according to [1]Shigionoth.
2 O Yahweh, I have [a]heard
[1]the report about You,
*and* [2]I [b]fear.
O Yahweh, [c]revive [d]Your work
in the midst of the years;
In the midst of the years
make it known;
In rage
remember [e]compassion.

3 God comes from [a]Teman,
And the Holy One
from Mount [b]Paran. Selah.
His [c]splendor covers
the heavens,
And the [d]earth is full
of His praise.
4 *His* [a]brightness is
like the sunlight;
He has rays *flashing*
from His hand,
And there is the hiding
of His [b]strength.
5 Before Him goes [a]pestilence,
And [b]plague comes [1]after Him.
6 He stood and [1]measured
out the earth;
He looked and [a]startled
the nations.
So the perpetual mountains
were shattered;
The ancient hills [2]collapsed.
His ways are [b]everlasting.
7 I saw the tents of Cushan
under [a]wickedness;
The tent curtains of the land
of [b]Midian were trembling.

8 Did Yahweh’s *fury* burn
against the [a]rivers,

---

**2:17** [b]Ps 55:23; Hab 2:8 [c]Jer 51:35; Hab 2:8 [2]Lit which *terrified them* [3]Lit *of the land* **2:18** [a]Is 42:17; 44:9; Jer 2:27, 28 [b]Jer 10:8, 14; Zec 10:2 [c]Ps 115:4, 8 [1]Lit *a lie* **2:19** [a]Jer 2:27, 28; 10:3 [b]1Ki 18:26-29 [c]Ps 135:15-18; Jer 10:4, 9, 14 [d]Ps 135:17 **2:20** [a]Mic 1:2 [b]Zep 1:7; Zec 2:13 [1]Lit *Hush before Him, all the earth* ◆ **3:1** [1]Possibly a wild, passionate, and animated song **3:2** [a]Job 42:5 [b]Ps 119:120; Jer 10:7 [c]Ps 71:20; 85:6 [d]Ps 44:1-8; Hab 1:5 [e]Nu 14:19; 2Sa 24:15-17; Is 54:8 [1]Or *Your report* [2]Or *I stand in awe of Your work, O Yahweh; In the midst of the years revive it,* **3:3** [a]Jer 49:7; Am 1:12; Ob 9 [b]Ge 21:21; Dt 33:2 [c]Ps 113:4; 148:13 [d]Ps 48:10 **3:4** [a]Ps 18:12 [b]Job 26:14 **3:5** [a]Ex 12:29, 30; Nu 16:46-49 [b]Nu 11:1-3; Ps 18:12, 13 [1]Lit *at His feet* **3:6** [a]Job 21:18; Ps 35:5 [b]Hab 1:12 [1]Or *shook* [2]Or *sank down*; lit *bowed* **3:7** [a]Ex 15:14-16 [b]Nu 31:7, 8; Jdg 7:24, 25; 8:12 **3:8** [a]Ex 7:19, 20; Jos 3:16; Is 50:2

Or *was* Your anger
against the rivers,
Or *was* Your wrath
against the [b]sea,
That You [c]rode on Your horses,
On Your [d]chariots of salvation?
9 Your [a]bow was made bare;
Rods were sworn *unto*
*battle* by word. Selah.
You [b]split the earth with rivers.
10 The mountains saw
You *and* writhed;
The downpour
of waters passed by.
The deep [a]gave forth its voice;
It lifted high its hands.
11 [a]Sun *and* moon stood
in their lofty places;
They went away at the
[b]light of Your arrows,
At the brightness
of Your flashing spear.
12 In indignation You [a]marched
through the earth;
In anger You [b,1]trampled
the nations.
13 You went forth for the
[a]salvation of Your people,
For salvation
with Your [b]anointed.
You crushed the [c]head
of the house of the wicked
To lay him bare
from [1]thigh to neck. Selah.
14 You pierced with his [a]own
*sharpened* rods
The head of his [1]throngs.
They [b]stormed in to scatter [2]us;
Their exultation *was* like those
Who [c]devour the afflicted
in secret.
15 You [a]tread on the sea
with Your horses,
On the [b]surge of many waters.

16 I heard, and my [1]inward
parts [a]trembled;
At the sound my lips tingled.
Decay enters my [b]bones,
And in my place I tremble.
Because I must [c]wait quietly
for the day of distress,
[2]For the [d]people to arise
*who* will invade us.
17 Though the [a]fig tree
should not blossom
And there be no produce
on the vines,
*Though* the yield
of the [b]olive should fail
And the fields yield no food,
Though the [c]flock should
be cut off from the fold
And there be [d]no cattle
in the stalls,
18 Yet I will [a]exult in Yahweh;
I will [b]rejoice in the [c]God
of my salvation.
19 Yahweh, the Lord,
is my [a,1]strength,
And [b]He has set my feet
like hinds' *feet*
And makes me tread
on my [c]high places.
[2]For the choir director, on my stringed instruments.

**3:8** [b]Ex 14:16, 21; Ps 114:3, 5 [c]Dt 33:26; Ps 18:10; Hab 3:15 [d]Ps 68:17 **3:9** [a]Ps 7:12, 13; Hab 3:11 [b]Ps 78:16; 105:41 **3:10** [a]Ps 93:3; 98:7, 8 **3:11** [a]Jos 10:12-14 [b]Ps 18:14 **3:12** [a]Ps 68:7 [b]Is 41:15; Jer 51:33; Mic 4:13 [1]Or *thresh* **3:13** [a]Ex 15:2; 2Sa 5:20; Ps 68:19, 20 [b]Ps 20:6; 28:8 [c]Ps 68:21; 110:6 [1]Lit *foundation* **3:14** [a]Jdg 7:22 [b]Da 11:40; Zec 9:14 [c]Ps 10:8; 64:2-5 [1]Or *warriors, villagers* [2]Lit *me* **3:15** [a]Ps 77:19; Hab 3:8 [b]Ex 15:8 **3:16** [a]Da 10:8; Hab 3:2 [b]Job 30:17, 30; Jer 23:9 [c]Lk 21:19 [d]Jer 5:15 [1]Lit *belly* [2]Or *To come upon the people* who *will* **3:17** [a]Joel 1:10-12; Am 4:9; 2Co 4:8, 9 [b]Mic 6:15 [c]Joel 1:18 [d]Jer 5:17 **3:18** [a]Ex 15:1, 2; Job 13:15; Is 61:10; Ro 5:2, 3 [b]Ps 46:1-5; Php 4:4 [c]Ps 25:5; 27:1; Is 12:2 **3:19** [a]Ps 18:32, 33; 27:1; 46:1; Is 45:24 [b]2Sa 22:34 [c]Dt 33:29 [1]Lit *valor* [2]Belonging to the choir director's anthology

*The Book of*

# ZEPHANIAH

### *Yahweh Will End All Things*

1 The word of [1]Yahweh which came
to Zephaniah son of Cushi, son
of Gedaliah, son of Amariah, son of
Hezekiah, in the days of [a]Josiah son
of [b]Amon, king of Judah:

2 "I will completely
[a]end all *things*
From the face of the ground,"
declares Yahweh.
3 "I will end [a]man and beast;
I will end the [b]birds of the sky
And the fish of the sea
And the [c,1]ruins
along with the wicked;
And I will cut off man
from the face of the
ground," declares Yahweh.
4 "So I will [a]stretch out My
hand against Judah
And against all the
inhabitants of Jerusalem.
And I will [b]cut off
the remnant of Baal
from this place,
*And* the names of the
[c]idolatrous priests
along with the priests,
5 And those who worship
on the [a]housetops the
host of heaven,
And those who worship *and*
[b]swear to Yahweh and
*yet* swear by [c,1]Milcom,
6 And those who have [a]turned
back from following Yahweh,
And those who have
[b]not sought Yahweh or
inquired of Him."

### *The Day of Yahweh Is Near*

7 [a,1]Be silent
before Lord Yahweh!
For the [b]day of Yahweh
is near,
For Yahweh has prepared
a [c]sacrifice;
He has [d]set apart His guests.
8 "Then it will be on the day
of Yahweh's sacrifice
That I will [a]punish the
princes, the king's sons,
And all who clothe themselves
with [b]foreign garments.
9 "And I will punish on that
day all who leap on the
*temple* threshold,
Who fill the house
of their [1]Lord
with [a]violence and deceit.
10 "And it will be in that day,"
declares Yahweh,
"*That* there will be the sound
of a cry from the [a]Fish Gate
And a wail from the
[b,1]Second Quarter
And a great destruction
from the [c]hills.

---

◆ **1:1** [a]2Ki 22:1, 2; 2Chr 34:1-33; Jer 1:2; 22:11 [b]2Ki 21:18-26; 2Chr 33:20-25 [1]The personal covenant name of God, a form of I AM WHO I AM, cf. Ex 3:14-15 **1:2** [a]Ge 6:7; Jer 7:20; Eze 33:27, 28 **1:3** [a]Is 6:11, 12 [b]Jer 4:25; 9:10 [c]Eze 7:19; 14:3, 4, 8 [1]Or *stumbling blocks* **1:4** [a]Jer 6:12; Eze 6:14 [b]Mic 5:13 [c]2Ki 23:5; Hos 10:5 **1:5** [a]2Ki 23:12; Jer 19:13 [b]Jer 5:2, 7; 7:9, 10 [c]1Ki 11:5, 33; Jer 49:1 [1]Or *their king*; M.T. *Malcam*, probably a variant spelling of Milcom **1:6** [a]Is 1:4; Hos 7:10 [b]Is 9:13 **1:7** [a]Hab 2:20; Zec 2:13 [b]Zep 1:14 [c]Is 34:6; Jer 46:10 [d]1Sa 16:5; Is 13:3 [1]Lit *Hush* **1:8** [a]Is 24:21; Hab 1:10 [b]Is 2:6 **1:9** [a]Jer 5:27; Am 3:10 [1]Or *lord* **1:10** [a]2Chr 33:14; Ne 3:3; 12:39 [b]2Chr 34:22 [c]Eze 6:13 [1]A district of Jerusalem

11 “Wail, O inhabitants
of the [1]Mortar,
For all the [2]people
of [a]Canaan will be silenced;
All who weigh out [b]silver
will be cut off.
12 “And it will be at that time
That I will [a]search
Jerusalem with lamps,
And I will punish the men
Who are [b,1]stagnant in spirit,
Who say in their hearts,
‘Yahweh will [c]not do
good or evil!’
13 “And it will be that their
wealth will become [a]spoil
And their houses desolate;
Indeed, [b]they will build
houses but not inhabit *them*,
And plant vineyards
but not drink their wine.”

14 Near is the [a]great
[b]day of Yahweh,
Near and coming very quickly;
O the sound, the day
of Yahweh!
[1]In it the mighty man
[c]cries out bitterly.
15 A day of fury is that day,
A day of [a]trouble and distress,
A day of destruction
and desolation,
A day of [b]darkness and
thick darkness,
A day of clouds and
dense gloom,
16 A day of [a]trumpet and
loud shouting
Against the [b]fortified cities
And the high corner towers.
17 I will bring [a]distress on men
So that they will walk
[b]like the blind
Because they have sinned
against Yahweh;
And their [c]blood will be
poured out like dust
And their [d]flesh like dung.
18 Neither their [a]silver
nor their gold
Will be able to deliver them
On the day of the
fury of Yahweh;
And [b]all the earth will
be devoured
In the fire of His jealousy,
For He will [c]make a
complete destruction,
Indeed a terrifying one,
Of all the inhabitants
of the earth.

### *Seek Yahweh Before His Day of Anger*

2 Gather yourselves together,
indeed, [a]gather,
O nation [b]without [1]shame,
2 Before the decree
[1]takes effect—
The day passes
[a]like the chaff—
Before the [b]burning anger
of Yahweh comes upon you,
Before the [c]day of Yahweh’s
anger comes upon you.
3 [a]Seek Yahweh,
All you [b]humble of the [1]earth
Who have worked His justice;

**1:11** [a]Zep 2:5; Zec 14:21 [b]Job 27:16, 17; Hos 9:6 [1]A district of Jerusalem [2]Or merchant people will
**1:12** [a]Jer 16:16, 17; Eze 9:4-11; Am 9:1-3 [b]Jer 48:11; Am 6:1 [c]Eze 8:12; 9:9 [1]Lit *thickening on their lees*
**1:13** [a]Jer 15:13; 17:3 [b]Am 5:11; Mic 6:15 **1:14** [a]Jer 30:7; Joel 2:11; Mal 4:5 [b]Eze 7:7, 12; 30:3; Joel 1:15; 3:14; Zep 1:7 [c]Eze 7:16-18 [1]Lit *There* **1:15** [a]Is 22:5 [b]Joel 2:2, 31; Am 5:18-20 **1:16** [a]Is 27:13; Jer 4:19 [b]Is 2:12-15
**1:17** [a]Jer 10:18 [b]Dt 28:29 [c]Eze 24:7, 8 [d]Jer 8:2; 9:22 **1:18** [a]Eze 7:19 [b]Zep 3:8 [c]Ge 6:7; Eze 7:5-7
◆ **2:1** [a]2Chr 20:4; Joel 1:14 [b]Jer 3:3; 6:15 [1]Or *longing* **2:2** [a]Is 17:13; Hos 13:3 [b]Lam 4:11; Na 1:6 [c]Zep 1:18 [1]Lit *is born* **2:3** [a]Ps 105:4; Am 5:6 [b]Ps 22:26; Is 11:4 [1]Or *land*

[c]Seek righteousness,
seek humility.
Perhaps you will be [d]hidden
In the day of Yahweh's anger.

4 For [a]Gaza will be [1]forsaken
And Ashkelon a desolation;
[a]Ashdod will be driven
out at noon,
And [a]Ekron will be uprooted.
5 Woe to the inhabitants
of the seacoast,
The nation of the [a,1]Cherethites!
The word of Yahweh
is [b]against you,
O [c]Canaan, land
of the Philistines;
And I will [d]make you perish
So that there will be
[e]no inhabitant.
6 So the seacoast will
be [a]pastures,
*With* [1]caves for shepherds
and folds for flocks.
7 And the coast will be
For the [a]remnant of the
house of Judah;
They will [b]feed upon it.
In the houses
of Ashkelon they will lie
down at evening;
For Yahweh their God
will [c]care for them
And [d]restore their fortune.

8 "I have heard the
[a]reproach of Moab
And the [b]revilings of the
sons of Ammon,
With which they have
reproached My people
And [c]magnified *themselves*
against their territory.
9 "Therefore, as I live,"
declares Yahweh of hosts,
The God of Israel,
"Surely [a]Moab will be
like [b]Sodom
And the sons of [c]Ammon
like [d]Gomorrah—
A place possessed
by nettles and salt pits,
And a perpetual desolation.
The remnant of My people
will [e]plunder them,
And the remainder of My
nation will inherit them."
10 This they will have in return for
their [a]pride because they have [b]re-
proached and magnified *themselves*
against the people of Yahweh of hosts.
11 Yahweh will be [a]fearsome to them,
for He will [1]starve [b]all the gods of
the earth; and all the [c]coastlands of
the nations will [d]bow down to Him,
everyone from his *own* place.
12 "You also, O [a]Ethiopians,
will be slain by My sword."
13 And He will [a]stretch out His
hand against the north
And cause [b]Assyria
to perish,
And He will make [c]Nineveh
a desolation,
Parched like the wilderness.
14 Flocks will lie down
in her midst,
All the beasts of the nation;

**2:3** [c]Am 5:14, 15 [d]Ps 57:1; Is 26:20 **2:4** [a]Am 1:7, 8; Zec 9:5-7 [1]Heb *Azabah*, sounds like Gaza **2:5** [a]Eze 25:16 [b]Am 3:1 [c]Zep 1:11 [d]Is 14:29, 30 [e]Zep 3:6 [1]A segment of the Philistines with roots in Crete **2:6** [a]Is 5:17; 7:25 [1]Or *meadows, wells* **2:7** [a]Is 11:16 [b]Is 32:14 [c]Ex 4:31; Ps 80:14 [d]Jer 32:44; Zep 3:20 **2:8** [a]Eze 25:8 [b]Eze 25:3 [c]Am 1:13 **2:9** [a]Is 15:1-9; Jer 48:1-47; Am 2:1-3 [b]Ge 19:24 [c]Jer 49:1-6; Eze 25:1-10 [d]Dt 29:23 [e]Is 11:14 **2:10** [a]Is 16:6 [b]Zep 2:8 **2:11** [a]Joel 2:11 [b]Zep 1:4 [c]Is 24:15 [d]Ps 72:8-11; Zep 3:9 [1]Lit *make lean* **2:12** [a]Is 18:1-7; 20:4, 5; Eze 30:4-9 **2:13** [a]Is 14:26; Zep 1:4 [b]Is 10:16; Mic 5:6 [c]Na 3:7

Both the [a,1]pelican and
the hedgehog
Will lodge in [2]the tops
of her pillars;
Their voice will sing
in the window,
Ruin *will be* on the threshold;
For He has laid bare
the cedar work.
15 This is the [a]exultant city
Which [b]inhabits securely,
Who says in her heart,
"[c]I am, and there is no
one besides me."
How she has become an
object of [d]horror,
A resting place for beasts!
[e]Everyone who passes
by her will hiss
*And* wave his hand
*in contempt.*

### *The Unjust Knows No Shame*

3 Woe to her who is
[a]rebellious and [b]defiled,
The oppressive [c]city!
2 She [a]did not listen
to *any* voice;
She [b]did not receive discipline.
She did not [c]trust in Yahweh;
She did not [d]draw
near to her God.
3 Her [a]princes in her midst
are roaring lions;
Her judges are [b]wolves
at evening;
They *leave* nothing
to gnaw for the morning.
4 Her prophets are [a]reckless,
treacherous men;
Her [b]priests have profaned
the sanctuary.
They have done violence
to the law.
5 Yahweh is [a]righteous
[b]in her midst;
He will [c]do no injustice.
[d]Every morning He brings
His justice to light;
[1]He does not fail.
But the unjust [e]knows
no shame.
6 "I have cut off nations;
Their corner towers
are desolate.
I have made their
streets [a]a waste,
With no one passing by;
Their [b]cities are laid waste,
Without a man,
[c]without an inhabitant.
7 "I said, 'Surely you will fear Me,
[a]Receive discipline.'
So her abode will
[b]not be cut off
*According to* all that I have
appointed concerning her.
But they were eager
to [c]corrupt all their deeds.

### *Yahweh Will Pour Out His Anger*

8 "Therefore [a]wait for Me,"
declares Yahweh,
"For the day when I rise
up as a witness.
Indeed, My judgment is
to [b]assemble nations,
To gather kingdoms,
To pour out on them
My indignation,

---

**2:14** [a]Is 14:23; 34:11 [1]Or *owl, jackdaw* [2]Lit *her capitals* **2:15** [a]Is 22:2 [b]Is 32:9, 11; 47:8 [c]Is 47:8; Eze 28:2, 9 [d]Is 32:14 [e]Jer 18:16; 19:8 ◆ **3:1** [a]Jer 5:23 [b]Eze 23:30 [c]Jer 6:6 **3:2** [a]Jer 7:23-28 [b]Jer 2:30; 5:3; 2Ti 3:16 [c]Ps 78:22; Jer 13:25 [d]Ps 73:28 **3:3** [a]Eze 22:27 [b]Jer 5:6; Hab 1:8 **3:4** [a]Jdg 9:4 [b]Eze 22:26; Mal 2:7, 8 **3:5** [a]Dt 32:4 [b]Zep 3:15, 17 [c]Ps 92:15 [d]Job 7:18 [e]Zep 2:1 [1]Lit *It is never missing* **3:6** [a]Jer 9:12; Zec 7:14; Mt 23:38 [b]Lv 26:31; Is 6:11 [c]Zep 2:5 **3:7** [a]Job 36:10; Ps 32:8; 1Ti 1:5 [b]Jer 7:7 [c]Hos 9:9 **3:8** [a]Ps 27:14; Is 30:18; Hab 2:3 [b]Eze 38:14-23; Joel 3:2

All My burning anger;
For [c]all the earth will
be devoured
By the fire of My zeal.
9 "For then I will change *them* to
peoples with [a]purified lips,
That all of them may [b]call
on the name of Yahweh,
To serve Him [1]shoulder
to shoulder.
10 "From beyond the rivers
of [a,1]Ethiopia
My [2]worshipers,
[3]My scattered ones,
Will [b]bring My offerings.
11 "In that day you will
[a]feel no shame
Because of all your deeds
By which you have
transgressed against Me;
For then I will remove
from your midst
Your [b]proud, exulting ones,
And you will never
again be haughty
On My [c]holy mountain.
12 "But I will cause to remain
in your midst
A [a,1]lowly and poor people,
And they will [b]take refuge
in the name of Yahweh.
13 "The [a]remnant of Israel
will [b]do no injustice
And [c]not speak falsehood,
Nor will a deceitful *tongue*
Be found in their mouths;
For they will [d]feed
and lie down
With no one to make
them tremble."

### *Yahweh's Joy in Restoring Israel*

14 Sing for joy, O daughter
of Zion!
[a]Make a loud shout, O Israel!
Be glad and exult
with all *your* heart,
O daughter of Jerusalem!
15 Yahweh has taken away [a]*His*
judgments against you;
He has cleared away
your enemies.
The King of Israel, Yahweh,
is [b]in your midst;
You will [c]fear evil no more.
16 [a]In that day it will be
said to Jerusalem:
"[b]Do not fear, O Zion;
[c]Do not let your
hands fall limp.
17 "Yahweh your God is
[a]in your midst,
A [b]mighty one who will save.
He will [c]be joyful
over you with gladness;
He will [1]be quiet in His love;
He will rejoice over you
with joyful singing.
18 "I will assemble those who
[a]grieve about
the appointed feasts—
They were from you, *O Zion*;
*The* reproach *of exile* is
a burden on [1]them.
19 "Behold, I am going
to deal at that time

**3:8** [c]Zep 1:18 **3:9** [a]Is 19:18; 57:19 [b]Ps 22:27; 86:9; Hab 2:14; Zep 2:11 [1]Lit *with one shoulder* **3:10** [a]Ps 68:31; Is 18:1 [b]Is 60:6, 7 [1]Or *Cush*, cf. Ge 10:6 [2]Or *suppliants* [3]Lit *the daughter of My scattered ones* **3:11** [a]Is 45:17; 54:4; Joel 2:26, 27 [b]Is 2:12; 5:15 [c]Is 11:9; 56:7; Eze 20:40 **3:12** [a]Is 14:30 [b]Is 14:32; 50:10; Na 1:7; Zec 13:8, 9 [1]Or *humble, afflicted* **3:13** [a]Is 10:20-22; Mic 4:7; Zep 2:7 [b]Ps 119:3; Jer 31:33; Zep 3:5 [c]Zec 8:3, 16; Rev 14:5 [d]Eze 34:13-15 **3:14** [a]Zec 9:9 **3:15** [a]Ps 19:9; Jn 5:30; Rev 18:20 [b]Eze 37:26-28; Zep 3:5 [c]Is 54:14 **3:16** [a]Is 25:9 [b]Is 35:3, 4 [c]Job 4:3; Heb 12:12 **3:17** [a]Zep 3:5, 15 [b]Is 63:1 [c]Is 62:5 [1]Some ancient versions *renew* you *in* **3:18** [a]Ps 42:2-4; Eze 9:4 [1]Lit *her*

With all those who [a]afflict you,
And I will save the [b]lame
And gather the banished,
And I will turn them—
in their [c]shame—
into [d]praise and a name
In all the earth.
20 "At that time I will
[a]bring you in,
Even at the time when I
gather you together;
Indeed, I will give you
*to be* a [b]name and praise
Among all the peoples
of the earth,
When I [c]restore your fortunes
before your eyes,"
Says Yahweh.

*The Book of*

# HAGGAI

### *The Commission to Rebuild the Temple*

1 In the [a]second year of Darius the
king, on the first day of the sixth
month, the word of [1]Yahweh came
by the hand of [b]Haggai the prophet
to [c]Zerubbabel the son of Shealtiel,
[d]governor of Judah, and to [e]Joshua
the son of Jehozadak, the high priest,
saying, **2** "Thus says Yahweh of [1]hosts,
'This people says, "The time has not
come, *even* the time for the house of
Yahweh to be rebuilt."'" **3** Then the
word of Yahweh came by the hand
of Haggai the prophet, saying, **4** "Is it
time for you yourselves to live in your
paneled houses while this house [a]*lies*
waste?" **5** So now, thus says Yahweh
of hosts, "Set your heart *to consider*
your ways! **6** You have [a]sown much,
but bring in little; *you* eat, but *there is*
not *enough* to be satisfied; *you* drink,
but *there is* [1]not *enough* to become
drunk; *you* put on clothing, but no
one is warm *enough*; and he who
earns, earns wages *to put* into a bag
with holes."
**7** Thus says Yahweh of hosts, "Set
your heart *to consider* your ways! **8** Go
up to the [1]mountains and bring wood
and [a]rebuild the house *of God*, that I
may be [b]pleased with it and be [c]glori-
fied," says Yahweh. **9** "[a]*You* look for
much, but behold, *it comes* to little;
and you bring *it* home, and I [b]blow
it *away*. Why?" declares Yahweh of
hosts, "Because of My house which
[c]*lies* waste, while each of you runs to
his own house. **10** Therefore, because
of you the [a]sky has restrained [1]its dew
and the earth has restrained its pro-
duce. **11** And I called for a [a,1]drought
on the land, on the mountains, on
the grain, on the new wine, on the oil,
on what the ground brings forth, on
[b]men, on cattle, and on [c]all the labor
of [2]your hands."

***3:19*** [a]*Is 60:14* [b]Eze 34:16; Mic 4:6 [c]Eze 16:27, 57 [d]Is 60:18; 62:7; Zec 8:23 **3:20** [a]Eze 37:12, 21 [b]Dt 26:18, 19; Is 56:5; 66:22 [c]*Jer 29:14; Joel 3:1; Zep 2:7* ◆ **1:1** [a]Ezr 4:24 [b]Ezr 5:1; 6:14; Hag 1:3, 12, 13; 2:1, 10, 20 [c]Ezr 2:2; Ne 7:7; Hag 1:12, 14; Zec 4:6; Mt 1:12, 13 [d]1Ki 10:15; Ezr 5:3 [e]Zec 6:11 [1]The personal covenant name of God, a form of I AM WHO I AM, cf. Ex 3:14-15 **1:2** [1]Lit *hosts, saying* **1:4** [a]Jer 33:10, 12; Hag 1:9 **1:6** [a]Dt 28:38-40; Hos 8:7; Hag 1:9, 10; 2:16, 17 [1]Lit *not becoming drunk* **1:8** [a]1Ki 6:1 [b]Ps 132:13, 14 [c]Hag 2:7, 9 [1]Lit *mountain* **1:9** [a]Pr 27:20; Ecc 1:8 [b]Is 40:7 [c]Hag 1:4 **1:10** [a]Dt 28:23, 24; 1Ki 17:1; Joel 1:18-20 [1]Lit *from dew* **1:11** [a]Jer 14:2-6; Mal 3:9, 11 [b]Dt 28:22 [c]Hag 2:17 [1]Or *waste*, cf. 1:4, 9 [2]Lit *the palms*

**12** Then [a]Zerubbabel the son of
Shealtiel, and [b]Joshua the son of
Jehozadak, the high priest, with all
the remnant of the people, [c]listened
to the voice of Yahweh their God and
the words of Haggai the prophet, as
Yahweh their God had sent him. And
the people [d]feared Yahweh. **13** Then
Haggai, the [a]messenger of Yahweh,
spoke by the commissioned message
of Yahweh to the people saying, "'[b]I
am with you,' declares Yahweh."
**14** So Yahweh stirred up the spirit
of [a]Zerubbabel the son of Shealtiel,
[a]governor of Judah, and the spirit
of Joshua the son of Jehozadak, the
high priest, and the spirit of all the
[b]remnant of the people; and they
came and [c]did work on the house of
Yahweh of hosts, their God, **15** on the
twenty-fourth day of the sixth month
in the second year of Darius the king.

### *The Glory of Yahweh Will Fill the Temple*

**2** On the twenty-first of the seventh
month, the word of Yahweh came
by the hand of [a]Haggai the prophet
saying, **2** "Speak now to [a]Zerubba-
bel the son of Shealtiel, [a]governor
of Judah, and to [a]Joshua the son of
Jehozadak, the high priest, and to
the [b]remnant of the people saying,
**3** 'Who among you [a]remains who saw
this house in its [b]former glory? And
how do you see it now? Does it not
seem like nothing in your eyes? **4** But
now, [a]be strong, Zerubbabel,' de-
clares Yahweh, 'be strong also, Joshua
son of Jehozadak, the high priest, and
all you people of the land, be strong,'
declares Yahweh, 'and work; for [b]I
am with you,' declares Yahweh of
hosts. **5** 'As for the [a,1]promise which
I cut with you when you came out of
Egypt, [2]My [b]Spirit is standing in your
midst; [c]do not fear!' **6** For thus says
Yahweh of hosts, '[a]Once more—[1]in
a [b]little while—I am going to [c]shake
the heavens and the earth, the sea
also and the dry land. **7** And I will
shake [a]all the nations; and [1]they will
come with the [b]desirable things of
all nations, and I will [c]fill this house
with glory,' says Yahweh of hosts.
**8** 'The [a]silver is Mine, and the gold
is Mine,' declares Yahweh of hosts.
**9** 'The latter [a]glory of this house will
be greater than the [b]former,' says
Yahweh of hosts, 'and in this place
I will give [c]peace,' declares Yahweh
of hosts."

**10** On the [a]twenty-fourth of the
ninth *month*, in the second year of
Darius, the word of Yahweh came to
Haggai the prophet, saying, **11** "Thus
says Yahweh of hosts, '[a]Ask now the
priests *about the* law: **12** If a man
carries [a]holy meat in the [1]fold of
his garment and touches bread with
[2]this fold or cooked food, wine, oil,
or any *other* food, will it become
holy?'" And the priests answered,
"No." **13** Then Haggai said, "[a]If one

---

**1:12** [a]Hag 1:1 [b]Hag 1:14; 2:2 [c]Is 1:19; 1Th 2:13 [d]Dt 31:12, 13; Ps 112:1; Is 50:10 **1:13** [a]Is 44:26; Eze 3:17; Mal 2:7; 3:1 [b]Ps 46:11; Is 41:10; 43:2 **1:14** [a]Hag 1:1; 2:2, 21 [b]Hag 1:12 [c]Ezr 5:2; Ne 4:6 ◆ **2:1** [a]Hag 1:1 **2:2** [a]Hag 1:1 [b]Hag 1:12 **2:3** [a]Ezr 3:12 [b]Hag 2:9 **2:4** [a]Dt 31:23; 1Chr 22:13; 28:20; Zec 8:9; Eph 6:10 [b]2Sa 5:10; Ac 7:9 **2:5** [a]Ex 19:4-6; 29:45, 46; 33:12-14; 34:8-10 [b]Ne 9:20; Is 63:11, 14 [c]Is 41:10, 13; Zec 8:13 [1]Lit *word* [2]Or *while...was standing* **2:6** [a]Heb 12:26 [b]Is 10:25; 29:17 [c]Hag 2:21 [1]Lit *it is a little* **2:7** [a]Da 2:44; Joel 3:9, 16 [b]Is 60:4-9 [c]1Ki 8:11; Is 60:7 [1]Or *the desire of all nations will come* **2:8** [a]1Chr 29:14, 16; Is 60:17 **2:9** [a]Zec 2:5 [b]Hag 2:3 [c]Is 9:6, 7; 66:12 **2:10** [a]Hag 2:20 **2:11** [a]Dt 17:8-11; Mal 2:7 **2:12** [a]Ex 29:37; Lv 6:27, 29; 7:6; Eze 44:19; Mt 23:19 [1]Lit *wing* [2]Lit *his wing* **2:13** [a]Lv 22:4-6; Nu 19:22

who is unclean from a [1]corpse
touches any of these, will *the latter*
become unclean?" And the priests
answered, "It will become unclean."
**14** Then Haggai answered and said,
"'[a]So is this people. And so is this
nation before Me,' declares Yahweh,
'and so is every work of their hands;
and what they bring near *to Me* there
is unclean. **15** But now, [a]oh set your
heart *to consider* from this day
[1]onward: from before one [b]stone
was set on another in the temple of
Yahweh, **16** [1]from when it was that
one came to a *grain* heap of twenty
*measures*, then there would be only
ten; and *from when* one came to the
wine vat to draw fifty troughs full,
then there would be *only* twenty. **17** I
struck you *and* every work of your
hands with [a]scorching wind, mildew,
and hail; [1]yet you *did* not *come back*
to Me,' declares Yahweh. **18** '[a]Oh set
your heart *to consider* from this day
[1]onward, from the [b]twenty-fourth
day of the ninth *month*; from the
day when the temple of Yahweh was
[c]founded, set your heart *to consider*:
**19** Is the seed still in the barn? Even
including the vine, the fig tree, the
pomegranate, and the olive tree, it
has not borne *fruit*. Yet from this
day on I will [a]bless *you*.'"

### *Yahweh Chooses Zerubbabel*

**20** Then the word of Yahweh came
a second time to Haggai on the
[a]twenty-fourth *day* of the month,
saying, **21** "Speak to [a]Zerubbabel
governor of Judah, saying, 'I am going
to [b]shake the heavens and the earth.
**22** I will [a]overthrow the thrones of
kingdoms and destroy the [b]strength
of the kingdoms of the [1]nations; and
I will [c]overthrow the chariots and
their riders, and the [d]horses and their
riders will go down, [e]everyone by the
sword of another.' **23** 'On that day,'
declares Yahweh of hosts, 'I will take
you, Zerubbabel, son of Shealtiel, My
servant,' declares Yahweh, 'and I will
make you like a [a,1]signet *ring*, for [b]I
have chosen you,'" declares Yahweh
of hosts.

**2:13** [1]Lit *soul* **2:14** [a]Pr 15:8; Is 1:11-15 **2:15** [a]Hag 1:5, 7; 2:18 [b]Ezr 3:10; 4:24 [1]Or *backward*
**2:16** [1]Lit *since they were* **2:17** [a]Dt 28:22; 1Ki 8:37; Am 4:9 [1]Or *but what did we have in common?*
**2:18** [a]Dt 32:29; Hag 2:15 [b]Hag 2:10 [c]Ezr 5:1, 2; Zec 8:9, 12 [1]Or *backward* **2:19** [a]Ps 128:1-6; Jer 31:12, 14; Mal 3:10 **2:20** [a]Hag 2:10 **2:21** [a]Ezr 5:2; Hag 1:1; Zec 4:6-10 [b]Hag 2:6; Heb 12:26, 27 **2:22** [a]Eze 26:16; Zep 3:8 [b]Mic 7:16 [c]Ps 46:9; Eze 39:20; Mic 5:10 [d]Am 2:15 [e]Jdg 7:22; 2Chr 20:23 [1]Or *Gentiles*
**2:23** [a]SS 8:6; Jer 22:24 [b]Is 42:1; 43:10 [1]Or *seal*

## *The Book of*
# ZECHARIAH

### *Return to Me, Declares Yahweh*

**1** In the eighth month of the sec-
ond year of [a]Darius, the word of
[1]Yahweh came to [b]Zechariah the
prophet, the son of Berechiah, the
son of [c]Iddo, saying, **2** "Yahweh was
very [a]wrathful against your fathers.
**3** Therefore say to them, 'Thus says
Yahweh of hosts, "[a]Return to Me,"
declares Yahweh of hosts, "that I
may return to you," says Yahweh of
hosts. **4** "Do not be [a]like your fathers,
to whom the [b]former prophets called
out, saying, 'Thus says Yahweh of
hosts, "[c]Return now from your evil
ways and from your evil deeds."'
But they did [d]not listen or give heed
to Me," declares Yahweh. **5** "Your
[a]fathers, where are they? And the
[b]prophets, do they live forever? **6** But
did not My words and My statutes,
which I commanded My slaves the
prophets, [a]overtake your fathers?
Then they [1]returned and said, '[b]As
Yahweh of hosts purposed to do to us
in accordance with our ways and our
deeds, so He has done with us.'"'"

### *A Man on a Red Horse*

**7** On the twenty-fourth day of
the eleventh month, *which is the
month* Shebat, in the second year
of Darius, the word of Yahweh came
to Zechariah the prophet, the son of
Berechiah, the son of Iddo, saying,
**8** I saw at night, and behold, a man
was riding on a [a]red horse, and he
was standing among the [b]myrtle
trees which were in the ravine, with
red, sorrel, and [c]white horses behind
him. **9** Then I said, "My [a]lord, what
are these?" And the [b]angel who was
speaking with me said to me, "I will
show you what these are." **10** And
the man who was standing among
the myrtle trees answered and said,
"These are those whom Yahweh has
sent to [a,1]patrol the earth." **11** So they
answered the angel of Yahweh who
was [a]standing among the myrtle
trees and said, "We have [1]patrolled
the earth, and behold, [b]all the earth
is sitting *still* and quiet."

**12** Then the angel of Yahweh an-
swered and said, "O Yahweh of hosts,
[a]how long will You [b]have no com-
passion for Jerusalem and the cities
of Judah, with which You have been
[c]indignant these [d]seventy years?"
**13** Yahweh answered the [a]angel who
was speaking with me with good
words, [b]comforting words. **14** So the
angel who was speaking with me said
*to me*, "[a]Call out, saying, 'Thus says
Yahweh of hosts, "I am [b]exceedingly
jealous for Jerusalem and Zion. **15** But

---

◆ **1:1** [a]Ezr 4:24; 6:15; Hag 1:15; 2:10; Zec 1:7; 7:1 [b]Ezr 5:1; 6:14; Zec 7:1; Mt 23:35; Lk 11:51 [c]Ne 12:4, 16 [1]The personal covenant name of God, a form of I AM WHO I AM, cf. Ex 3:14-15 **1:2** [a]2Chr 36:16; Jer 44:6; Eze 8:18; Zec 1:15 **1:3** [a]Is 31:6; 44:22; Mal 3:7 **1:4** [a]Ps 78:8; 106:6, 7 [b]2Chr 24:19; 36:15 [c]Is 1:16-19; Jer 4:1; Eze 33:11 [d]Jer 6:17; 11:7, 8 **1:5** [a]Lam 5:7 [b]Jn 8:52 **1:6** [a]Jer 12:16, 17; 44:28, 29; Am 9:10 [b]Lam 2:17 [1]Or *repented* **1:8** [a]Zec 6:2; Rev 6:4 [b]Ne 8:15; Is 41:19; 55:13; Zec 1:10, 11 [c]Zec 6:3; Rev 6:2 **1:9** [a]Zec 1:19; 4:4, 5, 13; 6:4 [b]Zec 2:3; 5:5 **1:10** [a]Job 1:7; Zec 1:11; 4:10; 6:5-8 [1]Lit *walk about through* **1:11** [a]Zec 1:8, 10 [b]Is 14:7 [1]Lit *walked about through* **1:12** [a]Ps 74:10; Jer 12:4; Hab 1:2 [b]Ps 102:13; Jer 30:18 [c]Ps 102:10; Jer 15:17 [d]Jer 25:11; 29:10; Da 9:2; Zec 7:5 **1:13** [a]Zec 1:9; 4:1 [b]Is 40:1, 2; 57:18 **1:14** [a]Is 40:2, 6; Zec 1:17 [b]Zec 8:2

I am very [a]wrathful with the nations
who are [b]at ease; for I was only a little
wrathful, but they [c]helped *increase*
the calamity." **16** Therefore thus says
Yahweh, "I will [a]return to Jerusalem
with compassion; My [b]house will
be built in it," declares Yahweh of
hosts, "and a measuring [c]line will be
stretched over Jerusalem."' **17** Again,
call out, saying, 'Thus says Yahweh of
hosts, "My [a]cities will again overflow
with good, and Yahweh will again
[b]comfort Zion and again [c]choose
Jerusalem."'"

### *Four Horns and Craftsmen*

**18** [1]Then I lifted up my eyes and saw,
and behold, *there were* four horns.
**19** So I said to the angel who was
speaking with me, "What are these?"
And he said to me, "These are the
[a]horns which have scattered Judah,
Israel, and Jerusalem." **20** Then Yah-
weh showed me four [a]craftsmen.
**21** And I said, "What are these coming
to do?" And he said, "These are the
[a]horns which have scattered Judah
so that no man lifts up his head; but
these *craftsmen* have come to cause
them to tremble, to [b]throw down the
horns of the nations who have lifted
up *their* horns against the land of
Judah in order to scatter it."

### *A Man with a Measuring Cord*

**2** [1]Then I lifted up my eyes and saw,
and behold, *there was* a man with
a [a]measuring cord in his hand. **2** So I
said, "Where are you going?" And he
said to me, "To [a]measure Jerusalem,
to see how wide it is and how long
it is." **3** And behold, the [a]angel who
was speaking with me was going
out, and another angel was coming
out to meet him **4** and said to him,
"Run, speak to that [a]young man,
saying, '[b]Jerusalem will be inhab-
ited [c,1]without walls because of the
[d]multitude of men and cattle within
it. **5** Indeed I,' declares Yahweh, 'will
be a [a]wall of fire [1]around her, and I
will be the [b]glory in her midst.'"
**6** "[1]Ho there! [a]Flee from the land
of the north," declares Yahweh, "for
I have [b]dispersed you as the four
winds of the heavens," declares
Yahweh. **7** "Woe, Zion! [a]Escape, you
who are living with the daughter of
Babylon." **8** For thus says Yahweh of
hosts, "After [a,1]glory He has sent Me
against the nations which have taken
you as spoil, for he who touches you,
touches the [b,2]apple of His eye. **9** For
behold, I will [a]wave My hand over
them so that they will be [b]spoil for
their slaves. Then you will know that
Yahweh of hosts has sent Me. **10** [a]Sing
for joy and be glad, O daughter of
Zion; for behold, I am coming and I
will [b]dwell in your midst," declares
Yahweh. **11** "[a]And many nations will
join themselves to Yahweh in that day
and will become My people. Then I
will [b]dwell in your midst, and you
will [c]know that Yahweh of hosts has
sent Me to you. **12** Then Yahweh will

---

**1:15** [a]Zec 1:2 [b]Ps 123:4; Jer 48:11 [c]Am 1:11 **1:16** [a]Is 54:8-10; Zec 2:10, 11 [b]Ezr 6:14, 15; Zec 4:9 [c]Jer 31:39; Zec 2:2, 4 **1:17** [a]*Is 44:26; 61:4* [b]*Is 51:3* [c]Zec 2:12 **1:18** [1]Ch 2:1 in Heb **1:19** [a]1Ki 22:11; Ps 75:4, 5; Am 6:13 mg **1:20** [a]Is 44:12; 54:16 **1:21** [a]Zec 1:19 [b]Ps 75:10 ◆ **2:1** [a]*Jer 31:39; Eze 40:3; 47:3;* Zec 1:16 [1]Ch 2:5 in Heb **2:2** [a]Jer 31:39; Eze 40:3; Rev 21:15-17 **2:3** [a]Zec 1:9 **2:4** [a]Jer 1:6; Da 1:4; 1Ti 4:12 [b]Zec 1:17; 8:4 [c]Eze 38:11 [d]Is 49:20; Jer 30:19; 33:22 [1]Or like *open country*; lit like *unwalled villages* **2:5** [a]Is 4:5; 26:1; 60:18 [b]Hag 2:9; Zec 2:10, 11 [1]Lit *to her* **2:6** [a]Jer 3:18 [b]Jer 31:10; Eze 11:16 [1]Lit *Ho! Ho!, Woe! Woe!*; cf. 2:7 **2:7** [a]Is 48:20; Jer 51:6 **2:8** [a]Is 60:7-9 [b]Dt 32:10; Ps 17:8 [1]Or *the glory* [2]Lit *pupil* **2:9** [a]Is 19:16 [b]Is 14:2 **2:10** [a]Is 65:18, 19; Zec 9:9 [b]Zec 2:5; 8:3 **2:11** [a]Mic 4:2 [b]Zec 2:5, 10 [c]Zec 2:9

[a]inherit Judah as His portion in the
holy land and will again [b]choose
Jerusalem.
**13** "[a,1]Be silent, all flesh, before
Yahweh; for He is [b]aroused from
His holy habitation."

### *The High Priest and a Branch*

**3** Then he showed me [a]Joshua
the high priest standing before
the angel of Yahweh, and [b,1]Satan
standing at his right hand to accuse
him. **2** And Yahweh said to Satan,
"[a]Yahweh rebuke you, Satan! Indeed,
Yahweh who has [b]chosen Jerusalem
rebuke you! Is this not a [c]brand de-
livered from the fire?" **3** Now Joshua
was clothed with [a]filthy garments
and standing before the angel. **4** And
he answered and spoke to those who
were standing before him, saying,
"[a]Remove the filthy garments from
him." Again he said to him, "See, I
have [b]made your iniquity pass away
from you and [1]will [c]clothe you with
festal robes." **5** Then I said, "Let them
put a clean [a]turban on his head." So
they put a clean turban on his head
and clothed him with garments,
while the angel of Yahweh was
standing by.
**6** And the angel of Yahweh testi-
fied to Joshua, saying, **7** "Thus says
Yahweh of hosts, 'If you will [a]walk
in My ways and if you will keep the
*responsibility given by* Me, then you
will also [b]render justice in My house
and also keep My [c]courts, and I will
grant you [1]access to walk among
these who are standing *here.* **8** Now
listen, Joshua the high priest, you and
your friends who are sitting in front
of you—indeed they are men who
are a [a]wondrous sign, for behold, I
am going to bring in My servant the
[b,1]Branch. **9** For behold, the stone
that I have put before Joshua; on one
stone are [a]seven eyes. Behold, I will
engrave an inscription on it,' declares
Yahweh of hosts, 'and I will [b]remove
the iniquity of that land in one day.
**10** In that day,' declares Yahweh of
hosts, 'every one of you will call for
his neighbor to *sit* under *his* [a]vine
and under *his* fig tree.'"

### *The Golden Lampstand*

**4** Then [a]the angel who was
speaking with me returned and
[b]roused me, as a man who is roused
from his sleep. **2** And he said to me,
"[a]What do you see?" And I said, "I
see, and behold, a [b]lampstand all
of gold with its bowl on the top of
it, and its [c]seven lamps on it with
seven spouts belonging to each of
the lamps which are on the top of
it, **3** also [a]two olive trees by it, one
on the right side of the bowl and
the other on its left side." **4** Then I
answered and said to the angel who
was speaking with me saying, "What
are these, [a]my lord?" **5** So [a]the angel
who was speaking with me answered
and said to me, "[b]Do you not know
what these are?" And I said, "No, my

---

**2:12** [a]Dt 32:9; Ps 33:12; Jer 10:16 [b]2Chr 6:6; Ps 132:13, 14; Zec 1:17 **2:13** [a]Hab 2:20; Zep 1:7 [b]Ps 78:65; Is 51:9 [1]Lit *Hush* ◆ **3:1** [a]Ezr 5:2; Hag 1:1; Zec 6:11 [b]1Chr 21:1; Job 1:6; Ps 109:6; Rev 12:10 [1]Or the *Adversary, Accuser* **3:2** [a]Mk 9:25; Jd 9 [b]Zec 2:12 [c]Am 4:11; Jd 23 **3:3** [a]Ezr 9:15; Is 4:4; 64:6 **3:4** [a]Is 43:25; Eze 36:25 [b]Mic 7:18, 19; Zec 3:9 [c]Is 52:1; 61:10 [1]Lit *to clothe* **3:5** [a]Job 29:14; Is 3:23 **3:7** [a]1Ki 3:14 [b]Dt 17:9, 12 [c]Is 62:9 [1]Lit *goings* **3:8** [a]Is 8:18; 20:3; Eze 12:11 [b]Is 11:1; 53:2; Jer 23:5; 33:15; Zec 6:12 [1]Lit *Sprout* **3:9** [a]Zec 4:10 [b]Jer 31:34; 50:20; Zec 3:4 **3:10** [a]1Ki 4:25; Is 36:16; Mic 4:4 ◆ **4:1** [a]Zec 1:9 [b]1Ki 19:5-7; Jer 31:26 **4:2** [a]Jer 1:13; Zec 5:2 [b]Ex 25:31, 37; Jer 52:19 [c]Rev 4:5 **4:3** [a]Zec 4:11; Rev 11:4 **4:4** [a]Zec 1:9; 4:5, 13; 6:4 **4:5** [a]Zec 1:9; 4:1 [b]Zec 4:13

lord." **6** Then he answered and spoke to me, saying, "This is the word of Yahweh to [a]Zerubbabel, saying, '[b]Not by [1]might nor by power, but by My [c]Spirit,' says Yahweh of hosts. **7** 'What are you, O great [a]mountain? Before Zerubbabel *you will become* a plain; and he will bring forth the top stone with [b]shouts of "Grace, grace to it!"'"

**8** Also the word of Yahweh came to me, saying, **9** "The hands of Zerubbabel have [a]laid the foundation of this house, and his hands will [b]finish *it*. Then you will know that Yahweh of hosts has sent me to [1]you. **10** For who has despised the day of [a]small things? [1]But these [b]seven will be glad when they see the [c,2]plumb line in the hand of Zerubbabel—*these are* the [d]eyes of Yahweh which [e]roam to and fro throughout the earth."

**11** Then I answered and said to him, "What are these [a]two olive trees on the right of the lampstand and on its left?" **12** And I answered the second time and said to him, "What are the two olive [1]branches which are beside the two golden pipes, which empty the golden *oil* from themselves?" **13** So he spoke to me, saying, "[a]Do you not know what these are?" And I said, "No, [b]my lord." **14** Then he said, "These are the two [a,1]anointed ones who are [b]standing by the [c]Lord of all the earth."

### *A Flying Scroll*

**5** Then I lifted up my eyes again and saw, and behold, a flying [a]scroll. **2** And he said to me, "[a]What do you see?" And I said, "I see a flying scroll; its length is [1]twenty cubits and its width ten cubits." **3** Then he said to me, "This is the [a]curse that is going forth over the face of the whole [1]land; surely everyone who [b]steals will be [2]purged away according to [3]the writing on one side, and everyone who [c]swears will be [2]purged away according to the writing on the other side. **4** I will [a]make it go forth," declares Yahweh of hosts, "and it will [b]enter the house of the [c]thief and the house of the one who swears falsely by My name; and it will spend the night within that house and [d]consume it with its timber and stones."

### *A Woman in an Ephah*

**5** Then [a]the angel who was speaking with me went out and said to me, "Lift up now your eyes and see what this is going forth." **6** So I said, "What is it?" And he said, "This is the [a,1]ephah going forth." Again he said, "This is their [2]appearance in all the [3]land **7** (and behold, a lead cover was lifted up); and this is a woman sitting inside the ephah." **8** Then he said, "This is [a]Wickedness!" And he threw her down into the middle of the ephah and threw the lead weight

**4:6** [a]Ezr 5:2; Hag 2:4, 5 [b]Is 11:2-4; 30:1; Hos 1:7 [c]2Chr 32:7, 8; Eph 6:17 [1]Lit *valor* **4:7** [a]Ps 114:4, 6; Is 40:4; Jer 51:25; Na 1:5; Zec 14:4, 5 [b]Ezr 3:10, 11; Ps 84:11 **4:9** [a]Ezr 3:8-10; 5:16; Hag 2:18 [b]Ezr 6:14, 15; Zec 6:12, 13 [1]Lit *you* (plural) **4:10** [a]Ne 4:2-4; Am 7:2, 5; Hag 2:3 [b]Zec 3:9; Rev 8:2 [c]Am 7:7, 8 [d]2Chr 16:9; Pr 15:3; Jer 16:17 [e]Zec 1:10; Rev 5:6 [1]Or *But they will rejoice when they see...Zerubbabel. These seven are the eyes of Yahweh* [2]Lit *plummet stone* **4:11** [a]Zec 4:3; Rev 11:4 **4:12** [1]Or *clusters* **4:13** [a]Zec 4:5 [b]Zec 4:4, 5 **4:14** [a]Ex 29:7; 40:15; 1Sa 16:1, 12, 13; Is 61:1-3; Da 9:24-26 [b]Zec 3:1-7 [c]Mic 4:13 [1]Lit *sons of fresh oil* ◆**5:1** [a]Jer 36:2; Eze 2:9; Rev 5:1 **5:2** [a]Zec 4:2 [1]Approx. 30 ft. long and 15 ft. wide or 9 m and 4.5 m **5:3** [a]Is 24:6; 43:28; Jer 26:6 [b]Ex 20:15; Lv 19:11; Mal 3:8, 9 [c]Lv 19:12; Is 48:1; Jer 5:2; Zec 5:4 [1]Or *earth* [2]Lit *free* (from covenant community), cf. Ge 24:8, 41 [3]Lit *it* **5:4** [a]Mal 3:5 [b]Hos 4:2, 3 [c]Jer 2:26 [d]Lv 14:34, 35; Job 18:15 **5:5** [a]Zec 1:9 **5:6** [a]Lv 19:36; Am 8:5 [1]A vessel containing approx. 21 qt. or 23 l [2]Lit *eye*; some ancient versions *iniquity* [3]Or *earth* **5:8** [a]Hos 12:7; Am 8:5; Mic 6:11

on its [1]opening. **9** Then I lifted up my
eyes and saw, and behold, two wom-
en were coming out with the wind in
their wings; and they had wings like
the wings of a [a]stork, and they lifted
up the ephah between the earth and
the heavens. **10** And I said to the angel
who was speaking with me, "Where
are they taking the ephah?" **11** Then
he said to me, "To build a [1]house for
her in the land of [a]Shinar; and when
it is prepared, she will be set there on
her own pedestal."

### *Four Chariots*

**6** Then I lifted up my eyes again
and saw, and behold, [a]four
chariots were coming forth from
between the two mountains; and
the mountains *were* bronze moun-
tains. **2** With the first chariot *were*
[a]red horses, with the second chariot
[b]black horses, **3** with the third chariot
[a]white horses, and with the fourth
chariot [b]dappled horses—*all of them*
mighty. **4** Then I answered and said to
the angel who was speaking with me,
"[a]What are these, my lord?" **5** And
the angel answered and said to me,
"These are the [a]four spirits of heav-
en, going forth after standing before
the Lord of all the earth, **6** with one
of which the black horses are going
forth to the [a]north country; and the
white ones go forth after them, and
the dappled ones go forth to the
[b]south country. **7** Now the mighty
ones went out, and they sought to
go to [a,1]patrol the earth." And He
said, "Go, [1]patrol the earth." So they
[2]patrolled the earth. **8** Then He cried
out to me and spoke to me saying,
"See, those who are going to the land
of the north have [a]caused My Spirit
to have rest in the land of the north."

### *The Crown and the Temple*

**9** And the [a]word of Yahweh came
to me, saying, **10** "[a]Take *an offering*
from the exiles, from Heldai, Tobi-
jah, and Jedaiah; and you come the
same day and come into the house of
Josiah the son of Zephaniah, where
they have come from Babylon. **11** And
take silver and gold, make an *ornate*
[a]crown, and set *it* on the head of
[b]Joshua the son of Jehozadak, the
high priest. **12** Then you will say to
him, 'Thus says Yahweh of hosts, "Be-
hold, a man whose name is [a,1]Branch,
and He will [b,2]branch out from where
He is; and He will [c]build the temple
of Yahweh. **13** Indeed, it is He who
will build the temple of Yahweh, and
He who will [a]bear the splendor and
sit and [b]rule on His throne. Thus,
He will be a [c]priest on His throne,
and the counsel of peace will be
between the two [1]offices."' **14** Now
the [a]crown will become a memorial
in the temple of Yahweh to Helem,
Tobijah, Jedaiah, and [1]Hen the son
of Zephaniah. **15** [a]And those who
are far off will come and [1]build the
temple of Yahweh." Then you will
[b]know that Yahweh of hosts has sent

**5:8** [1]Lit *mouth* **5:9** [a]Lv 11:13, 19; Ps 104:17; Jer 8:7 **5:11** [a]Ge 10:10; 11:2; 14:1; Is 11:11; Da 1:2 [1]Or *temple*
◆**6:1** [a]Da 7:3; 8:22; Zec 1:18; 6:5 **6:2** [a]Zec 1:8; Rev 6:4 [b]Rev 6:5 **6:3** [a]Rev 6:2 [b]Rev 6:8
**6:4** [a]Zec 1:9 **6:5** [a]Jer 49:36; Eze 37:9; Da 7:2; 11:4; Mt 24:31; Rev 7:1 **6:6** [a]Jer 1:14, 15; 4:6; 6:1; 25:9; 46:10; Eze 1:4 [b]Is 43:6; Da 11:5 **6:7** [a]Zec 1:10 [1]Lit *walk about through* [2]Lit *walked about through* **6:8** [a]Eze 5:13; 24:13; Zec 1:15 **6:9** [a]Zec 1:1; 7:1; 8:1 **6:10** [a]Ezr 7:14-16; 8:26-30; Jer 28:6
**6:11** [a]2Sa 12:30; Ps 21:3; SS 3:11 [b]Ezr 3:2; Hag 1:1; Zec 3:1 **6:12** [a]Is 4:2; 11:1; Jer 23:5; 33:15; Zec 3:8 [b]Is 53:2 [c]Ezr 3:8, 10; Am 9:11; Zec 4:6-9 [1]Lit *Sprout* [2]Lit *sprout up* **6:13** [a]Is 9:6; 11:10; 22:24; 49:5, 6 [b]Is 9:7 [c]Ps 110:1, 4 [1]Lit *of them* **6:14** [a]Zec 6:11 [1]Josiah **6:15** [a]Is 56:6-8; 60:10 [b]Zec 2:9-11; 4:9 [1]Lit *build in*

me to you. And it will happen if you
utterly [c]listen to the voice of Yahweh
your God.

### *The People's Hard Hearts*

7 Now it happened that in the fourth
year of King Darius, the word of
Yahweh came to Zechariah on the
fourth *day* of the ninth month, *which*
*is* [a]Chislev. **2** And *the town of* Bethel
sent Sharezer and Regemmelech and
[1]their men to [a,2]entreat the favor of
Yahweh, **3** speaking to the [a]priests,
who belong to the house of Yahweh
of hosts, and to the prophets, saying,
"Shall I weep in the [b]fifth month [1]and
abstain, as I have done these many
years?" **4** Then the word of Yahweh
of hosts came to me, saying, **5** "Speak
to all the people of the land and to
the priests, saying, 'When you fasted
and mourned in the fifth and seventh
months [1]these [a]seventy years, was
it actually for [b]Me that you fasted?
**6** And when you eat and when you
drink, [1]are you not eating for your-
selves and are you not drinking for
yourselves? **7** Are not *these* the words
which Yahweh [a]called out by the
hand of the former prophets, when
Jerusalem was inhabited and [b]at ease
along with its cities around it, and
the [c,1]Negev and the [2]Shephelah were
inhabited?'"
**8** Then the word of Yahweh came
to Zechariah saying, **9** "Thus has
Yahweh of hosts said, '[a]Judge with
true justice and show [b]lovingkind-
ness and compassion each to his
brother; **10** and [a]do not oppress the
widow or the [1]orphan, the sojourner
or the afflicted; and do [b]not devise
evil in your hearts against one anoth-
er.' **11** But they [a]refused to give heed
and [b,1]turned a stubborn shoulder
and [c,2]dulled their ears from hear-
ing. **12** And they made their [a]hearts
[b,1]diamond-hard [2]so that they could
not hear the law and the [c]words
which Yahweh of hosts had sent by
His Spirit by the hand of the [d]former
prophets; therefore great [e]wrath
came from Yahweh of hosts. **13** And it
happened that just as [a]He called and
they would not listen, so [b]they called
and I would not listen," says Yahweh
of hosts; **14** "but I [a,1]scattered them
with a [b]storm wind among all the
nations whom they have not known.
Thus the land is [c]desolated behind
them [2]so that [d]no one was passing
through and returning, for they
[e]made the pleasant land desolate."

### *Jerusalem, the City of Truth*

8 Then the word of Yahweh of
hosts came, saying, **2** "Thus says
Yahweh of hosts, '[1]I am [a]jealous with
great jealousy for Zion, and with
great wrath I am jealous for her.'
**3** Thus says Yahweh, 'I will return
to Zion and will [a]dwell in the midst

**6:15** [c]Is 58:10-14; Jer 7:23; Zec 3:7 ◆**7:1** [a]Ne 1:1 **7:2** [a]1Ki 13:6; Jer 26:19; Zec 8:21 [1]Lit *his* [2]Lit *soften the face of* **7:3** [a]Ezr 3:10-12 [b]Zec 8:19 [1]Or *dedicating myself*; lit *abstaining* **7:5** [a]Zec 1:12 [b]Is 1:11, 12; 58:5 [1]Lit *and these* **7:6** [1]Lit *is it not you who eat and you who drink* **7:7** [a]Is 1:16-20; Jer 7:5, 23; Zec 1:4 [b]Jer 22:21 [c]Jer 13:19; 32:44 [1]South country [2]Or lowland **7:9** [a]Eze 18:8; 45:9; Zec 8:16 [b]2Sa 9:7; Job 6:14; Mic 6:8 **7:10** [a]Ex 22:22; Ps 72:4; Jer 7:6 [b]Ps 21:11; Mic 2:1; Zec 8:17 [1]Or *fatherless* **7:11** [a]Jer 5:3; 8:5; 11:10 [b]Jer 7:26; 17:23 [c]Ps 58:4; Jer 5:21 [1]Lit *gave* [2]Lit *heavy, hardened*; cf. Ex 8:15; 1Sa 6:6 **7:12** [a]2Chr 36:13; Eze 2:4; 3:7-9 [b]Jer 17:1; Eze 3:9 [c]Zec 7:7 [d]Ne 9:30 [e]2Chr 36:16; Da 9:11, 12 [1]Lit *corundum* [2]Lit *from hearing* **7:13** [a]Jer 11:10, 14; 14:12 [b]Pr 1:24-28; Is 1:15 **7:14** [a]Dt 4:27; 28:64 [b]Jer 23:19 [c]Jer 44:6 [d]Is 60:15 [e]Jer 12:10 [1]Lit *stormed them away upon all* [2]Lit *from passing and from returning* ◆**8:2** [a]Zec 1:14 [1]Or *I am exceedingly jealous*, cf. 1:14 **8:3** [a]Zec 2:10, 11

of Jerusalem. Then Jerusalem will be called the City of [b]Truth, and the mountain of Yahweh of hosts *will be called* the Holy Mountain.' **4** Thus says Yahweh of hosts, '[a]Old men and old women will again sit in the [1]streets of Jerusalem, each man with his staff in his hand because of [2]age. **5** And the [1]streets of the city will be filled with [a]boys and girls playing in its [1]streets.' **6** Thus says Yahweh of hosts, 'If it is [a,1]too difficult in the sight of the remnant of this people in those days, will it also be [b,1]too difficult in My sight?' declares Yahweh of hosts. **7** Thus says Yahweh of hosts, 'Behold, I am going to save My people from the land where the [a,1]*sun* rises and from the land where the [2]sun sets; **8** and I will [a]bring them *back*, and they will [b]dwell in the midst of Jerusalem; and they shall be [c]My people, and I will be their God in [1]truth and righteousness.'

**9** "Thus says Yahweh of hosts, 'Let your hands be [a]strong, you who are listening in these days to these words from the mouth of the [b]prophets, *those* who *spoke* in the day that the foundation of the house of Yahweh of hosts was laid, to the end that the temple might be built. **10** For before those days there was [a]no wage for man or any wage for animal; and for him who went out or came in there was no [b,1]peace because of the adversary, and I [c]set all men one against another. **11** But now I will [a]not [1]treat the remnant of this people as in the former days,' declares Yahweh of hosts. **12** 'For *there will be* [a]peace for the seed: the vine will yield its fruit, the land will yield its produce, and the heavens will give their [b]dew; and I will cause the remnant of this people to inherit [c]all these *things*. **13** And it will be that just as you were a [a]curse among the nations, O house of Judah and house of Israel, so I will save you that you may become a [b]blessing. Do not fear; let your [c]hands be strong.'

**14** "For thus says Yahweh of hosts, 'Just as I [a]purposed to bring about evil to you when your fathers provoked Me to wrath,' says Yahweh of hosts, 'and I have not [b]relented, **15** so I have again purposed in these days to [a]do good to Jerusalem and to the house of Judah. [b]Do not fear! **16** These are the things which you should do: speak the [a]truth to one another; [b]judge with truth and judgment for peace in your [1]gates. **17** Also let none of you [a]devise evil in your heart against another, and do not love [b,1]false oaths; for all these are what I [c]hate,' declares Yahweh."

**18** Then the word of Yahweh of hosts came to me, saying, **19** "Thus says Yahweh of hosts, 'The fast of the [a]fourth, the fast of the [b]fifth, the fast

**8:3** [b]Zec 8:16, 19 **8:4** [a]Is 65:20 [1]Or *squares* [2]Lit *the multitude of days* **8:5** [a]Jer 30:19, 20; 31:12, 13 [1]Or *squares* **8:6** [a]Ps 118:23; 126:1-3 [b]Jer 32:17, 27 [1]Or *marvelous*, cf. Ge 18:14 **8:7** [a]Ps 107:3; Is 11:11; 27:12, 13; 43:5 [1]Or *east* [2]Or *west* **8:8** [a]Zep 3:20; Zec 10:10 [b]Jer 3:17; Eze 37:25 [c]Eze 11:20; 36:28; Zec 2:11 [1]Or *faithfulness* **8:9** [a]1Chr 22:13; Is 35:4; Hag 2:4 [b]Ezr 5:1; 6:14 **8:10** [a]Hag 2:15-19 [b]2Chr 15:5 [c]Is 19:2; Am 3:6; 9:4 [1]Or *safety* **8:11** [a]Ps 103:9; Is 12:1; Hag 2:19 [1]Lit *be to the* **8:12** [a]Lv 26:3-6 [b]Ge 27:28; Dt 33:13, 28; Hos 13:3 [c]Is 61:7; Ob 17 **8:13** [a]Jer 29:18; Da 9:11 [b]Ps 72:17; Is 19:24, 25; Eze 34:26; Zec 14:11 [c]Zec 8:9 **8:14** [a]Jer 31:28 [b]Jer 4:28; Eze 24:14 **8:15** [a]Jer 29:11; Mic 7:18-20 [b]Zec 8:13 **8:16** [a]Ps 15:2; Pr 12:17-19; Zec 8:3; Eph 4:25 [b]Is 9:7; 11:4, 5; Zec 7:9 [1]The place where court was held **8:17** [a]Pr 3:29; Jer 4:14; Zec 7:10 [b]Zec 5:4; Mal 3:5 [c]Pr 6:16-19; Hab 1:13 [1]Lit *lying*, cf. Ex 20:16 **8:19** [a]2Ki 25:3, 4; Jer 39:2 [b]Zec 7:3, 5

of the [c]seventh, and the fast of the
[d]tenth *months* will become [e]joy, glad-
ness, and [1]merry appointed feasts for
the house of Judah; so [f]love truth and
peace.'
**20** "Thus says Yahweh of hosts, '*It*
*will* yet *be* that [a]peoples will come,
even the inhabitants of many cities.
**21** The inhabitants of one will go to
another, saying, "Let us go at once
to [a,1]entreat the favor of Yahweh and
to seek Yahweh of hosts; [2]I will also
go." **22** So [a]many peoples and mighty
nations will come to seek Yahweh of
hosts in Jerusalem and to [b,1]entreat
the favor of Yahweh.' **23** Thus says
Yahweh of hosts, 'In those days ten
men from every tongue of the na-
tions will [a,1]take hold of the [2]garment
of a Jew, saying, "Let us go with you,
for we have heard that God is with
you."'"

### *Yahweh's Oracle Against Israel's Enemies*

**9** The [1]oracle of the word of Yahweh
is against the land of Hadrach,
with [a]Damascus as its resting place
(for the eyes of men, especially of
all the tribes of Israel, are toward
Yahweh),

**2** And [a]Hamath also,
which borders on it;
[b]*And* Tyre and [c]Sidon,
[1]because [2]they are
[b]very wise.
**3** So Tyre built herself
a [a]tight fortification
And [b]tied up silver like dust
And [c]fine gold
like the mire of the streets.
**4** Behold, the Lord will
[a]dispossess her
And strike her wealth
down into the sea;
And she will be
[b]consumed with fire.
**5** Ashkelon will see *it*
and be afraid.
Gaza too will writhe
in great pain;
Also Ekron, for her hope
has been put to shame.
Moreover, the king will
perish from Gaza,
And Ashkelon will not
be inhabited.
**6** And those of illegitimate
birth will inhabit [a]Ashdod,
And I will cut off the pride
of the Philistines.
**7** And I will remove their
blood from their mouth
And their detestable things
from between their teeth.
Then they also will be
a remnant for our God,
And be like a [1]clan in Judah,
And Ekron like a Jebusite.
**8** But I will camp
around My house
[1]because of an army,
Because of [a]him who
passes by and returns;
And [b]no taskmaster will
pass over them anymore,
For now I have seen
with My eyes.

**8:19** [c]2Ki 25:25; Zec 7:5 [d]Jer 52:4 [e]Ps 30:11; Is 12:1 [f]Zec 8:16; Lk 1:74, 75 [1]Or *goodly* **8:20** [a]Ps 117:1; Jer 16:19; Mic 4:2, 3; Zec 2:11; 14:16 **8:21** [a]Zec 7:2 [1]Lit *soften the face of* [2]Or *let me go too* **8:22** [a]Is 2:2, 3; 25:7; 49:6, 22, 23; 60:3-12 [b]Zec 8:21 [1]Lit *soften the face of* **8:23** [a]Is 45:14, 24; 60:14 [1]Lit *grasp, and they will grasp* [2]Or *corner of the garment* ◆ **9:1** [a]Is 17:1; Jer 49:23-27; Am 1:3-5 [1]Or *burden* **9:2** [a]Jer 49:23 [b]Eze 28:2-5, 12 [c]Eze 28:21 [1]Or *though* [2]They think they are **9:3** [a]Jos 19:29; 2Sa 24:7 [b]Job 27:16; Eze 27:33; 28:4, 5 [c]1Ki 10:21, 27 **9:4** [a]Eze 26:3-5 [b]Eze 28:18 **9:6** [a]Am 1:8; Zep 2:4 **9:7** [1]Or *chief* **9:8** [a]Is 52:1 [b]Is 54:14; 60:18 [1]Or *as a guard, so that none will go back and forth*

### The Coming King of Zion

9 [a]Rejoice greatly,
O daughter of Zion!
Make a loud shout,
O daughter of Jerusalem!
Behold, your [b]king is
coming to you;
He is [c,1]righteous and
[d]endowed with salvation,
[e,2]Lowly and mounted
on a donkey,
Even on a [f,3]colt, the [4]foal
of a pack animal.
10 I will [a]cut off the chariot
from Ephraim
And the [b]horse
from Jerusalem;
And the [c]bow of war
will be cut off.
And He will speak [d]peace
to the nations;
And His [e]reign will be
from sea to sea
And from the [1]River
to the ends of the earth.

11 As for you also, because of
the [a]blood of your covenant,
I have set your [b]prisoners free
from the [1]waterless pit.
12 Return to the [a,1]stronghold,
O prisoners [2]who
have the [b]hope;
This very day I am
declaring that I will
return [c]double to you.
13 For I will [a]bend Judah
[1]as My bow;
I will fill the bow
with Ephraim.
And I will rouse up your
sons, O Zion, against
your sons, O [b,2]Greece;
And I will make you like
a [c]mighty man's sword.
14 Then Yahweh will
appear [a]over them,
And His [b]arrow will go
forth like lightning;
And Lord Yahweh will
blow the [c]trumpet
And will go in the [d]storm
winds of the south.
15 [a]Yahweh of hosts will
defend them.
And they will [b]consume
and trample
on the [c]stones of a sling;
And they will drink *and*
[d]roar as with wine;
And they will be filled
like a *sacrificial* bowl,
*Drenched* like the
[e]corners of the altar.
16 And Yahweh their God will
[a]save them in that day
As the flock of His people;
For *they are as* the
stones of a [b]crown,
[1]Sparkling in His land.
17 For what [a]goodness
and [b]what beauty
*will be* [1]theirs!
Grain will make the choice
men flourish, and new
wine the virgins.

---

**9:9** [a]Zep 3:14, 15; Zec 2:10 [b]Ps 110:1; Is 9:6, 7; Jer 23:5, 6; Mt 21:5; Jn 12:15 [c]Zep 3:5 [d]Is 43:3, 11 [e]Is 57:15 [f]Jdg 10:4; Is 30:6 [1]Or *vindicated and victorious* [2]Or *humble, afflicted* [3]Or *foal,* cf. Ge 49:11 [4]Or *donkey's colt,* cf. Ge 49:11; lit *son of a female donkey* **9:10** [a]Hos 1:7 [b]Mic 5:10 [c]Hos 2:18 [d]Is 57:19; Mic 4:2-4 [e]Ps 72:8; Is 60:12 [1]The Euphrates River **9:11** [a]Ex 24:8; Heb 10:2 [b]Is 24:22; 51:14 [1]Lit *cistern in which there is no water* **9:12** [a]Jer 16:19; Joel 3:16 [b]Jer 14:8; 17:13; Heb 6:18, 19 [c]Is 61:7 [1]Or *Stronghold* [2]Lit *of the hope* **9:13** [a]Jer 51:20 [b]Joel 3:6 [c]Ps 45:3 [1]Lit *for Me* [2]Lit *Javan* **9:14** [a]Is 31:5; Zec 2:5 [b]Ps 18:14; Hab 3:11 [c]Is 27:13 [d]Is 21:1; 66:15 **9:15** [a]Is 37:35; Zec 12:8 [b]Zec 12:6 [c]Job 41:28 [d]Ps 78:65 [e]Ex 27:2 **9:16** [a]Jer 31:10, 11 [b]Is 62:3 [1]Or *Displayed over* **9:17** [a]Jer 31:12, 14 [b]Ps 27:4; Is 33:17 [1]Lit *his*

### *Yahweh Will Redeem Judah and Israel*

**10** Ask [a]rain from Yahweh at
the time of the [1]late rain—
Yahweh who [b]makes
the [2]storm clouds;
And He will give them
[c]showers of rain, *the* plant
in the field to *each* man.
2 For the [a]teraphim
speak wickedness,
And the [b]diviners behold
[1]false visions
And speak [c]worthless dreams;
They comfort in vain.
Therefore *the people*
journey like [d]sheep;
They are afflicted because
there is no shepherd.
3 "My [a]anger burns
against the shepherds,
And I will visit *punishment*
upon the [1]male goats;
For Yahweh of hosts has
[b]visited His flock, the
house of Judah,
And will make them like His
splendid horse in battle.
4 "From [1]them will come
the [a]cornerstone,
From [1]them the tent peg,
From [1]them the bow of [b,2]battle,
From [1]them every *good*
[3]taskmaster, *all*
*of them* together.
5 "And they will be
as mighty men,
[a]Treading down *the*
*enemy* in the mire
of the streets in battle;
And they will battle, for
Yahweh *will be* with them;
And the [b]riders on horses
will be put to shame.
6 "I will [a]make the house
of Judah mighty,
And I will [b]save the
house of Joseph,
And I will [c,1]cause
them to return,
Because I have had
[d]compassion on them;
And they will be as though I
had [e]not rejected them,
For I am Yahweh their God,
and I will [f]answer them.
7 "And Ephraim will be
like a mighty man,
And their heart will be
glad as if *from* wine;
Indeed, their [a]children
will see *it* and be glad;
[1]Their heart will rejoice
in Yahweh.
8 "I will [a]whistle for them
to gather them together,
For I have redeemed them;
And they will be as [b]numerous
as they [c]were [1]before.
9 "And I will sow them
among the peoples,
And they will [a]remember
Me in far countries,
And they with their children
will live and turn back.
10 "Then I will cause them
to [a]return from the land
of Egypt
And gather them from Assyria;

◆ **10:1** [a]Joel 2:23 [b]Jer 10:13 [c]Is 30:23 [1]Spring [2]Or *thunderbolts* **10:2** [a]Eze 21:21; Hos 3:4 [b]Jer 27:9 [c]Jer 23:32 [d]Eze 34:5, 8; Mt 9:36; Mk 6:34 [1]Lit a *lie* **10:3** [a]Jer 25:34-36 [b]Eze 34:12 [1]Or *leaders* **10:4** [a]Lk 20:17; Eph 2:20; 1Pe 2:6 [b]Jer 51:20; Zec 9:10 [1]Lit *him* [2]Or *war*, cf. 9:10 [3]Or *oppressor* **10:5** [a]2Sa 22:43 [b]Am 2:15; Hag 2:22 **10:6** [a]Zec 10:12 [b]Zec 8:7; 9:16 [c]Zec 8:8 [d]Is 54:8; Zec 1:16 [e]Is 54:4 [f]Zec 13:9 [1]Or *make them dwell* **10:7** [a]Is 54:13; Eze 37:25 [1]Or *Let their heart rejoice* **10:8** [a]Is 5:26; 7:18, 19 [b]Jer 33:22; Rev 7:9 [c]Jer 30:20; Eze 36:11 [1]Lit *numerous* **10:9** [a]1Ki 8:47, 48; Eze 6:9 **10:10** [a]Is 11:11

And I will bring them into the
land of [b]Gilead and Lebanon
[1]Until [c]no *room* can be
found for them.
11 “And [1]they will pass
through the [a]sea *of* distress,
And He will strike the
waves in the sea,
So that all the depths
of the [b]Nile will dry up;
And the pride of [c]Assyria
will be brought down,
And the scepter
of [d]Egypt will depart.
12 “And I will [a]make them
mighty in Yahweh,
And in His name [b]they will
walk,” declares Yahweh.

### *Woe to the Worthless Shepherd*

11 Open your doors,
O Lebanon,
That a [a]fire may consume
your [b]cedars.
2 Wail, O [1]cypress, for the
cedar has fallen,
Because the mighty *trees*
have been destroyed;
Wail, O oaks of Bashan,
For the [2]impenetrable
forest has come down.
3 There is a sound
of the shepherds’ [a]wail,
For their might is destroyed;
There is a [b]sound of the
young lions’ roar,
For the [1]pride of the
Jordan is destroyed.

4 Thus says Yahweh my God,
“Shepherd the flock *doomed* to
[a]slaughter. 5 Those who buy them
slaughter them and are not [a]held
guilty, and *each of* those who sell
them says, ‘Blessed be Yahweh.
Indeed, [b]I have become rich!’ And
their [c]own shepherds do not spare
them. 6 For I will [a]no longer spare
the inhabitants of the land,” declares
Yahweh; “but behold, I will [b]cause
the men to [1]fall, each into another’s
hand and into the hand of his king;
and they will crush the land, and
I will [c]not deliver *them* from their
hand.”
7 So I [a]shepherded the flock
*doomed* to slaughter—[1]hence the
[b]afflicted of the flock. And I took
for myself two [c]staffs: the one I
called [d,2]Favor, and the other I called
[e,3]Union; so I shepherded the flock.
8 Then I annihilated the three shep-
herds in [a]one month, for my soul was
impatient with them, and their soul
also [1]was weary of me. 9 Then I said,
“I will not shepherd you. What is to
[a]die, [1]let it die, and what is to be an-
nihilated, [2]let it be annihilated; and
[3]let those who remain consume one
another’s flesh.” 10 And I took my staff
[a,1]Favor and cut it in pieces, to [b,2]break
my covenant which I had cut with
all the peoples. 11 So it was [1]broken
on that day, and [2]thus the [a]afflicted
of the flock who were watching me
knew that it was the word of Yahweh.
12 And I said to them, “If it is good in

**10:10** [b]Jer 50:19 [c]Is 49:19, 20 [1]Lit *And* **10:11** [a]Is 51:9, 10 [b]Is 19:5-7 [c]Zep 2:13 [d]Eze 30:13 [1]Or *He*
**10:12** [a]Zec 10:6 [b]Mic 4:5 ◆ **11:1** [a]Jer 22:6, 7 [b]Eze 31:3 **11:2** [1]Or *juniper* [2]Or *forest of the vintage*
**11:3** [a]Jer 25:34-36 [b]Jer 2:15; 50:44 [1]Or *jungle* **11:4** [a]Ps 44:22; Zec 11:7 **11:5** [a]Jer 50:7 [b]Hos 12:8; 1Ti 6:9 [c]Eze 34:2, 3 **11:6** [a]Jer 13:14 [b]Is 9:19-21; Mic 7:2-6; Zec 14:13 [c]Ps 50:22; Mic 5:8 [1]Lit *find*
**11:7** [a]Zec 11:4 [b]Jer 39:10; Zep 3:12 [c]Eze 37:16 [d]Ps 27:4; 90:17; Zec 11:10 [e]Ps 133:1; Eze 37:16-23; Zec 11:14 [1]Or *for the sheep dealers* [2]Or *Pleasantness* [3]Or *Cords* **11:8** [a]Hos 5:7 [1]Or *detested* **11:9** [a]Jer 15:2 [1]Or *will die* [2]Or *will be annihilated* [3]Or *those...will eat* **11:10** [a]Zec 11:7 [b]Ps 89:39; Jer 14:21 [1]Or *Pleasantness* [2]Or *annul* **11:11** [a]Zep 3:12 [1]Or *annulled* [2]Or *the sheep dealers who*

your sight, give *me* my [a]wages; but if
not, [1]never mind!" So they weighed
out [b]thirty [2]*shekels* of silver as my
wages. **13** Then Yahweh said to me,
"Throw it to the [a]potter, *that* valuable
price at which I was valued by them."
So I took the thirty *shekels* of silver
and threw them to the potter in the
house of Yahweh. **14** Then I cut in
pieces my second staff [a,1]Union, to
[b]break the brotherhood between
Judah and Israel.

**15** Then Yahweh said to me, "Take
again for yourself the equipment of
a [a,1]foolish shepherd. **16** For behold,
I am going to raise up a shepherd
in the land who will [a]not care for
those who face annihilation, seek the
young, heal the broken, or sustain
the one standing, but will [b]consume
the flesh of the fat *sheep* and tear off
their hoofs.

**17** "[a]Woe to the worthless
shepherd
Who forsakes the flock!
A [b]sword will be on his arm
And on his right eye!
His [c]arm will be
totally dried up,
And his right eye will be
utterly dimmed."

### *Yahweh Will Save*

**12** The oracle of the word of Yah-
weh concerning Israel.
*Thus* declares Yahweh who
[a]stretches out the heavens, [b]lays
the foundation of the earth, and
[c]forms the spirit of man within him,
**2** "Behold, I am going to make Jerusa-
lem a [a]cup [1]that causes reeling to all
the peoples all around. Now *the one*
in siege against Jerusalem will also
*be* against [b]Judah. **3** But it will be in
that day, *that* I will make Jerusalem
a heavy [a]stone for all the peoples;
all who heave it up will be [b]severely
[1]injured. And all the [c]nations of the
earth will be gathered against it. **4** In
that day," declares Yahweh, "I will
strike every horse with bewilderment
and his rider with madness. But I
will open my eyes *to watch* over the
house of Judah, while I strike every
horse of the peoples with blindness.
**5** Then the clans of Judah will say in
their hearts, '[1]A strong support for
us are the inhabitants of Jerusalem
through Yahweh of hosts, their God.'

**6** "In that day I will make the
clans of Judah like a [a]fiery laver
among pieces of wood and a fiery
torch among sheaves, so they will
consume on the right hand and on
the left all the surrounding peoples,
while Jerusalem will again be [b]inhab-
ited in its own place—in Jerusalem.
**7** Yahweh also will [a]save the tents of
Judah first so that the glory of the
house of [b]David and the glory of
the inhabitants of Jerusalem will
not be magnified above Judah. **8** In
that day Yahweh will [a]defend the
inhabitants of Jerusalem, and the one
who [b]stumbles among them in that
day will be like David, and the house
of David *will be* like [c]God, like the
[d]angel of Yahweh before them. **9** And

**11:12** [a]1Ki 5:6; Mal 3:5 [b]Ge 37:28; Ex 21:32; Mt 26:15; 27:9, 10 [1]Lit *cease* [2]A shekel was approx. 0.4 oz. or 11 gm **11:13** [a]Mt 27:3-10; Ac 1:18, 19 **11:14** [a]Zec 11:7 [b]Is 9:21; Zec 11:6 [1]Or *Cords* **11:15** [a]Is 6:10-12; Zec 11:17 [1]Lit *ignorant foolish* **11:16** [a]Jer 23:2 [b]Eze 34:2-6 **11:17** [a]Jer 23:1; Zec 10:2; 11:15 [b]Jer 50:35-37 [c]Eze 30:21, 22 ◆ **12:1** [a]Is 42:5; 44:24; Jer 51:15 [b]Job 26:7; Ps 102:25, 26; Heb 1:10-12 [c]Is 57:16; Heb 12:9 **12:2** [a]Ps 75:8; Is 51:22, 23 [b]Zec 14:14 [1]Lit *of reeling* **12:3** [a]Da 2:34, 35, 44, 45 [b]Mt 21:44 [c]Zec 14:2 [1]Lit *scratched* **12:5** [1]Lit *My strength is* **12:6** [a]Is 10:17, 18; Ob 18; Zec 11:1 [b]Zec 2:4; 8:3-5 **12:7** [a]Jer 30:18 [b]Am 9:11 **12:8** [a]Joel 3:16; Zec 9:14, 15 [b]Lv 26:8; Jos 23:10; Mic 7:8 [c]Ps 8:5; 82:6 [d]Ex 14:19; 33:2

it will be in that day, *that* I will [a]seek
to destroy all the nations that come
against Jerusalem.

### *Mourning for the Pierced One*

**10** "And I will [a]pour out on the house
of David and on the inhabitants of
Jerusalem [1]the Spirit of grace and of
supplication, so that they will look
on Me whom they have [b]pierced;
and they will mourn for Him, as
one [c]mourns for an only son, and
they will weep bitterly over Him like
the bitter weeping over a firstborn.
**11** In that day there will be great
[a]mourning in Jerusalem, like the
mourning of Hadadrimmon in the
[1]plain of [2]Megiddo. **12** And the land
will mourn, each family alone; the
family of the house of David alone
and their wives alone; the family
of the house of Nathan alone and
their wives alone; **13** the family of the
house of Levi alone and their wives
alone; the family of the Shimeites
alone and their wives alone; **14** all
the families that remain, each family
alone and their wives alone.

### *Jerusalem Refined and Tested*

**13** "In that day a [a]fountain will be
opened for the house of David
and for the inhabitants of Jerusalem,
for [b]sin and for [c]impurity.
**2** "And it will be in that day," de-
clares Yahweh of hosts, "*that* I will
[a]cut off the names of the idols from
the land, and they will no longer be
remembered; and I will also cause the
[b]prophets and the [c]unclean spirit to
pass away from the land. **3** And it will
be that if anyone still [a]prophesies,
then his father and mother who gave
birth to him will say to him, 'You shall
[b]not live, for you have spoken [c]falsely
in the name of Yahweh'; and his
[d]father and mother who gave birth
to him will pierce him through when
he prophesies. **4** And it will be in that
day, *that* the prophets will each be
[a]ashamed of his vision when he
prophesies, and they will not put on
a [b]hairy mantle in order to deceive;
**5** but he will say, 'I am [a]not a prophet;
I am a cultivator of the ground, for a
man [1]sold me as a slave in my youth.'
**6** And one will say to him, 'What are
these wounds struck *here* [a]between
your [1]arms?' Then he will say, '*Those*
with which I was struck in the house
of [2]my friends.'

**7** "Awake, O [a]sword,
  against My [b]Shepherd
And against the man,
  My [c]Associate,"
Declares Yahweh of hosts.
"[d]Strike the Shepherd that
  the sheep may be scattered;
And I will [e]turn My hand
  [1]against the little ones.

**8** "And it will be in all the land,"
Declares Yahweh,
"That [a]two parts in it will
  be cut off *and* breathe
  their last;
But the third will be left in it.

**9** "And I will bring the third
  part through the [a]fire

---

**12:9** [a]Zec 14:2, 3 **12:10** [a]Is 44:3; Eze 39:29; Joel 2:28, 29 [b]Jn 19:37; Rev 1:7 [c]Jer 6:26; Am 8:10 [1]Or *a spirit* **12:11** [a]Mt 24:30; Rev 1:7 [1]Or *broad valley* [2]Heb *Megiddon* ◆ **13:1** [a]Jer 2:13; 17:13 [b]Ps 51:2, 7; Is 1:16-18; Jn 1:29 [c]Nu 19:17; Is 4:4; Eze 36:25 **13:2** [a]Ex 23:13; Hos 2:17 [b]Jer 23:14, 15 [c]1Ki 22:22; Eze 36:25, 29 **13:3** [a]Jer 23:34 [b]Dt 18:20; Eze 14:9 [c]Jer 23:25 [d]Dt 13:6-11; Mt 10:37 **13:4** [a]Jer 6:15; 8:9; Mic 3:7 [b]2Ki 1:8; Is 20:2; Mt 3:4 **13:5** [a]Am 7:14 [1]Lit *caused another to buy me* **13:6** [a]2Ki 9:24 [1]Lit *hands* [2]Lit *those who love me* **13:7** [a]Jer 47:6; Eze 21:3-5 [b]Is 40:11; Eze 34:23, 24; 37:24; Mic 5:2, 4 [c]Ps 2:2; Jer 23:5, 6 [d]Is 53:4, 5, 10; Mt 26:31; Mk 14:27 [e]Is 1:25 [1]Or *upon* **13:8** [a]Is 6:13; Eze 5:2-4, 12 **13:9** [a]Is 48:10; Mal 3:3

And refine them
as silver is refined
And test them as gold is tested.
[1]They will [b]call on My name,
And I will [c]answer them;
I will say, 'They are
[d]My people,'
And they will say,
'Yahweh is my God.'"

### *Yahweh Will Battle the Nations*

**14** Behold, a [a]day is coming for
Yahweh when [b]the spoil *taken*
from you will be divided among you.
**2** Indeed, I will [a]gather all the nations
against Jerusalem to battle, and the
city will be captured, the [b]houses
plundered, the women ravished, and
half of the city will go forth in exile,
but those left of the people will not be
cut off from the city. **3** Then Yahweh
will go forth and [a]fight against those
nations, as the day when He fights
on a day of battle. **4** And in that day
His feet will [a]stand on the Mount of
Olives, which is in front of Jerusalem
on the east; and the Mount of Olives
will be [b]split in its middle from east to
west by a very large valley so that half
of the mountain will move toward
the north and the other half toward
the south. **5** And you will flee by the
valley of My mountains, for the valley
of the mountains will reach to Azel;
indeed, you will flee just as you fled
before the [a]earthquake in the days of
Uzziah king of Judah. [b]Then Yahweh,
my God, will come, *and* all the holy
ones with [1]Him!
**6** And it will be in that day, *that*
there will be [a]no light; the [1]lumi-
naries will dwindle. **7** And it will be
[a]a [1]unique day which is [b]known to
Yahweh, neither day nor night, but
it will be that at [c]evening time there
will be light.
**8** And it will be in that day, [a]*that*
living waters will flow out of Jerusa-
lem, half of them toward the eastern
sea and the other half toward the
western sea; it will be in summer as
well as in winter.

### *Yahweh Will Be King over All*

**9** And Yahweh will be [a]king over all
the earth; in that day Yahweh will be
*the only* [b]one, and His name one.
**10** All the land will be changed into
a plain from [a]Geba to [b]Rimmon south
of Jerusalem; but [1]Jerusalem will [c]rise
and [d]inhabit its site from [e]Benjamin's
Gate as far as the place of the First
Gate to the [f]Corner Gate, and from
the [g]Tower of Hananel to the king's
wine presses. **11** And [1]people will
inhabit it, and there will [a]no longer
be *anything* devoted to destruction,
for Jerusalem will [b]be inhabited in
security.
**12** Now this will be the plague
with which Yahweh will plague
all the peoples who have gone to
war against Jerusalem; their flesh
will [a]rot while they stand on their

---

**13:9** [b]Ps 34:15-17; 50:15; Zec 12:10 [c]Is 58:9; 65:24; Jer 29:11-13; Zec 10:6 [d]Hos 2:23 [1]Lit *He* ◆ **14:1** [a]Is 13:6, *9; Joel 2:1;* Mal 4:1 [b]Zec 14:14 **14:2** [a]Zec 12:2, 3 [b]Is 13:16 **14:3** [a]Zec 9:14, 15 **14:4** [a]Eze 11:23 [b]Is 64:1, *2; Eze 47:1-10; Mic 1:3, 4; Hab 3:6; Zec 4:7; 14:8* **14:5** [a]*Is 29:6;* Am 1:1 [b]Ps 96:13; Is 66:15, 16; Mt 16:27; 25:31 [1]As in the ancient versions; Heb *You* **14:6** [a]Is 13:10; Jer 4:23; Eze 32:7, 8; Joel 2:30, 31; Ac 2:16, 19 [1]Lit *glorious ones will congeal* **14:7** [a]Jer 30:7; Am 8:9 [b]Is 45:21; Ac 15:18 [c]Is 58:10; Rev 22:5 [1]Lit *day one,* cf. Ge 1:5 **14:8** [a]Eze 47:1-12; Joel 3:18; Jn 7:38; Rev 22:1, 2 **14:9** [a]Is 2:2-4; 45:23; Zec 9:9; 14:16, 17 [b]Dt 6:4; Is 45:21-24 **14:10** [a]1Ki 15:22 [b]Jos 15:32; Jdg 20:45, 47 [c]Is 2:2; Am 9:11 [d]Jer 30:18; Zec 12:6 [e]Jer 37:13; 38:7 [f]2Ki 14:13 [g]Jer 31:38 [1]Lit *it* **14:11** [a]Zec 8:13; Rev 22:3 [b]Jer 23:5, 6; Eze 34:25-28 [1]Lit *they* **14:12** [a]Lv 26:16; Dt 28:21, 22

feet, and their eyes will rot in their
sockets, and their tongue will rot
in their mouth. **13** And it will be in
that day, *that* abundant confusion
from Yahweh will [1]fall on them; and
they will [a]take hold of one another's
hand, and the hand of one will [2]go up
against the hand of another. **14** [a]And
Judah also will fight at Jerusalem; and
the [b]wealth of all the surrounding
nations will be gathered, gold and
silver and garments in great abun-
dance. **15** And in the same way, [a]the
plague on the horse, the mule, the
camel, the donkey, and all the cattle
that will be in those camps will be
like this plague.

**16** Then it will be that any who
are left of all the nations that went
against Jerusalem will [a]go up from
year to year to worship the King,
Yahweh of hosts, and to celebrate
the [b]Feast of Booths. **17** And it will
be that whichever of the families of
the earth does not go up to Jerusa-
lem to worship the [a]King, Yahweh
of hosts, there will be [b]no rain on
them. **18** And if the family of Egypt
does not go up or enter, then no
*rain will fall* on them; it will be the
[a]plague with which Yahweh plagues
the nations who do not go up to cele-
brate the Feast of Booths. **19** This will
be the [1]punishment of Egypt, and the
[1]punishment of all the nations who
do not go up to celebrate the Feast
of Booths.

**20** In that day there will *be in-
scribed* on the bells of the horses,
"[a]Holy to Yahweh." And the [b]pots
in the house of Yahweh will be like
the bowls before the altar. **21** And
every pot in Jerusalem and in Judah
will be [a]holy to Yahweh of hosts; and
all who sacrifice will come and take
of them and boil in them. And there
will no longer be a [b,1]Canaanite in the
house of Yahweh of hosts in that day.

*The Book of*

# MALACHI

### *Yahweh's Love for Jacob*

**1** The [a,1]oracle of the word of
[2]Yahweh to [b]Israel by the hand of
[3]Malachi.

**2** "I have [a]loved you," says Yahweh.
But you say, "How have You loved
us?" "*Was* not Esau Jacob's brother?"
declares Yahweh. "Yet I [b]have loved
Jacob; **3** but I have hated Esau, and I
have [a]set his mountains *to be* a des-
olation and his inheritance for the
jackals of the wilderness." **4** Though
Edom says, "We have been [a]demol-
ished, but we will [b,1]return and build
up the waste places"; thus says Yah-
weh of hosts, "They may [c]build, but
I will pull down; and *men* will call
them a [2]territory of wickedness, and

**14:13** [a]Zec 11:6 [1]Lit *be among* [2]Lit *rise up* **14:14** [a]Zec 12:2, 5 [b]Is 23:18; Zec 14:1 **14:15** [a]Zec 14:12 **14:16** [a]Is 60:6-9; 66:18-21, 23 [b]Lv 23:34-44 **14:17** [a]Zec 14:9, 16 [b]Jer 14:3-6; Am 4:7 **14:18** [a]Zec 14:12, 15 **14:19** [1]Lit *sin* **14:20** [a]Ex 28:36-38 [b]Eze 46:20 **14:21** [a]Ne 8:10; Ro 14:6, 7; 1Co 10:31 [b]Zep 1:11 [1]Or *merchant* ◆ **1:1** [a]Is 13:1; Na 1:1; Hab 1:1; Zec 9:1 [b]Mal 2:11 [1]Or *burden* [2]The personal covenant name of God, a form of I AM WHO I AM, cf. Ex 3:14-15 [3]Lit *My messenger* **1:2** [a]Dt 4:37; 7:8; 23:5; Is 41:8, 9; Jer 31:3; Jn 15:12 [b]Ro 9:13 **1:3** [a]Jer 49:10, 16-18; Eze 35:3, 4, 7, 8, 15 **1:4** [a]Jer 5:17 [b]Is 9:9, 10 [c]Am 3:15; 5:11; 6:11 [1]Or *rebuild the ruins* [2]Lit *border of wickedness*

the people [3]toward whom Yahweh
is indignant [d]forever." **5** And your
eyes will see this, and you will say,
"[a]Yahweh [1]be magnified beyond the
[2]territory of Israel!"

### *The Priests Defile Yahweh*

**6** "'A son [a]honors *his* father, and
a slave his master. Then if I am a
[b]father, where is My honor? And if
I am a master, where is the fear of
Me?' says Yahweh of hosts to you,
O [c]priests who despise My name. But
you say, 'How have we despised Your
name?' **7** *You* are presenting [a]defiled
[b,1]food upon My altar. But you say,
'How have we defiled You?' In that
you say, 'The [c]table of Yahweh is to
be despised.' **8** But when you present
the [a]blind for sacrifice, is it not evil?
And when you present the lame and
sick, is it not evil? Please, bring it
near to your [b]governor! Would he
accept you? Or would he lift up your
face?" says Yahweh of hosts. **9** "But
now, [a,1]entreat God's favor, that He
may be gracious to us! With this
thing which is from your hand, will
He [b]lift up any of your faces?" says
Yahweh of hosts. **10** "Oh that there
were one among you who would
[a]shut the [1]gates, that you might not
light a *fire on* My altar in vain! I have
no delight in you," says Yahweh of
hosts, "[b]nor will I accept an offering
from your hand. **11** For from the
[a]rising of the sun even to its setting,
[b]My name *will be* [c]great among the
nations, and in every place [d]incense
is going to be presented to My name,
as well as a grain offering *that is*
clean; for My name *will be* [e]great
among the nations," says Yahweh
of hosts. **12** "But you are [a]profaning
it, in that you say, 'The table of the
Lord is defiled, and as for its fruit,
its food is to be despised.' **13** You
also say, 'Behold, *how* [a]tiresome
it is!' And you disdainfully sniff at
it," says Yahweh of hosts, "and you
bring what was taken by [b]robbery
and *what is* [c]lame or sick; so you
bring the offering! Should I [d]accept
that from your hand?" says Yahweh.
**14** "But cursed be the [a]swindler who
has a male in his flock and vows it,
but sacrifices a [b,1]blemished animal
to the Lord, for I am a great [c]King,"
says Yahweh of hosts, "and My name
is [d,2]feared among the [3]nations."

### *I Will Curse Your Blessings*

**2** "And now this commandment
is for you, O priests. **2** If you do
[a]not listen, and if you do not set it
upon *your* heart to give [1]honor to
My name," says Yahweh of hosts,
"then I will send the [b]curse upon
you, and I will curse your blessings;
and indeed, I have [c]cursed them
*already* because you are not setting
*it* upon *your* heart. **3** Behold, I am
going to [a]rebuke your seed, and I
will [b]spread [1]refuse on your faces,
the [1]refuse of your [c]feasts; and you
will be taken away [2]with it. **4** Then

---

**1:4** [d]Eze 35:9; Ob 10 [3]Or *whom Yahweh has cursed* **1:5** [a]Ps 35:27; Mic 5:4 [1]Or *will be great* [2]Or *border* **1:6** [a]Ex 20:12; Pr 30:11, 17 [b]Dt 1:31; Is 1:2; Jer 3:4; Mal 2:10 [c]Zep 3:4; Mal 2:1-9 **1:7** [a]Mal 1:8, 13 [b]Lv 3:11; 21:6, 8 [c]Mal 1:12 [1]Lit *bread* **1:8** [a]Lv 22:22; Dt 15:21 [b]Hag 1:1 **1:9** [a]Jer 27:18; Joel 2:12-14 [b]Am 5:22 [1]Lit *soften the face of* **1:10** [a]Is 1:13 [b]Jer 14:10, 12; Hos 5:6 [1]Or *doors* **1:11** [a]Is 45:6 [b]Ps 111:9 [c]Is 66:18, 19 [d]Is 60:6 [e]Is 12:4, 5; 54:5; Jer 10:6, 7 **1:12** [a]Mal 1:7 **1:13** [a]Is 43:22 [b]Lv 6:4; Is 61:8 [c]Mal 1:8 [d]Mal 1:10 **1:14** [a]Ac 5:1-4 [b]Lv 22:18-20 [c]Zec 14:9 [d]Zep 2:11 [1]Or *ruined* [2]Or *reverenced* [3]Or *Gentiles*
◆ **2:2** [a]Lv 26:14, 15; Dt 28:15 [b]Dt 28:16-20 [c]Mal 3:9 [1]Or *glory* **2:3** [a]Lv 26:16; Dt 28:38 [b]Na 3:6 [c]Ex 29:14 [1]Or *vomit* [2]Lit *to*

you will know that I have sent
this commandment to you, [1]that
My [a]covenant may [2]continue with
Levi," says Yahweh of hosts. **5** "My
covenant with him was *one of* life
and [a]peace, and I gave them to him
*as something to be* [1]feared; so he
[b]feared Me and stood in [2]awe of My
name. **6** [a,1]Instruction of truth was
in his mouth, and unrighteousness
was not found on his lips; he walked
[b]with Me in peace and uprightness,
and he [c]turned many back from in-
iquity. **7** For the lips of a priest should
keep [a]knowledge, and [1]men should
[b]seek [2]instruction from his mouth;
for he is the [c]messenger of Yahweh
of hosts. **8** But as for you, you have
turned aside from the way; you have
caused many to [a]stumble [1]by the
instruction; you have [b,2]corrupted
the covenant of Levi," says Yahweh
of hosts. **9** "So [a]I also have made you
despised and [b]low [1]before all the
people, just as you are not keeping
My ways but are showing [c]partiality
in the [2]instruction.

### *Judah Profaned Yahweh's Sanctuary*

**10** "Do we not all have [a]one father?
[b]Has not one God created us? Why
do we deal [c]treacherously each
against his brother so as to profane
the [d]covenant of our fathers? **11** Ju-
dah has dealt [a]treacherously, and
an abomination has been done in
Israel and in Jerusalem; for Judah has
[b]profaned the sanctuary of Yahweh
[1]which He loves and has married the
daughter of a foreign god. **12** *As* for
the man who does this, may [a]Yahweh
cut off from the tents of Jacob *every-
one* who awakes and answers or who
[b]presents [1]an offering to Yahweh of
hosts.

**13** "And this is a second thing you
do: you cover the altar of Yahweh
with tears, with weeping, and with
groaning because He [a]no longer
regards the [1]offering or receives
*it as* acceptable from your hand.
**14** But you say, 'For what reason?'
Because Yahweh has been a witness
between you and the [a]wife of your
youth, against whom you have
dealt [b]treacherously, though she is
your companion and your wife by
covenant. **15** [1]But not one has [a]done
*so*, even *one* who has a remnant of
the Spirit. And [2]what did *that* one *do*
while he was seeking a [b]godly seed?
Be careful then to keep your spirit,
and let no one deal [c]treacherously
against the wife of your youth. **16** For
[1]I hate [a,2]divorce," says Yahweh, the
God of Israel, "and [3]him who covers
his garment with [b,4]wrong," says
Yahweh of hosts. "Be careful then to
keep your spirit, that you do not deal
treacherously."

**17** You have [a]wearied Yahweh with
your words. But you say, "How have

**2:4** [a]Nu 3:11-13, 45; 18:21; Ne 13:29; Mal 3:1 [1]Or *to be My covenant with* [2]Lit *be* **2:5** [a]Nu 25:12 [b]Nu 25:7, 8, 13 [1]Or *reverenced* [2]Lit *terror* **2:6** [a]Ps 119:142, 151, 160 [b]Dt 33:8, 9; Ps 37:37 [c]Jer 23:22 [1]Or *Law* **2:7** [a]Lv 10:11; Ne 8:7 [b]Nu 27:21; Dt 17:8-11; Jer 18:18; Eze 7:26 [c]Hag 1:13 [1]Lit *they* [2]Or *law* **2:8** [a]Jer 18:15 [b]Nu 25:12, 13; Ne 13:29; Eze 44:10 [1]Or *in the law* [2]Or *violated* **2:9** [a]Na 3:6 [b]Eze 7:26 [c]Dt 1:17; Mic 3:11 [1]Lit *to* [2]Or *law* **2:10** [a]Is 63:16; 64:8; Jer 31:9; 1Co 8:6; Eph 4:6 [b]Ac 17:24f [c]Jer 9:4, 5 [d]Ex 19:4-6; 24:3, 7, 8 **2:11** [a]Jer 3:7-9 [b]Ezr 9:1, 2 [1]Or *in that He has loved and married* **2:12** [a]Eze 24:21; Hos 9:12 [b]Mal 1:10, 13 [1]Or *a grain offering* **2:13** [a]Jer 11:14; 14:12 [1]Or *grain offering* **2:14** [a]Is 54:6 [b]Jer 9:2; Mal 3:5 **2:15** [a]Ge 2:24; Mt 19:4, 5 [b]Ru 4:12; 1Sa 2:20 [c]Ex 20:14; Lv 20:10 [1]Or *Did He not make one, although He had the remnant* [2]Or *why one? He sought a godly offspring.* **2:16** [a]Dt 24:1; Mt 5:31; 19:6-8 [b]Ps 73:6; Is 59:6 [1]Lit *He hates* [2]Lit *sending away* [3]Lit *he covers* [4]Or *violence* **2:17** [a]Is 43:22, 24

we wearied *Him*?" In that you say,
"[b]Everyone who does evil is good in
the sight of Yahweh, and He [c]delights
in them," or, "[d]Where is the God of
[e]justice?"

### *The Messenger and the Lord*

**3** "[a]Behold, I am going to send [b]My
[1]messenger, and he will [c,2]prepare
the way before Me. And the Lord,
whom you seek, will suddenly come
to His temple; [3]and the [d,1]messen-
ger of the covenant, in whom you
delight, behold, He is coming," says
Yahweh of hosts. **2** "But who can
[a]endure the day of His coming? And
who can stand when He appears? For
He is like a [b]smelter's fire and like
[1]fullers' soap. **3** And He will sit as a
smelter and purifier of silver, and
He will [a]purify the sons of Levi and
refine them like gold and silver, so
that they may [b]present to Yahweh
[1]offerings in righteousness. **4** Then
the [1]offering of Judah and Jerusalem
will be [a]pleasing to Yahweh as in the
[b]ancient days and as in former years.
**5** "Then I will draw near to you for
judgment; and I will be a swift witness
against the [a]sorcerers and against the
[b]adulterers and against those who
[c]swear falsely and against those who
oppress the [d]wage earner in his wag-
es, the [e]widow and the [1]orphan, and
those who turn aside the [f]sojourner
and do not [2]fear Me," says Yahweh
of hosts. **6** "For [1]I, Yahweh, [a]do not
change; therefore you, O sons of
Jacob, [2]are not consumed.

### *You Have Robbed God*

**7** "From the [a]days of your fathers you
have turned aside from My statutes
and have not kept *them*. [b]Return to
Me, and I will return to you," says
Yahweh of hosts. "But you say, 'How
shall we return?'
**8** "Will a man [1]rob God? Yet you are
robbing Me! But you say, 'How have we
robbed You?' In [a]tithes and [2]contribu-
tions. **9** You are [a]cursed with a curse,
for you are [1]robbing Me, the whole
nation *of you*! **10** [a]Bring the whole
tithe into the storehouse, so that there
may be [1]food in My house, and test Me
now in this," says Yahweh of hosts, "if
I will not [b]open for you the windows
of heaven and [c]empty out for you a
blessing until [d,2]it is beyond enough.
**11** Then I will rebuke the [a]devourer for
you so that it will not corrupt the fruits
of the ground; nor will your vine in the
field [1]fail to bear," says Yahweh of hosts.
**12** "[a]So all the nations will call you
blessed, for you shall be a [b]delightful
land," says Yahweh of hosts.

### *Arrogant Words*

**13** "Your words have been strong
against Me," says Yahweh. "But you
say, 'What have we spoken against
You?' **14** You have said, 'It is [a]worth-
less to serve God; and what [b]gain is
it that we have kept His charge and

---

**2:17** [b]Is 5:20; Zep 1:12 [c]Job 9:24 [d]2Pe 3:4 [e]Is 5:19; Jer 17:15 ◆ **3:1** [a]Mt 11:10, 14; Mk 1:2; Lk 1:76; 7:27 [b]Hag 1:13; Jn 1:6, 7 [c]Is 40:3 [d]Is 63:9 [1]Or *angel* [2]Or *clear* [3]Or *even* **3:2** [a]Is 33:14; Eze 22:14; Rev 6:17 [b]Zec 13:9; Mt 3:10-12; 1Co 3:13-15 [1]Lit *laundrymen's* **3:3** [a]Is 1:25; Da 12:10 [b]Ps 4:5; 51:19 [1]Or *grain offerings* **3:4** [a]Ps 51:17-19 [b]2Chr 7:1-3, 12 [1]Or *grain offering* **3:5** [a]Dt 18:10; Jer 27:9, 10 [b]Eze 22:9-11 [c]Jer 5:2; 7:9; Zec 5:4 [d]Lv 19:13 [e]Ex 22:22-24 [f]Dt 27:19 [1]Or *fatherless* [2]Or *reverence* **3:6** [a]Nu 23:19; Jas 1:17 [1]Or *I am Yahweh; I do not* [2]Or *have not come to an end* **3:7** [a]Jer 7:25, 26; 16:11, 12 [b]Zec 1:3 **3:8** [a]Ne 13:11, 12 [1]Or *defraud* [2]Or *heave offerings* **3:9** [a]Mal 2:2 [1]Or *defrauding* **3:10** [a]Lv 27:30; Nu 18:21-24; Dt 12:6; 14:22-29; Ne 13:12 [b]Ps 78:23-29 [c]Eze 34:26 [d]Lv 26:3-5 [1]Lit *prey* [2]Or *there is not* room *enough* **3:11** [a]Joel 1:4; 2:25 [1]Lit *be bereaved* **3:12** [a]Is 61:9 [b]Is 62:4 **3:14** [a]Jer 2:25; 18:12 [b]Is 58:3

that we have walked in mourning before Yahweh of hosts? **15** So now we [a]call the arrogant blessed; not only are the doers of wickedness built up, but they also test God and [b]escape.'"

### *The Book of Remembrance*

**16** Then those who [1]feared Yahweh spoke to one another, and Yahweh [a]gave heed and heard *it*, and a [b]book of remembrance was written before Him for those who [1]fear Yahweh and who think upon His name. **17** "And they will be [a]Mine," says Yahweh of hosts, "on the [b]day that I [1]prepare *My* [c,2]own treasured possession, and I will [3]spare them as a man [d,4]spares his own son who serves him." **18** So you will return and [a]see *the distinction* between the righteous and the wicked, between one who serves God and one who does not serve Him.

### *The Great Day of Yahweh*

**4** "[1]For behold, the day is coming, [a]burning like a furnace; and all the arrogant and every worker of wickedness will be [b]chaff; and the day that is coming will [c]set them aflame," says Yahweh of hosts, "so that it will leave them neither root nor branch." **2** "But for you who [1]fear My name, the [a]sun of righteousness will rise with [b]healing in its wings; and you will go forth and [c]skip about like calves from the stall. **3** And you will [a]tread down the wicked, for they will be [b]ashes under the soles of your feet [c]on the day [1]which I am preparing," says Yahweh of hosts.

**4** "[a,1]Remember the law of Moses My servant, *even the* statutes and judgments which I commanded him in Horeb for all Israel.

**5** "Behold, I am going to send you [a]Elijah the prophet before the coming of the great and awesome day of Yahweh. **6** And he will [a]turn the hearts of the fathers to *their* children and the hearts of the children to their fathers, lest I come and [b]strike the land, [1]devoting it to destruction."

**3:15** [a]Is 2:22; Mal 4:1 [b]Jer 7:10 **3:16** [a]Ps 34:15; Jer 31:18-20 [b]Is 4:3; Da 12:1 [1]Or *reverence(d)* **3:17** [a]Is 43:1 [b]Is 4:2 [c]Ex 19:5; Dt 7:6; Is 43:21; 1Pe 2:9 [d]Ps 103:13 [1]Lit *make* [2]Or *special treasure* [3]Or *have compassion on* [4]Or *has compassion on* **3:18** [a]Ge 18:25; Am 5:15 ◆ **4:1** [a]Ps 21:9; Na 1:5, 6; Mal 3:2, 3; 2Pe 3:7 [b]Is 5:24; Ob 18 [c]Is 9:18, 19 [1]Ch 3:19 in Heb **4:2** [a]2Sa 23:4; Is 30:26; 60:1 [b]Jer 30:17; 33:6 [c]Is 35:6 [1]Or *reverence(d)* **4:3** [a]Job 40:12; Is 26:6; Mic 5:8 [b]Eze 28:18 [c]Mal 3:17 [1]Or *when I act* **4:4** [a]Dt 4:23; 8:11, 19 [1]Ch 3:22 in Heb **4:5** [a]Mt 11:14; 17:10-13; Mk 9:11-13; Lk 1:17; Jn 1:21 **4:6** [a]Lk 1:17 [b]Is 11:4; Rev 19:15 [1]Or *with a curse, with the ban*

that we have walked in mourning
before Yahweh of hosts? 15 So now we
call the arrogant blessed; not only
are the doers of wickedness built up,
but they also test God and escape.'"

### The Book of Remembrance

16 Then those who feared Yahweh
spoke to one another, and Yahweh
gave heed and heard it, and a book
of remembrance was written before
Him for those who fear Yahweh and
who think upon His name. 17 "And
they will be Mine," says Yahweh of
hosts, "on the day that I prepare
My own treasured possession, and
I will spare them as a man spares
his own son who serves him." 18 So
you will return and see the distinc-
tion between the righteous and the
wicked, between one who serves God
and one who does not serve Him.

### The Great Day of Yahweh

4 "For behold, the day is coming,
burning like a furnace; and all
the arrogant and every worker of
wickedness will be chaff; and the
day that is coming will set them
aflame," says Yahweh of hosts, "so
that it will leave them neither root
nor branch." 2 "But for you who
fear My name, the sun of righ-
teousness will rise with healing
in its wings; and you will go forth
and skip about like calves from the
stall. 3 And you will tread down
the wicked, for they will be ashes
under the soles of your feet on the
day which I am preparing," says
Yahweh of hosts.
4 "Remember the law of Moses
My servant, even the statutes and
judgments which I commanded him
in Horeb for all Israel.
5 "Behold, I am going to send
you Elijah the prophet before the
coming of the great and awesome
day of Yahweh. 6 And he will turn
the hearts of the fathers to their
children and the hearts of the chil-
dren to their fathers, lest I come
and strike the land, devoting it to
destruction."

3:15 Is 2:22; Mal 4:1 Jer 7:10 3:16 Ps 34:15; Jer 31:18-20 Is 4:3; Dan 12:1 Or reverence(d) 3:17 Is 43:21 Is 4:2 Ex 19:5; Dt 7:6; Is 43:21 Ps 2:3 Ps 103:13 Lit make Or special treasure Or have compassion on Or has compassion on 3:18 Gen 18:25; Amos 5:15 4:1 Ps 21:9; Nah 1:5, 6; Mal 3:2, 3 Obad 18 Is 5:24; Obad 18 Is 9:18, 19 Ch 3:19 in Heb 4:2 2 Sam 23:4; Is 30:26; 60:1 Jer 30:17; 33:6 Is 35:6 Or revere(d) 4:3 Job 40:12; Is 26:6; Mic 5:8 Ezek 28:18 Mal 3:17 Or when I act 4:4 Dt 4:23; 8:11, 19 Ch 3:22 in Heb 4:5 Matt 11:14; 17:10-13; Mark 9:11-13; Luke 1:17; John 1:21 4:6 Luke 1:17 Is 11:4; Rev 19:15 Or with a curse, with the ban

# THE NEW TESTAMENT

LEGACY STANDARD BIBLE

*The Gospel According to*

# MATTHEW

### *The Genealogy of Jesus Christ*

1 The book of the genealogy of [1]Jesus [2]Christ, [a]the son of David,
[b]the son of Abraham:
2 Abraham [1]was the father
of Isaac,
and Isaac was the father
of Jacob,
and Jacob was the father
of [2]Judah and his brothers.
3 And Judah was the father
of Perez and Zerah by Tamar,
and [a]Perez was the father
of Hezron,
and Hezron was the father
of [1]Ram.
4 And Ram was the father
of Amminadab,
and Amminadab was
the father of Nahshon,
and Nahshon was the father
of Salmon.
5 And Salmon was the father
of Boaz by Rahab,
and Boaz was the father
of Obed by Ruth,
and Obed was the father
of Jesse.
6 And Jesse was the father
of David the king.
And David [a]was the father
of Solomon by [1]the *wife*
of Uriah.
7 And Solomon [a]was the father
of Rehoboam,
and Rehoboam was
the father of Abijah,
and Abijah was the father
of [1]Asa.
8 And Asa was the father
of Jehoshaphat,
and Jehoshaphat was
the father of [1]Joram,
and Joram was the father
of Uzziah.
9 And Uzziah was the father
of [1]Jotham,
and Jotham was the father
of Ahaz,
and Ahaz was the father
of Hezekiah.
10 And Hezekiah was the father
of Manasseh,
and Manasseh was
the father of [1]Amon,
and Amon was the [a]father
of Josiah.
11 And Josiah was the father
of [1]Jeconiah and his brothers,
at the time of the [a]deportation
to Babylon.

12 And after the [a]deportation
to Babylon:
Jeconiah was the father
of [1]Shealtiel,
and Shealtiel was the father
of Zerubbabel.
13 And Zerubbabel was
the father of [1]Abihud,

---

◆ **1:1** [a]2Sa 7:12-16; Ps 89:3f; 132:11; Is 9:6f; 11:1; Mt 9:27; Lk 1:32, 69; Jn 7:42; Ac 13:23; Ro 1:3; Rev 22:16 [b]Mt 1:1-6: *Lk 3:32-34;* Ge 22:18; Ga 3:16 [1]Heb *Yeshua* (*Joshua*), meaning *Yahweh saves* [2]Messiah **1:2** [1]Lit *fathered*, so in genealogy [2]Gr *Judas*; names of people in the Old Testament are given in their Old Testament form **1:3** [a]Ru 4:18-22; 1Chr 2:1-15; Mt 1:3-6 [1]Gr *Aram* **1:6** [a]2Sa 11:27; 12:24 [1]Lit *her of Uriah* **1:7** [a]1Chr 3:10ff [1]Gr *Asaph* **1:8** [1]Also Gr for *Jehoram* in 2Ki 8:16, cf. 1Chr 3:11 **1:9** [1]Gr *Joatham* **1:10** [a]1Chr 3:14 [1]Gr *Amos* **1:11** [a]2Ki 24:14f; Jer 27:20; Mt 1:17 [1]*Jehoiachin* in 2Ki 24:15 **1:12** [a]2Ki 24:14f; Jer 27:20; Mt 1:17 [1]Gr *Salathiel* **1:13** [1]Gr *Abioud*, usually spelled *Abiud*

and Abihud was the father
of Eliakim,
and Eliakim was the father
of Azor.
**14** And Azor was the father
of Zadok,
and Zadok was the father
of Achim,
and Achim was the father
of Eliud.
**15** And Eliud was the father
of Eleazar,
and Eleazar was the father
of Matthan,
and Matthan was the father
of Jacob.
**16** And Jacob was the father of
Joseph the husband of Mary,
by whom Jesus was born,
[a]who is called [1]Christ.

**17** Therefore all the generations
from Abraham to David are fourteen
generations; and from David to the
[a]deportation to Babylon, fourteen
generations; and from the [a]depor-
tation to Babylon to [1]the Christ,
fourteen generations.

### *The Conception and Birth of Jesus*

**18** Now the birth of Jesus [1]Christ
was as follows: when His [a]mother
Mary had been [2]betrothed to Joseph,
before they came together she was
[b]found to be with child by the Holy
Spirit. **19** And Joseph her husband,
being a righteous man and not
wanting to disgrace her, planned
[a,1]to send her away secretly. **20** But
when he had considered this, behold,
an angel of the [1]Lord appeared to him
in a dream, saying, "[a]Joseph, son of
David, do not be afraid to take Mary
as your wife; for [2]the One who has
been [3]conceived in her is of the Holy
Spirit. **21** And she will bear a Son; and
[a]you shall call His name Jesus, for
[1]He [b]will save His people from their
sins." **22** Now all this [1]took place in
order that what was [a]spoken by the
[2]Lord through the prophet would be
fulfilled, saying, **23** "[a]BEHOLD, THE
VIRGIN SHALL BE WITH [b]CHILD AND
SHALL BEAR A SON, AND THEY SHALL
CALL HIS NAME [1]IMMANUEL," which
translated means, "[c]GOD WITH US."
**24** And Joseph got up from his sleep
and did as the angel of the [1]Lord
commanded him, and took *Mary* as
his wife, **25** [1]but kept her a virgin until
she [a,2]gave birth to a Son; and [b]he
called His name Jesus.

### *The Visit of the Magi*

**2** Now after Jesus was [a]born in
Bethlehem of Judea in the days
of [b]Herod the king, behold, [1]magi
from the east arrived in Jerusalem,
saying, **2** "Where is He who has
been born [a]King of the Jews? For we
saw [b]His star in the east and have
come to worship Him." **3** And when
Herod the king heard *this*, he was

**1:16** [a]Mt 27:17, 22; Lk 2:11; Jn 4:25 [1]Messiah **1:17** [a]2Ki 24:14f; Jer 27:20; Mt 1:11, 12 [1]Messiah
**1:18** [a]Mt 12:46; Lk 1:27 [b]Lk 1:35 [1]The Messiah [2]The first stage of marriage in ancient Jewish culture, usually lasting for a year before the wedding night, more legal than an engagement **1:19** [a]Dt 22:20-24; *24:1-4; Jn 8:4, 5* [1]*Or to divorce her* **1:20** [a]Lk 2:4 [1]In OT, Yahweh, cf. 2Ki 1:3 [2]Lit *that which* [3]Lit *begotten* **1:21** [a]Lk 1:31; 2:21 [b]Lk 2:11; Jn 1:29; Ac 4:12; 5:31; 13:23, 38, 39; Col 1:20-23 [1]Lit *He Himself*
**1:22** [a]Lk 24:44; Ro 1:2-4 [1]Lit *has happened* [2]In OT, Yahweh, cf. Is 7:10 **1:23** [a]Is 7:14 [b]Is 9:6, 7 [c]Is 8:10 [1]Or *Emmanuel* **1:24** [1]In OT, Yahweh, cf. 2Ki 1:3 **1:25** [a]Lk 2:7 [b]Mt 1:21; Lk 2:21 [1]Lit *and was not knowing her* [2]Or *bore a Son*, cf. 1:21, 23 ◆ **2:1** [a]Mic 5:2; Lk 2:4-7 [b]Lk 1:5 [1]A class of wise men specializing in astronomy, astrology, and natural science **2:2** [a]Jer 23:5; 30:9; Zec 9:9; Mt 27:11; Lk 19:38; 23:38; Jn 1:49 [b]Nu 24:17

troubled, and all Jerusalem with him.
**4** And gathering together all the chief
priests and scribes of the people, he
was inquiring of them where the
[1]Christ was to be born. **5** And they
said to him, "[a]In Bethlehem of Judea;
for this is what has been written [1]by
the prophet:

**6** '[a]AND YOU, BETHLEHEM,
LAND OF JUDAH,
ARE BY NO MEANS LEAST AMONG
THE LEADERS OF JUDAH;
FOR OUT OF YOU SHALL
COME FORTH A LEADER
WHO WILL [b]SHEPHERD
MY PEOPLE ISRAEL.'"

**7** Then Herod secretly called the
magi and carefully determined from
them [1]the time [a]the star appeared.
**8** And he sent them to Bethlehem
and said, "Go and search carefully for
the Child; and when you have found
*Him*, report to me, so that I too may
come and worship Him." **9** Now after
hearing the king, they went their way;
and behold, the star, which they had
seen in the east, was going on before
them until it came and stood over *the
place* where the Child was. **10** And
when they saw the star, they rejoiced
exceedingly with great joy. **11** And after
coming into the house they saw the
Child with [a]Mary His mother; and they
[1]fell to the ground and [b]worshiped
Him. Then, opening their treasures,
they presented to Him gifts of gold,
frankincense, and myrrh. **12** And hav-
ing been [a]warned [b]in a dream not to
return to Herod, the magi departed for
their own country by another way.

### *The Flight to Egypt*

**13** Now when they had departed,
behold, an [a]angel of the [1]Lord *[b]ap-
peared to Joseph in a dream, saying,
"Get up! Take the Child and His moth-
er and flee to Egypt, and remain there
until I tell you; for Herod is going to
search for the Child to destroy Him."
**14** So [1]Joseph got up and took the
Child and His mother while it was still
night, and departed for Egypt. **15** And
he [1]remained there until the death of
Herod, in order that what had been
spoken by the [2]Lord through the
prophet would be fulfilled, saying,
"[a]OUT OF EGYPT I CALLED [b]MY SON."

### *Herod Slaughters Children*

**16** Then when Herod saw that he
had been tricked by [a]the magi, he
became very enraged, and sent and
[b]slew all the male children who were
in Bethlehem and all its vicinity, from
two years old and under, according to
the time which he had carefully de-
termined from the magi. **17** Then what
had been spoken through Jeremiah
the prophet was fulfilled, saying,

**18** "[a]A VOICE WAS HEARD IN RAMAH,
WEEPING AND GREAT
MOURNING,
RACHEL WEEPING
FOR HER CHILDREN;
AND SHE WAS REFUSING
TO BE COMFORTED,
BECAUSE THEY WERE NO MORE."

**19** But when Herod died, behold,
an angel of the [1]Lord *[a]appeared in
a dream to Joseph in Egypt, saying,
**20** "Get up, take the Child and His

---

**2:4** [1]Messiah **2:5** [a]Jn 7:42 [1]Or *through* **2:6** [a]Mic 5:2; Jn 7:42 [b]Jn 21:16 **2:7** [a]Nu 24:17 [1]Lit *the time of the appearing star* **2:11** [a]Mt 1:18; 12:46 [b]Mt 14:33 [1]Face down in a prone position to indicate worship; lit *prostrated* **2:12** [a]Mt 2:13, 19, 22; Lk 2:26; Ac 10:22; Heb 8:5; 11:7 [b]Job 33:15, 16; Mt 1:20 **2:13** [a]Ac 5:19; 10:7; 12:7-11 [b]Mt 2:12, 19 [1]In OT, Yahweh, cf. 2Ki 1:3 **2:14** [1]Lit *he* **2:15** [a]Hos 11:1; Nu 24:8 [b]Ex 4:22f [1]Lit *was* [2]In OT, Yahweh, cf. Hos 1:1 **2:16** [a]Mt 2:1 [b]Is 59:7 **2:18** [a]Jer 31:15 **2:19** [a]Mt 1:20; 2:12, 13, 22 [1]In OT, Yahweh, cf. 2Ki 1:3

mother, and go into the land of Isra-
el; for those who sought the Child's
life are dead." **21** So [1]Joseph got up,
took the Child and His mother, and
came into the land of Israel. **22** But
when he heard that Archelaus was
reigning over Judea in place of his
father Herod, he was afraid to go
there. Then after being [a]warned *by*
*God* in a dream, he departed for the
district of Galilee, **23** and came and
lived in a city called [a]Nazareth, so
that what was spoken through the
prophets would be fulfilled: "He shall
be called a [b]Nazarene."

### *The Preaching of John the Baptist*

**3** Now [a]in those days [b,1]John the
Baptist *[2]came, [3]preaching in the
[c]wilderness of Judea, saying, **2** "[a]Re-
pent, for [b]the kingdom of heaven [1]is
at hand." **3** For this is the [a]one referred
to [1]by Isaiah the prophet, saying,

"[b]The voice of one [2]crying
in the wilderness,
'[c]Make ready the way
of the [3]Lord,
Make His paths straight!'"

**4** Now John himself had [a,1]a garment
of camel's hair and a leather belt
around his waist; and his food was
[b]locusts and wild honey. **5** Then
Jerusalem [a]was going out to him,
and all Judea, and all [b]the district
around the Jordan; **6** and they were
being [a]baptized by him in the Jordan
River, as they confessed their sins.

**7** But when he saw many of the
[a]Pharisees and [b]Sadducees coming
for his baptism, he said to them,
"You [c]brood of vipers, who warned
you to flee from [d]the wrath to come?
**8** [a]Therefore bear fruit [b]in keeping
with repentance; **9** and do not suppose
that you can say to yourselves, '[a]We
have Abraham for our father'; for I say
to you that from these stones God is
able to raise up children to Abraham.
**10** And the [a]axe is already laid at the
root of the trees; therefore [b]every tree
that does not bear good fruit is cut
down and thrown into the fire.

**11** "As for me, [a]I baptize you with
water for repentance, but He who is
coming after me is mightier than I,
and I am not fit to remove His san-
dals; [b]He will baptize you with the
Holy Spirit and fire. **12** His [a]winnow-
ing fork is in His hand, and He will
thoroughly clear His threshing floor;
and He will [b]gather His wheat into
the barn, but He will burn up the
[c]chaff with [d]unquenchable fire."

### *The Baptism of Jesus*

**13** [a]Then Jesus *arrived [b]from Galilee
at the Jordan *coming* to John to be
baptized by him. **14** But John tried to
prevent Him, saying, "I have need to
be baptized by You, and do You come
to me?" **15** But Jesus answered and

---

**2:21** [1]Lit *he* **2:22** [a]Mt 2:12, 13, 19 **2:23** [a]Lk 1:26; 2:39; Jn 1:45, 46 [b]Mk 1:24; Jn 18:5, 7; 19:19
◆ **3:1** [a]Mt 3:1-12: *Mk 1:3-8; Lk 3:2-17;* Jn 1:6-8, 19-28 [b]Mt 11:11-14; 16:14 [c]Jos 15:61; Jdg 1:16 [1]Gr *Joannes*, Heb *Johanan*; so in Matt [2]Or *arrived, appeared* [3]Or *proclaiming as a herald* **3:2** [a]Mt 4:17 [b]Da 2:44; Mt 4:17, 23; 6:10; 10:7; Mk 1:15; Lk 10:9f; 11:20; 21:31 [1]Lit *has come near* **3:3** [a]Lk 1:17, 76 [b]Is 40:3 [c]Jn 1:23 [1]Or *through* [2]Or *shouting* [3]In OT, Yahweh, cf. Is 40:3 **3:4** [a]2Ki 1:8; Zec 13:4; Mt 11:8; Mk 1:6 [b]Lv 11:22 [1]Lit *his garment* **3:5** [a]Mk 1:5 [b]Lk 3:3 **3:6** [a]Mt 3:11, 13-16; Mk 1:5; Jn 1:25, 26; 3:23; Ac 1:5; 2:38-41; 10:37 **3:7** [a]Mt 16:1ff; 23:13, 15 [b]Mt 22:23; Ac 4:1; 5:17; 23:6ff [c]Mt 12:34; 23:33 [d]1Th 1:10 **3:8** [a]Lk 3:8; Eph 5:8, 9 [b]Ac 26:20 **3:9** [a]Lk 3:8; 16:24; Jn 8:33, 39, 53; Ac 13:26; Ro 4:1; 9:7, 8; Ga 3:29 **3:10** [a]Lk 3:9 [b]Ps 92:12-14; Mt 7:19; Jn 15:2 **3:11** [a]Mk 1:4, 8; Lk 3:16; Jn 1:26f; Ac 1:5; 8:36, 38; 11:16 [b]Jn 1:33; Ac 2:3, 4; Tit 3:5 **3:12** [a]Is 30:24; 41:16; Jer 15:7; 51:2; Lk 3:17 [b]Mt 13:30 [c]Ps 1:4 [d]Is 66:24; Jer 7:20; Mt 13:41, 42; Mk 9:43, 48 **3:13** [a]Mt 3:13-17: *Mk 1:9-11; Lk 3:21, 22;* Jn 1:31-34 [b]Mt 2:22

said to him, “Permit *it* at this time; for
in this way it is fitting for us [a]to fulfill
all righteousness.” Then he *permit-
ted Him. **16** And after being baptized,
Jesus came up immediately from
the water; and behold, the heavens
were opened, and [a,1]he saw the Spirit
of God descending like a dove *and*
coming upon Him, **17** and behold,
*there was* a voice out of the heavens
saying, “[a]This is [1]My beloved Son, in
whom I am well-pleased.”

### *The Temptation of Jesus*

**4** [a]Then Jesus was led up by the
Spirit into the wilderness [b]to be
tempted by the devil. **2** And after He
had [a]fasted forty days and forty nights,
He [1]then became hungry. **3** And [a]the
tempter came and said to Him, “If
You are the [b]Son of God, command
that these stones become bread.” **4** But
He answered and said, “It is written,
‘[a]MAN SHALL NOT LIVE ON BREAD ALONE,
BUT ON EVERY WORD THAT PROCEEDS OUT
OF THE MOUTH OF GOD.’”

**5** Then the devil *took Him into
[a]the holy city and had Him stand
on the pinnacle of the temple, **6** and
*said to Him, “If You are the Son of
God, throw Yourself down; for it is
written,

‘[a]HE WILL COMMAND HIS
ANGELS CONCERNING YOU’;

and

‘ON *their* HANDS THEY
WILL BEAR YOU UP,
LEST YOU STRIKE YOUR FOOT
AGAINST A STONE.’”

**7** Jesus said to him, “Again, it is writ-
ten, ‘[a]YOU SHALL NOT PUT THE [1]LORD
YOUR GOD TO THE TEST.’”

**8** [a]Again, the devil *took Him to
a very high mountain and *showed
Him all the kingdoms of the world
and their glory; **9** and he said to
Him, “[a]All these things I will give
You, if You fall down and [1]worship
me.” **10** Then Jesus *said to him, “Go,
Satan! For it is written, ‘[a]YOU SHALL
WORSHIP THE [1]LORD YOUR GOD, AND
[2]SERVE HIM ONLY.’” **11** Then the devil
*left Him; and behold, [a]angels came
and *began to* minister to Him.

### *Jesus Begins His Ministry*

**12** Now when *Jesus* heard that [a]John
had been taken into custody, [b]He
departed into Galilee; **13** and leaving
Nazareth, He came and [a]lived in
Capernaum, which is by the sea, in
the region of Zebulun and Naphtali,
**14** in order that what was spoken
through Isaiah the prophet would
be fulfilled, saying,

**15** “[a]THE LAND OF ZEBULUN AND
THE LAND OF NAPHTALI,
[1]BY THE WAY OF THE SEA,
BEYOND THE JORDAN, GALILEE
OF THE [2]GENTILES—

**16** [a]THE PEOPLE WHO WERE
SITTING IN DARKNESS
SAW A GREAT LIGHT,

---

**3:15** [a]Ps 40:7, 8; Jn 4:34; 8:29 **3:16** [a]Mk 1:10; Lk 3:22; Jn 1:32; Ac 7:56 [1]Or *He* **3:17** [a]Ps 2:7; Is 42:1; Mt 12:18; 17:5; Mk 9:7; Lk 9:35; Jn 12:28 [1]Or *My Son, the Beloved* ◆ **4:1** [a]Mt 4:1-11: *Mk 1:12, 13; Lk 4:1-13* [b]Heb 4:15; Jas 1:14 **4:2** [a]Ex 34:28; 1Ki 19:8 [1]Or *afterward became*; lit *later became* **4:3** [a]1Th 3:5 [b]Mt 14:33; 26:63; Mk 3:11; 5:7; Lk 1:35; 4:41; Jn 1:34, 49; Ac 9:20 **4:4** [a]Dt 8:3 **4:5** [a]Ne 11:1, 18; Da 9:24; Mt 27:53 **4:6** [a]Ps 91:11, 12 **4:7** [a]Dt 6:16 [1]In OT, Yahweh, cf. Dt 6:16 **4:8** [a]Mt 16:26; 1Jn 2:15-17 **4:9** [a]1Co 10:20f [1]Lit *prostrate Yourself* **4:10** [a]Dt 6:13; 10:20 [1]In OT, Yahweh, cf. Dt 6:13 [2]Or *fulfill religious duty to Him* **4:11** [a]Mt 26:53; Lk 22:43; Heb 1:14 **4:12** [a]Mt 14:3; Mk 1:14; Lk 3:20; Jn 3:24 [b]Mk 1:14; Lk 4:14; Jn 1:43; 2:11 **4:13** [a]Mt 11:23; Mk 1:21; 2:1; Lk 4:23, 31; Jn 2:12; 4:46f **4:15** [a]Is 9:1 [1]Or *Toward the sea* [2]Lit *nations*, usually non-Jewish **4:16** [a]Is 9:2; 60:1-3; Lk 2:32

AND THOSE WHO WERE
SITTING IN THE LAND AND
SHADOW OF DEATH,
UPON THEM A LIGHT DAWNED."
17 [a]From that time Jesus began to
[1]preach and say, "[b]Repent, for the
kingdom of heaven is at hand."

### *The First Disciples*

18 [a]Now as *Jesus* was walking by [b]the
Sea of Galilee, He saw two brothers,
[c]Simon who was called Peter, and
Andrew his brother, casting a net
into the sea; for they were fishermen.
19 And He *said to them, "[1]Follow Me,
and I will make you fishers of men."
20 And immediately they left their
nets and followed Him. 21 And going
on from there He saw two other
brothers, [a,1]James the *son* of Zebedee,
and John his brother, in the boat with
Zebedee their father, mending their
nets; and He called them. 22 And
immediately they left the boat and
their father, and followed Him.

### *Ministry in Galilee*

23 And Jesus was going [a]throughout
all Galilee, [b]teaching in their syna-
gogues and [c]preaching the [1]gospel
of the kingdom, and [d]healing every
kind of disease and every kind of
sickness among the people.
24 And the news about Him spread
[a]throughout all Syria; and they brought
to Him all who were ill, those suffer-
ing with various diseases and pains,
[b]demoniacs, [c,1]epileptics, [d]paralytics;
and He healed them. 25 And large
crowds [a]followed Him from Galilee
and [b]the Decapolis and Jerusalem and
Judea and *from* [c]beyond the Jordan.

### *The Sermon on the Mount; The Beatitudes*

5 [a]Now when Jesus saw the crowds,
He went up on [b]the [1]mountain; and
after He sat down, His disciples came
to Him. 2 [a]And He opened His mouth
and *began to* teach them, saying,
3 "[a,1]Blessed are the [2]poor in
spirit, for [b]theirs is the king-
dom of heaven.

4 Blessed are [a]those who
mourn, for they shall be
comforted.

5 Blessed are [a]the [1]lowly, for
they shall inherit the earth.

6 Blessed are [a]those who hunger
and thirst for righteousness,
for they shall be satisfied.

7 Blessed are [a]the merciful, for
they shall receive mercy.

8 Blessed are [a]the pure in heart,
for [b]they shall see God.

---

**4:17** [a]Mk 1:14, 15 [b]Mt 3:2 [1]Or *proclaim* **4:18** [a]Mt 4:18-22: *Mk 1:16-20;* Lk 5:2-11; Jn 1:40-42 [b]Mt 15:29; Mk 7:31; Lk 5:1; Jn 6:1 [c]Mt 10:2; 16:18; Jn 1:40-42 **4:19** [1]Lit *Come here after Me* **4:21** [a]Mt 10:2; 20:20 [1]Or *Jacob*; James is the Eng form of Jacob; so in Matt **4:23** [a]Mk 1:39; Lk 4:14, 44 [b]Mt 9:35; 13:54; Mk 1:21; 6:2; 10:1; Lk 4:15; 6:6; 13:10; Jn 6:59; 18:20 [c]Mt 3:2; 9:35; 24:14; Mk 1:14; Lk 4:43; 8:1; 16:16; Ac 20:25; 28:31 [d]Mt 8:16; 9:35; 14:14; 15:30; 19:2; 21:14; Mk 1:34; 3:10; Lk 4:40; 7:21; Ac 10:38 [1]Or *good news* **4:24** [a]Mk 7:26; Lk 2:2; Ac 15:23; 18:18; 20:3; 21:3; Ga 1:21 [b]Mt 8:16, 28, 33; 9:32; 12:22; 15:22; Mk 1:32; 5:15, 16, 18; Lk 8:36; Jn 10:21 [c]Mt 17:15 [d]Mt 8:6; 9:2, 6; Mk 2:3-5, 9; Lk 5:24 [1]Lit *moonstruck*; Gr *seleniazo* **4:25** [a]Mk 3:7, 8; Lk 6:17 [b]Mk 5:20; 7:31 [c]Mt 4:15 ◆**5:1** [a]Matt ch 5-7; Lk 6:20-49 [b]Mk 3:13; Lk 6:17; 9:28; Jn 6:3, 15 [1]Or *hill* **5:2** [a]Mt 13:35; Ac 8:35; 10:34; 18:14 **5:3** [a]Mt 5:3-12: *Lk 6:20-23* [b]Mt 5:10; 19:14; 25:34; Mk 10:14; Lk 6:20; 22:29f [1]Fortunate or prosperous, so through v 11 [2]Those who are not spiritually arrogant **5:4** [a]Is 61:2; Jn 16:20; Rev 7:17 **5:5** [a]Ps 37:11 [1]Or *humble, meek* **5:6** [a]Is 55:1, 2; Jn 4:14; 6:48ff; 7:37 **5:7** [a]Pr 11:17; Mt 6:14, 15; 18:33-35 **5:8** [a]Ps 24:4 [b]Heb 12:14; 1Jn 3:2; Rev 22:4

9 Blessed are the peacemakers,
for [a]they shall be called sons
of God.

10 Blessed are those who have
been [a]persecuted for the sake
of righteousness, for [b]theirs is
the kingdom of heaven.

11 "Blessed are you when *people*
[a]insult you and persecute you, and
falsely say all kinds of evil against
you because of Me. 12 Rejoice and
be glad, for your reward in heaven
is great; for [a]in the same way they
persecuted the prophets who were
before you.

### *Salt and Light*

13 "You are the salt of the earth; but
[a]if the salt has become tasteless, how
will it be made salty *again*? It is no
longer good for anything, except to
be thrown out to be trampled under
foot by men.

14 "You are [a]the light of the world.
A city set on a [1]hill cannot be hidden;
15 [a]nor does *anyone* light a lamp and
put it under a [1]basket, but on the
lampstand, and it gives light to all
who are in the house. 16 Let your light
shine before men in such a way that
they may [a]see your good works, and
[b]glorify your Father who is in heaven.

17 "Do not think that I came to
abolish the [a]Law or the Prophets; I
did not come *to abolish* but to fulfill.
18 For truly I say to you, [a]until heaven
and earth pass away, not [1]the small-
est letter or stroke shall pass from
the Law until all is accomplished.
19 Whoever then annuls one of the
least of these commandments, and
teaches [1]others *to do* the same, shall
be called least [a]in the kingdom of
heaven; but whoever does and
teaches *them*, he shall be called great
in the kingdom of heaven.

20 "For I say to you that unless
your [a]righteousness surpasses *that*
of the scribes and Pharisees, you will
not enter the kingdom of heaven.

### *Personal Relationships*

21 "[a]You have heard that [1]the ancients
were told, '[b]YOU SHALL NOT MURDER'
and 'Whoever murders shall be guilty
before [c]the court.' 22 But I say to you
that everyone who is angry with his
brother shall be guilty before [a]the
court; and whoever says to his broth-
er, '[1]Raca,' shall be guilty before the
[b,2]Sanhedrin; and whoever says, 'You
fool,' shall be guilty *enough to go* into
the [c,3]fiery hell. 23 Therefore if you
are [a]presenting your [1]offering at the
altar, and there remember that your
brother has something against you,
24 leave your [1]offering there before
the altar and go; first be [a]reconciled
to your brother, and then come and
present your [1]offering. 25 [a]Make
friends quickly with your opponent

---

**5:9** [a]Mt 5:45; Lk 6:35; Ro 8:14 **5:10** [a]1Pe 3:14 [b]Mt 5:3; 19:14; 25:34; Mk 10:14; Lk 6:20; 22:29f **5:11** [a]1Pe 4:14 **5:12** [a]2Chr 36:16; Mt 23:37; Ac 7:52; 1Th 2:15; Heb 11:33ff; Jas 5:10 **5:13** [a]Mk 9:50; Lk 14:34f **5:14** [a]Pr 4:18; Jn 8:12; 9:5; 12:36 [1]Or *mountain* **5:15** [a]Mk 4:21; Lk 8:16; 11:33; Php 2:15 [1]Or *peck-measure* **5:16** [a]1Pe 2:12 [b]Mt 9:8 **5:17** [a]Mt 7:12 **5:18** [a]Mt 24:35; Lk 16:17 [1]Or *one projection of a letter* (serif); lit *one iota* (Heb yodh) **5:19** [a]Mt 11:11 [1]Gr *anthropoi* **5:20** [a]Lk 18:11, 12
**5:21** [a]Mt 5:27, 33, 38, 43 [b]Ex 20:13; Dt 5:17 [c]Dt 16:18; 2Chr 19:5f [1]Lit *it was said to the ancients*
**5:22** [a]Dt 16:18; 2Chr 19:5f [b]Mt 10:17; 26:59; Mk 13:9; 14:55; 15:1; Lk 22:66; Jn 11:47; Ac 4:15; 5:21; 6:12; 22:30; 23:1; 24:20 [c]Mt 5:29f; 10:28; 18:9; 23:15, 33; Mk 9:43ff; Lk 12:5; Jas 3:6 [1]Or *empty-head*; from Aram *reqa* [2]Or *Council* [3]Lit *Gehenna of fire* **5:23** [a]Mt 5:24 [1]Or *gift* **5:24** [a]Ro 12:17, 18 [1]Or *gift*
**5:25** [a]Pr 25:8f; Lk 12:58

at law while you are with him on
the way, so that your opponent may
not hand you over to the judge, and
the judge to the officer, and you be
thrown into prison. **26** Truly I say
to you, [a]you will not come out of
there until you have paid up the last
[1]quadrans.
**27** "[a]You have heard that it was said,
'[b]YOU SHALL NOT COMMIT ADULTERY';
**28** but I say to you that everyone who
looks at a woman [a]to lust for her has
already committed adultery with her
in his heart. **29** [a]But if your right eye
makes you [1]stumble, tear it out and
throw it from you; for it is better for
you [2]to lose one of the parts of your
body, [3]than for your whole body to
be thrown into [b,4]hell. **30** [a]And if your
right hand makes you [1]stumble, cut
it off and throw it from you; for it
is better for you [2]to lose one of the
parts of your body, [3]than for your
whole body to go into [b,4]hell.
**31** "Now it was said, '[a]WHOEVER
SENDS HIS WIFE AWAY, LET HIM GIVE
HER A CERTIFICATE OF DIVORCE'; **32** [a]but
I say to you that everyone who
[1]divorces his wife, except for the
reason of sexual immorality, makes
her commit adultery; and whoever
marries a [2]divorced woman commits
adultery.
**33** "Again, [a]you have heard that
[1]the ancients were told, '[b,2]YOU SHALL
NOT [3]MAKE FALSE VOWS, BUT SHALL
FULFILL YOUR [4]VOWS TO THE [5]LORD.'
**34** But I say to you, [a]make no oath
at all, either by heaven, for it is [b]the
throne of God, **35** or by the earth, for
it is the [a]footstool of His feet, or [1]by
Jerusalem, for it is [b]THE CITY OF THE
GREAT KING. **36** Nor shall you make
an oath by your head, for you cannot
make one hair white or black. **37** But
let your statement be, 'Yes, yes' *or*
'No, no'; anything beyond these is
[1]of [a]the evil one.
**38** "[a]You have heard that it was
said, '[b]AN EYE FOR AN EYE, AND A
TOOTH FOR A TOOTH.' **39** But I say to
you, do not resist an evil person; but
[a]whoever slaps you on your right
cheek, turn the other to him also.
**40** And if anyone wants to sue you
and take your [1]tunic, let him have
your [2]garment also. **41** And whoever
[1]forces you to go one mile, go with
him two. **42** [a]Give to him who asks
of you, and do not turn away from
him who wants to borrow from you.
**43** "[a]You have heard that it was
said, '[b]YOU SHALL LOVE YOUR NEIGH-
BOR [c]and hate your enemy.' **44** But I
say to you, [a]love your enemies and
pray for those who persecute you,
**45** so that you may [1]be [a]sons of
your Father who is in heaven; for
He causes His sun to rise on *the* evil
and *the* good, and sends rain on *the*

**5:26** [a]Lk 12:59 [1]A Roman copper coin, approx. 1/64 of a laborer's daily wage **5:27** [a]Mt 5:21, 33, 38, 43 [b]Ex 20:14; Dt 5:18 **5:28** [a]2Sa 11:2-5; Job 31:1; Mt 15:19; Jas 1:14, 15 **5:29** [a]Mt 18:9; Mk 9:47 [b]Mt 5:22 [1]Sin [2]Lit *that one...be lost* [3]Lit *not your whole body* [4]Gr *Gehenna* **5:30** [a]Mt 18:8; Mk 9:43 [b]Mt 5:22 [1]Sin [2]Lit *that one...be lost* [3]Lit *not your whole body* [4]Gr *Gehenna* **5:31** [a]Dt 24:1, 3; Jer 3:1; Mt 19:7; Mk 10:4 **5:32** [a]Mt 19:9; Mk 10:11f; Lk 16:18; 1Co 7:11f [1]Or *sends away* [2]Or *sent away* **5:33** [a]*Mt 5:21, 27, 38, 43;* 23:16ff [b]Lv 19:12; Nu 30:2; Dt 23:21, 23 [1]Lit it was said to *the ancients* [2]*you* and *your* are singular here [3]Or *break your vows* [4]Lit *oaths* [5]In OT, Yahweh, cf. Dt 23:21 **5:34** [a]Jas 5:12 [b]Is 66:1; Mt 23:22 **5:35** [a]Is 66:1; Ac 7:49 [b]Ps 48:2 [1]Or *toward* **5:37** [a]Mt 6:13; 13:19, 38; Jn 17:15; 2Th 3:3; 1Jn 2:13f; 3:12; 5:18f [1]Or *from evil* **5:38** [a]Mt 5:21, 27, 33, 43 [b]Ex 21:24; Lv 24:20; Dt 19:21 **5:39** [a]Mt 5:39-42: *Lk 6:29, 30;* 1Co 6:7 **5:40** [1]A garment worn next to the body [2]An outer garment **5:41** [1]Lit *will force* **5:42** [a]Dt 15:7-11; Lk 6:34f; 1Ti 6:18 **5:43** [a]Mt 5:21, 27, 33, 38 [b]Lv 19:18 [c]Dt 23:3-6 **5:44** [a]Lk 6:27f; 23:34; Ac 7:60; Ro 12:20 **5:45** [a]Mt 5:9; Lk 6:35; Ac 14:17 [1]Or *show yourselves to be*

righteous and *the* unrighteous. **46** For
[a]if you love those who love you, what
reward do you have? Do not even the
tax collectors do the same? **47** And if
you greet only your brothers, what
more are you doing *than others*? Do
not even the Gentiles do the same?
**48** Therefore [a,1]you are to be perfect,
as your heavenly Father is perfect.

### *Giving to the Poor and Prayer*

**6** "Beware of doing your righteous-
ness before men [a]to be noticed by
them; otherwise you have no reward
with your Father who is in heaven.
**2** "Therefore, when you [1]give to
the poor, do not sound a trumpet
before you, as the hypocrites do in
the synagogues and in the streets, so
that they [a]may be glorified by men.
[b]Truly I say to you, they have their
reward in full. **3** But when you [1]give
to the poor, do not let your left hand
know what your right hand is doing,
**4** so that your [1]giving will be in secret;
and [a]your Father who sees *what is
done* in secret will reward you.
**5** "And when you pray, you are not
to be like the hypocrites; for they love
to [a]stand and pray in the synagogues
and on the street corners [b,1]so that
they may be seen by men. [c]Truly I say
to you, they have their reward in full.
**6** But you, when you pray, [a]go into
your inner room, and when you have
shut your door, pray to your Father
who is in secret, and [b]your Father
who sees *what is done* in secret will
reward you.
**7** "And when you are praying, do
not use meaningless repetition as the
Gentiles do, for they suppose that
they will be heard for their [a]many
words. **8** Therefore, do not be like
them; for [a]your Father knows what
you need before you ask Him.
**9** "[a]Pray, then, in this way:
'Our Father who is in heaven,
Hallowed be Your name.
**10** '[a]Your kingdom come.
[b]Your will be done,
On earth as it is in heaven.
**11** '[a]Give us this day [1]our
daily bread.
**12** 'And [a]forgive us our
debts, as we also have
forgiven our debtors.
**13** 'And do not lead us into
temptation, but [a]deliver
us from [b,1]the evil one.
[2][For Yours is the kingdom
and the power and the
glory forever. Amen.']
**14** "[a]For if you forgive [1]others for their
transgressions, your heavenly Father
will also forgive you. **15** But [a]if you do
not forgive [1]others, then your Father
will not forgive your transgressions.

### *Fasting*

**16** "[a]Now whenever you fast, do not
put on a gloomy face as the hypocrites
*do*, for they [1]neglect their appearance
so that they will be noticed by men

---

**5:46** [a]Lk 6:32 **5:48** [a]Lv 19:2; Dt 18:13; 2Co 7:1; Php 3:12-15 [1]Lit *you shall be* ◆ **6:1** [a]Mt 6:5, 16; 23:5 **6:2** [a]Mt 6:5, 16; 23:5 [b]Mt 6:5, 16; Lk 6:24 [1]Or *give alms* **6:3** [1]Or *give alms* **6:4** [a]Jer 17:10; Mt 6:6, 18; Heb 4:13 [1]Or *alms* **6:5** [a]Mk 11:25; Lk 18:11, 13 [b]Mt 6:1, 16 [c]Mt 6:2, 16; Lk 6:24 [1]Lit *to be apparent to men* **6:6** [a]Is 26:20; Mt 26:36-39; Ac 9:40 [b]Mt 6:4, 18 **6:7** [a]1Ki 18:26f **6:8** [a]Ps 38:9; 69:17-19; Mt 6:32; Lk 12:30 **6:9** [a]Mt 6:9-13: *Lk 11:2-4* **6:10** [a]Mt 3:2; 4:17 [b]Mt 26:42; Lk 22:42; Ac 21:14 **6:11** [a]Pr 30:8; Is 33:16; Lk 11:3 [1]Or *our bread for tomorrow* **6:12** [a]Ex 34:7; Ps 32:1; 130:4; Mt 9:2; 26:28; Eph 1:7; 1Jn 1:7-9 **6:13** [a]Jn 17:15; 1Co 10:13; 2Th 3:3; 2Ti 4:18; 2Pe 2:9; 1Jn 5:18 [b]Mt 5:37 [1]Or *evil* [2]Early mss omit bracketed portion **6:14** [a]Mt 7:2; Mk 11:25f; Eph 4:32; Col 3:13 [1]Gr *anthropoi* **6:15** [a]Mt 18:35 [1]Gr *anthropoi* **6:16** [a]Is 58:5 [1]Discolor their faces with makeup; lit *distort their faces*

when they are fasting. [b]Truly I say
to you, they have their reward in full.
**17** But you, when you fast, [a]anoint
your head and wash your face **18** so
that your fasting will not be noticed
by men, but by your Father who is
in secret; and your [a]Father who sees
*what is done* in secret will reward you.

### *Treasures in Heaven*

**19** "[a]Do not store up for *yourselves*
treasures on earth, where moth and
rust destroy, and where thieves break
in and steal. **20** But store up for your-
selves [a]treasures in heaven, where
neither moth nor rust destroys, and
where thieves do not break in or
steal; **21** for [a]where your treasure is,
there your heart will be also.
**22** "[a]The eye is the lamp of the
body; so then if your eye is [1]clear,
your whole body will be full of light.
**23** But if [a]your eye is [1]bad, your whole
body will be full of darkness. If then
the light that is in you is darkness,
how great is the darkness!
**24** "[a]No one can [1]serve two mas-
ters; for either he will hate the one
and love the other, or he will be
devoted to one and despise the other.
You cannot [1]serve God and [b,2]wealth.

### *Do Not Worry*

**25** "[a]For this reason I say to you, [1]do
not be [b]worried about your [2]life,
*as to* what you will eat or what you
will drink; nor for your body, *as to*
what you will put on. Is not life more
than food, and the body more than
clothing? **26** [a]Look at the birds of the
[1]air, that they do not sow, nor reap
nor gather into barns, and *yet* your
heavenly Father feeds them. Are you
not worth much more than they?
**27** And which of you by [a]worrying
can [b]add a single [1]cubit to his [2]life
span? **28** And why are you [a]worried
about clothing? Observe how the
lilies of the field grow; they do not
toil nor do they spin, **29** yet I say to
you that not even [a]Solomon in all
his glory clothed himself like one of
these. **30** But if God so clothes the
[a]grass of the field, which is *alive*
today and tomorrow is thrown into
the furnace, *will He* not much more
*clothe* you? [b]You of little faith! **31** Do
not [a]worry then, saying, 'What will
we eat?' or 'What will we drink?' or
'What will we wear for clothing?'
**32** For all these things the Gentiles
eagerly seek; for [a]your heavenly
Father knows that you need all these
things. **33** But [1]seek first [2]His kingdom
and His righteousness, and [a]all these
things will be [3]added to you.
**34** "So do not [a]worry about tomor-
row; for tomorrow will worry about
itself. [1]Each day has enough trouble
of its own.

**6:16** [b]Mt 6:2 **6:17** [a]Ru 3:3; 2Sa 12:20 **6:18** [a]Mt 6:4, 6 **6:19** [a]Pr 23:4; Mt 19:21; Lk 12:21, 33; 18:22; 1Ti 6:9, 10; Heb 13:5; Jas 5:2 **6:20** [a]Mt 19:21; Lk 12:33; 1Ti 6:19 **6:21** [a]Lk 12:34 **6:22** [a]Mt 6:22, 23: *Lk 11:34, 35* [1]Or *healthy, sincere* **6:23** [a]Mt 20:15; Mk 7:22 [1]Or *evil* **6:24** [a]1Ki 18:21; Lk 16:13; Ga 1:10; Jas 4:4 [b]Lk 16:9, 11, 13 [1]Or *be a slave to* [2]Gr *mamonas*, from Aram *mamon* (mammon); wealth, etc., personified as an object of worship **6:25** [a]Mt 6:25-33: *Lk 12:22-31* [b]Mt 6:27, 28, 31, 34; Lk 10:41; 12:11, 22; Php 4:6; 1Pe 5:7 [1]Or *stop being worried* [2]Lit *soul* **6:26** [a]Job 35:11; 38:41; Ps 104:27, 28; Mt 10:29ff; Lk 12:24 [1]Lit *heaven* **6:27** [a]Mt 6:25, 28, 31, 34; Lk 10:41; 12:11, 22; Php 4:6; 1Pe 5:7 [b]Ps 39:5 [1]A cubit was approx. 18 in. or 45 cm [2]Or *height* **6:28** [a]Mt 6:25, 27, 31, 34; Lk 10:41; 12:11, 22; Php 4:6; 1Pe 5:7 **6:29** [a]1Ki 10:4-7; 2Chr 9:4-6, 20-22 **6:30** [a]Jas 1:10, 11; 1Pe 1:24 [b]Mt 8:26; 14:31; 16:8 **6:31** [a]Mt 6:25, 27, 28, 34; Lk 10:41; 12:11, 22; Php 4:6; 1Pe 5:7 **6:32** [a]Mt 6:8; Php 4:19 **6:33** [a]Mt 19:28; Mk 10:29f; Lk 18:29f; 1Ti 4:8 [1]Or *continually seek* [2]Or *the kingdom* [3]Or *provided* **6:34** [a]Mt 6:25, 27, 28, 31; Lk 10:41; 12:11, 22; Php 4:6; 1Pe 5:7 [1]Lit *Sufficient for the day is its evils*

### *Judging Others*

7 "[a]Do not judge, so that you will not be judged. **2** For with what judgment you judge, you will be judged; and [a]with what measure you measure, it will be measured to you. **3** And why do you [a]look at the speck that is in your brother's eye, but do not notice the log that is in your own eye? **4** [a]Or how [1]can you say to your brother, 'Let me take the speck out of your eye,' and behold, the log is in your own eye? **5** You hypocrite, first take the log out of your own eye, and then you will see clearly to take the speck out of your brother's eye.

**6** "[a]Do not give what is holy to dogs, and do not throw your pearls before swine, lest they trample them under their feet, and turn and tear you to pieces.

### *Ask, and It Will Be Given*

**7** "[a,1]Ask, and [b]it will be given to you; [2]seek, and you will find; [3]knock, and it will be opened to you. **8** For everyone who asks receives, and he who seeks finds, and to him who knocks it will be opened. **9** Or what man is there among you [1]who, when his son asks for a loaf, [2]will give him a stone? **10** Or [1]if he asks for a fish, he will not give him a snake, will he? **11** If you then, being evil, know how to give good gifts to your children, [a]how much more will your Father *who is in* heaven give *what is* good to those who ask Him!

**12** "[a]Therefore, in all things, whatever you want people to do for you, so do for them, for [b]this is the Law and the Prophets.

### *The Narrow Gate*

**13** "[a]Enter through the narrow gate; for the gate is wide and the way is broad that leads to destruction, and there are many who enter through it. **14** For the gate is narrow and the way is constricted that leads to life, and there are few who find it.

### *A Tree and Its Fruit*

**15** "Beware of the [a]false prophets, who come to you in sheep's clothing, but inwardly are [b]ravenous wolves. **16** You will [a,1]know them by their fruits. [2]Are grapes gathered from thorn bushes or figs from thistles? **17** Even so, [a]every good tree bears good fruit, but the bad tree bears bad fruit. **18** A good tree cannot bear bad fruit, nor can a bad tree bear good fruit. **19** [a]Every tree that does not bear good fruit is cut down and thrown into the fire. **20** So then, you will [1]know them [a]by their fruits.

**21** "[a]Not everyone who says to Me, 'Lord, Lord,' will enter the kingdom of heaven, but he who does the will of My Father who is in heaven *will enter*. **22** [a]Many will say to Me on [b]that day, 'Lord, Lord, in Your name did we not prophesy, and in Your name cast out demons, and in Your name do

◆ **7:1** [a]Mt 7:1-5: *Lk 6:37f, 41f;* Ro 14:10, 13 **7:2** [a]Mk 4:24; Lk 6:38 **7:3** [a]Ro 2:1 **7:4** [a]Lk 6:42 [1]Lit *will* **7:6** [a]Mt 15:26 **7:7** [a]Mt 7:7-11: *Lk 11:9-13* [b]Mt 18:19; 21:22; Mk 11:24; Jn 14:13; 15:7, 16; 16:23f; Jas 1:5f; 1Jn 3:22; 5:14f [1]Or *Keep asking* [2]Or *keep seeking* [3]Or *keep knocking* **7:9** [1]Lit *whom his son will ask* [2]Lit *he will not give him a stone, will he?* **7:10** [1]Lit *also will ask* **7:11** [a]Ps 84:11; Is 63:7; Ro 8:32; Jas 1:17 **7:12** [a]Lk 6:31 [b]Mt 22:40; Ro 13:8ff; Ga 5:14 **7:13** [a]Lk 13:24 **7:15** [a]Mt 24:11, 24; Mk 13:22; Lk 6:26; Ac 13:6; 2Pe 2:1; 1Jn 4:1; Rev 16:13; 19:20; 20:10 [b]Eze 22:27; Jn 10:12; Ac 20:29 **7:16** [a]Mt 7:20; 12:33; Lk 6:44; Jas 3:12 [1]Or *recognize* [2]Lit *They do not gather* **7:17** [a]Mt 12:33, 35 **7:19** [a]Mt 3:10; Lk 3:9; 13:7; Jn 15:2, 6 **7:20** [a]Mt 7:16; 12:33; Lk 6:44; Jas 3:12 [1]Or *recognize* **7:21** [a]Lk 6:46 **7:22** [a]Mt 25:11f; Lk 13:25ff [b]Mt 10:15

many [1]miracles?' **23** And then I will
declare to them, 'I never knew you;
[a]DEPART FROM ME, YOU WHO PRACTICE
LAWLESSNESS.'

### *Build Your House on the Rock*

**24** "Therefore [a]everyone who hears
these words of Mine and does them,
[1]may be compared to a wise man who
built his house on the rock. **25** And
the rain descended, and the rivers
came, and the winds blew and fell
against that house; and *yet* it did not
fall, for it had been founded on the
rock. **26** And everyone hearing these
words of Mine and not doing them,
may be compared to a foolish man
who built his house on the sand.
**27** And the rain descended, and the
rivers came, and the winds blew and
slammed against that house; and it
fell—and great was its fall."

**28** [a,1]Now it happened that when
Jesus had finished these words, [b]the
crowds were astonished at His teach-
ing; **29** for He was teaching them as
*one* having authority, and not as their
scribes.

### *Jesus Cleanses a Leper*

**8** Now when [1]Jesus came down
from the [2]mountain, [3]large
crowds followed Him. **2** And be-
hold, [a]a leper came to Him and
[b,1]was bowing down before Him,
and said, "Lord, if You are willing,
You can make me clean." **3** And
Jesus stretched out His hand and
touched him, saying, "I am willing;
be cleansed." And immediately his
[a]leprosy was cleansed. **4** And Jesus
*said to him, "[a]See that you tell no
one; but [b]go, [c]show yourself to the
priest and present the [1]offering that
Moses commanded, as a testimony
to them."

### *The Centurion's Faith*

**5** And [a]when [1]Jesus entered Caper-
naum, a centurion came to Him,
pleading *with* Him, **6** and saying,
"[1]Lord, my [2]servant is [3]lying [a]para-
lyzed at home, fearfully tormented."
**7** And Jesus *said to him, "I will come
and heal him." **8** But the centurion
said, "[1]Lord, I am not good enough
for You to come under my roof, but
just [2]say the word, and my [3]servant
will be healed. **9** For I also am a man
under [a]authority, with soldiers under
me; and I say to this man, 'Go!' and he
goes, and to another, 'Come!' and he
comes, and to my slave, 'Do this!' and
he does *it*." **10** Now when Jesus heard
*this*, He marveled and said to those
who were following, "Truly I say to
you, I have not found such great faith
[1]with anyone in Israel. **11** And I say to
you that many [a]will come from east
and west, and [1]recline *at the table*
with Abraham, Isaac, and Jacob in the
kingdom of heaven; **12** but [a]the sons
of the kingdom will be cast out into
[b]the outer darkness; in that place
[c]there will be weeping and gnash-
ing of teeth." **13** And Jesus said to

---

**7:22** [1]Or *works of power* **7:23** [a]Ps 6:8; Mt 25:41; Lk 13:27 **7:24** [a]Mt 7:24-27: *Lk 6:47-49;* Mt 16:18; Jas 1:22-25 [1]Lit *will* **7:28** [a]Mt 11:1; 13:53; 19:1; 26:1 [b]Mt 13:54; 22:33; Mk 1:22; 6:2; 11:18; Lk 4:32; Jn 7:46 [1]Lit *And* ◆ **8:1** [1]Lit *He* [2]Or *hill* [3]Lit *many* **8:2** [a]Mt 8:2-4: *Mk 1:40-44; Lk 5:12-14* [b]Mt 9:18; 15:25; 18:26; 20:20; Jn 9:38; Ac 10:25 [1]Or *worshiped* **8:3** [a]Mt 11:5; Lk 4:27 **8:4** [a]Mt 9:30; 12:16; 17:9; Mk 1:44; 3:12; 5:43; 7:36; 8:30; 9:9; Lk 4:41; 8:56; 9:21 [b]Mk 1:44; Lk 5:14; 17:14 [c]Lv 13:49; 14:2ff [1]Lit *gift* **8:5** [a]Mt 8:5-13: *Lk 7:1-10* [1]Lit *He* **8:6** [a]Mt 4:24 [1]Or *Sir* [2]Lit *boy* [3]Lit *thrown down* **8:8** [1]Or *Sir* [2]Lit *say with a word* [3]Lit *boy* **8:9** [a]Mk 1:27; Lk 9:1 **8:10** [1]One early ms *not even in Israel* **8:11** [a]Is 49:12; 59:19; Mal 1:11; Lk 13:29 [1]Or *dine* **8:12** [a]Mt 13:38 [b]Mt 22:13; 25:30 [c]Mt 13:42, 50; 22:13; 24:51; 25:30; Lk 13:28

the centurion, "Go; [1]it shall be done
for you [a]as you have believed." And
the [2]servant was healed that *very*
[3]moment.

### *Peter's Mother-in-Law and Many Others Healed*

**14** [a]When Jesus came into Peter's
[1]home, He saw his mother-in-law
lying sick in bed with a fever. **15** And
He touched her hand, and the fever
left her; and she got up and *began*
[1]waiting on Him. **16** Now when
evening came, they brought to Him
many [a]who were demon-possessed;
and He cast out the spirits with a
word, and [b]healed all who were ill
**17** in order to fulfill what was spoken
through Isaiah the prophet, saying,
"[a]HE HIMSELF TOOK OUR INFIRMITIES
AND [1]CARRIED AWAY OUR DISEASES."

### *The Cost of Following Jesus*

**18** Now when Jesus saw a crowd
around Him, [a]He gave orders to
depart to the other side *of the sea.*
**19** [a]Then a scribe came and said
to Him, "Teacher, I will follow You
wherever You go." **20** And Jesus *said
to him, "The foxes have holes and the
birds of the [1]air *have* [2]nests, but [a]the
Son of Man has nowhere to lay His
head." **21** And another of the disciples
said to Him, "Lord, permit me first to
*go and bury* my father." **22** But Jesus
*said to him, "[a]Follow Me, and allow
the dead to bury their own dead."

### *Jesus Calms a Storm*

**23** [a]And when He got into the boat,
His disciples followed Him. **24** And
behold, there arose [1]a great storm on
the sea, so that the boat was being
covered with the waves; but Jesus
Himself was sleeping. **25** And they
came to *Him* and got Him up, saying,
"[a]Save *us,* Lord; we are perishing!"
**26** And He *said to them, "Why are
you *so* cowardly, [a]you men of little
faith?" Then He got up and rebuked
the winds and the sea, and [1]it became
perfectly calm. **27** And the men mar-
veled, and said, "What kind of a man
is this, that even the winds and the
sea obey Him?"

### *Jesus Saves Men from Demons*

**28** [a]And when He came to the other
side, into the region of the Gadarenes,
two men who were [b]demon-possessed
met Him as they were coming out of
the tombs. *They were* so extremely
violent that no one could pass by
that way. **29** And behold, they cried
out, saying, "[a,1]What do we have to
do with You, Son of God? Have You
come here to torment us before the
[2]time?" **30** Now there was a herd of
many swine feeding at a distance
from them. **31** And the demons *began*
*to* plead with Him, saying, "If You *are*
*going* to cast us out, send us into the
herd of swine." **32** And He said to
them, "Go!" And coming out, they

---

**8:13** [a]Mt 9:22, 29 [1]Or *let it be done*; Gr imperative [2]Lit *boy* [3]Lit *hour* **8:14** [a]Mt 8:14-16: *Mk 1:29-34; Lk 4:38-41* [1]Or *house* **8:15** [1]Or *serving Him* **8:16** [a]Mt 4:24 [b]Mt 4:23; 8:33 **8:17** [a]Is 53:4 [1]Or *removed* **8:18** [a]Mk 4:35; Lk 8:22 **8:19** [a]Mt 8:19-22: *Lk 9:57-60* **8:20** [a]Da 7:13; Mt 9:6; 12:8, 32, 40; 13:41; 16:13, 27f; 17:9; 19:28; 26:64; Mk 8:38; Lk 12:8; 18:8; 21:36; Jn 1:51; 3:13f; 6:27; 12:34; Ac 7:56 [1]Or *sky* [2]Or *roosting places* **8:22** [a]Mt 9:9; Mk 2:14; Lk 9:59, 60; Jn 1:43; 21:19 **8:23** [a]Mt 8:23-27: *Mk 4:36-41; Lk 8:22-25* **8:24** [1]Lit *a shaking* **8:25** [a]Mt 8:2; 9:18 **8:26** [a]Mt 6:30; 14:31; 16:8; 17:20 [1]Lit *a great calm occurred* **8:28** [a]Mt 8:28-34: *Mk 5:1-17; Lk 8:26-37* [b]Mt 4:24 **8:29** [a]Jdg 11:12; 2Sa 16:10; 19:22; 1Ki 17:18; 2Ki 3:13; 2Chr 35:21; Mk 1:24; 5:7; Lk 4:34; 8:28; Jn 2:4 [1]Lit *What is to us and to you* (a Heb idiom) [2]Appointed time of judgment

went into the swine; and behold, the
whole herd rushed down the steep
bank into the sea and perished in
the waters. **33** Now the herdsmen
ran away, and went to the city and
reported everything, [1]including what
had happened to the [a]demoniacs.
**34** And behold, the whole city came
out to meet Jesus; and when they saw
Him, [a]they pleaded with Him to leave
their region.

### *Jesus Heals a Paralytic*

**9** And getting into a boat, Jesus
crossed over *the sea* and came
to [a]His own city.
**2** [a]And behold, they brought to
Him a [b]paralytic lying on a bed.
Seeing their faith, Jesus said to the
paralytic, "[c]Take courage, [1]son; [d]your
sins are forgiven." **3** And behold,
some of the scribes said [1]to themselves,
"This man [a]blasphemes."
**4** And Jesus [a]knowing their thoughts
said, "Why are you thinking evil in
your hearts? **5** For which is easier,
to say, '[a]Your sins are forgiven,' or
to say, 'Get up and walk'? **6** But so
that you may know that [a]the Son
of Man has authority on earth to
forgive sins"—then He *said to the
[b]paralytic, "Get up, pick up your
bed and go home." **7** And he got up
and [1]went home. **8** But when the
crowds saw *this*, they were afraid,
and [a]glorified God, who had given
such authority to men.

### *Matthew and Sinners Called*

**9** [a]And as Jesus went on from there,
He saw a man called [b]Matthew, sitting
in the tax office; and He *said to
him, "[c]Follow Me!" And he stood up
and followed Him.
**10** [1]Then it happened that as [2]Jesus
was reclining *at the table* in the
house, behold, many tax collectors
and [3]sinners came and were dining
with Jesus and His disciples. **11** And
when the Pharisees saw *this*, they
said to His disciples, "[a]Why is your
Teacher eating with the tax collectors
and sinners?" **12** But when Jesus heard
*this*, He said, "*It is* not [a]those who are
healthy who need a physician, but
those who are sick. **13** But go and
learn [a,1]what this means: '[b]I DESIRE
[2]COMPASSION, [3]AND NOT SACRIFICE,'
for [c]I did not come to call the righteous,
but sinners."

### *A Question About Fasting*

**14** Then the disciples of John *came to
Him, [1]asking, "Why do we and [a]the
Pharisees fast, but Your disciples
do not fast?" **15** And Jesus said to
them, "Can the [1]attendants of the
bridegroom mourn as long as the
bridegroom is with them? But the days
will come when the bridegroom is
taken away from them, and then they
will fast. **16** But no one puts [1]a patch
of unshrunk cloth on an old garment;
for [2]the patch pulls away from the
garment, and a worse tear results.

---

**8:33** [a]Mt 4:24 [1]Lit *and the things of* **8:34** [a]Am 7:12; Ac 16:39 ◆**9:1** [a]Mt 4:13; Mk 5:21 **9:2** [a]Mt 9:2-8: *Mk 2:3-12; Lk 5:18-26* [b]Mt 4:24; 9:6 [c]*Mt 9:22; 14:27; Mk 6:50; 10:49; Jn 16:33; Ac 23:11* [d]Mk 2:5, 9; Lk 5:20, 23; 7:48 [1]Lit *child* **9:3** [a]Mk 3:28, 29 [1]Lit *among* **9:4** [a]Mt 12:25; Lk 6:8; 9:47 **9:5** [a]Mt 9:2, 6; Mk 2:5, 9; Lk 5:20, 23; 7:48 **9:6** [a]Mt 8:20; Jn 5:27 [b]Mt 4:24; 9:2 **9:7** [1]Or *departed* **9:8** [a]Mt 5:16; 15:31; Mk 2:12; Lk 2:20; 5:25, 26; 7:16; 13:13; 17:15; 23:47; Jn 15:8; Ac 4:21; 11:18; 21:20; 2Co 9:13; Ga 1:24 **9:9** [a]Mt 9:9-17: *Mk 2:14-22; Lk 5:27-38* [b]Mt 10:3; Mk 2:14; 3:18; Lk 6:15; Ac 1:13 [c]Mt 8:22 **9:10** [1]Lit *And* [2]Lit *He* [3]Irreligious Jews **9:11** [a]Mt 11:19; Mk 2:16; Lk 5:30; 15:2 **9:12** [a]Mk 2:17; Lk 5:31 **9:13** [a]Mt 12:7 [b]Hos 6:6 [c]Mk 2:17; Lk 5:32; 1Ti 1:15 [1]Lit *what is* [2]Or *mercy* [3]More than **9:14** [a]Lk 18:12 [1]Lit *saying* **9:15** [1]Lit *sons of the bridal chamber* **9:16** [1]Lit *that which is put on* [2]Lit *that which fills up*

17 Nor do *people* put new wine into old
wineskins; otherwise the wineskins
burst, and the wine pours out and
the wineskins are ruined; but they
put new wine into fresh wineskins,
and both are preserved."

### *Miracles of Healing*

18 [a]While He was saying these things
to them, behold, [1]a *synagogue* [2]offi-
cial came and [b,3]was bowing down
before Him, and said, "My daughter
has just died; but come and lay Your
hand on her, and she will live." 19 And
Jesus got up and *began to* follow him,
and *so did* His disciples.

20 And behold, a woman who had
been suffering from a hemorrhage
for twelve years, came up behind
Him and touched [a]the [1]fringe of His
[2]garment; 21 for she was saying [1]to
herself, "If I only [a]touch His garment,
I will [2]be saved *from this*." 22 But
Jesus turning and seeing her said,
"Daughter, [a]take courage; [b]your faith
has [1]saved you." [2]At once the woman
was [3]saved *from her hemorrhage*.

23 And when Jesus came into
the [1]official's house, and saw [a]the
flute-players and the crowd in noisy
disorder, 24 He was saying, "Leave;
for the girl [a]has not died, but is
asleep." And they *began* laughing
at Him. 25 But [a]when the crowd had
been sent out, coming in, He [b]took
her by the hand, and the girl [1]got up.
26 [a]And this news spread throughout
all that land.

27 And as Jesus went on from
there, two blind men followed Him,
[1]crying out, "Have mercy on us, [a]Son
of David!" 28 And when He entered
the house, the blind men came up
to Him, and Jesus *said to them,
"Do you believe that I am able to
do this?" They *said to Him, "Yes,
Lord." 29 Then He touched their
eyes, saying, "[1]It shall be done to
you [a]according to your faith." 30 And
their eyes were opened. And Jesus
[a]sternly warned them, saying, "See
that no one knows *about this*!" 31 But
they went out and [a]spread the news
about Him throughout all that land.

32 Now as they were going out,
behold, [a]a mute, [b]demon-possessed
man [1]was brought to Him. 33 And
after the demon was cast out, the
mute man spoke; and the crowds
marveled, saying, "[a]Nothing like
this has [1]ever been seen in Israel."
34 But the Pharisees were saying, "He
[a]casts out the demons by the ruler of
the demons."

35 And Jesus was going through all
the cities and villages, [a]teaching in
their synagogues, and preaching the
gospel of the kingdom, and healing
every kind of disease and every kind
of sickness.

36 [a]And seeing the crowds, He felt
compassion for them, [b]because they

**9:18** [a]Mt 9:18-26: *Mk 5:22-43; Lk 8:41-56* [b]Mt 8:2 [1]Or *one* [2]Lit *ruler* [3]Or *worshiped* **9:20** [a]Nu 15:38; Dt 22:12; Mt 14:36; 23:5 [1]Tassel fringe [2]Or *outer garment* **9:21** [a]Mt 14:36; Mk 3:10; Lk 6:19 [1]Lit *in herself* [2]Or *get well* **9:22** [a]Mt 9:2 [b]Mt 9:29; 15:28; Mk 5:34; 10:52; Lk 7:50; 8:48; 17:19; 18:42 [1]Or *made you well* [2]Lit *From that hour* [3]Or *made well* **9:23** [a]2Chr 35:25; Jer 9:17; 16:6; Eze 24:17 [1]Lit *ruler's* **9:24** [a]Jn 11:13; Ac 20:10 **9:25** [a]Ac 9:40 [b]Mk 9:27 [1]Or *was raised up* **9:26** [a]Mt 4:24; 9:31; 14:1; Mk 1:28, 45; Lk 4:14, 37; 5:15; 7:17 **9:27** [a]Mt 1:1; 12:23; 15:22; 20:30, 31; 21:9, 15; 22:42; Mk 10:47, 48; 12:35; Lk 18:38, 39; 20:41f [1]Lit *crying out and saying* **9:29** [a]Mt 8:13; 9:22 [1]Or *Let it be done*; Gr imperative **9:30** [a]Mt 8:4 **9:31** [a]Mt 4:24; 9:26; 14:1; Mk 1:28, 45; Lk 4:14, 37; 5:15; 7:17 **9:32** [a]Mt 12:22, 24 [b]Mt 4:24 [1]Lit *they brought* **9:33** [a]Mk 2:12 [1]Lit *ever appeared* **9:34** [a]Mt 12:24; Mk 3:22; Lk 11:15; Jn 7:20f **9:35** [a]Mt 4:23; Mk 1:14 **9:36** [a]Mt 14:14; 15:32; Mk 6:34; 8:2 [b]Nu 27:17; Eze 34:5; Zec 10:2; Mk 6:34

were [1]distressed and [2]downcast like sheep [3]without a shepherd. **37** Then He *said to His disciples, "[a]The harvest is plentiful, but the workers are few. **38** Therefore pray earnestly to the Lord of the harvest to send out workers into His harvest."

### *Jesus Appoints the Twelve*

**10** [a]And summoning His twelve disciples, *Jesus* gave them authority over unclean spirits, to cast them out, and to [b]heal every kind of disease and every kind of sickness.

**2** [a]Now the names of the twelve apostles are these: The first, [b]Simon, who is called Peter, and [b]Andrew his brother; and [c]James the son of Zebedee, and John his brother; **3** [a]Philip and [1]Bartholomew; [b]Thomas and [c]Matthew the tax collector; [d]James the son of Alphaeus, and [e]Thaddaeus; **4** Simon the [1]Zealot, and [a]Judas Iscariot, the one who betrayed Him.

### *The Twelve Disciples Sent Out*

**5** [a]These twelve Jesus sent out after instructing them, saying, "Do not [1]go [2]in the way of the Gentiles, and do not enter *any* city of the [b]Samaritans; **6** but rather go to [a]the lost sheep of the house of Israel. **7** And as you go, [1]preach, saying, '[a]The kingdom of heaven [2]is at hand.' **8** Heal *the* sick, raise *the* dead, cleanse *the* lepers, cast out demons. Freely you received, freely give. **9** [a]Do not acquire gold, or silver, or copper for your money belts, **10** or a [1]bag for *your* journey, or even two [2]tunics, or sandals, or a staff; for [a]the worker is worthy of his [3]support. **11** And whatever city or village you enter, inquire who is worthy in it, and stay there until you leave. **12** Now as you enter the [1]house, [a]give it your [2]greeting. **13** And if the house is worthy, let your peace come upon it. But if it is not worthy, let your peace return to you. **14** And whoever does not receive you, nor heed your words, as you leave that house or that city, [a]shake the dust off your feet. **15** Truly I say to you, [a]it will be more tolerable for the land of [b]Sodom and Gomorrah in [c]the day of judgment than for that city.

### *The Promise of Persecution*

**16** "[a]Behold, I send you out as sheep in the midst of wolves; so [1]be [b]shrewd as serpents and [c]innocent as doves. **17** But beware of men, for they will deliver you over to the [a]courts and flog you [b]in their synagogues; **18** and you will even be brought before governors and kings for My sake, as a testimony to them and to the Gentiles. **19** [a]But when they deliver you over, [b]do not worry about how or what you are to say; for it will be given to you in that

---

**9:36** [1]Or *harassed* [2]Lit *thrown down* [3]Lit *not having* **9:37** [a]Lk 10:2 ◆**10:1** [a]Mk 3:13-15; 6:7 [b]Mt 9:35; Lk 9:1 **10:2** [a]Mt 10:2-4: *Mk 3:16-19; Lk 6:14-16; Ac 1:13* [b]Mt 4:18 [c]Mt 4:21 **10:3** [a]Jn 1:43ff [b]Jn 11:16; 14:5; 20:24ff; 21:2 [c]Mt 9:9 [d]Mk 15:40 [e]Mk 3:18; Lk 6:16; Ac 1:13 [1]Son of Talmai (Aram) **10:4** [a]Mt 26:14; Lk 22:3; Jn 6:71; 13:2, 26 [1]Or *Cananaean* **10:5** [a]Mk 6:7; Lk 9:2 [b]2Ki 17:24ff; Lk 9:52; 10:33; 17:16; Jn 4:9, 39f; 8:48; Ac 8:25 [1]Or *go off* [2]Or *on the road of* **10:6** [a]Mt 15:24 **10:7** [a]Mt 3:2 [1]Or *proclaim* [2]Lit *has come near* **10:9** [a]Mt 10:9-15: *Mk 6:8-11; Lk 9:3-5; 10:4-12;* Lk 22:35 **10:10** [a]1Co 9:14; 1Ti 5:18 [1]Or *knapsack, beggar's bag* [2]Gr *khiton*, the garment worn next to the skin [3]Lit *nourishment* **10:12** [a]1Sa 25:6; Ps 122:7, 8 [1]Or *household* [2]The familiar Heb blessing, "Peace be to this house!" **10:14** [a]Ac 13:51 **10:15** [a]Mt 11:22, 24 [b]Mt 11:24; 2Pe 2:6; Jd 7 [c]Mt 7:22; 11:22, 24; 12:36; Ac 17:31; 1Th 5:4; Heb 10:25; 2Pe 2:9; 3:7; 1Jn 4:17; Jd 6 **10:16** [a]Lk 10:3 [b]Ge 3:1; Mt 24:25; Ro 16:19 [c]Hos 7:11 [1]Or *show yourselves to be* **10:17** [a]Mt 5:22 [b]Mt 23:34; Mk 13:9; Lk 12:11; Ac 5:40; 22:19; 26:11 **10:19** [a]Mt 10:19-22: *Mk 13:11-13; Lk 21:12-17* [b]Mt 6:25; Lk 12:11, 12

hour what you are to say. 20 For [a]it is
not you who speak, but the Spirit of
your Father who speaks in you.

21 "[a]And brother will betray broth-
er to death, and a father *his* child;
and [b]children will rise up against
parents and [1]cause them to be put
to death. 22 [a]And you will be hated
by all because of My name, but [b]it is
the one who has endured to the end
who will be saved.

23 "But whenever they [a]persecute
you in this city, flee to [1]the next; for
truly I say to you, you will not finish
*going through* the cities of Israel
[b]until the Son of Man comes.

### *The Meaning of Discipleship*

24 "[a]A [1]disciple is not above his
teacher, nor a slave above his master.
25 It is enough for the disciple that he
become like his teacher, and the slave
like his master. [a]If they have called
the head of the house [b,1]Beelzebul,
how much more the members of his
household!

26 "Therefore do not [a]fear them,
[b]for there is nothing concealed that
will not be revealed, and hidden that
will not be known. 27 [a]What I tell you
in the darkness, speak in the light;
and what you hear *whispered* in *your*
ear, proclaim [b]upon the housetops.
28 And do not fear those who kill the
body but are unable to kill the soul;
but rather [a]fear Him who is able to
destroy both soul and body in [b,1]hell.
29 [a]Are not two sparrows sold for an
[1]assarion? And *yet* not one of them
will fall to the ground apart from
your Father. 30 But [a]the very hairs
of your head are all numbered. 31 So
do not fear; [a]you are more valuable
than many sparrows.

32 "Therefore [a]everyone who
[1]confesses Me before men, I will also
confess [2]him before My Father who
is in heaven. 33 But [a]whoever [1]denies
Me before men, I will also deny him
before My Father who is in heaven.

34 "[a]Do not think that I came to
[1]bring peace on the earth; I did not
come to bring peace, but a sword.
35 For I came to [a]SET A MAN AGAINST
HIS FATHER, AND A DAUGHTER AGAINST
HER MOTHER, AND A DAUGHTER-IN-LAW
AGAINST HER MOTHER-IN-LAW; 36 and
[a]A MAN'S ENEMIES WILL BE THE MEM-
BERS OF HIS HOUSEHOLD.

37 "[a]He who loves father or mother
more than Me is not worthy of Me;
and he who loves son or daughter
more than Me is not worthy of Me.
38 And [a]he who does not take his
cross and follow after Me is not wor-
thy of Me. 39 [a]He who has found his
[1]life will lose it, and he who has lost
his [1]life for My sake will find it.

### *The Reward of Service*

40 "[a]He who receives you receives
Me, and [b]he who receives Me receives

**10:20** [a]Lk 12:12; Ac 4:8; 13:9; 2Co 13:3 **10:21** [a]Mt 10:35, 36; Mk 13:12 [b]Mic 7:6 [1]Lit *put them to death* **10:22** [a]Mt 24:9; Lk 21:17; Jn 15:18ff [b]Mt 24:13; Mk 13:13 **10:23** [a]Mt 23:34 [b]Mt 16:27f [1]Lit *the other* **10:24** [a]Lk 6:40; Jn 13:16; 15:20 [1]Or *student* **10:25** [a]Mt 9:34 [b]2Ki 1:2; Mt 12:24, 27; Mk 3:22; Lk 11:15, 18, 19 [1]Ruler of demons; or *Beezebul* **10:26** [a]Mt 10:26-33: *Lk 12:2-9* [b]Mk 4:22; Lk 8:17; 12:2; 1Co 4:5 **10:27** [a]Lk 12:3 [b]Mt 24:17; Ac 5:20 **10:28** [a]Heb 10:31 [b]Mt 5:22; Lk 12:5 [1]Gr *Gehenna* **10:29** [a]Lk 12:6 [1]A Roman copper coin, approx. 1/16 of a laborer's daily wage **10:30** [a]1Sa 14:45; 2Sa 14:11; 1Ki 1:52; Lk 21:18; Ac 27:34 **10:31** [a]Mt 12:12 **10:32** [a]Lk 12:8; Rev 3:5 [1]Lit *will confess in Me* [2]Lit *in him* **10:33** [a]Mk 8:38; Lk 9:26; 2Ti 2:12 [1]Lit *will deny* **10:34** [a]Mt 10:34, 35: *Lk 12:51-53* [1]Lit *cast* **10:35** [a]Mic 7:6; Mt 10:21; Lk 12:53 **10:36** [a]Mic 7:6; Mt 10:21 **10:37** [a]Dt 33:9; Lk 14:26 **10:38** [a]Mt 16:24; Mk 8:34; Lk 9:23; 14:27 **10:39** [a]Mt 16:25; Mk 8:35; Lk 9:24; 17:33; Jn 12:25 [1]Or *soul* **10:40** [a]Mt 18:5; Lk 10:16; Jn 13:20; Ga 4:14 [b]Mk 9:37; Lk 9:48; Jn 12:44

Him who sent Me. **41** [a]He who receives
a prophet in the name of a prophet
shall receive a prophet's reward; and
he who receives a righteous man in
the name of a righteous man shall
receive a righteous man's reward.
**42** And [a]whoever in the name of a
disciple gives to one of these [1]little
ones even a cup of cold water to
drink, truly I say to you, he shall not
lose his reward."

### *Questions from John the Baptist*

**11** [a,1]Now it happened that when
Jesus had finished [2]giving
instructions to His twelve disciples,
He departed from there [b]to teach and
[3]preach in their cities.
**2** [a]Now when [b]John in prison heard
of the works of Christ, he sent *word*
by his disciples **3** and said to Him, "Are
You [a]the One who is to come, or shall
we look for someone else?" **4** And
Jesus answered and said to them, "Go
and report to John what you hear and
see: **5** [a]*the* BLIND RECEIVE SIGHT and
*the* lame walk, *the* lepers are cleansed
and *the* deaf hear, *the* dead are raised
up, and *the* [b]POOR HAVE THE [1]GOSPEL
PREACHED TO THEM. **6** And blessed is he
[1]who [a]does not [2]take offense at Me."

### *Jesus' Tribute to John the Baptist*

**7** Now as these men were going *away*,
Jesus began to speak to the crowds
about John, "What did you go out
into [a]the wilderness to see? A reed
shaken by the wind? **8** [1]But what did
you go out to see? A man dressed
in soft *clothing*? Behold, those who
wear soft *clothing* are in kings'
[2]palaces! **9** [1]But what did you go out
to see? [a]A prophet? Yes, I tell you,
and one who is more than a prophet.
**10** This is the one about whom it [1]is
written,

'[a]BEHOLD, I SEND MY
MESSENGER [2]AHEAD OF YOU,
WHO WILL PREPARE YOUR
WAY BEFORE YOU.'

**11** "Truly I say to you, among those
born of women there has not arisen
*anyone* greater than John the Bap-
tist! Yet the one who is [1]least in the
kingdom of heaven is greater than
he. **12** [a]And from the days of John
the Baptist until now the kingdom of
heaven [1]suffers violence, and violent
men [2]take it by force. **13** For all the
prophets and the Law prophesied
until John. **14** And if you are willing
to accept *it*, John himself is [a]Elijah
who [1]was to come. **15** [a]He who has
ears to hear, [1]let him hear.
**16** "But to what shall I compare this
generation? It is like children sitting
in the marketplaces, who call out to
the other *children*, **17** and say, 'We
played the flute for you, and you did
not dance; we sang a dirge, and you
did not [1]mourn.' **18** For John came
neither [a]eating nor [b]drinking, and
they say, '[c]He has a demon!' **19** The
Son of Man came eating and drinking,

---

**10:41** [a]Mt 25:44, 45 **10:42** [a]Mt 25:40; Mk 9:41 [1]Possibly someone of low social standing ◆ **11:1** [a]Mt 7:28 [b]Mt 9:35; Lk 23:5 [1]Lit *And* [2]Or *commanding* [3]Or *proclaim* **11:2** [a]Mt 11:2-19: *Lk 7:18-35;* Mt 4:12 [b]Mt 14:3; Mk 6:17; Lk 9:7ff **11:3** [a]Ps 118:26; Mt 11:10; Jn 6:14; 11:27; Heb 10:37 **11:5** [a]Is 35:5f; Mt 8:3; 12:13 [b]Is 61:1; Lk 4:18 [1]Or *good news* **11:6** [a]Mt 5:29; 13:57; 24:10; 26:31; Mk 6:3; Jn 6:61; 16:1 [1]Lit *whoever* [2]Or *stumble over Me* **11:7** [a]Mt 3:1 **11:8** [1]Or *Well then,* [2]Lit *houses* **11:9** [a]Mt 14:5; 21:26; Lk 1:76; 20:6 [1]Or *Well then,* **11:10** [a]Mal 3:1; Mk 1:2 [1]Lit *has been written* [2]Lit *before your face* **11:11** [1]Or *less* **11:12** [a]Lk 16:16 [1]Or *is forcibly entered* [2]Or *seize it for themselves* **11:14** [a]Mal 4:5; Mt 17:10-13; Mk 9:11-13; Lk 1:17; Jn 1:21 [1]Or *is going to come* **11:15** [a]Mt 13:9, 43; Mk 4:9, 23; Lk 8:8; 14:35; Rev 2:7, 11, 17, 29; 3:6, 13, 22; 13:9 [1]Or *hear!, listen!*, Gr imperative **11:17** [1]Lit *beat the breast* **11:18** [a]Mt 3:4 [b]Lk 1:15 [c]Mt 9:34; Jn 7:20; 8:48f, 52; 10:20

and they say, 'Behold, a gluttonous
man and a [1]drunkard, [a]a friend of tax
collectors and [2]sinners!' Yet wisdom
is vindicated [3]by her deeds."

### *Woe to Unrepentant Cities*

20 Then He began to denounce the
cities in which most of His [a,1]miracles
were done, because they did not
repent. 21 "[a]Woe to you, Chorazin!
Woe to you, [b]Bethsaida! For if the
[1]miracles had occurred in [c]Tyre
and [c]Sidon which occurred in you,
they would have repented long ago
in [d,2]sackcloth and ashes. 22 Never-
theless I say to you, [a]it will be more
tolerable for Tyre and Sidon in [b]the
day of judgment than for you. 23 And
[a]Capernaum, will you be exalted to
heaven? You will [b]descend to [c]Hades;
for if the [1]miracles had occurred in
[d]Sodom which occurred in you, it
would have remained to this day.
24 Nevertheless I say to you that [a]it
will be more tolerable for the land
of [b]Sodom in the day of judgment,
than for you."

### *Come to Me*

25 [a]At that [1]time Jesus said, "I praise
You, [b]Father, Lord of heaven and
earth, that [c]You have hidden these
things from *the* wise and intelligent
and have revealed them to infants.
26 Yes, [a]Father, for this way was
well-pleasing in Your sight. 27 [a]All
things have been handed over to
Me by My Father; and no one knows
the Son except the Father; nor does
anyone know the Father [b]except the
Son, and anyone to whom the Son
wills to reveal *Him*.
28 "[a]Come to Me, all [1]who are wea-
ry and heavy-laden, and I will give
you rest. 29 Take My yoke upon you
and [a]learn from Me, for I am [1]gentle
and humble in heart, and [b]YOU WILL
FIND REST FOR YOUR SOULS. 30 For [a]My
yoke is [1]easy and My burden is light."

### *Lord of the Sabbath*

12 [a]At that [1]time Jesus went
through the grainfields on the
Sabbath, and His disciples became
hungry and began to [b]pick the
heads of grain and eat. 2 But when
the Pharisees saw *this*, they said to
Him, "Look, Your disciples do what
[a]is not lawful to do on a Sabbath."
3 But He said to them, "Have you not
read what David did when he became
hungry, he and his companions,
4 how he entered the house of God,
and [a]they ate the [1]consecrated bread,
which was not lawful for him to eat
nor for those with him, but for the
priests alone? 5 Or have you not
read in the Law, that on the Sabbath
the priests in the temple [1]break the
Sabbath and are innocent? 6 But I say

**11:19** [a]Mt 9:11; Lk 5:29-32; 15:2 [1]Or *wine-drinker* [2]Irreligious Jews [3]Or *from* **11:20** [a]Lk 10:13-15 [1]Or *works of power* **11:21** [a]Mt 11:21-23: *Lk 10:13-15* [b]Mk 6:45; 8:22; Lk 9:10; Jn 1:44; 12:21 [c]Mt 11:22; 15:21; Mk 3:8; 7:24, 31; Lk 4:26; 6:17; Ac 12:20; 27:3 [d]Rev 11:3 [1]Or *works of power* [2]Symbols of mourning **11:22** [a]Mt 10:15; 11:24 [b]Mt 10:15; 12:36; Rev 20:11, 12 **11:23** [a]Mt 4:13 [b]Is 14:13, 15; Eze 26:20; 31:14; 32:18, 24 [c]Mt 16:18; Lk 10:15; 16:23; Ac 2:27, 31; Rev 1:18; 6:8; 20:13f [d]Mt 10:15 [1]Or *works of power* **11:24** [a]Mt 10:15; 11:22 [b]Mt 10:15 **11:25** [a]Mt 11:25-27: *Lk 10:21, 22* [b]Lk 22:42; 23:34; Jn 11:41; 12:27, 28 [c]Ps 8:2; 1Co 1:26ff [1]Or *occasion* **11:26** [a]Lk 22:42; 23:34; Jn 11:41; 12:27, 28 **11:27** [a]Mt 28:18; Jn 3:35; 13:3; 17:2 [b]Jn 7:29; 10:15; 17:25 **11:28** [a]Jer 31:25; Jn 7:37 [1]Or *who work to exhaustion* **11:29** [a]Jn 13:15; Eph 4:20; Php 2:5; 1Pe 2:21; 1Jn 2:6 [b]Jer 6:16 [1]Lit *lowly* **11:30** [a]1Jn 5:3 [1]Or *comfortable, pleasant* ◆ **12:1** [a]Mt 12:1-8: *Mk 2:23-28; Lk 6:1-5* [b]Dt 23:25 [1]Or *occasion* **12:2** [a]Mt 12:10; Lk 13:14; 14:3; Jn 5:10; 7:23; 9:16 **12:4** [a]1Sa 21:6 [1]Or *showbread*; lit *loaves of presentation* **12:5** [1]Or *profane*

to you that something [a]greater than
the temple is here. 7 But if you had
known what this [1]means, '[a]I DESIRE
[2]COMPASSION, AND NOT A SACRIFICE,'
you would not have condemned the
innocent. 8 For [a]the Son of Man is
Lord of the Sabbath."

### *Jesus Heals a Man on the Sabbath*

9 [a]And departing from there, He
went into their synagogue. 10 And
behold, a man *was there* whose hand
was withered. And they questioned
[1]Jesus, saying, "[a]Is it lawful to heal
on the Sabbath?"—so that they
might accuse Him. 11 And He said to
them, "[a]What man [1]is there among
you who has a sheep, and if it falls
into a pit on the Sabbath, will not
take hold of it and lift it out? 12 [a]How
much more valuable then is a man
than a sheep! So then, it is lawful to
do [1]good on the Sabbath." 13 Then
He *said to the man, "Stretch out
your hand!" [a]He stretched it out,
and it was restored to [1]normal,
like the other. 14 But going out, the
Pharisees [a]took counsel together
against Him, *as to* how they might
destroy Him.

15 But Jesus, [1]aware *of this*, with-
drew from there. Many followed
Him, and [a]He healed them all,
16 and [a]warned them not to make
Him known, 17 in order that what was
spoken through Isaiah the prophet
would be fulfilled, saying,

18 "[a]BEHOLD, MY [1]SERVANT
WHOM I [2]HAVE CHOSEN;
[b]MY BELOVED IN WHOM MY
SOUL [3]IS WELL-PLEASED;
[c]I WILL PUT MY SPIRIT UPON HIM,
[a]AND HE SHALL PROCLAIM
[4]JUSTICE TO THE [5]GENTILES.
19 "[a]HE WILL NOT QUARREL,
NOR CRY OUT;
NOR WILL ANYONE HEAR HIS
VOICE IN THE STREETS.
20 "[a]A BATTERED REED HE
WILL NOT BREAK OFF,
AND A SMOLDERING WICK
HE WILL NOT PUT OUT,
UNTIL HE [1]LEADS [2]JUSTICE
TO VICTORY.
21 "[a]AND IN HIS NAME THE
[1]GENTILES WILL HOPE."

### *A Kingdom Divided*

22 [a]Then a [b]demon-possessed man
*who was* blind and mute was brought
to [1]Jesus, and He healed him, so that
the mute man spoke and saw. 23 And
all the crowds were astounded, and
were saying, "Can this man *really*
be the [a]Son of David?" 24 But when
the Pharisees heard *this*, they said,
"This man does not [a]cast out demons
except by [1]Beelzebul the ruler of the
demons."

25 [a]And [b]knowing their thoughts
He said to them, "[1]Any kingdom di-
vided against itself is laid waste; and
[2]any city or house divided against
itself will not stand. 26 And if [a]Satan

---

**12:6** [a]2Chr 6:18; Is 66:1, 2; Mt 12:41, 42 **12:7** [a]Hos 6:6; Mt 9:13 [1]Lit *is* [2]Or *mercy* **12:8** [a]Mt 8:20; 12:32, 40
**12:9** [a]Mt 12:9-14: *Mk 3:1-6; Lk 6:6-11* **12:10** [a]Mt 12:2; Lk 13:14; 14:3; Jn 5:10; 7:23; 9:16 [1]Lit *Him*
**12:11** [a]Lk 14:5 [1]Lit *will be from you* **12:12** [a]Mt 10:31; Lk 14:1-6 [1]Lit *well* **12:13** [a]Mt 8:3; Ac 28:8 [1]Lit *health* **12:14** [a]Mt 26:4; Mk 14:1; Lk 22:2; Jn 7:30, 44; 8:59; 10:31, 39; 11:53 **12:15** [a]Mt 4:23 [1]Lit *knowing*
**12:16** [a]Mt 8:4; 9:30; 17:9 **12:18** [a]Is 42:1 [b]Mt 3:17; 17:5 [c]Lk 4:18; Jn 3:34 [1]Lit *Child* [2]Lit *chose* [3]Or *took pleasure* [4]Or *judgment* [5]Or *nations* **12:19** [a]Is 42:2 **12:20** [a]Is 42:3 [1]Or *puts forth* [2]Or *judgment*
**12:21** [a]Ro 15:12 [1]Or *nations* **12:22** [a]Mt 12:22, 24: *Lk 11:14, 15;* Mt 9:32, 34 [b]Mt 4:24; 2Th 2:9 [1]Lit *Him*
**12:23** [a]Mt 9:27 **12:24** [a]Mt 9:34 [1]Or *Beezebul* **12:25** [a]Mt 12:25-29: *Mk 3:23-27; Lk 11:17-22* [b]Mt 9:4
[1]Lit *Every* [2]Lit *every* **12:26** [a]Mt 4:10; 13:19

casts out Satan, he [1]is divided against
himself; how then will his kingdom
stand? **27** And if I [a]by [1]Beelzebul cast
out demons, [b]by whom do your sons
cast *them* out? For this reason they
will be your judges. **28** But [a]if I cast
out demons by the Spirit of God, then
the kingdom of God has come upon
you. **29** Or how can anyone enter the
strong man's house and carry off
his property, unless he first binds
the strong man? And then he will
plunder his house.

### *Blasphemy Against the Holy Spirit*

**30** "[a]He who is not with Me is against
Me; and he who does not gather with
Me scatters.

**31** "[a]Therefore I say to you, any
sin and blasphemy shall be forgiven
people, but the blasphemy against the
Spirit shall not be forgiven. **32** [a]And
whoever [1]speaks a word against the
Son of Man, it shall be forgiven him;
but whoever [1]speaks against the Holy
Spirit, it shall not be forgiven him, ei-
ther in [b]this age or in the *age* to come.

### *The Heart Is Revealed by Words*

**33** "Either make the tree good and its
fruit good, or make the tree bad and
its fruit bad; for [a]the tree is known
by its fruit. **34** [a]You brood of vipers,
how can you, being evil, speak [1]what
is good? [b]For the mouth speaks out
of that which fills the heart. **35** [a]The
good man brings out of *his* good trea-
sure [1]what is good; and the evil man
brings out of *his* evil treasure [2]what
is evil. **36** But I tell you that every
[1]careless word that people [2]speak,
they shall give an accounting for it in
[a]the day of judgment. **37** For [1]by your
words you will be justified, and [1]by
your words you will be condemned."

### *The Sign of Jonah*

**38** Then some of the scribes and
Pharisees answered and said to
Him, "Teacher, [a]we want to see [1]a
sign from You." **39** But He answered
and said to them, "[a]An evil and adul-
terous generation eagerly seeks for a
sign; and *yet* no sign will be given to
it but the sign of Jonah the prophet;
**40** for just as [a]JONAH WAS THREE DAYS
AND THREE NIGHTS IN THE BELLY OF
THE SEA MONSTER, so will [b]the Son of
Man be [c]three days and three nights
in the heart of the earth. **41** [a]The men
of Nineveh will stand up with this
generation at the judgment, and will
condemn it because [b]they repented
at the preaching of Jonah; and be-
hold, [c]something greater than Jonah
is here. **42** [a]The Queen of the South
will rise up with this generation at
the judgment and will condemn it,
because she came from the ends
of the earth to hear the wisdom of
Solomon; and behold, [b]something
greater than Solomon is here.

**43** "[a]Now when the unclean spirit
goes out of a man, it passes through

**12:26** [1]Lit *was* **12:27** [a]Mt 9:34 [b]Ac 19:13 [1]v 24, note 1 **12:28** [a]1Jn 3:8 **12:30** [a]Mk 9:40; Lk 9:50; 11:23 **12:31** [a]Mt 12:31, 32: *Mk 3:28-30;* Lk 12:10 **12:32** [a]Lk 12:10 [b]Mt 13:22, 39; Mk 10:30; Lk 16:8; 18:30; 20:34, 35; Eph 1:21; 1Ti 6:17; 2Ti 4:10; Tit 2:12; Heb 6:5 [1]Lit *will speak* **12:33** [a]Mt 7:16-18; Lk 6:43, 44; Jn 15:4-7 **12:34** [a]Mt 3:7; 23:33; Lk 3:7 [b]1Sa 24:13; Is 32:6; Mt 12:34, 35: *Lk 6:45;* Mt 15:18; Eph 4:29; Jas 3:2-12 [1]Lit *good things* **12:35** [a]Pr 10:20, 21; 25:11, 12; Mt 13:52; Col 4:6 [1]Lit *good things* [2]Lit *evil things* **12:36** [a]Mt 10:15 [1]Or *useless* [2]Lit *will speak* **12:37** [1]Or *in accordance with* **12:38** [a]Mt 16:1; Mk 8:11, 12; Lk 11:16; Jn 2:18; 6:30; 1Co 1:22 [1]Or *an attesting miracle* **12:39** [a]Mt 12:39-42: *Lk 11:29-32;* Mt 16:4 **12:40** [a]Jon 1:17 [b]Mt 8:20 [c]Mt 16:21 **12:41** [a]Jon 1:2 [b]Jon 3:5 [c]Mt 12:6, 42 **12:42** [a]1Ki 10:1; 2Chr 9:1 [b]Mt 12:6, 41 **12:43** [a]Mt 12:43-45: *Lk 11:24-26*

waterless places seeking rest, and
does not find *it.* 44 Then it says, 'I
will return to my house from which
I came'; and when it comes, it finds *it*
unoccupied, swept, and put in order.
45 Then it goes and takes along with
it seven other spirits more wicked
than itself, and they go in and live
there; and [a]the last state of that man
becomes worse than the first. That is
the way it will also be with this evil
generation."

### *Jesus' Mother and Brothers*

46 [a]While He was still speaking to
the crowds, behold, His [b]mother and
[c]brothers were standing outside,
seeking to speak to Him. 47 [1]Now
someone said to Him, "Behold,
Your mother and Your brothers are
standing outside seeking to speak
to You." 48 But [1]Jesus answered the
one who was telling Him and said,
"Who is My mother and who are
My brothers?" 49 And stretching out
His hand toward His disciples, He
said, "Behold My mother and My
brothers! 50 For whoever does the
will of My Father who is in heaven,
he is My brother and sister and
mother."

### *The Parable of the Sower*

13 On that day Jesus went out of
[a]the house and was sitting [b]by
the sea. 2 And [1]large crowds gathered
to Him, so [a]He got into a boat and
sat down, and the whole crowd was
standing on the beach.
3 And He spoke many things to
them in [a]parables, saying, "Behold,
the sower went out to sow; 4 and
as he sowed, some *seeds* fell beside
the road, and the birds came and
ate them up. 5 And others fell on
the rocky places, where they did not
have much soil; and immediately
they sprang up, because they had
no depth of soil. 6 But when the
sun had risen, they were scorched;
and because they had no root, they
withered away. 7 And others fell
[1]among the thorns, and the thorns
came up and choked them out.
8 And others fell on the good soil
and were yielding [1]a crop, some a
[a]hundredfold, some sixty, and some
thirty. 9 [a]He who has ears, [1]let him
hear."

### *The Purpose of the Parables*

10 And the disciples came and said
to Him, "Why do You speak to them
in parables?" 11 And [1]Jesus answered
and said to them, "[a]To you it has been
given to know the mysteries of the
kingdom of heaven, but to them it has
not been given. 12 [a]For whoever has,
to him *more* shall be given, and he
will have an abundance; but whoever
does not have, even what he has shall
be taken away from him. 13 Therefore
I speak to them in parables; because
while [a]seeing they do not see, and
while hearing they do not hear, nor
do they understand. 14 And in them
the prophecy of Isaiah is being ful-
filled, which says,

**12:45** [a]Mk 5:9; Lk 11:26; *Heb 6:4-8; 2Pe 2:20* **12:46** [a]*Mt 12:46-50: Mk 3:31-35; Lk 8:19-21* [b]Mt 1:18; 2:11ff; 13:55; Lk 1:43; 2:33f, 48, 51; Jn 2:1, 5, 12; 19:25f; Ac 1:14 [c]Mt 13:55; Mk 6:3; Jn 2:12; 7:3, 5, 10; Ac 1:14; 1Co 9:5; Ga 1:19 **12:47** [1]This verse is not found in early mss **12:48** [1]Lit *He* ◆ **13:1** [a]Mt 9:28; 13:36 [b]Mt 13:1-15: *Mk 4:1-12; Lk 8:4-10;* Mk 2:13 **13:2** [a]Lk 5:3 [1]Lit *many* **13:3** [a]Mt 13:10ff; Mk 4:2ff **13:7** [1]Lit *upon* **13:8** [a]Ge 26:12; Mt 13:23 [1]Lit *fruit* **13:9** [a]Mt 11:15; Rev 2:7, 11, 17, 29; 3:6, 13, 22 [1]Or *hear!, listen!*; Gr imperative **13:11** [a]Mt 19:11; 20:23; Jn 6:65; 1Co 2:10; Col 1:27; 1Jn 2:20, 27 [1]Lit *He* **13:12** [a]Mt 25:29; Mk 4:25; Lk 8:18; 19:26 **13:13** [a]Dt 29:4; Is 42:19, 20; Jer 5:21; Eze 12:2

'[a,1]YOU WILL KEEP ON HEARING,
[2]BUT WILL NOT UNDERSTAND;
[3]YOU WILL KEEP ON SEEING,
BUT WILL NOT PERCEIVE;
15 [a]FOR THE HEART OF THIS
PEOPLE HAS BECOME DULL,
AND WITH THEIR EARS
THEY SCARCELY HEAR,
AND THEY HAVE CLOSED
THEIR EYES,
LEST THEY WOULD SEE
WITH THEIR EYES,
HEAR WITH THEIR EARS,
AND UNDERSTAND WITH THEIR
HEART AND RETURN,
AND I WOULD HEAL THEM.'

16 "[a]But blessed are your eyes,
because they see; and your ears,
because they hear. 17 For truly I say
to you that [a]many prophets and righ-
teous men desired to see what you
see, and did not see *it*, and to hear
what you hear, and did not hear *it*.

### *The Parable of the Sower Explained*

18 "[a]Hear then the parable of the
sower. 19 When anyone hears [a]the
word of the kingdom and does not
understand it, [b]the evil one comes
and snatches away what has been
sown in his heart. This is the one
on whom seed was sown beside the
road. 20 And the one on whom seed
was sown on the rocky places, this
is the man who hears the word and
immediately receives it with joy;
21 yet he has no root in himself, but is
*only* temporary, and when affliction
or persecution arises because of the
word, immediately he [a,1]falls away.
22 And the one on whom seed was
sown among the thorns, this is the
one who hears the word, and the
worry of [a]the [1]world and the [b]deceit-
fulness of wealth choke the word,
and it becomes unfruitful. 23 And the
one on whom seed was sown on the
good soil, this is the man who hears
the word and understands it; who
indeed bears fruit and brings forth,
some [a]a hundredfold, some sixty,
and some thirty."

### *The Parable of Tares Among Wheat*

24 He presented another parable
to them, saying, "[a]The kingdom of
heaven [1]may be compared to a man
who sowed good seed in his field.
25 But while his men were sleeping,
his enemy came and sowed [1]tares
among the wheat, and went away.
26 But when the [1]wheat sprouted and
bore grain, then the tares became
evident also. 27 The slaves of the
landowner came and said to him, 'Sir,
did you not sow good seed in your
field? [1]How then does it have tares?'
28 And he said to them, 'An [1]enemy
has done this!' The slaves *said to
him, 'Do you want us, then, to go and
gather them up?' 29 But he *said, 'No;
for while you are gathering up the
tares, you may uproot the wheat with
them. 30 Allow both to grow together
until the harvest; and in the time of
the harvest I will say to the reapers,

---

**13:14** [a]Is 6:9; Mk 4:12; Lk 8:10; Jn 12:40; Ac 28:26, 27; Ro 10:16; 11:8 [1]Lit *With a hearing you will hear* [2]Lit *and* [3]Lit *Seeing you will see* **13:15** [a]Is 6:10; Ps 119:70; Zec 7:11; Lk 19:42; Jn 8:43, 44; 2Ti 4:4; Heb 5:11 **13:16** [a]Mt 13:16, 17: *Lk 10:23, 24;* Mt 16:17; Jn 20:29 **13:17** [a]Jn 8:56; Heb 11:13; 1Pe 1:10-12 **13:18** [a]Mt 13:18-23: *Mk 4:13-20; Lk 8:11-15* **13:19** [a]Mt 4:23 [b]Mt 5:37 **13:21** [a]Mt 11:6 [1]Lit *is caused to stumble* **13:22** [a]Mt 12:32; 13:39; Mk 4:19; Ro 12:2; 1Co 1:20; 2:6, 8; 3:18; 2Co 4:4; Ga 1:4; Eph 2:2 [b]Mt 19:23; 1Ti 6:9, 10, 17 [1]Or *age* **13:23** [a]Mt 13:8 **13:24** [a]Mt 13:31, 33, 45, 47; 18:23; 20:1; 22:2; 25:1; Mk 4:26-30; Lk 13:18, 20 [1]Lit *was compared to* **13:25** [1]Or *darnel*, a weed resembling wheat **13:26** [1]Lit *grass* **13:27** [1]Lit *From where* **13:28** [1]Lit *enemy man*

"First gather up the tares and bind
them in bundles to burn them up; but
[a]gather the wheat into my barn."'"

### *Parables of the Mustard Seed and Leaven*

**31** He presented another parable
to them, saying, "[a]The kingdom
of heaven is like [b]a mustard seed,
which a man took and sowed in his
field; **32** and this is the [1]smallest of all
seeds, but when it is fully grown, it is
the [2]largest of the garden plants and
becomes a tree, so that [a]THE BIRDS
OF THE [3]AIR come and NEST IN ITS
BRANCHES."
**33** He spoke another parable to
them, "[a]The kingdom of heaven is
like leaven, which a woman took and
hid in [b,1]three sata of flour until it was
all leavened."
**34** All these things Jesus spoke to
the crowds in parables, and He was
not speaking to them [a]without a
parable **35** so that what was spoken
through the prophet might be fulfilled, saying,

"[a]I WILL OPEN MY MOUTH
IN PARABLES;
I WILL UTTER THINGS HIDDEN
SINCE THE FOUNDATION
OF THE WORLD."

### *The Parable of Tares Explained*

**36** Then He left the crowds and went
into [a]the house. And His disciples
came to Him and said, "[b]Explain to
us the parable of the [1]tares of the
field." **37** And He answered and said,
"The one who sows the good seed is
[a]the Son of Man, **38** and the field is the
world; and *as for* the good seed, these
are [a]the sons of the kingdom; and the
tares are [b]the sons of [c]the evil one;
**39** and the enemy who sowed them is
the devil, and the harvest is [a]the [1]end
of the age; and the reapers are angels.
**40** So just as the tares are gathered up
and burned with fire, so shall it be at
[a]the [1]end of the age. **41** [a]The Son of
Man [b]will send forth His angels, and
they will gather out of His kingdom
[1]all [c]stumbling blocks, and those
who commit lawlessness, **42** and [a]will
throw them into the fiery furnace;
in that place [b]there will be weeping
and gnashing of teeth. **43** [a]Then THE
RIGHTEOUS WILL SHINE FORTH AS THE
SUN in the kingdom of their Father.
[b]He who has ears, [1]let him hear.

### *A Hidden Treasure*

**44** "[a]The kingdom of heaven is like a
treasure hidden in the field, which a
man found and hid *again*; and from
joy over it he goes and [b]sells all that
he has and buys that field.

### *A Costly Pearl*

**45** "Again, [a]the kingdom of heaven is
like a merchant seeking fine pearls,
**46** and upon finding one pearl of
great value, he went and sold all that
he had and bought it.

---

**13:30** [a]Mt 3:12 **13:31** [a]Mt 13:31, 32: *Mk 4:30-32; Lk 13:18, 19;* Mt 13:24 [b]Mt 17:20; Lk 17:6
**13:32** [a]Eze 17:23; Ps 104:12; Eze 31:6; Da 4:12 [1]Lit *smaller* [2]Lit *larger* [3]Or *sky* **13:33** [a]Mt 13:33: *Lk 13:21; Mt 13:24* [b]*Ge 18:6; Jdg 6:19;* 1Sa 1:24 [1]Approx. 48 lb. or 39 l, a saton was approx. 16 lb. or 13 l
**13:34** [a]Mk 4:34; Jn 10:6; 16:25 **13:35** [a]Ps 78:2 **13:36** [a]Mt 13:1 [b]Mt 15:15 [1]Or *darnel*, a weed resembling wheat **13:37** [a]Mt 8:20 **13:38** [a]Mt 8:12 [b]Jn 8:44; Ac 13:10; 1Jn 3:10 [c]Mt 5:37
**13:39** [a]Mt 12:32; 13:22, 40, 49; 24:3; 28:20; 1Co 10:11; Heb 9:26 [1]Or *consummation* **13:40** [a]Mt 12:32; 13:22, 39, 49; 24:3; 28:20; 1Co 10:11; Heb 9:26 [1]Or *consummation* **13:41** [a]Mt 8:20 [b]Mt 24:31 [c]Zep 1:3 [1]Or *everything that is offensive* **13:42** [a]Mt 13:50 [b]Mt 8:12 **13:43** [a]Da 12:3 [b]Mt 11:15 [1]Or *hear!, listen!*; Gr imperative **13:44** [a]Mt 13:24 [b]Mt 13:46 **13:45** [a]Mt 13:24

### *A Dragnet*

**47** “Again, [a]the kingdom of heaven is
like a dragnet cast into the sea, and
gathering *fish* of every kind; **48** and
when it was filled, they drew it up
on the beach; and they sat down and
gathered the good *fish* into contain-
ers, but the bad they threw away.
**49** So it will be at [a]the [1]end of the
age; the angels will come forth and
[2]take out the wicked from among the
righteous, **50** and [a]will throw them
into the fiery furnace; in that place
[b]there will be weeping and gnashing
of teeth.
**51** “Have you understood all these
things?” They *said to Him, “Yes.”
**52** And He said to them, “Therefore
every scribe who has become a disci-
ple of the kingdom of heaven is like a
head of a household, who brings out
of his treasure things new and old.”

### *Jesus Rejected at Nazareth*

**53** [a,1]Now it happened that when
Jesus had finished these parables,
He departed from there. **54** [a]And He
came to [1]His hometown and [b]*began*
teaching them in their synagogue, so
that [c]they were astonished, and said,
“Where *did* this man *get* this wisdom
and *these* [2]miraculous powers? **55** Is
not this the carpenter’s son? Is not
[a]His mother called Mary, and His
[a]brothers, James and Joseph and Si-
mon and Judas? **56** And [a]His sisters,
are they not all with us? Where then
*did* this man *get* all these things?”
**57** And they were taking [a]offense
at Him. But Jesus said to them,
“[b]A prophet is not without honor
except in his [1]hometown and in his
*own* household.” **58** And He did not
do many [1]miracles there because of
their unbelief.

### *John the Baptist Beheaded*

**14** [a]At that [1]time [b]Herod the
tetrarch heard the news about
Jesus, **2** and said to his servants, “[a]This
is John the Baptist; [1]he has risen from
the dead, and that is why miraculous
powers are at work in him.”
**3** For when [a]Herod had John ar-
rested, he bound him and put him [b]in
prison because of [c]Herodias, the wife
of his brother Philip. **4** For John had
been saying to him, “[a]It is not lawful
for you to have her.” **5** And although
Herod wanted to put him to death,
he feared the crowd, because they
were regarding [1]John as [a]a prophet.
**6** But when Herod’s birthday came,
the daughter of [a]Herodias danced
[1]before *them* and pleased [b]Herod,
**7** so *much* that he promised with
an oath to give her whatever she
asked. **8** Now having been prompted
by her mother, she *said, “Give me
here on a platter the head of John
the Baptist.” **9** And although he was
grieved, the king commanded *it* to
be given because of his oaths, and
because of [1]his dinner guests. **10** And

**13:47** [a]Mt 13:44 **13:49** [a]Mt 13:39, 40 [1]Or *consummation* [2]Or *separate* **13:50** [a]Mt 13:42 [b]Mt 8:12 **13:53** [a]Mt 7:28 [1]Lit *And* **13:54** [a]Mt 13:54-58: *Mk 6:1-6* [b]Mt 4:23 [c]Mt 7:28 [1]Or *His own part of the country* [2]Or *miracles* **13:55** [a]Mt 12:46 **13:56** [a]Mk 6:3 **13:57** [a]Mt 11:6 [b]Mk 6:4; Lk 4:24; Jn 4:44 [1]Or *own part of the country* **13:58** [1]Or *works of power* ◆ **14:1** [a]Mt 14:1-12: *Mk 6:14-29;* Mt 14:1, 2: *Lk 9:7-9* [b]Mk 8:15; Lk 3:1, 19; 8:3; 13:31; 23:7f, 11f, 15; Ac 4:27; 12:1 [1]Or *occasion* **14:2** [a]Mt 16:14; Mk 6:14; Lk 9:7 [1]Or *he, himself* **14:3** [a]Mt 14:1-12: *Mk 6:14-29;* Mk 8:15; Lk 3:1, 19; 8:3; 13:31; 23:7f, 11f, 15; Ac 4:27; 12:1 [b]Mt 4:12; 11:2 [c]Mt 14:6; Mk 6:17, 19, 22; Lk 3:19f **14:4** [a]Lv 18:16; 20:21 **14:5** [a]Mt 11:9 [1]Lit *him* **14:6** [a]Mt 14:3; Mk 6:17, 19, 22; Lk 3:19 [b]Mt 14:1-12: *Mk 6:14-29;* Mk 8:15; Lk 3:1, 19; 8:3; 13:31; 23:7f, 11f, 15; Ac 4:27; 12:1 [1]Lit *in the midst* **14:9** [1]Lit *those who reclined* at the table *with him*

he sent and had John beheaded in the prison. **11** And his head was brought on a platter and given to the girl, and she brought it to her mother. **12** And his disciples came and took away the body and buried [1]it; and they went and reported to Jesus.

### *Jesus Feeds Five Thousand*

**13** [a]Now when Jesus heard *about John,* He withdrew from there in a boat to a desolate place by Himself; and when the crowds heard *of this,* they followed Him on foot from the cities. **14** And when He went [1]ashore, He [a]saw a large crowd, and felt compassion for them and [b]healed their sick.

**15** Now when it was evening, the disciples came to Him and said, "This place is desolate and the hour is already [1]late; so send the crowds away, that they may go into the villages and buy food for themselves." **16** But Jesus said to them, "They do not need to go away; you give them *something* to eat!" **17** But they *said to Him, "We have here only [a]five loaves and two fish." **18** And He said, "Bring them here to Me." **19** And ordering the crowds to [1]sit down on the grass, He took the five loaves and the two fish, and looking up toward heaven, He [a]blessed *the food.* And breaking the loaves, He gave them to the disciples, and the disciples *gave them* to the crowds, **20** and they all ate and were satisfied. They picked up what was left over of the broken pieces, twelve full [a]baskets. **21** And there were about five thousand men who ate, besides women and children.

### *Jesus Walks on the Sea*

**22** [a]Immediately He [1]made the disciples get into the boat and go ahead of Him to the other side, while He sent the crowds away. **23** And after He had sent the crowds away, [a]He went up on the mountain by Himself to pray; and when it was evening, He was there alone. **24** But the boat was already many [1]stadia away from the land, [2]being battered by the waves; for the wind was [a,3]against *them.* **25** And in [a]the [1]fourth watch of the night He came to them, walking on the sea. **26** Now when the disciples saw Him walking on the sea, they were terrified, and said, "It is [a]a ghost!" And they cried out [1]in fear. **27** But immediately Jesus spoke to them, saying, "[a]Take courage, [1]it is I; [b]do not be afraid."

**28** And Peter answered and said to Him, "Lord, if it is You, command me to come to You on the water." **29** And He said, "Come!" And getting out of the boat, Peter walked on the water and came toward Jesus. **30** But seeing the wind, he became frightened, and beginning to sink, he cried out, saying, "Lord, save me!" **31** And immediately Jesus stretched out His hand and took hold of him, and *said to him, "[a]You of little faith, why did

---

**14:12** [1]Lit *him* **14:13** [a]Mt 14:13-21: *Mk 6:32-44; Lk 9:10-17; Jn 6:1-13;* Mt 15:32-38 **14:14** [a]Mt 9:36 [b]Mt 4:23 [1]Lit *out* **14:15** [1]Lit *past* **14:17** [a]Mt 16:9 **14:19** [a]1Sa 9:13; Mt 15:36; 26:26; Mk 6:41; 8:7; 14:22; Lk 24:30; Ac 27:35; Ro 14:6 [1]Lit *recline* **14:20** [a]Mt 16:9; Mk 6:43; 8:19; Lk 9:17; Jn 6:13 **14:22** [a]Mt 14:22-33: *Mk 6:45-51; Jn 6:15-21* [1]Lit *compelled* **14:23** [a]Mk 6:46; Lk 6:12; 9:28; Jn 6:15 **14:24** [a]Ac 27:4 [1]A stadion was approx. 607 ft. or 185 m [2]Lit *tormented* [3]Lit *contrary* **14:25** [a]Mt 24:43; Mk 13:35 [1]3-6 a.m. **14:26** [a]Lk 24:37 [1]Lit *from* **14:27** [a]Mt 9:2 [b]Mt 17:7; 28:5, 10; Mk 6:50; Lk 1:13, 30; 2:10; 5:10; 12:32; Jn 6:20; Rev 1:17 [1]Or *I am* He, cf. Jn 4:26; 8:18, 24, 28; 13:19; 18:5, 6 **14:31** [a]Mt 6:30; 8:26; 16:8

you doubt?" **32** And when they got
into the boat, the wind stopped.
**33** And those who were in the boat
worshiped Him, saying, "You are
truly [a]God's Son!"
**34** [a]And when they had crossed
over, they came to land at [b]Gen-
nesaret. **35** And when the men of
that place [1]recognized Him, they
sent *word* into all that surrounding
district and brought to Him all who
were sick; **36** and they were pleading
*with* Him that they might just touch
[a]the fringe of His garment; and as
many as [b]touched *it* were cured.

### *God's Commandments, Man's Traditions*

**15** [a]Then some Pharisees and
scribes *came to Jesus [b]from
Jerusalem and said, **2** "Why do Your
disciples break the tradition of the
elders? For they [a]do not wash their
hands when they eat bread." **3** And
He answered and said to them, "Why
do you yourselves transgress the
commandment of God for the sake
of your tradition? **4** For God said,
'[a]HONOR YOUR FATHER AND MOTHER,'
and, '[b]HE WHO SPEAKS EVIL OF FATHER
OR MOTHER IS TO [1]BE PUT TO DEATH.'
**5** But you say, 'Whoever says to *his* fa-
ther or mother, "Whatever you might
benefit from me [1]is given *to God*,"
**6** he need not [1]honor his father.' And
*by this* you invalidated the word of
God for the sake of your tradition.
**7** You hypocrites, rightly did Isaiah
prophesy of you:

**8** '[a]THIS PEOPLE HONORS ME
WITH THEIR LIPS,
BUT THEIR HEART IS
FAR AWAY FROM ME.
**9** 'BUT IN VAIN DO THEY
WORSHIP ME,
TEACHING AS [a]DOCTRINES
THE COMMANDS OF MEN.'"

**10** After Jesus called the crowd
to Him, He said to them, "Hear and
understand. **11** [a]*It is* not what enters
into the mouth *that* defiles the man,
but what proceeds out of the mouth,
this defiles the man."
**12** Then the disciples *came and
*said to Him, "Do You know that
the Pharisees were [1]offended when
they heard this statement?" **13** But
He answered and said, "[a]Every plant
which My heavenly Father did not
plant shall be uprooted. **14** Let them
alone; [a]they are blind guides [1]of the
blind. And [b]if a blind man guides a
blind man, both will fall into a pit."

### *The Heart of Man*

**15** Now Peter answered and said to
Him, "[a]Explain the parable to us."
**16** And [1]Jesus said, "Are you still
lacking in understanding also?
**17** Do you not understand that ev-
erything that goes into the mouth
passes into the stomach, and goes
into the sewer? **18** But [a]the things
that proceed out of the mouth come
from the heart, and those defile the
man. **19** [a]For out of the heart come
evil thoughts, murders, adulteries,
sexual immoralities, thefts, false

---

**14:33** [a]Mt 4:3 **14:34** [a]Mt 14:34-36: *Mk 6:53-56;* Jn 6:24, 25 [b]Mk 6:53; Lk 5:1 **14:35** [1]Or *knew*
**14:36** [a]Mt 9:20 [b]Mt 9:21; Mk 3:10; 6:56; 8:22; Lk 6:19 ◆ **15:1** [a]Mt 15:1-20: *Mk 7:1-23* [b]Mk 3:22; 7:1; Jn 1:19; Ac 25:7 **15:2** [a]Lk 11:38 **15:4** [a]Ex 20:12; Dt 5:16 [b]Ex 21:17; Lv 20:9 [1]Lit *die the death*
**15:5** [1]An offering; lit *a gift* **15:6** [1]By supporting them with it **15:8** [a]Is 29:13 **15:9** [a]Col 2:22
**15:11** [a]Mt 15:18; Ac 10:14, 15; 1Ti 4:3 **15:12** [1]Lit *caused to stumble* **15:13** [a]Is 60:21; 61:3; Jn 15:2; 1Co 3:9 **15:14** [a]Mt 23:16, 24 [b]Lk 6:39 [1]Some mss omit *of the blind* **15:15** [a]Mt 13:36 **15:16** [1]Lit *He*
**15:18** [a]Mt 12:34; Mk 7:20 **15:19** [a]Ga 5:19ff

witness, slanders. 20 These are the
things which defile the man; but to
eat with unwashed hands does not
defile the man."

### *The Canaanite Woman*

21 [a]And going away from there,
Jesus withdrew into the district of
[b]Tyre and [b]Sidon. 22 And behold, a
Canaanite woman from that region
came out and *began to* cry out,
saying, "Have mercy on me, Lord,
[a]Son of David; my daughter is cru-
elly [b]demon-possessed." 23 But He
did not answer her a word. And His
disciples came and were pleading
with Him, saying, "Send her away,
because she keeps shouting [1]at us."
24 But He answered and said, "I was
not sent except to [a]the lost sheep of
the house of Israel." 25 But she came
and [a,1]was bowing down before Him,
saying, "Lord, help me!" 26 And He
answered and said, "It is not [1]good to
take the children's bread and throw
it to the dogs." 27 But she said, "Yes,
Lord; [1]but even the dogs feed on the
crumbs which fall from their masters'
table." 28 Then Jesus answered and
said to her, "O woman, [a]your faith is
great; it shall be done for you as you
wish." And her daughter was healed
[1]at once.

### *Jesus Heals the Crowds*

29 [a]And departing from there, Jesus
went along by [b]the Sea of Galilee,
and having gone up on the mountain,
He was sitting there. 30 And [1]large
crowds came to Him, bringing with
them *those who were* lame, crippled,
blind, mute, and many others, and
they laid them down at His feet; and
[a]He healed them. 31 So the crowd
marveled as they saw the mute
speaking, the crippled [1]restored,
and the lame walking, and the blind
seeing; and they [a]glorified the God
of Israel.

### *Jesus Feeds Four Thousand*

32 [a]And Jesus called His disciples to
Him, and said, "[b]I feel compassion
for the crowd, because they [1]have
remained with Me now three days
and have nothing to eat; and I do
not want to send them away hungry,
lest they faint on the way." 33 And
the disciples *said to Him, "Where
would we get so many loaves in *this*
desolate place to satisfy such a large
crowd?" 34 And Jesus *said to them,
"How many loaves do you have?"
And they said, "Seven, and a few
small fish." 35 And He directed the
crowd to [1]sit down on the ground;
36 and He took the seven loaves and
the fish; and [a]giving thanks, He
broke them and kept giving them to
the disciples, and the disciples *gave
them* to the crowds. 37 And they
all ate and were satisfied, and they
picked up what was left over of the
broken pieces, seven *large* [a]baskets
full. 38 And those who ate were four
thousand men, besides women and
children.

39 And sending away the crowds,
Jesus got into [a]the boat and came to
the region of [b]Magadan.

---

**15:21** [a]Mt 15:21-28: *Mk 7:24-30* [b]Mt 11:21 **15:22** [a]Mt 9:27 [b]Mt 4:24 **15:23** [1]Lit *behind us*
**15:24** [a]Mt 10:6 **15:25** [a]Mt 8:2 [1]Or *worshiped* **15:26** [1]Or *proper* **15:27** [1]Lit *for* **15:28** [a]Mt 9:22
[1]Lit *from that hour* **15:29** [a]Mt 15:29-31: *Mk 7:31-37* [b]Mt 4:18 **15:30** [a]Mt 4:23 [1]Lit *many*
**15:31** [a]Mt 9:8 [1]Or *healthy* **15:32** [a]Mt 15:32-39: *Mk 8:1-10;* Mt 14:13-21 [b]Mt 9:36 [1]Lit *are remaining*
**15:35** [1]Lit *recline* **15:36** [a]Mt 14:19; 26:27; Lk 22:17, 19; Jn 6:11, 23; Ac 27:35; Ro 14:6 **15:37** [a]Mt 16:10;
Mk 8:8, 20; Ac 9:25 **15:39** [a]Mk 3:9 [b]Mk 8:10

### The Pharisees and Sadducees Test Jesus

16 [a]And the [b]Pharisees and
Sadducees came, and testing
Him, they [c]asked Him to show them
[1]a sign from heaven. 2 But He replied
to them, "[a,1]When it is evening, you
say, '*It will be* fair weather, for the sky
is red.' 3 And in the morning, '*There*
*will be* a storm today, for the sky is
red and threatening.' [a]Do you know
how to discern the [1]appearance of the
sky, but cannot *discern* the signs of
the times? 4 [a]An evil and adulterous
generation eagerly seeks for [1]a sign;
and [1]a sign will not be given it, except
the [2]sign of Jonah." And He left them
and went away.
5 And coming to the other side *of*
*the sea*, the disciples had forgotten
to bring bread. 6 And Jesus said to
them, "Watch out and [a]beware of the
[1]leaven of the [b]Pharisees and Saddu-
cees." 7 Now they *began to* discuss
*this* among themselves, saying, "*He*
*said that* because we did not bring
bread." 8 But Jesus, aware of this, said,
"[a]You men of little faith, why do you
discuss among yourselves that you
have no bread? 9 Do you not yet
understand or remember [a]the five
loaves of the five thousand, and
how many baskets *full* you picked
up? 10 Or [a]the seven loaves of the
four thousand, and how many *large*
baskets *full* you picked up? 11 How
is it that you do not understand that
I did not speak to you concerning
bread? But [a]beware of the [1]leaven
of the [b]Pharisees and Sadducees."
12 Then they understood that He
did not say to beware of the leaven
of bread, but of the teaching of the
[a]Pharisees and Sadducees.

### Peter Confesses Jesus Is the Christ

13 [a]Now when Jesus came into the
district of [b]Caesarea Philippi, He was
asking His disciples, saying, "Who do
people say that [c]the Son of Man is?"
14 And they said, "Some *say* [a]John
the Baptist; and others, [b,1]Elijah; but
still others, [2]Jeremiah, or one of the
prophets." 15 He *said to them, "But
who do you say that I am?" 16 And
Simon Peter answered and said, "You
are [a,1]the Christ, [b]the Son of [c]the liv-
ing God." 17 And Jesus answered and
said to him, "Blessed are you, [a]Simon
[1]Bar-Jonah, because [b]flesh and blood
did not reveal *this* to you, but My
Father who is in heaven. 18 And I
also say to you that you are [a,1]Peter,
and upon this [2]rock I will build My
church; and the gates of [b]Hades will
not overpower it. 19 I will give you
[a]the keys of the kingdom of heaven;
and [b]whatever you bind on earth
[1]shall have been bound in heaven,
and whatever you loose on earth
[1]shall have been loosed in heaven."
20 [a]Then He [1]warned the disciples

◆**16:1** [a]Mt 16:1-12: *Mk 8:11-21* [b]Mt 3:7; 16:6, 11, 12 [c]Mt 12:38; Lk 11:16 [1]Or *an attesting miracle*
**16:2** [a]Lk 12:54f [1]Early mss omit rest of v 2 and v 3 **16:3** [a]Lk 12:56 [1]Lit *face* **16:4** [a]Mt 12:39; Lk 11:29 [1]Or *an attesting miracle* [2]Or *attesting miracle* **16:6** [a]Mk 8:15; Lk 12:1 [b]Mt 3:7 [1]Or *yeast*
**16:8** [a]Mt 6:30; 8:26; 14:31 **16:9** [a]Mt 14:17-21 **16:10** [a]Mt 15:34-38 **16:11** [a]Mt 16:6; Mk 8:15; Lk 12:1 [b]Mt 3:7; 16:6, 12 [1]Or *yeast* **16:12** [a]Mt 3:7; 5:20 **16:13** [a]Mt 16:13-16: *Mk 8:27-29; Lk 9:18-20* [b]Mk 8:27 [c]Mt 8:20; 16:27, 28 **16:14** [a]Mt 14:2 [b]Mt 17:10; Mk 6:15; Lk 9:8; Jn 1:21 [1]Gr *Elias* [2]Gr *Jeremias*
**16:16** [a]Mt 1:16; 16:20; Jn 11:27 [b]Mt 4:3 [c]Ps 42:2; Mt 26:63; Ac 14:15; Ro 9:26; 2Co 3:3; 6:16; 1Th 1:9; 1Ti 3:15; 4:10; Heb 3:12; 9:14; 10:31; 12:22; Rev 7:2 [1]The Messiah **16:17** [a]Jn 1:42; 21:15-17 [b]1Co 15:50; Ga 1:16; Eph 6:12; Heb 2:14 [1]Lit *son of Jonah* **16:18** [a]Mt 4:18 [b]Mt 11:23 [1]Gr *Petros*, a stone [2]Gr *petra*, a large rock or bed-rock **16:19** [a]Is 22:22; Rev 1:18; 3:7 [b]Mt 18:18; Jn 20:23 [1]Gr fut. pft. pass. tense
**16:20** [a]Mt 8:4; Mk 8:30; Lk 9:21 [1]Or *strictly admonished*

that they should tell no one that He
was the [b,2]Christ.

### *Jesus Foretells His Death and Resurrection*

21 [a]From that time [1]Jesus began to
show His disciples that He must go
to Jerusalem, and [b]suffer many things
from the elders and chief priests and
scribes, and be killed, and be raised
up on the third day. 22 And Peter took
Him aside and began to rebuke Him,
saying, "[1]God forbid *it*, Lord! This
shall never [2]happen to You." 23 But He
turned and said to Peter, "Get behind
Me, [a]Satan! You are a stumbling block
to Me; for you are not setting your
mind on [1]God's interests, but man's."

### *Take Up Your Cross*

24 Then Jesus said to His disciples, "If
anyone wishes to come after Me, let
him deny himself, and [a]take up his
cross and follow Me. 25 For [a]whoever
wishes to save his [1]life will lose it; but
whoever loses his [1]life for My sake
will find it. 26 For what will it profit a
man if he gains the whole world and
forfeits his soul? Or what will a man
give in exchange for his soul? 27 For
the [a]Son of Man [b]is going to come
in the glory of His Father with His
angels, and [c]WILL THEN [1]REPAY EACH
ONE ACCORDING TO HIS [2]DEEDS.
28 "Truly I say to you, there are
some of those who are standing here
who will not taste death until they
see the [a]Son of Man [b]coming in His
kingdom."

### *The Transfiguration*

17 And [a]six days later Jesus
*brought with Him [b]Peter and
James and John his brother, and *led
them up on a high mountain by them-
selves. 2 And He was transfigured
before them; and His face shone like
the sun, and His garments became as
white as light. 3 And behold, Moses
and Elijah appeared to them, talking
with Him. 4 And Peter answered and
said to Jesus, "Lord, it is good for us
to be here; if You wish, [a]I will make
three [1]booths here, one for You, and
one for Moses, and one for Elijah."
5 While he was still speaking, behold,
a bright cloud overshadowed them,
and behold, [a]a voice out of the cloud
said, "[b]This is My beloved Son, with
whom I am well-pleased; listen to
Him!" 6 And when the disciples heard
*this*, they fell on their faces and were
terrified. 7 And Jesus came to *them*
and touched them and said, "Get up,
and [a]do not be afraid." 8 And lifting
up their eyes, they saw no one except
Jesus Himself alone.
9 [a]And as they were coming down
from the mountain, Jesus command-
ed them, saying, "[b]Tell the vision to
no one until [c]the Son of Man has
[d]risen from the dead." 10 And His

**16:20** [b]Mt 1:16; 16:16; Jn 11:27 [2]Messiah **16:21** [a]Mt 16:21-28: *Mk 8:31-9:1; Lk 9:22-27* [b]Mt 12:40; 17:9, 12, 22f; 20:18f; 27:63; Mk 9:12, 31; Lk 17:25; 18:32; 24:7; Jn 2:19 [1]Two early mss *Jesus Christ* **16:22** [1]Lit (God be) *merciful to You* [2]Lit *be* **16:23** [a]Mt 4:10 [1]Lit *the things of God* **16:24** [a]Mt 10:38; Lk 14:27 **16:25** [a]Mt 10:39 [1]Or *soul* **16:27** [a]Mt 8:20 [b]Mt 10:23; 24:3, 27, 37, 39; 26:64; Mk 8:38; 13:26; Lk 21:27; *Jn 21:22; Ac 1:11; 1Co 15:23; 1Th 1:10*; 4:16; 2Th 1:7, 10; 2:1, 8; Jas 5:7f; 2Pe 1:16; 3:4, 12; 1Jn 2:28; Rev 1:7 [c]Ps 62:12; Pr 24:12; Ro 2:6; 14:12; 1Co 3:13; 2Co 5:10; Eph 6:8; Col 3:25; Rev 2:23; 20:12; 22:12 [1]Or *recompense* [2]Lit *doing* **16:28** [a]Mt 8:20 [b]Mt 10:23; 24:3, 27, 37, 39; 26:64; Mk 8:38; 13:26; Lk 21:27; Jn 21:22; Ac 1:11; 1Co 15:23; 1Th 1:10; 4:16; 2Th 1:7, 10; 2:1, 8; Jas 5:7f; 2Pe 1:16; 3:4, 12; 1Jn 2:28; Rev 1:7 ◆ **17:1** [a]Mt 17:1-8: *Mk 9:2-8; Lk 9:28-36* [b]Mt 26:37; Mk 5:37; 13:3 **17:4** [a]Mk 9:5; Lk 9:33 [1]Or *tents, tabernacles*, cf. Lv 23:34-43; Dt 16:13-15; Zec 14:16-19 **17:5** [a]Mk 1:11; Lk 3:22; 2Pe 1:17f [b]Is 42:1; Mt 3:17; 12:18 **17:7** [a]Mt 14:27 **17:9** [a]Mt 17:9-13: *Mk 9:9-13* [b]Mt 8:4 [c]Mt 8:20; 17:12, 22 [d]Mt 16:21

disciples asked Him, saying, "Why
then do the scribes say that [a]Elijah
must come first?" **11** And He answered
and said, "Elijah is coming and will
restore all things; **12** but I say to you
that Elijah already came, and they
did not recognize him, but did [1]to
him whatever they wished. So also
[a]the Son of Man is going to suffer [2]at
their hands." **13** Then the disciples
understood that He had spoken to
them about John the Baptist.

### *Jesus Casts Out a Demon*

**14** [a]And when they came to the
crowd, a man came up to Jesus, falling
on his knees before Him and saying,
**15** "[1]Lord, have mercy on my son, for
he has [a,2]seizures and suffers terribly;
for he often falls into the fire and
often into the water. **16** And I brought
him to Your disciples, and they could
not cure him." **17** And Jesus answered
and said, "O you unbelieving and
perverse generation, how long shall
I be with you? How long shall I put
up with you? Bring him here to Me."
**18** And Jesus rebuked him, and the
demon came out of him, and the boy
was cured [1]at once.

**19** Then the disciples came to Jesus
privately and said, "Why could we
not cast it out?" **20** And He *said to
them, "Because of your little faith; for
truly I say to you, [a]if you have faith
[1]the size of [b]a mustard seed, you will
say to [c]this mountain, 'Move from
here to there,' and it will move; and
[d]nothing will be impossible to you.
**21** [1][[a]But this kind does not go out
except by prayer and fasting."]

**22** [a]And while they were gathering
together in Galilee, Jesus said to
them, "The Son of Man is going to
be [1]delivered into the hands of men;
**23** and [a]they will kill Him, and He will
be raised on the third day." And they
were deeply grieved.

### *The Temple Tax*

**24** Now when they came to Caper-
naum, those who collected [a]the
[1]two-drachma *tax* came to Peter
and said, "Does your teacher not
pay [a]the [1]two-drachma *tax*?" **25** He
*said, "Yes." And when he came into
the house, Jesus spoke to him first,
saying, "What do you think, Simon?
From whom do the kings of the
earth collect [a]tolls or [b]taxes, from
their sons or from strangers?" **26** And
when Peter said, "From strangers,"
Jesus said to him, "Then the sons
are [1]exempt. **27** However, so that we
do not [a,1]offend them, go to the sea
and throw in a hook, and take the
first fish that comes up; and when
you open its mouth, you will find a
[2]stater. Take that and give it to them
for Me and you."

### *Who Is Greatest in Heaven?*

**18** [a]At that [1]time the disciples
came to Jesus and said, "[b]Who
then is greatest in the kingdom of
heaven?" **2** And He called a child to

**17:10** [a]Mal 4:5; Mt 11:14; 16:14 **17:12** [a]Mt 8:20; 17:9, 22 [1]Or *in his case*; lit *in him* [2]Lit *by them* **17:14** [a]Mt 17:14-19: *Mk 9:14-28;* Mt 17:14-18: *Lk 9:37-42* **17:15** [a]Mt 4:24 [1]Or *Sir* [2]Lit *moonstruck*; Gr *seleniazo* **17:18** [1]Lit *from that hour* **17:20** [a]Mt 21:21f; Mk 11:23f; Lk 17:6 [b]Mt 13:31; Lk 17:6 [c]Mt 17:9; 1Co 13:2 [d]Mk 9:23; Jn 11:40 [1]Lit *as* **17:21** [a]Mk 9:29 [1]Early mss omit this v **17:22** [a]Mt 17:22, 23: *Mk 9:30-32; Lk 9:44, 45* [1]Or *betrayed* **17:23** [a]Mt 16:21; 17:9 **17:24** [a]Ex 30:13; 38:26 [1]A Greek silver coin, approx. a laborer's daily wage **17:25** [a]Ro 13:7 [b]Mt 22:17, 19 **17:26** [1]Or *free* **17:27** [a]Mt 5:29, 30; 18:6, 8, 9; Mk 9:42, 43, 45, 47; Lk 17:2; Jn 6:61; 1Co 8:13 [1]Lit *cause them to stumble* [2]Lit *standard coin*, approx. 4 days of a laborer's wages ◆ **18:1** [a]Mt 18:1-5: *Mk 9:33-37; Lk 9:46-48* [b]Lk 22:24 [1]Lit *hour*

Himself and set him [1]before them,
**3** and said, "Truly I say to you, unless
you [1]are converted and [a]become
like children, you will never enter
the kingdom of heaven. **4** Whoever
therefore will humble himself as
this child, he is the greatest in the
kingdom of heaven. **5** And whoever
receives one such child in My name
receives Me; **6** but [a]whoever [b]causes
one of these little ones who believe in
Me to stumble, it is better for him that
a [1]heavy millstone be hung around
his neck, and that he be drowned in
the depth of the sea.

### *Stumbling Blocks*

**7** "Woe to the world because of *its*
stumbling blocks! For [a]it is inevitable that stumbling blocks come;
nevertheless, woe to that man
through whom the stumbling block
comes!

**8** "[a]And if your hand or your foot
causes you to stumble, cut it off and
throw it from you; it is better for you
to enter life crippled or lame, than,
having two hands or two feet, to
be cast into the eternal fire. **9** [a]And
if your eye causes you to stumble,
tear it out and throw it from you. It
is better for you to enter life with one
eye, than, having two eyes, to be cast
into the [b,1]fiery hell.

**10** "See that you do not despise
one of these little ones, for I say to
you that [a]their angels in heaven
continually see the face of My Father
who is in heaven. **11** [1][[a]For the Son
of Man has come to save that which
was lost.]

### *The Parable of the Lost Sheep*

**12** "What do you think? [a]If any man
has one hundred sheep, and one of
them has gone astray, does he not
leave the ninety-nine on the mountains and go and search for the one
that is straying? **13** And if it turns out
that he finds it, truly I say to you, he
rejoices over it more than over the
ninety-nine which have not gone
astray. **14** In this way, it is not the will
[1]of your Father who is in heaven that
one of these little ones perish.

### *If Your Brother Sins*

**15** "[a]Now if your brother sins[1], go and
[2]show him his fault, between you and
him alone; if he listens to you, you
have won your brother. **16** But if he
does not listen *to you*, take one or
two more with you, so that [a]BY THE
MOUTH OF TWO OR THREE WITNESSES
EVERY [1]FACT MAY BE CONFIRMED. **17** And
if he refuses to listen to them, [a]tell it
to the church; and if he refuses to
listen even to the church, [b]let him
be to you as the Gentile and the
tax collector. **18** Truly I say to you,
[a]whatever you [1]bind on earth [2]shall
have been bound in heaven; and
whatever you [3]loose on earth [2]shall
have been loosed in heaven.

**19** "Again I say to you, that if two
of you agree on earth about anything
that they may ask, [a]it shall be done
for them [1]by My Father who is in

***18:2*** [1]*Lit in their midst* **18:3** [a]Mt 19:14; Mk 10:15; Lk 18:17; 1Co 14:20; 1Pe 2:2 [1]Lit *are turned* **18:6** [a]Mk 9:42; Lk 17:2; 1Co 8:12 [b]Mt 17:27 [1]Lit *millstone turned by a donkey* **18:7** [a]Lk 17:1; 1Co 11:19; 1Ti 4:1 **18:8** [a]Mt 5:30; Mk 9:43 **18:9** [a]Mt 5:29; Mk 9:47 [b]Mt 5:22 [1]Lit *Gehenna of fire* **18:10** [a]Lk 1:19; Ac 12:15; Rev 8:2 **18:11** [a]Lk 19:10 [1]Early mss omit this v **18:12** [a]Mt 18:12-14: *Lk 15:4-7* **18:14** [1]Lit *before* **18:15** [a]Lv 19:17; Lk 17:3; Ga 6:1; 2Th 3:15; Jas 5:19 [1]Later mss add *against you* [2]Or *reprove him,* **18:16** [a]Dt 19:15; Jn 8:17; 2Co 13:1; 1Ti 5:19; Heb 10:28 [1]Lit *word* **18:17** [a]1Co 6:1ff [b]2Th 3:6, 14f **18:18** [a]Mt 16:19; Jn 20:23 [1]Or *forbid* [2]Gr fut. pft. pass. [3]Or *permit* **18:19** [a]Mt 7:7 [1]Lit *from*

heaven. **20** For where two or three
have gathered together in My name,
[a]I am there in their midst."

### *Forgiveness*

**21** Then Peter came and said to Him,
"Lord, [a]how often shall my brother
sin against me and I forgive him?
Up to [b]seven times?" **22** Jesus *said
to him, "I do not say to you, up to
seven times, but up to [a]seventy times
seven.

**23** "For this reason [a]the kingdom
of heaven [1]may be compared to a king
who wished to [b]settle accounts with
his slaves. **24** When he had begun to
settle *them,* one who owed him ten
thousand [1]talents was brought to
him. **25** But since he [a,1]did not have *the
means* to repay, his lord commanded
him [b]to be sold, along with his wife
and children and all that he had, and
repayment to be made. **26** Therefore,
the slave fell *to the ground* and [a]was
prostrating himself before him,
saying, 'Have patience with me and
I will repay you everything.' **27** And
feeling compassion, the lord of that
slave released him and [a]forgave him
the [1]debt. **28** But that slave went out
and found one of his fellow slaves
who owed him one hundred [1]denar-
ii; and he seized him and *began to*
choke *him,* saying, 'Pay back what
you owe.' **29** So, his fellow slave fell
*to the ground* and was pleading with
him, saying, 'Have patience with me
and I will repay you.' **30** But he was
unwilling [1]and went and threw him
in prison until he should pay back
what was owed. **31** So, when his fel-
low slaves saw what had happened,
they were deeply grieved and came
and reported to their lord all that
had happened. **32** Then summoning
him, his lord *said to him, 'You
wicked slave, I forgave you all that
debt because you pleaded with me.
**33** [a]Should you not also have had
mercy on your fellow slave, in the
same way that I had mercy on you?'
**34** And his lord, moved with anger,
handed him over to the torturers
until he should repay all that was
owed him. **35** [a]My heavenly Father
will also do the same to you, if each
of you does not forgive his brother
from your hearts."

### *Teaching About Divorce*

**19** [a,1]Now it happened that when
Jesus had finished these words,
He departed from Galilee and [b]came
into the region of Judea beyond the
Jordan; **2** and [1]large crowds followed
Him, and [a]He healed them there.

**3** And *some* Pharisees came to
[1]Jesus, testing Him and saying, "[a]Is
it lawful *for a man* to [2]divorce his
wife for any reason at all?" **4** And He
answered and said, "Have you not
read [a]that He who created *them* from
the beginning MADE THEM MALE AND
FEMALE, **5** and said, '[a]FOR THIS REASON
A MAN SHALL LEAVE HIS FATHER AND
MOTHER AND BE JOINED TO HIS WIFE,
AND [b]THE TWO SHALL BECOME ONE
FLESH'? **6** So they are no longer two,

---

**18:20** [a]Mt 28:20 **18:21** [a]Mt 18:15 [b]Lk 17:4 **18:22** [a]Ge 4:24 **18:23** [a]Mt 13:24 [b]Mt 25:19 [1]Lit *was compared to* **18:24** [1]A talent was approx. worth more than 15 years of a laborer's wages **18:25** [a]Lk 7:42 [b]Ex 21:2; Lv 25:39; 2Ki 4:1; Ne 5:5 [1]Or *was unable to* **18:26** [a]Mt 8:2 **18:27** [a]Lk 7:42 [1]Or *loan* **18:28** [1]A Roman silver coin, approx. a laborer's daily wage **18:30** [1]Lit *but* **18:33** [a]Mt 6:12; Eph 4:32 **18:35** [a]Mt 6:14 ◆ **19:1** [a]Mt 7:28 [b]Mt 19:1-9: *Mk 10:1-12* [1]Lit *And* **19:2** [a]Mt 4:23 [1]Lit *many* **19:3** [a]Mt 5:31 [1]Lit *Him* [2]Or *send away* **19:4** [a]Ge 1:27; 5:2 **19:5** [a]Ge 2:24; Eph 5:31 [b]1Co 6:16

but one flesh. What therefore God
has joined together, let no man sep-
arate." **7** They *said to Him, "[a]Why
then did Moses command to GIVE
HER A CERTIFICATE OF DIVORCE AND
SEND *her* AWAY?" **8** He *said to them,
"Because of your hardness of heart
Moses permitted you to [1]divorce
your wives; but from the beginning
it has not been this way. **9** And I say
to you, [a]whoever [1]divorces his wife,
except for sexual immorality, and
marries another woman [2]commits
adultery[3]."

**10** The disciples *said to Him, "If
the relationship of the man with
his wife is like this, it is better not
to marry." **11** But He said to them,
"[a]Not all men *can* accept this state-
ment, but [b]*only* those to whom it has
been given. **12** For there are eunuchs
who were born that way from their
mother's womb; and there are eu-
nuchs who were made eunuchs by
men; and there are *also* eunuchs who
made themselves eunuchs for the
sake of the kingdom of heaven. He
who is able to accept *this*, let him
accept *it*."

### *Jesus Blesses Children*

**13** [a]Then *some* children were brought
to Him so that He might lay His
hands on them and pray; and the
disciples rebuked them. **14** But Jesus
said, "[a,1]Let the children alone, and
do not hinder them from coming
to Me; for [b]the kingdom of heaven
belongs to such as these." **15** And
after laying His hands on them, He
departed from there.

### *The Rich Young Ruler*

**16** [a]And behold, someone came to
Him and said, "Teacher, what good
thing shall I do that I may have
[b]eternal life?" **17** And He said to him,
"Why are you asking Me about what is
good? There is *only* One who is good;
but [a]if you wish to enter into life,
keep the commandments." **18** *Then*
he *said to Him, "Which ones?" And
Jesus said, "[a]YOU SHALL NOT MURDER;
YOU SHALL NOT COMMIT ADULTERY;
YOU SHALL NOT STEAL; YOU SHALL NOT
BEAR FALSE WITNESS; **19** [a]HONOR YOUR
FATHER AND MOTHER; and [b]YOU SHALL
LOVE YOUR NEIGHBOR AS YOURSELF."
**20** The young man *said to Him, "All
these things I have kept; what am I
still lacking?" **21** Jesus said to him,
"If you wish to be [1]complete, go *and*
[a]sell your possessions and give to the
poor, and you will have [b]treasure in
heaven; and come, follow Me." **22** But
when the young man heard this
statement, he went away grieving;
for he was one who owned much
property.

**23** And Jesus said to His disciples,
"Truly I say to you, [a]it is hard for a
rich man to enter the kingdom of
heaven. **24** And again I say to you, [a]it
is easier for a camel to go through the
eye of a needle, than for a rich man
to enter the kingdom of God." **25** And
when the disciples heard *this*, they
were very astonished and said, "Then

***19:7*** [a]*Dt 24:1-4;* Mt 5:31 **19:8** [1]Or *send away* **19:9** [a]Mt 5:32 [1]Or *sends away* [2]Some early mss *makes her commit adultery* [3]Some early mss add *and he who marries a divorced woman commits adultery* **19:11** [a]1Co 7:7ff [b]Mt 13:11 **19:13** [a]Mt 19:13-15: *Mk 10:13-16; Lk 18:15-17* **19:14** [a]Mt 18:3; Mk 10:15; Lk 18:17; 1Co 14:20; 1Pe 2:2 [b]Mt 5:3 [1]Or *Permit the children* **19:16** [a]Mt 19:16-29: *Mk 10:17-30; Lk 18:18-30;* Lk 10:25-28 [b]Mt 25:46 **19:17** [a]Lv 18:5; Ne 9:29; Eze 20:21 **19:18** [a]Ex 20:13-16; Dt 5:17-20 **19:19** [a]Ex 20:12; Dt 5:16 [b]Lv 19:18 **19:21** [a]Lk 12:33; 16:9; Ac 2:45; 4:34f [b]Mt 6:20 [1]Or *perfect* **19:23** [a]Mt 13:22; Mk 10:23f; Lk 18:24 **19:24** [a]Mk 10:25; Lk 18:25

who can be saved?" **26** And looking
at *them* Jesus said to them, "[a]With
people this is impossible, but with
God all things are possible."

### *Many Who Are First Will Be Last*

**27** Then Peter answered and said to
Him, "Behold, we have left every-
thing and followed You; what then
will there be for us?" **28** And Jesus
said to them, "Truly I say to you, that
you who have followed Me, in the
regeneration when [a]the Son of Man
will sit on [1]His glorious throne, [b]you
also shall sit upon twelve thrones,
judging the twelve tribes of Israel.
**29** And [a]everyone who has left
houses or brothers or sisters or father
or mother [1]or children or farms for
My name's sake, will receive [2]one
hundred times as much, and will
inherit eternal life. **30** [a]But many *who
are* first will be last; and *the* last, first.

### *Laborers in the Vineyard*

**20** "For [a]the kingdom of heaven
is like [1]a landowner who
went out early in the morning to
hire laborers for his [b]vineyard.
**2** Now when he had agreed with the
laborers for a [1]denarius for the day,
he sent them into his vineyard. **3** And
he went out about the [1]third hour
and saw others standing idle in the
marketplace; **4** and to those he said,
'You also go into the vineyard, and
whatever is right I will give you.'
And *so* they went. **5** Again he went
out about the [1]sixth and the ninth
hour, and did [2]the same thing. **6** And
about the [1]eleventh *hour* he went out
and found others standing *around*;
and he *said to them, 'Why have you
been standing here idle all day long?'
**7** They *said to him, 'Because no one
hired us.' He *said to them, 'You go
into the vineyard too.'
**8** "Now when [a]evening came, the
[1]owner of the vineyard *said to his
[b,2]foreman, 'Call the laborers and pay
them their wages, beginning with the
last *group* to the first.' **9** And when
those *hired* about the eleventh hour
came, each one received a [1]denarius.
**10** And when those *hired* first came,
they supposed that they would re-
ceive more; [1]but each of them also
received a denarius. **11** Now when
they received it, they were grumbling
at the landowner, **12** saying, 'These
last men have worked *only* one hour,
and you have made them equal to
us who have borne the burden of
the day and the [a]scorching heat.'
**13** But he answered and said to one
of them, '[a]Friend, I am doing you no
wrong; did you not agree with me for
a denarius? **14** Take what is yours and
go, but I wish to give to this last man
the same as to you. **15** Is it not lawful
for me to do what I wish with what
is my own? Or is your [a]eye [1]envious
because I am [2]generous?' **16** So [a]the
last shall be first, and the first last."

**19:26** [a]Ge 18:14; Job 42:2; Jer 32:17; Zec 8:6; Mk 10:27; Lk 1:37; 18:27 **19:28** [a]Mt 25:31 [b]Lk 22:30; Rev 3:21; 4:4; 11:16; 20:4 [1]Lit *the throne of His glory* **19:29** [a]Mt 6:33; Mk 10:29f; Lk 18:29f [1]One early ms adds *or wife* [2]Some mss *many times as much* **19:30** [a]Mt 20:16; Mk 10:31; Lk 13:30
◆ **20:1** [a]Mt 13:24 [b]Mt 21:28, 33 [1]Lit *a man, a landowner* **20:2** [1]A Roman silver coin, approx. a laborer's daily wage **20:3** [1]9 a.m. **20:5** [1]Noon and 3 p.m. [2]Lit *similarly* **20:6** [1]5 p.m. **20:8** [a]Lv 19:13; Dt 24:15 [b]Lk 8:3 [1]Or *lord* [2]Or *manager*, cf. Lk 8:3 **20:9** [1]A Roman silver coin, approx. a laborer's daily wage **20:10** [1]Lit *each one a denarius* **20:12** [a]Jon 4:8; Lk 12:55; Jas 1:11 **20:13** [a]Mt 22:12; 26:50 **20:15** [a]Dt 15:9; Mt 6:23; Mk 7:22 [1]Lit *evil* [2]Lit *good* **20:16** [a]Mt 19:30; Mk 10:31; Lk 13:30

### *Jesus Again Foretells His Death and Resurrection*

**17** [a]And as Jesus was about to go up
to Jerusalem, He took the twelve
*disciples* aside by themselves, and on
the way He said to them, **18** "Behold,
we are going up to Jerusalem; and
the Son of Man [a]will be betrayed to
the chief priests and scribes, and
they will condemn Him to death,
**19** and [a]will deliver Him over to the
Gentiles to mock and flog and crucify
*Him*, and on [b]the third day He will be
raised up."

### *A Request for Status*

**20** [a]Then the mother of [b]the sons of
Zebedee came to Him with her sons,
[c]bowing down and making a request
of Him. **21** And He said to her, "What
do you wish?" She *said to Him,
"Command that in Your kingdom
these two sons of mine [a]may sit one
on Your right and one on Your left."
**22** But Jesus answered and said, "You
do not know what you are asking. Are
you able [a]to drink the cup that I am
about to drink?" They *said to Him,
"We are able." **23** He *said to them,
"[a]My cup you shall drink; but to sit
on My right and on *My* left, this is
not Mine to give, [b]but it is for those
for whom it has been [c]prepared by
My Father."

**24** And hearing *this*, the ten
became indignant with the two
brothers. **25** [a]But Jesus called them
to Himself and said, "You know that
the rulers of the Gentiles lord it over
them, and *their* great men exercise
authority over them. **26** It is not
this way among you, [a]but whoever
wishes to become great among you
shall be your servant, **27** and whoever
wishes to be first among you shall be
your slave; **28** just as [a]the Son of Man
[b]did not come to be served, but to
serve, and to give His [1]life a ransom
for many."

### *Sight for the Blind*

**29** [a]And as they were leaving Jericho,
a large crowd followed Him. **30** And
behold, two blind men sitting by the
road, hearing that Jesus *was passing
by, cried out, saying, "Lord, [a]have
mercy on us, [b]Son of David!" **31** But
the crowd sternly told them to be
quiet, but they cried out all the more,
saying, "Lord, [a]Son of David, have
mercy on us!" **32** And Jesus stopped
and called them, and said, "What do
you want Me to do for you?" **33** They
*said to Him, "Lord, that our eyes be
opened." **34** And moved with com-
passion, Jesus touched their eyes;
and immediately they regained their
sight and followed Him.

### *The Triumphal Entry*

**21** [a]And when they had ap-
proached Jerusalem and came
to Bethphage, at [b]the Mount of Olives,
then Jesus sent two disciples, **2** saying
to them, "Go into the village opposite
you, and immediately you will find

---

**20:17** [a]Mt 20:17-19: *Mk 10:32-34; Lk 18:31-33* **20:18** [a]Mt 16:21 **20:19** [a]Mt 27:2; Ac 2:23; 3:13; *4:27; 21:11* [b]*Mt 16:21; 17:23;* Lk 18:32f **20:20** [a]Mt 20:20-28: *Mk 10:35-45* [b]Mt 4:21; 10:2 [c]Mt 8:2 **20:21** [a]Mt 19:28 **20:22** [a]Is 51:17, 22; Jer 49:12; Mt 26:39, 42; Lk 22:42; Jn 18:11 **20:23** [a]Ac 12:2; Rev 1:9 [b]Mt 13:11 [c]Mt 25:34 **20:25** [a]Mt 20:25-28: *Lk 22:25-27* **20:26** [a]Mt 23:11; Mk 9:35; 10:43; Lk 22:26 **20:28** [a]Mt 8:20 [b]Mt 26:28; Jn 13:13ff; 2Co 8:9; Php 2:7; 1Ti 2:6; Tit 2:14; Heb 9:28; Rev 1:5 [1]Or *soul* **20:29** [a]Mt 20:29-34: *Mk 10:46-52; Lk 18:35-43;* Mt 9:27-31 **20:30** [a]Mt 9:27 [b]Mt 20:31 **20:31** [a]Mt 9:27 ◆ **21:1** [a]Mt 21:1-9: *Mk 11:1-10; Lk 19:29-38* [b]Mt 24:3; 26:30; Mk 11:1; 13:3; 14:26; Lk 19:29, 37; 21:37; 22:39; Jn 8:1; Ac 1:12

a donkey tied *there* and a colt with
her; untie them and bring them to Me.
3 And if anyone says anything to you,
you shall say, 'The Lord has need of
them,' and immediately he will send
them." 4 [a]And this [1]took place in
order that what was spoken through
the prophet would be fulfilled, saying,

5 "[a]SAY TO THE DAUGHTER OF ZION,
'BEHOLD YOUR KING IS
COMING TO YOU,
LOWLY, AND MOUNTED
ON A DONKEY,
AND ON A COLT, THE FOAL
OF A PACK ANIMAL.'"

6 And the disciples went and did just
as Jesus had instructed them, 7 and
brought the donkey and the colt, and
laid their garments on them; and He
sat on [1]the garments. 8 And most of
the crowd [a]spread their garments
in the road, and others were cutting
branches from the trees and spreading
them in the road. 9 And the crowds
going ahead of Him, and those who
followed, were crying out, saying,

"Hosanna to the [a]Son of David;
[b]BLESSED IS HE WHO COMES
IN THE NAME OF THE [1]LORD;
Hosanna [c]in the highest!"

10 And when He had entered Jerusa-
lem, all the city was stirred, saying,
"Who is this?" 11 And the crowds
were saying, "This is [a]the prophet
Jesus, from [b]Nazareth in Galilee."

### *Cleansing the Temple*

12 [a]And Jesus entered the temple
and drove out all those who were
buying and selling in the temple, and
overturned the tables of the [b]money
changers and the seats of those who
were selling [c]doves. 13 And He *said
to them, "It is written, '[a]MY HOUSE
SHALL BE CALLED A HOUSE OF PRAYER';
but you are making it a [b]ROBBERS'
[1]DEN."

14 And the blind and the lame came
to Him in the temple, and [a]He healed
them. 15 But when the chief priests
and the scribes saw the marvelous
things which He had done, and the
children who were shouting in the
temple, saying, "Hosanna to the [a]Son
of David," they became indignant
16 and said to Him, "Do You hear what
these *children* are saying?" And Jesus
*said to them, "Yes; have you never
read, '[a]OUT OF THE MOUTH OF INFANTS
AND NURSING BABIES YOU HAVE PRE-
PARED PRAISE FOR YOURSELF'?" 17 And
He left them and went out of the city
to [a]Bethany, and spent the night there.

### *The Barren Fig Tree*

18 [a]Now in the morning, when He
was returning to the city, He became
hungry. 19 And seeing a lone [a]fig tree
by the road, He came to it and found
nothing on it except leaves only; and
He *said to it, "No longer shall there
ever be *any* fruit from you." And at
once the fig tree withered.

20 And seeing *this*, the disciples
marveled, saying, "How did the fig
tree wither *all* at once?" 21 And Jesus
answered and said to them, "Truly
I say to you, [a]if you have faith and

**21:4** [a]Mt 21:4-9: *Mk 11:7-10; Lk 19:35-38; Jn 12:12-15* [1]Lit *has happened* **21:5** [a]Is 62:11; Zec 9:9 **21:7** [1]Lit *them* **21:8** [a]2Ki 9:13 **21:9** [a]Mt 9:27 [b]Ps 118:26 [c]Lk 2:14 [1]In OT, Yahweh, cf. Ps 118:26 **21:11** [a]Mt 21:26; Mk 6:15; Lk 7:16, 39; 13:33; 24:19; Jn 1:21, 25; 4:19; 6:14; 7:40; 9:17; Ac 3:22f; 7:37 [b]Mt 2:23 **21:12** [a]Mt 21:12-16: *Mk 11:15-18; Lk 19:45-47;* Mt 21:12, 13: *Jn 2:13-16* [b]Ex 30:13 [c]Lv 1:14; 5:7; 12:8 **21:13** [a]Is 56:7 [b]Jer 7:11 [1]Lit *cave* **21:14** [a]Mt 4:23 **21:15** [a]Mt 9:27 **21:16** [a]Ps 8:2; Mt 11:25 **21:17** [a]Mt 26:6; Mk 11:1, 11, 12; 14:3; Lk 19:29; 24:50; Jn 11:1, 18; 12:1 **21:18** [a]Mt 21:18-22: *Mk 11:12-14, 20-24* **21:19** [a]Lk 13:6-9 **21:21** [a]Mt 17:20; Mk 11:23; Lk 17:6; Jas 1:6

do not doubt, you will not only do
what was done to the fig tree, but
even if you say to this mountain, 'Be
taken up and cast into the sea,' it will
happen. 22 And [a]all things you ask in
prayer, believing, you will receive."

### *The Authority of Jesus Challenged*

23 [a]And when He entered the temple,
the chief priests and the elders of the
people came to Him [b]while He was
teaching, and said, "By what author-
ity are You doing these things, and
who gave You this authority?" 24 And
Jesus answered and said to them, "I
will also ask you one [1]thing, which
if you tell Me, I will also tell you by
what authority I do these things.
25 The baptism of John was from
what *source*, from heaven or from
men?" And they *began* reasoning
among themselves, saying, "If we
say, 'From heaven,' He will say to us,
'Then why did you not believe him?'
26 But if we say, 'From men,' we fear
the crowd; for they all regard John as
[a]a prophet." 27 And they answered
Jesus and said, "We do not know."
He also said to them, "Neither will I
tell you by what authority I do these
things.

### *Parable of Two Sons*

28 "But what do you think? A man
had two sons, and he came to the
first and said, 'Son, go work today in
the [a]vineyard.' 29 And he answered
and said, 'I will not'; but afterward he
regretted it and went. 30 And the man
came to the second and said the same
*thing; and he answered* and said, 'I
*will*, sir'; but he did not go. 31 Which
of the two did the will of his father?"
They *said, "The first." Jesus *said to
them, "Truly I say to you that [a]the
tax collectors and prostitutes [1]will
get into the kingdom of God before
you. 32 For John came to you in the
way of righteousness and you did not
believe him; but [a]the tax collectors
and prostitutes did believe him; and
you, seeing *this*, did not even regret
afterward so as to believe him.

### *Parable of the Vine-Growers*

33 "Listen to another parable. [a]There
was a [1]landowner who [b]PLANTED A
[c]VINEYARD AND PUT A [2]WALL AROUND
IT AND DUG A WINE PRESS IN IT, AND
BUILT A TOWER, and rented it out to
[3]vine-growers and [d]went on a jour-
ney. 34 Now when the [1]harvest time
approached, he [a]sent his slaves to
the vine-growers to receive his fruit.
35 And the vine-growers took his
slaves and beat one, and killed an-
other, and stoned a third. 36 Again he
[a]sent another group of slaves larger
than the first; and they did the same
thing to them. 37 But afterward he
sent his son to them, saying, 'They
will respect my son.' 38 But when the
vine-growers saw the son, they said
among themselves, 'This is the heir;
come, let us kill him and seize his in-
heritance.' 39 And they took him, and
threw him out of the vineyard and
killed him. 40 Therefore when the
[1]owner of the vineyard comes, what
will he do to those vine-growers?"
41 They **said to* Him, "He will bring
those wretches to a wretched end,

**21:22** [a]Mt 7:7 **21:23** [a]Mt 21:23-27: *Mk 11:27-33; Lk 20:1-8* [b]Mt 26:55 **21:24** [1]Lit *word*
**21:26** [a]Mt 11:9; Mk 6:20 **21:28** [a]Mt 20:1; 21:33 **21:31** [a]Lk 7:29, 37-50 [1]Lit *are getting into*
**21:32** [a]Lk 3:12; 7:29f **21:33** [a]Mt 21:33-46: *Mk 12:1-12; Lk 20:9-19* [b]Is 5:1, 2 [c]Mt 20:1; 21:28 [d]Mt 25:14
[1]Lit *man, head of a household* [2]Or *fence* [3]Or *tenant farmers*, so in vv 34, 35, 38, 40 **21:34** [a]Mt 22:3
[1]Lit *fruit season* **21:36** [a]Mt 22:4 **21:40** [1]Lit *lord*

and [a]will rent out the vineyard to
other vine-growers who will pay him
the proceeds at the *proper* seasons."
**42** Jesus *said to them, "Did you
never read in the Scriptures,

'[a]THE STONE WHICH THE
BUILDERS REJECTED,
THIS HAS BECOME THE
CHIEF CORNER *stone*;
THIS CAME ABOUT FROM
THE [1]LORD,
AND IT IS MARVELOUS
IN OUR EYES'?

**43** "Therefore I say to you, the king-
dom of God will be taken away from
you and given to a nation, producing
the fruit of it. **44** And [a]he who falls on
this stone will be broken to pieces;
but on whomever it falls, it will
scatter him like dust."
**45** And when the chief priests and
the Pharisees heard His parables,
they understood that He *was speak-
ing about them. **46** And although
they were seeking to seize Him, they
[a]feared the crowds, because they
were regarding Him to be a [b]prophet.

### *Parable of the Wedding Feast*

**22** And Jesus answered and spoke
to them again in parables, say-
ing, **2** "[a]The kingdom of heaven [1]may
be compared to [2]a king who [3]gave a
[b]wedding feast for his son. **3** And he
[a]*sent out* his slaves to call those who
had been called to the wedding feast,
and they were unwilling to come.
**4** Again he [a]sent out other slaves say-
ing, 'Tell those who have been called,
"Behold, I have prepared my dinner;
my oxen and my fattened livestock
are *all* butchered and everything is
ready; come to the wedding feast."'
**5** But they paid no attention and went
their way, one to his own [1]farm, an-
other to his business, **6** and the rest
seized his slaves and mistreated them
and killed them. **7** But the king was
enraged, and he sent his armies and
destroyed those murderers and set
their city on fire. **8** Then he *said to
his slaves, 'The wedding is ready,
but those who were called were not
worthy. **9** Go therefore to [a]the main
highways, and as many as you find
*there*, call to the wedding feast.'
**10** And those slaves went out into the
streets and gathered together all they
found, both evil and good; and the
wedding hall was filled with [1]dinner
guests.
**11** "But when the king came in to
look over the dinner guests, he saw
[a]a man there who was not dressed in
wedding clothes, **12** and he *said to
him, '[a]Friend, how did you come in
here without wedding clothes?' And
the man was speechless. **13** Then the
king said to the servants, 'Bind him
hand and foot, and throw him into
[a]the outer darkness; in that place
there will be weeping and gnashing
of teeth.' **14** For many are [a,1]called, but
few *are* [a]chosen."

### *Taxes to Caesar*

**15** [a]Then the Pharisees went and took
counsel together about how they
might trap Him [1]in what He said.
**16** And they *sent their disciples to

---

**21:41** [a]Mt 8:11f; Ac 13:46; 18:6; 28:28 **21:42** [a]Ps 118:22f; Ac 4:11; Ro 9:33; 1Pe 2:7 [1]In OT, Yahweh, cf. Ps 118:23 **21:44** [a]Is 8:14, 15 **21:46** [a]Mt 21:26 [b]Mt 21:11 ◆ **22:2** [a]Mt 13:24; 22:2-14; Lk 14:16-24 [b]Lk 12:36; Jn 2:2 [1]Lit *was compared to* [2]Lit *a man, a king* [3]Lit *made* **22:3** [a]Mt 21:34 **22:4** [a]Mt 21:36 **22:5** [1]Or *field* **22:9** [a]Eze 21:21; Ob 14 **22:10** [1]Lit *those reclining* at the table **22:11** [a]2Ki 10:22; Zec 3:3, 4 **22:12** [a]Mt 20:13; 26:50 **22:13** [a]Mt 8:12; 25:30; Lk 13:28 **22:14** [a]Mt 24:22; 2Pe 1:10; Rev 17:14 [1]Or *invited* **22:15** [a]Mt 22:15-22: *Mk 12:13-17; Lk 20:20-26* [1]Lit *in word*

Him, along with the [a]Herodians,
saying, "Teacher, we know that You
are truthful and teach the way of God
in truth, and [1]defer to no one; for You
are not partial to any. **17** Therefore,
tell us, what do You think? Is it
[1]lawful to give a [a]tax to [b]Caesar,
or not?" **18** But Jesus, knowing their
wickedness, said, "Why are you
testing Me, you hypocrites? **19** Show
Me the [a]coin *used* for the tax." And
they brought Him a [1]denarius. **20** And
He *said to them, "Whose likeness
and inscription is this?" **21** They *said
to Him, "Caesar's." Then He *said to
them, "[a]Therefore, render to Caesar
the things that are Caesar's; and to
God the things that are God's." **22** And
hearing *this*, they marveled, and
[a]leaving Him, they went away.

### *The Sadducees and the Resurrection*

**23** [a]On that day *some* [b]Sadducees
(who say [c]there is no resurrection)
came to Jesus and asked Him a ques-
tion, **24** saying, "Teacher, Moses said,
'[a]IF A MAN DIES HAVING NO CHILDREN,
HIS BROTHER AS NEXT OF KIN SHALL
MARRY HIS WIFE AND RAISE UP A SEED
FOR HIS BROTHER.' **25** Now there were
seven brothers with us; and the first
married and died, and having no
[1]seed, he left his wife to his brother;
**26** so also the second, and the third,
down to the seventh. **27** And last of
all, the woman died. **28** In the resur-
rection, therefore, whose wife of the
seven will she be? For they all had
*married* her."

**29** But Jesus answered and said
to them, "You are mistaken, [a]not
[1]understanding the Scriptures nor
the power of God. **30** For in the res-
urrection they neither [a]marry nor
are given in marriage, but are like
angels in heaven. **31** But regarding
the resurrection of the dead, have
you not read what was spoken to you
by God, saying, **32** '[a]I AM THE GOD OF
ABRAHAM, AND THE GOD OF ISAAC, AND
THE GOD OF JACOB'? He is not the God
of the dead but of the living." **33** And
when the crowds heard *this*, [a]they
were astonished at His teaching.

### *The Foremost Commandment*

**34** [a]But when the Pharisees heard
that Jesus had silenced [b]the Sad-
ducees, they gathered themselves
together. **35** And one of them, [a]a
scholar of the Law, asked *Him* a
question, testing Him, **36** "Teacher,
which is the great commandment
in the Law?" **37** And He said to him,
"'[a]YOU SHALL LOVE THE [1]LORD YOUR
GOD WITH ALL YOUR HEART, AND
WITH ALL YOUR SOUL, AND WITH ALL
YOUR MIND.' **38** This is the great and
[1]foremost commandment. **39** And the
second is like it, '[a]YOU SHALL LOVE
YOUR NEIGHBOR AS YOURSELF.' **40** [a]On
these two commandments hang the
whole Law and the Prophets."

**41** [a]Now while the Pharisees were
gathered together, Jesus asked them
a question, **42** saying, "What do you
think about [1]the Christ, whose son is
He?" They *said to Him, "[a]*The son* of

---

**22:16** [a]Mk 3:6; 8:15; 12:13 [1]*Lit it is not a concern to You about anyone;* **22:17** [a]Mt 17:25 [b]Lk 2:1; 3:1 [1]Or *permissible* **22:19** [a]Mt 17:25 [1]A Roman silver coin, approx. a laborer's daily wage **22:21** [a]Mk 12:17; Lk 20:25; Ro 13:7 **22:22** [a]Mk 12:12 **22:23** [a]Mt 22:23-33: *Mk 12:18-27; Lk 20:27-40* [b]Mt 3:7 [c]Ac 23:8 **22:24** [a]Dt 25:5 **22:25** [1]Or *offspring* **22:29** [a]Jn 20:9 [1]Or *knowing* **22:30** [a]Mt 24:38; Lk 17:27 **22:32** [a]Ex 3:6 **22:33** [a]Mt 7:28 **22:34** [a]Mt 22:34-40: *Mk 12:28-31;* Lk 10:25-37 [b]Mt 3:7 **22:35** [a]Lk 7:30; 10:25; 11:45, 46, 52; 14:3; Tit 3:13 **22:37** [a]Dt 6:5 [1]In OT, Yahweh, cf. Dt 6:5 **22:38** [1]Or *first* **22:39** [a]Lv 19:18; Mt 19:19; Ga 5:14 **22:40** [a]Mt 7:12 **22:41** [a]Mt 22:41-46: *Mk 12:35-37; Lk 20:41-44* **22:42** [a]Mt 9:27 [1]Messiah

David." **43** He *said to them, "Then
how does David [a,1]in the Spirit call
Him 'Lord,' saying,

**44** '[a]THE [1]LORD SAID TO MY LORD,
"SIT AT MY RIGHT HAND,
UNTIL I PUT YOUR ENEMIES
BENEATH YOUR FEET"'?

**45** "Therefore, if David calls Him
'Lord,' how is He his son?" **46** [a]And
no one was able to answer Him a
word, nor did anyone dare from that
day on to ask Him [1]another question.

### *The Scribes and Pharisees Denounced*

**23** [a]Then Jesus spoke to the
crowds and to His disciples,
**2** saying: "[a]The scribes and the Phar-
isees have seated themselves in the
chair of Moses; **3** therefore all that
they tell you, do and keep, but do
not do according to their deeds; for
they say *things* and do not do *them.*
**4** [a]And they tie up heavy burdens
and lay them on men's shoulders,
but they themselves are unwilling to
move them with *so much as* a finger.
**5** But they do all their deeds [a]to be
noticed by men; for they [b]broaden
their [1]phylacteries and lengthen [c]the
tassels *of their garments.* **6** And they
[a]love the place of honor at banquets
and the best seats in the synagogues,
**7** and respectful greetings in the mar-
*ketplaces,* and being called [a]Rabbi by
men. **8** But [a]do not be called [b]Rabbi;
for One is your Teacher, and you are
all brothers. **9** And do not call *anyone*
on earth your father; for [a]One is your
Father, He who is in heaven. **10** Do
not be called instructors; for One is
your Instructor, *that is,* Christ. **11** [a]But
the greatest among you shall be your
servant. **12** [a]And whoever exalts him-
self shall be humbled; and whoever
humbles himself shall be exalted.

### *Woes to the Scribes and Pharisees*

**13** "[a]But woe to you, scribes and
Pharisees, hypocrites, [b]because you
shut off the kingdom of heaven [1]from
[2]people; for you do not enter in your-
selves, nor do you allow those who
are entering to go in. **14** [1][Woe to you,
scribes and Pharisees, hypocrites, be-
cause [a]you devour widows' houses,
and for a pretense you make long
prayers; therefore you will receive
greater condemnation.]

**15** "Woe to you, scribes and Phar-
isees, hypocrites, because you travel
around on sea and land to make one
[a,1]proselyte; and when he becomes
one, you make him twice as much a
son of [b,2]hell as yourselves.

**16** "Woe to you, [a]blind guides,
who say, '[b]Whoever swears by the
[1]sanctuary, *that* is nothing; but
whoever swears by the gold of the
[1]sanctuary is obligated.' **17** You fools
and blind men! For [a]which is [1]more
important, the gold or the sanctuary

**22:43** [a]2Sa 23:2; Rev 1:10; 4:2 [1]Or *by inspiration* **22:44** [a]Ps 110:1; Mt 26:64; Mk 16:19; Ac 2:34f; 1Co 15:25; Heb 1:13; 10:13 [1]In OT, Yahweh, cf. Ps 110:1 **22:46** [a]Mk 12:34; Lk 14:6; 20:40 [1]Lit *any longer*
◆ **23:1** [a]Mt 23:1-7: *Mk 12:38, 39; Lk 20:45, 46* **23:2** [a]Dt 33:3f; Ezr 7:6, 25; Ne 8:4 **23:4** [a]Lk 11:46; Ac 15:10 **23:5** [a]Mt 6:1, 5, 16 [b]Ex 13:9; Dt 6:8; 11:18 [c]Mt 9:20 [1]Small cases containing Scripture texts worn on the left arm and forehead for religious purposes **23:6** [a]Lk 11:43; 14:7; 20:46 **23:7** [a]Mt 23:8; 26:25, 49; Mk 9:5; 10:51; 11:21; Jn 1:38, 49; 3:2, 26; 4:31; 6:25; 9:2; 11:8; 20:16 **23:8** [a]Jas 3:1 [b]Mt 23:7; 26:25, 49; Mk 9:5; 10:51; 11:21; 14:45; Jn 1:38, 49; 3:2, 26; 4:31; 6:25; 9:2; 11:8; 20:16 **23:9** [a]Mt 6:9; 7:11 **23:11** [a]Mt 20:26 **23:12** [a]Lk 14:11; 18:14 **23:13** [a]Mt 23:15, 16, 23, 25, 27, 29 [b]Lk 11:52 [1]Lit *in front of* [2]Gr *anthropoi* **23:14** [a]Mk 12:40; Lk 20:47 [1]Early mss omit this v **23:15** [a]Ac 2:10; 6:5; 13:43 [b]Mt 5:22 [1]Or *convert* [2]Gr *Gehenna* **23:16** [a]Mt 15:14; 23:24 [b]Mt 5:33-35 [1]The inner part of the temple **23:17** [a]Ex 30:29 [1]Lit *greater*

that sanctified the gold? 18 And,
'Whoever swears by the altar, *that*
is nothing, but whoever swears by
the [1]offering on it, he is obligated.'
19 You blind men, [a]which is [1]more
important, the [2]offering, or the
altar that sanctifies the [2]offering?
20 Therefore, [1]whoever swears by the
altar, swears *both* by [2]the altar and
by everything on it. 21 And [1]whoever
swears by the sanctuary, swears *both*
by the [2]sanctuary and by Him who
[a]dwells within it. 22 And [1]whoever
swears by heaven, [a]swears *both* by
the throne of God and by Him who
sits upon it.

23 "[a]Woe to you, scribes and
Pharisees, hypocrites! For you tithe
mint and dill and [1]cumin, and have
neglected the weightier provisions of
the Law: justice and mercy and faith-
fulness; but these are the things you
should have done without neglecting
the others. 24 You [a]blind guides, who
strain out a gnat but swallow a camel!

25 "Woe to you, scribes and Phar-
isees, hypocrites! For [a]you clean the
outside of the cup and of the dish,
but inside they are full [1]of robbery
and self-indulgence. 26 You blind
Pharisee, first [a]clean the inside of
the cup and of the dish, so that the
outside of it may become clean also.

27 "[a]Woe to you, scribes and Phar-
isees, hypocrites! For you are like
whitewashed tombs which on the
outside appear beautiful, but inside
they are full of dead men's bones
and all uncleanness. 28 In this way,
you also outwardly appear righteous
to men, but inwardly you are full of
hypocrisy and lawlessness.

29 "[a]Woe to you, scribes and Phar-
isees, hypocrites! For you build the
tombs of the prophets and adorn the
monuments of the righteous, 30 and
say, 'If we had been *living* in the days
of our fathers, we would not have
been partners with them in *shedding*
the blood of the prophets.' 31 So you
bear witness against yourselves,
that you [a]are [1]sons of those who
murdered the prophets. 32 Fill up,
then, the measure *of the guilt* of your
fathers. 33 You serpents, [a]you brood
of vipers, how [1]will you escape the
[2]sentence of [b,3]hell?

34 "[a]On account of this, behold, [b]I
am sending you prophets and wise
men and scribes; some of them you
will kill and crucify, and some of
them you will [c]flog in your syna-
gogues, and [d]persecute from city to
city, 35 so that upon you may fall *the*
*guilt of* all the righteous blood shed
on earth, from the blood of righteous
[a]Abel to the blood of Zechariah,
the [b]son of Berechiah, whom [c]you
murdered between the sanctuary
and the altar. 36 Truly I say to you,
all these things will come upon [a]this
generation.

### *Lament over Jerusalem*

37 "[a]Jerusalem, Jerusalem, who [b]kills
the prophets and stones those who
are sent to her! How often I wanted
to gather your children together, [c]the

**23:18** [1]Or *gift* **23:19** [a]Ex 29:37 [1]Lit *greater* [2]Or *gift* **23:20** [1]Lit *he who* [2]Lit *it* **23:21** [a]1Ki 8:13; Ps 26:8; 132:14 [1]Lit *he who* [2]Lit *it* **23:22** [a]Is 66:1; Mt 5:34 [1]Lit *he who* **23:23** [a]Mt 23:13; Lk 11:42 [1]Similar to caraway seeds **23:24** [a]Mt 23:16 **23:25** [a]Mk 7:4; Lk 11:39f [1]Or *as a result of* **23:26** [a]Mk 7:4; Lk 11:39f **23:27** [a]Lk 11:44; Ac 23:3 **23:29** [a]Lk 11:47f **23:31** [a]Mt 23:34, 37; Ac 7:51f [1]Or *descendants* **23:33** [a]Mt 3:7; Lk 3:7 [b]Mt 5:22 [1]Lit *would* [2]Or *judgment* [3]Gr *Gehenna* **23:34** [a]Mt 23:34-36; Lk 11:49-51 [b]2Chr 36:15, 16 [c]Mt 10:17 [d]Mt 10:23 **23:35** [a]Ge 4:8ff; Heb 11:4 [b]Zec 1:1 [c]2Chr 24:21 **23:36** [a]Mt 10:23; 24:34 **23:37** [a]Mt 23:37-39: *Lk 13:34, 35* [b]Mt 5:12 [c]Ru 2:12

way a hen gathers her chicks under
her wings, and you did not want *it.*
**38** Behold, [a]your house is being left to
you desolate! **39** For I say to you, from
now on you will not see Me until you
say, '[a]BLESSED IS HE WHO COMES IN
THE NAME OF THE [1]LORD!'"

### *Signs of Christ's Return*

**24** [a]And coming [b]out from the
temple, Jesus was going along,
and His disciples came up to point out
the temple buildings to Him. **2** And
He answered and said to them, "Do
you not see all these things? Truly I
say to you, [a]not one stone here will
be left upon another, which will not
be torn down."
**3** Now as He was sitting on [a]the
Mount of Olives, the disciples came
to Him privately, saying, "Tell us,
when will these things happen, and
what *will be* the sign of [b]Your coming
and of the [1]end of the age?"
**4** And Jesus answered and said
to them, "[a]See to it that no one de-
ceives you. **5** For [a]many will come in
My name, saying, 'I am the [1]Christ,'
and will deceive many. **6** And you are
going to hear of [a]wars and rumors of
wars. See that you are not alarmed,
for *those things* must take place, but
*that* is not yet the end. **7** For [a]nation
will rise against nation, and kingdom
against kingdom, and in various
places there will be [b]famines and
earthquakes. **8** [a]But all these things
are *merely* the beginning of birth
pains.
**9** "[a]Then they will deliver you to
tribulation, and will kill you, and
[b]you will be hated by all nations
because of My name. **10** And at that
time many will [a,1]fall away and will
[2]betray one another and hate one
another. **11** Many [a]false prophets will
arise and will deceive many. **12** And
because lawlessness is multiplied,
[1]most people's love will grow cold.
**13** [a]But the one who endures to the
end, he will be saved. **14** And this
[a]gospel of the kingdom [b]shall be
proclaimed in the whole [c,1]world as
a witness to all the nations, and then
the end will come.

### *Abomination of Desolation and the Tribulation*

**15** "Therefore when you see the
[a]ABOMINATION OF DESOLATION which
was spoken of through Daniel the
prophet, standing in [b]the holy place
([c]let the reader understand), **16** then
those who are in Judea must flee to
the mountains. **17** [1]Whoever is on
[a]the housetop must not go down
to get the things out that are in his
house. **18** And [1]whoever is in the field
must not turn back to get his garment.
**19** But [a]woe to those who are preg-
nant and to those who are nursing
babies in those days! **20** But pray that
your flight will not be in the winter,
or on a Sabbath. **21** For then there will

**23:38** [a]1Ki 9:7f; Jer 22:5 **23:39** [a]Ps 118:26; Mt 21:9 [1]In OT, Yahweh, cf. Ps 118:26 ◆ **24:1** [a]Mt 24:1-51: *Mk 13; Lk 21:5-36* [b]Mt 21:23 **24:2** [a]Lk 19:44 **24:3** [a]Mt 21:1 [b]Mt 16:27f; 24:27, 37, 39 [1]Or *consummation* **24:4** [a]Jer 29:8 **24:5** [a]Mt 24:11, 24; Ac 5:36f; 1Jn 2:18; 4:3 [1]Messiah **24:6** [a]Rev 6:4 **24:7** [a]2Chr 15:6; Is 19:2; Rev 6:8, 12 [b]Ac 11:28; Rev 6:5, 6 **24:8** [a]Mt 24:8-20: *Lk 21:12-24* **24:9** [a]Mt 10:17; Jn 16:2 [b]Mt 10:22; Jn 15:18ff **24:10** [a]Mt 11:6; 13:21 [1]Lit *be caused to stumble* [2]Or *hand over* **24:11** [a]Mt 7:15; 24:24 **24:12** [1]Lit *the love of many* **24:13** [a]Mt 10:22 **24:14** [a]Mt 4:23 [b]Ro 10:18; Col 1:6, 23 [c]Lk 2:1; 4:5; Ac 11:28; 17:6, 31; 19:27; Ro 10:18; Heb 1:6; 2:5; Rev 3:10; 16:14 [1]Lit *inhabited earth* **24:15** [a]Da 9:27; 11:31; 12:11 [b]Mk 13:14; Lk 21:20; Jn 11:48; Ac 6:13f; 21:28 [c]Mk 13:14; Rev 1:3 **24:17** [a]1Sa 9:25; 2Sa 11:2; Mt 10:27; Lk 5:19; 12:3; 17:31; Ac 10:9 [1]Lit *He who* **24:18** [1]Lit *He who* **24:19** [a]Lk 23:29

be a [a]great tribulation, such as has
not occurred since the beginning of
the world until now, nor ever will.
**22** And unless those days had been
cut short, no [1]life would have been
saved; but for [a]the sake of the [2]elect
those days will be cut short. **23** [a]Then
if anyone says to you, 'Behold, here
is the [1]Christ,' or '[2]There *He is,*' do
not believe *him.* **24** For false christs
and [a]false prophets will arise and will
[1]show great [b,2]signs and wonders, so
as to deceive, if possible, even [c]the
[3]elect. **25** Behold, I have told you in
advance. **26** Therefore, if they say to
you, 'Behold, He is in the wilderness,'
do not go out, *or,* 'Behold, He is in the
inner rooms,' do not believe *them.*
**27** [a]For just as the lightning comes
from the east and appears even to the
west, so will the [b]coming of the [c]Son
of Man be. **28** [a]Wherever the corpse
is, there the [1]vultures will gather.

### *The Coming of the Son of Man*

**29** "But immediately after the [a]tribu-
lation of those days [b]THE SUN WILL BE
DARKENED, AND THE MOON WILL NOT
GIVE ITS LIGHT, AND [c]THE STARS WILL
FALL from [1]the sky, and the POWERS
OF [1]THE HEAVENS will be shaken.
**30** And then [a]the sign of the Son of
Man will appear in the sky, and then
all the tribes of the earth will mourn,
and they will see [b]the SON OF MAN
COMING ON THE CLOUDS OF THE SKY
with power and great glory. **31** And
[a]He will send forth His angels with
[b]A GREAT TRUMPET and THEY WILL
GATHER TOGETHER His [c,1]elect from
[d]the four winds, from one end of the
sky to the [2]other.

### *The Parable of the Fig Tree*

**32** "Now learn the parable from the
fig tree: when its branch has already
become tender and puts forth its
leaves, you know that summer is
near; **33** so, you too, when you see
all these things, [1]recognize that [2]He
is near, *right* [a]at the [3]door. **34** Truly
I say to you, [a]this [1]generation will
not pass away until all these things
take place. **35** [a]Heaven and earth will
pass away, but My words will not pass
away.

**36** "But [a]of that day and hour no
one knows, not even the angels of
heaven, nor the Son, but the Father
alone. **37** For [a]just as the days of Noah
were, so the [b]coming of the Son of
Man will be. **38** For as in those days
before the flood they were eating
and drinking, [a]marrying and giv-
ing in marriage, until the day that
[b]Noah entered the ark, **39** and they
did not [1]understand until the flood
came and took them all away; so will
the [a]coming of the Son of Man be.
**40** Then there will be two in the field;
one [1]will be taken, and one [1]will be
left. **41** [a]Two women *will be* grinding

**24:21** [a]Da 12:1; Joel 2:2; Mt 24:29 **24:22** [a]Mt 22:14; 24:24, 31; Lk 18:7 [1]Lit *flesh* [2]Or *chosen ones* **24:23** [a]Lk 17:23f [1]Messiah [2]Lit *Here* **24:24** [a]Mt 7:15; 24:11 [b]Jn 4:48; 2Th 2:9 [c]Mt 22:14; 24:22, 31; Lk 18:7 [1]Lit *give* [2]Or *attesting miracles* [3]Or *chosen ones* **24:27** [a]Lk 17:24 [b]Mt 24:3, 37, 39 [c]Mt 8:20 **24:28** [a]Job 39:30; Eze 39:17; Hab 1:8; Lk 17:37 [1]Or *eagles* **24:29** [a]Mt 24:21 [b]Is 13:10; 24:23; Eze 32:7; Joel 2:10, 31; 3:15f; Am 5:20; 8:9; Zep 1:15; Mt 24:29-35; Ac 2:20; Rev 6:12-17; 8:12 [c]Is 34:4; Rev 6:13 [1]Or *heaven* **24:30** [a]Mt 24:3; Rev 1:7 [b]Da 7:13; Mt 16:27; 24:3, 37, 39 **24:31** [a]Mt 13:41 [b]Ex 19:16; Dt 30:4; Is 27:13; Zec 9:14; 1Co 15:52; 1Th 4:16; Heb 12:19; Rev 8:2; 11:15 [c]Mt 24:22 [d]Da 7:2; Zec 2:6; Rev 7:1 [1]Or *chosen ones* [2]Lit *their end* **24:33** [a]Jas 5:9; Rev 3:20 [1]Or *know* [2]Or *it* [3]Lit *doors* **24:34** [a]Mt 10:23; 16:28; 23:36 [1]Or *race* **24:35** [a]Mt 5:18; Mk 13:31; Lk 21:33 **24:36** [a]Mk 13:32; Ac 1:7 **24:37** [a]Ge 6:5; 7:6-23; Lk 17:26f [b]Mt 16:27; 24:3, 30, 39 **24:38** [a]Mt 22:30 [b]Ge 7:7 **24:39** [a]Mt 16:27; 24:3, 30, 37 [1]Lit *know* **24:40** [1]Lit *is* **24:41** [a]Lk 17:35

*grain* at the [b,1]mill; one [2]will be taken
and one [2]will be left.

### *Be Ready for His Coming*

**42** "Therefore [a]stay awake, for you
do not know which day your Lord is
coming. **43** But [1]be sure of this, that
[a]if the head of the house had known
[b]at what time of the night the thief
was coming, he would have stayed
awake and would not have allowed
his house to be [2]broken into. **44** For
this reason [a]you also must be ready;
for [b]the Son of Man is coming at an
hour when you do not think *He will.*
**45** "[a]Who then is the [b]faithful and
[c]prudent slave whom his [1]master
[d]put in charge of his household to
give them their food at the proper
time? **46** Blessed is that slave whom
his [1]master finds so doing when he
comes. **47** Truly I say to you that [a]he
will put him in charge of all his posses-
sions. **48** But if that evil slave says in his
heart, 'My [1]master [2]is not coming for
a long time,' **49** and begins to beat his
fellow slaves and eat and drink with
drunkards; **50** the [1]master of that slave
will come on a day when he does not
expect *him* and at an hour which he
does not know, **51** and will [1]cut him in
pieces and [2]assign him a place with
the hypocrites; in that place there will
be [a]weeping and gnashing of teeth.

### *Parable of Ten Virgins*

**25** "Then [a]the kingdom of heav-
en may be compared to ten
virgins, who took their [b]lamps and
went out to meet the bridegroom.
**2** Now five of them were foolish,
and five were [a]prudent. **3** For when
the foolish took their lamps, they
took no oil with them, **4** but the
[a]prudent took oil in flasks along
with their lamps. **5** Now while the
bridegroom was delaying, they all got
drowsy and *began to* sleep. **6** But at
midnight there was a shout, 'Behold,
the bridegroom! Come out to meet
him.' **7** Then all those virgins rose
and trimmed their lamps. **8** And the
foolish said to the prudent, 'Give
us some of your oil, for our lamps
are going out.' **9** But the [a]prudent
answered, saying, 'No, there will
not be enough for us and you *too*;
go instead to the dealers and buy
*some* for yourselves.' **10** And while
they were going away to make the
purchase, the bridegroom came, and
those who were [a]ready went in with
him to [b]the wedding feast; and [c]the
door was shut. **11** And later the other
virgins also *came, saying, '[a]Lord,
lord, open up for us.' **12** But he an-
swered and said, 'Truly I say to you, I
do not know you.' **13** [a]Therefore, stay
awake, for you do not know the day
nor the hour.

### *Parable of the Talents*

**14** "[a]For *it is* just like a man [b]*about* to
go on a journey, who called his own
slaves and handed over his posses-
sions to them. **15** And to one he gave

**24:41** [b]Ex 11:5; Dt 24:6; Is 47:2 [1]Handmill [2]Lit *is* **24:42** [a]Mt 24:43, 44; 25:10, 13; Lk 12:39f; 21:36 **24:43** [a]Mt 24:42, 44; 25:10, 13; Lk 12:39f; 21:36 [b]Mt 14:25; Mk 6:48; 13:35; Lk 12:38 [1]Lit *know this* [2]Lit *dug through* **24:44** [a]Mt 24:42, 43; 25:10, 13; Lk 12:39f; 21:36 [b]Mt 24:27 **24:45** [a]Mt 24:45-51: *Lk 12:42-46* [b]Mt 25:21, 23; Lk 16:10 [c]Mt 7:24; 10:16; 25:2ff [d]Mt 25:21, 23 [1]Or *lord* **24:46** [1]Or *lord* **24:47** [a]Mt 25:21, 23 **24:48** [1]Or *lord* [2]Lit *lingers* **24:50** [1]Or *lord* **24:51** [a]Mt 8:12 [1]Or *severely scourge him* [2]Lit *appoint his portion* ◆ **25:1** [a]Mt 13:24 [b]Jn 18:3; Ac 20:8; Rev 4:5; 8:10 **25:2** [a]Mt 7:24; 10:16; 25:2ff **25:4** [a]Mt 7:24; 10:16; 25:2ff **25:9** [a]Mt 7:24; 10:16; 25:2ff **25:10** [a]Mt 24:42ff [b]Lk 12:35f [c]Mt 7:21ff; Lk 13:25 **25:11** [a]Mt 7:21ff; Lk 13:25 **25:13** [a]Mt 24:42ff **25:14** [a]Mt 25:14-30: *Lk 19:12-27* [b]Mt 21:33

five [a,1]talents, to another, two, and
to another, one, each according to
his own ability; and he [b]went on his
journey. **16** Immediately the one who
had received the five [a]talents went
and traded with them, and gained
five more talents. **17** In the same
manner the one who *had received* the
two *talents* gained two more. **18** But
he who received the one *talent* went
away, and dug *a hole* in the ground
and hid his [1]master's money.

**19** "Now after a long time the
master of those slaves *came and
*[a]settled accounts with them. **20** And
the one who had received the five
[a]talents came up and brought five
more talents, saying, 'Master, you
handed five talents over to me. See,
I have gained five more talents.' **21** His
master said to him, 'Well done, good
and [a]faithful slave. You were faithful
with a few things, I will [b]put you in
charge of many things; enter into the
joy of your [1]master.'

**22** "Also the one who *had received*
the two [a]talents came up and said,
'Master, you handed two talents over
to me. See, I have gained two more
talents.' **23** His master said to him,
'Well done, good and [a]faithful slave.
You were faithful with a few things, I
will put you in charge of many things;
enter into the joy of your master.'

**24** "And the one also who had
received the one [a]talent came up
and said, 'Master, I knew you to be
a hard man, reaping where you did
not sow and gathering where you
scattered no *seed.* **25** And I was afraid,
and went away and hid your talent
in the ground. See, you have what
is yours.'

**26** "But his master answered and
said to him, 'You wicked, lazy slave,
you knew that I reap where I did not
sow and gather where I scattered no
*seed.* **27** Therefore, you ought to have
put my money [1]in the bank, and on
my arrival I would have received my
*money* back with interest. **28** There-
fore take away the talent from him,
and give it to the one who has the
ten talents.'

**29** "[a]For to everyone who has,
*more* shall be given, and he will have
an abundance; but from the one who
does not have, even what he does
have shall be taken away. **30** And
throw out the worthless slave into
[a]the outer darkness; in that place
there will be weeping and gnashing
of teeth.

### *The Final Judgment*

**31** "But when [a]the Son of Man comes
in His glory, and all the angels with
Him, then [b]He will sit on His glorious
throne. **32** And all the nations will be
[a]gathered before Him; and He will
separate them from one another, [b]as
the shepherd separates the sheep
from the goats; **33** and He will put the
sheep [a]on His right, and the goats
[b]on the left.

**34** "Then the King will say to those
on His right, 'Come, you who are
blessed of My Father, [a]inherit the

**25:15** [a]Mt 18:24; Lk 19:13 [b]*Mt 21:33* [1]*A* talent was worth more than 15 years of a laborer's *wages* **25:16** [a]Mt 18:24; Lk 19:13 **25:18** [1]Or *lord's* **25:19** [a]Mt 18:23 **25:20** [a]Mt 18:24; Lk 19:13 **25:21** [a]Mt 24:45, 47; 25:23 [b]Lk 12:44; 22:29; Rev 3:21; 21:7 [1]Or *lord* **25:22** [a]Mt 18:24; Lk 19:13 **25:23** [a]Mt 24:45, 47; 25:21 **25:24** [a]Mt 18:24; Lk 19:13 **25:27** [1]Lit *to the bankers* **25:29** [a]Mt 13:12; Mk 4:25; Lk 8:18; Jn 15:2 **25:30** [a]Mt 8:12; 22:13; Lk 13:28 **25:31** [a]Mt 16:27f; 1Th 4:16; 2Th 1:7; Heb 9:28; Jd 14; Rev 1:7 [b]Mt 19:28 **25:32** [a]Mt 13:49; 2Co 5:10 [b]Eze 34:17, 20 **25:33** [a]1Ki 2:19; Ps 45:9 [b]Ecc 10:2 **25:34** [a]Mt 5:3; 19:29; Lk 12:32; 1Co 6:9; 15:50; Ga 5:21; Jas 2:5

kingdom, which has been prepared for you [b]from the foundation of the world. **35** For [a]I was hungry, and you gave Me *something* to eat; I was thirsty, and you gave Me *something* to drink; [b]I was a stranger, and you invited Me in; **36** [a]naked, and you clothed Me; I was sick, and you [b]visited Me; [c]I was in prison, and you came to Me.' **37** Then the righteous will answer Him, saying, 'Lord, when did we see You hungry, and feed You, or thirsty, and give You *something* to drink? **38** And when did we see You a stranger, and invite You in, or naked, and clothe You? **39** And when did we see You sick, or in prison, and come to You?' **40** [a]And the King will answer and say to them, 'Truly I say to you, [b]to the extent that you did it to one of these brothers of Mine, *even* the least *of them*, you did it to Me.'

**41** "Then He will also say to those on His left, '[a]Depart from Me, accursed ones, into the [b]eternal fire which has been prepared for [c]the devil and his angels; **42** for I was hungry, and you gave Me *nothing* to eat; I was thirsty, and you gave Me nothing to drink; **43** I was a stranger, and you did not invite Me in; naked, and you did not clothe Me; sick, and in prison, and you did not visit Me.' **44** Then they themselves also will answer, saying, 'Lord, when did we see You hungry, or thirsty, or a stranger, or naked, or sick, or in prison, and did not [1]take care of You?' **45** Then He will answer them, saying, 'Truly I say to you, to the extent that you did not do it to one of the least of these, you did not do it to Me.' **46** And these will go away into [a]eternal punishment, but the righteous into [b]eternal life."

### *The Plot to Kill Jesus*

**26** [a,1]Now it happened that when Jesus had finished all these words, He said to His disciples, **2** "[a]You know that after two days [b]the Passover is coming, and the Son of Man is *to be* [c]delivered over for crucifixion."

**3** [a]Then the chief priests and the elders of the people were gathered together in [b]the court of the high priest, named [c]Caiaphas; **4** and they [a]plotted together to seize Jesus by stealth and kill Him. **5** But they were saying, "Not during the festival, [a]lest a riot occur among the people."

### *The Costly Perfume*

**6** [a]Now when Jesus was in [b]Bethany, at the home of Simon the leper, **7** [a]a woman came to Him with an alabaster jar of very costly perfume, and she poured it on His head as He reclined *at the table.* **8** But when the disciples saw *this*, they were indignant, saying, "Why this waste? **9** For this *perfume* might have been sold for a high price and *the money* given to the poor." **10** But Jesus, aware

---

**25:34** [b]Mt 13:35; Lk 11:50; Jn 17:24; Eph 1:4; Heb 4:3; 9:26; 1Pe 1:20; Rev 13:8; 17:8 **25:35** [a]Is 58:7; Eze 18:7, 16; Jas 2:15, 16 [b]Job 31:32; Heb 13:2 **25:36** [a]Is 58:7; Eze 18:7, 16; Jas 2:15, 16 [b]Jas 1:27 [c]2Ti 1:16f **25:40** [a]Mt 25:34; Lk 19:38; Rev 17:14; 19:16 [b]Pr 19:17; Mt 10:42; Heb 6:10 **25:41** [a]Mt 7:23 [b]Mk 9:48; Lk 16:24; Jd 7 [c]Mt 4:10; Rev 12:9 **25:44** [1]Or *serve* **25:46** [a]Da 12:2; Jn 5:29; Ac 24:15 [b]Mt 19:29; Jn 3:15f, 36; 5:24; 6:27, 40, 47, 54; 17:2f; Ac 13:46, 48; Ro 2:7; 5:21; 6:23; Ga 6:8; 1Jn 5:11 ◆ **26:1** [a]Mt 7:28 [1]Lit *And* **26:2** [a]Mt 26:2-5: *Mk 14:1, 2; Lk 22:1, 2* [b]Jn 11:55; 13:1 [c]Mt 10:4 **26:3** [a]Jn 11:47 [b]Mt 26:58, 69; 27:27; Mk 14:54, 66; 15:16; Lk 22:55; Jn 18:15 [c]Mt 26:57; Lk 3:2; Jn 11:49; 18:13, 14, 24, 28; Ac 4:6 **26:4** [a]Mt 12:14 **26:5** [a]Mt 27:24 **26:6** [a]Mt 26:6-13: *Mk 14:3-9;* Lk 7:37-39; Jn 12:1-8 [b]Mt 21:17 **26:7** [a]Lk 7:37f

of this, said to them, "Why do you
bother the woman? For she has done
a good work to Me. **11** For you always
have [a]the poor with you; but you do
not always have Me. **12** For when she
poured this perfume on My body,
she did it [a]to prepare Me for burial.
**13** Truly I say to you, [a]wherever this
gospel is proclaimed in the whole
world, what this woman has done
will also be spoken of in memory of
her."

### *Judas Looks to Betray Jesus*

**14** [a]Then one of the twelve, named
[b]Judas Iscariot, went to the chief
priests **15** and said, "What are you
willing to give me [1]to [a]deliver Him to
you?" And [b]they weighed out [2]thirty
pieces of silver to him. **16** And from
then on he *began* looking for a good
opportunity to [1]betray [2]Jesus.

### *The Passover Meal*

**17** [a]Now on the first *day* of [b]Unleav-
ened Bread the disciples came to
Jesus, saying, "Where do You want
us to prepare for You to eat the
Passover?" **18** And He said, "Go into
the city to [a]a certain man, and say to
him, 'The Teacher says, "[b]My time
is near; I am keeping the Passover
at your house with My disciples."'"
**19** And the disciples did as Jesus had
directed them; and they prepared the
Passover.

**20** [a]Now when evening came, Jesus
was reclining *at the table* with the
twelve disciples. **21** And as they were
eating, He said, "[a]Truly I say to you
that one of you will betray Me." **22** And
being deeply grieved, they [1]each one
began to say to Him, "Surely not I,
Lord?" **23** And He answered and said,
"[a]He who dipped his hand with Me in
the bowl is the one who will betray Me.
**24** The Son of Man is going, [a]just as it is
written of Him; but woe to that man by
whom the Son of Man is betrayed! [b]It
would have been good [1]for that man if
he had not been born." **25** And [a]Judas,
who was betraying Him, answered and
said, "Surely not I, [b]Rabbi?" Jesus *said
to him, "[c]You yourself said *it*."

### *The Lord's Supper*

**26** [a]Now while they were eating, Jesus
took *some* bread, and [b,1]after a bless-
ing, He broke *it*. And giving *it* to the
disciples, He said, "Take, eat; this is
My body." **27** And when He had taken
a cup and given thanks, He gave *it* to
them, saying, "Drink from it, all of
you; **28** for [a]this is My blood of the
covenant, which is poured out for
[b]many for forgiveness of sins. **29** But
I say to you, I will not drink of this
fruit of the vine from now on until
that day when I drink it new with you
in My Father's kingdom."

**30** [a]And after singing a hymn, they
went out to [b]the Mount of Olives.

---

**26:11** [a]Dt 15:11; Mk 14:7; Jn 12:8 **26:12** [a]Jn 19:40 **26:13** [a]Mk 14:9 **26:14** [a]Mt 26:14-16: *Mk 14:10, 11; Lk 22:3-6* [b]Mt 10:4; 26:25, 47; 27:3; Jn 6:71; 12:4; 13:26; Ac 1:16 **26:15** [a]Mt 10:4 [b]Ex 21:32; Zec 11:12 [1]Lit *and I will* [2]Silver shekels, approx. 120 days of a laborer's wages **26:16** [1]Or *deliver* [2]Lit *Him* ***26:17*** *[a]Mt 26:17-19: Mk 14:12-16; Lk 22:7-13* [b]Ex 12:18-20 **26:18** [a]Mk 14:13; Lk 22:10 [b]Jn 7:6, 8 **26:20** [a]Mt 26:20-24: *Mk 14:17-21* **26:21** [a]Lk 22:21-23; Jn 13:21f **26:22** [1]Or *one after another* **26:23** [a]Ps 41:9; Jn 13:18, 26 **26:24** [a]Mt 26:31, 54, 56; Mk 9:12; Lk 24:25-27, 46; Ac 17:2f; 26:22f; 1Co 15:3; 1Pe 1:10f [b]Mt 18:7; Mk 14:21 [1]Lit *for him if that man had not been born* **26:25** [a]Mt 26:14 [b]Mt 23:7; 26:49 [c]Mt 26:64; 27:11; Lk 22:70 **26:26** [a]Mt 26:26-29: *Mk 14:22-25; Lk 22:17-20; 1Co 11:23-25;* 1Co 10:16 [b]Mt 14:19 [1]Lit *having blessed* **26:28** [a]Ex 24:8; Heb 9:20 [b]Mt 20:28 **26:30** [a]Mt 26:30-35: *Mk 14:26-31; Lk 22:31-34* [b]Mt 21:1

31 Then Jesus *said to them, "You
will all [a,1]fall away because of Me this
night, for it is written, '[b]I WILL STRIKE
DOWN THE SHEPHERD, AND THE SHEEP
OF THE FLOCK SHALL BE [c]SCATTERED.'
32 But after I have been raised, [a]I will
go ahead of you to Galilee." 33 But Pe-
ter answered and said to Him, "*Even*
though all may [1]fall away because of
You, I will never fall away." 34 Jesus
said to him, "[a]Truly I say to you that
[b]this *very* night, before a rooster
crows, you will deny Me three times."
35 Peter *said to Him, "[a]Even if I have
to die with You, I will not deny You."
All the disciples said the same thing
too.

### *Jesus Prays in Gethsemane*

36 [a]Then Jesus *came with them to a
place called [b]Gethsemane, and *said
to His disciples, "Sit here while I go
over there and pray." 37 And He took
with Him [a]Peter and the two sons
of Zebedee, and began to be grieved
and distressed. 38 Then He *said to
them, "[a]My soul is deeply grieved,
to the point of death; remain here
and [b]keep watch with Me."
39 And He went a little beyond
*them*, and fell on His face and prayed,
saying, "My Father, if it is possible,
let [a]this cup pass from Me; [b]yet not
as I will, but as You will." 40 And He
*came to the disciples and *found
them sleeping, and *said to Peter, "So,
you *men* could not [a]keep watch with
Me for one hour? 41 [a]Keep watching
and praying that you may not enter
into temptation; [b]the spirit is willing,
but the flesh is weak."
42 He went away again a second
time and prayed, saying, "My Father,
if this [a]cannot pass away unless I
drink it, [b]Your will be done." 43 And
again He came and found them
sleeping, for their eyes were heavy.
44 And He left them again, and went
away and prayed a third time, saying
the same thing once more. 45 Then
He *came to the disciples and *said
to them, "[1]Are you still sleeping and
resting? Behold, [a]the hour is at hand
and the Son of Man is being betrayed
into the hands of sinners. 46 Get up,
let us go; behold, the one who betrays
Me is at hand!"

### *The Betrayal and Arrest of Jesus*

47 [a]And while He was still speaking,
behold, [b]Judas, one of the twelve,
came up, and with him *was* a large
crowd with swords and clubs, *who
came* from the chief priests and
elders of the people. 48 Now he who
was betraying Him gave them a sign,
saying, "Whomever I kiss, He is the
one; seize Him." 49 And immedi-
ately Judas went to Jesus and said,
"Greetings, [a]Rabbi!" and kissed Him.
50 And Jesus said to him, "[a]Friend, *do*
what you have come for." Then they
came and laid hands on Jesus and
seized Him.
51 And behold, [a]one of those who
were with Jesus stretched out his hand
and drew out his [b]sword and struck
the [a]slave of the high priest and [1]cut

**26:31** [a]Mt 11:6 [b]Zec 13:7 [c]Jn 16:32 [1]Or *stumble* **26:32** [a]Mt 28:7, 10, 16; Mk 16:7 **26:33** [1]Or *stumble* **26:34** [a]Mt 26:75; Jn 13:38 [b]Mk 14:30 **26:35** [a]Jn 13:37 **26:36** [a]Mt 26:36-46: *Mk 14:32-42; Lk 22:40-46* [b]Mk 14:32; Lk 22:39; Jn 18:1 **26:37** [a]Mt 4:21; 17:1; Mk 5:37 **26:38** [a]Jn 12:27 [b]Mt 26:40, 41 **26:39** [a]Mt 20:22 [b]Mt 26:42; Mk 14:36; Lk 22:42; Jn 6:38 **26:40** [a]Mt 26:38 **26:41** [a]Mt 26:38 [b]Mk 14:38 **26:42** [a]Mt 20:22 [b]Mt 26:39; Mk 14:36; Lk 22:42; Jn 6:38 **26:45** [a]Mk 14:41; Jn 12:27; 13:1 [1]Or *Keep on sleeping therefore* **26:47** [a]Mt 26:47-56: *Mk 14:43-50; Lk 22:47-53; Jn 18:3-11* [b]Mt 26:14 **26:49** [a]Mt 23:7; 26:25 **26:50** [a]Mt 20:13; 22:12 **26:51** [a]Mk 14:47; Lk 22:50; Jn 18:10 [b]Lk 22:38 [1]Lit *took off*

off his ear. 52 Then Jesus *said to him,
"Put your sword back into its place;
for [a]all those who take up the sword
shall perish by the sword. 53 Or do
you think that I cannot appeal to My
Father, and He will at once put at My
disposal more than twelve [a,1]legions
of [b]angels? 54 Therefore, how will
[a]the Scriptures be fulfilled, *which
say* that it must happen this way?"
55 At that time Jesus said to the
crowds, "Have you come out with
swords and clubs to arrest Me as *you
would* against a robber? [a]Every day
I used to sit in the temple teaching
and you did not seize Me. 56 But all
this has taken place in order that [a]the
Scriptures of the prophets would be
fulfilled." Then all the disciples left
Him and fled.

### *Jesus Before Caiaphas*

57 [a]Now those who had seized Jesus
led Him away to [b]Caiaphas, the
high priest, where the scribes and
the elders were gathered together.
58 But [a]Peter was following Him at a
distance as far as the [b]courtyard of
the high priest, and entered in, and
sat down with the [c,1]officers to see
the outcome.
59 Now the chief priests and
the whole [a]Sanhedrin kept trying
to obtain false testimony against
Jesus, so that they might put Him to
death. 60 And they did not find *any*,
even though many false witnesses
came forward. But later on [a]two
came forward, 61 and said, "This
man stated, '[a]I am able to destroy
the [1]sanctuary of God and to rebuild
it [2]in three days.'" 62 And the high
priest stood up and said to Him, "Do
You not answer? What are these men
testifying against You?" 63 But [a]Jesus
kept silent. [b]And the high priest said
to Him, "[c]I put You under oath by
[d]the living God, that You tell us
whether You are the [1]Christ, [e]the
Son of God." 64 Jesus *said to him,
"[a]You yourself said *it*; nevertheless I
tell you, [1]hereafter you will see [b]THE
SON OF MAN SITTING AT THE RIGHT
HAND OF POWER and [c]COMING ON THE
CLOUDS OF HEAVEN."
65 Then the high priest [a]tore his
garments and said, "He has blas-
phemed! What further need do we
have of witnesses? Behold, you have
now heard the blasphemy; 66 what do
you think?" They answered and said,
"[a]He deserves death!"
67 [a]Then they [b]spat in His face
and beat Him with their fists; and
others [1]slapped *Him*, 68 and said,
"[a]Prophesy to us, O [1]Christ; who is
the one who hit You?"

### *Peter's Denials*

69 [a]Now Peter was sitting outside in
the [b]courtyard, and a servant-girl
came to him and said, "You too were

---

**26:52** [a]Ge 9:6; Rev 13:10 **26:53** [a]Mk 5:9, 15; Lk 8:30 [b]Mt 4:11 [1]A legion equaled 4,000-6,000 soldiers
**26:54** [a]Mt 26:24 **26:55** [a]Mk 12:35; 14:49; Lk 4:20; 19:47; 20:1; 21:37; Jn 7:14, 28; 8:2, 20; 18:20
**26:56** [a]Mt 26:24 **26:57** [a]Mt 26:57-68: *Mk 14:53-65; Jn 18:12f, 19-24* [b]Mt 26:3 **26:58** [a]Jn 18:15
[b]*Mt 26:3* [c]*Mt 5:25; Jn 7:32, 45f*; 19:6; Ac 5:22, 26 [1]Or *servants* **26:59** [a]Mt 5:22 **26:60** [a]Dt 19:15
**26:61** [a]Mt 27:40; Mk 14:58; 15:29; Jn 2:19; Ac 6:14 [1]The inner part of the temple [2]Or *after*
**26:63** [a]Mt 27:12, 14; Jn 19:9 [b]Mt 26:63-66: *Lk 22:67-71* [c]Lv 5:1 [d]Mt 16:16 [e]Mt 4:3 [1]Messiah
**26:64** [a]Mt 26:25 [b]Ps 110:1; Mk 14:62 [c]Da 7:13; Mt 16:27f [1]Or *from now on* **26:65** [a]Nu 14:6; Mk 14:63;
Ac 14:14 **26:66** [a]Lv 24:16; Jn 19:7 **26:67** [a]Is 50:6; Mt 26:67, 68: *Lk 22:63-65; Jn 18:22* [b]Mt 27:30;
Mk 10:34 [1]Or *beat Him with rods* **26:68** [a]Mk 14:65; Lk 22:64 [1]Messiah **26:69** [a]Mt 26:69-75:
*Mk 14:66-72; Lk 22:55-62; Jn 18:16-18, 25-27* [b]Mt 26:3

with Jesus the Galilean." **70** But he
denied *it* before them all, saying, "I
do not know what you are talking
about." **71** And when he had gone out
to the gateway, another *servant-girl*
saw him and *said to those who were
there, "This man was with Jesus of
Nazareth." **72** And again he denied
*it* with an oath, "I do not know the
man." **73** A little later the bystanders
came up and said to Peter, "Surely
you too are *one* of them; [a]for even
the way you talk [1]gives you away."
**74** Then he began to curse and swear,
"I do not know the man!" And imme-
diately a rooster crowed. **75** And Peter
remembered the word which Jesus
had said, "[a]Before a rooster crows,
you will deny Me three times." And
he went out and cried bitterly.

### *Judas' Remorse*

**27** [a]Now when morning came, all
the chief priests and the elders
of the people took counsel together
against Jesus to put Him to death;
**2** and they bound Him, and led Him
away and [a]delivered Him to [b]Pilate
the governor.

**3** Then when [a]Judas, who had
betrayed Him, saw that He had been
condemned, he felt remorse and re-
turned [b]the [1]thirty pieces of silver to
the chief priests and elders, **4** saying,
"I have sinned by betraying innocent
blood." But they said, "What is that
to us? [a]See *to that* yourself!" **5** And
he threw the pieces of silver into
[a]the [1]sanctuary and departed; and
[b]he went away and hanged himself.
**6** And the chief priests took the pieces
of silver and said, "It is not lawful to
put them into the temple treasury,
since it is the price of blood." **7** And
taking counsel together, they bought
[1]with the money the Potter's Field
as a burial place for strangers. **8** [a]For
this reason that field has been called
the Field of Blood to this day. **9** Then
that which was spoken through
Jeremiah the prophet was fulfilled,
saying, "[a]AND [1]THEY TOOK THE THIRTY
PIECES OF SILVER, THE PRICE OF THE
ONE WHOSE PRICE HAD BEEN SET by
the sons of Israel; **10** [a]AND [1]THEY GAVE
THEM FOR THE POTTER'S FIELD, AS THE
[2]LORD DIRECTED ME."

### *Jesus Before Pilate*

**11** [a]Now Jesus stood before the gov-
ernor, and the governor questioned
Him, saying, "Are You the [b]King of the
Jews?" And Jesus said to him, "[c]You
yourself say *it*." **12** And while He was
being accused by the chief priests and
elders, [a]He did not answer. **13** Then
Pilate *said to Him, "Do You not hear
how many things they testify against
You?" **14** And [a]He did not answer him
with regard to even a *single* [1]charge,
so the governor marveled greatly.

**15** [a]Now at the feast the governor
was accustomed to release for the
crowd *any* one prisoner whom they
wanted. **16** And at that time they
were holding a notorious prisoner,

---

**26:73** [a]Mk 14:70; Lk 22:59; Jn 18:26 [1]Lit *makes you evident* **26:75** [a]Mt 26:34 ◆ **27:1** [a]Mk 15:1; Lk 22:66; Jn 18:28 **27:2** [a]Mt 20:19 [b]Lk 3:1; 13:1; 23:12; Ac 3:13; 4:27; 1Ti 6:13 **27:3** [a]Mt 26:14 [b]Mt 26:15 [1]Silver shekels, approx. 120 days of a laborer's wages **27:4** [a]Mt 27:24 **27:5** [a]Mt 26:61; Lk 1:9, 21 [b]Ac 1:18 [1]The inner part of the temple **27:7** [1]Lit *from them* **27:8** [a]Ac 1:19 **27:9** [a]Zec 11:12 [1]Or *I took*, cf. Zec 11:13 **27:10** [a]Zec 11:13 [1]Some early mss *I gave* [2]In OT, Yahweh, cf. Zec 11:13 **27:11** [a]Mt 27:11-14: *Mk 15:2-5; Lk 23:2, 3; Jn 18:29-38* [b]Mt 2:2 [c]Mt 26:25 **27:12** [a]Mt 26:63; Jn 19:9 **27:14** [a]Mt 27:12; Mk 15:5; Lk 23:9; Jn 19:9 [1]Lit *word* **27:15** [a]Mt 27:15-26: *Mk 15:6-15; Lk 23:17-25;* Jn 18:39-19:16

called Barabbas. 17 So when the
people gathered together, Pilate
said to them, "Whom do you want
me to release for you? [1]Barabbas, or
Jesus [a]who is called [2]Christ?" 18 For
he knew that because of envy they
had delivered Him over.

19 [a]Now while he was sitting on
the judgment seat, his wife sent him
*a message*, saying, "Have nothing to
do with that [b]righteous Man; for [1]last
night I suffered greatly [c]in a dream
because of Him." 20 But the chief
priests and the elders persuaded the
crowds to [a]ask for Barabbas and to
put Jesus to death. 21 But the governor
answered and said to them, "Which
of the two do you want me to release
for you?" And they said, "Barabbas."
22 Pilate *said to them, "Then, what
shall I do with Jesus [a]who is called
[1]Christ?" They all *said, "Let Him
be crucified!" 23 And he said, "Why,
what evil did He do?" But they were
crying out all the more, saying, "Let
Him be crucified!"

24 Now when Pilate saw that he
was accomplishing nothing, but
rather that [a]a riot was starting, he
took water and [b]washed his hands
in front of the crowd, saying, "I
am innocent of [c]this man's blood;
[d]see *to that* yourselves." 25 And
all the people answered and said,
"[a]His blood be on us and on our
children!" 26 Then he released
Barabbas [1]for them; but after having
Jesus [a]scourged, he delivered Him
over to be crucified.

### *Jesus Is Mocked*

27 [a]Then when the soldiers of
the governor took Jesus into [b]the
[1]Praetorium, they gathered the whole
*Roman* [c,2]cohort around Him. 28 And
they stripped Him and [a]put a scarlet
robe on Him. 29 [a]And after twisting
together a crown of thorns, they put
it on His head, and a [1]reed in His right
hand; and they knelt down before
Him and mocked Him, saying, "[b]Hail,
King of the Jews!" 30 [a]And they spat
on Him, and took the reed and *began*
*to* beat Him on the head. 31 [a]When
they had mocked Him, they took the
*scarlet* robe off Him and put His *own*
garments back on Him, and led Him
away to crucify Him.

32 [a]And as they were coming out,
they found a man of [b]Cyrene named
Simon, [1]whom they pressed into ser-
vice to bear His cross.

### *The Crucifixion*

33 [a]And when they came to a place
called [b]Golgotha, which means Place
of a Skull, 34 [a]they gave Him [b]wine
to drink mixed with gall; and after
tasting *it*, He did not want to drink.

35 And when they had crucified
Him, [a]they divided up His garments
among themselves by casting [1]lots.
36 And sitting down, they *began to*
[a]keep watch over Him there. 37 And

---

**27:17** [a]Mt 1:16; 27:22 [1]Some mss *Jesus Barabbas* [2]Messiah **27:19** [a]Jn 19:13; Ac 12:21; 18:12, 16f; 25:6, 10, 17 [b]Mt 27:24 [c]Ge 20:6; 31:11; Nu 12:6; Job 33:15; Mt 1:20; 2:12f, 19, 22 [1]Lit *today* **27:20** [a]Ac 3:14 **27:22** [a]Mt 1:16 [1]Messiah **27:24** [a]Mt 26:5 [b]Dt 21:6-8 [c]Mt 27:19 [d]Mt 27:4 **27:25** [a]Jos 2:19; Ac 5:28 **27:26** [a]Mk 15:15; Lk 23:16; Jn 19:1 [1]Or *to them* **27:27** [a]Mt 27:27-31: *Mk 15:16-20* [b]Mt 26:3; Jn 18:28, 33; 19:9 [c]Ac 10:1 [1]Governor's official residence [2]Normally 600 men (the number varied); or *battalion* **27:28** [a]Mk 15:17; Jn 19:2 **27:29** [a]Mk 15:17; Jn 19:2 [b]Mk 15:18; Jn 19:3 [1]Or *staff* **27:30** [a]Mt 26:67; Mk 10:34; 14:65; 15:19 **27:31** [a]Mk 15:20 **27:32** [a]Mt 27:32: *Mk 15:21; Lk 23:26;* Jn 19:17 [b]Ac 2:10; 6:9; 11:20; 13:1 [1]Lit *this one* **27:33** [a]Mt 27:34-44: *Mk 15:22-32; Lk 23:33-43; Jn 19:17-24* [b]Lk 23:33; Jn 19:17 **27:34** [a]Ps 69:21 [b]Mk 15:23 **27:35** [a]Ps 22:18 [1]Lit *a lot* **27:36** [a]Mt 27:54

above His head they put up the charge
against Him [1]which read, "[a]THIS IS
JESUS THE KING OF THE JEWS."
38 At that time two robbers *were
crucified with Him, one on the right
and one on the left. 39 And those
passing by were blaspheming Him,
[a]shaking their heads 40 and saying,
"[a]You who *are going to* destroy the
sanctuary and rebuild it in three
days, save Yourself! [b]If You are the
Son of God, come down from the
cross." 41 In the same way the chief
priests also, along with the scribes
and elders, were mocking *Him* and
saying, 42 "[a]He saved others; [1]He
cannot save Himself. [b]He is the King
of Israel; let Him now come down
from the cross, and we will believe in
Him. 43 [a]HE TRUSTS IN GOD; LET GOD
RESCUE *Him* now, IF HE [1]DELIGHTS IN
HIM; for He said, 'I am the Son of
God.'" 44 [a]And the robbers who had
been crucified with Him were also
insulting Him with the same words.
45 [a]Now from the [1]sixth hour
darkness [2]fell upon all the land until
the [3]ninth hour. 46 And about the
ninth hour Jesus cried out with a
loud voice, saying, "[a]ELI, ELI, LAMA
SABACHTHANI?" that is, "MY GOD, MY
GOD, WHY HAVE YOU FORSAKEN ME?"
47 And some of those who were
standing there, when they heard it,
*began* saying, "This man is calling
for Elijah." 48 [a]And immediately one
of them ran, and taking a sponge, he
filled it with sour wine and put it on
a reed, and gave Him a drink. 49 But
the rest *of them* were saying, "[1]Let us
see whether Elijah will come to save
Him[2]." 50 And Jesus [a]cried out again
with a loud voice, and yielded up
His spirit. 51 [a]And behold, [b]the [1]veil
of the sanctuary was torn in two from
top to bottom; and [c]the earth shook
and the rocks were split. 52 And the
tombs were opened, and many bodies
of the [1]saints who had [a]fallen asleep
were raised; 53 and coming out of the
tombs after His resurrection they
entered [a]the holy city and appeared
to many. 54 [a]Now the centurion, and
those who were with him [b]keeping
guard over Jesus, when they saw [c]the
earthquake and the things that were
happening, became very frightened
and said, "Truly this was [d]God's Son!"
55 [a]And many women were there
looking on from a distance, who had
followed Jesus from Galilee while
[b,1]ministering to Him. 56 Among
them was [a]Mary Magdalene, and
Mary the mother of James and Jo-
seph, and [b]the mother of the sons
of Zebedee.

### *Jesus Is Buried*

57 [a]Now when it was evening, there
came a rich man from Arimathea,
named Joseph, who himself had also
become a disciple of Jesus. 58 This

**27:37** [a]Mk 15:26; Lk 23:38; Jn 19:19 [1]Lit *written* **27:39** [a]Job 16:4; Ps 22:7; 109:25; Lam 2:15; Mk 15:29 **27:40** [a]Mt 26:61; Jn 2:19 [b]Mt 27:42 **27:42** [a]Mk 15:31; Lk 23:35 [b]Mt 27:37; Lk 23:37; Jn 1:49; 12:13 [1]Or *can He not save Himself?* **27:43** [a]Ps 22:8 [1]Or *takes pleasure in, cares for* **27:44** [a]Lk 23:39-43 **27:45** [a]Mt 27:45-56: *Mk 15:33-41; Lk 23:44-49* [1]Noon [2]Or *occurred* [3]3 p.m. **27:46** [a]Ps 22:1 **27:48** [a]Ps 69:21; Mk 15:36; Lk 23:36; Jn 19:29 **27:49** [1]Lit *Permit that we see* [2]Some early mss add *And another took a spear and pierced His side, and there came out water and blood*, cf. Jn 19:34 **27:50** [a]Mk 15:37; Lk 23:46; Jn 19:30 **27:51** [a]Mt 27:51-56: *Mk 15:38-41;* Lk 23:47-49 [b]Ex 26:31ff; Mk 15:38; Lk 23:45; Heb 9:3 [c]Mt 27:54 [1]Or *curtain* **27:52** [a]Ac 7:60 [1]Or *holy ones* **27:53** [a]Mt 4:5 **27:54** [a]Mk 15:39; Lk 23:47 [b]Mt 27:36 [c]Mt 27:51 [d]Mt 4:3; 27:43 **27:55** [a]Mk 15:40f; Lk 23:49; Jn 19:25 [b]Mk 15:41; Lk 8:2, 3 [1]Or *caring for Him* **27:56** [a]Mt 28:1; Mk 15:40, 47; 16:9; Lk 8:2; Jn 19:25; 20:1, 18 [b]Mt 20:20 **27:57** [a]Mt 27:57-61: *Mk 15:42-47; Lk 23:50-56; Jn 19:38-42*

man went to Pilate and asked for the
body of Jesus. Then Pilate ordered
it to be given *to him.* **59** And Joseph
took the body and wrapped it in a
clean linen cloth, **60** and laid it in his
own new tomb, which he had hewn
out in the rock; and he rolled [a]a large
stone against the entrance of the
tomb and went away. **61** And [a]Mary
Magdalene was there, and the other
Mary, sitting opposite the grave.
**62** Now on the next day, [1]the day
after [a]the [2]Preparation, the chief
priests and the Pharisees gathered
together with Pilate, **63** and said, "Sir,
we remember that when He was still
alive that deceiver said, '[a]After three
days I *am to* rise again.' **64** Therefore,
order for the grave to be made secure
until the third day, lest His disciples
come and steal Him away and say to
the people, 'He has risen from the
dead,' and the last deception will be
worse than the first." **65** Pilate said to
them, "You have a [a]guard; go, make it
*as* secure as you know how." **66** And
they went and made the grave secure,
and along with [a]the guard they set a
[b]seal on [c]the stone.

### *Jesus Is Risen!*

**28** [a]Now after the Sabbath, as it
began to dawn toward the first
*day* of the week, [b]Mary Magdalene
and the other Mary came to look at
the grave. **2** And behold, there was a
great earthquake, for [a]an angel of the
[1]Lord descended from heaven and
came and rolled away [b]the stone and
sat upon it. **3** And [a]his appearance
was like lightning, and his clothing
as white as snow. **4** And the guards
quaked from fear of him and became
like dead men. **5** And the angel an-
swered and said to the women, "[a,1]Do
not be afraid; for I know that you
are looking for Jesus who has been
crucified. **6** He is not here, for He has
risen, [a]just as He said. Come, see the
place where He was lying. **7** And go
quickly and tell His disciples that He
has risen from the dead; and behold,
He is going ahead of you [a]into Gali-
lee, there you will see Him; behold,
I have told you."
**8** And they left the tomb quickly
with fear and great joy and ran to
report it to His disciples. **9** And
behold, Jesus met them and said,
"Greetings!" And they came up and
took hold of His feet and worshiped
Him. **10** Then Jesus *said to them,
"[a,1]Do not be afraid; go and report
to [b]My brothers to leave [c]for Galilee,
and there they will see Me."
**11** Now while they were on their
way, behold, some of [a]the guard
came into the city and reported
to the chief priests all that had
happened. **12** And when they had
assembled with the elders and took
counsel together, they gave a large
sum of money to the soldiers, **13** and
said, "You are to say, 'His disciples
came by night and stole Him away
while we were asleep.' **14** And if this

---

**27:60** [a]Mt 27:66; 28:2; Mk 16:4 **27:61** [a]Mt 27:56; 28:1 **27:62** [a]Mk 15:42; Lk 23:54; Jn 19:14, 31, 42 [1]Lit *which is after* [2]Preparation for the Sabbath **27:63** [a]Mt 16:21; 17:23; 20:19; Mk 8:31; 9:31; 10:34; Lk 9:22; 18:31-33 **27:65** [a]Mt 27:66; 28:11 **27:66** [a]Mt 27:65; 28:11 [b]Da 6:17 [c]Mt 27:60; 28:2; Mk 16:4
◆ **28:1** [a]Mt 28:1-8: *Mk 16:1-8; Lk 24:1-10;* Jn 20:1-8 [b]Mt 27:56, 61 **28:2** [a]Lk 24:4; Jn 20:12 [b]Mt 27:66; Mk 16:4 [1]In OT, Yahweh, cf. 2Ki 1:3 **28:3** [a]Da 7:9; 10:6; Mk 9:3; Jn 20:12; Ac 1:10 **28:5** [a]Mt 14:27; 28:10; Rev 1:17 [1]Or *Stop being afraid* **28:6** [a]Mt 12:40; 16:21; 27:63 **28:7** [a]Mt 26:32; 28:10, 16; Mk 16:7 **28:10** [a]Mt 14:27; 28:5 [b]Jn 20:17; Ro 8:29; Heb 2:11f, 17 [c]Mt 26:32; 28:7, 16 [1]Or *Stop being afraid* **28:11** [a]Mt 27:65, 66

is heard before [a]the governor, we will win him over and [1]keep you out of trouble." **15** And they took the money and did as they had been instructed; and this story was widely [a]spread among the Jews, *and is* [b]to this day.

### *The Great Commission*

**16** But the eleven disciples proceeded [a]to Galilee, to the mountain which Jesus had designated. **17** And when they saw Him, they worshiped *Him;* but [a]some doubted. **18** And Jesus came up and spoke to them, saying, "[a]All authority has been given to Me in heaven and on earth. **19** [a,1]Go therefore and [b]make disciples of [c]all the nations, [d]baptizing them in the name of the Father and the Son and the Holy Spirit, **20** teaching them to keep all that I commanded you; and behold, [a]I am with you [1]always, even to [b]the end of the age."

**28:14** [a]Mt 27:2 [1]Lit *make you free from care* **28:15** [a]Mt 9:31; Mk 1:45 [b]Mt 27:8 **28:16** [a]Mt 26:32; 28:7, 10; Mk 15:41; 16:7 **28:17** [a]Mk 16:11 **28:18** [a]Da 7:13f; Mt 11:27; 26:64; Ro 14:9; Eph 1:20-22; Php 2:9f; Col 2:10; 1Pe 3:22 **28:19** [a]Mk 16:15f [b]Mt 13:52; Ac 1:8; 14:21 [c]Mt 25:32; Lk 24:47 [d]Ac 2:38; 8:16; Ro 6:3; 1Co 1:13, 15ff; Ga 3:27 [1]Or *Having gone*; Gr aorist part. **28:20** [a]Mt 18:20; Ac 18:10 [b]Mt 13:39 [1]Lit *all the days*

## *The Gospel According to*

# MARK

### *The Preaching of John the Baptist*

**1** The beginning of the gospel of
Jesus Christ, [a]the Son of God.
**2** [a]As it is written in Isaiah the
prophet:
"[b]BEHOLD, I SEND MY
MESSENGER [1]AHEAD OF YOU,
WHO WILL PREPARE YOUR WAY;
**3** [a]THE VOICE OF ONE CRYING
IN THE WILDERNESS,
'MAKE READY THE WAY
OF THE [1]LORD,
MAKE HIS PATHS STRAIGHT.'"
**4** [1]John the Baptist appeared in the
wilderness [a,2]preaching a baptism of
repentance for the [b]forgiveness of
sins. **5** And all the region of Judea was
going out to him, and all the people
of Jerusalem; and they were being
baptized by him in the Jordan River,
confessing their sins. **6** And John was
clothed with camel's hair and *wore* [a]a
leather belt around his waist and was
eating locusts and wild honey. **7** And
he was [1]preaching, saying, "After me
One is coming who is mightier than
I, and I am not fit to stoop down
and untie the strap of His sandals.
**8** I baptized you with water; but He
will baptize you with the Holy Spirit."

### *The Baptism of Jesus*

**9** [a,1]Now it happened that in those
days Jesus [b]came from Nazareth in
Galilee and was baptized by John
in the Jordan. **10** And immediately
coming up out of the water, He
saw the heavens [1]opening, and the
Spirit like a dove descending upon
Him; **11** and a voice came out of the
heavens: "[a]You are My beloved Son,
in You I am well-pleased."
**12** [a]And immediately the Spirit
*drove Him *to go* out into the wilder-
ness. **13** And He was in the wilderness
forty days being tempted by [a]Satan;
and He was with the wild beasts, and
the angels were ministering to Him.

### *Jesus Preaches in Galilee*

**14** [a]Now after John had been deliv-
ered up *into custody*, Jesus came
into Galilee, [b,1]preaching the gospel
of God, **15** and saying, "[a]The time is
fulfilled, and the kingdom of God [1]is
at hand; [b]repent and [2]believe in the
gospel."
**16** [a]As He was going along by
the Sea of Galilee, He saw Simon
and Andrew, the brother of Simon,
casting a net in the sea; for they
were fishermen. **17** And Jesus said to
them, "Follow Me, and I will make
you become fishers of men." **18** And
immediately they left their nets and
followed Him. **19** And going on a
little farther, He saw [1]James the son
of Zebedee, and John his brother,

---

◆ **1:1** [a]Mt 4:3 **1:2** [a]Mk 1:2-8: *Mt 3:1-11; Lk 3:2-16* [b]Mal 3:1; Mt 11:10; Lk 7:27 [1]Lit *before your face* **1:3** [a]Is 40:3; Mt 3:3; Lk 3:4; Jn 1:23 [1]In OT, Yahweh, cf. *Is 40:3* **1:4** [a]Ac 13:24 [b]Lk 1:77 [1]Gr *Joannes*, Heb *Johanan*; so in Mark [2]Or *proclaiming* **1:6** [a]2Ki 1:8 **1:7** [1]Or *proclaiming* **1:9** [a]Mk 1:9-11: *Mt 3:13-17; Lk 3:21, 22* [b]Mt 2:23; Lk 2:51 [1]Lit *And* **1:10** [1]Or *being parted, being torn apart*, cf. 15:38 **1:11** [a]Ps 2:7; Is 42:1; Mt 3:17; 12:18; Mk 9:7; Lk 3:22 **1:12** [a]Mk 1:12, 13: *Mt 4:1-11; Lk 4:1-13* **1:13** [a]Mt 4:10 **1:14** [a]Mt 4:12 [b]Mt 4:23 [1]Or *proclaiming* **1:15** [a]Ga 4:4; Eph 1:10; 1Ti 2:6; Tit 1:3 [b]Mt 3:2; Ac 20:21 [1]Lit *has come near* [2]Or *put your trust in* **1:16** [a]Mk 1:16-20: *Mt 4:18-22;* Lk 5:2-11; Jn 1:40-42 **1:19** [1]Or *Jacob*; James is the Eng form of Jacob; so in Mark

who were also in the boat mending
the nets. **20** And immediately He
called them; and they left their father
Zebedee in the boat with the hired
servants, and went away [1]to follow
Him.

**21** [a]And they *went into Caper-
naum; and immediately on the
Sabbath [b]He entered the synagogue
and *began to* teach. **22** [a]And they
were astonished at His teaching;
for He was teaching them as *one*
having authority, and not as the
scribes. **23** And immediately there
was a man in their synagogue with
an unclean spirit; and he cried out,
**24** saying, "[a]What [1]do we have to do
with You, Jesus the [b]Nazarene? Have
You come to destroy us? I know who
You are—[c]the Holy One of God!"
**25** And Jesus rebuked him, saying, "Be
quiet, and come out of him!" **26** And
throwing him into convulsions, the
unclean spirit cried out with a loud
voice and came out of him. **27** And
they were all [a]amazed, so that they
were arguing among themselves,
saying, "What is this? A new teaching
with authority! He commands even
the unclean spirits, and they obey
Him." **28** And immediately the news
about Him spread everywhere into
all the surrounding district of Galilee.

### *Simon's Mother-in-Law and Many Others Healed*

**29** [a]And immediately after they came
[b]out of the synagogue, they came
into the house of Simon and Andrew,
with James and John. **30** Now Simon's
mother-in-law was lying sick with a
fever; and immediately they *spoke
to [1]Jesus about her. **31** And He came
to her and raised her up, taking her
by the hand, and the fever left her,
and she [1]*began* waiting on them.

**32** [a]Now when evening came,
[b]after the sun had set, they *began*
bringing to Him all who were ill and
those who were [c]demon-possessed.
**33** And the whole [a]city had gathered
at the door. **34** And He [a]healed many
who were ill with various diseases,
and cast out many demons; and He
was not permitting the demons to
speak, because they knew who He
was.

**35** [a]And in the early morning,
while it was still dark, Jesus rose
up, went out of *the house*, and went
away to a desolate place, and [b]was
praying there. **36** And Simon and
his companions searched for Him;
**37** and they found Him, and *said to
Him, "Everyone is looking for You."
**38** And He *said to them, "Let us go
elsewhere, to the towns nearby, so
that I may [1]preach there also; for that
is what I came out for." **39** [a]And He
went, [1]preaching in their synagogues
throughout all Galilee and casting
out the demons.

**40** [a]And a leper *came to [1]Jesus,
pleading with Him and [b]falling on
his knees before Him, and saying,
"If You are willing, You can make
me clean." **41** And moved with com-
passion, He stretched out His hand

**1:20** [1]Lit *after Him* **1:21** [a]Mk 1:21-28: *Lk 4:31-37* [b]Mt 4:23; Mk 1:39; 10:1 **1:22** [a]Mt 7:28
**1:24** [a]Mt 8:29 [b]Mt 2:23; Mk 10:47; 14:67; 16:6; Lk 4:34; 24:19; Ac 24:5 [c]Lk 1:35; 4:34; Jn 6:69; Ac 3:14 [1]Lit *What to us and to You* (a Heb idiom) **1:27** [a]Mk 10:24, 32; 16:5, 6 **1:29** [a]Mk 1:29-31: *Mt 8:14, 15; Lk 4:38, 39* [b]Mk 1:21, 23 **1:30** [1]Lit *Him* **1:31** [1]Or *served* **1:32** [a]Mk 1:32-34: *Mt 8:16, 17; Lk 4:40, 41* [b]Mt 8:16; Lk 4:40 [c]Mt 4:24 **1:33** [a]Mk 1:21 **1:34** [a]Mt 4:23 **1:35** [a]Mk 1:35-38: *Lk 4:42, 43* [b]Mt 14:23; Lk 5:16
**1:38** [1]Or *proclaim* **1:39** [a]Mt 4:23; 9:35; Mk 1:23; 3:1 [1]Or *proclaiming* **1:40** [a]Mk 1:40-44: *Mt 8:2-4; Lk 5:12-14* [b]Mt 8:2; Mk 10:17; Lk 5:12 [1]Lit *Him*

and touched him, and *said to him,
"I am willing; be cleansed." 42 And
immediately the leprosy left him and
he was cleansed. 43 And He sternly
warned him and immediately sent
him away, 44 and He *said to him,
"[a]See that you say nothing to anyone;
but [a]go, show yourself to the priest
and [b]offer for your cleansing what
Moses commanded, as a testimony to
them." 45 But he went out and began
to [a]proclaim it freely and to [a]spread
the news around, to such an extent
that [1]Jesus could no longer publicly
enter a city, but [2]stayed out in desolate areas; and [b]they were coming to
Him from everywhere.

### *Jesus Heals a Paralytic*

2 And when He had come back to
Capernaum several days afterward, it was heard that He was at
home. 2 And [a]many were gathered
together, so that there was no longer
room, not even near the door; and
He was speaking the word to them.
3 [a]And they *came, bringing to Him a
[b]paralytic, carried by four men. 4 And
being unable to bring *him* to [1]Jesus
because of the crowd, they [a]removed
the roof *over* where He was; and
when they had dug an opening, they
let down the mat where the [b]paralytic was lying. 5 And Jesus seeing their
faith *said to the paralytic, "Child,
[a]your sins are forgiven." 6 But some
of the scribes were sitting there and
reasoning in their hearts, 7 "Why
does this man speak that way? He
is blaspheming; [a]who can forgive
sins [1]but God alone?" 8 Immediately
Jesus, aware [1]in His spirit that they
were reasoning that way within
themselves, *said to them, "Why are
you reasoning about these things in
your hearts? 9 Which is easier, to
say to the [a]paralytic, 'Your sins are
forgiven'; or to say, 'Get up, and pick
up your mat and walk'? 10 But so that
you may know that the Son of Man
has authority on earth to forgive
sins"—He *said to the paralytic, 11 "I
say to you, get up, pick up your mat,
and go to your home." 12 And he got
up and immediately picked up the
mat and went out before everyone,
so that they were all amazed and
[a]were glorifying God, saying, "[b]We
have never seen anything like this."
13 And He went out again by the
seashore; and [a]the entire crowd was
coming to Him, and He was teaching
them.

### *Levi and Sinners Called*

14 [a]And as He passed by, He saw
[b,1]Levi the *son* of Alphaeus sitting in
the tax office, and He *said to him,
"[c]Follow Me!" And he stood up and
followed Him.
15 And it *[1]happened that as He
was reclining *at the table* in his
house, many tax collectors and
[2]sinners [3]were reclining with Jesus
and His disciples. For there were
many of them, and they were following Him. 16 And when [a]the scribes of
the Pharisees saw that He was eating
with the sinners and tax collectors,
they were saying to His disciples,
"[b]He is eating and drinking with
tax collectors and [1]sinners!" 17 And

**1:44** [a]Mt 8:4 [b]Lv 14:1-32 **1:45** [a]Mt 28:15; Lk 5:15 [b]Mk 2:2, 13; 3:7; Lk 5:17; Jn 6:2 [1]Lit *He* [2]Lit *was*
◆ **2:2** [a]Mk 1:45; 2:13 **2:3** [a]Mk 2:3-12: *Mt 9:2-8; Lk 5:18-26* [b]Mt 4:24 **2:4** [a]Lk 5:19 [b]Mt 4:24 [1]Lit *Him*
**2:5** [a]Mt 9:2 **2:7** [a]Is 43:25 [1]Lit *if not one, God* **2:8** [1]Lit *by* **2:9** [a]Mt 4:24 **2:12** [a]Mt 9:8 [b]Mt 9:33
**2:13** [a]Mk 1:45 **2:14** [a]Mk 2:14-17: *Mt 9:9-13; Lk 5:27-32* [b]Mt 9:9 [c]Mt 8:22 [1]Also called Matthew
**2:15** [1]Lit *happens* [2]Irreligious Jews [3]Or *dining* **2:16** [a]Lk 5:30; Ac 23:9 [b]Mt 9:11 [1]Irreligious Jews

hearing *this*, Jesus *said to them,
"[a]Those who are healthy do not have
need for a physician, but *only* those
who are sick; I did not come to call
the righteous, but sinners."

18 [a]And John's disciples and the
Pharisees were fasting; and they
*came and *said to Him, "Why do
John's disciples and the disciples
of the Pharisees fast, but Your
disciples do not fast?" 19 And Jesus
said to them, "Can [1]the attendants
of the bridegroom fast when the
bridegroom is with them? So long as
they have the bridegroom with them,
they cannot fast. 20 But the [a]days will
come when the bridegroom is taken
away from them, and then they will
fast in that day.

21 "No one sews [1]a piece of un-
shrunk cloth on an old garment;
otherwise [2]that patch pulls away
from it, the new from the old, and
a worse tear results. 22 And no one
puts new wine into old wineskins;
otherwise the wine will burst the
skins, and the wine is lost and the
skins *as well*; but *one puts* new wine
into fresh wineskins."

### *Lord of the Sabbath*

23 [a]And it happened that He was
passing through the grainfields on the
Sabbath, and His disciples began to
make their way along while [b]picking
the heads *of grain*. 24 And the Phari-
sees were saying to Him, "Look, [a]why
are they doing what is not lawful on
the Sabbath?" 25 And He *said to them,
"Have you never read what David did
when he was in need and he and his
companions became hungry; 26 how
he entered the house of God around
the time of [a]Abiathar the high priest,
and ate the [1]consecrated bread, which
[b]is not lawful for *anyone* to eat except
the priests, and he also gave it to those
who were with him?" 27 And Jesus was
saying to them, "[a]The Sabbath [1]was
made [2]for man, and [b]not man [2]for the
Sabbath. 28 Consequently the Son of
Man is Lord even of the Sabbath."

### *Jesus Heals a Man on the Sabbath*

3 [a]And He [b]entered again into a
synagogue; and a man was there
with a withered hand. 2 [a]And they
were watching Him *to see* if He
would heal him on the Sabbath,
[b]so that they might accuse Him.
3 And He *said to the man with the
withered hand, "[1]Get up and come
forward!" 4 And He *said to them,
"Is it lawful to do good or to do harm
on the Sabbath, to save a life or to
kill?" But they kept silent. 5 And after
[a]looking around at them with anger,
grieved at their hardness of heart,
He *said to the man, "Stretch out
your hand." And he stretched it out,
and his hand was restored. 6 And the
Pharisees went out and immediately
*began* taking counsel together with
the [a]Herodians against Him, *as* to
how they might destroy Him.

7 [a]And Jesus withdrew to the
sea with His disciples; and [b]a great
multitude from Galilee followed; and

---

**2:17** [a]Mt 9:12, 13; Lk 5:31, 32 **2:18** [a]Mk 2:18-22: *Mt 9:14-17; Lk 5:33-38* **2:19** [1]Lit *sons of the bridal chamber* **2:20** [a]Mt 9:15; Lk 17:22 **2:21** [1]Lit *that which is put on* [2]Lit *that which fills up* **2:23** [a]Mk 2:23-28: *Mt 12:1-8; Lk 6:1-5* [b]Dt 23:25 **2:24** [a]Mt 12:2 **2:26** [a]1Sa 21:1; 2Sa 8:17; 1Chr 24:6 [b]Lv 24:9 [1]Or *showbread*; lit *loaves of presentation* **2:27** [a]Ex 23:12; Dt 5:14 [b]Col 2:16 [1]Or *came into being* [2]Lit *for the sake of* ◆ **3:1** [a]Mk 3:1-6: *Mt 12:9-14; Lk 6:6-11* [b]Mk 1:21, 39 **3:2** [a]Lk 6:7; 14:1; 20:20 [b]Mt 12:10; Lk 6:7; 11:54 **3:3** [1]Lit *Arise into the midst* **3:5** [a]Lk 6:10 **3:6** [a]Mt 22:16; Mk 12:13 **3:7** [a]Mk 3:7-12: *Mt 12:15, 16; Lk 6:17-19* [b]Mt 4:25; Lk 6:17

from Judea, **8** and from Jerusalem,
and from [a]Idumea, and beyond the
Jordan, and the vicinity of [b]Tyre and
Sidon, a great number of people
heard of all that He was doing and
came to Him. **9** [a]And He told His
disciples that a boat should stand
ready for Him because of the crowd,
so that they would not crowd Him;
**10** for He had [a]healed many, with the
result that all those who had [b]afflic-
tions pressed around Him in order
to [c]touch Him. **11** And whenever the
unclean spirits were seeing Him, they
would fall down before Him and cry
out, saying, "You are [a]the Son of
God!" **12** And He [a]earnestly warned
them not to [1]tell who He was.

### *Jesus Appoints the Twelve*

**13** And He *went up on [a]the moun-
tain and *[b]summoned those whom
He Himself wanted, and they came
to Him. **14** And He appointed twelve
[1](whom He also named apostles) to
be with Him and to send them out
to preach, **15** and to have authority
to cast out the demons. **16** And He
appointed the twelve: [a]Simon (to
whom He gave the name Peter),
**17** and James, the *son* of Zebedee,
and John the brother of James (to
them He gave the name Boanerges,
which means, "Sons of Thunder");
**18** and Andrew, and Philip, and
Bartholomew, and Matthew, and
Thomas, and James the son of Al-
phaeus, and Thaddaeus, and Simon
the [1]Zealot; **19** and Judas Iscariot,
who also betrayed Him.

**20** And He *came [a,1]home, and the
[b]crowd *gathered again, [c]so that they
could not even eat [2]a meal. **21** And
when [a]His own [1]people heard *this,*
they went out to take custody of Him;
for they were saying, "[b]He has lost
His senses." **22** And the scribes who
came down [a]from Jerusalem were
saying, "He is possessed by [b,1]Beelze-
bul," and "[c]He casts out the demons
by the ruler of the demons." **23** [a]And
He called them to Himself and *began*
speaking to them in [b]parables, "How
can [c]Satan cast out Satan? **24** And if
a kingdom is divided against itself,
that kingdom cannot stand. **25** And
if a house is divided against itself,
that house will not be able to stand.
**26** And if [a]Satan has risen up against
himself and is divided, he cannot
stand, but [1]he is finished! **27** [a]But no
one can enter the strong man's house
and plunder his property unless he
first binds the strong man, and then
he will plunder his house.

**28** "[a]Truly I say to you, all sins
shall be forgiven the sons of men,
and whatever blasphemies they
utter; **29** but [a]whoever blasphemes
against the Holy Spirit never has
forgiveness, but is guilty of an eternal
sin"— **30** because they were saying,
"He has an unclean spirit."

**31** [a]Then His mother and His
brothers *arrived, and standing
outside they sent *word* to Him,

**3:8** [a]*Jos 15:1, 21; Eze 35:15; 36:5* [b]Mt 11:21 **3:9** [a]Mk 4:1; Lk 5:1-3 **3:10** [a]Mt 4:23 [b]Mk 5:29, 34; Lk 7:21 [c]Mt 9:21; 14:36; Mk 6:56; 8:22 **3:11** [a]Mt 4:3 **3:12** [a]Mt 8:4 [1]Lit *make Him known* **3:13** [a]Mt 5:1; Lk 6:12 [b]Mt 10:1; Mk 6:7; Lk 9:1 **3:14** [1]Some mss omit this phrase **3:16** [a]Mk 3:16-19: *Mt 10:2-4; Lk 6:14-16;* Ac 1:13 **3:18** [1]Or *Cananaean* **3:20** [a]Mk 2:1; 7:17; 9:28 [b]Mk 1:45; 3:7 [c]Mk 6:31 [1]Lit *into a house* [2]Lit *bread* **3:21** [a]Mk 3:31f [b]Jn 10:20; Ac 26:24 [1]Or *kinsmen* **3:22** [a]Mt 15:1 [b]Mt 10:25; 11:18 [c]Mt 9:34 [1]Or *Beezebul*; some mss *Beelzebub* **3:23** [a]Mk 3:23-27: *Mt 12:25-29; Lk 11:17-22* [b]Mt 13:3ff; Mk 4:2ff [c]Mt 4:10 **3:26** [a]Mt 4:10 [1]Lit *he has an end* **3:27** [a]Is 49:24, 25 **3:28** [a]Mk 3:28-30: *Mt 12:31, 32; Lk 12:10* **3:29** [a]Lk 12:10 **3:31** [a]Mk 3:31-35: *Mt 12:46-50; Lk 8:19-21*

calling Him. 32 And a crowd was sitting around Him, and they *said to Him, "Behold, Your mother and Your brothers are outside looking for You." 33 And answering them, He *said, "Who are My mother and My brothers?" 34 And looking about at those who were sitting around Him, He *said, "[a]Behold My mother and My brothers! 35 For whoever [a]does the will of God, he is My brother and sister and mother."

### *The Parable of the Sower*

4 [a]And He began to teach again [b]by the sea. And such a very large crowd gathered to Him that [c]He got into a boat in the sea and sat down; and the whole crowd was by the sea on the land. 2 And He was teaching them many things in [a]parables, and was saying to them in His teaching, 3 "Listen *to this*! Behold, the sower went out to sow; 4 and it happened that as he was sowing, some *seed* fell beside the road, and the birds came and ate it up. 5 And other *seed* fell on the rocky *ground* where it did not have much soil; and immediately it sprang up because it had no depth of soil. 6 And after the sun rose, it was scorched; and because it had no root, it withered away. 7 And other *seed* fell among the thorns, and the thorns came up and choked it, and it yielded no [1]crop. 8 And other *seeds* fell into the good soil, and as they grew up and increased, they were yielding a [1]crop and produced thirty, sixty, and a hundredfold." 9 And He was saying, "[a]He who has ears to hear, [1]let him hear."

10 And when He was alone, [1]His followers, along with the twelve, *began* asking Him *about* the parables. 11 And He was saying to them, "To you has been given the mystery of the kingdom of God, but to [a]those who are outside, everything comes [b]in parables, 12 so that [a]WHILE SEEING, THEY MAY SEE AND NOT PERCEIVE, AND WHILE HEARING, THEY MAY HEAR AND NOT UNDERSTAND, LEST THEY RETURN AND BE FORGIVEN."

### *The Parable of the Sower Explained*

13 [a]And He *said to them, "Do you not understand this parable? How will you understand all the parables? 14 The sower sows the word. 15 And these are the ones who are beside the road where the word is sown: when they hear, immediately [a]Satan comes and takes away the word which has been sown in them. 16 And in a similar way, these are the ones being sown on the rocky *places*: those who, when hearing the word, immediately receive it with joy; 17 and they have no root in themselves, but are *only* temporary; then, when affliction or persecution arises because of the word, immediately they [1]fall away. 18 And others are those being sown among the thorns; these are the ones who have heard the word, 19 but the worries of [a]the [1]world, and the [b]deceitfulness of riches, and the desires for anything else enter in and choke the word, and it becomes

**3:34** [a]Mt 12:49 **3:35** [a]Eph 6:6; Heb 10:36; 1Pe 4:2; 1Jn 2:17 ◆ **4:1** [a]Mk 4:1-12: *Mt 13:1-15; Lk 8:4-10* [b]Mk 2:13; 3:7 [c]Lk 5:1-3 **4:2** [a]Mt 13:3ff; Mk 3:23; 4:2ff **4:7** [1]Lit *fruit* **4:8** [1]Lit *fruit* **4:9** [a]Mt 11:15; Mk 4:23; Rev 2:7, 11, 17, 29 [1]Or *hear!, listen!*; Gr imperative **4:10** [1]Lit *those about Him* **4:11** [a]1Co 5:12f; Col 4:5; 1Th 4:12; 1Ti 3:7 [b]Mk 3:23; 4:2 **4:12** [a]Is 6:9f; 43:8; Jer 5:21; Eze 12:2; Mt 13:14; Lk 8:10; Jn 12:40; Ro 11:8 **4:13** [a]Mk 4:13-20: *Mt 13:18-23; Lk 8:11-15* **4:15** [a]Mt 4:10f; 1Pe 5:8; Rev 20:2, 3, 7-10 **4:17** [1]Lit *are caused to stumble* **4:19** [a]Mt 13:22; Ro 12:2; Eph 2:2; 6:12 [b]Pr 23:4; 1Ti 6:9, 10, 17 [1]Or *age*

unfruitful. **20** And those are the ones
which were sown on the good soil:
they who hear the word and accept
it and [a]are bearing fruit, thirty, sixty,
and a hundredfold."

**21** And He was saying to them,
"[a]Is a lamp brought to be put under
a [1]basket or under a bed? Is it not
to be put on the lampstand? **22** [a]For
nothing is hidden, except to be
revealed; nor has *anything* been
secret, but that it would come to
light. **23** [a]If anyone has ears to hear,
let him hear." **24** And He was saying
to them, "Beware what you listen
to. [a,1]By your standard of measure it
will be measured to you, and more
will be given to you. **25** [a]For whoever
has, to him *more* shall be given; and
whoever does not have, even what he
has shall be taken away from him."

### *The Parable of the Seed*

**26** And He was saying, "The kingdom
of God is like a man who casts seed
upon the soil; **27** and he sleeps and
rises, night and day, and the seed
sprouts and grows—how, he himself
does not know. **28** The soil produces
crops by itself; first the blade, then
the head, then the mature grain in the
head. **29** But when the grain [1]is ripe,
he immediately [a,2]puts in the sickle,
because the harvest has come."

### *The Parable of the Mustard Seed*

**30** [a]And He was saying, "How shall
we [b]compare the kingdom of God,
or by what parable shall we present
it? **31** *It is* like a mustard seed, which,
when sown upon the soil, though it
is [1]smallest of all the seeds that are
upon the soil, **32** yet when it is sown,
it grows up and becomes [1]largest of
all the garden plants and forms large
branches; so that [a]THE BIRDS OF THE
[2]AIR CAN NEST UNDER ITS SHADE."

**33** And with many such parables
He was speaking the word to them,
as they were able to hear *it*; **34** and He
was not speaking to them [a]without
a parable; but He was [b]explaining
everything privately to His own
disciples.

### *Jesus Calms a Storm*

**35** [a]And on that day, when evening
came, He *said to them, "Let us go
over to the other side." **36** [1]And leav-
ing the crowd, they *took Him along
with them [a]in the boat, just as He
was; and other boats were with Him.
**37** And a great windstorm *arose, and
the waves were breaking into the boat
so that the boat was already filling
up. **38** And Jesus Himself was in the
stern, sleeping on the cushion; and
they *got Him up and *said to Him,
"Teacher, do You not care that we are
perishing?" **39** And He woke up and
[a]rebuked the wind and said to the
sea, "Silence! Be still." And the wind
died down and [1]it became [2]perfectly
calm. **40** And He said to them, "Why
are you *so* cowardly? [a]Do you still
have no faith?" **41** And they became

---

**4:20** [a]Jn 15:2ff; Ro 7:4 **4:21** [a]Mt 5:15; Lk 8:16; 11:33 [1]Or *peck-measure* **4:22** [a]Mt 10:26; Lk 8:17; 12:2 **4:23** [a]Mt 11:15; 13:9, 43; Mk 4:9; Lk 8:8; 14:35; Rev 3:6, 13, 22; 13:9 **4:24** [a]Mt 7:2; Lk 6:38 [1]Lit *By what measure you measure* **4:25** [a]Mt 13:12; 25:29; Lk 8:18; 19:26 **4:29** [a]Joel 3:13 [1]Lit *permits* [2]Lit *sends forth* **4:30** [a]Mk 4:30-32: *Mt 13:31, 32; Lk 13:18, 19* [b]Mt 13:24 **4:31** [1]Lit *smaller* **4:32** [a]Eze 17:23; Ps 104:12; Eze 31:6; Da 4:12 [1]Lit *larger* [2]Or *sky* **4:34** [a]Mt 13:34; Jn 10:6; 16:25 [b]Lk 24:27 **4:35** [a]Mk 4:35-41: *Mt 8:18, 23-27; Lk 8:22, 25* **4:36** [a]Mk 3:9; 4:1; 5:2, 21 [1]Or *Sending away* **4:39** [a]Ps 65:7; 89:9; 107:29; Mt 8:26; Lk 8:24 [1]Lit *a great calm occurred* [2]Or *greatly*, cf. 4:37 **4:40** [a]Mt 14:31; Lk 8:25

[1]very afraid and were saying to one
another, “Who then is this, that even
the wind and the sea obey Him?”

### *Jesus Saves a Man with Many Demons*

**5** [a]Then they came to the other
side of the sea, into the region
of the Gerasenes. **2** And when He
got out of [a]the boat, immediately a
man from the tombs [b]with an un-
clean spirit met Him, **3** who had his
dwelling among the tombs. And no
one was able to bind him anymore,
even with a chain; **4** because he had
often been bound with shackles and
chains, and the chains had been
torn apart by him and the shackles
broken in pieces, and no one was
strong enough to subdue him. **5** And
constantly, night and day, among the
tombs and in the mountains, he was
crying out and gashing himself with
stones. **6** And seeing Jesus from a
distance, he ran up and bowed down
before Him; **7** and crying out with a
loud voice, he *said, “[a,1]What do I
have to do with You, Jesus, [b]Son of
[c]the Most High God? I implore You
by God, do not torment me!” **8** For He
had been saying to him, “Come out of
the man, you unclean spirit!” **9** And
He was asking him, “What is your
name?” And he *said to Him, “My
name is [a]Legion; for we are many.”
**10** And he *began* pleading with Him
earnestly not to send them out of
the region. **11** Now there was a large
herd of swine feeding [1]nearby on the
mountain. **12** *And the demons* pleaded
with Him, saying, “Send us into the
swine so that we may enter them.”
**13** And Jesus gave them permission.
And coming out, the unclean spirits
entered the swine; and the herd
rushed down the steep bank into the
sea, about two thousand *of them*; and
they were drowned in the sea.
**14** And their herdsmen ran away
and reported it in the city and in the
countryside. And *the people* came to
see what it was that had happened.
**15** And they *came to Jesus and *ob-
served the [a]demon-possessed man
sitting down, [b]clothed and [c]in his
right mind, the very man who had the
“[d]legion”; and they became fright-
ened. **16** And those who had seen
it recounted to them how *this* had
happened to the [a]demon-possessed
man, and *all* about the swine. **17** And
they began to [a]plead with Him to
leave their region. **18** [a]And as He
was getting into the boat, the man
who had been [b]demon-possessed
was pleading with Him that he might
[1]accompany Him. **19** And He did not
let him, but He *said to him, “[a]Go
home to your people and report to
them [1]what great things the Lord has
done for you, and *how* He had mercy
on you.” **20** And he went away and
began to [a]preach in the [b]Decapolis
[1]what great things Jesus had done for
him; and everyone was marveling.

### *Jesus Heals a Woman and Jairus’ Daughter*

**21** [a]And when Jesus had crossed over
again in [b]the boat to the other side,

**4:41** [1]Or *greatly*, cf. 4:37 ◆ **5:1** [a]Mk 5:1-17: *Mt 8:28-34; Lk 8:26-37* **5:2** [a]Mk 3:9; 4:1, 36; 5:21 [b]Mk 1:23 **5:7** [a]Mt 8:29 [b]Mt 4:3 [c]Lk 8:28; Ac 16:17; Heb 7:1 [1]Lit *What to me and to you* (a Heb idiom) **5:9** [a]Mt 26:53; Mk 5:15; Lk 8:30 **5:11** [1]Lit *there* **5:15** [a]Mt 4:24; Mk 5:16, 18 [b]Lk 8:27 [c]Lk 8:35 [d]Mk 5:9 **5:16** [a]Mt 4:24; Mk 5:15 **5:17** [a]Mt 8:34; Ac 16:39 **5:18** [a]Mk 5:18-20: *Lk 8:38, 39* [b]Mt 4:24; Mk 5:15, 16 [1]Lit *be with Him* **5:19** [a]Lk 8:39 [1]Or *everything that* **5:20** [a]Ps 66:16 [b]Mt 4:25; Mk 7:31 [1]Or *everything that* **5:21** [a]Mt 9:1; Lk 8:40 [b]Mk 4:36

a large crowd gathered around Him;
and so He [1]stayed [c]by the seashore.
22 [a]And one of [b]the synagogue [1]offi-
cials named Jairus *came up, and on
seeing Him, *fell at His feet 23 and
*pleaded with Him earnestly, saying,
"My little daughter is at the point of
death; *please come,* that by coming,
[a]You may lay Your hands on her,
so that she will [1]be saved and live."
24 And He went off with him; and a
large crowd was following Him and
pressing in on Him.

25 And a woman—who had a hem-
orrhage for twelve years 26 and had
endured much at the hands of many
physicians, and had spent all that she
had and was not helped at all, but
rather had grown worse— 27 after
hearing about Jesus, she came up in
the crowd behind *Him* and touched
His garment. 28 For she was saying,
"If I just touch His garments, I will
[1]be saved *from this.*" 29 And imme-
diately the flow of her blood was
dried up; and she knew within her
body that she had been healed of
her [a]affliction. 30 And immediately
Jesus, perceiving in Himself that
[a]the power *proceeding* from Him
had gone forth, turned around in
the crowd and was saying, "Who
touched My garments?" 31 And His
disciples were saying to Him, "You
see the crowd pressing in on You, and
You say, 'Who touched Me?'" 32 And
He was looking around to see the
woman who had done this. 33 But
the woman fearing and trembling,
aware of what had happened to her,
came and fell down before Him and
told Him the whole truth. 34 And He
said to her, "Daughter, [a]your faith
has [1]saved you; [b]go in peace and be
healed of your [c]affliction."

35 While He was still speaking,
they *came from the *house of* the
[a]synagogue official, saying, "Your
daughter has died; why trouble the
Teacher anymore?" 36 But Jesus,
overhearing what had been spoken,
*said to the [a]synagogue official, "[b]Do
not be afraid, only [1]believe." 37 And
He allowed no one to accompany
Him, except [a]Peter and James and
John the brother of James. 38 And
they *came to the house of the
[a]synagogue official; and He *saw
a commotion, and *people* loudly
crying and wailing. 39 And entering
in, He *said to them, "Why are you
making a commotion and crying?
The child has not died, but is asleep."
40 And they *began* laughing at Him.
But putting them all out, He *took
along the child's father and mother
and His own companions, and
*entered *the room* where the child
was. 41 And taking the child by the
hand, He *said to her, "Talitha kum!"
(which translated means, "Little girl,
[a]I say to you, arise!"). 42 And imme-
diately the little girl stood up and
*began to* walk, for she was twelve
years old. And immediately they
were completely astounded. 43 And
He [a]gave them strict orders that no
one should know about this, and He
said that *some food* should be given
to her to eat.

---

**5:21** [c]Mk 4:1 [1]Lit *was* **5:22** [a]Mk 5:22-43: *Mt 9:18-26; Lk 8:41-56* [b]Mt 9:18; Mk 5:35, 36, 38; Lk 8:49; 13:14; Ac 13:15; 18:8, 17 [1]Or *rulers* **5:23** [a]Mk 6:5; 7:32; 8:23; 16:18; Lk 4:40; 13:13; Ac 6:6; 9:17; 28:8 [1]Or *get well* **5:28** [1]Or *get well* **5:29** [a]Mk 3:10; 5:34 **5:30** [a]Lk 5:17 **5:34** [a]Mt 9:22 [b]Lk 7:50; 8:48; Ac 16:36; Jas 2:16 [c]Mk 3:10; 5:29 [1]Or *made you well* **5:35** [a]Mk 5:22 **5:36** [a]Mk 5:22 [b]Lk 8:50 [1]Or *keep on believing* **5:37** [a]Mt 17:1; 26:37 **5:38** [a]Mk 5:22 **5:41** [a]Lk 7:14; Ac 9:40 **5:43** [a]Mt 8:4

### *Jesus Rejected at Nazareth*

6 [a]And Jesus went out from there
and *came into [b,1]His hometown;
and His disciples *followed Him.
2 And when the Sabbath came, He
began [a]to teach in the synagogue;
and [b]many listeners were astonished,
saying, "Where did this man *get* these
things, and what is *this* wisdom given
to this man, and such [1]miracles as
these performed by His hands? 3 Is
this man not [a]the carpenter, [b]the
son of Mary, and brother of James
and Joses and Judas and Simon? Are
not [c]His sisters here with us?" And
they were taking [d]offense at Him.
4 And Jesus was saying to them, "[a]A
prophet is not without honor except
in [b,1]his hometown and among his
*own* relatives and in his *own* house-
hold." 5 And He could do no [1]miracle
there except that He [a]laid His hands
on a few sick people and healed
them. 6 And He was marveling at
their unbelief.

[a]And He was going around the
villages teaching.

### *The Twelve Sent Out*

7 [a]And [b]He *summoned the twelve
and began to send them out [c]in
pairs, and was giving them authority
over the unclean spirits; 8 [a]and He
instructed them that they should
take nothing for *their* journey, except
a staff only—no bread, no [1]bag, no
money in their belt— 9 but [1]*to* wear
sandals; and *He added*, "Do not
put on two [2]tunics." 10 And He was
saying to them, "Wherever you enter
a house, stay there until you [1]leave
town. 11 And any place that does
not receive you or listen to you, as
you go out from there, [a]shake the
dust [1]off the soles of your feet for
a testimony against them." 12 [a]And
they went out and [1]preached that
*men* should repent. 13 And they were
casting out many demons and [a]were
anointing with oil many sick people
and healing them.

### *The Death of John the Baptist*

14 [a]And King Herod heard *it*, for His
name had become well known; and
*people* were saying, "[b]John the Bap-
tist has risen from the dead, and that
is why these miraculous powers are
at work in Him." 15 But others were
saying, "He is [a]Elijah." And others
were saying, "*He is* [b]a prophet, like
one of the prophets *of old*." 16 But
when Herod heard *it*, he kept saying,
"John, whom I beheaded, has risen!"

17 For Herod himself had sent
and had John arrested and bound in
prison on account of [a]Herodias, the
wife of his brother Philip, because
he had married her. 18 For John had
been saying to Herod, "[a]It is not
lawful for you to have your brother's
wife." 19 [a]Now Herodias was holding
a grudge against him and was want-
ing to put him to death and was not

---

◆ **6:1** [a]Mk 6:1-6: *Mt 13:54-58* [b]Mt 13:54, 57; Lk 4:16, 23 [1]Or *His own part of the country*
**6:2** [a]Mt 4:23; Mk 10:1 [b]Mt 7:28 [1]Or *works of power* **6:3** [a]Mt 13:55 [b]Mt 12:46 [c]Mt 13:56 [d]Mt 11:6
**6:4** [a]Mt 13:57; Jn 4:44 [b]Mk 6:1 [1]Or *his own part of the country* **6:5** [a]Mk 5:23 [1]Or *work of power*
**6:6** [a]Mt 9:35; Mk 1:39; 10:1; Lk 13:22 **6:7** [a]Mk 6:7-11: *Mt 10:1, 9-14; Lk 9:1, 3-5;* Lk 10:4-11 [b]Mt 10:1, 5; Mk 3:13; Lk 9:1 [c]Lk 10:1 **6:8** [a]Mt 10:10 [1]Or *knapsack, beggar's bag* **6:9** [1]Lit *being shod with*
[2]Or *inner garments* **6:10** [1]Lit *go out from there* **6:11** [a]Mt 10:14; Ac 13:51 [1]Lit *under your feet*
**6:12** [a]Mt 11:1; Lk 9:6 [1]Or *proclaimed as a herald* **6:13** [a]Jas 5:14 **6:14** [a]Mk 6:14-29: *Mt 14:1-12;* Mk 6:14-16: *Lk 9:7-9* [b]Mt 14:2; Lk 9:19 **6:15** [a]Mt 16:14; Mk 8:28 [b]Mt 21:11 **6:17** [a]Mt 14:3; Lk 3:19
**6:18** [a]Mt 14:4 **6:19** [a]Mt 14:3

able; **20** for [a]Herod was afraid of John,
knowing that he was a righteous and
holy man, and he was keeping him
safe. And when he heard him, he
was very perplexed; [1]but he [2]used
to enjoy listening to him. **21** And a
strategic day came when Herod on
his birthday [a]gave a banquet for
his great men and [1]military com-
manders and the leading men [b]of
Galilee; **22** and when the daughter
of [a]Herodias herself came in and
danced, she pleased Herod and [1]his
dinner guests; and the king said to
the girl, "Ask me for whatever you
want and I will give it to you." **23** And
he swore to her, "Whatever you ask
of me, I will give it to you; up to [a]half
of my kingdom." **24** And she went out
and said to her mother, "What shall I
ask for?" And she said, "The head of
John the Baptist." **25** And immediate-
ly she came in a hurry to the king and
asked, saying, "I want you to give me
at once the head of John the Baptist
on a platter." **26** And although the
king was very sorry, *yet* because of
his oaths and because of [1]his dinner
guests, he did not want to refuse her.
**27** And immediately the king sent an
executioner and commanded *him*
to bring *back* his head. And he went
and beheaded him in the prison,
**28** and brought his head on a platter,
and gave it to the girl; and the girl
gave it to her mother. **29** And when
his disciples heard *this*, they came
and took away his body and laid it
in a tomb.

**30** [a]And the [b]apostles *gathered
together with Jesus; and they
reported to Him all that they had
done and taught. **31** And He *said to
them, "Come away by yourselves to a
desolate place and rest a while." (For
there were many *people* coming and
going, and [a]they did not even have
time to eat.) **32** [a]And they went away
in [b]the boat to a desolate place by
themselves.

### *Jesus Feeds Five Thousand*

**33** And *the people* saw them going,
and many recognized *them* and ran
there together on foot from all the
cities, and got there ahead of them.
**34** And when Jesus went [1]ashore, He
[a]saw a large crowd, and He felt com-
passion for them because [b]they were
like sheep without a shepherd; and
He began to teach them many things.
**35** And when it was already quite late,
His disciples came to Him and *began*
saying, "[1]This place is desolate and
it is already quite late; **36** send them
away so that they may go into the
surrounding countryside and villages
and buy themselves [1]something to
eat." **37** But He answered and said
to them, "You give them *something*
to eat!" [a]And they *said to Him,
"Shall we go and spend two hun-
dred [b,1]denarii on bread and give
them *something* to eat?" **38** And He
*said to them, "How many loaves do
you have? Go look!" And when they
found out, they *said, "Five, and two
fish." **39** And He commanded them

---

**6:20** [a]Mt 21:26 [1]Lit *and* [2]Lit *was hearing him gladly* **6:21** [a]Es 1:3; 2:18 [b]Lk 3:1 [1]Military leader over 1,000 soldiers **6:22** [a]Mt 14:3 [1]Lit *those who reclined at the table with him* **6:23** [a]Es 5:3, 6; 7:2 **6:26** [1]Lit *those reclining at the table* **6:30** [a]Lk 9:10 [b]Mt 10:2; Mk 3:14; Lk 6:13; 9:10; 17:5; 22:14; 24:10; Ac 1:2, 26 **6:31** [a]Mk 3:20 **6:32** [a]Mk 6:32-44: *Mt 14:13-21; Lk 9:10-17; Jn 6:5-13;* Mk 8:2-9 [b]Mk 3:9; 4:36; 6:45 **6:34** [a]Mt 9:36 [b]Nu 27:17; 1Ki 22:17; 2Chr 18:16; Zec 10:2 [1]Lit *out* **6:35** [1]Lit *The* **6:36** [1]Lit *what they may eat* **6:37** [a]Jn 6:7 [b]Mt 18:28; Lk 7:41 [1]A Roman silver coin, approx. a laborer's daily wage

all to [1]sit down by [2]groups on the
green grass. **40** And they [1]sat down
in groups of hundreds and of fifties.
**41** And He took the five loaves and
the two fish, and looking up toward
heaven, He [a]blessed *the food* and
broke the loaves. And He kept giving
*them* to the disciples to set before
them, and He divided up the two fish
among them all. **42** And they all ate
and were satisfied, **43** and they picked
up twelve full [a]baskets of the broken
pieces, and also of the fish. **44** And
there were [a]five thousand men who
ate the loaves.

### *Jesus Walks on the Sea*

**45** [a]And immediately Jesus made His
disciples get into [b]the boat and go
ahead of *Him* to the other side to
[c]Bethsaida, while He Himself was
sending the crowd away. **46** And after
[a]bidding them farewell, He left [b]for
the mountain to pray.

**47** And when it was evening, the
boat was in the middle of the sea,
and He was alone on the land. **48** And
seeing them [1]straining at the oars, for
the wind was against them, at about
the [a,2]fourth watch of the night He
*came to them, walking on the sea;
and He was intending to pass by
them. **49** But when they saw Him
walking on the sea, they thought that
it was a ghost, and cried out; **50** for
they all saw Him and were [1]terrified.
But immediately He spoke with them
and *said to them, "[a]Take courage;
it is I, [b]do not be afraid." **51** Then He
got into [a]the boat with them, and the
wind stopped; and they were [1]utterly
amazed, **52** for [a]they [1]had not gained
any insight about the loaves, but their
[2]heart [b]was hardened.

### *Many Healed at Gennesaret*

**53** [a]And when they had crossed over
they came to land at Gennesaret, and
moored to the shore. **54** And when
they got out of the boat, immediately
*the people* recognized Him, **55** and ran
about that whole region and began to
carry here and there on their mats
those who were sick, to [1]the place
they heard He was. **56** And wherever
He was entering villages, or cities,
or countryside, they were laying the
sick in the marketplaces, and plead-
ing with Him that they might just
[a]touch [b]the fringe of His garment;
and as many as touched it were being
[1]saved *from their sicknesses.*

### *God's Commandments, Man's Traditions*

**7** [a]And the Pharisees and some
of the scribes *gathered around
Him when they had come [b]from
Jerusalem, **2** and had seen that some
of His disciples were eating their
bread with [a]defiled hands, that is,
unwashed. **3** (For the Pharisees and
all the Jews do not eat unless they
[1]carefully wash their hands, *thus*
observing the [a]tradition of the el-
ders; **4** and *when they come* from the

**6:39** [1]Lit *recline* [2]Lit *dining-groups* **6:40** [1]Lit *reclined* **6:41** [a]Mt 14:19 **6:43** [a]Mt 14:20
**6:44** [a]Mt 14:21 **6:45** [a]Mk 6:45-51: *Mt 14:22-32; Jn 6:15-21* [b]Mk 6:32 [c]Mt 11:21; Mk 8:22
**6:46** [a]Ac 18:18, 21; 2Co 2:13 [b]Mt 14:23 **6:48** [a]Mt 24:43; Mk 13:35 [1]Lit *harassed in rowing*
[2]3-6 a.m. **6:50** [a]Mt 9:2 [b]Mt 14:27 [1]Or *troubled* **6:51** [a]Mk 6:32 [1]Lit *utterly amazed in themselves*
**6:52** [a]Mk 8:17ff [b]Ro 11:7 [1]Lit *had not understood on the basis of* [2]Or *mind* **6:53** [a]Mk 6:53-56:
*Mt 14:34-36;* Jn 6:24, 25 **6:55** [1]Lit *where they were hearing that He was* **6:56** [a]Mk 3:10 [b]Mt 9:20;
Nu 15:37-40 [1]Or *cured* ◆ **7:1** [a]Mk 7:1-23: *Mt 15:1-20* [b]Mt 15:1 **7:2** [a]Mt 15:2; Mk 7:5; Lk 11:38; Ac 10:14,
28; 11:8; Ro 14:14; Heb 10:29; Rev 21:27 **7:3** [a]Mk 7:5, 8, 9, 13; Ga 1:14 [1]Lit *with the fist*

marketplace, they do not eat unless
they [1]wash themselves; and there are
many other things which they have
received in order to observe, such as
the washing of [a]cups and pitchers
and copper pots.) **5** And the Pharisees
and the scribes *asked Him, "Why do
Your disciples not walk according to
the [a]tradition of the elders, but eat
their bread with [b]defiled hands?"
**6** And He said to them, "Rightly did
Isaiah prophesy of you hypocrites,
as it is written:

'[a]THIS PEOPLE HONORS ME
WITH THEIR LIPS,
BUT THEIR HEART IS FAR
AWAY FROM ME.
**7** '[a]BUT IN VAIN DO THEY
WORSHIP ME,
TEACHING AS DOCTRINES THE
COMMANDS OF MEN.'

**8** "Leaving the commandment of
God, you hold to the [a]tradition of
men."

**9** And He was also saying to them,
"You are good at setting aside the
commandment of God in order to
keep your [a]tradition. **10** For Moses
said, '[a]HONOR YOUR FATHER AND YOUR
MOTHER'; and, '[b]HE WHO SPEAKS EVIL
OF FATHER OR MOTHER, IS TO [1]BE PUT
TO DEATH'; **11** but you say, 'If a man
says to *his* father or *his* mother,
whatever you might benefit from
me is [a]Corban (that is to say, [1]given
*to God*),' **12** you no longer leave him
to do anything for *his* father or *his*
mother; **13** *thus* invalidating the word
of God by your [a]tradition which you
have handed down; and you do many
things such as that."

### *The Heart of Man*

**14** And after He called the crowd to
Him again, He *began* saying to them,
"Listen to Me, all of you, and under-
stand: **15** there is nothing outside the
man which can defile him if it goes
into him; but the things which pro-
ceed out of the man are what defile
the man. **16** [1][And if anyone has ears
to hear, let him hear."]

**17** And when He had left the
crowd *and* entered [a]the house, [b]His
disciples were asking Him about the
parable. **18** And He *said to them, "Are
you lacking understanding in this
way as well? Do you not [1]perceive
that whatever goes into the man
from outside cannot defile him,
**19** because it does not go into his
heart, but into his stomach, and goes
to the sewer?" (*Thus He* declared [a]all
foods [b]clean.) **20** And He was saying,
"[a]That which proceeds out of the
man, that is what defiles the man.
**21** For from within, out of the heart
of men, proceed the evil thoughts,
sexual immoralities, thefts, murders,
adulteries, **22** coveting, wickedness,
deceit, sensuality, [a,1]envy, slander,
[2]pride, *and* foolishness. **23** All these
evil things proceed from within and
defile the man."

### *A Gentile Woman's Faith*

**24** [a]Now Jesus stood up and went away
from there to the region of [b]Tyre[1].

---

**7:4** [a]Mt 23:25 [1]Ceremonial cleansing; lit *baptizing* **7:5** [a]Mk 7:3, 8, 9, 13; Ga 1:14 [b]Mk 7:2
**7:6** [a]Is 29:13 **7:7** [a]Is 29:13 **7:8** [a]Mk 7:3, 5, 9, 13; Ga 1:14 **7:9** [a]Mk 7:3, 5, 8, 13; Ga 1:14
**7:10** [a]Ex 20:12; Dt 5:16 [b]Ex 21:17; Lv 20:9 [1]Lit *die the death* **7:11** [a]Lv 1:2; Mt 27:6 [1]An offering; or *a gift*
**7:13** [a]Mk 7:3, 5, 8, 9; Ga 1:14 **7:16** [1]Early mss omit this v **7:17** [a]Mk 2:1; 3:20; 9:28 [b]Mt 15:15
**7:18** [1]Or *understand*; see Mt 15:17, but cf. Mk 8:17 **7:19** [a]Ro 14:1-12; Col 2:16 [b]Lk 11:41; Ac 10:15; 11:9
**7:20** [a]Mt 15:18; Mk 7:23 **7:22** [a]Mt 6:23; 20:15 [1]Lit *an evil eye* [2]Or *arrogance* **7:24** [a]Mk 7:24-30:
*Mt 15:21-28* [b]Mt 11:21; Mk 7:31 [1]Two early mss add *and Sidon*

And when He had entered a house,
He was wanting no one to know *of*
*it;* [2]yet He could not escape notice.
25 But after hearing of Him, a woman
whose little daughter had an unclean
spirit immediately came and fell at
His feet. 26 Now the woman was a
[1]Greek, of Syrophoenician descent.
And she kept asking Him to cast the
demon out of her daughter. 27 And He
was saying to her, "Let the children
be satisfied first, for it is not [1]good to
take the children's bread and throw
it to the dogs." 28 But she answered
and *said to Him, "Yes, Lord, *but*
even the dogs under the table feed
on the children's crumbs." 29 And He
said to her, "Because of this [1]answer
go; the demon has gone out of your
daughter." 30 And going back to her
home, she found the child [1]lying on
the bed, the demon having left.

### *The Deaf Hear, the Mute Speak*

31 [a]And again He went out from the
region of [b]Tyre, and came through
Sidon to [c]the Sea of Galilee, within
the region of the [d]Decapolis. 32 And
they *brought to Him one who was
deaf and spoke with difficulty, and
they *pleaded with Him to [a]lay His
hand on him. 33 [a]And Jesus took him
aside from the crowd, by himself,
and put His fingers into his ears,
and after [a]spitting, He touched his
tongue; 34 and looking up to heav-
en with a [a]sigh, He *said to him,
"Ephphatha!" that is, "Be opened!"
35 And his ears were opened, and
the [1]impediment of his tongue [2]was
removed, and he *began* speaking
plainly. 36 And [a]He gave them orders
not to tell anyone; but the more He
was ordering them, the more wide-
ly they [b]continued to proclaim it.
37 And they were utterly astonished,
saying, "He has done all things well;
He makes even the deaf to hear and
the mute to speak."

### *Jesus Feeds Four Thousand*

8 In those days, when there was
again a large crowd and they
had nothing to eat, [a]Jesus called His
disciples and *said to them, 2 "[a]I feel
compassion for the crowd because
they have remained with Me now
three days and have nothing to eat.
3 And if I send them away hungry to
their homes, they will faint on the
way; and some of them have come
from a great distance." 4 And His
disciples answered Him, "Where
will anyone be able *to find enough*
[1]bread here in *this* desolate place to
satisfy these people?" 5 And He was
asking them, "How many loaves do
you have?" And they said, "Seven."
6 And He *directed the crowd to [1]sit
down on the ground; and taking the
seven loaves, He gave thanks and
broke them. And He kept giving them
to His disciples to [2]serve to them, and
they served them to the crowd. 7 And
they also had a few small fish; and
[a]after He blessed them, He ordered
these to be [1]served as well. 8 And
they ate and were satisfied; and they
picked up seven *large* [a]baskets full
of what was left over of the broken
pieces. 9 Now about four thousand
were *there*, and He sent them away.

---

**7:24** [2]Lit *and* **7:26** [1]Or *Gentile* **7:27** [1]Or *proper* **7:29** [1]Lit *word* **7:30** [1]Lit *thrown*
**7:31** [a]Mk 7:31-37: *Mt 15:29-31* [b]Mt 11:21; Mk 7:24 [c]Mt 4:18 [d]Mt 4:25; Mk 5:20 **7:32** [a]Mk 5:23
**7:33** [a]Mk 8:23 **7:34** [a]Mk 8:12 **7:35** [1]Or *bond* [2]Lit *was loosed* **7:36** [a]Mt 8:4 [b]Mk 1:45
◆ **8:1** [a]Mk 8:1-9: *Mt 15:32-39;* Mk 6:34-44 **8:2** [a]Mt 9:36; Mk 6:34 **8:4** [1]Lit *loaves* **8:6** [1]Lit *recline*
[2]Lit *set before* **8:7** [a]Mt 14:19 [1]Lit *set before them* **8:8** [a]Mt 15:37; Mk 8:20

**10** And immediately He entered the
boat with His disciples and came to
the district of [a]Dalmanutha.
**11** [a]And the Pharisees came out and
began to argue with Him, [b]seeking
from Him [1]a sign from heaven, test-
ing Him. **12** [a]And sighing deeply [1]in
His spirit, He *said, "Why does this
generation seek [2]a sign? Truly I say
to you, [b,3]no [4]sign will be given to this
generation." **13** And leaving them, He
again embarked and went away to the
other side.
**14** And they had forgotten to take
bread, and did not have more than
one loaf in the boat with them.
**15** And He was giving orders to
them, saying, "[a]Watch out! Beware
of the leaven of the Pharisees and
the leaven of [b]Herod." **16** And they
*began to* discuss with one another
*the fact* that they had no bread.
**17** And Jesus, aware of this, *said to
them, "Why do you discuss *the fact*
that you have no bread? [a]Do you not
yet perceive or understand? Do you
have a hardened heart? **18** [a]HAVING
EYES, DO YOU NOT SEE? AND HAVING
EARS, DO YOU NOT HEAR? And do you
not remember, **19** when I broke [a]the
five loaves for the five thousand,
how many [b]baskets full of broken
pieces you picked up?" They *said to
Him, "Twelve." **20** "When *I broke* [a]the
seven for the four thousand, how
many *large* [b]baskets full of broken
pieces did you pick up?" And they
*said to Him, "Seven." **21** And He
was saying to them, "[a]Do you not
yet understand?"
**22** And they *came to [a]Bethsaida.
And they *brought a blind man to
Jesus and *pleaded with Him to
[b]touch him. **23** And taking the blind
man by the hand, He [a]brought him
out of the village; and after [a]spitting
on his eyes and [b]laying His hands on
him, He was asking him, "Do you see
anything?" **24** And he [1]looked up and
was saying, "I see men, for [2]I see *them*
like trees, walking around." **25** Then
again He laid His hands on his eyes;
and he looked intently and was re-
stored, and *began to* see everything
clearly. **26** And He sent him to his
home, saying, "Do not even enter
[a]the village."

### *Peter Confesses Jesus Is the Christ*

**27** [a]And Jesus went out, along with His
disciples, to the villages of [b]Caesarea
Philippi; and on the way He was asking
His disciples, saying to them, "Who
do people say that I am?" **28** [a]And they
told Him, saying, "John the Baptist;
and others *say* Elijah; but others, one
of the prophets." **29** And He *continued*
asking them, "But who do you say
that I am?" [a]Peter *answered and
*said to Him, "You are the [1]Christ."
**30** And [a]He [1]warned them to tell no
one about Him.
**31** [a]And He began to teach them
that [b]the Son of Man must suffer
many things and be rejected by the
elders and the chief priests and the

**8:10** [a]Mt 15:39 **8:11** [a]Mk 8:11-21: *Mt 16:1-12* [b]Mt 12:38 [1]Or *an attesting miracle* **8:12** [a]Mk 7:34 [b]Mt 12:39 [1]Or *to Himself* [2]Or *an attesting miracle* [3]Lit *if a sign shall be given* [4]Or *attesting miracle* **8:15** [a]Mt 16:6; Lk 12:1 [b]Mt 14:1; 22:16 **8:17** [a]Mk 6:52 **8:18** [a]Jer 5:21; Eze 12:2; Mk 4:12 **8:19** [a]Mk 6:41-44 [b]Mt 14:20 **8:20** [a]Mk 8:6-9 [b]Mk 8:8 **8:21** [a]Mk 6:52 **8:22** [a]Mt 11:21; Mk 6:45 [b]Mk 3:10 **8:23** [a]Mk 7:33 [b]Mk 5:23 **8:24** [1]Or *gained sight* [2]Or *they look to me* **8:26** [a]Mk 8:23 **8:27** [a]Mk 8:27-29: *Mt 16:13-16; Lk 9:18-20* [b]Mt 16:13 **8:28** [a]Mk 6:14; Lk 9:7, 8 **8:29** [a]Jn 6:68, 69 [1]Messiah **8:30** [a]Mt 8:4; 16:20; Lk 9:21 [1]Or *strictly admonished* **8:31** [a]Mk 8:31-9:1: *Mt 16:21-28; Lk 9:22-27* [b]Mt 16:21

scribes, and be killed, and after three
days rise again. **32** And He was stating
the matter [a]openly. And Peter took
Him aside and began to rebuke Him.
**33** But turning around and seeing His
disciples, He rebuked Peter and *said,
"Get behind Me, [a]Satan! For you are
not setting your mind on [1]God's
interests, but man's."

### *Take Up Your Cross*

**34** And He summoned the crowd with
His disciples, and said to them, "If
anyone wishes to [1]come after Me,
he must deny himself, and [a]take
up his cross and follow Me. **35** For
[a]whoever wishes to save his [1]life will
lose it, but whoever loses his [1]life for
My sake and the gospel's will save it.
**36** For what does it profit a man to
gain the whole world, and forfeit his
soul? **37** For what will a man give in
exchange for his soul? **38** For [a]whoev-
er is ashamed of Me and My words in
this adulterous and sinful generation,
[b]the Son of Man will also be ashamed
of him when He [c]comes in the glory
of His Father with the holy angels."

### *The Transfiguration*

**9** And Jesus was saying to them,
"[a]Truly I say to you, there are
some of those who are standing here
who will not taste death until they
see the kingdom of God having come
in power."
**2** [a]And six days later, Jesus *took
with Him [b]Peter and James and John,
and *brought them up on a high
mountain alone by themselves. And
He was transfigured before them;
**3** and [a]His garments were shining
intensely white, as no launderer on
earth can whiten them. **4** And Elijah
appeared to them along with Moses
and they were conversing with Jesus.
**5** And Peter answered and *said to
Jesus, "[a]Rabbi, it is good for us to
be here; [b]let us make three [1]booths,
one for You, and one for Moses, and
one for Elijah." **6** For he did not know
what to answer; for they became
terrified. **7** Then a cloud [1]formed,
overshadowing them, and [a]a voice
[1]came out of the cloud, "[b]This is My
beloved Son, [2]listen to Him!" **8** And
all at once when they looked around,
they saw no one with them anymore,
except Jesus alone.
**9** [a]And as they were coming down
from the mountain, He [b]gave them
orders not to recount to anyone
what they had seen, [1]until the Son
of Man rose from the dead. **10** And
they [1]seized upon [2]that statement,
arguing with one another [3]what
rising from the dead meant. **11** And
they *began* asking Him, saying, "*Why
is it* that the scribes say that [a]Elijah
must come first?" **12** And He said to
them, "Elijah does first come and
restore all things. And *yet* how is
it written of [a]the Son of Man that
[b]He will suffer many things and be
treated with contempt? **13** But I say
to you that Elijah has [1]indeed come,

---

**8:32** [a]Jn 10:24; 11:14; 16:25, 29; 18:20 **8:33** [a]Mt 4:10 [1]Lit *the things of God* **8:34** [a]Mt 10:38; Lk 14:27 [1]Some mss *follow* **8:35** [a]Mt 10:39; Lk 17:33; Jn 12:25 [1]Or *soul* **8:38** [a]Mt 10:33; Lk 9:26; Heb 11:16 [b]Mt 8:20 [c]Mt 16:27; Mk 13:26; Lk 9:26 ◆ **9:1** [a]Mt 16:28; Mk 13:26; Lk 9:27 **9:2** [a]Mk 9:2-8: *Mt 17:1-8; Lk 9:28-36* [b]Mk 5:37 **9:3** [a]Mt 28:3 **9:5** [a]Mt 23:7 [b]Mt 17:4; Lk 9:33 [1]Or *tents, tabernacles*, cf. Lv 23:34-43; Dt 16:13-15; Zec 14:16-19 **9:7** [a]2Pe 1:17f [b]Mt 3:17; Mk 1:11; Lk 3:22 [1]Or *occurred* [2]Or *give constant heed* **9:9** [a]Mk 9:9-13: *Mt 17:9-13* [b]Mt 8:4; Mk 5:43; 7:36; 8:30 [1]Lit *except when* **9:10** [1]Or *kept to themselves* [2]Lit *the statement* [3]Lit *what was the rising from the dead* **9:11** [a]Mal 4:5; Mt 11:14 **9:12** [a]Mk 9:31 [b]Mt 16:21; 26:24 **9:13** [1]Lit *also*

and they did to him whatever they
wished, just as it is written of him."

### *I Believe, Help My Unbelief*

**14** [a]And when they came *back* to the
disciples, they saw a large crowd
around them, and scribes arguing
with them. **15** And immediately, when
the entire crowd saw Him, they were
[a]amazed. And as they ran up, they
were greeting Him. **16** And He asked
them, "What are you arguing with
them?" **17** And one of the crowd an-
swered Him, "Teacher, I brought You
my son, possessed with a spirit which
makes him mute; **18** and [1]whenever
it seizes him, it [2]slams him *to the
ground* and he foams *at the mouth*,
and grinds his teeth and [3]becomes
rigid. I told Your disciples to cast it
out, and they could not *do it*." **19** And
He *answered them and *said, "O un-
believing generation, how long shall I
be with you? How long shall I put up
with you? Bring him to Me!" **20** And
they brought [1]the boy to Him. When
he saw Him, immediately the spirit
threw him into a convulsion, and fall-
ing to the ground, he *began* rolling
around, foaming *at the mouth*. **21** And
He asked his father, "How long has
this been happening to him?" And he
said, "From childhood. **22** And it has
often thrown him both into the fire
and into the water to destroy him.
But if You can do anything, take pity
on us and help us!" **23** And Jesus said
to him, "'If You can?' [a]All things are
possible to him who believes." **24** Im-
mediately the boy's father cried out
and was saying, "I do believe; help
my unbelief." **25** Now when Jesus saw
that [a]a crowd was [1]rapidly gathering,
He rebuked the unclean spirit, saying
to it, "You mute and deaf spirit, [2]I
command you, come out of him and
do not enter him [3]again." **26** And after
crying out and throwing him into
terrible convulsions, it came out; and
*the boy* became so much like a corpse
that most *of them* said, "He is dead!"
**27** But Jesus took him by the hand and
raised him; and he stood up. **28** And
when He came [a]into the house, His
disciples *began* questioning Him
privately, "Why could we not cast it
out?" **29** And He said to them, "This
kind cannot come out by anything
but prayer."

### *Jesus Foretells His Death and Resurrection*

**30** [a]From there they went out and
were going through Galilee, and He
was not wanting anyone to know
*about it*. **31** For He was teaching His
disciples and telling them, "[a]The
Son of Man is to be [1]delivered into
the hands of men, and they will kill
Him; and when He has been killed,
He will rise again three days later."
**32** But [a]they [1]did not understand *this*
statement, and they were afraid to
ask Him.

**33** [a]And they came to Capernaum;
and when He [1]was in [b]the house, He
*began to* question them, "What were
you discussing on the way?" **34** But
they kept silent, for on the way [a]they
had discussed with one another which

**9:14** [a]Mk 9:14-28: *Mt 17:14-19; Lk 9:37-42* **9:15** [a]Mk 14:33; 16:5, 6 **9:18** [1]Or *wherever* [2]Or *tears him* [3]Or *withers away* **9:20** [1]Lit *him* **9:23** [a]Mt 17:20; Jn 11:40 **9:25** [a]Mk 9:15 [1]Or *running together* [2]Or *I Myself command* [3]Or *from now on* **9:28** [a]Mk 2:1; 7:17 **9:30** [a]Mk 9:30-32: *Mt 17:22, 23; Lk 9:43-45* **9:31** [a]Mt 16:21; Mk 8:31; 9:12 [1]Or *betrayed* **9:32** [a]Lk 2:50; 9:45; 18:34; Jn 12:16 [1]Lit *were not knowing* **9:33** [a]Mk 9:33-37: *Mt 18:1-5; Lk 9:46-48* [b]Mk 3:19 [1]Lit *had come* **9:34** [a]Mt 18:4; Mk 9:50; Lk 22:24

*of them was* the greatest. **35** And sitting
down, He called the twelve and *said
to them, "[a]If anyone wants to be first,
[1]he shall be last of all and servant of
all." **36** And taking a child, He set him
[1]before them. And taking him in His
arms, He said to them, **37** "[a]Whoever
receives [1]one child like this in My
name receives Me; and whoever
receives Me does not receive Me, but
Him who sent Me."

### *Warnings About Discipleship*

**38** [a]John said to Him, "Teacher, we
saw someone casting out demons in
Your name, and [b]we tried to hinder
him because he was not following
us." **39** But Jesus said, "Do not hinder
him, for there is no one who will per-
form a miracle in My name, and be
able soon afterward to speak evil of
Me. **40** [a]For he who is not against us
is [1]for us. **41** For [a]whoever gives you
a cup of water to drink in *My* name
because you are of Christ, truly I say
to you, he will not lose his reward.
**42** "[a]And whoever causes one
of these [1]little ones who believe
to stumble, it [2]would be better for
him if, with a heavy millstone hung
around his neck, he [3]had been cast
into the sea. **43** [a]And if your hand
causes you to stumble, cut it off; it
is better for you to enter life crippled,
than, having your two hands, to go
into [b,1]hell, into the [c]unquenchable
fire, **44** [1][and where THEIR WORM
DOES NOT DIE, AND THE FIRE IS NOT
QUENCHED.] **45** And if your foot causes
you to stumble, cut it off; it is better
for you to enter life lame, than, having
your two feet, to be cast into [a,1]hell,
**46** [1][and where THEIR WORM DOES NOT
DIE, AND THE FIRE IS NOT QUENCHED.]
**47** [a]And if your eye causes you to
stumble, gouge it out; it is better for
you to enter the kingdom of God with
one eye, than, having two eyes, to
be cast into [b,1]hell, **48** [a]where THEIR
WORM DOES NOT DIE, AND [b]THE FIRE
IS NOT QUENCHED.
**49** "For everyone will be salted
with fire. **50** Salt is good; but [a]if the
salt becomes unsalty, with what will
you [1]make it salty *again*? [b]Have salt
in yourselves, and [c]be at peace with
one another."

### *Teaching About Divorce*

**10** [a]And standing up, He *went
from there to the region of
Judea and beyond the Jordan; crowds
*gathered around Him again, and,
[b]according to His custom, He once
more *began to* teach them.
**2** And *some* Pharisees came up
to Jesus, testing Him, and *began to*
question Him whether it was lawful
for a man to [1]divorce a wife. **3** And He
answered and said to them, "What did
Moses command you?" **4** And they
said, "[a]Moses permitted *a man* TO
WRITE A CERTIFICATE OF DIVORCE AND
[1]SEND *her* AWAY." **5** But Jesus said to

**9:35** [a]Mt 20:26; 23:11; Mk 10:43, 44; Lk 22:26 [1]Or *let him be* **9:36** [1]Lit *in their midst* **9:37** [a]Mt 10:40; Lk 10:16; Jn 13:20 [1]Lit *one of such children* **9:38** [a]Mk 9:38-40: *Lk 9:49, 50* [b]Nu 11:27-29 **9:40** [a]Mt 12:30; Lk 11:23 [1]Or *on our side* **9:41** [a]Mt 10:42 **9:42** [a]Mt 18:6; Lk 17:2; 1Co 8:12 [1]Humble [2]Lit *is better for him if a millstone turned by a donkey is hung* [3]Lit *has been thrown* **9:43** [a]Mt 5:30; 18:8 [b]Mt 5:22 [c]Mt 3:12; 25:41 [1]Gr *Gehenna* **9:44** [1]vv 44 and 46, which are identical to v 48, are not found in the early mss **9:45** [a]Mt 5:22 [1]Gr *Gehenna* **9:46** [1]See v 44, note 1 **9:47** [a]Mt 5:29; 18:9 [b]Mt 5:22 [1]Gr *Gehenna* **9:48** [a]Is 66:24 [b]Mt 3:12; 25:41 **9:50** [a]Mt 5:13; Lk 14:34f [b]Col 4:6 [c]Mk 9:34; Ro 12:18; 2Co 13:11; 1Th 5:13 [1]Lit *season it* ◆ **10:1** [a]Mk 10:1-12: *Mt 19:1-9* [b]Mt 4:23; 26:55; Mk 1:21; 2:13; 4:2; 6:2, 6, 34; 12:35; 14:49 **10:2** [1]Or *send away* **10:4** [a]Dt 24:1, 3; Mt 5:31 [1]Or *divorce* her

them, "[a][1]Because of your hardness of
heart he wrote for you this command-
ment. **6** But [a]from the beginning of
creation, *God* [b]MADE THEM MALE AND
FEMALE. **7** [a]FOR THIS REASON A MAN
SHALL LEAVE HIS FATHER AND MOTHER[1],
**8** [a]AND THE TWO SHALL BECOME ONE
FLESH; so they are no longer two, but
one flesh. **9** What therefore God has
joined together, let no man separate."
**10** And in the house the disciples
*began* questioning Him about this
again. **11** And He *said to them,
"[a]Whoever [1]divorces his wife and
marries another woman commits
adultery against her; **12** and [a]if she
herself [1]divorces her husband and
marries another man, she is com-
mitting adultery."

### *Jesus Blesses Little Children*

**13** [a]And they were bringing children
to Him so that He might touch them;
but the disciples rebuked them.
**14** But when Jesus saw this, He was
indignant and said to them, "Permit
the children to come to Me; do not
hinder them; [a]for the kingdom
of God belongs to such as these.
**15** Truly I say to you, [a]whoever does
not receive the kingdom of God like
a child will not enter it *at all*." **16** And
He [a]took them in His arms and *began*
blessing them, laying His hands on
them.

### *The Rich Young Ruler*

**17** [a]And as He was setting out on a
journey, a man ran up to Him and
[b]knelt before Him, and *began* asking
Him, "Good Teacher, what shall I do
to [c]inherit eternal life?" **18** And Jesus
said to him, "Why do you call Me
good? No one is good except God
alone. **19** You know the command-
ments, '[a]DO NOT MURDER, DO NOT
COMMIT ADULTERY, DO NOT STEAL,
DO NOT BEAR FALSE WITNESS, Do not
defraud, HONOR YOUR FATHER AND
MOTHER.'" **20** And he said to Him,
"Teacher, I have kept [a]all these
things from my youth up." **21** And
looking at him, Jesus loved him and
said to him, "One thing you lack: go
and sell all you possess and give to
the poor, and you will have [a]treasure
in heaven; and come, follow Me."
**22** But at these words [1]he was sad-
dened, and he went away grieving,
for he was one who owned much
property.
**23** And Jesus, looking around,
*said to His disciples, "[a]How hard it
will be for those who are wealthy to
enter the kingdom of God!" **24** And
the disciples [a]were amazed at His
words. But Jesus *answered again
and *said to them, "Children, how
hard it is to enter the kingdom of
God! **25** [a]It is easier for a camel to go
through the eye of a needle than for
a rich man to enter the kingdom of
God." **26** And they were even more
astonished, saying to [1]Him, "[2]Then
who can be saved?" **27** Looking at
them, Jesus *said, "[a]With people it
is impossible, but not with God; for
all things are possible with God."

---

**10:5** [a]Mt 19:8 [1]Or *With reference to* **10:6** [a]Mk 13:19; 2Pe 3:4 [b]Ge 1:27; 5:2 **10:7** [a]Ge 2:24 [1]Many late mss add *and shall cling to his wife* **10:8** [a]Ge 2:24 **10:11** [a]Mt 5:32 [1]Or *sends away* **10:12** [a]1Co 7:11, 13 [1]Or *sends away* **10:13** [a]Mk 10:13-16: *Mt 19:13-15; Lk 18:15-17* **10:14** [a]Mt 5:3 **10:15** [a]Mt 18:3; 19:14; Lk 18:17; 1Co 14:20; 1Pe 2:2 **10:16** [a]Mk 9:36 **10:17** [a]Mk 10:17-31: *Mt 19:16-30; Lk 18:18-30* [b]Mk 1:40 [c]Mt 25:34; Lk 10:25; 18:18; Ac 20:32; Eph 1:18; 1Pe 1:4 **10:19** [a]Ex 20:12-16; Dt 5:16-20 **10:20** [a]Mt 19:20 **10:21** [a]Mt 6:20 **10:22** [1]Or *he became gloomy* **10:23** [a]Mt 19:23 **10:24** [a]Mk 1:27 **10:25** [a]Mt 19:24 **10:26** [1]Some mss *each other* [2]Lit *And* **10:27** [a]Mt 19:26

**28** [a]Peter began to say to Him,
"Behold, we have left everything and
followed You." **29** Jesus said, "Truly
I say to you, [a]there is no one who
has left house or brothers or sisters
or mother or father or children or
farms, for My sake and for the gos-
pel's sake, **30** [1]except *one who* will
receive one hundred times as much
now in [2]the present age—houses and
brothers and sisters and mothers
and children and farms, *along* with
persecutions—and in [a]the age to
come, eternal life. **31** But [a]many *who
are* first will be last, and the last,
first."

### *Jesus Again Foretells His Death and Resurrection*

**32** [a]And they were on the road going
up to Jerusalem, and Jesus was walk-
ing on ahead of them; and they [b]were
amazed, and those who followed
were fearful. And again He took the
twelve aside and began to tell them
what was going to happen to Him:
**33** "Behold, we are going up to Jeru-
salem, and [a]the Son of Man will be
betrayed to the chief priests and the
scribes; and they will condemn Him
to death and will deliver Him over to
the Gentiles. **34** And they will mock
Him and [a]spit on Him, and flog Him
and kill *Him,* and three days later He
will rise again."

### *A Request for Status*

**35** [a]Then James and John, the two
sons of Zebedee, *came up to Jesus,
saying to Him, "Teacher, we want You
to do for us whatever we ask of You."
**36** And He said to them, "What do
you want Me to do for you?" **37** And
they said to Him, "[1]Grant that we
[a]may sit, one on Your right and one
on *Your* left, in Your glory." **38** But
Jesus said to them, "You do not
know what you are asking. Are you
able [a]to drink the cup that I drink,
or [b]to be baptized with the baptism
with which I am baptized?" **39** And
they said to Him, "We are able." And
Jesus said to them, "The cup that I
drink [a]you shall drink; and you shall
be baptized with the baptism with
which I am baptized. **40** But to sit
on My right or on *My* left, *this* is not
Mine to give; [a]but it is for those for
whom it has been prepared."
**41** [a]And hearing *this,* the ten
began to feel indignant with James
and John. **42** And calling them to
Himself, Jesus *said to them, "You
know that those who are recognized
as rulers of the Gentiles lord it over
them; and their great men exercise
authority over them. **43** But it is not
this way among you, [a]but whoever
wishes to become great among you
shall be your servant; **44** and whoever
wishes to be first among you shall
be slave of all. **45** For even the Son
of Man [a]did not come to be served,
but to serve, and to give His [1]life a
ransom for many."

### *Bartimaeus Regains His Sight*

**46** [a]Then they *came to Jericho. And
[b]as He was leaving Jericho with His
disciples and a large crowd, a blind

**10:28** [a]Mt 4:20-22 **10:29** [a]Mt 6:33; 19:29; Lk 18:29f **10:30** [a]Mt 12:32 [1]Lit *if not* [2]Lit *this time*
**10:31** [a]Mt 19:30; 20:16; Lk 13:30 **10:32** [a]Mk 10:32-34: *Mt 20:17-19; Lk 18:31-33* [b]Mk 1:27
**10:33** [a]Mk 8:31; 9:12 **10:34** [a]Mt 16:21; 26:67; 27:30; Mk 9:31; 14:65 **10:35** [a]Mk 10:35-45: *Mt 20:20-28*
**10:37** [a]Mt 19:28 [1]Lit *Give to us* **10:38** [a]Mt 20:22 [b]Lk 12:50 **10:39** [a]Ac 12:2; Rev 1:9
**10:40** [a]Mt 13:11 **10:41** [a]Mk 10:42-45; Lk 22:25-27 **10:43** [a]Mt 20:26; 23:11; Mk 9:35; Lk 22:26
**10:45** [a]Mt 20:28 [1]Or *soul* **10:46** [a]Mk 10:46-52: *Mt 20:29-34; Lk 18:35-43* [b]Lk 18:35; 19:1

beggar *named* Bartimaeus, the
son of Timaeus, was sitting by the
road. **47** And when he heard that it
was Jesus the [a]Nazarene, he began
to cry out and say, "Jesus, [b]Son of
David, have mercy on me!" **48** And
many were sternly telling him to be
quiet, but he kept crying out all the
more, "[a]Son of David, have mercy on
me!" **49** And Jesus stopped and said,
"Call him *here*." So they *called the
blind man, saying to him, "[a]Take
courage, get up! He is calling for
you." **50** And throwing off his *outer*
garment, he jumped up and came
to Jesus. **51** And Jesus answered him
and said, "What do you want Me to
do for you?" And the blind man said
to Him, "[a,1]Rabboni, *I want* to regain
my sight!" **52** And Jesus said to him,
"Go; [a]your faith has [1]saved you."
Immediately he regained his sight
and *began* following Him on the road.

### *The Triumphal Entry*

**11** [a]And as they *approached
Jerusalem, at Bethphage and
[b]Bethany, near [c]the Mount of Olives,
He *sent two of His disciples, **2** and
*said to them, "Go into the village
opposite you, and immediately as
you enter it, you will find a colt tied
*there*, on which no one yet has ever
sat; untie it and bring it *here*. **3** And
if anyone says to you, 'Why are you
doing this?' you say, 'The Lord has
need of it'; and immediately he [1]will
send it back here." **4** And they went
away and found a colt tied at the door,
outside in the street; and they *untied
it. **5** And some of the bystanders were
saying to them, "What are you doing,
untying the colt?" **6** And they spoke
to them just as Jesus had told *them*,
and they gave them permission.
**7** [a]And they *brought the colt to Jesus
and put their garments on it; and He
sat on it. **8** And many spread their gar-
ments in the road, and others *spread*
leafy branches, having cut *them* from
the fields. **9** And those who went in
front and those who followed were
shouting:

"Hosanna!
[a]BLESSED IS HE WHO COMES
IN THE NAME OF THE [1]LORD;
**10** Blessed *is* the coming kingdom
of our father David;
Hosanna [a]in the highest!"

**11** [a]And Jesus entered Jerusalem
*and came* into the temple; and after
looking around at everything, [b]He
left for Bethany with the twelve,
since it was already late.

### *The Barren Fig Tree*

**12** [a]And on the next day, when they
had left Bethany, He became hungry.
**13** And seeing at a distance a fig tree
that had leaves, He went *to see* if
perhaps He would find anything on
it; and when He came to it, He found
nothing but leaves, for it was not the
season for figs. **14** And He answered
and said to it, "May no one ever
eat fruit from you again!" And His
disciples were listening.

### *Jesus Drives Merchants from the Temple*

**15** [a]Then they *came to Jerusalem.
And He entered the temple and

**10:47** [a]Mk 1:24 [b]Mt 9:27 **10:48** [a]Mt 9:27 **10:49** [a]Mt 9:2 **10:51** [a]Mt 23:7; Jn 20:16 [1]Lit *My Master* **10:52** [a]Mt 9:22 [1]Or *made you well* ◆ **11:1** [a]Mk 11:1-10: *Mt 21:1-9; Lk 19:29-38* [b]Mt 21:17 [c]Mt 21:1 **11:3** [1]Lit *sends* **11:7** [a]Mk 11:7-10: *Mt 21:4-9; Lk 19:35-38; Jn 12:12-15* **11:9** [a]Ps 118:26; Mt 21:9 [1]In OT, Yahweh, cf. Ps 118:26 **11:10** [a]Mt 21:9 **11:11** [a]Mt 21:12 [b]Mt 21:17 **11:12** [a]Mk 11:12-14, 20-24: *Mt 21:18-22* **11:15** [a]Mk 11:15-18: *Mt 21:12-16; Lk 19:45-47;* Jn 2:13-16

began to drive out those who were
buying and selling in the temple, and
overturned the tables of the money
changers and the seats of those
who were selling [1]doves; **16** and He
was not permitting anyone to carry
[1]merchandise through the temple.
**17** And He *began to* teach and say to
them, "Is it not written, '[a]MY HOUSE
SHALL BE CALLED A HOUSE OF PRAYER
FOR ALL THE NATIONS'? [b]But you have
made it a ROBBERS' [1]DEN." **18** And the
chief priests and the scribes heard
*this*, and [a]*began* seeking how to
destroy Him; for they were afraid
of Him, for [b]the whole crowd was
astonished at His teaching.
**19** [a]And when evening came, [1]they
were going out of the city.
**20** [a]And as they were passing by
in the morning, they saw the fig
tree withered from the roots. **21** And
being reminded, Peter *said to Him,
"[a]Rabbi, look, the fig tree which You
cursed has withered." **22** And Jesus
answered and *said to them, "[a]Have
faith in God. **23** [a]Truly I say to you,
whoever says to this mountain, 'Be
taken up and cast into the sea,' and
does not doubt in his heart, but be-
lieves that what he says [1]is going to
happen, it will be *granted* him. **24** For
this reason I say to you, [a]all things for
which you pray and ask, believe that
you have received them, and they will
be *granted* to you. **25** And whenever
you [a]stand praying, [b]forgive, if you
have anything against anyone, so
that your Father who is in heaven will
also forgive you your transgressions.
**26** [1][[a]But if you do not forgive, neither
will your Father who is in heaven
forgive your transgressions."]

### *The Authority of Jesus Challenged*

**27** Then they *came again to Jeru-
salem. [a]And as He was walking in
the temple, the chief priests and the
scribes and the elders *came to Him,
**28** and *began* saying to Him, "By what
authority are You doing these things,
or who gave You this authority to do
these things?" **29** And Jesus said to
them, "I will ask you one question,
and you answer Me, and *then* I will
tell you by what authority I do these
things. **30** Was the baptism of John
from heaven, or from men? Answer
Me." **31** And they *began* reasoning
among themselves, saying, "If we
say, 'From heaven,' He will say, 'Then
why did you not believe him?' **32** But
if we say, 'From men'?"—they were
afraid of the crowd, for everyone
was regarding John to have been a
real prophet. **33** And answering Jesus,
they *said, "We do not know." And
Jesus *said to them, "Neither [1]will I
tell you by what authority I do these
things."

### *Parable of the Vine-Growers*

**12** [a]And He began to speak to them
in parables: "[b]A man [c]PLANTED
A VINEYARD AND PUT A [1]WALL AROUND
IT, AND DUG A VAT UNDER THE WINE
PRESS AND BUILT A TOWER, and rented
it out to [2]vine-growers and went on
a journey. **2** And at the *harvest* time
he sent a slave to the vine-growers, in

**11:15** [1]Lit *the doves* **11:16** [1]Lit *a vessel* **11:17** [a]Is 56:7 [b]Jer 7:11 [1]Lit *cave* **11:18** [a]Mt 21:46; Mk 12:12; Lk 20:19; Jn 7:1 [b]Mt 7:28 **11:19** [a]Mt 21:17; Mk 11:11; Lk 21:37 [1]Jesus and His disciples **11:20** [a]Mk 11:12-14, 20-24: *Mt 21:19-22* **11:21** [a]Mt 23:7 **11:22** [a]Mt 17:20; 21:21f **11:23** [a]Mt 17:20; 1Co 13:2 [1]Lit *is happening* **11:24** [a]Mt 7:7f **11:25** [a]Mt 6:5 [b]Mt 6:14 **11:26** [a]Mt 6:15; 18:35 [1]Early mss omit this v **11:27** [a]Mk 11:27-33: *Mt 21:23-27; Lk 20:1-8* **11:33** [1]Lit *do I tell* ◆ **12:1** [a]Mk 3:23; 4:2ff [b]Mk 12:1-12: *Mt 21:33-46; Lk 20:9-19* [c]Is 5:1, 2 [1]Or *fence* [2]Or *tenant farmers*, so in vv 2, 7, 9

order to receive *some* of the fruit of
the vineyard from the vine-growers.
**3** And they took him, and beat him
and sent him away empty-handed.
**4** And again he sent them another
slave, and they wounded him in the
head, and treated him shamefully.
**5** And he sent another, and that one
they killed; and *so with* many others,
beating some and killing others. **6** He
had one more, a beloved son; he sent
him last *of all* to them, saying, 'They
will respect my son.' **7** But those vine-
growers said to one another, 'This is
the heir; come, let us kill him, and the
inheritance will be ours!' **8** And they
took him, and killed him and threw
him out of the vineyard. **9** What will
the [1]owner of the vineyard do? He
will come and destroy the vine-
growers, and will give the vineyard
to others. **10** Have you not even read
this Scripture:

'[a]THE STONE WHICH THE
BUILDERS REJECTED,
THIS HAS BECOME THE
CHIEF CORNER *stone*;
**11** [a]THIS CAME ABOUT
FROM THE [1]LORD,
AND IT IS MARVELOUS
IN OUR EYES'?"

**12** [a]And they were seeking to seize
Him, and *yet* they feared the crowd,
for they understood that He spoke
the parable against them. And *so*
[b]they left Him and went away.

### *Taxes to Caesar*

**13** [a]Then they *sent some of the
Pharisees and [b]Herodians to Him in
order to [c]trap Him in a statement.
**14** And they *came and *said to
Him, "Teacher, we know that You
are truthful and [1]defer to no one;
for You are not partial to any, but
teach the way of God in truth. Is it
[2]lawful to pay a tax to Caesar, or not?
**15** Shall we pay or shall we not pay?"
But He, knowing their hypocrisy,
said to them, "Why are you testing
Me? Bring Me a [1]denarius to look
at." **16** And they brought *one*. And
He *said to them, "Whose likeness
and inscription is this?" And they
said to Him, "Caesar's." **17** And Jesus
said to them, "[a]Render to Caesar the
things that are Caesar's, and to God
the things that are God's." And they
[1]were amazed at Him.

### *The Sadducees and the Resurrection*

**18** [a]Then *some* Sadducees (who say
that there is no resurrection) *came
to Jesus, and *began* questioning Him,
saying, **19** "Teacher, Moses wrote for
us that [a]IF A MAN'S BROTHER DIES and
leaves behind a wife AND LEAVES NO
CHILD, HIS BROTHER SHOULD [1]MARRY
THE WIFE AND RAISE UP A SEED FOR HIS
BROTHER. **20** There were seven broth-
ers; and the first [1]married a wife, and
died leaving no [2]seed. **21** And the
second one [1]married her, and died
leaving behind no seed; and the third
likewise; **22** and *so* [1]all seven left no
seed. Last of all the woman died also.
**23** In the resurrection, [1]when they rise
again, whose wife will she be? For [2]all
seven [3]had married her." **24** Jesus said
to them, "Is this not the reason you

---

***12:9*** [1]Lit *lord* **12:10** [a]Ps 118:22 **12:11** [a]Ps 118:23 [1]In OT, Yahweh, cf. Ps 118:23 **12:12** [a]Mk 11:18 [b]Mt 22:22 **12:13** [a]Mk 12:13-17: *Mt 22:15-22; Lk 20:20-26* [b]Mt 22:16 [c]Lk 11:54 **12:14** [1]You do not seek anyone's favor; lit *it is not a concern to You about anyone* [2]Or *permissible* **12:15** [1]A Roman silver coin, approx. a laborer's daily wage **12:17** [a]Mt 22:21 [1]Or *were greatly marveling* **12:18** [a]Mk 12:18-27: *Mt 22:23-33; Lk 20:27-38;* Ac 23:8 **12:19** [a]Dt 25:5 [1]Lit *take* **12:20** [1]Lit *took* [2]Or *offspring* **12:21** [1]Lit *took* **12:22** [1]Lit *the seven* **12:23** [1]Early mss omit *when they rise again* [2]Lit *the seven* [3]Lit *had her as a wife*

are mistaken, that you do not [1]under-
stand the Scriptures nor the power
of God? 25 For when they rise from
the dead, they neither marry nor are
given in marriage, but are like angels
in heaven. 26 But [1]regarding the fact
that the dead are raised, have you not
read in the book of Moses, [a]in the
*passage* about *the burning* bush, how
God spoke to him, saying, '[b]I AM THE
GOD OF ABRAHAM, AND THE GOD OF
ISAAC, AND THE GOD OF JACOB'? 27 [a]He
is not the God of the dead, but of the
living; you are greatly mistaken."

### *The Foremost Commandment*

28 [a]And when one of the scribes
came and heard them arguing, he
[b]recognized that He had answered
them well and asked Him, "What
commandment is the [1]foremost
of all?" 29 Jesus answered, "The
foremost is, '[a]HEAR, O ISRAEL! THE
[1]LORD OUR GOD IS ONE [1]LORD; 30 [a]AND
YOU SHALL LOVE THE [1]LORD YOUR GOD
WITH ALL YOUR HEART, AND WITH ALL
YOUR SOUL, AND WITH ALL YOUR MIND,
AND WITH ALL YOUR STRENGTH.' 31 The
second is this, '[a]YOU SHALL LOVE YOUR
NEIGHBOR AS YOURSELF.' There is no
other commandment greater than
these." 32 And the scribe said to
Him, "Right, Teacher; You have truly
stated that [a]HE IS ONE, AND THERE IS
NO ONE ELSE BESIDES HIM; 33 [a]AND TO
LOVE HIM WITH ALL THE HEART AND
WITH ALL THE UNDERSTANDING AND
WITH ALL THE STRENGTH, AND TO LOVE
ONE'S NEIGHBOR AS HIMSELF, [b]is much
more than all burnt offerings and
sacrifices." 34 And when Jesus saw
that he had answered thoughtfully,
He said to him, "You are not far from
the kingdom of God." [a]After that, no
one would dare to ask Him any more
questions.

35 [a]And Jesus *began to* say, as He
[b]taught in the temple, "How *is it that*
the scribes say that the [1]Christ is the
[c]son of David? 36 David himself said
[1]in the Holy Spirit,

'[a]THE [2]LORD SAID TO MY LORD,
"SIT AT MY RIGHT HAND,
UNTIL I PUT YOUR ENEMIES
BENEATH YOUR FEET."'

37 "David himself calls Him 'Lord';
so in what sense is He his son?" And
[a]the large crowd [1]enjoyed listening
to Him.

38 [a]And in His teaching He was
saying: "Beware of the scribes who
want to walk around in long robes,
and *want* [b]respectful greetings in the
marketplaces, 39 and best seats in the
synagogues and places of honor at
banquets, 40 [a]who devour widows'
houses, and for appearance's sake
offer long prayers; these will receive
greater condemnation."

### *The Widow's Offering*

41 [a]And He sat down opposite [b]the
treasury, and *began* observing how
the crowd was [c]putting [1]money into
the treasury; and many rich people
were putting in large sums. 42 And

**12:24** [1]Or *know* **12:26** [a]Lk 20:37; Ro 11:2 [b]Ex 3:6 [1]Lit *concerning the dead, that they rise*
**12:27** [a]Mt 22:32; Lk 20:38 **12:28** [a]Mk 12:28-34: *Mt 22:34-40;* Lk 10:25-28; 20:39f [b]Mt 22:34; Lk 20:39
[1]Or *first* **12:29** [a]Dt 6:4 [1]In OT, Yahweh, cf. Dt 6:4 **12:30** [a]Dt 6:5 [1]In OT, Yahweh, cf. Dt 6:5
**12:31** [a]Lv 19:18 **12:32** [a]Dt 4:35 **12:33** [a]Dt 6:5 [b]1Sa 15:22; Hos 6:6; Mic 6:6-8; Mt 9:13; 12:7
**12:34** [a]Mt 22:46 **12:35** [a]Mk 12:35-37: *Mt 22:41-46; Lk 20:41-44* [b]Mt 26:55; Mk 10:1 [c]Mt 9:27 [1]Messiah
**12:36** [a]Ps 110:1 [1]Or *by* [2]In OT, Yahweh, cf. Ps 110:1 **12:37** [a]Jn 12:9 [1]Lit *was gladly hearing Him*
**12:38** [a]Mk 12:38-40: *Mt 23:1-7; Lk 20:45-47* [b]Mt 23:7; Lk 11:43 **12:40** [a]Lk 20:47 **12:41** [a]Mk 12:41-44:
*Lk 21:1-4* [b]Jn 8:20 [c]2Ki 12:9 [1]Copper coins

a poor widow came and put in two
[1]lepta, which amount to a [2]quadrans.
**43** And calling His disciples to Him,
He said to them, "Truly I say to you,
this poor widow put in more than
all those putting *money* into the
treasury; **44** for they all put in out
of their [1]surplus, but she, out of her
poverty, put in all she owned, [2]all she
had [a]to live on."

### *Signs of Christ's Return*

**13** [a]And as He was going out of
the temple, one of His disci-
ples *said to Him, "Teacher, behold
[1]what wonderful stones and [1]what
wonderful buildings!" **2** And Jesus
said to him, "Do you see these great
buildings? [a]Not one stone will be left
upon another which will not be torn
down."
**3** And as He was sitting on [a]the
Mount of Olives opposite the temple,
[b]Peter and James and John and Andrew
were questioning Him privately, **4** "Tell
us, when will these things be, and what
*will be* the [1]sign when all these things
are going to be fulfilled?" **5** And Jesus
began to say to them, "See to it that no
one deceives you. **6** Many will come
in My name, saying, '[a]I am *He!*' and
will mislead many. **7** And when you
hear of wars and rumors of wars, do
not be alarmed; *those things* must take
place; but *that is* not yet the end. **8** For
nation will rise up against nation, and
kingdom against kingdom; there will
be earthquakes in various places; there
will *also* be famines. These things are
*merely* the beginning of birth pains.
**9** "But see to yourselves; for they
will [a]deliver you to *the* [1]courts, and
you will be beaten [a]in *the* synagogues,
and you will stand before governors
and kings for My sake, as a witness to
them. **10** [a]And the gospel must first be
proclaimed to all the nations. **11** [a]And
when they lead you away, delivering
you up, do not worry beforehand
about what you are to say, but say
whatever is given to you in that hour;
for it is not you who speak, but *it is*
the Holy Spirit. **12** And brother will
betray brother to death, and a father
*his* child; and children will rise up
against parents and [1]have them put to
death. **13** [a]And you will be hated by all
because of My name, but the one who
endures to the end, he will be saved.

### *The Abomination of Desolation and the Tribulation*

**14** "But [a]when you see the [b]ABOMINA-
TION OF DESOLATION standing where
it should not be (let the reader under-
stand), then those who are in Judea
must flee to the mountains. **15** [a]And
the one who is on the housetop must
not go down, or go in to get anything
out of his house; **16** and the one who
is in the field must not turn back to
get his garment. **17** But woe to those
who are pregnant and to those who
are nursing babies in those days!
**18** But pray that it may not happen
in the winter. **19** For those days will
be a *time of* tribulation such as has
not occurred [a]since the beginning of
the creation which God created until
now, and never will. **20** And unless

---

**12:42** [1]Smallest Greek copper coin, approx. 1/128 of a laborer's daily wage [2]A Roman copper coin, approx. 1/64 of a laborer's daily wage **12:44** [a]Lk 8:43; 15:12, 30; 21:4 [1]Or *abundance* [2]Lit *her whole livelihood* ◆**13:1** [a]Mk 13:1-37: *Mt 24; Lk 21:5-36* [1]Lit *how great* **13:2** [a]Lk 19:44 **13:3** [a]Mt 21:1 [b]Mt 17:1 **13:4** [1]Or *attesting miracle* **13:6** [a]Jn 8:24 **13:9** [a]Mt 10:17 [1]Or *Sanhedrin, Council* **13:10** [a]Mt 24:14 **13:11** [a]Mk 13:11-13: *Mt 10:19-22; Lk 21:12-17* **13:12** [1]Lit *put them to death* **13:13** [a]Mt 10:22; Jn 15:21 **13:14** [a]Mt 24:15f [b]Da 9:27; 11:31; 12:11 **13:15** [a]Lk 17:31 **13:19** [a]Da 12:1; Mk 10:6

the Lord had shortened *those* days,
no [1]life would have been saved; but
for the sake of the [2]elect, whom He
chose, He shortened the days. **21** And
then if anyone says to you, 'Behold,
here is the [1]Christ'; or, 'Behold, *He is*
there'; do not believe *him*; **22** for false
christs and [a]false prophets will arise,
and will show [b,1]signs and [b]wonders,
in order to lead astray, if possible, the
elect. **23** But as for you, see! I have
told you everything in advance.

### *The Coming of the Son of Man*

**24** "But in those days, after that tribula-
tion, [a]THE SUN WILL BE DARKENED AND
THE MOON WILL NOT GIVE ITS LIGHT,
**25** [a]AND THE STARS WILL BE FALLING
from heaven, AND THE POWERS THAT
ARE IN [1]THE HEAVENS will be shaken.
**26** And then they will see [a]THE SON
OF MAN [b]COMING IN CLOUDS with great
power and glory. **27** And then He will
send forth the angels, and [a]will gath-
er together His [1]elect from the four
winds, [b]from the farthest end of the
earth to the farthest end of heaven.

### *The Parable of the Fig Tree*

**28** "Now learn the parable from the
fig tree: when its branch has already
become tender and puts forth its
leaves, you know that summer is
near. **29** Even so, you too, when
you see these things happening,
[1]recognize that [2]He is near, *right* at
the [3]door. **30** Truly I say to you, this
[1]generation will not pass away until
all these things take place. **31** Heaven
and earth will pass away, but My
words will not pass away. **32** [a]But of
that day or hour no one knows, not
even the angels in heaven, nor the
Son, but the Father *alone*.

**33** "See to it, [a]keep on the alert; for
you do not know when the *appointed*
time [1]will come. **34** [a]*It is* like a man
away on a journey, *who*, leaving
his house and giving authority to
his slaves—each one his task, also
commanded the doorkeeper to stay
awake. **35** Therefore, [a]stay awake—for
you do not know when the [1]master of
the house is coming, whether in the
evening, at midnight, or [b]when the
rooster crows, or [c]in the morning—
**36** lest he come suddenly and find you
[a]sleeping. **37** And what I say to you I
say to all, '[a]Stay awake!'"

### *The Plot to Kill Jesus*

**14** [a]Now [b]the Passover and Un-
leavened Bread were two days
away; and the chief priests and the
scribes [c]were seeking how, after
seizing Him in secret, they might
kill *Him*; **2** for they were saying, "Not
during the festival, lest there be a riot
of the people."

### *The Costly Perfume*

**3** [a]And while He was in [b]Bethany at
the home of Simon the leper, and
reclining *at the table*, there came a
woman with an alabaster jar of per-
fume of very [c]costly pure [1]nard; *and*

**13:20** [1]Lit *flesh* [2]Or *chosen ones* **13:21** [1]Messiah **13:22** [a]Mt 7:15 [b]Mt 24:24; Jn 4:48 [1]Or *attesting miracles* **13:24** [a]Is 13:10; Eze 32:7; Joel 2:10, 31; 3:15; Rev 6:12 **13:25** [a]Is 34:4; Rev 6:13 [1]Or *heaven* **13:26** [a]Da 7:13; Rev 1:7 [b]Mt 16:27; Mk 8:38 **13:27** [a]Dt 30:4 [b]Zec 2:6 [1]Or *chosen ones* **13:29** [1]Or *know* [2]Or *it* [3]Lit *doors* **13:30** [1]Or *race* **13:32** [a]Mt 24:36; Ac 1:7 **13:33** [a]Eph 6:18; Col 4:2 [1]Lit *is* **13:34** [a]Lk 12:36-38 **13:35** [a]Mt 24:42; Mk 13:37 [b]Mk 14:30 [c]Mt 14:25; Mk 6:48 [1]Lit *lord* **13:36** [a]Ro 13:11 **13:37** [a]Mt 24:42; Mk 13:35 ◆**14:1** [a]Mk 14:1, 2: *Mt 26:2-5; Lk 22:1, 2* [b]Ex 12:1-27; Mk 14:12; Jn 11:55; 13:1 [c]Mt 12:14 **14:3** [a]Mk 14:3-9: *Mt 26:6-13;* Lk 7:37-39; Jn 12:1-8 [b]Mt 21:17 [c]Mt 26:6f; Jn 12:3 [1]An aromatic oil extracted from an East Indian plant

she broke the jar and poured it over
His head. **4** But some were indignant-
ly *remarking* to one another, "Why
has this perfume been wasted? **5** For
this perfume might have been sold
for over three hundred [1]denarii and
given to the poor." And they were
scolding her. **6** But Jesus said, "Let
her alone; why do you bother her?
She did a good work to Me. **7** For you
always have [a]the poor with you, and
whenever you wish you can do good
to them; but you do not always have
Me. **8** She has done what she could;
[a]she anointed My body beforehand
for the burial. **9** And truly I say to you,
[a]wherever the gospel is proclaimed
in the whole world, what this woman
did will also be spoken of in memory
of her."

**10** [a]Then Judas Iscariot, [b]who was
one of the twelve, went away to the
chief priests in order to [1]betray Him
to them. **11** And when they heard *this*,
they were glad and promised to give
him money. And he *began* seeking
how to betray Him at an opportune
time.

### *The Passover Meal*

**12** [a]And on the first day of [b]Unleav-
ened Bread, when [1]the Passover lamb
was being [c]sacrificed, His disciples
*said to Him, "Where do You want us
to go and prepare for You to eat the
Passover?" **13** And He *sent two of
His disciples and *said to them, "Go
into the city, and a man will meet you
carrying a pitcher of water; follow
him; **14** and wherever he enters, say to
the owner of the house, 'The Teacher
says, "Where is My [a]guest room in
which I may eat the Passover with
My disciples?"' **15** And he himself
will show you a large upper room
furnished *and* ready; prepare for us
there." **16** And the disciples went out
and came to the city, and found *it*
just as He had told them; and they
prepared the Passover.

**17** [a]And when it was evening He
*came with the twelve. **18** And as they
were reclining *at the table* and eating,
Jesus said, "Truly I say to you that one
of you will [1]betray Me—the one who
is eating with Me." **19** They began to
be grieved and to say to Him one by
one, "Surely not I?" **20** And He said
to them, "*It is* one of the twelve, the
one who dips with Me in the bowl.
**21** For the Son of Man *is to* go just as
it is written of Him; but woe to that
man [1]by whom the Son of Man is be-
trayed! *It would have been* good [2]for
that man if he had not been born."

### *The Lord's Supper*

**22** [a]And while they were eating,
He took *some* bread, and [1]after a
[b]blessing, He broke *it*, and gave *it* to
them, and said, "Take *it*; this is My
body." **23** And when He had taken
a cup *and* given thanks, He gave *it*
to them, and they all drank from it.
**24** And He said to them, "This is My
[a]blood of the [b]covenant, which is
poured out for many. **25** Truly I say
to you, I will never again drink of the

---

**14:5** [1]A denarius was approx. a laborer's daily wage **14:7** [a]Dt 15:11; Mt 26:11; Jn 12:8 **14:8** [a]Jn 19:40
**14:9** [a]Mt 26:13 **14:10** [a]Mk 14:10, 11: *Mt 26:14-16; Lk 22:3-6* [b]Jn 6:71 [1]Or *hand Him over*
**14:12** [a]Mk 14:12-16: *Mt 26:17-19; Lk 22:7-13* [b]Mt 26:17 [c]Dt 16:5; Mk 14:1; Lk 22:7; 1Co 5:7 [1]Lit *they were sacrificing the Passover,* **14:14** [a]Lk 22:11 **14:17** [a]Mk 14:17-21: *Mt 26:20-24; Lk 22:14, 21-23;* Jn 13:18ff **14:18** [1]Or *deliver Me over* **14:21** [1]Or *through* [2]Lit *for him if that man had not been born*
**14:22** [a]Mk 14:22-25: *Mt 26:26-29; Lk 22:17-20; 1Co 11:23-25;* Mk 10:16 [b]Mt 14:19 [1]Lit *having blessed*
**14:24** [a]Ex 24:8 [b]Jer 31:31-34

fruit of the vine until that day when I drink it new in the kingdom of God."

**26** [a]And after singing a hymn, they went out to [b]the Mount of Olives.

**27** [a]And Jesus *said to them, "You will all [1]fall away, because it is written, '[b]I WILL STRIKE DOWN THE SHEPHERD, AND THE SHEEP SHALL BE SCATTERED.' **28** But after I have been raised, [a]I will go ahead of you to Galilee." **29** But Peter said to Him, "*Even* though all may [1]fall away, yet I will not." **30** And Jesus *said to him, "Truly I say to you, that [a]today, this *very* night, before [b]a rooster crows twice, you yourself will deny Me three times." **31** But *Peter* kept saying insistently, "If I have to die with You, I will not deny You!" And they all were saying the same thing also.

### *Jesus Prays in Gethsemane*

**32** [a]Then they *came to a place named Gethsemane; and He *said to His disciples, "Sit here until I have prayed." **33** And He *took with Him Peter and James and John, and began to be very [a]distressed and troubled. **34** And He *said to them, "[a]My soul is deeply grieved to the point of death; remain here and keep watch." **35** And He went a little beyond *them*, and fell to the ground and *began to* pray that if it were possible, [a]the hour might pass from Him. **36** And He was saying, "[a]Abba! Father! All things are possible for You; remove this cup from Me; [b]yet not what I will, but what You will." **37** And He *came and *found them sleeping, and *said to Peter, "Simon, are you sleeping? Could you not keep watch for one hour? **38** [a]Keep watching and praying that you may not come into temptation; the spirit is willing, but the flesh is weak." **39** And again He went away and prayed, saying the same [1]words. **40** And again He came and found them sleeping, for their eyes were very heavy; and they did not know what to answer Him. **41** And He *came the third time, and *said to them, "[1]Are you still sleeping and resting? It is enough; [a]the hour has come; behold, the Son of Man is being [2]betrayed into the hands of sinners. **42** Get up, let us go; behold, the one who betrays Me is at hand!"

### *The Betrayal and Arrest of Jesus*

**43** [a]And immediately while He was still speaking, Judas, one of the twelve, *came up, and with him *was* a crowd with swords and clubs, *who were* from the chief priests and the scribes and the elders. **44** Now he who was betraying Him had given them a signal, saying, "Whomever I kiss, He is the one; seize Him and lead Him away [1]under guard." **45** And after coming, *Judas*, having immediately gone to Him, *said, "[a]Rabbi!" and kissed Him. **46** And they laid hands on Him and seized Him. **47** But one of those who stood by drew his sword, and struck the slave of the high priest and [1]cut off his ear. **48** And Jesus answered and said to them, "Have you come out with swords and clubs to arrest Me, as *you would* against a

**14:26** [a]Mt 26:30 [b]Mt 21:1 **14:27** [a]Mk 14:27-31: *Mt 26:31-35* [b]Zec 13:7 [1]Or *stumble* **14:28** [a]Mt 28:16 **14:29** [1]Or *stumble* **14:30** [a]Mt 26:34 [b]Mk 14:68, 72; Jn 13:38 **14:32** [a]Mk 14:32-42: *Mt 26:36-46; Lk 22:40-46* **14:33** [a]Mk 9:15; 16:5, 6 **14:34** [a]Mt 26:38; Jn 12:27 **14:35** [a]Mt 26:45; Mk 14:41 **14:36** [a]Ro 8:15; Ga 4:6 [b]Mt 26:39 **14:38** [a]Mt 26:41 **14:39** [1]Lit *word* **14:41** [a]Mk 14:35 [1]Or *Keep on sleeping therefore* [2]Or *delivered* **14:43** [a]Mk 14:43-50: *Mt 26:47-56; Lk 22:47-53; Jn 18:3-11* **14:44** [1]Lit *safely* **14:45** [a]Mt 23:7 **14:47** [1]Lit *took off*

robber? **49** Every day I was with you
[a]in the temple teaching, and you did
not seize Me; but *this has taken place*
in order that the Scriptures would
be fulfilled." **50** And they all left Him
and fled.

**51** And a young man was following
Him, wearing *nothing but* a linen
sheet over *his* naked *body*; and they
*seized him. **52** But he [1]pulled free of
the linen sheet and escaped naked.

### *Jesus Before His Accusers*

**53** [a]Then they led Jesus away to the
high priest; and all the chief priests
and the elders and the scribes *gath-
ered together. **54** And Peter followed
Him at a distance, [a]right into [b]the
courtyard of the high priest; and
he was sitting with the [1]officers
and [c]warming himself at the [2]fire.
**55** Now the chief priests and the
whole [a,1]Sanhedrin were seeking
to obtain testimony against Jesus
to put Him to death, and they were
not finding any. **56** For many were
giving false testimony against Him,
but their testimony was not consis-
tent. **57** And some, standing up, were
giving false testimony against Him,
saying, **58** "We ourselves heard Him
say, '[a]I will destroy this [1]sanctuary
made with hands, and in three days
I will build another made without
hands.'" **59** And not even in this
way was their testimony consistent.
**60** And the high priest stood up in
*their* midst and questioned Jesus,
saying, "You answer nothing? What
are these men testifying against
You?" **61** [a]But He kept silent and did
not answer. [b]Again the high priest
was questioning Him and *said to
Him, "Are You the [1]Christ, the Son
of the Blessed *One*?" **62** And Jesus
said, "I am; and you shall see [a]THE
SON OF MAN SITTING AT THE RIGHT
HAND OF THE POWER, and [b]COMING
WITH THE CLOUDS OF HEAVEN."
**63** [a]And tearing his tunics, the high
priest *said, "What further need
do we have of witnesses? **64** You
have heard the [a]blasphemy; how
does it seem to you?" And they all
condemned Him to be deserving of
death. **65** And some began to [a]spit
at Him, and [b,1]to blindfold Him, and
to beat Him with their fists, and to
say to Him, "[c]Prophesy!" And the
officers [2]received Him with [3]slaps
*in the face*.

### *Peter's Denials*

**66** [a]And as Peter was below in [b]the
courtyard, one of the servant-girls
of the high priest *came, **67** and
seeing Peter [a]warming himself, she
looked at him and *said, "You also
were with the [b]Nazarene, Jesus."
**68** But he denied *it*, saying, "I neither
know nor understand what you are
talking about." And he [a]went out
into the entryway.[1] **69** And when the
servant-girl saw him, she began once
more to say to the bystanders, "This
is *one* of them!" **70** But again [a]he was

---

**14:49** [a]Mk 12:35; Lk 19:47; 21:37 **14:52** [1]Lit *left behind* **14:53** [a]Mk 14:53-65: *Mt 26:57-68; Jn 18:12f, 19-24* **14:54** [a]Mk 14:68 [b]Mt 26:3 [c]Mk 14:67; Jn 18:18 [1]Or *servants* [2]Lit *light* **14:55** [a]Mt 5:22 [1]Or *Council* **14:58** [a]Mt 26:61; Mk 15:29; Jn 2:19 [1]The inner part of the temple **14:61** [a]Mt 26:63 [b]Mk 14:61-63: *Mt 26:63ff; Lk 22:67-71* [1]Messiah **14:62** [a]Ps 110:1; Mk 13:26 [b]Da 7:13 **14:63** [a]Nu 14:6; Mt 26:65; Ac 14:14 **14:64** [a]Lv 24:16 **14:65** [a]Mt 26:67; Mk 10:34 [b]Es 7:8 [c]Mt 26:68; Lk 22:64 [1]Or *cover over His face* [2]Or *treated* [3]Or *blows with rods* **14:66** [a]Mk 14:66-72: *Mt 26:69-75; Lk 22:56-62; Jn 18:16-18, 25-27* [b]Mk 14:54 **14:67** [a]Mk 14:54 [b]Mk 1:24 **14:68** [a]Mk 14:54 [1]Later mss add *and a rooster crowed* **14:70** [a]Mk 14:68

denying it. And after a little while
the bystanders were again saying to
Peter, "Surely you are *one* of them,
[b]for you are also a Galilean." **71** But
he began to [1]curse and swear, "I do
not know this man you are talking
about!" **72** And immediately a rooster
crowed a second time. And Peter
remembered how Jesus had said the
statement to him, "Before [a]a rooster
crows twice, you will deny Me three
times." [1]And throwing himself down,
he *began to* cry.

### *Jesus Before Pilate*

**15** [a]And early in the morning the
chief priests with the elders
and scribes and the whole [b]Sanhe-
drin, immediately held council; and
binding Jesus, led Him away and
delivered *Him* to Pilate. **2** [a]And Pilate
questioned Him, "Are You the King
of the Jews?" And He answered him
and *said, "You yourself say *it*." **3** And
the chief priests *began to* accuse
Him of many things. **4** Then Pilate
was questioning Him again, saying,
"You answer nothing? See how many
accusations they bring against You!"
**5** But Jesus [a]made no further answer;
so Pilate marveled.

**6** [a]Now at the feast he used to
release for them *any* one prisoner
whom they requested. **7** And the
man named Barabbas had been im-
prisoned with the insurrectionists
who had committed murder in the
insurrection. **8** And the crowd went
up and began asking him *to do* as
he had been accustomed to do for
them. **9** And Pilate answered them,
saying, "Do you want me to release
for you the King of the Jews?" **10** For
he was aware that the chief priests
had delivered Him over because of
envy. **11** But the chief priests stirred
up the crowd [a]*to ask* him to release
Barabbas for them instead. **12** And
answering again, Pilate was saying
to them, "Then what shall I do with
Him whom you call the King of the
Jews?" **13** And they shouted again,
"Crucify Him!" **14** But Pilate was
saying to them, "Why? What evil
did He do?" But they shouted all the
more, "Crucify Him!" **15** And wishing
to satisfy the crowd, Pilate released
Barabbas for them, and after having
Jesus [a]scourged, he delivered Him
over to be crucified.

### *Jesus Is Mocked*

**16** [a]So the soldiers took Him away
into [b]the [1]palace (that is, the [2]Praeto-
rium), and they *called together the
whole *Roman* [c,3]cohort. **17** And they
*dressed Him up in purple, and after
twisting a crown of thorns, they *put
it on Him; **18** and they began to greet
Him, "Hail, King of the Jews!" **19** And
they kept beating His head with a
[1]reed, and spitting on Him; and
kneeling, they were bowing down
before Him. **20** And after they had
mocked Him, they took the purple
robe off Him and put His *own* gar-
ments on Him. And they *led Him
out to crucify Him.

**21** [a]And they *pressed into ser-
vice a passer-by coming from the

---

**14:70** [b]Mt 26:73; Lk 22:59 **14:71** [1]Or *put himself under a curse* **14:72** [a]Mk 14:30, 68 [1]Or *Thinking of this, he began weeping* ◆ **15:1** [a]Mt 27:1 [b]Mt 5:22 **15:2** [a]Mk 15:2-5: *Mt 27:11-14; Lk 23:2, 3; Jn 18:29-38* **15:5** [a]Mt 27:12 **15:6** [a]Mk 15:6-15: *Mt 27:15-26; Lk 23:18-25; Jn 18:39-19:16* **15:11** [a]Ac 3:14 **15:15** [a]Mt 27:26 **15:16** [a]Mk 15:16-20: *Mt 27:27-31* [b]Mt 26:3; 27:27 [c]Ac 10:1 [1]Or *court* [2]Governor's official residence [3]Normally 600 men (the number varied); or *battalion* **15:19** [1]Or *staff* (made of a reed) **15:21** [a]Mk 15:21: *Mt 27:32; Lk 23:26*

countryside, Simon of Cyrene (the
father of Alexander and [b]Rufus), to
[1]carry His cross.

### *The Crucifixion*

22 [a]Then they *brought Him to the
place [b]Golgotha, which is translated,
Place of a Skull. 23 And they tried to
give Him [a]wine mixed with myrrh;
but He did not take it. 24 And they
*crucified Him, and *[a]divided up
His garments among themselves,
casting [1]lots for them *to decide* who
should take what. 25 Now it was the
[a,1]third hour, and they crucified Him.
26 And the inscription of the charge
against Him [1]read, "[a]THE KING OF
THE JEWS."

27 And they *crucified two robbers
with Him, one on His right and one
on His left. 28 [1][And the Scripture
was fulfilled which says, "And He
was numbered with transgressors."]
29 And those passing by were
blaspheming Him, [a]shaking their
heads, and saying, "Ha! You who
*are going to* [b]destroy the [1]sanctuary
and rebuild it in three days, 30 save
Yourself by coming down from the
cross!" 31 In the same way, mock-
ing *Him* to one another, the chief
priests also, along with the scribes,
were saying, "[a]He saved others; [1]He
cannot save Himself. 32 Let *this*
[1]Christ, [a]the King of Israel, now
come down from the cross, so that
we may see and believe!" [b]Those
who were crucified with Him were
also insulting Him.

33 [a]And when the [b,1]sixth hour
came, darkness [2]fell over the whole
land until the [b,3]ninth hour. 34 And
at the [a]ninth hour Jesus cried out
with a loud voice, "[b]ELOI, ELOI, LAMA
SABACHTHANI?" which is translated,
"MY GOD, MY GOD, WHY HAVE YOU
FORSAKEN ME?" 35 And when some
of the bystanders heard it, they
*began* saying, "Look, He is calling
for Elijah." 36 And someone ran
and filled a sponge with sour wine,
put it on a reed, and gave Him a
drink, saying, "[1]Let us see whether
Elijah will come to take Him down."
37 [a]And Jesus, uttering a loud cry,
breathed His last. 38 [a]And the veil
of the sanctuary was torn in two
from top to bottom. 39 [a]And when
the centurion, who was standing
[1]right in front of Him, saw [2]the way
He breathed His last, he said, "Truly
this man was God's Son!"

40 [a]And there were also *some*
women looking on from a distance,
among whom *were* Mary Magda-
lene, and Mary the mother of James
[b]the [1]Less and Joses, and [c]Salome,
41 who, when He was in Galilee,
were following Him and [a,1]serving
Him; and *there were* many other
women who came up with Him to
Jerusalem.

---

**15:21** [b]Ro 16:13 [1]Or *bear*, cf. Mt 27:32 **15:22** [a]Mk 15:22-32: *Mt 27:33-44; Lk 23:33-43; Jn 19:17-24* [b]Lk 23:33; Jn 19:17 **15:23** [a]Mt 27:34 **15:24** [a]Ps 22:18; Jn 19:24 [1]Lit *a lot upon* **15:25** [a]Mk 15:33 [1]9 a.m. **15:26** [a]Mt 27:37 [1]Lit *had been inscribed* **15:28** [1]Early mss omit this v **15:29** [a]Ps 22:7; 109:25; Mt 27:39 [b]Mk 14:58; Jn 2:19 [1]The inner part of the temple **15:31** [a]Mt 27:42; Lk 23:35 [1]Or *can He not save Himself?* **15:32** [a]Mt 27:42; Mk 15:26 [b]Mt 27:44; Mk 15:27; Lk 23:39-43 [1]Messiah **15:33** [a]Mk 15:33-41: *Mt 27:45-56; Lk 23:44-49* [b]Mt 27:45f; Mk 15:25; Lk 23:44 [1]Noon [2]Or *occurred* [3]3 p.m. **15:34** [a]Mt 27:45f; Mk 15:25; Lk 23:44 [b]Ps 22:1; Mt 27:46 **15:36** [1]Or *Hold off, let us see*; lit *Permit that we see* **15:37** [a]Mt 27:50; Lk 23:46; Jn 19:30 **15:38** [a]Ex 26:31-33; Mt 27:51; Lk 23:45 **15:39** [a]Mt 27:54; Mk 15:45; Lk 23:47 [1]Or *opposite Him* [2]Lit *that He thus* **15:40** [a]Mk 15:40, 41: *Mt 27:55f;* Lk 23:49; Jn 19:25 [b]Lk 19:3 [c]Mk 16:1 [1]Lit *little* (either in stature or age) **15:41** [a]Mt 27:55f [1]Or *waiting on*

### *Jesus Is Buried*

**42** [a]And when evening had already
come, because it was [b,1]Preparation
day, that is, the day before the Sab-
bath, **43** Joseph of Arimathea came, a
[a]prominent [1]Council member, who
himself was [b]waiting for the kingdom
of God; and he [c]gathered up courage
and went in before Pilate, and asked
for the body of Jesus. **44** And Pilate
wondered if He had died by this time,
and summoning the centurion, he
questioned him as to whether He
already died. **45** And ascertaining this
from [a]the centurion, he granted the
body to Joseph. **46** And when Joseph
had bought a linen cloth and took
Him down, he wrapped Him in the
linen cloth and laid Him in a tomb
which had been hewn out in the rock.
And he rolled a stone against the
entrance of the tomb. **47** [a]And Mary
Magdalene and Mary the *mother* of
Joses were looking on *to see* where
He had been laid.

### *Jesus Is Risen!*

**16** [a]And when the Sabbath passed,
[b]Mary Magdalene, and Mary the
*mother* of James, and Salome, [c]bought
spices, so that they might come and
anoint Him. **2** And very early on the
first day of the week, they *came to
the tomb when the sun had risen.
**3** *And they* were saying to one another,
"Who will roll away [a]the stone for us
from the entrance of the tomb?" **4** And
looking up, they *saw that the stone
had been rolled away, [1]although it was
very large. **5** [a]And entering the tomb,
they saw a young man sitting on the
right side, wearing a white robe; and
they [b]were amazed. **6** And he *said to
them, "[a]Do not be amazed; you are
looking for Jesus the [b]Nazarene, who
has been crucified. [c]He has risen; He is
not here; behold, the place where they
laid Him. **7** But go, tell His disciples and
Peter, '[a]He is going ahead of you to
Galilee; there you will see Him, just as
He told you.'" **8** And they went out and
fled from the tomb, for trembling and
astonishment were gripping them;
and they said nothing to anyone, for
they were afraid.

**9** [1][Now after He had risen early
on the first day of the week, He first
appeared to [a]Mary Magdalene, from
whom He had cast out seven demons.
**10** [a]She went and reported to those
who had been with Him, while they
were mourning and crying. **11** And
when they heard that He was alive
and had been seen by her, [a]they
refused to believe it.

**12** After that, [a]He appeared in a
different form [b]to two of them while
they were walking along on their way
to the countryside. **13** And they went
away and reported it to the others,
but they [a]did not believe them either.

### *The Great Commission*

**14** Afterward [a]He appeared [b]to
the eleven themselves as they
were reclining *at the table*; and He

---

**15:42** [a]Mk 15:42-47: *Mt 27:57-61; Lk 23:50-56; Jn 19:38-42* [b]Mt 27:62 [1]Preparation for the Sabbath
**15:43** [a]Mt 27:57; Lk 23:50, 51; Ac 13:50; 17:12 [b]Mt 27:57; Lk 2:25, 38; 23:51; Jn 19:38 [c]Jn 19:38 [1]The Sanhedrin
**15:45** [a]Mk 15:39 **15:47** [a]Mt 27:56; Mk 15:40; 16:1 ◆ **16:1** [a]Mk 16:1-8: *Mt 28:1-8; Lk 24:1-10;* Jn 20:1-8
[b]Mk 15:47 [c]Lk 23:56; Jn 19:39f **16:3** [a]Mt 27:60; Mk 15:46; 16:4 **16:4** [1]Lit *for* **16:5** [a]Jn 20:11, 12
[b]Mk 9:15 **16:6** [a]Mk 9:15 [b]Mk 1:24 [c]Mt 28:6; Lk 24:6 **16:7** [a]Mt 26:32; Mk 14:28 **16:9** [a]Mt 27:56;
Jn 20:14 [1]Later mss add vv 9-20 **16:10** [a]Jn 20:18 **16:11** [a]Mt 28:17; Mk 16:13, 14; Lk 24:11, 41;
Jn 20:25 **16:12** [a]Mk 16:14; Jn 21:1, 14 [b]Lk 24:13-35 **16:13** [a]Mt 28:17; Mk 16:11, 14; Lk 24:11, 41; Jn 20:25
**16:14** [a]Mk 16:12; Jn 21:1, 14 [b]Lk 24:36; Jn 20:19, 26; 1Co 15:5

reproached them for their [c]unbelief
and hardness of heart, because they
had not believed those who had
seen Him after He had risen. **15** And
He said to them, "[a]Go into all the
world and preach the gospel to all
creation. **16** [a]He who has believed
and has been baptized shall be
saved; but he who has disbelieved
shall be condemned. **17** And these
[1]signs will accompany those who
have believed: [a]in My name they will
cast out demons, they will [b]speak
with new tongues; **18** and they will
[a]pick up serpents, and if they drink
any deadly *poison*, it will not hurt
them; they will [b]lay hands on the
sick, and they will recover."
**19** So then, the Lord Jesus, after
He had [a]spoken to them, [b]was tak-
en up into heaven and [c]sat down at
the right hand of God. **20** And they
went out and preached everywhere,
while the Lord worked with them,
and confirmed the word by the [1]signs
that followed.]

[2][*And they promptly reported all these instructions to Peter and his companions. And after that, Jesus Himself sent out through them from east to west the sacred and imperishable preaching of eternal salvation.*]

**16:14** [c]Mt 28:17; Mk 16:11, 13; Lk 24:11, 41; Jn 20:25 **16:15** [a]Mt 28:19; Ac 1:8 **16:16** [a]Jn 3:18, 36; Ac 16:31 **16:17** [a]Mk 9:38; Lk 10:17; Ac 5:16; 8:7; 16:18; 19:12 [b]Ac 2:4; 10:46; 19:6; 1Co 12:10, 28, 30; 13:1; 14:2 [1]Or *attesting miracles* **16:18** [a]Lk 10:19; Ac 28:3-5 [b]Mk 5:23 **16:19** [a]Ac 1:3 [b]Lk 9:51; 24:51; Jn 6:62; 20:17; Ac 1:2, 9-11; 1Ti 3:16 [c]Ps 110:1; Lk 22:69; Ac 7:55f; Ro 8:34; Eph 1:20; Col 3:1; Heb 1:3; 8:1; 10:12; 12:2; 1Pe 3:22 **16:20** [1]Or *attesting miracles* [2]A few late mss and versions contain this paragraph, usually after v 8; a few have it at the end of ch

The Gospel According to

# LUKE

### *Luke's Account of Things Fulfilled*

**1** Inasmuch as many have under-
taken to compile an account of
the things that [a,1]have been fulfilled
among us, **2** just as those, who [a]from
the beginning [1]were [b]eyewitnesses and
[c,2]servants of [d]the [3]word, handed *them*
down to us, **3** it seemed fitting for me as
well, [a]having [1]investigated everything
carefully from the beginning, to write
*it* out for you [b]in orderly sequence,
[c]most excellent [d]Theophilus, **4** so that
you may know the certainty about the
things you have been [a,1]taught.

### *John the Baptist's Birth Foretold*

**5** [a]In the days of Herod, king of Judea,
there was a priest named Zechariah,
of the [b]division of [1]Abijah, and he had
a wife [2]from the daughters of Aaron,
and her name was Elizabeth. **6** And
they were both [a]righteous in the sight
of God, walking [b]blamelessly in all
the commandments and righteous
requirements of the [1]Lord. **7** But they
had no child, because Elizabeth was
barren, and they were both advanced
in [1]years.

**8** Now it happened that while [a]he
was performing his priestly service
before God in the order of his divi-
sion, **9** according to the custom of
the priestly office, he was chosen by
lot [a]to enter the [1]sanctuary of the
[2]Lord and burn incense. **10** And the
whole multitude of the people were
praying [a]outside at the hour of the
incense offering. **11** And [a]an angel of
the [1]Lord appeared to him, standing
to the right of the altar of incense.
**12** And Zechariah was troubled when
he saw *the angel*, and [a]fear fell upon
him. **13** But the angel said to him, "[a]Do
not be afraid, Zechariah, for your
prayer has been heard, and your wife
Elizabeth will [1]bear you a son, and
[b]you will call his name [2]John. **14** And
you will have joy and gladness, and
many will rejoice at his birth. **15** For he
will be great in the sight of the [1]Lord;
and [a]HE WILL NOT DRINK ANY WINE OR
STRONG DRINK, and he will be filled
with the Holy Spirit [2]while yet in his
mother's womb. **16** And he will [a]turn
many of the sons of Israel back to the
[1]Lord their God. **17** And he will [a]go
before Him in the spirit and power
of [b]Elijah, [c]TO TURN THE HEARTS OF
THE FATHERS BACK TO THE CHILDREN,
and the disobedient to the attitude
of the righteous, to [a]make ready a
people prepared for the [1]Lord."

**18** And Zechariah said to the angel,
"How will I know this? For [a]I am an

---

◆ **1:1** [a]Ro 4:21; 14:5; Col 2:2; 4:12; 1Th 1:5; 2Ti 4:17; Heb 6:11; 10:22 [1]Or *on which there is full conviction* **1:2** [a]Jn 15:27; Ac 1:21f [b]2Pe 1:16; 1Jn 1:1 [c]Ac 26:16; 1Co 4:1; Heb 2:3 [d]Mk 4:14; 16:20; Ac 8:4; 14:25; 16:6; 17:11 [1]Lit *became* [2]Or *ministers* [3]Gospel **1:3** [a]1Ti 4:6 [b]Ac 11:4; 18:23 [c]Ac 23:26; 24:3; 26:25 [d]Ac 1:1 [1]Or *followed* **1:4** [a]Ac 18:25; Ro 2:18; 1Co 14:19; Ga 6:6 [1]Or *orally instructed in* **1:5** [a]Mt 2:1 [b]1Chr 24:10 [1]Gr *Abia* [2]Of priestly descent **1:6** [a]Ge 7:1; Ac 2:25; 8:21 [b]Php 2:15; 3:6; 1Th 3:13 [1]In OT, Yahweh, cf. Dt 4:1 **1:7** [1]Lit *days* **1:8** [a]1Chr 24:19; 2Chr 8:14; 31:2 **1:9** [a]Ex 30:7f [1]The inner part of the temple [2]In OT, Yahweh, cf. 2Ki 18:16 **1:10** [a]Lv 16:17 **1:11** [a]Lk 2:9; Ac 5:19 [1]In OT, Yahweh, cf. 2Ki 1:3 **1:12** [a]Lk 2:9 **1:13** [a]Mt 14:27; Lk 1:30 [b]Lk 1:60, 63 [1]Or *give birth to*, cf. 1:14, 57 [2]Gr *Joannes*, Heb *Johanan*; so in Luke **1:15** [a]Nu 6:3; Jdg 13:4; Mt 11:18; Lk 7:33 [1]In OT, Yahweh, cf. Is 49:5 [2]Lit *from* **1:16** [a]Mt 3:2, 6; Lk 3:3 [1]In OT, Yahweh, cf. Ex 10:7 **1:17** [a]Lk 1:76 [b]Mt 11:14 [c]Mal 4:6 [1]In OT, Yahweh, cf. Is 40:1-3; Mal 4:6 **1:18** [a]Ge 17:17

old man and my wife is advanced in
[1]years." **19** And the angel answered
and said to him, "I am [a]Gabriel, who
[b]stands before God, and I was sent
to speak to you and to bring you
this good news. **20** And behold, you
shall be silent and unable to speak
until the day when these things take
place, because you did not believe my
words, which will be fulfilled in their
proper time."

**21** And the people were waiting
for Zechariah, and were wondering
at his delay in the sanctuary. **22** But
when he came out, he was unable
to speak to them, and they realized
that he had seen a vision in the sanc-
tuary. And he [a]kept [1]making signs
to them, and remained mute. **23** And
it happened that when the days of
his priestly service were fulfilled, he
went back home.

**24** After these days Elizabeth his
wife conceived, and she [1]kept herself
in seclusion for five months, saying,
**25** "This is the way the Lord has dealt
with me in the days when He looked
upon *me* to [a]take away my disgrace
among men."

### *Jesus' Birth Foretold*

**26** Now in the sixth month the angel
[a]Gabriel was sent from God to a city
in Galilee called [b]Nazareth, **27** to [a]a
virgin betrothed to a man whose
name was Joseph, [b]of the [1]house
of David, and the virgin's name was
[2]Mary. **28** And coming in, he said to
her, "Greetings, [1]favored one! The
Lord [2]*is* with you." **29** But she [a]was
very perplexed at *this* statement, and
was pondering what kind of greeting
this was. **30** And the angel said to her,
"[a]Do not be afraid, Mary, for you have
found favor with God. **31** And behold,
you will conceive in *your* womb and
bear a son, and you [a]shall name Him
Jesus. **32** [1]He will be great and will be
called the Son of [a]the Most High, and
the [2]Lord God will give Him [b]the
throne of His father David, **33** [a]and
He will reign over the house of Jacob
forever, [b]and there will be no end of
His kingdom." **34** But Mary said to
the angel, "How will this be, since I
[1]am a virgin?" **35** The angel answered
and said to her, "[a]The Holy Spirit will
come upon you, and the power of
[b]the Most High will overshadow
you; and for that reason [c,1]the holy
Child shall be called [d]the Son of God.
**36** And behold, your relative Eliza-
beth has also conceived a son in her
old age; and this is the sixth month
for her who was called barren. **37** For
[a,1]nothing will be impossible with
God." **38** And Mary said, "Behold, the
slave of the [1]Lord; may it be done to
me according to your word." And the
angel departed from her.

### *Mary Visits Elizabeth*

**39** Now [1]at this time Mary arose and
went in a hurry to [a]the hill country,
to a city of Judah, **40** and entered
the house of Zechariah and greeted

---

**1:18** [1]Lit *days* **1:19** [a]Da 8:16; 9:21; Lk 1:26 [b]Mt 18:10 **1:22** [a]Lk 1:62 [1]Or *beckoning to, nodding to* **1:24** [1]*Lit was hidden* **1:25** [a]Ge 30:23; Is 4:1; 25:8 **1:26** [a]Lk 1:19 [b]Mt 2:23 **1:27** [a]Mt 1:18 [b]Mt 1:16, 20; Lk 2:4 [1]Or *descendants* [2]Gr *Mariam*, Heb *Miriam*; so in Luke **1:28** [1]Or *woman richly blessed* [2]Or *be* **1:29** [a]Lk 1:12 **1:30** [a]Mt 14:27; Lk 1:13 **1:31** [a]Is 7:14; Mt 1:21, 25; Lk 2:21 **1:32** [a]Mk 5:7; Lk 1:35, 76; 6:35; Ac 7:48 [b]2Sa 7:12, 13, 16; Is 9:7 [1]Lit *This One* [2]In OT, Yahweh, cf. 2Sa 7:11 **1:33** [a]Mt 1:1 [b]2Sa 7:13, 16; Ps 89:36, 37; Da 2:44; 7:14, 18, 27; Mt 28:18 **1:34** [1]Lit *know no man* **1:35** [a]Mt 1:18 [b]Lk 1:32 [c]Mk 1:24 [d]Mt 4:3; Jn 1:34, 49; 20:31 [1]Lit *the holy thing begotten* **1:37** [a]Ge 18:14; Jer 32:17; Mt 19:26 [1]Lit *not any word* **1:38** [1]In OT, Yahweh, cf. Dt 34:5 **1:39** [a]Jos 20:7; 21:11; Lk 1:65 [1]Lit *in these days*

Elizabeth. **41** And it happened that
when Elizabeth heard Mary's greet-
ing, the baby leaped in her womb, and
Elizabeth was [a]filled with the Holy
Spirit. **42** And she cried out with a
loud voice and said, "Blessed *are* you
among women, and blessed *is* the
fruit of your womb! **43** And [1]how has
it *happened* to me, that the mother of
[a]my Lord would come to me? **44** For
behold, when the sound of your
greeting reached my ears, the baby
leaped in my womb for joy. **45** And
[a]blessed *is* she who believed [1]that
there would be a fulfillment of what
had been spoken to her [2]by the [3]Lord."

### *Mary Magnifies the Lord*

**46** And Mary said:
"[a]My soul [b]magnifies the [1]Lord,
**47** And [a]my spirit has rejoiced
in [b]God my Savior.
**48** "For [a]He has looked upon the
humble state of His slave,
For behold, from this time
on, all generations will
count me [b]blessed.
**49** "For the Mighty One has
done great things for me,
And holy is His name.
**50** "[a]AND HIS MERCY IS
[1]UPON GENERATION
AFTER GENERATION
TOWARD THOSE WHO FEAR HIM.
**51** "[a]He has done a mighty
deed with His arm;
He has scattered *those
who were* proud in the
[1]thoughts of their heart.
**52** "He has brought down rulers
from *their* thrones,
And has [a]exalted those
who were humble.
**53** "[a]HE HAS FILLED THE HUNGRY
WITH GOOD THINGS,
And sent away the rich
empty-handed.
**54** "He has given help
to Israel His servant,
[1]In remembrance of His mercy,
**55** [a]As He spoke to our fathers,
[b]To Abraham and his
seed forever."

**56** And Mary stayed with her about
three months, and *then* returned to
her home.

### *John the Baptist Is Born*

**57** Now the time was fulfilled for
Elizabeth to [1]give birth, and she gave
birth to a son. **58** And her neighbors
and her relatives heard that the Lord
had [a]magnified His great mercy to-
ward her, and they were rejoicing
with her.

**59** And it happened that on [a]the
eighth day they came to circumcise
the child, and they were going to call
him Zechariah, after the name of his
father. **60** But his mother answered
and said, "No, but [a]he shall be called
John." **61** And they said to her, "There
is no one among your relatives who
is called by this name." **62** And they
[a]were making signs to his father, as
to what he wanted him called. **63** And
he asked for a tablet and wrote as
follows, "[a]His name is John." And

**1:41** [a]Lk 1:67; Ac 2:4; 4:8; 9:17 **1:43** [a]Lk 2:11 [1]Lit *from where this to me* **1:45** [a]Lk 1:20, 48 [1]Or *because there will be* [2]Lit *from* [3]In OT, Yahweh, cf. Ge 12:4 **1:46** [a]Lk 1:46-53: *1Sa 2:1-10* [b]Ps 34:2f [1]In OT, Yahweh, cf. 1Sa 2:1 **1:47** [a]Ps 35:9; Hab 3:18 [b]1Ti 1:1; 2:3; Tit 1:3; 2:10; 3:4; Jd 25 **1:48** [a]Ps 138:6 [b]Lk 1:45 **1:50** [a]Ps 103:17 [1]Lit *unto generations and generations* **1:51** [a]Ps 98:1; 118:15 [1]Lit *thought* **1:52** [a]Job 5:11 **1:53** [a]Ps 107:9 **1:54** [1]Lit *So as to remember* **1:55** [a]Ge 17:19; Ps 132:11; Ga 3:16 [b]Ge 17:7 **1:57** [1]Or *bear* **1:58** [a]Ge 19:19 **1:59** [a]Ge 17:12; Lv 12:3; Lk 2:21; Php 3:5 **1:60** [a]Lk 1:13, 63 **1:62** [a]Lk 1:22 **1:63** [a]Lk 1:13, 60

they all marveled. **64** [a]And at once
his mouth was opened and his tongue
*loosed*, and he *began to* speak, bless-
ing God. **65** And fear came on all those
living around them, and all these
matters were being talked about in
all [a]the hill country of Judea. **66** And
all who heard *these things* put *them*
in their heart, saying, "What then will
this child be?" For [a]the hand of the
[1]Lord was indeed with him.

### *Zechariah's Prophecy*

**67** And his father Zechariah [a]was
filled with the Holy Spirit, and
[b]prophesied, saying:

**68** "[a]Blessed *be* the [1]Lord
God of Israel,
For He visited and
accomplished [b]redemption
for His people,
**69** And raised up a [a]horn
of salvation for us
In the house of David
[b]His servant—
**70** [a]As He spoke by the mouth
of His holy prophets
[b]from of old—
**71** [a,1]Salvation [b]FROM
OUR ENEMIES,
And FROM THE HAND
OF ALL WHO HATE US,
**72** [a]To show mercy
toward our fathers,
[b]And to remember His
holy covenant,
**73** [a]The oath which He swore
to Abraham our father,
**74** To grant us that we, being
rescued from the hand
of our enemies,
Might serve Him without fear,
**75** [a]In holiness and righteousness
before Him all our days.
**76** "And you, child, will be
called the [a]prophet
of [b]the Most High,
For you will go on
[c]BEFORE THE [1]LORD
TO [d]MAKE READY HIS WAYS,
**77** To give to His people *the*
knowledge of salvation
[1]By [a]the forgiveness
of their sins,
**78** Because of the tender
mercy of our God,
With which [a]the Sunrise
from on high will visit us,
**79** [a]TO SHINE UPON THOSE WHO
SIT IN DARKNESS AND THE
SHADOW OF DEATH,
To direct our feet
into the [b]way of peace."

**80** [a]And the child continued to grow
and to become strong in spirit, and he
lived in the desolate regions until the
day of his public appearance to Israel.

### *Jesus Is Born in Bethlehem*

**2** Now it happened that in those
days a decree went out from
[a]Caesar Augustus for a census to be
taken of [b]all [1]the inhabited earth.
**2** [1]This was the first census taken
while [2]Quirinius was governor of
[a]Syria. **3** And everyone was going

**1:64** [a]Lk 1:20 **1:65** [a]Lk 1:39 **1:66** [a]Ac 11:21 [1]In OT, Yahweh, cf. Ex 9:3 **1:67** [a]Lk 1:41; Ac 2:4, 8; 9:17 [b]Joel 2:28 **1:68** [a]1Ki 1:48; Ps 41:13; 72:18; 106:48 [b]Lk 1:71; 2:38; Heb 9:12 [1]In OT, Yahweh, cf. 1Sa 25:32 **1:69** [a]1Sa 2:1, 10; Ps 18:2; 89:17; 132:17; Eze 29:21 [b]Mt 1:1 **1:70** [a]Ro 1:2 [b]Ac 3:21 **1:71** [a]Lk 1:68 [b]Ps 106:10 [1]Or *Deliverance* **1:72** [a]Mic 7:20 [b]Ps 105:8f, 42; 106:45 **1:73** [a]Ge 22:16ff; Heb 6:13 **1:75** [a]Eph 4:24 **1:76** [a]Mt 11:9 [b]Lk 1:32 [c]Mal 3:1; Mt 11:10; Mk 1:2; Lk 7:27 [d]Lk 1:17 [1]In OT, Yahweh, cf. Is 40:1-3; Mal 3:1 **1:77** [a]Jer 31:34; Mk 1:4 [1]Or *Consisting in* **1:78** [a]Mal 4:2; Eph 5:14; 2Pe 1:19 **1:79** [a]Is 9:2 [b]Is 59:8; Mt 4:16 **1:80** [a]Lk 2:40 ◆ **2:1** [a]Mt 22:17; Lk 3:1 [b]Mt 24:14 [1]The Roman empire **2:2** [a]Mt 4:24 [1]Or *This took place as a first census* [2]Gr *Kyrenios*

to be registered for the census, each
to his own city. 4 And Joseph also
went up from Galilee, from the city
of Nazareth, to Judea, to the city of
David, which is called Bethlehem,
because [a]he was of the house and
family of David, 5 in order to register
along with Mary, who was betrothed
to him, *and* was with child. 6 Now it
happened that while they were there,
the days were fulfilled for her to give
birth. 7 And she [a]gave birth to her
firstborn son; and she wrapped Him
in cloths, and laid Him in a [1]manger,
because there was no place for them
in the [2]guest room.

8 In the same region there were
*some* shepherds staying out in the
fields and keeping watch over their
flock by night. 9 And [a]an angel of
the [1]Lord [b]stood before them, and
the glory of the [1]Lord shone around
them; and they were terribly fright-
ened. 10 But the angel said to them,
"[a]Do not be afraid; for behold, I bring
you good news of great joy which will
be for all the people. 11 For today in
the city of David there has been born
for you a [a]Savior, who is [b,1]Christ [c]the
Lord. 12 [a]And this *will be* the sign for
you: you will find a baby wrapped in
cloths and lying in a [1]manger." 13 And
suddenly there appeared with the
angel a multitude of the heavenly
host praising God and saying,

14 "[a]Glory to God in the highest,
And on earth peace among
men [b,1]with whom
He is pleased."

15 And it happened that when the
angels had gone away from them
into heaven, the shepherds *began*
saying to one another, "Let us go to
Bethlehem then, and see this thing
that has happened which the Lord
has made known to us." 16 So they
went in a hurry and found their way
to Mary and Joseph, and the baby ly-
ing in the [1]manger. 17 And when they
had seen this, they made known the
statement which had been told them
about this Child. 18 And all who heard
it marveled at the things which were
told them by the shepherds. 19 But
Mary [a]was treasuring all these things,
pondering them in her heart. 20 And
the shepherds went back, [a]glorifying
and praising God for all that they had
heard and seen, just as was told them.

### *Jesus Presented at the Temple*

21 And when [a]eight days were ful-
filled so that *they* could circumcise
Him, [b]His name was called Jesus, the
name given by the angel before He
was conceived in the womb.

22 [a]And when the days for their
cleansing according to the Law of
Moses were fulfilled, they brought
Him up to Jerusalem to present Him
to the [1]Lord 23 (as it is written in the
Law of the [1]Lord, "[a]EVERY *firstborn*
MALE THAT OPENS THE WOMB SHALL BE
CALLED HOLY TO THE [1]LORD"), 24 and
to offer a sacrifice according to what
was said in the Law of the [1]Lord, "[a]A
PAIR OF TURTLEDOVES OR TWO YOUNG
PIGEONS."

**2:4** [a]Lk 1:27 **2:7** [a]Mt 1:25 [1]Or *feeding trough* [2]Gr *kataluma*, cf. 22:11; some versions *inn* **2:9** [a]Lk 1:11; Ac 5:19 [b]Lk 24:4; Ac 12:7 [1]In OT, Yahweh, cf. Ex 40:34; 2Ki 1:3 **2:10** [a]Mt 14:27 **2:11** [a]Mt 1:21; Jn 4:42; Ac 5:31 [b]Mt 1:16; 16:16, 20; Jn 11:27 [c]Lk 1:43; Ac 2:36; 10:36 [1]Messiah **2:12** [a]1Sa 2:34; 2Ki 19:29; 20:8f; Is 7:11, 14 [1]Or *feeding trough* **2:14** [a]Mt 21:9; Lk 19:38 [b]Lk 3:22; Eph 1:9; Php 2:13 [1]Or *of good will*; lit *of good pleasure* **2:16** [1]Or *feeding trough* **2:19** [a]Lk 2:51 **2:20** [a]Mt 9:8 **2:21** [a]Ge 17:12; Lv 12:3; Lk 1:59 [b]Mt 1:21, 25; Lk 1:31 **2:22** [a]Lv 12:6-8 [1]In OT, Yahweh, cf. Lv 14:11 **2:23** [a]Ex 13:2, 12; Nu 3:13; 8:17 [1]In OT, Yahweh, cf. Ps 19:7; Ex 13:2 **2:24** [a]Lv 5:11; 12:8 [1]In OT, Yahweh, cf. Ps 19:7

**25** And behold, there was a man in
Jerusalem whose name was Simeon,
and this man was [a]righteous and de-
vout, [b]waiting for the [c,1]comfort of
Israel, and the Holy Spirit was upon
him. **26** And [a]it had been revealed to
him by the Holy Spirit that he would
not [b]see death before he had seen the
[1]Lord's [2]Christ. **27** And he came in
the Spirit into the temple, and when
the parents brought in the child Jesus
[a,1]to carry out for Him the custom of
the Law, **28** then he took Him into his
arms and blessed God, and said,

**29** "Now Master, You are releasing
Your slave in peace,
[a]According to Your word.
**30** For my eyes have [a]seen
Your salvation,
**31** Which You prepared in the
presence of all peoples,
**32** [a]A LIGHT FOR REVELATION
TO THE GENTILES,
And for the glory
of Your people Israel."

**33** And His father and [a]mother
were marveling at the things which
were being said about Him. **34** And
Simeon blessed them and said to
Mary [a]His mother, "Behold, this
*Child* is appointed for [b]the fall and
[1]rise of many in Israel, and for a sign
to be opposed— **35** and a sword will
pierce through your own soul as
well—that the thoughts from many
hearts may be revealed."
**36** And there was a [a]prophetess,
[1]Anna the daughter of Phanuel,
of [b]the tribe of Asher. She was
advanced in [2]years [c]having lived
with *her* husband seven years from
*when she was* a virgin, **37** and then as
a widow to the age of eighty-four. She
never left the temple, serving night
and day with [a]fastings and prayers.
**38** And at that very [1]moment she
came up and *began* giving thanks to
God, and continued to speak of Him
to all those who were [a]waiting for the
redemption of Jerusalem.

### The Return to Nazareth

**39** And when they had finished
everything according to the Law of
the [1]Lord, they returned to Galilee, to
[a]their own city of Nazareth. **40** [a]Now
the Child continued to grow and
become strong, being filled with
wisdom; and the grace of God was
upon Him.

### The Boy Jesus in the Temple

**41** And His parents would go to Jeru-
salem every year at [a]the Feast of the
Passover. **42** And when He became
twelve years *old*, they went up *there*
according to the custom of the Feast;
**43** and as they were returning, after
finishing the [a]days *of the Feast*, the
boy Jesus stayed behind in Jerusalem.
But His parents did not know. **44** But
supposing Him to be in the caravan,
they went a day's journey, and they
*began* searching for Him among
their relatives and acquaintances.
**45** When they did not find Him, they
returned to Jerusalem searching for
Him. **46** And it happened that after

---

**2:25** [a]Lk 1:6 [b]Mk 15:43; Lk 2:38; 23:51 [c]Is 40:1 [1]Or *consolation* **2:26** [a]Mt 2:12 [b]Ps 89:48; Jn 8:51; Heb 11:5 [1]In OT, Yahweh, cf. 1Sa 2:10 [2]Messiah **2:27** [a]Lk 2:22 [1]Lit *to do for Him according to*
**2:29** [a]Lk 2:26 **2:30** [a]Ps 119:166, 174; Is 52:10; Lk 3:6 **2:32** [a]Is 9:2; 42:6; 49:6, 9; 51:4; 60:1-3; Mt 4:16; Ac 13:47; 26:23 **2:33** [a]Mt 12:46 **2:34** [a]Mt 12:46 [b]Mt 21:44; 1Co 1:23; 2Co 2:16; 1Pe 2:8 [1]Or *resurrection*
**2:36** [a]Lk 2:38; Ac 21:9 [b]Jos 19:24 [c]1Ti 5:9 [1]Or *Hannah* [2]Lit *days* **2:37** [a]Lk 5:33; Ac 13:3; 14:23; 1Ti 5:5 **2:38** [a]Lk 1:68; 2:25 [1]Lit *hour* **2:39** [a]Mt 2:23; Lk 1:26; 2:51; 4:16 [1]In OT, Yahweh, cf. Ps 19:7
**2:40** [a]Lk 1:80; 2:52 **2:41** [a]Ex 12:11; 23:15; Dt 16:1-6 **2:43** [a]Ex 12:15

three days they found Him in the
temple, sitting in the midst of the
teachers, both listening to them and
asking them questions. **47** And all
who heard Him [a]were astounded at
His understanding and His answers.
**48** When they saw Him, they were
astonished, and [a]His mother said to
Him, "Child, why have You treated us
this way? Behold, [b]Your father and I
[1]have been anxiously searching for
You." **49** And He said to them, "Why
is it that you were searching for Me?
Did you not know that [a]I had to be
in My Father's [1]*house*?" **50** But [a]they
did not understand the statement
which He had spoken to them. **51** And
He went down with them and came
to [a]Nazareth, and He continued in
subjection to them, and [b]His mother
[c]was treasuring all *these* [1]things in
her heart.

**52** And Jesus was advancing in
wisdom and [1]stature, and in [a]favor
with God and men.

### *The Preaching of John the Baptist*

**3** Now in the fifteenth year of the
reign of Tiberius Caesar, when
[a]Pontius Pilate was governor of
Judea, and [b]Herod was tetrarch of
Galilee, and his brother Philip was
tetrarch of the region of Ituraea
and Trachonitis, and Lysanias was
*tetrarch* of Abilene, **2** during the high
priesthood of [a]Annas and [b]Caiaphas,
[c]the word of God came to John, the
son of Zechariah, in the wilderness.
**3** And he came into all [a]the district
around the Jordan, preaching a bap-
tism of repentance for the forgiveness
of sins; **4** as it is written in the book
of the words of Isaiah the prophet,

"[a]The voice of one crying
in the wilderness,
'Make ready the way
of the [1]Lord,
Make His paths straight.
**5** '[a]Every ravine will be filled,
And every mountain and hill
will be [1]brought low;
The crooked will be straight,
And the rough roads smooth.
**6** [a]And all [1]flesh will [b]see
the salvation of God.'"

**7** So he was saying to the crowds
who were going out to be baptized
by him, "[a]You brood of vipers, who
warned you to flee from the wrath
to come? **8** Therefore bear fruits in
keeping with repentance, and [a]do
not begin to say [1]to yourselves, '[b]We
have Abraham for our father,' for I say
to you that from these stones God is
able to raise up children to Abraham.
**9** But indeed the axe is already laid at
the root of the trees; therefore, [a]every
tree that does not bear good fruit is
cut down and thrown into the fire."

**10** And the crowds were question-
ing him, saying, "[a]Then what should
we do?" **11** And he would answer and
say to them, "The man who has two
[1]tunics is to [a]share with him who has
none; and he who has food is to do
likewise." **12** And [a]tax collectors also

**2:47** [a]Mt 7:28; 13:54; 22:33; Mk 1:22; 6:2; 11:18; Lk 4:32; Jn 7:15 **2:48** [a]Mt 12:46 [b]Lk 2:49; 3:23; 4:22 [1]Lit *are anxiously looking* **2:49** [a]Jn 4:34; 5:36 [1]Or *affairs*; lit *in the things of My Father* **2:50** [a]Mk 9:32; Lk 9:45; 18:34 **2:51** [a]Lk 2:39 [b]Mt 12:46 [c]Lk 2:19 [1]Lit *words* **2:52** [a]Lk 2:40 [1]Or *age* ◆ **3:1** [a]Mt 27:2 [b]Mt 14:1 **3:2** [a]Jn 18:13, 24; Ac 4:6 [b]Mt 26:3 [c]Lk 3:3-10: *Mt 3:1-10; Mk 1:3-5* **3:3** [a]Mt 3:5 **3:4** [a]Is 40:3 [1]In OT, Yahweh, cf. Is 40:3 **3:5** [a]Is 40:4 [1]Or *leveled* **3:6** [a]Is 40:5 [b]Lk 2:30 [1]Or *mankind* **3:7** [a]Mt 12:34; 23:33 **3:8** [a]Lk 5:21; 13:25, 26; 14:9 [b]Jn 8:33 [1]Or *in* **3:9** [a]Mt 7:19; Lk 13:6-9 **3:10** [a]Lk 3:12, 14; Ac 2:37, 38 **3:11** [a]Is 58:7; 1Ti 6:17, 18; Jas 2:14-20 [1]Gr *khiton*, the garment worn next to the skin **3:12** [a]Lk 7:29

came to be baptized, and they said to
him, "Teacher, what should we do?"
13 And he said to them, "[1]Collect
no more than what you have been
ordered to." 14 And soldiers were
also questioning him, saying, "What
should we also do?" And he said to
them, "Do not take money from any-
one by force, or [a]extort *anyone,* and
[b]be content with your wages."
15 Now while the people were in
a state of expectation and all were
reasoning in their hearts about John,
[a]as to whether he was the [1]Christ,
16 [a]John answered, saying to them all,
"As for me, I baptize you with water,
but One is coming who is mightier
than I, and I am not fit to untie the
strap of His sandals; He will baptize
you with the Holy Spirit and fire.
17 His [a]winnowing fork is in His hand
to thoroughly clear His threshing
floor and to gather the wheat into His
barn, but He will burn up the chaff
with [b]unquenchable fire."
18 So with many other exhor-
tations he proclaimed the gospel
to the people. 19 But when [a]Herod
the tetrarch was reproved by him
because of [a]Herodias, his brother's
wife, and because of all the wicked
things which [b]Herod had done,
20 Herod also added this to them all:
[a]he locked John up in prison.

### *The Baptism of Jesus*

21 [a]Now it happened that when all
the people were being baptized, Jesus
was also baptized, and while He was
[b]praying, heaven was opened, 22 and
the Holy Spirit descended upon Him
in bodily form like a dove, and a voice
came out of heaven, "[a]You are My be-
loved Son, in You I am well-pleased."

### *The Genealogy of Jesus*

23 [a]When He began His ministry,
Jesus Himself was about thirty years
of age, being, [1]as was supposed,
the son of [b]Joseph,
[2]the son of [3]Eli,
24 the son of Matthat,
the son of Levi,
the son of Melchi,
the son of Jannai,
the son of Joseph,
25 the son of Mattathias,
the son of Amos,
the son of Nahum,
the son of [1]Hesli,
the son of Naggai,
26 the son of Maath,
the son of Mattathias,
the son of Semein,
the son of Josech,
the son of Joda,
27 the son of Joanan,
the son of Rhesa,
[a]the son of Zerubbabel,
the son of [1]Shealtiel,
the son of Neri,
28 the son of Melchi,
the son of Addi,
the son of Cosam,
the son of Elmadam,
the son of Er,
29 the son of [1]Joshua,
the son of Eliezer,

---

**3:13** [1]Or *Exact* **3:14** [a]Ex 20:16; 23:1 [b]Php 4:11 **3:15** [a]Jn 1:19f [1]Messiah **3:16** [a]Lk 3:16, 17: *Mt 3:11, 12; Mk 1:7, 8* **3:17** [a]Is 30:24 [b]Mk 9:43, 48 **3:19** [a]Mt 14:3; Mk 6:17 [b]Mt 14:1; Lk 3:1 **3:20** [a]Jn 3:24 **3:21** [a]Lk 3:21, 22: *Mt 3:13-17; Mk 1:9-11* [b]Mt 14:23; Lk 5:16; 9:18, 28f **3:22** [a]Ps 2:7; Is 42:1; Mt 3:17; 17:5; Mk 1:11; Lk 9:35; 2Pe 1:17 **3:23** [a]Mt 4:17; Ac 1:1 [b]Lk 3:23-27: *Mt 1:16* [1]Lit *as it was being thought* [2]Lit *of Eli,* so in genealogy [3]Also spelled *Heli* **3:25** [1]Also spelled *Esli* **3:27** [a]Mt 1:12 [1]Gr *Salathiel;* names of people in the Old Testament are given in their Old Testament form through v 38
**3:29** [1]Gr *Jesus*

the son of Jorim,
the son of Matthat,
the son of Levi,
**30** the son of Simeon,
the son of [1]Judah,
the son of Joseph,
the son of Jonam,
the son of Eliakim,
**31** the son of Melea,
the son of Menna,
the son of Mattatha,
the son of Nathan,
the son of David,
**32** [a]the son of Jesse,
the son of Obed,
the son of Boaz,
the son of [1]Salmon,
the son of [2]Nahshon,
**33** the son of Amminadab,
the son of Admin,
the son of [1]Ram,
the son of Hezron,
the son of Perez,
the son of Judah,
**34** the son of Jacob,
the son of Isaac,
[a]the son of Abraham,
the son of Terah,
the son of Nahor,
**35** the son of Serug,
the son of [1]Reu,
the son of Peleg,
the son of [2]Heber,
the son of Shelah,
**36** the son of Cainan,
the son of Arphaxad,
the son of Shem,
[a]the son of Noah,
the son of Lamech,
**37** the son of Methuselah,
the son of Enoch,
the son of Jared,
the son of Mahalaleel,
the son of Cainan,
**38** the son of Enosh,
the son of Seth,
the son of Adam,
the son of God.

### *The Temptation of Jesus*

**4** [a]Now Jesus, full of the Holy
Spirit, [b]returned from the Jor-
dan and was being led around [1]by
the Spirit in the wilderness **2** for
[a]forty days, being tempted by the
devil. And He ate nothing during
those days, and when they had
finished, He was hungry. **3** And the
devil said to Him, "If You are the Son
of God, tell this stone to become
bread." **4** And Jesus answered him,
"It is written, '[a]MAN SHALL NOT LIVE
ON BREAD ALONE.'"
**5** [a]And he led Him up and showed
Him all the kingdoms of [b,1]the world
in a moment of time. **6** And the devil
said to Him, "I will give You all this
[a,1]dominion and [2]its glory, [b]for it has
been handed over to me, and I give
it to whomever I wish. **7** Therefore
if You [1]worship before me, it shall
all be Yours." **8** And Jesus answered
and said to him, "It is written, '[a]YOU
SHALL WORSHIP THE [1]LORD YOUR GOD
AND SERVE HIM ONLY.'"
**9** [a]And he led Him to Jerusalem
and had Him stand on the pinnacle of
the temple, and said to Him, "If You
are the Son of God, throw Yourself
down from here, **10** for it is written,

---

**3:30** [1]Gr *Judas* **3:32** [a]Lk 3:32-34: *Mt 1:1-6* [1]Gr *Sala* [2]Gr *Naasson* **3:33** [1]Gr *Arni* **3:34** [a]Lk 3:34-36: *Ge 11:26-30; 1Chr 1:24-27* **3:35** [1]Gr *Ragau* [2]Gr *Eber* **3:36** [a]Lk 3:36-38: *Ge 5:3-32; 1Chr 1:1-4*
◆ **4:1** [a]Lk 4:1-13: *Mt 4:1-11; Mk 1:12, 13* [b]Lk 3:3 [1]Or *under the influence of*; lit *in* **4:2** [a]Ex 34:28; 1Ki 19:8
**4:4** [a]Dt 8:3 **4:5** [a]Mt 4:8-10 [b]Mt 24:14 [1]Lit *the inhabited earth* **4:6** [a]Da 7:14 [b]1Jn 5:19 [1]Or *authority*, but cf. Da 7:14 [2]Lit *their* (referring to the kingdoms in v 5) **4:7** [1]Or *bow down before*
**4:8** [a]Dt 6:13; 10:20; Mt 4:10 [1]In OT, Yahweh, cf. Dt 6:13 **4:9** [a]Mt 4:5-7

'[a]HE WILL COMMAND HIS
ANGELS CONCERNING
YOU TO GUARD YOU,'
11 and,
'[a]ON *their* HANDS THEY
WILL BEAR YOU UP,
LEST YOU STRIKE YOUR FOOT
AGAINST A STONE.'"
12 And Jesus answered and said to
him, "It is said, '[a]YOU SHALL NOT PUT
THE [1]LORD YOUR GOD TO THE TEST.'"
13 And when the devil had finished
every temptation, he left Him until
an opportune time.

### *Jesus Begins His Ministry*

14 And [a]Jesus returned to Galilee in
the power of the Spirit, and [b]news
about Him spread through all the
surrounding district. 15 And He was
[a]teaching in their synagogues, being
glorified by all.

### *Jesus Rejected at Nazareth*

16 And He came to [a]Nazareth, where
He had been brought up, and as was
His custom, [b]He entered the syna-
gogue on the Sabbath and [c]stood
up to read. 17 And the scroll of the
prophet Isaiah was handed to Him.
And He opened the scroll and found
the place where it was written,
18 "[a]THE SPIRIT OF THE
[1]LORD IS UPON ME,
BECAUSE HE ANOINTED
ME TO PREACH THE
GOSPEL TO THE POOR.
HE HAS SENT ME TO PROCLAIM
RELEASE TO THE CAPTIVES,
AND RECOVERY OF SIGHT
TO THE BLIND,
TO SET FREE THOSE WHO
ARE OPPRESSED,
19 [a]TO PROCLAIM THE FAVORABLE
YEAR OF THE [1]LORD."
20 And He [a]closed the scroll, gave it
back to the attendant and [b]sat down,
and the eyes of all in the synagogue
were fixed on Him. 21 And He began
to say to them, "Today this Scripture
has been fulfilled in your [1]hearing."
22 And all were [1]speaking well of Him
and marveling at the [2]gracious words
which were coming forth from His
lips, and they were saying, "[a]Is this
not Joseph's son?" 23 And He said
to them, "No doubt you will quote
this proverb to Me, 'Physician, heal
yourself! Whatever we heard took
place [a]at Capernaum, do also here in
[b]your hometown as well.'" 24 And He
said, "Truly I say to you, [a]no prophet
is welcome in his hometown. 25 But I
say to you in truth, there were many
widows in Israel [a]in the days of Elijah,
when the sky was shut up for three
years and six months, when a great
famine came over all the land, 26 and
yet Elijah was sent to none of them,
but [a]only to [1]Zarephath, *in the land* of
[b]Sidon, to a woman who was a widow.
27 And there were many lepers in Is-
rael in the time of Elisha the prophet,
and none of them was cleansed, but
[a]only Naaman the Syrian." 28 And all
*the people* in the synagogue were filled
with rage as they heard these things,
29 and they stood up and [a]drove Him

**4:10** [a]Ps 91:11 **4:11** [a]Ps 91:12 **4:12** [a]Dt 6:16 [1]In OT, Yahweh, cf. Dt 6:16 **4:14** [a]Mt 4:12 [b]Mt 9:26; Lk 4:37 **4:15** [a]Mt 4:23 **4:16** [a]Lk 2:39, 51 [b]Mt 13:54; Mk 6:1f [c]Ac 13:14-16 **4:18** [a]Is 61:1; Mt 11:5; 12:18; Jn 3:34 [1]In OT, Yahweh, cf. Is 61:1 **4:19** [a]Is 61:2; Lv 25:10 [1]In OT, Yahweh, cf. Is 61:2 **4:20** [a]Lk 4:17 [b]Mt 26:55 **4:21** [1]Lit *ears* **4:22** [a]Mt 13:55; Mk 6:3; Jn 6:42 [1]Or *testifying* [2]Or *words of grace* **4:23** [a]Mt 4:13; Mk 1:21ff; 2:1ff; Lk 4:35ff; Jn 4:46ff [b]Mk 6:1; Lk 2:39, 51; 4:16 **4:24** [a]Mt 13:57; Mk 6:4; Jn 4:44 **4:25** [a]1Ki 17:1; 18:1; Jas 5:17 **4:26** [a]1Ki 17:9 [b]Mt 11:21 [1]Gr *Sarepta* **4:27** [a]2Ki 5:1-14 **4:29** [a]Nu 15:35; Ac 7:58; Heb 13:12

out of the city, and led Him to the edge
of the hill on which their city had been
built, in order to throw Him down the
cliff. **30** But [a]passing through their
midst, He went on His way.

### *Jesus Casts Out an Unclean Demon*

**31** And [a]He came down to [b]Caper-
naum, a city of Galilee, and He was
teaching them on the Sabbath; **32** and
[a]they were amazed at His teaching,
for [b]His [1]message was with author-
ity. **33** And in the synagogue there
was a man [1]possessed by the spirit
of an unclean demon, and he cried
out with a loud voice, **34** "[1]Let us
alone! [a2]What do we have to do with
You, Jesus the [b]Nazarene? Have You
come to destroy us? I know who You
are—[b]the Holy One of God!" **35** But
Jesus [a]rebuked it, saying, "Be quiet
and come out of him!" And when the
demon had thrown him down in the
midst *of the people,* it came out of him
without doing him any harm. **36** And
amazement came upon them all, and
they were talking with one another
saying, "What is [1]this message? For
[a]with authority and power He com-
mands the unclean spirits and they
come out." **37** And [a]the report about
Him was spreading into every place
in the surrounding district.

### *Peter's Mother-in-Law and Many Others Healed*

**38** [a]Then He stood up and *left* the
synagogue, and entered Simon's
home. Now Simon's mother-in-law
was [b]suffering from a high fever, and
they asked Him [1]to help her. **39** And
standing over her, He [a]rebuked the
fever, and it left her. Immediately
she stood up and [1]*began* waiting on
them.

**40** [a]And while [b]the sun was set-
ting, all those who had any *who were*
sick with various diseases brought
them to Him, and [c]laying His hands
on each one of them, He was [d]healing
them. **41** And demons also were
coming out of many, shouting and
saying, "You are [a]the Son of God!"
But [b]rebuking *them,* He was [c]not
allowing them to speak, because they
knew Him to be the [1]Christ.

**42** [a]When day came, Jesus left
and went to a secluded place; and
the crowds were eagerly seeking
for Him, and came to Him and tried
to keep Him from going away from
them. **43** But He said to them, "I
must proclaim the good news of the
kingdom of God to the other cities
also, [a]for I was sent for this purpose."

**44** So He kept on preaching in the
synagogues [a]of [1]Judea.

### *The First Disciples*

**5** [a]Now it happened that while the
crowd was pressing around Him
and listening to the word of God,
He was standing at the edge of [b]the
lake of Gennesaret; **2** and He saw two
boats lying at the edge of the lake,
and the fishermen, having gotten out

---

**4:30** [a]Jn 10:39 **4:31** [a]Lk 4:31-37: *Mk 1:21-28* [b]Mt 4:13; Lk 4:23 **4:32** [a]Mt 7:28 [b]Lk 4:36; Jn 7:46 [1]Lit *word* **4:33** [1]Lit *having a spirit* **4:34** [a]Mt 8:29 [b]Mk 1:24 [1]Lit *Ah!* [2]Lit *What to us and to you* (a Heb idiom) **4:35** [a]Mt 8:26; Mk 4:39; Lk 4:39, 41; 8:24 **4:36** [a]Lk 4:32 [1]Or *this word, that with authority...come out?* **4:37** [a]Lk 4:14 **4:38** [a]Lk 4:38, 39: *Mt 8:14, 15; Mk 1:29-31* [b]Mt 4:24 [1]Lit *about her* **4:39** [a]Lk 4:35, 41 [1]Or *served* **4:40** [a]Lk 4:40, 41: *Mt 8:16, 17; Mk 1:32-34* [b]Mk 1:32 [c]Mk 5:23 [d]Mt 4:23 **4:41** [a]Mt 4:3 [b]Lk 4:35 [c]Mt 8:16; Mk 1:34 [1]Messiah **4:42** [a]Lk 4:42, 43: *Mk 1:35-38* **4:43** [a]Mk 1:38 **4:44** [a]Mt 4:23 [1]The country of the Jews (including Galilee) ◆ **5:1** [a]Mt 4:18-22; Mk 1:16-20; Lk 5:1-11; Jn 1:40-42 [b]Nu 34:11; Dt 3:17; Jos 12:3; 13:27; Mt 4:18

of them, were washing their nets.
**3** [a]And He got into one of the boats,
which was Simon's, and asked him
to put out a little way from the land.
And He sat down and *began* teach-
ing the crowds from the boat. **4** And
when He had finished speaking, He
said to Simon, "Put out into the deep
water and [a]let down your nets for a
catch." **5** Simon answered and said,
"[a]Master, [b]we labored all night and
caught nothing, but at Your word, I
will let down the nets." **6** And when
they had done this, [a]they enclosed a
great quantity of fish. And their nets
*began to* break; **7** so they signaled to
their partners in the other boat for
them to come and help them. And
they came and filled both of the boats,
so that they began to sink. **8** But when
Simon Peter saw *this*, he fell down at
Jesus' knees, saying, "Go away from
me Lord, for I am a sinful man!" **9** For
amazement had seized him and all
his companions because of the catch
of fish which they had taken, **10** and
[1]James and John, sons of Zebedee,
who were partners with Simon, *were*
also likewise *amazed*. And Jesus said
to Simon, "[a]Do not fear, from now on
you will be [b]catching men." **11** And
when they had brought their boats
to land, [a]they left everything and
followed Him.

### *Jesus Heals a Leper*

**12** [a]And it happened that while He
was in one of the cities, behold, *there
was* a man [1]covered with leprosy; and
when he saw Jesus, he fell on his face
and begged Him, saying, "Lord, if You
are willing, You can make me clean."
**13** And He stretched out His hand and
touched him, saying, "I am willing;
be cleansed." And immediately the
leprosy left him. **14** And He directed
him to tell no one, "But go and [a]show
yourself to the priest and make an
offering for your cleansing, just as
Moses commanded, as a testimony
to them." **15** But [a]the news about Him
was spreading even farther, and large
crowds were gathering to hear *Him*
and to be healed of their sicknesses.
**16** But He Himself would *often* slip
away [1]to the desolate regions and
[a]pray.

### *Jesus Heals a Paralytic*

**17** And it happened that [1]one day He
was teaching; and [a]there were *some*
Pharisees and [b]teachers of the law
sitting *there*, who had [c]come from
every village of Galilee and Judea and
*from* Jerusalem, and [d]the power of the
Lord was *present* for Him to perform
healing. **18** [a]And behold, *some* men
*were* carrying on a stretcher a man
who was paralyzed; and they were
trying to bring him in and to set him
down before Him. **19** But not finding
any *way* to bring him in because of
the crowd, they went up on [a]the roof
and let him down [b]through the tiles
with his stretcher, into the middle *of
the crowd*, in front of Jesus. **20** And
seeing their faith, He said, "[1]Friend,
[a]your sins are forgiven you." **21** The
scribes and the Pharisees [a]began to
reason, saying, "[b]Who is this who

---

**5:3** [a]Mt 13:2; Mk 3:9, 10; 4:1 **5:4** [a]Jn 21:6 **5:5** [a]Lk 8:24; 9:33, 49; 17:13 [b]Jn 21:3 **5:6** [a]Jn 21:6
**5:10** [a]Mt 14:27 [b]2Ti 2:26 [1]Or *Jacob*; James is the Eng form of Jacob; so in Luke **5:11** [a]Mt 4:20, 22; 19:29; Mk 1:18, 20; Lk 5:28 **5:12** [a]Lk 5:12-14: *Mt 8:2-4; Mk 1:40-44* [1]Lit *full of* **5:14** [a]Lv 13:49; 14:2ff
**5:15** [a]Mt 9:26 **5:16** [a]Mt 14:23; Mk 1:35; Lk 6:12 [1]Lit *in* **5:17** [a]Mt 15:1 [b]Lk 2:46 [c]Mk 1:45 [d]Mk 5:30; Lk 6:19; 8:46 [1]Lit *on one of the days* **5:18** [a]Lk 5:18-26: *Mt 9:2-8; Mk 2:3-12* **5:19** [a]Mt 24:17 [b]Mk 2:4
**5:20** [a]Mt 9:2 [1]Lit *Man* **5:21** [a]Lk 3:8 [b]Lk 7:49

speaks blasphemies? [c]Who can forgive sins, but God alone?" **22** But Jesus, [1]knowing their reasonings, answered and said to them, "Why are you reasoning in your hearts? **23** Which is easier, to say, 'Your sins have been forgiven you,' or to say, 'Get up and walk'? **24** But, so that you may know that the Son of Man has authority on earth to forgive sins,"—He said to the [a]paralytic—"I say to you, get up, and, picking up your stretcher, go home." **25** And immediately he rose up before them, and picked up what he had been lying on, and went home [a]glorifying God. **26** And astonishment seized them all and they *began* [a]glorifying God; and they were filled [b]with fear, saying, "We have seen remarkable things today."

### *Levi and Sinners Called*

**27** [a]And after that He went out and noticed a tax collector named [b,1]Levi sitting in the tax office, and He said to him, "Follow Me." **28** And he [a]left everything behind, and rose up and *began to* follow Him.

**29** And [a]Levi gave a big reception for Him in his house; and there was a great crowd of [b]tax collectors and other *people* who were reclining *at the table* with them. **30** [a]And the Pharisees and their scribes *began grumbling* at His disciples, saying, "Why do you eat and drink with the tax collectors and [1]sinners?" **31** And Jesus answered and said to them, "[a]*It is* not those who are well who need a physician, but those who are sick. **32** I have not come to call the righteous but sinners to repentance."

**33** And they said to Him, "[a]The disciples of John often fast and offer prayers, the *disciples* of the Pharisees also do likewise, but Yours eat and drink." **34** And Jesus said to them, "Can you make the [1]attendants of the bridegroom fast while the bridegroom is with them? **35** [a]But *the* days will come; and when the bridegroom is taken away from them, then they will fast in those days." **36** And He was also telling them a parable: "No one tears a piece of cloth from a new garment and puts it on an old garment; otherwise he will both tear the new and the piece from the new will not match the old. **37** And no one puts new wine into old wineskins; otherwise the new wine will burst the skins and it will be spilled out, and the skins will be ruined. **38** But new wine must be put into fresh wineskins. **39** And no one, after drinking old *wine* wishes for new; for he says, 'The old is good enough.'"

### *Lord of the Sabbath*

**6** [a]Now it happened that on a Sabbath He was passing through *some* grainfields, and His disciples [b]were picking and eating the heads of grain, rubbing them in their hands. **2** But some of the Pharisees said, "Why do you do what [a]is not lawful on the Sabbath?" **3** And Jesus answered and said to them, "Have you never read [a]what David did when he was hungry, he and those who were with him, **4** how he entered

**5:21** [c]Is 43:25 **5:22** [1]Or *perceiving* **5:24** [a]Mt 4:24 **5:25** [a]Mt 9:8 **5:26** [a]Mt 9:8 [b]Lk 1:65; 7:16 **5:27** [a]Lk 5:27-39: *Mt 9:9-17; Mk 2:14-22* [b]Mt 9:9 [1]Also called Matthew **5:28** [a]Lk 5:11 **5:29** [a]Mt 9:9 [b]Lk 15:1 **5:30** [a]Mk 2:16; Lk 15:2; Ac 23:9 [1]Irreligious Jews **5:31** [a]Mt 9:12, 13; Mk 2:17 **5:33** [a]Mt 9:14; Mk 2:18 **5:34** [1]Lit *sons of the bridal chamber* **5:35** [a]Mt 9:15; Mk 2:20; Lk 17:22 ◆ **6:1** [a]Lk 6:1-5: *Mt 12:1-8; Mk 2:23-28* [b]Dt 23:25 **6:2** [a]Mt 12:2 **6:3** [a]1Sa 21:6

the house of God, and took and
ate the [1]consecrated bread which
[a]is not lawful for any to eat except
the priests alone, and gave it to his
companions?" **5** And He was saying
to them, "The Son of Man is Lord of
the Sabbath."

### *Jesus Heals a Man on the Sabbath*

**6** [a]Now it happened that on another
Sabbath He entered [b]the synagogue
and was teaching; and there was a
man there [1]whose right hand was
withered. **7** And the scribes and the
Pharisees [a]were watching Him close-
ly *to see* if He heals on the Sabbath, so
that they might find *reason* to accuse
Him. **8** But He [a]knew [1]what they were
thinking, and He said to the man
with the withered hand, "Get up and
[2]come forward!" And he stood up and
[3]came forward. **9** And Jesus said to
them, "I ask you, is it lawful to do
good or to do harm on the Sabbath,
to save a life or to destroy it?" **10** And
after [a]looking around at them all, He
said to him, "Stretch out your hand!"
And he did *so*, and his hand was re-
stored. **11** But they themselves were
filled with [1]rage, and were discussing
together what they might do to Jesus.

### *Jesus Appoints the Twelve*

**12** Now it happened that [1]at this time
He went off to [a]the mountain to [b]pray,
and He was spending the whole night
in prayer to God. **13** And when day
came, [a]He called His disciples to Him
and chose twelve of them, whom He
also named as [b]apostles: **14** Simon,
whom He also named Peter, and
Andrew his brother; and James and
John; and Philip and Bartholomew;
**15** and [a]Matthew and Thomas; James
*the son* of Alphaeus, and Simon who
was called the Zealot; **16** Judas *the son*
of James, and Judas Iscariot, who
became a traitor.

**17** And Jesus [a]came down with
them and stood on a level place;
and *there was* [b]a large crowd of His
disciples, and a great multitude of
people from all Judea and Jerusalem
and the coastal region of [c]Tyre and
Sidon, **18** who had come to hear Him
and to be healed of their diseases;
and those who were troubled with
unclean spirits were being cured.
**19** And all the crowd was trying to
[a]touch Him, for [b]power was coming
from Him and healing *them* all.

### *The Beatitudes*

**20** And turning His gaze toward His
disciples, He *began to* say,

"[a]Blessed *are* the poor, for [b]yours
is the kingdom of God.
**21** Blessed *are* those who hunger
now, for you shall be satisfied.
Blessed *are* those who cry
now, for you shall laugh.
**22** [a]Blessed are you when men
hate you, and [b]exclude you,
and insult you, and scorn your
name as evil, for the sake of
the Son of Man.

**23** "Be glad in that day and [a]leap *for
joy*, for behold, your reward is great in
heaven. For [b]their fathers were doing
the same things to the prophets.

---

**6:4** [a]Lv 24:9 [1]Or *showbread*; lit *loaves of presentation* **6:6** [a]Lk 6:6-11: *Mt 12:9-14; Mk 3:1-6;* Lk 6:1 [b]Mt 4:23 [1]Lit *and his* **6:7** [a]Mk 3:2 **6:8** [a]Mt 9:4 [1]Lit *their thoughts* [2]Lit *stand into the middle* [3]Lit *stood* **6:10** [a]Mk 3:5 **6:11** [1]Lit *folly* **6:12** [a]Mt 5:1 [b]Mt 14:23; Lk 5:16; 9:18, 28 [1]Lit *in these days* **6:13** [a]Lk 6:13-16: *Mt 10:2-4; Mk 3:16-19; Ac 1:13* [b]Mk 6:30 **6:15** [a]Mt 9:9 **6:17** [a]Lk 6:12 [b]Mt 4:25; Mk 3:7, 8 [c]Mt 11:21 **6:19** [a]Mt 9:21; 14:36; Mk 3:10 [b]Lk 5:17 **6:20** [a]Lk 6:20-23: *Mt 5:3-12* [b]Mt 5:3 **6:22** [a]1Pe 4:14 [b]Jn 9:22; 16:2 **6:23** [a]Mal 4 [b]2Chr 36:16; Ac 7:52

### *Jesus Pronounces Woes*

24 "But woe to [a]you who are rich,
for [b]you are receiving your
comfort in full.
25 Woe to you who [1]are well-fed
now, for you shall be hungry.
Woe *to you* who laugh now, for
you shall mourn and cry.
26 Woe *to you* when all men
speak well of you, for their
fathers were doing the same
things to the [a]false prophets.

### *Love Your Enemies*

27 "But I say to you who hear, [a]love
your enemies, do good to those who
hate you, 28 bless those who curse
you, [a]pray for those who disparage
you. 29 [a]Whoever hits you on the
cheek, offer him the other also; and
whoever takes away your garment,
do not withhold your [1]tunic from
him either. 30 Give to everyone who
asks of you, and whoever takes away
what is yours, do not demand it back.
31 And [a,1]treat others the same way
you want [2]them to treat you. 32 [a]And
if you love those who love you, what
credit is *that* to you? For even sinners
love those who love them. 33 And if
you do good to those who do good to
you, what credit is *that* to you? For
even sinners do the same. 34 [a]And if
you lend to those from whom you
expect to receive, what credit is *that*
to you? Even sinners lend to sinners
in order to receive back the same
*amount*. 35 But [a]love your enemies,
and do good, and lend, [1]expecting
nothing in return; and your reward
will be great, and you will be [b]sons
of [c]the Most High; for He Himself
is kind to the ungrateful and evil.
36 [1]Be merciful, just as your Father
is merciful.

### *Do Not Judge*

37 "[a]And do not judge, and you will
not be judged; and do not condemn,
and you will not be condemned;
[b,1]pardon, and you will be [2]pardoned.
38 Give, and it will be given to you.
They will [1]pour [a]into your lap a
[b]good measure—pressed down,
shaken together, running over. For
by your standard of measure it will
be measured to you in return."

39 And He also spoke a parable
to them: "[a]Can a blind man guide a
blind man? Will they not both fall
into a pit? 40 [a]A [1]student is not above
his teacher; but everyone, after he
has been fully trained, will [2]be like
his teacher. 41 And why do you look
at the speck that is in your brother's
eye, but do not notice the log that
is in your own eye? 42 How can you
say to your brother, 'Brother, let me
take out the speck that is in your eye,'
when you yourself do not see the log
that is in your own eye? You hypo-
crite, first take the log out of your
own eye, and then you will see clearly
to take out the speck that is in your
brother's eye. 43 [a]For there is no good
tree which produces bad fruit, nor,
[1]on the other hand, a bad tree which
produces good fruit. 44 [a]For each tree

---

**6:24** [a]Lk 16:25; Jas 5:1 [b]Mt 6:2 **6:25** [1]Lit *having been filled* **6:26** [a]Mt 7:15 **6:27** [a]Mt 5:44; Lk 6:35 **6:28** [a]Mt 5:44; Lk 6:35 **6:29** [a]Lk 6:29, 30: *Mt 5:39-42* [1]Gr *khiton*, the garment worn next to the skin **6:31** [a]Mt 7:12 [1]Lit *do to* [2]Lit *people* **6:32** [a]Mt 5:46 **6:34** [a]Mt 5:42 **6:35** [a]Lk 6:27 [b]Mt 5:9 [c]Lk 1:32 [1]Or *not despairing at all* **6:36** [1]Or *Become* **6:37** [a]Lk 6:37-42: *Mt 7:1-5* [b]Mt 6:14; Lk 23:16; Ac 3:13 [1]Lit *release* [2]Lit *released* **6:38** [a]Mk 4:24 [b]Ps 79:12; Is 65:6, 7; Jer 32:18 [1]Lit *give* **6:39** [a]Mt 15:14 **6:40** [a]Mt 10:24; Jn 13:16; 15:20 [1]Or *disciple* [2]Or *reach his teacher's level* **6:43** [a]Lk 6:43, 44: *Mt 7:16, 18, 20* [1]Lit *again* **6:44** [a]Mt 7:16; 12:33

is known by its own fruit. For men
do not gather figs from thorns, nor
do they pick grapes from a bramble
bush. **45** [a]The good man out of the
good [1]treasure of his heart brings
forth what is good; and the evil *man*
out of the evil *treasure* brings forth
what is evil. [b]For his mouth speaks
from the abundance of his heart.

### *Build Your House on the Rock*

**46** "[a]Now why do you call Me, 'Lord,
Lord,' and do not do what I say?
**47** [a]Everyone who comes to Me and
hears My words and does them, I will
show you whom he is like: **48** he is like
a man building a house, who dug and
went deep, and laid a foundation on
the rock; and when a flood occurred,
the river burst against that house and
could not shake it, because it had
been well built. **49** But the one who
heard and did not do *accordingly*, is
like a man who built a house on the
ground without any foundation; and
the river burst against it and imme-
diately it collapsed, and the ruin of
that house was great."

### *The Centurion's Faith*

**7** [a]When He had completed all
His words in the hearing of the
people, [b]He went to Capernaum.
**2** And a centurion's slave, [1]who
was highly regarded by him, was
sick and about to die. **3** Now when
he heard about Jesus, [a]he sent some
[1]Jewish elders asking Him to come
and [2]save the life of his slave. **4** And
when they came to Jesus, they were
earnestly pleading with Him, saying,
"He is worthy for You to grant this to
him; **5** for he loves our nation and it
was he who built us our synagogue."
**6** Now Jesus was going on His way
with them; and when He was not far
from the house, the centurion sent
friends, saying to Him, "[1]Lord, do not
trouble Yourself further, for I am not
good enough for You to come under
my roof. **7** For this reason I did not
even consider myself worthy to come
to You, but *just* [1]say the word, and my
[2]servant will be healed. **8** For I also
am a man placed under authority,
with soldiers under me; and I say to
this one, 'Go!' and he goes, and to
another, 'Come!' and he comes, and
to my slave, 'Do this!' and he does
it." **9** Now when Jesus heard this, He
marveled at him. And He turned to
the crowd that was following Him
and said, "I say to you, [a]not even in
Israel have I found such great faith."
**10** And when those who had been
sent returned to the house, they
found the slave in good health.

**11** And it happened that soon after-
wards He went to a city called Nain,
and His disciples were going along
with Him, [1]accompanied by a large
crowd. **12** Now as He approached the
gate of the city, behold, [1]a dead man
was being carried out, the [2]only son
of his mother, and she was a widow.
And a sizeable crowd from the city
was with her. **13** And when [a]the Lord
saw her, He felt compassion for her
and said to her, "Do not cry." **14** And
He came up and touched the coffin,
and the bearers came to a halt. And
He said, "Young man, I say to you,

---

**6:45** [a]Mt 12:35 [b]Mt 12:34 [1]Or *treasury, storehouse* **6:46** [a]Mal 1:6; Mt 7:21 **6:47** [a]Lk 6:47-49: *Mt 7:24-27;* Jas 1:22ff ◆ **7:1** [a]Mt 7:28 [b]Lk 7:1-10: *Mt 8:5-13* **7:2** [1]Lit *to whom he was honorable* **7:3** [a]Mt 8:5 [1]Lit *elders of the Jews* [2]Or *cure* **7:6** [1]Or *Sir* **7:7** [1]Lit *say with a word* [2]Or *boy* **7:9** [a]Mt 8:10; Lk 7:50 **7:11** [1]Lit *and* **7:12** [1]Lit *one who had died* [2]Or *only begotten* **7:13** [a]Lk 7:19; 10:1; 11:1, 39; 12:42; 13:15; 17:5, 6; 18:6; 19:8; 22:61; 24:34; Jn 4:1; 6:23; 11:2

arise!" **15** And the [1]dead man sat up
and began to speak. And *Jesus* gave
him back to his mother. **16** [a]And fear
gripped them all, and they *began*
[b]glorifying God, saying, "A great
[c]prophet has arisen among us!"
and, "God has [1]visited His people!"
**17** [a]And this report concerning Him
went out all over Judea and in all the
surrounding district.

### *Questions from John the Baptist*

**18** [a]And the disciples of John report-
ed to him about all these things.
**19** Summoning [1]two of his disciples,
John sent them to [a]the Lord, saying,
"Are You the One who is to come, or
should we look for someone else?"
**20** When the men came to Him,
they said, "John the Baptist has
sent us to You, saying, 'Are You the
One who is to come, or should we
look for someone else?'" **21** At that
[1]very time He [a]cured many *people*
of diseases and [b]afflictions and evil
spirits, and He granted sight to many
*who were* blind. **22** And He answered
and said to them, "Go and report to
John what you have seen and heard:
*the* [a]BLIND RECEIVE SIGHT, *the* lame
walk, *the* lepers are cleansed, and *the*
deaf hear, *the* dead are raised up, *the*
[b]POOR HAVE THE GOSPEL PREACHED TO
THEM. **23** Blessed is he [1]who does not
take offense at Me."

**24** And when the messengers of
John had left, He began to speak to
the crowds about John, "What did you
go out into the wilderness to behold?
A reed shaken by the wind? **25** [1]But
what did you go out to see? A man
dressed in soft garments? Behold,
those who are splendidly clothed
and live in luxury are *found* in royal
palaces! **26** But what did you go out to
see? A prophet? Yes, I say to you, and
even more than a prophet. **27** This is
*the one* about whom it is written,

> '[a]BEHOLD, I SEND MY
> MESSENGER [1]AHEAD OF YOU,
> WHO WILL PREPARE YOUR
> WAY BEFORE YOU.'

**28** "I say to you, among those born
of women there is no one greater
than John; yet he who is [1]least in
the kingdom of God is greater than
he." **29** And when all the people
and the tax collectors heard *this*,
they [1]acknowledged [a]God's justice,
[b]having been baptized with [c]the
baptism of John. **30** But the Pharisees
and the [a]scholars of the Law rejected
God's purpose for themselves, not
having been baptized by [1]John.

**31** "To what then shall I compare
the men of this generation, and
what are they like? **32** They are like
children, sitting in the marketplace
and calling to one another, who say,
'We played the flute for you, and
you did not dance; we sang a dirge,
and you did not cry.' **33** For John the
Baptist has come [a]eating no bread
and drinking no wine, and you say,
'He has a demon!' **34** The Son of Man
has come eating and drinking, and
you say, 'Behold, a gluttonous man
and a [1]drunkard, a friend of tax col-
lectors and [2]sinners!' **35** Yet wisdom
[a]is vindicated [1]by all her children."

---

**7:15** [1]Or *corpse* **7:16** [a]Lk 5:26 [b]Mt 9:8 [c]Mt 21:11; Lk 7:39 [1]Or *cared for* **7:17** [a]Mt 9:26
**7:18** [a]Lk 7:18-35: *Mt 11:2-19* **7:19** [a]Lk 7:13; 10:1; 11:1, 39; 12:42; 13:15; 17:5, 6; 18:6; 19:8; 22:61; 24:34; Jn 4:1; 6:23; 11:2 [1]Lit *a certain two* **7:21** [a]Mt 4:23 [b]Mk 3:10 [1]Lit *hour* **7:22** [a]Is 35:5 [b]Is 61:1 **7:23** [1]Lit *whoever* **7:25** [1]Or *Well then, what* **7:27** [a]Mal 3:1; Mt 11:10; Mk 1:2 [1]Lit *before Your face* **7:28** [1]Or *less* **7:29** [a]Lk 7:35 [b]Mt 21:32; Lk 3:12 [c]Ac 18:25; 19:3 [1]Or *justified God* **7:30** [a]Mt 22:35 [1]Lit *him*
**7:33** [a]Lk 1:15 **7:34** [1]Or *wine-drinker* [2]Irreligious Jews **7:35** [a]Lk 7:29 [1]Or *from*

**36** Now one of the Pharisees was
asking Him to eat with him, and
He entered the Pharisee's house
and reclined *at the table.* **37** [a]And
behold, there was a woman in the
city who was a [1]sinner. And when
she learned that He was reclining *at
the table* in the Pharisee's house, she
brought an alabaster jar of perfume.
**38** And standing behind *Him* at His
feet, crying, she began to wet His feet
with her tears. And she kept wiping
them with the hair of her head, and
kissing His feet and anointing them
with the perfume. **39** Now when the
Pharisee, who had invited Him, saw
this, he said to himself, saying, "If
this man were [a]a prophet He would
know who and what sort of person
this woman is who is touching Him,
that she is a sinner."

### *Parable of Two Debtors*

**40** And Jesus answered and said to
him, "Simon, I have something to
say to you." And he [1]replied, "Say
it, Teacher." **41** "A moneylender
had two debtors: one owed five
hundred [a,1]denarii, and the other
fifty. **42** When they [a]were unable to
repay, he graciously forgave them
both. So which of them will love him
more?" **43** Simon answered and said,
"I suppose the one whom he gra-
ciously forgave more." And He said
to him, "You have judged correctly."
**44** And turning toward the woman,
He said to Simon, "Do you see this
woman? I entered your house; you
[a]gave Me no water for My feet, but
she has wet My feet with her tears
and wiped them with her hair. **45** You
[a]gave Me no kiss; but she, since the
time I came in, has not ceased to
kiss My feet. **46** [a]You did not anoint
My head with oil, but she anointed
My feet with perfume. **47** For this
reason I say to you, her sins, which
are many, have been forgiven, for she
loved much. But he who is forgiven
little, loves little." **48** Then He said to
her, "[a]Your sins have been forgiven."
**49** And those who were reclining *at
the table* with Him began to say [1]to
themselves, "[a]Who is this *man* who
even forgives sins?" **50** And He said
to the woman, "[a]Your faith has saved
you; [b]go in peace."

### *Many Women Contribute to Jesus' Ministry*

**8** And it happened that soon
afterward He was going around
from one city and village to anoth-
er, [a]preaching and proclaiming the
good news of the kingdom of God.
The twelve were with Him, **2** and
*also* [a]some women who had been
healed of evil spirits and sicknesses:
[b]Mary who was called Magdalene,
from whom seven demons had gone
out, **3** and Joanna the wife of Chuza,
[a]Herod's [b]manager, and Susanna,
and many others who were minister-
ing to them from their possessions.

### *The Parable of the Sower*

**4** [a]Now when a large crowd was
coming together, and those from
the *various* cities were journeying

---

**7:37** [a]Lk 7:37-39: *Mt 26:6-13; Mk 14:3-9; Jn 12:1-8* [1]An immoral woman **7:39** [a]Lk 7:16; Jn 4:19
**7:40** [1]Lit *says* **7:41** [a]Mt 18:28; Mk 6:37 [1]A Roman silver coin, approx. a laborer's daily wage
**7:42** [a]Mt 18:25 **7:44** [a]Ge 18:4; 19:2; 43:24; Jdg 19:21; 1Ti 5:10 **7:45** [a]2Sa 15:5 **7:46** [a]2Sa 12:20;
Ps 23:5; Ecc 9:8; Da 10:3 **7:48** [a]Mt 9:2; Mk 2:5, 9; Lk 5:20, 23 **7:49** [a]Lk 5:21 [1]Or *among*
**7:50** [a]Mt 9:22; Lk 17:19; 18:42 [b]Mk 5:34; Lk 8:48 ◆ **8:1** [a]Mt 4:23 **8:2** [a]Mt 27:55; Mk 15:40, 41;
Lk 23:49, 55 [b]Mt 27:56; Mk 16:9 **8:3** [a]Mt 14:1 [b]Mt 20:8 **8:4** [a]Lk 8:4-8: *Mt 13:2-9; Mk 4:1-9*

to Him, He spoke by way of a parable: **5** "The sower went out to sow his seed. And as he sowed, some fell beside the road, and it was trampled under foot and the birds of the ʹair ate it up. **6** And other *seed* fell on rock and as soon as it grew up, it withered away, because it had no moisture. **7** And other *seed* fell among the thorns, and when the thorns grew up with it, they choked it out. **8** And other *seed* fell into the good soil; and growing up, it produced a crop one hundred times as great." As He said these things, He would call out, "[a]He who has ears to hear, ʹlet him hear."

### *The Parable of the Sower Explained*

**9** [a]And His disciples *began* questioning Him as to what this parable meant. **10** And He said, "[a]To you it has been granted to know the mysteries of the kingdom of God, but to the rest *it is* in parables, so that [b]SEEING THEY MAY NOT SEE, AND HEARING THEY MAY NOT UNDERSTAND.

**11** "Now the parable is this: [a]the seed is the word of God. **12** And those beside the road are those who have heard; then the devil comes and takes away the word from their heart, so that they will not believe and be saved. **13** And those on the rock are those who, when they hear, receive the word with joy, and these have no root; ʹthey believe for a while, and in time of temptation fall away. **14** And the *seed* which fell among the thorns, these are the ones who have heard, and as they go on their way they are choked with worries and riches and pleasures of life, and do not bear ripe fruit. **15** But the *seed* in the good soil, these are the ones who have heard the word in an honest and good heart, and hold it fast, and bear fruit with ʹperseverance.

### *A Lampstand and the Light*

**16** "Now [a]no one after lighting a lamp covers it with a container or puts it under a bed, but he puts it on a lampstand, so that those who come in may see the light. **17** [a]For nothing is hidden that will not become evident, nor *anything* secret that will not be known and come to light. **18** So beware how you listen, [a]for whoever has, to him *more* shall be given; and whoever does not have, even what he ʹthinks he has shall be taken away from him."

### *Jesus' Mother and Brothers*

**19** [a]And His mother and brothers came to Him, and they were unable to get to Him because of the crowd. **20** And it was reported to Him, "Your mother and Your brothers are standing outside, wishing to see You." **21** But He answered and said to them, "My mother and My brothers are these [a]who hear the word of God and do it."

### *Jesus Calms a Storm*

**22** [a]Now it happened that on one of *those* days He and His disciples got into a boat, and He said to them, "Let us go over to the other side of [b]the lake." So they set sail. **23** But as they were sailing along, He fell asleep, and

**8:5** ʹLit *heaven* **8:8** [a]Mt 11:15; Mk 7:16; Lk 14:35; Rev 2:7, 11, 17, 29; 3:6, 13, 22; 13:9 ʹOr *hear!, listen!*; Gr imperative **8:9** [a]Lk 8:9-15: *Mt 13:10-23; Mk 4:10-20* **8:10** [a]Mt 13:11 [b]Is 6:9; Mt 13:14; Ac 28:26 **8:11** [a]1Pe 1:23 **8:13** ʹLit *who believe* **8:15** ʹOr *steadfastness* **8:16** [a]Mt 5:15; Mk 4:21; Lk 11:33 **8:17** [a]Mt 10:26; Mk 4:22; Lk 12:2 **8:18** [a]Mt 13:12; 25:29; Lk 19:26 ʹOr *seems to have* **8:19** [a]Lk 8:19-21: *Mt 12:46-50; Mk 3:31-35* **8:21** [a]Lk 11:28 **8:22** [a]Lk 8:22-25: *Mt 8:23-27; Mk 4:36-41* [b]Lk 5:1f; 8:23

a windstorm descended on [a]the lake, and they *began to* be swamped and in danger. **24** And they came to Him and woke Him up, saying, "[a]Master, Master, we are perishing!" And He woke up and [b]rebuked the wind and the surging waves, and they stopped, and [1]it became calm. **25** And He said to them, "Where is your faith?" They were fearful and marveled, saying to one another, "Who then is this, that He commands even the winds and the water, and they obey Him?"

### *Jesus Saves a Man from Many Demons*

**26** [a]Then they sailed to the region of the Gerasenes, which is opposite Galilee. **27** And when He came out onto the land, a man from the city met Him, one who was possessed with demons and had not put on any garment for a long time, and was not living in a house, but in the tombs. **28** Now seeing Jesus, he cried out and fell before Him, and said in a loud voice, "[a,1]What do I have to do with You, Jesus, Son of [b]the Most High God? I beg You, do not torment me." **29** For He had commanded the unclean spirit to come out of the man. For it had seized him many times, and he was bound with chains and shackles, being kept under guard. And *yet* breaking his bonds, he was driven by the demon into the desolate regions. **30** And Jesus asked him, "What is your name?" And he said, "[a]Legion," for many demons had entered him. **31** And they were pleading with Him not to command them to go away into [a]the abyss.

**32** Now there was a herd of many swine feeding there on the mountain, and *the demons* pleaded with Him to permit them to enter [1]the swine. And He gave them permission. **33** And when the demons came out of the man, they entered the swine, and the herd rushed down the steep bank into [a]the lake and was drowned.

**34** And when the herdsmen saw what had happened, they ran away and reported it in the city and in the countryside. **35** And *the people* went out to see what had happened, and they came to Jesus, and found the man from whom the demons had gone out, sitting down [a]at the feet of Jesus, clothed and in his right mind. And they were afraid. **36** And those who had seen *it* reported to them how the man who was [a]demon-possessed had been [1]saved. **37** And all the people of the country of the Gerasenes and the surrounding district asked Him to leave them, for they were gripped with great fear. And He got into a boat and returned. **38** [a]But the man from whom the demons had gone out was begging Him that he might [1]accompany Him. But He sent him away, saying, **39** "Return to your house and recount what great things God has done for you." So he went away, proclaiming throughout the whole city what great things Jesus had done for him.

### *Jesus Heals a Woman and Jairus' Daughter*

**40** [a]And as Jesus returned, the crowd welcomed Him, for they had all been

**8:23** [a]Lk 5:1f; 8:22 **8:24** [a]Lk 5:5 [b]Lk 4:39 [1]Lit *a calm occurred* **8:26** [a]Lk 8:26-37: *Mt 8:28-34; Mk 5:1-17* **8:28** [a]Mt 8:29 [b]Mk 5:7 [1]Lit *What to me and to you* (a Heb idiom) **8:30** [a]Mt 26:53 **8:31** [a]Ro 10:7; Rev 9:1f, 11; 11:7; 17:8; 20:1, 3 **8:32** [1]Lit *them* **8:33** [a]Lk 5:1f; 8:22 **8:35** [a]Lk 10:39 **8:36** [a]Mt 4:24 [1]Or *made well* **8:38** [a]Lk 8:38, 39: *Mk 5:18-20* [1]Lit *be with* **8:40** [a]Mt 9:1; Mk 5:21

waiting for Him. **41** [a]And behold,
there came a man named Jairus, and
he was [b,1]an official of the synagogue.
And falling at Jesus' feet, he *began to*
plead with Him to come to his house,
**42** for he had an [1]only daughter, about
twelve years old, and she was dying.
But as He went, the crowds were
pressing against Him.
**43** And a woman who had a hem-
orrhage for twelve years, and could
not be healed by anyone, **44** came up
behind Him and touched the fringe
of His garment, and immediately
her hemorrhage stopped. **45** And
Jesus said, "Who is the one who
touched Me?" And while they were
all denying it, Peter said, "[a]Master,
the crowds are surrounding and
pressing in on You." **46** But Jesus said,
"Someone did touch Me, for I knew
that [a]power had gone out of Me."
**47** And when the woman saw that
she had not escaped notice, she came
trembling. And falling down before
Him, she declared in the presence
of all the people the reason why she
had touched Him and how she had
been immediately healed. **48** And He
said to her, "Daughter, [a]your faith
has [1]saved you; [b]go in peace."
**49** While He was still speaking,
someone *came from *the house of*
[a]the synagogue official, saying, "Your
daughter has died; do not trouble
the Teacher anymore." **50** But when
Jesus heard *this,* He answered him,
"[a]Do not be afraid *any longer*; only
believe, and she will be [1]saved." **51** So
when He came to the house, He did
not allow anyone to enter with Him,
except Peter and John and James, and
the girl's father and mother. **52** Now
they were all crying and [a]lamenting
for her, but He said, "Stop crying,
for she has not died, but [b]is asleep."
**53** And they *began* laughing at Him,
knowing that she had died. **54** He,
however, took her by the hand and
called, saying, "Child, arise!" **55** And
her spirit returned, and she stood
up immediately. And He gave orders
for *something* to be given her to eat.
**56** And her parents were astounded,
but He [a]directed them to tell no one
what had happened.

### *The Twelve Disciples Sent Out*

**9** [a]And calling the twelve together,
He gave them power and author-
ity over all the demons and to heal
diseases. **2** And He sent them out to
[a]preach the kingdom of God and to
heal the sick. **3** And He said to them,
"[a]Take nothing for *your* journey,
[b]neither a staff, nor a [1]bag, nor bread,
nor money; nor have two [2]tunics
apiece. **4** And whatever house you
enter, stay there [1]until you leave that
city. **5** And as for those who do not
receive you, as you go out from that
city, [a]shake the dust off your feet as
a testimony against them." **6** And de-
parting, they were going [1]throughout
the villages, [a]proclaiming the gospel
and healing everywhere.
**7** [a]Now [b]Herod the tetrarch heard
of all that was happening, and he was

---

**8:41** [a]Lk 8:41-56: *Mt 9:18-26; Mk 5:22-43* [b]Mk 5:22; Lk 8:49 [1]Lit *a ruler* **8:42** [1]Or *only begotten*
**8:45** [a]Lk 5:5 **8:46** [a]Lk 5:17 **8:48** [a]Mt 9:22 [b]Mk 5:34; Lk 7:50 [1]Or *made you well* **8:49** [a]Lk 8:41
**8:50** [a]Mk 5:36 [1]Or *made well* **8:52** [a]Mt 11:17; Lk 23:27 [b]Jn 11:13 **8:56** [a]Mt 8:4 ◆ **9:1** [a]Mt 10:5;
Mk 6:7 **9:2** [a]Mt 10:7 **9:3** [a]Lk 9:3-5: *Mt 10:9-15; Mk 6:8-11;* Lk 10:4-12; 22:35 [b]Mt 10:10; Mk 6:8;
Lk 22:35f [1]Or *knapsack, beggar's bag* [2]Gr *khiton*, the garment worn next to the skin **9:4** [1]Lit *and
leave from there* **9:5** [a]Lk 10:11; Ac 13:51 **9:6** [a]Mk 6:12; Lk 8:1 [1]Or *from village to village*
**9:7** [a]Lk 9:7-9: *Mt 14:1, 2;* Mk 6:14f [b]Mt 14:1; Lk 3:1; 13:31; 23:7

greatly perplexed, because it was said
by some that [c]John had risen from
the dead, **8** and by some that [a]Elijah
had appeared, and by others that one
of the prophets of old had risen again.
**9** And Herod said, "I myself had John
beheaded, but who is this man about
whom I hear such things?" And [a]he
kept trying to see Him.
**10** [a]And when the apostles re-
turned, they recounted to Him all
that they had done. [b]Taking them
with Him, He slipped away by Him-
self to a city called [c]Bethsaida. **11** But
when the crowds became aware of
this, they followed Him; and welcom-
ing them, He *began* speaking to them
about the kingdom of God and curing
those who had need of healing.

### *Jesus Feeds Five Thousand*

**12** Now the day [1]was ending, and the
twelve came and said to Him, "Send
the crowd away, that they may go
into the surrounding villages and
countryside and obtain lodging and
find provisions, for here we are in
a desolate place." **13** But He said to
them, "You give them *something* to
eat!" And they said, "We have no
more than five loaves and two fish,
unless perhaps we go and buy food
for all these people." **14** (For there
were about five thousand men.) And
He said to His disciples, "Have them
[1]sit down [a]in groups of about fifty
each." **15** And they did so, and had
them all [1]sit down. **16** Then He took
the five loaves and the two fish, and
looking up to heaven, He blessed
them. And He broke *them* and kept
giving *them* to the disciples to set
before the crowd. **17** And they all ate
and were satisfied; and [1]the broken
pieces which they had left over were
picked up, twelve [a]baskets *full*.

### *Peter Confesses Jesus Is the Christ*

**18** [a]And it happened that while He
was [b]praying alone, the disciples
were with Him, and He questioned
them, saying, "Who do the crowds
say that I am?" **19** And they answered
and said, "John the Baptist, and
others *say* Elijah, but others, that
one of the prophets of old has risen
again." **20** And He said to them, "But
who do you say that I am?" And Peter
answered and said, "[a]The [1]Christ
of God." **21** But He [a,1]warned them
and directed *them* not to tell this
to anyone, **22** [a]saying, "[b]The Son of
Man must suffer many things and
be rejected by the elders and chief
priests and scribes, and be killed and
be raised up on the third day."

### *Take up Your Cross*

**23** And He was saying to *them* all, "[a]If
anyone wishes to come after Me, let
him deny himself, and take up his
cross daily and follow Me. **24** For
[a]whoever wishes to save his [1]life will
lose it, but whoever loses his [1]life for
My sake, he is the one who will save
it. **25** For what is a man profited if he
gains the whole world, and [a]loses or
forfeits himself? **26** [a]For whoever is
ashamed of Me and My words, the
Son of Man will be ashamed of him

**9:7** [c]Mt 14:2 **9:8** [a]Mt 16:14 **9:9** [a]Lk 23:8 **9:10** [a]Mk 6:30 [b]Lk 9:10-17: *Mt 14:13-21; Mk 6:32-44; Jn 6:5-13* [c]Mt 11:21 **9:12** [1]Lit *began to decline* **9:14** [a]Mk 6:39 [1]Lit *recline* **9:15** [1]Lit *recline* **9:17** [a]Mt 14:20 [1]Lit *that which was left over to them of the broken pieces was* **9:18** [a]Lk 9:18-20: *Mt 16:13-16; Mk 8:27-29* [b]Mt 14:23; Lk 6:12; 9:28 **9:20** [a]Jn 6:68f [1]Messiah **9:21** [a]Mt 8:4; 16:20; Mk 8:30 [1]Or *strictly admonished* **9:22** [a]Lk 9:22-27: *Mt 16:21-28; Mk 8:31-9:1* [b]Mt 16:21; Lk 9:44 **9:23** [a]Mt 10:38; Lk 14:27 **9:24** [a]Mt 10:39; Lk 17:33; Jn 12:25 [1]Or *soul* **9:25** [a]Heb 10:34 **9:26** [a]Mt 10:33; Lk 12:9

when He comes in His glory, and *the*
*glory* of the Father and of the holy
angels. **27** But I say to you truthfully,
[a]there are some of those standing
here who will not taste death until
they see the kingdom of God."

### *The Transfiguration*

**28** [a]Now it happened some eight
days after these words, that taking
along [b]Peter and John and James, He
[c]went up on the mountain [d]to pray.
**29** And it happened that while He was
[a]praying, the appearance of His face
[b]became different, and His clothing
*became* white *and* [1]gleaming. **30** And
behold, two men were talking with
Him, and they were Moses and Eli-
jah, **31** who, appearing in [1]glory, were
speaking of His [a,2]departure which
He was about to fulfill at Jerusalem.
**32** Now Peter and his companions
[a]had been overcome with sleep, but
when they were fully awake, they saw
His glory and the two men standing
with Him. **33** And it happened that
as they were leaving Him, Peter said
to Jesus, "[a]Master, it is good for us to
be here; [b]let us make three [1]booths:
one for You, and one for Moses, and
one for Elijah"—[c]not realizing what
he was saying. **34** While he was saying
this, a cloud [1]formed and *began to*
overshadow them; and they were
afraid as they entered the cloud.
**35** Then [a]a voice came out of the
cloud, saying, "[b]This is My Son, *My*
Chosen One; listen to Him!" **36** And
when the voice [1]had spoken, Jesus
was found alone. And [a]they kept
silent, and reported to no one in
those days any of the things which
they had seen.

### *Jesus Casts Out a Demon*

**37** [a]Now it happened on the next day,
that when they came down from the
mountain, a large crowd met Him.
**38** And behold, a man from the crowd
shouted, saying, "Teacher, I beg You
to look at my son, for he is my [1]only
*one*, **39** and behold, a spirit seizes
him, and he suddenly screams, and
it throws him into a convulsion with
foaming *at the mouth*, and only with
difficulty does it leave him, mauling
him *as it leaves*. **40** And I begged Your
disciples to cast it out, and they could
not." **41** And Jesus answered and
said, "You unbelieving and perverse
generation, how long shall I be with
you and put up with you? Bring your
son here." **42** Now while he was still
approaching, the demon [1]slammed
him *to the ground* and threw him
into a convulsion. But Jesus rebuked
the unclean spirit and healed the
boy and gave him back to his father.
**43** And they were all astonished at
the [a]majesty of God.

### *Jesus Foretells His Death and Resurrection*

[b]But while everyone was marveling
at all that He was doing, He said to
His disciples, **44** "Put these words
into your ears; [a]for the Son of Man
is going to be [1]delivered into the

**9:27** [a]Mt 16:28 **9:28** [a]Lk 9:28-36: *Mt 17:1-8; Mk 9:2-8* [b]Mt 17:1 [c]Mt 5:1 [d]Lk 3:21; 5:16; 6:12; 9:18 **9:29** [a]Lk 3:21; 5:16; 6:12; 9:18 [b]Mk 16:12 [1]Lit *flashing like lightning* **9:31** [a]2Pe 1:15 [1]Or *splendor* [2]Or *exodus*, cf. 2Pe 1:15 **9:32** [a]Mt 26:43; Mk 14:40 **9:33** [a]Lk 5:5; 9:49 [b]Mt 17:4; Mk 9:5 [c]Mk 9:6 [1]Or *tents, tabernacles*, cf. Lv 23:34-43; Dt 16:13-15; Zec 14:16-19 **9:34** [1]Lit *occurred* **9:35** [a]2Pe 1:17f [b]Is 42:1; Mt 3:17; 12:18; Mk 1:11; Lk 3:22 **9:36** [a]Mt 17:9; Mk 9:9f [1]Lit *occurred* **9:37** [a]Lk 9:37-42: *Mt 17:14-18; Mk 9:14-27* **9:38** [1]Or *only begotten* **9:42** [1]Or *tore him* **9:43** [a]2Pe 1:16 [b]Lk 9:43-45: *Mt 17:22f; Mk 9:30-32* **9:44** [a]Lk 9:22 [1]Or *betrayed*

hands of men." 45 But [a]they [1]did
not understand this statement, and
it was concealed from them so that
they would not perceive it, and they
were afraid to ask Him about this
statement.

### *Who Is the Greatest?*

46 [a]Now an argument [1]started among
them as to which of them might be
the greatest. 47 But Jesus, [a]knowing
[1]what they were thinking in their
heart, took a child and stood him
by His side, 48 and said to them,
"[a]Whoever receives this child in My
name receives Me, and whoever re-
ceives Me receives Him who sent Me;
[b]for the one who is least among all
of you, this is the one who is great."
49 [a]And John answered and said,
"[b]Master, we saw someone casting
out demons in Your name, and we
tried to hinder him because he does
not follow along with us." 50 But Jesus
said to him, "Do not hinder *him*, [a]for
he who is not against you is [1]for you."
51 Now it happened that when
the days for [a]Him to be taken up
were soon to be fulfilled, He set
His face [b]to go to Jerusalem; 52 and
He sent messengers on ahead of
Him, and they went and entered a
village of the [a]Samaritans to [1]make
arrangements for Him. 53 But they
did not receive Him, [a]because [1]He
was journeying with His face toward
Jerusalem. 54 And when His disciples
[a]James and John saw *this*, they said,
"Lord, do You want us to [b]command
fire to come down from heaven and
consume them?" 55 But He turned
and rebuked them, [1][and said, "You
do not know what kind of spirit you
are of, 56 for the Son of Man did not
come to destroy men's lives, but to
save them."] And they went on to
another village.

### *The Cost of Following Jesus*

57 [a]And as they were going along
the road, [b]someone said to Him, "I
will follow You wherever You go."
58 And Jesus said to him, "The foxes
have holes and the birds of the [1]air
*have* [2]nests, but [a]the Son of Man has
nowhere to lay His head." 59 And He
said to another, "[a]Follow Me." But
he said, "Lord, permit me first to
go and bury my father." 60 But He
said to him, "Allow the dead to bury
their own dead; but as for you, go and
[a]proclaim everywhere the kingdom
of God." 61 Another also said, "I will
follow You, Lord, but [a]first permit
me to say farewell to those at home."
62 But Jesus said to him, "[a]No one, af-
ter putting his hand to the plow and
looking back, is fit for the kingdom
of God."

### *The Seventy Sent Out*

10 Now after this [a]the Lord
appointed [1]seventy [b]others,
and sent them [c]in pairs ahead of
Him to every city and place where
He Himself was going to come. 2 And

---

**9:45** [a]Mk 9:32 [1]Lit *were not knowing* **9:46** [a]Lk 9:46-48: *Mt 18:1-5; Mk 9:33-37;* Lk 22:24 [1]Lit *entered in* **9:47** [a]Mt 9:4 [1]Or *the argument*; lit *the reasoning* **9:48** [a]Mt 10:40; Lk 10:16; Jn 13:20 [b]Lk 22:26 **9:49** [a]Lk 9:49, 50: *Mk 9:38-40* [b]Lk 5:5; 9:33 **9:50** [a]Mt 12:30; Lk 11:23 [1]Or *on your side* **9:51** [a]Mk 16:19 [b]Lk 13:22; 17:11; 18:31; 19:11, 28 **9:52** [a]Mt 10:5; Lk 10:33; 17:16; Jn 4:4 [1]Or *prepare* **9:53** [a]Jn 4:9 [1]Lit *His face was proceeding toward* **9:54** [a]Mk 3:17 [b]2Ki 1:9-16 **9:55** [1]Early mss omit bracketed portion **9:57** [a]Lk 9:51 [b]Lk 9:57-60: *Mt 8:19-22* **9:58** [a]Mt 8:20 [1]Or *sky* [2]Or *roosting places* **9:59** [a]Mt 8:22 **9:60** [a]Mt 4:23 **9:61** [a]1Ki 19:20 **9:62** [a]Php 3:13 ◆ **10:1** [a]Lk 7:13 [b]Lk 9:1f, 52 [c]Mk 6:7 [1]Some mss *seventy-two*

He was saying to them, "[a]The harvest
is plentiful, but the laborers are few;
therefore pray earnestly to the Lord
of the harvest to send out laborers
into His harvest. **3** Go! [a]Behold, I
send you out as lambs in the midst
of wolves. **4** [a]Carry no money belt,
no bag, no sandals, and greet no
one on the way. **5** Whatever house
you enter, first say, 'Peace *be* to this
house.' **6** And if a [1]man of peace is
there, your peace will rest on him,
but if not, it will return to you. **7** Stay
in [1]that house, eating and drinking
[2]what they give you; for [a]the laborer
is worthy of his wages. Do not keep
moving from house to house. **8** And
whatever city you enter and they re-
ceive you, [a]eat what is set before you;
**9** and heal those in it who are sick,
and say to them, '[a]The kingdom of
God has come near to you.' **10** But in
whatever city you enter and they do
not receive you, go out into its streets
and say, **11** '[a]Even the dust of your city
which clings to our feet we wipe off
against you; yet know this, that [b]the
kingdom of God is at hand.' **12** I say to
you, [a]it will be more tolerable in that
day for [b]Sodom than for that city.
**13** "[a]Woe to you, [b]Chorazin! Woe to
you, [b]Bethsaida! For if the [1]miracles
had been performed in [b]Tyre and
Sidon which occurred in you, they
would have repented long ago, sitting
*in* [c,2]sackcloth and ashes. **14** But it will
be more tolerable for [a]Tyre and Sidon
in the judgment than for you. **15** And
you, [a]Capernaum, will you be exalted
to heaven? You will be brought down
to Hades!
**16** "[a]The one who listens to you
listens to Me, and [b]the one who
rejects you rejects Me. And he who
rejects Me rejects the One who sent
Me."

### *The Joyful Results*

**17** Now the [1]seventy returned with
joy, saying, "Lord, even [a]the demons
are subject to us in Your name."
**18** And He said to them, "I was
watching [a]Satan fall from heaven
like lightning. **19** Behold, I have given
you authority to [a]tread on serpents
and scorpions, and over all the power
of the enemy, and nothing will injure
you. **20** Nevertheless do not rejoice
in this, that the spirits are subject to
you, but rejoice that [a]your names are
recorded in heaven."
**21** [a]At that very [1]time He rejoiced
greatly in the Holy Spirit, and said, "I
[2]praise You, O Father, Lord of heaven
and earth, that You have hidden these
things from *the* wise and intelligent
and have revealed them to infants.
Yes, Father, for this way was well-
pleasing in Your sight. **22** [a]All things
have been handed over to Me by My
Father, and [b]no one knows who the
Son is except the Father, and who the
Father is except the Son, and anyone
to whom the Son wills to reveal *Him*."

**10:2** [a]Mt 9:37, 38; Jn 4:35 **10:3** [a]Mt 10:16 **10:4** [a]Mt 10:9-14; Mk 6:8-11; Lk 9:3-5; 10:4-12 **10:6** [1]Lit *son of peace* **10:7** [a]Mt 10:10; 1Co 9:14; 1Ti 5:18 [1]Lit *the house itself* [2]Lit *the things from them* **10:8** [a]1Co 10:27 **10:9** [a]Mt 3:2; 10:7; Lk 10:11 **10:11** [a]Mt 10:14; Mk 6:11; Lk 9:5; Ac 13:51 [b]Mt 3:2; 10:7; Lk 10:9 **10:12** [a]Ge 19:24-28; Mt 10:15; 11:24 [b]Mt 10:15 **10:13** [a]Lk 10:13-15: *Mt 11:21-23* [b]Is 23:1-18; Eze 26:1-28:26; Joel 3:4-8; Mt 11:21 [c]Rev 11:3 [1]Or *works of power* [2]Symbols of mourning **10:14** [a]Mt 11:21 **10:15** [a]Is 14:13-15; Mt 4:13; 11:23 **10:16** [a]Mt 10:40; Mk 9:37; Lk 9:48; Jn 13:20; Ga 4:14 [b]Jn 12:48; 1Th 4:8 **10:17** [a]Mk 16:17 [1]Some mss *seventy-two* **10:18** [a]Mt 4:10 **10:19** [a]Ps 91:13; Mk 16:18 **10:20** [a]Ex 32:32; Ps 69:28; Is 4:3; Eze 13:9; Da 12:1; Php 4:3; Heb 12:23; Rev 3:5; 13:8; 17:8; 20:12, 15; 21:27 **10:21** [a]Lk 10:21, 22: *Mt 11:25-27* [1]Lit *hour* [2]Or *acknowledge to You* **10:22** [a]Jn 3:35 [b]Jn 10:15

**23** [a]And turning to the disciples,
He said privately, "Blessed *are*
the eyes which see the things you
see, **24** for I say to you, that many
prophets and kings wished to see
the things which you see, and did
not see *them*, and to hear the things
which you hear, and did not hear
*them*."

### *The Good Samaritan*

**25** [a]And behold, a [b]scholar of the Law
stood up and was putting Him to the
test, saying, "Teacher, what shall I
do to inherit eternal life?" **26** And He
said to him, "What is written in the
Law? How do you read *it*?" **27** And he
answered and said, "[a]YOU SHALL LOVE
THE [1]LORD YOUR GOD WITH ALL YOUR
HEART, AND WITH ALL YOUR SOUL, AND
WITH ALL YOUR STRENGTH, AND WITH
ALL YOUR MIND; AND YOUR NEIGHBOR
AS YOURSELF." **28** And He said to
him, "You have answered correctly;
[a]DO THIS AND YOU WILL LIVE." **29** But
wishing [a]to justify himself, he said
to Jesus, "And who is my neighbor?"
**30** Jesus replied and said, "A man
was [a]going down from Jerusalem to
Jericho, and fell among robbers, and
they stripped him and [1]beat him, and
went away leaving him half dead.
**31** And a priest happened to be going
down on that road, and when he
saw him, he passed by on the other
side. **32** Likewise a Levite also, when
he came to the place and saw him,
passed by on the other side. **33** But a
[a]Samaritan, who was on a journey,
came upon him, and when he saw
him, he felt compassion. **34** And he
came to him and bandaged up his
wounds, pouring oil and wine on
*them*, and he put him on his own
animal, and brought him to an inn
and took care of him. **35** And on the
next day he took out two [1]denarii
and gave them to the innkeeper and
said, 'Take care of him, and whatever
more you spend, when I return I will
repay you.' **36** Which of these three
do you think proved to be a neighbor
to the man who fell into the robbers'
*hands*?" **37** And he said, "The one
who showed mercy toward him."
Then Jesus said to him, "Go and do
[1]the same."

### *Martha and Mary*

**38** Now as they were traveling along,
He entered a village; and a woman
named [a]Martha welcomed Him into
her home. **39** And she had a sister
called [a]Mary, who was also [b]seated at
the Lord's feet, listening to His word.
**40** But [a]Martha was distracted with
[1]all her preparations; and she came
up *to Him* and said, "Lord, do You
not care that my sister has left me
to do all the [2]preparations alone?
Then tell her to help me." **41** But
the Lord answered and said to her,
"[a]Martha, Martha, you are [b]worried
and bothered about so many things,
**42** [a]but *only* one thing is necessary,
for [b]Mary has chosen the good part,
which shall not be taken away from
her."

---

**10:23** [a]Lk 10:23, 24: *Mt 13:16, 17* **10:25** [a]Lk 10:25-28: *Mt 22:34-40; Mk 12:28-31;* Mt 19:16-19 [b]Mt 22:35
**10:27** [a]Dt 6:5; Lv 19:18 [1]In OT, Yahweh, cf. Dt 6:5 **10:28** [a]Lv 18:5; Eze 20:11; Mt 19:17 **10:29** [a]Lk 16:15
**10:30** [a]Lk 18:31; 19:28 [1]Lit *laid blows upon* **10:33** [a]Mt 10:5; Lk 9:52 **10:35** [1]A denarius was a laborer's daily wage **10:37** [1]Or *likewise* **10:38** [a]Lk 10:40f; Jn 11:1, 5, 19ff, 30, 39; 12:2
**10:39** [a]Lk 10:42; Jn 11:1f, 19f, 28, 31f, 45; 12:3 [b]Lk 8:35; Ac 22:3 **10:40** [a]Lk 10:38, 41; Jn 11:1, 5, 19ff, 30, 39; 12:2 [1]Lit *much service* [2]Lit *serving* **10:41** [a]Lk 10:38, 40; Jn 11:1, 5, 19ff, 30, 39; 12:2 [b]Mt 6:25
**10:42** [a]Ps 27:4; Jn 6:27 [b]Lk 10:39; Jn 11:1f, 19f, 28, 31f, 45; 12:3

### *The Lord's Prayer*

11 And it happened that while
[1]Jesus was praying in a certain
place, after He had finished, one
of His disciples said to Him, "Lord,
teach us to pray just as John also
taught his disciples." **2** And He said
to them, "[a]When you pray, say:
'[1]Father, hallowed be
Your name.
Your kingdom come.
**3** 'Give us [a]each day our
[1]daily bread.
**4** 'And forgive us our sins,
For we ourselves also
forgive everyone who
[a]is indebted to us.
And lead us not
into temptation.'"
**5** Then He said to them, "Which of
you has a friend and will go to him
at midnight and say to him, 'Friend,
lend me three loaves, **6** for a friend of
mine has come to me from a journey,
and I have nothing to set before him';
**7** and from inside he answers and
says, 'Do not bother me; the door has
already been shut and my children
[1]and I are in bed; I cannot rise up and
give you *anything*.' **8** I tell you, even
though he will not arise and give him
*anything* because he is his friend, yet
[a]because of his [1]persistence he will
get up and give him as much as he
needs.
**9** "So I say to you, [a,1]ask, and it will
be given to you; [2]seek, and you will
find; [3]knock, and it will be opened
to you. **10** For everyone who asks, re-
ceives; and he who seeks, finds; and
to him who knocks, it will be opened.
**11** But what father among you, *if* his
son asks for a [1]fish, will give him a
snake instead of a fish? **12** Or, *if his
son* asks for an egg, will give him a
scorpion? **13** [a]If you then, being evil,
know how to give good gifts to your
children, how much more will *your*
[1]heavenly Father give the Holy Spirit
to those who ask Him?"

### *A Kingdom Divided*

**14** [a]And He was casting out a demon,
and it was mute. Now it happened
that when the demon had gone out,
the mute man spoke, and the crowds
marveled. **15** But some of them said,
"He casts out demons [a]by [b]Beelze-
bul, the ruler of the demons." **16** And
others, testing *Him*, [a]were seeking
from Him [1]a sign from heaven. **17** [a]But
He knew their thoughts and said to
them, "[1]Any kingdom divided against
itself is laid waste, and a house *divid-
ed* against [2]itself falls. **18** But if [a]Satan
also is divided against himself, how
will his kingdom stand? For you say
that I cast out demons by [b]Beelze-
bul. **19** And if I by [a]Beelzebul cast
out demons, by whom do your sons
cast them out? For this reason, they
will be your judges. **20** But if I cast
out demons by the [a]finger of God,
then [b]the kingdom of God has come
upon you. **21** When [1]a strong *man*,
fully armed, guards his own house,

◆ **11:1** [1]Lit *He* **11:2** [a]Lk 11:2-4: *Mt 6:9-13* [1]Later mss add phrases from Mt 6:9-13 to make the two passages closely similar **11:3** [a]Ac 17:11 [1]Or *bread for the coming day* **11:4** [a]Lk 13:4 mg **11:7** [1]Lit *with me* **11:8** [a]Lk 18:1-5 [1]Lit *shamelessness* **11:9** [a]Lk 11:9-13: *Mt 7:7-11* [1]Or *keep asking* [2]Or *keep seeking* [3]Or *keep knocking* **11:11** [1]Two early mss insert *loaf, he will not give him a stone, will he, or for a...* **11:13** [a]Mt 7:11; Lk 18:7f [1]Lit *Father from heaven* **11:14** [a]Lk 11:14, 15: *Mt 12:22, 24;* Mt 9:32-34 **11:15** [a]Mt 9:34 [b]Mt 10:25 **11:16** [a]Mt 12:38; 16:1; Mk 8:11 [1]Or *an attesting miracle* **11:17** [a]Lk 11:17-22: *Mt 12:25-29; Mk 3:23-27* [1]Lit *Every* [2]Lit *a house* **11:18** [a]Mt 4:10 [b]Mt 10:25 **11:19** [a]Mt 10:25 **11:20** [a]Ex 8:19 [b]Mt 3:2 **11:21** [1]Lit *the*

his possessions are [2]undisturbed.
**22** But when someone stronger than
he attacks him and overpowers him,
he takes away from him all his armor
on which he had relied and distrib-
utes his plunder. **23** [a]He who is not
with Me is against Me and he who
does not gather with Me, scatters.

**24** "[a]When the unclean spirit goes
out of [1]a man, it passes through wa-
terless places seeking rest, and not
finding any, it says, 'I will return to
my house from which I came.' **25** And
when it comes, it finds it swept and
put in order. **26** Then it goes and takes
along seven other spirits more evil
than itself, and they go in and live
there, and the last state of that man
becomes worse than the first."

**27** Now it happened that while
[1]Jesus was saying these things, one
of the women in the crowd raised
her voice and said to Him, "[a]Blessed
is the womb that bore You and the
breasts at which You nursed." **28** But
He said, "On the contrary, blessed
are [a]those who hear the word of God
and keep it."

### *The Sign of Jonah*

**29** Now as the crowds were increas-
ing, He began to say, "[a]This genera-
tion is a wicked generation; it [b]seeks
[1]a sign, and *yet* no [2]sign will be given
to it but the [2]sign of Jonah. **30** For
just as [a]Jonah became [1]a sign to the
Ninevites, so will the Son of Man be
to this generation. **31** The [a]Queen of
the South will rise up at the judgment
with the men of this generation and
condemn them, because she came
from the ends of the earth to hear
the wisdom of Solomon. And behold,
something greater than Solomon is
here. **32** The men of Nineveh will
stand up at the judgment with this
generation and condemn it, because
[a]they repented at the preaching of Jo-
nah. And behold, something greater
than Jonah is here.

**33** "[a]No one, after lighting a lamp,
puts it away in a cellar nor under a
basket, but on the lampstand, so that
those who enter may see the light.
**34** [a]The eye is the lamp of your body;
when your eye is [1]clear, your whole
body also is full of light, but when
it is [2]bad, your body also is full of
darkness. **35** Therefore watch out that
the light in you is not darkness. **36** If
therefore your whole body is full of
light, with no dark part in it, it will be
wholly illumined, as when the lamp
illumines you with its rays."

### *Woes to the Pharisees and Lawyers*

**37** Now when He had spoken, a Phar-
isee *asked Him to have a meal with
him. And He went in and reclined *at
the table.* **38** But when the Pharisee
saw it, he marveled that He had not
first [a,1]ceremonially washed before
the [2]meal. **39** But [a]the Lord said to
him, "Now [b]you Pharisees clean the
outside of the cup and of the plat-
ter, but [1]inside of you, you are full
of robbery and wickedness. **40** [a]You
foolish ones, did not He who made
the outside make the inside also?
**41** But [a]give that which is within

**11:21** [2]Lit *in peace* **11:23** [a]Mt 12:30; Mk 9:40 **11:24** [a]Lk 11:24-26: *Mt 12:43-45* [1]Lit *the*
**11:27** [a]Lk 23:29 [1]Lit *He* **11:28** [a]Lk 8:21 **11:29** [a]Lk 11:29-32: *Mt 12:39-42;* Mt 16:4; Mk 8:12 [b]Mt 12:38; Lk 11:16 [1]Or *an attesting miracle* [2]Or *attesting miracle* **11:30** [a]Jon 3:4 [1]Or *an attesting miracle*
**11:31** [a]1Ki 10:1-10; 2Chr 9:1-12 **11:32** [a]Jon 3:5 **11:33** [a]Mt 5:15; Mk 4:21; Lk 8:16 **11:34** [a]Lk 11:34, 35: *Mt 6:22, 23* [1]Or *healthy* [2]Or *evil* **11:38** [a]Mt 15:2; Mk 7:3f [1]Lit *baptized* [2]Or *lunch* **11:39** [a]Lk 7:13 [b]Mt 23:25f [1]Lit *your inside is full* **11:40** [a]Lk 12:20; 1Co 15:36 **11:41** [a]Lk 12:33; 16:9

as charity, and [1]then all things are
[b]clean for you.
42 "[a]But woe to you Pharisees! For
you [b]pay tithe of mint and rue and
every *kind of* garden herb, and *yet*
disregard justice and the love of God,
but these are the things you should
have done without neglecting the
others. 43 Woe to you Pharisees! For
you [a]love the best seat in the syna-
gogues and the respectful greetings
in the marketplaces. 44 [a]Woe to you!
For you are like [1]concealed tombs,
and the people who walk over *them*
are unaware *of it*."
45 Now one of the [a]scholars of
the Law answered and said to Him,
"Teacher, when You say these things,
You insult us too." 46 But He said,
"Woe to you [a]scholars of the Law as
well! For [b]you weigh men down with
burdens hard to bear, and you your-
selves will not even touch the burdens
with one of your fingers. 47 [a]Woe to
you! For you build the [1]tombs of the
prophets, but your fathers killed
them. 48 So you are witnesses and
approve the deeds of your fathers;
because it was they who killed them,
and you build *their tombs*. 49 For this
reason also [a]the wisdom of God said,
'[b]I will send to them prophets and
apostles, and *some* of them they will
kill and *some* they will [1]persecute,
50 so that the blood of all the proph-
ets, shed [a]since the foundation of
the world, may be [1]charged against
this generation, 51 from [a]the blood of
Abel to [b]the blood of Zechariah, who
was killed between the altar and the
house *of God;* yes, I tell you, it shall
be [1]charged against this generation.'
52 Woe to you, [a]scholars of the Law!
For you have taken away the key of
knowledge; [b]you yourselves did not
enter, and you hindered those who
were entering."
53 And when He left there, the
scribes and the Pharisees began to
be very hostile and to question Him
closely on many subjects, 54 [a]plotting
[b]to catch [1]Him in something He
might say.

### *Fear Only God*

12 At this time, after [1]so many
thousands of the crowd had
gathered together that they were
trampling on one another, He began
saying to His disciples first, "[a]Be on
your guard for the leaven of the Phar-
isees, which is hypocrisy. 2 [a]But there
is nothing covered up that will not
be revealed, and hidden that will not
be known. 3 Accordingly, whatever
you have said in the dark will be
heard in the light, and what you have
[1]whispered in the inner rooms will
be proclaimed upon [a]the housetops.
4 "But I say to you, [a]My friends,
do not fear those who kill the body
and after that have no more that
they can do. 5 But I will show you
whom to fear: [a]fear the One who,
after He has killed, has authority to
cast into [b,1]hell; yes, I tell you, fear

**11:41** [b]Mk 7:19; Tit 1:15 [1]Lit *behold* **11:42** [a]Mt 23:23 [b]Lv 27:30; Lk 18:12 **11:43** [a]Mt 23:6f; Mk 12:38f; Lk 14:7; 20:46 **11:44** [a]Mt 23:27 [1]Or *indistinct* **11:45** [a]Mt 22:35; Lk 11:46, 52 **11:46** [a]Mt 22:35; Lk 11:45, 52 [b]Mt 23:4 **11:47** [a]Mt 23:29ff [1]Or *monuments to* **11:49** [a]1Co 1:24, 30; Col 2:3 [b]Mt 23:34-36 [1]Or *drive out* **11:50** [a]Mt 25:34 [1]Or *required of* **11:51** [a]Ge 4:8 [b]2Chr 24:20, 21 [1]Or *required of* **11:52** [a]Mt 22:35; Lk 11:45, 46 [b]Mt 23:13 **11:54** [a]Mk 3:2; Lk 20:20; Ac 23:21 [b]Mk 12:13 [1]Lit *something out of His mouth* ◆ **12:1** [a]Mt 16:6, 11f; Mk 8:15 [1]Lit *myriads* **12:2** [a]Lk 12:2-9: *Mt 10:26-33;* Mt 10:26; Mk 4:22; Lk 8:17 **12:3** [a]Mt 10:27; 24:17 [1]Lit *spoken in the ear* **12:4** [a]Jn 15:13-15 **12:5** [a]Heb 10:31 [b]Mt 5:22 [1]Gr *Gehenna*

Him! **6** Are not [a]five sparrows sold
for two [1]assaria? *Yet* not one of them
is forgotten before God. **7** [a]Indeed,
the *very* hairs of your head are all
numbered. Do not fear; you are more
valuable than many sparrows.

### *Blasphemy Against the Holy Spirit*

**8** "And I say to you, everyone who
[a]confesses Me before men, the Son of
Man will confess him also before the
angels of God, **9** but [a]he who denies
Me before men will be denied [b]before
the angels of God. **10** [a]And everyone
who [1]speaks a word against the Son
of Man, it will be forgiven him, but
he who blasphemes against the Holy
Spirit, it will not be forgiven him.
**11** Now when they bring you before
[a]the synagogues and the rulers and
the authorities, do not [b]worry about
how or what you are to speak in your
defense, or what you are to say, **12** for
[a]the Holy Spirit will teach you in that
very hour what you ought to say."

### *Parable of the Rich Fool*

**13** And someone from the crowd said
to Him, "Teacher, tell my brother to
divide the *family* inheritance with
me." **14** But He said to him, "[a]Man,
who appointed Me a judge or arbi-
trator over you?" **15** Then He said
to them, "[a]Watch out and be on
your guard against every form of
greed, for not *even* when one has an
abundance does his life consist of his
possessions." **16** And He told them a
parable, saying, "The land of a rich
man was very productive. **17** And he
*began* reasoning to himself, saying,
'What shall I do, since I have no place
to store my crops?' **18** Then he said,
'This is what I will do: I will tear down
my barns and build larger ones, and
there I will store all my grain and my
goods. **19** And I will say to my soul,
"Soul, [a]you have many goods laid up
for many years *to come*; take your
ease, eat, drink *and* be merry."' **20** But
God said to him, '[a]You fool! This *very*
night [b,1]your soul is required of you;
and [c]*now* who will own what you pre-
pared?' **21** So is the one who [a]stores
up treasure for himself, and is not
rich toward God."

### *Do Not Worry*

**22** And He said to His disciples, "[a]For
this reason I say to you, [1]do not worry
about *your* [2]life, *as to* what you will
eat; nor for your body, *as to* what
you will put on. **23** For life is more
than food, and the body more than
clothing. **24** Consider the [a]ravens, for
they neither sow nor reap; they have
no storeroom nor [b]barn, and *yet* God
feeds them; how much more valuable
you are than the birds! **25** And which
of you by worrying can add a *single*
[a,1]cubit to his [2]life span? **26** Therefore,
if you cannot do even a very little
thing, why do you worry about other
matters? **27** Consider the lilies, how
they grow: they neither toil nor spin,
but I tell you, not even [a]Solomon in
all his glory clothed himself like one
of these. **28** But if God so clothes

**12:6** [a]Mt 10:29 [1]A Roman copper coin, approx. 1/16 of a laborer's daily wage **12:7** [a]Mt 10:30
**12:8** [a]Mt 10:32; Lk 15:10; Ro 10:9 **12:9** [a]Mt 10:33; Lk 9:26 [b]Lk 15:10 **12:10** [a]Mt 12:31, 32; Mk 3:28-30
[1]Lit *will speak* **12:11** [a]Mt 10:17 [b]Mt 6:25; 10:19; Mk 13:11; Lk 12:22; 21:14 **12:12** [a]Mt 10:20; Lk 21:15
**12:14** [a]Mic 6:8; Ro 2:1, 3; 9:20 **12:15** [a]1Ti 6:6-10 **12:19** [a]Ecc 11:9 **12:20** [a]Jer 17:11; Lk 11:40 [b]Job 27:8
[c]Ps 39:6 [1]Lit *they are demanding your soul from you* **12:21** [a]Lk 12:33 **12:22** [a]Lk 12:22-31: *Mt 6:25-33*
[1]Or *stop being worried* [2]Lit *soul* **12:24** [a]Job 38:41 [b]Lk 12:18 **12:25** [a]Ps 39:5 [1]A cubit was approx. 18
in. or 45 cm [2]Or *height* **12:27** [a]1Ki 10:4-7; 2Chr 9:3-6

the grass in the field, which is *alive* today and tomorrow is thrown into the furnace, how much more *will He clothe* you? [a]You of little faith! **29** And do not seek what you will eat and what you will drink, and do not [a]keep worrying. **30** For [1]all these things the nations of the world eagerly seek, but your Father knows that you need these things. **31** But seek His kingdom, and [a]these things will be added to you. **32** [a]Do not fear, [b]little flock, for [c]your Father is well pleased to give you the kingdom.

**33** "[a]Sell your possessions and give *it* as charity; make yourselves money belts which do not wear out, [b]an unfailing treasure in heaven, where no thief comes near nor moth destroys. **34** For [a]where your treasure is, there your heart will be also.

### *Be Ready for His Coming*

**35** "[a]GIRD UP [b]YOUR LOINS, and *keep* your lamps lit. **36** And be like men who are waiting for their master when he returns from the wedding feast, so that they may immediately open *the door* to him when he comes and knocks. **37** Blessed are those slaves whom the master will find [a]awake when he comes; truly I say to you, that [b]he will gird himself *to serve*, and have them recline *at the table*, and will come up and wait on them. **38** [a]Whether he comes in the [1]second watch, or even in the [2]third, and finds *them* so, blessed are those *slaves*.

**39** "[a]But [1]be sure of this, that if the head of the house had known at what hour the thief was coming, he would not have allowed his house to be [b,2]broken into. **40** [a]You too, be ready, for the Son of Man is coming at an hour that you do not [1]expect."

**41** Now Peter said, "Lord, are You addressing this parable to us, or [a]to everyone *else* as well?" **42** And [a]the Lord said, "[b]Who then is the faithful and prudent [c]steward, whom his master will put in charge of his [1]servants, to give them their rations at the proper time? **43** Blessed is that [a]slave whom his [1]master finds so doing when he comes. **44** Truly I say to you that he will put him in charge of all his possessions. **45** But if that slave says in his heart, 'My master [1]will be a long time in coming,' and begins to beat the male and female servants, and to eat and drink and get drunk, **46** the master of that slave will come on a day when he does not expect and at an hour he does not know, and will cut him in pieces, and assign him a place with the unbelievers. **47** And that slave who knew his master's will and did not get ready or act in accord with his will, will [a]receive many beatings, **48** but the one who did not [a]know *it*, and committed deeds worthy of a beating, will receive but a few. [b]From everyone who has been given much, much will be required, and to whom they entrusted much, of him they will ask all the more.

---

**12:28** [a]Mt 6:30 **12:29** [a]Mt 6:31 **12:30** [1]Or *these things all the nations of the world* **12:31** [a]Mt 6:33 **12:32** [a]Mt 14:27 [b]Jn 21:15-17 [c]Eph 1:5, 9 **12:33** [a]Mt 19:21; Lk 11:41; 18:22 [b]Mt 6:20; Lk 12:21 **12:34** [a]Mt 6:21 **12:35** [a]Ex 12:11 [b]Eph 6:14; 1Pe 1:13 **12:37** [a]Mt 24:42 [b]Lk 17:8; Jn 13:4 **12:38** [a]Mt 24:43 [1]9 p.m. to midnight [2]Midnight to 3 a.m. **12:39** [a]Lk 12:39, 40: *Mt 24:43, 44* [b]Mt 6:19 [1]Lit *know* [2]Lit *dug through* **12:40** [a]Mk 13:33; Lk 21:36 [1]Lit *think* **12:41** [a]Lk 12:47, 48 **12:42** [a]Lk 7:13 [b]Lk 12:42-46: *Mt 24:45-51* [c]Mt 24:45; Lk 16:1ff [1]Lit *service* **12:43** [a]Lk 12:42 [1]Or *lord* **12:45** [1]Lit *is delaying to come* **12:47** [a]Dt 25:2; Jas 4:17 **12:48** [a]Lv 5:17; Nu 15:29f [b]Mt 13:12

### *Not Peace, but Division*

**49** "I [1]have come to cast fire upon the
earth, and [2]how I wish it were already
kindled! **50** But I have a [a]baptism to
[1]undergo, and how distressed I am
until it is finished! **51** [a]Do you think
that I came to grant peace on earth?
I tell you, no, but rather division;
**52** for from now on five *members* in
one household will be divided, three
against two and two against three.
**53** They will be divided, [a]father against
son and son against father, mother
against daughter and daughter against
mother, mother-in-law against her
daughter-in-law and daughter-in-law
against mother-in-law."

**54** And He was also saying to the
crowds, "[a]When you see a cloud
rising in the west, immediately you
say, 'A shower is coming,' and so
it happens. **55** And when *you see* a
south wind blowing, you say, 'It will
be a [a]hot day,' and it happens. **56** You
hypocrites! [a]You know how to exam-
ine the appearance of the earth and
the sky, but [1]why do you not examine
this present time?

**57** "And [a]why do you not even
judge for yourselves what is right?
**58** For [a]while you are going with
your opponent to appear before the
magistrate, on *your* way *there* make
an effort to [1]settle with him, so that
he may not drag you before the judge,
and the judge turn you over to the
officer, and the officer throw you into
prison. **59** I say to you, you will not get
out of there until you have paid the
last [a,1]lepton."

### *Repent or Perish*

**13** Now at that same time there
were some present who were
reporting to Him about the Galileans
whose blood [a]Pilate had [1]mixed with
their sacrifices. **2** And Jesus answered
and said to them, "[a]Do you think that
these Galileans were *greater* sinners
than all *other* Galileans because they
suffered these things? **3** I tell you, no,
but unless you [1]repent, you will all
likewise perish. **4** Or do you think
that those eighteen on whom the
tower in [a]Siloam fell and killed them
were *worse* [b,1]offenders than all the
men who live in Jerusalem? **5** I tell
you, no, but unless you repent, you
will all likewise perish."

### *The Parable of the Barren Fig Tree*

**6** And He was telling this parable: "A
man had [a]a fig tree which had been
planted in his vineyard; and he came
seeking fruit on it and did not find
any. **7** And he said to the vineyard-
keeper, 'Behold, for three years I
have come seeking fruit on this fig
tree [1]without finding any. [a]Cut it
down! Why does it even use up the
ground?' **8** And he answered and said
to him, 'Let it alone, sir, for this year
too, until I dig around it and put in
manure, **9** and if it bears fruit next
year, *fine*, but if not, cut it down.'"

### *A Woman Healed on the Sabbath*

**10** And He was [a]teaching in one of the
synagogues on the Sabbath. **11** And
behold, there was a woman who
for eighteen years had [a,1]a sickness

---

**12:49** [1]Or *came* [2]Lit *what do I wish if...?* **12:50** [a]Mk 10:38 [1]Lit *be baptized with* **12:51** [a]Lk 12:51-53: *Mt 10:34-36* **12:53** [a]Mic 7:6; Mt 10:21 **12:54** [a]Mt 16:2f **12:55** [a]Mt 20:12 **12:56** [a]Mt 16:3 [1]Lit *how* **12:57** [a]Lk 21:30 **12:58** [a]Lk 12:58, 59: *Mt 5:25, 26* [1]Lit *be released from him* **12:59** [a]Mk 12:42 [1]Smallest Greek copper coin, approx. 1/128 of a laborer's daily wage ◆ **13:1** [a]Mt 27 [1]Shed **13:2** [a]Jn 9:2f **13:3** [1]Or *are repentant* **13:4** [a]Ne 3:15; Is 8:6; Jn 9:7, 11 [b]Mt 6:12; Lk 11:4 [1]Lit *debtors* **13:6** [a]Mt 21:19 **13:7** [a]Mt 3:10; 7:19; Lk 3:9 [1]Lit *and I do not find* **13:10** [a]Mt 4:23 **13:11** [a]Lk 13:16 [1]Lit *a spirit of sickness*

caused by a spirit, and she was bent
double, and could not straighten
up at all. **12** But when Jesus saw her,
He called her over and said to her,
"Woman, you are freed from your
sickness." **13** And He [a]laid His hands
on her, and immediately she was
made erect again and *began* [b]glori-
fying God. **14** But [a]the synagogue
official, indignant because Jesus
[b]healed on the Sabbath, answered
and was saying to the crowd, "[c]There
are six days in which work should
be done; so come during them and
get healed, and not on the Sabbath
day." **15** But [a]the Lord answered him
and said, "You hypocrites, [b]does not
each of you on the Sabbath release
his ox or his donkey from the stall
and lead it away to water *it*? **16** And
this woman, [a]being a daughter of
Abraham, whom [b]Satan has bound
for—behold—eighteen years, should
she not have been released from this
bond on the Sabbath day?" **17** And as
He said this, all His opponents were
being put to shame; and [a]the entire
crowd was rejoicing over all the
glorious things being done by Him.

### *The Parables of the Mustard Seed and the Leaven*

**18** Therefore, [a]He was saying, "[b]What
is the kingdom of God like, and to
what shall I compare it? **19** It is like
a mustard seed, which a man took
and threw into his own garden,
and it grew and became a tree, and
[a]THE BIRDS OF THE [1]AIR NESTED IN ITS
BRANCHES."
**20** And again He said, "[a]To what
shall I compare the kingdom of God?
**21** [a]It is like leaven, which a woman
took and hid in [b,1]three sata of flour
until it was all leavened."

### *The Narrow Door*

**22** And He was passing through
from one city and village to another,
teaching, and [a]proceeding on His
way to Jerusalem. **23** And someone
said to Him, "Lord, are there *just* a
few who are being saved?" And He
said to them, **24** "[a]Strive to enter
through the narrow door, for many,
I tell you, will seek to enter and will
not be able. **25** Once the head of the
house gets up and [a]shuts the door,
and you begin to stand outside and
knock on the door, saying, '[b]Lord,
open up to us!' then He will answer
and say to you, '[c]I do not know where
you are from.' **26** Then you will
[a]begin to say, 'We ate and drank in
Your presence, and You taught in our
streets.' **27** And He will say, 'I tell you,
[a]I do not know where you are from;
[b]DEPART FROM ME, ALL YOU WORKERS
OF UNRIGHTEOUSNESS.' **28** [a]In that
place there will be weeping and
gnashing of teeth when you see
Abraham and Isaac and Jacob and all
the prophets in the kingdom of God,
but yourselves being cast out. **29** And
they [a]will come from east and west
and from north and south, and will
recline *at the table* in the kingdom
of God. **30** And behold, [a]*some* are last
who will be first and *some* are first
who will be last."

---

**13:13** [a]Mk 5:23 [b]Mt 9:8 **13:14** [a]Mk 5:22 [b]Mt 12:2; Lk 14:3 [c]Ex 20:9; Dt 5:13 **13:15** [a]Lk 7:13 [b]Lk 14:5 **13:16** [a]Lk 19:9 [b]Mt 4:10; Lk 13:11 **13:17** [a]Lk 18:43 **13:18** [a]Lk 13:18, 19: *Mt 13:31, 32; Mk 4:30-32* [b]Mt 13:24; Lk 13:20 **13:19** [a]Eze 17:23 [1]Or *sky* **13:20** [a]Mt 13:24; Lk 13:18 **13:21** [a]Lk 13:20, 21: *Mt 13:33* [b]Mt 13:33 [1]Approx. 48 lb. or 39 l, a saton was approx. 16 lb. or 13 l **13:22** [a]Lk 9:51 **13:24** [a]Mt 7:13 **13:25** [a]Mt 25:10 [b]Mt 7:22; 25:11 [c]Mt 7:23; 25:12; Lk 13:27 **13:26** [a]Lk 3:8 **13:27** [a]Lk 13:25 [b]Ps 6:8; Mt 25:41 **13:28** [a]Mt 8:12; 22:13; 25:30 **13:29** [a]Mt 8:11 **13:30** [a]Mt 19:30; 20:16; Mk 10:31

### *Lament over Jerusalem*

**31** Just at that time some Pharisees
approached, saying to Him, "Leave
and go from here, for [a]Herod wants
to kill You." **32** And He said to them,
"Go and tell that fox, 'Behold, I cast
out demons and perform cures today
and tomorrow, and on the third *day* I
[a][1]finish.' **33** Nevertheless [a]I must jour-
ney on today and tomorrow and the
next *day*, for it is not possible that a
[b]prophet would perish outside of Jeru-
salem. **34** [a]O Jerusalem, Jerusalem, *the
city* that kills the prophets and stones
those sent to her! How often I wanted
to gather your children together, [b]just
as a hen *gathers* her brood under
her wings, and you did not want *it*!
**35** Behold, your house is left to you
*desolate*, and I say to you, you will not
see Me until *the time* comes when you
say, '[a]BLESSED IS HE WHO COMES IN THE
NAME OF THE [1]LORD!'"

### *Jesus Heals on the Sabbath*

**14** And it happened that when
He went into the house of one
of the [1]leaders of the Pharisees on
*the* Sabbath to eat bread, [a]they were
watching Him closely. **2** And behold,
in front of Him was a man suffering
from dropsy. **3** And Jesus answered
and spoke to the [a]scholars of the Law
and Pharisees, saying, "[b]Is it lawful
to heal on the Sabbath, or not?" **4** But
they were silent. And He took hold of
him, healed him, and sent him away.
**5** And He said to them, "[a][1]Which one
of you will have a son or an ox fall into
a well, and will not immediately pull
him out on a Sabbath day?" **6** [a]And
they could make no reply to this.

### *Parable of the Wedding Feast*

**7** And He was telling a parable to the
invited guests when He noticed how
[a]they were picking out the places of
honor *at the table*, saying to them,
**8** "When you are invited by someone
to a wedding feast, [a]do not recline at
the place of honor, lest someone more
highly regarded than you be invited
by him, **9** and he who invited you both
will come and say to you, 'Give *your*
place to this man,' and then [a]in shame
you [1]proceed to occupy the last place.
**10** But when you are invited, go and
recline at the last place, so that when
the one who has invited you comes,
he may say to you, 'Friend, [a]move up
higher'; then you will have honor in
the sight of all who recline at the table
with you. **11** [a]For everyone who exalts
himself will be humbled, and he who
humbles himself will be exalted."

**12** And He also went on to say to the
one who had invited Him, "When you
give a luncheon or a dinner, do not
invite your friends or your brothers
or your relatives or rich neighbors,
lest they also invite you in return and
*that* will be your repayment. **13** But
when you give a [1]reception, invite
*the* poor, *the* crippled, *the* lame, *the*
blind, **14** and you will be blessed,
since they [1]do not have *the means* to
repay you; for it will be repaid to you
at [a]the resurrection of the righteous."

**15** But when one of those who
were reclining *at the table* with Him

---

**13:31** [a]Mt 14:1; Lk 3:1; 9:7; 23:7 **13:32** [a]Heb 2:10; 5:9; 7:28 [1]Or *am perfected* **13:33** [a]Jn 11:9 [b]Mt 21:11 **13:34** [a]Lk 13:34, 35: *Mt 23:37-39;* Lk 19:41 [b]Mt 23:37 **13:35** [a]Ps 118:26; Mt 21:9; Lk 19:38 [1]In OT, Yahweh, cf. Ps 118:26 ◆ **14:1** [a]Mk 3:2 [1]Members of the Sanhedrin **14:3** [a]Mt 22:35 [b]Mt 12:2; Lk 13:14 **14:5** [a]Mt 12:11; Lk 13:15 [1]Lit *Whose son of you...will fall* **14:6** [a]Mt 22:46; Lk 20:40 **14:7** [a]Mt 23:6 **14:8** [a]Pr 25:6, 7 **14:9** [a]Lk 3:8 [1]Lit *begin* **14:10** [a]Pr 25:6, 7 **14:11** [a]2Sa 22:28; Pr 29:23; Mt 23:12; Lk 1:52; 18:14; Jas 4:10 **14:13** [1]Or *banquet* **14:14** [a]Jn 5:29; Ac 24:15; Rev 20:4, 5 [1]Or *are unable to*

heard this, he said to Him, “[a]Blessed
is everyone who will eat bread in the
kingdom of God!”

*Parable of the Dinner*

**16** And He said to him, “[a]A man was
giving a big dinner, and he invited
many. **17** And at the dinner hour he
sent his slave to say to those who had
been invited, ‘Come, for everything is
ready now.’ **18** But they all alike began
to make excuses. The first one said to
him, ‘I have bought a [1]piece of land
and I need to go out and look at it. I
ask you, consider me excused.’ **19** And
another one said, ‘I have bought five
yoke of oxen, and I am going to try
them out. I ask you, consider me
excused.’ **20** And another one said,
‘[a]I have married a wife, and for that
reason I cannot come.’ **21** And when
the slave came *back*, he reported
these things to his master. Then
the head of the household became
angry and said to his slave, ‘Go out
at once into the streets and lanes of
the city and bring in here the poor
and crippled and blind and lame.’
**22** And the slave said, ‘Master, what
you commanded has been done,
and still there is room.’ **23** And the
master said to the slave, ‘Go out into
the highways and along the [1]fences,
and compel *them* to come in, so that
my house may be filled. **24** For I tell
you, none of those men who were
invited shall taste of my dinner.’”

*The Cost of Discipleship*

**25** Now many crowds were going
along with Him, and He turned and
said to them, **26** “[a]If anyone comes to
Me, and does not [1]hate his own father
and mother and wife and children and
brothers and sisters, yes, and even his
own life, he cannot be My disciple.
**27** Whoever does not [a]carry his own
cross and come after Me cannot
be My disciple. **28** For which one of
you, when he wants to build a tower,
does not first sit down and calculate
the cost to see if he has enough to
complete it? **29** Lest, when he has laid
a foundation and is not able to finish,
all who observe it begin to ridicule
him, **30** saying, ‘This man began to
build and was not able to finish.’ **31** Or
what king, when he sets out to meet
another king in battle, will not first
sit down and [a]consider whether he
is strong enough with ten thousand
*men* to encounter the one coming
against him with twenty thousand?
**32** Or else, while the other is still far
away, he sends [1]a delegation and asks
for terms of peace. **33** So then, none
of you can be My disciple who [a]does
not give up all his own possessions.

**34** “Therefore, salt is good, but
[a]if even salt has become tasteless,
with what will it be seasoned? **35** It
is useless either for the soil or for the
manure pile; it is thrown out. [a]He who
has ears to hear, [1]let him hear.”

*The Parable of the Lost Sheep*

**15** Now all the [a]tax collectors and
the [1]sinners were coming near
Him to listen to Him. **2** And both the
Pharisees and the scribes were grum-
bling, saying, “This man receives
sinners and [a]eats with them.”

**14:15** [a]Rev 19:9 **14:16** [a]Lk 14:16-24: *Mt 22:2-14* **14:18** [1]Or *field* **14:20** [a]Dt 24:5; 1Co 7:33
**14:23** [1]Or *lanes* **14:26** [a]Mt 10:37 [1]In comparison to his love for Me **14:27** [a]Mt 10:38; 16:24; Mk 8:34;
Lk 9:23 **14:31** [a]Pr 20:18 **14:32** [1]Or *an embassy* **14:33** [a]Php 3:7; Heb 11:26 **14:34** [a]Mt 5:13; Mk 9:50
**14:35** [a]Mt 11:15 [1]Or *hear!, listen!*; Gr imperative ◆ **15:1** [a]Lk 5:29 [1]Irreligious Jews **15:2** [a]Mt 9:11

**3** So He told them this parable, saying, **4** "[a]What man among you, if he has one hundred sheep and has lost one of them, does not leave the ninety-nine in the [1]open pasture and go after the one which is lost until he finds it? **5** And when he has found it, he lays it on his shoulders, rejoicing. **6** And when he comes home, he calls together his friends and his neighbors, saying to them, 'Rejoice with me, for I have found my sheep which was lost!' **7** I tell you that in the same way, there will be *more* joy in heaven over one sinner who repents than over ninety-nine righteous persons who need no repentance.

### *The Parable of the Lost Drachma*

**8** "Or what woman, if she has ten [1]drachmas and loses one [1]drachma, does not light a lamp and sweep the house and search carefully until she finds it? **9** And when she has found it, she calls together her friends and neighbors, saying, 'Rejoice with me, for I have found the [1]drachma which I had lost!' **10** In the same way, I tell you, there is joy [a]in the presence of the angels of God over one sinner who repents."

### *The Parable of the Prodigal Son*

**11** And He said, "A man had two sons. **12** And the younger of them said to his father, 'Father, give me [a]the share of the estate that falls *to me.*' So he divided his [b,1]wealth between them. **13** And not many days later, the younger son gathered everything together and went on a journey into a distant country, and there he squandered his estate living recklessly. **14** Now when he had spent everything, a severe famine occurred in that country, and he began to be impoverished. **15** So he went and [1]hired himself out to one of the citizens of that country, and he sent him into his fields to feed swine. **16** And he was desiring to be fed with the [1]pods that the swine were eating, and no one was giving *anything* to him. **17** But when he came to himself, he said, 'How many of my father's hired men have more than enough bread, but I am dying here with hunger! **18** I will rise up and go to my father, and will say to him, "Father, I have sinned against heaven, and before you. **19** I am no longer worthy to be called your son; make me as one of your hired men."' **20** So he rose up and came to [1]his father. But while he was still a long way off, his father saw him and felt compassion, and ran and [a,2]embraced him and kissed him. **21** And the son said to him, 'Father, I have sinned against heaven and before you. I am no longer worthy to be called your son.' **22** But the father said to his slaves, 'Quickly bring out [a]the best robe and put it on him, and [b]put a ring on his hand and sandals on his feet, **23** and bring the fattened calf, slaughter it, and let us eat and celebrate, **24** for this son of mine was [a]dead and has come to life again; he was lost and has been found.' And they began to celebrate.

**25** "Now his older son was in the field, and when he came and approached the house, he heard music

---

**15:4** [a]Lk 15:4-7: *Mt 18:12-14* [1]Lit *wilderness* **15:8** [1]A Greek silver coin, approx. a laborer's daily wage **15:9** [1]A Greek silver coin, approx. a laborer's daily wage **15:10** [a]Mt 10:32; Lk 15:7 **15:12** [a]Dt 21:17 [b]Mk 12:44; Lk 15:30 [1]Lit *living* **15:15** [1]Lit *was joined to* **15:16** [1]Of the carob tree **15:20** [a]Ge 45:14; 46:29; Ac 20:37 [1]Lit *his own* [2]Lit *fell on his neck* **15:22** [a]Zec 3:4; Rev 6:11 [b]Ge 41:42 **15:24** [a]Mt 8:22; Lk 9:60; 15:32; Ro 11:15; Eph 2:1, 5; 5:14; Col 2:13; 1Ti 5:6

and dancing. **26** And summoning one
of the servants, he *began* inquiring
what these things could be. **27** And
he said to him, 'Your brother has
come, and your father has killed the
fattened calf because he has received
him back safe and sound.' **28** But he
became angry and was not wanting
to go in, and his father came out
and *began* pleading with him. **29** But
he answered and said to his father,
'Look! For so many years I have
been serving you and never have I
[1]neglected a command of yours. And
*yet* never have you given me a young
goat, so that I might celebrate with
my friends. **30** But when this son of
yours came, who has devoured your
[a,1]wealth with prostitutes, you killed
the fattened calf for him.' **31** And he
said to him, 'Child, you are always
with me, and all that is mine is yours.
**32** But we had to celebrate and rejoice,
for this brother of yours was [a]dead
and is alive, and *was* lost and has
been found.'"

### *The Parable of the Unrighteous Steward*

**16** Now He was also saying to the
disciples, "There was a rich
man who had a steward, and this
*steward* was [1]reported to him as
[a]squandering his possessions. **2** And
he called for him and said to him,
'What is this I hear about you? Give
an accounting of your stewardship,
for you can no longer be steward.'
**3** And the steward said to himself,
'What shall I do, since my [1]master
is taking the stewardship away from
me? I am not strong enough to dig; I
am ashamed to beg. **4** I know what I
shall do, so that when I am removed
from the stewardship people will
[1]take me into their homes.' **5** And he
summoned each one of his [1]master's
debtors, and he *began* saying to the
first, 'How much do you owe my
master?' **6** And he said, 'One hundred
[1]baths of oil.' And he said to him, 'Take
your bill, and sit down quickly and
write fifty.' **7** Then he said to another,
'And how much do you owe?' And he
said, 'One hundred [1]kors of wheat.'
He *said to him, 'Take your bill,
and write eighty.' **8** And his [1]master
praised the unrighteous steward
because he had acted shrewdly, for
the sons of [a]this age are more shrewd
in relation to their own [2]kind than
the [b]sons of light. **9** And I say to you,
[a]make friends for yourselves from
the [b,1]wealth of unrighteousness, so
that when it fails, [c]they will [2]take you
into the eternal dwellings.
**10** "[a]He who is faithful in a very lit-
tle thing is faithful also in much, and
he who is unrighteous in a very little
thing is unrighteous also in much.
**11** Therefore if you have not been
faithful in the *use of* unrighteous
[a,1]wealth, who will entrust the true
*riches* to you? **12** And if you have not
been faithful in *the use of* that which
is another's, who will give you that
which is your own? **13** [a]No [1]servant
can [2]serve two masters; for either he
will hate the one and love the other,
or else he will be devoted to one and

---

**15:29** [1]Or *disobeyed* **15:30** [a]Pr 29:3; Lk 15:12 [1]Lit *living* **15:32** [a]Lk 15:24 ◆ **16:1** [a]Lk 15:13 [1]Or *accused* **16:3** [1]Or *lord* **16:4** [1]Or *receive* **16:5** [1]Or *lord's* **16:6** [1]A bath was approx. 6 gal. or 23 l **16:7** [1]A kor was approx. 6.5 bu. or 230 l **16:8** [a]Mt 12:32; Lk 20:34 [b]Jn 12:36; Eph 5:8; 1Th 5:5 [1]Or *lord* [2]Lit *generation* **16:9** [a]Mt 19:21; Lk 11:41; 12:33 [b]Mt 6:24; Lk 16:11, 13 [c]Lk 16:4 [1]Gr *mamonas* (mammon); wealth personified as an object of worship [2]Or *receive* **16:10** [a]Mt 25:21, 23 **16:11** [a]Lk 16:9 [1]Gr *mamonas* (mammon); wealth personified as an object of worship **16:13** [a]Mt 6:24 [1]Or *house-servant* [2]Or *be a slave to*

despise the other. You cannot [2]serve God and [b,3]wealth."

**14** Now the Pharisees, who were [a]lovers of money, were listening to all these things and [b]were scoffing at Him. **15** And He said to them, "You are those who [a]justify yourselves [1]in the sight of men, but [b]God knows your hearts, for that which is highly esteemed among men is detestable [1]in the sight of God.

**16** "[a]The Law and the Prophets were until John; [1]since that time [b]the good news of the kingdom of God is proclaimed, and everyone is forcing his way into it. **17** [a]But it is easier for heaven and earth to pass away than for one [1]stroke of a letter of the Law to fail.

**18** "[a]Everyone who [1]divorces his wife and marries another commits adultery, and he who marries a woman who is [2]divorced from a husband commits adultery.

### *The Rich Man and Lazarus*

**19** "Now there was a rich man, and he habitually dressed in purple and fine linen, joyously living in splendor every day. **20** But a poor man named Lazarus [a]was laid at his gate, covered with sores, **21** and desiring to be fed with the *crumbs* which were falling from the rich man's table; besides, even the dogs were coming and licking his sores. **22** Now it happened that the poor man died and was carried away by the angels to [a]Abraham's bosom, and the rich man also died and was buried. **23** And in [a]Hades he lifted up his eyes, being in torment, and *saw Abraham far away and Lazarus in his bosom. **24** And he cried out and said, '[a]Father Abraham, have mercy on me, and send Lazarus so that he may dip the tip of his finger in water and cool off my tongue, for I am in agony in [b]this flame.' **25** But Abraham said, 'Child, remember that [a]during your life you received your good things, and likewise Lazarus bad things. But now he is being comforted here, and you are in agony. **26** And [1]besides all this, between us and you there is a great chasm fixed, so that those who wish to come over from here to you are not able, and none may cross over from there to us.' **27** And he said, 'Then I am asking you, father, that you send him to my father's house— **28** for I have five brothers—in order that he may [a]warn them, so that they will not also come to this place of torment.' **29** But Abraham *said, 'They have [a]Moses and the Prophets; let them hear them.' **30** But he said, 'No, [a]father Abraham, but if someone goes to them from the dead, they will repent!' **31** But he said to him, 'If they do not listen to Moses and the Prophets, they will not be persuaded even if someone rises from the dead.'"

### *Do All Which Jesus Commands*

**17** Now He said to His disciples, "[a]It is [1]inevitable that [2]stumbling blocks come, but woe to him through

**16:13** [b]Lk 16:9 [2]Or *be a slave to* [3]Gr *mamonas* (mammon); wealth personified as an object of worship **16:14** [a]2Ti 3:2 [b]Lk 23:35 **16:15** [a]Lk 10:29; 18:9, 14 [b]1Sa 16:7; Pr 21:2; Ac 1:24; Ro 8:27 [1]Lit *before* **16:16** [a]Mt 11:12f [b]Mt 4:23 [1]Lit *from then* **16:17** [a]Mt 5:18 [1]Projection of a letter (serif) **16:18** [a]Mt 5:32; 1Co 7:10, 11 [1]Or *sends away* [2]Or *sent away* **16:20** [a]Ac 3:2 **16:22** [a]Jn 1:18; 13:23 **16:23** [a]Mt 11:23 **16:24** [a]Lk 3:8; 16:30; 19:9 [b]Mt 25:41 **16:25** [a]Lk 6:24 **16:26** [1]Lit *in all these things* **16:28** [a]Ac 2:40; 8:25; 10:42; 18:5; 20:21ff; 23:11; 28:23; Ga 5:3; Eph 4:17; 1Th 2:11; 4:6 **16:29** [a]Lk 4:17; Jn 5:45-47; Ac 15:21 **16:30** [a]Lk 3:8; 16:24; 19:9 ◆ **17:1** [a]Mt 18:7; 1Co 11:19; 1Ti 4:1 [1]Lit *impossible that stumbling blocks not come* [2]Or *temptations to sin*

whom they come! **2** [a]It [1]would be bet-
ter for him if a millstone were hung
around his neck and he were thrown
into the sea, than that he would cause
one of these little ones to stumble.
**3** [1]Be on your guard! [a]If your brother
sins, rebuke him; and if he repents,
forgive him. **4** And if he sins against
you [a]seven times a day, and returns
to you seven times, saying, 'I repent,'
[1]forgive him."

**5** [a]And the apostles said to [b]the
Lord, "Increase our faith!" **6** And [a]the
Lord said, "If you have faith like [b]a
mustard seed, you would say to this
[c]mulberry tree, 'Be uprooted and
be planted in the sea'; and it would
[1]obey you.

**7** "But which of you, having a slave
plowing or tending sheep, will say
to him when he has come in from
the field, 'Come immediately and [1]sit
down to eat'? **8** But will he not say to
him, '[a]Prepare something for me to
eat, and, [1]clothing yourself *properly*,
serve me while I eat and drink; and
[2]afterward you [3]may eat and drink'?
**9** Is he grateful to the slave because
he did the things which were com-
manded? **10** In this way, you also,
when you do all the things which
are commanded of you, say, 'We are
unworthy slaves; we have done *only*
that which we ought to have done.'"

### *Jesus Cleanses Ten Lepers*

**11** And it happened that while He was
[a]on the way to Jerusalem, [b]He was
passing through Samaria and Galilee.
**12** And as He entered a village, ten
leprous men who [a]stood at a dis-
tance met Him. **13** And they raised
their voices, saying, "Jesus, [a]Master,
have mercy on us!" **14** When He saw
them, He said to them, "[a]Go and
show yourselves to the priests." And
it happened that as they were going,
they were cleansed. **15** Now one of
them, when he saw that he had been
healed, turned back, [a]glorifying God
with a loud voice, **16** and he fell on his
face at His feet, giving thanks to Him.
And he was a [a]Samaritan. **17** Then
Jesus answered and said, "Were there
not ten cleansed? But the nine—
where are they? **18** [1]Was there no
one found who turned back to [a]give
glory to God, except this foreigner?"
**19** And He said to him, "Stand up and
go; [a]your faith has [1]saved you."

**20** Now having been questioned
by the Pharisees [a]as to when the
kingdom of God was coming, He an-
swered them and said, "The kingdom
of God is not coming with [b,1]*signs to
be* observed, **21** nor will [a]they say,
'Look, here!' or, 'There!' For behold,
the kingdom of God is in your midst."

### *The Coming of the Son of Man*

**22** And He said to the disciples, "[a]The
days will come when you will long to
see one of the days of the Son of Man,
and you will not see it. **23** [a]And they
will say to you, 'Look there! Look
here!' Do not go away, and do not run
after *them*. **24** [a]For just like the light-
ning, when it flashes out of one part

---

**17:2** [a]Mt 18:6; Mk 9:42; 1Co 8:12 [1]Lit *is* **17:3** [a]Mt 18:15 [1]Lit *Take heed to yourselves* **17:4** [a]Mt 18:21f [1]Lit *you shall forgive* **17:5** [a]Mk 6:30 [b]Lk 7:13 **17:6** [a]Lk 7:13 [b]Mt 13:31; 17:20; Mk 4:31; Lk 13:19 [c]Lk 19:4 [1]Lit *have obeyed* **17:7** [1]Lit *recline* **17:8** [a]Lk 12:37 [1]Lit *gird* [2]Lit *after these things* [3]Lit *will* **17:11** [a]Lk 9:51 [b]Lk 9:52ff; Jn 4:3f **17:12** [a]Lv 13:45f **17:13** [a]Lk 5:5 **17:14** [a]Lv 14:1-32; Mt 8:4; Lk 5:14 **17:15** [a]Mt 9:8 **17:16** [a]Mt 10:5 **17:18** [a]Mt 9:8 [1]Lit *Were there not found those who* **17:19** [a]Mt 9:22; Lk 18:42 [1]Or *made you well* **17:20** [a]Lk 19:11; Ac 1:6 [b]Lk 14:1 [1]Lit *observation* **17:21** [a]Lk 17:23 **17:22** [a]Mt 9:15; Mk 2:20; Lk 5:35 **17:23** [a]Mt 24:23; Mk 13:21; Lk 21:8 **17:24** [a]Mt 24:27

[1]of the sky, shines to the other part
[1]of the sky, so will the Son of Man
be in His day. 25 [a]But first He must
suffer many things and be rejected
by this generation. 26 [a]And just as it
was [b]in the days of Noah, so it will be
also in the days of the Son of Man:
27 they were eating, they were drink-
ing, they were marrying, they were
being given in marriage, until the day
that Noah entered the ark, and the
flood came and destroyed them all.
28 [1]It was the same as in [a]the days
of Lot—they were eating, they were
drinking, they were buying, they
were selling, they were planting, they
were building; 29 but on the day that
Lot went out from Sodom it rained
fire and [1]brimstone from heaven and
destroyed them all. 30 It will be [1]just
the same on the day that the Son of
Man [a]is revealed. 31 On that day, the
one who is [a]on the housetop and
whose goods are in the house must
not go down to take them out, and
likewise the one who is in the field
must not turn back. 32 [a]Remember
Lot's wife. 33 [a]Whoever seeks to keep
his [1]life will lose it, and whoever loses
*his life* will preserve it. 34 I tell you,
on that night there will be two in one
bed; one will be taken and the other
will be left. 35 [a]There will be two
women grinding *grain* at the same
place; one will be taken and the other
will be left. 36 [1][[a]Two men will be in
the field; one will be taken and the
other will be left."] 37 And answering
they *said to Him, "Where, Lord?"
And He said to them, "[a]Where the
body *is*, there also the [1]vultures will
be gathered."

### *Parables on Prayer*

18 Now He was telling them a
parable to show that at all
times they [a]ought to pray and not
to [b]lose heart, 2 saying, "In a certain
city there was a certain judge who
did not fear God and did not [a]respect
man. 3 Now there was a widow in
that city, and she kept coming to
him, saying, 'Give me justice from
my opponent.' 4 And for a while he
was unwilling; but afterward he said
to himself, 'Even though I do not fear
God nor [a]respect man, 5 yet [a]because
this widow is bothering me, I will
give her justice, lest by continually
coming she [b,1]wears me out.'" 6 And
[a]the Lord said, "Hear what the un-
just judge *said. 7 Now, will God not
[a]bring about justice for His [b]elect
who cry to Him day and night, [1]and
will He [c]delay long over them? 8 I tell
you that He will bring about justice
for them quickly. However, when the
Son of Man comes, [a]will He find that
faith on the earth?"
9 And He also told this parable
to some people who [a]trusted in
themselves that they were righteous,
and [b]viewed others with contempt:
10 "Two men [a]went up into the tem-
ple to pray, one a Pharisee and the
other a tax collector. 11 The Pharisee

---

**17:24** [1]Lit *under heaven* **17:25** [a]Mt 16:21; Lk 9:22 **17:26** [a]Lk 17:26, 27: *Mt 24:37-39* [b]Ge 6:5-8; 7
**17:28** [a]Ge 19 [1]Lit *In the same way as* **17:29** [1]Burning sulfur **17:30** [a]Mt 16:27; 1Co 1:7; Col 3:4;
2Th 1:7; 1Pe 1:7; 4:13; 1Jn 2:28 [1]Lit *according to the same things* **17:31** [a]Mt 24:17, 18; Mk 13:15f; Lk 21:21
**17:32** [a]Ge 19:26 **17:33** [a]Mt 10:39 [1]Or *soul* **17:35** [a]Mt 24:41 **17:36** [a]Mt 24:40 [1]Early mss omit
this v **17:37** [a]Mt 24:28 [1]Or *eagles* ◆ **18:1** [a]Lk 11:5-10 [b]2Co 4:1 **18:2** [a]Lk 18:4; 20:13; Heb 12:9
**18:4** [a]Lk 18:2; 20:13; Heb 12:9 **18:5** [a]Lk 11:8 [b]1Co 9:27 [1]Lit *hit me under the eye* **18:6** [a]Lk 7:13
**18:7** [a]Rev 6:10 [b]Mt 24:22; Ro 8:33; Col 3:12; 2Ti 2:10; Tit 1:1 [c]2Pe 3:9 [1]Or *and yet He is very patient
toward them* **18:8** [a]Lk 17:26ff **18:9** [a]Lk 16:15 [b]Ro 14:3, 10 **18:10** [a]1Ki 10:5; 2Ki 20:5, 8; Ac 3:1

[a]stood and was praying these things
to himself: 'God, I thank You that I
am not like other people: swindlers,
unjust, adulterers, or even like this
tax collector. **12** I [a]fast twice a week;
I [b]pay tithes of all that I get.' **13** But
the tax collector, [a]standing some
distance away, [b]was even unwilling
to lift up his eyes to heaven, but [c]was
[1]beating his chest, saying, 'God, be
[2]merciful to me, the sinner!' **14** I
tell you, this man went down to his
house justified rather than the other,
[a]for everyone who exalts himself will
be humbled, but he who humbles
himself will be exalted."

**15** [a]And they were bringing even
their babies to Him so that He would
touch them, but when the disciples
saw it, they were rebuking them.
**16** But Jesus called for them, saying,
"Permit the children to come to Me,
and do not hinder them, for the
kingdom of God belongs to such as
these. **17** Truly I say to you, [a]whoever
does not receive the kingdom of God
like a child will never enter it."

### *The Rich Young Ruler*

**18** [a]And a ruler questioned Him, say-
ing, "Good Teacher, what shall I do to
inherit eternal life?" **19** And Jesus said
to him, "Why do you call Me good?
No one is good except God alone.
**20** You know the commandments,
'[a]DO NOT COMMIT ADULTERY, DO NOT
MURDER, DO NOT STEAL, DO NOT BEAR
FALSE WITNESS, HONOR YOUR FATHER
AND MOTHER.'" **21** And he said, "All
these things I have kept from *my*
youth." **22** And when Jesus heard
*this*, He said to him, "One thing you
still lack: [a]sell all that you possess
and distribute it to the poor, and
you shall have [b]treasure in heaven.
And come, follow Me." **23** But when
he heard these things, he became
very sad, for he was extremely rich.
**24** And Jesus looked at him and said,
"[a]How hard it is for those who are
wealthy to enter the kingdom of God!
**25** For [a]it is easier for a camel to [1]go
through the eye of a needle than for
a rich man to enter the kingdom of
God." **26** And those who heard it said,
"Then who can be saved?" **27** But He
said, "[a]The things that are impossible
with people are possible with God."

**28** And Peter said, "Behold, [a]we
have left *all that is* our own and
followed You." **29** And He said to
them, "Truly I say to you, [a]there is
no one who has left house or wife
or brothers or parents or children,
for the sake of the kingdom of God,
**30** who will not receive many times
more at this time and in [a]the age to
come, eternal life."

**31** [a]But when He took the twelve
aside, He said to them, "Behold, [b]we
are going up to Jerusalem, and [c]all
things which are written through
the prophets about the Son of Man
will be [1]completed. **32** [a]For He will
be [1]delivered over to the Gentiles,
and will be mocked and mistreated

---

**18:11** [a]Mt 6:5; Mk 11:25; Lk 22:41 **18:12** [a]Mt 9:14 [b]Lk 11:42 **18:13** [a]Mt 6:5; Mk 11:25; Lk 22:41 [b]Ezr 9:6 [c]Lk 23:48 [1]A traditional sign of mourning or contrition [2]Or *propitious* **18:14** [a]Mt 23:12; Lk 14:11 **18:15** [a]Lk 18:15-17: *Mt 19:13-15; Mk 10:13-16* **18:17** [a]Mt 18:3; 19:14; Mk 10:15; 1Co 14:20; 1Pe 2:2 **18:18** [a]Lk 18:18-30: *Mt 19:16-29; Mk 10:17-30;* Lk 10:25-28 **18:20** [a]Ex 20:12-16; Dt 5:16-20 **18:22** [a]Mt 19:21; Lk 12:33 [b]Mt 6:20 **18:24** [a]Mt 19:23; Mk 10:23f **18:25** [a]Mt 19:24; Mk 10:25 [1]Lit *enter* **18:27** [a]Mt 19:26 **18:28** [a]Lk 5:11 **18:29** [a]Mt 6:33; 19:29; Mk 10:29f **18:30** [a]Mt 12:32 **18:31** [a]Lk 18:31-33: *Mt 20:17-19; Mk 10:32-34* [b]Lk 9:51 [c]Ps 22; Is 53 [1]Or *finished*, cf. 12:50 **18:32** [a]Mt 16:21 [1]Or *betrayed*

and spit upon, **33** and after they have
flogged Him, they will kill Him, and
the third day He will rise again." **34** But
[a]the disciples understood none of
these things, and this statement was
hidden from them, and they did not
comprehend the things that were said.

### *Bartimaeus Regains His Sight*

**35** [a]Now it happened that as [b,1]Jesus
was approaching Jericho, a blind
man was sitting by the road begging.
**36** Now hearing a crowd going by,
he *began to* inquire what this was.
**37** They reported to him, "Jesus of
Nazareth is passing by." **38** And he
called out, saying, "Jesus, [a]Son of
David, have mercy on me!" **39** And
those who went ahead were rebuking
him so that he would be quiet, but he
kept crying out all the more, "[a]Son of
David, have mercy on me!" **40** And
Jesus stopped and commanded that
he be brought to Him, and when
he came near, He questioned him,
**41** "What do you want Me to do for
you?" And he said, "Lord, *I want* to
regain my sight!" **42** And Jesus said
to him, "[1]Receive your sight; [a]your
faith has [2]saved you." **43** Immediately
he regained his sight and *began* fol-
lowing Him, [a]glorifying God. And
when [b]all the people saw it, they
gave praise to God.

### *Zaccheus Is Saved*

**19** And He [a]entered Jericho and
was passing through. **2** And
behold, there was a man called by
the name of Zaccheus; he was a chief
tax collector and he was rich. **3** And
Zaccheus was trying to see who Jesus
was, and was unable because of the
crowd, for he was small in stature.
**4** So he ran on before and climbed
up into a [a,1]sycamore tree in order to
see Him, for He was about to pass
through that way. **5** And when Jesus
came to the place, He looked up and
said to him, "Zaccheus, hurry and
come down, for today I must stay
at your house." **6** And he hurried
and came down and received Him
[1]gladly. **7** And when they saw it, they
all *began to* grumble, saying, "He has
gone [1]to be the guest of a man who
is a sinner." **8** But Zaccheus stopped
and said to [a]the Lord, "Behold, half
of my possessions, Lord, I [1]will give
to the poor, and if I have [b]extorted
anyone of anything, I [1]will give back
[c]four times as much." **9** And Jesus said
to him, "Today salvation has come to
this house, because he, too, is [a]a son
of Abraham. **10** For [a]the Son of Man
has come to seek and to save the lost."

### *Parable of the Ten Minas*

**11** Now while they were listening to
these things, Jesus went on to tell a
parable, because [a]He was near Jeru-
salem, and they thought that [b]the
kingdom of God was going to appear
immediately. **12** So He said, "[a]A no-
bleman went to a distant country to
receive a kingdom for himself, and
*then* return. **13** And he called ten of
his slaves, and gave them ten [1]minas

---

**18:34** [a]Mk 9:32; Lk 9:45 **18:35** [a]Lk 18:35-43: *Mt 20:29-34; Mk 10:46-52* [b]Mt 20:29; Mk 10:46; Lk 19:1 [1]Lit *He* **18:38** [a]Mt 9:27; Lk 18:39 **18:39** [a]Lk 18:38 **18:42** [a]Mt 9:22 [1]Lit *Regain* [2]Or *made you well* **18:43** [a]Mt 9:8 [b]Lk 9:43; 13:17; 19:37 ◆ **19:1** [a]Lk 18:35 **19:4** [a]1Ki 10:27; 1Chr 27:28; 2Chr 1:15; 9:27; Ps 78:47; Is 9:10; Lk 17:6 [1]Fig-mulberry **19:6** [1]Lit *rejoicing* **19:7** [1]Or *to find lodging* **19:8** [a]Lk 7:13 [b]Lk 3:14 [c]Ex 22:1; Lv 6:5; Nu 5:7; 2Sa 12:6 [1]Lit *am giving* **19:9** [a]Lk 3:8; 13:16; Ro 4:16; Ga 3:7 **19:10** [a]Mt 18:11 **19:11** [a]Lk 9:51 [b]Lk 17:20 **19:12** [a]Lk 19:12-27: *Mt 25:14-30* **19:13** [1]Gr monetary unit worth approx. 100 days of a laborer's wages

and said to them, 'Engage in business
[2]until I come *back.*' **14** But his citizens
hated him and sent [1]a delegation
after him, saying, 'We do not want
this man to reign over us.' **15** And it
happened that when he returned,
after receiving the kingdom, he
ordered that these slaves, to whom
he had given the money, be called
to him so that he might know how
much they had made in business.
**16** So the first appeared, saying,
'[1]Master, your [2]mina has made ten
minas more.' **17** And he said to him,
'Well done, good slave, because you
have been [a]faithful in a very little
thing, you are to be in authority
over ten cities.' **18** Then the second
came, saying, 'Your [1]mina, [2]master,
has made five minas.' **19** And he said
to him also, 'And you are to be over
five cities.' **20** Then another came,
saying, 'Master, here is your mina,
which I kept put away in a cloth; **21** for
I was afraid of you, because you are a
strict man; you take up what you did
not lay down and reap what you did
not sow.' **22** He *said to him, 'From
your own mouth I will judge you, you
worthless slave. Did you know that
I am a strict man, taking up what I
did not lay down and reaping what
I did not sow? **23** Then why did you
not put my money in the bank, and
having come, I would have collected
it with interest?' **24** Then he said
to the bystanders, 'Take the mina
away from him and give it to the
one who has the ten minas.' **25** And
they said to him, 'Master, he has ten
minas *already*.' **26** '[a]I tell you that
to everyone who has, more shall be
given, but from the one who does not
have, even what he does have shall be
taken away. **27** But [a]these enemies of
mine, who did not want me to reign
over them, bring them here and [b]slay
them in my presence.'"

### *The Triumphal Entry*

**28** And after He had said these things,
He [a]was going on ahead, [b]going up
to Jerusalem.
**29** [a]And it happened that when
He approached Bethphage and
[b]Bethany, near the mount called "of
[c]Olives," He sent two of the disciples,
**30** saying, "Go into the village ahead
of *you*; in which, as you enter, you
will find a colt tied, on which no one
yet has ever sat; untie it and bring
it *here*. **31** And if anyone asks you,
'Why are you untying it?' you shall
say this: 'Because the Lord has need
of it.'" **32** So when those who were
sent departed, they found it just as
He had told them. **33** And as they
were untying the colt, its [1]owners
said to them, "Why are you untying
the colt?" **34** And they said, "The Lord
has need of it." **35** And they brought
it to Jesus, [a]and after they threw
their garments on the colt, they put
Jesus *on it*. **36** And as He was going,
they were spreading their garments
on the road. **37** Now as soon as He
was approaching, near the descent
of [a]the Mount of Olives, the whole
multitude of the disciples began to
[b]praise God, rejoicing with a loud
voice for all the [1]miracles which they
had seen, **38** saying,

---

**19:13** [2]Lit *while I am coming* **19:14** [1]Or *an embassy* **19:16** [1]Lit *Lord*, so in ch [2]v 13, note 1
**19:17** [a]Lk 16:10 **19:18** [1]v 13, note 1 [2]Lit *lord* **19:26** [a]Mt 13:12; Mk 4:25; Lk 8:18 **19:27** [a]Lk 19:14
[b]Mt 22:7; Lk 20:16 **19:28** [a]Mk 10:32 [b]Lk 9:51 **19:29** [a]Lk 19:29-38: *Mt 21:1-9; Mk 11:1-10*
[b]Mt 21:17 [c]Lk 21:37; Ac 1:12 **19:33** [1]Lit *lords* **19:35** [a]Lk 19:35-38: *Mt 21:4-9; Mk 11:7-10; Jn 12:12-15*
**19:37** [a]Mt 21:1; Lk 19:29 [b]Lk 18:43 [1]Or *works of power*

"[a]BLESSED IS THE [b]KING
WHO COMES IN THE
NAME OF THE [1]LORD.
Peace in heaven and [c]glory
in the highest!"
**39** [a]And some of the Pharisees [1]in
the crowd said to Him, "Teacher,
rebuke Your disciples." **40** But Jesus
answered and said, "I tell you, if these
were silent, [a]the stones will cry out!"

### *Lament over Jerusalem*

**41** And as He approached *Jerusalem*
and saw the city, He [a]cried over it,
**42** saying, "If you knew in this day,
even you, the things which make
for peace! But now they have been
hidden from your eyes. **43** For the
days will come upon you [1]when your
enemies will [a]throw up a [2]barricade
against you, and [b]surround you and
hem you in on every side, **44** and they
will level you to the ground and your
children within you, and [a]they will
not leave in you one stone upon an-
other, because you did not [1]recognize
[b]the time of your visitation."

### *Jesus Drives Merchants from the Temple*

**45** [a]And Jesus entered the temple
and began to drive out those who
were selling, **46** saying to them, "It is
written, '[a]AND MY HOUSE SHALL BE
A HOUSE OF PRAYER,' [b]but you have
made it a ROBBERS' [1]DEN."
**47** And [a]He was teaching daily in the
temple, but the chief priests and the
scribes and the leading men among the
people [b]were trying to destroy Him,
**48** and they could not find [1]anything
that they might do, for all the people
hung upon [2]every word He said.

### *The Authority of Jesus Challenged*

**20** [a]And it happened that on one
of the days while [b]He was
teaching the people in the temple
and [c]proclaiming the gospel, the
chief priests and the scribes with
the elders [d]came up to *Him,* **2** and
they spoke, saying to Him, "Tell us
by what authority You are doing
these things, or who is the one who
gave You this authority?" **3** And Jesus
answered and said to them, "I will
also ask you a [1]question, and you tell
Me: **4** Was the baptism of John from
heaven or from men?" **5** And they
reasoned among themselves, saying,
"If we say, 'From heaven,' He will say,
'Why did you not believe him?' **6** But
if we say, 'From men,' all the people
will stone us to death, for they are
convinced that John was a [a]prophet."
**7** So they answered that they did not
know where *it came* from. **8** And Jesus
said to them, "Neither [1]will I tell you
by what authority I do these things."

### *Parable of the Vine-Growers*

**9** [a]And He began to tell the people this
parable: "A man planted a vineyard
and rented it out to [1]vine-growers,
and went on a journey for a long time.
**10** And at the *harvest* time he sent a

---

**19:38** [a]Ps 118:26 [b]Mt 2:2; 25:34 [c]Mt 21:9; Lk 2:14 [1]In OT, Yahweh, cf. Ps 118:26 **19:39** [a]Mt 21:15f [1]Lit *from* **19:40** [a]Hab 2:11 **19:41** [a]Lk 13:34, 35 **19:43** [a]Ecc 9:14; Is 29:3; 37:33; Jer 6:6; Eze 4:2; 26:8 [b]Lk 21:20 [1]Lit *and* [2]A dirt wall or mound for siege purposes **19:44** [a]Mt 24:2; Mk 13:2; Lk 21:6 [b]1Pe 2:12 [1]Lit *know*, cf. 19:42 **19:45** [a]Lk 19:45, 46: *Mt 21:12, 13; Mk 11:15-17;* Jn 2:13-16 **19:46** [a]Is 56:7; Jer 7:11; Mt 21:13; Mk 11:17 [b]Jer 7:11 [1]Lit *cave* **19:47** [a]Mt 26:55; Lk 21:37 [b]Lk 20:19 **19:48** [1]Lit *what they would do* [2]Lit *Him, listening* ◆ **20:1** [a]Lk 20:1-8: *Mt 21:23-27; Mk 11:27-33* [b]Mt 26:55 [c]Lk 8:1 [d]Ac 4:1; 6:12 **20:3** [1]Lit *word* **20:6** [a]Mt 11:9; Lk 7:29, 30 **20:8** [1]Lit *do I tell* **20:9** [a]Lk 20:9-19: *Mt 21:33-46; Mk 12:1-12* [1]Or *tenant farmers*, so in vv 10, 14, 16

slave to the vine-growers, so that they
would give him *some* of the fruit of the
vineyard. But the vine-growers sent
him away empty-handed having beat-
en him. **11** And he proceeded to send
another slave; and when they beat
him also and treated him shamefully,
they sent him away empty-handed.
**12** And he proceeded to send a third;
and this one also they wounded
and cast out. **13** Now the [1]owner of
the vineyard said, 'What shall I do?
I will send my beloved son; perhaps
they will [a]respect him.' **14** But when
the vine-growers saw him, they were
reasoning with one another, saying,
'This is the heir; let us kill him so that
the inheritance will be ours.' **15** So
they threw him out of the vineyard
and killed him. What, then, will the
[1]owner of the vineyard do to them?
**16** He will come and [a]destroy these
vine-growers and will give the vine-
yard to others." When they heard *this*,
they said, "[b]May it never be!" **17** But
when [1]Jesus looked at them, He said,
"What then is this that is written:

'[a]THE STONE WHICH THE
BUILDERS REJECTED,
THIS HAS BECOME [b]THE
CHIEF CORNER *stone*'?

**18** "[a]Everyone who falls on that
stone will be broken to pieces, but
on whomever it falls, it will scatter
him like dust."

### *Taxes to Caesar*

**19** And the scribes and the chief
priests [a]tried to lay hands on Him
that very hour, but they feared the
people. For they understood that
He spoke this parable against them.
**20** [a]So they watched Him, and sent
spies who [1]pretended to be righteous,
so [b]that they might [2]catch Him in
some statement, in order to deliver
Him to the rule and the author-
ity of [c]the governor. **21** And they
questioned Him, saying, "Teacher,
we know that You speak and teach
correctly, and You [1]are not partial
to any, but teach the way of God in
truth. **22** Is it [1]lawful for us [a]to pay
taxes to Caesar, or not?" **23** But He
perceived their craftiness and said
to them, **24** "Show Me a [1]denarius.
Whose [2]likeness and inscription does
it have?" They said, "Caesar's." **25** And
He said to them, "Then [a]render to
Caesar the things that are Caesar's,
and to God the things that are God's."
**26** And they were unable to [a,1]catch
Him in a word in the presence of the
people; and marveling at His answer,
they became silent.

### *The Sadducees Ask About the Resurrection*

**27** [a]Now some of the [b]Sadducees
(who say that there is no resurrection)
came to Him, **28** and they questioned
Him, saying, "Teacher, Moses wrote
for us that [a]IF A MAN'S BROTHER DIES,
having a wife, AND HE IS CHILDLESS,
HIS BROTHER SHOULD [1]MARRY THE WIFE
AND RAISE UP [2]SEED FOR HIS BROTHER.
**29** Now there were seven brothers;
and the first married a wife and died

**20:13** [a]Lk 18:2 [1]Lit *lord* **20:15** [1]Lit *lord* **20:16** [a]Mt 21:41; Mk 12:9; Lk 19:27 [b]Ro 3:4, 6, 31; 6:2, 15; 7:7, 13; 9:14; 11:1, 11; 1Co 6:15; Ga 2:17; 3:21; 6:14 **20:17** [a]Ps 118:22 [b]Eph 2:20; 1Pe 2:6 [1]Lit *He* **20:18** [a]Mt 21:44 **20:19** [a]Lk 19:47 **20:20** [a]Lk 20:20-26: *Mt 22:15-22; Mk 12:13-17;* Mk 3:2 [b]Lk 11:54; 20:26 [c]Mt 27:2 [1]Lit *falsely represented themselves* [2]Lit *take hold of His word* **20:21** [1]Lit *do not receive a face* **20:22** [a]Mt 17:25; Lk 23:2 [1]Or *permissible* **20:24** [1]A Roman silver coin, approx. a laborer's daily wage [2]Lit *image* **20:25** [a]Mt 22:21; Mk 12:17 **20:26** [a]Lk 11:54 [1]Lit *catch His statement* **20:27** [a]Lk 20:27-40: *Mt 22:23-33; Mk 12:18-27* [b]Ac 23:8 **20:28** [a]Dt 25:5 [1]Lit *take* [2]Or *descendant*

childless, **30** and the second **31** and
the third [1]married her; and in the
same way, [2]all seven [3]died, leaving no
children. **32** Finally the woman died
also. **33** Therefore, this woman—in
the resurrection—whose wife will
she be? For all seven had her as a
wife."

**34** And Jesus said to them, "The
sons of [a]this age marry and are giv-
en in marriage, **35** but those who are
considered worthy to attain to [a]that
age and the resurrection from the
dead, neither marry nor are given in
marriage. **36** For they cannot even die
anymore, because they are like angels
and are [a]sons of God, being sons of
the resurrection. **37** But that the
dead are raised, even Moses showed
in [a]the *passage about the burning*
bush, where he calls the [1]Lord [b]THE
GOD OF ABRAHAM, AND THE GOD OF
ISAAC, AND THE GOD OF JACOB. **38** [a]Now
He is not the God of the dead but of
the living; for [b]all live to Him." **39** And
some of the scribes answered and
said, "Teacher, You have spoken well."
**40** For [a]they did not dare to question
Him any longer about anything.

**41** [a]Then He said to them, "How *is
it that* they say the [1]Christ is [b]David's
son? **42** For David himself says in the
book of Psalms,

'[a]THE [1]LORD SAID TO MY LORD,
"SIT AT MY RIGHT HAND,
**43** [a]UNTIL I PUT YOUR ENEMIES
AS A FOOTSTOOL FOR
YOUR FEET."'

**44** "Therefore David calls Him 'Lord,'
so how is He his son?"

**45** [a]And while all the people were
listening, He said to the disciples,
**46** "Beware of the scribes, [a]who want
to walk around in long robes, and
love greetings in the marketplaces,
and best seats in the synagogues
and places of honor at banquets,
**47** who devour widows' houses, and
for appearance's sake offer long
prayers. These will receive greater
condemnation."

### *The Widow's Offering*

**21** [a]And He looked up and saw the
rich putting their gifts into the
treasury. **2** And He saw a poor widow
putting [1]in [a]two [2]lepta. **3** And He said,
"Truly I say to you, this poor widow
put in more than all *of them*. **4** For
they all put in their gifts out of their
abundance; but she, out of what she
lacked, put in all [1]that she had [a]for
living."

**5** [a]And while some were talking
about the temple, that it had been
adorned with beautiful stones and
dedicated gifts, He said, **6** "*As for*
these things which you are looking
at, the days will come in which [a]there
will not be left one stone upon an-
other which will not be torn down."

**7** So they questioned Him, saying,
"Teacher, when therefore will these
things happen? And what *will be* the
[1]sign when these things are about to
take place?" **8** And He said, "See to it

---

**20:31** [1]Lit *took* [2]Lit *the seven also* [3]Lit *left no children, and died* **20:34** [a]Mt 12:32; Lk 16:8
***20:35*** [a]*Mt 12:32; Lk 16:8* **20:36** [a]Ro 8:16f; 1Jn 3:1, 2 **20:37** [a]Mk 12:26 [b]Ex 3:6 [1]In OT, Yahweh,
cf. Ex 3:6 **20:38** [a]Mt 22:32; Mk 12:27 [b]Ro 14:8 **20:40** [a]Mt 22:46; Lk 14:6 **20:41** [a]Lk 20:41-44:
*Mt 22:41-46; Mk 12:35-37* [b]Mt 9:27 [1]Messiah **20:42** [a]Ps 110:1 [1]In OT, Yahweh, cf. Ps 110:1
**20:43** [a]Ps 110:1 **20:45** [a]Lk 20:45-47: *Mt 23:1-7; Mk 12:38-40* **20:46** [a]Lk 11:43; 14:7 ♦ **21:1** [a]Lk 21:1-4:
*Mk 12:41-44* **21:2** [a]Mk 12:42 [1]Lit *there* [2]Smallest Greek copper coin, approx. 1/128 of a laborer's daily
wage **21:4** [a]Mk 12:44 [1]Lit *the living that she had* **21:5** [a]Lk 21:5-36: *Mt 24; Mk 13* **21:6** [a]Lk 19:44
**21:7** [1]Or *attesting miracle*

that you are not deceived; for many
will come in My name, saying, '[a]I am
*He*,' and, 'The time is at hand.' [b]Do
not go after them. 9 And when you
hear of wars and disturbances, do
not be terrified; for these things must
take place first, but the end *does* not
*follow* immediately."

### *Signs of Christ's Return*

10 Then He continued saying to them,
"Nation will rise against nation and
kingdom against kingdom, 11 and
there will be great earthquakes,
and in various places famines and
plagues; and there will be terrors and
great [1]signs from heaven.

12 "But before all these things,
[a]they will lay their hands on you
and will persecute you, delivering
you to the synagogues and prisons,
[1]bringing you before kings and
governors for My name's sake. 13 [a]It
will result in [1]an opportunity for your
testimony. 14 [a]So set in your hearts
not to prepare beforehand to defend
yourselves; 15 for [a]I will give you a
mouth and wisdom which none of
your opponents will be able to resist
or refute. 16 But you will be betrayed
even by parents and brothers and
relatives and friends, and they will
put *some* of you to death, 17 and you
will be hated by all because of My
name. 18 Yet [a]not a hair of your head
will perish. 19 [a]By your perseverance
you will gain your [1]lives.

20 "But when you see Jerusalem
[a]surrounded by armies, then know
that its desolation is at hand. 21 Then
those who are in Judea must flee to
the mountains, and those who are in
the midst of [1]the city must leave, and
[a]those who are in the countryside
must not enter [1]the city; 22 because
these are [a]days of vengeance, so that
all things which are written will be
fulfilled. 23 Woe to those who are
pregnant and to those who are nurs-
ing babies in those days; for [a]there will
be great distress upon the [1]land and
wrath against this people, 24 and they
will fall by [a]the edge of the sword, and
will be led captive into all the nations,
and [b]Jerusalem will be [c]trampled
under foot by the Gentiles until [d]the
times of the Gentiles are fulfilled.

### *When Christ Returns*

25 "And there will be [1]signs in sun
and moon and stars, and on the
earth anguish among nations, in
perplexity at the roaring of the sea
and the waves, 26 men fainting from
fear and the expectation of the things
which are coming upon the [1]world;
for the POWERS OF [2]THE HEAVENS will
be shaken. 27 [a]And then they will see
[b]THE SON OF MAN COMING IN A CLOUD
with power and great glory. 28 But
when these things begin to take
place, straighten up and lift up your
heads, because [a]your redemption is
drawing near."

### *The Parable of the Fig Tree*

29 Then He told them a parable:
"Behold the fig tree and all the trees;

**21:8** [a]Jn 8:24 [b]Lk 17:23 **21:11** [1]Or *attesting miracles* **21:12** [a]Lk 21:12-17: *Mt 10:19-22; Mk 13:11-13* [1]Lit *being brought* **21:13** [a]Php 1:12 [1]Lit *a testimony for you* **21:14** [a]Lk 12:11 **21:15** [a]Lk 12:12 **21:18** [a]Mt 10:30; Lk 12:7 **21:19** [a]Mt 10:22; 24:13; Ro 2:7; 5:3f; Heb 10:36; Jas 1:3; 2Pe 1:6 [1]Lit *souls* **21:20** [a]Lk 19:43 **21:21** [a]Lk 17:31 [1]Lit *her* **21:22** [a]Is 63:4; Da 9:24-27; Hos 9:7 **21:23** [a]Da 8:19; 1Co 7:26 [1]Or *earth* **21:24** [a]Ge 34:26; Ex 17:13; Heb 11:34 [b]Is 63:18; Da 8:13 [c]Rev 11:2 [d]Ro 11:25 **21:25** [1]Or *attesting miracles* **21:26** [1]Lit *inhabited earth* [2]Or *heaven* **21:27** [a]Mt 16:27; 24:30; 26:64; Mk 13:26 [b]Da 7:13; Rev 1:7 **21:28** [a]Lk 18:7

**30** as soon as they put forth *leaves* and you see it for yourselves, [a]know that summer is now near. **31** So you also, when you see these things happening, know that [a]the kingdom of God is near. **32** Truly I say to you, this [1]generation will not pass away until all things take place. **33** [a]Heaven and earth will pass away, but My words will never pass away.

**34** "[a]But be on guard, so that your hearts will not be overcome with dissipation and drunkenness and the worries of life, and that day will not come on you suddenly like a trap; **35** for it will come upon all those who inhabit the face of all the earth. **36** But [a]keep on the alert at all times, praying earnestly that you may have strength to escape all these things that are about to take place, and to [b]stand before the Son of Man."

**37** Now [1]during the day He was [a]teaching in the temple, but [b,2]during the night He would go out and spend it on [c,3]the mount called "of [4]Olives." **38** And all the people would get up [a]early in the morning *to come* to Him in the temple to listen to Him.

### *The Plot to Kill Jesus*

**22** [a]Now the Feast of Unleavened Bread, which is called the [b]Passover, was drawing near. **2** And the chief priests and the scribes [a]were seeking how they might put Him to death; for they were afraid of the people.

**3** [a]And [b]Satan entered into Judas who was called Iscariot, who [1]belonged to the number of the twelve. **4** And he went away and discussed with the chief priests and [a]officers how he might betray Him to them. **5** And they were glad and agreed to give him money. **6** So he consented, and *began* seeking a good opportunity to betray Him to them [1]apart from the crowd.

### *The Passover Meal*

**7** [a]Then came the *first* day of Unleavened Bread on which [b]the Passover lamb had to be sacrificed. **8** And *Jesus* sent [a]Peter and John, saying, "Go and prepare the Passover for us, so that we may eat it." **9** And they said to Him, "Where do You want us to prepare it?" **10** And He said to them, "Behold, after you have entered the city, a man will meet you carrying a pitcher of water; follow him into the house that he enters. **11** And you shall say to the owner of the house, 'The Teacher says to you, "Where is the guest room in which I may eat the Passover with My disciples?"' **12** And he will show you a large, furnished upper room; prepare it there." **13** And they left and found *everything* just as He had told them; and they prepared the Passover.

### *The Lord's Supper*

**14** [a]And when the hour had come, He reclined *at the table*, and [b]the apostles with Him. **15** And He said to

---

***21:30*** [a]*Lk 12:57* **21:31** [a]Mt 3:2 **21:32** [1]Or *race* **21:33** [a]Mt 5:18; Lk 16:17 **21:34** [a]Mt 24:42-44; Mk 4:19; Lk 12:40, 45; 1Th 5:2ff **21:36** [a]Mk 13:33; Lk 12:40 [b]Lk 1:19; Rev 7:9; 8:2; 11:4 **21:37** [a]Mt 26:55; Lk 19:47 [b]Mk 11:19 [c]Mt 21:1 [1]Lit *days* [2]Lit *nights* [3]Or *the hill* [4]Or *Olive Grove* **21:38** [a]Jn 8:2
◆ **22:1** [a]Lk 22:1, 2: *Mt 26:2-5; Mk 14:1, 2;* Ex 12:1-27 [b]Jn 11:55; 13:1 **22:2** [a]Mt 12:14 **22:3** [a]Lk 22:3-6: *Mt 26:14-16; Mk 14:10, 11* [b]Mt 4:10; Jn 13:2, 27 [1]Lit *being of* **22:4** [a]1Chr 9:11; Ne 11:11; Lk 22:52; Ac 4:1; 5:24, 26 **22:6** [1]Or *without a disturbance* **22:7** [a]Lk 22:7-13: *Mt 26:17-19; Mk 14:12-16* [b]Mk 14:12
**22:8** [a]Ac 3:1, 11; 4:13, 19; 8:14; Ga 2:9 **22:14** [a]Mt 26:20; Mk 14:17 [b]Mk 6:30

them, "I have earnestly desired to eat
this Passover with you before I suffer;
16 for I say to you, I shall never again
eat it [a]until it is fulfilled in the king-
dom of God." 17 [a]And when He had
taken a cup *and* [b]given thanks, He
said, "Take this and share it among
yourselves. 18 For [a]I say to you, I will
not drink of the fruit of the vine from
now on until the kingdom of God
comes." 19 And when He had taken
*some* bread *and* [a]given thanks, He
broke it and gave it to them, saying,
"This is My body which is given for
you. Do this in remembrance of Me."
20 And in the same way *He took* the
cup after they had eaten, saying,
"This cup which is [a]poured out for
you is the [b]new covenant in My
blood. 21 [a]But behold, the hand of the
one betraying Me is with Me on the
table. 22 For indeed, the Son of Man
is going [a]as it has been determined;
but woe to that man by whom He
is betrayed!" 23 And they began to
argue among themselves which one
of them it might be who was going
to do this thing.

### *Who Is Greatest?*

24 And there arose also [a]a dispute
among them *as to* which one of them
was regarded to be greatest. 25 [a]And
He said to them, "The kings of the
Gentiles lord it over them, and those
who have authority over them are
called 'Benefactors.' 26 But not so
with you; [a]rather the one who is the
greatest among you must become like
[b]the youngest, and the leader like the
servant. 27 For [a]who is greater, the one
who reclines *at the table* or the one
who serves? Is it not the one who
reclines? But [b]I am among you as
the one who serves.

28 "Now you are those who have
stood by Me in My [a]trials, 29 and I
grant you a [a]kingdom, just as My
Father granted *one* to Me, 30 that
you may [a]eat and drink at My table
in My [b]kingdom, and [c]you will sit on
thrones judging the twelve tribes of
Israel.

31 "Simon, Simon, behold, [a]Satan
has [1]demanded to [b]sift *all of* you like
wheat. 32 But I [a]have prayed earnestly
for you, that your faith may not fail;
and you, once you have returned,
[b]strengthen your brothers." 33 [a]But
he said to Him, "Lord, with You I
am ready to go both to prison and
to death!" 34 And He said, "I say to
you, Peter, the rooster will not crow
today until you have denied three
times that you know Me."

35 And He said to them, "[a]When
I sent you out without money belt
and bag and sandals, did you lack
anything?" They said, "Not a thing."
36 And He said to them, "But now,
[1]whoever has a money belt is to take
it along, likewise also a bag, and
[1]whoever has no sword should sell
his garment and buy one. 37 For I tell

**22:16** [a]Lk 14:15; 22:18, 30; Rev 19:9 **22:17** [a]Lk 22:17-20: *Mt 26:26-29; Mk 14:22-25; 1Co 11:23-25;* 1Co 10:16 [b]Mt 14:19 **22:18** [a]Mt 26:29; Mk 14:25 **22:19** [a]Mt 14:19 **22:20** [a]Mt 26:28; Mk 14:24 [b]Ex 24:8; Jer 31:31; 1Co 11:25; 2Co 3:6; Heb 8:8, 13; 9:15 **22:21** [a]Lk 22:21-23: *Mt 26:21-24; Mk 14:18-21;* Ps 41:9; Jn 13:18, 21, 22, 26 **22:22** [a]Ac 2:23; 4:28; 10:42; 17:31 **22:24** [a]Mk 9:34; Lk 9:46 **22:25** [a]Lk 22:25-27: *Mt 20:25-28; Mk 10:42-45* **22:26** [a]Mt 23:11; Mk 9:35; Lk 9:48 [b]1Pe 5:5 **22:27** [a]Lk 12:37 [b]Mt 20:28; Jn 13:12-15 **22:28** [a]Heb 2:18; 4:15 **22:29** [a]Mt 5:3; 2Ti 2:12 **22:30** [a]Lk 22:16 [b]Mt 5:3; 2Ti 2:12 [c]Mt 19:28 **22:31** [a]Job 1:6-12; 2:1-6; Mt 4:10 [b]Am 9:9 [1]Or *obtained by asking* **22:32** [a]Jn 17:9, 15 [b]Jn 21:15-17 **22:33** [a]Lk 22:33, 34: *Mt 26:33-35; Mk 14:29-31; Jn 13:37, 38* **22:35** [a]Mt 10:9f; Mk 6:8; Lk 9:3ff; 10:4 **22:36** [1]Lit *he who*

you that this which is written must
be [1]completed in Me, '[a]AND HE WAS
NUMBERED WITH TRANSGRESSORS';
for [b]that which refers to Me has
*its* [2]completion." **38** And they said,
"Lord, look, here are two [a]swords."
And He said to them, "It is enough."

### *Jesus Prays in Gethsemane*

**39** [a]And He came out and went [b]as was
His custom to [c]the Mount of Olives;
and the disciples also followed Him.
**40** [a]Now when He arrived at the place,
He said to them, "[b]Pray that you may
not enter into temptation." **41** And He
withdrew from them about a stone's
throw, and He [a]knelt down and *began*
*to* pray, **42** saying, "Father, if You are
willing, remove this [a]cup from Me,
[b]yet not My will, but Yours be done."
**43** [1]Now an [a]angel from heaven ap-
peared to Him, strengthening Him.
**44** And [a]being in agony He was praying
very fervently, and His sweat became
like drops of blood, falling down upon
the ground. **45** And when He rose from
prayer, He came to the disciples and
found them sleeping from sorrow,
**46** and said to them, "Why are you
sleeping? Rise up and [a]pray that you
may not enter into temptation."

### *The Betrayal and Arrest of Jesus*

**47** [a]While He was still speaking, be-
hold, a crowd *came*, and the one called
Judas, one of the twelve, was coming
ahead of them, and he approached
Jesus to kiss Him. **48** But Jesus said
to him, "Judas, are you betraying
the Son of Man with a kiss?" **49** And
when those around Him saw what
was going to happen, they said, "Lord,
shall we strike with the [a]sword?"
**50** And one of them struck the slave
of the high priest and cut off his
right ear. **51** But Jesus answered and
said, "[1]Stop! No more of this." And
He touched his ear and healed him.
**52** Then Jesus said to the chief priests
and [a]officers of the temple and elders
who had come against Him, "Have
you come out with swords and clubs
[b]as against a robber? **53** While I was
with you daily in the temple, you did
not stretch out your hands against
Me, but [1]this hour and the authority
of darkness are yours."

**54** [a]Now having arrested Him, they
led Him *away* and brought Him to the
house of the high priest, but [b]Peter
was following at a distance. **55** [a]And
after they had kindled a fire in the
middle of [b]the courtyard and had
sat down together, Peter was sitting
among them. **56** And a servant-girl,
seeing him as he sat in the firelight
and looking intently at him, said,
"This man was with Him too." **57** But
he denied *it*, saying, "Woman, I do
not know Him." **58** A little later,
[a]another saw him and said, "You
are *one* of them too!" But Peter said,
"Man, I am not!" **59** And after about
an hour had passed, another man
*began to* insist, saying, "Certainly
this man was with Him too, [a]for he

---

**22:37** [a]Is 53:12 [b]Jn 17:4; 19:30 [1]Or *finished,* cf. 12:50 [2]Lit *end* **22:38** [a]Lk 22:36, 49 **22:39** [a]Mt 26:30; *Mk 14:26; Jn 18:1* [b]Lk 21:37 [c]Mt 21:1 **22:40** [a]Lk 22:40-46: *Mt 26:36-46; Mk 14:32-42* [b]Mt 6:13; Lk 22:46 **22:41** [a]Mt 26:39; Mk 14:35; Lk 18:11 **22:42** [a]Mt 20:22 [b]Mt 26:39 **22:43** [a]Mt 4:11 [1]Some early mss omit vv 43-44 **22:44** [a]Heb 5:7 **22:46** [a]Lk 22:40 **22:47** [a]Lk 22:47-53: *Mt 26:47-56; Mk 14:43-50; Jn 18:3-11* **22:49** [a]Lk 22:38 **22:51** [1]Or *"Let them do this," and He touched* **22:52** [a]Lk 22:4 [b]Lk 22:37 **22:53** [1]Lit *this is your hour and power of darkness* **22:54** [a]Mt 26:57; Mk 14:53 [b]Mt 26:58; Mk 14:54; Jn 18:15 **22:55** [a]Lk 22:55-62: *Mt 26:69-75; Mk 14:66-72; Jn 18:16-18, 25-27* [b]Mt 26:3 **22:58** [a]Jn 18:26 **22:59** [a]Mt 26:73; Mk 14:70

also is a Galilean." **60** But Peter said,
"Man, I do not know what you are
talking about." Immediately, while he
was still speaking, a rooster crowed.
**61** [a]And the Lord turned and looked
at Peter. And Peter remembered the
word of the Lord, how He had told
him, "[b]Before a rooster crows today,
you will deny Me three times." **62** And
he went out and cried bitterly.
**63** [a]Now the men who were hold-
ing [1]Jesus in custody were mocking
Him while they beat Him, **64** and they
blindfolded Him and were asking
Him, saying, "[a]Prophesy, who is the
one who hit You?" **65** And they were
saying many other things against
Him, [a]blaspheming.

### *Jesus Before the Sanhedrin*

**66** [a]And as the day came, [b]the
Council of elders of the people
assembled, both chief priests and
scribes, and they led Him away to
their [c]Sanhedrin, saying, **67** "[a]If You
are the [1]Christ, tell us." But He said
to them, "If I tell you, you will not
believe, **68** and if I ask a question, you
will not answer. **69** [a]But from now
on [b]THE SON OF MAN WILL BE SEATED
AT THE RIGHT HAND of the power OF
[1]GOD." **70** And they all said, "Are You
[a]the Son of God, then?" And He said
to them, "[b]You yourselves say that I
am." **71** Then they said, "What further
need do we have of testimony? For
we have heard it ourselves from His
own mouth."

### *Jesus Before Pilate*

**23** Then their whole assembly
rose up and [a]brought Him
before Pilate. **2** [a]And they began to
accuse Him, saying, "We found this
man [b]misleading our nation and
[c]forbidding to pay taxes to Caesar,
and saying that He Himself is [1]Christ,
a King." **3** So Pilate asked Him, saying,
"Are You the King of the Jews?" And
He answered him and said, "[a]You
yourself say *it*." **4** Then Pilate said to
the chief priests and the crowds, "[a]I
find no guilt in this man." **5** But they
kept on insisting, saying, "He stirs up
the people, teaching all over Judea,
[a]starting from Galilee even as far as
this place."
**6** Now when Pilate heard *this*, he
asked whether the man was a Gali-
lean. **7** And when he learned that He
belonged to Herod's jurisdiction, he
sent Him to [a]Herod, who himself
also was in Jerusalem in those days.

### *Jesus Before Herod*

**8** Now when Herod saw Jesus, he re-
joiced greatly; for [a]he had wanted to
see Him for a long time, because he
had been hearing about Him and was
hoping to see some [1]sign performed
by Him. **9** And he questioned Him
[1]at some length, but [a]He answered
him nothing. **10** And the chief priests
and the scribes were standing there,
vehemently accusing Him. **11** And
Herod with his soldiers, after treating
Him with contempt and mocking

**22:61** [a]Lk 7:13 [b]Lk 22:34 **22:63** [a]Mt 26:67f; Mk 14:65; Jn 18:22f [1]Lit *Him* **22:64** [a]Mt 26:68; Mk 14:65
**22:65** [a]Mt 27:39 **22:66** [a]Mt 27:1f; Mk 15:1; Jn 18:28 [b]Ac 22:5 [c]Mt 5:22 **22:67** [a]Lk 22:67-71: *Mt 26:63-66; Mk 14:61-63; Jn 18:19-21* [1]Messiah **22:69** [a]Mt 26:64; Mk 14:62; 16:19 [b]Ps 110:1 [1]In OT, Yahweh, cf. Ps 110:1 **22:70** [a]Mt 4:3 [b]Mt 26:64; 27:11; Lk 23:3 ◆ **23:1** [a]Mt 27:2; Mk 15:1; Jn 18:28
**23:2** [a]Lk 23:2, 3: *Mt 27:11-14; Mk 15:2-5; Jn 18:29-37* [b]Lk 23:14 [c]Lk 20:22; Jn 18:33ff; 19:12; Ac 17:7 [1]Messiah
**23:3** [a]Lk 22:70 **23:4** [a]Mt 27:23; Mk 15:14; Lk 23:14, 22; Jn 18:38; 19:4, 6 **23:5** [a]Mt 4:12 **23:7** [a]Mt 14:1; Mk 6:14; Lk 3:1; 9:7; 13:31 **23:8** [a]Lk 9:9 [1]Or *attesting miracle* **23:9** [a]Mt 27:12, 14; Mk 15:5; Jn 19:9 [1]Lit *in many words*

Him, [a]dressed Him in a bright robe
and sent Him back to Pilate. 12 Now
[a]Herod and Pilate became friends
with one another that very day; for
before they had been at enmity with
each other.

### *Pilate Grants the Crowd's Request*

13 And Pilate summoned the chief
priests and the [a]rulers and the
people, 14 and said to them, "You
brought this man to me as one who
[a1]incites the people to rebellion, and
behold, having examined Him before
you, I [b]have found in this man no
guilt of what you are accusing Him.
15 No, nor has [a]Herod, for he sent
Him back to us; and behold, nothing
deserving death has been done by
Him. 16 Therefore I will [a]punish Him
and release Him." 17 [1][Now he was
obliged to release to them at the feast
one prisoner.]

18 But they cried out all together,
saying, "[a]Away with this man, and
release for us Barabbas!" 19 (He
had been thrown into prison for
an insurrection made in the city
and for murder.) 20 But again Pilate
addressed them, wanting to release
Jesus, 21 but they kept on calling
out, saying, "Crucify, crucify Him!"
22 And he said to them a third time,
"Why, what evil has this man done?
I have found in Him no guilt *worthy
of* death; therefore I will [a]punish
Him and release Him." 23 But they
were insistent, with loud voices
asking that He be crucified. And
their voices were prevailing. 24 And
Pilate pronounced sentence that
their demand be granted. 25 And he
released the man they were asking
for who had been thrown into prison
for insurrection and murder, but he
delivered Jesus to their will.

### *Simon Carries the Cross*

26 [a]And when they led Him away,
they took hold of a man, Simon of
[b]Cyrene, coming in from the country,
and placed on him the cross to carry
behind Jesus.

27 And following Him was a large
multitude of the people, and of
women who were [a1]mourning and
lamenting Him. 28 But Jesus, turning
to them, said, "Daughters of Jerusa-
lem, stop crying for Me, but cry for
yourselves and for your children.
29 For behold, the days are coming
when they will say, '[a]Blessed are the
barren, and the wombs that never
bore, and the breasts that never
nursed.' 30 Then they will begin TO
[a]SAY TO THE MOUNTAINS, 'FALL ON US,'
AND TO THE HILLS, 'COVER US.' 31 For if
they do these things [1]when the tree
is green, what will happen [2]when it
is dry?"

32 [a]Now two others also, who were
criminals, were being led away to be
put to death with Him.

### *The Crucifixion*

33 [a]And when they came to the
place called [1]The Skull, there they
crucified Him and the criminals,

**23:11** [a]Mt 27:28 **23:12** [a]Ac 4:27 **23:13** [a]Lk 23:35; Jn 7:26, 48; 12:42; Ac 3:17; 4:5, 8; 13:27
**23:14** [a]Lk 23:2 [b]Lk 23:4 [1]Lit *turns away* **23:15** [a]Lk 9:9 **23:16** [a]Mt 27:26; Mk 15:15; Lk 23:22; Jn 19:1;
Ac 16:37 **23:17** [1]Early mss omit this v **23:18** [a]Lk 23:18-25: *Mt 27:15-26; Mk 15:6-15;* Jn 18:39-19:16
**23:22** [a]Lk 23:16 **23:26** [a]Lk 23:26: *Mt 27:32; Mk 15:21;* Jn 19:17 [b]Mt 27:32 **23:27** [a]Lk 8:52 [1]Lit *beating
the breast* **23:29** [a]Mt 24:19; Lk 11:27; 21:23 **23:30** [a]Hos 10:8; Is 2:19, 20; Rev 6:16 **23:31** [1]Lit *in
the green tree* [2]Lit *in the dry* **23:32** [a]Mt 27:38; Mk 15:27; Jn 19:18 **23:33** [a]Lk 23:33-43: *Mt 27:33-44;
Mk 15:22-32; Jn 19:17-24* [1]In Lat *Calvarius*; or *Calvary*

one on the right and the other on
the left. **34** [1]But Jesus was saying,
"[a]Father, forgive them; for they do
not know what they are doing." [b]AND
THEY CAST LOTS, DIVIDING UP HIS GAR-
MENTS AMONG THEMSELVES. **35** And
the people stood by, looking on.
And even the [a]rulers were scoffing
at Him, saying, "He saved others; [b]let
Him save Himself if this is the [1]Christ
of God, His Chosen One." **36** And the
soldiers also mocked Him, coming
up to Him, [a]offering Him sour wine,
**37** and saying, "[a]If You are the King of
the Jews, save Yourself!" **38** Now there
was also an inscription above Him,
"[a]THIS IS THE KING OF THE JEWS."

**39** [a]And one of the criminals hang-
ing *there* was blaspheming Him, say-
ing, "Are You not the [1]Christ? [b]Save
Yourself and us!" **40** But the other
answered, and rebuking him said,
"Do you not even fear God, since
you are under the same sentence of
condemnation? **41** And we indeed *are
suffering* justly, for we are receiving
[1]what we deserve for what we have
done; but this man has done nothing
wrong." **42** And he was saying, "Jesus,
remember me when You come [1]in
Your kingdom!" **43** And He said to
him, "Truly I say to you, today you
shall be with Me in [a]Paradise."

**44** [a]And it was now about [b,1]the
sixth hour, and darkness [2]fell over
the whole land until [3]the ninth hour,
**45** [1]because the sun was obscured.
And [a]the veil of the [2]sanctuary was
torn [3]in two. **46** And Jesus, [a]crying
out with a loud voice, said, "Father,
[b]INTO YOUR HANDS I COMMIT MY
SPIRIT." Having said this, He breathed
His last. **47** [a]Now when the centurion
saw what had happened, he *began*
[b]praising God, saying, "Certainly
this man was righteous." **48** And all
the crowds who came together for
this spectacle, when they observed
what had happened, were returning,
[a,1]beating their chests. **49** [a]And all His
acquaintances and [a]the women who
accompanied Him from Galilee were
standing at a distance, watching
these things.

### *Jesus Is Buried*

**50** [a]And behold, a man named Jo-
seph, who was a [b]Council member,
a good and righteous man **51** (he had
not consented to their counsel and
action), *a man* from Arimathea, a city
of the Jews, who was [a]waiting for the
kingdom of God; **52** this man went to
Pilate and asked for the body of Jesus.
**53** And he took it down and wrapped
it in a linen cloth, and laid Him in a
tomb cut into the rock, where no one
had ever lain. **54** It was [a,1]Preparation
day, and the Sabbath was about to
[2]begin. **55** Now [a]the women, who
had come with Him from Galilee,
followed and beheld the tomb and

---

**23:34** [a]Mt 11:25; Lk 22:42 [b]Ps 22:18; Jn 19:24 [1]Some early mss omit *But Jesus was saying...doing* **23:35** [a]Lk 23:13 [b]Mt 27:43 [1]Messiah **23:36** [a]Mt 27:48 **23:37** [a]Mt 27:43 **23:38** [a]Mt 27:37; Mk 15:26; Jn 19:19 **23:39** [a]Lk 23:39-43: *Mt 27:44; Mk 15:32* [b]Lk 23:35, 37 [1]Messiah **23:41** [1]Lit *things worthy of* **23:42** [1]Or *into* **23:43** [a]2Co 12:4; Rev 2:7 **23:44** [a]Lk 23:44-49: *Mt 27:45-56; Mk 15:33-41* [b]Jn 19:14 [1]Noon [2]Or *occurred* [3]3 p.m. **23:45** [a]Ex 26:31-33; Mt 27:51 [1]Lit *the sun failing* [2]The inner part of the temple [3]Lit *in the middle* **23:46** [a]Mt 27:50; Mk 15:37; Jn 19:30 [b]Ps 31:5 **23:47** [a]Mt 27:54; Mk 15:39 [b]Mt 9:8 **23:48** [a]Lk 8:52; 18:13 [1]A traditional sign of mourning or contrition **23:49** [a]Mt 27:55f; Mk 15:40f; Lk 8:2; Jn 19:25 **23:50** [a]Lk 23:50-56: *Mt 27:57-61; Mk 15:42-47; Jn 19:38-42* [b]Mk 15:43 **23:51** [a]Mk 15:43; Lk 2:25 **23:54** [a]Mt 27:62; Mk 15:42 [1]Preparation for the Sabbath [2]Lit *dawn* **23:55** [a]Lk 23:49

how His body was laid. **56** Then after
they returned, they [a]prepared spices
and perfumes.

And [b]on the Sabbath they rested
according to the commandment.

### *Jesus Is Risen!*

**24** [a]Now on the first day of the
week, at early dawn, they
came to the tomb bringing the spices
which they had prepared. **2** And they
found the stone rolled away from
the tomb, **3** but when they entered,
they did not find the body of [a]the
Lord Jesus. **4** And it happened that
while they were perplexed about this,
behold, [a]two men suddenly [b]stood
near them in dazzling clothing, **5** and
when *the women* were terrified and
bowed their faces to the ground, *the
men* said to them, "Why do you seek
the living One among the dead? **6** He
is not here, but He [a]has [1]risen. Re-
member how He spoke to you [b]while
He was still in Galilee, **7** saying that
[a]the Son of Man must be delivered
into the hands of sinful men, and
be crucified, and the third day rise
again." **8** And [a]they remembered His
words, **9** and when they returned
from the tomb, they reported all
these things to the eleven and to all
the rest. **10** Now [a]Mary Magdalene
and Joanna and Mary the *mother* of
James and the rest of the women with
them were *there*; they were telling
these things to [b]the apostles. **11** But
these words appeared [1]to them as
nonsense, and they [a]were not be-
lieving them. **12** But Peter stood up
and [a]ran to the tomb; and stooping to
look in, he *saw the linen wrappings
[1]only. And he went away [b]by himself,
marveling at what had happened.

### *The Road to Emmaus*

**13** And behold, [a]two of them were
going that same day to a village
named Emmaus, which was [1]sixty
stadia from Jerusalem. **14** And they
were conversing with each other
about all these things which had
happened. **15** And it happened that
while they were conversing and
debating, Jesus Himself approached
and was going with them. **16** But
[a]their eyes were prevented from
recognizing Him. **17** And He said to
them, "What are these words that
you are discussing with one another
as you are walking?" And they stood
still, looking sad. **18** And one *of them*,
named Cleopas, answered and said to
Him, "Are You [1]the only one visiting
Jerusalem and unaware of the things
which have happened here in these
days?" **19** And He said to them, "What
things?" And they said to Him, "The
things about [a]Jesus the Nazarene,
who was a mighty [b]prophet in deed
and word in the sight of God and
all the people, **20** and how the chief
priests and our [a]rulers delivered
Him to the sentence of death, and
crucified Him. **21** But we were hop-
ing that it was He who was going to
[a]redeem Israel. Indeed, besides all
this, it is the third day since these
things happened. **22** But also some
women among us astounded us.

---

**23:56** [a]Mk 16:1; Lk 24:1 [b]Ex 20:10f; Dt 5:14 ◆ **24:1** [a]Lk 24:1-10: *Mt 28:1-8; Mk 16:1-8;* Jn 20:1-8
**24:3** [a]Lk 7:13; Ac 1:21 **24:4** [a]Jn 20:12 [b]Lk 2:9; Ac 12:7 **24:6** [a]Mk 16:6 [b]Mt 17:22f; Mk 9:30f; Lk 9:44; 24:44 [1]Or *been raised* **24:7** [a]Mt 16:21; Lk 24:46 **24:8** [a]Jn 2:22 **24:10** [a]Mt 27:56 [b]Mk 6:30
**24:11** [a]Mk 16:11 [1]Lit *in their sight* **24:12** [a]Jn 20:3-6 [b]Jn 20:10 [1]Or *by themselves* **24:13** [a]Mk 16:12 [1]Approx. 7 mi. or 11 km, a stadion was approx. 607 ft. or 185 m **24:16** [a]Lk 24:31; Jn 20:14; 21:4
**24:18** [1]Or *visiting Jerusalem alone* **24:19** [a]Mk 1:24 [b]Mt 21:11 **24:20** [a]Lk 23:13 **24:21** [a]Lk 1:68

[a]When they were at the tomb early
in the morning, **23** and not finding
His body, they came, saying that they
had also seen a vision of angels who
said that He was alive. **24** Some of
those who were with us went to the
tomb and found it just exactly as the
women also said, but Him they did
not see." **25** And He said to them,
"O foolish ones and slow of heart to
believe in all that [a]the prophets have
spoken! **26** [a]Was it not necessary for
the [1]Christ to suffer these things
and to enter into His glory?" **27** Then
beginning [1]with [a]Moses and [1]with
all the [b]prophets, He interpreted to
them the things concerning Himself
in all the Scriptures.

**28** And they approached the village
where they were going, and [a]He acted
as though He were going farther.
**29** But they urged Him strongly,
saying, "Stay with us, for it is toward
evening, and the day [1]is now nearly
over." So He went in to stay with them.
**30** And it happened that when He had
reclined *at the table* with them, He
took the bread and [a]blessed *it*, and
after breaking *it*, He was giving *it* to
them. **31** Then their [a]eyes were opened
and they recognized Him. And He
vanished from [1]their sight. **32** And
they said to one another, "[1]Were not
our hearts burning within us while
He was speaking to us on the road,
while He [a]was opening the Scriptures
to us?" **33** And they stood up that very
hour and returned to Jerusalem, and
[a]found gathered together the eleven
and [b]those with them, **34** who were
saying, "[a]The Lord has really risen and
[b]has appeared to Simon." **35** And they
were relating [1]their experiences on
the road and how [a]He was recognized
by them in the breaking of the bread.

### *Jesus Appears to His Disciples*

**36** Now while they were telling these
things, [a]He Himself stood in their
midst and *said to them, "Peace to
you." **37** But being startled and fright-
ened, they were thinking that they
were seeing [a]a spirit. **38** And He said
to them, "Why are you troubled, and
why do doubts arise in your [1]hearts?
**39** [a]See My hands and My feet, that it
is I Myself; [b]touch Me and see, for a
spirit does not have flesh and bones
as you see that I have." **40** And when
He had said this, He showed them
His hands and His feet. **41** And while
they still [a]were not believing because
of their joy and were *still* marveling,
He said to them, "[b]Have you anything
here to eat?" **42** They gave Him a piece
of a broiled fish, **43** and He took it and
[a]ate *it* before them.

**44** Now He said to them, "[a]These
are My words which I spoke to you
while I was still with you, that all
things which are written about Me in
the [b]Law of Moses and the Prophets
and [c]the Psalms must be fulfilled."
**45** Then He [a]opened their [1]minds to

**24:22** [a]Lk 24:1ff **24:25** [a]Mt 26:24 **24:26** [a]Lk 24:7, 44ff; Heb 2:10; 1Pe 1:11 [1]Messiah **24:27** [a]Ge 3:15; 12:3; Nu 21:9 [Jn 3:14]; Dt 18:15 [Jn 1:45]; Jn 5:46 [b]2Sa 7:12-16; Is 7:14 [Mt 1:23]; Is 9:1f [Mt 4:15f]; Is 42:1 [Mt 12:18ff]; Is 53:4 [Mt 8:17; Lk 22:37]; Da 7:13 [Mt 24:30]; Mic 5:2 [Mt 2:6]; Zec 9:9 [Mt 21:5]; Ac 13:27 [1]Lit *from* **24:28** [a]Mk 6:48 **24:29** [1]Lit *has now declined* **24:30** [a]Mt 14:19 **24:31** [a]Lk 24:16 [1]Lit *them* **24:32** [a]Lk 24:45 [1]Lit *Was not our heart* **24:33** [a]Mk 16:13 [b]Ac 1:14 **24:34** [a]Lk 24:6 [b]1Co 15:5 **24:35** [a]Lk 24:30f [1]Lit *the things* **24:36** [a]Mk 16:14 **24:37** [a]Mt 14:26; Mk 6:49 **24:38** [1]Lit *heart* **24:39** [a]Jn 20:20, 27 [b]Jn 20:27; 1Jn 1:1 **24:41** [a]Lk 24:11 [b]Jn 21:5 **24:43** [a]Ac 10:41 **24:44** [a]Lk 9:22, 44f; 18:31-34; 22:37 [b]Lk 24:27 [c]Ps 2:7ff [Ac 13:33]; Ps 16:10 [Ac 2:27]; Ps 22:1-18 [Mt 27:34-46]; Ps 69:1-21 [Jn 19:28ff]; Ps 72; 110:1 [Mt 22:43f]; Ps 118:22f [Mt 21:42] **24:45** [a]Lk 24:32; Ac 16:14; 1Jn 5:20 [1]Lit *mind*

understand the Scriptures, **46** and He
said to them, “[a]Thus it is written, that
the [1]Christ would suffer and [b]rise again
from the dead the third day, **47** and that
[a]repentance [1]for forgiveness of sins
would be proclaimed [2]in His name to
[b]all the nations, beginning from Jeru-
salem. **48** You are [a]witnesses of these
things. **49** And behold, [a]I am sending
the promise of My Father upon you,
but [b]you are to stay in the city until you
are clothed with power from on high.”

### *The Ascension*

**50** And He led them out as far as
[a]Bethany, and lifting up His hands,
He blessed them. **51** And it happened
that while He was blessing them, He
parted from them and was carried
up into heaven. **52** And they, after
worshiping Him, returned to Jeru-
salem with great joy, **53** and were
continually in the temple blessing
God.

---

**24:46** [a]Lk 24:26, 44 [b]Lk 24:7 [1]Messiah **24:47** [a]Ac 5:31; 10:43; 13:38; 26:18 [b]Mt 28:19 [1]Later mss *and forgiveness* [2]Or *on the basis of* **24:48** [a]Ac 1:8, 22; 2:32; 3:15; 4:33; 5:32; 10:39, 41; 13:31; 1Pe 5:1
**24:49** [a]Jn 14:26 [b]Ac 1:4 **24:50** [a]Mt 21:17; Ac 1:12

*The Gospel According to*

# JOHN

### *The Deity of Jesus Christ*

**1** [a]In the beginning was [b]the Word,
and the Word was [c]with God, and
[d]the Word was God. **2** [1]He was in the
beginning with God. **3** [a]All things
came into being through Him, and
apart from Him nothing came into
being that has come into being. **4** [a]In
Him was life, and the life was [b]the
Light of men. **5** [a]And the Light shines
in the darkness, and the darkness did
not overtake it.

### *The Witness of John the Baptist*

**6** There was a man having been sent
from God, whose name was [a,1]John.
**7** [1]He came [a,2]as a witness, to bear
witness about the Light, [b]so that all
might believe through him. **8** [a,1]He
was not the Light, but *he came* to
bear witness about the Light.
**9** There was [a]the true Light [1]which,
coming into the world, enlightens
everyone. **10** He was in the world,
and [a]the world [1]was made through
Him, and the world did not know
Him. **11** He came to what was His
[1]own, and those who were His own
did not receive Him. **12** But as many
as received Him, to them He gave
the right to become [a]children of
God, *even* [b]to those who believe in
His name, **13** [a]who were [1]born, not
of [2]blood nor of the will of the flesh
nor of the will of man, but of God.

### *The Word Became Flesh*

**14** And [a]the Word [b]became flesh, and
[c,1]dwelt among us, and [d]we beheld
His glory, glory as of the [2]only begot-
ten from the Father, full of [e]grace and
[f]truth. **15** John *[a]bore witness about
Him and cried out, saying, "This was
He of whom I said, '[b]He who comes
after me [1]has been ahead of me, [c]for
He existed before me.'" **16** For of His
[a]fullness [1]we have all received, and
grace [2]upon grace. **17** For [a]the Law
was given through Moses; [b]grace and
[c]truth came through Jesus Christ.
**18** [a]No one has seen God at any
time; [b]the only begotten God who
is [c]in the bosom of the Father, [d]He
has explained *Him*.

### *A Voice in the Wilderness*

**19** And this is [a]the witness of John,
when [b]the [1]Jews sent to him priests
and Levites [c]from Jerusalem to ask
him, "Who are you?" **20** And he

◆ **1:1** [a]Ge 1:1; Col 1:17; 1Jn 1:1 [b]Jn 1:14; Rev 19:13 [c]Jn 17:5; 1Jn 1:2 [d]Php 2:6 **1:2** [1]Lit *This one* **1:3** [a]Jn 1:10; 1Co 8:6; Col 1:16; Heb 1:2 **1:4** [a]Jn 5:26; 11:25; 14:6 [b]Jn 8:12; 9:5; 12:46 **1:5** [a]Jn 3:19 **1:6** [a]Mt 3:1 [1]Gr *Joannes*, Heb *Johanan*; so in John **1:7** [a]Jn 1:15, 19, 32; 3:26; 5:33 [b]Jn 1:12; Ac 19:4; Ga 3:26 [1]Lit *This one* [2]Lit *for testimony* **1:8** [a]Jn 1:20 [1]Lit *That one* **1:9** [a]1Jn 2:8 [1]Or *which enlightens every person coming into the world* **1:10** [a]1Co 8:6; Col 1:16; Heb 1:2 [1]Or *came into being*, cf. Jn 1:3 **1:11** [1]Or *own things* **1:12** [a]Jn 11:52; Ga 3:26 [b]Jn 1:7; 3:18; 1Jn 3:23; 5:13 **1:13** [a]Jn 3:5f; Jas 1:18; 1Pe 1:23; 1Jn 2:29; 3:9 [1]Or *begotten* [2]Lit *bloods* **1:14** [a]Rev 19:13 [b]Ro 1:3; Ga 4:4; Php 2:7f; 1Ti 3:16; Heb 2:14; 1Jn 1:1f; 4:2; 2Jn 7 [c]Rev 21:3 [d]Lk 9:32; Jn 2:11; 17:22, 24; 2Pe 1:16f; 1Jn 1:1 [e]Jn 1:17; Ro 5:21; 6:14 [f]Jn 8:32; 14:6; 18:37 [1]Or *tabernacled, dwelt temporarily* [2]Or *unique, only one of His kind* **1:15** [a]Jn 1:7 [b]Mt 3:11; Jn 1:27, 30 [c]Jn 1:30 [1]Or *has a higher rank than* **1:16** [a]Eph 1:23; 3:19; 4:13; Col 1:19; 2:9 [1]Lit *we all received* [2]Lit *for* **1:17** [a]Jn 7:19 [b]Jn 1:14; Ro 5:21; 6:14 [c]Jn 8:32; 14:6; 18:37 **1:18** [a]Ex 33:20; Jn 6:46; Col 1:15; 1Ti 6:16; 1Jn 4:12 [b]Jn 3:16, 18; 1Jn 4:9 [c]Lk 16:22; Jn 13:23 [d]Jn 3:11 **1:19** [a]Jn 1:7 [b]Jn 2:18, 20; 5:10, 15f, 18; 6:41, 52; 7:1, 11, 13, 15, 35; 8:22, 48, 52, 57; 9:18, 22; 10:24, 31, 33 [c]Mt 15:1 [1]Often refers to Jewish leaders in John's gospel

confessed and did not deny, but confessed, "[a]I am not the [1]Christ." **21** And they asked him, "What then? Are you [a]Elijah?" And he *said, "I am not." "Are you [b]the Prophet?" And he answered, "No." **22** Therefore, they said to him, "Who are you, so that we may give an answer to those who sent us? What do you say about yourself?" **23** He said, "I am [a]A VOICE OF ONE CRYING IN THE WILDERNESS, 'MAKE STRAIGHT THE WAY OF THE [1]LORD,' as Isaiah the prophet said."

**24** Now they had been sent from the Pharisees. **25** And they asked him, and said to him, "Why then are you baptizing, if you are not the [1]Christ, nor Elijah, nor [a]the Prophet?" **26** John answered them, saying, "[a]I baptize with water, *but* among you stands One whom you do not know. **27** *This One is* [a]He who comes after me, of whom I am not worthy to untie the [b]strap of His sandal." **28** These things took place in Bethany [a]beyond the Jordan, where John was baptizing.

**29** On the next day, he *saw Jesus coming to him and *said, "Behold, [a]the Lamb of God who [b]takes away the sin of the world! **30** This is He of whom I said, '[a]After me comes a man who has been [1]ahead of me, [b]for He existed before me.' **31** I did not know [1]Him, but so that He might be manifested to Israel, I came baptizing with water." **32** And John [a]bore witness saying, "[b]I have beheld the Spirit descending as a dove out of heaven, and He abided on Him. **33** And I did not know [1]Him, but He who sent me to baptize with water said to me, 'The One upon whom you see the Spirit descending and abiding on Him, [a]this is the One who baptizes with the Holy Spirit.' **34** And I myself have seen, and have borne witness that this is [a]the Son of God."

### *Behold, the Lamb of God*

**35** [a]On the next day, John again was standing [1]with two of his disciples, **36** and he looked at Jesus as He walked, and *said, "Behold, [a]the Lamb of God!" **37** And the two disciples heard him speak and followed Jesus. **38** And when Jesus turned and noticed them following, He *said to them, "What do you seek?" They said to Him, "[a]Rabbi (which translated means Teacher), where are You staying?" **39** He *said to them, "Come, and you will see." So they came and saw where He was staying; and they stayed with Him that day. It was about the [1]tenth hour. **40** [a]One of the two who heard John *speak* and followed Him, was Andrew, Simon Peter's brother. **41** He first *found his own brother Simon and *said to him, "We have found the [a]Messiah" (which translated means [1]Christ). **42** He brought him to Jesus. When Jesus looked at him, He said, "You are Simon the son of [a]John; you shall be called [b]Cephas" (which is translated [c,1]Peter).

---

**1:20** [a]Lk 3:15f; Jn 3:28 [1]Messiah **1:21** [a]Mt 11:14; 16:14 [b]Dt 18:15, 18; Mt 21:11; Jn 1:25 **1:23** [a]Is 40:3; Mt 3:3; Mk 1:3; Lk 3:4 [1]In OT, Yahweh, cf. Is 40:3 **1:25** [a]Dt 18:15, 18; Mt 21:11; Jn 1:21 [1]Messiah **1:26** [a]Mt 3:11; Mk 1:8; Lk 3:16; Ac 1:5 **1:27** [a]Mt 3:11; Jn 1:30 [b]Mt 3:11; Mk 1:7; Lk 3:16 **1:28** [a]Jn 3:26; 10:40 **1:29** [a]Is 53:7; Jn 1:36; Ac 8:32; 1Pe 1:19; Rev 5:6, 8, 12f; 6:1 [b]Mt 1:21; 1Jn 3:5 **1:30** [a]Mt 3:11; Jn 1:27 [b]Jn 1:15 [1]Or *has a higher rank than* **1:31** [1]As the Messiah **1:32** [a]Jn 1:7 [b]Mt 3:16; Mk 1:10; Lk 3:22 **1:33** [a]Mt 3:11; Mk 1:8; Lk 3:16; Ac 1:5 [1]As the Messiah **1:34** [a]Mt 4:3; Jn 1:49 **1:35** [a]Jn 1:29 [1]Lit *and* **1:36** [a]Jn 1:29 **1:38** [a]Mt 23:7f; Jn 1:49 **1:39** [1]10 a.m. **1:40** [a]Mt 4:18-22; Mk 1:16-20; Lk 5:2-11; Jn 1:40-42 **1:41** [a]Da 9:25; Jn 4:25 [1]Gr *Christos*; lit *Anointed One* **1:42** [a]Mt 16:17; Jn 21:15-17 [b]1Co 1:12; 3:22; 9:5; 15:5; Ga 1:18; 2:9, 11, 14 [c]Mt 16:18 [1]Gr *Petros*; lit *stone*

**43** [a]On the next day, He desired to go into [b]Galilee, and He *found [c]Philip. And Jesus *said to him, "[d]Follow Me." **44** Now [a]Philip was from [b]Bethsaida, the city of Andrew and Peter. **45** [a]Philip *found [b]Nathanael and *said to him, "We have found Him of whom [c]Moses in the Law and *also* [c]the Prophets wrote—Jesus of [d]Nazareth, [e]the son of Joseph." **46** And Nathanael said to him, "[a]Can any good thing come out of Nazareth?" [b]Philip *said to him, "Come and see." **47** Jesus saw Nathanael coming to Him, and *said about him, "Behold, truly an [a]Israelite in whom there is no deceit!" **48** Nathanael *said to Him, "From where do You know me?" Jesus answered and said to him, "Before [a]Philip called you, when you were under the fig tree, I saw you." **49** Nathanael answered Him, "[a]Rabbi, You are [b]the Son of God; You are the [c]King of Israel." **50** Jesus answered and said to him, "Because I said to you that I saw you under the fig tree, do you believe? You will see greater things than these." **51** And He *said to him, "Truly, truly, I say to you, you will see [a]THE HEAVENS OPENED AND [b]THE ANGELS OF GOD ASCENDING AND DESCENDING on [c]the Son of Man."

### *The Wedding at Cana*

**2** And on [a]the third day there was a wedding in [b]Cana of Galilee, and the [c]mother of Jesus was there; **2** and both Jesus and His [a]disciples were invited to the wedding. **3** And when the wine ran out, the mother of Jesus *said to Him, "They have no wine." **4** And Jesus *said to her, "[a]Woman, [b,1]what do I have to do with you? [c]My hour has not yet come." **5** His [a]mother *said to the servants, "Whatever He says to you, do *it*." **6** Now there were six stone water jars set there [a]for the Jewish custom of purification, containing [1]two or three measures each. **7** Jesus *said to them, "Fill the water jars with water." So they filled them up to the brim. **8** And He *said to them, "Draw *some* out now and take it to the headwaiter." So they took it *to him*. **9** Now when the headwaiter tasted the water [a]which had become wine, and did not know where it came from (but the servants who had drawn the water knew), the headwaiter *called the bridegroom, **10** and *said to him, "Every man serves the good wine first, and when *the people* [a]have [1]drunk freely, *then* the inferior *wine*; *but* you have kept the good wine until now." **11** Jesus did this in Cana of [a]Galilee as the beginning of *His* [b,1]signs, and manifested His [c]glory, and His disciples believed in Him.

**12** After this He went down to [a]Capernaum, He and His [b]mother

**1:43** [a]Jn 1:29, 35 [b]Mt 4:12; Jn 1:28; 2:11 [c]Mt 10:3; Jn 1:44-48; 6:5, 7; 12:21f; 14:8f [d]Mt 8:22 **1:44** [a]Mt 10:3; Jn 1:44-48; 6:5, 7; 12:21f; 14:8f [b]Mt 11:21 **1:45** [a]Mt 10:3; Jn 1:44-48; 6:5, 7; 12:21f; 14:8f [b]Jn 1:46-49; 21:2 [c]Lk 24:27 [d]Mt 2:23 [e]Lk 2:48; 3:23; 4:22; Jn 6:42 **1:46** [a]Jn 7:41, 52 [b]Mt 10:3; Jn 1:44-48; 6:5, 7; 12:21f; 14:8f **1:47** [a]Ro 9:4 **1:48** [a]Mt 10:3; Jn 1:44-48; 6:5, 7; 12:21f; 14:8f **1:49** [a]Jn 1:38 [b]Jn 1:34 [c]Mt 2:2; 27:42; Mk 15:32; Jn 12:13 **1:51** [a]Eze 1:1; Mt 3:16; Lk 3:21; Ac 7:56; 10:11; Rev 19:11 [b]Ge 28:12 [c]Mt 8:20 ◆ **2:1** [a]Jn 1:29, 35, 43 [b]Jn 2:11; 4:46; 21:2 [c]Mt 12:46 **2:2** [a]Jn 1:40-49; 2:12, 17, 22; 3:22; 4:2, 8, 27; 6:8, 12, 16, 22, 24, 60f, 66; 7:3; 8:31 **2:4** [a]Jn 19:26 [b]Mt 8:29 [c]Jn 7:6, 8, 30; 8:20 [1]Lit *what to Me and to you* (a Heb idiom) **2:5** [a]Mt 12:46 **2:6** [a]Mk 7:3f; Jn 3:25 [1]Approx. 20-30 gal. or 75-115 l, a measure was approx. 10 gal. or 38 l **2:9** [a]Jn 4:46 **2:10** [a]Mt 24:49; Lk 12:45; Ac 2:15; 1Co 11:21; Eph 5:18; 1Th 5:7; Rev 17:2, 6 [1]Or *have become drunk* **2:11** [a]Jn 1:43 [b]Jn 2:23; 3:2; 4:54; 6:2, 14, 26, 30; 7:31; 9:16; 10:41; 11:47; 12:18, 37; 20:30 [c]Jn 1:14 [1]Or *attesting miracles* **2:12** [a]Mt 4:13 [b]Mt 12:46

and *His* [b]brothers and His [c]disciples;
and they stayed there a few days.

### *Jesus Cleanses the Temple*

**13** [a]And the Passover of the Jews was
near, and Jesus [b]went up to Jerusalem.
**14** [a]And He found in the temple those
who were selling oxen and sheep
and doves, and the money changers
seated *at their tables.* **15** And He
made a scourge of cords, and drove
*them* all out of the temple, with the
sheep and the oxen; and He poured
out the coins of the money changers
and overturned their tables; **16** and to
those who were selling [a]the doves
He said, "Take these things away;
stop making [b]My Father's house a
[1]place of business." **17** His [a]disciples
remembered that it was written,
"[b]ZEAL FOR YOUR HOUSE WILL CON-
SUME ME." **18** [a]The Jews then said to
Him, "[b]What sign do You show us
[1]as your authority for doing these
things?" **19** Jesus answered them,
"[a]Destroy this [1]sanctuary, and in
three days I will raise it up." **20** [a]The
Jews then said, "It took [b]forty-six
years to build this sanctuary, and will
You raise it up in three days?" **21** But
He was speaking about [a]the sanctu-
ary of His body. **22** So when He was
raised from the dead, His [a]disciples
[b]remembered that He said this; and
they believed [c]the Scripture and the
word which Jesus had spoken.

**23** Now when He was in Jerusalem
at [a]the Passover, during the feast,
many believed in His name, [b]when
they saw His signs which He was do-
ing. **24** But Jesus, [1]on His part, was not
entrusting Himself to them, for [a]He
knew all men, **25** and because He had
no need that anyone bear witness
concerning man, [a]for He Himself
knew what was in man.

### *You Must Be Born Again*

**3** Now there was a man of the Phari-
sees, named [a]Nicodemus, a [b]ruler
of the Jews; **2** this man came to Jesus
by night and said to Him, "[a]Rabbi,
we know that You have come from
God *as* a teacher; for no one can do
these [b,1]signs that You do unless [c]God
is with him." **3** Jesus answered and
said to him, "Truly, truly, I say to you,
unless one [a]is born [1]again he cannot
see [b]the kingdom of God."

**4** Nicodemus *said to Him, "How
can a man be born when he is old?
Can he enter a second time into
his mother's womb and be born?"
**5** Jesus answered, "Truly, truly, I say
to you, unless one is born of [a]water
and the Spirit he cannot enter into
[b]the kingdom of God. **6** [a]That which
has been born of the flesh is flesh,
and that which has been born of
the Spirit is spirit. **7** Do not marvel
that I said to you, 'You must be born
[1]again.' **8** [a]The wind blows where it

---

**2:12** [b]Mt 12:46 [c]Jn 2:2 **2:13** [a]Dt 16:1-6; Jn 5:1; 6:4; 11:55 [b]Lk 2:41; Jn 2:23 **2:14** [a]Jn 2:14-16: *Mt 21:12ff; Mk 11:15, 17; Lk 19:45f;* Mal 3:1ff **2:16** [a]Mt 21:12 [b]Lk 2:49 [1]Lit *house* **2:17** [a]Jn 2:2 [b]Ps 69:9 ***2:18*** [a]*Jn 1:19* [b]Mt 12:38 [1]Lit *that You do these* **2:19** [a]Mt 26:61; 27:40; Mk 14:58; 15:29; Ac 6:14 [1]The inner part of the temple **2:20** [a]Jn 1:19 [b]Ezr 5:16 **2:21** [a]1Co 6:19 **2:22** [a]Jn 2:2 [b]Lk 24:8; Jn 2:17; 12:16; 14:26 [c]Ps 16:10; Lk 24:26f; Jn 20:9; Ac 13:33 **2:23** [a]Jn 2:13 [b]Jn 2:11 **2:24** [a]Ac 1:24; 15:8 [1]Lit *Himself* **2:25** [a]Mt 9:4; Jn 1:42, 47; 6:61, 64; 13:11 ◆**3:1** [a]Jn 7:50; 19:39 [b]Lk 23:13; Jn 7:26, 48 **3:2** [a]Mt 23:7; Jn 3:26 [b]Jn 2:11 [c]Jn 9:33; 10:38; 14:10f; Ac 2:22; 10:38 [1]Or *attesting miracles* **3:3** [a]2Co 5:17; 1Pe 1:23 [b]Mt 19:24; 21:31; Mk 9:47; 10:14f; Jn 3:5 [1]Or *from above* **3:5** [a]Eze 36:25-27; Eph 5:26; Tit 3:5 [b]Mt 19:24; 21:31; Mk 9:47; 10:14f; Jn 3:3 **3:6** [a]Jn 1:13; 1Co 15:50 **3:7** [1]Or *from above* **3:8** [a]Ps 135:7; Ecc 11:5; Eze 37:9

wishes and you hear its sound, but do
not know where it comes from and
where it is going; so is everyone who
has been born of the Spirit."
**9** Nicodemus answered and said
to Him, "How can these things be?"
**10** Jesus answered and said to him,
"Are you [a]the teacher of Israel and do
not understand these things? **11** Truly,
truly, I say to you, [a]we speak of what
we know and [b]bear witness of what
we have seen, and [b]you do not accept
our witness. **12** If I told you earthly
things and you do not believe, how
will you believe if I tell you heavenly
things? **13** [a]And no one has ascended
into heaven, but [b]He who descended
from heaven, [c]the Son of Man. **14** And
as [a]Moses lifted up the serpent in
the wilderness, even so must [b]the
Son of Man [c]be lifted up; **15** so that
whoever believes will [a]in Him have
eternal life.
**16** "For God [1]so [a]loved the world,
that He [b]gave His [c,2]only begotten
Son, that whoever [d]believes in Him
shall not perish, but have eternal
life. **17** For God [a]did not send the Son
into the world [b]to judge the world,
but that the world might be saved
through Him. **18** [a]He who believes
in Him is not judged; he who does
not believe has been judged already,
because he has not believed in the
name of [b]the [1]only begotten Son of
God. **19** And this is the judgment, that
[a]the Light has come into the world,
and men loved the darkness rather
than the Light, for [b]their deeds were
evil. **20** [a]For everyone who does evil
hates the Light, and does not come to
the Light lest his deeds be exposed.
**21** But he who [a]practices the truth
comes to the Light, so that his deeds
may be manifested as having been
done by God."

### *John the Baptist's Last Witness*

**22** After these things Jesus and His
[a]disciples came into the land of
Judea, and there He was spending
time with them and [b]baptizing.
**23** And John also was baptizing in
Aenon near Salim, because there was
much water there; and *people* were
coming and were being baptized—
**24** for [a]John had not yet been thrown
into prison.
**25** Therefore there arose a de-
bate between John's disciples and
a Jew about [a]purification. **26** And
they came to John and said to him,
"[a]Rabbi, He who was with you
[b]beyond the Jordan, to whom you
[c]have borne witness, behold, He is
baptizing and all are coming to Him."
**27** John answered and said, "[a]A man
can receive nothing unless it [b]has
been given him from heaven. **28** You
yourselves [1]are my witnesses that I
said, '[a]I am not the [2]Christ,' but, 'I
have been sent ahead of Him.' **29** He
who has the bride is [a]the bridegroom;
but the friend of the bridegroom,

---

**3:10** [a]Lk 2:46; 5:17; Ac 5:34 **3:11** [a]Jn 1:18; 7:16f; 8:26, 28; 12:49; 14:24 [b]Jn 3:32 **3:13** [a]Dt 30:12; Pr 30:4; Ac 2:34; Ro 10:6; Eph 4:9 [b]Jn 3:31; 6:38, 42 [c]Mt 8:20 **3:14** [a]Nu 21:9 [b]Mt 8:20 [c]Jn 8:28; 12:34 **3:15** [a]Jn 20:31; 1Jn 5:11-13 **3:16** [a]Ro 5:8; Eph 2:4; 2Th 2:16; 1Jn 4:10; Rev 1:5 [b]Ro 8:32; 1Jn 4:9 [c]Jn 1:18; 3:18; 1Jn 4:9 [d]Jn 3:36; 6:40; 11:25f [1]Or *in this way* [2]Or *unique*, only one of His kind **3:17** [a]Jn 3:34; 5:36, 38; 6:29, 38, 57; 7:29; 8:42; 10:36; 11:42; 17:3, 8, 18, 21, 23, 25; 20:21 [b]Lk 19:10; Jn 8:15; 12:47; 1Jn 4:14 **3:18** [a]Mk 16:16; Jn 5:24 [b]Jn 1:18; 1Jn 4:9 [1]Or *unique*, only one of His kind **3:19** [a]Jn 1:4; 8:12; 9:5; 12:46 [b]Jn 7:7 **3:20** [a]Jn 3:20, 21; Eph 5:11, 13 **3:21** [a]1Jn 1:6 **3:22** [a]Jn 2:2 [b]Jn 4:1, 2 **3:24** [a]Mt 4:12; 14:3; Mk 6:17; Lk 3:20 **3:25** [a]Jn 2:6 **3:26** [a]Mt 23:7; Jn 3:2 [b]Jn 1:28 [c]Jn 1:7 **3:27** [a]1Co 4:7; Heb 5:4 [b]Jas 1:17 **3:28** [a]Jn 1:20, 23 [1]Lit *testify for me* [2]Messiah **3:29** [a]Mt 9:15; 25:1

who stands and hears him, rejoices
greatly because of the bridegroom's
voice. So this [b]joy of mine has been
made full. **30** He must increase, but I
must decrease.

**31** "[a]He who comes from above
is above all, [b]he who is of the earth
is from the earth and speaks of the
earth. [a]He who comes from heaven
is above all. **32** What He has seen and
heard, of that He [a]bears witness; and
[a]no one receives His witness. **33** He
who has received His witness [a]has
set his seal to *this*, that God is true.
**34** For He whom God has [a]sent speaks
the words of God; [b,1]for He gives the
Spirit without measure. **35** [a]The
Father loves the Son and [b]has given
all things into His hand. **36** He who
[a]believes in the Son has eternal life;
but he who [b]does not [1]obey the Son
will not see life, but the wrath of God
abides on him."

### *Jesus Goes to Galilee*

**4** Therefore when [a]Jesus knew that
the Pharisees had heard that Jesus
was making and [b]baptizing more dis-
ciples than John **2** (although [a]Jesus
Himself was not baptizing, but His
[b]disciples *were*), **3** He left [a]Judea and
went away [b]again into Galilee. **4** And
He had to pass through [a]Samaria.
**5** So He *came to a city of [a]Samaria
called Sychar, near [b]the field that
[c]Jacob gave to his son Joseph; **6** and
Jacob's well was there. So Jesus, being
wearied from His journey, was sitting
thus by the well. It was about [1]the
sixth hour.

### *Jesus and the Samaritan Woman*

**7** A woman of Samaria *came to draw
water. Jesus *said to her, "Give Me a
drink." **8** For His [a]disciples had gone
away into [b]the city to buy food.
**9** Therefore the [a]Samaritan woman
*said to Him, "How do You, being a
Jew, ask for a drink from me, being
a Samaritan woman?" (For [b]Jews
have no dealings with Samaritans.)
**10** Jesus answered and said to her,
"If you knew the gift of God, and
who it is who says to you, 'Give Me
a drink,' you would have asked Him,
and He would have given you [a]living
water." **11** She *said to Him, "[1]Sir, You
have nothing to draw with and the
well is deep. Where then do You get
that [a]living water? **12** Are You greater
than our father Jacob, who [a]gave us
this well, and drank of it himself
and his sons and his cattle?" **13** Jesus
answered and said to her, "Everyone
who drinks of this water will thirst
again; **14** but whoever drinks of the
water that I will give him [a]will never
thirst—ever; but the water that I will
give him will become in him a well of
water springing up to [b]eternal life."
**15** The woman *said to Him, "[1]Sir,
[a]give me this water, so I will not
be thirsty nor come *back* here to
draw." **16** He *said to her, "Go, call

---

**3:29** [b]Jn 15:11; 16:24; 17:13; Php 2:2; 1Jn 1:4; 2Jn 12 **3:31** [a]Mt 28:18; Jn 3:13; 8:23 [b]1Co 15:47; 1Jn 4:5
**3:32** [a]Jn 3:11 **3:33** [a]Jn 6:27; Ro 4:11; 15:28; 1Co 9:2; 2Co 1:22; Eph 1:13; 4:30; 2Ti 2:19; Rev 7:3-8
**3:34** [a]Jn 3:17 [b]Mt 12:18; Lk 4:18; Ac 1:2; 10:38 [1]Lit *because He does not give the Spirit by measure*
**3:35** [a]Mt 28:18; Jn 5:20; 17:2 [b]Mt 11:27; Lk 10:22 **3:36** [a]Jn 3:16 [b]Ac 14:2; Heb 3:18 [1]Or *believe*
◆ **4:1** [a]Lk 7:13 [b]Jn 3:22, 26; 1Co 1:17 **4:2** [a]Jn 3:22, 26; 1Co 1:17 [b]Jn 2:2 **4:3** [a]Jn 3:22 [b]Jn 2:11f
**4:4** [a]Lk 9:52 **4:5** [a]Lk 9:52 [b]Ge 33:19; Jos 24:32 [c]Ge 48:22; Jn 4:12 **4:6** [1]Perhaps 6 p.m. Roman time
or noon Jewish time **4:8** [a]Jn 2:2 [b]Jn 4:5, 39 **4:9** [a]Lk 9:52 [b]Ezr 4:3-6, 11ff; Mt 10:5; Jn 8:48; Ac 10:28
**4:10** [a]Jer 2:13; Jn 4:14; 7:37f; Rev 7:17; 21:6; 22:1, 17 **4:11** [a]Jer 2:13; Jn 4:14; 7:37f; Rev 7:17; 21:6; 22:1, 17
[1]Or *Lord* **4:12** [a]Jn 4:6 **4:14** [a]Jn 6:35; 7:38 [b]Mt 25:46; Jn 6:27 **4:15** [a]Jn 6:35 [1]Or *Lord*

your husband and come *back* here."
17 The woman answered and said,
"I have no husband." Jesus *said to
her, "You have correctly said, 'I have
no husband'; 18 for you had five hus-
bands, and the one you now have is
not your husband; this you have said
truly." 19 The woman *said to Him,
"[1]Sir, I see that You are [a]a prophet.
20 [a]Our fathers worshiped on [b]this
mountain, and you *people* say that
[c]in Jerusalem is the place where men
ought to worship." 21 Jesus *said to
her, "Woman, believe Me, [a]an hour
is coming when [b]neither in this
mountain nor in Jerusalem will you
worship the Father. 22 [a]You worship
what you do not know; we worship
what we know, for [b]salvation is from
the Jews. 23 But [a]an hour is coming,
and now is, when the true worshipers
will worship the Father [b]in spirit and
truth; for such people the Father
seeks to be His worshipers. 24 God
is [1]spirit, and those who worship Him
must worship [a]in spirit and truth."
25 The woman *said to Him, "I know
that [a]Messiah is coming ([b]He who is
called [1]Christ); when He comes, He
will declare all things to us." 26 Jesus
*said to her, "[a]I who speak to you
am *He*."
27 And at this point His [a]disciples
came, and they were marveling that
He was speaking with a woman, yet
no one said, "What do You seek?" or,
"Why are You speaking with her?"
28 So the woman left her water jar,
and went into the city and *said to the
men, 29 "Come, see a man [a]who told
me all the things that I *have* done; [b]is
this not the [1]Christ?" 30 They went
out of the city, and were coming to
Him.
31 Meanwhile the disciples were
urging Him, saying, "[a]Rabbi, eat."
32 But He said to them, "I have food
to eat that you do not know about."
33 So the [a]disciples were saying to
one another, "Has anyone brought
Him *anything* to eat?" 34 Jesus *said
to them, "My food is to [a]do the will of
Him who sent Me and to [b]finish His
work. 35 Do you not say, 'There are
yet four months, and *then* comes the
harvest'? Behold, I say to you, lift up
your eyes and look on the fields, that
they are white [a]for harvest. 36 Even
now he who reaps is receiving [a]wages
and is gathering [b]fruit for [c]life eter-
nal; so that he who sows and he who
reaps may rejoice together. 37 For in
this *case* the saying is true, '[a]One
sows and another reaps.' 38 I sent
you to reap that for which you have
not labored; others have labored and
you have entered into their labor."

### *Many Samaritans Believe*

39 From [a]that city many of the Samar-
itans believed in Him because of the
word of the woman who bore witness,
"[b]He told me all the things that I *have*
done." 40 So when the Samaritans
came to Jesus, they were asking Him
to stay with them; and He stayed

**4:19** [a]Mt 21:11; Lk 7:16, 39; 24:19; Jn 6:14; 7:40; 9:17 [1]Or *Lord* **4:20** [a]Ge 33:20; Jn 4:12 [b]Dt 11:29; Jos 8:33 [c]Lk 9:53 **4:21** [a]Jn 4:23; 5:25, 28; 16:2, 32 [b]Mal 1:11; 1Ti 2:8 **4:22** [a]2Ki 17:28-41 [b]Is 2:3; Ro 3:1f; 9:4f **4:23** [a]Jn 4:21; 5:25, 28; 16:2, 32 [b]Php 3:3 **4:24** [a]Php 3:3 [1]Or *Spirit* **4:25** [a]Da 9:25; Jn 1:41 [b]Mt 1:16; 27:17, 22; Lk 2:11 [1]Gr *Christos*; lit *Anointed One* **4:26** [a]Jn 8:24, 28, 58; 9:37; 13:19 **4:27** [a]Jn 4:8 **4:29** [a]Jn 4:17f [b]Mt 12:23; Jn 7:26, 31 [1]Messiah **4:31** [a]Mt 23:7; 26:25, 49; Mk 9:5; 11:21; 14:45; Jn 1:38, 49; 3:2, 26; 6:25; 9:2; 11:8 **4:33** [a]Lk 6:13-16; Jn 1:40-49; 2:2 **4:34** [a]Jn 5:30; 6:38 [b]Jn 5:36; 17:4; 19:28, 30 **4:35** [a]Mt 9:37, 38; Lk 10:2 **4:36** [a]Pr 11:18; 1Co 9:17f [b]Ro 1:13 [c]Mt 19:29; Jn 3:36; 4:14; 5:24; Ro 2:7; 6:23 **4:37** [a]Job 31:8; Mic 6:15 **4:39** [a]Jn 4:5, 30 [b]Jn 4:29

there two days. **41** And many more
believed because of His word; **42** and
they were saying to the woman, "It is
no longer because of what you said
that we believe, for we have heard for
ourselves and know that this One is
truly [a]the Savior of the world."
**43** And after [a]the two days He went
from there into Galilee. **44** For Jesus
Himself bore witness that [a]a prophet
has no honor in his own country.
**45** So when He came to Galilee, the
Galileans received Him, [a]having seen
all the things that He did in Jerusalem
at the feast; for they themselves also
went to the feast.

### *Jesus Heals a Royal Official's Son*

**46** Then He came again to [a]Cana of
Galilee [b]where He had made the water wine. And there was a royal official
whose son was sick at [c]Capernaum.
**47** When he heard that Jesus had come
[a]out of Judea into Galilee, he went
to Him and was asking *Him* to come
down and heal his son; for he was
about to die. **48** So Jesus said to him,
"Unless you *people* see [a,1]signs and
[a]wonders, you will never believe."
**49** The royal official *said to Him,
"[1]Sir, come down before my child
dies." **50** Jesus *said to him, "[a]Go; your
son lives." The man believed the word
that Jesus spoke to him and started
on his way. **51** And while he was still
going down, his slaves met him,
saying that his [1]son was alive. **52** So
he inquired of them the hour when he
began to get better. Then they said to
him, "Yesterday at the [1]seventh hour
the fever left him." **53** So the father
knew that *it was* at that hour in which
Jesus said to him, "Your son lives";
and he himself believed and [a]his
whole household. **54** This is again a
[a]second [1]sign that Jesus did when He
had [b]come out of Judea into Galilee.

### *The Healing at Bethesda*

**5** After these things there was [a]a
feast of the Jews, and Jesus went
up to Jerusalem.
**2** Now there is in Jerusalem by [a]the
sheep *gate* a pool, which is called [b]in
[1]Hebrew [2]Bethesda, having five porticoes. **3** In these lay a multitude of
those who were sick, blind, lame, and
withered, [1][waiting for the moving of
the waters; **4** for an angel of the Lord
went down at certain seasons into
the pool and stirred up the water;
whoever then first, after the stirring
up of the water, stepped in was
made well from whatever sickness
with which he was afflicted.] **5** And
a man was there who had been sick
for thirty-eight years. **6** When Jesus
saw him lying *there* and knew that
he had already been *sick* a long time,
He *said to him, "Do you wish to get
well?" **7** The sick man answered Him,
"Sir, I have no man to put me into
the pool when [a]the water is stirred
up, but while I am coming, another
steps down before me." **8** Jesus *said
to him, "[a]Get up, pick up your mat

---

**4:42** [a]Mt 1:21; Lk 2:11; Jn 1:29; Ac 5:31; 13:23; 1Ti 4:10; 1Jn 4:14 **4:43** [a]Jn 4:40 **4:44** [a]Mt 13:57; Mk 6:4; Lk 4:24 **4:45** [a]Jn 2:23 **4:46** [a]Jn 2:1 [b]Jn 2:9 [c]Lk 4:23; Jn 2:12 **4:47** [a]Jn 4:3, 54 **4:48** [a]Da 4:2f; 6:27; Mt 24:24; Mk 13:22; Ac 2:19, 22, 43; 4:30; 5:12; 6:8; 7:36; 14:3; 15:12; Ro 15:19; 1Co 1:22; 2Co 12:12; 2Th 2:9; Heb 2:4 [1]Or *attesting miracles* **4:49** [1]Or *Lord* **4:50** [a]Mt 8:13 **4:51** [1]Or *boy* **4:52** [1]Perhaps 7 p.m. Roman time or 1 p.m. Jewish time **4:53** [a]Ac 11:14 **4:54** [a]Jn 2:11 [b]Jn 4:45f [1]Or *attesting miracle*
◆ **5:1** [a]Dt 16:1; Jn 2:13 **5:2** [a]Ne 3:1, 32; 12:39 [b]Jn 19:13, 17, 20; 20:16; Ac 21:40; Rev 9:11; 16:16 [1]Jewish Aramaic [2]Some early mss *Bethsaida, Bethzatha* **5:3** [1]Early mss omit rest of v 3, and v 4 **5:7** [a]Jn 5:4 **5:8** [a]Mt 9:6; Mk 2:11; Lk 5:24

and walk." 9 And immediately the
man became well, and picked up his
mat and *began to* walk.

[a]Now it was the Sabbath on that
day. 10 So [a]the Jews were saying to
the man who had been healed, "It
is the Sabbath, and [b]it is not lawful
for you to carry your mat." 11 But he
answered them, "He who made me
well was the one who said to me,
'Pick up your mat and walk.'" 12 They
asked him, "Who is the man who said
to you, 'Pick up *your mat* and walk'?"
13 But the man who was healed did
not know who it was, for Jesus had
slipped away while there was a crowd
in *that* place. 14 Afterward Jesus
*found him in the temple and said to
him, "Behold, you have become well;
do not [a]sin anymore, [b]so that noth-
ing worse happens to you." 15 The
man went away, and disclosed to [a]the
Jews that it was Jesus who had made
him well. 16 And for this reason [a]the
Jews were persecuting Jesus, because
He was doing these things on the
Sabbath. 17 But He answered them,
"My Father is working until now, and
I Myself am working."

### *Jesus' Equality with the Father*

18 For this reason therefore [a]the
Jews [b]were seeking all the more to
kill Him, because He not only was
breaking the Sabbath, but also was
calling God His own Father, [c]making
Himself equal with God.

19 Therefore Jesus answered and
was saying to them, "Truly, truly, I
say to you, [a]the Son can do nothing
from Himself, unless *it is* something
He sees the Father doing; for whatev-
er [1]the Father does, these things the
Son also does in the same manner.
20 [a]For the Father loves the Son, and
shows Him all things that He Himself
is doing; and *the Father* will show
Him [b]greater works than these, so
that you will marvel. 21 For just as
the Father raises the dead and [a]gives
*them* life, even so [b]the Son also gives
life to whom He wishes. 22 For not
even the Father judges anyone, but
[a]He has given all judgment to the
Son, 23 so that all will honor the Son
even as they honor the Father. [a]He
who does not honor the Son does
not honor the Father who sent Him.

24 "Truly, truly, I say to you, he
who hears My word, and [a]believes
Him who sent Me, has eternal life,
and [b]does not come into judgment,
but has [c]passed out of death into life.

### *Two Resurrections*

25 "Truly, truly, I say to you, [a]an hour
is coming and now is, when [b]the dead
will hear the voice of the Son of God,
and those who [c]hear will live. 26 For
just as the Father has life in Himself,
even so He [a]gave to the Son also to
have life in Himself; 27 and He gave
Him authority to [a]execute judgment,
because He is [1]the Son of Man. 28 Do
not marvel at this; for [a]an hour is
coming, in which [b]all who are in the
tombs will hear His voice, 29 and will
come forth; [a]those who did the good

**5:9** [a]Jn 9:14 **5:10** [a]Jn 1:19; 5:15, 16, 18 [b]Ne 13:19; Jer 17:21f; Mt 12:2; Lk 6:2; Jn 7:23; 9:16 **5:14** [a]Mk 2:5; Jn 8:11 [b]Ezr 9:14 **5:15** [a]Jn 1:19; 5:16, 18 **5:16** [a]Jn 1:19; 5:10, 15, 18 **5:18** [a]Jn 1:19; 5:15, 16 [b]Jn 5:16; 7:1 [c]Jn 10:33; 19:7 **5:19** [a]Mt 26:39; Jn 5:30; 6:38; 8:28; 12:49; 14:10 [1]Lit *that One* **5:20** [a]Mt 3:17; Jn 3:35; 2Pe 1:17 [b]Jn 14:12 **5:21** [a]Ro 4:17; 8:11 [b]Jn 11:25 **5:22** [a]Jn 5:27; 9:39; Ac 10:42; 17:31 **5:23** [a]Lk 10:16; 1Jn 2:23 **5:24** [a]Jn 3:18; 12:44; 20:31; 1Jn 5:13 [b]Jn 3:18 [c]1Jn 3:14 **5:25** [a]Jn 4:21, 23; 5:28 [b]Lk 15:24 [c]Jn 6:60; 8:43, 47; 9:27 **5:26** [a]Jn 1:4; 6:57 **5:27** [a]Jn 9:39; Ac 10:42; 17:31 [1]Or *a son of man* **5:28** [a]Jn 4:21 [b]Jn 11:24; 1Co 15:52 **5:29** [a]Da 12:2; Mt 25:46; Ac 24:15

deeds to a resurrection of life, those
who committed the evil deeds to a
resurrection of judgment.
**30** "[a]I can do nothing from Myself.
As I hear, I judge; and [b]My judgment
is righteous, because I do not seek My
own will, but [c]the will of Him who
sent Me.
**31** "[a]If I *alone* bear witness about
Myself, My witness is not [1]true.
**32** There is [a]another who bears
witness about Me, and I know that
the witness which He gives about Me
is true.

### *Witnesses to Jesus: The Father and the Scriptures*

**33** "You have sent to John, and he [a]has
borne witness to the truth. **34** But
[a]the witness I receive is not from
man, but I say these things so that
you may be saved. **35** He was [a]the
lamp that was burning and shining
and you [b]were willing to rejoice for [1]a
while in his light. **36** But the witness
I have is greater than *the witness
of* John; for [a]the works which the
Father has given Me [b]to finish—the
very works that I do—bear witness
about Me, that the Father [c]has sent
Me. **37** And the Father who sent Me,
[a]He has borne witness about Me.
You have neither heard His voice at
any time nor seen His form. **38** And
you do not have [a]His word abiding
in you, for you do not believe Him
whom He [b]sent. **39** [a,1]You search the
Scriptures because you think that
in them you have eternal life; it is
[b]these that bear witness about Me;
**40** and you are unwilling to come to
Me so that you may have life. **41** [a]I do
not receive glory from men; **42** but
I know you, that you do not have
the love of God in yourselves. **43** I
have come in My Father's name, and
you do not receive Me; [a]if another
comes in his own name, you will
receive him. **44** How can you believe,
when you [a]receive [1]glory from one
another and you do not seek [b]the
[1]glory that is from [c]the only God?
**45** Do not think that I will accuse you
to the Father; the one who accuses
you is [a]Moses, in whom you have
set your hope. **46** For if you believed
Moses, you would believe Me, for
[a]he wrote about Me. **47** But [a]if you
do not believe his writings, how will
you believe My words?"

### *Jesus Feeds Five Thousand*

**6** After these things [a]Jesus went
away to the other side of [b]the Sea
of Galilee (or [c]Tiberias). **2** Now a large
crowd was following Him, because
they were seeing the [a,1]signs which
He was doing on those who were
sick. **3** Then [a]Jesus went up on the
mountain, and there He was sitting
down with His disciples. **4** Now [a]the
Passover, the feast of the Jews, was
near. **5** Therefore Jesus, lifting up His
eyes and seeing that a large crowd

---

**5:30** [a]Jn 5:19 [b]Jn 8:16 [c]Jn 4:34; 6:38 **5:31** [a]Jn 8:14 [1]Admissible as legal evidence **5:32** [a]Jn 5:37 ***5:33*** [a]Jn 1:7, 15, 19, 32; 3:26-30 **5:34** [a]Jn 5:32; 1Jn 5:9 **5:35** [a]2Sa 21:17; 2Pe 1:19 [b]Mk 1:5 [1]Lit *an hour* **5:36** [a]Mt 11:4; Jn 2:23; 10:25, 38; 14:11; 15:24 [b]Jn 4:34 [c]Jn 3:17 **5:37** [a]Mt 3:17; Mk 1:11; Lk 3:22; 24:27; Jn 8:18; 1Jn 5:9 **5:38** [a]1Jn 2:14 [b]Jn 3:17 **5:39** [a]Jn 7:52; Ro 2:17ff [b]Lk 24:25, 27; Ac 13:27 [1]Or *Search the Scriptures!*, Gr imperative **5:41** [a]Jn 5:44; 7:18; 1Th 2:6 **5:43** [a]Mt 24:5 **5:44** [a]Jn 5:41 [b]Ro 2:29 [c]Jn 17:3; 1Ti 1:17 [1]Or *honor* or *fame* **5:45** [a]Jn 9:28; Ro 2:17ff **5:46** [a]Lk 24:27 **5:47** [a]Lk 16:29, 31 ◆ **6:1** [a]Jn 6:1-13: *Mt 14:13-21; Mk 6:32-44; Lk 9:10-17* [b]Mt 4:18; Lk 5:1 [c]Jn 6:23; 21:1 **6:2** [a]Jn 2:11, 23; 3:2; 6:14, 30; 11:47; 12:18, 37; 20:30 [1]Or *attesting miracles* **6:3** [a]Mt 5:1; Mk 3:13; Lk 6:12; 9:28; Jn 6:15 **6:4** [a]Dt 16:1; Jn 2:13

was coming to Him, *said to [a]Philip,
"Where should we buy bread, so that
these people may eat?" 6 And this
He was saying to [a]test him, for He
Himself knew what He was going to
do. 7 [a]Philip answered Him, "[b]Two
hundred [1]denarii worth of bread is
not sufficient for them, for every-
one to receive a little." 8 One of His
[a]disciples, [b]Andrew, Simon Peter's
brother, *said to Him, 9 "There is a
boy here who has five barley loaves
and two [a]fish, but what are these
for so many people?" 10 Jesus said,
"Have the people [1]sit down." Now
there was [a]much grass in the place.
So the men [1]sat down, in number
about [b]five thousand. 11 Jesus then
took the loaves, and [a]having given
thanks, He distributed *them* to those
who were seated; likewise also of
the [b]fish, as much as they wanted.
12 And when they were filled, He
*said to His [a]disciples, "Gather up
the leftover pieces so that nothing
will be lost." 13 So they gathered
them up, and filled twelve [a]baskets
with pieces of the five barley loaves
left over by those who had eaten.
14 Therefore when the people saw
the [1]sign which He had done, they
were saying, "This is truly the
[a]Prophet who is to come into the
world."

### *Jesus Walks on the Sea*

15 So Jesus, knowing that they were
going to come and take Him by force
[a]to make Him king, [b]withdrew again
to [c]the mountain by Himself alone.
16 Now when evening came, His
[a]disciples went down to the sea,
17 and after getting into a boat,
they *began to* cross the sea [a]to
Capernaum. It had already become
dark, and Jesus had not yet come to
them. 18 And the sea *was stirred up
because a strong wind was blowing.
19 Then, when they had rowed about
[1]twenty-five or thirty stadia, they
*saw Jesus walking on the sea and
drawing near to the boat; and they
were frightened. 20 But He *said to
them, [1]"It is I; [a,2]do not be afraid."
21 So they were willing to receive Him
into the boat, and immediately the
boat was at the land to which they
were going.

22 On the next day, [a]the crowd
which stood on the other side of the
sea saw that there was no other small
boat there, except one, and that Jesus
[b]had not entered with His disciples
into the boat, but *that* His disciples
had gone away alone. 23 Other small
boats came from [a]Tiberias near to
the place where they ate the bread
after the [b]Lord [c]had given thanks.
24 So when the crowd saw that Jesus
was not there, nor His disciples, they
themselves got into the small boats,
and [a]came to Capernaum seeking
Jesus. 25 And when they found Him
on the other side of the sea, they said
to Him, "[a]Rabbi, when did You come
here?"

---

**6:5** [a]Jn 1:43 **6:6** [a]2Co 13:5; Rev 2:2 **6:7** [a]Jn 1:43 [b]Mk 6:37 [1]A Roman silver coin, approx. a laborer's daily wage **6:8** [a]Jn 2:2 [b]Jn 1:40 **6:9** [a]Jn 6:11; 21:9, 10, 13 **6:10** [a]Mk 6:39 [b]Mt 14:21 [1]Lit *recline(d)* **6:11** [a]Mt 15:36; Jn 6:23 [b]Jn 6:9; 21:9, 10, 13 **6:12** [a]Jn 2:2 **6:13** [a]Mt 14:20 **6:14** [a]Mt 11:3; 21:11; Jn 1:21 [1]Or *attesting miracle* **6:15** [a]Jn 18:36f [b]Jn 6:15-21: *Mt 14:22-33; Mk 6:45-51* [c]Jn 6:3 **6:16** [a]Jn 2:2 **6:17** [a]Mk 6:45; Jn 6:24, 59 **6:19** [1]Approx. 2.8-3.5 mi. or 4.6-5.5 km; a stadion was about 607 ft. or 185 m **6:20** [a]Mt 14:27 [1]Or *I am* He, cf. 4:26; 8:18, 24, 28; 13:19; 18:5, 6 [2]Or *stop being afraid* **6:22** [a]Jn 6:2 [b]Jn 6:15ff **6:23** [a]Jn 6:1 [b]Lk 7:13 [c]Jn 6:11 **6:24** [a]Mt 14:34; Mk 6:53; Jn 6:17, 59 **6:25** [a]Mt 23:7

### *I Am the Bread of Life*

26 Jesus answered them and said,
"Truly, truly, I say to you, you [a]seek
Me, not because you saw [b]signs, but
because you ate of the loaves and
were filled. 27 Do not [a]work for the
food which perishes, but for the
food which endures to [b]eternal life,
which [c]the Son of Man will give to
you, for on Him the Father, God, [d]set
His seal." 28 Therefore they said to
Him, "What should we do, so that
we may work the works of God?"
29 Jesus answered and said to them,
"This is [a]the work of God, that you
believe in Him whom He [b]has sent."
30 So they said to Him, "[a]What then
do You do for a [b]sign so that we may
see, and believe You? What work
do You perform? 31 [a]Our fathers ate
the manna in the wilderness; as it is
written, '[b]HE GAVE THEM BREAD FROM
HEAVEN TO EAT.'" 32 Jesus then said
to them, "Truly, truly, I say to you,
Moses has not given you the bread
from heaven, but My Father gives you
the true bread from heaven. 33 For the
bread of God is [1]that which [a]comes
down from heaven and gives life to
the world." 34 Then they said to Him,
"Lord, always [a]give us this bread."
35 Jesus said to them, "[a]I am the
bread of life. He who comes to Me
will never hunger, and he who be-
lieves in Me [b]will never thirst. 36 But
[a]I said to you that you have seen Me,
and yet do not believe. 37 [a]All that the
Father gives Me will come to Me, and
the one who comes to Me I will never
cast out. 38 For [a]I have come down
from heaven, [b]not to do My own will,
but [c]the will of Him who [d]sent Me.
39 Now this is the will of Him who
sent Me, that of [a]all that He has given
Me I [b]lose nothing, but [c]raise it up on
the last day. 40 For this is the will of
My Father, that everyone who [a]sees
the Son and [b]believes in Him will
have eternal life, and I Myself will
[c]raise him up on the last day."

### *Words to the Jews*

41 [a]Therefore the Jews were grum-
bling about Him, because He said, "I
am the bread that [b]came down from
heaven." 42 They were saying, "[a]Is not
this Jesus, the son of Joseph, whose
father and mother [b]we know? How
does He now say, '[c]I have come down
from heaven'?" 43 Jesus answered and
said to them, "Stop grumbling among
yourselves. 44 No one can come to
Me unless the Father who sent Me
[a]draws him; and I will [b]raise him up
on the last day. 45 It is written [a]in the
prophets, '[b]AND THEY SHALL ALL BE
[c]TAUGHT BY GOD.' Everyone who has
heard and learned from the Father
comes to Me. 46 [a]Not that anyone
has seen the Father, except the One
who is from God; He has seen the
Father. 47 Truly, truly, I say to you, he
who believes [a]has eternal life. 48 [a]I
am the bread of life. 49 [a]Your fathers

---

**6:26** [a]Jn 6:24 [b]Jn 6:2, 14, 30 **6:27** [a]Is 55:2 [b]Jn 3:15f; 4:14; 6:40, 47, 54; 10:28; 17:2f [c]Mt 8:20; Jn 6:53, 62 [d]*Jn 3:33* **6:29** [a]1Th 1:3; Jas 2:22; 1Jn 3:23; Rev 2:26 [b]Jn 3:17 **6:30** [a]Mt 12:38 [b]Jn 6:2, 14, 26 **6:31** [a]Ex 16:4, 15, 21; Nu 11:8; Jn 6:49, 58 [b]Ps 78:24; Ex 16:4, 15; Ne 9:15; Ps 105:40 **6:33** [a]Jn 6:41, 50 [1]Or *He who comes* **6:34** [a]Jn 4:15 **6:35** [a]Jn 6:48, 51 [b]Jn 4:14 **6:36** [a]Jn 6:26 **6:37** [a]Jn 6:39; 17:2, 24 **6:38** [a]Jn 3:13 [b]Mt 26:39 [c]Jn 4:34; 5:30 [d]Jn 6:29 **6:39** [a]Jn 6:37; 17:2, 24 [b]Jn 17:12; 18:9 [c]Mt 10:15; Jn 6:40, 44, 54; 11:24 **6:40** [a]Jn 12:45; 14:17, 19 [b]Jn 3:16 [c]Mt 10:15; Jn 6:39, 44, 54; 11:24 **6:41** [a]Jn 1:19; 6:52 [b]Jn 6:33, 51, 58 **6:42** [a]Lk 4:22 [b]Jn 7:27f [c]Jn 6:38, 62 **6:44** [a]Jer 31:3; Hos 11:4; Jn 6:65; 12:32 [b]Jn 6:39 **6:45** [a]Ac 7:42; 13:40; Heb 8:11 [b]Is 54:13; Jer 31:34 [c]Php 3:15; 1Th 4:9; 1Jn 2:27 **6:46** [a]Jn 1:18 **6:47** [a]Jn 3:36; 5:24; 6:51, 58; 11:26 **6:48** [a]Jn 6:35, 51 **6:49** [a]Jn 6:31, 58

ate the manna in the wilderness, and
they died. **50** This is the bread which
[a]comes down from heaven, so that
one may eat of it and [b]not die. **51** [a]I
am the living bread that [b]came down
from heaven; if anyone eats of this
bread, [c]he will live forever; and also
the bread which I will give [d]for the
life of the world is [e]My flesh."
**52** [a]Then the Jews [b]*began to* argue
with one another, saying, "How can
this man give us *His* flesh to eat?"
**53** So Jesus said to them, "Truly, truly,
I say to you, unless you eat the flesh
of [a]the Son of Man and drink His
blood, you have no life in yourselves.
**54** He who eats My flesh and drinks
My blood has eternal life, and I will
[a]raise him up on the last day. **55** For
My flesh is true food, and My blood
is true drink. **56** He who eats My flesh
and drinks My blood [a]abides in Me,
and I in him. **57** As the [a]living Father
[b]sent Me, and I live because of the
Father, so he who eats Me, he also will
live because of Me. **58** This is the bread
which [a]came down out of heaven, not
as [b]the fathers ate and died. He who
eats this bread [c]will live forever."

### *Words to the Disciples*

**59** These things He said [a]in the syn-
agogue as He taught [b]in Capernaum.
**60** Therefore many of His [a]disci-
ples, when they heard *this* said,
"[b]*This is a difficult statement; who*
*can listen to it?*" **61** But Jesus, [a]know-
ing in Himself that His disciples were
grumbling at this, said to them,
"Does this [b]cause you to stumble?
**62** *What* then if you see [a]the Son of
Man [b]ascending to where He was
before? **63** [a]The Spirit is the One who
gives life; the flesh profits nothing;
[b]the words that I have spoken to you
are spirit and are life. **64** But there are
[a]some of you who do not believe."
For Jesus [b]knew from the beginning
who they were who did not believe,
and [c]who it was that would [1]betray
Him. **65** And He was saying, "For this
reason I have [a]said to you, that no
one can come to Me unless [b]it has
been granted him from the Father."

### *Peter Confesses Jesus Is the Christ*

**66** As a result of this many of His
[a]disciples [b,1]went away and were
not walking with Him anymore.
**67** So Jesus said to [a]the twelve, "Do
you also want to go?" **68** [a]Simon Peter
answered Him, "Lord, to whom shall
we go? You have [b]words of eternal
life. **69** And we have believed and
have come to know that You are [a]the
Holy One of God." **70** Jesus answered
them, "[a]Did I Myself not choose you,
[b]the twelve, and *yet* one of you is [c]a
devil?" **71** Now He was speaking of
Judas [a]*the son* of Simon Iscariot, for
he, [b]one of [c]the twelve, [1]was going
to betray Him.

---

**6:50** [a]Jn 6:33 [b]Jn 3:36; 5:24; 6:47, 51, 58; 11:26 **6:51** [a]Jn 6:35, 48 [b]Jn 6:41, 58 [c]Jn 3:36; 5:24; 6:47, 58; 11:26 [d]Jn 1:29; 3:14f; Heb 10:10; 1Jn 4:10 [e]Jn 6:53-56 **6:52** [a]Jn 1:19; 6:41 [b]Jn 9:16; 10:19 **6:53** [a]Mt 8:20; Jn 6:27, 62 **6:54** [a]Jn 6:39 **6:56** [a]Jn 15:4f; 17:23; 1Jn 2:24; 3:24; 4:15f **6:57** [a]Mt 16:16; Jn 5:26 [b]Jn 3:17; 6:29, 38 **6:58** [a]Jn 6:33, 41, 51 [b]Jn 6:31, 49 [c]Jn 3:36; 5:24; 6:47, 51; 11:26 **6:59** [a]Mt 4:23 [b]Jn 6:24 **6:60** [a]Jn 2:2; 6:66; 7:3 [b]Jn 6:52 **6:61** [a]Jn 6:64 [b]Mt 11:6 **6:62** [a]Mt 8:20; Jn 6:27, 53 [b]Mk 16:19; Jn 3:13 **6:63** [a]2Co 3:6 [b]Jn 6:68 **6:64** [a]Jn 6:60, 66 [b]Jn 2:25 [c]Mt 10:4; Jn 6:71; 13:11 [1]Or *hand Him over* **6:65** [a]Jn 6:37, 44 [b]Mt 13:11; Jn 3:27 **6:66** [a]Jn 2:2; 7:3 [b]Jn 6:60, 64 [1]Lit *went away to what was previous* **6:67** [a]Mt 10:2; Jn 2:2; 6:70f; 20:24 **6:68** [a]Mt 16:16 [b]Jn 6:63; 12:49f; 17:8 **6:69** [a]Mk 1:24; 8:29; Lk 9:20 **6:70** [a]Jn 15:16, 19 [b]Mt 10:2; Jn 2:2; 6:71; 20:24 [c]Jn 8:44; 13:2, 27; 17:12 **6:71** [a]Jn 12:4; 13:2, 26 [b]Mk 14:10 [c]Mt 10:2; Jn 2:2; 6:70; 20:24 [1]Or *was intending to*

### *Jesus Teaches at the Feast of Booths*

7 And after these things Jesus [a]was
walking in Galilee, for He was
unwilling to walk in Judea because
[b]the Jews [c]were seeking to kill Him.
2 Now the feast of the Jews, [a]the Feast
of Booths, was near. 3 Therefore
His [a]brothers said to Him, "Leave
here and go into Judea, so that Your
[b]disciples also may see Your works
which You are doing. 4 For no one
does anything in secret [1]when he
himself seeks to be *known* openly.
If You do these things, show Yourself
publicly to the world." 5 For not even
His [a]brothers were believing in Him.
6 So Jesus *said to them, "[a]My time is
not yet here, but your time is always
here. 7 [a]The world cannot hate you,
but it hates Me because I bear witness
about it, that [b]its deeds are evil. 8 Go
up to the feast yourselves; I am not
[1]yet going up to this feast because
[a]My time has not yet been fulfilled."
9 Having said these things to them,
He stayed in Galilee.

10 But when His [a]brothers had
gone up to the feast, then He Himself
also went up, not publicly, but as in
secret. 11 [a]So the Jews [b]were seeking
Him at the feast and saying, "Where
is He?" 12 And there was much grum-
bling among the crowds concerning
Him; [a]some were saying, "He is a
good man"; others were saying, "No,
on the contrary, He leads the crowd
astray." 13 Yet no one was speaking
openly about Him for [a]fear of the
Jews.

14 But when it was now the mid-
dle of the feast Jesus went up into
the temple, and *began to* [a]teach.
15 [a]The Jews then were marveling,
saying, "How has this man [b]become
learned, not having been educated?"
16 So Jesus answered them and said,
"[a]My teaching is not Mine, but from
Him who sent Me. 17 [a]If anyone is
willing to do His will, he will know
about the teaching, whether it is of
God or I speak from Myself. 18 He
who speaks from himself [a]seeks his
own glory; but He who is seeking the
glory of the One who sent Him, He is
true, and there is no unrighteousness
in Him.

19 "[a]Did not Moses give you the
Law? And *yet* none of you does the
Law. Why do you [b]seek to kill Me?"
20 The crowd answered, "[a]You have
a demon! Who seeks to kill You?"
21 Jesus answered them, "I did [a]one
work, and you all marvel. 22 For
this reason [a]Moses has given you
circumcision (not because it is from
Moses, but from [b]the fathers), and
on *the* Sabbath you circumcise a
man. 23 [a]If a man receives circum-
cision on the Sabbath so that the
Law of Moses will not be broken, are
you angry with Me because I made
an entire man well on *the* Sabbath?
24 Do not [a]judge according to ap-
pearance, but [1]judge with righteous
judgment."

---

◆ **7:1** [a]Jn 4:3; 6:1; 11:54 [b]Jn 1:19; 7:11, 13, 15, 35 [c]Jn 5:18; 7:19; 8:37, 40; 11:53 **7:2** [a]Lv 23:34; Dt 16:13, 16; Zec 14:16-19 **7:3** [a]Mt 12:46; Mk 3:21; Jn 7:5, 10 [b]Jn 6:60 **7:4** [1]Lit *and* **7:5** [a]Mt 12:46; Mk 3:21; Jn 7:3, 10 **7:6** [a]Mt 26:18; Jn 2:4; 7:8, 30 **7:7** [a]Jn 15:18f [b]Jn 3:19f **7:8** [a]Jn 7:6 [1]Some early mss omit *yet* **7:10** [a]Mt 12:46; Mk 3:21; Jn 7:3, 5 **7:11** [a]Jn 7:13, 15, 35 [b]Jn 11:56 **7:12** [a]Jn 7:40-43 **7:13** [a]Jn 9:22; 12:42; 19:38; 20:19 **7:14** [a]Mt 26:55; Jn 7:28 **7:15** [a]Jn 1:19; 7:11, 13, 35 [b]Ac 26:24 **7:16** [a]Jn 3:11 **7:17** [a]Ps 25:9, 14; Pr 3:32; Da 12:10; Jn 3:21; 8:43f **7:18** [a]Jn 5:41; 8:50, 54; 12:43 **7:19** [a]Jn 1:17 [b]Mk 11:18; Jn 7:1 **7:20** [a]Mt 11:18; Jn 8:48f, 52; 10:20 **7:21** [a]Jn 5:2-9, 16; 7:23 **7:22** [a]Lv 12:3 [b]Ge 17:10ff; 21:4; Ac 7:8 **7:23** [a]Mt 12:2; Jn 5:9, 10 **7:24** [a]Lv 19:15; Is 11:3; Zec 7:9; Jn 8:15 [1]Lit *judge the righteous judgment*

25 So some of the people of Jeru-
salem were saying, "Is this not the
man whom they are seeking to kill?
26 And look, He is speaking openly,
and they are saying nothing to Him.
[a]Do the rulers truly know that this is
the [1]Christ? 27 However, [a]we know
where this man is from; but when-
ever the Christ comes, no one knows
where He is from." 28 Then Jesus
cried out in the temple, [a]teaching
and saying, "[b]You both know Me
and know where I am from; and [c]I
have not come of Myself, but He who
sent Me is true, whom you do not
know. 29 [a]I know Him, because [b]I am
from Him, and [c]He sent Me." 30 So
they [a]were seeking to seize Him;
[1]yet no man laid his hand on Him,
because His [b]hour had not yet come.
31 But [a]many of the crowd believed in
Him; and they were saying, "[b]When
the [1]Christ comes, will He do more
[c,2]signs than this man did?"
32 The Pharisees heard the crowd
[1]whispering these things about
Him, and the chief priests and the
Pharisees sent [a]officers to [b]seize
Him. 33 Therefore Jesus said, "[a]For a
little while longer I am with you, then
[b]I go to Him who sent Me. 34 [a]You
will seek Me, and will not find Me;
and where I am, you cannot come."
35 [a]The Jews then said to one anoth-
er, "[b]Where does this man intend to
go that we will not find Him? Is He
intending to go to [c]the Dispersion
among [d]the Greeks and teach the
Greeks? 36 What is this statement
that He said, '[a]You will seek Me, and
will not find Me; and where I am, you
cannot come'?"
37 Now on [a]the last day, the great
*day* of the feast, Jesus stood and cried
out, saying, "[b,1]If anyone is thirsty,
[2]let him come to Me and drink. 38 He
who believes in Me, [a]as the Scripture
said, 'From [1]his innermost being will
flow rivers of [b]living water.'" 39 But
this He spoke [a]of the Spirit, whom
those who believed in Him were
going to receive; for [b]the Spirit was
not yet *given*, because Jesus was not
yet [c]glorified.

### *Division of People over Jesus*

40 *Some* of the crowd therefore, when
they heard these words, were saying,
"This truly is [a]the Prophet." 41 Others
were saying, "This is the [1]Christ." Still
others were saying, "[a]*No*, for is the
[1]Christ going to come from Galilee?
42 Has not the Scripture said that the
Christ comes from [a]the seed of David
and from Bethlehem, the village
where David was?" 43 So [a]a division
occurred in the crowd because of
Him. 44 [a]Some of them were wanting
to seize Him, but no one laid hands
on Him.
45 The [a]officers then came to the
chief priests and Pharisees, and they

**7:26** [a]Lk 23:13; Jn 3:1 [1]Messiah **7:27** [a]Jn 6:42; 7:41f; 9:29 **7:28** [a]Jn 7:14 [b]Jn 6:42; 7:14f; 9:29 [c]Jn 8:42 **7:29** [a]Mt 11:27; Jn 8:55; 17:25 [b]Jn 6:46 [c]Jn 3:17 **7:30** [a]Mt 21:46; Jn 7:32, 44; 10:39 [b]Jn 7:6; 8:20 [1]Lit *and* **7:31** [a]Jn 2:23; 8:30; 10:42; 11:45; 12:11, 42 [b]Jn 7:26 [c]Jn 2:11 [1]Messiah [2]Or *attesting miracles* **7:32** [a]Mt 26:58; Jn 7:45f [b]Mt 12:14 [1]Or *grumbling* **7:33** [a]Jn 12:35; 13:33; 14:19; 16:16-19 [b]Jn 14:12, 28; 16:5, 10, 17, 28; 20:17 **7:34** [a]Jn 7:36; 8:21; 13:33 **7:35** [a]Jn 7:1 [b]Jn 8:22 [c]Ps 147:2; Is 11:12; 56:8; Zep 3:10; Jas 1:1; 1Pe 1:1 [d]Jn 12:20; Ac 14:1; 17:4; 18:4; Ro 1:16 **7:36** [a]Jn 7:34; 8:21; 13:33 **7:37** [a]Lv 23:36; Nu 29:35; Ne 8:18 [b]Jn 4:10, 14; 6:35 [1]vv 37-38 may also be read: *If anyone is thirsty,...let him come..., he who believes in me as...* [2]Or *let him keep coming to Me and let him keep drinking* **7:38** [a]Is 44:3; 55:1; 58:11 [b]Jn 4:10 [1]Lit *out of his belly* **7:39** [a]Joel 2:28; Jn 1:33 [b]Jn 20:22; Ac 1:4f; 2:4, 33; 19:2 [c]Jn 12:16, 23; 13:31f; 16:14; 17:1 **7:40** [a]Mt 21:11; Jn 1:21 **7:41** [a]Jn 1:46; 7:52 [1]Messiah **7:42** [a]Ps 89:4; Mic 5:2; Mt 1:1; 2:5f; Lk 2:4ff **7:43** [a]Jn 9:16; 10:19 **7:44** [a]Jn 7:30 **7:45** [a]Jn 7:32

said to them, "Why did you not bring
Him?" **46** The [a]officers answered,
"[b]Never has a man spoken like this!"
**47** The Pharisees then answered
them, "[a]Have you also been led
astray? **48** [a]Have any of [b]the rulers
or Pharisees believed in Him? **49** But
this crowd which does not know the
Law is accursed." **50** [a]Nicodemus (he
who came to Him before), being one
of them, *said to them, **51** "[a]Does our
Law judge a man unless it first hears
from him and knows what he is do-
ing?" **52** They answered him, "[a]Are
you also from Galilee? Search and see
that no prophet arises out of Galilee."
**53** [1][Everyone went to his home.

### *An Adulteress Forgiven*

**8** But Jesus went to [a]the Mount of
Olives. **2** Early in the morning
He came again into the temple, and
all the people were coming to Him;
and [a]He sat down and *began to* teach
them. **3** The scribes and the Pharisees
*brought a woman caught in adultery,
and having set her in the center *of the
court,* **4** they *said to Him, "Teacher,
this woman has been caught in
adultery, in the very act. **5** Now in the
Law [a]Moses commanded us to stone
such women; what then do You say?"
**6** They were saying this, [a]testing Him,
[b]so that they might have *evidence* to
accuse Him. But Jesus stooped down
and with His finger wrote on the
ground. **7** But when they persisted
in asking Him, [a]He straightened
up and said to them, "[b]Let him
who is without sin among you *be
the* [c]first to throw a stone at her."
**8** Again He stooped down and wrote
on the ground. **9** When they heard
it, they began *to* go out one by one,
beginning with the older ones, and
He was left alone, and the woman,
where she was, in the center *of the
court.* **10** [a]Straightening up, Jesus said
to her, "Woman, where are they? Did
no one condemn you?" **11** She said,
"No one, [1]Lord." And Jesus said, "[a]I
do not condemn you, either. Go, and
from now on [b]sin no more."]

### *I Am the Light of the World*

**12** Then Jesus again spoke to them,
saying, "[a]I am the Light of the world;
[b]he who follows Me will never walk
in the darkness, but will have the
Light of life." **13** So the Pharisees said
to Him, "[a]You are bearing witness
about Yourself; Your witness is not
[1]true." **14** Jesus answered and said to
them, "[a]Even if I bear witness about
Myself, My witness is [1]true, for I know
[b]where I came from and where I am
going; but [c]you do not know where
I come from or where I am going.
**15** [a]You judge [1]according to the flesh;
[b]I am not judging anyone. **16** But even
[a]if I do judge, My judgment is true;
for I am not alone *in it,* but I and
the Father who sent Me. **17** Even in
[a]your law it has been written that
the witness of [b]two men is [1]true.
**18** I am He who bears witness about

**7:46** [a]Jn 7:32 [b]Mt 7:28 **7:47** [a]Jn 7:12 **7:48** [a]Jn 12:42 [b]Lk 23:13; Jn 7:26 **7:50** [a]Jn 3:1; 19:39 **7:51** [a]Ex 23:1; Dt 17:6; 19:15; Pr 18:13; Ac 23:3 **7:52** [a]Jn 1:46; 7:41 **7:53** [1]Later mss add the story of the adulterous woman, numbering it as Jn 7:53–8:11 ◆ **8:1** [a]Mt 21:1 **8:2** [a]Mt 26:55; Jn 8:20 **8:5** [a]Lv 20:10; Dt 22:22f **8:6** [a]Mt 16:1; 19:3; 22:18, 35; Mk 8:11; 10:2; 12:15; Lk 10:25; 11:16 [b]Mk 3:2 **8:7** [a]Jn 8:10 [b]Mt 7:1; Ro 2:1 [c]Dt 17:7 **8:10** [a]Jn 8:7 **8:11** [a]Jn 3:17 [b]Jn 5:14 [1]Or *Sir* **8:12** [a]Jn 1:4; 9:5; 12:35 [b]Mt 5:14 **8:13** [a]Jn 5:31 [1]Or *valid* **8:14** [a]Jn 18:37; Rev 1:5; 3:14 [b]Jn 8:42; 13:3; 16:28 [c]Jn 7:28; 9:29 [1]Or *valid* **8:15** [a]1Sa 16:7; Jn 7:24 [b]Jn 3:17 [1]By a carnal standard **8:16** [a]Jn 5:30 **8:17** [a]Dt 17:6; 19:15 [b]Mt 18:16 [1]Valid or admissible

Myself, and [a]the Father who sent
Me bears witness about Me." **19** So
they were saying to Him, "Where is
Your Father?" Jesus answered, "You
know neither Me nor My Father;
[a]if you knew Me, you would know
My Father also." **20** These words He
spoke in [a]the treasury, as [b]He was
teaching in the temple; and no one
seized Him, because [c]His hour had
not yet come.

**21** Then He said again to them, "I
am going away, and [a]you will seek Me,
and [b]will die in your sin. Where I am
going, you cannot come." **22** So [a]the
Jews were saying, "Surely He will not
kill Himself, since He says, '[b]Where
I am going, you cannot come'?"
**23** And He was saying to them, "[a]You
are from below, I am from above.
[b]You are of this world, [c]I am not of
this world. **24** Therefore I said to you
that you [a]will die in your sins. For
unless you believe that [b,1]I am *He*,
[a]you will die in your sins." **25** So they
were saying to Him, "Who are You?"
Jesus said to them, "[1]What have I been
saying to you *from* the beginning? **26** I
have many things to say and to judge
concerning you, but [a]He who sent
Me is true; and [b]the things which I
heard from Him, these I am saying to
the world." **27** They did not know that
He had been speaking to them about
the Father. **28** So Jesus said, "When
you [a]lift up the Son of Man, then
you will know that [b,1]I am *He*, and [c]I
do nothing from Myself, but I speak
these things as the Father taught
Me. **29** And He who sent Me is with
Me; [a]He [1]has not left Me alone, for [b]I
always do the things that are pleasing
to Him." **30** As He was speaking these
things, [a]many believed in Him.

### *The Son Will Make You Free*

**31** So Jesus was saying to those Jews
who had believed Him, "[a]If you abide
in My word, *then* you are truly My
[b]disciples; **32** and [a]you will know the
truth, and [b]the truth will make you
free." **33** They answered Him, "[a]We
are Abraham's seed and have never
yet been enslaved to anyone. How
is it that You say, 'You will become
free'?"

**34** Jesus answered them, "Truly,
truly, I say to you, [a]everyone who
commits sin is the slave of sin.
**35** [a]And the slave does not remain in
the house forever; [b]the son does re-
main forever. **36** So if the Son [a]makes
you free, you will be free indeed. **37** I
know that you are [a]Abraham's seed;
yet [b]you are seeking to kill Me, be-
cause My word [1]has no place in you.
**38** I speak the things which I have
seen [1]with *My* Father; therefore you
also do the things which you heard
from [a]*your* father."

**39** They answered and said to Him,
"Abraham is [a]our father." Jesus *said

**8:18** [a]Jn 5:37; 1Jn 5:9 **8:19** [a]Jn 7:28; 8:55; 14:7, 9; 16:3 **8:20** [a]Mk 12:41, 43; Lk 21:1 [b]Jn 7:14; 8:2 [c]Jn 7:30 **8:21** [a]Jn 7:34 [b]Jn 8:24 **8:22** [a]Jn 1:19; 8:48, 52, 57 [b]Jn 7:35 **8:23** [a]Jn 3:31 [b]1Jn 4:5 [c]Jn 17:14, 16 **8:24** [a]Jn 8:21 [b]Mt 24:5; Mk 13:6; Lk 21:8; Jn 4:26; 8:28, 58; 13:19 [1]Cf. Ex 3:14; Is 43:10 *I AM HE* **8:25** [1]Or *That which I have been saying to you from the beginning* **8:26** [a]Jn 3:33; 7:28 [b]Jn 8:40; 12:49; 15:15 **8:28** [a]Jn 3:14; 12:32 [b]Mt 24:5; Mk 13:6; Lk 21:8; Jn 4:26; 8:24, 58; 13:19 [c]Jn 3:11; 5:19 [1]Lit *I AM* (v 24 note) **8:29** [a]Jn 8:16; 16:32 [b]Jn 4:34 [1]Or *did not leave* **8:30** [a]Jn 7:31 **8:31** [a]Jn 15:7; 2Jn 9 [b]Jn 2:2 **8:32** [a]Jn 1:14, 17 [b]Jn 8:36; Ro 8:2; 2Co 3:17; Ga 5:1, 13; Jas 2:12; 1Pe 2:16 **8:33** [a]Mt 3:9; Lk 3:8; Jn 8:37, 39 **8:34** [a]Ro 6:16; 2Pe 2:19 **8:35** [a]Ge 21:10; Ga 4:30 [b]Lk 15:31 **8:36** [a]Jn 8:32 **8:37** [a]Mt 3:9; Jn 8:39 [b]Jn 7:1; 8:40 [1]Or *makes no progress* **8:38** [a]Jn 8:41, 44 [1]Or *in the presence of* **8:39** [a]Mt 3:9; Jn 8:37

to them, "[b]If you are Abraham's
children, you would do the deeds
of Abraham. **40** But now [a]you are
seeking to kill Me, a man who has
[b]told you the truth, which I heard
from God. This Abraham did not do.
**41** You are doing the deeds of [a]your
father." They said to Him, "We were
not born of sexual immorality; [b]we
have one Father: God." **42** Jesus said
to them, "If God were your Father,
[a]you would love Me, [b]for I proceeded
forth and have come from God, for I
have [c]not even come of Myself, but
[d,1]He sent Me. **43** Why do you not
understand [a,1]what I am saying? *It is*
because you cannot [b]hear My word.
**44** [a]You are of [b]*your* father the devil,
and [c]you want to do the desires of
your father. [d]He was a murderer from
the beginning, and does not stand in
the truth because [e]there is no truth
in him. Whenever he speaks [1]a lie, he
[f]speaks from his own *nature*, for he
is a liar and the father of [2]lies. **45** But
because [a]I speak the truth, you do
not believe Me. **46** Which one of you
convicts Me of sin? If [a]I speak truth,
why do you not believe Me? **47** [a]He
who is of God hears the words of
God; for this reason you do not hear
*them*, because you are not of God."

**48** [a]The Jews answered and said
to Him, "Do we not say rightly that
You are a [b]Samaritan and [c]have a
demon?" **49** Jesus answered, "I do
not [a]have a demon, but I honor
My Father, and you dishonor Me.
**50** But [a]I do not seek My glory;
there is One who seeks and judges.
**51** Truly, truly, I say to you, if anyone
[a]keeps My word he will never [b]see
death—ever." **52** [a]The Jews said to
Him, "Now we know that You [b]have
a demon. Abraham died, and the
prophets *also*; and You say, 'If anyone
[c]keeps My word, he will never [d]taste
of death—ever.' **53** Surely You [a]are
not greater than our father Abraham
who died? The prophets died too;
whom do You make Yourself out *to
be*?" **54** Jesus answered, "[a]If I glorify
Myself, My glory is nothing; [b]it is My
Father who glorifies Me, of whom
you say, 'He is our God'; **55** and [a]you
have not known Him, [b]but I know
Him; and if I say that I do not know
Him, I will be [c]a liar like you, [b]but I
do know Him and [d]keep His word.
**56** [a]Your father Abraham [b]rejoiced
[1]to see My day, and he saw *it* and was
glad." **57** [a]So the Jews said to Him,
"You are not yet fifty years old, and
have You seen Abraham?" **58** Jesus
said to them, "Truly, truly, I say to
you, before Abraham was, [a]I am."
**59** Therefore they [a]picked up stones
to throw at Him, but Jesus [b,1]hid
Himself and went out of the temple.

### *Jesus Heals a Man Born Blind*

**9** As He passed by, He saw a man
blind from birth. **2** And His disci-
ples asked Him, saying, "[a]Rabbi, who

**8:39** [b]Ro 9:7; Ga 3:7 **8:40** [a]Jn 7:1; 8:37 [b]Jn 8:26 **8:41** [a]Jn 8:38, 44 [b]Dt 32:6; Is 63:16; 64:8
***8:42*** [a]1Jn 5:1 [b]Jn 13:3; 16:28, 30; 17:8 [c]Jn 7:28 [d]Jn 3:17 [1]Lit *that One* **8:43** [a]Jn 8:33, 39, 41 [b]Jn 5:25
[1]Or *My way of speaking* **8:44** [a]1Jn 3:8 [b]Jn 8:38, 41 [c]Jn 7:17 [d]Ge 3:4; 1Jn 3:8, 15 [e]1Jn 2:4 [f]Mt 12:34
[1]Lit *the lie* [2]Lit *it* **8:45** [a]Jn 18:37 **8:46** [a]Jn 18:37 **8:47** [a]1Jn 4:6 **8:48** [a]Jn 1:19 [b]Mt 10:5; Jn 4:9
[c]Jn 7:20 **8:49** [a]Jn 7:20 **8:50** [a]Jn 5:41; 8:54 **8:51** [a]Jn 8:55; 14:23; 15:20; 17:6 [b]Mt 16:28; Lk 2:26;
Jn 8:52; Heb 2:9; 11:5 **8:52** [a]Jn 1:19 [b]Jn 7:20 [c]Jn 8:55; 14:23; 15:20; 17:6 [d]Jn 8:51 **8:53** [a]Jn 4:12
**8:54** [a]Jn 8:50 [b]Jn 7:39 **8:55** [a]Jn 8:19; 15:21 [b]Jn 7:29 [c]Jn 8:44 [d]Jn 8:51; 15:10 **8:56** [a]Jn 8:37, 39
[b]Mt 13:17; Heb 11:13 [1]Lit *in order that he might see* **8:57** [a]Jn 1:19 **8:58** [a]Ex 3:14; Jn 1:1; 17:5, 24
**8:59** [a]Mt 12:14; Jn 10:31; 11:8 [b]Jn 12:36 [1]Lit *was hidden* ◆ **9:2** [a]Mt 23:7

sinned, [b]this man or his [c]parents, that he would be born blind?" **3** Jesus answered, "Neither this man nor his parents sinned, but *this was* so [a]that the works of God might be manifested in him. **4** We must work the works of Him who sent Me [a]as long as it is day; night is coming when no one can work. **5** While I am in the world, I am [a]the light of the world." **6** When He had said this, He [a]spat on the ground, made clay of the saliva, and rubbed the clay on his eyes, **7** and said to him, "Go, wash in [a]the pool of Siloam" (which is translated, Sent). So he went away and [b]washed, and [c]came *back* seeing. **8** Therefore the neighbors, and those who previously saw him as a beggar, were saying, "Is not this the one who used to [a]sit and beg?" **9** Others were saying, "This is he," *still* others were saying, "No, but he is like him." [1]He kept saying, "I am the one." **10** So they were saying to him, "How then were your eyes opened?" **11** He answered, "The man who is called Jesus made clay, and rubbed my eyes, and said to me, 'Go to [a]Siloam and wash'; so when I went away and washed, I received sight." **12** And they said to him, "Where is He?" He *said, "I do not know."

### *Controversy over the Man Born Blind*

**13** They *brought to the Pharisees the man who was formerly blind. **14** [a]Now it was a Sabbath on the day when Jesus made the clay and opened his eyes. **15** [a]So the Pharisees also were asking him again how he received his sight. And he said to them, "He applied clay to my eyes, and I washed, and I see." **16** So then some of the Pharisees were saying, "This man is not from God, because He [a]does not keep the Sabbath." But others were saying, "How can a sinful man do such [b,1]signs?" And [c]there was a division among them. **17** Therefore, they *said to the blind man [a]again, "What do you say about Him, since He opened your eyes?" And he said, "He is a [b]prophet."

**18** [a]Then, the Jews did not believe *it* of him that he was blind and had received sight, until they called the parents of the very one who had received his sight, **19** and questioned them, saying, "Is this your son, who you say was born blind? Then how does he now see?" **20** So his parents answered and said, "We know that this is our son, and that he was born blind; **21** but how he now sees, we do not know; or who opened his eyes, we do not know. Ask him; he is of age, he will speak for himself." **22** His parents said this because they [a]were afraid of the Jews; for the Jews [b]had already agreed that if anyone confessed Him to be [1]Christ, [c]he was to be put out of the synagogue. **23** For this reason his parents said, "[a]He is of age; ask him."

**24** Therefore, a second time they called the man who had been blind, and said to him, "[a]Give glory to God; we know that [b]this man is a sinner." **25** He then answered, "Whether He is a sinner, I do not know; one thing I do

---

**9:2** [b]Lk 13:2; Jn 9:34; Ac 28:4 [c]Ex 20:5 **9:3** [a]Jn 11:4 **9:4** [a]Jn 7:33; 11:9; 12:35; Ga 6:10 **9:5** [a]Mt 5:14; Jn 1:4; 8:12; 12:46 **9:6** [a]Mk 7:33; 8:23 **9:7** [a]Ne 3:15; Is 8:6; Lk 13:4; Jn 9:11 [b]2Ki 5:13f [c]Is 29:18; 35:5; 42:7; Mt 11:5; Jn 11:37 **9:8** [a]Ac 3:2, 10 **9:9** [1]Lit *That one* **9:11** [a]Jn 9:7 **9:14** [a]Jn 5:9 **9:15** [a]Jn 9:10 **9:16** [a]Mt 12:2; Lk 13:14; Jn 5:10; 7:23 [b]Jn 2:11 [c]Jn 6:52; 7:12, 43; 10:19 [1]Or *attesting miracles* **9:17** [a]Jn 9:15 [b]Dt 18:15; Mt 21:11 **9:18** [a]Jn 1:19; 9:22 **9:22** [a]Jn 7:13 [b]Jn 7:45-52 [c]Lk 6:22; Jn 12:42; 16:2 [1]The Messiah **9:23** [a]Jn 9:21 **9:24** [a]Jos 7:19; Ezr 10:11; Rev 11:13 [b]Jn 9:16

know, that though I was blind, now
I see." **26** So they said to him, "What
did He do to you? How did He open
your eyes?" **27** He answered them,
"[a]I told you already and you did not
[b]listen. Why do you want to listen
again? Do you want to become His
disciples too?" **28** And they reviled
him and said, "You are His disciple,
but [a]we are disciples of Moses. **29** We
know that God has spoken to Mo-
ses, but as for this man, [a]we do not
know where He is from." **30** The man
answered and said to them, "Well,
here is a marvelous thing, that you
do not know where He is from, and
He opened my eyes. **31** We know that
[a]God does not listen to sinners; but if
anyone is God-fearing and does His
will, He listens to him. **32** [1]Since the
beginning of time it has never been
heard that anyone opened the eyes
of a person born blind. **33** [a]If this
man were not from God, He could
do nothing." **34** They answered and
said to him, "[a]You were born entirely
in sins, and are you teaching us?" So
they [b]put him out.

### *Jesus Affirms His Deity*

**35** Jesus heard that they had [a]put him
out, and after finding him, He said,
"Do you believe in the [b]Son of Man?"
**36** He answered and said, "[a]Who is
He, [1]Lord, that I may believe in Him?"
**37** Jesus said to him, "You have both
seen Him, and [a]He is the one who
is talking with you." **38** And he said,
"Lord, I believe." And he [a]worshiped
Him. **39** And Jesus said, "[a]For judg-
ment I came into this world, so that
[b]those who do not see may see, and
that [c]those who see may become
blind." **40** Some of the Pharisees who
were with Him heard these things
and said to Him, "[a]Are we blind too?"
**41** Jesus said to them, "[a]If you were
blind, you would have no sin; but
now *that* you say, '[b]We see,' your
sin remains.

### *I Am the Good Shepherd*

**10** "Truly, truly, I say to you, he
who does not enter by the door
into the fold of the sheep, but climbs
up some other way, he is [a]a thief and
a robber. **2** But he who enters by the
door is [a]a shepherd of the sheep. **3** To
him the doorkeeper opens, and the
sheep hear [a]his voice, and he calls
his own sheep by name and [b]leads
them out. **4** When he brings all his
own out, he goes ahead of them, and
the sheep follow him because they
know [a]his voice. **5** A stranger they
will never follow, but will flee from
him, because they do not know [a]the
voice of strangers." **6** This [a]figure of
speech Jesus spoke to them, but they
did not understand what those things
were which He had been saying to
them.

**7** So Jesus said to them again, "Tru-
ly, truly, I say to you, I am [a]the door
of the sheep. **8** All who came before
Me are [a]thieves and robbers, but the
sheep did not hear them. **9** [a]I am the
door; if anyone enters through Me, he

---

**9:27** [a]Jn 9:15 [b]Jn 5:25 **9:28** [a]Jn 5:45; Ro 2:17 **9:29** [a]Jn 8:14 **9:31** [a]Job 27:8f; 35:13; Ps 34:15f; 66:18; 145:19; Pr 15:29; 28:9; Is 1:15; Jas 5:16ff **9:32** [1]Lit *From the age it was not heard* **9:33** [a]Jn 3:2; 9:16 **9:34** [a]Jn 9:2 [b]Jn 9:22, 35; 3Jn 10 **9:35** [a]Jn 9:22, 34; 3Jn 10 [b]Mt 4:3 **9:36** [a]Ro 10:14 [1]Or *Sir* **9:37** [a]Jn 4:26 **9:38** [a]Mt 8:2 **9:39** [a]Jn 3:19; 5:22, 27 [b]Lk 4:18 [c]Mt 13:13; 15:14 **9:40** [a]Ro 2:19 **9:41** [a]Jn 15:22, 24 [b]Pr 26:12 ♦ **10:1** [a]Jn 10:8 **10:2** [a]Jn 10:11f **10:3** [a]Jn 10:4f, 16, 27 [b]Jn 10:9 **10:4** [a]Jn 10:5, 16, 27 **10:5** [a]Jn 10:4, 16, 27 **10:6** [a]Jn 16:25, 29; 2Pe 2:22 **10:7** [a]Jn 10:1f, 9 **10:8** [a]Jer 23:1f; Eze 34:2ff; Jn 10:1 **10:9** [a]Jn 10:1f, 9

will be saved, and will go in and out and find pasture. **10** The thief comes only to steal and kill and destroy; I came that they [a]may have life, and [1]have *it* abundantly.

**11** "[a]I am the good shepherd; the good shepherd [b]lays down His life for the sheep. **12** He who is a hired hand, and not a [a]shepherd, who is not the owner of the sheep, sees the wolf coming, and leaves the sheep and flees—and the wolf snatches and scatters them— **13** because he is a hired hand and is not concerned about the sheep. **14** [a]I am the good shepherd, and [b]I know My own and My own know Me, **15** even as [a]the Father knows Me and I know the Father; and [b]I lay down My life for the sheep. **16** And I have [a]other sheep, which are not from this fold; I must bring them also, and they will hear My voice; and they will become [b]one flock *with* [c]one shepherd. **17** For this reason the Father loves Me, because I [a]lay down My life so that I may take it again. **18** [a]No one [1]takes it away from Me, but from Myself, I [b]lay it down. I have authority to lay it down, and I have authority to take it up again. [c]This commandment I received from My Father."

**19** [a]A division occurred again among the Jews because of these words. **20** And many of them were saying, "He [a]has a demon and [b]is insane. Why do you listen to Him?" **21** Others were saying, "These are not the words of someone [a]demon-possessed. [b]Can a demon open the eyes of the blind?"

### *I and the Father Are One*

**22** At that time the Feast of the Dedication took place at Jerusalem; **23** it was winter, and Jesus was walking in the temple in the Portico of [a]Solomon. **24** [a]The Jews then gathered around Him, and were saying to Him, "How long [1]will You keep us in suspense? If You are the [2]Christ, tell us [b]openly." **25** Jesus answered them, "[a]I told you, and you do not believe; [b]the works that I do in My Father's name, these bear witness of Me. **26** But you do not believe because [a]you are not of My sheep. **27** My sheep [a]hear My voice, and [b]I know them, and they follow Me; **28** and I give [a]eternal life to them, and they will never perish—ever; and [b]no one will snatch them out of My hand. **29** [1]My Father, who has given *them* to Me, is greater than all; and no one is able to snatch *them* out of the Father's hand. **30** [a]I and the Father are [1]one."

**31** The Jews [a]picked up stones again to stone Him. **32** Jesus answered them, "I showed you many good works from the Father; for which of them are you stoning Me?" **33** The Jews answered Him, "For a good work we do not stone You, but for [a]blasphemy; and because You,

**10:10** [a]Jn 5:40 [1]Or *have abundance* **10:11** [a]Is 40:11; Eze 34:11-16, 23; Jn 10:14; Heb 13:20; 1Pe 5:4; Rev 7:17 [b]Jn 10:15, 17, 18; 15:13; 1Jn 3:16 **10:12** [a]Jn 10:2 **10:14** [a]Jn 10:11 [b]Jn 10:27 **10:15** [a]Mt 11:27; Lk 10:22 [b]Jn 10:11, 17, 18 **10:16** [a]Is 56:8 [b]Jn 11:52; 17:20f; Eph 2:13-18; 1Pe 2:25 [c]Eze 34:23; 37:24 **10:17** [a]Jn 10:11, 15, 18 **10:18** [a]Mt 26:53; Jn 2:19; 5:26 [b]Jn 10:11, 15, 17 [c]Jn 14:31; 15:10; Php 2:8; Heb 5:8 [1]Some mss *has taken* **10:19** [a]Jn 7:43; 9:16 **10:20** [a]Jn 7:20 [b]Mk 3:21 **10:21** [a]Mt 4:24 [b]Ex 4:11; Jn 9:32f **10:23** [a]Ac 3:11; 5:12 **10:24** [a]Jn 1:19; 10:31, 33 [b]Lk 22:67; Jn 16:25 [1]Lit *do You lift up our soul* [2]Messiah **10:25** [a]Jn 8:56, 58 [b]Jn 5:36; 10:38 **10:26** [a]Jn 8:47 **10:27** [a]Jn 10:4, 16 [b]Jn 10:14 **10:28** [a]Jn 17:2f; 1Jn 2:25; 5:11 [b]Jn 6:37, 39 **10:29** [1]One early ms *What My Father has given Me is greater than all* **10:30** [a]Jn 17:21ff [1]Or *a unity, one essence* **10:31** [a]Jn 8:59 **10:33** [a]Lv 24:16

being a man, [b]make Yourself God."
**34** Jesus answered them, "Has it not
been written in [a]your [b]Law, '[c]I SAID,
YOU ARE GODS'? **35** If he called them
gods, to whom the word of God
came (and the Scripture cannot be
broken), **36** do you say of Him, whom
the Father [a]sanctified and [b]sent into
the world, 'You are blaspheming,'
because I said, '[c]I am the Son of
God'? **37** [a]If I do not do the works of
My Father, do not believe Me; **38** but if
I do them, though you do not believe
Me, believe [a]the works, so that you
may know and continue knowing
that [b]the Father is in Me, and I in
the Father." **39** Therefore [a]they were
seeking again to seize Him, and [b]He
eluded their grasp.

**40** And He went away [a]again be-
yond the Jordan to the place where
John was first baptizing, and He was
staying there. **41** And many came
to Him and were saying, "While
John did no [a]sign, yet [b]everything
John said about this man was true."
**42** [a]And many believed in Him there.

### *The Death and Resurrection of Lazarus*

**11** Now a certain man was sick,
Lazarus from [a]Bethany, the vil-
lage of Mary and her sister [b]Martha.
**2** And it was *the* Mary who [a]anointed
[b]the Lord with perfume, and wiped
His feet with her hair, whose brother
Lazarus was sick. **3** So the sisters sent
to Him, saying, "[a]Lord, behold, [b]he
whom You love is sick." **4** But when
Jesus heard *this*, He said, "This
sickness is not to end in death, but
is for [a]the glory of God, so that the
Son of God may be glorified by it."
**5** Now Jesus loved [a]Martha and her
sister and Lazarus. **6** So when He
heard that he was sick, He then
stayed two days in the place where
He was. **7** Then after this He *said
to the disciples, "[a]Let us go to Judea
again." **8** The disciples *said to Him,
"[a]Rabbi, the Jews were just now seek-
ing [b]to stone You, and are You going
there again?" **9** Jesus answered, "[a]Are
there not twelve hours in the day? If
anyone walks in the day, he does not
stumble, because he sees the light
of this world. **10** But if anyone walks
in the night, he stumbles, because
the light is not in him." **11** He said
these things, and after that He *said
to them, "Our [a]friend Lazarus [b]has
fallen asleep; but I go, so that I may
awaken him." **12** The disciples then
said to Him, "Lord, if he has fallen
asleep, he will [1]be saved *from his
sickness*." **13** Now [a]Jesus had spoken
of his death, but they thought that
He was speaking of [1]actual sleep.
**14** So Jesus then said to them [1]plainly,
"Lazarus is dead, **15** and I am glad for
your sakes that I was not there, so
that you may believe; but let us go to
him." **16** [a]Therefore Thomas, who is
called [b,1]Didymus, said to *his* fellow
disciples, "Let us also go, so that we
may die with Him."

---

**10:33** [b]Jn 5:18 **10:34** [a]Jn 8:17 [b]Jn 12:34; 15:25; Ro 3:19; 1Co 14:21 [c]Ps 82:6 **10:36** [a]Jer 1:5; Jn 6:69 [b]Jn 3:17 [c]Jn 5:17f; 10:30 **10:37** [a]Jn 10:25; 15:24 **10:38** [a]Jn 10:25; 14:11 [b]Jn 14:10f, 20; 17:21, 23 **10:39** [a]Jn 7:30 [b]Lk 4:30; Jn 8:59 **10:40** [a]Jn 1:28 **10:41** [a]Jn 2:11 [b]Jn 1:27, 30, 34; 3:27-30 **10:42** [a]Jn 7:31 ◆**11:1** [a]Mt 21:17; Jn 11:18 [b]Lk 10:38; Jn 11:5, 19ff **11:2** [a]Jn 12:3 [b]Lk 7:13; Jn 11:3, 21, 32; 13:13f **11:3** [a]Lk 7:13; Jn 11:2, 21, 32; 13:13f [b]Jn 11:5, 11, 36 **11:4** [a]Jn 9:3; 10:38; 11:40 **11:5** [a]Jn 11:1 **11:7** [a]Jn 10:40 **11:8** [a]Mt 23:7 [b]Jn 8:59; 10:31 **11:9** [a]Lk 13:33; Jn 9:4; 12:35 **11:11** [a]Jn 11:3 [b]Mt 27:52; Mk 5:39; Jn 11:13; Ac 7:60 **11:12** [1]Or *recover* **11:13** [a]Mt 9:24; Lk 8:52 [1]Lit *the slumber of sleep* **11:14** [1]Or *openly* **11:16** [a]Mt 10:3; Mk 3:18; Lk 6:15; Jn 14:5; 20:26-28; Ac 1:13 [b]Jn 20:24; 21:2 [1]The Twin

17 So when Jesus came, He found
that he had already been in the tomb
[a]four days. 18 Now [a]Bethany was near
Jerusalem, about [1]fifteen stadia away;
19 and many of [a]the Jews had come
to [b]Martha and Mary, [c]to console
them about their brother. 20 [a]Martha
therefore, when she heard that Jesus
was coming, went to meet Him, but
[a]Mary was sitting in the house.
21 Martha then said to Jesus, "[a]Lord,
[b]if You had been here, my brother
would not have died. 22 But even now
I know that [a]whatever You ask from
God, God will give You." 23 Jesus *said
to her, "Your brother will rise again."
24 Martha *said to Him, "[a]I know that
he will rise again in the resurrection
on the last day." 25 Jesus said to her,
"[a]I am the resurrection and the life;
he who believes in Me will live even
if he dies, 26 and everyone who
lives and believes in Me [a]will never
die—ever. Do you believe this?"
27 She *said to Him, "Yes, Lord; I have
believed that You are [a]the [1]Christ, the
Son of God, [b,2]the One who comes
into the world."

28 And when she had said this,
she [a]went away and called Mary her
sister, saying secretly, "[b]The Teacher
is here and is calling for you." 29 And
when she heard it, she *got up quick-
ly and was coming to Him.

30 Now Jesus had not yet come into
the village, but [a]was still in the place
where Martha met Him. 31 [a]Then the
Jews—who were with her in the
house and [b]consoling her—when
they saw that Mary rose up quickly
and went out, they followed her,
thinking that she was going to the
tomb to cry there. 32 Therefore,
when Mary came where Jesus was,
she saw Him, and fell at His feet,
saying to Him, "[a]Lord, [b]if You had
been here, my brother would not
have died." 33 When Jesus therefore
saw her crying, and [a]the Jews who
came with her *also* crying, He [b]was
[1]deeply moved in spirit and [c,2]was
troubled, 34 and said, "Where have
you laid him?" They *said to Him,
"Lord, come and see." 35 Jesus [a]wept.
36 So [a]the Jews were saying, "See
how He [b]loved him!" 37 But some
of them said, "Could not this man,
who [a]opened the eyes of the blind
man, [1]have kept this man also from
dying?"

38 So Jesus, again being [1]deeply
moved within, *came to the tomb.
Now it was a [a]cave, and a stone
was lying against it. 39 Jesus *said,
"Remove the stone." Martha, the
sister of the deceased, *said to Him,
"Lord, by this time he smells, for he
has been *dead* [a]four days." 40 Jesus
*said to her, "[a]Did I not say to you
that if you believe, you will see the
glory of God?" 41 So they removed
the [a]stone. Then Jesus [b]raised His
eyes, and said, "[c]Father, I thank You
that You have heard Me. 42 And I

**11:17** [a]Jn 11:39 **11:18** [a]Jn 11:1 [1]Approx. 1.7 mi. or 2.7 km, a stadion was approx. 607 ft. or 185 m **11:19** [a]Jn 1:19; 11:8 [b]Jn 11:1 [c]1Sa 31:13; 1Chr 10:12; Job 2:11; Jn 11:31 **11:20** [a]Lk 10:38-42 **11:21** [a]Jn 11:2 [b]Jn 11:32, 37 **11:22** [a]Jn 9:31; 11:41f **11:24** [a]Da 12:2; Jn 5:28f; Ac 24:15 **11:25** [a]Jn 1:4; 5:26; 6:39f; Rev 1:18 **11:26** [a]Jn 6:47, 50, 51; 8:51 **11:27** [a]Mt 16:16; Lk 2:11 [b]Jn 6:14 [1]Messiah [2]Or *the Coming One* **11:28** [a]Jn 11:30 [b]Mt 26:18; Mk 14:14; Lk 22:11; Jn 13:13 **11:30** [a]Jn 11:20 **11:31** [a]Jn 11:19, 33 [b]Jn 11:19 **11:32** [a]Jn 11:2 [b]Jn 11:21 **11:33** [a]Jn 11:19 [b]Jn 11:38 [c]Jn 12:27; 13:21 [1]Or *indignant* [2]Or *disturbed* **11:35** [a]Lk 19:41; Jn 11:33 **11:36** [a]Jn 11:19 [b]Jn 11:3 **11:37** [a]Jn 9:7 [1]Lit *have caused that this man also not die* **11:38** [a]Mt 27:60; Mk 15:46; Lk 24:2; Jn 20:1 [1]Or *indignant* **11:39** [a]Jn 11:17 **11:40** [a]Jn 11:4, 23ff **11:41** [a]Mt 27:60; Mk 15:46; Lk 24:2; Jn 20:1 [b]Jn 17:1; Ac 7:55 [c]Mt 11:25

knew that You always hear Me; but
[a]because of the crowd standing
around I said this, so that they may
believe that [b]You sent Me." **43** And
when He had said these things, He
cried out with a loud voice, "Lazarus,
come forth." **44** The man who had
died came forth, [a]bound hand and
foot with wrappings, and [b]his face
was wrapped around with a cloth.
Jesus *said to them, "Unbind him,
and let him go."

**45** [a]Therefore many of the Jews
[b]who came to Mary, and [c]saw what
He had done, believed in Him. **46** But
some of them went to the [a]Pharisees
and told them the things which Jesus
had done.

### *The Leaders Plot to Kill Jesus*

**47** Therefore [a]the chief priests and
the Pharisees [b]gathered the [c,1]San-
hedrin together, and were saying,
"What are we doing? For this man
is doing many [d,2]signs. **48** If we let
Him *go on* like this, all will believe
in Him, and the Romans will come
and take away both our [a]place and
our nation." **49** But one of them,
[a]Caiaphas, [b]who was high priest
that year, said to them, "You know
nothing at all, **50** nor do you take
into account that [a]it is better for
you that one man should die for the
people, and that the whole nation
not perish." **51** Now he did not say
this from himself, but [a]being high
priest that year, he prophesied that
Jesus was going to die for the nation,
**52** and not for the nation only, but
in order that He might also [a]gather
together into one the children of God
who are scattered abroad. **53** So from
that day on they [a]planned together
to kill Him.

**54** Therefore Jesus [a]no longer
continued to walk openly among the
Jews, but went away from there to
the region near the wilderness, into
a city called [b]Ephraim; and there He
stayed with the disciples.

**55** Now [a]the Passover of the Jews
was near, and many went up to Je-
rusalem from the region before the
Passover [b]to purify themselves. **56** So
they [a]were seeking Jesus, and were
saying to one another as they stood
in the temple, "What do you think?
That He will not come to the feast at
all?" **57** Now [a]the chief priests and
the Pharisees had given orders that if
anyone knew where He was, he was
to report it, so that they might seize
Him.

### *Mary Anoints Jesus with Costly Perfume*

**12** [a]Jesus, therefore, six days
before [b]the Passover, came to
[c]Bethany where Lazarus was, whom
Jesus had raised from the dead. **2** So
they made Him a supper there, and
[a]Martha was serving; and Lazarus
was one of those reclining *at the
table* with Him. **3** [a]Mary then took
a [1]litra of [b]perfume of very costly
pure nard, and anointed the feet of
Jesus and wiped His feet with her

**11:42** [a]Jn 12:30; 17:21 [b]Jn 3:17 **11:44** [a]Jn 19:40 [b]Jn 20:7 **11:45** [a]Jn 7:31 [b]Jn 11:19; 12:17f [c]Jn 2:23
**11:46** [a]Jn 7:32, 45; 11:57 **11:47** [a]Jn 7:32, 45; 11:57 [b]Mt 26:3 [c]Mt 5:22 [d]Jn 2:11 [1]Or *Council* [2]Or *attesting miracles* **11:48** [a]Mt 24:15 **11:49** [a]Mt 26:3 [b]Jn 11:51; 18:13 **11:50** [a]Jn 18:14 **11:51** [a]Jn 18:13
**11:52** [a]Jn 10:16 **11:53** [a]Mt 26:4 **11:54** [a]Jn 7:1 [b]2Chr 13:19 mg **11:55** [a]Mt 26:1f; Mk 14:1; Lk 22:1; Jn 2:13; 12:1; 13:1 [b]Nu 9:10; 2Chr 30:17f; Jn 18:28 **11:56** [a]Jn 7:11 **11:57** [a]Jn 11:47 ◆ **12:1** [a]Jn 12:1-8: *Mt 26:6-13; Mk 14:3-9; Lk 7:37-39* [b]Jn 11:55; 12:20 [c]Mt 21:17; Jn 11:43f **12:2** [a]Lk 10:38 **12:3** [a]Lk 7:37f; Jn 11:2 [b]Mk 14:3 [1]A Roman pound, approx. 12 oz. or 340 gm

hair; and the house was filled with
the fragrance of the perfume. **4** But
[a]Judas Iscariot, one of His disciples,
who was going to [1]betray Him, *said,
**5** "Why was this perfume not sold for
[1]three hundred denarii and given to
the poor?" **6** Now he said this, not
because he was concerned about the
poor, but because he was a thief, and
as he [a]had the money box, he used
to take from [b]what was put into it.
**7** Therefore Jesus said, "Let her alone,
so that she may keep it for [a]the day
of My burial. **8** [a]For you always have
the poor with you, but you do not
always have Me."

**9** Then the [a]large crowd from the
Jews learned that He was there. And
they came, not because of Jesus only,
but that they might also see Lazarus,
[b]whom He raised from the dead.
**10** But the chief priests planned to put
Lazarus to death also; **11** because [a]on
account of him [b]many of the Jews
were going away and were believing
in Jesus.

### *The Triumphal Entry*

**12** On the next day [a]the large crowd
who had come to [b]the feast, when
they heard that Jesus was coming to
Jerusalem, **13** took the branches of
the palm trees and went out to meet
Him, and *began to* shout, "[a]Hosan-
na! BLESSED IS HE WHO COMES IN THE
NAME OF THE [1]LORD, even the [b]King of
Israel." **14** And Jesus, finding a young
donkey, sat on it; as it is written,
**15** "[a]FEAR NOT, DAUGHTER OF ZION;
BEHOLD, YOUR KING IS COMING, SEATED
ON A DONKEY'S COLT." **16** [a]These things
His disciples did not understand at
the first; but when Jesus [b]was glo-
rified, then they remembered that
these things were written about Him,
and that they had done these things
to Him. **17** So [a]the crowd, who was
with Him when He called Lazarus
out of the tomb and raised him from
the dead, continued to bear witness
*about Him.* **18** [a]For this reason
also the crowd went and met Him,
[b]because they heard that He had
done this [1]sign. **19** So the Pharisees
said to one another, "You see that
you are gaining nothing; look, the
world has gone after Him."

### *Some Greeks Seek Jesus*

**20** Now there were some [a]Greeks
among those who were going up
to worship at [b]the feast; **21** these
then came to [a]Philip, who was from
[b]Bethsaida of Galilee, and *began
to* ask him, saying, "Sir, we wish
to see Jesus." **22** Philip *came and
*told [a]Andrew; Andrew and Philip
*came and *told Jesus. **23** And Jesus
*answered them, saying, "[a]The hour
has come for the Son of Man to [b]be
glorified. **24** Truly, truly, I say to you,
[a]unless a grain of wheat falls into the
earth and dies, it remains alone; but
if it dies, it bears much fruit. **25** [a]He
who loves his [1]life loses it, and he
who [b]hates his [1]life in this world will

---

**12:4** [a]Jn 6:71 [1]Or *hand Him over* **12:5** [1]Approx. 11 months' wages, a denarius was a laborer's daily wage **12:6** [a]Jn 13:29 [b]Lk 8:3 **12:7** [a]Jn 19:40 **12:8** [a]Dt 15:11; Mt 26:11; Mk 14:7 **12:9** [a]Mk 12:37; Jn 12:12 mg [b]Jn 11:43f; 12:1, 17f **12:11** [a]Jn 11:45f; 12:18 [b]Jn 7:31; 11:42 **12:12** [a]Jn 12:12-15: *Mt 21:4-9; Mk 11:7-10; Lk 19:35-38* [b]Jn 12:1 **12:13** [a]Ps 118:26 [b]Jn 1:49 [1]In OT, Yahweh, cf. Ps 118:26 **12:15** [a]Zec 9:9 **12:16** [a]Mk 9:32; Jn 2:22; 14:26 [b]Jn 7:39; 12:23 **12:17** [a]Jn 11:42 **12:18** [a]Lk 19:37; Jn 12:12 [b]Jn 12:11 [1]Or *attesting miracle* **12:20** [a]Jn 7:35 [b]Jn 12:1 **12:21** [a]Jn 1:44 [b]Mt 11:21 **12:22** [a]Jn 1:44 **12:23** [a]Mt 26:45; Mk 14:35, 41; Jn 13:1; 17:1 [b]Jn 7:39; 12:16; 13:32 **12:24** [a]Ro 14:9; 1Co 15:36 **12:25** [a]Mt 10:39; 16:25; Mk 8:35; Lk 9:24; 17:33 [b]Lk 14:26 [1]Lit *soul*

keep it to life eternal. **26** If anyone
[1]serves Me, he must follow Me; and
[a]where I am, there My servant will be
also; if anyone [1]serves Me, the Father
will [b]honor him.

### *The Son of Man Must Be Lifted Up*

**27** "[a]Now [b]MY SOUL HAS BECOME DIS-
MAYED; and what shall I say, '[c]Father,
[d]SAVE ME from [e]this hour'? But for
this purpose I came to this hour.
**28** [a]Father, glorify Your name." Then
a [b]voice came from heaven: "I have
both glorified it, and will glorify it
again." **29** So the crowd *of people* who
stood by and heard it were saying that
it had thundered; others were say-
ing, "[a]An angel has spoken to Him."
**30** Jesus answered and said, "[a]This
voice has not come for My sake, but
for your sake. **31** [a]Now judgment is
upon this world; now [b]the ruler of
this world will be cast out. **32** And
I, if I [a]am lifted up from the earth,
will [b]draw all men to Myself." **33** But
He was saying this [a]to indicate the
kind of death by which He was about
to die. **34** The crowd then answered
Him, "We have heard from [a]the Law
that [b]the [1]Christ is to remain forev-
er; and how do You say, 'The [c]Son
of Man must be [d]lifted up'? Who is
this [c]Son of Man?" **35** So Jesus said to
them, "[a]For a little while longer [b]the
Light is among you. [c]Walk while you
have the Light, so that darkness will
not overtake you; he who [d]walks in
the darkness does not know where
he goes. **36** While you have the Light,
[a]believe in the Light, so that you may
become [b]sons of Light."

These things Jesus spoke, and He
went away and [c,1]hid Himself from
them. **37** But though He had done so
many [1]signs before them, they *still*
were not believing in Him, **38** so that
the word of Isaiah the prophet might
be fulfilled, which he spoke: "[a,1]LORD,
WHO HAS BELIEVED OUR REPORT? AND
TO WHOM HAS THE ARM OF THE [1]LORD
BEEN REVEALED?" **39** For this reason
they could not believe, for Isaiah said
again, **40** "[a]HE HAS BLINDED THEIR
EYES AND HE [b]HARDENED THEIR HEART,
LEST THEY SEE WITH THEIR EYES AND
UNDERSTAND WITH THEIR HEART, AND
RETURN AND I HEAL THEM." **41** These
things Isaiah said because [a]he saw
His glory, and [b]he spoke about Him.
**42** Nevertheless [a]many even of [b]the
rulers believed in Him, but [c]because
of the Pharisees they were not con-
fessing *Him*, [1]for fear that they would
be [d]put out of the synagogue; **43** [a]for
they loved the glory of men rather
than the glory of God.

**44** And Jesus cried out and said,
"[a]He who believes in Me, does not
believe in Me but in Him who sent
Me. **45** [a]And he who sees Me sees the
One who sent Me. **46** [a]I have come *as*
Light into the world, so that everyone

---

**12:26** [a]Jn 14:3; 17:24; 2Co 5:8; Php 1:23; 1Th 4:17 [b]1Sa 2:30; Ps 91:15; Lk 12:37 [1]Or *is serving*
**12:27** [a]Mt 26:38; Mk 14:34; Jn 11:33 [b]Ps 6:3 [c]Mt 11:25 [d]Ps 6:4 [e]Jn 12:23 **12:28** [a]Mt 11:25 [b]Mt 3:17; 17:5; Mk 1:11; 9:7; Lk 3:22; 9:35 **12:29** [a]Ac 23:9 **12:30** [a]Jn 11:42 **12:31** [a]Jn 3:19; 9:39; 16:11 [b]Jn 14:30; *16:11; 2Co 4:4; Eph 2:2; 6:12; 1Jn 4:4; 5:19* **12:32** [a]Jn 3:14; 8:28; 12:34 [b]Jn 6:44 **12:33** [a]Jn 18:32; 21:19 **12:34** [a]Jn 10:34 [b]Ps 110:4; Is 9:7; Eze 37:25; Da 7:14 [c]Mt 8:20 [d]Jn 3:14; 8:28; 12:32 [1]Messiah
**12:35** [a]Jn 7:33; 9:4 [b]Jn 12:46; 1Jn 2:10 [c]Ga 6:10; Eph 5:8 [d]1Jn 1:6; 2:11 **12:36** [a]Jn 12:46 [b]Lk 16:8; Jn 8:12 [c]Jn 8:59 [1]Lit *was hidden* **12:37** [1]Or *attesting signs* **12:38** [a]Is 53:1; Ro 10:16 [1]In OT, Yahweh, cf. Is 53:1
**12:40** [a]Is 6:10; Mt 13:14f [b]Mk 6:52 **12:41** [a]Is 6:1ff [b]Lk 24:27 **12:42** [a]Jn 7:48; 12:11 [b]Lk 23:13 [c]Jn 7:13 [d]Jn 9:22 [1]Lit *lest* **12:43** [a]Jn 5:41, 44 **12:44** [a]Mt 10:40; Jn 5:24 **12:45** [a]Jn 14:9 **12:46** [a]Jn 1:4; 3:19; 8:12; 9:5; 12:35f

who believes in Me will not remain in
darkness. **47** And if anyone hears My
words and does not keep them, I do
not judge him; for [a]I did not come to
judge the world, but to save the world.
**48** [a]He who rejects Me and does not
receive My words, has one who judges
him; [b]the word I spoke is what will
judge him on [c]the last day. **49** [a]For I
did not speak from Myself, but the
Father Himself who sent Me [b]has
given Me a commandment—what to
say and what to speak. **50** And I know
that [a]His commandment is eternal
life; therefore the things I speak, I
speak [b]just as the Father has told Me."

### *The Lord's Supper*

**13** Now before the Feast of [a]the
Passover, Jesus knowing that
[b]His hour had come that He would
depart out of this world [c]to the Fa-
ther, having loved His own who were
in the world, He loved them [1]to the
end. **2** And during supper, [a]the devil
having already put into the heart of
[b]Judas Iscariot, *the son* of Simon, to
betray Him, **3** *Jesus,* [a]knowing that
the Father had given all things into
His hands, and that [b]He had come
forth from God and was going back
to God, **4** *got up from supper, and
*laid aside His garments; and taking
a towel, He [a]tied it around Himself.

### *Jesus Washes the Disciples' Feet*

**5** Then He *poured water into the
washbasin, and began to [a]wash the
disciples' feet and to wipe them with
the towel which He had tied around
*Himself.* **6** So He *came to Simon
Peter. He *said to Him, "Lord, are You
going to wash my feet?" **7** Jesus an-
swered and said to him, "What I am
doing you do not realize now, but you
will understand [a]afterwards." **8** Peter
*said to Him, "You will never wash
my feet—ever!" Jesus answered him,
"[a]If I do not wash you, [b]you have no
part with Me." **9** Simon Peter *said
to Him, "Lord, not only my feet, but
also my hands and my head." **10** Jesus
*said to him, "He who has bathed
needs only to wash his feet, but is
completely clean; and [a]you are clean,
but not all *of you.*" **11** For [a]He knew
the one who was betraying Him; for
this reason He said, "Not all of you
are clean."

**12** So when He had washed their
feet, and [a]taken His garments and
reclined *at the table* again, He said
to them, "Do you know what I have
done to you? **13** You call Me [a]Teacher
and [b]Lord; and [1]you are right, for *so*
I am. **14** If I then, [a]the Lord and the
Teacher, washed your feet, you also
ought to wash one another's feet.
**15** For I gave you [a]an example that
you also should do as I did to you.
**16** Truly, truly, I say to you, [a]a slave
is not greater than his master, nor
*is* [b]one who is sent greater than the
one who sent him. **17** If you know
these things, you are [a]blessed if you
do them. **18** [a]I do not speak about

**12:47** [a]Jn 3:17; 8:15f **12:48** [a]Lk 10:16 [b]Dt 18:18f; Jn 5:45ff; 8:47 [c]Mt 10:15; Jn 6:39; Ac 17:31; 1Pe 1:5; 2Pe 3:3, 7; Heb 10:25 **12:49** [a]Jn 3:11; 7:16; 8:26, 28, 38; 14:10, 24 [b]Jn 14:31; 17:8 **12:50** [a]Jn 6:68 [b]Jn 5:19; 8:28 ◆ **13:1** [a]Jn 2:13; 11:55 [b]Jn 12:23 [c]Jn 13:3; 16:28 [1]Or *completely* **13:2** [a]Jn 6:70; 13:27 [b]Jn 6:71 **13:3** [a]Jn 3:35 [b]Jn 8:42 **13:4** [a]Lk 12:37; 17:8 **13:5** [a]Ge 18:4; 19:2; 43:24; Jdg 19:21; Lk 7:44; 1Ti 5:10 **13:7** [a]Jn 13:12ff **13:8** [a]Ps 51:2, 7; Eze 36:25; Ac 22:16; 1Co 6:11; Heb 10:22 [b]Dt 12:12; 2Sa 20:1; 1Ki 12:16 **13:10** [a]Jn 15:3; Eph 5:26 **13:11** [a]Jn 6:64; 13:2 **13:12** [a]Jn 13:4 **13:13** [a]Jn 11:28 [b]Jn 11:2; 1Co 12:3; Php 2:11 [1]Lit *you say well* **13:14** [a]Jn 11:2; 1Co 12:3; Php 2:11 **13:15** [a]1Pe 5:3 **13:16** [a]Mt 10:24; Lk 6:40; Jn 15:20 [b]2Co 8:23; Php 2:25 **13:17** [a]Mt 7:24ff; Lk 11:28; Jas 1:25 **13:18** [a]Jn 13:10f

all of you. I know the ones I have
[b]chosen; but [c]that the Scripture
may be fulfilled, '[d]HE WHO EATS MY
BREAD HAS LIFTED UP HIS HEEL AGAINST
ME.' **19** From now on [a]I am telling you
before *it* occurs, so that when it does
occur, you may believe that [b]I am *He.*
**20** Truly, truly, I say to you, [a]he who
receives anyone I send receives Me;
and he who receives Me receives Him
who sent Me."

### *Jesus Predicts His Betrayal*

**21** When Jesus had said these things,
He [a]became troubled in spirit, and
bore witness and said, "Truly, truly,
I say to you, that [b]one of you will
[1]betray Me." **22** The disciples *began*
looking at one another, [a]perplexed
about whom He *spoke. **23** There
was reclining on [a]Jesus' bosom one
of His disciples, [b]whom Jesus loved.
**24** So Simon Peter *gestured to him
to inquire, "Who is the one of whom
He is speaking?" **25** He, [a]leaning back
thus on Jesus' bosom, *said to Him,
"Lord, who is it?" **26** Jesus *answered,
"He is the one for whom I shall dip
the piece of bread and give it to him."
So when He had dipped the piece of
bread, He *took and *gave it to Judas,
[a]*the son* of Simon Iscariot. **27** And
after the piece of bread, [a]Satan
then [b]entered into him. Therefore
Jesus *said to him, "What you do,
do quickly." **28** Now no one of those
reclining *at the table* knew for what
purpose He had said this to him.
**29** For some were thinking, because
Judas [a]had the money box, that Jesus
was saying to him, "Buy the things we
have need of [b]for the feast"; or else,
that he should [c]give something to the
poor. **30** So after receiving the piece
of bread, he went out immediately.
And [a]it was night.

**31** Therefore when he had gone
out, Jesus *said, "Now [1]is [a]the Son
of Man [b]glorified, and [c]God [1]is glo-
rified in Him; **32** [1]if God is glorified
in Him, [a]God will also glorify Him
in Himself, and will glorify Him
immediately. **33** [a]Little children, I
am with you [b]a little while longer.
[c]You will seek Me; and as I said to the
Jews, now I also say to you, 'Where
I am going, you cannot come.' **34** A
[a]new commandment I give to you,
[b]that you love one another, [c]even as
I have loved you, that you also love
one another. **35** [a]By this all will know
that you are My disciples, if you have
love for one another."

**36** Simon Peter *said to Him,
"Lord, where are You going?" Jesus
answered, "[a]Where I go, you cannot
follow Me now; but [b]you will follow
later." **37** Peter *said to Him, "Lord,
why can I not follow You right now?
[a]I will lay down my life for You."
**38** Jesus *answered, "Will you lay
down your life for Me? Truly, truly,
I say to you, [a]a rooster will not crow
until you deny Me three times.

---

**13:18** [b]Jn 6:70; 15:16, 19 [c]Jn 15:25; 17:12; 18:32; 19:24, 36 [d]Ps 41:9; Mt 26:21ff; Mk 14:18f; Lk 22:21ff; Jn 13:21, 22, 26 **13:19** [a]Jn 14:29; 16:4 [b]Jn 8:24 **13:20** [a]Mt 10:40; Mk 9:37; Lk 9:48; 10:16; Ga 4:14 **13:21** [a]Jn 11:33 [b]Mt 26:21f; Mk 14:18ff; Lk 22:21ff; Jn 13:18, 22, 26 [1]Or *hand Me over* **13:22** [a]Mt 26:21ff; Mk 14:18ff; Lk 22:21ff; Jn 13:18, 21, 26 **13:23** [a]Jn 1:18 [b]Jn 19:26; 20:2; 21:7, 20 **13:25** [a]Jn 21:20 **13:26** [a]Jn 6:71 **13:27** [a]Mt 4:10 [b]Lk 22:3; Jn 13:2 **13:29** [a]Jn 12:6 [b]Jn 13:1 [c]Jn 12:5 **13:30** [a]Lk 22:53 **13:31** [a]Mt 8:20 [b]Jn 7:39 [c]Jn 14:13; 17:4; 1Pe 4:11 [1]Or *was* **13:32** [a]Jn 17:1 [1]Most early mss omit this phrase **13:33** [a]1Jn 2:1 [b]Jn 7:33 [c]Jn 7:34 **13:34** [a]Jn 15:12, 17; 1Jn 2:7f; 3:11, 23; 2Jn 5 [b]Lv 19:18; Mt 5:44; Ga 5:14; 1Th 4:9; Heb 13:1; 1Pe 1:22; 1Jn 4:7 [c]Eph 5:2; 1Jn 4:10f **13:35** [a]1Jn 3:14; 4:20 **13:36** [a]Jn 13:33; 14:2; 16:5 [b]Jn 21:18f; 2Pe 1:14 **13:37** [a]Jn 13:37, 38: *Mt 26:33-35; Mk 14:29-31; Lk 22:33-34* **13:38** [a]Mk 14:30; Jn 18:27

### *I Am the Way, the Truth, and the Life*

14 "[a]Do not let your heart be trou-
bled; [1]believe in God, believe
also in Me. 2 In My Father's house are
many dwelling places; if it were not
so, I would have told you; for [a]I go to
prepare a place for you. 3 And if I go
and prepare a place for you, [a]I will
come again and receive you to Myself,
that [b]where I am, *there* you may be
also. 4 And you know the way where
I am going." 5 [a]Thomas *said to Him,
"Lord, we do not know where You are
going. How do we know the way?"
6 Jesus *said to him, "I am [a]the way,
and [b]the truth, and [c]the life. No one
comes to the Father but through Me.

### *Oneness with the Father*

7 "[a]If you have come to know Me, you
will know My Father also; from now
on you [b]know Him, and have [c]seen
Him."
8 [a]Philip *said to Him, "Lord, show
us the Father, and it is enough for
us." 9 Jesus *said to him, "Have I
been with you all so long and have
you not come to know Me, Philip?
[a]He who has seen Me has seen the
Father; how *can* you say, 'Show us the
Father'? 10 Do you not believe that
[a]I am in the Father, and the Father
is in Me? [b]The words that I say to
you I do not speak from Myself, but
the Father abiding in Me does His
works. 11 Believe Me that [a]I am in
the Father and the Father is in Me;
otherwise [b]believe because of the
works themselves. 12 Truly, truly, I
say to you, he who believes in Me,
the works that I do, he will do also;
and [a]greater *works* than these he
will do because [b]I go to the Father.
13 [a]Whatever you ask in My name,
this will I do, so that [b]the Father may
be glorified in the Son. 14 If you ask
Me anything [a]in My name, I will do *it*.
15 "[a]If you love Me, you will keep
My commandments.

### *Jesus Promises the Holy Spirit*

16 "And I will ask the Father, and He
will give you another [a,1]Advocate,
that He may be with you forever;
17 [a]the Spirit of truth, [b]whom the
world cannot receive, because it does
not see Him or know Him. You know
Him because He abides with you and
will be in you.
18 "I will not leave you as orphans;
[a]I will come to you. 19 [a,1]After a little
while [b]the world will no longer see
Me, but you *will* see Me; [c]because I
live, you will live also. 20 [a]On that
day you will know that [b]I am in My
Father, and you in Me, and I in you.
21 [a]He who has My commandments
and keeps them is the one who loves
Me; and [b]he who loves Me will be
loved by My Father, and I will love
him and will [c]disclose Myself to him."
22 [a]Judas (not Iscariot) *said to Him,
"Lord, what then has happened [b]that
You are going to disclose Yourself to

---

◆ **14:1** [a]Jn 14:27; 16:22, 24 [1]Or *you believe in God* **14:2** [a]Jn 13:33, 36 **14:3** [a]Jn 14:18, 28 [b]Jn 12:26 **14:5** [a]Jn 11:16 **14:6** [a]Jn 10:9; Ro 5:2; Eph 2:18; Heb 10:20 [b]Jn 1:14 [c]Jn 1:4; 11:25; 1Jn 5:20 **14:7** [a]Jn 8:19 [b]1Jn 2:13 [c]Jn 6:46 **14:8** [a]Jn 1:43 **14:9** [a]Jn 1:14; 12:45; Col 1:15; Heb 1:3 **14:10** [a]Jn 10:38; 14:11, 20 [b]Jn 5:19; 14:24 **14:11** [a]Jn 10:38; 14:10, 20 [b]Jn 5:36 **14:12** [a]Jn 4:37f; 5:20 [b]Jn 7:33; 14:28 **14:13** [a]Mt 7:7 [b]Jn 13:31 **14:14** [a]Jn 15:16; 16:23f **14:15** [a]Jn 14:21, 23; 15:10; 1Jn 5:3; 2Jn 6 **14:16** [a]Jn 7:39; 14:26; 15:26; 16:7; Ro 8:26; 1Jn 2:1 [1]Gr *parakletos*, one called alongside as a helper **14:17** [a]Jn 15:26; 16:13; 1Jn 4:6; 5:7 [b]1Co 2:14 **14:18** [a]Jn 14:3, 28 **14:19** [a]Jn 7:33 [b]Jn 16:16, 22 [c]Jn 6:57 [1]Lit *Yet a little and the world* **14:20** [a]Jn 16:23, 26 [b]Jn 10:38; 14:11 **14:21** [a]Jn 14:15, 23; 15:10; 1Jn 5:3; 2Jn 6 [b]Jn 14:23; 16:27 [c]Ex 33:18f; Pr 8:17 **14:22** [a]Lk 6:16; Ac 1:13 [b]Ac 10:40, 41

us and not to the world?" 23 Jesus an-
swered and said to him, "[a]If anyone
loves Me, he will [b]keep My word; and
[c]My Father will love him, and We [d]will
come to him and make Our dwelling
with him. 24 He who does not love Me
[a]does not keep My words; and [b]the
word which you hear is not Mine, but
the Father's who sent Me.
25 "These things I have spoken to
you while abiding with you. 26 But the
[a]Advocate, the Holy Spirit, [b]whom
the Father will send in My name, [c]He
will teach you all things, and [d]bring
to your remembrance all that I said
to you. 27 [a]Peace I leave with you; My
peace I give to you; not as the world
gives do I give to you. [b]Do not let your
heart be troubled, nor let it be fearful.
28 [a]You heard that I said to you, 'I go
away, and [b]I will come to you.' If you
loved Me, you would have rejoiced
because [c]I go to the Father, for [d]the
Father is greater than I. 29 And now
[a]I have told you before it happens,
so that when it happens, you may
believe. 30 I will not speak much more
with you, for [a]the ruler of the world
is coming, and he has nothing in Me;
31 but so that the world may know
that I love the Father, [1]I do exactly as
[a]the Father commanded Me. Get up,
[b]let us go from here.

### *I Am the True Vine*

15 "[a]I am the true vine, and My
Father is the [b]vine-grower.
2 Every branch in Me that does not
bear fruit, He takes away; and every
*branch* that bears fruit, He [1]cleans
it so that it may bear more fruit.
3 [a]You are already [1]clean because
of the word which I have spoken to
you. 4 [a]Abide in Me, and I in you. As
the branch cannot bear fruit from
itself unless it abides in the vine, so
neither *can* you unless you abide
in Me. 5 I am the vine, you are the
branches; he who abides in Me and
I in him, he [a]bears much fruit, for
apart from Me you can do nothing.
6 If anyone does not abide in Me,
he is [a]thrown away as a branch and
dries up; and they gather them, and
cast them into the fire and they are
burned. 7 If you abide in Me, and My
words abide in you, [a]ask whatever
you wish, and it will be done for you.
8 My [a]Father is glorified by this, that
you bear much fruit, and *so* [b,1]prove
to be My disciples. 9 Just as [a]the Fa-
ther has loved Me, I have also loved
you; abide in My love. 10 [a]If you keep
My commandments, you will abide
in My love; just as [b]I have kept My
Father's commandments and abide
in His love. 11 [a]These things I have
spoken to you so that My joy may
be in you, and *that* your [b]joy may be
complete.

### *Jesus' Commandment Is Love*

12 "This is [a]My commandment, that
you love one another, just as I have

**14:23** [a]Jn 14:15, 21; 15:10; 1Jn 5:3; 2Jn 6 [b]Jn 8:51; 1Jn 2:5 [c]Jn 14:21 [d]2Co 6:16; Eph 3:17; 1Jn 2:24; Rev 3:20; 21:3 **14:24** [a]Jn 14:23 [b]Jn 7:16; 14:10 **14:26** [a]Jn 14:16 [b]Lk 24:49; Jn 1:33; 15:26; 16:7; Ac 2:33 [c]Jn 16:13f; 1Jn 2:20, 27 [d]Jn 2:22 **14:27** [a]Jn 16:33; 20:19; Php 4:7; Col 3:15 [b]Jn 14:1 **14:28** [a]Jn 14:2-4 [b]Jn 14:3, 18 [c]Jn 14:12 [d]Jn 10:29; Php 2:6 **14:29** [a]Jn 13:19 **14:30** [a]Jn 12:31 **14:31** [a]Jn 10:18; 12:49 [b]Jn 13:1; 18:1 [1]Lit *and as the Father...so I do* ◆ **15:1** [a]Ps 80:8ff; Is 5:1ff; Eze 19:10ff; Mt 21:33ff [b]Mt 15:13; Ro 11:17; 1Co 3:9 **15:2** [1]Prunes **15:3** [a]Jn 13:10; 17:17; Eph 5:26 [1]Pruned like a branch **15:4** [a]Jn 6:56; 15:4-7; 1Jn 2:6 **15:5** [a]Jn 15:16 **15:6** [a]Jn 15:2 **15:7** [a]Mt 7:7; Jn 15:16 **15:8** [a]Mt 5:16 [b]Jn 8:31 [1]Or *become My disciples* **15:9** [a]Jn 3:35; 17:23, 24, 26 **15:10** [a]Jn 14:15 [b]Jn 8:29 **15:11** [a]Jn 17:13 [b]Jn 3:29 **15:12** [a]Jn 13:34; 15:17; 1Jn 3:23; 2Jn 5

loved you. **13** [a]Greater love has no one
than this, that one [b]lay down his life
for his friends. **14** You are My [a]friends
if [b]you do what I command you. **15** No
longer do I call you slaves, for the slave
does not know what his master is
doing; but I have called you friends,
for [a]all things that I have heard from
My Father I have made known to you.
**16** [a]You did not choose Me but I chose
you, and appointed you that you would
go and [b]bear fruit, and *that* your fruit
would abide, so that [c]whatever you
ask of the Father in My name He may
give to you. **17** This [a]I command you,
that you love one another.

### *If the World Hates You*

**18** "[a]If the world hates you, [1]know that
it has hated Me before *it hated* you.
**19** If you were of the world, the world
would love its own; but because you
are not of the world, but [a]I chose you
out of the world, [b]because of this the
world hates you. **20** Remember the
word that I said to you, '[a]A slave is
not greater than his master.' If they
persecuted Me, [b]they will also perse-
cute you; if they [c]kept My word, they
will keep yours also. **21** But all these
things they will do to you [a]for My
name's sake, [b]because they do not
know the One who sent Me. **22** [a]If I
had not come and spoken to them,
they would not have [1]sin, but now they
have no excuse for their sin. **23** He who
hates Me hates My Father also. **24** [a]If I
had not done among them [b]the works
which no one else did, they would not
have [1]sin; but now they have both seen
and hated Me and My Father as well.
**25** But *this happened* to fulfill the word
that is written in their [a]Law, '[b]THEY
HATED ME WITHOUT CAUSE.'

**26** "When the [a,1]Advocate comes,
[b]whom I will send to you from the
Father, [c]the Spirit of truth who pro-
ceeds from the Father, [d]He will bear
witness about Me, **27** [1]and [a]you *will*
bear witness also, because you have
been with Me [b]from the beginning.

### *Jesus' Warning*

**16** "[a]These things I have spoken
to you so that you may be kept
from [b]stumbling. **2** They will [a]put
you out of the synagogue, but [b]an
hour is coming for everyone [c]who
kills you to think that he is offering
service to God. **3** These things they
will do [a]because they did not know
the Father or Me. **4** But these things
I have spoken to you, [a]so that when
their hour comes, you [1]may remem-
ber that I told you of them. These
things I did not say to you [b]at the
beginning, because I was with you.

### *The Spirit Is Promised Again*

**5** "But now [a]I am going to Him who
sent Me; and none of you asks Me,
'[b]Where are You going?' **6** But because

---

**15:13** [a]Ro 5:7f [b]Jn 10:11 **15:14** [a]Lk 12:4 [b]Mt 12:50 **15:15** [a]Jn 8:26; 16:12 **15:16** [a]Jn 6:70; 13:18; 15:19 [b]Jn 15:5 [c]Jn 14:13; 15:7; 16:23 **15:17** [a]Jn 15:12 **15:18** [a]Jn 7:7; 1Jn 3:13 [1]Or *you know*; Gr indicative **15:19** [a]Jn 15:16 [b]Mt 10:22; 24:9; Jn 17:14 **15:20** [a]Mt 10:24; Jn 13:16 [b]1Co 4:12; 2Co 4:9; 2Ti 3:12 [c]Jn 8:51 **15:21** [a]Mt 10:22; 24:9; Mk 13:13; Lk 21:12, 17; Ac 4:17; 5:41; 9:14; 26:9; 1Pe 4:14; Rev 2:3 [b]Jn 8:19, 55; 16:3; 17:25; Ac 3:17; 1Jn 3:1 **15:22** [a]Jn 9:41; 15:24 [1]Guilt **15:24** [a]Jn 9:41; 15:21 [b]Jn 5:36; 10:37 [1]Guilt **15:25** [a]Jn 10:34 [b]Ps 35:19; 69:4 **15:26** [a]Jn 14:16 [b]Jn 14:26 [c]Jn 14:17 [d]1Jn 5:7 [1]Gr *parakletos*, one called alongside as a helper **15:27** [a]Lk 24:48; Jn 19:35; 21:24; 1Jn 1:2; 4:14 [b]Lk 1:2 [1]Or *and bear witness!*; Gr imperative ◆**16:1** [a]Jn 15:18-27 [b]Mt 11:6 **16:2** [a]Jn 9:22 [b]Jn 4:21; 16:25 [c]Is 66:5; Ac 26:9-11; Rev 6:9 **16:3** [a]Jn 8:19, 55; 15:21; 17:25; Ac 3:17; 1Jn 3:1 **16:4** [a]Jn 13:19 [b]Lk 1:2 [1]Or *will remember them, that I told you* **16:5** [a]Jn 7:33; 16:10, 17, 28 [b]Jn 13:36; 14:5

I have said these things to you, [a]sorrow
has filled your heart. **7** But I tell you
the truth, it is to your advantage that
I go away; for if I do not go away, the
[a,1]Advocate will not come to you; but
if I go, [b]I will send Him to you. **8** And
He, when He comes, will convict the
world concerning sin and righteous-
ness and judgment; **9** concerning sin,
[a]because they do not believe in Me;
**10** and concerning [a]righteousness,
because [b]I go to the Father and you
no longer see Me; **11** [a]and concerning
judgment, because the ruler of this
world has been judged.

**12** "I still have many more things
to say to you, but you cannot bear
*them* now. **13** But when He, [a]the Spirit
of truth, comes, He will [b]guide you
into all the truth; for He will not
speak from Himself, but whatever
He hears, He will speak; and He will
disclose to you what is to come. **14** He
will [a]glorify Me, for He will take of
Mine and will disclose *it* to you.
**15** [a]All things that the Father has are
Mine; therefore I said that He takes
of Mine and will disclose *it* to you.

### *Sorrow Turned to Joy*

**16** "[a]A little while, and [b]you will no
longer see Me; and again a little
while, and [c]you will see Me." **17** *Some*
of His disciples then said to one
another, "What is this He is telling
us, '[a]A little while, and you will not
see Me; and again a little while, and
you will see Me'; and, 'because [b]I
go to the Father'?" **18** So they were
saying, "What is this that He says, 'A
little while'? We do not know what
He is talking about." **19** [a]Jesus knew
that they were wishing to question
Him, and He said to them, "Are you
deliberating together about this, that
I said, 'A little while, and you will not
see Me, and again a little while, and
you will see Me'? **20** Truly, truly, I say
to you, that [a]you will cry and lament,
but the world will rejoice; you will be
sorrowful, but [b]your sorrow will be
turned into joy. **21** [a]Whenever a wom-
an is in labor she has sorrow, because
her hour has come; but when she
gives birth to the child, she no longer
remembers the suffering because of
the joy that a [1]child has been born
into the world. **22** Therefore [a]you too
have sorrow now; but [b]I will see you
again, and your heart will rejoice, and
no one *will* take your joy away from
you.

### *I Have Overcome the World*

**23** "[a]And on that day [b]you will not
question Me about anything. Truly,
truly, I say to you, [c]if you ask the
Father for anything in My name, He
will give it to you. **24** [a]Until now you
have asked for nothing in My name;
ask and you will receive, so that your
[b]joy may be made complete.

**25** "These things I have spoken to
you in [a]figures of speech; [b]an hour is
coming when I will no longer speak
to you in figures of speech, but will
tell you openly of the Father. **26** [a]On
that day [b]you will ask in My name,

---

**16:6** [a]Jn 14:1; 16:22 **16:7** [a]Jn 14:16 [b]Jn 14:26 [1]Gr *parakletos*, one called alongside as a helper
**16:9** [a]Jn 15:22, 24 **16:10** [a]Ac 3:14; 7:52; 17:31; 1Pe 3:18 [b]Jn 16:5 **16:11** [a]Jn 12:31 **16:13** [a]Jn 14:17
[b]Jn 14:26 **16:14** [a]Jn 7:39 **16:15** [a]Jn 17:10 **16:16** [a]Jn 7:33 [b]Jn 14:18-24; 16:16-24 [c]Jn 16:22
**16:17** [a]Jn 16:16 [b]Jn 16:5 **16:19** [a]Mk 9:32; Jn 6:61 **16:20** [a]Mk 16:10; Lk 23:27 [b]Jn 20:20
**16:21** [a]Is 13:8; 21:3; 26:17; 66:7; Hos 13:13; Mic 4:9; 1Th 5:3 [1]Lit *human being* **16:22** [a]Jn 16:6
[b]Jn 16:16 **16:23** [a]Jn 14:20; 16:26 [b]Jn 16:19, 30 [c]Jn 15:16 **16:24** [a]Jn 14:14; 1Jn 1:4 [b]Jn 3:29; 15:11
**16:25** [a]Mt 13:34; Jn 10:6; 16:29 [b]Jn 16:2 **16:26** [a]Jn 14:20; 16:23 [b]Jn 16:19, 30

and I do not say to you that I will
request of the Father on your behalf;
**27** for [a]the Father Himself loves you,
because you have loved Me and
[b]have believed that [c]I came forth
from the Father. **28** [a]I came forth
from the Father and have come into
the world; I am leaving the world
again and [b]going to the Father."
**29** His disciples *said, "Behold,
now You are speaking openly and
are not [1]using [a]a figure of speech.
**30** Now we know that You know all
things, and have no need for anyone
to question You; by this we [a]believe
that You [b]came from God." **31** Jesus
answered them, "Do you now be-
lieve? **32** Behold, [a]an hour is coming,
and has *already* come, for [b]you to be
scattered, each to [c]his own *home*, and
to leave Me alone; and *yet* [d]I am not
alone, because the Father is with Me.
**33** These things I have spoken to you,
so that [a]in Me you may have peace.
[b]In the world you have tribulation,
but [c]take courage; [d]I have overcome
the world."

### *The High Priestly Prayer*

**17** Jesus spoke these things; and
[a]lifting up His eyes to heaven,
He said, "Father, the hour has come;
[b]glorify Your Son, that the Son may
glorify You, **2** even as [a]You gave Him
authority over all flesh, that [b]to [1]all
whom You have given Him, [c]He may
give eternal life. **3** And this is eternal
life, that they may know You, [a]the
only true God, and Jesus Christ whom
[b]You have sent. **4** [a]I glorified You on
the earth, [b,1]having finished the work
which You have given Me to do.
**5** Now, Father, [a]glorify Me together
with Yourself, with the glory which I
had [b]with You before the world was.

### *Jesus Prays for His Disciples*

**6** "[a]I have manifested Your name to
the men whom [b]You gave Me out
of the world; they were [c]Yours and
You gave them to Me, and they have
[d]kept Your word. **7** Now they have
come to know that everything You
have given Me is from You; **8** for [a]the
words which You gave Me [b]I have giv-
en to them; and they received *them*
and truly understood that [c]I came
forth from You, and they believed
that [d]You sent Me. **9** [a]I ask on their
behalf; [b]I do not ask on behalf of
the world but of those whom [c]You
have given Me; for [d]they are Yours;
**10** and [a]all things that are Mine are
Yours, and Yours are Mine; and I have
been glorified in them. **11** And I am
no longer in the world; and *yet* [a]they
themselves are in the world, and [b]I
come to You. [c]Holy Father, keep them
in Your name, *the name* [d]which You
have given Me, that [e]they may be one
even as We *are*. **12** While I was with
them, I was keeping them in Your

**16:27** [a]Jn 14:21, 23 [b]Jn 2:11; 16:30 [c]Jn 8:42 **16:28** [a]Jn 8:42; 16:30 [b]Jn 13:1, 3; 16:5, 10, 17
**16:29** [a]Mt 13:34; Jn 10:6; 16:25 [1]Lit *saying a proverb* **16:30** [a]Jn 2:11; 16:27 [b]Jn 8:42; 16:28
**16:32** [a]Jn 4:23; 16:2, 25 [b]Zec 13:7; Mt 26:31 [c]Jn 19:27 [d]Jn 8:29 **16:33** [a]Jn 14:27 [b]Jn 15:18ff [c]Mt 9:2 [d]Ro 8:37; 2Co 2:14; 4:7ff; 6:4ff; Rev 3:21; 12:11 ◆**17:1** [a]Jn 11:41 [b]Jn 7:39; 13:31f **17:2** [a]Jn 3:35 [b]Jn 10:28 [c]Jn 6:37, 39; 17:6, 9, 24 [1]Lit *everything that You have given Him, to them He may* **17:3** [a]Jn 5:44 [b]Jn 3:17; 17:8, 21, 23, 25 **17:4** [a]Jn 13:31 [b]Lk 22:37; Jn 4:34 [1]Or *by accomplishing* **17:5** [a]Jn 17:1 [b]Jn 1:1; 8:58; 17:24; Php 2:6 **17:6** [a]Jn 17:26 [b]Jn 6:37, 39; 17:2, 9, 24 [c]Jn 17:9 [d]Jn 8:51 **17:8** [a]Jn 6:68; 12:49 [b]Jn 15:15; 17:14, 26 [c]Jn 8:42; 16:27, 30 [d]Jn 3:17; 17:18, 21, 23, 25 **17:9** [a]Lk 22:32; Jn 14:16 [b]Lk 23:34; Jn 17:20f [c]Jn 6:37, 39; 17:2, 6, 24 [d]Jn 17:6 **17:10** [a]Jn 16:15 **17:11** [a]Jn 13:1 [b]Jn 7:33; 17:13 [c]Jn 17:25 [d]Jn 17:6; Php 2:9; Rev 19:12 [e]Jn 17:21f; Ro 12:5; Ga 3:28

name [a]which You have given Me; and
I guarded them and [b]not one of them
perished but [c]the [1]son of perdition,
so that the [d]Scripture would be ful-
filled. **13** But now [a]I come to You; and
[b]these things I speak in the world so
that they may have My [c]joy made full
in themselves. **14** I have given them
Your word; and [a]the world has hated
them, because [b]they are not of the
world, even as I am not of the world.
**15** I do not ask You to take them out
of the world, but to keep them [1]from
[a,2]the evil one. **16** [a]They are not of the
world, even as I am not of the world.
**17** [a]Sanctify them by the truth; Your
word is truth. **18** As [a]You sent Me into
the world, [b]I also sent them into the
world. **19** For their sake I [a]sanctify
Myself, that they themselves also
may be [b]sanctified [c]in truth.
**20** "I do not ask on behalf of these
alone, but for those also who believe
in Me through their word; **21** that
they may all be one; [a]even as You,
Father, *are* in Me and I in You, that
they also may be in Us, [b]so that the
world may [1]believe that [c]You sent Me.
**22** The [a]glory which You have given
Me I have given to them, that they
may be one, just as We are one; **23** [a]I
in them and You in Me, that they
may be [1]perfected [2]in unity, so that
the world may [3]know that [b]You sent
Me, and [c]loved them, even as You
have loved Me. **24** Father, I desire that
[a]they also, whom You have given Me,
[b]be with Me where I am, so that they
may see My [c]glory which You have
given Me, for You loved Me before
[d]the foundation of the world.
**25** "O [a]righteous Father, [1]although
[b]the world has not known You, yet
I have known You; and these have
known that [c]You sent Me; **26** and
[a]I have made Your name known to
them, and will make it known, so that
[b]the love with which You loved Me
may be in them, and I in them."

### *Jesus Betrayed and Arrested*

**18** When Jesus had spoken these
words, [a]He went forth with His
disciples to the other side of [b]the
Kidron Valley, where there was [c]a
garden, into which He entered [1]with
His disciples. **2** Now Judas also, who
was [1]betraying Him, knew the place,
for Jesus had [a]often gathered there
with His disciples. **3** [a]Judas then,
having received [b]the *Roman* [1]cohort
and [c]officers from the chief priests
and the Pharisees, *came there with
lanterns and [d]torches and weapons.
**4** So Jesus, [a]knowing all the things
that were coming upon Him, went
forth and *said to them, "[b]Whom
do you seek?" **5** They answered
Him, "Jesus the Nazarene." He *said
to them, "I am *He*." And Judas also,

**17:12** [a]Jn 17:6; Php 2:9; Rev 19:12 [b]Jn 6:39; 18:9 [c]Jn 6:70 [d]Ps 41:9; Jn 13:18 [1]Heb idiom for one destined to perish **17:13** [a]Jn 7:33; 17:11 [b]Jn 15:11 [c]Jn 3:29 **17:14** [a]Jn 15:19 [b]Jn 8:23; 17:16 **17:15** [a]Mt 5:37 [1]Or *out of* the power of [2]Or *evil* **17:16** [a]Jn 17:14 **17:17** [a]Jn 15:3 **17:18** [a]Jn 3:17; 17:3, 8, 21, 23, 25 [b]Mt 10:5; Jn 4:38; 20:21 **17:19** [a]Jn 15:13 [b]Jn 15:3 [c]2Co 7:14; Col 1:6; 1Jn 3:18 **17:21** [a]Jn 10:38; 17:11, 23 [b]Jn 17:8 [c]Jn 3:17; 17:3, 8, 18, 23, 25 [1]Gr tense indicates *continually believe* **17:22** [a]Jn 1:14; 17:24 **17:23** [a]Jn 10:38; 17:11, 21 [b]Jn 3:17; 17:3, 8, 18, 21, 25 [c]Jn 16:27 [1]Lit *finished* [2]Lit *into one* [3]Gr tense indicates *continually know* **17:24** [a]Jn 17:2 [b]Jn 12:26 [c]Jn 1:14; 17:22 [d]Mt 25:34; Jn 17:5 **17:25** [a]Jn 17:11; 1Jn 1:9 [b]Jn 7:29; 15:21 [c]Jn 3:17; 17:3, 8, 18, 21, 23 [1]Lit *even the world* **17:26** [a]Jn 17:6 [b]Jn 15:9 ◆ **18:1** [a]Mt 26:30, 36; Mk 14:26, 32; Lk 22:39 [b]2Sa 15:23; 1Ki 2:37; 15:13; 2Ki 23:4, 6, 12; 2Chr 15:16; 29:16; 30:14; Jer 31:40 [c]Mt 26:36; Mk 14:32; Jn 18:26 [1]Lit *and* **18:2** [a]Lk 21:37; 22:39 [1]Or *handing Him over* **18:3** [a]Jn 18:3-11: *Mt 26:47-56; Mk 14:43-50; Lk 22:47-53* [b]Jn 18:12; Ac 10:1 [c]Jn 7:32; 18:12, 18 [d]Mt 25:1 [1]Normally 600 men (the number varied); or *battalion* **18:4** [a]Jn 6:64; 13:1, 11 [b]Jn 18:7

who was betraying Him, was stand-
ing with them. **6** So when He said
to them, "I am *He*," they drew back
and fell to the ground. **7** Therefore
He again asked them, "[a]Whom do
you seek?" And they said, "Jesus the
Nazarene." **8** Jesus answered, "I told
you that I am *He*; so if you seek Me,
let these go their way," **9** in order that
the word which He spoke would be
fulfilled, "[a]Of those whom You have
given Me, I lost not one." **10** Simon
Peter then, [a]having a sword, drew it
and struck the high priest's slave, and
cut off his right ear; and the slave's
name was Malchus. **11** So Jesus said to
Peter, "Put the sword into the sheath;
[a]the cup which the Father has given
Me, shall I not drink it?"

### *Jesus Before the Priests; Peter Denies Jesus*

**12** [a]So [b]the *Roman* [1]cohort and the
[2]commander and the [b]officers of the
Jews, arrested Jesus and bound Him,
**13** and led Him to [a]Annas first; for
he was father-in-law of [b]Caiaphas,
who was high priest that year. **14** Now
Caiaphas was the one who had
advised the Jews that [a]it was better
for one man to die on behalf of the
people.
**15** [a]And Simon Peter was following
Jesus, and *so was* another disciple.
Now that disciple was known to the
high priest, and entered with Jesus
into [b]the court of the high priest,
**16** [a]but Peter was standing at the door
outside. So the other disciple, who
was known to the high priest, went
out and spoke to the doorkeeper,
and brought Peter in. **17** [a]Then the
servant-girl who kept the door *said
to Peter, "[b]Are you not also *one* of
this man's disciples?" He *said, "I
am not." **18** Now the slaves and the
[a]officers were standing *there*, having
made [b]a charcoal fire, for it was cold
and they were [c]warming themselves;
and Peter was also with them, stand-
ing and warming himself.
**19** [a]The high priest then questioned
Jesus about His disciples, and about
His teaching. **20** Jesus answered him,
"I [a]have spoken openly to the world;
I always [b]taught in [1]synagogues and
[c]in the temple, where all the Jews
come together; and I spoke nothing
in secret. **21** Why do you question
Me? Question those who have heard
what I spoke to them; behold, they
know what I said." **22** And when He
had said this, one of the [a]officers
standing nearby [b]gave Jesus a slap,
saying, "Is that the way You answer
the high priest?" **23** [a]Jesus answered
him, "If I have spoken wrongly, bear
witness of the wrong; but if rightly,
why do you strike Me?" **24** [a]So Annas
sent Him bound to [a]Caiaphas the
high priest.
**25** [a]Now [b]Simon Peter was stand-
ing and warming himself. So they
said to him, "[c]You are not also *one*
of His disciples, are you?" He denied
*it*, and said, "I am not." **26** One of

---

**18:7** [a]Jn 18:4 **18:9** [a]Jn 17:12 **18:10** [a]Mt 26:51; Mk 14:47 **18:11** [a]Mt 20:22; 26:39; Mk 14:36; Lk 22:42
**18:12** [a]Jn 18:12f: *Mt 26:57ff* [b]Jn 18:3 [1]v 3, note 1 [2]Military leader over 1,000 soldiers **18:13** [a]Lk 3:2; Jn 18:24 [b]Mt 26:3; Jn 11:49, 51 **18:14** [a]Jn 11:50 **18:15** [a]Mt 26:58; Mk 14:54; Lk 22:54 [b]Mt 26:3; Jn 18:24, 28 **18:16** [a]Jn 18:16-18: *Mt 26:69f; Mk 14:66-68; Lk 22:55-57* **18:17** [a]Ac 12:13 [b]Jn 18:25
**18:18** [a]Jn 18:3 [b]Jn 21:9 [c]Mk 14:54, 67 **18:19** [a]Jn 18:19-24: *Mt 26:59-68; Mk 14:55-65; Lk 22:63-71*
**18:20** [a]Jn 7:26; 8:26 [b]Mt 4:23; Jn 6:59 [c]Mt 26:55 [1]Lit *a synagogue* **18:22** [a]Jn 18:3 [b]Jn 19:3
**18:23** [a]Mt 5:39; Ac 23:2-5 **18:24** [a]Jn 18:13 **18:25** [a]Jn 18:25-27: *Mt 26:71-75; Mk 14:69-72; Lk 22:58-62* [b]Jn 18:18 [c]Jn 18:17

the slaves of the high priest, being a
relative of the one [a]whose ear Peter
cut off, *said, "Did I not see you in
[b]the garden with Him?" **27** Peter then
denied *it* again, and immediately [a]a
rooster crowed.

### *Jesus Before Pilate*

**28** [a]Then they *led Jesus from
[b]Caiaphas into [c]the [1]Praetorium,
and it was early; and they themselves
did not enter into [c]the [1]Praetorium so
that [d]they would not be defiled, but
might eat the Passover. **29** [a]Therefore
Pilate went out to them and *said,
"What accusation do you bring
against this man?" **30** They answered
and said to him, "If this man were
not an evildoer, we would not have
delivered Him to you." **31** So Pilate
said to them, "Take Him yourselves,
and judge Him according to your
law." The Jews said to him, "It is not
lawful for us to put anyone to death,"
**32** in order that [a]the word of Jesus
which He spoke would be fulfilled,
signifying by what kind of death He
was about to die.
**33** Therefore Pilate [a]entered again
into the Praetorium, and summoned
Jesus and said to Him, "[b]Are You the
King of the Jews?" **34** Jesus answered,
"Are you saying this from yourself, or
did others tell you about Me?" **35** Pilate answered, "Am I a Jew? Your own
nation and the chief priests delivered
You to me; what did You do?" **36** Jesus
answered, "[a]My kingdom [1]is not of
this world. If My kingdom were of
this world, then My servants would
be fighting so that I would not be
delivered over to the Jews; but as it
is, My kingdom is not [2]from here."
**37** Therefore Pilate said to Him, "So
You are a king?" Jesus answered,
"[a]You yourself said I am a king. For
this I have been born, and for this I
have come into the world, [b]to bear
witness to the truth. [c]Everyone who
is of the truth hears My voice." **38** Pilate *said to Him, "What is truth?"
And when he had said this, he
[a]went out again to the Jews and
*said to them, "[b]I find no guilt in
Him. **39** [a]But you have a custom that
I release someone [1]for you at the
Passover; do you wish then that I
release [1]for you the King of the Jews?"
**40** So they cried out again, saying,
"[a]Not this man, but Barabbas." Now
Barabbas was a robber.

### *Jesus Flogged and Rejected as King*

**19** Pilate then took Jesus and
[a,1]flogged Him. **2** [a]And when
the soldiers twisted together a crown
of thorns, they put it on His head,
and put a purple [1]robe on Him; **3** and
they were coming to Him and saying,
"[a]Hail, King of the Jews!" and were
[b]giving Him slaps *in the face.* **4** And
Pilate [a]came out again and *said to
them, "Behold, I am bringing Him
out to you so that you may know
that [b]I find no guilt in Him." **5** Jesus
then came out, [a]wearing the crown

---

**18:26** [a]Jn 18:10 [b]Jn 18:1 **18:27** [a]Jn 13:38 **18:28** [a]Mt 27:2; Mk 15:1; Lk 23:1 [b]Jn 18:13 [c]Mt 27:27; *Jn 18:33; 19:9* [d]Jn 11:55; Ac 11:3 [1]Governor's official residence **18:29** [a]Jn 18:29-38: *Mt 27:11-14; Mk 15:2-5; Lk 23:2, 3* **18:32** [a]Mt 20:19; 26:2; Mk 10:33f; Lk 18:32f; Jn 3:14; 8:28; 12:32f **18:33** [a]Jn 18:28, 29; 19:9 [b]Lk 23:3; Jn 19:12 **18:36** [a]Mt 26:53; Lk 17:21; Jn 6:15 [1]Or *is not derived from* [2]From this realm **18:37** [a]Mt 27:11; Mk 15:2; Lk 22:70; 23:3 [b]Jn 1:14; 3:32; 8:14 [c]Jn 8:47; 1Jn 4:6 **18:38** [a]Jn 18:33; 19:4 [b]Lk 23:4; Jn 19:4, 6 **18:39** [a]Jn 18:39-19:16: *Mt 27:15-26; Mk 15:6-15; Lk 23:18-25* [1]Or *to you* **18:40** [a]Ac 3:14 ◆ **19:1** [a]Mt 27:26 [1]Or *had Him flogged* **19:2** [a]Mt 27:27-30: *Mk 15:16-19* [1]Lit *garment* **19:3** [a]Mt 27:29; Mk 15:18 [b]Jn 18:22 **19:4** [a]Jn 18:33, 38 [b]Lk 23:4; Jn 18:38; 19:6 **19:5** [a]Jn 19:2

of thorns and the purple [1]robe. *Pilate*
*said to them, "Behold, the man!"
**6** So when the chief priests and the
[a]officers saw Him, they cried out
saying, "Crucify, crucify!" Pilate *said
to them, "Take Him yourselves and
crucify Him, for [b]I find no guilt in
Him." **7** The Jews answered him, "[a]We
have a law, and by that law He ought
to die because He [b]made Himself out
*to be* the Son of God."
**8** Therefore when Pilate heard this
statement, he became more afraid;
**9** and he [a]entered into the [1]Praetori-
um again and *said to Jesus, "Where
are You from?" But [b]Jesus gave him
no answer. **10** So Pilate *said to Him,
"You do not speak to me? Do You not
know that I have authority to release
You, and I have authority to crucify
You?" **11** Jesus answered, "[a]You would
have no authority [1]over Me, unless it
had been given you from above; for
this reason [b]he who delivered Me to
you has *the* greater sin." **12** As a result
of this Pilate kept seeking to release
Him, but the Jews cried out saying,
"[a]If you release this man, you are no
friend of Caesar; everyone who makes
himself *to be* a king [1]opposes Caesar."
**13** Therefore when Pilate heard these
words, he brought Jesus out, and [a]sat
down on the judgment seat at a place
called [1]The Stone Pavement, but [b]in
[2]Hebrew, Gabbatha. **14** Now it was [a]the
day of [1]Preparation for the Passover;
it was about the [b,2]sixth hour. And he
*said to the Jews, "Behold, [c]your King!"
**15** So they cried out, "[a]Away with *Him*!
Away with *Him*! Crucify Him!" Pilate
*said to them, "Shall I crucify your
King?" The chief priests answered,
"We have no king but Caesar."

### *The Crucifixion*

**16** So he then [a]delivered Him over to
them to be crucified.
**17** [a]They took Jesus, therefore,
and He went out, [b,1]bearing His own
cross, to the place called [c]the Place of
a Skull, which is called [d]in [2]Hebrew,
Golgotha. **18** There they crucified
Him, and with Him [a]two other
men, one on either side, and Jesus
in between. **19** And Pilate also wrote
an inscription and put it on the cross.
It was written, "[a]JESUS THE NAZA-
RENE, [b]THE KING OF THE JEWS."
**20** Therefore many of the Jews read
this inscription, for the place where
Jesus was crucified was near the city;
and it was written [a]in [1]Hebrew, Latin,
*and* in Greek. **21** So the chief priests
of the Jews were saying to Pilate, "Do
not write, '[a]The King of the Jews;'
but that He said, 'I am [a]King of the
Jews.'" **22** Pilate answered, "[a]What I
have written I have written."
**23** Then [a]the soldiers, when they
had crucified Jesus, took His gar-
ments and made [b]four parts, a part
to each soldier and *also* His [1]tunic;

---

**19:5** [1]Lit *garment* **19:6** [a]Mt 26:58; Jn 18:3 [b]Lk 23:4; Jn 18:38; 19:4 **19:7** [a]Lv 24:16; Mt 26:63-66 [b]Jn 5:18; 10:33 **19:9** [a]Jn 18:33 [b]Mt 26:63; 27:12, 14; Jn 18:34-37 [1]Governor's official residence **19:11** [a]Ro 13:1 [b]Jn 18:13f, 28ff; Ac 3:13 [1]Lit *against* **19:12** [a]Lk 23:2; Jn 18:33ff [1]Or *speaks against* **19:13** [a]Mt 27:19 [b]Jn 5:2; 19:17, 20 [1]Gr *The Lithostrotos* [2]Jewish Aramaic **19:14** [a]Mt 27:62; Jn 19:31, 42 [b]Mt 27:45; Mk 15:25 [c]Jn 19:19, 21 [1]Preparation for the Sabbath [2]6 a.m. **19:15** [a]Lk 23:18 **19:16** [a]Mt 27:26; Mk 15:15; Lk 23:25 **19:17** [a]Jn 19:17-24: *Mt 27:33-44; Mk 15:22-32; Lk 23:33-43* [b]Mt 27:32; Mk 15:21; Lk 14:27; 23:26 [c]Lk 23:33 [d]Jn 19:13 [1]Lit *bearing the cross for Himself* [2]Jewish Aramaic **19:18** [a]Lk 23:32 **19:19** [a]Mt 27:37; Mk 15:26; Lk 23:38 [b]Jn 19:14, 21 **19:20** [a]Jn 19:13 [1]Jewish Aramaic **19:21** [a]Jn 19:14, 19 **19:22** [a]Ge 43:14; Es 4:16 **19:23** [a]Mt 27:35; Mk 15:24; Lk 23:34 [b]Ac 12:4 [1]Gr *khiton*, the garment worn next to the skin

now that tunic was seamless, woven
in one piece from the top. **24** So they
said to one another, "[a]Let us not
tear it, but cast lots for it, *to decide*
whose it shall be;" [b]*this was* in order
that the Scripture would be fulfilled:
"THEY [c]DIVIDED MY GARMENTS AMONG
THEM, AND FOR MY CLOTHING THEY
CAST [1]LOTS." **25** Therefore the soldiers
did these things.

[a]But standing by the cross of Jesus
were [b]His mother, and His mother's
sister, Mary the *wife* of Clopas, and
[c]Mary Magdalene. **26** When Jesus
then saw His mother, and [a]the disci-
ple whom He loved standing nearby,
He *said to His mother, "[b]Woman,
behold, your son!" **27** Then He *said
to the disciple, "Behold, your moth-
er!" From that hour the disciple took
her into [a]his *home*.

### *Scripture Fulfilled—It Is Finished*

**28** After this, Jesus, [a]knowing that all
things had already been finished, [b]in
order [1]to finish the Scripture, *said,
"[c]I am thirsty." **29** A jar full of sour
wine was standing there; so [a]they put
a sponge full of the sour wine upon
*a branch of* hyssop and brought it
up to His mouth. **30** Therefore when
Jesus had received the sour wine, He
said, "[a]It is finished!" And bowing
His head, He [b]gave up His spirit.

**31** Then the Jews, because it was
[a]the day of Preparation, so that
[b]the bodies would not remain on
the cross on the Sabbath ([1]for that
Sabbath was a [c]high day), asked Pi-
late that their legs might be broken,
and *that* they might be taken away.
**32** So the soldiers came, and broke
the legs of the first man and of the
other who was [a]crucified with Him;
**33** but coming to Jesus, when they
saw that He was already dead, they
did not break His legs. **34** But one of
the soldiers pierced His side with a
spear, and immediately [a]blood and
water came out. **35** And he who has
seen has [a]borne witness, and his
witness is true; and he knows that
he is telling the truth, so that you also
may believe. **36** For these things came
to pass [a]in order that the Scripture
would be fulfilled, "[b]NOT A BONE OF
HIM SHALL BE [1]BROKEN." **37** And again
another Scripture says, "[a]THEY SHALL
LOOK ON HIM WHOM THEY PIERCED."

### *Jesus Is Buried*

**38** [a]Now after these things Joseph of
Arimathea, being a disciple of Jesus,
but [b]secretly because of his [c]fear of
the Jews, asked Pilate that he might
take away the body of Jesus; and Pi-
late granted permission. So he came
and took away His body. **39** [a]And
Nicodemus, who had first come to
Him by night, also came, [b]bringing
a [1]mixture of [c]myrrh and aloes,
*weighing* about [2]one [d]hundred litras.
**40** So they took the body of Jesus and
[a]bound it in [b]linen wrappings with

---

**19:24** [a]Ex 28:32; Mt 27:35; Mk 15:24; Lk 23:34 [b]Jn 19:28, 36f [c]Ps 22:18 [1]Lit *a lot* **19:25** [a]Mt 27:55f; Mk 15:40f; Lk 23:49 [b]Mt 12:46 [c]Lk 8:2; Jn 20:1, 18 **19:26** [a]Jn 13:23 [b]Jn 2:4 **19:27** [a]Lk 18:28; Jn 1:11; 16:32; Ac 21:6 **19:28** [a]Jn 13:1; 17:4 [b]Jn 19:24, 36f [c]Ps 69:21 [1]Lit *Scripture would be finished* **19:29** [a]Jn 19:29, 30: *Mt 27:48, 50; Mk 15:36f; Lk 23:36* **19:30** [a]Jn 17:4 [b]Mt 27:50; Mk 15:37; Lk 23:46 **19:31** [a]Jn 19:14, 42 [b]Dt 21:23; Jos 8:29; 10:26f [c]Ex 12:16 [1]Lit *for the day of that Sabbath was great* **19:32** [a]Jn 19:18 **19:34** [a]1Jn 5:6, 8 **19:35** [a]Jn 15:27; 21:24 **19:36** [a]Jn 19:24, 28 [b]Ex 12:46; Nu 9:12; Ps 34:20 [1]Or *crushed, shattered* **19:37** [a]Zec 12:10; Rev 1:7 **19:38** [a]Jn 19:38-42: *Mt 27:57-61; Mk 15:42-47; Lk 23:50-56* [b]Mk 15:43 [c]Jn 7:13 **19:39** [a]Jn 3:1 [b]Mk 16:1 [c]Ps 45:8; Pr 7:17; SS 4:14; Mt 2:11 [d]Jn 12:3 [1]Two early mss *package of* [2]Approx. 75 lb. or 34 kg **19:40** [a]Mt 26:12; Mk 14:8; Jn 11:44 [b]Lk 24:12; Jn 20:5, 7

the spices, as is the burial custom of
the Jews. **41** Now in the place where
He was crucified there was a garden,
and in the garden a [a]new tomb [b]in
which no one had yet been laid.
**42** Therefore because of the Jewish
day of [a]Preparation, since the tomb
was [b]nearby, they laid Jesus there.

### *The Empty Tomb*

**20** [a]Now on the first *day* of
the week, [b]Mary Magdalene
*came early to the tomb, while it *was
still dark, and *saw [c]the stone *already*
taken away from the tomb. **2** So she
*ran and *came to Simon Peter and
to the other [a]disciple whom Jesus
loved, and *said to them, "[b]They
have taken away the Lord out of the
tomb, and we do not know where
they have laid Him." **3** [a]So Peter and
the other disciple went forth, and they
were going to the tomb. **4** And the
two were running together; and the
other disciple ran ahead faster than
Peter and came to the tomb first;
**5** and [a]stooping and looking in, he
*saw the [b]linen wrappings lying
*there*; but he did not go in. **6** And so
Simon Peter also *came, following
him, and entered the tomb; and
he *saw the linen wrappings lying
there, **7** and [a]the face-cloth which
had been on His head, not lying with
the [b]linen wrappings, but folded up
in a place by itself. **8** So the other
disciple who [a]had first come to the
tomb then also entered, and he saw
and believed. **9** For as yet [a]they did
not understand the Scripture, [b]that
He must rise again from the dead.
**10** So the disciples went away again
[a]to where they were staying.

### *Jesus Appears to Mary Magdalene*

**11** [a]But Mary was standing outside
the tomb crying; and so, as she was
crying, she [b]stooped to look into the
tomb; **12** and she *saw [a]two angels
in white sitting, one at the head and
one at the feet, where the body of
Jesus had been lying. **13** And they
*said to her, "[a]Woman, why are you
crying?" She *said to them, "Because
[b]they have taken away my Lord, and
I do not know where they have laid
Him." **14** When she had said this,
she turned around and *[a]saw Jesus
standing *there*, and [b]did not know
that it was Jesus. **15** Jesus *said to
her, "[a]Woman, why are you crying?
Whom are you seeking?" Thinking
Him to be the gardener, she *said
to Him, "Sir, if you have carried
Him away, tell me where you have
laid Him, and I will take Him away."
**16** Jesus *said to her, "Mary!" She
turned and *said to Him [a]in [1]Hebrew,
"[b]Rabboni!" (which means, Teacher).
**17** Jesus *said to her, "Stop clinging
to Me, for I have not yet ascended to
the Father; but go to [a]My brothers
and say to them, 'I [b]ascend to My
Father and your Father, and My God
and your God.'" **18** [a]Mary Magdalene
*came, [b]announcing to the disciples,
"I have seen the Lord," and *that* He
had said these things to her.

---

**19:41** [a]Mt 27:60 [b]Lk 23:53 **19:42** [a]Jn 19:14, 31 [b]Jn 19:20, 41 ◆ **20:1** [a]Jn 20:1-8: *Mt 28:1-8; Mk 16:1-8; Lk 24:1-10* [b]Jn 19:25; 20:18 [c]Mt 27:60, 66; 28:2; Mk 15:46; 16:3f; Lk 24:2; Jn 11:38 **20:2** [a]Jn 13:23 [b]Jn 20:13 **20:3** [a]Jn 20:3-10: *Lk 24:12* **20:5** [a]Jn 20:11 [b]Jn 19:40 **20:7** [a]Jn 11:44 [b]Jn 19:40 **20:8** [a]Jn 20:4 **20:9** [a]Mt 22:29; Jn 2:22 [b]Lk 24:26ff, 46 **20:10** [a]Lk 24:12 **20:11** [a]Mk 16:5 [b]Jn 20:5 **20:12** [a]Mt 28:2f; Mk 16:5; Lk 24:4 **20:13** [a]Jn 20:15 [b]Jn 20:2 **20:14** [a]Mt 28:9; Mk 16:9 [b]Jn 21:4 **20:15** [a]Jn 20:13 **20:16** [a]Jn 5:2 [b]Mt 23:7; Mk 10:51 [1]Jewish Aramaic **20:17** [a]Mt 28:10 [b]Mk 12:26; 16:19; Jn 7:33 **20:18** [a]Jn 20:1 [b]Mk 16:10; Lk 24:10, 23

### *Jesus Appears to His Disciples*

**19** So while it was evening on that day,
the first *day* of the week, and while
the doors were shut where the disci-
ples were, for [a]fear of the Jews, Jesus
came and stood in their midst and
*said to them, "[b,1]Peace *be* with you."
**20** And when He had said this, [a]He
showed them both His hands and
His side. The disciples then [b]rejoiced
when they saw the Lord. **21** So Jesus
said to them again, "[a]Peace *be* with
you; [b]as the Father has sent Me, I
also send you." **22** And when He had
said this, He [a]breathed on *them* and
*said to them, "Receive the Holy
Spirit. **23** [a]If you forgive the sins of
any, *their sins* [1]have been forgiven
them; if you retain the *sins* of any,
they have been retained."

**24** But [a]Thomas, one of [b]the twelve,
called [a,1]Didymus, was not with them
when Jesus came. **25** So the other
disciples were saying to him, "We
have seen the Lord!" But he said to
them, "Unless I see in [a]His hands the
imprint of the nails, and put my finger
into the place of the nails, and put my
hand into His side, [b]I will not believe."

**26** And [1]after eight days His disci-
ples were again inside, and Thomas
with them. Jesus *came, the doors
having been [2]shut, and stood in
their midst and said, "[a]Peace *be* with
you." **27** Then He *said to Thomas,
"[a]Bring your finger here, and see
My hands; and bring your hand
*here* and put it into My side; and do
not be unbelieving, but believing."
**28** Thomas answered and said to Him,
"My Lord and my God!" **29** Jesus *said
to him, "Because you have seen Me,
have you believed? [a]Blessed *are* those
who did not see, and *yet* believed."

### *Why This Gospel Was Written*

**30** [a]Therefore many other [b,1]signs
Jesus also did in the presence of the
disciples, which are not written in
this book; **31** but these have been
written [a]so that you may believe that
Jesus is the [1]Christ, [b]the Son of God;
and that [c]believing you may have life
in His name.

### *Jesus Appears at the Sea of Galilee*

**21** After these things Jesus [a,1]man-
ifested Himself [b]again to the
disciples at the [c]Sea of Tiberias, and
He manifested *Himself* in this way.
**2** Simon Peter, and [a]Thomas called
[1]Didymus, and [b]Nathanael of [c]Cana
in Galilee, and [d]the *sons* of Zebedee,
and two others of His disciples were
together. **3** Simon Peter *said to them,
"I am going fishing." They *said to
him, "We will also come with you."
They went out and got into the boat;
and [a]that night they caught nothing.
**4** But when the day was now break-
ing, Jesus stood on the beach; yet the
disciples did not [a]know that it was
Jesus. **5** So Jesus *said to them, "Chil-
dren, [a]do you have [1]any fish?" They
answered Him, "No." **6** And He said to
them, "[a]Cast the net on the right side

---

**20:19** [a]Jn 7:13 [b]Lk 24:36; Jn 14:27; 20:21, 26 [1]Lit *Peace to you* **20:20** [a]Lk 24:39, 40; Jn 19:34 [b]*Jn 16:20, 22* **20:21** [a]Lk 24:36; Jn 14:27; 20:19, 26 [b]Jn 17:18 **20:22** [a]Ge 2:7 **20:23** [a]Mt 16:19; 18:18 [1]Have previously been forgiven **20:24** [a]Jn 11:16 [b]Jn 6:67 [1]The Twin **20:25** [a]Jn 20:20 [b]Mk 16:11 **20:26** [a]Lk 24:36; Jn 14:27; 20:19, 21 [1]Or *A week later* [2]Or *locked* **20:27** [a]Lk 24:40; Jn 20:25 **20:29** [a]1Pe 1:8 **20:30** [a]Jn 21:25 [b]Jn 2:11 [1]Or *attesting miracles* **20:31** [a]Jn 19:35 [b]Mt 4:3 [c]Jn 3:15 [1]Messiah ◆ **21:1** [a]Mk 16:12; Jn 21:14 [b]Jn 20:19, 26 [c]Jn 6:1 [1]Or *made Himself visible* **21:2** [a]Jn 11:16 [b]Jn 1:45ff [c]Jn 2:1 [d]Mt 4:21; Mk 1:19; Lk 5:10 [1]The Twin **21:3** [a]Lk 5:5 **21:4** [a]Lk 24:16; Jn 20:14 **21:5** [a]Lk 24:41 [1]Or *something eaten with bread* **21:6** [a]Lk 5:4ff

of the boat and you will find *some*."
So they cast, and then they were not
able to haul it in because of the great
number of fish. **7** [a]Therefore that
disciple whom Jesus loved *said to
Peter, "It is the Lord." So when Simon
Peter heard that it was the Lord, he
put his outer garment on (for he was
stripped *for work*), and cast himself
into the sea. **8** But the other disciples
came in the little boat, for they were
not far from the land, but about [1]two
hundred cubits away, dragging the
net *full* of fish.
**9** So when they got out on the land,
they *saw a charcoal [a]fire in place and
[b]fish placed on it, and bread. **10** Jesus
*said to them, "Bring some of the
[a]fish which you have now caught."
**11** Simon Peter went up and drew the
net to land, full of large fish, 153; and
although there were so many, the net
was not torn.

### *Jesus Provides Breakfast*

**12** Jesus *said to them, "Come, have
[a]breakfast." None of the disciples
dared to question Him, "Who are
You?" knowing that it was the Lord.
**13** Jesus *came and *took [a]the bread
and *gave *it* to them, and the [b]fish
likewise. **14** This is now the [a]third
time that Jesus [1]was manifested to
the disciples, after He was raised
from the dead.

### *Peter's Restoration and Commission*

**15** So when they had [a]finished
breakfast, Jesus *said to Simon Peter,
"Simon, *son* of John, do you [b,1]love Me
more than these?" He *said to Him,
"Yes, Lord; You know that I [2]love
You." He *said to him, "Tend [c]My
lambs." **16** He *said to him again a
second time, "Simon, *son* of John, do
you [1]love Me?" He *said to Him, "Yes,
Lord; You know that I [2]love You." He
*said to him, "[a]Shepherd My sheep."
**17** He *said to him the third time,
"Simon, *son* of John, do you [1]love
Me?" Peter was grieved because He
said to him [a]the third time, "Do you
[1]love Me?" And he said to Him, "Lord,
[b]You know all things; You know that I
[1]love You." Jesus *said to him, "[c]Tend
My sheep. **18** Truly, truly, I say to you,
when you were younger, you used
to gird yourself and walk wherever
you wished; but when you grow old,
you will stretch out your hands and
someone else will gird you, and bring
you where you do not wish to *go*."
**19** Now this He said, [a]signifying by
[b]what kind of death he would glorify
God. And when He had spoken this,
He *said to him, "[c]Follow Me!"

### *Jesus' Command to Follow Him*

**20** Peter, turning around, *saw the
[a]disciple whom Jesus loved following
*them*; the one who also had [b]leaned
back on His bosom at the supper
and said, "Lord, who is the one who
betrays You?" **21** So Peter seeing him
*said to Jesus, "Lord, and what about
this man?" **22** Jesus *said to him, "If
I want him to remain [a]until I come,
what *is that* to you? You [b]follow

---

**21:7** [a]Jn 13:23; 21:20 **21:8** [1]Approx. 100 yd. or 91 m, a cubit was approx. 18 in. or 45 cm
**21:9** [a]Jn 18:18 [b]Jn 6:9, 11; 21:10, 13 **21:10** [a]Jn 6:9, 11; 21:9, 13 **21:12** [a]Jn 21:15 **21:13** [a]Jn 21:9 [b]Jn 6:9, 11; 21:9, 10 **21:14** [a]Jn 20:19, 26 [1]Or *made Himself visible* **21:15** [a]Jn 21:12 [b]Mt 26:33; Mk 14:29; Jn 13:37 [c]Lk 12:32 [1]Gr *agapao* [2]Gr *phileo* **21:16** [a]Mt 2:6; Ac 20:28; 1Pe 5:2; Rev 7:17 [1]Gr *agapao* [2]Gr *phileo*
**21:17** [a]Jn 13:38 [b]Jn 16:30 [c]Jn 21:15, 16 [1]Gr *phileo* **21:19** [a]Jn 12:33; 18:32 [b]2Pe 1:14 [c]Mt 8:22; 16:24; Jn 21:22 **21:20** [a]Jn 21:7 [b]Jn 13:25 **21:22** [a]Mt 16:27f; 1Co 4:5; 11:26; Jas 5:7; Rev 2:25 [b]Mt 8:22; 16:24; Jn 21:19

Me!" **23** Therefore this saying went
out among [a]the brothers that this
disciple would not die; yet Jesus did
not say to him that he would not die,
but *only*, "If I want him to remain
[b]until I come, what *is that* to you?"

**24** This is the disciple who [a]is
bearing witness to these things and
wrote these things, and we know that
his witness is true.

**25** And there are also [a]many other
things which Jesus did, which if they
*were written one after the other, I
suppose that even the world itself
*could not contain the books that
*would be written.

# THE ACTS
## *of the Apostles*

### *The Promise of the Holy Spirit*

**1** The first account, O [a]Theophi-
lus, I [1]composed, about all that
Jesus [b]began to do and teach, **2** until
the day when He [a]was taken up *to*
*heaven*, after He [b]had [1]by the Holy
Spirit given orders to [c]the apostles
whom He had [d]chosen, **3** to whom
[a]He also presented Himself alive
after His suffering by many convinc-
ing proofs, appearing to them over
forty days and speaking about [b]the
things concerning the kingdom of
God. **4** And [1]gathering them togeth-
er, He commanded them [a]not to
leave Jerusalem, but to wait for the
[b]promise of the Father, "Which," *He*
*said*, "you heard of from Me; **5** for
[a,1]John baptized with water, but you
will be baptized [2]with the Holy Spirit
[b,3]not many days from now."

**6** So when they had come together,
they were asking Him, saying, "Lord,
[a]is it at this time You are restoring the
kingdom to Israel?" **7** But He said to
them, "It is not for you to know times
or seasons which [a]the Father has set
by His own authority; **8** but you will
receive power [a]when the Holy Spirit
has come upon you; and you shall be
[b]My witnesses both in Jerusalem, and
in all Judea and [c]Samaria, and even
to [d,1]THE END OF THE EARTH."

### *The Ascension*

**9** And after He had said these things,
[a]He was lifted up while they were
looking on, and a cloud received Him
out of their sight. **10** And as they were
gazing intently into [1]the sky while
He was going, behold, [a]two men in
white clothing stood beside them.
**11** They also said, "[a]Men of Galilee,
why do you stand looking toward
heaven? This Jesus, who [b]has been
taken up from you into heaven, will

**21:23** [a]Ac 1:15 [b]Mt 16:27f; 1Co 4:5; 11:26; Jas 5:7; Rev 2:25 **21:24** [a]Jn 15:27 **21:25** [a]Jn 20:30
◆**1:1** [a]Lk 1:3 [b]Lk 3:23 [1]Lit *made* **1:2** [a]Mk 16:19; Ac 1:9, 11, 22 [b]Mt 28:19f; Mk 16:15; Jn 20:21f; Ac 10:42 [c]*Mk 6:30* [d]*Jn 13:18*; Ac 10:41 [1]Or *through* **1:3** [a]Mt 28:17; Mk 16:12, 14; Lk 24:34, 36; Jn 20:19, 26; 21:1, 14; 1Co 15:5-7 [b]Ac 8:12; 19:8; 28:23, 31 **1:4** [a]Lk 24:49 [b]Jn 14:16, 26; 15:26; Ac 2:33 [1]Or *eating with, lodging with* **1:5** [a]Mt 3:11; Mk 1:8; Lk 3:16; Jn 1:33; Ac 11:16 [b]Ac 2:1-4 [1]Gr *Joannes*, Heb *Johanan*; so in Acts [2]Or *in* [3]Lit *not* long *after these many days* **1:6** [a]Mt 17:11; Mk 9:12; Lk 17:20; 19:11 **1:7** [a]Mt 24:36; Mk 13:32 **1:8** [a]Ac 2:1-4 [b]Lk 24:48; Jn 15:27 [c]Ac 8:1, 5, 14 [d]Mt 28:19; Mk 16:15; Ro 10:18; Col 1:23 [1]Cf. Is 42:6; 49:6; Ac 13:47 **1:9** [a]Lk 24:50, 51; Ac 1:2 **1:10** [a]Lk 24:4; Jn 20:12 [1]Or *heaven* **1:11** [a]Ac 2:7; 13:31 [b]Mk 16:19; Ac 1:9, 22

[c]come in just the same way as you
have watched Him go into heaven."

### *Matthias Chosen to Replace Judas*

**12** Then they [a]returned to Jerusalem
from the [b,1]mount called [2]Olivet,
which is near Jerusalem, a [3]Sabbath
day's journey away. **13** And when
they had entered *the city*, they went
up to [a]the upper room where they
were staying; [b]that is, Peter and John
and [1]James and Andrew, Philip and
Thomas, Bartholomew and Matthew,
James *the son* of Alphaeus, and
Simon the Zealot, and [c]Judas *the*
[2]*son* of James. **14** These all with one
accord [a]were continually devoting
themselves to prayer, along with
[b]*the* women, and Mary the [c]mother
of Jesus, and His [c]brothers.

**15** And in those days, Peter stood
up in the midst of [a]the brothers (a
crowd of about 120 [1]persons was
there together), and said, **16** "Men,
brothers, [a]the Scripture had to
be fulfilled, which the Holy Spirit
foretold by the mouth of David con-
cerning Judas, [b]who became a guide
to those who arrested Jesus. **17** For he
was [a]counted among us and received
his share in [b]this ministry." **18** (Now
this man [a]acquired a field with [b]the
price of his unrighteousness, and
falling headlong, he burst open in the
*middle* and all his intestines gushed
out. **19** And it became known to all
who were living in Jerusalem; so that
in [a]their own language that field was
called Hakeldama, that is, Field of
Blood.) **20** "For it is written in the
book of Psalms,

'[a]LET HIS RESIDENCE BE
MADE DESOLATE,
AND LET NO ONE DWELL IN IT';
and,
'[b]LET ANOTHER MAN
TAKE HIS [1]OFFICE.'

**21** "Therefore it is necessary that of the
men who have accompanied us all the
time that [a]the Lord Jesus went in and
out [1]among us— **22** [a]beginning [1]with
the baptism of John until the day that
He [b]was taken up from us—one of
these *must* become a [c]witness with us
of His resurrection." **23** And they put
forward two men, Joseph called Bar-
sabbas (who was also called Justus),
and [a]Matthias. **24** And they [a]prayed
and said, "You, Lord, [b]who know
the hearts of all men, show which
one of these two You have chosen
**25** to take the place of [a]this ministry
and [b]apostleship from which Judas
turned aside to go to his own place."
**26** And they [a,1]cast lots for them, and
the lot fell [2]to [b]Matthias; and he was
[3]added to [c]the eleven apostles.

### *The Holy Spirit Comes at Pentecost*

**2** And when [a]the day of Pentecost
[1]had fully come, they were all to-
gether in one place. **2** And suddenly

**1:11** [c]Mt 16:27f; Ac 3:21 **1:12** [a]Lk 24:52 [b]Mt 21:1 [1]Or *hill* [2]Or *Olive Grove* [3]Approx. 0.6 mi. or 1 km **1:13** [a]Mk 14:15; Lk 22:12; Ac 9:37, 39; 20:8 [b]Ac 1:13: *Mt 10:2-4; Mk 3:16-19; Lk 6:14-16* [c]Jn 14:22 [1]Or *Jacob*; James is the Eng form of Jacob; so in Acts [2]Or brother **1:14** [a]Ac 2:42; 6:4; Ro 12:12; Eph 6:18; Col 4:2 [b]Lk 8:2f [c]Mt 12:46 **1:15** [a]Jn 21:23; Ac 6:3; 9:30; 10:23; 11:1, 12, 26, 29; 12:17; 14:2; 15:1, 3, 22, 23, 32f, 40; 16:2, 40; 17:6, 10, 14; 18:18, 27; 21:7, 17; 22:5; 28:14f; Ro 1:13 [1]Lit *names* **1:16** [a]Jn 13:18; 17:12; Ac 1:20 [b]Mt 26:47; Mk 14:43; Lk 22:47; Jn 18:3 **1:17** [a]Jn 6:70f [b]Ac 1:25; 20:24; 21:19 **1:18** [a]Mt 27:3-10 [b]Mt 26:14f **1:19** [a]Mt 27:8; Ac 21:40 **1:20** [a]Ps 69:25 [b]Ps 109:8 [1]Lit *position as overseer* **1:21** [a]Lk 24:3 [1]Lit *to us* **1:22** [a]Mt 3:16; Mk 1:1-4, 9; Lk 3:21 [b]Mk 16:19; Ac 1:2 [c]Ac 1:8; 2:32 [1]Lit *from* **1:23** [a]Ac 1:26 **1:24** [a]Ac 6:6; 13:3; 14:23 [b]1Sa 16:7; Jer 17:10; Ac 15:8; Ro 8:27 **1:25** [a]Ac 1:17 [b]Ro 1:5; 1Co 9:2; Ga 2:8 **1:26** [a]Lv 16:8; Jos 14:2; 1Sa 14:41f; Ne 10:34; 11:1; Pr 16:33 [b]Ac 1:23 [c]Ac 2:14 [1]Lit *gave* [2]Or *upon* [3]Lit *voted together with* ◆ **2:1** [a]Lv 23:15f; Ac 20:16; 1Co 16:8 [1]Lit *was being fulfilled*

there came from heaven a noise
like a violent rushing [a]wind, and it
filled [b]the whole house where they
were sitting. **3** And there appeared to
them tongues like fire [a,1]distributing
themselves, and [2]they [3]rested on
each one of them. **4** And they were
all [a]filled with the Holy Spirit and
began to [b]speak with other [1]tongues,
as the Spirit was giving them [2]utter-
ance.
**5** Now there were Jews living in
Jerusalem, [a]devout men from every
nation under heaven. **6** And when
[a]this sound occurred, the multitude
came together, and were bewildered
because each one of them was hearing
them speak in his own [1]language. **7** [a]So
they were astounded and marveling,
saying, "Behold, are not all these who
are speaking [b]Galileans? **8** And how is
it that we each hear *them* in our own
[1]language in which we were born?
**9** Parthians and Medes and Elamites,
and residents of Mesopotamia, Judea
and [a]Cappadocia, [b]Pontus and [c,1]Asia,
**10** [a]Phrygia and [b]Pamphylia, Egypt
and the district of Libya around
[c]Cyrene, and [d,1]visitors from Rome,
both Jews and [e,2]proselytes, **11** Cretans
and Arabs—we hear them in our *own*
tongues speaking of the mighty deeds
of God." **12** And [a]they all continued in
astonishment and great perplexity,
saying to one another, "What does
this mean?" **13** But others, mocking,
were saying, "[a]They are full of new
wine."

### *Peter's Sermon at Pentecost*

**14** But Peter, [1]taking his stand with
[a]the eleven, raised his voice and
declared to them: "Men of Judea and
all you who live in Jerusalem, let this
be known to you and give heed to
my words. **15** For these men are not
drunk, as you suppose, [a]for it is the
[1]third hour of the day; **16** but this is
what was spoken through the prophet
Joel:

**17** '[a]AND IT SHALL BE IN THE
LAST DAYS,' God says,
'THAT I WILL POUR OUT MY
SPIRIT ON ALL [1]MANKIND;
AND YOUR SONS AND YOUR
DAUGHTERS SHALL PROPHESY,
AND YOUR YOUNG MEN
SHALL SEE VISIONS,
AND YOUR OLD MEN SHALL
DREAM DREAMS;
**18** EVEN ON MY MALE SLAVES
AND FEMALE SLAVES,
I WILL IN THOSE DAYS
POUR OUT MY SPIRIT
And they shall prophesy.
**19** 'AND I WILL PUT WONDERS
IN THE SKY ABOVE
AND SIGNS ON THE
EARTH BELOW,
BLOOD, AND FIRE,
AND VAPOR OF SMOKE.
**20** 'THE SUN WILL BE TURNED
INTO DARKNESS
AND THE MOON INTO BLOOD,
BEFORE THE GREAT AND
AWESOME DAY OF THE
[1]LORD COMES.

---

**2:2** [a]Ge 2:7 [b]Ac 4:31 **2:3** [a]Ge 10:25 [1]Or *being distributed* [2]Lit *it* [3]Or *sat* **2:4** [a]Mt 10:20; Ac 1:5, 8; 4:8, 31; 6:3, 5; 7:55; 8:17; 9:17; 11:15; 13:9, 52 [b]Mk 16:17; 1Co 12:10f; 14:21 [1]Or *languages* [2]Or *ability to speak out* **2:5** [a]Lk 2:25; Ac 8:2 **2:6** [a]Ac 2:2 [1]Or *dialect* **2:7** [a]Ac 2:12 [b]Mt 26:73; Ac 1:11 **2:8** [1]Or *dialect* **2:9** [a]1Pe 1:1 [b]Ac 18:2; 1Pe 1:1 [c]Ac 6:9; 16:6; 19:10; 20:4; 21:27; 24:18; 27:2; Ro 16:5; 1Co 16:19; 2Co 1:8; 2Ti 1:15; Rev 1:4 [1]West coast province of Asia Minor **2:10** [a]Ac 16:6; 18:23 [b]Ac 13:13; 14:24; 15:38; 27:5 [c]Mt 27:32 [d]Ac 17:21 [e]Mt 23:15 [1]Lit *the sojourning Romans* [2]Gentile converts to Judaism **2:12** [a]Ac 2:7 **2:13** [a]1Co 14:23 **2:14** [a]Ac 1:26 [1]Or *being put forward* as spokesman **2:15** [a]1Th 5:7 [1]9 a.m. **2:17** [a]Joel 2:28-32 [1]Lit *flesh* **2:20** [1]In OT, Yahweh, cf. Joel 2:31

21 'And it will be that [a]everyone
who calls on the name of
the [1]Lord will be saved.'
22 "Men of Israel, listen to these
words: [a]Jesus the Nazarene, [b]a man
[1]attested to you by God with [2]miracles
and [c]wonders and [3]signs which God
did through Him in your midst, just as
you yourselves know— 23 this *Man*,
delivered over by the [a]predetermined
plan and foreknowledge of God, [b]you
nailed to a cross by the hands of law-
less men and put *Him* to death. 24 [1]But
[a]God raised Him up again, putting an
end to the [2]agony of death, since it
[b]was impossible for Him to be held
[3]in its power. 25 For David says of Him,
'[a]I saw the [1]Lord
continually before me;
Because He is at my right
hand, so that I will
not be shaken.
26 'Therefore my heart was glad
and my tongue exulted;
Moreover my flesh also
will live in hope;
27 Because You will not forsake
my soul to [a]Hades,
[b]Nor give Your [1]Holy One
over to see corruption.
28 'You have made known
to me the ways of life;
You will make me
full of gladness
with Your presence.'

29 "Men, brothers, I may confident-
ly say to you regarding the [a]patriarch
David that he both [b]died and [c]was
buried, and [d]his tomb is [1]with us to
this day. 30 And so, because he was
[a]a prophet and knew that [b]God had
sworn to him with an oath to set
*one* of the fruit [1]of his body on his
throne, 31 he looked ahead and spoke
of the resurrection of the [1]Christ, that
[a]He was neither forsaken to Hades,
nor did His flesh see corruption.
32 This Jesus [a]God raised up again,
to which we are all [b]witnesses.
33 Therefore having been exalted [a,1]to
the right hand of God, and [b]having
received from the Father [c]the promise
of the Holy Spirit, He has [d]poured
out this which you both see and hear.
34 For David did not ascend into the
heavens, but he himself says:
'[a]The [1]Lord said to my Lord,
"Sit at My right hand,
35 Until I put Your enemies as a
footstool for Your feet."'
36 "Therefore let all the [a]house of
Israel know for certain that God has
made Him both [b]Lord and [1]Christ—
this Jesus [c]whom you crucified."

### *About Three Thousand Souls Saved*

37 Now when they heard *this*, they
were [1]pierced to the heart, and said
to Peter and the rest of the apostles,
"Men, brothers, [a]what should we do?"

---

**2:21** [a]Ro 10:13 [1]In OT, Yahweh, cf. Joel 2:32 **2:22** [a]Ac 3:6; 4:10; 10:38 [b]Jn 3:2 [c]Jn 4:48; Ac 2:19, 43 [1]Or *exhibited, accredited* [2]Or *works of power* [3]Or *attesting miracles* **2:23** [a]Lk 22:22; Ac 3:18; 4:28; 1Pe 1:20 [b]Mt 27:35; Mk 15:24; Lk 23:33; 24:20; Jn 19:18; Ac 3:13 **2:24** [a]Mt 28:5, 6; Mk 16:6; Lk 24:5, 6; Ac 2:32; 3:15, 26; 4:10; 5:30; 10:40; 13:30, 33, 34, 37; 17:31; Ro 4:24; 6:4; 8:11; 10:9; 1Co 6:14; 15:15; 2Co 4:14; Ga 1:1; Eph 1:20; Col 2:12; 1Th 1:10; Heb 13:20; 1Pe 1:21 [b]Jn 20:9 [1]Lit *Whom God raised up* [2]Lit *birth pains* [3]Lit *by it* **2:25** [a]Ps 16:8-11 [1]In OT, Yahweh, cf. Ps 16:8 **2:27** [a]Mt 11:23; Ac 2:31 [b]Ac 13:35 [1]Or *devout, pious* **2:29** [a]Ac 7:8f; Heb 7:4 [b]Ac 13:36 [c]1Ki 2:10 [d]Ne 3:16 [1]Lit *among* **2:30** [a]Mt 22:43 [b]Ps 132:11; 2Sa 7:12f; Ps 89:3f [1]Offspring; lit *of his loins* **2:31** [a]Mt 11:23; Ac 2:27 [1]Messiah **2:32** [a]Ac 2:24; 3:15, 26; 4:10; 5:30; 10:40; 13:30, 33, 34, 37; 17:31; Ro 4:24; 6:4; 8:11; 10:9; 1Co 6:14; 15:15; 2Co 4:14; Ga 1:1; Eph 1:20; Col 2:12; 1Th 1:10; Heb 13:20; 1Pe 1:21 [b]Ac 1:8 **2:33** [a]Mk 16:19; Ac 5:31 [b]Ac 1:4 [c]Jn 7:39; Ga 3:14 [d]Ac 2:17; 10:45 [1]Or *by* **2:34** [a]Ps 110:1; Mt 22:44f [1]In OT, Yahweh, cf. Ps 110:1 **2:36** [a]Eze 36:22, 32, 37; 45:6 [b]Ac 2:23 [c]Lk 2:11 [1]Messiah **2:37** [a]Lk 3:10, 12, 14 [1]Or *wounded in conscience*

**38** And Peter *said* to them, "[a]Repent,
and each of you be [b]baptized in the
name of Jesus Christ [1]for the forgive-
ness of your sins; and you will receive
the gift of the Holy Spirit. **39** For [a]the
promise is for you and your children
and for all who are [b]far off, as many as
the Lord our God will call to Himself."
**40** And with many other words he
solemnly [a]bore witness and kept on
exhorting them, saying, "[1]Be saved
from this [b]crooked generation!"
**41** So then, those who had received
his word were baptized; and that
day there were added about three
thousand [a]souls. **42** And they were
[a]continually devoting themselves
to the apostles' teaching and to the
fellowship, to [b]the breaking of bread
and [a]to the prayers.

**43** And fear came upon every
soul; and many [a]wonders and
[1]signs were taking place through
the apostles. **44** And all those who
had believed [1]were together and
[a]had all things in common; **45** and
they [a]*began* selling their property
and possessions and were [b]dividing
them up with all, as anyone might
have need. **46** [a]And daily devoting
themselves with one accord in the
temple and [b]breaking bread [1]from
house to house, they were taking
their [2]meals together with gladness
and [3]sincerity of heart, **47** praising
God and [a]having favor with all the
people. And the Lord [b]was adding
[1]to their number daily [c]those who
were being saved.

### *The Lame Beggar Healed*

**3** Now [a]Peter and John were going
up to the temple at the [1]ninth
*hour*, [b]the hour of prayer. **2** And [a]a
man who had been lame from his
mother's womb was being carried,
whom they [b]used to set down daily
at the gate of the temple which is
called Beautiful, [c]in order to beg
[1]alms of those who were entering
the temple. **3** When he saw [a]Peter
and John about to go into the temple,
he *began* asking to receive alms. **4** But
when Peter, along with John, [a]fixed
his gaze on him, he said, "Look at
us!" **5** And he *began to* give them his
attention, expecting to receive some-
thing from them. **6** But Peter said, "I
do not possess silver and gold, but
what I do have I give to you: [a]In the
name of Jesus Christ the Nazarene—
walk!" **7** And seizing him by the
right hand, he raised him up; and
immediately his feet and his ankles
were strengthened. **8** [a]And leaping
up, he stood upright and *began to*
walk; and he entered the temple
with them, walking and leaping and
praising God. **9** And [a]all the people
saw him walking and praising God;
**10** and they were recognizing him,
that he was the one who used to [a]sit
at the Beautiful Gate of the temple to
*beg* alms, and they were filled with

---

**2:38** [a]Mk 1:15; Lk 24:47; Ac 3:19; 5:31; 20:21 [b]Mk 16:16; Ac 8:12, 16; 22:16 [1]Or *because of* **2:39** [a]Is 44:3; 54:13; 57:19; Joel 2:32; Ro 9:4; Eph 2:12 [b]Eph 2:13, 17 **2:40** [a]Lk 16:28 [b]Dt 32:5; Mt 17:17; Php 2:15 [1]Or *Escape* **2:41** [a]Ac 3:23; 7:14; 27:37; Ro 13:1; 1Pe 3:20; Rev 16:3 **2:42** [a]Ac 1:14 [b]Lk 24:30; Ac 2:46; 20:7; 1Co 10:16 **2:43** [a]Ac 2:22 [1]Or *attesting miracles* **2:44** [a]Ac 4:32, 37; 5:2 [1]One early ms omits *were* and *and* **2:45** [a]Mt 19:21; Ac 4:34 [b]Ac 2:3 **2:46** [a]Ac 5:42 [b]Lk 24:30; Ac 2:42; 20:7; 1Co 10:16 [1]Or *in the various private homes* [2]Lit *food* [3]Or *simplicity* **2:47** [a]Ac 5:13 [b]Ac 2:41; 4:4; 5:14; 6:1, 7; 9:31, 35, 42; 11:21, 24; 14:1, 21; 16:5; 17:12 [c]1Co 1:18 [1]Lit *together* ◆ **3:1** [a]Lk 22:8; Ac 3:3, 4, 11 [b]Ps 55:17; Mt 27:45; Ac 10:30 [1]3 p.m. **3:2** [a]Ac 14:8 [b]Lk 16:20 [c]Jn 9:8; Ac 3:10 [1]Or *a gift of charity* **3:3** [a]Lk 22:8; Ac 3:1, 4, 11 **3:4** [a]Ac 10:4 **3:6** [a]Ac 2:22; 3:16; 4:10 **3:8** [a]Ac 14:10 **3:9** [a]Ac 4:16, 21 **3:10** [a]Jn 9:8; Ac 3:2

wonder and amazement at what had
happened to him.

### *Peter's Sermon in Solomon's Portico*

**11** And while he was clinging to [a]Peter
and John, all the people ran togeth-
er to them at the [b,1]portico called
Solomon's, full of wonder. **12** But
when Peter saw *this*, he replied to
the people, "Men of Israel, why do
you marvel at this, or why do you
gaze at us, as if by our own power or
piety we had made him walk? **13** [a]The
God of Abraham, Isaac, and Jacob,
[b]the God of our fathers, has glori-
fied His [c]Servant Jesus, whom [d]you
delivered and denied in the presence
of [e]Pilate, when he had [f]decided to
release Him. **14** But you denied [a]the
Holy and Righteous One and [b]asked
for a murderer to be granted to you,
**15** but put to death the [a]Author of life,
whom [b]God raised from the dead,
*a fact* to which we are [c]witnesses.
**16** And on the basis of faith [a]in His
name, *it is* [1]the name of Jesus which
has strengthened this man whom
you see and know; and the faith
which *is* through Him has given him
this perfect health in the presence of
you all.

**17** "And now, brothers, I know
that you acted [a]in ignorance, just as
your [b]rulers did also. **18** But the things
which [a]God announced beforehand
by the mouth of all the prophets,
[b]that His [1]Christ would suffer, He has
thus fulfilled. **19** Therefore [a]repent
and return, so that your sins may be
wiped away, in order that [b,1]times of
refreshing may come from the pres-
ence of the Lord; **20** and that He may
send Jesus, the [1]Christ appointed for
you, **21** [a]whom heaven must receive
until *the* [1]period of [b]restoration of
all things about which [c]God spoke
by the mouth of His holy prophets
from ancient time. **22** Moses said,
'[a]THE [1]LORD GOD WILL RAISE UP
FOR YOU A PROPHET [2]LIKE ME FROM
YOUR BROTHERS; TO HIM YOU SHALL
LISTEN to everything He says to you.
**23** [a]AND IT WILL BE THAT EVERY [b]SOUL
THAT DOES NOT HEED THAT PROPHET
[c]SHALL BE UTTERLY DESTROYED FROM
AMONG THE PEOPLE.' **24** And likewise,
[a]all the prophets who have spoken,
from Samuel and *his* successors
onward, also proclaimed these days.
**25** It is you who are [a]the sons of the
prophets and of the [b]covenant which
God [1]made with your fathers, saying
to Abraham, '[c]AND IN YOUR SEED ALL
THE FAMILIES OF THE EARTH SHALL BE
BLESSED.' **26** For you [a]first, God [b]raised
up His [1]Servant and sent Him to bless
you by turning every one *of you* from
your wicked ways."

### *Peter and John Arrested*

**4** Now as they were speaking to
the people, the priests and [a]the
captain of the temple *guard* and [b]the
Sadducees [c]came up to them, **2** being

---

**3:11** [a]Lk 22:8; Ac 3:3, 4 [b]Jn 10:23; Ac 5:12 [1]Or *colonnade* **3:13** [a]Mt 22:32 [b]Ex 3:13, 15; Ac 5:30; 7:32; 22:14 [c]Is 52:13; Ac 3:26; 4:27, 30 [d]Mt 20:19; Jn 19:11; Ac 2:23 [e]Mt 27:2 [f]Lk 23:4 **3:14** [a]Mk 1:24; Ac 4:27; 7:52; 2Co 5:21 [b]Mt 27:20; Mk 15:11; Lk 23:18, 25 **3:15** [a]Ac 5:31; Heb 2:10; 12:2 [b]Ac 2:24 [c]Lk 24:48 **3:16** [a]Ac 3:6 [1]Lit *His name* **3:17** [a]Lk 23:34; Jn 15:21; Ac 13:27; 26:9; Eph 4:18 [b]Lk 23:13 **3:18** [a]Ac 2:23 [b]Lk 24:27; Ac 17:3; 26:23 [1]Or *Anointed One*; Messiah **3:19** [a]Ac 2:38; 26:20 [b]2Th 1:7; Heb 4:1ff [1]Or *seasons*, cf. 1:7 **3:20** [1]Or *Anointed One*; Messiah **3:21** [a]Ac 1:11 [b]Mt 17:11; Ro 8:21 [c]Lk 1:70 [1]Or *times*, cf. 1:7 **3:22** [a]Dt 18:15, 18; Ac 7:37 [1]In OT, Yahweh, cf. Dt 18:15 [2]Or *as* He raised up **3:23** [a]Dt 18:19 [b]Ac 2:41 [c]Lv 23:29 **3:24** [a]Lk 24:27; Ac 17:3; 26:23 **3:25** [a]Ac 2:39 [b]Ro 9:4f [c]Ge 22:18 [1]Lit *covenanted* **3:26** [a]Mt 15:24; Jn 4:22; Ac 13:46; Ro 1:16; 2:9f [b]Ac 2:24 [1]Or *Son* ◆ **4:1** [a]Lk 22:4 [b]Mt 3:7 [c]Lk 20:1; Ac 6:12

greatly agitated because they were
teaching the people and proclaiming
[a,1]in Jesus the resurrection from the
dead. **3** And they laid hands on them
and [a]put them in jail until the next
day, for it was already evening. **4** But
many of those who had heard the
[1]message believed, and [a]the number
of the men came to be about five
thousand.

**5** Now it happened that on the
next day, their [a]rulers and elders
and scribes were gathered together
in Jerusalem; **6** and [a]Annas the high
priest *was there*, and [b]Caiaphas
and John and Alexander, and all
who were of high-priestly descent.
**7** And when they had placed them
in their midst, they *began to* inquire,
"By what power, or in what name,
have you done this?" **8** Then Peter,
[a,1]filled with the Holy Spirit, said to
them, "[b,2]Rulers and elders of the
people, **9** if we are [1]being examined
today for [a]a good deed *done* to a sick
man, [2]as to how this man has been
[3]saved *from his sickness*, **10** let it be
known to all of you and to all the
people of Israel, that [a,1]by the name
of Jesus Christ the Nazarene, whom
you crucified, whom [b]God raised
from the dead—[1]by [2]this *name* this
man stands here before you in good
health. **11** [a,1]He is the [b]STONE WHICH
WAS [c]REJECTED by you, THE BUILDERS,
*but* WHICH BECAME THE CHIEF CORNER
*stone*. **12** And there is salvation in [a]no
one else, for there is no other name
under heaven that has been given
among men by which we must be
saved."

### *Peter and John Threatened and Released*

**13** Now as they observed the
[a]confidence of [b]Peter and John and
comprehended that they were uned-
ucated and ordinary men, they were
marveling, and [c]*began to* recognize
them [1]as having been with Jesus.
**14** And seeing the man who had been
healed standing with them, they had
nothing to say in reply. **15** But when
they had ordered them to leave the
[a,1]Sanhedrin, they *began to* confer
with one another, **16** saying, "[a]What
should we do with these men? For
the fact that a [b]noteworthy [1]sign has
happened through them is apparent
to all who live in Jerusalem, and we
cannot deny it. **17** But lest it spread
any further among the people, let
us warn them to speak no longer
to any man [a]in this name." **18** And
when they had summoned them,
they [a]commanded them not to speak
or teach at all [1]in the name of Jesus.
**19** But [a]Peter and John answered and
said to them, "[b]Whether it is right in
the sight of God to hear you rather
than God, you be the judge; **20** for
[a]we cannot stop speaking about what
we have seen and heard." **21** And
when they had threatened them
further, they let them go (finding no
basis on which to punish them) [a]on
account of the people, because they
were all [b]glorifying God for what had

---

**4:2** [a]Ac 3:15; 17:18 [1]Or *in the case of* **4:3** [a]Ac 5:18 **4:4** [a]Ac 2:41 [1]Lit *word* **4:5** [a]Lk 23:13; Ac 4:8
**4:6** [a]Lk 3:2 [b]Mt 26:3 **4:8** [a]Ac 2:4; 13:9 [b]Lk 23:13; Ac 4:5 [1]Or *having* just *been filled* [2]Lit *Rulers of the people and elders* **4:9** [a]Ac 3:7f [1]Or *on trial* [2]Or *by whom* [3]Or *made well* **4:10** [a]Ac 2:22; 3:6
[b]Ac 2:24 [1]Or *in* [2]Or *Him* **4:11** [a]Mt 21:42 [b]Ps 118:22 [c]Mk 9:12 [1]Lit *This One* **4:12** [a]Mt 1:21; Ac 10:43; 1Ti 2:5 **4:13** [a]Ac 4:31 [b]Lk 22:8; Ac 4:19 [c]Jn 7:15 [1]Lit *that they had been* **4:15** [a]Mt 5:22 [1]Or *Council*
**4:16** [a]Jn 11:47 [b]Ac 3:7-10 [1]Or *attesting miracle* **4:17** [a]Jn 15:21 **4:18** [a]Ac 5:28f [1]Or *on the basis of*
**4:19** [a]Ac 4:13 [b]Ac 5:28f **4:20** [a]1Co 9:16 **4:21** [a]Ac 5:26 [b]Mt 9:8

happened; 22 for the man was more
than forty years old on whom this
sign of healing had occurred.
23 So when they were released,
they went to their own *companions*
and reported all that the chief priests
and the elders had said to them.
24 And when they heard *this*, they
lifted their voices to God with one
accord and said, "O Master, it is You
who [a]MADE THE HEAVEN AND THE
EARTH AND THE SEA, AND ALL THAT IS
IN THEM, 25 who [a]by the Holy Spirit,
*through* the mouth of our father
David Your servant, said,

'[b]WHY DID THE [1]GENTILES RAGE,
AND THE PEOPLES DEVISE
VAIN THINGS?
26 '[a]THE KINGS OF THE EARTH
[1]TOOK THEIR STAND,
AND THE RULERS WERE
GATHERED TOGETHER
AGAINST THE LORD AND
AGAINST HIS [b,2]CHRIST.'

27 "For truly in this city there were
gathered together against Your holy
[a,1]Servant Jesus, whom You anointed,
both [b]Herod and [c]Pontius Pilate,
along with [d]the [2]Gentiles and the
peoples of Israel, 28 to do whatever
Your hand and [a]Your purpose pre-
destined to occur. 29 And [1]now, Lord,
take note of their threats, and grant
that Your slaves may [a]speak Your
word with all [b]confidence, 30 while
You extend Your hand to heal, and
[a,1]signs and wonders happen through
the name of Your holy [b,2]Servant
Jesus." 31 And when they had prayed
earnestly, the [a]place where they had
gathered together was shaken, and
they were all [b]filled with the Holy
Spirit and *began to* [c]speak the word
of God with [d]confidence.

### *Distribution Among Needy Believers*

32 And the [1]congregation of those
who believed were of one heart and
soul, and not one was saying that any
of his possessions was his own, but,
for them, [a]everything was common.
33 And [a]with great power the apostles
were bearing [b]witness to the resur-
rection of the Lord Jesus, and great
grace was upon them all. 34 For there
was not a needy person among them,
for all who were owners of land or
houses [a]would sell them and bring
the [1]proceeds of the sales 35 and [a]lay
them at the apostles' feet, and they
would be [b]distributed to each as any
had need.
36 Now Joseph, a Levite of [a]Cyprian
birth, who was also called [b]Barnabas
by the apostles (which translated
means Son of [c,1]Encouragement),
37 and who owned a field, sold it and
brought the money and [a]laid it at the
apostles' feet.

### *Ananias and Sapphira*

5 But a man named Ananias, with
his wife Sapphira, sold a piece of
property, 2 and [a]kept back *some* of the

**4:24** [a]Ex 20:11; Ne 9:6; Ps 146:6 **4:25** [a]Ac 1:16 [b]Ps 2:1 [1]Or *nations* **4:26** [a]Ps 2:2 [b]Da 9:24f; Lk 4:18; Ac 10:38; Heb 1:9 [1]Or *approached* [2]Or *Anointed One*; Messiah, cf. Ps 2:2; Ac 4:27 **4:27** [a]Ac 3:13; 4:30 [b]Mt 14:1; Lk 23:7-11 [c]Mt 27:2; Mk 15:1; Lk 23:1, 12; Jn 18:28, 29 [d]Mt 20:19 [1]Or *Son* [2]Or *nations* **4:28** [a]Ac 2:23 **4:29** [a]Php 1:14 [b]Ac 4:13, 31; 14:3 [1]Or *as for the present situation* **4:30** [a]Jn 4:48 [b]Is 52:13; Ac 3:13; 4:27 [1]Or *attesting miracles* [2]Or *Son* **4:31** [a]Ac 2:1 [b]Ac 2:4 [c]Php 1:14 [d]Ac 4:13; 14:3 **4:32** [a]Ac 2:44 [1]Or *multitude* **4:33** [a]Ac 1:8 [b]Lk 24:48 **4:34** [a]Mt 19:21; Ac 2:45 [1]Lit *the prices of the things being sold* **4:35** [a]Ac 4:37; 5:2 [b]Ac 2:45; 6:1 **4:36** [a]Ac 11:19f; 13:4; 15:39; 21:3, 16; 27:4 [b]Ac 9:27; 11:22, 30; 12:25; 13:1, 2, 7; 1Co 9:6; Ga 2:1, 9, 13; Col 4:10 [c]Ac 2:40; 11:23; 13:15; 1Co 14:3; 1Th 2:3 [1]Or *Exhortation, Consolation* **4:37** [a]Ac 4:35; 5:2 ◆ **5:2** [a]Ac 5:3

price for himself, with his wife's [1]full knowledge. And bringing a portion of it, he [b]laid it at the apostles' feet. **3** But Peter said, "Ananias, why has [a]Satan filled your heart to lie [b]to the Holy Spirit and to [c]keep back *some* of the price of the land? **4** While it remained *unsold,* did it not remain your own? And after it was sold, was it not [1]under your authority? Why is it that you laid this deed in your heart? You have not lied to men but [a]to God." **5** And as he heard these words, Ananias [a]fell down and breathed his last; and [b]great fear came over all who heard. **6** And the young men rose up and [a]wrapped him up, and after carrying him out, they buried him.

**7** Now there was an interval of about three hours, and his wife came in, not knowing what had happened. **8** And Peter responded to her, "Tell me whether you were paid [a]this much for the land?" And she said, "Yes, that much." **9** Then Peter *said* to her, "Why is it that you have agreed together to [a]put [b]the Spirit of the [1]Lord to the test? Behold, the feet of those who buried your husband are at the door, and they will carry you out *as well.*" **10** And immediately she [a]fell at his feet and breathed her last, and the young men came in and found her dead, and they carried her out and buried her beside her husband. **11** And [a]great fear came over the whole church, and over all who heard these things.

**12** Now [1]at the hands of the apostles many [a]signs and wonders were happening among the people, and they were all with one accord in [b]Solomon's Portico. **13** But none of the rest dared to associate with them; however, [a]the people were holding them in high esteem. **14** And more than ever [a]believers in the Lord were [b]added to *their number,* multitudes of men and women, **15** to such an extent that they even carried the sick out into the streets and laid them on cots and mats, so that when Peter came by [a]at least his shadow might fall on any one of them. **16** Also the multitude from the cities in the vicinity of Jerusalem were coming together, bringing people who were sick [1]or afflicted with unclean spirits, and they were all being healed.

### *The Apostles Jailed and Freed*

**17** But the high priest rose up and those with him (that is [a]the sect of [b]the Sadducees), and they were filled with jealousy. **18** And they laid hands on the apostles and [a]put them in a public jail. **19** But during the night [a]an angel of the [1]Lord opened the doors of the prison, and taking them out, he said, **20** "Go, stand and [1]speak to the people in the temple [a,2]the whole message of this Life." **21** Upon hearing *this,* they entered into the temple [a]about daybreak and *began to* teach.

Now when [b]the high priest and those with him came, they called [c]the Sanhedrin together, even all

**5:2** [b]Ac 4:35, 37 [1]*Or collusion* **5:3** [a]Mt 4:10; Lk 22:3; Jn 13:2, 27 [b]Ac 5:4, 9 [c]Ac 5:2 **5:4** [a]Ac 5:3, 9 [1]Or *in* **5:5** [a]Eze 11:13; Ac 5:10 [b]Ac 2:43; 5:11 **5:6** [a]Jn 19:40 **5:8** [a]Ac 5:2 **5:9** [a]Ac 15:10 [b]Ac 5:3, 4 [1]In OT, Yahweh, cf. Jdg 3:10 **5:10** [a]Eze 11:13; Ac 5:5 **5:11** [a]Ac 2:43; 5:5 **5:12** [a]Jn 4:48 [b]Jn 10:23; Ac 3:11 [1]Lit *through* **5:13** [a]Ac 2:47; 4:21 **5:14** [a]2Co 6:15 [b]Ac 2:47; 11:24 **5:15** [a]Ac 19:12 **5:16** [1]Lit *and* **5:17** [a]Ac 15:5 [b]Mt 3:7; Ac 4:1 **5:18** [a]Ac 4:3 **5:19** [a]Mt 1:20, 24; 2:13, 19; 28:2; Lk 1:11; 2:9; Ac 8:26; 10:3; 12:7, 23; 27:23 [1]In OT, Yahweh, cf. 2Ki 1:3 **5:20** [a]Jn 6:63, 68 [1]Or *continue to speak* [2]Lit *all the words* **5:21** [a]Jn 8:2 [b]Ac 4:6 [c]Mt 5:22; Ac 5:27, 34, 41

the Council of the sons of Israel,
and sent *orders* to the jailhouse
for them to be brought. **22** But [a]the
officers who came did not find them
in the prison, and they returned and
reported back, **23** saying, "We found
the jailhouse locked quite securely
and the guards standing at the doors,
but we opened it and found no one
inside." **24** Now when [a]the captain
of the temple *guard* and the chief
priests heard these words, they were
greatly perplexed about them as to
what [1]would come of this. **25** But
someone came and reported to them,
"The men whom you put in prison are
standing in the temple and teaching
the people!" **26** Then [a]the captain
went along with [b]the officers and
*proceeded* to bring them *back* without
violence (for [c]they were afraid of the
people, that they might be stoned).

**27** And when they had brought
them, they stood them [1]before [a]the
Sanhedrin. And the high priest
questioned them, **28** saying, "We
[a]strictly commanded you not to
continue teaching in this name, and
[1]yet, you have filled Jerusalem with
your teaching and [b]intend to bring
this man's blood upon us." **29** But
Peter and the apostles answered
and said, "[a]We must obey God
rather than men. **30** [a]The God of
our fathers [b]raised up Jesus, [1]whom
you [c]put to death by hanging Him
on a tree. **31** [a]This One God exalted
[1]to His right hand as [2]a [b]Leader and
a [c]Savior, to grant [d]repentance to
Israel, and forgiveness of sins. **32** And
we are [a]witnesses [1]of these things,
and [b]*so is* the Holy Spirit, whom God
gave to those who obey Him."

### *Gamaliel's Counsel*

**33** But when they heard this, they
became [a]furious and intended to
kill them. **34** But a Pharisee named
[a]Gamaliel, a [b]teacher of the Law,
respected by all the people, stood up
in [c]the Sanhedrin and gave orders
to put the men outside for a short
time. **35** And he said to them, "Men of
Israel, take care what you propose to
do with these men. **36** For some time
ago Theudas rose up, [a]claiming to be
somebody, and a group of about four
hundred men joined up with him.
[1]But he was killed, and all who [2]were
following him were dispersed and
came to nothing. **37** After this man,
Judas the Galilean rose up in the days
of [a]the census and drew away people
after him. He too perished, and all
those who [1]were following him were
scattered. **38** So in the present case, I
also say to you, stay away from these
men and let them alone, for if this
plan or [1]action [a]is of men, it will be
overthrown; **39** but if it is of God, you
will not be able to overthrow them;
or you may even be found [a]fighting
against God."

**40** So they [1]followed his advice.
And after calling the apostles in *and*
[a]beating them, they commanded

---

**5:22** [a]Mt 26:58; Ac 5:26 **5:24** [a]Ac 4:1; 5:26 [1]Lit *this would become* **5:26** [a]Ac 5:24 [b]Ac 5:22 [c]Ac 4:21; 5:13 **5:27** [a]Mt 5:22; Ac 5:21, 34, 41 [1]Lit *in* **5:28** [a]Ac 4:18 [b]Mt 23:35; 27:25; Ac 2:23, 36; 3:14f; 7:52 [1]Lit *behold* **5:29** [a]Ac 4:19 **5:30** [a]Ac 3:13 [b]Ac 2:24 [c]Ac 10:39; 13:29; Ga 3:13; 1Pe 2:24 [1]Or *on whom you had laid violent hands* **5:31** [a]Ac 2:33 [b]Ac 3:15 [c]Lk 2:11 [d]Lk 24:47; Ac 2:38 [1]Or *by* [2]Or *an Author* **5:32** [a]Lk 24:48 [b]Jn 15:26; Ac 15:28; Ro 8:16; Heb 2:4 [1]One early ms adds *in Him* **5:33** [a]Ac 2:37; 7:54 **5:34** [a]Ac 22:3 [b]Lk 2:46; 5:17 [c]Ac 5:21 **5:36** [a]Ac 8:9; Ga 2:6; 6:3 [1]Lit *Who was killed* [2]Lit *were obeying* **5:37** [a]Lk 2:2 [1]Lit *were obeying* **5:38** [a]Mk 11:30 [1]Or *work* **5:39** [a]Pr 21:30; Ac 11:17 **5:40** [a]Mt 10:17 [1]Lit *were persuaded by him*

them not to [2]speak in the name of
Jesus, and *then* released them. **41** So
they went on their way from the pres-
ence of the [a]Sanhedrin, [b]rejoicing
that they had been considered wor-
thy to suffer shame [c]for the Name.
**42** [a]And every day, in the temple and
[1]from house to house, they did not
cease teaching and [b]proclaiming the
good news that Jesus *is* the [2]Christ.

### *Selection of the Seven*

**6** Now in those days, while the
[a]disciples were [b]multiplying
*in number*, there was grumbling
from the [c,1]Hellenists against the
[d]Hebrews, because their [e]widows
were being overlooked in [f]the daily
serving *of food.* **2** So the twelve
summoned the [1]congregation of the
disciples and said, "It is not pleasing
*to God* for us to neglect the word of
God in order to serve tables. **3** There-
fore, [a]brothers, select from among
you seven men of good reputation,
[b]full of the Spirit and of wisdom,
whom we may put in charge of this
need. **4** But we will [a]devote ourselves
to prayer and to the service of the
word." **5** And this word pleased the
whole [1]congregation, and they chose
[a]Stephen, a man [b]full of faith and of
the Holy Spirit, and [c]Philip, Procho-
rus, Nicanor, Timon, Parmenas, and
Nicolas, a [d,2]proselyte from [e]Antioch.
**6** And these they stood before the
apostles, and after [a]praying, they
[b]laid their hands on them.
**7** [a]And the word of God kept on
spreading, and [b]the number of the
disciples continued to multiply great-
ly in Jerusalem, and a great [1]many of
the priests were becoming obedient
to [c]the faith.

### *Stephen Accused of Blasphemy*

**8** And Stephen, full of grace and
power, was doing great [a]wonders
and [1]signs among the people. **9** But
some men from what was called the
Synagogue of the Freedmen, *includ-
ing* both [a]Cyrenians and [b]Alexan-
drians, and some from [c]Cilicia and
[d,1]Asia, rose up and were arguing
with Stephen. **10** But they were
unable to oppose the wisdom and
the Spirit by whom he was speaking.
**11** Then they secretly induced men
to say, "We have heard him speak
blasphemous words against Moses
and God." **12** And they stirred up the
people, the elders, and the scribes,
and they [a]came up to him, dragged
him away, and brought him to [b]the
Sanhedrin. **13** And they put forward
[a]false witnesses who said, "This man
never ceases speaking words against
this [b]holy place and the Law; **14** for
we have heard him say that [a]this
Jesus the Nazarene will destroy this
place and alter [b]the customs which
Moses handed down to us." **15** And

---

**5:40** [2]Lit *be speaking* **5:41** [a]Ac 5:21 [b]1Pe 4:14, 16 [c]Jn 15:21 **5:42** [a]Ac 2:46 [b]Ac 8:35; 11:20; 17:18; Ga 1:16 [1]Lit *according to home* [2]Messiah ◆ **6:1** [a]Ac 11:26 [b]Ac 2:47; 6:7 [c]Ac 9:29; 11:20 [d]2Co 11:22; Php 3:5 [e]Ac 9:39, 41; 1Ti 5:3 [f]Ac 4:35; 11:29 [1]*Jews who adopted the Gr language and much of Gr culture through acculturation* ***6:2*** [1]*Lit multitude* **6:3** [a]Jn 21:23; Ac 1:15 [b]Ac 2:4 **6:4** [a]Ac 1:14 **6:5** [a]Ac 6:8ff; 11:19; 22:20 [b]Ac 6:3; 11:24 [c]Ac 8:5ff; 21:8 [d]Mt 23:15 [e]Ac 11:19 [1]Lit *multitude* [2]A Gentile convert to Judaism **6:6** [a]Ac 1:24 [b]Nu 8:10; 27:18; Dt 34:9; Mk 5:23; Ac 8:17ff; 9:17; 13:3; 19:6; 1Ti 4:14; 2Ti 1:6; Heb 6:2 **6:7** [a]Ac 12:24; 19:20 [b]Ac 6:1 [c]Ac 13:8; 14:22; Ga 1:23; 6:10; Jd 3, 20 [1]Lit *crowd* **6:8** [a]Jn 4:48 [1]Or *attesting miracles* **6:9** [a]Mt 27:32; Ac 2:10 [b]Ac 18:24 [c]Ac 15:23, 41; 21:39; 22:3; 23:34; 27:5; Ga 1:21 [d]Ac 16:6; 19:10; 21:27; 24:18 [1]West coast province of Asia Minor **6:12** [a]Lk 20:1; Ac 4:1 [b]Mt 5:22 **6:13** [a]Mt 26:59-61; Ac 7:58 [b]Mt 24:15; Ac 21:28; 25:8 **6:14** [a]Mt 26:61 [b]Ac 15:1; 21:21; 26:3; 28:17

fixing their gaze on him, all who were
sitting in the [a]Sanhedrin saw his face
like the face of an angel.

### *Stephen's Defense*

**7** And the high priest said, "Are
these things so?"
**2** And he said, "Hear me, [a]brothers
and fathers! [b]The God of glory [c]ap-
peared to our father Abraham when he
was in Mesopotamia, before he lived
in [1]Haran, **3** and said to him, '[a]LEAVE
YOUR COUNTRY AND YOUR RELATIVES,
AND COME INTO THE LAND THAT I WILL
SHOW YOU.' **4** [a]Then he left the land of
the Chaldeans and settled in [1]Haran.
[b]From there, after his father died,
*God* had him move to this country in
which you are now living. **5** But He
gave him no inheritance in it, not even
a foot of ground, and [a]He promised
that HE WOULD GIVE IT TO HIM AS A
POSSESSION, AND TO HIS SEED AFTER
HIM, even when he had no child. **6** But
[a]God spoke in this way, that his SEED
WOULD BE SOJOURNERS IN A FOREIGN
LAND, AND THAT THEY WOULD [1]BE
ENSLAVED AND MISTREATED FOR FOUR
HUNDRED YEARS. **7** 'AND I MYSELF WILL
JUDGE THE NATION TO WHICH THEY WILL
BE ENSLAVED,' said God, 'AND [a]AFTER
THAT THEY WILL COME OUT AND [1]SERVE
ME IN THIS PLACE.' **8** And He [a]gave him
[1]the covenant of circumcision; and so
[b]*Abraham* was the father of Isaac, and
circumcised him on the eighth day;
and [c]Isaac *was the father of* Jacob, and
[d]Jacob *of* the twelve [e]patriarchs.
**9** "And the patriarchs, [a]becoming
jealous of Joseph, sold him into
Egypt. *Yet* God was with him, **10** and
rescued him from all his afflictions,
and [a]granted him favor and wisdom
in the sight of Pharaoh, king of Egypt,
and he appointed him governor over
Egypt and all his household.
**11** "Now [a]a famine came over
all Egypt and Canaan, and great
affliction *with it*, and our fathers
[1]could find no food. **12** But [a]when
Jacob heard that there was grain
in Egypt, he sent our fathers *there*
the first time. **13** And on the second
*visit* [a]Joseph [1]made himself known
to his brothers, and [b]Joseph's family
was disclosed to Pharaoh. **14** Then
[a]Joseph sent *word* and invited Jacob
his father and all his relatives to come
to him, [b]seventy-five [c,1]persons *in all.*
**15** And [a]Jacob went down to Egypt
and *there* he and our fathers died.
**16** *And from there* they were removed
to [a,1]Shechem and placed in the tomb
which Abraham had purchased for
a sum of money from the sons of
[2]Hamor in [1]Shechem.
**17** "But as the [a]time of the promise
was drawing near which God had
assured to Abraham, [b]the people
increased and multiplied in Egypt,
**18** until [a]ANOTHER KING AROSE OVER
EGYPT WHO DID NOT KNOW ABOUT
JOSEPH. **19** It was he who [a]deceitfully
took advantage of our family and
mistreated our fathers to [b,1]set their
infants outside so that they would

---

**6:15** [a]Mt 5:22 ◆**7:2** [a]Ac 22:1 [b]Ps 29:3; 1Co 2:8 [c]Ge 11:31; 15:7 [1]Gr *Charran* **7:3** [a]Ge 12:1
**7:4** [a]Ge 11:31; 15:7 [b]Ge 12:4, 5 [1]Gr *Charran* **7:5** [a]Ge 12:7; 13:15; 15:18; 17:8 **7:6** [a]Ge 15:13f [1]Lit *enslave them and mistreat them* **7:7** [a]Ex 3:12 [1]Or *worship* **7:8** [a]Ge 17:10ff [b]Ge 21:2-4 [c]Ge 25:26 [d]Ge 29:31ff; 30:5ff; 35:23ff [e]Ac 2:29 [1]Or *a* **7:9** [a]Ge 37:11, 28; 39:2, 21f; 45:4 **7:10** [a]Ge 39:21; 41:40-46; Ps 105:21
**7:11** [a]Ge 41:54f; 42:5 [1]Lit *were not finding* **7:12** [a]Ge 42:2 **7:13** [a]Ge 45:1-4 [b]Ge 45:16 [1]Or *was made known* **7:14** [a]Ge 45:9, 10, 17, 18 [b]Ge 46:26f; Ex 1:5; Dt 10:22 [c]Ac 2:41 [1]Lit *souls* **7:15** [a]Ge 46:1-7; 49:33; Ex 1:6 **7:16** [a]Ge 23:16; 33:19; 50:13; Jos 24:32 [1]Gr *Sychem* [2]Gr *Emmor* **7:17** [a]Ge 15:13 [b]Ex 1:7f
**7:18** [a]Ex 1:8 **7:19** [a]Ex 1:10f, 16ff [b]Ex 1:22 [1]Or *put out to die*

not survive. **20** It was at this time that
[a]Moses was born, and he was lovely
[1]in the sight of God, and he was
nurtured three months in his father's
home. **21** And after he had been set
outside, [a]Pharaoh's daughter [1]took
him away and nurtured him as her
own son. **22** And Moses was educated
in all [a]the wisdom of the Egyptians,
and he was powerful in words and
deeds. **23** But when he was approach-
ing the age of forty, [a]it entered his
heart to visit his brothers, the sons
of Israel. **24** And when he saw one
*of them* being treated unjustly, he
defended him and took justice for
the oppressed by striking down the
Egyptian. **25** And he supposed that
his brothers understood that God was
granting them salvation [1]through
him, but they did not understand.
**26** [a]On the following day he appeared
to them as they were fighting togeth-
er, and he tried to reconcile them in
peace, saying, 'Men, you are brothers,
why are you treating one another
unjustly?' **27** But the one who was
treating his neighbor unjustly pushed
him away, saying, '[a]WHO MADE YOU
A RULER AND JUDGE OVER US? **28** [a]DO
YOU INTEND TO KILL ME AS YOU KILLED
THE EGYPTIAN YESTERDAY?' **29** At this
remark, [a]MOSES FLED AND BECAME A
SOJOURNER IN THE LAND OF [1]MIDIAN,
where he [b]was the father of two sons.
**30** "And after forty years had passed,
[a]AN ANGEL APPEARED TO HIM IN THE
WILDERNESS OF MOUNT Sinai, IN THE
FLAME OF A BURNING BUSH. **31** When
Moses saw it, he was marveling at the
sight; and as he approached to look
*more* closely, there came the voice of
the [1]Lord: **32** '[a]I AM THE GOD OF YOUR
FATHERS, THE GOD OF ABRAHAM AND
ISAAC AND JACOB.' Moses trembled
with fear and would not dare to
look. **33** [a]BUT THE [1]LORD SAID TO HIM,
'[b]REMOVE THE SANDALS FROM YOUR
FEET, FOR THE PLACE ON WHICH YOU
ARE STANDING IS HOLY GROUND. **34** [a]I
HAVE SURELY SEEN THE OPPRESSION OF
MY PEOPLE IN EGYPT AND HAVE HEARD
THEIR GROANS, AND I HAVE COME DOWN
TO DELIVER THEM; [b,1]COME NOW, AND I
WILL SEND YOU TO EGYPT.'
**35** "This Moses whom they
[a]disowned, saying, 'WHO MADE YOU
A RULER AND A JUDGE?' is the one
whom God [1]sent *to be* both a ruler
and a deliverer with the [2]help of the
angel who appeared to him in the
bush. **36** [a]This man led them out,
doing [b]wonders and [1]signs in the
land of Egypt and in the Red Sea and
in the [c]wilderness for forty years.
**37** This is the Moses who said to the
sons of Israel, '[a]GOD WILL RAISE UP
FOR YOU A PROPHET [1]LIKE ME FROM
YOUR BROTHERS.' **38** This is the one
who, in [a]the [1]congregation in the
wilderness, was with [b]the angel who
was speaking to him on Mount Sinai
and with our fathers; the one who
received [c]living [d]oracles to pass on
to you. **39** Our fathers were unwilling
to be obedient to him, but [a]rejected

---

**7:20** [a]Ex 2:2; Heb 11:23 [1]Lit *to God* **7:21** [a]Ex 2:5f, 10 [1]Or *adopted him* **7:22** [a]1Ki 4:30; Is 19:11
**7:23** [a]*Ex 2:11f; Heb 11:24-26* **7:25** [1]*Lit through his hand* **7:26** [a]Ex 2:13f **7:27** [a]Ex 2:14; Ac 7:35
**7:28** [a]Ex 2:14 **7:29** [a]Ex 2:15, 22 [b]Ex 18:3, 4 [1]Gr *Madiam* **7:30** [a]Ex 3:1f; Is 63:9 **7:31** [1]In
OT, Yahweh, cf. Ex 3:4 **7:32** [a]Ex 3:6; Mt 22:32 **7:33** [a]Ex 3:5 [b]Jos 5:15 [1]In OT, Yahweh, cf.
Ex 3:4 **7:34** [a]Ex 3:7f [b]Ex 3:10 [1]Lit *and now come!* **7:35** [a]Ex 2:14; Ac 7:27 [1]Lit *has sent* [2]Lit *hand*
**7:36** [a]Ex 12:41; 33:1; Heb 8:9 [b]Ex 7:3; 14:21; Jn 4:48 [c]Ex 16:35; Nu 14:33; Ps 95:8-10; Ac 7:42; 13:18; Heb 3:8f
[1]Or *attesting miracles* **7:37** [a]Dt 18:15, 18; Ac 3:22 [1]Or *as* He raised up *me* **7:38** [a]Ex 19:17 [b]Ac 7:53
[c]Dt 32:47; Heb 4:12 [d]Ro 3:2; Heb 5:12; 1Pe 4:11 [1]Gr *ekklesia* **7:39** [a]Nu 14:3f

him and in their hearts turned back
to Egypt, 40 [a]Saying to Aaron,
'Make for us gods who will go
before us; for this Moses who led
us out of the land of Egypt—we
do not know what has become of
him.' 41 [1]At that time [a]they made
a [2]calf and brought a sacrifice to
the idol, and were rejoicing in [b]the
works of their hands. 42 But God
[a]turned away and delivered them
up to [1]serve the [2]host of heaven;
as it is written in the book of the
prophets, '[b]Did you present Me
with slain beasts and sacrifices
[c]forty years in the wilderness,
O house of Israel? 43 [a]You also
took along the tabernacle of
Moloch and the star of the god
[1]Rompha, the images which you
made to worship. I also will re-
move you beyond Babylon.'

44 "Our fathers had [a]the taberna-
cle of testimony in the wilderness,
just as He, who spoke to Moses,
directed *him* to make it [b]according
to the pattern which he had seen.
45 And having received it in their
turn, our fathers [a]brought it in with
[1]Joshua when they dispossessed the
[2]nations whom God drove out before
our fathers, until the time of David.
46 [a]*David* found favor in the sight of
God, and [b]asked that he might find a
dwelling place for the [1]God of Jacob.
47 But [a]Solomon built a house for
Him. 48 However, [a]the Most High
does not dwell in *houses* made by
*human* hands, as the prophet says:

49 '[a]Heaven is My throne,
And earth is the
footstool of My feet.
What kind of house will you
build for Me?' says the Lord,
'Or what place is there
for My rest?
50 '[a]Was it not My hand which
made all these things?'

51 "You men—[a]stiff-necked and
uncircumcised in heart and ears—are
always resisting the Holy Spirit. As
your fathers did, so do you. 52 [a]And
which one of the prophets did your
fathers not persecute? They killed
those who had previously announced
the coming of [b]the Righteous One,
whose betrayers and murderers
[c]you have now become; 53 you who
received the Law as [a]ordained by
angels, and *yet* did not observe it."

### *Stephen Is Stoned to Death*

54 Now when they heard this, they
became [a]furious in their hearts, and
they *began* gnashing their teeth at
him. 55 But being [a]full of the Holy
Spirit, he [b]gazed intently into heaven
and saw the glory of God, and Jesus
standing [c]at the right hand of God;
56 and he said, "Behold, I see the
[a]heavens opened up and [b]the Son
of Man standing at the right hand
of God." 57 But crying out with a
loud voice, they covered their ears

**7:40** [a]Ex 32:1, 23 **7:41** [a]Ex 32:4, 6 [b]Rev 9:20 [1]Lit *in those days* [2]Or *young bull* **7:42** [a]Jos 24:20; Is 63:10; Jer 19:13; Eze 20:39 [b]Am 5:25 [c]Ac 7:36 [1]Or *worship* [2]Heavenly bodies **7:43** [a]Am 5:26, 27 [1]Other mss spell it: *Romphan*, or *Rempham*, or *Raiphan*, or *Rephan* **7:44** [a]Ex 25:8, 9; 38:21 [b]Ex 25:40 **7:45** [a]Dt 32:49; Jos 3:14ff; 18:1; 23:9; 24:18; Ps 44:2f [1]Gr *Jesus* [2]Or *Gentiles* **7:46** [a]2Sa 7:8ff; Ps 132:1-5; Ac 13:22 [b]2Sa 7:1-16; 1Chr 17:1-14 [1]As in LXX; the earliest mss *house* **7:47** [a]1Ki 6:1-38; 8:20; 2Chr 3:1-17 **7:48** [a]Lk 1:32 **7:49** [a]Is 66:1; Mt 5:34f **7:50** [a]Is 66:2 **7:51** [a]Ex 32:9; 33:3, 5; Lv 26:41; Nu 27:14; Is 63:10; Jer 6:10; 9:26 **7:52** [a]2Chr 36:15f; Mt 5:12; 23:31, 37 [b]Ac 3:14; 22:14; 1Jn 2:1 [c]Ac 3:14; 5:28 **7:53** [a]Dt 33:2; Ac 7:38; Ga 3:19; Heb 2:2 **7:54** [a]Ac 5:33 **7:55** [a]Ac 2:4 [b]Jn 11:41 [c]Mk 16:19 **7:56** [a]Jn 1:51 [b]Mt 8:20

and rushed at him with one accord.
**58** And when they had [a]driven him
out of the city, they *began* stoning
*him;* and [b]the witnesses [c]laid aside
their garments at the feet of [d]a young
man named Saul. **59** They went on
stoning Stephen as he [a]was calling
out and saying, "Lord Jesus, receive
my spirit!" **60** Then [a]falling on his
knees, he cried out with a loud voice,
"Lord, [b]do not hold this sin against
them!" And having said this, he [c,1]fell
asleep.

### *Saul Persecutes the Church*

**8** [a]Now Saul was in hearty agree-
ment with putting him to death.
And on that day a great persecu-
tion [1]began against [b]the church in Je-
rusalem, and they were all [c]scattered
throughout the regions of Judea and
[d]Samaria, except the apostles. **2** And
*some* devout men buried Stephen
and made loud lamentation over
him. **3** But [a]Saul *began* ravaging the
church, entering house after house,
and [b]dragging off men and women,
he was delivering them into prison.

### *Philip Preaches in Samaria*

**4** Therefore, those [a]who had been
scattered went about, [b]proclaiming
the good news of the word. **5** [a]Now
Philip went down to the city of Sa-
maria and *began* preaching [1]Christ
to them. **6** And the crowds with one
accord were giving attention to what
was being said by Philip, as they
heard and saw the [1]signs which he
was doing. **7** For *in the case of* many
who had [a]unclean spirits, they were
coming out *of them* shouting with a
loud voice; and many who had been
[b]paralyzed and lame were healed.
**8** So there was [a]great joy in that city.
**9** Now there was a man named
Simon, who formerly was practicing
[a]magic in the city and astounding
the people of Samaria, [b]claiming to
be someone great; **10** and they all,
from smallest to greatest, were giving
attention to him, saying, "[a]This man
is what is called the Great Power of
God." **11** And they were giving him
attention because he had for a long
time astounded them with his [a]magic
arts. **12** But when they believed Philip
[a]proclaiming the good news about
the kingdom of God and the name
of Jesus Christ, they were being
[b]baptized, both men and women.
**13** Even Simon himself believed; and
after being baptized, he continued
on with Philip, and as he observed
[a]signs and [b]great miracles taking
place, he was constantly astounded.
**14** Now when [a]the apostles in
Jerusalem heard that Samaria had
received the word of God, they sent
them [b]Peter and John, **15** who came
down and prayed for them [a]that
they might receive the Holy Spirit.
**16** For He had [a]not yet fallen upon
any of them; they had simply been
[b]baptized [1]in the name of the Lord
Jesus. **17** Then they [a]*began* laying

---

**7:58** [a]Lv 24:14, 16; Lk 4:29 [b]Dt 13:9f; 17:7; Ac 6:13 [c]Ac 22:20 [d]Ac 8:1; 22:20; 26:10 **7:59** [a]Ac 9:14, 21; *22:16; Ro 10:12-14; 1Co 1:2; 2Ti 2:22* **7:60** [a]Lk 22:41 [b]Mt 5:44; Lk 23:34 [c]Da 12:2; Mt 27:52; Jn 11:11f; Ac 13:36; 1Co 15:6, 18, 20; 1Th 4:13ff; 2Pe 3:4 [1]Died ◆ **8:1** [a]Ac 7:58; 22:20; 26:10 [b]Ac 9:31 [c]Ac 8:4; 11:19 [d]Ac 1:8; 8:5, 14; 9:31 [1]Lit *occurred* **8:3** [a]Ac 9:1, 13, 21; 22:4, 19; 26:10f; 1Co 15:9; Ga 1:13; Php 3:6; 1Ti 1:13 [b]Jas 2:6 **8:4** [a]Ac 8:1 [b]Ac 8:12; 15:35 **8:5** [a]Ac 6:5; 8:26, 30 [1]The Messiah **8:6** [1]Or *attesting miracles* **8:7** [a]Mk 16:17 [b]Mt 4:24 **8:8** [a]Jn 4:40-42; Ac 8:39 **8:9** [a]Ac 8:11; 13:6 [b]Ac 5:36 **8:10** [a]Ac 14:11; 28:6 **8:11** [a]Ac 8:9; 13:6 **8:12** [a]Ac 1:3; 8:4 [b]Ac 2:38 **8:13** [a]Ac 8:6 [b]Ac 19:11 **8:14** [a]Ac 8:1 [b]Lk 22:8 **8:15** [a]Ac 2:38; 19:2 **8:16** [a]Mt 28:19; Ac 19:2 [b]Ac 2:38; 10:48 [1]Lit *into* **8:17** [a]Mk 5:23; Ac 6:6

their hands on them, and they were
[b]receiving the Holy Spirit. 18 Now
when Simon saw that the Spirit had
been bestowed through the laying
on of the apostles' hands, he offered
them money, 19 saying, "Give this au-
thority to me as well, so that everyone
on whom I lay my hands may receive
the Holy Spirit." 20 But Peter said to
him, "May your silver perish with
you, because you supposed you could
[a]obtain the gift of God with money!
21 You have [a]no part or portion in this
[1]matter, for your heart is not [b]right
before God. 22 Therefore repent of
this wickedness of yours, and pray
earnestly to the Lord that, [a]if possi-
ble, the intention of your heart may
be forgiven you. 23 For I see that you
are in the gall of bitterness and in
[a]the [1]bondage of unrighteousness."
24 But Simon answered and said,
"[a]Pray earnestly to the Lord for me
yourselves, so that nothing of what
you have said may come upon me."

### *An Ethiopian Receives Christ*

25 So, when they had solemnly [a]borne
witness and spoken [b]the word of the
Lord, they started back to Jerusalem,
and were [c]proclaiming the gospel to
many villages of the [d]Samaritans.
26 But [a]an angel of the [1]Lord spoke
to [b]Philip saying, "Rise up and go
south to the road that descends from
Jerusalem to [c]Gaza." ([2]This is a desert
*road.*) 27 So he rose up and went; and
behold, [a]there was an Ethiopian
eunuch, a court official of Candace,
queen of the Ethiopians, who was
in charge of all her treasure; and he
[b]had come to Jerusalem to worship,
28 and he was returning and sitting
in his [1]chariot, and was reading the
prophet Isaiah. 29 Then [a]the Spirit
said to Philip, "Go over and join this
[1]chariot." 30 And Philip ran up and
heard him reading Isaiah the prophet,
and said, "Do you understand what
you are reading?" 31 And he said,
"Well, how could I, unless someone
guides me?" And he invited Philip to
come up and sit with him. 32 Now the
passage of Scripture which he was
reading was this:

"[a]AS A SHEEP IS LED
TO SLAUGHTER;
AND AS A LAMB BEFORE ITS
SHEARER IS SILENT,
SO HE DOES NOT OPEN
HIS MOUTH.
33 "[a]IN HUMILIATION HIS
JUDGMENT WAS TAKEN AWAY;
WHO WILL [1]RECOUNT
HIS [2]GENERATION?
FOR HIS LIFE IS REMOVED
FROM THE EARTH."

34 And the eunuch answered Philip
and said, "I ask you earnestly, of
whom does the prophet say this?
Of himself or of someone else?"
35 Then Philip [a]opened his mouth,
and [b]beginning from this Scripture
he [c]proclaimed the good news
about Jesus to him. 36 And as they
went along the road they came to
some water; and the eunuch *said,
"Look! Water! [a]What prevents me

**8:17** [b]Ac 2:4 **8:20** [a]2Ki 5:16; Is 55:1; Da 5:17; Mt 10:8; Ac 2:38 **8:21** [a]Dt 10:9; 12:12; Eph 5:5 [b]Ps 78:37 [1]Or *teaching*; lit *word* **8:22** [a]Is 55:7 **8:23** [a]Is 58:6 [1]Lit *bond* **8:24** [a]Ge 20:7; Ex 8:8; Nu 21:7; Jas 5:16 **8:25** [a]Lk 16:28 [b]Ac 13:12 [c]Ac 8:40 [d]Mt 10:5 **8:26** [a]Ac 5:19; 8:29 [b]Ac 8:5 [c]Ge 10:19 [1]In OT, Yahweh, cf. Ge 16:7 [2]Or *This city is deserted* **8:27** [a]Ps 68:31; 87:4; Is 56:3ff [b]1Ki 8:41f; Jn 12:20 **8:28** [1]Or *carriage* **8:29** [a]Ac 8:39; 10:19; 11:12; 13:2; 16:6, 7; 20:23; 21:11; 28:25; Heb 3:7 [1]Or *carriage* **8:32** [a]Is 53:7 **8:33** [a]Is 53:8 [1]Or *describe* [2]Or *family, origin* **8:35** [a]Mt 5:2 [b]Lk 24:27; Ac 17:2; 18:28; 28:23 [c]Ac 5:42 **8:36** [a]Ac 10:47

from being baptized?" **37** [1][And Philip
said, "If you believe with all your
heart, you may." And he answered
and said, "I believe that Jesus Christ
is the Son of God."] **38** And he ordered
the [1]chariot to stop, and they both
went down into the water, Philip as
well as the eunuch, and he baptized
him. **39** When they came up out of
the water, [a]the Spirit of the Lord
snatched Philip away, and the eunuch
no longer saw him, [1]but went on his
way rejoicing. **40** But Philip [1]found
himself at [a][2]Azotus, and as he passed
through he [b]kept proclaiming the
gospel to all the cities until he came
to [c]Caesarea.

### *The Conversion of Saul*

**9** [a]Now [1]Saul, still [b]breathing
[2]threats and murder against the
disciples of the Lord, went to the
high priest, **2** and asked for [a]letters
from him to [b]the synagogues at
[c]Damascus, so that if he found any
belonging to [d]the Way, both men and
women, he might bring them bound
to Jerusalem. **3** And as he was travel-
ing, it happened that when he was
approaching Damascus, [a]suddenly
a light from heaven flashed around
him; **4** and [a]falling to the ground, he
heard a voice saying to him, "Saul,
Saul, why are you persecuting Me?"
**5** And he said, "Who are You, Lord?"
And He *said*, "I am Jesus whom you
are persecuting, **6** but rise up and
enter the city, and [a]it will be told
you what you must do." **7** And the
men who traveled with him [a]stood
speechless, [b]hearing the [1]voice but
seeing no one. **8** And Saul got up
from the ground, and [a]though his
eyes were open, he [1]could see noth-
ing. Leading him by the hand, they
brought him into [b]Damascus. **9** And
he was three days without sight, and
neither ate nor drank.

**10** Now there was a disciple at
[a]Damascus named [b]Ananias, and
the Lord said to him in [c]a vision,
"Ananias." And he said, "Here I am,
Lord." **11** And the Lord *said* to him,
"Rise up and go to the street called
Straight, and inquire at the house of
Judas for a man from [a]Tarsus named
Saul, for behold, he is praying, **12** and
he has seen [1]in a vision a man named
Ananias come in and [a]lay his hands
on him, so that he might regain his
sight." **13** But Ananias answered,
"Lord, I have heard from many about
this man, [a]how much harm he did
to [b]Your [1]saints at Jerusalem. **14** And
here he [a]has authority from the chief
priests to bind all who [b]call on Your
name." **15** But the Lord said to him,
"Go, for [a]he is a chosen [1]instrument
of Mine, to bear My name before
[b]the Gentiles and [c]kings and the
sons of Israel; **16** for [a]I will show
him how much he must suffer for

---

**8:37** [1]Early mss omit this v **8:38** [1]Or *carriage* **8:39** [a]1Ki 18:12; 2Ki 2:16; Eze 3:12, 14; 8:3; 11:1, 24; 43:5; 2Co 12:2 [1]Lit *for he was going* **8:40** [a]Jos 11:22; 1Sa 5:1 [b]Ac 8:25 [c]Ac 9:30; 10:1, 24; 11:11; 12:19; 18:22; 21:8, 16; 23:23, 33; 25:1, 4, 6, 13 [1]Or *was found* [2]In OT, Ashdod ◆ **9:1** [a]Ac 9:1-22; 22:3-16; 26:9-18 [b]Ac 8:3; 9:13-21 [1]Later called Paul [2]Lit *threat* **9:2** [a]Ac 9:14, 21; 22:5; *26:10* [b]*Mt 10:17* [c]Ge 14:15; 2Co 11:32; Ga 1:17 [d]Jn 14:6; *Ac 18:25f; 19:9, 23; 22:4; 24:14, 22* **9:3** [a]1Co 15:8 **9:4** [a]Ac 22:7; 26:14 **9:6** [a]Ac 9:16 **9:7** [a]Ac 26:14 [b]Jn 12:29f; Ac 22:9 [1]Or *sound* **9:8** [a]Ac 9:18; 22:11 [b]Ge 14:15; 2Co 11:32; Ga 1:17 [1]Lit *was seeing nothing* **9:10** [a]Ge 14:15; 2Co 11:32; Ga 1:17 [b]Ac 22:12 [c]Ac 10:3, 17, 19; 11:5; 12:9; 16:9f; 18:9 **9:11** [a]Ac 9:30; 11:25; 21:39; 22:3 **9:12** [a]Mk 5:23; Ac 6:6; 9:17 [1]Some early mss omit *in a vision* **9:13** [a]Ac 8:3 [b]Ac 9:32, 41; 26:10; Ro 1:7; 15:25, 26, 31; 16:2, 15; 1Co 1:2 [1]Or *holy ones* **9:14** [a]Ac 9:2, 21 [b]Ac 7:59 **9:15** [a]Ac 13:2; Ro 1:1; 9:23; Ga 1:15; Eph 3:7 [b]Ac 22:21; 26:17; Ro 1:5; 11:13; 15:16; Ga 1:16; 2:7ff; Eph 3:1, 8; 1Ti 2:7; 2Ti 4:17 [c]Ac 25:22f; 26:1, 32; 2Ti 4:17 [1]Or *vessel* **9:16** [a]Ac 20:23; 21:4, 11, 13; 2Co 6:4f; 11:23-27; 1Th 3:3

My name." **17** So Ananias departed and entered the house. And he [a]laid his hands on him and said, "[b]Brother Saul, the Lord sent me—*that is* Jesus who appeared to you on the road by which you were coming—so that you may regain your sight and be [c]filled with the Holy Spirit." **18** And immediately there fell from his eyes something like scales, and he regained his sight, and he rose up and was baptized; **19** and he took food and was strengthened.

### *Saul Begins to Preach Christ*

Now [a]for several days he was with [b]the disciples who were at Damascus, **20** and immediately he *began to* proclaim Jesus [a]in the synagogues, [1]saying, "He is [b]the Son of God." **21** And all those hearing him continued to be astounded, and were saying, "Is this not the one who in Jerusalem [a]destroyed those that [b]called on this name, and *who* had come here for the purpose of bringing them bound before the chief priests?" **22** But Saul kept increasing in strength and confounding the Jews who lived at Damascus by proving that this One is the [1]Christ.

**23** And when [a]many days had elapsed, [b]the Jews plotted together to put him to death, **24** but [a]their plot became known to Saul. [b]They were also watching the gates day and night so that they might put him to death; **25** but his disciples took him by night and let him down through the wall, lowering him in a *large* basket.

**26** [a]And when he came to Jerusalem, he was trying to associate with the disciples, [1]but they were all afraid of him, not believing that he was a disciple. **27** But [a]Barnabas took him and brought him to the apostles and recounted to them how he had [b]seen the Lord on the road, and that He had talked to him, and how [c]at Damascus he had [d]spoken out boldly in the name of Jesus. **28** So he was with them, [1]moving about freely in Jerusalem, [a]speaking out boldly in the name of the Lord. **29** And he was talking and arguing with the [a,1]Hellenistic *Jews*, but they were attempting to put him to death. **30** But when [a]the brothers learned *of it*, they brought him down to [b]Caesarea and [c]sent him away to [d]Tarsus.

**31** So [a]the church throughout all Judea and Galilee and Samaria was having peace, being built up. And going on in the fear of the Lord and in the encouragement of the Holy Spirit, it continued to multiply.

### *Peter Heals Aeneas*

**32** Now it happened that as Peter was traveling through all *those regions*, he came down also to [a]the [1]saints who lived at [b,2]Lydda. **33** And there he found a man named Aeneas, who had been bedridden eight years, for he was paralyzed. **34** And Peter said to him, "Aeneas, Jesus Christ heals you. Rise up and make your bed."

**9:17** [a]Mk 5:23; Ac 6:6; 9:12 [b]Ac 22:13 [c]Ac 2:4 **9:19** [a]Ac 26:20 [b]Ac 9:26, 38; 11:26 **9:20** [a]Ac 13:5, 14; 14:1; 16:13; 17:2, 10; 18:4, 19; 19:8 [b]Mt 4:3; Ac 9:22; 13:33 [1]Lit *that* **9:21** [a]Ac 8:3; 9:13; Ga 1:13, 23 [b]Ac 9:14 **9:22** [1]Messiah **9:23** [a]Ga 1:17, 18 [b]1Th 2:16 **9:24** [a]Ac 20:3, 19; 23:12, 30; 25:3 [b]2Co 11:32f **9:26** [a]Ac 22:17-20; 26:20 [1]Lit *and* **9:27** [a]Ac 4:36 [b]Ac 9:3-6 [c]Ac 9:20, 22 [d]Ac 4:13, 29; 9:29 **9:28** [a]Ac 4:13, 29; 9:29 [1]Lit *going in and going out* **9:29** [a]Ac 6:1 [1]Jews who adopted the Gr language and much of Gr culture through acculturation **9:30** [a]Ac 1:15 [b]Ac 8:40 [c]Ga 1:21 [d]Ac 9:11 **9:31** [a]Ac 5:11; 8:1; 16:5 **9:32** [a]Ac 9:13 [b]1Chr 8:12; Ezr 2:33; Ne 7:37; 11:35 [1]Or *holy ones* [2]OT: Lod

Immediately he rose up. **35** And all
who lived at [a,1]Lydda and [b]Sharon
saw him, and they [c]turned to the
Lord.

### *Peter Raises Tabitha to Life*

**36** Now in [a]Joppa there was a disciple
named Tabitha (which translated is
called [1]Dorcas). This woman was full
of good works and charity which she
continually did. **37** And it happened
[1]at that time that she fell sick and
died; and when they had washed
her body, they laid it in an [a]upper
room. **38** Now since Lydda was near
[a]Joppa, [b]the disciples, having heard
that Peter was there, sent two men
to him, pleading with him, "Do not
delay in coming to us." **39** So Peter
arose and went with them. When he
arrived, they brought him into the
[a]upper room; and all the [b]widows
stood beside him, crying and show-
ing all the [1]tunics and garments that
Dorcas used to make while she was
with them. **40** But Peter [a]sent them
all out and [b]knelt down and prayed,
and turning to the body, he said,
"[c]Tabitha, arise." And she opened
her eyes, and when she saw Peter, she
sat up. **41** And he gave her his hand
and raised her up. And calling [a]the
[1]saints and [b]widows, he presented
her alive. **42** And it became known
all over [a]Joppa, and [b]many believed
in the Lord. **43** And it happened that
he stayed many days in [a]Joppa with
[b]a tanner *named* Simon.

### *Cornelius' and Peter's Visions*

**10** Now *there was* a man at
[a]Caesarea named Cornelius,
a centurion of what was [b]called the
Italian [1]cohort, **2** a devout man and
[a]one who feared God with all his
household, and [b]gave many [1]alms
to the people and prayed to God
continually. **3** About [a]the [1]ninth
hour of the day he clearly saw [b]in
a vision [c]an angel of God who had
come in and said to him, "Cornelius!"
**4** And [a]looking intently on him and
becoming afraid, he said, "What is
it, Lord?" And he said to him, "Your
prayers and [1]alms [b]have ascended [c]as
a memorial before God. **5** Now send
*some* men to [a]Joppa and summon
a man *named* Simon, who is also
called Peter; **6** he is lodging with a
tanner *named* [a]Simon, whose house
is by the sea." **7** And when the angel
who was speaking to him had left,
he called two of his servants and a
devout soldier of those who were
his personal attendants, **8** and after
he explained everything to them, he
sent them to [a]Joppa.

**9** And on the next day, as they were
on their way and approaching the
city, [a]Peter went up on [b]the housetop
about [c]the [1]sixth hour to pray. **10** But
he became hungry and was desiring

**9:35** [a]1Chr 8:12; Ezr 2:33; Ne 7:37; 11:35 [b]1Chr 5:16; 27:29; Is 33:9; 35:2; 65:10 [c]Ac 2:47; 9:42; 11:21 [1]OT: Lod **9:36** [a]Jos 19:46; 2Chr 2:16; Ezr 3:7; Jon 1:3; Ac 9:38, 42f; 10:5, 8, 23, 32; 11:5, 13 [1]Gr for Gazelle **9:37** [a]Ac 1:13; 9:39 [1]Lit *in those days* **9:38** [a]Jos 19:46; 2Chr 2:16; Ezr 3:7; Jon 1:3; Ac 9:36, 42f; 10:5, 8, 23, 32; 11:5, 13 [b]Ac 11:26 **9:39** [a]Ac 1:13; 9:37 [b]Ac 6:1 [1]Or *inner garments* **9:40** [a]Mt 9:25 [b]Lk 22:41; Ac 7:60 [c]Mk 5:41 **9:41** [a]Ac 9:13, 32 [b]Ac 6:1 [1]Or *holy ones* **9:42** [a]Jos 19:46; 2Chr 2:16; Jon 1:3; Ac 9:38, 42f; 10:5, 8, 23, 32; 11:5, 13 [b]Ac 9:35 **9:43** [a]Jos 19:46; 2Chr 2:16; Ezr 3:7; Jon 1:3; Ac 9:38, 42f; 10:5, 8, 23, 32; 11:13, 15 [b]Ac 10:6 ◆ **10:1** [a]Ac 8:40; 10:24 [b]Mt 27:27; Mk 15:16; Jn 18:3, 12; Ac 21:31; 27:1 [1]Normally 600 men (the number varied); or *battalion* **10:2** [a]Ac 10:22, 35; 13:16, 26 [b]Lk 7:4f [1]Or *gifts of charity* **10:3** [a]Ac 3:1 [b]Ac 9:10; 10:17, 19 [c]Ac 5:19 [1]3 p.m. **10:4** [a]Ac 3:4 [b]Rev 8:4 [c]Mt 26:13; Php 4:18; Heb 6:10 [1]Or *gifts of charity* **10:5** [a]Ac 9:36 **10:6** [a]Ac 9:43 **10:8** [a]Ac 9:36 **10:9** [a]Ac 10:9-32; 11:5-14 [b]Jer 19:13; 32:29; Zep 1:5; Mt 24:17 [c]Ps 55:17; Ac 10:3 [1]Noon

to eat. And while they were making
preparations, he [a]fell into a trance
**11** and *saw [a]heaven opened up, and
[1]an object like a great sheet coming
down, lowered by four corners to
the ground, **12** and there were in it
all *kinds of* four-footed animals and
crawling creatures of the earth and
birds of the [1]sky. **13** And a voice came
to him, "Rise up, Peter, [1]slaughter and
eat!" **14** But Peter said, "By no means,
[a]Lord, for [b]I have never eaten any-
thing defiled and unclean." **15** Again
a voice *came* to him a second time,
"[a]What God has cleansed, no *longer*
consider defiled." **16** And this hap-
pened three times and immediately
the [1]object was taken up into heaven.
**17** Now while Peter was greatly
perplexed in [1]mind as to what [a]the
vision which he had seen might be,
behold, [b]the men who had been sent
by Cornelius, having asked directions
for Simon's house, appeared at the
gate; **18** and calling out, they were
asking whether Simon, who was
also called Peter, was lodging there.
**19** And while Peter was reflecting on
[a]the vision, [b]the Spirit said to him,
"Behold, [1]three men are looking for
you. **20** But rise up, go down and [a]ac-
company them without taking issue
at all, for I have sent them Myself."
**21** And Peter went down to the men
and said, "Behold, I am the one you
are looking for; what is the reason
for which you have come?" **22** And
they said, "Cornelius, a centurion,
a righteous and [a]God-fearing man
well spoken of by the entire nation
of the Jews, [b]was directed by a [c]holy
angel to summon you to his house
and hear [d,1]a message from you."
**23** So he invited them in and gave
them lodging.

### *Peter at Caesarea*

And on the next day he rose up and
went away with them, and [a]some of
[b]the brothers from [c]Joppa went with
him. **24** And on the following day he
entered [a]Caesarea. Now Cornelius
was waiting for them and had called
together his relatives and close
friends. **25** And when Peter entered,
Cornelius met him, and fell at his feet
and [a,1]worshiped *him*. **26** But Peter
raised him up, saying, "[a]Stand up;
I too am *just* a man." **27** As he talked
with him, he entered and *found
[a]many people assembled. **28** And he
said to them, "You yourselves know
how [a]unlawful it is for a man who is
a Jew to associate with a foreigner or
to visit him; and *yet* [b]God has shown
me that I should not call any man
defiled or unclean. **29** That is why
I came without even raising any
objection when I was summoned.
So I ask for what reason you have
summoned me."
**30** And Cornelius said, "[a]Four days
ago to this hour, I was praying in my
house during [b]the [1]ninth hour; and
behold, [c]a man stood before me in
shining garments, **31** and he *said,

**10:10** [a]Ac 11:5; 22:17 **10:11** [a]Jn 1:51 [1]Or *a vessel* **10:12** [1]Or *heaven* **10:13** [1]Or *sacrifice*
**10:14** [a]Mt 8:2ff; Jn 4:11ff; Ac 9:5; 22:8 [b]Lv 11:20-25; Dt 14:4-20; Eze 4:14; Da 1:8; Ac 10:28
**10:15** [a]Mt 15:11; Mk 7:19; Ro 14:14; 1Co 10:25ff; 1Ti 4:4f; Tit 1:15 **10:16** [1]Or *vessel* **10:17** [a]Ac 10:3
[b]Ac 10:8 [1]Lit *himself* **10:19** [a]Ac 10:3 [b]Ac 8:29 [1]One early ms *two* **10:20** [a]Ac 15:7-9
**10:22** [a]Ac 10:2 [b]Mt 2:12 [c]Mk 8:38; Lk 9:26; Rev 14:10 [d]Ac 11:14 [1]Lit *words* **10:23** [a]Ac 10:45; 11:12
[b]Ac 1:15 [c]Ac 9:36 **10:24** [a]Ac 8:40; 10:1 **10:25** [a]Mt 8:2 [1]Or *prostrated himself in reverence*
**10:26** [a]Ac 14:15; Rev 19:10; 22:8f **10:27** [a]Ac 10:24 **10:28** [a]Jn 4:9; 18:28; Ac 11:3 [b]Ac 10:14f, 35; 15:9
**10:30** [a]Ac 10:9, 22f [b]Ac 3:1; 10:3 [c]Ac 10:3-6, 30-32 [1]3 p.m.

'Cornelius, your prayer has been
heard and your [1]alms have been re-
membered before God. **32** Therefore
send to [a]Joppa and invite Simon, who
is also called Peter, to come to you;
he is lodging at the house of Simon
*the* tanner by the sea.' **33** So I sent for
you immediately, and you have [1]been
kind enough to come. Now then, we
are all here present before God to
hear all that you have been ordered
by the Lord."

### *The Holy Spirit Poured Out on the Gentiles*

**34** [a]And opening his mouth, Peter
said:

"I most truly comprehend *now* that
[b]God is not one to show partiality,
**35** but [a]in every nation the one who
[b,1]fears Him and does righteousness
is welcome to Him. **36** As for the word
which He sent to the sons of Israel,
[a]proclaiming the good news of [b]peace
through Jesus Christ—He is [c]Lord of
all— **37** you yourselves know the
thing which happened throughout
all Judea, starting from Galilee, after
the baptism which John proclaimed.
**38** [1]*You know of* [a]Jesus of Nazareth,
how God [b]anointed Him with the
Holy Spirit and with power, [c,2]and
*how* He went about doing good and
healing all who were oppressed by the
devil, for [d]God was with Him. **39** And
we are [a]witnesses of all the things
He did both in the [1]land of the Jews
and in Jerusalem. They also [b]put Him
to death by hanging Him on a tree.
**40** [a]God raised Him up on the third day
and granted that He appear, **41** [a]not to
all the people, but to [b]witnesses who
were chosen beforehand by God, *that
is,* to us [c]who ate and drank with Him
after He arose from the dead. **42** And
He [a]commanded us to [1]preach to the
people, and solemnly to [b]bear witness
that this is the One who has been
[c]designated by God as [d]Judge of the
living and the dead. **43** Of Him [a]all the
prophets bear witness that through
[b]His name everyone who believes in
Him receives forgiveness of sins."

**44** While Peter was still speaking
these things, [a]the Holy Spirit fell
upon all those who were listening to
the word. **45** [a]And all the [1]circumcised
believers who came with Peter were
astounded that the gift of the Holy
Spirit had been [b]poured out on the
Gentiles also. **46** For they were hearing
them [a]speaking with tongues and
magnifying God. Then Peter answered,
**47** "[a]Can anyone refuse water for these
to be baptized who [b]have received the
Holy Spirit just as we *did*?" **48** And he
[a]ordered them to be baptized [b]in the
name of Jesus Christ. Then they asked
him to remain for a few days.

### *Peter's Report in Jerusalem*

**11** Now the apostles and [a]the
brothers who were throughout
Judea heard that the Gentiles also

**10:31** [1]Or *deeds of charity* **10:32** [a]Jn 4:9; 18:28; Ac 11:3 **10:33** [1]Lit *done well in coming*
**10:34** [a]Mt 5:2 [b]Dt 10:17; 2Chr 19:7; Ro 2:11; Ga 2:6; Eph 6:9; Col 3:25; 1Pe 1:17 **10:35** [a]Ac 10:28
[b]Ac 10:2 [1]Or *reverences* **10:36** [a]Ac 13:32 [b]Lk 1:79; 2:14; Ro 5:1; Eph 2:17 [c]Mt 28:18; Ac 2:36; Ro 10:12
**10:38** [a]Ac 2:22 [b]Ac 4:26 [c]Mt 4:23 [d]Jn 3:2 [1]Or *How God anointed Jesus of Nazareth* [2]Lit *who went*
**10:39** [a]Lk 24:48; Ac 10:41 [b]Ac 5:30 [1]Or *countryside* **10:40** [a]Ac 2:24 **10:41** [a]Jn 14:19, 22; 15:27
[b]Lk 24:48; Ac 10:39 [c]Lk 24:43; Ac 1:4 mg **10:42** [a]Ac 1:2 [b]Lk 16:28 [c]Lk 22:22 [d]Jn 5:22, 27; Ac 17:31;
2Ti 4:1; 1Pe 4:5 [1]Or *proclaim* **10:43** [a]Ac 3:18 [b]Lk 24:47; Ac 2:38; 4:12 **10:44** [a]Ac 11:15; 15:8
**10:45** [a]Ac 10:23 [b]Ac 2:33, 38 [1]Lit *believers from among the circumcision* **10:46** [a]Mk 16:17; Ac 2:4; 19:6
**10:47** [a]Ac 8:36 [b]Ac 2:4; 10:44f; 11:17; 15:8 **10:48** [a]1Co 1:14-17 [b]Ac 2:38; 8:16; 19:5 ◆ **11:1** [a]Ac 1:15

had received the word of God. **2** And
when Peter came up to Jerusalem,
[a,1]those who were circumcised took
issue with him, **3** saying, "[a]You [1]went
to uncircumcised men and ate with
them." **4** But Peter began *speaking*
[1]and *proceeded* to explain to them
[a]in orderly sequence, saying, **5** "[a]I
was in the city of Joppa praying;
and in a trance I saw [b]a vision, [1]an
object coming down like a great sheet
lowered by four corners from heaven,
and it came right down to me, **6** and
when looking closely at it, I was
observing it and saw the four-footed
animals of the earth and the wild
beasts and the crawling creatures
and the birds of the [1]sky. **7** And I
also heard a voice saying to me, 'Rise
up, Peter; [1]slaughter and eat.' **8** But I
said, 'By no means, Lord, for nothing
defiled or unclean has ever entered
my mouth.' **9** But a voice from heaven
answered a second time, '[a]What God
has cleansed, no longer consider
defiled.' **10** And this happened three
times, and everything was drawn
back up into heaven. **11** And behold,
immediately three men appeared at
the house in which we were, having
been sent to me from [a]Caesarea.
**12** [a]And the Spirit told me to go with
them [b,1]without taking issue at all.
[c]These six brothers also went with
me and we entered the man's house.
**13** And he reported to us how he
had seen the angel [1]standing in his
house, and saying, 'Send to Joppa and
summon Simon, who is also called
Peter; **14** and he will speak [a]words to
you by which you will be saved, you
and [b]all your household.' **15** And as I
began to speak, [a]the Holy Spirit fell
upon them just [b]as *He did* upon us at
the beginning. **16** And I remembered
the word of the Lord, how He used to
say, '[a]John baptized with water, but
you will be baptized [1]with the Holy
Spirit.' **17** Therefore if [a]God gave to
them the same gift as *He gave* to us
also after believing in the Lord Jesus
Christ, [b]who was I that I could pre-
vent God's way?" **18** And when they
heard this, they [1]quieted down and
[a]glorified God, saying, "Well then,
God has granted to the Gentiles also
the [b]repentance *that leads* to life."

### *The Church in Antioch*

**19** [a]So then those who were scattered
because of the [1]persecution that oc-
curred in connection with Stephen
made their way [2]to [b]Phoenicia and
[c]Cyprus and [d]Antioch, speaking the
word to no one except to Jews alone.
**20** But there were some of them, men
of [a]Cyprus and [b]Cyrene, who came to
[c]Antioch and *began* speaking to the
[d,1]Greeks also, [e]proclaiming the good
news of the Lord Jesus. **21** And [a]the
hand of the Lord was with them, and
[b]a large number who believed turned

**11:2** [a]Ac 10:45 [1]Lit *those of the circumcision* **11:3** [a]Mt 9:11; Ac 10:28; Ga 2:12 [1]Or *entered the house of* **11:4** [a]Lk 1:3 [1]Lit *and was explaining* **11:5** [a]Ac 10:9-32; 11:5-14 [b]Ac 9:10 [1]Or *a vessel* **11:6** [1]Or *heaven* **11:7** [1]Or *sacrifice* **11:9** [a]Ac 10:15 **11:11** [a]Ac 8:40 **11:12** [a]Ac 8:29 [b]Ac 15:9; Ro 3:22 [c]Ac 10:23 [1]Or *without making any distinction* **11:13** [1]Or *after he had stood in his house and said* **11:14** [a]Ac 10:22 [b]Jn 4:53; Ac 10:2; 16:15, 31-34; 18:8; 1Co 1:16 **11:15** [a]Ac 10:44 [b]Ac 2:4 **11:16** [a]Ac 1:5 [1]Or *in* **11:17** [a]Ac 10:45, 47 [b]Ac 5:39 **11:18** [a]Mt 9:8 [b]2Co 7:10 [1]Lit *became silent* **11:19** [a]Ac 8:1, 4 [b]Ac 15:3; 21:2 [c]Ac 4:36 [d]Ac 6:5; 11:20, 22, 27; 13:1; 14:26; 15:22f, 30, 35; 18:22; Ga 2:11 [1]Lit *tribulation* [2]Lit *as far as* **11:20** [a]Ac 4:36 [b]Mt 27:32; Ac 2:10; 6:9; 13:1 [c]Ac 6:5; 11:19, 22, 27; 13:1; 14:26; 15:22f, 30, 35; 18:22; Ga 2:11 [d]Jn 7:35; Ac 6:1 [e]Ac 5:42 [1]Lit *Hellenists*; people who lived by Gr customs and culture **11:21** [a]Lk 1:66 [b]Ac 2:47

to the Lord. **22** Now the [1]news about them [2]reached the ears of the church at Jerusalem, and they sent [a]Barnabas off [3]to [b]Antioch, **23** who, when he arrived and saw [a]the grace of God, rejoiced and *began to* encourage them all with a purposeful heart to remain *true* to the Lord; **24** for he was a good man, and [a]full of the Holy Spirit and of faith. And a [b]considerable crowd was [1]brought to the Lord. **25** And he left for [a]Tarsus to search for Saul; **26** and when he found him, he brought him to [a]Antioch. And it happened that for an entire year they [1]met with the church and taught a considerable crowd. And [b]the disciples were first called [c]Christians in [a]Antioch.

**27** Now in those days, [a]some prophets came down from Jerusalem to [b]Antioch. **28** And one of them named [a]Agabus stood up and indicated [1]by the Spirit that there was going to be a great famine [b]all over the [2]world. [3]And this took place in the *reign* of [c]Claudius. **29** And as any of [a]the disciples had means, each of them determined to send *a contribution* for the service of [b]the brothers living in Judea. **30** [a]And this they did, sending it [1]in charge of [b]Barnabas and Saul to the [c]elders.

### *An Angel Frees Peter from Prison*

**12** Now about that time [1]Herod the king laid hands on some who belonged to the church in order to harm them. **2** And he [a]had James the brother of John [b]put to death with a sword. **3** And when he saw that it [a]pleased the Jews, he proceeded to arrest Peter also. Now [1]it was during [b]the days of Unleavened Bread. **4** When he had seized him, he put him in prison, delivering him to four [a,1]squads of soldiers to guard him, intending after [b]the Passover to bring him out before the people. **5** So Peter was kept in the prison, but prayer for him was being made fervently by the church to God.

**6** Now on [1]the very night when Herod was about to bring him forward, Peter was sleeping between two soldiers, [a]bound with two chains, and guards in front of the door were watching over the prison. **7** And behold, [a]an angel of the Lord suddenly [b]appeared and a light shone in the cell; and he struck Peter's side and woke him up, saying, "Rise up quickly." And [c]his chains fell off his hands. **8** And the angel said to him, "Gird yourself and [1]put on your sandals." And he did so. And he *said to him, "Wrap your garment around yourself and follow me." **9** And he went out and continued to follow, and he did not know that what was being done by the angel was real, but was thinking he was seeing [a]a vision. **10** And when they had passed the first and second

**11:22** [a]Ac 4:36 [b]Ac 6:5; 11:19, 20, 27; 13:1; 18:22; Ga 2:11 [1]Lit *word* [2]Lit *was heard in* [3]Lit *as far as*
**11:23** [a]Ac 13:43; 14:26; 15:40; 20:24, 32 **11:24** [a]Ac 2:4 [b]Ac 2:47; 5:14; 11:21 [1]Lit *added* **11:25** [a]Ac 9:11
**11:26** [a]Ac 6:5; 11:20, 22, 27 [b]Jn 2:2; Ac 1:15 [c]Ac 26:28; 1Pe 4:16 [1]Or *were gathered together*
**11:27** [a]Lk 11:49; Ac 2:17; 13:1; 1Co 12:10, 28f [b]Ac 6:5; 11:20, 22, 26; 13:1; 14:26; 15:22f, 30, 35; 18:22; Ga 2:11
**11:28** [a]Ac 21:10 [b]Mt 24:14 [c]Ac 18:2 [1]Or *through* [2]Lit inhabited earth [3]Lit Which **11:29** [a]Jn 2:2; Ac 1:15; 6:1f; 9:19, 25, 26, 38; 11:26; 13:52; 14:20, 22, 28 [b]Ac 11:1 **11:30** [a]Ac 12:25 [b]Ac 4:36 [c]Ac 14:23; 15:2, 4, 6, 22f; 16:4; 20:17; 21:18; 1Ti 5:17, 19; Tit 1:5; Jas 5:14; 1Pe 5:1; 2Jn 1; 3Jn 1 [1]Lit *by the hand of*
◆ **12:1** [1]Herod Agrippa I **12:2** [a]Mt 4:21; 20:23 [b]Mk 10:39 **12:3** [a]Ac 24:27; 25:9 [b]Ex 12:15; 23:15; Ac 20:6 [1]Lit *they were the days* **12:4** [a]Jn 19:23 [b]Ex 12:1-27; Mk 14:1; Ac 12:3 [1]Lit *quaternions*; a quaternion was composed of four soldiers **12:6** [a]Ac 21:33 [1]Lit *that night* **12:7** [a]Ac 5:19 [b]Lk 2:9; 24:4 [c]Ac 16:26
**12:8** [1]Lit *bind* **12:9** [a]Ac 9:10

guard posts, they came to the iron
gate that leads into the city, which
[a]opened for them by itself; and they
went out and went along one street,
and immediately the angel departed
from him. **11** When Peter [a]came [1]to
himself, he said, "Now truly I know
that [b]the Lord has sent His angel and
rescued me from the hand of Herod
and from all [2]that the Jewish people
were expecting." **12** And when he
realized *this,* he went to the house
of Mary, the mother of [a]John who
was also called Mark, where many
were gathered together and [b]were
praying. **13** And when he knocked at
the door of the gate, [a]a servant-girl
named Rhoda came to answer. **14** And
when she recognized Peter's voice,
[a]because of her joy she did not open
the gate. But she ran in and reported
that Peter was standing in front of
the gate. **15** And they said to her, "You
are out of your mind!" But she kept
insisting that it was so. They kept
saying, "It is [a]his angel." **16** But Peter
continued knocking, and when they
opened *the door,* they saw him and
were astounded. **17** But [a]motioning
to them with his hand to be silent,
he recounted to them how the Lord
had led him out of the prison. And he
said, "Report these things to [b]James
and [c]the brothers." Then he left and
went to another place.
**18** Now when day came, there
was no small disturbance among
the soldiers *as to* what [1]had become
of Peter. **19** And when Herod had
searched for him and had not found
him, he examined the guards and
ordered that they [a]be led away *to
execution.* Then he went down from
Judea to [b]Caesarea and was spending
time there.

### *The Death of Herod*

**20** Now he was very angry with the
people of [a]Tyre and Sidon; and with
one accord they came to him, and
having won over Blastus the king's
chamberlain, they were asking for
peace, because [b]their country was
fed by the king's country. **21** And on
an appointed day Herod, having put
on his royal apparel and sitting on
the judgment seat, *began* delivering
an address to them. **22** And the as-
sembly kept crying out, "The voice
of a god and not of a man!" **23** And
immediately [a]an angel of the [1]Lord
struck him because he did not give
God the glory, and he was eaten by
worms and breathed his last.
**24** But [a]the word of the Lord con-
tinued to grow and to be multiplied.
**25** And [a]Barnabas and [a]Saul
[1]returned [2]to Jerusalem, [b]fulfilling
their ministry, taking along with *them*
[c]John, who was also called Mark.

### *Barnabas and Saul Sent from Antioch by the Holy Spirit*

**13** Now there were at [a]Antioch,
in the [b]church that was *there,*
[c]prophets and [d]teachers: [e]Barnabas,

**12:10** [a]Ac 5:19; 16:26 **12:11** [a]Lk 15:17 [b]Da 3:28; 6:22 [1]Lit *in himself* [2]Lit *the expectation of the people of the Jews* **12:12** [a]Ac 12:25; 13:5, 13; 15:37, 39; Col 4:10; 2Ti 4:11; Phm 24; 1Pe 5:13 [b]Ac 12:5 **12:13** [a]Jn 18:16f **12:14** [a]Lk 24:41 **12:15** [a]Mt 18:10 **12:17** [a]Ac 13:16; 19:33; 21:40 [b]Mk 6:3; Ac 15:13; 21:18; 1Co 15:7; Ga 1:19; 2:9, 12 [c]Ac 1:15 **12:18** [1]Lit *therefore had become* **12:19** [a]Ac 16:27; 27:42 [b]Ac 8:40 **12:20** [a]Mt 11:21 [b]1Ki 5:11; Ezr 3:7; Eze 27:17 **12:23** [a]2Sa 24:16; 2Ki 19:35; Ac 5:19 [1]In OT, Yahweh, cf. 2Ki 1:3 **12:24** [a]Ac 6:7; 19:20 **12:25** [a]Ac 4:36; 13:1ff [b]Ac 11:30 [c]Ac 12:12 [1]Or *returned, fulfilling their ministry in Jerusalem* [2]Later mss *from* ◆ **13:1** [a]Ac 11:19 [b]Ac 11:26 [c]Ac 11:27; 15:32; 19:6; 21:9; 1Co 11:4f; 13:2, 8f; 14:29, 32, 37 [d]Ro 12:6f; 1Co 12:28f; Eph 4:11; Jas 3:1 [e]Ac 4:36

and Simeon who was called Niger,
and Lucius of [f]Cyrene, and Manaen
who had been brought up with
[g]Herod the tetrarch, and Saul. **2** And
while they were ministering to the
Lord and fasting, [a]the Holy Spirit
said, “Set apart for Me [b]Barnabas and
Saul for [c]the work to which I have
called them.” **3** Then, when they had
fasted and [a]prayed and [b]laid their
hands on them, [c]they sent them
away.

### *On Cyprus*

**4** So, being [a]sent out by the Holy
Spirit, they went down to Seleu-
cia and from there they sailed to
[b]Cyprus. **5** And when they reached
Salamis, they *began to* proclaim the
word of God in [a]the synagogues of
the Jews, and they also had [b]John as
their helper. **6** And when they had
gone through the whole island as far
as Paphos, they found a [a]magician,
a Jewish [b]false prophet whose name
was Bar-Jesus, **7** who was with the
[a]proconsul, Sergius Paulus, a man
of intelligence. This man summoned
Barnabas and Saul and sought to hear
the word of God. **8** But Elymas the
[a]magician (for so his name is trans-
lated) was opposing them, seeking to
turn the [b]proconsul away from [c]the
faith. **9** But Saul, who was also *known
as* Paul, [a,1]filled with the Holy Spirit,
fixed his gaze on him, **10** and said,
“You who are full of all deceit and
fraud, you [a]son of the devil, you en-
emy of all righteousness, will you not
cease to make crooked [b]the straight
ways of the [1]Lord? **11** Now, behold,
[a]the hand of the [1]Lord is upon you,
and you will be blind and not see the
sun for a time.” And immediately a
mist and a darkness fell upon him,
and he went about seeking those
who would lead him by the hand.
**12** Then the [a]proconsul believed
when he saw what had happened,
being astonished at [b]the teaching of
the Lord.

### *In Pisidian Antioch*

**13** Now after Paul and his compan-
ions set sail from [a]Paphos, they came
to [b]Perga in [c]Pamphylia, but [d]John
left them and returned to Jerusalem.
**14** But going on from Perga, they
arrived at [a]Pisidian [b]Antioch. And
on [c]the Sabbath day, they went into
[d]the synagogue and sat down. **15** And
after [a]the reading of the Law and [b]the
Prophets [c]the synagogue officials
sent to them, saying, “Brothers, if you
have any word of exhortation for the
people, say it.” **16** So Paul stood up,
and [a]motioning with his hand said,
“Men of Israel, and [b]you who
fear God, listen: **17** The God of this
people Israel [a]chose our fathers
and [b,1]lifted up the people during
their stay in the land of Egypt, and
with an uplifted arm [c]He led them
out from it. **18** And for [a]a period of

**13:1** [f]Mt 27:32; Ac 11:20 [g]Mt 14:1 **13:2** [a]Ac 8:29; 13:4 [b]Ac 4:36 [c]Ac 9:15 **13:3** [a]Ac 1:24 [b]Ac 6:6 [c]Ac 13:4; 14:26 **13:4** [a]Ac 13:2f [b]Ac 4:36 **13:5** [a]Ac 9:20; 13:14 [b]Ac 12:12 **13:6** [a]Ac 8:9 [b]Mt 7:15 ***13:7*** *[a]Ac 13:8, 12; 18:12; 19:38* **13:8** [a]Ac 8:9 [b]Ac 13:7, 12; 18:12; 19:38 [c]Ac 6:7 **13:9** [a]Ac 2:4; 4:8 [1]Or *having* just *been filled* **13:10** [a]Mt 13:38; Jn 8:44 [b]Hos 14:9; 2Pe 2:15 [1]In OT, Yahweh, cf. Is 40:3 **13:11** [a]Ex 9:3; 1Sa 5:6f; Job 19:21; Ps 32:4; Heb 10:31 [1]In OT, Yahweh, cf. Ex 9:3 **13:12** [a]Ac 13:7, 8; 18:12; 19:38 [b]Ac 8:25; 13:49; 15:35f; 19:10, 20 **13:13** [a]Ac 13:6 [b]Ac 14:25 [c]Ac 2:10; 14:24; 15:38; 27:5 [d]Ac 12:12 **13:14** [a]Ac 14:24 [b]Ac 14:19, 21; 2Ti 3:11 [c]Ac 13:42, 44; 16:13; 17:2; 18:4 [d]Ac 9:20; 13:5 **13:15** [a]Ac 15:21; 2Co 3:14f [b]Ac 13:27 [c]Mk 5:22 **13:16** [a]Ac 12:17 [b]Ac 10:2; 13:26 **13:17** [a]Ex 6:1, 6; 13:14, 16; Dt 7:6-8; Ac 7:17ff [b]Ex 1:7 [c]Ex 12:51 [1]Or *exalted* **13:18** [a]Nu 14:34; Ac 7:36

about forty years [b]He put up with
them in the wilderness. **19** [a]And
when He destroyed [b]seven nations in
the land of Canaan, He [c]distributed
their land as an inheritance—*all of
which took* [d]about 450 years. **20** After
these things He [a]gave *them* judges
until [b]Samuel the prophet. **21** Then
they [a]asked for a king, and God gave
them [b]Saul the son of Kish, a man of
the tribe of Benjamin, for forty years.
**22** And after He had [a]removed him,
He raised up David to be their king,
about whom He also said, bearing
witness, '[b]I HAVE FOUND DAVID the
son of Jesse, A MAN AFTER MY HEART,
who will do all My [1]will.' **23** [a]From
the seed of this man, [b]according to
promise, God has brought to Israel
[c]a Savior, Jesus, **24** after [a]John had
preached before [1]His coming a
[b]baptism of repentance to all the
people of Israel. **25** And as John [a]was
fulfilling his course, [b]he kept saying,
'What do you suppose that I am? I am
not *He*. But behold, one is coming
after me of whom I am not worthy
to untie the sandals of His feet.'

**26** "Brothers, sons of Abraham's
family, and those among you who
fear God, to us the word of [a]this
salvation was sent. **27** For those who
live in Jerusalem, and their [a]rulers,
[b]recognizing neither Him nor the [1]ut-
terances of [c]the prophets which are
[d]read every Sabbath, fulfilled *them*
by condemning *Him*. **28** And though
they found no ground for death, they
[a]asked Pilate that He be [1]executed.
**29** And when they had [a]finished all
that was written concerning Him,
[b]they took Him down from [c]the
tree and [d]laid Him in a tomb. **30** But
God [a]raised Him from the dead;
**31** and for many days [a]He appeared
to those who came up with Him
from Galilee to Jerusalem, the very
ones who are now [b]His witnesses to
the people. **32** And we [a]proclaim to
you the good news of [b]the promise
made to the fathers, **33** that God has
fulfilled this *promise* [1]to our children
in that He [a]raised up Jesus, as it is also
written in the second Psalm, '[b]YOU
ARE MY SON; TODAY I HAVE BEGOTTEN
YOU.' **34** *But* that He [a]raised Him up
from the dead, no longer to return
to corruption, He has spoken in
this way: '[b]I WILL GIVE YOU THE HOLY
*and* [1]FAITHFUL *lovingkindnesses* OF
DAVID.' **35** Therefore He also says in
another *Psalm*, '[a]YOU WILL NOT GIVE
YOUR [1]HOLY ONE OVER TO SEE COR-
RUPTION.' **36** For [a]David, after he had
[1]served [b]the purpose of God in his
own generation, [c]fell asleep and was
laid among his fathers and saw cor-
ruption; **37** but He whom God [a]raised
did not see corruption. **38** Therefore
let it be known to you, brothers,
that [a]through [1]Him forgiveness of
sins is proclaimed to you, **39** and that

**13:18** [b]Dt 1:31 **13:19** [a]Ac 7:45 [b]Dt 7:1 [c]Jos 14:1; 19:51; Ps 78:55 [d]Jdg 11:26; 1Ki 6:1 **13:20** [a]Jdg 2:16 [b]1Sa 3:20; Ac 3:24 **13:21** [a]1Sa 8:5 [b]1Sa 9:1f; 10:1, 21 **13:22** [a]1Sa 15:23, 26, 28; 16:1, 13 [b]1Sa 13:14; Ps 89:20; Ac 7:46 [1]Lit *wishes* **13:23** [a]Mt 1:1 [b]Ac 13:32f [c]Lk 2:11; Jn 4:42 **13:24** [a]Mk 1:1-4; Ac 1:22; 19:4 [b]Lk 3:3 [1]Lit *the face of His entering* **13:25** [a]Ac 20:24 [b]Mt 3:11; Mk 1:7; Lk 3:16; Jn 1:20, 27 **13:26** [a]Jn 6:68; Ac 4:12; 5:20; 13:46; 28:28 **13:27** [a]Lk 23:13 [b]Ac 3:17 [c]Lk 24:27 [d]Ac 13:15 [1]Lit *voices* **13:28** [a]Mt 27:22, 23; Mk 15:13, 14; Lk 23:21-23; Jn 19:15; Ac 3:14 [1]Lit *destroyed* **13:29** [a]Ac 26:22 [b]Lk 23:53 [c]Ac 5:30 [d]Mt 27:57-61; Mk 15:42-47; Lk 23:50-56; Jn 19:38-42 **13:30** [a]Ac 2:24; 13:33, 34, 37 **13:31** [a]Ac 1:3 [b]Lk 24:48 **13:32** [a]Ac 5:42; 14:15 [b]Ac 13:23; 26:6; Ro 1:2; 4:13; 9:4 **13:33** [a]Ac 2:24; 13:30, 34, 37 [b]Ps 2:7 [1]Late mss *to us their children* **13:34** [a]Ac 2:24; 13:30, 33, 37 [b]Is 55:3 [1]Lit *trustworthy* **13:35** [a]Ps 16:10; Ac 2:27 [1]Or *Devout, Pious* **13:36** [a]Ac 2:29 [b]Ac 13:22; 20:27 [c]1Ki 2:10; Ac 8:1 [1]Or *served his own generation by the purpose of God* **13:37** [a]Ac 2:24; 13:30, 33, 34 **13:38** [a]Lk 24:47; Ac 2:38 [1]Lit *this One*

in Him, [a]everyone who believes is
justified from all things which you
could not be justified from [1]through
the Law of Moses. **40** Therefore watch
out, so that the thing spoken of [a]in
the Prophets may not come upon *you*:
**41** '[a]LOOK, YOU SCOFFERS, AND
MARVEL, AND [1]PERISH;
FOR I AM ACCOMPLISHING
A WORK IN YOUR DAYS,
A WORK WHICH YOU WILL NEVER
BELIEVE, THOUGH SOMEONE
SHOULD RECOUNT IT TO YOU.'"
**42** And as [1]Paul and Barnabas were
leaving, the people kept pleading that
these words might be spoken to them
the next [a]Sabbath. **43** Now when *the
meeting of* the synagogue had bro-
ken up, many of the Jews and of the
[a]God-fearing [b,1]proselytes followed
Paul and Barnabas, who, speaking to
them, were urging them to continue
in [c]the grace of God.

### *Many Gentiles Believe*

**44** And the next [a]Sabbath, nearly
the whole city assembled to hear
the word of [1]the [2]Lord. **45** But when
[a]the Jews saw the crowds, they were
filled with jealousy and *began* con-
tradicting the things spoken by Paul,
[1]blaspheming. **46** Paul and Barnabas
spoke out boldly and said, "It was
necessary that the word of God be
spoken to you [a]first. Since you reject
it and judge yourselves unworthy of
eternal life, behold, [b]we are turning
to the Gentiles. **47** For so the [1]Lord has
commanded us,
'[a]I HAVE PLACED YOU AS A
[b]LIGHT FOR THE GENTILES,
THAT YOU MAY [2]BRING
SALVATION TO THE END
OF THE EARTH.'"
**48** And when the Gentiles heard
this, they *began* rejoicing and glori-
fying [a]the word of [1]the [2]Lord, and as
many as [b]had been appointed to eter-
nal life believed. **49** And [a]the word of
the [1]Lord was being spread through
the whole region. **50** But [a]the Jews
incited the [b,1]God-fearing women [c]of
prominence and the leading men of
the city, and instigated a persecution
against Paul and Barnabas, and
drove them out of their [2]district.
**51** But [a]having shaken off the dust of
their feet against them, they went to
[b]Iconium. **52** And the disciples were
continually [a]filled with joy and with
the Holy Spirit.

### *In Iconium*

**14** Now it happened that in [a]Iconi-
um [b]they entered the syna-
gogue of the Jews together and spoke
in such a manner [c]that a large number
of people believed, both of Jews and of
[d]Greeks. **2** But [a]the [b,1]unbelieving Jews
instigated and embittered the [2]minds
of the Gentiles against [c]the brothers.
**3** Therefore they spent a long time

---

**13:39** [a]Ac 10:43; Ro 3:28; 10:4 [1]Lit *by* **13:40** [a]Lk 24:44; Jn 6:45; Ac 7:42 **13:41** [a]Hab 1:5 [1]Lit *disappear* **13:42** [a]Ac 13:14 [1]Lit *they* **13:43** [a]Ac 13:50; 16:14; 17:4, 17; 18:7 [b]Mt 23:15 [c]Ac 11:23 [1]Gentile converts to Judaism **13:44** [a]Ac 13:14 [1]One early ms *God* [2]In OT, Yahweh, cf. Is 1:10 **13:45** [a]Ac 13:50; 14:2, 4, 5, 19; 1Th 2:16 [1]Or *slandering him* **13:46** [a]Ac 3:26; 9:20; 13:5, 14 [b]Ac 18:6; 19:9; 22:21; 26:20; 28:28 **13:47** [a]Is 42:6; 49:6 [b]Lk 2:32 [1]In OT, Yahweh, cf. Is 42:6 [2]Lit *be for salvation* **13:48** [a]Ac 13:12 [b]Ro 8:28ff; Eph 1:4f, 11 [1]Two early mss *God* [2]In OT, Yahweh, cf. Is 1:10 **13:49** [a]Ac 13:12 [1]In OT, Yahweh, cf. Is 1:10 **13:50** [a]Ac 13:45; 14:2, 4, 5, 19; 1Th 2:14ff [b]Ac 13:43; 16:14; 17:4, 17; 18:7 [c]Mk 15:43 [1]Or *worshiping* [2]Lit *boundaries* **13:51** [a]Mt 10:14; Mk 6:11; Lk 9:5; 10:11; Ac 18:6 [b]Ac 14:1, 19, 21; 16:2; 2Ti 3:11 **13:52** [a]Ac 2:4 ◆ **14:1** [a]Ac 13:51; 14:19, 21; 16:2; 2Ti 3:11 [b]Ac 13:5 [c]Ac 2:47 [d]Jn 7:35; Ac 18:4 **14:2** [a]Ac 13:45, 50; 14:4, 5, 19; 1Th 2:14ff [b]Jn 3:36 [c]Ac 1:15 [1]Or *disobeying* [2]Lit *souls*

*there* [a]speaking boldly *with reliance*
upon the Lord, who was testifying to
the word of His grace, granting that
[b,1]signs and wonders be done through
their hands. **4** [a]But the multitude of
the city was divided; and some [1]sided
with [b]the Jews, and some with [c]the
apostles. **5** And when an attempt was
made by both the Gentiles and [a]the
Jews with their rulers to mistreat and
to [b]stone them, **6** they became aware
of it and fled to the cities of [a]Lyca-
onia, [b]Lystra and [c]Derbe, and the
surrounding region; **7** and there they
continued to [a]proclaim the gospel.

### *In Lystra and Derbe*

**8** And at [a]Lystra [b]a man was sitting
who had no strength in his feet, lame
from his mother's womb, who had
never walked. **9** This man listened
to Paul as he spoke, who, [a]when
he fixed his gaze on him and saw
that he had [b]faith to be [1]saved *from
being lame*, **10** said with a loud voice,
"Stand upright on your feet." [a]And he
leaped up and *began to* walk. **11** And
when the crowds saw what Paul had
done, they raised their voice, saying
in the [a]Lycaonian language, "[b]The
gods have become like men and have
come down to us." **12** And they *began*
calling Barnabas, [1]Zeus, and Paul,
[2]Hermes, because he was [3]the chief
speaker. **13** And the priest of Zeus,
whose *temple* was [1]just outside the
city, brought oxen and garlands to
the gates, and [a]was wanting to offer
sacrifice with the crowds. **14** But
when [a]the apostles Barnabas and
Paul heard of it, they [b]tore their gar-
ments and rushed out into the crowd,
crying out **15** and saying, "Men, why
are you doing these things? We are
also [a]men of the same nature as you,
[b]proclaiming the gospel to you that
you should turn from these [c,1]vain
things to a [d]living God, [e]WHO MADE
THE HEAVEN AND THE EARTH AND THE
SEA AND ALL THAT IS IN THEM. **16** [1]In
the generations gone by He [a]permit-
ted all the [2]nations to [b]go their own
ways; **17** and yet [a]He did not leave
Himself without witness, in that He
did good and [b]gave you rains from
heaven and fruitful seasons, filling
your hearts with food and gladness."
**18** And saying these things, with dif-
ficulty they restrained the crowds
from offering sacrifice to them.

**19** But [a]Jews came from [b]Antioch
and [c]Iconium, and after winning
over the crowds and [d]stoning Paul,
they were dragging him out of the
city, supposing him to be dead. **20** But
while [a]the disciples stood around
him, he rose up and entered the city.
The next day he went away with Bar-
nabas to [b]Derbe. **21** And after they had
[a]proclaimed the gospel to that city

**14:3** [a]Ac 4:29f; 20:32; Heb 2:4 [b]Jn 4:48 [1]Or *attesting miracles* **14:4** [a]Ac 17:4f; 19:9; 28:24 [b]Ac 13:45, 50; 14:2, 5, 19; 1Th 2:14ff [c]Ac 14:14 [1]Lit *were* **14:5** [a]Ac 13:45, 50; 14:2, 4, 19; 1Th 2:14ff [b]Ac 14:19 **14:6** [a]Ac 14:11 [b]Ac 14:8, 21; 16:1f; 2Ti 3:11 [c]Ac 14:20; 16:1; 20:4 **14:7** [a]Ac 14:15, 21; 16:10 **14:8** [a]Ac 14:6, 21; 16:1f; 2Ti 3:11 [b]Ac 3:2 **14:9** [a]Ac 3:4; 10:4 [b]Mt 9:28 [1]Or *made well* **14:10** [a]Ac 3:8 **14:11** [a]Ac 14:6 [b]Ac 8:10; 28:6 **14:12** [1]In Lat *Jupiter*, the chief pagan god [2]In Lat *Mercury*, considered the messenger or spokesman for the pagan gods of Greece and Rome [3]Lit *the leader of the speaking* **14:13** [a]Da 2:46 [1]Lit *in front of* **14:14** [a]Ac 14:4 [b]Nu 14:6; Mt 26:65; Mk 14:63 **14:15** [a]Ac 10:26; Jas 5:17 [b]Ac 13:32; 14:7, 21 [c]Dt 32:21; 1Sa 12:21; Jer 8:19; 14:22; 1Co 8:4 [d]Mt 16:16 [e]Ex 20:11; Ps 146:6; Ac 4:24; 17:24; Rev 14:7 [1]Idols **14:16** [a]Ac 17:30 [b]Ps 81:12; Mic 4:5 [1]Lit *Who in the generations gone by permitted* [2]Or *Gentiles* **14:17** [a]Ac 17:26f; Ro 1:19f [b]Dt 11:14; Job 5:10; Ps 65:10f; Eze 34:26f; Joel 2:23 **14:19** [a]Ac 13:45, 50; 14:2, 4, 5; 1Th 2:14ff [b]Ac 13:14; 14:21, 26 [c]Ac 13:51; 14:1, 21 [d]Ac 14:5; 2Co 11:25; 2Ti 3:11 **14:20** [a]Ac 11:26; 14:22, 28 [b]Ac 14:6 **14:21** [a]Ac 14:7

and had [b]made many disciples, they
returned to [c]Lystra and to [d]Iconium
and to [e]Antioch, **22** strengthening the
souls of [a]the disciples, encouraging
them to continue in [b]the faith, and
*saying,* "[c]Through many afflictions
we must enter the kingdom of God."
**23** And when [a]they had appointed
[b]elders for them in every church,
having [c]prayed with fasting, they
[d]commended them to the Lord in
whom they had believed.

### *The Return to Antioch*

**24** And when they passed through
[a]Pisidia, they came into [b]Pamphylia.
**25** And when they had spoken the
word in [a]Perga, they went down to
Attalia. **26** And from there they sailed
to [a]Antioch, from [b]where they had
been [c]committed to the grace of God
for the work that they had fulfilled.
**27** And when they had arrived and
gathered the church together, they
*began to* [a]report all things that God
had done with them and [1]how He
had opened a [b]door of faith to the
Gentiles. **28** And they spent not a
little time with [a]the disciples.

### *The Jerusalem Council*

**15** [a]Some men came down from
Judea and *began* teaching [b]the
brothers, "Unless you are [c]circum-
cised according to [d]the custom of
Moses, you cannot be saved." **2** And
when Paul and Barnabas had not a
little dissension and [a]debate with
them, [b]*the brothers* determined that
Paul and Barnabas and some others
of them should go up to Jerusalem to
the [c]apostles and elders concerning
this issue. **3** Therefore, being [a]sent on
their way by the church, they were
passing through both [b]Phoenicia and
Samaria, [c]recounting in detail the
conversion of the Gentiles, and were
bringing great joy to all [d]the brothers.
**4** When they arrived at Jerusalem,
they were received by the church
and [a]the apostles and the elders, and
they [b]reported all that God had done
with them. **5** But some of [a]the sect
of the [b]Pharisees who had believed
stood up, saying, "It is necessary to
[c]circumcise them and to command
them to keep the Law of Moses."

**6** [a]Both the apostles and the elders
came together to [1]look into this
[2]matter. **7** And after there had been
much [a]debate, Peter stood up and
said to them, "Brothers, you know
that [1]in the early days [b]God made a
choice among you, that by my mouth
the Gentiles would hear the word of
[c]the gospel and believe. **8** And God,
[a]who knows the heart, testified to
them [b]giving them the Holy Spirit,
just as He also did to us; **9** and [a]He
made no distinction between us
and them, [b]cleansing their hearts
by faith. **10** Now therefore why do

---

**14:21** [b]Ac 2:47 [c]Ac 14:6 [d]Ac 13:51; 14:1, 19 [e]Ac 13:14; 14:19, 26 **14:22** [a]Ac 11:26; 14:28 [b]Ac 6:7 [c]Mk 10:30; Jn 15:18, 20; 16:33; Ac 9:16; 1Th 3:3; 2Ti 3:12; 1Pe 2:21; Rev 1:9 **14:23** [a]2Co 8:19; Tit 1:5 [b]Ac 11:30 [c]Ac 1:24; 13:3 [d]Ac 20:32 **14:24** [a]Ac 13:14 [b]Ac 13:13 **14:25** [a]Ac 13:13 **14:26** [a]Ac 11:19 *[b]Ac 13:3 [c]Ac 11:23; 15:40* **14:27** [a]Ac 15:3, 4, 12; 21:19 [b]1Co 16:9; 2Co 2:12; Col 4:3; Rev 3:8 [1]Lit *that* **14:28** [a]Ac 11:26; 14:22 ◆ **15:1** [a]Ac 15:24 [b]Ac 1:15; 15:3, 22, 32 [c]Lv 12:3; Ac 15:5; 1Co 7:18; Ga 2:11, 14; 5:2f [d]Ac 6:14 **15:2** [a]Ac 15:7 [b]Ga 2:2 [c]Ac 11:30; 15:4, 6, 22, 23; 16:4 **15:3** [a]Ac 20:38; 21:5; Ro 15:24; 1Co 16:6, 11; 2Co 1:16; Tit 3:13; 3Jn 6 [b]Ac 11:19 [c]Ac 14:27; 15:4, 12 [d]Ac 1:15; 15:22, 32 **15:4** [a]Ac 11:30; 15:6, 22, 23; 16:4 [b]Ac 14:27; 15:12 **15:5** [a]Ac 5:17; 24:5, 14; 26:5; 28:22 [b]Mt 3:7; Ac 26:5 [c]1Co 7:18; Ga 2:11, 14; 5:2f **15:6** [a]Ac 11:30; 15:4, 22, 23; 16:4 [1]Lit *see about* [2]Lit *word* **15:7** [a]Ac 15:2 [b]Ac 10:19f [c]Ac 20:24 [1]Lit *from days of old* **15:8** [a]Ac 1:24 [b]Ac 2:4; 10:44, 47 **15:9** [a]Ac 10:28, 34; 11:12 [b]Ac 10:43

you [a]put God to the test by placing
upon the neck of the disciples a yoke
which [b]neither our fathers nor we
have been able to bear? 11 But we
believe that we are saved through
[a]the grace of the Lord Jesus, in the
same way as they also are."
12 And all the multitude kept silent,
and they were listening to Barnabas
and Paul as they were [a]relating what
[b]signs and wonders God had done
through them among the Gentiles.

### *James Issues a Judgment*

13 Now after they had stopped
speaking, [a]James answered, saying,
"Brothers, listen to me. 14 [a]Simeon
has related how God first concerned
Himself about taking from among
the Gentiles a people for His name.
15 And with this the words of [a]the
Prophets agree, just as it is written,

16 '[a]AFTER THESE THINGS
[b]I will return,
AND I WILL REBUILD THE
[c]FALLEN [1]BOOTH OF DAVID,
AND I WILL REBUILD ITS RUINS,
AND I WILL RESTORE IT,
17 [a]SO THAT THE REST
OF [1]MANKIND MAY
SEEK THE LORD,
AND ALL THE GENTILES [b,2]WHO
ARE CALLED BY MY NAME,'
18 [a]SAYS THE [1]LORD, WHO
[b,2]MAKES THESE THINGS
KNOWN FROM LONG AGO.

19 "Therefore [a]I judge that we do not
trouble those who are turning to God
from among the Gentiles, 20 but that
we write to them that they abstain
from [a]things contaminated by idols
and from [b]sexual immorality and
from [c]what is strangled and from
blood. 21 For from ancient genera-
tions, [a]Moses has those who preach
him in every city, since [1]he is read in
the synagogues every Sabbath."
22 Then it seemed good to [a]the
apostles and the elders, with the
whole church, to choose men from
among them—Judas called Barsab-
bas, and [b]Silas, leading men among
[c]the brothers—to send to [d]Antioch
with Paul and Barnabas, 23 and they
[1]sent this letter by them,

"[a]The apostles and the brothers
who are elders, to [b]the brothers
in [c]Antioch and [d]Syria and
[e]Cilicia who are from the
Gentiles, [f]greetings. 24 Since we
have heard that [a]some of us, to
whom we gave no instruction,
have gone out and [b]disturbed
you with *their* words, unsettling
your souls, 25 [a]it seemed
good to us, having [1]come to
one accord, to select men to
send to you with our beloved
Barnabas and Paul, 26 men
who have [a,1]risked their lives
for the name of our Lord Jesus
Christ. 27 Therefore we have

**15:10** [a]Ac 5:9 [b]Mt 23:4; Ga 5:1 **15:11** [a]Ro 3:24; 5:15; 2Co 13:14; Eph 2:5-8 **15:12** [a]Ac 14:27; 15:3, 4 [b]Jn 4:48 **15:13** [a]Ac 12:17 **15:14** [a]Ac 15:7; 2Pe 1:1 **15:15** [a]Ac 13:40 **15:16** [a]Am 9:11 [b]Jer 12:15 [c]Is 16:5 [1]Or *tent* **15:17** [a]Am 9:12 [b]Dt 28:10; Is 63:19; Jer 14:9; Da 9:19; Jas 2:7 [1]Gr *anthropoi* [2]Lit *upon whom My name is called* **15:18** [a]Am 9:12 [b]Is 45:21 [1]In OT, Yahweh, cf. Am 9:12 [2]Or *does these things which were known* **15:19** [a]Ac 15:28; 21:25 **15:20** [a]Ex 34:15-17; Da 1:8; Ac 15:29; 1Co 8:7, 13; 10:7f, 14-28; Rev 2:14, 20 [b]Lv 18:6-23 [c]Ge 9:4; Lv 3:17; 7:26; 17:10, 14; 19:26; Dt 12:16, 23; 15:23; 1Sa 14:33 **15:21** [a]Ac 13:15; 2Co 3:14f [1]The books of Moses, Gen-Deut **15:22** [a]Ac 15:2 [b]Ac 15:27, 32, 40; 16:19, 25, 29; 17:4, 10, 14f; 18:5; 2Co 1:19; 1Th 1:1; 2Th 1:1; 1Pe 5:12 [c]Ac 15:1 [d]Ac 11:20 **15:23** [a]Ac 15:2 [b]Ac 15:1 [c]Ac 11:20 [d]Mt 4:24; Ac 15:41; Ga 1:21 [e]Ac 6:9 [f]Ac 23:26; Jas 1:1; 2Jn 10f [1]Lit *wrote by their hand* **15:24** [a]Ac 15:1 [b]Ga 1:7; 5:10 **15:25** [a]Ac 15:28 [1]Or *met together* **15:26** [a]Ac 9:23ff; 14:19 [1]Lit *given over*

sent [a]Judas and [b]Silas, and they
themselves will report the same
things by word *of mouth.* **28** For
[a]it seemed good to [b]the Holy
Spirit and to [c]us to lay upon
you no greater burden than
these essentials: **29** that you
abstain from [a]things sacrificed
to idols and from [a]blood and
from [a]things strangled and
from [a]sexual immorality, from
which if you keep yourselves,
you will do well. Farewell."
**30** So when they were sent away,
[a]they went down to Antioch; and
having gathered the [1]congregation
together, they delivered the letter.
**31** And when they had read it, they
rejoiced because of its [1]encouragement.
**32** [a]And both Judas and [b]Silas,
also being [c]prophets themselves,
[1]encouraged and strengthened [d]the
brothers with a lengthy message.
**33** And after they had spent time
*there,* they were sent away from the
brothers [a]in peace to those who had
[b]sent them. **34** [1][But it seemed good
to Silas to remain there.] **35** But [a]Paul
and Barnabas spent a long time in
Antioch, teaching and [b,1]preaching
with many others also, [c]the word of
the Lord.

### *Disagreement Between Paul and Barnabas*

**36** Now after some days Paul said to
Barnabas, "Let us return and visit
the brothers in [a]every city in which
we proclaimed [b]the word of the
Lord, *and see* how they are." **37** And
Barnabas wanted to take [a]John,
called Mark, along with them also.
**38** But Paul kept insisting that they
should not take him along who
had [a]deserted them [1]in Pamphylia
and had not gone with them to the
work. **39** And there was such a sharp
disagreement that they separated
from one another, and Barnabas took
[a]Mark with him and sailed away to
[b]Cyprus. **40** But Paul chose [a]Silas and
left, being [b]committed by the brothers
to the grace of the Lord. **41** And
he was traveling through [a]Syria and
[b]Cilicia, strengthening the churches.

### *Timothy Joins Paul and Silas*

**16** Now Paul also arrived at [a]Derbe
and at [a]Lystra. And behold, a
disciple was there, named [b]Timothy,
the son of a [c]Jewish woman who was
a believer, but his father was a Greek,
**2** and he was well spoken of by [a]the
brothers who were in [b]Lystra and
[c]Iconium. **3** Paul wanted this man
to [1]go with him, and he [a]took him
and circumcised him because of the
Jews who were in those parts, for
they all knew that his father was a
Greek. **4** Now while they were passing
through the cities, they were delivering
[a]the decrees which had been
decided upon by [b]the apostles and
[c]elders who were in Jerusalem, for

---

**15:27** [a]Ac 15:22, 32 [b]Ac 15:22 **15:28** [a]Ac 15:25 [b]Ac 5:32; 15:8 [c]Ac 15:19, 25 **15:29** [a]Ac 15:20 **15:30** [a]Ac 15:22f [1]Or *multitude* **15:31** [1]Or *exhortation* **15:32** [a]Ac 15:22, 27 [b]Ac 15:22 [c]Ac 13:1 [d]*Ac 15:1* [1]*Or exhorted* **15:33** [a]*Mk 5:34; Ac 16:36;* 1Co 16:11; Heb 11:31 [b]Ac 15:22 **15:34** [1]Early mss omit this v **15:35** [a]Ac 12:25 [b]Ac 8:4 [c]Ac 13:12 [1]Lit *proclaiming as good news* **15:36** [a]Ac 13:4, 13, 14, 51; 14:6, 24f [b]Ac 13:12 **15:37** [a]Ac 12:12 **15:38** [a]Ac 13:13 [1]Lit *from* **15:39** [a]Ac 12:12; 15:37; Col 4:10 [b]Ac 4:36 **15:40** [a]Ac 15:22 [b]Ac 11:23; 14:26 **15:41** [a]Mt 4:24; Ac 15:23 [b]Ac 6:9 ◆ **16:1** [a]Ac 14:6 [b]Ac 17:14f; 18:5; 19:22; 20:4; Ro 16:21; 1Co 4:17; 16:10; 2Co 1:1, 19; Php 1:1; 2:19; Col 1:1; 1Th 1:1; 3:2, 6; 2Th 1:1; 1Ti 1:2, 18; 6:20; 2Ti 1:2; Phm 1; Heb 13:23 [c]2Ti 1:5; 3:15 **16:2** [a]Ac 16:40 [b]Ac 14:6 [c]Ac 13:51 **16:3** [a]Ga 2:3 [1]Lit *go out* **16:4** [a]Ac 15:28f [b]Ac 15:2 [c]Ac 11:30

them to keep. **5** So [a]the churches were
being strengthened [1]in the faith, and
were [b]abounding in number daily.

### *The Macedonian Vision*

**6** And they passed through the
[a,1]Phrygian and [b]Galatian region,
having been forbidden by the Holy
Spirit to speak the word in [c,2]Asia;
**7** and after they came to [a]Mysia, they
were trying to go into [b]Bithynia, and
the [c]Spirit of Jesus did not permit
them; **8** and passing by [a]Mysia, they
came down to [b]Troas. **9** [a]And a vi-
sion appeared to Paul in the night:
a man of [b]Macedonia was standing
and appealing to him, and saying,
"Come over to Macedonia and help
us." **10** And when he had seen [a]the
vision, immediately [b]we sought to
[1]go into Macedonia, concluding that
God had called us to [c]proclaim the
gospel to them.

### *Lydia's Conversion in Philippi*

**11** So setting sail from [a]Troas, we ran
[b]a straight course to Samothrace, and
on the day following to Neapolis;
**12** and from there to [a]Philippi, which
is a leading city of the district of
[b]Macedonia, [c]a Roman colony; and
we were staying in this city for some
days. **13** And on [a]the Sabbath day we
went outside the gate to a riverside,
where we were supposing that there
would be a place of prayer; and sit-
ting down, we *began* speaking to the
women who had assembled. **14** And a
woman named Lydia, from the city of
[a]Thyatira, a seller of purple fabrics,
[b]a worshiper of God, was listening,
whose heart the Lord [c]opened to
pay attention to the things spoken
by Paul. **15** And when she and [a]her
household had been baptized, she
urged us, saying, "If you have judged
me to be faithful to the Lord, come
into my house and stay." And she
prevailed upon us.

### *Paul and Silas in Prison*

**16** Now it happened that as we
were going to [a]the place of prayer,
a servant-girl having [b]a spirit of
divination met us, who was bringing
her masters much profit by fortune-
telling. **17** Following after Paul and
us, she kept crying out, saying,
"These men are slaves of [a]the Most
High God, who are proclaiming to
you [1]the way of salvation." **18** And
she continued doing this for many
days. But being greatly annoyed,
Paul turned and said to the spirit, "I
command you [a]in the name of Jesus
Christ to leave her!" And it left at that
very [1]moment.

**19** But when her masters saw that
their hope of [a]profit had left, they
seized [b]Paul and Silas and [c]dragged
them into the marketplace before
the authorities, **20** and when they
had brought them to the chief mag-
istrates, they said, "These men are

**16:5** [a]Ac 9:31 [b]Ac 2:47 [1]Or *in faith* **16:6** [a]Ac 2:10; 18:23 [b]Ac 18:23; 1Co 16:1; Ga 1:2; 3:1; 2Ti 4:10; 1Pe 1:1 [c]Ac 2:9 [1]Or *Phrygia and the Galatian region* [2]West coast province of Asia Minor **16:7** [a]Ac 16:8 [b]1Pe 1:1 [c]Lk 24:49; Ac 8:29; Ro 8:9; Ga 4:6; Php 1:19; 1Pe 1:11 **16:8** [a]Ac 16:7 [b]Ac 16:11; 20:5f; 2Co 2:12; 2Ti 4:13 **16:9** [a]Ac 9:10 [b]Ac 16:10, 12; 18:5; 19:21f, 29; 20:1, 3; 27:2; Ro 15:26 **16:10** [a]Ac 9:10 [b]Ac 16:10-17; 20:5-15; 21:1-18; 27:1-28:16 [c]Ac 14:7 [1]Lit *go out* **16:11** [a]Ac 16:8; 20:5f; 2Co 2:12; 2Ti 4:13 [b]Ac 21:1 **16:12** [a]Ac 20:6; Php 1:1; 1Th 2:2 [b]Ac 16:9, 10; 18:5; 19:21f, 29; 20:1, 3; 27:2; Ro 15:26 [c]Ac 16:21 **16:13** [a]Ac 13:14 **16:14** [a]Rev 1:11; 2:18, 24 [b]Ac 13:43; 18:7 [c]Lk 24:45 **16:15** [a]Ac 11:14 **16:16** [a]Ac 16:13 [b]Lv 19:31; 20:6, 27; Dt 18:11; 1Sa 28:3, 7; 2Ki 21:6; 1Chr 10:13; Is 8:19 **16:17** [a]Mk 5:7 [1]Lit *a way* **16:18** [a]Mk 16:17 [1]Lit *hour* **16:19** [a]Ac 16:16; 19:25f [b]Ac 15:22, 40; 16:25, 29 [c]Ac 8:3; 17:6f; 21:30; Jas 2:6

throwing our city into confusion,
being Jews, **21** and [a]are proclaiming
customs that are not lawful for
us to accept or to observe, being
[b]Romans." **22** And the crowd joined
together to attack them, and the
chief magistrates, tearing their
garments off of them, proceeded to
order *them* to be [a]beaten with rods.
**23** And when they had inflicted them
with many wounds, they threw them
into prison, commanding [a]the jailer
to guard them securely, **24** who,
having received such a command,
threw them into the inner prison and
fastened their feet in [a]the [1]stocks.

### *The Philippian Jailer Converted*

**25** But about midnight [a]Paul and
Silas were praying and [b]singing
hymns of praise to God, and the
prisoners were listening to them.
**26** And suddenly [a]there came a great
earthquake, so that the foundations
of the jailhouse were shaken; and
immediately [b]all the doors were
opened and everyone's [c]chains were
unfastened. **27** And when [a]the jailer
awoke and saw the prison doors
opened, he drew his sword and was
about [b]to kill himself, supposing that
the prisoners had escaped. **28** But
Paul cried out with a loud voice,
saying, "Do not harm yourself, for
we are all here!" **29** And he called for
lights and rushed in, and trembling
with fear he fell down before [a]Paul
and Silas, **30** and after he brought
them out, he said, "Sirs, [a]what must
I do to be saved?" **31** And they said,
"[a]Believe in the Lord Jesus, and you
will be saved, you and [b]your house."
**32** And they spoke the word of [1]the
Lord to him together with all who
were in his household. **33** And he
took them [a]that *very* hour of the
night and washed their wounds, and
immediately he was baptized, he and
all his *household.* **34** And he brought
them into his house and set [1]food
before them, and rejoiced [2]greatly
with [a]his whole household, because
he had believed in God.
**35** Now when day came, the chief
magistrates sent their policemen,
saying, "Release those men." **36** And
[a]the jailer reported these words to
Paul, *saying*, "The chief magistrates
have sent to release you. Therefore
come out now and go [b]in peace."
**37** But Paul said to them, "Having
beaten us in public without trial,
[a]men who are Romans, they have
thrown us into prison. And now are
they sending us away secretly? No
indeed! But let them come them-
selves and bring us out." **38** And the
policemen reported these words to
the chief magistrates. [a]They were
afraid when they heard that they
were Romans, **39** and they came and
appealed to them, and when they
had brought them out, they kept
requesting them [a]to leave the city.
**40** And they went out of the prison
and entered *the house of* [a]Lydia, and
when they saw [b]the brothers, they
[1]encouraged them and left.

---

***16:21*** [a]*Es 3:8* [b]*Ac 16:12* **16:22** [a]2Co 11:25; 1Th 2:2 **16:23** [a]Ac 16:27, 36 **16:24** [a]Job 13:27; 33:11; Jer 20:2f; 29:26 [1]Lit *wood* **16:25** [a]Ac 16:19 [b]Eph 5:19 **16:26** [a]Ac 4:31 [b]Ac 12:10 [c]Ac 12:7 **16:27** [a]Ac 16:23, 36 [b]Ac 12:19 **16:29** [a]Ac 16:19 **16:30** [a]Ac 2:37; 22:10 **16:31** [a]Mk 16:16 [b]Ac 11:14; 16:15 **16:32** [1]Two early mss *God* **16:33** [a]Ac 16:25 **16:34** [a]Ac 11:14; 16:15 [1]Lit *a table* [2]Or *greatly with his whole household, having believed in God* **16:36** [a]Ac 16:27 [b]Ac 15:33 **16:37** [a]Ac 22:25-29 **16:38** [a]Ac 22:29 **16:39** [a]Mt 8:34 **16:40** [a]Ac 16:14 [b]Ac 1:15; 16:2 [1]Or *exhorted*

### *Paul and Silas in Thessalonica*

**17** Now when they had traveled
through Amphipolis and Apol-
lonia, they came to [a]Thessalonica,
where there was a synagogue of the
Jews. **2** And [a]according to Paul's cus-
tom, he went to them, and for three
[b]Sabbaths reasoned with them from
[c]the Scriptures, **3** [1]explaining and
setting before them that the [2]Christ
[a]had to suffer and [b]rise again from
the dead, and *saying*, "[c]This Jesus
whom I am proclaiming to you is that
[2]Christ." **4** [a]And some of them were
persuaded and joined [b]Paul and Silas,
[1]along with a great multitude of the
[c]God-fearing [d]Greeks and not a few of
the [e]leading women. **5** But [a]the Jews,
becoming jealous, taking along some
wicked men from the marketplace,
and forming a mob, set the city in
an uproar. And attacking the house
of [b]Jason, they were seeking to bring
them out to the assembly. **6** And when
they did not find them, they *began*
[a]dragging Jason and some brothers
before the city authorities, shouting,
"These men who have upset [b,1]the
world have come here also; **7** [1]and
Jason [a]has welcomed them, and
they all act [b]contrary to the decrees
of Caesar, saying that there is another
king, Jesus." **8** And they disturbed the
crowd and the city authorities who
*heard* these things. **9** And when they
had received the bond from [a]Jason
and the others, they released them.

### *In Berea*

**10** [a]And the brothers immediately
sent [b]Paul and Silas away by night
to [c]Berea, [1]and when they arrived,
they went into [d]the synagogue of the
Jews. **11** Now these were more noble-
minded than those in [a]Thessalonica,
[1]for they received the word with
[2]great eagerness, [3]examining the
Scriptures daily *to see* whether these
things were so. **12** Therefore [a]many
of them believed, along with not
a few [b]prominent Greek [c]women
and men. **13** But when the Jews of
[a]Thessalonica found out that the
word of God had been proclaimed by
Paul in [b]Berea also, they came there
as well, shaking up and disturbing
the crowds. **14** Then immediately
[a]the brothers sent Paul out to go as
far as the sea; and [b]Silas and [c]Timo-
thy remained there. **15** Now [a]those
who escorted Paul brought him as
far as [b]Athens; and after receiving
a command for [c]Silas and Timothy
to [d]come to him as soon as possible,
they left.

### *In Athens*

**16** Now while Paul was waiting for
them at [a]Athens, his spirit was be-
ing provoked within him as he was
observing the city full of idols. **17** So
he was reasoning [a]in the synagogue
with the Jews and [b]the God-fearing
*Gentiles*, and in the marketplace
every day with those who happened

◆ **17:1** [a]Ac 17:11, 13; 20:4; 27:2; Php 4:16; 1Th 1:1; 2Th 1:1; 2Ti 4:10 **17:2** [a]Ac 9:20; 17:10, 17 [b]Ac 13:14 [c]Ac 8:35 **17:3** [a]Ac 3:18 [b]Jn 20:9 [c]Ac 9:22; 18:5, 28 [1]Lit *opening* [2]Messiah **17:4** [a]Ac 14:4 [b]Ac 15:22, 40; 17:10, 14f [c]Ac 13:43; 17:17 [d]Jn 7:35 [e]Ac 13:50 [1]Lit *and a large* **17:5** [a]Ac 17:13; 1Th 2:14ff [b]Ac 17:6, 7, 9; Ro 16:21 **17:6** [a]Ac 16:19f [b]Mt 24:14; Ac 17:31 [1]Lit *the inhabited earth* **17:7** [a]Lk 10:38; Jas 2:25 [b]Lk 23:2 [1]Lit *whom Jason has welcomed* **17:9** [a]Ac 17:5 **17:10** [a]Ac 1:15; 17:6, 14f [b]Ac 17:4 [c]Ac 17:13; 20:4 [d]Ac 17:1f [1]Lit *who* **17:11** [a]Ac 17:1 [1]Lit *who received* [2]Lit *all* [3]Or *inquiring about the Scriptures* **17:12** [a]Ac 2:47 [b]Mk 15:43 [c]Ac 13:50 **17:13** [a]Ac 17:1 [b]Ac 17:10; 20:4 **17:14** [a]Ac 1:15; 17:6, 10 [b]Ac 15:22; 17:4, 10 [c]Ac 16:1 **17:15** [a]Ac 15:3 [b]Ac 17:16, 21f; 18:1; 1Th 3:1 [c]Ac 17:14 [d]Ac 18:5 **17:16** [a]Ac 17:15, 21f; 18:1; 1Th 3:1 **17:17** [a]Ac 9:20; 17:2 [b]Ac 17:4

to be present. **18** And also some of the Epicurean and Stoic philosophers were [1]conversing with him. Some were saying, "What would [a]this [2]idle babbler wish to say?" Others, "He seems to be a proclaimer of strange deities,"—because he was proclaiming the good news of [b]Jesus and the resurrection. **19** And they [a]took him and brought him [1]to the [b,2]Areopagus, saying, "May we know what [c]this new teaching is [3]which you are speaking? **20** For you are bringing some strange things to our ears. So we want to know what these things mean." **21** (Now all the Athenians and the strangers [a]visiting there used to spend their time in nothing other than telling or hearing something newer.)

**22** So Paul stood in the midst of the [1]Areopagus and said, "Men of [a]Athens, I observe that you are very [b]religious in all respects. **23** For while I was passing through and examining the [a]objects of your worship, I also found an altar with this inscription, 'TO AN UNKNOWN GOD.' Therefore what [b]you worship in ignorance, this I proclaim to you. **24** [a]The God who made the world and all things in it, since He is [b]Lord of heaven and earth, does not [c]dwell in temples made with hands; **25** nor is He served by human hands, [a]as though He needed anything, since He Himself gives to all *people* life and breath and all things; **26** and [a]He made from one *man* every nation of mankind to inhabit all the face of the earth, having [b]determined *their* appointed times and the boundaries of their habitation, **27** that they would seek God, if perhaps they might grope for Him and find Him, [a]though He is not far from each one of us; **28** for [a]in Him we live and move and [1]exist, as even some of your own poets have said, 'For we also are His offspring.' **29** Being then the offspring of God, we [a]ought not to suppose that the Divine Nature is like gold or silver or stone, an image formed by the craft and thought of man. **30** Therefore having [a]overlooked [b]the times of ignorance, God is [c]now commanding men that everyone everywhere should repent, **31** because He has fixed [a]a day in which [b]He will judge [c,1]the world in righteousness [2]through a Man whom He [d]determined, having furnished proof to all [3]by [e]raising Him from the dead."

**32** Now when they heard about [a]the resurrection of the dead, some *began to* sneer, but others said, "We shall hear you [1]again concerning this." **33** In this way, Paul went out of their midst. **34** But some men joined him and believed, among whom also were Dionysius the [a]Areopagite and a woman named Damaris and others with them.

---

**17:18** [a]1Co 1:20; 4:10 [b]Ac 4:2; 17:31f [1]Or *disputing* [2]One who makes his living by picking up scraps **17:19** [a]Ac 23:19 [b]Ac 17:22 [c]Mk 1:27 [1]Or *before* [2]Or *Hill of Ares*; Greek god of war [3]Lit *which is being spoken by you* **17:21** [a]Ac 2:10 **17:22** [a]Ac 17:15 [b]Ac 25:19 [1]Or *the Council of the Areopagus* **17:23** [a]2Th 2:4 [b]Jn 4:22 **17:24** [a]Is 42:5; Ac 14:15 [b]Dt 10:14; Ps 115:16; Mt 11:25 [c]1Ki 8:27; Ac 7:48 **17:25** [a]Job 22:2; Ps 50:10-12 **17:26** [a]Mal 2:10 [b]Dt 32:8; Job 12:23 **17:27** [a]Dt 4:7; Jer 23:23f; Ac 14:17 **17:28** [a]Job 12:10; Da 5:23 [1]Lit *are* **17:29** [a]Is 40:18ff; Ro 1:23 **17:30** [a]Ac 14:16; Ro 3:25 [b]Ac 17:23 [c]Lk 24:47; Ac 26:20; Tit 2:11f **17:31** [a]Mt 10:15 [b]Ps 9:8; 96:13; 98:9; Jn 5:22, 27; Ac 10:42 [c]Mt 24:14; Ac 17:6 [d]Lk 22:22 [e]Ac 2:24 [1]Lit *the inhabited earth* [2]Or *in*; lit *by* [3]Or *when He raised* **17:32** [a]Ac 17:18, 31 [1]Lit *also again* **17:34** [a]Ac 17:19, 22

### *In Corinth*

18 After these things he departed
[a]Athens and went to [b]Corinth.
**2** And he found a Jew named [a]Aquila,
a native of [b]Pontus, and his wife [a]Pris-
cilla, who recently came from [c]Italy
because [d]Claudius had commanded
all the Jews to depart from Rome. He
came to them, **3** and because he was
of the same trade, he was staying with
them and [a]they were working, for by
trade they were tent-makers. **4** And he
was reasoning [a]in the synagogue ev-
ery [b]Sabbath and trying to persuade
both [c]Jews and Greeks.

**5** But when [a]Silas and Timothy
[b]came down from [c]Macedonia, Paul
*began* devoting himself completely
to the word, solemnly [d]bearing
witness to the Jews that [e]Jesus is the
[1]Christ. **6** But when they resisted
and blasphemed, he [a]shook out his
garments and said to them, "Your
[b]blood *be* on your own heads! I am
clean. From now on I will go [c]to the
Gentiles." **7** Then he left there and
went to the house of a man named
[1]Titius Justus, a [a]God-fearer, whose
house was next to the synagogue.
**8** [a]And Crispus, [b]the leader of the
synagogue, believed in the Lord [c]with
all his household, and many of the
[d]Corinthians when they heard were
believing and being baptized. **9** And
the Lord said to Paul in the night by
[a]a vision, "Do not be afraid, but go on
speaking and do not be silent; **10** for
I am with you, and no man will lay *a*
*hand* on you in order to harm you,
for I have many people in this city."
**11** And he stayed *there* a year and six
months, teaching the word of God
among them.

**12** But while Gallio was [a]proconsul
of [b]Achaia, [c]the Jews with one accord
rose up against Paul and brought him
before [d]the judgment seat, **13** saying,
"This man persuades men to worship
God contrary to [a]the law." **14** But
when Paul was about to [a]open his
mouth, Gallio said to the Jews, "If it
were a wrongdoing or vicious crime,
O Jews, it would be reasonable for me
to put up with you; **15** but if there are
[a]questions about words and names
and your own law, see to it yourselves;
I am not willing to be a judge of these
matters." **16** And he drove them away
from [a]the judgment seat. **17** And they
all took hold of [a]Sosthenes, [b]the
leader of the synagogue, and *began*
beating him in front of [c]the judgment
seat. But Gallio was not concerned
about any of these things.

### *Priscilla, Aquila, and Apollos*

**18** And Paul, having remained many
days longer, [a]took leave of [b]the broth-
ers and put out to sea for [c]Syria, and
with him were [d]Priscilla and [d]Aquila.
In [e]Cenchreae [1]he [f]had his hair cut,
for he was keeping a vow. **19** And they

◆ **18:1** [a]Ac 17:15 [b]Ac 18:8; 19:1; 1Co 1:2; 2Co 1:1, 23; 6:11; 2Ti 4:20 **18:2** [a]Ac 18:18, 26; Ro 16:3; 1Co 16:19; 2Ti 4:19 [b]Ac 2:9 [c]Ac 27:1, 6; Heb 13:24 [d]Ac 11:28 **18:3** [a]Ac 20:34; 1Co 4:12; 9:14f; 2Co 11:7; 12:13; 1Th 2:9; 4:11; 2Th 3:8 **18:4** [a]Ac 9:20; 18:19 [b]Ac 13:14 [c]Ac 14:1 **18:5** [a]Ac 15:22; 16:1; 17:14 [b]Ac 17:15 [c]Ac 16:9 [d]Lk 16:28; Ac 20:21 [e]Ac 17:3; 18:28 [1]Messiah **18:6** [a]Ne 5:13; Ac 13:51 [b]2Sa 1:16; 1Ki 2:33; Eze 18:13; 33:4, 6, 8; Mt 27:25; Ac 20:26 [c]Ac 13:46 **18:7** [a]Ac 13:43; 16:14 [1]One early ms *Titus*; two other early mss omit the name **18:8** [a]1Co 1:14 [b]Mk 5:22 [c]Ac 11:14 [d]Ac 18:1; 19:1; 1Co 1:2; 2Co 1:1, 23; 6:11; 2Ti 4:20 **18:9** [a]Ac 9:10 **18:12** [a]Ac 13:7 [b]Ac 18:27; 19:21; Ro 15:26; 1Co 16:15; 2Co 1:1; 9:2; 11:10; 1Th 1:7f [c]1Th 2:14ff [d]Mt 27:19 **18:13** [a]Jn 19:7; Ac 18:15 **18:14** [a]Mt 5:2 **18:15** [a]Ac 23:29; 25:19 **18:16** [a]Mt 27:19 **18:17** [a]1Co 1:1 [b]Ac 18:8 [c]Mt 27:19 **18:18** [a]Mk 6:46 [b]Ac 1:15; 18:27 [c]Mt 4:24 [d]Ac 18:2, 26 [e]Ro 16:1 [f]Nu 6:2, 5, 9, 18; Ac 21:24 [1]Lit *having his hair cut*

arrived at [a]Ephesus, and he left them there. Now he himself entered [b]the synagogue and reasoned with the Jews. **20** When they asked him to stay for a longer time, he did not consent, **21** but [a]taking leave of them and saying, "I will return to you again [b]if God wills," he set sail from [c]Ephesus.

**22** And when he had landed at [a]Caesarea, he went up and greeted the church, and went down to [b]Antioch. **23** And having spent some time *there,* he left and passed successively through the [a]Galatian region and Phrygia, strengthening all the disciples.

**24** Now a Jew named [a]Apollos, an [b]Alexandrian by birth, [1]an eloquent man, arrived at [c]Ephesus; and he was mighty in the Scriptures. **25** This man had been instructed in [a]the way of the Lord; and being fervent in spirit, he was speaking and teaching accurately the things concerning Jesus, being acquainted only with [b]the baptism of John; **26** and [1]he began to speak out boldly in the synagogue. But when [a]Priscilla and Aquila heard him, they took him aside and explained to him [b]the way of God more accurately. **27** And when he wanted to go across to [a]Achaia, [b]the brothers encouraged him and wrote to [c]the disciples to welcome him; and when he had arrived, he greatly [1]helped those who had believed through grace, **28** for he powerfully refuted the Jews in public, demonstrating [a]by the Scriptures that [b]Jesus is the [1]Christ.

### *Paul in Ephesus*

**19** Now it happened that while [a]Apollos was at [b]Corinth, Paul passed through the [c]upper regions and came to [d]Ephesus and found some disciples. **2** And he said to them, "[a]Did you receive the Holy Spirit when you believed?" And they *said* to him, "No, [b]we have not even heard if the Holy Spirit is *being received.*" **3** And he said, "Into what then were you baptized?" And they said, "[a]Into John's baptism." **4** Then Paul said, "[a]John baptized with the baptism of repentance, telling the people [b]to believe in Him who was coming after him, that is, in Jesus." **5** And when they heard this, they were [a]baptized [1]in the name of the Lord Jesus. **6** And when Paul had [a]laid his hands upon them, the Holy Spirit came on them, and they *began* [b]speaking with tongues and [c]prophesying. **7** Now there were in all about twelve men.

**8** And after he entered [a]the synagogue, he continued speaking out boldly for three months, reasoning and persuading *them* [b]about the kingdom of God. **9** But when [a]some were becoming hardened and were not believing, speaking evil of [b]the

---

**18:19** [a]Ac 18:21, 24; 19:1, 17, 26, 28, 34f; 20:16f; 21:29; 1Co 15:32; 16:8; Eph 1:1; 1Ti 1:3; 2Ti 1:18; 4:12; Rev 1:11; 2:1 [b]Ac 18:4 **18:21** [a]Mk 6:46 [b]Ro 1:10; 15:32; 1Co 4:19; 16:7; Heb 6:3; Jas 4:15; 1Pe 3:17 [c]Ac 18:19, 24; 19:1, 17, 26, 28, 34f; 20:16f; 21:29; 1Co 15:32; 16:8; Eph 1:1; 1Ti 1:3; 2Ti 1:18; 4:12; Rev 1:11; 2:1 **18:22** [a]Ac 8:40 [b]Ac 11:19 **18:23** [a]Ac 16:6 **18:24** [a]Ac 19:1; 1Co 1:12; 3:5, 6, 22; 4:6; 16:12; Tit 3:13 [b]Ac 6:9 [c]Ac 18:19 [1]Or *a learned man* **18:25** [a]Ac 9:2; 18:26 [b]Lk 7:29; Ac 19:3 **18:26** [a]Ac 18:2, 18 [b]Ac 18:25 [1]Lit *this man* **18:27** [a]Ac 18:12; 19:1 [b]Ac 18:18 [c]Ac 11:26 [1]Or *helped greatly through grace those who had believed* **18:28** [a]Ac 8:35 [b]Ac 18:5 [1]Messiah ◆ **19:1** [a]Ac 18:24; 1Co 1:12; 3:5, 6, 22; 4:6; 16:12; Tit 3:13 [b]Ac 18:1 [c]Ac 18:23 [d]Ac 18:21, 24; 19:17, 26, 28, 34f; 20:16f; 21:29; 1Co 15:32; 16:8; Eph 1:1; 1Ti 1:3; 2Ti 1:18; 4:12; Rev 1:11; 2:1 **19:2** [a]Ac 8:15f; 11:16f [b]Jn 7:39 **19:3** [a]Lk 7:29; Ac 18:25 **19:4** [a]Mt 3:11; Mk 1:4, 7, 8; Lk 3:16; Jn 1:26, 27; Ac 13:24 [b]Jn 1:7 **19:5** [a]Ac 8:12, 16; 10:48 [1]Lit *into* **19:6** [a]Ac 6:6; 8:17 [b]Mk 16:17; Ac 2:4; 10:46 [c]Ac 13:1 **19:8** [a]Ac 9:20; 18:26 [b]Ac 1:3 **19:9** [a]Ac 14:4 [b]Ac 9:2; 19:23

Way before the multitude, he left them and took away [c]the disciples, reasoning daily in the school of Tyrannus. **10** This took place for [a]two years, so that all who lived in [b,1]Asia heard [c]the word of the Lord, both Jews and Greeks.

### *Miracles in Ephesus*

**11** And God was doing [a]extraordinary [1]miracles by the hands of Paul, **12** [a]so that cloths or aprons were even carried from his body to the sick, and the diseases left them and [b]the evil spirits went out. **13** But also some of the Jewish [a]exorcists, who went from place to place, attempted to invoke over those who had the evil spirits the name of the Lord Jesus, saying, "I implore you by Jesus whom Paul preaches." **14** Now seven sons of one *named* Sceva, a Jewish chief priest, were doing this. **15** And the evil spirit answered and said to them, "I recognize Jesus, and I know about Paul, but who are you?" **16** And the man, in whom was the evil spirit, leaped on them, subdued all of them, and utterly prevailed against them, so that they fled out of that house naked and wounded. **17** And this became known to all, both Jews and Greeks, who lived in [a]Ephesus; and fear fell upon them all and the name of the Lord Jesus was being magnified. **18** Also, many of those who had believed kept coming, confessing and disclosing their practices. **19** And many of those who practiced magic brought their books together and were burning them in the sight of everyone; and they counted up the price of them and found it fifty thousand [a,1]pieces of silver. **20** So [a,1]the word of the Lord [b]was growing mightily and prevailing.

### *Riots in Ephesus*

**21** Now after these things were finished, Paul purposed in the [1]Spirit to [a]go to Jerusalem [b]after he had passed through [c]Macedonia and [d]Achaia, saying, "After I have been there, [e]I must also see Rome." **22** And having sent into [a]Macedonia two of [b]those who ministered to him, [c]Timothy and [d]Erastus, he himself stayed in [e,1]Asia for a while.

**23** Now about that time there occurred no small disturbance concerning [a]the Way. **24** For a man named Demetrius, a silversmith, who made silver shrines of [1]Artemis, [a]was bringing no little [2]business to the craftsmen; **25** these he gathered together with the workers of similar *trades*, and said, "Men, you know that our prosperity is from this business. **26** And you see and hear that not only in [a]Ephesus, but in almost all of [b]Asia, this Paul has persuaded and turned away a considerable crowd, saying that [c]things made with hands are not gods. **27** And not only is there

**19:9** [c]Ac 11:26; 19:30 **19:10** [a]Ac 19:8; 20:31 [b]Ac 16:6; 19:22, 26, 27 [c]Ac 13:12; 19:20 [1]West coast province of Asia Minor **19:11** [a]Ac 8:13 [1]Or *works of power* **19:12** [a]Ac 5:15 [b]Mk 16:17 **19:13** [a]Mt 12:27; Lk 11:19 **19:17** [a]Ac 18:19 **19:19** [a]Lk 15:8 [1]A silver piece was approx. a laborer's daily wage **19:20** [a]Ac 19:10 [b]Ac 6:7; 12:24 [1]Or *according to the power of the Lord the word was growing* **19:21** [a]Ac 20:16, 22; 21:15; Ro 15:25; 2Co 1:16 [b]Ac 20:1; 1Co 16:5 [c]Ac 16:9; 19:22, 29; Ro 15:26; 1Th 1:7f [d]Ac 18:12 [e]Ac 23:11; Ro 15:24, 28 [1]Or *spirit* **19:22** [a]Ac 16:9; 19:21, 29 [b]Ac 13:5; 19:29; 20:34; 2Co 8:19 [c]Ac 16:1 [d]Ro 16:23; 2Ti 4:20 [e]Ac 19:10 [1]West coast province of Asia Minor **19:23** [a]Ac 19:9 **19:24** [a]Ac 16:16, 19f [1]Lat *Diana* [2]Or *profit* **19:26** [a]Ac 18:19 [b]Ac 19:10 [c]Dt 4:28; Ps 115:4; Is 44:10-20; Jer 10:3ff; Ac 17:29; 1Co 8:4; 10:19; Rev 9:20

danger that this trade of ours fall into
disrepute, but also that the temple
of the great goddess [1]Artemis be
considered as worthless and that she,
whom all of [a]Asia and [b]the [2]world
worship, is even about to be brought
down from her majesty."
**28** When they heard *this* and were
filled with rage, they *began* crying
out, saying, "Great is [1]Artemis of
the [a]Ephesians!" **29** And the city
was filled with the confusion, and
they rushed [1]with one accord into
the theater, dragging along [a]Gaius
and [b]Aristarchus, Paul's traveling
[c]companions from [d]Macedonia.
**30** And when Paul wanted to go into
the [1]assembly, [a]the disciples would
not let him. **31** Also some of the
[1]Asiarchs who were friends of his
sent to him and repeatedly urged him
not to [2]venture into the theater. **32** [a]So
then, some were shouting one thing
and some another, for the [1]meeting
was in confusion and the majority
did not know [2]for what reason they
had come together. **33** And some of
the crowd [1]concluded *it was* Alex-
ander, since the Jews had put him
forward; and having [a]motioned with
his hand, Alexander was intending
to make a defense to the [2]assembly.
**34** But when they recognized that
he was a Jew, a single cry arose from
them all as they shouted for about
two hours, "Great is Artemis of the
Ephesians!" **35** Now after calming the
crowd, the city clerk *said, "Men of
[a]Ephesus, what man is there after
all who does not know that the city
of the Ephesians is guardian of the
temple of the great Artemis and of
the *image* which fell down from
heaven? **36** So, since these are unde-
niable facts, you ought to keep calm
and to do nothing rash. **37** For you
have brought these men *here* who
are neither [a]robbers of temples nor
blasphemers of our goddess. **38** So
then, if Demetrius and the craftsmen
who are with him have a complaint
against anyone, the courts are in ses-
sion and [a,1]proconsuls are *available*;
let them bring charges against one
another. **39** But if you want anything
beyond this, it shall be settled in the
[1]lawful meeting. **40** For indeed we are
in danger of being accused of a riot
in connection with today's events,
since there is no cause for which
we can give as an account for this
disorderly gathering." **41** After saying
this he dismissed the meeting.

### *Through Macedonia and Greece*

**20** Now after the uproar had
ceased, Paul having summoned
and exhorted [a]the disciples, said
farewell and left [b]to go to [c]Macedo-
nia. **2** And when he had gone through
those districts and had given them
much exhortation, he came to Greece.
**3** And *there* he spent three months, and
when [a]a plot was formed against him
by the Jews as he was about to set sail
for [b]Syria, he decided to return through
[c]Macedonia. **4** And he was accom-
panied by Sopater of [a]Berea, *the son*

**19:27** [a]Ac 19:10 [b]Mt 24:14 [1]Lat *Diana* [2]Lit *the inhabited earth* **19:28** [a]Ac 18:19 [1]Lat *Diana* **19:29** [a]Ac 20:4 [b]Ac 20:4; 27:2; Col 4:10; Phm 24 [c]Ac 13:5; 19:22; 20:34; 2Co 8:19 [d]Ac 16:9; 19:22 [1]Or *together* **19:30** [a]Ac 19:9 [1]Lit *people* **19:31** [1]Political or religious officials of the province of Asia [2]Lit *give himself* **19:32** [a]Ac 21:34 [1]Gr *ekklesia* [2]Or *on whose account* **19:33** [a]Ac 12:17 [1]Or *advised Alexander* [2]Lit *people* **19:35** [a]Ac 18:19 **19:37** [a]Ro 2:22 **19:38** [a]Ac 13:7 [1]Or *provincial governors* **19:39** [1]Or *regular* ◆ **20:1** [a]Ac 11:26 [b]Ac 19:21 [c]Ac 16:9; 20:3 **20:3** [a]Ac 9:23f; 20:19 [b]Mt 4:24 [c]Ac 16:9; 20:1 **20:4** [a]Ac 17:10

of Pyrrhus, and by [b]Aristarchus and
Secundus of the [c]Thessalonians, and
[b]Gaius of [d]Derbe, and [e]Timothy,
and [f]Tychicus and [g]Trophimus of
[h,1]Asia. **5** But these had gone on ahead
and were waiting for [a]us at [b]Troas.
**6** [a]And we sailed from [b]Philippi after
[c]the days of Unleavened Bread, and
came to them at [d]Troas within five
days; and there we stayed seven days.

### *Eutychus Raised from the Dead in Troas*

**7** And on [a]the first day of the week,
when [b]we were gathered together to
[c]break bread, Paul *began* speaking to
them, intending to leave the next day,
and he prolonged his [1]message until
midnight. **8** Now there were many
[a]lamps in the [b]upper room where we
were gathered together. **9** And there
was a young man named [1]Eutychus
sitting on the windowsill, sinking
into a deep sleep. And as Paul kept
on talking, he sunk into that sleep
and fell down from the third floor
and was picked up dead. **10** But Paul
went down and [a]fell upon him, and
after embracing him, he [b]said, "[1]Do
not be troubled, for his life is in him."
**11** And when he had gone *back* up and
had [a]broken the bread and [1]eaten, he
talked with them a long while until
daybreak, and then left. **12** And they
took away the boy alive, and were not
a little comforted.

### *Paul's Farewell to the Ephesian Elders*

**13** But [a]we, going ahead to the ship,
set sail for Assos, intending from
there to take Paul on board; for so
he had arranged it, intending himself
to go [1]by land. **14** And when he met
us at Assos, we took him on board
and came to Mitylene. **15** And sailing
from there, we arrived the following
day opposite Chios; and the next day
we crossed over to Samos; and the
day following we came to [a]Miletus.
**16** For Paul had decided to sail past
[a]Ephesus so that he would not have
to spend time in [b,1]Asia; for he was
hurrying [c]to be in Jerusalem, if pos-
sible, [d]on the day of Pentecost.

**17** Now from Miletus he sent to
[a]Ephesus and called to him [b]the el-
ders of the church. **18** And when they
had come to him, he said to them,

"You yourselves know, [a]from
the first day that I set foot in Asia,
how I was with you the whole time,
**19** serving the Lord with all humility
and with tears and with trials which
came upon me [1]through [a]the plots
of the Jews; **20** how I [a]did not shrink
from declaring to you anything that
was profitable, and teaching you
publicly and [1]from house to house,
**21** solemnly [a]testifying to both Jews
and Greeks about [b]repentance to-
ward God and [c]faith in our Lord Jesus
Christ. **22** And now, behold, bound

---

**20:4** [b]Ac 19:29 [c]Ac 17:1 [d]Ac 14:6 [e]Ac 16:1 [f]Eph 6:21; Col 4:7; 2Ti 4:12; Tit 3:12 [g]Ac 21:29; 2Ti 4:20 [h]Ac 16:6; 20:16, 18 [1]West coast province of Asia Minor **20:5** [a]Ac 16:10; 20:5-15 [b]Ac 16:8 **20:6** [a]Ac 16:10; 20:5-15 [b]Ac 16:12 [c]Ac 12:3 [d]Ac 16:8 **20:7** [a]1Co 16:2; Rev 1:10 [b]Ac 16:10; 20:5-15 [c]Ac 2:42; 20:11 [1]Lit *word, speech* **20:8** [a]Mt 25:1 [b]Ac 1:13 **20:9** [1]*Eutychus* means *good fortune*; 'lucky' **20:10** [a]1Ki 17:21; 2Ki 4:34 [b]Mt 9:23f; Mk 5:39 [1]Or *Stop being troubled* **20:11** [a]Ac 2:42; 20:7 [1]Lit *tasted* **20:13** [a]Ac 16:10; 20:5-15 [1]Or *on foot* **20:15** [a]Ac 20:17; 2Ti 4:20 **20:16** [a]Ac 18:19 [b]Ac 16:6; 20:4, 18 [c]Ac 19:21; 20:6, 22; 1Co 16:8 [d]Ac 2:1 [1]West coast province of Asia Minor **20:17** [a]Ac 18:19 [b]Ac 11:30 **20:18** [a]Ac 18:19; 19:1, 10; 20:4, 16 **20:19** [a]Ac 20:3 [1]Lit *by* **20:20** [a]Ac 20:27 [1]Or *in the various private homes* **20:21** [a]Lk 16:28; Ac 18:5; 20:23, 24 [b]Ac 2:38; 11:18; 26:20 [c]Ac 24:24; 26:18; Eph 1:15; Col 2:5; Phm 5

by the [1]Spirit, [a]I am on my way to
Jerusalem, not knowing what will
happen to me there, **23** except that
[a]the Holy Spirit solemnly [b]testifies to
me in every city, saying that [c]chains
and afflictions await me. **24** But [a]I do
not make my life of any account nor
dear to myself, so that I may [b]finish
my course and [c]the ministry which
I received from the Lord Jesus, to
[d]testify solemnly of the gospel of
[e]the grace of God.

**25** "And now, behold, I know that
all of you, among whom I went
about [a]preaching the kingdom, will
no longer see my face. **26** Therefore,
I [1]testify to you this day that [a]I am
[2]innocent of the blood of all. **27** For
I [a]did not shrink from declaring to
you the whole [b]purpose of God. **28** Be
on guard for yourselves and for all
[a]the flock, among which the Holy
Spirit has made you [1]overseers, to
shepherd [b]the church of God which
[c]He [2]purchased [3]with His own blood.
**29** I know that after my departure
[a]savage wolves will come in among
you, not sparing [b]the flock; **30** and
from among your own selves men
will arise, speaking perverse things,
to draw away [a]the disciples after
them. **31** Therefore be watchful, re-
membering that night and day for a
period of [a]three years I did not cease
to admonish each one [b]with tears.
**32** And now I [a]commend you to God
and to [b]the word of His grace, which
is able to [c]build *you* up and to give
*you* [d]the inheritance among all those
who have been sanctified. **33** [a]I have
coveted no one's silver or gold or
clothes. **34** You yourselves know that
[a]these hands ministered to my *own*
needs and to those [b]who were with
me. **35** In everything I showed you
that by laboring in this manner you
must help the weak and remember
the words of the Lord Jesus, that He
Himself said, 'It is more blessed to
give than to receive.'"

**36** And when he had said these
things, he [a]knelt down and prayed
with them all. **37** And [1]they *began*
to weep aloud and [a]falling on Paul's
neck, they were kissing him, **38** being
in agony especially over [a]the word
which he had spoken, that they
would not see his face again. And
they were [b]accompanying him to
the ship.

### *Paul Sets Out for Jerusalem*

**21** Now when [a]we had parted
from them and had set sail,
we came by [b]a straight course to Cos
and the next day to Rhodes and from
there to Patara; **2** and having found
a ship crossing over to [a]Phoenicia,
we went aboard and set sail. **3** And
when we came in sight of [a]Cyprus,
leaving it on the left, we kept sailing
to [b]Syria and landed at [c]Tyre; for

---

**20:22** [a]Ac 17:16; 20:16 [1]Or *in spirit* **20:23** [a]Ac 8:29 [b]Lk 16:28; Ac 18:5; 20:21, 24 [c]Ac 9:16; 21:33
**20:24** [a]Ac 21:13 [b]Ac 13:25; 2Ti 4:7 [c]Ac 1:17 [d]Lk 16:28; Ac 18:5; 20:21 [e]Ac 11:23; 20:32 **20:25** [a]Mt 4:23;
Ac 28:31 **20:26** [a]Ac 18:6 [1]Or *call you to witness* [2]Lit *pure from* **20:27** [a]Ac 20:20 [b]Ac 13:36
***20:28*** [a]Lk 12:32; Jn 21:15-17; Ac 20:29; 1Pe 5:2f [b]Mt 16:18; Ro 16:16; 1Co 10:32 [c]Eph 1:7, 14; Tit 2:14; 1Pe 1:19;
2:9; Rev 5:9 [1]Or *bishops* [2]Lit *acquired* [3]Lit *through* **20:29** [a]Eze 22:27; Mt 7:15 [b]Lk 12:32; Jn 21:15-17;
Ac 20:28; 1Pe 5:2f **20:30** [a]Ac 11:26 **20:31** [a]Ac 19:8, 10; 24:17 [b]Ac 20:19 **20:32** [a]Ac 14:23 [b]Ac 14:3;
20:24 [c]Ac 9:31 [d]Ac 26:18; Eph 1:14; 5:5; Col 1:12; 3:24; Heb 9:15; 1Pe 1:4 **20:33** [a]1Co 9:4-18; 2Co 11:7-12;
12:14-18; 1Th 2:5f **20:34** [a]Ac 18:3 [b]Ac 19:22 **20:36** [a]Ac 9:40; 21:5; Lk 22:41 **20:37** [a]Lk 15:20 [1]Lit
*a considerable weeping of all occurred* **20:38** [a]Ac 20:25 [b]Ac 15:3 ◆ **21:1** [a]Ac 16:10; 21:1-18 [b]Ac 16:11
**21:2** [a]Ac 11:19; 21:3 **21:3** [a]Ac 4:36; 21:16 [b]Mt 4:24 [c]Ac 12:20; 21:7

there the ship was to unload its cargo.
**4** And after looking up [a]the disciples,
we stayed there seven days; and
they kept telling Paul [b]through the
Spirit not to set foot in Jerusalem.
**5** And when [1]our days there were
ended, we left and started on our
journey, while they all, with wives
and children, [a]escorted us until *we*
*were* out of the city. After [b]kneeling
down on the beach and praying, we
said farewell to one another. **6** Then
we went on board the ship, and they
returned [a]home again.

**7** And when we had finished the
voyage from [a]Tyre, we arrived at
Ptolemais, and after greeting [b]the
brothers, we stayed with them for a
day. **8** And on the next day we left and
came to [a]Caesarea, and entering the
house of [b]Philip the [c]evangelist, who
was [b]one of the seven, we stayed with
him. **9** Now this man had four virgin
daughters who [a]prophesied. **10** And
as we were staying there for some
days, a prophet named [a]Agabus came
down from Judea. **11** And coming to
us, he [a]took Paul's belt and bound
his own feet and hands, and said,
"This [b]is what the Holy Spirit says:
'In this way the Jews at Jerusalem will
[c]bind the man who owns this belt
and [d]deliver him into the hands of
the Gentiles.'" **12** And when we had
heard this, we as well as the local
residents *began* begging him [a]not
to go up to Jerusalem. **13** Then Paul
answered, "What are you doing,
crying and breaking my heart? For
[a]I am ready not only to be bound,
but even to die at Jerusalem for [b]the
name of the Lord Jesus." **14** And since
he would not be persuaded, we fell
silent, saying, "[a]The will of the Lord
be done!"

**15** Now after these days we got
ready and [a]started on our way up to
Jerusalem. **16** And *some* of [a]the disci-
ples from [b]Caesarea also came with
us, taking us to Mnason of [c]Cyprus,
an [d]early disciple with whom we
were to lodge.

### *In Jerusalem*

**17** And after we arrived in Jerusalem,
[a]the brothers welcomed us gladly.
**18** And the following day Paul went
in with us to [a]James, and all [b]the
elders were present. **19** And after he
had greeted them, he [a]*began to* relate
one by one the things which God
did among the Gentiles through his
[b]ministry. **20** And when they heard
it they *began* [a]glorifying God; and
they said to him, "You see, brother,
how many [1]thousands there are
among the Jews of those who have
believed, and they are all [b]zealous for
the Law; **21** and they have been told
about you, that you are [a]teaching all
the Jews who are among the Gentiles
to forsake Moses, telling them [b]not
to circumcise their children nor to
[1]walk according to [c]the customs.
**22** What, *then, is to be done*? They
will certainly hear that you have
come. **23** Therefore do this that we
tell you. We have four men who

---

**21:4** [a]Ac 11:26; 21:16 [b]Ac 20:23; 21:11 **21:5** [a]Ac 15:3 [b]Lk 22:41; Ac 9:40; 20:36 [1]Lit *we had completed the days* **21:6** [a]Jn 19:27 **21:7** [a]Ac 12:20; 21:3 [b]Ac 1:15; 21:17 **21:8** [a]Ac 8:40; 21:16 [b]Ac 6:5; 8:5 [c]Eph 4:11; 2Ti 4:5 **21:9** [a]Lk 2:36; Ac 13:1; 1Co 11:5 **21:10** [a]Ac 11:28 **21:11** [a]1Ki 22:11; Is 20:2; Jer 13:1-11; 19:1, 11; Jn 18 [b]Ac 8:29 [c]Ac 9:16; 21:33 [d]Mt 20:19 **21:12** [a]Ac 21:15 **21:13** [a]Ac 20:24 [b]Ac 5:41; 9:16 **21:14** [a]Lk 22:42 **21:15** [a]Ac 21:12 **21:16** [a]Ac 21:4 [b]Ac 8:40 [c]Ac 4:36; 21:3 [d]Ac 15:7 **21:17** [a]Ac 1:15; 21:7 **21:18** [a]Ac 12:17 [b]Ac 11:30 **21:19** [a]Ac 14:27 [b]Ac 1:17 **21:20** [a]Mt 9:8 [b]Ac 15:1; 22:3; Ro 10:2; Ga 1:14 [1]Lit *ten thousands* **21:21** [a]Ac 21:28 [b]Ac 15:19ff; 1Co 7:18f [c]Ac 6:14 [1]Observe or live by

[a,1]are under a vow; **24** take them and
[a]purify yourself along with them,
and [1]pay their expenses so that they
may [b]shave their [2]heads. Then all
will know that there is nothing to
the things which they have been
told about you, but that you yourself
also walk orderly, keeping the Law.
**25** But concerning the Gentiles who
have believed, we wrote, [a]having
decided that they should keep from
[1]meat sacrificed to idols and from
blood and from what is strangled
and from sexual immorality." **26** Then
Paul [1]took the men, and the next day,
[a]purifying himself along with them,
[b]went into the temple giving notice
of the completion of the days of
purification, until the sacrifice was
offered for each one of them.

### *Paul Is Arrested*

**27** Now when [a]the seven days were
almost over, [b]the Jews from [c,1]Asia,
upon noticing him in the temple,
*began to* throw all the crowd into
confusion and laid hands on him,
**28** crying out, "Men of Israel, help!
[a]This is the man who teaches to
everyone everywhere against our
people and the Law and this place;
and besides, he has even brought
Greeks into the temple and has
[b]defiled this holy place." **29** For they
had previously seen [a]Trophimus the
[b]Ephesian in the city with him, and
they supposed that Paul had brought
him into the temple. **30** Then all the
city was stirred, and [1]the people
rushed together, and taking hold of
Paul they [a]dragged him out of the
temple, and immediately the doors
were shut. **31** While they were seeking
to kill him, a report came up to the
[1]commander of the [a]*Roman* [2]cohort
that all Jerusalem was in confusion.
**32** At once he [a]took along soldiers
and centurions and ran down
to them; and when they saw the
commander and the soldiers, they
stopped beating Paul. **33** Then the
commander came up and took hold
of him, and ordered him to be [a]bound
with [b]two chains; and he *began*
asking who he was and what he had
done. **34** But among the crowd [a]some
were shouting one thing *and* some
another, and when he could not find
out the [1]facts because of the uproar,
he ordered him to be brought into
[b]the barracks. **35** And when he got to
[a]the stairs, he actually was carried by
the soldiers because of the violence
of the crowd; **36** for the multitude
of the people kept following them,
shouting, "[a]Away with him!"

### *Paul's Defense Before the Jews*

**37** As Paul was about to be brought
into [a]the barracks, he said to the
commander, "May I say something
to you?" And he *said, "Do you
know Greek? **38** Then you are not
[a]the Egyptian who some [1]time ago

**21:23** [a]Nu 6:13-21; Ac 18:18 [1]Lit *have a vow on them* **21:24** [a]Jn 11:55; Ac 21:26; 24:18 [b]Ac 18:18 [1]Lit *spend on them* [2]Lit *head* **21:25** [a]Ac 15:19f, 29 [1]Lit *the thing* **21:26** [a]Jn 11:55; Ac 21:24; 24:18 [b]Nu 6:13; Ac 24:18 [1]Or *took the men the next day, and purifying himself* **21:27** [a]Nu 6:9, 13-20 [b]Ac 20:19; 24:18 [c]Ac 16:6 [1]West coast province of Asia Minor **21:28** [a]Ac 6:13 [b]Mt 24:15; Ac 6:13f; 24:6 **21:29** [a]Ac 20:4 [b]Ac 18:19 **21:30** [a]2Ki 11:15; Ac 16:19; 26:21 [1]Lit *a running together of the people occurred* **21:31** [a]Ac 10:1 [1]Military leader over 1,000 soldiers [2]Normally 600 men (the number varied); or *battalion* **21:32** [a]Ac 23:27 **21:33** [a]Ac 20:23; 21:11; 22:29; 26:29; 28:20; Eph 6:20; 2Ti 1:16; 2:9 [b]Ac 12:6 **21:34** [a]Ac 19:32 [b]Ac 21:37; 22:24; 23:10, 16, 32 [1]Lit *certainty* **21:35** [a]Ac 21:40 **21:36** [a]Lk 23:18; Jn 19:15; Ac 22:22 **21:37** [a]Ac 21:34; 22:24; 23:10, 16, 32 **21:38** [a]Ac 5:36 [1]Lit *days*

raised a revolt and led the four thou-
sand men of the Assassins out [b]into
the wilderness?" **39** But Paul said,
"[a]I am a Jew of Tarsus in [b]Cilicia, a
citizen of no insignificant city; and
I beg you, allow me to speak to the
people." **40** And when he had given
him permission, Paul, standing on
[a]the stairs, [b]motioned to the peo-
ple with his hand; and when there
[1]was a great hush, he spoke to them
in the [c]Hebrew language, saying,

**22** "[a]Men, brothers, and fathers,
hear my defense which I now
*offer* to you."

**2** And when they heard that he
was addressing them in the [a]Hebrew
language, they became even quieter;
and he *said,

**3** "[a]I am [b]a Jew, born in [c]Tarsus of
[d]Cilicia, but having been brought up
in this city, having been instructed
at the feet of [e]Gamaliel according
to the [f]strictness of the law of our
fathers, being zealous for God just
as [g]you all are today, **4** [a]I persecuted
this [b]Way to the death, binding and
delivering both men and women
into prisons, **5** as also [a]the high
priest and all [b]the Council of the
elders [1]can testify. From them I also
[c]received letters to [d]the brothers,
and started off for [c]Damascus in
order to bring even those who were
there to Jerusalem [2]as prisoners to
be punished.

**6** "[a]But it happened that as I was
on my way, approaching Damascus
about noontime, a very bright light
suddenly flashed from heaven all
around me, **7** and I fell to the ground
and heard a voice saying to me,
'Saul, Saul, why are you persecuting
Me?' **8** And I answered, 'Who are
You, Lord?' And He said to me, 'I am
[a]Jesus the Nazarene, whom you are
persecuting.' **9** And those who were
with me [a]beheld the light, to be
sure, but [b]did not [1]understand the
voice of the One who was speaking
to me. **10** And I said, '[a]What should I
do, Lord?' And the Lord said to me,
'Rise up and go on into Damascus,
and there you will be told of all that
has been determined for you to do.'
**11** But since I [a]could not see because
of the glory of that light, being led by
the hand by those who were with me,
I came into Damascus.

**12** "Now a certain [a]Ananias, a man
who was devout by the standard of
the Law, *and* [b]well spoken of by all
the Jews who lived there, **13** came to
me, and standing near, said to me,
'[a]Brother Saul, regain your sight!'
And [b,1]at that very hour I regained
my sight and *saw* him. **14** And he
said, '[a]The God of our fathers has
[b]appointed you to know His will and
to [c]see the [d]Righteous One and to
hear a [1]voice from His mouth. **15** For
you will be [a]a witness for Him to all
men of [b]what you have seen and
heard. **16** Now why do you delay?
[a]Rise up and be baptized, and [b]wash
away your sins, [c]calling on His name.'

---

**21:38** [b]Mt 24:26 **21:39** [a]Ac 9:11; 22:3 [b]Ac 6:9 **21:40** [a]Ac 21:35 [b]Ac 12:17 [c]Jn 5:2; Ac 1:19; 22:2; 26:14 [1]Lit *occurred* ◆ **22:1** [a]Ac 7:2 **22:2** [a]Ac 21:40 **22:3** [a]Ac 9:1-22; 22:3-16; 26:9-18 [b]Ac 21:39 [c]Ac 9:11 [d]Ac 6:9 [e]Ac 5:34 [f]Ac 23:6; 26:5; Php 3:6 [g]Ac 21:20 **22:4** [a]Ac 8:3; 22:19f; 26:9-11 [b]Ac 9:2 **22:5** [a]Ac 9:1 [b]Lk 22:66; Ac 5:21; 1Ti 4:14 [c]Ac 9:2 [d]Ac 2:29; 3:17; 13:26; 23:1; 28:17, 21; Ro 9:3 [1]Lit *testifies for me* [2]Lit *having been bound* **22:6** [a]Ac 22:6-11: *Ac 9:3-8; 26:12-18* **22:8** [a]Ac 26:9 **22:9** [a]Ac 26:13 [b]Ac 9:7 [1]Or *hear (with comprehension)* **22:10** [a]Ac 16:30 **22:11** [a]Ac 9:8 **22:12** [a]Ac 9:10 [b]Ac 6:3; 10:22 **22:13** [a]Ac 9:17 [b]Ac 9:18 [1]Or *instantly* **22:14** [a]Ac 3:13 [b]Ac 9:15; 26:16 [c]Ac 9:17; 26:16; 1Co 9:1; 15:8 [d]Ac 7:52 [1]Or *message* **22:15** [a]Ac 23:11; 26:16 [b]Ac 22:14 **22:16** [a]Ac 9:18 [b]Ac 2:38; 1Co 6:11; Eph 5:26; Heb 10:22 [c]Ac 7:59

**17** "Now it happened when I
[a]returned to Jerusalem and was
praying in the temple, that I [b]fell into
a trance, **18** and I saw Him saying to
me, '[a]Hurry and get out of Jerusalem
quickly, because they will not accept
your witness about Me.' **19** And I said,
'Lord, they themselves understand
that in one synagogue after another
[a]I used to imprison and [b]beat those
who believed in You. **20** And [a]when
the blood of Your witness Stephen
was being shed, I also was standing
by approving, and guarding the
garments of those who were slaying
him.' **21** And He said to me, 'Go!
For I will send you far away [a]to the
Gentiles.'"

### *Paul, a Citizen of Rome*

**22** And they were listening to him
up to this statement, and *then* they
raised their voices and said, "[a]Away
with such a fellow from the earth, for
[b]he should not be allowed to live!"
**23** And as they were crying out and
[a]throwing off their garments and
[b]tossing dust into the air, **24** the
[1]commander ordered him to be
brought into [a]the barracks, stating
that he should be [b]examined by
flogging so that he might find out
the reason why they were shouting
against him that way. **25** But when
they stretched him out [1]with leather
straps, Paul said to the centurion who
was standing by, "Is it [2]lawful for you
to flog [a]a man who is a Roman and
uncondemned?" **26** And when the
centurion heard *this*, he went to the
commander and reported to him,
saying, "What are you about to do?
For this man is a Roman." **27** And
the commander came and said to
him, "Tell me, are you a Roman?"
And he said, "Yes." **28** And the
commander answered, "I acquired
this citizenship with a large sum of
money." And Paul said, "But I have
been born *a citizen*." **29** Therefore
those who were about to [a]examine
him immediately withdrew from
him; and the commander also [b]was
afraid when he learned that he was a
Roman, and because he had [c]bound
him.

### *Paul Before the Sanhedrin*

**30** But on the next day, [a]wishing to
know for certain why he had been
accused by the Jews, he [b]released
him and ordered the chief priests and
all [c]the Sanhedrin to come together,
and brought Paul down and set him
before them.

**23** Now Paul, looking intently at
[a]the Sanhedrin, said, "[b]Brothers,
[c]I have [1]lived my life in all good
conscience before God up to this
day." **2** And the high priest [a]Ananias
commanded those standing beside
him [b]to strike him on the mouth.
**3** Then Paul said to him, "God is going
to strike you, [a]you whitewashed wall!
Do you [b]sit to try me according to
the Law, and in violation of the Law
order me to be struck?" **4** But those
standing nearby said, "Do you revile

***22:17*** [a]*Ac 9:26; 26:20* [b]Ac 10:10 **22:18** [a]Ac 9:29 **22:19** [a]Ac 8:3; 22:4 [b]Mt 10:17; Ac 26:11
**22:20** [a]Ac 7:58f; 8:1; 26:10 **22:21** [a]Ac 9:15 **22:22** [a]Ac 21:36; 1Th 2:16 [b]Ac 25:24 **22:23** [a]Ac 7:58
[b]2Sa 16:13 **22:24** [a]Ac 21:34 [b]Ac 22:29 [1]Military leader over 1,000 soldiers **22:25** [a]Ac 16:37 [1]Or *for the whip* [2]Interrogation by torture was a procedure used with slaves **22:29** [a]Ac 22:24 [b]Ac 16:38
[c]Ac 21:33 **22:30** [a]Ac 23:28 [b]Ac 21:33 [c]Mt 5:22 ◆**23:1** [a]Ac 22:30; 23:6, 15, 20, 28 [b]Ac 22:5 [c]Ac 24:16;
2Co 1:12; 2Ti 1:3 [1]Or *conducted myself as a citizen* **23:2** [a]Ac 24:1 [b]Jn 18:22 **23:3** [a]Mt 23:27 [b]Lv 19:15;
Dt 25:2; Jn 7:51

the high priest of God?" **5** And Paul said, "I was not aware, brothers, that he was high priest; for it is written, '[a]YOU SHALL NOT SPEAK EVIL OF A RULER OF YOUR PEOPLE.'"

**6** But knowing that one group were [a]Sadducees and the other Pharisees, Paul *began* crying out in [b]the Sanhedrin, "[c]Brothers, [d]I am a Pharisee, a son of Pharisees; I am on trial for [e]the hope and resurrection of the dead!" **7** As he said this, there was dissension between the Pharisees and Sadducees, and the assembly was divided. **8** For [a]the Sadducees say that there is no resurrection, nor an angel, nor a spirit, but the Pharisees acknowledge them all. **9** And there occurred a great outcry; and some of [a]the scribes of the Pharisaic party stood up and *began to* argue heatedly, saying, "[b]We find nothing wrong with this man. [c]Suppose a spirit or an angel has spoken to him?" **10** And as a great dissension was developing, because the [1]commander was afraid Paul would be torn to pieces by them, he ordered the troops to go down and take him away from them by force, and bring him into [a]the barracks.

**11** But on [a]that very night, the Lord stood at his side and said, "[b]Take courage; for [c]as you have [d]solemnly borne witness to My cause at Jerusalem, so you must bear witness at Rome also."

### *A Plot to Kill Paul*

**12** Now when it was day, [a]the Jews formed a [1]conspiracy and [b]bound themselves under a curse, saying that they would neither eat nor drink until they had killed Paul. **13** And there were more than forty who formed this scheme. **14** They came to the chief priests and the elders and said, "We have [a]bound ourselves under a curse to taste nothing until we have killed Paul. **15** So now you, along with [a]the Sanhedrin, notify the commander to bring him down to you, as though you were going to determine his case more carefully; and we for our part are ready to slay him before he comes near."

**16** But when the son of Paul's sister heard of their ambush, [1]he came and entered [a]the barracks and reported *it* to Paul. **17** And Paul called one of the centurions to him and said, "Lead this young man to the commander, for he has something to report to him." **18** So he took him and led him to the [1]commander and *said, "Paul [a]the prisoner called me to him and asked me to lead this young man to you since he has something to tell you." **19** And the [1]commander took him by the hand and stepping aside, *began to* inquire of him privately, "What is it that you have to report to me?" **20** And he said, "[a]The Jews have agreed to ask you to bring Paul down tomorrow to [b]the Sanhedrin, as though they were going to inquire somewhat more carefully about him. **21** So do not be persuaded by them, for more than forty of them—who have [a]bound themselves under a

---

**23:5** [a]Ex 22:28 **23:6** [a]Mt 3:7; 22:23 [b]Ac 22:30; 23:1, 15, 20, 28 [c]Ac 22:5 [d]Ac 26:5; Php 3:5 [e]Ac 24:15, 21; 26:8 **23:8** [a]Mt 22:23; Mk 12:18; Lk 20:27 **23:9** [a]Mk 2:16; Lk 5:30 [b]Ac 23:29 [c]Jn 12:29; Ac 22:6ff **23:10** [a]Ac 21:34; 23:16, 32 [1]Military leader over 1,000 soldiers **23:11** [a]Ac 18:9 [b]Mt 9:2 [c]Ac 19:21 [d]Lk 16:28; Ac 28:23 **23:12** [a]Ac 9:23; 23:30; 1Th 2:16 [b]Ac 23:14, 21 [1]Or *mob* **23:14** [a]Ac 23:12, 21 **23:15** [a]Ac 22:30; 23:1, 6, 20, 28 **23:16** [a]Ac 21:34; 23:10, 32 [1]Or *having been present* with them, **23:18** [a]Eph 3:1 [1]v 10, note 1 **23:19** [1]v 10, note 1 **23:20** [a]Ac 23:14f [b]Ac 22:30; 23:1, 6, 15, 28 **23:21** [a]Ac 23:12, 14

curse not to eat or drink until they
slay him—are [b]lying in wait for him
and now they are ready and waiting
for the promise from you." **22** So
the commander let the young man
go, instructing him, "Tell no one
that you have notified me of these
things."

### *Paul Is Brought to Caesarea*

**23** And when he called to him two
of the centurions, he said, "Make
ready two hundred soldiers, [1]sev-
enty horsemen, and two hundred
[2]spearmen to proceed to [a]Caesarea
by the [3]third hour of the night,
**24** and provide mounts to put Paul
on and bring him safely to [a]Felix the
governor." **25** And he wrote a letter
having this form:
**26** "Claudius Lysias, to the
[a]most excellent governor
Felix, [b]greetings.

**27** "When this man was arrested
by the Jews and was about to
be slain by them, [a]I came up
to them with the troops and
rescued him, [b]having learned
that he was a Roman. **28** And
[a]wanting to ascertain the
charge for which they were
accusing him, I [b]brought him
down to their [c]Sanhedrin;
**29** and I found him to be
accused over [a]questions
about their Law, but [1]under
[b]no accusation deserving
death or [2]imprisonment.
**30** "And when I was [a]informed
that there would be [b]a plot
against the man, I sent him to
you at once, also instructing
[c]his accusers to speak
against him before you."

**31** So the soldiers, according to their
orders, took Paul and brought him
by night to Antipatris. **32** But the
next day, leaving [a]the horsemen to
go on with him, they returned to [b]the
barracks. **33** When these had come to
[a]Caesarea and delivered the letter to
[b]the governor, they also presented
Paul to him. **34** And when he had read
it, he asked from what [a]province he
was, and when he learned that [b]he
was from Cilicia, **35** he said, "I will
give you a hearing after your [a]accus-
ers arrive also," giving orders for him
to be [b]kept in Herod's [1]Praetorium.

### *Paul's Trial Before Felix the Governor*

**24** Now after [a]five days the high
priest [b]Ananias came down
with some elders, [1]with an [2]attorney
*named* Tertullus, and they [3]brought
charges to [c]the governor against
Paul. **2** And after *Paul* had been sum-
moned, Tertullus began to accuse
him, saying,
"As we have attained much peace
through you—and because by your
provision reforms are being carried
out for this nation— **3** we welcome
*this* in every way and everywhere,
[a]most excellent Felix, with all
thankfulness. **4** But, that I may not

***23:21*** [b]*Lk 11:54* **23:23** [a]Ac 8:40; 23:33 [1]Lit *and* [2]Or *slingers, bowmen* [3]9 p.m. **23:24** [a]Ac 23:26, 33; 24:1, 3, 10; 25:14 **23:26** [a]Lk 1:3; Ac 24:3; 26:25 [b]Ac 15:23 **23:27** [a]Ac 21:32f [b]Ac 22:25-29 **23:28** [a]Ac 22:30 [b]Ac 23:10 [c]Ac 23:1 **23:29** [a]Ac 18:15; 25:19 [b]Ac 23:9; 25:25; 26:31; 28:18 [1]Lit *having* [2]Lit *bonds* **23:30** [a]Ac 23:20f [b]Ac 9:24; 23:12 [c]Ac 23:35; 24:19; 25:16 **23:32** [a]Ac 23:23 [b]Ac 23:10 **23:33** [a]Ac 8:40; 23:23 [b]Ac 23:24, 26; 24:1, 3, 10; 25:14 **23:34** [a]Ac 25:1 [b]Ac 6:9; 21:39 **23:35** [a]Ac 23:30; 24:19; 25:16 [b]Ac 24:27 [1]Governor's official residence ◆ **24:1** [a]Ac 24:11 [b]Ac 23:2 [c]Ac 23:24 [1]Lit *and* [2]Lit *orator* [3]Or *presented their evidence* **24:3** [a]Ac 23:26; 26:25

weary you any further, I plead with
you by your forbearance to hear us
briefly. **5** For we have found this man
a real pest and a fellow who stirs
up dissension among all the Jews
throughout [1]the world, and a ring-
leader of the [a]sect of the Nazarenes.
**6** And he even tried to [a]desecrate the
temple; and [1]then we arrested him.
[2][We wanted to judge him according
to our own Law. **7** But Lysias the
commander came along, and with
much violence took him out of our
hands, **8** ordering his accusers to
come before you.] By examining
him yourself concerning all these
matters you will be able to ascertain
the things of which we accuse him."
**9** [a]And the Jews also joined in the
attack, asserting that these things
were so.

**10** And when [a]the governor had
nodded for him to speak, Paul an-
swered:

"Knowing that for many years you
have been a judge to this nation, I
cheerfully make my defense, **11** since
you are able to ascertain the fact
that no more than [a]twelve days ago
I went up to Jerusalem to worship.
**12** [a]And neither in the temple, nor
in the synagogues, nor across the
city did they find me carrying on a
discussion with anyone or [b]causing
[1]a riot. **13** [a]Nor are they able to prove
to you of what they are now accusing
me. **14** But this I confess to you, that
according to [a]the Way, which they
call a [b]sect, I do serve [c,1]the God of
our fathers, [d]believing everything
that is in accordance with the Law
and that is written in the Prophets;
**15** having a hope in God, for which
[a]these men are waiting, that there
shall certainly be a resurrection
of both the righteous and the un-
righteous. **16** In view of this, [a]I also
[1]do my best to maintain always a
conscience without fault *both* before
God and before men. **17** Now [a]after
several years I [b]came to bring [1]alms
to my nation and offerings; **18** in
which they found me, having been
[a]purified in the temple, without *any*
[b]crowd or uproar. But *there were*
some [c]Jews from [1]Asia— **19** who
ought to have been present before
you and to [a]make accusation, if they
should have anything against me.
**20** Or else let these men themselves
tell what wrongdoing they found
when I stood before [a]the Sanhedrin,
**21** other than for this one statement
which [a]I shouted out while standing
among them, 'For the resurrection
of the dead I am on trial before you
today.'"

**22** But Felix, having a more ac-
curate knowledge about [a]the Way,
put them off, saying, "When Lysias
the [1]commander comes down, I will
decide your case." **23** Then he gave
orders to the centurion for him to be
[a]kept in custody and *yet* [b]have *some*
rest, and not to prevent any of [c]his
friends from ministering to him.

---

**24:5** [a]Ac 15:5; 24:14 [1]Lit *the inhabited earth* **24:6** [a]Ac 21:28 [1]Lit *also* [2]The early mss omit rest of v 6, v 7, and first part of v 8 **24:9** [a]1Th 2:16 **24:10** [a]Ac 23:24 **24:11** [a]Ac 21:18, 27; 24:1 **24:12** [a]Ac 25:8 [b]Ac 24:18 [1]Lit *an attack of a mob* **24:13** [a]Ac 25:7 **24:14** [a]Ac 9:2; 24:22 [b]Ac 15:5; 24:5 [c]Ac 3:13 [d]Ac 25:8; 26:4ff, 22f; 28:23 [1]Lit *the ancestral God* **24:15** [a]Da 12:2; Jn 5:28f; 11:24; Ac 23:6 **24:16** [a]Ac 23:1 [1]Lit *practice myself* **24:17** [a]Ac 20:31 [b]Ac 11:29f; Ro 15:25-28; 1Co 16:1-4; 2Co 8:1-4; 9:1, 2, 12; Ga 2:10 [1]Or *gifts to charity* **24:18** [a]Ac 21:26 [b]Ac 24:12 [c]Ac 21:27 [1]West coast province of Asia Minor **24:19** [a]Ac 23:30 **24:20** [a]Mt 5:22 **24:21** [a]Ac 23:6; 24:15 **24:22** [a]Ac 24:14 [1]Military leader over 1,000 soldiers **24:23** [a]Ac 23:35 [b]Ac 28:16 [c]Ac 23:16; 27:3

24 But some days later Felix
arrived with Drusilla, his [1]wife
who was a Jewess, and summoned
Paul and heard him *speak* about
[a]faith in Christ Jesus. 25 But as he
was discussing [a]righteousness,
[b]self-control, and [c]the judgment to
come, Felix became frightened and
answered, "Go away for the present,
and when I find time I will call for
you." 26 At the same time, he was
also hoping that [a]money would be
given him by Paul; therefore he also
used to summon for him quite often
and converse with him. 27 But after
two years had passed, Felix [1]was
succeeded by Porcius [a]Festus, and
[b]wishing to do the Jews a favor, Felix
left Paul [c]imprisoned.

### *Paul Before Festus*

25 Festus then, having arrived in
[a]the province, after three days
went up to Jerusalem from [b]Caesa-
rea. 2 And the chief priests and the
leading men of the Jews [a]brought
charges against Paul, and they were
pleading with him, 3 requesting a fa-
vor against [1]Paul, that he might [2]have
him brought to Jerusalem (while they
[a]set an ambush to kill him on the
way). 4 Festus then [a]answered that
Paul [b]was being kept in custody at
[c]Caesarea and that he himself was
about to leave shortly. 5 "Therefore,"
he *said, "let the influential men
among you go down there with me,
and if there is anything wrong [1]about
the man, let them accuse him."

6 And after he had spent not
more than eight or ten days among
them, he went down to [a]Caesarea,
and on the next day he took his seat
on [b]the judgment seat and ordered
Paul to be brought. 7 And after Paul
arrived, the Jews who had come
down from Jerusalem stood around
him, bringing [a]many and serious
charges against him [b]which they
could not prove, 8 while Paul said in
his own defense, "[a]I have committed
no sin either against the Law of the
Jews or against the temple or against
Caesar." 9 But Festus, [a]wishing to do
the Jews a favor, answered Paul and
said, "[b]Are you willing to go up to
Jerusalem and to be tried before
me on these *matters*?" 10 But Paul
said, "I am standing before Caesar's
[a]judgment seat, where I ought to be
tried. I have done no wrong to *the*
Jews, as you also very well know. 11 If,
then, I am a wrongdoer and have
committed anything worthy of death,
I do not refuse to die; but if none of
those things is *true* of which these
men accuse me, no one can hand me
over to them. I [a]appeal to Caesar."
12 Then when Festus had conferred
with [1]his council, he answered, "You
have appealed to Caesar, to Caesar
you shall go."

### *Festus and Agrippa Discuss Paul's Trial*

13 Now when several days had
passed, King Agrippa and Bernice
arrived at [a]Caesarea [1]and greeted

***24:24*** *[a]Ac 20:21* *[1]Lit own wife* **24:25** [a]Tit 2:12 [b]Ga 5:23; Tit 1:8; 2Pe 1:6 [c]Ac 10:42 **24:26** [a]Ac 24:17 **24:27** [a]Ac 25:1, 4, 9, 12; 26:24f, 32 [b]Ac 12:3; 25:9 [c]Ac 23:35; 25:14 [1]Lit *received a successor, Porcius Festus* ◆ **25:1** [a]Ac 23:34 [b]Ac 8:40; 25:4, 6, 13 **25:2** [a]Ac 24:1; 25:15 **25:3** [a]Ac 9:24 [1]Lit *him* [2]Lit *send for him to Jerusalem* **25:4** [a]Ac 25:16 [b]Ac 24:23 [c]Ac 8:40; 25:1, 6, 13 **25:5** [1]Lit *in* **25:6** [a]Ac 8:40; 25:1, 4, 13 [b]Mt 27:19; Ac 25:10, 17 **25:7** [a]Ac 24:5f [b]Ac 24:13 **25:8** [a]Ac 6:13; 24:12; 28:17 **25:9** [a]Ac 12:3; 24:27 [b]Ac 25:20 **25:10** [a]Mt 27:19; Ac 25:6, 17 **25:11** [a]Ac 25:21, 25; 26:32; 28:19 **25:12** [1]A different group from that mentioned in Ac 4:15 and 24:20 **25:13** [a]Ac 8:40; 25:1, 4, 6 [1]Lit *greeting Festus*

Festus. **14** And while they were spending many days there, Festus laid Paul's case before the king, saying, "There is a man who was [a]left as a prisoner by Felix; **15** and when I was at Jerusalem, the chief priests and the elders of the Jews [a]brought charges against him, asking for a sentence of condemnation against him. **16** I [a]answered them that it is not the custom of the Romans to hand over any man before [b]the accused meets his accusers face to face and has an opportunity to make his defense against the charges. **17** So after they had assembled here, I did not delay, but on the next day took my seat on [a]the judgment seat and ordered the man to be brought before me. **18** When the accusers stood up, they were not bringing any charges against him for the evil deeds I was expecting, **19** but they had some [a]points of disagreement with him about their own [b,1]religion and about a certain Jesus, a dead man whom Paul asserted to be alive. **20** [a]And being perplexed about how to investigate [1]such matters, I was asking whether he was willing to go to Jerusalem and there to be tried on these matters. **21** But when Paul [a]appealed to be held in custody for [1]the Emperor's decision, I ordered him to be kept in *custody until I send him* to Caesar." **22** Then [a]Agrippa *said* to Festus, "I also would like to hear the man myself." "Tomorrow," he *said, "you shall hear him."

### *Paul Before Agrippa and Bernice*

**23** So, on the next day when [a]Agrippa came [1]together with [a]Bernice amid great pomp, and entered the hall [2]accompanied by the [3]commanders and the prominent men of the city, at the order of Festus, Paul was brought in. **24** And Festus *said, "King Agrippa, and all you gentlemen here present with us, you see this man about whom [a]all the people of the Jews appealed to me, both at Jerusalem and here, loudly declaring that [b]he ought not to live any longer. **25** But I found that he had committed [a]nothing worthy of death, and since he himself [b]appealed to [1]the Emperor, I decided to send him. **26** [1]Yet I have nothing definite about him to write to my lord. Therefore I have brought him before you *all* and especially before you, King Agrippa, so that after the investigation has taken place, I may have something to write. **27** For it seems absurd to me in sending a prisoner, not to indicate also the charges against him."

**26** [a]Now Agrippa said to Paul, "You are permitted to speak for yourself." Then Paul, stretching out his hand, *began to* make his defense:

**2** "Concerning all the things of which I am accused by the Jews, I regard myself blessed, King Agrippa, that I am about to make my defense before you today; **3** [1]especially because you are an expert in all [a]customs and [2]questions among *the* Jews; therefore I beg you to listen to me patiently.

**25:14** [a]Ac 24:27 **25:15** [a]Ac 24:1; 25:2 **25:16** [a]Ac 25:4f [b]Ac 23:30 **25:17** [a]Mt 27:19; Ac 25:6, 10 **25:19** [a]Ac 18:15; 23:29 [b]Ac 17:22 [1]Or *superstition* **25:20** [a]Ac 25:9 [1]Lit *these* **25:21** [a]Ac 25:11f [1]Lit *the Augustus'* (in this case Nero) **25:22** [a]Ac 9:15 **25:23** [a]Ac 25:13; 26:30 [1]Lit *and Bernice* [2]Lit *and with* [3]Military leader over 1,000 soldiers **25:24** [a]Ac 25:2, 7 [b]Ac 22:22 **25:25** [a]Lk 23:4; Ac 23:29 [b]Ac 25:11f [1]v 21, note 1 **25:26** [1]Lit *About whom I have nothing definite* ◆ **26:1** [a]Ac 9:15 **26:3** [a]Ac 6:14; 25:19; 26:7 [1]Or *because you are especially expert* [2]Or *controversial issues*

4 "So then, all Jews know [a]my
manner of life from my youth, which
from the beginning was spent among
my *own* nation and at Jerusalem;
5 since they have known about me
for a long time, if they are willing
to testify, that I lived *as* a [a]Pharisee
[b]according to the strictest [c]sect of
our religion. 6 And now I am stand-
ing here being tried [a]for the hope of
[b]the promise made by God to our
fathers; 7 *the promise* [a]to which our
twelve tribes hope to attain, as they
earnestly serve *God* night and day.
And for this [b]hope, O King, I am
being [c]accused by Jews. 8 Why is it
considered unbelievable among all
of you [a]if God does raise the dead?

9 "So then, [a]I thought to myself that
I had to do many things hostile to [b]the
name of Jesus the Nazarene. 10 And
this is [1]just what I [a]did in Jerusalem;
not only did I lock up many of the
[2]saints in prisons, having [b]received
authority from the chief priests, but
also when they were being put to
death I [c]cast my vote against them.
11 And [a]as I punished them often in all
the synagogues, I tried to force them
to blaspheme; and being [b]furiously
enraged at them, I kept pursuing
them [c]even to [1]foreign cities.

### *Paul Tells of His Conversion*

12 "[1]While so engaged [a]as I was
journeying to Damascus with the au-
thority and commission of the chief
priests, 13 at midday, O King, I saw on
the way a light from heaven, [1]brighter
than the sun, shining all around me
and those who were journeying with
me. 14 And when we had [a]all fallen to
the ground, I heard a voice saying to
me in the [b,1]Hebrew language, 'Saul,
Saul, why are you persecuting Me?
[2]It is hard for you to kick against the
goads.' 15 And I said, 'Who are You,
Lord?' And the Lord said, 'I am Jesus
whom you are persecuting. 16 But
rise up and [a]stand on your feet;
for this purpose I have appeared to
you, to [b]appoint you a [c]servant and
[d]a witness not only to the things
which you have [1]seen, but also to
the things in which I will appear to
you; 17 [a]rescuing you [b]from the *Jew-
ish* people and from the Gentiles, to
whom I am sending you, 18 to [a]open
their eyes so that they may turn from
[b]darkness to light and from the au-
thority of [c]Satan to God, that they
may receive [d]forgiveness of sins and
an [e]inheritance among those who
have been sanctified by [f]faith in Me.'

19 "So, King Agrippa, I did not
prove disobedient to the heavenly
vision, 20 but *kept* declaring both [a]to
those of Damascus first, and *also* [b]at
Jerusalem and *then* throughout all
the region of Judea, and *even* [c]to the
Gentiles, that they should [d]repent
and turn to God, practicing deeds
[e]appropriate to repentance. 21 For this
reason *some* Jews [a]seized me in the

---

**26:4** [a]Ga 1:13f; Php 3:5 **26:5** [a]Ac 23:6; Php 3:5 [b]Ac 22:3 [c]Ac 15:5 **26:6** [a]Ac 24:15; 28:20 [b]Ac 13:32 **26:7** [a]Jas 1:1 [b]Ac 24:15; 28:20 [c]Ac 26:2 **26:8** [a]Ac 23:6 **26:9** [a]Jn 16:2; 1Ti 1:13 [b]Jn 15:21 **26:10** [a]Ac 8:3; 9:13 [b]Ac 9:1f [c]Ac 22:20 [1]Lit *also* [2]Or *holy ones* **26:11** [a]Mt 10:17; Ac 22:19 [b]Ac 9:1 [c]Ac 22:5 [1]Or *outlying* **26:12** [a]Ac 26:12-18: *9:3-8; 22:6-11* [1]Lit *In which things* **26:13** [1]Lit *above the brightness of* **26:14** [a]Ac 9:7 [b]Ac 21:40 [1]Jewish Aramaic [2]An idiom referring to an animal's futile resistance to being prodded with goads **26:16** [a]Eze 2:1; Da 10:11 [b]Ac 22:14 [c]Lk 1:2 [d]Ac 22:15 [1]Two early mss *seen Me* **26:17** [a]Jer 1:8, 19 [b]1Chr 16:35; Ac 9:15 **26:18** [a]Is 35:5; 42:7, 16; Eph 5:8; Col 1:13; 1Pe 2:9 [b]Jn 1:5; Eph 5:8; Col 1:12f; 1Th 5:5; 1Pe 2:9 [c]Mt 4:10 [d]Lk 24:47; Ac 2:38 [e]Ac 20:32 [f]Ac 20:21 **26:20** [a]Ac 9:19ff [b]Ac 9:26-29; 22:17-20 [c]Ac 9:15; 13:46 [d]Ac 3:19 [e]Mt 3:8; Lk 3:8 **26:21** [a]Ac 21:27, 30

temple and were trying [b]to put me to
death. **22** Therefore, having obtained
help from God to this day, I stand here
[a]bearing witness both to small and
great, stating nothing but what [b]the
Prophets and Moses said was going
to take place; **23** [a,1]that the [2]Christ was
[3]to suffer, *and* [1]that [b]as first of the
resurrection from the dead, He was
going to proclaim [c]light both to the
*Jewish* people and to the Gentiles."

**24** Now while [1]Paul was saying
this in his defense, Festus *said in a
loud voice, "Paul, you are out of your
mind! [2]Great [a]learning is driving
you out of your mind." **25** But Paul
*said, "I am not out of my mind,
[a]most excellent Festus, but I utter
words [1]of sober truth. **26** For the king
[a,1]knows about these matters, and I
speak to him also with confidence,
since I am persuaded that none of
these things escape his notice; for
this has not been done in a [2]corner.
**27** King Agrippa, do you believe
the Prophets? I know you believe."
**28** But Agrippa *replied* to Paul, "[1]In
*such* short time [2]are you persuading
me to become a [a]Christian?" **29** And
Paul *said*, "I would pray to God, that
whether [1]in a short or long time, not
only you, but also all who hear me
this day, might become such as I am,
except for these [a]chains."

**30** [a]And the king stood up and the
governor *and Bernice*, and those who
were sitting with them, **31** and when
they had gone aside, they *began*
talking to one another, saying, "[a]This
man is not doing anything worthy
of death or [1]imprisonment." **32** And
Agrippa said to Festus, "This man
could have been [a]set free if he had
not [b]appealed to Caesar."

### *Paul Is Sent to Rome*

**27** Now when it was decided that
[a]we [b]would sail for [c]Italy, they
proceeded to deliver Paul and some
other prisoners to a centurion of the
Augustan [d,1]cohort named Julius.
**2** And getting aboard an Adramyttian
ship, which was about to sail to the
regions along the coast of [a,1]Asia, we
set sail accompanied by [b]Aristarchus,
a [c]Macedonian of [d]Thessalonica.
**3** The next day we put in at [a]Sidon,
and Julius [b]treated Paul with consid-
eration and [c]allowed him to go to his
friends and receive care. **4** And from
there we set sail and sailed under
the shelter of [a]Cyprus because [b]the
winds were against *us*. **5** And when
we had sailed through the sea along
the coast of [a]Cilicia and [b]Pamphylia,
we landed at Myra in Lycia. **6** There
the centurion found an [a]Alexandrian
ship sailing for [b]Italy, and he put us
aboard it. **7** And when we had sailed
slowly for a good many days, and
with difficulty had arrived off Cni-
dus, [a]since the wind did not permit

---

**26:21** [b]Ac 21:31 **26:22** [a]Lk 16:28 [b]Ac 10:43; 24:14 **26:23** [a]Mt 26:24; Ac 3:18 [b]1Co 15:20, 23; Col 1:18; Rev 1:5 [c]Is 42:6; 49:6; Lk 2:32; 2Co 4:4 [1]Lit *whether* [2]Messiah [3]Lit *subject to suffering* **26:24** [a]Jn 7:15; 2Ti 3:15 [1]Lit *he* [2]Lit *The many letters* **26:25** [a]Ac 23:26; 24:3 [1]Lit *of truth and rationality* **26:26** [a]Ac 26:3 [1]Or *understands* [2]A hidden or secret place **26:28** [a]Ac 11:26 [1]Or *With a little* [2]Or *you are persuading me to become a Christian* **26:29** [a]Ac 21:33 [1]Or *with a little or with much* **26:30** [a]Ac 25:23 **26:31** [a]Ac 23:29 [1]Lit *bonds* **26:32** [a]Ac 28:18 [b]Ac 25:11 ◆ **27:1** [a]Ac 16:10; 27:1-28 [b]Ac 25:12, 25 [c]Ac 18:2; 27:6 [d]Ac 10:1 [1]Normally 600 men (the number varied); or *battalion* **27:2** [a]Ac 2:9 [b]Ac 19:29 [c]Ac 16:9 [d]Ac 17:1 [1]West coast province of Asia Minor **27:3** [a]Mt 11:21 [b]Ac 27:43 [c]Ac 24:23 **27:4** [a]Ac 4:36 [b]Ac 27:7 **27:5** [a]Ac 6:9 [b]Ac 13:13 **27:6** [a]Ac 28:11 [b]Ac 18:2; 27:1 **27:7** [a]Ac 27:4

us to go farther, we sailed under the
shelter of [b]Crete, off Salmone; **8** and
with difficulty, we [a]sailed past it and
came to a place called Fair Havens,
near which was the city of Lasea.

**9** And when considerable time
had passed and the voyage was
now dangerous, since even [a]the
[1]Fast was already over, Paul *began*
*to* advise them, **10** and said to them,
"Men, I perceive that the voyage will
certainly be with [a]damage and great
loss, not only of the cargo and the
ship, but also of our lives." **11** But the
centurion was being more persuaded
by the [a]pilot and the [1]captain of the
ship than by what was being said
by Paul. **12** And because the harbor
was not suitable for wintering, the
majority reached a decision to set sail
from there, if somehow they could
arrive at Phoenix, a harbor of [a]Crete
facing southwest and northwest, to
spend the winter *there*.

**13** And when a moderate [1]south
wind came up, thinking that they had
attained their purpose, they weighed
anchor and *began* [a]sailing along [2]the
shore of [b]Crete.

### *The Storm at Sea*

**14** But before very long there [a]rushed
down from [1]the land a violent wind,
called [2]Euraquilo; **15** and when the
ship was caught *in it* and could not
face the wind, we gave way *to it* and
let ourselves be carried along. **16** And
running under the shelter of a small
island called Clauda, we were scarce-
ly able to get the *ship's* [1]boat under
control. **17** After they had hoisted it
up, they used [1]supporting cables in
undergirding the ship. Fearing that
they might [a]run aground on *the shal-*
*lows* of Syrtis, they let down the [2]sea
anchor and in this way let themselves
be carried along. **18** And the next day
as we were being violently storm-
tossed, [1]they *began to* [a]jettison the
cargo; **19** and on the third day they
cast the ship's tackle overboard
with their own hands. **20** And since
neither sun nor stars appeared for
many days, and no small storm was
assailing *us*, from then on all hope
of our being saved was gradually
abandoned.

**21** And [1]when they had gone a long
time without food, then Paul stood up
in their midst and said, "[a]Men, you
ought to have [2]followed my advice to
not set sail from [b]Crete and to [3]avoid
this [a]damage and loss. **22** And now I
advise you to [a]be cheerful, for there
will be no loss of life among you,
but *only* of the ship. **23** For this very
night [a]an angel of the God to whom
I belong and [b]whom I serve [c]stood
before me, **24** saying, 'Do not be
afraid, Paul; [a]you must stand before
Caesar; and behold, God has granted
you [b]all those who are sailing with
you.' **25** Therefore, [a]be cheerful, men,
for I believe God that [1]it will turn out

---

**27:7** [b]Ac 2:11; 27:12f, 21; Tit 1:5, 12 **27:8** [a]Ac 27:13 **27:9** [a]Lv 16:29-31; 23:27-29; Nu 29:7 [1]Day of Atonement in September or October, which was a dangerous time of year for navigation **27:10** [a]Ac 27:21 **27:11** [a]Rev 18:17 [1]Or *owner* **27:12** [a]Ac 2:11; 27:13, 21; Tit 1:5, 12 **27:13** [a]Ac 27:8 [b]Ac 2:11; 27:12f, 21; Tit 1:5, 12 [1]Lit *south wind having gently blown* [2]Lit *closer* **27:14** [a]Mk 4:37 [1]Lit *it* [2]A northeaster **27:16** [1]Or *skiff*: a small boat in tow or carried on board for emergency use, transportation to and from shore, etc. **27:17** [a]Ac 27:26, 29 [1]Lit *helps* [2]Or *gear* **27:18** [a]Jon 1:5; Ac 27:38 [1]Lit *they were doing a throwing out* **27:21** [a]Ac 27:10 [b]Ac 27:7 [1]Or *when they had lost their appetite for a long time* [2]Lit *obeyed me* [3]Lit *gained* **27:22** [a]Ac 27:25, 36 **27:23** [a]Ac 5:19 [b]Ro 1:9 [c]Ac 18:9; 23:11; 2Ti 4:17 **27:24** [a]Ac 23:11 [b]Ac 27:31, 42, 44 **27:25** [a]Ac 27:22, 36 [1]Lit *it will be* exactly as I have been told. **26** But we must [a]run aground on some [b]island."

**27** But when the fourteenth night came, as we were being carried about in the Adriatic Sea, about midnight the sailors *began to* suspect that some land was approaching them. **28** And when they took soundings, they found *it to be* [1]twenty fathoms; and a little farther on they took another sounding and found *it to be* [2]fifteen fathoms. **29** And fearing that we might [a]run aground somewhere on the [1]rocks, they cast four anchors from the stern and were praying for daybreak. **30** But as the sailors were trying to escape from the ship and had let down [a]the *ship's* boat into the sea, on the pretense of intending to lay out anchors from the bow, **31** Paul said to the centurion and to the soldiers, "Unless these men remain in the ship, you yourselves cannot [1]be saved." **32** Then the soldiers cut away the [a]ropes of the *ship's* boat and let it fall away.

**33** Until the day was about to dawn, Paul was encouraging them all to take some food, saying, "Today is the fourteenth day that you have been constantly watching and going without eating, having taken nothing. **34** Therefore I encourage you to take some food, for this is for your [1]salvation, for [a]not a hair from the head of any of you will perish." **35** And having said these things, he took bread and [a]gave thanks to God in the presence of all. And he broke it and began to eat. **36** And all [a]of them became cheerful and they themselves also took food. **37** And all of us in the ship were 276 [a,1]persons. **38** And when they had eaten enough, they *began to* lighten the ship by [a]throwing out the wheat into the sea.

### *The Shipwreck*

**39** Now when day came, [a]they [1]could not recognize the land; but they were noticing a bay with a beach, and they were resolving to drive the ship onto it if they could. **40** And casting off [a]the anchors, they left them in the sea while at the same time they were loosening the ropes of the rudders. And hoisting the foresail to the wind, they were heading for the beach. **41** But striking a [1]reef where two seas met, they ran the vessel aground; and the bow stuck fast and remained immovable, but the stern *began to* be broken up by the force *of the waves*. **42** Now the soldiers' plan was to [a]kill the prisoners, so that none *of them* would swim away and escape; **43** but the centurion, [a]wanting to bring Paul safely through, kept them from their intention, and ordered that those who could swim should [1]jump overboard first and get to land, **44** and the rest *should follow*, some on planks, and others on various things from the ship. And so it happened that [a]they all were brought safely to land.

### *On the Island of Malta*

**28** And when [a]they had been brought safely through *to shore*, [b]then we learned that [c]the

**27:26** [a]Ac 27:17, 29 [b]Ac 28:1 **27:28** [1]Approx. 120 ft. or 36 m, a fathom was approx. 6 ft. or 1.8 m [2]Approx. 90 ft. or 27 m **27:29** [a]Ac 27:17, 26 [1]Lit *rough places* **27:30** [a]Ac 27:16 **27:31** [1]Or *survive* **27:32** [a]Jn 2:15 **27:34** [a]Mt 10:30 [1]Or *survival* **27:35** [a]Mt 14:19 **27:36** [a]Ac 27:22, 25 **27:37** [a]Ac 2:41 [1]Lit *souls* **27:38** [a]Jon 1:5; Ac 27:18 **27:39** [a]Ac 28:1 [1]Lit *were not recognizing* **27:40** [a]Ac 27:29 **27:41** [1]Lit *place* **27:42** [a]Ac 12:19 **27:43** [a]Ac 27:3 [1]Lit *throw themselves* **27:44** [a]Ac 27:22, 31 ◆ **28:1** [a]Ac 16:10; 27:1 [b]Ac 27:39 [c]Ac 27:26

island was called [1]Malta. **2** [a]And the
[1]natives showed us extraordinary
affection; for because of the rain that
had set in and because of the cold,
they kindled a fire and [b]received us
all. **3** But when Paul had gathered a
bundle of sticks and laid them on
the fire, a viper came out [1]because
of the heat and fastened itself on his
hand. **4** And when [a]the [1]natives saw
the creature hanging from his hand,
they *began* saying to one another,
"[b]Undoubtedly this man is a mur-
derer, and though he has been saved
from the sea, [2]Justice has not allowed
him to live." **5** However [a]he shook the
creature off into the fire and suffered
no harm. **6** But they were waiting for
him to soon swell up or suddenly fall
down dead. But after they had waited
a long time and had seen nothing
unusual happen to him, changing
their minds, they [a]*began to* say that
he was a god.

**7** Now in the areas around that
place were lands belonging to the
leading man of the island, named
Publius, who welcomed us and en-
tertained us courteously three days.
**8** And it happened that the father
of Publius was lying afflicted with
fever and dysentery; and Paul, going
*to see* him and having [a]prayed, [b]laid
his hands on him and healed him.
**9** And after this had happened, the
rest of the people on the island who
had diseases were coming to him and
being healed. **10** They also bestowed
on us many honors of respect; and
when we were setting sail, they
[1]supplied *us* with [2]all we needed.

### *Paul Arrives in Rome*

**11** Now at the end of three months
we set sail on [a]an Alexandrian ship
which had wintered at the island,
and which had [1]the Twin Brothers
for its figurehead. **12** After we put into
Syracuse, we stayed there for three
days. **13** From there we sailed around
and arrived at Rhegium, and after a
day when a south wind sprang up, on
the second day we came to Puteoli.
**14** [1]There we found *some* [a]brothers,
and were invited to stay with them
for seven days; and thus we came to
Rome. **15** And the [a]brothers, when
they heard about us, came from there
as far as the [1]Market of Appius and
[2]Three Inns to meet us. When Paul
saw them, he thanked God and took
courage.

**16** And when we entered Rome,
Paul was [a]allowed to stay by himself,
with the soldier who was guarding
him.

### *Paul's Ministry in Rome*

**17** And it happened that after three
days [1]Paul called together those who
were [a]the leading men of the Jews,
and when they came together, he
*began* saying to them, "[b]Brothers,
[c]though I had done nothing against
our people or [d]the customs of our
[2]fathers, yet I was delivered as a

---

**28:1** [1]Or *Melita* **28:2** [a]Ac 28:4; Ro 1:14; 1Co 14:11; Col 3:11 [b]Ro 14:1 [1]Lit *barbarians* **28:3** [1]Or *from the heat* **28:4** [a]Ac 28:2 [b]Lk 13:2, 4 [1]Lit *barbarians* [2]The personification of a goddess **28:5** [a]Mk 16:18 **28:6** [a]Ac 14:11 **28:8** [a]Ac 9:40; Jas 5:14f [b]Mt 9:18; Mk 5:23; 6:5 **28:10** [1]Or *put on board* [2]Lit *the things pertaining to the needs* **28:11** [a]Ac 27:6 [1]Gr *Dioscuri*; Castor and Pollux, twin sons of Zeus **28:14** [a]Jn 21:23; Ac 1:15; 6:3; 9:30; 28:15; Ro 1:13 [1]Lit *Where* **28:15** [a]Ac 1:15; 10:23; 11:1, 12, 29; 12:17 [1]Lat *Appii Forum*, a station approx. 43 miles from Rome [2]Lat *Tres Tabernae*, a station approx. 33 miles from Rome **28:16** [a]Ac 24:23 **28:17** [a]Ac 13:50; 25:2 [b]Ac 22:5 [c]Ac 25:8 [d]Ac 6:14 [1]Lit *he* [2]Or *forefathers*

prisoner from Jerusalem into the
hands of the Romans. **18** And when
they had [a]examined me, they [b]were
willing to release me because there
was [c]no ground [1]for putting me to
death. **19** But when the Jews [1]objected,
I was forced to [a]appeal to Caesar, not
that I had any accusation against my
nation. **20** For this reason, therefore,
I [1]requested to see you and to speak
with you, for I am wearing [a]this
chain for [b]the sake of the hope of
Israel." **21** And they said to him, "We
have neither received letters from
Judea concerning you, nor have any
of [a]the brothers come here and re-
ported or spoken anything bad about
you. **22** But we desire to hear from
you what you think; for concerning
this [a]sect, it is known to us that [b]it is
spoken against everywhere."

**23** And when they had set a day
for Paul, they came to him at [a]his
lodging in large numbers; and he
was explaining to them by solemnly
[b]bearing witness about the kingdom
of God and trying to persuade them
concerning Jesus, [c]from both the Law
of Moses and from the Prophets, from
morning until evening. **24** [a]And some
were being persuaded by the things
spoken, but others were not believ-
ing. **25** And when they disagreed with
one another, they *began* leaving after
Paul had spoken one word, "The Holy
Spirit rightly spoke through Isaiah
the prophet to your fathers, **26** saying,

'[a]GO TO THIS PEOPLE AND SAY,
"[b,1]YOU WILL KEEP ON
HEARING, [2]BUT WILL
NOT UNDERSTAND;
AND [3]YOU WILL KEEP ON SEEING,
BUT WILL NOT PERCEIVE;
**27** [a]FOR THE HEART OF THIS
PEOPLE HAS BECOME DULL,
AND WITH THEIR EARS
THEY SCARCELY HEAR,
AND THEY HAVE CLOSED
THEIR EYES;
LEST THEY MIGHT SEE
WITH THEIR EYES,
AND HEAR WITH THEIR EARS,
AND UNDERSTAND WITH THEIR
HEART AND RETURN,
AND I HEAL THEM."'

**28** "Therefore let it be known to you
that [a]this salvation of God was sent
[b]to the Gentiles—they will also
hear." **29** [1][When he had spoken these
words, the Jews departed, having a
great dispute among themselves.]

**30** And he stayed two full years
[1]in his own rented quarters and was
welcoming all who came to him,
**31** [a,1]preaching the kingdom of God
and teaching concerning the Lord
Jesus Christ [b]with all confidence,
unhindered.

---

***28:18*** [a]*Ac 22:24* [b]*Ac 26:32* [c]Ac 23:29; 25:25; 26:31 [1]Lit *of death in me* **28:19** [a]Ac 25:11, 21, 25; 26:32 [1]Lit *spoke against* **28:20** [a]Ac 21:33 [b]Ac 26:6f [1]Or *invited you to see me and speak with me* **28:21** [a]Ac 3:17; 22:5; 28:14; Ro 9:3 **28:22** [a]Ac 24:14 [b]1Pe 2:12; 3:16; 4:14, 16 **28:23** [a]Phm 22 [b]Lk 16:28; Ac 1:3; 23:11 [c]Ac 8:35 **28:24** [a]Ac 14:4 **28:26** [a]Is 6:9 [b]Mt 13:14f [1]Lit *with a hearing* [2]Lit *and* [3]Lit *seeing you will see* **28:27** [a]Is 6:10 **28:28** [a]Ps 98:3; Lk 2:30; Ac 13:26 [b]Ac 9:15; 13:46 **28:29** [1]Early mss omit this v **28:30** [1]Or *at his own expense* **28:31** [a]Mt 4:23; Ac 20:25; 28:23 [b]2Ti 2:9 [1]Or *proclaiming*

*The Letter of Paul to the*

# ROMANS

### *The Gospel Exalted*

**1** Paul, a slave of Christ Jesus,
[a,1]called *as* an apostle, having
been [b]set apart for [c]the gospel of
God, **2** which He [a]promised before-
hand through His [b]prophets in the
holy Scriptures, **3** concerning His
Son, who was born [a]of the seed of
David [b]according to the flesh, **4** who
was designated as [a]the Son of God
in power, according to the [1]Spirit of
holiness, [2]by the resurrection from
the dead, Jesus Christ our Lord,
**5** through whom we received grace
and [a]apostleship for *the* [b]obedience
of faith among [c]all the Gentiles
for the sake of His name, **6** among
whom you also are the [a]called of
Jesus Christ;

**7** to all who are [a]beloved of God in
Rome, called *as* [b,1]saints: [c]Grace to
you and peace from God our Father
and the Lord Jesus Christ.

**8** First, [a]I thank my God through
Jesus Christ [1]for you all, because
[b]your faith is being proclaimed
throughout the whole world. **9** For
[a]God, whom I [b]serve in my spirit in
the gospel of His Son, is my witness
*as to* how without ceasing [c]I make
mention of you, **10** always in my
prayers earnestly asking, if perhaps
now at last by [a]the will of God I may
succeed in coming to you. **11** For [a]I
long to see you so that I may impart
some spiritual gift to you, that you
may be strengthened; **12** that is, to be
mutually encouraged, *while* among
you, by each other's faith, both yours
and mine. **13** [a]I do not want you to
be unaware, [b]brothers, that often I
[c]have planned to come to you (and
have been prevented so far) so that
I may have some [d]fruit among you
also, even as among the rest of the
Gentiles. **14** [a]I am [1]under obligation
both to Greeks and to [b]barbarians,
both to the wise and to the foolish.
**15** In this way, for my part, I am eager
to [a]proclaim the gospel to you also
who are in Rome.

**16** For I am not [a]ashamed of the
gospel, for [b]it is the power of God for
salvation to everyone who believes,
to the [c]Jew first and also to [d]the Greek.
**17** For in it [a]*the* righteousness of God
is revealed [1]from faith to faith; as it is
written, "[b,2]BUT THE RIGHTEOUS WILL
LIVE BY FAITH."

### *God's Wrath on Unrighteousness*

**18** For [a]the wrath of God is revealed
from heaven against all ungodliness
and unrighteousness of men who

---

◆ **1:1** [a]1Co 1:1; 9:1; 2Co 1:1 [b]Ac 9:15; 13:2; Ga 1:15 [c]Mk 1:14; Ro 15:16 [1]Lit *a called apostle* **1:2** [a]Tit 1:2 [b]Lk 1:70; Ro 3:21; 16:26 **1:3** [a]Mt 1:1 [b]Jn 1:14; Ro 4:1; 9:3, 5; 1Co 10:18 **1:4** [a]Mt 4:3 [1]Or *spirit* [2]Or *as a result of* **1:5** [a]Ac 1:25; Ga 1:16 [b]Ac 6:7; Ro 16:26 [c]Ac 9:15 **1:6** [a]Jd 1; Rev 17:14 **1:7** [a]Ro 5:5ff; 8:39 [b]Ac 9:13; Ro 8:28ff; 1Co 1:2, 24 [c]Nu 6:25f; 1Co 1:3; 2Co 1:2; Ga 1:3; Eph 1:2; Php 1:2; Col 1:2; 1Th 1:1; 2Th 1:2 [1]Or *holy ones* **1:8** [a]1Co 1:4; Eph 1:15f; Php 1:3f; Col 1:3f; 1Th 1:2; 2:13 [b]Ac 28:22; Ro 16:19 [1]Or *concerning you all, that...* **1:9** [a]Ro 9:1 [b]Ac 24:14; 2Ti 1:3 [c]Eph 1:16; Php 1:3f **1:10** [a]Ac 18:21; Ro 15:32 **1:11** [a]Ac 19:21; Ro 15:23 **1:13** [a]Ro 11:25; 1Co 10:1; 12:1; 2Co 1:8; 1Th 4:13 [b]Ac 1:15; Ro 7:1; 1Co 1:10; 14:20, 26; Ga 3:15 [c]Ac 19:21; Ro 15:22f [d]Jn 4:36; 15:16; Php 1:22; Col 1:6 **1:14** [a]1Co 9:16 [b]Ac 28:2 [1]Lit *debtor* **1:15** [a]Ro 15:20 **1:16** [a]Mk 8:38; 2Ti 1:8, 12, 16 [b]1Co 1:18, 24 [c]Ac 3:26; Ro 2:9 [d]Jn 7:35 **1:17** [a]Ro 3:21; 9:30; Php 3:9 [b]Hab 2:4; Ga 3:11; Heb 10:38 [1]Or *by* [2]Or *But he who is righteous by faith shall live* **1:18** [a]Ro 5:9; Eph 5:6; Col 3:6

[b]suppress the truth [1]in unrighteous-
ness, **19** because [a]that which is known
about God is evident [1]within them; for
God made it evident to them. **20** For
[a]since the creation of the world His
invisible attributes, both His eternal
power and divine nature, have been
clearly seen, [b]being understood
through what has been made, so that
they are without excuse. **21** For even
though they knew God, they did not
glorify Him as God or give thanks, but
they became [a]futile in their thoughts,
and their foolish heart was darkened.
**22** [a]Professing to be wise, they became
fools, **23** and [a]exchanged the glory of
the incorruptible God for an image in
the likeness of corruptible man and
of birds and four-footed animals and
crawling creatures.

**24** Therefore [a]God gave them
over in the lusts of their hearts to
impurity, so that their bodies would
be [b]dishonored among them. **25** For
they exchanged the truth of God for
[1]a [a]lie, and worshiped and served
the creature rather than the Creator,
[b]who is blessed [2]forever. Amen.

**26** For this reason [a]God gave them
over to [b]dishonorable passions; for
their [c]females exchanged the natural
function for that which is [1]unnat-
ural, **27** and in the same way also
the [a]males abandoned the natural
function of the female and burned
in their desire toward one another,
[b]males with males committing
[1]indecent acts and receiving in [2]their
own persons the due penalty of their
error.

**28** And just as they did not see fit [1]to
acknowledge God, [a]God gave them
over to an unfit mind, to do those
things which are not proper, **29** having
been filled with all unrighteousness,
wickedness, greed, evil; full of envy,
murder, strife, deceit, malice; *they*
*are* [a]gossips, **30** slanderers, [a,1]haters
of God, violent, arrogant, boastful,
inventors of evil, [b]disobedient to
parents, **31** without understanding,
untrustworthy, [a]unloving, unmer-
ciful; **32** and although they know
the righteous requirement of God,
that those who practice such things
are worthy of [a]death, they not only
do the same, but also [b]give hearty
approval to those who practice *them*.

### *God's Righteous Judgment*

**2** Therefore you are [a]without
excuse, [b]O man, everyone who
passes judgment, for in that which
[c]you judge another, you condemn
yourself; for you who judge practice
the same things. **2** And we know that
the judgment of God [1]rightly falls
upon those who practice such things.
**3** But do you presume this, [a]O man—
who passes judgment on those who
practice such things and does the
same—that you will escape the
judgment of God? **4** Or do you think
lightly of [a]the riches of His [b]kindness

---

**1:18** [b]2Th 2:6f [1]Or *by* **1:19** [a]Ac 14:17; 17:24ff [1]Or *among* **1:20** [a]Mk 10:6 [b]Job 12:7-9; Ps 19:1-6; Jer 5:21f **1:21** [a]2Ki 17:15; Jer 2:5; Eph 4:17f **1:22** [a]Jer 10:14; 1Co 1:20 **1:23** [a]Dt 4:16-18; Ps 106:20; Jer 2:11; Ac 17:29 **1:24** [a]Ro 1:26, 28; Eph 4:19 [b]Eph 2:3 **1:25** [a]Is 44:20; Jer 10:14; 13:25; 16:19 [b]Ro 9:5; 2Co 11:31 [1]Lit *the lie* [2]Lit *to the ages* **1:26** [a]Ro 1:24 [b]1Th 4:5 [c]Ge 1:27 [1]Lit *against nature* **1:27** [a]Ge 1:27 [b]Lv 18:22; 20:13; 1Co 6:9 [1]Lit *the shameless deed* [2]Lit *themselves* **1:28** [a]Ro 1:24 [1]Lit *to have God in knowledge* **1:29** [a]2Co 12:20 **1:30** [a]Ps 5:5 [b]2Ti 3:2 [1]Or *hateful to God* **1:31** [a]2Ti 3:3 **1:32** [a]Ro 6:21 [b]Lk 11:48; Ac 8:1; 22:20 ◆ **2:1** [a]Ro 1:20 [b]Lk 12:14; Ro 2:3; 9:20 [c]2Sa 12:5-7; Mt 7:1; Lk 6:37; Ro 14:22 **2:2** [1]Lit *is according to truth against* **2:3** [a]Lk 12:14; Ro 2:1; 9:20 **2:4** [a]Ro 9:23; 11:33; 2Co 8:2; Eph 1:7, 18; 2:7; Php 4:19; Col 1:27; 2:2; Tit 3:6 [b]Ro 11:22

and [c]forbearance and [d]patience,
not knowing that the kindness of
God leads you to repentance? **5** But
[1]because of your stubbornness and
unrepentant heart [a]you are storing
up wrath for yourself [b]in the day of
wrath and revelation of the righteous
judgment of God, **6** [a]who WILL REPAY
TO EACH ACCORDING TO HIS WORKS: **7** to
those who by [a]perseverance in doing
good seek for [b]glory and honor and
[c]immortality, [d]eternal life; **8** but to
those who are [a]selfishly ambitious
and [b]do not obey the truth, but obey
unrighteousness, wrath and anger.
**9** *There will be* [a]affliction and turmoil
[1]for every soul of man who works out
evil, of the Jew [b]first and also of the
Greek, **10** but [a]glory and honor and
peace to everyone who works good,
to the Jew [b]first and also to the Greek.
**11** For [a]there is no partiality with God.

**12** For all who have sinned [a,1]with-
out the Law will also perish [1]without
the Law, and all who have sinned
[2]under the Law will be judged [3]by the
Law. **13** For *it is* [a]not the hearers [1]of
the Law *who* are [2]just before God, but
the doers [1]of the Law will be justified.
**14** For when Gentiles who do not have
[1]the Law [a]naturally do the things of
the Law, these, not having [1]the Law,
are a law to themselves, **15** in that
they demonstrate [a]the work of the
Law written in their hearts, their
conscience bearing witness and their
thoughts alternately accusing or else
defending them, **16** on the day when,
[a]according to my gospel, [b]God will
judge the secrets of men through
Christ Jesus.

### *The Jew Is Judged by the Law*

**17** But if you bear the name "Jew" and
[a]rely [1]upon the Law and boast in God,
**18** and know *His* will and [a,1]approve
the things that are essential, being
instructed out of the Law, **19** and are
confident that you yourself are a
guide to the blind, a light to those
who are in darkness, **20** a [1]corrector
of the foolish, a teacher of [2]the
immature, having in the Law [a]the
embodiment of knowledge and of
the truth, **21** you, therefore, [a]who
teach another, do you not teach
yourself? You who [1]preach that one
shall not steal, do you steal? **22** You
who say that one should not commit
adultery, do you commit adultery?
You who abhor idols, do you [a]rob
temples? **23** You who [a]boast [1]in the
Law, through your transgression of
the Law, do you dishonor God? **24** For
"[a]THE NAME OF GOD IS BLASPHEMED
AMONG THE GENTILES [b]BECAUSE OF
YOU," just as it is written.

**25** For indeed circumcision is
of value if you [a]practice [1]the Law,
but if you are a transgressor [2]of
the Law, [b]your circumcision has
become uncircumcision. **26** [a]So if

**2:4** [c]Ro 3:25 [d]Ex 34:6; Ro 9:22; 1Ti 1:16; 1Pe 3:20; 2Pe 3:9, 15 **2:5** [a]Dt 32:34f; Pr 1:18 [b]Ps 110:5; 2Co 5:10; 2Th 1:5; Jd 6 [1]Or *in accordance with* **2:6** [a]Ps 62:12; Pr 24:12; Mt 16:27 **2:7** [a]Lk 8:15; Heb 10:36 [b]Ro 2:10; Heb 2:7; 1Pe 1:7 [c]1Co 15:42, 50, 53f; Eph 6:24; 2Ti 1:10 [d]Mt 25:46 **2:8** [a]2Co 12:20; Ga 5:20; Php 1:17; 2:3; Jas 3:14, 16 [b]2Th 2:12 **2:9** [a]Ro 8:35 [b]Ac 3:26; Ro 1:16; 1Pe 4:17 [1]Lit *upon* **2:10** [a]Ro 2:7; Heb 2:7; 1Pe 1:7 [b]Ro 2:9 **2:11** [a]*Dt 10:17; Ac 10:34* **2:12** [a]Ac 2:23; 1Co 9:21 [1]Or *without law* [2]Or *under law* [3]Or *by law* **2:13** [a]Mt 7:21, 24ff; Jn 13:17; Jas 1:22f, 25 [1]Or *of law* [2]Or *righteous* **2:14** [a]Ac 10:35; Ro 1:19; 2:15 [1]Or *law* **2:15** [a]Ro 2:14, 27 **2:16** [a]Ro 16:25; 1Co 15:1; Ga 1:11; 1Ti 1:11; 2Ti 2:8 [b]Ac 10:42; 17:31; Ro 3:6; 14:10 **2:17** [a]Mic 3:11; Jn 5:45; Ro 2:23; 9:4 [1]Or *upon law* **2:18** [a]Php 1:10 [1]Or *distinguish between the things which differ* **2:20** [a]Ro 3:31; 2Ti 1:13 [1]Or *instructor* [2]Lit *infants* **2:21** [a]Mt 23:3ff [1]Or *proclaim* **2:22** [a]Ac 19:37 **2:23** [a]Mic 3:11; Jn 5:45; Ro 2:17; 9:4 [1]Or *in law* **2:24** [a]Is 52:5; Eze 36:20ff [b]2Pe 2:2 **2:25** [a]Ro 2:13f, 27 [b]Jer 4:4; 9:25f [1]Or *law* [2]Or *of law* **2:26** [a]1Co 7:19

[b]the [1]uncircumcised man [c]observes
the righteous requirements of the
Law, will not his uncircumcision be
counted as circumcision? **27** And [a]he
who is physically uncircumcised, if
he [1]fulfills the Law, will he not [b]judge
you who, through the letter *of the*
*Law* and circumcision, are a trans-
gressor [2]of the Law? **28** For [a]he is not
a Jew who is one outwardly, nor is
circumcision that which is outward
in the flesh. **29** But [a]he is a Jew who
is one inwardly; and [b]circumcision
is that which is of the heart, by the
[c]Spirit, not by the letter; [d]and his
praise is not from men, but from God.

### *There Is None Righteous*

**3** Then what advantage has the Jew?
Or what is the value of circumci-
sion? **2** Great in every respect. First
of all, that [a]they were entrusted with
the [b]oracles of God. **3** What then? If
[a]some [1]did not believe, does their
[2]unbelief abolish the faithfulness of
God? **4** [a]May it never be! Rather, let
God be true and every man [b]a liar, as
it is written,

"[c]THAT YOU MAY BE JUSTIFIED
IN YOUR WORDS,
AND OVERCOME
WHEN YOU [1]ARE JUDGED."

**5** But if our unrighteousness [a][1]dem-
onstrates the righteousness of God,
[b]what shall we say? Is the God who
*inflicts* wrath unrighteous? ([c]I am
speaking in human terms.) **6** [a]May
it never be! For otherwise, how will
[b]God judge the world? **7** But if through
my lie [a]the truth of God abounded to
His glory, [b]why am I also still being
judged as a sinner? **8** And why not *say*
(as we are slanderously reported and
as some claim that we say), "[a]Let us
do evil that good may come"? [1]Their
condemnation is just.

**9** What then? [a]Are we [1]better? Not
at all; for we have already charged
that both [b]Jews and [c]Greeks are [d]all
under sin; **10** as it is written,

"[a]THERE IS NONE RIGHTEOUS,
NOT EVEN ONE;
**11** THERE IS NONE
WHO UNDERSTANDS,
THERE IS NONE WHO
SEEKS FOR GOD;
**12** ALL HAVE TURNED ASIDE,
TOGETHER THEY HAVE
BECOME WORTHLESS;
THERE IS NONE WHO
DOES GOOD,
THERE IS NOT EVEN ONE."
**13** "[a]THEIR THROAT IS AN
OPEN TOMB,
WITH THEIR TONGUES THEY
KEEP DECEIVING,"
"[b]THE POISON OF ASPS IS
UNDER THEIR LIPS";
**14** "[a]WHOSE MOUTH IS FULL
OF CURSING AND BITTERNESS";
**15** "[a]THEIR FEET ARE SWIFT
TO SHED BLOOD,
**16** DESTRUCTION AND MISERY
ARE IN THEIR PATHS,
**17** AND THE PATH OF PEACE
THEY HAVE NOT KNOWN."

---

**2:26** [b]Ro 3:30; Eph 2:11 [c]Ro 2:25, 27; 8:4 [1]Lit *uncircumcision* **2:27** [a]Ro 3:30; Eph 2:11 [b]Mt 12:41 [1]Or *completes*, cf. Jas 2:8 [2]Or *of law* **2:28** [a]Jn 8:39; Ro 2:17; 9:6; Ga 6:15 **2:29** [a]Php 3:3; Col 2:11 [b]Dt 30:6 [c]Ro 2:27; 7:6; 2Co 3:6 [d]Jn 5:44; 12:43; 1Co 4:5; 2Co 10:18 ◆ **3:2** [a]Dt 4:8; Ps 147:19; Ro 9:4 [b]Ac 7:38 **3:3** [a]Ro 10:16; Heb 4:2 [1]Or *were unfaithful* [2]Or *unfaithfulness* **3:4** [a]Lk 20:16; Ro 3:6, 31 [b]Ps 116:11; Ro 3:7 [c]Ps 51:4 [1]Lit *in Your judging* **3:5** [a]Ro 5:8; 2Co 6:4; 7:11 [b]Ro 4:1; 7:7; 8:31; 9:14, 30 [c]Ro 6:19; 1Co 9:8; 15:32; Ga 3:15 [1]Or *commends* **3:6** [a]Lk 20:16; Ro 3:4, 31 [b]Ro 2:16 **3:7** [a]Ro 3:4 [b]Ro 9:19 **3:8** [a]Ro 6:1 [1]Lit *Whose* **3:9** [a]Ro 3:1 [b]Ro 2:1-29 [c]Ro 1:18-32 [d]Ro 3:19, 23; 11:32; Ga 3:22 [1]Or *worse* **3:10** [a]Ps 14:1-3; 53:1-3 **3:13** [a]Ps 5:9 [b]Ps 140:3 **3:14** [a]Ps 10:7 **3:15** [a]Is 59:7f

**18** “[a]THERE IS NO FEAR OF GOD
BEFORE THEIR EYES.”

**19** Now we know that whatever the [a]Law says, it speaks to [b]those who are in the Law, so that every mouth may be shut and [c]all the world may become accountable to God; **20** because [a]by the works [1]of the Law NO FLESH WILL BE JUSTIFIED IN HIS SIGHT, for [b,2]through the Law *comes* the knowledge of sin.

### *The Righteousness of God through Faith*

**21** But now apart [1]from the Law [a]*the* righteousness of God has been manifested, being [b]witnessed by the Law and the Prophets, **22** even *the* [a]righteousness of God through [b]faith [c]in Jesus Christ for [d]all those [1]who believe; for [e]there is no distinction; **23** for all [a,1]have sinned and fall short of the glory of God, **24** being justified as a gift [a]by His grace through [b]the redemption which is in Christ Jesus; **25** whom God displayed publicly as [a]a [1]propitiation [b,2]in His blood through faith, for a demonstration of His righteousness, [3]because in the [c]forbearance of God He [d]passed over the sins previously committed; **26** for the demonstration of His righteousness at the present time, so that He would be just and the justifier of the one who [1]has faith in Jesus.

**27** Where then is [a]boasting? It is excluded. By [b]what kind of law? Of works? No, but by a law of faith. **28** [1]For [a]we maintain that a man is justified by faith apart from works [2]of the Law. **29** Or [a]is God *the God* of Jews only? Is He not *the God* of Gentiles also? Yes, of Gentiles also, **30** since indeed [a]God, [b]who will justify the [1]circumcised [2]by faith and the [3]uncircumcised through that faith, [c]is one.

**31** Do we then abolish [1]the Law through faith? [a]May it never be! On the contrary, we [b]establish the Law.

### *Abraham and David’s Faith Counted as Righteousness*

**4** What then shall we say that Abraham, [1]our forefather [a]according to the flesh, has found? **2** For if Abraham was justified [1]by works, he has something to boast about—but [a]not [2]before God! **3** For what does the Scripture say? “[a]ABRAHAM BELIEVED GOD, AND IT WAS COUNTED TO HIM AS RIGHTEOUSNESS.” **4** Now to the one who [a]works, his wage is not counted according to grace, but according to what is due. **5** But to the one who does not work, but [a]believes upon Him who justifies the ungodly, his

**3:18** [a]Ps 36:1 **3:19** [a]Jn 10:34 [b]Ro 2:12 [c]Ro 3:9 **3:20** [a]Ps 143:2; Ac 13:39; Ga 2:16 [b]Ro 4:15; 5:13, 20; 7:7 [1]Or *of law* [2]Or *through law* **3:21** [a]Ro 1:17; 9:30 [b]Ac 10:43; Ro 1:2 [1]Or *from law* **3:22** [a]Ro 1:17; 9:30 [b]Ro 4:5 [c]Ac 3:16; Ga 2:16, 20; 3:22; Eph 3:12 [d]Ro 4:11, 16; 10:4 [e]Ro 10:12; Ga 3:28; Col 3:11 [1]Or *who believe. For there is no distinction, since they all have sinned...and are being justified* **3:23** [a]Ro 3:9 [1]Or *sinned* **3:24** [a]Ro 4:4f, 16; Eph 2:8 [b]1Co 1:30; Eph 1:7; Col 1:14; Heb 9:15 **3:25** [a]1Jn 2:2; 4:10 [b]1Co 5:7; Heb 9:14, 28; 1Pe 1:19; Rev 1:5 [c]Ro 2:4 [d]Ac 14:16; 17:30 [1]Or *propitiatory sacrifice* [2]Or *by* [3]Lit *because of the passing over of the sins previously committed in the forbearance of God* **3:26** [1]Lit is of the faith of Jesus **3:27** [a]Ro 2:17, 23; 4:2; 1Co 1:29ff [b]Ro 9:31 **3:28** [a]Ac 13:39; Ro 3:20, 21; Eph 2:9; Jas 2:20, 24, 26 [1]One early ms *Therefore* [2]Or *of law* **3:29** [a]Ac 10:34f; Ro 9:24; 10:12; 15:9; Ga 3:28 **3:30** [a]Ro 10:12; Ga 3:20 [b]Ro 3:22; 4:11f, 16; Ga 3:8 [c]Dt 6:4 [1]Lit *circumcision* [2]Lit *out of* [3]Lit *uncircumcision* **3:31** [a]Lk 20:16; Ro 3:4 [b]Mt 5:17; Ro 3:4, 6; 8:4 [1]Or *law* ◆ **4:1** [a]Ro 1:3 [1]Or *our forefather, has found according to the flesh* **4:2** [a]1Co 1:31 [1]Lit *out of* [2]Lit *toward* **4:3** [a]Ge 15:6; Ro 4:9, 22; Ga 3:6; Jas 2:23 **4:4** [a]Ro 11:6 **4:5** [a]Jn 6:29; Ro 3:22

faith is counted as righteousness,
6 just as David also speaks of the
blessing on the man to whom God
counts righteousness apart from
works:

7 “[a]BLESSED ARE THOSE
WHOSE LAWLESS DEEDS
HAVE BEEN FORGIVEN,
AND WHOSE SINS HAVE
BEEN COVERED.
8 “[a]BLESSED IS THE MAN WHOSE
SIN THE [1]LORD WILL NOT
[b]TAKE INTO ACCOUNT.”

9 Therefore, is this blessing
on [a,1]the circumcised, or on [2]the
uncircumcised also? For [b]we say,
“[c]FAITH WAS COUNTED TO ABRAHAM
AS RIGHTEOUSNESS.” 10 How then
was it counted? While he was
[1]circumcised, or [2]uncircumcised?
Not while [1]circumcised, but while
[2]uncircumcised; 11 and he [a]received
the sign of circumcision, [b]a seal of
the righteousness of the faith which
[1]he had while uncircumcised, so that
he might be [c]the father of [d]all who
believe without being circumcised,
that righteousness might be counted
to them, 12 and the father of circum-
cision to those who not only are
of the circumcision, but who also
follow in the steps of the faith of our
father Abraham which [1]he had while
uncircumcised.

13 For [a]the promise to Abraham or
to his seed [b]that he would be heir of
the world was not [1]through the Law,
but through the righteousness of
faith. 14 For [a]if those who are [1]of the
Law are heirs, faith has been made
empty and the promise has been
abolished; 15 for [a]the Law brings
about wrath, but [b]where there is no
law, there also is no trespass.

16 For this reason *it is* [1]by faith,
in order that *it may be* according
to [a]grace, so that the promise will
be guaranteed to [b]all the seed, not
only to [2]those who are of the Law,
but also to [c,2]those who are of the
faith of Abraham, who is [d]the father
of us all— 17 as it is written, “[a]A FA-
THER OF MANY NATIONS HAVE I MADE
YOU”—in the presence of Him whom
he believed, *even* God, [b]who gives
life to the dead and [c,1]calls into being
[d]that which does not exist. 18 In hope
against hope he believed, so that he
might become [a]a father of many
nations according to that which had
been spoken, “[b]SO SHALL YOUR SEED
BE.” 19 And without becoming weak
in faith he contemplated his own
body, now [a]as good as dead since
[b]he was about a hundred years old,
and [c]the deadness of Sarah’s womb;
20 yet, with respect to the promise of
God, he did not waver in unbelief but
grew strong in faith, [a]giving glory to
God, 21 and [a]being fully assured that
[b]what God had promised, He was able
also to do. 22 Therefore [a]IT WAS ALSO
COUNTED TO HIM AS RIGHTEOUSNESS.
23 Now [a]not for his sake only was it
written THAT IT WAS COUNTED TO HIM,
24 but for our sake also, to whom it

---

**4:7** [a]Ps 32:1 **4:8** [a]Ps 32:2 [b]2Co 5:19 [1]In OT, Yahweh, cf. Ps 32:2 **4:9** [a]Ro 3:30 [b]Ro 4:3 [c]Ge 15:6 [1]Lit *circumcision* [2]Lit *uncircumcision* **4:10** [1]Lit *in circumcision* [2]Lit *in uncircumcision* **4:11** [a]Ge 17:10f [b]Jn 3:33 [c]Lk 19:9; Ro 4:16f [d]Ro 3:22; 4:16 [1]Lit *was in uncircumcision* **4:12** [1]Lit *was in uncircumcision* **4:13** [a]Ro 9:8; Ga 3:16, 29 [b]Ge 17:4-6; 22:17f [1]Or *through law* **4:14** [a]Ga 3:18 [1]Or *of law* **4:15** [a]Ro 7:7, 10-25; 1Co 15:56; Ga 3:10 [b]Ro 3:20 **4:16** [a]Ro 3:24 [b]Ro 4:11; 9:8; 15:8 [c]Ga 3:7 [d]Lk 19:9; Ro 4:11 [1]Or *out of* [2]Lit *that which is* **4:17** [a]Ge 17:5 [b]Jn 5:21 [c]Is 48:13; 51:2 [d]1Co 1:28 [1]Lit *calls the things which do not exist as existing* **4:18** [a]Ro 4:17 [b]Ge 15:5 **4:19** [a]Heb 11:12 [b]Ge 17:17 [c]Ge 18:11 **4:20** [a]Mt 9:8 **4:21** [a]Ro 14:5 [b]Ge 18:14; Heb 11:19 **4:22** [a]Ge 15:6; Ro 4:3 **4:23** [a]Ro 15:4; 1Co 9:9f; 10:11; 2Ti 3:16f

will be counted, as those [a]who be-
lieve upon Him who [b]raised Jesus
our Lord from the dead, **25** *He* who
was [a]delivered over on account of
our transgressions, and was [b]raised
on account of our justification.

### *Results of Justification by Faith*

**5** [a]Therefore, having been justi-
fied by faith, [b,1]we have peace
with God through our Lord Jesus
Christ, **2** through whom also we have
[a]obtained our introduction by faith
into this grace [b]in which we stand;
and [1]we boast in hope of the glory
of God. **3** [a]And not only this, but
[1]we also [b]boast in our afflictions,
knowing that affliction brings about
[c]perseverance; **4** and [a]perseverance,
[b]proven character; and proven char-
acter, hope; **5** and hope [a]does not put
to shame, because the love of God
has been [b]poured out within our
hearts through the Holy Spirit who
was given to us.
**6** For while we were still [a]weak,
[b]at the right time [c]Christ died for the
ungodly. **7** For one will hardly die for
a righteous man, [1]though perhaps for
the good man someone would dare
even to die. **8** But God [a]demonstrates
[b]His own love toward us, in that
while we were yet sinners, [c]Christ
died for us. **9** Much more then, having
now been justified [a,1]by His blood, we
shall be saved [b]from the wrath *of God*
through Him. **10** For if while we were
[a]enemies we were reconciled to God
through the death of His Son, much
more, having been reconciled, we
shall be saved [b,1]by His life. **11** [a]And
not only this, [1]but we also boast in
God through our Lord Jesus Christ,
through whom we have now received
[b]the reconciliation.

### *The Gift of Righteousness in Christ*

**12** Therefore, just as through [a]one man
sin entered into the world, and [b]death
through sin, and [c]so death spread to
all men, because all sinned— **13** for
[1]until the Law sin was in the world,
but [a]sin is not imputed when there is
no law. **14** Nevertheless death reigned
from Adam until Moses, even over
those who had not sinned [a]in the
likeness of the trespass of Adam, who
is a [b,1]type of Him who was to come.
**15** But [1]the gracious gift is not like
the transgression. For if by the trans-
gression of [a]the one [b]the many died,
much more did the grace of God and
the gift by [c]the grace of the one Man,
Jesus Christ, abound to the many.
**16** And the gift is not like *that which
came* through the one who sinned; for
on the one hand [a]the judgment *arose*
from one *transgression* [1]resulting in
condemnation, but on the other hand
the gracious gift *arose* from many
transgressions [2]resulting in justifi-
cation. **17** For if by the transgression of

---

**4:24** [a]Ro 10:9; 1Pe 1:21 [b]Ac 2:24 **4:25** [a]Is 53:4, 5; Ro 5:6, 8; 8:32; Ga 2:20; Eph 5:2 [b]Ro 5:18; 1Co 15:17; 2Co 5:15 ◆ **5:1** [a]Ro 3:28 [b]Ro 5:11 [1]Two early mss *let us have* **5:2** [a]Eph 2:18; 3:12; Heb 10:19f; 1Pe 3:18 [b]1Co 15:1 [1]Or *let us boast* **5:3** [a]Ro 5:11; 8:23; 9:10; 2Co 8:19 [b]Mt 5:12; Jas 1:2f [c]Lk 21:19 [1]Or *let us also boast* **5:4** [a]Lk 21:19 [b]Php 2:22; Jas 1:12 **5:5** [a]Ps 119:116; Ro 9:33; Heb 6:18f [b]Ac 2:33; 10:45; Ga 4:6; Tit 3:6 **5:6** [a]Ro 5:8, 10 [b]Ga 4:4 [c]Ro 4:25; 5:8; 8:32; Ga 2:20; Eph 5:2 **5:7** [1]Lit *for* **5:8** [a]Ro 3:5 [b]Jn 3:16; 15:13; Ro 8:39 [c]Ro 4:25; 5:6; 8:32; Ga 2:20; Eph 5:2 **5:9** [a]Ro 3:25 [b]Ro 1:18; 1Th 1:10 [1]Or *in* **5:10** [a]Ro 11:28; 2Co 5:18f; Eph 2:3; Col 1:21f [b]Ro 8:34; Heb 7:25; 1Jn 2:1 [1]Or *in* **5:11** [a]Ro 5:3; 8:23; 9:10; 2Co 8:19 [b]Ro 5:10; 11:15; 2Co 5:18f [1]Lit *but also exulting* **5:12** [a]Ge 2:17; 3:6, 19; Ro 5:15-17; 1Co 15:21f [b]Ro 6:23; 1Co 15:56; Jas 1:15 [c]Ro 5:14, 19, 21; 1Co 15:22 **5:13** [a]Ro 4:15 [1]Or *until law* **5:14** [a]Hos 6:7 [b]1Co 15:45 [1]Or *foreshadowing* **5:15** [a]Ro 5:12, 18, 19 [b]Ro 5:19 [c]Ac 15:11 [1]Lit *not as the transgression, so also is the gracious gift* **5:16** [a]1Co 11:32 [1]Lit *to condemnation* [2]Lit *to an act of righteousness*

the one, death reigned [a]through the
one, much more those who receive
the abundance of grace and of the
gift of righteousness will [b]reign in life
through the One, Jesus Christ.
**18** So then as through [a]one
transgression [1]there resulted
condemnation to all men, even so
through one [b]act of righteousness
[2]there resulted [c]justification of life
to all men. **19** For as through the one
man's disobedience [a]the many [b]were
appointed sinners, even so through
[c]the obedience of the One [a]the many
will be appointed righteous. **20** Now
[a,1]the Law came in so that the trans-
gression would increase, but where
sin increased, [b]grace abounded all
the more, **21** so that, as [a]sin reigned
in death, even so [b]grace would reign
through righteousness to eternal life
through Jesus Christ our Lord.

### *Dead to Sin, Alive to God*

**6** [a]What shall we say then? Are
we to [b]continue in sin so that
grace may increase? **2** [a]May it never
be! How shall we who [b]died to sin
still live in it? **3** Or do you not know
that all of us who were [a]baptized into
[b]Christ Jesus were baptized into His
death? **4** Therefore we were [a]buried
with Him through baptism into
death, so that as Christ was [b]raised
from the dead through the [c]glory of
the Father, so we too might walk in
[d]newness of life. **5** For [a]if we have
become [1]united with *Him* in the
likeness of His death, certainly we
shall also be [2]*in the likeness* of His
resurrection, **6** knowing this, that our
[a]old man was [b]crucified with *Him*, in
order that our [c]body of sin might be
[1]done away with, so that we would no
longer be slaves to sin; **7** for [a]he who
has died has been [1]justified from sin.
**8** Now [a]if we died with Christ, we
believe that we shall also live with
Him, **9** knowing that Christ, having
been [a]raised from the dead, [1]is never
to die again; [b]death no longer is mas-
ter over Him. **10** For the death that
He died, He died to sin once for all,
but the life that He lives, He lives to
God. **11** Even so consider yourselves
to be [a]dead to sin, but alive to God
in Christ Jesus.
**12** Therefore do not let sin [a]reign in
your mortal body so that you obey its
lusts, **13** and do not go on [a]presenting
your members to sin *as* [1]instruments
of unrighteousness, but [b]present
yourselves to God as those alive
from the dead, and your members
*as* [1]instruments of righteousness to
God. **14** For [a]sin shall not [b]be master
over you, for [c]you are not under law
but [d]under grace.

### *Slaves of Righteousness*

**15** What then? [a]Shall we sin because
we are not under law but under grace?

**5:17** [a]Ge 2:17; 3:6, 19; Ro 5:12, 15, 16; 1Co 15:21f [b]2Ti 2:12; Rev 22:5 **5:18** [a]Ro 5:12, 15 [b]Ro 3:25 [c]Ro 4:25 [1]Lit *to condemnation* [2]Lit *to justification* **5:19** [a]Ro 5:15, 18 [b]Ro 5:12; 11:32 [c]Php 2:8 **5:20** [a]Ro 3:20; 7:7f; Ga 3:19 [b]Ro 6:1; 1Ti 1:14 [1]Or *law* **5:21** [a]Ro 5:12, 14 [b]Jn 1:17; Ro 6:23 ◆ **6:1** [a]Ro 3:5 [b]Ro 3:8; 6:15 **6:2** [a]Lk 20:16; Ro 6:15 [b]Ro 6:11; 7:4, 6; Ga 2:19; Col 2:20; 3:3; 1Pe 2:24 **6:3** [a]Mt 28:19 [b]Ac 2:38; 8:16; 19:5; Ga 3:27 **6:4** [a]Col 2:12 [b]Ac 2:24; Ro 6:9 [c]Jn 11:40; 2Co 13:4 [d]Ro 7:6; 2Co 5:17; Ga 6:15; Eph 4:23f; Col 3:10 **6:5** [a]2Co 4:10; Php 3:10f; Col 2:12; 3:1 [1]Or *united with the likeness* [2]Or *with* **6:6** [a]Eph 4:22; Col 3:9 [b]Ga 2:20; 5:24; 6:14 [c]Ro 7:24 [1]Or *made powerless* **6:7** [a]1Pe 4:1 [1]Or *acquitted* **6:8** [a]Ro 6:4; 2Co 4:10; 2Ti 2:11 **6:9** [a]Ac 2:24; Ro 6:4 [b]Rev 1:18 [1]Lit *no longer dies* **6:11** [a]Ro 6:2; 7:4, 6; Ga 2:19; Col 2:20; 3:3; 1Pe 2:24 **6:12** [a]Ro 6:14 **6:13** [a]Ro 6:16, 19; 7:5; Col 3:5 [b]Ro 12:1; 2Co 5:14f; 1Pe 2:24 [1]Or *weapons* **6:14** [a]Ro 8:2, 12 [b]Ro 6:12 [c]Ro 5:18; 7:4, 6; Ga 4:21 [d]Ro 5:17, 21 **6:15** [a]Ro 6:1

[b]May it never be! **16** Do you not [a]know
that when you go on presenting
yourselves to someone *as* [b]slaves for
obedience, you are slaves of the one
whom you obey, either of [c]sin [1]leading
to death, or of obedience [2]leading to
righteousness? **17** But [a]thanks be to
God that *though* you were slaves of
sin, you obeyed from the heart that
[b]pattern of teaching to which you
were [c]given over, **18** and having been
[a]freed from sin, you became slaves
of righteousness. **19** [a]I am speaking
in human terms because of the weak-
ness of your flesh. For just [b]as you
presented your members as slaves to
impurity and to lawlessness, [1]leading
to *further* lawlessness, so now present
your members as slaves to righteous-
ness, [2]leading to sanctification.

**20** For [a]when you were slaves of sin,
you were free in regard to righteous-
ness. **21** Therefore what [a,1]benefit were
you then having [2]from the things of
which you are now ashamed? For the
end of those things is [b]death. **22** But
now having been [a]freed from sin
and [b]enslaved to God, you have your
[c,1]benefit, [2]leading to sanctification,
and [d]the end, eternal life. **23** For the
wages of [a]sin is death, but the gra-
cious gift of God is [b]eternal life in
Christ Jesus our Lord.

### *Released from the Law*

**7** Or do you not know, [a]brothers—
for I am speaking to those who
know the law—that the law is
master over a person as long as he
lives? **2** For [a]the married woman has
been bound by law to her [1]husband
while he is living, but if her husband
dies, she is released from the law
[2]concerning the husband. **3** So then,
if while her husband is living she
is joined to another man, she shall
be called an adulteress. But if her
husband dies, she is free from the
law, so that she is not an adulteress
though she is joined to another
man.

**4** So, my brothers, you also were
[a]made to die [b]to the Law [c]through
the body of Christ, so that you
might be joined to another, to Him
who was raised from the dead, in
order that we might bear fruit for
God. **5** For while we were [a]in the
flesh, the sinful passions, which
were [b]*aroused* by the Law, were at
work [c]in our members to bear fruit
for death. **6** But now we have been
[a]released from the Law, having
[b]died to that by which we were
constrained, so that we serve in
[c]newness of [d,1]the Spirit and not in
oldness of the letter.

**7** [a]What shall we say then? Is the
Law sin? [b]May it never be! Rather,
[c]I would not have come to know sin
except [1]through the Law. For I would
not have known about [2]coveting if
the Law had not said, "[d]YOU SHALL
NOT [2]COVET." **8** But sin, [a]taking

---

**6:15** [b]Lk 20:16; Ro 6:2 **6:16** [a]Ro 11:2; 1Co 3:16; 5:6; 6:2, 3, 9, 15, 16, 19; 9:13, 24 [b]Jn 8:34; 2Pe 2:19 [c]Ro 6:21, 23 [1]Lit *to death* [2]Lit *to righteousness* **6:17** [a]Ro 1:8; 2Co 2:14 [b]2Ti 1:13 [c]Ro 1:24, 26, 28 **6:18** [a]Jn 8:32; Ro 6:22; 8:2 **6:19** [a]Ro 3:5 [b]Ro 6:13 [1]Lit *to lawlessness* [2]Lit *to sanctification* **6:20** [a]Mt 6:24; Ro 6:16 **6:21** [a]Jer 12:13; Eze 16:63; Ro 7:5 [b]Ro 1:32; 5:12; 6:16, 23; 8:6, 13; Ga 6:8 [1]Or *fruit*, cf. 7:4, 5 [2]Lit *in* **6:22** [a]Jn 8:32; Ro 6:18; 8:2 [b]1Co 7:22; 1Pe 2:16 [c]Ro 7:4 [d]1Pe 1:9 [1]Or *fruit*, cf. 7:4, 5 [2]Lit *to sanctification* **6:23** [a]Ro 1:32; 5:12; 6:16, 21; 8:6, 13; Ga 6:8 [b]Mt 25:46; Ro 5:21; 8:38, 39 ◆ **7:1** [a]Ro 1:13 **7:2** [a]1Co 7:39 [1]Lit *living husband* [2]Lit *of* **7:4** [a]Ro 6:2; 7:6 [b]Ro 8:2; Ga 2:19; 5:18 [c]Col 1:22 **7:5** [a]Ro 8:8f; 2Co 10:3 [b]Ro 7:7f [c]Ro 6:13, 21, 23 **7:6** [a]Ro 7:2 [b]Ro 6:2 [c]Ro 6:4 [d]Ro 2:29 [1]Or *spirit* **7:7** [a]Ro 3:5 [b]Lk 20:16 [c]Ro 3:20; 4:15; 5:20 [d]Ex 20:17; Dt 5:21 [1]Or *through law* [2]Or *lust* **7:8** [a]Ro 7:11

opportunity [b]through the commandment, worked out in me [1]coveting of every kind. For [c]apart [2]from the Law sin *is* dead. **9** Now I was once alive apart [1]from the Law, but when the commandment came, sin revived and I died; **10** and this commandment, which was [a,1]to lead to life, was found [2]to lead to death for me. **11** For sin, [a]taking an opportunity [b]through the commandment, [c]deceived me and through it killed me. **12** [a]So, the Law is holy, and the commandment is holy and righteous and good.

### *The Conflict of Two Natures*

**13** Therefore did that which is good become *a cause of* death for me? [a]May it never be! Rather it was sin, in order that it might be shown to be sin by working out my death through that which is good, so that through the commandment sin would [1]become utterly sinful.

**14** For we know that the Law is [a]spiritual, but I am [a]fleshly, [b]having been sold [c,1]into bondage under sin. **15** For what I am working out, [a]I do not understand; for I am not practicing [b]what I *would* like to *do*, but I am doing the very thing I hate. **16** But if I do the very thing I do not want, I agree with [a]the Law, that it is good. **17** So now, [a]no longer am I the one *working it out*, but sin which dwells in me. **18** For I know that nothing good dwells in me, that is, in my [a]flesh; for the willing is present in me, but the working out of the good *is* not. **19** For [a]the good that I want, I do not do, but I practice the very evil that I do not want. **20** But if I am doing the very thing I do not want, [a]I am no longer the one working it out, but sin which dwells in me.

**21** I find then [a]the [1]principle that in me evil is present—in me who wants to do good. **22** For I joyfully concur with the law of God [1]in [a]the inner man, **23** but I see [a]a different law in my members, waging war against the [b]law of my mind and making me a captive [1]to [c]the law of sin which is in my members. **24** Wretched man that I am! Who will deliver me from [a,1]the body of this [b]death? **25** [a,1]Thanks be to God through Jesus Christ our Lord! So then, on the one hand I myself with my mind am serving the law of God, but on the other, with my flesh [b]the law of sin.

### *The Spirit of God Dwells in You*

**8** Therefore there is now no [a]condemnation for those who are [b]in [c]Christ Jesus. **2** For [a]the law of the Spirit of life [1]in [b]Christ Jesus [c]has set you free from the law of sin and of death. **3** For [a]what the Law could not do, [b,1]weak as it was through the flesh, God *did*: sending His own Son in [c]the likeness of [2]sinful flesh and *as*

**7:8** [b]Ro 3:20; 7:11 [c]1Co 15:56 [1]Or *lust* [2]Or *from law* **7:9** [1]Or *from law* **7:10** [a]Lv 18:5; Lk 10:28; Ro 10:5; Ga 3:12 [1]Lit *to life* [2]Lit *to death* **7:11** [a]Ro 7:8 [b]Ro 3:20; 7:8 [c]Ge 3:13 **7:12** [a]Ro 7:16; 1Ti 1:8 **7:13** [a]Lk 20:16 [1]Or *prove to be* **7:14** [a]1Co 3:1 [b]1Ki 21:20, 25; 2Ki 17:17; Ro 6:6; Ga 4:3 [c]Ro 3:9 [1]Lit *under sin* **7:15** [a]Jn 15:15 [b]Ro 7:19; Ga 5:17 **7:16** [a]Ro 7:12; 1Ti 1:8 **7:17** [a]Ro 7:20 **7:18** [a]Jn 3:6; Ro 7:25; 8:3 **7:19** [a]Ro 7:15 **7:20** [a]Ro 7:17 **7:21** [a]Ro 7:23, 25; 8:2 [1]Lit *law* **7:22** [a]2Co 4:16; Eph 3:16; 1Pe 3:4 [1]Or *concerning* **7:23** [a]Ro 6:19; Ga 5:17; Jas 4:1; 1Pe 2:11 [b]Ro 7:25 [c]Ro 7:21, 25; 8:2 [1]Lit *in* **7:24** [a]Ro 6:6; Col 2:11 [b]Ro 8:2 [1]Or *this body of death* **7:25** [a]1Co 15:57 [b]Ro 7:21, 23; 8:2 [1]Lit *Grace*; with gratitude ◆ **8:1** [a]Ro 5:16; 8:34 [b]Ro 8:9f [c]Ro 8:2, 11, 39; 16:3 **8:2** [a]1Co 15:45 [b]Ro 8:1, 11, 39; 16:3 [c]Jn 8:32, 36; Ro 6:14, 18; 7:4 [1]Or *has set you free in Christ Jesus* **8:3** [a]Ac 13:39; Heb 10:1ff [b]Ro 7:18f; Heb 7:18 [c]Php 2:7; Heb 2:14, 17; 4:15 [1]Lit *in which it was weak* [2]Lit *flesh of sin*

*an offering* for sin, He condemned sin
in the flesh, **4** so that the [a]righteous
requirement of the Law might be
fulfilled in us, who [b]do not walk
according to the flesh but according
to the Spirit. **5** For those who are
according to the flesh set their minds
on [a]the things of the flesh, but those
who are according to the Spirit, [b]the
things of the Spirit. **6** [a]For the mind
set on the flesh is [b]death, but the
mind set on the Spirit is life and peace,
**7** because the mind set on the flesh is
[a]*at* enmity toward God, for it does not
subject itself to the law of God, for it
is not even able *to do so,* **8** and those
who are [a]in the flesh are not able to
please God.

**9** However, you are not [a]in the
flesh but in the Spirit, if indeed the
Spirit of God [b]dwells in you. But [c]if
anyone does not have the Spirit of
Christ, he does not belong to Him.
**10** [a]But if Christ is in you, though the
body is dead because of sin, yet the
spirit is [1]alive because of righteous-
ness. **11** But if the Spirit of Him who
[a]raised Jesus from the dead dwells
in you, [b]He who raised [c]Christ Jesus
from the dead will also give life to
your mortal bodies [1]through His
Spirit who dwells in you.

**12** So then, brothers, we are under
obligation, not to the flesh, to live
according to the flesh— **13** for [a]if you
are living according to the flesh, you
[1]must die, but if by the Spirit you are
[b]putting to death the [c]practices of the
body, you will live. **14** For as many as
are [a]being led by the Spirit of God,
these are [b]sons of God. **15** For you
[a]have not received a spirit of slavery
[1]leading to fear again, but you [b]have
received *the* Spirit of adoption as sons
by whom we cry out, "[c]Abba! Father!"
**16** The Spirit Himself [a]testifies with
our spirit that we are [b]children of
God, **17** and if children, also [a]heirs,
heirs of God and fellow heirs with
Christ, [b]if indeed we suffer with *Him*
so that we may also be glorified with
*Him.*

### *Present Suffering and Future Glory*

**18** For I consider that the sufferings of
this present time [a]are not worthy to
be compared with the [b]glory that is to
be revealed to us. **19** For the [a]anxious
longing of the creation eagerly waits
for [b]the revealing of the [c]sons of God.
**20** For the creation [a]was subjected to
[b]futility, not willingly, but [c]because
of Him who subjected it, in hope
**21** [1]that [a]the creation itself also will
be set free from its slavery to corrup-
tion into the freedom of the glory of
the children of God. **22** For we know
that the whole creation [a]groans
and suffers the pains of childbirth
together until now. **23** [a]And not only

**8:4** [a]Lk 1:6; Ro 2:26 [b]Ga 5:16, 25 **8:5** [a]Ga 5:19-21 [b]Ga 5:22-25 **8:6** [a]Ga 6:8 [b]Ro 6:21; 8:13 **8:7** [a]Jas 4:4 **8:8** [a]Ro 7:5 **8:9** [a]Ro 7:5 [b]Jn 14:23; Ro 8:11; 1Co 3:16; 6:19; 2Co 6:16; Ga 4:6; Php 1:19; 2Ti 1:14; 1Jn 4:13 [c]Jn 14:17 **8:10** [a]Jn 17:23; Ga 2:20; Eph 3:17; Col 1:27 [1]Lit *life* **8:11** [a]Ac 2:24; Ro 6:4 [b]Jn 5:21 [c]Ro 8:1, 2, 39; 16:3 [1]One early ms *because of* **8:13** [a]Ro 8:6 [b]Col 3:5 [c]Col 3:9 [1]Or *are going to* **8:14** [a]Ga 5:18 [b]Hos 1:10; Mt 5:9; Jn 1:12; Ro 8:16, 19; 9:8, 26; 2Co 6:18; Ga 3:26; 1Jn 3:1; Rev 21:7 **8:15** [a]2Ti 1:7; Heb 2:15 [b]Ro 8:23; Ga 4:5f [c]Mk 14:36; Ga 4:6 [1]Lit *for fear again* **8:16** [a]Ac 5:32 [b]Hos 1:10; Mt 5:9; Jn 1:12; Ro 8:14, 19; 9:8, 26; 2Co 6:18; Ga 3:26; 1Jn 3:1; Rev 21:7 **8:17** [a]Ac 20:32; Ga 3:29; 4:7; Eph 3:6; Tit 3:7; Heb 1:14; Rev 21:7 [b]2Co 1:5, 7; Php 3:10; Col 1:24; 2Ti 2:12; 1Pe 4:13 **8:18** [a]2Co 4:17; 1Pe 4:13 [b]Col 3:4; Tit 2:13; 1Pe 1:5; 5:1 **8:19** [a]Php 1:20 [b]Ro 8:18; 1Co 1:7f; Col 3:4; 1Pe 1:7, 13; 1Jn 3:2 [c]Hos 1:10; Mt 5:9; Jn 1:12; Ro 8:14, 16; 9:8, 26; 2Co 6:18; Ga 3:26; 1Jn 3:1; Rev 21:7 **8:20** [a]Ge 3:17-19 [b]Ps 39:5f; Ecc 1:2 [c]Ge 3:17; 5:29 **8:21** [a]Ac 3:21; 2Pe 3:13; Rev 21:1 [1]Or *because* **8:22** [a]Jer 12:4, 11 **8:23** [a]Ro 5:3

this, but also we ourselves, having
[b]the first fruits of the Spirit, even we
ourselves [c]groan within ourselves,
[d]eagerly waiting for *our* adoption as
sons, [e]the redemption of our body.
**24** For [a]in hope we were saved, but
[b]hope that is seen is not hope, for
who hopes for what he *already* sees?
**25** But [a]if we hope for what we do not
see, with perseverance we eagerly
wait for it.

**26** And in the same way the Spirit
also helps our weakness, for [a]we do
not know how to pray as we should,
but [b]the Spirit Himself intercedes
for *us* with groanings too deep for
words; **27** and [a]He who searches the
hearts knows what [b]the mind of the
Spirit is, because He [c]intercedes for
the [1]saints according to *the will of*
God.

**28** And we know that for those who
love God [a,1]all things work together
for good, for those who are [b]called
according to *His* purpose. **29** Because
those whom He [a]foreknew, He also
[b]predestined *to become* [c]conformed
to the image of His Son, so that He
would be the [d]firstborn among many
brothers; **30** and those whom He
[a]predestined, He also [b]called; and
those whom He called, He also [c]justi-
fied; and those whom He justified,
He also [d]glorified.

### *God Is for Us*

**31** [a]What then shall we say to these
things? [b]If God *is* for us, who *is*
against us? **32** He who indeed [a]did
not spare His own Son, but [b]deliv-
ered Him over for us all, how will
He not also with Him graciously
give us all things? **33** Who will bring
a charge against [a]God's elect? [b]God
is the one who justifies; **34** who is the
one who [a]condemns? Christ Jesus is
He who [b]died, yes, rather who was
[c,1]raised, who is [d]at the right hand
of God, who also [e]intercedes for us.
**35** Who will separate us from [a]the
love of [1]Christ? Will [b]affliction, or
turmoil, or [c]persecution, or [c]famine,
or [c]nakedness, or [c]peril, or sword?
**36** Just as it is written,

"[a]FOR YOUR SAKE WE ARE
BEING PUT TO DEATH
ALL DAY LONG;
WE WERE COUNTED AS SHEEP
FOR *the* SLAUGHTER."

**37** But in all these things we over-
whelmingly [a]conquer through [b]Him
who loved us. **38** For I am convinced
that neither [a]death, nor life, nor
[b]angels, nor rulers, nor [a]things
present, nor things to come, nor
powers, **39** nor height, nor depth, nor
any other created thing, will be able
to separate us from [a]the love of God,
which is [b]in Christ Jesus our Lord.

---

**8:23** [b]Ro 8:16; 2Co 1:22 [c]2Co 5:2, 4 [d]Ro 8:15, 19, 25; Ga 5:5 [e]Ro 7:24 **8:24** [a]Ro 8:20; 1Th 5:8; Tit 3:7 [b]Ro 4:18; 2Co 5:7; Heb 11:1 **8:25** [a]1Th 1:3 **8:26** [a]Mt 20:22; 2Co 12:8 [b]Jn 14:16; Ro 8:15f; Eph 6:18 **8:27** [a]Ps 139:1f; Lk 16:15; Ac 1:24; Rev 2:23 [b]Ro 8:6 [c]Ro 8:34 [1]Or *holy ones* **8:28** [a]Ro 8:32 [b]Ro 8:30; 9:24; 11:29; 1Co 1:9; Ga 1:6, 15; 5:8; Eph 1:11; 3:11; 2Th 2:14; Heb 9:15; 1Pe 2:9; 3:9 [1]Some mss *God works all things together for good* **8:29** [a]Ro 11:2; 1Co 8:3; 2Ti 1:9; 1Pe 1:2, 20 [b]Ro 9:23; 1Co 2:7; Eph 1:5, 11 [c]1Co 15:49; Php 3:21 [d]Col 1:18; Heb 1:6 **8:30** [a]Ro 9:23; 11:29; 1Co 2:7; Eph 1:5, 11 [b]Ro 8:28; 9:24; 1Co 1:9; Ga 1:6, 15; 5:8; Eph 1:11; 3:11; 2Th 2:14; Heb 9:15; 1Pe 2:9; 3:9 [c]1Co 6:11 [d]Jn 17:22; Ro 8:21; 9:23 **8:31** [a]Ro 3:5; 4:1 [b]Ps 118:6; Mt 1:23 **8:32** [a]Jn 3:16; Ro 5:8 [b]Ro 4:25 **8:33** [a]Lk 18:7 [b]Is 50:8f **8:34** [a]Ro 8:1 [b]Ro 5:6f [c]Ac 2:24 [d]Mk 16:19 [e]Ro 8:27; Heb 7:25 [1]One early ms *raised from the dead* **8:35** [a]Ro 8:37f [b]Ro 2:9; 2Co 4:8 [c]1Co 4:11; 2Co 11:26f [1]Two early mss *God* **8:36** [a]Ps 44:22; Ac 20:24; 1Co 4:9; 15:30f; 2Co 1:9; 4:10f; 6:9; 11:23 **8:37** [a]Jn 16:33; 1Co 15:57 [b]Ga 2:20; Eph 5:2; Rev 1:5 **8:38** [a]1Co 3:22 [b]1Co 15:24; Eph 1:21; 1Pe 3:22 **8:39** [a]Ro 5:8 [b]Ro 8:1

### *God's Chosen People, Israel*

**9** [a]I am telling the truth in Christ,
I am not lying, my conscience
testifies with me in the Holy Spirit,
**2** that I have great sorrow and unceas-
ing grief in my heart. **3** For [a]I could
[1]wish that I myself were [b]accursed,
*separated* from Christ for the sake of
my brothers, my kinsmen [c]according
to the flesh, **4** who are [a]Israelites, to
whom belongs [b]the adoption as sons,
and [c]the glory and [d]the covenants
and [e]the giving of the Law and [f]the
*temple* service and [g]the promises,
**5** whose are [a]the fathers, and [b]from
whom is the [1]Christ according to the
flesh, [c]who is [d]God over all, [e]blessed
[2]forever. Amen.

**6** But *it is* not as though [a]the word
of God has failed. [b]For they are not all
Israel who are *descended* from Israel;
**7** nor are they all children [a]because
they are Abraham's seed, but:
"[b,1]THROUGH ISAAC YOUR SEED WILL
BE NAMED." **8** That is, the children
of the flesh are not the [a]children of
God, but the [b]children of the promise
are considered as seed. **9** For this is
the word of promise: "[a]AT THIS TIME
I WILL COME, AND SARAH SHALL HAVE
A SON." **10** [a]And not only this, but
there was [b]Rebekah also, when she
had conceived *twins* by one man, our
father Isaac; **11** for though *the twins*
were not yet born and had not done
anything good or bad, so that the
[a]purpose of God according to *His*
choice would [1]stand, not [2]because
of works but [2]because of Him who
calls, **12** it was said to her, "[a]THE OLD-
ER SHALL SERVE THE YOUNGER." **13** Just
as it is written, "[a]JACOB I LOVED, BUT
ESAU I HATED."

**14** [a]What shall we say then? [b]Is
there any unrighteousness with God?
[c]May it never be! **15** For He says to Mo-
ses, "[a]I WILL HAVE MERCY ON WHOM I
HAVE MERCY, AND I WILL HAVE COMPAS-
SION ON WHOM I HAVE COMPASSION."
**16** So then it *does* not *depend* on the
one who wills or the one who [a]runs,
but on [b]God who has mercy. **17** For
the Scripture says to Pharaoh, "[a]FOR
THIS VERY PURPOSE I RAISED YOU UP,
IN ORDER TO DEMONSTRATE MY POWER
IN YOU, AND IN ORDER THAT MY NAME
MIGHT BE PROCLAIMED [1]THROUGHOUT
THE WHOLE EARTH." **18** So then He has
mercy on whom He desires, and He
[a]hardens whom He desires.

**19** [a]You will say to me then, "[b]Why
does He still find fault? For [c]who
resists His will?" **20** On the contrary,
who are you, [a]O man, who [b]answers
back to God? [c]WILL THE THING MOLD-
ED SAY TO THE MOLDER, "WHY DID YOU
MAKE ME LIKE THIS"? **21** Or does not the
potter have authority over the clay, to
make from the same lump one vessel
[1]for honorable use and another [2]for
dishonorable use? **22** And [1]what if
God, wanting to demonstrate His

---

◆ **9:1** [a]2Co 11:10; Ga 1:20; 1Ti 2:7 **9:3** [a]Ex 32:32 [b]1Co 12:3; 16:22; Ga 1:8f [c]Ro 1:3; 11:14; Eph 6:5 [1]Lit *pray* **9:4** [a]Dt 7:6; 14:1f; Ro 9:6 [b]Ex 4:22; Ro 8:15 [c]Ex 40:34; 1Ki 8:11; Eze 1:28; Heb 9:5 [d]Ge 17:2; Dt 29:14; Lk 1:72; Ac 3:25; Eph 2:12 [e]Dt 4:13f; Ps 147:19 [f]Heb 9:1, 6 [g]Ac 2:39; 13:32; Eph 2:12 **9:5** [a]Ac 3:13; Ro 11:28 [b]Mt 1:1-16; Ro 1:3 [c]Col 1:16-19 [d]Jn 1:1 [e]Ro 1:25 [1]Messiah [2]Lit *to the ages* **9:6** [a]Nu 23:19 [b]Jn 1:47; Ro 2:28f; Ga 6:16 **9:7** [a]Jn 8:33, 39; Ga 4:23 [b]Ge 21:12; Heb 11:18 [1]Lit *in* **9:8** [a]Ro 8:14 [b]Ro 4:13, 16; Ga 3:29; 4:28; Heb 11:11 **9:9** [a]Ge 18:10 **9:10** [a]Ro 5:3 [b]Ge 25:21 **9:11** [a]Ro 4:17; 8:28 [1]Lit *remain* [2]Lit *from* **9:12** [a]Ge 25:23 **9:13** [a]Mal 1:2f **9:14** [a]Ro 3:5 [b]2Chr 19:7; Ro 2:11 [c]Lk 20:16 **9:15** [a]Ex 33:19 **9:16** [a]Ga 2:2 [b]Eph 2:8 **9:17** [a]Ex 9:16 [1]Lit *in* **9:18** [a]Ex 4:21; 7:3; 9:12; 10:20, 27; 11:10; 14:4, 17; Dt 2:30; Jos 11:20; Jn 12:40; Ro 11:7, 25 **9:19** [a]Ro 11:19; 1Co 15:35; Jas 2:18 [b]Ro 3:7 [c]2Chr 20:6; Job 9:12; Da 4:35 **9:20** [a]Ro 2:1 [b]Job 33:13 [c]Is 29:16; 45:9; 64:8; Jer 18:6; Ro 9:22f; 2Ti 2:20 **9:21** [1]Lit *for honor* [2]Lit *for dishonor* **9:22** [1]Lit *But*

wrath and to make His power known,
endured with much [a]patience vessels
of wrath [b]having been prepared for
destruction, **23** and in order that He
might make known [a]the riches of
His glory upon [b]vessels of mercy,
which He [c]prepared beforehand for
glory— **24** *even* us, whom He also
[a]called, [b]not from among Jews only,
but also from among Gentiles? **25** As
He says also in Hosea,

"[a]I WILL CALL THOSE WHO WERE
NOT MY PEOPLE, 'MY PEOPLE,'
AND HER WHO WAS NOT
BELOVED, 'BELOVED.'"

**26** "[a]AND IT SHALL BE THAT
IN THE PLACE WHERE
IT WAS SAID TO THEM,
'YOU ARE NOT MY PEOPLE,'
THERE THEY SHALL BE CALLED
SONS OF [b]THE LIVING GOD."

**27** And Isaiah cries out concerning
Israel, "[a]THOUGH THE NUMBER OF THE
SONS OF ISRAEL BE [b]LIKE THE SAND OF
THE SEA, IT IS [c]THE REMNANT THAT
WILL BE SAVED; **28** [a]FOR THE LORD
WILL EXECUTE HIS WORD ON THE LAND,
[1]THOROUGHLY AND [2]QUICKLY." **29** And
just as Isaiah foretold,

"[a]UNLESS [b]THE LORD
OF [1]SABAOTH HAD LEFT
TO US A SEED,
[c]WE WOULD HAVE BECOME
LIKE SODOM, AND WOULD HAVE
[2]RESEMBLED GOMORRAH."

**30** [a]What shall we say then? That
Gentiles, who did not pursue righ-
teousness, laid hold of righteousness,
even [b]the righteousness which is [1]by
faith; **31** but Israel, [a]pursuing a law of
righteousness, did not [b]attain *that*
law. **32** Why? Because *they did* not
*pursue it* [1]by faith, but as though *it*
*were* [1]by works. They stumbled over
[a]the stumbling stone, **33** just as it is
written,

"[a]BEHOLD, I AM LAYING IN ZION
[b]A STONE OF STUMBLING
AND A ROCK OF OFFENSE,
[c]AND THE ONE WHO BELIEVES
UPON HIM [d]WILL NOT
BE PUT TO SHAME."

**10** Brothers, my heart's desire and
my prayer to God for them is
for *their* salvation. **2** For I testify
about them that they have [a]a zeal
for God, but not according to knowl-
edge. **3** For not knowing about the
[a]righteousness of God and [b]seeking
to establish their own, they did
not subject themselves to the righ-
teousness of God. **4** For [a]Christ is the
[1]end of the law for righteousness to
[b]everyone who believes.

### *Faith Comes by Hearing*

**5** For Moses writes about the righ-
teousness which is of law: "[a]THE MAN
WHO DOES THESE THINGS SHALL LIVE
BY THEM." **6** But [a]the righteousness
of faith speaks in this way: "[b]DO
NOT SAY IN YOUR HEART, 'WHO WILL
GO UP INTO HEAVEN?' (that is, to
bring Christ down), **7** or 'WHO WILL
GO DOWN INTO THE [a]ABYSS?' (that is,
to [b]bring Christ up from the dead)."

**9:22** [a]Ro 2:4 [b]Pr 16:4; 1Pe 2:8 **9:23** [a]Ro 2:4; Eph 3:16 [b]Ac 9:15 [c]Ro 8:29f **9:24** [a]Ro 8:28 [b]Ro 3:29 **9:25** [a]Hos 2:23; 1Pe 2:10 **9:26** [a]Hos 1:10 [b]Mt 16:16 **9:27** [a]Is 10:22 [b]Ge 22:17; Hos 1:10 [c]Ro 11:5 **9:28** [a]Is 10:23 [1]Lit *finishing it* [2]Lit *cutting it short* **9:29** [a]Is 1:9 [b]Jas 5:4 [c]Dt 29:23; Is 13:19; Jer 49:18; 50:40; Am 4:11 [1]Hosts [2]Lit *been made like* **9:30** [a]Ro 9:14 [b]Ro 1:17; 3:21f; 10:6; Ga 2:16; 3:24; Php 3:9; Heb 11:7 [1]Lit *out of* **9:31** [a]Is 51:1; Ro 9:30; 10:2f, 20; 11:7 [b]Ga 5:4 **9:32** [a]Is 8:14; 1Pe 2:6, 8 [1]Lit *out of* **9:33** [a]Is 28:16 [b]Is 8:14 [c]Ro 10:11 [d]Ro 5:5 ◆ **10:2** [a]Ac 21:20 **10:3** [a]Ro 1:17 [b]Is 51:1; Ro 10:2f, 20; 11:7 **10:4** [a]Ro 7:1-4; Ga 3:24; 4:5 [b]Ro 3:22 [1]Or *goal* **10:5** [a]Lv 18:5; Ne 9:29; Eze 20:11, 13, 21; Ro 7:10 **10:6** [a]Ro 9:30 [b]Dt 30:12 **10:7** [a]Lk 8:31 [b]Heb 13:20

8 But what does it say? "[a]THE WORD
IS NEAR YOU, IN YOUR MOUTH AND IN
YOUR HEART"—that is, the word of
faith which we are preaching, 9 [1]that
[a]if you confess with your mouth
Jesus *as* Lord, and [b]believe in your
heart that [c]God raised Him from
the dead, you will be saved; 10 for
with the heart a person believes,
[1]leading to righteousness, and with
the mouth he confesses, [2]leading to
salvation. 11 For the Scripture says,
"[a]WHOEVER BELIEVES UPON HIM WILL
NOT BE PUT TO SHAME." 12 For [a]there
is no distinction between Jew and
Greek, for the same *Lord* is [b]Lord of
[c]all, abounding in riches for all who
call on Him, 13 for "[a]WHOEVER CALLS
ON THE NAME OF THE LORD WILL BE
SAVED."

14 How then will they call on Him
in whom they have not believed?
How will they believe in Him [a]whom
they have not heard? And how will
they hear without [b]a preacher?
15 And how will they preach unless
they are sent? Just as it is written,
"[a]HOW BEAUTIFUL ARE THE FEET OF
THOSE WHO [b]PROCLAIM GOOD NEWS
OF GOOD THINGS!"

16 However, they [a]did not all
heed the [1]good news, for Isaiah
says, "[b]LORD, WHO HAS BELIEVED
OUR REPORT?" 17 So faith *comes* from
[a]hearing, and hearing by [b]the word
[1]of Christ.

18 But I say, have they never heard?
On the contrary, they have;

"[a]THEIR VOICE HAS GONE OUT
INTO ALL THE EARTH,
AND THEIR WORDS TO THE
ENDS OF THE [1]WORLD."

19 But I say, did Israel not know? First
Moses says,

"[a]I WILL [b]MAKE YOU JEALOUS BY
THAT WHICH IS NOT A NATION,
BY A NATION WITHOUT
UNDERSTANDING WILL
I ANGER YOU."

20 And Isaiah is very bold and says,

"[a]I WAS FOUND BY THOSE
WHO DID NOT SEEK ME,
I BECAME MANIFEST TO THOSE
WHO DID NOT ASK FOR ME."

21 But as for Israel He says, "[a]ALL
DAY LONG I HAVE STRETCHED OUT MY
HANDS TO A DISOBEDIENT AND OBSTI-
NATE PEOPLE."

### *God Has Not Rejected Israel*

11 I say then, has God [a]rejected
His people? [b]May it never be!
For [c]I too am an Israelite, a seed of
Abraham, of the tribe of Benjamin.
2 [a,1]GOD HAS NOT REJECTED HIS PEOPLE
whom He [b]foreknew. [c]Or do you not
know what the Scripture says in *the*
*passage about* Elijah, how he appeals
to God against Israel? 3 "Lord, [a]THEY
HAVE KILLED YOUR PROPHETS, THEY
HAVE TORN DOWN YOUR ALTARS, AND I
ALONE AM LEFT, AND THEY ARE SEEKING
MY LIFE." 4 But what does the divine
response say to him? "[a]I HAVE LEFT
for Myself SEVEN THOUSAND MEN WHO
HAVE NOT BOWED THE KNEE TO BAAL."

---

**10:8** [a]Dt 30:14 **10:9** [a]Mt 10:32; Lk 12:8; Ro 14:9; 1Co 12:3; Php 2:11 [b]Ac 16:31; Ro 4:24 [c]Ac 2:24 [1]Or *because* **10:10** [1]Lit *to righteousness* [2]Lit *to salvation* **10:11** [a]Is 28:16; Ro 9:33 **10:12** [a]Ro 3:22, 29 [b]Ac 10:36 [c]Ro 3:29 **10:13** [a]Joel 2:32; Ac 2:21 **10:14** [a]Eph 2:17; 4:21 [b]Ac 8:31; Tit 1:3 **10:15** [a]Is 52:7 [b]Ro 1:15; 15:20 **10:16** [a]Ro 3:3 [b]Is 53:1; Jn 12:38 [1]Or *gospel* **10:17** [a]Ga 3:2, 5 [b]Col 3:16 [1]Or *concerning Christ* **10:18** [a]Ps 19:4; Ro 1:8; Col 1:6, 23; 1Th 1:8 [1]Or *inhabited earth* **10:19** [a]Dt 32:21 [b]Ro 11:11, 14 **10:20** [a]Is 65:1; Ro 9:30 **10:21** [a]Is 65:2 ◆ **11:1** [a]1Sa 12:22; Jer 31:37; 33:24-26 [b]Lk 20:16 [c]2Co 11:22; Php 3:5 **11:2** [a]Ps 94:14 [b]Ro 8:29 [c]Ro 6:16 [1]In OT, Yahweh, cf. Ps 94:14 **11:3** [a]1Ki 19:10, 14 **11:4** [a]1Ki 19:18

5 In this way then, at the present
time, [a]a remnant according to *God's*
[1]gracious choice has also come to
be. 6 But [a]if it is by grace, it is no
longer of works, otherwise grace is
no longer grace.

7 What then? What [a]Israel is
seeking, it has not obtained, but the
chosen obtained it, and the rest were
[b]hardened; 8 just as it is written,

> "[a,1]GOD GAVE THEM
> A SPIRIT OF STUPOR,
> EYES TO SEE NOT AND
> EARS TO HEAR NOT,
> DOWN TO THIS VERY DAY."

9 And David says,

> "[a]LET THEIR TABLE BECOME
> A SNARE AND A TRAP,
> AND A STUMBLING BLOCK AND
> A RETRIBUTION TO THEM.

10 "[a]LET THEIR EYES BE
> DARKENED TO SEE NOT,
> AND BEND THEIR
> BACKS FOREVER."

### *Gentiles Grafted In*

11 [a]I say then, did they stumble so as
to fall? [b]May it never be! But by their
transgression [c]salvation *has come* to
the Gentiles, to [d]make them jealous.
12 Now if their transgression is riches
for the world and their failure is
riches for the Gentiles, how much
more will their [a,1]fullness be! 13 But I
am speaking to you who are Gentiles.
Inasmuch then as [a]I am an apostle of
Gentiles, I magnify my ministry, 14 if
somehow I might [a]move to jealousy
[b]my [1]fellow countrymen and [c]save
some of them. 15 For if their rejection
is the [a]reconciliation of the world,
what will *their* acceptance be but
[b]life from the dead? 16 And if the
[a]first piece *of dough* is holy, the
lump is also; and if the root is holy,
the branches are too.

17 But if some of the [a]branches
were broken off, and [b]you, being a
wild olive, were grafted in among
them and became a partaker with
them of the [1]rich root of the olive
tree, 18 do not boast against the
branches. But if you do boast against
*them, remember that* [a]it is not you
who supports the root, but the root
*supports* you. 19 [a]You will say then,
"Branches were broken off so that I
might be grafted in." 20 Quite right!
They were broken off for their unbe-
lief, but you [a]stand by your faith. [b]Do
not be haughty, but fear, 21 for if God
did not spare the natural branches,
He will not spare you, either. 22 Be-
hold then the kindness and severity
of God; to those who fell, severity,
but to you, God's [a]kindness, [b]if you
continue in His kindness; otherwise
you also [c]will be cut off. 23 And they
also, [a]if they do not continue in their
unbelief, will be grafted in, for God
is able to graft them in again. 24 For
if you were cut off from what is by
nature a wild olive tree, and were
grafted contrary to nature into a
cultivated olive tree, how much
more will these who are the natural
*branches* be grafted into their own
olive tree?

---

**11:5** [a]2Ki 19:4; Ro 9:27 [1]Lit *choice of grace* **11:6** [a]Ro 4:4 **11:7** [a]Ro 9:31 [b]Mk 6:52; Ro 9:18; 11:25; 2Co 3:14 **11:8** [a]Dt 29:4; Is 29:10; Mt 13:13f [1]In OT, Yahweh, cf. Is 29:10 **11:9** [a]Ps 69:22 **11:10** [a]Ps 69:23 **11:11** [a]Ro 11:1 [b]Lk 20:16 [c]Ac 28:28 [d]Ro 11:14 **11:12** [a]Ro 11:25 [1]Or *fulfillment* **11:13** [a]Ac 9:15 **11:14** [a]Ro 11:11 [b]Ge 29:14; 2Sa 19:12f; Ro 9:3 [c]1Co 1:21; 7:16; 9:22; 1Ti 1:15; 2:4; 2Ti 1:9; Tit 3:5 [1]Lit *flesh* **11:15** [a]Ro 5:11 [b]Lk 15:24, 32 **11:16** [a]Nu 15:18ff; Ne 10:37; Eze 44:30 **11:17** [a]Jer 11:16; Jn 15:2 [b]Eph 2:11ff [1]Lit *root of the fatness* **11:18** [a]Jn 4:22 **11:19** [a]Ro 9:19 **11:20** [a]Ro 5:2; 1Co 10:12; 2Co 1:24 [b]Ro 12:16; 1Ti 6:17; 1Pe 1:17 **11:22** [a]Ro 2:4 [b]1Co 15:2; Heb 3:6, 14 [c]Jn 15:2 **11:23** [a]2Co 3:16

### *All Israel Will Be Saved*

**25** For [a]I do not want you, brothers, to
be uninformed of this [b]mystery—so
that you will not be [c]wise in your own
estimation—that a partial [d]harden-
ing has happened to Israel until the
[e]fullness of the Gentiles has come in;
**26** and so all Israel will be saved; just
as it is written,

"[a]THE DELIVERER WILL
COME FROM ZION,
HE WILL REMOVE UNGODLINESS
FROM JACOB."

**27** "[a]AND THIS IS [1]MY
COVENANT WITH THEM,
[b]WHEN I TAKE AWAY
THEIR SINS."

**28** [1]From the standpoint of the gospel
they are [a]enemies for your sake, but
[2]from the standpoint of *God's* choice
they are beloved for [b]the sake of the
fathers; **29** for the gifts and the [a]call-
ing of God [b]are irrevocable. **30** For
just as you once were disobedient
to God, but now have been shown
mercy because of their disobedience,
**31** so these also now have been dis-
obedient, that because of the mercy
shown to you they also may now be
shown mercy. **32** For [a]God has shut
up all in disobedience so that He may
show mercy to all.
**33** Oh, the depth of [a]the riches
and [b]wisdom and knowledge of
God! [c]How unsearchable are His
judgments and unfathomable His
ways! **34** For [a]WHO HAS KNOWN THE
MIND OF THE LORD, OR WHO BECAME
HIS COUNSELOR? **35** Or [a]WHO HAS
FIRST GIVEN TO HIM [1]THAT IT MIGHT
BE REPAID TO HIM? **36** For [a]from Him
and through Him and to Him are all
things. [b]To Him *be* the glory [1]forever.
Amen.

### *A Living and Holy Sacrifice*

**12** Therefore [a]I exhort you,
brothers, by the mercies of
God, to [b]present your bodies as a
sacrifice—living, holy, *and* pleasing
to God, *which is* your [1]spiritual
service of worship. **2** And do not
[a]be conformed to [b]this [1]world, but
be transformed by the [c]renewing of
your mind, so that you may [d]approve
what the will of God is, that which is
good and pleasing and [2]perfect.
**3** For through [a]the grace given to
me I say to each one among you [b]not
to think more highly of himself than
he ought to think; but to think so as
to have sound thinking, as God has
allotted to [c]each a measure of faith.
**4** For [a]just as we have many members
in one body and all the members
do not have the same function, **5** so
we, [a]who are many, are [b]one body
in Christ, and individually members
one of another, **6** but having gifts
that [a]differ according to the grace

---

**11:25** [a]Ro 1:13 [b]Mt 13:11; Ro 16:25; 1Co 2:7-10; Eph 3:3-5, 9 [c]Ro 12:16 [d]Ro 11:7 [e]Lk 21:24; Jn 10:16; Ro 11:12
**11:26** [a]Is 59:20 **11:27** [a]Is 59:21; Jer 31:33, 34; Heb 8:10 [b]Is 27:9; Heb 8:12 [1]Lit *the covenant from Me*
**11:28** [a]Ro 5:10 [b]Dt 7:8; 10:15; Ro 9:5 [1]Lit *According to the gospel* [2]Lit *according to the election*
**11:29** [a]Ro 8:28; 1Co 1:26; Eph 1:18; 4:1, 4; Php 3:14; 2Th 1:11; 2Ti 1:9; Heb 3:1; 2Pe 1:10 [b]Heb 7:21
**11:32** [a]Ro 3:9; Ga 3:22f **11:33** [a]Ro 2:4; Eph 3:8 [b]Eph 3:10; Col 2:3 [c]Job 5:9; 11:7; 15:8 **11:34** [a]Is 40:13f; 1Co 2:16 **11:35** [a]Job 35:7; 41:11 [1]Lit *and it will be paid back* **11:36** [a]1Co 8:6; 11:12; Col 1:16; Heb 2:10 [b]Ro 16:27; Eph 3:21; Php 4:20; 1Ti 1:17; 2Ti 4:18; 1Pe 4:11; 5:11; 2Pe 3:18; Jd 25; Rev 1:6; 5:13; 7:12 [1]Lit *to the ages*
◆ **12:1** [a]1Co 1:10; 2Co 10:1-4; Eph 4:1; 1Pe 2:11 [b]Ro 6:13, 16, 19; 1Co 6:20; Heb 13:15; 1Pe 2:5 [1]Or *rational*
**12:2** [a]1Pe 1:14 [b]Mt 13:22; Ga 1:4; 1Jn 2:15 [c]Eph 4:23; Tit 3:5 [d]Eph 5:10, 17; Col 1:9 [1]Or *age* [2]Or *complete*
**12:3** [a]Ro 1:5; 15:15; 1Co 3:10; 15:10; Ga 2:9; Eph 3:7f [b]Ro 11:20; 12:16 [c]1Co 7:17; 2Co 10:13; Eph 4:7; 1Pe 4:11
**12:4** [a]1Co 12:12-14; Eph 4:4, 16 **12:5** [a]1Co 10:17, 33 [b]1Co 12:20, 27; Eph 4:12, 25 **12:6** [a]Ro 12:3; 1Co 7:7; 12:4; 1Pe 4:10

given to us: whether [b]prophecy,
[1]in agreement with the faith; **7** or
[a,1]service, in his serving; or he
who [b]teaches, in his teaching; **8** or
he who [a]exhorts, in his exhortation;
he who gives, with [b,1]generosity; [c]he
who [2]leads, with diligence; he who
shows mercy, with [d]cheerfulness.

**9** *Let* [a]love *be* without hypocrisy—
by [b]abhorring what is evil, clinging
to what is good, **10** *being* [a]devoted to
one another in brotherly love, [1]giving
preference to one another [b]in honor,
**11** not lagging behind in diligence,
being [a]fervent in spirit, [b]serving the
Lord, **12** [a]rejoicing in hope, [b]persever-
ing in affliction, being [c]devoted to
prayer, **13** [a]contributing to the needs
of the [1]saints, [b]pursuing hospitality.

**14** [a]Bless those who persecute
[1]you; bless, and do not curse.
**15** [a]Rejoice with those who rejoice;
weep with those who weep, **16** by
[a]being of the same mind toward one
another, [b]not being haughty in mind,
but [1]associating with the humble.
[c]Do not be wise in your own mind.
**17** [a]Never paying back evil for evil to
anyone, [b,1]respecting what is good
in the sight of all men, **18** if possible,
[a]so far as it depends on you, [b]being at
peace with all men, **19** [a]never taking
your own revenge, beloved—instead
[1]leave room for the wrath *of God.* For
it is written, "[b]VENGEANCE IS MINE, I
WILL REPAY," says the Lord. **20** "[a]BUT IF
YOUR ENEMY IS HUNGRY, FEED HIM, AND
IF HE IS THIRSTY, GIVE HIM A DRINK; FOR
IN SO DOING YOU WILL HEAP BURNING
COALS ON HIS HEAD." **21** Do not be
overcome by evil, but overcome evil
with good.

### *Be Subject to Government*

**13** Every [a,1]person is to be in
[b]subjection to the governing
authorities. For [c]there is no authority
except [2]from God, and those which
exist have been appointed by God.
**2** Therefore [1]whoever resists that au-
thority has opposed the ordinance of
God; and they who have opposed will
receive condemnation upon them-
selves. **3** For [a]rulers are not *a cause
of* fear for [1]good behavior, but for
evil. Do you want to have no fear of
that authority? Do what is good, and
you will have praise from the same;
**4** for it is a minister of God to you for
good. But if you do what is evil, be
afraid; for it does not bear the sword
in vain, for it is a minister of God, an
[a]avenger who brings wrath on the
one who practices evil. **5** Therefore
it is necessary to be in subjection,
not only because of that wrath, but
also because of [a]conscience. **6** For
because of this you also pay taxes,
for *rulers* are servants of God, de-
voting themselves to this very thing.

---

**12:6** [b]Ac 13:1; 1Co 12:10 [1]Or *according to the proportion of his faith* **12:7** [a]Ac 6:1; 1Co 12:5, 28 [b]Ac 13:1; 1Co 12:28; 14:26 [1]Or *office of service* **12:8** [a]Ac 4:36; 11:23; 13:15 [b]2Co 8:2; 9:11, 13 [c]1Co 12:28; 1Ti 5:17 [d]2Co 9:7 [1]Or *simplicity*, without false motives [2]Or *gives aid* **12:9** [a]2Co 6:6; 1Ti 1:5 [b]1Th 5:21f **12:10** [a]Jn 13:34; 1Th 4:9; Heb 13:1; 2Pe 1:7 [b]Ro 13:7; Php 2:3; 1Pe 2:17 [1]Or *outdo one another in showing honor* **12:11** [a]Ac 18:25 [b]Ac 20:19 **12:12** [a]Ro 5:2 [b]Heb 10:32, 36 [c]Ac 1:14 **12:13** [a]Ro 15:25; 1Co 16:15; 2Co 9:1; Heb 6:10 [b]Mt 25:35; 1Ti 3:2 [1]Or *holy ones* **12:14** [a]Mt 5:44; Lk 6:28; 1Co 4:12 [1]Two early mss omit *you* **12:15** [a]Job 30:25; Heb 13:3 **12:16** [a]Ro 15:5; 2Co 13:11; Php 2:2; 4:2; 1Pe 3:8 [b]Ro 11:20; 12:3 [c]Pr 3:7; Ro 11:25 [1]Or *accommodate yourself to lowly things* **12:17** [a]Pr 20:22; 24:29; Ro 12:19 [b]2Co 8:21 [1]Lit *take thought for* **12:18** [a]Ro 1:15 [b]Mk 9:50; Ro 14:19 **12:19** [a]Pr 20:22; 24:29; Ro 12:17 [b]Dt 32:35; Ps 94:1; 1Th 4:6; Heb 10:30 [1]Lit *give a place* **12:20** [a]2Ki 6:22; Pr 25:21f; Mt 5:44; Lk 6:27 ◆ **13:1** [a]Ac 2:41 [b]Tit 3:1; 1Pe 2:13f [c]Da 2:21; 4:17; Jn 19:11 [1]Or *soul* [2]Lit *by* **13:2** [1]Lit *he who* **13:3** [a]1Pe 2:14 [1]Lit *good work* **13:4** [a]1Th 4:6 **13:5** [a]Ecc 8; 1Pe 2:13, 19

**7** [a]Render to all what is due them:
[b]tax to whom tax *is due*; [c]custom to
whom custom; fear to whom fear;
honor to whom honor.

**8** Owe nothing to anyone except to
love one another; for [a]he who loves
[1]his neighbor has fulfilled *the* law.
**9** For this, "[a]YOU SHALL NOT COMMIT
ADULTERY, YOU SHALL NOT MURDER, YOU
SHALL NOT STEAL, YOU SHALL NOT COV-
ET," and if there is any other command-
ment, it is summed up in this word,
"[b]YOU SHALL LOVE YOUR NEIGHBOR AS
YOURSELF." **10** Love does not work evil
against a neighbor; therefore [a]love is
the fulfillment of *the* Law.

**11** And *do* this, knowing the time,
that it is [a]already the hour for you to
[b]awaken from sleep; for now [1]salvation
is nearer to us than when we believed.
**12** [a]The night is almost gone, and [b]the
day is at hand. Therefore let us lay aside
[c]the deeds of darkness and put on [d]the
armor of light. **13** Let us [a]walk properly
as in the day, [b]not in carousing and
drunkenness, not in sexual promis-
cuity and sensuality, not in strife and
jealousy. **14** But [a]put on the Lord Jesus
Christ, and make no provision for the
flesh [b]in regard to *its* lusts.

### *Do Not Pass Judgment on One Another*

**14** Now [a]accept the one who is
[b]weak in faith, *but* not for
*the purpose of* passing judgment
on opinions. **2** [a]One person has
faith that he may eat all things, but
he who is [b]weak eats vegetables
*only*. **3** The one who eats must not
[a]view the one who does not eat
with contempt, and the one who
does not eat must not [b]judge the
one who eats, for God [c]accepted
him. **4** [a]Who are you to judge the
[1]servant of another? To his own
[2]master he stands or falls; and he
will stand, for the Lord is able to
make him stand.

**5** [a]One person judges one day
above another, another judges ev-
ery day *alike*. Each person must be
[b]fully convinced in his own mind.
**6** He who regards the day, regards it
for the Lord, and he who eats, eats
for the Lord, for he [a]gives thanks to
God; and he who does not eat, for
the Lord he does not eat and gives
thanks to God. **7** For not one of us
[a]lives for himself, and not one dies
for himself; **8** for if we live, we live
for the Lord, or if we die, we die for
the Lord; therefore [a]whether we live
or die, we are the Lord's. **9** For to this
end [a]Christ died and lived again, that
He might be [b]Lord both of the dead
and of the living.

**10** But you, why do you judge your
brother? Or you again, why do you
[a]view your brother with contempt?

---

**13:7** [a]Mt 22:21; Mk 12:17; Lk 20:25 [b]Lk 20:22; 23:2 [c]Mt 17:25 **13:8** [a]Mt 7:12; 22:39f; Jn 13:34; Ro 13:10; Ga 5:14; Jas 2:8 [1]Lit *the other* **13:9** [a]Ex 20:13ff; Dt 5:17ff [b]Lv 19:18; Mt 19:19 **13:10** [a]Mt 7:12; 22:39f; Jn 13:34; Ro 13:8; Ga 5:14; Jas 2:8 **13:11** [a]1Co 7:29f; 10:11; Jas 5:8; 1Pe 4:7; 2Pe 3:9, 11; 1Jn 2:18; Rev 1:3; 22:10 [b]Mk 13:37; 1Co 15:34; Eph 5:14; 1Th 5:6 [1]Or *our salvation is nearer than when* **13:12** [a]1Co 7:29f; 10:11; Jas 5:8; 1Pe 4:7; 2Pe 3:9, 11; 1Jn 2:18; Rev 1:3; 22:10 [b]Heb 10:25; 1Jn 2:8; Rev 1:3; 22:10 [c]Eph 5:11 [d]2Co 6:7; 10:4; Eph 6:11, 13; 1Th 5:8 **13:13** [a]1Th 4:12 [b]Lk 21:34; Ga 5:21; Eph 5:18; 1Pe 4:3 **13:14** [a]Job 29:14; Ga 3:27; Eph 4:24; Col 3:10, 12 [b]Ga 5:16; 1Pe 2:11 ◆ **14:1** [a]Ac 28:2; Ro 11:15; 14:3; 15:7 [b]Ro 14:2; 15:1; 1Co 8:9ff; 9:22 **14:2** [a]Ro 14:14 [b]Ro 14:1; 15:1; 1Co 8:9ff; 9:22 **14:3** [a]Lk 18:9; Ro 14:10 [b]Ro 14:10, 13; Col 2:16 [c]Ac 28:2; Ro 11:15; 14:1; 15:7 **14:4** [a]Ro 9:20; Jas 4:12 [1]Or *house-servant* [2]Lit *lord* **14:5** [a]Ga 4:10 [b]Lk 1:1; Ro 4:21; 14:23 **14:6** [a]Mt 14:19; 15:36; 1Co 10:30; 1Ti 4:3f **14:7** [a]Ro 8:38f; 2Co 5:15; Ga 2:20; Php 1:20f **14:8** [a]Lk 20:38; Php 1:20; 1Th 5:10; Rev 14:13 **14:9** [a]Rev 1:18; 2:8 [b]Mt 28:18; Jn 12:24; Php 2:11; 1Th 5:10 **14:10** [a]Lk 18:9; Ro 14:3

For [b]we will all stand before the judgment seat of God. **11** For it is written,

"[a]As I LIVE, SAYS THE [1]LORD,
[b]TO ME EVERY KNEE SHALL BOW,
AND EVERY TONGUE SHALL
CONFESS TO GOD."

**12** So then [a]each one of us will give an account of himself to God.

**13** Therefore let us not [a]judge one another anymore, but rather judge this—[b]not to put a stumbling block or offense before a brother. **14** I know and am convinced [1]in the Lord Jesus that [a]nothing is defiled in itself; but to him who [b]considers anything to be defiled, to him it is defiled. **15** For if because of food your brother is grieved, you are no longer [a]walking according to love. [b]Do not destroy with your food him for whom Christ died. **16** Therefore [a]do not let what is for you a good thing be [1]slandered; **17** for the kingdom of God [a]is not eating and drinking, but righteousness and [b]peace and [b]joy in the Holy Spirit. **18** For he who in this *way* [a]serves Christ is [b]pleasing to God and approved by men. **19** So then [1]let us [a]pursue the things which make for peace and the [b]building up of one another. **20** [a]Do not tear down the work of God for the sake of food. [b]All things indeed are clean, but [c]they are evil for the man who eats [1]and gives offense. **21** [a]It is good not to eat meat or to drink wine, or *to do anything* by which your brother stumbles. **22** The faith which you have, have [1]as your own conviction before God. Blessed is he who [a]does not judge himself in what he approves. **23** But [a]he who doubts is condemned if he eats, because *his eating is* not from faith; and whatever is not from faith is sin.

### *Bearing the Weaknesses of Others*

**15** Now we who are strong ought to bear the weaknesses of [a]those without strength and not *just* please ourselves. **2** Each of us is to [a]please his neighbor [1]for his good, to his [b]building up. **3** For even [a]Christ did not please Himself; but as it is written, "[b]THE REPROACHES OF THOSE WHO REPROACHED YOU FELL ON ME." **4** For [a]whatever was written in earlier times was written for our instruction, so that through the perseverance and the encouragement of the Scriptures we might have hope. **5** Now may the [a]God of perseverance and encouragement grant you [b]to be of the same mind with one another according to Christ Jesus, **6** so that with one accord you may with one [1]voice glorify [a]the God and Father of our Lord Jesus Christ.

### *Christ, the Hope of Jews and Gentiles*

**7** Therefore, [a]accept one another, just as Christ also accepted [1]us to the glory of God. **8** For I say that Christ

---

**14:10** [b]Ro 2:16; 2Co 5:10 **14:11** [a]Is 45:23 [b]Php 2:10f [1]In OT, Yahweh, cf. Is 45:23 **14:12** [a]Mt 12:36; 16:27; 1Pe 4:5 **14:13** [a]Mt 7:1; Ro 14:3 [b]1Co 8:13 **14:14** [a]Ac 10:15; Ro 14:2, 20 [b]1Co 8:7 [1]Lit *through* **14:15** [a]Eph 5:2 [b]Ro 14:20; 1Co 8:11 **14:16** [a]1Co 10:30; Tit 2:5 [1]Or *blasphemed* **14:17** [a]1Co 8:8 [b]Ro 15:13; Ga 5:22 **14:18** [a]Ro 16:18 [b]2Co 8:21; Php 4:8; 1Pe 2:12 **14:19** [a]Ps 34:14; Ro 12:18; 1Co 7:15; 2Ti 2:22; Heb 12:14 [b]Ro 15:2; 1Co 10:23; 14:3f, 26; 2Co 12:19; Eph 4:12, 29 [1]Some mss *we pursue* **14:20** [a]Ro 14:15 [b]Ac 10:15; Ro 14:2, 14 [c]1Co 8:9-12 [1]Lit *through stumbling*, cf. 14:13, 21 **14:21** [a]1Co 8:13 **14:22** [a]1Jn 3:21 [1]Lit *according to yourself* **14:23** [a]Ro 14:5 ◆**15:1** [a]Ro 14:1; Ga 6:2; 1Th 5:14 **15:2** [a]1Co 9:22; 10:24, 33; 2Co 13:9 [b]Ro 14:19; 1Co 10:23; 14:3f, 26; 2Co 12:19; Eph 4:12, 29 [1]Lit *for what is good to edification* **15:3** [a]2Co 8:9 [b]Ps 69:9 **15:4** [a]Ro 4:23f; 2Ti 3:16 **15:5** [a]2Co 1:3 [b]Ro 12:16 **15:6** [a]Rev 1:6 [1]Lit *mouth* **15:7** [a]Ro 14:1 [1]One early ms *you*

has become a servant to [a]the cir-
cumcision on behalf of the truth of
God to confirm [b]the promises *given*
to the fathers, **9** and for [a]the Gentiles
to [b]glorify God for His mercy; as it is
written,

"[c]THEREFORE I WILL [1]GIVE PRAISE
TO YOU AMONG THE GENTILES,
AND I WILL SING
TO YOUR NAME."

**10** And again he says,

"[a]REJOICE, O GENTILES,
WITH HIS PEOPLE."

**11** And again,

"[a]PRAISE THE [1]LORD ALL
YOU GENTILES,
AND LET ALL THE PEOPLES
PRAISE HIM."

**12** And again Isaiah says,

"[a]THERE SHALL COME
[b]THE ROOT OF JESSE,
AND HE WHO ARISES TO RULE
OVER THE GENTILES,
[c]IN HIM SHALL THE
GENTILES HOPE."

**13** Now may the God of hope fill you
with all [a]joy and peace in believing,
so that you will abound in hope [b]by
the power of the Holy Spirit.

### *Paul's Ministry Plans*

**14** But I myself am also convinced
about you, my brothers, that you
yourselves are full of [a]goodness,
having been filled with [b]all knowl-
edge and being able also to admonish
one another. **15** But I have written
very boldly to you on some points
so as to remind you again, because of
[a]the grace that was given me [1]by God
**16** for me to be [a]a minister of Christ
Jesus to the Gentiles, ministering as a
priest the [b]gospel of God, so that *my*
[c]offering of the Gentiles may become
acceptable, having been sanctified by
the Holy Spirit. **17** Therefore in Christ
Jesus I have [a]reason for boasting in
[b]things pertaining to God. **18** For I
will not be bold to speak of anything
[1]except what [a]Christ has brought
about through me, [2]leading to the
obedience of the Gentiles by word
and deed, **19** in the power of [a,1]signs
and wonders, [b]in the power of the
Spirit; so that [c]from Jerusalem and
all around as [d]far as Illyricum I have
[2]fully preached the gospel of Christ.
**20** And in this way I make it my am-
bition to [a]proclaim the gospel, not
where Christ was *already* named, [b]so
that I would not build on another
man's foundation; **21** but as it is
written,

"[a]THEY WHO HAD NO
DECLARATION OF HIM
SHALL SEE,
AND THEY WHO HAVE NOT
HEARD SHALL UNDERSTAND."

**22** For this reason [a]I have often
been prevented from coming to you;
**23** but now, with no further place
for me in these regions, and since I
[a]have had for many years a longing
to come to you **24** whenever I [a]go to
Spain—for I hope, passing through,
to see you, and to be [b]helped on my

---

**15:8** [a]Mt 15:24; Ac 3:26 [b]Ro 4:16; 2Co 1:20 **15:9** [a]Ro 3:29; 11:30f [b]Mt 9:8 [c]2Sa 22:50; Ps 18:49 [1]Or *confess* **15:10** [a]Dt 32:43 **15:11** [a]Ps 117:1 [1]In OT, Yahweh, cf. Ps 117:1 **15:12** [a]Is 11:10 [b]Rev 5:5; 22:16 [c]Mt 12:21 **15:13** [a]Ro 14:17 [b]Ro 15:19; 1Co 2:4; 1Th 1:5 **15:14** [a]Eph 5:9; 2Th 1:11 [b]1Co 1:5; 8:1, 7, 10; 12:8; 13:2 **15:15** [a]Ro 12:3 [1]Some early mss *from* **15:16** [a]Ac 9:15; Ro 11:13 [b]Ro 1:1; 15:19, 20 [c]Ro 12:1; Eph 5:2; Php 2:17 **15:17** [a]Php 3:3 [b]Heb 2:17; 5:1 **15:18** [a]Ac 15:12; 21:19; Ro 1:5; 2Co 3:5 [1]Lit *which Christ has not accomplished* [2]Lit *to the obedience* **15:19** [a]Jn 4:48 [b]Ro 15:13; 1Co 2:4; 1Th 1:5 [c]Ac 22:17-21 [d]Ac 20:1f [1]Or *attesting miracles* [2]Lit *fulfilled* **15:20** [a]Ro 1:15; 10:15; 15:16 [b]1Co 3:10; 2Co 10:15f **15:21** [a]Is 52:15 **15:22** [a]Ro 1:13; 1Th 2:18 **15:23** [a]Ac 19:21; Ro 1:10f; 15:29, 32 **15:24** [a]Ro 15:28 [b]Ac 15:3

way there by you, when I have first
[c]enjoyed your company [1]for a while.
**25** But now [a]I am going to Jerusalem to
[b]serve the [1]saints. **26** For [a]Macedonia
and [b]Achaia were pleased to [1]share
with the poor among the saints in
Jerusalem. **27** Yes, they were pleased
*to do so,* and they are indebted
to them. For [a]if the Gentiles have
shared in their spiritual things, they
are indebted to minister to them also
in material things. **28** Therefore,
when I have completed this and
[a]have [1]put my seal on this fruit of
theirs, I will [b]go on by way of you
to Spain. **29** And I know that when
[a]I come to you, I will come in the
fullness of the blessing of Christ.

**30** Now I urge you, brothers, by
our Lord Jesus Christ and by [a]the
love of the Spirit, to [b]strive together
with me in your prayers to God for
me, **31** that I may be [a]rescued from
those who are disobedient in Judea,
and *that* my [b]service for Jerusalem
may prove acceptable to the [c,1]saints;
**32** so that [a]I may come to you in joy
by [b]the will of God and find rest in
your company. **33** Now may [a]the God
of peace be with you all. Amen.

### Final Instructions and Greetings

**16** Now I [a]commend to you our
sister Phoebe, who is a [1]servant
of the church which is at [b]Cenchrea;
**2** that you [a]receive her in the Lord in
a manner worthy of the [b,1]saints, and
that you help her in whatever matter
she may have need of you; for she
herself has also been a benefactor of
many, [2]and of myself as well.

**3** Greet [a]Prisca and Aquila,
my fellow workers [b]in
[c]Christ Jesus,
**4** who for my life risked their
own necks, to whom not only
do I give thanks, but also all
the churches of the Gentiles;
**5** also *greet* [a]the church that is
in their house.
Greet Epaenetus, my beloved,
who is the [b]first convert to
Christ from [c,1]Asia.
**6** Greet Mary, who has labored
much for you.
**7** Greet Andronicus and
[1]Junia, my [a]kinsmen and my
[b]fellow prisoners, who are
outstanding to the apostles,
who also [2]were [c]in Christ
before me.
**8** Greet Ampliatus, my beloved
in the Lord.
**9** Greet Urbanus, our fellow
worker [a]in Christ, and Stachys
my beloved.
**10** Greet Apelles, the approved [a]in
Christ. Greet those who are of
the *household* of Aristobulus.
**11** Greet Herodion, my [a]kinsman.
Greet those of the *household* of
Narcissus, who are in the Lord.

**15:24** [c]Ro 1:12 [1]Lit *in part* **15:25** [a]Ac 19:21 [b]Ac 24:17 [1]Or *holy ones* **15:26** [a]Ac 16:9; 1Co 16:5; 2Co 1:16; 2:13; 7:5; 8:1; 9:2, 4; 11:9; Php 4:15; 1Th 1:7f; 4:10; 1Ti 1:3 [b]Ac 18:12; 19:21 [1]Lit *make fellowship* **15:27** [a]1Co 9:11 **15:28** [a]Jn 3:33 [b]Ro 15:24 [1]Lit *sealed to them this fruit* **15:29** [a]Ac 19:21; Ro 1:10f; 15:23, 32 **15:30** [a]Ga 5:22; Col 1:8 [b]2Co 1:11; Col 4:12 **15:31** [a]2Co 1:10; 2Th 3:2; 2Ti 3:11; 4:17 [b]Ro 15:25f; 2Co 8:4; 9:1 [c]Ac 9:13, 15 [1]Or *holy ones* **15:32** [a]Ro 15:23 [b]Ac 18:21; Ro 1:10 **15:33** [a]Ro 16:20; 2Co 13:11; Php 4:9; 1Th 5:23; 2Th 3:16; Heb 13:20 ◆ **16:1** [a]2Co 3:1 [b]Ac 18:18 [1]Or *deaconess* **16:2** [a]Php 2:29 [b]Ac 9:13, 15 [1]Or *holy ones* [2]Lit *and of me, myself* **16:3** [a]Ac 18:2 [b]Ro 8:11ff; 16:7, 9, 10; 2Co 5:17; 12:2; Ga 1:22 [c]Ro 8:1 **16:5** [a]1Co 16:19; Col 4:15; Phm 2 [b]1Co 16:15 [c]Ac 16:6 [1]West coast province of Asia Minor **16:7** [a]Ro 9:3; 16:11, 21 [b]Col 4:10; Phm 23 [c]Ro 8:11ff; 16:3, 9, 10; 2Co 5:17; 12:2; Ga 1:22 [1]Or *Junias* [2]Lit *have become* **16:9** [a]Ro 8:11ff; 16:3, 7, 10; 2Co 5:17; 12:2; Ga 1:22 **16:10** [a]Ro 8:11ff; 16:3, 7, 9; 2Co 5:17; 12:2; Ga 1:22 **16:11** [a]Ro 9:3; 16:7, 21

12 Greet Tryphaena and
Tryphosa, laborers in the Lord.
Greet Persis the beloved, who
labored much in the Lord.
13 Greet [a]Rufus, a choice man
in the Lord, also his mother
and mine.
14 Greet Asyncritus, Phlegon,
Hermes, Patrobas, Hermas
and the brothers with them.
15 Greet Philologus and Julia,
Nereus and his sister, and
Olympas, and all [a]the [1]saints
who are with them.
16 [a]Greet one another with
a holy kiss.
All the churches of Christ
greet you.

17 Now I urge you, brothers, to keep
your eye on those who cause dissen-
sions and stumblings [a]contrary to
the teaching which you learned, and
[b]turn away from them. 18 For such
men are [a]slaves, not of our Lord
Christ but of [b]their own [1]stomach,
and by their [c]smooth and flattering
speech they deceive the hearts of
the unsuspecting. 19 For the report
of your obedience [a]has reached to
all. Therefore I am rejoicing over you,
but [b]I want you to be wise in what is
good and innocent in what is evil.
20 [a]And the God of peace will soon
crush [b]Satan under your feet.

[c]The grace of our Lord Jesus be
with you.

21 [a]Timothy my fellow worker
greets you, and *so do* [b]Lucius and
[c]Jason and [d]Sosipater, my [e]kinsmen.
22 I, Tertius, who [a]wrote this letter,
greet you in the Lord.
23 [a]Gaius, host to me and to the
whole church, greets you. [b]Erastus,
the city treasurer greets you, and
Quartus, the brother. 24 [1][The grace
of our Lord Jesus Christ be with you
all. Amen.]

25 [a]Now to Him who is able to
strengthen you [b]according to my
gospel and the preaching of Jesus
Christ, according to the revelation
of [c]the mystery which has been kept
secret for [d]long ages past, 26 but now
is manifested, and by [a]the Scriptures
of the prophets, according to the
commandment of the eternal God,
has been made known to all the Gen-
tiles, *leading* to [b]obedience of faith;
27 to the only wise God, through Jesus
Christ, [a]be the glory forever. Amen.

**16:13** [a]Mk 15:21 **16:15** [a]Ro 16:2, 14 [1]v 2, note 1 **16:16** [a]1Co 16:20; 2Co 13:12; 1Th 5:26; 1Pe 5:14
**16:17** [a]1Ti 1:3; 6:3 [b]Mt 7:15; Ga 1:8f; 2Th 3:6, 14; Tit 3:10; 2Jn 10 **16:18** [a]Ro 14:18 [b]Php 3:19 [c]Col 2:4; 2Pe 2:3 [1]Lit *belly* **16:19** [a]Ro 1:8 [b]Jer 4:22; Mt 10:16; 1Co 14:20 **16:20** [a]Ro 15:33 [b]Mt 4:10 [c]1Co 16:23; 2Co 13:14; Ga 6:18; Php 4:23; 1Th 5:28; 2Th 3:18; Rev 22:21 **16:21** [a]Ac 16:1 [b][Ac 13:1] [c][Ac 17:5] [d][Ac 20:4] [e]Ro 9:3; 16:7, 11 **16:22** [a]1Co 16:21; Ga 6:11; Col 4:18; 2Th 3:17; Phm 19 **16:23** [a][Ac 19:29; 20:4]; 1Co 1:14 [b]Ac 19:22; 2Ti 4:20 **16:24** [1]Early mss omit this v **16:25** [a]Eph 3:20; Jd 24 [b]Ro 2:16 [c]Mt 13:35; Ro 11:25; 1Co 2:1, 7; 4:1; Eph 1:9; 3:3, 9; 6:19; Col 1:26f; 2:2; 4:3; 1Ti 3:16 [d]2Ti 1:9; Tit 1:2 **16:26** [a]Ro 1:2 [b]Ro 1:5
**16:27** [a]Ro 11:36

The First Letter of Paul to the

# CORINTHIANS

### Christ Is Undivided

1 Paul, [a]called *as* an apostle of Jesus
Christ [1]by [b]the will of God, and
[c]Sosthenes our [d]brother,
2 To [a]the church of God which is
at [b]Corinth, to those who have been
sanctified in Christ Jesus, [c]called as
[1]saints, with all who in every place
[d]call on the name of our Lord Jesus
Christ, their *Lord* and ours:
3 [a]Grace to you and peace from God
our Father and the Lord Jesus Christ.
4 [a]I thank [1]my God always concern-
ing you for the grace of God which
was given you in Christ Jesus, 5 that
in everything you were [a]enriched in
Him, in all [b]word and [b]all knowledge,
6 even as [a]the witness about Christ
was confirmed [1]in you, 7 so that you
are not lacking in any gift, [a]eagerly
awaiting the revelation of our Lord
Jesus Christ, 8 [a]who will also confirm
you to the end, beyond reproach in
[b]the day of our Lord Jesus Christ.
9 [a]God is faithful, through whom
you were [b]called into [c]fellowship
with His Son, Jesus Christ our Lord.
10 Now [a]I exhort you, [b]brothers,
by the name of our Lord Jesus Christ,
that you all [1]agree and that there be
no [c,2]divisions among you, but that
you be [3]made complete in [d]the same
mind and in the same judgment. 11 For
I have been informed concerning
you, my brothers, by Chloe's *people*,
that there are quarrels among you.
12 Now I mean this, that [a]each one
of you is saying, "I am of Paul," and
"I of [b]Apollos," and "I of [c]Cephas,"
and "I of Christ." 13 [1]Has Christ
been divided? Was Paul crucified
for you? Or were you [a]baptized [2]in
the name of Paul? 14 [1]I thank God
that I [a]baptized none of you except
[a]Crispus and [b]Gaius, 15 so that no
one would say you were baptized
[1]in my name. 16 Now I did baptize
also the [a]household of Stephanas;
beyond that, I do not know whether
I baptized any other. 17 [a]For Christ
did not send me to baptize, but to
proclaim the gospel, [b]not in wisdom
of word, so that the cross of Christ
will not be made empty.

### Christ the Power and Wisdom of God

18 For the word of the cross is [a]fool-
ishness to [b]those who [1]are perishing,
but to us who [2]are being saved, it is
[c]the power of God. 19 For it is written,

"[a]I WILL DESTROY THE
WISDOM OF THE WISE,
AND THE CLEVERNESS OF THE
CLEVER I WILL SET ASIDE."

---

◆ **1:1** [a]Ro 1:1 [b]Ro 1:10; 2Ti 1:1 [c]Ac 18:17 [d]Ac 1:15 [1]Lit *through* **1:2** [a]1Co 10:32 [b]Ac 18:1 [c]Ro 1:7; 8:28 [d]Ac 7:59 [1]Or *holy ones* **1:3** [a]Ro 1:7 **1:4** [a]Ro 1:8 [1]Two early mss omit *my* **1:5** [a]2Co 9:11 [b]Ro 15:14; 2Co 8:7 **1:6** [a]2Th 1:10; 1Ti 2:6; 2Ti 1:8; Rev 1:2 [1]Or *among* **1:7** [a]Lk 17:30; Ro 8:19, 23; Php 3:20; 2Pe 3:12 **1:8** [a]Ro 8:19; Php 1:6; Col 2:7; 1Th 3:13; 5:23 [b]Lk 17:24, 30; 1Co 5:5; 2Co 1:14; Php 1:6, 10; 2:16; 1Th 5:2; 2Th 2:2 **1:9** [a]Dt 7:9; Is 49:7; 1Co 10:13; 2Co 1:18; 1Th 5:24; 2Th 3:3 [b]Ro 8:28 [c]1Jn 1:3 **1:10** [a]Ro 12:1 [b]Ro 1:13 [c]1Co 11:18 [d]Ro 12:16; Php 1:27 [1]Lit *speak the same thing* [2]Lit *schisms* [3]Or *united* **1:12** [a]Mt 23:8-10; 1Co 3:4 [b]Ac 18:24; 1Co 3:22 [c]Jn 1:42; 1Co 3:22; 9:5; 15:5 **1:13** [a]Mt 28:19; Ac 2:38 [1]Or *Christ has been divided!* or *Christ is divided!* [2]Lit *into* **1:14** [a]Ac 18:8 [b]Ro 16:23 [1]Two early mss *I give thanks that* **1:15** [1]Lit *into* **1:16** [a]1Co 16:15, 17 **1:17** [a]Jn 4:2; Ac 10:48 [b]1Co 2:1, 4, 13; 2Co 10:10; 11:6 **1:18** [a]1Co 1:21, 23, 25; 2:14; 4:10 [b]Ac 2:47; 2Co 2:15; 4:3; 2Th 2:10 [c]Ro 1:16; 1Co 1:24 [1]Or *perish* [2]Or *are saved* **1:19** [a]Is 29:14

**20** [a]Where is the wise man? Where is
the scribe? Where is the debater of
[b]this age? Has not God [c]made fool-
ish the wisdom of [d]the world? **21** For
since, in the wisdom of God, [a]the
world through its wisdom did not
*come to* know God, [b]God was well-
pleased, through the [c]foolishness of
the [1]message preached, to [d]save those
who believe. **22** For indeed [a]Jews
ask for [1]signs and Greeks search for
wisdom, **23** but we preach [a,1]Christ
crucified, [b]to Jews a stumbling block
and to Gentiles [c]foolishness, **24** but to
those who are [a]the called, both Jews
and Greeks, Christ [b]the power of God
and [c]the wisdom of God. **25** Because
the [a]foolishness of God is wiser than
men, and [b]the weakness of God is
stronger than men.

**26** For [1]consider your [a]calling,
brothers, that there were [b]not many
wise according to [2]the flesh, not
many mighty, not many noble. **27** But
[a]God has chosen the foolish things
of [b]the world to shame the wise, and
God has chosen the weak things of
[b]the world to shame the things which
are strong, **28** and the base things of
[a]the world and the despised God has
chosen, [b]the things that are not, so
that He may [c]abolish the things that
are, **29** so that [a]no flesh may boast
before God. **30** But by His doing you
are in [a]Christ Jesus, who became
to us [b]wisdom from God, [1]and
[c]righteousness and [d]sanctification,
and [e]redemption, **31** so that, just as
it is written, "[a]LET HIM WHO BOASTS,
BOAST IN THE [1]LORD."

### *Paul's Reliance upon the Spirit*

**2** And when I came to you,
brothers, I [a]did not come with
superiority of word or of wisdom,
proclaiming to you [b]the [1]witness
of God. **2** For I determined to know
nothing among you except [a]Jesus
Christ, and Him crucified. **3** And I
was with you in [a]weakness and in
[b]fear and in much trembling, **4** and
my word and my preaching were [a]not
in persuasive words of wisdom, but
in demonstration of [b]the Spirit and
of power, **5** so that your faith would
not be in the wisdom of men, but in
[a]the power of God.

**6** Yet we do speak wisdom among
those who are [a]mature, a wisdom,
however, not of [b]this age nor of the
rulers of [b]this age, who are [c]being
abolished. **7** But we speak God's
wisdom in a [a]mystery, the *wisdom*
which has been hidden, which God
[b]predestined before the [c]ages to our
glory, **8** [a]which none of the rulers of
[b]this age has understood; for if they
had understood it, they would not
have crucified [c]the Lord of glory.
**9** But just as it is written,

---

**1:20** [a]Job 12:17; Is 19:11f; 33:18 [b]Mt 13:22; 1Co 2:6, 8; 3:18, 19 [c]Ro 1:20ff [d]Jn 12:31; 1Co 1:27f; 6:2; 11:32; Jas 4:4 **1:21** [a]Jn 12:31; 1Co 1:27f; 6:2; 11:32; Jas 4:4 [b]Lk 12:32; Ga 1:15; Col 1:19 [c]1Co 1:18, 23, 25; 2:14; 4:10 [d]Ro 11:14; Jas 5:20 [1]Lit *preaching* **1:22** [a]Mt 12:38 [1]Or *attesting miracles* **1:23** [a]1Co 2:2; Ga 3:1; 5:11 [b]Lk 2:34; 1Pe 2:8 [c]1Co 1:18, 21, 25; 2:14; 4:10 [1]Messiah **1:24** [a]Ro 8:28 [b]Ro 1:16; 1Co 1:18 [c]Lk 11:49; 1Co 1:30 **1:25** [a]1Co 1:18, 21, 23; 2:14; 4:10 [b]2Co 13:4 **1:26** [a]Ro 11:29 [b]Mt 11:25; 1Co 1:20; 2:8 [1]Lit *see* [2]*Human standards* **1:27** [a]*Jas 2:5* [b]1Co 1:20 **1:28** [a]1Co 1:20 [b]Ro 4:17 [c]Job 34:19; 1Co 2:6; 2Th 2:8; Heb 2:14 **1:29** [a]Eph 2:9 **1:30** [a]Ro 8:1; 1Co 4:15 [b]1Co 1:24 [c]Jer 23:5f; 33:16; 2Co 5:21; Php 3:9 [d]1Co 1:2; 6:11; 1Th 5:23 [e]Ro 3:24; Eph 1:7, 14; Col 1:14 [1]Or *both* **1:31** [a]Jer 9:23f; 2Co 10:17 [1]In OT, Yahweh, cf. Jer 9:24
◆ **2:1** [a]1Co 1:17; 2:4, 13 [b]1Co 2:7 [1]Some early mss *mystery* **2:2** [a]1Co 1:23; Ga 6:14 **2:3** [a]1Co 4:10; 2Co 11:30; 12:5, 9f; 13:9 [b]Is 19:16; 2Co 7:15; Eph 6:5 **2:4** [a]1Co 1:17; 2:1, 13 [b]Ro 15:19; 1Co 4:20 **2:5** [a]2Co 4:7; 6:7; 12:9 **2:6** [a]Eph 4:13; Php 3:15; Heb 5:14; 6:1 [b]Mt 13:22; 1Co 1:20 [c]1Co 1:28 **2:7** [a]Ro 11:25; 16:25f; 1Co 2:1 [b]Ro 8:29f [c]Heb 1:2; 11:3 **2:8** [a]1Co 1:26; 2:6 [b]Mt 13:22; 1Co 1:20 [c]Ac 7:2; Jas 2:1

"[a]THINGS WHICH EYE HAS
NOT SEEN AND EAR
HAS NOT HEARD,
AND *which* HAVE NOT
ENTERED THE HEART
OF MAN,
ALL THAT GOD HAS PREPARED
FOR THOSE WHO LOVE HIM."
**10** [a,1]But to us God revealed *them*
[b]through the Spirit, for the Spirit
searches all things, even the [c]depths
of God. **11** For who among men knows
the *depths* of a man except the [a]spirit
of the man which is in him? Even
so the *depths* of God no one knows
except the Spirit of God. **12** Now we
[a]have received, not the spirit of [b]the
world, but the Spirit who is from
God, so that we may know the *depths*
graciously given to us by God, **13** of
which *depths* we also speak, [a]not
in words taught by human wisdom,
but in those taught by the Spirit,
[1]combining spiritual *depths* with
spiritual *words.*
**14** But [1]a [a]natural man [b]does not
accept the *depths* of the Spirit of God,
for they are [c]foolishness to him, and
he cannot understand them, because
[d]they are spiritually examined. **15** But
he who is [a]spiritual examines all
things, yet he himself is examined
by no one. **16** For [a]WHO HAS KNOWN
THE MIND OF THE [1]LORD, THAT HE WILL
DIRECT HIM? But [b]we have the mind
of Christ.

### *Jesus Christ, Our Foundation*

**3** And I, brothers, was not able to
speak to you as to [a]spiritual men,
but as to [b]fleshly men, as to [c]infants
in Christ. **2** I gave you [a]milk to drink,
not solid food, for you [b]were not yet
able *to receive it.* Indeed, even now
you are still not able, **3** for you are still
fleshly. For since there is [a]jealousy
and strife among you, are you not
fleshly, and are you not walking [b,1]like
mere men? **4** For when [a]one says, "I
am of Paul," and another, "I am of
Apollos," are you not *mere* [b]men?
**5** What then is Apollos? And what
is Paul? [a]Servants through whom
you believed, even [b]as the Lord gave
to each one. **6** [a]I planted, [b]Apollos
watered, but [c]God was causing the
growth. **7** So then neither the one
who plants nor the one who waters
is anything, but God who causes the
growth. **8** Now he who plants and he
who waters are one, but each will
[a]receive his own [1]reward according
to his own labor. **9** For we are God's
[a]fellow workers; you are God's [b,1]field,
God's [c]building.
**10** According to [a]the grace of God
which was given to me, like a wise
master builder [b]I laid a foundation,
and [c]another is building on it. But
each man must be careful how he
builds on it. **11** For no one can lay a
[a]foundation other than the one which
is laid, which is Jesus Christ. **12** Now

**2:9** [a]Is 64:4; 65:17 **2:10** [a]Mt 11:25; 13:11; 16:17; Ga 1:12; Eph 3:3, 5 [b]Jn 14:26 [c]Ro 11:33ff [1]Some early mss *For* **2:11** [a]Pr 20:27 **2:12** [a]Ro 8:15 [b]1Co 1:27 **2:13** [a]1Co 1:17; 2:1, 4 [1]Or *interpreting spiritual things for spiritual* men **2:14** [a]1Co 15:44, 46; Jas 3:15; Jd 19 mg [b]Jn 14:17 [c]1Co 1:18 [d]Ac 17:11 [1]Or *an unspiritual* **2:15** [a]1Co 3:1; 14:37; Ga 6:1 **2:16** [a]Is 40:13; Ro 11:34 [b]Jn 15:15 [1]In OT, Yahweh, cf. Is 40:13 ◆ **3:1** [a]1Co 2:15; 14:37; Ga 6:1 [b]Ro 7:14; 1Co 2:14 [c]1Co 2:6; Eph 4:14; Heb 5:13 **3:2** [a]Heb 5:12f; 1Pe 2:2 [b]Jn 16:12 **3:3** [a]Ro 13:13; 1Co 1:10f; 11:18 [b]1Co 3:4 [1]Lit *according to man* **3:4** [a]1Co 1:12 [b]1Co 3:3 **3:5** [a]Ro 15:16; 2Co 3:3, 6; 4:1; 5:18; 6:4; Eph 3:7; Col 1:25; 1Ti 1:12 [b]Ro 12:6; 1Co 3:10 **3:6** [a]1Co 4:15; 9:1; 15:1; 2Co 10:14f [b]Ac 18:24-27; 1Co 1:12 [c]1Co 15:10 **3:8** [a]1Co 3:14; 4:5; 9:17; Ga 6:4 [1]Or *wages* **3:9** [a]Mk 16:20; 2Co 6:1 [b]Is 61:3; Mt 15:13 [c]1Co 3:16; Eph 2:20-22; Col 2:7; 1Pe 2:5 [1]Or *cultivated land* **3:10** [a]Ro 12:3; 1Co 15:10 [b]Ro 15:20; 1Co 3:11f [c]1Th 3:2 **3:11** [a]Is 28:16; Eph 2:20; 1Pe 2:4ff

if anyone builds on the foundation with gold, silver, [1]precious stones, wood, hay, straw, **13** [a]each man's work will become evident, for [b]the day will indicate it because it is revealed with fire, and the fire itself will test [1]the quality of each man's work. **14** If any man's work which he has built on it remains, he will [a]receive a reward. **15** If any man's work is burned up, he will suffer loss, but he himself will be saved, yet [a]so as through fire.

**16** [a]Do you not know that [b]you are a [1]sanctuary of God and *that* the Spirit of God dwells in you? **17** If any man destroys the [1]sanctuary of God, God will destroy him, for the [1]sanctuary of God is holy, and [2]that is what you are.

**18** [a]Let no man deceive himself. [b]If any man among you thinks that he is wise in [c]this age, he must become foolish, so that he may become wise. **19** For [a]the wisdom of this world is foolishness before God. For it is written, "*He is* [b]THE ONE WHO CATCHES THE WISE IN THEIR CRAFTINESS"; **20** and again, "[a]THE LORD KNOWS THE REASONINGS of the wise, THAT THEY ARE USELESS." **21** So then [a]let no one boast in men. For [b]all things belong to you, **22** [a]whether Paul or Apollos or Cephas or the world or [b]life or death or things present or things to come; all things belong to you, **23** and [a]you belong to Christ, and [b]Christ belongs to God.

### *Servants of Christ*

**4** Let a man consider us in this manner, as [a]servants of Christ and [b]stewards of [c]the mysteries of God. **2** In this case, moreover, it is required [1]of stewards that one be found faithful. **3** But to me it is a very small thing that I may be examined by you, or by *any* human [1]court. In fact, I do not even examine myself. **4** For I [a]am conscious of nothing against myself, yet I am not by this [b]acquitted. But the one who examines me is the Lord. **5** Therefore [a]do not go on [1]passing judgment before [2]the time, *but wait* [b]until the Lord comes who will both [c]bring to light the things hidden in the darkness and make manifest the motives of hearts. And then each one's [d]praise will come to him from God.

**6** Now these things, brothers, I have applied to myself and Apollos for your sakes, so that in us you may learn not to go beyond [a]what is written, so that no one of you will [b]become puffed up [c]on behalf of one against the other. **7** For who regards you as superior? [a]What do you have that you did not receive? And if you did receive it, why do you boast as if you had not received it?

**8** You are [a]already filled, you have already become rich, you have ruled without us—and *how I* wish that you had ruled indeed so that we also might rule with you. **9** For, I think that

**3:12** [1]Or *costly* **3:13** [a]1Co 4:5 [b]Mt 10:15; 1Co 1:8; 2Th 1:7-10; 2Ti 1:12, 18; 4:8 [1]Lit *of what sort each man's work is* **3:14** [a]1Co 3:8; 4:5; 9:17; Ga 6:4 **3:15** [a]Job 23:10; Ps 66:10, 12; Jd 23 **3:16** [a]Ro 6:16 [b]Ro 8:9; 1Co 6:19; 2Co 6:16; Eph 2:21f [1]The inner part of the temple **3:17** [1]The inner part of the temple [2]Lit *who you are* **3:18** [a]Is 5:21 [b]1Co 8:2; Ga 6:3 [c]1Co 1:20 **3:19** [a]1Co 1:20 [b]Job 5:13 **3:20** [a]Ps 94:11 **3:21** [a]1Co 4:6 [b]Ro 8:32 **3:22** [a]1Co 1:12; 3:5, 6 [b]Ro 8:38 **3:23** [a]1Co 15:23; 2Co 10:7; Ga 3:29 [b]1Co 11:3; 15:28 ◆ **4:1** [a]Lk 1:2 [b]1Co 9:17; Tit 1:7; 1Pe 4:10 [c]Ro 11:25; 16:25 **4:2** [1]Lit *in* **4:3** [1]Lit *day* **4:4** [a]Ac 23:1; 2Co 1:12 [b]Ps 143:2; Ro 2:13 **4:5** [a]Mt 7:1; Ro 2:1 [b]Jn 21:22; Ro 2:16 [c]1Co 3:13 [d]Ro 2:29; 1Co 3:8; 2Co 10:18 [1]Lit *judging anything* [2]The appointed time of judgment **4:6** [a]1Co 1:19, 31; 3:19f [b]1Co 4:18f; 8:1; 13:4 [c]1Co 1:12; 3:4 **4:7** [a]Jn 3:27; Ro 12:3, 6; 1Pe 4:10 **4:8** [a]Rev 3:17f

God has exhibited us apostles last of
all, as men [a]condemned to death, be-
cause we [b]have become a spectacle to
the world, and to angels, and to men.
**10** We are [a]fools for the sake of Christ,
but [b]you are prudent in Christ! [c]We
are weak, but you are strong! You are
glorious, but we are without honor!
**11** To this present hour we [a]hunger
and thirst, and are poorly clothed,
and roughly treated, and homeless;
**12** and we labor, [a]working with our
own hands; when we are [b]reviled, we
bless; when we are [c]persecuted, we
endure; **13** when we are slandered,
we try to plead; we have [a]become as
the scum of the world, the grime of
all things, *even* until now.

**14** I do not write these things to
[a]shame you, but to admonish you
as my beloved [b]children. **15** For if
you were to have countless [a]tutors
in Christ, yet *you would* not *have*
many fathers, for in [b]Christ Jesus
I [c]became your father through the
[d]gospel. **16** Therefore I exhort you, be
[a]imitators of me. **17** For this reason I
[a]have sent to you [b]Timothy, who is
my [c]beloved and faithful child in the
Lord, and who will remind you of my
ways which are in Christ, [d]just as I
teach everywhere in every church.
**18** Now some have become [a]puffed
up, as though I were not [b]coming
to you. **19** But I [a]will come to you
soon, [b]*if* the Lord wills, and I shall
know, not the [1]words of those who
are [c]puffed up but their power. **20** For
the kingdom of God does [a]not con-
sist in [1]words but in power. **21** What
do you desire? [a]Shall I come to you
with a rod, or with love and a spirit
of gentleness?

### *Sexual Immorality in the Church*

**5** It is actually reported that there
is sexual immorality among you,
and sexual immorality of such a kind
as does not exist even among the
Gentiles, that someone has [a]his fa-
ther's wife. **2** And [1]you [a]have become
puffed up and [2]have not [b]mourned
instead, so that the one who had
done this deed would be [c]removed
from your midst.

**3** For I, on my part, though [a]absent
in body but present in spirit, have
already judged him who has so
committed this, as though I were
present: **4** [a]in the name of our Lord
Jesus, when you are assembled, and
[1]I with you in spirit, [b]with the power
of our Lord Jesus, **5** [a]deliver such a
one to [b]Satan for the destruction of
his flesh, so that his spirit may be
saved in [c]the day of [1]the Lord.

**6** [a]Your boasting is not good. [b]Do
you not know that [c]a little leaven
leavens the whole lump? **7** Clean out
the old leaven so that you may be a
new lump, just as you are *in fact* un-
leavened. For Christ, our [a]Passover

---

**4:9** [a]Ro 8:36; 1Co 15:31; 2Co 11:23 [b]Heb 10:33 **4:10** [a]Ac 17:18; 26:24; 1Co 1:18 [b]1Co 1:19f; 3:18; 2Co 11:19 [c]1Co 2:3; 2Co 13:9 **4:11** [a]Ro 8:35; 2Co 11:23-27 **4:12** [a]Ac 18:3 [b]1Pe 3:9 [c]Jn 15:20; Ro 8:35 **4:13** [a]Lam 3:45 **4:14** [a]1Co 6:5; 15:34 [b]2Co 6:13; 12:14; 1Th 2:11; 1Jn 2:1; 3Jn 4 **4:15** [a]Ga 3:24f [b]1Co 1:30 [c]Nu 11:12; 1Co 3:8; Ga 4:19; Phm 10 [d]1Co 9:12, 14, 18, 23; 15:1 **4:16** [a]1Co 11:1; Php 3:17; 4:9; 1Th 1:6; 2Th 3:9 **4:17** [a]1Co 16:10 [b]Ac 16:1 [c]1Co 4:14; 1Ti 1:2, 18; 2Ti 1:2 [d]1Co 7:17; 14:33; 16:1; Tit 1:5 **4:18** [a]1Co 4:6 [b]1Co 4:21 **4:19** [a]Ac 19:21; 20:2; 1Co 11:34; 16:5f; 16:7-9; 2Co 1:15f [b]Ac 18:21 [c]1Co 4:6 [1]Lit *word* **4:20** [a]1Co 2:4 [1]Lit *word* **4:21** [a]2Co 1:23; 2:1, 3; 12:20; 13:2, 10 ◆ **5:1** [a]Lv 18:8; Dt 22:30; 27:20 **5:2** [a]1Co 4:6 [b]2Co 7:7-10 [c]1Co 5:13 [1]Or *have you...?* [2]Or *have you...?* **5:3** [a]Col 2:5; 1Th 2:17 **5:4** [a]2Th 3:6 [b]Jn 20:23; 2Co 2:10; 13:3, 10 [1]Lit *my spirit, with the power* **5:5** [a]Pr 23:14; Lk 22:31; 1Ti 1:20 [b]Mt 4:10 [c]1Co 1:8 [1]Some mss *Jesus, Jesus Christ* **5:6** [a]1Co 5:2; Jas 4:16 [b]Ro 6:16 [c]Hos 7:4; Mt 16:6, 12; Ga 5:9 **5:7** [a]Mk 14:12; 1Pe 1:19

lamb, also was sacrificed. **8** Therefore
let us celebrate the feast, [a]not with
old leaven, nor with the leaven of
malice and wickedness, but with the
unleavened bread of sincerity and
truth.

**9** I wrote you in my letter [a]not
to associate with sexually immoral
people; **10** I *did* not at all *mean* with
the sexually immoral people of
this world, or with the greedy and
swindlers, or with [a]idolaters, for
then you would have to go out of
the world. **11** But now I am writing
to you not to associate [1]with any
so-called [a]brother if he is a sexually
immoral person, or greedy, or [b]an
idolater, or a reviler, or a drunkard,
or a swindler—not even to eat with
such a one. **12** For what have I to do
with judging [a]outsiders? [b]Are you
not to judge those who are within *the*
*church*? **13** But those who are outside,
God will judge. [a]REMOVE THE WICKED
MAN FROM AMONG YOURSELVES.

### *Lawsuits Among Believers*

**6** Does any one of you, when he
has a [1]case against another, dare
to be tried before the unrighteous
and [a]not before the [2]saints? **2** Or
[a]do you not know that [b]the [1]saints
will judge [c]the world? If the world
is judged by you, are you not wor-
thy *to* [2]*constitute* the smallest law
courts? **3** [a]Do you not know that we
will judge angels? How much more
matters of this life? **4** So if you have
law courts dealing with matters of
this life, do you appoint those who
are of no account in the church as
judges? **5** [a]I say *this* to your shame.
*Is it really* this way: there is not one
wise man among you who will be
able to pass judgment between his
[b]brothers? **6** On the contrary, brother
is tried with brother, and that before
[a]unbelievers!

**7** Actually, then, it is already a
failure for you, that you have lawsuits
with one another. [a]Why not rather
be wronged? Why not rather be
defrauded? **8** On the contrary, you
yourselves wrong and defraud. *You*
*do* this even to *your* [a]brothers.

**9** Or [a]do you not know that the
unrighteous will not [b]inherit the
kingdom of God? [c]Do not be de-
ceived; [d]neither *the* sexually immoral,
nor idolaters, nor adulterers, nor
[1]effeminate, nor homosexuals, **10** nor
thieves, nor *the* greedy, nor drunk-
ards, nor revilers, nor swindlers, will
[a]inherit the kingdom of God. **11** [a]And
such were some of you; but you were
[b]washed, but you were [c]sanctified,
but you were [d]justified in the name
of the Lord Jesus Christ and in the
Spirit of our God.

### *Flee Sexual Immorality*

**12** [a]All things are lawful for me, but
not all things are profitable. All
things are lawful for me, but I will not

---

**5:8** [a]Ex 12:19; 13:7; Dt 16:3 **5:9** [a]2Co 6:14; Eph 5:11; 2Th 3:6 **5:10** [a]1Co 10:27 **5:11** [a]Ac 1:15; 2Th 3:6 [b]1Co 10:7, 14, 20f [1]Lit *together if any man called a brother is* **5:12** [a]Mk 4:11 [b]1Co 5:3-5; 6:1-4 **5:13** [a]Dt 13:5; 17:7, 12; 21:21; 22:21; 1Co 5:2 ◆**6:1** [a]Mt 18:17 [1]Lit *matter* [2]Or *holy ones* **6:2** [a]Ro 6:16 [b]Da 7:18, 22, 27; Mt 19:28 [c]1Co 1:20 [1]v 1, note 2 [2]Or try *the trivial cases?* **6:3** [a]Ro 6:16 **6:5** [a]1Co 4:14; 15:34 [b]Ac 1:15; 9:13; 1Co 6:1 **6:6** [a]2Co 6:14f; 1Ti 5:8 **6:7** [a]Mt 5:39f **6:8** [a]1Th 4:6 **6:9** [a]Ro 6:16 [b]Ac 20:32; 1Co 15:50; Ga 5:21; Eph 5:5 [c]Lk 21:8; 1Co 15:33; Ga 6:7; Jas 1:16; 1Jn 3:7 [d]Ro 13:13; 1Co 5:11; Ga 5:19-21; Eph 5:5; 1Ti 1:10; Rev 21:8; 22:15 [1]Effeminate by perversion **6:10** [a]Ac 20:32; 1Co 15:50; Ga 5:21; Eph 5:5 **6:11** [a]1Co 12:2; Eph 2:2f; Col 3:5-7; Tit 3:3-7 [b]Ac 22:16; Eph 5:26 [c]1Co 1:2, 30 [d]Ro 8:30 **6:12** [a]1Co 10:23

be mastered by anything. **13** [a]Food is
for the [1]stomach and the [1]stomach is
for food, but God will [b]do away with
both [2]of them. Yet the body is not
for sexual immorality, but [c]for the
Lord, and [d]the Lord is for the body.
**14** Now God has not only [a]raised
the Lord, but [b]will also raise us up
through His power. **15** [a]Do you not
know that [b]your bodies are members
of Christ? Shall I then take away the
members of Christ and make them
members of a prostitute? [c]May it
never be! **16** Or [a]do you not know
that the one who joins himself to a
prostitute is one body *with her*? For
He says, "[b]THE TWO SHALL BECOME
ONE FLESH." **17** But the one who joins
himself to the Lord is [a]one spirit *with
Him.* **18** [a]Flee sexual immorality. Ev-
ery *other* sin that a man commits is
outside the body, but the [1]sexually
immoral man sins against his own
body. **19** Or [a]do you not know that
[b]your body is a [1]sanctuary of the
Holy Spirit who is in you, whom
you have from [2]God, and that [c]you
are not your own? **20** For [a]you were
bought with a price: therefore glorify
God in [b]your body.

### *Concerning Marriage and Singleness*

**7** Now concerning the things about
which you wrote, it is [a]good for
a man not to touch a woman. **2** But
because of sexual immoralities, each
man is to have his own wife, and each
woman is to have her own husband.
**3** The husband must [1]fulfill his duty
to his wife, and likewise also the wife
to her husband. **4** The wife does not
have authority over her own body, but
the husband *does*; and likewise also
the husband does not have authority
over his own body, but the wife *does*.
**5** [a]Stop depriving one another, except
by agreement for a time, so that you
may devote yourselves to prayer, and
[1]come together again so that [b]Satan
will not tempt you because of your
lack of self-control. **6** But this I say
as a concession, [a]not as a command.
**7** [1]Yet I wish that all men were [a]even
as I myself am. However, [b]each man
has his own gift from God, one this
way, and another that.

**8** But I say to the unmarried and
to widows that it is [a]good for them
if they remain [b]even as I. **9** But if they
do not have self-control, [a]let them
marry, for it is better to marry than
to burn *with passion*.

**10** But to the married I give instruc-
tions, [a]not I, but the Lord, that the
wife should not [1]leave her husband
**11** (but if she does leave, she must
remain unmarried, or else be recon-
ciled to her husband), and that the
husband should not [1]divorce his wife.

**12** But to the rest [a]I say, not the
Lord, that if any brother has a wife
who is an unbeliever, and she con-
sents to live with him, he must not
[1]divorce her. **13** And a woman who

**6:13** [a]Mt 15:17 [b]Col 2:22 [c]1Co 6:15, 19 [d]Ga 5:24; Eph 5:23 [1]Lit *belly* [2]Lit *it and them* **6:14** [a]Ac 2:24 [b]Jn 6:39f; 1Co 15:23 **6:15** [a]1Co 6:3 [b]Ro 12:5; 1Co 6:13; 12:27; Eph 5:30 [c]Lk 20:16 **6:16** [a]1Co 6:3 [b]Ge 2:24; Mt 19:5; Mk 10:8; Eph 5:31 **6:17** [a]Jn 17:21-23; Ro 8:9-11; 1Co 6:15; Ga 2:20 **6:18** [a]1Co 6:9; 2Co 12:21; Eph 5:3; Col 3:5; Heb 13:4 [1]Or *one who practices sexual immorality* **6:19** [a]1Co 6:3 [b]Jn 2:21; 1Co 3:16; 2Co 6:16 [c]Ro 14:7f [1]The inner part of the temple [2]Or *God? And you are not your own.* **6:20** [a]Ac 20:28; 1Co 7:23; 1Pe 1:18f; 2Pe 2:1; Rev 5:9 [b]Ro 12:1; Php 1:20 ◆**7:1** [a]1Co 7:8, 26 **7:3** [1]Lit *render* **7:5** [a]Ex 19:15; 1Sa 21:5 [b]Mt 4:10 [1]Lit *be* **7:6** [a]2Co 8:8 **7:7** [a]1Co 7:8; 9:5 [b]Mt 19:11f; Ro 12:6; 1Co 12:4, 11 [1]One early ms *For* **7:8** [a]1Co 7:1, 26 [b]1Co 7:7; 9:5 **7:9** [a]1Ti 5:14 **7:10** [a]Mal 2:16; Mt 5:32; 19:3-9; Mk 10:2-12; Lk 16:18; 1Co 7:6 [1]Lit *depart from* **7:11** [1]Or *leave his wife* **7:12** [a]1Co 7:6; 2Co 11:17 [1]Or *leave her*

has an unbelieving husband, and he
consents to live with her, she must
not divorce her husband. **14** For the
unbelieving husband is sanctified
through his wife, and the unbeliev-
ing wife is sanctified through [1]her
believing husband. For otherwise
your children are unclean, but now
they are [a]holy. **15** Yet if the unbeliev-
ing one leaves, let him leave. The
brother or the sister is not enslaved
in such *cases*, but God has called [1]us
[a,2]to peace. **16** For how do you know,
O wife, whether you will [a]save your
husband? Or how do you know,
O husband, whether you will save
your wife?

**17** Only, [a]as the Lord has assigned
to each one, as God has called each,
in this manner let him walk. And [b]so
I direct in [c]all the churches. **18** Was
any man called *when he was already*
circumcised? He is not to become
uncircumcised. Has anyone been
called in uncircumcision? [a]He is not
to be circumcised. **19** [a]Circumcision
is nothing, and uncircumcision is
nothing, but *what matters is* [b]the
keeping of the commandments of
God. **20** [a]Each man must remain
in that [1]condition in which he was
called.

**21** Were you called while a slave?
[1]Do not worry about it. But if you
are able also to become free, rather
[2]do that. **22** For he who was called
in the Lord while a slave, is [a]the
Lord's freedman. Likewise he who
was called while free, is [b]Christ's
slave. **23** [a]You were bought with a
price; do not become slaves of men.
**24** Brothers, [a]each one is to remain
with God in that *condition* in which
he was called.

**25** Now concerning virgins I have
[a]no command of the Lord, but I give
an opinion as one who [b,1]by the
mercy of the Lord is trustworthy.
**26** I think then that this is good
because of the [1]present [a]distress,
that [b]it is good for a man [2]to remain
as he is. **27** Are you bound to a wife?
Do not seek to be released. Are you
released from a wife? Do not seek a
wife. **28** But if you marry, you have
not sinned. And if a virgin marries,
she has not sinned. Yet such will
have [1]trouble in this life, and I am
trying to spare you. **29** But this I
say, brothers, [a]the time has been
shortened, so that from now on
those who have wives should be as
though they had none; **30** and those
who cry, as though they did not cry;
and those who rejoice, as though
they did not rejoice; and those who
buy, as though they did not possess;
**31** and those who use the world, as
though they did not [a]make full use
of it. For [b]the form of this world is
passing away.

**32** But I want you to be free from
concern. One who is [a]unmarried
is concerned about the things of
the Lord, how he may please the
Lord. **33** But one who is married

**7:14** [a]Ezr 9:2; Mal 2:15 [1]Lit *the brother* **7:15** [a]Ro 14:19 [1]One early ms *you* [2]Lit *in* **7:16** [a]Ro 11:14; 1Pe 3:1 **7:17** [a]Ro 12:3 [b]1Co 4:17 [c]1Co 11:16; 14:33; 2Co 8:18; 11:28; Ga 1:22; 1Th 2:14; 2Th 1:4
**7:18** [a]Ac 15:1ff **7:19** [a]Ro 2:27, 29; Ga 3:28; 5:6; 6:15; Col 3:11 [b]Ro 2:25 **7:20** [a]1Co 7:24 [1]Lit *calling*
**7:21** [1]Lit *Let it not be a care to you* [2]Lit *use* **7:22** [a]Jn 8:32, 36; Phm 16 [b]Eph 6:6; Col 3:24; 1Pe 2:16
**7:23** [a]1Co 6:20 **7:24** [a]1Co 7:20 **7:25** [a]1Co 7:6 [b]2Co 4:1; 1Ti 1:13, 16 [1]Lit *has had mercy shown on him by the Lord to be trustworthy* **7:26** [a]Lk 21:23; 2Th 2:2 [b]1Co 7:1, 8 [1]Or *impending* [2]Lit *so to be*
**7:28** [1]Lit *affliction in the flesh* **7:29** [a]Ro 13:11f; 1Co 7:31 **7:31** [a]1Co 9:18 [b]1Co 7:29; 1Jn 2:17
**7:32** [a]1Ti 5:5

is concerned about the things of
the world, how he may please his
wife, **34** and *his interests* have been
divided. The woman who is unmar-
ried, and the virgin, is concerned
about the things of the Lord, that
she may be holy both in body and
spirit. But one who is married is
concerned about the things of the
world, how she may please her
husband. **35** Now this I say for your
own benefit, not to put a restraint
upon you, but [1]to promote propri-
ety and undistracted devotion to
the Lord.

**36** But if any man thinks that he
is acting unbecomingly toward his
virgin *daughter*, if she is past her
youth, and if it must be so, let him
do what he wishes, he does not sin;
let [1]her marry. **37** But he who stands
firm in his heart, [1]being under no
compulsion, but has authority [2]over
his own will, and has decided this in
his own heart, to keep his own virgin
*daughter*, he will do well. **38** So then
both he who gives his own virgin
*daughter* in marriage does well, and
he who does not give her in marriage
will do better.

**39** [a]A wife is bound as long as her
husband lives; but if her husband
has [1]fallen asleep, she is free to be
married to whom she wishes, only
[b]in the Lord. **40** But [a]in my opinion
she is happier if she remains as she
is. And I think that I also have the
Spirit of God.

### *Take Care with Your Liberty*

**8** Now concerning [a]things sacri-
ficed to idols, we know that we all
have [b]knowledge. Knowledge [c]puffs
up, but love [d]builds up. **2** [a]If anyone
thinks that he has known anything,
he has not yet [b]known as he ought
to know; **3** but if anyone loves God,
he [a]has been known by Him.

**4** Therefore, concerning the eat-
ing of [a]things sacrificed to idols, we
know that [1]an idol is [b]nothing in the
world, and that [c]there is no God but
one. **5** For even if [a]there are so-called
gods whether in heaven or on earth,
as indeed there are many gods and
many lords, **6** yet for us [a]there is one
God, [b]the Father, [c]from whom are all
things and we *exist* for Him, and [d]one
Lord, Jesus Christ, [e]by whom are all
things, and we *exist* through Him.

**7** However, not all men [a]have
this knowledge; but [b]some, being
accustomed to the idol until now,
eat *food* as if it were sacrificed to
an idol; and their conscience, being
weak, is defiled. **8** But [a]food will not
[1]commend us to God. We neither lack
if we do not eat, nor abound if we do
eat. **9** But [a]see *to it* that this [1]authority
of yours does not somehow become
a stumbling block to the [b]weak.
**10** For if someone sees you, who
have [a]knowledge, dining in an idol's
temple, will not his conscience, if he
is weak, be built up to eat [b]things sac-
rificed to idols? **11** For through [a]your
knowledge he who is weak [b]is ruined,

---

**7:35** [1]Lit *for what is seemly* **7:36** [1]Lit *them*; the virgin daughter and her fiancé **7:37** [1]Lit *having no necessity* [2]Lit *pertaining to* **7:39** [a]Ro 7:2 [b]2Co 6:14 [1]Or *died* **7:40** [a]1Co 7:6, 25 ◆ **8:1** [a]Ac 15:20; 1Co 8:4, 7, 10 [b]Ro 15:14; 1Co 8:7, 10; 10:15 [c]1Co 4:6 [d]Ro 14:19 **8:2** [a]1Co 3:18 [b]1Co 13:8-12; 1Ti 6:4 **8:3** [a]Ps 1:6; Jer 1:5; Am 3:2; Ro 8:29; 11:2; Ga 4:9 **8:4** [a]Ac 15:20; 1Co 8:1, 7, 10 [b]Ac 14:15; 1Co 10:19; Ga 4:8 [c]Dt 4:35, 39; 6:4; 1Co 8:6 [1]An idol has no real existence **8:5** [a]2Th 2:4 **8:6** [a]Dt 4:35, 39; 6:4; Is 46:9; Jer 10:6, 7; 1Co 8:4 [b]Mal 2:10; Eph 4:6 [c]Ro 11:36 [d]Jn 13:13; 1Co 1:2; Eph 4:5; 1Ti 2:5 [e]Jn 1:3; Col 1:16 **8:7** [a]1Co 8:4ff [b]Ro 14:14, 22f **8:8** [a]Ro 14:17 [1]Or *present* **8:9** [a]Ro 14:13, 21; 1Co 10:28; Ga 5:13 [b]Ro 14:1; 1Co 8:10f [1]Or *liberty* **8:10** [a]1Co 8:4ff [b]Ac 15:20; 1Co 8:1, 4, 7 **8:11** [a]1Co 8:4ff [b]Ro 14:15, 20

the brother for whose sake Christ
died. **12** [a]And in that way, by sinning
against the brothers and wounding
their conscience when it is weak, you
sin [b]against Christ. **13** Therefore, [a]if
food causes my brother to stumble,
I will never eat meat again—ever, so
that I will not cause my brother to
stumble.

### *Paul Gives Up His Rights*

**9** Am I not [a]free? Am I not an
[b]apostle? Have I not [c]seen Jesus
our Lord? Are you not [d]my work in
the Lord? **2** If to others I am not an
apostle, at least I am to you, for you
are the [a]seal of my [b]apostleship in
the Lord.

**3** My defense to those who ex-
amine me is this: **4** [a]Do we not have
authority to eat and drink? **5** [a]Do we
not have authority to take along a
[1]believing wife, even as the rest of
the apostles and the [b]brothers of
the Lord and [c]Cephas? **6** Or do only
[a,1]Barnabas and I not have authority
to refrain from working? **7** Who at
any time serves [a]as a soldier at his
own expense? Who [b]plants a vine-
yard and does not [1]consume the fruit
of it? Or who shepherds a flock and
does not [1]consume the milk of the
flock?

**8** Am I speaking these things
[a]according to [1]human judgment?
Or does not the Law also say these
things? **9** For it is written in the Law
of Moses, "[a]YOU SHALL NOT MUZZLE
THE OX WHILE IT IS THRESHING." Is God
*merely* concerned about [b]oxen? **10** Or
is He speaking altogether for our
sake? Yes, [a]for our sake it was writ-
ten, because [b]the plowman ought
to plow in hope, and the thresher *to
thresh* in hope of sharing *the crops.*
**11** [a]If we sowed spiritual things in
you, is it too much if we reap material
things from you? **12** If others share
this authority over you, do we not
more? Nevertheless, we [a]did not
use this authority, but we endure
all things [b]so that we will cause no
hindrance to the [c]gospel of Christ.
**13** [a]Do you not know that those who
[b]perform sacred services eat the *food*
of the temple, *and* those who attend
regularly to the altar have their share
[1]from the altar? **14** So also [a]the Lord
directed those who proclaim the
[b]gospel to [c]get their living from the
gospel.

**15** But I have [a]used none of these
things. And I am not writing these
things so that it will be done so in
my case, for it would be better for
me to die than have anyone make
[b]my boast an empty one. **16** For if I
proclaim the gospel, I have nothing
to boast, for [a]I am under compulsion.
For woe is me if I do not proclaim [b]the
gospel. **17** For if I do this voluntarily,
I have a [a]reward; but if against my

---

**8:12** [a]Mt 18:6; Ro 14:20 [b]Mt 25:45 **8:13** [a]Ro 14:21; 1Co 10:32; 2Co 6:3; 11:29 ◆ **9:1** [a]1Co 9:19; 10:29 [b]Ac 14:14; Ro 1:1; 2Co 12:12; 1Th 2:6; 1Ti 2:7; 2Ti 1:11 [c]Ac 9:3, 17; 18:9; 22:14, 18; 23:11; 1Co 15:8 [d]1Co 3:6; 4:15 **9:2** [a]Jn 3:33; 2Co 3:2f [b]Ac 1:25 **9:4** [a]1Co 9:14; 1Th 2:6, 9; 2Th 3:8f **9:5** [a]1Co 7:7f [b]Mt 12:46 [c]Mt 8:14; Jn 1:42 [1]Lit *sister, as wife* **9:6** [a]Ac 4:36 [1]Lit *I and Barnabas* **9:7** [a]2Co 10:4; 1Ti 1:18; 2Ti 2:3f [b]Dt 20:6; Pr 27:18; 1Co 3:6, 8 [1]Lit *eat of* **9:8** [a]Ro 3:5 [1]Lit *man* **9:9** [a]Dt 25:4; 1Ti 5:18 [b]Dt 22:1-4; Pr 12:10 **9:10** [a]Ro 4:23f [b]2Ti 2:6 **9:11** [a]Ro 15:27; 1Co 9:14 **9:12** [a]Ac 18:3; 20:33; 1Co 9:15, 18 [b]2Co 6:3; 11:12 [c]1Co 4:15; 9:14, 16, 18, 23; 2Co 2:12 **9:13** [a]Ro 6:16 [b]Lv 6:16, 26; 7:6, 31ff; Nu 5:9f; 18:8-20, 31; Dt 18:1 [1]Lit *with* **9:14** [a]Mt 10:10; Lk 10:7; 1Ti 5:18 [b]1Co 4:15; 9:12, 16, 18, 23; 2Co 2:12 [c]Lk 10:8; 1Co 9:4 **9:15** [a]Ac 18:3; 20:33; 1Co 9:12, 18 [b]2Co 11:10 **9:16** [a]Ac 9:15; Ro 1:14 [b]1Co 4:15; 9:12, 14, 18, 23; 2Co 2:12 **9:17** [a]Jn 4:36; 1Co 3:8; 9:18

will, I have a [b]stewardship entrusted
to me. **18** What then is my [a]reward?
That, when I proclaim the gospel, I
may offer the gospel [b]without charge,
so as [c]not to make full use of my au-
thority in the gospel.

**19** For though I am [a]free from all,
I have made myself [b]a slave to all,
so that I may [c]win more. **20** [a]And to
the Jews I became as a Jew, so that
I might win Jews. To those who are
under [1]the Law, as under [1]the Law
though [b]not being myself under [1]the
Law, so that I might win those who
are under [1]the Law. **21** To those who
are [a]without law, [b]as without law,
though not being without the law
of God but [c]under the law of Christ,
so that I might win those who are
without law. **22** To the [a]weak I
became weak, that I might win the
weak. I have become [b]all things to
all men, [c]so that I may by all means
save some. **23** So I do all things for
the sake of the gospel, so that I may
become a fellow partaker of it.

**24** [a]Do you not know that those
who run in a [1]race all run, but *only*
one receives [b]the prize? [c]Run
in such a way that you may win.
**25** Now everyone who [a]competes in
the games exercises self-control in
all things. They then *do it* to receive
a corruptible [b]crown, but we an
incorruptible. **26** Therefore I [a]run
in such a way, as not without aim;
I box in such a way, as not [b]beating
the air; **27** but I [1]discipline [a]my body
and make it my slave, so that, after I
have preached to others, I myself will
not be disqualified.

### *Temptation and God's Faithfulness*

**10** For [a]I do not want you to be
unaware, brothers, that our
fathers were all [b]under the cloud
and all [c]passed through the sea;
**2** and all were [a]baptized into Moses
in the cloud and in the sea; **3** and all
[a]ate the same spiritual food; **4** and all
[a]drank the same spiritual drink, for
they were drinking from a spiritual
rock which followed them, and the
rock was [1]Christ. **5** Nevertheless,
with most of them God was not well-
pleased. For [a]THEY WERE [1]STRUCK
DOWN IN THE WILDERNESS. **6** Now
these things happened as [a]examples
for us, so that we would not crave evil
things as [b]they also craved.

**7** Do not be [a]idolaters, as some of
them were. As it is written, "[b]THE
PEOPLE SAT DOWN TO EAT AND DRINK,
AND STOOD UP TO [c]PLAY." **8** Nor let us
act in sexual immorality, as [a]some
of them [1]did, and [b]twenty-three
thousand fell in one day. **9** Nor let
us put Christ to the test, as [a]some
of them [1]did, and were destroyed
by the serpents. **10** Nor [a]grumble,
as some of them [1]did, and [b]were
destroyed by the [c]destroyer. **11** Now

---

**9:17** [b]1Co 4:1; Ga 2:7; Eph 3:2; Php 1:16; Col 1:25 **9:18** [a]Jn 4:36; 1Co 3:8; 9:17 [b]Ac 18:3; 2Co 11:7; 12:13 [c]1Co 7:31; 9:12 **9:19** [a]1Co 9:1 [b]2Co 4:5; Ga 5:13 [c]Mt 18:15; 1Pe 3:1 **9:20** [a]Ac 16:3; 21:23-26; Ro 11:14 [b]Ga 2:19 [1]Or *law* **9:21** [a]Ro 2:12, 14 [b]Ga 2:3; 3:2 [c]1Co 7:22; Ga 6:2 **9:22** [a]Ro 14:1; 15:1; 2Co 11:29 [b]1Co 10:33 [c]Ro 11:14 **9:24** [a]1Co 9:13 [b]Php 3:14; Col 2:18 [c]Ga 2:2; 2Ti 4:7; Heb 12:1 [1]Lit *stadium* **9:25** [a]Eph 6:12; 1Ti 6:12; 2Ti 2:5; 4:7 [b]2Ti 4:8; Jas 1:12; 1Pe 5:4; Rev 2:10; 3:11 **9:26** [a]Ga 2:2; 2Ti 4:7; Heb 12:1 [b]1Co 14:9 **9:27** [a]Ro 8:13 [1]Lit *bruise* ◆ **10:1** [a]Ro 1:13 [b]Ex 13:21; Ps 105:39 [c]Ex 14:22, 29; Ne 9:11; Ps 66:6 **10:2** [a]Ro 6:3; 1Co 1:13; Ga 3:27 **10:3** [a]Ex 16:4, 35; Dt 8:3; Ne 9:15, 20; Ps 78:24f; Jn 6:31 **10:4** [a]Ex 17:6; Nu 20:11; Ps 78:15 [1]Messiah **10:5** [a]Nu 14:16, 29ff, 37; 26:65; Heb 3:17; Jd 5 [1]Lit *scattered about* **10:6** [a]1Co 10:11 [b]Nu 11:4, 34; Ps 106:14 **10:7** [a]Ex 32:4; 1Co 5:11; 10:14 [b]Ex 32:6 [c]Ex 32:19 **10:8** [a]Nu 25:1ff [b]Nu 25:9 [1]Lit *acted immorally* **10:9** [a]Nu 21:5f [1]Lit *made trial* **10:10** [a]Nu 16:41; 17:5, 10 [b]Nu 16:49 [c]Ex 12:23; 2Sa 24:16; 1Chr 21:15; Heb 11:28 [1]Lit *grumbled*

these things happened to them as an
[a]example, and [b]they were written
for our instruction, upon whom
[c]the ends of the ages have arrived.
12 Therefore let him who [a]thinks he
stands take heed that he does not
fall. 13 No temptation has overtaken
you but such as is common to man,
but [a]God is faithful, who will not
allow you to be [b]tempted beyond
what you are able, but with the
temptation will provide the way of
escape also, so that you will be able
to endure it.
14 Therefore, my [a]beloved, flee
from [b]idolatry. 15 I speak as to pru-
dent people. You judge what I say.
16 Is not the [a]cup of blessing which
we bless a sharing in the blood of
Christ? Is not the [b,1]bread which we
break a sharing in the body of Christ?
17 Since there is one [1]bread, we [a]who
are many are one body, for we all
partake of the one [1]bread. 18 Look
at [1]the nation [a]Israel. Are not those
who [b]eat the sacrifices sharers in the
altar? 19 What do I mean then? That
a thing sacrificed to idols is anything,
or [a]that an idol is anything? 20 *No*,
but *I say* that the things which the
Gentiles sacrifice, they [a]SACRIFICE
TO DEMONS AND NOT TO GOD. And I
do not want you to become sharers
in demons. 21 [a]You cannot drink
the cup of the Lord and the cup of
demons. You cannot partake of the
table of the Lord and [b]the table of
demons. 22 Or do we [a]PROVOKE THE
[1]LORD TO JEALOUSY? Are we [b]stronger
than He?
23 [a]All things are lawful, but not
all things are profitable. All things
are lawful, but not all things [b]build
up. 24 Let no one [a]seek his own *good*,
but that of the other person. 25 [a]Eat
anything that is sold in the meat
market without asking questions
for conscience' sake. 26 [a]FOR THE
EARTH IS THE [1]LORD'S, AS WELL AS ITS
FULLNESS. 27 If [a]one of the unbeliev-
ers invites you and you want to go,
[b]eat anything that is set before you
without asking questions for con-
science' sake. 28 But [a]if anyone says
to you, "This is meat consecrated to
idols," do not eat *it*, for the sake of
the one who informed *you*, and for
conscience' sake. 29 I do not mean
your own conscience, but the other
*person's*. For [a]why is my freedom
judged by another's conscience? 30 If I
partake with gratefulness, [a]why am I
slandered concerning that for which
I [b]give thanks?
31 Whether, then, you eat or drink
or [a]whatever you do, do all to the
glory of God. 32 [a]Give no offense ei-
ther to Jews or to Greeks or to [b]the
church of God; 33 just as I also [a]please
all men in all things, [b]not seeking my
own profit but the *profit* of the many,
[c]so that they may be saved.

---

**10:11** [a]1Co 10:6 [b]Ro 4:23 [c]Ro 13:11 **10:12** [a]Ro 11:20; 2Pe 3:17 **10:13** [a]1Co 1:9 [b]2Pe 2:9 **10:14** [a]Heb 6:9 [b]1Co 10:7, 19f; 1Jn 5:21 **10:16** [a]Mt 26:27f; Mk 14:23f; Lk 22:20; 1Co 11:25 [b]Mt 26:26; Lk 22:19; Ac 2:42; 1Co 11:23f [1]Lit *loaf* **10:17** [a]Ro 12:5; 1Co 12:12f, 27; Eph 4:4, 16; Col 3:15 [1]Lit *loaf* **10:18** [a]Ro 1:3 [b]Lv 7:6, 14f; Dt 12:17f [1]Lit *Israel according to the flesh* **10:19** [a]1Co 8:4 **10:20** [a]Dt 32:17; Ps 106:37; Ga 4:8; Rev 9:20 **10:21** [a]2Co 6:16 [b]Is 65:11 **10:22** [a]Dt 32:21 [b]Ecc 6:10; Is 45:9 [1]In OT, Yahweh, cf. Dt 32:19-21 **10:23** [a]1Co 6:12 [b]Ro 14:19 **10:24** [a]Ro 15:2; 1Co 10:33; 13:5; 2Co 12:14; Php 2:21 **10:25** [a]Ac 10:15; 1Co 8:7 **10:26** [a]Ps 24:1; 50:12; 1Ti 4:4 [1]In OT, Yahweh, cf. Ps 24:1 **10:27** [a]1Co 5:10 [b]Lk 10:8 **10:28** [a]1Co 8:7, 10-12 **10:29** [a]Ro 14:16; 1Co 9:19 **10:30** [a]1Co 9:1 [b]Ro 14:6 **10:31** [a]Col 3:17; 1Pe 4:11 **10:32** [a]Ac 24:16; 1Co 8:13 [b]Ac 20:28; 1Co 1:2; 7:17; 11:22; 15:9; 2Co 1:1; Ga 1:13; Php 3:6; 1Ti 3:5, 15 **10:33** [a]Ro 15:2; 1Co 9:22; Ga 1:10 [b]Ro 15:2; 1Co 13:5; 2Co 12:14; Php 2:21 [c]Ro 11:14; 1Th 2:16

11 [a]Be imitators of me, just as I
also am of Christ.

### *Head Coverings*

2 Now [a]I praise you because you
[b]remember me in everything and
[c]hold firmly to the traditions, just as
I delivered them to you. 3 But I want
you to understand that [1]Christ is the
[a]head of every man, and [b]the man is
the head of a woman, and God is the
[c]head of [1]Christ. 4 Every man who has
*something* on his head while praying
or [a]prophesying, shames his head.
5 But every [a]woman who has her head
uncovered while praying or prophe-
sying, shames her head, for she is one
and the same as the woman [1]whose
head is [b]shaved. 6 For if a woman
does not cover [1]her head, let her also
[2]have her hair cut short. But if it is
disgraceful for a woman to [2]have her
hair cut short or [1]her head shaved, let
her cover [1]her head. 7 For a man ought
not to have his head covered, since
he is the [a]image and glory of God,
but the woman is the glory of man.
8 For [a]man [1]does not originate from
woman, but woman from man. 9 For
indeed man was not created for the
woman's sake, but [a]woman for the
man's sake. 10 Therefore the woman
ought to have *a symbol of* authority
on her head, because of the angels.
11 Nevertheless, in the Lord, neither
is woman [1]independent of man, nor
is man [1]independent of woman. 12 For
as the woman [1]originates from the
man, so also the man *has his birth*
through the woman, but [a]all things
[2]originate [b]from God. 13 [a]Judge [1]for
yourselves: is it proper for a woman to
pray to God *with her head* uncovered?
14 Does not even nature itself teach
you that if a man has long hair, it is
a dishonor to him, 15 but if a woman
has long hair, it is a glory to her? For
her hair is given to her for a covering.
16 But if one is inclined to be conten-
tious, [a]we have no [1]other practice, nor
have [b]the churches of God.

### *The Lord's Supper*

17 But in giving this instruction, [a]I
do not praise you, because you come
together not for the better but for the
worse. 18 For, in the first place, when
you come together [1]as a church, I hear
that [a,2]divisions exist among you, and
in part I believe it. 19 For there [a]must
also be factions among you, [b]so that
those who are approved may become
[1]evident among you. 20 Therefore
when you meet together in the
same *place*, it is not to eat the Lord's
Supper, 21 for in your eating each one
takes his own supper first, and one is
hungry and [a]another is drunk. 22 For
do you not have houses in which to
eat and drink? Or do you despise the
[a]church of God and [b]shame those
who have nothing? What shall I say
to you? Shall [c]I praise you? In this I
will not praise you.

23 For [a]I received from the Lord
that which I also delivered to you,

---

◆ **11:1** [a]1Co 4:16; Php 3:17 **11:2** [a]1Co 11:17, 22 [b]1Co 4:17; 15:2; 1Th 1:6; 3:6 [c]2Th 2:15; 3:6 **11:3** [a]Eph 1:22; 4:15; 5:23; Col 1:18; 2:19 [b]Ge 3:16; Eph 5:23 [c]1Co 3:23 [1]Messiah **11:4** [a]Ac 13:1; 1Th 5:20 **11:5** [a]Lk 2:36; Ac 21:9; 1Co 14:34 [b]Dt 21:12 [1]Lit *who is shaved* **11:6** [1]Lit *herself* [2]Lit *shear herself* **11:7** [a]Ge 1:26; 5:1; 9:6; Jas 3:9 **11:8** [a]Ge 2:21-23; 1Ti 2:13 [1]Lit *is not from* **11:9** [a]Ge 2:18 **11:11** [1]Lit *without* **11:12** [a]2Co 5:18 [b]Ro 11:36 [1]Lit *is* [2]Lit *are* **11:13** [a]Lk 12:57 [1]Lit *in* **11:16** [a]1Co 4:5; 9:1-3, 6 [b]1Co 7:17 [1]Lit *such* **11:17** [a]1Co 11:2, 22 **11:18** [a]1Co 1:10; 3:3 [1]Lit *in church* [2]Lit *schisms* **11:19** [a]Mt 18:7; Lk 17:1; 1Ti 4:1; 2Pe 2:1 [b]Dt 13:3; 1Jn 2:19 [1]Or *manifest* **11:21** [a]Jd 12 **11:22** [a]1Co 10:32 [b]Jas 2:6 [c]1Co 11:2, 17 **11:23** [a]1Co 15:3; Ga 1:12; Col 3:24

that [b]the Lord Jesus in the night in
which He was being betrayed took
bread, **24** and when He had given
thanks, He broke it and said, "This
is My body, which is for you. Do
this in remembrance of Me." **25** In
the same way *He took* [a]the cup also
after supper, saying, "This cup is the
[b]new covenant in My blood; do this,
as often as you drink *it*, in remem-
brance of Me." **26** For as often as you
eat this bread and drink the cup, you
proclaim the death of the Lord [a]until
He comes.

**27** Therefore whoever eats the
bread or drinks the cup of the Lord
in an unworthy manner, shall be
[a]guilty of the body and the blood
of the Lord. **28** But a man must [a]test
himself, and in so doing he is to eat of
the bread and drink of the cup. **29** For
he who eats and drinks, eats and
drinks judgment to himself if he does
not judge the body rightly. **30** For this
reason many among you are weak
and sick, and a number [a,1]sleep.
**31** But if we judged ourselves rightly,
we would not be judged. **32** But when
we are judged, we are [a]disciplined
by the Lord so that we will not be
condemned along with [b]the world.

**33** So then, my brothers, when you
come together to eat, wait for one
another. **34** If anyone is [a]hungry, let
him eat [b]at home, so that you will
not come together for judgment.
The remaining matters I will [c]direct
[d]when I come.

### *Concerning Spiritual Gifts*

**12** Now concerning [a]spiritual
*gifts*, brothers, [b]I do not want
you to be ignorant. **2** [a]You know that
when you were pagans, *you were*
[b]being led astray to the [c]mute idols,
however you were led. **3** Therefore
I make known to you that no one
speaking [a,1]by the Spirit of God says,
"Jesus is [b,2]accursed," and no one can
say, "Jesus is [c]Lord," except [a,1]by the
Holy Spirit.

**4** Now there are [a]varieties of gifts,
but the same Spirit. **5** And there
are varieties of ministries, and the
same Lord. **6** And there are varieties
of workings, but the same [a]God
who works everything in everyone.
**7** But to each one is given the man-
ifestation of the Spirit [a]for what
is profitable. **8** For to one is given
the word of [a]wisdom through the
Spirit, and to another the word of
[b]knowledge according to the same
Spirit; **9** to someone else [a]faith [1]by
the same Spirit, and to another
[b]gifts of [2]healing [1]by the one Spirit,
**10** and to another the workings of
[a]miracles, and to another [b]prophecy,
and to another the [c,1]distinguishing
of spirits, to someone else *various*
[d]kinds of tongues, and to another
the [e,2]translation of tongues. **11** But

---

**11:23** [b]1Co 11:23-25: *Mt 26:26-28; Mk 14:22-24; Lk 22:17-20;* 1Co 10:16 **11:25** [a]1Co 10:16 [b]Ex 24:6-8; Lk 22:20; 2Co 3:6 **11:26** [a]Jn 21:22; 1Co 4:5 **11:27** [a]Heb 10:29 **11:28** [a]Mt 26:22; 2Co 13:5; Ga 6:4 **11:30** [a]Ac 7:60 [1]Are dead **11:32** [a]2Sa 7:14; Ps 94:12; Heb 12:7-10; Rev 3:19 [b]1Co 1:20 **11:34** [a]1Co 11:21 [b]*1Co 11:22* [c]*1Co 4:17; 7:17; 16:1* [d]*1Co 4:19* ◆ **12:1** [a]*1Co 12:4; 14:1* [b]*Ro 1:13* **12:2** [a]1Co 6:11; Eph 2:11f; 1Pe 4:3 [b]1Th 1:9 [c]Ps 115:5; Is 46:7; Jer 10:5; Hab 2:18f **12:3** [a]Mt 22:43; 1Jn 4:2f; Rev 1:10 [b]Ro 9:3 [c]Jn 13:13; Ro 10:9 [1]Or *in* [2]Gr *anathema* **12:4** [a]Ro 12:6f; 1Co 12:11; Eph 4:4ff, 11; Heb 2:4 **12:6** [a]1Co 15:28; Eph 1:23; 4:6 **12:7** [a]1Co 12:12-30; 14:26; Eph 4:12 **12:8** [a]1Co 2:6; 2Co 1:12 [b]Ro 15:14; 1Co 2:11, 16; 2Co 2:14; 4:6; 8:7; 11:6 **12:9** [a]1Co 13:2; 2Co 4:13 [b]1Co 12:28, 30 [1]Or *in* [2]Lit *healings* **12:10** [a]1Co 12:28f; Ga 3:5 [b]1Co 11:4; 13:2, 8 [c]1Co 14:29; 1Jn 4:1 [d]Mk 16:17; 1Co 12:28, 30; 13:1; 14:2ff [e]1Co 12:30; 14:26 [1]Lit *distinguishings* [2]Or *interpretation*

one and the same Spirit works all
these things, [a]distributing to each
one individually just as He wills.
**12** For even [a]as the body is one and
*yet* has many members, and all the
members of the body, though they
are many, are one body, [b]so also is
Christ. **13** For also [a,1]by one Spirit
we were all baptized into one body,
whether [b]Jews or Greeks, whether
slaves or free, and we were all made
to [c]drink of one Spirit.
**14** For also [a]the body is not one
member, but many. **15** If the foot
says, "Because I am not a hand, I am
not *a part* of the body," it is not for
this reason [1]any the less *a part* of the
body. **16** And if the ear says, "Because
I am not an eye, I am not *a part* of the
body," it is not for this reason [1]any the
less *a part* of the body. **17** If the whole
body were an eye, where would the
hearing be? If the whole were hear-
ing, where would the sense of smell
be? **18** But now God has [a]appointed
the members, each one of them, in
the body, [b]just as He desired. **19** And
if they were all one member, where
would the body be? **20** But now
[a]there are many members, but one
body. **21** And the eye cannot say to
the hand, "I have no need of you"; or
again the head to the feet, "I have no
need of you." **22** On the contrary, *how*
much more is it that the members of
the body which seem to be weaker
are necessary, **23** and those *members*
of the body which we think as less
honorable, [1]on these we bestow
more abundant honor, and our
less presentable members become
much more presentable, **24** whereas
our more presentable members
have no *such* need. But God has *so*
composed the body, giving more
abundant honor to that *member*
which lacked, **25** so that there may be
no [1]division in the body, but *that* the
members may have the same care for
one another. **26** And if one member
suffers, all the members suffer with
it; if *one* member is [1]honored, all the
members rejoice with it.
**27** Now you are [a]Christ's body, and
[b]individually members of it. **28** And
God has [a,1]appointed in [b]the church,
first [c]apostles, second [d]prophets,
third [e]teachers, then [f,2]miracles, then
[g]gifts of healings, helps, [h]adminis-
trations, *various* [i]kinds of tongues.
**29** Are all apostles? Are all prophets?
Are all teachers? Are all *workers of*
[1]miracles? **30** Do all have gifts of heal-
ings? Do all speak with tongues? Do
all [a,1]translate? **31** But [1]you [a]earnestly
desire the greater gifts.
And I will yet show you a more
excellent way.

### The Excellence of Love

**13** If I speak with the [a]tongues of
men and of [b]angels, but do not
have love, I have become a noisy gong
or a [c]clanging cymbal. **2** And if I have
*the gift of* [a]prophecy, and know all
[b]mysteries and all [c]knowledge; and

**12:11** [a]1Co 12:4 **12:12** [a]Ro 12:4f; 1Co 10:17 [b]1Co 12:27 **12:13** [a]Eph 2:18 [b]Ro 3:22; Ga 3:28; Eph 2:13-18; Col 3:11 [c]Jn 7:37-39 [1]Or *in* **12:14** [a]1Co 12:20 **12:15** [1]Lit *not* a part **12:16** [1]Lit *not* a part **12:18** [a]1Co 12:28 [b]Ro 12:6; 1Co 12:11 **12:20** [a]1Co 12:12, 14 **12:23** [1]Or *these we clothe with* **12:25** [1]Lit *schism* **12:26** [1]Lit *glorified* **12:27** [a]1Co 1:2; 12:12; Eph 1:23; 4:12; Col 1:18, 24; 2:19 [b]Ro 12:5; Eph 5:30 **12:28** [a]1Co 12:18 [b]1Co 10:32 [c]Eph 4:11 [d]Ac 13:1; Eph 2:20; 3:5 [e]Ac 13:1 [f]1Co 12:10, 29 [g]1Co 12:9, 30 [h]Ro 12:8 [i]1Co 12:10 [1]Lit *set some in* [2]Or *works of power* **12:29** [1]Or *works of power* **12:30** [a]1Co 12:10 [1]Or *interpret* **12:31** [a]1Co 14:1, 39 [1]Or *earnestly desire* ◆ **13:1** [a]1Co 12:10 [b]2Co 12:4; Rev 14:2 [c]Ps 150:5 **13:2** [a]Mt 7:22; Ac 13:1; 1Co 11:4; 13:8; 14:1, 39 [b]1Co 14:2; 15:51 [c]Ro 15:14

if I have [d]all faith, so as to [e]remove
mountains, but do not have love, I
am nothing. **3** And if I [a]give all my
possessions to feed *the poor*, and if
I [b]surrender my body [1]to be burned,
but do not have love, it profits me
nothing.
**4** Love [a]is patient, love is kind,
[b]is not jealous, does not brag, is not
[c]puffed up; **5** it does not act unbe-
comingly, [a]does not seek its own, is
not provoked, [b]does not take into
account a wrong *suffered*; **6** [a]it does
not rejoice in unrighteousness, but
[b]rejoices with the truth; **7** [a,1]it bears
all things, believes all things, hopes
all things, endures all things.
**8** Love never fails, but if *there are
gifts of* [a,1]prophecy, they will be done
away; if *there are* [b]tongues, they will
cease; if *there is* knowledge, it will
be done away. **9** For we [a]know in
part and we prophesy in part, **10** but
when the [1]perfect comes, the partial
will be done away. **11** When I was a
child, I used to speak like a child,
think like a child, reason like a child.
When I [1]became a man, I did away
with childish things. **12** For now we
[a]see in a mirror [1]dimly, but then
[b]face to face. Now I know in part,
but then I will know fully just as I
also [c]have been fully known. **13** But
now abide faith, hope, love—these
three; but the [1]greatest of these
is [a]love.

### *Prophecy and Tongues*

**14** [a]Pursue love, yet [b]earnestly
desire [c]spiritual *gifts*, but
especially that you may [d]prophesy.
**2** For one who [a]speaks in a tongue
does not speak to men but to God,
for no one [1]understands, but [2]in *his*
spirit he speaks [b]mysteries. **3** But one
who prophesies speaks to men for
[a]edification and [b]exhortation and
encouragement. **4** One who [a]speaks
in a tongue [b]edifies himself; but
one who [c]prophesies [b]edifies the
church. **5** But I wish that you all
[a]spoke in tongues, but [b]*even* more
that you would prophesy. And greater
is one who prophesies than one
who [a]speaks in tongues, unless he
[1]translates, so that the church may
receive [c]edification.
**6** But now, brothers, if I come to
you speaking in tongues, what will
I profit you unless I speak to you
either by way of [a]revelation or of
[b]knowledge or of [c]prophecy or of
[d]teaching? **7** Yet *even* lifeless things,
either flute or harp, in producing
a sound, if they do not produce a
distinction in the tones, how will it
be known what is played on the flute
or on the harp? **8** For if [a]the trumpet
produces an indistinct sound, who
will prepare himself for battle? **9** So
also you, unless you utter by the
tongue a word that is clear, how
will it be known what is spoken?

**13:2** [d]1Co 12:9 [e]Mt 17:20; 21:21; Mk 11:23 **13:3** [a]Mt 6:2 [b]Da 3:28 [1]Some early mss *that I may boast*
**13:4** [a]Pr 10:12; 17:9; 1Th 5:14; 1Pe 4:8 [b]Ac 7:9 [c]1Co 4:6 **13:5** [a]1Co 10:24; Php 2:21 [b]2Co 5:19
**13:6** [a]2Th 2:12 [b]2Jn 4; 3Jn 3f **13:7** [a]1Co 9:12 [1]Or *covers* **13:8** [a]1Co 13:2 [b]1Co 13:1 [1]Lit *prophecies*
**13:9** [a]1Co 8:2; 13:12 **13:10** [1]Or *mature* **13:11** [1]Lit *have become...have done away with*
**13:12** [a]2Co 5:7; Php 3:12; Jas 1:23 [b]Ge 32:30; Nu 12:8; 1Jn 3:2 [c]1Co 8:3 [1]Lit *in a riddle* **13:13** [a]Ga 5:6
[1]Lit *greater* ◆**14:1** [a]1Co 16:14 [b]1Co 12:31; 14:39 [c]1Co 12:1 [d]1Co 13:2 **14:2** [a]Mk 16:17; 1Co 12:10, 28,
30; 13:1; 14:18ff [b]1Co 13:2 [1]Lit *hears* [2]Or *by the Spirit* **14:3** [a]Ro 14:19; 1Co 14:5, 12, 17, 26 [b]Ac 4:36
**14:4** [a]Mk 16:17; 1Co 12:10, 28, 30; 13:1; 14:18ff, 26f [b]Ro 14:19; 1Co 14:5, 12, 17, 26 [c]1Co 13:2
**14:5** [a]Mk 16:17; 1Co 12:10, 28, 30; 13:1; 14:18ff, 26f [b]Nu 11:29 [c]Ro 14:19; 1Co 14:4, 12, 17, 26 [1]Or *interprets*
**14:6** [a]1Co 14:26; Eph 1:17 [b]1Co 12:8 [c]1Co 13:2 [d]Ac 2:42; Ro 6:17; 1Co 14:26 **14:8** [a]Nu 10:9; Jer 4:19;
Eze 33:3-6; Joel 2:1

For you will be [a]speaking into the
air. 10 There are, perhaps, a great
many kinds of sounds in the world,
and none is without meaning. 11 If
then I do not know the meaning of
the sound, I will be to the one who
speaks a [a,1]barbarian, and the one
who speaks will be a [1]barbarian [2]to
me. 12 So also you, since you are
zealous for [1]spiritual *gifts*, seek to
abound for the [a]edification of the
church.

13 Therefore let one who speaks in
a tongue pray that he may [1]translate.
14 For if I pray in a tongue, my spirit
prays, but my mind is unfruitful.
15 [a]What is *the outcome* then? I will
pray with the spirit and I will pray
with the mind also; I will [b]sing with
the spirit and I will sing with the mind
also. 16 Otherwise if you bless [1]in the
spirit *only*, how will the one who fills
the place of the [2]uninformed say [a]the
"Amen" at your [b]giving of thanks,
since he does not know what you are
saying? 17 For you are giving thanks
well enough, but the other person
is not [a]edified. 18 I thank God that I
speak in tongues more than you all;
19 however, in the church I desire to
speak five words with my mind so
that I may instruct others also, rather
than ten thousand words in a tongue.

20 [a]Brothers, [b]do not be children
in your thinking; rather in evil [c]be
infants, but in your thinking be
mature. 21 In [a]the Law it is written,
"[b]BY MEN OF STRANGE TONGUES AND
BY THE LIPS OF STRANGERS I WILL SPEAK
TO THIS PEOPLE, AND EVEN SO THEY
WILL NOT LISTEN TO ME," says the
[1]Lord. 22 So then tongues are for a
sign, not to those who believe but
to unbelievers; but [a]prophecy *is for
a sign* not to unbelievers but to those
who believe. 23 Therefore if the whole
church assembles together and all
speak in tongues, and [1]uninformed
men or unbelievers enter, will they
not say that [a]you are out of your
mind? 24 But if all [a]prophesy, and
an unbeliever or an [1]uninformed
man enters, he is [b]convicted by all,
he is called to account by all; 25 [a]the
secrets of his heart are disclosed;
and so he will [b]fall on his face and
worship God, declaring that [c]SURELY
GOD IS AMONG YOU.

### *Orderly Worship*

26 [a]What is *the outcome* then, [b]broth-
ers? When you assemble, [c]each one
has a [d]psalm, has a [e]teaching, has
a [e]revelation, has a [f]tongue, has a
[g,1]translation. Let [h]all things be done
for edification. 27 If anyone speaks in
a [a]tongue, *it should be* by two or at
the most three, and *each* in turn, and
one must [b,1]translate; 28 but if there
is no [1]translator, he must keep silent
in the church, and let him speak to
himself and to God. 29 And let two
or three [a]prophets speak, and let
the others [b]pass judgment. 30 But if

**14:9** [a]1Co 9:26 **14:11** [a]Ac 28:2 [1]Or *foreigner* [2]Or *in my estimation* **14:12** [a]Ro 14:19; 1Co 14:4, 5, 17, 26 [1]Lit *spirits* **14:13** [1]Or *interpret* **14:15** [a]Ac 21:22; 1Co 14:26 [b]Eph 5:19; Col 3:16 **14:16** [a]Dt 27:15-26; 1Chr 16:36; Ne 5:13; 8:6; Ps 106:48; Jer 11:5; 28:6; Rev 5:14; 7:12 [b]Mt 15:36 [1]Or *with the* [2]Unversed in spiritual gifts **14:17** [a]Ro 14:19; 1Co 14:4, 5, 12, 26 **14:20** [a]Ro 1:13 [b]Eph 4:14; Heb 5:12f [c]Ps 131:2; Mt 18:3; Ro 16:19; 1Pe 2:2 **14:21** [a]Jn 10:34; 1Co 14:34 [b]Is 28:11f [1]In OT, Yahweh, cf. Is 28:13 **14:22** [a]1Co 14:1 **14:23** [a]Ac 2:13 [1]v 16, note 2 **14:24** [a]1Co 14:1 [b]Jn 16:8 [1]v 16, note 2 **14:25** [a]Jn 4:19 [b]Lk 17:16 [c]Is 45:14; Da 2:47; Zec 8:23; Ac 4:13 **14:26** [a]1Co 14:15 [b]Ro 1:13 [c]1Co 12:8-10 [d]Eph 5:19 [e]1Co 14:6 [f]1Co 14:2 [g]1Co 12:10; 14:5, 13, 27f [h]Ro 14:19 [1]Or *an interpretation* **14:27** [a]1Co 14:2 [b]1Co 12:10; 14:5, 13, 26ff [1]Or *interpret* **14:28** [1]Or *interpreter* **14:29** [a]1Co 13:2; 14:32, 37 [b]1Co 12:10

a revelation is made to another who
is seated, the first one must keep
silent. **31** For you can all prophesy one
by one, so that all may learn and all
may be exhorted. **32** And the spirits
of prophets are subject to prophets;
**33** for God is not *a God* of [a]confusion
but of [1]peace, as in [b]all the churches
of the [c]saints.

**34** The women are to [a]keep silent
in the churches, for they are not per-
mitted to speak, but [b]are to subject
themselves, just as [c]the Law also says.
**35** But if they desire to learn anything,
let them ask their own husbands at
home, for it is disgraceful for a wom-
an to speak in church. **36** [1]Was it from
you that the word of God *first* went
forth? Or has it arrived to you only?

**37** [a]If anyone thinks he is a prophet
or [b]spiritual, let him recognize that
the things which I write to you [c]are
the Lord's commandment. **38** But if
anyone remains ignorant about *this*,
he [1]is ignored *by God*.

**39** Therefore, my brothers, [a]ear-
nestly desire to [b]prophesy, and do
not forbid to speak in tongues. **40** But
[a]all things must be done properly
and in an orderly manner.

### *The Resurrection of Christ*

**15** Now [a]I make known to you,
brothers, the [b]gospel which
I proclaimed as good news to you,
which also you received, [c]in which
also you stand, **2** by which also you
are saved, [a]if you hold fast [1]the
word which I proclaimed to you as
good news, [b]unless you believed for
nothing.

**3** For [a]I delivered to you [1]as of first
importance what I also received, that
Christ died [b]for our sins [c]according
to the Scriptures, **4** and that He was
buried, and that He was [a]raised
on the third day [b]according to the
Scriptures, **5** and that [a]He appeared
to [b]Cephas, then [c]to the twelve. **6** Af-
ter that He appeared to more than
five hundred brothers at one time,
most of whom remain until now, but
some [a]have fallen asleep. **7** After that,
He appeared to [a,1]James, then to [b]all
the apostles, **8** and last of all, as [1]to
one untimely born, [a]He appeared to
me also. **9** For I am [a]the least of the
apostles, [1]and not worthy to be called
an apostle, because I [b]persecuted the
church of God. **10** But by [a]the grace
of God I am what I am, and His grace
toward me did not prove vain; but I
[b]labored even more than all of them,
yet [c]not I, but the grace of God with
me. **11** Whether then *it was* I or they,
so we preach and so you believed.

### *The Resurrection of the Dead*

**12** Now if Christ is preached, that He
has been raised from the dead, how
do some among you say that there [a]is
no resurrection of the dead? **13** But if

---

**14:33** [a]1Co 14:40 [b]1Co 4:17; 7:17 [c]Ac 9:13 [1]Or *peace. As in all...saints, let* **14:34** [a]1Co 11:5, 13 [b]1Ti 2:11f; 1Pe 3:1 [c]1Co 14:21 **14:36** [1]Lit *Or was* **14:37** [a]2Co 10:7 [b]1Co 2:15 [c]1Jn 4:6 **14:38** [1]Two early *mss is not to be recognized* **14:39** [a]1Co 12:31 [b]1Co 13:2; 14:1 **14:40** [a]1Co 14:33 ◆ **15:1** [a]Ro 2:16; Ga 1:11 [b]Ro 2:16; 1Co 3:6; 4:15 [c]Ro 5:2; 11:20; 2Co 1:24 **15:2** [a]Ro 11:22 [b]Ga 3:4 [1]Lit *to what word I* **15:3** [a]1Co 11:23 [b]Jn 1:29; Ga 1:4; Heb 5:1, 3; 1Pe 2:24 [c]Is 53:5-12; Mt 26:24; Lk 24:25-27; Ac 8:32f; 17:2f; 26:22 [1]Lit *among the first* **15:4** [a]Mt 16:21; Jn 2:20ff; Ac 2:24 [b]Ps 16:8ff; Ac 2:31; 26:22f **15:5** [a]Lk 24:34 [b]1Co 1:12 [c]Mk 16:14; Lk 24:36; Jn 20:19 **15:6** [a]Ac 7:60; 1Co 15:18, 20 **15:7** [a]Ac 12:17 [b]Lk 24:33, 36f; Ac 1:3f [1]Or *Jacob*; James is the Eng form of Jacob **15:8** [a]Ac 9:3-8; 22:6-11; 26:12-18; 1Co 9:1 [1]Lit *to an untimely birth* **15:9** [a]2Co 12:11; Eph 3:8; 1Ti 1:15 [b]Ac 8:3 [1]Lit *who am* **15:10** [a]Ro 12:3 [b]2Co 11:23; Col 1:29; 1Ti 4:10 [c]1Co 3:6; 2Co 3:5; Php 2:13 **15:12** [a]Ac 17:32; 23:8; 2Ti 2:18

there is no resurrection of the dead,
not even Christ has been raised.
**14** And [a]if Christ has not been raised,
then our preaching is vain, your faith
also is vain. **15** Moreover we are even
found *to be* false witnesses of God,
because we bore witness [1]against
God that He [a]raised [2]Christ, whom
He did not raise, if in fact the dead
are not raised. **16** For if the dead are
not raised, not even Christ has been
raised. **17** And if Christ has not been
raised, your faith is worthless; [a]you
are still in your sins. **18** Then those
also who [a]have fallen asleep in Christ
have perished. **19** If we have hoped in
Christ in this life only, we are [a]of all
men most to be pitied.

**20** But now Christ [a]has been raised
from the dead, the [b]first fruits of
those who have [c]fallen asleep. **21** For
since [a]by a man *came* death, by a
man also *came* the resurrection of
the dead. **22** For [a]as in Adam all die,
so also in [1]Christ all will be made
alive. **23** But each in his own order:
Christ [a]the first fruits, after that
[b]those who are Christ's at [c]His com-
ing. **24** Then *comes* the end, when He
hands over [a]the kingdom to the [b]God
and Father, when He has abolished
[c]all rule and all authority and power.
**25** For He must reign [a]UNTIL HE HAS
PUT ALL HIS ENEMIES UNDER HIS FEET.
**26** *The last enemy* to be [a]abolished is
death. **27** For [a]HE HAS PUT ALL THINGS
IN SUBJECTION UNDER HIS FEET. But
when He says, "[b]All things are put
in subjection," it is evident that He
is excepted who put all things in
subjection to Him. **28** And when [a]all
things are subjected to Him, then the
Son Himself also will be subjected to
the One who subjected all things to
Him, so that [b]God may be all in all.

**29** Otherwise, what will those do
who are baptized [1]for the dead? If
the dead are not raised at all, why
then are they baptized for them?
**30** Why are we also [a]in danger every
hour? **31** I affirm, brothers, by the
boasting in you which I have in
Christ Jesus our Lord, [a]I die daily.
**32** If [1]from human motives I [a]fought
with wild beasts at [b]Ephesus, what
does it profit me? If the dead are not
raised, [c]LET US EAT AND DRINK, FOR
TOMORROW WE DIE. **33** [a]Do not be de-
ceived: "Bad company corrupts good
morals." **34** [a]Become righteously
sober-minded, and stop sinning; for
some have [b]no knowledge of God. [c]I
speak *this* to your shame.

### *The Resurrection Body*

**35** But [a]someone will say, "How are
[b]the dead raised? And with what
kind of body do they come?" **36** [a]You
fool! That which you [b]sow does not
come to life unless it dies; **37** and that
which you sow, you do not sow the
body which is to be, but a bare grain,
perhaps of wheat or of [1]something
else. **38** But God gives it a body just

**15:14** [a]1Th 4:14 **15:15** [a]Ac 2:24 [1]Or *concerning* [2]Messiah **15:17** [a]Ro 4:25 **15:18** [a]1Co 15:6; 1Th 4:16; Rev 14:13 **15:19** [a]1Co 4:9; 2Ti 3:12 **15:20** [a]Ac 2:24; 1Pe 1:3 [b]Ac 26:23; 1Co 15:23; Rev 1:5 [c]1Co 15:6; 1Th 4:16; Rev 14:13 **15:21** [a]Ro 5:12 **15:22** [a]Ro 5:14-18 [1]Messiah **15:23** [a]Ac 26:23; 1Co 15:20; Rev 1:5 [b]1Co 6:14; 15:52; 1Th 4:16 [c]1Th 2:19 **15:24** [a]Da 2:44; 7:14, 27; 2Pe 1:11 [b]Eph 5:20 [c]Ro 8:38 **15:25** [a]Ps 110:1; Mt 22:44 **15:26** [a]2Ti 1:10; Rev 20:14; 21:4 **15:27** [a]Ps 8:6 [b]Mt 11:27; 28:18; Eph 1:22; Heb 2:8 **15:28** [a]Php 3:21 [b]1Co 3:23; 12:6 **15:29** [1]Or *because of* **15:30** [a]2Co 11:26 **15:31** [a]Ro 8:36 **15:32** [a]2Co 1:8 [b]Ac 18:19; 1Co 16:8 [c]Is 22:13; 56:12; Lk 12:19 [1]Lit *according to man* **15:33** [a]1Co 6:9 **15:34** [a]Ro 13:11 [b]Mt 22:29; Ac 26:8 [c]1Co 6:5 **15:35** [a]Ro 9:19 [b]Eze 37:3 **15:36** [a]Lk 11:40 [b]Jn 12:24 **15:37** [1]Lit *some of the rest*

as He wished, and [a]to each of the
seeds a body of its own. **39** All flesh
is not the same flesh, but there is one
*flesh* of men, and another flesh of
beasts, and another flesh of birds,
and another of fish. **40** There are also
heavenly bodies and earthly bodies,
but the glory of the heavenly is one,
and the *glory* of the earthly is anoth-
er. **41** There is one glory of the sun,
and another glory of the moon, and
another glory of the stars; for star
differs from star in glory.

**42** [a]So also is the resurrection of
the dead. It is sown [b,1]a corruptible
*body*, it is raised [c2]an incorruptible
*body*; **43** it is sown in dishonor, it
is raised in [a]glory; it is sown in
weakness, it is raised in power; **44** it
is sown a [a]natural body, it is raised
a [b]spiritual body. If there is a natural
body, there is also a spiritual *body*.
**45** So also it is written, "The first
[a]MAN, Adam, BECAME A LIVING SOUL."
The [b]last Adam *became* a [c]life-giving
spirit. **46** However, the spiritual is
not first, but the natural; then the
spiritual. **47** The first man is [a]from
the earth, [b,1]earthy; the second man
is from heaven. **48** As is the earthy,
so also are those who are earthy; and
as is the heavenly, [a]so also are those
who are heavenly. **49** And just as we
have [a]borne the image of the earthy,
[1]we [b]will also bear the image of the
heavenly.

**50** Now I say this, brothers, that
[a]flesh and blood cannot [b]inherit
the kingdom of God, nor does the
corruptible inherit [c]the incorrupt-
ible. **51** Behold, I tell you a [a]mystery:
we will not all sleep, but we will all
be [b]changed, **52** in a moment, in the
twinkling of an eye, at the last trum-
pet. For [a]the trumpet will sound, and
[b]the dead will be raised incorrupt-
ible, and [c]we will be changed. **53** For
this corruptible must put on [a]the
incorruptible, and this [b]mortal must
put on immortality. **54** But when this
corruptible puts on the incorruptible,
and this mortal puts on immortality,
then will come about the word that is
written, "[a]DEATH IS SWALLOWED UP in
victory. **55** [a]O DEATH, WHERE IS YOUR
VICTORY? O DEATH, WHERE IS YOUR
STING?" **56** Now the sting of [a]death
is sin, and [b]the power of sin is the
law; **57** but [a]thanks be to God, who
gives us the [b]victory through our
Lord Jesus Christ!

**58** [a]Therefore, my beloved broth-
ers, be steadfast, immovable, always
abounding in [b]the work of the Lord,
knowing that your labor is not *in* vain
in the Lord.

### *The Collection of Gifts*

**16** Now concerning [a]the col-
lection for [b]the saints, as [c]I
directed the churches of [d]Galatia,
so do you also. **2** On [a]the first day of
every week each one of you is to [1]set
*something* aside, saving whatever he
has prospered, so that [b]no collections
be made when I come. **3** And when I

---

***15:38*** [a]*Ge 1:11* ***15:42*** [a]*Da 12:3; Mt 13:43* [b]Ro 8:21; 1Co 15:50; Ga 6:8 [c]Ro 2:7 [1]Lit *in corruption* [2]Lit *in incorruption* **15:43** [a]Php 3:21; Col 3:4 **15:44** [a]1Co 2:14 [b]1Co 15:50 **15:45** [a]Ge 2:7 [b]Ro 5:14 [c]Jn 5:21; 6:57f; Ro 8:2 **15:47** [a]Jn 3:31 [b]Ge 2:7; 3:19 [1]Lit *made of dust* **15:48** [a]Php 3:20f **15:49** [a]Ge 5:3 [b]Ro 8:29 [1]Two early mss *let us also* **15:50** [a]Mt 16:17; Jn 3:5f [b]1Co 6:9 [c]Ro 2:7 **15:51** [a]1Co 13:2 [b]2Co 5:2, 4 **15:52** [a]Mt 24:31 [b]Jn 5:28 [c]1Th 4:15, 17 **15:53** [a]Ro 2:7 [b]2Co 5:4 **15:54** [a]Is 25:8 **15:55** [a]Hos 13:14 **15:56** [a]Ro 5:12 [b]Ro 3:20; 4:15; 7:8 **15:57** [a]Ro 7:25; 2Co 2:14 [b]Ro 8:37; Heb 2:14f; 1Jn 5:4; Rev 21:4 **15:58** [a]2Pe 3:14 [b]1Co 16:10 ◆ **16:1** [a]Ac 24:17; Ro 15:25f [b]Ac 9:13 [c]1Co 4:17 [d]Ac 16:6 **16:2** [a]Ac 20:7 [b]2Co 9:4f [1]Lit *put by himself*

arrive, [a]whomever you may approve,
I will send them with letters to carry
your gracious gift to Jerusalem, **4** and
if it is fitting for me to go also, they
will go with me.
**5** But I [a]will come to you after I go
through [b]Macedonia, for I [c]am going
through Macedonia; **6** and perhaps
I will stay with you, or even spend
the winter, so that you may [a]send me
on my way wherever I may go. **7** For
I do not wish to see you now [a]*just* in
passing, for I hope to remain with
you for some time, [b]if the Lord permits.
**8** But I will remain in [a]Ephesus
until [b]Pentecost, **9** for a [a]wide and
effective door has opened to me, and
[b]there are many adversaries.
**10** Now if [a]Timothy comes, take
care that he is with you without fear,
for he is doing [b]the Lord's work, as
I also am. **11** [a]So let no one despise
him. But [b]send him on his way [c]in
peace, so that he may come to me,
for I expect him with the brothers.
**12** Now concerning [a]Apollos our
brother, I encouraged him greatly to
come to you with the brothers, and
it was not at all *his* desire to come
now, but he will come when he has
opportunity.

### *Final Instructions and Greetings*

**13** [a]Be watchful, [b]stand firm in the
faith, [c]act like men, [d]be strong. **14** Let
all that you do be done [a]in love.
**15** Now I exhort you, brothers (you
know the [a]household of Stephanas,
that [1]they were the [b]first fruits of
[c]Achaia, and that they have devoted
themselves for [d]service to [e]the
saints), **16** that [a]you also be in subjection
to such men and to everyone
who helps in the work and labors.
**17** And I rejoice over the [a,1]coming of
Stephanas and Fortunatus and Achaicus,
because they have [2]supplied
[b]what was lacking on your part.
**18** For they [a]have refreshed my spirit
and yours. Therefore [b]recognize such
men.
**19** The churches of [a]Asia greet you.
[b]Aquila and Prisca greet you heartily
in the Lord, with [c]the church that
is in their house. **20** All the brothers
greet you. [a]Greet one another with
a holy kiss.
**21** The greeting is in [a]my own
hand—[1]Paul. **22** If anyone does not
love the Lord, he is to be [a,1]accursed.
[b,2]Maranatha. **23** [a]The grace of the
Lord Jesus be with you. **24** My love
be with you all in Christ Jesus. Amen.

---

**16:3** [a]2Co 3:1; 8:18f **16:5** [a]1Co 4:19 [b]Ro 15:26 [c]Ac 19:21 **16:6** [a]Ac 15:3; 1Co 16:11 **16:7** [a]2Co 1:15f [b]Ac 18:21 **16:8** [a]Ac 18:19 [b]Ac 2:1 **16:9** [a]Ac 14:27 [b]Ac 19:9 **16:10** [a]Ac 16:1; 1Co 4:17; 2Co 1:1 [b]1Co 15:58 **16:11** [a]1Ti 4:12; Tit 2:15 [b]Ac 15:3; 1Co 16:6 [c]Ac 15:33 **16:12** [a]Ac 18:24; 1Co 1:12; 3:5f **16:13** [a]Mt 24:42 [b]1Co 15:1; Ga 5:1; Php 1:27; 4:1; 1Th 3:8; 2Th 2:15 [c]1Sa 4:9; 2Sa 10:12 [d]Ps 31:24; Eph 3:16; 6:10; Col 1:11 **16:14** [a]1Co 14:1 **16:15** [a]1Co 1:16 [b]Ro 16:5 [c]Ac 18:12 [d]Ro 15:31 [e]1Co 16:1 [1]Lit *it was* **16:16** [a]1Th 5:12; Heb 13:17 **16:17** [a]2Co 7:6f [b]2Co 11:9; Php 2:30 [1]Or *presence* [2]Or *made up for your absence* **16:18** [a]2Co 7:13; Phm 7, 20 [b]Php 2:29; 1Th 5:12 **16:19** [a]Ac 16:6 [b]Ac 18:2 [c]Ro 16:5 **16:20** [a]Ro 16:16 **16:21** [a]Ro 16:22; Ga 6:11; Col 4:18; 2Th 3:17; Phm 19 [1]Lit *Paul's* **16:22** [a]Ro 9:3 [b]Php 4:5; Rev 22:20 [1]Gr *anathema* [2]O [our] Lord come! **16:23** [a]Ro 16:20

*The Second Letter of Paul to the*

# CORINTHIANS

### *God of All Comfort*

**1** Paul, [a]an apostle of [b]Christ Jesus
[c]by the will of God, and [d]Timothy
*our* brother,
To [e]the church of God which is at
[f]Corinth with all the [1]saints who are
throughout [g]Achaia:
**2** [a]Grace to you and peace from
God our Father and the Lord Jesus
Christ.
**3** [a]Blessed *be* the God and Father
of our Lord Jesus Christ, the Father
of mercies and [b]God of all comfort,
**4** who [a]comforts us in all our afflic-
tion so that we will be able to comfort
those who are in [1]any affliction with
the comfort with which we ourselves
are comforted by God. **5** For just [a]as
the sufferings of Christ abound to us,
so also our comfort abounds through
Christ. **6** But whether we are afflicted,
it is [a]for your comfort and salvation;
or whether we are comforted, it is
for your comfort, which is working
in *your* perseverance in the same
sufferings which we also suffer. **7** And
our hope for you is firmly grounded,
knowing that [a]as you are sharers of
our sufferings, so also you are *sharers*
of our comfort.
**8** For [a]we do not want you to be
unaware, brothers, of our [b]affliction
which came *to us* in [c,1]Asia, that we
were burdened excessively, beyond
our strength, so that we despaired
even to live. **9** [1]Indeed, we had the
sentence of death within ourselves so
that we would not have confidence
in ourselves, but in God who raises
the dead; **10** who [a]rescued us from
so great a *peril of* death, and will
rescue *us*, [1]He [b]on whom we have
set our hope. And He will yet rescue
us, **11** you also joining in [a]helping *us*
through your prayers on our behalf,
so that thanks may be given on our
behalf by [b]many persons for the
gracious gift bestowed on us through
*the prayers of* many.

### *Paul's Change of Plans*

**12** For our boasting is this: the tes-
timony of [a]our conscience, that in
[1]holiness and [b]godly sincerity, [c]not
in fleshly wisdom but in the grace of
God, we have conducted ourselves in
the world, and especially toward you.
**13** For we write nothing else to you
than what you read and understand,
and I hope you will understand [a]until
the end, **14** just as you also partially
did understand us, that we are your
reason for boasting as you also are
ours, in [a]the day of our Lord Jesus.
**15** And in this confidence I intend-
ed at first to [a]come to you, so that
you might receive [b,1]grace twice;
**16** [1]that is, to [a]pass [2]your way into

◆ **1:1** [a]Ro 1:1; Ga 1:1; Eph 1:1; Col 1:1; 2Ti 1:1; Tit 1:1 [b]Ga 3:26 [c]1Co 1:1 [d]Ac 16:1; 1Co 16:10; 2Co 1:19 [e]1Co 10:32 [f]Ac 18:1 [g]Ac 18:12 [1]Or *holy ones* **1:2** [a]Ro 1:7 **1:3** [a]Eph 1:3; 1Pe 1:3 [b]Ro 15:5 **1:4** [a]Is 51:12; 66:13; 2Co 7:6, 7, 13 [1]Lit *every* **1:5** [a]2Co 4:10; Php 3:10; Col 1:24 **1:6** [a]2Co 4:15; 12:15; Eph 3:1, 13; 2Ti 2:10 **1:7** [a]Ro 8:17 **1:8** [a]Ro 1:13 [b]Ac 19:23; 1Co 15:32 [c]Ac 16:6 [1]West coast province of Asia Minor **1:9** [1]Lit *But we ourselves* **1:10** [a]Ro 15:31 [b]1Ti 4:10 [1]One early ms *on whom we have set our hope that He will also* **1:11** [a]Ro 15:30; Php 1:19; Phm 22 [b]2Co 4:15; 9:11f **1:12** [a]Ac 23:1; 1Th 2:10; Heb 13:18 [b]2Co 2:17 [c]1Co 1:17; Jas 3:15 [1]Some mss *simplicity*, cf. 11:3 **1:13** [a]1Co 1:8 **1:14** [a]1Co 1:8 **1:15** [a]1Co 4:19 [b]Ro 1:11; 15:29 [1]One early ms *joy* **1:16** [a]Ac 19:21; 1Co 16:5-7 [1]Lit *and* [2]Lit *through you into*

[b]Macedonia, and again from Mace-
donia to come to you, and by you to
be [c]helped on my journey to Judea.
**17** Therefore, was I vacillating when
I intended to do this? Or what I pur-
pose, do I purpose [a]according to the
flesh, so that with me there will be
yes, yes and no, no *at the same time*?
**18** But as [a]God is faithful, [b]our word
to you is not yes and no. **19** For [a]the
Son of God, Jesus Christ, who was
preached among you by us—by me
and [b]Silvanus and [c]Timothy—was
not yes and no, but has become yes
[d]in Him. **20** For [a]as many as are the
promises of God, [b]in Him they are yes.
Therefore also through Him is [c]our
Amen to the glory of God through
us. **21** Now He who [a]establishes us
with you in Christ and [b]anointed us
is God, **22** who also [a]sealed us and
[b]gave the [1]pledge of the Spirit in our
hearts.
**23** But [a]I call God as witness [1]to
my soul, that [b]to spare you I did not
come again to [c]Corinth. **24** Not that
we [a]lord it over your faith, but are
workers with you for your joy; for
in your faith you are [b]standing firm.
**2** But I determined this [1]for my own
sake, that I [a]would not come to
you again in sorrow. **2** For if I [a]cause
you sorrow, who then makes me glad
but the one whom I made sorrowful?
**3** And this is the very thing I [a]wrote
you, so that [b]when I came, I would
not have sorrow from those who
ought to make me rejoice; having
[c]confidence in you all that my joy
would be *the joy* of you all. **4** For
out of much affliction and anguish
of heart I [a]wrote to you with many
tears; not so that you would be made
sorrowful, but that you might know
the love which I have abundantly for
you.

### *Forgive and Love the Sinner*

**5** But [a]if any has caused sorrow, he
has caused sorrow not to me, but in
some degree—[1]in order not to say
too much—to all of you. **6** Sufficient
for such a one is [a]this punishment
which *was inflicted* by the majority,
**7** so that on the contrary you should
rather [a]graciously forgive and com-
fort *him*, lest such a one be swallowed
up by excessive sorrow. **8** Therefore
I encourage you to reaffirm *your*
love for him. **9** For to this end also
[a]I wrote, so that I might [b]know
your proven character, whether you
are [c]obedient in all things. **10** But
one whom you graciously forgive
anything, I *graciously forgive* also.
For indeed what I have graciously
forgiven, if I have graciously forgiven
anything, *I did it* for your sakes [a]in
the presence of Christ, **11** so that no
advantage would be taken of us by
[a]Satan, for [b]we are not ignorant of
his schemes.
**12** Now when I came to [a]Troas for
the [b]gospel of Christ and when a

**1:16** [b]Ac 19:21; Ro 15:26 [c]Ac 15:3; 1Co 16:6, 11 **1:17** [a]2Co 10:2f; 11:18 **1:18** [a]1Co 1:9 [b]2Co 2:17
**1:19** [a]Mt 4:3; 16:16; 26:63 [b]Ac 15:22; 1Th 1:1; 2Th 1:1; 1Pe 5:12 [c]Ac 18:5; 2Co 1:1 [d]Heb 13:8 **1:20** [a]Ro 15:8
[b]Heb 13:8 [c]1Co 14:16; Rev 3:14 **1:21** [a]1Co 1:8 [b]1Jn 2:20, 27 **1:22** [a]Jn 3:33 [b]Ro 8:16; 2Co 5:5; Eph 1:14
[1]Or *down payment* **1:23** [a]Ro 1:9; Ga 1:20 [b]1Co 4:21; 2Co 2:1, 3 [c]2Co 1:1 [1]Lit *upon* **1:24** [a]2Co 4:5;
11:20; 1Pe 5:3 [b]Ro 11:20; 1Co 15:1 ◆ **2:1** [a]1Co 4:21; 2Co 12:21 [1]Or *as far as I am concerned* **2:2** [a]2Co 7:8
**2:3** [a]2Co 2:9; 7:8, 12 [b]1Co 4:21; 2Co 12:21 [c]Ga 5:10; 2Th 3:4; Phm 21 **2:4** [a]2Co 2:9; 7:8, 12 **2:5** [a]1Co 5:1f
[1]Lit *so that I not be burdensome* **2:6** [a]1Co 5:4f; 2Co 7:11 **2:7** [a]Ga 6:1; Eph 4:32 **2:9** [a]2Co 2:3f
[b]2Co 8:2; Php 2:22 [c]2Co 7:15; 10:6 **2:10** [a]1Co 5:4; 2Co 4:6 **2:11** [a]Mt 4:10 [b]Lk 22:31; 2Co 4:4; 1Pe 5:8
**2:12** [a]Ac 16:8 [b]Ro 1:1; 2Co 4:3, 4; 8:18; 9:13; 10:14; 11:4, 7; 1Th 3:2

[c]door was opened for me in the
Lord, **13** I [a]had no rest for my spirit,
not finding [b]Titus my brother. But
[c]saying farewell to them, I went on
to [d]Macedonia.
**14** [a]But thanks be to God, who always
[b]leads us in triumphal procession in
Christ, and manifests through us the
[c]aroma of the [d]knowledge of Him in
every place. **15** For we are a [a]fragrance
of Christ to God among [b]those who
are being saved and among those who
are perishing; **16** [a]to the one an aroma
from death to death, to the other an
aroma from life to life. And who is
[b]sufficient for these things? **17** For
we are not like many, [a,1]peddling the
word of God, but [b]as from sincerity,
but as from God, [c]in the sight of God,
we speak in Christ.

### *Ministers of a New Covenant*

**3** Are we beginning to [a]commend
ourselves again? Or do we need,
as some, [b]letters of commendation to
you or from you? **2** [a]You are our letter,
having been written in our hearts,
known and read by all men, **3** being
manifested that you are a letter of
Christ, [a]ministered to by us, having
been written not with ink but with
the Spirit of [b]the living God, not on
[c]tablets of stone but on [d]tablets of
hearts of [e]flesh.
**4** And such [a]confidence we have
through Christ toward God. **5** Not
that we are sufficient in ourselves
to consider anything as *coming*
from ourselves, but [a]our sufficiency
is from God, **6** who also made us
sufficient *as* [a]ministers of a [b]new
covenant, not of [c]the letter but of
the Spirit; for the letter kills, but
[d]the Spirit gives life.
**7** But if the [a]ministry of death,
[b]in letters having been engraved on
stones, came [1]with glory, [c]so that the
sons of Israel could not look intently
at the face of Moses because of the
glory of his face, which was being
brought to an end, **8** how will the
ministry of the Spirit not be even
more in glory? **9** For if [a]the ministry of
condemnation has glory, much more
does the [b]ministry of righteousness
abound in glory. **10** For indeed what
had been glorious, in this case has
no glory because of the glory that
surpasses *it.* **11** For if that which was
being brought to an end *was* [1]with
glory, much more that which remains
*is* in glory.
**12** [a]Therefore having such a hope,
[b]we use great boldness, **13** and *are*
not like Moses, [a]*who* used to put a
veil over his face so that the sons
of Israel would not look intently
at the consequence of what was
being brought to an end. **14** But their
minds were [a]hardened; for until this
very day at the [b]reading of [c]the old
covenant the same veil [1]remains

---

**2:12** [c]Ac 14:27 **2:13** [a]2Co 7:5 [b]2Co 7:6, 13f; 8:6, 16, 23; 12:18; Ga 2:1, 3; 2Ti 4:10; Tit 1:4 [c]Mk 6:46 [d]Ro 15:26 **2:14** [a]Ro 1:8; 6:17; 1Co 15:57; 2Co 8:16; 9:15 [b]Col 2:15 [c]SS 1:3; Eze 20:41; Eph 5:2; Php 4:18 [d]1Co 12:8 **2:15** [a]SS 1:3; Eze 20:41; Eph 5:2; Php 4:18 [b]1Co 1:18 **2:16** [a]Lk 2:34; Jn 9:39; 1Pe 2:7f [b]2Co 3:5f *2:17* *[a]2Co 4:2; Ga 1:6-9* [b]1Co 5:8; 2Co 1:12; 1Th 2:4; 1Pe 4:11 [c]2Co 12:19 [1]Or *corrupting* ◆ **3:1** [a]2Co 5:12; 10:12, 18; 12:11 [b]Ac 18:27; 1Co 16:3 **3:2** [a]1Co 9:2 **3:3** [a]2Co 3:6 [b]Mt 16:16 [c]Ex 24:12; 31:18; 32:15f; 2Co 3:7 [d]Pr 3:3; 7:3; Jer 17:1 [e]Jer 31:33; Eze 11:19; 36:26 **3:4** [a]Eph 3:12 **3:5** [a]1Co 15:10 **3:6** [a]1Co 3:5 [b]Jer 31:31; Lk 22:20 [c]Ro 2:29 [d]Jn 6:63; Ro 7:6 **3:7** [a]Ro 4:15; 5:20; 7:5f; 2Co 3:9; Ga 3:10, 21f [b]Ex 24:12; 31:18; 32:15f; 2Co 3:3 [c]Ex 34:29-35; 2Co 3:13 [1]Or *in glory* **3:9** [a]Dt 27:26; 2Co 3:7; Heb 12:18-21 [b]Ro 1:17; 3:21f **3:11** [1]Lit *through* **3:12** [a]2Co 7:4 [b]Ac 4:13, 29; 2Co 7:4; Eph 6:19; 1Th 2:2 **3:13** [a]Ex 34:33-35; 2Co 3:7 **3:14** [a]Ro 11:7; 2Co 4:4 [b]Ac 13:15 [c]2Co 3:6 [1]Or *remains, it not being revealed that it is done away in Christ*

unlifted, because it is brought to
an end in Christ. **15** But to this day
whenever Moses is read, a veil lies
over their heart, **16** but [a]WHENEVER
a person TURNS TO THE [1]LORD, THE
VEIL IS TAKEN AWAY. **17** Now the Lord
is the Spirit, and where [a]the Spirit of
the Lord is, [b]*there* is freedom. **18** But
we all, with unveiled face, [a]beholding
as in a mirror the [b]glory of the Lord,
are being [c]transformed into the same
image from glory to glory, just as
from [d]the Lord, the Spirit.

### *The Gospel of the Glory of Christ*

**4** Therefore, since we have this
[a]ministry, as we [b]received mer-
cy, we [c]do not lose heart, **2** but we
have renounced the [a]hidden things
of shame, not walking in craftiness
or [b]adulterating the word of God,
but by the manifestation of truth
[c]commending ourselves to every
man's conscience in the sight of God.
**3** And even if our [a]gospel is [b]veiled, it
is veiled [1]to [c]those who are perishing,
**4** in whose case [a]the god of [b]this age
has [c]blinded the minds of the unbe-
lieving [1]so that they might not see
the [d]light of the gospel of the [e]glory
of Christ, who is the [f]image of God.
**5** For we [a]do not preach ourselves but
Jesus Christ as Lord, and ourselves
as your slaves [1]for the sake of Jesus.
**6** For God, who said, "[a]Light shall
shine out of darkness," is the One
who has [b]shone in our hearts to give
the [c]Light of the knowledge of the
glory of God in the face of Christ.
**7** But we have this treasure in
[a]earthen vessels, so that the surpass-
ing greatness of [b]the power will be
of God and not from ourselves; **8** [a]in
every way afflicted, but not [b]crushed;
[c]perplexed, but not despairing;
**9** [a]persecuted, but not [b]forsaken;
[c]struck down, but not destroyed;
**10** [a]always carrying about in the
body the dying of Jesus, so that [b]the
life of Jesus also may be manifested
in our body. **11** For we who live are
constantly being delivered over to
death for Jesus' sake, so that the life
of Jesus also may be manifested in
our mortal flesh. **12** So death works
in us, but life in you.
**13** But having the same [a]spirit of
faith, according to what is written,
"[b]I BELIEVED, THEREFORE I SPOKE," we
also believe, therefore we also speak,
**14** knowing that He who [a]raised the
Lord Jesus [b]will raise us also with
Jesus and will [c]present us with you.
**15** For all things *are* [a]for your sakes,
so that the grace which is [b,1]spreading
to more and more people may cause
the giving of thanks to abound to the
glory of God.
**16** Therefore we [a]do not lose heart,
but though our outer man is decaying,
yet our [b]inner man is [c]being renewed
day by day. **17** For our momentary,

---

**3:16** [a]Ex 34:34; Ro 11:23 [1]In OT, Yahweh, cf. Ex 34:34 **3:17** [a]Is 61:1f; Ga 4:6 [b]Jn 8:32; Ga 5:1, 13 **3:18** [a]1Co 13:12 [b]Jn 17:22, 24; 2Co 4:4, 6 [c]Ro 8:29 [d]2Co 3:17 ◆ **4:1** [a]1Co 3:5 [b]1Co 7:25 [c]Lk 18:1; 2Co 4:16; Ga 6:9; Eph 3:13; 2Th 3:13 **4:2** [a]Ro 6:21; 1Co 4:5 [b]2Co 2:17 [c]2Co 5:11f **4:3** [a]2Co 2:12 [b]1Co 2:6ff; 2Co 3:14 [c]1Co 1:18; 2Co 2:15 [1]Lit *in* **4:4** [a]Jn 12:31 [b]Mt 13:22 [c]2Co 3:14 [d]Ac 26:18; 2Co 4:6 [e]2Co 3:18; 4:6 [f]Jn 1:18; Php 2:6; Col 1:15; Heb 1:3 [1]Or *that the light...image of God, would not dawn* upon them **4:5** [a]1Co 4:15f; 1Th 2:6f [1]Two early mss *through Jesus* **4:6** [a]Ge 1:3 [b]2Pe 1:19 [c]Ac 26:18; 2Co 4:4 **4:7** [a]Job 4:19; 10:9; 33:6; Lam 4:2; 2Co 5:1; 2Ti 2:20 [b]Jdg 7:2; 1Co 2:5 **4:8** [a]2Co 1:8; 7:5 [b]2Co 6:12 [c]Ga 4:20 **4:9** [a]Jn 15:20; Ro 8:35f [b]Ps 129:2; Heb 13:5 [c]Ps 37:24; Pr 24:16; Mic 7:8 **4:10** [a]Ro 6:5; 8:36; Ga 6:17 [b]Ro 6:8 **4:13** [a]1Co 12:9 [b]Ps 116:10 **4:14** [a]Ac 2:24 [b]1Th 4:14 [c]Lk 21:36; Eph 5:27; Col 1:22; Jd 24 **4:15** [a]Ro 8:28; 2Co 1:6 [b]1Co 9:19; 2Co 1:11 [1]Lit *being multiplied through the many* **4:16** [a]2Co 4:1 [b]Ro 7:22 [c]Is 40:29, 31; Col 3:10

[a]light affliction is working out for us
an eternal weight of glory far beyond
all comparison, **18** while we [a]look not
at the things which are seen, but at
the things which are not seen; for the
things which are seen are temporal,
but the things which are not seen are
eternal.

### *The Temporal and Eternal*

**5** For we know that if [1]the [a]earthly
[b]tent which is our house is torn
down, we have a building from God, a
house [c]not made with hands, eternal
in the heavens. **2** For indeed in this
we [a]groan, longing to be [b]clothed
with our dwelling from heaven,
**3** inasmuch as we, having put it
on, will not be found naked. **4** For
indeed while we are in this tent, we
[a]groan, being burdened, because we
do not want to be unclothed but to
be [b]clothed, so that what is [c]mortal
will be swallowed up by life. **5** Now
He who prepared us for this very
purpose is God, who [a]gave to us the
Spirit as a [1]pledge.

**6** Therefore, being always of good
courage, and knowing that [a]while we
are at home in the body we are absent
from the Lord— **7** for [a]we walk by
faith, not by [1]sight— **8** we are of
good courage and [a]prefer rather to
be absent from the body and [b]to be at
home with the Lord. **9** Therefore we
also have as our ambition, whether
at home or absent, to be [a]pleasing to
Him. **10** For we must all appear before
[a]the judgment seat of Christ, so that
each one may be recompensed for
[1]his deeds in the body, according to
what he has done, whether good or
bad.

**11** So then, knowing the [a]fear of
the Lord, we persuade men, but we
[1]have been made manifest to God;
and I hope that we [1]have been [b]made
manifest also in your consciences.
**12** We are not [a]again commending
ourselves to you but *are* giving you
an [b]opportunity to boast of us, so
that you will have *an answer* for
those who boast in appearance and
not in heart. **13** For if we [1]are [a]out of
our mind, it is for God, or if we are
of right mind, it is for you. **14** For the
love of Christ [a]controls us, having
concluded this, that [b]one died for
all, therefore all died. **15** And He died
for all, so that they who live would
no longer [a]live for themselves, but
for Him who died and rose again on
their behalf.

**16** Therefore from now on we
recognize no one [a,1]according to the
flesh; even though we have known
Christ [1]according to the flesh, yet
now we know *Him in this way* no
longer. **17** Therefore if anyone is [a]in
Christ, *he is* [b]a new creation; [c]the
old things passed away; behold,
new things have come. **18** Now [a]all
*these* things are from God, [b]who
reconciled us to Himself through

---

**4:17** [a]Ro 8:18 **4:18** [a]Ro 8:24; 2Co 5:7; Heb 11:1, 13 ◆ **5:1** [a]Job 4:19; 1Co 15:47; 2Co 4:7 [b]2Pe 1:13f [c]Mk 14:58; Ac 7:48; Heb 9:11, 24 [1]Lit *our earthly house of the tent* **5:2** [a]Ro 8:23; 2Co 5:4 [b]1Co 15:53f; 2Co 5:4 **5:4** [a]2Co 5:2 [b]1Co 15:53f; 2Co 5:2 [c]1Co 15:54 **5:5** [a]Ro 8:23; 2Co 1:22 [1]Or *down payment* **5:6** [a]Heb 11:13f **5:7** [a]1Co 13:12; 2Co 4:18 [1]Or *appearance* **5:8** [a]Php 1:23 [b]Jn 12:26; Php 1:23 **5:9** [a]Ro 14:18; Col 1:10; 1Th 4:1 **5:10** [a]Mt 16:27; Ac 10:42; Ro 2:16; 14:10, 12; Eph 6:8 [1]Lit *the things through the body* **5:11** [a]Heb 10:31; 12:29; Jd 23 [b]2Co 4:2 [1]Or *have appeared* **5:12** [a]2Co 3:1 [b]2Co 1:14; Php 1:26 **5:13** [a]Mk 3:21; 2Co 11:1, 16ff; 12:11 [1]Lit *were* **5:14** [a]Ac 18:5 [b]Ro 5:15; 6:6f; Ga 2:20; Col 3:3 **5:15** [a]Ro 14:7-9 **5:16** [a]Jn 8:15; 2Co 11:18; Php 3:4 [1]By what he is in the flesh **5:17** [a]Ro 16:7 [b]Jn 3:3; Ro 6:4; Ga 6:15 [c]Is 43:18f; 65:17; Eph 4:24; Rev 21:4f **5:18** [a]1Co 11:12 [b]Ro 5:10; Col 1:20

Christ and gave us the [c]ministry of
reconciliation, **19** namely, that [a]God
was in Christ reconciling the world
to Himself, [b]not counting their
transgressions against them, and
[1]He has [2]committed to us the word
of reconciliation.
**20** So then, we are [a]ambassadors
for Christ, [b]as God is pleading
through us. We beg you on behalf of
Christ, be [c]reconciled to God. **21** He
made Him who [a]knew no sin *to be*
[b]sin on our behalf, so that we might
become the [c]righteousness of God
in Him.

### *Commendable Ministers of God*

**6** And [a]working together *with Him,*
[b]we also plead with you not to
receive [c]the grace of God in vain—
**2** for He says,

"[a]AT THE ACCEPTABLE TIME
I LISTENED TO YOU,
AND ON THE DAY
OF SALVATION I HELPED YOU."

Behold, now is "THE ACCEPTABLE
TIME," behold, now is "THE DAY OF
SALVATION"— **3** [a]giving no cause for
offense in anything, so that the min-
istry will not be discredited, **4** but in
everything [a]commending ourselves
as [b]ministers of God, [c]in much perse-
verance, in afflictions, in distresses,
in hardships, **5** in [a]beatings, in impris-
onments, in [b]disturbances, in labors,
in sleeplessness, in [c]hunger, **6** in
purity, in [a]knowledge, in [b]patience,
in kindness, in the [c]Holy Spirit, in
[d]unhypocritical love, **7** in [a]the word
of truth, in [b]the power of God; by
[c]the weapons of righteousness for
the right hand and the left, **8** by glory
and [a]dishonor, by [b]evil report and
good report; *regarded* as [c]deceivers
and *yet* [d]true; **9** as unknown and
*yet* well-known, as [a]dying and *yet*
behold, [b]we live; as [1]punished and
*yet* not put to death, **10** as [a]sorrowful
but always [a]rejoicing, as [b]poor but
making many rich, as [c]having noth-
ing and *yet* possessing [d]all things.
**11** [a]Our mouth [1]has spoken
freely to you, O Corinthians, our
[b]heart is opened wide. **12** You are
not restrained [1]by us, but [a]you are
restrained in your own [2]affections.
**13** Now in a like [a]exchange—I speak
as to [b]children—open wide *to us*
also.
**14** [a]Do not be unequally yoked with
[b]unbelievers; for what [c]partnership
have righteousness and lawlessness,
or what fellowship has light with
darkness? **15** Or what [a]harmony has
Christ with [1]Belial, or [2]what has a
[b]believer in common with an [c]unbe-
liever? **16** Or [a]what agreement has a
[1]sanctuary of God with idols? For we
are [b]a sanctuary of [c]the living God;
just as God said,

---

**5:18** [c]1Co 3:5 **5:19** [a]Col 2:9 [b]Ro 4:8; 1Co 13:5 [1]Lit *having* [2]Lit *placed in us* **5:20** [a]Mal 2:7; Eph 6:20 [b]2Co 6:1 [c]Ro 5:10; Col 1:20 **5:21** [a]Ac 3:14; Heb 4:15; 7:26; 1Pe 2:22; 1Jn 3:5 [b]Ro 3:25; 4:25; 8:3; Ga 3:13 [c]Ro 1:17; 3:21f; 1Co 1:30 ◆ **6:1** [a]1Co 3:9 [b]2Co 5:20 [c]Ac 11:23 **6:2** [a]Is 49:8 **6:3** [a]1Co 8:9, 13; 9:12 **6:4** [a]Ro 3:5 [b]1Co 3:5; 2Ti 2:24f [c]Ac 9:16; 2Co 4:8-11; 6:4ff; 11:23-27; 12:10 **6:5** [a]Ac 16:23 [b]Ac 19:23ff [c]1Co 4:11 **6:6** [a]1Co 12:8; 2Co 11:6 [b]2Co 1:23; 2:10; 13:10 [c]1Co 2:4; 1Th 1:5 [d]Ro 12:9 **6:7** [a]2Co 2:17; 4:2 [b]1Co 2:5 [c]Ro 13:12; 2Co 10:4; Eph 6:11ff **6:8** [a]1Co 4:10 [b]Ro 3:8; 1Co 4:13; 2Co 12:16 [c]Mt 27:63 [d]2Co 1:18; 4:2; 1Th 2:3f **6:9** [a]Ro 8:36 [b]2Co 1:8, 10; 4:11 [1]Or *disciplined* **6:10** [a]Jn 16:22; 2Co 7:4; Php 2:17; 4:4; Col 1:24; 1Th 1:6 [b]1Co 1:5; 2Co 8:9 [c]Ac 3:6 [d]Ro 8:32; 1Co 3:21 **6:11** [a]Eze 33:22; Eph 6:19 [b]Is 60:5; 2Co 7:3 [1]Lit *is open to you* **6:12** [a]2Co 7:2 [1]Or *in us* [2]Lit *inward parts* **6:13** [a]Ga 4:12 [b]1Co 4:14 **6:14** [a]Dt 22:10; 1Co 5:9f [b]1Co 6:6 [c]Eph 5:7, 11; 1Jn 1:6 **6:15** [a]1Co 10:21 [b]Ac 5:14; 1Pe 1:21 [c]1Co 6:6 [1]Gr *Beliar* [2]Lit *what part has a believer with an unbeliever* **6:16** [a]1Co 10:21 [b]1Co 3:16; 6:19 [c]Mt 16:16 [1]The innermost part of the temple

“[d]I WILL [e]DWELL IN THEM AND
[f]WALK AMONG THEM;
AND I WILL BE THEIR GOD, AND
THEY SHALL BE MY PEOPLE.
17 “[a]Therefore, [b]COME OUT
FROM THEIR MIDST AND BE
SEPARATE,” says the [1]Lord.
“AND DO NOT TOUCH
WHAT IS UNCLEAN;
And I will welcome you.
18 “[a]AND I WILL BE
A FATHER TO YOU,
And you shall be [b]sons
and daughters to Me,”
SAYS THE [1]LORD ALMIGHTY.

7 Therefore, having these prom-
ises, [a]beloved, [b]let us cleanse
ourselves from all defilement of flesh
and spirit, perfecting holiness in the
fear of God.

### *Godly Sorrow Produces Repentance*

2 [a]Make room for us *in your hearts.*
We wronged no one, we corrupted
no one, we took advantage of no one.
3 I do not speak to condemn you, for
I have said [a]before that you are [b]in
our hearts to die together and to live
together. 4 Great is my [a]boldness to-
ward you; great is my [b]boasting on
your behalf. I have been filled with
[c]comfort; I am overflowing with [d]joy
in all our affliction.
5 For even when we came into
[a]Macedonia our flesh had no rest,
but we were [b]afflicted on every
side—[c]conflicts without, fears
within. 6 But [a]God, who comforts
the humbled, [b]comforted us by the
coming of [c]Titus; 7 and not only by
his coming, but also by the comfort
with which he was comforted in you,
as he reported to us your longing,
your mourning, your zeal for me,
so that I rejoiced even more. 8 For
though I [a]caused you sorrow by
my letter, I do not regret it, though
I did regret it—*for* I see that that
letter caused you sorrow, though
only for a while— 9 I now rejoice,
not that you were made sorrowful,
but that you were made sorrowful
to repentance. For you were made to
have [1]godly sorrow, so that you might
not suffer loss in anything [2]through
us. 10 For [1]godly sorrow produces a
[a]repentance [2]without regret, *leading*
to salvation, but the sorrow of the
world brings about death. 11 For
behold what earnestness this very
thing—this [1]godly sorrow—has
brought about in you: what vindica-
tion of yourselves, what indignation,
what fear, what [a]longing, what zeal,
what [b]avenging of wrong! In every-
thing you [c]demonstrated yourselves
to be innocent in the matter. 12 So
although [a]I wrote to you, *it was* not
for the sake of [b]the offender nor for
the sake of the one offended, but that
your earnestness on our behalf might
be manifested to you in the sight of
God. 13 For this reason we have been
[a]comforted.
And besides our comfort, we
rejoiced even much more for the

**6:16** [d]Ex 29:45; Lv 26:12; Jer 31:1; Eze 37:27 [e]Ex 25:8; Jn 14:23 [f]Rev 2:1 **6:17** [a]Is 52:11 [b]Rev 18:4 [1]In OT, *Yahweh, cf. Is 52:11* **6:18** [a]2Sa 7:14; 1Chr 17:13; Is 43:6; Hos 1:10 [b]Ro 8:14 [1]In OT, Yahweh, cf. 1Chr 17:7; Hos 1:9 ◆ **7:1** [a]Heb 6:9 [b]1Pe 1:15f **7:2** [a]2Co 6:12f; 12:15 **7:3** [a]2Co 6:11f [b]Php 1:7 **7:4** [a]2Co 3:12 [b]2Co 7:14; 8:24; 9:2f; 10:8; Php 1:26; 2Th 1:4 [c]2Co 1:4 [d]2Co 6:10 **7:5** [a]Ro 15:26; 2Co 2:13 [b]2Co 4:8 [c]Dt 32:25 **7:6** [a]2Co 1:3f [b]2Co 7:13 [c]2Co 2:13; 7:13f **7:8** [a]2Co 2:2 **7:9** [1]Lit *sorrow according to God* [2]Lit *from* **7:10** [a]Ac 11:18 [1]Lit *sorrow according to God* [2]Or leading *to a salvation without regret* **7:11** [a]2Co 7:7 [b]2Co 2:6 [c]Ro 3:5 [1]Lit *sorrow according to God* **7:12** [a]2Co 2:3, 9; 7:8 [b]1Co 5:1f **7:13** [a]2Co 7:6

joy of [b]Titus, because his [c]spirit has
been refreshed by you all. **14** For if
in anything I have [a]boasted to him
about you, I was not put to shame,
but as we spoke all things to you in
truth, so also our boasting before
[b]Titus proved to be *the* truth. **15** And
his [1]affection abounds all the more
toward you, as he remembers the
[a]obedience of you all, how you re-
ceived him with [b]fear and trembling.
**16** I rejoice that in everything [a]I am
encouraged about you.

### *Generosity and Grace*

**8** Now brothers, we make known
to you the grace of God which
has been [a]given in the churches of
[b]Macedonia, **2** that in a great testing
by affliction their abundance of joy
and their deep poverty abounded
unto the [a]richness of their [1]gener-
osity. **3** For I testify that [a]according
to their ability, and beyond their
ability, *they gave* of their own accord,
**4** begging us with much urging for
the [a]grace [1]of sharing in the [b]minis-
try to the saints, **5** and *this,* not as we
had [1]expected, but they first [a]gave
themselves to the Lord and to us by
[b]the will of God. **6** So we [a]encour-
aged [b]Titus that as he had previously
[c]made a beginning, so he would also
complete in you [d]this gracious work
as well.
**7** But just as you [a]abound [b]in
everything, in faith and word and
knowledge and in all earnestness
and in [1]the love we inspired in you,
*see* that you [a]abound in this gracious
work also. **8** I [a]am not speaking *this* as
a command, but as proving through
the earnestness of others the sincer-
ity of your love also. **9** For you know
[a]the grace of our Lord Jesus Christ,
that [b]though being rich, yet for your
sake He became poor, so that you
through His poverty might become
rich. **10** And I [a]give *my* opinion in this
matter, for this is profitable for you,
who were the first to begin [b]a year
ago not only to do *this,* but also to
desire *to do it.* **11** But now complete
[1]doing it also, so that just as *there was*
the [a]readiness to desire it, so *there*
*may be* also the completion of it from
what you have. **12** For if the readiness
is present, it is acceptable [a]according
to what *a person* has, not according
to what he does not have. **13** For *this*
is not for the relief of others *and* for
your affliction, but by way of equal-
ity— **14** at this present time your
abundance *being a supply* for [a]their
need, so that their abundance also
may become *a supply* for [a]your need,
that there may be equality. **15** As it is
written, "[a]HE WHO *gathered* MUCH
DID NOT HAVE TOO MUCH, AND HE WHO
*gathered* LITTLE HAD NO LACK."
**16** But [a,1]thanks be to God who
[b]puts the same earnestness on your
behalf in the heart of [c]Titus. **17** For
he not only accepted our [a]plea, but

---

**7:13** [b]2Co 2:13; 7:6, 14 [c]1Co 16:18 **7:14** [a]2Co 7:4; 8:24; 9:2f; 10:8; Php 1:26; 2Th 1:4 [b]2Co 2:13; 7:6, 13 **7:15** [a]2Co 2:9 [b]1Co 2:3; Php 2:12 [1]Lit *inward parts* **7:16** [a]2Co 2:3 ◆ **8:1** [a]2Co 8:5 [b]Ac 16:9 **8:2** [a]Ro 2:4 [1]Or *simplicity*; without false motives **8:3** [a]1Co 16:2; 2Co 8:11 **8:4** [a]Ac 24:17; Ro 15:25f [b]Ro 15:31; 2Co 8:19f; 9:1, 12f [1]Lit *and* **8:5** [a]2Co 8:1 [b]1Co 1:1 [1]Lit *hoped* **8:6** [a]2Co 8:17; 12:18 [b]2Co 2:13; 8:16, 23 [c]2Co 8:10 [d]Ac 24:17; Ro 15:25f **8:7** [a]2Co 9:8 [b]Ro 15:14; 1Co 1:5; 12:8 [1]Lit *the love from us in you*; one early ms *your love for us* **8:8** [a]1Co 7:6 **8:9** [a]2Co 13:14 [b]Mt 20:28; 2Co 6:10; Php 2:6f **8:10** [a]1Co 7:25, 40 [b]1Co 16:2f; 2Co 9:2 **8:11** [a]2Co 8:12, 19; 9:2 [1]Lit *the doing* **8:12** [a]Mk 12:43f; Lk 21:3, 4; 2Co 9:7 **8:14** [a]Ac 4:34; 2Co 9:12 **8:15** [a]Ex 16:18 **8:16** [a]2Co 2:14 [b]Rev 17:17 [c]2Co 2:13; 8:6, 23 [1]With gratitude; lit *grace* **8:17** [a]2Co 8:6; 12:18

being himself very earnest, he has
gone out to you of his own accord.
**18** And we have sent along with him
[a]the brother whose praise in *the*
*things of* the [b]gospel is throughout
[c]all the churches. **19** [a]And not only
*this,* but he has also been [b]appointed
by the churches to travel with us in
[c]this gracious work that is being min-
istered by us for the glory of the Lord
Himself, and *to show* our [d]readiness,
**20** [1]taking precaution lest anyone
discredits us in our ministering of
this generous gift, **21** for we [a]respect
what is good, not only in [b]the sight of
the Lord, but also in the sight of men.
**22** And we have sent with them our
brother, whom we have often tested
and found earnest in many things,
but now even more earnest because
of *his* great confidence in you. **23** As
for [a]Titus, *he is* my [b]partner and
fellow worker [1]among you; as for
our [c]brothers, *they are* [d,2]messen-
gers of the churches, [e]a glory to
Christ. **24** Therefore [1]openly before
the churches, [2]show them the proof
of your love and of our [a]reason for
boasting about you.

### *God Loves a Cheerful Giver*

**9** For [a]it is superfluous for me to
write to you about this [b]ministry
to the [1]saints; **2** for I know your readi-
ness, of which I [a]boast about you to
the [b]Macedonians, that [c]Achaia has
been prepared since [d]last year, and
your zeal stirred up most of them.
**3** But I have sent the brothers, in
order that our [a]boasting about you
may not be made empty in this case,
so that, [b]as I was saying, you may be
prepared; **4** lest if any [a]Macedonians
come with me and find you unpre-
pared, we—not to speak of you—be
put to shame in this certainty *of*
*ours.* **5** So I regarded it necessary
to encourage the [a]brothers that
they would go on ahead to you and
arrange beforehand your previously
promised [b]blessing, so that the same
would be ready as a [c]blessing and not
as a [d,1]begrudging obligation.
**6** Now this *I say,* [a]he who sows
sparingly will also reap sparingly,
and he who sows with blessing will
also reap with blessing. **7** Each one
*must do* just as he has purposed in
his heart, not [a]grudgingly or under
compulsion, for [b]God loves a cheer-
ful giver. **8** And [a]God is able to make
every grace abound to you, so that
in everything at every time having
every sufficiency, you may have an
abundance for every good deed; **9** as
it is written,

"[a]HE SCATTERED ABROAD,
HE GAVE TO THE NEEDY,
HIS RIGHTEOUSNESS
[1]STANDS FOREVER."

**10** Now He who supplies [a]SEED TO
THE SOWER AND BREAD FOR FOOD will
supply and multiply your seed and
[b]increase the harvest of your righ-
teousness; **11** you will be [a]enriched
in everything for all generosity,

---

**8:18** [a]1Co 16:3; 2Co 12:18 [b]2Co 2:12 [c]1Co 4:17; 7:17 **8:19** [a]Ro 5:3 [b]Ac 14:23; 1Co 16:3f [c]2Co 8:4, 6 [d]*2Co 8:11, 12; 9:2* ***8:20*** [1]Lit *avoiding this* **8:21** [a]Ro 12:17 [b]Pr 3:4; Ro 14:18 **8:23** [a]2Co 8:6 [b]Phm 17 [c]2Co 8:18, 22 [d]Jn 13:16; Php 2:25 [e]1Co 11:7 [1]Lit *for you* [2]Lit *apostles* **8:24** [a]2Co 7:4 [1]Lit *in the face of the churches* [2]Or *show the proof...for boasting to them about you* ♦ **9:1** [a]1Th 4:9 [b]2Co 8:4 [1]Or *holy ones* **9:2** [a]2Co 7:4 [b]Ro 15:26 [c]Ac 18:12 [d]2Co 8:10 **9:3** [a]2Co 7:4 [b]1Co 16:2 **9:4** [a]Ro 15:26 **9:5** [a]2Co 9:3 [b]Ge 33:11; Jdg 1:15; 2Co 9:6 [c]Php 4:17 [d]2Co 12:17f [1]Lit *covetousness* **9:6** [a]Pr 11:24f; 22:9; Ga 6:7, 9 **9:7** [a]Dt 15:10; 1Chr 29:17; Ro 12:8; 2Co 8:12 [b]Pr 22:9; Ex 25:2 **9:8** [a]Eph 3:20 **9:9** [a]Ps 112:9 [1]Lit *abides* **9:10** [a]Is 55:10 [b]Hos 10:12 **9:11** [a]1Co 1:5

which through us is bringing about
[b]thanksgiving to God. **12** For the min-
istry of this service is not only fully
supplying [a]the needs of the [1]saints,
but is also abounding [b]through many
thanksgivings to God. **13** Because of
the proven character given by this
[a]ministry, they will [b]glorify God for
*your* obedience to your [c]confession
of the [d]gospel of Christ and for the
[1]generosity of your [2]fellowship to-
ward them and toward all, **14** while
they also, by prayer on your behalf,
long for you because of the surpass-
ing grace of God on you. **15** [a,1]Thanks
be to God for His indescribable [b]gift!

### *Paul Defends His Authority*

**10** Now [a]I, Paul, myself [b]plead
with you by the [c]gentleness
and forbearance of Christ—I who
[d]am humble when face-to-face
with you, but courageous toward
you when absent! **2** But I beg that
[a]when I am present I *need* not act
*so* courageously with the confidence
that I consider to daringly *use* against
[b]some, who consider us as if we
walked [c]according to the flesh. **3** For
though we walk in the flesh, we do
not war [a]according to the flesh, **4** for
the [a]weapons of our warfare are not
of the flesh, but [1]divinely powerful
[b]for the tearing down of strongholds,
**5** as we tear down speculations and
every [a]lofty thing raised up against
the knowledge of God, and take every
thought captive to the [b]obedience
of Christ, **6** and are ready to punish
all disobedience, whenever [a]your
obedience is fulfilled.
**7** [a,1]You are looking at [2]things
as they are outwardly. [b]If anyone
is confident in himself that he is
Christ's, let him consider this again
within himself, that just as he is
Christ's, [c]so also are we. **8** For even
if [a]I boast somewhat [1]further about
our [b]authority, which the Lord
gave for building you up and not
for tearing you down, I will not be
put to shame, **9** [1]for I do not wish to
seem as if I would terrify you by my
letters. **10** For they say, "His letters are
weighty and strong, but his [1]personal
presence is [a]weak and [b]his [2]words
contemptible." **11** Let such a person
consider this, that what we are in
word by letters when absent, such
persons we are also in deed when
present.
**12** For we do not dare to classify
or compare ourselves with [1]some of
those who [a]commend themselves,
but when they measure themselves
by themselves and compare them-
selves with themselves, they are
without understanding. **13** But we will
not boast [a]beyond *our* measure, but
[b,1]within the measure of the area of
influence which God apportioned to
us as a measure, to reach even as far

---

**9:11** [b]2Co 1:11 **9:12** [a]2Co 8:14 [b]2Co 1:11 [1]Or *holy ones* **9:13** [a]Ro 15:31; 2Co 8:4 [b]Mt 9:8 [c]1Ti 6:12f; Heb 3:1; 4:14; 10:23 [d]2Co 2:12 [1]Or *simplicity*; without false motives [2]Or *sharing*, cf. Ro 15:26
**9:15** [a]2Co 2:14 [b]Ro 5:15f [1]Lit *Grace*; with gratitude ◆**10:1** [a]Ga 5:2; Eph 3:1; Col 1:23 [b]Ro 12:1 [c]Mt 11:29; 1Co 4:21; Php 4:5 [d]1Co 2:3f; 2Co 10:10 **10:2** [a]1Co 4:21; 2Co 13:2, 10 [b]1Co 4:18f [c]Ro 8:4; 2Co 1:17
**10:3** [a]Ro 8:4; 2Co 1:17 **10:4** [a]1Co 9:7; 2Co 6:7; 1Ti 1:18 [b]Jer 1:10; 2Co 10:8; 13:10 [1]Or *mighty before God*
**10:5** [a]Is 2:11f [b]2Co 9:13 **10:6** [a]2Co 2:9 **10:7** [a]Jn 7:24; 2Co 5:12 [b]1Co 1:12; 14:37 [c]1Co 9:1; 2Co 11:23; Ga 1:12 [1]Or *Look at...* or *Do you look at...?* [2]Lit *what is before your face* **10:8** [a]2Co 7:4 [b]2Co 13:10 [1]Or *more abundantly* **10:9** [1]Lit *so that I may not seem* **10:10** [a]1Co 2:3; 2Co 12:7; Ga 4:13f [b]1Co 1:17; 2Co 11:6 [1]Lit *bodily presence is weak* [2]Lit *word* **10:12** [a]2Co 3:1; 10:18 [1]Or *any* **10:13** [a]2Co 10:15 [b]Ro 12:3; 2Co 10:15f [1]Lit *according to the measure*

as you. **14** For we are not overextending ourselves, as if we did not reach you, (for [a]we were the first to come even as far as you in the [b]gospel of Christ), **15** not boasting [a]beyond *our* measure in [b]other men's labors, but having the hope—that as [c]your faith grows—to be [d]enlarged even more by you [1]within our area of influence, **16** so as to [a]proclaim the gospel even to [b]the regions beyond you, *and* not to boast [c][1]in what has been accomplished in the area of influence of another. **17** But [a]HE WHO BOASTS IS TO BOAST IN THE LORD. **18** For it is not the one who [a]commends himself that is approved, but the one [b]whom the Lord commends.

### *Paul Defends His Apostleship*

**11** I wish that you would [a]bear with me in a little [b]foolishness, but [1]indeed you are bearing with me. **2** For I am jealous for you with a godly jealousy, for I [a]betrothed you to one husband, so that I might [b]present you *as* a pure virgin to Christ. **3** But I fear that, as the [a]serpent deceived Eve by his craftiness, your minds will be corrupted from the simplicity and purity *of devotion* to Christ. **4** For if [1]one comes and preaches [a]another Jesus whom we did not preach, or you receive a [b]different spirit which you did not receive, or a [c]different gospel which you did not accept, you [d]bear *this* [e]beautifully. **5** For I consider myself [a]in no way inferior to the [1]most-eminent apostles. **6** But even if I am [a]unskilled in word, yet I am not *so* in [b]knowledge; in fact, in every way we have [c]made *this* evident to you in all things.

**7** Or [a]did I commit a sin in humbling myself so that you might be exalted, because I proclaimed the [b]gospel of God to you [c]without charge? **8** I robbed other churches by [a]taking wages *from them* to minister to you. **9** And when I was present with you and was in need, I was [a]not a burden to anyone; for when [b]the brothers came from [c]Macedonia they fully supplied my need, and in everything I kept and will keep myself from [a]being a burden to you. **10** [a]As the truth of Christ is in me, [b]this boasting of mine will not be stopped in the regions of [c]Achaia. **11** Why? [a]Because I do not love you? [b]God knows *I do*!

**12** But what I am doing I will continue to do, [a]so that I may cut off opportunity from those who desire an opportunity to be found just as we are in the matter about which they are boasting. **13** For such men are [a]false apostles, [b]deceitful workers, disguising themselves as apostles of Christ. **14** And no wonder, for even [a]Satan disguises himself as an [b]angel of light. **15** Therefore it is not surprising if his ministers also

---

**10:14** [a]1Co 3:6 [b]2Co 2:12 **10:15** [a]2Co 10:13 [b]Ro 15:20 [c]2Th 1:3 [d]Ac 5:13 [1]Lit *according to our area of influence* **10:16** [a]2Co 11:7 [b]Ac 19:21 [c]Ro 15:20 [1]Lit *to the things prepared in the* **10:17** [a]Jer 9:24; 1Co 1:31 **10:18** [a]2Co 10:12 [b]Ro 2:29; 1Co 4:5 ◆ **11:1** [a]Mt 17:17; 2Co 11:4, 16, 19f [b]2Co 5:13; 11:17, 21 [1]Or *do indeed bear with me* **11:2** [a]Hos 2:19f; Eph 5:26f [b]2Co 4:14 **11:3** [a]Ge 3:4, 13; Jn 8:44; 1Th 3:5; 1Ti 2:14; Rev 12:9, 15 **11:4** [a]1Co 3:11 [b]Ro 8:15 [c]Ga 1:6 [d]2Co 11:1 [e]Mk 7:9 [1]Lit *the one who comes preaches* **11:5** [a]2Co 12:11; Ga 2:6 [1]Or *super-apostles* **11:6** [a]1Co 1:17 [b]1Co 12:8; Eph 3:4 [c]2Co 4:2 **11:7** [a]2Co 12:13 [b]Ro 1:1; 2Co 2:12 [c]Ac 18:3; 1Co 9:18 **11:8** [a]1Co 4:12; 9:6; Php 4:15, 18 **11:9** [a]2Co 12:13f, 16 [b]Ac 18:5 [c]Ro 15:26; Php 4:15-18 **11:10** [a]Ro 1:9; 9:1; 2Co 1:23; Ga 2:20 [b]1Co 9:15 [c]Ac 18:12 **11:11** [a]2Co 12:15 [b]Ro 1:9; 2Co 2:17; 11:31; 12:2f **11:12** [a]1Co 9:12 **11:13** [a]Ac 20:30; Ga 1:7; 2:4; Php 1:15; Tit 1:10f; 2Pe 2:1; Rev 2:2 [b]Php 3:2 **11:14** [a]Mt 4:10; Eph 6:12; Col 1:13 [b]Col 1:12

disguise themselves as ministers of
righteousness, [a]whose end will be
according to their deeds.
**16** [a]Again I say, let no one think me
foolish; but if *you do,* receive me even
as foolish, so that I also may boast a
little. **17** What I am saying, I am not
saying [a,1]according to the Lord, but
as [b]in foolishness, in this confidence
of boasting. **18** Since [a]many boast
[b]according to the flesh, I will boast
also. **19** For you, [a]being *so* wise, are
bearing the foolish gladly. **20** For
you bear it if anyone [a]enslaves you,
anyone [b]devours you, anyone [c]takes
advantage of you, anyone [d]exalts
himself, anyone [e]hits you in the face.
**21** To *my* [a]shame I *must* say that we
have been [b]weak *by comparison.*

But in whatever respect anyone
*else* [c]is daring—I [d]speak in foolish-
ness—I am just as daring myself.
**22** Are they [a]Hebrews? [b]So am I. Are
they [c]Israelites? [c]So am I. Are they
Abraham's [d]seed? [e]So am I. **23** Are
they [a]ministers of Christ?—I speak
as if insane—I more so; in [b,1]far more
labors, in [c,1]far more imprisonments,
in [d]beatings without number, in fre-
quent [e]danger of death. **24** Five times
I received from the Jews [a]forty *lashes*
less one. **25** Three times I was [a]beaten
with rods, once I was [b]stoned, three
times I was shipwrecked—a night
and a day I have spent in the deep.
**26** *I have been* on frequent journeys,
in dangers from rivers, dangers from
robbers, dangers from *my* [a]country-
men, dangers from the [b]Gentiles,
dangers in the [c]city, dangers in the
desolate places, dangers on the sea,
dangers among [d]false brothers. **27** *I
have been* in [a]labor and hardship, in
many sleepless nights, in [b]starvation
and thirst, often [c]hungry, in cold and
[d,1]without enough clothing. **28** Apart
from *such* [1]external things, there is
the daily pressure on me *of* con-
cern for [a]all the churches. **29** Who
is [a]weak without my being weak?
Who is made to stumble [1]without
my burning concern?

**30** If I have to boast, I will boast
of what pertains to my [a]weakness.
**31** The God and Father of the Lord
Jesus, [a]He who is blessed forever,
[b]knows that I am not lying. **32** In
[a]Damascus the ethnarch under
Aretas the king was [b]guarding the
city of the Damascenes in order to
seize me, **33** and I was let down in
a basket [a]through a window [1]in the
wall, and *so* escaped his hands.

### *A Vision of Paradise*

**12** [a]It is necessary to boast, though
it is not profitable, but I will
go on to visions and [b]revelations [1]of
the Lord. **2** I know a man [a]in Christ
who fourteen years ago—whether in
the body I do not know, or out of the
body I do not know, [b]God knows—

**11:15** [a]Ro 2:6; 3:8 **11:16** [a]2Co 11:1 **11:17** [a]1Co 7:12, 25 [b]2Co 11:21 [1]Or *as the Lord would*
**11:18** [a]Php 3:3f [b]2Co 5:16 **11:19** [a]1Co 4:10 **11:20** [a]2Co 1:24; Ga 2:4; 4:3, 9; 5:1 [b]Mk 12:40 [c]2Co 11:3; 12:16 [d]2Co 10:5 [e]1Co 4:11 **11:21** [a]2Co 6:8 [b]2Co 10:10 [c]2Co 10:2 [d]2Co 11:17 **11:22** [a]Ac 6:1 [b]Php 3:5 [c]Ro 9:4 [d]Ga 3:16 [e]Ro 11:1 **11:23** [a]1Co 3:5; 2Co 3:6; 10:7 [b]1Co 15:10 [c]2Co 6:5 [d]Ac 16:23; 2Co 6:5 [e]Ro 8:36 [1]Lit *more abundant* **11:24** [a]Dt 25:3 **11:25** [a]Ac 16:22 [b]Ac 14:19 **11:26** [a]Ac 9:23; 13:45, 50; 14:5; 17:5, 13; 18:12; 20:3, 19; 21:27; 23:10, 12; 25:3; 1Th 2:15 [b]Ac 14:5, 19; 19:23ff; 27:42 [c]Ac 21:31 [d]Ga 2:4
**11:27** [a]1Th 2:9; 2Th 3:8 [b]1Co 4:11; Php 4:12 [c]2Co 6:5 [d]1Co 4:11 [1]Lit *nakedness* **11:28** [a]1Co 7:17 [1]Or *the things unmentioned* **11:29** [a]1Co 8:9, 13; 9:22 [1]Lit *and I do not burn* **11:30** [a]1Co 2:3 **11:31** [a]Ro 1:25 [b]2Co 11:11 **11:32** [a]Ac 9:2 [b]Ac 9:24 **11:33** [a]Ac 9:25 [1]Lit *through* ◆**12:1** [a]2Co 11:16, 18, 30; 12:5, 9 [b]1Co 14:6; 2Co 12:7; Ga 1:12; 2:2; Eph 3:3 [1]Or *from* **12:2** [a]Ro 16:7 [b]2Co 11:11

such a man was [c]caught up to the
[d]third heaven. **3** And I know how
such a man—whether in the body
or apart from the body I do not know,
[a]God knows— **4** was [a]caught up into
[b]Paradise and heard inexpressible
words, which a man is not permitted
to speak. **5** [a]On behalf of such a man
I will boast, but on my own behalf I
will not boast, except in [b]weaknesses.
**6** For if I do wish to boast I will not be
[a]foolish, [b]for I will be speaking the
truth; but I refrain *from this,* so that
no one will consider me beyond what
he sees *in* me or hears from me.

### A Thorn in the Flesh

**7** Because of the surpassing greatness
of the [a]revelations, for this reason, to
keep me from exalting myself, there
was given me a [b]thorn in the flesh,
a [c]messenger of Satan to [1]torment
me—to keep me from exalting my-
self! **8** Concerning this I pleaded with
the Lord [a]three times that it might
leave me. **9** And He has said to me,
"My grace is sufficient for you, for
[a]power is perfected in weakness."
Most gladly, therefore, I will rather
[b]boast in my weaknesses, so that
the power of Christ may dwell in
me. **10** Therefore [a]I am well content
with weaknesses, with [1]insults, with
[b]distresses, with [c]persecutions and
[b]hardships, [d]for the sake of Christ, for
[e]when I am weak, then I am strong.

### Concern for the Corinthian Church

**11** I have become [a]foolish; you your-
selves compelled me. For I ought to
have been commended by you, for
[b]in no respect was I inferior to the
[1]most-eminent apostles, even if [c]I
am nothing. **12** The [a,1]signs [2]of a true
apostle were worked out among you
with all perseverance, by [1]signs and
wonders and [3]miracles. **13** For in what
respect were you treated as less than
the rest of the churches, except that
[a]I myself did not become a burden to
you? [1]Forgive me [b]this wrong!
**14** Here [a]for this third time I am
ready to come to you, and I [b]will not
be a burden to you; for I [c]do not seek
what is yours, but [d]you. For [e]children
ought not to save up for *their* parents,
but [f]parents for *their* children. **15** So I
will [a]most gladly spend and be fully
spent for your souls. If [b]I love you
more, am I to be loved less? **16** But be
that as it may, I [a]did not burden you
myself. Nevertheless, crafty fellow
that I am, I [b]took you in by deceit.
**17** [a]Have I taken advantage of you
through any of those whom I have
sent to you? **18** I [a]encouraged [b]Titus
*to go,* and I sent [c]the brother with
him. Did Titus take any advantage
of you? Did we not walk [1]in the same
[d]spirit—[e]in the very same steps?
**19** All this time [1]you think we
are defending ourselves to you. We
speak in Christ [a]in the sight of God.

**12:2** [c]Eze 8:3; Ac 8:39; 2Co 12:4; 1Th 4:17; Rev 12:5 [d]Dt 10:14; Ps 148:4; Eph 4:10; Heb 4:14 **12:3** [a]2Co 11:11 **12:4** [a]Eze 8:3; Ac 8:39; 2Co 12:2; 1Th 4:17; Rev 12:5 [b]Lk 23:43 **12:5** [a]2Co 12:1 [b]1Co 2:3; 2Co 12:9f **12:6** [a]2Co 5:13; 11:16f; 12:11 [b]2Co 7:14 **12:7** [a]2Co 12:1 [b]Nu 33:55; Eze 28:24; Hos 2:6 [c]Job 2:6; Mt 4:10; 1Co 5:5 [1]Lit *beat* **12:8** [a]Mt 26:44 **12:9** [a]1Co 2:5; Eph 3:16; Php 4:13 [b]1Co 2:3; 2Co 12:5 **12:10** [a]Ro 5:3; 8:35 [b]2Co 6:4 [c]2Th 1:4; 2Ti 3:11 [d]2Co 5:15, 20 [e]2Co 13:4 [1]Or *mistreatment* **12:11** [a]2Co 5:13; 11:16f; 12:6 [b]1Co 15:10; 2Co 11:5 [c]1Co 3:7; 13:2; 15:9 [1]Or *super-apostles* **12:12** [a]Jn 4:48; Ro 15:19; 1Co 9:1 [1]Or *attesting miracles* [2]Lit *of the apostle* [3]Or *works of power* **12:13** [a]1Co 9:12, 18; 2Co 11:9; 12:14 [b]2Co 11:7 [1]Or *Graciously forgive* **12:14** [a]2Co 1:15; 13:1, 2 [b]1Co 9:12, 18; 2Co 11:9; 12:13 [c]1Co 10:24, 33 [d]1Co 9:19 [e]1Co 4:14f; Ga 4:19 [f]Pr 19:14; Eze 34:2 **12:15** [a]Ro 9:3; 2Co 1:6; Php 2:17; Col 1:24; 1Th 2:8; 2Ti 2:10 [b]2Co 11:11 **12:16** [a]2Co 11:9 [b]2Co 11:20 **12:17** [a]2Co 9:5 **12:18** [a]2Co 8:6 [b]2Co 2:13 [c]2Co 8:18 [d]1Co 4:21 [e]Ro 4:12 [1]Or *by the same Spirit* **12:19** [a]Ro 9:1; 2Co 2:17 [1]Or *have you been thinking...building up?*

[b]And all *these* things, [c]beloved, are
for your building up. **20** For I am
afraid that perhaps [a]when I come I
may find you to be not what I wish
and may be found by you to be not
what you wish; that perhaps *there*
*will be* [b]strife, jealousy, [c]outbursts of
anger, [d]selfish ambition, [e]slanders,
[f]gossip, [g]arrogance, [h]disturbances.
**21** *I am afraid that* when I come again
my God may humiliate me before
you, and I may mourn over many of
those who have [a]sinned in the past
and not repented of the [b]impurity,
sexual immorality, and sensuality
which they have practiced.

### *Examine Yourselves*

**13** [a]This is the third time I am
coming to you. [b]BY THE MOUTH
OF TWO OR THREE WITNESSES EVERY
[1]MATTER SHALL BE CONFIRMED. **2** I
have previously said when present
the second time, and though now
absent I say in advance to those who
have [a]sinned in the past and to all
the rest *as well*, that [b]if I come again
I will not [c]spare *anyone*, **3** since
you are [a]seeking proof that [b]Christ
speaks in me; He is not weak toward
you, but [c]mighty in you. **4** For in-
deed He was [a]crucified because of
weakness, yet He lives [b]because of
the power of God. For we also are
[c]weak [1]in Him, yet [d]we will live with
Him because of the power of God
toward you.
**5** [a]Test yourselves *to see* if you are
in the faith; [b]examine yourselves!
Or do you not recognize about
yourselves that Jesus Christ is in
you—unless indeed you [c,1]fail the
test? **6** But I hope that you will realize
that we ourselves [1]do not fail the test.
**7** Now we pray to God that you do no
wrong, not that we ourselves may
appear approved, but that you may
do what is right, even though we
may [1]appear unapproved. **8** For we
can do nothing against the truth, but
*only* for the truth. **9** For we rejoice
when we ourselves are [a]weak but you
are strong. This we also pray for, [1]that
you be [b]restored. **10** For this reason I
am writing these things while absent,
so that when present [a]I *need* not use
[b]severity, in accordance with the
[c]authority which the Lord gave me
for building up and not for tearing
down.
**11** [a]Finally, brothers, [1]rejoice,
[b,2]be restored, be comforted, [c]be
like-minded, [d]live in peace, and [e]the
God of love and peace will be with
you. **12** [a]Greet one another with a
holy kiss. **13** [a]All the [1]saints greet you.
**14** [a]The grace of the Lord Jesus
Christ, and the [b]love of God, and
the [c]fellowship of the Holy Spirit,
be with you all.

---

**12:19** [b]Ro 14:19; 2Co 10:8; 1Th 5:11 [c]Heb 6:9 **12:20** [a]1Co 4:21; 2Co 2:1-4 [b]1Co 1:11; 3:3 [c]Ga 5:20 [d]Ro 2:8; 1Co 11:19 [e]Ro 1:30; Jas 4:11; 1Pe 2:1 [f]Ro 1:29 [g]1Co 4:6, 18; 5:2 [h]1Co 14:33 **12:21** [a]2Co 13:2 [b]1Co 6:9, 18; Ga 5:19; Col 3:5 ◆**13:1** [a]2Co 12:14 [b]Dt 17:6; 19:15; Mt 18:16 [1]Lit *word* **13:2** [a]2Co 12:21 [b]1Co 4:21; 2Co 13:10 [c]2Co 1:23; 10:11 **13:3** [a]2Co 10:1, 10 [b]Mt 10:20; 1Co 5:4; 7:40 [c]2Co 9:8; 10:4 **13:4** [a]Php 2:7f; 1Pe 3:18 [b]Ro 1:4; 6:4; 1Co 6:14 [c]1Co 2:3; 2Co 13:9 [d]Ro 6:8 [1]One early ms *with Him* **13:5** [a]Jn 6:6 [b]1Co 11:28 [c]1Co 9:27 [1]Lit *are unapproved* **13:6** [1]Lit *are not unapproved* **13:7** [1]Lit *be as* **13:9** [a]2Co 12:10; 13:4 [b]1Co 1:10; 2Co 13:11; Eph 4:12; 1Th 3:10 [1]Lit *your completion* **13:10** [a]2Co 2:3 [b]Tit 1:13 [c]1Co 5:4; 2Co 10:8 **13:11** [a]1Th 4:1; 2Th 3:1 [b]1Co 1:10; 2Co 13:9; Eph 4:12; 1Th 3:10 [c]Ro 12:16 [d]Mk 9:50 [e]Ro 15:33; Eph 6:23 [1]Or *farewell* [2]Or *put yourselves in order* **13:12** [a]Ro 16:16 **13:13** [a]Php 4:22 [1]Or *holy ones* **13:14** [a]Ro 16:20; 2Co 8:9 [b]Ro 5:5; Jd 21 [c]Php 2:1

*The Letter of Paul to the*

# GALATIANS

### *Greetings and Grace*

1 Paul, [a]an apostle—[b]not *sent*
from men nor through man, but
[c]through Jesus Christ and God the
Father, who [d]raised Him from the
dead— **2** and all [a]the brothers who
are with me,

To [b]the churches of Galatia:

**3** [a]Grace to you and peace from
[1]God our Father and the Lord Jesus
Christ, **4** who [a]gave Himself for our
sins so that He might rescue us from
[b]this present evil [1]age, according to
the will of [c]our God and Father, **5** [a]to
whom *be* the glory forever and ever.
Amen.

### *Distorting the Gospel*

**6** I marvel that you are so quickly de-
serting [a]Him who called you [1]by the
grace of Christ for a [b]different gospel,
**7** which is *really* not another, only
there are some who are [a]disturbing
you and want to distort the gospel of
Christ. **8** But even if we, or [a]an angel
from heaven, should proclaim to
you a gospel [1]contrary to the gospel
we have proclaimed to you, let him
be [b,2]accursed! **9** As we [a]have said
before, so I say again now, [b]if any
man is proclaiming to you a gospel
[1]contrary to what you received, let
him be [c,2]accursed!

**10** For am I now [a]seeking the favor
of men, or of God? Or am I striving
to please men? If I were still trying to
please men, I would not be a [b]slave
of Christ.

### *Paul Called by God*

**11** For [a]I make known to you, brothers,
that the gospel which I am proclaim-
ing as good news is [b]not according
to man. **12** For [a]I neither received it
from man, nor was I taught it, but *I
received it* through a [b]revelation of
Jesus Christ.

**13** For you have heard of [a]my
former conduct in Judaism, how I
[b]used to persecute [c]the church of God
beyond measure and [d]tried to destroy
it. **14** And I [a]was advancing in Judaism
beyond many of my contemporaries
among my countrymen, being far
more zealous for the traditions of my
[b]fathers. **15** But when God, who had
set me apart from my mother's womb
and [a]called me through His grace, was
pleased **16** to reveal His Son in me so
that I might [a]proclaim Him as good
news among the Gentiles, [b]I did not
immediately consult with [c,1]flesh and
blood, **17** [a]nor did I go up to Jerusalem
to those who were apostles before
me, but I went away to Arabia, and
returned once more to [b]Damascus.

◆**1:1** [a]2Co 1:1 [b]Ga 1:11f [c]Ac 9:15; Ga 1:15f [d]Ac 2:24 **1:2** [a]Php 4:21 [b]Ac 16:6; 1Co 16:1 **1:3** [a]Ro 1:7 [1]Two early mss *God the Father, and our Lord Jesus Christ* **1:4** [a]Ga 2:20 [b]Mt 13:22; Ro 12:2; 2Co 4:4 [c]Php 4:20 [1]*Or world* **1:5** [a]Ro 11:36 **1:6** [a]Ro 8:28; Ga 1:15; 5:8 [b]2Co 11:4; Ga 1:7, 11; 2:2, 7; 5:14; 1Ti 1:3 [1]Lit *in* **1:7** [a]Ac 15:24; Ga 5:10 **1:8** [a]2Co 11:14 [b]Ro 9:3 [1]Or *other than, more than* [2]Gr *anathema* **1:9** [a]Ac 18:23 [b]Ro 16:17 [c]Ro 9:3 [1]Or *other than, more than* [2]Gr *anathema* **1:10** [a]1Co 10:33; 1Th 2:4 [b]Ro 1:1; Php 1:1 **1:11** [a]Ro 2:16; 1Co 15:1 [b]1Co 3:4; 9:8 **1:12** [a]1Co 11:23; Ga 1:1 [b]1Co 2:10; 2Co 12:1; Ga 1:16; 2:2 **1:13** [a]Ac 26:4f [b]Ac 8:3; 22:4, 5 [c]1Co 10:32 [d]Ac 9:21 **1:14** [a]Ac 22:3 [b]Jer 9:14; Mt 15:2; Mk 7:3; Col 2:8 **1:15** [a]Is 49:1, 5; Jer 1:5; Ac 9:15; Ro 1:1; Ga 1:6 **1:16** [a]Ac 9:15; Ga 2:9 [b]Ac 9:20 [c]Mt 16:17 [1]Human beings **1:17** [a]Ac 9:19-22 [b]Ac 9:2

**18** Then [a]three years later I went up
[b]to Jerusalem to [1]become acquainted
with [c]Cephas, and stayed with him
fifteen days. **19** But I did not see any
other of the apostles except [a][1]James,
the Lord's brother. **20** (Now in what
I am writing to you, [1]I assure you
[a]before God that I am not lying!)
**21** Then [a]I went into the regions of
[b]Syria and [c]Cilicia. **22** And I was *still*
unknown by [1]sight to [a]the churches
of Judea which are [b]in Christ; **23** but
only, they kept hearing, "He who once
persecuted us is now proclaiming the
good news of [a]the faith which he
once [b]tried to destroy." **24** And they
[a]were glorifying God [1]because of me.

### *Paul Accepted by the Apostles*

**2** Then after fourteen years I
[a]went up again to Jerusalem
with [b]Barnabas, taking [c]Titus along
also. **2** And I went up [1]because of a
[a]revelation, and I laid out to them
the [b]gospel which I preach among
the Gentiles, but *I did so* in private
to those who were of reputation, lest
somehow I might be [c]running, or had
run, in vain. **3** But not even [a]Titus,
who was with me, though he was a
Greek, was [b]compelled to be circum-
cised. **4** But *this was* because of the
[a]false brothers secretly brought in,
who [b]had sneaked in to spy out our
[c]freedom which we have in Christ
Jesus, in order to [d]enslave us. **5** But we
did not yield in subjection to them for
even [1]a moment, so that [a]the truth of
the gospel would remain with you.
**6** But from those who [1]were of high
[a]reputation (what they were makes
no difference to me; [b]God [2]shows no
partiality)—well, those who were
of reputation contributed nothing
to me. **7** But on the contrary, seeing
that I had been [a]entrusted with the
[b]gospel [1]to the uncircumcised, just as
[c]Peter *had been* [2]to the circumcised
**8** (for He who worked in Peter unto
*his* [a]apostleship [1]to the circumcised
worked in me also unto the Gentiles),
**9** and recognizing [a]the grace that had
been given to me, [b]James and [c]Cephas
and [1]John, who were [d]reputed to be
[e]pillars, gave to me and [f]Barnabas the
[g]right [2]hand of fellowship, so that we
*might* [h]*go* to the Gentiles and they to
the circumcised. **10** Only *they asked*
us to remember the poor—[a]the very
thing I also was eager to do.

### *Paul Opposes Peter (Cephas)*

**11** But when [a]Cephas came to
[b]Antioch, I opposed him to his face,
because he [1]stood condemned. **12** For
prior to the coming of certain men
from [a]James, he used to [b]eat with
the Gentiles, but when they came,

**1:18** [a]Ac 9:22f [b]Ac 9:26 [c]Jn 1:42; Ga 2:9, 11, 14 [1]Or *visit Cephas* **1:19** [a]Mt 12:46; Ac 12:17 [1]Or *Jacob*; James is the Eng form of Jacob; so in Gal **1:20** [a]Ro 9:1; 2Co 1:23; 11:31 [1]Lit *behold before God* **1:21** [a]Ac 9:30 [b]Ac 15:23, 41 [c]Ac 6:9 **1:22** [a]1Co 7:17; 1Th 2:14 [b]Ro 16:7 [1]Lit *face* **1:23** [a]Ac 6:7; Ga 6:10 [b]Ac 9:21 **1:24** [a]Mt 9:8 [1]Lit *in me* ◆ **2:1** [a]Ac 15:2 [b]Ac 4:36; Ga 2:9, 13 [c]2Co 2:13; Ga 2:3 **2:2** [a]Ac 15:2; Ga 1:12 [b]Ga 1:6 [c]Ro 9:16; 1Co 9:24ff; Ga 5:7; Php 2:16; 2Ti 4:7; Heb 12:1 [1]Lit *according to revelation* **2:3** [a]2Co 2:13; Ga 2:1 [b]Ac 16:3; 1Co 9:21 **2:4** [a]Ac 15:1, 24; 2Co 11:13, 26; Ga 1:7 [b]2Pe 2:1; Jd 4 [c]Ga 5:1, 13; Jas 1:25 [d]Ro 8:15; 2Co 11:20 **2:5** [a]Ga 1:6; 2:14; Col 1:5 [1]Lit *an hour* **2:6** [a]2Co 11:5; 12:11; Ga 2:9; 6:3 [b]Ac 10:34 [1]Lit *seemed to be something* [2]Lit *does not receive a face* **2:7** [a]1Co 9:17; 1Th 2:4; 1Ti 1:11 [b]Ac 9:15; Ga 1:16 [c]Ga 1:18; 2:9, 11, 14 [1]Lit *of the uncircumcision* [2]Lit *of the circumcision* **2:8** [a]Ac 1:25 [1]Lit *of the circumcision* **2:9** [a]Ro 12:3 [b]Ac 12:17; Ga 2:12 [c]Lk 22:8; Ga 1:18; 2:7, 11, 14 [d]2Co 11:5; 12:11; Ga 2:2, 6; 6:3 [e]1Ti 3:15; Rev 3:12 [f]Ac 4:36; Ga 2:1, 13 [g]2Ki 10:15 [h]Ga 1:16 [1]Gr *Joannes*, Heb *Johanan* [2]Lit *hands* **2:10** [a]Ac 24:17 **2:11** [a]Ga 1:18; 2:7, 9, 14 [b]Ac 11:19; 15:1 [1]Or *was to be condemned* **2:12** [a]Ac 12:17; Ga 2:9 [b]Ac 11:3

he *began to* shrink back and sepa-
rate himself, [c]fearing [1]the party of
the circumcision. **13** And the rest of
the Jews joined him in hypocrisy,
with the result that even [a]Barnabas
was carried away by their hypocrisy.
**14** But when I saw that they [a]were not
[1]straightforward about [b]the truth of
the gospel, I said to [c]Cephas before
everyone, "If you, being a Jew, [d]live
like the Gentiles and not like the
Jews, how *is it that* you compel the
Gentiles to live like Jews? [2]

**15** "We *are* [a]Jews by nature and not
[b]sinners from among the Gentiles;
**16** nevertheless [1]knowing that [a]a man
is not justified by the works of the
Law but through faith in Jesus Christ,
even we have believed in Christ Jesus,
so that we may be justified by [b]faith
in Christ and not by the works of the
Law; since [c]by the works of [2]the Law
no [3]flesh will be justified. **17** But if,
while seeking to be justified in Christ,
we ourselves have also been found
[a]sinners, is Christ then a minister
of sin? [b]May it never be! **18** For if I
rebuild what I have *once* destroyed,
I [a]prove myself to be a transgressor.
**19** For through [1]the Law I [a]died to [1]the
Law, so that I might live to God. **20** I
have been [a]crucified with Christ, and
it is no longer I who live, but [b]Christ
lives in me. And the *life* which I
now live in the flesh I live by faith
in [c]the Son of God, who [d]loved me
and [e]gave Himself up for me. **21** I do
not set aside the grace of God, for
[a]if righteousness *comes* through [1]the
Law, then Christ died needlessly."

### *The Righteous Shall Live by Faith*

**3** O foolish [a]Galatians, who be-
witched you, before whose eyes
Jesus Christ [b]was publicly portrayed
*as* crucified? **2** This is the only thing
I want to learn from you: did you re-
ceive the Spirit by the works of [1]the
Law, or by [a,2]hearing with faith? **3** Are
you so foolish? Having begun [1]by the
Spirit, are you now [2]being perfected
by the flesh? **4** Did you [1]suffer so
many things for nothing—[a]if indeed
it was for nothing? **5** So then, does He
who [a]provides you with the Spirit
and [b]works [1]miracles among you,
do it by the works of [2]the Law, or by
[c,3]hearing with faith?

**6** Just as [a]Abraham [b]BELIEVED GOD
AND IT WAS COUNTED TO HIM AS RIGH-
TEOUSNESS, **7** so know that [a]those
who are of faith, those are [b]sons
of Abraham. **8** And the Scripture,
foreseeing that God [1]would justify
the [2]Gentiles by faith, proclaimed
the gospel beforehand to Abraham,
*saying*, "[a]ALL THE NATIONS WILL BE
BLESSED IN YOU." **9** So then [a]those
who are of faith are blessed with
[1]Abraham, the believer.

---

**2:12** [c]Ac 11:2 [1]Or converts *from the circumcised*; lit *those from the circumcision* **2:13** [a]Ac 4:36; Ga 2:1, 9 **2:14** [a]Heb 12:13 [b]Ga 1:6; 2:5; Col 1:5 [c]Ga 1:18; 2:7, 9, 11 [d]Ac 10:28; Ga 2:12 [1]Or *progressing toward*; lit *walking straightly* [2]Some translations close the direct quotation here, others extend it through v 21 **2:15** [a]Php 3:4f [b]1Sa 15:18; Lk 24:7 **2:16** [a]Ac 13:39; Ga 3:11 [b]Ro 3:22; 9:30 [c]Ps 143:2; Ro 3:20 [1]Or *although we* supposedly *knew that a man is not justified by the works of the law except through faith in Jesus Christ* [2]Or *law* [3]Or *mortal man* **2:17** [a]Ga 2:15 [b]Lk 20:16; Ga 3:21 **2:18** [a]Ro 3:5 **2:19** [a]Ro 6:2; 7:4; 1Co 9:20 [1]Or *law* **2:20** [a]Ro 6:6; Ga 5:24; 6:14 [b]Ro 8:10 [c]Mt 4:3 [d]Ro 8:37 [e]Ga 1:4 **2:21** [a]Ga 3:21 [1]Or *law* ◆ **3:1** [a]Ga 1:2 [b]1Co 1:23; Ga 5:11 **3:2** [a]Ro 10:17 [1]Or *law* [2]Lit *the hearing of faith* **3:3** [1]Or *with* [2]Or *ending with* **3:4** [a]1Co 15:2 [1]Or *experience* **3:5** [a]2Co 9:10; Php 1:19 [b]1Co 12:10 [c]Ro 10:17 [1]Or *works of power* [2]Or *law* [3]Lit *the hearing of faith* **3:6** [a]Ro 4:3 [b]Ge 15:6 **3:7** [a]Ro 4:16; Ga 3:9 [b]Lk 19:9; Ga 6:16 **3:8** [a]Ge 12:3 [1]Lit *justifies* [2]Lit *nations* **3:9** [a]Ga 3:7 [1]Lit *the believing Abraham*

**10** For as many as are of the works
of [1]the Law are under a curse, for it
is written, "[a]CURSED IS EVERYONE
WHO DOES NOT ABIDE BY ALL THINGS
WRITTEN IN THE BOOK OF THE LAW,
TO DO THEM." **11** Now that [a]no one is
justified [1]by [2]the Law before God is
evident, [3]for "[b]THE RIGHTEOUS SHALL
LIVE BY FAITH." **12** [1]However, the Law
is not [2]of faith; rather, "[a]HE WHO
DOES THEM SHALL LIVE [3]BY THEM."
**13** Christ [a]redeemed us from the
curse of the Law, having become
a curse for us—for it is written,
"[b]CURSED IS EVERYONE WHO HANGS
ON [c]A [1]TREE"— **14** in order that [a]in
Christ Jesus the blessing of Abraham
might [1]come to the Gentiles, so that
we [b]would receive [c]the promise of
the Spirit through faith.

### *The Promise by Faith*

**15** [a]Brothers, [b]I speak [1]in human
terms: [c]even though it is *only* a
man's [2]covenant, yet when it has
been ratified, no one sets it aside or
adds [3]conditions to it. **16** Now the
promises were spoken [a]to Abraham
and to his seed. He does not say, "And
to seeds," as *referring* to many, but
*rather* to one, "And [b]TO YOUR SEED,"
that is, Christ. **17** And what I am
saying is this: the Law, which came
[a]430 years later, does not invalidate
*a covenant* previously ratified by
God, so as to abolish the promise.
**18** For [a]if the inheritance is by law,
it is no longer by promise, but [b]God
has granted it to Abraham through
promise.

**19** [a]Why the Law then? It was
added [1]because of trespasses, hav-
ing been [b]ordained through angels
[c]by the hand of a mediator, until
[d]the seed would come to whom the
promise had been made. **20** Now
[a]a mediator is not [1]for one *person*
*only*, whereas God is one. **21** Is the
Law then contrary to the promises
of God? [a]May it never be! For [b]if a
law had been given which was able to
impart life, then righteousness would
indeed be by law. **22** But the Scripture
has [a]shut up [1]everyone under sin,
so that the promise by faith in Jesus
Christ might be given to those who
believe.

**23** But before faith came, we were
held in custody under the Law,
[a]being shut up for the coming faith
to be revealed. **24** Therefore the Law
has become our [a]tutor unto Christ,
so that [b]we may be justified by faith.
**25** But now that faith has come, we
are no longer under a [a,1]tutor. **26** For
you are all [a]sons of God through
faith in [b]Christ Jesus. **27** For all of
you who were [a]baptized into Christ
have [b]clothed yourselves with Christ.
**28** [a]There is neither Jew nor Greek,
there is neither slave nor free man,
there is no [b]male and female, for [c]you

---

**3:10** [a]Dt 27:26 [1]Or *law* **3:11** [a]Ga 2:16 [b]Hab 2:4; Ro 1:17; Heb 10:38 [1]Or *in* [2]Or *law* [3]Or *but he who is righteous by faith shall live* **3:12** [a]Lv 18:5; Ro 10:5 [1]Or *And* [2]Or *based on* [3]Or *in* **3:13** [a]Ga 4:5 [b]Dt 21:23 [c]Ac 5:30 [1]Or *cross;* lit *wood* **3:14** [a]Ro 4:9, 16; Ga 3:28 [b]Ga 3:2 [c]Ac 2:33; Eph 1:13 [1]Or *occur* **3:15** [a]Ac 1:15; Ro 1:13; Ga 6:18 [b]Ro 3:5 [c]Heb 6:16 [1]Lit *according to man* [2]Or *will* or *testament* [3]Or *a codicil* **3:16** [a]Lk 1:55; Ro 4:13, 16; 9:4 [b]Ge 17:7; Ac 3:25 **3:17** [a]Ge 15:13f; Ex 12:40; Ac 7:6 **3:18** [a]Ro 4:14 [b]Heb 6:14 **3:19** [a]Ro 5:20 [b]Ac 7:53 [c]Ex 20:19; Dt 5:5 [d]Ga 3:16 [1]Or *for the sake of defining* **3:20** [a]1Ti 2:5; Heb 8:6; 9:15; 12:24 [1]Lit *of one* **3:21** [a]Lk 20:16; Ga 2:17 [b]Ga 2:21 **3:22** [a]Ro 11:32 [1]Lit *all things* **3:23** [a]Ro 11:32 **3:24** [a]1Co 4:15 [b]Ga 2:16 **3:25** [a]1Co 4:15 [1]Lit *child-conductor* **3:26** [a]Ro 8:14; Ga 4:5 [b]Ro 8:1; Ga 3:28; 4:14; 5:6, 24; Eph 1:1; Php 1:1; Col 1:4; 1Ti 1:12; 2Ti 1:1; Tit 1:4 **3:27** [a]Mt 28:19; Ro 6:3; 1Co 10:2 [b]Ro 13:14 **3:28** [a]Ro 3:22; 1Co 12:13; Col 3:11 [b]Ge 1:27 [c]Jn 17:11; Eph 2:15

are all one in [d]Christ Jesus. **29** And if
[a]you [1]belong to Christ, then you are
Abraham's [2]seed, heirs according to
[b]promise.

### *Sonship in Christ*

**4** Now I say, as long as the heir is
a [1]child, he does not differ at all
from a slave although he is [2]owner of
everything, **2** but he is under guard-
ians and stewards until the date set
by the father. **3** So also we, while we
were children, were [a]enslaved under
the [b,1]elemental things of the world.
**4** But when [a]the fullness of the time
came, God sent forth His Son, [b]born
of a woman, born [c]under [1]the Law,
**5** so that He might redeem those who
were under [1]the Law, that we might
receive the adoption as [a]sons. **6** And
because you are sons, [a]God sent forth
the Spirit of His Son into our hearts,
crying, "[b]Abba! Father!" **7** Therefore
you are no longer a slave, but a son;
and [a]if a son, then an heir [1]through
God.

**8** However at that time, [a]when you
did not know God, you were [b]slaves
to [c]those which by nature are no
gods. **9** But now, having known God,
or rather having been [a]known by
God, [b]how is it that you turn back
again to the weak and worthless
[c,1]elemental things, to which you
want to be enslaved all over again?
**10** You [a]observe days and months and
seasons and years. **11** I fear for you,
that perhaps I have labored [1]over you
for nothing.

**12** I beg of you, [a]brothers, [b]become
as I *am*, for I also *have become* as you
*are*. You have done me no wrong.
**13** But you know that it was because
of a [1]bodily illness that I proclaimed
the gospel to you the [2]first time;
**14** and that which was a [1]trial to
you in my [2]bodily condition you
did not despise or [3]loathe, but [a]you
received me as an angel of God, as
[b]Christ Jesus *Himself*. **15** Where then
is [1]that sense of blessing you had? For
I testify to you that, if possible, you
would have plucked out your eyes
and given them to me. **16** So have I
become your enemy [a]by [1]telling you
the truth? **17** They zealously seek
you, not commendably, but they
wish to shut you out so that you
will zealously seek them. **18** But it is
good always to be zealously sought
in a commendable [1]manner, and [a]not
only when I am present with you.
**19** [a]My children, with whom [b]I am
again in labor until [c]Christ is formed
in you— **20** but I could wish to be
present with you now and to change
my tone, because [a]I am perplexed
about you.

### *An Allegory of Two Covenants*

**21** Tell me, you who want to be under
law, do you not [a]listen to the Law?

---

**3:28** [d]Ro 8:1; Ga 3:26; 4:14; 5:6, 24; Eph 1:1; Php 1:1; Col 1:4; 1Ti 1:12; 2Ti 1:1; Tit 1:4 **3:29** [a]Ro 4:13; 1Co 3:23 [b]Ro 9:8; Ga 3:18; 4:28 [1]Lit *are Christ's* [2]Or *descendants* ◆ **4:1** [1]Or *minor* [2]Lit *lord* **4:3** [a]Ga 2:4; 4:8f, 24f [b]Ga 4:9; Col 2:8, 20; Heb 5:12 [1]Or *rudimentary teachings, principles* **4:4** [a]Mk 1:15 [b]Jn 1:14; Ro 1:3; 8:3; Php 2:7 [c]Lk 2:21f, 27 [1]Or *law* **4:5** [a]Ro 8:14; Ga 3:26 [1]Or *law* **4:6** [a]Ac 16:7; Ro 5:5; 8:9, 16; 2Co 3:17 [b]Mk 14:36; Ro 8:15 **4:7** [a]Ro 8:17 [1]Through the gracious act of **4:8** [a]1Co 1:21; Eph 2:12; 1Th 4:5; 2Th 1:8 [b]Ga 4:3 [c]2Chr 13:9; Is 37:19; Jer 2:11; 1Co 8:4f; 10:20 **4:9** [a]1Co 8:3 [b]Col 2:20 [c]Ga 4:3 [1]Or *rudimentary teachings, principles* **4:10** [a]Ro 14:5; Col 2:16 **4:11** [1]Or *for* **4:12** [a]Ga 6:18 [b]2Co 6:11, 13 **4:13** [1]Lit *weakness of the flesh* [2]Or *former* **4:14** [a]Mt 10:40; 1Th 2:13 [b]Ga 3:26 [1]Or *temptation* [2]Lit *flesh* [3]Lit *spit out at* **4:15** [1]Lit *the congratulation of yourselves* **4:16** [a]Am 5:10 [1]Or *dealing truthfully with you* **4:18** [a]Ga 4:13f [1]Or *thing* **4:19** [a]1Jn 2:1 [b]1Co 4:15 [c]Eph 4:13 **4:20** [a]2Co 4:8 **4:21** [a]Lk 16:29

**22** For it is written that Abraham had
two sons, [a]one by the servant-woman
and [b]one by the free woman. **23** But
[a]the son by the servant-woman had
been born according to the flesh,
while [b]the son by the free woman
through the promise. **24** [a,1]This is
[2]spoken with allegory, for these
women are two covenants: one from
[b]Mount Sinai bearing children into
[c]slavery; [3]she is Hagar. **25** Now this
Hagar is Mount Sinai in Arabia and
corresponds to the present Jerusalem,
for she is in slavery with her children.
**26** But [a]the Jerusalem above is free;
[1]she is our mother. **27** For it is written,

"[a]REJOICE, BARREN WOMAN
WHO DOES NOT GIVE BIRTH;
BREAK FORTH AND SHOUT, YOU
WHO ARE NOT IN LABOR;
FOR MORE NUMEROUS
ARE THE CHILDREN
OF THE DESOLATE ONE
THAN OF THE ONE WHO
HAS A HUSBAND."

**28** And you brothers, [a]in accordance
with Isaac, are [b]children of promise.
**29** But as at that time [a]he who was
born according to the flesh [b]was per-
secuting him *who was born* according
to the Spirit, [c]so it is now also. **30** But
what does the Scripture say?

"[a]CAST OUT THE SERVANT-
WOMAN AND HER SON,
FOR [b]THE SON OF THE SERVANT-
WOMAN SHALL NOT BE
AN HEIR WITH THE SON
OF THE FREE WOMAN."

**31** So then, brothers, we are not chil-
dren of a servant-woman, [1]but of the
free woman.

### *Christ Set Us Free*

**5** [a,1]It was for freedom that Christ
set us free. Therefore, [b]stand firm
and do not be subject again to a [c]yoke
of slavery.

**2** Behold I, [a]Paul, say to you that if
you receive [b]circumcision, Christ will
be of no benefit to you. **3** And I [a]testify
again to every man who receives
[b]circumcision, that he is under obliga-
tion to [c]keep the whole Law. **4** You have
been [1]severed from Christ, you who
are being justified by law; you have
[a]fallen from grace! **5** For we [1]through
the Spirit, [2]by faith, are [a]eagerly wait-
ing for the hope of righteousness. **6** For
in [a]Christ Jesus [b]neither circumcision
nor uncircumcision means anything,
but [c]faith working through love.

**7** You were [a]running well; who
hindered you from [1]obeying the
truth? **8** This persuasion *is* not from
[a]Him who calls you. **9** [a]A little leaven
leavens the whole lump. **10** [a]I have
confidence [1]in you in the Lord that
you [b]will adopt no other view. But the
one who is [c]disturbing you will bear
his judgment, whoever he is. **11** But I,
brothers, if I still preach circumcision,
why am I still [a]persecuted? Then [b]the

---

**4:22** [a]Ge 16:15 [b]Ge 21:2 **4:23** [a]Ro 9:7; Ga 4:29 [b]Ge 17:16ff; 18:10ff; 21:1; Ga 4:28; Heb 11:11 **4:24** [a]1Co 10:11 [b]Dt 33:2 [c]Ga 4:3 [1]Lit *Which* [2]Or *written* [3]Lit *which* **4:26** [a]Heb 12:22; Rev 3:12; 21:2, 10 [1]Lit *which* **4:27** [a]Is 54:1 **4:28** [a]Ga 4:23 [b]Ro 9:7ff; Ga 3:29 **4:29** [a]Ga 4:23 [b]Ge 21:9 [c]Ga 5:11 **4:30** [a]Ge 21:10, 12 [b]Jn 8:35 **4:31** [1]Ch 5:1, note 1 ◆ **5:1** [a]Jn 8:32, 36; Ro 8:15; 2Co 3:17; Ga 2:4; 5:13 [b]1Co 16:13 [c]Ac 15:10; Ga 2:4 [1]Some authorities prefer to join this sentence with 4:31 and render *but with the freedom of the free woman Christ set us free* **5:2** [a]2Co 10:1 [b]Ac 15:1; Ga 5:3, 6, 11 **5:3** [a]Lk 16:28 [b]Ac 15:1; Ga 5:2, 6, 11 [c]Ro 2:25 **5:4** [a]Heb 12:15; 2Pe 3:17 [1]Lit *abolished*, cf. 5:11 **5:5** [a]Ro 8:23; 1Co 1:7 [1]Lit *by* [2]Lit *out of* **5:6** [a]Ga 3:26 [b]1Co 7:19; Ga 6:15 [c]Col 1:4f; 1Th 1:3; Jas 2:18, 20, 22 **5:7** [a]Ga 2:2 [1]Or *being persuaded by*, cf. 5:8, 10 **5:8** [a]Ro 8:28; Ga 1:6 **5:9** [a]1Co 5:6 **5:10** [a]2Co 2:3 [b]Ga 5:7; Php 3:15 [c]Ga 1:7; 5:12 [1]Lit *toward* **5:11** [a]Ga 4:29; 6:12 [b]Ro 9:33; 1Co 1:23

stumbling block of the cross would
have been abolished. **12** I wish that
[a]those who are upsetting you would
even [b,1]mutilate themselves.
**13** For you were called to [a]freedom,
brothers; [b]only *do* not *turn* your free-
dom into an opportunity for the flesh,
but through love [c]serve one another.
**14** For [a]the whole Law is fulfilled in
one word, in this: "[b]YOU SHALL LOVE
YOUR NEIGHBOR AS YOURSELF." **15** But
if you [a]bite and devour one another,
beware that you are not consumed
by one another.

### *Walk by the Spirit*

**16** But I say, [a]walk by the Spirit and
you will not carry out [b]the desire of
the flesh. **17** For [a]the flesh [1]sets its
desire against the Spirit, and the
Spirit against the flesh; for these are
in opposition to one another, [b]so that
you do not do the things that you
want. **18** But if you are [a]led by the
Spirit, [b]you are not under the Law.
**19** Now the deeds of the flesh are
evident, which are: [a]sexual immoral-
ity, impurity, sensuality, **20** idolatry,
[a]sorcery, enmities, [b]strife, jealousy,
outbursts of anger, [c]selfish ambition,
dissensions, [d,1]factions, **21** envying,
[a]drunkenness, carousing, and things
like these, of which I forewarn you,
just as I have forewarned you, that
those who practice such things
will not [b]inherit the kingdom of
God. **22** But [a]the fruit of the Spirit is
[b]love, joy, peace, patience, kindness,
goodness, faithfulness, **23** gentleness,
[a]self-control. Against such things
[b]there is no law. **24** Now those who
[1]belong to [a]Christ Jesus [b]crucified the
flesh with its passions and [c]desires.
**25** If we live by the Spirit, let us also
[1]walk in step with [a]the Spirit. **26** Let
us not become *those* with [a]vain glory,
challenging one another, envying
one another.

### *Bear One Another's Burdens*

**6** [a]Brothers, even if [1]anyone is
caught in any transgression, you
who are [b]spiritual, [c]restore such a
one [d]in a spirit of gentleness, *each
of you* looking to yourself, so that
you too will not be tempted. **2** [a]Bear
one another's burdens, and so fulfill
[b]the law of Christ. **3** For [a]if anyone
thinks he is something when he is
nothing, he deceives himself. **4** But
each one must [a]examine his own
work, and then he will have *reason
for* [b]boasting in regard to himself
alone, and not in regard to another.
**5** For [a]each one will bear his own
load.
**6** [a]And the one who is instructed
in [b]the word is to share in all good
things with the one who instructs
*him*. **7** [a]Do not be deceived, [b]God is
not mocked, for [c]whatever a man
sows, this he will also reap. **8** [a]For

---

**5:12** [a]Ga 2:4; 5:10 [b]Dt 23:1 [1]Or *cut themselves off, castrate* **5:13** [a]Ga 5:1 [b]1Co 8:9; 1Pe 2:16 [c]1Co 9:19; Eph 5:21 **5:14** [a]Mt 7:12; 22:40; Ro 13:8, 10; Ga 6:2 [b]Lv 19:18; Mt 19:19; Jn 13:34 **5:15** [a]Ga 5:20; Php 3:2 **5:16** [a]Ro 8:4; 13:14; Ga 5:24f [b]Ro 13:14; Eph 2:3 **5:17** [a]Ro 7:18, 23; 8:5ff [b]Ro 7:15ff [1]Lit *lusts against* ***5:18*** *[a]Ro 8:14 [b]Ro 6:14; 7:4; 1Ti 1:9* **5:19** [a]1Co 6:9, 18; 2Co 12:21 **5:20** [a]Rev 21:8 [b]2Co 12:20 [c]Ro 2:8; Jas 3:14ff [d]1Co 11:19 [1]Or *heresies* **5:21** [a]Ro 13:13 [b]1Co 6:9 **5:22** [a]Mt 7:16ff; Eph 5:9 [b]Ro 5:1-5; 1Co 13:4; Col 3:12-15 **5:23** [a]Ac 24:25 [b]Ga 5:18 **5:24** [a]Ga 3:26 [b]Ro 6:6; Ga 2:20; 6:14 [c]Ga 5:16f [1]Lit *are of* **5:25** [a]Ga 5:16 [1]Lit *following in line* **5:26** [a]Php 2:3 ◆ **6:1** [a]Ga 6:18; 1Th 4:1 [b]1Co 2:15 [c]2Co 2:7; 2Th 3:15; Heb 12:13; Jas 5:19f [d]1Co 4:21 [1]Gr *anthropos* **6:2** [a]Ro 15:1 [b]Ro 8:2; 1Co 9:21; Jas 1:25; 2:12; 2Pe 3:2 **6:3** [a]Ac 5:36; 1Co 3:18; 2Co 12:11 **6:4** [a]1Co 11:28 [b]Php 1:26 **6:5** [a]Pr 9:12; Ro 14:12; 1Co 3:8 **6:6** [a]1Co 9:11, 14 [b]2Ti 4:2 **6:7** [a]1Co 6:9 [b]Job 13:9 [c]2Co 9:6 **6:8** [a]Job 4:8; Hos 8:7; Ro 6:21

the one who sows to his own flesh
will from the flesh reap [b]corruption,
but [c]the one who sows to the Spirit
will from the Spirit reap eternal life.
**9** [a]And let us not lose heart in doing
good, for in due time we will reap if
we [b]do not grow weary. **10** So then,
[a,1]while we have opportunity, let us
do good to all people, and especially
to those who are of the [b]household
of [c]the faith.

**11** See with what large letters I
[1]am writing to you [a]with my own
hand! **12** As many as are wanting
[a]to make a good showing in the
flesh, these are trying to [b]compel
you to be circumcised, simply so
that they [c]will not be persecuted
[1]for the cross of Christ. **13** For those
who [1]are circumcised do not even
[a]keep [2]the Law themselves, but they
want to have you circumcised so
that they may [b]boast in your flesh.
**14** But [a]may it never be that I would
boast, [b]except in the cross of our
Lord Jesus Christ, [c]through [1]which
the world has been crucified to me,
and [d]I to the world. **15** For [a]neither
is circumcision anything, nor un-
circumcision, but a [b]new [1]creation.
**16** And those who will [1]walk in step
with this rule, peace and mercy *be*
upon them, and upon the [a]Israel of
God.

**17** From now on let no one cause
trouble for me, for I bear on my body
the [a]marks of Jesus.

**18** [a]The grace of our Lord Jesus
Christ be [b]with your spirit, [c]brothers.
Amen.

*The Letter of Paul to the*

# EPHESIANS

### *Spiritual Blessings in Christ*

**1** Paul, [a]an apostle of [b]Christ Jesus
[c,1]by the will of God,

To the [d,2]saints who are [3]at
[e]Ephesus and [f]*who are* faithful in
[b]Christ Jesus: **2** [a]Grace to you and
peace from God our Father and the
Lord Jesus Christ.

**3** [a]Blessed *be* the God and Father
of our Lord Jesus Christ, who has
blessed us with every spiritual bless-
ing in [b]the heavenly *places* in Christ,
**4** just as [a]He chose us in Him before
[b]the foundation of the world, that we
would be [c]holy and blameless before
[1]Him [d]in love, **5** by [a]predestining us
to [b]adoption as sons through Jesus
Christ to Himself, [c]according to
the good pleasure of His will, **6** [a]to
the praise of the glory of His grace,

**6:8** [b]1Co 15:42 [c]Ro 8:11; Jas 3:18 **6:9** [a]1Co 15:58; 2Co 4:1 [b]Mt 10:22; Heb 12:3, 5; Jas 5:7f **6:10** [a]Pr 3:27; Jn 12:35 [b]Eph 2:19; Heb 3:6; 1Pe 2:5; 4:17 [c]Ac 6:7; Ga 1:23 [1]Or *as* **6:11** [a]1Co 16:21 [1]Or *have written* **6:12** [a]Mt 23:27f [b]Ac 15:1 [c]Ga 5:11 [1]Or *because of* **6:13** [a]Ro 2:25 [b]Php 3:3 [1]Two early mss *have been* [2]Or *law* **6:14** [a]Lk 20:16; Ga 2:17; 3:21 [b]1Co 2:2 [c]Ga 2:20; Col 2:20 [d]Ro 6:2, 6; Ga 2:19f; 5:24 [1]Or *whom* **6:15** [a]Ro 2:26, 28; 1Co 7:19; Ga 5:6 [b]2Co 5:17; Eph 2:10, 15; 4:24; Col 3:10 [1]Or *creature* **6:16** [a]Ro 9:6; Ga 3:7, 29; Php 3:3 [1]Lit *following in line* **6:17** [a]Is 44:5; Eze 9:4; 2Co 4:10; 11:23; Rev 13:16 **6:18** [a]Ro 16:20 [b]2Ti 4:22 [c]Ac 1:15; Ro 1:13; Ga 3:15; 4:12, 28, 31 ◆ **1:1** [a]2Co 1:1 [b]Ro 8:1 [c]1Co 1:1 [d]Ac 9:13 [e]Ac 18:19 [f]Col 1:2 [1]Lit *through* [2]Or *holy ones* [3]Three early mss omit *at Ephesus* **1:2** [a]Ro 1:7 **1:3** [a]2Co 1:3 [b]Eph 1:20; 2:6; 3:10; 6:12 **1:4** [a]Eph 2:10; 2Th 2:13f [b]Mt 25:34 [c]Eph 5:27; Col 1:22 [d]Eph 4:2, 15, 16; 5:2 [1]Or *Him, in love* **1:5** [a]Ac 13:48; Ro 8:29f [b]Ro 8:14ff [c]Php 2:13; Col 1:19 **1:6** [a]Eph 1:12, 14

which He graciously bestowed on us
in [b]the Beloved. **7** [a]In [1]Him we have
[b]redemption [c]through His blood, the
[d]forgiveness of our transgressions,
according to [e]the riches of His grace
**8** which He caused to abound to us
in all wisdom and insight, **9** [a]making
known to us the mystery of His will,
[b]according to His good pleasure
which He [c]purposed in Him **10** for
an administration of [a]the fullness
of the times, *that is,* [b]the summing
up of all things in Christ, things [1]in
the heavens and things on the earth
in Him. **11** In [1]Him, we also [a][2]have
been made an inheritance, having
been [b]predestined [c]according to the
purpose of Him who works all things
[d]according to the counsel of His will,
**12** to the end that we who first have
hoped in [1]Christ would be [a]to the
praise of His glory. **13** In [1]Him, you
also, after listening to [a]the word of
truth, the gospel of your salvation—
having also [2]believed, you were
[b]sealed in [1]Him with [c]the Holy
Spirit of promise, **14** who is [a][1]given
as a pledge of [b]our inheritance, unto
the [c]redemption of [d]*God's own* possession, [e]to the praise of His glory.
**15** For this reason I too, [a]having
heard of the faith in the Lord Jesus
which *exists* among you and [1]your
love for [b]all the [2]saints, **16** [a]do
not cease giving thanks for you,
[b]while making mention *of you* in
my prayers: **17** that the [a]God of our
Lord Jesus Christ, [b]the Father of
glory, may give to you *the* [1]Spirit of
[c]wisdom and of [d]revelation in the
[2]full knowledge of Him, **18** so that
you—[a]the eyes of your heart having
been enlightened—will know what
is the [b]hope of His [c]calling, what
are [d]the riches of the glory of [e]His
inheritance in [f]the [1]saints, **19** and
what is the surpassing greatness of
His power toward us who believe
[a]according to the working of the
[b]might of His strength, **20** which He
worked in Christ, by [a]raising Him
from the dead and [b]seating Him
at His right hand in [c]the heavenly
*places,* **21** far above [a]all rule and
authority and power and dominion,
and every [b]name that is named, not
only in [c]this age but also in the one
to come. **22** And [a]HE PUT ALL THINGS
IN SUBJECTION UNDER HIS FEET, and
gave Him as [b]head over all things to
the church, **23** which is His [a]body, the
[b]fullness of Him who [c]fills [d]all in all.

### *By Grace Through Faith*

**2** And you [1]were [a]dead [2]in your
transgressions and sins, **2** in
which you [a]formerly walked
according to the [1]course of [b]this
world, according to [c]the ruler of
the power of the air, the spirit that

---

**1:6** [b]Mt 3:17 **1:7** [a]Col 1:14 [b]Ro 3:24; 1Co 1:30; Eph 1:14 [c]Ac 20:28; Ro 3:25 [d]Ac 2:38 [e]Ro 2:4; Eph 1:18; 2:7; 3:8, 16 [1]Lit *whom* **1:9** [a]Ro 11:25; Eph 3:3 [b]1Co 1:21; Ga 1:15 [c]Ro 8:28; Eph 1:11 **1:10** [a]Mk 1:15 [b]Eph 3:15; Php 2:9f; Col 1:16, 20 [1]Lit *upon* **1:11** [a]Dt 4:20; Eph 1:14; Tit 2:14 [b]Eph 1:5 [c]Ro 8:28f; Eph 3:11 [d]Ro 9:11; Heb 6:17 [1]Lit *whom* [2]Or *obtained an inheritance* **1:12** [a]Eph 1:6, 14 [1]Messiah **1:13** [a]Eph 4:21; Col 1:5 [b]Eph 4:30 [c]Ac 2:33 [1]Lit *whom* [2]Or *believed in Him* **1:14** [a]2Co 1:22 [b]Ac 20:32 [c]Eph 1:7 [d]Eph 1:11 [e]Eph 1:6, 12 [1]Or *a down payment* **1:15** [a]Col 1:4; Phm 5 [b]Eph 1:1; 3:18 [1]Three early mss omit *your love* [2]Or *holy ones* **1:16** [a]Ro 1:8f; Col 1:9 [b]Ro 1:9 **1:17** [a]Jn 20:17; Ro 15:6 [b]Ac 7:2; 1Co 2:8 [c]Col 1:9 [d]1Co 14:6 [1]Or *spirit* [2]Or *true knowledge* **1:18** [a]Ac 26:18; 2Co 4:6; Heb 6:4 [b]Eph 4:4 [c]Ro 11:29 [d]Eph 1:7 [e]Eph 1:11 [f]Col 1:12 [1]Or *holy ones* **1:19** [a]Eph 3:7; Col 1:29 [b]Eph 6:10 **1:20** [a]Ac 2:24 [b]Mk 16:19 [c]Eph 1:3 **1:21** [a]Mt 28:18; Col 1:16 [b]Php 2:9; Rev 19:12 [c]Mt 12:32 **1:22** [a]Ps 8:6; 1Co 15:27 [b]1Co 11:3; Eph 4:15; Col 1:18 **1:23** [a]1Co 12:27; Eph 4:12; Col 1:18, 24 [b]Jn 1:16; Eph 3:19 [c]Eph 4:10 [d]Col 3:11 ◆ **2:1** [a]Eph 2:5; Col 2:13 [1]Lit *being* [2]Or *by reason of* **2:2** [a]1Co 6:11; Eph 2:3 [b]Eph 1:21 [c]Jn 12:31; Eph 6:12 [1]Lit *age*

is now working in [d]the sons of
disobedience, **3** among whom we all
also [a]formerly conducted ourselves
in [b]the lusts of our flesh, doing the
desires of the flesh and of the [1]mind,
and were [c]by nature [d]children of
wrath, [e]even as the rest. **4** But God,
being [a]rich in mercy because of [b]His
great love with which He loved us,
**5** even when we were [a]dead [1]in our
transgressions, made us alive togeth-
er [2]with Christ—[b]by grace you have
been saved— **6** and [a]raised us up
with Him, and [b]seated us with Him
in [c]the heavenly *places* in [d]Christ
Jesus, **7** so that in the ages to come He
might show the surpassing [a]riches
of His grace in [b]kindness toward us
in Christ Jesus. **8** For [a]by grace you
have been saved [b]through faith, and
[1]this not of yourselves, *it is* [c]the gift
of God; **9** [a]not of works, so that [b]no
one may boast. **10** For we are His
workmanship, [a]created in [b]Christ
Jesus for [c]good works, which God
[d]prepared beforehand so that we
would [e]walk in them.

**11** Therefore, remember that
[a]formerly [b]you—the Gentiles in the
flesh, who are called "[c]Uncircumci-
sion" by the so-called "[c]Circumci-
sion," *which is* performed in the flesh
by *human* hands— **12** *remember*
that you were at that time without
Christ, [a]alienated from the citi-
zenship of Israel, and strangers to
[b]the covenants of promise, having
[c]no hope and [d]without God in the
world. **13** But now in [a]Christ Jesus you
who [b]formerly were [c]far off [1]have
[c]been brought near [d]by the blood
of Christ. **14** For He Himself is [a]our
peace, [b]who made both *groups* one
and broke down the dividing wall of
the partition **15** [1]by [a]abolishing in His
flesh the enmity, [b]the Law of com-
mandments *contained* in ordinances,
so that in Himself He might [c]create
the two into [d]one new man, making
[e]peace, **16** and might [a]reconcile them
both in [b]one body to God through
the cross, having in Himself [c]put to
death the enmity. **17** AND [a]HE CAME
AND PREACHED [b]THE GOOD NEWS OF
PEACE TO YOU WHO WERE [c]FAR AWAY,
AND PEACE TO THOSE WHO WERE
[c]NEAR; **18** for through Him we both
have [a]our access in [b]one Spirit to [c]the
Father. **19** So then you are no longer
[a]strangers and sojourners, but you
are [b]fellow citizens with the [1]saints,
and are of [c]God's household, **20** hav-
ing been [a]built on [b]the foundation of
[c]the apostles and prophets, [d]Christ
Jesus Himself being the [e]corner
*stone*, **21** [a]in whom the whole build-
ing, being joined together, is growing
into [b]a holy [1]sanctuary in the Lord,

**2:2** [d]Eph 5:6 **2:3** [a]Eph 2:2 [b]Ga 5:16f [c]Ro 2:14; Ga 2:15 [d]Ro 5:9; Col 1:21; 2Pe 2:14 [e]Ro 5:12 [1]Lit *thoughts* **2:4** [a]Eph 1:7 [b]Jn 3:16 **2:5** [a]Eph 2:1 [b]Ac 15:11 [1]Or *by reason of* [2]Two early mss *in Christ* **2:6** [a]Col 2:12 [b]Eph 1:20 [c]Eph 1:3 [d]Eph 1:1; 2:10, 13 **2:7** [a]Ro 2:4; Eph 1:7 [b]Tit 3:4 **2:8** [a]Ac 15:11; Eph 2:5 [b]1Pe 1:5 [c]Jn 4:10 [1]This salvation **2:9** [a]Ro 3:28; 2Ti 1:9 [b]1Co 1:29 **2:10** [a]Eph 2:15; 4:24; Col 3:10 [b]Eph 1:1; 2:6, 13 [c]Tit 2:14 [d]Eph 1:4 [e]Eph 4:1 **2:11** [a]Eph 2:2 [b]1Co 12:2; Eph 5:8 [c]Ro 2:28f; Col 2:11 **2:12** [a]Ro 9:4; Col 1:21 [b]Ga 3:17; Heb 8:6 [c]1Th 4:13 [d]Ga 4:8; 1Th 4:5 **2:13** [a]Eph 1:1; 2:6 [b]Eph 2:2 [c]Is 57:19; Ac 2:39; Eph 2:17 [d]Ro 3:25; Col 1:20 [1]Or *were made*; lit *became* **2:14** [a]Is 9:6; Eph 2:15; Col 3:15 [b]1Co 12:13; Ga 3:28; Col 3:11 **2:15** [a]Eph 2:16; Col 1:21f [b]Col 2:14, 20 [c]Ga 3:28; Eph 2:10; Col 3:10, 11 [d]Ga 3:28; Col 3:10f [e]Is 9:6; Eph 2:14; Col 3:15 [1]Or *the enmity, by abolishing in His flesh the Law* **2:16** [a]2Co 5:18; Col 1:20, 22 [b]1Co 10:17; Eph 4:4 [c]Eph 2:15 **2:17** [a]Is 57:19; Ro 10:14 [b]Ac 10:36; Eph 2:14 [c]Eph 2:13 **2:18** [a]Ro 5:2; Eph 3:12 [b]1Co 12:13; Eph 4:4 [c]Col 1:12 **2:19** [a]Eph 2:12; Heb 11:13; 1Pe 2:11 [b]Php 3:20; Heb 12:22f [c]Ga 6:10 [1]Or *holy ones* **2:20** [a]1Co 3:9 [b]Mt 16:18; 1Co 3:10; Rev 21:14 [c]1Co 12:28; Eph 3:5 [d]1Co 3:11 [e]Ps 118:22; Lk 20:17 **2:21** [a]Eph 4:15f; Col 2:19 [b]1Co 3:16f [1]The innermost part of the temple

**22** in whom you also are being [a]built
together into a [b]dwelling of God in
the Spirit.

### *The Mystery of Christ Revealed*

**3** For this reason I, Paul, [a]the pris-
oner of [b]Christ Jesus [c]on behalf
of you [d]Gentiles— **2** if indeed you
heard of the [a]stewardship of God's
grace which was given to me for
you; **3** [a]that [b]by revelation there was
[c]made known to me [d]the mystery, [e]as
I wrote before in brief. **4** About which,
when you read you can understand
[a]my insight [1]into the [b]mystery of
Christ, **5** which in other generations
was not made known to the sons of
men, as it was now revealed to His
holy [a]apostles and prophets [1]in the
Spirit: **6** that the Gentiles are [a]fellow
heirs and [b]fellow members of the
body, and [c]fellow partakers of the
promise in [d]Christ Jesus through
the gospel, **7** [a]of which I was made
a [b]minister, according to the gift of
[c]God's grace which was given to me
[d]according to the working of His
power. **8** To me, [a]the very least of
all [1]saints, this grace was given, to
[b]proclaim to the Gentiles the good
news of the unfathomable [c]riches
of Christ, **9** and to bring to light for
all what is the administration of
the [a]mystery which for ages has
been [b]hidden in God [c]who created
all things; **10** so that the manifold
[a]wisdom of God might now be
[b]made known through the church
to the [c]rulers and the authorities in
[d]the heavenly *places.* **11** *This was* in
[a]accordance with the [1]eternal pur-
pose which He [2]carried out in [b]Christ
Jesus our Lord, **12** in whom we have
boldness and [a,1]confident [b]access
through faith [2]in Him. **13** Therefore
I ask [1]you not [a]to lose heart at my
afflictions [b]on your behalf, which are
your glory.

### *Prayer for Spiritual Power*

**14** For this reason I [a]bow my knees
before the Father, **15** from whom
[1]every family in heaven and on earth
is named, **16** that He would give you,
according to [a]the riches of His glo-
ry, to be [b]strengthened with power
through His Spirit in [c]the inner man,
**17** so that [a]Christ may dwell in your
hearts through faith; *and* that you,
being firmly [b]rooted and [c]grounded
in love, **18** may be able to comprehend
with [a]all the [1]saints what is [b]the
breadth and length and height and
depth, **19** and to know [a]the love of
Christ which [b]surpasses knowledge,
that you may be [c]filled up to all the
[d]fullness of God.

**20** [a]Now to Him who is [b]able to do
far more abundantly beyond all that
we ask or understand, [c]according to

---

**2:22** [a]1Co 3:9, 16; 2Co 6:16 [b]Eph 3:17 ◆ **3:1** [a]Ac 23:18; Eph 4:1; 2Ti 1:8; Phm 1, 9, 23 [b]Ga 5:24 [c]2Co 1:6; Eph 3:13 [d]Eph 3:8 **3:2** [a]Eph 1:10; 3:9; Col 1:25; 1Ti 1:4 **3:3** [a]Ac 22:17, 21; 26:16ff [b]Ga 1:12 [c]Eph 1:9; 3:4, 6, 9 [d]Ro 11:25; 16:25; Eph 3:4, 9; 6:19; Col 1:26f; 4:3 [e]Eph 1:9f; Heb 13:22; 1Pe 5:12 **3:4** [a]2Co 11:6 [b]Ro 11:25; 16:25; Eph 3:3, 9; 6:19; Col 1:26f; 4:3 [1]Lit *in* **3:5** [a]1Co 12:28; Eph 2:20 [1]Or *by* **3:6** [a]Ga 3:29 [b]Eph 2:16 [c]Eph 5:7 [d]Ga 5:24 **3:7** [a]Col 1:23, 25 [b]1Co 3:5 [c]Ac 9:15; Ro 12:3; Eph 3:2 [d]Eph 1:19; 3:20 **3:8** [a]1Co 15:9 *[b]Ac 9:15; Eph 3:1f [c]Ro 2:4; Eph 1:7; 3:16* [1]Or *holy ones* **3:9** [a]Ro 11:25; 16:25; Eph 3:3, 4; 6:19; Col 1:26f; 4:3 [b]Col 3:3 [c]Rev 4:11 **3:10** [a]Ro 11:33; 1Co 2:7 [b]Eph 1:23; 1Pe 1:12 [c]Eph 1:21; 6:12; Col 2:10, 15 [d]Eph 1:3 **3:11** [a]Eph 1:11 [b]Ga 5:24; Eph 3:1 [1]Lit *purpose of the ages* [2]Lit *did* **3:12** [a]2Co 3:4; Heb 4:16; 10:19, 35; 1Jn 2:28; 3:21 [b]Eph 2:18 [1]Lit *access in confidence* [2]Lit *of Him* **3:13** [a]2Co 4:1 [b]Eph 3:1 [1]Or *that I may not lose* **3:14** [a]Php 2:10 **3:15** [1]Or *the whole* **3:16** [a]Eph 1:18; 3:8 [b]1Co 16:13; Php 4:13; Col 1:11 [c]Ro 7:22 **3:17** [a]Jn 14:23; Ro 8:9f; 2Co 13:5; Eph 2:22 [b]1Co 3:6; Col 2:7 [c]Col 1:23 **3:18** [a]Eph 1:15 [b]Job 11:8f [1]v 8, note 1 **3:19** [a]Ro 8:35, 39 [b]Php 4:7 [c]Col 2:10 [d]Eph 1:23 **3:20** [a]Ro 16:25 [b]2Co 9:8 [c]Eph 3:7

the power that works within us, **21** [a]to
Him *be* the glory in the church and
in Christ Jesus to all generations
[1]forever and ever. Amen.

### *Unity of the Spirit*

**4** Therefore I, [a]the prisoner in
the Lord, [b]exhort you to [c]walk
worthy of the [d]calling with which
you have been [e]called, **2** with all
[a]humility and gentleness, with
patience, bearing with one another
[b]in love, **3** being diligent to keep the
unity of the Spirit in the [a]bond of
peace. **4** *There is* [a]one body and one
Spirit, just as also you were called
in one [b]hope of your calling; **5** [a]one
Lord, one faith, one baptism; **6** one
God and Father of all [a]who is over
all and through all and in all.
**7** But [a]to each one of us [b]grace was
given [c]according to the measure of
Christ's gift. **8** Therefore [1]it says,

"[a]WHEN HE ASCENDED
ON HIGH,
HE [b]LED CAPTIVE A HOST
OF CAPTIVES,
*And* HE GAVE GIFTS TO MEN."

**9** (Now this *expression*, "He [a]ascend-
ed," what [1]does it mean except
that He also [2]descended into [b]the
lower parts of the earth? **10** He who
descended is Himself also He who
ascended [a]far above all the heavens,
so that He might [b]fill all things.)
**11** And He Himself [a]gave [b]some *as*
apostles, and some *as* prophets, and
some *as* [c]evangelists, and some *as*
pastors and [d]teachers, **12** [a]for the
equipping of the [1]saints for the work
of service, to the building up of [b]the
body of Christ, **13** until we all attain
to [a]the unity of the faith, and of the
[b,1]full knowledge of the Son of God,
to a [c]mature man, to the measure
of the stature [2]which belongs to the
[d]fullness of Christ, **14** so that we are
[a]no longer to be children, [b]tossed
here and there by waves and carried
about by every wind of doctrine, by
the trickery of men, by [c]craftiness [1]in
[d]deceitful scheming, **15** but [1]speaking
the truth [a]in love, [2]we are to [b]grow
up in all *aspects* into Him who is the
[c]head, *that is* Christ, **16** from whom
[a]the whole body, being joined and
held together [1]by what every joint
supplies, according to the properly
[b]measured working of each individ-
ual part, causes the growth of the
body for the building up of itself [c]in
love.

### *Put On the New Man*

**17** [a]Therefore this I say, and testify in
the Lord, [b]that you walk no longer
just as the Gentiles also walk, in
the [c]futility of their mind, **18** being
[a]darkened in their mind, [b]alienated
from the life of God because of the
[c]ignorance that is in them, because of
the [d]hardness of their heart. **19** *And*

---

**3:21** [a]Ro 11:36 [1]Lit *of the age of the ages* ◆ **4:1** [a]Eph 3:1 [b]Ro 12:1 [c]Eph 2:10; Col 1:10; 2:6; 1Th 2:12 [d]Ro 11:29 [e]Ro 8:28f **4:2** [a]Col 3:12f [b]Eph 1:4 **4:3** [a]Col 3:14f **4:4** [a]1Co 12:4ff; Eph 2:16, 18 [b]Eph 1:18 **4:5** [a]1Co 8:6 **4:6** [a]Ro 11:36 **4:7** [a]1Co 12:7, 11 [b]Eph 3:2 [c]Ro 12:3 **4:8** [a]Ps 68:18 [b]Col 2:15 [1]Or *He* **4:9** [a]Jn 3:13 [b]Is 44:23 [1]Lit *is it except* [2]One early ms *had first descended* **4:10** [a]Eph 1:20f; Heb 4:14; 7:26 [b]Eph 1:23 **4:11** [a]Eph 4:8 [b]Ac 13:1; 1Co 12:28 [c]Ac 21:8 [d]Ac 13:1 **4:12** [a]2Co 13:9 [b]1Co 12:27; Eph 1:23 [1]Or *holy ones* **4:13** [a]Eph 4:3, 5 [b]Jn 6:69; Eph 1:17; Php 3:10 [c]1Co 14:20; Col 1:28; Heb 5:14 [d]Jn 1:16; Eph 1:23 [1]Or *true knowledge* [2]Lit *of the fullness* **4:14** [a]1Co 14:20 [b]Jas 1:6; Jd 12 [c]1Co 3:19; 2Co 4:2; 11:3 [d]Eph 6:11 [1]Lit *with regard to the scheming of deceit* **4:15** [a]Eph 1:4 [b]Eph 2:21 [c]Eph 1:22 [1]Or *holding to, being truthful in* [2]Or *let us grow up* **4:16** [a]Ro 12:4f; Col 2:19 [b]Eph 4:7 [c]Eph 1:4 [1]Lit *through every joint of the supply* **4:17** [a]Col 2:4 [b]Eph 2:2; 4:22 [c]Ro 1:21; Col 2:18; 1Pe 1:18; 2Pe 2:18 **4:18** [a]Ro 1:21 [b]Eph 2:1, 12 [c]Ac 3:17; 17:30; 1Co 2:8; Heb 5:2; 9:7; 1Pe 1:14 [d]Mk 3:5; Ro 11:7, 25; 2Co 3:14

they, having [a]become callous, [b]have
given themselves over to [c]sensuality
[1]for the practice of every kind of im-
purity with greediness. **20** But you did
not [a]learn [1]Christ in this way— **21** if
indeed you [a]heard Him and were
[b]taught in Him, just as truth is in
Jesus, **22** [1]to [a]lay aside, in reference to
your former conduct, the [b]old man,
which is being corrupted in accor-
dance with the [c]lusts of deceit, **23** and
to be [a]renewed in the spirit of your
mind, **24** and to [a]put on the [b]new
man, which [c,1]in *the likeness of* God
has been created in righteousness
and holiness of the truth.

**25** Therefore, [a]laying aside false-
hood, [b]SPEAK TRUTH EACH ONE *of*
*you* WITH HIS NEIGHBOR, for we are
[c]members of one another. **26** [a]BE
ANGRY, AND *yet* DO NOT SIN; do not
let the sun go down on your anger,
**27** and do not [a]give the devil [1]an op-
portunity. **28** He who steals must steal
no longer, but rather [a]he must labor,
[b]performing with his own hands
what is good, [c]so that he will have
*something* to share with [1]one who
has need. **29** Let no [a,1]unwholesome
word proceed from your mouth,
but only such *a word* as is good for
[b]building up [2]what is needed, so that
it will give grace to those who hear.
**30** [a]And do not grieve the Holy Spirit
of God, [1]by whom you were [b]sealed
for the day of redemption. **31** [a]Let all
bitterness and anger and wrath and
shouting and slander be [b]put away
from you, along with all [c]malice.
**32** [a]Instead, be kind to one another,
tender-hearted, graciously forgiving
each other, [b]just as God in Christ also
has graciously forgiven [1]you.

### *Be Imitators of God*

**5** [a]Therefore be imitators of God, as
beloved children, **2** and [a]walk in
love, just as Christ also [b]loved [1]us and
[c]gave Himself up for us, an [d]offering
and a sacrifice to God [2]as a [e]fragrant
aroma.

**3** But [a]sexual immorality [1]or any
impurity or greed must not even
be named among you, as is proper
among [2]saints; **4** *nor* [a]filthiness and
foolish talk, or coarse jesting, which
[b]are not fitting, but rather [c]giving
of thanks. **5** For this you know with
certainty, that [a]no one sexually im-
moral or impure or greedy, who is an
idolater, has an inheritance in the
kingdom [b]of Christ and God.

**6** [a]Let no one deceive you with
empty words, for because of these
things [b]the wrath of God comes
upon [c]the sons of disobedience.
**7** Therefore do not be [a]partakers
with them, **8** for [a]you were formerly

**4:19** [a]1Ti 4:2 [b]Ro 1:24 [c]Col 3:5 [1]Or *greedy for the practice of every kind of impurity* **4:20** [a]Mt 11:29 [1]Messiah **4:21** [a]Ro 10:14; Eph 1:13; 2:17; Col 1:5 [b]Col 2:7 **4:22** [a]Eph 4:25, 31; Col 3:8; Heb 12:1; Jas 1:21; 1Pe 2:1 [b]Ro 6:6 [c]2Co 11:3; Heb 3:13 [1]Lit *for you* **4:23** [a]Ro 12:2 **4:24** [a]Ro 13:14 [b]Ro 6:4; 7:6; 12:2; 2Co 5:17; Col 3:10 [c]Eph 2:10 [1]Lit *according to God* **4:25** [a]Eph 4:22, 31; Col 3:8; Heb 12:1; Jas 1:21; 1Pe 2:1 [b]Zec 8:16; Eph 4:15; Col 3:9 [c]Ro 12:5 **4:26** [a]Ps 4:4 **4:27** [a]Ro 12:19; Jas 4:7 [1]Lit *a place* **4:28** [a]Ac 20:35; 1Co 4:12; Ga 6:10 [b]1Th 4:11; 2Th 3:8, 11f; Tit 3:8, 14 [c]Lk 3:11; 1Th 4:12 [1]Lit *the one* **4:29** [a]Mt 12:34; Eph 5:4; Col 3:8 [b]Ecc 10:12; Ro 14:19; Col 4:6 [1]Lit *rotten* [2]Or *according to the need* **4:30** [a]Is 63:10; 1Th 5:19 [b]Jn 3:33; Eph 1:13 [1]Lit *in* **4:31** [a]Ro 3:14; Col 3:8, 19 [b]Eph 4:22 [c]1Pe 2:1 **4:32** [a]1Co 13:4; Col 3:12f; 1Pe 3:8 [b]Mt 6:14f; 2Co 2:10 [1]Two early mss *us* ◆**5:1** [a]Mt 5:48; Lk 6:36; Eph 4:32 **5:2** [a]Ro 14:15; Col 3:14 [b]Jn 13:34; Ro 8:37 [c]Jn 6:51; Ro 4:25; Ga 2:20; Eph 5:25 [d]Heb 7:27; 9:14; 10:10, 12 [e]Ex 29:18, 25; 2Co 2:14 [1]Some mss *you* [2]Lit *for an odor of fragrance* **5:3** [a]Col 3:5 [1]Lit *and all* [2]Or *holy ones* **5:4** [a]Mt 12:34; Eph 4:29; Col 3:8 [b]Ro 1:28 [c]Eph 5:20 **5:5** [a]1Co 6:9; Col 3:5 [b]Col 1:13 **5:6** [a]Col 2:8 [b]Ro 1:18; Col 3:6 [c]Eph 2:2 **5:7** [a]Eph 3:6 **5:8** [a]Eph 2:2

[b]darkness, but now you are light in
the Lord; walk as [c]children of light
9 (for [a]the fruit of that light *consists*
in all [b]goodness and righteousness
and truth), 10 [a,1]trying to learn what
is pleasing to the Lord. 11 [a]And do not
participate in the unfruitful [b]works
of [c]darkness, but instead even
[d,1]expose them. 12 For it is disgraceful
even to speak of the things which
are done by them in secret. 13 But all
things become visible [a]when they are
[1]exposed by the light, for everything
that becomes visible is light. 14 For
this reason [1]it says,

"[a]AWAKE, SLEEPER,
And arise from [b]the dead,
And Christ [c]will shine on you."

15 Therefore look carefully how
you [a]walk, not [b]as unwise but as wise,
16 [a]redeeming the time, because [b]the
days are evil. 17 On account of this,
do not be foolish, but [a]understand
what the will of the Lord is. 18 And
[a]do not get drunk with wine, [1]for
that is [b]dissipation, but be [c]filled
with the Spirit, 19 [a]speaking to [1]one
another in [b]psalms and [c]hymns and
spiritual [d]songs, [e]singing and making
melody with your heart to the Lord;
20 [a]always giving thanks for all things
in the name of our Lord Jesus Christ
to [b,1]God, even the Father; 21 [a,1]and
being subject to one another in the
[b,2]fear of Christ.

### *Wives and Husbands*

22 [a]Wives, [b]*be subject* to your own
husbands, [c]as to the Lord. 23 For
[a]the husband is the head of the
wife, as Christ also is the [b]head
of the church, He Himself [c]*being*
the Savior of the body. 24 But as
the church is subject to Christ, so
also the wives *ought to be* to their
husbands in everything.

25 [a]Husbands, love your wives,
just as Christ also loved the church
and [b]gave Himself up for her, 26 [a]so
that He might sanctify her, having
[b]cleansed her by the [c]washing of
water with [d]the word, 27 that He
might [a]present to Himself the
church [1]in all her glory, having no
spot or wrinkle or any such thing,
but that she would be [b]holy and
blameless. 28 So husbands ought
also to [a]love their own wives as their
own bodies. He who loves his own
wife loves himself; 29 for no one ever
hated his own flesh, but nourishes
and cherishes it, just as Christ also
*does* the church, 30 because we are
[a]members of His [b]body. 31 [a]FOR
THIS REASON A MAN SHALL LEAVE HIS
FATHER AND MOTHER AND BE JOINED
TO HIS WIFE, AND THE TWO SHALL
BECOME ONE FLESH. 32 This mystery
is great, but I am speaking with
reference to Christ and the church.
33 Nevertheless, each individual

---

**5:8** [b]Ac 26:18; Col 1:12f [c]Jn 12:36; Ro 13:12 **5:9** [a]Ga 5:22 [b]Ro 15:14 **5:10** [a]Ro 12:2 [1]Lit *proving what* **5:11** [a]1Co 5:9; 2Co 6:14 [b]Ro 13:12 [c]Ac 26:18; Col 1:12f [d]1Ti 5:20 [1]Or *reprove* **5:13** [a]Jn 3:20f [1]Or *reproved* **5:14** [a]Is 26:19; 51:17; 52:1; 60:1; Ro 13:11 [b]Eph 2:1 [c]Lk 1:78f [1]Or *He* **5:15** [a]Eph 5:2 [b]Col 4:5 **5:16** [a]Col 4:5 [b]Ga 1:4; Eph 6:13 **5:17** [a]Ro 12:2; Col 1:9; 1Th 4:3 **5:18** [a]Pr 20:1; 23:31f; Ro 13:13; 1Co 5:11; 1Th 5:7 [b]Tit 1:6; 1Pe 4:4 [c]Lk 1:15 [1]Lit *in which is* **5:19** [a]Col 3:16 [b]1Co 14:26 [c]Ac 16:25 [d]Rev 5:9 [e]1Co 14:15 [1]Or *yourselves* **5:20** [a]Ro 1:8; Eph 5:4; Col 3:17 [b]1Co 15:24 [1]Lit *the God and Father* **5:21** [a]Ga 5:13; Php 2:3; 1Pe 5:5 [b]2Co 5:11 [1]Lit *being subject* [2]Or *reverence* **5:22** [a]Eph 5:22-6:9: *Col 3:18-4:1* [b]1Co 14:34f; Tit 2:5; 1Pe 3:1 [c]Eph 6:5 **5:23** [a]1Co 11:3 [b]Eph 1:22 [c]1Co 6:13 **5:25** [a]Eph 5:28, 33; Col 3:19; 1Pe 3:7 [b]Eph 5:2 **5:26** [a]Tit 2:14; Heb 10:10, 14, 29; 13:12 [b]2Pe 1:9 [c]Ac 22:16; 1Co 6:11; Tit 3:5 [d]Jn 15:3; 17:17; Ro 10:8f; Eph 6:17 **5:27** [a]2Co 4:14; 11:2; Col 1:22 [b]Eph 1:4 [1]Lit *glorious* **5:28** [a]Eph 5:25, 33; 1Pe 3:7 **5:30** [a]1Co 6:15; 12:27 [b]Eph 1:23 **5:31** [a]Ge 2:24; Mt 19:5; Mk 10:7f

among you also is to [a]love his own
wife even as himself, and the wife
must *see to it* that she [b,1]respects her
husband.

### *Children and Parents*

6 [a]Children, obey your parents
in the Lord, for this is right.
2 [a]HONOR YOUR FATHER AND MOTHER
(which is the first commandment
with a promise), 3 SO THAT IT MAY BE
WELL WITH YOU, AND THAT YOU MAY
LIVE LONG IN THE LAND.
4 [a]Fathers, do not provoke your
children to anger, but [b]bring them
up in the discipline and instruction
of the Lord.
5 [a]Slaves, be obedient to those
who are your [1]masters according to
the flesh, with [b]fear and trembling,
in the [2]integrity of your heart, [c]as to
Christ; 6 [a]not [1]by way of eyeservice,
as [b]men-pleasers, but as [c]slaves of
Christ, [d]doing the will of God from
the [2]heart, 7 serving with good will
[a]as to the Lord, and not to men,
8 [a]knowing that [b]whatever good
thing each one does, this he will re-
ceive back from the Lord, [c]whether
slave or free.
9 And masters, do the same things
to them, [a]giving up threatening,
knowing that [b]both their Master
and yours is in heaven, and there is
[c]no partiality with Him.

### *The Armor of God*

10 Finally, [a]be strong in the Lord and
in [b]the might of His strength. 11 [a]Put
on the full armor of God, so that you
will be able to stand firm against
the [b]schemes of the devil. 12 For our
[a]struggle is not against [b,1]flesh and
blood, but [c]against the rulers, against
the authorities, against the [d]world
forces of this [e]darkness, against the
[f]spiritual *forces* of wickedness in [g]the
heavenly *places*. 13 Therefore, take up
[a]the full armor of God, so that you
will be able to [b]resist in [c]the evil day,
and having done everything, to stand
firm. 14 Stand firm therefore, [a]HAVING
GIRDED YOUR LOINS WITH TRUTH, and
HAVING [b]PUT ON THE BREASTPLATE OF
RIGHTEOUSNESS, 15 and having [a]shod
YOUR FEET WITH THE PREPARATION OF
THE GOSPEL OF PEACE. 16 [1]In addition
to all, having taken up the [a]shield of
faith with which you will be able to
extinguish all the [b]flaming arrows of
[c]the evil one, 17 also receive [a]THE HEL-
MET OF SALVATION, and the [b]sword of
the Spirit, which is [c]the word of God,
18 [a]praying at all times [1]with all
[b]prayer and petition [c]in the Spirit,
and to this end, [d]being on the alert
with all [e]perseverance and [f]petition
for all the saints, 19 as well as [a]on my
behalf, that [1]words may be given to
me [b]in the opening of my mouth, to
make known with [c]boldness [d]the

---

**5:33** [a]Eph 5:25, 28; 1Pe 3:7 [b]1Pe 3:2, 5f [1]Lit *fear*, cf. 5:21 ◆ **6:1** [a]Pr 6:20; 23:22; Col 3:20 **6:2** [a]Ex 20:12; Dt 5:16 **6:4** [a]Col 3:21 [b]Ge 18:19; Dt 6:7; 11:19; Ps 78:4; Pr 22:6; 2Ti 3:15 **6:5** [a]Col 3:22; 1Ti 6:1; Tit 2:9 [b]1Co 2:3 [c]Eph 5:22 [1]Earthly masters [2]Lit *simplicity* **6:6** [a]Col 3:22 [b]Ga 1:10 [c]1Co 7:22 [d]Mk 3:35 [1]Lit *according to* [2]Lit *soul* **6:7** [a]Col 3:23 **6:8** [a]Col 3:24 [b]Mt 16:27; 2Co 5:10; Col 3:24f [c]1Co 12:13; Col 3:11 **6:9** [a]Lv 25:43 [b]Job 31:13ff; Jn 13:13; Col 4:1 [c]Dt 10:17; Ac 10:34; Col 3:25 **6:10** [a]1Co 16:13; 2Ti 2:1 [b]Eph 1:19 **6:11** [a]Ro 13:12; Eph 6:13 [b]Eph 4:14 **6:12** [a]1Co 9:25 [b]Mt 16:17 [c]Eph 1:21; 2:2; 3:10 [d]Jn 12:31 [e]Ac 26:18; Col 1:13 [f]Eph 3:10 [g]Eph 1:3 [1]Lit *blood and flesh* **6:13** [a]Eph 6:11 [b]Jas 4:7 [c]Eph 5:16 **6:14** [a]Is 11:5; Lk 12:35; 1Pe 1:13 [b]Is 59:17; Ro 13:12; Eph 6:13; 1Th 5:8 **6:15** [a]Is 52:7; Ro 10:15 **6:16** [a]1Th 5:8 [b]Ps 7:13; 120:4 [c]Mt 5:37 [1]Lit *In all* **6:17** [a]Is 59:17 [b]Is 49:2; Hos 6:5; Heb 4:12 [c]Eph 5:26; Heb 6:5 **6:18** [a]Lk 18:1; Col 1:3; 4:2; 1Th 5:17 [b]Php 4:6 [c]Ro 8:26f [d]Mk 13:33 [e]Ac 1:14 [f]1Ti 2:1 [1]Lit *through* **6:19** [a]Col 4:3; 1Th 5:25 [b]2Co 6:11 [c]2Co 3:12 [d]Eph 3:3 [1]Lit *word*

mystery of the gospel— **20** for which
I am an [a]ambassador [b]in [1]chains—so
that [2]in *proclaiming* it I may speak
[c]boldly, [d]as I ought to speak.
**21** [a]But that you also may know
about all my affairs, [1]how I am do-
ing, [b]Tychicus, [c]the beloved brother
and faithful servant in the Lord,
will make everything known to you.
**22** [a,1]I have sent him to you for this
very purpose, so that you may know
[2]our circumstances, and that he may
[b]encourage your hearts.
**23** [a]Peace be to the brothers, and
[b]love with faith, from God the Father
and the Lord Jesus Christ. **24** Grace
be with all those who love our Lord
Jesus Christ [1]with incorruptible *love.*

*The Letter of Paul to the*

# PHILIPPIANS

### *Thanksgiving*

**1** [a]Paul and [b]Timothy, [c]slaves of
[d]Christ Jesus,
To [e]all the [f,1]saints in Christ Jesus
who are in [g]Philippi, with the [h]over-
seers and [i]deacons: **2** [a]Grace to you
and peace from God our Father and
the Lord Jesus Christ.
**3** [a]I thank my God in all my re-
membrance of you, **4** always offering
prayer with joy in [a]my every prayer
for you all, **5** because of your [a,1]fellow-
ship in the [b]gospel [c]from the first day
until now. **6** *For I am* confident of this
very thing, that He who began a good
work in you will perfect it until [a]the
day of Christ Jesus. **7** [1]For [a]it is only
right for me to think this way about
you all, because I [b]have you in my
heart, since both in my [c]chains and
in the [d]defense and confirmation of
the [e]gospel, you all are fellow partak-
ers with me in this grace. **8** For [a]God
is my witness, how I long for you all
with the [1]affection of [b]Christ Jesus.
**9** And this I pray, that [a]your love may
abound still more and more in [b]full
knowledge and all discernment, **10** so
that you may [a,1]approve the things
that are excellent, in order to be sin-
cere and without fault [2]until [b]the day
of Christ, **11** having been filled with
the [a]fruit of righteousness which
*comes* through Jesus Christ, to the
glory and praise of God.

### *The Progress of the Gospel*

**12** Now I want you to know, brothers,
that my circumstances [a]have turned
out for the greater progress of the
[b]gospel, **13** so that my [a]chains in
Christ have become well known

**6:20** [a]2Co 5:20; Phm 9 mg [b]Ac 21:33; 28:20; Eph 3:1; Php 1:7; Col 4:3 [c]2Co 3:12 [d]Col 4:4 [1]Lit *a chain* [2]Two early mss *I may speak it boldly* **6:21** [a]Eph 6:21, 22: *Col 4:7-9* [b]Ac 20:4; 2Ti 4:12 [c]Col 4:7 [1]Lit *what* **6:22** [a]Col 4:8 [b]Col 2:2; 4:8 [1]Lit *Whom I have sent to you* [2]Lit *the things about us* **6:23** [a]Ro 15:33; Ga 6:16; 2Th 3:16; 1Pe 5:14 [b]Ga 5:6; 1Th 5:8 **6:24** [1]Lit *in incorruption* ◆ **1:1** [a]2Co 1:1 [b]Ac 16:1 [c]Ro 1:1; Ga 1:10 [d]Ga 3:26 [e]2Co 1:1; Col 1:2 [f]Ac 9:13 [g]Ac 16:12 [h]Ac 20:28; 1Ti 3:1f; Tit 1:7 [i]1Ti 3:8ff [1]Or *holy ones* **1:2** [a]Ro 1:7 **1:3** [a]Ro 1:8 **1:4** [a]Ro 1:9 **1:5** [a]Ac 2:42; Php 4:15 [b]Php 1:7; 2:22; 4:3, 15 [c]Ac 16:12-40; Php 2:12; 4:15 [1]Or *partnership in the preaching of the gospel* **1:6** [a]1Co 1:8; Php 1:10; 2:16 **1:7** [a]2Pe 1:13 [b]2Co 7:3 [c]Ac 21:33; Eph 6:20; Php 1:13f, 17 [d]Php 1:16 [e]Php 1:5, 12, 16, 27; 2:22; 4:3, 15 [1]Lit *Just as it is right* **1:8** [a]Ro 1:9 [b]Ga 3:26 [1]Lit *inward parts* **1:9** [a]1Th 3:12 [b]Col 1:9 **1:10** [a]Ro 2:18 [b]1Co 1:8; Php 1:6; 2:16 [1]Or *discover, distinguish between the things which differ* [2]Or *for* **1:11** [a]Jas 3:18 **1:12** [a]Lk 21:13 [b]Php 1:5, 7, 16, 27; 2:22; 4:3, 15 **1:13** [a]Php 1:7; 2Ti 2:9

throughout the whole [1]praetorian
guard and to [b]everyone else, **14** and
that most of the [1]brothers, having
become confident in the Lord be-
cause of my [a]chains, have [b]far more
courage to speak the word of God
without fear. **15** [a]Some, to be sure,
are preaching Christ even [1]from envy
and strife, but some also [1]from good
will; **16** the latter *do it* out of love,
knowing that I am appointed for the
defense of the [a]gospel; **17** the former
proclaim Christ [a]out of selfish ambi-
tion [1]rather than from pure motives,
thinking to cause me affliction in my
[b]chains. **18** What then? Only that in
every way, whether in pretense or
in truth, Christ is proclaimed, and
in this I rejoice.

Yes, and I will rejoice, **19** for I know
that [a]THIS WILL TURN OUT FOR MY SAL-
VATION [b]through your [1]prayers and
the provision of [c]the Spirit of Jesus
Christ, **20** according to my [a]earnest
expectation and [b]hope, that I will not
be put to shame in anything, but *that*
with [c]all boldness, Christ will even
now, as always, be [d]magnified in my
body, [e]whether by life or by death.

### *To Live Is Christ*

**21** For to me, [a]to live is Christ and to
die is gain. **22** [1]But if *I am* to live *on*
in the flesh, this *will mean* [a]fruitful
labor for me; and I do not know
what I will choose. **23** But I am hard-
pressed [1]between the two, having the
[a]desire to depart and [b]be with Christ,
for *that* is very much better, **24** yet
to remain on in the flesh is more
necessary for your sake. **25** [a]And
convinced of this, I know that I will
remain and continue with you all for
your progress and joy [1]in the faith,
**26** so that your reason for [a]boasting
may abound in Christ Jesus in me,
through my coming to you again.

**27** Only [1]live your lives in a manner
[a]worthy of the [b]gospel of Christ, so
that whether I come and see you
or remain absent, I will hear about
your circumstances, that you are
[c]standing firm in [d]one spirit, with
one [2]mind [e]contending together for
the faith of the gospel, **28** in no way
alarmed by *your* opponents—which
is a [a]sign of destruction for them,
but of salvation for you, and that
*too*, from God. **29** For to you [a]it has
been granted for Christ's sake, not
only to believe in Him, but also to
[b]suffer for His sake, **30** having the
same [a]struggle which [b]you saw in
me, and now hear *to be* in me.

### *Christ's Humility and Exaltation*

**2** Therefore if there is any en-
couragement in Christ, if there
is any consolation of love, if there
is any [a]fellowship of the Spirit, if
any [b,1]affection and compassion,
**2** [a]fulfill my joy, that [b]you think

**1:13** [b]Ac 28:30 [1]Or *governor's palace* **1:14** [a]Php 1:7; 2Ti 2:9 [b]Ac 4:31; 2Co 3:12; 7:4; Php 1:20 [1]Or *brothers in the Lord, trusting because of my chains* **1:15** [a]2Co 11:13 [1]Lit *because of* **1:16** [a]Php 1:5, 7, 12, 27; 2:22; 4:3, 15 **1:17** [a]Ro 2:8; Php 2:3 [b]Php 1:7; 2Ti 2:9 [1]Lit *not sincerely* **1:19** [a]Job 13:16 [b]2Co 1:11 [c]Ac 16:7 [1]Lit *supplication* **1:20** [a]Ro 8:19 [b]Ro 5:5; 1Pe 4:16 [c]Ac 4:31; 2Co 3:12; 7:4; Php 1:14 [d]1Co 6:20 [e]Ro 14:8 **1:21** [a]Ga 2:20 **1:22** [a]Ro 1:13 [1]Or *But if to live in the flesh, this will be fruitful labor for me, then I* **1:23** [a]2Co 5:8; 2Ti 4:6 [b]Jn 12:26 [1]Lit *from* **1:25** [a]Php 2:24 [1]Lit *of* **1:26** [a]2Co 5:12; 7:4; Php 2:16 **1:27** [a]Eph 4:1 [b]Php 1:5 [c]1Co 16:13; Php 4:1 [d]Ac 4:32 [e]Jd 3 [1]To lead one's life as a citizen, cf. 3:20 [2]Lit *soul* **1:28** [a]2Th 1:5 **1:29** [a]Mt 5:11, 12 [b]Ac 14:22 **1:30** [a]Col 1:29; 2:1; 1Th 2:2; 1Ti 6:12; 2Ti 4:7; Heb 10:32; 12:1 [b]Ac 16:19-40; Php 1:13 ◆ **2:1** [a]2Co 13:14 [b]Col 3:12 [1]Lit *inward parts* **2:2** [a]Jn 3:29 [b]Ro 12:16; Php 4:2

the same *way*, by maintaining the
same love, *being* united in spirit,
thinking on one purpose, **3** doing
nothing [1]from [a,2]selfish ambition
or [b]vain glory, but with humility of
mind [c]regarding one another as more
important than yourselves, **4** [a]not
*merely* looking out for your own
personal interests, but also for the
interests of others. **5** [a]Have this *way*
*of* thinking [1]in yourselves which was
also in [b]Christ Jesus, **6** who, although
[a]existing in the [b]form of God, [c]did
not regard equality with God a thing
[1]to be grasped, **7** but [a,1]emptied Him-
self, by taking the form of a [b]slave,
by [c]being made in the likeness of
men. **8** Being found in appearance
as a man, [a]He humbled Himself by
becoming [b]obedient to the point
of death, even [c]death [1]on a cross.
**9** [a]Therefore, God also [b]highly ex-
alted Him, and bestowed on Him [c]the
name which is above every name,
**10** so that at the name of Jesus [a]EVERY
KNEE WILL BOW, of [b]those who are in
heaven and on earth and under the
earth, **11** and that [a]EVERY TONGUE WILL
CONFESS that Jesus Christ is [b,1]LORD,
to the glory of God the Father.

**12** So then, my beloved, [a]just as
you have always obeyed, not as in
my presence only, but now much
more in my absence, work out your
[b]salvation with [c]fear and trembling;
**13** for it is [a]God who is at work in you,
both to will and to work [b]for *His* good
pleasure.

**14** Do all things without [a]grumbling
or disputing, **15** so that you will be
[a]blameless and innocent, [b]children
of God without blemish in the midst
of a [c]crooked and perverse gener-
ation, among whom you [d]shine as
[1]lights in the world, **16** holding [1]fast
the word of life, so that in [a]the day
of Christ I will have reason to boast
because I did not [b]run in vain nor
[c]labor in vain. **17** But even if I am be-
ing [a]poured out as a drink offering
upon [b]the sacrifice and service of
your faith, I rejoice and share my joy
with you all. **18** And you also, rejoice
in the same way and share your joy
with me.

### *Timothy and Epaphroditus Sent*

**19** But I hope in the Lord Jesus to [a]send
[b]Timothy to you shortly, so that I also
may be in good spirits when I learn
of your circumstances. **20** For I have
no one *else* [a]of kindred spirit who
will genuinely be concerned about
your circumstances. **21** For they all
[a]seek after their own interests, not
those of Christ Jesus. **22** But you know
[a]of his proven worth, that [b]he served
with me in the furtherance of the
gospel [c]like a child *serving* his father.
**23** [a]Therefore I hope to send him
immediately, as soon as I [1]evaluate
my own circumstances, **24** and [a]I am

**2:3** [a]Ro 2:8; Php 1:17 [b]Ga 5:26 [c]Ro 12:10; Eph 5:21 [1]Lit *according to* [2]Or *contentiousness* **2:4** [a]Ro 15:1f **2:5** [a]Mt 11:29; Ro 15:3 [b]Php 1:1 [1]Or *among* **2:6** [a]Jn 1:1 [b]2Co 4:4 [c]Jn 5:18; 10:33; 14:28 [1]Or *of which to be taken advantage* **2:7** [a]2Co 8:9 [b]Mt 20:28 [c]Jn 1:14; Ro 8:3; Ga 4:4; Heb 2:17 [1]Laid aside His privileges **2:8** [a]2Co 8:9 [b]Mt 26:39; Jn 10:18; Ro 5:19; Heb 5:8 [c]Heb 12:2 [1]Lit *of* **2:9** [a]Heb 1:9 [b]Mt 28:18; Ac 2:33; Heb 2:9 [c]Eph 1:21 **2:10** [a]Is 45:23; Ro 14:11 [b]Eph 1:10 **2:11** [a]Is 45:23-25 [b]Jn 13:13; Ro 10:9; 14:9 [1]In OT, Yahweh, cf. Is 45:23-25 **2:12** [a]Php 1:5, 6; 4:15 [b]Heb 5:9 [c]2Co 7:15 **2:13** [a]Ro 12:3; 1Co 12:6; 15:10; Heb 13:21 [b]Eph 1:5 **2:14** [a]1Co 10:10; 1Pe 4:9 **2:15** [a]Lk 1:6; Php 3:6 [b]Mt 5:45; Eph 5:1 [c]Dt 32:5; Ac 2:40 [d]Mt 5:14-16 [1]Or *luminaries, stars* **2:16** [a]Php 1:6 [b]Ga 2:2 [c]Is 49:4; Ga 4:11; 1Th 3:5 [1]Or *forth* **2:17** [a]2Co 12:15; 2Ti 4:6 [b]Nu 28:6, 7; Ro 15:16 **2:19** [a]Php 2:23 [b]Php 1:1 **2:20** [a]1Co 16:10; 2Ti 3:10 **2:21** [a]1Co 10:24; 13:5; Php 2:4 **2:22** [a]Ro 5:4; Ac 16:2 [b]Ac 16:3; 1Co 16:10; 2Ti 3:10 [c]1Co 4:17 **2:23** [a]Php 2:19 [1]Or *see about* **2:24** [a]Php 1:25

confident in the Lord that I myself
also will be coming shortly. **25** But
I regarded it necessary to send to
you [a]Epaphroditus, my brother and
[b]fellow worker and [c]fellow soldier,
who is also your [d,1]messenger and
[a]minister to my need; **26** because
he was longing [1]for you all and was
distressed because you had heard
that he was sick. **27** For indeed he
was sick to the point of death, but
God had mercy on him, and not on
him only but also on me, so that I
would not have sorrow upon sorrow.
**28** Therefore I have sent him all the
more eagerly so that when you see
him again you may rejoice and I may
be less concerned. **29** [a]Receive him
then in the Lord with all joy, and
[b]hold men like him in high regard
**30** because he came close to death
[a,1]for the work of Christ, risking his
life to [b]fulfill [2]what was lacking in
your service to me.

### *Righteousness Through Faith in Christ*

**3** Finally, my brothers, [a]rejoice in
the Lord. To write the same things
*again* is no trouble to me, and it is a
safeguard for you.
**2** Beware of the [a]dogs! Beware of the
[b]evil workers! Beware of the [1]mutila-
tion! **3** For [a]we are the [1]circumcision,
who [b]worship [2]in the Spirit of God
and [c]boast in [d]Christ Jesus and put
no confidence in the flesh, **4** although
[a]I myself might have confidence even
in the flesh. If anyone else has a mind
to put confidence in the flesh, I far
more: **5** [a]circumcised the eighth day,
of the [b]nation of Israel, of the [c]tribe
of Benjamin, a [b]Hebrew of Hebrews;
as to the Law, [d]a Pharisee; **6** as to zeal,
[a]a persecutor of the church; as to the
[b]righteousness which is in the Law,
found [c]blameless.
**7** But [a]whatever things were gain
to me, those things I have counted
as loss for the sake of Christ. **8** More
than that, I count all things to be loss
because of the surpassing value of
[a,1]knowing [b]Christ Jesus my Lord, [2]for
whom I have suffered the loss of all
things, and count them but rubbish so
that I may gain Christ **9** and be found
in Him, not having [a]a righteousness
of my own which is from *the* Law, but
that which is through faith in Christ,
[b]the righteousness which *is* from God
upon faith, **10** that I may [a]know Him
and [b]the power of His resurrection
and [c,1]the fellowship of His sufferings,
being [d]conformed to His death, **11** [1]in
order that I may [a]attain to the resur-
rection from the dead.

### *Pressing On Toward the Goal*

**12** Not that I have already [a]obtained *it*
or have already [b]become perfect, but
I press on [1]so that I may [c]lay hold of
that [2]for which also I [d]was laid hold of

---

**2:25** [a]Php 4:18 [b]Ro 16:3, 9, 21; Php 4:3; Phm 1, 24 [c]Phm 2 [d]Jn 13:16; 2Co 8:23 [1]Lit *apostle* **2:26** [1]One early ms *to see you all* **2:29** [a]Ro 16:2 [b]1Co 16:18 **2:30** [a]Ac 20:24 [b]1Co 16:17; Php 4:10 [1]Lit *because of* [2]Lit *your deficiency of service* ◆ **3:1** [a]Php 2:18; 4:4 **3:2** [a]Ps 22:16, 20; Ga 5:15; Rev 22:15 [b]2Co 11:13 [1]*Or false circumcision* **3:3** [a]Ro 2:29; 9:6; Ga 6:15 [b]Ga 5:25 [c]Ro 15:17; Ga 6:14 [d]Ro 8:39; Php 1:1; 3:12 [1]Gr *peritome* [2]Or *by* **3:4** [a]2Co 5:16; 11:18 **3:5** [a]Lk 1:59 [b]Ro 11:1; 2Co 11:22 [c]Ro 11:1 [d]Ac 22:3; 23:6; 26:5 **3:6** [a]Ac 8:3; 22:4, 5; 26:9-11 [b]Php 3:9 [c]Php 2:15 **3:7** [a]Lk 14:33 **3:8** [a]Jer 9:23f; Jn 17:3; Eph 4:13; Php 3:10; 2Pe 1:3 [b]Ro 8:39; Php 1:1; 3:12 [1]Lit *the knowledge of* [2]Lit *because of* **3:9** [a]Ro 10:5; Php 3:6 [b]Ro 9:30; 1Co 1:30 **3:10** [a]Jer 9:23f; Jn 17:3; Eph 4:13; Php 3:8; 2Pe 1:3 [b]Ro 6:5 [c]Ro 8:17 [d]Ro 6:5; 8:36; Ga 6:17 [1]Or *participation in* **3:11** [a]Ac 26:7; 1Co 15:23; Rev 20:5f [1]Lit *if somehow* **3:12** [a]1Co 9:24f; 1Ti 6:12, 19 [b]1Co 13:10 [c]1Ti 6:12, 19 [d]Ac 9:5f [1]Lit *if I may even* [2]Or *because also*

by [e]Christ Jesus. **13** Brothers, I do not
consider myself as having laid hold of
*it* yet, but one thing *I do*: [a]forgetting
what *lies* behind and reaching for-
ward to what *lies* ahead, **14** I [a]press
on toward the goal for the prize of
the [b]upward call of God in [c]Christ
Jesus. **15** Let us therefore, as many as
are [a,1]perfect, think this way; and if
in anything you [b]think differently,
[c]God will reveal that also to you.
**16** However, *let us* keep [a,1]walking in
step with the same *standard* to which
we have attained.

**17** Brothers, [a]join in following my
example, and [b]look for those who
walk according to the [c]pattern you
have in us. **18** For [a]many walk—of
whom I often told you, and now tell
you even [b]crying—as enemies of
[c]the cross of Christ, **19** whose end is
destruction, whose god is *their* [a]stom-
ach and [b]glory is in their shame, who
[c]set their thoughts on earthly things.
**20** For [a]our [1]citizenship is in heaven,
from which also we eagerly [b]wait
for a Savior, the Lord Jesus Christ,
**21** who will [a]transform [1]the body of
our humble state into [b]conformity
with [2]the [c]body of His glory, [d]by His
working through which He is able to
even [e]subject all things to Himself.

### *Rejoice in the Lord Always*

**4** Therefore my brothers, loved and
[a]longed for, my joy and crown, in
this way [b]stand firm in the Lord, my
beloved.

**2** I urge Euodia and I urge Syntyche
to [a]think the same way in the Lord.
**3** Indeed, I ask you also, genuine com-
panion, help these women who have
contended together alongside of me
in the gospel, with also Clement and
the rest of my [a]fellow workers, whose
[b]names are in the book of life.

**4** [a]Rejoice in the Lord always; again
I will say, rejoice! **5** Let your consid-
erate *spirit* be known to all men.
[a]The Lord is [1]near. **6** [a]Be anxious for
nothing, but in everything by [b]prayer
and petition with thanksgiving let
your requests be made known to
God. **7** And [a]the peace of God, which
surpasses all [1]comprehension, will
[b]guard your hearts and your [c]minds
in [d]Christ Jesus.

**8** Finally, brothers, [a]whatever is
true, whatever is dignified, whatever
is right, whatever is pure, whatever
is [1]lovely, whatever is commendable,
if there is any excellence and if
anything worthy of praise, consider
these things. **9** The things you have
learned and received and heard and
seen [a]in me, practice these things,
and [b]the God of peace will be with
you.

### *God Will Fill Your Needs*

**10** But I rejoiced in the Lord greatly,
that now at last [a]you have revived

---

**3:12** [e]Ro 8:39; Php 1:1; 3:3, 8 **3:13** [a]Lk 9:62 **3:14** [a]1Co 9:24; Heb 6:1 [b]Ro 8:28; 11:29; 2Ti 1:9 [c]Php 3:3 **3:15** [a]Mt 5:48; 1Co 2:6 [b]Ga 5:10 [c]Jn 6:45; Eph 1:17; 1Th 4:9 [1]Or *mature* **3:16** [a]Ga 6:16 [1]Lit *following in line* **3:17** [a]1Co 4:16; 11:1; Php 4:9 [b]Php 2:4 [c]1Pe 5:3 **3:18** [a]2Co 11:13 [b]Ac 20:31 [c]Ga 6:14 **3:19** [a]Ro 16:18; Tit 1:12 [b]Ro 6:21; Jd 13 [c]Ro 8:5f; Col 3:2 **3:20** [a]Eph 2:19; Php 1:27; Col 3:1; Heb 12:22 [b]1Co 1:7 [1]Lit *commonwealth* **3:21** [a]1Co 15:43-53 [b]Ro 8:29; Col 3:4 [c]1Co 15:43, 49 [d]Eph 1:19 [e]1Co 15:28 [1]Or *our lowly body* [2]Or *His glorious body* ◆ **4:1** [a]Php 1:8 [b]1Co 16:13; Php 1:27 **4:2** [a]Php 2:2 **4:3** [a]Php 2:25 [b]Lk 10:20 **4:4** [a]Php 3:1 **4:5** [a]1Co 16:22 mg; Heb 10:37; Jas 5:8f [1]Or *at hand* **4:6** [a]Mt 6:25 [b]Eph 6:18; 1Ti 2:1; 5:5 **4:7** [a]Is 26:3; Jn 14:27; Php 4:9; Col 3:15 [b]1Pe 1:5 [c]2Co 10:5 [d]Php 1:1; 4:19, 21 [1]Lit *mind* **4:8** [a]Ro 14:18; 1Pe 2:12 [1]Or *lovable and gracious* **4:9** [a]Php 3:17 [b]Ro 15:33 **4:10** [a]2Co 11:9; Php 2:30

thinking about me; indeed, you
were thinking about me *before*, but
you lacked opportunity. **11** Not that
I speak [1]from want, for I learned to be
[a,2]content in whatever circumstances
I am. **12** I know how to get along with
humble means, and I also know how
to live in abundance; in any and all
things I have learned the secret of
being filled and going [a]hungry, both
of having abundance and [b]suffering
need. **13** I can do all things [1]through
Him who [a]strengthens me. **14** Nev-
ertheless, you have done well to
[a]fellowship *with me* in my affliction.
**15** And you yourselves also know,
Philippians, that at the [a,1]first preach-
ing of the gospel, after I left [b]Macedo-
nia, no church [c]fellowshipped with
me in the matter of giving and
receiving but you alone. **16** For even in
[a]Thessalonica you sent *a gift* more
than once for my needs. **17** [a]Not that
I seek the gift itself, but I seek the fruit
which increases to your account. **18** But
I have received everything in full and
have an abundance; I have been filled,
having received from [a]Epaphroditus
[1]what you have sent, [b,2]a fragrant aro-
ma, an acceptable sacrifice, pleasing
to God. **19** And [a]my God will fulfill [1]all
your needs according to His [b]riches in
glory in Christ Jesus. **20** Now to [a]our
God and Father [b]*be* the glory [1]forever
and ever. Amen.
**21** Greet every [1]saint in Christ
Jesus. [a]The brothers who are with
me greet you. **22** [a]All the [b,1]saints
greet you, especially those of Caesar's
household.
**23** [a]The grace of the Lord Jesus
Christ [b]be with your spirit.

*The Letter of Paul to the*

# COLOSSIANS

### *Thanksgiving and Prayer*

**1** [a]Paul, [b]an apostle of Christ Jesus
[c,1]by the will of God, and [d]Timothy
[2]our brother,
**2** To the [a,1]saints and faithful broth-
ers in Christ in Colossae: [b]Grace to
you and peace from God our Father.
**3** [a]We give thanks to God, [b]the
Father of our Lord Jesus Christ,
praying always for you, **4** [a]since we
heard of your faith in Christ Jesus and
the [b]love which you have [1]for [c]all the
[2]saints, **5** because of the [a]hope [b]laid
up for you in [1]heaven, of which you
previously [c]heard in the word of
truth, [2]the gospel **6** which has come
to you, just as [a,1]in all the world also
it is constantly bearing [b]fruit and
[2]multiplying, just as *it has been doing*
in you also since the day you [c]heard

---

**4:11** [a]2Co 9:8; 1Ti 6:6, 8; Heb 13:5 [1]Lit *according to* [2]Or *self-sufficient* **4:12** [a]1Co 4:11 [b]2Co 11:9 **4:13** [a]2Co 12:9; Eph 3:16; Col 1:11 [1]Lit *in* **4:14** [a]Heb 10:33; Rev 1:9 **4:15** [a]Php 1:5 [b]Ro 15:26 [c]2Co 11:9 [1]*Lit beginning of* **4:16** [a]Ac 17:1; 1Th 2:9 **4:17** [a]1Co 9:11f; 2Co 9:5 **4:18** [a]Php 2:25 [b]Ex 29:18; 2Co 2:14; Eph 5:2 [1]Lit *the things from you* [2]Lit *an odor of fragrance* **4:19** [a]2Co 9:8 [b]Ro 2:4 [1]Or *every need of yours* **4:20** [a]Ga 1:4 [b]Ro 11:36 [1]Lit *to the ages of the ages* **4:21** [a]Ga 1:2 [1]Or *holy one* **4:22** [a]2Co 13:13 [b]Ac 9:13 [1]v 21, note 1 **4:23** [a]Ro 16:20 [b]2Ti 4:22 ◆**1:1** [a]Php 1:1 [b]2Co 1:1 [c]1Co 1:1 [d]2Co 1:1; 1Th 3:2 [1]Lit *through* [2]Lit *the* **1:2** [a]Ac 9:13 [b]Ro 1:7 [1]Or *holy ones* **1:3** [a]Ro 1:8 [b]Ro 15:6; 2Co 1:3 **1:4** [a]Eph 1:15; Phm 5 [b]Ga 5:6 [c]Eph 6:18 [1]Or *toward* [2]Or *holy ones* **1:5** [a]Ac 23:6 [b]2Ti 4:8 [c]Eph 1:13 [1]Lit *the heavens* [2]Or *of the gospel* **1:6** [a]Ro 10:18 [b]Ro 1:13 [c]Eph 4:21 [1]Or *it is in the world* [2]Or *growing*, cf. 2:19

and [3]understood the grace of God
in truth; **7** just as you learned *it* from
[a]Epaphras, our [b]beloved fellow slave,
who is a faithful servant of Christ on
our behalf, **8** who also informed us of
your [a]love in the Spirit.

**9** For this reason also, [a]since the
day we heard, [b]we have not ceased to
pray for you and to ask that you may
be filled with the [c,1]full knowledge
of His will in all spiritual [d]wisdom
and understanding, **10** so that you
may [a]walk in a manner worthy
of the Lord, [b,1]to please *Him* in all
respects, [c]bearing fruit in every
good work and [2]multiplying in the
[3]full knowledge of God; **11** [a]being
strengthened with all power, ac-
cording to [1]His glorious might, [2]for
the attaining of all steadfastness and
[3]patience; [b]joyously **12** giving thanks
to [a]the Father, who has qualified us
[1]to share in [b]the inheritance of the
[2]saints in [c]light. **13** Who rescued us
from the [a]authority of darkness, and
transferred us to the kingdom of [b]the
Son of His love, **14** [a]in whom we have
redemption, the forgiveness of sins.

### *The Firstborn of All Creation*

**15** [1]Who is the [a]image
of the [b]invisible God,
the [c]firstborn of all creation.
**16** For [a,1]in Him all things were
created, [a]*both* in the heavens
and on earth, visible
and invisible, whether
[b]thrones or dominions or
rulers or authorities—[c]all
things have been created
through Him and for Him.

**17** And He [a,1]is before all things,
And in Him all things
[2]hold together.
**18** And He is the [a]head
of [b]the body, the church;

Who is [c]the beginning,
[d]the firstborn from the
dead, so that He Himself
will come to have first
place in everything.
**19** For in Him [1]all [a]the fullness
*of God* [b]was pleased to dwell,
**20** And through Him
to [a]reconcile all things
to Himself, having made
[b]peace through [c]the blood
of His cross—through Him—
[d]whether things on earth
or things in [1]heaven.

**21** And although you were
[a]formerly alienated and enemies in
mind *and* in evil deeds, **22** but now
He [a]reconciled you in the [b]body of
His flesh through death, in order to
[c]present you before Him [d]holy and
blameless and beyond reproach—
**23** if indeed you continue in [1]the faith
firmly [a]grounded and steadfast, and
not moved away from the [b]hope of

**1:6** [3]Or *came really to know* **1:7** [a]Col 4:12 [b]Col 4:7 **1:8** [a]Ro 15:30 **1:9** [a]Col 1:4 [b]Eph 1:16 [c]Php 1:9 [d]Eph 1:17 [1]Or *true knowledge* **1:10** [a]Eph 4:1 [b]Eph 5:10 [c]Ge 1:26-28; Ro 1:13 [1]Lit *to all pleasing* [2]Or *growing*, cf. 2:19 [3]Or *true knowledge* **1:11** [a]1Co 16:13 [b]Eph 4:2 [1]Lit *the might of His glory* [2]Lit *unto all* [3]Or *patience with joy* **1:12** [a]Eph 2:18 [b]Ac 20:32 [c]Ac 26:18 [1]Lit *unto the portion of* [2]Or *holy ones* **1:13** [a]Eph 6:12 [b]Eph 1:6 **1:14** [a]Ro 3:24 **1:15** [a]2Co 4:4 [b]Jn 1:1 [c]Ro 8:29 [1]vv 15-20 are formatted to show the chiastic structure of the poem **1:16** [a]Eph 1:10 [b]Eph 1:20f; Col 2:15 [c]Jn 1:3; Ro 11:36; 1Co 8:6 [1]Or *by* **1:17** [a]Jn 1:1; 8:58 [1]Or *has existed prior to* [2]Or *endure* **1:18** [a]Eph 1:22 [b]Eph 1:23; Col 1:24; 2:19 [c]Rev 3:14 [d]Ac 26:23 **1:19** [a]Jn 1:16 [b]Eph 1:5 [1]Or God *was pleased for all the fullness to dwell* **1:20** [a]2Co 5:18; Eph 2:16 [b]Ro 5:1; Eph 2:14 [c]Eph 2:13 [d]Col 1:16 [1]Lit *the heavens* **1:21** [a]Ro 5:10; Eph 2:3, 12 **1:22** [a]2Co 5:18; Eph 2:16 [b]Ro 7:4 [c]Eph 5:27; Col 1:28 [d]Eph 1:4 **1:23** [a]Eph 3:17; Col 2:7 [b]Col 1:5 [1]Or *in faith*

the gospel, which you have heard,
which was proclaimed [c]in all creation
under heaven, [d]and of which I, Paul,
[2]was made a [e,3]minister.

**24** [a]Now I rejoice in my sufferings
for your sake, and [b]I fill up what is
lacking of Christ's afflictions in my
flesh, on behalf of [c]His body, which
is the church, **25** [a]of which I [1]was
made a minister according to the
[b]stewardship from God given to me
for you, so that I might [2]fully carry
out *the preaching of* the word of
God, **26** *that is,* [a]the mystery which
has been hidden from the *past* ages
and generations, but has now been
manifested to His [1]saints, **27** to whom
[a]God willed to make known what is
[b]the riches of the glory of this mys-
tery among the Gentiles, which is
[c]Christ in you, the [d]hope of glory.
**28** Him we proclaim, [a]admonishing
every man and teaching every man
[1]with all [b]wisdom, so that we may
[c]present every man [d,2]complete in
Christ. **29** For this purpose I also
[a]labor, [b]striving [c]according to His
working, which He works in me in
power.

### *Alive with Christ*

**2** For I want you to understand
how great a [a]struggle I have on
your behalf and for those who are at
[b]Laodicea, and for all those who have
not seen my face in the flesh, **2** so that
their [a]hearts may be encouraged,
having been [b]held together in love,
even unto all [c]the wealth of the full
assurance of understanding, unto the
[d]full knowledge of [e]God's mystery,
*that is,* Christ *Himself,* **3** in whom are
hidden all [a]the treasures of wisdom
and knowledge. **4** [a]I say this so that
no one will delude you with [b]persua-
sive argument. **5** For even though I
am [a]absent in body, nevertheless I
am with you in spirit, rejoicing [1]to see
your [b]good order and the [c]stability of
your faith in Christ.

**6** Therefore as you received [a]Christ
Jesus the Lord, *so* [b,1]walk in Him,
**7** having been firmly [a]rooted and
being [b]built up in Him, and having
been [c]established [1]in your faith—
just as you [d]were instructed—*and*
abounding [2]with thanksgiving.

**8** [a]See to it that no one takes you
captive through [b]philosophy and
empty deception, according to the
tradition of men, according to the
[c]elementary principles of the world,
and not according to Christ. **9** For in
Him all the [a]fullness of Deity dwells
bodily, **10** and in Him you have been
[a]filled, [b]who is the head [1]over all
[c]rule and authority; **11** in whom
[a]you were also circumcised with a
circumcision made without hands,
in the removal of [b]the body of the
flesh, in the circumcision of Christ,
**12** having been [a]buried with Him

---

**1:23** [c]Mk 16:15; Ac 2:5; Col 1:6 [d]Eph 3:7; Col 1:25 [e]1Co 3:5 [2]Lit *became* [3]Or *servant* **1:24** [a]Ro 8:17; 2Co 1:5; 12:15; Php 2:17 [b]2Ti 1:8; 2:10 [c]Col 1:18 **1:25** [a]Col 1:23 [b]Eph 3:2 [1]Lit *became* [2]Lit *make full the word of God* **1:26** [a]Ro 16:25f; Eph 3:3f; Col 2:2; 4:3 [1]Or *holy ones* **1:27** [a]Mt 13:11 [b]Eph 1:7, 18; 3:16 [c]Ro 8:10 [d]1Ti 1:1 **1:28** [a]Ac 20:31; Col 3:16 [b]1Co 2:6f; Col 2:3 [c]Col 1:22 [d]Mt 5:48; Eph 4:13 [1]Lit *in* [2]Or *perfect* ***1:29*** [a]*1Co 15:10* [b]Col 2:1; 4:12 [c]Eph 1:19; Col 2:12 ◆ **2:1** [a]Col 1:29; 4:12 [b]Col 4:13, 15f; Rev 1:11 **2:2** [a]1Co 14:31; Eph 6:22; Col 4:8 [b]Col 2:19 [c]Eph 1:7, 18; 3:16 [d]Mt 13:11 [e]Ro 16:25f; Eph 3:3f; Col 1:26; 4:3 **2:3** [a]Is 11:2; Ro 11:33 **2:4** [a]Eph 4:17 [b]Ro 16:18 **2:5** [a]1Co 5:3 [b]1Co 14:40 [c]1Pe 5:9 [1]Lit *and seeing* **2:6** [a]Ga 3:26 [b]Col 1:10 [1]Or *lead your life* **2:7** [a]Eph 3:17 [b]1Co 3:9; Eph 2:20 [c]1Co 1:8 [d]Eph 4:21 [1]Or *by* [2]One early ms *in it with* **2:8** [a]1Co 8:9; 10:12; Ga 5:15; Heb 3:12 [b]Eph 5:6; Col 2:23; 1Ti 6:20 [c]Ga 4:3; Col 2:20 **2:9** [a]2Co 5:19; Col 1:19 **2:10** [a]Eph 3:19 [b]Eph 1:21f [c]1Co 15:24; Eph 3:10; Col 2:15 [1]Lit *of* **2:11** [a]Ro 2:29; Eph 2:11 [b]Ro 6:6; 7:24; Ga 5:24; Col 3:5 **2:12** [a]Ro 6:4f

in baptism, in which you were also
[b]raised up with Him through faith
in the working of God, who [c]raised
Him from the dead. **13** And you being
[a]dead [1]in your transgressions and
the uncircumcision of your flesh, He
[b]made you alive with Him, having
graciously forgiven us all our trans-
gressions. **14** Having canceled out
[a]the certificate of debt consisting of
decrees against us which was hostile
to us, [b]He also has taken it out of the
way, having nailed it to the cross.
**15** Having [a,1]disarmed the [b]rulers
and authorities, He [a]made a public
display of them, having [c]triumphed
over them in [2]Him.

**16** Therefore, no one is to [a]judge you
in [b]food and [b]drink, or in respect to a
[c]festival or a [d]new moon or a [e]Sabbath
[1]day— **17** things which are *only* a
[a]shadow of what is to come; but the
[1]substance [2]belongs to Christ. **18** Let
no one keep [a,1]defrauding you of your
prize by [b]delighting in [2]self-abasement
and the worship of the angels, going
into detail about *visions* he has seen,
[c]being puffed up for nothing by his
[d]fleshly mind, **19** and not holding fast
to [a]the head, from whom [b]the entire
body, being supplied and held togeth-
er by the joints and [1]ligaments, grows
with a growth [2]that is from God.

**20** [a]If you have died with Christ
[1]to the [b]elementary principles of the
world, [c]why, as if you were living in
the world, do you submit yourself
to [d]decrees: **21** "Do not handle, nor
taste, nor touch"? **22** Which [1]deal with
everything [a]destined to perish [2]with
use, *which are* in accordance with the
[b]commands and teachings of men;
**23** which are matters having, to be
sure, a [1]word of wisdom in [a,2]self-
made religion and self-abasement
and [b]severe treatment of the body,
*but are* of no value against [c]fleshly
indulgence.

### *Put On the New Man*

**3** Therefore, if you have been
[a]raised up with Christ, keep
seeking the things above, where
Christ is, [b]seated at the right hand
of God. **2** [a,1]Set your mind on the
things above, not on the things that
are on earth. **3** For you [a]died and your
life has been hidden with Christ in
God. **4** When Christ, [a]who is our life,
is manifested, [b]then you also will be
manifested with Him in glory.

**5** [a]Therefore, [1]consider [b]the mem-
bers of your earthly body as dead to
[c]sexual immorality, impurity, pas-
sion, evil desire, and greed, which is
idolatry. **6** On account of these things,
[a]the wrath of God is coming [1]upon
the sons of disobedience, **7** and [a]in
them you also once walked, when
you were living [1]in them. **8** But now

---

**2:12** [b]Ro 6:5; Eph 2:6; Col 2:13; 3:1 [c]Ac 2:24 **2:13** [a]Eph 2:1 [b]Eph 2:5; Col 2:12 [1]Or *by reason of* **2:14** [a]Eph 2:15; Col 2:20 [b]1Pe 2:24 **2:15** [a]Eph 4:8 [b]Jn 12:31; 1Co 15:24; Eph 3:10; Col 2:10 [c]2Co 2:14 [1]Or *divested Himself of* [2]Or *it*; the cross **2:16** [a]Ro 14:3 [b]Mk 7:19; Ro 14:17; Heb 9:10 [c]Lv 23:2; Ro 14:5 [d]1Chr 23:31; 2Chr 31:3; Ne 10:33 [e]Mk 2:27f; Ga 4:10 [1]Or *days* **2:17** [a]Heb 8:5; 10:1 [1]Lit *body* [2]Lit *of Christ* **2:18** [a]1Co 9:24; Php 3:14 [b]Col 2:23 [c]1Co 4:6 [d]Ro 8:7 [1]Or *deciding against you* [2]Or *humility* **2:19** [a]Eph 1:22 [b]Eph 1:23; 4:16 [1]Lit *bonds* [2]Lit *of God* **2:20** [a]Ro 6:2 [b]Col 2:8 [c]Ga 4:9 [d]Col 2:14, 16 [1]Lit *from* **2:22** [a]1Co 6:13 [b]Is 29:13; Mt 15:9; Tit 1:14 [1]Lit *are* [2]Or *by being consumed* **2:23** [a]Col 2:18 [b]1Ti 4:3 [c]Ro 13:14; 1Ti 4:8 [1]Or *message* [2]Or *would-be religion* ◆ **3:1** [a]Col 2:12 [b]Ps 110:1; Mk 16:19 **3:2** [a]Mt 16:23; Php 3:19, 20 [1]Or *Be intent on* **3:3** [a]Ro 6:2; 2Co 5:14; Col 2:20 **3:4** [a]Jn 11:25; Ga 2:20 [b]1Co 1:7; Php 3:21; 1Pe 1:13; 1Jn 2:28; 3:2 **3:5** [a]Ro 8:13 [b]Col 2:11 [c]Mk 7:21f; 1Co 6:9f, 18; 2Co 12:21; Ga 5:19f; Eph 4:19; 5:3, 5 [1]Or *put to death the members which are upon the earth* **3:6** [a]Ro 1:18; Eph 5:6 [1]Two early mss omit final clause **3:7** [a]Eph 2:2 [1]Or *among these*

you also, [a]lay them all aside: [b]wrath,
anger, malice, slander, *and* [c]abusive
speech from your mouth. **9** [a,1]Do not
lie to one another, since you [b]put off
the old man with its *evil* practices,
**10** and have [a]put on the new man
who is being [b,1]renewed to a full
knowledge [c]according to the image
of the One who [d]created him—
**11** *a renewal* in which [a]there is no
*distinction between* Greek and Jew,
[b]circumcised and uncircumcised,
[c,1]barbarian, Scythian, [d]slave, *and*
freeman, but [e]Christ is all and in all.
**12** So, as the [a]elect of God, holy and
beloved, [b]put on a [c]heart of compas-
sion, kindness, [d]humility, gentleness,
*and* [e,1]patience; **13** [a]bearing with one
another, and [b]graciously forgiving
each other, whoever has a complaint
against anyone, [b]just as the Lord gra-
ciously forgave you, so also should
you. **14** Above all these things *put on*
love, which is [a,1]the perfect bond of
[b]unity. **15** And let [a]the peace of Christ
[1]rule in your hearts, to which [2]indeed
you were called in [b]one body, and [3]be
thankful. **16** Let [a]the word of [1]Christ
dwell in you richly, [2]with all wisdom
[b]teaching and admonishing [3]one
another [c]with psalms *and* hymns
*and* spiritual songs, [d]singing [4]with
gratefulness in your hearts to God.
**17** [a]And whatever you do in word or
deed, *do* all in the name of the Lord
Jesus, [b]giving thanks to God the
Father through Him.

### *Family and Work*

**18** [a]Wives, [b]be subject to your
husbands, as is fitting in the Lord.
**19** [a]Husbands, love your wives and
do not be embittered against them.
**20** [a]Children, obey your parents in
all things, for this is pleasing [1]to the
Lord. **21** [a]Fathers, do not exasperate
your children, so that they will not
lose heart.
**22** [a]Slaves, in all things obey those
who are your masters [1]according to the
flesh, [b]not with eyeservice, as men-
pleasers, but with [2]integrity of heart,
fearing the Lord. **23** Whatever you do,
do your work [1]heartily, [a]as for the Lord
[2]rather than for men, **24** [a]knowing that
from the Lord you will receive the
reward [1]of [b]the inheritance. [c,2]Serve
the Lord Christ. **25** For [a]he who does
wrong will receive the consequences
of the wrong which he has done, and
[b,1]that without partiality.

### *Final Instructions and Greetings*

**4** Masters, show to your slaves
what is right and fair, [a]knowing
that you too have a Master in heaven.
**2** [a]Devote yourselves to prayer, be-
ing watchful in it with thanksgiving;

**3:8** [a]Eph 4:22 [b]Eph 4:31 [c]Eph 4:29 **3:9** [a]Eph 4:25 [b]Eph 4:22 [1]Or *Stop lying* **3:10** [a]Eph 4:24 [b]Ro 12:2; 2Co 4:16; Eph 4:23 [c]Ge 1:26; Ro 8:29 [d]Eph 2:10 [1]Lit *renovated* **3:11** [a]Ro 10:12; 1Co 12:13; Ga 3:28 [b]1Co 7:19; Ga 5:6 [c]Ac 28:2 [d]Eph 6:8 [e]Eph 1:23 [1]Those who were not Greeks, either by birth or by culture **3:12** [a]Lk 18:7 [b]Eph 4:24 [c]Lk 1:78; Ga 5:22f; Php 2:1 [d]Eph 4:2; Php 2:3 [e]1Co 13:4; 2Co 6:6 [1]Forbearance toward others **3:13** [a]Eph 4:2 [b]Ro 15:7; Eph 4:32 **3:14** [a]Eph 4:3 [b]Jn 17:23; Heb 6:1 [1]Lit *the uniting bond of perfection* **3:15** [a]Jn 14:27 [b]Eph 2:16 [1]Or *act as arbiter* [2]Lit *also* [3]Or *show yourselves thankful* **3:16** [a]Ro 10:17; Eph 5:26; 1Th 1:8 [b]Col 1:28 [c]Eph 5:19 [d]1Co 14:15 [1]One early ms *the Lord* [2]Or *in* [3]Or *one another, singing with psalms* [4]Or *by*; lit *in His grace* **3:17** [a]1Co 10:31 [b]Eph 5:20; Col 3:15 **3:18** [a]Col 3:18-4:1: *Eph 5:22-6:9* [b]Eph 5:22 **3:19** [a]Eph 5:25; 1Pe 3:7 **3:20** [a]Eph 6:1 [1]Lit *in* **3:21** [a]Eph 6:4 **3:22** [a]Eph 6:5 [b]Eph 6:6 [1]Or *on earth* [2]Lit *simplicity* **3:23** [a]Eph 6:7 [1]Lit *from the soul* [2]Lit *and not* **3:24** [a]Eph 6:8 [b]Ac 20:32; 1Pe 1:4 [c]1Co 7:22 [1]Consisting of [2]Or *You serve the Lord Christ* **3:25** [a]Eph 6:8 [b]Dt 10:17; Ac 10:34; Eph 6:9 [1]Lit *there is no partiality* ◆ **4:1** [a]Eph 6:9 **4:2** [a]Ac 1:14; Eph 6:18

**3** praying at the same time [a]for us
as well, that God will open up to us
a [b]door for [c]the word, so that we
may speak [d]the mystery of Christ,
for which I have also [e]been bound,
**4** that I may make it [a]manifest [b]in the
way I ought to speak.
**5** [a]Walk in wisdom toward [b]outsid-
ers, [c]redeeming the time. **6** [a]Let your
[1]words always be [2]with grace, seasoned
with [b]salt, so that you will know how
you should [c]answer each person.
**7** [a]Tychicus, *our* [b]beloved brother
and faithful servant and fellow slave
in the Lord, will make known to you
[c]all my affairs, **8** [a]whom I have sent
to you for this very purpose, that you
may know about our circumstances
and that he may [b]encourage your
hearts; **9** [1]and with him [a]Onesimus,
*our* faithful and [b]beloved brother,
[c]who is one of you. They will inform
you about the whole situation here.
**10** [a]Aristarchus, my [b]fellow pris-
oner, sends you his greetings; and
*also* Mark, the cousin of [c]Barnabas
(about whom you received [1]instruc-
tions; [d]if he comes to you, welcome
him); **11** and *also* Jesus who is called
Justus. These are the only [a]fellow
workers for the kingdom of God
[b]who are from the circumcision, and
they have proved to be a comfort to
me. **12** [a]Epaphras, [b]who is one of your
number, a slave of Christ Jesus, sends
you his greetings, always [c]striving
for you in his prayers, that you may
stand [d,1]complete and [e]fully assured
in all the will of God. **13** For I testify
for him that he has [1]a deep concern
for you and for those who are in
[a]Laodicea and Hierapolis. **14** [a]Luke,
the beloved physician, sends you his
greetings, and *also* [b]Demas. **15** Greet
the brothers who are in [a]Laodicea
and also [1]Nympha and [b]the church
that is in [2]her house. **16** [a]And when
[1]this letter is read among you, have
it also read in the church of the
Laodiceans; and you, for your part
[a]read [1]my letter *that is coming* from
[b]Laodicea. **17** And say to [a]Archippus,
"Take heed to the [b]ministry which
you have received in the Lord, that
you may [1]fulfill it."
**18** [a]The greeting is in my own
hand—[1]Paul. [b]Remember my [c]chains.
[d]Grace be with you.

---

**4:3** [a]Eph 6:19 [b]Ac 14:27 [c]2Ti 4:2 [d]Eph 3:3, 4; 6:19 [e]Eph 6:20 **4:4** [a]Col 1:26; 3:4 [b]Eph 6:20
**4:5** [a]Eph 5:15 [b]Mk 4:11 [c]Eph 5:16 **4:6** [a]Eph 4:29 [b]Mk 9:50 [c]1Pe 3:15 [1]Lit *word* [2]Or *gracious*
**4:7** [a]Ac 20:4; 2Ti 4:12 [b]Eph 6:21; Col 1:7 [c]Col 4:7-9: *Eph 6:21, 22* **4:8** [a]Eph 6:22 [b]Col 2:2 **4:9** [a]Phm 10
[b]Col 1:7 [c]Col 4:12 [1]Lit *along with Onesimus* **4:10** [a]Ac 19:29; 27:2; Phm 24 [b]Ro 16:7 [c]Ac 4:36; 12:12,
25; 15:37, 39 [d]2Ti 4:11 [1]Or *commands* **4:11** [a]Ro 16:3 [b]Ac 11:2 **4:12** [a]Col 1:7; Phm 23 [b]Col 4:9
[c]Ro 15:30 [d]Col 1:28 [e]Col 2:2 [1]Or *firm* **4:13** [a]Col 2:1; 4:15f [1]Or *much toil, great pain* **4:14** [a]2Ti 4:11;
Phm 24 [b]2Ti 4:10; Phm 24 **4:15** [a]Col 2:1; 4:13, 16 [b]Ro 16:5 [1]Or *Nymphas* (masc) [2]One early ms
*their* **4:16** [a]1Th 5:27; 2Th 3:14 [b]Col 2:1; 4:13, 15 [1]Lit *the* **4:17** [a]Phm 2 [b]2Ti 4:5 [1]Or *continually fulfill*
**4:18** [a]1Co 16:21 [b]Heb 13:3 [c]Php 1:7; Col 4:3 [d]1Ti 6:21; 2Ti 4:22; Tit 3:15; Heb 13:25 [1]Lit *Paul's*

*The First Letter of Paul to the*

# THESSALONIANS

### *Thanksgiving*

**1** [a]Paul and [b]Silvanus and [c]Timothy, To the [d]church of the Thessalonians in God the Father and the Lord Jesus Christ: [e]Grace to you and peace.

**2** [a]We give thanks to God always for all of you, [b]making mention *of you* in our prayers; **3** remembering without ceasing your [a]work of faith and labor of [b]love and [c,1]steadfastness of hope [2]in our Lord Jesus Christ before [d]our God and Father, **4** knowing, [a]brothers beloved by God, [b]your election, **5** for our [a]gospel did not come to you in word only, but also [b]in power and in the Holy Spirit and with [c]full assurance; just as you know [d]what kind of men we [1]proved to be among you for your sake. **6** You also became [a]imitators of us and of the Lord, [b]having received [c]the word in much affliction with the [d]joy of the Holy Spirit, **7** so that you became a model to all the believers in [a]Macedonia and in [b]Achaia. **8** For [a]the word of the Lord has [b]sounded forth from you, not only in [c]Macedonia and [d]Achaia, but also [e]in every place your faith toward God has gone forth, so that we have no need to say anything. **9** For they themselves report about us what kind of an [a]entrance we had [1]with you, and how you [b]turned to God [c]from [2]idols to serve [d,3]a living and true God, **10** and to [a]wait for His Son from [1]heaven, whom He [b]raised from the dead, Jesus, who [c]rescues us from [d]the wrath to come.

### *Entrusted with the Gospel*

**2** For you yourselves know, brothers, that our [a]entrance to you [b]was not in vain, **2** but after we had already suffered and been [a]mistreated in [b]Philippi, as you know, we had the boldness in our God [c]to speak to you the [d]gospel of God amid much [e]struggle. **3** For our [a]exhortation does not *come* from [b]error or [c]impurity or [1]by way of [d]deceit; **4** [a]but just as we have been approved by God to be [b]entrusted with the gospel, so we speak, [c]not as pleasing men, but God who [d,1]examines our hearts. **5** For we never came with a flattering word, as you know, nor with [a]a pretext for greed—[b]God is witness— **6** nor [a]seeking glory from men, either from you or from others, even though as [b]apostles of Christ we [1]could have been a burden to *you*. **7** But we [1]proved to be [a,2]gentle [3]among you, [b]as a nursing *mother* [4]tenderly cares for her own children. **8** In this way,

---

◆ **1:1** [a]2Th 1:1 [b]2Co 1:19 [c]Ac 16:1 [d]Ac 17:1 [e]Ro 1:7 **1:2** [a]Ro 1:8; 2Th 1:3 [b]Ro 1:9 **1:3** [a]Jn 6:29 [b]1Co 13:13 [c]Ro 8:25; 15:4 [d]Ga 1:4 [1]Or *perseverance* [2]Lit *of* **1:4** [a]Ro 1:7; 2Th 2:13 [b]2Pe 1:10 **1:5** [a]1Co 9:14 [b]Ro 15:19 [c]Lk 1:1; Col 2:2 [d]1Th 2:10 [1]Or *became* **1:6** [a]1Co 4:16; 11:1f [b]Ac 17:5-10 [c]2Ti 4:2 [d]Ac 13:52; 2Co 6:10; Ga 5:22 **1:7** [a]Ro 15:26 [b]*Ac 18:12* **1:8** [a]*Col* 3:16; 2Th 3:1 [b]Ro 10:18 [c]Ro 15:26 [d]*Ac 18:12* [e]*Ro 1:8*; 16:19; 2Co 2:14 **1:9** [a]1Th 2:1 [b]Ac 14:15 [c]1Co 12:2 [d]Mt 16:16 [1]Lit *to* [2]Or *the idols* [3]Or *the* **1:10** [a]Mt 16:27f; 1Co 1:7 [b]Ac 2:24 [c]Ro 5:9 [d]Mt 3:7; 1Th 2:16; 5:9 [1]Lit *the heavens*

◆ **2:1** [a]1Th 1:9 [b]2Th 1:10 **2:2** [a]Ac 14:5; 16:19-24; Php 1:30 [b]Ac 16:22-24 [c]Ac 17:1-9 [d]Ro 1:1 [e]Php 1:30 **2:3** [a]Ac 13:15 [b]2Th 2:11 [c]1Th 4:7 [d]2Co 4:2 [1]Lit *in deceit* **2:4** [a]2Co 2:17 [b]Ga 2:7 [c]Ga 1:10 [d]Ro 8:27 [1]Or *approves* **2:5** [a]Ac 20:33; 2Pe 2:3 [b]Ro 1:9; 1Th 2:10 **2:6** [a]Jn 5:41, 44; 2Co 4:5 [b]1Co 9:1f [1]Lit *are able to be* **2:7** [a]2Ti 2:24 [b]Ga 4:19; 1Th 2:11 [1]Or *became gentle* [2]Three early mss *babes* [3]Lit *in the midst of you* [4]Or *cherishes*

having fond affection for you, we
were pleased to [a]impart to you not
only the [b]gospel of God but also our
own [1]lives, because you had become
beloved to us.
**9** For you remember, brothers, our
[a]labor and hardship, *how* [b]working
night and day so as not to be a
[c]burden to any of you, we proclaimed
to you the [d]gospel of God. **10** You
are witnesses, and *so is* [a]God, of
[b]how devoutly and righteously and
blamelessly we [1]behaved toward you
[2]believers; **11** just as you know how
we *were* [a]exhorting and encouraging
and [b]bearing witness to each one
of you as [c]a father *would* his own
children, **12** so that you would [a]walk
in a manner worthy of the God who
[b]calls you into His own kingdom and
[c]glory.
**13** And for this reason we also
[a]thank God without ceasing that
when you received the [b]word of
God which you heard from us, you
accepted *it* [c]not *as* the word of men,
but *for* what it really is, the word of
God, [d]which also is at work in you
who believe. **14** For you, brothers,
became [a]imitators of [b]the churches
of God in Christ Jesus that are [c]in
Judea, for [d]you also suffered the
same things at the hands of your own
countrymen, [e]even as they *did* from
the Jews, **15** [a]who both killed the Lord
Jesus and [b]the prophets, and [1]drove
us out, and do not please God, and
*are* hostile to all men, **16** [a]hindering
us from speaking to the Gentiles
[b]so that they may be saved; with the
result that they always [c]fill up the
measure of their sins. But [d]wrath has
come upon them [1]to the utmost.
**17** But we, brothers, having been
taken away from you for a [1]short
while—[a]in face but not in heart—
were all the more eager with great
desire [b]to see your face. **18** [1]For [a]we
wanted to come to you—I, Paul,
[b,2]more than once—and *yet* [c]Satan
[d]hindered us. **19** For who is our hope
or [a]joy or crown of boasting? Is it not
even you, before our Lord Jesus at
His [b,1]coming? **20** For you are [a]our
glory and joy.

### *Timothy's Good Report*

**3** Therefore [a]when we could endure
*it* no longer, we were pleased to
be left behind at [b]Athens alone, **2** and
we sent [a]Timothy, our brother and
God's fellow worker in the gospel of
Christ, to strengthen and encourage
you as to your faith, **3** so that no one
would be shaken by these afflictions,
for you yourselves know that [a]we
have been destined for this. **4** For
indeed when we were with you, we
*kept* telling you in advance that we
were going to suffer affliction, [a]just
as it happened and *as* you know. **5** For
this reason, [a]when I could endure

**2:8** [a]2Co 12:15; 1Jn 3:16 [b]Ro 1:1 [1]Or *souls* **2:9** [a]Php 4:16; 2Th 3:8 [b]Ac 18:3 [c]1Co 9:4f; 2Co 11:9 [d]Ro 1:1 **2:10** [a]1Th 2:5 [b]2Co 1:12; 1Th 1:5 [1]Lit *became* [2]Or who *believe* **2:11** [a]1Th 5:14 [b]Lk 16:28; 1Th 4:6 [c]1Co 4:14; 1Th 2:7 **2:12** [a]Eph 4:1 [b]Ro 8:28; 1Th 5:24; 2Th 2:14 [c]2Co 4:6; 1Pe 5:10 **2:13** [a]Ro 1:8; 1Th 1:2 [b]Ro 10:17; Heb 4:2 [c]Mt 10:20; Ga 4:14 [d]Heb 4:12 **2:14** [a]1Th 1:6 [b]1Co 7:17; 10:32 [c]Ga 1:22 [d]Ac 17:5; 1Th 3:4; 2Th 1:4f [e]Heb 10:33f **2:15** [a]Lk 24:20; Ac 2:23 [b]Mt 5:12; Ac 7:52 [1]Or *persecuted us* **2:16** [a]Ac 9:23; 13:45, 50; 14:2, 5, 19; 17:5, 13; 18:12; 21:21f, 27; 25:2, 7 [b]1Co 10:33 [c]Ge 15:16; Da 8:23; Mt 23:32 [d]1Th 1:10 [1]Or *forever*; lit *to the end* **2:17** [a]1Co 5:3 [b]1Th 3:10 [1]Lit *occasion of an hour* **2:18** [a]Ro 15:22 [b]Php 4:16 [c]Mt 4:10 [d]Ro 1:13; 15:22 [1]Or *Because* [2]Lit *both once and twice* **2:19** [a]Php 4:1 [b]Mt 16:27; Mk 8:38; Jn 21:22; 1Th 3:13; 4:15; 5:23 [1]Or *presence* **2:20** [a]2Co 1:14 ◆ **3:1** [a]1Th 3:5 [b]Ac 17:15f **3:2** [a]2Co 1:1; Col 1:1 **3:3** [a]Ac 9:16; 14:22 **3:4** [a]1Th 2:14 **3:5** [a]Php 2:19; 1Th 3:1

*it* no longer, I also [b]sent to know
about your faith, lest somehow [c]the
tempter has tempted you, and [d]our
labor be in vain.
**6** But now that [a]Timothy has come
to us from you, and has brought us
good news of [b]your faith and love,
and that you always [c]remember
us kindly, longing to see us just as
we also long to see you, **7** for this
reason, brothers, in all our distress
and affliction we were comforted
about you through your faith; **8** for
now we *really* live, if you [a]stand firm
in the Lord. **9** For [a]what thanks can
we render to God for you in return
for all the joy with which we rejoice
before our God because of you, **10** as
we [a]night and day keep praying most
earnestly that we may [b]see your face,
and may [c]complete what is lacking in
your faith?
**11** [a]Now may [b]our God and Father
[c]Himself and Jesus our Lord [d]direct
our way to you, **12** and may the Lord
cause you to increase and [a]abound
in love for one another, and for all
people, just as we also *do* for you,
**13** so that He may [a]strengthen your
hearts [b]blameless in holiness, before
[c]our God and Father, at the [d,1]coming
of our Lord Jesus [e]with all His [2]saints.

### *Sanctification and Love*

**4** [a]Finally then, [b]brothers, we ask
and exhort you in the Lord Jesus,
that as you received from us as to
how you ought to [c,1]walk and [d]please
God (just as you actually do [1]walk),
that you [e]excel still more. **2** For you
know what commandments we gave
you through the Lord Jesus. **3** For this
is the will of God, your sanctifica-
tion: that you [a]abstain from [1]sexual
immorality; **4** that [a]each of you know
how to [1]possess his own [b,2]vessel in
sanctification and [c]honor, **5** not in
[a,1]lustful passion, like the Gentiles
who [b]do not know God; **6** *and* that
no man transgress and [a]defraud his
brother [b]in the matter because [c]the
Lord is *the* avenger in all these things,
just as we also [d]told you before and
solemnly warned *you*. **7** For [a]God
did not call us to [b]impurity, but [1]in
sanctification. **8** Consequently, he
who sets *this* aside is not setting
aside man but the God who [a]gives
His Holy Spirit to you.
**9** Now concerning [a]love of the
brothers, you [b]have no need for
*anyone* to write to you, for you
yourselves are [c]taught by God to
love one another, **10** for indeed
[a]you do practice it toward all the
brothers who are in all Macedonia.
But we urge you, brothers, to [b]excel
still more, **11** and to make it your
ambition [a]to lead a quiet life and
[b]attend to your own business and
[c]work with your hands, just as we
commanded you, **12** so that you will

---

**3:5** [b]1Th 3:2 [c]Mt 4:3 [d]2Co 6:1; Php 2:16 **3:6** [a]Ac 18:5 [b]1Th 1:3 [c]1Co 11:2 **3:8** [a]1Co 16:13
**3:9** [a]1Th 1:2 **3:10** [a]2Ti 1:3 [b]1Th 2:17 [c]2Co 13:9 **3:11** [a]2Th 2:16 [b]Ga 1:4; 1Th 3:13 [c]1Th 4:16; 5:23; 2Th 2:16; 3:16; Rev 21:3 [d]2Th 3:5 **3:12** [a]*Php 1:9; 1Th 4:1, 10; 2Th 1:3* **3:13** [a]1Co 1:8; 1Th 3:2 [b]*Lk 1:6* [c]*Ga 1:4; 1Th 3:11* [d]*1Th 2:19* [e]*Mt 25:31*; Mk 8:38; 1Th 4:17; 2Th 1:7 [1]Or *presence* [2]Or *holy ones*
◆ **4:1** [a]2Co 13:11; 2Th 3:1 [b]Ga 6:1; 1Th 5:12; 2Th 1:3; 2:1; 3:1, 13 [c]Eph 4:1 [d]2Co 5:9 [e]Php 1:9; 1Th 3:12; 4:10; 2Th 1:3 [1]Or *conduct yourselves* **4:3** [a]1Co 6:18 [1]Or *fornication* **4:4** [a]1Co 7:2, 9 [b]2Co 4:7; 1Pe 3:7 [c]Ro 1:24 [1]Or *acquire* [2]Body, wife **4:5** [a]Ro 1:26 [b]Ga 4:8 [1]Lit *passion of lust* **4:6** [a]1Co 6:8 [b]2Co 7:11 [c]Ro 12:19; 13:4; Heb 13:4 [d]Lk 16:28; 1Th 2:11; Heb 2:6 **4:7** [a]1Pe 1:15 [b]1Th 2:3 [1]In the state or sphere of **4:8** [a]Ro 5:5; 2Co 1:22; Ga 4:6; 1Jn 3:24 **4:9** [a]Jn 13:34; Ro 12:10 [b]2Co 9:1; 1Th 5:1 [c]Jer 31:33f; Jn 6:45; 1Jn 2:27 **4:10** [a]1Th 1:7 [b]1Th 3:12 **4:11** [a]2Th 3:12 [b]1Pe 4:15 [c]Ac 18:3; Eph 4:28; 2Th 3:10-12

[a]walk properly toward [b]outsiders
and [c,1]not be in any need.

### *The Dead in Christ Will Rise*

13 But [a]we do not want you to be
uninformed, brothers, about those
who [b]are asleep, so that you will not
grieve as do [c]the rest who have [d]no
hope. 14 For if we believe that Jesus
died and rose again, [a]even so God
will bring with Him [b]those who have
fallen asleep [1]in Jesus. 15 For this we
say to you [a]by the word of the Lord,
that [b]we who are alive [1]and remain
until [c]the coming of the Lord, will
not precede [d]those who have fallen
asleep. 16 For the Lord [a]Himself [b]will
descend from heaven with a [c,1]shout,
with the voice of [d]*the* archangel and
with the [e]trumpet of God, and [f]the
dead in Christ will rise first. 17 Then
[a]we who are alive [1]and remain will
be [b]caught up together with them
[c]in the clouds to meet the Lord in
the air, and so we shall always [d]be
with the Lord. 18 Therefore comfort
one another with these words.

### *The Day of the Lord*

5 Now concerning the [a]times and
the seasons, brothers, you [b]have
no need of anything to be written to
you. 2 For you yourselves know full
well that [a]the day of the Lord [1]will
come [b]just like a thief in the night.
3 While they are saying, "[a]Peace and
safety!" then [b,1]destruction [2]will come
upon them suddenly like [c]labor pains
upon a woman who is pregnant, and
they will never escape. 4 But you,
brothers, are not in [a]darkness, that
the day would overtake you [b,1]like a
thief, 5 for you are all [a]sons of light
and sons of day. We are not of night
nor of [b]darkness; 6 so then let us not
[a]sleep as [b,1]others do, but let us be
awake and [c,2]sober. 7 For those who
sleep, sleep at night, and those who
get drunk, get [a]drunk at night. 8 But
since [a]we are of *the* day, let us [b]be
[1]sober, having put on the [c]breastplate
of [d]faith and love, and as a [e]helmet,
the [f]hope of salvation. 9 For God has
not appointed us for [a]wrath, but for
[b]obtaining salvation through our
Lord Jesus Christ, 10 [a]who died for
us, so that whether we are awake
or asleep, we will live together with
Him. 11 Therefore, [1]comfort one
another and [a]build up one another,
just as you also are doing.

### *Admonishment and Instruction*

12 But we ask of you, brothers, that
you [a]know those [b]who labor among
you, and [c]lead you in the Lord and
admonish you, 13 and that you regard
them very highly in love because of
their work. [a]Live in peace with one
another. 14 And we urge you, brothers,

**4:12** [a]Ro 13:13; Col 4:5 [b]Mk 4:11 [c]Eph 4:28 [1]Lit *have need of nothing* **4:13** [a]Ro 1:13 [b]Ac 7:60 [c]Eph 2:3; 1Th 5:6 [d]Eph 2:12 **4:14** [a]Ro 14:9; 2Co 4:14 [b]1Co 15:18; 1Th 4:13 [1]Lit *through* **4:15** [a]1Ki 13:17f; 20:35; 2Co 12:1; Ga 1:12 [b]1Co 15:52; 1Th 5:10 [c]1Th 2:19 [d]1Co 15:18; 1Th 4:13 [1]Lit *who* **4:16** [a]1Th 3:11 [b]1Th 1:10; 2Th 1:7 [c]Joel 2:11 [d]Jd 9 [e]Mt 24:31 [f]1Co 15:23; 2Th 2:1; Rev 14:13 [1]Or *cry of command* **4:17** [a]1Co 15:52; 1Th 5:10 [b]2Co 12:2 [c]Da 7:13; Ac 1:9; Rev 11:12 [d]Jn 12:26 [1]Lit *who* ◆**5:1** [a]Ac 1:7 [b]1Th 4:9 **5:2** [a]1Co 1:8 [b]Lk 21:34; 1Th 5:4; 2Pe 3:10; Rev 3:3; 16:15 [1]Lit *is coming* **5:3** [a]Jer 6:14; 8:11; Eze 13:10 [b]2Th 1:9 [c]Jn 16:21 [1]Or *sudden destruction* [2]Lit *comes upon* **5:4** [a]Ac 26:18; 1Jn 2:8 [b]Lk 21:34; 1Th 5:2; 2Pe 3:10; Rev 3:3; 16:15 [1]One early ms *like thieves* **5:5** [a]Lk 16:8 [b]Ac 26:18; 1Jn 2:8 **5:6** [a]Ro 13:11; 1Th 5:10 [b]Eph 2:3; 1Th 4:13 [c]1Pe 1:13 [1]Lit *the remaining ones* [2]Or *self-controlled* **5:7** [a]Ac 2:15; 2Pe 2:13 **5:8** [a]1Th 5:5 [b]1Pe 1:13 [c]Is 59:17; Eph 6:14 [d]Eph 6:23 [e]Eph 6:17 [f]Ro 8:24 [1]Or *self-controlled* **5:9** [a]1Th 1:10 [b]2Th 2:13f **5:10** [a]Ro 14:9 **5:11** [a]Eph 4:29 [1]Or *encourage* **5:12** [a]1Co 16:18; 1Ti 5:17 [b]Ro 16:6, 12; 1Co 15:10; 16:16 [c]Heb 13:17 **5:13** [a]Mk 9:50

admonish [a]the [1]unruly, encourage
[b]the fainthearted, help [c]the weak, be
[d]patient with everyone. **15** See that
[a]no one repays another with evil for
evil, but always [b]seek after that which
is good for one another and for all
people. **16** [a]Rejoice always; **17** [a]pray
without ceasing; **18** in everything
[a]give thanks, for this is God's will for
you in Christ Jesus. **19** [a]Do not quench
the Spirit; **20** do not despise [a]prophe-
cies, **21** but [a]examine all things; [b]hold
fast to that which is good; **22** abstain
from every [1]form of evil.

**23** Now [a]may the God of peace
[b]Himself sanctify you entirely, and
may your [c]spirit and soul and body
be preserved complete, [d]without
blame at [e]the coming of our Lord
Jesus Christ. **24** [a]Faithful is He who
[b]calls you, who also will do it.
**25** Brothers, [a]pray for us[1].
**26** [a]Greet all the brothers with
a holy kiss. **27** I implore you by the
Lord to [a]have this letter read to all
the [b]brothers.
**28** [a]The grace of our Lord Jesus
Christ be with you.

*The Second Letter of Paul to the*

# THESSALONIANS

### *Greetings of Grace and Thanksgiving*

**1** [a]Paul and [b]Silvanus and [c]Timothy,
To the [d]church of the Thessa-
lonians in God our Father and the
Lord Jesus Christ: **2** [a]Grace to you and
peace from God the Father and the
Lord Jesus Christ.
**3** We ought always [a]to give thanks
to God for you, [b]brothers, as is *only*
fitting, because your faith is growing
abundantly, and the [c]love of each
one of you all toward one another
increases *all the more*, **4** so that we
ourselves [a]boast about you among
[b]the churches of God for your [1]perse-
verance and faith [b]in the midst of
all your persecutions and afflictions
which you endure.

### *God's Righteous Judgment*

**5** *This is* a [a]plain indication of God's
righteous judgment so that you will be
[b]considered worthy of the kingdom of
God, for which indeed you are suf-
fering. **6** [1]Since [a]it is right [2]for God to
repay with affliction those who afflict
you, **7** and *to give* rest to you who are
afflicted [1]and to us as well [a]at the rev-
elation of the Lord Jesus [b]from heaven
[c]with [2]His mighty angels [d]in flaming
fire, **8** executing vengeance on those
who [a]do not know God and to those

---

**5:14** [a]2Th 3:6, 7, 11 [b]Is 35:4 [c]Ro 14:1f; 1Co 8:7ff; Ro 15:1 [d]1Co 13:4 [1]Or *undisciplined* **5:15** [a]Mt 5:44; Ro 12:17; 1Pe 3:9 [b]Ro 12:9; Ga 6:10; 1Th 5:21 **5:16** [a]Php 4:4 **5:17** [a]Eph 6:18 **5:18** [a]Eph 5:20 **5:19** [a]Eph 4:30 **5:20** [a]Ac 13:1; 1Co 14:31 **5:21** [a]1Co 14:29; 1Jn 4:1 [b]Ro 12:9; Ga 6:10; 1Th 5:15 **5:22** [1]Or *appearance* **5:23** [a]Ro 15:33 [b]1Th 3:11 [c]Lk 1:46f; Heb 4:12 [d]Jas 1:4; 2Pe 3:14 [e]1Th 2:19 **5:24** [a]1Co 1:9; 2Th 3:3 [b]1Th 2:12 **5:25** [a]Eph 6:19; 2Th 3:1; Heb 13:18 [1]Two early mss add *also* **5:26** [a]Ro 16:16 **5:27** [a]Col 4:16 [b]Ac 1:15 **5:28** [a]Ro 16:20; 2Th 3:18 ◆ **1:1** [a]1Th 1:1 [b]2Co 1:19 [c]Ac 16:1 [d]Ac 17:1; 1Th 1:1 **1:2** [a]Ro 1:7 **1:3** [a]Ro 1:8; Eph 5:20; 1Th 1:2; 2Th 2:13 [b]1Th 4:1; 2Th 2:1 [c]1Th 3:12 **1:4** [a]2Co 7:4; 1Th 2:19 [b]1Co 7:17; 1Th 2:14 [1]Or *steadfastness* **1:5** [a]Php 1:28 [b]Lk 20:35; 2Th 1:11 **1:6** [a]Ex 23:22; Col 3:25; Heb 6:10 [1]Lit *If indeed* [2]Or *in the sight of* **1:7** [a]Lk 17:30 [b]1Th 4:16 [c]Jd 14 [d]Ex 3:2; 19:18; Is 66:15; Eze 1:13; Da 7:9; Mt 25:41; 1Co 3:13; Heb 10:27; 12:29; 2Pe 3:7; Jd 7; Rev 14:10 [1]Lit *along with us* [2]Lit *the angels of His power* **1:8** [a]Ga 4:8

who [b]do not obey the gospel of our
Lord Jesus. **9** These will pay the penal-
ty of [a]eternal destruction, [b]AWAY FROM
THE PRESENCE OF THE [1]LORD AND FROM
THE GLORY OF HIS MIGHT, **10** when He
comes to be [a]glorified [1]in His [2]saints
on that [b]day, and to be marveled at
among all who have believed—for
our [c]witness to you was believed. **11** To
this end also we [a]pray for you always,
that our God will [b,1]count you worthy
of your [c]calling, and fulfill all *your*
[c]good pleasure for [d]goodness and
the [e]work of faith with power, **12** so
that the [a]name of our Lord Jesus will
be glorified in you, and you in Him,
according to the grace of our God and
*the* Lord Jesus Christ.

### *The Man of Lawlessness*

**2** Now we ask you, [a]brothers, with
regard to the [b,1]coming of our
Lord Jesus Christ and our [c]gathering
together to Him, **2** that you not be
quickly shaken in your mind or be
alarmed whether by a [a]spirit or a
[b]word or a [c]letter as if from us, to the
effect that [d]the day of the Lord [e]has
come. **3** [a]Let no one in any way deceive
you, for *it has not come* unless the
[b,1]apostasy comes first, and the [c]man
of lawlessness is revealed, the [d]son of
destruction, **4** who opposes and exalts
himself above [a,1]every so-called god
or object of worship, so that he takes
his seat in the [2]sanctuary of God,
[b]exhibiting himself as being God.
**5** Do you not remember that [a]while
I was still with you, I was telling you
these things? **6** And you know [a]what
restrains him now, so that in his time
he will be revealed. **7** For [a]the mystery
of lawlessness is already at work; only
[b]he who now restrains *will do so* until
he is taken out of the way. **8** And then
that lawless one [a]will be revealed—
whom the Lord [1]Jesus [b]WILL SLAY
WITH THE BREATH OF HIS MOUTH and
bring to an end by the [c]appearance
of His [2]coming— **9** whose [1]coming
is in accord with the working of
[a]Satan, with all power and [b,2]signs
and false wonders, **10** and with [1]all
the deception of unrighteousness for
[a]those who perish, because they did
not receive the love of [b]the truth so
as to be saved. **11** And for this reason
[a]God sends upon them a [b,1]deluding
influence so that they will believe
[2]what is false, **12** in order that they
all may be [1]judged who [a]did not be-
lieve the truth, but [b,2]took pleasure in
unrighteousness.

**13** [a]But we should always give
thanks to God for you, [b]brothers
beloved by the Lord, because [c]God
has chosen you [1]as the first fruits [d]for
salvation [e]through sanctification [2]by

---

**1:8** [b]Ro 2:8 **1:9** [a]Php 3:19; 1Th 5:3 [b]Is 2:10, 19, 21; 2Th 2:8 [1]In OT, Yahweh, cf. Is 2:10, 19, 21
**1:10** [a]Is 49:3; Jn 17:10; 1Th 2:12 [b]Is 2:11ff; 1Co 3:13 [c]1Co 1:6; 1Th 2:1 [1]Or *in the persons of* [2]Or *holy ones*
**1:11** [a]Col 1:9 [b]2Th 1:5 [c]Ro 11:29; 2Th 2:12 [d]Ro 15:14 [e]1Th 1:3 [1]Or *make* **1:12** [a]Is 24:15; 66:5; Mal 1:11;
Php 2:9ff ◆ **2:1** [a]2Th 1:3 [b]1Th 2:19 [c]Mk 13:27; 1Th 4:15-17 [1]Or *presence* **2:2** [a]1Co 14:32; 1Jn 4:1
[b]1Th 5:2; 2Th 2:15 [c]2Th 3:17 [d]1Co 1:8 [e]1Co 7:26 **2:3** [a]Eph 5:6 [b]1Ti 4:1 [c]Da 7:25; 8:25; 11:36; 2Th 2:8;
Rev 13:5ff [d]Jn 17:12 [1]Or *falling away* from the faith **2:4** [a]1Co 8:5 [b]Is 14:14; Eze 28:2 [1]Or *everyone
who is called God* [2]The innermost part of the temple **2:5** [a]1Th 3:4 **2:6** [a]2Th 2:7 **2:7** [a]Rev 17:5, 7
[b]2Th 2:6 **2:8** [a]Da 7:25; 8:25; 11:36; 2Th 2:3; Rev 13:5ff [b]Is 11:4; Rev 2:16; 19:15 [c]1Ti 6:14; 2Ti 1:10; 4:1, 8;
Tit 2:13 [1]Some mss omit *Jesus* [2]Or *presence* **2:9** [a]Mt 4:10 [b]Mt 24:24; Jn 4:48 [1]Or *presence*
[2]Or *attesting miracles* **2:10** [a]1Co 1:18 [b]2Th 2:12, 13 [1]Or *every deception* **2:11** [a]1Ki 22:22; Ro 1:28
[b]1Th 2:3; 2Ti 4:4 [1]Lit *work of delusion*, cf. 2:7, 9 [2]Or *the lie* **2:12** [a]Ro 2:8 [b]Ro 1:32; 1Co 13:6; 2Th 1:11
[1]Or *condemned* [2]Or *approved* **2:13** [a]2Th 1:3 [b]1Th 1:4 [c]Eph 1:4ff [d]1Co 1:21; 1Th 2:12; 5:9; 1Pe 1:5
[e]1Th 4:7; 1Pe 1:2 [1]Some mss *from the beginning* [2]Lit *of*

the Spirit and faith in the truth. **14** [1]It was for this He [a]called you through [b]our gospel, [2]that you may obtain the glory of our Lord Jesus Christ. **15** So then, brothers, [a]stand firm and [b]hold to the traditions which you were taught, whether [c]by word *of mouth* or [c]by letter [1]from us.

**16** [a]Now may our Lord Jesus Christ [a]Himself and God our Father, who has [b]loved us and given us eternal comfort and [c]good hope by grace, **17** [a]encourage your hearts and [b]strengthen *them* in every good work and word.

### *Disobedient Brothers*

**3** [a]Finally, brothers, [b]pray for us that [c]the word of the Lord will [1]spread rapidly and be glorified, just as *it did* also with you; **2** and that we will be [a]rescued from [1]perverse and evil men, for not all have [2]faith. **3** But [a]the Lord is faithful, who will strengthen and guard you [1]from [b]the evil one. **4** And we have [a]confidence in the Lord about you, that you [b]are doing and will *continue to* do what we command. **5** And may the Lord [a]direct your hearts into the love of God and into the steadfastness of Christ.

**6** Now we command you, brothers, [a]in the name of our Lord Jesus Christ, that you [b,1]keep away from every brother who walks in an [c,2]unruly manner and not according to [d]the tradition which [3]they received from us. **7** For you yourselves know how you ought to [a]imitate us, because we did not act in an unruly manner among you, **8** nor did we [a]eat [1]anyone's bread [2]without paying for it, but with [b]labor and hardship we *kept* [c]working night and day so that we would not be a burden to any of you; **9** not because we do not have [a]the authority, but in order to offer ourselves [b]as a model for you, so that you would imitate us. **10** For even [a]when we were with you, we used to command this to you: [b]if anyone is not willing to work, neither let him eat. **11** For we hear that some among you are [a]walking in an unruly manner, doing no work at all, but acting like [b]busybodies. **12** Now such persons we command and [a]exhort in the Lord Jesus Christ, that [b]working with quietness, they eat their own bread. **13** But as for you, [a]brothers, [b]do not lose heart in doing good.

**14** And if anyone does not obey our word [a,1]in this letter, take special note of that person [b]to not associate with him, so that he will be [c]put to shame. **15** And *yet* [a]do not regard him as an enemy, but [b,1]admonish him as a [c]brother.

**16** Now [a]may the Lord of peace [b]Himself continually give you peace in every [1]circumstance. [c]The Lord be with you all!

---

**2:14** [a]1Th 2:12 [b]1Th 1:5 [1]Some mss *And* [2]Lit *to the gaining of* **2:15** [a]1Co 16:13 [b]1Co 11:2; 2Th 3:6 [c]2Th 2:2 [1]Lit *of* **2:16** [a]1Th 3:11 [b]Jn 3:16 [c]Tit 3:7; 1Pe 1:3 **2:17** [a]1Th 3:2, 13 [b]2Th 3:3 ◆ **3:1** [a]1Th 4:1 [b]1Th 5:25 [c]1Th 1:8 [1]Lit *run* **3:2** [a]Ro 15:31 [1]Lit *improper* [2]Or *the faith* **3:3** [a]1Co 1:9; 1Th 5:24 [b]Mt 5:37 [1]Or *from evil* **3:4** [a]2Co 2:3 [b]1Th 4:10 **3:5** [a]1Th 3:11 **3:6** [a]1Co 5:4 [b]Ro 16:17; 1Co 5:11; 2Th 3:14 [c]1Th 5:14; 2Th 3:7, 11 [d]1Co 11:2; 2Th 2:15 [1]Or *avoid* [2]Or *undisciplined* [3]Some mss *you* **3:7** [a]1Th 1:6; 2Th 3:9 **3:8** [a]1Co 9:4 [b]1Th 2:9 [c]Ac 18:3; Eph 4:28 [1]Lit *from anyone* [2]Lit *freely* **3:9** [a]1Co 9:4ff [b]2Th 3:7 **3:10** [a]1Th 3:4 [b]1Th 4:11 **3:11** [a]2Th 3:6 [b]1Ti 5:13; 1Pe 4:15 **3:12** [a]1Th 4:1 [b]1Th 4:11 **3:13** [a]1Th 4:1 [b]2Co 4:1; Ga 6:9 **3:14** [a]Col 4:16 [b]2Th 3:6 [c]1Co 4:14 [1]Lit *through* **3:15** [a]Ga 6:1 [b]1Th 5:14 [c]2Th 3:6, 13 [1]Or *keep admonishing* **3:16** [a]Ro 15:33 [b]1Th 3:11 [c]Ru 2:4 [1]Lit *way*

**17** The greeting [a]is in my own
hand—[1]Paul, which is a distinguish-
ing mark in every letter; this is the
way I write. **18** [a]The grace of our Lord
Jesus Christ be with you all.

*The First Letter of Paul to*

# TIMOTHY

### *Instructions in Doctrine and Living*

**1** Paul, [a]an apostle of [b]Christ Jesus
[c]according to the commandment
of [c]God our Savior, and of [b]Christ
Jesus, our [d]hope,
**2** To [a]Timothy, [a]*my* genuine child
in *the* faith: [b]Grace, mercy, *and* peace
from God the Father and [c]Christ Jesus
our Lord.
**3** As I exhorted you when going to
[a]Macedonia, [1]remain on at [b]Ephesus
so that you may command certain
ones not to [c]teach a different
doctrine, **4** nor to [1]pay attention to
[a]myths and endless [b]genealogies,
which give rise to mere [c]speculation
rather than *furthering* [d]the stew-
ardship from God which is by faith.
**5** But the goal of our [a]command is
love [b]from a pure heart and a [c]good
conscience and an unhypocritical
[d]faith. **6** For some, straying from these
things, have turned aside to [a]fruitless
discussion, **7** [a]wanting to be [b]teachers
of the Law, even though they do not
understand either what they are
saying or the matters about which
they make confident assertions.
**8** But we know that [a]the Law is
good, if one uses it lawfully, **9** know-
ing this, that [a]law is not made for a
righteous person, but for those who
are lawless and [b]rebellious, for the
[c]ungodly and sinners, for the unholy
and [d]godless, for those who kill their
fathers or mothers, for murderers,
**10** for [a]sexually immoral persons, for
[b]homosexuals, for [c]kidnappers, for
[d]liars, for [e]perjurers, and whatever
else is contrary to [f]sound teaching,
**11** according to [a]the gospel of the glo-
ry of [b]the blessed God, with which I
have been [c]entrusted.
**12** I am grateful to [a]Christ Jesus
our Lord, who has [b]strengthened
me, because He regarded me faith-
ful, [c]putting me into service, **13** even
though I was formerly a blasphem-
er and a [a]persecutor and a violent
aggressor. Yet I was [b]shown mercy
because [c]I acted ignorantly in un-
belief; **14** and the [a]grace of our Lord
was more than abundant, with the
[b]faith and love which *are* in Christ
Jesus. **15** [a]It is a trustworthy saying
and deserving full acceptance: that

---

**3:17** [a]1Co 16:21 [1]Lit *Paul's* **3:18** [a]Ro 16:20; 1Th 5:28 ◆ **1:1** [a]2Co 1:1 [b]1Ti 1:12 [c]Tit 1:3 [d]Col 1:27
**1:2** [a]2Ti 1:2 [b]Ro 1:7; 2Ti 1:2; Tit 1:4 [c]1Ti 1:12 **1:3** [a]Ro 15:26 [b]Ac 18:19 [c]Ro 16:17; 2Co 11:4; Ga 1:6f; 1Ti 6:3
[1]Lit *to remain* **1:4** [a]1Ti 4:7; 2Ti 4:4; Tit 1:14; 2Pe 1:16 [b]Tit 3:9 [c]2Ti 2:23 [d]Eph 3:2 [1]Or *occupy themselves with* **1:5** [a]1Ti 1:18 [b]2Ti 2:22 [c]1Ti 1:19; 3:9; 2Ti 1:3; 1Pe 3:16, 21 [d]2Ti 1:5 **1:6** [a]Tit 1:10 **1:7** [a]Jas 3:1
[b]Lk 2:46 **1:8** [a]Ro 7:12, 16 **1:9** [a]Ga 5:23 [b]Tit 1:6, 10 [c]1Pe 4:18; Jd 15 [d]1Ti 4:7; 6:20; Heb 12:16
**1:10** [a]1Co 6:9 [b]Lv 18:22 [c]Ex 21:16; Rev 18:13 [d]Rev 21:8, 27; 22:15 [e]Mt 5:33 [f]1Ti 4:6; 6:3; 2Ti 4:3;
Tit 1:9, 13; 2:1, 2 **1:11** [a]2Co 4:4 [b]1Ti 6:15 [c]Ga 2:7 **1:12** [a]Ga 3:26 [b]Ac 9:22; Php 4:13; 2Ti 4:17 [c]Ac 9:15
**1:13** [a]Ac 8:3 [b]1Co 7:25 [c]Ac 26:9 **1:14** [a]Ro 5:20; 1Co 3:10; 2Co 4:15; Ga 1:13-16 [b]1Th 1:3; 1Ti 2:15; 4:12; 6:11;
2Ti 1:13; 2:22; Tit 2:2 **1:15** [a]1Ti 3:1; 4:9; 2Ti 2:11; Tit 3:8

[b]Christ Jesus came into the world
to [c]save sinners, among whom [d]I
am foremost. **16** Yet for this reason
I [a]was shown mercy, so that in me
as the foremost, Christ Jesus might
[b]demonstrate all His patience as an
example for those [1]who are going to
believe upon Him for eternal life.
**17** Now to the [a]King of the [1]ages,
[b]immortal, [c]invisible, the [d]only
God, [e]*be* honor and glory [2]forever
and ever. Amen.

**18** This [a]command I entrust to
you, Timothy, [b]*my* child, in accor-
dance with the [c]prophecies previ-
ously made concerning you, that
by them you may [d]fight the good
fight, **19** keeping [a]faith and a good
conscience, which some, having re-
jected, suffered shipwreck in regard
to [b,1]their faith. **20** [1]Among these
are [a]Hymenaeus and [b]Alexander,
whom I have [c]handed over to Satan,
so that they will be [d]taught not to
blaspheme.

### *Exhortation to Prayer*

**2** First of all, then, I exhort that
[a]petitions *and* prayers, requests
*and* thanksgivings, be made for all
men, **2** [a]for kings and all who are in
[1]authority, so that we may lead a tran-
quil and quiet life in all godliness and
[2]dignity. **3** This is good and accept-
able in the sight of [a]God our Savior,
**4** [a]who desires all men to be [b]saved
and to [c]come to the [1]full knowledge
of the truth. **5** For there is [a]one God,
*and* [b]one mediator also between God
and men, *the* [c]man Christ Jesus, **6** who
[a]gave Himself as a ransom for all, the
[b]witness for [c,1]this proper time. **7** [a]For
this I was appointed a [1]preacher and
[b]an apostle ([c]I am telling the truth,
I am not lying) as a teacher of [d]the
Gentiles in faith and truth.

**8** Therefore [a]I want the men [b]in
every place to pray, [c]lifting up [d]holy
hands, without wrath and dissension.

### *Instructions for Women*

**9** Likewise, *I want* [a]women to adorn
themselves with proper clothing,
with modesty and self-restraint, not
with braided hair and gold or pearls
or costly clothing, **10** but rather by
means of good works, as is proper
for women professing godliness. **11** [a]A
woman must learn in quietness,
in all submission. **12** [a]But I do not
allow a woman to teach or exercise
authority over a man, but to remain
quiet. **13** [a]For it was Adam who was
first formed, *and* then Eve. **14** And
*it was* not Adam *who* was deceived,
but [a]the woman being deceived, [1]fell
into trespass. **15** But she will be [1]saved
through the bearing of children, if
they continue in [a]faith and love and
sanctification with self-restraint.

---

**1:15** [b]Mk 2:17; Lk 15:2ff; 19:10 [c]Ro 11:14 [d]1Co 15:9; Eph 3:8 **1:16** [a]1Co 7:25; 1Ti 1:13 [b]Eph 2:7 [1]Or *destined to* **1:17** [a]Rev 15:3 [b]1Ti 6:16 [c]Col 1:15 [d]Jn 5:44; 1Ti 6:15; Jd 25 [e]Ro 2:7, 10; 11:36; Heb 2:7 [1]Or *eternal* [2]Lit *to the ages of the ages* **1:18** [a]1Ti 1:5 [b]1Ti 1:2 [c]1Ti 4:14 [d]2Co 10:4; 1Ti 6:12; 2Ti 2:3f; 4:7 **1:19** [a]1Ti 1:5 [b]1Ti 6:12, 21; 2Ti 2:18 [1]Lit *the* **1:20** [a]2Ti 2:17 [b]2Ti 4:14 [c]1Co 5:5 [d]1Co 11:32; Heb 12:5ff [1]Lit *Of* ◆ **2:1** [a]Eph 6:18 **2:2** [a]Ezr 6:10; Ro 13:1 [1]Or *a high position* [2]Or *seriousness* **2:3** [a]Lk 1:47; 1Ti 1:1; 4:10 **2:4** [a]Eze 18:23, 32; Jn 3:17; 1Ti 4:10; Tit 2:11; 2Pe 3:9 [b]Ro 11:14 [c]2Ti 2:25; 3:7; Tit 1:1; Heb 10:26 [1]Or *recognition* **2:5** [a]Ro 3:30; 10:12; 1Co 8:4 [b]1Co 8:6; Ga 3:20 [c]Mt 1:1; Ro 1:3 **2:6** [a]Mt 20:28; Ga 1:4 [b]1Co 1:6 [c]Mk 1:15; Ga 4:4; 1Ti 6:15; Tit 1:3 [1]Lit *its own times* **2:7** [a]Eph 3:8; 1Ti 1:11; 2Ti 1:11 [b]1Co 9:1 [c]Ro 9:1 [d]Ac 9:15 [1]Or *herald* **2:8** [a]Php 1:12; 1Ti 5:14; Tit 3:8 [b]Jn 4:21; 1Co 1:2; 2Co 2:14; 1Th 1:8 [c]Ps 63:4; Lk 24:50 [d]Ps 24:4; Jas 4:8 **2:9** [a]1Pe 3:3 **2:11** [a]1Co 14:34; Tit 2:5 **2:12** [a]1Co 14:34; Tit 2:5 **2:13** [a]Ge 2:7, 22; 3:16; 1Co 11:8ff **2:14** [a]Ge 3:6, 13; 2Co 11:3 [1]Lit *has come* **2:15** [a]1Ti 1:14 [1]Or *vindicated*, cf. 4:16

### *Overseers and Deacons*

3 [a]It is a trustworthy saying: if
any man aspires to the [b]office of
[1]overseer, he desires a good work.
**2** [a,1]An overseer, then, must be above
reproach, [b]the husband of one wife,
[c]temperate, sensible, respectable,
[d]hospitable, [e]able to teach, **3** [a]not
addicted to wine [1]or pugnacious, but
considerate, peaceable, [b]free from
the love of money; **4** [a]leading his own
household well, having his children
in submission with all dignity **5** (but
if a man does not know how to lead
his own household, how will he take
care of [a]the church of God?), **6** *and*
not a new convert, so that he will not
become [a]conceited and fall into the
[b]condemnation of the devil. **7** And he
must [a]have a good reputation with
[b]those outside *the church,* so that
he will not fall into reproach and [c]the
snare of the devil.
**8** [a]Deacons likewise *must be* dig-
nified, not [1]double-tongued, [b]not
indulging in much wine, [c]not fond
of dishonest gain, **9** [a]*but* holding to
the mystery of the faith with a clear
conscience. **10** [a]And these men must
also first be tested; then let them
serve as deacons if they are beyond
reproach. **11** [1]Women *must* likewise
*be* dignified, [a]not malicious gossips,
but [b]temperate, faithful in all things.
**12** [a]Deacons must be [b]husbands of
*only* one wife, [c]leading *their* children
and their own households well. **13** For
those who have served well as dea-
cons [a]obtain for themselves a [1]high
standing and great boldness in the
faith that is in Christ Jesus.
**14** I am writing these things to you,
hoping to come to you soon, **15** but [1]in
case I am delayed, *I write* so that you
will know how [2]one ought to conduct
himself in [a]the household of God,
which is the [b]church of [c]the living
God, the [d]pillar and support of the
truth. **16** And by common confession,
great is [a]the mystery of godliness:

He who was [b]manifested
  in the flesh,
Was [c,1]vindicated [2]in the Spirit,
[d]Seen by angels,
[e]Proclaimed among
  the nations,
[f]Believed on in the world,
[g]Taken up in glory.

### *Some Will Fall Away*

4 But [a]the Spirit explicitly says
that [b]in later times some will [1]fall
away from the faith, paying attention
to [c]deceitful spirits and [d]doctrines of
demons, **2** by the hypocrisy of liars,
who have been [a]seared in their own
conscience, **3** who [a]forbid marriage
*and advocate* [b]abstaining from foods
which [c]God created to be shared in
[d]with thanksgiving by those who
believe and know the truth. **4** For
[a]everything created by God is good,

◆ **3:1** [a]1Ti 1:15 [b]Ac 20:28; Php 1:1 [1]Or *bishop* **3:2** [a]1Ti 3:2-4; Tit 1:6-8 [b]Lk 2:36f; 1Ti 5:9; Tit 1:6 [c]1Ti 3:8, 11; Tit 2:2 [d]Ro 12:13; Tit 1:8; Heb 13:2; 1Pe 4:9 [e]2Ti 2:24 [1]Lit *The* **3:3** [a]Tit 1:7 [b]1Ti 3:8; 6:10; Tit 1:7; Heb 13:5 [1]Lit *not* **3:4** [a]1Ti 3:12 **3:5** [a]1Co 10:32; 1Ti 3:15 **3:6** [a]1Ti 6:4; 2Ti 3:4 [b]1Ti 3:7 **3:7** [a]2Co 8:21 [b]Mk 4:11 [c]1Ti 6:9; 2Ti 2:26 **3:8** [a]Php 1:1; 1Ti 3:12 [b]1Ti 5:23; Tit 2:3 [c]1Ti 3:3; Tit 1:7; 1Pe 5:2 [1]Or *given to double-talk* **3:9** [a]1Ti 1:5, 19 **3:10** [a]1Ti 5:22 **3:11** [a]2Ti 3:3; Tit 2:3 [b]1Ti 3:2 [1]Either deacons' wives or deaconesses **3:12** [a]Php 1:1; 1Ti 3:8 [b]1Ti 3:2 [c]1Ti 3:4 **3:13** [a]Mt 25:21 [1]Lit *good* **3:15** [a]1Co 3:16; 2Co 6:16; Eph 2:21f; 1Pe 2:5; 4:17 [b]1Ti 3:5 [c]Mt 16:16; 1Ti 4:10 [d]Ga 2:9; 2Ti 2:19 [1]Lit *if I delay* [2]Or *you ought to conduct yourself* **3:16** [a]Ro 16:25 [b]Jn 1:14; 1Pe 1:20; 1Jn 3:5, 8 [c]Ro 3:4 [d]Lk 2:13; 24:4; 1Pe 1:12 [e]Ro 16:26; 2Co 1:19; Col 1:23 [f]2Th 1:10 [g]Mk 16:19; Ac 1:9 [1]Or *justified* [2]Or *by* ◆ **4:1** [a]Jn 16:13; Ac 20:23; 21:11; 1Co 2:10f [b]2Th 2:3ff; 2Ti 3:1; 2Pe 3:3; Jd 18 [c]1Jn 4:6 [d]Jas 3:15 [1]Apostatize **4:2** [a]Eph 4:19 **4:3** [a]Heb 13:4 [b]Col 2:16, 23 [c]Ge 1:29; 9:3 [d]Ro 14:6; 1Co 10:30f; 1Ti 4:4 **4:4** [a]1Co 10:26

and nothing is to be rejected if it is
[b]received with thanksgiving, **5** for it
is sanctified by [a]the word of God and
prayer.

### *A Good Minister's Discipline*

**6** In pointing out these things to [a]the
brothers, you will be a good [b]servant
of Christ Jesus, being nourished on
the words of the faith and of the
[c,1]sound doctrine which you [d]have
been following. **7** But refuse [a]godless
[b]myths fit only for old women. On
the other hand, train yourself for the
purpose of [c]godliness, **8** for [a]bodily
training is only of little profit, but
[b]godliness is profitable for all
things, since it [c]holds promise for
the [d]present life and *also* for the *life*
to come. **9** [a]It is a trustworthy saying
and deserving full acceptance. **10** For
it is for this we labor and strive, be-
cause we have fixed [a]our hope on
[b]the living God, who is [c]the Savior
of all men, especially of believers.
**11** [a]Command and teach these
things. **12** [a]Let no one look down on
your youthfulness, but show yourself
as [b]a model to those who believe in
word, conduct, [c]love, faith, *and* purity.
**13** [a]Until I come, give attention to the
public [b]reading *of Scripture,* to exhor-
tation and teaching. **14** Do not neglect
the gift within you, which was given
to you through [a]prophetic utterance
with [b]the laying on of hands by the
[c]council of elders. **15** Take pains with
these things; be *absorbed* in them, so
that your progress will be evident to
all. **16** [a]Pay close attention to yourself
and to your teaching; persevere in
these things, for as you do this you
will [b]save both yourself and those
who hear you.

### *Honor Widows*

**5** [a]Do not sharply rebuke an [b]older
man, but *rather* plead with *him*
as a father, *to* [c]the younger men
as brothers, **2** the older women as
mothers, *and* the younger women
as sisters, in all purity.
**3** Honor widows who are [a]widows
indeed, **4** but if any widow has chil-
dren or grandchildren, [a]they must
first learn to practice piety in regard
to their own family and to [1]make
some return to their parents; for this
is [b]acceptable in the sight of God.
**5** Now she who is a [a]widow indeed
and who has been left alone, [b]has
fixed her hope on God and continues
in [c]petitions and prayers night and
day. **6** But she who [a]lives in self-
indulgence is [b]dead even while she
lives. **7** [a]And command these things
as well, so that they may be above
reproach. **8** But if anyone does not
provide for his own, and especially
for those of his household, he has
[a]denied the faith and is worse than
an unbeliever.
**9** A widow is to be [a]put on the
list only if she is not less than sixty

---

**4:4** [b]Ro 14:6; 1Co 10:30f; 1Ti 4:3 **4:5** [a]Ge 1:25, 31; Heb 11:3 **4:6** [a]Ac 1:15 [b]2Co 11:23 [c]1Ti 1:10 [d]Lk 1:3; Php 2:20, 22; 2Ti 3:10 [1]Lit *good* **4:7** [a]*1Ti 1:9* [b]*1Ti 1:4* [c]1Ti 4:8; 6:3, 5f; 2Ti 3:5 **4:8** [a]Col 2:23 [b]*1Ti 4:7; 6:3, 5f; 2Ti 3:5* [c]Ps 37:9, 11; Pr 19:23; 22:4; Mt 6:33 [d]Mt 6:33; 12:32; Mk 10:30 **4:9** [a]1Ti 1:15 **4:10** [a]2Co 1:10; 1Ti 6:17 [b]1Ti 3:15 [c]Jn 4:42; 1Ti 2:4 **4:11** [a]1Ti 5:7; 6:2 **4:12** [a]1Co 16:11; Tit 2:15 [b]1Ti 1:14 [c]Tit 2:7; 1Pe 5:3 **4:13** [a]1Ti 3:14 [b]2Ti 3:15ff **4:14** [a]1Ti 1:18 [b]Ac 6:6; 1Ti 5:22; 2Ti 1:6 [c]Ac 11:30 **4:16** [a]Ac 20:28 [b]1Co 1:21 ◆ **5:1** [a]Lv 19:32 [b]Tit 2:2 [c]Tit 2:6 **5:3** [a]Ac 6:1; 9:39, 41; 1Ti 5:5, 16 **5:4** [a]Eph 6:2 [b]1Ti 2:3 [1]Lit *give back recompenses* **5:5** [a]Ac 6:1; 9:39, 41; 1Ti 5:3, 16 [b]1Co 7:34; 1Pe 3:5 [c]Lk 2:37; 1Ti 2:1; 2Ti 1:3 **5:6** [a]Jas 5:5 [b]Lk 15:24; 2Ti 3:6; Rev 3:1 **5:7** [a]1Ti 4:11 **5:8** [a]2Ti 2:12; Tit 1:16; 2Pe 2:1; Jd 4 **5:9** [a]1Ti 5:16

years old, *having been* [b]the wife of
one man, **10** having a reputation for
[a]good works; if she has brought up
children, if she has [b]shown hospital-
ity to strangers, if she [c]has washed
the [1]saints' feet, if she has [d]assisted
those in affliction, if she has devoted
herself to every good work. **11** But
refuse *to put* younger widows *on
the list*, for when they feel [a]sensual
desires in disregard of Christ, they
want to get married, **12** *thus* incurring
condemnation, because they have set
aside their previous [1]pledge. **13** And
at the same time they also learn
*to be* idle, as they go around from
house to house. And not merely idle,
but also [a]gossips and [b]busybodies,
talking about [c]things not proper
*to mention.* **14** Therefore, I want
younger *widows* to get [a]married,
bear children, [b]keep house, *and*
[c]give the enemy no opportunity for
reviling, **15** for some [a]have already
turned aside after [b]Satan. **16** If any
believing woman [a]has widows, she
must [b]assist them and the church
must not be burdened, so that it may
assist those who are [c]widows indeed.

### *Honoring the Elders*

**17** [a]The elders who [b]lead well are
to be considered worthy of double
honor, especially those who [c]labor
[1]at *preaching* the word and teach-
ing. **18** For the Scripture says, "[a]YOU
SHALL NOT MUZZLE THE OX WHILE IT
IS THRESHING," and "[b]THE LABORER IS
WORTHY OF HIS WAGES." **19** Do not re-
ceive an accusation against an [a]elder
except on the basis of [b]two or three
witnesses. **20** Those who continue in
sin, [a]reprove in the presence of all,
[b]so that the rest also will be fearful.
**21** [a]I solemnly charge you in the
presence of God and of Christ Jesus
and of *His* elect angels, to observe
these *instructions* without bias,
doing nothing in partiality. **22** [a]Do
not lay hands upon anyone hastily
and [1]thereby share [b]*responsibility
for* the sins of others; keep yourself
pure.

**23** No longer drink water *only*, but
[a]use a little wine for the sake of your
stomach and your frequent ailments.

**24** The sins of some men are
quite evident, going before them
to judgment; for others, their *sins*
[a]follow after. **25** So also good works
are quite evident, and [a]those which
are otherwise cannot be concealed.

### *Instructions to Those Who Serve*

**6** [a]All who are under the yoke as
slaves are to regard their own
masters as worthy of all honor
so [b]that the name of God and *our*
doctrine will not be [1]slandered. **2** But
those who have believers as their
masters must not be disrespectful
to them because they are [a]brothers,
but must serve them all the more,
because those who [1]partake of the
benefit are believers and beloved.
[b]Teach and exhort these *things*.

---

**5:9** [b]1Ti 3:2 **5:10** [a]Ac 9:36; 1Ti 6:18; Tit 2:7; 3:8; 1Pe 2:12 [b]1Ti 3:2 [c]Lk 7:44; Jn 13:14 [d]1Ti 5:16 [1]Or *holy ones'* **5:11** [a]Rev 18:7 **5:12** [1]Lit *faith* **5:13** [a]3Jn 10 [b]2Th 3:11 [c]Tit 1:11 **5:14** [a]1Co 7:9; 1Ti 4:3 [b]Tit 2:5 [c]1Ti 6:1 **5:15** [a]1Ti 1:20 [b]Mt 4:10 **5:16** [a]1Ti 5:4 [b]1Ti 5:10 [c]1Ti 5:3 **5:17** [a]Ac 11:30; 1Ti 4:14; 5:19 [b]Ro 12:8 [c]1Th 5:12 [1]Lit *in word* **5:18** [a]Dt 25:4; 1Co 9:9 [b]Lv 19:13; Dt 24:15; Mt 10:10; Lk 10:7; 1Co 9:14 **5:19** [a]Ac 11:30; 1Ti 4:14; 5:17 [b]Dt 17:6; 19:15; Mt 18:16 **5:20** [a]Ga 2:14; Eph 5:11; 2Ti 4:2 [b]2Co 7:11 **5:21** [a]Lk 9:26; 1Ti 6:13; 2Ti 2:14; 4:1 **5:22** [a]1Ti 3:10; 4:14 [b]Eph 5:11; 1Ti 3:2-7 [1]Lit *do not share* **5:23** [a]1Ti 3:8 **5:24** [a]Rev 14:13 **5:25** [a]Pr 10:9 ◆ **6:1** [a]Eph 6:5; Tit 2:9; 1Pe 2:18 [b]Tit 2:5 [1]Or *blasphemed* **6:2** [a]Ac 1:15; Ga 3:28; Phm 16 [b]1Ti 4:11 [1]Or *devote themselves to kindness*

**3** If anyone [a]teaches a different
doctrine and does not [1]agree with
[b]sound words—those of our Lord
Jesus Christ—and with the doctrine
[c]conforming to godliness, **4** he is
[a]conceited, understanding nothing
but [1]having a morbid interest in [b]con-
troversial questions and [c]disputes
about words, out of which arise envy,
strife, slander, evil suspicions, **5** and
constant friction between [a]men of
depraved mind and deprived of the
truth, who [b]suppose that [1]godliness
is a means of gain. **6** [a]But godliness
*actually* is a means of [b]great gain,
when accompanied by [c]contentment.
**7** For [a]we have brought nothing into
the world, so we cannot take any-
thing out of it either. **8** And if we
[a]have food and covering, with these
we shall be content. **9** [a]But those who
want to get rich fall into temptation
and [b]a snare and many foolish and
harmful desires which plunge men
into ruin and destruction. **10** For [a]the
love of money is a root of all [1]sorts of
evils, and some by aspiring to it have
[b]wandered away from the faith and
pierced themselves with many griefs.

**11** But you, O [a]man of God, [b]flee
from these things, and pursue righ-
teousness, godliness, [c]faith, [d]love,
[1]perseverance, gentleness. **12** [a]Fight the
good fight of [b]faith. [c]Take hold of the
eternal life [d]to which you were called,
and you made the good [e]confession in
the presence of [f]many witnesses. **13** [a]I
charge you in the presence of God,
who [1]gives life to all things, and of
[b]Christ Jesus, who testified the [c]good
confession [d]before Pontius Pilate,
**14** that you keep the commandment
without stain or reproach until the
[a]appearing of our Lord Jesus Christ,
**15** which He will [1]bring about at [a]the
proper time—He who is [b]the blessed
and [c]only Sovereign, [d]the King of
[2]kings and [e]Lord of [3]lords, **16** [a]who
alone has immortality and [b]dwells in
unapproachable light, [c]whom no man
has seen or can see. [a]To Him *be* honor
and eternal might! Amen.

**17** Command those who are rich in
[a]this present age [b]not to be haughty
or to [c]set their hope on the uncertain-
ty of riches, but on God, [d]who richly
supplies us with all things to enjoy.
**18** *Command them* to do good, to be
rich in [a]good [1]works, [b]to be generous
and ready to share, **19** [a]storing up for
themselves the treasure of a good
foundation for the future, so that
they may [b]take hold of that which
is life indeed.

**20** O [a]Timothy, guard [b]what has
been entrusted to you, turning aside
from [c]godless *and* empty chatter *and*
the opposing arguments of what is
falsely called knowledge— **21** which
some, while professing, have [a]gone
astray [1]from [b]the faith.

[c]Grace be with [2]you.

---

**6:3** [a]1Ti 1:3 [b]1Ti 1:10 [c]Tit 1:1 [1]Or *come with;* lit *come to* **6:4** [a]1Ti 3:6 [b]1Ti 1:4 [c]Ac 18:15; 2Ti 2:14 [1]Lit *is sick about* **6:5** [a]2Ti 3:8; Tit 1:15 [b]Tit 1:11; 2Pe 2:3 [1]Or *religion* **6:6** [a]Lk 12:15-21; 1Ti 6:6-10 [b]1Ti 4:8 [c]Php 4:11; Heb 13:5 **6:7** [a]Job 1:21; Ecc 5:15 **6:8** [a]Pr 30:8 **6:9** [a]Pr 15:27; 23:4; 28:20; Lk 12:21; 1Ti 6:17 [b]1Ti 3:7 **6:10** [a]Col 3:5; 1Ti 3:3; 6:9 [b]Jas 5:19 [1]Lit *the evils* **6:11** [a]2Ti 3:17 [b]2Ti 2:22 [c]1Ti 1:14 [d]2Ti 3:10 [1]Or *steadfastness* **6:12** [a]1Co 9:25f; Php 1:30; 1Ti 1:18 [b]1Ti 1:19 [c]Php 3:12; 1Ti 6:19 [d]Col 3:15 [e]2Co 9:13; 1Ti 6:13 [f]1Ti 4:14; 2Ti 2:2 **6:13** [a]1Ti 5:21 [b]Ga 3:26; 1Ti 1:12, 15; 2:5 [c]2Co 9:13; 1Ti 6:12 [d]Mt 27:2; Jn 18:37 [1]Or *preserves alive* **6:14** [a]2Th 2:8 **6:15** [a]1Ti 2:6 [b]1Ti 1:11 [c]1Ti 1:17 [d]Dt 10:17; Rev 17:14; 19:16 [e]Ps 136:3 [1]Lit *show* [2]Lit *those who reign as kings* [3]Lit *those who rule as lords* **6:16** [a]1Ti 1:17 [b]Ps 104:2; Jas 1:17; 1Jn 1:5 [c]Jn 1:18 **6:17** [a]Mt 12:32; 2Ti 4:10; Tit 2:12 [b]Ps 62:10; Lk 12:20; Ro 11:20; 1Ti 6:9 [c]1Ti 4:10 [d]Ac 14:17 **6:18** [a]1Ti 5:10 [b]Ro 12:8; Eph 4:28 [1]Or *deeds* **6:19** [a]Mt 6:20 [b]1Ti 6:12 **6:20** [a]1Ti 1:2 [b]2Ti 1:12, 14 [c]1Ti 1:9; 2Ti 2:16 **6:21** [a]2Ti 2:18 [b]1Ti 1:19 [c]Col 4:18 [1]Lit *concerning* [2]Lit *you* (plural)

*The Second Letter of Paul to*
# TIMOTHY

### *Guard the Treasure Entrusted to You*

**1** Paul, [a]an apostle of [b]Christ Jesus
[c,1]by the will of God, according to
the promise of [d]life in Christ Jesus,
**2** To [a]Timothy, my beloved [b]child:
[c]Grace, mercy, *and* peace from God
the Father and Christ Jesus our Lord.
**3** [a]I am grateful to God, whom I
[b]serve with a [c]clear conscience [1]the
way my forefathers did, [d]as I unceas-
ingly remember you in my [2]prayers
night and day, **4** [a]longing to see you,
[b]having remembered your tears, so
that I may be filled with joy, **5** [1]being
reminded of the [a]unhypocritical faith
within you, which first dwelt in your
grandmother Lois and [b]your mother
Eunice, and I am convinced that *it
is* in you as well. **6** For this reason
I remind you to kindle afresh [a]the
gift of God which is in you through
[a]the laying on of my hands. **7** For
God has not given us a [a]spirit of
[1]timidity, but of power and love and
[2]self-discipline.
**8** Therefore [a]do not be ashamed of
either the [b]witness about our Lord or
me [c]His prisoner, but join with *me* in
[d]suffering for the [e]gospel according
to the power of God, **9** who has
[a]saved us and [b]called us with a holy
[c]calling, [d]not according to our works,
but according to His own [b]purpose
and grace which was given to us
in [e]Christ Jesus from [f]all eternity,
**10** but [a]now has been manifested by
the [b]appearing of our Savior [c]Christ
Jesus, who [d]abolished death and
brought life and immortality to light
through the gospel, **11** [a]for which I
was appointed a preacher and an
apostle and a teacher. **12** For this rea-
son I also suffer these things, but [a]I
am not ashamed; for I know [b]whom
I have believed and I am convinced
that He is able to [c]guard what I have
entrusted to Him [1]until [d]that day.
**13** [a,1]Hold to the [b]standard of [c]sound
words [d]which you have heard from
me, in the [e]faith and love which are
in [f]Christ Jesus. **14** Guard, through
the Holy Spirit who [a]dwells in us, the
[b,1]treasure which has been entrusted
to *you.*
**15** You are aware of this: that all
who are in [a]Asia [b]turned away from
me, among whom are Phygelus and
Hermogenes. **16** The Lord give mercy
to [a]the house of Onesiphorus, for
he often refreshed me and [b]was not
ashamed of my [c,1]chains, **17** but when
he was in Rome, he eagerly searched
for me and found me— **18** the Lord
[1]grant to him to find mercy from the

---

◆**1:1** [a]2Co 1:1 [b]Ga 3:26 [c]1Co 1:1 [d]1Ti 6:19 [1]Lit *through* **1:2** [a]Ac 16:1; 1Ti 1:2 [b]1Ti 1:2; 2Ti 2:1; Tit 1:4 [c]Ro 1:7 **1:3** [a]Ro 1:8 [b]Ac 24:14 [c]Ac 23:1; 24:16; 1Ti 1:5 [d]Ro 1:9 [1]Lit *from my forefathers* [2]Or *petitions* **1:4** [a]2Ti 4:9, 21 [b]Ac 20:37 **1:5** [a]1Ti 1:5 [b]Ac 16:1; 2Ti 3:15 [1]Lit *receiving remembrance of* **1:6** [a]1Ti 4:14 **1:7** [a]Jn 14:27; Ro 8:15 [1]Or *cowardice* [2]Or *sound judgment* **1:8** [a]Mk 8:38; Ro 1:16; 2Ti 1:12, 16 [b]1Co 1:6 [c]Eph 3:1; 2Ti 1:16 [d]2Ti 2:3, 9; 4:5 [e]2Ti 1:10; 2:8 **1:9** [a]Ro 11:14 [b]Ro 8:28ff [c]Ro 11:29 [d]Eph 2:9 [e]2Ti 1:1 [f]Ro 16:25; Eph 1:4; Tit 1:2 **1:10** [a]Ro 16:26 [b]2Th 2:8; 2Ti 4:1, 8; Tit 2:11 [c]2Ti 1:1 [d]1Co 15:26; Heb 2:14f **1:11** [a]1Ti 2:7 **1:12** [a]2Ti 1:8, 16 [b]Tit 3:8 [c]1Ti 6:20; 2Ti 1:14 [d]1Co 1:8; 3:13; 2Ti 1:18; 4:8 [1]Or *for* **1:13** [a]2Ti 3:14; Tit 1:9 [b]Ro 2:20; 6:17 [c]1Ti 1:10 [d]2Ti 2:2 [e]1Ti 1:14 [f]2Ti 1:1 [1]Or *Hold the example* **1:14** [a]Ro 8:9 [b]1Ti 6:20; 2Ti 1:12 [1]Lit *good deposit* **1:15** [a]Ac 2:9 [b]2Ti 4:10, 11, 16 **1:16** [a]2Ti 4:19 [b]2Ti 1:8 [c]Eph 6:20 [1]Lit *chain* **1:18** [1]Or *give*, cf. 1:16

Lord on [a]that day—and you know
very well what services he rendered
at [b]Ephesus.

### *Remember Jesus Christ*

**2** You therefore, my [a]child, [b]be
strong in the grace that is in
[c]Christ Jesus. **2** And the things
[a]which you have heard from me in
the presence of [b]many witnesses,
[c]entrust these to [d]faithful men who
will be [e]able to teach others also.
**3** [a]Suffer hardship with *me*, as a good
[b]soldier of [c]Christ Jesus. **4** No soldier
in active service [a]entangles himself
in the affairs of everyday life, so that
he may please the one who enlisted
him as a soldier. **5** And also if anyone
[a]competes as an athlete, he is not
crowned unless he competes accord-
ing to the rules. **6** [a]The hard-working
farmer ought to be the first to receive
his share of the crops. **7** Understand
what I say, for the Lord will give you
insight in everything.

**8** Remember Jesus Christ, [a]risen
from the dead, of the [b]seed of David,
[c]according to my gospel, **9** [1]for which
I [a]endure hardship even to [b]chains
as a [c]criminal. But [d]the word of God
[e]has not been chained. **10** For this
reason [a]I endure all things for [b]the
sake of the elect, [c]so that they also
may obtain the [d]salvation, which is
in [e]Christ Jesus, with [f]eternal glory.
**11** [a]It is a trustworthy saying:

For [b]if we died with Him,
we will also live with Him;
**12** If we endure, [a]we will
also reign with Him;
If we [b]will deny Him,
He also will deny us;
**13** If we are faithless,
[a]He remains faithful, for
[b]He cannot deny Himself.

### *Accurately Handle the Word of Truth*

**14** Remind *them* of these things,
solemnly [a]charging *them* in the
presence of God not to [b]dispute
about words, which is useless *and
leads* to the ruin of the hearers.
**15** Be diligent to [a]present yourself
approved to God as a workman who
does not need to be ashamed, accu-
rately handling [b]the word of truth.
**16** But [a]avoid [b]godless *and* empty
chatter, for [1]it will lead to further
ungodliness, **17** and their word will
spread like [1]gangrene. Among them
are [a]Hymenaeus and Philetus, **18** who
have gone astray from the truth say-
ing that [a]the resurrection has already
taken place, and they upset [b]the faith
of some. **19** Nevertheless, the [a]firm
foundation of God stands, having
this [b]seal, "[c]THE [1]LORD KNOWS THOSE
WHO ARE HIS," and, "[d]EVERYONE WHO
NAMES THE NAME OF THE [2]LORD is to
[e]DEPART FROM WICKEDNESS."
**20** Now in a large house there are
not only gold and silver vessels, but

---

**1:18** [a]1Co 1:8; 3:13; 2Ti 1:12; 4:8 [b]Ac 18:19; 1Ti 1:3 ◆ **2:1** [a]2Ti 1:2 [b]Eph 6:10 [c]2Ti 1:1 **2:2** [a]2Ti 1:13 [b]1Ti 6:12 [c]1Ti 1:18 [d]1Ti 1:12 [e]2Co 2:14ff; 3:5 **2:3** [a]2Ti 1:8 [b]1Co 9:7; 1Ti 1:18 [c]2Ti 1:1 **2:4** [a]2Pe 2:20 **2:5** [a]1Co 9:25 **2:6** [a]1Co 9:10 **2:8** [a]*Ac 2:24* [b]*Mt 1:1* [c]*Ro 2:16* **2:9** [a]*2Ti 1:8; 2:3* [b]Php 1:7 [c]Lk 23:32 [d]*1Th 1:8* [e]*Ac 28:31; 2Ti 4:17* [1]Lit *in which* **2:10** [a]Col 1:24 [b]Lk 18:7; Tit 1:1 [c]2Co 1:6; 1Th 5:9 [d]1Co 1:21 [e]2Ti 1:1; 2:1, 3 [f]2Co 4:17; 1Pe 5:10 **2:11** [a]1Ti 1:15 [b]Ro 6:8; 1Th 5:10 **2:12** [a]Mt 19:28; Lk 22:29; Ro 5:17; 8:17 [b]Mt 10:33; Lk 12:9; 1Ti 5:8 **2:13** [a]Ro 3:3; 1Co 1:9 [b]Nu 23:19; Tit 1:2 **2:14** [a]1Ti 5:21; 2Ti 4:1 [b]1Ti 6:4; 2Ti 2:23; Tit 3:9 **2:15** [a]Ro 6:13; Jas 1:12 [b]Eph 1:13; Jas 1:18 **2:16** [a]Tit 3:9 [b]1Ti 1:9; 6:20 [1]Lit *they will make further progress in ungodliness* **2:17** [a]1Ti 1:20 [1]Or *cancer* **2:18** [a]1Co 15:12 [b]1Ti 1:19; Tit 1:11 **2:19** [a]Is 28:16f; 1Ti 3:15 [b]Jn 3:33 [c]Nu 16:5; Jn 10:14; 1Co 8:3 [d]Joel 2:23; Lk 13:27; 1Co 1:2 [e]Nu 16:26-27 [1]In OT, Yahweh, cf. Nu 16:5 [2]In OT, Yahweh, cf. Joel 2:23

also vessels of wood and of clay, and [a]some to honor and some to dishonor. **21** Therefore, if anyone cleanses himself from [a]these *things*, he will be a vessel for honor, sanctified, useful to the Master, having been [b]prepared for every good work. **22** Now [a]flee from youthful lusts and pursue righteousness, [b]faith, love, *and* peace, with those who [c]call on the Lord [d]from a pure heart. **23** But refuse foolish and ignorant [a]speculations, knowing that they [b]produce [1]quarrels. **24** [a]And the Lord's slave must not be quarrelsome, but be kind to all, [b]able to teach, patient when wronged, **25** [a]with gentleness correcting those who are in opposition, [b]if perhaps God may give them repentance leading to [c]the full knowledge of the truth, **26** and they may come to their senses *and escape* from [a]the snare of the devil, having been [b]held captive [1]by him to do his will.

### *Difficult Times Will Come*

**3** But know this, that [a]in the last days difficult times will come. **2** For men will be [a]lovers of self, [b]lovers of money, [c]boastful, [c]arrogant, [d]blasphemers, [c]disobedient to parents, [e]ungrateful, [f]unholy, **3** [a]unloving, irreconcilable, [b,1]malicious gossips, without self-control, without gentleness, [c]without love for good, **4** [a]treacherous, [b]reckless, [c]conceited, [d]lovers of pleasure rather than lovers of God, **5** holding to a form of [a,1]godliness, but having [b]denied its power. [c]Keep away from such men as these. **6** For among them are those who [a,1]enter into households and take captive [b,2]weak women weighed down with sins, being led on by [c]various desires, **7** always learning and never able to [a]come to the [1]full knowledge of the truth. **8** Just as [a]Jannes and Jambres [b]opposed Moses, so these *men* also oppose the truth, [c]men of depraved mind, disqualified in regard to the faith. **9** But they will not make further progress, for their [a]folly will be obvious to all, just [b]as theirs was also.

**10** But you [a]followed my teaching, conduct, purpose, faith, patience, [b]love, [1]perseverance, **11** [a]persecutions, *and* [b]sufferings, such as happened to me at [c]Antioch, at [d]Iconium, *and* at [e]Lystra. What [f]persecutions I endured, and out of them all [g]the Lord rescued me! **12** Indeed, all who desire to live godly in Christ Jesus [a]will be persecuted.

**13** But evil men and impostors [a]will proceed *from bad* to worse, [b]deceiving and being deceived.

**14** But you, [a]continue in the things you learned and became convinced of, knowing from whom you learned *them*, **15** and that [a]from childhood

---

**2:20** [a]Ro 9:21 **2:21** [a]1Ti 6:11; 2Ti 2:16-18 [b]2Co 9:8; Eph 2:10; 2Ti 3:17 **2:22** [a]1Ti 6:11 [b]1Ti 1:14 [c]Nu 16:5; Ac 7:59 [d]Joel 2:23; 1Ti 1:5 **2:23** [a]1Ti 6:4; 2Ti 2:14; Tit 3:9 [b]Tit 3:9; Jas 4:1 [1]Lit *conflicts* **2:24** [a]1Ti 3:3; Tit 1:7 [b]1Ti 3:2 **2:25** [a]Ga 6:1; Tit 3:2; 1Pe 3:15 [b]Ac 8:22 [c]1Ti 2:4 **2:26** [a]1Ti 3:7 [b]Lk 5:10 [1]Or *by him, to do His will* ◆ **3:1** [a]1Ti 4:1 **3:2** [a]Php 2:21 [b]Lk 16:14; 1Ti 3:3; 6:10 [c]Ro 1:30 [d]2Pe 2:10-12 [e]Lk 6:35 [f]1Ti 1:9 **3:3** [a]Ro 1:31 [b]1Ti 3:11 [c]Tit 1:8 [1]Or *devilish* **3:4** [a]Ac 7:52 [b]Ac 19:36 [c]1Ti 3:6 [d]Php 3:19 **3:5** [a]1Ti 4:7 [b]1Ti 5:8 [c]Mt 7:15; 2Th 3:6 [1]Or *religion* **3:6** [a]Jd 4 [b]1Ti 5:6; Tit 3:3 [c]Tit 3:3 [1]Or *creep* [2]Or *idle* **3:7** [a]2Ti 2:25 [1]Or *recognition* **3:8** [a]Ex 7:11 [b]Ac 13:8 [c]1Ti 6:5 **3:9** [a]Lk 6:11 [b]Ex 7:11, 12; 8:18; 9:11 **3:10** [a]Php 2:20, 22; 1Ti 4:6 [b]1Ti 6:11 [1]Or *steadfastness* **3:11** [a]2Co 12:10 [b]2Co 1:5, 7 [c]Ac 13:14, 45, 50 [d]Ac 14:1-7, 19 [e]Ac 14:8-20 [f]2Co 11:23-27 [g]Ro 15:31 **3:12** [a]Jn 15:20; Ac 14:22; 2Co 4:9f **3:13** [a]2Ti 2:16 [b]Tit 3:3 **3:14** [a]2Ti 1:13; Tit 1:9 **3:15** [a]2Ti 1:5

you have known [b]the sacred writings
which are able to [c]make you wise
unto [d]salvation through faith which
is in [e]Christ Jesus. **16** [a]All Scripture
is [1]God-breathed and profitable for
teaching, for reproof, for correc-
tion, for [2]training in righteousness,
**17** so that [a]the man of God may be
equipped, having been [b]thoroughly
equipped for every good work.

### *Preach the Word*

**4** [a]I solemnly charge *you* in the
presence of God and of Christ
Jesus, who is to [b]judge the living
and the dead, and by His [c]appear-
ing and His kingdom: **2** preach [a]the
word; be ready in season *and* out of
season; [b]reprove, rebuke, exhort,
with [1]great [c]patience and teaching.
**3** For [a]the time will come when they
will not endure [b]sound doctrine, but
*wanting* to have [1]their ears tickled,
they will accumulate for themselves
teachers in accordance to their own
desires, **4** and [a]will turn away their
ears from the truth and [b]will turn
aside to myths.

**5** But you, [a]be sober in all things,
[b]endure hardship, do the work of an
[c]evangelist, fulfill your [d]ministry.

**6** For I am already being [a]poured
out as a drink offering, and the time
of [b]my departure has come. **7** [a]I have
fought the good fight, I have finished
[b]the course, I have kept [c]the faith.
**8** In the future there [a]is laid up for me
[b]the crown of righteousness, which
the Lord, the righteous Judge, will
award to me on [c]that day, and not
only to me, but also to [d]all who have
loved His [e]appearing.

### *Personal Concerns*

**9** [a]Be diligent to come to me soon,
**10** for [a]Demas, having loved [b]this
present age, has deserted me and
gone to [c]Thessalonica; Crescens
*has gone* to [d,1]Galatia, [e]Titus to
Dalmatia. **11** [a]Only [b]Luke is with
me. Pick up [c]Mark and bring him
with you, [d]for he is useful to me for
service. **12** But [a]Tychicus I sent to
[b]Ephesus. **13** When you come bring
the cloak which I left at [a]Troas with
Carpus, and the scrolls, especially
the parchments. **14** [a]Alexander the
coppersmith showed me much harm;
[b]the Lord will award him according to
his deeds. **15** Be on guard against him
yourself, for he vigorously opposed
our words.

**16** At my first defense no one
supported me, but all deserted me.
[a]May it not be counted against them.
**17** But the Lord stood with me and
[a]strengthened me, so that through me
[b]the preaching might be [c]fulfilled, and
that all [d]the Gentiles might hear. And I
was [e]rescued out of [f]the lion's mouth.
**18** The Lord will rescue me from every
evil deed, and will [a]save me unto His

---

**3:15** [b]Jn 5:47; Ro 2:27 [c]Ps 119:98f [d]1Co 1:21 [e]2Ti 1:1 **3:16** [a]Ro 4:23f; 15:4; 2Pe 1:20f [1]Or *inspired by God* [2]Lit *training which is in* **3:17** [a]1Ti 6:11 [b]2Ti 2:21; Heb 13:21 ◆ **4:1** [a]1Ti 5:21; 2Ti 2:14 [b]Ac 10:42 [c]2Th 2:8; 2Ti 1:10; 4:8 **4:2** [a]Ga 6:6; Col 4:3; 1Th 1:6 [b]1Ti 5:20; Tit 1:13; 2:15 [c]2Ti 3:10 [1]Lit *all* **4:3** [a]2Ti 3:1 [b]1Ti 1:10; 2Ti 1:13 [1]Or *itching ears* **4:4** [a]2Th 2:11; Tit 1:14 [b]1Ti 1:4 **4:5** [a]1Pe 1:13 [b]2Ti 1:8 [c]*Ac 21:8* [d]*Eph 4:12; Col* 4:17 **4:6** [a]Php 2:17 [b]Php 1:23; 2Pe 1:14 **4:7** [a]1Co 9:25f; Php 1:30; 1Ti 1:18; 6:12 [b]Ac 20:24; 1Co 9:24 [c]2Ti 3:10 **4:8** [a]Col 1:5; 1Pe 1:4 [b]1Co 9:25; 2Ti 2:5; Jas 1:12 [c]2Ti 1:12 [d]Php 3:11 [e]2Ti 4:1 **4:9** [a]2Ti 1:4; 4:21; Tit 3:12 **4:10** [a]Col 4:14 [b]1Ti 6:17 [c]Ac 17:1 [d]Ac 16:6 [e]2Co 2:13; 8:23; Ga 2:3; Tit 1:4 [1]One early ms *Gaul* **4:11** [a]2Ti 1:15 [b]Col 4:14; Phm 24 [c]Ac 12:12, 25; 15:37-39; Col 4:10 [d]2Ti 2:21 **4:12** [a]Ac 20:4; Eph 6:21, 22; Col 4:7f [b]Ac 18:19 **4:13** [a]Ac 16:8 **4:14** [a]Ac 19:33; 1Ti 1:20 [b]Ps 62:12; Ro 2:6; 12:19 **4:16** [a]Ac 7:60; 1Co 13:5 **4:17** [a]1Ti 1:12; 2Ti 2:1 [b]Tit 1:3; 2Ti 4:2 [c]2Ti 4:5 [d]Ac 9:15; Php 1:12ff [e]Ro 15:31; 2Ti 3:11 [f]1Sa 17:37; Ps 22:21 **4:18** [a]1Co 1:21

[b]heavenly kingdom; [c]to [1]Him *be* the
glory forever and ever. Amen.
19 Greet Prisca and [a]Aquila, and
[b]the household of Onesiphorus.
20 [a]Erastus remained at [b]Corinth, but
[c]Trophimus I left sick at [d]Miletus.
21 [a]Be diligent to come before [b]win-
ter. Eubulus greets you, also Pudens
and Linus and Claudia and all the
brothers.
22 [a]The Lord be with your spirit.
[b]Grace be with [1]all of you.

*The Letter of Paul to*

# TITUS

### *Greetings and Grace*

1 Paul, [a]a slave of God and an [b]apos-
tle of Jesus Christ, [1]for the faith of
God's [c]elect and [d]the full knowledge
of the truth which is [e]according to
godliness, 2 in [a]the hope of eternal
life, which the God [b]who cannot lie
[c]promised [d,1]from all eternity, 3 but
[a]at the proper time manifested His
word in [b]preaching, [c]with which I
was entrusted [d]according to the
commandment of [e]God our Savior,
4 To [a]Titus, [b]my genuine child ac-
cording to our [c]common faith: [d]Grace
and peace from God the Father and
[e]Christ Jesus our Savior.

### *Qualifications of Elders*

5 For this reason I left you in [a]Crete,
that you would set in order what re-
mains and [b]appoint [c]elders in every
city as I directed you, 6 *namely*, [a]if any
man is beyond reproach, the [b]husband
of one wife, having faithful children,
*who are* not accused of [c]dissipation,
or [d]rebellious. 7 For the [a,1]overseer
must be beyond reproach as [b]God's
steward, not [c]self-willed, not quick-
tempered, not [d]addicted to wine, not
pugnacious, [e]not fond of dishonest
gain, 8 but [a]hospitable, [b]loving what
is good, sensible, righteous, holy, self-
controlled, 9 [a]holding fast the faithful
word which is in accordance with the
teaching, so that he will be able both
to exhort in [b]sound doctrine and to
reprove those who contradict.
10 [a]For there are many [b]rebellious
men, [c]empty talkers and deceivers,
especially [d]those of the circumcision,
11 who must be silenced because they
are upsetting [a]whole families, teach-
ing [b]things they should not *teach* [c]for
the sake of dishonest gain. 12 One of
themselves, a prophet of their own,
said, "[a]Cretans are always liars, evil
beasts, lazy gluttons." 13 This testi-
mony is true. For this reason [a]reprove

---

**4:18** [b]1Co 15:50; 2Ti 4:1; Heb 11:16; 12:22 [c]Ro 11:36; 2Pe 3:18 [1]Lit *Whom* **4:19** [a]Ac 18:2 [b]2Ti 1:16 **4:20** [a]Ac 19:22; Ro 16:23 [b]Ac 18:1 [c]Ac 20:4; 21:29 [d]Ac 20:15 **4:21** [a]2Ti 4:9 [b]Tit 3:12 **4:22** [a]Ga 6:18; Php 4:23; Phm 25 [b]Col 4:18 [1]Or *you* (plural) ◆ **1:1** [a]Ro 1:1; Jas 1:1; Rev 1:1 [b]2Co 1:1 [c]Lk 18:7 [d]1Ti 2:4 [e]1Ti 6:3 [1]Or *according to* **1:2** [a]2Ti 1:1; Tit 3:7 [b]2Ti 2:13; Heb 6:18 [c]Ro 1:2 [d]2Ti 1:9 [1]Lit *before times eternal* **1:3** [a]1Ti 2:6 [b]Ro 16:25; 2Ti 4:17 [c]1Ti 1:11 [d]1Ti 1:1 [e]Lk 1:47; 1Ti 1:1; Tit 2:10; 3:4 **1:4** [a]2Co 2:13; 8:23; Ga 2:3; 2Ti 4:10 [b]2Ti 1:2 [c]2Pe 1:1 [d]Ro 1:7 [e]1Ti 1:12; 2Ti 1:1 **1:5** [a]Ac 27:7; Tit 1:12 [b]Ac 14:23 [c]Ac 11:30 **1:6** [a]1Ti 3:2-4; Tit 1:6-8 [b]1Ti 3:2 [c]Eph 5:18 [d]Tit 1:10 **1:7** [a]1Ti 3:2 [b]1Co 4:1 [c]2Pe 2:10 [d]1Ti 3:3 [e]1Ti 3:3, 8 [1]Or *bishop* **1:8** [a]1Ti 3:2 [b]2Ti 3:3 **1:9** [a]2Th 2:15; 1Ti 1:19; 2Ti 1:13 [b]1Ti 1:10; Tit 2:1 **1:10** [a]2Co 11:13 [b]Tit 1:6 [c]1Ti 1:6 [d]Ac 11:2 **1:11** [a]1Ti 5:4; 2Ti 3:6 [b]1Ti 5:13 [c]1Ti 6:5 **1:12** [a]Ac 2:11; 27:7 **1:13** [a]1Ti 5:20; 2Ti 4:2; Tit 2:15

them [b]severely so that they may be
[c]sound in the faith, **14** not paying
attention to Jewish [a]myths and
[b]commandments of men who [c]turn
away from the truth. **15** [a]To the pure,
all things are pure, but [b]to those who
are defiled and unbelieving, nothing
is pure, but both their [c]mind and their
conscience are defiled. **16** [a]They pro-
fess to know God, but by *their* works
they [b]deny *Him*, being [c]detestable
and [d]disobedient and [e]unfit [f]for any
good work.

### *Instructions for the Older and Younger*

**2** But as for you, speak the things
which are proper for [a]sound doc-
trine. **2** [a]Older men are to be [b]temper-
ate, dignified, sensible, [c]sound [d]in
faith, in love, in [1]perseverance.
**3** Older women likewise are to
be reverent in their behavior, [a]not
malicious gossips nor [b]enslaved to
much wine, teaching what is good,
**4** so that they may instruct the young
women in sensibility: to love their
husbands, to love their children,
**5** *to be* sensible, pure, [a]workers at
home, kind, being [b]subject to their
own husbands, [c]so that the word of
God will not be slandered.
**6** Likewise urge [a]the younger men to
be [1]sensible; **7** in all things show your-
self to be [a]a model of good works, *with*
[1]purity in doctrine, dignified, **8** sound *in*
word which is irreproachable, so [a]that
the opponent will be put to shame,
having nothing bad to say about us.
**9** *Urge* [a]slaves to be subject to
their own masters in everything,
to be pleasing, not contradicting,
**10** not pilfering, but demonstrating
all good faith so that they will adorn
the doctrine of [a]God our Savior in
everything.
**11** For the grace of God has [a]ap-
peared, [b,1]bringing salvation to all
men, **12** [1]instructing us that, denying
ungodliness and [a]worldly desires, we
should [b]live sensibly, righteously, and
godly [c]in the present age, **13** looking
for the blessed hope and the [a]appear-
ing of the glory of [b,1]our great God
and Savior, Jesus Christ, **14** who [a]gave
Himself for us [b]that He might redeem
us from all lawlessness, and [c]purify
for Himself a [d]people for His own
possession, [e]zealous for good works.
**15** These things speak and [a]exhort
and [a]reprove with all [1]authority. [b]Let
no one disregard you.

### *Be Ready for Every Good Work*

**3** [a]Remind them [b]to be subject to
rulers, to authorities, to be obedi-
ent, to be [c]ready for every good work,
**2** to slander no one, [a]to be peaceable,
[a]considerate, [b]demonstrating all gen-
tleness to all men. **3** [a]For we ourselves
also once were foolish, [b]disobedient,
[c]deceived, [d]enslaved to [e]various lusts

**1:13** [b]2Co 13:10 [c]Tit 2:2 **1:14** [a]1Ti 1:4 [b]Col 2:22 [c]2Ti 4:4 **1:15** [a]Lk 11:41; Ro 14:20 [b]Ro 14:14, 23 [c]1Ti 6:5 **1:16** [a]1Jn 2:4 [b]1Ti 5:8 [c]Rev 21:8 [d]Tit 3:3 [e]2Ti 3:8 [f]2Ti 3:17; Tit 3:1 ◆ **2:1** [a]Tit 1:9 **2:2** [a]Phm 9 [b]1Ti 3:2 [c]Tit 1:13 [d]1Ti 1:2, 14 [1]Or *steadfastness* **2:3** [a]1Ti 3:11 [b]1Ti 3:8 **2:5** [a]1Ti 5:14 [b]Eph 5:22 [c]1Ti 6:1 **2:6** [a]1Ti 5:1 [1]Or *sensible in all things; show* **2:7** [a]1Ti 4:12 [1]Or *soundness;* lit *incorruptness* **2:8** [a]2Th 3:14; 1Pe 2:12 **2:9** [a]Eph 6:5; 1Ti 6:1 **2:10** [a]Tit 1:3 **2:11** [a]2Ti 1:10; Tit 3:4 [b]1Ti 2:4 [1]Or *to all men, bringing* **2:12** [a]1Ti 6:9; Tit 3:3 [b]2Ti 3:12 [c]1Ti 6:17 [1]Or *disciplining* **2:13** [a]2Th 2:8 [b]1Ti 1:1; 2Ti 1:2; Tit 1:4; 2Pe 1:1 [1]Or *the great God and our Savior* **2:14** [a]1Ti 2:6 [b]Ps 130:8; 1Pe 1:18f [c]Eze 37:23; Heb 1:3; 9:14; 1Jn 1:7 [d]Ex 19:5; Dt 4:20; 7:6; 14:2; Eph 1:11; 1Pe 2:9 [e]Eph 2:10; Tit 3:8; 1Pe 3:13 **2:15** [a]1Ti 4:13; 5:20; 2Ti 4:2 [b]1Ti 4:12 [1]Lit *command* ◆ **3:1** [a]2Ti 2:14 [b]Ro 13:1 [c]2Ti 2:21 **3:2** [a]1Ti 3:3; 1Pe 2:18 [b]2Ti 2:25 **3:3** [a]Ro 11:30; Col 3:7 [b]Tit 1:16 [c]2Ti 3:13 [d]Ro 6:6, 12 [e]2Ti 3:6; Tit 2:12

and pleasures, spending our life in
[f]malice and [f]envy, despicable, hating
one another. **4** But when the [a]kindness
and affection of [b]God our Savior [c]ap-
peared, **5** [a]He saved us, [b]not by works
which we did in righteousness, but
[c]according to His mercy, through the
[d]washing of regeneration and [e]renew-
ing by the Holy Spirit, **6** [a]whom He
poured out upon us [b]richly through
Jesus Christ our Savior, **7** so that having
been justified by His grace, we would
become [a]heirs [1]according to *the* hope
of eternal life. **8** [a]This is a trustworthy
saying. And concerning these things
I [b]want you to speak confidently, so
that those who have [c]believed God
will be intent to [d]lead in good works.
These things are good and profit-
able for men. **9** But [a]avoid [b]foolish
controversies and [c]genealogies and
strife and [d]conflicts about the Law,
for they are [e]unprofitable and worth-
less. **10** [a]Reject a [b]factious man [c]after a
first and second warning, **11** knowing
that such a man is [a]perverted and is
sinning, being self-condemned.

### *Personal Instructions and Greetings*

**12** When I send Artemas or [a]Tychi-
cus to you, [b]be diligent to come to
me at Nicopolis, for I have decided
to [c]spend the winter there. **13** Dili-
gently help send Zenas the [a]lawyer
and [b]Apollos on their way so that
nothing is lacking for them. **14** [a]And
our people must also learn to [b]lead in
good [1]works to meet [c]pressing needs,
so that they will not be [d]unfruitful.

**15** [a]All who are with me greet you.
Greet those who love us [b]in *the* faith.
[c]Grace be with you all.

*The Letter of Paul to*

# PHILEMON

### *Philemon's Love and Faith*

**1** [a]Paul, [b]a prisoner of [c]Christ Jesus,
and [d]Timothy [1]our brother,
To Philemon our beloved *brother*
and [e]fellow worker, **2** and to Apphia
[a,1]our sister, and to [b]Archippus our
[c]fellow soldier, and to [d]the church
in your house: **3** [a]Grace to you and
peace from God our Father and the
Lord Jesus Christ.

**4** [a]I thank my God, always mak-
ing mention of you in my prayers,
**5** because I [a]hear of your love and of
the faith which you have toward the
Lord Jesus and toward all the [1]saints;
**6** *and I pray* that the fellowship of
your faith may become effective
[1]through the [a]full knowledge of ev-
ery good thing which is in you [2]for
the sake of Christ. **7** For I have come

**3:3** [f]Ro 1:29 **3:4** [a]Ro 2:4; Eph 2:7; 1Pe 2:3 [b]Tit 2:10 [c]Tit 2:11 **3:5** [a]Ro 11:14; 2Ti 1:9 [b]Eph 2:9 [c]Eph 2:4; 1Pe 1:3 [d]Jn 3:5; Eph 5:26; 1Pe 3:21 [e]Ro 12:2 **3:6** [a]Ro 5:5 [b]Ro 2:4; 1Ti 6:17 **3:7** [a]Mt 25:34; Mk 10:17; Ro 8:17, 24; Tit 1:2 [1]Or *of eternal life according to hope* **3:8** [a]1Ti 1:15 [b]1Ti 2:8 [c]2Ti 1:12 [d]Tit 2:7, 14; 3:14 **3:9** [a]2Ti 2:16 [b]1Ti 1:4; 2Ti 2:23 [c]1Ti 1:4 [d]Jas 4:1 [e]2Ti 2:14 **3:10** [a]2Jn 10 [b]Ro 16:17 [c]Mt 18:15f **3:11** [a]Tit 1:14 **3:12** [a]Ac 20:4; Eph 6:21f; Col 4:7f; 2Ti 4:12 [b]2Ti 4:9 [c]2Ti 4:21 **3:13** [a]Mt 22:35 [b]Ac 18:24; 1Co 16:12 **3:14** [a]Tit 2:8 [b]Tit 3:8 [c]Ro 12:13; Php 4:16 [d]Mt 7:19; Php 1:11; Col 1:10 [1]Or *occupations* **3:15** [a]Ac 20:34 [b]1Ti 1:2 [c]Col 4:18 ◆ **1** [a]Php 1:1 [b]Eph 3:1 [c]Ga 3:26 [d]2Co 1:1; Col 1:1 [e]Php 2:25; Phm 24 [1]Lit *the* **2** [a]Ro 16:1 [b]Col 4:17 [c]Php 2:25; 2Ti 2:3 [d]Ro 16:5 [1]Lit *the* **3** [a]Ro 1:7 **4** [a]Ro 1:8f **5** [a]Eph 1:15; Col 1:4; 1Th 3:6 [1]Or *holy ones* **6** [a]Php 1:9; Col 1:9; 3:10 [1]Or *in* [2]Lit *toward Christ*

to have much [a]joy and comfort in
your love, because the [1]hearts of the
[2]saints have been [b]refreshed through
you, brother.
**8** Therefore, [a]though I have much
boldness in Christ to command you *to*
*do* what is [b]proper, **9** yet for love's sake
I rather [a]plead with *you*—since I am
such a person as Paul, [1]the [b]aged, and
now also [c]a prisoner of [d]Christ Jesus—

### *Plea for Onesimus*

**10** I [a]plead with you for my [b]child
[c,1]Onesimus, of whom I became a
[2]father in my chains, **11** who formerly
was useless to you, but now is useful
both to you and to me. **12** I have sent
him back to you in person, that is,
my very heart, **13** whom I intended
to keep with me, so that on your
behalf he might minister to me in
my [a]chains for the gospel, **14** but
without your consent I did not want
to do anything, so that your goodness
would [a]not be, in effect, by compul-
sion but voluntary. **15** For perhaps
[a]he was for this reason separated
*from you* for a while, that you would
have him back forever, **16** [a]no longer
as a slave, but more than a slave, [b]a
beloved brother, especially to me, but
how much more to you, both [c]in the
flesh and in the Lord.
**17** If then you regard me a [a]partner,
accept him as *you would accept* me.
**18** But if he has wronged you in any
way or owes you anything, charge
that to my account. **19** [a]I, Paul, am
writing this with my own hand, I will
repay it ([b]not to [1]mention to you that
you owe to me even your own self as
well). **20** Yes, brother, let me benefit
from you in the Lord. [a]Refresh my
heart in Christ!
**21** [a]Having confidence in your obe-
dience, I write to you, since I know
that you will do even more than what
I say.
**22** And at the same time also
prepare me a [a]lodging, for [b]I hope
that through [c]your prayers [d]I will be
graciously given to you.
**23** [a]Epaphras, my [b]fellow prisoner
in Christ Jesus, greets you, **24** *as do*
[a]Mark, [b]Aristarchus, [c]Demas, [c]Luke,
my [d]fellow workers.
**25** [a]The grace of the Lord Jesus
Christ be [b]with your spirit.[1]

---

**7** [a]2Co 7:4, 13 [b]1Co 16:18; Phm 20 [1]Lit *inward parts* [2]Or *holy ones* **8** [a]2Co 3:12; 1Th 2:6 [b]Eph 5:4
**9** [a]Ro 12:1 [b]Tit 2:2 [c]Phm 1 [d]Ga 3:26; 1Ti 1:12; Phm 23 [1]Or *an ambassador* **10** [a]Ro 12:1 [b]1Co 4:14f
[c]Col 4:9 [1]Useful [2]Or *begotten* **13** [a]Php 1:7; Phm 10 **14** [a]2Co 9:7; 1Pe 5:2 **15** [a]Ge 45:5, 8
**16** [a]1Co 7:22 [b]Mt 23:8; 1Ti 6:2 [c]Eph 6:5; Col 3:22 **17** [a]2Co 8:23 **19** [a]1Co 16:21; 2Co 10:1; Ga 5:2
[b]2Co 9:4 [1]Lit *say* **20** [a]Phm 7 **21** [a]2Co 2:3 **22** [a]Ac 28:23 [b]Php 1:25; 2:24 [c]2Co 1:11 [d]Ac 27:24;
Heb 13:19 **23** [a]Col 1:7; 4:12 [b]Ro 16:7; Phm 1 **24** [a]Ac 12:12, 25; 15:37-39; Col 4:10 [b]Ac 19:29; 27:2; Col 4:10
[c]Col 4:14; 2Ti 4:10f [d]Phm 1 **25** [a]Ga 6:18 [b]2Ti 4:22 [1]One early ms adds *Amen*

*The Letter to the*

# HEBREWS

### *God's Final Word in His Son*

**1** God, having [a]spoken long ago to
the fathers in [b]the prophets in
many portions and [c]in many ways,
**2** [a,1]in these last days [b]spoke to us [2]in
[c]*His* Son, whom He appointed [d]heir
of all things, [e]through whom also
He made the [f,3]worlds, **3** who is the
radiance of His glory and the exact
[a]representation of His nature, and
[b,1]upholds all things by the word of
His power; who, having accomplished
[c]cleansing for sins, [d]sat down at the
right hand of the [e]Majesty on high,
**4** having become so much better
than the angels, as He has inherited
a more excellent [a]name than they.
**5** For to which of the angels did He
ever say,

"[a]You are My Son,
Today I have begotten You"?

And again,

"[b]I will be a Father to Him
And He shall be a Son to Me"?

**6** And [1]when He again [a]brings the
firstborn into [b,2]the world, He says,

"[c]And let all the angels
of God worship Him."

**7** And of the angels He says,

"[a]Who makes His
angels winds,
And His ministers
flaming fire."

**8** But of the Son *He says,*

"[a]Your throne, O God,
is forever and ever,
And the scepter of
uprightness is the scepter
of [1]Your kingdom.

**9** "[a]You have loved
righteousness and
hated lawlessness;
[b]Therefore God, Your God,
has [c]anointed You
With the oil of gladness
above Your companions."

**10** And,

"[a]You, Lord, in the beginning
founded the earth,
And the heavens are
the works of Your hands;

**11** [a]They will perish,
but You remain;
[b]And they all will wear
out like a garment,

**12** [a]And like a mantle You
will roll them up;
Like a garment they will
also be changed.
But You are [b]the same,
And Your years will not
come to an end."

**13** But to which of the angels has He
ever said,

"[a]Sit at My right hand,
[b]Until I put Your enemies
As a footstool
for Your feet"?

---

◆**1:1** [a]Jn 9:29; 16:13; Heb 2:2f; 3:5; 4:8; 5:5; 11:18; 12:25 [b]Ac 2:30; 3:21 [c]Nu 12:6, 8; Joel 2:28
**1:2** [a]Mt 13:39; 1Pe 1:20 [b]Jn 9:29 [c]Jn 5:26, 27; Heb 3:6; 5:8; 7:28 [d]Ps 2:8; Mt 28:18; Mk 12:7; Ro 8:17; Heb 2:8 [e]Jn 1:3; 1Co 8:6; Col 1:16 [f]1Co 2:7; Heb 11:3 [1]Or *at the end of these days* [2]Lit *in Son* [3]Lit *ages*
**1:3** [a]2Co 4:4 [b]Col 1:17 [c]Tit 2:14; Heb 9:14 [d]Mk 16:19; Heb 8:1; 10:12; 12:2 [e]2Pe 1:17 [1]Lit *upholding*
**1:4** [a]Eph 1:21 **1:5** [a]Ps 2:7; Ac 13:33; Heb 5:5 [b]2Sa 7:14 **1:6** [a]Heb 10:5 [b]Mt 24:14 [c]Ps 97:7 [1]Or *again when He brings* [2]Lit *the inhabited earth* **1:7** [a]Ps 104:4 **1:8** [a]Ps 45:6 [1]Some mss *His* **1:9** [a]Ps 45:7 [b]Jn 10:17; Php 2:9; Heb 2:9 [c]Is 61:1, 3 **1:10** [a]Ps 102:25 **1:11** [a]Ps 102:26 [b]Is 51:6; Heb 8:13
**1:12** [a]Ps 102:26, 27 [b]Heb 13:8 **1:13** [a]Ps 110:1; Mt 22:44; Heb 1:3 [b]Jos 10:24; Heb 10:13

**14** Are they not all [a]ministering spirits, sent to render service for the sake of those who will [b]inherit [c]salvation?

### *Warning Against Neglecting Salvation*

**2** For this reason we must pay much
closer attention to [1]what we have
heard, lest [a]we drift away. **2** For if
the word [a]spoken through [b]angels
proved [1]unalterable, and [c]every
trespass and disobedience received a
just [d,2]penalty, **3** [a]how will we escape
if we neglect so great a [b]salvation?
That *salvation*, first [c]spoken by the
Lord, was [d]confirmed to us by those
who heard, **4** God also testifying with
them, both by [a]signs and wonders
and by [b]various [1]miracles and by
[c,2]gifts of the Holy Spirit [d]according
to His own will.

### *Jesus, the Author of Salvation*

**5** For He did not subject to angels
[a,1]the world to come, concerning
which we are speaking. **6** But one has
testified [a]somewhere, saying,

"[b]What is man, that You
remember him?
Or the son of man, that You
are concerned about him?
7 "[a]You have made [1]him
for a little while lower
than the angels;
You have crowned him
with glory and honor,
[2]And have appointed
him over the works
of Your hands;
8 [a]You have put all things in
subjection under his feet."

For in subjecting all things to him,
He left nothing that is not subject to
him. But now [b]we do not yet see all
things subjected to him. **9** But we do
see Him who was [a]made [1]for a little
while lower than the angels—Jesus,
[b]because of the suffering of death
[c]crowned with glory and honor, so
that [d]by the grace of God He might
[e]taste death [f]for everyone.

**10** For [a]it was fitting for Him, [b]for
whom are all things, and through
whom are all things, in bringing many
sons to glory, to [c]perfect the [d,1]author
of their salvation through sufferings.
**11** For both He who [a]sanctifies and
those who [b]are being sanctified are
all [c]of One; for which reason He is
not ashamed to call them [d]brothers,
**12** saying,

"[a]I will recount Your
name to My brothers,
In the midst of the assembly
I will sing Your praise."

**13** And again,

"[a]I will put My trust in Him."

And again,

"[b]Behold, I and the children
whom God has given Me."

**14** Therefore, since the children
share in [a,1]flesh and blood, [b]He

---

**1:14** [a]Ps 103:20f; Da 7:10 [b]Mt 25:34; Mk 10:17; Tit 3:7; Heb 6:12 [c]Ro 11:14; 1Co 1:21; Heb 2:3; 5:9; 9:28
◆ **2:1** [a]Pr 3:21 [1]Lit *the things that have been heard* **2:2** [a]Heb 1:1 [b]Ac 7:53 [c]Heb 10:28 [d]Heb 10:35; 11:26 [1]Or *steadfast* [2]Or *recompense* **2:3** [a]Heb 10:29; 12:25 [b]Ro 11:14; 1Co 1:21; Heb 1:14; 5:9; 9:28 [c]Heb 1:1 [d]Mk 16:20; Lk 1:2; 1Jn 1:1 **2:4** [a]Jn 4:48 [b]Mk 6:14 [c]1Co 12:4, 11; Eph 4:7 [d]Eph 1:5 [1]Or *works of power* [2]Lit *distributions* **2:5** [a]Mt 24:14; Heb 6:5 [1]Lit *the inhabited earth* **2:6** [a]Heb 4:4 [b]Ps 8:4 **2:7** [a]Ps 8:5, 6 [1]Or *...him a little lower than...* [2]Two early mss omit *And...hands* **2:8** [a]Ps 8:6; 1Co 15:27 [b]1Co 15:25 **2:9** [a]Heb 2:7 [b]Ac 2:33; 3:13; 1Pe 1:21 [c]Php 2:9; Heb 1:9 [d]Jn 3:16 [e]Mt 16:28; Jn 8:52 [f]Heb 7:25 [1]Or *a little lower* **2:10** [a]Lk 24:26 [b]Ro 11:36 [c]Heb 5:9; 7:28 [d]Ac 3:15; 5:31 [1]Or *leader* **2:11** [a]Heb 13:12 [b]Heb 10:10 [c]Ac 17:28 [d]Mt 25:40; Mk 3:34f; Jn 20:17 **2:12** [a]Ps 22:22 **2:13** [a]Is 8:17 [b]Is 8:18 **2:14** [a]Mt 16:17 [b]Jn 1:14 [1]Lit *blood and flesh*

Himself likewise also partook of
the same, that [c]through death He
might render powerless [d]him who
had the [2]power of death, that is, the
devil, **15** and might free those who
through [a]fear of death were sub-
ject to slavery all their lives. **16** For
assuredly He does not [1]give help to
angels, but He gives help to the seed
of Abraham. **17** Therefore, He [1]had
[a]to be made like His brothers in all
things, so that He might [b]become a
merciful and faithful [c]high priest in
[d]things pertaining to God, to [e]make
propitiation for the sins of the people.
**18** For since He Himself was [a]tempted
in that which He has suffered, He is
able to come to help those who are
tempted.

### *Jesus Greater than Moses*

**3** Therefore, [a]holy brothers, partak-
ers of a [b]heavenly calling, consid-
er [c]the Apostle and [d]High Priest of
our [e]confession—Jesus, **2** who was
faithful to Him who appointed Him,
as [a]Moses also was in all His house.
**3** [a]For He has been counted worthy
of more glory than Moses, in so much
as the builder of the house has more
honor than the house. **4** For every
house is built by someone, but the
builder of all things is God. **5** Now
[a]MOSES WAS FAITHFUL IN ALL HIS
HOUSE AS [b]A SERVANT, [c]for a testimony
of those things [d]which were to be
spoken later, **6** but Christ *was faithful*
as [a]a Son over His house—[b]whose
house we are, [c]if we hold fast our
[d]confidence and the boast of our
[e]hope.

**7** Therefore, just as [a]the Holy Spirit
says,

"[b]TODAY IF YOU HEAR HIS VOICE,
**8** [a]DO NOT HARDEN YOUR
HEARTS AS [1]WHEN THEY
PROVOKED ME,
AS IN THE DAY OF TRIAL
IN THE WILDERNESS,
**9** [a]WHERE YOUR FATHERS TRIED
*ME* BY TESTING *ME*,
AND SAW MY WORKS
FOR [b]FORTY YEARS.
**10** "[a]THEREFORE I WAS ANGRY
WITH THIS GENERATION,
AND SAID, 'THEY ALWAYS GO
ASTRAY IN THEIR HEART,
AND THEY DID NOT
KNOW MY WAYS';
**11** [a]AS I SWORE IN MY WRATH,
'THEY SHALL NOT ENTER
MY REST.'"

### *Warning Against Unbelief*

**12** [a]See *to it* brothers, that there not
be in any one of you an evil, unbe-
lieving heart [1]that falls away from
[b]the living God. **13** But [a]encourage
one another day after day, as long
as it is *still* called "TODAY," so that
none of you will be hardened by the
[b]deceitfulness of sin. **14** For we have

**2:14** [c]1Co 15:54-57; 2Ti 1:10 [d]Jn 12:31; 1Jn 3:8 [2]Lit *might* **2:15** [a]Ro 8:15 **2:16** [1]Lit *take hold of angels, but He takes hold of* **2:17** [a]Php 2:7; Heb 2:14 [b]Heb 4:15f; 5:2 [c]Heb 3:1; 4:14f; 5:5, 10; 6:20; 7:26, 28; 8:1, 3; 9:11; 10:21 [d]Ro 15:17; Heb 5:1 [e]Da 9:24; 1Jn 2:2; 4:10 [1]Lit *was obligated to be* **2:18** [a]Heb 4:15
◆ **3:1** [a]Ac 1:15; Heb 2:11; 3:12; 10:19; 13:22 [b]Php 3:14 [c]Jn 17:3 [d]Heb 2:17; 4:14f; 5:5, 10; 6:20; 7:26, 28; 8:1, 3; 9:11; 10:21 [e]2Co 9:13; Heb 4:14; 10:23 **3:2** [a]Ex 40:16; Nu 12:7; Heb 3:5 **3:3** [a]2Co 3:7-11 **3:5** [a]Ex 40:16; Nu 12:7; Heb 3:2 [b]Ex 14:31; Nu 12:7 [c]Dt 18:18f [d]Heb 1:1 **3:6** [a]Heb 1:2 [b]1Co 3:16; 1Ti 3:15 [c]Ro 11:22; Heb 3:14; 4:14 [d]Eph 3:12; Heb 4:16; 10:19, 35 [e]Heb 6:11; 7:19; 10:23; 11:1; 1Pe 1:3 **3:7** [a]Ac 28:25; Heb 9:8; 10:15 [b]Ps 95:7; Heb 3:15; 4:7 **3:8** [a]Ps 95:8 [1]Lit *in the provocation* **3:9** [a]Ps 95:9-11 [b]Ac 7:36 **3:10** [a]Ps 95:10 **3:11** [a]Ps 95:11; Heb 4:3, 5 **3:12** [a]Col 2:8; Heb 12:25 [b]Mt 16:16; Heb 9:14; 10:31; 12:22 [1]Lit *in falling* **3:13** [a]Heb 10:24f [b]Eph 4:22

become partakers of Christ, [a]if we
hold fast the beginning of our [b]as-
surance firm until the end, **15** while
it is said,

> "[a]TODAY IF YOU HEAR HIS VOICE,
> DO NOT HARDEN YOUR
> HEARTS, AS [1]WHEN THEY
> PROVOKED ME."

**16** For who [a]provoked *Him* when they
had heard? Indeed, [b]did not all those
who came out of Egypt *led* by Moses?
**17** And with whom was He angry for
forty years? Was it not with those
who sinned, [a]whose corpses fell in
the wilderness? **18** And to whom
did He swear [a]that they would not
enter His rest, but to those who were
[b]disobedient? **19** *So* we see that they
were not able to enter because of
[a]unbelief.

### *The Believer's Rest*

**4** Therefore, let us fear, lest, while a
promise remains of entering His
rest, any one of you may seem to have
[a]fallen short of it. **2** For indeed we
have had good news proclaimed to
us, just as they also; but [a]the word
[1]that was heard did not profit those
[2]who were not united with faith
among those who heard. **3** For we
who have believed enter that rest,
just as He has said,

> "[a]AS I SWORE IN MY WRATH,
> THEY SHALL NOT
> ENTER MY REST,"

although His works were finished
[b]from the foundation of the world.
**4** For He has spoken [a]somewhere in
this way concerning the seventh *day*:
"[b]AND GOD [c]RESTED ON THE SEVENTH
DAY FROM ALL HIS WORKS"; **5** and again
in this *passage*, "[a]THEY SHALL NOT
ENTER MY REST." **6** Therefore, since
it remains for some to enter it, and
those who formerly had good news
proclaimed to them failed to enter
because of [a]disobedience, **7** He again
determines a certain day, "TODAY,"
saying [1]through David after so long
a time just [a]as has been said before,

> "[b]TODAY IF YOU HEAR
> HIS VOICE,
> DO NOT HARDEN
> YOUR HEARTS."

**8** For [a]if [1]Joshua had given them rest,
He would not have spoken of another
day after that. **9** So there remains a
Sabbath rest for the people of God.
**10** For the one who has entered His
rest has himself also [a]rested from
his works, as [b]God did from His.
**11** Therefore let us be diligent to
enter that rest, lest anyone fall into
the same [a]example of [b]disobedience.
**12** For [a]the word of God is [b]living and
[c]active and sharper than any two-
edged [d]sword, and piercing as far as
the division of [e]soul and [e]spirit, of
both joints and marrow, and [f]able to
judge the thoughts and intentions of
the heart. **13** And [a]there is no creature
hidden from His sight, but all things
are [b,1]uncovered and laid bare to the
eyes of Him to whom we have an
account *to give*.

---

**3:14** [a]Heb 3:6 [b]Heb 11:1 **3:15** [a]Ps 95:7f; Heb 3:7; 4:7 [1]Lit *in the rebellion* **3:16** [a]Jer 32:29; 44:3, 8 [b]*Nu 14:2, 11, 30; Dt 1:35, 36, 38* **3:17** [a]Nu 14:29; 1Co 10:5 **3:18** [a]Nu 14:23; Dt 1:34f; Heb 4:2 [b]Ro 11:30-32; Heb 4:6, 11 **3:19** [a]Jn 3:18, 36; Ro 11:23; Heb 3:12 ◆ **4:1** [a]2Co 6:1; Ga 5:4; Heb 12:15 **4:2** [a]Ro 10:17; Ga 3:2; 1Th 2:13 [1]Lit *of hearing* [2]Some mss *because it was not united with faith* **4:3** [a]Ps 95:11; Heb 3:11 [b]Mt 25:34 **4:4** [a]Heb 2:6 [b]Ge 2:2 [c]Ex 20:11; 31:17 **4:5** [a]Ps 95:11; Heb 3:11 **4:6** [a]Heb 3:18; 4:11 **4:7** [a]Heb 3:7f [b]Ps 95:7f [1]Or *in* **4:8** [a]Jos 22:4 [1]Gr *Jesus* **4:10** [a]Rev 14:13 [b]Ge 2:2; Heb 4:4 **4:11** [a]2Pe 2:6 [b]Heb 3:18; 4:6 **4:12** [a]Jer 23:29; Eph 5:26; Heb 6:5; 1Pe 1:23 [b]Ac 7:38 [c]1Th 2:13 [d]Eph 6:17 [e]1Th 5:23 [f]Jn 12:48; 1Co 14:24f **4:13** [a]2Chr 16:9; Ps 33:13-15 [b]Job 26:6 [1]Lit *naked*

### *Jesus Our Great High Priest*

**14** Therefore, since we have a great
[a]high priest who has [b]passed through
the heavens, Jesus [c]the Son of God,
let us take hold of our [d]confession.
**15** For we do not have [a]a high priest
who cannot sympathize with our
weaknesses, but One who has been
[b]tempted in all things like *we are,*
*yet* [c]without sin. **16** Therefore let
us [a]draw near with [b]confidence to
the throne of grace, so that we may
receive mercy and find grace to help
in time of need.

**5** For every high priest [a]taken
from among men is appointed
on behalf of men in [b]things per-
taining to God, in order to [c]offer
both gifts and sacrifices [d]for sins,
**2** [a]being able to deal gently with
the [b]ignorant and [c]misguided,
since he himself also is [d,1]beset with
weakness; **3** and because of it, he is
obligated, [a]just as for the people,
to also offer *sacrifices* [b]for sins in
the same way for himself. **4** And [a]no
one takes this honor to himself, but
*receives it* when he is called by God,
even [b]as Aaron was.
**5** In this way also Christ [a]did not
glorify Himself to become a [b]high
priest, but He who [c]said to Him,

"[d]YOU ARE MY SON,
TODAY I HAVE
BEGOTTEN YOU";

**6** just as He says also in another
*passage,*

"[a]YOU ARE A
PRIEST FOREVER
ACCORDING TO [b]THE ORDER
OF MELCHIZEDEK."

**7** He, [1]in the days of His flesh,
[a,2]offered up both prayers and suppli-
cations with [b]loud crying and tears
to the One [c]able to save Him [3]from
death, and He [4]was heard because
of His [d]reverence. **8** Although He
was [a]a Son, He learned [b]obedience
from the things which He suffered.
**9** And having been made [a]perfect,
He became to all those who obey
Him the source of eternal salvation,
**10** being designated by God as [a]a
high priest according to [b]the order
of Melchizedek.
**11** Concerning [1]him we have much
to say, and *it is* hard to explain, since
you have become dull of hearing.
**12** For though [1]by this time you
ought to be teachers, you have need
again for someone to teach you [a]the
[b,2]elementary principles of the [c]ora-
cles of God, and you have come to
need [d]milk and not solid food. **13** For
everyone who partakes *only* of milk
is not accustomed to the word of
righteousness, for he is an [a]infant.
**14** But solid food is for [a]the [1]mature,
who because of practice have their
senses [b]trained to [c]discern both good
and evil.

**4:14** [a]Heb 2:17 [b]Eph 4:10; Heb 6:20; 8:1; 9:24 [c]Mt 4:3; Heb 1:2; 6:6; 7:3; 10:29 [d]Heb 3:1 **4:15** [a]Heb 2:17 [b]Heb 2:18 [c]2Co 5:21; Heb 7:26 **4:16** [a]Heb 7:19 [b]Heb 3:6 ◆ **5:1** [a]Ex 28:1 [b]Heb 2:17 [c]Heb 7:27; 8:3f; 9:9; 10:11 [d]1Co 15:3; Heb 7:27; 10:12 **5:2** [a]Heb 2:18; 4:15 [b]Eph 4:18; Heb 9:7 mg [c]Jas 5:19; 1Pe 2:25 [d]Heb 7:28 [1]Or *subject to weakness* **5:3** [a]Lv 9:7; 16:6; Heb 7:27; 9:7 [b]1Co 15:3; Heb 7:27; 10:12 **5:4** [a]Nu 16:40; 18:7; 2Chr 26:18 [b]Ex 28:1; 1Chr 23:13 **5:5** [a]Jn 8:54 [b]Heb 2:17; 5:10 [c]Heb 1:1, 5 [d]Ps 2:7 **5:6** [a]Ps 110:4; Heb 7:17 [b]Heb 5:10; 6:20; 7:11, 17 **5:7** [a]Mt 26:39, 42, 44; Mk 14:36, 39; Lk 22:41, 44 [b]Mt 27:46, 50; Mk 15:34, 37; Lk 23:46 [c]Mk 14:36 [d]Heb 11:7; 12:28 [1]During Christ's earthly life [2]Lit *who having offered up* [3]Or *out of* [4]Lit *having been heard* **5:8** [a]Heb 1:2 [b]Php 2:8 **5:9** [a]Heb 2:10 **5:10** [a]Heb 2:17; 5:5 [b]Heb 5:6 **5:11** [1]Lit *whom, which* **5:12** [a]Ga 4:3 [b]Heb 6:1 [c]Ac 7:38 [d]1Co 3:2; 1Pe 2:2 [1]Lit *because of the time* [2]Lit *elementary principles of the beginning* **5:13** [a]1Co 3:1; 14:20; 1Pe 2:2 **5:14** [a]1Co 2:6; Eph 4:13; Heb 6:1 [b]1Ti 4:7 [c]Ro 14:1ff [1]Or *perfect*, cf. 5:9

### *Warning Against Falling Away*

**6** Therefore [a]leaving [b]the [1]elemen-
tary teaching about the [2]Christ,
let us press on to [c,3]maturity, not
laying again a foundation of repen-
tance from [d]dead works and of faith
toward God, **2** of [a]teaching about
washings and [b]laying on of hands,
and the [c]resurrection of the dead
and [c]eternal judgment. **3** And this
we will do, [a]if God permits. **4** For in
the case of those once having been
[a]enlightened and having tasted of
[b]the heavenly gift and having be-
come [c]partakers of the Holy Spirit,
**5** and having [a]tasted the good [b]word
of God and the powers of [c]the age to
come, **6** and having fallen away, it is
[a]impossible to renew them again to
repentance, [b,1]since they again cruci-
fy to themselves the Son of God and
put Him to open shame. **7** For ground
that drinks the rain which often [1]falls
on it and brings forth vegetation use-
ful to those [a]for whose sake it is also
tilled, receives a blessing from God;
**8** but if it yields thorns and thistles,
it is unfit and [a]close [1]to being cursed,
and its end is to be burned.

### *The Inheritance of the Promises*

**9** But we are convinced about you,
[a]beloved, of things that are better and
that belong to salvation, though we are
speaking in this way. **10** For [a]God is not
unrighteous so as to forget [b]your work
and the love which you have shown
toward His name, in having [c]minis-
tered and continuing to minister to
the [1]saints. **11** And we desire that each
one of you show the same diligence
[1]so as to realize the [a]full assurance
of [b]hope until the end, **12** so that you
may not become dull, but [a]imitators
of those who through [b]faith and
patience [c]inherit the promises.

**13** For [a]when God made the promise
to Abraham, since He could swear by
no one greater, He [b]swore by Himself,
**14** saying, "[a]I WILL GREATLY BLESS YOU
AND I WILL GREATLY MULTIPLY YOU."
**15** And so, [a]having patiently waited,
he obtained the promise. **16** [a]For men
swear by [1]one greater *than themselves*,
and with them [b]an oath *given* as con-
firmation is an end of every dispute.
**17** [1]In the same way God, desiring
even more to show to [a]the heirs of
the promise [b]the unchangeableness
of His purpose, guaranteed *it* with an
oath, **18** so that by two unchangeable
things in which [a]it is impossible for
God to lie, we who have taken refuge
would have strong encouragement to
take hold of [b]the hope set before us.
**19** [1]This [a]hope we have as an anchor
of the soul, a *hope* both sure and con-
firmed and one which [b]enters [2]within
the veil, **20** [a]where a forerunner has
entered for us—Jesus, having become
a [b]high priest forever according to the
order of Melchizedek.

---

◆ **6:1** [a]Php 3:13f [b]Heb 5:12 [c]Heb 5:14 [d]Heb 9:14 [1]Lit *word of the beginning* [2]Messiah [3]Or *perfection*, cf. 5:9, 14 **6:2** [a]Jn 3:25; Ac 19:3f [b]Ac 6:6 [c]Ac 17:31f **6:3** [a]Ac 18:21 **6:4** [a]2Co 4:4, 6; Heb 10:32 [b]Jn 4:10; Eph 2:8 [c]Ga 3:2; Heb 2:4 **6:5** [a]1Pe 2:3 [b]Eph 6:17 [c]Heb 2:5 **6:6** [a]Mt 19:26; Heb 10:26f; 2Pe 2:21; 1Jn 5:16 [b]Heb 10:29 [1]Or *while* **6:7** [a]2Ti 2:6 [1]Lit *comes* **6:8** [a]Ge 3:17f; Dt 29:22ff [1]Lit *near to a curse* **6:9** [a]1Co 10:14; 2Co 7:1; 12:19; 1Pe 2:11; 2Pe 3:1; 1Jn 2:7; Jd 3 **6:10** [a]Pr 19:17; Mt 10:42; 25:40; Ac 10:4 [b]1Th 1:3 [c]Ro 15:25; Heb 10:32-34 [1]Or *holy ones* **6:11** [a]Heb 10:22 [b]Heb 3:6 [1]Lit *to the full* **6:12** [a]Heb 13:7 [b]2Th 1:4; Jas 1:3; Rev 13:10 [c]Heb 1:14 **6:13** [a]Ga 3:15, 18 [b]Ge 22:16; Lk 1:73 **6:14** [a]Ge 22:17 **6:15** [a]Ge 12:4; 21:5 **6:16** [a]Ga 3:15 [b]Ex 22:11 [1]Or *Him who is greater* **6:17** [a]Heb 11:9 [b]Ps 110:4; Pr 19:21; Heb 6:18 [1]Lit *In which* **6:18** [a]Nu 23:19; Tit 1:2 [b]Heb 3:6; 7:19 **6:19** [a]Ps 39:7; 62:5; Ac 23:6; Ro 4:18; 5:4, 5; 1Co 13:13; Col 1:27; 1Pe 1:3 [b]Lv 16:2, 15; Heb 9:3, 7 [1]Lit *Which* hope *we have* [2]Or *inside* **6:20** [a]Jn 14:2; Heb 4:14 [b]Ps 110:4; Heb 2:17; 5:6

### *The Priesthoods of Melchizedek and Christ*

7 For this [a]Melchizedek, king of
Salem, priest of the [b]Most High
God, who met Abraham as he was
returning from the slaughter of
the kings and blessed him, **2** [a]to
whom also Abraham apportioned
a tenth part of all, was first of all,
by the translation *of his name*, king
of righteousness, and then also king
of Salem, which is king of peace.
**3** Without father, without mother,
[a]without genealogy, having neither
beginning of days nor end of life,
but made like [b]the Son of God, he
remains a priest continually.
**4** Now observe how great this man
was to whom Abraham, the [a]patri-
arch, [b]gave a tenth of the spoils.
**5** And those indeed of [a]the sons of
Levi, who receive the priest's office,
have a commandment [1]in the Law
to collect [2]a tenth from the people,
that is, from their brothers, although
these [3]are descended from Abraham.
**6** But the one [a]whose genealogy is
not traced from them had [b]collected
[1]a tenth from Abraham and [b,2]blessed
the one who [c]had the promises. **7** But
without any dispute the lesser is
blessed by the greater. **8** And in this
case mortal men receive tithes, but
in that case one *receives them*, [a]of
whom it is witnessed that he lives on.
**9** And, so to speak, through Abraham
even Levi, who received tithes, paid
tithes, **10** for he was still in the loins
of his father when Melchizedek met
him.
**11** [a]Now if perfection was through
the Levitical priesthood (for on the
basis of it [b]the people received the
Law), what further need *was there*
for another priest to arise [c]according
to the order of Melchizedek, and not
be designated according to the order
of Aaron? **12** For when the priesthood
is changed, of necessity there takes
place a change of law also. **13** For [a]the
one concerning whom [b]these things
are spoken belongs to another tribe,
from which no one has officiated at
the altar. **14** For it is evident that our
Lord [1]was [a]descended from Judah, a
tribe with reference to which Moses
spoke nothing concerning priests.
**15** And this is clearer still, if another
priest arises according to the likeness
of Melchizedek, **16** who has become
*such* not according to a law of [a,1]phys-
ical requirement, but according to
the power of [b]an indestructible life.
**17** For it is witnessed *about Him*,

"[a]You are a priest forever
According to the order
of Melchizedek."

**18** For, on the one hand, there is a
setting aside of a former command-
ment [a]because of its weakness and
uselessness **19** (for [a]the Law made
nothing perfect), and on the other
hand there is a bringing in of a bet-
ter [b]hope, through which we [c]draw
near to God. **20** And inasmuch as *it*
*was* not without an oath **21** (for they

---

◆ **7:1** [a]Ge 14:18-20; Heb 7:6 [b]Mk 5:7 **7:2** [a]Ge 14:20 **7:3** [a]Heb 7:6 [b]Mt 4:3; Heb 7:1, 28 **7:4** [a]Ac 2:29; 7:8f [b]Ge 14:20 **7:5** [a]Nu 18:21, 26; 2Chr 31:4f [1]Lit *according to* [2]Or *tithes* [3]Lit *have come out of the loins of* **7:6** [a]Heb 7:3 [b]Heb 7:1f [c]Ro 4:13 [1]Or *tithes* [2]Lit *has blessed* **7:8** [a]Heb 5:6; 6:20 **7:11** [a]Heb 7:18f; 8:7 [b]Heb 9:6; 10:1 [c]Heb 5:6; 7:17 **7:13** [a]Heb 7:14 [b]Heb 7:11 **7:14** [a]Nu 24:17; Is 11:1; Mic 5:2; Mt 2:6; Rev 5:5 [1]Lit *has arisen from* **7:16** [a]Heb 9:10 [b]Heb 9:14 [1]To be a descendant of Levi; lit *fleshly commandment* **7:17** [a]Ps 110:4; Heb 5:6; 6:20; 7:21 **7:18** [a]Ro 8:3; Ga 3:21; Heb 7:11 **7:19** [a]Ac 13:39; Ro 3:20; 7:7f; Ga 2:16; 3:21; Heb 9:9; 10:1 [b]Heb 3:6 [c]Lam 3:57; Heb 4:16; 7:25; 10:1, 22; Jas 4:8

indeed became priests without an
oath, but He with an oath through
the One who said to Him,

"[a]THE [1]LORD HAS SWORN
AND [b]WILL NOT CHANGE
HIS MIND,
'YOU ARE A PRIEST [c]FOREVER'");

**22** so much more Jesus also has
become the [a]guarantee of [b]a better
covenant.

**23** And [1]the *former* priests, on the
one hand, existed in greater num-
bers because they were prevented
by death from continuing, **24** but
*Jesus*, on the other hand, because He
continues [a]forever, holds His priest-
hood permanently. **25** Therefore He
is able also to [a]save [1]forever those
who [b]draw near to God through
Him, since He always lives to [c]make
intercession for them.

**26** For it was fitting for us to have
such a [a]high priest, [b]holy, [c]innocent,
undefiled, separated from sinners
and [d]exalted above the heavens;
**27** who does not need daily, like those
high priests, to [a]offer up sacrifices,
[b]first for His own sins and then
for the *sins* of the people, because
this He did [c]once for all when He
[d]offered up Himself. **28** For the Law
appoints men as high priests [a]who
are weak, but the word of the oath,
which came after the Law, *appoints*
[b]a Son, who has been [c]made perfect
forever.

### *Jesus, High Priest of a New Covenant*

**8** Now the main point in what is
being said *is this*: we have such
a [a]high priest, who sat down at
[b]the right hand of the throne of the
[b]Majesty in the heavens, **2** a [a]minister
[1]in the [2]holy places and [1]in the [b]true
[3]tabernacle, which the Lord [c]pitched,
not man. **3** For every [a]high priest is
appointed [b]to offer both gifts and
sacrifices; so it is necessary that this
*high priest* also have something to
offer. **4** Now if He were on earth, He
would not be a priest at all, since
there are those who [a]offer the gifts
according to the Law; **5** who serve [a]a
copy and [b]shadow of the heavenly
things, just as Moses [1]was [c]warned
*by God* when he was about to erect
the tabernacle; for, "[d]SEE," He says,
"THAT YOU MAKE all things ACCORDING
TO THE PATTERN WHICH WAS SHOWN
YOU ON THE MOUNTAIN." **6** But now
He has obtained a more excellent
ministry, by as much as He is also
the [a]mediator of [b]a better covenant,
which has been enacted on better
promises. **7** For [a]if that first *covenant*
had been faultless, there would have
been no occasion sought for a sec-
ond. **8** For finding fault with them,
He says,

"[a]BEHOLD, DAYS ARE COMING,
SAYS THE [1]LORD,
[2]WHEN I WILL COMPLETE
[b]A NEW COVENANT

---

**7:21** [a]Ps 110:4; Heb 5:6; 7:17 [b]Nu 23:19; 1Sa 15:29; Ro 11:29 [c]Heb 7:23f, 28 [1]In OT, Yahweh, cf. Ps 110:4
**7:22** [a]Ps 119:122; Is 38:14 [b]Heb 8:6 **7:23** [1]Lit *the greater number have become priests...* **7:24** [a]Is 9:7; Jn 12:34; Ro 9:5; Heb 7:23f, 28 **7:25** [a]1Co 1:21 [b]Heb 7:19 [c]Ro 8:34; Heb 9:24 [1]Or *completely*
***7:26*** *[a]Heb 2:17* [b]2Co 5:21; Heb 4:15 [c]1Pe 2:22 [d]Heb 4:14 **7:27** [a]Heb 5:1 [b]Lv 9:7; Heb 5:3 [c]Heb 9:12, 28; 10:10 [d]Eph 5:2; Heb 9:14, 28; 10:10, 12 **7:28** [a]Heb 5:2 [b]Heb 1:2 [c]Heb 2:10 ◆ **8:1** [a]Col 3:1; Heb 2:17; 3:1 [b]Ps 110:1; Heb 1:3 **8:2** [a]Heb 10:11 [b]Heb 9:11, 24 [c]Ex 33:7 [1]Or *of* [2]The holy places within the sanctuary, cf. 9:2-3 [3]Or *sacred tent* **8:3** [a]Heb 2:17 [b]Ro 4:25; 5:6, 8; Ga 2:20; Eph 5:2; Heb 5:1; 8:4 **8:4** [a]Heb 5:1; 7:27; 8:3; 9:9; 10:11 **8:5** [a]Heb 9:23 [b]Col 2:17; Heb 10:1 [c]Mt 2:12; Heb 11:7; 12:25 [d]Ex 25:40 [1]Lit *has been*
**8:6** [a]1Ti 2:5 [b]Lk 22:20; Heb 7:22; 8:8; 9:15; 12:24 **8:7** [a]Heb 7:11 **8:8** [a]Jer 31:31 [b]Lk 22:20; 2Co 3:6; Heb 7:22; 8:6, 13; 9:15; 12:24 [1]In OT, Yahweh, cf. Jer 31:31 [2]Lit *And*

With the house of Israel and
With the house of Judah;
9 [a]Not like the covenant
Which I made
With their fathers
In the day when I took
Them by the hand
To lead them out
Of the land of Egypt;
For they did not continue
In My covenant,
And I did not care for them,
Says the [1]Lord.
10 “[a]For this is the covenant
That I will make
With the house of Israel
After those days,
Says the [1]Lord:
[2]I will put My laws
Into their minds,
And [b]upon their hearts
I will write them.
And I will be their God,
And they shall be My people.
11 “[a]And they shall not
Teach everyone his
Fellow citizen,
And everyone his brother,
Saying, ‘Know the Lord,’
For [b]all will know Me,
From [1]the least to the
Greatest of them.
12 “[a]For I will be merciful
To their iniquities,
[b]And I will remember
Their sins no more.”

13 [1]When He said, “[a]A new *covenant,*”
He has made the first obsolete. [b]But
whatever is becoming obsolete and
growing old is [2]ready to disappear.

### *The Old Covenant*

9 Now even the first *covenant* had
[a]requirements of divine worship
and [b]the earthly sanctuary. 2 For there
was [a]a tabernacle prepared: the first
part, in which *were* [b]the lampstand
and [c]the table and [d]the [1]sacred bread,
which is called the holy place. 3 And
behind [a]the second veil there was a
tabernacle which is called the [b]Holy
of Holies, 4 having a golden [a,1]altar of
incense and [b]the ark of the covenant
covered on all sides with gold, in
which was [c]a golden jar holding the
manna, and [d]Aaron’s rod which bud-
ded, and [e]the tablets of the covenant.
5 And above it *were* the [a]cherubim
of glory [b]overshadowing the [1]mercy
seat. Of these things we cannot now
speak in detail.
6 Now when these things have
been so prepared, the priests [a]are
continually entering the first part *of
the* tabernacle performing the divine
worship, 7 but into [a]the second, only
[b]the high priest *enters* [c]once a year,
[d]not without *taking* blood, which he
[e]offers for himself and for the [f,1]sins
of the people committed in igno-
rance. 8 [a]The Holy Spirit *is* indicat-
ing this, [b]that the way into the holy

**8:9** [a]Ex 19:5; 24:6-8; Dt 5:2, 3; Jer 31:32 [1]In OT, Yahweh, cf. Jer 31:32 **8:10** [a]Jer 31:33; Ro 11:27; Heb 10:16 [b]2Co 3:3 [1]In OT, Yahweh, cf. Jer 31:31 [2]Lit *Putting my laws into* **8:11** [a]Jer 31:34 [b]Is 54:13; Jn 6:45; 1Jn 2:27 [1]Lit *small to great of them* **8:12** [a]Is 43:25; Jer 31:34; 50:20; Mic 7:18, 19 [b]Heb 10:17 **8:13** [a]Lk 22:20; 2Co 3:6; Heb 7:22; 8:6, 8; 9:15; 12:24 [b]2Co 5:17; Heb 1:11 [1]Or *In His saying* [2]Or *near*
◆ **9:1** [a]Heb 9:10 [b]Ex 25:8; Heb 8:2; 9:11, 24 **9:2** [a]Ex 25:8, 9; 26:1-30 [b]Ex 25:31-39 [c]Ex 25:23-29 [d]Ex 25:30; Lv 24:5ff; Mt 12:4 [1]Lit *loaves of presentation* **9:3** [a]Ex 26:31-33; 40:3 [b]Ex 26:33 **9:4** [a]Ex 30:1-5; 37:25f [b]Ex 25:10ff; 37:1ff [c]Ex 16:32f [d]Nu 17:10 [e]Ex 25:16; 31:18; 32:15; Dt 9:9, 11, 15; 10:3-5 [1]Or *censer* **9:5** [a]Ex 25:18ff [b]Ex 25:17, 20; Lv 16:2; 1Ki 8:7 [1]Or *propitiatory seat, place of atonement* **9:6** [a]Nu 18:2-6; 28:3 **9:7** [a]Heb 9:3 [b]Lv 16:12ff [c]Ex 30:10; Lv 16:34; Heb 10:3 [d]Lv 16:11, 14 [e]Heb 5:3 [f]Nu 15:25; Heb 5:2 [1]Lit *ignorance of the people* **9:8** [a]Heb 3:7 [b]Jn 14:6; Heb 10:20

places has not yet been manifested
while that first part *of the* tabernacle
is still standing, **9** which *is* a symbol
for the present time. Accordingly
[a]both gifts and sacrifices are offered
which [b]cannot make the worshiper
perfect in conscience, **10** since they
*relate* only to [a]food and [b]drink and
various [c]washings, [d]requirements for
the [1]body imposed until [e]a time of
reformation.

### *The New Covenant*

**11** But when Christ appeared *as* a
[a]high priest of the [b]good things [1]to
come, *He entered* through [c]the great-
er and more perfect tabernacle, [d]not
made with hands, that is to say, [e]not
of this creation, **12** and not through
[a]the blood of goats and calves, but
[b]through His own blood, He [c]entered
the holy places [d]once for all, [1]having
obtained [e]eternal redemption. **13** For
if [a]the blood of goats and bulls and
[b]the ashes of a heifer sprinkling
those who have been defiled sanctify
for the [1]cleansing of the flesh, **14** how
much more will [a]the blood of Christ,
who through [b,1]the eternal Spirit
[c]offered Himself without blemish to
God, [d]cleanse [2]your conscience from
[e]dead works to serve [f]the living God?
**15** And for this reason [a]He is the
[b]mediator of a [c]new covenant, so
that, since a death has taken place
for the redemption of the trespasses
that were *committed* under the first
covenant, those who have been
[d]called may [e]receive the promise
of [f]the eternal inheritance. **16** For
where a [1]covenant is, there must of
necessity [2]be the death of the one
who made it. **17** For a [1]covenant is
valid *only* when [2]men are dead, [3]for
it is never in force while the one who
made it lives. **18** Therefore not even
the first *covenant* was inaugurated
without blood. **19** For when every
commandment had been [a]spoken
by Moses to all the people according
to the Law, [b]he took the [c]blood of the
calves and the goats, with [d]water and
scarlet wool and hyssop, and sprin-
kled both [e]the book itself and all
the people, **20** saying, "[a]THIS IS THE
BLOOD OF THE COVENANT WHICH GOD
COMMANDED YOU." **21** And in the same
way, both the tabernacle and all the
vessels of the ministry he [a]sprinkled
with the blood. **22** And according to
the [1]Law, *one may* [a]almost *say*, all
things are cleansed with blood, and
[b]without shedding of blood there is
no forgiveness.

**23** Therefore it was necessary
for the [a]copies of the things in the
heavens to be cleansed with these,
but [a]the heavenly things themselves
with better sacrifices than these.
**24** For Christ [a]did not enter holy
places made with hands, *mere* copies
of [b]the true ones, but into [c]heaven

---

**9:9** [a]Heb 5:1 [b]Heb 7:19 **9:10** [a]Lv 11:2ff; Col 2:16 [b]Nu 6:3 [c]Lv 11:25; Nu 19:13; Mk 7:4 [d]Heb 7:16 [e]Heb 7:12 [1]Lit *flesh* **9:11** [a]Heb 2:17 [b]Heb 10:1 [c]Heb 8:2; 9:24 [d]Mk 14:58; 2Co 5:1 [e]2Co 4:18; Heb 12:27; 13:14 [1]Two early mss *that have come* **9:12** [a]Lv 4:3; 16:6, 15; Heb 9:19 [b]Heb 9:14; 13:12 [c]Heb 9:24 [d]Heb 7:27 [e]Heb 5:9; 9:15 [1]Or *obtaining* **9:13** [a]Lv 16:15; Heb 9:19; 10:4 [b]Nu 19:9, 17f [1]Lit *purity* **9:14** [a]Heb 9:12; 13:12 [b]1Co 15:45; 1Pe 3:18 [c]Eph 5:2; Heb 7:27; 10:10, 12 [d]Ac 15:9; Tit 2:14; Heb 1:3; 10:2, 22 [e]Heb 6:1 [f]Mt 16:16; Heb 3:12 [1]Or His *eternal spirit* [2]One early ms *our* **9:15** [a]Ro 3:24 [b]1Ti 2:5; Heb 8:6; 12:24 [c]Heb 8:8 [d]Mt 22:3ff; Ro 8:28f; Heb 3:1 [e]Heb 6:15; 10:36; 11:39 [f]Ac 20:32 **9:16** [1]Or *testament* [2]Lit *be brought* **9:17** [1]Or *testament* [2]Lit *over the dead* [3]Two early mss *for is it then...lives?* **9:19** [a]Heb 1:1 [b]Ex 24:6ff [c]Heb 9:12 [d]Lv 14:4, 7; Nu 19:6, 18 [e]Ex 24:7 **9:20** [a]Ex 24:8; Mt 26:28 **9:21** [a]Ex 24:6; 40:9; Lv 8:15, 19; 16:14-16 **9:22** [a]Lv 5:11f [b]Lv 17:11 [1]Or *Law, almost all things* **9:23** [a]Heb 8:5 **9:24** [a]Heb 4:14; 9:12 [b]Heb 8:2 [c]Heb 9:12

itself, now [d]to appear in the presence
of God for us; **25** nor was it that He
would offer Himself often, as [a]the
high priest enters [b]the holy places
[a]year by year with blood that is not
his own. **26** Otherwise, He would
have needed to suffer often since
[a]the foundation of the world; but
now [b]once at [c]the consummation of
the ages He has been [d]manifested
to put away sin [e,1]by the sacrifice of
Himself. **27** And inasmuch as [a]it is
[1]appointed for men to die once and
after this [b]*comes* judgment, **28** so
Christ also, having been [a]offered
once to [b]bear the sins of many, will
appear [c]a second time for [d]salvation
[e]without *reference to* sin, to those
who [f]eagerly await Him.

### *Christ's Sacrifice Once for All*

**10** For the Law, since it has *only*
[a]a shadow of [b]the good things
to come *and* not the very [1]form of
things, [2]can [c]never, by the same
sacrifices which they offer contin-
ually year by year, [d]make perfect
those who draw near. **2** Otherwise,
would they not have ceased to be
offered, because the worshipers,
having once been cleansed, would
no longer have [a]consciousness of
sins? **3** But [a]in [1]those *sacrifices* there
is a reminder of sins year by year.
**4** For it is [a]impossible for the [b]blood
*of bulls* and goats to take away sins.
**5** Therefore, [a]when He comes into
the world, He says,

"[b]SACRIFICE AND OFFERING
YOU HAVE NOT DESIRED,
BUT [c]A BODY YOU HAVE
PREPARED FOR ME;
**6** [a]IN BURNT OFFERINGS AND
*sacrifices* FOR SIN YOU HAVE
TAKEN NO PLEASURE.
**7** "[a]THEN I SAID, 'BEHOLD,
I HAVE COME,
IN [b]THE SCROLL OF THE BOOK
IT IS WRITTEN OF ME,
TO DO YOUR WILL, O GOD.'"

**8** After saying above, "[a]SACRIFICES
AND OFFERINGS AND [b]BURNT OFFER-
INGS AND *sacrifices* [c]FOR SIN YOU HAVE
NOT DESIRED, NOR HAVE YOU TAKEN
PLEASURE *in them*" (which are offered
according to the Law), **9** then He
[1]said, "[a]BEHOLD, I HAVE COME TO DO
YOUR WILL." He takes away the first in
order to establish the second. **10** By
[1]this will we have been [a]sanctified
through [b]the offering of [c]the body
of Jesus Christ [d]once for all.
**11** And every priest stands daily
ministering and [a]offering time after
time the same sacrifices, which [b]can
never take away sins; **12** but He, hav-
ing offered one sacrifice [a]for [1]sins
[b]for all time, [c]SAT DOWN AT THE RIGHT
HAND OF GOD, **13** waiting from that
time [a]UNTIL HIS ENEMIES ARE PUT AS A
FOOTSTOOL FOR HIS FEET. **14** For by one
offering He has [a]perfected [b]for all

**9:24** [d]Mt 18:10; Heb 7:25 **9:25** [a]Heb 9:7 [b]Heb 9:2; 10:19 **9:26** [a]Mt 25:34; Heb 4:3 [b]Heb 7:27; 9:12 [c]Mt 13:39; Heb 1:2 [d]1Jn 3:5, 8 [e]Heb 9:12, 14 [1]Or *by His sacrifice* **9:27** [a]Ge 3:19 [b]2Co 5:10; 1Jn 4:17 [1]Lit *laid up* **9:28** [a]Heb 7:27 [b]Is 53:12; 1Pe 2:24 [c]Ac 1:11 [d]Heb 5:9 [e]Heb 4:15 [f]1Co 1:7; Tit 2:13 ◆**10:1** [a]Heb 8:5 [b]Heb 9:11 [c]Ro 8:3; Heb 9:9; 10:4, 11 [d]Heb 7:19 [1]Lit *image* [2]Two early mss *they can* **10:2** [a]1Pe 2:19 **10:3** [a]Heb 9:7 [1]Lit *them there is* **10:4** [a]Heb 10:1, 11 [b]Heb 9:12f **10:5** [a]Heb 1:6 [b]Ps 40:6 [c]Heb 2:14; 5:7; 1Pe 2:24 **10:6** [a]Ps 40:6 **10:7** [a]Ps 40:7, 8 [b]Ezr 6:2; Jer 36:2; Eze 2:9; 3:1f **10:8** [a]Ps 40:6; Heb 10:5f [b]Mk 12:33 [c]Ro 8:3 **10:9** [a]Ps 40:7, 8; Heb 10:7 [1]Lit *has said* **10:10** [a]Jn 17:19; Eph 5:26; Heb 2:11; 10:14, 29; 13:12 [b]Jn 6:51; Eph 5:2; Heb 7:27; 9:14, 28; 10:12 [c]Heb 2:14; 5:7; 1Pe 2:24 [d]Heb 7:27 [1]Lit *which* **10:11** [a]Heb 5:1 [b]Mic 6:6-8; Heb 10:1, 4 **10:12** [a]Heb 5:1 [b]Heb 10:14 [c]Ps 110:1; Heb 1:3 [1]Or *sins, forever sat down* **10:13** [a]Ps 110:1; Heb 1:13 **10:14** [a]Heb 10:1 [b]Heb 10:12

time those who are being sanctified.
**15** And [a]the Holy Spirit also testifies
to us, for after saying,

**16** "[a]THIS IS THE COVENANT
THAT I WILL MAKE WITH THEM
AFTER THOSE DAYS,
SAYS THE [1]LORD:
I WILL PUT MY LAWS
UPON THEIR HEART,
AND ON THEIR MIND I
WILL WRITE THEM,"

*He then says,*

**17** "[a]AND THEIR SINS AND
THEIR LAWLESS DEEDS
I WILL REMEMBER NO MORE."

**18** Now where there is forgiveness of
these things, there is no longer *any*
offering for sin.

### *A New and Living Way*

**19** Therefore, brothers, since we [a]have
confidence to [b]enter the holy places
by the blood of Jesus, **20** by [a]a new
and living way which He inaugurated
for us through [b]the veil, that is, His
flesh, **21** and since *we have* [a]a great
priest [b]over the house of God, **22** let
us [a]draw near with a [1]sincere heart
in [b]full assurance of faith, having
our hearts [c]sprinkled from an evil
conscience and our bodies [d]washed
with pure water. **23** Let us hold fast
the [a]confession of our [b]hope without
wavering, for [c]He who promised is
faithful. **24** And let us consider how
[a]to stimulate one another to love
and [b]good deeds, **25** not forsaking
our own [a]assembling together, as is
the habit of some, but [b]encouraging
*one another*, and all the more as you
see [c]the day drawing near.

### *Warning Against Willful Sin*

**26** For if we go on [a]sinning willfully
after receiving [b]the knowledge of
the truth, there no longer remains a
sacrifice for sins, **27** but a terrifying
expectation of [a]judgment and [b]THE
FURY OF A FIRE WHICH WILL CONSUME
THE ADVERSARIES. **28** [a]Anyone who
has set aside the Law of Moses dies
without mercy by *the mouth of* two
or three witnesses. **29** [a]How much
worse punishment do you think
he will deserve [b]who has trampled
underfoot the Son of God, and has
regarded as defiled [c]the blood of the
covenant [d]by which he was sancti-
fied, and has [e]insulted the Spirit of
grace? **30** For we know Him who said,
"[a]VENGEANCE IS MINE, I WILL REPAY."
And again, "[b]THE [1]LORD WILL JUDGE
HIS PEOPLE." **31** It is a [a]terrifying thing
to fall into the hands of the [b]living
God.

**32** But remember [a]the former
days, [1]when, after being [b]enlight-
ened, you endured a great [c]conflict
of sufferings, **33** partly by being
[a]made a public spectacle through
reproaches and afflictions, and partly
by becoming [b]sharers with those
who were so treated. **34** For you also
[a]showed sympathy to the prisoners

---

**10:15** [a]Heb 3:7 **10:16** [a]Jer 31:33; Heb 8:10 [1]In OT, Yahweh, cf. Jer 31:33 **10:17** [a]Jer 31:34; Heb 8:12
**10:19** [a]Heb 3:6; 10:35 [b]Heb 9:25 **10:20** [a]Heb 9:8 [b]Heb 6:19; 9:3 **10:21** [a]Heb 2:17 [b]1Ti 3:15; Heb 3:6
**10:22** [a]Heb 7:19; 10:1 [b]Heb 6:11 [c]Eze 36:25; Heb 9:19; 12:24; 1Pe 1:2 [d]Ac 22:16; 1Co 6:11; Eph 5:26; Tit 3:5;
1Pe 3:21 [1]Lit *true* **10:23** [a]Heb 3:1 [b]Heb 3:6 [c]1Co 1:9; 10:13; Heb 11:11 **10:24** [a]Heb 13:1 [b]Tit 3:8
**10:25** [a]Ac 2:42 [b]Heb 3:13 [c]1Co 3:13 **10:26** [a]Nu 15:30; Heb 6:4-8; 2Pe 2:20f [b]1Ti 2:4 **10:27** [a]Jn 5:29;
Heb 9:27 [b]Is 26:11; 2Th 1:7 **10:28** [a]Dt 17:2-6; 19:15; Mt 18:16; Heb 2:2 **10:29** [a]Heb 2:3 [b]Heb 6:6
[c]Ex 24:8; Mt 26:28; Heb 13:20 [d]Eph 5:26; Heb 9:13f; Rev 1:5 [e]1Co 6:11; Eph 4:30; Heb 6:4 **10:30** [a]Dt 32:35;
Ro 12:19 [b]Dt 32:36 [1]In OT, Yahweh, cf. Dt 32:36 **10:31** [a]2Co 5:11 [b]Mt 16:16; Heb 3:12 **10:32** [a]Heb 5:12
[b]Heb 6:4 [c]Php 1:30 [1]Lit *in which* **10:33** [a]1Co 4:9; Heb 12:4 [b]Php 4:14; 1Th 2:14 **10:34** [a]Heb 13:3

and accepted with [b]joy the seizure
of your possessions, knowing that
you have for yourselves [c]a better and
lasting possession. 35 Therefore, do
not throw away that [a]confidence of
yours, which has a great [b]reward.
36 For you have need of [a]endurance,
so that when you have [b]done the will
of God, you may [c]receive the promise.
37 [a]FOR YET IN A VERY
LITTLE WHILE,
[b]HE WHO IS COMING WILL
COME, AND WILL NOT DELAY.
38 [a]BUT MY RIGHTEOUS ONE
SHALL LIVE BY FAITH,
AND IF HE SHRINKS
BACK, MY SOUL HAS NO
PLEASURE IN HIM.
39 But [1]we are not of those who shrink
back to destruction, but of those who
have faith to the [2]preserving of the
soul.

### *By Faith*

11 Now faith is the [a,1]assurance of
*things* [b,2]hoped for, the [3]convic-
tion of [c]things not seen. 2 For by it the
[a,1]men of old [b,2]gained approval.
3 By faith we understand that
the [a,1]worlds were prepared [b]by the
word of God, so that what is seen
[c]was not made out of things which
are visible. 4 By faith [a]Abel offered
to God a better sacrifice than Cain,
through which he [b]was approved as
being righteous—God approving [1]his
[c]gifts—and through [2]faith, though
[d]he is dead, he still speaks. 5 By
faith [a]Enoch was taken up so that
he would not [b]see death; AND HE WAS
NOT FOUND BECAUSE GOD TOOK HIM
UP; for prior to being taken up, he was
approved as being pleasing to God.
6 And without faith it is impossible to
please *Him*, for he who [a]draws near
to God must believe that He is and
*that* He is a rewarder of those who
seek Him. 7 By faith [a]Noah, being
[b]warned about [c]things not yet seen,
[d,1]in reverence [e]prepared an ark for
the salvation of his household, by
which he condemned the world, and
became an heir of [f]the righteousness
which is according to faith.
8 By faith [a]Abraham, when he
was called, obeyed [1]by going out
to a place which he was to [b]receive
for an inheritance; and he went
out, not knowing where he was
going. 9 By faith he sojourned in
[a]the land of promise, as in a foreign
*land*, [b]dwelling in tents with Isaac
and Jacob, [c]fellow heirs of the same
promise, 10 for he was looking for
[a]the city which has [b]foundations,
[c]whose architect and builder is
God. 11 By faith even [a]Sarah herself
[1]received [2]ability to conceive, even
beyond the proper time of life, since
she regarded Him [b]faithful who had
promised. 12 Therefore there were
born even of one man, and [a]him as

**10:34** [b]Mt 5:12 [c]Heb 9:15; 11:16; 13:14; 1Pe 1:4f **10:35** [a]Heb 10:19 [b]Heb 2:2 **10:36** [a]Lk 21:19; Heb 12:1 [b]Mk 3:35 [c]Heb 9:15 **10:37** [a]Hab 2:3; Heb 10:25; Rev 22:20 [b]Mt 11:3 **10:38** [a]Hab 2:4; Ro 1:17; Ga 3:11 **10:39** [1]Lit *we are not of shrinking back...but of faith* [2]Or *possessing* ◆ **11:1** [a]Heb 3:14 [b]Heb 3:6 [c]Ro 8:24; 2Co 4:18; 5:7; Heb 11:7, 27 [1]Or *substance* [2]Or *expected* [3]Or *evidence* **11:2** [a]Heb 1:1 [b]Heb 11:4, 39 [1]Lit *elders* [2]Lit *obtained a* good *testimony* **11:3** [a]Jn 1:3; Heb 1:2 [b]Gen ch 1; Ps 33:6, 9; Heb 6:5; 2Pe 3:5 [c]Ro 4:17 [1]Lit *ages* **11:4** [a]Ge 4:4; Mt 23:35; 1Jn 3:12 [b]Heb 11:2 [c]Heb 5:1 [d]Ge 4:8-10; Heb 12:24 [1]By receiving his gifts [2]Lit *it* **11:5** [a]Ge 5:21-24 [b]Lk 2:26; Jn 8:51; Heb 2:9 **11:6** [a]Heb 4:16; 7:19, 25; 10:1 **11:7** [a]Ge 6:13-22 [b]Heb 8:5 [c]Heb 11:1 [d]Heb 5:7 [e]1Pe 3:20 [f]Ge 6:9; Eze 14:14, 20; Ro 4:13; 9:30 [1]Lit *having become reverent* **11:8** [a]Ge 12:1-4; Ac 7:2-4 [b]Ge 12:7 [1]Lit *to go out* **11:9** [a]Ac 7:5 [b]Ge 12:8; 13:3, 18; 18:1, 9 [c]Heb 6:17 **11:10** [a]Heb 12:22; 13:14 [b]Rev 21:14ff [c]Heb 11:16 **11:11** [a]Ge 17:19; 18:11-14; 21:2 [b]Heb 10:23 [1]Some mss add *being barren* [2]Lit *power for the laying down of seed* **11:12** [a]Ro 4:19

good as dead [1]at that, *as many* [b]AS
THE STARS OF HEAVEN IN NUMBER, AND
INNUMERABLE AS THE SAND WHICH IS
BY THE SEASHORE.
**13** [a]All these died in faith, [b]without
receiving the promises, but [c]having
seen them and having welcomed
them from a distance, and [d]having
confessed that they were strangers
and exiles on the earth. **14** For those
who say such things make it clear
that they are seeking a country of
their own. **15** And indeed if they had
been remembering that *country* from
which they went out, [a]they would
have had opportunity to return.
**16** But now, they aspire to a better
*country*, that is, a [a]heavenly one.
Therefore [b]God is not [1]ashamed to
be [c]called their God, for [d]He prepared
a city for them.
**17** By faith [a]Abraham, when he
was tested, offered up Isaac, and he
who had [b]received the promises was
offering up his only *son*, **18** to whom it
was said, "[a]IN ISAAC YOUR SEED SHALL
BE CALLED." **19** [1]He considered that
[a]God is able to raise *people* even from
the dead, from which, [b,2]figuratively
speaking, he also received him back.
**20** By faith [a]Isaac blessed Jacob and
Esau, even regarding things to come.
**21** By faith [a]Jacob, as he was dying,
blessed each of the sons of Joseph,
and [b]WORSHIPED, *leaning* ON THE
TOP OF HIS STAFF. **22** By faith [a]Joseph,
when he was dying, made mention
of the exodus of the sons of Israel,
and gave commands concerning his
bones.
**23** By faith [a]Moses, when he was
born, was hidden for three months
by his parents, because they saw he
was a beautiful child, and they were
not afraid of the [b]king's edict. **24** By
faith Moses, [a]when he had grown up,
refused to be called the son of Phar-
aoh's daughter, **25** choosing rather
to [a]be mistreated with the people
of God than to enjoy the passing
pleasures of sin, **26** [a]regarding the
reproach of [1]Christ greater riches
than the treasures of Egypt; for he
was looking to the [b]reward. **27** By
faith he [a]left Egypt, not [b]fearing the
rage of the king; for he endured, as
[c]seeing Him who is unseen. **28** By
faith he [a,1]kept the Passover and
the sprinkling of the blood, so that
[b]he who destroyed the firstborn
would not touch them. **29** By faith
they [a]passed through the Red Sea
as though *they were passing* through
dry land, and the Egyptians, when
they attempted it, were [1]drowned.
**30** By faith [a]the walls of Jericho
fell down [b]after they had been en-
circled for seven days. **31** By faith
[a]Rahab the harlot did not perish
along with those who were disobe-
dient, after welcoming the spies [1]in
peace.
**32** And what more shall I say? For
time will fail me if I recount [a]Gideon,

---

**11:12** [b]Ge 15:5; 22:17; 32:12 [1]Lit *in these things* **11:13** [a]Mt 13:17 [b]Heb 11:39 [c]Jn 8:56; Heb 11:27 [d]Ge 23:4; 47:9; 1Chr 29:15; Ps 39:12; Eph 2:19; 1Pe 1:1; 2:11 **11:15** [a]Ge 24:6-8 **11:16** [a]2Ti 4:18 [b]Mk 8:38; Heb 2:11 [c]Ge 26:24; 28:13; Ex 3:6, 15; 4:5 [d]Heb 11:10; Rev 21:2 [1]Lit *ashamed of them, to be* **11:17** [a]Ge 22:1-10; Jas 2:21 [b]Heb 11:13 **11:18** [a]Ge 21:12; Ro 9:7 **11:19** [a]Ro 4:21 [b]Heb 9:9 [1]Lit *Considering* [2]Lit *in a parable* **11:20** [a]Ge 27:27-29, 39f **11:21** [a]Ge 48:1, 5, 16, 20 [b]Ge 47:31; 1Ki 1:47 **11:22** [a]Ge 50:24f; Ex 13:19 **11:23** [a]Ex 2:2 [b]Ex 1:16, 22 **11:24** [a]Ex 2:10, 11ff **11:25** [a]Heb 11:37 **11:26** [a]Lk 14:33; Php 3:7f [b]Heb 2:2 [1]Messiah **11:27** [a]Ex 2:15; 12:50f; 13:17f [b]Ex 2:14; 10:28f [c]Col 1:15; Heb 11:1, 13 **11:28** [a]Ex 12:21ff [b]Ex 12:23, 29f; 1Co 10:10 [1]Lit *has kept* **11:29** [a]Ex 14:22-29 [1]Lit *swallowed up* **11:30** [a]Jos 6:20 [b]Jos 6:15f **11:31** [a]Jos 2:9ff; 6:23; Jas 2:25 [1]Lit *with* **11:32** [a]Judg ch 6-8

[b]Barak, [c]Samson, [d]Jephthah, as
well as [e]David and [f]Samuel and
the prophets, **33** who through faith
[a]conquered kingdoms, [b]performed
righteousness, [c]obtained prom-
ises, [d]shut the mouths of lions,
**34** [a]quenched the power of fire,
[b]escaped the edge of the sword,
were made strong from weakness,
[c]became mighty in war, [c]put foreign
armies to flight. **35** [a]Women received
*back* their dead by resurrection; and
others were tortured, not accepting
their [1]release, so that they might
obtain a better resurrection; **36** and
others [1]experienced mockings and
floggings, yes, also [a]chains and im-
prisonment. **37** They were [a]stoned,
they were [b]sawn in two, [1]they were
tempted, they were [c]put to death
with the sword. They went about
[d]in sheepskins, in goatskins, being
destitute, afflicted, [e]mistreated **38** (of
whom the world was not worthy),
[a]wandering in desolate places and
mountains and caves and holes [1]in
the ground.
**39** And all these, having [a,1]gained
approval through their faith, [b]did
not receive [2]what was promised,
**40** because God had [1]provided
[a]something better for us, so that
[b]apart from us they would not be
made perfect.

### *Jesus, the Author and Perfecter of Faith*

**12** Therefore, since we have so
great a cloud of witnesses
surrounding us, [a]laying aside
every weight and the sin which so
easily entangles us, let us [b]run with
[c]endurance the race that is set before
us, **2** [1]fixing our eyes on Jesus, the
[a,2]author and perfecter of faith, who
for the joy set before Him [b]endured
the cross, [c]despising the shame, and
has [d]sat down at the right hand of the
throne of God.
**3** For [a]consider Him who has
endured such hostility by sinners
against Himself, so that you will not
grow weary, [b]fainting [1]in heart.

### *The Father's Discipline*

**4** [a]You have not yet resisted [b,1]to
the point of shedding blood in your
striving against sin. **5** And you have
forgotten the exhortation which is
addressed to you as sons,

"[a]My son, do not regard
lightly the discipline
of the [1]Lord,
Nor [b]faint when you
are reproved by Him;
**6** [a]For those [b]whom the [1]Lord
loves He disciplines,
And He flogs every son
whom He receives."

**11:32** [b]Judg ch 4, 5 [c]Judg ch 13-16 [d]Judg ch 11, 12 [e]1Sa 16:1, 13 [f]1Sa 1:20 **11:33** [a]Judg ch 4, 7, 11, 14; 2Sa 5:17-20; 8:1f; 10:12 [b]1Sa 12:4; 2Sa 8:15 [c]2Sa 7:11f [d]Jdg 14:6; 1Sa 17:34ff; Da 6:22 **11:34** [a]Da 3:23ff [b]Ex 18:4; 1Sa 18:11; 19:10; 1 Kin ch 19; 2 Kin ch 6; Ps 144:10 [c]Jdg 7:21; 15:8, 15f; 1Sa 17:51f; 2Sa 8:1-6; 10:15ff **11:35** [a]1Ki 17:23; 2Ki 4:36f [1]Lit *redemption* **11:36** [a]Ge 39:20; 1Ki 22:27; 2Chr 18:26; Jer 20:2; 37:15 [1]Lit *received the trial of* **11:37** [a]1Ki 21:13; 2Chr 24:21 [b]2Sa 12:31; 1Chr 20:3 [c]1Ki 19:10; Jer 26:23 [d]1Ki 19:13, 19; 2Ki 2:8, 13f; Zec 13:4 [e]Heb 11:25; 13:3 [1]One early ms omits *they were tempted* **11:38** [a]1Ki 18:4, 13; 19:9 [1]Lit *of* **11:39** [a]Heb 11:2 [b]Heb 10:36; 11:13 [1]Lit *obtained a testimony* [2]Lit *the promise* **11:40** [a]Heb 11:16 [b]Rev 6:11 [1]Or *foreseen* ◆ **12:1** [a]Ro 13:12; Eph 4:22 [b]1Co 9:24; Ga 2:2 [c]Heb 10:36 **12:2** [a]Heb 2:10 [b]Php 2:8f; Heb 2:9 [c]1Co 1:18, 23; Heb 13:13 [d]Heb 1:3 [1]Lit *looking to* [2]Or *leader* **12:3** [a]Rev 2:3 [b]Ga 6:9; Heb 12:5 [1]Lit *souls* **12:4** [a]Heb 10:32ff; 13:13 [b]Php 2:8 [1]Lit *as far as blood* **12:5** [a]Job 5:17; Pr 3:11 [b]Heb 12:3 [1]In OT, Yahweh, cf. Pr 3:11 **12:6** [a]Pr 3:12 [b]Ps 119:75; Rev 3:19 [1]In OT, Yahweh, cf. Pr 3:12

**7** It is for discipline that you endure;
[a]God deals with you as with sons; for
what son is there whom *his* father
does not discipline? **8** But if you are
without discipline, [a]of which all have
become partakers, then you are ille-
gitimate children and not sons. **9** Fur-
thermore, we [1]had [2]earthly fathers
to discipline us, and we [a]respected
them. Shall we not much rather be
subject to [b]the Father of [3]spirits, and
[c]live? **10** For they disciplined us for a
short time as seemed best to them,
but He *disciplines us* for our benefit,
[a]so that we may share His holiness.
**11** And all discipline [a]for the moment
seems not to be joyful, but sorrowful,
but to those who have been trained by
it, afterwards it yields the [b]peaceful
fruit of righteousness.

**12** Therefore, [a,1]STRENGTHEN THE
HANDS THAT ARE WEAK AND THE
KNEES THAT ARE FEEBLE, **13** and [a]make
straight paths for your feet, so that
what is lame may not be put out of
joint, but rather [b]be healed.

**14** [a]Pursue peace with all men, and
the [b]sanctification without which no
one will [c]see the Lord, **15** seeing to it
that no one [a]falls short of the grace
of God; that no [b]ROOT OF BITTERNESS
SPRINGING UP CAUSES TROUBLE, and by
it many be [c]defiled; **16** that *also there
be* no [a]sexually immoral or [b]godless
person like Esau, [c]who sold his own
birthright for a *single* meal. **17** For you
know that even afterwards, [a]when
he desired to inherit the blessing, he
was rejected, for he found no place
for repentance, though he sought for
it with tears.

### *Contrast of Sinai and Zion*

**18** [a]For you have not come to [b]*a
mountain* that can be touched and
to a blazing fire, and to darkness and
gloom and whirlwind, **19** and to the
[a]blast of a trumpet and the [b]sound of
words which *was such that* those who
heard [c]begged that no further word
be spoken to them. **20** For they could
not bear what was being command-
ed, "[a]IF EVEN A BEAST TOUCHES THE
MOUNTAIN, IT WILL BE STONED." **21** And
so terrible was what appeared, *that*
Moses said, "[a]I AM FULL OF FEAR and
trembling." **22** But [a]you have come to
Mount Zion and to [b]the city of [c]the
living God, [d]the heavenly Jerusalem,
and to [e]myriads of [1]angels, **23** to the
festal gathering and [a]assembly of
the firstborn who [b]are enrolled in
heaven, and to God, [c]the Judge of all,
and to the [d]spirits of *the* righteous
made perfect, **24** and to Jesus, the
[a]mediator of a new covenant, and to
the [b]sprinkled blood, which speaks
better than [c]*the blood* of Abel.

### *An Unshakable Kingdom*

**25** [a]See to it that you do not refuse
Him who is [b]speaking. For [c]if those

---

**12:7** [a]Dt 8:5; 2Sa 7:14; Pr 13:24; 19:18; 23:13f **12:8** [a]1Pe 5:9 **12:9** [a]Lk 18:2 [b]Nu 16:22; 27:16; Rev 22:6 [c]Is 38:16 [1]Lit *were having* [2]Lit *fathers of our flesh* [3]Or *our spirits* **12:10** [a]2Pe 1:4 **12:11** [a]1Pe 1:6 [b]Is 32:17; 2Ti 4:8; Jas 3:17f **12:12** [a]Is 35:3 [1]Lit *make straight* **12:13** [a]Pr 4:26; Ga 2:14 [b]Ga 6:1; Jas 5:16 **12:14** [a]Ro 14:19 [b]Ro 6:22; Heb 12:10 [c]Mt 5:8; Heb 9:28 **12:15** [a]2Co 6:1; Ga 5:4; Heb 4:1 [b]Dt 29:18 [c]Tit 1:15 **12:16** [a]Ge 26:34-35; Heb 13:4 [b]1Ti 1:9 [c]Ge 25:33f **12:17** [a]Ge 27:30-40 **12:18** [a]2Co 3:7-13; Heb 12:18ff [b]Ex 19:12, 16ff; 20:18; Dt 4:11; 5:22 **12:19** [a]Ex 19:16, 19; 20:18; Mt 24:31 [b]Ex 19:19; Dt 4:12 [c]Ex 20:19; Dt 5:25; 18:16 **12:20** [a]Ex 19:12f **12:21** [a]Dt 9:19 **12:22** [a]Rev 14:1 [b]Eph 2:19; Php 3:20; Heb 11:10; Rev 21:2 [c]Heb 3:12 [d]Ga 4:26; Heb 11:16 [e]Rev 5:11 [1]Or *angels in festive gathering, and to the church* **12:23** [a]Ex 4:22; Heb 2:12 [b]Lk 10:20 [c]Ge 18:25; Ps 50:6; 94:2 [d]Heb 11:40; Rev 6:9, 11 **12:24** [a]1Ti 2:5; Heb 8:6; 9:15 [b]Heb 9:19; 10:22; 1Pe 1:2 [c]Ge 4:10; Heb 11:4 **12:25** [a]Heb 3:12 [b]Heb 1:1 [c]Heb 2:2f; 10:28f

did not escape when they [d]refused
him who [e]warned *them* on earth,
[1]much less *will* we *escape* who turn
away from Him who [e]*warns* from
heaven. **26** And [a]His voice shook the
earth then, but now He has promised,
saying, "[b]YET ONCE MORE I WILL SHAKE
NOT ONLY THE EARTH, BUT ALSO THE
HEAVEN." **27** Now this *expression*, "Yet
once more," indicates [a]the removing
of those things which can be shaken,
as of created things, so that those
things which cannot be shaken may
remain. **28** Therefore, since we are
receiving a [a]kingdom which cannot
be shaken, let us [1]show gratitude, by
which we may [b]offer to God an accept-
able service with reverence and awe;
**29** for [a]OUR GOD IS A CONSUMING FIRE.

### *Sacrifices Pleasing to God*

**13** Let [a]love of the brothers
continue. **2** Do not neglect to
[a]show hospitality to strangers, for by
this some have [b]entertained angels
without knowing it. **3** [a]Remember
[b]the prisoners, as though in prison
with them, *and* those who are mis-
treated, since you yourselves also
are in the body. **4** [a]Marriage *is to be*
*held* in honor among all, and the
*marriage* bed *is to be* undefiled, [b]for
the sexually immoral and adulterers
God will judge. **5** *Make sure that* your
way *of life* is [a]free from the love of
money, [b]being content with what
you have; for He Himself has said,
"[c]I WILL NEVER DESERT YOU, NOR WILL
I EVER FORSAKE YOU," **6** so that we
confidently say,

"[a]THE [1]LORD IS MY HELPER,
I WILL NOT BE AFRAID.
WHAT WILL MAN DO TO ME?"

**7** Remember your [a]leaders, who
spoke [b]the word of God to you;
and considering the [1]result of
their conduct, [c]imitate their faith.
**8** [a]Jesus Christ *is* the same yesterday
and today and forever. **9** [a]Do not be
carried away by varied and strange
teachings; for it is good for the heart
to [b]be strengthened by grace, not by
[c]foods, [d]through which those who
[1]were so occupied were not benefit-
ed. **10** We have an altar [a]from which
those [b]who serve the tabernacle
have no authority to eat. **11** For [a]the
bodies of those animals whose blood
is brought into the holy places by
the high priest *as an offering* for
sin, are burned outside the camp.
**12** Therefore Jesus also, [a]that He
might sanctify the people [b]through
His own blood, suffered [c]outside the
gate. **13** So, let us go out to Him out-
side the camp, [a]bearing His reproach.
**14** For here [a]we do not have a lasting
city, but we are seeking [b]*the one* to
come. **15** [a]Through Him then, let us
continually offer up a [b]sacrifice of
praise to God, that is, [c]the fruit of lips
that confess His name. **16** And do not

---

**12:25** [d]Heb 12:19 [e]Ex 20:22; Heb 8:5; 11:7 [1]Lit *much rather we* will not escape... **12:26** [a]Ex 19:18; Jdg 5:4f [b]Hag 2:6 **12:27** [a]Is 34:4; 54:10; 65:17; Ro 8:19, 21; 1Co 7:31; Heb 1:10ff **12:28** [a]Da 2:44 [b]Heb 13:15, 21 [1]Lit *have* **12:29** [a]Dt 4:24; 9:3; Is 33:14; 2Th 1:7; Heb 10:27, 31 ◆ **13:1** [a]Ro 12:10; 1Th 4:9; 1Pe 1:22 **13:2** [a]Mt 25:35; Ro 12:13; 1Pe 4:9 [b]Ge 13:1ff; 19:1f **13:3** [a]Col 4:18 [b]Mt 25:36; Heb 10:34 **13:4** [a]1Co 7:38; 1Ti 4:3 [b]1Co 6:9; Ga 5:19, 21; 1Th 4:6 **13:5** [a]Eph 5:3; Col 3:5; 1Ti 3:3 [b]Php 4:11 [c]Dt 31:6, 8; Jos 1:5 **13:6** [a]Ps 118:6 [1]In OT, Yahweh, cf. Ps 118:6 **13:7** [a]Heb 13:17, 24 [b]Lk 5:1 [c]Heb 6:12 [1]Or *end of their life* **13:8** [a]2Co 1:19; Heb 1:12 **13:9** [a]Eph 4:14; 5:6; Jd 12 [b]2Co 1:21; Col 2:7 [c]Col 2:16 [d]Heb 9:10 [1]Lit *walked* **13:10** [a]1Co 10:18 [b]Heb 8:5 **13:11** [a]Ex 29:14; Lv 4:12, 21; 9:11; 16:27; Nu 19:3, 7 **13:12** [a]Eph 5:26; Heb 2:11 [b]Heb 9:12 [c]Jn 19:17 **13:13** [a]Lk 9:23; Heb 11:26; 12:2 **13:14** [a]Heb 10:34; 12:27 [b]Eph 2:19; Heb 2:5; 11:10, 16; 12:22 **13:15** [a]1Pe 2:5 [b]Lv 7:12 [c]Is 57:19; Hos 14:2

neglect doing good and [a]sharing, for [b]with such sacrifices God is pleased.

**17** [a]Obey your leaders and submit *to them*—for [b]they keep watch over your souls as those who will give an account—so that they will do this with joy and not with groaning, for this would be unprofitable for you.

**18** [a]Pray for us, for we are convinced that we have a [b]good conscience, desiring to conduct ourselves well in all things. **19** And I urge *you* all the more to do this, [a]so that I may be restored to you the sooner.

### *Benediction*

**20** Now [a]the God of peace, who [b]brought up from the dead the [c]great Shepherd of the sheep [1]through [d]the blood of the [e]eternal covenant, our Lord Jesus, **21** [a]equip you in every good thing to do His will, by [b]doing in us [c]what is pleasing in His sight, through Jesus Christ, [d]to whom *be* the glory forever and ever. Amen.

**22** But [a]I urge you, [b]brothers, [1]bear with [2]this [b]word of exhortation, for [c]I have written to you briefly. **23** Know that [a]our brother Timothy has been released, with whom, if he comes soon, I will see you. **24** Greet [a]all of your leaders and all the [b,1]saints. Those from [c]Italy greet you.

**25** [a]Grace be with you all.

# *The Letter of* JAMES

### *Testing Your Faith*

**1** [a,1]James, a [b]slave of God and [c]of the Lord Jesus Christ,

To [d]the twelve tribes who are in the [e]Dispersion: [f]Greetings.

**2** [a]Consider it all joy, my brothers, when you encounter [b]various [1]trials, **3** knowing that [a]the testing of your [b]faith brings about [c]perseverance. **4** And let [a]perseverance have *its* perfect work, so that you may be [b,1]perfect and complete, lacking in nothing.

**5** But if any of you [a]lacks wisdom, let him ask of God, who gives to all generously and [1]without reproach, and [b]it will be given to him. **6** But he must [a]ask in faith, [b]doubting nothing, for the one who doubts is like the surf of the sea, [c]driven and tossed by the wind. **7** For that man ought not to expect that he will receive anything from the Lord, **8** *being* a [a,1]double-minded man, [b]unstable in all his ways.

---

**13:16** [a]Ro 12:13 [b]Php 4:18 **13:17** [a]1Co 16:16; Heb 13:7, 24 [b]Is 62:6; Eze 3:17; Ac 20:28 **13:18** [a]1Th 5:25 [b]Ac 24:16; 1Ti 1:5 **13:19** [a]Phm 22 **13:20** [a]Ro 15:33 [b]Ac 2:24; Ro 10:7 [c]Is 63:11; Jn 10:11; 1Pe 2:25 [d]Zec 9:11; Heb 10:29 [e]Is 55:3; Jer 32:40; Eze 37:26 [1]Lit *in* **13:21** [a]1Pe 5:10 [b]Php 2:13 [c]Heb 12:28; 1Jn 3:22 [d]Ro 11:36 **13:22** [a]Ac 13:15; Heb 3:13; 10:25; 12:5; 13:19 [b]Heb 3:1 [c]1Pe 5:12 [1]Or *listen to* [2]Lit *the* **13:23** [a]Ac 16:1; Col 1:1 **13:24** [a]1Co 16:16; Heb 13:7, 17 [b]Ac 9:13 [c]Ac 18:2 [1]Or *holy ones* **13:25** [a]Col 4:18 ◆ **1:1** [a]Ac 12:17 [b]Tit 1:1 [c]Ro 1:1 [d]Lk 22:30 [e]Jn 7:35 [f]Ac 15:23 [1]Or *Jacob*; James is the Eng form of Jacob **1:2** [a]Mt 5:12; Jas 1:12; 5:11 [b]1Pe 1:6 [1]Or *temptations* **1:3** [a]1Pe 1:7 [b]Heb 6:12 [c]Lk 21:19 **1:4** [a]Lk 21:19 [b]Mt 5:48; Col 4:12 [1]Or *mature* **1:5** [a]1Ki 3:9ff; Jas 3:17 [b]Mt 7:7 [1]Lit *does not reproach* **1:6** [a]Mt 21:21 [b]Mk 11:23; Ac 10:20 [c]Mt 14:28-31; Eph 4:14 **1:8** [a]Jas 4:8 [b]2Pe 2:14 [1]Or *doubting, hesitating*

9 [a]But the [1]brother of humble
circumstances is to boast in his high
position; 10 and the rich man *is to
boast* in his humiliation, because
[a]like [1]flowering grass he will pass
away. 11 For the sun rises with [a,1]a
scorching heat and [b]withers the
grass; and its flower falls off and the
beauty of its appearance is destroyed;
so too the rich man in the midst of
his pursuits will fade away.

12 [a]Blessed is a man who perseveres
under trial; for once he has [1]been ap-
proved, he will receive [b]the crown of
life which *the Lord* [c]has promised to
those who [d]love Him. 13 Let no one
say when he is tempted, "[a]I am being
tempted [1]by God"; for God cannot be
tempted [2]by evil, and He Himself does
not tempt anyone. 14 But each one is
tempted when he is carried away and
enticed by his own lust. 15 Then [a]when
lust has conceived, it gives birth to
sin, and when [b]sin is fully matured,
it brings forth death. 16 [a]Do not be
[1]deceived, [b]my beloved brothers.
17 Every good thing given and every
perfect gift is [a]from above, coming
down from [b]the Father of lights, [c]with
whom there is no variation or [1]shifting
shadow. 18 In the exercise of [a]His will
He [b]brought us forth by [c]the word of
truth, so that we would be [1]a kind of
[d]first fruits [2]among His creatures.

### *Doers of the Word*

19 [a,1]Know *this*, [b]my beloved broth-
ers. But everyone must be quick
to hear, [c]slow to speak *and* [d]slow
to anger; 20 for [a]the anger of man
does not achieve the righteousness
of God. 21 Therefore, [a]laying aside
all filthiness and *all* [1]that remains
of wickedness, in gentleness receive
[b]the implanted word, which is able to
save your souls. 22 [a]But become doers
of the word, and not merely hearers
who delude themselves. 23 For if
anyone is a hearer of the word and
not a doer, he is like a man who looks
at his [1]natural face [a]in a mirror; 24 for
*once* he looked at himself and has
gone away, [1]he immediately forgot
what kind of person he was. 25 But
one who looks intently at the perfect
law, [a]the *law* of freedom, and abides
by it, not having become a forgetful
hearer but a doer of the work, this
man will be [b]blessed in [1]what he
does.

26 If anyone thinks himself to
be religious while not [a,1]bridling
his tongue but deceiving his *own*
heart, this man's religion is worth-
less. 27 Pure and undefiled religion
[a]before *our* God and Father is this:
to [b]visit [c]orphans and widows in
their affliction, *and* to keep oneself
unstained [1]by [d]the world.

---

**1:9** [a]Lk 14:11 [1]Church member **1:10** [a]1Co 7:31; 1Pe 1:24 [1]Lit *the flower of the grass* **1:11** [a]Mt 20:12 [b]Ps 102:4, 11; Is 40:7f [1]Lit *the* **1:12** [a]Lk 6:22; Jas 5:11; 1Pe 3:14; 4:14 [b]1Co 9:25 [c]Ex 20:6; Jas 2:5 [d]1Co 2:9; 8:3 [1]Or *passed the test* **1:13** [a]Ge 22:1 [1]Lit *from* [2]Lit *of evil things* **1:15** [a]Job 15:35; Ps 7:14; Is 59:4 [b]Ro 5:12; 6:23 **1:16** [a]1Co 6:9 [b]Ac 1:15; Jas 1:2, 19; 2:1, 5, 14; 3:1, 10; 4:11; 5:12, 19 [1]Or *misled* **1:17** [a]Jn 3:3; Jas 3:15, 17 [b]Ps 136:7; 1Jn 1:5 [c]Mal 3:6 [1]Lit *shadow of turning* **1:18** [a]Jn 1:13 [b]Jas 1:15; 1Pe 1:3, 23 [c]2Co 6:7; Eph 1:13; 2Ti 2:15 [d]Jer 2:3; Rev 14:4 [1]Or *a certain first fruits* [2]Lit *of* **1:19** [a]1Jn 2:21 [b]Ac 1:15; Jas 1:2, 16; 2:1, 5, 14; 3:1, 10; 4:11; 5:12, 19 [c]Pr 10:19; 17:27 [d]Pr 16:32; Ecc 7:9 [1]Or This *you know* **1:20** [a]Mt 5:22; Eph 4:26 **1:21** [a]Eph 4:22; 1Pe 2:1 [b]Eph 1:13; 1Pe 1:22f [1]Lit *abundance of malice* **1:22** [a]Mt 7:24-27; Lk 6:46-49; Ro 2:13; Jas 1:22-25; 2:14-20 **1:23** [a]1Co 13:12 [1]Or *nature*; lit *the face of his birth* **1:24** [1]Lit *and he* **1:25** [a]Jn 8:32; Ro 8:2; Ga 2:4; 6:2; Jas 2:12; 1Pe 2:16 [b]Jn 13:17 [1]Lit *his doing* **1:26** [a]Ps 39:1; 141:3; Jas 3:2-12 [1]Or *controlling* **1:27** [a]Ro 2:13; Ga 3:11 [b]Mt 25:36 [c]Dt 14:29; Job 31:16, 17, 21; Ps 146:9; Is 1:17, 23 [d]Mt 12:32; Eph 2:2; Tit 2:12; Jas 4:4; 2Pe 1:4; 2:20; 1Jn 2:15-17 [1]Lit *from*

### *The Sin of Favoritism*

**2** [a]My brothers, [b]do not hold your
faith in our [c,1]glorious Lord Jesus
Christ with *an attitude of* [d]personal
favoritism. **2** For if a man comes into
your [1]assembly with a gold ring
and dressed in [a]bright clothes, and
there also comes in a poor man in
[b]dirty clothes, **3** and you [1]pay special
attention to the one who is wearing
the [a]bright clothes, and say, "You sit
here in a good place," and you say to
the poor man, "You stand over there,
or sit down by my footstool," **4** have
you not made distinctions among
yourselves, and become judges [a]with
evil thoughts? **5** Listen, [a]my beloved
brothers: did not [b]God choose the
poor [1]of this world *to be* [c]rich in faith
and [d]heirs of the kingdom which He
[e]promised to those who love Him?
**6** But you have dishonored the poor
man. Is it not the rich who oppress
you and they themselves [a]drag you
into [1]court? **7** [a]Do they not blaspheme
the good name [1]by which you have
been called?

**8** If, however, you [a]are fulfilling the
[1]royal law according to the Scripture,
"[b]YOU SHALL LOVE YOUR NEIGHBOR
AS YOURSELF," you are doing well.
**9** But if you [a]show partiality, you
are committing sin, being convicted
by the [1]law as transgressors. **10** For
whoever keeps the whole [1]law and
yet [a]stumbles in one *point*, he has
become [b]guilty of all. **11** For He who
said, "[a]DO NOT COMMIT ADULTERY,"
also said, "[b]DO NOT MURDER." Now
if you do not commit adultery, but
murder, you have become a trans-
gressor of the [1]law. **12** So speak and so
act as those who are to be judged by
[a]*the* law of freedom. **13** For [a]judgment
*will be* merciless to one who has
shown no mercy. Mercy [1]triumphs
over judgment.

### *Faith and Works*

**14** [a]What use is it, [b]my brothers, if
someone says he has faith but he has
no works? Can [1]that faith save him?
**15** [a]If a brother or sister is without
clothing and in need of daily food,
**16** and one of you says to them, "[a]Go
in peace, [1]be warmed and be filled,"
and yet you do not give them what
is necessary for *their* body, what use
is that? **17** Even so [a]faith, if it has no
works, is [1]dead by itself.

**18** [a]But someone will say, "You
have faith; and I have works. Show
me your [b]faith without the works,
and I will [c]show you my faith [d]by my
works." **19** You believe that [a,1]God is
one. [b]You do well; [c]the demons also
believe, and shudder. **20** But are you
willing to recognize, [a]you foolish
fellow, that [b]faith without works is
useless? **21** [a]Was not Abraham our
father justified by works when he
offered up Isaac his son on the altar?

◆ **2:1** [a]Jas 1:16 [b]Heb 12:2 [c]Ac 7:2; 1Co 2:8 [d]Ac 10:34; Jas 2:9 [1]Or *Lord Jesus Christ, the glorious one* **2:2** [a]Lk 23:11; Jas 2:3 [b]Zec 3:3f [1]Or *synagogue* **2:3** [a]Lk 23:11 [1]Lit *look at* **2:4** [a]Lk 18:6; Jn 7:24 **2:5** [a]Jas 1:16 [b]Job 34:19; 1Co 1:27f [c]Lk 12:21; Rev 2:9 [d]Mt 5:3; 25:34 [e]Jas 1:12 [1]Lit *to the* **2:6** [a]Ac 8:3; 16:19 [1]Lit *courts* **2:7** [a]Ac 11:26; 1Pe 4:16 [1]Lit *which has been called upon you* **2:8** [a]Mt 7:12 [b]Lv 19:18 [1]Or *law of* our *King* **2:9** [a]Ac 10:34; Jas 2:1 [1]Or *Law* **2:10** [a]Jas 3:2; 2Pe 1:10; Jd 24 [b]Mt 5:19; Ga 5:3 [1]Or *Law* **2:11** [a]Ex 20:14; Dt 5:18 [b]Ex 20:13; Dt 5:17 [1]Or *Law* **2:12** [a]Jas 1:25 **2:13** [a]Pr 21:13; Mt 5:7; 18:32-35; Lk 6:37f [1]Lit *boasts against* **2:14** [a]Jas 1:22ff [b]Jas 1:16 [1]Lit *the* **2:15** [a]Mt 25:35f; Lk 3:11 **2:16** [a]1Jn 3:17f [1]Or *warm yourselves and fill yourselves* **2:17** [a]Ga 5:6; Jas 2:20, 26 [1]Or *dead by its own standards* **2:18** [a]Ro 9:19 [b]Ro 3:28; 4:6; Heb 11:33 [c]Jas 3:13 [d]Mt 7:16f; Ga 5:6 **2:19** [a]Dt 6:4; Mk 12:29 [b]Jas 2:8 [c]Mt 8:29; Mk 1:24; 5:7; Lk 4:34; Ac 19:15 [1]One early ms *there is one God* **2:20** [a]Ro 9:20; 1Co 15:36 [b]Ga 5:6; Jas 2:17, 26 **2:21** [a]Ge 22:9, 10, 12, 16-18

**22** You see that [a]faith was working
with his works, and [1]as a result of the
[b]works, faith was [2]perfected. **23** And
the Scripture was fulfilled which
says, "[a]AND ABRAHAM BELIEVED
GOD, AND IT WAS COUNTED TO HIM AS
RIGHTEOUSNESS," and he was called
[b]the friend of God. **24** You see that a
man is justified by works and not by
faith alone. **25** And in the same way,
was not [a]Rahab the harlot also jus-
tified by works [b]when she received
the messengers and sent them out by
another way? **26** For just as the body
without *the* spirit is dead, so also
[a]faith without works is dead.

### *The Tongue Is a Fire*

**3** [a]Do not, many *of you*, become
teachers, [b]my brothers, knowing
that we will receive a [1]stricter judg-
ment. **2** For we all [a]stumble in many
*ways.* [b]If anyone does not stumble in
[1]what he says, he is a [c]perfect man,
able to [d]bridle the entire body as
well. **3** Now [a]if we put the bits into
the horses' mouths so that they will
obey us, we direct their entire body as
well. **4** Look at the ships also, though
they are so great and are driven by
strong winds, they are still directed
by a very small rudder wherever the
inclination of the pilot wills. **5** So also
the tongue is a small part of the body,
and *yet* it [a]boasts of great things.
[b]Behold how great a forest is set
aflame by such a small fire! **6** And
[a]the tongue is a fire, the *very* world
of unrighteousness; the tongue is set
among our members as that which
[b]defiles the entire body, and sets on
fire the course of *our* [1]existence, and
is set on fire by [c,2]hell. **7** For every kind
of beasts and birds, of reptiles and
creatures of the sea, is tamed and has
been tamed by mankind. **8** But no one
can tame the tongue; *it is* a restless
evil *and* full of [a]deadly poison. **9** With
it we bless [a]*our* Lord and Father, and
with it we curse men, [b]who have been
made in the likeness of God. **10** From
the same mouth come blessing and
cursing. My brothers, these things
ought not to be so. **11** Does a fountain
pour forth from the same opening
[1]fresh and bitter *water*? **12** [a]Can a fig
tree, my brothers, produce olives, or a
vine produce figs? Nor *can* saltwater
produce [1]fresh.

### *Wisdom from Above*

**13** Who among you is wise and
understanding? [a]Let him show by
his [b]good conduct his works in the
gentleness of wisdom. **14** But if you
have bitter [a]jealousy and [1]selfish
ambition in your heart, do not be
arrogant and *so* lie against [b]the truth.
**15** This wisdom is not coming down
[a]from above, but is [b]earthly, [c,1]natu-
ral, [d]demonic. **16** For where [a]jealousy
and [1]selfish ambition exist, [2]there is
disorder and every evil practice.
**17** But the wisdom [a]from above is first

---

**2:22** [a]Jn 6:29; Heb 11:17 [b]1Th 1:3 [1]Or *by the deeds* [2]Or *completed* **2:23** [a]Ge 15:6; Ro 4:3 [b]2Chr 20:7; Is 41:8 **2:25** [a]Heb 11:31 [b]Jos 2:4, 6, 15 **2:26** [a]Ga 5:6; Jas 2:17, 20 ◆ **3:1** [a]Mt 23:8; Ro 2:20f; 1Ti 1:7 [b]Jas 1:16; 3:10 [1]Or *greater condemnation* **3:2** [a]Jas 2:10 [b]Mt 12:34-37; Jas 3:2-12 [c]Jas 1:4 [d]Jas 1:26 [1]Lit *word* **3:3** [a]Ps 32:9 **3:5** [a]Ps 12:3f; 73:8f [b]Pr 26:20f **3:6** [a]Ps 120:2, 3; Pr 16:27 [b]Mt 12:36f; 15:11, 18f [c]Mt 5:22 [1]Or *birth* [2]Gr *Gehenna* **3:8** [a]Ps 140:3; Ecc 10:11; Ro 3:13 **3:9** [a]Jas 1:27 [b]Ge 1:26; 1Co 11:7 **3:11** [1]Lit *sweet* **3:12** [a]Mt 7:16 [1]v 11, note 1 **3:13** [a]Jas 2:18 [b]1Pe 2:12 **3:14** [a]Ro 2:8; 2Co 12:20; Jas 3:16 [b]1Ti 2:4; Jas 1:18; 5:19 [1]Or *strife* **3:15** [a]Jas 1:17 [b]1Co 2:6; 3:19 [c]2Co 1:12; Jd 19 [d]2Th 2:9f; 1Ti 4:1; Rev 2:24 [1]Or *unspiritual* **3:16** [a]Ro 2:8; 2Co 12:20; Jas 3:14 [1]v 14, note 1 [2]In that place **3:17** [a]Jas 1:17

[b]pure, then [c]peaceable, [d]considerate,
submissive, [e]full of mercy and good
fruits, [f]without doubting, without
[g]hypocrisy. **18** And the fruit of righ-
teousness [a]is sown in peace [1]by those
who make peace.

### *Draw Near to God*

**4** [1]What is the source of quarrels
and [a]conflicts among you? [2]Is
not the source your pleasures that
wage [b]war in your members? **2** You
lust and do not have, *so* you [a]murder.
You are envious and cannot obtain,
*so* you fight and quarrel. You do not
have because you do not ask. **3** You
ask and [a]do not receive, because
you ask [1]with wrong motives, so that
you may spend *it* [2]on your pleasures.
**4** You [a]adulteresses, do you not know
that friendship with [b]the world is
[c]enmity *toward* God? [d]Therefore,
whoever wishes to be a friend of
the world sets himself as an enemy
of God. **5** Or do you think that the
Scripture [a]speaks to no purpose: "[1]He
[2]jealously desires [b]the Spirit which
He has made to dwell in us"? **6** But
[a]He gives a greater grace. Therefore *it*
says, "[b]GOD IS OPPOSED TO THE PROUD,
BUT GIVES GRACE TO THE HUMBLE."
**7** [a]Be subject therefore to God. [b]Resist
the devil and he will flee from you.
**8** [a]Draw near to God and He will draw
near to you. [b]Cleanse your hands,
you sinners, and [c]purify your hearts,
you [d]double-minded. **9** [a]Be miserable
and mourn and cry. Let your laughter
be turned into mourning and your
joy to gloom. **10** [a]Humble yourselves
in the presence of the Lord, and He
will exalt you.
**11** [a]Do not slander one another,
[b]brothers. He who slanders a brother
or [c]judges his brother, slanders [d]the
law and judges the law; but if you
judge the law, you are not [e]a doer
of the law but a judge *of it.* **12** There
is *only* one [a]Lawgiver and Judge,
the One who is [b]able to save and to
destroy. But [c]who are you who judge
your neighbor?

### *Life Is a Vapor*

**13** [a]Come now, you who say, "[b]Today
or tomorrow we will go to such and
such a city, and spend a year there
and engage in business and make
a profit." **14** [1]Yet you do not know
[2]what your life will be like tomor-
row. [a]You are a vapor that appears
for a little while and then vanishes
away. **15** [1]Instead, you ought to say,
"[a]If the Lord wills, we will live and
also do this or that." **16** But as it is,
you boast in your [1]arrogance. [a]All
such boasting is evil. **17** Therefore,
[a]to one who knows to do *the* [1]right
thing and does not do it, to him it
is sin.

---

**3:17** [b]2Co 7:11; Jas 4:8 [c]Mt 5:9; Heb 12:11 [d]Tit 3:2 [e]Lk 6:36; Jas 2:13 [f]Jas 2:4 [g]Ro 12:9; 2Co 6:6 **3:18** [a]Pr 11:18; Is 32:17; Hos 10:12; Am 6:12; Ga 6:8; Php 1:11 [1]Or *for* ◆ **4:1** [a]Tit 3:9 [b]Ro 7:23 [1]Lit *From where wars and from where fightings* [2]Lit Are they *not from here*, from your **4:2** [a]Jas 5:6; 1Jn 3:15 **4:3** [a]1Jn 3:22; 5:14 [1]Lit *wickedly* [2]Lit *in* **4:4** [a]Jer 2:2; Eze 16:32 [b]Jas 1:27 [c]Ro 8:7; 1Jn 2:15 [d]Mt 6:24; Jn 15:19 **4:5** [a]Nu 23:19 [b]1Co 6:19; 2Co 6:16 [1]Or *The spirit which He has made to dwell in us lusts with envy* [2]Lit *desires to jealousy* **4:6** [a]Is 54:7f; Mt 13:12 [b]Ps 138:6; Pr 3:34; Mt 23:12; 1Pe 5:5 **4:7** [a]1Pe 5:6 [b]Eph 4:27; 6:11f; 1Pe 5:8f **4:8** [a]2Chr 15:2; Zec 1:3; Mal 3:7; Heb 7:19 [b]Job 17:9; Is 1:16; 1Ti 2:8 [c]Jer 4:14; Jas 3:17; 1Pe 1:22; 1Jn 3:3 [d]Jas 1:8 **4:9** [a]Ne 8:9; Pr 14:13; Lk 6:25 **4:10** [a]Job 5:11; Eze 21:26; Lk 1:52; Jas 4:6 **4:11** [a]2Co 12:20; Jas 5:9; 1Pe 2:1 [b]Jas 1:16; 5:7, 9, 10 [c]Mt 7:1; Ro 14:4 [d]Jas 2:8 [e]Jas 1:22 **4:12** [a]Is 33:22; Jas 5:9 [b]Mt 10:28 [c]Ro 14:4 **4:13** [a]Jas 5:1 [b]Pr 27:1; Lk 12:18-20 **4:14** [a]Job 7:7; Ps 39:5; 102:3; 144:4 [1]Lit *Who do not* [2]Or *what* will happen *tomorrow. What kind of life is yours?* **4:15** [a]Ac 18:21 [1]Lit *Instead of your saying* **4:16** [a]1Co 5:6 [1]Or *pretensions* **4:17** [a]Lk 12:47; Jn 9:41; 2Pe 2:21 [1]Or *good*

### *Miseries of the Rich*

5 [a]Come now, [b]you rich, [c]cry,
howling over your miseries
which are coming upon you. **2** [a]Your
riches have rotted and your garments
have become moth-eaten. **3** Your gold
and your silver have rusted, and their
corrosion will be a witness against
you and will consume your flesh like
fire. You have stored up *such* treasure
[a]in the last days! **4** Behold, [a]the pay
of the laborers who mowed your
fields—that which has been withheld by you—cries out *against you;*
and [b]the outcries of those who did
the harvesting have reached the ears
of [c]the [1]Lord of [2]Sabaoth. **5** You have
[a]lived luxuriously on the earth and
lived in self-indulgence. You have
[1]fattened your hearts in a [b]DAY OF
SLAUGHTER. **6** You have condemned
and [a]murdered [b]the righteous *man;*
[1]he does not resist you.

### *Patience and Perseverance*

**7** Therefore be patient, [a]brothers,
[b]until the coming of the Lord. Behold, [c]the farmer waits for the precious fruit of the soil, being patient
about it, until [1]it receives [d]the early
and late rains. **8** [a]You too be patient;
[b]strengthen your hearts, for [c]the
coming of the Lord is [d]at hand. **9** [a]Do
not groan, [b]brothers, against one
another, so that you yourselves may
not be judged. Behold, [c]the Judge is
standing [d,1]right at the [2]door. **10** As
an example, [a]brothers, of suffering
and patience, take [b]the prophets
who spoke in the name of the Lord.
**11** Behold, we count those [a]blessed
who persevere. You have heard of
[b]the [1]perseverance of Job and have
seen [c]the [2]outcome of the Lord's
dealings, that [d]the Lord is full of
compassion and *is* merciful.

**12** But above all, [a]my brothers,
[b]do not swear, either by heaven or
by earth or with any other oath. But
let [1]your yes be yes, and your no,
no, so that you may not fall under
judgment.

**13** Is anyone among you [a]suffering? [b]*Then* he must pray. Is anyone
cheerful? He is to [c]sing praises. **14** Is
anyone among you sick? *Then* he must
call for [a]the elders of the church and
they are to pray over him, [b,1]anointing
him with oil in the name of the Lord.
**15** And the [a]prayer [1]offered in faith
will [b]save the one who is sick, and the
Lord will [c]raise him up, and if he has
committed sins, [2]they will be forgiven
him. **16** Therefore, [a]confess your sins
to one another, and pray for one another so that you may be [b]healed. [c]The
effective [1]prayer of a righteous man
can accomplish much. **17** Elijah was
[a]a man with a nature like ours, and
[b]he prayed [1]earnestly that it would not

◆ **5:1** [a]Jas 4:13 [b]Lk 6:24; 1Ti 6:9 [c]Is 13:6; 15:3; Eze 30:2 **5:2** [a]Job 13:28; Is 50:9; Mt 6:19f **5:3** [a]Jas 5:7, 8 **5:4** [a]Lv 19:13; Job 24:10f; Jer 22:13; Mal 3:5 [b]Ex 2:23; Dt 24:15; Job 31:38f [c]Ro 9:29; Is 5:9 [1]In OT, Yahweh, cf. Is 5:9 [2]Hosts **5:5** [a]Eze 16:49; Lk 16:19; 1Ti 5:6; 2Pe 2:13 [b]Is 30:25; Jer 12:3; 25:34 [1]Lit *nourished* **5:6** [a]Jas 4:2 [b]Heb 10:38; 1Pe 4:18 [1]Or *does He not resist you?*, cf. 4:6 **5:7** [a]Jas 4:11; 5:9, 10 [b]Jn 21:22; 1Th 2:19 [c]Ga 6:9 [d]Dt 11:14; Jer 5:24; Joel 2:23 [1]Or *he* **5:8** [a]Lk 21:19 [b]1Th 3:13 [c]Jn 21:22; 1Th 2:19 [d]Ro 13:11, 12; 1Pe 4:7 **5:9** [a]Jas 4:11 [b]Jas 5:7, 10 [c]1Co 4:5; Jas 4:12; 1Pe 4:5 [d]Mt 24:33; Mk 13:29 [1]Lit *before* [2]Lit *doors* **5:10** [a]Jas 4:11; 5:7, 9 [b]Mt 5:12 **5:11** [a]Mt 5:10; 1Pe 3:14 [b]Job 1:21f; 2:10 [c]Job 42:10, 12 [d]Ex 34:6; Ps 103:8 [1]Or *steadfastness* [2]Lit *end of the Lord* **5:12** [a]Jas 1:16 [b]Mt 5:34-37 [1]Lit *yours is to be yes, yes, and no, no* **5:13** [a]Jas 5:10 [b]Ps 50:15 [c]1Co 14:15; Col 3:16 **5:14** [a]Ac 11:30 [b]Mk 6:13; 16:18 [1]Lit *having anointed* **5:15** [a]Jas 1:6 [b]1Co 1:21; Jas 5:20 [c]Jn 6:39; 2Co 4:14 [1]Lit *of* [2]Lit *it* **5:16** [a]Mt 3:6; Mk 1:5; Ac 19:18 [b]Heb 12:13; 1Pe 2:24 [c]Ge 18:23-32; Jn 9:31 [1]Lit *supplication* **5:17** [a]Ac 14:15 [b]1Ki 17:1; 18:1 [1]Lit *with prayer*

rain, and it did not rain on the earth for
[c]three years and six months. **18** Then
he [a]prayed again, and [b]the [1]sky gave
rain and the earth produced its fruit.
**19** My brothers, [a]if any among you
strays from [b]the truth and one turns
him back, **20** let him know that [1]he
who turns a sinner from the error
of his way will [a]save his soul from
death and will [b]COVER A MULTITUDE
OF SINS.

# *The First Letter of* PETER

### *A Living Hope*

**1** [a]Peter, an apostle of Jesus Christ,
To those who reside as [b]exiles,
[c]scattered throughout [d]Pontus,
[e]Galatia, [d]Cappadocia, [d]Asia, and
[f]Bithynia, [g]who are chosen **2** ac-
cording to the [a]foreknowledge of
God the Father, [b]by the sanctifying
work of the Spirit, to the [c]obedience
of Jesus Christ and the [d]sprinkling of
His blood: [e]May grace and peace be
multiplied to you.
**3** [a]Blessed be the God and Father of
our Lord Jesus Christ, who [b]accord-
ing to His great mercy [c]has caused
us to be born again to [d]a living hope
through the [e]resurrection of Jesus
Christ from the dead, **4** to *obtain*
an [a]inheritance incorruptible and
undefiled and [b]unfading, having
been [c]kept in heaven for you, **5** who
are [a]protected by the power of God
[b]through faith for [c]a salvation ready
[d]to be revealed in the last time. **6** [a]In
this you greatly rejoice, even though
now [b]for a little while, [c]if necessary,
you have been grieved by [d]various
[1]trials, **7** so that the [a,1]proof of your
faith, *being* more precious than gold
which [2]is perishable, [b]even though
tested by fire, [c]may be found to result
in praise and glory and honor at [d]the
revelation of Jesus Christ. **8** And
[a]though you have not seen Him,
you [b]love Him, and though you do
not see Him now, but believe in Him,
you rejoice with joy inexpressible
and [1]full of glory, **9** receiving as [a]the
outcome of your faith the salvation
of [1]your souls.
**10** [a]Concerning this salvation,
the prophets, who [b]prophesied of
the [c]grace that *would come* to you,
made careful searches and inquiries,
**11** [1]inquiring to know what *time* or
what kind of time [a]the Spirit of
Christ within them was indicating
as He was [b]predicting the sufferings
of Christ and the glories [2]to follow.
**12** It was revealed to them that they

---

**5:17** [c]Lk 4:25 **5:18** [a]1Ki 18:42 [b]1Ki 18:45 [1]Lit *heaven* **5:19** [a]Mt 18:15; Ga 6:1 [b]Jas 3:14 **5:20** [a]Ro 11:14; 1Co 1:21; Jas 1:21 [b]Pr 10:12; 1Pe 4:8 [1]Lit *he who has turned* ◆ **1:1** [a]2Pe 1:1 [b]1Pe 2:11 [c]Jas 1:1 [d]Ac 2:9 [e]Ac 16:6 [f]Ac 16:7 [g]Mt 24:22; Lk 18:7 **1:2** [a]Ro 8:29; 1Pe 1:20 [b]2Th 2:13 [c]1Pe 1:14, 22 [d]Heb 10:22; 12:24 [e]2Pe 1:2 **1:3** [a]2Co 1:3 [b]Ga 6:16; Tit 3:5 [c]Jas 1:18; 1Pe 1:23 [d]1Pe 1:13, 21; 3:5, 15; 1Jn 3:3 [e]1Co 15:20; 1Pe 3:21 **1:4** [a]Ac 20:32; Ro 8:17; Col 3:24 [b]1Pe 5:4 [c]2Ti 4:8 **1:5** [a]Jn 10:28; Php 4:7 [b]Eph 2:8 [c]1Co 1:21; 2Th 2:13 [d]1Pe 4:13; 5:1 **1:6** [a]Ro 5:2 [b]1Pe 5:10 [c]1Pe 3:17 [d]Jas 1:2; 1Pe 4:12 [1]Or *temptations* **1:7** [a]Jas 1:3 [b]1Co 3:13 [c]Ro 2:7 [d]Lk 17:30; 1Pe 1:13; 4:13 [1]Or *genuineness* [2]Lit *perishes* **1:8** [a]Jn 20:29 [b]Eph 3:19 [1]Lit *glorified* **1:9** [a]Ro 6:22 [1]One early ms omits *your* **1:10** [a]Mt 13:17; Lk 10:24 [b]Mt 26:24 [c]1Pe 1:13 **1:11** [a]2Pe 1:21 [b]Mt 26:24 [1]Or *seeking* [2]Lit *after these*

were not serving themselves, but
you, in these things which now
have been declared to you through
those who [a]proclaimed the gospel
to you by [b]the Holy Spirit sent from
heaven—things into which [c]angels
long to [1]look.
**13** Therefore, having [a,1]girded your
minds for action, [b,2]being sober *in*
*spirit*, fix your [c]hope completely on
the [d]grace [3]to be brought to you at
[e]the revelation of Jesus Christ. **14** As
[a,1]obedient children, not [b,2]being
conformed to the former lusts *which*
*were yours* in your [c]ignorance, **15** but
[a,1]like the Holy One who called you,
[b,2]be holy yourselves also [c]in all *your*
conduct; **16** because it is written,
"[a]YOU SHALL BE HOLY, FOR I AM HOLY."
**17** And if you [a]address as Father
the One who [b]impartially [c]judges
according to each one's work, con-
duct yourselves [d,1]in fear during the
time of your [e]sojourn, **18** knowing
that you were not [a,1]redeemed with
corruptible things like silver or gold
from your [b]futile conduct inherited
from your forefathers, **19** but with
precious [a]blood, as of a [b]lamb un-
blemished and spotless, *the blood* of
Christ. **20** He was [a]foreknown before
[b]the foundation of the world, but
[c]appeared [1]in these last times [d]for
the sake of you **21** who through Him
are [a]believers in God, who raised
Him from the dead and [b]gave Him
glory, so that your faith and [c]hope
are in God.
**22** Since you have [a]in obedience
to the truth [b]purified your souls
for a love of the brothers [c]without
hypocrisy, fervently love one another
from [1]the heart, **23** for you have been
[a]born again [b]not of corruptible seed
but incorruptible, *that is*, through
the living and enduring [c]word of
God. **24** For,

"[a]ALL FLESH IS LIKE GRASS,
AND ALL ITS GLORY
LIKE THE FLOWER OF GRASS.
THE GRASS WITHERS,
AND THE FLOWER FALLS OFF,
**25** [a]BUT THE WORD
OF THE LORD
ENDURES FOREVER."

And this is [b]the word which was
[1]proclaimed to you as good news.

### *As Living Stones, God's Chosen Family*

**2** Therefore, [a]laying aside all [1]mal-
ice and all deceit and [2]hypocrisy
and [2]envy and all [b,2]slander, **2** [a]like
newborn babies, long for the [b,1]pure
[2]milk of the word, so that by it you
may [c]grow [3]in respect to salvation,
**3** if you have [a]TASTED [b,1]THE KINDNESS
OF THE [2]LORD.

---

**1:12** [a]1Pe 1:25; 4:6 [b]Ac 2:2-4 [c]1Ti 3:16 [1]Or *gain a clear glimpse* **1:13** [a]Eph 6:14 [b]1Th 5:6, 8; 2Ti 4:5; 1Pe 4:7; 5:8 [c]1Pe 1:3 [d]1Pe 1:10 [e]1Pe 1:7 [1]Lit *gird the loins of your mind* [2]Lit *be sober* [3]Or *which is announced* **1:14** [a]1Pe 1:2 [b]Ro 12:2; 1Pe 4:2f [c]Eph 4:18 [1]Lit *children of obedience* [2]Or *conforming yourselves* **1:15** [a]1Th 4:7; 1Jn 3:3 [b]2Co 7:1 [c]Jas 3:13 [1]Lit *according to* [2]Or *become* **1:16** [a]Lv 11:44f; 19:2; 20:7 **1:17** [a]Ps 89:26; Jer 3:19; Mt 6:9 [b]Ac 10:34 [c]Mt 16:27 [d]2Co 7:1; Heb 12:28; 1Pe 3:15 [e]1Pe 2:11 [1]Or *with reverence* **1:18** [a]Is 52:3; 1Co 6:20; Tit 2:14; Heb 9:12 [b]Eph 4:17 [1]Or *ransomed* **1:19** [a]Ac 20:28; 1Pe 1:2 [b]Jn 1:29 **1:20** [a]Ac 2:23; Eph 1:4; 1Pe 1:2; Rev 13:8 [b]Mt 25:34 [c]Heb 9:26 [d]Heb 2:14 [1]Lit *at the end of the times* **1:21** [a]Ro 4:24; 10:9 [b]Jn 17:5, 24; 1Ti 3:16; Heb 2:9 [c]1Pe 1:3 **1:22** [a]1Pe 1:2 [b]Jas 4:8 [c]Jn 13:34; Ro 12:10; Heb 13:1; 1Pe 2:17; 3:8 [1]Two early mss *a clean heart* **1:23** [a]Jn 3:3; 1Pe 1:3 [b]Jn 1:13 [c]Heb 4:12 **1:24** [a]Is 40:6ff; Jas 1:10f **1:25** [a]Is 40:8 [b]Heb 6:5 [1]Lit *preached as good news to you*
◆ **2:1** [a]Eph 4:22, 25, 31; Jas 1:21 [b]Jas 4:11 [1]Or *wickedness* [2]Plural nouns **2:2** [a]Mt 18:3; 19:14; Mk 10:15; Lk 18:17; 1Co 14:20 [b]1Co 3:2 [c]Eph 4:15f [1]Or *unadulterated* [2]Or *spiritual* (Gr *logikos*) *milk* [3]Or *up to salvation* **2:3** [a]Heb 6:5 [b]Ps 34:8; Tit 3:4 [1]Lit *that the Lord is kind* [2]In OT, Yahweh, cf. Ps 34:8

**4** *And* coming to Him as to a living
stone which has been [a]rejected by
men, but is [1]choice and precious in
the sight of God, **5** [a]you also, as living
stones, [1]are being built up as a [b]spiritual
house for a holy [c]priesthood, to
[d]offer up spiritual sacrifices acceptable
to God through Jesus Christ.
**6** For *this* is contained in [1]Scripture:

"[a]BEHOLD, I LAY IN ZION A
CHOICE STONE,
A [b]PRECIOUS CORNER *STONE*,
AND HE WHO BELIEVES
UPON [2]HIM WILL NOT
BE PUT TO SHAME."

**7** [a]This precious value, then, is for
you who believe; but for those who
disbelieve,

"[b]THE STONE WHICH THE
BUILDERS [c]REJECTED,
THIS HAS BECOME THE
CHIEF CORNER *stone*,"

**8** and,

"[a]A STONE OF STUMBLING
AND A ROCK OF OFFENSE."

[b]They stumble because they are
disobedient to the word, [c]and to this
*stumbling* they were also appointed.
**9** But you are [a]A CHOSEN FAMILY, A
royal [b]PRIESTHOOD, A [c]HOLY NATION,
[d]A PEOPLE FOR *God's* OWN POSSESSION,
so that you may proclaim the excellencies
of Him who has called you
[e]out of darkness into His marvelous
light; **10** [a]for you once were NOT A
PEOPLE, but now you are THE PEOPLE
OF GOD; you had NOT RECEIVED MERCY,
but now you have RECEIVED MERCY.
**11** [a]Beloved, [b]I urge you as
[c]sojourners and exiles to abstain
from [d]fleshly lusts which wage [e]war
against the soul, **12** [a]by keeping
your conduct excellent among the
Gentiles, so that in the thing which
they [b]slander you as evildoers, they
may [1]because of your good works, as
they observe *them*, [c]glorify God [d]in
the DAY OF [2]VISITATION.

### *Be Subject to Authority*

**13** [a]Be subject for the sake of the Lord
to every human institution, whether
to a king as the one in authority, **14** or to
governors as sent [1]by him [a]for the
punishment of evildoers and the
[b]praise of those who do good. **15** For
[a,1]such is the will of God that by doing
good you may [b]silence the ignorance
of foolish men. **16** *Act* as [a]free people,
and [1]do not use your freedom as a
covering for evil, but *use it* as [b]slaves
of God. **17** [a]Honor all people, [b]love
the [1]brethren, [c]fear God, [d]honor the
[2]king.
**18** [a]Servants, be subject to your
masters with all fear, not only to
those who are good and [b]considerate,
but also to those who are
[1]crooked. **19** For this *finds* [1]favor, if
for the sake of [a]conscience toward

---

**2:4** [a]1Pe 2:7 [1]Or *elect*; lit *chosen* **2:5** [a]1Co 3:9 [b]Ga 6:10; 1Ti 3:15 [c]Is 61:6; 66:21; 1Pe 2:9; Rev 1:6 [d]Ro 15:16; Heb 13:15 [1]Or *allow yourselves to be built up, build yourselves up* **2:6** [a]Is 28:16; Ro 9:32, 33; 10:11; 1Pe 2:8 [b]Eph 2:20 [1]Or *a scripture* [2]Or *it* **2:7** [a]2Co 2:16; 1Pe 2:7, 8 [b]Ps 118:22; Mt 21:42; Lk 2:34 [c]1Pe 2:4 **2:8** [a]Is 8:14 [b]1Co 1:23; Ga 5:11 [c]Ro 9:22 **2:9** [a]Is 43:20f; Dt 10:15 [b]Is 61:6; 66:21; 1Pe 2:5; Rev 1:6 [c]Ex 19:6; Dt 7:6 [d]Ex 19:5; Dt 4:20; 14:2; Tit 2:14 [e]Is 9:2; 42:16; Ac 26:18; 2Co 4:6 **2:10** [a]Hos 1:10; 2:23; Ro 9:25; 10:19 **2:11** [a]Heb 6:9; 1Pe 4:12 [b]Ro 12:1 [c]Lv 25:23; Ps 39:12; Eph 2:19; Heb 11:13; 1Pe 1:17 [d]Ro 13:14; Ga 5:16, 24 [e]Jas 4:1 **2:12** [a]2Co 8:21; Php 2:15; Tit 2:8; 1Pe 2:15; 3:16 [b]Ac 28:22 [c]Mt 5:16; 9:8; Jn 13:31; 1Pe 4:11, 16 [d]Is 10:3; Lk 19:44 [1]Or *as a result of* [2]Christ's coming again in judgment **2:13** [a]Ro 13:1 **2:14** [a]Ro 13:4 [b]Ro 13:3 [1]Lit *through* **2:15** [a]1Pe 3:17 [b]1Pe 2:12 [1]Lit *so* **2:16** [a]Jn 8:32; Jas 1:25 [b]Ro 6:22; 1Co 7:22 [1]Lit *not having* **2:17** [a]Ro 12:10; 13:7 [b]1Pe 1:22 [c]Pr 24:21 [d]Mt 22:21; 1Pe 2:13 [1]Or *brotherhood* [2]Or *emperor* **2:18** [a]Eph 6:5 [b]Jas 3:17 [1]Or *unreasonable* **2:19** [a]Ro 13:5; 1Pe 3:14, 16f [1]Or *grace*

God a person bears up under sorrows
when suffering unrighteously. **20** For
what credit is there if, when you sin
and are harshly treated, you endure?
But if [a]when you do good and suffer
*for it,* you endure, this *finds* favor
with God.

### *Christ, Our Example*

**21** For to this [a]you have been called,
[b]since Christ also suffered for you,
leaving you [c]an example that you
should follow in His steps, **22** WHO
[a]DID NO SIN, NOR WAS ANY DECEIT
FOUND IN HIS MOUTH; **23** who being
[a]reviled, was not reviling in return;
while suffering, He was uttering no
threats, but kept entrusting *Himself*
to Him who judges righteously.
**24** Who Himself [a,1]bore our sins
in His body on the [b]tree, so that
[c]having died to [2]sin, we might live
to righteousness; [d]by His [3]WOUNDS
YOU WERE [e]HEALED. **25** For you were
[a]continually straying like sheep,
but now you have returned to the
[b]Shepherd and Overseer of your
souls.

### *Wives and Husbands*

**3** [a]In the same way, you wives,
[b]be subject to your own hus-
bands so that even if any *of them*
are disobedient to the word, they
may be [c]won without a word by
the conduct of their wives, **2** as they
observe your pure conduct with
fear. **3** [a]Your adornment must not
be *merely* external—braiding the
hair, and wearing gold jewelry, or
putting on garments; **4** but *let it be*
[a]the hidden person of the heart, with
the incorruptible quality of a lowly
and quiet spirit, which is precious in
the sight of God. **5** For in this way in
former times the holy women also,
[a]who hoped in God, used to adorn
themselves, being subject to their
own husbands, **6** just as Sarah obeyed
Abraham, [a]calling him lord. You have
become her children if you do good,
[b,1]NOT FEARING ANY INTIMIDATION.

**7** [a]You husbands in the same
way, live with *your wives* in an un-
derstanding way, as with a weaker
[b]vessel, since she is a woman; and
show her honor as a fellow heir of
the grace of life, so that your prayers
will not be hindered.

**8** [1]Now to sum up, [a]all of you be
like-minded, sympathetic, [b]brother-
ly, [c]tender-hearted, and [d]humble in
spirit; **9** [a]not returning evil for evil
or [b]reviling for reviling, but [1]giving
a [c]blessing instead, for [d]you were
called for the very purpose that you
might [e]inherit a blessing. **10** For,

"[a]THE ONE WHO DESIRES LIFE,
TO LOVE AND SEE GOOD DAYS,
MUST KEEP HIS TONGUE
FROM EVIL AND HIS LIPS
FROM SPEAKING DECEIT.
**11** "[a]HE MUST TURN AWAY
FROM EVIL AND DO GOOD;
HE MUST SEEK PEACE
AND PURSUE IT.

---

**2:20** [a]1Pe 3:17 **2:21** [a]Ac 14:22; 1Pe 3:9 [b]1Pe 3:18; 4:1, 13 [c]Mt 11:29; 16:24 **2:22** [a]Is 53:9; 2Co 5:21
**2:23** [a]Is 53:7; Heb 12:3; 1Pe 3:9 **2:24** [a]Is 53:4, 11; 1Co 15:3; Heb 9:28 [b]Dt 21:22-23; Ac 5:30 [c]Ro 6:2, 13
[d]Is 53:5 [e]Heb 12:13; Jas 5:16 [1]Or *carried...up to the cross* [2]Lit *sins* [3]Or *bruise*; lit *wound* **2:25** [a]Is 53:6
[b]Jn 10:11; 1Pe 5:4 ◆ **3:1** [a]1Pe 3:7 [b]Eph 5:22; Col 3:18 [c]1Co 9:19 **3:3** [a]Is 3:18ff; 1Ti 2:9 **3:4** [a]Ro 7:22
**3:5** [a]1Ti 5:5; 1Pe 1:3 **3:6** [a]Ge 18:12 [b]Pr 3:25; 1Pe 3:14 [1]Lit *and are not* **3:7** [a]Eph 5:25; Col 3:19 [b]1Th 4:4
**3:8** [a]Ro 12:16 [b]1Pe 1:22 [c]Eph 4:32 [d]Eph 4:2; Php 2:3; 1Pe 5:5 [1]Or *Finally* **3:9** [a]Ro 12:17; 1Th 5:15
[b]1Co 4:12; 1Pe 2:23 [c]Lk 6:28; Ro 12:14; 1Co 4:12 [d]1Pe 2:21 [e]Ga 3:14; Heb 6:14; 12:17 [1]Lit *blessing instead*
**3:10** [a]Ps 34:12, 13 **3:11** [a]Ps 34:14

12 “[a]FOR THE EYES OF THE [1]LORD
ARE TOWARD THE RIGHTEOUS,
AND HIS EARS ATTEND
TO THEIR PRAYER,
BUT THE FACE OF THE
[1]LORD IS AGAINST THOSE
WHO DO EVIL.”

### *Suffering for Righteousness*

13 [a]And who is [1]there to [2]harm you if
you prove zealous for what is good?
14 But even if you should [a]suffer for
the sake of righteousness, [b]you [1]are
blessed. [c]AND DO NOT FEAR THEIR
FEAR, AND DO NOT BE TROUBLED, 15 but
[1]sanctify [a]Christ as Lord in your
hearts, always *being* ready [b]to make
[2]a defense to everyone who asks you
to give an account for the [a]hope that
is in you, yet [c]with gentleness and
[d]fear, 16 having a [a]good conscience
so that in the thing in which [b]you
are slandered, those who disparage
your good conduct in Christ will be
put to shame. 17 For [a]it is better, [b]if
[1]God should will it so, that you suffer
for doing good rather than for doing
wrong. 18 For [a]Christ also suffered for
sins [b]once for all, *the* righteous for *the*
unrighteous, so that He might [c]bring
you to God, having been put to death
[d]in the flesh, but made alive [e]in the
[1]spirit; 19 in [1]which also He went and
made proclamation to the spirits *now*
in prison, 20 who once were disobedi-
ent, when the [a]patience of God [b]kept
waiting in the days of Noah, during
the construction of [c]the ark, in which
a few, that is, [d]eight [e]persons, were
brought safely through *the* [1]water.
21 [a]Corresponding to that, baptism
now saves you—[b]not the removal
of dirt from the flesh, but an appeal
[1]of a [c]good conscience to God—
through [d]the resurrection of Jesus
Christ, 22 [a]who is at the right hand of
God, [b]having gone into heaven, [c]after
angels and authorities and powers
had been subjected to Him.

### *Keep Fervent in Your Love*

4 Therefore, since [a]Christ has
[1]suffered in the flesh, [b]arm your-
selves also with the same purpose—
because [c]he who has [1]suffered in the
flesh has ceased from sin— 2 [a]so as
to no longer live [b]the rest of the time
in the flesh for the lusts of men, but
for the [c]will of God. 3 For [a]the time
already past is sufficient *for you* to
have worked out the desire of the
Gentiles, [b,1]having pursued a course
of sensuality, lusts, drunkenness,
carousing, drinking parties, and
[2]abominable idolatries. 4 In *all* this,
they are surprised that you do not
run with *them* into the same excesses
of [a]dissipation, [b]maligning *you*, 5 but
they will give account to Him who
is ready to judge [a]the living and the
dead. 6 For to this [a]the gospel has
been [1]proclaimed even to those who

**3:12** [a]Ps 34:15, 16 [1]In OT, Yahweh, cf. Ps 34:15 **3:13** [a]Pr 16:7 [1]Lit *the one who will harm you* [2]Or *do evil against you*, cf. 3:9, 10, 11, 12 **3:14** [a]Mt 5:10; 1Pe 2:19ff; 4:15f [b]Jas 5:11 [c]Is 8:12f; 1Pe 3:6 [1]Or *would be* **3:15** [a]1Pe 1:3 [b]Col 4:6 [c]2Ti 2:25 [d]1Pe 1:17 [1]Set apart [2]Or *an argument, an explanation* **3:16** [a]1Ti 1:5; Heb 13:18; 1Pe 3:21 [b]1Pe 2:12, 15 **3:17** [a]1Pe 2:20; 4:15f [b]Ac 18:21; 1Pe 1:6; 2:15; 4:19 [1]Lit *the will of God* **3:18** [a]1Pe 2:21 [b]Heb 9:26, 28; 10:10 [c]Ro 5:2; Eph 3:12 [d]Col 1:22; 1Pe 4:1 [e]1Pe 4:6 [1]Or *Spirit* **3:19** [1]Or *whom* **3:20** [a]Ro 2:4 [b]Ge 6:3, 5, 13f [c]Heb 11:7 [d]Ge 8:18; 2Pe 2:5 [e]Ac 2:41; 1Pe 1:9, 22; 2:25; 4:19 [1]The great flood **3:21** [a]Ac 16:33; Tit 3:5 [b]Heb 9:14; 10:22 [c]1Ti 1:5; Heb 13:18; 1Pe 3:16 [d]1Pe 1:3 [1]Or *for* **3:22** [a]Mk 16:19 [b]Heb 4:14; 6:20 [c]Ro 8:38f; Heb 1:6 ◆ **4:1** [a]1Pe 2:21 [b]Eph 6:13 [c]Ro 6:7 [1]Suffered death **4:2** [a]Ro 6:2; Col 3:3 [b]1Pe 1:14 [c]Mk 3:35 **4:3** [a]1Co 12:2 [b]Ro 13:13; Eph 2:2; 4:17ff [1]Lit *having gone in* [2]Lit *lawless* **4:4** [a]Eph 5:18 [b]1Pe 3:16 **4:5** [a]Ac 10:42; Ro 14:9; 2Ti 4:1 **4:6** [a]1Pe 3:18 [1]Proclaimed in their lifetimes

are *now* dead, so that though they
were judged in the flesh as men, they
live in the spirit according to *the will
of* God.
**7** [a]The end of all things is at hand;
therefore, [b]be of sound thinking
and sober *spirit* for the purpose of
[1]prayer. **8** Above all, [a]keep fervent in
your love for one another, because
[b]LOVE COVERS A MULTITUDE OF SINS.
**9** [a]Be hospitable to one another with-
out [b]grumbling. **10** [a]As each one has
received a gift, employ it in serving
one another as good [b]stewards of the
manifold grace of God— **11** [a]whoever
speaks, [1]as one *speaking* the [b]ora-
cles of God; whoever serves, as one
*serving* [c,2]by the strength which
God supplies; so that [d]in all things
God may be glorified through Jesus
Christ, [e]to whom belongs the glory
and might forever and ever. Amen.

### *Sharing the Suffering of Christ*

**12** [a]Beloved, do not be surprised at
the [b]fiery trial among you, which
comes upon you for your testing,
as though some strange thing were
happening to you. **13** But to the de-
gree you are [a]sharing the sufferings
of Christ, keep on rejoicing, so that
also at the [b]revelation of His glory
[c]you may rejoice with exultation.
**14** If you are insulted [a,1]for the name
of Christ, [b]you are blessed, [c]because
the Spirit of glory and of God rests
on you. **15** Make sure that [a]none of
you suffers as a murderer, or thief,
or evildoer, or a [b,1]troublesome
meddler; **16** but if *anyone suffers* as
a [a]Christian, he is not to be put to
shame, but is to [b]glorify God in this
name. **17** For *it is* time for judgment
[a]to begin [1]with [b]the house of God;
and if *it* [c]*begins* with us first, what
*will be* the outcome for those [d]who
do not obey the [e]gospel of God?
**18** [a]AND IF IT IS WITH DIFFICULTY THAT
THE RIGHTEOUS IS SAVED, [1]WHAT WILL
BECOME OF THE [b]GODLESS MAN AND
THE SINNER? **19** Therefore, those also
who suffer according to [a]the will of
God must entrust their souls to a
faithful Creator in doing good.

### *Shepherd the Flock of God*

**5** [a]Therefore, I exhort the elders
among you, as *your* [b]fellow el-
der and [c]witness of the sufferings of
Christ, and a [d]partaker also of the
glory that is to be revealed, **2** shep-
herd [a]the flock of God among you,
overseeing [b]not under compulsion,
but willingly, according to God; and
[c]not for dishonest gain, but with
eagerness; **3** nor yet as [a]lording it
over [1]those allotted to you, but being
[b]examples to the flock. **4** And when
the Chief [a]Shepherd appears, you
will receive the [b]unfading [c,1]crown of
glory. **5** [a]You younger men, likewise,
[b]be subject to *your* elders. And all of

**4:7** [a]Ro 13:11; Heb 9:26; Jas 5:8; 1Jn 2:18 [b]1Pe 1:13 [1]Lit *prayers* **4:8** [a]1Pe 1:22 [b]Pr 10:12; 1Co 13:4ff; Jas 5:20 **4:9** [a]1Ti 3:2; Heb 13:2 [b]Php 2:14 **4:10** [a]Ro 12:6f [b]1Co 4:1 **4:11** [a]1Th 2:4; Tit 2:1, 15; Heb 13:7 [b]Ac 7:38 [c]Eph 1:19; 6:10 [d]1Co 10:31; 1Pe 2:12 [e]Ro 11:36; 1Pe 5:11; Rev 1:6; 5:13 [1]Lit *as utterances* [2]Lit *from* **4:12** [a]1Pe 2:11 [b]1Pe 1:6f **4:13** [a]Ro 8:17; 2Co 1:5; 4:10; Php 3:10 [b]2Ti 2:12 [c]1Pe 1:7; 5:1 **4:14** [a]Jn 15:21; Heb 11:26; 1Pe 4:16 [b]Mt 5:11; Lk 6:22; Ac 5:41 [c]2Co 4:10f, 16 [1]Lit *in* **4:15** [a]1Pe 2:19f; 3:17 [b]1Th 4:11; 2Th 3:11; 1Ti 5:13 [1]Lit *one who oversees others' affairs* **4:16** [a]Ac 5:41; 28:22; Jas 2:7 [b]1Pe 4:11 **4:17** [a]Jer 25:29; Eze 9:6; Am 3:2 [b]1Ti 3:15; Heb 3:6; 1Pe 2:5 [c]Ro 2:9 [d]2Th 1:8 [e]Ro 1:1 [1]Lit *from* **4:18** [a]Pr 11:31; Lk 23:31 [b]1Ti 1:9 [1]Lit *where will appear* **4:19** [a]1Pe 3:17 ◆ **5:1** [a]Ac 11:30 [b]2Jn 1; 3Jn 1 [c]Lk 24:48; Heb 12:1 [d]1Pe 1:5, 7; 4:13; Rev 1:9 **5:2** [a]Jn 21:16; Ac 20:28 [b]Phm 14 [c]1Ti 3:8 **5:3** [a]Eze 34:4; Mt 20:25f [b]Jn 13:15; Php 3:17; 1Th 1:7; 2Th 3:9; 1Ti 4:12; Tit 2:7 [1]Lit *the allotments* **5:4** [a]1Pe 2:25 [b]1Pe 1:4 [c]1Co 9:25 [1]Lit *wreath* **5:5** [a]Lk 22:26; 1Ti 5:1 [b]Eph 5:21

you, clothe yourselves with [c]humility
toward one another, for [d]GOD IS OP-
POSED TO THE PROUD, BUT GIVES GRACE
TO THE HUMBLE.
**6** Therefore [a]humble yourselves
under the mighty hand of God, that
He may exalt you at the proper time,
**7** [a]CASTING ALL YOUR ANXIETY ON
HIM, because He cares for you. **8** [a]Be
of sober *spirit,* [b]be watchful. Your
adversary, [c]the devil, prowls around
like a roaring [d]lion, seeking someone
to devour. **9** [a,1]But resist him, [b]firm
in the faith, knowing that [c]the same
experiences of suffering are being
accomplished among your [2]brethren
who are in the world. **10** And after
you have suffered [a]for a little while,
the [b]God of all grace, who [c]called
you to His [d]eternal glory in Christ,
will Himself [e]restore, [f]strengthen,
confirm, *and* ground you. **11** [a]To Him
*be* might forever and ever. Amen.
**12** Through [a]Silvanus, our faith-
ful brother as I regard *him,* [b]I have
written to you briefly, exhorting and
bearing witness that this is [c]the true
grace of God. [d]Stand firm in it! **13** She
who is in Babylon, chosen together
with you, sends you greetings, and
*so does* my son, [a]Mark. **14** [a]Greet one
another with a kiss of love.
[b]Peace be to you all who are in
Christ.

*The Second Letter of*

# PETER

### *Precious and Magnificent Promises*

**1** [1]Simeon Peter, a [a]slave and
[b]apostle of Jesus Christ,
To those who have received [c]the
same [2]kind of faith as ours, [3]by
[d]the righteousness of [e]our God and
Savior, Jesus Christ: **2** [a]Grace and
peace be multiplied to you in [b]the
full knowledge of God and of Jesus
our Lord; **3** seeing that His [a]divine
power has granted to us everything
pertaining to life and godliness,
through the [b]full knowledge of Him
who [c]called us [1]by His own glory
and [2]excellence. **4** [1]For by these He
has granted to us His precious and
magnificent [a]promises, so that by
them you may become [b]partakers
of *the* divine nature, having [c]escaped
the [d]corruption that is in [e]the world
by lust. **5** Now for this very reason
also, applying all diligence, in your
faith [a]supply [b]moral [1]excellence,
and in *your* moral excellence,
[c]knowledge, **6** and in *your* knowl-
edge, [a]self-control, and in *your*

---

**5:5** [c]1Pe 3:8 [d]Pr 3:34; Jas 4:6 **5:6** [a]Mt 23:12; Lk 14:11; 18:14; Jas 4:10 **5:7** [a]Ps 55:22; Mt 6:25 **5:8** [a]1Pe 1:13 [b]Mt 24:42 [c]Jas 4:7 [d]2Ti 4:17 **5:9** [a]Jas 4:7 [b]Col 2:5 [c]Ac 14:22 [1]Lit *Whom resist* [2]Or *brotherhood* **5:10** [a]1Pe 1:6 [b]1Pe 4:10 [c]1Co 1:9; 1Th 2:12 [d]2Co 4:17; 2Ti 2:10 [e]1Co 1:10; Heb 13:21 [f]*Ro 16:25; 2Th 2:17; 3:3* **5:11** [a]Ro 11:36; 1Pe 4:11 **5:12** [a]2Co 1:19 [b]Heb 13:22 [c]Ac 11:23; 1Pe 1:13; 4:10 [d]1Co 15:1 **5:13** [a]Ac 12:12, 25; 15:37, 39; Col 4:10; Phm 24 **5:14** [a]Ro 16:16 [b]Eph 6:23 ◆**1:1** [a]Ro 1:1; Php 1:1; Jas 1:1; Jd 1 [b]1Pe 1:1 [c]Ro 1:12; 2Co 4:13; Tit 1:4 [d]Ro 3:21-26 [e]Tit 2:13 [1]Cf. Ac 15:14 [2]Or *value* [3]Or *in* **1:2** [a]Ro 1:7; 1Pe 1:2 [b]Jn 17:3; Php 3:8; 2Pe 1:3, 8; 2:20; 3:18 **1:3** [a]1Pe 1:5 [b]Jn 17:3; Php 3:8; 2Pe 1:2, 8; 2:20; 3:18 [c]1Th 2:12; 2Th 2:14; 1Pe 5:10 [1]Or *to* [2]Or *virtue* **1:4** [a]2Pe 3:9, 13 [b]Eph 4:13, 24; Heb 12:10; 1Jn 3:2 [c]2Pe 2:18, 20 [d]2Pe 2:19 [e]Jas 1:27 [1]Lit *Through which* (things) **1:5** [a]2Pe 1:11 [b]2Pe 1:3 [c]Col 2:3; 2Pe 1:2 [1]Or *virtue* **1:6** [a]Ac 24:25

self-control, [b]perseverance, and
in *your* perseverance, [c]godliness,
**7** and in *your* godliness, [a,1]brotherly
kindness, and in *your* [1]brotherly
kindness, [2]love. **8** For if these things
are yours and are increasing, they
render you neither useless nor
[a]unfruitful in the [b]full knowledge
of our Lord Jesus Christ. **9** For in
whom these things are not present,
*that one* is [a]blind, being nearsighted,
having [1]forgotten the [b]purification
from his former sins. **10** Therefore,
brothers, be all the more diligent to
make your [a]calling and [b]choosing
sure; for in doing these things, you
will never [c]stumble; **11** for in this
way the entrance into [a]the eternal
kingdom of our [b]Lord and Savior
Jesus Christ will be [c]abundantly
[d]supplied to you.

**12** Therefore, [a]I will always be
ready to remind you of these things,
even though you *already* know *them*,
and have been strengthened in [b]the
truth which is present with *you*. **13** I
consider it [a]right, as long as I am in
[b]this *earthly* dwelling, to [c]stir you
up by way of reminder, **14** knowing
that [a]the laying aside of my *earthly*
dwelling is imminent, [b]as also our
Lord Jesus Christ has indicated to me.
**15** And I will also be diligent that at
any time after my [a,1]departure you
will be able to call these things to
mind.

### *Eyewitnesses of Jesus*

**16** For we did not make known to
you the [a]power and coming of our
Lord Jesus Christ, following cleverly
devised [b]myths, but being [c]eyewit-
nesses of His majesty. **17** For when He
received honor and glory from God
the Father, such an [a,1]utterance as this
was [2]made to Him by the [b]Majestic
Glory, "This is My beloved Son with
whom I am well-pleased"— **18** and
we ourselves heard this [1]utterance
made from heaven when we were
with Him on the [a]holy mountain.

**19** [1]And we have as more [a]sure [b]the
prophetic word, to which you do well
to pay attention as to [c]a lamp shining
in a dark place, until the [d]day dawns
and the [e]morning star arises [f]in your
hearts. **20** [a]Know this first of all, that
[b]no prophecy of Scripture comes by
one's own interpretation. **21** For [a]no
prophecy was ever made by the will
of man, but men being [b]moved by
the Holy Spirit spoke from God.

### *The Rise of False Prophets*

**2** But [a]false prophets also arose
among the people, just as there
will also be [b]false teachers [c]among
you, who will [d]secretly introduce
[e]destructive heresies, even [f]deny-
ing the [g]Master who [h]bought them,
bringing swift destruction upon
themselves. **2** And many will follow
their [a]sensuality, and because of

---

**1:6** [b]Lk 21:19 [c]2Pe 1:3 **1:7** [a]Ro 12:10; 1Pe 1:22 [1]Gr *philadelphia* [2]Gr *agape* **1:8** [a]Col 1:10 [b]Jn 17:3; Php 3:8; 2Pe 1:2, 3; 2:20; 3:18 **1:9** [a]1Jn 2:11 [b]Eph 5:26; Tit 2:14 [1]Or *escaped their notice*, cf. 3:5, 8 **1:10** [a]Mt 22:14; Ro 11:29; 2Pe 1:3 [b]1Th 1:4 [c]Jas 2:10; 2Pe 3:17; Jd 24 **1:11** [a]2Ti 4:18 [b]2Pe 2:20; 3:18 [c]Ro 2:4; 1Ti 6:17 [d]2Pe 1:5 **1:12** [a]Php 3:1; 1Jn 2:21; Jd 5 [b]Col 1:5f; 2Jn 2 **1:13** [a]Php 1:7 [b]2Co 5:1, 4; 2Pe 1:14 [c]2Pe 3:1 **1:14** [a]2Co 5:1; 2Ti 4:6 [b]Jn 13:36; 21:19 **1:15** [a]Lk 9:31 [1]Or *exodus*, cf. Lk 9:31 **1:16** [a]Mk 13:26; 14:62; 1Th 2:19 [b]1Ti 1:4; 2Pe 2:3 [c]Mt 17:1ff; Mk 9:2ff; Lk 9:28ff **1:17** [a]Mt 17:5; Mk 9:7; Lk 9:35 [b]Heb 1:3 [1]Lit *voice* [2]Lit *brought* **1:18** [a]Ex 3:5; Jos 5:15 [1]Lit *voice brought* **1:19** [a]Heb 2:2 [b]1Pe 1:10f [c]Ps 119:105 [d]Lk 1:78 [e]Rev 22:16 [f]2Co 4:6 [1]Or *We have the prophetic word* made *more sure* **1:20** [a]2Pe 3:3 [b]Ro 12:6 **1:21** [a]Jer 23:26; 2Ti 3:16 [b]2Sa 23:2; Lk 1:70; Ac 1:16; 3:18; 1Pe 1:11 ◆ **2:1** [a]Dt 13:1ff; Jer 6:13 [b]2Co 11:13 [c]Mt 7:15; 1Ti 4:1 [d]Ga 2:4; Jd 4 [e]1Co 11:19; Ga 5:20 [f]Jd 4 [g]Rev 6:10 [h]1Co 6:20 **2:2** [a]Ge 19:5ff; 2Pe 2:7, 18; Jd 4

them [b]the way of the truth will be
[c]maligned. **3** And in *their* [a]greed they
will [b]exploit you with [c]false words,
[d]their judgment from long ago is
not idle, and their destruction is not
asleep.
**4** For [a]if God did not spare angels
who sinned, but cast them into
the [1]pit and [b]delivered them to
chains of darkness, being kept for
judgment; **5** and did not spare [a]the
ancient world, but preserved [b]Noah,
a [1]preacher of righteousness, with
seven others, when He brought a
[c]flood upon the world of the ungodly;
**6** and *if* He [a]condemned the cities of
Sodom and Gomorrah to destruction
by reducing *them* to ashes, having
made them an [b]example to those who
would [c]live ungodly *lives* thereafter;
**7** and *if* He [a]rescued righteous Lot,
oppressed by the [b]sensual conduct of
[c]unprincipled men **8** (for by what he
saw and heard *that* [a]righteous man,
while living among them, felt *his*
righteous soul tormented day after
day by *their* lawless deeds), **9** [a]*then*
the Lord knows how to rescue the
godly from [1]trial, and to keep the un-
righteous under punishment for the
[b]day of judgment, **10** and especially
those who [a]go after the flesh in *its*
corrupt lust and [b]despise authority.
Daring, [c]self-willed, they do not
tremble when they [b]blaspheme [1]glo-
rious ones, **11** [a]whereas angels who
are greater in strength and power do
not bring a reviling judgment against
them before the Lord. **12** But [a]these,
like unreasoning animals, [b]born as
creatures of instinct to be captured
and killed, blaspheming where they
have no knowledge, will in [1]the de-
struction of those creatures also be
destroyed, **13** suffering unrighteous-
ness as [a]the wages of *their* unrigh-
teousness, considering it a pleasure
to [b]revel in the [c]daytime—*they are*
stains and blemishes, [b]reveling in
their [1]deceptions, as they [d]feast with
you, **14** having eyes full of adultery
and unceasing sin, [a]enticing [b]unsta-
ble souls, having a heart trained in
[c]greed—*they are* [d]accursed children.
**15** Forsaking [a]the right way, they have
gone astray, having followed [b]the
way of Balaam, the *son* of Beor, who
loved [c]the wages of unrighteousness,
**16** but he received a rebuke for his
own lawlessness, [a]*for* a mute don-
key, speaking out with a voice of a
man, restrained the madness of the
prophet.
**17** These are [a]springs without
water and mists driven by a storm,
[b]for whom the [1]black darkness
has been kept. **18** For speaking out
[a]arrogant *words* of [b]vanity, they
[c]entice by [d]sensual lusts of the flesh,
those who barely [e]escape from the
ones who conducted themselves in
error, **19** promising them freedom
while they themselves are slaves
of corruption; for [a]by what a man

---

**2:2** [b]Ac 16:17; 22:4; 24:14 [c]Ro 2:24 **2:3** [a]1Ti 6:5; 2Pe 2:14; Jd 16 [b]2Co 2:17; 1Th 2:5 [c]Ro 16:18; 2Pe 1:16 [d]Dt 32:35 **2:4** [a]Jd 6 [b]Rev 20:1f [1]Gr *tartarus* **2:5** [a]Eze 26:20; 2Pe 3:6 [b]Ge 6:8, 9; 1Pe 3:20 [c]2Pe 3:6 [1]Or *herald* **2:6** [a]Ge 19:24; Jd 7 [b]Is 1:9; Mt 10:15; 11:23; Ro 9:29; Jd 7 [c]Jd 15 **2:7** [a]Ge 19:16, 29 [b]Ge 19:5ff; 2Pe 2:2, 18; Jd 4 [c]2Pe 3:17 **2:8** [a]Heb 11:4 **2:9** [a]1Co 10:13; Rev 3:10 [b]Mt 10:15; Jd 6 [1]Or *temptation* **2:10** [a]2Pe 3:3; Jd 16, 18 [b]Ex 22:28; Jd 8 [c]Tit 1:7 [1]Angels **2:11** [a]Jd 9 **2:12** [a]Jd 10 [b]Jer 12:3; Col 2:22 [1]Lit *their destruction also* **2:13** [a]2Pe 2:15 [b]Ro 13:13 [c]1Th 5:7 [d]1Co 11:21; Jd 12 [1]One early ms *love feasts* **2:14** [a]2Pe 2:18 [b]Jas 1:8; 2Pe 3:16 [c]2Pe 2:3 [d]Eph 2:3 **2:15** [a]Ac 13:10 [b]Nu 22:5, 7; Dt 23:4; Ne 13:2; Jd 11; Rev 2:14 [c]2Pe 2:13 **2:16** [a]Nu 22:21, 23, 28, 30ff **2:17** [a]Jd 12 [b]Jd 13 [1]Lit *blackness of darkness* **2:18** [a]Jd 16 [b]Eph 4:17 [c]2Pe 2:14 [d]2Pe 2:2 [e]2Pe 1:4; 2:20 **2:19** [a]Jn 8:34; Ro 6:16

is overcome, by this he is enslaved.
**20** For if they are overcome, having
*both* [a]escaped the defilements of the
world by [b]the knowledge of the [c]Lord
and Savior Jesus Christ and having
again been [d]entangled in them, *then*
[e]the last state has become worse for
them than the first. **21** [a]For it would
be better for them not to have known
the way of righteousness, than
having known it, to turn away from
[b]the holy commandment [c]handed
on to them. **22** The [1]*message* of the
true proverb has happened to them,
"[a]A DOG RETURNS TO ITS OWN VOMIT,"
and, "A sow, after washing, *returns* to
wallowing in the mire."

### *The Day of the Lord Will Come*

**3** This is now, [a]beloved, the sec-
ond letter I am writing to you in
which I am [b]stirring up your sincere
mind by way of reminder, **2** that you
should [a]remember the words spoken
beforehand by [b]the holy prophets
and [c]the commandment of the Lord
and Savior *spoken* by your apostles,
**3** [a]knowing this first of all, that [b]in
the last days [c]mockers will come with
*their* mocking, [d]following after their
own lusts, **4** and saying, "[a]Where is
the promise of His [b]coming? For
since the fathers [c]fell asleep, all
continues just as it was [d]from the be-
ginning of creation." **5** For [1]when they
maintain this, it escapes their notice
that [a]by the word of God *the* heavens
existed long ago and *the* earth was
[b]formed out of water and by water,
**6** through which [a]the world at that
time was [b]destroyed, being deluged
with water. **7** But by His word [a]the
present heavens and earth are being
reserved for [b]fire, being kept for [c]the
day of judgment and destruction of
ungodly men.

**8** But do not let this one *fact* escape
your notice, [a]beloved, that with the
Lord one day is like a thousand years,
and [b]a thousand years like one day.
**9** [a]The Lord is not slow about His
promise, as some consider slowness,
but [b]is patient toward you, [c]not willing
for any to perish but for all to come to
repentance. **10** But [a]the day of the Lord
[b]will come like a thief, in which [c]the
heavens [d]will pass away with a roar
and the [e]elements will be destroyed
with intense heat, and [f]the earth and
[1]its works will be [2]found *out*.

**11** Since all these things are to
be destroyed in this way, what sort
of people ought you to be in holy
conduct and godliness, **12** [a]looking
for and hastening the coming of the
day of God, because of which [b]the
heavens burning will be destroyed,
and the [c]elements will melt with
intense heat! **13** But according to His
[a]promise we are looking for [b]NEW
HEAVENS AND A NEW EARTH, [c]in which
righteousness dwells.

**2:20** [a]2Pe 2:18 [b]2Pe 1:2 [c]2Pe 1:11; 3:18 [d]2Ti 2:4 [e]Mt 12:45; Lk 11:26 **2:21** [a]Eze 18:24; Heb 6:4ff; 10:26f; Jas 4:17 [b]Ga 6:2; 1Ti 6:14; 2Pe 3:2 [c]Jd 3 **2:22** [a]Pr 26:11 [1]Lit *thing* ◆ **3:1** [a]1Pe 2:11; 2Pe 3:8, 14, 17 [b]2Pe 1:13 **3:2** [a]Jd 17 [b]Lk 1:70; Ac 3:21; Eph 3:5 [c]Ga 6:2; 1Ti 6:14; 2Pe 2:21 **3:3** [a]2Pe 1:20 [b]1Ti 4:1; Heb 1:2 [c]Jd 18 [d]2Pe 2:10 **3:4** [a]Is 5:19; Jer 17:15; Eze 11:3; 12:22, 27; Mal 2:17; Mt 24:48 [b]1Th 2:19; 2Pe 3:12 [c]Ac 7:60 [d]Mk 10:6 **3:5** [a]Ge 1:6, 9; Heb 11:3 [b]Ps 24:2; 136:6 [1]Or *they are willfully ignorant of this fact, that* **3:6** [a]2Pe 2:5 [b]Ge 7:11, 12, 21f **3:7** [a]2Pe 3:10, 12 [b]Is 66:15; Da 7:9f; 2Th 1:7; Heb 12:29 [c]Mt 10:15; 1Co 3:13; Jd 7 **3:8** [a]2Pe 3:1 [b]Ps 90:4 **3:9** [a]Hab 2:3; Ro 13:11; Heb 10:37 [b]Ro 2:4; Rev 2:21 [c]1Ti 2:4; Rev 2:21 **3:10** [a]1Co 1:8 [b]Mt 24:43; Lk 12:39; 1Th 5:2; Rev 3:3; 16:15 [c]Is 34:4; 2Pe 3:7, 12 [d]Mt 24:35; Rev 21:1 [e]Is 24:19; Mic 1:4 [f]2Pe 3:7 [1]Lit *the works in it* [2]Some mss *burned up* **3:12** [a]1Co 1:7 [b]2Pe 3:10 [c]Is 24:19; 34:4; Mic 1:4 **3:13** [a]Is 65:17; 66:22 [b]Is 65:17; Ro 8:21; Rev 21:1 [c]Is 60:21; 65:25; Rev 21:27

### *Be on Your Guard*

14 [a]Therefore, [b]beloved, since you
are looking for these things, be
diligent to be [c]found by Him in
peace, [d]spotless and blameless,
15 and consider the [a]patience of our
Lord *as* salvation, just as also [b]our
beloved brother Paul, [c]according to
the wisdom given him, wrote to you,
16 as also in all *his* letters, speaking
in them of [a]these things, [b]in which
are some things hard to understand,
which the untaught and [c]unstable
distort, as *they do* also [d]the rest of the
Scriptures, to their own destruction.
17 You therefore, [a]beloved, knowing
this beforehand, [b]be on your guard
lest you, having been carried away by
[c]the error of [d]unprincipled men, [e]fall
from your own steadfastness, 18 but
grow in the grace and [a]knowledge
of our [b]Lord and Savior Jesus Christ.
[c]To Him *be* the glory, both now and
to the day of eternity. Amen.

# *The First Letter of* JOHN

### *The Word of Life*

1 What was [a]from the beginning,
what we have [b]heard, what we
have [c]seen with our eyes, what
we [d]beheld and [e]touched with
our hands, concerning the [f]Word
of Life— 2 and [a]the life was man-
ifested, and we have [b]seen and
[c]bear witness and proclaim to you
[d]the eternal life, which was [e]with
the Father and was [a]manifested
to us— 3 what we have [a]seen and
[b]heard we proclaim to you also, so
that you may also have fellowship
with us; and indeed our [c]fellowship
is with the Father, and with His Son
Jesus Christ. 4 [a]And these things we
are writing, so that our [b]joy may be
made complete.

### *God Is Light*

5 [a]And this is the message we have
heard from Him and declare to you,
that [b]God is Light, and in Him there
is no darkness at all. 6 [a]If we say
that we have fellowship with Him
and *yet* walk in the darkness, we [b]lie
and [c]do not do the truth; 7 but if we
[a]walk in the Light as [b]He Himself
is in the Light, we have fellowship
with one another, and [c]the blood of
Jesus His Son cleanses us from all
sin. 8 [a]If we say that we have no sin,
we deceive ourselves and the [b]truth
is not in us. 9 [a]If we confess our
sins, He is faithful and righteous to
forgive us our sins and [b]to cleanse
us from all unrighteousness. 10 [a]If
we say that we have not sinned, we

---

**3:14** [a]1Co 15:58; 2Pe 1:10 [b]2Pe 3:1 [c]1Pe 1:7 [d]Php 2:15; 1Th 5:23; 1Ti 6:14; Jas 1:27 **3:15** [a]2Pe 3:9 [b]Ac 9:17; 15:25; 2Pe 3:2 [c]1Co 3:10; Eph 3:3 **3:16** [a]2Pe 3:14 [b]Heb 5:11 [c]2Pe 2:14 [d]2Pe 3:2 **3:17** [a]2Pe 3:1 [b]1Co 10:12 [c]2Pe 2:18 [d]2Pe 2:7 [e]Rev 2:5 **3:18** [a]2Pe 1:2 [b]2Pe 1:11; 2:20 [c]Ro 11:36; 2Ti 4:18; Rev 1:6
♦ **1:1** [a]Jn 1:1f; 1Jn 2:13, 14 [b]Ac 4:20; 1Jn 1:3 [c]Jn 19:35; 2Pe 1:16; 1Jn 1:2 [d]Jn 1:14; 1Jn 4:14 [e]Lk 24:39; Jn 20:27 [illegible]n 1:1, 4 **1:2** [a]Jn 1:4; 1Jn 3:5, 8; 5:20 [b]Jn 19:35; 1Jn 1:1 [c]Jn 15:27; 1Jn 4:14 [d]Jn 10:28; 17:3; 1Jn 2:25; 5:11, [illegible]20 [e]Jn 1:1 **1:3** [a]Jn 19:35; 2Pe 1:16; 1Jn 1:1 [b]Ac 4:20; 1Jn 1:1 [c]Jn 17:3, 21; 1Co 1:9 **1:4** [a]1Jn 2:1 [b]Jn 3:29 [illegible] [a]Jn 1:19; 1Jn 3:11 [b]1Ti 6:16; Jas 1:17 **1:6** [a]Jn 8:12; 1Jn 2:11 [b]Jn 8:55; 1Jn 2:4; 4:20 [c]Jn 3:21 **1:7** [a]Is 2:5 [illegible] 6:16 [c]Tit 2:14 **1:8** [a]Job 15:14; Pr 20:9; Ro 3:10ff; Jas 3:2 [b]Jn 8:44; 1Jn 2:4 **1:9** [a]Ps 32:5; Pr 28:13 [illegible] 2:14 **1:10** [a]Job 15:14

[b]make Him a liar and [c]His word is not in us.

### *Jesus Christ Our Advocate*

**2** [a]My little children, I am [b]writing these things to you so that you may not sin. And if anyone sins, [c]we have an [d,1]Advocate with the Father, Jesus Christ the righteous; **2** and He Himself is [a]the [1]propitiation for our sins, and not for ours only, but also [b]for *those of* the whole world.

**3** [a]And by this we know that we have come to [b]know Him, if we [c]keep His commandments. **4** The one who says, "[a]I have come to [b]know Him," and does not keep His commandments, is a [c]liar, and [d]the truth is not in him; **5** but whoever [a]keeps His word, truly in him the [b]love of God has been perfected. [c]By this we know that we are in Him: **6** the one who says he [a]abides in Him [b]ought himself to walk in the same manner as He walked.

**7** [a]Beloved, I am [b]not writing a new commandment to you, but an old commandment which you have had [c]from the beginning; the old commandment is the word which you have heard. **8** [1]On the other hand, I am writing [a]a new commandment to you, which is true in Him and in you, because [b]the darkness is passing away and [c]the true Light is already shining. **9** The one who says he is in the Light and *yet* [a]hates his [b]brother is in the darkness until now. **10** [a]The one who loves his brother abides in the Light and there is no cause for stumbling in him. **11** But the one who [a]hates his brother is in the darkness and [b]walks in the darkness, and does not know where he is going because the darkness [c]blinded his eyes.

**12** I am writing to you, [a]little children, because [b]your sins have been forgiven you for His name's sake. **13** I am writing to you, fathers, because you have known Him [a]who has been from the beginning. I am writing to you, young men, because [b]you have overcome [c]the evil one. I have written to you, children, because [d,1]you have known the Father. **14** I have written to you, fathers, because you have known Him [a]who has been from the beginning. I have written to you, young men, because you are [b]strong, and the [c]word of God abides in you, and [d]you have overcome the evil one.

### *Do Not Love the World*

**15** Do not love [a]the world nor the things in the world. [b]If anyone loves the world, the love of the Father is not in him. **16** For all that is in the world, [a]the lust of the flesh and [b]the lust of the eyes and [c]the boastful pride of life, is not from the Father, but is from the world. **17** [a]And the world is passing away, and *also* its lusts, but

---

**1:10** [b]Jn 3:33; 1Jn 5:10 [c]1Jn 2:14 ◆ **2:1** [a]Jn 13:33; Ga 4:19; 1Jn 2:12, 28; 3:7, 18; 4:4; 5:21 [b]1Jn 1:4 [c]Ro 8:34; 1Ti 2:5; Heb 7:25; 9:24 [d]Jn 14:16 [1]Gr *Paracletos*, one called alongside to help; or *Intercessor* **2:2** [a]Ro 3:25; Heb 2:17; 1Jn 4:10 [b]Jn 4:42; 11:51f; 1Jn 4:14 [1]Or *satisfaction* **2:3** [a]1Jn 2:5; 3:24; 4:13; 5:2 [b]1Jn 2:4; 3:6; 4:7f [c]Jn 14:15; 15:10; 1Jn 3:22, 24; 5:3; Rev 12:17; 14:12 **2:4** [a]Tit 1:10 [b]1Jn 3:6; 4:7f [c]1Jn 1:6 [d]1Jn 1:8 **2:5** [a]Jn 14:23 [b]1Jn 4:12 [c]1Jn 2:3; 3:24; 4:13; 5:2 **2:6** [a]Jn 15:4 [b]Jn 13:15; 15:10; 1Pe 2:21 **2:7** [a]Heb 6:9; 1Jn 3:2, 21; 4:1, 7, 11 [b]Jn 13:34; 1Jn 3:11, 23; 4:21; 2Jn 5 [c]1Jn 2:24; 3:11; 2Jn 5, 6 **2:8** [a]Jn 13:34 [b]Ro 13:12; Eph 5:8; 1Th 5:4f [c]Jn 1:9 [1]Lit *Again* **2:9** [a]1Jn 2:11; 3:15; 4:20 [b]Ac 1:15; 1Jn 3:10, 16; 4:20f **2:10** [a]Jn 11:9; 1Jn 2:10, 11 **2:11** [a]1Jn 2:9; 3:15; 4:20 [b]Jn 12:35; 1Jn 1:6 [c]2Co 4:4; 2Pe 1:9 **2:12** [a]1Jn 2:1 [b]Ac 13:38; 1Co 6:11 **2:13** [a]1Jn 1:1 [b]Jn 16:33; 1Jn 2:14; 4:4; 5:4f; Rev 2:7 [c]Mt 5:37; 1Jn 2:14; 3:12; 5:18f [d]Jn 14:7; 1Jn 2:3 [1]Or *you have come to know* **2:14** [a]1Jn 1:1 [b]Eph 6:10 [c]Jn 5:38; 8:37; 1Jn 1:10 [d]1Jn 2:1?, **2:15** [a]Ro 12:2; Jas 1:27 [b]Jas 4:4 **2:16** [a]Ro 13:14; Eph 2:3; 1Pe 2:11 [b]Pr 27:20 [c]Jas 4:16 **2:17** [a]1Co 7:?

the one who [b]does the will of God abides forever.

**18** Children, [a]it is the last hour; and just as you heard that [b]antichrist is coming, [c]even now many antichrists have appeared. From this we know that it is the last hour. **19** [a]They went out from us, but they were not *really* of us; for if they were of us, they would have remained with us; but *they went out*, [b]so that [1]it would be manifested that they all are not of us. **20** [1]But you have an [a]anointing from [b]the Holy One, and [c]you all know. **21** I have not written to you because you do not know the truth, but [a]because you do know it, and [1]because no lie is [b]of the truth. **22** Who is the liar but [a]the one who denies that Jesus is the [1]Christ? This is [b]the [2]antichrist, the one who denies the Father and the Son. **23** [a]Everyone who denies the Son does not have the Father; the one who confesses the Son has the Father also. **24** As for you, let that which you heard [a]from the beginning abide in you. If what you heard from the beginning abides in you, you also [b]will abide in the Son and in the Father. **25** [a]And this is the promise which He Himself [1]made to us: eternal life.

**26** These things I have written to you about those who are trying to [a]deceive you. **27** And as for you, the [a]anointing whom you received from Him abides in you, and you have no need for anyone to teach you. But as His anointing [b]teaches you about all things, and is [c]true and is not a lie, and just as He has taught you, [1]abide in Him.

**28** And now, [a]little children, abide in Him, so that when He [b]is manifested, we may have [c]confidence and [d]not [1]shrink away from Him in shame [2]at His [e]coming. **29** If you know that [a]He is righteous, you know that everyone also who does righteousness [b]has been [1]born of Him.

### *Children of God, Love One Another*

**3** See [a,1]how great a love the Father has given to us, that we would be called [b]children of God; and we are. For this reason the world does not know us, because [c]it did not know Him. **2** [a]Beloved, now we are [b]children of God, and [c]it has not been manifested as yet what we will be. We know that when He [d]is manifested, we will be [e]like Him, because we will [f]see Him just as He is. **3** And everyone who has this [a]hope *fixed* on Him [b]purifies himself, just as He is pure.

**4** Everyone who does sin also does lawlessness; and [a]sin is lawlessness. **5** And you know that He [a]was

---

**2:17** [b]Mk 3:35 **2:18** [a]Ro 13:11; 1Ti 4:1; 1Pe 4:7 [b]Mt 24:5, 24; 1Jn 2:22; 4:3; 2Jn 7 [c]Mk 13:22; 1Jn 4:1, 3 **2:19** [a]Ac 20:30 [b]1Co 11:19 [1]Lit *they would be revealed* **2:20** [a]2Co 1:21; 1Jn 2:27 [b]Mk 1:24; Ac 10:38 [c]Pr 28:5; Mt 13:11; Jn 14:26; 1Co 2:15f; 1Jn 2:27 [1]Lit *And* **2:21** [a]Jas 1:19; 2Pe 1:12; Jd 5 [b]Jn 8:44; 18:37; 1Jn 3:19 [1]Or know *that* **2:22** [a]1Jn 4:3; 2Jn 7 [b]Mt 24:5, 24; 1Jn 2:18; 4:3; 2Jn 7 [1]Or *Anointed One*, cf. 2:27 [2]Or *one against the Anointed One*, cf. 2:27 **2:23** [a]Jn 8:19; 16:3; 17:3; 1Jn 4:15; 5:1; 2Jn 9 **2:24** [a]1Jn 2:7 [b]Jn 14:23; 1Jn 1:3; 2Jn 9 **2:25** [a]Jn 3:15; 6:40; 1Jn 1:2 [1]Lit *promised us* **2:26** [a]1Jn 3:7; *2Jn 7* ***2:27*** *[a]Jn 14:16; 1Jn 2:20* [b]Jn 14:26; 1Co 2:12; 1Th 4:9 [c]Jn 14:17 [1]Or *you abide in Him*; Gr indicative **2:28** [a]1Jn 2:1 [b]Lk 17:30; Col 3:4; 1Jn 3:2 [c]Eph 3:12; 1Jn 3:21; 4:17; 5:14 [d]Mk 8:38 [e]1Th 2:19 [1]Lit *be put to shame from Him* [2]Or *in His presence* **2:29** [a]Jn 7:18; 1Jn 3:7 [b]Jn 1:13; 3:3; 1Jn 3:9; 4:7; 5:1, 4, 18; 3Jn 11 [1]Or *begotten* ◆ **3:1** [a]Jn 3:16; 1Jn 4:10 [b]Jn 1:12; 11:52; Ro 8:16; 1Jn 3:2, 10 [c]Jn 15:18, 21; 16:3 [1]Lit *what kind of love* **3:2** [a]1Jn 2:7 [b]Jn 1:12; 11:52; Ro 8:16; 1Jn 3:1, 10 [c]Ro 8:19, 23f [d]Lk 17:30; Col 3:4; 1Jn 2:28 [e]Ro 8:29; 2Pe 1:4 [f]Jn 17:24; 2Co 3:18 **3:3** [a]Ro 15:12; 1Pe 1:3 [b]Jn 17:19; 2Co 7:1 **3:4** [a]Ro 4:15; 1Jn 5:17 **3:5** [a]1Jn 1:2; 3:8

manifested in order to [b]take away
sins, and [c]in Him there is no sin. **6** No
one who abides in Him [a]sins; no one
who sins has seen Him or [b][1]has come
to know Him. **7** [a]Little children, let
no one [b]deceive you. [c]The one who
does righteousness is righteous, just
as He is righteous. **8** The one who
does sin is [a]of the devil, because
the devil sins from the beginning.
[b]The Son of God [c]was manifested for
this purpose, [d]to destroy the works
of the devil. **9** Everyone who has
been [a][1]born of God [b]does not sin,
because His seed abides in him; and
he cannot sin, because he has been
[1]born of God. **10** By this the [a]children
of God and the [b]children of the devil
are manifested: everyone who does
not do righteousness is not of God,
as well as the one who [c]does not love
his [d]brother.

**11** [a]For this is the message [b]which
you have heard from the beginning,
[c]that we should love one another;
**12** not as [a]Cain, *who* was of [b]the evil
one and slew his brother. And for
what reason did he slay him? Because
[c]his deeds were evil, and his brother's
were righteous.

**13** Do not marvel, brothers, if [a]the
world hates you. **14** We know that
we have [a]passed out of death into
life, [b]because we love the brothers.
The one who does not love abides
in death. **15** Everyone who [a]hates his
brother is a murderer, and you know
that [b]no murderer has eternal life
abiding in him. **16** By this we have
known love, that [a]He laid down
His life for us; and [b]we ought to lay
down our lives for the [c]brothers.
**17** But [a]whoever has the world's
goods, and sees his brother in need
and [b]closes his [1]heart [2]against him,
[c]how does the love of God abide in
him? **18** [a]Little children, let us not
love with word or with tongue, but
in deed and [b]truth. **19** And by this we
will know that we are [a]of the truth,
and will [1]assure our heart before
Him **20** [1]in whatever our heart
condemns us; for God is greater
than our heart and knows all things.
**21** [a]Beloved, if our heart does not
condemn us, we have [b]confidence
[1]before God; **22** and [a]whatever we
ask we receive from Him, because
we [b]keep His commandments and
do [c]the things that are pleasing in
His sight.

**23** And this is His commandment,
that we [a][1]believe in [b]the name of His
Son Jesus Christ, and love one anoth-
er, just as [c]He gave a commandment
to us. **24** And the one who [a]keeps His
commandments [b]abides in Him, and
He in him. [c]We know by this that [d]He
abides in us, by the Spirit whom He
gave us.

---

**3:5** [b]Jn 1:29; 1Pe 1:18-20; 1Jn 2:2 [c]2Co 5:21; 1Jn 2:29 **3:6** [a]1Jn 3:9 [b]1Jn 2:3; 3Jn 11 [1]Or *has known* **3:7** [a]1Jn 2:1 [b]1Jn 2:26 [c]1Jn 2:29 **3:8** [a]Mt 13:38; Jn 8:44; 1Jn 3:10 [b]Mt 4:3 [c]1Jn 3:5 [d]Jn 12:31; 16:11 **3:9** [a]Jn 1:13; 3:3; 1Jn 2:29; 4:7; 5:1, 4, 18; 3Jn 11 [b]1Pe 1:23; 1Jn 3:6; 5:18 [1]Or *begotten* **3:10** [a]Jn 1:12; 11:52; Ro 8:16; 1Jn 3:1, 2 [b]Mt 13:38; Jn 8:44; 1Jn 3:8 [c]Ro 13:8ff; Col 3:14; 1Ti 1:5; 1Jn 4:8 [d]1Jn 2:9 **3:11** [a]1Jn 1:5 [b]1Jn 2:7 [c]Jn 13:4f; 15:12; 1Jn 4:7, 11f, 21; 2Jn 5 **3:12** [a]Ge 4:8 [b]Mt 5:37; 1Jn 2:13f [c]Ps 38:20; Pr 29:10; Jn 8:40, 41 **3:13** [a]Jn 15:18; 17:14 **3:14** [a]Jn 5:24 [b]Jn 13:35; 1Jn 2:10 **3:15** [a]Mt 5:21f; Jn 8:44 [b]Ga 5:20f; Rev 21:8 **3:16** [a]Jn 10:11; 15:13 [b]Php 2:17; 1Th 2:8 [c]1Jn 2:9 **3:17** [a]Jas 2:15f [b]Dt 15:7 [c]1Jn 4:20 [1]Lit *inward parts* [2]Lit *from* **3:18** [a]1Jn 2:1; 3:7 [b]2Jn 1; 3Jn 1 **3:19** [a]1Jn 2:21 [1]Lit *persuade* **3:20** [1]Or *that if our heart condemns us, that God...* **3:21** [a]1Jn 3:2 [b]1Jn 2:28; 5:14 [1]Lit *toward* **3:22** [a]Job 22:26f; Mt 7:7; 21:22; Jn 9:31 [b]1Jn 2:3 [c]Jn 8:29; Heb 13:21 **3:23** [a]Jn 6:29 [b]Jn 1:12; 2:23; 3:18 [c]Jn 13:34; 15:12; 1Jn 2:8 [1]Or *believe the name* **3:24** [a]1Jn 2:3 [b]Jn 6:56; 10:38; 1Jn 2:6, 24; 4:15 [c]Jn 14:17; Ro 8:9, 14, 16; 1Th 4:8; 1Jn 4:13 [d]1Jn 2:5

### *Test the Spirits*

4 [a]Beloved, do not believe every
[b]spirit, but test the spirits to see
whether they are from God, because
[c]many false prophets have gone out
into the world. **2** By this you know
the Spirit of God: [a]every spirit that
[b]confesses that [c]Jesus Christ has
come in the flesh is from God, **3** and
every spirit that [a]does not confess
Jesus is not from God. This is the
*spirit* of the [b]antichrist, of which
you have heard that it is coming,
and [c]now it is already in the world.
**4** You are from God, [a]little children,
and [b]have overcome them; because
[c]greater is He who is in you than [d]he
who is in the world. **5** [a]They are from
the world; therefore they speak *as*
from the world, and the world hears
them. **6** [a]We are from God. [b]The one
who knows God hears us; [c]the one
who is not from God does not hear
us. From this we know [d]the spirit of
truth and [e]the spirit of error.

### *God Is Love*

**7** [a]Beloved, let us [b]love one another,
for love is from God; and [c]everyone
who loves has been [d,1]born of God
and [e]knows God. **8** The one who does
not love does not know God, because
[a]God is love. **9** By this the love of God
was manifested [a,1]in us, that [b]God
has sent His [2]only begotten Son
into the world so that we might live
through Him. **10** In this is love, [a]not
that we have loved God, but that [b]He
loved us and sent His Son *to be* [c]the
propitiation for our sins. **11** [a]Beloved,
if God so loved us, [b]we also ought
to love one another. **12** [a]No one has
beheld God at any time; if we love
one another, God abides in us, and
His [b]love is perfected in us. **13** [a]By
this we know that we abide in Him
and He in us, because He has given
us of His Spirit. **14** We have beheld
and [a]bear witness that the Father has
[b]sent the Son *to be* the Savior of the
world.
**15** [a]Whoever confesses that [b]Jesus
is the Son of God, God [c]abides in
him, and he in God. **16** [a]And we have
come to know and have believed the
love which God has [b]in us. [c]God
is love, and the one who [d]abides in
love abides in God, and God abides
in him. **17** By this, [a]love has been per-
fected with us, so that we may have
[b]confidence in [c]the day of judgment,
because [d]as He is, so also are we in
this world. **18** There is no fear in love;
but [a]perfect love casts out fear, be-
cause fear [1]involves punishment, and
the one who fears is not [b]perfected
in love. **19** [a]We love, because He first
loved us. **20** [a]If someone says, "I love
God," and [b]hates his brother, he is
a [c]liar; for [d]the one who does not
love his brother whom he has seen,
[e]cannot love God whom he has not

---

◆ **4:1** [a]3Jn 11 [b]Jer 29:8; 1Co 12:10; 1Th 5:20f; 2Th 2:2 [c]Jer 14:14; 2Pe 2:1; 1Jn 2:18 **4:2** [a]1Co 12:3 [b]1Jn 2:23 [c]Jn 1:14; 1Jn 1:2 **4:3** [a]1Jn 2:22; 2Jn 7 [b]1Jn 2:18, 22 [c]2Th 2:3-7; 1Jn 2:18 **4:4** [a]1Jn 2:1 [b]1Jn 2:13 [c]Ro 8:31; 1Jn 3:20 [d]Jn 12:31 **4:5** [a]*Jn 15:19; 17:14, 16* **4:6** [a]Jn 8:23; 1Jn 4:4 [b]Jn 8:47; 10:3ff; 18:37 [c]1Co 14:37 [d]Jn 14:17 [e]1Ti 4:1 **4:7** [a]1Jn 2:7 [b]1Jn 3:11 [c]1Jn 5:1 [d]1Jn 2:29 [e]1Co 8:3; 1Jn 2:3 [1]Or *begotten* **4:8** [a]1Jn 4:7, 16 **4:9** [a]Jn 9:3; 1Jn 4:16 [b]Jn 3:16f; 1Jn 4:10; 5:11 [1]Or *in our case* [2]Or *unique, only one of His kind* **4:10** [a]Ro 5:8, 10; 1Jn 4:19 [b]Jn 3:16f; 1Jn 4:9; 5:11 [c]1Jn 2:2 **4:11** [a]1Jn 2:7 [b]1Jn 4:7 **4:12** [a]Jn 1:18; 1Ti 6:16; 1Jn 4:20 [b]1Jn 2:5; 4:17f **4:13** [a]Ro 8:9; 1Jn 3:24 **4:14** [a]Jn 15:27; 1Jn 1:2 [b]Jn 3:17; 4:42; 1Jn 2:2 **4:15** [a]1Jn 2:23 [b]Ro 10:9; 1Jn 3:23; 4:2; 5:1, 5 [c]1Jn 2:24; 3:24 **4:16** [a]Jn 6:69 [b]Jn 9:3; 1Jn 4:9 [c]1Jn 4:7, 8 [d]1Jn 4:12f **4:17** [a]1Jn 2:5; 4:12 [b]1Jn 2:28 [c]Mt 10:15 [d]Jn 17:22; 1Jn 2:6; 3:1, 7, 16 **4:18** [a]Ro 8:15 [b]1Jn 4:12 [1]Lit *has* **4:19** [a]1Jn 4:10 **4:20** [a]1Jn 1:6, 8, 10; 2:4 [b]1Jn 2:9, 11 [c]1Jn 1:6 [d]1Jn 3:17 [e]1Pe 1:8; 1Jn 4:12

seen. **21** And [a]this commandment we
have from Him, that the one who
loves God [b]should love his brother
also.

### *Overcoming the World*

**5** [a]Everyone who believes that Jesus
is the [1]Christ has been [b,2]born of
God, and everyone who loves the
[3]One who gives *new* birth [c]loves
also the one who has been [2]born of
Him. **2** [a]By this we know that [b]we love
the children of God, when we love
God and do His commandments.
**3** For [a]this is the love of God, that we
[b]keep His commandments; and [c]His
commandments are not burdensome.
**4** For everything that has been [a,1]born
of God [b]overcomes the world; and
this is the overcoming that has over-
come the world—our faith.

**5** Who is the one who overcomes
the world, but he who [a]believes
that Jesus is the Son of God? **6** This
is the One who came [a]by water and
blood, Jesus Christ; not [1]with the
water only, but [1]with the water and
[1]with the blood. It is [b]the Spirit who
bears witness, because the Spirit is
the truth. **7** For there are [a]three that
bear witness: **8** [1]the Spirit and the
water and the blood; and the three
are [2]in agreement. **9** [a]If we receive the
witness of men, the witness of God is
greater; for the witness of God is this,
that [b]He has borne witness about His
Son. **10** The one who believes in the
Son of God [a]has this witness in him-
self. The one who does not believe
God has [b]made Him a liar, because
he has not believed in the witness
which God has borne witness about
His Son. **11** And the witness is this,
that God gave us [a]eternal life, and
[b]this life is in His Son. **12** [a]He who has
the Son has the life; he who does not
have the Son of God does not have
that life.

### *That You May Know*

**13** [a]These things I have written to you
who [b]believe in the name of the Son
of God, so that you may know that
you have [c]eternal life. **14** And this
is [a]the confidence which we have
[1]before Him, that, [b]if we ask anything
according to His will, He hears us.
**15** And if we know that He hears us
*in* whatever we ask, [a]we know that
we have the requests which we have
asked from Him.

**16** If anyone sees his brother
[1]committing a sin not *leading* to
death, [a]he shall ask and [2]*God* will
for him give life to those who commit
sin not *leading* to death. [b]There is
a sin *leading* to death; [c]I do not say
that he should make request for this.
**17** [a]All unrighteousness is sin, and
[b]there is a sin not *leading* to death.

**18** [a]We know that [b]no one who has
been [1]born of God sins; but He who

---

**4:21** [a]Lv 19:18; Mt 5:43f; 22:37ff; Jn 13:34 [b]1Jn 3:11 ◆ **5:1** [a]1Jn 2:22f; 4:2, 15 [b]Jn 1:3; 3:3; 1Jn 2:29; 5:4, 18 [c]Jn 8:42 [1]Messiah [2]Or *begotten* [3]Lit *one who begets* **5:2** [a]1Jn 2:5 [b]1Jn 3:14 **5:3** [a]Jn 14:15; 2Jn 6 [b]1Jn 2:3 [c]Mt 11:30; 23:4 **5:4** [a]Jn 1:13; 3:3; 1Jn 2:29; 5:1, 18 [b]1Jn 2:13; 4:4 [1]Or *begotten* **5:5** [a]1Jn 4:15; 5:1 **5:6** [a]Jn 19:34 [b]Mt 3:16f; Jn 15:26; 16:13-15 [1]Lit *in* **5:7** [a]Mt 18:16 **5:8** [1]A few late mss add ...*in heaven, the Father, the Word, and the Holy Spirit, and these three are one. And there are three that testify on earth, the Spirit* [2]Lit *for the one thing* **5:9** [a]Jn 5:34, 37; 8:18 [b]Mt 3:17; Jn 5:32, 37 **5:10** [a]Ro 8:16; Ga 4-6; Rev 12:17 [b]Jn 3:18, 33; 1Jn 1:10 **5:11** [a]Jn 3:36; 1Jn 1:2; 2:25; 4:9; 5:13, 20 [b]Jn 1:4 **5:12** [a]Jn 3:15f, 36 **5:13** [a]Jn 20:31 [b]1Jn 3:23 [c]1Jn 1:2; 2:25; 4:9; 5:11, 20 **5:14** [a]1Jn 2:28; 3:21f [b]Mt 7:7; Jn 14:13; 1Jn 3:22 [1]Lit *toward* **5:15** [a]1Jn 5:18-20 **5:16** [a]Jas 5:15 [b]Nu 15:30; Heb 6:4-6; 10:26 [c]Jer 7:16; 14:11 [1]Lit *sinning* [2]Or *God will give him life*, that is, *to those who...* **5:17** [a]1Jn 3:4 [b]1Jn 2:1f; 5:16 **5:18** [a]1Jn 5:15, 19, 20 [b]1Jn 3:9 [1]Or *begotten*

was [2]begotten of God [c]keeps him,
and [d]the evil one does not [e]touch
him. **19** [a]We know that [b]we are of
God, and that [c]the whole world lies in
*the power of* the evil one. **20** And [a]we
know that [b]the Son of God has come,
and has [c]given us understanding so
that we may know [d]Him who is true;
and we [e]are in Him who is true, in
His Son Jesus Christ. [f]This is the true
God and [g]eternal life.
**21** [a]Little children, guard your-
selves from [b]idols.

# *The Second Letter of* JOHN

### *Walk in Truth and Love*

**1** [a]The elder to the [b]elect [c]lady and
her children, whom I [d]love in
truth, and not only I, but also all who
[e]know the truth, **2** for [a]the sake of the
truth which abides [b]in us and will be
[c]with us forever: **3** [a]Grace, mercy, *and*
peace will be with us, from God the
Father and from Jesus Christ, the Son
of the Father, in truth and love.
**4** [a]I rejoiced greatly to find *some* of
your children walking in truth, just as
we received commandment from the
Father. **5** Now I ask you, lady, [a]not as
though *I were* writing to you a new
commandment, but the one which
we have had [a]from the beginning,
that we [b]love one another. **6** And
[a]this is love, that we walk according
to His commandments. This is the
commandment, [b]just as you have
heard [c]from the beginning, that you
should walk in it.
**7** For [a]many deceivers have [b]gone
out into the world, those who [c]do
not confess Jesus Christ *as* coming
in the flesh. This is [a]the deceiver
and the [d]antichrist. **8** [a]See to your-
selves, [b]that you do not lose what
we accomplished, but that you may
receive a full reward. **9** [1]Anyone who
[2]goes too far and [a]does not abide
in the teaching of Christ, does not
have God. The one who abides
in the teaching, he has both the
Father and the Son. **10** If anyone
comes to you and does not bring
this teaching, [a]do not receive him
into *your* house, and do not give
him a greeting, **11** for the one who
gives him a greeting [a,1]participates
in his evil deeds.
**12** [a]Though I have many things
to write to you, I do not want to *do
so* with paper and ink; but I hope
to come to you and speak face to
face, so that [1]your [b]joy may be made
complete.
**13** The children of your [a]elect
sister greet you.

---

**5:18** [c]Jas 1:27; Jd 21 [d]1Jn 2:13 [e]Jn 14:30 [2]Or *born* **5:19** [a]1Jn 5:15, 18, 20 [b]1Jn 4:6 [c]Jn 12:31; 17:15; Ga 1:4 **5:20** [a]1Jn 5:15, 18, 19 [b]Jn 8:42; 1Jn 5:5 [c]Lk 24:45 [d]Jn 17:3; Rev 3:7 [e]Jn 1:18; 14:9; 1Jn 2:23; Rev 3:7 [f]1Jn 1:2 [g]1Jn 5:11 **5:21** [a]1Jn 2:1 [b]1Co 10:7, 14; 1Th 1:9 ◆ **1** [a]Ac 11:30; 1Pe 5:1; 3Jn 1 [b]Ro 16:13; 1Pe 5:13; 2Jn 13 [c]2Jn 5 [d]1Jn 3:18; 2Jn 3; 3Jn 1 [e]Jn 8:32; 1Ti 2:4 **2** [a]2Pe 1:12 [b]1Jn 1:8 [c]Jn 14:16 **3** [a]Ro 1:7; 1Ti 1:2 **4** [a]3Jn 3f **5** [a]1Jn 2:7 [b]Jn 13:34, 35; 15:12, 17; 1Jn 3:11; 4:7, 11 **6** [a]1Jn 2:5; 5:3 [b]1Jn 2:24 [c]1Jn 2:7 **7** [a]1Jn 2:26 [b]1Jn 2:19; 4:1 [c]1Jn 4:2f [d]1Jn 2:18 **8** [a]Mk 13:9 [b]1Co 3:8; Heb 10:35 **9** [a]Jn 7:16; 8:31; 1Jn 2:23 [1]Lit *Everyone* [2]Lit *goes on ahead* **10** [a]1Ki 13:16f; Ro 16:17; 2Th 3:6, 14; Tit 3:10 **11** [a]Eph 5:11; 1Ti 5:22; Jd 23 [1]Lit *fellowships* **12** [a]3Jn 13, 14 [b]Jn 3:29; 1Jn 1:4 [1]One early ms *our* **13** [a]2Jn 1

# The Third Letter of JOHN

### *Walking in the Truth*

**1** [a]The elder to the beloved [b]Gaius,
whom I [c]love in truth.
**2** Beloved, I pray that in all respects
you may prosper and be in good
health, just as your soul prospers.
**3** For I [a]rejoiced greatly when [b]broth-
ers came and bore witness to your
truth, *that is,* how you [a]are walking
in truth. **4** I have no greater joy than
[1]this, to hear that [a]my children are
[b]walking in the truth.

**5** Beloved, you are acting faith-
fully in whatever [1]work you do for
the [a]brothers, and *are doing* this
*though they are* [b]strangers; **6** and
they bore witness to your love be-
fore the church. You will do well to
[a]send them on their way in a manner
[b]worthy of God. **7** For they went out
for the sake of [a]the Name, [b]receiving
nothing from the Gentiles. **8** There-
fore we ought to [1]support such men,
so that we may [2]be fellow workers
[3]with the truth.

**9** I wrote something to the church,
but Diotrephes, who loves to [a]be
first among them, does not welcome
[1]what we say. **10** For this reason, [a]if I
come, I will bring to remembrance
his deeds which he does, unjustly
disparaging us with wicked words.
And not satisfied with this, he him-
self does not [b]welcome the [c]brothers
either, and he forbids those who
want *to do so* and [d]puts *them* out of
the church.

**11** Beloved, [a]do not imitate what
is evil, but what is good. [b]The one
who does good is of God; [c]the one
who does evil has not seen God.
**12** Demetrius [a]has received a *good*
witness from everyone, and from the
truth itself; and we add our witness,
and [b]you know that our witness is
true.

**13** [a]I had many things to write to
you, but I am not willing to write
*them* to you with pen and ink; **14** but
I hope to see you shortly, and we will
speak face to face.

**15** [a]Peace *be* to you. The friends
greet you. Greet the friends [b]by
name.

---

◆ **1** [a]2Jn 1 [b]Ac 19:29; 20:4; Ro 16:23; 1Co 1:14 [c]1Jn 3:18; 2Jn 1 **3** [a]2Jn 4 [b]Ac 1:15; Ga 6:10; 3Jn 5, 10 **4** [a]1Co 4:14f; 2Co 6:13; Ga 4:19; 1Th 2:11; 1Ti 1:2; 2Ti 1:2; Phm 10; 1Jn 2:1 [b]2Jn 4 [1]Lit *these things, that I hear* **5** [a]Ac 1:15; Ga 6:10; 3Jn 3, 10 [b]Ro 12:13; Heb 13:2 [1]Lit *work* **6** [a]Ac 15:3; Tit 3:13 [b]Col 1:10; 1Th 2:12 **7** [a]*Jn 15:21; Ac 5:41; Php 2:9* [b]Ac 20:33, 35 **8** [1]Or *receive such men as guests* [2]Or *prove ourselves to be* [3]Or *for* **9** [a]2Jn 9 [1]Lit *us* **10** [a]2Jn 12 [b]2Jn 10; 3Jn 5 [c]Ac 1:15; Ga 6:10; 3Jn 3, 5 [d]Jn 9:34 **11** [a]Ps 34:14; 37:27 [b]1Jn 2:29; 3:10 [c]1Jn 3:6 **12** [a]Ac 6:3; 1Ti 3:7 [b]Jn 19:35; 21:24 **13** [a]2Jn 12 **15** [a]Jn 20:19, 21, 26; Eph 6:23; 1Pe 5:14 [b]Jn 10:3

*The Letter of*

# JUDE

### *Contend Earnestly for the Faith*

**1** [a,1]Jude, a [b]slave of Jesus Christ,
and brother of [2]James,
To [c]those who are the called, be-
loved in God the Father, and [d]kept
for Jesus Christ: **2** [a]May mercy and
peace and love [b]be multiplied to you.
**3** [a]Beloved, while I was making
every effort to write you about our
[b]common salvation, I felt the neces-
sity to write to you exhorting that
you [c]contend earnestly for [d]the faith
which was once for all [e]handed down
to [f]the [1]saints. **4** For certain persons
have [a]crept in unnoticed, those who
were long beforehand [b,1]marked out
for this condemnation, ungodly
persons who turn [c]the grace of our
God into [d]sensuality and [e]deny our
only Master and Lord, Jesus Christ.
**5** Now I want to [a]remind you,
though [b]you know all things, that
[1]Jesus, [c]having once saved a people
out of the land of Egypt, [2]subse-
quently destroyed those who did not
believe. **6** And [a]angels who did not
keep their own domain, but aban-
doned their proper abode, He has
[b]kept in eternal bonds under dark-
ness for the judgment of the great
day, **7** just as [a]Sodom and Gomorrah
and the [b]cities around them, having
indulged in the same way as these in
gross sexual immorality and having
[c]gone after [1]strange flesh, are exhib-
ited as an [d,2]example in undergoing
the [e]punishment of eternal fire.
**8** Yet in the same way these men,
also by dreaming, [a]defile the flesh,
and reject authority, and blaspheme
[1]glorious ones. **9** But [a]Michael [b]the
archangel, when he, disputing
with the devil, was arguing about
[c]the body of Moses, did not dare
pronounce against him a blasphe-
mous judgment, but said, "[d]The
Lord rebuke you!" **10** But [a]these
men blaspheme the things which
they do not understand; and [b]the
things which they know by instinct,
[a]like unreasoning animals, by these
things they are [1]destroyed. **11** Woe
to them! For they have gone [a]the
way of Cain, and for pay they have
poured themselves into [b]the error
of Balaam, and [c]perished in the
rebellion of Korah. **12** These are the
men who are [1]hidden reefs [a]in your
love feasts when they feast with you
[b]without fear, caring for themselves;
[c]clouds without water, [d]carried along
by winds; autumn trees without fruit,
[2]doubly dead, [e]uprooted; **13** [a]wild
waves of the sea, casting up [b]their

---

◆**1** [a]Mt 13:55; Mk 6:3; [Lk 6:16; Jn 14:22; Ac 1:13] [b]Ro 1:1 [c]Ro 1:6f [d]Jn 17:11f; 1Pe 1:5; Jd 21 [1]Gr *Judas* [2]Or *Jacob*; James is the Eng form of Jacob **2** [a]Ga 6:16; 1Ti 1:2 [b]1Pe 1:2; 2Pe 1:2 **3** [a]Heb 6:9; Jd 1, 17, 20 [b]Tit 1:4 [c]1Ti 6:12 [d]Ac 6:7; Jd 20 [e]2Pe 2:21 [f]Ac 9:13 [1]Or *holy ones* **4** [a]Ga 2:4; 2Ti 3:6 [b]1Pe 2:8 [c]Ac 11:23 [d]2Pe 2:7 [e]2Ti 2:12; Tit 1:16; 2Pe 2:1; 1Jn 2:22 [1]Or *written about...long ago* **5** [a]2Pe 1:12f; 3:1f [b]1Jn 2:20 [c]Ex 12:51; 1Co 10:5-10; Heb 3:16f [1]Some mss *Lord* [2]Lit *the second time* **6** [a]2Pe 2:4 [b]2Pe 2:9 **7** [a]Ge 19:24f; 2Pe 2:6 [b]Dt 29:23; Hos 11:8 [c]2Pe 2:2 [d]2Pe 2:6 [e]Mt 25:41; 2Th 1:8f; 2Pe 3:7 [1]Or *other*; lit *different* [2]Or *example of eternal fire, in undergoing punishment* **8** [a]2Pe 2:10 [1]Angels **9** [a]Da 10:13, 21; 12:1; Rev 12:7 [b]1Th 4:16; 2Pe 2:11 [c]Dt 34:6 [d]Zec 3:2 **10** [a]2Pe 2:12 [b]Php 3:19 [1]Lit *corrupted* **11** [a]Ge 4:3-8; Heb 11:4; 1Jn 3:12 [b]Nu 31:16; 2Pe 2:15; Rev 2:14 [c]Nu 16:1-3, 31-35 **12** [a]1Co 11:20ff; 2Pe 2:13 and mg [b]Eze 34:2, 8, 10 [c]Pr 25:14; 2Pe 2:17 [d]Eph 4:14 [e]Mt 15:13 [1]Or *stains* [2]Lit *twice* **13** [a]Is 57:20 [b]Php 3:19

own [1]shame like foam; wandering
stars, [c]for whom the [2]black darkness
has been reserved forever.

**14** But [a]Enoch, *in* the seventh *gen-*
*eration* from Adam, also prophesied
about these men, saying, "[b]Behold,
the Lord came with [1]many thousands
of His holy ones, **15** [a]to execute
judgment upon all, and to convict
all the ungodly of all their ungodly
deeds which they have done in an
ungodly way, and of all the harsh
things which [b]ungodly sinners have
spoken against Him." **16** These are
[a]grumblers, finding fault, [b]following
after their *own* lusts; and their mouth
speaks [c]arrogantly, [1]flattering people
[d]for the sake of *their own* benefit.

### *Keep Yourselves in the Love of God*

**17** But you, [a]beloved, [b]must remem-
ber the words that were spoken
beforehand by [c]the apostles of our
Lord Jesus Christ, **18** that they were
saying to you, "[a]In the last time there
will be mockers, [b]following after
their own ungodly lusts." **19** These
are the ones who cause divisions,
[a,1]worldly-minded, not having the
Spirit. **20** But you, [a]beloved, [b]building
yourselves up on your most holy
[a]faith, [c]praying in the Holy Spirit,
**21** keep yourselves in the love of God,
[a]waiting for the mercy of our Lord
Jesus Christ to eternal life. **22** And on
some, who are doubting, have mercy;
**23** and for others, save, [a]snatching
them out of the fire; and on others
have mercy with fear, [b]hating even
the tunic polluted by the flesh.

**24** [a]Now to Him who is able to keep
you from stumbling, and to [b]make
you stand in the presence of His glory
blameless with [c]great joy, **25** to the
[a]only [b]God our Savior, through Jesus
Christ our Lord, [c]*be* glory, majesty,
might, and authority, [d]before all time
and now and [1]forever. Amen.

**13** [c]2Pe 2:17; Jd 6 [1]Or *shameless deeds* [2]Or *netherworld gloom*; lit *blackness of darkness* **14** [a]Ge 5:18, 21ff [b]Dt 33:2; Da 7:10; Mt 16:27; Heb 12:22 [1]Lit *His holy ten thousands* **15** [a]2Pe 2:6ff [b]1Ti 1:9 **16** [a]Nu 16:11, 41; 1Co 10:10 [b]2Pe 2:10; Jd 18 [c]2Pe 2:18 [d]2Pe 2:3 [1]Lit *marveling faces* **17** [a]Jd 3 [b]2Pe 3:2 [c]Heb 2:3 **18** [a]Ac 20:29; 1Ti 4:1; 2Ti 3:1f; 4:3; 2Pe 3:3 [b]Jd 4, 16 **19** [a]1Co 2:14f; Jas 3:15 [1]Or *merely natural* **20** [a]Jd 3 [b]Col 2:7; 1Th 5:11 [c]Eph 6:18 **21** [a]Tit 2:13; Heb 9:28; 2Pe 3:12 **23** [a]Am 4:11; Zec 3:2; 1Co 3:15 [b]Zec 3:3f; Rev 3:4 **24** [a]Ro 16:25 [b]2Co 4:14 [c]1Pe 4:13 **25** [a]Jn 5:44; 1Ti 1:17 [b]Lk 1:47 [c]Ro 11:36 [d]Heb 13:8 [1]Lit *to all the ages*

# THE REVELATION
## *to John*

### *The Revelation of Jesus Christ*

**1** The Revelation of Jesus Christ,
which [a]God gave Him to [b]show
to His slaves [c]the things which must
soon happen; and He indicated *this*
[d]by sending *it* through His angel to
His slave [e,1]John, **2** who bore witness
to [a]the word of God and to [b]the wit-
ness of Jesus Christ, *even* to all that
he saw. **3** [a]Blessed is he who reads
and those who hear the words of the
prophecy and keep the things which
are written in it, [b]for the time is near.

### *Message to the Seven Churches*

**4** [a]John to [b]the seven churches that
are in [c]Asia: [d]Grace to you and peace,
from [e]the One who is and who was
and who [1]is to come, and from [f]the
seven Spirits who are before His
throne, **5** and from Jesus Christ, [a]the
faithful witness, the [b]firstborn of the
dead, and the [c]ruler of the kings of
the earth. To Him who [d]loves us and
released us from our sins [1]by His
blood— **6** and He has made us *to be*
a [a]kingdom, [a]priests to [b,1]His God
and Father—[c]to Him *be* the glory and
the might forever and ever. Amen.
**7** [a]BEHOLD, HE IS COMING WITH THE
CLOUDS, and [b]EVERY EYE WILL SEE HIM,
EVEN THOSE WHO PIERCED HIM; and all
the tribes of the earth will [c]MOURN
OVER HIM. Yes, amen.
**8** "I am [a]the Alpha and the Ome-
ga," says the [b,1]Lord God, "[c]who is
and who was and who [2]is to come,
the Almighty."

### *The Vision of the Son of Man*

**9** [a]I, John, your [b]brother and [c]fellow
partaker in the tribulation and
[d]kingdom and [e,1]perseverance *which*
*are* in Jesus, was on the island called
Patmos [f]because of the word of God
and the witness of Jesus. **10** I was [a,1]in
the Spirit on [b]the Lord's day, and I
heard behind me a loud voice [c]like
a trumpet, **11** saying, "[a]Write in a
scroll what you see, and send *it* to
the [b]seven churches: to [c]Ephesus
and to [d]Smyrna and to [e]Pergamum
and to [f]Thyatira and to [g]Sardis and
to [h]Philadelphia and to [i]Laodicea."
**12** Then I turned to see the voice
that was speaking with me. And
having turned I saw [a]seven golden
lampstands; **13** and [a]in the middle of
the lampstands *I saw* one [b]like [1]a son
of man, [c]clothed in a robe reaching
to the feet, and [d]girded across His
chest with a golden sash. **14** And His
head and His [a]hair were white like
white wool, like snow; and [b]His eyes

◆ **1:1** [a]Jn 17:8; Rev 5:7 [b]Rev 22:6 [c]Da 2:28f; Rev 1:19 [d]Rev 17:1; 19:9f; 21:9; 22:16 [e]Rev 1:4, 9; 22:8 [1]Gr *Joannes*, Heb *Johanan*; so in Rev **1:2** [a]Rev 1:9; 6:9; 12:17; 20:4 [b]1Co 1:6; Rev 12:17 **1:3** [a]Lk 11:28; Rev 22:7 [b]Ro 13:11; Rev 3:11; 22:7, 10, 12 **1:4** [a]Rev 1:1, 9; 22:8 [b]Rev 1:11, 20 [c]Ac 2:9 [d]Ro 1:7 [e]Rev 1:8, 17; 4:8; 16:5 [f]Is 11:2; Rev 3:1; 4:5; 5:6; 8:2 [1]Or *is coming* **1:5** [a]Rev 3:14; 19:11 [b]1Co 15:20; Col 1:18 [c]Rev 17:14; 19:16 [d]*Ro 8:37* [1]*Or in* **1:6** [a]Rev 5:10; 20:6 [b]Ro 15:6 [c]Ro 11:36 [1]Or *God and His Father* **1:7** [a]Da 7:13; 1Th 4:17 [b]Zec 12:10-14; Jn 19:37 [c]Lk 23:28 **1:8** [a]Is 41:4; Rev 21:6; 22:13 [b]Rev 4:8; 11:17 [c]Rev 1:4 [1]In OT, Yahweh, cf. Is 41:4 [2]Or *is coming* **1:9** [a]Rev 1:1 [b]Ac 1:15 [c]Mt 20:23; Ac 14:22; 2Co 1:7; Php 4:14 [d]2Ti 2:12; Rev 1:6 [e]2Th 3:5; Rev 3:10 [f]Rev 1:2 [1]Or *steadfastness* **1:10** [a]Mt 22:43; Rev 4:2; 17:3; 21:10 [b]Ac 20:7 [c]Rev 4:1 [1]Or *in spirit* **1:11** [a]Rev 1:2, 19 [b]Rev 1:4, 20 [c]Rev 2:1 [d]Rev 2:8 [e]Rev 2:12 [f]Ac 16:14; Rev 2:18, 24 [g]Rev 3:1, 4 [h]Rev 3:7 [i]Col 2:1; Rev 3:14 **1:12** [a]Ex 25:37; 37:23; Zec 4:2; Rev 1:20; 2:1 **1:13** [a]Rev 2:1 [b]Eze 1:26; Da 7:13; 10:16; Rev 14:14 [c]Da 10:5 [d]Rev 15:6 [1]Or *the Son of Man* **1:14** [a]Da 7:9 [b]Da 7:9; 10:6; Rev 2:18; 19:12

were like a flame of fire. **15** His [a]feet
*were* like burnished bronze, when it
has been made to glow in a furnace,
and His [b]voice *was* like the sound
of many waters, **16** and having in His
right hand [a]seven stars, and a [b]sharp
two-edged sword which comes out
of His mouth, and His [c]face was like
[d]the sun [1]shining in its power.
**17** And when I saw Him, I [a]fell at His
feet like a dead man. And He [b]placed
His right hand on me, saying, "[c]Do not
fear; [d]I am the first and the last, **18** and
the [a]living One; and I [b,1]was dead, and
behold, I am alive forever and ever,
and I have [c]the keys of death and of
Hades. **19** Therefore [a]write [b]the things
which you have seen, and the things
which are, and the things which will
take place [c]after these things. **20** As
for the [a]mystery of the [b]seven stars
which you saw in My right hand,
and the [c]seven golden lampstands:
the [b]seven stars are the angels of
[d]the seven churches, and the seven
[e]lampstands are the seven churches.

### *To the Church in Ephesus*

**2** "To the angel of the church in
[a]Ephesus write:
This is what the One who holds
[b]the seven stars in His right hand, the
One who walks [c,1]among the seven
golden lampstands, says:
**2** '[a]I know your deeds and your
toil and perseverance, and that you
cannot bear with those who are evil,
and you [b]put to the test those who
call themselves [c]apostles, and they
are not, and you found them *to be*
false; **3** and you have perseverance
and have [1]endured [a]for My name's
sake, you also have not grown
weary. **4** But I have *this* against you,
that you have [a]left your first love.
**5** Therefore remember from where
you have fallen, and [a]repent and [b]do
the [1]deeds you did at first. But if not,
I am coming to you and will remove
your [c]lampstand out of its place,
unless you repent. **6** Yet this you do
have, that you hate the deeds of the
[a]Nicolaitans, which I also hate. **7** [a]He
who has an ear, let him hear what
the Spirit says to the churches. [b]To
him who overcomes, I will grant to
eat of [c]the tree of life which is in the
[d]Paradise of God.'

### *To the Church in Smyrna*

**8** "And to the angel of the church in
[a]Smyrna write:
[b]This is what THE FIRST AND THE
LAST, who [c,1]was dead, and has come
to life, says:
**9** 'I know your [a]tribulation and
your [b]poverty (but you are [b]rich),
and the blasphemy by those who
[c]say they are Jews and are not, but
are a synagogue of [d]Satan. **10** Do not
fear what you are about to suffer.
Behold, the devil is about to cast

**1:15** [a]Eze 1:7; Da 10:6; Rev 2:18 [b]Eze 1:24; 43:2; Rev 14:2; 19:6 **1:16** [a]Rev 1:20; 2:1; 3:1 [b]Is 49:2; Heb 4:12; Rev 2:12, 16; 19:15 [c]Mt 17:2; Rev 10:1 [d]Jdg 5:31 [1]Lit *shines* **1:17** [a]Da 8:17; 10:9, 10, 15 [b]Da 8:18; 10:10, 12 [c]Mt 14:27; 17:7 [d]Is 41:4; 44:6; 48:12; Rev 2:8; 22:13 **1:18** [a]Lk 24:5; Rev 4:9f [b]Ro 6:9; Rev 2:8; 10:6; 15:7 [c]Job 38:17; Mt 11:23; 16:19; Rev 9:1; 20:1 [1]Lit *became* **1:19** [a]Rev 1:11 [b]Rev 1:12-16 [c]Rev 4:1 **1:20** [a]Ro 11:25 [b]Rev 1:16; 2:1; 3:1 [c]Ex 25:37; 37:23; Zec 4:2; Rev 1:12; 2:1 [d]Rev 1:4, 11 [e]Mt 5:14f ◆**2:1** [a]Rev 1:11 [b]Rev 1:16 [c]Rev 1:12f [1]Lit *in the middle of* **2:2** [a]Rev 2:19; 3:1, 8, 15 [b]Jn 6:6; 1Jn 4:1 [c]2Co 11:13 **2:3** [a]Jn 15:21 [1]Lit *bear up*, cf. 2:2 **2:4** [a]Jer 2:2; Mt 24:12 **2:5** [a]Rev 2:16, 22; 3:3, 19 [b]Heb 10:32; Rev 2:2 [c]Mt 5:14ff; Php 2:15; Rev 1:20 [1]Lit *first deeds* **2:6** [a]Rev 2:15 **2:7** [a]Mt 11:15; Rev 2:11, 17; 3:6, 13, 22; 13:9 [b]Rev 2:11, 17, 26; 3:5, 12, 21; 21:7 [c]Ge 2:9; 3:22; Pr 3:18; 11:30; 13:12; 15:4; Rev 22:2, 14 [d]Eze 28:13; 31:8f; Lk 23:43 **2:8** [a]Rev 1:11 [b]Is 44:6; 48:12; Rev 1:17; 22:13 [c]Rev 1:18 [1]Lit *became* **2:9** [a]Rev 1:9 [b]2Co 6:10; 8:9; Jas 2:5 [c]Rev 3:9 [d]Mt 4:10; Rev 2:13, 24

some of you into prison, so that you
will be [a]tested, and you will have
tribulation [b]for ten days. [1]Be [c]faithful
until death, and I will give you [d]the
crown of life. **11** [a]He who has an ear,
let him hear what the Spirit says to
the churches. [b]He who overcomes
will never be hurt by the [c]second
death.'

### *To the Church in Pergamum*

**12** "And to the angel of the church in
[a]Pergamum write:
This is what the One who has [b]the
sharp two-edged sword says:
**13** 'I know where you dwell, where
[a]Satan's throne is; and you hold fast
My name, and did not deny [b]My
faith even in the days of Antipas,
My [c]witness, My [d]faithful one,
who was killed among you, [e]where
Satan dwells. **14** But [a]I have a few
things against you, that you have
there some who hold the [b]teaching
of Balaam, who kept teaching Balak
to put a stumbling block before the
sons of Israel, [c]to eat things sacrificed
to idols and to commit sexual immo-
rality. **15** So you also have some who
in the same way hold the teaching
of the [a]Nicolaitans. **16** Therefore
[a]repent. But if not, [b]I am coming
to you quickly, and I will make war
against them with [c]the sword of My
mouth. **17** [a]He who has an ear, let
him hear what the Spirit says to the
churches. [a]To him who overcomes,
to him I will give *some* of the hidden
[b]manna, and I will give him a white
stone, and a [c]new name written on
the stone [d]which no one knows but
he who receives it.'

### *To the Church in Thyatira*

**18** "And to the angel of the church in
[a]Thyatira write:
[b]This is what the Son of God, the
One [c]who has [1]eyes like a flame of
fire and His feet are like burnished
bronze, says:
**19** '[a]I know your deeds, and your
love and faith and service and perse-
verance, and that your last deeds are
greater than [1]at first. **20** But [a]I have
*this* against you, that you tolerate the
woman [b]Jezebel, who calls herself
a prophetess, and she teaches and
deceives My slaves so that they
[c]commit sexual immorality and eat
things sacrificed to idols. **21** [a]And I
gave her time to repent, and she
[b]does not wish to repent of her
sexual immorality. **22** Behold, I will
throw her [1]on a bed *of sickness*, and
those who [a]commit adultery with
her into great tribulation, unless
they repent of [2]her deeds. **23** And I
will kill her children with [1]pestilence,
and all the churches will know that
I am He who [a]searches the [2]minds
and hearts; and [b]I will give to each
one of you according to your deeds.

---

**2:10** [a]Rev 3:10; 13:14ff [b]Da 1:12, 14 [c]Rev 2:13; 12:11; 17:14 [d]1Co 9:25; Rev 3:11 [1]Or *Prove yourself faithful* **2:11** [a]Mt 11:15; Rev 2:7, 17, 29; 3:6, 13, 22; 13:9 [b]Rev 2:7, 17, 26; 3:5, 12, 21; 21:7 [c]Rev 20:6, 14; 21:8 **2:12** [a]*Rev 1:11* [b]*Rev 1:16; 2:16* ***2:13*** [a]*Mt 4:10; Rev 2:24* [b]1Ti 5:8; Rev 14:12 [c]Ac 22:20; Rev 1:5; 11:3; 17:6 [d]Rev 2:10; 12:11; 17:14 [e]Rev 2:9 **2:14** [a]Rev 2:20 [b]Nu 31:16; 2Pe 2:15 [c]Nu 25:1f; Ac 15:29; 1Co 10:20; Rev 2:20 **2:15** [a]Rev 2:6 **2:16** [a]Rev 2:5 [b]Rev 22:7, 20 [c]2Th 2:8; Rev 1:16 **2:17** [a]Rev 2:7 [b]Ex 16:33; Jn 6:49f [c]Is 56:5; 62:2; 65:15 [d]Rev 14:3; 19:12 **2:18** [a]Rev 1:11; 2:24 [b]Mt 4:3 [c]Rev 1:14f [1]Lit *His eyes* **2:19** [a]Rev 2:2 [1]Lit *the first* **2:20** [a]Rev 2:14 [b]1Ki 16:31; 21:25; 2Ki 9:7, 22, 30 [c]Ac 15:29; 1Co 10:20; Rev 2:14 **2:21** [a]Ro 2:4; 2Pe 3:9 [b]Ro 2:5; Rev 9:20f; 16:9, 11 **2:22** [a]Rev 17:2; 18:9 [1]Lit *into* [2]One early ms *their* **2:23** [a]Ps 7:9; 26:2; 139:1; Jer 11:20; 17:10; Mt 16:27; Lk 16:15; Ac 1:24; Ro 8:27 [b]Ps 62:12 [1]Lit *death* [2]Inner man; lit *kidneys*

**24** But I say to you, the rest who are
in [a]Thyatira, who do not have this
teaching, who have not known the
[b]deep things of Satan, as they call
them—I [c]place no other burden on
you. **25** Nevertheless [a]what you have,
hold fast [b]until I come. **26** [a]And he
who overcomes, and he who keeps
My deeds [b]until the end, [c]TO HIM I
WILL GIVE AUTHORITY OVER THE [1]NA-
TIONS; **27** AND HE SHALL [a,1]RULE THEM
WITH A ROD OF IRON, [b]AS THE VESSELS
OF THE POTTER ARE BROKEN TO PIECES,
as I also have received *authority* from
My Father; **28** and I will give him [a]the
morning star. **29** [a]He who has an ear,
let him hear what the Spirit says to
the churches.'

### *To the Church in Sardis*

**3** "And to the angel of the church
in [a]Sardis write:
This is what He who has [b]the
seven Spirits of God and [c]the seven
stars, says: '[d]I know your deeds, that
you have a name that you are alive,
[1]but you are [e]dead. **2** Wake up, and
strengthen the things that remain,
which were about to die, for I have
not found your deeds complete in
the sight of My God. **3** So [a]remember
[1]what you have received and heard;
and keep *it*, and [a]repent. Therefore
if you do not wake up, [a]I will come
[b]like a thief, and you will not know
at [c]what hour I will come to you.
**4** But you have a few [a,1]names in
[b]Sardis who have not [c]defiled their
garments, and they will walk with Me
[d]in white, for they are worthy. **5** [a]He
who overcomes will thus be clothed
in [b]white garments, and I will never
[c]erase his name from the book of life,
and [d]I will confess his name before
My Father and before His angels.
**6** [a]He who has an ear, let him hear
what the Spirit says to the churches.'

### *To the Church in Philadelphia*

**7** "And to the angel of the church in
[a]Philadelphia write:
[b]This is what He who is holy, [c]who
is true, who has [d]the key of David,
who opens and no one will shut, and
who shuts and no one opens, says:
**8** '[a]I know your [1]deeds. Behold, I
have given before you [b]an open door
which no one can shut, because you
have a little power, and have kept My
word, and [c]have not denied My name.
**9** Behold, I am giving *up those* of [a]the
synagogue of Satan, those who say
that they are Jews and are not, but
lie. Behold, I will make them [b]come
and bow down before your feet, and
*make them* know that [c]I have loved
you. **10** Because you have [a]kept the
word of [b]My perseverance, [c]I also will
keep you from the hour of [d,1]testing,
which is about to come upon the
whole [e,2]world, to [3]test [f]those who
dwell on the earth. **11** [a]I am coming

**2:24** [a]Rev 2:18 [b]1Co 2:10 [c]Ac 15:28 **2:25** [a]Rev 3:11 [b]Jn 21:22 **2:26** [a]Rev 2:7 [b]Mt 10:22; Heb 3:6 [c]Ps 2:8; Rev 3:21; 20:4 [1]Or *Gentiles* **2:27** [a]Ps 2:9; Rev 12:5; 19:15 [b]Is 30:14; Jer 19:11 [1]Lit *shepherd* **2:28** [a]1Jn 3:2; Rev 22:16 **2:29** [a]Rev 2:7 ◆ **3:1** [a]Rev 1:11 [b]Rev 1:4 [c]Rev 1:16 [d]Rev 2:2; 3:8, 15 [e]1Ti 5:6 [1]Lit *and* **3:3** [a]Rev 2:5 [b]1Th 5:2; 2Pe 3:10; Rev 16:15 [c]Mt 24:43; Lk 12:39f [1]Lit *how* **3:4** [a]Rev 11:13 [b]Rev 1:11 [c]Jd 23 [d]Ecc 9:8; Rev 3:5, 18; 4:4; 6:11; 7:9, 13f; 19:8, 14 [1]People **3:5** [a]Rev 2:7 [b]Rev 3:4 [c]Ex 32:32f; Ps 69:28; Lk 10:20; Rev 13:8; 17:8; 20:12, 15; 21:27 [d]Mt 10:32; Lk 12:8 **3:6** [a]Rev 2:7 **3:7** [a]Rev 1:11 [b]Rev 6:10 [c]1Jn 5:20; Rev 3:14; 19:11 [d]Job 12:14; Is 22:22; Mt 16:19; Rev 1:18 **3:8** [a]Rev 3:1 [b]Ac 14:27 [c]Rev 2:13 [1]Or *deeds (behold...shut), that you have* **3:9** [a]Rev 2:9 [b]Is 45:14; 49:23; 60:14 [c]Is 43:4; Jn 17:23 **3:10** [a]Jn 17:6; Rev 3:8 [b]Rev 1:9 [c]2Ti 2:12; 2Pe 2:9 [d]Rev 2:10 [e]Mt 24:14; Rev 16:14 [f]Rev 6:10; 8:13; 11:10; 13:8, 14; 17:8 [1]Or *temptation* [2]Lit *inhabited earth* [3]Or *tempt* **3:11** [a]Rev 1:3; 22:7, 12, 20

quickly; [b]hold fast what you have, so that no one will take your [c]crown. **12** [a]He who overcomes, I will make him a [b]pillar in the sanctuary of My God, and he will never go out from it anymore. And I will write on him the [c]name of My God, and [d]the name of the city of My God, [e]the new Jerusalem, which comes down out of heaven from My God, and My [f]new name. **13** [a]He who has an ear, let him hear what the Spirit says to the churches.'

### *To the Church in Laodicea*

**14** "And to the angel of the church in [a]Laodicea write:

[b]This is what the Amen, [c]the faithful and true Witness, [d]the [1]Beginning of the creation of God, says:

**15** '[a]I know your deeds, that you are neither cold nor hot. [b]I wish that you were cold or hot. **16** So because you are lukewarm, and neither hot nor cold, I will [1]spit you out of My mouth. **17** Because you say, "[a]I am rich, and have become wealthy, and have need of nothing," and you do not know that you are wretched and pitiable and poor and blind and naked. **18** I advise you to [a]buy from Me [b]gold refined by fire so that you may become rich, and [c]white garments so that you may clothe yourself, and *that* [d]the shame of your nakedness will not be manifested; and eye salve to anoint your eyes so that you may see. **19** [a]Those whom I love, I reprove and discipline. Therefore be zealous and [b]repent. **20** Behold, I stand [a]at the door and [b]knock. If anyone hears My voice and opens the door, [c]I will come in to him and will dine with him, and he with Me. **21** [a]He who overcomes, I will grant to him [b]to sit down with Me on My throne, as [c]I also overcame and sat down with My Father on His throne. **22** [a]He who has an ear, let him hear what the Spirit says to the churches.'"

### *The Throne in Heaven*

**4** After [a]these things I looked, and behold, [b]a door *standing* open in heaven, and the first voice which I had heard, [c]like *the sound* of a trumpet speaking with me, said, "[d]Come up here, and I will [e]show you what must take place after these things." **2** Immediately I was [a,1]in the Spirit, and behold, [b]a throne was standing in heaven, and [c]One sitting on the throne. **3** And He who was sitting *was* like a [a]jasper stone and a [b]sardius in appearance; and *there was* a [c,1]rainbow around the throne, like an [d]emerald in appearance. **4** [a]Around the throne *were* [b]twenty-four thrones, and upon those thrones *I saw* [c]twenty-four elders [d]sitting, clothed in [e]white garments, and [f]golden crowns on

---

**3:11** [b]Rev 2:25 [c]Rev 2:10 **3:12** [a]Rev 3:5 [b]1Ki 7:21; Jer 1:18; Ga 2:9 [c]Rev 14:1; 22:4 [d]Eze 48:35; Rev 21:2 [e]Ga 4:26; Heb 13:14; Rev 21:2, 10 [f]Is 62:2; Rev 2:17 **3:13** [a]Rev 3:6 **3:14** [a]Rev 1:11 [b]2Co 1:20 [c]Rev 1:5; 3:7 [d]Ge 49:3; Dt 21:17; Pr 8:22; Jn 1:3; Col 1:18; Rev 21:6; 22:13 [1]Origin or Source **3:15** [a]Rev 3:1 [b]Ro 12:11 ***3:16*** [1]*Lit vomit* **3:17** [a]Hos 12:8; Zec 11:5; Mt 5:3; 1Co 4:8 **3:18** [a]Is 55:1; Mt 13:44 [b]1Pe 1:7 [c]Rev 3:4 [d]Rev 16:15 **3:19** [a]Pr 3:12; 1Co 11:32; Heb 12:6 [b]Rev 2:5 **3:20** [a]Mt 24:33; Jas 5:9 [b]Lk 12:36; Jn 10:3 [c]Jn 14:23 **3:21** [a]Rev 2:7 [b]Mt 19:28; 2Ti 2:12; Rev 2:26; 20:4 [c]Jn 16:33; Rev 5:5; 6:2; 17:14 **3:22** [a]Rev 2:7 ◆ **4:1** [a]Rev 1:12ff, 19 [b]Eze 1:1; Rev 19:11 [c]Rev 1:10 [d]Rev 11:12 [e]Rev 1:19; 22:6 **4:2** [a]Rev 1:10 [b]1Ki 22:19; Is 6:1; Eze 1:26; Da 7:9; Rev 4:9f [c]Rev 4:9 [1]Or *in spirit* **4:3** [a]Rev 21:11 [b]Rev 21:20 [c]Eze 1:28; Rev 10:1 [d]Rev 21:19 [1]Or *halo* **4:4** [a]Rev 4:6; 5:11; 7:11 [b]Rev 11:16 [c]Rev 4:10; 5:6, 8, 14; 19:4 [d]Mt 19:28; Rev 20:4 [e]Rev 3:18 [f]Rev 4:10

their heads. **5** And out from the
throne come [a]flashes of lightning
and sounds and peals of thunder.
And *there were* [b]seven lamps of fire
burning before the throne, which
are [c]the seven Spirits of God. **6** And
before the throne *there was some-*
*thing* like a [a]sea of glass, like crystal.
And in the [1]center and [b]around the
throne, [c]four living creatures [d]full of
eyes in front and behind. **7** [a]And the
first creature *was* like a lion, and
the second creature like a calf, and
the third creature had a face like that
of a man, and the fourth creature *was*
like a flying eagle. **8** And the [a]four
living creatures, each one of them
having [b]six wings, are [c]full of eyes
around and within, and [d]day and
night [1]they do not cease to say,

"[e]HOLY, HOLY, HOLY *is* THE
[f,2]LORD GOD, THE ALMIGHTY,
[g]WHO WAS AND WHO IS
AND WHO [3]IS TO COME."

**9** And when the living creatures give
glory and honor and thanks to Him
who [a]sits on the throne, to [b]Him
who lives forever and ever, **10** the
[a]twenty-four elders will [b]fall down
before Him who [c]sits on the throne,
and will worship [d]Him who lives
forever and ever, and will cast their
[e]crowns before the throne, saying,

**11** "[a]Worthy are You, our Lord
and our God, to receive glory
and honor and power, for
You [b]created all things, and
because of Your will they
[1]existed, and were created."

### *The Scroll and the Lamb*

**5** Then I saw [1]in the right hand of
Him who [a]sits on the throne a
[b]scroll written inside and on the back,
[c]sealed up with seven seals. **2** Then I
saw a [a]strong angel proclaiming with
a loud voice, "Who is worthy to open
the scroll and to break its seals?"
**3** And no one [a]in heaven or on the
earth or under the earth was able
to open the scroll or to look into it.
**4** Then I was crying greatly because
no one was found worthy to open the
scroll or to look into it. **5** And one of
the elders *said to me, "Stop crying!
Behold, the [a]Lion that is [b]from the
tribe of Judah, the [c]Root of David,
has overcome so as to open the scroll
and its seven seals."

**6** Then I saw in the midst of the
throne and the four living creatures
and in the midst of [a]the elders a
[b]Lamb standing, as if [c]slain, having
seven [d]horns and [e]seven eyes, which
are [f]the seven Spirits of God, sent
out into all the earth. **7** And He came
and took [a]*the scroll* out of the right
hand of Him who [a]sits on the throne.
**8** And when He had taken the scroll,
the [a]four living creatures and the
[b]twenty-four elders [c]fell down before
the [d]Lamb, each one having a [e]harp

**4:5** [a]Ex 19:16; Rev 8:5; 11:19; 16:18 [b]Ex 25:37; Zec 4:2 [c]Rev 1:4 **4:6** [a]Eze 1:22; Rev 15:2; 21:18, 21 [b]Rev 4:4 [c]Eze 1:5; Rev 4:8f; 5:6; 6:1, 6; 7:11; 14:3; 15:7; 19:4 [d]Eze 1:18; 10:12 [1]Lit *middle of the throne and around* **4:7** [a]Eze 1:10; 10:14 **4:8** [a]Eze 1:5; Rev 4:6, 9; 5:6; 6:1, 6; 7:11; 14:3; 15:7; 19:4 [b]Is 6:2 [c]Eze 1:18; 10:12 [d]Rev 14:11 [e]Is 6:3 [f]Rev 1:8 [g]Rev 1:4 [1]Lit *they have no rest, saying,* [2]In OT, Yahweh, cf. Is 6:3 [3]Or *is coming* **4:9** [a]Ps 47:8; Is 6:1; Rev 4:2 [b]Dt 32:40; Da 4:34; 12:7; Rev 10:6; 15:7 **4:10** [a]Rev 4:4 [b]Rev 5:8, 14; 7:11; 11:16; 19:4 [c]Ps 47:8; Is 6:1; Rev 4:2 [d]Dt 32:40; Da 4:34; 12:7 [e]Rev 4:4; 10:6; 15:7 **4:11** [a]Rev 1:6; 5:12 [b]Ac 14:15; Rev 10:6; 14:7 [1]Lit *were* ◆ **5:1** [a]Rev 4:9; 5:7, 13 [b]Eze 2:9, 10 [c]Is 29:11; Da 12:4 [1]Lit *upon* **5:2** [a]Rev 10:1; 18:21 **5:3** [a]Php 2:10; Rev 5:13 **5:5** [a]Ge 49:9 [b]Heb 7:14 [c]Is 11:1, 10; Ro 15:12; Rev 22:16 **5:6** [a]Rev 4:4; 5:8, 14 [b]Jn 1:29; Rev 5:8, 12f; 13:8 [c]Rev 5:9, 12; 13:8 [d]Da 8:3f [e]Zec 3:9; 4:10 [f]Rev 1:4 **5:7** [a]Rev 5:1 **5:8** [a]Rev 4:6; 5:6, 11, 14 [b]Rev 4:4; 5:14 [c]Rev 4:10 [d]Jn 1:29; Rev 5:6, 12f; 13:8 [e]Rev 14:2; 15:2

and [f]golden bowls full of incense,
which are the [g]prayers of the [1]saints.
**9** And they *sang a [a]new song, saying,
> "[b]Worthy are You to take the
> scroll and to open its seals,
> because You were [c]slain and
> [d]purchased for God with Your
> blood *people* from [e]every
> tribe and tongue and people
> and nation. **10** And You made
> them *to be* a [a]kingdom and
> [a]priests to our God, and they
> will [b]reign upon the earth."

### *Angels Worship the Lamb*

**11** Then I looked, and I heard the
voice of many angels [a]around the
throne and the [b]living creatures
and the [c]elders; and the number of
them was [d]myriads of myriads, and
thousands of thousands, **12** saying
with a loud voice,
> "[a]Worthy is the [b]Lamb that
> was [b]slain to receive power
> and riches and wisdom
> and strength and honor
> and glory and blessing."

**13** And [a]every created thing which
is in heaven and on the earth and
under the earth and on the sea, and
all things in them, I heard saying,
> "To Him who [b]sits on the
> throne, and to the [c]Lamb,
> [d]*be* the blessing and the
> honor and the glory and the
> might forever and ever."

**14** And the [a]four living creatures kept
saying, "[b]Amen." And the [c]elders
[d]fell down and worshiped.

### *The Seven Seals*

**6** Then I looked when the [a]Lamb
opened one of the [b]seven seals,
and I heard one of the [c]four living
creatures saying as with a [d]voice of
thunder, "[1]Come." **2** Then I looked,
and behold, a [a]white horse, and
he who sits on it had a bow; and [b]a
crown was given to him, and he went
out [c]overcoming and to overcome.
**3** And when He opened the second
seal, I heard the [a]second living crea-
ture saying, "Come." **4** And another,
[a]a red horse, went out; and to him
who sits on it, it was given to him to
[b]take peace from the earth, and that
*men* would slay one another; and a
great sword was given to him.
**5** And when He opened the third
seal, I heard the [a]third living creature
saying, "Come." Then I looked, and
behold, a [b]black horse; and he who
sits on it had a [c]pair of scales in his
hand. **6** And I heard *something* like a
voice in the midst of the [a]four living
creatures saying, "One [1]choinix of
wheat for one [2]denarius, and three
[1]choinix of barley for one [2]denarius,
and [b]do not harm the oil and the
wine."
**7** And when He opened the fourth
seal, I heard the voice of the [a]fourth

---

**5:8** [f]Rev 15:7 [g]Ps 141:2; Rev 8:3f [1]Or *holy ones* **5:9** [a]Ps 33:3; 40:3; 98:1; 149:1; Is 42:10; Rev 14:3; 15:3 [b]Rev 4:11 [c]Rev 5:6, 12; 13:8 [d]1Co 6:20; Rev 14:3f [e]Da 3:4; 5:19; Rev 7:9; 10:11; 11:9; 13:7; 14:6; 17:15 **5:10** [a]Rev 1:6 [b]Rev 3:21; 20:4 **5:11** [a]Rev 4:4 [b]Rev 4:6; 5:6, 8, 14 [c]Rev 4:4; 5:6, 14 [d]Da 7:10; Heb 12:22; Jd 14; Rev 9:16 **5:12** [a]Rev 1:6; 4:11; 5:9 [b]Jn 1:29; Rev 5:6, 13; 13:8 **5:13** [a]Php 2:10; Rev 5:3 [b]Rev 5:1 [c]Jn 1:29; Rev 5:6, 12f; 13:8 [d]Ro 11:36; Rev 1:6 **5:14** [a]Rev 4:6; 5:6, 8, 11 [b]1Co 14:16; Rev 7:12; 19:4 [c]Rev 4:4; 5:6, 8 [d]Rev 4:10 ◆ **6:1** [a]Jn 1:29; Rev 5:6, 12f; 13:8 [b]Rev 5:1 [c]Rev 4:6; 5:6, 8, 11, 14 [d]Rev 14:2; 19:6 [1]One early ms adds *and see*, so in v 3, 5, 7 **6:2** [a]Zec 1:8; 6:3f; Rev 19:11 [b]Zec 6:11; Rev 9:7; 14:14; 19:12 [c]Rev 3:21; 13:7; 15:2 **6:3** [a]Rev 4:7 **6:4** [a]Zec 1:8; 6:2 [b]Mt 10:34 **6:5** [a]Rev 4:7 [b]Zec 6:2, 6 [c]Eze 4:16 **6:6** [a]Rev 4:6f [b]Rev 7:3; 9:4 [1]A choinix was approx. 1 qt. or 1 l [2]A Roman silver coin, approx. a laborer's daily wage **6:7** [a]Rev 4:7

living creature saying, "Come."
**8** Then I looked, and behold, a [a]pale
horse; and he who sits on it had
the name [b]Death, and [b]Hades was
following with him. Authority was
given to them over a fourth of the
earth, [c]to kill with sword and with
famine and with [1]pestilence and by
the wild beasts of the earth.
**9** And when He opened the fifth
seal, I saw [a]underneath the [b]altar the
[c]souls of those who had been slain
[d]because of the word of God, and
because of the [e]witness which they
had maintained; **10** and they cried
out with a loud voice, saying, "[a]How
long, O [b]Master, [c]holy and true? [1]Will
You not [d]judge and avenge our blood
on [e]those who dwell on the earth?"
**11** And [a]a white robe was given to
each of them; and it was told to them
that they should [b]rest for a little while
longer, [c]until *the number of* their
fellow slaves and their brothers who
were to be killed even as they had
been, would be [d]completed also.
**12** Then I looked when He opened
the sixth seal, and there was a great
[a]earthquake; and the [b]sun became
black as [c]sackcloth *made* of hair, and
the whole moon became like blood;
**13** and [a]the stars of the sky fell to the
earth, [b]as a fig tree casts its unripe
figs when shaken by a great wind.
**14** [a]And the sky was split apart like a
scroll when it is rolled up, and [b]every
mountain and island were moved out
of their places. **15** Then [a]the kings of
the earth and the great men and the
[1]commanders and the rich and the
strong and every slave and free man
[b]HID THEMSELVES IN THE CAVES and
among the rocks of the mountains;
**16** and they *[a]SAID TO THE MOUNTAINS
AND TO THE ROCKS, "FALL ON US AND
HIDE US from the [1]presence of Him
[b]who sits on the throne, and from
the [c,2]wrath of the Lamb, **17** for [a]the
great [b]DAY OF their [1]WRATH has come,
and [c]who is able to stand?"

### *The 144,000*

**7** After this I saw [a]four angels
standing at the [b]four corners of
the earth, holding back [c]the four
winds of the earth, [d]so that no wind
would blow on the earth or on the sea
or on any tree. **2** Then I saw another
angel ascending [a]from the rising of
the sun, having the [b]seal of [c]the liv-
ing God; and he cried out with a loud
voice to the [d]four angels to whom it
was granted to harm the earth and
the sea, **3** saying, "[a]Do not harm the
earth or the sea or the trees until we
have [b]sealed the slaves of our God on
their [c]foreheads."
**4** And I heard the [a]number of those
having been sealed, [b]144,000 sealed
from every tribe of the sons of Israel:

---

**6:8** [a]Zec 6:3 [b]Pr 5:5; Hos 13:14; Mt 11:23; Rev 1:18; 20:13f [c]Jer 14:12; 15:2f; 24:10; 29:17f; Eze 5:12, 17; 14:21; 29:5 [1]Or *death* **6:9** [a]Ex 29:12; Lv 4:7; Jn 16:2 [b]Rev 14:18; 16:7 [c]Rev 20:4 [d]Rev 1:2, 9 [e]Rev 12:17 **6:10** [a]Zec 1:12 [b]Lk 2:29; 2Pe 2:1 [c]Rev 3:7 [d]Dt 32:43; Ps 79:10; Lk 18:7; Rev 19:2 [e]Rev 3:10 [1]Lit *do You not judge and avenge* **6:11** [a]Rev 3:4, 5; 7:9 [b]2Th 1:7; Heb 4:10; Rev 14:13 [c]Heb 11:40 [d]Ac 20:24; 2Ti 4:7 **6:12** [a]Mt 24:7; Rev 8:5; 11:13; 16:18 [b]Is 13:10; Joel 2:10, 31; 3:15; Mt 24:29; Mk 13:24 [c]Is 50:3; Mt 11:21 **6:13** [a]Mt 24:29; Mk 13:25; Rev 8:10; 9:1 [b]Is 34:4 **6:14** [a]Is 34:4; 2Pe 3:10; Rev 20:11; 21:1 [b]Is 54:10; Jer 4:24; Eze 38:20; Na 1:5; Rev 16:20 **6:15** [a]Is 2:10f, 19, 21; 24:21; Rev 19:18 [b]Is 2:19 [1]Military leader over 1,000 soldiers **6:16** [a]Hos 10:8; Lk 23:30; Rev 9:6 [b]Rev 4:9; 5:1 [c]Mk 3:5 [1]Lit *face* [2]Or *rage* **6:17** [a]Is 63:4; Jer 30:7; Joel 1:15; 2:1f, 11, 31; Zep 1:14f; Rev 16:14 [b]Zep 1:15 [c]Ps 76:7; Na 1:6; Mal 3:2; Lk 21:36 [1]Or *rage* ◆ **7:1** [a]Rev 9:14 [b]Is 11:12; Eze 7:2; Rev 20:8 [c]Jer 49:36; Da 7:2; Zec 6:5; Mt 24:31 [d]Rev 7:3; 8:7; 9:4 **7:2** [a]Is 41:2 [b]Rev 7:3; 9:4 [c]Mt 16:16 [d]Rev 9:14 **7:3** [a]Rev 6:6 [b]Jn 3:33; Rev 7:3-8 [c]Eze 9:4, 6; Rev 13:16; 14:1, 9; 20:4; 22:4 **7:4** [a]Rev 9:16 [b]Rev 14:1, 3

5 from the tribe of Judah, 12,000
having been sealed,
from the tribe
of Reuben 12,000,
from the tribe
of Gad 12,000,
6 from the tribe
of Asher 12,000,
from the tribe
of Naphtali 12,000,
from the tribe
of Manasseh 12,000,
7 from the tribe
of Simeon 12,000,
from the tribe
of Levi 12,000,
from the tribe
of Issachar 12,000,
8 from the tribe
of Zebulun 12,000,
from the tribe
of Joseph 12,000,
from the tribe of Benjamin,
12,000 having been sealed.

### *A Multitude from Every Nation*

9 After these things I looked, and
behold, a great [1]multitude which
no one could count, from [a]every
nation and *all* tribes and peoples
and tongues, standing [b]before the
throne and [c]before the Lamb, clothed
in [d]white robes, and [e]palm branches
*were* in their hands; 10 and they cry
out with a loud voice, saying,
"[a]Salvation *belongs* to our God
[b]who sits on the throne, and to the
Lamb." 11 And all the angels were
standing [a]around the throne and
[a]the elders and the [b]four living
creatures, and they [c]fell on their faces
before the throne and worshiped
God, 12 saying,
"[a]Amen, [b]the blessing and the glory
and the wisdom and the thanksgiving
and the honor and the power and the
strength, *be* to our God forever and
ever. [a]Amen."
13 Then one of the elders [a]an-
swered, saying to me, "These, clothed
in the [b]white robes, who are they,
and from where have they come?"
14 And I [1]said to him, "My lord, you
know." And he said to me, "These
are the ones who come out of the
[a]great tribulation, and they [b]washed
their robes and made them [c]white in
the [d]blood of the Lamb. 15 For this
reason, they are [a]before the throne
of God; and they [b]serve Him day and
night in His [c,1]sanctuary; and [d]He
who sits on the throne will [e,2]dwell
over them. 16 [a]THEY WILL HUNGER NO
LONGER, NOR THIRST ANYMORE; NOR
WILL THE SUN [1]BEAT DOWN ON THEM,
NOR ANY HEAT; 17 for the Lamb at the
center of the throne will [a]shepherd
them and will guide them to springs
of the [b,1]water of life. And [c]God WILL
WIPE EVERY TEAR FROM THEIR EYES."

### *The Seventh Seal*

8 When He opened the [a]seventh
seal, there was silence in heaven
for about half an hour. 2 Then I saw
[a]the seven angels who stand before
God, and seven [b]trumpets were given
to them.

**7:9** [a]Rev 5:9 [b]Rev 7:15 [c]Rev 22:3 [d]Rev 6:11; 7:14 [e]Lv 23:40 [1]Lit *crowd* **7:10** [a]Ps 3:8; Rev 12:10; 19:1 [b]Rev 22:3 **7:11** [a]Rev 4:4 [b]Rev 4:6 [c]Rev 4:10 **7:12** [a]Rev 5:14 [b]Rev 5:12 **7:13** [a]Ac 3:12 [b]Rev 7:9 **7:14** [a]Da 12:1; Mt 24:21; Mk 13:19 [b]Zec 3:3-5; Rev 22:14 [c]Rev 6:11; 7:9 [d]Heb 9:14; 1Jn 1:7 [1]Lit *have said* **7:15** [a]Rev 7:9 [b]Rev 4:8f; 22:3 [c]Rev 11:19; 21:22 [d]Rev 4:9 [e]Lv 26:11; Eze 37:27; Jn 1:14; Rev 21:3 [1]The inner part of the temple [2]Or *tabernacle* **7:16** [a]Ps 121:5f; Is 49:10 [1]Lit *fall* **7:17** [a]Ps 23:1f; Mt 2:6; Jn 10:11 [b]Jn 4:14; Rev 21:6; 22:1 [c]Is 25:8; Mt 5:4; Rev 21:4 [1]Lit *waters* ◆**8:1** [a]Rev 5:1; 6:1, 3, 5, 7, 9, 12 **8:2** [a]Rev 1:4; 8:6-13; 9:1, 13; 11:15 [b]1Co 15:52; 1Th 4:16

**3** [a]And another angel came and
stood at the [b]altar, having a [c]golden
censer; and much [d]incense was given
to him, so that he might [1]add it to the
[d]prayers of all the saints on the [e]golden
altar which was before the throne.
**4** And [a]the smoke of the incense went
up [1]with the prayers of the saints, out
of the angel's hand, before God. **5** Then
the angel [1]took the censer and [a]filled it
with the fire of the altar, and [b]threw it
to the earth; and there followed [c]peals
of thunder and sounds and flashes of
lightning and an [d]earthquake.

### *The Seven Trumpets*

**6** [a]And the seven angels who had the
seven trumpets prepared themselves
to sound them.

**7** And the first sounded, and there
came [a]hail and fire, mixed with
blood, and they were thrown to the
earth; and [b]a third of the earth was
burned up, and [b]a third of the [c]trees
were burned up, and all the green
[c]grass was burned up.

**8** And the second angel sounded,
and *something* like a great [a]mountain
burning with fire was thrown into the
sea; and [b]a third of the [c]sea became
blood, **9** and [a]a third of the creatures
which were in the sea—those which
had life—died; and a third of the
[b]ships were destroyed.

**10** And the third angel sounded,
and a great star [a]fell from heaven,
burning like a torch, and it fell on
a [b]third of the rivers and on the
[c]springs of waters. **11** And the name
of the star is called Wormwood;
and a [a]third of the waters became
[b]wormwood, and many men died
from the waters, because they were
made bitter.

**12** And the fourth angel sounded,
and a [a]third of the [b]sun and a third
of the [b]moon and a [a]third of the
[b]stars were struck, so that a [a]third
of them would be darkened and the
day would not shine for a [a]third of it,
and the night in the same way.

**13** Then I looked, and I heard [1]an
eagle flying in [a]midheaven, saying
with a loud voice, "[b]Woe, woe, woe
to [c]those who dwell on the earth,
because of the remaining blasts of
the trumpet of the [d]three angels who
are about to sound!"

**9** Then the [a]fifth angel sounded.
Then I saw a [b]star from heaven
which had fallen to the earth, and
the [c]key of the [d]pit of the abyss was
given to him. **2** And he opened the
pit of the abyss and [a]smoke went
up out of the pit, like the smoke of
a great furnace, and [b]the sun and
the air were darkened by the smoke
of the pit. **3** Then out of the smoke
came [a]locusts [1]upon the earth,
and power was given them, as the
[b]scorpions of the earth have power.
**4** And they were told not to [a]hurt the

**8:3** [a]Rev 7:2 [b]Am 9:1; Rev 6:9 [c]Heb 9:4 [d]Ex 30:1; Rev 5:8 [e]Ex 30:3; Nu 4:11; Rev 8:5; 9:13 [1]Lit *give*
**8:4** [a]Ps 141:2 [1]Or *for* **8:5** [a]Lv 16:12 [b]Eze 10:2 [c]Ex 19:16; Rev 4:5; 11:19; 16:18 [d]Rev 6:12 [1]Lit *has taken*
**8:6** [a]Rev 8:2 **8:7** [a]Ex 9:23ff; Is 28:2; Eze 38:22; Joel 2:30 [b]Zec 13:8, 9; Rev 8:7-12; 9:15, 18; 12:4 [c]Rev 9:4
**8:8** [a]Jer 51:25 [b]Zec 13:8, 9; Rev 8:7-12; 9:15, 18; 12:4 [c]Ex 7:17ff; Rev 11:6; 16:3 **8:9** [a]Zec 13:8, 9; Rev 8:7-12; 9:15, 18; 12:4 [b]Is 2:16 **8:10** [a]Is 14:12; Rev 6:13; 9:1 [b]Zec 13:8, 9; Rev 8:7-12; 9:15, 18; 12:4 [c]Rev 14:7; 16:4
**8:11** [a]Zec 13:8, 9; Rev 8:7-12; 9:15, 18; 12:4 [b]Jer 9:15; 23:15 **8:12** [a]Zec 13:8, 9; Rev 8:7-12; 9:15, 18; 12:4 [b]Ex 10:21ff; Is 13:10; Eze 32:7; Joel 2:10, 31; 3:15; Rev 6:12f **8:13** [a]Rev 14:6; 19:17 [b]Rev 9:12; 11:14; 12:12 [c]Rev 3:10 [d]Rev 8:2 [1]Lit *one eagle* ◆ **9:1** [a]Rev 8:2 [b]Rev 8:10 [c]Rev 1:18 [d]Lk 8:31; Rev 9:2, 11
**9:2** [a]Ge 19:28; Ex 19:18 [b]Joel 2:2, 10 **9:3** [a]Ex 10:12-15; Rev 9:7 [b]2Chr 10:11, 14; Eze 2:6; Rev 9:5, 10 [1]Lit *into* **9:4** [a]Rev 6:6

[b]grass of the earth, nor any green
thing, nor any tree, but only the men
who do not have the [c]seal of God on
their foreheads. **5** And [1]they were
not permitted to kill [2]anyone, but
to torment for [a]five months, and
their torment was like the torment
of a [b]scorpion when it [3]stings a man.
**6** And in those days [a]men will seek
death and will never find it; they
will long to die, and death flees from
them.

**7** And the [a,1]appearance of the
locusts was like horses prepared for
battle. And on their heads appeared
to be crowns like gold, and their faces
were like the faces of men. **8** And they
had hair like the hair of women, and
their [a]teeth were like *the teeth* of li-
ons. **9** And they had breastplates like
breastplates of iron, and the [a]sound
of their wings was like the sound of
chariots, of many horses running
to battle. **10** And they have tails like
[a]scorpions, and stings; and in their
[b]tails is their power to hurt men for
[c]five months. **11** They have as king
over them, the angel of the [a]abyss.
His name in [b]Hebrew is [c,1]Abaddon,
and in the Greek he has the name
[2]Apollyon.

**12** [a]One woe is past; behold, two
woes are still coming after these
things.

**13** Then the sixth angel sounded,
and I heard [1]a voice from the [2]four
[a]horns of the [b]golden altar which is
before God, **14** one saying to the sixth
angel who had the trumpet, "Release
the [a]four angels who have been
bound at the [b]great river Euphrates."
**15** And the four angels were [a]released,
who had been prepared for the hour
and day and month and year, so that
they would kill a [b]third of [1]mankind.
**16** And the number of the armies of
the horsemen was [a]two hundred
million; [b]I heard the number of them.
**17** And [1]this is how I saw [a]in the vi-
sion the horses and those who sit on
them: *the riders* had breastplates *the
color* of fire and of hyacinth and of
[b,2]brimstone; and the heads of the
horses are like the heads of lions; and
[c]out of their mouths come fire and
smoke and [b,2]brimstone. **18** A [a]third
of [1]mankind was killed by these three
plagues, by the [b]fire and the smoke
and the [2]brimstone which came out
of their mouths. **19** For the power of
the horses is in their mouths and
in their tails; for their tails are like
serpents, having heads, and with
them they do harm.

**20** And the rest of [1]mankind, who
were not killed by these plagues,
[a]did not repent of [b]the works of
their hands, so as not to [c]worship
demons, and [d]the idols of gold and
of silver and of brass and of stone
and of wood, which can neither see
nor hear nor walk. **21** And they [a]did

**9:4** [b]Rev 8:7 [c]Eze 9:4; Rev 7:2, 3 **9:5** [a]Rev 9:10 [b]2Chr 10:11, 14; Eze 2:6; Rev 9:3, 10 [1]Lit *it was given to them that they might not kill them* [2]Lit *them* [3]Lit *strikes* **9:6** [a]Job 3:21; 7:15; Jer 8:3; Rev 6:16 **9:7** [a]Joel 2:4 [1]Lit *likenesses* **9:8** [a]Joel 1:6 **9:9** [a]Jer 47:3; Joel 2:5 **9:10** [a]2Chr 10:11, 14; Eze 2:6; Rev 9:3, 5 [b]Rev 9:19 [c]Rev 9:5 **9:11** [a]Lk 8:31; Rev 9:1, 2 [b]Jn 5:2; Rev 16:16 [c]Job 26:6; 28:22; 31:12; Ps 88:11 mg; Pr 15:11 [1]Destruction [2]Destroyer **9:12** [a]Rev 8:13; 11:14 **9:13** [a]Ex 30:2f, 10 [b]Rev 8:3 [1]Lit *one voice* [2]Two early mss omit *four* **9:14** [a]Rev 7:1 [b]Ge 15:18; Dt 1:7; Jos 1:4; Rev 16:12 **9:15** [a]Rev 20:7 [b]Rev 8:7; 9:18 [1]Gr *anthropoi* **9:16** [a]Rev 5:11 [b]Rev 7:4 **9:17** [a]Da 8:2; 9:21 [b]Rev 9:18; 14:10; 19:20; 20:10; 21:8 [c]Rev 11:5 [1]Lit *thus I saw* [2]Burning sulfur **9:18** [a]Rev 8:7; 9:15 [b]Rev 9:17 [1]Gr *anthropoi* [2]Burning sulfur **9:20** [a]Rev 2:21 [b]Dt 4:28; Jer 1:16; Mic 5:13; Ac 7:41 [c]1Co 10:20 [d]Ps 115:4-7; 135:15-17; Da 5:23 [1]Gr *anthropoi* **9:21** [a]Rev 9:20

not repent of their murders nor of
their [b]sorceries nor of their [c]sexual
immorality nor of their thefts.

### *The Angel and the Little Scroll*

**10** Then I saw another [a]strong
angel [b]coming down out of
heaven, clothed with a cloud, and
the [c]rainbow was upon his head,
and [d]his face was like the sun, and
his [e]feet like pillars of fire; **2** and he
had in his hand a [a]little scroll which
was open. He placed [b]his right foot
on the sea and his left on the earth,
**3** and he cried out with a loud voice,
[a]as when a lion roars. And when he
had cried out, the [b]seven peals of
thunder [1]uttered their voices. **4** And
when the seven peals of thunder had
spoken, [a]I was about to write; and I
[b]heard a voice from heaven saying,
"[c]Seal up the things which the seven
peals of thunder have spoken and do
not write them." **5** Then the angel,
whom I saw standing on the sea and
on the earth, [a]lifted up his right hand
to heaven, **6** [a]and swore by [b]Him who
lives forever and ever, [c]WHO CREATED
HEAVEN AND THE THINGS IN IT, AND
THE EARTH AND THE THINGS IN IT, AND
THE SEA AND THE THINGS IN IT, that
[d]there will be delay no longer, **7** but in
the days of the voice of the [a]seventh
angel, when he is about to sound,
then [b]the mystery of God is finished,
as He proclaimed good news to His
slaves, the prophets.
**8** Then [a]the voice which I heard
from heaven, *I heard* again speaking
with me, and saying, "Go, take [b]the
scroll which is open in the hand of
the angel who [b]stands on the sea and
on the earth." **9** So I went to the angel,
telling him to give me the little scroll.
And he *said to me, "[a]Take it and eat
it; it will make your stomach bitter,
but in your mouth it will be sweet as
honey." **10** And I took the little scroll
out of the angel's hand and ate it, and
in my mouth it was sweet as honey;
and when I had eaten it, my stomach
was made bitter. **11** And [a]they *said
to me, "You must [b]prophesy again
about [c]many peoples and nations
and tongues and [d]kings."

### *The Two Witnesses*

**11** Then a [a,1]measuring rod like a
staff was given to me, [b]saying,
"Get up and measure the sanctuary
of God and the altar, and those who
worship in it. **2** And [1]leave out the
[a]court which is outside the sanctu-
ary and do not measure it, for [b]it has
been given to the Gentiles, and they
will [b]trample [c]the holy city under
foot for [d]forty-two months. **3** And I
will give *authority* to my two [a]wit-
nesses, and they will prophesy for
[b]1,260 days, clothed in [c]sackcloth."
**4** These are the [a]two olive trees and
the two lampstands that stand before
the Lord of the earth. **5** And if anyone
wishes to harm them, [a]fire comes

---

**9:21** [b]Is 47:9, 12; Rev 18:23 [c]Rev 17:2, 4, 5 ◆**10:1** [a]Rev 5:2 [b]Rev 18:1; 20:1 [c]Rev 4:3 [d]Mt 17:2; Rev 1:16 [e]Rev 1:15 **10:2** [a]Rev 5:1; 10:8-10 [b]Rev 10:5, 8 **10:3** [a]Is 31:4; Hos 11:10 [b]Ps 29:3-9; Rev 4:5 [1]Or *spoke* **10:4** [a]Rev 1:11, 19 [b]Rev 10:8 [c]Da 8:26; 12:4, 9; Rev 22:10 **10:5** [a]Dt 32:40; Da 12:7 **10:6** [a]Ge 14:22; Ex 6:8; Nu 14:30; Eze 20:5 [b]Rev 4:9 [c]Ex 20:11; Rev 4:11 [d]Rev 6:11; 12:12; 16:17; 21:6 **10:7** [a]Rev 11:15 [b]Am 3:7; Ro 16:25 **10:8** [a]Rev 10:4 [b]Rev 10:2 **10:9** [a]Jer 15:16; Eze 2:8; 3:1-3 **10:11** [a]Rev 11:1 [b]Eze 37:4, 9 [c]Rev 5:9 [d]Rev 17:10, 12 ◆**11:1** [a]Eze 40:3-42:20; Zec 2:1; Rev 21:15f [b]Rev 10:11 [1]Lit *reed* **11:2** [a]Eze 40:17, 20 [b]Lk 21:24 [c]Is 52:1; Mt 4:5; 27:53; Rev 21:2, 10; 22:19 [d]Da 7:25; 12:7; Rev 12:6; 13:5 [1]Lit *Throw out* **11:3** [a]Rev 1:5; 2:13 [b]Da 7:25; 12:7; Rev 12:6; 13:5 [c]Ge 37:34; 2Sa 3:31; 1Ki 21:27; 2Ki 19:1f; Ne 9:1; Es 4:1; Ps 69:11; Joel 1:13; Jon 3:5f, 8 **11:4** [a]Ps 52:8; Jer 11:16; Zec 4:3, 11, 14 **11:5** [a]2Ki 1:10-12; Jer 5:14; Rev 9:17f

out of their mouth and devours their
enemies; so if anyone wishes to harm
them, [b]he must be killed in this way.
**6** These have the authority to [a]shut
up the sky, so that rain will not fall
during [b]the days of their prophesy-
ing; they also have authority over
the waters to [c]turn them into blood,
and [d]to strike the earth with every
plague, as often as they wish.
**7** And when they have finished
their witness, [a]the beast that comes
up out of the [b]abyss will [c]make war
with them and overcome them and
kill them. **8** And their dead bodies
*will lie* in the street of the [a]great city
which spiritually is called [b]Sodom
and [c]Egypt, where also their Lord
was crucified. **9** And those from
[a]the peoples and tribes and tongues
and nations *will* look at their dead
[1]bodies for three and a half days, and
[b,2]will not permit their dead bodies
to be laid in a tomb. **10** And [a]those
who dwell on the earth *will* rejoice
over them and celebrate and [b]send
gifts to one another, because these
two prophets tormented [a]those who
dwell on the earth.
**11** But after the three and a half
days, [a]the breath of life from God
came into them, and they stood on
their feet, and great fear fell upon
those who were watching them.
**12** And they heard a loud voice from
heaven saying to them, "[a]Come up
here." Then they [b]went up into heaven
in the cloud, and their enemies
watched them. **13** And in that hour
there was a great [a]earthquake, and a
tenth of the city fell; [1]seven thousand
people were killed in the earthquake,
and the rest were terrified and [b]gave
glory to the [c]God of heaven.
**14** The second [a]woe is past; behold,
the third woe is coming quickly.

### *The Seventh Trumpet*

**15** Then the [a]seventh angel sounded,
and there were [b]loud voices in heav-
en, saying,
"[c]The kingdom of the world has
become *the kingdom* of our Lord and
of [d]His [1]Christ, and [e]He will reign
forever and ever." **16** And the twenty-
four elders, who [a]sit on their thrones
before God, [b]fell on their faces and
worshiped God, **17** saying,
"We give You thanks, [a]O Lord God,
the Almighty, who is and who was,
because You have taken Your great
power and have begun to [b]reign.
**18** And [a]the nations were enraged,
and [b]Your rage came, and [c]the time
*came* for the dead to be judged, and
to give reward to Your [d]slaves—the
prophets and the saints and those
who fear Your name, [e]the small and
the great—and to destroy those who
destroy the earth."
**19** And [a]the sanctuary of God
which is in heaven was opened, and
[b]the ark of His covenant appeared in
His sanctuary, and there were flashes

---

**11:5** [b]Nu 16:29, 35 **11:6** [a]1Ki 17:1; Lk 4:25 [b]Rev 11:3 [c]Ex 7:17ff; Rev 8:8 [d]1Sa 4:8 **11:7** [a]Rev 13:1ff; 17:8 [b]Rev 9:1 [c]Da 7:21; Rev 13:7 **11:8** [a]Rev 14:8; 16:19; 17:18; 18:2, 10, 16, 18, 19, 21 [b]Is 1:9, 10; 3:9; Jer 23:14; Eze 16:46, 49 [c]Eze 23:3, 8, 19, 27 **11:9** [a]Rev 5:9; 10:11 [b]1Ki 13:22; Ps 79:2f [1]Lit *body* [2]Lit *do not permit* **11:10** [a]Rev 3:10 [b]Ne 8:10, 12; Es 9:19, 22 **11:11** [a]Eze 37:5, 9, 10, 14 **11:12** [a]Rev 4:1 [b]2Ki 2:11; Ac 1:9 **11:13** [a]Rev 6:12; 8:5; 11:19; 16:18 [b]Jn 9:24; Rev 14:7; 16:9; 19:7 [c]Rev 16:11 [1]Lit *names of people, seven thousand* **11:14** [a]Rev 8:13; 9:12 **11:15** [a]Rev 8:2; 10:7 [b]Rev 16:17; 19:1 [c]Rev 12:10 [d]Ps 2:2; Ac 4:26 [e]Ex 15:18; Da 2:44; 7:14, 27; Lk 1:33 [1]Messiah **11:16** [a]Mt 19:28; Rev 4:4 [b]Rev 4:10 **11:17** [a]Rev 1:8 [b]Rev 19:6 **11:18** [a]Ps 2:1 [b]Ps 2:5; 110:5 [c]Da 7:10; Rev 20:12 [d]Rev 10:7; 16:6 [e]Ps 115:13; Rev 13:16; 19:5 **11:19** [a]Rev 4:1; 15:5 [b]Heb 9:4

of [c]lightning and sounds and peals
of thunder and an earthquake and a
[d]great [1]hailstorm.

### *The Woman, the Child, and the Dragon*

**12** And a great [a]sign appeared [b]in
heaven: [c]a woman [d]clothed
with the sun, and the moon under
her feet, and on her head a crown of
twelve stars. **2** And she was with child,
and she *[a]cried out, being in labor and
in pain to give birth. **3** Then [a]another
sign appeared in heaven: and behold, a
great red [b]dragon having [c]seven heads
and [d]ten horns, and on his heads *were*
[e]seven diadems. **4** And his tail *swept
away a [a]third of the stars of heaven
and [b]threw them to the earth. And the
[c]dragon stood before the woman who
was about to give birth, so that when
she gave birth [d]he might devour her
child. **5** And [a]she gave birth to a son,
a male *child*, who is to [b,1]rule all the
[2]nations with a rod of iron; and her
child was [c]caught up to God and to
His throne. **6** Then the woman fled
into the wilderness where she *had a
place prepared by God, so that there
[1]she would be nourished for [a]1,260
days.

### *War in Heaven*

**7** And there was war in heaven,
[a]Michael and his angels waging war
with the [b]dragon. The dragon and
[c]his angels waged war, **8** and they
were not strong enough, and there
was no longer a place found for them
in heaven. **9** And the great [a]dragon
was thrown down, the [b]serpent of
old who is called the devil and [c]Satan,
who [d]deceives the whole [1]world. He
was [e]thrown down to the earth, and
his angels were thrown down with
him. **10** Then I heard [a]a loud voice
in heaven, saying,
"Now the [b]salvation, and the
power, and the [a]kingdom of our
God and the authority of His Christ
have come, for the [c]accuser of our
brothers has been thrown down, he
who accuses them before our God
day and night. **11** And they [a]overcame
him because of [b]the blood of the
Lamb and because of [c]the word of
their witness, and they [d]did not
love their life even to death. **12** For
this reason, [a]rejoice, O heavens and
[b]you who [1]dwell in them. [c]Woe to the
earth and the sea, because [d]the devil
has come down to you, having great
wrath, knowing that he has *only* [e]a
short time."
**13** And when the [a]dragon saw that
he was thrown down to the earth,
he persecuted [b]the woman who
gave birth to the male *child*. **14** But
the [a]two wings of the great eagle
were given to the woman, so that
she could fly [b]into the wilderness to
her place, where she *was nourished

---

**11:19** [c]Rev 4:5; 8:5; 16:18 [d]Rev 16:21 [1]Lit *hail* ◆ **12:1** [a]Mt 24:30; Rev 12:3 [b]Rev 11:19 [c]Ga 4:26 [d]Ps 104:2; SS 6:10 **12:2** [a]Is 26:17; 66:6-9; Mic 4:9f **12:3** [a]Rev 12:1; 15:1 [b]Is 27:1; Rev 12:4, 7, 9, 13, 16f; 13:2, 4, 11; 16:13; 20:2 [c]Rev 13:1; 17:3, 7, 9ff [d]Da 7:7, 20, 24; Rev 13:1; 17:12, 16 [e]Rev 13:1; 19:12 **12:4** [a]Rev 8:7, 12 [b]Da 8:10 [c]Is 27:1; Rev 12:3, 7, 9, 13, 16f; 13:2, 4, 11; 16:13; 20:2 [d]Mt 2:16 **12:5** [a]Is 66:7 [b]Ps 2:9; Rev 2:27 [c]2Co 12:2ff [1]Or *shepherd* [2]Or *Gentiles* **12:6** [a]Rev 11:3; 13:5 [1]Lit *they would nourish her for* **12:7** [a]Da 10:13, 21; 12:1; Jd 9 [b]Rev 12:3 [c]Mt 25:41 **12:9** [a]Rev 12:3 [b]Ge 3:1; 2Co 11:3; Rev 12:15; 20:2 [c]Mt 4:10; 25:41 [d]Rev 13:14; 20:3, 8, 10 [e]Lk 10:18; Jn 12:31 [1]Lit *inhabited earth* **12:10** [a]Rev 11:15 [b]Rev 7:10 [c]Job 1:11; 2:5; Zec 3:1; Lk 22:31; 1Pe 5:8 **12:11** [a]Jn 16:33; 1Jn 2:13; Rev 15:2 [b]Rev 7:14 [c]Rev 6:9 [d]Lk 14:26; Rev 2:10 **12:12** [a]Ps 96:11; Is 44:23; Rev 18:20 [b]Rev 13:6 [c]Rev 8:13 [d]Rev 12:9 [e]Rev 10:6 [1]Or *tabernacle* **12:13** [a]Rev 12:3 [b]Rev 12:5 **12:14** [a]Ex 19:4; Dt 32:11; Is 40:31 [b]Rev 12:6

for [c]a time and times and half a time,
from the [1]presence of the serpent.
**15** And the [a]serpent [1]poured water
like a river out of his mouth after
the woman, so that he might cause
her to be swept away with the flood.
**16** [1]But the earth helped the woman,
and the earth opened its mouth and
drank up the river which the dragon
[2]poured out of his mouth. **17** So the
dragon was enraged with the woman
and went off to [a]make war with the
rest of her [b]seed, who [c]keep the
commandments of God and [d]have
the witness of Jesus.

### *The Beast from the Sea*

**13** And the [1]dragon stood on the
sand of the [2]seashore.
Then I saw a [a]beast coming up out
of the sea, having [b]ten horns and
[b]seven heads, and on his horns *were*
[c]ten diadems, and on his heads *were*
[d]blasphemous names. **2** And the beast
which I saw was [a]like a leopard, and
his feet were like *those* of [b]a bear, and
his mouth like the mouth of [c]a lion.
And the [d]dragon gave him his power
and his [e]throne and great authority.
**3** And *I saw* one of his heads as if it
had been [1]slain fatally, and his [a]fatal
wound was healed. And the whole
earth [b]marveled *and followed* after
the beast. **4** And they worshiped the
[a]dragon because he [a]gave his author-
ity to the beast, and they worshiped
the beast, saying, "[b]Who is like the
beast, and who is able to wage war
with him?" **5** And there was given to
him a mouth [a]speaking [1]great boasts
and blasphemies, and authority to
act for [b]forty-two months was given
to him. **6** And he opened his mouth
in blasphemies against God, to blas-
pheme His name and His tabernacle,
*that is,* [a]those who [1]dwell in heaven.
**7** And it was also given to him to
[a]make war with the saints and to
overcome them, and authority over
[b]every tribe and people and tongue
and nation was given to him. **8** And all
who [a]dwell on the earth will worship
him, *everyone* [b]whose name has not
been [1]written [c]from the foundation
of the world in the [d]book of life of
[e]the Lamb who has been slain. **9** [a]If
anyone has an ear, let him hear. **10** [a]If
anyone [1]*is destined* for captivity, to
captivity he goes; [b]if anyone kills
with the sword, with the sword he
must be killed. Here is [c]the perse-
verance and the faith of the saints.

### *The Beast from the Earth*

**11** Then [a]I saw another beast coming
up out of the earth, and he had [b]two
horns like a lamb and he was speak-
ing as a [c]dragon. **12** And he [a]exercises
all the authority of the first beast [b,1]in
his presence. And he makes [c]the
earth and those who dwell in it to
[d]worship the first beast, whose [e]fatal

---

**12:14** [c]Da 7:25; 12:7 [1]Lit *face* **12:15** [a]Ge 3:1; 2Co 11:3; Rev 12:9; 20:2 [1]Lit *threw* **12:16** [1]Lit *And* [2]Lit *threw* **12:17** [a]Rev 11:7; 13:7 [b]Ge 3:15 [c]1Jn 2:3; Rev 14:12 [d]Rev 1:2; 6:9; 14:12; 19:10 ◆ **13:1** [a]Da 7:3; Rev 11:7; 13:14, 15; 15:2; 16:13; 17:8 [b]Rev 12:3 [c]Rev 12:3; 17:12 [d]Da 7:8; 11:36; Rev 17:3 [1]Lit *he* [2]Lit *sea* **13:2** [a]Da 7:6; Hos 13:7f [b]Da 7:5 [c]Da 7:4 [d]Rev 12:3; 13:4, 12 [e]Rev 2:13; 16:10 **13:3** [a]Rev 13:12, 14 [b]Rev 17:8 [1]Lit *slaughtered to death* **13:4** [a]Rev 12:3; 13:2, 12 [b]Ex 15:11; Is 46:5; Rev 18:18 **13:5** [a]Da 7:8, 11, 20, 25; 11:36; 2Th 2:3f [b]Rev 11:2 [1]Lit *great things* **13:6** [a]Rev 7:15; 12:12 [1]Or *tabernacle* **13:7** [a]Da 7:21; Rev 11:7 [b]Rev 5:9 **13:8** [a]Rev 3:10; 13:12, 14 [b]Rev 3:5 [c]Mt 25:34; Rev 17:8 [d]Ps 69:28 [e]Rev 5:6 [1]Or *written in the book...slain from the foundation of the world* **13:9** [a]Rev 2:7 **13:10** [a]Is 33:1; Jer 15:2; 43:11 [b]Ge 9:6; Mt 26:52; Rev 11:18 [c]Heb 6:12; Rev 14:12 [1]Or leads *into captivity* **13:11** [a]Rev 13:1; 16:13 [b]Da 8:3 [c]Rev 13:4 **13:12** [a]Rev 13:4 [b]Rev 13:14; 19:20 [c]Rev 13:8 [d]Rev 13:15; 14:9, 11; 16:2; 19:20; 20:4 [e]Rev 13:3 [1]Or *by his authority*

wound was healed. **13** And he [a]does
great signs, so that he even makes
[b]fire come down out of heaven to
the earth in the presence of men.
**14** And he [a]deceives [b]those who
dwell on the earth because of [c]the
signs which were given to him to do
[d,1]in the presence of the beast, telling
those who dwell on the earth to make
an image to the beast who *had the
[e]wound of the sword and has come
to life. **15** And it was given to him to
give breath to the image of the beast,
so that the image of the beast would
even [1]speak and cause [a]as many as do
not [b]worship the image of the beast
to be killed. **16** And he causes all, [a]the
small and the great, and the rich and
the poor, and the free men and the
slaves, that they [1]be given a [b]mark on
their right hand or on their forehead,
**17** and that no one will be able to buy
or to sell, except the one who has
the [a]mark, *either* [b]the name of the
beast or [c]the number of his name.
**18** [a]Here is wisdom. Let him who has
understanding calculate the number
of the beast, for it is the number [b]of
man; and his number is [1]666.

### *The Lamb and the 144,000*

**14** Then I looked, and behold, [a]the
Lamb *was* standing on [b]Mount
Zion, and with Him [c]144,000, having
[d]His name and the [d]name of His
Father written [e]on their foreheads.
**2** And I heard a voice from heaven,
like [a]the sound of many waters and
like the [b]sound of loud thunder, and
the voice which I heard *was* like *the
sound* of [c]harpists playing on their
harps. **3** And they *[1]sang [a]a new song
before the throne and before the
[b]four living creatures and the [c]elders.
And [d]no one could learn that song
except the [e]144,000 who had been
[a]purchased from the earth. **4** [a]These
are the ones who are not defiled with
women, for they are virgins. These
*are* the ones who [b]follow the Lamb
wherever He goes. These have been
[c]purchased from among men [d]as first
fruits to God and to the Lamb. **5** And
[a]NO LIE WAS FOUND IN THEIR MOUTH;
they are [b]blameless.

### *The Messages of the Three Angels*

**6** Then I saw another angel flying in
[a]midheaven, having [b]an eternal gos-
pel to proclaim to [c]those who [1]inhabit
the earth, and to [d]every nation and
tribe and tongue and people. **7** And
he said with a loud voice, "[a]Fear
God, and [b]give Him glory, because
the hour of His judgment has come;
worship Him who [c]made the heaven
and the earth and sea and [d]springs
of waters."

**8** And another angel, a second one,
followed, saying, "[a,1]FALLEN, FALLEN
IS [b]BABYLON THE GREAT, she who has
[c]made all the nations drink of the

**13:13** [a]Mt 24:24; Rev 16:14; 19:20 [b]1Ki 18:38; Lk 9:54; Rev 11:5; 20:9 **13:14** [a]Rev 12:9 [b]Rev 13:8 [c]2Th 2:9f [d]Rev 13:12; 19:20 [e]Rev 13:3 [1]Or *by the authority of* **13:15** [a]Da 3:3ff [b]Rev 13:12; 14:9, 11; 16:2; 19:20; 20:4 [1]One early ms *speak, and he will cause* **13:16** [a]Rev 11:18; 19:5, 18 [b]Ga 6:17; Rev 7:3; 14:9; 20:4 [1]Lit *that they give them a mark* **13:17** [a]Ga 6:17; Rev 7:3; 14:9; 20:4 [b]Rev 14:11 [c]Rev 15:2 **13:18** [a]Rev 17:9 [b]Rev 21:17 [1]One early ms *616* ◆ **14:1** [a]Rev 5:6 [b]Ps 2:6; Heb 12:22 [c]Rev 7:4; 14:3 [d]Rev 3:12 [e]Eze 9:4; Rev 7:3 **14:2** [a]Rev 1:15 [b]Rev 6:1 [c]Rev 5:8 **14:3** [a]Rev 5:9 [b]Rev 4:6 [c]Rev 4:4 [d]Rev 2:17 [e]Rev 7:4; 14:1 [1]Two early mss *sing* something *like a new song* **14:4** [a]Mt 19:12; 2Co 11:2; Eph 5:27; Rev 3:4 [b]Rev 3:4; 7:17; 17:14 [c]Rev 5:9 [d]Heb 12:23; Jas 1:18 **14:5** [a]Zep 3:13; Mal 2:6; Jn 1:47; 1Pe 2:22 [b]Heb 9:14; 1Pe 1:19; Jd 24 **14:6** [a]Rev 8:13 [b]1Pe 1:25; Rev 10:7 [c]Rev 3:10 [d]Rev 5:9 [1]Lit *sit on* **14:7** [a]Rev 15:4 [b]Rev 11:13 [c]Rev 4:11 [d]Rev 8:10 **14:8** [a]Is 21:9; Jer 51:8; Rev 18:2 [b]Da 4:30; Rev 16:19; 17:5; 18:10 [c]Jer 51:7 [1]Or *Babylon the great fell, fell*

[d]wine of the wrath of her [2]sexual
immorality."
**9** Then another angel, a third one,
followed them, saying with a loud
voice, "If anyone [a]worships the beast
and his [b]image, and receives a [c]mark
on his forehead or on his hand, **10** and
he also will drink of the [a]wine of the
wrath of God, which is mixed [1]in full
strength [b]in the cup of His rage, and
he will be tormented with [c]fire and
[2]brimstone in the presence of the
[d]holy angels and in the presence of
the Lamb. **11** And the [a]smoke of their
torment goes up forever and ever;
[b]they have no rest day and night,
those who [c]worship the beast and
his [c]image, and [1]whoever receives
the [d]mark of his name." **12** Here is
[a]the perseverance of the saints who
[b]keep the commandments of God
and [c,1]their faith in Jesus.
**13** And I heard a voice from heaven,
saying, "Write, '[a]Blessed are the dead
who [b]die in the Lord from now on!'"
"Yes," [c]says the Spirit, "so that they
may [d]rest from their labors, for their
[e]deeds follow with them."

### *Reaping the Earth's Harvest*

**14** Then I looked, and behold, a
[a]white cloud, and sitting on the
cloud *was* one [b]like [1]a son of man,
having a golden [c]crown on His head
and a sharp sickle in His hand.
**15** And another angel [a]came out of
the sanctuary, crying out with a loud
voice to Him who sits on the cloud,
"[b,1]Put in Your sickle and reap, for the
hour to reap has come, because the
[c]harvest of the earth [2]is ripe." **16** Then
He who sits on the cloud [1]swung His
sickle over the earth, and the earth
was reaped.
**17** And another angel [a]came out of
the sanctuary which is in heaven, and
he also had a sharp sickle. **18** Then
another angel, [a]the one who has
authority over fire, came out from
[b]the altar; and he called with a loud
voice to him who had the sharp sick-
le, saying, "[c,1]Put in your sharp sickle
and gather the clusters [2]from the vine
of the earth, [d]because her grapes are
ripe." **19** So the angel [1]swung his sickle
to the earth and gathered *the clusters*
*from* the vine of the earth, and threw
them into [a]the great wine press of
the wrath of God. **20** And [a]the wine
press was trodden [b]outside the city,
and [c]blood came out from the wine
press, up to the horses' bridles, [1]for a
distance of [2]1,600 stadia.

### *Seven Angels, Seven Plagues*

**15** Then I saw [a]another sign in
heaven, great and marvelous,
[b]seven angels who have [c]seven
plagues, *which are* [d]the last, because
in them the wrath of God is finished.

**14:8** [d]Rev 17:2, 4; 18:3 [2]Spiritual adulteries **14:9** [a]Rev 13:12; 14:11 [b]Rev 13:14f; 14:11 [c]Rev 13:16
**14:10** [a]Is 51:17; Jer 25:15f, 27; Rev 16:19; 19:15 [b]Ps 75:8; Rev 18:6 [c]Ge 19:24; Eze 38:22; 2Th 1:7; Rev 19:20; 20:10, 14f; 21:8 [d]Mk 8:38 [1]Lit *unmixed*; in ancient times wine was usually diluted with water [2]Burning sulfur **14:11** [a]Is 34:8-10; Rev 18:9, 18; 19:3 [b]Rev 4:8 [c]Rev 13:12; 14:9 [d]Rev 13:17 [1]Lit *if anyone*
**14:12** [a]Rev 13:10 [b]Rev 12:17 [c]Rev 2:13 [1]Lit *the faith of* **14:13** [a]Rev 20:6 [b]1Co 15:18; 1Th 4:16 [c]Rev 2:7; 22:17 [d]Heb 4:9ff; Rev 6:11 [e]1Ti 5:25 **14:14** [a]Mt 17:5 [b]Da 7:13; Rev 1:13 [c]Ps 21:3; Rev 6:2 [1]Or *the Son of Man* **14:15** [a]Rev 11:19; 14:17; 15:6; 16:17 [b]Joel 3:13; Mk 4:29; Rev 14:18 [c]Jer 51:33; Mt 13:39-41 [1]Lit *Send forth* [2]Lit *has become dry* **14:16** [1]Lit *cast* **14:17** [a]Rev 11:19; 14:15; 15:6; 16:17 **14:18** [a]Rev 16:8 [b]Rev 6:9; 8:3 [c]Joel 3:13; Mk 4:29; Rev 14:15 [d]Joel 3:13 [1]Lit *Send forth* [2]Lit *of* **14:19** [a]Is 63:2f; Rev 19:15 [1]Lit *cast* **14:20** [a]Is 63:3; Lam 1:15; Rev 19:15 [b]Heb 13:12; Rev 11:8 [c]Ge 49:11; Dt 32:14 [1]Lit *from* [2]Approx. 184 mi. or 296 km, a stadion was approx. 607 ft. or 185 m ◆ **15:1** [a]Rev 12:1, 3 [b]Rev 15:6-8; 16:1; 17:1; 21:9 [c]Lv 26:21 [d]Rev 9:20

**2** Then I saw something like a [a]sea
of glass mixed with fire, and those
who have [b]overcome [1]the [c]beast and
[d]his image and the [e]number of his
name, standing on the [a]sea of glass,
having [f]harps of God. **3** And they
*sang the [a]song of Moses, [b]the slave
of God, and the [c]song of the Lamb,
saying,

"[d]Great and marvelous
 are Your works,
[e]O [1]Lord God, the Almighty;
Righteous and true
 are Your ways,
[f]King of the [2]nations!

**4** "[a]Who will not fear, O [1]Lord,
 and glorify Your name?
For You alone are holy;
For [b]all the nations
 will come and worship
 before You,
For Your [c,2]righteous acts
 have been revealed."

**5** And after these things I looked,
and [a]the sanctuary of the [b]taber-
nacle of testimony in heaven was
opened, **6** and the [a]seven angels who
have the seven plagues [b]came out
of the sanctuary, clothed in [1]linen,
clean *and* bright, and [c]girded around
their chests with golden sashes.
**7** Then one of the [a]four living crea-
tures gave to the [b]seven angels seven
[c]golden bowls full of the [d]wrath of
God, who [e]lives forever and ever.
**8** And the sanctuary was filled with
[a]smoke from the glory of God and
from His power; and no one was
able to enter the sanctuary until the
seven plagues of the seven angels
were finished.

### *The Seven Bowls of God's Wrath*

**16** Then I heard a loud voice from
[a]the sanctuary, saying to the
[b]seven angels, "Go and [c]pour out
[1]on the earth the seven bowls of the
wrath of God."
**2** So the first *angel* went and
poured out his bowl [a,1]on the earth;
and it became a loathsome and ma-
lignant [b]sore on the [2]people [c]who
have the mark of the beast and who
worship his image.
**3** And the second *angel* poured out
his bowl [a]into the sea, and it became
blood like *that* of a dead man, and
every living [1]thing in the sea died.
**4** Then the third *angel* poured out
his bowl into the [a]rivers and the
springs of waters, and they [b]became
blood. **5** And I heard the angel of the
waters saying, "[a]Righteous are You,
[b]who is and who was, O [c]Holy One,
because You [d]judged these things;
**6** for they poured out [a]the blood of
saints and prophets, and You have
given them [b]blood to drink. They
[1]deserve it." **7** And I heard [a]the altar
saying, "Yes, O [b,1]Lord God, the Al-
mighty, [c]true and righteous are Your
judgments."

**15:2** [a]Rev 4:6 [b]Rev 12:11 [c]Rev 13:1 [d]Rev 13:14f [e]Rev 13:17 [f]Rev 5:8 [1]Lit *from* **15:3** [a]Ex 15:1ff [b]Jos 22:5; Heb 3:5 [c]Ps 98:2; Rev 5:9f, 12f [d]Dt 32:3f; Ps 111:2; 139:14 [e]Hos 14:9; Rev 1:8 [f]1Ti 1:17 [1]In OT, Yahweh, cf. Am 4:13 [2]Two early mss *ages* **15:4** [a]Jer 10:7; Rev 14:7 [b]Ps 86:9; Is 66:23 [c]Rev 19:8 [1]In OT, Yahweh, Jer 10:6 [2]Or *judgments* **15:5** [a]Rev 11:19 [b]Ex 38:21; Nu 1:50; Heb 8:5; Rev 13:6 **15:6** [a]Rev 15:1 [b]Rev 14:15 [c]Rev 1:13 [1]One early ms *stone* **15:7** [a]Rev 4:6 [b]Rev 15:1 [c]Rev 5:8 [d]Rev 14:10; 15:1 [e]Rev 4:9 **15:8** [a]Ex 19:18; 40:34f; Lv 16:2; 1Ki 8:10f; 2Chr 5:13f; Is 6:4 ◆ **16:1** [a]Rev 11:19 [b]Rev 15:1 [c]Ps 79:6; Jer 10:25; Eze 22:31; Zep 3:8; Rev 16:2ff [1]Lit *into* **16:2** [a]Rev 8:7 [b]Ex 9:9-11; Dt 28:35; Rev 16:11 [c]Rev 13:15-17; 14:9 [1]Lit *into* [2]Gr *anthropoi* **16:3** [a]Ex 7:17-21; Rev 8:8f; 11:6 [1]Lit *soul* **16:4** [a]Rev 8:10 [b]Ex 7:17-20; Ps 78:44; Rev 11:6 **16:5** [a]Jn 17:25 [b]Rev 11:17 [c]Rev 15:4 [d]Rev 6:10 **16:6** [a]Rev 17:6; 18:24 [b]Is 49:26; Lk 11:49-51 [1]Lit *are worthy* **16:7** [a]Rev 6:9; 14:18 [b]Rev 1:8 [c]Rev 15:3; 19:2 [1]In OT, Yahweh, cf. Am 4:13

**8** And the fourth *angel* poured out
his bowl upon [a]the sun, [b]and it was
given to it to scorch men with fire.
**9** And men were scorched with [1]fierce
heat, and they [a]blasphemed the
name of God who has the authority
over these plagues, and they [b]did not
repent so as to [c]give Him glory.
**10** Then the fifth *angel* poured
out his bowl on the [a]throne of the
beast, and his kingdom became
[b]darkened; and they gnawed their
tongues because of pain, **11** and they
[a]blasphemed the [b]God of heaven
because of their pains and their
[c]sores, and they [d]did not repent of
their deeds.
**12** And the sixth *angel* poured out
his bowl on the [a]great river, the Eu-
phrates, and [b]its water was dried up,
so that [c]the way would be prepared
for the kings [d]from the [1]east. **13** Then
I saw *coming* out of the mouth of
the [a]dragon and out of the mouth
of the [b]beast and out of the mouth of
the [c]false prophet, three [d]unclean
spirits like [e]frogs; **14** for they are
[a]spirits of demons, [b]doing signs,
which go out to the kings of the
[c]whole [1]world, to [d]gather them to-
gether for the war of the [e]great day
of God, the Almighty. **15** ("Behold, [a]I
am coming like a thief. [b]Blessed is the
one who stays awake and keeps his
garments, [c]so that he will not walk
about naked and men will not see
his shame.") **16** And they [a]gathered
them together to the place which [b]in
Hebrew is called [c,1]Har-Magedon.

### *The Seventh Bowl*

**17** Then the seventh *angel* poured out
his bowl upon [a]the air, and a [b]loud
voice came out of the [c]sanctuary
from the throne, saying, "[d]It is
done." **18** And there were flashes of
[a]lightning and sounds and peals
of thunder; and there was [b]a great
earthquake, [c]such as there had not
been since man came to be upon the
earth, so great an earthquake *was it,*
*and* so mighty. **19** [a]And the great city
was split into three parts, and the cit-
ies of the [1]nations fell. [b]Babylon the
great was [c]remembered before God,
to give her [d]the cup of the wine of
the wrath of His rage. **20** And [a]every
island fled away, and the moun-
tains were not found. **21** And [a]huge
[1]hailstones, about one [2]talent each,
*came down from heaven upon men;
and men [b]blasphemed God because
of the [c]plague of the hail, because its
plague *was extremely [3]severe.

### *The Woman and the Beast*

**17** [a]Then one of the [b]seven angels
who have the [c]seven bowls
came and spoke with me, saying,
"Come here, I will show you [d]the
judgment of the [e]great harlot who
[f]sits on many waters, **2** with whom

**16:8** [a]Rev 6:12 [b]Rev 14:18 **16:9** [a]Rev 16:11, 21 [b]Rev 2:21 [c]Rev 11:13 [1]Lit *great* **16:10** [a]Rev 13:2 [b]Ex 10:21f; Is 8:22; Rev 8:12; 9:2 **16:11** [a]Rev 16:9, 21 [b]Rev 11:13 [c]Rev 16:2 [d]Rev 2:21 **16:12** [a]Rev 9:14 [b]Is 11:15f; 44:27; Jer 51:36 [c]Is 41:2, 25; 46:11 [d]Rev 7:2 [1]Lit *rising of the sun* **16:13** [a]Rev 12:3 [b]Rev 13:1 [c]Rev 13:11, 14; 19:20; 20:10 [d]Rev 18:2 [e]Ex 8:6 **16:14** [a]1Ti 4:1 [b]Rev 13:13 [c]Rev 3:10 [d]1Ki 22:21-23; Rev 17:14; 19:19; 20:8 [e]Rev 6:17 [1]Lit *inhabited earth* **16:15** [a]Mt 24:43f; Lk 12:39f; Rev 3:3, 11 [b]Lk 12:37 [c]Rev 3:18 **16:16** [a]Rev 19:19 [b]Rev 9:11 [c]Jdg 5:19; 2Ki 23:29f; 2Chr 35:22; Zec 12:11 [1]Two early mss *Armagedon* **16:17** [a]Eph 2:2 [b]Rev 11:15 [c]Rev 14:15 [d]Rev 10:6; 21:6 **16:18** [a]Rev 4:5 [b]Rev 6:12 [c]Da 12:1; Mt 24:21 **16:19** [a]Rev 11:8; 17:18; 18:10, 18f, 21 [b]Rev 14:8 [c]Rev 18:5 [d]Rev 14:10 [1]Or *Gentiles* **16:20** [a]Rev 6:14; 20:11 **16:21** [a]Rev 8:7; 11:19 [b]Rev 16:9, 11 [c]Ex 9:18-25 [1]Lit *hail* [2]Approx. 100 lb. or 45 kg [3]Lit *great* ◆**17:1** [a]Rev 1:1; 21:9 [b]Rev 15:1 [c]Rev 15:7 [d]Rev 16:19 [e]Is 1:21; Jer 2:20; Na 3:4; Rev 17:5, 15f; 19:2 [f]Jer 51:13; Rev 17:15

[a]the kings of the earth committed
[1]sexual immorality, and [b]those
who dwell on the earth were [c]made
drunk with the wine of her [1]sexual
immorality." **3** And [a]he carried me
away [b,1]in the Spirit [c]into a wilder-
ness; then I saw a woman sitting on
a [d]scarlet beast, full of [e]blasphemous
names, having [f]seven heads and
ten horns. **4** And the woman [a]was
clothed in purple and scarlet, and
[1]adorned with gold and precious
[2]stones and pearls, having in her
hand [b]a gold cup full of abomina-
tions and of the unclean things of
her [3]sexual immorality, **5** and on
her forehead a name *was* written, a
[a]mystery, "[b]BABYLON THE GREAT,
THE MOTHER OF HARLOTS AND
OF [c]THE ABOMINATIONS OF THE
EARTH." **6** Then I saw the woman
drunk with [a]the blood of the saints,
and with the blood of the witnesses
of Jesus. When I saw her, I wondered
[1]greatly. **7** And the angel said to me,
"Why [1]do you wonder? I will tell you
the [a]mystery of the woman and of the
beast that carries her, which has the
[b]seven heads and the ten horns.

**8** "[a]The beast that you saw [b]was,
and is not, and is about to [c]come up
out of the [d]abyss and [e,1]go to destruc-
tion. And [f]those who dwell on the
earth, [g]whose name has not been
written in the book of life [h]from the
foundation of the world, will [i]wonder
when they see the beast, that he was
and is not and will come. **9** [a]Here is
the mind which has wisdom. The
[b]seven heads are seven mountains
on which the woman sits, **10** and they
are seven [a]kings; five have fallen, one
is, the other has not yet come; and
when he comes, he must remain a
little while. **11** And the beast which
[a]was and is not, is himself also an
eighth and is *one* of the seven, and
he [b]goes to destruction. **12** And the
[a]ten horns which you saw are ten
kings who have not yet received a
kingdom, but they receive authority
as kings with the beast [b]for one hour.
**13** These have [a]one [1]purpose, and
they give their power and authority
to the beast. **14** These will wage [a]war
against the Lamb, and the Lamb
will [b]overcome them, because He
is [c]Lord of lords and [c]King of kings,
and [d]those who are with Him *are the*
[e]called and elect and faithful."

**15** And he *said to me, "The [a]waters
which you saw where the harlot sits,
are [b]peoples and crowds and nations
and tongues. **16** And the [a]ten horns
which you saw, and the beast, these
will hate the harlot and will [b]lay
waste to her and make *her* [c]naked,
and will [d]eat her flesh and will [e]burn
her up with fire. **17** For [a]God gave *it*
in their hearts to do His [1]purpose
both [2]by [b]doing *their own* common
purpose and by giving their kingdom

**17:2** [a]Rev 2:22; 18:3, 9 [b]Rev 3:10; 17:8 [c]Rev 14:8 [1]Spiritual adulteries **17:3** [a]Rev 21:10 [b]Rev 1:10 [c]Rev 12:6, 14; 21:10 [d]Mt 27:28; Rev 18:12, 16 [e]Rev 13:1 [f]Rev 12:3; 17:7, 9, 12, 16 [1]Or *in spirit*
**17:4** [a]Eze 28:13; Rev 18:12, 16 [b]Jer 51:7; Rev 18:6 [1]Lit *gilded* [2]Lit *stone* [3]Spiritual adulteries
**17:5** [a]Da 4:27; 2Th 2:7; Rev 1:20; 17:7 [b]Rev 14:8; 16:19 [c]Rev 17:2 **17:6** [a]Rev 16:6 [1]Lit *with great wonder* **17:7** [a]2Th 2:7; Rev 1:20; 17:5 [b]Rev 17:3 [1]Lit *have you wondered* **17:8** [a]Da 7:7 [b]Rev 13:3, 12, 14; 17:11 [c]Rev 11:7; 13:1 [d]Rev 9:1; 13:1 [e]Rev 13:10; 17:11 [f]Rev 3:10 [g]Ps 69:28; Rev 3:5 [h]Mt 25:34; Rev 13:8 [i]Rev 13:3 [1]One early ms *is going* **17:9** [a]Rev 13:18 [b]Rev 17:3 **17:10** [a]Rev 10:11 **17:11** [a]Rev 13:3, 12, 14; 17:8 [b]Rev 13:10; 17:8 **17:12** [a]Da 7:24; Rev 12:3; 13:1; 17:16 [b]Rev 18:10, 17, 19 **17:13** [a]Rev 17:17 [1]Or *mind*
**17:14** [a]Rev 16:14 [b]Rev 3:21 [c]1Ti 6:15; Rev 19:16 [d]Rev 2:10f [e]Mt 22:14 **17:15** [a]Is 8:7; Jer 47:2; Rev 17:1 [b]Rev 5:9 **17:16** [a]Rev 17:12 [b]Rev 18:17, 19 [c]Eze 16:37, 39 [d]Rev 19:18 [e]Rev 18:8 **17:17** [a]2Co 8:16 [b]Rev 17:13 [1]Or *mind* [2]Lit *even to do one mind and to give*

to the beast, until the [c]words of God
will be finished. **18** And the woman
whom you saw is [a]the great city,
which has a kingdom over the kings
of the earth."

### *Fallen Is Babylon*

**18** After these things I saw anoth-
er [a]angel [b]coming down from
heaven, having great authority, and
the earth was [c]illumined with his glo-
ry. **2** And he cried out with a mighty
voice, saying, "[a,1]FALLEN, FALLEN IS
BABYLON THE GREAT! And she [b]has
become a dwelling place of demons
and a [2]prison of every [c]unclean spirit,
and a [2]prison of every unclean bird
[3]and a [2]prison of every unclean and
hateful beast. **3** For all the nations
[1]have drunk of the [a]wine of the wrath
of her sexual immorality, and [b]the
kings of the earth have committed
sexual immorality with her, and the
[c]merchants of the earth have become
rich by the power of her [d,2]sensual-
ity."
**4** And I heard another voice from
heaven, saying, "[a]Come out of her,
my people, so that you will not par-
ticipate in her sins and receive of her
plagues; **5** for her sins have [a,1]piled
up as high as heaven, and God has
[b]remembered her iniquities. **6** [a]Pay
her back even as she paid, and [1]give
*her* back double according to her
deeds; in the [b]cup which she has
mixed, mix double for her. **7** [a]To
the degree that she glorified herself
and [b]lived [1]sensuously, to the same
degree give her torment and mourn-
ing, for she says in her heart, '[c]I SIT
*as* A QUEEN AND I AM NOT A WIDOW,
and will never see mourning.' **8** For
this reason [a]in one day her plagues
will come, [1]pestilence and mourning
and famine, and she will be [b]burned
up with fire; for the Lord God who
judges her [c]is strong.
**9** "And [a]the kings of the earth,
who committed sexual immorality
and [b]lived [1]sensuously with her,
will [c]cry and lament over her when
they [d]see the smoke of her burning,
**10** [a]standing at a distance because
of the fear of her torment, saying,
'[b]Woe, woe, [c]the great city, Babylon,
the strong city! For in [d]one hour your
judgment has come.'
**11** "And the [a]merchants of the
earth [b]cry and mourn over her,
because no one buys their cargo any-
more— **12** cargo of [a]gold and silver
and precious [1]stones and pearls and
fine linen and purple and silk and
scarlet, and every *kind of* citron wood
and every article of ivory and every
article *made* from precious wood and
[2]bronze and iron and marble, **13** and
cinnamon and amomum and incense
and perfume and frankincense and
wine and olive oil and fine flour and
wheat and cattle and sheep, and *cargo*

---

**17:17** [c]Rev 10:7 **17:18** [a]Rev 11:8; 16:19 ◆ **18:1** [a]Rev 17:1, 7 [b]Rev 10:1 [c]Eze 43:2 **18:2** [a]Is 21:9; Jer 51:8; Rev 14:8 [b]Is 13:21f; 34:11, 13-15; Jer 50:39; 51:37; Zep 2:14f [c]Rev 16:13 [1]Lit *Babylon...fell, fell* [2]Or *haunt* [3]Some mss omit *and a prison of every unclean and hateful beast* **18:3** [a]Jer 51:7; Rev 14:8 [b]Rev 17:2; 18:9 [c]Eze 27:9-25; Rev 18:11, 15, 19, 23 [d]1Ti 5:11; Rev 18:7, 9 [1]Two early mss *have fallen by* [2]Or *luxury* **18:4** [a]Is 52:11; Jer 50:8; 51:6, 9, 45; 2Co 6:17 **18:5** [a]Jer 51:9 [b]Rev 16:19 [1]Lit *joined together* **18:6** [a]Ps 137:8; Jer 50:15, 29 [b]Rev 17:4 [1]Lit *double* to her **18:7** [a]Eze 28:2-8 [b]1Ti 5:11; Rev 18:3, 9 [c]Is 47:7f; Zep 2:15 [1]Or *luxuriously* **18:8** [a]Is 47:9; Jer 50:31f; Rev 18:10 [b]Rev 17:16 [c]Jer 50:34; Rev 11:17f [1]Lit *death* **18:9** [a]Rev 17:2; 18:3 [b]1Ti 5:11; Rev 18:3, 7 [c]Eze 26:16f; 27:35 [d]Rev 14:11; 18:18; 19:3 [1]Or *luxuriously* **18:10** [a]Rev 18:15, 17 [b]Rev 18:16, 19 [c]Rev 11:8; 16:19; 18:16, 18, 19, 21 [d]Rev 17:12; 18:8, 17, 19 **18:11** [a]Eze 27:9-25; Rev 18:3, 15, 19, 23 [b]Eze 27:27-34 **18:12** [a]Eze 27:12-22; Rev 17:4 [1]Lit *stone* [2]Or *brass*

of horses and carriages and [1]human
beings and [a,2]human lives. **14** And the
fruit [1]you long for has gone from you,
and all things that were splendid
and shining have passed away from
you and *men* will no longer find
them. **15** The [a]merchants of [b]these
things, who became rich from her,
will [c]stand at a distance because
of the fear of her torment, crying
and mourning, **16** saying, '[a]Woe,
woe, [b]the great city, she who [c]was
clothed in fine linen and purple and
scarlet, and [1]adorned with gold and
precious [2]stones and pearls; **17** for in
[a]one hour such great wealth has been
laid [b]waste!' And [c]every shipmaster
and every [1]passenger and sailor, and
as many as make their living by the
sea, [a]stood at a distance, **18** and were
[a]crying out as they [b]saw the smoke
of her burning, saying, '[c]What is like
[d]the great city?' **19** And they threw
[a]dust on their heads and were crying
out, crying and mourning, saying,
'[b]Woe, woe, the great city, in which
all who have ships at sea [c]became
rich by her [1]wealth, for in [b]one hour
she has been laid [d]waste!' **20** [a]Rejoice
over her, O heaven, and you saints
and [b]apostles and prophets, because
[c]God has [1]pronounced judgment for
you against her."

**21** Then [1]a [a]strong angel [b]picked
up a stone like a great millstone and
threw it into the sea, saying, "So will
Babylon, [c]the great city, be thrown
down with violence, and [d]will not
be found any longer. **22** And [a]the
sound of harpists and musicians and
flute-players and trumpeters will not
be heard in you any longer; and no
craftsman of any craft will be found
in you any longer; and the [b]sound of
a mill will not be heard in you any
longer; **23** and the light of a lamp
will not shine in you any longer; and
the [a]voice of the bridegroom and
bride will not be heard in you any
longer; for your [b]merchants were the
great men of the earth, because all
the nations were deceived [c]by your
sorcery. **24** And in her was found the
[a]blood of prophets and of saints and
of [b]all who have been slain on the
earth."

### *Hallelujah!*

**19** After these things I heard
something like a [a]loud voice
of a great crowd in heaven, saying,
"[b]Hallelujah! [c]Salvation and
[d]glory and power belong to our God;
**2** [a]BECAUSE HIS [b]JUDGMENTS ARE [c]TRUE
AND RIGHTEOUS; for He has judged
the [d]great harlot who was corrupting
the earth with her sexual immorality,
and HE HAS [e]AVENGED THE BLOOD OF
HIS SLAVES *shed* BY HER HAND." **3** And
a second time they said, "[a]Hallelu-
jah! [b]HER SMOKE RISES UP FOREVER
AND EVER." **4** And the [a]twenty-four

**18:13** [a]1Chr 5:21; Eze 27:13; 1Ti 1:10 [1]Lit *bodies* [2]Lit *souls of people* **18:14** [1]Lit *of your soul's desire*
**18:15** [a]Rev 18:3 [b]Rev 18:12, 13 [c]Rev 18:10 **18:16** [a]Rev 18:10, 19 [b]Rev 18:10, 18, 19, 21 [c]Rev 17:4 [1]Lit *gilded* [2]Lit *stone and pearl* **18:17** [a]Rev 18:10 [b]Rev 17:16; 18:19 [c]Eze 27:28f [1]Lit *one who sails to a place* **18:18** [a]Eze 27:30 [b]Rev 18:9 [c]Eze 27:32; Rev 13:4 [d]Rev 18:10 **18:19** [a]Jos 7:6; Job 2:12; Lam 2:10 [b]Rev 18:10 [c]Rev 18:3, 15 [d]Rev 17:16; 18:17 [1]Lit *costliness* **18:20** [a]Jer 51:48; Rev 12:12 [b]Lk 11:49f [c]Rev 6:10; 18:6ff; 19:2 [1]Lit *judged your judgment of her* **18:21** [a]Rev 5:2; 10:1 [b]Jer 51:63f [c]Rev 18:10 [d]Eze 26:21 [1]Lit *one* **18:22** [a]Is 24:8; Eze 26:13; Mt 9:23 [b]Ecc 12:4; Jer 25:10 **18:23** [a]Jer 7:34; 16:9 [b]Is 23:8; Rev 6:15; 18:3 [c]Na 3:4; Rev 9:21 **18:24** [a]Rev 16:6; 17:6 [b]Mt 23:35 ◆ **19:1** [a]Jer 51:48; Rev 11:15; 19:6 [b]Ps 104:35; Rev 19:3, 4, 6 [c]Rev 7:10 [d]Rev 4:11 **19:2** [a]Ps 19:9 [b]Rev 6:10 [c]Rev 16:7 [d]Rev 17:1 [e]Dt 32:43; 2Ki 9:7; Rev 16:6; 18:20 **19:3** [a]Ps 104:35; Rev 19:1, 4, 6 [b]Is 34:10; Rev 14:11 **19:4** [a]Rev 4:4, 10

elders and the [b]four living creatures
[c]fell down and worshiped God who
sits on the throne saying, "[d]Amen.
[e]Hallelujah!" **5** And a voice came
from the throne, saying,

"[a]Give praise to our God, all you
His slaves, [b]you who fear Him, the
small and the great." **6** Then I heard
*something* like [a]the voice of a great
crowd and like [b]the sound of many
waters and like the [c]sound of mighty
peals of thunder, saying,

"[a]Hallelujah! For the [d]Lord our
God, the Almighty, reigns.

### *The Marriage Supper of the Lamb*

**7** "Let us rejoice and be glad and [a]give
the glory to Him, for [b]the marriage of
the Lamb has come and His [c,1]bride
has made herself ready." **8** And it was
given to her to clothe herself in [a]fine
linen, bright *and* clean; for the fine
linen is the [b]righteous acts of the
saints.

**9** Then [a]he *said to me, "[b]Write,
'[c]Blessed are those who are invited
to the marriage supper of the Lamb.'"
And he *said to me, "[d]These are true
words of God." **10** Then [a]I fell at his
feet to worship him. [b]But he *said to
me, "[1]Do not do that! I am a [c]fellow
slave with you and your brothers who
[d]have the witness of Jesus. Worship
God! For the witness of Jesus is the
spirit of prophecy."

### *The Rider on a White Horse*

**11** Then I saw [a]heaven opened, and
behold, a [b]white horse, and He who
sits on it *is* called [c]Faithful and True,
and in [d]righteousness He judges and
wages war. **12** His [a]eyes *are* a flame
of fire, and on His head *are* many
[b]diadems; having a [c]name written
*on Him* which no one knows except
Himself, **13** and being clothed with
a [a]garment dipped in blood, His
name is also called [b]The Word of
God. **14** And the armies which are
in heaven, clothed in [a]fine linen,
[b]white *and* clean, were following
Him on white horses. **15** [a]And from
His mouth comes a sharp sword, so
that with it He may [b]STRIKE DOWN
THE NATIONS, and He will [c,1]RULE
THEM WITH A ROD OF IRON; and [d]HE
TREADS THE WINE PRESS OF THE WRATH
OF THE RAGE OF GOD, the Almighty.
**16** And He has on His garment and on
His thigh [a]a name written, "[b]KING
OF KINGS, AND LORD OF LORDS."

**17** Then I saw [1]an angel standing in
the sun, and he cried out with a loud
voice, saying to [a]all the birds which fly
in [b]midheaven, "[c]Come, assemble for
the great supper of God, **18** so that you
may [a]eat the flesh of kings and the
flesh of [1]commanders and the flesh
of strong men and the flesh of horses
and of those who sit on them and the
flesh of all men, [b]both free men and
slaves, and [c]small and great."

---

**19:4** [b]Rev 4:6 [c]Rev 4:10 [d]Ps 106:48; Rev 5:14 [e]Ps 104:35; Rev 19:3, 6 **19:5** [a]Ps 22:23; 115:13; 134:1; 135:1 [b]Rev 11:18 **19:6** [a]Jer 51:48; Rev 11:15; 19:1 [b]Eze 1:24; Rev 1:15 [c]Rev 6:1 [d]Ps 93:1; 97:1; 99:1; Rev 1:8 **19:7** [a]Rev 11:13 [b]Mt 22:2; 25:10; Lk 12:36; Jn 3:29; Eph 5:23, 32; Rev 19:9 [c]Mt 1:20; Rev 21:2, 9 [1]Lit *wife* **19:8** [a]Rev 15:6; 19:14 [b]Rev 15:4 **19:9** [a]Rev 17:1; 19:10 [b]Rev 1:19 [c]Mt 22:2f; Lk 14:15 [d]Rev 17:17; 21:5; 22:6 **19:10** [a]Rev 22:8 [b]Ac 10:26; Rev 22:9 [c]Rev 1:1f [d]Rev 12:17 [1]Lit *See to it not* **19:11** [a]Eze 1:1; Jn 1:51; Rev 4:1 [b]Rev 6:2; 19:19, 21 [c]Rev 3:14 [d]Ps 96:13; Is 11:4 **19:12** [a]Da 10:6; Rev 1:14 [b]Rev 6:2; 12:3 [c]Rev 2:17; 19:16 **19:13** [a]Is 63:3 [b]Jn 1:1 **19:14** [a]Rev 19:8 [b]Rev 3:4; 19:8 **19:15** [a]Rev 1:16; 19:21 [b]Is 11:4; 2Th 2:8 [c]Ps 2:9; Rev 2:27 [d]Is 63:3; Joel 3:13; Rev 14:19, 20 [1]Or *shepherd* **19:16** [a]Rev 2:17; 19:12 [b]Rev 17:14 **19:17** [a]Rev 19:21 [b]Rev 8:13 [c]1Sa 17:44; Jer 12:9; Eze 39:17 [1]Lit *one* **19:18** [a]Eze 39:18-20 [b]Rev 6:15 [c]Rev 11:18; 13:16; 19:5 [1]Military leader over 1,000 soldiers

**19** Then I saw [a]the beast and [b]the
kings of the earth and their armies
assembled to make war with Him
who [c]sits on the horse and with His
army.

### *The Beast and False Prophet Are Seized*

**20** And the beast was seized, and with
him the [a]false prophet who [b]did the
signs [c,1]in his presence, by which he
[d]deceived those who had received
the [e]mark of the beast and those who
[f]worshiped his image. These two
were thrown alive into the [g]lake of
[h]fire which burns with [2]brimstone.
**21** And the rest were killed with the
sword which [a]came from the mouth
of Him who [b]sits on the horse, and
[c]all the birds were filled with their
flesh.

### *Christ's Thousand Year Reign*

**20** Then I saw [a]an angel coming
down from heaven, having the
[b]key of the abyss and a great chain [1]in
his hand. **2** And he laid hold of the
[a]dragon, the serpent of old, who
is the devil and Satan, and [b]bound
him for a thousand years; **3** and he
threw him into the [a]abyss, and shut
*it* and [b]sealed *it* over him, so that he
would [c]not deceive the nations any
longer, until the thousand years were
finished. After these things he must
be released for a short time.

**4** Then I saw [a]thrones, and [b]they
sat on them, and [c]judgment was
given to them. And I *saw* [d]the souls
of those who had been beheaded
because of [1]their [e]witness of Jesus
and because of the word of God,
and who also had not [f]worshiped
the beast or his image, and had not
received the [g]mark on their forehead
and on their hand. And they [h]came
to life and [i]reigned with Christ for
a thousand years. **5** The rest of the
dead did not come to life until the
thousand years were finished. [a]This
is the first resurrection. **6** [a]Blessed
and holy is the one who has a part
in the first resurrection. Over these
the [b]second death has no authority,
but they will be [c]priests of God and
of Christ and will [d]reign with Him for
a thousand years.

### *The Defeat of Satan*

**7** And when the thousand years are
finished, Satan will be [a]released
from his prison, **8** and will come out
to [a]deceive the nations which are in
the [b]four corners of the earth, [c]Gog
and Magog, to [d]gather them together
for the war; the number of them is
like the [e]sand of the [1]seashore. **9** And
they [a]came up on the [1]broad plain of
the earth and surrounded the [b]camp
of the saints and the [c]beloved city,
and [d]fire came down from heaven
and devoured them. **10** And [a]the devil

---

**19:19** [a]Rev 11:7; 13:1 [b]Rev 16:14, 16 [c]Rev 19:11, 21 **19:20** [a]Rev 16:13 [b]Rev 13:13 [c]Rev 13:12 [d]Rev 13:14 [e]Rev 13:16f [f]Rev 13:12, 15 [g]Rev 20:10, 14f; 21:8 [h]Is 30:33; Da 7:11; Rev 14:10 [1]Or *by his authority* [2]Burning sulfur **19:21** [a]Rev 19:15 [b]Rev 19:11, 19 [c]Rev 19:17 ◆ **20:1** [a]Rev 10:1 [b]Rev 1:18; 9:1 [1]Lit *upon* **20:2** [a]Ge 3:1; Rev 12:9 [b]Is 24:22; 2Pe 2:4; Jd 6 **20:3** [a]Rev 20:1 [b]Da 6:17; Mt 27:66 [c]Rev 12:9; 20:8, 10 **20:4** [a]Da 7:9 [b]Mt 19:28; Rev 3:21 [c]Da 7:22; 1Co 6:2 [d]Rev 6:9 [e]Rev 1:9 [f]Rev 13:12, 15 [g]Rev 13:16f [h]Jn 14:19 [i]Rev 3:21; 5:10; 20:6; 22:5 [1]Lit *the* **20:5** [a]Lk 14:14; Php 3:11; 1Th 4:16 **20:6** [a]Rev 14:13 [b]Rev 2:11; 20:14 [c]Rev 1:6 [d]Rev 3:21; 5:10; 20:4; 22:5 **20:7** [a]Rev 20:2f **20:8** [a]Rev 12:9; 20:3, 10 [b]Eze 7:2; Rev 7:1 [c]Eze 38:2; 39:1, 6 [d]Rev 16:14 [e]Heb 11:12 [1]Lit *sea* **20:9** [a]Eze 38:9, 16 [b]Dt 23:14 [c]Ps 87:2 [d]Eze 38:22; 39:6; Rev 13:13 [1]Lit *breadth of the earth* **20:10** [a]Rev 20:2f

who [a]deceived them was thrown into
the [b]lake of fire and [1]brimstone,
where the [c]beast and the [c]false
prophet are also, and they will be
[d]tormented day and night forever
and ever.

### *The Great White Throne Judgment*

**11** Then I saw a great white [a]throne
and Him who sits upon it, from
whose [1]presence [b]earth and heaven
fled away, and [c]no place was found
for them. **12** Then I saw the dead,
the [a]great and the small, standing
before the throne, and [b,1]books
were opened; and another [2]book
was opened, which is [c]*the book* of
life. And the dead [a]were judged
from the things which were written
in the [1]books, [d]according to their
deeds. **13** And the sea gave up the
dead which were in it, and [a]death
and Hades [b]gave up the dead which
were in them, and they were judged,
every one *of them* [c]according to their
deeds. **14** Then [a]death and Hades
were thrown into [b]the lake of fire.
This is the [c]second death, the lake
of fire. **15** And if [1]anyone's name was
not found written in [a]the book of life,
he was thrown into the lake of fire.

### *The New Heaven and Earth*

**21** Then I saw [a]a new heaven
and a new earth; for [b]the
first heaven and the first earth
passed away, and there is no longer
*any* sea. **2** And I saw [a]the holy city,
[b]new Jerusalem, [c]coming down out
of heaven from God, [d]made ready as
a bride adorned for her husband.
**3** And I heard a loud voice from
the throne, saying, "Behold, [a]the
tabernacle of God is among men,
and He will [b,1]dwell among them,
and they shall be His people, and
God Himself will be among [2]them,
**4** and He will [a]WIPE AWAY EVERY TEAR
FROM THEIR EYES; and [b]there will no
longer be *any* death; [c]there will no
longer be *any* mourning, or crying,
or pain. [d]The first things passed
away."

**5** And [a]He who sits on the throne
said, "Behold, I am [b]making all things
new." And He *said, "Write, for [c]these
words are faithful and true." **6** Then
He said to me, "[a]They are done. I
am the [b]Alpha and the Omega, the
beginning and the end. [c]I will give to
the one who thirsts from the spring
of the [d]water of life without cost.
**7** [a]He who overcomes will inherit
these things, and [b]I WILL BE HIS GOD
AND HE WILL BE MY SON. **8** [a]But for
the cowardly and [1]unbelieving and
abominable and murderers and sex-
ually immoral persons and sorcerers
and idolaters and all liars, their part
*will be* in [b]the lake that burns with
fire and [2]brimstone, which is the
[c]second death."

**20:10** [a] Rev 20:2f [b]Rev 19:20; 20:14, 15 [c]Rev 16:13 [d]Rev 14:10f [1]Burning sulfur **20:11** [a]Rev 4:2 [b]Rev 6:14; 21:1 [c]Da 2:35; Rev 12:8 [1]Lit *face* **20:12** [a]Rev 11:18 [b]Da 7:10 [c]Rev 3:5; 20:15 [d]Mt 16:27; Rev 2:23; 20:13 [1]Or *scrolls* [2]Or *scroll* **20:13** [a]1Co 15:26; Rev 1:18; 6:8; 21:4 [b]Is 26:19 [c]Mt 16:27; Rev 2:23; 20:12 **20:14** [a]1Co 15:26; Rev 1:18; 6:8; 21:4 [b]Rev 19:20; 20:10, 15 [c]Rev 20:6 **20:15** [a]Rev 3:5; 20:12 [1]*Lit anyone was* ◆ ***21:1*** [a]*Is* 65:17; 66:22; 2Pe 3:13 [b]2Pe 3:10; Rev 20:11 **21:2** [a]Is 52:1; Rev 11:2; 21:10; 22:19 [b]Rev 3:12; 21:10 [c]Heb 11:10, 16; Rev 21:10 [d]Is 61:10; Rev 19:7; 21:9; 22:17 **21:3** [a]Lv 26:11f; Eze 37:27; 48:35; Heb 8:2; Rev 7:15 [b]Jn 14:23; 2Co 6:16 [1]Or *tabernacle* [2]One early ms adds and be *their God* **21:4** [a]Is 25:8; Rev 7:17 [b]1Co 15:26; Rev 20:14 [c]Is 35:10; 51:11; 65:19 [d]2Co 5:17; Heb 12:27 **21:5** [a]Rev 4:9; 20:11 [b]2Co 5:17; Heb 12:27 [c]Rev 19:9; 22:6 **21:6** [a]Rev 10:6; 16:17 [b]Rev 1:8; 22:13 [c]Is 55:1; Jn 4:10; Rev 7:17; 22:17 [d]Rev 7:17 **21:7** [a]Rev 2:7 [b]2Sa 7:14; Ps 89:26f; 2Co 6:16, 18; Rev 21:3 **21:8** [a]1Co 6:9; Ga 5:19-21; Rev 9:21; 21:27; 22:15 [b]Rev 19:20 [c]Rev 2:11 [1]Or *untrustworthy* [2]Burning sulfur

9 [a]Then one of the seven angels
who have the [b]seven bowls [1]full of
the [c]seven last plagues came and
spoke with me, saying, "[a]Come here,
I will show you the [d]bride, the wife
of the Lamb."

### *New Jerusalem, the Holy City*

10 And [a]he carried me away [b,1]in the
Spirit to a great and high mountain,
and showed me [c]the holy city, Jeru-
salem, coming down out of heaven
from God, 11 having [a]the glory of
God. Her [1]brilliance was like precious
stone, as a [b]stone of [c]crystal-clear
jasper. 12 [1]It had a great and high wall.
[1]It had [a]twelve [b]gates and at those
gates, twelve angels; and names
[2]have been written on *those gates,*
which are *the names* of the twelve
tribes of the sons of Israel. 13 *There
were* three gates on the east and three
gates on the north and three gates
on the south and three gates on the
west. 14 And the wall of the city had
[a]twelve foundation stones, and on
them *were* the twelve names of the
[b]twelve apostles of the Lamb.

15 And the one who spoke with
me had a [1]gold measuring [a]rod to
measure the city and its [b]gates and
its wall. 16 And the city is laid out as
a square, and its length is as great
as the width; and he measured the
city with the [1]rod, [2]12,000 stadia;
its length and width and height are
equal. 17 And he measured its wall,
[1]144 cubits, *according to* [a]human
[2]measurements, which are *also*
[b]angelic *measurements.* 18 And the
material of the wall was [a]jasper, and
the city was [b]pure gold, like pure
[c]glass. 19 [a]The foundation stones
of the city wall were adorned with
every kind of precious stone. The
first foundation stone was [b]jasper;
the second, sapphire; the third, chal-
cedony; the fourth, [c]emerald; 20 the
fifth, sardonyx; the sixth, [a]sardius;
the seventh, chrysolite; the eighth,
beryl; the ninth, topaz; the tenth,
chrysoprase; the eleventh, jacinth;
the twelfth, amethyst. 21 And the
twelve [a]gates were twelve [b]pearls;
each one of the gates was a single
pearl. And the street of the city was
[c]pure gold, like transparent [d]glass.

22 And I saw [a]no sanctuary in it,
for the [b]Lord God the Almighty and
the [c]Lamb are its sanctuary. 23 And
the city [a]has no need of the sun or
of the moon to shine on it, for [b]the
glory of God has illumined it, and
its lamp *is* the [c]Lamb. 24 [a]And the
nations will walk by its light, and the
[b]kings of the earth [1]will bring their
glory into it. 25 [a]And its gates [b]will
never be closed by day, for [c]there
will be no night there; 26 and [a]they
will bring the glory and the honor of
the nations into it. 27 And [a]nothing
defiled, and no one who practices

**21:9** [a]Rev 17:1 [b]Rev 15:7 [c]Rev 15:1 [d]Rev 19:7; 21:2 [1]Lit *who were full* **21:10** [a]Eze 40:2; Rev 17:3 [b]Rev 1:10 [c]Rev 21:2 [1]Or *in spirit* **21:11** [a]Is 60:1f; Eze 43:2; Rev 15:8; 21:23; 22:5 [b]Rev 4:3; 21:18, 19 [c]Rev 4:6 [1]Lit *luminary* **21:12** [a]Eze 48:31-34 [b]Rev 21:15, 21, 25; 22:14 [1]Lit *Having* [2]Lit *having been* **21:14** [a]Heb 11:10 [b]Ac 1:26 **21:15** [a]Eze 40:3; Rev 11:1 [b]Rev 21:12, 21, 25 [1]Lit *measure, a gold reed* **21:16** [1]Lit *reed* [2]Approx. 1,380 mi. or 2,220 km, a stadion was approx. 607 ft. or 185 m **21:17** [a]Dt 3:11; Rev 13:18 [b]Rev 21:9 [1]Approx. 216 ft. or 66 m, a cubit was approx. 18 in. or 45 cm [2]Lit *measure* **21:18** [a]Rev 21:11 [b]Rev 21:21 [c]Rev 4:6 **21:19** [a]Ex 28:17-20; Is 54:11f; Eze 28:13 [b]Rev 21:11 [c]Rev 4:3 **21:20** [a]Rev 4:3 **21:21** [a]Rev 21:12, 15, 25 [b]Rev 17:4 [c]Rev 21:18 [d]Rev 4:6 **21:22** [a]Mt 24:2; Jn 4:21 [b]Rev 1:8 [c]Rev 5:6; 7:17; 14:4 **21:23** [a]Is 24:23; 60:19, 20; Rev 21:25; 22:5 [b]Rev 21:11 [c]Rev 5:6; 7:17; 14:4 **21:24** [a]Is 60:3, 5 [b]Ps 72:10f; Is 49:23; 60:16; Rev 21:26 [1]Lit *bring* **21:25** [a]Rev 21:12, 15 [b]Is 60:11 [c]Zec 14:7; Rev 21:23; 22:5 **21:26** [a]Ps 72:10f; Is 49:23; 60:16 **21:27** [a]Is 52:1; Eze 44:9; Zec 14:21; Rev 22:14f

abomination and lying, shall ever
come into it, but only those [1]whose
names are [b]written in the Lamb's
book of life.

### *The River and the Tree of Life*

22 Then [a]he showed me a [b]river
of the [c]water of life, bright [d]as
crystal, coming from the throne of
God and of [1]the Lamb, 2 in the middle
of [a]its street. [b]On either side of the
river was [c]the tree of life, bearing
twelve [1]*kinds of* fruit, yielding its
fruit every month; and the leaves of
the tree were for the healing of the
nations. 3 [a]And there will no longer
be any curse; and [b]the throne of God
and of the Lamb will be in it, and His
slaves will [c]serve Him; 4 and they will
[a]see His face, and His [b]name *will be*
on their [c]foreheads. 5 And [a]there will
no longer be *any* night, and they [1]will
not have need [b]of the light of a lamp
nor the light of the sun, because the
Lord God will illumine them, and
they will [c]reign forever and ever.

6 And [a]he said to me, "[b]These
words are faithful and true"; and the
Lord, the [c]God of the spirits of the
prophets, [d]sent His angel to show
to His slaves the things which must
soon take place.

7 "And behold, [a]I am coming
quickly. [b]Blessed is he who keeps
[c]the words of the prophecy of this
book."

8 [a]I, John, am the one who was
hearing and seeing these things. And
when I heard and saw, [b]I fell down
to worship at the feet of the angel
who showed me these things. 9 But
[a]he *said to me, "[1]Do not do that! I
am a [b]fellow slave with you and your
brothers the prophets and with those
who keep the words of [c]this book.
Worship God!"

### *The Final Message: Come*

10 And he *said to me, "[a]Do not seal
up [b]the words of the prophecy of this
book, [c]for the time is near. 11 [a]Let the
one who does unrighteousness, still
do unrighteousness; and the one
who is filthy, still be filthy; and let
the one who is righteous, still do
righteousness; and the one who is
holy, still keep himself holy."

12 "Behold, [a]I am coming quick-
ly, and My [b]reward *is* with Me, [c]to
render to every man [1]according to
his work. 13 I am the [a]Alpha and the
Omega, [b]THE FIRST AND THE LAST, [c]the
beginning and the end."

14 Blessed are those who [a]wash
their robes, so that they may have
the authority to [b]the tree of life and
may [c]enter by the [d]gates into the city.
15 [a]Outside are the [b]dogs and the
sorcerers and the sexually immoral
persons and the murderers and the
idolaters, and everyone who loves
and practices lying.

---

**21:27** [b]Rev 3:5 [1]Lit *who have been* ◆ **22:1** [a]Rev 1:1; 21:9; 22:6 [b]Ps 46:4; Eze 47:1 [c]Zec 14:8; Rev 7:17; 22:17 [d]Rev 4:6 [1]Or *the Lamb. In the middle of its street, and on either side of the river, was* **22:2** [a]Rev 21:21 [b]Eze 47:12 [c]Ge 2:9; Rev 2:7; 22:14, 19 [1]Or crops of *fruit* **22:3** [a]Zec 14:11 [b]Rev 21:3 [c]Rev 7:15 **22:4** [a]Ps 17:15; 42:2; Mt 5:8 [b]Rev 14:1 [c]Rev 7:3 **22:5** [a]Zec 14:7; Rev 21:25 [b]Is 60:19; Rev 21:23 [c]Da 7:18, 27; Mt 19:28; Ro 5:17; Rev 20:4 [1]Lit *do not have* **22:6** [a]Rev 1:1; 21:9 [b]Rev 19:9; 21:5 [c]1Co 14:32; Heb 12:9 [d]Rev 1:1; 22:16 **22:7** [a]Rev 1:3; 3:3, 11; 16:15; 22:12, 20 [b]Rev 1:3; 16:15 [c]Rev 1:11; 22:9, 10, 18f **22:8** [a]Rev 1:1 [b]Rev 19:10 **22:9** [a]Rev 19:10 [b]Rev 1:1 [c]Rev 1:11; 22:10, 18f [1]Lit *See to it not* **22:10** [a]Da 8:26; Rev 10:4 [b]Rev 1:11; 22:9, 18f [c]Rev 1:3 **22:11** [a]Eze 3:27; Da 12:10 **22:12** [a]Rev 22:7 [b]Is 40:10; 62:11 [c]Ps 28:4; Jer 17:10; Mt 16:27; Rev 2:23 [1]Lit *as his work is* **22:13** [a]Rev 1:8 [b]Is 44:6; 48:12; Rev 1:17; 2:8 [c]Rev 21:6 **22:14** [a]Rev 7:14 [b]Ge 2:9; 3:22; Rev 22:2 [c]Rev 21:27 [d]Rev 21:12 **22:15** [a]Mt 8:12; 1Co 6:9f; Ga 5:19ff; Rev 21:8 [b]Dt 23:18; Mt 7:6; Php 3:2

16 "[a]I, Jesus, sent [b]My angel to bear
witness to you of these things [c,1]for
the churches. I am [d]the root and the
[e]descendant of David, the bright
[f]morning star."
17 And the [a]Spirit and the [b]bride
say, "Come." And let the one who
hears say, "Come." And [c]let the one
who is thirsty come. Let the one
who wishes receive the [d]water of life
without cost.
18 I bear witness to everyone who
hears [a]the words of the prophecy of
this book: If anyone [b]adds to them,
God will add to him [c]the plagues
which are written in [d]this book.
19 And if anyone [a]takes away from
the [b]words of the book of this proph-
ecy, God will take away his part from
[c]the tree of life and [1]from the holy
city, [d]which are written in this book.
20 He who [a]bears witness to these
things says, "Yes, [b]I am coming
quickly." Amen. [c]Come, Lord Jesus.
21 [a]The grace of the Lord Jesus be
with [1]all. Amen.

---

**22:16** [a]Rev 1:1 [b]Rev 1:1; 22:6 [c]Rev 1:4, 11; 3:22 [d]Rev 5:5 [e]Mt 1:1 [f]Mt 2:2; Rev 2:28 [1]Or *concerning* **22:17** [a]Rev 2:7; 14:13 [b]Rev 21:2, 9 [c]Is 55:1; Rev 21:6 [d]Rev 7:17; 22:1 **22:18** [a]Rev 22:7 [b]Dt 4:2; 12:32; Pr 30:6 [c]Rev 15:6-16:21 [d]Rev 22:7 **22:19** [a]Dt 4:2; 12:32; Pr 30:6 [b]Rev 22:7 [c]Rev 22:2 [d]Rev 21:10-22:5 [1]Lit *out of* **22:20** [a]Rev 1:2 [b]Rev 22:7 [c]1Co 16:22 **22:21** [a]Ro 16:20 [1]One early ms *the saints*

# MONETARY UNITS

| | |
|---|---|
| **Assarion** *(plural assaria)* | A Roman copper coin, approximately 1/16 of a laborer's daily wage |
| **Daric** | A Persian gold coin, weighing approximately 0.3 ounces or 8 grams |
| **Denarius** *(plural denarii)* | A Roman silver coin, approximately a laborer's daily wage |
| **Drachma** *(plural drachmas)* | A Greek silver coin, approximately a laborer's daily wage |
| **Lepton** *(plural lepta)* | Smallest Greek copper coin, approximately 1/128 of a laborer's daily wage |
| **Mina** *(plural minas)* | A Greek monetary unit worth approximately 100 days of a laborer's wages |
| **Quadrans** | A Roman copper coin, approximately 1/64 of a laborer's daily wage |
| **Shekel** | A coin weighing approximately 0.4 ounces or 11 grams |
| **Stater** | Literally "standard coin," approximately 4 days of a laborer's wages |
| **Talent** | Approximately worth more than 15 years of a laborer's wages |

This table contains values regarding monetary units, gathered from widely accepted historical and archeological research. These values are based on the most accurate information available.

# WEIGHTS AND MEASUREMENTS

| | |
|---|---|
| **Bath** | Approximately 6 gallons or 23 liters |
| **Choinix** | A dry measure, approximately 1 quart or 1 liter |
| **Cubit** | Approximately 18 inches or 45 centimeters |
| **Ephah** | A dry measure, approximately 21 quarts or 23 liters |
| **Fathom** | Approximately 6 feet or 1.8 meters |
| **Gerah** | Approximately 0.025 ounces or 0.7 grams |
| **Handbreadth** | Approximately 3 inches or .75 cemtimeters |
| **Hin** | A liquid measure, approximately 1 gallon or 3.8 liters |
| **Homer** | Approximately 6.5 bushels or 230 liters |
| **Kab** | Approximately 2 quarts or 1.9 liters |
| **Kor** | As a dry measure, 6.5 bushels or 230 liters; as a liquid measure, 61 gallons or 230 liters |
| **Litra** | A Roman pound, approximately 12 ounces or 340 grams |
| **Log** | A liquid measure, approximately 10 ounces or 300 milliliters |
| **Measure** | Approximately 10 gallons or 38 liters |
| **Omer** | A dry measure, approximately 2.1 quarts or 2.3 liters |
| **Sabbath Day's Journey** | Approximately 0.6 miles or 1 kilometer |
| **Saton** *(plural sata)* | Approximately 16 pounds or 13 liters |
| **Seah** | A dry measure, approximately 7 quarts or 7.7 liters |
| **Shekel** | The most common unit of weight in the OT, approximately 0.4 ounces or 11 grams |
| **Stadion** *(plural stadia)* | Approximately 607 feet or 185 meters |
| **Talent** | As an OT weight, approximately 75 pounds or 34 kilograms; as a NT weight, approximately 100 pounds or 45 kilograms |

This table contains data gathered from widely accepted historical and archeological research. The amounts listed as weights and measurements are not intended to be precise. Further discoveries may allow for more consistent and accurate data. Until then, these units remain approximations.

# Map 1: The Biblical World of the Patriarchs

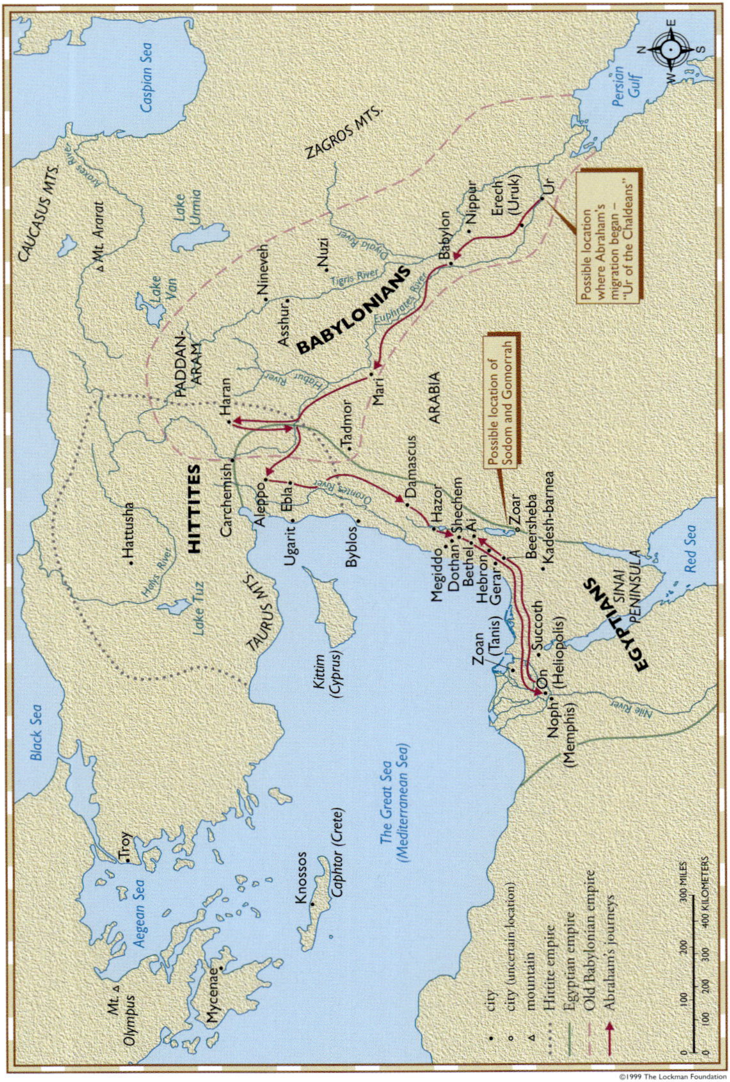

# Map 2: The Exodus Route and Conquest of Canaan

# MAP 3: THE TWELVE TRIBES OF ISRAEL

# MAP 4: THE DIVIDED KINGDOMS OF ISRAEL AND JUDAH

# MAP 5: THE HERODIAN KINGDOM IN THE TIME OF CHRIST

# Map 6a: Old Testament Jerusalem

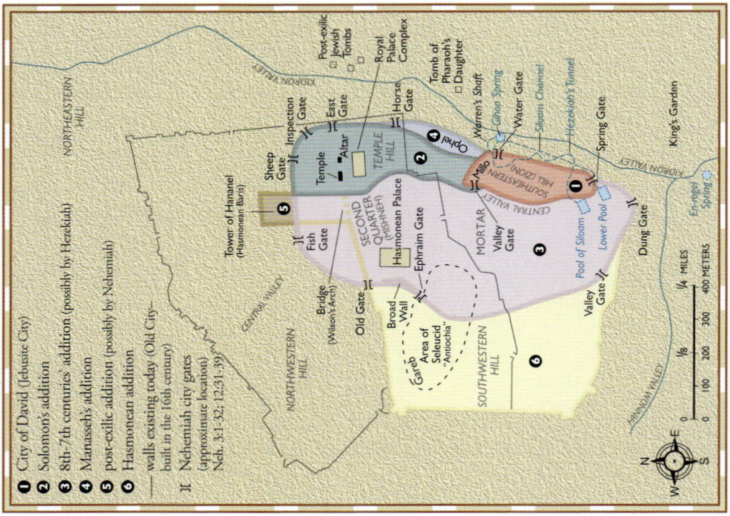


# Map 6b: New Testament Jerusalem

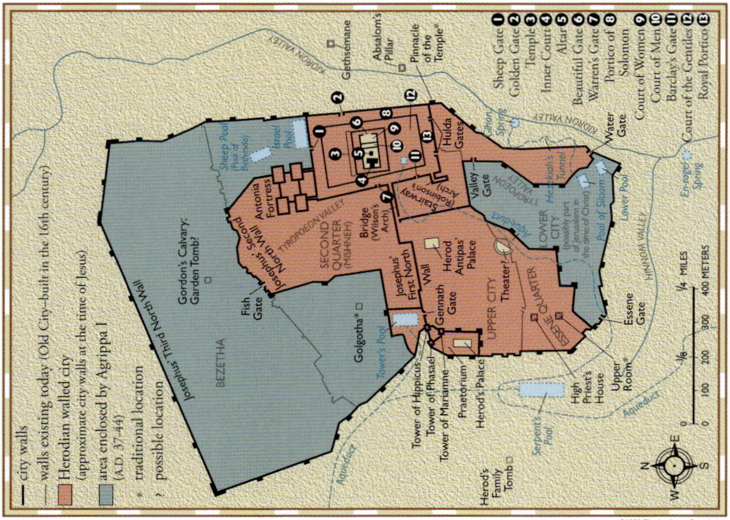

# MAP 7: THE MINISTRY OF JESUS

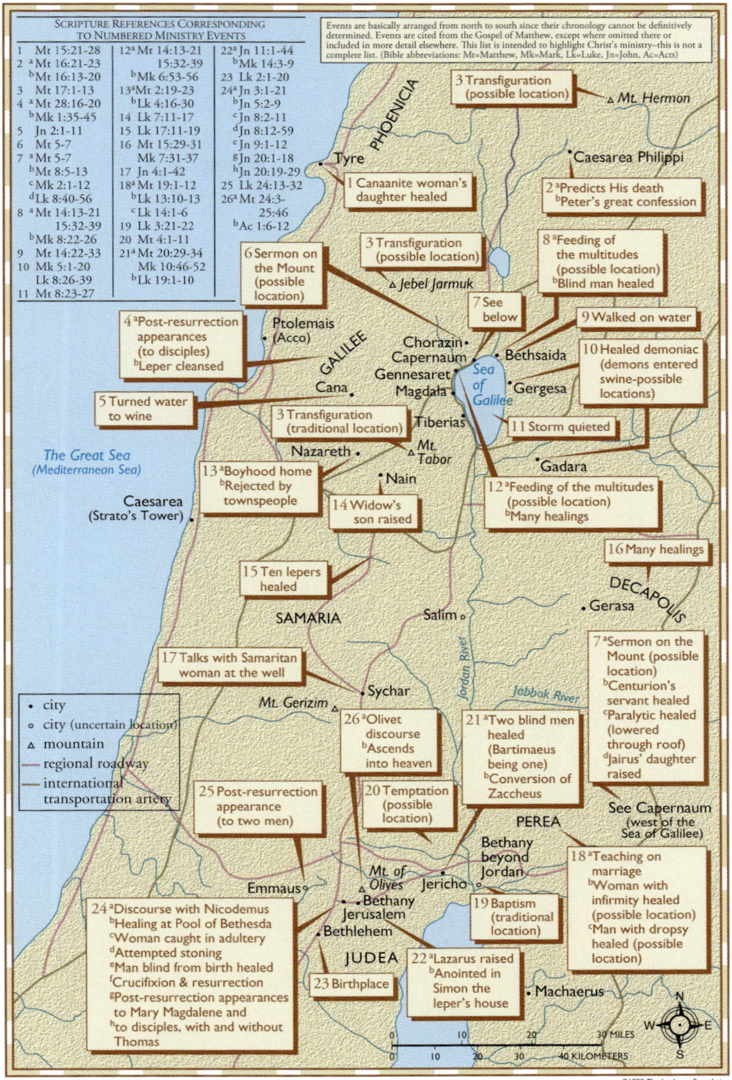

# MAP 8: THE MISSIONARY JOURNEYS OF PAUL

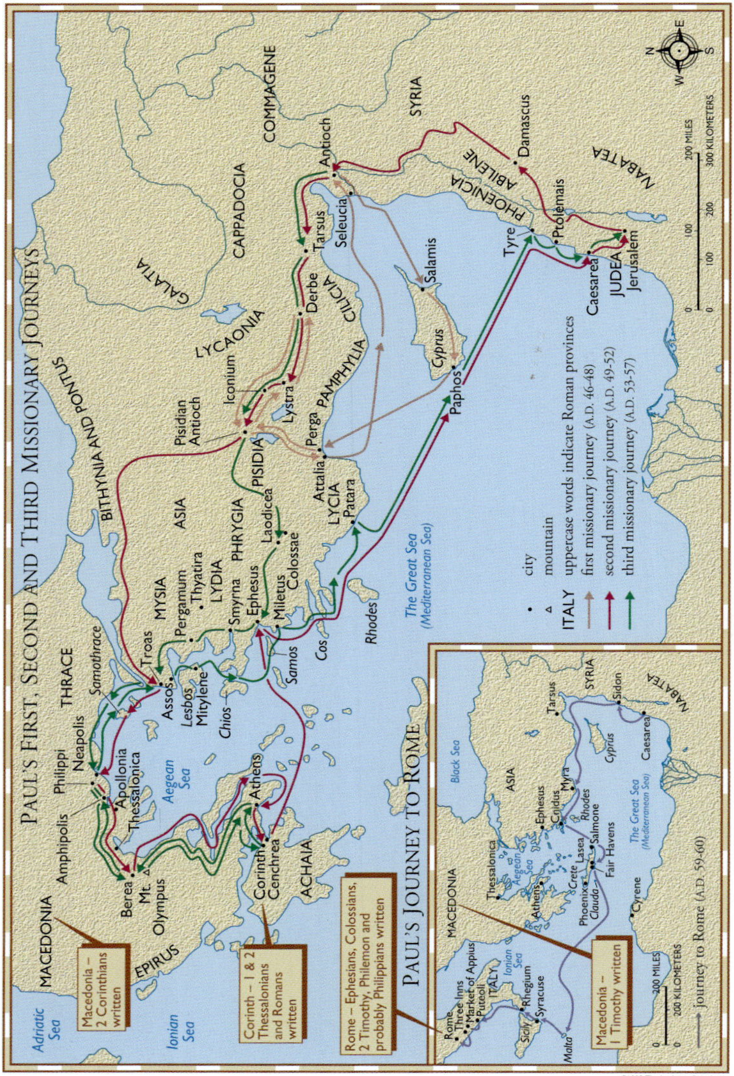